Peterson's Four-Year Colleges 2021

About Peterson's®

Peterson's® has been your trusted educational publisher for over 50 years. It's a milestone we're quite proud of, as we continue to offer the most accurate, dependable, high-quality educational content in the field, providing you with everything you need to succeed. No matter where you are on your academic or professional path, you can rely on Peterson's for its books, online information, expert test-prep tools, the most up-to-date education exploration data, and the highest quality career success resources—everything you need to achieve your education goals. For our complete line of products, visit **www.petersons.com**.

For more information about Peterson's range of educational products, contact Peterson's, 4380 S. Syracuse Street, Suite 200, Denver, CO 80237, or find us online at **www.petersons.com**.

Previous editions published as *Peterson's Annual Guide to Undergraduate Study* © 1970, 1971, 1972, 1973, 1974, 1975, 1976, 1977, 1978, 1979, 1980, 1981, 1982 and as *Peterson's Four-Year Colleges* © 1983, 1984, 1985, 1986, 1987, 1988, 1989, 1990, 1991, 1992, 1993, 1994, 1995, 1996, 1997, 1998, 1999, 2000, 2001, 2002, 2003, 2004, 2005, 2006, 2007, 2008, 2009, 2010, 2011, 2012, 2013, 2014, 2015, 2016, 2017, 2018, 2019

ISSN 1544-2330
ISBN 978-0-7689-4326-9

Printed in the United States of America

10 9 8 7 6 5 4 3 2 1   22 21 20

Fifty-first Edition

Contents

A Note from the Peterson's® Editors

For over fifty years, Peterson's® has given students and parents the most comprehensive, up-to-date information on undergraduate institutions in the United States and Canada. *Peterson's® Four-Year Colleges 2020* features advice and tips on the college search and selection process, such as how to consider the factors that truly make a difference during your search, how to understand the application process, and how to get financial aid. Each year, Peterson's researches the data published in *Peterson's® Four-Year Colleges*. The information is furnished by the colleges and is accurate at the time of publishing.

Opportunities abound for students, and this guide can help you find what you want in a number of ways:

- For application and admissions advice and guidance, just head to **THE ADVICE CENTER.** The "College Admissions Countdown Calendar" outlines pertinent month-by-month milestones. "Choosing Your Top Ten Colleges" gets you started on putting together the most important Top Ten list you have ever made. You'll find some excellent advice in the article, "Planning is Essential on the Road to College," by Sarah E. Gibbs, Director of Admissions at Grove City College. Next, "Surviving Standardized Tests" describes frequently used tests and what you need to know to succeed on them. Of course, part of the college selection process involves visiting the schools themselves, and "The Whys and Whats of College Visits" is the planner you need to make those trips well worth your while. Be sure to check out the articles on specific institutions and programs that may be just right for you, including "Honors Programs and Colleges: Smart Choices for an Undergraduate Education," "Public and Private Colleges and Universities—How to Choose," "Distance Education—It's Closer than You Think," and "Why Not Women's Colleges?" Next, "Applying 101" provides advice on how best to approach the application phase of the process. If you can't make sense out of the early decision/early action conundrum, "The 'Early Decision' Decision" may help clarify it for you. The article "Coming to America: Tips for International Students Considering Study in the U.S." offers helpful information and expert tips from professionals who work with international students at colleges and universities throughout the United States. For essential information on how to meet your education expenses, you'll find the "Financial Aid Countdown Calendar" followed by the articles "Who's Paying for This? Financial Aid Basics" and "Middle Income Families: Making the Financial Aid Process Work." Finally, you'll want to read through the "How to Use This Guide" section, which explains the information presented for each individual college, how Peterson's collects its data, and how Peterson's determines eligibility for inclusion in this guide.
- Next up is the **PROFILES** section. Here you'll find our unparalleled college profiles, arranged alphabetically by state, U.S. territories, and by country. They provide need-to-know information about accredited four-year colleges—including entrance difficulty, campus setting, total enrollment, student-faculty ratio, application deadlines, expenses, most frequently chosen baccalaureate fields, and academic programs. The contact information appears at the conclusion of each college profile. Display ads, which appear near some of the institutions' profiles, have been provided and paid for by those colleges or universities that wished to supplement their profile data with additional information about their institution.
- Over 100 two-page narrative descriptions appear as **COLLEGE CLOSE-UPS**—descriptions written by admissions or college officials that provide great detail about each school. They are edited to provide a consistent format across entries for your ease of comparison.
- If you already have specifics in mind, such as a particular major or institution, turn to the **INDEXES** section. Here you can search for a school based on major, entrance difficulty, cost ranges, and geography. If you already have colleges in mind that pique your interest, you can use the "Alphabetical Listing of Colleges and Universities" to search for these schools. Page numbers referring to all information presented about a college are conveniently referenced.

Peterson's publishes a full line of books—college and grad guides as well as books on education exploration, test preparation, financial aid, and career preparation. Peterson's® publications can be found at high school guidance offices, college libraries and career centers, and your local bookstore and library. Peterson's books are also available at **www.petersons.com**.

We welcome any comments or suggestions you may have about this publication. Your feedback will help us make educational dreams possible for you—and others like you.

Colleges will be pleased to know that Peterson's helped you in your selection. Admissions staff members are more than happy to answer questions, address specific problems, and help in any way they can. The editors at Peterson's wish you great success in your college search!

The Advice Center

College Admissions Countdown Calendar

This practical month-by-month calendar is designed to help you stay on top of the process of applying to college. For most students, the process begins in September of the junior year of high school and ends in June of the senior year. You may want to begin considering financial aid options, reviewing your academic schedule, and attending college fairs before your junior year.

FRESHMAN YEAR

- **Remember that college admissions decisions are most often based on a six semester transcript (your grades your Freshman, Sophomore, and Junior years) so instead of having four years to create your best GPA, you really only have three.**
- Get organized! Using a paper or digital planner, begin keeping up with your assignments in your classes, note when you have tests or quizzes coming up, and plan ahead. Staying organized in high school will help you continue these good study habits into your college years.
- Begin keeping records of your accomplishments and awards now to create your resume your senior year.
- You should begin evaluating your interests and join clubs and organizations specifically for those interests.
- Explore community service opportunities in your area. Most nonprofits will be glad to have a volunteer that works from a few hours a month to multiple hours a week and anywhere in between. Your continued participation in volunteer activities throughout your high school career speaks volumes about your character that a 30-minute interview might not provide.

SOPHOMORE YEAR

- Continue the above activities you started your freshman year.
- Begin building your preliminary college preference list
- Register for the PSAT®. This test provides a a great practice experience for the SAT, **but your PSAT test score only qualifies for the National Merit Scholarship Qualifying Competition in your JUNIOR year.**
- Check in with your counselor frequently and make sure you're signed up for classes that challenge you and will help you prepare for college. Sometimes the rigor of the curriculum on your high school transcript can mean the difference in receiving scholarships or even gaining admission into a college.
- For extra practice, sign up for the ACT® and/or the SAT® anytime this year and begin prepping for those tests using resources found at **actstudent.org**, **collegeboard.org**, and **petersons.com.**
- In the summer, spend time visiting colleges, interning, working, and/or volunteering. Depending on how busy you are during the school year, sometimes the summer months provide a valuable "break" for you to participate more in these activities.
- Ask your counselor about any **concurrent enrollment** opportunities available at your school. Most of these courses can be taken your Junior or Senior year in high school and are offered in partnership with local colleges or universities. Concurrent enrollment courses allow you to receive both high school and college credit for these courses.

JUNIOR YEAR

September

- Create an account at **www.commonapp.org** to begin adding your personal information and accomplishments to a Common Application that is accepted by many colleges and universities around the U.S.
- Check again with your counselor to make sure your course credits will meet college requirements.
- Be sure you are involved in one or two extracurricular activities.
- Explore opportunities to add community service hours to your list of activities for applications.
- Begin building your preferred college list (if you haven't already). Ideally, you should have fifteen to twenty colleges and/or universities on this list.
- If you plan to play college sports, register with the NCAA.

October

- Register for and take the PSAT/NMSQT®.

November

- Strive to get the best grades you can. A serious effort will provide you with the most options during the application process.

December

- If you haven't already, get involved in a community service activity.
- To familiarize yourself with current events, begin to read newspapers, reputable online news sources, and news magazines. This will prepare you for admissions and/or scholarship interviews where you might be asked your opinion on important happenings in the U.S. and around the world.
- Buy *Peterson's® SAT® Prep Guide*, or *Peterson's® ACT® Prep Guide* and begin to study for the tests.

January

- With your school counselor, decide when to take the ACT®, SAT®, and SAT Subject Tests™ (and which Subject Tests to take). If English is not your primary language and you are planning on attending a college in North America, decide when to take the TOEFL®.
- Keep your grades up!

February

- Plan a challenging schedule of classes for your senior year.
- Think about which teachers you will ask to write recommendations.
- Check **www.nacacfairs.org/exhibit/national-college-fairs/** and click on "College Fairs" for up-to-date schedules and locations of college fairs.

March

- Register for the tests you will take in the spring (ACT®, SAT®, SAT Subject Tests™, or the TOEFL®).
- Meet with your school counselor to discuss college choices.
- Review your transcript and test scores with your counselor to determine how competitive your range of choices should be.
- Narrow down your preferred colleges list to ten to fifteen colleges and universities.
- Start scheduling campus visits. The best time is when school is in session (but never during final exams). Summers are OK but will not show you what the college is really like. If possible, save your top college choices for the fall. Be aware, however, that fall is the busiest visit season, and you will need advance planning. Don't forget to write thank you letters to your interviewers.

April

- Take any standardized tests for which you have registered.
- Create a list of your potential college choices and begin to record personal and academic information that can be transferred later to your college applications.

May

- Plan college visits and make appointments.
- Structure your summer plans to include advanced academic work, travel, volunteer work, or a job.
- Confirm your academic schedule for the fall.

Summer

- Write to any colleges on your list that do not accept the Common Application to request application forms.
- Begin working on your application essays.

SENIOR YEAR

September

- Continue any appropriate activities from your freshman, sophomore, and junior years.
- DEADLINES! Note in your planner your preferred colleges' admissions deadlines, financial aid application due dates, ACT®/SAT® registration deadlines for testing, scholarship application deadlines, and any other related important dates in your planner.
- Begin asking your Junior year teachers for letters of recommendation now because they're the most familiar with your work and abilities.
- Register for the ACT®, SAT®, SAT Subject Tests™, or the TOEFL®, as necessary.
- Check with your school counselor for the fall visiting schedule of college reps.
- Ask appropriate teachers if they would write recommendations for you. Don't forget to write thank you letters when they accept.
- Meet with your counselor to compile your final list of colleges.

October

- Prepare the Free Application for Federal Student Aid (FAFSA®), available at **www.fafsa.ed.gov** or through your school counseling office. An estimated income tax statement (which can be corrected later) can be used. The sooner you apply for financial aid, the better your chances. For academic year 2019–2020, the FAFSA® application window opens October 1, 2018, and closes June 30, 2020.
- Mail or send early applications electronically after carefully checking them to be sure they are completely filled out.
- Photocopy or print extra copies of your applications to use as a backup.
- Take the tests for which you have registered.
- Don't be late! Keep track of all deadlines for transcripts, recommendations, financial aid, etc.

November

- Be sure that you have requested your ACT® and SAT® scores be sent to your colleges of choice.
- Complete and submit all applications. Print or photocopy an extra copy for your records.

December

- Take any necessary tests: ACT®, SAT®, SAT Subject Tests™, or the TOEFL®.
- Meet with your counselor to verify that all is in order and that transcripts were sent to colleges.

February

- Submit your FAFSA® either online or via U.S. mail.
- Be sure your midyear report has gone out to the colleges to which you've applied.
- Let colleges know of any new honors or accomplishments that were not in your original application.

March

- Register for any Advanced Placement® (AP®) tests you might take.
- Be sure you have received a FAFSA® acknowledgment.

April

- Review the acceptances and financial aid offers you receive.
- Go back to visit one or two of your top-choice colleges.
- Notify your college of choice that you have accepted its offer (and send in a deposit by May 1).
- Notify the colleges you have chosen not to attend of your decision.

May

- Take AP® tests.
- Graduate! Congratulations and best of luck.

Choosing Your Top Ten Colleges

By using all the information in the various sections of this guide, you will find colleges worthy of the most important top-ten list on the planet—yours.

The first thing you will need to do is decide what type of institution of higher learning you want to attend. Each of the thousands of four-year colleges and universities in the United States is as unique as the people applying to it. Although listening to the voices and media hype around you can make it sound as though there are only a few elite schools worth attending, this simply is not true. By considering some of the following criteria, you will soon find that the large pool of interesting colleges can be narrowed down to a more reasonable number.

SIZE AND CATEGORY

Schools come in all shapes and sizes, from tiny rural colleges of 400 students to massive state university systems serving 100,000 students or more. If you are coming from a small high school, a college with 3,500 students may seem large to you. If you are currently attending a high school with 3,000 students, selecting a college of a similar size may not feel like a new enough experience. Some students coming from very large impersonal high schools are looking for a place where they will be recognized from the beginning and offered a more personal approach. If you don't have a clue about what size might feel right to you, try visiting a couple of nearby colleges of varying sizes. You do not have to be seriously interested in them; just feel what impact the number of students on campus has on you.

Large Universities

Large universities offer a wide range of educational, athletic, and social experiences. Universities offer a full scope of undergraduate majors and award master's and doctoral degrees as well. Universities are usually composed of several smaller colleges. Depending on your interest in a major field or area of study, you would likely apply to a specific college within the university. Each college has the flexibility to set its own standards for admission, which may differ from the overall average of the university. The colleges within a university system also set their own course requirements for earning a degree.

Universities may be public or private. Some large private universities, such as Harvard, Yale, Princeton, University of Pennsylvania, New York University, Northwestern, and Stanford, are well-known for their high entrance standards, the excellence of their education, and the success rates of their graduates. These institutions place a great deal of emphasis on research and compete aggressively for grants from the federal government to fund these projects. Large public universities, such as the State University of New York (SUNY) System, University of Michigan, University of Texas, University of Illinois, University of Washington, and University of North Carolina, also support excellent educational programs, compete for and win research funding, and have successful graduates. Public universities usually offer substantially lower tuition rates to in-state students, although their tuition rates for out-of-state residents are often comparable to those of private institutions.

At many large universities, sports play a major role on campus. Athletics can dominate the calendar and set the tone year-round at some schools. Alumni travel from far and wide to attend their alma mater's football or basketball games, and the campus—and frequently the entire town—grinds to a halt when there is a home game. Athletes are heroes and dominate campus social life.

What are some other features of life on a university campus? Every kind of club imaginable, from literature to bioengineering and chorus to politics, can be found on most college campuses. You will be able to play the intramural version of almost every sport in which the university fields interscholastic teams and join fraternities, sororities, and groups dedicated to social action. You can become a member of a band, an orchestra, or perhaps a chamber music group or work on the newspaper, the literary magazine, or the website. The list can go on and on. You may want to try out a new interest or two or pursue what you have always been interested in and make like-minded friends along the way.

Take a look at the size of the classrooms in the larger universities and envision yourself sitting in that atmosphere. Would this offer a learning environment that would benefit you?

Liberal Arts Colleges

If you have considered large universities and come to the conclusion that all that action could be a distraction, a small liberal arts college might be right for you. Ideally tucked away on a picture-perfect campus, a liberal arts college generally has fewer than 5,000 students. The mission of most liberal arts schools is learning for the sake of learning, with a strong emphasis on creating lifelong learners who will be able to apply their education to any number of careers. This contrasts with objectives of the profession-based preparation of specialized colleges.

Liberal arts colleges cannot offer the breadth of courses provided by the large universities. As a result, liberal arts colleges try to create a niche for themselves. For instance, a college may place its emphasis on its humanities departments, whose professors are all well-known published authors and international presenters in their areas of expertise. A college may highlight its science departments by providing state-of-the-art-facilities where undergraduates conduct research side by side with top-notch professors and co-publish their findings in the most prestigious scientific journals in the country. The personal approach is very important at liberal arts colleges. Whether in advisement, course selection, athletic programs tailored to students' interests, or dinner with the department head at her home, liberal arts colleges emphasize that they get to know their students.

If they are so perfect, why doesn't everyone choose a liberal arts college? Well, the small size limits options. Fewer people may mean less diversity. The fact that many of these colleges encourage a study-abroad option (a student elects to spend a semester or a year studying in another country) reduces the number of students on campus even further. Some liberal arts colleges have a certain reputation that does not appeal to some students. You should ask yourself questions about the campus life that most appeals to you. Will you fit in with the campus culture? Will the small size mean that you go through your social options quickly? Check out the activities listed on the Student Center bulletin board. Does the student body look diverse enough for you? Will what is happening keep you busy and interested? Do the students have input into decision making? Do they create the social climate of the school?

Small Universities

Smaller universities often combine stringent admissions policies, handpicked faculty members, and attractive scholarship packages. These institutions generally have undergraduate enrollments of about 4,000 students. Some are more famous for their graduate and professional schools but have also established strong undergraduate colleges. Smaller universities balance the great majors options of large universities with a smaller campus community. They offer choices but not to the same extent as large universities. On the other hand, by limiting admissions and enrollment, they manage to cultivate some of the characteristics of a liberal arts college. Like a liberal arts college, a small university may emphasize a particular program and go out of its way to draw strong candidates in a specific area, such as premed, to its campus. Universities such as The Johns Hopkins University, University of Notre Dame, Vanderbilt University, Washington University in St. Louis, and Wesleyan University in Connecticut are a few examples of small universities.

Technical or Specialized Colleges

Another alternative to the liberal arts college or large university is the technical or otherwise specialized college. Its goal is to offer a specialized and saturated experience in a particular field of study. Such an institution might limit its course offerings to engineering and science, the performing or fine arts, or business. Schools such as California Institute of Technology, Carnegie Mellon University, Massachusetts Institute of Technology, and Rensselaer Polytechnic Institute concentrate on attracting the finest math and science students in the country. At other schools, like Bentley College in Massachusetts or Bryant College in Rhode Island, students eat, sleep, and breathe business. These institutions are purists at heart and strong believers in the necessity of focused, specialized study to produce excellence in their graduates' achievements. If you are certain about your chosen path in life and want to immerse yourself in subjects such as math, music, or business, you will fit right in.

Religious Colleges

Many private colleges have religious origins, and many of these have become secular institutions with virtually no trace of their religious roots. Others remain dedicated to a religious way of education. What sets religious colleges apart is the way they combine faith, learning, and student life. Faculty members and administrators are hired with faith as a criterion as much as their academic credentials.

Single-Gender Colleges

There are strong arguments that being able to pursue one's education without the distraction, competition, and stress caused by the presence of the opposite sex helps a student evolve a stronger sense of her or his self-worth, achieve more academically; have a more fulfilling, less pressured social schedule; and achieve more later in life. For various historic, social, and psychological reasons, there are many more all-women than all-men colleges. A strict single-sex environment is rare. Even though the undergraduate day college adheres to an all-female or all-male admissions policy, coeducational evening classes or graduate programs and coordinate facilities and classes shared with nearby coed or opposite-sex institutions can result in a good number of students of the opposite sex being found on campus. If you want to concentrate on your studies and hone your leadership qualities, a single-gender school is an option.

LOCATION

Location and distance from home are two other important considerations. If you have always lived in the suburbs, choosing an urban campus can be an adventure, but after a week of the urban experience, will you long for a grassy campus and open space? On the other hand, if you choose a college in a rural area, will you run screaming into the Student Center some night looking for noise, lights, and people? The location—urban, rural, or suburban—can directly affect how easy or how difficult adjusting to college life will be for you.

Don't forget to factor in distance from home. Everyone going off to college wants to think he or she won't be homesick, but sometimes it's nice to get a home-cooked meal or to do the laundry in a place that does not require quarters. Even your kid sister may seem like less of a nuisance after a couple of months away.

Here are some questions you might ask yourself as you go through the selection process: In what part of the country do I want to be? How far away from home do I want to be? What is the cost of returning home? Do I need to be close to a city? How close? How large of a city? Would city life distract me? Would I concentrate better in a setting that is more rural or more suburban?

ENTRANCE DIFFICULTY

Many students will look at a college's entrance difficulty as an indicator of whether or not they will be admitted. For instance, if you have an excellent academic record, you might wish to primarily consider those colleges that are highly competitive.

Although entrance difficulty does not translate directly to quality of education, it indicates which colleges are attracting large numbers of high-achieving students. A high-achieving student body usually translates into prestige for the college and its graduates. Prestige has some advantages but should definitely be viewed as a secondary factor that might tip the scales when all the other important factors are equal. Never base your decision on prestige alone!

The other principle to keep in mind when considering this factor is to not sell yourself short. If everything else tells you that a college might be right for you, but your numbers just miss that college's average range, apply there anyway. Your numbers—grades and test scores—are undeniably important in the admissions decision, but there are other considerations. First, lower grades in honors or AP® courses will impress colleges more than top grades in regular-track courses because they demonstrate that you are the kind of student willing to accept challenges. Second, admissions directors are looking for different qualities in students that can be combined to create a multifaceted class. For example, if you did poorly in your freshman and sophomore years but made a great improvement in your grades in later years, this usually will impress a college. If you are likely to contribute to your class because of your special personal qualities, a strong sense of commitment and purpose, unusual and valuable experiences, or special interests and talents, these factors can outweigh numbers that are weaker than average. Nevertheless, be practical. Overreach yourself in a few applications, but put the bulk of your effort into gaining admission to colleges where you have a realistic chance for admission.

THE PRICE OF AN EDUCATION

The price tag for higher education continues to rise, and it has become an increasingly important factor for people. While it is necessary to consider your family's resources when choosing a list of colleges to which you might apply, never eliminate a college solely because of cost. There are many ways to pay for college, including loans, and a college education will never depreciate in value, unlike other purchases. It is an investment in yourself and will pay back the expense many times over in your lifetime.

Surviving Standardized Tests

WHAT ARE STANDARDIZED TESTS?

Colleges and universities in the United States use tests to help evaluate applicants' readiness for admission or to place them in appropriate courses. The tests that are most frequently used by colleges are the ACT® Exam and the College Board's SAT® Exam. In addition, the Educational Testing Service (ETS) offers the TOEFL® test, which evaluates the English-language proficiency of nonnative speakers. The tests are offered at designated testing centers located at high schools and colleges throughout the United States and U.S. territories and at testing centers in various countries throughout the world.

Upon request, special accommodations for students with documented visual, hearing, physical, or learning disabilities are available. Examples of special accommodations include tests in Braille or large print and such aids as a reader, recorder, magnifying glass, or sign language interpreter. Additional testing time may be allowed in some instances. Contact the appropriate testing program or your guidance counselor for details on how to request special accommodations.

THE ACT® EXAM

The ACT® exam is a standardized college entrance examination that measures knowledge and skills in English, mathematics, reading comprehension, and science reasoning and the application of these skills to future academic tasks. The ACT® exam consists of four multiple-choice tests. The four tests and the content covered in each is as follows:

English Test (75 questions; 45 minutes)

- Usage and mechanics
- Rhetorical skills

Mathematics Test (60 questions; 60 minutes)

- Pre-algebra
- Elementary algebra
- Intermediate algebra
- Coordinate geometry
- Plane geometry
- Trigonometry

Reading Test (40 questions; 35 minutes)

- Literary narrative/Prose fiction
- Humanities
- Social studies
- Natural sciences

Science (40 questions; 35 minutes)

- Data representation
- Research summaries
- Conflicting viewpoints

Each section is scored from 1 to 36 and is scaled for slight variations in difficulty. Students are not penalized for incorrect responses. The composite score is the average of the four scaled scores. The ACT® Plus Writing includes the four multiple-choice tests and the 40-minute Writing Test, which measures writing skills emphasized in high school English classes and in entry-level college composition courses and does not count toward your final score.

To prepare for the ACT® Exam, ask your guidance counselor for a free guidebook, *Preparing for the ACT® Test*, or download it at **http://www.act.org/content/dam/act/unsecured/documents/Preparing-for-the-ACT.pdf**. Besides providing general test-preparation information and additional test-taking strategies, this guidebook provides a full-length practice exam including the Writing Test, instructions for taking the Writing Test, test-preparation strategies, and what to expect on test day.

DON'T FORGET TO . . .

- ❑ Take the SAT® Exam or ACT® Exam before application deadlines.
- ❑ Note that test registration deadlines precede test dates by about six weeks.
- ❑ Register to take the TOEFL® test if English is not your native language and you are planning on studying at a North American college.
- ❑ Contact the College Board or ACT, Inc., in advance if you need special accommodations when taking tests.

THE SAT® EXAM

The SAT® has these sections: Evidence-Based Reading and Writing, Math, and the SAT® Essay. It is based on 1600 points—the top scores for the Math section and the Evidence-Based Reading and Writing section will be 800, and the SAT® Essay score is reported separately.

Reading Test (52 questions; 65 minutes)

Passages in U.S. and world literature, history/social studies, and science are used to test the following skills:

- Command of Evidence
- Words in Context
- Analysis in History/Social Studies and in Science

Writing and Language Test (44 questions; 35 minutes)

Passages in careers, history/social studies, humanities, and science are used to test the following skills:

- Command of Evidence
- Words in Context
- Analysis in History/Social Studies and in Science
- Expression of ideas
- Standard English conventions

Math Test (58 questions; 80 minutes)

This test is divided into two sections: the no-calculator section (25 minutes) and the calculator section (55 minutes).

- Content includes algebra, problem solving and data analysis, advanced math, area and volume calculations, trigonometric functions, and lines, triangles, and circles using theorems.

SAT® Essay (Optional)

* 50 minutes

- Argument passage written for a general audience
- Analysis of argument in passage using text evidence
- Score: 3–12 (Reading: 1–4 scale, Analysis: 1–4 scale, Writing: 1–4 scale)

According to the College Board's website, the following are the "Key Content Features" of the SAT® exam:

- **Relevant Words in Context:** Students need to interpret the meaning of words based on the context of the passage in which they appear. The focus is on "relevant" words—not obscure ones.
- **Command of Evidence:** In addition to demonstrating writing skills, students need to show that they're able to interpret, synthesize, and use evidence found in a wide range of sources.
- **Essay Analyzing a Source:** Students read a passage and explain how the author builds an argument and supports their claims with actual data from the passage.
- **Math Focused on Three Key Areas:** Problem Solving and Data Analysis (using ratios, percentages, and proportional reasoning to solve problems in science, social science, and career contexts), the Heart of Algebra (mastery of linear equations and systems), and Passport to Advanced Math (more complex equations and the manipulation they require).
- **Problems Grounded in Real-World Contexts:** All of the questions are grounded in the real world, directly related to work performed in college.
- **Analysis in Science and in Social Studies:** Students need to apply reading, writing, language, and math skills to answer questions in contexts of science, history, and social studies.
- **Founding Documents and Great Global Conversation:** Students will find an excerpt from one of the Founding Documents—such as the Declaration of Independence, the Constitution, and the Bill of Rights—or a text from the "Great Global Conversation" about freedom, justice, and human dignity.
- **No Penalty for Wrong Answers:** Students earn points for the questions they answer correctly, and like the ACT® optional writing test, the optional SAT® Essay section does not count toward your final score.

Check out the College Board's website at **https://collegereadiness.collegeboard.org/sat-subject-tests/about/at-a-glance** for the most up-to-date information.

Top 10 Ways NOT to Take the Test

1. Cramming the night before the test.
2. Not becoming familiar with the directions before you take the test.
3. Not becoming familiar with the format of the test before you take it.
4. Not knowing how the test is graded.
5. Spending too much time on any one question.
6. Second-guessing yourself.
7. Not checking spelling, grammar, and sentence structure in essays.
8. Writing a one-paragraph essay.
9. Forgetting to take a deep breath—
10. and finally—Don't lose it!

SAT SUBJECT TESTS™

SAT Subject Tests™ are required by some institutions for admission and/or placement in freshman-level courses. Each Subject Test measures one's knowledge of a specific subject and the ability to apply that knowledge. Students should check with each institution for its specific requirements. In general, students are required to take three Subject Tests (one English, one mathematics, and one of their choice).

Subject Tests are given in the following areas: biology, chemistry, Chinese, French, German, Italian, Japanese, Korean, Latin, literature, mathematics, modern Hebrew, physics, Spanish, U.S. history, and world history. These tests are 1 hour long and are primarily multiple-choice tests. Three Subject Tests may be taken on one test date.

On the subject tests, students gain a point for each correct answer and lose a fraction of a point for each incorrect answer. The raw scores are then converted to scaled scores that range from 200 to 800 For more details about SAT Subject Tests™, visit **https://collegereadiness.collegeboard.org/sat-subject-tests/about/at-a-glance**.

THE TOEFL (IBT)® INTERNET-BASED TEST

The Test of English as a Foreign Language Internet-Based Test (TOEFL iBT®) is designed to help assess a student's grasp of English if it is not the student's first language. Performance on the TOEFL® test may help interpret scores on the critical reading sections of the SAT® exam. The test consists of four integrated sections: speaking, listening, reading, and writing. The TOEFL iBT® emphasizes integrated skills. The paper-based versions of the TOEFL® test will continue to be administered in certain countries where the internet-based version has not yet been introduced. For further information, visit **www.ets.org/toefl**.

WHAT OTHER TESTS SHOULD I KNOW ABOUT?

The AP® Program

The AP® program allows high school students to try college-level work and build valuable skills and study habits in the process. Subject matter is explored in more depth in AP courses than in other high school classes. A qualifying score on an AP test—which varies from school to school—can earn you college credit or advanced placement. Getting qualifying grades on enough exams can even earn you a full year's credit and sophomore standing at more than 1,500 higher-education institutions. There are more than thirty AP courses across multiple subject areas, including art history, biology, and computer science. Speak to your guidance counselor for information about your school's offerings. For more information about the AP® program, **visit www.apstudent.collegeboard.org/home**.

College-Level Examination Program (CLEP®)

The CLEP® exam enables students to earn college credit for what they already know, whether it was learned in school, through independent study, or through other experiences outside of the classroom. More than 2,900 colleges and universities now award credit for qualifying scores on one or more of the 33 CLEP exams. The exams, which are 90 minutes in length and are primarily multiple choice, are administered at participating colleges and universities. For more information, check out the website at **www.clep.collegeboard.org**.

WHAT CAN I DO TO PREPARE FOR THESE TESTS?

Know what to expect. Get familiar with how the tests are structured, how much time is allowed, and the directions for each type of question. Get plenty of rest the night before the test and eat breakfast that morning.

There are a variety of products, from books to software to videos, available to help you prepare for most standardized tests. Find the learning style that suits you best. As for which products to buy, there are two major categories—those created by the test-makers and those created by private companies. The best approach is to talk to someone who has been through the process and find out which product or products he or she recommends.

Some students report significant increases in scores after participating in coaching programs. Longer-term programs (40 hours) seem to raise scores more than short-term programs (20 hours), but beyond 40 hours, score gains are minor. Math scores appear to benefit more from coaching than critical reading scores.

Resources

There is a variety of ways to prepare for standardized tests—find a method that fits your schedule and your budget—but you should definitely prepare. Far too many students walk into these tests cold, either because they find standardized tests frightening or annoying or they just haven't found the time to study. The key is that these exams are standardized. That means these tests are largely the same from administration to administration; they always test the same concepts. They have to, or else you couldn't compare the scores of people who took the tests on different dates. The numbers or words may change, but the underlying content doesn't.

So how do you prepare? At the very least, you should review relevant material, such as math formulas and commonly used vocabulary words, and know the directions for each question type or test section. You should take at least one practice test and review your mistakes so you don't make them again on the test day. Beyond that, you know best how much preparation you need. You'll also find lots of material in libraries or bookstores to help you: books and software from the test-makers and from other publishers (including Peterson's) or live courses that range from national test-preparation companies to teachers at your high school who offer classes.

Planning is Essential on the Road to College

Sarah E. Gibbs, Director of Admissions
Grove City College

The road to college is much like an expedition. It can appear overwhelming, exciting, and at times too far away to be tangible. However, much like planning a trip out of town or across the globe, there is preparation involved, and it is always best to start that planning early. First, you must figure out where you want to go, then how you want to get there, and finally, what you want to do once you arrive. Each decision will require a different route—a route that may or may not look the same as that of your friends.

The same is true when considering college planning. If you start early—making short-term and long-term goals—it will help you determine your next steps. For instance, if you start your freshman year determining you want to graduate with a certain GPA, that decision will dictate your next steps, like studying, choosing to take harder curriculum, and prioritizing your involvement in activities.

Once you establish your short-term and long-term goals, you need to make wise decisions about those goals. For instance, if you do not do well in a certain class, don't make a rash decision to withdraw from that subject area. You may want to continue in that subject knowing that you may need to seek out help or tutors to help you achieve your goal.

In addition to thinking through your academic goals, you must also consider your personal interests and activities. Your interests may determine the type of college you would like to attend. Decide early on what your passion(s) are, and invest your time wisely in those pursuits. If you know those activities are ones you want to pursue in college, then visit college campuses that fulfill your desire to march in the band, compete in a varsity or intramural sport, or participate in a service organization.

Ask yourself the question that most students do not: Am I ready for college? If the answer is no, then ask yourself what you need to do to be ready, and work towards that goal.

When looking at applicants, most private colleges will look holistically at the student, taking into consideration his or her commitment, dedication, and character. These attributes, along with academic performance and specific major pursuit, indicate whether the student may succeed at a campus. Also, make sure you participate in any interview process through an admissions office. Interviewing with an Admission Counselor allows him/her to get to know you and become your advocate.

Ultimately, the sooner you start planning, the better prepared you will be for the journey you are about to take. Not only will you be prepared for the college planning process, you will be well equipped for attending college and achieving your goals and dreams for a successful future.

Sarah E. Gibbs has been serving families in higher education for several decades. She is currently the Director of Admissions at Grove City College in Grove City, Pennsylvania.

The Whys and Whats of College Visits

Dawn B. Sova, Ph.D.

The campus visit should not be a passive activity for you and your parents. Take the initiative and gather information beyond that provided in the official tour. You will see many important indicators during your visit that will tell you more about the true character of a college and its students than the tour guide will reveal. Know what to look for and how to assess the importance of such indicators.

WHAT SHOULD YOU ASK AND WHAT SHOULD YOU LOOK FOR?

Your first stop on a campus visit is the visitor center or admissions office, where you will probably have to wait to meet with a counselor. Colleges usually plan to greet visitors later than the appointed time in order to give them the opportunity to review some of the campus information that is liberally scattered throughout the visitor waiting room. Take advantage of the time to become even more familiar with the college by arriving 15 to 30 minutes before your appointment to observe the behavior of staff members and to browse through the yearbooks and student newspapers that will be available.

If you prepare in advance, you will have already reviewed the college catalog and map of the campus. These materials familiarize you with the academic offerings and the physical layout of the campus, but the true character of the college and its students emerges in other ways.

Begin your investigation with the visitor center staff members. As a student's first official contact with the college, they should make every effort to welcome prospective students and project a friendly image.

- How do they treat you and other prospective students who are waiting? Are they friendly and willing to speak with you, or do they try their hardest to avoid eye contact and conversation?
- Are they friendly with each other and with students who enter the office, or are they curt and unwilling to help?
- Does the waiting room have a friendly feeling or is it cold and sterile?

If the visitor center staff members seem indifferent to prospective students, there is little reason to believe that they will be warm and welcoming to current students. View such behavior as a warning to watch very carefully the interaction of others with you during the tour. An indifferent or unfriendly reception in the admissions office may be simply the first of many signs that attending this college will not be a pleasant experience.

Look through several yearbooks and see the types of activities that are actually photographed, as opposed to the activities that colleges promise in their promotional literature. Some questions are impossible to answer if the college is very large, but for small and moderately sized colleges the yearbook is a good indicator of campus activity.

- Has the number of clubs and organizations increased or decreased in the past five years?
- Do the same students appear repeatedly in activities?
- Do sororities and fraternities dominate campus activities?
- Are participants limited to one sex or one ethnic group, or is there diversity?
- Are all activities limited to the campus, or are students involved in activities in the community?

Use what you observe in the yearbooks as a means of forming a more complete understanding of the college, but don't base your entire impression on just one facet. If time permits, look through several copies of the school newspaper, which should reflect the major concerns and interests of the students. The paper is also a good way to learn about the campus social life.

- Does the paper contain a mix of national and local news?
- What products or services are advertised?
- How assertive are the editorials?
- With what topics are the columnists concerned?
- Are movies and concerts that meet your tastes advertised or reviewed?
- What types of ads appear in the classified section?

The newspaper should be a public forum for students, and, as such, should reflect the character of the campus and of the student body. A paper that deals only with seemingly safe and well-edited topics on the editorial page and in regular feature columns might indicate administrative censorship. A lack of ads for restaurants might indicate either a lack of good places to eat or that area restaurants do not welcome student business. A limited mention of movies, concerts, or other entertainment might reveal a severely limited campus social life. Even if ads and reviews are included, you should still balance how such activities reflect your tastes.

You will have only a limited amount of time to ask questions during your initial meeting with the admissions counselor, for very few schools include a formal interview in the initial campus visit or tour. Instead, this brief meeting is often just a nicety that allows the admissions office to begin a file for the student and to record some initial impressions. Save your questions for the tour guide and for students on campus you meet along the way.

HOW CAN YOU ASSESS THE TRUE CHARACTER OF A COLLEGE AND ITS STUDENTS?

Colleges do not train their tour guides to deceive prospective students, but they do caution guides to avoid unflattering topics and campus sites. Does this mean that you will see only a sugarcoated version of life on a particular college campus? Not at all, especially not if you are observant.

Most organized campus visits include such campus facilities as dormitories, dining halls, libraries, student activity and recreation centers, and the health and student services centers. Some may only be pointed out, while you will walk through others. Either way, you will find that many signs of the true character of the college emerge if you keep your eyes open.

Bulletin boards in dormitories and student centers contain a wealth of information about campus activities, student concerns, and campus groups. Read the posters, notices, and messages to learn what *really* interests students. Unlike ads in the school newspaper, posters put up by students advertise both on-and off-campus events, so they will give you an idea of what is also available in the surrounding community.

Review the notices, which may cover either campus-wide events or events that concern only small groups of students. The catalog may not mention a performance group, but an individual dormitory with its own small theater may offer regular productions. Poetry readings, jam sessions, writers' groups, and other activities may be announced and show diversity of student interests.

Even the brief bulletin board messages offering objects for sale and noting objects that people want to purchase reveal a lot about a campus. Are most of the items computer-related? Or do the messages specify audio equipment or musical instruments? Are offers to trade goods or services posted? Don't ignore the "ride wanted" messages. Students who want to share rides home during a break may specify widely diverse geographical locations. If so, then you know that the student body is not limited to only the immediate area or one locale. Other messages can also enhance your knowledge of the true character of the campus and its students.

As you walk through various buildings, examine their condition carefully.

- Is the paint peeling, and do the exteriors look worn?
- Are the exteriors and interiors of the building clean?
- Is the equipment in the classrooms up-to-date or outdated?

Pay particular attention to the residence halls, especially to factors that might affect your safety. Observe the appearance of the structure and ask about the security measures in and around the residence halls.

- Are the residence halls noisy or quiet?
- Do they seem crowded?
- How good is the lighting around each residence hall?
- Are the residence halls spread throughout the campus or are they clustered in one main area?
- Who has access to the residence halls in addition to students?
- How secure are the means by which students enter and leave the residence hall?

While you are on the subject of dormitory safety, you should also ask about campus safety. Don't expect that the guide will rattle off a list of crimes that have been committed in the past year. To obtain that information, access the recent year of issues of *The Chronicle of Higher Education* and locate its yearly report on campus crime. Also ask the guide about safety measures that the campus police take and those that students have initiated.

- Can students request escorts to their residences late at night?
- Do campus shuttle buses run at frequent intervals all night?
- Are "blue-light" telephones liberally placed throughout the campus for students to use to call for help?
- Do the campus police patrol the campus regularly?

If the guide does not answer your questions satisfactorily, wait until after the tour to contact the campus police or traffic office for answers.

Campus tours usually just point out the health services center without taking the time to walk through. Even if you don't see the inside of the building, you should take a close look at the location of the health services center and ask the guide questions about services.

- How far is the health center from the residence halls?
- Is a doctor always on call?
- Does the campus transport sick students from their dormitories or must they walk?
- What are the operating hours of the health center?
- Does the health center refer students to a nearby hospital?

If the guide can't answer your questions, visit the health center later and ask someone there.

Most campus tours take pride in showing students their activities centers, which may contain snack bars, game rooms, workout facilities, and other means of entertainment. Should you scrutinize this building as carefully as the rest? Of course. Outdated and poorly maintained activity equipment contributes to your total impression of the college. You should also ask about the hours, availability, and cost (no, the activities are usually not free) of using the bowling alleys, pool tables, air hockey tables, and other amenities.

As you walk through campus with the tour, also look carefully at the appearance of the students who pass. The way in which both men and women groom themselves, the way they dress, and even their physical bearing communicate a lot more than any guidebook can. If everyone seems to conform to the same look, you might feel that you would be uncomfortable at the college, however nonconformist that look might be. On the other hand, you might not feel comfortable on a campus that stresses diversity of dress and behavior, and your observations now can save you discomfort later.

- Does every student seem to wear a sorority or fraternity t-shirt or jacket?
- Is everyone of your sex sporting the latest fad haircut?
- Do all of the men or the women seem to be wearing expensive name-brand clothes?
- Do most of the students seem to be working hard to look outrageous with regards to clothing, hair color, and body art?
- Would you feel uncomfortable in a room full of these students?

Is appearance important to you? If it is, then you should consider very seriously if you answer *yes* to any of the questions above. You don't have to be the same as everyone else on campus, but standing out too much may make you unhappy.

As you observe the physical appearance of the students, also listen to their conversations as you pass them. What are they talking about? How are they speaking? Are their voices and accents all the same, or do you hear diversity in their speech? Are you offended by their language? Think how you will feel if surrounded by the same speech habits and patterns for four years.

WHERE SHOULD YOU VISIT ON YOUR OWN?

Your campus visit is not over when the tour ends because you will probably have many questions yet to be answered and many places to still be seen. Where you go depends upon the extent to which the organized tour covers the campus. Your tour should take you to view residential halls, health and student services centers, the gymnasium or field house, dining halls, the library, and recreational centers. If any of the facilities on this list have been omitted, visit them on your own and ask questions of the students and staff members you meet. In addition, you should step off campus and gain an impression of the surrounding community. You will probably become bored with life on campus and spend at least some time off campus. Make certain that you know what the surrounding area is like.

The campus tour leaves little time to ask impromptu questions of current students, but you can do so after the tour. Eat lunch in one of the dining halls. Most will allow visitors to pay cash to experience a typical student meal. Food may not be important to you now while you are living at home and can simply take anything you want from the refrigerator at any time, but it will be when you are away at college with only a meal ticket to feed you.

- How clean is the dining hall? Consider serving tables, floors, and seating.
- What is the quality of the food?
- How big are the portions?
- How much variety do students have at each meal?
- How healthy are the food choices?

While you are eating, try to strike up a conversation with students and tell them that you are considering attending their college. Their reactions and advice can be eye-opening. Ask them questions about the academic atmosphere and the professors.

- Are the classes large or small?
- Do the majority of the professors only lecture or are tutorials and seminars common?
- Is the emphasis of the faculty career-oriented or abstract?
- Are the teaching methods innovative and stimulating or boring and dull?
- Is the academic atmosphere pressured, lax, or somewhere in between?
- Which are the strong majors? The weak majors?
- Is the emphasis on grades or social life or a mix of both at the college?
- How hard do students have to work to receive high grades?

Current students can also give you the inside line on the true nature of the college social life. You may gain some idea through looking in the yearbook, in the newspaper, and on the bulletin boards, but students will reveal the true highs and lows of campus life. Ask them about drug use, partying, dating, drinking, and anything else that may affect your life as a student.

- Which are the most popular club activities?
- What do students do on weekends? Do most go home?
- How frequently do concerts occur on campus? Who has recently performed?
- How can you become involved in specific activities (name them)?
- How strictly are campus rules enforced and how severe are penalties?
- What counseling services are available?
- Are academic tutoring services available?
- Do they feel that the faculty really cares about students, especially freshmen?

You will receive the most valuable information from current students, but you will only be able to speak with them after the tour is over. And you might have to risk rejection as you try to initiate conversations with students who might not want to reveal how they feel about the campus. Still, the value of this information is worth the chance.

If you have the time, you should also visit the library to see just how accessible research materials are and to observe the physical layout. The catalog usually specifies the days and hours of operation, as well as the number of volumes contained in the library and the number of periodicals to which it subscribes. A library also requires accessibility, good lighting, an adequate number of study carrels, and lounge areas for students. Many colleges have created 24-hour study lounges for students who find the residence halls too noisy for studying, although most colleges claim that they designate areas of the residences as "quiet study" areas. You may not be interested in any of this information, but when you are a student you will have to make frequent use of the campus library so you should know what is available. You should at least ask how extensive their holdings are in your proposed major area. If they have virtually nothing, you will have to spend a lot of time ordering items via interlibrary loan or making copies, which can become expensive. The ready answer of students that they will obtain their information from the internet is unpleasantly countered by professors who demand journal articles with documentation.

Make a point of at least driving through the community surrounding the college because you will be spending time there shopping, dining, working in a part-time job, or attending events. Even the largest and best-stocked campus will not meet all of your social and personal needs. If you can spare the time, stop in several stores to see if they welcome college students.

- Is the surrounding community suburban, urban, or rural?
- Does the community offer stores of interest, such as bookstores, craft shops, and boutiques?
- Do the businesses employ college students?
- Does the community have a movie or stage theater?
- Are there several types of interesting restaurants?
- Do there seem to be any clubs that court a college clientele?
- Is the center of activity easy to walk to, or do you need other transportation?

You might feel that a day is not enough to answer all of your questions, but even answering some questions will provide you with a stronger basis for choosing a college. Many students visit a college campus several times before making their decision. Keep in mind that for the rest of your life you will be associated with the college that you attend. You will spend four years of your life at this college. The effort of spending several days to obtain the information to make your decision is worthwhile.

Dawn B. Sova, Ph.D., is a former newspaper reporter and columnist, as well as the author of 22 books and numerous magazine articles. She teaches creative and research writing, as well as scientific and technical writing, newswriting, and journalism.

Honors Programs and Colleges: Smart Choices for an Undergraduate Education

Dr. Joan Digby

In general, students and their parents are guided toward a narrow selection of colleges and universities based on reputation, conversations with friends, or promotional material. Few people think to approach the college search focused on honors opportunities. As a result, students with extraordinary talents and interests miss out on a rich variety of untapped financial resources and exciting college experiences.

The smarter approach is to seek out a distinctive education that caters to students' great diversity of intellectual and creative strengths. If you are a strong student filled with ideas, longing for creative expression and ready to take on career-shaping challenges, then an honors education is just for you. Honors programs and colleges offer some of the finest undergraduate degrees available at U.S. colleges and do it with students in mind. The essence of honors is personal attention, top faculty, enlightening seminars, illuminating study-travel experiences, research options, and career-building internships—all designed to enhance a classic education and prepare you for life achievements. And here is an eye-opening bonus: Honors programs and colleges may reward your past academic performance by giving you scholarships that will help you pay for your higher education!

Take your choice of institutions: community college, state or private, two- or four-year, college or large research university. There are honors opportunities in each. What they share is an unqualified commitment to academic excellence. Honors education teaches students to think and write clearly, be excited by ideas, and become independent, creative, self-confident learners. It prepares exceptional students for professional choices in every imaginable sphere of life: arts and sciences, engineering, business, health, education, medicine, theater, music, film, journalism, media, law, politics—invent your own professional goal and honors will guide you to it! Whichever honors program or college you choose, you can be sure to enjoy an extraordinarily fulfilling undergraduate education.

WHO ARE HONORS STUDENTS?

Who are you? Perhaps a high school junior filling out your first college application, a community college student seeking to transfer to a four-year college, or possibly a four-year college student doing better than you had expected. You might be an international student, a varsity athlete, captain of the debate team, or second violin in the orchestra. Whether you are the first person in your family to attend college or an adult with a grown family seeking a new career, honors might well be right for you. Honors programs admit students with every imaginable background and educational goal.

How does honors satisfy students and give them something special? Read what students in some honors programs and colleges say. Although they refer to particular honors colleges or programs, their experiences are typical of what students find exciting about honors education on hundreds of campuses around the country.

> "Being an honors program student has been a life-changing experience for me. I have gained tremendously in knowledge, experience, and self-esteem. I have learned so much more in the program than any textbook could teach about the value of encouraging support and positive thinking."
>
> *—Cheri, Mount Wachusett Community College*

> "I've been in a healing ceremony in Ecuador and have performed music on stage. I've guided my peers and Navajo children, hiked the Grand Canyon, and so much more. Sometimes, experience speaks for itself; always, it creates paths, opens eyes, and helps us find our places. Thanks to my honors program, I've experienced these wonders and accomplishments. Now I know that there are no greater lessons than how to learn and love discovery."
>
> *—April, University of North Florida*

> "The Honors College has been my home away from home. In the midst of a diverse, fairly large university, it has provided me with the intimacy that I needed... My freshman-year living situation on the honors floor... allowed me to find like-minded students early in my college career."
>
> *—Brian, Davidson Honors College, University of Montana*

"I was able to transition from an honors program at a two-year institution into an honors program at a four-year institution without any reservations or tribulations."

—Rachel, Harrisburg Area Community College

"Every single professor is in love with what they do and it shows in their research, their amazing teaching, and their interaction with students outside of the classroom. The undergraduate journey can be very difficult at times, but as an Honors College student, you're sure to have plenty of support every step of the way."

—Walteria, Wilkes Honors College, Florida Atlantic University

"The class size is perfect, and I've been able to make some of my closest relationships with students and teachers through the program. The majority of honors faculty I have encountered have been overwhelmingly helpful... and my favorite courses have been honors classes."

—Ellen, Eastern Illinois University

"Our professor met us at a local restaurant the last evening of class, and we shared a wonderful dinner. It had such a familiar feel to it because these are students I have known throughout my four years in the program."

—Betsy, University of La Verne

"For the last two years, I have investigated new synthetic methods under the direction of a professor emeritus. Through the University Honors College, I am able to pursue this interest in chemistry and other academic endeavors... that have allowed me to develop my academic potential and contribute to the scientific body of knowledge."

—Justin, University of Pittsburgh

"The most rewarding part of being a member of the honors program is the joy of doing creative, meaningful projects with faculty I love."

—Meleia, Hartwick College

"I would... like to add a word of praise for the way the curriculum is structured. It has deepened and enriched my thinking and helped me develop tools to negotiate the complex world we live in."

—Monideepa, Southeastern Louisiana University

"We have a better time... our discussions get rather heated. In a lot of classes, only one or two students will speak up, but in the honors classes, it's a free-for-all."

—Jonathan, Reinhardt College

"My internship at a major international bank gave me an in-depth look into the world of investment and accounting. Funded by the Honors College, I was able to study business and culture in Shanghai, China, for a month. These valuable experiences are helping me to develop professionally, academically, and personally."

—Jenny, Honors College, The College of Staten Island, CUNY

"The honors thesis was the key factor during the selection process at my future employer.... It helped me to get the job and have an advantage over others. It is a lot of work but, in the end, it is worth it."

—Olgierd, Lee Honors College, Western Michigan University

These portraits don't tell the whole story, but they should give you a sense of what it means to be part of an honors program or college. One of the great strengths of honors programs and colleges is that they are nurturing environments that encourage students to be well-rounded and help students make life choices.

WHAT IS AN HONORS PROGRAM?

An honors program is a sequence of courses designed specifically to encourage independent and creative learning. For more than half a century, honors education—given definition by the National Collegiate Honors Council—has been an institution on U.S. campuses. Although honors programs have many different designs, there are typical components. At two-year colleges, the programs often concentrate on special versions of general education courses and may have individual capstone projects that come out of students' special interests. At four-year colleges and universities, honors programs are generally designed for students of almost every major in every college on campus. In growing numbers, they are given additional prominence as honors colleges. Whether a program or a college, honors often includes a general education or "core" component followed by advanced courses (often called colloquia or seminars). Some programs have honors contracts that shape existing courses into honors components to suit the needs of individual students. Many have interdisciplinary or collaborative seminars that bring students of different majors together to discuss a complex topic with faculty members from different disciplines. A good number have final thesis, capstone, or creative projects, which may or may not be in the departmental major. Almost always, honors curriculum is incorporated within whatever number of credits is required of every student for graduation. Honors very rarely requires students to take additional credits. Students who complete an honors program or honors college curriculum frequently receive transcript and diploma notations as well as certificates, medallions, or other citations at graduation ceremonies.

In every case, catering to the student as an individual plays a central role in honors course design. Most honors classes are small (fewer than 20 students); most are discussion-oriented, giving students a chance to present their own interpretations of ideas and even teach a part of the course. Many classes are interdisciplinary, which means they are taught by faculty members from two or more departments, providing different perspectives on a subject. All honors classes help students develop and articulate their own perspectives by cultivating both verbal and written style. They help students mature intellectually, preparing them to engage in their own explorations and research. Some programs even extend the options for self-growth to study abroad and internships in science, government, the arts, or business related to the major. Other programs encourage or require community service as part of the honors experience. In every case, honors is an experiential education that deepens classroom learning and extends far beyond.

Despite their individual differences, all honors programs and honors colleges rely on faculty members who enjoy working with bright, independent students. The ideal honors faculty members are open-minded, encouraging master teachers. They want to see their students achieve at their highest capacity and are glad to spend time with students in discussions and laboratories, on field trips and at conferences, or online in e-mail. They often influence career decisions, are inspiring role models, and remain friends long after they have served as thesis advisers.

WHERE ARE HONORS PROGRAMS AND HONORS COLLEGES LOCATED?

Because honors programs and honors colleges include students from many different departments or colleges, they usually have their own offices and space on campus. Some have their own buildings. Most programs have honors centers or lounges, where students gather together for informal conversations, luncheons, discussions, lectures, and special projects.

Many honors students have cultivated strong personal interests that have nothing to do with classes. They may be multilingual; they may be fine artists or poets, musicians or racing car enthusiasts, mothers or fathers. Some volunteer in hospitals or do landscape gardening to pay for college. Many work in retail stores and in catering. Some are avid sports enthusiasts, while others collect antiques. When they get together in honors lounges, there is always an interesting mixture of ideas!

In the honors center, you will also find the honors director or dean. The honors director often serves as a personal adviser to all of the students in the program. Many programs also have peer counselors and mentors who are upperclass honors students and know the ropes from a student's perspective and experience. Some have specially assigned honors advisers who guide honors students through their degrees, assist in registration, and answer every imaginable question. The honors office area usually is a good place to meet people, ask questions, and solve problems.

In general, honors provides an environment in which students feel free to talk about their passionate interests and ideas knowing that they will find good listeners and, sometimes, even arguers. There is no end to conversations among honors students. Like many students in honors, you may feel a great relief in finding a sympathetic group that respects your intelligence and creativity. In honors, you can be eccentric; you can be yourself! Some lifelong friendships, even marriages, are the result of social relationships developed in honors programs.

ARE YOU READY FOR HONORS?

Admission to honors programs and honors colleges is generally based on a combination of several factors: high school or previous college grades, experience taking AP or IB courses, SAT or ACT scores, personal essay, and extracurricular achievements. To stay in honors, students need to maintain a certain grade point average (GPA) and show progress toward the completion of the specific honors program or college requirements. Since you have probably exceeded admissions standards all along, maintaining your GPA will not be as big a problem as it sounds. Your professors and your honors director are there to help you succeed in the program. Most honors programs have very low attrition rates because students enjoy classes and do well.

Of course, you must be careful about how you budget your time for studying. Honors encourages well-rounded, diversified students, so you should play a sport, work at the radio station, join clubs of interest, or pledge a sorority or fraternity. You might find a job in the student center or library that will help you pay for your car expenses and that also is reasonable. But remember, each activity takes time, and you must strike the balance that leaves you enough time to do your homework, write papers, prepare for seminar discussions, do your research, and do well on exams. Choose the jobs and activities that attract you, but never let them overshadow your primary purpose—which is to be a student.

Sometimes even the very best students who apply for admission into an honors program or college are frightened by the thought of speaking in front of a group, giving seminar papers, or writing a thesis. But if you understand how the programs work, you will see that there is nothing to fear. The basis of honors is confidence in the student and building the student's self-confidence. Admittance to an honors program means you have already demonstrated your academic achievement in high school or college classes. Once in the honors environment, you learn how to formulate and structure ideas so that you can apply critical judgment to sets of facts and opinions. In small seminar classes, you practice discussion and arguments, so by the time you come to the senior thesis or project, the method is second nature. For most honors students, the senior thesis, performance, or portfolio presentation is the project that gives them the greatest fulfillment and pride. In many honors programs and colleges, students present their work either to other students or to faculty members in their major departments. Students often present their work at regional and national honors conferences. Some students even publish their work jointly with their faculty mentors. These are great achievements, and they come naturally with the training. There is nothing to fear. Honors will prepare you for life.

Dr. Joan Digby is Director of the Honors Program and Professor of English at Long Island University, C.W. Post Campus. She was also President of the National Collegiate Honors Council from 1999 to 2000, and she received NCHC's prestigious Founders Award in 2018.

Public and Private Colleges and Universities—How to Choose

Debra Humphreys

As you survey the thousands of four-year colleges in the country and weigh the options before you, it is important to be aware of how colleges differ and what kind of educational experience each college offers you. In every state in the country, you will find both public and private colleges and universities. What are the differences between public and private colleges, and how should you approach the decision to attend one or the other? What are some common misconceptions regarding both public and private colleges that you should know about before you eliminate an entire category of institution from your list of prospective schools?

WHAT ARE THE BASIC CHARACTERISTICS OF PUBLIC AND PRIVATE INSTITUTIONS?

Over the course of the nation's history, what began as a small group of mostly church-affiliated colleges has grown in both size and complexity. Over the years, education in the United States became increasingly democratized, and more and more state-sponsored institutions and state systems of higher education emerged. These included small colleges, sometimes called "normal schools," designed to train school teachers for the expanding public school system; land-grant colleges and universities brought into existence with federal support in the mid-nineteenth century in order to prepare workers to expand the nation's agricultural and technological capacity; and large state systems that evolved in the twentieth century and now include two-year colleges, basic four-year institutions, and large research universities, all supported at least in part by state revenues.

While there are some clear distinctions to be made, even some of the core characteristics of public and private colleges vary from state to state. In general, a public institution receives at least part of its operating budget from state tax revenues, operates with a mandate and mission from the state where it is located, and is accountable to the elected officials of that state. Most private colleges and universities are independent, not-for-profit institutions. They operate with revenues from tuition; income from endowments; private gifts and bequests; and federal, private, or corporate foundation grants. These institutions are primarily accountable to a board of trustees, usually made up of local or national business and community leaders and esteemed alumni.

There are also a small but growing number of for-profit colleges whose operating revenues include tuition dollars but also might include investor financing. Some of these colleges are owned and operated by publicly traded corporations. Most of the following generalizations about private institutions however refer to the more familiar not-for-profit independent college previously described.

While the distinction between public and private institutions might seem clear at first, these two kinds of colleges and universities actually share many characteristics. All accredited colleges and universities in the country—whether public or private, for profit or not—are entitled to receive public funds from the federal government in the form of direct grants and loans for eligible students, support for student work-study programs, and competitive grants to support research or campus programs. In exchange for this federal support, all schools undergo a peer-reviewed accreditation process by a regional accreditor authorized by the federal government's Department of Education.

Whether a college is public or private, you should know if it is accredited and therefore an institution whose students are eligible for all available federal financial aid. Accreditation status also provides you with assurance that the school operates in a fiscally responsible manner and that its academic programs have been deemed sound by an outside group of educators from its peer institutions.

HOW ARE PUBLIC AND PRIVATE COLLEGES AND UNIVERSITIES RUN?

In many ways, your experience as a student will not differ significantly based on what type of governance system a college or university uses. However, some knowledge of this might be useful in making choices among the various options. Private colleges and universities tend to have more independence and autonomy in how they are run, with boards of trustees that oversee financial and other programs and life on campus at these schools. Public colleges and universities often have more complex governing structures with boards of regents or other types of oversight committees made up of politically appointed or elected officials exercising more or less oversight and intrusion into their day-to-day operations. New York, for instance, has a board of regents that oversees the system's campuses and is more actively involved in reviewing and revising curricular requirements that apply to institutions throughout the system. Other states have multiple public colleges, each with its own board overseeing each campus' operations with more or less intrusion into day-to-day operations.

Whether an institution is public or private, you will want to ask lots of questions about campus climate and academic programs in order to help you determine if a school is right for you. Being aware of some facts about public and private institutions will help you frame these questions to get truly useful answers.

ARE ALL PUBLIC COLLEGES AND UNIVERSITIES BIG AND IMPERSONAL?

Like private institutions, public colleges come in all shapes and sizes. Some are large institutions offering multiple degrees and majors to both undergraduate and graduate students alike. These institutions offer students many curricular options as well as access to leading scholars and an environment where cutting-edge academic research is conducted. While an institution of this size and scope might seem intimidating at first, remember that there are large institutions that do take very seriously their undergraduate programs. While you may receive less customized attention at a larger institution, many large public and private research universities offer options such as smaller honors programs, academic learning communities with smaller cohorts of students, or theme residence halls that can minimize the potential that you will get lost in the crowd.

If you are considering a large research institution—whether it is public or private—you should ask questions about the undergraduate program. What is the student-faculty ratio for undergraduates? What is the average class size, especially for introductory first-year courses? How many courses are taught by graduate students, and what sort of teacher training do those students receive? Are there opportunities for undergraduate students to participate in research projects with university faculty members?

In addition to the large, public research universities, there are many other smaller, state-funded regional institutions that still offer a wide range of both liberal arts and sciences fields as well as professional fields of study. Many states also offer small, public liberal arts colleges that share many of the defining characteristics of traditional, private liberal arts colleges. In 1987, some of these institutions formed the Council of Public Liberal Arts Colleges (COPLAC). COPLAC schools pride themselves on providing students of high ability and from all backgrounds access to a quality liberal education. These colleges and universities have been nationally recognized as outstanding in many ways. They offer small classes, innovations in teaching, personal interactions with faculty members, opportunities for faculty-supervised research, and supportive atmospheres. Most of them are located on campuses in rural or small-town settings. In addition to offering rigorous and well-integrated undergraduate programs, these institutions often charge far less tuition than many private colleges do. More information can be found at www.coplac.org.

These public liberal arts colleges, along with more traditional private liberal arts institutions, do offer unique learning environments that research suggests often lead to higher levels of student achievement. Liberal arts colleges tend to offer a high degree of student-faculty interaction, high levels of student engagement with both in-class and out-of-class experiences, and lots of opportunities for collaborative and innovative learning practices. Businesses are also increasingly asking for exactly the set of skills and capacities that a liberal education provides, whether offered in a traditional liberal arts college setting or within a larger university that grants degrees in both liberal arts and other fields. Many public liberal arts and more comprehensive colleges and universities also now offer students a rigorous liberal education while integrating liberal learning into professional degree programs, for instance in health sciences, engineering, or education.

ARE PUBLIC COLLEGES CHEAPER THAN PRIVATE COLLEGES?

The cost of college is not easy to calculate and is not limited simply to the advertised price of tuition. It is absolutely not the case that attending a public college will always cost a student less money than attending a private institution. It is true that the basic tuition for in-state or out-of-state students attending public colleges is on average less expensive than the advertised tuition rate at private institutions. It is very important, however, to note that many private colleges and universities offer significant amounts of financial aid—often beyond the basic federal loans and grants available to all students. Many, but not all, private colleges have large endowments that allow them to effectively discount the standard, published tuition rates for a great number of their students. The National Association of College and University Business Officers sampled a small group of private colleges and discovered that only 10 percent of entering students were paying the full, advertised tuition. Ninety percent of their students received price discounts in the form of scholarships or financial aid. In other words, don't write off a college simply because its tuition looks extremely high relative to other institutions.

Both private and public institutions, however, have been fiscally stressed in recent years because of declining values of stock portfolios in endowments or because of declining state revenues. It is safe to say that for many students in the coming years, it will become increasingly difficult to get large amounts of financial aid. Many institutions, however, remain committed to widening access to more students from less economically privileged backgrounds. In addition, students demonstrating high levels of academic achievement are being rewarded at both private and public institutions—both in terms of admission and financial aid.

It is important to look carefully at the tuition and the financial aid requirements and availability at each school you are considering, private or public. In-state and out-of-state tuitions and the difference between them varies substantially from state to state. Out-of-state tuition also varies from state to state but still tends to be lower than average private tuition levels.

Policies vary as well for determining state residency status. In many states, the policy for dependent students requires that their parents must have lived in the state for at least twelve months prior to attendance in order to qualify for in-state tuition. For independent students, the requirement of twelve months residence prior to enrollment applies to the student. Independent status must be verified and generally entails proof that a student receives no support from parents or other relatives living in or out of the state in question. As budgets have increasingly tightened, states have over the past several years made it increasingly difficult to establish in-state residence after matriculating at a school. Exceptions are sometimes made, however, for students from migrant, refugee, or military families.

IS IT EASIER TO GAIN ADMISSION TO A PUBLIC INSTITUTION ESPECIALLY AS A STATE RESIDENT?

Few public colleges and universities automatically admit students who graduate from a public high school in their state. Many, however, give preference in admissions and financial assistance to in-state residents. Moreover, some states have implemented policies that guarantee admission to at least one of the state's public institutions for all students graduating in a top percentage of their high school classes.

There are, indeed, more highly selective private than public institutions. Many public colleges and universities, however, do admit very few applicants. These highly selective institutions might draw their students from a national pool of applicants and can be among the most selective in the country. However, the national universities and liberal arts colleges with the lowest acceptance rates in the country are mostly all private institutions.

While some public institutions offer virtually open admissions to state residents, it is important for all prospective students to realize that even an open-admission institution will require incoming students to meet certain academic standards before being admitted to credit-bearing courses. In most cases, public and private institutions give incoming students a series of placement exams that determines at what level the student can begin his or her course work. Depending on the results of these exams, a student may be required to take and pass one or more remedial courses before being admitted to courses that will actually count towards a degree.

Since each state's requirements are different and shift often, you should not assume that, regardless of your academic background, admission is automatic to your local state college. In the current climate—with costs rising and competition across systems tightening—admission rates are dropping at many public institutions.

IS THE CLIMATE ON A PUBLIC COLLEGE CAMPUS SIGNIFICANTLY DIFFERENT THAN THAT ON A PRIVATE COLLEGE CAMPUS?

The social and academic climate at colleges and universities varies substantially, and public institutions do not necessarily offer a distinctively different climate than private institutions do. You can find, at some public institutions, the small, residential environment traditionally associated with private liberal arts colleges. You will also find the presence of fraternities and sororities at both public and private institutions. You should look carefully at whether a school in which you are interested has fraternities and sororities and how much influence the Greek system has on college life. At some institutions, fraternities and sororities dominate the entire social life of the campus.

One campus environment that can only be found at a private institution is a highly religious environment. Many early colleges and universities were founded by churches or religious orders. Some of these institutions no longer retain a strong affiliation with one church or denomination. Others do retain a strong affiliation, and church traditions can heavily influence the climate of these institutions. Usually, these campuses will admit a student from any religious background, but they may require students to attend chapel services and/or take religion or theology courses to graduate. In addition, some college missions and curricula are influenced by their religious affiliations. For instance, many Catholic institutions have a strong commitment to community service and social justice. Students may find, at these institutions, curricula related to social justice issues and requirements that they complete a community-service learning activity or course to graduate. Institutions with a strong mission are also often able to develop more coherent, cohesive, and innovative curricula for their students.

Finally, other important climate factors to consider include whether a college or university is in an urban or rural setting; what the diversity of the student body is in terms of geographic, religious, or racial/ethnic background; if most students live on campus or commute from home; and finally if the college dominates the life of the community in which it is located. Each of these options has advantages and disadvantages you will want to weigh in making your decisions.

ARE PRIVATE COLLEGES MORE ACADEMICALLY RIGOROUS THAN PUBLIC COLLEGES?

Private colleges and universities are not necessarily more academically rigorous than public institutions. You will find rigorous, intellectually challenging, and innovative academic programs at both private and public institutions. There is also a common misconception that schools that are more highly selective have the most effective or engaging academic programs. Research suggests that there is no connection between the selectivity of an institution and the presence of effective or innovative teaching and learning practices. There is, however, preliminary research that suggests that the academic quality of

Questions to Ask as You Evaluate Prospective Colleges and Universities

- Does the college offer a distinctive first-year experience?
- Does the college offer a small-size freshman seminar for all students?
- Are all students required to complete a senior project or assignment that allows them to integrate all that they have learned and demonstrate acquired skills and knowledge?
- Are students encouraged or required to complete internships and/or service-learning courses?
- Are students encouraged to study abroad? Is support for study abroad provided to all students and are study abroad experiences integrated into a student's overall curricula?
- Does the college offer learning communities, especially in the student's early years?
- Are students required to complete rigorous writing courses not only in the freshman year but also across the curriculum in whatever major he or she chooses to pursue?
- Are there opportunities for students to pursue independent research or creative projects under the supervision of a senior faculty member?

one's peers does seem to have an impact on the grade point averages of fellow students.

Nothing could be more important in your decision-making process than evaluating the nature of academic programs at prospective colleges or universities. Across both public and private institutions, there have been exciting and important changes in how colleges and universities are organizing undergraduate curricula. Many promising programs have been proven to result in higher levels of student retention, graduation, satisfaction, and academic achievement.

Many colleges and universities also now participate in the National Survey of Student Engagement. This survey asks students in both their first and last years about a series of effective educational practices and the degree to which they are engaged in the academic life of their school. Issues that are examined in the survey include the level of academic challenge, active and collaborative learning opportunities, the nature of student-faculty interactions, the number of enriching educational experiences available, and the supportive nature of the campus environment. Ask if the school you are considering participates in this survey and if you can see the results from recent classes of students.

THE PRIVATE/PUBLIC CHOICE

While there are distinct differences between public and private colleges and universities you should not limit your choice—whatever your background—to only one type of institution. There are wonderful opportunities at many different kinds of schools. The availability of many kinds of financial aid may bring private institutions with high-tuition levels within reach for you, whatever your financial background. Whether a school is highly selective or has open admissions, you should also be able to find a college or university that will challenge you academically and provide you with a supportive environment in which to live, learn, and pursue a college degree of lasting value.

Debra Humphreys is the Vice President of Strategic Engagement at the Lumina Foundation for the Association of American Colleges and Universities.

Distance Education—It's Closer Than You Think

You may not realize it, but as an incoming college student, you are joining a revolution that is radically changing education. It's called distance learning. From kindergarten up to postgraduate degrees, distance learning is fast becoming an essential teaching tool. Most of the colleges and universities you are considering for a bachelor's degree offer distance learning in one form or another. Most likely you will be a distance learner at some point, whether during college or graduate school or throughout your career.

In case you're not familiar with distance learning—or asynchronous learning, online learning, or distance education—it means you don't sit in a classroom facing a teacher. You can be hundreds of miles or minutes from the teacher and other students. Most often you connect through the internet to the teacher, fellow students, and study materials. However, increasingly sophisticated technologies, such as virtual laboratories, simulations, and interactive multimedia, are also used. You may run across the term "blended learning." Many institutions incorporate online learning into their face-to-face classes. In fact, a number of colleges require that a part of all classes is online.

FROM SNAIL-MAIL COURSES TO LEADING-EDGE TECHNOLOGY

Talk about change. Distance education began in the late 1800s, when schools mailed correspondence courses to farmers who wanted to learn how to grow better crops. As technology has advanced, distance learning has become accessible and widespread. At first educators were skeptical, but as name-plate universities began to incorporate it into their teaching methodology, distance education became accepted.

When brick-and-mortar colleges and universities first considered distance education, the goal was to make it as good as face-to-face education. Now, says Ray Schroeder, Professor Emeritus of Communication and Director of the Center for Online Learning, Research, and Service (COLRS), at the University of Illinois at Springfield, "Field research shows that online learning technologies are better than face-to-face learning in a number of ways." Having taught online, he has seen firsthand how students participate more in discussions and learn from one another. Peg Miller, Ph.D., former Coordinator of Academic Support for Distributed Learning, University of Central Florida, cites a survey she conducted every other semester that compares face-to-face and distance learners at her institution. She has found that students from face-to-face and online classes were almost identical in the grades they earned and in their satisfaction with the classes.

ON THE UPSWING

Today, a third of all college and university students are enrolled in at least one online course. Many reasons have caused the phenomenal growth of distance education. It's convenient and user-friendly, plus the scope of classes is stunning. Not that you'll likely begin your college years with classes in forensics or grading diamonds, but they are offered and indicate the enormous variety of courses. Along with many others in education, Michael P. Lambert, former executive director of the Distance Education Training Council, feels that online learning has transformed how people learn. "You no longer sit in a box with 35 other people where you might never raise your hand," he says. Adds Gerald Heeger, former President of the University of Maryland University College (UMUC), "Online learning gets rid of the limitations of geography and time. And as bandwidth increases, we will do more and more."

PROCEED WITH CAUTION

Now that you're convinced that distance education sounds great, and you're ready to say "sign me up," it's only fair to warn you that perhaps you shouldn't start your bachelor's degree totally online. Distance learning changes how you study, respond to your teachers, participate in class discussions, and take exams. If you're not prepared for the differences, you can easily fall behind and even fail. Though the age of online students continues to drop, many are older, have had some life experience since graduating from high school, and have the self-discipline, maturity, and self-motivation, that distance education demands. They know what they want from college and are willing to meet the rigors of online learning, which are considerable.

Of course, some students straight from high school do successfully start college as distance learners because they've already had some online learning experience. Some take online classes in high school or advanced-placement and college courses. At Stevens Institute of Technology's Web Campus, incoming freshmen brush up on math and precalculus online before their first fall semester. At first, Nathan Kahl, former instructor for the Euclid Program at Stevens Institute of Technology Web Campus, was skeptical that high school graduates could succeed in the online courses he taught, but he saw that "everyone quickly got into the swing of things." He admits that he underestimated the students' ability to learn online. Heeger agrees "There's no reason why a bright junior in high school who is ready to take college freshmen courses can't do it."

The University of Phoenix Online (parent company: Apollo Group, Inc.) has developed a bachelor's degree program specifically for incoming freshmen of any age—including those just out of high school. In today's job market, a college education is a necessity, yet many students have life situations that prevent them from attending. Notes former president of Apollo Group, Inc., Brian Mueller about the accommodations their program makes for students who are new to higher education, "It is our experience that if you create an online classroom, it must have all the features that incoming students need, which are small, highly interactive, and collaborative classes." Their freshman classes average 15 and require that the instructor has consistent contact with the students. New freshmen also get a tremendous amount of support in writing, math, and online research skills and have the help of an academic counselor who closely tracks them for ten weeks into their first semester. "We think there are more students coming out of high school who must have jobs, so we took the model for working adults and created an environment for traditional students that combines education and work," says Mueller.

However, not all educators have the same experience with incoming freshmen. Jimmy Reeves, Ph.D., Professor of Chemistry and Coordinator of the Tablet PC Initiative at the University of North Carolina at Wilmington, teaches both online and face-to-face classes and knows how students can react. Freshmen who fail his face-to-face class sometimes ask to take his class online. He says no because the discipline required is rare among 19-year-old students. "Junior and senior college students do well, but it has more to do with their level of maturity and the reasons why they're in college," he says, referring to the fact that many incoming college students want to experiment or come because their parents demand it. "Without any real desire to learn or sense of why they're in college, it's easy to get distracted in online classes," he notes. You can't hide in the back of a lecture hall half asleep on Monday morning and hope for the best on multiple-choice questions. In online classes, your active participation is noticed and taken into account for final grades.

Attending college isn't just about acquiring knowledge in a particular field in order to get a job. It's also about learning social skills and meeting people with different ideas from diverse backgrounds. "If you want to live in a dorm and have bull sessions on the meaning of life with the kids down the hall, then being a fully online freshman student isn't for you," advises Cynthia Davis, Acting Vice Provost and Dean of the Undergraduate School at the University of Maryland University College (UMUC). She adds that sometimes students mistakenly think getting a bachelor's degree online will take less time than physically attending classes or won't require as much work. But as she points out, online classes demand the same amount of effort, if not more, than face-to-face classes.

WHAT'S IT GOING TO BE LIKE?

Blended learning or mixed-mode classes, combining face-to-face and online instruction, are becoming a permanent fixture in higher education. Students might sit in a classroom on Monday but take the remaining two classes for that week online. Professors routinely post the syllabus, class calendar, or PowerPoint lectures online. Reeves says that it's rare to see college classes without some web-based materials. Davis comments that UMUC routinely enhances all of its face-to-face classes with companion online classrooms. Students can have optional online discussions or print copies of class materials.

"We find more students use online technology to enhance their studies and get better grades," comments Schroeder. Educators see a trend of students enrolling in one university and taking courses from other institutions. For instance, say you're in an art class but want to study German cathedral architecture, which your university doesn't have but another one offers online. It's only a matter of time before this will be a standard option for college students.

LOTS TO LOOK FOR, LOTS TO AVOID, LOTS TO ASK

Though much of distance education depends on the internet, you can't just type in "distance education" and see what comes up in a search for a college. You must seriously research and do background checks to make sure a diploma mill doesn't hand you a bachelor's degree that isn't credible. There are plenty of places to get information. Petersons.com offers a database of colleges and universities that have online courses, as well as totally online distance education providers. "You have to be a good consumer," recommends Heeger. "It's no different from getting a loan. You don't borrow money from people you never heard of. You shouldn't get degrees from people you never heard of." Schroeder suggests checking the course completion of online programs, their enrollment, and growth of programs. "Just as one checks with friends and colleagues about the quality of consumer services, such as computers and cars, one should check with students who are enrolled in online programs," he advises.

Is the Institution Accredited by a Valid Accrediting Body?

There are several kinds of accrediting organizations:

- The six regional accrediting agencies recognized by the U.S. Department of Education
- The Council for Higher Education Accreditation (**www.chea.org**)
- Other institutional accrediting agencies, such as the Accrediting Council for Independent Colleges and Schools and the Distance Education and Training Council
- Specialized accrediting agencies that cover schools offering everything from acupuncture to veterinary medicine
- Other discipline-based accrediting organizations, such as those for law and business schools

Can You Transfer Credits Received Online from One Institution to Another?

Policies vary greatly among universities and colleges. Though distance education is widely accepted, there are so many places where students can take bogus online courses that institutions are justifiably cautious. If students do decide they want to get a bachelor's degree completely online, they need to be sure the campus-based program and distance education program offer the same degree. At most institutions, both on-campus and online degrees are the same, but others do differentiate in the degrees conferred, and it will show up on your diploma.

Test-Drive an Online Class

Just like face-to-face instruction, online classes are different, depending on the course material and how each teacher chooses to structure the course, but here's a typical scenario of what it's like to be a distance learner.

Getting started. First you'll want to get to the general information page for the class, which you'll visit often. The professor's contact information, the class calendar, the syllabus, and announcements on quizzes and tests or links to other pages on which you'll find posted discussion questions may be found here. Some teachers will ask you to tell something about yourself to the other students in the class. Be sure to read the syllabus, which will outline the course and tell you when assignments are due and how grades are determined.

Responding to discussion questions. Those students who never raised their hands in face-to-face classes will get a shock in online courses. Responding with thoughtful answers to online discussion groups is mandatory. Usually the teacher will assign reading material and then post a discussion question. The material might be from your textbook or websites. You must respond to the question and possibly to the postings of other students in the class. Teachers will gauge your participation in the class and how well you learn the material.

Interacting with fellow students and your teacher. Ray Schroeder, Professor Emeritus of Communication and Director of the Center for Online Learning, Research, and Service (COLRS) at the University of Illinois at Springfield, gives talks about distance education. Often he'll ask his audience to recall their favorite class from elementary school up to college and what made it so memorable. Was it the textbook? The actual classroom? The view out the window? When he asks if it was the interaction among students and with the teacher, the audience realizes that's what made the class good. "Both in person and online, learning takes place in the interaction," says Schroeder. "Otherwise, we would do just as well to read a book or watch a video to learn." In online classes, interaction between you and the professor and other students is an enormous part of your success.

Nathan Kahl, former instructor for the Euclid Program at Stevens Institute of Technology Web Campus, explains, "Distance students expect that their teachers will be online at least as much as they are." The level of interaction expected from you will vary by school and course, but you should know that in online courses, you must be an active participant. On the flip side, teachers carefully monitor discussions to make sure the more talkative students don't dominate. Keith W. Miller, Professor of Computer Science at the University of Illinois at Springfield, interacts with his students in a variety of ways. "I make announcements to the whole class on the homepage. I send e-mails to the whole class. I enter into the electronic discussions on the bulletin board forums and post daily reminders and assignments to the course calendar. The students interact with me using e-mail, notes in their assignments, and via the bulletin boards. Now and then someone calls me at my office on the phone, but that's rare." He likes to answer his e-mails at least once a day, which means that his students get much more feedback than they would if he were physically in a classroom with them.

As do most online teachers, Cynthia Davis, Associate Dean of Academic Affairs in the School of Undergraduate Studies at the University of Maryland University College, gets students to participate with a weekly discussion topic. "If we're reading a novel," she says, "I ask them to discuss the role of the narrator or analyze a passage. The students respond individually and then respond to other students' comments."

Attending virtual lectures. Some online courses allow you to hear and see the professor or other guest speakers who are also online. If you want to ask a question, there's a button to indicate you want to speak. Everyone else can hear you as if you all were in the same room. Other professors add voice to PowerPoint lectures, which you can view when you want to, not at some prearranged time.

Taking quizzes and tests. No more waiting weeks to get your tests back. Online technology in some courses instantly zaps back the corrected test and notes that you missed question six and need to study page 54 of the textbook. Just like in face-to-face classes, you have an allotted amount of time to take the quiz. Some online courses may have automated components, such as instant quizzes and animated and interactive practice sessions. Others have mandatory proctored exams at a nearby community college or learning center for students who are off campus.

What Kind of Refund Policy Does the University Have for Distance Learners?

It might become painfully apparent for students that online learning is not for them, and they want to drop out. Find out ahead of time about the refund policy for online classes. What happens if you're ill during an online class? How can you make up the work? Even before taking any classes, you should find out if you're suited for online learning. Many institutions offer self-assessment tests on their websites.

What Online Services Does the College Provide?

Is the dorm wired? Can you get an e-mail address from the university? What about browsers and computer compatibility? Ask how the internet is part of face-to-face classes. To what extent is the library online, and is it available 24/7 for research? Ask about writing and math labs and help-desk support. Look for online tutorials that show students how to use the school's specific software. Is there a tech fee?

IF YOU'RE LEARNING ONLINE, YOU BETTER HAVE THESE

Since online learning is part of college, it's helpful to know what to expect ahead of time, rather than three weeks into the class, when you feel like throwing your laptop out the window and would happily settle for sitting in the back row of the nearest classroom. Here are the five skills and abilities that successful online students must have:

1. You must have the self-discipline to do things you don't want to do when you don't want to do them.

If you're a procrastinator, you'll find the catch-up tactics that served you well in face-to-face classes won't work online. "Students get the idea they can whiz by without studying, or they came from high schools where they weren't pushed," cautions Heeger. "Maybe they never got Fs in high school, but they do here." That's because they don't realize they're responsible for learning the material on their own. The burden is on you to keep up with the homework. It doesn't take long to fall far behind in online classes.

Typically, students in face-to-face and online classes need 2 hours for work outside of class for every hour in class. But online students often forget to add that hour. For every hour they would have to sit in a traditional classroom, they should be listening, studying, thinking, writing, responding to discussions, and getting ready for tests, plus the 2 hours outside of class. Three classes a week—that's 9 to 10 hours for one class. Online teachers keep students on track with weekly quizzes and homework assignments. If students start lagging, they're likely to get an e-mail from the professor asking what's going on. Claudine SchWeber, Ph.D., Chair of the Doctor of Management Program at the University of Maryland University College, has taught online for years and states, "My classes are structured by weekly readings, activities, and discussions. Students can't decide to get around to doing the work when they feel like it. It must be done at the instructor's pace. The first shot of online can be a shock to their system."

2. You must have the ability to manage your time without anyone telling you to do your homework NOW.

In high school, students usually can put off studying until the weekend. "That doesn't work in college. You can't write complex papers the night before," says Karen L. Kirkendall, Ph.D., Associate Professor of Liberal and Integrative Studies and Director of the Capitol Scholars Honors Program at the University of Illinois at Springfield. She teaches both online and face-to-face classes and has seen first-time online students who have never failed before start to slip and suddenly realize they are in big trouble. "My online classes are extraordinarily structured so I pretty much know when students aren't engaged, which I monitor by seeing how much they participate in online discussions," she notes.

3. You must have the skills to communicate your thoughts in writing.

"Online participation in class discussions isn't instant messaging. You are what you write in online classes," advises SchWeber. Most of the work in online classes is written, whether it's participation in discussions, homework, quizzes, papers, or tests.

Since you'll communicate by e-mail and post your thoughts, netiquette is essential. You need to think differently online than when speaking on the phone or face-to-face. "You can't

Distance Learning Myths

Myths regarding distance learning continue to persist even as distance education becomes more widely accepted and offered.

Distance learning is for people on ranches 200 miles from the nearest freeway. Geography is not a factor. Many distance learners who are located across the campus or a few miles away just don't want to deal with the commute or have a work schedule that conflicts with being in a class at a certain time. They appreciate the flexibility that distance education gives them.

Distance learning is easier than face-to-face classes. Once you start an online class, you'll knock that myth off the list. Still, some students think it will be easier. When they realize they must not only respond to discussion questions but also comment on the responses from other students, they wonder why they ever thought distance education was going to be easy. Online teachers normally keep track of how their students progress with frequent monitoring and quizzes.

I'll get a better education in face-to-face classes. Much research has been conducted comparing the two and consistently, online learning is equivalent or better. Teachers of online courses now have plenty of precedents to follow, training and research to help them teach better, and technology to prepare for classes and keep up with their students' progress.

I'll talk to a computer all day. Yes, you are in front of a computer as a distance learner, but you also interact with professors and other students much more than you ever would in a core freshman class of 200. Teachers have sophisticated software to facilitate interaction. Even though you don't physically see your teachers, they put a great deal of effort into class preparation and reading e-mails. Some get as many as 3,000 e-mails in a ten-week class. Distance learners often get to know fellow students much more easily online than they would walking in and out of a class.

I need to be a computer geek. If you can handle the simplest maneuvers around a computer, such as attaching documents to e-mails or going to a specified web address, you can be a distance learner. And you'll have tech support to help out if you run into problems.

Distance education is cheaper than face-to-face. Too bad this is a myth. It costs the same as a traditional college if you attend a recognized institution. Most students pay for distance education through student loans.

write a report that sounds like you are hanging out with friends," advises SchWeber. "When you are totally online, the only image people (including your professor) have of you is how you write." Kirkendall has reprimanded students who sent e-mails showing disrespect to the teacher because they were upset about something. Probably they would never respond that way if face-to-face. "Never hit the submit button when you're angry," Kirkendall cautions.

4. You must have the ability to research worthwhile information on the web.

You need to know what's junk and what's reliable. In addition, professors take plagiarism very seriously, especially because it's so easy to do.

5. You must have some computer skills and know some computer-speak.

Those who design the software and set up how a distance learning class is taught are careful to make sure the technology doesn't get in the way of learning; however, you should know the basics. "In some classes, certain downloads are required, such as Adobe Acrobat, but in general, the skills are not beyond the abilities used daily by most elementary school children," says Schroeder, pointing out that if distance programs use expensive or exotic technology, they defeat the purpose. He reports that most computers that are five years old have the speed, memory, and capability to support online learning. Some classes might require a microphone. You should be familiar with some of the computer jargon so that if you're asked to post something or use a drop box, add an attachment, or take part in a threaded discussion, you'll know what you need to do. Just about every distance learning provider has online tutorials to familiarize you with their particular online software. If you run into technical problems, help-desk support is available.

Why Not Women's Colleges?

Before we start talking about the many advantages that women's colleges offer, let's get some myths out of the way. It is almost certain that the minute you hear "women's colleges" in the same sentence with "choosing colleges" you immediately think: no boys, no fun, no way!

Maybe that is why some girls who visit Joan Jaffe's office at Mills College in San Francisco, California, rush in to tell her that they just saw some guys on the campus of this women's college. Jaffe, Associate Dean of Admission, frequently gets this reaction from the young women who visit the campus. That's because many think that if they go to a women's college they are never going to see a guy within 2 miles of the campus gates, which, by the way, will clang shut behind them, leaving them secluded inside a heavily guarded male-free zone.

KISS MYTH NUMBER ONE GOOD-BYE

Forget iron gates. The first myth to get rid of is the one that assumes attending a women's college means kissing your social life good-bye. In fact, as Patricia Gibbs, Vice President for Student Affairs, Dean of Students at Wesleyan College in Macon, Georgia, points out, "If you were a guy looking for a date, where would you go?" Not only that, the majority of women's colleges are near, if not next to, coed campuses. Most share activities with other colleges and universities, and many have reciprocal agreements so that guys can take classes at the women's college and vice versa.

When it comes to dating, women's colleges offer the best of both worlds. You can hang out with guys when you want to and then retreat to your own lovely environment (women's dorms usually are beautiful) and hang out with the girls. Julie Binder, who transferred from the University of Wisconsin to all-women's Barnard College in New York City, notes that there is open registration with Columbia University, which just happens to be right next door. "Campus life is shared. Sports are shared," she says.

As you dig deeper into this myth, you will find that attending a women's college is not about isolation, it's about options. You get to choose if you want to be in classes, clubs, and organizations only with women or mingle with the men.

SCRATCH MYTH NUMBER TWO

Women's colleges are just a bunch of catty, competitive females waiting for the right moment to claw each other's eyes out. Scratch that myth, too. Instead, women's colleges cultivate an environment of sisterhood—women who look out for one another. Most women's colleges encourage women in the upper-level classes to help their younger classmates. Talking to their "big sisters," newcomers can find out what classes to take and which professors are best, and they find a sympathetic ear for the problems that most first-year college students face.

The Rich Traditions in Women's Colleges

Tradition plays an important part of the experience women have in women's colleges. They run the gamut from solemn ceremonies of passing along the bond of sisterhood to the fun of secret surprises. "Women's colleges have a strong sense of tradition," says Amy Shaver, former Academic Dean at Stephens College in Columbia, Missouri. It's also a wonderful way to help women from all social, economic, religious, and ethnic backgrounds to share a common experience and pass it on to the next generation of students. "Traditions bond women over the generations," says Jennifer Rickard, former Dean of Admissions and Financial Aid at Bryn Mawr College, who notes that it's not unusual at all to have students today singing songs and participating in ceremonies that the class of 1945 did and which will be the same when today's students have their twenty-year reunion.

Here's a sampling of the many traditions you'll find on women's college campuses:

Lantern Night At Bryn Mawr's Lantern Night, women gather around a fountain on campus. Each woman is given a lantern as a symbol of knowledge and learning. Each class has a color, and as the lanterns are passed from the sophomores to the first-year students, songs are sung in Greek that are the same as the ones sung 100 years ago around the same fountain.

Senior Paint Night Mills College seniors get the okay to paint the campus in their class color. Along with brushes and cans of paint, they are given a few guidelines as to what can and cannot be painted, but the rest is up to them.

The Crossing of the Bridge As women students come to Stephens to begin their college education, they cross over a bridge on campus in a ceremony symbolizing their entrance into the world of academia. At graduation, they cross over another bridge on campus and are welcomed into the alumnae society.

Candlelight Induction Ceremony Spelman students dressed in white dresses and black shoes light candles and hear the charge to be the best they can be. While the candles are still lit, they sing the Spelman hymn.

Midnight Breakfast At Barnard, the night before finals, the president of the college, deans, and professors make breakfast for the students.

"The sense of community is very strong at women's colleges," observes Fran Samuels, former Director of College Counseling at The Master's School in Dobbs Ferry, New York. "The myth is that a women's college will be cliquish. In truth, the women are supportive of each other." The strong bonds of sisterhood that naturally develop connect students to their college, its history, and its students—past, present, and future. Many women's colleges designate a rotating color for each incoming class. For example, if the freshman class you enter is dubbed the golden hearts, by the time you graduate, you are connected to all the golden hearts who graduated ahead of you and all the golden hearts who will graduate after you.

TOSS MYTH NUMBER THREE

Another myth that should be tossed out is that women's colleges don't prepare you for the "real world." Well, try saying that to the 12 women members of Congress who graduated from women's colleges. Or to the 15 women on *Business Week*'s list of the rising stars in corporate America. Although you are not in a totally coed situation, on the other hand you are in an environment in which you can gain skills to think critically and learn to meet challenges. Becky Marsh, Director of Communications and Marketing at Whitfield School, in St. Louis, Missouri, points out that when you first ride a bike, training wheels allow you to learn how to balance. Once you are ready to race down the street, you take them off. Same with women's colleges. The focus is on your education and your strengths, and who you are. You graduate ready to take on the obstacles of the real world. "In high school, I had the feeling that boys were given more opportunities to share their knowledge. It was harder and more intimidating for me to share my opinions in a coed class," says Brittany Johnson, from Spelman College in Atlanta, Georgia. "Now I feel like I can do anything."

Graduates of women's colleges feel empowered and willing to confront any limits to their abilities. While in college, they have many opportunities to assume leadership roles and see women in leadership positions as professors and deans. "They don't doubt whether they can do anything. Instead, they ask, 'Why can't I do it now?'" reports Amy Shaver, former Academic Dean at Stephens College in Columbia, Missouri. Women can find their own voices and establish their own ways of approaching things that will ultimately make them successful in a male-dominated world. They learn from seeing other women students and professors engaged in the intellectual process.

THE ADVANTAGES

As more young women find out about the advantages that women's colleges offer them, they like what they see. Maybe that is why attendance at women's colleges is growing. Learning leadership skills tops the list of advantages. Says Shaver, "Women in a same-sex environment are more likely to take risks and speak up in class. They are more willing to stand up and voice an opinion." If you think about it, students get plenty of practice at a women's college because all the leadership roles go to women. From day one, you will see women leading the entire college or involved in interesting and significant research. You get more exposure to what leadership is and what to expect as a leader. "Leadership becomes ingrained," notes Jennifer Fondiller, Dean of Enrollment Management at Barnard College in New York City.

You might not realize it, but women react differently in classrooms with all women. They tend to speak up with confidence and test their ideas more readily when they are not competing with men. Researchers find that even as early as the fifth grade, girls are taught differently than boys. Teachers call on boys more frequently and don't ask girls the more thought-provoking questions or to critically analyze problems. In coed situations, the more aggressive and competitive guys take over, whereas in all-female classes, research indicates there is much more give-and-take and exchange of ideas.

Coming from a coed public school, Johnson realized that more attention was given to the guys in her classes, but at Spelman, she says, "Everyone is on the same path." Arlene Cash, former Vice President for Enrollment Management at Spelman, notes that women don't have to vie for attention or retreat into the intellectual background in all-women classes. In a coed class, the environment becomes more adversarial. "Women feel they have to perform. In women's colleges they become more academically involved and interact with faculty members more frequently," says Debbie Greenberg, former College Counselor at Whitfield School. Speaking of the rich interaction that occurs in her classes at Barnard, Binder says, "The diversity of experience around the discussion table is unparalleled."

YOU CAN SUCCEED

Shaver characterizes the environment in women's colleges as one in which there is no fear of failing when the social pressures and dynamics of men and women are removed from the classroom. Women's colleges give women the opportunity to explore different avenues without the fear of failing. "We challenge them to become what they want to become," says Gibbs from Wesleyan. "No one says, 'You can't do that because you are a woman.'" At the same time, you are interacting with other women who have the same goals as you, which reinforces who you are. Or, as Jennifer Rickard, former Dean of Admissions and Financial Aid at Bryn Mawr College, in Bryn Mawr, Pennsylvania, points out, women are not just sitting in classes to do well on exams and get good grades. They also are figuring out what they want to do with their education. "There's less expectation to conform to an external measure," she says.

Many women's colleges foster self-government and give their students responsibilities they might not find in a coed institution. At Bryn Mawr, for instance, students pay a self-government association fee as part of their tuition. This is put into a fund that is controlled by a student government that takes ownership of how the students want to govern themselves. "This isn't student government making only recommendations to the administration as to how to allocate the budget to the different student groups vying for funds," notes Rickard. "You have students dealing with real-world management issues, such as resource allocation."

Since women's colleges are smaller than big coed universities, women receive all the benefits that students get from a small liberal arts college in addition to the advantages that only a women's college offers. A big plus is interaction with professors and staff, which is hard to achieve when you are one of

What Made You Choose a Women's College?

When she got to the point of choosing which college to attend, Wisambi Loundu had plenty of options. Coming from San Diego, the California universities were a logical choice. Women's colleges were not on her list. In fact, she hardly knew they existed. Her first thought when someone suggested a women's college to her was, "I'm not going to a school full of girls minus boys." Her second thought was just as negative. "If it's all girls, they will always be fighting." The third and fourth thoughts assumed that a women's college wouldn't prepare her for the real world, plus she would be isolated.

But then her math teacher's daughter told her about Bryn Mawr, and as Wisambi started exploring the possibility, the advantages of a women's college started lining up. However, it wasn't until she visited Bryn Mawr that she really began to see herself there. "I fell in love with the campus," says Wisambi. "It was like nothing I'd ever seen before." Her stay in the dorm added to her steadily growing thoughts that Bryn Mawr might be it. "The girls I stayed with in the dorm were so friendly. At first I was suspicious, but I saw it was not a front. Plus, there were girls from all over the world."

But Wisambi didn't make her final decision just yet. She decided to look at other schools, like Wellesley and the University of California schools, as well as Stanford. Meanwhile, her friend told her more about Bryn Mawr. "She said I'd make lasting friends and she talked about how the academics would train me for the outside world even if there were no men on campus. Bryn Mawr would build my identity as a woman."

She still wasn't convinced and made a second visit, along with visits to Wellesley and Stanford, which she says were nice, but too big. It would be too hard to make friends there, she thought. When the time came to make her final selection, she chose Bryn Mawr.

Now at Bryn Mawr, how does Wisambi feel about her choice? The academics are more challenging than she anticipated but doable, and she is excited about the internships she will be able to access. She also finds that the staff and teachers at Bryn Mawr go out of their way to make her feel at home. "They match us up with a mentor and professor," she says.

How about dating? Since Bryn Mawr is part of a tri-college community, guys are around, though Wisambi says you have to make an effort to meet people on other campuses.

Talking to seniors who are getting ready to head out to the "real world," Wisambi can see that they are full of confidence and don't think for a minute that they won't do well. "And that's a positive," she says.

200 students in a lecture hall taught by a graduate student. Women's colleges tend to foster seminar-style classes taught by full professors, many of them women. "You have an expert teaching you," says Gibbs. Faculty members get to know their students and can challenge them intellectually on an individual basis. "Within two days, all my teachers knew my name," recalls Johnson, who says she was given each professor's e-mail address, home phone number, and all the contact information she needed and was encouraged to reach out to them.

Women are encouraged to achieve their intellectual goals. Professors often will point out specific programs that they know suit the student's interests. Add to this the opportunities to conduct research with a professor, and in many cases actually present research findings to a professional society, and you can see why women graduate with a terrific resume before they even start their careers. Rickard mentions the opportunity that Bryn Mawr students have to work on funded projects with professors during the summer and then present the results along with them at conferences. "It's a window into the academic world and the world of the intellectual," she notes. It's no surprise that women in women's colleges major in math and science at a higher national average than women in coed institutions.

Paid and unpaid internships, too, are more available for women at women's colleges, mainly because of the network of women graduates in business and industry who want to help their "sisters" at their alma maters. "I'm getting my professional edge now," says Binder, who is interested in TV production and had a paid internship as a production assistant while a sophomore at Barnard. "You will have an amazing resume by the time you graduate," she says.

Peggy Hock, Ph.D., former College Counselor at Notre Dame High School in San Jose, California, points out that colleges naturally rely on their alumni to come forward with networking opportunities for students; however, the alumnae of women's colleges tend to be more loyal and willing to give of their time. This translates into many more opportunities for internships, mentoring, and job possibilities. At Barnard, for example, the career office has an alumna mentor network. Students can call, ask questions, and get advice about career choices. At alumnae events, current students mix with the graduates. Binder takes full advantage of the web log of women who are working all over the world and willing to spend time online with Barnard students. She applied for a job at a public relations firm in New York after contacting a fellow Barnard graduate working there. She met with her and subsequently got a letter of recommendation.

HOW TO CHOOSE

Choosing a women's college isn't any different from choosing a coed college. You should definitely visit the campus and don't be afraid to ask lots of questions—even the ones that might make you uncomfortable. Because women's colleges are similar to small coed liberal arts colleges, make sure that you don't compare a women's campus to a big university.

Janet Ashley, former Interim Director for Admissions at Spelman College, advises high school women to ask what a women's college can give them academically. "Their choice depends on what their goals are," she says.

If you're worried about the dating scene, ask about the levels of interaction with guys and how close the relationships are with neighboring institutions.

"Look at the individuality of each women's college," suggests Rickard, "because each has its own personality."

Look at the school before looking at the fact that it's a women's college, and on the flip side, don't rule out a school just because it is a women's college. "So many students make quick decisions about where to apply," warns Fondiller, noting that sometimes the decision hinges on what schools a friend is applying to rather than if that institution really fits the student. Many women's colleges specialize in certain fields like science, math, or theater.

Famous Firsts from Women's Colleges

Do you know which college the first woman to be named Secretary of State graduated from? Or the woman scientist who identified the Hong Kong flu? Or the first woman executive vice president of the American Stock Exchange? Here's a big clue. They were all graduates of women's colleges.

SENATORS

- Barbara Mikulski (MD)—Mount Saint Agnes College
- Tammy Baldwin (WI)—Smith College

REPRESENTATIVES (Current and Former)

- Tammy Baldwin (WI)—Smith College
- Donna Christian-Christensen (VI)—St. Mary's College
- Rosa DeLauro (CT)—Marymount College
- Jane Harman (CA)—Smith College
- Gabrielle Giffords (AZ, 2007–12)—Scripps College
- Eddie Bernice Johnson (TX)—Saint Mary's College
- Barbara Lee (CA)—Mills College
- Nita Lowey (NY)—Mount Holyoke College
- Betty McCollum (MN)—College of Saint Catherine
- Nancy Pelosi (CA), first woman elected as Speaker of the House of Representatives—Trinity College
- Allyson Schwartz (PA)—Simmons College

FORMER SECRETARY OF STATE

- Hillary Rodham Clinton (NY)—Wellesley College

OTHER FAMOUS WOMEN FIRSTS

- Madeleine Albright, first woman to be named Secretary of State in the United States, appointed in 1997—Wellesley College
- Jane Amsterdam, first woman editor, the New York Post—Cedar Crest College
- Emily Green Balch, first woman to receive the Nobel Peace Prize in 1946—Bryn Mawr College
- Catherine Brewer Benson, first woman to receive a college bachelor's degree—Wesleyan College
- Earla Biekert, first scientist to identify the Hong Kong flu virus—Wesleyan College
- Cathleen Black, first woman leader of the American Newspaper Publishers Association—Trinity Washington University
- Sarah Porter Boehmler, first woman executive vice president of American Stock Exchange—Sweet Briar College
- Jane Matilda Bolin, first African American woman judge in the United States—Wellesley College
- Dorothy L. Brown, first African American woman general surgeon in the South—Bennett College for Women
- Pearl S. Buck, first American woman to win the Nobel Prize in Literature—Randolph-Macon Woman's College
- Ila Burdett, Georgia's first female Rhodes Scholar—Agnes Scott College
- Dorothy Vredenburgh Bush, first woman secretary of the Democratic National Party—Mississippi University for Women
- Hon. Audrey J. S. Carrion, first Hispanic woman judge Circuit Court for Baltimore City—College of Notre Dame of Maryland
- Rachel Carson, first environmentalist who awakened public consciousness through her book, *Silent Spring*—Chatham University
- Barbara Cassani, first woman CEO of a commercial airline—Mount Holyoke College
- Elaine L. Chao, U.S. Secretary of Labor, 2001; First Asian American woman appointed to a President's cabinet—Mount Holyoke College

Adapted from the website of the Women's College Coalition at http://www.womenscolleges.org.

Applying 101

The words "applying yourself" have several important meanings in the college application process. One meaning refers to the fact that you need to keep focused during this important time in your life, keep your priorities straight, and know the dates that your applications are due so you can apply on time. The phrase might also refer to the person who is really responsible for your application—you.

You are the only person who should compile your college application. You need to take ownership of this process. The guidance counselor is not responsible for completing your applications, and neither are your parents. College applications must be completed in addition to your normal workload at school, college visits, and SAT®, ACT®, or TOEFL® testing.

THE APPLICATION

The application is your way of introducing yourself to a college admissions office. As with any introduction, you want to make a good first impression. The first thing you should do in presenting your application is to find out what the college or university needs from you. Read the application carefully to find out the application fee and deadline, required standardized tests, number of essays, interview requirements, and anything else you can do or submit to help improve your chances for acceptance.

FOLLOW THESE TIPS WHEN FILLING OUT YOUR APPLICATIONS

- **Follow the directions to the letter.** You don't want to be in a position to ask an admissions officer for exceptions due to your inattentiveness.
- **Proofread all parts of your application,** including your essay. Again, the final product indicates to the admissions staff how meticulous and careful you are in your work.
- **Submit your application as early as possible,** provided all of the pieces are available. If there is a problem with your application, this will allow you to work through it with the admissions staff in plenty of time. If you wait until the last minute, it not only takes away that cushion but also reflects poorly on your sense of priorities.
- **Keep a copy of the completed application,** whether it is a photocopy or a copy saved on your computer.

(For more hands-on help with your application essays, pair up with a professional editor who can provide you with proofreading services as well as full critiques: www.essayedge.com)

Completing college applications yourself helps you learn more about the schools to which you are applying. The information a college asks for in its application can tell you much about the school. State university applications often tell you how they are going to view their applicants. Usually, they select students based on GPAs and test scores. Colleges that request an interview, ask you to respond to a few open-ended questions, or require an essay are interested in a more personal approach to the application process and may be looking for different types of students than those sought by a state school.

In addition to submitting the actual application, there are several other items that are commonly required. You will be responsible for ensuring that your standardized test scores and your high school transcript arrive at the colleges to which you apply. Most colleges will ask that you submit teacher recommendations as well. Select teachers who know you and your abilities well and allow them plenty of time to complete the recommendations. When all portions of the application have been completed and sent in, whether electronically or by mail, make sure you follow up with the college to ensure their receipt.

THE APPLICATION ESSAY

Whereas the other portions of your application—your transcript, test scores, and involvement in extracurricular activities—are a reflection of what you've accomplished up to this point, your application essay is an opportunity to present yourself in the here and now. The essay shows your originality and verbal skills and how you approach a topic or problem and express your opinion.

Some colleges may request one essay or a combination of essays and short-answer topics to learn more about who you are and how well you can communicate your thoughts. Common essay topics cover such simple themes as writing about yourself and your experiences or why you want to attend that particular school. Other colleges will ask that you show your imaginative or creative side by writing about a favorite author, for instance, or commenting on a hypothetical situation. In such cases, they will be looking at your thought processes and level of creativity.

Admissions officers, particularly those at small or mid-size colleges, use the essay to determine how you, as a student, will fit into life at that college. The essay, therefore, is a critical component of the application process. Here are some tips for writing a winning essay:

- Colleges are looking for an honest representation of who you are and what you think. Make sure that the tone of the essay reflects enthusiasm, maturity, creativity, the ability to communicate, talent, and your leadership skills.
- Be sure you set aside enough time to write the essay, revise it, and revise it *again.* Running "spell check" will only

detect a fraction of the errors you probably made on your first pass at writing it. Take a break and then come back to it and reread it. You will probably notice other style, content, and grammar problems—and ways that you can improve the essay overall.

- Always answer the question that is being asked, making sure that you are specific, clear, and true to your personality.
- Enlist the help of reviewers who know you well—friends, parents, teachers—since they are likely to be the most honest and will keep you on track in the presentation of your true self.

THE PERSONAL INTERVIEW

Although it is relatively rare that a personal interview is required, many colleges recommend that you take this opportunity for a face-to-face discussion with a member of the admissions staff. Read through the application materials to determine whether or not a college places great emphasis on the interview. If they strongly recommend that you have one, it may work against you to forego it.

In contrast to a group interview and some alumni interviews, which are intended to provide information about a college, the personal interview is viewed both as an information session and as further evaluation of your skills and strengths. You will meet with a member of the admissions staff who will be assessing your personal qualities, high school preparation, and your capacity to contribute to undergraduate life at the institution. On average, these meetings last about 45 minutes—a relatively short amount of time in which to gather information and leave the desired impression—so here are some suggestions on how to make the most of it.

Scheduling Your Visit

Generally, students choose to visit campuses in the summer or fall of their senior year. Both times have their advantages. A summer visit, when the campus is not in session, generally allows for a less hectic visit and interview. Visiting in the fall, on the other hand, provides the opportunity to see what campus life is like in full swing. If you choose the fall, consider arranging an overnight trip so that you can stay in one of the college dormitories. At the very least, you should make your way around campus to take part in classes, athletic events, and social activities. Always make an appointment and avoid scheduling more than two college interviews on any given day. Multiple interviews in a single day hinder your chances of making a good impression, and your impressions of the colleges will blur into each other as you hurriedly make your way from place to place.

Preparation

Know the basics about the college before going for your interview. Read the college catalog and website in addition to this guide. You will be better prepared to ask questions that are not answered in the literature and that will give you a better understanding of what the college has to offer. You should also spend some time thinking about your strengths and weaknesses and, in particular, what you are looking for in a college education. You will find that as you get a few interviews under your belt, they will get easier. You might consider starting with a college that is not a top contender on your list, so that the stakes are not as high.

Asking Questions

Inevitably, your interviewer will ask you, "Do you have any questions?" Not having one may suggest that you're unprepared or, even worse, not interested. When you do ask questions, make sure that they are ones that matter to you and that have a bearing on your decision about whether or not to attend that college. The questions that you ask will give the interviewer some insight into your personality and priorities. Avoid asking questions that are answered in the college literature—again, a sign of unpreparedness. Although the interviewer will undoubtedly pose questions to you, the interview should not be viewed merely as a question-and-answer session. If a conversation evolves out of a particular question, so much the better. Your interviewer can learn a great deal about you from how you sustain a conversation. Similarly, you will be able to learn a great deal about the college in a conversational format.

Separate the Interview from the Interviewer

Many students base their feelings about a college solely on their impressions of the interviewer. Try not to characterize a college based only on your personal reaction, however, since your impressions can be skewed by whether you and your interviewer hit it off. Pay lots of attention to everything else that you see, hear, and learn about a college. Once on campus, you may never see your interviewer again.

In the end, remember to relax and be yourself. Your interviewer will expect you to be somewhat nervous, which will relieve some of the pressure. Don't drink jitters-producing caffeinated beverages prior to the interview, and suppress nervous fidgets like leg-wagging, finger-drumming, or bracelet jangling. Consider your interview an opportunity to put forth your best effort and to enhance everything that the college knows about you up to this point.

THE FINAL DECISION

Once you have received your acceptance letters, it is time to go back and look at the whole picture. Provided you received more than one acceptance, you are now in a position to compare your options. The best way to do this is to compare your original list of important college-ranking criteria with what you've discovered about each college along the way. In addition, you and your family will need to factor in the financial aid component. You will need to look beyond these cost issues and the quantifiable pros and cons of each college, however, and know that you have a good feeling about your final choice. Before sending off your acceptance letter, you need to feel confident that the college will feel like home for the next four years. Once the choice is made, the only hard part will be waiting for an entire summer before heading off to college!

The "Early Decision" Decision

Maybe a senior you knew last year didn't get into the college he wanted. He said it was because he didn't apply "early decision." Maybe your friend's mom told your mom that unless students apply early decision, their chances of getting into top schools are slim to none, even though they have great grades and spectacular essays. Maybe you figure you'd better get in on the early decision action.

All of the above are true—well, sort of—because many students applying to college get the term "early decision" backwards. High school guidance and college counselors run into this kind of thinking all the time and suggest putting "decision" before "early"—as in making a wise decision about committing to a college before applying early. For some students, early decision is a great option. For others, early decision is loaded with pitfalls and dangers.

"When students come back in the fall of their senior year, I often hear 'I know I want to apply early. Can you help me choose the school?'" says Kathy Cleaver, Co-Director of College Counseling at Durham Academy in Durham, North Carolina. She compares that to saying, "I know I want to get married, please help me pick the man." Continues Cleaver, "First you have to fall in love with the school and know it's your first choice and then join the circus for early decision." She's referring to the media hype flying around high school halls about early decision—it's easy to fall prey to the early decision madness. Hot competition to get into "top" schools creates early decision anxiety. Michael "Mickey" Gilbert, Guidance Counselor at Passaic High School in Passaic, New Jersey, throws out some scary numbers that confirm that, yes, the competition for admittance to top schools is white-hot. There are about 30,000 high schools in the United States, and although the majority of high school seniors apply to institutions in their own states, there are still limited spaces in the "top" schools and the eight Ivy League schools. "No wonder kids think that early decision is the way to go," speculates Gilbert. Early decision panic sets in because students are convinced that if they get their applications in early, they have an edge. Sometimes early decision might make the difference, but there are many issues to consider before taking the early decision leap.

EARLY THIS, EARLY THAT

With all the buzz about early decision, do you really know what it means along with all the other early options, such as early action and early notification? And what about the variations of early decision? Each institution can have its own version of early decision, meaning that deadlines and criteria are different. There's the early decision that notifies students by December, there's the early decision round two, and then there is the early action/single choice.

Seeing the confusion, the National Association for College Admission Counseling (NACAC) developed a standard set of definitions. NACAC is an education association of secondary school counselors, college and university admissions and financial aid officers, counselors, and other individuals who work with students as they transition from high school to college. While each institution has its own variations of each early option, an understanding of the basic differences can help. The list that follows was adapted from the definitions found on the NACAC website (**www.nacacnet.org**).

Early Decision

- Early decision is the application process in which students make a commitment to a first-choice institution where, if admitted, they definitely will enroll. Should a student who applies for financial aid not be offered an award that makes attendance possible, the student may decline the offer of admission and be released from the early decision commitment.
- While pursuing admission under an early decision plan, students may apply to other institutions, but may have only one early decision application pending at any time.
- The institution must notify the applicant of the decision within a reasonable and clearly stated period of time after the early decision deadline. Usually, a nonrefundable deposit must be made well in advance of May 1.
- A student applying for financial aid must adhere to institutional early decision aid application deadlines.
- The institution will respond to an application for financial aid at or near the time of an offer of admission.
- The early decision application supercedes all other applications. Immediately upon acceptance of an offer of admission, a student must withdraw all other applications and make no subsequent applications.
- The application form will include a request for a parent and a counselor signature, in addition to the student's signature, indicating an understanding of the early decision commitment and agreement to abide by its terms.

Early Action

- Early action is the application process in which students make application to an institution of preference and receive a decision well in advance of the institution's regular response date. Students who are admitted under early action are not obligated to accept the institution's offer of admission or to submit a deposit until the regular reply date (not prior to May 1).

- A student may apply to other colleges without restriction.
- The institution must notify the applicant of the decision within a reasonable and clearly stated period of time after the early action deadline.
- A student applying for financial aid must adhere to institutional aid application deadlines.
- A student admitted under an early action plan may not be required to make a commitment prior to May 1 but may be encouraged to do so as soon as a final college choice is made. Colleges that solicit commitments to offers of early action admission and/or financial assistance prior to May 1 may do so provided those offers include a clear statement that written requests for extensions until May 1 will be granted, and that such requests will not jeopardize a student's status for admission or financial aid.

Regular Decision

- Regular decision is the application process in which a student submits an application to an institution by a specified date and receives a decision within a reasonable and clearly stated period of time, but not later than April 15.
- A student may apply to other colleges without restriction.
- The institution will state a deadline for completion of applications and will respond to completed applications by a specified date.
- A student applying for financial aid must adhere to institutional aid application deadlines.
- A student admitted under a regular decision plan may not be required to make a commitment prior to May 1 but may be encouraged to do so as soon as a final college choice is made. Colleges that solicit commitments to offers of admission and/or financial assistance prior to May 1 may do so provided those offers include a clear statement that written requests for extensions until May 1 will be granted, and that such requests will not jeopardize a student's status for admission or financial aid.

Rolling Admission

- Rolling admission is the application process in which an institution reviews applications as they are completed and renders admission decisions to students throughout the admission cycle.
- A student may apply to other colleges without restriction.
- The institution will respond to completed applications in a timely manner.
- A student applying for financial aid must adhere to institutional aid application deadlines.
- A student admitted under a rolling admission plan may not be required to make a commitment prior to May 1 but may be encouraged to do so as soon as a final college choice is made. Colleges that solicit commitments to offers of admission and/or financial assistance prior to May 1 may do so provided those offers include a clear statement that written requests for extensions until May 1 will be granted, and that such requests will not jeopardize a student's status for admission or financial aid.

Wait List

- Wait list is an admission decision option utilized by institutions to protect against shortfalls in enrollment. Wait lists are sometimes made necessary because of the uncertainty of the admission process, as students submit applications for admission to multiple institutions and may receive several offers of admission. By placing a student on the wait list, an institution does not initially offer or deny admission, but extends to a candidate the possibility of admission in the future before the institution's admission cycle is concluded.
- The institution will ensure that a wait list, if necessary, is of reasonable length and is maintained for a reasonable period of time, but never later than August 1.
- In the letter offering a wait list position, the institution should provide a past wait list history, which describes the number of students placed on the wait list(s), the number offered admission from the wait list, and the availability of financial aid. Students should be given an indication of when they can expect to be notified of a final admission decision.
- An institution must resolve final status and notify wait list candidates as soon after May 1 as possible.
- The institution will not require students to submit deposits to remain on a wait list or pressure students for a commitment to enroll prior to sending an official offer of admission in writing.

There is one more option, called early action/single choice (EASC), that some highly selective schools such as Harvard, Yale, Princeton, and Stanford have begun using. Early action/single choice is a nonbinding early admission option for freshman applicants that replaces early decision. With this change, students learn about their admission decision in December without being required to reply until May 1. This option allows students to apply to as many colleges as they want under a regular admission time frame. The difference is that the early action/single choice option does not allow a candidate to apply to other schools under any type of early action, early decision, or early notification program. Students are asked to sign a statement in their application agreeing to file only one early application.

Each of these options has variations, depending on the institution using them. Some schools have a November 1 deadline for early decision round one. Smaller schools have a deadline of November 15, while others have a December 1 deadline. Then there's an early decision round two. To make matters even more complicated, some schools with early decision say that students can't apply to other institutions if they've sent in an early decision application to their admissions office. Others say it's okay to apply to other schools at the same time you're

PARENTS, SOME ADVICE FOR YOU

Though guidance counselors stress that high school students should make the final decision about which college to attend, they also say that parents are a very important part of the decision equation. Parents can help as organizers of all the information and provide the support needed to make a good choice. "Little things like setting up file folders and keeping track of deadlines can keep a student on track," advises David Gibson, former College Advisor at St. Mary's Parish in Annapolis, Maryland.

Along with their children, parents also need to understand the basics of early option terminology as it applies to each institution being considered. Five different colleges might have five different early decision criteria. Read the fine print and make note of deadlines.

What really will help—you, your child, and your wallet—is to understand the basics about financial aid. Says Shawn Leftwich, Director of Undergraduate Admissions at Wheaton College in Illinois, "Have an in-depth discussion with the financial aid officer so that you are aware of the ramifications, restrictions, and implications of the financial aid offer."

If possible, make an appointment to visit with a financial aid officer at the college while your child is visiting the campus. Bring your tax forms and discuss the prospects of financial aid. "Financial aid people are straight shooters. It's not in their best interest to tell you one thing to get your foot in the door and then turn around and pull the rug out from under you," says Bill McClintick, Dean of College Relations and Outreach at Mercerburg Academy. "Parents might not like the answer they get from the financial aid officer, but they will get a candid assessment of their eligibility for financial aid."

Leftwich suggests having an honest discussion with your child early in the college selection process. Talk about what you can realistically afford, what colleges will appropriately challenge him or her, if location is a factor, and what kind of environment best suits your child. Whichever option your child uses to apply, you both will know the decision is an informed one.

applying early decision to them, but if they send you an acceptance, you must withdraw the other applications.

Just because two institutions have an application process called early decision or early action doesn't mean that their policies are identical. "There is no common terminology, even among the colleges that have early decision," says Christoph Guttentag, Dean of Undergraduate Admissions at Duke University in Durham, North Carolina. He also points out that just when you think you've got the definitions figured out, institutions change them. "Colleges are always balancing the needs of their institution and the needs of students," he comments.

EARLY DECISION: A MATCHMAKING TOOL OR A CLEVER STRATEGY?

Despite the differences in what actually constitutes early decision, it has become more of a strategy than a matchmaking tool, according to Bill McClintick, Director of College Relations and Outreach at Mercersburg Academy in Mercersburg, Pennsylvania. He also chairs the national steering committee on admissions standards for NACAC. The focus of early decision used to be on matching the student with the college and letting the admissions office know that that institution is where the student wants to be above all others. Today, early decision is misunderstood and misused. High school seniors think that they must use the early decision tactic to get an edge. The result, says McClintick is "at many of the top places, early decision applications have gone through the roof."

Though high school students may have exaggerated ideas of how much early decision can really help them, it is true that it does give a small segment of students applying at highly selective schools an advantage. Generally, the more selective the institution, the more small differences matter. "Even if it's a small increase, you need everything you can get," states John Latting, Ph.D., Emory University's Assistant Vice Provost for Undergraduate Enrollment and Dean of Admission.

"Remember," cautions McClintick, "we're only talking about a small slice of kids in the grand scheme of things." He mentions 5 percent of high school seniors nationally who aspire to the "top" institutions. State colleges and universities fill a much lower percentage of their freshman class with early decision applications. "I don't believe that more kids are chasing the same number of spots," says Jon Reider, Director of College Counseling at San Francisco University High School in San Francisco, California. "Students are applying to more and more schools, even with the early decision option on the side. This is inflating the selectivity of some colleges beyond what it used to be." In reality, 90 percent of students apply regular admission. Interest in early decision comes from a relatively small segment of the college applicant pool.

THE BENEFITS OF EARLY DECISION

There are clear benefits for students who apply for early decision. Aside from the fact that early decision does play a role in acceptance rates for a relatively small percentage of students at a small number of schools, early decision is a good option. The caveat is that students must know, without a shred of doubt, that one institution, above all others, is the best match for their goals and their likes and dislikes, and that based on grades and test scores, they solidly match the institution's criteria for admission. The option to go early decision should be taken after extensive research, multiple visits to the campus, and talking to a lot of people. "Early decision is for those who can put their hearts and souls into one application," advises Cleaver.

There are other advantages. You have to make only one choice, and you will know by December if you've been accepted. You have to fill out only one application. You are not chewing your nails over your list of possibilities during the winter break. Instead, you know where you're going and can sit back and enjoy the rest of your senior year, while others in your class are madly filling out applications, writing essays, and agonizing over the thin envelopes that arrive in the mail. Says Guttentag, "The advantage of having that challenging process over with is not insignificant."

Early decision is helpful for admissions officers at selective colleges because it allows them to make decisions between well-qualified students and select those who really want to be at their institution. As Shawn Leftwich, Director of Undergraduate Admissions at Wheaton College in Illinois, points out, early decision is for the students who are strongly committed. "We like you. You like us. We know you're coming, and we can fill our freshman class." However, on the flip side, she adds that some students aren't so sure about which college they want to attend, and early decision only makes the process more stressful.

Before you decide to go with early decision, consider early action. Many high school counselors lean toward early action, which is another good option. With early action you're able to apply later in the process. This means you will be able to take the SATs again. Your first-semester grades and AP classes taken in the first semester of your senior year can be used to evaluate your eligibility. You have September and October to visit several campuses while they are in session and plenty of time to do the research to put more than one school on your list.

THE PITFALLS OF EARLY DECISION

Though early decision has benefits, before you jump into it, look at the ramifications of that option. Advises Gilbert, "Early decision might give you an edge, but the tradeoff is not so great."

Perhaps the most compelling reason why students should seriously examine early decision before jumping at it is because they are bound by an agreement to attend that school if accepted. Students sign a pledge to attend that institution and are required to withdraw applications from all other schools. They also are obligated to accept the financial aid award that the institution gives them. An early decision is a binding decision. "Regardless," advises David Gibson, of David Gibson College Advising, LLC, in Annapolis, Maryland, "students don't learn about their financial aid awards until March or April, and if the award funding is not at all acceptable because the family's financial need was not met, they need to decline the offer and begin searching for a new college. March or April is not a good time to start applying to new colleges."

How binding is binding? Though no school can force a student to attend if they've signed an early decision agreement, students who decide not to attend that school hurt others with that decision. High school counselors have to sign the binding agreement, along with parents, and must state that they will not send out transcripts to other institutions. Many institutions will not accept the application of a student who applied early decision elsewhere and backed out of the agreement. Admissions officers may find out in May that an

QUESTIONS TO ASK YOURSELF BEFORE APPLYING EARLY DECISION

What if you don't get accepted early decision—then what? Speaking from the experience of seeing students deal with early decision rejection letters, Reider says, "Some of your friends are getting acceptance letters, and you get one thin envelope and the pain of rejection. You've given the early decision institution your best shot and you lost." Cleaver has seen kids in her high school end up thinking they won't get in anywhere. "This is the first time they've faced a big rejection and news they don't want to hear," she says, noting that because of the timetable of early decision, letters often come right around exam time in December.

When students apply regular decision, meaning they wait until well into their senior year and apply to several different institutions, it's "all or some," quips Latting. "With early decision, it's all or nothing." Many application deadlines for regular decision are in January. If you get that rejection letter from the school you were counting on, that doesn't give you much time to apply to other schools, much less visit them.

Are you ready to make such a drastic decision so early in your senior year? A lot can change in how you think about your future between the beginning of your senior year and graduation. With six or seven months behind you as a senior, you might be in a better position to compare colleges in April than you were back in September. Think about it—you're making the decision about where you want to spend the next four years of your life in early October of your senior year!

Have you given yourself enough time to pick one college above all others? If you want to apply early decision, you should start making plans to do so in your junior year. In order to apply early decision, you must have your ACT®s or SAT®s taken, campus visits done, a final choice made, a dynamite essay written, a stellar application filled out, and teacher recommendation letters collected. That's a lot to cram into the end of your junior year and a few months into your senior year.

Have you given an admissions office enough information to make a decision about you? The more information the admissions office has about grades and classes you took and activities and leadership positions you held, the better they can decide if you're a good match for them. Do you really want decisions being made about you based on sophomore and junior grades and activities? What happens to that AP English class you finally felt ready to take the beginning of your senior year? What about that calculus class you aced in the first semester of your senior year? Admissions won't be able to assess that on an early decision application.

early decision student is not coming, so they'll call the counselor and ask if the student applied to another school. If so, often a phone call to the other institution is made and acceptance denied. Sometimes the counselor loses a good reputation with that institution, putting applicants who follow in subsequent years at a disadvantage.

After the consequences of signing a binding agreement, the financial aspect of early decision is the next biggest pitfall. "You can't compare financial aid offers," says Latting. "You have only one offer." Students won't know if they're eligible for Pell grants or merit scholarships. Government FAFSA forms are not submitted until January, and students might not find out how much aid they can get until March or April, long after the early decision agreement was signed and sealed. "This means that if they are accepted, they are then obligated to a college that might not fund them to the level of their financial need," says Gibson. Students who apply early action or regular decision are in a better position to negotiate financial aid packages.

EARLY DECISION REJECTION

In case you haven't heard, "fat" is good, "thin" is bad. Thin envelopes from college admissions offices usually mean a single-page letter saying good luck, we wish you the best, but you're not going to be attending our school next fall. However stated, it's hard to be rejected, especially when you've applied early decision, which states to the college and to yourself that this is the college you've decided is the only one you really, really want to attend above all others.

But thin envelopes don't mean the end of the world. Cleaver advises to not let early decision get control of you. "There are too many choices of colleges for you not to get into college. You might not get into Princeton, but there are many other wonderful schools if you do the research to look for a good match. Early decision is a tool to use to apply, but it is not always the best tool."

Objecting to the term "perfect match," Reider asks, "Does it really matter what kind of car you drive? There are twenty different colleges that can get you where you want to go. You'll be successful in most places."

HOW TO DO EARLY DECISION THE RIGHT WAY

Taking the early decision option requires more than gathering information, filling out an application, writing an essay, and waiting for an envelope to come in the mail or an e-mail to hit your Inbox. If you're going to be serious about early decision, the time to start is in your junior year.

Research the institutions at the top of your list. Think through what you want out of college—not just in terms of a future career, but also factors such as location, size, distance from home, sports, and other activities. Think about who you want to be. "It has to be a love connection," says Cleaver. Tune out all the early decision talk and do your homework about each college. Then ask yourself if one stands out above all the others you've researched. Is this the one to which you can commit to a binding agreement? Are you in the competition to be admitted? Will you have the funds to attend this college?

"Admissions can tell if your application is from the heart," Cleaver cautions. Students ask her how to make their applications "look like they want to go there." She replies that what they put on an application and in an essay has to pour out of their hearts. Students who visit the campus and sit in on a class or a campus organization have the edge if something really clicked with them. They will write a convincing application. Perhaps they'll tell about how exciting the professor they heard was or how wonderful it is that the college has a chess club. Cleaver observes that kids usually write about an institution's sports team or about the ivy-covered walls of the campus on their application essay instead of writing about some interesting aspect of the university that spoke to them, which takes research, time, and reflection. "Don't make the mistake of chasing a name and not being a good consumer," cautions McClintick. Part of being a good consumer is to make sure you are a reasonably competitive applicant. This means looking at the school's admission criteria and statistics. What percentage of the freshman class is filled with early decision and early action students? If it's a high percentage, then you might want to reconsider where that school falls on your wish list. How many students return for their sophomore year? If more than 10 percent leave after their freshman year, that should tell you something about student satisfaction—and ultimately yours.

One of the most important ways to choose the right school is to visit the campus, perhaps multiple times and preferably with students on campus. "Campus visits are a critical time to talk with undergraduates and to find out what the academic, social, and physical climate is like," advises Guttentag. If you're staying in a dorm on Tuesday night during a visit, you can tell how serious kids are about their work. What kinds of conversations are they having? "Are these the kind of kids you want to spend four years of your life with?" asks McClintick.

After you've thoroughly investigated all the aspects of a college and decided it's at the absolute top of your list, after you are familiar with the early decision requirements at that institution, and after you've determined that you have a good chance of getting into that institution, then you can say early decision is for you. For those who are not so sure, fortunately, colleges and universities have plenty of other options for admission.

Coming to America: Tips for International Students Considering Study in the U.S.

Introduction: Why Study in the United States?

Are you thinking about going to a college or university in the United States? If you're looking at this book, you probably are! All around the world, students like you who are pursuing high education are considering that possibility. They envision themselves on modern, high-tech campuses in well-known cities, surrounded by American students, taking classes and having fun. A degree from a U.S. school would certainly lead to success and fortune, either back in your home country or perhaps even in the United States, wouldn't it?

It can be done—but becoming a student at a college or university in the U.S. requires academic talent, planning, time, effort, and money. While there may be only a small number of institutions of higher learning in your country, there are more than 2,900 four-year colleges and universities in the United States. Choosing one, being accepted, and then traveling and becoming a student in America is a big undertaking.

If this is your dream, here is some helpful information and expert tips from professionals who work with international students at colleges and universities throughout the United States.

Timing and Planning

The journey to a college or university in the U.S. often starts years in advance. Most international students choose to study in the U.S. because of the high quality of academics. Your family may also have a lot of input on this decision, too.

"We always tell students they should be looking in the sophomore year, visiting in the junior year, and applying in the senior year," says Father Francis E. Chambers, OSA, D.Min., Associate Director of International Admission at Villanova University. He stresses that prospective students need to be taking challenging courses in the years leading up to college. "We want to see academic rigor. Most admission decisions are based on the first six semesters—senior year is too late."

Heidi Gregori-Gahan, Assistant Provost for International Programs at the University of Southern Indiana agrees that it's important to start early. "Plan ahead and do your homework. There is so much to choose from—so many schools, programs, degrees, and experiences. It can be overwhelming."

While students in some countries may pay an agent to help them get into a school in the United States, Gregori-Gahan often directs potential international students to EducationUSA (**https://educationusa.state.gov**), a U.S. State Department network of over 400 international student advising centers in more than 170 countries. "They are there to provide unbiased information about studying in the United States and help you understand the process and what you need to do."

Two to three years of advance planning is also recommended by Daphne Durham, who has been an international student adviser at Harvard, Suffolk University, Valdosta State University, and the University of Georgia. She points out that the academic schedule in other countries is often different than that of the United States, so you need to synchronize your calendar accordingly.

You will have to take several tests in order to gain admission to a U.S. school, so it's important to know when those tests are given in your country, then register and take them so your scores will be available when you apply. Even if you have taken English in school, you will probably have to take The Test of English as a Foreign Language (TOEFL®), but some schools also accept the International English Language Testing System (IELTS). You will probably also have to take the SAT® or ACT® tests, which are achievement or aptitude tests, and are usually required of all students applying for admission, not just international students.

"Make sure you understand how the international admissions process works at the school or schools you want to attend," says Durham. "What test scores are needed and when? Does the school have a fixed calendar or rolling admissions?" Those are just some of the many factors that can impact your application and could make a difference in when you are able to start school.

"Every university is unique in what's required and what they need to do. Even navigating each school's different website can be challenging," explains Gregori-Gahan.

Searching for Schools

This book contains information on thousands of four-year colleges and universities, and it will be a valuable resource for you in your search and application process. But with so many options, how do you decide which school you should attend?

"Where I find a big difference with international students is if their parents don't recognize the school, they don't apply to the school," says Fr. Chambers. "They could be overlooking a lot of great schools. They have to look outside the box."

The school Gregori-Gahan represents is in Evansville, Indiana, and it probably isn't familiar to students abroad. "Not many people have heard of anything beyond New York and California and maybe Florida. I like to tell students that this is 'real America.' But happy international students on our campus have recruited others to come here."

She points out that internet technology has made a huge difference in the search process for international students. Websites full of information, live chat, webinars, virtual tours, and admission interviews via video chat have made it easier for potential students to connect with U.S. institutions, get more information, and be better able to visualize the campus.

One thing that will help narrow your search for a school is knowing specifically what you want to study. You need to know what the course of study is called in the United States, what it means, and what is required in order to study that subject. You also need to consider your future plans. What are your goals and objectives? What do you plan to do after earning your degree?

"If you're going to overcome the hurdles and get to a U.S. school, you have to have a directed path chosen," says Durham.

The other thing that could help your search process is finding a school that is a good fit.

Fit Is Important

You want your clothing and shoes to fit you properly and be comfortable, so a place where you will spend four or more years of your life studying should also be comfortable and appropriate for you. So how can you determine if a particular school is a good fit?

"We really recommend international students visit first. Yes, there are websites and virtual tours, but there's still nothing that beats an in-person visit," says Fr. Chambers. He estimates that 50 to 60 percent of Villanova's international students visited the campus before enrolling.

"It can be hard to get a sense of a place—you're so far away and you're probably not going to set foot on campus until you arrive," says Gregori-Gahan. "There is a high potential for culture shock."

You need to ask yourself what is important to you in a campus environment, then do some homework to ensure that the schools you are considering meet those needs. Here are some things to consider when it comes to fit:

- **Location:** Is it important for you to be in a well-known city or is a part of the United States that is unfamiliar a possibility? "Look at geographic areas, but also cost of living," recommends Durham. "Be sure to factor in transportation costs also, especially if you plan to return to your home country regularly."
- **Student population:** Some small schools have 1,000 students while larger ones may have 30,000 students or more.
- **Familiar faces:** Is it important for you to be at a school with others from your home nation or region?
- **Climate:** Some students want a climate similar to where they live now, but others are open and curious about seasons and weather conditions they may not have ever experienced. "We do have four seasons here," says Gregori-Gahan. "Sometimes students who come here from tropical regions are concerned about the winters. The first snow is so exciting, but after that, students may not be aware of how cold it really is."
- **Amenities:** Do you want to find your own housing or choose a school where the majority of students live on campus? Is there public transportation available or is it necessary to walk or have a bicycle or car? Does the school or community have access to things that are important to you culturally and meet the traditions you want to follow?
- **Campus size:** Some campuses are tightly compacted into a few city blocks, but others cover hundreds of acres of land. "International students are amazed by how green and spacious our campus is, with blooming flowers, trees, and lots of grass," says Gregori-Gahan.
- **Academic offerings:** Does this school offer the program you want to study? Can you complete it in four years or perhaps sooner? What sort of internship and career services are available?
- **Finances:** Can you afford to attend this school? Is there any sort of financial assistance available for international students?
- **Support services:** Durham suggests students look carefully at each school's offerings for international students. "Does the school have online guidance for getting your visa? Is ESL tutoring available? Does the school offer host family or community friend programs?" She also suggests you look for campus support groups for students from your country or region.

Looking at the listings and reading the in-depth descriptions in this book can help you search for a school that is a good fit for you.

Government Requirements

The one thing that every international student must have in order to study in the United States is a student visa. Having accurate advice and following all the necessary steps regarding the visa process is essential to being able to enter this country and start school.

As you schedule your tests and application deadlines, you must also consider how long it will take to get your visa. This varies depending on where you live; in some countries, extensive background checks are required. The subject you plan to study can also impact your visa status; it does help to have a major rather than be undeclared. The U.S. State Department website, **https://travel.state.gov/content/travel/en/us-visas/study.html**, can give you an idea of how long it will take.

In addition to the visa, you will also need a Form I-20, which is a U.S. government immigration form. You must have this form when you get to the United States.

"It's very different from being a tourist. You need to be prepared to meet with an immigration officer and be interviewed about your college," explains Durham. "Where you are going, why you are going, where the school is located, what you are studying, and so on."

You also need to keep in mind that there are reporting requirements once you are a student in the United States. Every semester, your adviser has to report to the government to confirm that you are enrolled in and attending school in order for you to stay.

Finances

Part of the visa process includes having the funds to pay for the cost of your schooling and support yourself. Finances are a huge hurdle in the process of becoming a college student in the United States.

"It's crucial. So many foreign systems offer 'free' higher education to students. How is your family going to handle the ongoing expense of attending college for four years or longer in the United States?" Durham reiterates that planning ahead is key because there are so many details. Student loans require a U.S.-based cosigner. Each school has its own financial aid deadlines. You have to factor in your own government's requirements, such currency exchange and fund transfers.

The notion that abundant funds are available to assist international students is not true. Sometimes state schools may offer diversity waivers or there may be special scholarship opportunities for international students. But attending school in the U.S. is still a costly venture.

"We do offer financial aid to international students, but they still have to be able to handle a large portion of the costs. Full-need scholarships are not likely," explained Fr. Chambers. "Sometimes students think that once they get here, it will all work out and the funds will be there. But the scenario for the first year has to be repeated each year they are on campus."

Once You Arrive...

You've taken your tests, researched schools, found a good fit, applied, got accepted, arranged the financing, gotten your visa and I-20, and made it to the campus in the United States. Now what?

You can expect the school where you have enrolled to be welcoming and helpful, but within reason. If you arrive on a weekend, or at a time outside of the time when international students are scheduled to arrive, the assistance you need may not be available to you.

Every school offers different levels of assistance to international students. For instance, Villanova offers a full-service office that can assist students with everything from visas, to employment, to finding a place for students to stay over breaks.

Fr. Chambers attends the international student orientation session to greet the students he's worked with through the recruitment and application process. "But I rarely see an international student after that. I think that bodes well for them being integrated into the entire university."

"Those of us who work with international students are really working to help them adjust," says Gregori-Gahan. "International students get here well before school starts so they can get over jet lag. We have orientation sessions and pair them with peer advisers who help them navigate the first few days, and we assure them that we are there for them."

Students should be open to their new setting, but they should be prepared that things may not be at all how they had envisioned during their planning and searching process. "While you may think you'll meet lots of Americans, don't underestimate the importance of community with your traditional home culture and people," says Durham.

Don't Make These Mistakes

The journey to college attendance in the United States is a long one, with many steps. Experts warn about avoiding common mistakes along the way and offer the following helpful advice:

"Not reading through everything thoroughly and not understanding what the program of study really is and what will it cost. You have to be really clear on the important details," says Gregori-Gahan.

"Every school does things differently," cautions Fr. Chambers. "International students must be aware of that as they are applying."

Durham stresses that going to school in the United States is too big a decision to leave to someone else. "Students need to know about their school—they have to be in charge of their application."

"It involves a lot of work to be successful and happy and not surprised by too many things," Gregori-Gahan says.

Hopefully now, you are more informed and better prepared to pursue your dream of studying at a college or university in the United States.

Financial Aid Countdown Calendar

JUNIOR YEAR

Fall

Now is the time to get serious about the colleges in which you are interested. Meet with your guidance counselor to help you narrow down your choices. Hopefully by the spring, your list will have five to ten solid choices. College visits are always a great idea—remember this will be the place you will call home for four years, so start your campus visits soon!

- ❑ Register for the PSAT/NMSQT®.
- ❑ Check out local financial aid nights in the area. Be sure to attend these valuable sessions, especially if this is the first time your family is sending someone off to college. Try to become familiar with common financial aid terms. Start reviewing the literature available and begin to familiarize yourself with the various programs. **https://studentaid.ed.gov/h/understand-aid**
- ❑ In October, take the PSAT/NMSQT®.
- ❑ Do some web browsing! There are many free scholarship search engines, such as **Petersons.com.** Also, head to the bookstore or library and pick up a copy of *Peterson's® Scholarships, Grants & Prizes,* which features details on aid from private sources, or *Best Scholarships for the Best Students,* which offers great info on scholarships, fellowships, and experiential learning programs for top students.
- ❑ Ask your parents to contact their employers, unions, and any religious and fraternal organizations with which they have a connection to learn about possible scholarship opportunities.
- ❑ Check with your high school guidance counselor for the qualifications and deadlines of local scholarship awards. Many guidance counselors report that there are few applicants for these awards.

Winter

- ❑ Keep checking for scholarships! Remember that this is the one area over which you have control. The harder you work, the better your chances for success!
- ❑ Register and study for the ACT® or SAT® and SAT Subject Tests™.

Spring

- ❑ Spring Break—a great time to visit colleges. Remember your top ten list? Time to start narrowing it down.
- ❑ Review the requirements for local scholarships. What can you do now and over the summer to improve your chances?
- ❑ Take the ACT® or SAT®. Good luck!
- ❑ Look for a summer job, especially one that ties in with your college plans. For example, if you want to major in premed, why not try to get a job at a hospital or with a laboratory?

Summer

- ❑ College visit time! Ask: Is this where I see myself getting my undergraduate degree? Can I adjust to the seasons, the town surrounding the campus, the distance from home, the college size? Does this school feel right for me?
- ❑ Why not get a jump on college (and maybe save some money!) and enroll for a college course at the local community college? Or, better yet, do some extra prep work for the ACT® or SAT®!

SENIOR YEAR

Fall

How's the college list coming? Can you get your list down to five or six choices? Your guidance counselor can help with this process. Once you have your top choices, make a list of what each college requires for admission and financial aid. Be sure your list includes all deadlines. Attend a financial aid night presentation with your parents. Some of these sessions offer help in completing forms; others offer a broader view of the process. Contact the presenter (usually a local college financial aid professional) to be sure you are getting the information you need.

- ❑ Do any of these colleges require the CSS/Financial Aid PROFILE® financial aid application? Many private colleges use this form for institutional aid. You need to file this comprehensive form in late September or early October. For more information or to find out which colleges use this supplemental form, go to **https://cssprofile.collegeboard.org/**. (Website registration is free; however, PROFILE® is a fee-based application).
- ❑ If you are planning on applying for federal student aid, you should complete and submit your FAFSA® Application as soon as possible. The application can be submitted as early as October 1 every year.
- ❑ Don't falter now in your scholarship search. Get the applications filed by the published deadlines.
- ❑ Register now if you are planning to retake the SAT®.
- ❑ Most important, start completing your college applications—the earlier, the better! If you are interested in early decision or early action, now is the time! Remember, accuracy and completeness are a must!

Winter

- ❑ Ensure all college applications are completed.
- ❑ Do you have questions? Call the local financial aid office. Many states have special toll-free call-in programs in January and February (Financial Aid Awareness Month). Be sure that you have completed each school's required forms.
- ❑ As the letters of admission start to arrive, the financial aid award letters should be right behind them. Important question for parents: What is the bottom line? Remember, aid at a lower-cost state school will be less than a higher-cost private college. But what will you be required to pay? This can be confusing, so consider gift aid (scholarships and grants), student loans, and parent loans. The school with the lowest sticker price (tuition, fees, and room and board) might not be the best bargain when you look at the overall financial aid package.

Spring

- ❑ Still not sure where to go? The financial aid package at your top choice just not enough? Call the financial aid office and the admissions office. Talk it over. While schools don't like to bargain, they are usually willing to take a second look. Is there something unusual about your family's financial situation that might impact your parents' ability to pay?
- ❑ By May 1, you must make your final decision. Notify your chosen college and find out what you need to do next. Tell the other colleges you are not accepting their offers of admission and financial aid.

Summer

- ❑ Time to crunch the numbers. Parents, get information from the college on the total charges for the coming fall term. Deduct the aid package and then plan for how the balance will be paid. Contact the college financial aid office for the best parental loan program. If you want to arrange for a payment plan, contact the business office for further information. Most schools have deferred payment plans available for a nominal fee.

Congratulations! Remember that you need to reapply for aid every year!

Who's Paying for This? Financial Aid Basics

A college education can be expensive—costing over $250,000 for four years at some of the higher priced private colleges and universities. Among the 10 most expensive private schools, the average tuition and fees in 2018-2019 was almost $56,900. Even at the lower-cost state colleges and universities, the cost of a four-year education can approach $60,000. Determining how you and your family will come up with the necessary funds to pay for your education requires planning, perseverance, and learning as much as you can about the options that are available to you. But before you get discouraged, College Board statistics show that 53 percent of full-time students attend four-year public and private colleges with tuition and fees less than $12,000, while 20 percent attend colleges that have tuition and fees more than $48,000. College costs tend to be less in the western states and higher in New England.

Paying for college should not be looked at as a four-year financial commitment. For many families, paying the total cost of a student's college education out of current income and savings is usually not realistic. For families that have planned ahead and have financial savings established for higher education, the burden is a lot easier. But for most, meeting the cost of college requires the pooling of current income and assets and investing in longer-term loan options. These family resources, together with financial assistance from state, federal, and institutional sources, enable millions of students each year to attend the institution of their choice.

FINANCIAL AID PROGRAMS

There are three types of financial aid:

1. Gift-aid—Scholarships and grants are funds that do not have to be repaid.
2. Loans—Loans must be repaid, usually after graduation; the amount you have to pay back is the total you've borrowed plus any accrued interest. This is considered a source of self-help aid.
3. Student employment—Student employment is a job arranged for you by the financial aid office. This is another source of self-help aid.

The federal government has four major grant programs—the Federal Pell Grant, the Federal Supplemental Educational Opportunity Grant, Academic Competitiveness Grants (ACG), and National SMART (Science and Mathematics Access to Retain Talent) grants. ACG and SMART grants are limited to students who qualify for a Pell Grant and are awarded to a select group of students. Overall, these grants are targeted to low-to-moderate income families with significant financial need. The federal government also sponsors a student employment program called the Federal Work-Study Program, which offers jobs both on and off campus, and several loan programs, including those for students and for parents of undergraduate students.

There are two types of student loan programs: subsidized and unsubsidized. The subsidized Federal Direct Loan and the Federal Perkins Loan are need-based, government-subsidized loans. Students who borrow through these programs do not have to pay interest on the loan until after they graduate or leave school. The unsubsidized Federal Direct Loan and the Federal Direct PLUS Loan Program are not based on need, and borrowers are responsible for the interest while the student is in school. These loans are administered by different methods. Once you choose your college, the financial aid office will guide you through this process.

After you've submitted your financial aid application and you've been accepted for admission, each college will send you a letter describing your financial aid award. Most award letters show estimated college costs, how much you and your family are expected to contribute, and the amount and types of aid you have been awarded. Most students are awarded aid from a combination of sources and programs. Hence, your award is often called a financial aid "package."

SOURCES OF FINANCIAL AID

Millions of students and families apply for financial aid each year. Financial aid from all sources exceeds $143 billion per year. The largest single source of aid is the federal government, which will award more than $100 billion this year.

The next largest source of financial aid is found in the college and university community. Most of this aid is awarded to students who have a demonstrated need based on the Federal Methodology. Some institutions use a different formula, the Institutional Methodology (IM), to award their own funds in conjunction with other forms of aid. Institutional aid may be either need-based or non-need based. Aid that is not based on need is usually awarded for a student's academic performance (merit awards), specific talents or abilities, or to attract the type of students a college seeks to enroll.

Another source of financial aid is from state government. All states offer grant and/or scholarship aid, most of which is need-based. However, more and more states are offering substantial merit-based aid programs. Most state programs award aid only to students attending college in their home state.

Other sources of financial aid include:

- Private agencies
- Foundations
- Corporations

- Clubs
- Fraternal and service organizations
- Civic associations
- Unions
- Religious groups that award grants, scholarships, and low-interest loans
- Employers that provide tuition reimbursement benefits for employees and their children

More information about these different sources of aid is available from high school guidance offices, public libraries, college financial aid offices, directly from the sponsoring organizations, and online at **https://www.petersons.com/scholarship-search.aspx**.

HOW NEED-BASED FINANCIAL AID IS AWARDED

When you apply for aid, your family's financial situation is analyzed using a government-approved formula called the Federal Methodology. This formula looks at five items:

1. Demographic information of the family
2. Income of the parents
3. Assets of the parents
4. Income of the student
5. Assets of the student

This analysis determines the amount you and your family are expected to contribute toward your college expenses, called your Expected Family Contribution, or EFC. If the EFC is equal to or more than the cost of attendance at a particular college, then you do not demonstrate financial need. However, even if you don't have financial need, you may still qualify for aid, as there are grants, scholarships, and loan programs that are not need-based.

If the cost of your education is greater than your EFC, then you do demonstrate financial need and qualify for assistance. The amount of your financial need that can be met varies from school to school. Some are able to meet your full need, while others can only cover a certain percentage of need. Here's the formula:

Cost of Attendance
− Expected Family Contribution
= Financial Need

The EFC remains constant, but your need will vary according to the costs of attendance at a particular college. In general, the higher the tuition and fees at a particular college, the higher the cost of attendance will be. Expenses for books and supplies, room and board, transportation, and other miscellaneous items are included in the overall cost of attendance. It is important to remember that you do not have to be low-income to qualify for financial aid. Many middle and upper-middle income families qualify for need-based financial aid.

APPLYING FOR FINANCIAL AID

Every student must complete the Free Application for Federal Student Aid (FAFSA) to be considered for financial aid. The FAFSA is available from your high school guidance office, many public libraries, colleges in your area, or directly from the U.S. Department of Education.

Students are encouraged to apply for federal student aid on the web. The electronic version of the FAFSA can be accessed at **http://www.fafsa.ed.gov**.

The NEW Federal Student Aid ID

In order for a student to complete the online FAFSA®, he or she will need a Federal Student Aid (FSA) ID. You can get this online at **https://fsaid.ed.gov/npas/index.htm**. Since May 2015, the FSA ID has replaced the previously used PIN system. Parents of dependent students also need to obtain their own FSA ID in order to sign their child's FAFSA® electronically online.

The FSA ID can be used to access several federal aid-related websites, including FAFSA.gov and StudentLoans.gov. It consists of a username and password and can be used to electronically sign Federal Student Aid documents, access your personal records, and make binding legal obligations. The FSA ID is beneficial in several ways:

- It removes your personal identifiable information (PII), such as your Social Security number, from your log-in credentials.
- It creates a more secure and efficient way to verify your information when you log in to access to your federal student aid information online.
- It gives you the ability to easily update your personal information.
- It allows you to easily retrieve your username and password by requesting a secure code be sent to your e-mail address or by answering challenge questions.

It's relatively simple to create an FSA ID and should only take a few minutes. In addition, you will have an opportunity to link your current Federal Student Aid PIN (if you already have one) to your FSA ID. The final step is to confirm your e-mail address. You will receive a secure code to the e-mail address you provided when you set up your FSA ID. Once you retrieve the code from your e-mail account and enter it—to confirm your e-mail address is valid—you will be able to use this e-mail address instead of your username to log in to any of the federal aid-related websites, making the log-in process EVEN simpler for you and your parents.

When you initially create your FSA ID, your information will need to be verified with the Social Security Administration. This process can take anywhere from one to three days. For that reason, it's a good idea to take care of setting up your FSA ID as early as possible, so it will be all set when you are ready to begin completing your FAFSA.

IMPORTANT NOTE: Since your FSA ID provides access to your personal information and is used to sign online documents, it's imperative that you protect this ID. Don't share it with *anyone* or write it down in an insecure location—you could place yourself at great risk for identify theft.

If Every College You're Applying to for Fall 2021 Requires the FAFSA

. . . then it's pretty simple: Complete the FAFSA after October 1, 2020, being certain to send it in before any college-imposed deadlines. Students will be required to report income information from an earlier tax year. For example, on the 2020-21 FAFSA, students (and parents, as appropriate) will report their 2019 income information, rather than their 2019 income information.

After you send in your FAFSA, you'll receive a Student Aid Report (SAR) that includes all of the information you reported and shows your EFC. If you provided an e-mail address, the SAR is sent to you electronically; otherwise, you will receive a SAR or SAR Acknowledgment in the mail, which lists your FAFSA information but may require you to make any corrections on the FAFSA website. Be sure to review the SAR, checking to see if the information you reported is accurately represented. If you used estimated numbers to complete the FAFSA, you may have to resubmit the SAR with any corrections to the data. The college(s) you have designated on the FAFSA will receive the information you reported and will use that data to make their decision.

The CSS/Financial Aid PROFILE®

To award their own funds, some colleges require an additional application, the CSS/Financial Aid PROFILE® form. The PROFILE asks supplemental questions that some colleges and awarding agencies feel provide a more accurate assessment of the family's ability to pay for college. It is up to the college to decide whether it will use only the FAFSA or both the FAFSA and the PROFILE. PROFILE applications are available from the high school guidance office and on the Web. Both the paper application and the website list those colleges and programs that require the PROFILE application.

If a College Requires the PROFILE

Step 1: Register for the CSS/Financial Aid PROFILE in the fall of your senior year in high school. You can apply for the PROFILE online at **https://cssprofile.collegeboard.org/**. Registration information with a list of the colleges that require the PROFILE is available in most high school guidance offices. There is a fee for using the Financial Aid PROFILE application ($25 for the first college, which includes the $9 application fee, and $16 for each additional college). You must pay for the service by credit card when you register. If you do not have a credit card, you will be billed. A limited number of fee waivers are automatically granted to first-time applicants based on the financial information provided on the PROFILE.

Step 2: Fill out your customized CSS/Financial Aid PROFILE. Once you register, your application will be immediately available online and will have questions that all students must complete, questions which must be completed by the student's parents (unless the student is independent and the colleges or programs selected do not require parental information), and *may* have supplemental questions needed by one or more of your schools or programs. If required, those will be found in Section Q of the application.

In addition to the PROFILE application you complete online, you may also be required to complete a Business/ Farm Supplement via traditional paper format. Completion of this form is not a part of the online process. If this form is required, instructions on how to download and print the supplemental form are provided. If your biological or adoptive parents are separated or divorced and your colleges and programs require it, your noncustodial parent may be asked to complete the Noncustodial PROFILE.

Once you complete and submit your PROFILE application, it will be processed and sent directly to your requested colleges and programs.

IF YOU DON'T QUALIFY FOR NEED-BASED AID

If you are not eligible for need-based aid, you can still find ways to lessen your burden.

Here are some suggestions:

- Search for merit scholarships. You can start at the initial stages of your application process. College merit awards are increasingly important as more and more colleges award these to students they especially want to attract. As a result, applying to a college at which your qualifications put you at the top of the entering class may give you a larger merit award. Another source of aid to look for is private scholarships that are given for special skills and talents. Additional information can be found at **www.finaid.org**.
- Seek employment during the summer and the academic year. The student employment office at your college can help you locate a school-year job. Many colleges and local businesses have vacancies remaining after they have hired students who are receiving Federal Work-Study Program financial aid.
- Borrow through the unsubsidized Federal Direct Loan program. This is generally available to all students. The terms and conditions are similar to the subsidized loans. The biggest difference is that the borrower is responsible for the interest while still in college, although the government permits students to delay paying the interest right away and add the accrued interest to the total amount owed. You must file the FAFSA to be considered.
- After you've secured what you can through scholarships, working, and borrowing, you and your parents will be expected to meet your share of the college bill (the Expected Family Contribution). Many colleges offer monthly payment plans that spread the cost over the academic year. If the monthly payments are too high, parents can borrow through the Federal Direct PLUS Loan Program, through one of the many private education loan programs available, or through home equity loans and lines of credit. Families seeking assistance in financing college expenses should inquire at the financial aid office about what programs are available at the college. Some families seek the advice of professional financial advisers and tax consultants.

How to Use This Guide

PROFILES

The **PROFILES** section contains basic data in capsule form for quick review and comparison. Organized by state, more than 2,600 colleges and universities are listed alphabetically, followed by their city and state and website URL.

The following outline of the format shows the section headings and the items that each section covers. Any item that does not apply to a particular college or for which no information was supplied is omitted from that college's listing. Display ads, which appear near some of the institutions' profiles, have been provided and paid for by those colleges and universities that chose to supplement their profile with additional information.

Category Overviews

Type of Institution

Private institutions are designated as *independent* (nonprofit), *proprietary* (profit-making), or *independent with a specific religious denomination or affiliation*. Nondenominational or interdenominational religious orientation is possible and would be indicated. Public institutions are designated by the source of funding. Designations include *federal, state, province, commonwealth* (Puerto Rico), *territory* (U.S. territories), *county, district* (an educational administrative unit often having boundaries different from units of local government), *city, state and local* (local may refer to county, district, or city), or *state-related* (funded primarily by the state but administratively autonomous). *Religious affiliation* may follow, along with year founded. Each institution is classified as one of the following:

- Primarily two-year: Awards baccalaureate degrees but majority of students are enrolled in two-year programs.
- Four-year: Awards baccalaureate degrees; may also award associate degrees; does not award graduate (postbaccalaureate) degrees.
- Five-year: Awards a five-year baccalaureate in a professional field such as architecture or pharmacy; does not award graduate degrees.
- Upper-level: Awards baccalaureate degrees but entering students must have at least two years of previous college-level credit; may also offer graduate degrees.
- Comprehensive: Awards baccalaureate degrees; may also award associate degrees; offers graduate degree programs, primarily at the master's, specialist's, or professional level, although one or two doctoral programs may be offered.
- University: Offers four years of undergraduate work, plus graduate degrees through the doctorate in more than two academic or professional fields.

Setting

Designated as *urban* (located within a major city), *suburban* (a residential area within commuting distance of a major city), *small town* (a small but compactly settled area not within commuting distance of a major city), or *rural* (a remote and sparsely populated area).

Endowment

The total dollar value of funds and/or property donated to the institution or the multicampus educational system of which the institution is a part.

Student Body

An institution is *coed* (coeducational—admits men and women), *primarily* (80 percent or more) *women, primarily men, women only,* or *men only.* A few schools are designated as *undergraduate: women only; graduate: coed* or *undergraduate: men only; graduate: coed.*

Entrance

The five levels of entrance difficulty (*most difficult, very difficult, moderately difficult, minimally difficult,* and *noncompetitive*) are based on the percentage of applicants who were accepted for fall 2018 freshman admission (or, in the case of upper-level schools, for entering-class admission) and on the high school class rank and standardized test scores of the accepted freshmen who actually enrolled in fall 2018. The colleges were asked to select the level that most closely corresponds to their entrance difficulty, according to these guidelines.

UNDERGRAD STUDENTS

Number of full-time or part-time undergraduates. Number of states and territories that students come from; percentages of undergraduates who are out-of-state; live on campus; Black or African American, non-Hispanic/Latino; Hispanic/Latino; Asian, non-Hispanic/Latino; Native Hawaiian or other Pacific Islander, non-Hispanic/Latino; American Indian or Alaska Native, non-Hispanic/Latino American Indian or Alaska Native, non-Hispanic/Latino; two or more races, non-Hispanic/Latino; race/ethnicity unknown; international; and percentage of students who transferred in are given.

Freshmen

Admission: Figures are given for the number of students who applied for fall 2018 admission, the number of those who were admitted, and the number who enrolled. *Average high school GPA:* Freshman statistics include the average high school GPA. *Test scores:* Percentage of freshmen who took the SAT® (not the Redesigned SAT) and received critical reading, math, and writing scores above 500, above 600, and above 700; as well as percentage of freshmen taking the ACT® who received a composite score of 18 or higher, 24 or higher, and 30 or higher.

Retention: The percentage of full-time freshmen who returned the following year for the fall semester/term.

FACULTY

Total: The total number of faculty members; percentage of full-time faculty members as of fall 2019; and percentage of total faculty members who hold terminal degrees. *Student/faculty ratio:* School's estimate of the ratio of matriculated undergraduate students to faculty members teaching undergraduate courses.

ACADEMICS

Calendar: Most colleges indicate one of the following: 4-1-4, 4-4-1, or a similar arrangement (two terms of equal length plus an abbreviated winter or spring term, with the numbers referring to months); semesters; trimesters; quarters; 3-3 (three courses for each of three terms); modular (the academic year is divided into small blocks of time; courses of varying lengths are assembled according to individual programs); or standard year (for most Canadian institutions). *Degrees:* This names the full range of levels of certificates, diplomas, and degrees, including prebaccalaureate, baccalaureate, graduate, and professional, that are offered by this institution.

Special study options: Details on study options available at each college, such as accelerated degree program, academic remediation for entering students, Advanced Placement credit, cooperative education programs, distance learning, double majors, English as a second language (ESL), and external degree programs. *ROTC:* Army, Naval, or Air Force Reserve Officers' Training Corps programs offered either on campus, at a branch campus [designated by a (b)], or at a cooperating host institution [designated by (c)].

Unusual degree programs: Information is offered here on any unique programs at the institution, such as 3-2 engineering, computer science, or business administration programs.

Computers: Information is provided on the numbers of computers/terminals available on campus for general student use, what computer technology is accessible to students, and availability of a campus-wide network and wireless campus network.

STUDENT LIFE

Housing options: Institution's policy about whether students are permitted to live off-campus or are required to live on campus for a specified period; whether freshmen only, coed, single-sex, cooperative, and disabled student housing options are available; whether campus housing is leased by the school and/or provided by a third party; whether freshman applicants are given priority for college housing. "College housing not available" indicates that no college-owned or -operated housing facilities are provided for undergraduates and that noncommuting students must arrange for their own accommodations.

Activities and organizations: Information on clubs and organizations, including sororities and fraternities.

Athletics: Membership in one or more of the following athletic associations is indicated by initials: NCAA: National Collegiate Athletic Association; NAIA: National Association of Intercollegiate Athletics; NCCAA: National Christian College Athletic Association; USCAA: United States Collegiate Athletic Association; and CIS: Canadian Interuniversity Sport. The overall NCAA division in which all or most intercollegiate teams compete is designated by I, II, or III. All teams that do not compete in this division are listed as exceptions.

Sports offered by the college are divided into two groups: *Intercollegiate* ("M" or "W" following the name of each sport indicates that it is offered for men or women) and *Intramural.* An "s" in parentheses following an "M" or "W" for an intercollegiate sport indicates that athletic scholarships (or grants-in-aid) are offered for men or women in that sport, and a "c" indicates a club team as opposed to a varsity team.

Campus security: Campus safety measures including 24-hour emergency response devices (phones and alarms) and patrols by trained security personnel, student patrols, late-night transport-escort service, and controlled dormitory access (key, security card, etc.).

Student services: Information indicates services offered to students by the college, such as legal services, health clinics, personal-psychological counseling, and women's centers.

COSTS & FINANCIAL AID

Costs: Costs are given for the 2020–21 academic year or for the 2019–20 academic year if 2020–21 figures were not yet available. *Tuition:* Annual expenses may be expressed as a comprehensive fee (including full-time tuition, mandatory fees, and college room and board) or as separate figures for full-time tuition, fees, room and board, or room only. For public institutions where tuition differs according to residence, separate figures are given for area or state residents and for nonresidents. Part-time tuition is expressed in terms of a per-unit rate (per credit, per semester hour, etc.).

The tuition structure at some institutions is complex in that freshmen and sophomores may be charged a different rate from that for juniors and seniors, a professional or vocational division may have a different fee structure from the liberal arts division of the same institution, or part-time tuition may be prorated on a sliding scale according to the number of credit hours taken. Tuition and fees may vary according to academic program, campus/location, class time (day, evening, weekend), course/credit load, course level, degree level, reciprocity agreements, and student level. *Room and board* charges are reported as an average for one academic year and may vary according to the board plan selected, campus/location, type of housing facility, or student level. *Payment plans* may include tuition prepayment, installment payments, and deferred payment. A tuition prepayment plan gives a student the option of locking in the current tuition rate for the entire term of enrollment by paying the full amount in advance rather than year by year. *Waivers:* availability of full or partial undergraduate tuition waivers to minority students, children of alumni, employees or their children, adult students, and senior citizens may be listed.

Financial Aid: This information represents aid awarded to undergraduates for the available academic year. Figures are given for the number of undergraduates who applied for aid, the number who were judged to have need, and the number who had their need met. The number of Federal Work-Study

Programs and/or part-time jobs and average earnings are listed, as well as the number of non-need-based awards. The *Average percent of need met* for those determined to have need, *Average financial aid package* awarded to undergraduates (the amount of scholarships, grants, work-study payments, or loans in the institutionally administered financial aid package divided by the number of students who received any financial aid-amounts used to pay the officially designated Expected Family Contribution (EFC), *Average need based loan, Average need-based gift aid,* and *Average non-need-based aid* are given. *Average indebtedness upon graduation,* which is the average per-borrower indebtedness of the last graduating undergraduate class from amounts borrowed at this institution through any loan programs, excluding parent loans, is listed last.

APPLYING

Standardized Tests

The most commonly required standardized tests are the ACT®, SAT®, and SAT Subject Tests™. These and other standardized tests may be used for selective admission, as a basis for counseling or course placement, or for both purposes. This section notes if a test is used for admission or placement and whether it is required, required for some, or recommended. In addition to the ACT and SAT, the following standardized entrance and placement examinations are referred to by their initials: ABLE (Adult Basic Learning Examination); ACT ASSET (ACT Assessment of Skills for Successful Entry and Transfer); ACT PEP (ACT Proficiency Examination Program); CAT (California Achievement Tests); CELT (Comprehensive English Language Test); CPAt (Career Programs Assessment); CPT (Computerized Placement Test); DAT (Differential Aptitude Test); LSAT (Law School Admission Test); MAPS (Multiple Assessment Program Service); MCAT (Medical College Admission Test); MMPI (Minnesota Multiphasic Personality Inventory); OAT (Optometry Admission Test); PAA (Prueba de Aptitud Académica—Spanish-language version of SAT); PCAT (Pharmacy College Admission Test); PSAT/NMSQT® (Preliminary SAT/National Merit Scholarship Qualifying Test); SCAT (Scholastic College Aptitude Test); TABE (Test of Adult Basic Education); TASP (Texas Academic Skills Program); TOEFL® (Test of English as a Foreign Language); WPCT (Washington Pre-College Test).

Options: This includes the following: Early admission—(highly qualified students may matriculate before graduating from high school); Early action—admission plan that allows students to apply and be notified of an admission decision well in advance of the regular notification dates (if accepted, the candidate is not committed to enroll; students may reply to the offer under the college's regular reply policy); Deferred entrance—practice of permitting accepted students to postpone enrollment, usually for a period of one academic term or year; Early decision deadline—plan that permits students to apply and be notified of an admission decision (and financial aid offer, if applicable) well in advance of the regular notification date, and applicants agree to accept an offer of admission and to withdraw their applications from other colleges.

Application fee: The fee required with an application is noted.

Required, Required for some, and Recommended: Other application requirements are grouped into three categories and may include an essay, standardized test scores, a high school transcript, a minimum high school grade point average (expressed as a number on a scale of 0 to 4.0, where 4.0 equals A, 3.0 equals B, etc.), letters of recommendation, an interview on campus or with local alumni, and, for certain types of schools or programs, special requirements such as a musical audition or an art portfolio.

Application deadlines and notification: Admission application deadlines and dates for notification of acceptance or rejection are given either as specific dates or as rolling and continuous. Rolling means that applications are processed as they are received, and qualified students are accepted as long as there are openings. Continuous means that applicants are notified of acceptance or rejection as applications are processed up until the date indicated or the actual beginning of classes. The application deadline and the notification date for transfers are given if they differ from the dates for freshmen. Early decision and early action application deadlines and notification dates are also indicated when relevant.

CONTACT

The name, title, mailing address, and phone number of the person to contact for further information are given at the end of the profile. The fax number and e-mail address may also be provided.

Additional Information

Each school that has a College Close-Up and a half-page display in this guide will have a cross-reference with the page numbers of the half-page display and Close-Up.

COLLEGE CLOSE-UPS

These two-page descriptions are more in-depth and provide an inside look at several colleges and universities. The descriptions provide a wealth of information that is crucial in the college decision-making process—components such as tuition, financial aid, and major fields of study. Prepared exclusively by college officials, the descriptions are designed to help give students a better sense of the individuality of each institution, in terms that include campus environment, student activities, and lifestyle. The absence of any college or university does not constitute an editorial decision on the part of Peterson's. In essence, these descriptions are an open forum for colleges and universities, on a voluntary basis, to communicate their particular message to prospective college students. The colleges included have paid a fee to Peterson's to provide this information. The College Close-Ups are edited to provide a consistent format across entries for your ease of comparison.

INDEXES

Here you'll find easy-to-use breakdowns of schools' majors, entrance difficulty, and cost ranges. In addition, you'll find an "Advertisers Index," a "Geographical Listing of College Close-Ups," and an "Alphabetical Listing of Colleges and Universities."

Majors

This listing presents hundreds of undergraduate fields of study that are currently offered, according to the colleges' responses on *Peterson's® Annual Survey of Undergraduate Institutions.* The majors appear in alphabetical order, each followed by an alphabetical list of the schools that offer a bachelor's-level program in that particular field. Liberal Arts and Sciences/ Liberal Studies indicates a general program with no specified major.

The terms used are those of the U.S. Department of Education Classification of Instructional Programs (CIP). Many institutions, however, use different terms. Although the term major is used in this guide, some colleges may use other terms, such as concentration, program of study, or field.

Entrance Difficulty

This listing groups colleges by their own assessment of their entrance difficulty level. The colleges were asked to select the level that most closely corresponds to their entrance difficulty. Institutions for which high school class rank and/or standardized test scores do not apply as admission criteria were asked to select the level that best indicates their entrance difficulty as compared to other institutions.

Cost Ranges

Colleges are grouped into ten price ranges, from under $2,000 to $30,000 and over.

DATA COLLECTION PROCEDURES

The data contained in the **PROFILES** and **INDEXES** sections were researched between winter 2019 and spring 2020 through *Peterson's® Annual Survey of Undergraduate Institutions.* Questionnaires were sent to the more than 4,500 colleges and universities that met the outlined inclusion criteria. All data included in this edition have been submitted by officials (usually admissions and financial aid officers, registrars, or institutional research personnel) at the colleges. Some of the institutions that submitted data were contacted directly by the Peterson's research staff to verify unusual figures, resolve discrepancies, or obtain additional data. All usable information received in time for publication has been included. The omission of any particular item from the **PROFILES** and **INDEXES** sections signifies that the information is either not applicable to that institution or not available. Because of Peterson's comprehensive editorial review and because all material comes directly from college officials, we believe that the information presented is accurate. You should check with a specific college or university at the time of application to verify such figures as tuition and fees, which may have changed since this guide's publication.

CRITERIA FOR INCLUSION IN THIS BOOK

The term "four-year college" is the commonly used designation for institutions that grant the baccalaureate degree. Four years is the expected amount of time required to earn this degree, although some bachelor's degree programs may be completed in three years, others require five years, and part-time programs may take considerably longer. Upper-level institutions offer only the junior and senior years and accept only students with two years of college-level credit. Therefore, "four-year college" is a conventional term that accurately describes most of the institutions included in this guide but should not be taken literally in all cases.

To be included in this guide, an institution must have full accreditation or be a candidate for accreditation (preaccreditation) status by an institutional or specialized accrediting body recognized by the U.S. Department of Education or the Council for Higher Education Accreditation (CHEA). Institutional accrediting bodies, which review each institution as a whole, include the six regional associations of schools and colleges (Middle States, New England, North Central, Northwest, Southern, and Western), each of which is responsible for a specified portion of the United States and its territories. Other institutional accrediting bodies are national in scope and accredit specific kinds of institutions (e.g., Bible colleges, independent colleges, and rabbinical and Talmudic schools). Program registration by the New York State Board of Regents is considered to be the equivalent of institutional accreditation, since the board requires that all programs offered by an institution meet its standards before recognition is granted. A Canadian institution must be chartered and authorized to grant degrees by the provincial government, affiliated with a chartered institution, or accredited by a recognized U.S. accrediting body. This guide also includes institutions outside the United States that are accredited by these U.S. accrediting bodies. There are recognized specialized or professional accrediting bodies in more than forty different fields, each of which is authorized to accredit institutions or specific programs in its particular field. For specialized institutions that offer programs in one field only, we designate this to be the equivalent of institutional accreditation. A full explanation of the accrediting process and complete information on recognized, institutional (regional and national) and specialized accrediting bodies can be found online at **www.chea.org** or at **www.ed.gov**.

Institutional Changes Since *Peterson's®* *Four-Year Colleges* 2020

The American Academy of Dramatic Arts (Los Angeles, CA): *name changed to The American Academy of Dramatic Arts*

American Academy of Dramatic Arts (New York, NY): *name changed to The American Academy of Dramatic Arts*

American National University (Charlottesville, VA): *closed.*

American National University (Danville, KY): *closed.*

American National University (Florence, KY): *closed.*

American National University (Harrisonburg, VA): *closed.*

American National University (Kettering, OH): *closed.*

American National University (Lexington, KY): *closed.*

American National University (Lynchburg, VA): *closed.*

American National University (Richmond, KY): *closed.*

American National University (Youngstown, OH): *closed.*

Antioch University (Midwest Yellow Springs, OH): *closed.*

Antonelli College (Cincinnati, OH): *closed.*

Antonelli College (Hattiesburg, MS): *closed.*

Antonelli College (Jackson, MS): *closed.*

Bethel College (Mishawaka, IN): *name changed to Bethel University*

Central Community College (Columbus, NE): *closed.*

Central Community College (Grand Island, NE): *closed.*

Central Community College (Hastings, NE): *closed.*

College America (Colorado Springs, CO): *closed*

Delaware Technical and Community College System (Dover, DE) *closed*

Florida Keys Community College (Key West, FL): *name changed to The College of the Florida Keys*

MacMurray College (Jacksonville, IL): *closed.*

Metro Business College (Jefferson City, MO): *closed.*

Metro Business College (Rolla, MO): *closed.*

Metro Business College (Cape Girardeau, MO): *closed.*

Nebraska Christian College of Hope International University (Papillion, NE): *closed.*

Notre Dame de Namur University (Belmont, CA): *closed.*

North Florida Community College (Madison, FL): *name changed to North Florida College*

Rochester College (Detroit, MI): *name changed to Rochester University*

Profiles

NOTICE: Certain portions of or information contained in this book have been submitted and paid for by the educational institution identified, and such institutions take full responsibility for the accuracy, timeliness, completeness and functionality of such content. Such portions or information include (i) each display ad in the "Profiles" section from pages 53 through 1037 that comprises a half or full page of information covering a single educational institution, and (ii) each two-page description in the "College Close-Up" section from pages 1039 through 1141.

ALABAMA

Alabama Agricultural and Mechanical University

Huntsville, Alabama

http://www.aamu.edu/

CONTACT

Dr. Evelyn Ellis, Interim Director of Admissions, Alabama Agricultural and Mechanical University, 4900 Meridian Street, Huntsville, AL 35811. *Phone:* 256-372-5245. *Toll-free phone:* 800-553-0816. *Fax:* 256-851-9747.

Alabama State University

Montgomery, Alabama

http://www.alasu.edu/

- **State-supported** university, founded 1867, part of Alabama Commission on Higher Education
- **Urban** 172-acre campus
- **Endowment** $89.3 million
- **Coed**
- **Minimally difficult** entrance level

FACULTY

Student/faculty ratio: 17:1.

ACADEMICS

Calendar: semesters. *Degrees:* certificates, bachelor's, master's, doctoral, post-master's, and postbachelor's certificates.

Library: Levi Watkins Learning Center plus 1 other. *Books:* 437,312 (physical), 69,796 (digital/electronic); *Serial titles:* 1,607 (physical), 6,084 (digital/electronic); *Databases:* 192. Weekly public service hours: 78; study areas open 24 hours, 5–7 days a week; students can reserve study rooms.

STUDENT LIFE

Housing options: men-only, women-only, special housing for students with disabilities. Campus housing is university owned.

Activities and organizations: drama/theater group, student-run newspaper, radio station, choral group, marching band, Alabama State University Marching Band, Alpha Kappa Alpha Sorority Inc, Empower Ministry, Nu Alpha Nu Service Fraternity Inc, Delta Sigma Theta Sorority Inc, national fraternities, national sororities.

Athletics Member NCAA. All Division I.

Campus security: 24-hour emergency response devices and patrols, late-night transport/escort service.

Student services: health clinic, personal/psychological counseling.

FINANCIAL AID

Financial Aid Of all full-time matriculated undergraduates who enrolled in 2019, 3,350 applied for aid, 3,280 were judged to have need, 1,269 had their need fully met. In 2019, 58 non-need-based awards were made. ***Average percent of need met:*** 71. ***Average financial aid package:*** $16,730. ***Average need-based loan:*** $4104. ***Average need-based gift aid:*** $5472. ***Average non-need-based aid:*** $9822. ***Average indebtedness upon graduation:*** $3486.

APPLYING

Standardized Tests *Required:* SAT or ACT (for admission).

Options: electronic application, early admission, deferred entrance.

Application fee: $25.

Required: high school transcript, minimum 2.0 GPA. ***Recommended:*** essay or personal statement, interview.

CONTACT

Mr. Freddie Williams, Director of Admissions and Recruitment, Alabama State University, 915 South Jackson Street, Montgomery, AL 36101-0271. *Phone:* 334-229-4291. *Toll-free phone:* 800-253-5037. *Fax:* 334-229-4984. *E-mail:* fwilliams@alasu.edu.

Amridge University

Montgomery, Alabama

http://www.amridgeuniversity.edu/

- **Independent** university, founded 1967, affiliated with Church of Christ
- **Urban** 10-acre campus
- **Endowment** $8.0 million
- **Coed**
- **Minimally difficult** entrance level

FACULTY

Student/faculty ratio: 12:1.

ACADEMICS

Calendar: semesters. *Degrees:* associate, bachelor's, master's, and doctoral.

Library: Southern Christian University Library. *Books:* 90,000 (physical); *Databases:* 12. Weekly public service hours: 50.

STUDENT LIFE

Housing options: college housing not available.

Activities and organizations: Amridge University Student Advisory Committee.

Campus security: 24-hour emergency response devices, security guards.

FINANCIAL AID

Financial Aid Of all full-time matriculated undergraduates who enrolled in 2018, 77 applied for aid, 77 were judged to have need, 69 had their need fully met. ***Average financial aid package:*** $8734. ***Average need-based loan:*** $5423. ***Average need-based gift aid:*** $2871. ***Average indebtedness upon graduation:*** $11,179.

APPLYING

Standardized Tests *Required:* ACT (for admission). *Required for some:* SAT or ACT (for admission).

Options: electronic application, early admission.

Application fee: $50.

Required: high school transcript, minimum 2.0 GPA.

CONTACT

Mrs. Elaine Tarence, Registrar, Amridge University, 1200 Taylor Road, Montgomery, AL 36117. *Phone:* 334-387-3877 Ext. 7528. *Toll-free phone:* 888-790-8080. *Fax:* 334-387-3878. *E-mail:* registrar@amridgeuniversity.edu.

Athens State University

Athens, Alabama

http://www.athens.edu/

- **State-supported** upper-level, founded 1822
- **Small-town** 45-acre campus
- **Coed** 2,778 undergraduate students, 43% full-time, 68% women, 32% men
- **Noncompetitive** entrance level

UNDERGRAD STUDENTS

1,194 full-time, 1,584 part-time. Students come from 22 states and territories; 3 other countries; 4% are from out of state; 13% Black or African American, non-Hispanic/Latino; 4% Hispanic/Latino; 0.7% Asian, non-Hispanic/Latino; 0.1% Native Hawaiian or other Pacific Islander, non-Hispanic/Latino; 0.8% American Indian or Alaska Native, non-Hispanic/Latino; 3% Two or more races, non-Hispanic/Latino; 3% Race/ethnicity unknown; 22% transferred in.

FACULTY

Total: 189, 47% full-time, 38% with terminal degrees.

Student/faculty ratio: 15:1.

ACADEMICS

Calendar: semesters. *Degrees:* certificates, bachelor's, and master's.

Special study options: adult/continuing education programs, advanced placement credit, cooperative education, distance learning, double majors, independent study, internships, off-campus study, part-time degree program, study abroad, summer session for credit.

Computers: 210 computers/terminals are available on campus for general student use. Students can access the following: computer help desk, free student e-mail accounts, online (class) grades, online (class) registration, online (class) schedules, transcripts, e-mail. Campuswide network is available. Wireless service is available via entire campus.
Library: Athens State University Library. *Books:* 83,092 (physical), 255,950 (digital/electronic); *Serial titles:* 289 (physical), 296,023 (digital/electronic); *Databases:* 23,955. Students can reserve study rooms.

STUDENT LIFE
Housing options: college housing not available.

Activities and organizations: drama/theater group, student-run newspaper, SGA, Accounting, Art, PE.

Campus security: 24-hour emergency response devices and patrols.

Student services: personal/psychological counseling, veterans affairs office.

COSTS & FINANCIAL AID
Costs (2019–20) ***Tuition:*** state resident $6180 full-time; nonresident $12,360 full-time. ***Required fees:*** $1530 full-time. ***Payment plan:*** installment. ***Waivers:*** senior citizens and employees or children of employees.

Financial Aid Of all full-time matriculated undergraduates who enrolled in 2018, 990 applied for aid, 878 were judged to have need, 46 had their need fully met. In 2018, 14 non-need-based awards were made. ***Average percent of need met:*** 44. ***Average financial aid package:*** $10,504. ***Average need-based loan:*** $3312. ***Average need-based gift aid:*** $4543. ***Average non-need-based aid:*** $1256.

APPLYING
Options: electronic application, deferred entrance.

Application fee: $30.

Notification: continuous (transfers).

CONTACT
Athens State University, 300 North Beaty Street, Athens, AL 35611. *Phone:* 256-233-8151. *Toll-free phone:* 800-522-0272.

Auburn University

Auburn University, Alabama

http://www.auburn.edu/

- **State-supported** university, founded 1856
- **Small-town** 1875-acre campus with easy access to Atlanta, Birmingham
- **Endowment** $768.1 million
- **Coed** 24,594 undergraduate students, 92% full-time, 48% women, 52% men
- **Moderately difficult** entrance level, 81% of applicants were admitted

UNDERGRAD STUDENTS
22,527 full-time, 2,067 part-time. 37% are from out of state; 5% Black or African American, non-Hispanic/Latino; 3% Hispanic/Latino; 2% Asian, non-Hispanic/Latino; 0.1% Native Hawaiian or other Pacific Islander, non-Hispanic/Latino; 0.3% American Indian or Alaska Native, non-Hispanic/Latino; 3% Two or more races, non-Hispanic/Latino; 0.3% Race/ethnicity unknown; 6% international; 4% transferred in; 19% live on campus.

Freshmen:
Admission: 20,205 applied, 16,300 admitted, 4,808 enrolled. ***Average high school GPA:*** 3.9. ***Test scores:*** SAT evidence-based reading and writing scores over 500: 99%; SAT math scores over 500: 98%; ACT scores over 18: 100%; SAT evidence-based reading and writing scores over 600: 62%; SAT math scores over 600: 60%; ACT scores over 24: 84%; SAT evidence-based reading and writing scores over 700: 9%; SAT math scores over 700: 16%; ACT scores over 30: 35%.
Retention: 91% of full-time freshmen returned.

FACULTY
Total: 1,644, 87% full-time, 85% with terminal degrees.

Student/faculty ratio: 20:1.

ACADEMICS
Calendar: semesters. *Degrees:* certificates, bachelor's, master's, doctoral, post-master's, and postbachelor's certificates.

Special study options: accelerated degree program, adult/continuing education programs, advanced placement credit, distance learning, double majors, English as a second language, freshman honors college, honors programs, independent study, internships, off-campus study, part-time degree program, services for LD students, study abroad, summer session for credit. ***ROTC:*** Army (b), Navy (b), Air Force (b).

Unusual degree programs: 3-2 engineering.

Computers: 1,722 computers/terminals are available on campus for general student use. Students can access the following: computer help desk, free student e-mail accounts, online (class) grades, online (class) registration, bursar payments, course materials. Campuswide network is available. 100% of college-owned or -operated housing units are wired for high-speed Internet access. Wireless service is available via entire campus.
Library: R. B. Draughon Library plus 3 others. *Books:* 4.6 million (physical), 1.0 million (digital/electronic); *Serial titles:* 76,345 (physical), 94,890 (digital/electronic); *Databases:* 245. Study areas open 24 hours, 5–7 days a week.

STUDENT LIFE
Housing options: coed, men-only, women-only, special housing for students with disabilities. Campus housing is university owned.

Activities and organizations: drama/theater group, student-run newspaper, radio and television station, choral group, marching band, Student Government Association, University Program Council, IMPACT (volunteer opportunities), International Student Organization, student media (AU Plainsman newspaper, WEGL radio, Glomerata yearbook, Eagle Eye television, AU Circle literary journal), national fraternities, national sororities.

Athletics Member NCAA. All Division I except football (Division I-A). ***Intercollegiate sports:*** baseball M(s), basketball M(s)/W(s), cheerleading M/W, cross-country running M(s)/W(s), equestrian sports W(s), golf M(s)/W(s)(c), gymnastics W(s), soccer W(s), softball W(s), swimming and diving M(s)/W(s), tennis M(s)/W(s), track and field M(s)/W(s), volleyball W(s). ***Intramural sports:*** basketball M/W, crew M(c)/W(c), football M, golf M/W, ice hockey M(c)/W(c), lacrosse M(c)/W(c), racquetball M/W, rugby M(c), sailing M(c)/W(c), sand volleyball M(c)/W(c), skiing (downhill) M(c)/W(c), soccer M/W, softball M/W, swimming and diving M/W, table tennis M/W, tennis M/W, track and field M/W, ultimate Frisbee M/W, volleyball M/W, water polo M(c)/W(c), wrestling M(c)/W(c).

Campus security: 24-hour emergency response devices and patrols, late-night transport/escort service, controlled dormitory access.

Student services: health clinic, personal/psychological counseling, veterans affairs office.

COSTS & FINANCIAL AID
Costs (2020–21) ***Tuition:*** area resident $9816 full-time, $409 per credit hour part-time; state resident $9816 full-time, $409 per credit hour part-time; nonresident $29,448 full-time, $1227 per credit hour part-time. Full-time tuition and fees vary according to program and reciprocity agreements. Part-time tuition and fees vary according to course load, program, and reciprocity agreements. ***Required fees:*** $1676 full-time. ***Room and board:*** $13,600; room only: $8014. Room and board charges vary according to board plan and housing facility. ***Payment plan:*** installment. ***Waivers:*** employees or children of employees.

Financial Aid Of all full-time matriculated undergraduates who enrolled in 2018, 14,813 applied for aid, 7,788 were judged to have need, 1,025 had their need fully met. 142 Federal Work-Study jobs (averaging $4539). In 2018, 4618 non-need-based awards were made. ***Average percent of need met:*** 45. ***Average financial aid package:*** $10,961. ***Average need-based loan:*** $4224. ***Average need-based gift aid:*** $8343. ***Average non-need-based aid:*** $7706. ***Average indebtedness upon graduation:*** $29,331.

APPLYING
Standardized Tests *Required:* SAT or ACT (for admission).

Options: electronic application, early admission, early action.

Application fee: $50.

Notification: 2/1 (freshmen), continuous (transfers).

CONTACT
Cindy Singley, Director, University Recruitment, Auburn University, Quad Center, Auburn, AL 36849. *Phone:* 334-844-4080. *Toll-free phone:* 800-AUBURN9. *E-mail:* admissions@auburn.edu.

Auburn University at Montgomery

Montgomery, Alabama

http://www.aum.edu/

- **State-supported** comprehensive, founded 1967, part of Auburn University
- **Urban** 500-acre campus
- **Endowment** $50.1 million
- **Coed** 4,523 undergraduate students, 77% full-time, 65% women, 35% men
- **Moderately difficult** entrance level, 90% of applicants were admitted

UNDERGRAD STUDENTS
3,505 full-time, 1,018 part-time. Students come from 39 states and territories; 41 other countries; 6% are from out of state; 42% Black or African American, non-Hispanic/Latino; 1% Hispanic/Latino; 2% Asian, non-Hispanic/Latino; 0.1% Native Hawaiian or other Pacific Islander, non-Hispanic/Latino; 0.4% American Indian or Alaska Native, non-Hispanic/Latino; 4% Two or more races, non-Hispanic/Latino; 1% Race/ethnicity unknown; 6% international; 10% transferred in; 29% live on campus.

Freshmen:
Admission: 4,109 applied, 3,716 admitted, 626 enrolled. ***Average high school GPA:*** 3.4. ***Test scores:*** SAT evidence-based reading and writing scores over 500: 74%; SAT math scores over 500: 83%; ACT scores over 18: 99%; SAT evidence-based reading and writing scores over 600: 24%; SAT math scores over 600: 21%; ACT scores over 24: 24%; ACT scores over 30: 2%.

Retention: 66% of full-time freshmen returned.

FACULTY
Total: 343, 64% full-time, 66% with terminal degrees.

Student/faculty ratio: 16:1.

ACADEMICS
Calendar: semesters. *Degrees:* bachelor's, master's, doctoral, and post-master's certificates.

Special study options: academic remediation for entering students, advanced placement credit, cooperative education, distance learning, double majors, English as a second language, honors programs, independent study, internships, off-campus study, part-time degree program, services for LD students, study abroad, summer session for credit. ***ROTC:*** Army (b), Air Force (c).

Computers: 500 computers/terminals are available on campus for general student use. Students can access the following: computer help desk, free student e-mail accounts, online (class) grades, online (class) registration, online (class) schedules. Campuswide network is available. 100% of college-owned or -operated housing units are wired for high-speed Internet access. Wireless service is available via entire campus.
Library: Auburn University at Montgomery Library. *Books:* 343,407 (physical), 1.2 million (digital/electronic). Weekly public service hours: 84; students can reserve study rooms.

STUDENT LIFE
Housing options: coed, special housing for students with disabilities. Campus housing is university owned.

Activities and organizations: drama/theater group, student-run newspaper, choral group, Student Government Association, Campus Activities Board, Panhellenic Association, Accounting Club, national fraternities, national sororities.

Athletics Member NCAA. All Division II. ***Intercollegiate sports:*** baseball M(s), basketball M(s)/W(s), cheerleading M(s)/W(s), cross-country running M(s)/W(s), soccer M(s)/W(s), softball W(s), tennis M(s)/W(s), volleyball W(s). ***Intramural sports:*** badminton M/W, table tennis M/W, tennis M/W, ultimate Frisbee M/W, volleyball M/W.

Campus security: 24-hour emergency response devices and patrols, student patrols, late-night transport/escort service, controlled dormitory access.

Student services: health clinic, personal/psychological counseling, veterans affairs office.

COSTS & FINANCIAL AID
Costs (2020–21) ***One-time required fee:*** $125. ***Tuition:*** state resident $7992 full-time, $333 per credit hour part-time; nonresident $17,952 full-time, $748 per credit hour part-time. Full-time tuition and fees vary according to course load and degree level. Part-time tuition and fees vary according to course load and degree level. ***Required fees:*** $868 full-time. ***Room and board:*** $7268; room only: $4580. Room and board charges vary according to board plan and housing facility. ***Payment plan:*** installment. ***Waivers:*** employees or children of employees.

Financial Aid Of all full-time matriculated undergraduates who enrolled in 2018, 2,786 applied for aid, 2,454 were judged to have need, 160 had their need fully met. 64 Federal Work-Study jobs (averaging $3458). In 2018, 404 non-need-based awards were made. ***Average percent of need met:*** 56. ***Average financial aid package:*** $9176. ***Average need-based loan:*** $3329. ***Average need-based gift aid:*** $4815. ***Average non-need-based aid:*** $2927. ***Average indebtedness upon graduation:*** $30,138.

APPLYING
Standardized Tests *Required:* SAT or ACT (for admission).

Options: electronic application, early admission.

Required: high school transcript, minimum 2.3 GPA.

Notification: continuous (freshmen), continuous (transfers).

CONTACT
Auburn University at Montgomery, PO Box 244023, Montgomery, AL 36124-4023. *Phone:* 334-244-3615. *Toll-free phone:* 800-227-2649.

Birmingham-Southern College

Birmingham, Alabama

http://www.bsc.edu/

- **Independent Methodist** 4-year, founded 1856
- **Urban** 196-acre campus with easy access to Birmingham, AL
- **Endowment** $51.7 million
- **Coed** 1,209 undergraduate students, 99% full-time, 53% women, 47% men
- **Moderately difficult** entrance level, 54% of applicants were admitted

UNDERGRAD STUDENTS
1,201 full-time, 8 part-time. Students come from 33 states and territories; 18 other countries; 35% are from out of state; 14% Black or African American, non-Hispanic/Latino; 3% Hispanic/Latino; 2% Asian, non-Hispanic/Latino; 0.2% American Indian or Alaska Native, non-Hispanic/Latino; 0.9% Two or more races, non-Hispanic/Latino; 1% international; 5% transferred in; 78% live on campus.

Freshmen:
Admission: 3,384 applied, 1,821 admitted, 332 enrolled. ***Average high school GPA:*** 3.7. ***Test scores:*** SAT evidence-based reading and writing scores over 500: 98%; SAT math scores over 500: 91%; ACT scores over 18: 99%; SAT evidence-based reading and writing scores over 600: 57%; SAT math scores over 600: 48%; ACT scores over 24: 59%; SAT evidence-based reading and writing scores over 700: 14%; SAT math scores over 700: 17%; ACT scores over 30: 16%.

Retention: 80% of full-time freshmen returned.

FACULTY
Total: 133, 72% full-time, 71% with terminal degrees.

Student/faculty ratio: 12:1.

ACADEMICS
Calendar: 4-1-4. *Degree:* bachelor's.

Special study options: advanced placement credit, cooperative education, double majors, honors programs, independent study, internships, off-campus study, part-time degree program, student-designed majors, study abroad, summer session for credit. ***ROTC:*** Army (c), Air Force (c).

Unusual degree programs: 3-2 engineering with Washington University in St. Louis, University of Alabama at Birmingham; nursing with University of Alabama at Birmingham; environmental management with Duke University, forestry with Duke, law with Cumberland School of Law.

Computers: 306 computers/terminals and 306 ports are available on campus for general student use. Students can access the following: campus intranet, computer help desk, free student e-mail accounts, online (class) grades, online (class) registration, online (class) schedules. Campuswide network is available. 100% of college-owned or -operated housing units are wired for high-speed Internet access. Wireless service is available via entire campus.
Library: Charles Andrew Rush Learning Center/N. E. Miles Library. Students can reserve study rooms.

STUDENT LIFE
Housing options: on-campus residence required for freshman year; coed, men-only, women-only, special housing for students with disabilities. Campus housing is university owned. Freshman campus housing is guaranteed.

Activities and organizations: drama/theater group, student-run newspaper, choral group, marching band, Student Government Association, Quest II Event Programming, Black Student Union, Multi-Cultural Awareness Organization, Reformed University Fellowship, national fraternities, national sororities.

Athletics Member NCAA. All Division III. ***Intercollegiate sports:*** baseball M, basketball M/W, cheerleading M/W, cross country running M/W, football M, golf M/W, lacrosse M/W, soccer M/W, softball W, swimming and diving M/W, tennis M/W, track and field M/W, volleyball W. ***Intramural sports:*** basketball M/W, football M/W, racquetball M/W, soccer M/W, softball M, table tennis M/W, tennis M/W, ultimate Frisbee M/W, volleyball M/W, water polo M/W.

Campus security: 24-hour emergency response devices and patrols, late-night transport/escort service, controlled dormitory access, vehicle safety inspections for students, emergency phone stations throughout campus.

Student services: health clinic, personal/psychological counseling.

FINANCIAL AID
Financial Aid Of all full-time matriculated undergraduates who enrolled in 2018, 872 applied for aid, 694 were judged to have need, 154 had their need fully met. In 2018, 483 non-need-based awards were made. ***Average percent of need met:*** 56. ***Average financial aid package:*** $16,057. ***Average need-based loan:*** $4230. ***Average need-based gift aid:*** $6401. ***Average non-need-based aid:*** $7946. ***Average indebtedness upon graduation:*** $28,007.

APPLYING
Standardized Tests *Recommended:* SAT or ACT (for admission).

Options: electronic application, early decision, early action, deferred entrance.

Application fee: $50.

Required: high school transcript, minimum 2.5 GPA, 1 letter of recommendation. ***Required for some:*** interview. ***Recommended:*** essay or personal statement, interview.

Early decision deadline: 11/1.

Notification: 3/1 (freshmen), 12/1 (early decision), 12/15 (early action).

CONTACT
Birmingham-Southern College, 900 Arkadelphia Road, Birmingham, AL 35254. *Toll-free phone:* 800-523-5793.

Columbia Southern University
Orange Beach, Alabama
http://www.columbiasouthern.edu/

- **Proprietary** comprehensive, founded 1993
- **Small-town** campus
- **Coed**
- **Noncompetitive** entrance level

FACULTY
Student/faculty ratio: 70:1.

ACADEMICS
Calendar: Non-standard Term: 9-weeks of instruction, LifePace Learning: 10-week courses that are self-paced. *Degrees:* certificates, associate, bachelor's, master's, doctoral, post-master's, and postbachelor's certificates (offers only distance learning degree programs).
Library: CSU Online Library.

STUDENT LIFE
Housing options: college housing not available.
Activities and organizations: Student Veteran Association, American Criminal Justice Association, Delta Epsilon Tou (DET) - Alumni Honor Society.
Campus security: 24-hour emergency response devices, On-line Institutions.

COSTS
Costs (2019–20) ***Tuition:*** $5520 full-time, $230 per credit hour part-time. ***Required fees:*** $135 full-time.

APPLYING
Options: electronic application.

CONTACT
Columbia Southern University, 21982 University Lane, PO Box 3110, Orange Beach, AL 36561. *Toll-free phone:* 800-977-8449.

Faulkner University
Montgomery, Alabama
http://www.faulkner.edu/

CONTACT
Mr. Neil Scott, Director of Admissions, Faulkner University, 5345 Atlanta Highway, Montgomery, AL 36109-3398. *Phone:* 334-386-7200. *Toll-free phone:* 800-879-9816. *Fax:* 334-386-7137. *E-mail:* nscott@faulkner.edu.

Heritage Christian University
Florence, Alabama
http://www.hcu.edu/

CONTACT
Mr. Brad McKinnon, Dean of Students, Heritage Christian University, PO Box HCU, Florence, AL 35630. *Phone:* 256-766-6610 Ext. 305. *Toll-free phone:* 800-367-3565. *Fax:* 256-766-9289. *E-mail:* bmckinnon@hcu.edu.

Herzing University
Birmingham, Alabama
http://www.herzing.edu/birmingham/

CONTACT
Ms. Tess Anderson, Admissions Coordinator, Herzing University, 280 West Valley Avenue, Birmingham, AL 35209. *Phone:* 205-916-2800. *Toll-free phone:* 800-596-0724. *E-mail:* admiss@bhm.herzing.edu.

Huntingdon College
Montgomery, Alabama
http://www.huntingdon.edu/

CONTACT
Office of Admission, Huntingdon College, 1500 East Fairview Avenue, Montgomery, AL 36106-2148. *Phone:* 334-833-4497. *Toll-free phone:* 800-763-0313. *Fax:* 334-833-4347. *E-mail:* admiss@hawks.huntingdon.edu.

Huntsville Bible College
Huntsville, Alabama
http://www.huntsvillebiblecollege.org/

CONTACT
Huntsville Bible College, 904 Oakwood Avenue, Huntsville, AL 35811-1632.

Jacksonville State University

Jacksonville, Alabama

http://www.jsu.edu/

- **State-supported** comprehensive, founded 1883
- **Small-town** 459-acre campus with easy access to Birmingham
- **Coed** 7,749 undergraduate students, 77% full-time, 59% women, 41% men
- **Moderately difficult** entrance level, 55% of applicants were admitted

UNDERGRAD STUDENTS

5,942 full-time, 1,807 part-time. 19% are from out of state; 19% Black or African American, non-Hispanic/Latino; 0.8% Hispanic/Latino; 0.7% Asian, non-Hispanic/Latino; 0.1% Native Hawaiian or other Pacific Islander, non-Hispanic/Latino; 0.4% American Indian or Alaska Native, non-Hispanic/Latino; 6% Race/ethnicity unknown; 2% international; 8% transferred in; 23% live on campus.

Freshmen:

Admission: 10,187 applied, 5,581 admitted, 1,493 enrolled. ***Average high school GPA:*** 3.5. ***Test scores:*** SAT evidence-based reading and writing scores over 500: 67%; SAT math scores over 500: 67%; ACT scores over 18: 80%; SAT evidence-based reading and writing scores over 600: 22%; SAT math scores over 600: 11%; ACT scores over 24: 30%; ACT scores over 30: 4%.

Retention: 76% of full-time freshmen returned.

FACULTY

Total: 495, 69% full-time.

Student/faculty ratio: 18:1.

ACADEMICS

Calendar: semesters. *Degrees:* bachelor's, master's, doctoral, post-master's, and postbachelor's certificates.

Special study options: academic remediation for entering students, adult/continuing education programs, advanced placement credit, cooperative education, distance learning, double majors, English as a second language, freshman honors college, honors programs, independent study, internships, part-time degree program, services for LD students, student-designed majors, study abroad, summer session for credit. ***ROTC:*** Army (b).

Computers: 350 computers/terminals are available on campus for general student use. Students can access the following: computer help desk, free student e-mail accounts, online (class) grades, online (class) registration, online (class) schedules. Campuswide network is available. Wireless service is available via entire campus.

Library: Houston Cole Library. *Books:* 711,815 (physical), 32,128 (digital/electronic); *Databases:* 307. Weekly public service hours: 87.

STUDENT LIFE

Housing options: on-campus residence required for freshman year; coed, men-only, women-only, special housing for students with disabilities. Campus housing is university owned.

Activities and organizations: drama/theater group, student-run newspaper, radio and television station, choral group, marching band, Student Government Association, Archaeology Club, Campus Fellowship Clubs, Computer Science Club, Biology Club, national fraternities, national sororities.

Athletics Member NCAA. All Division I except football (Division I-AA). ***Intercollegiate sports:*** baseball M(s), basketball M(s)/W(s), cross-country running M(s)/W(s), golf M(s)/W(s), riflery M(s)/W(s), soccer W(s), softball W(s), tennis M(s)/W(s), volleyball W(s). ***Intramural sports:*** badminton M(c)/W(c), basketball M(c)/W(c), bowling M(c)/W(c), football M(c), golf M(c)/W(c), racquetball M(c)/W(c), soccer M(c)/W(c), softball M(c)/W(c), table tennis M(c)/W(c), tennis M(c)/W(c), volleyball M(c)/W(c).

Campus security: 24-hour emergency response devices and patrols, student patrols, late-night transport/escort service, controlled dormitory access, night security officer in female residence halls.

Student services: health clinic, personal/psychological counseling, veterans affairs office.

COSTS & FINANCIAL AID

Costs (2020–21) ***Tuition:*** area resident $9720 full-time, $3 per credit hour part-time; state resident $9720 full-time, $324 per credit hour part-time; nonresident $19,440 full-time, $648 per credit hour part-time. ***Required fees:*** $1400 full-time. ***Room and board:*** $8000.

Financial Aid Of all full-time matriculated undergraduates who enrolled in 2018, 4,853 applied for aid, 4,781 were judged to have need. ***Average financial aid package:*** $10,971. ***Average need-based loan:*** $3061. ***Average need-based gift aid:*** $5680.

APPLYING

Standardized Tests *Required:* SAT or ACT (for admission).

Options: electronic application, deferred entrance.

Application fee: $35.

Required: high school transcript.

Application deadlines: rolling (freshmen), rolling (transfers).

Notification: continuous (freshmen), continuous (transfers).

CONTACT

Mr. Andrew Green, Director of Admission, Jacksonville State University, 700 Pelham Road North, Jacksonville, AL 36265. *Phone:* 256-782-5363. *Toll-free phone:* 800-231-5291. *Fax:* 256-782-5291. *E-mail:* info@jsu.edu.

Judson College

Marion, Alabama

http://www.judson.edu/

CONTACT

Ms. Layne Hoggle, Executive Director of Enrollment Services, Judson College, 302 Bibb Street, Marion, AL 36756. *Phone:* 334-683-5110. *Toll-free phone:* 800-447-9472. *Fax:* 334-683-5282. *E-mail:* admissions@judson.edu.

Miles College

Fairfield, Alabama

http://www.miles.edu/

CONTACT

Mr. Christopher Robertson, Director of Admissions and Recruitment, Miles College, 5500 Myron Massey Boulevard, Bell Building, Fairfield, AL 35064. *Phone:* 205-929-1657. *Toll-free phone:* 800-445-0708. *Fax:* 205-929-1627. *E-mail:* admissions@miles.edu.

Oakwood University

Huntsville, Alabama

http://www.oakwood.edu/

- **Independent Seventh-day Adventist** comprehensive, founded 1896
- 1200-acre campus
- **Coed**
- **Minimally difficult** entrance level

FACULTY

Student/faculty ratio: 14:1.

ACADEMICS

Calendar: semesters. *Degrees:* associate, bachelor's, master's, and postbachelor's certificates.

Library: Eva B. Dykes Library.

STUDENT LIFE

Housing options: on-campus residence required for freshman year; men-only, women-only. Campus housing is university owned. Freshman applicants given priority for college housing.

Activities and organizations: student-run newspaper, radio station, choral group, United Student Movement.

Campus security: 24-hour patrols, student patrols, late-night transport/escort service.

Student services: health clinic, personal/psychological counseling.

FINANCIAL AID

Financial Aid Of all full-time matriculated undergraduates who enrolled in 2001, 1,422 applied for aid, 1,422 were judged to have need, 131 had their need fully met. ***Average percent of need met:*** 77. ***Average financial aid package:*** $6500. ***Average need-based loan:*** $4500. ***Average need-***

based gift aid: $2500. ***Average non-need-based aid:*** $2000. ***Average indebtedness upon graduation:*** $15,000.

APPLYING
Standardized Tests *Required:* SAT or ACT (for admission).

Options: early action, deferred entrance.

Application fee: $25.

Required: high school transcript, minimum 2.0 GPA. ***Required for some:*** essay or personal statement.

CONTACT
Mr. Jason McCracken, Director of Enrollment Management, Oakwood University, 7000 Adventist Boulevard, NW, Huntsville, AL 35896. *Phone:* 256-726-7354. *Toll-free phone:* 800-824-5312. *Fax:* 256-726-7154. *E-mail:* admission@oakwood.edu.

Remington College–Mobile Campus

Mobile, Alabama

http://www.remingtoncollege.edu/

CONTACT
Remington College–Mobile Campus, 828 Downtowner Loop West, Mobile, AL 36609. *Phone:* 251-343-8200. *Toll-free phone:* 800-323-8122.

Samford University

Birmingham, Alabama

http://www.samford.edu/

- **Independent Baptist** university, founded 1841
- **Suburban** 212-acre campus
- **Endowment** $347.1 million
- **Coed** 3,591 undergraduate students, 98% full-time, 67% women, 33% men
- **Moderately difficult** entrance level, 83% of applicants were admitted

UNDERGRAD STUDENTS
3,509 full-time, 82 part-time. Students come from 41 states and territories; 24 other countries; 68% are from out of state; 7% Black or African American, non-Hispanic/Latino; 3% Hispanic/Latino; 1% Asian, non-Hispanic/Latino; 0.2% American Indian or Alaska Native, non-Hispanic/Latino; 2% Two or more races, non-Hispanic/Latino; 0.3% Race/ethnicity unknown; 1% international; 2% transferred in; 65% live on campus.

Freshmen:
Admission: 3,912 applied, 3,259 admitted, 901 enrolled. ***Average high school GPA:*** 3.8. ***Test scores:*** SAT evidence-based reading and writing scores over 500: 92%; SAT math scores over 500: 86%; ACT scores over 18: 100%; SAT evidence-based reading and writing scores over 600: 47%; SAT math scores over 600: 33%; ACT scores over 24: 72%; SAT evidence-based reading and writing scores over 700: 8%; SAT math scores over 700: 5%; ACT scores over 30: 22%.

Retention: 89% of full-time freshmen returned.

FACULTY
Total: 559, 66% full-time, 78% with terminal degrees.

Student/faculty ratio: 13:1.

ACADEMICS
Calendar: 4-1-4. *Degrees:* certificates, bachelor's, master's, doctoral, post-master's, and postbachelor's certificates.

Special study options: accelerated degree program, adult/continuing education programs, distance learning, double majors, honors programs, independent study, internships, off-campus study, part-time degree program, services for LD students, study abroad, summer session for credit. ***ROTC:*** Army (c), Air Force (b).

Unusual degree programs: 3-2 engineering with The University of Alabama at Birmingham, Auburn University, Mercer University.

Computers: 330 computers/terminals and 400 ports are available on campus for general student use. Students can access the following: campus intranet, computer help desk, free student e-mail accounts, online (class) grades, online (class) registration, online (class) schedules, free online storage and tech support. Campuswide network is available. 100% of college-owned or -operated housing units are wired for high-speed Internet access. Wireless service is available via entire campus.

Library: University Library plus 2 others. *Books:* 569,940 (physical), 389,971 (digital/electronic); *Serial titles:* 6,045 (physical), 118,182 (digital/electronic); *Databases:* 302. Weekly public service hours: 99; students can reserve study rooms.

STUDENT LIFE
Housing options: on-campus residence required through sophomore year; men-only, women-only. Campus housing is university owned. Freshman campus housing is guaranteed.

Activities and organizations: student-run newspaper, choral group, Student Government Association, Greek Chapters and councils, Campus Ministries, national fraternities, national sororities.

Athletics Member NCAA. All Division I. ***Intercollegiate sports:*** baseball M(s), basketball M(s)/W(s), cross-country running M(s)/W(s), football M(s), golf M(s)/W(s), soccer W(s), softball W(s), tennis M(s)/W(s), track and field M(s)/W(s), volleyball W(s). ***Intramural sports:*** basketball M/W, crew M(c)/W(c), equestrian sports M(c)/W(c), football M/W, golf M(c)/W(c), lacrosse M(c), sand volleyball M/W, soccer M(c)/W(c), ultimate Frisbee M/W, volleyball M/W.

Campus security: 24-hour emergency response devices and patrols, late-night transport/escort service.

Student services: health clinic, personal/psychological counseling, veterans affairs office.

COSTS & FINANCIAL AID
Costs (2019–20) ***Comprehensive fee:*** $43,830 includes full-time tuition ($32,000), mandatory fees ($850), and room and board ($10,980). Full-time tuition and fees vary according to course load and program. Part-time tuition: $1070 per credit. Part-time tuition and fees vary according to course load and program. ***Required fees:*** $355 per term part-time. ***College room only:*** $5970. Room and board charges vary according to board plan and housing facility. ***Payment plan:*** installment. ***Waivers:*** employees or children of employees.

Financial Aid Of all full-time matriculated undergraduates who enrolled in 2018, 2,050 applied for aid, 1,439 were judged to have need, 353 had their need fully met. 564 Federal Work-Study jobs (averaging $2958). 783 state and other part-time jobs (averaging $1571). In 2018, 1668 non-need-based awards were made. ***Average percent of need met:*** 71. ***Average financial aid package:*** $21,460. ***Average need-based loan:*** $3859. ***Average need-based gift aid:*** $17,128. ***Average non-need-based aid:*** $12,221. ***Average indebtedness upon graduation:*** $29,676.

APPLYING
Standardized Tests *Required:* SAT or ACT (for admission).

Options: electronic application, early admission, deferred entrance.

Application fee: $40.

Required: essay or personal statement, high school transcript, 1 letter of recommendation. ***Required for some:*** interview.

Application deadlines: 2/15 (freshmen), 2/15 (out-of-state freshmen), rolling (transfers).

Notification: continuous until 11/1 (freshmen), continuous until 11/1 (out-of-state freshmen), continuous (transfers).

CONTACT
Mr. Brian L. Kennedy, Director of Recruitment, Samford University, 800 Lakeshore Drive, Samford Hall, Birmingham, AL 35229-0002. *Phone:* 205-726-4176. *Toll-free phone:* 800-888-7218. *E-mail:* blkenned@samford.edu.

Selma University

Selma, Alabama

http://www.selmauniversity.edu/

CONTACT
Selma University, 1501 Lapsley Street, Selma, AL 36701-5299. *Phone:* 334-872-2533 Ext. 116.

South University - Montgomery

Montgomery, Alabama

http://www.southuniversity.edu/montgomery/

CONTACT
South University - Montgomery, 5355 Vaughn Road, Montgomery, AL 36116-1120. *Phone:* 334-395-8800. *Toll-free phone:* 866-629-2962.

Spring Hill College

Mobile, Alabama

http://www.shc.edu/

- **Independent Roman Catholic (Jesuit)** comprehensive, founded 1830
- **Suburban** 450-acre campus
- **Coed** 1,187 undergraduate students, 99% full-time, 63% women, 37% men
- **Moderately difficult** entrance level, 50% of applicants were admitted

UNDERGRAD STUDENTS
1,170 full-time, 17 part-time. 58% are from out of state; 14% Black or African American, non-Hispanic/Latino; 4% Hispanic/Latino; 1% Asian, non-Hispanic/Latino; 0.3% Native Hawaiian or other Pacific Islander, non-Hispanic/Latino; 0.3% American Indian or Alaska Native, non-Hispanic/Latino; 3% Two or more races, non-Hispanic/Latino; 5% Race/ethnicity unknown; 4% international; 4% transferred in; 70% live on campus.

Freshmen:
Admission: 7,616 applied, 3,791 admitted, 290 enrolled. ***Average high school GPA:*** 3.6. ***Test scores:*** SAT evidence-based reading and writing scores over 500: 84%; SAT math scores over 500: 87%; ACT scores over 18: 95%; SAT evidence-based reading and writing scores over 600: 29%; SAT math scores over 600: 23%; ACT scores over 24: 41%; SAT evidence-based reading and writing scores over 700: 2%; SAT math scores over 700: 7%; ACT scores over 30: 8%.

Retention: 70% of full-time freshmen returned.

FACULTY
Total: 126, 67% full-time, 75% with terminal degrees.

Student/faculty ratio: 13:1.

ACADEMICS
Calendar: semesters. *Degrees:* certificates, bachelor's, master's, post-master's, and postbachelor's certificates.

Special study options: academic remediation for entering students, accelerated degree program, adult/continuing education programs, advanced placement credit, distance learning, double majors, external degree program, honors programs, independent study, internships, off-campus study, part-time degree program, services for LD students, student-designed majors, study abroad, summer session for credit. ***ROTC:*** Army (c), Air Force (c).

Unusual degree programs: 3-2 engineering with Marquette University, University of Alabama at Birmingham, University of Florida, Auburn University, Texas A&M University, University of South Alabama.

Computers: Students can access the following: campus intranet, computer help desk, free student e-mail accounts, online (class) grades, online (class) registration, online (class) schedules. Campuswide network is available. 100% of college-owned or -operated housing units are wired for high-speed Internet access. Wireless service is available via computer centers, computer labs, dorm rooms, libraries, student centers.
Library: Marnie and John Burke Memorial Library plus 1 other.

STUDENT LIFE
Housing options: on-campus residence required through senior year; coed. Campus housing is university owned. Freshman campus housing is guaranteed.

Activities and organizations: drama/theater group, student-run newspaper, choral group, Fraternities and sororities, SHAPe, National Society of Leadership and Success, Peer One Project, Chemistry Club, national fraternities, national sororities.

Athletics Member NCAA. All Division II. ***Intercollegiate sports:*** baseball M(s), basketball M(s)/W(s), cross-country running M(s)/W(s), golf M(s), soccer M(s)/W(s), softball W(s), tennis M(s)/W(s), track and field M(s)/W(s), volleyball W(s). ***Intramural sports:*** basketball M/W, bowling M(c)/W(c), football M/W, racquetball M/W, rugby M(c)/W(c), soccer M/W, ultimate Frisbee M/W, volleyball M/W.

Campus security: 24-hour emergency response devices and patrols, late-night transport/escort service, controlled dormitory access.

Student services: health clinic, personal/psychological counseling.

COSTS & FINANCIAL AID
Costs (2019–20) ***Comprehensive fee:*** $54,300 includes full-time tuition ($38,190), mandatory fees ($2458), and room and board ($13,652). Full-time tuition and fees vary according to course load. Part-time tuition: $1126 per credit hour. Part-time tuition and fees vary according to course load. ***Required fees:*** $57 per credit hour part-time. ***College room only:*** $7108. Room and board charges vary according to board plan and housing facility. ***Payment plan:*** installment. ***Waivers:*** employees or children of employees.

Financial Aid Of all full-time matriculated undergraduates who enrolled in 2019, 943 applied for aid, 836 were judged to have need, 377 had their need fully met. In 2019, 283 non-need-based awards were made. ***Average percent of need met:*** 84. ***Average financial aid package:*** $36,757. ***Average need-based loan:*** $4465. ***Average need-based gift aid:*** $9185. ***Average non-need-based aid:*** $22,061.

APPLYING
Standardized Tests *Required:* SAT or ACT (for admission).

Options: electronic application, early admission, deferred entrance.

Application fee: $25.

Required: essay or personal statement, high school transcript, 1 letter of recommendation. ***Recommended:*** minimum 2.5 GPA, interview.

Notification: continuous (freshmen), continuous (out-of-state freshmen), continuous (transfers).

CONTACT
Ms. Britney Finley, Admissions Counselor, Spring Hill College, 4000 Dauphin Street, Mobile, AL 36608-1791. *Phone:* 251-380-3032. *Toll-free phone:* 800-SHC-6704. *Fax:* 251-460-2186. *E-mail:* bfinley@shc.edu.

Stillman College

Tuscaloosa, Alabama

http://www.stillman.edu/

- **Independent** 4-year, founded 1876, affiliated with Presbyterian Church (U.S.A.)
- **Urban** 100-acre campus with easy access to Birmingham
- **Endowment** $18.2 million
- **Coed**
- **Minimally difficult** entrance level

FACULTY
Student/faculty ratio: 18:1.

ACADEMICS
Calendar: semesters. *Degree:* bachelor's.
Library: Sheppard Library.

STUDENT LIFE
Housing options: on-campus residence required for freshman year; men-only, women-only. Campus housing is university owned. Freshman campus housing is guaranteed.

Activities and organizations: drama/theater group, student-run newspaper, choral group, marching band, Stillman Blue Pride Marching Band, Sophisticated Unlimited Modeling Troupe, Christian Student Association, Student Government Association, Students in Free Enterprise (SIFE), national fraternities, national sororities.

Athletics Member NCAA. All Division II.

Campus security: 24-hour patrols.

Student services: health clinic, personal/psychological counseling.

COSTS & FINANCIAL AID
Costs (2019–20) ***Tuition:*** $9548 full-time. ***Required fees:*** $1774 full-time. ***Room only:*** $5984.

Financial Aid Of all full-time matriculated undergraduates who enrolled in 2016, 580 applied for aid, 580 were judged to have need, 125 had their need fully met. 173 Federal Work-Study jobs (averaging $1152). 173 state and other part-time jobs (averaging $1152). In 2016, 7 non-need-based awards were made. ***Average percent of need met:*** 75. ***Average financial***

aid package: $23,110. *Average need-based loan:* $3500. *Average need-based gift aid:* $5815. *Average non-need-based aid:* $10,589. *Average indebtedness upon graduation:* $30,429. *Financial aid deadline:* 6/1.

APPLYING

Standardized Tests *Required:* SAT and SAT Subject Tests or ACT (for admission). *Recommended:* SAT (for admission), ACT (for admission), SAT Subject Tests (for admission).

Options: electronic application, early admission, early decision, deferred entrance.

Application fee: $15.

Required: high school transcript, minimum 2.5 GPA. *Recommended:* essay or personal statement, interview.

CONTACT

Stillman College, PO Drawer 1430, 3600 Stillman Boulevard, Tuscaloosa, AL 35403-9990. *Phone:* 205-366-8837. *Toll-free phone:* 800-841-5722.

Strayer University - Birmingham

Birmingham, Alabama

http://www.strayer.edu/alabama/birmingham/

CONTACT

Strayer University - Birmingham, 3570 Grandview Parkway, Suite 200, Birmingham, AL 35243. *Toll-free phone:* 888-311-0355.

Strayer University–Huntsville Campus

Huntsville, Alabama

http://www.strayer.edu/alabama/huntsville/

CONTACT

Strayer University–Huntsville Campus, 4955 Corporate Drive, Huntsville, AL 35805. *Toll-free phone:* 888-311-0355.

Talladega College

Talladega, Alabama

http://www.talladega.edu/

CONTACT

Talladega College, 627 West Battle Street, Talladega, AL 35160-2354. *Phone:* 256-761-6175. *Toll-free phone:* 866-540-3956.

Troy University

Troy, Alabama

http://www.troy.edu/

- **State-supported** comprehensive, founded 1887, part of Troy University System
- **Small-town** 906-acre campus
- **Endowment** $104.4 million
- **Coed** 12,995 undergraduate students, 67% full-time, 63% women, 37% men
- 88% of applicants were admitted

UNDERGRAD STUDENTS

8,741 full-time, 4,254 part-time. 30% are from out of state; 31% Black or African American, non-Hispanic/Latino; 4% Hispanic/Latino; 0.8% Asian, non-Hispanic/Latino; 0.1% Native Hawaiian or other Pacific Islander, non-Hispanic/Latino; 0.3% American Indian or Alaska Native, non-Hispanic/Latino; 3% Two or more races, non-Hispanic/Latino; 3% Race/ethnicity unknown; 5% international; 11% transferred in; 15% live on campus.

Freshmen:

Admission: 6,146 applied, 5,382 admitted, 1,679 enrolled. *Average high school GPA:* 3.4. *Test scores:* SAT evidence-based reading and writing scores over 500: 62%; SAT math scores over 500: 54%; ACT scores over 18: 84%; SAT evidence-based reading and writing scores over 600: 15%; SAT math scores over 600: 4%; ACT scores over 24: 30%; SAT evidence-based reading and writing scores over 700: 1%; SAT math scores over 700: 1%; ACT scores over 30: 5%.

Retention: 75% of full-time freshmen returned.

FACULTY

Total: 1,118, 47% full-time, 55% with terminal degrees.

Student/faculty ratio: 17:1.

ACADEMICS

Calendar: semesters. *Degrees:* certificates, associate, bachelor's, master's, doctoral, post-master's, and postbachelor's certificates.

Special study options: academic remediation for entering students, accelerated degree program, advanced placement credit, distance learning, double majors, English as a second language, honors programs, independent study, internships, part-time degree program, services for LD students, study abroad, summer session for credit. *ROTC:* Army (b), Air Force (b).

Computers: 1,935 computers/terminals and 21,221 ports are available on campus for general student use. Students can access the following: campus intranet, computer help desk, free student e-mail accounts, online (class) grades, online (class) registration, online (class) schedules. Campuswide network is available. Wireless service is available via classrooms, dorm rooms, libraries.

Library: Lurleen B. Wallace Library (Troy Campus) plus 2 others. *Books:* 603,904 (physical), 277,690 (digital/electronic); *Serial titles:* 213 (physical), 134,396 (digital/electronic); *Databases:* 261.

STUDENT LIFE

Housing options: on-campus residence required for freshman year; coed, men-only, women-only, special housing for students with disabilities. Campus housing is university owned. Freshman campus housing is guaranteed.

Activities and organizations: drama/theater group, student-run newspaper, radio and television station, choral group, marching band, T-Day/Athletic Events (Homecoming), Activities Council, Pep Rallies, national fraternities, national sororities.

Athletics Member NCAA. All Division I except football (Division I-A). *Intercollegiate sports:* baseball M(s), basketball M(s)/W(s), cross-country running M(s)/W(s), golf M(s)/W(s), soccer W(s), softball W(s), tennis M(s)/W(s), track and field M(s)/W(s), volleyball W(s). *Intramural sports:* basketball M/W, bowling M/W, cross-country running M/W, football M, golf M/W, soccer W, softball W, tennis M/W, track and field M/W, volleyball W.

Campus security: 24-hour emergency response devices and patrols, student patrols, late-night transport/escort service, controlled dormitory access.

Student services: health clinic, personal/psychological counseling.

FINANCIAL AID

Financial Aid Of all full-time matriculated undergraduates who enrolled in 2018, 6,383 applied for aid, 5,805 were judged to have need. In 2018, 392 non-need-based awards were made. *Average financial aid package:* $3573. *Average need-based loan:* $3007. *Average need-based gift aid:* $4600. *Average non-need-based aid:* $3822. *Average indebtedness upon graduation:* $26,144.

APPLYING

Standardized Tests *Required:* SAT or ACT (for admission).

Options: electronic application, early admission, deferred entrance.

Application fee: $30.

Required: high school transcript, rigor of secondary school record.

Application deadlines: rolling (freshmen), rolling (transfers).

CONTACT

Mr. Buddy Starling, Associate Vice Chancellor for Enrollment Management, Troy University, University Avenue, Troy, AL 36082. *Phone:* 334-670-3243. *Toll-free phone:* 800-551-9716. *Fax:* 334-670-3733. *E-mail:* bstar@troy.edu.

Tuskegee University

Tuskegee, Alabama

http://www.tuskegee.edu/

- **Independent** comprehensive, founded 1881
- **Small-town** 5000-acre campus
- **Endowment** $113.7 million
- **Coed**
- **Moderately difficult** entrance level

FACULTY

Student/faculty ratio: 14:1.

ACADEMICS

Calendar: semesters. *Degrees:* bachelor's, master's, and doctoral.
Library: Hollis B. Frissell Library plus 3 others. *Books:* 370,430 (physical), 2,330 (digital/electronic); *Serial titles:* 1,810 (physical), 836 (digital/electronic); *Databases:* 175. Students can reserve study rooms.

STUDENT LIFE

Housing options: on-campus residence required through sophomore year; coed, men-only, women-only. Campus housing is university owned. Freshman applicants given priority for college housing.

Activities and organizations: drama/theater group, student-run newspaper, television station, choral group, marching band, Student Government, Marching Band, State Clubs, Fraternities, Sororities, national fraternities, national sororities.

Athletics Member NCAA. All Division II.

Campus security: 24-hour emergency response devices and patrols, late-night transport/escort service.

Student services: health clinic, personal/psychological counseling.

FINANCIAL AID

Financial Aid Of all full-time matriculated undergraduates who enrolled in 2017, 2,618 applied for aid, 2,221 were judged to have need, 1,050 had their need fully met. 625 Federal Work-Study jobs (averaging $2610). 225 state and other part-time jobs (averaging $2000). In 2017, 728 non-need-based awards were made. ***Average percent of need met:*** 85. ***Average financial aid package:*** $20,500. ***Average need-based loan:*** $6000. ***Average need-based gift aid:*** $950. ***Average non-need-based aid:*** $6500. ***Average indebtedness upon graduation:*** $26,500.

APPLYING

Standardized Tests *Required:* SAT or ACT (for admission). *Recommended:* SAT (for admission).

Options: electronic application, early admission.

Application fee: $25.

Required: high school transcript, minimum 3.0 GPA.

CONTACT

Hon. Courtney L. Griffin, Executive Director of Enrollment Management, Tuskegee University, 1200 Old Montgomery Road, Margaret Murray Hall, Admissions, Tuskegee, AL 36088. *Phone:* 334-724-4828. *Toll-free phone:* 800-622-6531. *Fax:* 334-727-5750. *E-mail:* cgriffin@mytu.tuskegee.edu.

United States Sports Academy

Daphne, Alabama

http://www.ussa.edu/

CONTACT

United States Sports Academy, One Academy Drive, Daphne, AL 36526-7055. *Phone:* 251-626-3303 Ext. 7147. *Toll-free phone:* 800-223-2668.

The University of Alabama

Tuscaloosa, Alabama

http://www.ua.edu/

- **State-supported** university, founded 1831, part of University of Alabama System
- **Suburban** 1026-acre campus with easy access to Birmingham
- **Endowment** $845.9 million
- **Coed** 32,795 undergraduate students, 89% full-time, 56% women, 44% men
- **Moderately difficult** entrance level, 83% of applicants were admitted

UNDERGRAD STUDENTS

29,135 full-time, 3,660 part-time. Students come from 52 states and territories; 58 other countries; 61% are from out of state; 10% Black or African American, non-Hispanic/Latino; 5% Hispanic/Latino; 1% Asian, non-Hispanic/Latino; 0.1% Native Hawaiian or other Pacific Islander, non-Hispanic/Latino; 0.4% American Indian or Alaska Native, non-Hispanic/Latino; 4% Two or more races, non-Hispanic/Latino; 0.5% Race/ethnicity unknown; 2% international; 5% transferred in; 25% live on campus.

Freshmen:

Admission: 38,505 applied, 31,835 admitted, 6,764 enrolled. ***Average high school GPA:*** 3.8. ***Test scores:*** SAT evidence-based reading and writing scores over 500: 94%; SAT math scores over 500: 92%; ACT scores over 18: 100%; SAT evidence-based reading and writing scores over 600: 51%; SAT math scores over 600: 45%; ACT scores over 24: 69%; SAT evidence-based reading and writing scores over 700: 15%; SAT math scores over 700: 21%; ACT scores over 30: 39%.

Retention: 87% of full-time freshmen returned.

FACULTY

Total: 1,955, 75% full-time, 79% with terminal degrees.

Student/faculty ratio: 20:1.

ACADEMICS

Calendar: semesters. *Degrees:* bachelor's, master's, doctoral, and post-master's certificates.

Special study options: academic remediation for entering students, accelerated degree program, adult/continuing education programs, advanced placement credit, cooperative education, distance learning, double majors, English as a second language, external degree program, freshman honors college, honors programs, independent study, internships, off-campus study, part-time degree program, services for LD students, student-designed majors, study abroad, summer session for credit. ***ROTC:*** Army (b), Air Force (b).

Computers: 2,500 computers/terminals and 14,000 ports are available on campus for general student use. Students can access the following: campus intranet, computer help desk, free student e-mail accounts, online (class) grades, online (class) registration, online (class) schedules. Campuswide network is available. 100% of college-owned or -operated housing units are wired for high-speed Internet access. Wireless service is available via entire campus.
Library: Amelia Gayle Gorgas Library plus 8 others. *Books:* 3.3 million (physical), 1.8 million (digital/electronic); *Serial titles:* 137,451 (physical), 203,341 (digital/electronic); *Databases:* 580. Weekly public service hours: 141; study areas open 24 hours, 5–7 days a week; students can reserve study rooms.

STUDENT LIFE

Housing options: on-campus residence required for freshman year; coed, men-only, women-only, special housing for students with disabilities. Campus housing is university owned. Freshman campus housing is guaranteed.

Activities and organizations: drama/theater group, student-run newspaper, radio station, choral group, marching band, ABXY Gaming Network, Residence Hall Association, International Student Association, Student Government Association, Black Student Union, national fraternities, national sororities.

Athletics Member NCAA. All Division I except football (Division I-A). ***Intercollegiate sports:*** badminton M(c)/W(c), baseball M(s), basketball M(s)/W(s), bowling M(c)/W(c), cheerleading M(s)/W(s), crew M(c)/W(s), cross-country running M(s)/W(s), equestrian sports M(c)/W(c), field hockey W(c), golf M(s)/W(s), gymnastics W(s), ice hockey M(c), lacrosse M(c)/W(c), rugby M(c)/W(c), soccer M(s)(c)/W, softball W(s), swimming and diving M(s)/W(s), table tennis M(c)/W(c), tennis M(s)/W(s), track and field M(s)/W(s), triathlon M(c)/W(c), ultimate Frisbee M(c)/W(c), volleyball M(c)/W(s), water polo M(c), wrestling M(c). ***Intramural sports:*** basketball M/W, soccer M/W, tennis M/W, ultimate Frisbee M/W, volleyball M/W.

Campus security: 24-hour emergency response devices and patrols, late-night transport/escort service, controlled dormitory access, 24-hour patrols by University of Alabama Police (UAPD), certified law enforcement personnel.

Student services: health clinic, personal/psychological counseling, women's center, legal services, veterans affairs office.

COSTS & FINANCIAL AID

Costs (2019–20) ***Tuition:*** state resident $10,780 full-time; nonresident $30,250 full-time. Full-time tuition and fees vary according to course load. Part-time tuition and fees vary according to course load. ***Room and board:*** $10,836; room only: $6900. Room and board charges vary according to board plan, housing facility, and location. ***Payment plans:*** installment, deferred payment. ***Waivers:*** employees or children of employees.

Financial Aid Of all full-time matriculated undergraduates who enrolled in 2018, 16,585 applied for aid, 12,792 were judged to have need, 2,527 had their need fully met. 641 Federal Work-Study jobs (averaging $2863). In 2018, 8187 non-need-based awards were made. ***Average percent of need met:*** 54. ***Average financial aid package:*** $15,217. ***Average need-based loan:*** $4134. ***Average need-based gift aid:*** $13,730. ***Average non-need-based aid:*** $16,843. ***Average indebtedness upon graduation:*** $34,975.

APPLYING

Standardized Tests *Required:* SAT or ACT (for admission).

Options: electronic application, early admission, deferred entrance.

Application fee: $40.

Required: high school transcript, minimum 3.0 GPA. ***Required for some:*** essay or personal statement, 2 letters of recommendation, interview.

Application deadlines: 5/1 (freshmen), 5/1 (out-of-state freshmen), 3/1 (transfers).

Notification: continuous (freshmen), continuous (out-of-state freshmen), continuous (transfers).

CONTACT

Dr. Matthew McLendon, Assistant Vice President for Enrollment Management, The University of Alabama, Box 870132, Tuscaloosa, AL 35487. *Phone:* 205-348-8666. *Toll-free phone:* 800-933-BAMA. *Fax:* 205-348-9046. *E-mail:* admissions@ua.edu.

The University of Alabama at Birmingham

Birmingham, Alabama

http://www.uab.edu/

- **State-supported** university, founded 1969, part of University of Alabama System
- **Urban** 636-acre campus with easy access to Birmingham, AL
- **Endowment** $403.3 million
- **Coed** 13,836 undergraduate students, 75% full-time, 61% women, 39% men
- 175% of applicants were admitted

UNDERGRAD STUDENTS

10,315 full-time, 3,521 part-time. Students come from 53 states and territories; 78 other countries; 13% are from out of state; 24% Black or African American, non-Hispanic/Latino; 6% Hispanic/Latino; 7% Asian, non-Hispanic/Latino; 0.2% American Indian or Alaska Native, non-Hispanic/Latino; 4% Two or more races, non-Hispanic/Latino; 0.6% Race/ethnicity unknown; 2% international; 10% transferred in; 23% live on campus.

Freshmen:

Admission: 5,236 applied, 9,174 admitted, 2,346 enrolled. ***Average high school GPA:*** 3.8. ***Test scores:*** SAT evidence-based reading and writing scores over 500: 93%; SAT math scores over 500: 92%; ACT scores over 18: 99%; SAT evidence-based reading and writing scores over 600: 63%; SAT math scores over 600: 53%; ACT scores over 24: 62%; SAT evidence-based reading and writing scores over 700: 17%; SAT math scores over 700: 21%; ACT scores over 30: 24%.

Retention: 83% of full-time freshmen returned.

FACULTY

Total: 1,180, 76% full-time, 81% with terminal degrees.

Student/faculty ratio: 19:1.

ACADEMICS

Calendar: semesters. *Degrees:* certificates, bachelor's, master's, doctoral, and post-master's certificates.

Special study options: academic remediation for entering students, accelerated degree program, advanced placement credit, cooperative education, distance learning, double majors, English as a second language, freshman honors college, honors programs, independent study, internships, off-campus study, part-time degree program, services for LD students, student-designed majors, study abroad, summer session for credit. ***ROTC:*** Army (b), Air Force (c).

Unusual degree programs: 3-2 business administration with accounting; engineering with biomedical engineering, civil engineering, electrical and computer engineering, electrical engineering, mechanical engineering, materials engineering; biotechnology, biology, environmental health, epidemiology, health behavior, health care organization and policy, health informatics, mathematics, public health, occupational therapy.

Computers: Students can access the following: campus intranet, computer help desk, free student e-mail accounts, online (class) grades, online (class) registration, online (class) schedules. Campuswide network is available. Wireless service is available via entire campus.

Library: Lister Hill Library plus 2 others. *Books:* 1.5 million (physical), 510,501 (digital/electronic); *Databases:* 451. Students can reserve study rooms.

STUDENT LIFE

Housing options: on-campus residence required for freshman year; coed. Campus housing is university owned. Freshman campus housing is guaranteed.

Activities and organizations: drama/theater group, student-run newspaper, radio station, choral group, marching band, Active Minds at UAB, Black Student Awareness Committee, Public Health Student Association, American Red Cross Club at UAB, Good Games UAB, national fraternities, national sororities.

Athletics Member NCAA. All Division I. ***Intercollegiate sports:*** baseball M(s), basketball M(s)/W(s), bowling W(s), cross-country running W(s), football M(s), golf M(s)/W(s), soccer M(s)/W(s), table tennis M(s), tennis W(s), track and field W(s), volleyball W(s). ***Intramural sports:*** badminton M/W, basketball M/W, football M/W, soccer M/W, softball M/W, ultimate Frisbee M/W, volleyball M/W.

Campus security: 24-hour emergency response devices and patrols, late-night transport/escort service, controlled dormitory access.

Student services: health clinic, personal/psychological counseling, veterans affairs office.

COSTS & FINANCIAL AID

Costs (2019–20) ***Tuition:*** state resident $10,710 full-time, $357 per credit hour part-time; nonresident $25,500 full-time, $850 per credit hour part-time. Full-time tuition and fees vary according to course load, degree level, program, and reciprocity agreements. Part-time tuition and fees vary according to course load, degree level, program, and reciprocity agreements. ***Room and board:*** $10,910; room only: $6600. Room and board charges vary according to board plan and housing facility. ***Payment plan:*** installment. ***Waivers:*** employees or children of employees.

Financial Aid Of all full-time matriculated undergraduates who enrolled in 2019, 7,404 applied for aid, 6,077 were judged to have need, 894 had their need fully met. In 2019, 2403 non-need-based awards were made. ***Average percent of need met:*** 55. ***Average financial aid package:*** $12,330. ***Average need-based loan:*** $3914. ***Average need-based gift aid:*** $4950. ***Average non-need-based aid:*** $8304. ***Average indebtedness upon graduation:*** $29,941.

APPLYING

Standardized Tests *Required:* SAT or ACT (for admission).

Options: electronic application, deferred entrance.

Application fee: $30.

Required: high school transcript.

Application deadlines: rolling (freshmen), rolling (out-of-state freshmen), rolling (transfers).

Notification: continuous until 8/1 (freshmen), 8/1 (out-of-state freshmen), continuous until 8/1 (transfers).

CONTACT
Kathleen Stallings, Director of Undergraduate Admissions, The University of Alabama at Birmingham, Office of Undergraduate Admission, 1720 2nd Avenue South, Birmingham, AL 35294-4600. *Phone:* 800-4218743. *Toll-free phone:* 800-421-8743. *Fax:* 205-9757114. *E-mail:* khstall@uab.edu.

The University of Alabama in Huntsville

Huntsville, Alabama

http://www.uah.edu/

- **State-supported** university, founded 1950, part of University of Alabama System
- **Suburban** 400-acre campus
- **Endowment** $66.9 million
- **Coed** 7,989 undergraduate students, 84% full-time, 42% women, 58% men
- **Moderately difficult** entrance level, 81% of applicants were admitted

UNDERGRAD STUDENTS
6,749 full-time, 1,240 part-time. 20% are from out of state; 9% Black or African American, non-Hispanic/Latino; 6% Hispanic/Latino; 4% Asian, non-Hispanic/Latino; 0.1% Native Hawaiian or other Pacific Islander, non-Hispanic/Latino; 1% American Indian or Alaska Native, non-Hispanic/Latino; 4% Two or more races, non-Hispanic/Latino; 4% Race/ethnicity unknown; 2% international; 10% transferred in; 28% live on campus.

Freshmen:
Admission: 4,543 applied, 3,674 admitted, 1,497 enrolled. ***Average high school GPA:*** 3.9. ***Test scores:*** SAT evidence-based reading and writing scores over 500: 88%; SAT math scores over 500: 75%; ACT scores over 18: 100%; SAT evidence-based reading and writing scores over 600: 75%; SAT math scores over 600: 50%; ACT scores over 24: 84%; SAT evidence-based reading and writing scores over 700: 38%; SAT math scores over 700: 13%; ACT scores over 30: 49%.

Retention: 83% of full-time freshmen returned.

FACULTY
Total: 619, 59% full-time, 62% with terminal degrees.

Student/faculty ratio: 18:1.

ACADEMICS
Calendar: semesters. *Degrees:* certificates, bachelor's, master's, doctoral, post-master's, and postbachelor's certificates.

Special study options: academic remediation for entering students, advanced placement credit, cooperative education, distance learning, double majors, English as a second language, freshman honors college, honors programs, independent study, internships, off-campus study, part-time degree program, services for LD students, student-designed majors, study abroad, summer session for credit. ***ROTC:*** Army (c).

Unusual degree programs: 3-2 engineering with Oakwood College, Morehouse College, Clark Atlanta University, Spelman College.

Computers: 1,227 computers/terminals and 5,330 ports are available on campus for general student use. Students can access the following: campus intranet, computer help desk, free student e-mail accounts, online (class) grades, online (class) registration, online (class) schedules. Campuswide network is available. 100% of college-owned or -operated housing units are wired for high-speed Internet access. Wireless service is available via classrooms, computer centers, computer labs, dorm rooms, learning centers, libraries, student centers.

Library: Louis Salmon Library. *Books:* 239,503 (physical), 387,481 (digital/electronic); *Serial titles:* 3,441 (physical), 42,868 (digital/electronic); *Databases:* 133.

STUDENT LIFE
Housing options: on-campus residence required through sophomore year; coed, cooperative, special housing for students with disabilities. Campus housing is university owned. Freshman campus housing is guaranteed.

Activities and organizations: drama/theater group, student-run newspaper, choral group, Student Government Association, Student Run Sports, International Student Association, CRU, Blue Crew, national fraternities, national sororities.

Athletics Member NCAA. All Division II except ice hockey (Division I). ***Intercollegiate sports:*** baseball M(s), basketball M(s)/W(s), cheerleading M(s)/W(s), crew M(c)/W(c), cross-country running M(s)/W(s), ice hockey M(s), lacrosse M(c)/W(c), soccer M(s)/W(s), softball W(s), tennis M(s)/W(s), track and field M(s)/W(s), volleyball W(s). ***Intramural sports:*** basketball M/W, football M/W, racquetball M/W, soccer M/W, softball M/W, tennis M/W, ultimate Frisbee M/W, volleyball M/W.

Campus security: 24-hour emergency response devices and patrols, late-night transport/escort service, controlled dormitory access, 24/7 dispatch center, community policing efforts.

Student services: health clinic, personal/psychological counseling, veterans affairs office.

COSTS & FINANCIAL AID
Costs (2020–21) ***Tuition:*** state resident $9730 full-time, $437 per credit hour part-time; nonresident $22,126 full-time, $1058 per credit hour part-time. Full-time tuition and fees vary according to course load and program. Part-time tuition and fees vary according to course load and program. ***Required fees:*** $1392 full-time. ***Room and board:*** $10,632. Room and board charges vary according to board plan and housing facility. ***Payment plan:*** installment. ***Waivers:*** employees or children of employees.

Financial Aid Of all full-time matriculated undergraduates who enrolled in 2018, 3,939 applied for aid, 3,220 were judged to have need, 1,042 had their need fully met. 54 Federal Work-Study jobs (averaging $4449). In 2018, 1826 non-need-based awards were made. ***Average percent of need met:*** 73. ***Average financial aid package:*** $16,187. ***Average need-based loan:*** $7319. ***Average need-based gift aid:*** $9348. ***Average non-need-based aid:*** $10,741. ***Average indebtedness upon graduation:*** $27,929. ***Financial aid deadline:*** 7/31.

APPLYING
Standardized Tests *Required:* SAT or ACT (for admission).

Options: electronic application, deferred entrance.

Application fee: $30.

Required: high school transcript.

Application deadlines: 8/17 (freshmen), 8/17 (transfers).

Notification: continuous (freshmen), continuous (out-of-state freshmen), continuous (transfers).

CONTACT
Ms. Peggy Masters, Director of Undergraduate Admissions, The University of Alabama in Huntsville, Enrollment Services, 301 Sparkman Drive, Huntsville, AL 35899. *Phone:* 256-824-2771. *Toll-free phone:* 800-UAH-CALL. *Fax:* 256-824-4539. *E-mail:* uahadmissions@uah.edu.

University of Mobile

Mobile, Alabama

http://www.umobile.edu/

CONTACT
Mrs. Hali Givens, Director of Enrollment, University of Mobile, 5735 College Parkway, Mobile, AL 36613-2842. *Phone:* 251-442-2222. *Toll-free phone:* 800-946-7267. *E-mail:* hgivens@umobile.edu.

University of Montevallo

Montevallo, Alabama

http://www.montevallo.edu/

- **State-supported** comprehensive, founded 1896
- **Small-town** 160-acre campus with easy access to Birmingham
- **Endowment** $21.9 million
- **Coed** 2,242 undergraduate students, 89% full-time, 65% women, 35% men
- **Moderately difficult** entrance level, 53% of applicants were admitted

UNDERGRAD STUDENTS
1,997 full-time, 245 part-time. Students come from 35 states and territories; 26 other countries; 13% are from out of state; 16% Black or African American, non-Hispanic/Latino; 5% Hispanic/Latino; 0.9% Asian, non-Hispanic/Latino; 0.2% Native Hawaiian or other Pacific Islander, non-Hispanic/Latino; 0.3% American Indian or Alaska Native, non-Hispanic/Latino; 4% Two or more races, non-Hispanic/Latino; 2%

Race/ethnicity unknown; 3% international; 8% transferred in; 48% live on campus.

Freshmen:
Admission: 5,553 applied, 2,955 admitted, 493 enrolled. ***Average high school GPA:*** 3.6. ***Test scores:*** ACT scores over 18: 98%; ACT scores over 24: 48%; ACT scores over 30: 10%.

Retention: 74% of full-time freshmen returned.

FACULTY
Total: 230, 69% full-time, 77% with terminal degrees.

Student/faculty ratio: 13:1.

ACADEMICS
Calendar: semesters. *Degrees:* bachelor's, master's, and post-master's certificates.

Special study options: academic remediation for entering students, accelerated degree program, advanced placement credit, distance learning, double majors, honors programs, independent study, internships, part-time degree program, services for LD students, study abroad, summer session for credit. ***ROTC:*** Army (c), Air Force (c).

Unusual degree programs: 3-2 engineering with Auburn University, University of Alabama at Birmingham.

Computers: 340 computers/terminals are available on campus for general student use. Students can access the following: campus intranet, computer help desk, free student e-mail accounts, online (class) grades, online (class) registration, online (class) schedules. Campuswide network is available. 100% of college-owned or -operated housing units are wired for high-speed Internet access. Wireless service is available via classrooms, computer centers, computer labs, dorm rooms, libraries, student centers.
Library: Carmichael Library. Students can reserve study rooms.

STUDENT LIFE
Housing options: on-campus residence required for freshman year; coed, men-only, women-only. Campus housing is university owned. Freshman campus housing is guaranteed.

Activities and organizations: drama/theater group, student-run newspaper, television station, choral group, Student Government Association, University Programming Council, Campus Ministries, Greek Life, Environmental Club, national fraternities, national sororities.

Athletics Member NCAA. All Division II except golf (Division I). ***Intercollegiate sports:*** baseball M(s), basketball M(s)/W(s), cheerleading W, cross-country running M/W, golf M(s)/W(s), lacrosse M/W, soccer M(s)/W(s), softball W, swimming and diving M/W, tennis M/W(s), track and field M/W, volleyball W(s). ***Intramural sports:*** basketball M/W, bowling M, football M, golf M, tennis M/W, volleyball M/W.

Campus security: 24-hour emergency response devices and patrols, late-night transport/escort service, controlled dormitory access.

Student services: health clinic, personal/psychological counseling.

COSTS & FINANCIAL AID
Costs (2020–21) ***Tuition:*** area resident $12,090 full-time; state resident $12,090 full-time, $403 per credit hour part-time; nonresident $25,110 full-time, $837 per credit hour part-time. Full-time tuition and fees vary according to course load and program. Part-time tuition and fees vary according to course load and program. ***Required fees:*** $1620 full-time. ***Room and board:*** $9810; room only: $6596. Room and board charges vary according to housing facility. ***Payment plan:*** installment. ***Waivers:*** employees or children of employees.

Financial Aid Of all full-time matriculated undergraduates who enrolled in 2019, 1,638 applied for aid, 1,357 were judged to have need, 286 had their need fully met. 118 Federal Work-Study jobs (averaging $2303). In 2019, 502 non-need-based awards were made. ***Average percent of need met:*** 57. ***Average financial aid package:*** $12,666. ***Average need-based loan:*** $4038. ***Average need-based gift aid:*** $10,154. ***Average non-need-based aid:*** $13,133. ***Average indebtedness upon graduation:*** $29,968.

APPLYING
Standardized Tests *Required:* SAT or ACT (for admission).

Options: electronic application, early admission, deferred entrance.

Application fee: $30.

Required: high school transcript, minimum 2.0 GPA. ***Recommended:*** interview.

Application deadlines: 8/15 (freshmen), rolling (transfers).
Notification: 9/1 (freshmen).

CONTACT
Audrey Crawford, Director of Admissions, University of Montevallo, Office of Admissions, Station 6030, Montevallo, AL 35115-6030. *Phone:* 205-665-6030. *Toll-free phone:* 800-292-4349. *Fax:* 205-665-6032. *E-mail:* admissions@montevallo.edu.

University of North Alabama

Florence, Alabama

http://www.una.edu/

- **State-supported** comprehensive, founded 1830
- **Urban** 200-acre campus with easy access to Huntsville
- **Endowment** $32.6 million
- **Coed**
- **Minimally difficult** entrance level

FACULTY
Student/faculty ratio: 19:1.

ACADEMICS
Calendar: semesters. *Degrees:* bachelor's, master's, post-master's, and postbachelor's certificates.
Library: Collier Library plus 3 others. *Books:* 225,076 (physical), 469,260 (digital/electronic); *Serial titles:* 4,070 (physical), 55,929 (digital/electronic); *Databases:* 182. Weekly public service hours: 98; students can reserve study rooms.

STUDENT LIFE
Housing options: on-campus residence required for freshman year; coed, men-only, women-only, special housing for students with disabilities. Campus housing is university owned and is provided by a third party. Freshman campus housing is guaranteed.

Activities and organizations: drama/theater group, student-run newspaper, choral group, marching band, Phi Mu, Alpha Gamma Delta, Zeta Tau Alpha, Alpha Delta Pi, Student Government Association, national fraternities, national sororities.

Athletics Member NCAA. All Division II.

Campus security: 24-hour emergency response devices and patrols, student patrols, late-night transport/escort service, controlled dormitory access.

Student services: health clinic, personal/psychological counseling, women's center, veterans affairs office.

COSTS & FINANCIAL AID
Costs (2019–20) ***Tuition:*** state resident $9600 full-time, $320 per credit hour part-time; nonresident $19,200 full-time, $640 per credit hour part-time. Full-time tuition and fees vary according to course load and program. Part-time tuition and fees vary according to course load and program. ***Required fees:*** $1200 full-time, $320 per credit hour part-time. ***Room and board:*** $7830. Room and board charges vary according to board plan, housing facility, and student level.

Financial Aid Of all full-time matriculated undergraduates who enrolled in 2017, 3,958 applied for aid, 3,911 were judged to have need, 144 had their need fully met. In 2017, 427 non-need-based awards were made. ***Average percent of need met:*** 50. ***Average financial aid package:*** $8629. ***Average need-based loan:*** $3852. ***Average need-based gift aid:*** $3677. ***Average non-need-based aid:*** $2870. ***Average indebtedness upon graduation:*** $28,283.

APPLYING
Standardized Tests *Required:* SAT or ACT (for admission).

Options: electronic application, early admission, deferred entrance.

Application fee: $35.

Required: high school transcript, minimum 2.0 GPA, 13 approved units from high school academic core.

CONTACT
Mrs. Julie Taylor, Interim Director of Admissions, University of North Alabama, One Harrison Plaza, Florence, AL 35632-0001. *Phone:* 256-765-4680. *Toll-free phone:* 800-TALK-UNA. *Fax:* 256-765-4329. *E-mail:* admissions@una.edu.

University of South Alabama

Mobile, Alabama

http://www.southalabama.edu/

- **State-supported** university, founded 1963
- **Suburban** 1225-acre campus
- **Endowment** $428.0 million
- **Coed** 9,601 undergraduate students, 84% full-time, 60% women, 40% men
- **Moderately difficult** entrance level, 78% of applicants were admitted

UNDERGRAD STUDENTS

8,065 full-time, 1,536 part-time. Students come from 38 states and territories; 49 other countries; 18% are from out of state; 22% Black or African American, non-Hispanic/Latino; 4% Hispanic/Latino; 3% Asian, non-Hispanic/Latino; 0.1% Native Hawaiian or other Pacific Islander, non-Hispanic/Latino; 0.7% American Indian or Alaska Native, non-Hispanic/Latino; 4% Two or more races, non-Hispanic/Latino; 3% Race/ethnicity unknown; 2% international; 7% transferred in; 21% live on campus.

Freshmen:

Admission: 6,495 applied, 5,047 admitted, 1,617 enrolled. ***Average high school GPA:*** 3.7. ***Test scores:*** SAT evidence-based reading and writing scores over 500: 82%; SAT math scores over 500: 79%; ACT scores over 18: 99%; SAT evidence-based reading and writing scores over 600: 37%; SAT math scores over 600: 27%; ACT scores over 24: 49%; SAT evidence-based reading and writing scores over 700: 8%; SAT math scores over 700: 7%; ACT scores over 30: 12%.

Retention: 74% of full-time freshmen returned.

FACULTY

Total: 1,060, 55% full-time, 62% with terminal degrees.

Student/faculty ratio: 17:1.

ACADEMICS

Calendar: semesters. *Degrees:* certificates, bachelor's, master's, doctoral, post-master's, and postbachelor's certificates.

Special study options: academic remediation for entering students, accelerated degree program, adult/continuing education programs, advanced placement credit, cooperative education, distance learning, double majors, English as a second language, external degree program, freshman honors college, honors programs, independent study, internships, part-time degree program, services for LD students, student-designed majors, study abroad, summer session for credit. ***ROTC:*** Army (b), Air Force (b).

Computers: Students can access the following: campus intranet, computer help desk, free student e-mail accounts, online (class) grades, online (class) registration, online (class) schedules. Campuswide network is available. 100% of college-owned or -operated housing units are wired for high-speed Internet access. Wireless service is available via entire campus.

Library: Marx Library plus 4 others.

STUDENT LIFE

Housing options: coed, special housing for students with disabilities. Campus housing is university owned.

Activities and organizations: drama/theater group, student-run newspaper, radio and television station, choral group, marching band, Student Government Association, African American Student Association, Council of International Student Organizations, Alpha Epsilon Delta Pre-Health Professions, Panhellenic Council, national fraternities, national sororities.

Athletics Member NCAA. All Division I. ***Intercollegiate sports:*** baseball M(s), basketball M(s)/W(s), cross-country running M(s)/W(s), football M(s), golf M(s)/W(s), soccer W(s), softball W(s), tennis M(s)/W(s), track and field M(s)/W(s), volleyball W(s). ***Intramural sports:*** archery M(c)/W(c), basketball M/W, cheerleading M(c)/W(c), football M(c)/W(c), rock climbing M(c)/W(c), rugby M(c), soccer M/W, softball M/W, ultimate Frisbee M(c)/W(c), volleyball M/W, water polo M/W.

Campus security: 24-hour emergency response devices and patrols, late-night transport/escort service, controlled dormitory access.

Student services: health clinic, personal/psychological counseling, women's center, legal services, veterans affairs office.

COSTS & FINANCIAL AID

Costs (2020–21) ***One-time required fee:*** $200. ***Tuition:*** area resident $9870 full-time; state resident $9870 full-time, $329 per credit hour part-time; nonresident $19,740 full-time, $658 per credit hour part-time. Full-time tuition and fees vary according to course load, degree level, and program. Part-time tuition and fees vary according to course load, degree level, and program. ***Required fees:*** $200 full-time, $210 per term part-time. ***Room and board:*** $7800; room only: $4100. Room and board charges vary according to board plan and housing facility. ***Payment plan:*** installment. ***Waivers:*** employees or children of employees.

Financial Aid Of all full-time matriculated undergraduates who enrolled in 2015, 7,167 applied for aid, 5,829 were judged to have need, 487 had their need fully met. In 2015, 1146 non-need-based awards were made. ***Average percent of need met:*** 50. ***Average financial aid package:*** $9708. ***Average need-based loan:*** $4348. ***Average need-based gift aid:*** $6606. ***Average non-need-based aid:*** $5321.

APPLYING

Standardized Tests *Required for some:* SAT or ACT (for admission).

Options: electronic application, early admission, deferred entrance.

Application fee: $45.

Required: high school transcript. ***Required for some:*** essay or personal statement, minimum 3.5 GPA, 1 letter of recommendation, minimum high school GPA of 3.0 for Accelerated College Enrollment Program, minimum high school GPA of 3.5 for Early Admission. ***Recommended:*** minimum 2.5 GPA.

Application deadlines: 7/15 (freshmen), 7/15 (out-of-state freshmen), 7/15 (transfers).

Notification: continuous (freshmen), continuous (out-of-state freshmen), continuous (transfers).

CONTACT

Ms. Adrienne Gannon, Associate Director, New Student Recruitment, University of South Alabama, 390 Alumni Circle, 2500 Meisler Hall, Mobile, AL 36688-0002. *Phone:* 251-460-7719. *Toll-free phone:* 800-872-5247. *Fax:* 251-460-7876. *E-mail:* recruitment@southalabama.edu.

The University of West Alabama

Livingston, Alabama

http://www.uwa.edu/

- **State-supported** comprehensive, founded 1835
- **Small-town** 514-acre campus
- **Endowment** $59,125
- **Coed** 2,239 undergraduate students, 84% full-time, 61% women, 39% men
- **Minimally difficult** entrance level, 35% of applicants were admitted

UNDERGRAD STUDENTS

1,883 full-time, 356 part-time. Students come from 30 states and territories; 27 other countries; 18% are from out of state; 41% Black or African American, non-Hispanic/Latino; 2% Hispanic/Latino; 0.3% Asian, non-Hispanic/Latino; 0.5% American Indian or Alaska Native, non-Hispanic/Latino; 2% Two or more races, non-Hispanic/Latino; 5% Race/ethnicity unknown; 4% international; 17% transferred in; 50% live on campus.

Freshmen:

Admission: 7,569 applied, 2,644 admitted, 322 enrolled. ***Test scores:*** ACT scores over 18: 81%; ACT scores over 24: 16%; ACT scores over 30: 2%.

Retention: 66% of full-time freshmen returned.

FACULTY

Total: 314, 39% full-time, 62% with terminal degrees.

Student/faculty ratio: 14:1.

ACADEMICS

Calendar: semesters. *Degrees:* certificates, associate, bachelor's, master's, doctoral, and post-master's certificates.

Special study options: academic remediation for entering students, accelerated degree program, advanced placement credit, cooperative education, distance learning, double majors, English as a second language, freshman honors college, honors programs, independent study, internships, part-time degree program, services for LD students, student-designed majors, study abroad, summer session for credit. ***ROTC:*** Air Force (c).

Unusual degree programs: 3-2 engineering with Auburn University, The University of Alabama at Birmingham, Mississippi State University, The University of Alabama; forestry with Auburn University; social work with University of Alabama; wildlife with Auburn University.

Computers: 400 computers/terminals are available on campus for general student use. Students can access the following: campus intranet, computer help desk, free student e-mail accounts, online (class) grades, online (class) registration, online (class) schedules. Campuswide network is available. 100% of college-owned or -operated housing units are wired for high-speed Internet access. Wireless service is available via entire campus.

Library: Julia Tutwiler Library plus 1 other. *Books:* 209,776 (physical), 2,121 (digital/electronic); *Serial titles:* 41,804 (physical), 108,967 (digital/electronic); *Databases:* 174. Weekly public service hours: 96; students can reserve study rooms.

STUDENT LIFE

Housing options: on-campus residence required for freshman year; coed. Campus housing is university owned. Freshman campus housing is guaranteed.

Activities and organizations: drama/theater group, student-run newspaper, television station, choral group, marching band, Wesley Campus Ministries, UWA Rotoract, Active Minds, Phi Mu, Alpha Sigma Alpha, national fraternities, national sororities.

Athletics Member NCAA. All Division II. ***Intercollegiate sports:*** baseball M(s), basketball M(s)/W(s), cross-country running M(s)/W(s), football M(s), softball W(s), tennis M(s)/W(s), track and field M(s)/W(s), volleyball W(s). ***Intramural sports:*** basketball M/W, bowling M/W, football M/W, soccer M/W, softball M/W, table tennis M/W, tennis M/W, ultimate Frisbee M/W, volleyball M/W.

Campus security: 24-hour emergency response devices and patrols, controlled dormitory access.

Student services: health clinic, personal/psychological counseling.

COSTS & FINANCIAL AID

Costs (2020–21) ***Tuition:*** state resident $9100 full-time, $325 per credit hour part-time; nonresident $18,200 full-time, $650 per credit hour part-time. Full-time tuition and fees vary according to course load. Part-time tuition and fees vary according to course load. ***Required fees:*** $1890 full-time. ***Room and board:*** $7510; room only: $4760. Room and board charges vary according to board plan, housing facility, and student level. ***Payment plan:*** installment. ***Waivers:*** employees or children of employees.

Financial Aid Of all full-time matriculated undergraduates who enrolled in 2018, 1,643 applied for aid, 1,471 were judged to have need, 53 had their need fully met. 135 Federal Work-Study jobs (averaging $1869). In 2018, 38 non-need-based awards were made. ***Average percent of need met:*** 22. ***Average financial aid package:*** $10,889. ***Average need-based gift aid:*** $5839. ***Average non-need-based aid:*** $5102. ***Average indebtedness upon graduation:*** $24,408.

APPLYING

Standardized Tests *Required:* SAT or ACT (for admission).

Options: electronic application, deferred entrance.

Application fee: $40.

Required: high school transcript, minimum 2.0 GPA.

Application deadlines: rolling (freshmen), rolling (transfers).

Notification: continuous (freshmen), continuous (transfers).

CONTACT

Mrs. Brenda Edwards, Coordinator of Admissions Operations, The University of West Alabama, Station 4, Livingston, AL 35470. *Phone:* 205-652-3699. *Toll-free phone:* 888-636-8800. *Fax:* 205-652-3881. *E-mail:* belliott@uwa.edu.

ALASKA

Alaska Bible College

Palmer, Alaska

http://www.akbible.edu/

- **Independent nondenominational** 4-year, founded 1966
- **Small-town** 2-acre campus with easy access to Anchorage, AK
- **Coed**
- **Minimally difficult** entrance level

FACULTY

Student/faculty ratio: 4:1.

ACADEMICS

Calendar: semesters. *Degrees:* certificates, associate, and bachelor's.

Library: Alaska Bible College Ball Memorial Library. *Books:* 32,000 (physical); *Serial titles:* 46 (physical). Weekly public service hours: 40.

STUDENT LIFE

Housing options: men-only, women-only. Campus housing is university owned. Freshman applicants given priority for college housing.

Student services: veterans affairs office.

FINANCIAL AID

Financial Aid Of all full-time matriculated undergraduates who enrolled in 2018, 4 Federal Work-Study jobs (averaging $1250).

APPLYING

Standardized Tests *Required:* SAT or ACT (for admission).

Options: electronic application, deferred entrance.

Application fee: $35.

Required: essay or personal statement, high school transcript, minimum 2.0 GPA, 3 letters of recommendation.

CONTACT

Justin Archuletta, Director of Admissions, Alaska Bible College, 248 E. Elmwood Avenue, Palmer, AK 99645. *Phone:* 907-745-3201 Ext. 111. *Toll-free phone:* 800-478-7884. *Fax:* 907-745-3210. *E-mail:* admissions@akbible.edu.

Alaska Pacific University

Anchorage, Alaska

http://www.alaskapacific.edu/

CONTACT

Ms. Kate Hillenbrand, Director of Admissions, Alaska Pacific University, 4101 University Drive, Anchorage, AK 99508. *Phone:* 907-564-8300. *Toll-free phone:* 800-252-7528. *Fax:* 907-564-8317. *E-mail:* admissions@alaskapacific.edu.

Charter College

Anchorage, Alaska

http://www.chartercollege.edu/

CONTACT

Ms. Lily Sirianni, Vice President, Charter College, 2221 East Northern Lights Boulevard, Suite 120, Anchorage, AK 99508. *Phone:* 907-277-1000. *Toll-free phone:* 888-200-9942.

University of Alaska Anchorage

Anchorage, Alaska

http://www.uaa.alaska.edu/

- **State-supported** comprehensive, founded 1954, part of University of Alaska System
- **Urban** 428-acre campus
- **Coed**
- **Noncompetitive** entrance level

FACULTY

Student/faculty ratio: 12:1.

ACADEMICS
Calendar: semesters. *Degrees:* certificates, associate, bachelor's, master's, doctoral, post-master's, and postbachelor's certificates.
Library: Consortium Library.

STUDENT LIFE
Housing options: coed, special housing for students with disabilities.

Activities and organizations: drama/theater group, student-run newspaper, radio station, choral group, Accounting Club, African-American Students Association, Association of Latin-American Spanish Students, Inter-Varsity Christian Fellowship, Student Nurses Association, national fraternities, national sororities.

Athletics Member NCAA. All Division II.

Campus security: 24-hour emergency response devices and patrols, student patrols, late-night transport/escort service, controlled dormitory access.

Student services: health clinic, personal/psychological counseling, women's center.

FINANCIAL AID
Financial Aid Of all full-time matriculated undergraduates who enrolled in 2019, 3,723 applied for aid, 2,691 were judged to have need, 533 had their need fully met. In 2019, 458 non-need-based awards were made. ***Average percent of need met:*** 73. ***Average financial aid package:*** $10,955. ***Average need-based loan:*** $4077. ***Average need-based gift aid:*** $3629. ***Average non-need-based aid:*** $2417. ***Average indebtedness upon graduation:*** $24,866.

APPLYING
Options: electronic application, deferred entrance.

Application fee: $50.

Required: minimum 2.0 GPA. ***Required for some:*** high school transcript.

CONTACT
Enrollment Services, University of Alaska Anchorage, PO Box 141629, 3901 Old Seward Highway, Anchorage, AK 99508-8046. *Phone:* 907-786-1480. *Fax:* 907-786-4888. *E-mail:* enroll@uaa.alaska.edu.

University of Alaska Anchorage, Kenai Peninsula College

Soldotna, Alaska

http://www.kpc.alaska.edu/

- **State-supported** primarily 2-year, founded 1964, part of University of Alaska
- **Rural** 360-acre campus
- **Coed** 2,142 undergraduate students, 33% full-time, 64% women, 36% men
- **Noncompetitive** entrance level

UNDERGRAD STUDENTS
702 full-time, 1,440 part-time. Students come from 40 states and territories; 4 other countries; 2% Black or African American, non-Hispanic/Latino; 6% Hispanic/Latino; 4% Asian, non-Hispanic/Latino; 2% Native Hawaiian or other Pacific Islander, non-Hispanic/Latino; 6% American Indian or Alaska Native, non-Hispanic/Latino; 9% Two or more races, non-Hispanic/Latino; 16% Race/ethnicity unknown; 1% international.

FACULTY
Total: 117, 28% full-time.

Student/faculty ratio: 18:1.

ACADEMICS
Calendar: semesters. *Degrees:* certificates, associate, and bachelor's.

Special study options: academic remediation for entering students, adult/continuing education programs, advanced placement credit, cooperative education, distance learning, double majors, English as a second language, independent study, internships, part-time degree program, services for LD students.

Computers: Students can access the following: computer help desk, free student e-mail accounts, online (class) grades, online (class) registration, online (class) schedules. Campuswide network is available. Wireless service is available via entire campus.
Library: Kenai Peninsula College Library.

STUDENT LIFE
Housing options: college housing not available.

Campus security: 24-hour emergency response devices.

Student services: health clinic, personal/psychological counseling, veterans affairs office.

COSTS
Costs (2020–21) ***Tuition:*** state resident $5616 full-time, $234 per credit hour part-time; nonresident $5616 full-time, $234 per credit hour part-time. ***Required fees:*** $828 full-time. ***Waivers:*** senior citizens and employees or children of employees.

APPLYING
Options: electronic application.

Application fee: $40.

Required: high school transcript.

Application deadlines: rolling (freshmen), rolling (out-of-state freshmen), rolling (transfers).

Notification: continuous (freshmen), continuous (out-of-state freshmen), continuous (transfers).

CONTACT
Ms. Ginger Rose, Admission and Student Records Coordinator, University of Alaska Anchorage, Kenai Peninsula College, 156 College Road, Soldotna, AK 99669. *Phone:* 907-262-0311. *Toll-free phone:* 877-262-0330. *E-mail:* glrose@alaska.edu.

University of Alaska Fairbanks

Fairbanks, Alaska

http://www.uaf.edu/

- **State-supported** university, founded 1917, part of University of Alaska System
- **Small-town** 2250-acre campus
- **Endowment** $98.9 million
- **Coed** 6,284 undergraduate students, 41% full-time, 60% women, 40% men
- **Minimally difficult** entrance level, 76% of applicants were admitted

UNDERGRAD STUDENTS
2,596 full-time, 3,688 part-time. 15% are from out of state; 4% Black or African American, non-Hispanic/Latino; 9% Hispanic/Latino; 2% Asian, non-Hispanic/Latino; 0.8% Native Hawaiian or other Pacific Islander, non-Hispanic/Latino; 13% American Indian or Alaska Native, non-Hispanic/Latino; 11% Two or more races, non-Hispanic/Latino; 10% Race/ethnicity unknown; 1% international; 6% transferred in.

Freshmen:
Admission: 1,383 applied, 1,051 admitted, 686 enrolled. ***Average high school GPA:*** 3.4. ***Test scores:*** SAT evidence-based reading and writing scores over 500: 84%; SAT math scores over 500: 78%; ACT scores over 18: 74%; SAT evidence-based reading and writing scores over 600: 45%; SAT math scores over 600: 38%; ACT scores over 24: 33%; SAT evidence-based reading and writing scores over 700: 10%; SAT math scores over 700: 8%; ACT scores over 30: 7%.
Retention: 73% of full-time freshmen returned.

FACULTY
Total: 855, 53% full-time, 55% with terminal degrees.

Student/faculty ratio: 8:1.

ACADEMICS
Calendar: semesters. *Degrees:* certificates, associate, bachelor's, master's, doctoral, and postbachelor's certificates.

Special study options: academic remediation for entering students, accelerated degree program, advanced placement credit, cooperative education, distance learning, double majors, English as a second language, external degree program, honors programs, independent study, internships, off-campus study, part-time degree program, services for LD students, student-designed majors, study abroad, summer session for credit. ***ROTC:*** Army (b).

Unusual degree programs: 3-2 engineering; computer science.

Computers: 125 computers/terminals and 22 ports are available on campus for general student use. Students can access the following: campus intranet, computer help desk, free student e-mail accounts, online (class) grades, online (class) registration, online (class) schedules, university portal. Campuswide network is available. 100% of college-owned or -operated housing units are wired for high-speed Internet access. Wireless service is available via entire campus.

Library: Rasmuson Library plus 1 other. *Books:* 533,679 (physical), 324,260 (digital/electronic); *Serial titles:* 222,847 (physical), 30,490 (digital/electronic); *Databases:* 175. Weekly public service hours: 87; students can reserve study rooms.

STUDENT LIFE

Activities and organizations: drama/theater group, student-run newspaper, radio station, choral group, Chi Alpha, Yoga Club, Aurora Aerial Arts, Festival of Native Arts, Gender and Sexuality Alliance.

Athletics Member NCAA. All Division II except ice hockey (Division I). ***Intercollegiate sports:*** basketball M(s)/W(s), cross-country running M(s)/W(s), ice hockey M(s), riflery M(s)/W(s), skiing (cross-country) M(s)/W(s), swimming and diving W(s), volleyball W(s). ***Intramural sports:*** badminton M(c)/W(c), basketball M/W, cross-country running M(c)/W(c), fencing M(c)/W(c), ice hockey M/W, soccer M/W, ultimate Frisbee M/W, volleyball M/W.

Campus security: 24-hour emergency response devices and patrols, student patrols, late-night transport/escort service, controlled dormitory access, ID check at door of residence halls, crime prevention and safety workshops.

Student services: health clinic, personal/psychological counseling, legal services, veterans affairs office.

COSTS & FINANCIAL AID

Costs (2020–21) ***Tuition:*** area resident $8460 full-time, $282 per credit hour part-time; state resident $8460 full-time, $282 per credit hour part-time; nonresident $25,440 full-time, $848 per credit hour part-time. ***Required fees:*** $1848 full-time. ***Room and board:*** $10,440; room only: $6000.

Financial Aid Of all full-time matriculated undergraduates who enrolled in 2018, 2,232 applied for aid, 1,546 were judged to have need, 232 had their need fully met. In 2018, 339 non-need-based awards were made. ***Average percent of need met:*** 54. ***Average financial aid package:*** $9230. ***Average need-based loan:*** $3774. ***Average need-based gift aid:*** $8101. ***Average non-need-based aid:*** $3768. ***Average indebtedness upon graduation:*** $26,406. ***Financial aid deadline:*** 7/1.

APPLYING

Standardized Tests *Required:* SAT or ACT (for admission).

Options: electronic application, early admission, deferred entrance.

Application fee: $50.

Required: high school transcript, minimum 2.5 GPA.

Application deadlines: 6/15 (freshmen), 6/15 (transfers).

Notification: continuous (freshmen), continuous (out-of-state freshmen), continuous (transfers).

CONTACT

University of Alaska Fairbanks, PO Box 757500, Fairbanks, AK 99775-7520. *Toll-free phone:* 800-478-1823.

University of Alaska Southeast

Juneau, Alaska

http://www.uas.alaska.edu/

- **State-supported** comprehensive, founded 1972, part of University of Alaska System
- **Small-town** 198-acre campus
- **Coed** 1,886 undergraduate students, 31% full-time, 67% women, 33% men
- **Noncompetitive** entrance level, 61% of applicants were admitted

UNDERGRAD STUDENTS

588 full-time, 1,298 part-time. 11% are from out of state; 0.8% Black or African American, non-Hispanic/Latino; 9% Hispanic/Latino; 2% Asian, non-Hispanic/Latino; 3% Native Hawaiian or other Pacific Islander, non-Hispanic/Latino; 10% American Indian or Alaska Native, non-Hispanic/Latino; 11% Two or more races, non-Hispanic/Latino; 8% Race/ethnicity unknown; 0.4% international; 10% transferred in; 15% live on campus.

Freshmen:

Admission: 492 applied, 298 admitted, 172 enrolled.

Retention: 59% of full-time freshmen returned.

FACULTY

Total: 169, 55% full-time, 34% with terminal degrees.

Student/faculty ratio: 9:1.

ACADEMICS

Calendar: semesters. *Degrees:* certificates, associate, bachelor's, master's, and post-master's certificates.

Special study options: academic remediation for entering students, adult/continuing education programs, advanced placement credit, cooperative education, distance learning, double majors, independent study, internships, off-campus study, part-time degree program, services for LD students, student-designed majors, study abroad, summer session for credit.

Computers: Students can access the following: campus intranet, computer help desk, free student e-mail accounts, online (class) grades, online (class) registration, online (class) schedules. Campuswide network is available. 100% of college-owned or -operated housing units are wired for high-speed Internet access. Wireless service is available via entire campus.

Library: Egan Memorial Library. *Books:* 152,804 (physical), 197,031 (digital/electronic); *Serial titles:* 3,473 (physical), 78,178 (digital/electronic); *Databases:* 124.

STUDENT LIFE

Housing options: coed, special housing for students with disabilities. Campus housing is university owned. Freshman applicants given priority for college housing.

Activities and organizations: student-run newspaper, radio station, Gaming Club, Wooch.een, Sustainability Club, Southeast Alaska Prospective Accountants, Human Resources Management Club.

Athletics ***Intercollegiate sports:*** riflery M(c)/W(c). ***Intramural sports:*** basketball M/W, rock climbing M(c)/W(c), skiing (cross-country) M(c)/W(c), skiing (downhill) M(c)/W(c), soccer M/W, softball M/W, ultimate Frisbee M/W, volleyball M/W.

Campus security: 24-hour emergency response devices, student patrols, late-night transport/escort service, controlled dormitory access.

Student services: health clinic, personal/psychological counseling, veterans affairs office.

COSTS & FINANCIAL AID

Costs (2020–21) ***Tuition:*** area resident $6192 full-time, $258 per credit hour part-time; state resident $6192 full-time, $258 per credit hour part-time; nonresident $19,776 full-time, $258 per credit hour part-time. Full-time tuition and fees vary according to course level, course load, degree level, and location. Part-time tuition and fees vary according to course level, course load, degree level, and location. ***Required fees:*** $1368 full-time. ***Room and board:*** $8900; room only: $5600. Room and board charges vary according to housing facility and location. ***Payment plans:*** tuition prepayment, installment. ***Waivers:*** senior citizens and employees or children of employees.

Financial Aid Of all full-time matriculated undergraduates who enrolled in 2018, 446 applied for aid, 334 were judged to have need, 70 had their need fully met. In 2018, 29 non-need-based awards were made. ***Average percent of need met:*** 64. ***Average financial aid package:*** $19,091. ***Average need-based loan:*** $8360. ***Average need-based gift aid:*** $6778. ***Average non-need-based aid:*** $3490. ***Average indebtedness upon graduation:*** $33,869.

APPLYING

Standardized Tests *Required for some:* SAT (for admission).

Options: electronic application, deferred entrance.

Application fee: $50.

Required: high school transcript, minimum 2.0 GPA.

Application deadlines: 8/15 (freshmen), 8/15 (transfers).

Notification: continuous (freshmen), continuous (out-of-state freshmen), continuous (transfers).

CONTACT

Admissions Clerk, University of Alaska Southeast, 11120 Glacier Highway, Juneau, AK 99801-8625. *Phone:* 907-796-6294 Ext. 6100. *Toll-*

free phone: 877-465-4827. *Fax:* 907-796-6365. *E-mail:* admissions@uas.alaska.edu.

University of Alaska Southeast, Sitka Campus

Sitka, Alaska

http://www.uas.alaska.edu/sitka/

CONTACT

Ms. Teal Gordon, Admissions Representative, University of Alaska Southeast, Sitka Campus, UAS Sitka, 1332 Seward Avenue, Sitka, AK 99835. *Phone:* 907-747-7726. *Toll-free phone:* 800-478-6653. *Fax:* 907-747-7731. *E-mail:* ktgordon@uas.alaska.edu.

ARIZONA

Argosy University, Phoenix

Phoenix, Arizona

http://www.argosy.edu/phoenix-arizona/default.aspx

CONTACT

Argosy University, Phoenix, 2233 West Dunlap Avenue, Phoenix, AZ 85021. *Phone:* 602-216-2600. *Toll-free phone:* 866-216-2777.

Arizona Christian University

Glendale, Arizona

http://arizonachristian.edu/

- **Independent Conservative Baptist** 4-year, founded 1960
- **Urban** 19-acre campus with easy access to Phoenix
- **Coed** 870 undergraduate students, 82% full-time, 38% women, 62% men
- 65% of applicants were admitted

UNDERGRAD STUDENTS

713 full-time, 157 part-time. 41% are from out of state; 15% Black or African American, non-Hispanic/Latino; 24% Hispanic/Latino; 1% Asian, non-Hispanic/Latino; 0.2% Native Hawaiian or other Pacific Islander, non-Hispanic/Latino; 0.7% American Indian or Alaska Native, non-Hispanic/Latino; 5% Two or more races, non-Hispanic/Latino; 3% Race/ethnicity unknown; 4% international; 15% transferred in; 50% live on campus.

Freshmen:

Admission: 421 applied, 274 admitted, 222 enrolled. ***Average high school GPA:*** 3.0. ***Test scores:*** SAT evidence-based reading and writing scores over 500: 50%; SAT math scores over 500: 54%; ACT scores over 18: 55%; SAT evidence-based reading and writing scores over 600: 9%; SAT math scores over 600: 8%; ACT scores over 24: 8%; SAT math scores over 700: 1%.

Retention: 57% of full-time freshmen returned.

FACULTY

Total: 92, 25% full-time, 35% with terminal degrees.

Student/faculty ratio: 16:1.

ACADEMICS

Calendar: semesters. *Degrees:* certificates, associate, bachelor's, and postbachelor's certificates.

Special study options: academic remediation for entering students, adult/continuing education programs, advanced placement credit, distance learning, double majors, external degree program, independent study, internships, part-time degree program, services for LD students, study abroad, summer session for credit. ***ROTC:*** Air Force (c).

Computers: 37 computers/terminals are available on campus for general student use. Students can access the following: free student e-mail accounts, online (class) grades, online (class) registration, online (class) schedules. 100% of college-owned or -operated housing units are wired for high-speed Internet access. Wireless service is available via entire campus.

Library: R. S. Beal Library. *Books:* 28,496 (physical), 19,581 (digital/electronic); *Serial titles:* 471 (physical), 32 (digital/electronic); *Databases:* 18. Weekly public service hours: 76.

STUDENT LIFE

Housing options: on-campus residence required through sophomore year; men-only, women-only, special housing for students with disabilities. Campus housing is university owned. Freshman campus housing is guaranteed.

Activities and organizations: drama/theater group, choral group, Joseph Story Pre-Law Society, International Student Association, Pre-Medicine Club, Flock Council and Flock Leaders, Reason and Religion.

Athletics Member NAIA, NCCAA. ***Intercollegiate sports:*** baseball M(s), basketball M(s)/W(s), cross-country running M(s)/W(s), football M(s), golf M(s)/W(s), soccer M(s)/W(s), softball W(s), swimming and diving W(s), tennis M(s)/W(s), track and field M(s)/W(s), volleyball W(s). ***Intramural sports:*** basketball M/W, bowling M(c)/W(c), cheerleading W(c), soccer M/W, table tennis M/W, volleyball M/W.

Campus security: 24-hour emergency response devices, student patrols, late-night transport/escort service, controlled dormitory access, 20-hour patrol with a guard on call on weekdays, 24-hour patrol by trained security personnel on weekends.

Student services: personal/psychological counseling.

COSTS & FINANCIAL AID

Costs (2020–21) ***Comprehensive fee:*** $42,624 includes full-time tuition ($28,874), mandatory fees ($1750), and room and board ($12,000). Part-time tuition: $1203 per credit hour.

Financial Aid Of all full-time matriculated undergraduates who enrolled in 2018, 601 applied for aid, 491 were judged to have need, 47 had their need fully met. In 2018, 165 non-need-based awards were made. ***Average percent of need met:*** 32. ***Average financial aid package:*** $9070. ***Average need-based loan:*** $3581. ***Average need-based gift aid:*** $8275. ***Average non-need-based aid:*** $15,167.

APPLYING

Standardized Tests *Required:* SAT or ACT (for admission).

Options: deferred entrance.

Required: essay or personal statement, high school transcript, minimum 2.0 GPA, 1 letter of recommendation.

CONTACT

Lambert Cruz, Registrar and Assistant Dir Enrollment Management, Arizona Christian University, 2625 E. Cactus Road, Phoenix, AZ 85032. *Phone:* 602-386-4160. *Toll-free phone:* 800-247-2697. *Fax:* 602-404-2159. *E-mail:* lambert.cruz@arizonachristian.edu.

Arizona College–Mesa

Mesa, Arizona

http://www.arizonacollege.edu/

CONTACT

Arizona College–Mesa, 163 N Dobson Road, Mesa, AZ 85201.

Arizona State University at the Downtown Phoenix campus

Phoenix, Arizona

http://campus.asu.edu/downtown/

- **State-supported** university, founded 2006
- **Urban** 18-acre campus with easy access to Phoenix
- **Coed** 8,513 undergraduate students, 92% full-time, 69% women, 31% men
- **Moderately difficult** entrance level, 82% of applicants were admitted

UNDERGRAD STUDENTS

7,827 full-time, 686 part-time. Students come from 31 other countries; 26% are from out of state; 6% Black or African American, non-Hispanic/Latino; 34% Hispanic/Latino; 6% Asian, non-Hispanic/Latino; 0.3% Native Hawaiian or other Pacific Islander, non-Hispanic/Latino; 2% American Indian or Alaska Native, non-Hispanic/Latino; 5% Two or more races, non-Hispanic/Latino; 0.6% Race/ethnicity unknown; 2% international; 9% transferred in; 22% live on campus.

Freshmen:
Admission: 7,752 applied, 6,345 admitted, 1,676 enrolled. ***Average high school GPA:*** 3.5. ***Test scores:*** SAT evidence-based reading and writing scores over 500: 90%; SAT math scores over 500: 89%; ACT scores over 18: 88%; SAT evidence-based reading and writing scores over 600: 50%; SAT math scores over 600: 41%; ACT scores over 24: 46%; SAT evidence-based reading and writing scores over 700: 7%; SAT math scores over 700: 7%; ACT scores over 30: 8%.

Retention: 85% of full-time freshmen returned.

FACULTY
Total: 1,138, 56% full-time, 54% with terminal degrees.

Student/faculty ratio: 14:1.

ACADEMICS
Calendar: semesters. *Degrees:* certificates, bachelor's, master's, doctoral, post-master's, and postbachelor's certificates.

Special study options: accelerated degree program, advanced placement credit, distance learning, double majors, freshman honors college, honors programs, independent study, internships, off-campus study, part-time degree program, services for LD students, student-designed majors, study abroad, summer session for credit. ***ROTC:*** Army (c), Navy (c), Air Force (c).

Computers: 486 computers/terminals are available on campus for general student use. Students can access the following: campus intranet, computer help desk, free student e-mail accounts, online (class) grades, online (class) registration, online (class) schedules. Campuswide network is available. 100% of college-owned or -operated housing units are wired for high-speed Internet access. Wireless service is available via classrooms, computer centers, computer labs, dorm rooms, learning centers, libraries, student centers.

Library: Downtown Phoenix campus Library. *Books:* 2.4 million (physical), 1.5 million (digital/electronic); *Serial titles:* 65,552 (physical), 112,025 (digital/electronic); *Databases:* 685. Weekly public service hours: 149; study areas open 24 hours, 5–7 days a week; students can reserve study rooms.

STUDENT LIFE
Housing options: on-campus residence required for freshman year; coed, special housing for students with disabilities. Campus housing is university owned. Freshman campus housing is guaranteed.

Activities and organizations: student-run newspaper, radio and television station, Student Nurses Association, American Medical Student Association, Student Health Outreach for Wellness, Student Nutrition Council, Physical Therapy Club.

Athletics Member NCAA. All Division I. ***Intercollegiate sports:*** baseball M(s), basketball M(s)/W(s), cross-country running M(s)/W(s), football M(s), golf M(s)/W(s), gymnastics W(s), ice hockey M(s), lacrosse W(s), sand volleyball W(s), soccer W(s), softball W(s), swimming and diving M(s)/W(s), tennis M(s)/W(s), track and field M(s)/W(s), triathlon W(s), volleyball W(s), water polo W(s), wrestling M(s). ***Intramural sports:*** baseball M(c)/W(c), basketball M/W, cheerleading M(c)/W(c), crew M(c), equestrian sports M(c)/W(c), fencing M(c)/W(c), golf M(c)/W(c), gymnastics M(c)/W(c), ice hockey M(c)/W(c), lacrosse M(c)/W(c), racquetball M(c)/W(c), rowing M(c)/W(c), rugby M(c)/W(c), sailing M(c)/W(c), soccer M(c)/W(c), softball M/W, squash M(c)/W(c), table tennis M/W, tennis M(c)/W(c), triathlon M(c)/W(c), ultimate Frisbee M(c)/W(c), volleyball M(c)/W(c), water polo M(c)/W(c), weight lifting M(c)/W(c), wrestling M(c)/W(c).

Campus security: 24-hour emergency response devices and patrols, late-night transport/escort service, controlled dormitory access, LiveSafe smart phone application, surveillance camera in some residence halls.

Student services: health clinic, personal/psychological counseling, veterans affairs office.

COSTS & FINANCIAL AID
Costs (2019–20) ***Tuition:*** state resident $10,710 full-time, $765 per credit hour part-time; nonresident $28,800 full-time, $1200 per credit hour part-time. Full-time tuition and fees vary according to program. Part-time tuition and fees vary according to program. ***Required fees:*** $628 full-time, $157 per term part-time. ***Room and board:*** $14,924; room only: $9750. Room and board charges vary according to board plan. ***Payment plan:*** installment. ***Waivers:*** employees or children of employees.

Financial Aid Of all full-time matriculated undergraduates who enrolled in 2018, 6,394 applied for aid, 5,414 were judged to have need, 964 had their need fully met. 443 Federal Work-Study jobs (averaging $2952). 1,208 state and other part-time jobs (averaging $3118). In 2018, 1321 non-need-based awards were made. ***Average percent of need met:*** 60. ***Average financial aid package:*** $15,792. ***Average need-based loan:*** $3923. ***Average need-based gift aid:*** $11,434. ***Average non-need-based aid:*** $8827. ***Average indebtedness upon graduation:*** $25,136.

APPLYING
Standardized Tests *Required for some:* SAT or ACT (for admission), SAT Subject Tests (for admission). *Recommended:* SAT or ACT (for admission).

Options: electronic application, deferred entrance.

Application fee: $50.

Required: high school transcript, minimum 3.0 GPA. ***Required for some:*** essay or personal statement, letters of recommendation, additional requirements for Honors College and certain majors.

Application deadlines: rolling (freshmen), rolling (transfers).

Notification: continuous until 8/1 (freshmen), continuous (transfers).

CONTACT
Admission Services Applicant Processing, Arizona State University at the Downtown Phoenix campus, PO Box 871004, Tempe, AZ 85287-1004. *Phone:* 480-965-7788. *Fax:* 480-965-3610. *E-mail:* admissions@asu.edu.

Arizona State University at the Polytechnic campus

Mesa, Arizona

http://campus.asu.edu/polytechnic

- **State-supported** university, founded 1996
- **Suburban** 575-acre campus with easy access to Phoenix
- **Coed** 4,611 undergraduate students, 87% full-time, 33% women, 67% men
- **Moderately difficult** entrance level, 84% of applicants were admitted

UNDERGRAD STUDENTS
4,030 full-time, 581 part-time. Students come from 45 other countries; 21% are from out of state; 5% Black or African American, non-Hispanic/Latino; 24% Hispanic/Latino; 7% Asian, non-Hispanic/Latino; 0.5% Native Hawaiian or other Pacific Islander, non-Hispanic/Latino; 2% American Indian or Alaska Native, non-Hispanic/Latino; 4% Two or more races, non-Hispanic/Latino; 0.9% Race/ethnicity unknown; 6% international; 10% transferred in; 22% live on campus.

Freshmen:
Admission: 3,328 applied, 2,786 admitted, 659 enrolled. ***Average high school GPA:*** 3.5. ***Test scores:*** SAT evidence-based reading and writing scores over 500: 90%; SAT math scores over 500: 94%; ACT scores over 18: 93%; SAT evidence-based reading and writing scores over 600: 52%; SAT math scores over 600: 59%; ACT scores over 24: 51%; SAT evidence-based reading and writing scores over 700: 7%; SAT math scores over 700: 14%; ACT scores over 30: 10%.

Retention: 87% of full-time freshmen returned.

FACULTY
Total: 313, 59% full-time, 63% with terminal degrees.

Student/faculty ratio: 22:1.

ACADEMICS
Calendar: semesters. *Degrees:* certificates, bachelor's, master's, doctoral, and postbachelor's certificates.

Special study options: accelerated degree program, advanced placement credit, cooperative education, distance learning, double majors, freshman honors college, honors programs, independent study, internships, off-campus study, part-time degree program, services for LD students, student-designed majors, study abroad, summer session for credit. ***ROTC:*** Army (c), Navy (c), Air Force (c).

Computers: 591 computers/terminals are available on campus for general student use. Students can access the following: campus intranet, computer help desk, free student e-mail accounts, online (class) grades, online (class) registration, online (class) schedules. Campuswide network is available. 100% of college-owned or -operated housing units are wired for

high-speed Internet access. Wireless service is available via classrooms, computer centers, computer labs, dorm rooms, learning centers, libraries, student centers.
Library: Polytechnic campus Library. *Books:* 2.4 million (physical), 1.5 million (digital/electronic); *Serial titles:* 65,552 (physical), 112,025 (digital/electronic); *Databases:* 385. Weekly public service hours: 149; study areas open 24 hours, 5–7 days a week; students can reserve study rooms.

STUDENT LIFE
Housing options: on-campus residence required for freshman year; coed, special housing for students with disabilities. Campus housing is university owned. Freshman campus housing is guaranteed.

Activities and organizations: student-run newspaper, Dev Club, AIGA Polytechnic, Environmental Resource Management Club, Programming and Activities Board, Poly Photo Club.

Athletics Member NCAA. All Division I. ***Intercollegiate sports:*** baseball M(s), basketball M(s)/W(s), cross-country running M(s)/W(s), football M(s), golf M(s)/W(s), gymnastics W(s), ice hockey M(s), lacrosse W(s), sand volleyball W(s), soccer W(s), softball W(s), swimming and diving M(s)/W(s), tennis M(s)/W(s), track and field M(s)/W(s), triathlon W(s), volleyball W(s), water polo W(s), wrestling M(s). ***Intramural sports:*** baseball M(c)/W(c), basketball M/W, cheerleading M(c)/W(c), crew M(c), equestrian sports M(c)/W(c), fencing M(c)/W(c), golf M(c)/W(c), gymnastics M(c)/W(c), ice hockey M(c)/W(c), lacrosse M(c)/W(c), racquetball M(c)/W(c), rowing M(c)/W(c), rugby M(c)/W(c), sailing M(c)/W(c), sand volleyball M/W, soccer M(c)/W(c), softball M/W, squash M(c)/W(c), tennis M(c)/W(c), triathlon M(c)/W(c), ultimate Frisbee M(c)/W(c), volleyball M(c)/W(c), water polo M(c)/W(c), weight lifting M(c)/W(c), wrestling M(c)/W(c).

Campus security: 24-hour emergency response devices and patrols, late-night transport/escort service, controlled dormitory access, LiveSafe smart phone application, surveillance camera in some residence halls.

Student services: health clinic, personal/psychological counseling, veterans affairs office.

COSTS & FINANCIAL AID
Costs (2019–20) ***Tuition:*** state resident $10,175 full-time, $727 per credit hour part-time; nonresident $27,360 full-time, $1140 per credit hour part-time. Full-time tuition and fees vary according to program. Part-time tuition and fees vary according to program. ***Required fees:*** $628 full-time, $157 per term part-time. ***Room and board:*** $12,728; room only: $7554. Room and board charges vary according to board plan and housing facility. ***Payment plan:*** installment. ***Waivers:*** employees or children of employees.

Financial Aid Of all full-time matriculated undergraduates who enrolled in 2018, 2,924 applied for aid, 2,412 were judged to have need, 444 had their need fully met. 186 Federal Work-Study jobs (averaging $3026). 808 state and other part-time jobs (averaging $3810). In 2018, 613 non-need-based awards were made. ***Average percent of need met:*** 59. ***Average financial aid package:*** $14,674. ***Average need-based loan:*** $4127. ***Average need-based gift aid:*** $9993. ***Average non-need-based aid:*** $7428. ***Average indebtedness upon graduation:*** $26,096.

APPLYING
Standardized Tests *Required for some:* SAT or ACT (for admission), SAT Subject Tests (for admission). *Recommended:* SAT or ACT (for admission).

Options: electronic application, deferred entrance.

Application fee: $50.

Required: high school transcript, minimum 3.0 GPA. ***Required for some:*** essay or personal statement, letters of recommendation, additional requirements for Honors College and certain majors.

Application deadlines: rolling (freshmen), rolling (transfers).

Notification: continuous until 8/1 (freshmen), continuous (transfers).

CONTACT
Admission Services Applicant Processing, Arizona State University at the Polytechnic campus, PO Box 871004, Tempe, AZ 85287-1004. *Phone:* 480-965-7788. *Fax:* 480-965-3610. *E-mail:* admissions@asu.edu.

Arizona State University at the Tempe campus

Tempe, Arizona

http://www.asu.edu/

- **State-supported** university, founded 1885
- **Urban** 664-acre campus with easy access to Phoenix
- **Coed** 44,461 undergraduate students, 93% full-time, 45% women, 55% men
- **Moderately difficult** entrance level, 86% of applicants were admitted

UNDERGRAD STUDENTS
41,182 full-time, 3,279 part-time. Students come from 99 other countries; 27% are from out of state; 4% Black or African American, non-Hispanic/Latino; 23% Hispanic/Latino; 9% Asian, non-Hispanic/Latino; 0.2% Native Hawaiian or other Pacific Islander, non-Hispanic/Latino; 1% American Indian or Alaska Native, non-Hispanic/Latino; 5% Two or more races, non-Hispanic/Latino; 0.8% Race/ethnicity unknown; 9% international; 7% transferred in; 27% live on campus.

Freshmen:
Admission: 34,188 applied, 29,562 admitted, 10,044 enrolled. ***Average high school GPA:*** 3.5. ***Test scores:*** SAT evidence-based reading and writing scores over 500: 94%; SAT math scores over 500: 94%; ACT scores over 18: 95%; SAT evidence-based reading and writing scores over 600: 60%; SAT math scores over 600: 60%; ACT scores over 24: 61%; SAT evidence-based reading and writing scores over 700: 14%; SAT math scores over 700: 22%; ACT scores over 30: 18%.

Retention: 88% of full-time freshmen returned.

FACULTY
Total: 2,897, 79% full-time, 79% with terminal degrees.

Student/faculty ratio: 20:1.

ACADEMICS
Calendar: semesters. *Degrees:* certificates, bachelor's, master's, doctoral, and postbachelor's certificates (profile includes data for the West, Polytechnic and Downtown Phoenix campuses).

Special study options: accelerated degree program, advanced placement credit, cooperative education, distance learning, double majors, English as a second language, freshman honors college, honors programs, independent study, internships, off-campus study, part-time degree program, services for LD students, student-designed majors, study abroad, summer session for credit. ***ROTC:*** Army (b), Navy (b), Air Force (b).

Computers: 2,524 computers/terminals are available on campus for general student use. Students can access the following: campus intranet, computer help desk, free student e-mail accounts, online (class) grades, online (class) registration, online (class) schedules. Campuswide network is available. 100% of college-owned or -operated housing units are wired for high-speed Internet access. Wireless service is available via classrooms, computer centers, computer labs, dorm rooms, learning centers, libraries, student centers.
Library: Hayden plus 4 others. *Books:* 2.4 million (physical), 1.5 million (digital/electronic); *Serial titles:* 65,552 (physical), 112,025 (digital/electronic); *Databases:* 685. Weekly public service hours: 149; study areas open 24 hours, 5–7 days a week; students can reserve study rooms.

STUDENT LIFE
Housing options: on-campus residence required for freshman year; coed, special housing for students with disabilities. Campus housing is university owned. Freshman campus housing is guaranteed.

Activities and organizations: drama/theater group, student-run newspaper, choral group, marching band, Arizona Outdoors club, Software Developers Association, Tempe American Medical Student Association, Snow Devils, Women in Computer Science, national fraternities, national sororities.

Athletics Member NCAA. All Division I. ***Intercollegiate sports:*** baseball M(s), basketball M(s)/W(s), cross-country running M(s)/W(s), football M(s), golf M(s)/W(s), gymnastics W(s), ice hockey M(s), lacrosse W(s), sand volleyball W(s), soccer W(s), softball W(s), swimming and diving M(s)/W(s), tennis M(s)/W(s), track and field M(s)/W(s), triathlon W(s), volleyball W(s), water polo W(s), wrestling M(s). ***Intramural sports:*** badminton M/W, baseball M(c)/W(c), basketball M/W, cheerleading

M(c)/W(c), crew M(c), equestrian sports M(c)/W(c), fencing M(c)/W(c), golf M(c)/W(c), gymnastics M(c)/W(c), ice hockey M(c)/W(c), lacrosse M(c)/W(c), racquetball M(c)/W(c), rowing M(c)/W(c), rugby M(c)/W(c), sailing M(c)/W(c), sand volleyball M/W, soccer M(c)/W(c), softball M/W, squash M(c)/W(c), table tennis M/W, tennis M(c)/W(c), triathlon M(c)/W(c), ultimate Frisbee M(c)/W(c), volleyball M(c)/W(c), water polo M(c)/W(c), weight lifting M(c)/W(c), wrestling M(c)/W(c).

Campus security: 24-hour emergency response devices and patrols, late-night transport/escort service, controlled dormitory access, LiveSafe smart phone application, surveillance cameras in some residence halls.

Student services: health clinic, personal/psychological counseling, veterans affairs office.

COSTS & FINANCIAL AID

Costs (2019–20) ***Tuition:*** state resident $10,710 full-time, $765 per credit hour part-time; nonresident $28,800 full-time, $1200 per credit hour part-time. Full-time tuition and fees vary according to program. Part-time tuition and fees vary according to program. ***Required fees:*** $628 full-time, $157 per term part-time. ***Room and board:*** $13,164; room only: $7990. Room and board charges vary according to board plan and housing facility. ***Payment plan:*** installment. ***Waivers:*** employees or children of employees.

Financial Aid Of all full-time matriculated undergraduates who enrolled in 2018, 26,961 applied for aid, 21,158 were judged to have need, 4,176 had their need fully met. 1,214 Federal Work-Study jobs (averaging $2844). 6,324 state and other part-time jobs (averaging $3418). In 2018, 10530 non-need-based awards were made. ***Average percent of need met:*** 63. ***Average financial aid package:*** $15,878. ***Average need-based loan:*** $3959. ***Average need-based gift aid:*** $11,690. ***Average non-need-based aid:*** $8977. ***Average indebtedness upon graduation:*** $23,711.

APPLYING

Standardized Tests *Required for some:* SAT or ACT (for admission), SAT Subject Tests (for admission). *Recommended:* SAT or ACT (for admission).

Options: electronic application, deferred entrance.

Application fee: $50.

Required: high school transcript, minimum 3.0 GPA. ***Required for some:*** essay or personal statement, letters of recommendation, additional requirements for Honors College and certain majors.

Application deadlines: rolling (freshmen), rolling (transfers).

Notification: continuous until 8/1 (freshmen), continuous (transfers).

CONTACT

Admission Services Applicant Processing, Arizona State University at the Tempe campus, PO Box 871004, Tempe, AZ 85287-1004. *Phone:* 480-965-7788. *Fax:* 480-965-3610. *E-mail:* admissions@asu.edu.

Arizona State University at the West campus

Glendale, Arizona

http://campus.asu.edu/west

- **State-supported** university, founded 1984
- **Urban** 278-acre campus with easy access to Phoenix
- **Coed** 4,601 undergraduate students, 89% full-time, 62% women, 38% men
- **Moderately difficult** entrance level, 82% of applicants were admitted

UNDERGRAD STUDENTS

4,076 full-time, 525 part-time. 14% are from out of state; 5% Black or African American, non-Hispanic/Latino; 38% Hispanic/Latino; 6% Asian, non-Hispanic/Latino; 0.3% Native Hawaiian or other Pacific Islander, non-Hispanic/Latino; 1% American Indian or Alaska Native, non-Hispanic/Latino; 3% Two or more races, non-Hispanic/Latino; 0.9% Race/ethnicity unknown; 4% international; 15% transferred in; 15% live on campus.

Freshmen:

Admission: 3,376 applied, 2,760 admitted, 789 enrolled. ***Average high school GPA:*** 3.5. ***Test scores:*** SAT evidence-based reading and writing scores over 500: 87%; SAT math scores over 500: 82%; ACT scores over 18: 87%; SAT evidence-based reading and writing scores over 600: 42%; SAT math scores over 600: 36%; ACT scores over 24: 36%; SAT evidence-based reading and writing scores over 700: 7%; SAT math scores over 700: 7%; ACT scores over 30: 6%.

Retention: 86% of full-time freshmen returned.

ACADEMICS

Calendar: semesters. *Degrees:* certificates, bachelor's, master's, doctoral, and postbachelor's certificates.

Special study options: accelerated degree program, advanced placement credit, cooperative education, distance learning, double majors, English as a second language, freshman honors college, honors programs, independent study, internships, off-campus study, part-time degree program, services for LD students, student-designed majors, study abroad, summer session for credit. ***ROTC:*** Army (c), Navy (c), Air Force (c).

Computers: 612 computers/terminals are available on campus for general student use. Students can access the following: campus intranet, computer help desk, free student e-mail accounts, online (class) grades, online (class) registration, online (class) schedules. Campuswide network is available. 100% of college-owned or -operated housing units are wired for high-speed Internet access. Wireless service is available via classrooms, computer centers, computer labs, dorm rooms, learning centers, libraries, student centers.

Library: Fletcher Library at the West campus. *Books:* 3.0 million (physical), 963,136 (digital/electronic); *Serial titles:* 72,649 (physical), 73,043 (digital/electronic); *Databases:* 650. Weekly public service hours: 149; study areas open 24 hours, 5–7 days a week; students can reserve study rooms.

STUDENT LIFE

Housing options: on-campus residence required for freshman year; coed, special housing for students with disabilities. Campus housing is university owned. Freshman campus housing is guaranteed.

Activities and organizations: drama/theater group, student-run newspaper, choral group, Hispanic Honor Society, Teachers of the Future, Business to Business, W. P. Carey MBA Association, American Medical Student Association.

Athletics Member NCAA. All Division I. ***Intercollegiate sports:*** baseball M(s), basketball M(s)/W(s), cross-country running M(s)/W(s), football M(s), golf M(s)/W(s), gymnastics W(s), ice hockey M(s), lacrosse W(s), sand volleyball W(s), soccer W(s), softball W(s), swimming and diving M(s)/W(s), tennis M(s)/W(s), track and field M(s)/W(s), triathlon W(s), volleyball W(s), water polo W(s), wrestling M(s). ***Intramural sports:*** baseball M(c), basketball M/W, cheerleading M(c)/W(c), equestrian sports M(c)/W(c), fencing M(c)/W(c), golf M(c)/W(c), gymnastics M(c)/W(c), ice hockey M(c)/W(c), lacrosse M(c)/W(c), racquetball M(c)/W(c), rowing M(c)/W(c), rugby M(c)/W(c), sailing M(c)/W(c), soccer M(c)/W(c), softball M/W, table tennis M/W, tennis M(c)/W(c), triathlon M(c)/W(c), ultimate Frisbee M(c)/W(c), volleyball M(c)/W(c), water polo M(c)/W(c), weight lifting M(c)/W(c).

Campus security: 24-hour emergency response devices and patrols, late-night transport/escort service, controlled dormitory access, LiveSafe smart phone application, surveillance camera in some residence halls.

Student services: health clinic, personal/psychological counseling, veterans affairs office.

COSTS & FINANCIAL AID

Costs (2019–20) ***Tuition:*** state resident $10,175 full-time, $727 per credit hour part-time; nonresident $27,360 full-time, $1140 per credit hour part-time. Full-time tuition and fees vary according to program. Part-time tuition and fees vary according to program. ***Required fees:*** $628 full-time, $157 per term part-time. ***Room and board:*** $11,914; room only: $6740. Room and board charges vary according to board plan. ***Payment plan:*** installment. ***Waivers:*** employees or children of employees.

Financial Aid Of all full-time matriculated undergraduates who enrolled in 2018, 2,944 applied for aid, 2,604 were judged to have need, 352 had their need fully met. 188 Federal Work-Study jobs (averaging $2730). 543 state and other part-time jobs (averaging $2922). In 2018, 380 non-need-based awards were made. ***Average percent of need met:*** 60. ***Average financial aid package:*** $13,747. ***Average need-based loan:*** $4152. ***Average need-based gift aid:*** $10,523. ***Average non-need-based aid:*** $6974. ***Average indebtedness upon graduation:*** $25,021.

APPLYING

Standardized Tests *Required for some:* SAT or ACT (for admission), SAT Subject Tests (for admission). *Recommended:* SAT or ACT (for admission).

Options: electronic application, deferred entrance.

Application fee: $50.

Required: high school transcript, minimum 3.0 GPA. ***Required for some:*** essay or personal statement, letters of recommendation, additional requirements for Honors College and certain majors.

Application deadlines: rolling (freshmen), rolling (transfers).

Notification: continuous until 9/1 (freshmen), continuous (transfers).

CONTACT
Arizona State University at the West campus, PO Box 870112, Tempe, AZ 85287-0112. *Phone:* 480-965-7788. *Fax:* 480-965-3610. *E-mail:* admissions@asu.edu.

Brookline College - Phoenix Campus

Phoenix, Arizona

http://brooklinecollege.edu/

CONTACT
Ms. Theresa Dean, Director of Admissions, Brookline College - Phoenix Campus, 2445 West Dunlap Avenue, Suite 100, Phoenix, AZ 85021. *Phone:* 602-242-6265. *Toll-free phone:* 800-793-2428. *Fax:* 602-973-2572. *E-mail:* tdean@brooklinecollege.edu.

Brookline College - Tempe Campus

Tempe, Arizona

http://brooklinecollege.edu/

CONTACT
Ms. Cheryl Kindred, Campus Director, Brookline College - Tempe Campus, 1140-1150 South Priest Drive, Tempe, AZ 85281. *Phone:* 480-545-8755. *Toll-free phone:* 888-886-2428. *Fax:* 480-926-1371. *E-mail:* ckindred@brooklinecollege.edu.

Chamberlain College of Nursing - Phoenix

Phoenix, Arizona

http://www.chamberlain.edu/

CONTACT
Admissions, Chamberlain College of Nursing - Phoenix, 2149 West Dunlap Avenue, Phoenix, AZ 85021. *Phone:* 602-331-2720. *Toll-free phone:* 877-751-5783.

CollegeAmerica–Flagstaff

Flagstaff, Arizona

http://www.collegeamerica.edu/

CONTACT
CollegeAmerica–Flagstaff, 399 South Malpais Lane, Flagstaff, AZ 86001. *Phone:* 928-213-6060 Ext. 1402. *Toll-free phone:* 800-622-2894.

CollegeAmerica–Phoenix

Phoenix, Arizona

http://www.collegeamerica.edu/

CONTACT
CollegeAmerica–Phoenix, 9801 North Metro Parkway East, Phoenix, AZ 85051. *Toll-free phone:* 800-622-2894.

DeVry University–Phoenix Campus

Phoenix, Arizona

http://www.devry.edu/

- **Proprietary** comprehensive, founded 1967, part of DeVry University
- **Urban** campus
- **Coed**
- **Minimally difficult** entrance level

FACULTY
Student/faculty ratio: 11:1.

ACADEMICS
Calendar: semesters. *Degrees:* associate, bachelor's, master's, and postbachelor's certificates.
Library: Learning Resource Center.

STUDENT LIFE
Housing options: college housing not available.

APPLYING
Options: deferred entrance.

Application fee: $30.

Required: high school transcript, interview.

CONTACT
DeVry University–Phoenix Campus, 2149 West Dunlap Avenue, Phoenix, AZ 85021. *Phone:* 602-870-9222. *Toll-free phone:* 866-338-7934.

Dunlap-Stone University

Phoenix, Arizona

http://www.dunlap-stone.edu/

CONTACT
Dunlap-Stone University, 19820 North 7th Street, Suite #100, Phoenix, AZ 85024. *Phone:* 602-648-5750. *Toll-free phone:* 800-474-8013.

Embry-Riddle Aeronautical University–Prescott

Prescott, Arizona

http://www.prescott.erau.edu/

- **Independent** comprehensive, founded 1978
- **Small-town** 547-acre campus with easy access to Phoenix
- **Endowment** $40.6 million
- **Coed**
- **Moderately difficult** entrance level

FACULTY
Student/faculty ratio: 17:1.

ACADEMICS
Calendar: semesters. *Degrees:* bachelor's and master's.
Library: Christine & Steven F. Udvar-Hazy Library & Learning Center. *Books:* 26,008 (physical), 249,693 (digital/electronic); *Serial titles:* 137 (physical), 54,540 (digital/electronic); *Databases:* 90. Students can reserve study rooms.

STUDENT LIFE
Housing options: on-campus residence required for freshman year; coed. Campus housing is university owned. Freshman campus housing is guaranteed.

Activities and organizations: student-run newspaper, choral group, Hawaii Club, Strike Eagles, Theta XI, American Institute of Aeronautics and Astronautics (AIAA), Arnold Air Society, national fraternities, national sororities.

Athletics Member NCAA, NAIA. All NCAA Division II.

Campus security: 24-hour emergency response devices and patrols, student patrols, late-night transport/escort service, controlled dormitory access.

Student services: health clinic, personal/psychological counseling, women's center, veterans affairs office.

COSTS & FINANCIAL AID
Costs (2019–20) ***One-time required fee:*** $150. ***Comprehensive fee:*** $48,426 includes full-time tuition ($35,424), mandatory fees ($1284), and room and board ($11,718). Part-time tuition: $1476 per credit hour. ***Required fees:*** $642 per term part-time. ***College room only:*** $6882.

Financial Aid Of all full-time matriculated undergraduates who enrolled in 2018, 1,788 applied for aid, 1,523 were judged to have need. In 2018, 656 non-need-based awards were made. ***Average financial aid package:*** $19,115. ***Average need-based loan:*** $4242. ***Average need-based gift aid:*** $16,568. ***Average non-need-based aid:*** $15,683.

APPLYING
Standardized Tests *Recommended:* SAT or ACT (for admission).

Options: electronic application, deferred entrance.

Application fee: $50.

Required: high school transcript, minimum 2.0 GPA, medical examination for flight students. ***Recommended:*** essay or personal statement, minimum 3.0 GPA, 2 letters of recommendation, interview.

CONTACT
Ms. Sara K. Bofferding, Director, Prescott Admissions, Embry-Riddle Aeronautical University–Prescott, 3700 Willow Creek Road, Prescott, AZ 86301-3720. *Phone:* 800-888-3728. *Toll-free phone:* 800-888-3728. *Fax:* 928-777-6606. *E-mail:* prescott@erau.edu.

Grand Canyon University

Phoenix, Arizona

http://www.gcu.edu/

CONTACT
Enrollment, Grand Canyon University, 3300 West Camelback Road, PO Box 11097, Phoenix, AZ 86017-3030. *Phone:* 800-486-7085. *Toll-free phone:* 800-800-9776. *E-mail:* admissionsonline@gcu.edu.

International Baptist College and Seminary

Chandler, Arizona

http://www.ibcs.edu/

CONTACT
Director of Admissions, International Baptist College and Seminary, 2211 West Germann Road, Chandler, AZ 85286. *Phone:* 480-245-7970. *Toll-free phone:* 800-422-4858. *E-mail:* admissions@ibconline.edu.

National Paralegal College

Phoenix, Arizona

http://nationalparalegal.edu/

- **Proprietary** comprehensive, founded 2003
- **Coed**
- 85% of applicants were admitted

FACULTY
Student/faculty ratio: 28:1.

ACADEMICS
Calendar: continuous new session each month. *Degrees:* certificates, associate, bachelor's, and master's.
Library: Jones eGlobal Library. *Books:* 27,803 (digital/electronic); *Databases:* 56. Weekly public service hours: 168.

APPLYING
Options: electronic application.

Required for some: high school transcript. ***Recommended:*** essay or personal statement, interview.

CONTACT
Ms. Dana Wasserstrom, Admissions Director, National Paralegal College, 717 East Maryland Avenue, Phoenix, AZ 85014. *Phone:* 800-371-6105 Ext. 126. *Toll-free phone:* 800-371-6105. *E-mail:* danielle@nationalparalegal.edu.

Northern Arizona University

Flagstaff, Arizona

http://www.nau.edu/

- **State-supported** university, founded 1899, part of Arizona University System
- **Small-town** 829-acre campus
- **Endowment** $33.7 million
- **Coed** 26,513 undergraduate students, 82% full-time, 61% women, 39% men
- **Moderately difficult** entrance level, 85% of applicants were admitted

UNDERGRAD STUDENTS
21,731 full-time, 4,782 part-time. Students come from 53 states and territories; 57 other countries; 31% are from out of state; 3% Black or African American, non-Hispanic/Latino; 25% Hispanic/Latino; 2% Asian, non-Hispanic/Latino; 0.3% Native Hawaiian or other Pacific Islander, non-Hispanic/Latino; 3% American Indian or Alaska Native, non-Hispanic/Latino; 6% Two or more races, non-Hispanic/Latino; 2% Race/ethnicity unknown; 4% international; 9% transferred in; 37% live on campus.

Freshmen:
Admission: 36,855 applied, 31,313 admitted, 5,455 enrolled. ***Average high school GPA:*** 3.6. ***Test scores:*** SAT evidence-based reading and writing scores over 500: 87%; SAT math scores over 500: 85%; ACT scores over 18: 87%; SAT evidence-based reading and writing scores over 600: 38%; SAT math scores over 600: 31%; ACT scores over 24: 33%; SAT evidence-based reading and writing scores over 700: 5%; SAT math scores over 700: 4%; ACT scores over 30: 4%.

Retention: 78% of full-time freshmen returned.

FACULTY
Total: 1,758, 65% full-time, 60% with terminal degrees.

Student/faculty ratio: 19:1.

ACADEMICS
Calendar: semesters. *Degrees:* certificates, bachelor's, master's, doctoral, post-master's, and postbachelor's certificates.

Special study options: accelerated degree program, advanced placement credit, cooperative education, distance learning, double majors, English as a second language, freshman honors college, honors programs, independent study, internships, off-campus study, part-time degree program, services for LD students, study abroad, summer session for credit. ***ROTC:*** Army (b), Air Force (b).

Unusual degree programs: 3-2 business administration; engineering; forestry; social work; Athletic Training, Communication, Communication Sciences and Disorders, Criminology and Criminal Justice, Education: Career and Technical Education, English, â€Geography, Planning and Recreationâ?History, Psychological Sciences, Sociology, Spanish, Sustainable Communities.

Computers: 2,675 computers/terminals and 2,150 ports are available on campus for general student use. Students can access the following: campus intranet, computer help desk, free student e-mail accounts, online (class) grades, online (class) registration, online (class) schedules, computer repair service available on campus. Campuswide network is available. 100% of college-owned or -operated housing units are wired for high-speed Internet access. Wireless service is available via entire campus.

Library: Cline Library plus 1 other. *Books:* 570,569 (physical), 233,285 (digital/electronic); *Serial titles:* 6,146 (physical), 152,078 (digital/electronic); *Databases:* 181. Weekly public service hours: 150; study areas open 24 hours, 5–7 days a week; students can reserve study rooms.

STUDENT LIFE
Housing options: coed, special housing for students with disabilities. Campus housing is university owned. Freshman campus housing is guaranteed.

Activities and organizations: drama/theater group, student-run newspaper, radio and television station, choral group, marching band, Louie's Cupboard, Kappa Delta, NAU Feral Cat Alliance, Pi Beta Phi, Delta Delta Delta, national fraternities, national sororities.

Athletics Member NCAA. All Division I. ***Intercollegiate sports:*** basketball M(s)/W(s), cross-country running M(s)/W(s), football M(s), golf W(s), soccer W(s), swimming and diving W(s), tennis M(s)/W(s), track and field M(s)/W(s), volleyball W(s). ***Intramural sports:*** archery M(c)/W(c), badminton M(c)/W(c), baseball M, basketball M(c)/W, bowling M(c)/W(c), cross-country running M(c)/W(c), equestrian sports M(c)/W(c), gymnastics M(c)/W(c), ice hockey M(c), lacrosse M(c)/W(c), racquetball M(c)/W(c), rugby M(c)/W(c), sand volleyball M(c)/W(c), skiing (downhill) M(c)/W(c), soccer M(c)/W(c), softball M/W(c), swimming and diving M/W, tennis M(c)/W(c), track and field M(c)/W(c), triathlon M(c)/W(c), ultimate Frisbee M(c)/W(c), volleyball M(c)/W(c), water polo M(c).

Campus security: 24-hour emergency response devices and patrols, student patrols, late-night transport/escort service, controlled dormitory access.

Student services: health clinic, personal/psychological counseling, legal services, veterans affairs office.

COSTS & FINANCIAL AID
Costs (2020–21) ***Tuition:*** area resident $10,650 full-time, $761 per credit hour part-time; state resident $10,650 full-time, $761 per credit hour part-time; nonresident $25,270 full-time, $1053 per credit hour part-time. Full-time tuition and fees vary according to course load, location, and reciprocity agreements. Part-time tuition and fees vary according to course load, location, and reciprocity agreements. No tuition increase for student's term of enrollment. ***Required fees:*** $1246 full-time, $14 per credit hour part-time, $434 per term part-time. ***Room and board:*** $10,780; room only: $5830. Room and board charges vary according to board plan and housing facility. ***Payment plans:*** installment, deferred payment. ***Waivers:*** employees or children of employees.

Financial Aid Of all full-time matriculated undergraduates who enrolled in 2018, 16,623 applied for aid, 13,590 were judged to have need, 1,855 had their need fully met. In 2018, 4586 non-need-based awards were made. ***Average percent of need met:*** 64. ***Average financial aid package:*** $13,228. ***Average need-based loan:*** $4046. ***Average need-based gift aid:*** $7348. ***Average non-need-based aid:*** $6697. ***Average indebtedness upon graduation:*** $23,560.

APPLYING
Standardized Tests *Recommended:* SAT or ACT (for admission).

Options: electronic application, deferred entrance.

Application fee: $25.

Required: high school transcript, minimum 2.5 GPA, 16 college preparatory courses with minimum 2.0 in each subject.

Application deadlines: 8/1 (freshmen), rolling (transfers).

Notification: continuous until 6/1 (freshmen), continuous (transfers).

CONTACT
Undergraduate Admissions, Northern Arizona University, Box 4084, Flagstaff, AZ 86011. *Phone:* 928-523-5511. *Toll-free phone:* 888-628-2968. *Fax:* 928-523-6023. *E-mail:* Undergraduate.Admissions@nau.edu.

See below for display ad and page 1092 for the College Close-Up.

Penn Foster College

Scottsdale, Arizona

http://www.pennfostercollege.edu/

CONTACT
Admissions, Penn Foster College, 14300 North Northsight Boulevard, Suite 120, Scottsdale, AZ 85260. *Phone:* 888-427-1000. *Toll-free phone:* 800-471-3232.

Pima Medical Institute - Mesa

Mesa, Arizona

http://www.pmi.edu/

CONTACT
Admissions Office, Pima Medical Institute - Mesa, 957 South Dobson Road, Mesa, AZ 85202. *Phone:* 480-644-0267 Ext. 225. *Toll-free phone:* 800-477-PIMA.

Pima Medical Institute - Tucson

Tucson, Arizona

http://www.pmi.edu/

CONTACT
Admissions Office, Pima Medical Institute - Tucson, 3350 East Grant Road, Tucson, AZ 85716. *Phone:* 520-326-1600 Ext. 5112. *Toll-free phone:* 800-477-PIMA.

Prescott College

Prescott, Arizona

http://www.prescott.edu/

CONTACT

Nancy Simmons, Admissions Coordinator, Prescott College, 220 Grove Avenue, Prescott, AZ 86301. *Phone:* 928-350-2100. *Toll-free phone:* 877-350-2100. *Fax:* 928-776-5242. *E-mail:* admissions@prescott.edu.

Southwest University of Visual Arts

Tucson, Arizona

http://www.suva.edu/

CONTACT

Robert Mairs, Director of Admissions, Southwest University of Visual Arts, 2525 North Country Club Road, Tucson, AZ 85716-2505. *Phone:* 520-325-0123. *Toll-free phone:* 800-825-8753. *Fax:* 520-325-5535.

University of Advancing Technology

Tempe, Arizona

http://www.uat.edu/

CONTACT

Admissions Office, University of Advancing Technology, 2625 West Baseline Road, Tempe, AZ 85283-1042. *Phone:* 602-383-8228. *Toll-free phone:* 800-658-5744. *Fax:* 602-383-8222. *E-mail:* admissions@uat.edu.

The University of Arizona

Tucson, Arizona

http://www.arizona.edu/

- **State-supported** university, founded 1885, part of Arizona Board of Regents
- **Urban** 392-acre campus with easy access to Tucson
- **Endowment** $928.0 million
- **Coed** 35,801 undergraduate students, 82% full-time, 53% women, 47% men
- **Moderately difficult** entrance level, 85% of applicants were admitted

UNDERGRAD STUDENTS

29,454 full-time, 6,347 part-time. Students come from 52 states and territories; 120 other countries; 33% are from out of state; 4% Black or African American, non-Hispanic/Latino; 27% Hispanic/Latino; 5% Asian, non-Hispanic/Latino; 0.2% Native Hawaiian or other Pacific Islander, non-Hispanic/Latino; 1% American Indian or Alaska Native, non-Hispanic/Latino; 5% Two or more races, non-Hispanic/Latino; 2% Race/ethnicity unknown; 6% international; 7% transferred in; 20% live on campus.

Freshmen:

Admission: 40,854 applied, 34,558 admitted, 7,683 enrolled. ***Average high school GPA:*** 3.4. ***Test scores:*** SAT evidence-based reading and writing scores over 500: 92%; SAT math scores over 500: 92%; ACT scores over 18: 91%; SAT evidence-based reading and writing scores over 600: 59%; SAT math scores over 600: 58%; ACT scores over 24: 58%; SAT evidence-based reading and writing scores over 700: 16%; SAT math scores over 700: 23%; ACT scores over 30: 21%.

Retention: 83% of full-time freshmen returned.

FACULTY

Total: 2,488, 85% full-time, 91% with terminal degrees.

Student/faculty ratio: 15:1.

ACADEMICS

Calendar: semesters. *Degrees:* certificates, bachelor's, master's, doctoral, post-master's, and postbachelor's certificates.

Special study options: academic remediation for entering students, accelerated degree program, adult/continuing education programs, advanced placement credit, cooperative education, distance learning, double majors, English as a second language, freshman honors college, honors programs, independent study, internships, off-campus study, part-time degree program, services for LD students, study abroad, summer session for credit. ***ROTC:*** Army (b), Navy (b), Air Force (b).

Unusual degree programs: 3-2 business administration; engineering.

Computers: 951 computers/terminals are available on campus for general student use. Students can access the following: campus intranet, computer help desk, free student e-mail accounts, online (class) grades, online (class) registration, online (class) schedules. Campuswide network is available. 100% of college-owned or -operated housing units are wired for high-speed Internet access. Wireless service is available via entire campus.

Library: University of Arizona Main Library plus 4 others. *Books:* 2.7 million (physical), 2.1 million (digital/electronic); *Serial titles:* 4,025 (physical), 251,334 (digital/electronic); *Databases:* 1,135. Weekly public service hours: 90; study areas open 24 hours, 5–7 days a week; students can reserve study rooms.

STUDENT LIFE

Housing options: coed, women-only, special housing for students with disabilities. Campus housing is university owned. Freshman applicants given priority for college housing.

Activities and organizations: drama/theater group, student-run newspaper, radio and television station, choral group, marching band, national fraternities, national sororities.

Athletics Member NCAA. All Division I except rugby (Division I-A). ***Intercollegiate sports:*** baseball M(s), basketball M(s)/W(s), cross-country running M(s)/W(s), equestrian sports M(c)/W(c), football M(s), golf M(s)/W(s), gymnastics W(s), lacrosse M(c)/W(c), rugby M/W, sand volleyball W(s), soccer M(c)/W(s), softball W(s), swimming and diving M(s)/W(s), tennis M(s)/W(s), track and field M(s)/W(s), triathlon M(c)/W(c), ultimate Frisbee M(c)/W(c), volleyball M(c)/W(s), water polo M(c)/W(c), wrestling M(c)/W(c). ***Intramural sports:*** archery M(c)/W(c), badminton M(c)/W(c), baseball M(c), basketball M/W, cheerleading M(c)/W(c), equestrian sports M(c)/W(c), fencing M(c)/W(c), lacrosse M(c)/W(c), rugby M(c)/W(c), sand volleyball M/W, soccer M(c)/W(c), softball M/W, table tennis M(c)/W(c), tennis M(c)/W(c), triathlon M(c)/W(c), ultimate Frisbee M(c)/W(c), volleyball M(c)/W(c), water polo M(c)/W(c), wrestling M(c)/W(c).

Campus security: 24-hour emergency response devices and patrols, student patrols, late-night transport/escort service, controlled dormitory access.

Student services: health clinic, personal/psychological counseling, women's center, legal services, veterans affairs office.

COSTS & FINANCIAL AID

Costs (2020–21) ***One-time required fee:*** $425. ***Tuition:*** area resident $10,990 full-time, $785 per credit hour part-time; state resident $10,990 full-time, $785 per credit hour part-time; nonresident $33,273 full-time, $1386 per credit hour part-time. Full-time tuition and fees vary according to location. Part-time tuition and fees vary according to location. No tuition increase for student's term of enrollment. ***Required fees:*** $1389 full-time. ***Room and board:*** $13,050; room only: $8050. Room and board charges vary according to board plan and housing facility. ***Payment plan:*** installment. ***Waivers:*** employees or children of employees.

Financial Aid Of all full-time matriculated undergraduates who enrolled in 2018, 18,696 applied for aid, 14,998 were judged to have need, 2,019 had their need fully met. 1,403 Federal Work-Study jobs (averaging $3247). 7,170 state and other part-time jobs (averaging $3495). In 2018, 6895 non-need-based awards were made. ***Average percent of need met:*** 61. ***Average financial aid package:*** $14,300. ***Average need-based loan:*** $4074. ***Average need-based gift aid:*** $11,716. ***Average non-need-based aid:*** $8921. ***Average indebtedness upon graduation:*** $26,414.

APPLYING

Standardized Tests *Required for some:* SAT or ACT (for admission).

Options: electronic application.

Application fee: $50.

Required: high school transcript. ***Recommended:*** essay or personal statement.

Application deadlines: 5/1 (freshmen), 5/1 (out-of-state freshmen), 7/1 (transfers).

Notification: continuous until 9/1 (freshmen), continuous until 9/1 (out-of-state freshmen), continuous (transfers).

CONTACT

The University of Arizona, 1200 E University Blvd, Tucson, AZ 85721. *Phone:* 520-621-3237. *E-mail:* admissions@arizona.edu.

University of Arizona South
Sierra Vista, Arizona
http://www.uas.arizona.edu/

CONTACT
University of Arizona South, 1140 North Colombo Avenue, Sierra Vista, AZ 85635.

University of Phoenix–Online Campus
Phoenix, Arizona
http://www.phoenix.edu/

CONTACT
Marc Booker, Senior Director, Office of Admissions and Evaluation, University of Phoenix–Online Campus, 4035 South Riverpoint Parkway, Mail Stop CF-L101, Phoenix, AZ 85040. *Phone:* 602-557-4609. *Toll-free phone:* 866-766-0766. *Fax:* 480-643-1156.

University of Phoenix–Phoenix Campus
Tempe, Arizona
http://www.phoenix.edu/

CONTACT
Marc Booker, Senior Director, Office of Admissions and Evaluation, University of Phoenix–Phoenix Campus, 4035 South Riverpoint Parkway, Mail Stop CF-L101, Phoenix, AZ 85040. *Phone:* 602-557-4609. *Toll-free phone:* 866-766-0766. *Fax:* 480-643-1156.

ARKANSAS

Arkansas Baptist College
Little Rock, Arkansas
http://www.arkansasbaptist.edu/

CONTACT
Arkansas Baptist College, 1621 Dr. Martin Luther King, Jr. Drive, Little Rock, AR 72202-6067. *Phone:* 501-244-5104 Ext. 5124.

Arkansas State University
Jonesboro, Arkansas
http://www.astate.edu/

- **State-supported** comprehensive, founded 1909, part of Arkansas State University System
- **Small-town** 1376-acre campus with easy access to Memphis
- **Endowment** $54.9 million
- **Coed**
- **Moderately difficult** entrance level

FACULTY
Student/faculty ratio: 16:1.

ACADEMICS
Calendar: semesters. *Degrees:* associate, bachelor's, master's, doctoral, post-master's, and postbachelor's certificates.
Library: Dean B. Ellis Library. *Books:* 386,049 (physical), 452,194 (digital/electronic); *Serial titles:* 353 (physical), 40,469 (digital/electronic); *Databases:* 163. Weekly public service hours: 103; students can reserve study rooms.

STUDENT LIFE
Housing options: on-campus residence required for freshman year; coed, men-only, women-only. Campus housing is university owned.

Activities and organizations: drama/theater group, student-run newspaper, radio and television station, choral group, marching band, Honors College, Volunteer A-State, Baptist Collegiate Ministry, Black Student Association, Student Activities Board, national fraternities, national sororities.

Athletics Member NCAA. All Division I except football (Division I-A).

Campus security: 24-hour emergency response devices and patrols, student patrols, late-night transport/escort service, controlled dormitory access, check-in desk, video surveillance cameras.

Student services: health clinic, personal/psychological counseling, veterans affairs office.

FINANCIAL AID
Financial Aid Of all full-time matriculated undergraduates who enrolled in 2015, 6,564 applied for aid, 6,304 were judged to have need, 3,463 had their need fully met. 190 Federal Work-Study jobs (averaging $3500). 380 state and other part-time jobs (averaging $3900). In 2015, 748 non-need-based awards were made. ***Average percent of need met:*** 51. ***Average financial aid package:*** $10,500. ***Average need-based loan:*** $8200. ***Average need-based gift aid:*** $10,000. ***Average non-need-based aid:*** $5600. ***Average indebtedness upon graduation:*** $27,400. ***Financial aid deadline:*** 7/1.

APPLYING
Standardized Tests *Required:* SAT or ACT (for admission). *Required for some:* ACT ASSET; ACT Compass; TOEFL, IELTS, PTE, iTEP, or Proof of English Proficiency for international students. *Recommended:* ACT (for admission).

Options: electronic application, early admission.

Application fee: $30.

Required: high school transcript, minimum 2.8 GPA, minimum ACT composite score of 21, immunization, Selective Service.

CONTACT
Ms. Tracy Finch, Director of Admissions, Records, and Registration, Arkansas State University, PO Box 1570, State University, AR 72467. *Phone:* 870-972-2031. *Toll-free phone:* 800-382-3030. *Fax:* 870-972-3406. *E-mail:* admissions@astate.edu.

Arkansas Tech University
Russellville, Arkansas
http://www.atu.edu/

- **State-supported** comprehensive, founded 1909
- **Small-town** 559-acre campus
- **Endowment** $43.6 million
- **Coed** 11,015 undergraduate students, 60% full-time, 55% women, 45% men
- **Moderately difficult** entrance level, 95% of applicants were admitted

UNDERGRAD STUDENTS
6,584 full-time, 4,431 part-time. Students come from 40 states and territories; 45 other countries; 4% are from out of state; 8% Black or African American, non-Hispanic/Latino; 8% Hispanic/Latino; 1% Asian, non-Hispanic/Latino; 0.1% Native Hawaiian or other Pacific Islander, non-Hispanic/Latino; 0.6% American Indian or Alaska Native, non-Hispanic/Latino; 5% Two or more races, non-Hispanic/Latino; 3% international; 3% transferred in; 30% live on campus.

Freshmen:
Admission: 7,228 applied, 6,848 admitted, 2,091 enrolled. ***Average high school GPA:*** 3.3. ***Test scores:*** SAT math scores over 500: 65%; ACT scores over 18: 82%; SAT math scores over 600: 30%; ACT scores over 24: 38%; ACT scores over 30: 7%.

Retention: 70% of full-time freshmen returned.

FACULTY
Total: 582, 59% full-time, 46% with terminal degrees.

Student/faculty ratio: 18:1.

ACADEMICS
Calendar: semesters. *Degrees:* certificates, associate, bachelor's, master's, doctoral, post-master's, and postbachelor's certificates.

Special study options: academic remediation for entering students, accelerated degree program, adult/continuing education programs, advanced placement credit, distance learning, double majors, English as a second language, honors programs, independent study, internships, off-campus study, part-time degree program, services for LD students, study abroad, summer session for credit. ***ROTC:*** Army (c).

Computers: 1,168 computers/terminals are available on campus for general student use. Students can access the following: campus intranet, computer help desk, free student e-mail accounts, online (class) grades, online (class) registration, online (class) schedules. Campuswide network is available. 100% of college-owned or -operated housing units are wired for high-speed Internet access. Wireless service is available via classrooms, computer centers, computer labs, dorm rooms, learning centers, libraries, student centers.
Library: Ross Pendergraft Library and Technology Center. *Books:* 156,543 (physical), 459,680 (digital/electronic); *Serial titles:* 6,649 (physical), 86,255 (digital/electronic); *Databases:* 336. Students can reserve study rooms.

STUDENT LIFE
Housing options: on-campus residence required through sophomore year; coed, men-only, women-only, special housing for students with disabilities. Campus housing is university owned. Freshman campus housing is guaranteed.

Activities and organizations: drama/theater group, student-run newspaper, radio and television station, choral group, marching band, national fraternities, national sororities.

Athletics Member NCAA. All Division II except golf (Division I). ***Intercollegiate sports:*** baseball M(s), basketball M(s)/W(s), cheerleading M(s)/W(s), cross-country running W(s), football M(s), golf M(s)/W(s), softball W(s), tennis W(s), volleyball W(s). ***Intramural sports:*** basketball M/W, bowling M/W, golf M(c)/W(c), racquetball M/W, soccer M/W, softball M/W, table tennis M/W, tennis M/W, ultimate Frisbee M/W, volleyball M/W.

Campus security: 24-hour emergency response devices and patrols, student patrols, late-night transport/escort service, controlled dormitory access.

Student services: health clinic, personal/psychological counseling.

COSTS & FINANCIAL AID
Costs (2020–21) ***Tuition:*** state resident $232 per credit hour part-time; nonresident $464 per credit hour part-time. Full-time tuition and fees vary according to course load and location. Part-time tuition and fees vary according to course load and location. ***Required fees:*** $88 per credit hour part-time. ***Room and board:*** Room and board charges vary according to board plan, housing facility, and location. ***Payment plans:*** installment, deferred payment. ***Waivers:*** senior citizens and employees or children of employees.

Financial Aid Of all full-time matriculated undergraduates who enrolled in 2018, 5,812 applied for aid, 4,393 were judged to have need, 492 had their need fully met. In 2018, 1054 non-need-based awards were made. ***Average percent of need met:*** 62. ***Average financial aid package:*** $10,702. ***Average need-based loan:*** $3622. ***Average need-based gift aid:*** $5002. ***Average non-need-based aid:*** $6915. ***Average indebtedness upon graduation:*** $24,142.

APPLYING
Standardized Tests *Required:* SAT or ACT (for admission).

Options: electronic application, early action, deferred entrance.

Required: high school transcript, minimum 2.0 GPA.

Notification: continuous (freshmen), continuous (transfers).

CONTACT
Ms. Jessica Brock, Director of Admissions, Arkansas Tech University, Brown Hall, Suite 104, 105 West O Street, Russellville, AR 72801. *Phone:* 479-968-0343. *Toll-free phone:* 800-582-6953. *Fax:* 479-964-0522. *E-mail:* tech.enroll@atu.edu.

Central Baptist College

Conway, Arkansas

http://www.cbc.edu/

- **Independent Baptist** 4-year, founded 1952
- **Small-town** 11-acre campus
- **Coed**
- **Minimally difficult** entrance level

FACULTY
Student/faculty ratio: 12:1.

ACADEMICS
Calendar: semesters. *Degrees:* associate and bachelor's.
Library: Story Library. Students can reserve study rooms.

STUDENT LIFE
Housing options: on-campus residence required through senior year; coed.

Activities and organizations: drama/theater group, student-run newspaper, radio station, choral group.

Athletics Member NCCAA.

Campus security: controlled dormitory access.

Student services: personal/psychological counseling.

APPLYING
Standardized Tests *Required:* SAT or ACT (for admission).

Options: electronic application, early admission.

Required: high school transcript.

CONTACT
Central Baptist College, 1501 College Avenue, Conway, AR 72032. *Toll-free phone:* 800-205-6872.

Crowley's Ridge College

Paragould, Arkansas

http://www.crc.edu/

CONTACT
Crowley's Ridge College, 100 College Drive, Paragould, AR 72450-9731. *Toll-free phone:* 800-264-1096.

Ecclesia College

Springdale, Arkansas

http://www.ecollege.edu/

- **Independent Christian** comprehensive, founded 1995
- **Small-town** 200-acre campus with easy access to Northwest Arkansas
- **Coed** 211 undergraduate students, 80% full-time, 44% women, 56% men
- **Noncompetitive** entrance level, 63% of applicants were admitted

UNDERGRAD STUDENTS
169 full-time, 42 part-time. Students come from 12 states and territories; 5 other countries; 70% are from out of state; 10% Black or African American, non-Hispanic/Latino; 21% Hispanic/Latino; 1% Asian, non-Hispanic/Latino; 0.5% American Indian or Alaska Native, non-Hispanic/Latino; 0.5% Two or more races, non-Hispanic/Latino; 0.5% Race/ethnicity unknown; 7% international; 10% transferred in; 75% live on campus.

Freshmen:
Admission: 108 applied, 68 admitted, 61 enrolled.

Retention: 54% of full-time freshmen returned.

FACULTY
Total: 75, 24% full-time, 36% with terminal degrees.

Student/faculty ratio: 10:1.

ACADEMICS
Calendar: semesters. *Degrees:* associate, bachelor's, and master's.

Special study options: distance learning, double majors, English as a second language, independent study, internships.

Computers: Students can access the following: campus intranet, computer help desk, free student e-mail accounts, online (class) grades, online (class) schedules. Campuswide network is available. 90% of college-owned or -operated housing units are wired for high-speed Internet access. Wireless service is available via entire campus.
Library: Ecclesia College Library.

STUDENT LIFE
Housing options: men-only, women-only. Campus housing is university owned. Freshman campus housing is guaranteed.

Activities and organizations: drama/theater group, choral group, Service Learning, Student Council, Worship Team, Missions.

Athletics Member NCCAA. ***Intercollegiate sports:*** baseball M(s), basketball M(s)/W(s), cross-country running M(s)/W(s), soccer M(s)/W(s), softball W(s).

Campus security: student patrols.

Student services: personal/psychological counseling, veterans affairs office.

COSTS

Costs (2020–21) ***Comprehensive fee:*** $21,410 includes full-time tuition ($15,000), mandatory fees ($1100), and room and board ($5310). Full-time tuition and fees vary according to course load. Part-time tuition: $500 per credit hour. Part-time tuition and fees vary according to course load. ***College room only:*** $2460. ***Payment plan:*** installment. ***Waivers:*** employees or children of employees.

APPLYING

Standardized Tests *Recommended:* SAT or ACT (for admission).

Options: electronic application.

Application fee: $35.

Required: essay or personal statement, high school transcript, minimum 2.0 GPA, 1 letter of recommendation, interview.

Application deadlines: rolling (freshmen), rolling (transfers).

Notification: continuous (freshmen), continuous (transfers).

CONTACT

Ecclesia College, 9653 Nations Drive, Springdale, AR 72762. *Phone:* 479-248-7236 Ext. 223.

Harding University

Searcy, Arkansas

http://www.harding.edu/

- **Independent** university, founded 1924, affiliated with Church of Christ
- **Small-town** 350-acre campus with easy access to Little Rock
- **Endowment** $128.7 million
- **Coed** 3,974 undergraduate students, 94% full-time, 54% women, 46% men
- **Moderately difficult** entrance level, 68% of applicants were admitted

UNDERGRAD STUDENTS

3,742 full-time, 232 part-time. Students come from 54 states and territories; 49 other countries; 72% are from out of state; 4% Black or African American, non-Hispanic/Latino; 4% Hispanic/Latino; 0.8% Asian, non-Hispanic/Latino; 0.3% American Indian or Alaska Native, non-Hispanic/Latino; 3% Two or more races, non-Hispanic/Latino; 0.1% Race/ethnicity unknown; 6% international; 3% transferred in; 91% live on campus.

Freshmen:

Admission: 1,927 applied, 1,309 admitted, 857 enrolled. ***Average high school GPA:*** 3.6. ***Test scores:*** SAT evidence-based reading and writing scores over 500: 90%; SAT math scores over 500: 86%; ACT scores over 18: 96%; SAT evidence-based reading and writing scores over 600: 52%; SAT math scores over 600: 42%; ACT scores over 24: 64%; SAT evidence-based reading and writing scores over 700: 11%; SAT math scores over 700: 9%; ACT scores over 30: 21%.

Retention: 85% of full-time freshmen returned.

FACULTY

Total: 403, 76% full-time, 61% with terminal degrees.

Student/faculty ratio: 14:1.

ACADEMICS

Calendar: semesters. *Degrees:* bachelor's, master's, doctoral, and post-master's certificates.

Special study options: academic remediation for entering students, accelerated degree program, adult/continuing education programs, advanced placement credit, cooperative education, distance learning, double majors, English as a second language, freshman honors college, honors programs, independent study, internships, part-time degree program, services for LD students, student-designed majors, study abroad, summer session for credit. ***ROTC:*** Army (c).

Computers: 512 computers/terminals and 3,200 ports are available on campus for general student use. Students can access the following: campus intranet, computer help desk, free student e-mail accounts, online (class) grades, online (class) registration, online (class) schedules. Campuswide network is available. 100% of college-owned or -operated housing units are wired for high-speed Internet access. Wireless service is available via entire campus.

Library: Brackett Library plus 1 other. *Books:* 178,520 (physical), 222,895 (digital/electronic); *Serial titles:* 464 (physical), 86,289 (digital/electronic); *Databases:* 188. Weekly public service hours: 88; students can reserve study rooms.

STUDENT LIFE

Housing options: on-campus residence required through senior year; men-only, women-only, special housing for students with disabilities. Campus housing is university owned. Freshman campus housing is guaranteed.

Activities and organizations: drama/theater group, student-run newspaper, radio and television station, choral group, marching band, Bisons for Christ, Harding in Action, Spring Break Campaigns, HUmanity.

Athletics Member NCAA. All Division II except golf (Division I). ***Intercollegiate sports:*** baseball M(s), basketball M(s)/W(s), cheerleading W, cross-country running M(s)/W(s), football M(s), golf M(s)/W(s), lacrosse M(c), rugby M(c), soccer M(s)/W(s), tennis M(s)/W(s), track and field M(s)/W(s), ultimate Frisbee M(c)/W(c), volleyball W(s). ***Intramural sports:*** basketball M/W, cross-country running M/W, football M/W, golf M/W, racquetball M/W, soccer M/W, softball M/W, swimming and diving M/W, table tennis M/W, tennis M/W, track and field M/W, ultimate Frisbee M/W, volleyball M/W, weight lifting M/W.

Campus security: 24-hour emergency response devices and patrols, student patrols, late-night transport/escort service, controlled dormitory access.

Student services: health clinic, personal/psychological counseling, veterans affairs office.

COSTS & FINANCIAL AID

Costs (2020–21) ***Comprehensive fee:*** $28,978 includes full-time tuition ($21,000), mandatory fees ($540), and room and board ($7438). Full-time tuition and fees vary according to course load. Part-time tuition: $700 per credit hour. Part-time tuition and fees vary according to course load. ***Required fees:*** $35 per credit hour part-time, $35 per credit hour part-time. ***College room only:*** $3888. Room and board charges vary according to board plan and housing facility. ***Payment plans:*** tuition prepayment, installment. ***Waivers:*** senior citizens and employees or children of employees.

Financial Aid Of all full-time matriculated undergraduates who enrolled in 2017, 3,066 applied for aid, 2,533 were judged to have need, 335 had their need fully met. 603 Federal Work-Study jobs (averaging $1279). 1,268 state and other part-time jobs (averaging $1349). In 2017, 1142 non-need-based awards were made. ***Average percent of need met:*** 76. ***Average financial aid package:*** $13,086. ***Average need-based loan:*** $4947. ***Average need-based gift aid:*** $9795. ***Average non-need-based aid:*** $7270. ***Average indebtedness upon graduation:*** $33,954.

APPLYING

Standardized Tests *Required:* SAT or ACT (for admission).

Options: electronic application, early admission, early action, deferred entrance.

Application fee: $50.

Required: essay or personal statement, high school transcript, 3 letters of recommendation.

Application deadlines: rolling (freshmen), rolling (transfers).

Notification: continuous (freshmen), continuous (transfers).

CONTACT

Mr. Scott Hannigan, Senior Director of Admissions, Harding University, 915 E. Market Avenue, Box 12255, Searcy, AR 72149-5615. *Phone:* 501-279-4407. *Toll-free phone:* 800-477-4407. *Fax:* 501-279-4129. *E-mail:* admissions@harding.edu.

Henderson State University

Arkadelphia, Arkansas

http://www.hsu.edu/

CONTACT
Dr. Brandie Benton, Associate Provost Enrollment Services and Admissions, Henderson State University, 1100 Henderson Street, PO Box 7560, Arkadelphia, AR 71999-0001. *Phone:* 870-230-5203. *Toll-free phone:* 800-228-7333. *Fax:* 870-230-5066. *E-mail:* bentonb@hsu.edu.

Hendrix College

Conway, Arkansas

http://www.hendrix.edu/

CONTACT
Hendrix College, 1600 Washington Avenue, Conway, AR 72032. *Phone:* 501-450-1362. *Toll-free phone:* 800-277-9017. *Fax:* 501-450-3843. *E-mail:* adm@hendrix.edu.

John Brown University

Siloam Springs, Arkansas

http://www.jbu.edu/

- **Independent interdenominational** comprehensive, founded 1919
- **Small-town** 200-acre campus
- **Endowment** $113.3 million
- **Coed** 1,608 undergraduate students, 78% full-time, 57% women, 43% men
- **Moderately difficult** entrance level, 76% of applicants were admitted

UNDERGRAD STUDENTS
1,262 full-time, 346 part-time. 58% are from out of state; 1% Black or African American, non-Hispanic/Latino; 8% Hispanic/Latino; 1% Asian, non-Hispanic/Latino; 0.1% Native Hawaiian or other Pacific Islander, non-Hispanic/Latino; 1% American Indian or Alaska Native, non-Hispanic/Latino; 5% Two or more races, non-Hispanic/Latino; 2% Race/ethnicity unknown; 8% international; 8% transferred in; 60% live on campus.

Freshmen:
Admission: 1,176 applied, 891 admitted, 319 enrolled. ***Average high school GPA:*** 3.8. ***Test scores:*** SAT evidence-based reading and writing scores over 500: 90%; SAT math scores over 500: 87%; ACT scores over 18: 100%; SAT evidence-based reading and writing scores over 600: 47%; SAT math scores over 600: 27%; ACT scores over 24: 75%; SAT evidence-based reading and writing scores over 700: 10%; SAT math scores over 700: 7%; ACT scores over 30: 21%.

Retention: 82% of full-time freshmen returned.

FACULTY
Total: 181, 48% full-time, 59% with terminal degrees.

Student/faculty ratio: 13:1.

ACADEMICS
Calendar: semesters. *Degrees:* associate, bachelor's, master's, and post-master's certificates.

Special study options: academic remediation for entering students, accelerated degree program, adult/continuing education programs, distance learning, double majors, English as a second language, honors programs, independent study, internships, part-time degree program, services for LD students, student-designed majors, study abroad. ***ROTC:*** Army (c), Air Force (c).

Computers: 250 computers/terminals are available on campus for general student use. Students can access the following: campus intranet, computer help desk, free student e-mail accounts, online (class) grades, online (class) registration, online (class) schedules. Campuswide network is available. 100% of college-owned or -operated housing units are wired for high-speed Internet access. Wireless service is available via entire campus.

Library: Arutunoff Learning Resource Center plus 4 others. *Books:* 105,116 (physical), 329,913 (digital/electronic); *Serial titles:* 1,032 (physical), 67,078 (digital/electronic); *Databases:* 144. Weekly public service hours: 110; students can reserve study rooms.

STUDENT LIFE
Housing options: on-campus residence required through junior year; coed, men-only, women-only, special housing for students with disabilities. Campus housing is university owned. Freshman campus housing is guaranteed.

Activities and organizations: drama/theater group, student-run newspaper, radio and television station, choral group, Student Government Association, Student Ministries Organization, Student Activities Club, Student Missionary Fellowship, Enactus.

Athletics Member NAIA. ***Intercollegiate sports:*** basketball M(s)/W(s), cross-country running M(s)/W(s), rugby M(c)/W(c), soccer M(s)/W(s), tennis M(s)/W(s), ultimate Frisbee M(c)/W(c), volleyball W(s). ***Intramural sports:*** basketball M/W, football M/W, soccer M/W, softball M/W, volleyball M/W.

Campus security: 24-hour emergency response devices and patrols, late-night transport/escort service, controlled dormitory access.

Student services: health clinic, personal/psychological counseling.

COSTS & FINANCIAL AID
Costs (2019–20) ***Comprehensive fee:*** $37,124 includes full-time tuition ($26,458), mandatory fees ($1210), and room and board ($9456). Full-time tuition and fees vary according to course load and degree level. Part-time tuition: $882 per credit hour. Part-time tuition and fees vary according to course load and degree level. ***Required fees:*** $303 per term part-time. ***College room only:*** $4536. Room and board charges vary according to board plan and housing facility. ***Payment plan:*** installment. ***Waivers:*** employees or children of employees.

Financial Aid Of all full-time matriculated undergraduates who enrolled in 2018, 1,150 applied for aid, 1,002 were judged to have need, 175 had their need fully met. In 2018, 458 non-need-based awards were made. ***Average percent of need met:*** 70. ***Average financial aid package:*** $20,410. ***Average need-based loan:*** $3021. ***Average need-based gift aid:*** $14,144. ***Average non-need-based aid:*** $11,260. ***Average indebtedness upon graduation:*** $25,593.

APPLYING
Standardized Tests *Required for some:* SAT or ACT (for admission).

Options: electronic application, deferred entrance.

Application fee: $25.

Required: essay or personal statement, high school transcript, minimum 2.5 GPA, 2 letters of recommendation. ***Recommended:*** interview.

Application deadlines: rolling (freshmen), rolling (transfers).

Notification: continuous (freshmen), continuous (transfers).

CONTACT
Mr. Jared Burgess, Director of Visitation Program, John Brown University, 2000 West University, Siloam Springs, AR 72761. *Phone:* 479-524-7190. *Toll-free phone:* 877-JBU-INFO. *Fax:* 479-524-4196. *E-mail:* jburgess@jbu.edu.

Lyon College

Batesville, Arkansas

http://www.lyon.edu/

CONTACT
Office of Enrollment Services, Lyon College, 2300 Highland Road, Batesville, AR 72501. *Phone:* 870-307-7250. *Toll-free phone:* 800-423-2542. *Fax:* 870-307-7542. *E-mail:* admissions@lyon.edu.

Ouachita Baptist University

Arkadelphia, Arkansas

http://www.obu.edu/

- **Independent Baptist** 4-year, founded 1886
- **Small-town** 200-acre campus with easy access to Little Rock
- **Endowment** $118,705
- **Coed**
- **Moderately difficult** entrance level

FACULTY
Student/faculty ratio: 12:1.

ACADEMICS
Calendar: semesters. *Degrees:* associate and bachelor's.

Library: Riley-Hickingbotham Library plus 2 others. *Books:* 160,398 (physical), 12,821 (digital/electronic); *Serial titles:* 1,723 (physical), 41,230 (digital/electronic); *Databases:* 150. Weekly public service hours: 80; students can reserve study rooms.

STUDENT LIFE
Housing options: on-campus residence required through senior year; men-only, women-only, special housing for students with disabilities. Campus housing is university owned and leased by the school. Freshman campus housing is guaranteed.

Activities and organizations: drama/theater group, student-run newspaper, television station, choral group, marching band, Phi Beta Lambda, Student Foundation, Student Education Association, Campus Activities Board, International Club.

Athletics Member NCAA. All Division II.

Campus security: 24-hour emergency response devices and patrols, controlled dormitory access.

Student services: health clinic, personal/psychological counseling.

COSTS & FINANCIAL AID
Costs (2019–20) ***Comprehensive fee:*** $35,900 includes full-time tuition ($27,280), mandatory fees ($620), and room and board ($8000). Full-time tuition and fees vary according to degree level and location. Part-time tuition: $725 per credit hour. Part-time tuition and fees vary according to degree level and location. ***College room only:*** $4000. Room and board charges vary according to housing facility.

Financial Aid Of all full-time matriculated undergraduates who enrolled in 2019, 1,261 applied for aid, 960 were judged to have need, 526 had their need fully met. 378 Federal Work-Study jobs (averaging $1900). 147 state and other part-time jobs (averaging $1900). In 2019, 516 non-need-based awards were made. ***Average percent of need met:*** 91. ***Average financial aid package:*** $29,837. ***Average need-based loan:*** $4012. ***Average need-based gift aid:*** $19,174. ***Average non-need-based aid:*** $15,571. ***Average indebtedness upon graduation:*** $24,157.

APPLYING
Standardized Tests *Required:* SAT or ACT (for admission).

Options: deferred entrance.

Required: high school transcript, minimum 2.8 GPA. ***Recommended:*** interview.

CONTACT
Mrs. Lori Motl, Director of Admissions Counseling, Ouachita Baptist University, OBU Box 3776, Arkadelphia, AR 71998-0001. *Phone:* 870-245-5110. *Toll-free phone:* 800-342-5628. *Fax:* 870-245-5500. *E-mail:* motll@obu.edu.

Philander Smith College

Little Rock, Arkansas

http://www.philander.edu/

- **Independent United Methodist** 4-year, founded 1877
- **Urban** 25-acre campus
- **Coed**
- **Minimally difficult** entrance level

FACULTY
Student/faculty ratio: 17:1.

ACADEMICS
Calendar: semesters. *Degree:* bachelor's.
Library: D. W. Reynolds Library & Technology Center. *Books:* 74,152 (physical), 20,575 (digital/electronic); *Serial titles:* 190 (physical), 166 (digital/electronic); *Databases:* 47. Weekly public service hours: 81; students can reserve study rooms.

STUDENT LIFE
Housing options: on-campus residence required for freshman year; coed. Campus housing is university owned. Freshman campus housing is guaranteed.

Activities and organizations: drama/theater group, choral group, Student Government Association, Panther Programming Council, Panther Dolls, Panther Newscast, Religious Life Council, national fraternities, national sororities.

Athletics Member NAIA.

Campus security: 24-hour emergency response devices and patrols, student patrols, controlled dormitory access.

Student services: health clinic, personal/psychological counseling.

COSTS & FINANCIAL AID
Costs (2019–20) ***Comprehensive fee:*** $21,114 includes full-time tuition ($11,804), mandatory fees ($1060), and room and board ($8250). Full-time tuition and fees vary according to program. Part-time tuition: $495 per credit hour. Part-time tuition and fees vary according to course load. ***Required fees:*** $530 per term part-time. ***Room and board:*** Room and board charges vary according to board plan and housing facility. ***Payment plans:*** installment, deferred payment.

Financial Aid Of all full-time matriculated undergraduates who enrolled in 2016, 690 applied for aid, 668 were judged to have need, 36 had their need fully met. 88 Federal Work-Study jobs (averaging $2600). In 2016, 31 non-need-based awards were made. ***Average percent of need met:*** 51. ***Average financial aid package:*** $13,134. ***Average need-based loan:*** $3653. ***Average need-based gift aid:*** $9917. ***Average non-need-based aid:*** $13,673. ***Average indebtedness upon graduation:*** $46,965.

APPLYING
Standardized Tests *Required:* SAT or ACT (for admission).

Options: electronic application, deferred entrance.

Application fee: $25.

Required: high school transcript.

CONTACT
Mr. Maurice Osbourne, Director of Admissions, Philander Smith College, 900 West Daisy Bates Drive, Little Rock, AR 72202. *Phone:* 501-370-5221. *Toll-free phone:* 800-446-6772. *Fax:* 501-370-5225.

Southern Arkansas University–Magnolia

Magnolia, Arkansas

http://www.saumag.edu/

- **State-supported** comprehensive, founded 1909, part of Southern Arkansas University System
- **Small-town** 1390-acre campus
- **Endowment** $44.3 million
- **Coed** 3,585 undergraduate students, 84% full-time, 56% women, 44% men
- **Moderately difficult** entrance level, 70% of applicants were admitted

UNDERGRAD STUDENTS
3,003 full-time, 582 part-time. Students come from 30 states and territories; 15 other countries; 23% are from out of state; 25% Black or African American, non-Hispanic/Latino; 4% Hispanic/Latino; 0.9% Asian, non-Hispanic/Latino; 0.6% American Indian or Alaska Native, non-Hispanic/Latino; 2% international; 5% transferred in; 54% live on campus.

Freshmen:
Admission: 3,604 applied, 2,518 admitted, 833 enrolled. ***Average high school GPA:*** 3.4. ***Test scores:*** SAT evidence-based reading and writing scores over 500: 67%; SAT math scores over 500: 84%; ACT scores over 18: 81%; SAT evidence-based reading and writing scores over 600: 50%; SAT math scores over 600: 17%; ACT scores over 24: 31%; ACT scores over 30: 5%.

Retention: 67% of full-time freshmen returned.

FACULTY
Total: 301, 53% full-time, 45% with terminal degrees.

Student/faculty ratio: 17:1.

ACADEMICS
Calendar: semesters. *Degrees:* certificates, associate, bachelor's, master's, and post-master's certificates.

Special study options: academic remediation for entering students, accelerated degree program, adult/continuing education programs, advanced placement credit, distance learning, double majors, English as a second language, freshman honors college, honors programs, independent study, internships, part-time degree program, services for LD students, study abroad, summer session for credit.

Unusual degree programs: 3-2 business administration.

Computers: 199 computers/terminals and 199 ports are available on campus for general student use. Students can access the following: campus intranet, computer help desk, free student e-mail accounts, online (class) grades, online (class) registration, online (class) schedules. Campuswide network is available. 100% of college-owned or -operated housing units are wired for high-speed Internet access. Wireless service is available via computer centers, computer labs, dorm rooms, libraries, student centers.

Library: Magale Library. *Books:* 149,415 (physical), 14,006 (digital/electronic); *Serial titles:* 96 (physical), 82 (digital/electronic); *Databases:* 188. Weekly public service hours: 87.

STUDENT LIFE

Housing options: on-campus residence required through sophomore year; coed, men-only, women-only. Campus housing is university owned. Freshman campus housing is guaranteed.

Activities and organizations: drama/theater group, student-run newspaper, radio station, choral group, marching band, Student Government Association, Student Activities Board, Resident Hall Association, Residential College, International Student Association, national fraternities, national sororities.

Athletics Member NCAA. All Division II except golf (Division I). ***Intercollegiate sports:*** baseball M(s), basketball M(s)/W(s), cheerleading M(s)(c)/W(s)(c), cross-country running M(s)/W(s), football M(s), golf M/W, softball W(s), tennis W(s), track and field M(s)/W(s), volleyball W(s). ***Intramural sports:*** badminton M/W, basketball M/W, football M, golf M/W, sand volleyball M/W, soccer M/W, softball M/W, swimming and diving M/W, table tennis M/W, tennis M/W, ultimate Frisbee M/W, volleyball M/W.

Campus security: 24-hour emergency response devices, student patrols, late-night transport/escort service, controlled dormitory access.

Student services: health clinic, personal/psychological counseling, veterans affairs office.

COSTS & FINANCIAL AID

Costs (2019–20) ***Tuition:*** state resident $6420 full-time, $214 per credit hour part-time; nonresident $10,920 full-time, $364 per credit hour part-time. Full-time tuition and fees vary according to course load and program. Part-time tuition and fees vary according to course load and program. ***Required fees:*** $2560 full-time, $84 per credit hour part-time, $84 per credit hour part-time. ***Room and board:*** $6520; room only: $3266. Room and board charges vary according to board plan and housing facility. ***Payment plan:*** installment. ***Waivers:*** children of alumni, senior citizens, and employees or children of employees.

Financial Aid ***Average indebtedness upon graduation:*** $22,616.

APPLYING

Standardized Tests *Required:* SAT or ACT (for admission). *Recommended:* ACT (for admission).

Options: electronic application, early admission, deferred entrance.

Required: high school transcript. ***Required for some:*** interview.

Application deadlines: 8/27 (freshmen), 8/27 (transfers).

CONTACT

Southern Arkansas University–Magnolia, 100 East University, Magnolia, AR 71753. *Phone:* 870-235-4040. *Toll-free phone:* 800-332-7286.

Strayer University–Little Rock Campus

Little Rock, Arkansas

http://www.strayer.edu/arkansas/little-rock/

CONTACT

Strayer University–Little Rock Campus, 10825 Financial Centre Parkway, Suite 400, Little Rock, AR 72211. *Toll-free phone:* 888-311-0355.

University of Arkansas

Fayetteville, Arkansas

http://www.uark.edu/

- **State-supported** university, founded 1871, part of University of Arkansas System
- **Urban** 718-acre campus
- **Coed** 23,025 undergraduate students, 89% full-time, 54% women, 46% men
- **Moderately difficult** entrance level, 77% of applicants were admitted

UNDERGRAD STUDENTS

20,559 full-time, 2,466 part-time. Students come from 49 states and territories; 80 other countries; 46% are from out of state; 4% Black or African American, non-Hispanic/Latino; 9% Hispanic/Latino; 3% Asian, non-Hispanic/Latino; 0.1% Native Hawaiian or other Pacific Islander, non-Hispanic/Latino; 0.9% American Indian or Alaska Native, non-Hispanic/Latino; 4% Two or more races, non-Hispanic/Latino; 0.7% Race/ethnicity unknown; 3% international; 5% transferred in; 25% live on campus.

Freshmen:

Admission: 17,913 applied, 13,809 admitted, 4,601 enrolled. ***Average high school GPA:*** 3.7. ***Test scores:*** SAT evidence-based reading and writing scores over 500: 96%; SAT math scores over 500: 96%; ACT scores over 18: 100%; SAT evidence-based reading and writing scores over 600: 57%; SAT math scores over 600: 50%; ACT scores over 24: 72%; SAT evidence-based reading and writing scores over 700: 10%; SAT math scores over 700: 10%; ACT scores over 30: 26%.

Retention: 84% of full-time freshmen returned.

FACULTY

Total: 1,443, 84% full-time, 77% with terminal degrees.

Student/faculty ratio: 18:1.

ACADEMICS

Calendar: semesters. *Degrees:* certificates, bachelor's, master's, doctoral, post-master's, and postbachelor's certificates.

Special study options: academic remediation for entering students, accelerated degree program, adult/continuing education programs, advanced placement credit, cooperative education, distance learning, double majors, English as a second language, freshman honors college, honors programs, independent study, internships, off-campus study, part-time degree program, services for LD students, student-designed majors, study abroad, summer session for credit. ***ROTC:*** Army (b), Air Force (b).

Unusual degree programs: 3-2 business administration; law.

Computers: 675 computers/terminals and 24 ports are available on campus for general student use. Students can access the following: campus intranet, computer help desk, free student e-mail accounts, online (class) grades, online (class) registration, online (class) schedules. Campuswide network is available. 100% of college-owned or -operated housing units are wired for high-speed Internet access. Wireless service is available via entire campus.

Library: David W. Mullins Library plus 4 others. *Books:* 2.0 million (physical), 703,745 (digital/electronic); *Serial titles:* 60,187 (physical), 173,320 (digital/electronic); *Databases:* 331. Weekly public service hours: 109.

STUDENT LIFE

Housing options: on-campus residence required for freshman year; coed, women-only, special housing for students with disabilities. Campus housing is university owned. Freshman campus housing is guaranteed.

Activities and organizations: drama/theater group, student-run newspaper, radio and television station, choral group, marching band, Associated Student Government, Catholic Campus Ministry, Chinese Students and Scholars, Alpha Lambda Delta, Student Alumni Association, national fraternities, national sororities.

Athletics Member NCAA. All Division I except football (Division I-A). ***Intercollegiate sports:*** baseball M(s), basketball M(s)/W(s), cross-country running M(s)/W(s), golf M(s)/W(s)(c), gymnastics W(s), soccer W(s), softball W(s), swimming and diving W(s), tennis M(s)/W(s), track and field M(s)/W(s), volleyball W(s). ***Intramural sports:*** badminton M/W, baseball M(c), basketball M/W, cross-country running M(c)/W(c), golf M(c)/W(c), ice hockey M(c), lacrosse M(c)/W(c), racquetball M(c)/W(c), riflery M(c)/W(c), rugby M(c)/W(c), sand volleyball M/W, soccer

M(c)/W(c), softball M/W, swimming and diving M(c)/W(c), table tennis M/W, tennis M(c)/W(c), track and field M/W, triathlon M(c)/W(c), ultimate Frisbee M(c)/W(c), volleyball M(c)/W(c).

Campus security: 24-hour emergency response devices and patrols, controlled dormitory access, Safe Ride.

Student services: health clinic, personal/psychological counseling, women's center, legal services, veterans affairs office.

COSTS & FINANCIAL AID

Costs (2019–20) ***Tuition:*** $313 per credit hour part-time; state resident $7568 full time, $313 per credit hour part-time; nonresident $24,056 full-time, $862 per credit hour part-time. Full-time tuition and fees vary according to course load, location, and program. Part-time tuition and fees vary according to course load, location, and program. ***Required fees:*** $1816 full-time, $61 per credit hour part-time. ***Room and board:*** $11,330; room only: $7290. Room and board charges vary according to board plan, housing facility, and location. ***Payment plan:*** installment. ***Waivers:*** senior citizens and employees or children of employees.

Financial Aid Of all full-time matriculated undergraduates who enrolled in 2019, 13,193 applied for aid, 8,459 were judged to have need, 1,271 had their need fully met. 872 Federal Work-Study jobs (averaging $2801). In 2019, 3158 non-need-based awards were made. ***Average percent of need met:*** 59. ***Average financial aid package:*** $10,337. ***Average need-based loan:*** $4348. ***Average need-based gift aid:*** $8253. ***Average non-need-based aid:*** $5399. ***Average indebtedness upon graduation:*** $27,123.

APPLYING

Standardized Tests *Required:* SAT or ACT (for admission).

Options: electronic application, early action.

Application fee: $40.

Required: high school transcript, minimum 3.0 GPA, minimum ACT Composite score of 20 or SAT total (math and EBRW only) of 1030, completion of 16 core academic units. ***Required for some:*** essay or personal statement.

Application deadlines: 8/1 (freshmen), 8/1 (out-of-state freshmen), 8/1 (transfers), 11/1 (early action).

Notification: continuous until 9/1 (freshmen), continuous until 9/1 (out-of-state freshmen), continuous (transfers), 12/15 (early action).

CONTACT

Wendy Stouffer, Associate Vice Provost for Enrollment Services and Assistant Dean of Admissions and Financial Aid, University of Arkansas, 232 Silas H. Hunt Hall, Office of Admissions, Fayetteville, AR 72701-1201. *Phone:* 479-575-6870. *Toll-free phone:* 800-377-8632. *Fax:* 479-575-7515. *E-mail:* uofa@uark.edu.

University of Arkansas at Little Rock

Little Rock, Arkansas

http://www.ualr.edu/

- **State-supported** university, founded 1927, part of University of Arkansas System
- **Urban** 229-acre campus
- **Coed** 7,615 undergraduate students, 51% full-time, 64% women, 36% men
- **Minimally difficult** entrance level, 64% of applicants were admitted

UNDERGRAD STUDENTS

3,847 full-time, 3,768 part-time. 6% are from out of state; 27% Black or African American, non-Hispanic/Latino; 4% Hispanic/Latino; 2% Asian, non-Hispanic/Latino; 0.4% American Indian or Alaska Native, non-Hispanic/Latino; 13% Two or more races, non-Hispanic/Latino; 0.3% Race/ethnicity unknown; 4% international; 9% transferred in.

Freshmen:

Admission: 2,325 applied, 1,481 admitted, 584 enrolled. ***Average high school GPA:*** 3.3. ***Test scores:*** ACT scores over 18: 83%; ACT scores over 24: 36%; ACT scores over 30: 7%.

Retention: 66% of full-time freshmen returned.

ACADEMICS

Calendar: semesters. *Degrees:* certificates, associate, bachelor's, master's, doctoral, post-master's, and postbachelor's certificates.

Special study options: academic remediation for entering students, accelerated degree program, adult/continuing education programs, advanced placement credit, cooperative education, distance learning, double majors, English as a second language, external degree program, freshman honors college, honors programs, independent study, internships, part-time degree program, student-designed majors, study abroad, summer session for credit.

Computers: Students can access the following: campus intranet, computer help desk, free student e-mail accounts, online (class) grades, online (class) registration, online (class) schedules. Campuswide network is available. Wireless service is available via entire campus.

Library: Ottenheimer Library.

STUDENT LIFE

Housing options: college housing not available.

Activities and organizations: drama/theater group, student-run newspaper, radio station, choral group, Student Government, University Program Council, Housing Activities Council, International Student Organization, Panhellenic Council, national fraternities, national sororities.

Athletics Member NCAA. All Division I. ***Intercollegiate sports:*** baseball M(s), basketball M(s)/W, cross-country running M(s)/W(s), golf M(s)/W(s), soccer M/W(s), swimming and diving W, track and field M/W(s), volleyball W(s). ***Intramural sports:*** archery M/W, badminton M/W, basketball M, bowling M/W, football M/W, golf M/W, swimming and diving M/W, table tennis M/W, tennis M/W, volleyball M/W.

Campus security: 24-hour emergency response devices and patrols, student patrols, late-night transport/escort service, controlled dormitory access.

Student services: health clinic.

FINANCIAL AID

Financial Aid Of all full-time matriculated undergraduates who enrolled in 2016, 3,875 applied for aid, 2,520 were judged to have need. ***Average financial aid package:*** $13,138. ***Average need-based gift aid:*** $4482.

APPLYING

Standardized Tests *Required:* SAT or ACT (for admission).

Options: electronic application, deferred entrance.

Application fee: $40.

Required: high school transcript, minimum 2.5 GPA, proof of immunization.

CONTACT

Ms. Tammy Harrison, Director of Admissions, University of Arkansas at Little Rock, 2801 South University Avenue, Little Rock, AR 72204-1099. *Phone:* 501-569-3127. *Toll-free phone:* 800-482-8892. *Fax:* 501-569-8956. *E-mail:* twharrison@ualn.edu.

University of Arkansas at Monticello

Monticello, Arkansas

http://www.uamont.edu/

- **State-supported** comprehensive, founded 1909, part of University of Arkansas System
- **Small-town** 1600-acre campus
- **Endowment** $2.5 million
- **Coed**
- **Noncompetitive** entrance level

FACULTY

Student/faculty ratio: 16:1.

ACADEMICS

Calendar: semesters. *Degrees:* certificates, associate, bachelor's, master's, and postbachelor's certificates.

Library: Fred J. Taylor Library and Technology Center.

STUDENT LIFE

Housing options: coed, men-only, women-only. Campus housing is university owned.

Activities and organizations: drama/theater group, student-run newspaper, choral group, marching band, national fraternities, national sororities.

Athletics Member NCAA. All Division II.

Campus security: 24-hour emergency response devices and patrols.

Student services: health clinic, personal/psychological counseling.

FINANCIAL AID
Financial Aid Of all full-time matriculated undergraduates who enrolled in 2006, 166 Federal Work-Study jobs (averaging $1159). 292 state and other part-time jobs (averaging $1388).

APPLYING
Options: early admission, deferred entrance.

Required: high school transcript, proof of immunization.

CONTACT
Ms. Mary Whiting, Director of Admissions, University of Arkansas at Monticello, 346 University Drive, Monticello, AR 71656. *Phone:* 870-460-1026. *Toll-free phone:* 800-844-1826. *E-mail:* admissions@uamont.edu.

University of Arkansas at Pine Bluff

Pine Bluff, Arkansas

http://www.uapb.edu/

- **State-supported** comprehensive, founded 1873, part of University of Arkansas System
- **Urban** 327-acre campus
- **Endowment** $3.5 million
- **Coed**
- 46% of applicants were admitted

FACULTY
Student/faculty ratio: 15:1.

ACADEMICS
Calendar: semesters. *Degrees:* certificates, associate, bachelor's, master's, and doctoral.
Library: John Brown Watson Memorial Library plus 4 others.

STUDENT LIFE
Housing options: men-only, women-only. Campus housing is university owned.

Activities and organizations: drama/theater group, student-run newspaper, choral group, marching band, Union Programming Board, Student Government Association, Pan Hellenic Council, Lion Year Book, Arkansawyer Newspaper, national fraternities, national sororities.

Athletics Member NCAA, NAIA. All NCAA Division I except football (Division I-AA).

Campus security: 24-hour emergency response devices and patrols.

Student services: health clinic, personal/psychological counseling, veterans affairs office.

FINANCIAL AID
Financial Aid Of all full-time matriculated undergraduates who enrolled in 2005, 2,825 applied for aid, 2,825 were judged to have need, 1,200 had their need fully met. 328 Federal Work-Study jobs (averaging $1000). ***Average percent of need met:*** 70. ***Average financial aid package:*** $8121. ***Average need-based loan:*** $4500. ***Average need-based gift aid:*** $1000.

APPLYING
Standardized Tests *Required:* SAT or ACT (for admission).

Options: electronic application, early admission, deferred entrance.

Required: high school transcript, minimum 2.0 GPA.

CONTACT
University of Arkansas at Pine Bluff, 1200 North University Drive, Pine Bluff, AR 71601-2799. *Phone:* 870-575-8492. *Toll-free phone:* 800-264-6585.

University of Arkansas for Medical Sciences

Little Rock, Arkansas

http://www.uams.edu/

CONTACT
University of Arkansas for Medical Sciences, 4301 West Markham, Little Rock, AR 72205-7199.

University of Arkansas-Fort Smith

Fort Smith, Arkansas

http://uafs.edu/

- **State and locally supported** comprehensive, founded 1928, part of University of Arkansas System
- **Suburban** 170-acre campus
- **Endowment** $79.4 million
- **Coed**
- **Minimally difficult** entrance level

FACULTY
Student/faculty ratio: 18:1.

ACADEMICS
Calendar: semesters. *Degrees:* certificates, associate, bachelor's, and master's.
Library: Boreham Library.

STUDENT LIFE
Housing options: coed, special housing for students with disabilities. Campus housing is university owned.

Activities and organizations: drama/theater group, student-run newspaper, choral group, Campus Activities Board, Phi Beta Lambda, Student Alumni Association, Non-Traditional Students, Grand Avenue Baptist College Ministry (Reach), national fraternities, national sororities.

Athletics Member NCAA. All Division II.

Campus security: 24-hour emergency response devices and patrols, student patrols, late-night transport/escort service, controlled dormitory access.

Student services: health clinic, personal/psychological counseling, veterans affairs office.

FINANCIAL AID
Financial Aid Of all full-time matriculated undergraduates who enrolled in 2004, 2,564 applied for aid, 2,232 were judged to have need, 215 had their need fully met. 110 Federal Work-Study jobs (averaging $3000). 94 state and other part-time jobs (averaging $3000). In 2004, 350 non-need-based awards were made. ***Average percent of need met:*** 62. ***Average financial aid package:*** $5568. ***Average need-based loan:*** $3183. ***Average need-based gift aid:*** $3504. ***Average non-need-based aid:*** $2643. ***Average indebtedness upon graduation:*** $7339.

APPLYING
Standardized Tests *Required:* SAT, ACT or ACT Compass (for admission).

Options: electronic application, deferred entrance.

Required: high school transcript, minimum 2.0 GPA.

CONTACT
Ms. Kelly Westeen, Director of Admissions, University of Arkansas-Fort Smith, 5210 Grand Avenue, PO Box 3649, Fort Smith, AR 72913-3649. *Phone:* 479-788-7106. *Toll-free phone:* 888-512-5466. *Fax:* 479-424-6106. *E-mail:* kelly.westeen@uafortsmith.edu.

University of Central Arkansas

Conway, Arkansas

http://www.uca.edu/

- **State-supported** university, founded 1907
- **Small-town** 356-acre campus
- **Coed** 9,425 undergraduate students, 83% full-time, 60% women, 40% men
- **Moderately difficult** entrance level, 91% of applicants were admitted

UNDERGRAD STUDENTS
7,863 full-time, 1,562 part-time. Students come from 45 states and territories; 72 other countries; 10% are from out of state; 7% transferred in; 40% live on campus.

Freshmen:

Admission: 5,541 applied, 5,048 admitted, 2,033 enrolled. ***Average high school GPA:*** 3.5.

Retention: 74% of full-time freshmen returned.

ACADEMICS
Calendar: semesters. *Degrees:* certificates, bachelor's, master's, doctoral, post-master's, and postbachelor's certificates.

Special study options: academic remediation for entering students, accelerated degree program, advanced placement credit, cooperative education, distance learning, double majors, English as a second language, freshman honors college, honors programs, independent study, internships, part-time degree program, services for LD students, study abroad, summer session for credit. ***ROTC:*** Army (b).

Unusual degree programs: 3-2 engineering with Arkansas Tech University.

Computers: 610 computers/terminals are available on campus for general student use. Students can access the following: campus intranet, computer help desk, free student e-mail accounts, online (class) grades, online (class) registration, online (class) schedules. Campuswide network is available. 100% of college-owned or -operated housing units are wired for high-speed Internet access. Wireless service is available via entire campus.
Library: Torreyson Library plus 1 other. Study areas open 24 hours, 5–7 days a week; students can reserve study rooms.

STUDENT LIFE
Housing options: on-campus residence required for freshman year; coed, men-only, women-only, special housing for students with disabilities. Campus housing is university owned. Freshman campus housing is guaranteed.

Activities and organizations: drama/theater group, student-run newspaper, radio and television station, choral group, marching band, Bears Den, Greek Organizations, national fraternities, national sororities.

Athletics ***Intercollegiate sports:*** baseball M(s), basketball M(s)/W(s), cheerleading M(s)(c)/W(s)(c), cross-country running M(s)/W(s), football M(s), golf M(s)/W(s)(c), soccer M(s)/W(s), softball W(s), tennis W(s), track and field M(s)/W(s), volleyball W(s). ***Intramural sports:*** basketball M/W, soccer M/W, softball M/W, tennis W, track and field M/W, volleyball M/W.

Campus security: 24-hour emergency response devices and patrols, student patrols, late-night transport/escort service, controlled dormitory access.

Student services: health clinic, personal/psychological counseling, women's center, veterans affairs office.

COSTS
Costs (2019–20) ***Tuition:*** state resident $6810 full-time, $227 per credit hour part-time; nonresident $13,620 full-time, $454 per credit hour part-time. Full-time tuition and fees vary according to course load. Part-time tuition and fees vary according to course load. ***Required fees:*** $2378 full-time. ***Room and board:*** $7198. Room and board charges vary according to board plan and housing facility. ***Payment plan:*** installment. ***Waivers:*** senior citizens and employees or children of employees.

APPLYING
Standardized Tests *Required:* SAT or ACT (for admission).

Options: electronic application, early admission, deferred entrance.

Application fee: $25.

Required: high school transcript. ***Required for some:*** minimum 2.75 GPA, minimum ACT score of 21 or SAT score of 1450.

Application deadlines: rolling (freshmen), rolling (transfers).

Notification: continuous (freshmen), continuous (transfers).

CONTACT
University of Central Arkansas, 201 Donaghey Avenue, Conway, AR 72035-0001. *Phone:* 501-450-3185. *Toll-free phone:* 800-243-8245.

University of the Ozarks
Clarksville, Arkansas
http://www.ozarks.edu/

CONTACT
Ms. Jana Hart, Dean of Admission and Financial Aid, University of the Ozarks, 415 North College Avenue, Clarksville, AR 72830-2880. *Phone:* 479-979-1227. *Toll-free phone:* 800-264-8636. *Fax:* 479-979-1417. *E-mail:* admiss@ozarks.edu.

Williams Baptist College
Walnut Ridge, Arkansas
http://www.wbcoll.edu/

CONTACT
Mr. Andrew Watson, Director of Admissions, Williams Baptist College, PO Box 3737, Walnut Ridge, AR 72476. *Phone:* 870-759-4118. *Toll-free phone:* 800-722-4434. *Fax:* 870-759-4163. *E-mail:* awatson@wbcoll.edu.

CALIFORNIA

Abraham Lincoln University
Los Angeles, California
http://www.alu.edu/

- **Proprietary** comprehensive
- **Urban** campus with easy access to Los Angeles
- **Coed**

ACADEMICS
Degrees: certificates, diplomas, bachelor's, master's, and doctoral.

CONTACT
Abraham Lincoln University, 3530 Wilshire Boulevard, Suite 1430, Los Angeles, CA 90010.

Academy of Art University
San Francisco, California
http://www.academyart.edu/

- **Proprietary** comprehensive, founded 1929
- **Urban** 3-acre campus
- **Coed** 6,694 undergraduate students, 56% full-time, 57% women, 43% men
- **Noncompetitive** entrance level, 100% of applicants were admitted

UNDERGRAD STUDENTS
3,758 full-time, 2,936 part-time. Students come from 50 states and territories; 99 other countries; 39% are from out of state; 6% Black or African American, non-Hispanic/Latino; 11% Hispanic/Latino; 5% Asian, non-Hispanic/Latino; 0.5% Native Hawaiian or other Pacific Islander, non-Hispanic/Latino; 0.5% American Indian or Alaska Native, non-Hispanic/Latino; 3% Two or more races, non-Hispanic/Latino; 33% Race/ethnicity unknown; 26% international; 14% transferred in; 14% live on campus.

Freshmen:
Admission: 2,396 applied, 2,396 admitted, 803 enrolled.

Retention: 72% of full-time freshmen returned.

FACULTY
Total: 1,059, 21% full-time, 17% with terminal degrees.

Student/faculty ratio: 14:1.

ACADEMICS
Calendar: semesters. *Degrees:* certificates, associate, bachelor's, and master's.

Special study options: academic remediation for entering students, adult/continuing education programs, distance learning, English as a second language, independent study, internships, part-time degree program, services for LD students, study abroad, summer session for credit. ***ROTC:*** Army (c).

Computers: 900 computers/terminals are available on campus for general student use. Students can access the following: free student e-mail accounts, online (class) grades, online (class) registration, online (class) schedules, support for students taking online courses. Campuswide network is available. 100% of college-owned or -operated housing units are wired for high-speed Internet access. Wireless service is available via entire campus.
Library: Academy of Art University Library. *Books:* 30,674 (physical), 9,600 (digital/electronic); *Serial titles:* 792 (physical), 2

(digital/electronic); *Databases:* 20. Weekly public service hours: 83; students can reserve study rooms.

STUDENT LIFE
Housing options: coed, men-only, women-only. Campus housing is university owned. Freshman campus housing is guaranteed.

Activities and organizations: drama/theater group, student-run newspaper, radio and television station, choral group, Tea Time Animation, Beyond the Front Row, Drawaholics Anonymous Crew, Comics and Concept Art Club, Chinese Student Association, national fraternities, national sororities.

Athletics Member NCAA. All Division II except golf (Division I). ***Intercollegiate sports:*** baseball M(s), basketball M(s)/W(s), cross-country running M(s)/W(s), golf M(s)/W(s), soccer M(s)/W(s), softball W(s), tennis W(s), track and field M(s)/W(s), volleyball W(s).

Campus security: 24-hour emergency response devices and patrols, late-night transport/escort service, controlled dormitory access.

COSTS & FINANCIAL AID
Costs (2020–21) ***Comprehensive fee:*** $49,016 includes full-time tuition ($30,330), mandatory fees ($300), and room and board ($18,386). Full-time tuition and fees vary according to course load. Part-time tuition: $1011 per credit hour. Part-time tuition and fees vary according to course load. ***Required fees:*** $1011 per credit hour part-time. ***College room only:*** $12,328. Room and board charges vary according to board plan and housing facility. ***Payment plan:*** installment.

Financial Aid Of all full-time matriculated undergraduates who enrolled in 2018, 1,872 applied for aid, 1,740 were judged to have need, 51 had their need fully met. In 2018, 181 non-need-based awards were made. ***Average percent of need met:*** 35. ***Average financial aid package:*** $13,401. ***Average need-based loan:*** $3853. ***Average need-based gift aid:*** $12,104. ***Average non-need-based aid:*** $4486. ***Average indebtedness upon graduation:*** $31,360.

APPLYING
Options: electronic application, deferred entrance.

Application fee: $50.

Required: high school transcript. ***Recommended:*** interview.

Application deadlines: rolling (freshmen), rolling (transfers).

Notification: continuous (freshmen), continuous (transfers).

CONTACT
Academy of Art University, 79 New Montgomery Street, San Francisco, CA 94105-3410. *Toll-free phone:* 800-544-ARTS.

Alliant International University - San Diego

San Diego, California

http://www.alliant.edu/

CONTACT
Ms. Ashley Carter, Director of Admissions, Alliant International University - San Diego, 10455 Pomerado Road, San Diego, CA 92131-1799. *Phone:* 866-825-5426. *Toll-free phone:* 866-825-5426. *E-mail:* admissions@alliant.edu.

AMDA College and Conservatory of the Performing Arts, Los Angeles Campus

Los Angeles, California

http://www.amda.edu/

CONTACT
Mr. Joseph Siriano, Director of Admissions, AMDA College and Conservatory of the Performing Arts, Los Angeles Campus, 6305 Yucca Street, Los Angeles, CA 90028. *Phone:* 323-603-5999. *Toll-free phone:* 888-474-9444. *E-mail:* admissionsteam@amda.edu.

America Evangelical University

Los Angeles, California

http://www.aeu.edu/

CONTACT
America Evangelical University, 1818 South Western Avenue, Los Angeles, CA 90006.

American University of Health Sciences

Signal Hill, California

http://www.auhs.edu/

CONTACT
American University of Health Sciences, 1600 East Hill Street, Building #1, Signal Hill, CA 90755.

Angeles College

Los Angeles, California

http://www.angelescollege.edu/

CONTACT
Angeles College, 3440 Wilshire Boulevard, Suite 310, Los Angeles, CA 90010.

Antelope Valley College

Lancaster, California

http://www.avc.edu/

CONTACT
Welcome Center, Antelope Valley College, 3041 West Avenue K, SSV Building, Lancaster, CA 93536. *Phone:* 661-722-6300 Ext. 6331.

Antioch University Los Angeles

Culver City, California

http://www.antioch.edu/los-angeles/

CONTACT
Admissions, Antioch University Los Angeles, 400 Corporate Pointe, Culver City, CA 90230. *Phone:* 310-578-1080 Ext. 100. *Toll-free phone:* 800-726-8462. *Fax:* 310-822-4824. *E-mail:* admissions@antiochla.edu.

Antioch University Santa Barbara

Santa Barbara, California

http://www.antioch.edu/santa-barbara/

- **Independent** upper-level, founded 1977, part of Antioch University
- **Urban** campus
- **Coed** 74 undergraduate students, 61% full-time, 69% women, 31% men
- **Moderately difficult** entrance level

UNDERGRAD STUDENTS
45 full-time, 29 part-time. Students come from 8 states and territories; 1 other country; 3% are from out of state; 3% Black or African American, non-Hispanic/Latino; 24% Hispanic/Latino; 1% Asian, non-Hispanic/Latino; 1% American Indian or Alaska Native, non-Hispanic/Latino; 1% Two or more races, non-Hispanic/Latino; 18% Race/ethnicity unknown; 15% international.

FACULTY
Total: 78, 12% full-time.

ACADEMICS
Calendar: quarters. *Degrees:* certificates, bachelor's, master's, and doctoral.

Special study options: academic remediation for entering students, accelerated degree program, cooperative education, distance learning, external degree program, independent study, internships, off-campus study, part-time degree program, services for LD students, student-designed majors, summer session for credit.

Computers: 16 computers/terminals are available on campus for general student use. Students can access the following: computer help desk, free student e-mail accounts, online (class) grades, online (class) registration, online (class) schedules. Campuswide network is available. Wireless service is available via entire campus.
Library: Sage Library.

STUDENT LIFE
Housing options: college housing not available.

Activities and organizations: student-run newspaper.

Campus security: late-night transport/escort service.

COSTS
Costs (2020–21) ***Tuition:*** $17,820 full-time, $495 per credit hour part-time. Full-time tuition and fees vary according to course load, degree level, and program. Part-time tuition and fees vary according to course load, degree level, and program. ***Required fees:*** $400 full-time. ***Payment plan:*** installment. ***Waivers:*** employees or children of employees.

APPLYING
Standardized Tests *Required for some:* TOEFL for international students.

Options: electronic application, deferred entrance.

Application fee: $60.

Notification: continuous (transfers).

CONTACT
Antioch University Santa Barbara, 602 Anacapa Street, Santa Barbara, CA 93101-1581. *Toll-free phone:* 866-526-8462.

Argosy University, Los Angeles

Los Angeles, California

http://www.argosy.edu/locations/los-angeles/

CONTACT
Argosy University, Los Angeles, 5230 Pacific Concourse, Suite 200, Los Angeles, CA 90045. *Phone:* 310-531-9700. *Toll-free phone:* 866-505-0332.

Argosy University, Orange County

Orange, California

http://www.argosy.edu/locations/los-angeles-orange-county/

CONTACT
Argosy University, Orange County, 601 South Lewis Street, Orange, CA 92868. *Phone:* 714-620-3700. *Toll-free phone:* 800-716-9598.

ArtCenter College of Design

Pasadena, California

http://www.artcenter.edu/

CONTACT
Ms. Kit Baron, Vice President, Admissions and Enrollment Management, ArtCenter College of Design, 1700 Lida Street, Pasadena, CA 91103. *Phone:* 626-396-2322. *Fax:* 626-795-0578. *E-mail:* kit.baron@artcenter.edu.

The Art Institute of California–Hollywood, a campus of Argosy University

North Hollywood, California

http://www.artinstitutes.edu/hollywood/

CONTACT
The Art Institute of California–Hollywood, a campus of Argosy University, 5250 Lankershim Boulevard, North Hollywood, CA 91601. *Phone:* 818-299-5100. *Toll-free phone:* 877-468-6232.

Ashford University

San Diego, California

http://www.ashford.edu/

- **Proprietary** comprehensive, founded 1918
- **Small-town** 24-acre campus with easy access to Chicago
- **Endowment** $1.4 million
- **Coed**
- **Minimally difficult** entrance level

FACULTY
Student/faculty ratio: 37:1.

ACADEMICS
Calendar: semesters. *Degrees:* associate, bachelor's, master's, and postbachelor's certificates.
Library: The Franciscan University of the Prairies Library.

STUDENT LIFE
Housing options: on-campus residence required through junior year; coed. Campus housing is university owned. Freshman campus housing is guaranteed.

Activities and organizations: drama/theater group, student-run newspaper, choral group, Student Senate, Student Ambassadors, Hall Council, Black Student Union, Student Iowa State Education Association.

Athletics Member NAIA.

Campus security: 24-hour emergency response devices and patrols, student patrols, late-night transport/escort service, controlled dormitory access, self-defense education, lighted pathways.

Student services: health clinic, personal/psychological counseling.

FINANCIAL AID
Financial Aid Of all full-time matriculated undergraduates who enrolled in 2007, 14 state and other part-time jobs (averaging $1650).

APPLYING
Standardized Tests *Required for some:* SAT or ACT (for admission).

Options: electronic application, early admission, deferred entrance.

Application fee: $20.

Required: high school transcript. ***Required for some:*** interview. ***Recommended:*** minimum 2.0 GPA, interview.

CONTACT
Ms. Waunita M. Sullivan, Director of Enrollment, Ashford University, 8620 Spectrum Center Boulevard, San Diego, CA 92123. *Phone:* 563-242-4023 Ext. 3401. *Toll-free phone:* 866-711-1700. *E-mail:* admissns@tfu.edu.

Azusa Pacific University

Azusa, California

http://www.apu.edu/

- **Independent nondenominational** university, founded 1899
- **Suburban** 103-acre campus with easy access to Los Angeles
- **Endowment** $94.0 million
- **Coed** 5,657 undergraduate students, 88% full-time, 66% women, 34% men
- **Moderately difficult** entrance level, 69% of applicants were admitted

UNDERGRAD STUDENTS
5,003 full-time, 654 part-time. 20% are from out of state; 6% Black or African American, non-Hispanic/Latino; 33% Hispanic/Latino; 10% Asian, non-Hispanic/Latino; 1% Native Hawaiian or other Pacific Islander, non-Hispanic/Latino; 0.3% American Indian or Alaska Native, non-Hispanic/Latino; 7% Two or more races, non-Hispanic/Latino; 2% Race/ethnicity unknown; 3% international; 6% transferred in; 62% live on campus.

Freshmen:
Admission: 9,832 applied, 6,736 admitted, 1,005 enrolled. ***Average high school GPA:*** 3.7. ***Test scores:*** SAT evidence-based reading and writing scores over 500: 83%; SAT math scores over 500: 77%; ACT scores over 18: 92%; SAT evidence-based reading and writing scores over 600: 38%; SAT math scores over 600: 33%; ACT scores over 24: 53%; SAT evidence-based reading and writing scores over 700: 5%; SAT math scores over 700: 8%; ACT scores over 30: 13%.

Retention: 81% of full-time freshmen returned.

FACULTY
Total: 1,235, 40% full-time, 27% with terminal degrees.

Student/faculty ratio: 11:1.

ACADEMICS
Calendar: semesters. *Degrees:* certificates, bachelor's, master's, doctoral, post-master's, and postbachelor's certificates.

Special study options: academic remediation for entering students, accelerated degree program, adult/continuing education programs, advanced placement credit, cooperative education, distance learning, double majors, English as a second language, freshman honors college, honors programs, independent study, internships, off-campus study, part-time degree program, services for LD students, study abroad, summer session for credit. ***ROTC:*** Army (b), Air Force (c).

Unusual degree programs: 3-2 business administration; engineering; nursing; social work.

Computers: Students can access the following: campus intranet, computer help desk, free student e-mail accounts, online (class) grades, online (class) registration, online (class) schedules. Campuswide network is available. Wireless service is available via entire campus.

Library: Marshburn Memorial Library plus 3 others. Students can reserve study rooms.

STUDENT LIFE
Housing options: on-campus residence required through sophomore year; coed, women-only. Campus housing is university owned. Freshman applicants given priority for college housing.

Activities and organizations: drama/theater group, student-run newspaper, radio and television station, choral group, marching band, Pacific Islanders Organization (PIO), Boundless Brilliance, The Dream Project, Free the Captives, Allies for Change.

Athletics Member NCAA, NAIA. All NCAA Division II. ***Intercollegiate sports:*** baseball M(s), basketball M(s)/W(s), cross-country running M(s)/W(s), football M(s), gymnastics W(s), soccer M(s)/W(s), softball W(s), swimming and diving W(s), tennis M(s)/W(s), track and field M(s)/W(s), volleyball W(s), water polo W. ***Intramural sports:*** basketball M/W, cheerleading W(c), rugby M(c), skiing (downhill) M/W, soccer M/W, softball M/W, tennis M/W, ultimate Frisbee M/W, volleyball M/W.

Campus security: 24-hour emergency response devices and patrols, student patrols, late-night transport/escort service, controlled dormitory access.

Student services: health clinic, personal/psychological counseling, women's center, veterans affairs office.

COSTS & FINANCIAL AID
Costs (2020–21) ***Comprehensive fee:*** $51,486 includes full-time tuition ($40,830), mandatory fees ($580), and room and board ($10,076). Full-time tuition and fees vary according to course load and degree level. Part-time tuition: $1596 per unit. Part-time tuition and fees vary according to course load and degree level. ***Required fees:*** $1596 per unit part-time. ***College room only:*** $6016. Room and board charges vary according to board plan and housing facility. ***Payment plan:*** installment. ***Waivers:*** employees or children of employees.

Financial Aid Of all full-time matriculated undergraduates who enrolled in 2018, 4,658 applied for aid, 3,544 were judged to have need, 1,040 had their need fully met. In 2018, 1017 non-need-based awards were made. ***Average percent of need met:*** 61. ***Average financial aid package:*** $24,723. ***Average need-based loan:*** $3612. ***Average need-based gift aid:*** $5535. ***Average non-need-based aid:*** $10,296. ***Average indebtedness upon graduation:*** $24,867.

APPLYING
Standardized Tests *Required:* SAT or ACT (for admission).

Options: electronic application, early action.

Application fee: $45.

Required: essay or personal statement, high school transcript, minimum 3.0 GPA, 1 letter of recommendation, SAT composite of 990 (writing excluded) or ACT composite 19. ***Required for some:*** interview.

Application deadlines: 6/1 (freshmen), 7/1 (transfers), 11/15 (early action).

Notification: continuous until 10/1 (freshmen), continuous (transfers), 1/15 (early action).

CONTACT
Emily Belsey, Associate Director of Data Operations, Azusa Pacific University, 901 East Alosta Avenue, PO Box 7000, Undergraduate Admissions, 7221, Azusa, CA 91702-7000. *Phone:* 626-8123016. *Toll-free phone:* 800-TALK-APU. *Fax:* 626-812-3096. *E-mail:* admissions@apu.edu.

Bergin University of Canine Studies

Rohnert Park, California

http://www.berginu.edu/

CONTACT
Bergin University of Canine Studies, 5860 Labath Avenue, Rohnert Park, CA 94928.

Bethesda University

Anaheim, California

http://www.buc.edu/

- **Independent** comprehensive, founded 1978, affiliated with Full Gospel World Mission
- **Suburban** campus with easy access to Los Angeles
- **Coed** 232 undergraduate students
- **Minimally difficult** entrance level, 95% of applicants were admitted

Freshmen:
Admission: 19 applied, 18 admitted.

ACADEMICS
Calendar: semesters. *Degrees:* certificates, bachelor's, master's, and doctoral.

Special study options: accelerated degree program, adult/continuing education programs, double majors, English as a second language, independent study, internships, part-time degree program, study abroad, summer session for credit.
Library: Library plus 1 other.

STUDENT LIFE
Housing options: college housing not available.

Campus security: student patrols, late-night transport/escort service, 24-hour security monitor.

Student services: personal/psychological counseling.

FINANCIAL AID
Financial Aid Of all full-time matriculated undergraduates who enrolled in 2010, 50 applied for aid, 45 were judged to have need, 30 had their need fully met. In 2010, 20 non-need-based awards were made. ***Average percent of need met:*** 80. ***Average financial aid package:*** $5000. ***Average need-based loan:*** $4000. ***Average need-based gift aid:*** $4000. ***Average non-need-based aid:*** $500. ***Average indebtedness upon graduation:*** $2500.

APPLYING
Options: early admission.

Application fee: $35.

Required: essay or personal statement, high school transcript, minimum 2.0 GPA, 2 letters of recommendation, interview, 2 photographs.

Notification: continuous until 8/25 (freshmen).

CONTACT
Bethesda University, 730 North Euclid Street, Anaheim, CA 92801. *Phone:* 714-517-1945.

Beverly Hills Design Institute

Beverly Hills, California

http://www.bhdi.edu/

CONTACT
Beverly Hills Design Institute, 8484 Wilshire Boulevard, Suite 730, Beverly Hills, CA 90211. *Phone:* 310-360-8888.

Biola University

La Mirada, California

http://www.biola.edu/

- **Independent interdenominational** university, founded 1908
- **Suburban** 95-acre campus with easy access to Los Angeles
- **Coed** 4,043 undergraduate students, 93% full-time, 63% women, 37% men
- **Moderately difficult** entrance level, 71% of applicants were admitted

UNDERGRAD STUDENTS

3,772 full-time, 271 part-time. 24% are from out of state; 3% Black or African American, non-Hispanic/Latino; 21% Hispanic/Latino; 15% Asian, non-Hispanic/Latino; 0.8% Native Hawaiian or other Pacific Islander, non-Hispanic/Latino; 0.2% American Indian or Alaska Native, non-Hispanic/Latino; 6% Two or more races, non-Hispanic/Latino; 4% Race/ethnicity unknown; 5% international; 7% transferred in; 63% live on campus.

Freshmen:

Admission: 4,149 applied, 2,927 admitted, 841 enrolled. ***Average high school GPA:*** 3.6. ***Test scores:*** SAT evidence-based reading and writing scores over 500: 91%; SAT math scores over 500: 88%; ACT scores over 18: 93%; SAT evidence-based reading and writing scores over 600: 54%; SAT math scores over 600: 47%; ACT scores over 24: 59%; SAT evidence-based reading and writing scores over 700: 12%; SAT math scores over 700: 12%; ACT scores over 30: 17%.

Retention: 83% of full-time freshmen returned.

FACULTY

Total: 525, 54% full-time, 46% with terminal degrees.

Student/faculty ratio: 14:1.

ACADEMICS

Calendar: 4-1-4. *Degrees:* diplomas, bachelor's, master's, doctoral, post-master's, and postbachelor's certificates.

Special study options: adult/continuing education programs, advanced placement credit, cooperative education, distance learning, double majors, English as a second language, honors programs, independent study, internships, off-campus study, part-time degree program, services for LD students, study abroad, summer session for credit. ***ROTC:*** Army (c), Air Force (c).

Unusual degree programs: 3-2 engineering.

Computers: Students can access the following: campus intranet, computer help desk, free student e-mail accounts, online (class) grades, online (class) registration, online (class) schedules. Campuswide network is available. 100% of college-owned or -operated housing units are wired for high-speed Internet access. Wireless service is available via entire campus.

Library: Biola University Library plus 1 other. *Books:* 550,000 (physical); *Databases:* 259. Weekly public service hours: 100; students can reserve study rooms.

STUDENT LIFE

Housing options: coed, men-only, women-only, special housing for students with disabilities. Campus housing is university owned. Freshman campus housing is guaranteed.

Activities and organizations: drama/theater group, student-run newspaper, radio and television station, choral group, Adventure Club, Guerilla Film Society, Biola Cross-Fit, Xopoc Dance Team, Lacrosse Club.

Athletics Member NCAA, NAIA. All NCAA Division II. ***Intercollegiate sports:*** baseball M(s), basketball M(s)/W(s), cross-country running M(s)/W(s), golf M(s)/W(s), soccer M(s)/W(s), softball W(s), swimming and diving M(s)/W(s), tennis M(s)/W(s), track and field M(s)/W(s), volleyball W(s). ***Intramural sports:*** archery M(c)/W(c), basketball M/W, bowling M/W, cheerleading W(c), football M/W, lacrosse M(c)/W(c), rugby M(c), soccer M/W, softball M/W, tennis M/W, ultimate Frisbee M/W, volleyball M(c)/W, water polo M(c)/W(c).

Campus security: 24-hour emergency response devices and patrols, late-night transport/escort service, controlled dormitory access.

Student services: health clinic, personal/psychological counseling, veterans affairs office.

COSTS & FINANCIAL AID

Costs (2020–21) ***Comprehensive fee:*** $65,004 includes full-time tuition ($41,976), mandatory fees ($11,514), and room and board ($11,514). Full-time tuition and fees vary according to course load and degree level. Part-time tuition: $1749 per credit hour. Part-time tuition and fees vary according to course load and degree level. ***Room and board:*** Room and board charges vary according to board plan and housing facility. ***Payment plan:*** installment. ***Waivers:*** employees or children of employees.

Financial Aid Of all full-time matriculated undergraduates who enrolled in 2018, 2,794 applied for aid, 2,507 were judged to have need, 219 had their need fully met. In 2018, 1142 non-need-based awards were made. ***Average percent of need met:*** 55. ***Average financial aid package:*** $25,339. ***Average need-based loan:*** $3129. ***Average need-based gift aid:*** $19,347. ***Average non-need-based aid:*** $11,917. ***Average indebtedness upon graduation:*** $36,330.

APPLYING

Standardized Tests *Required:* SAT or ACT (for admission).

Options: electronic application, early action, deferred entrance.

Application fee: $45.

Required: essay or personal statement, high school transcript. ***Required for some:*** interview. ***Recommended:*** minimum 3.0 GPA.

Application deadlines: 3/1 (freshmen), 3/1 (transfers), 1/15 (early action).

Notification: 4/1 (freshmen), 4/1 (out-of-state freshmen), 4/1 (transfers), 2/15 (early action).

CONTACT

Mrs. Michelle Reider, Associate Director of Undergraduate Freshman Admissions, Biola University, 13800 Biola Avenue, La Mirada, CA 90639. *Phone:* 562-903-4752. *Toll-free phone:* 800-652-4652. *E-mail:* admissions@biola.edu.

Brandman University

Irvine, California

http://www.brandman.edu/

- **Independent** comprehensive, founded 1958, part of Chapman University System
- **Suburban** 7-acre campus with easy access to Greater Los Angeles Area
- **Coed**
- 79% of applicants were admitted

FACULTY

Student/faculty ratio: 15:1.

ACADEMICS

Calendar: trimesters. *Degrees:* certificates, associate, bachelor's, master's, doctoral, post-master's, and postbachelor's certificates.

Library: Leatherby Library plus 1 other. *Books:* 300,000 (physical), 17,000 (digital/electronic); *Serial titles:* 265 (physical), 71,000 (digital/electronic); *Databases:* 300. Weekly public service hours: 65; study areas open 24 hours, 5–7 days a week; students can reserve study rooms.

STUDENT LIFE

Housing options: college housing not available.

Activities and organizations: Social Work Student Association, Society for Human Resource Management, Nursing Honor Society, Early Childhood Education Leadership, Pi Alpha Honor Society for Social Workers.

Campus security: late-night transport/escort service.

Student services: personal/psychological counseling, veterans affairs office.

APPLYING

Options: electronic application, deferred entrance.

Required: high school transcript, minimum 2.0 GPA. ***Required for some:*** essay or personal statement, 3 letters of recommendation, CPR certification, immunizations, professional liability insurance, RN licensure, and prerequisite coursework for RN-BSN program.

CONTACT
Andy LeCompte, Admissions Office, Brandman University, 16355 Laguna Canyon Drive, Irvine, CA 92618. *Phone:* 949-341-9839. *Toll-free phone:* 800-746-0082. *E-mail:* lecompte@brandman.edu.

California Baptist University

Riverside, California

http://www.calbaptist.edu/

- **Independent Southern Baptist** comprehensive, founded 1950
- **Suburban** 160-acre campus with easy access to Los Angeles
- **Endowment** $41.8 million
- **Coed** 8,190 undergraduate students, 90% full-time, 62% women, 38% men
- **Moderately difficult** entrance level, 78% of applicants were admitted

UNDERGRAD STUDENTS
7,333 full-time, 857 part-time. Students come from 47 states and territories; 31 other countries; 8% are from out of state; 6% Black or African American, non-Hispanic/Latino; 36% Hispanic/Latino; 6% Asian, non-Hispanic/Latino; 1% Native Hawaiian or other Pacific Islander, non-Hispanic/Latino; 0.6% American Indian or Alaska Native, non-Hispanic/Latino; 6% Two or more races, non-Hispanic/Latino; 3% Race/ethnicity unknown; 2% international; 12% transferred in; 42% live on campus.

Freshmen:
Admission: 8,241 applied, 6,451 admitted, 1,523 enrolled. ***Average high school GPA:*** 3.6. ***Test scores:*** SAT evidence-based reading and writing scores over 500: 76%; SAT math scores over 500: 71%; ACT scores over 18: 79%; SAT evidence-based reading and writing scores over 600: 26%; SAT math scores over 600: 22%; ACT scores over 24: 28%; SAT evidence-based reading and writing scores over 700: 3%; SAT math scores over 700: 3%; ACT scores over 30: 5%.

Retention: 77% of full-time freshmen returned.

FACULTY
Total: 857, 41% full-time, 55% with terminal degrees.

Student/faculty ratio: 15:1.

ACADEMICS
Calendar: 2-4-4-2. *Degrees:* associate, bachelor's, master's, and doctoral.

Special study options: academic remediation for entering students, accelerated degree program, adult/continuing education programs, advanced placement credit, distance learning, double majors, English as a second language, honors programs, internships, off-campus study, part-time degree program, services for LD students, study abroad, summer session for credit. ***ROTC:*** Army (b), Air Force (c).

Computers: 279 computers/terminals are available on campus for general student use. Students can access the following: campus intranet, computer help desk, free student e-mail accounts, online (class) grades, online (class) registration, online (class) schedules, online course evaluations. Campuswide network is available. 100% of college-owned or -operated housing units are wired for high-speed Internet access. Wireless service is available via entire campus.
Library: Annie Gabriel Library. *Books:* 126,845 (physical), 280,092 (digital/electronic); *Serial titles:* 15,127 (physical), 45,466 (digital/electronic); *Databases:* 105. Weekly public service hours: 101; students can reserve study rooms.

STUDENT LIFE
Housing options: on-campus residence required for freshman year; men-only, women-only. Campus housing is university owned. Freshman applicants given priority for college housing.

Activities and organizations: drama/theater group, student-run newspaper, choral group, International Service Projects, United States Service Projects, CBU Crazies (Campus Spirit), Summer of Service, Associated Students of California Baptist University (government and leadership).

Athletics Member NCAA. All Division I. ***Intercollegiate sports:*** baseball M(s), basketball M(s)/W(s), cheerleading W(s), cross-country running M(s)/W(s), golf M(s)/W(s), soccer M(s)/W(s), softball W(s), swimming and diving M(s)/W(s), track and field M(s)/W(s), volleyball W(s), water polo M(s)/W(s), wrestling M(s). ***Intramural sports:*** basketball M/W, football M/W, rock climbing M/W, sand volleyball M/W, soccer M/W, softball M/W, table tennis M/W, ultimate Frisbee M/W, volleyball M/W.

Campus security: 24-hour emergency response devices and patrols, late-night transport/escort service, controlled dormitory access.

Student services: health clinic, personal/psychological counseling, veterans affairs office.

COSTS & FINANCIAL AID
Costs (2020–21) ***One-time required fee:*** $310. ***Comprehensive fee:*** $48,940 includes full-time tuition ($33,930), mandatory fees ($2410), and room and board ($12,600). Full-time tuition and fees vary according to course load, location, and program. Part-time tuition: $1305 per unit. Part-time tuition and fees vary according to course load, location, and program. ***Required fees:*** $180 per term part-time. ***College room only:*** $6710. Room and board charges vary according to board plan and housing facility. ***Payment plan:*** installment. ***Waivers:*** employees or children of employees.

Financial Aid Of all full-time matriculated undergraduates who enrolled in 2019, 7,010 applied for aid, 6,574 were judged to have need, 1,092 had their need fully met. 366 Federal Work-Study jobs (averaging $2588). In 2019, 534 non-need-based awards were made. ***Average percent of need met:*** 33. ***Average financial aid package:*** $21,442. ***Average need-based loan:*** $4501. ***Average need-based gift aid:*** $11,198. ***Average non-need-based aid:*** $12,096. ***Average indebtedness upon graduation:*** $36,383.

APPLYING
Standardized Tests *Required:* SAT or ACT (for admission). *Recommended:* SAT and SAT Subject Tests or ACT (for admission).

Options: electronic application, early action, deferred entrance.

Application fee: $45.

Required: essay or personal statement, minimum 2.0 GPA. ***Required for some:*** high school transcript. ***Recommended:*** high school transcript.

Application deadlines: rolling (freshmen), rolling (transfers).

Notification: continuous (freshmen), continuous (transfers).

CONTACT
Mr. Bryce Burditt, Associate Director of Undergraduate Admissions, California Baptist University, 8432 Magnolia Avenue, Riverside, CA 92504-3297. *Phone:* 951-343-4476. *Toll-free phone:* 877-228-8866. *Fax:* 951-343-4525. *E-mail:* admissions@calbaptist.edu.

California Christian College

Fresno, California

http://www.calchristiancollege.edu/

- **Independent Free Will Baptist** 4-year
- **Urban** campus
- **Endowment** $166,018
- **Coed** 12 undergraduate students, 75% full-time, 25% women, 75% men
- **Noncompetitive** entrance level, 100% of applicants were admitted

UNDERGRAD STUDENTS
9 full-time, 3 part-time. Students come from 2 states and territories; 9% are from out of state; 18% Black or African American, non-Hispanic/Latino; 45% Hispanic/Latino; 18% Asian, non-Hispanic/Latino; 8% transferred in; 9% live on campus.

Freshmen:
Admission: 1 applied, 1 admitted, 1 enrolled.

Retention: 100% of full-time freshmen returned.

FACULTY
Total: 11, 18% full-time, 27% with terminal degrees.

Student/faculty ratio: 1:1.

ACADEMICS
Calendar: semesters. *Degrees:* associate and bachelor's.

Special study options: academic remediation for entering students, cooperative education, distance learning, independent study, part-time degree program.

Computers: 12 computers/terminals and 5 ports are available on campus for general student use. Students can access the following: free student e-mail accounts, online (class) grades. Campuswide network is available. 100% of college-owned or -operated housing units are wired for high-speed Internet access. Wireless service is available via entire campus.

Library: Cortese Library. *Books:* 17,572 (physical); *Serial titles:* 12 (physical). Weekly public service hours: 15.

STUDENT LIFE
Housing options: men-only, women-only. Campus housing is university owned.

Student services: personal/psychological counseling.

COSTS & FINANCIAL AID
Costs (2020–21) ***Comprehensive fee:*** $16,800 includes full-time tuition ($9360), mandatory fees ($690), and room and board ($6750). Part-time tuition: $390 per credit. ***College room only:*** $4950. ***Payment plan:*** installment.

Financial Aid Of all full-time matriculated undergraduates who enrolled in 2018, 7 applied for aid, 7 were judged to have need. 3 Federal Work-Study jobs (averaging $1658). ***Average percent of need met:*** 58. ***Average financial aid package:*** $11,433. ***Average need-based loan:*** $7395. ***Average need-based gift aid:*** $8610.

APPLYING
Standardized Tests *Required:* math and English exams (for admission). *Recommended:* SAT or ACT (for admission).

Options: electronic application.

Application fee: $40.

Required: essay or personal statement, high school transcript, minimum 2.0 GPA, 2 letters of recommendation, statement of faith, moral/ethical statement. ***Recommended:*** interview.

Application deadlines: rolling (freshmen), rolling (transfers).

Notification: continuous (freshmen), continuous (transfers).

CONTACT
Ms. Violet Douglas, Admissions Recruiter, California Christian College, 5364 E. Belmont Avenue, Fresno, CA 93727. *Phone:* 559-251-4215 Ext. 1002. *Fax:* 559-385-2329. *E-mail:* admissions@calchristiancollege.edu.

California Coast University

Santa Ana, California

http://www.calcoast.edu/

CONTACT
California Coast University, 925 North Spurgeon Street, Santa Ana, CA 92701. *Phone:* 714-547-9625. *Toll-free phone:* 888-CCU-UNIV.

California College of the Arts

San Francisco, California

http://www.cca.edu/

CONTACT
Mr. Arnold Icasiano, Director of Admissions, California College of the Arts, 1111 Eighth Street, San Francisco, CA 94107. *Phone:* 415-703-9523 Ext. 9532. *Toll-free phone:* 800-447-1ART. *Fax:* 415-703-9539. *E-mail:* enroll@cca.edu.

California College San Diego

National City, California

http://www.cc-sd.edu/

CONTACT
California College San Diego, 700 Bay Marina Drive, Suite 100, National City, CA 91950. *Toll-free phone:* 800-622-3188.

California College San Diego

San Diego, California

http://www.cc-sd.edu/

CONTACT
Tana Sanderson, Director of Admission, California College San Diego, 6602 Convoy Court, Suite 100, San Diego, CA 92111. *Phone:* 619-295-5785. *Toll-free phone:* 800-622-3188. *E-mail:* tana.sanderson@cc-sd.edu.

California College San Diego

San Marcos, California

http://www.cc-sd.edu/

CONTACT
California College San Diego, 277 Rancheros Drive, Suite 200, San Marcos, CA 92069. *Toll-free phone:* 800-622-3188.

California Institute of Integral Studies

San Francisco, California

http://www.ciis.edu/

- **Independent** upper-level, founded 1968
- **Urban** campus with easy access to San Francisco
- **Endowment** $1.9 million
- **Coed** 69 undergraduate students, 91% full-time, 74% women, 28% men
- **Minimally difficult** entrance level

UNDERGRAD STUDENTS
63 full-time, 7 part-time. Students come from 9 states and territories; 4 other countries; 16% are from out of state; 9% Black or African American, non-Hispanic/Latino; 17% Hispanic/Latino; 4% Asian, non-Hispanic/Latino; 7% Two or more races, non-Hispanic/Latino; 1% Race/ethnicity unknown; 1% international; 68% transferred in.

FACULTY
Total: 201, 29% full-time.

Student/faculty ratio: 11:1.

ACADEMICS
Calendar: semesters. *Degrees:* bachelor's, master's, doctoral, and postbachelor's certificates.

Special study options: accelerated degree program, adult/continuing education programs, distance learning, external degree program, independent study, summer session for credit.

Computers: 25 computers/terminals are available on campus for general student use. Students can access the following: campus intranet, free student e-mail accounts, online (class) grades, online (class) registration, online (class) schedules. Campuswide network is available. Wireless service is available via classrooms, libraries, student centers.
Library: The Laurance S. Rockefeller Library plus 1 other.

STUDENT LIFE
Housing options: college housing not available.

Activities and organizations: drama/theater group, Student Alliance, People of Color, Queer@CIIS, International Students and Friends, AWARE - Awaking to Whiteness and Racism Everywhere.

Student services: personal/psychological counseling, veterans affairs office.

COSTS & FINANCIAL AID
Costs (2019–20) ***Tuition:*** $20,500 full-time, $855 per unit part-time. ***Required fees:*** $480 full-time, $240 per term part-time. ***Payment plans:*** installment, deferred payment. ***Waivers:*** employees or children of employees.

Financial Aid Of all full-time matriculated undergraduates who enrolled in 2015, 86 applied for aid, 86 were judged to have need, 4 had their need fully met. 6 Federal Work-Study jobs (averaging $3208). ***Average percent of need met:*** 22. ***Average financial aid package:*** $18,625. ***Average need-based loan:*** $5799. ***Average need-based gift aid:*** $6193.

APPLYING
Options: electronic application.

Application fee: $65.

CONTACT
Admissions Counselor, California Institute of Integral Studies, 1453 Mission Street, San Francisco, CA 94103. *Phone:* 415-575-6156. *Fax:* 415-575-1268. *E-mail:* admissions@ciis.edu.

California Institute of Technology
Pasadena, California
http://www.caltech.edu/

- **Independent** university, founded 1891
- **Suburban** 124-acre campus with easy access to Los Angeles
- **Endowment** $2.9 billion
- **Coed**
- **Most difficult** entrance level

FACULTY
Student/faculty ratio: 3:1.

ACADEMICS
Calendar: quarters. *Degrees:* bachelor's, master's, doctoral, and post-master's certificates.
Library: Sherman Fairchild Library plus 5 others. *Books:* 276,995 (physical), 74,744 (digital/electronic); *Serial titles:* 6,183 (physical), 5,495 (digital/electronic); *Databases:* 197. Weekly public service hours: 168; study areas open 24 hours, 5–7 days a week; students can reserve study rooms.

STUDENT LIFE
Housing options: on-campus residence required for freshman year; coed, special housing for students with disabilities. Campus housing is university owned. Freshman campus housing is guaranteed.

Activities and organizations: drama/theater group, student-run newspaper, choral group, Instrumental music groups, Entrepreneur's Club, Glee Club, Theater Arts, Ultimate Disc Club.

Athletics Member NCAA. All Division III.

Campus security: 24-hour emergency response devices and patrols, late-night transport/escort service, controlled dormitory access.

Student services: health clinic, personal/psychological counseling, women's center.

COSTS & FINANCIAL AID
Costs (2019–20) ***One-time required fee:*** $500. ***Comprehensive fee:*** $71,244 includes full-time tuition ($52,506), mandatory fees ($2094), and room and board ($16,644). ***College room only:*** $9615.

Financial Aid Of all full-time matriculated undergraduates who enrolled in 2019, 562 applied for aid, 469 were judged to have need, 469 had their need fully met. 215 Federal Work-Study jobs (averaging $2985). 34 state and other part-time jobs (averaging $2448). In 2019, 1 non-need-based awards were made. ***Average percent of need met:*** 100. ***Average financial aid package:*** $53,090. ***Average need-based loan:*** $2874. ***Average need-based gift aid:*** $50,058. ***Average non-need-based aid:*** $5000. ***Average indebtedness upon graduation:*** $20,192.

APPLYING
Standardized Tests *Required:* SAT or ACT (for admission), SAT and SAT Subject Tests or ACT (for admission), SAT Subject Tests (for admission).

Options: electronic application, early admission, early action, deferred entrance.

Application fee: $75.

Required: essay or personal statement, high school transcript, 2 letters of recommendation.

CONTACT
Mr. Jarrid James Whitney, Executive Director of Admissions, California Institute of Technology, 383 South Hill Avenue, Mail Code 10-90, Pasadena, CA 91125. *Phone:* 626-395-6341. *Fax:* 626-683-3026.

California Institute of the Arts
Valencia, California
http://www.calarts.edu/

- **Independent** comprehensive, founded 1961
- **Suburban** 60-acre campus with easy access to Los Angeles
- **Endowment** $101.6 million
- **Coed** 1,021 undergraduate students, 99% full-time, 55% women, 45% men
- **Very difficult** entrance level, 25% of applicants were admitted

UNDERGRAD STUDENTS
1,011 full-time, 10 part-time. 42% are from out of state; 4% Black or African American, non-Hispanic/Latino; 13% Hispanic/Latino; 11% Asian, non-Hispanic/Latino; 0.1% Native Hawaiian or other Pacific Islander, non-Hispanic/Latino; 0.4% American Indian or Alaska Native, non-Hispanic/Latino; 6% Two or more races, non-Hispanic/Latino; 4% Race/ethnicity unknown; 21% international; 10% transferred in; 36% live on campus.

Freshmen:
Admission: 2,267 applied, 573 admitted, 216 enrolled.
Retention: 86% of full-time freshmen returned.

FACULTY
Total: 400, 42% full-time, 60% with terminal degrees.
Student/faculty ratio: 7:1.

ACADEMICS
Calendar: semesters. *Degrees:* certificates, bachelor's, master's, and doctoral.

Special study options: advanced placement credit, external degree program, independent study, internships, services for LD students, student-designed majors, study abroad, summer session for credit.

Computers: 42 computers/terminals and 1,000 ports are available on campus for general student use. Students can access the following: campus intranet, computer help desk, free student e-mail accounts, online (class) grades, online (class) registration, online (class) schedules. Campuswide network is available. 100% of college-owned or -operated housing units are wired for high-speed Internet access. Wireless service is available via libraries, student centers.
Library: Division of Library and Information Resources.

STUDENT LIFE
Housing options: coed, special housing for students with disabilities. Campus housing is university owned.

Activities and organizations: drama/theater group, student-run radio station, choral group, Student Council, FISK - Graphic Arts Club, Soccer Club, Korean Bible Study, Black Student Union.

Campus security: 24-hour emergency response devices and patrols, late-night transport/escort service, controlled dormitory access.

Student services: health clinic, personal/psychological counseling.

COSTS & FINANCIAL AID
Costs (2020–21) ***Comprehensive fee:*** $65,601 includes full-time tuition ($52,850), mandatory fees ($616), and room and board ($12,135). ***College room only:*** $7040.

Financial Aid Of all full-time matriculated undergraduates who enrolled in 2016, 637 applied for aid, 553 were judged to have need, 64 had their need fully met. 280 Federal Work-Study jobs (averaging $2188). In 2016, 78 non-need-based awards were made. ***Average percent of need met:*** 75. ***Average financial aid package:*** $35,000. ***Average need-based loan:*** $10,500. ***Average need-based gift aid:*** $17,500. ***Average non-need-based aid:*** $8800. ***Average indebtedness upon graduation:*** $31,293.

APPLYING
Options: electronic application.

Application fee: $70.

Required: essay or personal statement, high school transcript, 2 letters of recommendation, portfolio or audition. ***Required for some:*** 3 letters of recommendation, interview.

Application deadlines: 1/5 (freshmen), rolling (out-of-state freshmen), 1/5 (transfers).

Notification: continuous until 4/1 (freshmen), continuous until 4/1 (transfers).

CONTACT
Molly Ryan, Director of Admissions, California Institute of the Arts, 24700 McBean Parkway, Valencia, CA 91355-2340. *Phone:* 661-255-1050. *Toll-free phone:* 800-545-2787. *Fax:* 661-253-7710. *E-mail:* admiss@calarts.edu.

California Intercontinental University

Irvine, California

http://caluniversity.edu/

CONTACT

John Ramsay, Director of Admission, California Intercontinental University, 17310 Red Hill Avenue, #200, Irvine, CA 92614. *Phone:* 909-396-6090. *Toll-free phone:* 866-687-2258. *Fax:* 909-804-5151. *E-mail:* admissions@caluniversity.com.

California Jazz Conservatory

Berkeley, California

http://www.cjc.edu/

CONTACT

California Jazz Conservatory, 2087 Addison Street, Berkeley, CA 94704.

California Lutheran University

Thousand Oaks, California

http://www.callutheran.edu/

- **Independent Lutheran** comprehensive, founded 1959
- **Suburban** 290-acre campus with easy access to Los Angeles
- **Endowment** $112.0 million
- **Coed** 3,078 undergraduate students, 97% full-time, 56% women, 44% men
- **Moderately difficult** entrance level, 71% of applicants were admitted

UNDERGRAD STUDENTS

2,971 full-time, 107 part-time. Students come from 39 states and territories; 32 other countries; 11% are from out of state; 4% Black or African American, non-Hispanic/Latino; 37% Hispanic/Latino; 5% Asian, non-Hispanic/Latino; 0.5% Native Hawaiian or other Pacific Islander, non-Hispanic/Latino; 0.2% American Indian or Alaska Native, non-Hispanic/Latino; 7% Two or more races, non-Hispanic/Latino; 3% Race/ethnicity unknown; 3% international; 7% transferred in; 53% live on campus.

Freshmen:

Admission: 6,175 applied, 4,406 admitted, 647 enrolled. ***Average high school GPA:*** 3.8. ***Test scores:*** SAT evidence-based reading and writing scores over 500: 94%; SAT math scores over 500: 90%; ACT scores over 18: 96%; SAT evidence-based reading and writing scores over 600: 44%; SAT math scores over 600: 38%; ACT scores over 24: 56%; SAT evidence-based reading and writing scores over 700: 5%; SAT math scores over 700: 6%; ACT scores over 30: 9%.

Retention: 84% of full-time freshmen returned.

FACULTY

Total: 480, 41% full-time, 59% with terminal degrees.

Student/faculty ratio: 15:1.

ACADEMICS

Calendar: semesters. *Degrees:* certificates, bachelor's, master's, doctoral, post-master's, and postbachelor's certificates.

Special study options: accelerated degree program, adult/continuing education programs, advanced placement credit, cooperative education, double majors, honors programs, independent study, internships, off-campus study, part-time degree program, services for LD students, student-designed majors, study abroad, summer session for credit. ***ROTC:*** Army (c), Air Force (c).

Computers: 553 computers/terminals are available on campus for general student use. Students can access the following: campus intranet, computer help desk, free student e-mail accounts, online (class) grades, online (class) registration, online (class) schedules. Campuswide network is available. 100% of college-owned or -operated housing units are wired for high-speed Internet access. Wireless service is available via entire campus.

Library: Pearson Library. *Books:* 94,908 (physical), 276,800 (digital/electronic); *Serial titles:* 63 (physical), 71,300 (digital/electronic); *Databases:* 154. Weekly public service hours: 105; students can reserve study rooms.

STUDENT LIFE

Housing options: on-campus residence required through junior year; coed, special housing for students with disabilities. Campus housing is university owned. Freshman campus housing is guaranteed.

Activities and organizations: drama/theater group, student-run newspaper, radio and television station, choral group, Student Government, Recreation or Club Sports related, Service Organizations, Campus Ministry or other religiously affiliated organization, Multicultural Organizations.

Athletics Member NCAA. All Division III. ***Intercollegiate sports:*** baseball M, basketball M/W, cheerleading M/W, cross-country running M/W, football M, golf M/W, lacrosse W, soccer M/W, softball W, swimming and diving M/W, tennis M/W, track and field M/W, volleyball M/W, water polo M/W. ***Intramural sports:*** basketball M/W, equestrian sports M(c)/W(c), football M/W, golf M(c)/W(c), ice hockey M(c)/W(c), lacrosse M(c)/W(c), rugby M(c)/W(c), skiing (downhill) M(c)/W(c), soccer M/W, tennis M(c)/W(c), ultimate Frisbee M(c)/W(c), volleyball M/W, wrestling M(c)/W(c).

Campus security: 24-hour emergency response devices and patrols, late-night transport/escort service, controlled dormitory access, Escort and shuttle services.

Student services: health clinic, personal/psychological counseling, women's center, veterans affairs office.

COSTS & FINANCIAL AID

Costs (2020–21) ***Comprehensive fee:*** $60,577 includes full-time tuition ($45,500), mandatory fees ($482), and room and board ($14,595). Part-time tuition: $1470 per credit. ***College room only:*** $7890.

Financial Aid Of all full-time matriculated undergraduates who enrolled in 2017, 2,771 applied for aid, 2,065 were judged to have need, 452 had their need fully met. 260 Federal Work-Study jobs (averaging $2500). In 2017, 688 non-need-based awards were made. ***Average percent of need met:*** 79. ***Average financial aid package:*** $36,600. ***Average need-based loan:*** $4840. ***Average need-based gift aid:*** $27,600. ***Average non-need-based aid:*** $18,860. ***Average indebtedness upon graduation:*** $34,220.

APPLYING

Standardized Tests *Required:* SAT or ACT (for admission).

Options: electronic application, early action, deferred entrance.

Application fee: $25.

Required: essay or personal statement, high school transcript, minimum 2.8 GPA, 1 letter of recommendation. ***Recommended:*** minimum 3.0 GPA, interview.

Application deadlines: 1/1 (freshmen), 6/1 (transfers).

Notification: 4/1 (freshmen), continuous (transfers), 1/15 (early action).

CONTACT

Dr. Michael Elgarico, Dean of Undergraduate Enrollment, California Lutheran University, Office of Admission, #1350, Thousand Oaks, CA 91360. *Phone:* 805-493-3135. *Toll-free phone:* 877-258-3678. *Fax:* 805-493-3114. *E-mail:* cluadm@clunet.edu.

California Miramar University

San Diego, California

http://www.calmu.edu/

CONTACT

Jean Van Slyke, Director of Admissions, California Miramar University, 3550 Camino Del Rio North, Suite 208, San Diego, CA 92108. *Phone:* 858-653-3000. *Toll-free phone:* 877-570-5678. *Fax:* 858-653-6786. *E-mail:* admissions@calmu.edu.

California Polytechnic State University, San Luis Obispo

San Luis Obispo, California

http://www.calpoly.edu/

- **State-supported** comprehensive, founded 1901, part of California State University System
- **Suburban** 6000-acre campus
- **Coed** 20,454 undergraduate students, 96% full-time, 48% women, 52% men
- **Moderately difficult** entrance level, 28% of applicants were admitted

UNDERGRAD STUDENTS

19,635 full-time, 819 part-time. 15% are from out of state; 0.8% Black or African American, non-Hispanic/Latino; 18% Hispanic/Latino; 14% Asian, non-Hispanic/Latino; 0.2% Native Hawaiian or other Pacific Islander, non-Hispanic/Latino; 0.1% American Indian or Alaska Native, non-Hispanic/Latino; 8% Two or more races, non-Hispanic/Latino; 4% Race/ethnicity unknown; 2% international; 4% transferred in; 35% live on campus.

Freshmen:

Admission: 54,072 applied, 15,366 admitted, 4,613 enrolled. ***Average high school GPA:*** 4.0. ***Test scores:*** SAT evidence-based reading and writing scores over 500: 100%; SAT math scores over 500: 100%; ACT scores over 18: 100%; SAT evidence-based reading and writing scores over 600: 85%; SAT math scores over 600: 85%; ACT scores over 24: 90%; SAT evidence-based reading and writing scores over 700: 26%; SAT math scores over 700: 42%; ACT scores over 30: 49%.

Retention: 94% of full-time freshmen returned.

FACULTY

Total: 1,487, 66% full-time, 58% with terminal degrees.

Student/faculty ratio: 18:1.

ACADEMICS

Calendar: quarters. *Degrees:* bachelor's, master's, and postbachelor's certificates.

Special study options: academic remediation for entering students, advanced placement credit, cooperative education, distance learning, double majors, English as a second language, honors programs, internships, off-campus study, part-time degree program, services for LD students, study abroad, summer session for credit. ***ROTC:*** Army (b).

Computers: Students can access the following: campus intranet, free student e-mail accounts, online (class) grades, online (class) registration, online (class) schedules. Campuswide network is available. Wireless service is available via classrooms, computer centers, computer labs, dorm rooms, learning centers, libraries, student centers.

Library: Robert E. Kennedy Library.

STUDENT LIFE

Housing options: on-campus residence required for freshman year; coed, special housing for students with disabilities. Campus housing is university owned.

Activities and organizations: drama/theater group, student-run newspaper, radio and television station, choral group, marching band, national fraternities, national sororities.

Athletics Member NCAA. All Division I except football (Division I-AA). ***Intercollegiate sports:*** baseball M(s), basketball M(s)/W(s), bowling M(s)/W(s), cross-country running M(s)/W(s), golf M(s)/W(s)(c), soccer M(s)/W(s), softball W(s), swimming and diving M(s)/W(s), tennis M(s)/W(s), track and field M(s)/W(s), volleyball W(s), wrestling M(s). ***Intramural sports:*** badminton M/W, basketball M/W, football M, racquetball M/W, sand volleyball M/W, soccer M/W, softball M/W, table tennis M/W, tennis M/W, volleyball M/W.

Campus security: 24-hour emergency response devices and patrols, student patrols, late-night transport/escort service.

Student services: health clinic, personal/psychological counseling, women's center, legal services, veterans affairs office.

COSTS & FINANCIAL AID

Costs (2019–20) ***Tuition:*** state resident $5742 full-time, $3330 per year part-time; nonresident $19,632 full-time, $8082 per year part-time. Full-time tuition and fees vary according to course load, degree level, and program. Part-time tuition and fees vary according to course load, degree level, and program. ***Required fees:*** $4201 full-time, $3185 per year part-time. ***Room and board:*** $14,208; room only: $8719. Room and board charges vary according to board plan and housing facility. ***Payment plan:*** installment. ***Waivers:*** employees or children of employees.

Financial Aid Of all full-time matriculated undergraduates who enrolled in 2019, 12,356 applied for aid, 8,315 were judged to have need, 704 had their need fully met. In 2019, 2525 non-need-based awards were made. ***Average percent of need met:*** 55. ***Average financial aid package:*** $10,774. ***Average need-based loan:*** $4133. ***Average need-based gift aid:*** $3159. ***Average non-need-based aid:*** $1943. ***Average indebtedness upon graduation:*** $22,411.

APPLYING

Standardized Tests *Required:* SAT or ACT (for admission).

Options: electronic application.

Application fee: $55.

Required: high school transcript.

Application deadlines: 11/30 (freshmen), 11/30 (transfers).

Notification: 4/1 (freshmen), 4/1 (transfers).

CONTACT

Mr. James Maraviglia, Vice Provost for Enrollment Development and Chief Marketing Officer, California Polytechnic State University, San Luis Obispo, Admissions Office, 1 Grand Avenue, San Luis Obispo, CA 93407-0031. *Phone:* 805-756-2913. *Fax:* 805-756-5911. *E-mail:* admissions@calpoly.edu.

California State Polytechnic University, Pomona

Pomona, California

http://www.cpp.edu/

- **State-supported** comprehensive, founded 1938, part of California State University System
- **Urban** 1400-acre campus with easy access to Los Angeles
- **Endowment** $101.6 million
- **Coed** 26,455 undergraduate students, 89% full-time, 47% women, 53% men
- **Moderately difficult** entrance level, 55% of applicants were admitted

UNDERGRAD STUDENTS

23,597 full-time, 2,858 part-time. Students come from 39 states and territories; 103 other countries; 2% are from out of state; 3% Black or African American, non-Hispanic/Latino; 47% Hispanic/Latino; 22% Asian, non-Hispanic/Latino; 0.2% Native Hawaiian or other Pacific Islander, non-Hispanic/Latino; 0.1% American Indian or Alaska Native, non-Hispanic/Latino; 4% Two or more races, non-Hispanic/Latino; 3% Race/ethnicity unknown; 6% international; 13% transferred in; 10% live on campus.

Freshmen:

Admission: 39,726 applied, 21,687 admitted, 3,696 enrolled. ***Average high school GPA:*** 3.6. ***Test scores:*** SAT evidence-based reading and writing scores over 500: 81%; SAT math scores over 500: 82%; ACT scores over 18: 85%; SAT evidence-based reading and writing scores over 600: 36%; SAT math scores over 600: 39%; ACT scores over 24: 45%; SAT evidence-based reading and writing scores over 700: 5%; SAT math scores over 700: 12%; ACT scores over 30: 13%.

Retention: 89% of full-time freshmen returned.

FACULTY

Total: 1,452, 44% full-time, 53% with terminal degrees.

Student/faculty ratio: 24:1.

ACADEMICS

Calendar: quarters. *Degrees:* bachelor's, master's, and doctoral.

Special study options: academic remediation for entering students, adult/continuing education programs, advanced placement credit, cooperative education, distance learning, double majors, English as a second language, external degree program, freshman honors college, honors programs, internships, off-campus study, part-time degree program, services for LD students, study abroad, summer session for credit. ***ROTC:*** Army (b).

Computers: 2,117 computers/terminals and 3,588 ports are available on campus for general student use. Students can access the following: campus intranet, computer help desk, free student e-mail accounts, online (class) grades, online (class) schedules. Campuswide network is available. 100% of college-owned or -operated housing units are wired for high-speed Internet access. Wireless service is available via entire campus.
Library: University Library. *Books:* 517,449 (physical), 314,565 (digital/electronic); *Serial titles:* 14,240 (physical), 66,509 (digital/electronic); *Databases:* 197. Weekly public service hours: 92; study areas open 24 hours, 5–7 days a week; students can reserve study rooms.

STUDENT LIFE
Housing options: on-campus residence required for freshman year; coed, special housing for students with disabilities. Campus housing is university owned. Freshman applicants given priority for college housing.

Activities and organizations: drama/theater group, student-run newspaper, choral group, Rose Float Club, Mexican American Student Association (MASA), Barkada - Filipino American Student Association, American Marketing Association, Cal Poly Society of Accountants, national fraternities, national sororities.

Athletics Member NCAA. All Division II. ***Intercollegiate sports:*** baseball M(s), basketball M(s)/W(s), cross-country running M(s)/W(s), soccer M(s)/W(s), track and field M(s)/W(s), volleyball W(s). ***Intramural sports:*** basketball M/W, bowling M/W, football M/W, softball M/W, volleyball M/W.

Campus security: 24-hour emergency response devices and patrols, student patrols, late-night transport/escort service, controlled dormitory access, video camera surveillance.

Student services: health clinic, personal/psychological counseling, women's center, veterans affairs office.

COSTS & FINANCIAL AID
Costs (2020–21) ***Tuition:*** area resident $5742 full-time; state resident $5472 full-time; nonresident $17,622 full-time, $396 per credit hour part-time. ***Required fees:*** $1654 full-time. ***Room and board:*** $15,791; room only: $10,363. Room and board charges vary according to board plan and housing facility. ***Waivers:*** employees or children of employees.

Financial Aid Of all full-time matriculated undergraduates who enrolled in 2019, 17,142 applied for aid, 15,042 were judged to have need, 595 had their need fully met. In 2019, 17 non-need-based awards were made. ***Average percent of need met:*** 52. ***Average financial aid package:*** $10,629. ***Average need-based loan:*** $4483. ***Average need-based gift aid:*** $9847. ***Average non-need-based aid:*** $2197. ***Average indebtedness upon graduation:*** $21,730.

APPLYING
Standardized Tests *Required:* SAT or ACT (for admission).

Options: electronic application.

Application fee: $70.

Required: high school transcript, minimum 2.0 GPA.

Application deadlines: 12/1 (freshmen), 11/30 (transfers).

Notification: continuous (freshmen), 5/1 (transfers).

CONTACT
Mr. Brandon Tuck, Interim Executive Director, Admissions & Enrollment Planning, California State Polytechnic University, Pomona, 3801 W Temple Avenue, 121E, 2nd Floor, Pomona, CA 91768. *Phone:* 909-869-3310. *E-mail:* hbtuck@cpp.edu.

California State University, Bakersfield

Bakersfield, California

http://www.csub.edu/

- **State-supported** comprehensive, founded 1970, part of California State University System
- **Urban** 575-acre campus
- **Coed** 9,796 undergraduate students, 85% full-time, 62% women, 38% men
- 79% of applicants were admitted

UNDERGRAD STUDENTS
8,292 full-time, 1,504 part-time. 1% are from out of state; 5% Black or African American, non-Hispanic/Latino; 61% Hispanic/Latino; 6% Asian, non-Hispanic/Latino; 0.2% Native Hawaiian or other Pacific Islander, non-Hispanic/Latino; 0.5% American Indian or Alaska Native, non-Hispanic/Latino; 2% Two or more races, non-Hispanic/Latino; 8% Race/ethnicity unknown; 2% international; 12% transferred in; 4% live on campus.

Freshmen:
Admission: 10,931 applied, 8,661 admitted, 1,434 enrolled. ***Average high school GPA:*** 3.4. ***Test scores:*** SAT evidence-based reading and writing scores over 500: 47%; SAT math scores over 500: 52%; ACT scores over 18: 52%; SAT evidence-based reading and writing scores over 600: 9%; SAT math scores over 600: 9%; ACT scores over 24: 9%; SAT math scores over 700: 1%; ACT scores over 30: 1%.

Retention: 77% of full-time freshmen returned.

FACULTY
Total: 777, 40% full-time, 41% with terminal degrees.

Student/faculty ratio: 21:1.

ACADEMICS
Calendar: semesters. *Degrees:* bachelor's, master's, and doctoral.

Special study options: adult/continuing education programs, external degree program, part-time degree program.

Computers: Students can access the following: online (class) registration. Campuswide network is available.
Library: Walter W. Stiern Library.

STUDENT LIFE
Housing options: coed.

Athletics Member NCAA. All Division II except wrestling (Division I). ***Intercollegiate sports:*** basketball M(s), golf M(s), soccer M(s), softball W(s), swimming and diving M(s)/W(s), tennis W(s), track and field M(s)/W(s), volleyball W(s), water polo W(s), wrestling M(s). ***Intramural sports:*** archery M/W, badminton M/W, baseball M/W, basketball M/W, fencing M, field hockey W, football M/W, golf M/W, gymnastics M/W, racquetball M/W, riflery M/W, soccer M, softball M/W, swimming and diving M/W, tennis W, volleyball M/W, weight lifting M/W, wrestling M/W.

Campus security: 24-hour emergency response devices and patrols, late-night transport/escort service.

FINANCIAL AID
Financial Aid Of all full-time matriculated undergraduates who enrolled in 2019, 6,989 applied for aid, 6,632 were judged to have need, 94 had their need fully met. In 2019, 36 non-need-based awards were made. ***Average percent of need met:*** 58. ***Average financial aid package:*** $11,343. ***Average need-based loan:*** $4036. ***Average need-based gift aid:*** $9977. ***Average non-need-based aid:*** $1817. ***Average indebtedness upon graduation:*** $18,941.

APPLYING
Standardized Tests *Required for some:* SAT or ACT (for admission).

Options: electronic application.

Application fee: $70.

Required: high school transcript.

CONTACT
Debra Blowers, Assistant Director, Admissions and Evaluations, California State University, Bakersfield, 9001 Stockdale Highway, Balersfield, CA 93311-1099. *Phone:* 661-664-3036. *Toll-free phone:* 800-788-2782. *E-mail:* admissions@csub.edu.

California State University Channel Islands

Camarillo, California

http://www.csuci.edu/

CONTACT
Ms. Ginger Reyes, California State University Channel Islands, One University Drive, Camarillo, CA 93012. *Phone:* 805-437-8520. *Fax:* 805-437-8519. *E-mail:* prospective.student@csuci.edu.

California State University, Chico

Chico, California

http://www.csuchico.edu/

- **State-supported** comprehensive, founded 1887, part of California State University System
- **Small-town** 119-acre campus
- **Endowment** $64.7 million
- **Coed**
- **Moderately difficult** entrance level

FACULTY
Student/faculty ratio: 24:1.

ACADEMICS
Calendar: semesters. *Degrees:* certificates, bachelor's, master's, post-master's, and postbachelor's certificates.
Library: Meriam Library plus 1 other. *Books:* 544,345 (physical), 306,440 (digital/electronic); *Serial titles:* 72,555 (physical). Study areas open 24 hours, 5–7 days a week; students can reserve study rooms.

STUDENT LIFE
Housing options: coed, women only, special housing for students with disabilities. Campus housing is university owned. Freshman applicants given priority for college housing.

Activities and organizations: drama/theater group, student-run newspaper, radio station, choral group, Chico Snow Club, Chico State Nursing Club, Pre-Medical Association, Health Professionals Association, Exercise Physiology Majors Club, national fraternities, national sororities.

Athletics Member NCAA. All Division II except golf (Division I).

Campus security: 24-hour emergency response devices and patrols, student patrols, late-night transport/escort service, controlled dormitory access.

Student services: health clinic, personal/psychological counseling, women's center, legal services, veterans affairs office.

COSTS & FINANCIAL AID
Costs (2019–20) ***Tuition:*** area resident $7806 full-time, $5394 per term part-time; state resident $7806 full-time, $5394 per term part-time; nonresident $17,310 full-time, $10,146 per year part-time. Full-time tuition and fees vary according to degree level and program. Part-time tuition and fees vary according to course load, degree level, and program. ***Required fees:*** $15,612 full-time. ***Room and board:*** $13,422. Room and board charges vary according to board plan and housing facility. ***Payment plans:*** installment, deferred payment.

Financial Aid Of all full-time matriculated undergraduates who enrolled in 2016, 12,269 applied for aid, 10,577 were judged to have need, 1,606 had their need fully met. In 2016, 444 non-need-based awards were made. ***Average percent of need met:*** 74. ***Average financial aid package:*** $16,022. ***Average need-based loan:*** $4653. ***Average need-based gift aid:*** $10,134. ***Average non-need-based aid:*** $1429.

APPLYING
Standardized Tests *Required:* SAT or ACT (for admission).

Options: electronic application, deferred entrance.

Application fee: $55.

Required: high school transcript, GPA from 10th/11th grade college preparatory courses.

CONTACT
Kimberly Guanzon, Director, California State University, Chico, 400 West First Street, Chico, CA 95929-0722. *Phone:* 530-898-6322. *Toll-free phone:* 800-542-4426. *Fax:* 530-898-6456. *E-mail:* info@csuchico.edu.

California State University, Dominguez Hills

Carson, California

http://www.csudh.edu/

- **State-supported** comprehensive, founded 1960, part of California State University System
- **Urban** 350-acre campus with easy access to Los Angeles
- **Endowment** $11.0 million
- **Coed** 15,315 undergraduate students, 79% full-time, 62% women, 38% men
- **Moderately difficult** entrance level, 79% of applicants were admitted

UNDERGRAD STUDENTS
12,094 full-time, 3,221 part-time. Students come from 18 states and territories; 73 other countries; 11% Black or African American, non-Hispanic/Latino; 66% Hispanic/Latino; 7% Asian, non-Hispanic/Latino; 0.2% Native Hawaiian or other Pacific Islander, non-Hispanic/Latino; 0.1% American Indian or Alaska Native, non-Hispanic/Latino; 3% Two or more races, non-Hispanic/Latino; 3% Race/ethnicity unknown; 5% International; 23% transferred in; 4% live on campus.

Freshmen:
Admission: 20,351 applied, 16,066 admitted, 2,533 enrolled. ***Average high school GPA:*** 3.2. ***Test scores:*** SAT evidence-based reading and writing scores over 500: 38%; SAT math scores over 500: 33%; ACT scores over 18: 41%; SAT evidence-based reading and writing scores over 600: 5%; SAT math scores over 600: 4%; ACT scores over 24: 4%.

Retention: 77% of full-time freshmen returned.

FACULTY
Total: 1,086, 31% full-time, 49% with terminal degrees.

Student/faculty ratio: 29:1.

ACADEMICS
Calendar: semesters. *Degrees:* bachelor's, master's, doctoral, post-master's, and postbachelor's certificates.

Special study options: academic remediation for entering students, accelerated degree program, advanced placement credit, cooperative education, distance learning, double majors, external degree program, honors programs, independent study, off-campus study, part-time degree program, services for LD students, student-designed majors, study abroad, summer session for credit. ***ROTC:*** Army (b), Air Force (c).

Computers: 1,100 computers/terminals and 1,100 ports are available on campus for general student use. Students can access the following: campus intranet, computer help desk, free student e-mail accounts, online (class) grades, online (class) registration, online (class) schedules. Campuswide network is available. 100% of college-owned or -operated housing units are wired for high-speed Internet access. Wireless service is available via entire campus.
Library: Leo F. Cain Educational Resource Center. *Books:* 457,885 (physical), 300,523 (digital/electronic); *Serial titles:* 6,542 (physical), 75,366 (digital/electronic); *Databases:* 94. Weekly public service hours: 81; students can reserve study rooms.

STUDENT LIFE
Housing options: special housing for students with disabilities. Campus housing is university owned. Freshman applicants given priority for college housing.

Activities and organizations: drama/theater group, student-run newspaper, radio station, choral group, American Marketing Association, Phi Sigma Sigma, Organization of African Studies, Latino Student Business Association, Circle K, national fraternities, national sororities.

Athletics Member NCAA. All Division II. ***Intercollegiate sports:*** baseball M(s), basketball M(s)/W(s), golf M(s), soccer M(s)/W(s), softball W(s), track and field W(s), volleyball W(s). ***Intramural sports:*** basketball M/W, football M/W, soccer M/W, softball M/W, swimming and diving M/W, tennis M/W, volleyball M/W, weight lifting M/W.

Campus security: 24-hour emergency response devices and patrols, student patrols, late-night transport/escort service.

Student services: health clinic, personal/psychological counseling, women's center, veterans affairs office.

COSTS & FINANCIAL AID
Costs (2020–21) ***Tuition:*** state resident $6941 full-time, $4529 per term part-time; nonresident $16,445 full-time. ***Required fees:*** $1199 full-time, $1199 per term part-time. ***Room and board:*** $13,984. ***Waivers:*** senior citizens.

Financial Aid Of all full-time matriculated undergraduates who enrolled in 2018, 7,418 applied for aid, 7,180 were judged to have need, 92 had their need fully met. In 2018, 147 non-need-based awards were made. ***Average percent of need met:*** 31. ***Average financial aid package:*** $6204. ***Average need-based loan:*** $2357. ***Average need-based gift aid:*** $5277. ***Average non-need-based aid:*** $3772. ***Average indebtedness upon graduation:*** $14,585.

APPLYING
Standardized Tests *Required for some:* SAT or ACT (for admission).

Options: electronic application.

Application fee: $55.

Required: high school transcript.

Application deadlines: rolling (freshmen), rolling (transfers).

Notification: continuous (freshmen), continuous (transfers).

CONTACT
Information Center, California State University, Dominguez Hills, 1000 East Victoria Street, Carson, CA 90747-0001. *Phone:* 310-243-3696. *E-mail:* info@csudh.edu.

California State University, East Bay
Hayward, California
http://www.csueastbay.edu/

- **State-supported** comprehensive, founded 1957, part of California State University System
- **Suburban** 343-acre campus with easy access to San Francisco Bay Area
- **Coed**
- **Minimally difficult** entrance level

FACULTY
Student/faculty ratio: 22:1.

ACADEMICS
Calendar: quarters. *Degrees:* certificates, bachelor's, master's, doctoral, and postbachelor's certificates.
Library: Hayward Campus Library. *Books:* 630,855 (physical), 233,485 (digital/electronic); *Serial titles:* 10,905 (physical), 107,791 (digital/electronic); *Databases:* 133. Weekly public service hours: 101; students can reserve study rooms.

STUDENT LIFE
Housing options: coed, special housing for students with disabilities. Campus housing is university owned and leased by the school. Freshman applicants given priority for college housing.

Activities and organizations: drama/theater group, student-run newspaper, choral group, marching band, Tau Sigma Hour Society, East Bay Student Nursing Association, Golden Key Honor Society, Black Student Union, Sigma Sigma Sigma Society, national fraternities, national sororities.

Athletics Member NCAA, NAIA. All NCAA Division II.

Campus security: 24-hour emergency response devices and patrols, student patrols, late-night transport/escort service, controlled dormitory access.

Student services: health clinic, personal/psychological counseling, veterans affairs office.

FINANCIAL AID
Financial Aid Of all full-time matriculated undergraduates who enrolled in 2016, 7,847 applied for aid, 7,676 were judged to have need, 189 had their need fully met. ***Average percent of need met:*** 55. ***Average financial aid package:*** $10,778. ***Average need-based loan:*** $6352. ***Average need-based gift aid:*** $8545. ***Average indebtedness upon graduation:*** $19,149.

APPLYING
Standardized Tests *Required for some:* SAT or ACT (for admission).

Options: electronic application.

Application fee: $55.

Required: high school transcript, minimum 2.0 GPA, California State University eligibility index.

CONTACT
Dave Vasques, Associate Director for Admissions, California State University, East Bay, 25800 Carlos Bee Boulevard, Hayward, CA 94542-3000. *Phone:* 510-885-2029. *E-mail:* dave.vasquez@csueastbay.edu.

California State University, Fresno
Fresno, California
http://www.csufresno.edu/

- **State-supported** comprehensive, founded 1911, part of California State University System
- **Urban** 1399-acre campus
- **Coed** 21,462 undergraduate students, 88% full-time, 59% women, 41% men
- **Minimally difficult** entrance level, 58% of applicants were admitted

UNDERGRAD STUDENTS
18,838 full-time, 2,624 part-time. 0.7% are from out of state; 3% Black or African American, non-Hispanic/Latino; 55% Hispanic/Latino; 13% Asian, non-Hispanic/Latino; 0.2% Native Hawaiian or other Pacific Islander, non-Hispanic/Latino; 0.4% American Indian or Alaska Native, non-Hispanic/Latino; 3% Two or more races, non-Hispanic/Latino; 3% Race/ethnicity unknown; 5% international; 9% transferred in; 5% live on campus.

Freshmen:
Admission: 18,122 applied, 10,500 admitted, 3,060 enrolled. ***Test scores:*** SAT evidence-based reading and writing scores over 500: 62%; SAT math scores over 500: 63%; ACT scores over 18: 64%; SAT evidence-based reading and writing scores over 600: 17%; SAT math scores over 600: 15%; ACT scores over 24: 16%; SAT evidence-based reading and writing scores over 700: 1%; SAT math scores over 700: 2%; ACT scores over 30: 2%.

Retention: 83% of full-time freshmen returned.

FACULTY
Total: 1,377, 52% full-time.

Student/faculty ratio: 23:1.

ACADEMICS
Calendar: semesters. *Degrees:* bachelor's, master's, doctoral, post-master's, and postbachelor's certificates.

Special study options: academic remediation for entering students, accelerated degree program, adult/continuing education programs, advanced placement credit, cooperative education, distance learning, double majors, English as a second language, freshman honors college, honors programs, independent study, internships, off-campus study, part-time degree program, services for LD students, student-designed majors, study abroad, summer session for credit. ***ROTC:*** Army (b), Air Force (b).

Computers: Students can access the following: campus intranet, computer help desk, free student e-mail accounts, online (class) grades, online (class) registration, online (class) schedules. Campuswide network is available. Wireless service is available via classrooms, computer centers, computer labs, learning centers, libraries, student centers.
Library: Henry Madden Library.

STUDENT LIFE
Housing options: coed, men-only, women-only. Campus housing is university owned.

Activities and organizations: drama/theater group, student-run newspaper, radio station, choral group, marching band, national fraternities, national sororities.

Athletics Member NCAA. All Division I except football (Division I-A). ***Intercollegiate sports:*** baseball M(s), basketball M(s)/W(s), cross-country running M(s)/W(s), equestrian sports W(s), golf M(s)/W(s), lacrosse W(s), soccer W(s), softball W(s), swimming and diving W(s), tennis M(s)/W(s), track and field M(s)/W(s), volleyball W(s). ***Intramural sports:*** archery M/W, badminton M/W, baseball M, basketball M/W, bowling M/W, cross-country running M/W, equestrian sports W, fencing M/W, golf M/W, gymnastics M/W, racquetball M/W, tennis M/W, volleyball M/W.

Campus security: 24-hour emergency response devices and patrols, late-night transport/escort service, controlled dormitory access.

Student services: health clinic, personal/psychological counseling, women's center.

FINANCIAL AID
Financial Aid ***Average indebtedness upon graduation:*** $15,772.

APPLYING
Standardized Tests *Required:* SAT or ACT (for admission).

Options: electronic application.

Application fee: $70.

Required: high school transcript, minimum 2.0 GPA.

CONTACT
Mr. Andy Hernandez, Admissions Officer, California State University, Fresno, 5150 North Maple Avenue, M/S JA 57, Fresno, CA 93740-8026. *Phone:* 559-278-6115. *Fax:* 559-278-4812. *E-mail:* andyhe@csufresno.edu.

California State University, Fullerton

Fullerton, California

http://www.fullerton.edu/

- **State-supported** comprehensive, founded 1957, part of California State University System
- **Suburban** 236-acre campus with easy access to Los Angeles
- **Endowment** $52.6 million
- **Coed** 35,169 undergraduate students, 82% full-time, 57% women, 43% men
- **Moderately difficult** entrance level, 53% of applicants were admitted

UNDERGRAD STUDENTS
28,769 full-time, 6,400 part-time. 1% are from out of state; 2% Black or African American, non-Hispanic/Latino; 46% Hispanic/Latino; 21% Asian, non-Hispanic/Latino; 0.2% Native Hawaiian or other Pacific Islander, non-Hispanic/Latino; 0.1% American Indian or Alaska Native, non-Hispanic/Latino; 4% Two or more races, non-Hispanic/Latino; 3% Race/ethnicity unknown; 6% international; 12% transferred in; 2% live on campus.

Freshmen:
Admission: 50,105 applied, 26,398 admitted, 4,778 enrolled. ***Average high school GPA:*** 3.7. ***Test scores:*** SAT evidence-based reading and writing scores over 500: 83%; SAT math scores over 500: 84%; ACT scores over 18: 84%; SAT evidence-based reading and writing scores over 600: 29%; SAT math scores over 600: 29%; ACT scores over 24: 28%; SAT evidence-based reading and writing scores over 700: 2%; SAT math scores over 700: 4%; ACT scores over 30: 3%.

Retention: 89% of full-time freshmen returned.

FACULTY
Total: 2,115, 48% full-time, 59% with terminal degrees.

Student/faculty ratio: 25:1.

ACADEMICS
Calendar: semesters. *Degrees:* bachelor's, master's, doctoral, post-master's, and postbachelor's certificates.

Special study options: academic remediation for entering students, adult/continuing education programs, advanced placement credit, cooperative education, distance learning, double majors, honors programs, internships, off-campus study, part-time degree program, services for LD students, study abroad, summer session for credit. ***ROTC:*** Army (b).

Computers: 2,000 computers/terminals are available on campus for general student use. Students can access the following: campus intranet, computer help desk, free student e-mail accounts, online (class) grades, online (class) registration, online (class) schedules. Campuswide network is available. Wireless service is available via entire campus.
Library: Pollak Library.

STUDENT LIFE
Housing options: coed, men-only, women-only. Campus housing is university owned. Freshman applicants given priority for college housing.

Activities and organizations: drama/theater group, student-run newspaper, radio station, choral group, Pan-Hellenic Council, American Marketing Association, Lacrosse Club, Samaritans (volunteer service club), Human Services Student Association, national fraternities, national sororities.

Athletics Member NCAA. All Division I. ***Intercollegiate sports:*** archery M(c)/W(c), baseball M(s), basketball M(s)/W(s), bowling M(c)/W(c), cross-country running M(s)/W(s), equestrian sports M(c)/W(c), golf M(s)/W(s)(c), ice hockey M(c)/W(c), lacrosse M(c)/W(c), rugby M(c)/W(c), sailing M(c)/W(c), skiing (downhill) W(c), soccer M(s)/W(s), softball W(s), tennis W(s), track and field M(s)/W(s), ultimate Frisbee M(c)/W(c), volleyball M(c)/W(s), water polo M(c)/W(c). ***Intramural sports:*** badminton M/W, basketball M/W, bowling M/W, football M/W, racquetball M/W, soccer M/W, softball M/W, volleyball M/W.

Campus security: 24-hour emergency response devices and patrols, student patrols, late-night transport/escort service, controlled dormitory access.

Student services: health clinic, personal/psychological counseling, women's center, legal services.

COSTS & FINANCIAL AID
Costs (2020–21) ***Tuition:*** area resident $6927 full-time; state resident $6927 full-time; nonresident $16,431 full-time, $396 per credit hour part-time. ***Required fees:*** $1181 full-time.

Financial Aid Of all full-time matriculated undergraduates who enrolled in 2018, 21,570 applied for aid, 19,443 were judged to have need, 2,346 had their need fully met. In 2018, 846 non-need-based awards were made. ***Average percent of need met:*** 65. ***Average financial aid package:*** $10,485. ***Average need-based loan:*** $4057. ***Average need-based gift aid:*** $9299. ***Average non-need-based aid:*** $1562. ***Average indebtedness upon graduation:*** $7665.

APPLYING
Standardized Tests *Required:* SAT or ACT (for admission).

Options: electronic application.

Application fee: $70.

Application deadlines: 12/15 (freshmen), 11/30 (transfers).

Notification: continuous (freshmen), continuous (transfers).

CONTACT
Ms. Nancy J. Dority, Assistant Vice President of Enrollment Services, California State University, Fullerton, Office of Admissions and Records, PO Box 34080, Fullerton, CA 92834-9480. *Phone:* 657-278-3100. *Fax:* 657-278-7699. *E-mail:* admissions@fullerton.edu.

California State University, Long Beach

Long Beach, California

http://www.csulb.edu/

- **State-supported** comprehensive, founded 1949, part of California State University System
- **Suburban** 320-acre campus with easy access to Los Angeles
- **Endowment** $77.2 million
- **Coed** 32,784 undergraduate students, 87% full-time, 57% women, 43% men
- **Moderately difficult** entrance level, 39% of applicants were admitted

UNDERGRAD STUDENTS
28,584 full-time, 4,200 part-time. 4% Black or African American, non-Hispanic/Latino; 45% Hispanic/Latino; 21% Asian, non-Hispanic/Latino; 0.3% Native Hawaiian or other Pacific Islander, non-Hispanic/Latino; 0.1% American Indian or Alaska Native, non-Hispanic/Latino; 5% Two or more races, non-Hispanic/Latino; 3% Race/ethnicity unknown; 5% international; 15% transferred in; 8% live on campus.

Freshmen:
Admission: 71,297 applied, 28,019 admitted, 5,161 enrolled. ***Average high school GPA:*** 3.6. ***Test scores:*** SAT evidence-based reading and writing scores over 500: 83%; SAT math scores over 500: 82%; ACT scores over 18: 89%; SAT evidence-based reading and writing scores over 600: 37%; SAT math scores over 600: 39%; ACT scores over 24: 47%; SAT evidence-based reading and writing scores over 700: 4%; SAT math scores over 700: 8%; ACT scores over 30: 8%.

Retention: 87% of full-time freshmen returned.

FACULTY
Total: 2,372, 44% full-time, 59% with terminal degrees.

ACADEMICS
Calendar: semesters. *Degrees:* bachelor's, master's, doctoral, and postbachelor's certificates.

Special study options: adult/continuing education programs, double majors, English as a second language, honors programs, independent study, internships, part-time degree program, student-designed majors, study abroad.

Computers: 2,000 computers/terminals are available on campus for general student use. Students can access the following: campus intranet, computer help desk, free student e-mail accounts, online (class) grades, online (class) registration, online (class) schedules. Campuswide network is available. Wireless service is available via entire campus.
Library: CSULB University Library. *Books:* 681,649 (physical), 1.0 million (digital/electronic); *Serial titles:* 16,851 (physical), 105,038 (digital/electronic); *Databases:* 227. Weekly public service hours: 97.

STUDENT LIFE
Housing options: coed.

Activities and organizations: national fraternities, national sororities.

Athletics Member NCAA. All Division I. ***Intercollegiate sports:*** archery M(c)/W(c), baseball M(s), basketball M(s)/W(s), bowling M(c)/W(c), cheerleading M(c)/W(c), crew M(c)/W(c), cross-country running M(s)/W(s), golf M(s)/W(s)(c), rugby M(c)/W(c), sailing M(c)/W(c), sand volleyball W(s), skiing (downhill) W(c), soccer M/W(s), softball W(s), tennis W(s), track and field M(s)/W(s), triathlon M(c)/W(c), ultimate Frisbee M(c)/W(c), volleyball M(s)/W(s), water polo M(s)/W(s), weight lifting M(c)/W(c), wrestling M(c)/W(c). ***Intramural sports:*** basketball M/W, cheerleading M/W, racquetball M/W, sand volleyball W, softball W, tennis W.

Campus security: 24-hour emergency response devices and patrols, student patrols, late-night transport/escort service, controlled dormitory access.

Student services: health clinic, personal/psychological counseling, women's center, legal services.

COSTS & FINANCIAL AID
Costs (2020–21) ***Tuition:*** area resident $5742 full-time; state resident $5742 full-time; nonresident $16,038 full-time. Full-time tuition and fees vary according to course level, course load, degree level, and program. Part-time tuition and fees vary according to course level, course load, degree level, and program. ***Required fees:*** $1104 full-time. ***Room and board:*** $13,070; room only: $8360. Room and board charges vary according to board plan. ***Payment plan:*** installment. ***Waivers:*** senior citizens and employees or children of employees.

Financial Aid Of all full-time matriculated undergraduates who enrolled in 2019, 24,796 applied for aid, 22,436 were judged to have need, 9,955 had their need fully met. ***Average percent of need met:*** 76. ***Average financial aid package:*** $14,185. ***Average need-based loan:*** $4106. ***Average need-based gift aid:*** $8641. ***Average indebtedness upon graduation:*** $18,686.

APPLYING
Standardized Tests *Required:* SAT or ACT (for admission). *Recommended:* ACT (for admission).

Options: electronic application.

Application fee: $55.

Required: high school transcript. ***Required for some:*** minimum 3.0 GPA.

Notification: continuous (freshmen), continuous (transfers).

CONTACT
Mrs. Janice Miller, Director, Admin Ops and Policy, ES Admissions, California State University, Long Beach, Brotman Hall, 1250 Bellflower Boulevard, Long Beach, CA 90840. *Phone:* 562-985-7827. *E-mail:* janice.miller@csulb.edu.

California State University, Los Angeles

Los Angeles, California

http://www.calstatela.edu/

- **State-supported** comprehensive, founded 1947, part of California State University System
- **Urban** 175-acre campus with easy access to Los Angeles
- **Endowment** $42.5 million
- **Coed** 22,626 undergraduate students, 87% full-time, 58% women, 42% men
- **Moderately difficult** entrance level, 48% of applicants were admitted

UNDERGRAD STUDENTS
19,609 full-time, 3,017 part-time. 0.5% are from out of state; 3% Black or African American, non-Hispanic/Latino; 70% Hispanic/Latino; 12% Asian, non-Hispanic/Latino; 0.1% Native Hawaiian or other Pacific Islander, non-Hispanic/Latino; 0.1% American Indian or Alaska Native, non-Hispanic/Latino; 1% Two or more races, non-Hispanic/Latino; 2% Race/ethnicity unknown; 6% international; 13% transferred in; 10% live on campus.

Freshmen:
Admission: 33,641 applied, 16,084 admitted, 3,292 enrolled. ***Average high school GPA:*** 3.3. ***Test scores:*** SAT evidence-based reading and writing scores over 500: 49%; SAT math scores over 500: 50%; ACT scores over 18: 49%; SAT evidence-based reading and writing scores over 600: 9%; SAT math scores over 600: 9%; ACT scores over 24: 8%; SAT math scores over 700: 1%; ACT scores over 30: 1%.

Retention: 81% of full-time freshmen returned.

FACULTY
Total: 1,745, 37% full-time, 49% with terminal degrees.

Student/faculty ratio: 23:1.

ACADEMICS
Calendar: quarters. *Degrees:* certificates, bachelor's, master's, doctoral, post-master's, and postbachelor's certificates.

Special study options: academic remediation for entering students, accelerated degree program, adult/continuing education programs, advanced placement credit, cooperative education, distance learning, double majors, English as a second language, freshman honors college, honors programs, independent study, internships, off-campus study, part-time degree program, services for LD students, student-designed majors, study abroad, summer session for credit. ***ROTC:*** Army (c), Air Force (c).

Unusual degree programs: 3-2 nursing.

Computers: 1,500 computers/terminals are available on campus for general student use. Students can access the following: campus intranet, computer help desk, free student e-mail accounts, online (class) grades, online (class) registration, online (class) schedules. Campuswide network is available. 100% of college-owned or -operated housing units are wired for high-speed Internet access. Wireless service is available via entire campus.
Library: John F. Kennedy Memorial Library. *Books:* 537,271 (physical), 86,220 (digital/electronic); *Serial titles:* 7,843 (physical), 83,822 (digital/electronic); *Databases:* 230. Weekly public service hours: 99.

STUDENT LIFE
Housing options: special housing for students with disabilities. Campus housing is university owned.

Activities and organizations: drama/theater group, student-run newspaper, radio and television station, choral group, Phi Alpha Theta History Honor Society, National Student Speech Language, Student Dietetic Association, Film Productions, Child Development Association, national fraternities, national sororities.

Athletics Member NCAA. All Division II. ***Intercollegiate sports:*** baseball M(s), basketball M(s)/W(s), cheerleading M(c)/W(c), cross-country running M(s)/W(s), golf W(s), sand volleyball W(s), soccer M(s)/W(s), tennis W(s), track and field M(s)/W(s), volleyball W(s). ***Intramural sports:*** basketball M/W, bowling M/W, football M/W, gymnastics M/W, racquetball M/W, skiing (cross-country) M/W, soccer M/W, softball M/W, swimming and diving M/W, volleyball M/W, water polo M/W, wrestling M.

Campus security: 24-hour emergency response devices and patrols, student patrols, late-night transport/escort service, controlled dormitory access.

Student services: health clinic, personal/psychological counseling, women's center, legal services, veterans affairs office.

COSTS & FINANCIAL AID

Costs (2020–21) ***Tuition:*** area resident $5742 full-time; state resident $5742 full-time; nonresident $17,622 full-time, $396 per unit part-time. Full-time tuition and fees vary according to course load, degree level, and program. Part-time tuition and fees vary according to course load, degree level, and program. ***Required fees:*** $1026 full-time, $1026 per year part-time. ***Room and board:*** $15,992; room only: $11,859. Room and board charges vary according to board plan, housing facility, and location. ***Payment plans:*** installment, deferred payment. ***Waivers:*** employees or children of employees.

Financial Aid Of all full-time matriculated undergraduates who enrolled in 2019, 18,084 applied for aid, 17,471 were judged to have need, 667 had their need fully met. In 2019, 17 non-need-based awards were made. ***Average percent of need met:*** 64. ***Average financial aid package:*** $12,384. ***Average need-based loan:*** $4390. ***Average need-based gift aid:*** $10,875. ***Average non-need-based aid:*** $6661. ***Average indebtedness upon graduation:*** $13,458.

APPLYING

Standardized Tests *Required:* SAT or ACT (for admission).

Options: electronic application, early admission.

Application fee: $55.

Required: high school transcript.

Application deadlines: 11/30 (freshmen), 11/30 (out-of-state freshmen), 11/30 (transfers).

Early decision deadline: 11/30 (for plan 1), 11/30 (for plan 2).

Notification: 8/30 (freshmen), 4/1 (out-of-state freshmen), 8/30 (transfers).

CONTACT

Vince Lopez, Director of Outreach and Recruitment, California State University, Los Angeles, 5151 State University Drive, Los Angeles, CA 90032-8530. *Phone:* 323-343-3839. *E-mail:* admission@calstatela.edu.

California State University Maritime Academy

Vallejo, California

http://www.csum.edu/

- **State-supported** comprehensive, founded 1929, part of California State University System
- **Suburban** 64-acre campus with easy access to San Francisco
- **Coed**
- **Moderately difficult** entrance level

FACULTY

Student/faculty ratio: 14:1.

ACADEMICS

Calendar: semesters. *Degrees:* bachelor's and master's.

STUDENT LIFE

Housing options: on-campus residence required through senior year; coed. Campus housing is university owned. Freshman campus housing is guaranteed.

Activities and organizations: student-run newspaper, choral group, Sailing Club, Dive Club, drill team.

Athletics Member NAIA.

Campus security: 24-hour patrols, student patrols.

Student services: health clinic, personal/psychological counseling.

FINANCIAL AID

Financial Aid Of all full-time matriculated undergraduates who enrolled in 2019, 652 applied for aid, 454 were judged to have need, 17 had their need fully met. In 2019, 23 non-need-based awards were made. ***Average financial aid package:*** $12,576. ***Average need-based loan:*** $4155. ***Average need-based gift aid:*** $9592. ***Average non-need-based aid:*** $1169. ***Average indebtedness upon graduation:*** $30,292.

APPLYING

Standardized Tests *Required:* SAT or ACT (for admission).

Options: electronic application, early action.

Application fee: $55.

Required: high school transcript, minimum 2.0 GPA, health form.

CONTACT

California State University Maritime Academy, 200 Maritime Academy Drive, Vallejo, CA 94590. *Phone:* 707-654-1330. *Toll-free phone:* 800-561-1945.

California State University, Monterey Bay

Seaside, California

http://www.csumb.edu/

- **State-supported** comprehensive, founded 1994, part of California State University System
- **Small-town** 1387-acre campus with easy access to San Jose
- **Coed** 6,799 undergraduate students, 89% full-time, 61% women, 39% men
- **Moderately difficult** entrance level, 75% of applicants were admitted

UNDERGRAD STUDENTS

6,052 full-time, 742 part-time. 2% are from out of state; 4% Black or African American, non-Hispanic/Latino; 42% Hispanic/Latino; 6% Asian, non-Hispanic/Latino; 0.8% Native Hawaiian or other Pacific Islander, non-Hispanic/Latino; 0.7% American Indian or Alaska Native, non-Hispanic/Latino; 8% Two or more races, non-Hispanic/Latino; 5% Race/ethnicity unknown; 6% international; 16% transferred in.

Freshmen:

Admission: 12,316 applied, 9,272 admitted, 1,045 enrolled. ***Test scores:*** SAT evidence-based reading and writing scores over 500: 70%; SAT math scores over 500: 66%; ACT scores over 18: 68%; SAT evidence-based reading and writing scores over 600: 25%; SAT math scores over 600: 16%; ACT scores over 24: 21%; SAT evidence-based reading and writing scores over 700: 2%; SAT math scores over 700: 2%; ACT scores over 30: 4%.

Retention: 80% of full-time freshmen returned.

FACULTY

Total: 516, 36% full-time, 50% with terminal degrees.

Student/faculty ratio: 25:1.

ACADEMICS

Calendar: semesters. *Degrees:* bachelor's, master's, and postbachelor's certificates.

Special study options: academic remediation for entering students, accelerated degree program, advanced placement credit, cooperative education, distance learning, double majors, external degree program, independent study, internships, off-campus study, part-time degree program, services for LD students, student-designed majors, study abroad, summer session for credit. ***ROTC:*** Air Force (c).

Computers: Students can access the following: campus intranet, computer help desk, free student e-mail accounts, online (class) grades, online (class) registration, online (class) schedules. Campuswide network is available. 100% of college-owned or -operated housing units are wired for high-speed Internet access. Wireless service is available via entire campus.

Library: The Tanimura & Antle Family Memorial Library.

STUDENT LIFE

Housing options: on-campus residence required through sophomore year; coed, special housing for students with disabilities. Campus housing is university owned. Freshman applicants given priority for college housing.

Activities and organizations: drama/theater group, student-run newspaper, radio and television station, national fraternities, national sororities.

Athletics Member NCAA. All Division II. ***Intercollegiate sports:*** baseball M(s), basketball M(s)/W(s), cross-country running M(s)/W(s), golf M(s), sailing M/W, soccer M(s)/W(s), softball W(s), volleyball W(s), water polo W(s). ***Intramural sports:*** basketball M/W, football M, soccer M/W, softball M/W, ultimate Frisbee M/W, volleyball M/W.

Campus security: 24-hour emergency response devices and patrols, student patrols, late-night transport/escort service, controlled dormitory access.

Student services: health clinic, personal/psychological counseling, women's center.

COSTS & FINANCIAL AID

Costs (2020–21) ***Tuition:*** area resident $5742 full-time; state resident $5742 full-time; nonresident $17,622 full-time, $396 per credit hour part-time. ***Required fees:*** $1401 full-time. ***Room and board:*** $13,711.

Financial Aid ***Average indebtedness upon graduation:*** $19,962. ***Financial aid deadline:*** 8/30.

APPLYING

Standardized Tests *Required:* SAT or ACT (for admission).

Options: electronic application.

Application fee: $70.

Required: high school transcript, minimum 2.0 GPA.

CONTACT

California State University, Monterey Bay, 100 Campus Center, Seaside, CA 93955-8001.

California State University, Northridge

Northridge, California

http://www.csun.edu/

- **State-supported** comprehensive, founded 1958, part of California State University System
- **Urban** 356-acre campus with easy access to Los Angeles
- **Coed** 34,633 undergraduate students, 85% full-time, 55% women, 45% men
- **Moderately difficult** entrance level, 59% of applicants were admitted

UNDERGRAD STUDENTS

29,275 full-time, 5,358 part-time. 3% are from out of state; 5% Black or African American, non-Hispanic/Latino; 52% Hispanic/Latino; 9% Asian, non-Hispanic/Latino; 0.1% Native Hawaiian or other Pacific Islander, non-Hispanic/Latino; 0.1% American Indian or Alaska Native, non-Hispanic/Latino; 3% Two or more races, non-Hispanic/Latino; 3% Race/ethnicity unknown; 7% international; 17% transferred in.

Freshmen:

Admission: 30,637 applied, 18,180 admitted, 4,792 enrolled. ***Average high school GPA:*** 3.4. ***Test scores:*** SAT evidence-based reading and writing scores over 500: 58%; SAT math scores over 500: 58%; SAT evidence-based reading and writing scores over 600: 16%; SAT math scores over 600: 14%; SAT evidence-based reading and writing scores over 700: 1%; SAT math scores over 700: 2%.

Retention: 80% of full-time freshmen returned.

FACULTY

Total: 2,093, 43% full-time.

Student/faculty ratio: 27:1.

ACADEMICS

Calendar: semesters. *Degrees:* bachelor's, master's, and doctoral.

Special study options: academic remediation for entering students, adult/continuing education programs, advanced placement credit, distance learning, double majors, English as a second language, independent study, internships, off-campus study, part-time degree program, services for LD students, student-designed majors, study abroad, summer session for credit. ***ROTC:*** Army (c), Air Force (c).

Computers: Students can access the following: online (class) registration. Campuswide network is available.

Library: Oviatt Library plus 1 other. Students can reserve study rooms.

STUDENT LIFE

Activities and organizations: drama/theater group, student-run newspaper, radio station, choral group, national fraternities, national sororities.

Athletics Member NCAA. All Division I except football (Division II). ***Intercollegiate sports:*** baseball M(s), basketball M(s)/W(s), cross-country running M(s)/W(s), football M(s), golf M(s), soccer M(s), softball W(s), swimming and diving M(s)/W(s), tennis W(s), track and field M(s)/W(s), volleyball M(s)/W(s). ***Intramural sports:*** baseball M, basketball M/W, bowling M(c)/W(c), cross-country running M/W, football M/W, golf M, ice hockey M(c), racquetball M/W, rugby M(c), sailing M(c)/W(c), skiing (downhill) M(c)/W(c), soccer M/W, softball W, swimming and diving M/W, table tennis M(c)/W(c), tennis W, track and field M/W, volleyball M/W.

Campus security: 24-hour emergency response devices, late-night transport/escort service.

Student services: health clinic, personal/psychological counseling, women's center.

COSTS & FINANCIAL AID

Costs (2019–20) ***Tuition:*** state resident $6972 full-time; nonresident $12,516 full-time, $396 per unit part-time. ***Required fees:*** $1582 full-time. ***Room and board:*** $16,188. Room and board charges vary according to board plan and housing facility. ***Payment plan:*** installment. ***Waivers:*** senior citizens and employees or children of employees.

Financial Aid Of all full-time matriculated undergraduates who enrolled in 2018, 24,428 applied for aid, 23,670 were judged to have need. In 2018, 5202 non-need-based awards were made. ***Average financial aid package:*** $19,235. ***Average need-based loan:*** $6033. ***Average need-based gift aid:*** $17,316. ***Average non-need-based aid:*** $2570.

APPLYING

Standardized Tests *Required:* SAT or ACT (for admission).

Options: electronic application.

Application fee: $55.

Required: high school transcript.

Notification: continuous (freshmen), continuous (transfers).

CONTACT

California State University, Northridge, 18111 Nordhoff Street, Northridge, CA 91330. *Phone:* 818-677-3700.

California State University, Sacramento

Sacramento, California

http://www.csus.edu/

- **State-supported** comprehensive, founded 1947, part of California State University System
- **Urban** 300-acre campus
- **Coed** 28,251 undergraduate students, 85% full-time, 55% women, 45% men
- **Moderately difficult** entrance level, 82% of applicants were admitted

UNDERGRAD STUDENTS

23,907 full-time, 4,344 part-time. 0.8% are from out of state; 6% Black or African American, non-Hispanic/Latino; 34% Hispanic/Latino; 19% Asian, non-Hispanic/Latino; 0.9% Native Hawaiian or other Pacific Islander, non-Hispanic/Latino; 0.2% American Indian or Alaska Native, non-Hispanic/Latino; 6% Two or more races, non-Hispanic/Latino; 5% Race/ethnicity unknown; 3% international; 14% transferred in; 7% live on campus.

Freshmen:

Admission: 27,576 applied, 22,685 admitted, 4,160 enrolled. ***Average high school GPA:*** 3.4. ***Test scores:*** SAT evidence-based reading and writing scores over 500: 62%; SAT math scores over 500: 63%; ACT scores over 18: 65%; SAT evidence-based reading and writing scores over 600: 17%; SAT math scores over 600: 15%; ACT scores over 24: 18%; SAT evidence-based reading and writing scores over 700: 1%; SAT math scores over 700: 2%; ACT scores over 30: 1%.

Retention: 83% of full-time freshmen returned.

FACULTY

Total: 1,725, 48% full-time, 55% with terminal degrees.

Student/faculty ratio: 24:1.

ACADEMICS

Calendar: semesters. *Degrees:* bachelor's, master's, and doctoral.

Special study options: accelerated degree program, adult/continuing education programs, advanced placement credit, cooperative education, distance learning, double majors, English as a second language, external degree program, honors programs, independent study, internships, off-campus study, part-time degree program, services for LD students, student-designed majors, study abroad, summer session for credit. ***ROTC:*** Army (b), Air Force (b).

Computers: Students can access the following: computer help desk, free student e-mail accounts, online (class) grades, online (class) registration, online (class) schedules, online transcripts. Campuswide network is available. Wireless service is available via entire campus.
Library: California State University, Sacramento Library. Students can reserve study rooms.

STUDENT LIFE
Housing options: coed, cooperative, special housing for students with disabilities. Campus housing is university owned.

Activities and organizations: drama/theater group, student-run newspaper, radio station, choral group, marching band, national fraternities, national sororities.

Athletics Member NCAA. All Division I except football (Division I-AA). ***Intercollegiate sports:*** baseball M(s), basketball M(s)/W(s), bowling M(c)/W(c), cheerleading M/W, crew M(s)/W(s), cross-country running M(s)/W(s), golf M(s)/W, gymnastics W(s), ice hockey M(c), lacrosse M(c)/W(c), racquetball M(c)/W(c), rugby M(c), skiing (downhill) M(c)/W(c), soccer M(s)/W(s), softball W(s), tennis M(s)/W(s), track and field M(s)/W(s), volleyball M(c)/W(s). ***Intramural sports:*** basketball M/W, crew M/W, football M/W, golf M/W, ice hockey M, skiing (downhill) M/W, soccer M/W, softball M/W, table tennis M/W, tennis M/W, volleyball M/W, water polo M/W, weight lifting M/W.

Campus security: 24-hour emergency response devices and patrols, student patrols, late-night transport/escort service, controlled dormitory access.

Student services: health clinic, personal/psychological counseling, women's center, legal services, veterans affairs office.

COSTS & FINANCIAL AID
Costs (2020–21) ***Tuition:*** area resident $5742 full-time; state resident $5742 full-time; nonresident $17,622 full-time. ***Required fees:*** $1626 full-time. ***Room and board:*** $15,224; room only: $7744.

Financial Aid Of all full-time matriculated undergraduates who enrolled in 2018, 4,784 applied for aid, 4,418 were judged to have need, 415 had their need fully met. In 2018, 25 non-need-based awards were made. ***Average percent of need met:*** 55. ***Average financial aid package:*** $10,010. ***Average need-based loan:*** $4158. ***Average need-based gift aid:*** $7939. ***Average non-need-based aid:*** $1525. ***Average indebtedness upon graduation:*** $23,460. ***Financial aid deadline:*** 5/1.

APPLYING
Standardized Tests *Required for some:* SAT or ACT (for admission), SAT and SAT Subject Tests or ACT (for admission).

Options: electronic application.

Application fee: $55.

Required: minimum 2.0 GPA. ***Required for some:*** high school transcript.

Application deadlines: 11/30 (freshmen), 11/30 (transfers).

Notification: continuous until 3/1 (freshmen), 3/1 (transfers).

CONTACT
Brian Henley, Director of Admissions and Outreach, California State University, Sacramento, 6000 J Street, Lassen Hall, Sacramento, CA 95819-6048. *Phone:* 916-278-7766. *Fax:* 916-278-5603. *E-mail:* admissions@csus.edu.

California State University, San Bernardino

San Bernardino, California

http://www.csusb.edu/

- **State-supported** comprehensive, founded 1965, part of California State University System
- **Suburban** 430-acre campus with easy access to Los Angeles
- **Coed** 18,114 undergraduate students, 91% full-time, 61% women, 39% men
- **Moderately difficult** entrance level, 69% of applicants were admitted

UNDERGRAD STUDENTS
16,432 full-time, 1,682 part-time. 5% Black or African American, non-Hispanic/Latino; 66% Hispanic/Latino; 5% Asian, non-Hispanic/Latino; 0.1% Native Hawaiian or other Pacific Islander, non-Hispanic/Latino; 0.2% American Indian or Alaska Native, non-Hispanic/Latino; 2% Two or more races, non-Hispanic/Latino; 4% Race/ethnicity unknown; 7% international; 15% transferred in; 6% live on campus.

Freshmen:
Admission: 16,307 applied, 11,180 admitted, 2,885 enrolled. ***Average high school GPA:*** 3.4. ***Test scores:*** SAT evidence-based reading and writing scores over 500: 51%; SAT math scores over 500: 52%; ACT scores over 18: 48%; SAT evidence-based reading and writing scores over 600: 9%; SAT math scores over 600: 7%; ACT scores over 24: 5%.

Retention: 86% of full-time freshmen returned.

FACULTY
Total: 1,021, 46% full-time, 47% with terminal degrees.

Student/faculty ratio: 28:1.

ACADEMICS
Calendar: quarters. *Degrees:* certificates, bachelor's, master's, doctoral, and postbachelor's certificates.

Special study options: academic remediation for entering students, accelerated degree program, advanced placement credit, cooperative education, distance learning, double majors, honors programs, independent study, internships, off-campus study, part-time degree program, services for LD students, student-designed majors, study abroad, summer session for credit. ***ROTC:*** Army (b), Air Force (b).

Computers: Students can access the following: computer help desk, free student e-mail accounts, online (class) grades, online (class) registration, online (class) schedules. Campuswide network is available. Wireless service is available via entire campus.
Library: Pfau Library.

STUDENT LIFE
Housing options: coed, special housing for students with disabilities. Campus housing is university owned. Freshman applicants given priority for college housing.

Activities and organizations: drama/theater group, student-run newspaper, radio and television station, choral group, national fraternities, national sororities.

Athletics Member NCAA. All Division II. ***Intercollegiate sports:*** baseball M(s), basketball M(s)/W(s), cross-country running W, golf M(s), soccer M(s)/W(s), softball W(s), track and field W, volleyball W(s).

Campus security: 24-hour emergency response devices and patrols, student patrols, late-night transport/escort service.

Student services: health clinic, personal/psychological counseling, women's center, legal services, veterans affairs office.

COSTS & FINANCIAL AID
Costs (2020–21) ***Tuition:*** area resident $5742 full-time. ***Required fees:*** $1214 full-time. ***Room and board:*** $13,435; room only: $11,965. Room and board charges vary according to board plan and housing facility. ***Payment plan:*** installment. ***Waivers:*** senior citizens and employees or children of employees.

Financial Aid Of all full-time matriculated undergraduates who enrolled in 2019, 14,918 applied for aid, 14,035 were judged to have need, 1,336 had their need fully met. In 2019, 29 non-need-based awards were made. ***Average percent of need met:*** 61. ***Average financial aid package:*** $9640. ***Average need-based loan:*** $4320. ***Average need-based gift aid:*** $9723. ***Average non-need-based aid:*** $4251. ***Average indebtedness upon graduation:*** $18,294.

APPLYING
Standardized Tests *Recommended:* SAT or ACT (for admission).

Options: electronic application, early admission, early action.

Application fee: $55.

Required: high school transcript, minimum 2.0 GPA.

Application deadlines: rolling (freshmen), rolling (transfers).

Notification: continuous (freshmen), continuous (transfers).

CONTACT

Lisa Rubio, Director of Admissions and Evaluations, California State University, San Bernardino, 5500 University Parkway, University Hall, Room 116A, San Bernardino, CA 92407-2397. *Phone:* 909-537-3577. *E-mail:* lisa.rubio@csusb.edu.

California State University, San Marcos

San Marcos, California

http://www.csusm.edu/

- **State-supported** comprehensive, founded 1990, part of California State University System
- **Suburban** 304-acre campus with easy access to San Diego
- **Coed** 13,879 undergraduate students, 82% full-time, 60% women, 40% men
- **Moderately difficult** entrance level, 62% of applicants were admitted

UNDERGRAD STUDENTS

11,445 full-time, 2,434 part-time. 4% are from out of state; 3% Black or African American, non-Hispanic/Latino; 48% Hispanic/Latino; 9% Asian, non-Hispanic/Latino; 0.2% Native Hawaiian or other Pacific Islander, non-Hispanic/Latino; 0.3% American Indian or Alaska Native, non-Hispanic/Latino; 5% Two or more races, non-Hispanic/Latino; 4% Race/ethnicity unknown; 4% international; 14% transferred in; 80% live on campus.

Freshmen:

Admission: 17,343 applied, 10,696 admitted, 2,245 enrolled. ***Average high school GPA:*** 3.4. ***Test scores:*** SAT evidence-based reading and writing scores over 500: 67%; SAT math scores over 500: 66%; ACT scores over 18: 66%; SAT evidence-based reading and writing scores over 600: 17%; SAT math scores over 600: 14%; ACT scores over 24: 14%; SAT evidence-based reading and writing scores over 700: 1%; SAT math scores over 700: 1%; ACT scores over 30: 1%.

Retention: 79% of full-time freshmen returned.

FACULTY

Total: 900, 32% full-time.

Student/faculty ratio: 26:1.

ACADEMICS

Calendar: semesters. *Degrees:* bachelor's and master's.

Special study options: academic remediation for entering students, adult/continuing education programs, advanced placement credit, distance learning, double majors, English as a second language, independent study, internships, off-campus study, part-time degree program, services for LD students, student-designed majors, study abroad, summer session for credit. ***ROTC:*** Army (c), Navy (c), Air Force (c).

Computers: Students can access the following: computer help desk, free student e-mail accounts, online (class) registration. Campuswide network is available.

Library: Kellogg Library. *Books:* 215,402 (physical), 268,189 (digital/electronic); *Serial titles:* 3,130 (physical), 81,643 (digital/electronic); *Databases:* 100. Weekly public service hours: 100; students can reserve study rooms.

STUDENT LIFE

Housing options: special housing for students with disabilities. Campus housing is university owned.

Activities and organizations: drama/theater group, student-run newspaper, choral group, national fraternities, national sororities.

Athletics Member NCAA. All Division I. ***Intercollegiate sports:*** baseball M, basketball M/W, cross-country running M/W, golf M/W(c), soccer M/W, softball W, track and field M/W, volleyball W.

Campus security: 24-hour emergency response devices and patrols, student patrols, late-night transport/escort service.

Student services: health clinic, personal/psychological counseling, women's center, veterans affairs office.

COSTS & FINANCIAL AID

Costs (2020–21) ***Comprehensive fee:*** $25,164 includes mandatory fees ($7712) and room and board ($13,150). ***Required fees:*** $2433 per term part-time.

Financial Aid Of all full-time matriculated undergraduates who enrolled in 2018, 9,392 applied for aid, 8,242 were judged to have need, 388 had their need fully met. In 2018, 16 non-need-based awards were made. ***Average percent of need met:*** 45. ***Average financial aid package:*** $10,808. ***Average need-based loan:*** $4131. ***Average need-based gift aid:*** $9317. ***Average non-need-based aid:*** $2157. ***Average indebtedness upon graduation:*** $23,725.

APPLYING

Standardized Tests *Required:* SAT or ACT (for admission).

Options: electronic application.

Application fee: $70.

Required: high school transcript.

Notification: continuous (freshmen), continuous (transfers).

CONTACT

Scott Hagg, Director of Admissions, California State University, San Marcos, 333 South Twin Oaks Valley Road, San Marcos, CA 92096-0001. *Phone:* 760-750-4848. *Fax:* 760-750-3248. *E-mail:* apply@csusm.edu.

California State University, Stanislaus

Turlock, California

http://www.csustan.edu/

- **State-supported** comprehensive, founded 1957, part of California State University System
- **Suburban** 228-acre campus
- **Endowment** $11.6 million
- **Coed** 11,277 undergraduate students, 86% full-time, 70% women, 30% men
- **Moderately difficult** entrance level, 89% of applicants were admitted

UNDERGRAD STUDENTS

9,702 full-time, 1,575 part-time. Students come from 17 states and territories; 18 other countries; 0.3% are from out of state; 2% Black or African American, non-Hispanic/Latino; 56% Hispanic/Latino; 9% Asian, non-Hispanic/Latino; 0.4% Native Hawaiian or other Pacific Islander, non-Hispanic/Latino; 0.2% American Indian or Alaska Native, non-Hispanic/Latino; 3% Two or more races, non-Hispanic/Latino; 5% Race/ethnicity unknown; 4% international; 12% transferred in; 7% live on campus.

Freshmen:

Admission: 8,764 applied, 7,825 admitted, 1,568 enrolled. ***Average high school GPA:*** 3.4. ***Test scores:*** SAT evidence-based reading and writing scores over 500: 49%; SAT math scores over 500: 47%; ACT scores over 18: 50%; SAT evidence-based reading and writing scores over 600: 9%; SAT math scores over 600: 7%; ACT scores over 24: 9%; SAT evidence-based reading and writing scores over 700: 1%; SAT math scores over 700: 1%; ACT scores over 30: 1%.

Retention: 83% of full-time freshmen returned.

FACULTY

Total: 694, 51% full-time, 53% with terminal degrees.

Student/faculty ratio: 22:1.

ACADEMICS

Calendar: semesters. *Degrees:* bachelor's, master's, and doctoral.

Special study options: academic remediation for entering students, advanced placement credit, cooperative education, distance learning, double majors, English as a second language, external degree program, honors programs, independent study, internships, off-campus study, part-time degree program, services for LD students, student-designed majors, study abroad, summer session for credit.

Computers: 200 computers/terminals are available on campus for general student use. Students can access the following: computer help desk, free student e-mail accounts, online (class) grades, online (class) registration, online (class) schedules. Campuswide network is available. 100% of college-owned or -operated housing units are wired for high-speed Internet access. Wireless service is available via entire campus.

Library: Vasche Library. *Books:* 316,942 (physical), 192,737 (digital/electronic); *Serial titles:* 634 (physical), 60,803 (digital/electronic); *Databases:* 187. Weekly public service hours: 90; students can reserve study rooms.

STUDENT LIFE
Housing options: coed. Campus housing is university owned.

Activities and organizations: drama/theater group, student-run newspaper, radio station, choral group, Alpha Xi Delta, Phi Sigma Sigma, Kappa Sigma, Tau Kappa Epsilon, Theta Chi, national fraternities, national sororities.

Athletics Member NCAA. All Division II. ***Intercollegiate sports:*** baseball M(s), basketball M(s)/W(s), cross-country running M(s)/W(s), golf M(s), soccer M(s)/W(s), softball W(s), tennis W(s), track and field M(s)/W(s), volleyball W(s). ***Intramural sports:*** basketball M/W, cheerleading M(c)/W(c), football M/W, soccer M/W, ultimate Frisbee M/W, volleyball M/W.

Campus security: 24-hour emergency response devices and patrols, student patrols, late-night transport/escort service, controlled dormitory access.

Student services: health clinic, personal/psychological counseling, women's center.

COSTS & FINANCIAL AID
Costs (2020–21) ***Tuition:*** area resident $5742 full-time; state resident $5742 full-time; nonresident $396 per credit hour part-time. Full-time tuition and fees vary according to course load. Part-time tuition and fees vary according to course load. ***Required fees:*** $1842 full-time. ***Room and board:*** $10,950; room only: $7150. Room and board charges vary according to board plan, housing facility, and student level. ***Payment plan:*** installment. ***Waivers:*** employees or children of employees.

Financial Aid Of all full-time matriculated undergraduates who enrolled in 2019, 7,344 applied for aid, 6,798 were judged to have need, 1,059 had their need fully met. In 2019, 121 non-need-based awards were made. ***Average percent of need met:*** 78. ***Average financial aid package:*** $17,184. ***Average need-based loan:*** $4327. ***Average need-based gift aid:*** $9822. ***Average non-need-based aid:*** $2345. ***Average indebtedness upon graduation:*** $17,952.

APPLYING
Standardized Tests *Required for some:* SAT or ACT (for admission).

Options: electronic application.

Application fee: $55.

Required for some: high school transcript. ***Recommended:*** minimum 3.0 GPA.

Application deadlines: 11/30 (freshmen), 11/30 (transfers).

Notification: continuous (freshmen), continuous (transfers).

CONTACT
Student Outreach, California State University, Stanislaus, One University Circle, Turlock, CA 95382. *Phone:* 209-667-3070. *Toll-free phone:* 800-300-7420. *Fax:* 209-667-3394. *E-mail:* outreach_help_desk@csustan.edu.

California University of Management and Sciences

Anaheim, California

http://www.calums.edu/

CONTACT
California University of Management and Sciences, 721 North Euclid Street, Anaheim, CA 92801.

Chamberlain College of Nursing - Sacramento

Rancho Cordova, California

http://www.chamberlain.edu/

CONTACT
Chamberlain College of Nursing - Sacramento, 10971 Sun Center Drive, Rancho Cordova, CA 95670.

Chapman University

Orange, California

http://www.chapman.edu/

- **Independent** comprehensive, founded 1861, affiliated with Christian Church (Disciples of Christ)
- **Suburban** 78-acre campus with easy access to Los Angeles
- **Endowment** $352.6 million
- **Coed**
- **Very difficult** entrance level

FACULTY
Student/faculty ratio: 14:1.

ACADEMICS
Calendar: 4-1-4. *Degrees:* bachelor's, master's, and doctoral.
Library: Leatherby Libraries plus 1 other. *Books:* 339,051 (physical), 17,371 (digital/electronic); *Serial titles:* 267 (physical), 69,372 (digital/electronic); *Databases:* 287. Weekly public service hours: 127; students can reserve study rooms.

STUDENT LIFE
Housing options: coed, special housing for students with disabilities. Campus housing is university owned. Freshman campus housing is guaranteed.

Activities and organizations: drama/theater group, student-run newspaper, radio station, choral group, national fraternities, national sororities.

Athletics Member NCAA. All Division III.

Campus security: 24-hour emergency response devices and patrols, late-night transport/escort service, controlled dormitory access, full safety education program.

Student services: health clinic, personal/psychological counseling.

COSTS & FINANCIAL AID
Costs (2019–20) ***Comprehensive fee:*** $70,442 includes full-time tuition ($54,540), mandatory fees ($384), and room and board ($15,518). Part-time tuition: $1695 per credit hour. Part-time tuition and fees vary according to course load. ***Required fees:*** $147 per term part-time. ***College room only:*** $10,400. Room and board charges vary according to board plan and housing facility. ***Payment plans:*** tuition prepayment, installment, deferred payment.

Financial Aid Of all full-time matriculated undergraduates who enrolled in 2018, 4,337 applied for aid, 3,768 were judged to have need, 490 had their need fully met. 3,245 Federal Work-Study jobs (averaging $2881). In 2018, 481 non-need-based awards were made. ***Average percent of need met:*** 70. ***Average financial aid package:*** $35,854. ***Average need-based loan:*** $4475. ***Average need-based gift aid:*** $19,239. ***Average non-need-based aid:*** $18,152. ***Average indebtedness upon graduation:*** $27,117.

APPLYING
Standardized Tests *Required:* SAT or ACT (for admission). *Recommended:* SAT Subject Tests (for admission).

Options: electronic application, early decision, early action.

Application fee: $70.

Required: essay or personal statement, high school transcript, 1 letter of recommendation. ***Required for some:*** audition for music, dance, and theatre majors; portfolio for art and film majors; supplemental application for all talent-based majors.

CONTACT
Ms. Marcela Mejia-Martinez, Director of Undergraduate Admission, Chapman University, One University Drive, Orange, CA 92866. *Phone:* 714-997-6711. *Toll-free phone:* 888-CUAPPLY. *Fax:* 714-997-6713. *E-mail:* admit@chapman.edu.

Charles R. Drew University of Medicine and Science

Los Angeles, California

http://www.cdrewu.edu/

- **Independent** comprehensive, founded 1966
- **Urban** 11-acre campus with easy access to Los Angeles
- **Endowment** $90.0 million
- **Coed** 199 undergraduate students, 69% full-time, 67% women, 33% men
- **Moderately difficult** entrance level, 20% of applicants were admitted

UNDERGRAD STUDENTS

138 full-time, 61 part-time. 3% are from out of state; 39% Black or African American, non-Hispanic/Latino; 32% Hispanic/Latino; 11% Asian, non-Hispanic/Latino; 6% Two or more races, non-Hispanic/Latino; 6% Race/ethnicity unknown; 2% international.

Freshmen:

Admission: 208 applied, 41 admitted, 13 enrolled.

Retention: 70% of full-time freshmen returned.

FACULTY

Student/faculty ratio: 8:1.

ACADEMICS

Calendar: semesters. *Degrees:* certificates, associate, bachelor's, master's, doctoral, post-master's, and postbachelor's certificates.

Special study options: academic remediation for entering students, adult/continuing education programs, advanced placement credit, distance learning, independent study, part-time degree program, services for LD students, study abroad, summer session for credit.

Computers: 90 computers/terminals are available on campus for general student use. Students can access the following: computer help desk, free student e-mail accounts, online (class) grades, online (class) registration, online (class) schedules, Campus wide wireless network. Campuswide network is available. Wireless service is available via entire campus.

Library: Health Sciences Library. *Books:* 6,436 (physical), 3,500 (digital/electronic); *Serial titles:* 596 (physical), 11,765 (digital/electronic); *Databases:* 38. Weekly public service hours: 91; students can reserve study rooms.

STUDENT LIFE

Housing options: college housing not availableCampus housing is university owned.

Activities and organizations: Student Government, Critical Exploration of Academic Literature (CEAL), Charles R. Drew University Alumni Association, Pre-Health Society, Pre-Dental Society.

Campus security: 24-hour emergency response devices, late-night transport/escort service.

Student services: personal/psychological counseling.

COSTS & FINANCIAL AID

Costs (2020–21) ***Tuition:*** $17,340 full-time, $578 per credit hour part-time. Full-time tuition and fees vary according to course load, degree level, and program. Part-time tuition and fees vary according to course load, degree level, and program. ***Required fees:*** $100 full-time. ***Payment plan:*** installment.

Financial Aid Of all full-time matriculated undergraduates who enrolled in 2018, 110 applied for aid, 106 were judged to have need, 1 had their need fully met. In 2018, 5 non-need-based awards were made. ***Average percent of need met:*** 41. ***Average financial aid package:*** $14,566. ***Average need-based loan:*** $4804. ***Average need-based gift aid:*** $11,177. ***Average non-need-based aid:*** $4218.

APPLYING

Standardized Tests *Required for some:* SAT or ACT (for admission).

Options: electronic application, early action, deferred entrance.

Application fee: $50.

Required: essay or personal statement, high school transcript, minimum 2.0 GPA. ***Required for some:*** pre-admission assessment exams.

Application deadlines: 7/30 (freshmen), 7/30 (transfers).

Notification: continuous (freshmen), continuous (transfers).

CONTACT

Charles R. Drew University of Medicine and Science, 1731 East 120th Street, Los Angeles, CA 90059.

Claremont McKenna College

Claremont, California

http://www.cmc.edu/

- **Independent** comprehensive, founded 1946
- **Suburban** 69-acre campus with easy access to Los Angeles
- **Endowment** $863.3 million
- **Coed** 1,343 undergraduate students, 100% full-time, 49% women, 51% men
- **Most difficult** entrance level, 10% of applicants were admitted

UNDERGRAD STUDENTS

1,340 full-time, 3 part-time. Students come from 47 states and territories; 46 other countries; 55% are from out of state; 4% Black or African American, non-Hispanic/Latino; 15% Hispanic/Latino; 12% Asian, non-Hispanic/Latino; 0.1% Native Hawaiian or other Pacific Islander, non-Hispanic/Latino; 0.1% American Indian or Alaska Native, non-Hispanic/Latino; 7% Two or more races, non-Hispanic/Latino; 5% Race/ethnicity unknown; 16% international; 2% transferred in; 96% live on campus.

Freshmen:

Admission: 6,066 applied, 625 admitted, 328 enrolled. ***Test scores:*** SAT evidence-based reading and writing scores over 500: 100%; SAT math scores over 500: 100%; ACT scores over 18: 100%; SAT evidence-based reading and writing scores over 600: 99%; SAT math scores over 600: 98%; ACT scores over 24: 99%; SAT evidence-based reading and writing scores over 700: 53%; SAT math scores over 700: 74%; ACT scores over 30: 87%.

Retention: 95% of full-time freshmen returned.

FACULTY

Total: 171, 87% full-time, 98% with terminal degrees.

Student/faculty ratio: 8:1.

ACADEMICS

Calendar: semesters. *Degrees:* bachelor's and master's.

Special study options: advanced placement credit, double majors, honors programs, independent study, internships, off-campus study, services for LD students, student-designed majors, study abroad. ***ROTC:*** Army (b), Air Force (c).

Unusual degree programs: 3-2 engineering with Columbia University, Harvey Mudd College.

Computers: 220 computers/terminals are available on campus for general student use. Students can access the following: campus intranet, computer help desk, free student e-mail accounts, online (class) grades, online (class) registration, online (class) schedules. Campuswide network is available. 100% of college-owned or -operated housing units are wired for high-speed Internet access. Wireless service is available via entire campus.

Library: Claremont Colleges Library plus 2 others. *Books:* 1.0 million (physical), 2.2 million (digital/electronic); *Serial titles:* 28,182 (physical), 81,005 (digital/electronic); *Databases:* 490. Weekly public service hours: 111; students can reserve study rooms.

STUDENT LIFE

Housing options: on-campus residence required for freshman year; coed. Campus housing is university owned. Freshman campus housing is guaranteed.

Activities and organizations: drama/theater group, student-run newspaper, choral group, Associated Students of Claremont McKenna College, College Programming Board, Asian Pacific American Mentoring Program (APAM).

Athletics Member NCAA. All Division III. ***Intercollegiate sports:*** baseball M, basketball M/W, cross-country running M/W, equestrian sports M(c)/W(c), fencing M(c)/W(c), field hockey M(c)/W(c), football M, golf M/W, lacrosse M(c)/W, rock climbing M(c)/W(c), rugby M(c)/W(c), soccer M/W, softball W, swimming and diving M/W, tennis M/W, track and field M/W, ultimate Frisbee M(c)/W(c), volleyball M(c)/W, water polo M/W. ***Intramural sports:*** badminton M/W, basketball

M, football M, sand volleyball M/W, soccer M/W(c), table tennis M/W, tennis M/W, ultimate Frisbee M/W, volleyball M/W, water polo M/W.

Campus security: 24-hour emergency response devices and patrols, late-night transport/escort service, controlled dormitory access.

Student services: health clinic, personal/psychological counseling.

COSTS & FINANCIAL AID

Costs (2019–20) ***Comprehensive fee:*** $73,775 includes full-time tuition ($56,190), mandatory fees ($285), and room and board ($17,300). Part-time tuition: $9365 per course. Part-time tuition and fees vary according to course load. ***College room only:*** $9300. Room and board charges vary according to board plan and housing facility. ***Payment plan:*** installment. ***Waivers:*** employees or children of employees.

Financial Aid Of all full-time matriculated undergraduates who enrolled in 2018, 574 applied for aid, 532 were judged to have need, 529 had their need fully met. In 2018, 86 non-need-based awards were made. ***Average percent of need met:*** 100. ***Average financial aid package:*** $52,467. ***Average need-based loan:*** $4060. ***Average need-based gift aid:*** $48,754. ***Average non-need-based aid:*** $18,788. ***Average indebtedness upon graduation:*** $19,355. ***Financial aid deadline:*** 2/1.

APPLYING

Standardized Tests *Required:* SAT or ACT (for admission). *Required for some:* SAT Subject Tests (for admission), TOEFL or IELTS for students for whom English is not their first language and the primary language of instruction in high school was not English.

Options: electronic application, early decision, deferred entrance.

Application fee: $70.

Required: essay or personal statement, high school transcript, 2 letters of recommendation. ***Recommended:*** interview.

Early decision deadline: 11/1 (for plan 1), 1/5 (for plan 2).

Notification: 4/1 (freshmen), 12/15 (early decision plan 1), 2/15 (early decision plan 2).

CONTACT

Mr. Omar Zazueta, Director of Admission, Claremont McKenna College, Office of Admission and Financial Aid, 888 Columbia Avenue, Claremont, CA 91711. *Phone:* 909-621-8088. *Fax:* 909-621-8516. *E-mail:* admission@cmc.edu.

Cogswell Polytechnical College

San Jose, California

http://www.cogswell.edu/

- **Proprietary** comprehensive, founded 1887
- **Suburban** 2-acre campus with easy access to San Francisco, San Jose
- **Coed** 608 undergraduate students, 72% full-time, 29% women, 71% men
- **Moderately difficult** entrance level, 65% of applicants were admitted

UNDERGRAD STUDENTS

436 full-time, 172 part-time. Students come from 13 states and territories; 3 other countries; 7% are from out of state; 5% Black or African American, non-Hispanic/Latino; 20% Hispanic/Latino; 22% Asian, non-Hispanic/Latino; 1% Native Hawaiian or other Pacific Islander, non-Hispanic/Latino; 0.8% American Indian or Alaska Native, non-Hispanic/Latino; 7% Two or more races, non-Hispanic/Latino; 7% Race/ethnicity unknown; 2% international; 8% transferred in.

Freshmen:

Admission: 231 applied, 149 admitted, 72 enrolled. ***Average high school GPA:*** 3.1. ***Test scores:*** SAT math scores over 500: 90%; ACT scores over 18: 100%; SAT math scores over 600: 40%; ACT scores over 24: 75%; SAT math scores over 700: 12%; ACT scores over 30: 25%.

Retention: 78% of full-time freshmen returned.

FACULTY

Total: 89, 18% full-time, 22% with terminal degrees.

Student/faculty ratio: 13:1.

ACADEMICS

Calendar: semesters. *Degrees:* bachelor's and master's.

Special study options: academic remediation for entering students, adult/continuing education programs, advanced placement credit, cooperative education, distance learning, double majors, internships, part-time degree program, summer session for credit.

Computers: 224 computers/terminals are available on campus for general student use. Students can access the following: computer help desk, free student e-mail accounts, online (class) grades, online (class) registration, online (class) schedules. Campuswide network is available. Wireless service is available via entire campus.

Library: Cogswell College Library. *Books:* 5,007 (physical); *Serial titles:* 920 (physical); *Databases:* 14.

STUDENT LIFE

Housing options: coed. Campus housing is university owned. Freshman applicants given priority for college housing.

Activities and organizations: choral group, ASB, Game Development club, Audio Production and Engineering club, Comic Club, E-Sports.

Campus security: 24-hour emergency response devices.

Student services: personal/psychological counseling.

COSTS & FINANCIAL AID

Costs (2019–20) ***Tuition:*** $19,800 full-time, $825 per credit part-time. Full-time tuition and fees vary according to course load. Part-time tuition and fees vary according to course load. No tuition increase for student's term of enrollment. ***Required fees:*** $1000 full-time, $500 per term part-time. ***Room only:*** $11,990. Room and board charges vary according to housing facility. ***Payment plan:*** deferred payment. ***Waivers:*** employees or children of employees.

Financial Aid Of all full-time matriculated undergraduates who enrolled in 2015, 17 Federal Work-Study jobs (averaging $2328).

APPLYING

Standardized Tests *Recommended:* SAT or ACT (for admission).

Options: electronic application, deferred entrance.

Required: essay or personal statement, high school transcript, minimum 2.0 GPA. ***Required for some:*** letters of recommendation, portfolio for Digital Art and Animation, Digital Audio Technology and Game Design Art majors. ***Recommended:*** minimum 2.7 GPA, interview.

Application deadlines: rolling (freshmen), rolling (transfers).

Notification: continuous (freshmen), continuous (transfers).

CONTACT

Sheri Stein, VP of Admissions, Cogswell Polytechnical College, 191 Baypointe Parkway, San Jose, CA 95134. *Phone:* 408-498-5103 Ext. 103. *Toll-free phone:* 800-264-7955. *Fax:* 408-747-0764. *E-mail:* sstein@cogswell.edu.

The Colburn School Conservatory of Music

Los Angeles, California

http://www.colburnschool.edu/

CONTACT

Ms. Jessica Cameron, Manager of Admissions, The Colburn School Conservatory of Music, 200 South Grand Avenue, Los Angeles, CA 90012. *Phone:* 213-621-4534. *Fax:* 213-625-0371. *E-mail:* admissions@colburnschool.edu.

Columbia College Hollywood

Tarzana, California

http://www.columbiacollege.edu/

- **Independent** 4-year, founded 1952
- **Urban** 1-acre campus with easy access to Los Angeles
- **Coed**
- **Minimally difficult** entrance level

FACULTY

Student/faculty ratio: 33:1.

ACADEMICS

Calendar: quarters. *Degrees:* associate and bachelor's.

Library: Columbia College Hollywood Library plus 1 other.

STUDENT LIFE

Housing options: coed. Campus housing is provided by a third party.

Activities and organizations: drama/theater group.

Campus security: 24-hour emergency response devices and patrols, late-night transport/escort service.

Student services: personal/psychological counseling.

FINANCIAL AID

Financial Aid Of all full-time matriculated undergraduates who enrolled in 2016, 300 applied for aid, 200 were judged to have need. 10 Federal Work-Study jobs (averaging $2000). ***Average financial aid package:*** $6000. ***Average need-based loan:*** $1300. ***Average need-based gift aid:*** $2000.

APPLYING

Options: electronic application, deferred entrance.

Application fee: $50.

Required: essay or personal statement, high school transcript, minimum 2.0 GPA, 2 letters of recommendation, interview. ***Recommended:*** portfolio.

CONTACT

Carmen Munoz, Admissions Director, Columbia College Hollywood, 18618 Oxnard Street, Tarzana, CA 91356. *Phone:* 818-345-8414 Ext. 203. *Toll-free phone:* 800-785-0585. *Fax:* 818-345-9053. *E-mail:* admissions@columbiacollege.edu.

Concordia University Irvine

Irvine, California

http://www.cui.edu/

- **Independent** comprehensive, founded 1972, affiliated with Lutheran Church–Missouri Synod, part of The Concordia University System
- **Suburban** 70-acre campus with easy access to Los Angeles
- **Endowment** $35.1 million
- **Coed**
- **Moderately difficult** entrance level

FACULTY

Student/faculty ratio: 17:1.

ACADEMICS

Calendar: semesters. *Degrees:* associate, bachelor's, master's, doctoral, and postbachelor's certificates (associate's degree for international students only).

Library: Concordia University Library. *Books:* 72,408 (physical), 196,626 (digital/electronic); *Serial titles:* 42 (physical), 22,390 (digital/electronic); *Databases:* 40. Weekly public service hours: 89.

STUDENT LIFE

Housing options: on-campus residence required for freshman year; coed, women-only, special housing for students with disabilities. Campus housing is university owned. Freshman campus housing is guaranteed.

Activities and organizations: drama/theater group, student-run newspaper, choral group, intramurals, Screaming Eagles, Lacrosse, Abbey West, LEAD Student Activities.

Athletics Member NCAA. All Division II.

Campus security: 24-hour emergency response devices and patrols, student patrols, late-night transport/escort service.

Student services: health clinic, personal/psychological counseling.

COSTS & FINANCIAL AID

Costs (2019–20) ***Comprehensive fee:*** $48,610 includes full-time tuition ($35,990), mandatory fees ($750), and room and board ($11,870). Part-time tuition: $1056 per credit. ***College room only:*** $6840.

Financial Aid Of all full-time matriculated undergraduates who enrolled in 2018, 1,304 applied for aid, 1,144 were judged to have need, 161 had their need fully met. 76 Federal Work-Study jobs (averaging $2582). In 2018, 328 non-need-based awards were made. ***Average percent of need met:*** 63. ***Average financial aid package:*** $23,749. ***Average need-based loan:*** $4541. ***Average need-based gift aid:*** $21,116. ***Average non-need-based aid:*** $11,757. ***Average indebtedness upon graduation:*** $31,516. ***Financial aid deadline:*** 3/2.

APPLYING

Standardized Tests *Required:* SAT or ACT (for admission).

Options: electronic application, early action, deferred entrance.

Application fee: $50.

Required: high school transcript. ***Recommended:*** essay or personal statement, minimum 2.8 GPA, 1 letter of recommendation, interview.

CONTACT

Ms. Susan Park, Director of Undergraduate Admissions, Concordia University Irvine, 1530 Concordia West, Irvine, CA 92612-3299. *Phone:* 800-229-1200. *Toll-free phone:* 800-229-1200. *Fax:* 949-214-3520. *E-mail:* admission@cui.edu.

Design Institute of San Diego

San Diego, California

http://www.disd.edu/

- **Proprietary** 4-year, founded 1977
- **Urban** campus with easy access to San Diego
- **Coed** 126 undergraduate students, 63% full-time, 89% women, 11% men
- 50% of applicants were admitted

UNDERGRAD STUDENTS

80 full-time, 46 part-time. Students come from 28 states and territories; 5 other countries; 7% Black or African American, non-Hispanic/Latino; 17% Hispanic/Latino; 10% Asian, non-Hispanic/Latino; 0.8% Native Hawaiian or other Pacific Islander, non-Hispanic/Latino; 2% American Indian or Alaska Native, non-Hispanic/Latino; 0.8% Two or more races, non-Hispanic/Latino; 6% international; 10% transferred in.

Freshmen:

Admission: 14 applied, 7 admitted, 2 enrolled.

Retention: 75% of full-time freshmen returned.

FACULTY

Total: 26, 19% full-time.

Student/faculty ratio: 9:1.

ACADEMICS

Calendar: semesters. *Degree:* bachelor's.

Special study options: accelerated degree program, adult/continuing education programs, internships, part-time degree program, services for LD students, student-designed majors, study abroad, summer session for credit.

Computers: 64 computers/terminals are available on campus for general student use. Students can access the following: campus intranet, free student e-mail accounts, computer lab tutors and support from the IT Department. Campuswide network is available. Wireless service is available via entire campus.

Library: DISD Library. *Books:* 6,179 (physical); *Serial titles:* 84 (physical). Weekly public service hours: 56.

STUDENT LIFE

Housing options: college housing not available.

Activities and organizations: ASID Student Chapter, IIDA Student Chapter, Student Mentor Program, Student Ambassador.

Campus security: security guard patrols during the semester from 5:30 - 10:30 pm Monday through Thursday, no classes on Friday past 5:00 pm.

Student services: veterans affairs office.

COSTS

Costs (2019–20) ***One-time required fee:*** $139. ***Tuition:*** $25,500 full-time, $1050 per unit part-time. Full-time tuition and fees vary according to class time, course load, and program. Part-time tuition and fees vary according to class time, course load, and program. ***Required fees:*** $10 full-time, $10 per year part-time. ***Payment plans:*** installment, deferred payment. ***Waivers:*** employees or children of employees.

APPLYING

Options: electronic application, early decision.

Application fee: $25.

Required: essay or personal statement, high school transcript, 2 letters of recommendation. ***Required for some:*** official transcripts from all colleges attended. ***Recommended:*** minimum 2.0 GPA, interview.

Application deadlines: rolling (freshmen), rolling (out-of-state freshmen), rolling (transfers), rolling (early action).

Early decision deadline: rolling (for plan 1), rolling (for plan 2).

Notification: continuous (freshmen), continuous (out-of-state freshmen), continuous (transfers), rolling (early decision plan 1), rolling (early decision plan 2), rolling (early action).

CONTACT
Design Institute of San Diego, 8555 Commerce Avenue, San Diego, CA 92121. *Phone:* 858-566-1200 Ext. 1044. *Toll-free phone:* 800-619-4337.

DeVry University–Folsom Campus
Folsom, California
http://www.devry.edu/

CONTACT
DeVry University–Folsom Campus, 950 Iron Point Road, Folsom, CA 95630. *Toll-free phone:* 866-338-7934.

DeVry University–Fremont Campus
Fremont, California
http://www.devry.edu/

CONTACT
Admissions Office, DeVry University–Fremont Campus, 6600 Dumbarton Circle, Fremont, CA 94555. *Phone:* 510-574-1200. *Toll-free phone:* 866-338-7934.

DeVry University–Long Beach Campus
Long Beach, California
http://www.devry.edu/

CONTACT
Admissions Office, DeVry University–Long Beach Campus, 3880 Kilroy Airport Way, Long Beach, CA 90806. *Phone:* 562-427-0861. *Toll-free phone:* 866-338-7934.

DeVry University–Pomona Campus
Pomona, California
http://www.devry.edu/

- **Proprietary** comprehensive, founded 1983, part of DeVry University
- **Urban** campus
- **Coed**
- **Minimally difficult** entrance level

FACULTY
Student/faculty ratio: 19:1.

ACADEMICS
Calendar: semesters. *Degrees:* associate, bachelor's, master's, and postbachelor's certificates.

STUDENT LIFE
Housing options: college housing not available.

APPLYING
Options: deferred entrance.

Application fee: $30.

Required: high school transcript, interview.

CONTACT
DeVry University–Pomona Campus, 901 Corporate Center Drive, Pomona, CA 91768. *Phone:* 909-622-8866. *Toll-free phone:* 866-338-7934.

DeVry University–San Diego Campus
San Diego, California
http://www.devry.edu/

CONTACT
Admissions Office, DeVry University–San Diego Campus, 2655 Camino Del Rio North, Suite 350, San Diego, CA 92108-1633. *Phone:* 619-683-2446. *Toll-free phone:* 866-338-7934.

DeVry University–Sherman Oaks Campus
Sherman Oaks, California
http://www.devry.edu/

CONTACT
Admissions Office, DeVry University–Sherman Oaks Campus, 15301 Ventura Boulevard, D-100, Sherman Oaks, CA 91403. *Phone:* 818-713-8111. *Toll-free phone:* 866-338-7934.

Dominican University of California
San Rafael, California
http://www.dominican.edu/

- **Independent** comprehensive, founded 1890, affiliated with Roman Catholic Church
- **Suburban** 85-acre campus with easy access to San Francisco
- **Endowment** $28.3 million
- **Coed** 1,461 undergraduate students, 85% full-time, 69% women, 31% men
- **Moderately difficult** entrance level, 91% of applicants were admitted

UNDERGRAD STUDENTS
1,241 full-time, 220 part-time. 12% are from out of state; 5% Black or African American, non-Hispanic/Latino; 26% Hispanic/Latino; 27% Asian, non-Hispanic/Latino; 0.5% Native Hawaiian or other Pacific Islander, non-Hispanic/Latino; 0.3% American Indian or Alaska Native, non-Hispanic/Latino; 6% Two or more races, non-Hispanic/Latino; 5% Race/ethnicity unknown; 1% international; 8% transferred in; 35% live on campus.

Freshmen:
Admission: 2,041 applied, 1,857 admitted, 322 enrolled. ***Average high school GPA:*** 3.6. ***Test scores:*** SAT evidence-based reading and writing scores over 500: 86%; SAT math scores over 500: 82%; ACT scores over 18: 90%; SAT evidence-based reading and writing scores over 600: 35%; SAT math scores over 600: 34%; ACT scores over 24: 37%; SAT evidence-based reading and writing scores over 700: 5%; SAT math scores over 700: 6%; ACT scores over 30: 7%.

Retention: 93% of full-time freshmen returned.

FACULTY
Total: 348, 30% full-time.

Student/faculty ratio: 9:1.

ACADEMICS
Calendar: semesters. *Degrees:* bachelor's and master's.

Special study options: accelerated degree program, adult/continuing education programs, distance learning, double majors, honors programs, independent study, internships, off-campus study, part-time degree program, student-designed majors, study abroad.

Unusual degree programs: 3-2 business administration; nursing; occupational therapy.

Computers: 195 computers/terminals and 700 ports are available on campus for general student use. Students can access the following: computer help desk, free student e-mail accounts, online (class) grades, online (class) registration, online (class) schedules, office software. Campuswide network is available. 100% of college-owned or -operated housing units are wired for high-speed Internet access. Wireless service is available via entire campus.

Library: Archbishop Alemany Library. *Books:* 110,523 (physical); *Databases:* 84.

STUDENT LIFE
Housing options: coed. Campus housing is university owned. Freshman applicants given priority for college housing.

Activities and organizations: drama/theater group, student-run newspaper, radio station, choral group, Filipino Cultural Club, BSU, Perceptions, Global Ambassadors, Intramural Club/Programming.

Athletics Member NCAA. All Division II. ***Intercollegiate sports:*** basketball M(s)/W(s), cross-country running M(s)/W(s), golf M(s)/W(s), lacrosse M(s), soccer M(s)/W(s), softball W(s), tennis W(s), volleyball W(s). ***Intramural sports:*** badminton M/W, bowling M/W, cheerleading

W, sailing M/W, skiing (downhill) M/W, soccer M/W, softball M/W, table tennis M/W, tennis M/W, ultimate Frisbee M/W, volleyball M/W, weight lifting M/W.

Campus security: 24-hour patrols, late-night transport/escort service, controlled dormitory access.

Student services: health clinic, personal/psychological counseling.

COSTS & FINANCIAL AID

Costs (2020–21) ***Comprehensive fee:*** $63,504 includes full-time tuition ($47,190), mandatory fees ($680), and room and board ($15,634). Part-time tuition: $1970 per credit hour. ***College room only:*** $8702. Room and board charges vary according to board plan and housing facility. ***Payment plan:*** installment. ***Waivers:*** employees or children of employees.

Financial Aid Of all full-time matriculated undergraduates who enrolled in 2018, 1,113 applied for aid, 907 were judged to have need, 97 had their need fully met. In 2018, 197 non-need-based awards were made. ***Average percent of need met:*** 67. ***Average financial aid package:*** $32,288. ***Average need-based loan:*** $4610. ***Average need-based gift aid:*** $28,149. ***Average non-need-based aid:*** $18,529. ***Average indebtedness upon graduation:*** $31,978.

APPLYING

Standardized Tests *Required:* SAT or ACT (for admission).

Options: electronic application, deferred entrance.

Required: essay or personal statement, high school transcript, minimum 2.0 GPA, 1 letter of recommendation. ***Recommended:*** interview.

Application deadlines: 2/1 (freshmen), 2/1 (transfers).

Notification: continuous until 10/15 (freshmen), continuous (transfers).

CONTACT

Mr. Rich Toledo, Assistant Vice President, Undergraduate Admissions, Dominican University of California, 50 Acacia Avenue, San Rafael, CA 94901-2298. *Phone:* 415-485-3206. *Toll-free phone:* 888-323-6763. *Fax:* 415-485-3287. *E-mail:* rich.toledo@dominican.edu.

Epic Bible College

Sacramento, California

http://epic.edu/

CONTACT

Ms. Sheila Knoll, Assistant Director of Records, Epic Bible College, 4330 Auburn Boulevard, Sacramento, CA 95841. *Phone:* 916-348-4689. *E-mail:* kclarke@tlbc.edu.

Feather River College

Quincy, California

http://www.frc.edu/

- **District-supported** primarily 2-year, founded 1968, part of California Community College System
- **Rural** 420-acre campus
- **Endowment** $48,205
- **Coed** 1,990 undergraduate students, 23% full-time, 52% women, 48% men
- **Noncompetitive** entrance level, 100% of applicants were admitted

UNDERGRAD STUDENTS

460 full-time, 1,530 part-time. 9% are from out of state; 15% Black or African American, non-Hispanic/Latino; 23% Hispanic/Latino; 3% Asian, non-Hispanic/Latino; 2% Native Hawaiian or other Pacific Islander, non-Hispanic/Latino; 3% American Indian or Alaska Native, non-Hispanic/Latino; 0.2% Two or more races, non-Hispanic/Latino; 4% Race/ethnicity unknown; 0.5% international; 10% transferred in; 20% live on campus.

Freshmen:

Admission: 304 applied, 304 admitted, 302 enrolled.

Retention: 100% of full-time freshmen returned.

FACULTY

Total: 107, 24% full-time, 10% with terminal degrees.

Student/faculty ratio: 19:1.

ACADEMICS

Calendar: semesters plus summer and winter terms. *Degrees:* certificates, diplomas, associate, and bachelor's.

Special study options: academic remediation for entering students, adult/continuing education programs, advanced placement credit, cooperative education, distance learning, double majors, English as a second language, independent study, part-time degree program, services for LD students, summer session for credit.

Computers: 116 computers/terminals are available on campus for general student use. Students can access the following: computer help desk, free student e-mail accounts, online (class) grades, online (class) registration, online (class) schedules. Campuswide network is available. 100% of college-owned or -operated housing units are wired for high-speed Internet access. Wireless service is available via entire campus.

Library: Feather River College Library. *Databases:* 35. Weekly public service hours: 61; students can reserve study rooms.

STUDENT LIFE

Housing options: coed. Campus housing is university owned.

Activities and organizations: drama/theater group, choral group, Student Environmental Association, Horse Show Team, Prisoner and Student Social Justice Journalism Club, International, Cultural & Diversity Club, Black Student Union.

Athletics ***Intercollegiate sports:*** baseball M, basketball M/W, cross-country running W, equestrian sports M(s)/W(s), football M, sand volleyball W, soccer M/W, softball W, track and field W, volleyball W.

Campus security: student patrols, part-time private security company patrols.

Student services: health clinic, personal/psychological counseling.

COSTS & FINANCIAL AID

Costs (2019–20) ***Tuition:*** area resident $1461 full-time, $46 per credit part-time; state resident $1461 full-time, $46 per credit part-time; nonresident $9441 full-time, $312 per credit part-time. Full-time tuition and fees vary according to course load. Part-time tuition and fees vary according to course load. ***Required fees:*** $81 full-time, $2 per credit part-time, $18 per term part-time. ***Room only:*** $5350. Room and board charges vary according to housing facility. ***Payment plan:*** installment.

Financial Aid Of all full-time matriculated undergraduates who enrolled in 2018, 444 applied for aid, 384 were judged to have need, 3 had their need fully met.

APPLYING

Options: electronic application, deferred entrance.

CONTACT

Gretchen Baumgartner, Feather River College, 570 Golden Eagle Avenue, Quincy, CA 95971. *Phone:* 530-2830202 Ext. 285. *Toll-free phone:* 800-442-9799. *E-mail:* gbaumgartner@frc.edu.

FIDM/Fashion Institute of Design & Merchandising, Los Angeles Campus

Los Angeles, California

http://www.fidm.edu/

- **Proprietary** 4-year, founded 1969, part of FIDM/Fashion Institute of Design & Merchandising
- **Urban** campus with easy access to Los Angeles
- **Coed** 2,383 undergraduate students, 90% full-time, 83% women, 17% men
- **Moderately difficult** entrance level, 37% of applicants were admitted

UNDERGRAD STUDENTS

2,147 full-time, 236 part-time. Students come from 25 states and territories; 36% are from out of state; 7% Black or African American, non-Hispanic/Latino; 22% Hispanic/Latino; 11% Asian, non-Hispanic/Latino; 1% Native Hawaiian or other Pacific Islander, non-Hispanic/Latino; 0.9% American Indian or Alaska Native, non-Hispanic/Latino; 0.9% Two or more races, non-Hispanic/Latino; 5% Race/ethnicity unknown; 19% international.

Freshmen:

Admission: 2,014 applied, 737 admitted, 468 enrolled.

Retention: 81% of full-time freshmen returned.

FACULTY
Student/faculty ratio: 18:1.

ACADEMICS
Calendar: quarters. *Degrees:* associate, bachelor's, and master's (also includes Orange County Campus).

Special study options: academic remediation for entering students, accelerated degree program, adult/continuing education programs, advanced placement credit, cooperative education, distance learning, English as a second language, independent study, internships, off-campus study, part-time degree program, services for LD students, study abroad.

Computers: 433 computers/terminals and 20 ports are available on campus for general student use. Students can access the following: campus intranet, computer help desk, free student e-mail accounts, online (class) grades, online (class) registration, online (class) schedules. Campuswide network is available. Wireless service is available via entire campus.

Library: FIDM Los Angeles Campus Library. *Books:* 48,534 (physical), 2,778 (digital/electronic); *Serial titles:* 548 (physical); *Databases:* 39. Students can reserve study rooms.

STUDENT LIFE
Housing options: college housing not available.

Activities and organizations: Cross-Cultural Student Alliance, Fashion Industry Club, Phi Theta Kappa Honor Society, Student Council, FIDM MODE Magazine.

Campus security: 24-hour emergency response devices and patrols, late-night transport/escort service.

Student services: personal/psychological counseling, veterans affairs office.

COSTS
Costs (2019–20) ***Tuition:*** $31,015 full-time. Full-time tuition and fees vary according to program. ***Required fees:*** $1295 full-time. ***Payment plan:*** installment.

APPLYING
Standardized Tests *Recommended:* SAT and SAT Subject Tests or ACT (for admission).

Options: electronic application, deferred entrance.

Application fee: $25.

Required: essay or personal statement, high school transcript, minimum 2.5 GPA, 3 letters of recommendation, interview, major-determined project.

Application deadlines: rolling (freshmen), rolling (out-of-state freshmen), rolling (transfers).

Notification: continuous (freshmen), continuous (out-of-state freshmen), continuous (transfers).

CONTACT
Ms. Belinda Harding, Executive Director of Admissions, FIDM/Fashion Institute of Design & Merchandising, Los Angeles Campus, 919 South Grand Avenue, Los Angeles, CA 90015. *Phone:* 213-624-1200 Ext. 5150. *Toll-free phone:* 800-624-1200. *E-mail:* bharding@fidm.edu.

FIDM/Fashion Institute of Design & Merchandising, San Francisco Campus

San Francisco, California

http://www.fidm.edu/

- **Proprietary** 4-year, founded 1973, part of FIDM/Fashion Institute of Design & Merchandising
- **Urban** campus with easy access to San Francisco
- **Coed**
- **Moderately difficult** entrance level

FACULTY
Student/faculty ratio: 11:1.

ACADEMICS
Calendar: quarters. *Degrees:* associate and bachelor's.
Library: FIDM San Francisco Library. Students can reserve study rooms.

STUDENT LIFE
Housing options: college housing not available.

Activities and organizations: Cross-Cultural Student Alliance, Fashion Industry Club, Phi Theta Kappa- National Honor Society, Student Council, FIDM MODE Magazine.

Campus security: 24-hour emergency response devices and patrols, security escorts.

Student services: personal/psychological counseling, veterans affairs office.

APPLYING
Standardized Tests *Recommended:* SAT or ACT (for admission).

Options: electronic application, deferred entrance.

Application fee: $25.

Required: essay or personal statement, high school transcript, minimum 2.5 GPA, 3 letters of recommendation, interview, major-determined project.

CONTACT
Ms. Sheryl Badalamenti, Director of Admissions, FIDM/Fashion Institute of Design & Merchandising, San Francisco Campus, 55 Stockton Street, San Francisco, CA 94108-5829. *Phone:* 415-433-6691 Ext. 1550. *Toll-free phone:* 800-422-3436. *E-mail:* sbadalamenti@fidm.edu.

Fremont College

Cerritos, California

http://www.fremont.edu/

CONTACT
Natașha Dawson, Director of Admissions, Fremont College, 18000 Studebaker Road, Suite 900A, Cerritos, CA 90703. *Phone:* 562-809-5100. *Toll-free phone:* 800-373-6668. *Fax:* 562-809-5100. *E-mail:* info@fremont.edu.

Fresno Pacific University

Fresno, California

http://www.fresno.edu/

CONTACT
Andy Johnson, Director of Undergraduate Admissions, Fresno Pacific University, 1717 South Chestnut Avenue, Fresno, CA 93727. *Phone:* 559-453-2000. *Toll-free phone:* 800-660-6089. *Fax:* 559-453-2007. *E-mail:* andy.johnson@fresno.edu.

Gnomon School of Visual Effects

Hollywood, California

http://www.gnomon.edu/

CONTACT
Gnomon School of Visual Effects, 1015 N. Cahuenga Boulevard, Suite 54301, Hollywood, CA 90038.

Golden Gate University

San Francisco, California

http://www.ggu.edu/

CONTACT
Mr. Louis D. Riccardi Jr., Director of Enrollment Services, Golden Gate University, 536 Mission Street, San Francisco, CA 94105-2968. *Phone:* 415-442-7800. *Toll-free phone:* 800-448-3381. *Fax:* 415-442-7807. *E-mail:* info@ggu.edu.

Grace Mission University

Fullerton, California

http://www.gm.edu/

CONTACT
Grace Mission University, 1645 West Valencia Drive, Fullerton, CA 92833.

Gurnick Academy of Medical Arts

San Mateo, California

http://www.gurnick.edu/

CONTACT
Gurnick Academy of Medical Arts, 2121 South El Camino Real, Building C 2000, San Mateo, CA 94403.

Harvey Mudd College

Claremont, California

http://www.hmc.edu/

- **Independent** 4-year, founded 1955, part of The Claremont Colleges
- **Suburban** 33-acre campus with easy access to Los Angeles
- **Endowment** $298.9 million
- **Coed**
- **Most difficult** entrance level

FACULTY
Student/faculty ratio: 8:1.

ACADEMICS
Calendar: semesters. *Degree:* bachelor's.
Library: Claremont Colleges Library plus 1 other.

STUDENT LIFE
Housing options: on-campus residence required for freshman year; coed. Campus housing is university owned. Freshman campus housing is guaranteed.

Activities and organizations: drama/theater group, student-run newspaper, radio station, choral group, Claremont Colleges Ballroom Dance Company, Science Bus, Society of Women Engineers (SWE), Intervarsity Christian Fellowship, Gonzo Unicycle Madness (Unicycle Club).

Athletics Member NCAA. All Division III.

Campus security: 24-hour emergency response devices and patrols, late-night transport/escort service, controlled dormitory access.

Student services: health clinic, personal/psychological counseling, women's center.

COSTS & FINANCIAL AID
Costs (2019–20) ***One-time required fee:*** $250. ***Comprehensive fee:*** $77,339 includes full-time tuition ($58,359), mandatory fees ($301), and room and board ($18,679). Part-time tuition: $1824 per unit. Part-time tuition and fees vary according to course load. ***College room only:*** $10,234. Room and board charges vary according to board plan.

Financial Aid Of all full-time matriculated undergraduates who enrolled in 2018, 513 applied for aid, 430 were judged to have need, 430 had their need fully met. In 2018, 169 non-need-based awards were made. ***Average percent of need met:*** 100. ***Average financial aid package:*** $47,348. ***Average need-based loan:*** $4113. ***Average need-based gift aid:*** $45,010. ***Average non-need-based aid:*** $14,735. ***Average indebtedness upon graduation:*** $29,139. ***Financial aid deadline:*** 2/1.

APPLYING
Standardized Tests *Required:* SAT or ACT (for admission), SAT Subject Tests (for admission).

Options: electronic application, early admission, early decision, deferred entrance.

Application fee: $70.

Required: essay or personal statement, high school transcript, 3 letters of recommendation. ***Recommended:*** interview.

CONTACT
Harvey Mudd College, 301 Platt Boulevard, Claremont, CA 91711-5994.

Holy Names University

Oakland, California

http://www.hnu.edu/

CONTACT
Holy Names University, 3500 Mountain Boulevard, Oakland, CA 94619. *Phone:* 510-436-1351. *Toll-free phone:* 800-430-1321. *Fax:* 510-436-1325. *E-mail:* admissions@hnu.edu.

Homestead Schools

Torrance, California

http://www.homesteadschools.com/

CONTACT
Homestead Schools, 23844 Hawthorne Boulevard, Suite 200, Torrance, CA 90505.

Hope International University

Fullerton, California

http://www.hiu.edu/

- **Independent** comprehensive, founded 1928, affiliated with Christian Churches and Churches of Christ
- **Suburban** 16-acre campus with easy access to Los Angeles
- **Coed** 651 undergraduate students, 83% full-time, 55% women, 45% men
- **Moderately difficult** entrance level, 37% of applicants were admitted

UNDERGRAD STUDENTS
538 full-time, 113 part-time. Students come from 33 states and territories; 16 other countries; 18% are from out of state; 8% Black or African American, non-Hispanic/Latino; 29% Hispanic/Latino; 5% Asian, non-Hispanic/Latino; 2% Native Hawaiian or other Pacific Islander, non-Hispanic/Latino; 0.8% American Indian or Alaska Native, non-Hispanic/Latino; 12% Two or more races, non-Hispanic/Latino; 6% Race/ethnicity unknown; 15% transferred in; 48% live on campus.

Freshmen:
Admission: 685 applied, 252 admitted, 111 enrolled. ***Average high school GPA:*** 3.3. ***Test scores:*** SAT evidence-based reading and writing scores over 500: 53%; SAT math scores over 500: 49%; ACT scores over 18: 71%; SAT evidence-based reading and writing scores over 600: 12%; SAT math scores over 600: 10%; ACT scores over 24: 30%; SAT evidence-based reading and writing scores over 700: 1%; ACT scores over 30: 9%.

Retention: 71% of full-time freshmen returned.

FACULTY
Total: 91, 24% full-time, 38% with terminal degrees.

Student/faculty ratio: 13:1.

ACADEMICS
Calendar: 4-1-4. *Degrees:* certificates, associate, bachelor's, master's, and postbachelor's certificates.

Special study options: academic remediation for entering students, adult/continuing education programs, advanced placement credit, distance learning, double majors, English as a second language, independent study, internships, off-campus study, part-time degree program, services for LD students, study abroad. ***ROTC:*** Army (c).

Computers: 30 computers/terminals are available on campus for general student use. Students can access the following: computer help desk, free student e-mail accounts, online (class) grades, online (class) registration, online (class) schedules, 30 Internet hotspots on campus. Campuswide network is available. 100% of college-owned or -operated housing units are wired for high-speed Internet access. Wireless service is available via entire campus.
Library: Darling Library. *Books:* 72,000 (physical), 198,000 (digital/electronic); *Serial titles:* 28,000 (physical); *Databases:* 49. Weekly public service hours: 68.

STUDENT LIFE
Housing options: on-campus residence required through sophomore year; men-only, women-only. Campus housing is university owned. Freshman campus housing is guaranteed.

Activities and organizations: drama/theater group, student-run newspaper, choral group, Campus Ministries, International Student Organization, Musical Theater, Student Government, Student Publications.

Athletics Member NAIA, NCCAA. ***Intercollegiate sports:*** baseball M(s), basketball M(s)/W(s), cross-country running M(s)/W(s), golf M(s)/W(s), soccer M(s)/W(s), softball W(s), tennis M(s)/W(s), track and field M(s)/W(s), volleyball M(s)/W(s). ***Intramural sports:*** volleyball M/W.

Campus security: 24-hour emergency response devices and patrols, late-night transport/escort service, controlled dormitory access.

Student services: personal/psychological counseling.

COSTS & FINANCIAL AID
Costs (2020–21) ***Comprehensive fee:*** $45,500 includes full-time tuition ($33,250), mandatory fees ($1200), and room and board ($11,050). Full-time tuition and fees vary according to course level, course load, degree level, location, program, and reciprocity agreements. Part-time tuition: $1500 per credit hour. Part-time tuition and fees vary according to course level, course load, degree level, location, program, and reciprocity agreements. ***Required fees:*** $1200 per year part-time. ***College room only:*** $5150. Room and board charges vary according to board plan. ***Payment plan:*** installment. ***Waivers:*** employees or children of employees.

Financial Aid Of all full-time matriculated undergraduates who enrolled in 2018, 412 applied for aid, 383 were judged to have need, 10 had their need fully met. In 2018, 16 non-need-based awards were made. ***Average percent of need met:*** 33. ***Average financial aid package:*** $14,962. ***Average need-based loan:*** $3141. ***Average need-based gift aid:*** $12,842. ***Average non-need-based aid:*** $12,937. ***Average indebtedness upon graduation:*** $35,427.

APPLYING
Standardized Tests *Required:* SAT or ACT (for admission).

Options: electronic application, deferred entrance.

Application fee: $40.

Required: essay or personal statement, high school transcript, minimum 2.5 GPA, 2 letters of recommendation, rank in upper 50% of high school class. ***Required for some:*** interview.

Application deadlines: rolling (freshmen), rolling (out-of-state freshmen), rolling (transfers).

Notification: continuous (freshmen), continuous (out-of-state freshmen), continuous (transfers).

CONTACT
Michael Cruz, Director of Undergraduate Admissions, Hope International University, 2500 East Nutwood Avenue, Fullerton, CA 92831-3138. *Phone:* 714-8793901 Ext. 2294. *Toll-free phone:* 866-722-HOPE. *E-mail:* macruz@hiu.edu.

Humboldt State University

Arcata, California

http://www.humboldt.edu/

- **State-supported** comprehensive, founded 1913, part of California State University System
- **Rural** 161-acre campus
- **Coed**
- **Minimally difficult** entrance level

FACULTY
Student/faculty ratio: 22:1.

ACADEMICS
Calendar: semesters. *Degrees:* bachelor's, master's, post-master's, and postbachelor's certificates.
Library: Humbolot State University Library. *Books:* 487,338 (physical), 165,816 (digital/electronic); *Serial titles:* 34,235 (physical), 190 (digital/electronic); *Databases:* 89. Weekly public service hours: 100; students can reserve study rooms.

STUDENT LIFE
Housing options: coed. Campus housing is university owned. Freshman campus housing is guaranteed.

Activities and organizations: drama/theater group, student-run newspaper, radio station, choral group, marching band, Bicycle Learning Center, Campus Center for Appropriate Technology (CCAT), Youth Educational Services, HOLA, MECHA, national fraternities, national sororities.

Athletics Member NCAA. All Division II.

Campus security: 24-hour emergency response devices and patrols, late-night transport/escort service, controlled dormitory access.

Student services: health clinic, personal/psychological counseling, women's center, veterans affairs office.

COSTS & FINANCIAL AID
Costs (2019–20) ***Tuition:*** state resident $5742 full-time, $3330 per term part-time; nonresident $17,622 full-time, $396 per credit part-time. ***Required fees:*** $2038 full-time, $1674 part-time. ***Room and board:*** $13,562; room only: $6216. Room and board charges vary according to board plan and location.

Financial Aid Of all full-time matriculated undergraduates who enrolled in 2019, 5,330 applied for aid, 4,703 were judged to have need, 462 had their need fully met. In 2019, 501 non-need-based awards were made. ***Average percent of need met:*** 76. ***Average financial aid package:*** $15,980. ***Average need-based loan:*** $7623. ***Average need-based gift aid:*** $9422. ***Average non-need-based aid:*** $917. ***Average indebtedness upon graduation:*** $23,028.

APPLYING
Standardized Tests *Required for some:* SAT or ACT (for admission).

Options: electronic application, deferred entrance.

Application fee: $55.

Required: high school transcript, minimum 2.0 GPA.

CONTACT
Mr. Steven Ladwig, Associate Director of Admissions, Humboldt State University, 1 Harpst Street, Arcata, CA 95521. *Phone:* 707-826-4402. *Toll-free phone:* 866 850 9556. *Fax:* 707-826-6190. *E-mail:* hsuinfo@humboldt.edu.

Humphreys University

Stockton, California

http://www.humphreys.edu/

- **Independent** comprehensive, founded 1896
- **Suburban** 10-acre campus with easy access to San Francisco
- **Coed**
- **Noncompetitive** entrance level

FACULTY
Student/faculty ratio: 12:1.

ACADEMICS
Calendar: quarters. *Degrees:* associate, bachelor's, master's, and doctoral.
Library: Humphreys College Library plus 1 other.

STUDENT LIFE
Housing options: coed.

Activities and organizations: Business Club, Paralegal Club, Student Council, Collegiate Secretaries International.

Campus security: 24-hour patrols, late-night transport/escort service.

APPLYING
Options: early admission, deferred entrance.

Application fee: $40.

Required: high school transcript, minimum 2.0 GPA. ***Recommended:*** interview.

CONTACT
Humphreys University, 6650 Inglewood Avenue, Stockton, CA 95207-3896. *Phone:* 209-235-2901.

Interior Designers Institute

Newport Beach, California

http://www.idi.edu/

CONTACT
Interior Designers Institute, 1061 Camelback Road, Newport Beach, CA 92660.

John F. Kennedy University

Pleasant Hill, California

http://www.jfku.edu/

CONTACT
Ms. Jen Miller-Hogg, Director of Admissions, John F. Kennedy University, 100 Ellinwood Way, Pleasant Hill, CA 94523-4817. *Phone:* 925-969-3584. *Toll-free phone:* 800-696-JFKU. *E-mail:* jmhogg@jfku.edu.

John Paul the Great Catholic University

Escondido, California

http://www.jpcatholic.edu/

- **Independent** comprehensive, founded 2006, affiliated with Roman Catholic Church
- **Urban** 3-acre campus with easy access to San Diego
- **Coed**
- **Moderately difficult** entrance level

FACULTY
Student/faculty ratio: 15:1.

ACADEMICS
Calendar: quarters. *Degrees:* bachelor's and master's.
Library: John Paul the Great Catholic University Library. *Books:* 21,325 (physical).

STUDENT LIFE
Housing options: on-campus residence required through senior year; men-only, women-only. Campus housing is leased by the school. Freshman campus housing is guaranteed.

Activities and organizations: drama/theater group, student-run newspaper, choral group, Student government, Knights of Columbus, Flag football, Swing dance club, Gaming club.

Campus security: student patrols.

Student services: personal/psychological counseling.

COSTS & FINANCIAL AID
Costs (2019–20) ***Tuition:*** $26,100 full-time, $700 per credit part-time. No tuition increase for student's term of enrollment. ***Required fees:*** $900 full-time. ***Room only:*** $7710.

Financial Aid Of all full-time matriculated undergraduates who enrolled in 2017, 200 applied for aid, 178 were judged to have need, 13 had their need fully met. In 2017, 65 non-need-based awards were made. ***Average percent of need met:*** 46. ***Average financial aid package:*** $18,249. ***Average need-based loan:*** $4227. ***Average need-based gift aid:*** $14,829. ***Average non-need-based aid:*** $8447.

APPLYING
Standardized Tests *Required for some:* SAT or ACT (for admission).

Options: electronic application, deferred entrance.

Application fee: $50.

Required: essay or personal statement, high school transcript, minimum 2.6 GPA. ***Recommended:*** interview.

CONTACT
Mr. Martin Harold, Vice President of Admissions, John Paul the Great Catholic University, 220 W. Grand Avenue, Escondido, CA 92025. *Phone:* 858-653-6740 Ext. 1101. *Fax:* 858-653-3791. *E-mail:* mharold@jpcatholic.com.

Laguna College of Art & Design

Laguna Beach, California

http://www.lcad.edu/

CONTACT
Madison Keyes, Admissions Coordinator, Laguna College of Art & Design, 2222 Laguna Canyon Road, Laguna Beach, CA 92651. *Phone:* 949-376-6000 Ext. 248. *Toll-free phone:* 800-255-0762. *E-mail:* mkeyes@lcad.edu.

La Sierra University

Riverside, California

http://www.lasierra.edu/

- **Independent Seventh-day Adventist** comprehensive, founded 1922, part of Seventh-Day Adventist Education System
- **Suburban** 150-acre campus with easy access to Los Angeles
- **Endowment** $17.2 million
- **Coed** 1,842 undergraduate students, 89% full-time, 60% women, 40% men
- **Minimally difficult** entrance level, 49% of applicants were admitted

UNDERGRAD STUDENTS
1,647 full-time, 195 part-time. Students come from 48 states and territories; 138 other countries; 11% are from out of state; 7% Black or African American, non-Hispanic/Latino; 47% Hispanic/Latino; 17% Asian, non-Hispanic/Latino; 1% Native Hawaiian or other Pacific Islander, non-Hispanic/Latino; 0.3% American Indian or Alaska Native, non-Hispanic/Latino; 4% Two or more races, non-Hispanic/Latino; 0.1% Race/ethnicity unknown; 11% international; 8% transferred in; 25% live on campus.

Freshmen:
Admission: 4,688 applied, 2,306 admitted, 399 enrolled. ***Average high school GPA:*** 3.3.

Retention: 89% of full-time freshmen returned.

FACULTY
Total: 118, 80% full-time, 85% with terminal degrees.

Student/faculty ratio: 15:1.

ACADEMICS
Calendar: quarters. *Degrees:* certificates, bachelor's, master's, doctoral, post-master's, and postbachelor's certificates.

Special study options: academic remediation for entering students, accelerated degree program, adult/continuing education programs, advanced placement credit, distance learning, double majors, English as a second language, honors programs, independent study, internships, off-campus study, part-time degree program, services for LD students, student-designed majors, study abroad, summer session for credit.

Unusual degree programs: 3-2 business administration; criminal justice.

Computers: 300 computers/terminals are available on campus for general student use. Students can access the following: computer help desk, free student e-mail accounts, online (class) grades, online (class) registration, online (class) schedules, student portals. Campuswide network is available. Wireless service is available via entire campus.
Library: University Library plus 1 other. *Books:* 246,563 (physical), 155,250 (digital/electronic); *Serial titles:* 610 (physical); *Databases:* 121. Weekly public service hours: 76; students can reserve study rooms.

STUDENT LIFE
Housing options: coed, men-only, women-only, cooperative, special housing for students with disabilities. Campus housing is university owned. Freshman campus housing is guaranteed.

Activities and organizations: drama/theater group, student-run newspaper, choral group, Pre Dentistry, Pre Med, Enactus (SIFE), International Club, Black Student Association.

Athletics Member NAIA. ***Intercollegiate sports:*** basketball M/W, golf M, soccer M, softball W, volleyball W. ***Intramural sports:*** baseball M, basketball M/W, soccer M, softball W, volleyball W.

Campus security: 24-hour emergency response devices and patrols, student patrols, late-night transport/escort service, controlled dormitory access.

Student services: health clinic, personal/psychological counseling, women's center.

COSTS & FINANCIAL AID
Costs (2020–21) ***Comprehensive fee:*** $48,453 includes full-time tuition ($34,218), mandatory fees ($990), and room and board ($13,245). Full-time tuition and fees vary according to course load, location, and program. Part-time tuition: $951 per unit. Part-time tuition and fees vary according to course load, location, and program. ***College room only:*** $12,282. Room and board charges vary according to board plan. ***Payment plan:*** installment. ***Waivers:*** adult students and employees or children of employees.

Financial Aid ***Financial aid deadline:*** 8/15.

APPLYING
Standardized Tests *Required:* SAT or ACT (for admission).

Options: electronic application, deferred entrance.

Required: high school transcript, minimum 2.0 GPA, Eligibility Index Table (combination of GPA and test scores). ***Required for some:*** essay or personal statement, 1 letter of recommendation, interview. ***Recommended:*** minimum 2.0 GPA.

Application deadlines: 2/1 (freshmen), 7/1 (transfers).

Notification: continuous (freshmen), continuous (transfers).

CONTACT

Ms. Ivy Teheda, Associate Director of Admissions, La Sierra University, 4500 Riverwalk Parkway, Riverside, CA 92505. *Phone:* 951-785-2957. *Toll-free phone:* 800-874-5587. *Fax:* 951-785-2447. *E-mail:* iteheda@lasierra.edu.

Life Pacific College

San Dimas, California

http://www.lifepacific.edu/

CONTACT

Ms. Dorienne Elston, Director of Admissions, Life Pacific College, 1100 Covina Boulevard, San Dimas, CA 91773-3298. *Phone:* 909-599-5433 Ext. 314. *Toll-free phone:* 877-886-5433 Ext. 314. *Fax:* 909-706-3070. *E-mail:* adm@lifepacific.edu.

Lincoln University

Oakland, California

http://www.lincolnuca.edu/

CONTACT

Mr. Sunny Saggi, Admissions Officer, Lincoln University, 401 15th Street, Oakland, CA 94612. *Phone:* 510-628-8010 Ext. 8011. *Toll-free phone:* 888-810-9998. *Fax:* 510-628-8012. *E-mail:* admissions@lincolnuca.edu.

Loma Linda University

Loma Linda, California

http://www.llu.edu/

CONTACT

Admissions Office, Loma Linda University, 11139 Anderson Street, Loma Linda, CA 92350. *Phone:* 909-558-1000. *Toll-free phone:* 800-422-4558.

Los Angeles Academy of Figurative Art

Van Nuys, California

http://www.laafa.edu/

CONTACT

Los Angeles Academy of Figurative Art, 16926 Saticoy Street, Van Nuys, CA 91406.

Los Angeles Film School

Hollywood, California

http://www.lafilm.edu/

- **Proprietary** 4-year, founded 1999
- **Urban** campus with easy access to Hollywood
- **Coed** 4,500 undergraduate students, 100% full-time, 28% women, 72% men
- **Noncompetitive** entrance level

UNDERGRAD STUDENTS

4,500 full-time. Students come from 48 states and territories; 15 other countries; 45% are from out of state.

FACULTY

Total: 171, 89% full-time.

ACADEMICS

Calendar: continuous. *Degrees:* associate and bachelor's.

Special study options: accelerated degree program, adult/continuing education programs, advanced placement credit, cooperative education, distance learning, internships, services for LD students.

Computers: 8 computers/terminals are available on campus for general student use. Students can access the following: campus intranet, computer help desk, free student e-mail accounts, online (class) grades, online (class) schedules. Campuswide network is available. Wireless service is available via classrooms, computer centers, computer labs, libraries, student centers.

Library: Main Library plus 1 other.

STUDENT LIFE

Housing options: college housing not available.

Campus security: 24-hour patrols.

Student services: veterans affairs office.

APPLYING

Options: electronic application.

Application fee: $75.

Required: essay or personal statement, high school transcript, interview.

CONTACT

Los Angeles Film School, 6363 Sunset Boulevard, Hollywood, CA 90028. *Toll-free phone:* 877-952-3456.

Loyola Marymount University

Los Angeles, California

http://www.lmu.edu/

- **Independent Roman Catholic** comprehensive, founded 1911
- **Suburban** 142-acre campus with easy access to Los Angeles
- **Endowment** $476.2 million
- **Coed** 6,778 undergraduate students, 97% full-time, 55% women, 45% men
- 44% of applicants were admitted

UNDERGRAD STUDENTS

6,548 full-time, 230 part-time. Students come from 89 other countries; 33% are from out of state; 7% Black or African American, non-Hispanic/Latino; 23% Hispanic/Latino; 10% Asian, non-Hispanic/Latino; 0.2% Native Hawaiian or other Pacific Islander, non-Hispanic/Latino; 7% Two or more races, non-Hispanic/Latino; 11% international; 6% transferred in; 47% live on campus.

Freshmen:

Admission: 18,592 applied, 8,150 admitted, 1,467 enrolled. ***Average high school GPA:*** 3.9. ***Test scores:*** SAT evidence-based reading and writing scores over 500: 99%; SAT math scores over 500: 99%; ACT scores over 18: 99%; SAT evidence-based reading and writing scores over 600: 86%; SAT math scores over 600: 82%; ACT scores over 24: 94%; SAT evidence-based reading and writing scores over 700: 29%; SAT math scores over 700: 33%; ACT scores over 30: 45%.

Retention: 89% of full-time freshmen returned.

ACADEMICS

Calendar: semesters. *Degrees:* bachelor's, master's, doctoral, post-master's, and postbachelor's certificates.

Special study options: accelerated degree program, advanced placement credit, distance learning, double majors, honors programs, independent study, internships, part-time degree program, student-designed majors, study abroad. ***ROTC:*** Army (c), Air Force (b).

Unusual degree programs: 3-2 mechanical engineering, healthcare systems engineering, educational studies.

Computers: 820 computers/terminals are available on campus for general student use. Students can access the following: campus intranet, computer help desk, free student e-mail accounts, online (class) grades, online (class) registration, online (class) schedules. Campuswide network is available. 100% of college-owned or -operated housing units are wired for high-speed Internet access. Wireless service is available via entire campus.

Library: William H. Hannon Library. Study areas open 24 hours, 5–7 days a week; students can reserve study rooms.

STUDENT LIFE

Housing options: coed, men-only, women-only, special housing for students with disabilities. Campus housing is university owned. Freshman applicants given priority for college housing.

Activities and organizations: drama/theater group, student-run newspaper, radio and television station, choral group, national fraternities, national sororities.

Athletics Member NCAA. All Division I. ***Intercollegiate sports:*** baseball M(s), basketball M(s)/W(s), cheerleading M/W, crew M/W(s), cross-country running M(s)/W(s), golf M(s), sand volleyball W(s), soccer M(s)/W(s), softball W(s), swimming and diving W(s), tennis M(s)/W(s), track and field M/W, volleyball W(s), water polo M(s)/W(s). ***Intramural***

sports: baseball M(c), basketball M/W(c), football M/W, ice hockey M(c), lacrosse M(c)/W(c), rugby M(c), sand volleyball M/W, skiing (downhill) M(c)/W(c), soccer M(c)/W(c), table tennis M/W, tennis M(c)/W(c), ultimate Frisbee M(c)/W(c), volleyball M(c)/W(c).

Campus security: 24-hour emergency response devices and patrols, late-night transport/escort service, controlled dormitory access.

Student services: health clinic, personal/psychological counseling, veterans affairs office.

COSTS & FINANCIAL AID

Costs (2019–20) ***One-time required fee:*** $400. ***Comprehensive fee:*** $65,893 includes full-time tuition ($49,550), mandatory fees ($733), and room and board ($15,610). Full-time tuition and fees vary according to reciprocity agreements. Part-time tuition: $2068 per credit hour. Part-time tuition and fees vary according to course load. ***Required fees:*** $9 per unit part-time, $65 per term part-time. ***College room only:*** $11,110. Room and board charges vary according to board plan and housing facility. ***Payment plan:*** installment. ***Waivers:*** employees or children of employees.

Financial Aid Of all full-time matriculated undergraduates who enrolled in 2017, 4,310 applied for aid, 3,242 were judged to have need, 730 had their need fully met. 1,306 Federal Work-Study jobs (averaging $1932). 2,123 state and other part-time jobs (averaging $1986). In 2017, 1689 non-need-based awards were made. ***Average percent of need met:*** 66. ***Average financial aid package:*** $30,544. ***Average need-based loan:*** $6223. ***Average need-based gift aid:*** $22,088. ***Average non-need-based aid:*** $10,282. ***Average indebtedness upon graduation:*** $32,262.

APPLYING

Standardized Tests *Required:* SAT or ACT (for admission).

Options: electronic application, early admission, early decision, early action, deferred entrance.

Application fee: $60.

Required: essay or personal statement, high school transcript, 1 letter of recommendation. ***Required for some:*** portfolio or audition required for animation, dance, music, and theatre applicants; portfolio optional for production (film and television) and studio arts applicants. ***Recommended:*** portfolio or audition required for animation, dance, music, and theatre applicants; portfolio optional for production (film and television) and studio arts applicants.

Application deadlines: 1/15 (freshmen), 3/15 (transfers), 11/1 (early action).

Early decision deadline: 11/1.

Notification: continuous (freshmen), continuous (transfers), 12/1 (early decision), 12/20 (early action).

CONTACT

Loyola Marymount University, 1 LMU Drive, Los Angeles, CA 90045. *Phone:* 310-338-2750. *Toll-free phone:* 800-LMU-INFO.

Marymount California University

Rancho Palos Verdes, California

http://www.marymountcalifornia.edu/

- **Independent Roman Catholic** comprehensive, founded 1932
- **Suburban** 26-acre campus with easy access to Los Angeles
- **Endowment** $10.7 million
- **Coed** 602 undergraduate students, 97% full-time, 50% women, 50% men
- **Minimally difficult** entrance level, 86% of applicants were admitted

UNDERGRAD STUDENTS

586 full-time, 16 part-time. 7% are from out of state; 7% Black or African American, non-Hispanic/Latino; 44% Hispanic/Latino; 5% Asian, non-Hispanic/Latino; 0.3% Native Hawaiian or other Pacific Islander, non-Hispanic/Latino; 0.2% American Indian or Alaska Native, non-Hispanic/Latino; 6% Two or more races, non-Hispanic/Latino; 3% Race/ethnicity unknown; 14% international; 12% transferred in; 36% live on campus.

Freshmen:

Admission: 1,481 applied, 1,267 admitted, 117 enrolled. ***Average high school GPA:*** 3.1. ***Test scores:*** SAT evidence-based reading and writing scores over 500: 59%; SAT math scores over 500: 53%; ACT scores over 18: 75%; SAT evidence-based reading and writing scores over 600: 11%; SAT math scores over 600: 15%; ACT scores over 24: 33%; SAT evidence-based reading and writing scores over 700: 3%; SAT math scores over 700: 5%.

Retention: 65% of full-time freshmen returned.

FACULTY

Total: 46, 67% full-time, 54% with terminal degrees.

Student/faculty ratio: 17:1.

ACADEMICS

Calendar: semesters. *Degrees:* associate, bachelor's, and master's.

Special study options: academic remediation for entering students, accelerated degree program, adult/continuing education programs, advanced placement credit, cooperative education, distance learning, English as a second language, honors programs, independent study, internships, off-campus study, part-time degree program, services for LD students, study abroad, summer session for credit.

Unusual degree programs: 3-2 business administration.

Computers: 210 computers/terminals are available on campus for general student use. Students can access the following: campus intranet, computer help desk, free student e-mail accounts, online (class) grades, online (class) registration, online (class) schedules. Campuswide network is available. 100% of college-owned or -operated housing units are wired for high-speed Internet access. Wireless service is available via entire campus.

Library: College Library plus 1 other. *Books:* 23,246 (physical), 135,971 (digital/electronic); *Serial titles:* 255 (physical), 30,329 (digital/electronic); *Databases:* 51. Weekly public service hours: 60; students can reserve study rooms.

STUDENT LIFE

Housing options: coed, special housing for students with disabilities. Campus housing is university owned. Freshman applicants given priority for college housing.

Activities and organizations: drama/theater group, choral group, Latinos Unidos, Student Veterans Organization, Marymount Pride, Black Student Union, Society for Advancement of Management (SAM).

Athletics Member NAIA. ***Intercollegiate sports:*** baseball M(s), golf M(s), lacrosse M(s)/W(s), soccer M(s)/W(s), track and field M(s). ***Intramural sports:*** basketball M/W, golf M/W, lacrosse M/W, soccer M/W, softball M/W, swimming and diving M/W, track and field M/W, volleyball M/W.

Campus security: 24-hour emergency response devices and patrols, late-night transport/escort service, controlled dormitory access.

Student services: health clinic, personal/psychological counseling, veterans affairs office.

COSTS & FINANCIAL AID

Costs (2020–21) ***Tuition:*** $35,158 full-time, $1475 per credit hour part-time. ***Required fees:*** $2000 full-time. ***Room only:*** Room and board charges vary according to board plan and housing facility. ***Payment plan:*** installment. ***Waivers:*** senior citizens and employees or children of employees.

Financial Aid Of all full-time matriculated undergraduates who enrolled in 2019, 409 applied for aid, 381 were judged to have need, 67 had their need fully met. In 2019, 92 non-need-based awards were made. ***Average percent of need met:*** 73. ***Average financial aid package:*** $30,159. ***Average need-based loan:*** $4683. ***Average need-based gift aid:*** $17,744. ***Average non-need-based aid:*** $13,811. ***Average indebtedness upon graduation:*** $24,143. ***Financial aid deadline:*** 2/15.

APPLYING

Options: electronic application, deferred entrance.

Application fee: $50.

Required: high school transcript. ***Required for some:*** essay or personal statement, interview. ***Recommended:*** minimum 2.0 GPA.

Notification: continuous until 9/1 (freshmen), continuous until 9/1 (transfers).

CONTACT

Meshach Puerto, Assistant Director of Admissions, Marymount California University, 30800 Palos Verdes Drive East, Rancho Palos Verdes, CA 90275. *Phone:* 310-377-5501 Ext. 7378. *Fax:* 310-303-7698. *E-mail:* mpuerto@marymountcalifornia.edu.

The Master's University

Santa Clarita, California

http://www.masters.edu/

CONTACT

Mr. Dariu Dumitru, Director of Admissions, The Master's University, 21726 Placerita Canyon Road, Santa Clarita, CA 91321. *Phone:* 661-362-2363. *Toll-free phone:* 800-568-6248. *Fax:* 661-362-2718. *E-mail:* admissions@masters.edu.

Menlo College

Atherton, California

http://www.menlo.edu/

- **Independent** 4-year, founded 1927
- **Small-town** 45-acre campus with easy access to San Francisco
- **Endowment** $25.6 million
- **Coed**
- **Moderately difficult** entrance level

FACULTY

Student/faculty ratio: 14:1.

ACADEMICS

Calendar: semesters. *Degree:* bachelor's.
Library: Bowman Library. *Books:* 47,340 (physical), 17,379 (digital/electronic); *Serial titles:* 76 (physical); *Databases:* 42. Weekly public service hours: 95; students can reserve study rooms.

STUDENT LIFE

Housing options: on-campus residence required through sophomore year; coed, men-only, women-only. Campus housing is university owned.

Activities and organizations: student-run newspaper, International Club, Student Government, SERV, Finance Club, Hawaiian Club.

Athletics Member NAIA.

Campus security: 24-hour emergency response devices and patrols, controlled dormitory access.

Student services: personal/psychological counseling, women's center, veterans affairs office.

FINANCIAL AID

Financial Aid Of all full-time matriculated undergraduates who enrolled in 2014, 522 applied for aid, 478 were judged to have need, 54 had their need fully met. 345 Federal Work-Study jobs (averaging $1024). In 2014, 168 non-need-based awards were made. ***Average percent of need met:*** 66. ***Average financial aid package:*** $28,874. ***Average need-based loan:*** $3741. ***Average need-based gift aid:*** $25,073. ***Average non-need-based aid:*** $12,737. ***Average indebtedness upon graduation:*** $29,943.

APPLYING

Standardized Tests *Required:* SAT or ACT (for admission).

Options: electronic application, early admission, early action, deferred entrance.

Application fee: $40.

Required: essay or personal statement, high school transcript, 1 letter of recommendation. ***Recommended:*** minimum 2.5 GPA, interview.

CONTACT

Priscila DeSouza, Associate Dean of Enrollment Management, Menlo College, 1000 El Camino Real, Atherton, CA 94027. *Phone:* 650-543-3786. *Toll-free phone:* 800-556-3656. *Fax:* 650-543-4496. *E-mail:* admissions@menlo.edu.

Mills College

Oakland, California

http://www.mills.edu/

- **Independent** comprehensive, founded 1852
- **Urban** 135-acre campus with easy access to San Francisco
- **Endowment** $184.9 million
- **Undergraduate: women only; graduate: coed**
- **Moderately difficult** entrance level

FACULTY

Student/faculty ratio: 10:1.

ACADEMICS

Calendar: semesters. *Degrees:* certificates, bachelor's, master's, doctoral, and postbachelor's certificates.
Library: F. W. Olin Library. *Books:* 190,417 (physical), 156,636 (digital/electronic); *Serial titles:* 153 (physical), 51,607 (digital/electronic); *Databases:* 39. Weekly public service hours: 89; students can reserve study rooms.

STUDENT LIFE

Housing options: coed, women-only, cooperative, special housing for students with disabilities. Campus housing is university owned. Freshman campus housing is guaranteed.

Activities and organizations: drama/theater group, student-run newspaper, choral group, Associated Students of Mills College, The Campanil, The Mills Choir, Mujeres Unidas, Asian Pacific Islander Student Association.

Athletics Member NCAA. All Division III.

Campus security: 24-hour emergency response devices and patrols, late-night transport/escort service, controlled dormitory access.

Student services: health clinic, personal/psychological counseling, women's center.

FINANCIAL AID

Financial Aid Of all full-time matriculated undergraduates who enrolled in 2019, 660 applied for aid, 560 were judged to have need, 63 had their need fully met. In 2019, 100 non-need-based awards were made. ***Average percent of need met:*** 70. ***Average financial aid package:*** $53,604. ***Average need-based loan:*** $8935. ***Average need-based gift aid:*** $39,192. ***Average non-need-based aid:*** $13,337. ***Average indebtedness upon graduation:*** $49,333.

APPLYING

Options: electronic application, early admission, early action, deferred entrance.

Application fee: $50.

Required: essay or personal statement, high school transcript, 1 letter of recommendation, college transcripts. ***Recommended:*** interview.

CONTACT

Mrs. Robynne Royster, Director of Undergraduate Admissions, Mills College, 5000 MacArthur Boulevard, Oakland, CA 94613-1301. *Phone:* 510-430-2135. *Toll-free phone:* 800-87-MILLS. *Fax:* 510-430-3314. *E-mail:* admission@mills.edu.

MiraCosta College

Oceanside, California

http://www.miracosta.edu/

- **District-supported** primarily 2-year, founded 1934, part of California Community College System
- **Suburban** 131-acre campus with easy access to San Diego
- **Endowment** $14.1 million
- **Coed** 14,687 undergraduate students, 34% full-time, 56% women, 44% men
- **Noncompetitive** entrance level

UNDERGRAD STUDENTS

5,024 full-time, 9,663 part-time. 2% are from out of state; 3% Black or African American, non-Hispanic/Latino; 33% Hispanic/Latino; 6% Asian, non-Hispanic/Latino; 0.5% Native Hawaiian or other Pacific Islander, non-Hispanic/Latino; 0.3% American Indian or Alaska Native, non-Hispanic/Latino; 7% Two or more races, non-Hispanic/Latino; 2% Race/ethnicity unknown; 1% international.

Freshmen:
Admission: 2,768 enrolled.

FACULTY

Total: 634, 23% full-time.

Student/faculty ratio: 23:1.

ACADEMICS

Calendar: semesters. *Degrees:* certificates, diplomas, associate, and bachelor's.

Special study options: academic remediation for entering students, accelerated degree program, adult/continuing education programs, advanced placement credit, cooperative education, distance learning, double majors, English as a second language, honors programs, independent study, internships, part-time degree program, services for LD students, student-designed majors, study abroad, summer session for credit.

Computers: 1,000 computers/terminals are available on campus for general student use. Students can access the following: campus intranet, online (class) grades, online (class) registration, online (class) schedules. Campuswide network is available. Wireless service is available via entire campus.

Library: MiraCosta College Library.

STUDENT LIFE

Activities and organizations: drama/theater group, student-run newspaper, choral group, Inter Varsity Christian Fellowship, Accounting and Business Club, Backstage Players (Drama), Gay Straight Alliance, Puente Diversity Network.

Athletics ***Intercollegiate sports:*** basketball M/W, soccer M/W.

Campus security: 24-hour emergency response devices, student patrols, late-night transport/escort service, trained security personnel during class hours.

Student services: health clinic, personal/psychological counseling, veterans affairs office.

COSTS

Costs (2019–20) ***Tuition:*** $46 per credit hour part-time; state resident $46 per credit hour part-time; nonresident $311 per credit hour part-time. Full-time tuition and fees vary according to course load and degree level. Part-time tuition and fees vary according to course load and degree level. ***Required fees:*** $48 per term part-time, $48 per term part-time. ***Room and board:*** Room and board charges vary according to housing facility. ***Payment plans:*** installment, deferred payment.

APPLYING

Options: electronic application, early admission, deferred entrance.

Application deadlines: rolling (freshmen), rolling (transfers).

CONTACT

Jane Sparks, Interim Director of Admissions and Records, MiraCosta College, One Barnard Drive, Oceanside, CA 92057. *Phone:* 760-795-6620. *Toll-free phone:* 888-201-8480. *E-mail:* admissions@miracosta.edu.

Mount Saint Mary's University

Los Angeles, California

http://www.msmu.edu/

- **Independent Roman Catholic** comprehensive, founded 1925
- **Urban** 56-acre campus with easy access to Los Angeles
- **Endowment** $138.5 million
- **Coed, primarily women** 2,601 undergraduate students, 79% full-time, 94% women, 6% men
- 81% of applicants were admitted

UNDERGRAD STUDENTS

2,054 full-time, 547 part-time. Students come from 12 states and territories; 16 other countries; 3% are from out of state; 2% transferred in; 24% live on campus.

Freshmen:

Admission: 2,352 applied, 1,910 admitted, 496 enrolled. ***Average high school GPA:*** 3.4.

Retention: 76% of full-time freshmen returned.

ACADEMICS

Calendar: semesters. *Degrees:* associate, bachelor's, master's, doctoral, and post-master's certificates.

Special study options: academic remediation for entering students, accelerated degree program, advanced placement credit, cooperative education, distance learning, double majors, English as a second language, honors programs, independent study, internships, off-campus study, part-time degree program, services for LD students, student-designed majors, study abroad, summer session for credit.

Computers: 170 computers/terminals are available on campus for general student use. Students can access the following: campus intranet, computer help desk, free student e-mail accounts, online (class) grades, online (class) registration, online (class) schedules. Campuswide network is available. 100% of college-owned or -operated housing units are wired for high-speed Internet access. Wireless service is available via entire campus.

Library: Charles Willard Coe Library plus 1 other. Weekly public service hours: 91; study areas open 24 hours, 5–7 days a week.

STUDENT LIFE

Housing options: men-only, women-only. Campus housing is university owned. Freshman applicants given priority for college housing.

Activities and organizations: drama/theater group, student-run newspaper, choral group, Sakura Society, Pangkat Pilipino, MSMU Women in Film, Athenian Print, Na Pua O Ka'Aina (NPOKA), national sororities.

Athletics ***Intramural sports:*** basketball M/W, soccer M/W, softball M/W, swimming and diving M/W, tennis M/W, volleyball M/W.

Campus security: 24-hour emergency response devices and patrols, late-night transport/escort service, controlled dormitory access.

Student services: health clinic, personal/psychological counseling, women's center, veterans affairs office.

COSTS & FINANCIAL AID

Costs (2019–20) ***Comprehensive fee:*** $55,247 includes full-time tuition ($41,592), mandatory fees ($1200), and room and board ($12,455). Full-time tuition and fees vary according to course load, degree level, and program. Part-time tuition and fees vary according to course load, degree level, and program. ***Room and board:*** Room and board charges vary according to board plan and housing facility. ***Payment plan:*** installment. ***Waivers:*** employees or children of employees.

Financial Aid Of all full-time matriculated undergraduates who enrolled in 2019, 1,631 applied for aid, 1,559 were judged to have need, 81 had their need fully met. In 2019, 51 non-need-based awards were made. ***Average percent of need met:*** 61. ***Average financial aid package:*** $31,778. ***Average need-based loan:*** $3183. ***Average need-based gift aid:*** $26,860. ***Average non-need-based aid:*** $11,364. ***Average indebtedness upon graduation:*** $29,482.

APPLYING

Standardized Tests *Required for some:* SAT or ACT (for admission).

Options: electronic application, early admission, early action.

Required: essay or personal statement, high school transcript, minimum 2.5 GPA, 1 letter of recommendation. ***Recommended:*** 2 letters of recommendation, interview.

Application deadlines: 8/1 (freshmen), rolling (transfers), 12/1 (early action).

Notification: continuous (freshmen), continuous (transfers), 1/30 (early action).

CONTACT

Erika Yamasaki, Director of Admissions, Mount Saint Mary's University, 12001 Chalon Road, Los Angeles, CA 90049-1599. *Phone:* 800-999-9893. *Toll-free phone:* 800-999-9893. *Fax:* 310-954-4259. *E-mail:* admissions@msmu.edu.

Mt. Sierra College

Monrovia, California

http://www.mtsierra.edu/

CONTACT

Mt. Sierra College, 800 Royal Oaks Drive, Suite 101, Monrovia, CA 91016. *Phone:* 888-486-9818. *Toll-free phone:* 888-828-8800.

Musicians Institute

Hollywood, California

http://www.mi.edu/

CONTACT

Musicians Institute, 1655 North McCadden Place, Hollywood, CA 90028. *Phone:* 323-860-4345. *Toll-free phone:* 800-255-PLAY.

National University
La Jolla, California
http://www.nu.edu/

- **Independent** comprehensive, founded 1971, part of National University System
- **Urban** campus with easy access to San Diego
- **Coed** 7,735 undergraduate students, 37% full-time, 57% women, 43% men
- **Noncompetitive** entrance level

UNDERGRAD STUDENTS
2,884 full-time, 4,851 part-time. Students come from 52 states and territories; 75 other countries; 11% are from out of state; 10% Black or African American, non-Hispanic/Latino; 26% Hispanic/Latino; 9% Asian, non-Hispanic/Latino; 1% Native Hawaiian or other Pacific Islander, non-Hispanic/Latino; 0.5% American Indian or Alaska Native, non-Hispanic/Latino; 6% Two or more races, non-Hispanic/Latino; 12% Race/ethnicity unknown; 2% international; 43% transferred in.

Freshmen:
Admission: 20 enrolled.
Retention: 50% of full-time freshmen returned.

FACULTY
Total: 1,390, 19% full-time, 41% with terminal degrees.
Student/faculty ratio: 17:1.

ACADEMICS
Calendar: continuous. *Degrees:* certificates, associate, bachelor's, master's, doctoral, post-master's, and postbachelor's certificates.

Special study options: academic remediation for entering students, accelerated degree program, adult/continuing education programs, advanced placement credit, cooperative education, distance learning, double majors, English as a second language, independent study, internships, off-campus study, part-time degree program, services for LD students, study abroad, summer session for credit. ***ROTC:*** Army (c), Air Force (c).

Computers: 2,800 computers/terminals are available on campus for general student use. Students can access the following: computer help desk, free student e-mail accounts, online (class) grades, online (class) registration, online (class) schedules. Campuswide network is available. Wireless service is available via entire campus.
Library: National University Library. *Books:* 201,123 (physical), 368,486 (digital/electronic); *Serial titles:* 3,050 (physical), 95,256 (digital/electronic); *Databases:* 190. Weekly public service hours: 72; students can reserve study rooms.

STUDENT LIFE
Housing options: college housing not available.

Campus security: 24-hour emergency response devices and patrols, late-night transport/escort service.

Student services: veterans affairs office.

COSTS & FINANCIAL AID
Costs (2019–20) ***Tuition:*** $13,320 full-time, $370 per unit part-time.

Financial Aid Of all full-time matriculated undergraduates who enrolled in 2018, 5,599 applied for aid, 5,381 were judged to have need, 15 had their need fully met. 26 Federal Work-Study jobs (averaging $3095). In 2018, 36 non-need-based awards were made. ***Average percent of need met:*** 19. ***Average financial aid package:*** $5836. ***Average need-based loan:*** $4108. ***Average need-based gift aid:*** $5215. ***Average non-need-based aid:*** $1942. ***Average indebtedness upon graduation:*** $48,851.

APPLYING
Options: electronic application, deferred entrance.

Required: high school transcript, minimum 2.0 GPA. ***Required for some:*** essay or personal statement.

Application deadlines: rolling (freshmen), rolling (transfers).

Notification: continuous (freshmen), continuous (transfers).

CONTACT
National University, 11255 North Torrey Pines Road, La Jolla, CA 92037-1011. *Toll-free phone:* 800-628-8648.

NewSchool of Architecture and Design
San Diego, California
http://www.newschoolarch.edu/

CONTACT
Kirk Nielson, Director of Enrollment and Field Recruitment, NewSchool of Architecture and Design, 1249 F Street, San Diego, CA 92101. *Phone:* 619-684-8841. *Toll-free phone:* 800-490-7081. *E-mail:* knielson@newschoolarch.edu.

New York Film Academy
Burbank, California
http://www.nyfa.edu/

CONTACT
Admissions Office, New York Film Academy, 3300 Riverside Drive, Burbank, CA 91505. *Phone:* 818-333-3558. *Fax:* 818-333-3557. *E-mail:* studios@nyfa.edu.

Northcentral University
San Diego, California
http://www.ncu.edu/

CONTACT
Northcentral University, 2488 Historic Decatur Road, Suite 100, San Diego, CA 92106. *Phone:* 866-776-0331. *Toll-free phone:* 866-776-0331.

Northwestern Polytechnic University
Fremont, California
http://www.npu.edu/

CONTACT
Mr. Michael Tang, Admission Officer, Northwestern Polytechnic University, 47671 Westinghouse Drive, Fremont, CA 94539. *Phone:* 510-592-9688 Ext. 15. *Fax:* 510-657-8975. *E-mail:* admission@npu.edu.

Occidental College
Los Angeles, California
http://www.oxy.edu/

- **Independent** comprehensive, founded 1887
- **Urban** 120-acre campus with easy access to Los Angeles
- **Coed** 1,985 undergraduate students, 99% full-time, 57% women, 43% men
- **Very difficult** entrance level, 37% of applicants were admitted

UNDERGRAD STUDENTS
1,962 full-time, 23 part-time. Students come from 50 states and territories; 26 other countries; 59% are from out of state; 4% Black or African American, non-Hispanic/Latino; 14% Hispanic/Latino; 16% Asian, non-Hispanic/Latino; 0.2% Native Hawaiian or other Pacific Islander, non-Hispanic/Latino; 9% Two or more races, non-Hispanic/Latino; 2% Race/ethnicity unknown; 7% international; 2% transferred in; 82% live on campus.

Freshmen:
Admission: 7,501 applied, 2,752 admitted, 562 enrolled. ***Average high school GPA:*** 3.6. ***Test scores:*** SAT evidence-based reading and writing scores over 500: 100%; SAT math scores over 500: 100%; ACT scores over 18: 100%; SAT evidence-based reading and writing scores over 600: 96%; SAT math scores over 600: 91%; ACT scores over 24: 99%; SAT evidence-based reading and writing scores over 700: 45%; SAT math scores over 700: 46%; ACT scores over 30: 60%.

Retention: 93% of full-time freshmen returned.

FACULTY
Total: 260, 75% full-time, 88% with terminal degrees.
Student/faculty ratio: 10:1.

ACADEMICS
Calendar: semesters. *Degrees:* bachelor's and master's.

Special study options: advanced placement credit, double majors, honors programs, independent study, internships, off-campus study, services for LD students, student-designed majors, study abroad. ***ROTC:*** Army (c), Air Force (c).

Unusual degree programs: 3-2 engineering with California Institute of Technology, Columbia University; law with Columbia University, biotechnology with Keck Graduate Institute.

Computers: 200 computers/terminals are available on campus for general student use. Students can access the following: campus intranet, computer help desk, free student e-mail accounts, online (class) grades, online (class) registration, online (class) schedules. Campuswide network is available. 98% of college-owned or -operated housing units are wired for high-speed Internet access. Wireless service is available via entire campus.

Library: Mary Norton Clapp Library and Academic Commons plus 2 others. *Books:* 195,328 (physical); *Serial titles:* 3,805 (physical), 75,011 (digital/electronic). Study areas open 24 hours, 5–7 days a week; students can reserve study rooms.

STUDENT LIFE

Housing options: on-campus residence required through junior year; coed, women-only. Campus housing is university owned. Freshman campus housing is guaranteed.

Activities and organizations: drama/theater group, student-run newspaper, radio station, choral group, national fraternities, national sororities.

Athletics Member NCAA. All Division III. ***Intercollegiate sports:*** baseball M, basketball M/W, cross-country running M/W, football M, golf M/W, lacrosse M(c)/W, rugby M(c)/W(c), soccer M/W, softball W, swimming and diving M/W, tennis M/W, track and field M/W, ultimate Frisbee M(c)/W(c), volleyball W, water polo M/W. ***Intramural sports:*** basketball M/W, cheerleading W(c), soccer M/W.

Campus security: 24-hour emergency response devices and patrols, late-night transport/escort service, controlled dormitory access, Surveillance cameras; emergency notification system; blue light phones.

Student services: health clinic, personal/psychological counseling, women's center.

COSTS & FINANCIAL AID

Costs (2019–20) ***Comprehensive fee:*** $72,610 includes full-time tuition ($55,980), mandatory fees ($596), and room and board ($16,034). Part-time tuition: $2333 per unit. ***College room only:*** $9124. Room and board charges vary according to board plan. ***Payment plan:*** tuition prepayment.

Financial Aid Of all full-time matriculated undergraduates who enrolled in 2018, 1,335 applied for aid, 1,166 were judged to have need, 1,158 had their need fully met. 835 Federal Work-Study jobs (averaging $2778). 139 state and other part-time jobs (averaging $6647). In 2018, 261 non-need-based awards were made. ***Average percent of need met:*** 100. ***Average financial aid package:*** $51,273. ***Average need-based loan:*** $5674. ***Average need-based gift aid:*** $43,248. ***Average non-need-based aid:*** $13,274. ***Average indebtedness upon graduation:*** $29,306. ***Financial aid deadline:*** 1/10.

APPLYING

Standardized Tests *Required:* SAT or ACT (for admission).

Options: electronic application, early admission, early decision, deferred entrance.

Application fee: $65.

Required: essay or personal statement, high school transcript, 2 letters of recommendation. ***Recommended:*** interview.

Application deadlines: 1/10 (freshmen), 4/1 (transfers).

Early decision deadline: 11/15 (for plan 1), 1/1 (for plan 2).

Notification: 3/25 (freshmen), 5/1 (transfers).

CONTACT

Mr. Vince Cuseo, Vice President of Enrollment and Dean of Admission, Occidental College, 1600 Campus Road, Los Angeles, CA 90041. *Phone:* 323-259-2700. *Toll-free phone:* 800-825-5262. *Fax:* 323-341-4875. *E-mail:* admission@oxy.edu.

Otis College of Art and Design

Los Angeles, California

http://www.otis.edu/

- **Independent** comprehensive, founded 1918
- **Urban** 5-acre campus with easy access to Los Angeles
- **Endowment** $21.0 million
- **Coed** 1,125 undergraduate students, 99% full-time, 69% women, 31% men
- **Moderately difficult** entrance level, 78% of applicants were admitted

UNDERGRAD STUDENTS

1,109 full-time, 16 part-time. Students come from 34 states and territories; 37 other countries; 37% are from out of state; 5% Black or African American, non-Hispanic/Latino; 16% Hispanic/Latino; 21% Asian, non-Hispanic/Latino; 0.5% Native Hawaiian or other Pacific Islander, non-Hispanic/Latino; 0.2% American Indian or Alaska Native, non-Hispanic/Latino; 6% Two or more races, non-Hispanic/Latino; 3% Race/ethnicity unknown; 25% international; 7% transferred in; 37% live on campus.

Freshmen:

Admission: 2,442 applied, 1,909 admitted, 274 enrolled. ***Average high school GPA:*** 3.2. ***Test scores:*** ACT scores over 18: 100%; ACT scores over 24: 71%; ACT scores over 30: 25%.

Retention: 79% of full-time freshmen returned.

FACULTY

Total: 311, 16% full-time, 4% with terminal degrees.

Student/faculty ratio: 9:1.

ACADEMICS

Calendar: semesters. *Degrees:* bachelor's and master's.

Special study options: accelerated degree program, adult/continuing education programs, advanced placement credit, distance learning, honors programs, independent study, internships, part-time degree program, services for LD students, study abroad, summer session for credit.

Computers: 400 computers/terminals are available on campus for general student use. Students can access the following: campus intranet, computer help desk, free student e-mail accounts, online (class) grades, online (class) registration, online (class) schedules. Campuswide network is available. 100% of college-owned or -operated housing units are wired for high-speed Internet access. Wireless service is available via entire campus.

Library: Milliard Sheets Library plus 1 other. *Books:* 35,988 (physical), 122,951 (digital/electronic); *Serial titles:* 112 (physical), 5 (digital/electronic); *Databases:* 10. Students can reserve study rooms.

STUDENT LIFE

Housing options: coed, special housing for students with disabilities. Campus housing is university owned. Freshman applicants given priority for college housing.

Activities and organizations: Dungeons, Dragons and Diversity, Otis Comic League, Trading Cards Game Club, The Outdoor Club, Gardening Club.

Athletics ***Intramural sports:*** skiing (downhill) W, soccer M.

Campus security: 24-hour emergency response devices and patrols, late-night transport/escort service, controlled dormitory access, Lighted pathways/sidewalks.

Student services: personal/psychological counseling.

COSTS & FINANCIAL AID

Costs (2020–21) ***Tuition:*** $1507 per unit part-time. ***Room only:*** Room and board charges vary according to board plan and housing facility. ***Waivers:*** employees or children of employees.

Financial Aid Of all full-time matriculated undergraduates who enrolled in 2019, 990 applied for aid, 990 were judged to have need. 399 Federal Work-Study jobs (averaging $770,260). ***Average percent of need met:*** 51. ***Average financial aid package:*** $22,854. ***Average need-based loan:*** $4702. ***Average need-based gift aid:*** $31,378.

APPLYING

Options: electronic application, early action, deferred entrance.

Application fee: $50.

Required: essay or personal statement, high school transcript, minimum 2.5 GPA, Portfolio, TOEFL (Test of English as a Foreign Language). ***Recommended:*** interview.

Application deadlines: rolling (freshmen), rolling (transfers).

Notification: continuous (freshmen), continuous (transfers).

CONTACT
Otis College of Art and Design, 9045 Lincoln Boulevard, Los Angeles, CA 90045-9785. *Phone:* 310-665-6819. *Toll-free phone:* 800-527-OTIS.

Pacific College

Costa Mesa, California

http://www.pacific-college.edu/

- **Proprietary** 4-year
- **Coed**
- 60% of applicants were admitted

FACULTY
Student/faculty ratio: 18:1.

ACADEMICS
Degrees: diplomas, associate, and bachelor's.

CONTACT
Pacific College, 3160 Red Hill Avenue, Costa Mesa, CA 92626.

Pacific Oaks College

Pasadena, California

http://www.pacificoaks.edu/

- **Independent** upper-level, founded 1945, part of The Chicago School Education System
- **Small-town** 2-acre campus with easy access to Los Angeles, San Gabriel Valley
- **Endowment** $7.3 million
- **Coed, primarily women**
- 31% of applicants were admitted

FACULTY
Student/faculty ratio: 5:1.

ACADEMICS
Calendar: semesters summer sessions and 2 intensive sessions. *Degrees:* certificates, bachelor's, master's, and post-master's certificates.
Library: Andrew Norman Library plus 1 other.

STUDENT LIFE
Housing options: college housing not available.

Activities and organizations: Latina/o Support Group, Student Empowerment Group, Teacher Education Student Association, Marriage, Family Therapy Student Association.

FINANCIAL AID
Financial Aid Of all full-time matriculated undergraduates who enrolled in 2006, 11 Federal Work-Study jobs (averaging $5000).

APPLYING
Options: electronic application, deferred entrance.

Application fee: $55.

CONTACT
Ms. Augusta Pickens, Office of Admissions, Pacific Oaks College, 5 Westmoreland Place, Pasadena, CA 91103. *Phone:* 626-397-1349. *Toll-free phone:* 877-314-2380. *Fax:* 626-666-1220. *E-mail:* admissions@pacificoaks.edu.

Pacific States University

Los Angeles, California

http://www.psuca.edu/

- **Independent** comprehensive, founded 1928
- **Urban** 1-acre campus
- **Coed**
- **Noncompetitive** entrance level

FACULTY
Student/faculty ratio: 5:1.

ACADEMICS
Calendar: quarters. *Degrees:* certificates, diplomas, bachelor's, master's, doctoral, and postbachelor's certificates.
Library: University Library plus 1 other. Students can reserve study rooms.

STUDENT LIFE
Housing options: coed. Campus housing is university owned.

Campus security: patrols by trained security personnel during campus hours.

APPLYING
Standardized Tests *Required for some:* TOEFL or IELTS. *Recommended:* SAT or ACT (for admission).

Options: electronic application, deferred entrance.

Application fee: $50.

Required: high school transcript, minimum 2.5 GPA. ***Recommended:*** essay or personal statement.

CONTACT
Mr. Maawiya Ayeva, Director of Admissions, Pacific States University, 3424 Wilshire Boulevard, 12th Floor, Los Angeles, CA 90010. *Phone:* 323-731-2383 Ext. 202. *Toll-free phone:* 888-200-0383. *Fax:* 323-731-7276. *E-mail:* admissions@psuca.edu.

Pacific Union College

Angwin, California

http://www.puc.edu/

CONTACT
Mr. Craig Philpott, Associate Director, Admissions, Pacific Union College, Enrollment Services, One Angwin Avenue, Angwin, CA 94508. *Phone:* 800-862-7080. *Toll-free phone:* 800-862-7080. *Fax:* 707-965-6671. *E-mail:* enroll@puc.edu.

Palo Alto University

Palo Alto, California

http://www.paloaltou.edu/

CONTACT
Mr. Lenard Wilson, Assistant Director of Undergraduate Admissions, Palo Alto University, 1791 Arastradero Road, Palo Alto, CA 94304. *Phone:* 650-417-2050. *Toll-free phone:* 800-818-6136. *E-mail:* undergrad@paloaltou.edu.

Pepperdine University

Malibu, California

http://www.pepperdine.edu/

- **Independent** university, founded 1937, affiliated with Church of Christ
- **Suburban** 830-acre campus with easy access to Los Angeles
- **Endowment** $861.6 million
- **Coed** 3,583 undergraduate students, 93% full-time, 58% women, 42% men
- **Very difficult** entrance level, 32% of applicants were admitted

UNDERGRAD STUDENTS
3,320 full-time, 263 part-time. Students come from 52 states and territories; 66 other countries; 45% are from out of state; 5% Black or African American, non-Hispanic/Latino; 14% Hispanic/Latino; 11% Asian, non-Hispanic/Latino; 0.1% Native Hawaiian or other Pacific Islander, non-Hispanic/Latino; 0.4% American Indian or Alaska Native, non-Hispanic/Latino; 7% Two or more races, non-Hispanic/Latino; 2% Race/ethnicity unknown; 12% international; 4% transferred in; 60% live on campus.

Freshmen:
Admission: 12,764 applied, 4,049 admitted, 726 enrolled. ***Average high school GPA:*** 3.7. ***Test scores:*** SAT evidence-based reading and writing scores over 500: 99%; SAT math scores over 500: 99%; ACT scores over 18: 99%; SAT evidence-based reading and writing scores over 600: 82%; SAT math scores over 600: 84%; ACT scores over 24: 90%; SAT evidence-based reading and writing scores over 700: 27%; SAT math scores over 700: 42%; ACT scores over 30: 50%.

Retention: 91% of full-time freshmen returned.

FACULTY

Total: 802, 50% full-time, 72% with terminal degrees.

Student/faculty ratio: 13:1.

ACADEMICS

Calendar: semesters. *Degrees:* bachelor's, master's, doctoral, and postbachelor's certificates.

Special study options: adult/continuing education programs, advanced placement credit, distance learning, double majors, honors programs, independent study, internships, part-time degree program, services for LD students, student-designed majors, study abroad, summer session for credit. ***ROTC:*** Army (c), Air Force (c).

Unusual degree programs: 3-2 business administration; engineering with University of Southern California, Washington University in St. Louis.

Computers: 240 computers/terminals are available on campus for general student use. Students can access the following: campus intranet, computer help desk, free student e-mail accounts, online (class) grades, online (class) registration, online (class) schedules. Campuswide network is available. 100% of college-owned or -operated housing units are wired for high-speed Internet access. Wireless service is available via entire campus.

Library: Payson Library plus 6 others. *Books:* 311,392 (physical), 356,075 (digital/electronic); *Serial titles:* 312 (physical), 66,464 (digital/electronic); *Databases:* 128. Weekly public service hours: 112; students can reserve study rooms.

STUDENT LIFE

Housing options: on-campus residence required through sophomore year; men-only, women-only, special housing for students with disabilities. Campus housing is university owned. Freshman campus housing is guaranteed.

Activities and organizations: drama/theater group, student-run newspaper, radio and television station, choral group, Latino Student Association, Black Student Union, Interfraternity Council, International Justice Mission, national fraternities, national sororities.

Athletics Member NCAA. All Division I. ***Intercollegiate sports:*** baseball M(s), basketball M(s)/W(s), cross-country running M(s)/W(s), golf M(s)/W(s), soccer W(s), tennis M(s)/W(s), track and field M(s)/W(s), volleyball M(s)/W(s), water polo M(s). ***Intramural sports:*** basketball M/W, football M/W, golf M(c)/W(c), rugby M(c), soccer M/W, tennis M(c)/W(c), volleyball M/W.

Campus security: 24-hour emergency response devices and patrols, student patrols, late-night transport/escort service, controlled dormitory access, front gate security, 24-hour security in residence halls, controlled access, crime prevention programs.

Student services: health clinic, personal/psychological counseling.

COSTS & FINANCIAL AID

Costs (2019–20) ***Comprehensive fee:*** $71,562 includes full-time tuition ($55,640), mandatory fees ($252), and room and board ($15,670). Part-time tuition: $1745 per credit hour. ***Room and board:*** Room and board charges vary according to board plan and housing facility. ***Payment plan:*** installment. ***Waivers:*** employees or children of employees.

Financial Aid Of all full-time matriculated undergraduates who enrolled in 2018, 3,324 applied for aid, 1,755 were judged to have need, 360 had their need fully met. In 2018, 1027 non-need-based awards were made. ***Average percent of need met:*** 75. ***Average financial aid package:*** $41,879. ***Average need-based loan:*** $5156. ***Average need-based gift aid:*** $38,089. ***Average non-need-based aid:*** $20,438. ***Average indebtedness upon graduation:*** $34,711.

APPLYING

Standardized Tests *Required:* SAT or ACT (for admission).

Options: electronic application, early action.

Application fee: $65.

Required: essay or personal statement, high school transcript, 1 letter of recommendation, SAT I or ACT.

Application deadlines: 1/15 (freshmen), 1/15 (transfers).

Notification: 4/1 (freshmen), 4/1 (transfers).

CONTACT
Mr. Falone Serna, Director of Admission, Enrollment Management, Pepperdine University, 24255 Pacific Coast Highway, Malibu, CA 90263. *Phone:* 310-506-4392. *E-mail:* falone.serna@pepperdine.edu.

See below for display ad and page 1098 for the College Close-Up.

Pima Medical Institute - Chula Vista

Chula Vista, California

http://www.pmi.edu/

CONTACT
Admissions Office, Pima Medical Institute - Chula Vista, 780 Bay Boulevard, Chula Vista, CA 91910. *Phone:* 619-425-3200. *Toll-free phone:* 800-477-PIMA.

Pitzer College

Claremont, California

http://www.pitzer.edu/

- **Independent** 4-year, founded 1963, part of The Claremont Colleges
- **Suburban** 35-acre campus with easy access to Los Angeles
- **Endowment** $144.6 million
- **Coed** 1,119 undergraduate students, 98% full-time, 57% women, 43% men
- **Very difficult** entrance level, 14% of applicants were admitted

UNDERGRAD STUDENTS
1,094 full-time, 25 part-time. Students come from 45 states and territories; 29 other countries; 56% are from out of state; 6% Black or African American, non-Hispanic/Latino; 15% Hispanic/Latino; 8% Asian, non-Hispanic/Latino; 0.5% Native Hawaiian or other Pacific Islander, non-Hispanic/Latino; 0.2% American Indian or Alaska Native, non-Hispanic/Latino; 9% Two or more races, non-Hispanic/Latino; 5% Race/ethnicity unknown; 8% international; 3% transferred in; 75% live on campus.

Freshmen:
Admission: 4,415 applied, 605 admitted, 276 enrolled. ***Average high school GPA:*** 3.9. ***Test scores:*** SAT evidence-based reading and writing scores over 500: 100%; SAT math scores over 500: 100%; ACT scores over 18: 100%; SAT evidence-based reading and writing scores over 600: 94%; SAT math scores over 600: 94%; ACT scores over 24: 100%; SAT evidence-based reading and writing scores over 700: 57%; SAT math scores over 700: 63%; ACT scores over 30: 79%.

Retention: 93% of full-time freshmen returned.

FACULTY
Total: 126, 79% full-time, 90% with terminal degrees.

Student/faculty ratio: 10:1.

ACADEMICS
Calendar: semesters. *Degree:* bachelor's.

Special study options: adult/continuing education programs, advanced placement credit, cooperative education, double majors, English as a second language, honors programs, independent study, internships, off-campus study, part-time degree program, services for LD students, student-designed majors, study abroad, summer session for credit. ***ROTC:*** Army (c), Air Force (c).

Unusual degree programs: 3-2 business administration with Claremont Graduate University; Economics, Information Systems and Technology, Psychology, Public Policy, Education, Mathematics, Cultural Studies, English, History, Music, Philosophy, Religion, Women's Studies, Teacher Education with Claremont Graduate University; BA/DO linkage pr.

Computers: Students can access the following: campus intranet, computer help desk, free student e-mail accounts, online (class) grades, online (class) registration, online (class) schedules. Campuswide network is available. 100% of college-owned or -operated housing units are wired for high-speed Internet access. Wireless service is available via entire campus.

Library: Honnold Mudd Library plus 3 others. *Books:* 1.0 million (physical), 2.2 million (digital/electronic); *Serial titles:* 28,128 (physical), 81,005 (digital/electronic); *Databases:* 490. Weekly public service hours: 111; students can reserve study rooms.

STUDENT LIFE
Housing options: on-campus residence required for freshman year; coed, cooperative, special housing for students with disabilities. Campus housing is university owned. Freshman campus housing is guaranteed.

Activities and organizations: drama/theater group, student-run newspaper, radio station, choral group, Pitzer Outdoor Adventure, Live Your Best Life Records, First Generation Students, 5x5 Productions, Asian Pacific American Coalition.

Athletics Member NCAA. All Division III except golf (Division II). ***Intercollegiate sports:*** baseball M, basketball M/W, cross-country running M/W, football M, golf M/W, lacrosse W, soccer M/W, softball W, swimming and diving M/W, tennis M/W, track and field M/W, volleyball W, water polo M/W. ***Intramural sports:*** badminton M(c)/W(c), basketball M/W, equestrian sports M(c)/W(c), fencing M(c)/W(c), field hockey M(c)/W(c), football M, ice hockey M(c)/W(c), lacrosse M(c), rugby M(c)/W(c), soccer M/W(c), tennis M(c)/W(c), ultimate Frisbee M(c)/W(c), volleyball M(c)/W(c).

Campus security: 24-hour emergency response devices and patrols, late-night transport/escort service, controlled dormitory access.

Student services: health clinic, personal/psychological counseling, women's center.

COSTS & FINANCIAL AID
Costs (2019–20) ***Comprehensive fee:*** $73,450 includes full-time tuition ($55,734), mandatory fees ($284), and room and board ($17,432). Part-time tuition: $6967 per course. Part-time tuition and fees vary according to course load. ***Required fees:*** $284 per year part-time. ***College room only:*** $10,060. Room and board charges vary according to board plan and housing facility. ***Payment plans:*** installment, deferred payment. ***Waivers:*** employees or children of employees.

Financial Aid Of all full-time matriculated undergraduates who enrolled in 2019, 482 applied for aid, 420 were judged to have need, 392 had their need fully met. 335 Federal Work-Study jobs (averaging $2514). 14 state and other part-time jobs (averaging $1880). In 2019, 19 non-need-based awards were made. ***Average percent of need met:*** 100. ***Average financial aid package:*** $49,818. ***Average need-based loan:*** $4558. ***Average need-based gift aid:*** $45,553. ***Average non-need-based aid:*** $5567. ***Average indebtedness upon graduation:*** $26,489. ***Financial aid deadline:*** 1/1.

APPLYING
Standardized Tests *Required for some:* SAT or ACT (for admission).

Options: electronic application, early decision, deferred entrance.

Application fee: $70.

Required: essay or personal statement, high school transcript, minimum 2.0 GPA, 3 letters of recommendation. ***Recommended:*** interview.

Application deadlines: 1/1 (freshmen), 1/1 (out-of-state freshmen), 4/1 (transfers).

Early decision deadline: 11/15 (for plan 1), 1/1 (for plan 2).

Notification: 4/1 (freshmen), 4/1 (out-of-state freshmen), 5/15 (transfers), 12/18 (early decision plan 1), 2/15 (early decision plan 2).

CONTACT
Ms. Yvonne Berumen, Vice President for Admission and Financial Aid, Pitzer College, 1050 North Mills Avenue, Claremont, CA 91711-6101. *Phone:* 909-621-8129. *Toll-free phone:* 800-748-9371. *Fax:* 909-621-8770. *E-mail:* admission@pitzer.edu.

Platt College

Alhambra, California

http://www.plattcollege.edu/

CONTACT
Mr. Detroit Whiteside, Director of Admissions, Platt College, 1000 South Fremont A9W, Alhambra, CA 91803. *Phone:* 323-258-8050. *Toll-free phone:* 888-866-6697 (in-state); 888-80-PLATT (out-of-state).

Platt College

Ontario, California

http://www.plattcollege.edu/

CONTACT
Ms. Jennifer Abandonato, Director of Admissions, Platt College, 3700 Inland Empire Boulevard, Ontario, CA 91764. *Phone:* 909-941-9410. *Toll-free phone:* 888-80-PLATT.

Platt College

Riverside, California

http://www.plattcollege.edu/

CONTACT
Platt College, 6465 Sycamore Canyon Boulevard, Suite 100, Riverside, CA 92507. *Toll-free phone:* 888-807-5288.

Platt College San Diego

San Diego, California

http://www.platt.edu/

- **Proprietary** 4-year, founded 1879
- **Suburban** 1-acre campus with easy access to San Diego
- **Coed** 114 undergraduate students, 100% full-time, 34% women, 66% men

UNDERGRAD STUDENTS
114 full-time. 5% are from out of state; 11% Black or African American, non-Hispanic/Latino; 21% Hispanic/Latino; 15% Asian, non-Hispanic/Latino; 3% Native Hawaiian or other Pacific Islander, non-Hispanic/Latino; 2% American Indian or Alaska Native, non-Hispanic/Latino; 4% Two or more races, non-Hispanic/Latino; 7% Race/ethnicity unknown.

Freshmen:
Admission: 20 admitted, 20 enrolled.

FACULTY
Total: 27, 41% full-time, 4% with terminal degrees.

Student/faculty ratio: 21:1.

ACADEMICS
Calendar: continuous. *Degree:* certificates, diplomas, and bachelor's.

Special study options: academic remediation for entering students, accelerated degree program, cooperative education, study abroad.

Computers: 144 computers/terminals are available on campus for general student use. Students can access the following: campus intranet, free student e-mail accounts, online (class) grades, online (class) schedules. Campuswide network is available. Wireless service is available via entire campus.
Library: Platt College San Diego Library plus 1 other. Students can reserve study rooms.

STUDENT LIFE
Housing options: college housing not available.

Activities and organizations: Virtual Reality Group.

Campus security: 24-hour emergency response devices, surveillance cameras and closed gates.

Student services: personal/psychological counseling, veterans affairs office.

COSTS
Costs (2020–21) ***One-time required fee:*** $110. ***Tuition:*** $20,313 full-time. Full-time tuition and fees vary according to degree level and program. No tuition increase for student's term of enrollment. ***Required fees:*** $1406 full-time. ***Payment plan:*** installment.

APPLYING
Options: electronic application, early admission, deferred entrance.

Application fee: $110.

Required: essay or personal statement, high school transcript, interview.

Application deadlines: rolling (freshmen), rolling (out-of-state freshmen), rolling (transfers).

Notification: continuous (freshmen), continuous (out-of-state freshmen), continuous (transfers).

CONTACT
Mr. Steve Gallup, Director of Admissions, Platt College San Diego, 6250 El Cajon Boulevard, San Diego, CA 92115-3919. *Phone:* 619-265-0107. *Toll-free phone:* 866-752-8826. *Fax:* 619-265-8655. *E-mail:* sgallup@platt.edu.

Point Loma Nazarene University

San Diego, California

http://www.pointloma.edu/

- **Independent Nazarene** comprehensive, founded 1902
- **Suburban** 93-acre campus with easy access to San Diego
- **Coed** 3,203 undergraduate students, 82% full-time, 65% women, 35% men
- **Moderately difficult** entrance level, 74% of applicants were admitted

UNDERGRAD STUDENTS
2,611 full-time, 592 part-time. Students come from 40 states and territories; 20 other countries; 18% are from out of state; 2% Black or African American, non-Hispanic/Latino; 26% Hispanic/Latino; 7% Asian, non-Hispanic/Latino; 0.7% Native Hawaiian or other Pacific Islander, non-Hispanic/Latino; 0.4% American Indian or Alaska Native, non-Hispanic/Latino; 8% Two or more races, non-Hispanic/Latino; 2% Race/ethnicity unknown; 1% international; 11% transferred in; 55% live on campus.

Freshmen:
Admission: 3,277 applied, 2,414 admitted, 612 enrolled. ***Average high school GPA:*** 3.7. ***Test scores:*** SAT evidence-based reading and writing scores over 500: 98%; SAT math scores over 500: 95%; ACT scores over 18: 100%; SAT evidence-based reading and writing scores over 600: 65%; SAT math scores over 600: 53%; ACT scores over 24: 79%; SAT evidence-based reading and writing scores over 700: 9%; SAT math scores over 700: 11%; ACT scores over 30: 21%.

Retention: 88% of full-time freshmen returned.

FACULTY
Total: 474, 31% full-time, 46% with terminal degrees.

Student/faculty ratio: 14:1.

ACADEMICS
Calendar: semesters. *Degrees:* bachelor's, master's, doctoral, and post-master's certificates.

Special study options: academic remediation for entering students, accelerated degree program, adult/continuing education programs, advanced placement credit, distance learning, double majors, external degree program, honors programs, independent study, internships, off-campus study, part-time degree program, services for LD students, study abroad, summer session for credit. ***ROTC:*** Army (c), Navy (c), Air Force (c).

Computers: 346 computers/terminals and 5,320 ports are available on campus for general student use. Students can access the following: campus intranet, computer help desk, free student e-mail accounts, online (class) grades, online (class) registration, online (class) schedules. Campuswide network is available. 100% of college-owned or -operated housing units are wired for high-speed Internet access. Wireless service is available via entire campus.
Library: Ryan Library.

STUDENT LIFE
Housing options: on-campus residence required through sophomore year; coed, men-only, women-only, special housing for students with disabilities. Campus housing is university owned. Freshman campus housing is guaranteed.

Activities and organizations: drama/theater group, student-run newspaper, radio and television station, choral group.

Athletics Member NCAA. All Division II. ***Intercollegiate sports:*** baseball M(s), basketball M(s)/W(s), cross-country running W(s), soccer M(s)/W(s), tennis M(s)/W(s), track and field W(s), volleyball W(s). ***Intramural sports:*** basketball M/W, cheerleading M(c)/W(c), football M/W, rugby M(c)/W(c), soccer M/W, softball M/W, tennis M/W, ultimate Frisbee M/W, volleyball M/W.

Campus security: 24-hour patrols, student patrols, late-night transport/escort service.

Student services: health clinic, personal/psychological counseling, women's center, veterans affairs office.

COSTS & FINANCIAL AID

Costs (2019–20) ***Comprehensive fee:*** $47,600 includes full-time tuition ($36,350), mandatory fees ($600), and room and board ($10,650). Full-time tuition and fees vary according to course load and program. Part-time tuition: $1515 per credit hour. Part-time tuition and fees vary according to course load and program. ***Room and board:*** Room and board charges vary according to board plan. ***Payment plan:*** installment. ***Waivers:*** senior citizens and employees or children of employees.

Financial Aid Of all full-time matriculated undergraduates who enrolled in 2018, 2,101 applied for aid, 1,722 were judged to have need, 275 had their need fully met. In 2018, 600 non-need-based awards were made. ***Average percent of need met:*** 62. ***Average financial aid package:*** $25,229. ***Average need-based loan:*** $4625. ***Average need-based gift aid:*** $19,563. ***Average non-need-based aid:*** $12,355. ***Average indebtedness upon graduation:*** $35,374.

APPLYING

Standardized Tests *Required:* SAT or ACT (for admission). *Recommended:* SAT (for admission), ACT (for admission).

Options: electronic application, early action.

Application fee: $55.

Required: essay or personal statement, high school transcript, minimum 2.8 GPA, 2 letters of recommendation.

Application deadlines: 2/15 (freshmen), 11/15 (early action).

Notification: 4/1 (freshmen).

CONTACT

Shannon Hutchison, Director of Undergraduate Admissions, Point Loma Nazarene University, 3900 Lomaland Drive, San Diego, CA 92106. *Phone:* 619-849-2541. *Toll-free phone:* 800-733-7770. *Fax:* 619-849-2601. *E-mail:* admissions@pointloma.edu.

Pomona College

Claremont, California

http://www.pomona.edu/

- **Independent** 4-year, founded 1887
- **Suburban** 140-acre campus with easy access to Los Angeles
- **Endowment** $2.2 billion
- **Coed** 1,717 undergraduate students, 99% full-time, 53% women, 47% men
- **Most difficult** entrance level, 7% of applicants were admitted

UNDERGRAD STUDENTS

1,696 full-time, 21 part-time. 10% Black or African American, non-Hispanic/Latino; 17% Hispanic/Latino; 16% Asian, non-Hispanic/Latino; 0.4% Native Hawaiian or other Pacific Islander, non-Hispanic/Latino; 0.5% American Indian or Alaska Native, non-Hispanic/Latino; 7% Two or more races, non-Hispanic/Latino; 4% Race/ethnicity unknown; 11% international; 1% transferred in; 98% live on campus.

Freshmen:

Admission: 10,401 applied, 770 admitted, 417 enrolled. ***Test scores:*** SAT evidence-based reading and writing scores over 500: 100%; SAT math scores over 500: 100%; ACT scores over 18: 100%; SAT evidence-based reading and writing scores over 600: 99%; SAT math scores over 600: 99%; ACT scores over 24: 100%; SAT evidence-based reading and writing scores over 700: 72%; SAT math scores over 700: 80%; ACT scores over 30: 90%.

Retention: 97% of full-time freshmen returned.

FACULTY

Total: 250, 78% full-time, 91% with terminal degrees.

Student/faculty ratio: 8:1.

ACADEMICS

Calendar: semesters. *Degree:* bachelor's.

Special study options: advanced placement credit, double majors, external degree program, independent study, internships, off-campus study, services for LD students, student-designed majors, study abroad. ***ROTC:*** Army (c), Air Force (c).

Unusual degree programs: 3-2 engineering with California Institute of Technology, Washington University in St. Louis, Dartmouth College.

Computers: 180 computers/terminals are available on campus for general student use. Students can access the following: computer help desk, free student e-mail accounts, online (class) grades, online (class) registration, online (class) schedules. Campuswide network is available. 100% of college-owned or -operated housing units are wired for high-speed Internet access. Wireless service is available via entire campus.

Library: Honnold/Mudd Library plus 4 others.

STUDENT LIFE

Housing options: college housing not available; coed. Campus housing is university owned. Freshman campus housing is guaranteed.

Activities and organizations: drama/theater group, student-run newspaper, radio station, choral group, Student Government, music/choral organizations, service organizations, intramural sports, outdoor activities club.

Athletics Member NCAA. All Division III. ***Intercollegiate sports:*** baseball M, basketball M/W, cross-country running M/W, football M, golf M/W, lacrosse W, soccer M/W, softball W, swimming and diving M/W, tennis M/W, track and field M/W, ultimate Frisbee M(c)/W(c), volleyball M(c)/W, water polo M/W. ***Intramural sports:*** badminton M(c)/W(c), basketball M/W, crew W(c), cross-country running M/W, equestrian sports M(c)/W(c), fencing M/W, field hockey M(c)/W(c), football M, golf M/W, lacrosse M(c), racquetball M/W, rock climbing M/W, skiing (cross-country) M(c)/W(c), skiing (downhill) M(c)/W(c), soccer M/W, softball M/W, squash M/W, swimming and diving M/W, tennis M/W, track and field M/W, ultimate Frisbee M, volleyball M/W, water polo M/W.

Campus security: 24-hour emergency response devices and patrols, late-night transport/escort service, controlled dormitory access.

Student services: health clinic, personal/psychological counseling, women's center.

COSTS & FINANCIAL AID

Costs (2019–20) ***Comprehensive fee:*** $71,980 includes full-time tuition ($54,380), mandatory fees ($382), and room and board ($17,218). Part-time tuition: $963 per course. Part-time tuition and fees vary according to course load. ***Required fees:*** $191 per term part-time. ***College room only:*** $9956. Room and board charges vary according to board plan. ***Payment plan:*** deferred payment. ***Waivers:*** employees or children of employees.

Financial Aid Of all full-time matriculated undergraduates who enrolled in 2018, 1,099 applied for aid, 913 were judged to have need, 913 had their need fully met. In 2018, 3 non-need-based awards were made. ***Average percent of need met:*** 100. ***Average financial aid package:*** $57,279. ***Average need-based gift aid:*** $55,082. ***Average non-need-based aid:*** $5000. ***Average indebtedness upon graduation:*** $18,829.

APPLYING

Standardized Tests *Required:* SAT or ACT (for admission).

Options: electronic application, early decision, deferred entrance.

Application fee: $70.

Required: essay or personal statement, high school transcript, 2 letters of recommendation. ***Recommended:*** supplemental forms for visual and performing arts and science research.

Application deadlines: 1/1 (freshmen), 2/15 (transfers).

Early decision deadline: 11/1 (for plan 1), 1/1 (for plan 2).

Notification: 4/1 (freshmen), 4/1 (transfers), 12/15 (early decision plan 1), 2/15 (early decision plan 2).

CONTACT

Pomona College, 333 North College Way, Claremont, CA 91711.

Providence Christian College

Pasadena, California

http://www.providencecc.edu/

CONTACT

Providence Christian College, 1539 East Howard Street, Pasadena, CA 91124.

SAE Expression College

Emeryville, California

http://www.sae.edu/

CONTACT
SAE Expression College, 6601 Shellmound Street, Emeryville, CA 94608. *Toll-free phone:* 877-833-8800.

Saint Mary's College of California

Moraga, California

http://www.stmarys-ca.edu/

- **Independent Roman Catholic** upper-level, founded 1863
- **Suburban** 420-acre campus with easy access to San Francisco
- **Endowment** $181.3 million
- **Coed** 2,646 undergraduate students, 94% full-time, 57% women, 43% men
- **Moderately difficult** entrance level, 166% of applicants were admitted

UNDERGRAD STUDENTS
2,495 full-time, 151 part-time. Students come from 38 states and territories; 21 other countries; 13% are from out of state; 4% Black or African American, non-Hispanic/Latino; 28% Hispanic/Latino; 12% Asian, non-Hispanic/Latino; 2% Native Hawaiian or other Pacific Islander, non-Hispanic/Latino; 0.4% American Indian or Alaska Native, non-Hispanic/Latino; 8% Two or more races, non-Hispanic/Latino; 2% Race/ethnicity unknown; 3% international; 6% transferred in; 55% live on campus.

Freshmen:
Admission: 4,129 applied, 6,856 admitted.

FACULTY
Total: 373, 52% full-time, 51% with terminal degrees.

Student/faculty ratio: 10:1.

ACADEMICS
Calendar: 4-1-4. *Degrees:* certificates, bachelor's, master's, doctoral, and postbachelor's certificates.

Special study options: adult/continuing education programs, advanced placement credit, double majors, honors programs, independent study, internships, off-campus study, part-time degree program, services for LD students, student-designed majors, study abroad, summer session for credit. ***ROTC:*** Army (c), Air Force (c).

Unusual degree programs: 3-2 engineering with Washington University in St. Louis, University of Southern California; education.

Computers: 244 computers/terminals and 1,800 ports are available on campus for general student use. Students can access the following: campus intranet, computer help desk, free student e-mail accounts, online (class) grades, online (class) registration, online (class) schedules, student accounts. Campuswide network is available. 100% of college-owned or -operated housing units are wired for high-speed Internet access. Wireless service is available via entire campus.
Library: St. Albert Hall Library. *Books:* 181,352 (physical), 196,024 (digital/electronic); *Serial titles:* 605 (physical), 172,000 (digital/electronic); *Databases:* 212. Weekly public service hours: 108; study areas open 24 hours, 5–7 days a week; students can reserve study rooms.

STUDENT LIFE
Housing options: coed, men-only, women-only, special housing for students with disabilities. Campus housing is university owned. Freshman campus housing is guaranteed.

Activities and organizations: drama/theater group, student-run newspaper, radio station, choral group, Gael Force, Campus Activities Board, LASA-Latin American Student Association-Black Student Union, La Hermandad, Asian Pacific American Student Association.

Athletics Member NCAA. All Division I. ***Intercollegiate sports:*** baseball M(s), basketball M(s)/W(s), crew W(s), cross-country running M(s)/W(s), golf M(s), lacrosse M(c)/W(c), rugby M(c)/W(c), sand volleyball W(s), soccer M/W(s), softball W(s), tennis M(s)/W(s), track and field M(s)/W(s), volleyball W(s), water polo M(c)/W(c). ***Intramural sports:*** baseball M(c), basketball M/W, crew M(c), soccer M(c)/W(c), softball M/W, table tennis M/W, tennis M(c)/W(c), ultimate Frisbee M/W, volleyball M(c)/W(c).

Campus security: 24-hour emergency response devices and patrols, late-night transport/escort service.

Student services: health clinic, personal/psychological counseling, women's center.

COSTS & FINANCIAL AID
Costs (2020–21) ***Comprehensive fee:*** $66,366 includes full-time tuition ($50,460), mandatory fees ($200), and room and board ($15,706). Part-time tuition: $6308 per course. Part time tuition and fees vary according to course load and program. ***Required fees:*** $200 per term part-time. ***Room and board:*** Room and board charges vary according to board plan and housing facility. ***Payment plan:*** installment. ***Waivers:*** employees or children of employees.

Financial Aid Of all full-time matriculated undergraduates who enrolled in 2019, 1,833 applied for aid, 1,794 were judged to have need, 7 had their need fully met. 214 Federal Work-Study jobs (averaging $2631). In 2019, 568 non-need-based awards were made. ***Average percent of need met:*** 67. ***Average financial aid package:*** $37,988. ***Average need-based loan:*** $4657. ***Average need-based gift aid:*** $16,751. ***Average non-need-based aid:*** $22,272. ***Average indebtedness upon graduation:*** $30,693.

APPLYING
Standardized Tests *Required:* SAT or ACT (for admission).

Options: electronic application, early action, deferred entrance.

Application fee: $60.

Application deadlines: 7/1 (transfers), 11/15 (early action).

Notification: continuous (transfers), 1/1 (early action).

CONTACT
Sherie Gilmore-Cleveland, Dean of Admissions, Saint Mary's College of California, 1928 St. Mary's Road, P.M.B. 4800, Moraga, CA 94575. *Phone:* 925-631-4224. *Toll-free phone:* 800-800-4SMC. *Fax:* 925-376-7193. *E-mail:* smcadmit@stmarys-ca.edu.

Samuel Merritt University

Oakland, California

http://www.samuelmerritt.edu/

CONTACT
Samuel Merritt University, 3100 Telegraph Avenue, Oakland, CA 94609-3108. *Phone:* 510-869-1508. *Toll-free phone:* 800-607-6377.

San Diego Christian College

Santee, California

http://www.sdcc.edu/

CONTACT
Christine Roberts, Admissions Director, San Diego Christian College, 200 Riverview Parkway, Santee, CA 92017. *Phone:* 619-201-8760. *Toll-free phone:* 800-676-2242. *Fax:* 619-201-8749. *E-mail:* christine.roberts@sdcc.edu.

San Diego State University

San Diego, California

http://www.sdsu.edu/

- **State-supported** university, founded 1897, part of California State University System
- **Urban** 288-acre campus with easy access to San Diego
- **Endowment** $312.2 million
- **Coed** 30,612 undergraduate students, 90% full-time, 55% women, 45% men
- **Very difficult** entrance level, 34% of applicants were admitted

UNDERGRAD STUDENTS
27,579 full-time, 3,033 part-time. Students come from 52 states and territories; 117 other countries; 11% are from out of state; 4% Black or African American, non-Hispanic/Latino; 32% Hispanic/Latino; 13% Asian, non-Hispanic/Latino; 0.3% Native Hawaiian or other Pacific Islander, non-Hispanic/Latino; 0.3% American Indian or Alaska Native, non-Hispanic/Latino; 6% Two or more races, non-Hispanic/Latino; 4%

Race/ethnicity unknown; 7% international; 14% transferred in; 23% live on campus.

Freshmen:

Admission: 69,842 applied, 23,767 admitted, 5,275 enrolled. ***Average high school GPA:*** 3.8. ***Test scores:*** SAT evidence-based reading and writing scores over 500: 93%; SAT math scores over 500: 93%; ACT scores over 18: 95%; SAT evidence-based reading and writing scores over 600: 55%; SAT math scores over 600: 54%; ACT scores over 24: 63%; SAT evidence-based reading and writing scores over 700: 8%; SAT math scores over 700: 15%; ACT scores over 30: 20%.

Retention: 89% of full-time freshmen returned.

FACULTY

Total: 1,910, 50% full-time, 62% with terminal degrees.

Student/faculty ratio: 25:1.

ACADEMICS

Calendar: semesters. *Degrees:* bachelor's, master's, doctoral, and postbachelor's certificates.

Special study options: advanced placement credit, distance learning, double majors, English as a second language, external degree program, freshman honors college, honors programs, independent study, internships, off-campus study, part-time degree program, services for LD students, student-designed majors, study abroad, summer session for credit. ***ROTC:*** Army (b), Navy (c), Air Force (b).

Computers: 2,000 computers/terminals and 1,500 ports are available on campus for general student use. Students can access the following: computer help desk, free student e-mail accounts, online (class) grades, online (class) registration, online (class) schedules, learning management system. Campuswide network is available. 100% of college-owned or -operated housing units are wired for high-speed Internet access. Wireless service is available via entire campus.

Library: Malcolm A. Love Library. *Books:* 1.2 million (physical), 1.3 million (digital/electronic); *Serial titles:* 21,859 (physical), 246,435 (digital/electronic); *Databases:* 371. Weekly public service hours: 168; study areas open 24 hours, 5–7 days a week; students can reserve study rooms.

STUDENT LIFE

Housing options: on-campus residence required through sophomore year; coed, special housing for students with disabilities. Campus housing is university owned. Freshman campus housing is guaranteed.

Activities and organizations: drama/theater group, student-run newspaper, radio and television station, choral group, marching band, AB Samahan, Asian Pacific Student Alliance, Enviro-Business Society, M.E.Ch.A de SDSU, Social fraternities and sororities, including both general and culturally based organizations, national fraternities, national sororities.

Athletics Member NCAA. All Division I. ***Intercollegiate sports:*** baseball M(s), basketball M(s)/W(s), cross-country running W(s), football M(s), golf M(s)/W(s)(c), lacrosse W(s), rowing W(s), soccer M(s)/W(s), softball W(s), swimming and diving W(s), tennis M(s)/W(s), track and field W(s), volleyball W(s), water polo W(s). ***Intramural sports:*** basketball M/W, bowling M/W, football M/W, ice hockey M(c), lacrosse M(c)/W(c), rowing M(c)/W(c), rugby M(c), skiing (downhill) M(c)/W(c), soccer M(c)/W(c), softball M/W, tennis M(c)/W(c), triathlon M(c)/W(c), ultimate Frisbee M(c)/W(c), volleyball M(c)/W(c), water polo M(c)/W(c).

Campus security: 24-hour emergency response devices and patrols, student patrols, late-night transport/escort service, controlled dormitory access.

Student services: health clinic, personal/psychological counseling, women's center, veterans affairs office.

COSTS & FINANCIAL AID

Costs (2019–20) ***Tuition:*** area resident $5742 full-time; state resident $5742 full-time; nonresident $17,622 full-time. Full-time tuition and fees vary according to course load and location. Part-time tuition and fees vary according to course load and location. ***Required fees:*** $1768 full-time. ***Room and board:*** $17,752. Room and board charges vary according to board plan, housing facility, and student level. ***Payment plans:*** installment, deferred payment. ***Waivers:*** senior citizens and employees or children of employees.

Financial Aid Of all full-time matriculated undergraduates who enrolled in 2019, 18,100 applied for aid, 14,300 were judged to have need, 2,800 had their need fully met. 707 Federal Work-Study jobs (averaging $2393). In 2019, 2185 non-need-based awards were made. ***Average percent of need met:*** 66. ***Average financial aid package:*** $10,000. ***Average need-based loan:*** $4000. ***Average need-based gift aid:*** $10,100. ***Average non-need-based aid:*** $2000. ***Average indebtedness upon graduation:*** $21,172.

APPLYING

Standardized Tests *Required:* SAT or ACT (for admission).

Options: electronic application.

Application fee: $70.

Required: high school transcript.

Application deadlines: 11/30 (freshmen), 11/30 (transfers).

CONTACT

Office of Admissions, San Diego State University, 5500 Campanile Drive, San Diego, CA 92182-7455. *Phone:* 619-594-6336. *Toll-free phone:* 855-594-6336 (in-state); 855-594-3983 (out-of-state). *E-mail:* admissions@sdsu.edu.

San Diego State University–Imperial Valley Campus

Calexico, California

http://www.ivcampus.sdsu.edu/

CONTACT

Aracely Bororquez, Admissions Department, San Diego State University–Imperial Valley Campus, 720 Heber Avenue, Calexico, CA 92231. *Phone:* 760-768-5506. *Fax:* 760-768-5589. *E-mail:* transfer@mail.sdsu.edu.

San Francisco Art Institute

San Francisco, California

http://www.sfai.edu/

- **Independent** comprehensive, founded 1871
- **Urban** 4-acre campus with easy access to San Francisco
- **Endowment** $10.3 million
- **Coed** 220 undergraduate students, 94% full-time, 65% women, 35% men
- **Moderately difficult** entrance level, 90% of applicants were admitted

UNDERGRAD STUDENTS

207 full-time, 13 part-time. 35% are from out of state; 4% Black or African American, non-Hispanic/Latino; 15% Hispanic/Latino; 6% Asian, non-Hispanic/Latino; 0.5% Native Hawaiian or other Pacific Islander, non-Hispanic/Latino; 0.5% American Indian or Alaska Native, non-Hispanic/Latino; 6% Two or more races, non-Hispanic/Latino; 4% Race/ethnicity unknown; 27% international; 8% transferred in; 22% live on campus.

Freshmen:

Admission: 269 applied, 243 admitted, 32 enrolled.

Retention: 50% of full-time freshmen returned.

FACULTY

Total: 80, 16% full-time, 84% with terminal degrees.

Student/faculty ratio: 9:1.

ACADEMICS

Calendar: semesters. *Degrees:* bachelor's, master's, and postbachelor's certificates.

Special study options: academic remediation for entering students, distance learning, English as a second language, honors programs, independent study, internships, off-campus study, services for LD students, study abroad, summer session for credit.

Computers: 150 computers/terminals are available on campus for general student use. Students can access the following: computer help desk, free student e-mail accounts, online (class) grades, online (class) registration, online (class) schedules. Campuswide network is available. 100% of college-owned or -operated housing units are wired for high-speed Internet access. Wireless service is available via entire campus.

Library: Anne Bremer Memorial Library plus 1 other. *Books:* 32,775 (physical); *Serial titles:* 126 (physical), 791 (digital/electronic); *Databases:* 6. Weekly public service hours: 59.

STUDENT LIFE

Housing options: on-campus residence required for freshman year; coed. Campus housing is university owned. Freshman applicants given priority for college housing.

Activities and organizations: student-run newspaper, radio station, Student Union, LOGS (Legion of Graduate Students), Film Club, Photo Club, SFAeye.

Campus security: 24-hour patrols, security cameras.

Student services: personal/psychological counseling.

COSTS & FINANCIAL AID

Costs (2020–21) ***Comprehensive fee:*** $61,114 includes full-time tuition ($45,664), mandatory fees ($950), and room and board ($14,500). Full-time tuition and fees vary according to degree level. Part-time tuition: $2000 per credit. Part-time tuition and fees vary according to degree level. ***Room and board:*** Room and board charges vary according to housing facility. ***Payment plan:*** installment. ***Waivers:*** employees or children of employees.

Financial Aid Of all full-time matriculated undergraduates who enrolled in 2019, 106 applied for aid, 95 were judged to have need, 7 had their need fully met. In 2019, 97 non-need-based awards were made. ***Average percent of need met:*** 45. ***Average financial aid package:*** $18,707. ***Average need-based loan:*** $2346. ***Average need-based gift aid:*** $5583. ***Average non-need-based aid:*** $9119. ***Average indebtedness upon graduation:*** $28,432.

APPLYING

Options: electronic application, deferred entrance.

Application fee: $75.

Required: essay or personal statement, high school transcript, 1 letter of recommendation, portfolio and artist statement for BFA applicants, critical essay for BA applicants. ***Recommended:*** minimum 2.5 GPA, interview.

Application deadlines: rolling (freshmen), rolling (transfers).

Notification: continuous (freshmen), continuous (transfers).

CONTACT

Office of Admissions, San Francisco Art Institute, 800 Chestnut Street, San Francisco, CA 94133. *Phone:* 415-749-4500. *Toll-free phone:* 800-345-SFAI. *Fax:* 415-749-4592. *E-mail:* admissions@sfai.edu.

San Francisco Conservatory of Music

San Francisco, California

http://www.sfcm.edu/

CONTACT

Ms. Melissa Cocco-Mitten, Director of Admissions, San Francisco Conservatory of Music, 50 Oak Street, San Francisco, CA 94102. *Phone:* 415-503-6231. *Fax:* 415-503-6299. *E-mail:* admit@sfcm.edu.

San Francisco State University

San Francisco, California

http://www.sfsu.edu/

- **State-supported** university, founded 1899, part of California State University System
- **Urban** 142-acre campus
- **Endowment** $83.7 million
- **Coed** 25,917 undergraduate students, 84% full-time, 55% women, 45% men
- **Moderately difficult** entrance level, 67% of applicants were admitted

UNDERGRAD STUDENTS

21,663 full-time, 4,237 part-time. 1% are from out of state; 6% Black or African American, non-Hispanic/Latino; 35% Hispanic/Latino; 26% Asian, non-Hispanic/Latino; 0.5% Native Hawaiian or other Pacific Islander, non-Hispanic/Latino; 0.1% American Indian or Alaska Native, non-Hispanic/Latino; 6% Two or more races, non-Hispanic/Latino; 4% Race/ethnicity unknown; 7% international; 14% transferred in; 7% live on campus.

Freshmen:

Admission: 34,592 applied, 23,282 admitted, 3,688 enrolled. ***Average high school GPA:*** 3.3. ***Test scores:*** SAT evidence-based reading and writing scores over 500: 66%; SAT math scores over 500: 65%; ACT scores over 18: 69%; SAT evidence-based reading and writing scores over 600: 20%; SAT math scores over 600: 16%; ACT scores over 24: 22%; SAT evidence-based reading and writing scores over 700: 2%; SAT math scores over 700: 2%; ACT scores over 30: 2%.

Retention: 79% of full-time freshmen returned.

FACULTY

Total: 1,824, 38% full-time, 46% with terminal degrees.

ACADEMICS

Calendar: semesters. *Degrees:* certificates, bachelor's, master's, doctoral, post-master's, and postbachelor's certificates.

Special study options: academic remediation for entering students, accelerated degree program, adult/continuing education programs, advanced placement credit, cooperative education, distance learning, double majors, English as a second language, honors programs, independent study, internships, off-campus study, part-time degree program, services for LD students, student-designed majors, study abroad, summer session for credit. ***ROTC:*** Army (c), Air Force (c).

Computers: 2,000 computers/terminals and 800 ports are available on campus for general student use. Students can access the following: campus intranet, computer help desk, free student e-mail accounts, online (class) grades, online (class) registration, online (class) schedules. Campuswide network is available. 100% of college-owned or -operated housing units are wired for high-speed Internet access. Wireless service is available via entire campus.

Library: J. Paul Leonard Library. Study areas open 24 hours, 5–7 days a week; students can reserve study rooms.

STUDENT LIFE

Housing options: coed, women-only, special housing for students with disabilities. Campus housing is university owned. Freshman applicants given priority for college housing.

Activities and organizations: drama/theater group, student-run newspaper, radio and television station, choral group, national fraternities, national sororities.

Athletics Member NCAA. All Division II. ***Intercollegiate sports:*** baseball M(s), basketball M(s)/W(s), cross-country running M(s)/W(s), soccer M(s)/W(s), softball W(s), track and field W(s), volleyball W(s), wrestling M(s). ***Intramural sports:*** basketball M/W, cheerleading M(c)/W(c), ice hockey M(c)/W(c), rugby M(c)/W(c), soccer M/W, tennis M/W, volleyball M/W, water polo M(c)/W(c).

Campus security: 24-hour emergency response devices and patrols, student patrols, late-night transport/escort service, controlled dormitory access.

Student services: health clinic, personal/psychological counseling, women's center, legal services, veterans affairs office.

COSTS & FINANCIAL AID

Costs (2019–20) ***Tuition:*** area resident $5742 full-time; state resident $5742 full-time, $1665 per term part-time; nonresident $17,622 full-time, $4041 per term part-time. ***Required fees:*** $1524 full-time, $762 per term part-time. ***Room and board:*** $14,384.

Financial Aid Of all full-time matriculated undergraduates who enrolled in 2019, 16,879 applied for aid, 15,071 were judged to have need, 2,591 had their need fully met. In 2019, 285 non-need-based awards were made. ***Average percent of need met:*** 64. ***Average financial aid package:*** $15,435. ***Average need-based loan:*** $4440. ***Average need-based gift aid:*** $9509. ***Average non-need-based aid:*** $2975. ***Average indebtedness upon graduation:*** $5928.

APPLYING

Options: electronic application.

Application fee: $70.

Required: high school transcript.

Notification: 12/1 (freshmen), 12/1 (transfers).

CONTACT

San Francisco State University, 1600 Holloway Avenue, San Francisco, CA 94132-1722. *Phone:* 415-338-7211.

San Jose State University

San Jose, California

http://www.sjsu.edu/

- **State-supported** comprehensive, founded 1857, part of California State University System
- **Urban** 152-acre campus
- **Endowment** $208.3 million
- **Coed** 27,895 undergraduate students, 85% full-time, 50% women, 50% men
- **Moderately difficult** entrance level, 64% of applicants were admitted

UNDERGRAD STUDENTS

23,583 full-time, 4,312 part-time. Students come from 42 states and territories; 118 other countries; 1% are from out of state; 3% Black or African American, non-Hispanic/Latino; 29% Hispanic/Latino; 36% Asian, non-Hispanic/Latino; 0.5% Native Hawaiian or other Pacific Islander, non-Hispanic/Latino; 0.1% American Indian or Alaska Native, non-Hispanic/Latino; 5% Two or more races, non-Hispanic/Latino; 4% Race/ethnicity unknown; 8% international; 16% transferred in; 14% live on campus.

Freshmen:

Admission: 35,287 applied, 22,433 admitted, 3,959 enrolled. ***Average high school GPA:*** 3.5. ***Test scores:*** SAT evidence-based reading and writing scores over 500: 81%; SAT math scores over 500: 85%; ACT scores over 18: 82%; SAT evidence-based reading and writing scores over 600: 37%; SAT math scores over 600: 43%; ACT scores over 24: 41%; SAT evidence-based reading and writing scores over 700: 5%; SAT math scores over 700: 15%; ACT scores over 30: 13%.

Retention: 87% of full-time freshmen returned.

FACULTY

Total: 1,858, 39% full-time, 52% with terminal degrees.

Student/faculty ratio: 26:1.

ACADEMICS

Calendar: semesters. *Degrees:* certificates, bachelor's, master's, and doctoral.

Special study options: accelerated degree program, adult/continuing education programs, advanced placement credit, cooperative education, distance learning, double majors, honors programs, independent study, internships, off-campus study, part-time degree program, services for LD students, student-designed majors, study abroad, summer session for credit. ***ROTC:*** Army (c), Air Force (b).

Computers: Students can access the following: computer help desk, free student e-mail accounts, online (class) grades, online (class) registration, online (class) schedules. Campuswide network is available. 100% of college-owned or -operated housing units are wired for high-speed Internet access. Wireless service is available via entire campus.

Library: Dr. Martin Luther King Jr. Library plus 1 other. *Books:* 108,203 (physical), 899,231 (digital/electronic); *Serial titles:* 170,652 (physical), 170,652 (digital/electronic); *Databases:* 448. Weekly public service hours: 62; study areas open 24 hours, 5–7 days a week; students can reserve study rooms.

STUDENT LIFE

Housing options: on-campus residence required for freshman year; coed, men-only, women-only. Campus housing is university owned. Freshman applicants given priority for college housing.

Activities and organizations: drama/theater group, student-run newspaper, radio and television station, choral group, marching band, national fraternities, national sororities.

Athletics Member NCAA. All Division I. ***Intercollegiate sports:*** baseball M(s), basketball M(s)/W(s), cheerleading M(s)/W(s), cross-country running M(s)/W(s), football M(s), golf M(s)/W(s), gymnastics W(s), soccer M(s)/W(s), softball W(s), swimming and diving W(s), tennis W(s), track and field M(s)/W(s), volleyball W(s), water polo M(s)/W(s). ***Intramural sports:*** archery M(c)/W(c), badminton M(c)/W(c), baseball M(c)/W(c), basketball M(c), bowling M(c)/W(c), fencing M(c)/W(c), gymnastics M(c)/W(c), ice hockey M(c), lacrosse M(c)/W(c), rugby M(c)/W(c), soccer M(c)/W(c), swimming and diving M(c)/W(c), tennis M(c)/W(c), triathlon M(c)/W(c), ultimate Frisbee M(c), volleyball M(c)/W(c), water polo M(c)/W(c), wrestling M(c)/W(c).

Campus security: 24-hour emergency response devices and patrols, student patrols, late-night transport/escort service.

Student services: health clinic, personal/psychological counseling, women's center, veterans affairs office.

COSTS & FINANCIAL AID

Costs (2020–21) ***Tuition:*** area resident $5742 full-time, $1665 per term part-time; state resident $5742 full-time, $1665 per term part-time; nonresident $15,246 full-time, $4041 per term part-time. Part-time tuition and fees vary according to student level. ***Required fees:*** $2110 full-time, $1055 per term part-time. ***Room and board:*** $16,248; room only: $10,368. Room and board charges vary according to board plan, housing facility, and location. ***Payment plans:*** installment, deferred payment. ***Waivers:*** employees or children of employees.

Financial Aid Of all full-time matriculated undergraduates who enrolled in 2019, 16,689 applied for aid, 15,267 were judged to have need, 10,334 had their need fully met. In 2019, 53 non-need-based awards were made. ***Average percent of need met:*** 89. ***Average financial aid package:*** $19,319. ***Average need-based loan:*** $4480. ***Average need-based gift aid:*** $11,544. ***Average non-need-based aid:*** $1928. ***Average indebtedness upon graduation:*** $18,225. ***Financial aid deadline:*** 1/28.

APPLYING

Standardized Tests *Required:* SAT or ACT (for admission).

Options: electronic application.

Application fee: $55.

Required: high school transcript.

Application deadlines: 11/30 (freshmen), 11/30 (transfers).

Notification: continuous until 12/15 (freshmen), continuous until 12/15 (transfers).

CONTACT

San Jose State University, One Washington Square, San Jose, CA 95192-0001. *Phone:* 408-283-7500.

Santa Barbara Business College

Bakersfield, California

http://www.sbbcollege.edu/

CONTACT

Santa Barbara Business College, 5300 California Avenue, Bakersfield, CA 93309.

Santa Barbara Business College

Santa Maria, California

http://www.sbbcollege.edu/

CONTACT

Santa Barbara Business College, 303 East Plaza Drive, Santa Maria, CA 93454.

Santa Barbara Business College

Ventura, California

http://www.sbbcollege.edu/

CONTACT

Santa Barbara Business College, 4839 Market Street, Ventura, CA 93003.

Santa Clara University

Santa Clara, California

http://www.scu.edu/

- **Independent Roman Catholic (Jesuit)** university, founded 1851
- **Suburban** 106-acre campus with easy access to San Francisco, San Jose
- **Endowment** $1.0 billion
- **Coed** 5,694 undergraduate students, 98% full-time, 50% women, 50% men
- **Very difficult** entrance level, 49% of applicants were admitted

UNDERGRAD STUDENTS

5,586 full-time, 108 part-time. Students come from 46 states and territories; 27 other countries; 42% are from out of state; 3% Black or

African American, non-Hispanic/Latino; 18% Hispanic/Latino; 18% Asian, non-Hispanic/Latino; 0.2% Native Hawaiian or other Pacific Islander, non-Hispanic/Latino; 0.1% American Indian or Alaska Native, non-Hispanic/Latino; 8% Two or more races, non-Hispanic/Latino; 2% Race/ethnicity unknown; 4% international; 3% transferred in; 58% live on campus.

Freshmen:
Admission: 16,300 applied, 7,958 admitted, 1,391 enrolled. ***Average high school GPA:*** 3.7. ***Test scores:*** SAT evidence-based reading and writing scores over 500: 99%; SAT math scores over 500: 100%; ACT scores over 18: 100%; SAT evidence-based reading and writing scores over 600: 91%; SAT math scores over 600: 92%; ACT scores over 24: 98%; SAT evidence-based reading and writing scores over 700: 29%; SAT math scores over 700: 47%; ACT scores over 30: 61%.

Retention: 94% of full-time freshmen returned.

FACULTY
Total: 916, 62% full-time, 83% with terminal degrees.

Student/faculty ratio: 10:1.

ACADEMICS
Calendar: quarters. *Degrees:* bachelor's, master's, doctoral, post-master's, and postbachelor's certificates.

Special study options: advanced placement credit, cooperative education, double majors, honors programs, independent study, internships, off-campus study, services for LD students, student-designed majors, study abroad, summer session for credit. ***ROTC:*** Army (b), Air Force (c).

Computers: Students can access the following: campus intranet, computer help desk, free student e-mail accounts, online (class) grades, online (class) registration, online (class) schedules. Campuswide network is available. 100% of college-owned or -operated housing units are wired for high-speed Internet access. Wireless service is available via entire campus.

Library: University Library plus 1 other. *Books:* 571,201 (physical), 668,268 (digital/electronic); *Serial titles:* 13,614 (physical), 107,027 (digital/electronic); *Databases:* 283. Weekly public service hours: 121; students can reserve study rooms.

STUDENT LIFE
Housing options: coed, special housing for students with disabilities. Campus housing is university owned. Freshman applicants given priority for college housing.

Activities and organizations: drama/theater group, student-run newspaper, radio station, choral group.

Athletics Member NCAA. All Division I. ***Intercollegiate sports:*** baseball M(s), basketball M(s)/W(s), cross-country running M(s)/W(s), equestrian sports M(c)/W(c), field hockey W(c), golf M(s)/W(s), ice hockey M(c), lacrosse M(c)/W(c), rowing M/W, rugby M(c)/W(c), sailing M(c)/W(c), sand volleyball W, soccer M(s)/W(s), softball W(s), swimming and diving M(c)/W(c), tennis M(s)/W(s), track and field M(s)/W(s), triathlon M(c)/W(c), ultimate Frisbee M(c)/W(c), volleyball M(c)/W(s), water polo M(s)/W(s). ***Intramural sports:*** badminton M/W, basketball M/W, football M/W, soccer M/W, softball M/W, table tennis M/W, tennis M/W, volleyball M/W.

Campus security: 24-hour emergency response devices and patrols, late-night transport/escort service, controlled dormitory access.

Student services: health clinic, personal/psychological counseling, veterans affairs office.

COSTS & FINANCIAL AID
Costs (2020–21) ***Comprehensive fee:*** $71,601 includes full-time tuition ($54,987), mandatory fees ($642), and room and board ($15,972). Part-time tuition: $1527 per credit. Part-time tuition and fees vary according to course load. ***Room and board:*** Room and board charges vary according to board plan and housing facility. ***Payment plan:*** installment. ***Waivers:*** employees or children of employees.

Financial Aid Of all full-time matriculated undergraduates who enrolled in 2019, 3,337 applied for aid, 2,498 were judged to have need, 646 had their need fully met. 204 Federal Work-Study jobs (averaging $3969). In 2019, 1730 non-need-based awards were made. ***Average percent of need met:*** 74. ***Average financial aid package:*** $39,105. ***Average need-based loan:*** $4400. ***Average need-based gift aid:*** $32,076. ***Average non-need-based aid:*** $17,015. ***Average indebtedness upon graduation:*** $26,603.

APPLYING
Options: electronic application, early decision, early action, deferred entrance.

Application fee: $60.

Required: essay or personal statement, high school transcript, 1 letter of recommendation.

Application deadlines: 1/7 (freshmen), 4/15 (transfers), 11/1 (early action).

Early decision deadline: 11/1.

Notification: 4/1 (freshmen), continuous (transfers), 12/23 (early decision), 12/23 (early action).

CONTACT
Mrs. Eva Blanco Masias, Dean of Undergraduate Admissions, Santa Clara University, 500 El Camino Real, Santa Clara, CA 95053. *Phone:* 408-554-4700. *Fax:* 408-554-5255. *E-mail:* admission@scu.edu.

Scripps College

Claremont, California

http://www.scrippscollege.edu/

- **Independent** 4-year, founded 1926
- **Suburban** 32-acre campus with easy access to Los Angeles
- **Women only** 1,089 undergraduate students, 99% full-time
- **Very difficult** entrance level, 32% of applicants were admitted

UNDERGRAD STUDENTS
1,082 full-time, 7 part-time. Students come from 24 other countries; 56% are from out of state; 4% Black or African American, non-Hispanic/Latino; 14% Hispanic/Latino; 16% Asian, non-Hispanic/Latino; 0.2% Native Hawaiian or other Pacific Islander, non-Hispanic/Latino; 7% Two or more races, non-Hispanic/Latino; 2% Race/ethnicity unknown; 5% international; 2% transferred in; 94% live on campus.

Freshmen:
Admission: 3,022 applied, 967 admitted, 283 enrolled. ***Average high school GPA:*** 4.2. ***Test scores:*** SAT evidence-based reading and writing scores over 500: 100%; SAT math scores over 500: 100%; ACT scores over 18: 100%; SAT evidence-based reading and writing scores over 600: 97%; SAT math scores over 600: 96%; ACT scores over 24: 97%; SAT evidence-based reading and writing scores over 700: 60%; SAT math scores over 700: 56%; ACT scores over 30: 76%.

Retention: 93% of full-time freshmen returned.

FACULTY
Total: 136, 75% full-time, 95% with terminal degrees.

Student/faculty ratio: 10:1.

ACADEMICS
Calendar: semesters. *Degrees:* bachelor's and postbachelor's certificates.

Special study options: accelerated degree program, advanced placement credit, cooperative education, double majors, independent study, internships, off-campus study, services for LD students, student-designed majors, study abroad. ***ROTC:*** Army (c), Air Force (c).

Unusual degree programs: 3-2 business administration with Claremont Graduate University; engineering with Harvey Mudd College; American politics, economics, philosophy, public policy, international studies, religion with Claremont Graduate University.

Computers: Students can access the following: campus intranet, computer help desk, free student e-mail accounts, online (class) grades, online (class) registration, online (class) schedules, 2 ports per dorm room. Campuswide network is available. 100% of college-owned or -operated housing units are wired for high-speed Internet access. Wireless service is available via entire campus.

Library: Honnold/Mudd Library plus 2 others. *Books:* 1.0 million (physical), 2.2 million (digital/electronic); *Serial titles:* 28,182 (physical), 81,005 (digital/electronic); *Databases:* 490. Students can reserve study rooms.

STUDENT LIFE
Housing options: on-campus residence required for freshman year; women-only, special housing for students with disabilities. Campus housing is university owned. Freshman campus housing is guaranteed.

Activities and organizations: drama/theater group, student-run newspaper, radio station, choral group, Scripps Associated Students.

Athletics Member NCAA. All Division III. ***Intercollegiate sports:*** basketball W, cross-country running W, equestrian sports W(c), fencing W(c), golf W, lacrosse W, rugby W(c), skiing (downhill) W(c), soccer W, softball W, swimming and diving W, tennis W, track and field W, ultimate Frisbee W(c), volleyball W, water polo W. ***Intramural sports:*** basketball W, soccer W, softball W, volleyball W, water polo W.

Campus security: 24-hour emergency response devices and patrols, late-night transport/escort service, controlled dormitory access.

Student services: health clinic, personal/psychological counseling, women's center.

COSTS & FINANCIAL AID

Costs (2019–20) ***Comprehensive fee:*** $74,788 includes full-time tuition ($56,970), mandatory fees ($218), and room and board ($17,600). Full-time tuition and fees vary according to course load and degree level. Part-time tuition: $7121 per course. Part-time tuition and fees vary according to course load and degree level. ***College room only:*** $9584. Room and board charges vary according to board plan. ***Payment plans:*** tuition prepayment, installment. ***Waivers:*** employees or children of employees.

Financial Aid Of all full-time matriculated undergraduates who enrolled in 2018, 508 applied for aid, 393 were judged to have need, 393 had their need fully met. In 2018, 187 non-need-based awards were made. ***Average percent of need met:*** 100. ***Average financial aid package:*** $47,740. ***Average need-based loan:*** $4215. ***Average need-based gift aid:*** $39,007. ***Average non-need-based aid:*** $18,301. ***Average indebtedness upon graduation:*** $30,150.

APPLYING

Standardized Tests *Required:* SAT or ACT (for admission).

Options: electronic application, early decision, deferred entrance.

Application fee: $60.

Required: essay or personal statement, high school transcript, 2 letters of recommendation, school report completed by the student's secondary school counselor. ***Recommended:*** minimum 3.0 GPA, interview.

Early decision deadline: 11/15 (for plan 1), 1/3 (for plan 2).

Notification: 4/1 (freshmen), 12/15 (early decision plan 1), 2/15 (early decision plan 2).

CONTACT

Laura Stratton, Director of Admission, Scripps College, 1030 Columbia Avenue, Claremont, CA 91711. *Phone:* 909-621-8149. *Toll-free phone:* 800-770-1333. *Fax:* 909-607-7508. *E-mail:* admission@scrippscollege.edu.

Shasta Bible College

Redding, California

http://www.shasta.edu/

CONTACT

Connie Barton, Registrar, Shasta Bible College, 2951 Goodwater Avenue, Redding, CA 96002. *Phone:* 530-221-4275 Ext. 26. *Toll-free phone:* 800-800-4SBC. *Fax:* 530-221-6929. *E-mail:* registrar@shasta.edu.

Simpson University

Redding, California

http://www.simpsonu.edu/

CONTACT

Mr. Molly McKeever, Director of Undergraduate Admissions, Simpson University, 2211 College View Drive, Redding, CA 96003-8606. *Phone:* 530-226-5600. *Toll-free phone:* 888-9-SIMPSON. *Fax:* 530-226-4861. *E-mail:* admissions@simpsonu.edu.

Soka University of America

Aliso Viejo, California

http://www.soka.edu/

- **Independent** comprehensive, founded 1987
- **Suburban** 103-acre campus with easy access to Los Angeles, San Diego
- **Endowment** $1.2 billion
- **Coed**
- **Most difficult** entrance level

FACULTY

Student/faculty ratio: 8:1.

ACADEMICS

Calendar: semesters. *Degrees:* bachelor's and master's.

Library: Daisaku and Kaneko Ikeda Library. *Books:* 95,080 (physical), 261,022 (digital/electronic); *Serial titles:* 96 (physical), 7,563 (digital/electronic); *Databases:* 170. Study areas open 24 hours, 5–7 days a week; students can reserve study rooms.

STUDENT LIFE

Housing options: on-campus residence required through senior year; coed, men-only, women-only, cooperative, special housing for students with disabilities. Campus housing is university owned. Freshman campus housing is guaranteed.

Activities and organizations: choral group, Josho Daiko (Japanese Drum Club), Rhythmission (Hip Hop Dance Club), Sualseros (Salsa Dance Club), Ka Pilina Ho'olokahi (Hawaiian Dance Club), Soul Wings (Choir).

Athletics Member NAIA.

Campus security: 24-hour emergency response devices and patrols, student patrols, late-night transport/escort service, controlled dormitory access.

Student services: health clinic, personal/psychological counseling.

COSTS & FINANCIAL AID

Costs (2019–20) ***Comprehensive fee:*** $47,014 includes full-time tuition ($32,250), mandatory fees ($1732), and room and board ($13,032). Part-time tuition: $1344 per credit hour.

Financial Aid Of all full-time matriculated undergraduates who enrolled in 2017, 411 applied for aid, 350 were judged to have need, 249 had their need fully met. 34 Federal Work-Study jobs (averaging $1969). In 2017, 22 non-need-based awards were made. ***Average percent of need met:*** 88. ***Average financial aid package:*** $36,220. ***Average need-based loan:*** $4092. ***Average need-based gift aid:*** $24,414. ***Average non-need-based aid:*** $11,409. ***Average indebtedness upon graduation:*** $23,441. ***Financial aid deadline:*** 3/2.

APPLYING

Standardized Tests *Required:* SAT or ACT (for admission).

Options: electronic application, early admission, early action, deferred entrance.

Application fee: $45.

Required: essay or personal statement, high school transcript, 2 letters of recommendation, IERF evaluation for course work completed abroad. ***Recommended:*** interview.

CONTACT

Erica Espejo, Admission Operations Coordinator, Soka University of America, Enrollment Services, 1 University Drive, Aliso Viejo, CA 92656. *Phone:* 949-480-4151 Ext. 4151. *Toll-free phone:* 888-600-SOKA. *Fax:* 949-480-4151. *E-mail:* eespejo@soka.edu.

Sonoma State University

Rohnert Park, California

http://www.sonoma.edu/

- **State-supported** comprehensive, founded 1960, part of California State University System
- **Small-town** 280-acre campus with easy access to San Francisco
- **Endowment** $47.1 million
- **Coed**
- **Moderately difficult** entrance level

FACULTY

Student/faculty ratio: 23:1.

ACADEMICS
Calendar: semesters. *Degrees:* bachelor's and master's.
Library: Jean and Charles Schultz Information Center plus 1 other. Students can reserve study rooms.

STUDENT LIFE
Housing options: coed, special housing for students with disabilities. Campus housing is university owned. Freshman applicants given priority for college housing.

Activities and organizations: drama/theater group, student-run newspaper, radio station, choral group, national fraternities, national sororities.

Athletics Member NCAA. All Division II.

Campus security: 24-hour emergency response devices and patrols, student patrols, late-night transport/escort service, controlled dormitory access.

Student services: health clinic, personal/psychological counseling, women's center, legal services, veterans affairs office.

FINANCIAL AID
Financial Aid Of all full-time matriculated undergraduates who enrolled in 2018, 5,755 applied for aid, 4,706 were judged to have need, 64 had their need fully met. In 2018, 28 non-need-based awards were made. ***Average percent of need met:*** 58. ***Average financial aid package:*** $10,653. ***Average need-based loan:*** $2332. ***Average need-based gift aid:*** $8321. ***Average non-need-based aid:*** $2910. ***Average indebtedness upon graduation:*** $46,917.

APPLYING
Standardized Tests *Required:* SAT or ACT (for admission).

Options: electronic application, early admission.

Application fee: $55.

Required: high school transcript.

CONTACT
Ms. Natalie Kalogiannis, Director of Admissions, Sonoma State University, 1801 East Cotati Avenue, Rohnert Park, CA 94928-3609. *Phone:* 707-664-2874. *E-mail:* natalie.kalogiannis@sonoma.edu.

Southern California Institute of Architecture

Los Angeles, California

http://www.sciarc.edu/

CONTACT
Jamie Black, Admissions Counselor, Southern California Institute of Architecture, 960 East Third Street, Los Angeles, CA 90013. *Phone:* 213-356-5320. *Fax:* 213-613-2260. *E-mail:* admissions@sciarc.edu.

Southern California Institute of Technology

Anaheim, California

http://www.scitech.edu/

- **Proprietary** 4-year, founded 1987
- **Urban** campus with easy access to Anaheim, Los Angeles, San Diego
- **Coed** 511 undergraduate students, 100% full-time, 4% women, 96% men

UNDERGRAD STUDENTS
511 full-time. 4% Black or African American, non-Hispanic/Latino; 54% Hispanic/Latino; 12% Asian, non-Hispanic/Latino; 2% Native Hawaiian or other Pacific Islander, non-Hispanic/Latino; 0.2% American Indian or Alaska Native, non-Hispanic/Latino; 5% Two or more races, non-Hispanic/Latino; 1% Race/ethnicity unknown.

Freshmen:
Admission: 511 enrolled.

Retention: 79% of full-time freshmen returned.

FACULTY
Student/faculty ratio: 26:1.

ACADEMICS
Degrees: certificates, diplomas, associate, and bachelor's.

Special study options: accelerated degree program, adult/continuing education programs, double majors, English as a second language.

Computers: 300 computers/terminals are available on campus for general student use. Students can access the following: campus intranet. Campuswide network is available. Wireless service is available via entire campus.
Library: SCIT Library plus 1 other.

STUDENT LIFE
Housing options: college housing not available.
Campus security: late-night transport/escort service.

FINANCIAL AID
Financial Aid Of all full-time matriculated undergraduates who enrolled in 2018, 8 Federal Work-Study jobs (averaging $2800).

APPLYING
Standardized Tests *Required:* entrance exam (for admission).

Required: interview. ***Required for some:*** high school transcript.

CONTACT
Mrs. Sam Rokni, Southern California Institute of Technology, 525 N. Muller Street, Anaheim, CA 92801. *Phone:* 714-300-0300 Ext. 227. *Fax:* 714-300-0311. *E-mail:* admissions@scitech.edu.

Southern California Seminary

El Cajon, California

http://www.socalsem.edu/

CONTACT
Southern California Seminary, 2075 East Madison Avenue, El Cajon, CA 92019. *Phone:* 619-201-8959. *Toll-free phone:* 888-389-7244.

Southern States University

San Diego, California

http://www.ssu.edu/

CONTACT
Southern States University, 1094 Cudahy Place, Suite 120, San Diego, CA 92110.

Stanbridge University

Irvine, California

http://www.stanbridge.edu/

CONTACT
Stanbridge University, 2041 Business Center Drive, Irvine, CA 92612.

Stanford University

Stanford, California

http://www.stanford.edu/

- **Independent** university, founded 1891
- **Suburban** 8180-acre campus with easy access to San Francisco, San Jose
- **Coed** 6,996 undergraduate students, 100% full-time, 50% women, 50% men
- **Most difficult** entrance level, 4% of applicants were admitted

UNDERGRAD STUDENTS
6,996 full-time. 61% are from out of state; 7% Black or African American, non-Hispanic/Latino; 17% Hispanic/Latino; 23% Asian, non-Hispanic/Latino; 0.4% Native Hawaiian or other Pacific Islander, non-Hispanic/Latino; 0.8% American Indian or Alaska Native, non-Hispanic/Latino; 9% Two or more races, non-Hispanic/Latino; 0.4% Race/ethnicity unknown; 11% international; 0.3% transferred in; 93% live on campus.

Freshmen:
Admission: 47,498 applied, 2,062 admitted, 1,698 enrolled. ***Average high school GPA:*** 4.0. ***Test scores:*** SAT evidence-based reading and writing scores over 500: 100%; SAT math scores over 500: 100%; ACT scores over 18: 100%; SAT evidence-based reading and writing scores over 600: 98%; SAT math scores over 600: 98%; ACT scores over 24: 99%; SAT

evidence-based reading and writing scores over 700: 79%; SAT math scores over 700: 86%; ACT scores over 30: 88%.

Retention: 99% of full-time freshmen returned.

FACULTY

Total: 2,517, 67% full-time, 63% with terminal degrees.

Student/faculty ratio: 5:1.

ACADEMICS

Calendar: quarters. *Degrees:* bachelor's, master's, doctoral, and postbachelor's certificates.

Special study options: advanced placement credit, distance learning, double majors, English as a second language, honors programs, independent study, internships, off-campus study, services for LD students, student-designed majors, study abroad, summer session for credit. ***ROTC:*** Army (c), Navy (c), Air Force (c).

Computers: 1,000 computers/terminals are available on campus for general student use. Students can access the following: campus intranet, computer help desk, free student e-mail accounts, online (class) grades, online (class) registration, online (class) schedules. Campuswide network is available. 100% of college-owned or -operated housing units are wired for high-speed Internet access. Wireless service is available via entire campus.

Library: Green Library plus 20 others. *Books:* 9.5 million (physical), 1.5 million (digital/electronic); *Serial titles:* 77,000 (physical). Study areas open 24 hours, 5–7 days a week; students can reserve study rooms.

STUDENT LIFE

Housing options: on-campus residence required for freshman year; coed, women-only, cooperative, special housing for students with disabilities. Campus housing is university owned. Freshman campus housing is guaranteed.

Activities and organizations: drama/theater group, student-run newspaper, radio and television station, choral group, marching band, Ram's Head (theatre club), Axe Committee (athletic support), Business Association of Stanford Entrepreneurial Students, Asian-American Student Association, Stanford Daily, national fraternities, national sororities.

Athletics Member NCAA, NAIA. All NCAA Division I. ***Intercollegiate sports:*** archery M(c)/W(c), badminton M(c)/W(c), baseball M(s), basketball M(s)/W(s), cheerleading M(c)/W(c), crew M(s)/W(s), cross-country running M(s)/W(s), equestrian sports M(c)/W(c), fencing M(s)/W(s), field hockey W(s), football M(s), golf M(s)/W(s), gymnastics M(s)/W(s), ice hockey M(c), lacrosse M(c)/W(s), racquetball M(c)/W(c), rock climbing M(c)/W(c), rowing M(s)/W(s), rugby M(c)/W(c), sailing M/W, sand volleyball W, skiing (downhill) M(c)/W(c), soccer M(s)/W(s), softball W(s), squash M(c)/W(s), swimming and diving M(s)/W(s), tennis M(s)/W(s), track and field M(s)/W(s), triathlon M(c)/W(c), ultimate Frisbee M(c)/W(c), volleyball M(s)/W(s), water polo M(s)/W(s), wrestling M(s). ***Intramural sports:*** badminton M/W, baseball M(c), basketball M(c)/W(c), bowling M/W, cross-country running M(c)/W(c), football M/W, golf M(c)/W(c), lacrosse W(c), racquetball M/W, rock climbing M/W, sand volleyball M/W, soccer M(c)/W(c), softball M/W, swimming and diving M(c)/W(c), table tennis M(c)/W(c), tennis M(c)/W(c), track and field M/W, ultimate Frisbee M/W, volleyball M/W, water polo M/W.

Campus security: 24-hour emergency response devices and patrols, late-night transport/escort service, controlled dormitory access.

Student services: health clinic, personal/psychological counseling, women's center, legal services, veterans affairs office.

COSTS & FINANCIAL AID

Costs (2020–21) ***Comprehensive fee:*** $73,424 includes full-time tuition ($55,473), mandatory fees ($696), and room and board ($17,255). ***College room only:*** $10,725.

Financial Aid Of all full-time matriculated undergraduates who enrolled in 2018, 4,136 applied for aid, 3,446 were judged to have need, 3,054 had their need fully met. 546 Federal Work-Study jobs (averaging $2425). 1,883 state and other part-time jobs (averaging $2236). In 2018, 18 non-need-based awards were made. ***Average percent of need met:*** 100. ***Average financial aid package:*** $56,382. ***Average need-based loan:*** $3133. ***Average need-based gift aid:*** $52,823. ***Average non-need-based aid:*** $16,428. ***Average indebtedness upon graduation:*** $22,897.

APPLYING

Standardized Tests *Required:* SAT or ACT (for admission).

Options: electronic application, early action, deferred entrance.

Application fee: $90.

Required: essay or personal statement, high school transcript, 2 letters of recommendation.

Application deadlines: 1/3 (freshmen), 3/15 (transfers), 11/1 (early action).

Notification: 4/1 (freshmen), 5/15 (transfers), 12/15 (early action).

CONTACT

Stanford University, 450 Serra Mall, Stanford, CA 94305-2004.

Studio School

Los Angeles, California

http://www.studioschool.org/

CONTACT

Studio School, 1201 West 5th Street, Los Angeles, CA 90017.

SUM Bible College & Theological Seminary

Oakland, California

http://www.sum.edu/

CONTACT

Admissions, SUM Bible College & Theological Seminary, 735 105th Avenue, Oakland, CA 94603. *Phone:* 510-567-6174. *Toll-free phone:* 888-567-6174. *Fax:* 510-568-1024.

Theatre of Arts

Hollywood, California

http://www.toa.edu/

- **Proprietary** primarily 2-year, part of Campus Hollywood
- **Urban** campus with easy access to Los Angeles
- **Coed**

FACULTY

Total: 17.

ACADEMICS

Degree: bachelor's.

Computers: 4 computers/terminals are available on campus for general student use. Students can access the following: computer help desk. Campuswide network is available. Wireless service is available via entire campus.

Library: Jessica plus 1 other. Weekly public service hours: 40; study areas open 24 hours, 5–7 days a week.

STUDENT LIFE

Housing options: Campus housing is university owned.

Activities and organizations: drama/theater group.

COSTS

Costs (2020–21) ***One-time required fee:*** $75. ***Comprehensive fee:*** $76,376 includes full-time tuition ($39,996), mandatory fees ($19,800), and room and board ($16,580). No tuition increase for student's term of enrollment. ***College room only:*** $11,164. Room and board charges vary according to housing facility. ***Payment plans:*** installment, deferred payment.

APPLYING

Options: electronic application.

Required: high school transcript, interview.

CONTACT

Theatre of Arts, 1536 North Highland Avenue, Hollywood, CA 90028. *Phone:* 323-3371064.

Thomas Aquinas College - California

Santa Paula, California

http://www.thomasaquinas.edu/

CONTACT

Mr. Jonathan P. Daly, Director of Admissions, Thomas Aquinas College - California, 10000 Ojai Road, Santa Paula, CA 93060-9621. *Phone:* 805-525-4417 Ext. 5901. *Toll-free phone:* 800-634-9797. *Fax:* 805-421-5905. *E-mail:* admissions@thomasaquinas.edu.

Touro College Los Angeles

West Hollywood, California

http://www.touro.edu/losangeles/

CONTACT

Touro College Los Angeles, 1317 North Crescent Heights Boulevard, West Hollywood, CA 90046.

Touro University Worldwide

Los Alamitos, California

http://www.tuw.edu/

CONTACT

Touro University Worldwide, 10601 Calle Lee, Suite 179, Los Alamitos, CA 90720.

Trident University International

Cypress, California

http://www.trident.edu/

CONTACT

Trident University International, 5757 Plaza Drive, Suite 100, Cypress, CA 90630. *Phone:* 800-579-3197.

United States University

San Diego, California

http://www.usuniversity.edu/

CONTACT

Admissions, United States University, 7675 Mission Valley Road, San Diego, CA 92108. *Phone:* 619-477-6310. *Toll-free phone:* 888-422-3381. *Fax:* 619-477-7340.

University of Antelope Valley

Lancaster, California

http://www.uav.edu/

CONTACT

University of Antelope Valley, 44055 North Sierra Highway, Lancaster, CA 93534.

University of California, Berkeley

Berkeley, California

http://www.berkeley.edu/

- **State-supported** university, founded 1868, part of University of California System
- **Urban** 1232-acre campus with easy access to San Francisco
- **Coed** 31,780 undergraduate students, 94% full-time, 53% women, 46% men
- 17% of applicants were admitted

UNDERGRAD STUDENTS

29,904 full-time, 1,457 part-time. 16% are from out of state; 2% Black or African American, non-Hispanic/Latino; 16% Hispanic/Latino; 36% Asian, non-Hispanic/Latino; 0.2% Native Hawaiian or other Pacific Islander, non-Hispanic/Latino; 0.1% American Indian or Alaska Native, non-Hispanic/Latino; 6% Two or more races, non-Hispanic/Latino; 4% Race/ethnicity unknown; 13% international; 8% transferred in; 27% live on campus.

Freshmen:

Admission: 84,852 applied, 14,176 admitted, 6,397 enrolled. ***Average high school GPA:*** 3.9. ***Test scores:*** SAT evidence-based reading and writing scores over 500: 99%; SAT math scores over 500: 98%; ACT scores over 18: 98%; SAT evidence-based reading and writing scores over 600: 89%; SAT math scores over 600: 87%; ACT scores over 24: 88%; SAT evidence-based reading and writing scores over 700: 54%; SAT math scores over 700: 68%; ACT scores over 30: 69%.

Retention: 97% of full-time freshmen returned.

FACULTY

Total: 2,525, 65% full-time, 99% with terminal degrees.

Student/faculty ratio: 19:1.

ACADEMICS

Calendar: semesters. *Degrees:* bachelor's, master's, doctoral, and postbachelor's certificates.

Special study options: accelerated degree program, adult/continuing education programs, advanced placement credit, double majors, English as a second language, honors programs, independent study, internships, off-campus study, services for LD students, student-designed majors, study abroad, summer session for credit. ***ROTC:*** Army (b), Navy (b), Air Force (b).

Computers: Students can access the following: computer help desk, free student e-mail accounts, online (class) grades, online (class) registration, online (class) schedules. Campuswide network is available. Wireless service is available via classrooms, computer centers, computer labs, dorm rooms, learning centers, libraries, student centers.

Library: Doe Library.

STUDENT LIFE

Housing options: coed, women-only, cooperative, special housing for students with disabilities. Campus housing is university owned. Freshman campus housing is guaranteed.

Activities and organizations: drama/theater group, student-run newspaper, radio and television station, choral group, marching band, national fraternities, national sororities.

Athletics Member NCAA. All Division I. ***Intercollegiate sports:*** baseball M, basketball M/W, crew M/W, cross-country running M/W, field hockey W, football M, golf M/W, gymnastics M/W, lacrosse M/W, rugby M, soccer M/W, softball W, swimming and diving M/W, tennis M/W, track and field M/W, volleyball W, water polo M/W. ***Intramural sports:*** basketball M/W, soccer M/W, softball M/W, tennis M/W, ultimate Frisbee M/W, volleyball M/W.

Campus security: 24-hour emergency response devices and patrols, late-night transport/escort service, controlled dormitory access, Office of Emergency Preparedness.

Student services: health clinic, personal/psychological counseling, women's center, legal services.

COSTS & FINANCIAL AID

Costs (2019–20) ***Tuition:*** state resident $11,442 full-time; nonresident $41,196 full-time. ***Required fees:*** $2811 full-time. ***Room and board:*** $17,220. Room and board charges vary according to board plan and housing facility. ***Payment plan:*** installment.

Financial Aid Of all full-time matriculated undergraduates who enrolled in 2019, 17,340 applied for aid, 13,558 were judged to have need, 3,948 had their need fully met. In 2019, 1636 non-need-based awards were made. ***Average percent of need met:*** 83. ***Average financial aid package:*** $26,153. ***Average need-based loan:*** $7231. ***Average need-based gift aid:*** $22,420. ***Average non-need-based aid:*** $8717. ***Average indebtedness upon graduation:*** $19,773. ***Financial aid deadline:*** 3/2.

APPLYING

Standardized Tests *Required:* SAT or ACT (for admission). *Recommended:* SAT Subject Tests (for admission).

Options: electronic application, deferred entrance.

Application fee: $70.

Required: essay or personal statement.

CONTACT

University of California, Berkeley, Berkeley, CA 94720.

University of California, Davis

Davis, California

http://www.ucdavis.edu/

- **State-supported** university, founded 1908, part of University of California System
- **Suburban** 5300-acre campus with easy access to San Francisco
- **Coed**
- **Very difficult** entrance level

ACADEMICS
Calendar: quarters. *Degrees:* bachelor's, master's, doctoral, post-master's, and postbachelor's certificates.
Library: Peter J. Shields Library plus 6 others. *Books:* 4.9 million (physical), 1.3 million (digital/electronic); *Serial titles:* 106,593 (physical).

STUDENT LIFE
Housing options: coed, women-only, cooperative, special housing for students with disabilities. Campus housing is university owned, leased by the school and is provided by a third party. Freshman campus housing is guaranteed.
Activities and organizations: drama/theater group, student-run newspaper, radio and television station, choral group, marching band, national fraternities, national sororities.

Athletics Member NCAA. All Division I except football (Division I-AA).

Campus security: 24-hour emergency response devices and patrols, student patrols, late-night transport/escort service, controlled dormitory access, Campus Violence Prevention Program (CVPP).

Student services: health clinic, personal/psychological counseling, women's center, legal services, veterans affairs office.

COSTS & FINANCIAL AID
Costs (2019–20) ***Tuition:*** state resident $11,442 full-time; nonresident $40,434 full-time. ***Required fees:*** $3050 full-time. ***Room and board:*** $15,863. Room and board charges vary according to board plan.

Financial Aid Of all full-time matriculated undergraduates who enrolled in 2019, 20,853 applied for aid, 17,463 were judged to have need, 3,938 had their need fully met. In 2019, 1108 non-need-based awards were made. ***Average percent of need met:*** 80. ***Average financial aid package:*** $21,768. ***Average need-based loan:*** $6193. ***Average need-based gift aid:*** $18,987. ***Average non-need-based aid:*** $6954. ***Average indebtedness upon graduation:*** $18,985.

APPLYING
Standardized Tests *Required:* SAT or ACT (for admission).

Options: electronic application.

Application fee: $70.

Required: essay or personal statement, high school transcript, high school subject requirements.

CONTACT
Ebony Lewis, Executive Director, Admissions, University of California, Davis, One Shields Avenue, Davis, CA 95616. *Phone:* 530-754-0707. *E-mail:* ucdlewis@ucdavis.edu.

University of California, Irvine

Irvine, California

http://www.uci.edu/

- **State-supported** university, founded 1965, part of University of California System
- **Suburban** 1477-acre campus with easy access to Los Angeles
- **Coed** 30,382 undergraduate students, 98% full-time, 52% women, 48% men
- **Very difficult** entrance level, 27% of applicants were admitted

UNDERGRAD STUDENTS
29,796 full-time, 586 part-time. Students come from 46 states and territories; 78 other countries; 2% are from out of state; 2% Black or African American, non-Hispanic/Latino; 26% Hispanic/Latino; 36% Asian, non-Hispanic/Latino; 0.2% Native Hawaiian or other Pacific Islander, non-Hispanic/Latino; 0.1% American Indian or Alaska Native, non-Hispanic/Latino; 4% Two or more races, non-Hispanic/Latino; 1% Race/ethnicity unknown; 17% international; 10% transferred in; 38% live on campus.

Freshmen:
Admission: 95,568 applied, 25,361 admitted, 6,068 enrolled. ***Average high school GPA:*** 4.0. ***Test scores:*** SAT evidence-based reading and writing scores over 500: 94%; SAT math scores over 500: 94%; SAT evidence-based reading and writing scores over 600: 65%; SAT math scores over 600: 74%; SAT evidence-based reading and writing scores over 700: 22%; SAT math scores over 700: 43%.

Retention: 94% of full-time freshmen returned.

FACULTY
Total: 1,720, 82% full-time, 98% with terminal degrees.
Student/faculty ratio: 18:1.

ACADEMICS
Calendar: quarters. *Degrees:* bachelor's, master's, doctoral, and postbachelor's certificates.

Special study options: accelerated degree program, advanced placement credit, distance learning, double majors, English as a second language, honors programs, independent study, internships, off-campus study, services for LD students, study abroad, summer session for credit. ***ROTC:*** Army (b), Air Force (c).

Computers: 1,500 computers/terminals are available on campus for general student use. Students can access the following: campus intranet, computer help desk, free student e-mail accounts, online (class) grades, online (class) registration, online (class) schedules. Campuswide network is available. 100% of college-owned or -operated housing units are wired for high-speed Internet access. Wireless service is available via entire campus.
Library: Langson Library plus 4 others. *Books:* 2.0 million (physical), 1.3 million (digital/electronic); *Serial titles:* 4,309 (physical), 177,370 (digital/electronic); *Databases:* 1,652. Study areas open 24 hours, 5–7 days a week; students can reserve study rooms.

STUDENT LIFE
Housing options: coed, men-only, women-only, special housing for students with disabilities. Campus housing is university owned. Freshman campus housing is guaranteed.

Activities and organizations: drama/theater group, student-run newspaper, radio station, choral group, marching band, national fraternities, national sororities.

Athletics Member NCAA. All Division I. ***Intercollegiate sports:*** archery M(c)/W(c), badminton M(c)/W(c), baseball M(s), basketball M(s)/W(s), crew M(c)/W(c), cross-country running M(s)/W(s), fencing M(c)/W(c), golf M(s)/W(s)(c), lacrosse M(c)/W(c), rugby M(c)/W(c), sailing M(c)/W(c), soccer M(s)/W(s), table tennis M(c)/W(c), tennis M(s)/W(s), track and field M(s)/W(s), ultimate Frisbee M(c)/W(c), volleyball M(s)/W(s), water polo M(s)/W(s), wrestling M(c)/W(c). ***Intramural sports:*** basketball M/W, bowling M/W, football M/W, racquetball M/W, soccer M/W, softball M/W, swimming and diving M/W, table tennis M/W, tennis M/W, track and field M/W, ultimate Frisbee M/W, volleyball M/W, water polo M/W, wrestling M/W.

Campus security: 24-hour emergency response devices and patrols, student patrols, late-night transport/escort service, controlled dormitory access.

Student services: health clinic, personal/psychological counseling, veterans affairs office.

COSTS & FINANCIAL AID
Costs (2019–20) ***Tuition:*** state resident $11,442 full-time; nonresident $41,196 full-time. ***Required fees:*** $2285 full-time. ***Room and board:*** $16,135. Room and board charges vary according to board plan and housing facility. ***Payment plan:*** installment. ***Waivers:*** employees or children of employees.

Financial Aid Of all full-time matriculated undergraduates who enrolled in 2018, 20,425 applied for aid, 1,790 were judged to have need, 3,128 had their need fully met. In 2018, 635 non-need-based awards were made. ***Average percent of need met:*** 79. ***Average financial aid package:*** $23,096. ***Average need-based loan:*** $7215. ***Average need-based gift aid:*** $19,488. ***Average non-need-based aid:*** $8013. ***Average indebtedness upon graduation:*** $19,039. ***Financial aid deadline:*** 6/26.

APPLYING

Standardized Tests *Required:* SAT or ACT (for admission).

Options: electronic application.

Application fee: $70.

Required: essay or personal statement, high school transcript.

Application deadlines: 11/30 (freshmen), 11/30 (transfers).

Notification: 3/31 (freshmen), 4/30 (transfers).

CONTACT

University of California, Irvine, Irvine, CA 92697. *Phone:* 949-824-6701.

University of California, Los Angeles

Los Angeles, California

http://www.ucla.edu/

- **State-supported** university, founded 1919, part of University of California System
- **Urban** 419-acre campus with easy access to Los Angeles
- **Endowment** $3.6 billion
- **Coed** 31,543 undergraduate students, 98% full-time, 58% women, 41% men
- **Very difficult** entrance level, 12% of applicants were admitted

UNDERGRAD STUDENTS

30,872 full-time, 571 part-time. 13% are from out of state; 3% Black or African American, non-Hispanic/Latino; 22% Hispanic/Latino; 28% Asian, non-Hispanic/Latino; 0.2% Native Hawaiian or other Pacific Islander, non-Hispanic/Latino; 0.2% American Indian or Alaska Native, non-Hispanic/Latino; 6% Two or more races, non-Hispanic/Latino; 3% Race/ethnicity unknown; 11% international; 10% transferred in; 48% live on campus.

Freshmen:

Admission: 108,831 applied, 13,432 admitted, 5,910 enrolled. ***Average high school GPA:*** 3.9. ***Test scores:*** SAT evidence-based reading and writing scores over 500: 99%; SAT math scores over 500: 98%; ACT scores over 18: 100%; SAT evidence-based reading and writing scores over 600: 88%; SAT math scores over 600: 83%; ACT scores over 24: 87%; SAT evidence-based reading and writing scores over 700: 51%; SAT math scores over 700: 59%; ACT scores over 30: 65%.

Retention: 96% of full-time freshmen returned.

FACULTY

Total: 3,343, 93% full-time, 98% with terminal degrees.

Student/faculty ratio: 18:1.

ACADEMICS

Calendar: quarters. *Degrees:* bachelor's, master's, and doctoral.

Special study options: accelerated degree program, advanced placement credit, double majors, freshman honors college, independent study, internships, off-campus study, services for LD students, student-designed majors, study abroad, summer session for credit. ***ROTC:*** Army (b), Navy (b), Air Force (b).

Computers: 4,000 computers/terminals are available on campus for general student use. Students can access the following: campus intranet, computer help desk, free student e-mail accounts, online (class) grades, online (class) registration, online (class) schedules, 24/7 Chat with a Librarian. Campuswide network is available. 100% of college-owned or -operated housing units are wired for high-speed Internet access. Wireless service is available via entire campus.

Library: Charles E. Young Research Library plus 13 others. *Books:* 13.8 million (physical), 2.1 million (digital/electronic); *Serial titles:* 9,543 (physical), 99,598 (digital/electronic); *Databases:* 1,794. Weekly public service hours: 104; study areas open 24 hours, 5–7 days a week; students can reserve study rooms.

STUDENT LIFE

Housing options: coed, cooperative, special housing for students with disabilities. Campus housing is university owned. Freshman campus housing is guaranteed.

Activities and organizations: drama/theater group, student-run newspaper, radio and television station, choral group, marching band, national fraternities, national sororities.

Athletics Member NCAA. All Division I except football (Division I-A). ***Intercollegiate sports:*** baseball M(s), basketball M(s)/W(s), crew W(s), cross-country running M(s)/W(s), golf M(s)/W(s)(c), gymnastics W(s), soccer M(s)/W(s), softball W(s), swimming and diving W(s), tennis M(s)/W(s), track and field M(s)/W(s), volleyball M(s)/W(s), water polo M(s)/W(s). ***Intramural sports:*** archery M/W, badminton M/W, basketball M/W, bowling M/W, crew M/W, cross-country running M/W, fencing M/W, field hockey W, football M/W, golf M/W, gymnastics M/W, ice hockey M/W, lacrosse M/W, racquetball M/W, riflery M/W, rugby M/W, sailing M/W, skiing (cross-country) M/W, skiing (downhill) M/W, soccer M/W, softball M/W, squash M/W, swimming and diving M/W, table tennis M/W, tennis M/W, track and field M/W, ultimate Frisbee M/W, volleyball M/W, water polo M/W.

Campus security: 24-hour emergency response devices and patrols, student patrols, late-night transport/escort service, controlled dormitory access.

Student services: health clinic, personal/psychological counseling, women's center, legal services, veterans affairs office.

COSTS & FINANCIAL AID

Costs (2019–20) ***One-time required fee:*** $165. ***Tuition:*** state resident $11,442 full-time; nonresident $41,196 full-time. ***Required fees:*** $2122 full-time. ***Room and board:*** $16,625. Room and board charges vary according to board plan and housing facility.

Financial Aid Of all full-time matriculated undergraduates who enrolled in 2019, 17,449 applied for aid, 15,582 were judged to have need, 3,997 had their need fully met. 2,325 Federal Work-Study jobs (averaging $1911). 25 state and other part-time jobs (averaging $3500). In 2019, 1106 non-need-based awards were made. ***Average percent of need met:*** 82. ***Average financial aid package:*** $24,808. ***Average need-based loan:*** $7487. ***Average need-based gift aid:*** $21,402. ***Average non-need-based aid:*** $5901. ***Average indebtedness upon graduation:*** $21,441.

APPLYING

Standardized Tests *Required:* SAT or ACT (for admission). *Required for some:* SAT Subject Tests (for admission).

Options: electronic application.

Application fee: $70.

Required: essay or personal statement, high school transcript.

Application deadlines: 11/30 (freshmen), 11/30 (transfers).

Notification: 3/31 (freshmen), 4/30 (transfers).

CONTACT

University of California, Los Angeles, 405 Hilgard Avenue, Los Angeles, CA 90095. *Phone:* 310-825-3101.

University of California, Merced

Merced, California

http://www.ucmerced.edu/

- **State-supported** university, part of University of California System
- **Small-town** 815-acre campus with easy access to Fresno
- **Coed** 8,151 undergraduate students, 99% full-time, 52% women, 48% men
- **Moderately difficult** entrance level, 72% of applicants were admitted

UNDERGRAD STUDENTS

8,080 full-time, 71 part-time. 4% Black or African American, non-Hispanic/Latino; 56% Hispanic/Latino; 19% Asian, non-Hispanic/Latino; 0.6% Native Hawaiian or other Pacific Islander, non-Hispanic/Latino; 0.1% American Indian or Alaska Native, non-Hispanic/Latino; 3% Two or more races, non-Hispanic/Latino; 0.5% Race/ethnicity unknown; 8% international; 2% transferred in; 44% live on campus.

Freshmen:

Admission: 25,368 applied, 18,263 admitted, 2,107 enrolled. ***Average high school GPA:*** 3.6. ***Test scores:*** SAT evidence-based reading and writing scores over 500: 73%; SAT math scores over 500: 74%; ACT scores over 18: 75%; SAT evidence-based reading and writing scores over 600: 22%; SAT math scores over 600: 24%; ACT scores over 24: 20%; SAT evidence-based reading and writing scores over 700: 2%; SAT math scores over 700: 5%; ACT scores over 30: 3%.

Retention: 85% of full-time freshmen returned.

FACULTY

Total: 420, 93% full-time, 80% with terminal degrees.

Student/faculty ratio: 19:1.

ACADEMICS

Degrees: bachelor's, master's, and doctoral.

Special study options: academic remediation for entering students, advanced placement credit, double majors, independent study, internships, off-campus study, part-time degree program, services for LD students, study abroad, summer session for credit.

Computers: Students can access the following: campus intranet, computer help desk, free student e-mail accounts, online (class) grades, online (class) registration, online (class) schedules, student calendar, 10Gb online cloud storage, free office software. Campuswide network is available. 100% of college-owned or -operated housing units are wired for high-speed Internet access. Wireless service is available via entire campus.

Library: Kolligian Library. *Books:* 145,798 (physical), 2.0 million (digital/electronic); *Serial titles:* 99,476 (physical). Weekly public service hours: 97; students can reserve study rooms.

STUDENT LIFE

Housing options: coed, special housing for students with disabilities. Campus housing is university owned. Freshman campus housing is guaranteed.

Activities and organizations: drama/theater group, student-run newspaper, radio station, choral group, marching band, national fraternities, national sororities.

Athletics Member NAIA. ***Intercollegiate sports:*** basketball M(s)/W(s), cross-country running M(s)/W(s), golf M(c), soccer M(s)/W(s), volleyball M(s)/W(s). ***Intramural sports:*** archery M/W, baseball M(c), basketball M/W, cheerleading M(c)/W(c), football M/W, lacrosse M(c)/W(c), soccer M/W, softball M(c)/W(c), table tennis M(c)/W(c), ultimate Frisbee M/W, volleyball M/W, weight lifting M(c)/W(c), wrestling M(c)/W(c).

Campus security: 24-hour emergency response devices and patrols, student patrols, late-night transport/escort service, controlled dormitory access.

Student services: health clinic, personal/psychological counseling, women's center, legal services.

COSTS & FINANCIAL AID

Costs (2020–21) ***Tuition:*** state resident $11,442 full-time, $2860 per term part-time; nonresident $40,434 full-time, $10,108 per term part-time. Full-time tuition and fees vary according to course load. Part-time tuition and fees vary according to course load. ***Required fees:*** $2096 full-time, $2096 per year part-time. ***Room and board:*** $17,046. Room and board charges vary according to board plan. ***Payment plan:*** deferred payment. ***Waivers:*** employees or children of employees.

Financial Aid Of all full-time matriculated undergraduates who enrolled in 2019, 7,654 applied for aid, 7,237 were judged to have need, 1,597 had their need fully met. In 2019, 86 non-need-based awards were made. ***Average percent of need met:*** 84. ***Average financial aid package:*** $26,288. ***Average need-based loan:*** $5251. ***Average need-based gift aid:*** $22,327. ***Average non-need-based aid:*** $11,369. ***Average indebtedness upon graduation:*** $17,872.

APPLYING

Standardized Tests *Required:* SAT or ACT (for admission).

Options: electronic application.

Application fee: $70.

Required: essay or personal statement, high school transcript, minimum 3.0 high school GPA for California residents.

Notification: 3/1 (freshmen), 3/1 (transfers).

CONTACT

Mr. Ruben Lubers, Assistant Director, Admissions and Outreach, University of California, Merced, 5200 North Lake Road, Merced, CA 95343. *Phone:* 209-228-4241. *E-mail:* admissions@ucmerced.edu.

University of California, Riverside

Riverside, California

http://www.ucr.edu/

- **State-supported** university, founded 1954, part of University of California System
- **Suburban** 1200-acre campus with easy access to Los Angeles
- **Endowment** $259.8 million
- **Coed** 22,055 undergraduate students, 98% full-time, 54% women, 46% men
- **Very difficult** entrance level, 57% of applicants were admitted

UNDERGRAD STUDENTS

21,652 full-time, 403 part-time. Students come from 34 states and territories; 91 other countries; 0.5% are from out of state; 3% Black or African American, non-Hispanic/Latino; 42% Hispanic/Latino; 34% Asian, non-Hispanic/Latino; 0.1% Native Hawaiian or other Pacific Islander, non-Hispanic/Latino; 0.1% American Indian or Alaska Native, non-Hispanic/Latino; 6% Two or more races, non-Hispanic/Latino; 1% Race/ethnicity unknown; 4% international; 9% transferred in; 28% live on campus.

Freshmen:

Admission: 49,518 applied, 28,224 admitted, 4,778 enrolled. ***Average high school GPA:*** 3.8. ***Test scores:*** SAT evidence-based reading and writing scores over 500: 95%; SAT math scores over 500: 95%; ACT scores over 18: 99%; SAT evidence-based reading and writing scores over 600: 56%; SAT math scores over 600: 57%; ACT scores over 24: 75%; SAT evidence-based reading and writing scores over 700: 9%; SAT math scores over 700: 22%; ACT scores over 30: 31%.

Retention: 90% of full-time freshmen returned.

FACULTY

Total: 1,196, 84% full-time, 98% with terminal degrees.

Student/faculty ratio: 22:1.

ACADEMICS

Calendar: quarters. *Degrees:* bachelor's, master's, and doctoral.

Special study options: accelerated degree program, adult/continuing education programs, advanced placement credit, distance learning, double majors, honors programs, independent study, internships, off-campus study, part-time degree program, services for LD students, study abroad, summer session for credit. ***ROTC:*** Army (c), Air Force (c).

Unusual degree programs: 3-2 engineering.

Computers: Students can access the following: campus intranet, computer help desk, free student e-mail accounts, online (class) grades, online (class) registration, online (class) schedules, online viewing of financial information. Campuswide network is available. 100% of college-owned or -operated housing units are wired for high-speed Internet access. Wireless service is available via entire campus.

Library: Tomas Rivera Library plus 4 others. *Books:* 3.4 million (physical), 1.1 million (digital/electronic); *Serial titles:* 2,308 (physical), 116,178 (digital/electronic); *Databases:* 1,664. Weekly public service hours: 96; study areas open 24 hours, 5–7 days a week; students can reserve study rooms.

STUDENT LIFE

Housing options: coed, special housing for students with disabilities. Campus housing is university owned. Freshman campus housing is guaranteed.

Activities and organizations: drama/theater group, student-run newspaper, radio station, choral group, American Red Cross at University of California, Riverside, Project Sunshine, Vietnamese Student Association, Healthy Hearts, American Sign Language Club, national fraternities, national sororities.

Athletics Member NCAA. All Division I. ***Intercollegiate sports:*** baseball M(s), basketball M(s)/W(s), cross-country running M(s)/W(s), golf M(s)/W(s), soccer M(s)/W(s), softball W(s), tennis M(s)/W(s), track and field M(s)/W(s), volleyball W(s). ***Intramural sports:*** archery M(c)/W(c), badminton M/W, baseball M(c)/W(c), basketball M/W, cheerleading W(c), cross-country running M(c)/W(c), fencing M(c)/W(c), racquetball M/W, rugby M(c)/W(c), skiing (downhill) M(c)/W(c), soccer M/W, softball M/W, swimming and diving M/W, table tennis M(c)/W(c), tennis M/W, track and field M/W, ultimate Frisbee M(c)/W(c), volleyball M/W, water polo M(c)/W(c), wrestling M(c)/W(c).

Campus security: 24-hour emergency response devices and patrols, student patrols, late-night transport/escort service, controlled dormitory access.

Student services: health clinic, personal/psychological counseling, women's center, legal services, veterans affairs office.

COSTS & FINANCIAL AID

Costs (2019–20) ***Tuition:*** state resident $11,442 full-time, $5721 per year part-time; nonresident $41,196 full-time, $20,598 per year part-time. Full-time tuition and fees vary according to course load. Part-time tuition and fees vary according to course load. ***Required fees:*** $4184 full-time, $1395 per term part-time. ***Room and board:*** $17,350. Room and board charges vary according to board plan and housing facility. ***Payment plan:*** deferred payment.

Financial Aid Of all full-time matriculated undergraduates who enrolled in 2019, 18,411 applied for aid, 16,573 were judged to have need, 2,549 had their need fully met. 3,174 Federal Work-Study jobs (averaging $1598). In 2019, 763 non-need-based awards were made. ***Average percent of need met:*** 81. ***Average financial aid package:*** $21,726. ***Average need-based loan:*** $5849. ***Average need-based gift aid:*** $17,670. ***Average non-need-based aid:*** $9663. ***Average indebtedness upon graduation:*** $20,779.

APPLYING

Options: electronic application.

Application fee: $70.

Required: essay or personal statement, high school transcript, minimum 3.0 GPA.

Application deadlines: 11/30 (freshmen), 11/30 (out-of-state freshmen), 11/30 (transfers).

Notification: continuous until 3/1 (freshmen), continuous until 3/1 (out-of-state freshmen), continuous until 3/1 (transfers).

CONTACT

Ms. Emily D. Engelschall, Interim Associate Vice Chancellor, Enrollment Services, University of California, Riverside, 3221 Student Services, 900 University Avenue, Riverside, CA 92521. *Phone:* 951-827-3411. *Fax:* 951-827-6344. *E-mail:* admissions@ucr.edu.

University of California, San Diego

La Jolla, California

http://www.ucsd.edu/

- **State-supported** university, founded 1959, part of University of California System
- **Suburban** 1976-acre campus with easy access to San Diego
- **Coed** 30,794 undergraduate students, 98% full-time, 50% women, 50% men
- **Very difficult** entrance level, 32% of applicants were admitted

UNDERGRAD STUDENTS

30,257 full-time, 537 part-time. Students come from 52 states and territories; 110 other countries; 7% are from out of state; 3% Black or African American, non-Hispanic/Latino; 21% Hispanic/Latino; 36% Asian, non-Hispanic/Latino; 0.2% Native Hawaiian or other Pacific Islander, non-Hispanic/Latino; 0.4% American Indian or Alaska Native, non-Hispanic/Latino; 2% Race/ethnicity unknown; 18% international; 10% transferred in; 38% live on campus.

Freshmen:

Admission: 99,133 applied, 32,062 admitted, 6,023 enrolled. ***Average high school GPA:*** 4.1. ***Test scores:*** SAT evidence-based reading and writing scores over 500: 99%; SAT math scores over 500: 99%; ACT scores over 18: 99%; SAT evidence-based reading and writing scores over 600: 82%; SAT math scores over 600: 83%; ACT scores over 24: 80%; SAT evidence-based reading and writing scores over 700: 31%; SAT math scores over 700: 55%; ACT scores over 30: 50%.

Retention: 93% of full-time freshmen returned.

FACULTY

Total: 1,465, 84% full-time, 98% with terminal degrees.

Student/faculty ratio: 19:1.

ACADEMICS

Calendar: quarters. *Degrees:* bachelor's, master's, and doctoral.

Special study options: accelerated degree program, advanced placement credit, cooperative education, double majors, English as a second language, freshman honors college, honors programs, independent study, internships, off-campus study, services for LD students, student-designed majors, study abroad, summer session for credit. ***ROTC:*** Army (c), Navy (c), Air Force (c).

Computers: Students can access the following: campus intranet, computer help desk, free student e-mail accounts, online (class) grades, online (class) registration, online (class) schedules. Campuswide network is available. 100% of college-owned or -operated housing units are wired for high-speed Internet access. Wireless service is available via entire campus.

Library: Geisel Library plus 1 other. *Books:* 3.5 million (physical), 958,000 (digital/electronic). Study areas open 24 hours, 5–7 days a week; students can reserve study rooms.

STUDENT LIFE

Housing options: coed, special housing for students with disabilities. Campus housing is university owned. Freshman campus housing is guaranteed.

Activities and organizations: drama/theater group, student-run newspaper, radio and television station, choral group, marching band, national fraternities, national sororities.

Athletics Member NCAA. All Division II. ***Intercollegiate sports:*** baseball M, basketball M/W, crew M/W, cross-country running M/W, fencing M/W, golf M, soccer M/W, softball W, swimming and diving M/W, tennis M/W, track and field M/W, volleyball M/W, water polo M/W. ***Intramural sports:*** basketball M/W, bowling M/W, equestrian sports M(c)/W(c), football M(c)/W(c), ice hockey M, lacrosse M(c)/W(c), racquetball M/W, sailing M(c)/W(c), skiing (downhill) M(c)/W(c), soccer M/W, softball M/W, table tennis M/W, tennis M/W, ultimate Frisbee M(c)/W(c), volleyball M/W, water polo M/W.

Campus security: 24-hour emergency response devices and patrols, student patrols, late-night transport/escort service, crime prevention programs.

Student services: health clinic, personal/psychological counseling, women's center, legal services, veterans affairs office.

COSTS & FINANCIAL AID

Costs (2020–21) ***Tuition:*** state resident $12,570 full-time; nonresident $42,324 full-time. ***Required fees:*** $1910 full-time. ***Room and board:*** $14,295. Room and board charges vary according to board plan and housing facility.

Financial Aid Of all full-time matriculated undergraduates who enrolled in 2018, 19,315 applied for aid, 16,650 were judged to have need, 4,209 had their need fully met. In 2018, 601 non-need-based awards were made. ***Average percent of need met:*** 83. ***Average financial aid package:*** $23,550. ***Average need-based loan:*** $6433. ***Average need-based gift aid:*** $19,496. ***Average non-need-based aid:*** $11,201. ***Average indebtedness upon graduation:*** $21,061.

APPLYING

Standardized Tests *Required:* SAT or ACT (for admission), SAT and SAT Subject Tests or ACT (for admission), ACT Assessment with Writing or SAT Reasoning Test, plus two SAT Subject Tests (for admission).

Options: electronic application.

Application fee: $105.

Required: essay or personal statement, high school transcript, minimum 3.0 GPA. ***Required for some:*** minimum 3.4 GPA.

Notification: 3/31 (freshmen).

CONTACT

Ms. Adele Brumfield, Assistant Vice Chancellor, Enrollment Management, University of California, San Diego, 9500 Gilman Drive, 0021, La Jolla, CA 92093-0021. *Phone:* 858-534-3156. *E-mail:* admissionsreply@ucsd.edu.

See below for display ad and page 1118 for the College Close-Up.

University of California, Santa Barbara

Santa Barbara, California

http://www.ucsb.edu/

- **State-supported** university, founded 1909, part of University of California System
- **Suburban** 989-acre campus
- **Endowment** $155.0 million
- **Coed** 23,349 undergraduate students, 98% full-time, 54% women, 45% men
- **Very difficult** entrance level, 29% of applicants were admitted

UNDERGRAD STUDENTS

22,777 full-time, 497 part-time. Students come from 51 states and territories; 81 other countries; 6% are from out of state; 2% Black or African American, non-Hispanic/Latino; 26% Hispanic/Latino; 19% Asian, non-Hispanic/Latino; 0.3% Native Hawaiian or other Pacific Islander, non-Hispanic/Latino; 0.2% American Indian or Alaska Native, non-Hispanic/Latino; 6% Two or more races, non-Hispanic/Latino; 1% Race/ethnicity unknown; 14% international; 9% transferred in; 39% live on campus.

Freshmen:

Admission: 91,308 applied, 26,881 admitted, 4,914 enrolled. ***Average high school GPA:*** 4.2. ***Test scores:*** SAT evidence-based reading and writing scores over 500: 99%; SAT math scores over 500: 98%; ACT scores over 18: 98%; SAT evidence-based reading and writing scores over 600: 84%; SAT math scores over 600: 81%; ACT scores over 24: 80%; SAT evidence-based reading and writing scores over 700: 37%; SAT math scores over 700: 52%; ACT scores over 30: 51%.

Retention: 92% of full-time freshmen returned.

FACULTY

Total: 1,208, 86% full-time, 100% with terminal degrees.

Student/faculty ratio: 17:1.

ACADEMICS

Calendar: quarters plus 6-week summer term. *Degrees:* bachelor's, master's, doctoral, post-master's, and postbachelor's certificates.

Special study options: accelerated degree program, advanced placement credit, cooperative education, double majors, English as a second language, honors programs, independent study, internships, off-campus study, services for LD students, student-designed majors, study abroad, summer session for credit. ***ROTC:*** Army (b), Air Force (c).

Computers: Students can access the following: computer help desk, free student e-mail accounts, online (class) grades, online (class) registration, online (class) schedules. Campuswide network is available. 100% of college-owned or -operated housing units are wired for high-speed Internet access. Wireless service is available via classrooms, computer labs, dorm rooms, libraries, student centers.

Library: Davidson Library plus 1 other. Weekly public service hours: 96; study areas open 24 hours, 5–7 days a week; students can reserve study rooms.

STUDENT LIFE

Housing options: coed, cooperative. Campus housing is university owned. Freshman applicants given priority for college housing.

Activities and organizations: drama/theater group, student-run newspaper, radio and television station, choral group, national fraternities, national sororities.

Athletics Member NCAA. All Division I. ***Intercollegiate sports:*** baseball M(s), basketball M(s)/W(s), bowling M(c)/W(c), crew M(c)/W(c), cross-country running M(s)/W(s), equestrian sports M(c)/W(c), fencing M(c)/W(c), field hockey W(c), golf M(s), gymnastics M(s)/W(s), lacrosse M(c)/W(c), rugby M(c), sailing M(c)/W(c), skiing (downhill) M(c)/W(c), soccer M(s)/W(s), softball W(s), swimming and diving M(s)/W(s), tennis M(s)/W(s), track and field M(s)/W(s), ultimate Frisbee M(c)/W(c), volleyball M(s)/W(s), water polo M(s)/W(s). ***Intramural sports:*** badminton M/W, basketball M/W, bowling M/W, cross-country running M/W, football M/W, golf M/W, gymnastics M/W, racquetball M/W, soccer M/W, softball M/W, squash M/W, tennis M/W, ultimate Frisbee M/W, volleyball M/W, water polo M/W.

Campus security: 24-hour emergency response devices and patrols, student patrols, late-night transport/escort service, controlled dormitory access.

Student services: health clinic, personal/psychological counseling, women's center, legal services.

COSTS & FINANCIAL AID

Costs (2020–21) ***Tuition:*** state resident $11,442 full-time; nonresident $41,196 full-time. ***Required fees:*** $2949 full-time. ***Room and board:*** $15,389.

Financial Aid Of all full-time matriculated undergraduates who enrolled in 2019, 14,971 applied for aid, 12,358 were judged to have need, 11,618 had their need fully met. In 2019, 500 non-need-based awards were made. ***Average percent of need met:*** 99. ***Average financial aid package:*** $29,936. ***Average need-based loan:*** $7883. ***Average need-based gift aid:*** $21,037. ***Average non-need-based aid:*** $8362. ***Average indebtedness upon graduation:*** $18,995.

APPLYING

Standardized Tests *Required:* SAT or ACT (for admission). *Recommended:* SAT Subject Tests (for admission).

Options: electronic application.

Application fee: $70.

Required: essay or personal statement, high school transcript. ***Required for some:*** interview.

Application deadlines: 11/30 (freshmen), 11/30 (transfers).

Notification: 3/31 (freshmen), 5/1 (transfers).

CONTACT

Office of Admissions, University of California, Santa Barbara, 1210 Cheadle Hall, Santa Barbara, CA 93106-2014. *Phone:* 805-893-2881. *Fax:* 805-893-2676. *E-mail:* admissions@sa.ucsb.edu.

University of California, Santa Cruz

Santa Cruz, California

http://www.ucsc.edu/

- **State-supported** university, founded 1965, part of University of California System
- **Small-town** 2000-acre campus with easy access to San Francisco, San Jose
- **Endowment** $215.4 million
- **Coed** 17,539 undergraduate students, 97% full-time, 48% women, 52% men
- **Very difficult** entrance level, 51% of applicants were admitted

UNDERGRAD STUDENTS

16,994 full-time, 545 part-time. Students come from 45 states and territories; 55 other countries; 4% are from out of state; 2% Black or African American, non-Hispanic/Latino; 26% Hispanic/Latino; 22% Asian, non-Hispanic/Latino; 0.1% Native Hawaiian or other Pacific Islander, non-Hispanic/Latino; 0.1% American Indian or Alaska Native, non-Hispanic/Latino; 8% Two or more races, non-Hispanic/Latino; 2% Race/ethnicity unknown; 9% international; 8% transferred in; 51% live on campus.

Freshmen:

Admission: 53,809 applied, 27,615 admitted, 3,713 enrolled. ***Average high school GPA:*** 3.6. ***Test scores:*** SAT evidence-based reading and writing scores over 500: 99%; SAT math scores over 500: 99%; ACT scores over 18: 100%; SAT evidence-based reading and writing scores over 600: 73%; SAT math scores over 600: 75%; ACT scores over 24: 78%; SAT evidence-based reading and writing scores over 700: 18%; SAT math scores over 700: 33%; ACT scores over 30: 31%.

Retention: 89% of full-time freshmen returned.

FACULTY

Total: 866, 72% full-time, 98% with terminal degrees.

Student/faculty ratio: 25:1.

ACADEMICS

Calendar: quarters. *Degrees:* bachelor's, master's, doctoral, and postbachelor's certificates.

Special study options: accelerated degree program, advanced placement credit, cooperative education, double majors, freshman honors college, honors programs, independent study, internships, off-campus study, services for LD students, student-designed majors, study abroad, summer session for credit. ***ROTC:*** Army (c), Navy (c), Air Force (c).

Computers: Students can access the following: campus intranet, computer help desk, free student e-mail accounts, online (class) grades, online (class) registration, online (class) schedules. Campuswide network is available. 100% of college-owned or -operated housing units are wired for high-speed Internet access. Wireless service is available via entire campus.

Library: UCSC Library. *Books:* 1.5 million (physical), 1.1 million (digital/electronic); *Serial titles:* 73,472 (physical), 68,740 (digital/electronic); *Databases:* 9,138. Weekly public service hours: 98; students can reserve study rooms.

STUDENT LIFE

Housing options: coed, men-only, women-only, cooperative. Campus housing is university owned. Freshman campus housing is guaranteed.

Activities and organizations: drama/theater group, student-run newspaper, radio and television station, choral group, marching band, Bayanihan, Chinese Students & Scholars Association, College Panhellenic & Inter-Greek Council, Film Production Coalition, Indian Student Association, national fraternities, national sororities.

Athletics Member NCAA. All Division III. ***Intercollegiate sports:*** badminton M(c)/W(c), basketball M/W, cheerleading M(c)/W(c), cross-country running M/W, equestrian sports M(c)/W(c), fencing M(c)/W(c), golf W, ice hockey M(c)/W(c), lacrosse M(c)/W(c), racquetball M(c)/W(c), rugby M(c)/W(c), sailing M(c)/W(c), soccer M/W, softball W(c), swimming and diving M/W, tennis M/W, track and field M/W, triathlon M(c)/W(c), ultimate Frisbee M(c)/W(c), volleyball M/W, water polo M(c)/W(c). ***Intramural sports:*** basketball M/W, soccer M/W, softball M/W, ultimate Frisbee M/W, volleyball M/W, water polo M/W.

Campus security: 24-hour emergency response devices and patrols, late-night transport/escort service, controlled dormitory access.

Student services: health clinic, personal/psychological counseling, women's center.

COSTS & FINANCIAL AID

Costs (2019–20) ***Tuition:*** state resident $11,442 full-time; nonresident $40,434 full-time. Part-time tuition and fees vary according to course load. ***Required fees:*** $2612 full-time. ***Room and board:*** $16,916. Room and board charges vary according to board plan and housing facility. ***Payment plan:*** installment.

Financial Aid Of all full-time matriculated undergraduates who enrolled in 2019, 11,516 applied for aid, 9,428 were judged to have need, 2,301 had their need fully met. 1,066 Federal Work-Study jobs (averaging $1853). In 2019, 1644 non-need-based awards were made. ***Average percent of need met:*** 83. ***Average financial aid package:*** $25,453. ***Average need-based loan:*** $6673. ***Average need-based gift aid:*** $21,111. ***Average non-need-based aid:*** $6206. ***Average indebtedness upon graduation:*** $21,375. ***Financial aid deadline:*** 3/2.

APPLYING

Standardized Tests *Required:* SAT or ACT (for admission).

Options: electronic application.

Application fee: $70.

Required: essay or personal statement, high school transcript, minimum 3.0 GPA, minimum high school GPA of 3.0 for California residents, 3.4 for non-residents. ***Required for some:*** minimum 3.4 GPA.

Application deadlines: 11/30 (freshmen), 11/30 (transfers).

Notification: 3/31 (freshmen), 5/1 (transfers).

CONTACT

Blia Yang, Director, Admissions, University of California, Santa Cruz, 1156 High Street, Santa Cruz, CA 95064. *Phone:* 831-459-4008. *Fax:* 831-459-4452. *E-mail:* admissions@ucsc.edu.

University of La Verne

La Verne, California

http://www.laverne.edu/

- **Independent** university, founded 1891
- **Suburban** 66-acre campus with easy access to Los Angeles
- **Coed** 2,509 undergraduate students, 96% full-time, 57% women, 43% men
- **Moderately difficult** entrance level, 55% of applicants were admitted

UNDERGRAD STUDENTS
2,412 full-time, 97 part-time. Students come from 29 states and territories; 31 other countries; 5% are from out of state; 5% Black or African American, non-Hispanic/Latino; 57% Hispanic/Latino; 5% Asian, non-Hispanic/Latino; 0.4% Native Hawaiian or other Pacific Islander, non-Hispanic/Latino; 0.2% American Indian or Alaska Native, non-Hispanic/Latino; 5% Two or more races, non-Hispanic/Latino; 1% Race/ethnicity unknown; 8% international; 7% transferred in; 32% live on campus.

Freshmen:
Admission: 6,864 applied, 3,763 admitted, 495 enrolled. ***Average high school GPA:*** 3.6. ***Test scores:*** SAT evidence-based reading and writing scores over 500: 87%; SAT math scores over 500: 88%; ACT scores over 18: 85%; SAT evidence-based reading and writing scores over 600: 29%; SAT math scores over 600: 23%; ACT scores over 24: 35%; SAT evidence-based reading and writing scores over 700: 2%; SAT math scores over 700: 3%; ACT scores over 30: 6%.

Retention: 82% of full-time freshmen returned.

FACULTY
Total: 534, 44% full-time.

Student/faculty ratio: 12:1.

ACADEMICS
Calendar: 4-1-4. *Degrees:* certificates, bachelor's, master's, and doctoral (also offers continuing education program with significant enrollment not reflected in profile).

Special study options: academic remediation for entering students, adult/continuing education programs, advanced placement credit, distance learning, double majors, English as a second language, freshman honors college, honors programs, independent study, internships, off-campus study, part-time degree program, services for LD students, student-designed majors, study abroad, summer session for credit. ***ROTC:*** Army (c).

Computers: Students can access the following: computer help desk, free student e-mail accounts, online (class) grades, online (class) registration, online (class) schedules, MyLaVerne (online). Campuswide network is available. 100% of college-owned or -operated housing units are wired for high-speed Internet access. Wireless service is available via entire campus.

Library: Wilson Library. Students can reserve study rooms.

STUDENT LIFE
Housing options: coed, men-only, women-only. Campus housing is university owned.

Activities and organizations: drama/theater group, student-run newspaper, radio and television station, choral group, Associated Students of La Verne, Latino Student Forum, Black Student Union, Psi Chi, Voices in Action, national fraternities, national sororities.

Athletics Member NCAA. All Division III. ***Intercollegiate sports:*** baseball M, basketball M/W, cross-country running M/W, football M, golf M, soccer M/W, softball W, swimming and diving M/W, tennis M/W, track and field M/W, volleyball W, water polo M/W.

Campus security: 24-hour emergency response devices and patrols, late-night transport/escort service, controlled dormitory access.

Student services: health clinic, personal/psychological counseling, veterans affairs office.

COSTS & FINANCIAL AID
Costs (2020–21) ***Comprehensive fee:*** $58,350 includes full-time tuition ($43,440), mandatory fees ($1110), and room and board ($13,800). Part-time tuition: $1300 per semester hour.

Financial Aid Of all full-time matriculated undergraduates who enrolled in 2018, 2,385 applied for aid, 2,268 were judged to have need, 436 had their need fully met. In 2018, 359 non-need-based awards were made. ***Average percent of need met:*** 61. ***Average financial aid package:*** $29,047. ***Average need-based loan:*** $4207. ***Average need-based gift aid:*** $16,680. ***Average non-need-based aid:*** $12,916. ***Average indebtedness upon graduation:*** $33,384.

APPLYING
Options: electronic application, deferred entrance.

Application fee: $50.

Required: essay or personal statement, high school transcript, 2 letters of recommendation.

Application deadlines: 2/1 (freshmen), 4/1 (transfers).

Notification: continuous (freshmen), continuous (transfers).

CONTACT
University of La Verne, 1950 Third Street, La Verne, CA 91750. *Phone:* 800-876-4858. *Toll-free phone:* 800-876-4858. *Fax:* 909-392-2714. *E-mail:* admissions@ulv.edu.

University of Phoenix–Bay Area Campus

San Jose, California

http://www.phoenix.edu/

CONTACT
Marc Booker, Senior Director, Office of Admissions and Evaluation, University of Phoenix–Bay Area Campus, 4035 South Riverpoint Parkway, Mail Stop CF-L101, Phoenix, AZ 85040-1958. *Phone:* 602-557-4609. *Toll-free phone:* 866-766-0766. *Fax:* 480-643-1156.

University of Phoenix–Central Valley Campus

Fresno, California

http://www.phoenix.edu/

CONTACT
Marc Booker, Senior Director, Office of Admissions and Evaluation, University of Phoenix–Central Valley Campus, 4035 South Riverpoint Parkway, Mail Stop CF-L101, Phoenix, AZ 85040. *Phone:* 602-557-4609. *Toll-free phone:* 866-766-0766. *Fax:* 480-643-1156.

University of Phoenix–Sacramento Valley Campus

Sacramento, California

http://www.phoenix.edu/

CONTACT
Marc Booker, Senior Director, Office of Admissions and Evaluation, University of Phoenix–Sacramento Valley Campus, 4035 South Riverpoint Parkway, Mail Stop CF-L101, Phoenix, AZ 85040. *Phone:* 602-557-4609. *Toll-free phone:* 866-766-0766. *Fax:* 480-643-1156.

University of Phoenix–San Diego Campus

San Diego, California

http://www.phoenix.edu/

CONTACT
Marc Booker, Senior Director, Office of Admissions and Evaluation, University of Phoenix–San Diego Campus, 4035 South Riverpoint Parkway, Mail Stop CF-L101, Phoenix, AZ 85040. *Phone:* 602-557-4609. *Toll-free phone:* 866-766-0766. *Fax:* 480-643-1156.

University of Redlands

Redlands, California

http://www.redlands.edu/

CONTACT

Ms. Belinda Sandoval Zazueta, Director of Undergraduate Admission, University of Redlands, 1200 East Colton Avenue, PO Box 3080, Redlands, CA 92373-0999. *Phone:* 909-748-8074. *Toll-free phone:* 800-455-5064. *Fax:* 909-335-4089. *E-mail:* belinda_sandoval@redlands.edu.

University of Saint Katherine

San Marcos, California

http://www.usk.edu/

CONTACT

Dean Marina Karavokiris, Dean of Admissions and Registrar, University of Saint Katherine, 1637 Capalina Road, San Marcos, CA 92069. *Phone:* 760-471-1316 Ext. 307. *Fax:* 760-471-1314. *E-mail:* admissions@stkath.org.

University of San Diego

San Diego, California

http://www.sandiego.edu/

- **Independent Roman Catholic** university, founded 1949
- **Urban** 180-acre campus with easy access to San Diego
- **Endowment** $545.6 million
- **Coed** 5,919 undergraduate students, 97% full-time, 56% women, 44% men
- **Very difficult** entrance level, 49% of applicants were admitted

UNDERGRAD STUDENTS

5,761 full-time, 158 part-time. Students come from 53 states and territories; 60 other countries; 39% are from out of state; 3% Black or African American, non-Hispanic/Latino; 21% Hispanic/Latino; 7% Asian, non-Hispanic/Latino; 0.3% Native Hawaiian or other Pacific Islander, non-Hispanic/Latino; 0.2% American Indian or Alaska Native, non-Hispanic/Latino; 7% Two or more races, non-Hispanic/Latino; 3% Race/ethnicity unknown; 9% international; 6% transferred in; 44% live on campus.

Freshmen:
Admission: 13,755 applied, 6,697 admitted, 1,142 enrolled. ***Average high school GPA:*** 3.9. ***Test scores:*** SAT evidence-based reading and writing scores over 500: 98%; SAT math scores over 500: 98%; ACT scores over 18: 99%; SAT evidence-based reading and writing scores over 600: 76%; SAT math scores over 600: 72%; ACT scores over 24: 89%; SAT evidence-based reading and writing scores over 700: 16%; SAT math scores over 700: 20%; ACT scores over 30: 39%.

Retention: 92% of full-time freshmen returned.

FACULTY

Total: 967, 50% full-time, 76% with terminal degrees.

Student/faculty ratio: 13:1.

ACADEMICS

Calendar: 4-1-4. *Degrees:* bachelor's, master's, doctoral, and postbachelor's certificates.

Special study options: advanced placement credit, double majors, English as a second language, honors programs, independent study, internships, part-time degree program, services for LD students, study abroad, summer session for credit. ***ROTC:*** Army (c), Navy (b), Air Force (c).

Computers: 1,066 computers/terminals and 4,250 ports are available on campus for general student use. Students can access the following: campus intranet, computer help desk, free student e-mail accounts, online (class) grades, online (class) registration, online (class) schedules. Campuswide network is available. 100% of college-owned or -operated housing units are wired for high-speed Internet access. Wireless service is available via entire campus.

Library: Helen K. and James S. Copley Library plus 1 other. *Books:* 453,355 (physical), 899,809 (digital/electronic); *Serial titles:* 10,956 (physical), 150,056 (digital/electronic); *Databases:* 402. Weekly public service hours: 116; students can reserve study rooms.

STUDENT LIFE

Housing options: on-campus residence required through sophomore year; coed, men-only, women-only, special housing for students with disabilities. Campus housing is university owned. Freshman campus housing is guaranteed.

Activities and organizations: drama/theater group, student-run newspaper, radio and television station, choral group, marching band, American Marketing Association - USD Chapter, Asian Student Association, Black Student Union, Cool Kids Club, Entrepreneurship Club, national fraternities, national sororities.

Athletics Member NCAA. All Division I except football (Division I-AA). ***Intercollegiate sports:*** baseball M(s), basketball M(s)/W(s), crew M/W(s), cross-country running M(s)/W(s), golf M(s), ice hockey M(c), lacrosse M(c)/W(c), rugby M(c), soccer M(s)/W(s), softball W(s), swimming and diving W(s), tennis M(s)/W(s), track and field W(s), ultimate Frisbee M(c)/W(c), volleyball M(c)/W(s), water polo M(c). ***Intramural sports:*** baseball M(c), basketball M/W, cross-country running M(c)/W(c), football M/W, golf M(c)/W(c), rock climbing M(c)/W(c), soccer M(c)/W(c), softball M/W, swimming and diving W(c), tennis M(c)/W(c), ultimate Frisbee M/W, volleyball M/W(c), water polo W(c).

Campus security: 24-hour emergency response devices and patrols, late-night transport/escort service, controlled dormitory access.

Student services: health clinic, personal/psychological counseling, women's center, legal services, veterans affairs office.

COSTS & FINANCIAL AID

Costs (2020–21) ***Comprehensive fee:*** $68,020 includes full-time tuition ($52,120), mandatory fees ($744), and room and board ($15,156). Part-time tuition: $1798 per credit. Part-time tuition and fees vary according to course load. ***Required fees:*** $514 per year part-time. ***Room and board:*** Room and board charges vary according to board plan and housing facility. ***Payment plan:*** installment. ***Waivers:*** employees or children of employees.

Financial Aid Of all full-time matriculated undergraduates who enrolled in 2019, 3,506 applied for aid, 3,059 were judged to have need, 422 had their need fully met. In 2019, 1044 non-need-based awards were made. ***Average percent of need met:*** 75. ***Average financial aid package:*** $40,082. ***Average need-based loan:*** $6630. ***Average need-based gift aid:*** $33,446. ***Average non-need-based aid:*** $18,259. ***Average indebtedness upon graduation:*** $30,497.

APPLYING

Standardized Tests *Required:* SAT or ACT (for admission).

Options: electronic application, deferred entrance.

Application fee: $55.

Required: essay or personal statement, high school transcript, 1 letter of recommendation.

Application deadlines: 12/15 (freshmen), 12/15 (out-of-state freshmen), 3/1 (transfers).

Notification: 2/20 (freshmen), continuous until 2/20 (out-of-state freshmen), continuous until 6/30 (transfers).

CONTACT

Ms. Minh-Ha Hoang, Director of Admissions, University of San Diego, 5998 Alcala Park, San Diego, CA 92110. *Phone:* 619-260-4506. *Toll-free phone:* 800-248-4873. *Fax:* 619-260-6836. *E-mail:* admissions@sandiego.edu.

University of San Francisco

San Francisco, California

http://www.usfca.edu/

- **Independent Roman Catholic (Jesuit)** university, founded 1855
- **Urban** 55-acre campus with easy access to San Francisco Bay Area
- **Endowment** $390.0 million
- **Coed** 6,577 undergraduate students, 96% full-time, 62% women, 38% men
- **Moderately difficult** entrance level, 64% of applicants were admitted

UNDERGRAD STUDENTS

6,345 full-time, 232 part-time. Students come from 54 states and territories; 92 other countries; 33% are from out of state; 5% Black or African American, non-Hispanic/Latino; 22% Hispanic/Latino; 24% Asian, non-Hispanic/Latino; 0.5% Native Hawaiian or other Pacific

Islander, non-Hispanic/Latino; 0.1% American Indian or Alaska Native, non-Hispanic/Latino; 9% Two or more races, non-Hispanic/Latino; 2% Race/ethnicity unknown; 13% international; 6% transferred in; 34% live on campus.

Freshmen:

Admission: 21,867 applied, 14,086 admitted, 1,293 enrolled. ***Average high school GPA:*** 3.5. ***Test scores:*** SAT evidence-based reading and writing scores over 500: 94%; SAT math scores over 500: 97%; ACT scores over 18: 99%; SAT evidence-based reading and writing scores over 600: 61%; SAT math scores over 600: 58%; ACT scores over 24: 67%; SAT evidence-based reading and writing scores over 700: 11%; SAT math scores over 700: 17%; ACT scores over 30: 22%.

Retention: 85% of full-time freshmen returned.

FACULTY

Total: 1,139, 41% full-time, 64% with terminal degrees.

Student/faculty ratio: 13:1.

ACADEMICS

Calendar: 4-1-4. *Degrees:* certificates, bachelor's, master's, doctoral, post master's, and postbachelor's certificates.

Special study options: accelerated degree program, adult/continuing education programs, advanced placement credit, cooperative education, distance learning, double majors, English as a second language, external degree program, freshman honors college, honors programs, independent study, internships, off-campus study, part-time degree program, services for LD students, student-designed majors, study abroad, summer session for credit. ***ROTC:*** Army (b), Air Force (c).

Unusual degree programs: 3-2 engineering with University of Southern California.

Computers: 257 computers/terminals are available on campus for general student use. Students can access the following: campus intranet, computer help desk, free student e-mail accounts, online (class) grades, online (class) registration, online (class) schedules. Campuswide network is available. 100% of college-owned or -operated housing units are wired for high-speed Internet access. Wireless service is available via entire campus.

Library: Gleeson Library|Geschke Center plus 1 other. *Books:* 532,484 (physical), 758,493 (digital/electronic); *Serial titles:* 7,804 (physical), 146,187 (digital/electronic); *Databases:* 344. Weekly public service hours: 136; study areas open 24 hours, 5–7 days a week; students can reserve study rooms.

STUDENT LIFE

Housing options: on-campus residence required for freshman year; coed, women-only. Campus housing is university owned. Freshman campus housing is guaranteed.

Activities and organizations: drama/theater group, student-run newspaper, radio and television station, choral group, marching band, Kasamahan, Nursing Student Association, Black Student Union, Delta Zeta, Kappa Alpha Theta, national fraternities, national sororities.

Athletics Member NCAA. All Division I. ***Intercollegiate sports:*** baseball M(s), basketball M(s)/W(s), cross-country running M(s)/W(s), golf M(s)/W(s), soccer M(s)/W(s), tennis M(s)/W(s), track and field M(s)/W(s), volleyball W(s). ***Intramural sports:*** badminton M(c)/W(c), basketball M/W, equestrian sports M(c)/W(c), fencing M(c)/W(c), football M/W, golf M(c)/W(c), lacrosse M(c), riflery M(c)/W(c), rock climbing M/W, rugby M(c)/W(c), sailing M(c)/W(c), skiing (cross country) M(c)/W(c), skiing (downhill) W(c), soccer M/W, softball M(c)/W(c), swimming and diving M(c)/W(c), table tennis M/W, tennis M(c)/W(c), ultimate Frisbee M(c)/W(c), volleyball M/W, water polo M(c)/W(c).

Campus security: 24-hour emergency response devices and patrols, student patrols, late-night transport/escort service, controlled dormitory access.

Student services: health clinic, personal/psychological counseling, women's center.

COSTS & FINANCIAL AID

Costs (2020–21) ***Comprehensive fee:*** $68,472 includes full-time tuition ($51,930), mandatory fees ($552), and room and board ($15,990). Part-time tuition: $1850 per credit hour. ***Required fees:*** $276 per term part-time. ***College room only:*** $10,930. Room and board charges vary according to board plan and housing facility.

Financial Aid Of all full-time matriculated undergraduates who enrolled in 2019, 4,263 applied for aid, 3,742 were judged to have need, 273 had their need fully met. 1,063 Federal Work-Study jobs (averaging $5025). 605 state and other part-time jobs (averaging $4710). In 2019, 1578 non-need-based awards were made. ***Average percent of need met:*** 67. ***Average financial aid package:*** $35,618. ***Average need-based loan:*** $4122. ***Average need-based gift aid:*** $29,709. ***Average non-need-based aid:*** $18,498. ***Average indebtedness upon graduation:*** $33,752. ***Financial aid deadline:*** 1/15.

APPLYING
Standardized Tests *Required for some:* TOEFL, IELTS or PTE Academic if English is not the student's native language.

Options: electronic application, early admission, early decision, early action, deferred entrance.

Application fee: $70.

Required: essay or personal statement, high school transcript, 1 letter of recommendation. ***Recommended:*** minimum 2.5 GPA, interview.

Application deadlines: 1/15 (freshmen), 1/15 (out-of-state freshmen), rolling (transfers), 11/1 (early action).

Early decision deadline: 11/1.

Notification: continuous until 3/15 (freshmen), 3/15 (out-of-state freshmen), continuous until 4/1 (transfers), 12/1 (early decision), 12/14 (early action).

CONTACT
April Crabtree, Assistant Vice Provost, Undergraduate Admission, University of San Francisco, 2130 Fulton Street, San Francisco, CA 94117-1080. *Phone:* 415-422-5287. *Toll-free phone:* 800-CALL-USF. *E-mail:* admissions@usfca.edu.

See below for display ad and page 1130 for the College Close-Up.

University of Southern California

Los Angeles, California

http://www.usc.edu/

- **Independent** university, founded 1880
- **Urban** 229-acre campus with easy access to Los Angeles
- **Endowment** $4.6 billion
- **Coed**
- **Most difficult** entrance level

FACULTY
Student/faculty ratio: 9:1.

ACADEMICS
Calendar: semesters. *Degrees:* bachelor's, master's, doctoral, post-master's, and postbachelor's certificates.
Library: Doheny Memorial Library plus 23 others.

STUDENT LIFE
Housing options: coed, cooperative, special housing for students with disabilities. Campus housing is university owned and is provided by a third party. Freshman campus housing is guaranteed.

Activities and organizations: drama/theater group, student-run newspaper, radio and television station, choral group, marching band, national fraternities, national sororities.

Athletics Member NCAA. All Division I except football (Division I-A).

Campus security: 24-hour emergency response devices and patrols, student patrols, late-night transport/escort service, controlled dormitory access.

Student services: health clinic, personal/psychological counseling, women's center, legal services.

COSTS & FINANCIAL AID
Costs (2019–20) ***One-time required fee:*** $450. ***Comprehensive fee:*** $74,111 includes full-time tuition ($57,256), mandatory fees ($939), and room and board ($15,916). Full-time tuition and fees vary according to program. Part-time tuition: $1928 per credit hour. Part-time tuition and fees vary according to course load and program. ***College room only:*** $9616. Room and board charges vary according to board plan and housing facility. ***Payment plans:*** tuition prepayment, installment.

Financial Aid Of all full-time matriculated undergraduates who enrolled in 2018, 9,680 applied for aid, 7,356 were judged to have need, 6,615 had their need fully met. In 2018, 4270 non-need-based awards were made. ***Average percent of need met:*** 100. ***Average financial aid package:*** $53,612. ***Average need-based loan:*** $5322. ***Average need-based gift aid:*** $41,082. ***Average non-need-based aid:*** $19,114. ***Average indebtedness upon graduation:*** $28,434.

APPLYING
Standardized Tests *Required:* SAT or ACT (for admission).

Options: electronic application, deferred entrance.

Application fee: $85.

Required: essay or personal statement, high school transcript.

CONTACT
Timothy Brunold, Dean of Admission, University of Southern California, University Park Campus, Los Angeles, CA 90089. *Phone:* 213-740-6753. *Fax:* 213-821-0285. *E-mail:* admdean@usc.edu.

University of the Pacific

Stockton, California

http://www.pacific.edu/

- **Independent** university, founded 1851
- **Suburban** 175-acre campus with easy access to Sacramento
- **Coed** 3,640 undergraduate students, 97% full-time, 52% women, 48% men
- **Moderately difficult** entrance level, 66% of applicants were admitted

UNDERGRAD STUDENTS
3,536 full-time, 104 part-time. 8% are from out of state; 3% Black or African American, non-Hispanic/Latino; 21% Hispanic/Latino; 38% Asian, non-Hispanic/Latino; 0.5% Native Hawaiian or other Pacific Islander, non-Hispanic/Latino; 0.3% American Indian or Alaska Native, non-Hispanic/Latino; 4% Two or more races, non-Hispanic/Latino; 3% Race/ethnicity unknown; 7% international; 6% transferred in; 47% live on campus.

Freshmen:
Admission: 13,096 applied, 8,592 admitted, 808 enrolled. ***Average high school GPA:*** 3.6. ***Test scores:*** SAT evidence-based reading and writing scores over 500: 93%; SAT math scores over 500: 95%; ACT scores over 18: 97%; SAT evidence-based reading and writing scores over 600: 55%; SAT math scores over 600: 62%; ACT scores over 24: 69%; SAT evidence-based reading and writing scores over 700: 14%; SAT math scores over 700: 27%; ACT scores over 30: 34%.

Retention: 83% of full-time freshmen returned.

FACULTY
Total: 894, 48% full-time, 66% with terminal degrees.

Student/faculty ratio: 13:1.

ACADEMICS
Calendar: semesters. *Degrees:* bachelor's, master's, and doctoral.

Special study options: academic remediation for entering students, accelerated degree program, advanced placement credit, cooperative education, double majors, English as a second language, honors programs, independent study, internships, part-time degree program, services for LD students, student-designed majors, summer session for credit. ***ROTC:*** Air Force (c).

Computers: Students can access the following: campus intranet, computer help desk, free student e-mail accounts, online (class) grades, online (class) registration, online (class) schedules. Campuswide network is available. Wireless service is available via entire campus.
Library: University of the Pacific Library plus 1 other.

STUDENT LIFE
Housing options: on-campus residence required through sophomore year; coed, cooperative. Campus housing is university owned. Freshman campus housing is guaranteed.

Activities and organizations: drama/theater group, student-run newspaper, radio station, choral group, national fraternities, national sororities.

Athletics Member NCAA. All Division I. ***Intercollegiate sports:*** baseball M(s), basketball M(s)/W(s), cross-country running W(s), field hockey W(s), golf M(s), soccer W(s), softball W(s), swimming and diving M(s)/W(s), tennis M(s)/W(s), volleyball M(s)/W(s), water polo

M(s)/W(s). ***Intramural sports:*** badminton M(c)/W(c), basketball M/W, bowling M/W, football M/W, golf M, lacrosse M(c)/W(c), rugby M(c), soccer M(c)/W(c), tennis M/W, volleyball W.

Campus security: 24-hour emergency response devices and patrols, late-night transport/escort service, controlled dormitory access.

Student services: health clinic, personal/psychological counseling, legal services.

COSTS & FINANCIAL AID

Costs (2020–21) ***Comprehensive fee:*** $63,328 includes full-time tuition ($48,904), mandatory fees ($684), and room and board ($13,740). Full-time tuition and fees vary according to course load and program. Part-time tuition: $1687 per credit hour. Part-time tuition and fees vary according to course load and program. ***Room and board:*** Room and board charges vary according to board plan, housing facility, and student level. ***Payment plan:*** installment. ***Waivers:*** employees or children of employees.

Financial Aid Of all full-time matriculated undergraduates who enrolled in 2019, 2,744 applied for aid, 2,495 were judged to have need, 207 had their need fully met. In 2019, 608 non-need-based awards were made. ***Average percent of need met:*** 67. ***Average financial aid package:*** $38,616. ***Average need-based loan:*** $8035. ***Average need-based gift aid:*** $32,267. ***Average non-need-based aid:*** $17,087. ***Average indebtedness upon graduation:*** $29,929.

APPLYING

Standardized Tests *Required:* SAT or ACT (for admission).

Options: electronic application, early action, deferred entrance.

Required: essay or personal statement, high school transcript.

Application deadlines: 8/15 (freshmen), 8/15 (transfers), 11/15 (early action).

Notification: continuous (freshmen), continuous (transfers), 1/15 (early action).

CONTACT

Mr. Rich Toledo, Director of Admissions, University of the Pacific, 3601 Pacific Avenue, Stockton, CA 95211-0197. *Phone:* 209-946-2211. *Fax:* 209-946-2413. *E-mail:* admissions@pacific.edu.

University of the People

Pasadena, California

http://www.uopeople.edu/

CONTACT

University of the People, 225 South Lake Avenue, Suite 300, Pasadena, CA 91101.

University of the West

Rosemead, California

http://www.uwest.edu/

CONTACT

University of the West, 1409 Walnut Grove Avenue, Rosemead, CA 91770. *Phone:* 626-571-8811 Ext. 311.

Vanguard University of Southern California

Costa Mesa, California

http://www.vanguard.edu/

- **Independent** comprehensive, founded 1920, affiliated with Assemblies of God
- **Suburban** 38-acre campus with easy access to Los Angeles
- **Coed** 1,869 undergraduate students, 89% full-time, 67% women, 33% men
- **Moderately difficult** entrance level, 49% of applicants were admitted

UNDERGRAD STUDENTS

1,668 full-time, 201 part-time. Students come from 37 states and territories; 24 other countries; 12% are from out of state; 5% Black or African American, non-Hispanic/Latino; 43% Hispanic/Latino; 6% Asian, non-Hispanic/Latino; 0.8% Native Hawaiian or other Pacific Islander, non-Hispanic/Latino; 0.3% American Indian or Alaska Native, non-Hispanic/Latino; 2% Two or more races, non-Hispanic/Latino; 8% Race/ethnicity unknown; 0.9% international; 6% transferred in; 59% live on campus.

Freshmen:

Admission: 3,976 applied, 1,966 admitted, 485 enrolled. ***Average high school GPA:*** 3.4. ***Test scores:*** SAT evidence-based reading and writing scores over 500: 68%; SAT math scores over 500: 62%; ACT scores over 18: 73%; SAT evidence-based reading and writing scores over 600: 16%; SAT math scores over 600: 13%; ACT scores over 24: 23%; SAT evidence-based reading and writing scores over 700: 1%; ACT scores over 30: 3%.

Retention: 76% of full-time freshmen returned.

FACULTY

Total: 260, 27% full-time, 45% with terminal degrees.

Student/faculty ratio: 15:1.

ACADEMICS

Calendar: semesters. *Degrees:* certificates, associate, bachelor's, master's, post-master's, and postbachelor's certificates.

Special study options: accelerated degree program, adult/continuing education programs, advanced placement credit, distance learning, double majors, honors programs, independent study, internships, off-campus study, part-time degree program, services for LD students, study abroad, summer session for credit. ***ROTC:*** Army (c), Air Force (c).

Computers: 100 computers/terminals and 50 ports are available on campus for general student use. Students can access the following: computer help desk, free student e-mail accounts, online (class) grades, online (class) registration, online (class) schedules. Campuswide network is available. 100% of college-owned or -operated housing units are wired for high-speed Internet access. Wireless service is available via entire campus.

Library: O. Cope Budge Library. *Books:* 104,872 (physical), 209,791 (digital/electronic); *Serial titles:* 6,350 (physical), 45,649 (digital/electronic); *Databases:* 93. Weekly public service hours: 82; students can reserve study rooms.

STUDENT LIFE

Housing options: on-campus residence required through sophomore year; coed, men-only, women-only, special housing for students with disabilities. Campus housing is university owned. Freshman campus housing is guaranteed.

Activities and organizations: drama/theater group, student-run newspaper, choral group, Local outreach, Global Missions, Student organizations/clubs, Choral groups, national sororities.

Athletics Member NAIA. ***Intercollegiate sports:*** baseball M(s), basketball M(s)/W(s), cheerleading W(s), cross-country running M(s)/W(s), golf M(s)/W(s), soccer M(s)/W(s), softball W(s), track and field M(s)/W(s), volleyball M(s)/W(s), wrestling M(s). ***Intramural sports:*** basketball M/W, football M/W, soccer M/W, softball M/W, ultimate Frisbee M, volleyball M/W.

Campus security: 24-hour emergency response devices and patrols, student patrols, late-night transport/escort service, controlled dormitory access.

Student services: health clinic, personal/psychological counseling, women's center, veterans affairs office.

COSTS & FINANCIAL AID

Costs (2020–21) ***One-time required fee:*** $170. ***Comprehensive fee:*** $48,772 includes full-time tuition ($35,850), mandatory fees ($700), and room and board ($12,222). Part-time tuition: $1495 per credit hour. ***College room only:*** $6792.

Financial Aid Of all full-time matriculated undergraduates who enrolled in 2019, 1,496 applied for aid, 1,487 were judged to have need, 1,487 had their need fully met. In 2019, 1587 non-need-based awards were made. ***Average financial aid package:*** $15,700. ***Average need-based gift aid:*** $8283. ***Average non-need-based aid:*** $8978. ***Average indebtedness upon graduation:*** $18,769.

APPLYING

Standardized Tests *Required:* SAT or ACT (for admission).

Options: electronic application, early action, deferred entrance.

Application fee: $45.

Required: essay or personal statement, high school transcript, minimum 2.8 GPA, 2 letters of recommendation. ***Required for some:*** interview.

Application deadlines: 8/1 (freshmen), rolling (out-of-state freshmen), 12/1 (early action).

Notification: 5/1 (freshmen), continuous (transfers), 1/15 (early action).

CONTACT

Undergraduate Admissions, Vanguard University of Southern California, 55 Fair Drive, Costa Mesa, CA 92626. *Phone:* 800-722-6279 Ext. 4107. *Toll-free phone:* 800-722-6279. *Fax:* 714-966-5471. *E-mail:* admissions@vanguard.edu.

Westcliff University

Irvine, California

http://www.westcliff.edu/

CONTACT

David McKinney, Westcliff University, 16715 Von Karman Avenue, Irvine, CA 92606. *E-mail:* davidmckinney@westcliff.edu.

West Coast Ultrasound Institute

Beverly Hills, California

http://wcui.edu/

CONTACT

West Coast Ultrasound Institute, 291 S. La Cienega Boulevard, Suite 500, Beverly Hills, CA 90211.

West Coast University

Anaheim, California

http://westcoastuniversity.edu/

CONTACT

West Coast University, 1477 S. Manchester Avenue, Anaheim, CA 92802.

West Coast University

North Hollywood, California

http://www.westcoastuniversity.edu/

CONTACT

Mr. Roger A. Miller, Dean of Admissions and Registrar, West Coast University, 12215 Victory Boulevard, North Hollywood, CA 91606. *Phone:* 213-427-4400. *Toll-free phone:* 866-508-2684. *E-mail:* info@katz.wcula.edu.

West Coast University

Ontario, California

http://westcoastuniversity.edu/

CONTACT

West Coast University, 2855 E. Guasti Road, Ontario, CA 91761.

Westmont College

Santa Barbara, California

http://www.westmont.edu/

- **Independent nondenominational** 4-year, founded 1937
- **Suburban** 111-acre campus with easy access to Los Angeles
- **Endowment** $84.0 million
- **Coed** 1,277 undergraduate students, 99% full-time, 61% women, 39% men
- **Moderately difficult** entrance level, 65% of applicants were admitted

UNDERGRAD STUDENTS

1,266 full-time, 11 part-time. Students come from 41 states and territories; 20 other countries; 27% are from out of state; 2% Black or African American, non-Hispanic/Latino; 18% Hispanic/Latino; 8% Asian, non-Hispanic/Latino; 0.6% Native Hawaiian or other Pacific Islander, non-Hispanic/Latino; 0.2% American Indian or Alaska Native, non-Hispanic/Latino; 6% Two or more races, non-Hispanic/Latino; 6% Race/ethnicity unknown; 2% international; 4% transferred in; 95% live on campus.

Freshmen:
Admission: 3,074 applied, 1,992 admitted, 345 enrolled. ***Average high school GPA:*** 3.5. ***Test scores:*** SAT evidence-based reading and writing scores over 500: 93%; SAT math scores over 500: 91%; ACT scores over 18: 94%; SAT evidence-based reading and writing scores over 600: 59%; SAT math scores over 600: 51%; ACT scores over 24: 63%; SAT evidence-based reading and writing scores over 700: 19%; SAT math scores over 700: 16%; ACT scores over 30: 35%.

Retention: 82% of full-time freshmen returned.

FACULTY
Total: 154, 62% full-time, 69% with terminal degrees.

Student/faculty ratio: 11:1.

ACADEMICS
Calendar: semesters. *Degree:* bachelor's.

Special study options: academic remediation for entering students, accelerated degree program, advanced placement credit, double majors, honors programs, internships, off-campus study, services for LD students, student-designed majors, study abroad, summer session for credit. ***ROTC:*** Army (c), Air Force (c).

Unusual degree programs: 3-2 engineering with Washington University in St. Louis; Boston University; University of Southern California; University of California, Berkeley, Los Angeles, and Santa Barbara; California Polytechnic State University; Stanford University.

Computers: 100 computers/terminals and 100 ports are available on campus for general student use. Students can access the following: campus intranet, computer help desk, free student e-mail accounts, online (class) grades, online (class) registration, online (class) schedules. Campuswide network is available. 100% of college-owned or -operated housing units are wired for high-speed Internet access. Wireless service is available via entire campus.
Library: Roger John Voskuyl Library. *Books:* 129,978 (physical), 186,115 (digital/electronic); *Serial titles:* 418 (physical), 70,790 (digital/electronic); *Databases:* 68. Weekly public service hours: 102; study areas open 24 hours, 5–7 days a week; students can reserve study rooms.

STUDENT LIFE
Housing options: on-campus residence required through senior year; coed, cooperative, special housing for students with disabilities. Campus housing is university owned. Freshman campus housing is guaranteed.

Activities and organizations: drama/theater group, student-run newspaper, choral group, Student Ministries, Student Government, Competitive Athletics, Music, Art and Theater ensembles, Intramural Sports.

Athletics Member NAIA. ***Intercollegiate sports:*** baseball M(s), basketball M(s)/W(s), cross-country running M(s)/W(s), golf M(s)/W(s), rugby M(c), soccer M(s)/W(s), swimming and diving W(s), tennis M(s)/W(s), track and field M(s)/W(s), volleyball M(c)/W(s). ***Intramural sports:*** basketball M/W, cheerleading W(c), football M/W, rugby M(c), sailing M(c)/W(c), soccer M/W, ultimate Frisbee M(c), volleyball M/W, water polo M(c)/W(c).

Campus security: 24-hour emergency response devices and patrols, late-night transport/escort service, controlled dormitory access.

Student services: health clinic, personal/psychological counseling, women's center.

COSTS & FINANCIAL AID
Costs (2019–20) ***Comprehensive fee:*** $61,240 includes full-time tuition ($45,410), mandatory fees ($1184), and room and board ($14,646). Part-time tuition: $2120 per unit. ***College room only:*** $8996.

Financial Aid Of all full-time matriculated undergraduates who enrolled in 2019, 1,039 applied for aid, 893 were judged to have need, 256 had their need fully met. 321 Federal Work-Study jobs (averaging $1859). In 2019, 366 non-need-based awards were made. ***Average percent of need met:*** 84. ***Average financial aid package:*** $37,908. ***Average need-based loan:*** $5352. ***Average need-based gift aid:*** $29,075. ***Average non-need-based aid:*** $22,676. ***Average indebtedness upon graduation:*** $39,145.

APPLYING
Standardized Tests *Required:* SAT or ACT (for admission).

Options: electronic application, early action, deferred entrance.

Required: essay or personal statement, high school transcript, 1 letter of recommendation. ***Required for some:*** interview. ***Recommended:*** interview.

Application deadlines: rolling (freshmen), rolling (transfers), 11/1 (early action).

Notification: continuous (freshmen), continuous (transfers), 12/1 (early action).

CONTACT
Westmont College, 955 La Paz Road, Santa Barbara, CA 93108-1099. *Phone:* 805-565-6016. *Toll-free phone:* 800-777-9011.

See below for display ad and page 1136 for the College Close-Up.

Whittier College
Whittier, California
http://www.whittier.edu/

- **Independent** comprehensive, founded 1887
- **Suburban** 95-acre campus with easy access to Los Angeles
- **Endowment** $117.0 million
- **Coed**
- **Moderately difficult** entrance level

FACULTY
Student/faculty ratio: 12:1.

ACADEMICS
Calendar: 4-1-4. *Degrees:* bachelor's, master's, and doctoral.
Library: Bonnie Bell Wardman Library plus 1 other. *Books:* 180,054 (physical), 178,258 (digital/electronic); *Serial titles:* 2,730 (physical), 222,633 (digital/electronic); *Databases:* 67. Study areas open 24 hours, 5–7 days a week; students can reserve study rooms.

STUDENT LIFE
Housing options: on-campus residence required through junior year; coed, special housing for students with disabilities. Campus housing is university owned. Freshman campus housing is guaranteed.

Activities and organizations: drama/theater group, student-run newspaper, radio and television station, choral group, Hispanic Students Association, Hawaiian Islander Club, Black Student Union, Asian Students Association, Environment & Sustainability - Raising Awareness for the Environment / Urban Agriculture / Food Recovery Network.

Athletics Member NCAA. All Division III.

Campus security: 24-hour emergency response devices and patrols, late-night transport/escort service, controlled dormitory access.

Student services: health clinic, personal/psychological counseling, veterans affairs office.

COSTS & FINANCIAL AID
Costs (2019–20) ***Tuition:*** $48,924 full-time, $2039 per semester hour part-time. Full-time tuition and fees vary according to course load. Part-time tuition and fees vary according to course load. ***Required fees:*** $390 full-time, $2039 per semester hour part-time. ***Room only:*** Room and board charges vary according to board plan.

Financial Aid Of all full-time matriculated undergraduates who enrolled in 2019, 1,452 applied for aid, 1,333 were judged to have need, 201 had their need fully met. 251 Federal Work-Study jobs (averaging $2383). 590 state and other part-time jobs (averaging $1977). In 2019, 374 non-need-based awards were made. ***Average percent of need met:*** 78. ***Average financial aid package:*** $39,393. ***Average need-based loan:*** $5029. ***Average need-based gift aid:*** $37,228. ***Average non-need-based aid:*** $24,987. ***Average indebtedness upon graduation:*** $35,328. ***Financial aid deadline:*** 6/30.

APPLYING
Standardized Tests *Required for some:* SAT or ACT (for admission). *Recommended:* SAT Subject Tests (for admission).

Options: electronic application, early action, deferred entrance.

Application fee: $50.

Required: essay or personal statement, high school transcript, minimum 2.5 GPA, 2 letters of recommendation. ***Required for some:*** minimum 3.0 GPA. ***Recommended:*** minimum 2.5 GPA, interview.

CONTACT
Ms. Janine Bissic, Director of Admission, Whittier College, Office of Admission, 13406 East Philadelphia Street, Whittier, CA 90608-0634. *Phone:* 562-907-4238. *Fax:* 562-907-4870. *E-mail:* admission@whittier.edu.

William Jessup University

Rocklin, California

http://www.jessup.edu/

CONTACT
Traditional Undergraduate Admission, William Jessup University, 2121 University Avenue, Rocklin, CA 95765. *Phone:* 916-577-2222. *Fax:* 916-577-2220. *E-mail:* admissions@jessup.edu.

Woodbury University

Burbank, California

http://www.woodbury.edu/

- **Independent** comprehensive, founded 1884
- **Suburban** 22-acre campus with easy access to Los Angeles
- **Coed** 1,118 undergraduate students, 95% full-time, 52% women, 48% men
- **Moderately difficult** entrance level, 66% of applicants were admitted

UNDERGRAD STUDENTS
1,064 full-time, 54 part-time. 16% are from out of state; 4% Black or African American, non-Hispanic/Latino; 38% Hispanic/Latino; 10% Asian, non-Hispanic/Latino; 0.2% Native Hawaiian or other Pacific Islander, non-Hispanic/Latino; 0.3% American Indian or Alaska Native, non-Hispanic/Latino; 3% Two or more races, non-Hispanic/Latino; 0.2% Race/ethnicity unknown; 11% international; 12% transferred in; 17% live on campus.

Freshmen:
Admission: 1,907 applied, 1,265 admitted, 203 enrolled. ***Average high school GPA:*** 3.3. ***Test scores:*** SAT evidence-based reading and writing scores over 500: 71%; SAT math scores over 500: 70%; ACT scores over 18: 75%; SAT evidence-based reading and writing scores over 600: 34%; SAT math scores over 600: 28%; ACT scores over 24: 46%; SAT math scores over 700: 5%.

Retention: 84% of full-time freshmen returned.

FACULTY
Total: 214, 31% full-time, 65% with terminal degrees.

Student/faculty ratio: 9:1.

ACADEMICS
Calendar: semesters. *Degrees:* bachelor's and master's.

Special study options: academic remediation for entering students, accelerated degree program, advanced placement credit, double majors, independent study, internships, part-time degree program, services for LD students, student-designed majors, study abroad, summer session for credit.

Computers: Students can access the following: campus intranet, computer help desk, free student e-mail accounts, online (class) grades, online (class) registration, online (class) schedules. Campuswide network is available. 100% of college-owned or -operated housing units are wired for high-speed Internet access. Wireless service is available via entire campus.

Library: Los Angeles Times Library. *Books:* 58,266 (physical), 84,399 (digital/electronic); *Serial titles:* 328 (physical), 59,537 (digital/electronic); *Databases:* 53. Weekly public service hours: 74.

STUDENT LIFE
Housing options: coed. Campus housing is university owned. Freshman applicants given priority for college housing.

Activities and organizations: student-run radio station, national fraternities, national sororities.

Campus security: 24-hour patrols, late-night transport/escort service, controlled dormitory access.

Student services: health clinic, personal/psychological counseling.

COSTS & FINANCIAL AID
Costs (2020–21) ***Comprehensive fee:*** $55,927 includes full-time tuition ($41,102), mandatory fees ($1494), and room and board ($13,331). Full-time tuition and fees vary according to course load, degree level, and program. Part-time tuition: $1338 per credit hour. Part-time tuition and fees vary according to course load, degree level, and program. ***Required fees:*** $747 per term part-time. ***College room only:*** $8259. Room and board charges vary according to board plan, housing facility, and location. ***Payment plan:*** deferred payment. ***Waivers:*** employees or children of employees.

Financial Aid Of all full-time matriculated undergraduates who enrolled in 2019, 838 applied for aid, 796 were judged to have need, 35 had their need fully met. In 2019, 162 non-need-based awards were made. ***Average percent of need met:*** 63. ***Average financial aid package:*** $32,723. ***Average need-based loan:*** $9339. ***Average need-based gift aid:*** $24,981. ***Average non-need-based aid:*** $12,506. ***Average indebtedness upon graduation:*** $35,814.

APPLYING
Options: electronic application, deferred entrance.

Application fee: $85.

Required: high school transcript, minimum 2.3 GPA. ***Recommended:*** essay or personal statement, 1 letter of recommendation.

Application deadlines: rolling (freshmen), rolling (transfers).

Notification: continuous (freshmen), continuous (transfers).

CONTACT
Woodbury University, 7500 North Glenoaks Boulevard, Burbank, CA 91504-1052. *Phone:* 818-252-5225. *Toll-free phone:* 800-784-WOOD.

World Mission University

Los Angeles, California

http://www.wmu.edu/

CONTACT
World Mission University, 500 Shatto Place, Suite 600, Los Angeles, CA 90020.

Yeshiva Ohr Elchonon Chabad/West Coast Talmudical Seminary

Los Angeles, California

http://www.yoec.edu/

CONTACT
Rabbi Ezra Binyomin Schochet, Dean, Yeshiva Ohr Elchonon Chabad/West Coast Talmudical Seminary, 7215 Waring Avenue, Los Angeles, CA 90046-7660. *Phone:* 323-937-3763. *E-mail:* roshyeshiva@yoec.edu.

Zaytuna College

Berkeley, California

http://www.zaytuna.edu/

CONTACT
Yusuf Samara, Admissions, Zaytuna College, 2401 Le Conte Avenue, Berkeley, CA 94709. *Phone:* 510-900-3156. *E-mail:* admissions@zaytuna.org.

COLORADO

Adams State University

Alamosa, Colorado

http://www.adams.edu/

- **State-supported** comprehensive, founded 1921
- **Small-town** 90-acre campus with easy access to Pueblo
- **Endowment** $64,882
- **Coed** 1,959 undergraduate students, 70% full-time, 46% women, 54% men
- **Moderately difficult** entrance level, 99% of applicants were admitted

UNDERGRAD STUDENTS
1,363 full-time, 596 part-time. 42% are from out of state; 8% Black or African American, non-Hispanic/Latino; 35% Hispanic/Latino; 0.6% Asian, non-Hispanic/Latino; 0.7% Native Hawaiian or other Pacific Islander, non-Hispanic/Latino; 1% American Indian or Alaska Native, non-Hispanic/Latino; 4% Two or more races, non-Hispanic/Latino; 8% Race/ethnicity unknown; 1% international; 12% transferred in; 46% live on campus.

Freshmen:
Admission: 1,765 applied, 1,749 admitted, 398 enrolled. ***Average high school GPA:*** 3.1. ***Test scores:*** SAT evidence-based reading and writing scores over 500: 55%; SAT math scores over 500: 48%; ACT scores over 18: 68%; SAT evidence-based reading and writing scores over 600: 8%; SAT math scores over 600: 9%; ACT scores over 24: 13%; SAT math scores over 700: 1%; ACT scores over 30: 2%.

Retention: 58% of full-time freshmen returned.

FACULTY
Total: 187, 55% full-time, 35% with terminal degrees.

Student/faculty ratio: 12:1.

ACADEMICS
Calendar: semesters. *Degrees:* associate, bachelor's, master's, and doctoral.

Special study options: academic remediation for entering students, accelerated degree program, adult/continuing education programs, advanced placement credit, distance learning, double majors, external degree program, independent study, internships, off-campus study, part-time degree program, services for LD students, student-designed majors, study abroad, summer session for credit.

Computers: 322 computers/terminals are available on campus for general student use. Students can access the following: campus intranet, computer help desk, free student e-mail accounts, online (class) grades, online (class) registration, online (class) schedules. Campuswide network is available. 100% of college-owned or -operated housing units are wired for high-speed Internet access. Wireless service is available via entire campus.

Library: Nielsen Library. *Books:* 252 (physical), 891 (digital/electronic); *Serial titles:* 102 (physical), 372 (digital/electronic); *Databases:* 60. Weekly public service hours: 84.

STUDENT LIFE
Housing options: on-campus residence required through sophomore year; coed, men-only, women-only. Campus housing is university owned. Freshman campus housing is guaranteed.

Activities and organizations: drama/theater group, student-run newspaper, radio station, choral group, Student Programming Board, Student government, Semillas de la Tierra, Newman Club, Fellowship of Christian Athletes.

Athletics Member NCAA. All Division II except golf (Division I). ***Intercollegiate sports:*** baseball M(s), basketball M(s)/W(s), cross-country running M(s)/W(s), football M(s), golf M(s)/W(s), lacrosse M(s)/W(s), soccer M(s)/W(s), softball W(s), swimming and diving M(s)/W(s), track and field M(s)/W(s), volleyball W(s), wrestling M(s). ***Intramural sports:*** basketball M/W, bowling M/W, cheerleading M(c)/W(c), football M/W, golf M(c)/W(c), racquetball M/W, rock climbing M/W, rugby M(c)/W(c), skiing (cross-country) M/W, skiing (downhill) M/W, soccer M/W, softball M/W, swimming and diving M/W, volleyball M/W, water polo M/W.

Campus security: 24-hour emergency response devices and patrols, student patrols, late-night transport/escort service, controlled dormitory access.

Student services: personal/psychological counseling, veterans affairs office.

COSTS & FINANCIAL AID
Costs (2020–21) ***Tuition:*** area resident $5736 full-time, $333 per credit hour part-time; state resident $5736 full-time, $333 per credit hour part-time; nonresident $17,160 full-time, $715 per credit hour part-time. Full-time tuition and fees vary according to course load, location, program, and reciprocity agreements. Part-time tuition and fees vary according to course load, location, program, and reciprocity agreements. No tuition increase for student's term of enrollment. ***Required fees:*** $3704 full-time. ***Room and board:*** $8760; room only: $4200. Room and board charges vary according to board plan and housing facility. ***Payment plans:*** installment, deferred payment. ***Waivers:*** senior citizens and employees or children of employees.

Financial Aid Of all full-time matriculated undergraduates who enrolled in 2019, 1,353 applied for aid, 1,053 were judged to have need, 58 had their need fully met. ***Average percent of need met:*** 62. ***Average financial aid package:*** $14,004. ***Average need-based loan:*** $4018. ***Average need-based gift aid:*** $10,079. ***Average indebtedness upon graduation:*** $32.9 million.

APPLYING
Standardized Tests *Required:* SAT or ACT (for admission). *Recommended:* SAT (for admission), ACT (for admission).

Options: electronic application.

Application fee: $30.

Required: high school transcript, minimum 2.0 GPA. ***Required for some:*** essay or personal statement, audition for music majors, portfolio for art majors.

Application deadlines: rolling (freshmen), rolling (transfers).

Notification: continuous (freshmen), continuous (transfers).

CONTACT
Adams State University, 208 Edgemont Boulevard, Alamosa, CO 81101. *Phone:* 719-587-8124. *Toll-free phone:* 800-824-6494.

American Sentinel University

Aurora, Colorado

http://www.americansentinel.edu/

CONTACT
Natalie Nixon, Vice President of Admission, American Sentinel University, 2260 South Xanadu Way, Suite 310, Aurora, CO 80014. *Phone:* 800-729-2427. *Toll-free phone:* 800-729-2427. *Fax:* 866-505-2450. *E-mail:* natalie.nixon@americansentinel.edu.

Arapahoe Community College

Littleton, Colorado

http://www.arapahoe.edu/

- **State-supported** primarily 2-year, founded 1965, part of Colorado Community College and Occupational Education System
- **Suburban** 52-acre campus with easy access to Denver
- **Coed** 10,963 undergraduate students, 19% full-time, 56% women, 44% men
- **Noncompetitive** entrance level, 100% of applicants were admitted

UNDERGRAD STUDENTS
2,051 full-time, 8,912 part-time. Students come from 36 states and territories; 6% are from out of state; 3% Black or African American, non-Hispanic/Latino; 16% Hispanic/Latino; 4% Asian, non-Hispanic/Latino; 0.3% Native Hawaiian or other Pacific Islander, non-Hispanic/Latino; 0.6% American Indian or Alaska Native, non-Hispanic/Latino; 4% Two or more races, non-Hispanic/Latino; 5% Race/ethnicity unknown; 2% international; 6% transferred in.

Freshmen:
Admission: 1,956 applied, 1,956 admitted, 1,083 enrolled.

FACULTY
Total: 532, 19% full-time.

Student/faculty ratio: 20:1.

ACADEMICS
Calendar: semesters. *Degrees:* certificates, diplomas, associate, and bachelor's.

Special study options: academic remediation for entering students, accelerated degree program, adult/continuing education programs, advanced placement credit, cooperative education, distance learning, double majors, English as a second language, external degree program, independent study, internships, off-campus study, part-time degree program, services for LD students, study abroad, summer session for credit. ***ROTC:*** Army (c), Air Force (c).

Computers: Students can access the following: campus intranet, computer help desk, free student e-mail accounts, online (class) grades, online (class) registration, online (class) schedules. Campuswide network is available. Wireless service is available via entire campus.

Library: ACC Library & Learning Commons plus 1 other. *Books:* 30,246 (physical), 372,182 (digital/electronic); *Serial titles:* 550 (physical), 191,651 (digital/electronic); *Databases:* 77. Weekly public service hours: 69; students can reserve study rooms.

STUDENT LIFE
Housing options: college housing not available.

Activities and organizations: drama/theater group, student-run newspaper, choral group, National Society of Leadership and Success, Phi Theta Kappa, American Society of Interior Designers, History Club, STEM Club.

Campus security: 24-hour emergency response devices and patrols, late-night transport/escort service.

Student services: personal/psychological counseling, veterans affairs office.

COSTS & FINANCIAL AID
Costs (2019–20) ***Tuition:*** state resident $4467 full-time, $149 per credit hour part-time; nonresident $18,327 full-time, $611 per credit hour part-time. Full-time tuition and fees vary according to degree level, program, and reciprocity agreements. Part-time tuition and fees vary according to degree level, program, and reciprocity agreements. ***Required fees:*** $347 full-time, $12 per credit hour part-time, $24 per term part-time. ***Payment plan:*** installment. ***Waivers:*** employees or children of employees.

Financial Aid Of all full-time matriculated undergraduates who enrolled in 2018, 1,101 applied for aid. 50 Federal Work-Study jobs (averaging $2642). 142 state and other part-time jobs (averaging $3138).

APPLYING
Options: electronic application, early admission, deferred entrance.

Application deadlines: rolling (freshmen), rolling (out-of-state freshmen), rolling (transfers).

Notification: continuous (freshmen), continuous (out-of-state freshmen), continuous (transfers).

CONTACT
Arapahoe Community College, 5900 South Santa Fe Drive, PO Box 9002, Littleton, CO 80160-9002. *Phone:* 303-797-5623.

Aspen University
Denver, Colorado
http://www.aspen.edu/

- **Independent** comprehensive, founded 1987
- **Coed**
- **Moderately difficult** entrance level

FACULTY
Student/faculty ratio: 20:1.

ACADEMICS
Calendar: 5 terms per year. *Degrees:* certificates, bachelor's, master's, and doctoral.

APPLYING
Options: electronic application.

Application fee: $50.

CONTACT
Aspen University, 720 South Colorado Boulevard, Suite 1150N, Denver, CO 80246-1930. *Phone:* 303-333-4224. *Toll-free phone:* 800-441-4746.

CollegeAmerica–Fort Collins
Fort Collins, Colorado
http://www.collegeamerica.edu/

CONTACT
CollegeAmerica–Fort Collins, 4601 South Mason Street, Fort Collins, CO 80525. *Phone:* 970-223-6060 Ext. 8002. *Toll-free phone:* 800-622-2894.

Colorado Christian University
Lakewood, Colorado
http://www.ccu.edu/

CONTACT
Jo Leda Martin, Director of Admissions, Colorado Christian University, 8787 West Alameda Avenue, Lakewood, CO 80226. *Phone:* 303-963-3206. *Toll-free phone:* 800-44-FAITH. *Fax:* 303-963-3201. *E-mail:* jomartin@ccu.edu.

The Colorado College
Colorado Springs, Colorado
http://www.coloradocollege.edu/

- **Independent** comprehensive, founded 1874
- **Urban** 90-acre campus with easy access to Denver
- **Endowment** $807.8 million
- **Coed** 2,099 undergraduate students, 100% full-time, 55% women, 45% men
- **Very difficult** entrance level, 14% of applicants were admitted

UNDERGRAD STUDENTS
2,089 full-time, 10 part-time. Students come from 48 states and territories; 53 other countries; 83% are from out of state; 3% Black or African American, non-Hispanic/Latino; 9% Hispanic/Latino; 5% Asian, non-Hispanic/Latino; 0.1% Native Hawaiian or other Pacific Islander, non-Hispanic/Latino; 0.3% American Indian or Alaska Native, non-Hispanic/Latino; 8% Two or more races, non-Hispanic/Latino; 2% Race/ethnicity unknown; 8% international; 2% transferred in; 83% live on campus.

Freshmen:
Admission: 9,456 applied, 1,277 admitted, 535 enrolled. ***Test scores:*** SAT evidence-based reading and writing scores over 500: 100%; SAT math scores over 500: 100%; ACT scores over 18: 100%; SAT evidence-based reading and writing scores over 600: 94%; SAT math scores over 600: 89%; ACT scores over 24: 97%; SAT evidence-based reading and writing scores over 700: 48%; SAT math scores over 700: 53%; ACT scores over 30: 67%.

Retention: 96% of full-time freshmen returned.

FACULTY
Total: 246, 85% full-time, 94% with terminal degrees.

Student/faculty ratio: 10:1.

ACADEMICS
Calendar: 8 blocks of 3 1/2 week courses. *Degrees:* bachelor's and master's (master's degree in education only).

Special study options: advanced placement credit, double majors, English as a second language, independent study, internships, off-campus study, services for LD students, student-designed majors, study abroad, summer session for credit. ***ROTC:*** Army (c).

Unusual degree programs: 3-2 engineering with Rensselaer Polytechnic Institute, Washington University in St. Louis, University of Southern California, Columbia University.

Computers: 400 computers/terminals are available on campus for general student use. Students can access the following: campus intranet, computer help desk, free student e-mail accounts, online (class) grades, online (class) registration, online (class) schedules. Campuswide network is available. 100% of college-owned or -operated housing units are wired for

high-speed Internet access. Wireless service is available via entire campus.

Library: Tutt Library plus 1 other. *Books:* 390,309 (physical), 504,332 (digital/electronic); *Serial titles:* 4,204 (physical), 82,734 (digital/electronic); *Databases:* 329. Weekly public service hours: 114; students can reserve study rooms.

STUDENT LIFE

Housing options: on-campus residence required through junior year; coed, men-only, women-only. Campus housing is university owned. Freshman campus housing is guaranteed.

Activities and organizations: drama/theater group, student-run newspaper, choral group, national fraternities, national sororities.

Athletics Member NCAA. All Division III except ice hockey (Division I), soccer (Division I). ***Intercollegiate sports:*** baseball M(c), basketball M/W, cross-country running M/W, equestrian sports M(c)/W(c), ice hockey M(s)/W(c), lacrosse M/W, rugby M(c)/W(c), skiing (downhill) W(c), soccer M/W(s), softball W(c), swimming and diving M/W, tennis M/W, track and field M/W, ultimate Frisbee M(c)/W(c), volleyball W, water polo W(c). ***Intramural sports:*** basketball M/W, football M, ice hockey M/W, racquetball M/W, soccer M/W, softball M/W, table tennis M/W, ultimate Frisbee M/W, volleyball M/W.

Campus security: 24-hour emergency response devices and patrols, late-night transport/escort service, controlled dormitory access.

Student services: health clinic, personal/psychological counseling.

COSTS & FINANCIAL AID

Costs (2020–21) ***One-time required fee:*** $250. ***Comprehensive fee:*** $74,256 includes full-time tuition ($60,390), mandatory fees ($474), and room and board ($13,392). Full-time tuition and fees vary according to course load. Part-time tuition: $10,144 per course. Part-time tuition and fees vary according to course load. ***College room only:*** $7992. Room and board charges vary according to board plan and housing facility. ***Payment plan:*** installment. ***Waivers:*** employees or children of employees.

Financial Aid Of all full-time matriculated undergraduates who enrolled in 2019, 897 applied for aid, 831 were judged to have need, 831 had their need fully met. In 2019, 102 non-need-based awards were made. ***Average percent of need met:*** 100. ***Average financial aid package:*** $47,954. ***Average need-based loan:*** $3968. ***Average need-based gift aid:*** $48,600. ***Average non-need-based aid:*** $9763. ***Average indebtedness upon graduation:*** $23,579. ***Financial aid deadline:*** 1/15.

APPLYING

Standardized Tests *Required for some:* SAT or ACT (for admission).

Options: electronic application, early decision, early action, deferred entrance.

Required: essay or personal statement, high school transcript, 2 letters of recommendation. ***Recommended:*** interview.

Application deadlines: 1/15 (freshmen), 3/1 (transfers), 11/1 (early action).

Early decision deadline: 11/1 (for plan 1), 1/15 (for plan 2).

Notification: 3/13 (freshmen), 4/30 (transfers), 12/12 (early decision plan 1), 2/11 (early decision plan 2), 12/17 (early action).

CONTACT

Mr. Matthew Bonser, Director of Admission â?Systems, Operations, and International, The Colorado College, 14 East Cache La Poudre Street, Colorado Springs, CO 80903-3294. *Phone:* 719-389-6344. *Toll-free phone:* 800-542-7214. *Fax:* 719-389-6816. *E-mail:* admission@coloradocollege.edu.

Colorado Mesa University

Grand Junction, Colorado

http://www.coloradomesa.edu/

- **State-supported** comprehensive, founded 1925
- **Suburban** 90-acre campus
- **Endowment** $27.7 million
- **Coed**
- **Minimally difficult** entrance level

FACULTY

Student/faculty ratio: 20:1.

ACADEMICS

Calendar: semesters. *Degrees:* certificates, associate, bachelor's, master's, doctoral, and postbachelor's certificates.

Library: John U. Tomlinson Library. *Books:* 202,919 (physical), 162,000 (digital/electronic); *Databases:* 116. Weekly public service hours: 94; study areas open 24 hours, 5–7 days a week; students can reserve study rooms.

STUDENT LIFE

Housing options: on-campus residence required through junior year; coed, special housing for students with disabilities. Campus housing is university owned. Freshman applicants given priority for college housing.

Activities and organizations: drama/theater group, student-run newspaper, radio and television station, choral group, marching band, Environmental Club, Student Body Association, KMSA radio station, Rodeo Club, Campus Residents Association, national fraternities, national sororities.

Athletics Member NCAA. All Division II.

Campus security: 24-hour emergency response devices and patrols, late-night transport/escort service, controlled dormitory access.

Student services: health clinic, personal/psychological counseling, legal services, veterans affairs office.

COSTS & FINANCIAL AID

Costs (2019–20) ***Tuition:*** area resident $8343 full-time, $278 per credit hour part-time; state resident $8343 full-time, $278 per credit hour part-time; nonresident $22,200 full-time, $740 per credit hour part-time. ***Required fees:*** $963 full-time. ***Room and board:*** $11,168; room only: $6100.

Financial Aid Of all full-time matriculated undergraduates who enrolled in 2018, 5,696 applied for aid, 4,421 were judged to have need, 866 had their need fully met. In 2018, 583 non-need-based awards were made. ***Average percent of need met:*** 64. ***Average financial aid package:*** $10,393. ***Average need-based loan:*** $3705. ***Average need-based gift aid:*** $8047. ***Average non-need-based aid:*** $3639. ***Average indebtedness upon graduation:*** $27,269.

APPLYING

Standardized Tests *Required:* SAT or ACT (for admission).

Options: electronic application, deferred entrance.

Application fee: $30.

Required: high school transcript. ***Recommended:*** 2 letters of recommendation.

CONTACT

Admissions, Colorado Mesa University, 1100 North Avenue, Grand Junction, CO 81501. *Phone:* 970-248-1875. *Toll-free phone:* 800-982-MESA. *Fax:* 970-248-1973. *E-mail:* admissions@coloradomeas.edu.

Colorado Mountain College

Glenwood Springs, Colorado

http://www.coloradomtn.edu/

- **District-supported** 4-year, founded 1965, part of Colorado Mountain College District System
- **Rural** 680-acre campus
- **Coed**
- **Noncompetitive** entrance level

FACULTY

Student/faculty ratio: 11:1.

ACADEMICS

Calendar: semesters. *Degrees:* certificates, associate, and bachelor's.

Library: Quigley Library.

STUDENT LIFE

Housing options: on-campus residence required for freshman year; coed, special housing for students with disabilities. Campus housing is university owned. Freshman applicants given priority for college housing.

Activities and organizations: drama/theater group, student-run newspaper, Student Government, Outdoor activities, World Awareness Society, Peer Mentors, Student Activities Board.

Athletics Member NCAA, NJCAA. All NCAA Division I.

Campus security: 24-hour emergency response devices, student patrols, controlled dormitory access.

Student services: health clinic, personal/psychological counseling.

COSTS & FINANCIAL AID

Costs (2019–20) ***Tuition:*** area resident $2400 full-time, $80 per credit hour part-time; state resident $5400 full-time, $180 per credit hour part-time; nonresident $13,590 full-time, $453 per credit hour part-time. ***Required fees:*** $300 full-time. ***Room and board:*** $10,322; room only: $6000.

Financial Aid In 2016, 306 non-need-based awards were made. ***Average need-based gift aid:*** $1748. ***Average non-need-based aid:*** $1271.

APPLYING

Standardized Tests *Recommended:* SAT or ACT (for admission).

Options: electronic application, early admission, deferred entrance.

Required: high school transcript.

CONTACT

Vicky Butler, Admissions Assistant, Colorado Mountain College, 3000 CR 114, Glenwood Springs, CO 81601. *Phone:* 970-947-8276. *Toll-free phone:* 800-621-8559. *E-mail:* vvalentine@coloradomtn.edu.

Colorado Mountain College

Leadville, Colorado

http://www.coloradomtn.edu/

CONTACT

Ms. Mary Laing, Admissions Assistant, Colorado Mountain College, 901South Highway 24, Leadville, CO 80461. *Phone:* 719-486-4292. *Toll-free phone:* 800-621-8559. *E-mail:* joinus@coloradomtn.edu.

Colorado Mountain College

Steamboat Springs, Colorado

http://www.coloradomtn.edu/

CONTACT

Ms. Jackie Brazill, Admissions Assistant, Colorado Mountain College, 1275 Crawford Avenue, Steamboat Springs, CO 80487. *Phone:* 970-870-4417 Ext. 4417. *Toll-free phone:* 800-621-8559. *E-mail:* jbrazill@coloradomtn.edu.

Colorado School of Mines

Golden, Colorado

http://www.mines.edu/

- **State-supported** university, founded 1874
- **Small-town** 499-acre campus with easy access to Denver
- **Endowment** $289.0 million
- **Coed** 5,154 undergraduate students, 96% full-time, 31% women, 69% men
- **Very difficult** entrance level, 53% of applicants were admitted

UNDERGRAD STUDENTS

4,928 full-time, 226 part-time. 42% are from out of state; 1% Black or African American, non-Hispanic/Latino; 11% Hispanic/Latino; 5% Asian, non-Hispanic/Latino; 0.1% Native Hawaiian or other Pacific Islander, non-Hispanic/Latino; 0.3% American Indian or Alaska Native, non-Hispanic/Latino; 6% Two or more races, non-Hispanic/Latino; 3% Race/ethnicity unknown; 5% international; 4% transferred in; 11% live on campus.

Freshmen:

Admission: 11,756 applied, 6,240 admitted, 1,282 enrolled. ***Average high school GPA:*** 3.8. ***Test scores:*** SAT evidence-based reading and writing scores over 500: 100%; SAT math scores over 500: 100%; ACT scores over 18: 100%; SAT evidence-based reading and writing scores over 600: 88%; SAT math scores over 600: 94%; ACT scores over 24: 96%; SAT evidence-based reading and writing scores over 700: 32%; SAT math scores over 700: 54%; ACT scores over 30: 59%.

Retention: 92% of full-time freshmen returned.

FACULTY

Total: 594, 53% full-time, 60% with terminal degrees.

Student/faculty ratio: 15:1.

ACADEMICS

Calendar: semesters. *Degrees:* bachelor's, master's, doctoral, and post-master's certificates.

Special study options: accelerated degree program, advanced placement credit, cooperative education, double majors, honors programs, independent study, internships, off-campus study, services for LD students, study abroad, summer session for credit. ***ROTC:*** Army (b), Air Force (b).

Computers: 1,000 computers/terminals are available on campus for general student use. Students can access the following: campus intranet, computer help desk, free student e-mail accounts, online (class) grades, online (class) registration, online (class) schedules. Campuswide network is available. 100% of college-owned or -operated housing units are wired for high-speed Internet access. Wireless service is available via entire campus.

Library: Arthur Lakes Library. *Books:* 406,665 (physical), 822,340 (digital/electronic); *Serial titles:* 1,768 (physical), 116,813 (digital/electronic); *Databases:* 168. Weekly public service hours: 107; students can reserve study rooms.

STUDENT LIFE

Housing options: on-campus residence required for freshman year; coed. Campus housing is university owned. Freshman campus housing is guaranteed.

Activities and organizations: drama/theater group, student-run newspaper, radio station, choral group, marching band, Society of Women Engineers, Residence Hall Association, Associated Students of Colorado School of Mines, Student Professional Societies/ and/ Religious Organizations, Multicultural Engineering Program, national fraternities, national sororities.

Athletics Member NCAA. All Division II. ***Intercollegiate sports:*** baseball M(s), basketball M(s)/W(s), bowling M(c)/W(c), cross-country running M(s)/W(s), football M(s), golf M(s), ice hockey M(c), lacrosse M(c)/W(c), rugby M(c)/W(c), skiing (downhill) M(c)/W(c), soccer M(s)/W(s), softball W(s), swimming and diving M(s)/W(s), tennis M(c)/W(c), track and field M(s)/W(s), triathlon M(c)/W(c), ultimate Frisbee M(c)/W(c), volleyball M(c)/W(s), water polo M(c)/W(c), wrestling M(s). ***Intramural sports:*** badminton M/W, basketball M/W, bowling M/W, cross-country running M/W, field hockey M/W, football M/W, golf M/W, lacrosse M/W, racquetball M/W, rugby M, skiing (downhill) M/W, soccer M/W, softball M/W, swimming and diving M/W, table tennis M/W, tennis M/W, track and field M/W, ultimate Frisbee M/W, volleyball M/W, water polo M/W, wrestling M.

Campus security: 24-hour emergency response devices and patrols, late-night transport/escort service, controlled dormitory access, campus policy department.

Student services: health clinic, personal/psychological counseling, women's center, veterans affairs office.

COSTS & FINANCIAL AID

Costs (2019–20) ***Tuition:*** state resident $16,650 full-time, $555 per credit hour part-time; nonresident $37,350 full-time, $1245 per credit hour part-time. ***Required fees:*** $2412 full-time. ***Room and board:*** $14,211. Room and board charges vary according to board plan and housing facility. ***Payment plan:*** installment. ***Waivers:*** employees or children of employees.

Financial Aid Of all full-time matriculated undergraduates who enrolled in 2018, 3,168 applied for aid, 2,141 were judged to have need, 490 had their need fully met. 340 Federal Work-Study jobs (averaging $1666). 430 state and other part-time jobs (averaging $1551). In 2018, 1539 non-need-based awards were made. ***Average percent of need met:*** 58. ***Average financial aid package:*** $15,006. ***Average need-based loan:*** $4363. ***Average need-based gift aid:*** $6653. ***Average non-need-based aid:*** $8904. ***Average indebtedness upon graduation:*** $32,482.

APPLYING

Standardized Tests *Required:* SAT or ACT (for admission).

Options: electronic application, deferred entrance.

Application fee: $45.

Required: high school transcript. ***Required for some:*** essay or personal statement, interview. ***Recommended:*** minimum 3.8 GPA, rank in upper quartile of high school class.

Notification: continuous until 10/1 (freshmen), continuous until 10/1 (transfers).

CONTACT
Lori Kester, Associate Provost, Enrollment Management, Colorado School of Mines, Admissions Office, Starzer Welcome Center, 1812 Illinois Street, Golden, CO 80401. *Phone:* 303-273-3220. *Toll-free phone:* 800-446-9488 Ext. 3220. *E-mail:* admissions@mines.edu.

Colorado State University

Fort Collins, Colorado

http://www.colostate.edu/

- **State-supported** university, founded 1870, part of Colorado State University System
- **Urban** 4773-acre campus with easy access to Denver
- **Endowment** $356.0 million
- **Coed** 26,559 undergraduate students, 84% full-time, 53% women, 47% men
- **Moderately difficult** entrance level, 81% of applicants were admitted

UNDERGRAD STUDENTS
22,388 full-time, 4,171 part-time. 28% are from out of state; 2% Black or African American, non-Hispanic/Latino; 15% Hispanic/Latino; 3% Asian, non-Hispanic/Latino; 0.2% Native Hawaiian or other Pacific Islander, non-Hispanic/Latino; 0.5% American Indian or Alaska Native, non-Hispanic/Latino; 5% Two or more races, non-Hispanic/Latino; 0.8% Race/ethnicity unknown; 4% international; 6% transferred in; 24% live on campus.

Freshmen:
Admission: 28,319 applied, 23,038 admitted, 5,137 enrolled. ***Average high school GPA:*** 3.7. ***Test scores:*** SAT evidence-based reading and writing scores over 500: 92%; SAT math scores over 500: 90%; ACT scores over 18: 98%; SAT evidence-based reading and writing scores over 600: 51%; SAT math scores over 600: 44%; ACT scores over 24: 67%; SAT evidence-based reading and writing scores over 700: 9%; SAT math scores over 700: 10%; ACT scores over 30: 20%.

Retention: 85% of full-time freshmen returned.

FACULTY
Total: 1,870, 74% full-time, 80% with terminal degrees.

Student/faculty ratio: 16:1.

ACADEMICS
Calendar: semesters. *Degrees:* bachelor's, master's, doctoral, and postbachelor's certificates.

Special study options: accelerated degree program, adult/continuing education programs, advanced placement credit, cooperative education, distance learning, double majors, English as a second language, honors programs, independent study, internships, off-campus study, part-time degree program, services for LD students, study abroad, summer session for credit. ***ROTC:*** Army (b), Air Force (b).

Unusual degree programs: 3-2 engineering.

Computers: 1,700 computers/terminals and 3,000 ports are available on campus for general student use. Students can access the following: campus intranet, computer help desk, free student e-mail accounts, online (class) grades, online (class) registration, online (class) schedules, personalized portal services including transcripts and financials (billing, financial aid). Campuswide network is available. 100% of college-owned or -operated housing units are wired for high-speed Internet access. Wireless service is available via classrooms, computer centers, computer labs, dorm rooms, learning centers, libraries, student centers.
Library: William E. Morgan Library plus 1 other. *Books:* 1.2 million (physical), 1.1 million (digital/electronic); *Serial titles:* 45,581 (physical), 104,097 (digital/electronic); *Databases:* 345. Weekly public service hours: 108; study areas open 24 hours, 5–7 days a week; students can reserve study rooms.

STUDENT LIFE
Housing options: on-campus residence required for freshman year; coed, special housing for students with disabilities. Campus housing is university owned. Freshman campus housing is guaranteed.

Activities and organizations: drama/theater group, student-run newspaper, radio and television station, choral group, marching band, Photography at Colorado State University, Outdoor Club at CSU, Biomedical Student Association, Criminal Justice Organization, Colorado State University Zoology Club, national fraternities, national sororities.

Athletics Member NCAA. All Division I except football (Division I-A). ***Intercollegiate sports:*** baseball M(c), basketball M(s)/W(s), crew M(c)/W(c), cross-country running M(s)/W(s), field hockey M(c)/W(c), golf M(s)/W(s)(c), ice hockey M(c)/W(c), lacrosse M(c)/W(c), riflery M(c)/W(c), rock climbing M(c)/W(c), rowing M(c)/W(c), rugby M(c)/W(c), skiing (downhill) W(c), soccer M(c)/W(s), softball W(s), swimming and diving M(c)/W(s), table tennis M(c)/W(c), tennis M(c)/W(s), track and field M(s)/W(s), triathlon M(c)/W(c), ultimate Frisbee M(c)/W(c), volleyball M(c)/W(s), water polo M(c)/W(c), wrestling M(c)/W(c). ***Intramural sports:*** badminton M/W, basketball M/W, bowling M/W, golf M/W, racquetball M/W, sand volleyball M/W, soccer M/W, softball M/W, table tennis M/W, tennis M/W, track and field M/W, ultimate Frisbee M/W, volleyball M/W, water polo M/W.

Campus security: 24-hour emergency response devices and patrols, student patrols, late-night transport/escort service, controlled dormitory access.

Student services: health clinic, personal/psychological counseling, women's center, legal services, veterans affairs office.

COSTS & FINANCIAL AID
Costs (2019–20) ***Tuition:*** state resident $9426 full-time, $428 per credit hour part-time; nonresident $27,327 full-time, $1366 per credit hour part-time. ***Required fees:*** $2405 full-time, $59 per credit hour part-time, $296 per term part-time. ***Room and board:*** $11,964; room only: $5746.

Financial Aid Of all full-time matriculated undergraduates who enrolled in 2018, 16,332 applied for aid, 11,688 were judged to have need, 2,135 had their need fully met. In 2018, 4059 non-need-based awards were made. ***Average percent of need met:*** 65. ***Average financial aid package:*** $11,515. ***Average need-based loan:*** $6250. ***Average need-based gift aid:*** $8892. ***Average non-need-based aid:*** $6127. ***Average indebtedness upon graduation:*** $27,142.

APPLYING
Standardized Tests *Required:* SAT or ACT (for admission).

Options: electronic application, early action, deferred entrance.

Application fee: $50.

Required: essay or personal statement, high school transcript, 1 letter of recommendation.

Application deadlines: 7/1 (freshmen), 6/1 (transfers), 12/1 (early action).

Notification: continuous until 9/15 (freshmen), continuous (transfers), 1/1 (early action).

CONTACT
Kelly Nolin, Associate Director of Admission, Recruitment and Outreach, Colorado State University, Ammons Hall (1062), Fort Collins, CO 80523-1062. *Phone:* 970-491-6909. *Fax:* 970-491-7799. *E-mail:* admissions@colostate.edu.

Colorado State University–Global Campus

Greenwood Village, Colorado

http://csuglobal.edu/

- **State-supported** comprehensive, part of Colorado State University System
- **Suburban** campus with easy access to Denver
- **Coed** 8,114 undergraduate students, 22% full-time, 57% women, 43% men
- **Moderately difficult** entrance level, 93% of applicants were admitted

UNDERGRAD STUDENTS
1,796 full-time, 6,318 part-time. Students come from 7 states and territories; 24 other countries; 54% are from out of state; 7% Black or African American, non-Hispanic/Latino; 14% Hispanic/Latino; 4% Asian, non-Hispanic/Latino; 0.5% Native Hawaiian or other Pacific Islander, non-Hispanic/Latino; 1% American Indian or Alaska Native, non-Hispanic/Latino; 3% Two or more races, non-Hispanic/Latino; 3% Race/ethnicity unknown; 0.3% international; 1% transferred in.

Freshmen:
Admission: 353 applied, 329 admitted.

FACULTY
Total: 572, 5% full-time.

Student/faculty ratio: 24:1.

ACADEMICS
Degrees: certificates, bachelor's, and master's.

Special study options: academic remediation for entering students, cooperative education, external degree program, freshman honors college, honors programs, independent study, internships, off-campus study, part-time degree program, services for LD students, student-designed majors, study abroad.

Computers: Students can access the following: computer help desk, free student e-mail accounts, online (class) grades, online (class) registration, online (class) schedules.
Library: CSU Global Library. *Books:* 77,190 (digital/electronic); *Serial titles:* 6 (digital/electronic); *Databases:* 90.

COSTS
Costs (2020–21) ***Tuition:*** area resident $10,500 full-time, $350 per credit hour part-time; state resident $10,500 full-time, $350 per credit hour part-time; nonresident $10,500 full-time, $350 per credit hour part-time. Full-time tuition and fees vary according to course load. Part-time tuition and fees vary according to course load. No tuition increase for student's term of enrollment. ***Required fees:*** $350 per credit hour part-time. ***Payment plans:*** installment, deferred payment. ***Waivers:*** employees or children of employees.

APPLYING
Standardized Tests *Required for some:* SAT or ACT (for admission).

Options: electronic application.

Application fee: $25.

Required for some: essay or personal statement, high school transcript, minimum 2.8 GPA.

Application deadlines: rolling (freshmen), rolling (out-of-state freshmen), rolling (transfers).

Notification: continuous (freshmen), continuous (out-of-state freshmen), continuous (transfers).

CONTACT
Colorado State University–Global Campus, 8000 E. Maplewood Avenue, Greenwood Village, CO 80111. *Toll-free phone:* 800-920-6723.

Colorado State University-Pueblo

Pueblo, Colorado

http://www.csupueblo.edu/

- **State-supported** comprehensive, founded 1933, part of Colorado State University System
- **Small-town** 279-acre campus with easy access to Colorado Springs
- **Endowment** $18.2 million
- **Coed**
- **Minimally difficult** entrance level

FACULTY
Student/faculty ratio: 14:1.

ACADEMICS
Calendar: semesters. *Degrees:* bachelor's, master's, and doctoral.
Library: CSU-Pueblo University Library. *Books:* 183,220 (physical), 227,551 (digital/electronic); *Serial titles:* 2,882 (physical), 157,848 (digital/electronic); *Databases:* 426. Weekly public service hours: 93; students can reserve study rooms.

STUDENT LIFE
Housing options: on-campus residence required through sophomore year; coed. Campus housing is university owned. Freshman campus housing is guaranteed.

Activities and organizations: student-run newspaper, radio and television station, choral group, marching band, Fellowship of Christian Athletes, Black Student Union, Latinx Student Union, National Society of Leadership and Success, Southern Colorado Assoc. of Nursing Students (SCANS), national fraternities, national sororities.

Athletics Member NCAA. All Division II.

Campus security: 24-hour emergency response devices and patrols, student patrols, late-night transport/escort service, controlled dormitory access.

Student services: health clinic, personal/psychological counseling, veterans affairs office.

COSTS & FINANCIAL AID
Costs (2019–20) ***Tuition:*** area resident $7936 full-time, $265 per credit hour part-time; state resident $7936 full-time, $265 per credit hour part-time; nonresident $24,573 full-time, $819 per credit hour part-time. Full-time tuition and fees vary according to reciprocity agreements. Part-time tuition and fees vary according to reciprocity agreements. ***Required fees:*** $2509 full-time, $84 per credit hour part-time, $1255 per term part-time. ***Room and board:*** $10,740; room only: $6100. Room and board charges vary according to board plan and housing facility.

Financial Aid Of all full-time matriculated undergraduates who enrolled in 2015, 2,933 applied for aid, 2,521 were judged to have need, 168 had their need fully met. 686 Federal Work-Study jobs (averaging $3000). 1,109 state and other part-time jobs (averaging $3000). In 2015, 333 non-need-based awards were made. ***Average percent of need met:*** 51. ***Average financial aid package:*** $9865. ***Average need-based loan:*** $3723. ***Average need-based gift aid:*** $7340. ***Average non-need-based aid:*** $3361. ***Average indebtedness upon graduation:*** $28,914.

APPLYING
Standardized Tests *Required:* SAT or ACT (for admission).

Options: electronic application, deferred entrance.

Application fee: $25.

Required: minimum 2.0 GPA. ***Required for some:*** essay or personal statement, interview.

CONTACT
Tiffany Kingrey, Director of Admissions, Colorado State University-Pueblo, 2200 Bonforte Boulevard, Pueblo, CO 81001-4901. *Phone:* 719-549-2462. *Fax:* 719-549-2419. *E-mail:* info@csupueblo.edu.

Colorado Technical University Aurora

Aurora, Colorado

http://www.coloradotech.edu/

CONTACT
Rosaland Giboney, Associate Director of Admissions, Colorado Technical University Aurora, 3151 South Vaughn Way, Aurora, CO 80014. *Phone:* 888-404-7555. *Toll-free phone:* 888-309-6555. *E-mail:* rgiboney@coloradotech.edu.

Colorado Technical University Colorado Springs

Colorado Springs, Colorado

http://www.coloradotech.edu/

CONTACT
Beth Braaten, Vice President of Admissions, Colorado Technical University Colorado Springs, 4435 North Chestnut Street, Colorado Springs, CO 80907. *Phone:* 888-404-7555. *Toll-free phone:* 866-942-6555. *E-mail:* bbraaten@coloradotech.edu.

Colorado Technical University Online

Colorado Springs, Colorado

http://www.coloradotech.edu/

CONTACT
William Beckley, Chief Admission Officer, Colorado Technical University Online, 4435 North Chestnut Street, Colorado Springs, CO 80907. *Phone:* 888-404-7555. *Toll-free phone:* 866-813-1836.

Denver College of Nursing

Denver, Colorado

http://www.denvercollegeofnursing.edu/

CONTACT

Denver College of Nursing, 1401 19th Street, Denver, CO 80202. *Toll-free phone:* 888-479-5550.

DeVry University–Westminster Campus

Westminster, Colorado

http://www.devry.edu/

- **Proprietary** comprehensive, founded 1945
- **Urban** campus
- **Coed**

FACULTY

Student/faculty ratio: 14:1.

ACADEMICS

Calendar: semesters. *Degrees:* associate, bachelor's, master's, and postbachelor's certificates.

FINANCIAL AID

Financial Aid Of all full-time matriculated undergraduates who enrolled in 2007, 148 applied for aid, 136 were judged to have need, 6 had their need fully met. In 2007, 17 non-need-based awards were made. ***Average percent of need met:*** 37. ***Average financial aid package:*** $11,971. ***Average need-based loan:*** $8024. ***Average need-based gift aid:*** $6094. ***Average non-need-based aid:*** $13,350. ***Average indebtedness upon graduation:*** $11,071.

APPLYING

Options: deferred entrance.

Application fee: $30.

CONTACT

Admissions Office, DeVry University–Westminster Campus, 1870 West 122nd Avenue, Westminster, CO 80234-2010. *Phone:* 303-280-7400. *Toll-free phone:* 866-338-7934.

Fort Lewis College

Durango, Colorado

http://www.fortlewis.edu/

- **State-supported** comprehensive, founded 1911
- **Small-town** 350-acre campus
- **Endowment** $9.6 million
- **Coed** 3,229 undergraduate students, 89% full-time, 54% women, 46% men
- **Moderately difficult** entrance level, 90% of applicants were admitted

UNDERGRAD STUDENTS

2,865 full-time, 364 part-time. Students come from 47 states and territories; 15 other countries; 58% are from out of state; 1% Black or African American, non-Hispanic/Latino; 12% Hispanic/Latino; 0.6% Asian, non-Hispanic/Latino; 0.2% Native Hawaiian or other Pacific Islander, non-Hispanic/Latino; 29% American Indian or Alaska Native, non-Hispanic/Latino; 10% Two or more races, non-Hispanic/Latino; 2% Race/ethnicity unknown; 0.6% international; 9% transferred in; 43% live on campus.

Freshmen:

Admission: 3,757 applied, 3,393 admitted, 761 enrolled. ***Average high school GPA:*** 3.3. ***Test scores:*** SAT evidence-based reading and writing scores over 500: 76%; SAT math scores over 500: 69%; ACT scores over 18: 74%; SAT evidence-based reading and writing scores over 600: 32%; SAT math scores over 600: 21%; ACT scores over 24: 22%; SAT evidence-based reading and writing scores over 700: 4%; SAT math scores over 700: 3%; ACT scores over 30: 4%.

Retention: 62% of full-time freshmen returned.

FACULTY

Total: 253, 72% full-time, 72% with terminal degrees.

Student/faculty ratio: 15:1.

ACADEMICS

Calendar: semesters modified trimesters. *Degrees:* certificates, bachelor's, and master's.

Special study options: academic remediation for entering students, advanced placement credit, distance learning, double majors, honors programs, independent study, internships, services for LD students, student-designed majors, study abroad, summer session for credit.

Unusual degree programs: 3-2 social work with University of Denver.

Computers: 935 computers/terminals are available on campus for general student use. Students can access the following: campus intranet, computer help desk, free student e-mail accounts, online (class) grades, online (class) registration, online (class) schedules. Campuswide network is available. 100% of college-owned or -operated housing units are wired for high-speed Internet access. Wireless service is available via entire campus.

Library: John F. Reed Library plus 1 other. *Books:* 117,854 (physical), 217,517 (digital/electronic); *Serial titles:* 3 (physical), 138,779 (digital/electronic); *Databases:* 72. Weekly public service hours: 80; study areas open 24 hours, 5–7 days a week, students can reserve study rooms.

STUDENT LIFE

Housing options: on-campus residence required for freshman year; coed, special housing for students with disabilities. Campus housing is university owned. Freshman applicants given priority for college housing.

Activities and organizations: drama/theater group, student-run newspaper, radio station, KDUR - Campus/community radio, Environmental Center, Student Union Productions, Dance Co-Motion, Master Plan Ministries.

Athletics Member NCAA. All Division II. ***Intercollegiate sports:*** basketball M(s)/W(s), cross-country running M(s)/W(s), football M(s), golf M(s)/W(s), ice hockey M(c)/W(c), lacrosse M(c)/W(s), skiing (downhill) W(c), soccer M(s)/W(s), softball W(s), tennis M(c)/W(c), track and field M(s)/W(s), volleyball W(s). ***Intramural sports:*** badminton M/W, basketball M/W, cheerleading M/W, football M/W, rock climbing M/W, ultimate Frisbee M/W, volleyball M/W.

Campus security: 24-hour emergency response devices and patrols, late-night transport/escort service, controlled dormitory access.

Student services: health clinic, personal/psychological counseling, legal services.

COSTS & FINANCIAL AID

Costs (2019–20) ***Tuition:*** state resident $7065 full-time, $294 per credit hour part-time; nonresident $17,712 full-time, $738 per contact hour part-time. Full-time tuition and fees vary according to course load and reciprocity agreements. Part-time tuition and fees vary according to course load and reciprocity agreements. ***Required fees:*** $1816 full-time, $61 per credit hour part-time. ***Room and board:*** $9878; room only: $7496. Room and board charges vary according to board plan and housing facility. ***Payment plan:*** installment. ***Waivers:*** minority students, senior citizens, and employees or children of employees.

Financial Aid Of all full-time matriculated undergraduates who enrolled in 2018, 1,999 applied for aid, 1,655 were judged to have need, 334 had their need fully met. In 2018, 413 non-need-based awards were made. ***Average percent of need met:*** 91. ***Average financial aid package:*** $18,607. ***Average need-based loan:*** $3816. ***Average need-based gift aid:*** $5525. ***Average non-need-based aid:*** $5353. ***Average indebtedness upon graduation:*** $19,429.

APPLYING

Standardized Tests *Required:* SAT or ACT (for admission).

Options: electronic application, early action, deferred entrance.

Application fee: $40.

Required: high school transcript. ***Required for some:*** interview. ***Recommended:*** essay or personal statement, 2 letters of recommendation.

Application deadlines: 8/1 (out-of-state freshmen), 8/1 (transfers), 11/15 (early action).

Notification: continuous (out-of-state freshmen), continuous (transfers), 1/1 (early action).

CONTACT

Jess Savage, Director of Admissions, Fort Lewis College, 1000 Rim Drive, Admissions, Durango, CO 81301. *Phone:* 877-352-2656. *Toll-free phone:* 877-FLC-COLO. *Fax:* 970-247-7147. *E-mail:* admission@fortlewis.edu.

Front Range Community College

Westminster, Colorado

http://www.frontrange.edu/

- **State-supported** primarily 2-year, founded 1968, part of Community Colleges of Colorado System
- **Suburban** 90-acre campus with easy access to Denver
- **Endowment** $623,313
- **Coed** 18,880 undergraduate students, 26% full-time, 56% women, 44% men
- **Noncompetitive** entrance level, 100% of applicants were admitted

UNDERGRAD STUDENTS
4,999 full-time, 13,881 part-time. Students come from 43 states and territories; 85 other countries; 2% are from out of state; 2% Black or African American, non-Hispanic/Latino; 19% Hispanic/Latino; 3% Asian, non-Hispanic/Latino; 0.2% Native Hawaiian or other Pacific Islander, non-Hispanic/Latino; 0.7% American Indian or Alaska Native, non-Hispanic/Latino; 4% Two or more races, non-Hispanic/Latino; 4% Race/ethnicity unknown; 3% international; 10% transferred in.

Freshmen:
Admission: 4,793 applied, 4,793 admitted, 2,265 enrolled.
Retention: 59% of full-time freshmen returned.

FACULTY
Total: 1,247, 20% full-time.
Student/faculty ratio: 17:1.

ACADEMICS
Calendar: semesters. *Degrees:* certificates, associate, and bachelor's.
Special study options: academic remediation for entering students, advanced placement credit, cooperative education, distance learning, double majors, English as a second language, freshman honors college, honors programs, independent study, internships, off-campus study, part-time degree program, services for LD students, student-designed majors, study abroad, summer session for credit. ***ROTC:*** Army (c), Air Force (c).
Computers: Students can access the following: campus intranet, computer help desk, free student e-mail accounts, online (class) grades, online (class) registration, online (class) schedules. Campuswide network is available. Wireless service is available via entire campus.
Library: College Hill Library plus 2 others. *Books:* 32,801 (physical), 546 (digital/electronic); *Databases:* 12. Weekly public service hours: 54; students can reserve study rooms.

STUDENT LIFE
Housing options: college housing not available.
Activities and organizations: drama/theater group, student-run newspaper, Student Government Association, Student Colorado Registry of Interpreters for the Deaf, Students in Free Enterprise (SIFE), Gay-Straight Alliance, Recycling Club.
Campus security: 24-hour emergency response devices and patrols, late-night transport/escort service.
Student services: personal/psychological counseling, veterans affairs office.

COSTS
Costs (2019–20) ***Tuition:*** state resident $4372 full-time, $149 per credit hour part-time; nonresident $10,996 full-time, $611 per credit hour part-time. Full-time tuition and fees vary according to program. Part-time tuition and fees vary according to program. ***Required fees:*** $412 full-time, $206 per term part-time. ***Payment plan:*** installment. ***Waivers:*** employees or children of employees.

APPLYING
Options: electronic application, early admission, deferred entrance.

CONTACT
Ms. Miori Gidley, Registrar, Front Range Community College, Westminster, CO 80031. *Phone:* 303-404-5000. *Fax:* 303-439-2614. *E-mail:* miori.gidley@frontrange.edu.

Johnson & Wales University

Denver, Colorado

http://www.jwu.edu/denver/

CONTACT
Kim Medina, Director of Admissions, Johnson & Wales University, 7150 Montview Boulevard, Denver, CO 80220. *Phone:* 303-256-9300. *Toll-free phone:* 877-598-3368. *Fax:* 303-598-3368. *E-mail:* den@admissions.jwu.edu.

Metropolitan State University of Denver

Denver, Colorado

http://www.msudenver.edu/

- **State-supported** comprehensive, founded 1963
- **Urban** 175-acre campus with easy access to Denver
- **Endowment** $7.1 million
- **Coed**
- **Minimally difficult** entrance level

FACULTY
Student/faculty ratio: 17:1.

ACADEMICS
Calendar: semesters. *Degrees:* certificates, bachelor's, master's, and postbachelor's certificates.
Library: Auraria Library.

STUDENT LIFE
Housing options: college housing not available.
Activities and organizations: drama/theater group, student-run newspaper, radio and television station, choral group, national fraternities, national sororities.
Athletics Member NCAA. All Division II.
Campus security: 24-hour emergency response devices and patrols, late-night transport/escort service.
Student services: health clinic, personal/psychological counseling, women's center, legal services, veterans affairs office.

FINANCIAL AID
Financial Aid Of all full-time matriculated undergraduates who enrolled in 2016, 9,539 applied for aid, 8,141 were judged to have need, 459 had their need fully met. 157 Federal Work-Study jobs (averaging $3585). 698 state and other part-time jobs (averaging $3555). In 2016, 626 non-need-based awards were made. ***Average percent of need met:*** 56. ***Average financial aid package:*** $9130. ***Average need-based loan:*** $4089. ***Average need-based gift aid:*** $6697. ***Average non-need-based aid:*** $1779. ***Average indebtedness upon graduation:*** $25,805.

APPLYING
Standardized Tests *Required:* SAT or ACT (for admission). *Required for some:* SAT (for admission), ACT (for admission).
Options: electronic application, deferred entrance.
Application fee: $25.
Required: high school transcript. ***Recommended:*** minimum 2.0 GPA.

CONTACT
Associate Director of Admissions, Metropolitan State University of Denver, 890 Auraria Parkway, Denver, CO 80204. *Phone:* 303-556-2615.

Naropa University

Boulder, Colorado

http://www.naropa.edu/

- **Independent** comprehensive, founded 1974
- **Urban** 12-acre campus with easy access to Denver
- **Endowment** $7.6 million
- **Coed**
- **Moderately difficult** entrance level

FACULTY
Student/faculty ratio: 9:1.

ACADEMICS
Calendar: semesters. *Degrees:* bachelor's and master's.
Library: Allen Ginsberg Library plus 2 others. *Books:* 36,333 (physical), 177,800 (digital/electronic); *Serial titles:* 335 (physical), 33,467 (digital/electronic); *Databases:* 47. Weekly public service hours: 69.

STUDENT LIFE
Housing options: on-campus residence required for freshman year; coed, men-only, women-only. Campus housing is university owned. Freshman campus housing is guaranteed.

Activities and organizations: drama/theater group, choral group, Student Union of Naropa, ROOT: Reconnecting on Outdoor Terrain, Team Tapas (yoga club), Community of Color and Allies, Naropa Zazen.

Campus security: late-night transport/escort service, controlled dormitory access, foot and vehicle patrol 4:30 pm to midnight, 24 hour on-call Safety and Security Manager.

Student services: personal/psychological counseling.

COSTS & FINANCIAL AID
Costs (2019–20) ***Comprehensive fee:*** $43,128 includes full-time tuition ($32,900), mandatory fees ($170), and room and board ($10,058). Part-time tuition: $1090 per credit hour.

Financial Aid Of all full-time matriculated undergraduates who enrolled in 2015, 272 applied for aid, 251 were judged to have need, 1 had their need fully met. 168 Federal Work-Study jobs (averaging $3077). 11 state and other part-time jobs (averaging $2455). In 2015, 15 non-need-based awards were made. ***Average percent of need met:*** 90. ***Average financial aid package:*** $37,077. ***Average need-based loan:*** $11,519. ***Average need-based gift aid:*** $24,862. ***Average non-need-based aid:*** $6858. ***Average indebtedness upon graduation:*** $38,199.

APPLYING
Options: electronic application, deferred entrance.

Application fee: $25.

Required: high school transcript. ***Required for some:*** essay or personal statement, 1 letter of recommendation, interview.

CONTACT
Ms. Karen Wills, Assistant Dean of Undergraduate Admissions, Naropa University, 2130 Arapahoe Avenue, Boulder, CO 80302. *Phone:* 303-245-4693. *Toll-free phone:* 800-772-6951. *Fax:* 303-546-3536. *E-mail:* kwills@naropa.edu.

National American University
Centennial, Colorado
http://www.national.edu/

CONTACT
National American University, 8242 South University Boulevard, Suite 100, Centennial, CO 80122. *Toll-free phone:* 877-628-5211.

National American University
Colorado Springs, Colorado
http://www.national.edu/

CONTACT
National American University, 1079 Space Center Drive, Suite 140, Colorado Springs, CO 80915. *Toll-free phone:* 855-369-9397.

National American University
Colorado Springs, Colorado
http://www.national.edu/

CONTACT
Director of Admissions, National American University, 1915 Jamboree Drive, Suite 185, Colorado Springs, CO 80920. *Phone:* 719-590-8300. *Toll-free phone:* 855-369-9397. *E-mail:* csadmissions@national.edu.

Nazarene Bible College
Colorado Springs, Colorado
http://www.nbc.edu/

- **Independent** 4-year, founded 1967, affiliated with Church of the Nazarene
- **Coed** 698 undergraduate students, 3% full-time, 45% women, 55% men
- **Noncompetitive** entrance level, 11% of applicants were admitted

UNDERGRAD STUDENTS
23 full-time, 675 part-time. Students come from 47 states and territories; 6 other countries; 93% are from out of state; 6% Black or African American, non-Hispanic/Latino; 9% Hispanic/Latino; 1% Asian, non-Hispanic/Latino; 0.9% American Indian or Alaska Native, non-Hispanic/Latino; 3% Two or more races, non-Hispanic/Latino; 8% transferred in.

Freshmen:
Admission: 66 applied, 7 admitted, 14 enrolled. ***Average high school GPA:*** 2.4.

FACULTY
Total. 135, 6% full-time, 54% with terminal degrees.

ACADEMICS
Calendar: trimesters. *Degrees:* certificates, diplomas, associate, and bachelor's.

Special study options: academic remediation for entering students, accelerated degree program, advanced placement credit, distance learning, double majors, independent study, internships, part-time degree program, services for LD students, summer session for credit.

Computers: Students can access the following: free student e-mail accounts, online (class) grades, online (class) schedules. Campuswide network is available.
Library: Mabee Library. *Books:* 54,500 (physical), 1,298 (digital/electronic); *Serial titles:* 410 (physical), 5,034 (digital/electronic); *Databases:* 18. Weekly public service hours: 83.

STUDENT LIFE
Campus security: NBC is fully online without geophysical campus, thus no campus safety measures..

Student services: personal/psychological counseling.

COSTS & FINANCIAL AID
Costs (2020–21) ***Tuition:*** $8880 full-time, $370 per credit hour part-time. Full-time tuition and fees vary according to program and reciprocity agreements. Part-time tuition and fees vary according to program and reciprocity agreements. ***Required fees:*** $1200 full-time, $50 per credit hour part-time. ***Payment plan:*** installment. ***Waivers:*** employees or children of employees.

Financial Aid Of all full-time matriculated undergraduates who enrolled in 2018, 42 applied for aid, 42 were judged to have need. ***Average percent of need met:*** 78. ***Average financial aid package:*** $8268. ***Average need-based loan:*** $4525. ***Average need-based gift aid:*** $3411. ***Average indebtedness upon graduation:*** $36,370.

APPLYING
Options: electronic application, deferred entrance.

Required: official transcripts from all prior colleges. ***Required for some:*** high school transcript.

Application deadlines: rolling (freshmen), rolling (transfers).

Notification: continuous (freshmen), continuous (transfers).

CONTACT
Will Mackey, Director of Enrollment Management, Nazarene Bible College, 17001 Prairie Star Parkway Suite 300, Lenexa, KS 66220. *Phone:* 719-884-5031. *Toll-free phone:* 800-873-3873. *Fax:* 719-884-5039. *E-mail:* WEMackey@nbc.edu.

Pima Medical Institute - Denver

Denver, Colorado

http://www.pmi.edu/

CONTACT
Admissions Office, Pima Medical Institute - Denver, 7475 Dakin Street, Denver, CO 80221. *Phone:* 303-426-1800. *Toll-free phone:* 800-477-PIMA.

Platt College

Aurora, Colorado

http://www.plattcolorado.edu/

CONTACT
Admissions Office, Platt College, 3100 South Parker Road, Suite 200, Aurora, CO 80014-3141. *Phone:* 303-369-5151.

Pueblo Community College

Pueblo, Colorado

http://www.pueblocc.edu/

- **State-supported** primarily 2-year, founded 1933, part of Colorado Community College System
- **Urban** 35-acre campus
- **Endowment** $1.1 million
- **Coed**
- **Noncompetitive** entrance level

FACULTY
Student/faculty ratio: 16:1.

ACADEMICS
Calendar: semesters. *Degrees:* certificates, associate, and bachelor's.
Library: PCC Library. *Books:* 19,162 (physical), 33,004 (digital/electronic); *Serial titles:* 695 (physical), 7,707 (digital/electronic); *Databases:* 12. Weekly public service hours: 60.

STUDENT LIFE
Housing options: college housing not available.

Activities and organizations: drama/theater group, choral group, Phi Theta Kappa, Welding Club, Culinary Arts Club, Performing Arts Club, Art Club.

Campus security: 24-hour emergency response devices and patrols, late-night transport/escort service.

Student services: health clinic, personal/psychological counseling, veterans affairs office.

COSTS
Costs (2019–20) ***Tuition:*** state resident $4300 full-time, $180 per credit hour part-time; nonresident $15,060 full-time, $628 per credit hour part-time. ***Required fees:*** $750 full-time, $21 per credit hour part-time, $58 per term part-time.

APPLYING
Options: electronic application, early admission, deferred entrance.

CONTACT
Mrs. Barbara Benedict, Director of Admissions and Records, Pueblo Community College, 900 West Orman Avenue, Pueblo, CO 81004. *Phone:* 719-549-3039. *Toll-free phone:* 888-642-6017. *Fax:* 719-549-3012. *E-mail:* barbara.benedict@pueblocc.edu.

Regis University

Denver, Colorado

http://www.regis.edu/

- **Independent Roman Catholic (Jesuit)** comprehensive, founded 1877
- **Urban** 90-acre campus with easy access to Denver, Colorado
- **Endowment** $65.1 million
- **Coed**
- **Moderately difficult** entrance level

FACULTY
Student/faculty ratio: 13:1.

ACADEMICS
Calendar: semesters. *Degrees:* certificates, bachelor's, master's, doctoral, post-master's, and postbachelor's certificates.
Library: Dayton Memorial Library. *Books:* 247,545 (physical), 182,210 (digital/electronic); *Serial titles:* 1,558 (physical), 112,666 (digital/electronic); *Databases:* 260. Students can reserve study rooms.

STUDENT LIFE
Housing options: on-campus residence required for freshman year; coed, special housing for students with disabilities. Campus housing is university owned. Freshman applicants given priority for college housing.

Activities and organizations: drama/theater group, student-run newspaper, radio station, choral group.

Athletics Member NCAA. All Division II except golf (Division I).

Campus security: 24-hour emergency response devices and patrols, student patrols, late-night transport/escort service, controlled dormitory access.

Student services: health clinic, personal/psychological counseling.

FINANCIAL AID
Financial Aid Of all full-time matriculated undergraduates who enrolled in 2017, 1,861 applied for aid, 1,636 were judged to have need, 208 had their need fully met. 343 Federal Work-Study jobs (averaging $2222). 522 state and other part-time jobs (averaging $2314). In 2017, 511 non-need-based awards were made. ***Average percent of need met:*** 78. ***Average financial aid package:*** $29,824. ***Average need-based loan:*** $4469. ***Average need-based gift aid:*** $20,657. ***Average non-need-based aid:*** $16,121. ***Average indebtedness upon graduation:*** $24,531. ***Financial aid deadline:*** 8/15.

APPLYING
Standardized Tests *Required:* SAT or ACT (for admission).

Options: electronic application, deferred entrance.

Required: essay or personal statement, high school transcript. ***Required for some:*** 1 letter of recommendation, interview.

CONTACT
Ms. Sarah Engel, Director of Admissions, Regis University, 3333 Regis Boulevard, Mail Code A-12, Denver, CO 80221. *Phone:* 303-458-4938. *Toll-free phone:* 800-388-2366 Ext. 4900. *Fax:* 303-964-5534. *E-mail:* sengel@regis.edu.

Rocky Mountain College of Art + Design

Lakewood, Colorado

http://www.rmcad.edu/

CONTACT
Mr. Marc Abraham, Director of Admissions, Rocky Mountain College of Art + Design, 1600 Pierce Street, Lakewood, CO 80214. *Phone:* 321-256-9223. *Toll-free phone:* 800-888-ARTS. *E-mail:* mabraham@rmcad.edu.

United States Air Force Academy

Colorado Springs, Colorado

http://www.usafa.edu/

- **Federally supported** 4-year, founded 1954
- **Suburban** 18,000-acre campus with easy access to Colorado Springs, Denver
- **Endowment** $106.7 million
- **Coed**
- **Most difficult** entrance level

FACULTY
Student/faculty ratio: 7:1.

ACADEMICS
Calendar: semesters. *Degree:* bachelor's.
Library: McDermott Library plus 1 other. *Books:* 463,745 (physical), 74,225 (digital/electronic); *Serial titles:* 229 (physical), 325 (digital/electronic); *Databases:* 36. Weekly public service hours: 83.

STUDENT LIFE

Housing options: on-campus residence required through senior year; coed. Campus housing is university owned. Freshman campus housing is guaranteed.

Activities and organizations: drama/theater group, student-run radio station, choral group, marching band, Recreational Ski Club, Men's and Women's Rugby Club, Cycling Club, Aviation Club, Drum and Bugle Corps.

Athletics Member NCAA. All Division I.

Campus security: 24-hour emergency response devices and patrols, late-night transport/escort service, controlled dormitory access, self-defense education, well-lit campus, Charge of Quarters.

Student services: health clinic, personal/psychological counseling, women's center, legal services, veterans affairs office.

APPLYING

Standardized Tests *Required:* SAT or ACT (for admission).

Options: electronic application.

Required: essay or personal statement, high school transcript, 1 letter of recommendation, interview, authorized nomination, Candidate Fitness Assessment, medical examination.

CONTACT

Dr. Phillip Prosseda, CHIEF, Selections Division, United States Air Force Academy, HQ USAFA/RRS, 2304 Cadet Drive, Suite 2400, USAF Academy, CO 80840-5025. *Phone:* 800-443-9266. *Toll-free phone:* 800-443-9266. *Fax:* 719-333-3012.

University of Colorado Boulder

Boulder, Colorado

http://www.colorado.edu/

- **State-supported** university, founded 1876, part of University of Colorado System
- **Suburban** 600-acre campus with easy access to Denver
- **Endowment** $596.0 million
- **Coed** 31,101 undergraduate students, 93% full-time, 45% women, 55% men
- **Moderately difficult** entrance level, 78% of applicants were admitted

UNDERGRAD STUDENTS

28,834 full-time, 2,267 part-time. 42% are from out of state; 2% Black or African American, non-Hispanic/Latino; 13% Hispanic/Latino; 6% Asian, non-Hispanic/Latino; 0.1% Native Hawaiian or other Pacific Islander, non-Hispanic/Latino; 0.1% American Indian or Alaska Native, non-Hispanic/Latino; 6% Two or more races, non-Hispanic/Latino; 0.6% Race/ethnicity unknown; 6% international; 5% transferred in; 28% live on campus.

Freshmen:

Admission: 40,740 applied, 31,933 admitted, 7,113 enrolled. ***Average high school GPA:*** 3.7. ***Test scores:*** SAT evidence-based reading and writing scores over 500: 95%; SAT math scores over 500: 95%; ACT scores over 18: 98%; SAT evidence-based reading and writing scores over 600: 67%; SAT math scores over 600: 62%; ACT scores over 24: 82%; SAT evidence-based reading and writing scores over 700: 16%; SAT math scores over 700: 22%; ACT scores over 30: 35%.

Retention: 87% of full-time freshmen returned.

FACULTY

Total: 2,330, 72% full-time, 70% with terminal degrees.

Student/faculty ratio: 18:1.

ACADEMICS

Calendar: semesters. *Degrees:* bachelor's, master's, doctoral, and post-master's certificates.

Special study options: accelerated degree program, adult/continuing education programs, advanced placement credit, cooperative education, distance learning, double majors, English as a second language, freshman honors college, honors programs, independent study, internships, off-campus study, part-time degree program, services for LD students, student-designed majors, study abroad, summer session for credit. ***ROTC:*** Army (b), Navy (b), Air Force (b).

Computers: 1,689 computers/terminals and 60,000 ports are available on campus for general student use. Students can access the following: campus intranet, computer help desk, free student e-mail accounts, online (class) grades, online (class) registration, online (class) schedules, training, tutorials, workshops, seminars, standard and academic software, student government voting. Campuswide network is available. 100% of college-owned or -operated housing units are wired for high-speed Internet access. Wireless service is available via entire campus.
Library: Norlin Library plus 5 others. *Books:* 664,601 (physical), 984,952 (digital/electronic); *Databases:* 594. Students can reserve study rooms.

STUDENT LIFE
Housing options: on-campus residence required for freshman year; coed, special housing for students with disabilities. Campus housing is university owned. Freshman campus housing is guaranteed.

Activities and organizations: drama/theater group, student-run newspaper, radio and television station, choral group, marching band, Student Government, CU Gaming, Boulder Freeride, Neuroscience Club, Association of Holistic Wellness, national fraternities, national sororities.

Athletics Member NCAA. All Division I except football (Division I-A). ***Intercollegiate sports:*** baseball M(c)/W(c), basketball M(s)/W(s), cheerleading M/W, crew M(c)/W(c), cross-country running M(s)/W(s), equestrian sports M(c)/W(c), fencing M(c)/W(c), field hockey M(c)/W(c), golf M(s)/W(s), ice hockey M(c)/W(c), lacrosse M(c)/W(s), racquetball M(c)/W(c), rugby M(c)/W(c), skiing (cross-country) M(s)/W(s), skiing (downhill) M(s)/W(s), soccer M(c)/W(s), softball W(c), swimming and diving M(c)/W(c), tennis M(c)/W(s), track and field M(s)/W(s), triathlon M(c)/W(c), ultimate Frisbee M(c)/W(c), volleyball M(c)/W(s), water polo M(c)/W(c), wrestling M(c)/W(c). ***Intramural sports:*** badminton M/W, basketball M/W, ice hockey M/W, soccer M/W, tennis M/W, ultimate Frisbee M/W, volleyball M/W, water polo M/W.

Campus security: 24-hour patrols, student patrols, late-night transport/escort service, controlled dormitory access, University police department, LifeLine Response app connecting to police dispatch center.

Student services: health clinic, personal/psychological counseling, women's center, legal services, veterans affairs office.

COSTS & FINANCIAL AID
Costs (2019–20) ***One-time required fee:*** $232. ***Tuition:*** state resident $10,728 full-time; nonresident $36,546 full-time. Full-time tuition and fees vary according to program. Part-time tuition and fees vary according to course load and program. No tuition increase for student's term of enrollment. ***Required fees:*** $1772 full-time. ***Room and board:*** $14,778. Room and board charges vary according to board plan, housing facility, and location. ***Payment plan:*** installment. ***Waivers:*** senior citizens and employees or children of employees.

Financial Aid Of all full-time matriculated undergraduates who enrolled in 2019, 15,078 applied for aid, 10,053 were judged to have need, 3,912 had their need fully met. 738 Federal Work-Study jobs (averaging $1920). 879 state and other part-time jobs (averaging $3101). In 2019, 8732 non-need-based awards were made. ***Average percent of need met:*** 80. ***Average financial aid package:*** $17,962. ***Average need-based loan:*** $6206. ***Average need-based gift aid:*** $11,882. ***Average non-need-based aid:*** $9345. ***Average indebtedness upon graduation:*** $27,568.

APPLYING
Standardized Tests *Required:* SAT or ACT (for admission).

Options: electronic application, early action, deferred entrance.

Application fee: $50.

Required: essay or personal statement, high school transcript, 1 letter of recommendation. ***Required for some:*** audition for music program. ***Recommended:*** minimum 3.0 GPA.

Application deadlines: 1/15 (freshmen), 3/1 (transfers), 11/15 (early action).

Notification: 4/1 (freshmen), continuous until 3/1 (transfers), 2/1 (early action).

CONTACT
Admissions Office, University of Colorado Boulder, Regent Administrative Center 125, 552 UCB, Boulder, CO 80309. *Phone:* 303-492-6301. *Fax:* 303-735-2501. *E-mail:* apply@colorado.edu.

See below for display ad and page 1120 for the College Close-Up.

University of Colorado Colorado Springs

Colorado Springs, Colorado

http://www.uccs.edu/

- **State-supported** university, founded 1965, part of University of Colorado System
- **Urban** 532-acre campus with easy access to Colorado Springs
- **Endowment** $60.1 million
- **Coed** 10,196 undergraduate students, 80% full-time, 52% women, 48% men
- **Moderately difficult** entrance level, 87% of applicants were admitted

UNDERGRAD STUDENTS
8,181 full-time, 2,015 part-time. Students come from 49 states and territories; 66 other countries; 13% are from out of state; 4% Black or African American, non-Hispanic/Latino; 19% Hispanic/Latino; 3% Asian, non-Hispanic/Latino; 0.2% Native Hawaiian or other Pacific Islander, non-Hispanic/Latino; 0.3% American Indian or Alaska Native, non-Hispanic/Latino; 8% Two or more races, non-Hispanic/Latino; 1% Race/ethnicity unknown; 0.9% international; 10% transferred in; 16% live on campus.

Freshmen:
Admission: 7,906 applied, 6,897 admitted, 1,788 enrolled. ***Average high school GPA:*** 3.5. ***Test scores:*** SAT evidence-based reading and writing scores over 500: 84%; SAT math scores over 500: 80%; ACT scores over 18: 94%; SAT evidence-based reading and writing scores over 600: 36%; SAT math scores over 600: 29%; ACT scores over 24: 48%; SAT evidence-based reading and writing scores over 700: 4%; SAT math scores over 700: 5%; ACT scores over 30: 7%.

Retention: 70% of full-time freshmen returned.

FACULTY
Total: 792, 58% full-time, 50% with terminal degrees.

Student/faculty ratio: 17:1.

ACADEMICS
Calendar: semesters. *Degrees:* bachelor's, master's, doctoral, post-master's, and postbachelor's certificates.

Special study options: accelerated degree program, advanced placement credit, cooperative education, distance learning, double majors, English as a second language, honors programs, independent study, internships, off-campus study, part-time degree program, services for LD students, student-designed majors, study abroad, summer session for credit. ***ROTC:*** Army (b), Air Force (c).

Unusual degree programs: 3-2 engineering; chemistry, biochemistry, communication, criminal justice, electrical engineering, math, mechanical engineering, sociology.

Computers: Students can access the following: campus intranet, computer help desk, free student e-mail accounts, online (class) grades, online (class) registration, online (class) schedules, student portal, learning management system. Campuswide network is available. 100% of college-owned or -operated housing units are wired for high-speed Internet access. Wireless service is available via entire campus.
Library: Kraemer Family Library. *Books:* 330,823 (physical), 279,953 (digital/electronic); *Serial titles:* 1,326 (physical), 129,566 (digital/electronic); *Databases:* 166. Weekly public service hours: 108; students can reserve study rooms.

STUDENT LIFE
Housing options: on-campus residence required for freshman year; coed, special housing for students with disabilities. Campus housing is university owned.

Activities and organizations: drama/theater group, student-run newspaper, radio and television station, choral group, Global Medical Brigade, National Society for Leadership abd Success, Studnet Veteran Organization, Spectrum, Beth-El Student Nurses Association, national fraternities, national sororities.

Athletics Member NCAA. All Division II. ***Intercollegiate sports:*** baseball M(s), basketball M(s)/W(s), cross-country running M(s)/W(s), golf M(s)/W(s), lacrosse W(s), soccer M(s)/W(s), softball W(s), track and field M(s)/W(s), volleyball W(s).

Campus security: 24-hour emergency response devices and patrols, late-night transport/escort service, controlled dormitory access, emergency text messaging, state-authorized campus police and public safety department.

Student services: health clinic, personal/psychological counseling, veterans affairs office.

COSTS & FINANCIAL AID

Costs (2019–20) ***One-time required fee:*** $140. ***Tuition:*** state resident $8850 full-time, $345 per credit hour part-time; nonresident $23,970 full-time, $721 per credit hour part-time. Full-time tuition and fees vary according to course load, degree level, location, program, reciprocity agreements, and student level. Part-time tuition and fees vary according to course load, degree level, location, program, reciprocity agreements, and student level. ***Required fees:*** $1613 full-time. ***Room and board:*** $10,798. Room and board charges vary according to board plan, housing facility, and student level. ***Payment plan:*** installment. ***Waivers:*** employees or children of employees.

Financial Aid Of all full-time matriculated undergraduates who enrolled in 2018, 6,268 applied for aid, 5,072 were judged to have need, 273 had their need fully met. 153 Federal Work-Study jobs (averaging $2952). 238 state and other part-time jobs (averaging $3171). In 2018, 771 non-need-based awards were made. ***Average percent of need met:*** 45. ***Average financial aid package:*** $9041. ***Average need-based loan:*** $3993. ***Average need-based gift aid:*** $7976. ***Average non-need-based aid:*** $2611. ***Average indebtedness upon graduation:*** $23,805.

APPLYING

Standardized Tests *Required:* SAT or ACT (for admission).

Options: electronic application, deferred entrance.

Application fee: $50.

Required: high school transcript.

Application deadlines: rolling (freshmen), rolling (transfers).

Notification: continuous (freshmen), continuous (transfers).

CONTACT

Mr. Chris Beiswanger, Director of Admissions Services, University of Colorado Colorado Springs, 1420 Austin Bluffs Parkway, Colorado Springs, CO 80918. *Phone:* 719-255-3088. *Toll-free phone:* 800-990-8227 Ext. 3383. *E-mail:* cbeiswan@uccs.edu.

University of Colorado Denver

Denver, Colorado

http://www.ucdenver.edu/

- **State-supported** university, founded 1912, part of University of Colorado System
- **Urban** 171-acre campus with easy access to Denver, CO
- **Endowment** $595.8 million
- **Coed** 16,443 undergraduate students, 55% full-time, 55% women, 45% men
- **Moderately difficult** entrance level, 64% of applicants were admitted

UNDERGRAD STUDENTS

8,980 full-time, 7,463 part-time. 9% are from out of state; 5% Black or African American, non-Hispanic/Latino; 24% Hispanic/Latino; 10% Asian, non-Hispanic/Latino; 0.1% Native Hawaiian or other Pacific Islander, non-Hispanic/Latino; 0.3% American Indian or Alaska Native, non-Hispanic/Latino; 6% Two or more races, non-Hispanic/Latino; 1% Race/ethnicity unknown; 8% international; 9% transferred in.

Freshmen:

Admission: 11,315 applied, 7,200 admitted, 1,743 enrolled. ***Average high school GPA:*** 3.5.

Retention: 72% of full-time freshmen returned.

ACADEMICS

Calendar: semesters. *Degrees:* bachelor's, master's, doctoral, post-master's, and postbachelor's certificates.

Special study options: accelerated degree program, advanced placement credit, cooperative education, distance learning, double majors, English as a second language, honors programs, independent study, internships, off-campus study, part-time degree program, services for LD students, student-designed majors, study abroad, summer session for credit. ***ROTC:*** Army (c), Air Force (c).

Computers: 750 computers/terminals are available on campus for general student use. Students can access the following: campus intranet, computer help desk, free student e-mail accounts, online (class) grades, online (class) registration, online (class) schedules. Campuswide network is available. 100% of college-owned or -operated housing units are wired for high-speed Internet access. Wireless service is available via entire campus.

Library: Auraria Library plus 1 other. Weekly public service hours: 85; students can reserve study rooms.

STUDENT LIFE

Housing options: Campus housing is university owned.

Activities and organizations: drama/theater group, student-run newspaper, choral group, Veterans Student Organization (Service), Golden Key Honor Society (Academic), Minority Association for Pre-Health Students (Health), Future Doctors of Denver, Intercultural Club Beijing (Cultural and Social).

Athletics ***Intramural sports:*** basketball M(c)/W(c), cheerleading M(c)/W(c), cross-country running M(c)/W(c), golf M(c)/W(c), ice hockey M(c), lacrosse M(c)/W(c), soccer M(c)/W(c), tennis M(c)/W(c), ultimate Frisbee M(c)/W(c), volleyball W(c).

Campus security: 24-hour emergency response devices and patrols, student patrols, late-night transport/escort service.

Student services: health clinic, personal/psychological counseling, women's center, veterans affairs office.

COSTS & FINANCIAL AID

Costs (2020–21) ***Tuition:*** $330 per credit hour part-time; state resident $9900 full-time, $330 per credit hour part-time; nonresident $30,510 full-time, $1017 per credit hour part-time. ***Required fees:*** $1547 full-time. ***Room and board:*** $12,620; room only: $8800.

Financial Aid Of all full-time matriculated undergraduates who enrolled in 2018, 6,548 applied for aid, 5,538 were judged to have need, 59 had their need fully met. 370 Federal Work-Study jobs (averaging $5190). 344 state and other part-time jobs (averaging $5158). In 2018, 632 non-need-based awards were made. ***Average percent of need met:*** 49. ***Average financial aid package:*** $10,556. ***Average need-based loan:*** $3709. ***Average need-based gift aid:*** $8404. ***Average non-need-based aid:*** $2241. ***Average indebtedness upon graduation:*** $20,859.

APPLYING

Standardized Tests *Required:* SAT or ACT (for admission).

Options: electronic application, deferred entrance.

Application fee: $50.

Required: minimum 2.5 GPA. ***Required for some:*** minimum 3.0 GPA, audition, portfolio, entrance exam.

Application deadlines: rolling (out-of-state freshmen), 8/1 (transfers).

Notification: continuous (freshmen), continuous (out-of-state freshmen), continuous (transfers).

CONTACT

Catherine Wilson, Director of Undergraduate Admissions, University of Colorado Denver, PO Box 173364, Campus Box 167, Denver, CO 80217. *Phone:* 303-315-2601. *E-mail:* admissions@ucdenver.edu.

University of Denver

Denver, Colorado

http://www.du.edu/

- **Independent** university, founded 1864
- **Urban** 125-acre campus with easy access to Denver
- **Endowment** $786.4 million
- **Coed** 5,774 undergraduate students, 95% full-time, 54% women, 46% men
- **Moderately difficult** entrance level, 59% of applicants were admitted

UNDERGRAD STUDENTS

5,478 full-time, 296 part-time. Students come from 56 states and territories; 52 other countries; 63% are from out of state; 2% Black or African American, non-Hispanic/Latino; 12% Hispanic/Latino; 4% Asian, non-Hispanic/Latino; 0.1% Native Hawaiian or other Pacific Islander, non-Hispanic/Latino; 0.4% American Indian or Alaska Native, non-Hispanic/Latino; 5% Two or more races, non-Hispanic/Latino; 2% Race/ethnicity unknown; 6% international; 4% transferred in; 48% live on campus.

Freshmen:

Admission: 21,028 applied, 12,345 admitted, 1,351 enrolled. ***Average high school GPA:*** 3.7. ***Test scores:*** SAT evidence-based reading and writing scores over 500: 97%; SAT math scores over 500: 96%; ACT scores over 18: 100%; SAT evidence-based reading and writing scores over 600: 71%; SAT math scores over 600: 64%; ACT scores over 24: 90%; SAT evidence-based reading and writing scores over 700: 15%; SAT math scores over 700: 13%; ACT scores over 30: 37%.

Retention: 86% of full-time freshmen returned.

FACULTY

Total: 1,426, 51% full-time, 62% with terminal degrees.

Student/faculty ratio: 12:1.

ACADEMICS

Calendar: quarters semesters for law school. *Degrees:* certificates, bachelor's, master's, doctoral, post-master's, and postbachelor's certificates.

Special study options: accelerated degree program, adult/continuing education programs, advanced placement credit, cooperative education, distance learning, double majors, English as a second language, freshman honors college, honors programs, independent study, internships, off-campus study, part-time degree program, services for LD students, student-designed majors, study abroad, summer session for credit. ***ROTC:*** Army (c), Air Force (c).

Unusual degree programs: 3-2 business administration; engineering; social work; art history, public policy, accounting, international studies, education, environmental science, geography.

Computers: 150 computers/terminals and 36,000 ports are available on campus for general student use. Students can access the following: campus intranet, computer help desk, free student e-mail accounts, online (class) grades, online (class) schedules, Online (class) learning management system. Campuswide network is available. 100% of college-owned or -operated housing units are wired for high-speed Internet access. Wireless service is available via entire campus.

Library: Anderson Academic Commons plus 1 other. *Books:* 1.7 million (physical), 2.3 million (digital/electronic); *Serial titles:* 594,063 (physical), 218,954 (digital/electronic); *Databases:* 1,306. Weekly public service hours: 145; study areas open 24 hours, 5–7 days a week; students can reserve study rooms.

STUDENT LIFE

Housing options: on-campus residence required through sophomore year; coed, cooperative. Campus housing is university owned. Freshman campus housing is guaranteed.

Activities and organizations: drama/theater group, student-run newspaper, radio station, Club Sports Council, Alpine Club, DU Programs Board, Greek Life Council, Residence Hall Association, national fraternities, national sororities.

Athletics Member NCAA. All Division I. ***Intercollegiate sports:*** baseball M(c), basketball M(s)/W(s), cross-country running M(c)/W(c), equestrian sports M(c)/W(c), golf M(s)/W(s), gymnastics W(s), ice hockey M(s)/W(c), lacrosse M(s)/W(s), racquetball M(c)/W(c), skiing (cross-country) M(s)/W(s), skiing (downhill) M(s)/W(s), soccer M(s)/W(s), softball W(c), swimming and diving M(s)/W(s), tennis M(s)/W(s), volleyball W(s), water polo M(c)/W(c). ***Intramural sports:*** basketball

M/W, field hockey M(c)/W(c), football M/W, golf M(c)/W(c), gymnastics W(c), ice hockey M(c)/W(c), lacrosse M(c)/W(c), racquetball M(c)/W(c), rock climbing M(c)/W(c), rowing M(c), rugby M(c)/W(c), skiing (downhill) M(c)/W(c), soccer M(c)/W(c), softball M/W, swimming and diving M(c)/W(c), table tennis M/W, tennis M(c)/W(c), ultimate Frisbee M(c)/W(c), volleyball M(c)/W(c).

Campus security: 24-hour emergency response devices and patrols, late-night transport/escort service, controlled dormitory access, Emergency blue-light stations on campus.

Student services: health clinic, personal/psychological counseling, women's center, veterans affairs office.

COSTS & FINANCIAL AID

Costs (2020–21) ***Comprehensive fee:*** $67,953 includes full-time tuition ($52,596), mandatory fees ($1179), and room and board ($14,178). Full-time tuition and fees vary according to course load and program. Part-time tuition: $1461 per credit hour. Part-time tuition and fees vary according to course load and program. ***College room only:*** $8949. Room and board charges vary according to board plan and housing facility. ***Payment plans:*** installment, deferred payment. ***Waivers:*** senior citizens and employees or children of employees.

Financial Aid Of all full-time matriculated undergraduates who enrolled in 2017, 3,010 applied for aid, 2,333 were judged to have need, 782 had their need fully met. 471 Federal Work-Study jobs (averaging $2825). 195 state and other part-time jobs (averaging $3128). In 2017, 2197 non-need-based awards were made. ***Average percent of need met:*** 86. ***Average financial aid package:*** $40,587. ***Average need-based loan:*** $4291. ***Average need-based gift aid:*** $34,077. ***Average non-need-based aid:*** $18,280. ***Average indebtedness upon graduation:*** $31,526.

APPLYING

Options: electronic application, early admission, early decision, early action, deferred entrance.

Application fee: $65.

Required: essay or personal statement, high school transcript, 1 letter of recommendation. ***Recommended:*** 2 letters of recommendation.

Application deadlines: 1/15 (freshmen), rolling (transfers), 11/1 (early action).

Early decision deadline: 11/1 (for plan 1), 1/15 (for plan 2).

Notification: 3/15 (freshmen), continuous (transfers), 12/15 (early decision plan 1), 2/20 (early decision plan 2), 1/15 (early action).

CONTACT

Mr. Todd Rinehart, Vice Chancellor for Enrollment, University of Denver, 2197 South University Boulevard, Denver, CO 80208. *Phone:* 303-871-3125. *Toll-free phone:* 800-525-9495. *Fax:* 303-871-3301. *E-mail:* admission@du.edu.

See below for display ad and page 1122 for the College Close-Up.

University of Northern Colorado

Greeley, Colorado

http://www.unco.edu/

- **State-supported** university, founded 1890
- **Suburban** 237-acre campus with easy access to Denver
- **Endowment** $90.3 million
- **Coed** 9,876 undergraduate students, 81% full-time, 65% women, 35% men
- **Moderately difficult** entrance level, 91% of applicants were admitted

UNDERGRAD STUDENTS

8,047 full-time, 1,829 part-time. Students come from 49 states and territories; 39 other countries; 14% are from out of state; 4% Black or African American, non-Hispanic/Latino; 22% Hispanic/Latino; 2% Asian, non-Hispanic/Latino; 0.2% Native Hawaiian or other Pacific Islander, non-Hispanic/Latino; 0.4% American Indian or Alaska Native, non-Hispanic/Latino; 4% Two or more races, non-Hispanic/Latino; 2% Race/ethnicity unknown; 1% international; 7% transferred in; 34% live on campus.

Freshmen:

Admission: 8,294 applied, 7,527 admitted, 1,858 enrolled. ***Average high school GPA:*** 3.4. ***Test scores:*** SAT evidence-based reading and writing scores over 500: 76%; SAT math scores over 500: 73%; ACT scores over 18: 88%; SAT evidence-based reading and writing scores over 600: 29%; SAT math scores over 600: 19%; ACT scores over 24: 36%; SAT evidence-based reading and writing scores over 700: 3%; SAT math scores over 700: 2%; ACT scores over 30: 6%.

Retention: 72% of full-time freshmen returned.

ACADEMICS

Calendar: semesters. *Degrees:* bachelor's, master's, and doctoral.

Special study options: accelerated degree program, adult/continuing education programs, advanced placement credit, cooperative education, distance learning, double majors, English as a second language, external degree program, honors programs, independent study, internships, off-campus study, part-time degree program, services for LD students, student-designed majors, study abroad, summer session for credit. ***ROTC:*** Army (b), Air Force (b).

Computers: 1,723 computers/terminals and 825 ports are available on campus for general student use. Students can access the following: computer help desk, free student e-mail accounts, online (class) grades, online (class) registration, online (class) schedules. Campuswide network is available. 100% of college-owned or -operated housing units are wired for high-speed Internet access. Wireless service is available via entire campus.

Library: James A. Michener Library plus 2 others. Weekly public service hours: 97; students can reserve study rooms.

STUDENT LIFE

Housing options: on-campus residence required for freshman year; coed, women-only, special housing for students with disabilities. Campus housing is university owned. Freshman campus housing is guaranteed.

Activities and organizations: drama/theater group, student-run newspaper, choral group, marching band, Fraternities and Sororities, Club Sports, Campus Religious/Spiritual Organizations, Academic Clubs, Services Clubs, national fraternities, national sororities.

Athletics ***Intercollegiate sports:*** baseball M(s), basketball M(s)/W(s), cross-country running M(s)/W(s), football M(s), golf M(s)/W(s), soccer W(s), softball W(s), swimming and diving W(s), tennis M(s)/W(s), track and field M(s)/W(s), volleyball W(s), wrestling M(s). ***Intramural sports:*** basketball M/W, cross-country running M(c)/W(c), fencing M(c)/W(c), football M/W, golf M/W, ice hockey M(c), lacrosse M(c)/W(c), rugby M(c)/W(c), soccer M/W, softball M/W, swimming and diving M(c)/W(c), tennis M/W, ultimate Frisbee M(c)/W(c), volleyball M/W, water polo M/W, weight lifting M(c)/W(c).

Campus security: 24-hour emergency response devices and patrols, student patrols, late-night transport/escort service, controlled dormitory access.

Student services: health clinic, personal/psychological counseling, women's center, legal services, veterans affairs office.

COSTS & FINANCIAL AID

Costs (2020–21) ***One-time required fee:*** $250. ***Tuition:*** area resident $7830 full-time, $304 per credit hour part-time; state resident $7830 full-time, $304 per credit hour part-time; nonresident $19,902 full-time, $792 per credit hour part-time. ***Required fees:*** $2358 full-time, $111 per credit hour part-time. ***Room and board:*** $11,204; room only: $5304.

Financial Aid Of all full-time matriculated undergraduates who enrolled in 2019, 6,496 applied for aid, 4,842 were judged to have need, 1,476 had their need fully met. 218 Federal Work-Study jobs (averaging $1762). 551 state and other part-time jobs (averaging $2318). In 2019, 2001 non-need-based awards were made. ***Average percent of need met:*** 78. ***Average financial aid package:*** $15,328. ***Average need-based loan:*** $4218. ***Average need-based gift aid:*** $7553. ***Average non-need-based aid:*** $3354. ***Average indebtedness upon graduation:*** $23,967.

APPLYING

Standardized Tests *Required:* SAT or ACT (for admission).

Options: electronic application, deferred entrance.

Application fee: $50.

Required: high school transcript. ***Required for some:*** essay or personal statement.

Application deadlines: 8/1 (freshmen), 8/1 (out-of-state freshmen), 8/1 (transfers).

Notification: continuous (freshmen), 9/1 (out-of-state freshmen), continuous (transfers).

CONTACT
Sean Broghammer, Director of Admissions, University of Northern Colorado, Campus Box 10, Carter Hall 3006, Greeley, CO 80639. *Phone:* 970-351-2881. *Toll-free phone:* 888-700-4UNC. *Fax:* 970-351-2984. *E-mail:* admissions@unco.edu.

Western Colorado University

Gunnison, Colorado

http://www.western.edu/

- **State-supported** comprehensive, founded 1901
- **Rural** 381-acre campus
- **Coed** 3,040 undergraduate students, 58% full-time, 49% women, 51% men
- **Moderately difficult** entrance level, 84% of applicants were admitted

UNDERGRAD STUDENTS
1,762 full-time, 1,278 part-time. 29% are from out of state; 3% Black or African American, non-Hispanic/Latino; 11% Hispanic/Latino; 0.8% Asian, non-Hispanic/Latino; 0.2% Native Hawaiian or other Pacific Islander, non-Hispanic/Latino; 0.2% American Indian or Alaska Native, non-Hispanic/Latino; 4% Two or more races, non-Hispanic/Latino; 10% Race/ethnicity unknown; 0.5% international; 4% transferred in; 47% live on campus.

Freshmen:
Admission: 2,504 applied, 2,107 admitted, 454 enrolled. ***Average high school GPA:*** 3.4. ***Test scores:*** SAT evidence-based reading and writing scores over 500: 79%; SAT math scores over 500: 77%; ACT scores over 18: 89%; SAT evidence-based reading and writing scores over 600: 33%; SAT math scores over 600: 24%; ACT scores over 24: 45%; SAT evidence-based reading and writing scores over 700: 2%; SAT math scores over 700: 3%; ACT scores over 30: 6%.

Retention: 65% of full-time freshmen returned.

FACULTY
Total: 187, 69% full-time, 71% with terminal degrees.

Student/faculty ratio: 18:1.

ACADEMICS
Calendar: semesters. *Degrees:* certificates, bachelor's, master's, and postbachelor's certificates.

Special study options: academic remediation for entering students, adult/continuing education programs, advanced placement credit, double majors, honors programs, independent study, internships, off-campus study, part-time degree program, services for LD students, study abroad, summer session for credit.

Computers: 215 computers/terminals are available on campus for general student use. Students can access the following: computer help desk, free student e-mail accounts, online (class) grades, online (class) registration, online (class) schedules. Campuswide network is available. 100% of college-owned or -operated housing units are wired for high-speed Internet access. Wireless service is available via entire campus.
Library: Leslie J. Savage Library plus 1 other. *Books:* 200,544 (physical), 1,000 (digital/electronic); *Serial titles:* 4,031 (physical). Weekly public service hours: 101; students can reserve study rooms.

STUDENT LIFE
Housing options: on-campus residence required through sophomore year; coed, special housing for students with disabilities. Campus housing is university owned. Freshman campus housing is guaranteed.

Activities and organizations: drama/theater group, student-run newspaper, radio and television station, choral group, Mountain Search and Rescue Team, Student Government Association, Rodeo Club, wilderness pursuits, Peak Productions.

Athletics Member NCAA. All Division II. ***Intercollegiate sports:*** baseball M(c), basketball M(s)/W(s), cheerleading M(c)/W(c), cross-country running M(s)/W(s), football M(s), ice hockey M(c), lacrosse M(c)/W(c), rock climbing M(c)/W(c), rugby M(c)/W(c), skiing (cross-country) M(c)/W(c), skiing (downhill) W(c), soccer M(c)/W(s), swimming and diving W(s), track and field M(s)/W(s), volleyball M(c)/W(s), wrestling M(s)/W(c). ***Intramural sports:*** badminton M/W, basketball M/W, field hockey M/W, football M/W, golf M/W, soccer M/W, softball M/W, table tennis M/W, tennis M/W, ultimate Frisbee M/W, volleyball M/W.

Campus security: 24-hour emergency response devices and patrols, student patrols, late-night transport/escort service, controlled dormitory access.

Student services: health clinic, personal/psychological counseling.

COSTS & FINANCIAL AID
Costs (2020–21) ***Tuition:*** state resident $6624 full-time, $276 per credit hour part-time; nonresident $18,096 full-time, $754 per credit hour part-time. ***Required fees:*** $3813 full-time. ***Room and board:*** $9704; room only: $5030. Room and board charges vary according to board plan and housing facility. ***Waivers:*** senior citizens and employees or children of employees.

Financial Aid Of all full-time matriculated undergraduates who enrolled in 2019, 1,571 applied for aid, 983 were judged to have need, 28 had their need fully met. In 2019, 454 non-need-based awards were made. ***Average percent of need met:*** 69. ***Average financial aid package:*** $12,280. ***Average need-based loan:*** $4224. ***Average need-based gift aid:*** $9523. ***Average non-need-based aid:*** $5399. ***Average indebtedness upon graduation:*** $26,060.

APPLYING
Standardized Tests *Required:* SAT or ACT (for admission).

Options: electronic application, early action, deferred entrance.

Application fee: $30.

Required: essay or personal statement, high school transcript. ***Recommended:*** minimum 2.5 GPA.

Application deadlines: rolling (freshmen), rolling (transfers).

Notification: continuous until 10/1 (freshmen), continuous (transfers).

CONTACT
Western Colorado University, 600 North Adams Street, Gunnison, CO 81231. *Phone:* 970-943-2243. *Toll-free phone:* 800-876-5309.

CONNECTICUT

Albertus Magnus College

New Haven, Connecticut

http://www.albertus.edu/

- **Independent Roman Catholic** comprehensive, founded 1925
- **Suburban** 50-acre campus
- **Coed**
- **Moderately difficult** entrance level

FACULTY
Student/faculty ratio: 13:1.

ACADEMICS
Calendar: semesters. *Degrees:* certificates, diplomas, associate, bachelor's, master's, post-master's, and postbachelor's certificates.
Library: Rosary Hall. *Books:* 38,339 (physical), 148,500 (digital/electronic); *Databases:* 88.

STUDENT LIFE
Housing options: coed, men-only, women-only. Campus housing is university owned. Freshman applicants given priority for college housing.

Activities and organizations: drama/theater group, choral group, Student Alumni Association, Student Government Association, M.A.L.E.S Club, Service Club, Honors Club.

Athletics Member NCAA. All Division III.

Campus security: 24-hour emergency response devices and patrols, late-night transport/escort service, controlled dormitory access.

Student services: health clinic, personal/psychological counseling, veterans affairs office.

FINANCIAL AID
Financial Aid Of all full-time matriculated undergraduates who enrolled in 2019, 890 applied for aid, 863 were judged to have need, 49 had their need fully met. 64 Federal Work-Study jobs (averaging $2508). In 2019, 57 non-need-based awards were made. ***Average percent of need met:*** 50. ***Average financial aid package:*** $19,337. ***Average need-based loan:***

$3685. ***Average need-based gift aid:*** $9059. ***Average non-need-based aid:*** $19,435. ***Average indebtedness upon graduation:*** $34,935.

APPLYING
Standardized Tests *Required:* SAT or ACT (for admission). *Recommended:* SAT Subject Tests (for admission).

Options: electronic application, deferred entrance.

Application fee: $35.

Required: high school transcript, minimum 2.0 GPA, 1 letter of recommendation. ***Required for some:*** essay or personal statement, interview.

CONTACT
Anthony Reich, Director of Admission, Albertus Magnus College, 700 Prospect Street, New Haven, CT 06511-1189. *Phone:* 203-773-5032 Ext. 5032. *Toll-free phone:* 800-578-9160. *E-mail:* admissions@albertus.edu.

Bais Binyomin Academy

Stamford, Connecticut

CONTACT
Director of Admissions, Bais Binyomin Academy, 132 Prospect Street, Stamford, CT 06901-1202. *Phone:* 203-325-4351.

Central Connecticut State University

New Britain, Connecticut

http://www.ccsu.edu/

- **State-supported** comprehensive, founded 1849, part of Connecticut State Colleges & Universities (CSCU)
- **Suburban** 314-acre campus
- **Endowment** $72.7 million
- **Coed** 17,634 undergraduate students, 82% full-time, 47% women, 53% men
- **Moderately difficult** entrance level, 66% of applicants were admitted

UNDERGRAD STUDENTS
14,486 full-time, 3,148 part-time. Students come from 29 other countries; 4% are from out of state; 13% Black or African American, non-Hispanic/Latino; 16% Hispanic/Latino; 4% Asian, non-Hispanic/Latino; 0.1% Native Hawaiian or other Pacific Islander, non-Hispanic/Latino; 0.1% American Indian or Alaska Native, non-Hispanic/Latino; 3% Two or more races, non-Hispanic/Latino; 3% Race/ethnicity unknown; 2% international; 5% transferred in; 25% live on campus.

Freshmen:
Admission: 7,807 applied, 5,124 admitted, 1,377 enrolled. ***Average high school GPA:*** 3.2. ***Test scores:*** SAT evidence-based reading and writing scores over 500: 73%; SAT math scores over 500: 67%; ACT scores over 18: 64%; SAT evidence-based reading and writing scores over 600: 22%; SAT math scores over 600: 14%; ACT scores over 24: 24%; SAT evidence-based reading and writing scores over 700: 2%; SAT math scores over 700: 1%; ACT scores over 30: 6%.

Retention: 72% of full-time freshmen returned.

FACULTY
Total: 981, 45% full-time, 53% with terminal degrees.

Student/faculty ratio: 14:1.

ACADEMICS
Calendar: semesters. *Degrees:* bachelor's, master's, doctoral, post-master's, and postbachelor's certificates.

Special study options: academic remediation for entering students, adult/continuing education programs, advanced placement credit, cooperative education, distance learning, double majors, English as a second language, honors programs, independent study, internships, off-campus study, part-time degree program, services for LD students, student-designed majors, study abroad, summer session for credit. ***ROTC:*** Army (c), Air Force (c).

Computers: 450 computers/terminals and 2,200 ports are available on campus for general student use. Students can access the following: campus intranet, computer help desk, free student e-mail accounts, online (class) grades, online (class) registration, online (class) schedules. Campuswide network is available. 100% of college-owned or -operated housing units are wired for high-speed Internet access. Wireless service is available via entire campus.

Library: Elihu Burritt Library plus 1 other. *Books:* 449,293 (physical), 199,200 (digital/electronic); *Serial titles:* 6,833 (physical), 89,498 (digital/electronic); *Databases:* 151. Weekly public service hours: 84.

STUDENT LIFE
Housing options: coed, women-only, special housing for students with disabilities. Campus housing is university owned.

Activities and organizations: drama/theater group, student-run newspaper, radio and television station, choral group, Inter-Residence Council, student radio station, Program Board (C.A.N.), Student Government Association, A Cappella Society, national fraternities, national sororities.

Athletics Member NCAA. All Division I except football (Division I-AA). ***Intercollegiate sports:*** baseball M(s), basketball M(s)/W(s), lacrosse W(s), soccer M(s)/W(s), softball W(s), swimming and diving W(s), track and field M(s)/W(s), volleyball W(s). ***Intramural sports:*** archery M/W, basketball M/W, ice hockey M(c), soccer M/W, softball W, tennis M(c), volleyball M/W.

Campus security: 24-hour emergency response devices and patrols, student patrols, late-night transport/escort service, controlled dormitory access.

Student services: health clinic, personal/psychological counseling, women's center, veterans affairs office.

COSTS & FINANCIAL AID
Costs (2019–20) ***Tuition:*** area resident $5924 full-time, $247 per credit part-time; state resident $5924 full-time, $247 per credit part-time; nonresident $17,726 full-time, $247 per credit part-time. Part-time tuition and fees vary according to course load. ***Required fees:*** $5144 full-time, $298 per credit part-time, $78 per term part-time. ***Room and board:*** $12,528; room only: $7130. Room and board charges vary according to board plan and housing facility. ***Payment plan:*** installment. ***Waivers:*** senior citizens and employees or children of employees.

Financial Aid Of all full-time matriculated undergraduates who enrolled in 2019, 5,768 applied for aid, 4,950 were judged to have need, 184 had their need fully met. 325 Federal Work-Study jobs (averaging $2198). In 2019, 265 non-need-based awards were made. ***Average percent of need met:*** 46. ***Average financial aid package:*** $9868. ***Average need-based loan:*** $4469. ***Average need-based gift aid:*** $3686. ***Average non-need-based aid:*** $2856. ***Average indebtedness upon graduation:*** $29,709.

APPLYING
Standardized Tests *Required:* SAT or ACT (for admission).

Options: electronic application.

Application fee: $50.

Required: high school transcript, minimum 2.0 GPA, 2 letters of recommendation. ***Required for some:*** essay or personal statement, interview, high school class rank.

Notification: continuous until 10/15 (freshmen), continuous until 10/15 (transfers).

CONTACT
Lawrence Hall, Central Connecticut State University, 1615 Stanley Street, New Britain, CT 06050. *Phone:* 860-832-2285. *Toll-free phone:* 888-733-2278. *Fax:* 860-832-2522. *E-mail:* admissions@ccsu.edu.

Charter Oak State College

New Britain, Connecticut

http://www.charteroak.edu/

- **State-supported** comprehensive, founded 1973, part of Connecticut State Colleges & Universities (CSCU)
- **Suburban** campus with easy access to Hartford, CT
- **Coed** 1,547 undergraduate students, 25% full-time, 70% women, 30% men
- **Noncompetitive** entrance level

UNDERGRAD STUDENTS
387 full-time, 1,160 part-time. Students come from 36 states and territories; 17% are from out of state; 17% Black or African American, non-Hispanic/Latino; 16% Hispanic/Latino; 3% Asian, non-Hispanic/Latino; 0.3% American Indian or Alaska Native, non-

Hispanic/Latino; 3% Two or more races, non-Hispanic/Latino; 4% Race/ethnicity unknown; 0.6% international.

FACULTY
Total: 182.

Student/faculty ratio: 14:1.

ACADEMICS
Calendar: semesters. *Degrees:* certificates, associate, bachelor's, and master's (offers only external degree programs).

Special study options: accelerated degree program, adult/continuing education programs, advanced placement credit, distance learning, double majors, external degree program, independent study, off-campus study, part-time degree program, services for LD students, student-designed majors, summer session for credit.

Computers: Students can access the following: computer help desk, free student e-mail accounts, online (class) grades, online (class) registration, online (class) schedules. Campuswide network is available. Wireless service is available via entire campus.

STUDENT LIFE
Housing options: college housing not available.

COSTS
Costs (2020–21) ***Tuition:*** state resident $9570 full-time, $319 per credit part-time; nonresident $12,570 full-time, $419 per credit part-time. Full-time tuition and fees vary according to course load. Part-time tuition and fees vary according to course load. ***Required fees:*** $673 full-time, $299 per term part-time. ***Payment plan:*** installment.

APPLYING
Options: electronic application, deferred entrance.

Application fee: $50.

Application deadlines: rolling (freshmen), rolling (out-of-state freshmen), rolling (transfers).

Notification: continuous (freshmen), continuous (out-of-state freshmen), continuous (transfers).

CONTACT
Charter Oak State College, CT. *Phone:* 860-515-3858.

Connecticut College

New London, Connecticut

http://www.conncoll.edu/

- **Independent** 4-year, founded 1911
- **Small-town** 750-acre campus with easy access to Providence, RI
- **Endowment** $318.3 million
- **Coed**
- **Very difficult** entrance level

FACULTY
Student/faculty ratio: 9:1.

ACADEMICS
Calendar: semesters. *Degree:* bachelor's.
Library: Charles Shain Library plus 1 other. Weekly public service hours: 115.

STUDENT LIFE
Housing options: on-campus residence required through junior year; coed. Campus housing is university owned. Freshman campus housing is guaranteed.

Activities and organizations: drama/theater group, student-run newspaper, radio station, choral group.

Athletics Member NCAA. All Division III.

Campus security: 24-hour emergency response devices and patrols, late-night transport/escort service, controlled dormitory access.

Student services: health clinic, personal/psychological counseling, women's center.

COSTS & FINANCIAL AID
Costs (2019–20) ***Comprehensive fee:*** $72,590 includes full-time tuition ($56,540), mandatory fees ($350), and room and board ($15,700). Part-time tuition: $1683 per credit hour. ***College room only:*** $9070.

Financial Aid Of all full-time matriculated undergraduates who enrolled in 2019, 1,198 applied for aid, 1,070 were judged to have need, 1,070 had their need fully met. In 2019, 428 non-need-based awards were made. ***Average percent of need met:*** 100. ***Average financial aid package:*** $46,607. ***Average need-based loan:*** $4487. ***Average need-based gift aid:*** $43,639. ***Average non-need-based aid:*** $14,798. ***Average indebtedness upon graduation:*** $37,817.

APPLYING
Options: electronic application, early decision, deferred entrance.

Required: essay or personal statement, high school transcript, 2 letters of recommendation. ***Recommended:*** interview.

CONTACT
Andrew Strickler, Dean of Admission and Financial Aid, Connecticut College, 270 Mohegan Avenue, New London, CT 06320. *Phone:* 860-439-2200. *E-mail:* admission@conncoll.edu.

Eastern Connecticut State University

Willimantic, Connecticut

http://www.easternct.edu/

- **State-supported** comprehensive, founded 1889, part of Connecticut State Colleges & Universities (CSCU)
- **Small-town** 182-acre campus with easy access to Hartford
- **Endowment** $13.3 million
- **Coed**
- **Moderately difficult** entrance level

FACULTY
Student/faculty ratio: 16:1.

ACADEMICS
Calendar: semesters. *Degrees:* associate, bachelor's, and master's.
Library: J. Eugene Smith Library.

STUDENT LIFE
Housing options: coed. Campus housing is university owned. Freshman campus housing is guaranteed.

Activities and organizations: drama/theater group, student-run newspaper, radio and television station, choral group, Repertory Dance Troupe, Rugby Club, Biology Club, Education Club, Psychology Club.

Athletics Member NCAA. All Division III.

Campus security: 24-hour emergency response devices and patrols, student patrols, late-night transport/escort service, controlled dormitory access.

Student services: health clinic, personal/psychological counseling, women's center.

FINANCIAL AID
Financial Aid Of all full-time matriculated undergraduates who enrolled in 2015, 3,535 applied for aid, 2,863 were judged to have need, 299 had their need fully met. 85 Federal Work-Study jobs (averaging $2198). In 2015, 312 non-need-based awards were made. ***Average percent of need met:*** 61. ***Average financial aid package:*** $9669. ***Average need-based loan:*** $4301. ***Average need-based gift aid:*** $5743. ***Average non-need-based aid:*** $3726. ***Average indebtedness upon graduation:*** $30,566.

APPLYING
Options: electronic application, deferred entrance.

Application fee: $50.

Required: high school transcript. ***Required for some:*** interview. ***Recommended:*** essay or personal statement, rank in upper 50% of high school class.

CONTACT
Eastern Connecticut State University, CT. *Phone:* 860-465-4381.

Fairfield University

Fairfield, Connecticut

http://www.fairfield.edu/

- **Independent Roman Catholic (Jesuit)** comprehensive, founded 1942
- **Suburban** 200-acre campus with easy access to New York City
- **Endowment** $374.9 million
- **Coed** 4,303 undergraduate students, 97% full-time, 59% women, 41% men
- **Very difficult** entrance level, 57% of applicants were admitted

UNDERGRAD STUDENTS

4,160 full-time, 143 part-time. Students come from 39 states and territories; 50 other countries; 73% are from out of state; 2% Black or African American, non-Hispanic/Latino; 7% Hispanic/Latino; 3% Asian, non-Hispanic/Latino; 0.1% American Indian or Alaska Native, non-Hispanic/Latino; 2% Two or more races, non-Hispanic/Latino; 6% Race/ethnicity unknown; 4% international; 1% transferred in; 73% live on campus.

Freshmen:

Admission: 12,313 applied, 7,033 admitted, 1,176 enrolled. ***Average high school GPA:*** 3.6. ***Test scores:*** SAT evidence-based reading and writing scores over 500: 99%; SAT math scores over 500: 100%; ACT scores over 18: 100%; SAT evidence-based reading and writing scores over 600: 81%; SAT math scores over 600: 79%; ACT scores over 24: 95%; SAT evidence-based reading and writing scores over 700: 11%; SAT math scores over 700: 18%; ACT scores over 30: 32%.

Retention: 90% of full-time freshmen returned.

FACULTY

Total: 643, 47% full-time, 65% with terminal degrees.

Student/faculty ratio: 12:1.

ACADEMICS

Calendar: semesters. *Degrees:* bachelor's, master's, doctoral, post-master's, and postbachelor's certificates.

Special study options: accelerated degree program, adult/continuing education programs, advanced placement credit, distance learning, double majors, honors programs, independent study, internships, off-campus study, part-time degree program, services for LD students, student-designed majors, study abroad, summer session for credit. ***ROTC:*** Army (c), Air Force (c).

Computers: 150 computers/terminals are available on campus for general student use. Students can access the following: campus intranet, computer help desk, free student e-mail accounts, online (class) grades, online (class) registration, online (class) schedules. Campuswide network is available. 100% of college-owned or -operated housing units are wired for high-speed Internet access. Wireless service is available via entire campus.

Library: DiMenna-Nyselius Library. *Books:* 311,985 (physical), 1.0 million (digital/electronic); *Serial titles:* 86,612 (digital/electronic); *Databases:* 209. Weekly public service hours: 104; study areas open 24 hours, 5–7 days a week; students can reserve study rooms.

STUDENT LIFE

Housing options: coed, special housing for students with disabilities. Campus housing is university owned. Freshman campus housing is guaranteed.

Activities and organizations: drama/theater group, student-run newspaper, radio and television station, choral group, Fairfield University Student Association (FUSA), Inter-Residential Housing Associations (IRHA), Commuter Student Association (CSA), Play Like a Girl (PLAG), Intramural/Club Sports.

Athletics Member NCAA. All Division I. ***Intercollegiate sports:*** baseball M(s), basketball M(s)/W(s), crew M(s)/W(s), cross-country running M(s)/W(s), field hockey W(s), golf M(s)/W(s)(c), lacrosse M(s)/W(s), rowing M(s)/W(s), soccer M(s)/W(s), softball W(s), swimming and diving M(s)/W(s), tennis M(s)/W(s), volleyball W(s). ***Intramural sports:*** badminton M/W, baseball M(c), basketball M(c)/W(c), cheerleading M(c)/W(c), cross-country running M(c)/W(c), equestrian sports M(c)/W(c), field hockey M(c)/W(c), golf M(c)/W(c), ice hockey M(c), lacrosse M(c)/W(c), rugby M(c)/W(c), sailing M(c)/W(c), skiing (downhill) M(c)/W(c), soccer M(c)/W(c), softball M/W(c), swimming and diving M(c)/W(c), table tennis M/W, tennis M(c)/W(c), ultimate Frisbee M(c)/W(c), volleyball M(c)/W(c), wrestling M(c)/W(c).

Campus security: 24-hour emergency response devices and patrols, late-night transport/escort service, controlled dormitory access.

Student services: health clinic, personal/psychological counseling.

COSTS & FINANCIAL AID

Costs (2020–21) ***One-time required fee:*** $400. ***Comprehensive fee:*** $66,935 includes full-time tuition ($50,550), mandatory fees ($775), and room and board ($15,610). Full-time tuition and fees vary according to course load. Part-time tuition: $775 per credit hour. Part-time tuition and fees vary according to course load. ***Required fees:*** $50 per term part-time. ***College room only:*** $9560. Room and board charges vary according to board plan and housing facility. ***Payment plan:*** installment. ***Waivers:*** employees or children of employees.

Financial Aid Of all full-time matriculated undergraduates who enrolled in 2019, 2,231 applied for aid, 1,666 were judged to have need, 514 had their need fully met. 608 Federal Work-Study jobs (averaging $1633). In 2019, 1923 non-need-based awards were made. ***Average percent of need met:*** 87. ***Average financial aid package:*** $33,292. ***Average need-based loan:*** $4300. ***Average need-based gift aid:*** $31,834. ***Average non-need-based aid:*** $16,552. ***Average indebtedness upon graduation:*** $39,211. ***Financial aid deadline:*** 1/15.

APPLYING

Options: electronic application, early admission, early decision, early action, deferred entrance.

Application fee: $60.

Required: essay or personal statement, high school transcript, 1 letter of recommendation. ***Recommended:*** interview.

Application deadlines: 1/15 (freshmen), 4/1 (transfers), 11/1 (early action).

Early decision deadline: 11/15 (for plan 1), 1/15 (for plan 2).

Notification: 4/1 (freshmen), continuous (transfers), 12/15 (early decision plan 1), 2/15 (early decision plan 2), 12/20 (early action).

CONTACT

Alison Hildenbrand, Director of Admission, Fairfield University, 1073 North Benson Road, Fairfield, CT 06824. *Phone:* 203-254-4100. *Fax:* 203-254-4199. *E-mail:* admis@fairfield.edu.

Goodwin College

East Hartford, Connecticut

http://www.goodwin.edu/

CONTACT

Mr. Nicholas Lentino, Assistant Vice President for Admissions, Goodwin College, One Riverside Drive, East Hartford, CT 06118. *Phone:* 860-727-6765. *Toll-free phone:* 800-889-3282. *Fax:* 860-291-9550. *E-mail:* nlentino@goodwin.edu.

Holy Apostles College and Seminary

Cromwell, Connecticut

http://www.holyapostles.edu/

- **Independent Roman Catholic** comprehensive, founded 1956
- **Suburban** 17-acre campus with easy access to Hartford, New Haven
- **Coed** 202 undergraduate students, 39% full-time, 48% women, 52% men
- **Noncompetitive** entrance level, 100% of applicants were admitted

UNDERGRAD STUDENTS

79 full-time, 123 part-time. Students come from 37 states and territories; 2 other countries; 55% are from out of state; 1% Black or African American, non-Hispanic/Latino; 8% Hispanic/Latino; 3% Asian, non-Hispanic/Latino; 3% Two or more races, non-Hispanic/Latino; 3% Race/ethnicity unknown; 21% international; 13% transferred in.

Freshmen:

Admission: 15 applied, 15 admitted, 15 enrolled.

Retention: 88% of full-time freshmen returned.

FACULTY

Total: 83, 17% full-time, 63% with terminal degrees.

Student/faculty ratio: 2:1.

ACADEMICS
Calendar: semesters. *Degrees:* certificates, associate, bachelor's, master's, post-master's, and postbachelor's certificates.

Special study options: academic remediation for entering students, adult/continuing education programs, English as a second language, external degree program, independent study, part-time degree program, services for LD students, summer session for credit.

Computers: 10 computers/terminals are available on campus for general student use. Students can access the following: free student e-mail accounts, online (class) grades, online (class) registration, online (class) schedules. Campuswide network is available. 100% of college-owned or -operated housing units are wired for high-speed Internet access. Wireless service is available via entire campus.
Library: Holy Apostles College and Seminary Library. *Books:* 60,000 (physical); *Serial titles:* 145 (physical), 32 (digital/electronic); *Databases:* 5. Weekly public service hours: 70.

STUDENT LIFE
Housing options: college housing not available.

Activities and organizations: Pro-Life Organization.

COSTS
Costs (2020–21) ***Tuition:*** $8640 full-time, $360 per credit hour part-time. ***Required fees:*** $100 full-time, $50 part-time.

APPLYING
Standardized Tests *Required:* SAT or ACT (for admission). *Recommended:* SAT (for admission), ACT (for admission).

Options: deferred entrance.

Application fee: $50.

Required: high school transcript, 2 letters of recommendation. ***Required for some:*** interview.

Application deadlines: rolling (freshmen), rolling (out-of-state freshmen), rolling (transfers).

CONTACT
Dr. Elizabeth Rex, Director of Admissions, Holy Apostles College and Seminary, Holy Apostles College and Seminary, 33 Prospect Hill Road, Cromwell, CT 06416. *Phone:* 860-632-3056. *Fax:* 860-632-3083. *E-mail:* admissions@holyapostles.edu.

Mitchell College

New London, Connecticut

http://www.mitchell.edu/

CONTACT
Mr. Bob Martin, Director of Admissions, Mitchell College, 437 Pequot Avenue, New London, CT 06320. *Phone:* 860-701-5178. *Toll-free phone:* 800-443-2811. *Fax:* 860-444-1209. *E-mail:* admissions@mitchell.edu.

Paier College of Art, Inc.

Hamden, Connecticut

http://www.paiercollegeofart.edu/

- **Proprietary** 4-year, founded 1946
- **Suburban** 3-acre campus with easy access to New York City
- **Coed** 89 undergraduate students, 72% full-time, 70% women, 30% men
- 70% of applicants were admitted

UNDERGRAD STUDENTS
64 full-time, 25 part-time. Students come from 2 other countries; 25% Black or African American, non-Hispanic/Latino; 15% Hispanic/Latino; 1% Asian, non-Hispanic/Latino; 1% American Indian or Alaska Native, non-Hispanic/Latino; 2% international; 18% transferred in.

Freshmen:
Admission: 53 applied, 37 admitted, 18 enrolled.

Retention: 90% of full-time freshmen returned.

FACULTY
Total: 28, 21% full-time, 64% with terminal degrees.

Student/faculty ratio: 3:1.

ACADEMICS
Calendar: semesters plus 1 summer session. *Degree:* certificates, diplomas, and bachelor's.

Special study options: academic remediation for entering students, advanced placement credit, independent study, internships, part-time degree program, services for LD students, study abroad, summer session for credit.

Computers: 75 computers/terminals are available on campus for general student use. Students can access the following: online (class) grades, online (class) schedules. Wireless service is available via entire campus.
Library: Adele K. Paier Memorial Library. *Books:* 15,000 (physical), 200 (digital/electronic); *Serial titles:* 85 (physical).

STUDENT LIFE
Activities and organizations: student-run newspaper, Student Council, School Newspaper.

Student services: veterans affairs office.

COSTS & FINANCIAL AID
Costs (2020–21) ***One-time required fee:*** $25. ***Comprehensive fee:*** $23,170 includes full-time tuition ($19,200), mandatory fees ($470), and room and board ($3500). Part-time tuition: $600 per credit hour. Part-time tuition and fees vary according to course load. ***Required fees:*** $190 per term part-time. ***College room only:*** $1750. ***Payment plan:*** installment.

Financial Aid Of all full-time matriculated undergraduates who enrolled in 2018, 40 applied for aid, 34 were judged to have need, 3 had their need fully met. ***Average percent of need met:*** 48. ***Average financial aid package:*** $9366. ***Average need-based loan:*** $4137. ***Average need-based gift aid:*** $7273. ***Average indebtedness upon graduation:*** $37,318.

APPLYING
Options: early admission.

Application fee: $25.

Required: essay or personal statement, high school transcript, interview, portfolio.

Application deadlines: rolling (freshmen), rolling (out-of-state freshmen), rolling (transfers), rolling (early action).

Early decision deadline: rolling (for plan 1), rolling (for plan 2).

Notification: continuous (freshmen), continuous (out-of-state freshmen), continuous (transfers), rolling (early decision plan 1), rolling (early decision plan 2), rolling (early action).

CONTACT
Ms. Damary Rodriguez, Admissions Representative, Paier College of Art, Inc., 20 Gorham Avenue, Hamden, CT 06514. *Phone:* 203-287-3031. *Fax:* 203-287-3021. *E-mail:* drodriguez@paier.edu.

Post University

Waterbury, Connecticut

http://www.post.edu/

CONTACT
Post University, 800 Country Club Road, Waterbury, CT 06723-2540. *Toll-free phone:* 800-345-2562.

Quinnipiac University

Hamden, Connecticut

http://www.qu.edu/

- **Independent** comprehensive, founded 1929
- **Suburban** 600-acre campus with easy access to New Haven, Hartford
- **Endowment** $481.6 million
- **Coed**
- **Moderately difficult** entrance level

FACULTY
Student/faculty ratio: 16:1.

ACADEMICS
Calendar: semesters. *Degrees:* bachelor's, master's, doctoral, post-master's, and postbachelor's certificates.
Library: Arnold Bernhard Library plus 3 others. *Books:* 135,000 (physical), 500,000 (digital/electronic); *Databases:* 190. Weekly public

service hours: 93; study areas open 24 hours, 5–7 days a week; students can reserve study rooms.

STUDENT LIFE

Housing options: coed. Campus housing is university owned. Freshman campus housing is guaranteed.

Activities and organizations: drama/theater group, student-run newspaper, radio and television station, choral group, Student Government, Social Programming Board, Drama Club, Chronicle (student newspaper), dance company, national fraternities, national sororities.

Athletics Member NCAA. All Division I.

Campus security: 24-hour emergency response devices and patrols, late-night transport/escort service, controlled dormitory access, text message emergency notification system.

Student services: health clinic, personal/psychological counseling, women's center, veterans affairs office.

FINANCIAL AID

Financial Aid Of all full-time matriculated undergraduates who enrolled in 2018, 5,242 applied for aid, 4,468 were judged to have need, 736 had their need fully met. 1,767 Federal Work-Study jobs (averaging $2117). In 2018, 1991 non-need-based awards were made. ***Average percent of need met:*** 65. ***Average financial aid package:*** $29,097. ***Average need-based loan:*** $4477. ***Average need-based gift aid:*** $23,028. ***Average non-need-based aid:*** $17,552. ***Average indebtedness upon graduation:*** $48,544.

APPLYING

Standardized Tests *Required for some:* SAT or ACT (for admission).

Options: electronic application, early decision, deferred entrance.

Application fee: $65.

Required: essay or personal statement, high school transcript, 1 letter of recommendation. ***Required for some:*** minimum 3.0 GPA. ***Recommended:*** minimum 3.0 GPA, interview.

CONTACT

Ms. Carla Knowlton, Director of Admissions, Quinnipiac University, 275 Mount Carmel Avenue, Hamden, CT 06518. *Phone:* 203-582-8600. *Toll-free phone:* 800-462-1944. *Fax:* 203-582-8906. *E-mail:* admissions@qu.edu.

Sacred Heart University

Fairfield, Connecticut

http://www.sacredheart.edu/

- **Independent Roman Catholic** comprehensive, founded 1963
- **Suburban** 350-acre campus with easy access to New York City
- **Endowment** $167.6 million
- **Coed** 6,158 undergraduate students, 87% full-time, 66% women, 34% men
- **Moderately difficult** entrance level, 64% of applicants were admitted

UNDERGRAD STUDENTS

5,348 full-time, 810 part-time. 64% are from out of state; 5% Black or African American, non-Hispanic/Latino; 12% Hispanic/Latino; 2% Asian, non-Hispanic/Latino; 0.1% American Indian or Alaska Native, non-Hispanic/Latino; 2% Two or more races, non-Hispanic/Latino; 4% Race/ethnicity unknown; 1% international; 5% transferred in; 50% live on campus.

Freshmen:

Admission: 11,748 applied, 7,515 admitted, 1,601 enrolled. ***Average high school GPA:*** 3.6. ***Test scores:*** SAT evidence-based reading and writing scores over 500: 99%; SAT math scores over 500: 98%; ACT scores over 18: 100%; SAT evidence-based reading and writing scores over 600: 52%; SAT math scores over 600: 47%; ACT scores over 24: 74%; SAT evidence-based reading and writing scores over 700: 3%; SAT math scores over 700: 5%; ACT scores over 30: 12%.

Retention: 83% of full-time freshmen returned.

FACULTY

Total: 970, 34% full-time, 47% with terminal degrees.

Student/faculty ratio: 13:1.

ACADEMICS

Calendar: semesters. *Degrees:* certificates, associate, bachelor's, master's, doctoral, post-master's, and postbachelor's certificates (also offers part-time program with significant enrollment not reflected in profile).

Special study options: academic remediation for entering students, accelerated degree program, adult/continuing education programs, advanced placement credit, distance learning, double majors, English as a second language, external degree program, honors programs, independent study, internships, part-time degree program, services for LD students, study abroad, summer session for credit. ***ROTC:*** Air Force (c).

Unusual degree programs: 3-2 engineering with Columbia University, Rensselaer Polytechnic Institute; health professions and a law program with Seton Hall University, pre-pharmacy with University of St. Joseph's.

Computers: 499 computers/terminals are available on campus for general student use. Students can access the following: computer help desk, free student e-mail accounts, online (class) grades, online (class) registration. Campuswide network is available. 100% of college-owned or -operated housing units are wired for high-speed Internet access. Wireless service is available via entire campus.

Library: Ryan Matura Library plus 1 other. *Books:* 89,846 (physical), 228,647 (digital/electronic); *Serial titles:* 412 (physical), 62,191 (digital/electronic); *Databases:* 140. Weekly public service hours: 119; students can reserve study rooms.

STUDENT LIFE

Housing options: on-campus residence required through sophomore year; coed, special housing for students with disabilities. Campus housing is university owned. Freshman campus housing is guaranteed.

Activities and organizations: drama/theater group, student-run newspaper, radio and television station, choral group, marching band, Alpha Sigma Lambda Honor Society, Inter Resident Council, Student Nursing Association, Habitat for Humanity, Pre-PT Club, national fraternities, national sororities.

Athletics Member NCAA. All Division I except football (Division I-AA). ***Intercollegiate sports:*** baseball M(s), basketball M(s)/W(s), bowling W(s), cheerleading W(c), crew W(s), cross-country running M(s)/W(s), equestrian sports W(s), fencing M(s)/W(s), field hockey W(s), golf M(s)/W(s)(c), ice hockey M(s)/W(s), lacrosse M(s)/W(s), rowing W(s), rugby W(s), soccer M(s)/W(s), softball W(s), swimming and diving W(s), tennis M(s)/W(s), track and field M(s)/W(s), volleyball M(s)/W(s), wrestling M(s). ***Intramural sports:*** baseball M(c), basketball M(c)/W(c), bowling M(c)/W(c), cross-country running M(c)/W(c), fencing W(c), football M(c), golf M(c)/W(c), gymnastics M(c)/W(c), ice hockey M(c), lacrosse M(c)/W(c), rugby M(c), sailing M(c)/W(c), soccer M(c)/W(c), softball M(c)/W(c), swimming and diving W(c), tennis M(c)/W(c), ultimate Frisbee M(c), volleyball M(c)/W(c), weight lifting M(c)/W(c), wrestling M(c).

Campus security: 24-hour emergency response devices and patrols, late-night transport/escort service, controlled dormitory access, Bystander Intervention, Personal Safety Escort Program, Silent Witness Program, crime prevention announcements, SHU Safe App.

Student services: health clinic, personal/psychological counseling, veterans affairs office.

COSTS & FINANCIAL AID

Costs (2019–20) ***Comprehensive fee:*** $59,030 includes full-time tuition ($42,800), mandatory fees ($270), and room and board ($15,960). Part-time tuition: $625 per credit hour. Part-time tuition and fees vary according to course load. ***Required fees:*** $115 per term part-time. ***College room only:*** $10,900. Room and board charges vary according to board plan and housing facility. ***Payment plan:*** installment. ***Waivers:*** employees or children of employees.

Financial Aid Of all full-time matriculated undergraduates who enrolled in 2019, 4,184 applied for aid, 3,405 were judged to have need, 625 had their need fully met. 1,388 Federal Work-Study jobs (averaging $1945). 914 state and other part-time jobs (averaging $1525). In 2019, 1774 non-need-based awards were made. ***Average percent of need met:*** 58. ***Average financial aid package:*** $22,356. ***Average need-based loan:*** $4740. ***Average need-based gift aid:*** $18,140. ***Average non-need-based aid:*** $14,164. ***Average indebtedness upon graduation:*** $45,630. ***Financial aid deadline:*** 2/15.

APPLYING

Options: electronic application, early decision, early action, deferred entrance.

Application fee: $50.

Required: high school transcript, 1 letter of recommendation. ***Required for some:*** interview, interview for Early Decision candidates. ***Recommended:*** essay or personal statement.

Application deadlines: rolling (freshmen), 12/15 (early action).

Early decision deadline: 12/1.

Notification: continuous (freshmen), continuous (transfers), 12/15 (early decision), 1/31 (early action).

CONTACT

Ms. Pam Pillo, Executive Director of Undergraduate Admissions, Sacred Heart University, 5151 Park Avenue, Fairfield, CT 06825. *Phone:* 203-371-7880. *Fax:* 203-365-7607. *E-mail:* pillop@sacredheart.edu.

Southern Connecticut State University

New Haven, Connecticut

http://www.southernct.edu/

CONTACT

Mrs. Alexis S. Haakonsen, Director of Admissions, Southern Connecticut State University, Admissions House, 131 Farnham Avenue, New Haven, CT 06515-1202. *Phone:* 203-392-5652. *Fax:* 203-392-5727. *E-mail:* haakonsena1@southernct.edu.

Trinity College

Hartford, Connecticut

http://www.trincoll.edu/

- **Independent** comprehensive, founded 1823
- **Urban** 100-acre campus
- **Endowment** $551.8 million
- **Coed**
- **Most difficult** entrance level

FACULTY

Student/faculty ratio: 9:1.

ACADEMICS

Calendar: semesters. *Degrees:* bachelor's and master's.
Library: Trinity College Library plus 1 other.

STUDENT LIFE

Housing options: on-campus residence required for freshman year; coed, special housing for students with disabilities. Campus housing is university owned. Freshman campus housing is guaranteed.

Activities and organizations: drama/theater group, student-run newspaper, radio station, choral group, Friends Active in Community Engagement and Service (FACES), The Mill, Student Government Association, Relay for Life, Multi-Cultural Affairs Council, national fraternities, national sororities.

Athletics Member NCAA. All Division III.

Campus security: 24-hour emergency response devices and patrols, late-night transport/escort service, controlled dormitory access.

Student services: health clinic, personal/psychological counseling, women's center.

COSTS & FINANCIAL AID

Costs (2019–20) ***Comprehensive fee:*** $74,350 includes full-time tuition ($56,380), mandatory fees ($2670), and room and board ($15,300). ***College room only:*** $9960.

Financial Aid Of all full-time matriculated undergraduates who enrolled in 2018, 1,288 applied for aid, 1,049 were judged to have need, 1,026 had their need fully met. In 2018, 121 non-need-based awards were made. ***Average percent of need met:*** 100. ***Average financial aid package:*** $50,520. ***Average need-based loan:*** $4266. ***Average need-based gift aid:*** $47,156. ***Average non-need-based aid:*** $28,738. ***Average indebtedness upon graduation:*** $25,958. ***Financial aid deadline:*** 3/1.

APPLYING

Options: electronic application, early admission, early decision, deferred entrance.

Application fee: $65.

Required: essay or personal statement, high school transcript, 3 letters of recommendation. ***Recommended:*** interview.

CONTACT

Trinity College, 300 Summit Street, Hartford, CT 06106-3100. *Phone:* 860-297-2180.

United States Coast Guard Academy

New London, Connecticut

http://www.uscga.edu/

- **Federally supported** 4-year, founded 1876
- **Suburban** 103-acre campus with easy access to Providence, Hartford
- **Coed**
- **Very difficult** entrance level

FACULTY

Student/faculty ratio: 7:1.

ACADEMICS

Calendar: semesters. *Degree:* bachelor's.
Library: USCG Academy Library. Students can reserve study rooms.

STUDENT LIFE

Housing options: on-campus residence required through senior year; coed. Campus housing is university owned. Freshman campus housing is guaranteed.

Activities and organizations: drama/theater group, choral group, marching band, Club Sports, Musical activities, Multicultural Club, Officers Christian Fellowship, International Dance Club.

Athletics Member NCAA. All Division III.

Campus security: 24-hour patrols, late-night transport/escort service, controlled dormitory access, cadets staff a 24-hour Watch Office.

Student services: health clinic, personal/psychological counseling, legal services, veterans affairs office.

APPLYING

Standardized Tests *Required:* SAT or ACT (for admission).

Options: electronic application, early action, deferred entrance.

Required: essay or personal statement, high school transcript, 3 letters of recommendation, medical examination, physical fitness examination. ***Recommended:*** interview.

CONTACT

Mr. Daniel V. Pinch, Associate Director of Admissions for Outreach, United States Coast Guard Academy, 31 Mohegan Avenue, New London, CT 06320-4195. *Phone:* 860-701-6327. *Toll-free phone:* 800-883-8724. *Fax:* 860-701-6700. *E-mail:* daniel.v.pinch@uscga.edu.

University of Bridgeport

Bridgeport, Connecticut

http://www.bridgeport.edu/

CONTACT

Ms. Jessica N. Crowley Goddu, Director of Undergraduate Admissions, University of Bridgeport, 126 Park Avenue, Bridgeport, CT 06604. *Phone:* 203-576-4812. *Toll-free phone:* 800-EXCEL-UB. *Fax:* 203-576-4941. *E-mail:* admit@bridgeport.edu.

University of Connecticut

Storrs, Connecticut

http://www.uconn.edu/

- **State-supported** university, founded 1881
- **Rural** 4099-acre campus
- **Endowment** $367.0 million
- **Coed**
- **Moderately difficult** entrance level

FACULTY

Student/faculty ratio: 16:1.

ACADEMICS

Calendar: semesters. *Degrees:* associate, bachelor's, master's, doctoral, post-master's, and postbachelor's certificates.

Library: Homer Babbidge Library plus 3 others.

STUDENT LIFE

Housing options: coed, men-only, women-only, special housing for students with disabilities. Campus housing is university owned and is provided by a third party. Freshman campus housing is guaranteed.

Activities and organizations: drama/theater group, student-run newspaper, radio and television station, choral group, marching band, national fraternities, national sororities.

Athletics Member NCAA. All Division I except football (Division I-A).

Campus security: 24-hour emergency response devices, late-night transport/escort service.

Student services: health clinic, personal/psychological counseling, women's center.

COSTS & FINANCIAL AID

Costs (2019–20) ***Tuition:*** area resident $13,798 full-time, $575 per credit hour part-time; state resident $13,798 full-time, $575 per credit hour part-time; nonresident $36,466 full-time, $1520 per credit hour part-time. ***Required fees:*** $3428 full-time. ***Room and board:*** $13,258; room only: $7238.

Financial Aid Of all full-time matriculated undergraduates who enrolled in 2017, 12,774 applied for aid, 9,986 were judged to have need, 1,329 had their need fully met. In 2017, 2366 non-need-based awards were made. ***Average percent of need met:*** 59. ***Average financial aid package:*** $14,884. ***Average need-based loan:*** $4409. ***Average need-based gift aid:*** $11,306. ***Average non-need-based aid:*** $8338.

APPLYING

Standardized Tests *Required:* SAT or ACT (for admission).

Options: electronic application, deferred entrance.

Application fee: $80.

Required: essay or personal statement, high school transcript. ***Recommended:*** 2 letters of recommendation.

CONTACT

Nathan Fuerst, Director of Undergraduate Admissions, University of Connecticut, 2131 Hillside Road, U-88, Storrs, CT 06269. *Phone:* 860-486-3137. *Fax:* 860-486-1476. *E-mail:* beahusky@uconn.edu.

University of Hartford

West Hartford, Connecticut

http://www.hartford.edu/

- **Independent** comprehensive, founded 1877
- **Suburban** 320-acre campus with easy access to Hartford
- **Endowment** $182.8 million
- **Coed** 4,793 undergraduate students, 89% full-time, 52% women, 48% men
- **Moderately difficult** entrance level, 76% of applicants were admitted

UNDERGRAD STUDENTS

4,247 full-time, 546 part-time. Students come from 46 states and territories; 47 other countries; 50% are from out of state; 15% Black or African American, non-Hispanic/Latino; 13% Hispanic/Latino; 4% Asian, non-Hispanic/Latino; 0.2% American Indian or Alaska Native, non-Hispanic/Latino; 4% Two or more races, non-Hispanic/Latino; 5% Race/ethnicity unknown; 6% international; 4% transferred in; 60% live on campus.

Freshmen:

Admission: 13,233 applied, 10,103 admitted, 1,234 enrolled. ***Average high school GPA:*** 3.3. ***Test scores:*** SAT evidence-based reading and writing scores over 500: 84%; SAT math scores over 500: 82%; ACT scores over 18: 94%; SAT evidence-based reading and writing scores over 600: 35%; SAT math scores over 600: 31%; ACT scores over 24: 55%; SAT evidence-based reading and writing scores over 700: 4%; SAT math scores over 700: 5%; ACT scores over 30: 12%.

Retention: 75% of full-time freshmen returned.

FACULTY

Total: 816, 44% full-time.

Student/faculty ratio: 9:1.

ACADEMICS

Calendar: semesters. *Degrees:* certificates, diplomas, associate, bachelor's, master's, doctoral, post-master's, and postbachelor's certificates.

Special study options: academic remediation for entering students, adult/continuing education programs, advanced placement credit, cooperative education, distance learning, double majors, English as a second language, honors programs, independent study, internships, off-campus study, part-time degree program, services for LD students, student-designed majors, study abroad, summer session for credit. ***ROTC:*** Army (c), Air Force (c).

Computers: 400 computers/terminals are available on campus for general student use. Students can access the following: computer help desk, free student e-mail accounts, online (class) grades, online (class) registration, online (class) schedules, student Web pages. Campuswide network is available. 100% of college-owned or -operated housing units are wired for high-speed Internet access. Wireless service is available via entire campus.

Library: Mortensen Library plus 1 other. *Books:* 287,556 (physical), 4,624 (digital/electronic); *Serial titles:* 56,360 (digital/electronic); *Databases:* 213. Weekly public service hours: 104.

STUDENT LIFE

Housing options: on-campus residence required for freshman year; coed, women-only, special housing for students with disabilities. Campus housing is university owned. Freshman campus housing is guaranteed.

Activities and organizations: drama/theater group, student-run newspaper, radio and television station, choral group, Program Council, Brothers and Sisters United, Hillel, Student Government Association, Residence Hall Association, national fraternities, national sororities.

Athletics Member NCAA. All Division I. ***Intercollegiate sports:*** badminton M(c)/W(c), baseball M(s), basketball M(s)/W(s), cross-country running M(s)/W(s), golf M(s)/W(s), lacrosse M(s), racquetball M(c)/W(c), rugby M(c)/W(c), soccer M(s)/W(s), softball W(s), track and field M/W, volleyball M(c)/W(s). ***Intramural sports:*** badminton M/W, basketball M/W, football M/W, racquetball M/W, soccer M/W, softball M/W, tennis M/W, ultimate Frisbee M/W, volleyball M/W.

Campus security: 24-hour emergency response devices and patrols, late-night transport/escort service, controlled dormitory access, bicycle patrols.

Student services: health clinic, personal/psychological counseling, women's center, legal services.

COSTS & FINANCIAL AID

Costs (2020–21) ***Comprehensive fee:*** $56,760 includes full-time tuition ($40,490), mandatory fees ($3070), and room and board ($13,200). Full-time tuition and fees vary according to program. Part-time tuition: $580 per credit. Part-time tuition and fees vary according to course load and program. ***College room only:*** $8090. Room and board charges vary according to board plan and housing facility. ***Payment plans:*** tuition prepayment, installment. ***Waivers:*** senior citizens and employees or children of employees.

Financial Aid Of all full-time matriculated undergraduates who enrolled in 2018, 3,556 applied for aid, 3,266 were judged to have need, 455 had their need fully met. 546 Federal Work-Study jobs (averaging $1894). In 2018, 887 non-need-based awards were made. ***Average percent of need met:*** 69. ***Average financial aid package:*** $29,084. ***Average need-based loan:*** $4356. ***Average need-based gift aid:*** $23,538. ***Average non-need-based aid:*** $17,837.

APPLYING

Standardized Tests *Required:* SAT or ACT (for admission).

Options: electronic application, early admission, early action, deferred entrance.

Application fee: $35.

Required: high school transcript. ***Recommended:*** essay or personal statement, 2 letters of recommendation, interview.

Application deadlines: rolling (freshmen), rolling (transfers).

Notification: continuous (freshmen), continuous (transfers).

CONTACT

Mr. Richard Zeiser, Dean of Admissions, University of Hartford, 200 Bloomfield Avenue, West Hartford, CT 06117. *Phone:* 860-768-4296.

Toll-free phone: 800-947-4303. *Fax:* 860-768-4961. *E-mail:* admissions@hartford.edu.

University of New Haven

West Haven, Connecticut

http://www.newhaven.edu/

- **Independent** comprehensive, founded 1920
- **Suburban** 82-acre campus with easy access to New Haven
- **Coed** 4,912 undergraduate students, 94% full-time, 56% women, 44% men
- **Moderately difficult** entrance level, 83% of applicants were admitted

UNDERGRAD STUDENTS

4,625 full-time, 287 part-time. Students come from 39 states and territories; 31 other countries; 57% are from out of state; 12% Black or African American, non-Hispanic/Latino; 13% Hispanic/Latino; 4% Asian, non-Hispanic/Latino; 0.1% Native Hawaiian or other Pacific Islander, non-Hispanic/Latino; 0.3% American Indian or Alaska Native, non-Hispanic/Latino; 0.8% Two or more races, non-Hispanic/Latino; 3% Race/ethnicity unknown; 3% international; 4% transferred in; 55% live on campus.

Freshmen:

Admission: 10,997 applied, 9,126 admitted, 1,285 enrolled. ***Average high school GPA:*** 3.5. ***Test scores:*** SAT evidence-based reading and writing scores over 500: 86%; SAT math scores over 500: 84%; ACT scores over 18: 94%; SAT evidence-based reading and writing scores over 600: 33%; SAT math scores over 600: 28%; ACT scores over 24: 48%; SAT evidence-based reading and writing scores over 700: 3%; SAT math scores over 700: 4%; ACT scores over 30: 11%.

Retention: 77% of full-time freshmen returned.

FACULTY

Total: 652, 41% full-time, 60% with terminal degrees.

Student/faculty ratio: 16:1.

ACADEMICS

Calendar: 4-1-4. *Degrees:* certificates, associate, bachelor's, master's, doctoral, and postbachelor's certificates.

Special study options: academic remediation for entering students, accelerated degree program, adult/continuing education programs, advanced placement credit, cooperative education, distance learning, double majors, English as a second language, honors programs, independent study, internships, off-campus study, part-time degree program, services for LD students, study abroad, summer session for credit. ***ROTC:*** Army (b), Air Force (c).

Computers: Students can access the following: campus intranet, computer help desk, free student e-mail accounts, online (class) grades, online (class) registration, online (class) schedules, computer repair services. Campuswide network is available. Wireless service is available via entire campus.
Library: Marvin K. Peterson Library.

STUDENT LIFE

Housing options: coed, special housing for students with disabilities. Campus housing is university owned. Freshman campus housing is guaranteed.

Activities and organizations: drama/theater group, student-run newspaper, radio station, marching band, national fraternities, national sororities.

Athletics Member NCAA. All Division II. ***Intercollegiate sports:*** baseball M(s), basketball M(s)/W(s), cross-country running M(s)/W(s), field hockey W(s), football M(s), ice hockey M(c), lacrosse M(c)/W(s), rugby M(c), soccer M(s)/W(s), softball W(s), tennis W(s), track and field M(s)/W(s), ultimate Frisbee M(c)/W(c), volleyball M(c)/W(s), wrestling M(c). ***Intramural sports:*** basketball M/W, cheerleading M/W, racquetball M/W, soccer M/W, softball M/W, tennis M/W, volleyball M/W.

Campus security: 24-hour emergency response devices and patrols, student patrols, late-night transport/escort service, controlled dormitory access.

Student services: health clinic, personal/psychological counseling, veterans affairs office.

COSTS & FINANCIAL AID

Costs (2019–20) ***Comprehensive fee:*** $56,800 includes full-time tuition ($39,000), mandatory fees ($1440), and room and board ($16,360). Full-time tuition and fees vary according to course load and program. Part-time tuition: $1300 per credit hour. Part-time tuition and fees vary according to class time, course load, and program. ***Required fees:*** $145 per term part-time. ***College room only:*** $10,450. Room and board charges vary according to board plan and housing facility. ***Payment plan:*** installment. ***Waivers:*** senior citizens and employees or children of employees.

Financial Aid Of all full-time matriculated undergraduates who enrolled in 2019, 4,034 applied for aid, 3,636 were judged to have need, 558 had their need fully met. In 2019, 713 non-need-based awards were made. ***Average percent of need met:*** 59. ***Average financial aid package:*** $24,714. ***Average need-based loan:*** $4243. ***Average need-based gift aid:*** $21,357. ***Average non-need-based aid:*** $18,230. ***Average indebtedness upon graduation:*** $47,457. ***Financial aid deadline:*** 5/1.

APPLYING

Options: electronic application, early decision, early action.

Application fee: $50.

Required: essay or personal statement, high school transcript. ***Recommended:*** interview.

Application deadlines: rolling (freshmen), rolling (out-of-state freshmen), rolling (transfers), 12/15 (early action).

Early decision deadline: 12/1.

Notification: continuous (freshmen), continuous (out-of-state freshmen), continuous (transfers), 12/15 (early decision), 1/15 (early action).

CONTACT

Mr. Jason Riendeau, Executive Director of Undergraduate Admissions, University of New Haven, Bayer Hall, 300 Boston Post Road, West Haven, CT 06516. *Phone:* 203-931-2920. *Toll-free phone:* 800-342-5864. *E-mail:* jriendeau@newhaven.edu.

University of Saint Joseph

West Hartford, Connecticut

http://www.usj.edu/

- **Independent Roman Catholic** comprehensive, founded 1932
- **Suburban** 90-acre campus with easy access to Hartford
- **Coed, primarily women** 904 undergraduate students, 88% full-time, 81% women, 19% men
- **Moderately difficult** entrance level, 77% of applicants were admitted

UNDERGRAD STUDENTS

794 full-time, 110 part-time. Students come from 15 states and territories; 5% are from out of state; 14% Black or African American, non-Hispanic/Latino; 14% Hispanic/Latino; 5% Asian, non-Hispanic/Latino; 0.1% Native Hawaiian or other Pacific Islander, non-Hispanic/Latino; 0.3% American Indian or Alaska Native, non-Hispanic/Latino; 3% Two or more races, non-Hispanic/Latino; 4% Race/ethnicity unknown; 1% international; 6% transferred in; 70% live on campus.

Freshmen:

Admission: 1,646 applied, 1,261 admitted, 194 enrolled. ***Average high school GPA:*** 3.4. ***Test scores:*** SAT evidence-based reading and writing scores over 500: 77%; SAT math scores over 500: 80%; ACT scores over 18: 100%; SAT evidence-based reading and writing scores over 600: 27%; SAT math scores over 600: 23%; ACT scores over 24: 14%; SAT evidence-based reading and writing scores over 700: 3%; SAT math scores over 700: 6%.

Retention: 75% of full-time freshmen returned.

FACULTY

Total: 301, 45% full-time, 103% with terminal degrees.

Student/faculty ratio: 9:1.

ACADEMICS

Calendar: semesters. *Degrees:* certificates, bachelor's, master's, doctoral, post-master's, and postbachelor's certificates.

Special study options: accelerated degree program, adult/continuing education programs, advanced placement credit, distance learning, double majors, honors programs, independent study, internships, off-campus study, part-time degree program, services for LD students, student-designed majors, study abroad, summer session for credit.

Computers: 72 computers/terminals are available on campus for general student use. Students can access the following: campus intranet, computer help desk, free student e-mail accounts, online (class) grades, online (class) registration, online (class) schedules. Campuswide network is available. 100% of college-owned or -operated housing units are wired for high-speed Internet access. Wireless service is available via entire campus.
Library: Pope Pius XII Library. Students can reserve study rooms.

STUDENT LIFE
Housing options: coed, women-only, cooperative, special housing for students with disabilities. Campus housing is university owned.

Activities and organizations: drama/theater group, choral group.

Athletics Member NCAA. All Division III. ***Intercollegiate sports:*** basketball W, cross-country running W, lacrosse W, soccer W, softball W, swimming and diving W, tennis W, volleyball W. ***Intramural sports:*** badminton M/W, basketball M/W, cross-country running M(c)/W(c), field hockey W(c).

Campus security: 24-hour emergency response devices and patrols, late-night transport/escort service, controlled dormitory access.

Student services: health clinic, personal/psychological counseling.

COSTS & FINANCIAL AID
Costs (2020–21) ***Tuition:*** $644 per credit hour part-time. Full-time tuition and fees vary according to class time, course load, degree level, location, and program. Part-time tuition and fees vary according to class time, course load, degree level, location, and program. ***Required fees:*** $65 per credit hour part-time. ***Room only:*** $3448. Room and board charges vary according to board plan and location.

Financial Aid Of all full-time matriculated undergraduates who enrolled in 2018, 745 applied for aid, 740 were judged to have need. 214 Federal Work-Study jobs (averaging $2184). ***Average indebtedness upon graduation:*** $38,916.

APPLYING
Standardized Tests *Required for some:* SAT or ACT (for admission).

Options: electronic application, deferred entrance.

Application fee: $50.

Required: high school transcript, 1 letter of recommendation. ***Recommended:*** essay or personal statement, interview.

Application deadlines: rolling (freshmen), rolling (transfers).

Notification: continuous (freshmen), continuous (transfers).

CONTACT
University of Saint Joseph, 1678 Asylum Avenue, West Hartford, CT 06117-2700. *Toll-free phone:* 866-442-8752.

Wesleyan University
Middletown, Connecticut
http://www.wesleyan.edu/

- **Independent** university, founded 1831
- **Suburban** 316-acre campus with easy access to Hartford, CT; New Haven, CT; Springfield, MA
- **Endowment** $1.1 million
- **Coed** 3,018 undergraduate students, 97% full-time, 54% women, 46% men
- **Most difficult** entrance level, 16% of applicants were admitted

UNDERGRAD STUDENTS
2,937 full-time, 81 part-time. Students come from 46 states and territories; 56 other countries; 92% are from out of state; 5% Black or African American, non-Hispanic/Latino; 11% Hispanic/Latino; 7% Asian, non-Hispanic/Latino; 0.1% Native Hawaiian or other Pacific Islander, non-Hispanic/Latino; 6% Two or more races, non-Hispanic/Latino; 2% Race/ethnicity unknown; 14% international; 2% transferred in; 99% live on campus.

Freshmen:
Admission: 13,264 applied, 2,186 admitted, 771 enrolled. ***Test scores:*** SAT evidence-based reading and writing scores over 500: 99%; SAT math scores over 500: 99%; ACT scores over 18: 100%; SAT evidence-based reading and writing scores over 600: 93%; SAT math scores over 600: 90%; ACT scores over 24: 98%; SAT evidence-based reading and writing scores over 700: 53%; SAT math scores over 700: 64%; ACT scores over 30: 86%.
Retention: 97% of full-time freshmen returned.

FACULTY
Total: 430, 87% full-time, 87% with terminal degrees.
Student/faculty ratio: 8:1.

ACADEMICS
Calendar: semesters. *Degrees:* bachelor's, master's, doctoral, and post-master's certificates.

Special study options: accelerated degree program, advanced placement credit, double majors, honors programs, independent study, internships, off-campus study, part-time degree program, services for LD students, student-designed majors, study abroad, summer session for credit. ***ROTC:*** Air Force (c).

Unusual degree programs: 3-2 engineering with Columbia University, California Institute of Technology, Dartmouth College.

Computers: 118 computers/terminals and 7,200 ports are available on campus for general student use. Students can access the following: campus intranet, computer help desk, free student e-mail accounts, online (class) grades, online (class) registration, online (class) schedules, electronic portfolio, course drop/add, learning management system, software training. Campuswide network is available. 100% of college-owned or -operated housing units are wired for high-speed Internet access. Wireless service is available via entire campus.
Library: Olin Memorial Library plus 1 other. *Books:* 948,293 (physical), 1.2 million (digital/electronic); *Serial titles:* 8,132 (physical), 1.3 million (digital/electronic); *Databases:* 478. Weekly public service hours: 113; students can reserve study rooms.

STUDENT LIFE
Housing options: on-campus residence required through senior year; coed, men-only, women-only, special housing for students with disabilities. Campus housing is university owned. Freshman campus housing is guaranteed.

Activities and organizations: drama/theater group, student-run newspaper, radio station, choral group, Athletic Clubs, Dance and Performance Groups, The Wesleyan Student Assembly, Second Stage, Affinity Groups, national fraternities, national sororities.

Athletics Member NCAA. All Division III. ***Intercollegiate sports:*** badminton M(c)/W(c), baseball M, basketball M/W, crew M/W, cross-country running M/W, equestrian sports M(c)/W(c), fencing M(c)/W(c), field hockey W, football M, ice hockey M/W, lacrosse M/W, rugby M(c)/W(c), sailing M(c)/W(c), soccer M/W, softball W, squash M/W, swimming and diving M/W, tennis M/W, track and field M/W, ultimate Frisbee M(c)/W(c), volleyball W, water polo M(c)/W(c), wrestling M. ***Intramural sports:*** basketball M/W, golf M/W, ice hockey M/W, soccer M/W, softball M/W, squash M/W, ultimate Frisbee M/W, water polo M/W.

Campus security: 24-hour emergency response devices and patrols, late-night transport/escort service, controlled dormitory access, Self-defense classes offered by certified instructors.

Student services: health clinic, personal/psychological counseling, veterans affairs office.

COSTS & FINANCIAL AID
Costs (2019–20) ***Comprehensive fee:*** $72,728 includes full-time tuition ($56,704), mandatory fees ($300), and room and board ($15,724). ***Room and board:*** Room and board charges vary according to board plan and student level. ***Payment plan:*** installment.

Financial Aid Of all full-time matriculated undergraduates who enrolled in 2019, 1,281 applied for aid, 1,203 were judged to have need, 1,203 had their need fully met. 1,926 Federal Work-Study jobs (averaging $2.3 million). 314 state and other part-time jobs (averaging $2093). In 2019, 20 non-need-based awards were made. ***Average percent of need met:*** 100. ***Average financial aid package:*** $58,719. ***Average need-based loan:*** $4058. ***Average need-based gift aid:*** $52,284. ***Average non-need-based aid:*** $42,760. ***Average indebtedness upon graduation:*** $26,016.

APPLYING
Standardized Tests *Required for some:* SAT and SAT Subject Tests or ACT (for admission).

Options: electronic application, early admission, early decision, deferred entrance.

Application fee: $55.

Required: essay or personal statement, high school transcript, 2 letters of recommendation. ***Recommended:*** interview.

Application deadlines: 1/1 (freshmen), 3/15 (transfers).

Early decision deadline: 11/15.

Notification: 4/1 (freshmen), 5/15 (transfers), 12/15 (early decision).

CONTACT

Mr. Amin Abdul-Malik Gonzalez, Vice President and Dean of Admission and Financial Aid, Wesleyan University, 70 WYLLYS AVENUE, The Stewart M. Reid House, Office of Admission, MIDDLETOWN, CT 06459. *Phone:* 860-685-3000. *Fax:* 860-685-3001. *E-mail:* agonzalez03@wesleyan.edu.

Western Connecticut State University

Danbury, Connecticut

http://www.wcsu.edu/

- **State-supported** comprehensive, founded 1903, part of Connecticut State Colleges & Universities (CSCU)
- **Urban** 340-acre campus with easy access to New York City
- **Endowment** $19.1 million
- **Coed** 4,982 undergraduate students, 82% full-time, 53% women, 47% men
- **Moderately difficult** entrance level, 76% of applicants were admitted

UNDERGRAD STUDENTS

4,078 full-time, 904 part-time. Students come from 5 states and territories; 7 other countries; 16% are from out of state; 9% Black or African American, non-Hispanic/Latino; 22% Hispanic/Latino; 5% Asian, non-Hispanic/Latino; 0.1% American Indian or Alaska Native, non-Hispanic/Latino; 3% Two or more races, non-Hispanic/Latino; 3% Race/ethnicity unknown; 9% transferred in; 30% live on campus.

Freshmen:

Admission: 5,388 applied, 4,084 admitted, 840 enrolled. ***Average high school GPA:*** 3.4. ***Test scores:*** SAT evidence-based reading and writing scores over 500: 85%; SAT math scores over 500: 80%; ACT scores over 18: 85%; SAT evidence-based reading and writing scores over 600: 31%; SAT math scores over 600: 21%; ACT scores over 24: 35%; SAT evidence-based reading and writing scores over 700: 4%; SAT math scores over 700: 2%; ACT scores over 30: 5%.

Retention: 74% of full-time freshmen returned.

FACULTY

Total: 650, 34% full-time, 31% with terminal degrees.

Student/faculty ratio: 12:1.

ACADEMICS

Calendar: semesters. *Degrees:* associate, bachelor's, master's, doctoral, and post-master's certificates.

Special study options: advanced placement credit, cooperative education, distance learning, honors programs, independent study, internships, part-time degree program, services for LD students, student-designed majors, study abroad, summer session for credit. ***ROTC:*** Army (c), Air Force (c).

Computers: 1,042 computers/terminals and 1,065 ports are available on campus for general student use. Students can access the following: computer help desk, free student e-mail accounts, online (class) grades, online (class) registration, online (class) schedules, online payment. Campuswide network is available. 100% of college-owned or -operated housing units are wired for high-speed Internet access. Wireless service is available via entire campus.

Library: Ruth Haas Library plus 1 other. *Books:* 204,701 (physical), 240,140 (digital/electronic); *Serial titles:* 302 (physical), 67,162 (digital/electronic); *Databases:* 188. Weekly public service hours: 144; students can reserve study rooms.

STUDENT LIFE

Housing options: coed. Campus housing is university owned.

Activities and organizations: drama/theater group, student-run newspaper, radio station, choral group, National Society of Collegiate Scholars, Criminology Club, Jazz Club, American Marketing Club, Meteorology, national fraternities, national sororities.

Athletics Member NCAA. All Division III. ***Intercollegiate sports:*** baseball M, basketball M/W, cheerleading W(c), cross-country running M/W, field hockey W, football M, golf M, lacrosse M/W, soccer M/W, softball W, swimming and diving M/W, tennis M/W, volleyball W. ***Intramural sports:*** basketball M/W, football M, ice hockey M(c), rock climbing M(c)/W(c), rugby M(c), soccer M/W, softball W.

Campus security: 24-hour emergency response devices and patrols, student patrols, late-night transport/escort service, controlled dormitory access.

Student services: health clinic, personal/psychological counseling, women's center, veterans affairs office.

COSTS & FINANCIAL AID

Costs (2020–21) ***Tuition:*** state resident $6162 full-time, $257 per credit hour part-time; nonresident $18,436 full-time, $257 per credit hour part-time. ***Required fees:*** $5619 full-time, $303 per credit part-time, $60 per term part-time. ***Room and board:*** $13,921; room only: $8020. Room and board charges vary according to board plan and housing facility.

Financial Aid Of all full-time matriculated undergraduates who enrolled in 2019, 3,183 applied for aid, 2,216 were judged to have need, 282 had their need fully met. 130 Federal Work-Study jobs (averaging $1348). In 2019, 185 non-need-based awards were made. ***Average percent of need met:*** 41. ***Average financial aid package:*** $9582. ***Average need-based loan:*** $4103. ***Average need-based gift aid:*** $5639. ***Average non-need-based aid:*** $4947. ***Average indebtedness upon graduation:*** $38,657.

APPLYING

Standardized Tests *Recommended:* SAT (for admission), SAT or ACT (for admission).

Options: electronic application, deferred entrance.

Application fee: $50.

Required: high school transcript. ***Required for some:*** essay or personal statement, interview.

Application deadlines: rolling (freshmen), rolling (transfers).

Notification: continuous (freshmen), continuous (transfers).

CONTACT

Luis Santiago, Interim Director of Admissions, Western Connecticut State University, 181 White Street, Danbury, CT 06810-6885. *Phone:* 203-8379000. *Toll-free phone:* 877-837-WCSU.

Yale University

New Haven, Connecticut

http://www.yale.edu/

- **Independent** university, founded 1701
- **Urban** 342-acre campus with easy access to New York City
- **Coed** 6,092 undergraduate students, 100% full-time, 51% women, 49% men
- **Most difficult** entrance level, 6% of applicants were admitted

UNDERGRAD STUDENTS

6,088 full-time, 4 part-time. 92% are from out of state; 8% Black or African American, non-Hispanic/Latino; 14% Hispanic/Latino; 20% Asian, non-Hispanic/Latino; 0.1% Native Hawaiian or other Pacific Islander, non-Hispanic/Latino; 0.5% American Indian or Alaska Native, non-Hispanic/Latino; 7% Two or more races, non-Hispanic/Latino; 0.5% Race/ethnicity unknown; 10% international; 0.3% transferred in; 84% live on campus.

Freshmen:

Admission: 36,844 applied, 2,241 admitted, 1,550 enrolled. ***Test scores:*** SAT evidence-based reading and writing scores over 500: 100%; SAT math scores over 500: 100%; SAT evidence-based reading and writing scores over 600: 100%; SAT math scores over 600: 100%; SAT evidence-based reading and writing scores over 700: 83%; SAT math scores over 700: 90%.

Retention: 99% of full-time freshmen returned.

FACULTY

Total: 1,871, 66% full-time, 83% with terminal degrees.

Student/faculty ratio: 6:1.

ACADEMICS

Calendar: semesters. *Degrees:* bachelor's, master's, doctoral, and post-master's certificates.

Special study options: accelerated degree program, advanced placement credit, double majors, English as a second language, honors programs, independent study, internships, part-time degree program, services for LD students, student-designed majors, study abroad, summer session for credit. ***ROTC:*** Army (c), Navy (b), Air Force (b).

Computers: 450 computers/terminals are available on campus for general student use. Students can access the following: campus intranet, computer help desk, free student e-mail accounts, online (class) grades, online (class) registration, online (class) schedules. Campuswide network is available. 100% of college-owned or -operated housing units are wired for high-speed Internet access. Wireless service is available via classrooms, computer centers, computer labs, dorm rooms, learning centers, libraries, student centers.

Library: Sterling Memorial Library plus 15 others. *Books:* 13.8 million (physical), 1.8 million (digital/electronic). Weekly public service hours: 93; students can reserve study rooms.

STUDENT LIFE

Housing options: on-campus residence required through sophomore year; coed, special housing for students with disabilities. Campus housing is university owned. Freshman campus housing is guaranteed.

Activities and organizations: drama/theater group, student-run newspaper, radio and television station, choral group, marching band, national fraternities, national sororities.

Athletics Member NCAA. All Division I except football (Division I-AA). ***Intercollegiate sports:*** archery M(c)/W(c), badminton M(c)/W(c), baseball M, basketball M/W, cheerleading M(c)/W, crew M/W, cross-country running M/W, equestrian sports M(c)/W(c), fencing M/W, field hockey W, golf M/W, gymnastics W, ice hockey M/W, lacrosse M/W, riflery M(c)/W(c), rock climbing M(c)/W(c), rugby M(c)/W(c), sailing M/W, skiing (cross-country) M(c)/W(c), skiing (downhill) M(c)/W(c), soccer M/W, softball W, squash M/W, swimming and diving M/W, table tennis M(c)/W(c), tennis M/W, track and field M/W, ultimate Frisbee M(c)/W(c), volleyball M(c)/W, water polo M(c)/W(c), wrestling M(c)/W(c). ***Intramural sports:*** badminton M(c)/W(c), baseball M, basketball M/W, bowling M/W, crew M/W, cross-country running M/W, field hockey W, football M/W, golf M/W, ice hockey M/W, racquetball M/W, soccer M/W, softball M/W, squash M/W, swimming and diving M/W, table tennis M/W, tennis M/W, ultimate Frisbee M/W, volleyball M/W, water polo M/W.

Campus security: 24-hour emergency response devices and patrols, late-night transport/escort service, controlled dormitory access.

Student services: health clinic, personal/psychological counseling, women's center.

COSTS & FINANCIAL AID

Costs (2020–21) ***Comprehensive fee:*** $74,900 includes full-time tuition ($57,700) and room and board ($17,200). ***College room only:*** $9750. ***Payment plan:*** installment. ***Waivers:*** employees or children of employees.

Financial Aid Of all full-time matriculated undergraduates who enrolled in 2019, 3,519 applied for aid, 3,204 were judged to have need, 3,204 had their need fully met. ***Average percent of need met:*** 100. ***Average financial aid package:*** $61,610. ***Average need-based loan:*** $3108. ***Average need-based gift aid:*** $59,150. ***Average indebtedness upon graduation:*** $15,379. ***Financial aid deadline:*** 3/1.

APPLYING

Standardized Tests *Required:* SAT or ACT (for admission). *Recommended:* SAT Subject Tests (for admission).

Options: electronic application, early action, deferred entrance.

Application fee: $80.

Required: essay or personal statement, high school transcript, 3 letters of recommendation. ***Recommended:*** interview.

Application deadlines: 1/1 (freshmen), 3/1 (transfers), 11/1 (early action).

Notification: 4/1 (freshmen), 5/15 (transfers), 12/15 (early action).

CONTACT

Undergraduate Admissions, Yale University, PO Box 208234, New Haven, CT 06520. *Phone:* 203-432-9300. *E-mail:* student.questions@yale.edu.

DELAWARE

Delaware State University

Dover, Delaware

http://www.desu.edu/

- **State-supported** university, founded 1891, part of Delaware Higher Education Commission
- **Small-town** 400-acre campus
- **Coed**
- **Moderately difficult** entrance level

FACULTY

Student/faculty ratio: 15:1.

ACADEMICS

Calendar: semesters. *Degrees:* certificates, bachelor's, master's, and doctoral.

Library: William C. Jason Library.

STUDENT LIFE

Housing options: coed, men-only, women-only. Campus housing is university owned. Freshman applicants given priority for college housing.

Activities and organizations: drama/theater group, student-run newspaper, radio and television station, choral group, marching band, SGA, NPHC, Women's Senate, RHA, Men's Council, national fraternities, national sororities.

Athletics Member NCAA. All Division I except football (Division I-AA).

Campus security: 24-hour emergency response devices and patrols, student patrols, late-night transport/escort service, controlled dormitory access.

Student services: health clinic, personal/psychological counseling, women's center.

FINANCIAL AID

Financial Aid Of all full-time matriculated undergraduates who enrolled in 2016, 3,301 applied for aid, 2,971 were judged to have need, 467 had their need fully met. In 2016, 91 non-need-based awards were made. ***Average percent of need met:*** 77. ***Average financial aid package:*** $11,234. ***Average need-based loan:*** $3883. ***Average need-based gift aid:*** $5250. ***Average non-need-based aid:*** $4530. ***Average indebtedness upon graduation:*** $36,812.

APPLYING

Options: electronic application, early admission.

Application fee: $35.

Required: high school transcript, minimum 2.0 GPA.

CONTACT

Mrs. Erin Hill, Executive Director for Admissions, Delaware State University, 1200 North DuPont Highway, Dover, DE 19901-2277. *Phone:* 302-857-6351. *Toll-free phone:* 800-845-2544. *Fax:* 302-857-6352. *E-mail:* ehill@desu.edu.

Delaware Technical Community College

Dover, Delaware

https://www.dtcc.edu/

- **State-supported** 4-year, part of Delaware Technical & Community College System
- 14,029 undergraduate students, 29% full-time

UNDERGRAD STUDENTS

4,114 full-time, 9,915 part-time. 26% Black or African American, non-Hispanic/Latino; 14% Hispanic/Latino; 3% Asian, non-Hispanic/Latino; 0.2% Native Hawaiian or other Pacific Islander, non-Hispanic/Latino; 0.4% American Indian or Alaska Native, non-Hispanic/Latino; 4% Two or more races, non-Hispanic/Latino; 3% Race/ethnicity unknown; 1% international; 6% transferred in.

Freshmen:

Admission: 2,940 enrolled.

ACADEMICS
Degrees: certificates, diplomas, associate, and bachelor's.
ROTC: Air Force (c).

APPLYING
Options: deferred entrance.

CONTACT
Delaware Technical Community College, 100 Campus Drive, Dover, DE 19904.

Goldey-Beacom College

Wilmington, Delaware

http://www.gbc.edu/

CONTACT
Mr. Larry Eby, Director of Admissions, Goldey-Beacom College, 4701 Limestone Road, Wilmington, DE 19808. *Phone:* 302-225-6289. *Toll-free phone:* 800-833-4877. *Fax:* 302-996-5408. *E-mail:* admissions@gbc.edu.

University of Delaware

Newark, Delaware

http://www.udel.edu/

- **State-related** university, founded 1743
- **Small-town** 1000-acre campus with easy access to Philadelphia, Baltimore
- **Coed**
- **Moderately difficult** entrance level

FACULTY
Student/faculty ratio: 15:1.

ACADEMICS
Calendar: 4-1-4. *Degrees:* associate, bachelor's, master's, and doctoral.
Library: Hugh Morris Library.

STUDENT LIFE
Housing options: on-campus residence required for freshman year; coed, women-only, special housing for students with disabilities. Campus housing is university owned. Freshman campus housing is guaranteed.

Activities and organizations: drama/theater group, student-run newspaper, radio station, choral group, marching band, national fraternities, national sororities.

Athletics Member NCAA. All Division I except football (Division I-AA).

Campus security: 24-hour emergency response devices and patrols, student patrols, late-night transport/escort service, controlled dormitory access.

Student services: health clinic, personal/psychological counseling, women's center.

FINANCIAL AID
Financial Aid ***Average indebtedness upon graduation:*** $34,144. ***Financial aid deadline:*** 3/15.

APPLYING
Standardized Tests *Required:* SAT or ACT (for admission). *Required for some:* SAT Subject Tests (for admission). *Recommended:* SAT Subject Tests (for admission).

Options: electronic application, early admission, deferred entrance.

Application fee: $75.

Required: essay or personal statement, high school transcript, 1 letter of recommendation.

CONTACT
Dr. Douglas Zander, Director of Admissions, University of Delaware, 122 University Visitors Center, Newark, DE 19716. *Phone:* 302-831-8123. *Fax:* 302-831-6905. *E-mail:* admissions@udel.edu.

Wesley College

Dover, Delaware

http://www.wesley.edu/

- **Independent United Methodist** comprehensive, founded 1873
- **Small-town** 40-acre campus
- **Coed**
- **Moderately difficult** entrance level

FACULTY
Student/faculty ratio: 12:1.

ACADEMICS
Calendar: semesters. *Degrees:* certificates, associate, bachelor's, master's, post-master's, and postbachelor's certificates.
Library: Robert H. Parker Library.

STUDENT LIFE
Housing options: on-campus residence required for freshman year; coed, men-only, women-only. Campus housing is university owned. Freshman campus housing is guaranteed.

Activities and organizations: drama/theater group, student-run newspaper, choral group, Student Activity Board, Student Government Association, National Coeducation Community Service Organization, national fraternities, national sororities.

Athletics Member NCAA. All Division III.

Campus security: 24-hour patrols, controlled dormitory access.

Student services: health clinic, personal/psychological counseling.

FINANCIAL AID
Financial Aid Of all full-time matriculated undergraduates who enrolled in 2011, 1,265 applied for aid, 1,265 were judged to have need, 2 had their need fully met. ***Average percent of need met:*** 39. ***Average financial aid package:*** $13,896. ***Average need-based loan:*** $1858. ***Average need-based gift aid:*** $13,896.

APPLYING
Standardized Tests *Required:* SAT (for admission). *Required for some:* exam for nursing.

Options: electronic application.

Application fee: $25.

Required: essay or personal statement, high school transcript, minimum 2.2 GPA, 1 letter of recommendation. ***Recommended:*** interview.

CONTACT
Mr. Christopher Jester, Assistant Director of Undergraduate Admissions, Wesley College, 120 North State Street, Dover, DE 19901-3875. *Phone:* 302-736-2468. *Toll-free phone:* 800-937-5398. *E-mail:* christopher.jester@wesley.edu.

Wilmington University

New Castle, Delaware

http://www.wilmu.edu/

CONTACT
Ms. Laura Morris, Director of Admissions, Wilmington University, 320 North DuPont Highway, New Castle, DE 19720-6491. *Phone:* 302-295-1179. *Toll-free phone:* 877-967-5464. *E-mail:* undergradadmissions@wilmu.edu.

DISTRICT OF COLUMBIA

American University

Washington, District of Columbia

http://www.american.edu/

- **Independent Methodist** university, founded 1893
- **Suburban** 84-acre campus with easy access to Washington, DC
- **Endowment** $676.4 million
- **Coed** 8,527 undergraduate students, 96% full-time, 61% women, 39% men
- **Very difficult** entrance level, 36% of applicants were admitted

UNDERGRAD STUDENTS
8,207 full-time, 320 part-time. 80% are from out of state; 7% Black or African American, non-Hispanic/Latino; 13% Hispanic/Latino; 6% Asian, non-Hispanic/Latino; 0.1% Native Hawaiian or other Pacific Islander, non-Hispanic/Latino; 0.1% American Indian or Alaska Native, non-Hispanic/Latino; 5% Two or more races, non-Hispanic/Latino; 4% Race/ethnicity unknown; 10% international; 3% transferred in.

Freshmen:
Admission: 18,545 applied, 6,691 admitted, 1,754 enrolled. ***Test scores:*** SAT evidence-based reading and writing scores over 500: 100%; SAT math scores over 500: 98%; ACT scores over 18: 100%; SAT evidence-based reading and writing scores over 600: 87%; SAT math scores over 600: 72%; ACT scores over 24: 93%; SAT evidence-based reading and writing scores over 700: 31%; SAT math scores over 700: 22%; ACT scores over 30: 45%.

Retention: 87% of full-time freshmen returned.

FACULTY
Total: 1,566, 53% full-time, 50% with terminal degrees.

Student/faculty ratio: 11:1.

ACADEMICS
Calendar: semesters. *Degrees:* certificates, bachelor's, master's, doctoral, and postbachelor's certificates.

Special study options: accelerated degree program, distance learning, double majors, English as a second language, honors programs, independent study, internships, part-time degree program, student-designed majors, study abroad. ***ROTC:*** Army (c), Air Force (c).

Unusual degree programs: 3-2 engineering with University of Maryland, College Park.

Computers: 700 computers/terminals and 7,000 ports are available on campus for general student use. Students can access the following: campus intranet, computer help desk, free student e-mail accounts, online (class) grades, online (class) registration, online (class) schedules, online e-support through learning management system. Campuswide network is available. 100% of college-owned or -operated housing units are wired for high-speed Internet access. Wireless service is available via entire campus.
Library: Bender Library plus 1 other. *Books:* 700,000 (physical), 800,000 (digital/electronic); *Serial titles:* 650 (physical), 145,000 (digital/electronic); *Databases:* 500. Study areas open 24 hours, 5–7 days a week; students can reserve study rooms.

STUDENT LIFE
Housing options: coed. Campus housing is university owned. Freshman campus housing is guaranteed.

Activities and organizations: drama/theater group, student-run newspaper, radio and television station, choral group, Kennedy Political Union, Habitat for Humanity, Student government, Amnesty International, Multiple Ethnic and religious organizations, national fraternities, national sororities.

Athletics Member NCAA. All Division I. ***Intercollegiate sports:*** basketball M(s)/W(s), cross-country running M(s)/W(s), field hockey W(s), lacrosse W(s), soccer M(s)/W(s), swimming and diving M/W, track and field M(s)/W(s), volleyball W(s), wrestling M(s). ***Intramural sports:*** baseball M(c)/W(c), basketball M/W, crew M(c)/W(c), equestrian sports M(c)/W(c), fencing W(c), field hockey M(c), football M/W, golf M(c)/W(c), gymnastics M(c)/W(c), ice hockey M(c)/W(c), lacrosse M(c)/W(c), rugby M(c)/W(c), sailing M(c)/W(c), soccer M/W, table tennis M/W, tennis M/W, track and field M/W, ultimate Frisbee M(c)/W(c), volleyball M/W, water polo M/W, weight lifting M.

Campus security: 24-hour emergency response devices and patrols, late-night transport/escort service, controlled dormitory access.

Student services: health clinic, personal/psychological counseling, women's center, veterans affairs office.

COSTS & FINANCIAL AID
Costs (2020–21) ***Comprehensive fee:*** $66,341 includes full-time tuition ($50,542), mandatory fees ($819), and room and board ($14,980). Full-time tuition and fees vary according to course load. Part-time tuition: $1684 per credit hour. Part-time tuition and fees vary according to course load. ***College room only:*** $10,096. Room and board charges vary according to board plan, housing facility, and location. ***Payment plans:*** tuition prepayment, installment. ***Waivers:*** employees or children of employees.

Financial Aid Of all full-time matriculated undergraduates who enrolled in 2019, 4,458 applied for aid, 3,411 were judged to have need, 544 had their need fully met. 1,608 Federal Work-Study jobs (averaging $1885). In 2019, 360 non-need-based awards were made. ***Average percent of need met:*** 74. ***Average financial aid package:*** $35,880. ***Average need-based loan:*** $4358. ***Average need-based gift aid:*** $29,427. ***Average non-need-based aid:*** $12,939. ***Financial aid deadline:*** 1/15.

APPLYING
Options: electronic application, early decision, deferred entrance.

Application fee: $70.

Required: essay or personal statement, high school transcript. ***Recommended:*** 2 letters of recommendation.

Early decision deadline: 11/15 (for plan 1), 1/15 (for plan 2).

Notification: continuous (transfers), 12/31 (early decision plan 1), 2/15 (early decision plan 2).

CONTACT
Dr. Andrea Felder, Assistant Vice Provost, Undergraduate Admissions, American University, 4400 Massachusetts Avenue, NW, Washington, DC 20016-8001. *Phone:* 202-885-6000. *E-mail:* admissions@american.edu.

Bay Atlantic University
Washington, District of Columbia

- university
- **Urban** 1-acre campus with easy access to District of Columbia
- 130 undergraduate students, 100% full-time
- **Noncompetitive** entrance level, 58% of applicants were admitted

UNDERGRAD STUDENTS
130 full-time. Students come from 5 states and territories; 30 other countries; 14% are from out of state.

Freshmen:
Admission: 128 applied, 74 admitted, 43 enrolled. ***Average high school GPA:*** 3.1.

Retention: 80% of full-time freshmen returned.

FACULTY
Total: 25, 100% full-time.

Student/faculty ratio: 10:1.

ACADEMICS
Degrees: certificates, bachelor's, and master's.

Special study options: English as a second language, honors programs, internships, part-time degree program, study abroad, summer session for credit.

Computers: 15 computers/terminals are available on campus for general student use. Students can access the following: campus intranet, computer help desk, free student e-mail accounts, online (class) grades, online (class) registration, online (class) schedules. Campuswide network is available. Wireless service is available via entire campus.
Library: BAU Library. *Books:* 2,000 (physical), 450,000 (digital/electronic); *Databases:* 3.

STUDENT LIFE
Housing options: Campus housing is university owned. Freshman campus housing is guaranteed.

Activities and organizations: drama/theater group, Student Government/International Counsel, Master Networking, Book Club, Self Defense Club, Theater Club.

Campus security: 24-hour patrols, controlled dormitory access.

Student services: personal/psychological counseling.

APPLYING
Options: electronic application.

Required: essay or personal statement, high school transcript, minimum 1.8 GPA, 2 letters of recommendation.

CONTACT
Admissions, Bay Atlantic University, 1510 H St NW, Washington, DC 20005. *Phone:* 844-922-8228. *E-mail:* admissions@bau.edu.

The Catholic University of America

Washington, District of Columbia

http://www.catholic.edu/

- **Independent** university, founded 1887, affiliated with Roman Catholic Church
- **Urban** 176-acre campus with easy access to Washington DC
- **Coed** 3,279 undergraduate students, 97% full-time, 55% women, 45% men
- **Moderately difficult** entrance level, 85% of applicants were admitted

UNDERGRAD STUDENTS

3,168 full-time, 111 part-time. Students come from 48 states and territories; 35 other countries; 96% are from out of state; 4% Black or African American, non-Hispanic/Latino; 14% Hispanic/Latino; 3% Asian, non-Hispanic/Latino; 0.2% American Indian or Alaska Native, non-Hispanic/Latino; 4% Two or more races, non-Hispanic/Latino; 2% Race/ethnicity unknown; 5% international; 2% transferred in; 59% live on campus.

Freshmen:

Admission: 5,668 applied, 4,838 admitted, 818 enrolled. ***Average high school GPA:*** 3.5. ***Test scores:*** SAT evidence-based reading and writing scores over 500: 96%; SAT math scores over 500: 92%; ACT scores over 18: 96%; SAT evidence-based reading and writing scores over 600: 66%; SAT math scores over 600: 53%; ACT scores over 24: 78%; SAT evidence-based reading and writing scores over 700: 15%; SAT math scores over 700: 13%; ACT scores over 30: 23%.

Retention: 88% of full-time freshmen returned.

FACULTY

Total: 702, 54% full-time, 47% with terminal degrees.

Student/faculty ratio: 10:1.

ACADEMICS

Calendar: semesters. *Degrees:* certificates, bachelor's, master's, doctoral, post-master's, and postbachelor's certificates.

Special study options: accelerated degree program, adult/continuing education programs, advanced placement credit, cooperative education, distance learning, double majors, English as a second language, external degree program, honors programs, independent study, internships, off-campus study, part-time degree program, services for LD students, study abroad, summer session for credit. ***ROTC:*** Army (c), Navy (c), Air Force (c).

Unusual degree programs: 3-2 business administration; engineering; nursing; social work; architecture, accounting, education, psychology.

Computers: 542 computers/terminals and 13,403 ports are available on campus for general student use. Students can access the following: campus intranet, computer help desk, free student e-mail accounts, online (class) grades, online (class) registration, online (class) schedules. Campuswide network is available. 100% of college-owned or -operated housing units are wired for high-speed Internet access. Wireless service is available via entire campus.

Library: Mullen Library plus 1 other. *Books:* 754,067 (physical), 357,968 (digital/electronic); *Serial titles:* 14,610 (physical), 129,482 (digital/electronic); *Databases:* 232. Weekly public service hours: 97.

STUDENT LIFE

Housing options: on-campus residence required through sophomore year; men-only, women-only. Campus housing is university owned. Freshman campus housing is guaranteed.

Activities and organizations: drama/theater group, student-run newspaper, radio station, choral group, College Republicans, Habitat for Humanity, Student Nurse's Association, Cardinals for Life, College Democrats, national fraternities, national sororities.

Athletics Member NCAA. All Division III. ***Intercollegiate sports:*** baseball M, basketball M/W, crew M/W, cross-country running M/W, field hockey W, football M, golf M/W, lacrosse M/W, soccer M/W, softball W, swimming and diving M/W, tennis M/W, track and field M/W, volleyball W. ***Intramural sports:*** badminton M/W, basketball M/W, cheerleading M(c)/W(c), football M, ice hockey M(c), lacrosse M(c), racquetball M/W, rowing M(c)/W(c), rugby M(c)/W(c), sailing M(c)/W(c), soccer M/W, softball M/W, tennis M/W, track and field M/W, ultimate Frisbee M(c)/W(c), volleyball M/W.

Campus security: 24-hour emergency response devices and patrols, late-night transport/escort service, controlled dormitory access, controlled access of academic buildings.

Student services: health clinic, personal/psychological counseling, legal services.

COSTS & FINANCIAL AID

Costs (2020–21) ***Comprehensive fee:*** $65,236 includes full-time tuition ($48,600), mandatory fees ($816), and room and board ($15,820). Full-time tuition and fees vary according to degree level and program. Part-time tuition and fees vary according to degree level, program, and reciprocity agreements. ***Required fees:*** $1925 per credit hour part-time. ***Room and board:*** Room and board charges vary according to board plan and housing facility. ***Payment plan:*** installment. ***Waivers:*** employees or children of employees.

Financial Aid Of all full-time matriculated undergraduates who enrolled in 2019, 2,065 applied for aid, 1,747 were judged to have need, 735 had their need fully met. 313 Federal Work-Study jobs (averaging $1948). In 2019, 1114 non-need-based awards were made. ***Average percent of need met:*** 80. ***Average financial aid package:*** $33,655. ***Average need-based loan:*** $4413. ***Average need-based gift aid:*** $30,418. ***Average non-need-based aid:*** $22,783. ***Average indebtedness upon graduation:*** $46,702.

APPLYING

Options: electronic application, early decision, early action, deferred entrance.

Required: essay or personal statement, high school transcript, 1 letter of recommendation. ***Recommended:*** minimum 3.0 GPA, interview.

Application deadlines: 1/15 (freshmen), 6/1 (transfers), 11/1 (early action).

Early decision deadline: 11/15 (for plan 1), 1/15 (for plan 2).

Notification: 3/15 (freshmen), 12/20 (early decision plan 1), 2/15 (early decision plan 2), 12/20 (early action).

CONTACT

James Dewey-Rosenfeld, Dean of Undergraduate Admission, The Catholic University of America, 102 Father OâConnell Hall, 620 Michigan Avenue, NE, Washington, DC 20064. *Phone:* 202-319-5305. *Toll-free phone:* 800-673-2772. *Fax:* 202-319-6533. *E-mail:* cua-admissions@cua.edu.

Gallaudet University

Washington, District of Columbia

http://www.gallaudet.edu/

- **Independent** university, founded 1864
- **Urban** 99-acre campus
- **Coed** 1,075 undergraduate students, 93% full-time, 54% women, 46% men
- **Moderately difficult** entrance level, 61% of applicants were admitted

UNDERGRAD STUDENTS

1,005 full-time, 70 part-time. 96% are from out of state; 17% Black or African American, non-Hispanic/Latino; 15% Hispanic/Latino; 5% Asian, non-Hispanic/Latino; 0.9% Native Hawaiian or other Pacific Islander, non-Hispanic/Latino; 0.9% American Indian or Alaska Native, non-Hispanic/Latino; 3% Two or more races, non-Hispanic/Latino; 7% Race/ethnicity unknown; 5% international; 7% transferred in; 85% live on campus.

Freshmen:

Admission: 477 applied, 292 admitted, 183 enrolled. ***Average high school GPA:*** 3.2. ***Test scores:*** SAT evidence-based reading and writing scores over 500: 44%; SAT math scores over 500: 28%; ACT scores over 18: 38%; SAT evidence-based reading and writing scores over 600: 10%; SAT math scores over 600: 10%; ACT scores over 24: 10%; SAT evidence-based reading and writing scores over 700: 3%; ACT scores over 30: 1%.

Retention: 75% of full-time freshmen returned.

FACULTY

Total: 260, 73% full-time, 55% with terminal degrees.

Student/faculty ratio: 6:1.

ACADEMICS

Calendar: semesters. *Degrees:* bachelor's, master's, doctoral, post-master's, and postbachelor's certificates (Undergraduate programs are open primarily to the students with hearing-impairments).

Special study options: academic remediation for entering students, adult/continuing education programs, advanced placement credit, distance learning, double majors, honors programs, independent study, off-campus study, part-time degree program, services for LD students, student-designed majors, study abroad, summer session for credit.

Computers: 400 computers/terminals are available on campus for general student use. Students can access the following: campus intranet, computer help desk, free student e-mail accounts, online (class) grades, online (class) registration, online (class) schedules. Campuswide network is available. 100% of college-owned or -operated housing units are wired for high-speed Internet access. Wireless service is available via entire campus.

Library: Merrill Learning Center. *Books:* 121,359 (physical), 547,506 (digital/electronic); *Serial titles:* 4,142 (physical), 71,930 (digital/electronic); *Databases:* 79. Weekly public service hours: 90; students can reserve study rooms.

STUDENT LIFE

Housing options: coed. Campus housing is university owned.

Activities and organizations: drama/theater group, student-run newspaper, television station, Student Body Government, The Buff and Blue, Rainbow Society, Green Grow, national fraternities, national sororities.

Athletics Member NCAA. All Division III. ***Intercollegiate sports:*** baseball M, basketball M/W, cheerleading M(c)/W(c), cross-country running M/W, football M, soccer M/W, softball W, swimming and diving M/W, track and field M/W, volleyball W. ***Intramural sports:*** basketball M/W, football M/W, table tennis M/W, ultimate Frisbee M/W, volleyball M/W.

Campus security: 24-hour emergency response devices and patrols, late-night transport/escort service, controlled dormitory access.

Student services: health clinic, personal/psychological counseling.

COSTS & FINANCIAL AID

Costs (2020–21) ***Tuition:*** $16,512 full-time, $688 per credit hour part-time. Full-time tuition and fees vary according to course load. Part-time tuition and fees vary according to course load. ***Required fees:*** $526 full-time. ***Room only:*** $8000. Room and board charges vary according to board plan and housing facility. ***Payment plans:*** installment, deferred payment. ***Waivers:*** employees or children of employees.

Financial Aid Of all full-time matriculated undergraduates who enrolled in 2018, 1,020 applied for aid, 1,008 were judged to have need, 248 had their need fully met. In 2018, 52 non-need-based awards were made. ***Average percent of need met:*** 75. ***Average financial aid package:*** $25,111. ***Average need-based loan:*** $3922. ***Average need-based gift aid:*** $29,145. ***Average non-need-based aid:*** $5143. ***Average indebtedness upon graduation:*** $1.1 million.

APPLYING

Standardized Tests *Required:* SAT or ACT (for admission). *Recommended:* ACT (for admission).

Options: electronic application, deferred entrance.

Application fee: $50.

Required: essay or personal statement, high school transcript, 2 letters of recommendation, audiogram. ***Required for some:*** interview.

Notification: continuous (freshmen), continuous (transfers).

CONTACT

Gallaudet University, 800 Florida Avenue, NE, Washington, DC 20002-3625. *Phone:* 202-651-5750. *Toll-free phone:* 800-995-0550.

Georgetown University

Washington, District of Columbia

http://www.georgetown.edu/

- **Independent Roman Catholic (Jesuit)** university, founded 1789
- **Urban** 104-acre campus with easy access to Washington, DC
- **Coed** 7,459 undergraduate students, 94% full-time, 56% women, 44% men
- **Most difficult** entrance level, 14% of applicants were admitted

UNDERGRAD STUDENTS

6,990 full-time, 469 part-time. Students come from 52 states and territories; 105 other countries; 98% are from out of state; 6% Black or African American, non-Hispanic/Latino; 10% Hispanic/Latino; 9% Asian, non-Hispanic/Latino; 5% Two or more races, non-Hispanic/Latino; 5% Race/ethnicity unknown; 15% international; 1% transferred in; 77% live on campus.

Freshmen:

Admission: 22,764 applied, 3,269 admitted, 1,621 enrolled. ***Test scores:*** SAT evidence-based reading and writing scores over 500: 100%; SAT math scores over 500: 100%; ACT scores over 18: 100%; SAT evidence-based reading and writing scores over 600: 96%; SAT math scores over 600: 94%; ACT scores over 24: 98%; SAT evidence-based reading and writing scores over 700: 71%; SAT math scores over 700: 73%; ACT scores over 30: 87%.

Retention: 96% of full-time freshmen returned.

FACULTY

Total: 2,322, 49% full-time, 49% with terminal degrees.

Student/faculty ratio: 11:1.

ACADEMICS

Calendar: semesters. *Degrees:* certificates, bachelor's, master's, doctoral, post-master's, and postbachelor's certificates.

Special study options: academic remediation for entering students, adult/continuing education programs, advanced placement credit, distance learning, double majors, English as a second language, honors programs, independent study, internships, off-campus study, part-time degree program, services for LD students, student-designed majors, study abroad, summer session for credit. ***ROTC:*** Army (b), Navy (c), Air Force (c).

Unusual degree programs: 3-2 foreign service.

Computers: 430 computers/terminals and 1,000 ports are available on campus for general student use. Students can access the following: computer help desk, free student e-mail accounts, online (class) grades, online (class) registration, online (class) schedules. Campuswide network is available. 100% of college-owned or -operated housing units are wired for high-speed Internet access. Wireless service is available via entire campus.

Library: Joseph Mark Lauinger Memorial Library plus 6 others. *Books:* 2.4 million (physical), 1.9 million (digital/electronic); *Serial titles:* 52,479 (physical), 275,836 (digital/electronic); *Databases:* 1,556. Weekly public service hours: 100; study areas open 24 hours, 5–7 days a week; students can reserve study rooms.

STUDENT LIFE

Housing options: on-campus residence required through sophomore year; coed, special housing for students with disabilities. Campus housing is university owned. Freshman campus housing is guaranteed.

Activities and organizations: drama/theater group, student-run newspaper, radio and television station, choral group, Georgetown University Student Association (Student Government), International Relations Club, College Democrats, Georgetown University Grilling Society, Black Student Alliance.

Athletics Member NCAA. All Division I except football (Division I-AA). ***Intercollegiate sports:*** baseball M(s), basketball M(s)/W(s), crew M(s)/W(s), cross-country running M(s)/W(s), field hockey W(s), golf M(s)/W(s), ice hockey M(c), lacrosse M(s)/W(s), rugby M(c)/W(c), sailing M/W, soccer M(s)/W(s), softball W(s), swimming and diving M/W(s), tennis M/W(s), track and field M(s)/W(s), ultimate Frisbee M(c)/W(c), volleyball M(c)/W(s), water polo M(c). ***Intramural sports:*** basketball M/W, cross-country running M/W, football M/W, golf M/W, racquetball M/W, soccer M/W, softball M/W, squash M/W, table tennis M/W, tennis M/W, track and field M/W, ultimate Frisbee M, volleyball M/W.

Campus security: 24-hour emergency response devices and patrols, late-night transport/escort service, controlled dormitory access, student guards at residence halls and academic facilities.

Student services: health clinic, personal/psychological counseling, women's center, veterans affairs office.

COSTS & FINANCIAL AID

Costs (2019–20) ***Tuition:*** $55,440 full-time, $2310 per credit hour part-time. ***Required fees:*** $354 full-time. ***Room only:*** $11,404.

Financial Aid Of all full-time matriculated undergraduates who enrolled in 2019, 3,294 applied for aid, 2,642 were judged to have need, 2,642 had their need fully met. 2,545 Federal Work-Study jobs (averaging $2924). ***Average percent of need met:*** 100. ***Average financial aid package:*** $50,261. ***Average need-based loan:*** $4370. ***Average need-based gift aid:*** $46,304. ***Average indebtedness upon graduation:*** $26,759. ***Financial aid deadline:*** 2/1.

APPLYING
Standardized Tests *Required:* SAT or ACT (for admission). *Recommended:* SAT Subject Tests (for admission).

Options: electronic application, early action, deferred entrance.

Application fee: $75.

Required: essay or personal statement, high school transcript, 2 letters of recommendation, interview.

Application deadlines: 1/10 (freshmen), 3/1 (transfers), 11/1 (early action).

Notification: 4/1 (freshmen), 6/1 (transfers), 12/15 (early action).

CONTACT
Dean Charles A. Deacon, Dean of Undergraduate Admissions, Georgetown University, 37th and O Street, NW, Washington, DC 20057. *Phone:* 202-687-3600. *Fax:* 202-687-5084.

The George Washington University

Washington, District of Columbia

http://www.gwu.edu/

- **Independent** university, founded 1821
- **Urban** 36-acre campus
- **Coed** 12,484 undergraduate students, 89% full-time, 62% women, 38% men
- **Most difficult** entrance level, 41% of applicants were admitted

UNDERGRAD STUDENTS
11,102 full-time, 1,382 part-time. 96% are from out of state; 8% Black or African American, non-Hispanic/Latino; 11% Hispanic/Latino; 11% Asian, non-Hispanic/Latino; 0.1% Native Hawaiian or other Pacific Islander, non-Hispanic/Latino; 0.0% American Indian or Alaska Native, non-Hispanic/Latino; 4% Two or more races, non-Hispanic/Latino; 4% Race/ethnicity unknown; 12% international; 5% transferred in; 58% live on campus.

Freshmen:
Admission: 26,978 applied, 11,019 admitted, 2,619 enrolled. ***Test scores:*** SAT evidence-based reading and writing scores over 500: 100%; SAT math scores over 500: 100%; ACT scores over 18: 100%; SAT evidence-based reading and writing scores over 600: 87%; SAT math scores over 600: 90%; ACT scores over 24: 97%; SAT evidence-based reading and writing scores over 700: 38%; SAT math scores over 700: 52%; ACT scores over 30: 71%.

Retention: 92% of full-time freshmen returned.

FACULTY
Total: 2,658, 44% full-time.

Student/faculty ratio: 13:1.

ACADEMICS
Calendar: semesters. *Degrees:* certificates, associate, bachelor's, master's, doctoral, post-master's, and postbachelor's certificates.

Special study options: accelerated degree program, adult/continuing education programs, advanced placement credit, cooperative education, distance learning, double majors, honors programs, independent study, internships, off-campus study, part-time degree program, services for LD students, student-designed majors, study abroad, summer session for credit. ***ROTC:*** Army (c), Navy (b), Air Force (c).

Unusual degree programs: 3-2 business administration; engineering; chemical toxicology, art therapy, economics, engineering economics, operations research.

Computers: Campuswide network is available.

Library: Gelman Library.

STUDENT LIFE
Housing options: on-campus residence required through sophomore year; coed, women-only. Campus housing is university owned. Freshman campus housing is guaranteed.

Activities and organizations: drama/theater group, student-run newspaper, radio and television station, choral group, marching band, Program Board, Student Association, Residence Hall Association, College Democrats, College Republicans, national fraternities, national sororities.

Athletics Member NCAA. All Division I. ***Intercollegiate sports:*** baseball M(s), basketball M(s)/W(s), crew M(s)/W(s), cross-country running M(s)/W(s), golf M(s), gymnastics W(s), soccer M(s)/W(s), swimming and diving M(s)/W(s), tennis M(s)/W(s), volleyball W(s), water polo M(s). ***Intramural sports:*** badminton M(c)/W(c), basketball M/W, bowling M(c)/W(c), equestrian sports M(c)/W(c), fencing M(c)/W(c), football M/W, lacrosse M(c), racquetball M/W, rugby M(c), sailing M(c)/W(c), soccer M/W, softball M/W, squash M(c)/W, swimming and diving M/W, tennis M/W, volleyball M(c)/W, water polo M/W.

Campus security: 24-hour emergency response devices and patrols, late-night transport/escort service, controlled dormitory access.

Student services: health clinic, personal/psychological counseling, legal services.

COSTS & FINANCIAL AID
Costs (2019–20) ***Comprehensive fee:*** $71,235 includes full-time tuition ($56,845), mandatory fees ($90), and room and board ($14,300). Full-time tuition and fees vary according to student level. Part-time tuition: $1625 per credit hour. Part-time tuition and fees vary according to course load. No tuition increase for student's term of enrollment. ***Required fees:*** $3 per credit hour part-time. ***Room and board:*** Room and board charges vary according to housing facility. ***Payment plan:*** installment. ***Waivers:*** employees or children of employees.

Financial Aid Of all full-time matriculated undergraduates who enrolled in 2018, 6,476 applied for aid, 5,373 were judged to have need, 2,027 had their need fully met. In 2018, 3196 non-need-based awards were made. ***Average percent of need met:*** 84. ***Average financial aid package:*** $47,368. ***Average need-based loan:*** $7098. ***Average need-based gift aid:*** $32,089. ***Average non-need-based aid:*** $20,455. ***Average indebtedness upon graduation:*** $34,768. ***Financial aid deadline:*** 2/1.

APPLYING
Standardized Tests *Required for some:* SAT or ACT (for admission), SAT and SAT Subject Tests or ACT (for admission).

Options: electronic application, early admission, early decision, deferred entrance.

Application fee: $80.

Required: essay or personal statement, high school transcript, 2 letters of recommendation.

Early decision deadline: 11/1 (for plan 1), 1/1 (for plan 2).

Notification: 4/1 (freshmen), continuous (transfers), 12/15 (early decision plan 1), 2/1 (early decision plan 2).

CONTACT
The George Washington University, 2121 I Street, NW, Washington, DC 20052. *Phone:* 202-994-6040.

Howard University

Washington, District of Columbia

http://www.howard.edu/

- **Independent** university, founded 1867
- **Urban** 257-acre campus with easy access to Washington
- **Endowment** $692.3 million
- **Coed** 6,526 undergraduate students, 96% full-time, 71% women, 29% men
- **Moderately difficult** entrance level, 36% of applicants were admitted

UNDERGRAD STUDENTS
6,269 full-time, 257 part-time. Students come from 53 states and territories; 39 other countries; 98% are from out of state; 73% Black or African American, non-Hispanic/Latino; 6% Hispanic/Latino; 1% Asian, non-Hispanic/Latino; 0.2% Native Hawaiian or other Pacific Islander, non-Hispanic/Latino; 2% American Indian or Alaska Native, non-Hispanic/Latino; 3% Two or more races, non-Hispanic/Latino; 9%

Race/ethnicity unknown; 5% international; 3% transferred in; 78% live on campus.

Freshmen:

Admission: 21,006 applied, 7,578 admitted, 1,925 enrolled. ***Average high school GPA:*** 3.6. ***Test scores:*** SAT evidence-based reading and writing scores over 500: 99%; SAT math scores over 500: 98%; ACT scores over 18: 99%; SAT evidence-based reading and writing scores over 600: 62%; SAT math scores over 600: 44%; ACT scores over 24: 59%; SAT evidence-based reading and writing scores over 700: 8%; SAT math scores over 700: 7%; ACT scores over 30: 8%.

Retention: 86% of full-time freshmen returned.

FACULTY

Total: 1,114, 80% full-time, 88% with terminal degrees.

Student/faculty ratio: 10:1.

ACADEMICS

Calendar: semesters. *Degrees:* certificates, bachelor's, master's, doctoral, post-master's, and postbachelor's certificates.

Special study options: academic remediation for entering students, accelerated degree program, advanced placement credit, cooperative education, distance learning, double majors, honors programs, independent study, internships, off-campus study, part-time degree program, study abroad, summer session for credit. ***ROTC:*** Army (b), Air Force (b).

Unusual degree programs: 3-2 medicine.

Computers: 1,968 computers/terminals are available on campus for general student use. Students can access the following: campus intranet, computer help desk, free student e-mail accounts, online (class) grades, online (class) registration, online (class) schedules, student residential network. Campuswide network is available. 100% of college-owned or -operated housing units are wired for high-speed Internet access. Wireless service is available via entire campus.

Library: Howard University Libraries plus 7 others. *Books:* 1.5 million (physical), 442,313 (digital/electronic); *Serial titles:* 80,661 (physical), 4,338 (digital/electronic); *Databases:* 156. Weekly public service hours: 80; students can reserve study rooms.

STUDENT LIFE

Housing options: on-campus residence required through sophomore year; coed, women-only. Campus housing is university owned. Freshman campus housing is guaranteed.

Activities and organizations: drama/theater group, student-run newspaper, radio and television station, choral group, marching band, Howard University Student Association, Undergraduate Student Assembly, Campus Pals, International Student Organization, Entrepreneurial Society, Howard University, national fraternities, national sororities.

Athletics Member NCAA. All Division I except football (Division I-AA). ***Intercollegiate sports:*** basketball M(s)/W(s), bowling W(s), cross-country running M(s)/W(s), lacrosse W(s), soccer M(s)/W(s), softball W(s), swimming and diving M(s)/W(s), tennis M(s)/W(s), track and field M(s)/W(s), volleyball W(s). ***Intramural sports:*** basketball M/W, golf M(c)/W(c), soccer M/W, volleyball M/W, water polo M/W.

Campus security: 24-hour emergency response devices and patrols, student patrols, late-night transport/escort service, controlled dormitory access, security lighting.

Student services: health clinic, personal/psychological counseling, women's center, legal services, veterans affairs office.

COSTS & FINANCIAL AID

Costs (2020–21) ***Comprehensive fee:*** $40,820 includes full-time tuition ($26,464), mandatory fees ($1976), and room and board ($12,380). Part-time tuition: $1108 per credit hour. ***College room only:*** $9030. Room and board charges vary according to board plan and housing facility. ***Payment plan:*** installment. ***Waivers:*** children of alumni and employees or children of employees.

Financial Aid Of all full-time matriculated undergraduates who enrolled in 2015, 5,440 applied for aid, 4,942 were judged to have need, 324 had their need fully met. In 2015, 486 non-need-based awards were made. ***Average percent of need met:*** 62. ***Average financial aid package:*** $14,601. ***Average need-based loan:*** $4184. ***Average need-based gift aid:*** $8264. ***Average non-need-based aid:*** $27,095. ***Average indebtedness upon graduation:*** $26,181. ***Financial aid deadline:*** 5/1.

APPLYING

Standardized Tests *Required:* SAT (for admission), ACT (for admission), SAT or ACT (for admission), High School GPA (on a 4.0 scale) (for admission). *Recommended:* SAT and SAT Subject Tests or ACT (for admission).

Options: electronic application, early admission, early decision, early action, deferred entrance.

Application fee: $45.

Required: essay or personal statement, high school transcript, 2 letters of recommendation, Standardized test scores required; campus visit recommended. ***Recommended:*** Standardized test scores required; campus visit recommended.

Application deadlines: 2/15 (freshmen), 4/1 (transfers), 11/1 (early action).

Early decision deadline: 11/1.

Notification: continuous until 4/9 (freshmen), continuous (transfers), 12/20 (early action).

CONTACT

Mrs. LaTrice Byam, Executive Director of Admissions and Registrar, Howard University, 2400 Sixth Street NW, Washington, DC 20059. *Phone:* 202-806-2702. *Toll-free phone:* 800-822-6363. *Fax:* 202-806-4467. *E-mail:* latrice.byam@howard.edu.

National Intelligence University

Washington, District of Columbia

http://www.ni-u.edu/

- **Federally supported** upper-level, founded 1963
- **Coed**

FACULTY

Student/faculty ratio: 4:1.

ACADEMICS

Calendar: quarters.

CONTACT

National Intelligence University, Washington, DC 20340-5100.

Strayer University–Takoma Park Campus

Washington, District of Columbia

http://www.strayer.edu/district-columbia/takoma-park/

CONTACT

Strayer University–Takoma Park Campus, 6830 Laurel Street, NW, Washington, DC 20012. *Toll-free phone:* 888-311-0355.

Strayer University–Washington Campus

Washington, District of Columbia

http://www.strayer.edu/district-columbia/washington/

CONTACT

Strayer University–Washington Campus, 1133 15th Street, NW, Washington, DC 20025. *Toll-free phone:* 888-311-0355.

Trinity Washington University

Washington, District of Columbia

http://www.trinitydc.edu/

CONTACT

Director of Admissions, Trinity Washington University, 125 Michigan Avenue, NE, Washington, DC 20017-1094. *Phone:* 800-492-6882. *Toll-free phone:* 800-IWANTTC. *E-mail:* admissions@trinitydc.edu.

University of the District of Columbia
Washington, District of Columbia
http://www.udc.edu/

CONTACT
Ms. Nicole L. Daniels, Director of Undergraduate Recruitment and Admissions, University of the District of Columbia, 4200 Connecticut Avenue NW, Washington, DC 20008. *Phone:* 202-274-6430. *Fax:* 202-274-5553. *E-mail:* nicole.daniels@udc.edu.

University of the Potomac
Washington, District of Columbia
http://www.potomac.edu/

CONTACT
Gina Rice-Holland, Director of Admissions, University of the Potomac, 1401 H Street NW, Suite 100, Washington, DC 20005. *Phone:* 202-274-2338. *Toll-free phone:* 888-686-0876. *E-mail:* gina.riceholland@potomac.edu.

FLORIDA

AdventHealth University
Orlando, Florida
http://www.ahu.edu/

- **Independent** comprehensive, founded 1992
- **Urban** 9-acre campus with easy access to Orlando
- **Endowment** $8.6 million
- **Coed** 1,234 undergraduate students, 32% full-time, 79% women, 21% men
- **Minimally difficult** entrance level, 51% of applicants were admitted

UNDERGRAD STUDENTS
390 full-time, 844 part-time. Students come from 35 states and territories; 14 other countries; 23% are from out of state; 17% Black or African American, non-Hispanic/Latino; 32% Hispanic/Latino; 7% Asian, non-Hispanic/Latino; 0.5% Native Hawaiian or other Pacific Islander, non-Hispanic/Latino; 0.3% American Indian or Alaska Native, non-Hispanic/Latino; 4% Two or more races, non-Hispanic/Latino; 2% Race/ethnicity unknown; 3% international; 12% transferred in; 10% live on campus.

Freshmen:
Admission: 283 applied, 143 admitted, 64 enrolled. ***Test scores:*** SAT evidence-based reading and writing scores over 500: 81%; SAT math scores over 500: 75%; ACT scores over 18: 90%; SAT evidence-based reading and writing scores over 600: 27%; SAT math scores over 600: 16%; ACT scores over 24: 21%; SAT evidence-based reading and writing scores over 700: 2%; SAT math scores over 700: 2%.

Retention: 61% of full-time freshmen returned.

FACULTY
Total: 246, 37% full-time, 41% with terminal degrees.

Student/faculty ratio: 6:1.

ACADEMICS
Calendar: trimesters. *Degrees:* certificates, associate, bachelor's, master's, and doctoral.

Special study options: academic remediation for entering students, distance learning, double majors, freshman honors college, honors programs, independent study, internships, services for LD students, summer session for credit.

Computers: 51 computers/terminals are available on campus for general student use. Students can access the following: campus intranet, computer help desk, free student e-mail accounts, online (class) grades, online (class) registration, online (class) schedules. Campuswide network is available. 100% of college-owned or -operated housing units are wired for high-speed Internet access. Wireless service is available via entire campus.

Library: R. A. Williams Library. *Books:* 12,089 (physical), 21,228 (digital/electronic); *Serial titles:* 20 (physical), 44,390 (digital/electronic); *Databases:* 122. Weekly public service hours: 65; students can reserve study rooms.

STUDENT LIFE
Housing options: coed. Campus housing is university owned.

Activities and organizations: Student Nursing Association, Student Occupational Therapy Association, Pre Physician Assistant, Pre PT/OT, Campus Ministries.

Campus security: 24-hour emergency response devices and patrols, controlled dormitory access.

Student services: personal/psychological counseling.

COSTS & FINANCIAL AID
Costs (2020–21) ***Tuition:*** $15,750 full-time, $525 per credit hour part-time. ***Required fees:*** $600 full-time, $300 per term part-time. ***Room only:*** $4200. ***Payment plans:*** installment, deferred payment. ***Waivers:*** employees or children of employees.

Financial Aid Of all full-time matriculated undergraduates who enrolled in 2018, 498 applied for aid, 451 were judged to have need, 16 had their need fully met. In 2018, 19 non-need-based awards were made. ***Average percent of need met:*** 30. ***Average financial aid package:*** $9634. ***Average need-based loan:*** $3592. ***Average need-based gift aid:*** $7319. ***Average non-need-based aid:*** $2564. ***Average indebtedness upon graduation:*** $38,990. ***Financial aid deadline:*** 7/15.

APPLYING
Standardized Tests *Required:* SAT or ACT (for admission). *Recommended:* TOEFL; Recommended only for non-native English speakers.

Options: electronic application, early admission, early action, deferred entrance.

Application fee: $20.

Required: high school transcript, minimum 2.7 GPA, interview.

Application deadlines: 7/1 (freshmen), 7/1 (out-of-state freshmen), 7/1 (transfers), 5/1 (early action).

Notification: 7/15 (freshmen), 7/15 (out-of-state freshmen), 7/15 (transfers).

CONTACT
AdventHealth University, 671 Winyah Drive, Orlando, FL 32803. *Phone:* 407-303-7742. *Toll-free phone:* 800-500-7747.

Albizu University - Miami
Miami, Florida
http://www.albizu.edu/

CONTACT
Ms. Maria Elena Torres, Admissions Officer, Albizu University - Miami, 2173 NW 99 Avenue, Miami, FL 33172. *Phone:* 305-593-1223 Ext. 3134. *Toll-free phone:* 888-GO-TO-CAU (in-state); 800-GO-TO-CAU (out-of-state). *Fax:* 305-593-1854. *E-mail:* matorres@albizu.edu.

Altierus Career College - Tampa
Tampa, Florida
http://www.altierus.edu/

CONTACT
Altierus Career College - Tampa, 3319 West Hillsborough Avenue, Tampa, FL 33614. *Phone:* 813-879-6000 Ext. 129.

American College for Medical Careers
Orlando, Florida
http://www.acmc.edu/

CONTACT
American College for Medical Careers, 5959 Lake Ellenor Drive, Orlando, FL 32809. *Toll-free phone:* 888-599-7887.

Argosy University, Tampa

Tampa, Florida

http://www.argosy.edu/locations/tampa/

CONTACT
Argosy University, Tampa, 1403 North Howard Avenue, Tampa, FL 33607. *Phone:* 813-393-5290. *Toll-free phone:* 800-850-6488.

The Art Institute of Tampa, a branch of Miami International University of Art & Design

Tampa, Florida

http://www.artinstitutes.edu/tampa/

CONTACT
The Art Institute of Tampa, a branch of Miami International University of Art & Design, Parkside at Tampa Bay Park, 4401 North Himes Avenue, Suite 150, Tampa, FL 33614. *Phone:* 813-873-2112. *Toll-free phone:* 866-703-3277.

Atlantis University

Miami, Florida

http://www.atlantisuniversity.edu/

CONTACT
Atlantis University, 1442 Biscayne Boulevard, Miami, FL 33132.

Ave Maria University

Ave Maria, Florida

http://www.avemaria.edu/

CONTACT
Ave Maria University, 5050 Ave Maria Boulevard, Ave Maria, FL 34142. *Phone:* 239-280-2487. *Toll-free phone:* 877-283-8648. *Fax:* 239-280-2559.

The Baptist College of Florida

Graceville, Florida

http://www.baptistcollege.edu/

- **Independent Southern Baptist** comprehensive, founded 1943
- **Small-town** 250-acre campus
- **Endowment** $7.9 million
- **Coed** 427 undergraduate students, 52% full-time, 50% women, 50% men
- **Noncompetitive** entrance level, 94% of applicants were admitted

UNDERGRAD STUDENTS
224 full-time, 203 part-time. Students come from 3 states and territories; 2 other countries; 27% are from out of state; 7% Black or African American, non-Hispanic/Latino; 2% Hispanic/Latino; 1% Asian, non-Hispanic/Latino; 0.3% Native Hawaiian or other Pacific Islander, non-Hispanic/Latino; 0.7% American Indian or Alaska Native, non-Hispanic/Latino; 1% Two or more races, non-Hispanic/Latino; 10% Race/ethnicity unknown; 0.3% international; 9% transferred in; 41% live on campus.

Freshmen:
Admission: 78 applied, 73 admitted, 25 enrolled.
Retention: 47% of full-time freshmen returned.

FACULTY
Total: 68, 34% full-time, 56% with terminal degrees.
Student/faculty ratio: 8:1.

ACADEMICS
Calendar: semesters. *Degrees:* associate, bachelor's, and master's.
Special study options: academic remediation for entering students, advanced placement credit, distance learning, double majors, independent study, internships, part-time degree program, services for LD students, summer session for credit.
Computers: 25 computers/terminals are available on campus for general student use. Students can access the following: free student e-mail accounts, online (class) grades, online (class) registration, online (class) schedules. Campuswide network is available. Wireless service is available via entire campus.
Library: Ida J. MacMillan Library plus 1 other. *Books:* 87,455 (physical), 1,794 (digital/electronic); *Serial titles:* 50 (physical); *Databases:* 17. Weekly public service hours: 66.

STUDENT LIFE
Housing options: on-campus residence required through sophomore year; men-only, women-only, special housing for students with disabilities. Campus housing is university owned. Freshman campus housing is guaranteed.
Activities and organizations: choral group, Baptist Collegiate Ministry, College Choir, AACC.
Athletics ***Intramural sports:*** basketball M/W, football M/W, soccer M/W, ultimate Frisbee M/W, volleyball M/W.
Campus security: 24-hour emergency response devices, student patrols, patrols by police officers 11 pm to 7 am.
Student services: personal/psychological counseling, veterans affairs office.

COSTS & FINANCIAL AID
Costs (2020–21) ***Required fees:*** $900 full-time, $30 per credit hour part-time. ***Room and board:*** $4612. Room and board charges vary according to board plan and housing facility. ***Payment plan:*** installment. ***Waivers:*** employees or children of employees.
Financial Aid Of all full-time matriculated undergraduates who enrolled in 2019, 294 applied for aid, 257 were judged to have need, 7 had their need fully met. 26 Federal Work-Study jobs (averaging $2000). In 2019, 19 non-need-based awards were made. ***Average percent of need met:*** 32. ***Average financial aid package:*** $9263. ***Average need-based loan:*** $3241. ***Average need-based gift aid:*** $7190. ***Average non-need-based aid:*** $1939. ***Average indebtedness upon graduation:*** $18,945.

APPLYING
Standardized Tests *Required:* SAT or ACT (for admission).
Options: electronic application, deferred entrance.
Application fee: $25.
Required: high school transcript, minimum 2.5 GPA, 2 letters of recommendation, Christian/church member for 1 year minimum. ***Recommended:*** interview.
Application deadlines: 8/15 (freshmen), 8/15 (transfers).
Notification: continuous (freshmen), continuous (transfers).

CONTACT
The Baptist College of Florida, 5400 College Drive, Graceville, FL 32440. *Phone:* 850-263-3261 Ext. 460. *Toll-free phone:* 800-328-2660 Ext. 460.

Barry University

Miami Shores, Florida

http://www.barry.edu/

- **Independent Roman Catholic** university, founded 1940
- **Suburban** 122-acre campus with easy access to Miami
- **Coed** 3,747 undergraduate students, 80% full-time, 63% women, 37% men
- **Moderately difficult** entrance level, 51% of applicants were admitted

UNDERGRAD STUDENTS
3,015 full-time, 732 part-time. 16% are from out of state; 36% Black or African American, non-Hispanic/Latino; 36% Hispanic/Latino; 1% Asian, non-Hispanic/Latino; 0.1% Native Hawaiian or other Pacific Islander, non-Hispanic/Latino; 0.5% American Indian or Alaska Native, non-Hispanic/Latino; 2% Two or more races, non-Hispanic/Latino; 1% Race/ethnicity unknown; 7% international; 13% transferred in; 25% live on campus.

Freshmen:
Admission: 10,577 applied, 5,415 admitted, 717 enrolled. ***Test scores:*** SAT evidence-based reading and writing scores over 500: 64%; SAT math scores over 500: 48%; ACT scores over 18: 77%; SAT evidence-based

reading and writing scores over 600: 9%; SAT math scores over 600: 9%; ACT scores over 24: 21%; ACT scores over 30: 6%.

Retention: 65% of full-time freshmen returned.

FACULTY
Total: 1,083, 28% full-time.

Student/faculty ratio: 10:1.

ACADEMICS
Calendar: semesters. *Degrees:* certificates, bachelor's, master's, doctoral, post-master's, and postbachelor's certificates.

Special study options: academic remediation for entering students, accelerated degree program, adult/continuing education programs, advanced placement credit, distance learning, double majors, English as a second language, honors programs, independent study, internships, off-campus study, part-time degree program, services for LD students, study abroad, summer session for credit. ***ROTC:*** Army (c), Air Force (c).

Unusual degree programs: 3-2 engineering with University of Miami.

Computers: 368 computers/terminals are available on campus for general student use. Students can access the following: campus intranet, computer help desk, free student e-mail accounts, online (class) grades, online (class) registration, online (class) schedules, learning management system. Campuswide network is available. Wireless service is available via computer centers, computer labs, learning centers, student centers. **Library:** Monsignor William Barry Memorial Library plus 1 other.

STUDENT LIFE
Housing options: on-campus residence required for freshman year; coed, special housing for students with disabilities. Campus housing is university owned.

Activities and organizations: drama/theater group, student-run newspaper, radio and television station, choral group, Student Government Association, Campus Activities Board, SCUBA Society, Caribbean Students Association, Jamaican Association, national fraternities, national sororities.

Athletics Member NCAA. All Division II. ***Intercollegiate sports:*** baseball M(s), basketball M(s)/W(s), crew W(s), golf M(s)/W(s), soccer M(s)/W(s), softball W(s), tennis M(s)/W(s), volleyball W(s). ***Intramural sports:*** basketball M/W, football M/W, golf M/W, soccer M/W, softball M/W, volleyball M/W.

Campus security: 24-hour emergency response devices and patrols, late-night transport/escort service.

Student services: health clinic, personal/psychological counseling.

COSTS & FINANCIAL AID
Costs (2019–20) ***Comprehensive fee:*** $41,074 includes full-time tuition ($29,700), mandatory fees ($150), and room and board ($11,224). Part-time tuition: $925 per credit hour.

Financial Aid Of all full-time matriculated undergraduates who enrolled in 2019, 2,462 applied for aid, 2,339 were judged to have need, 108 had their need fully met. In 2019, 288 non-need-based awards were made. ***Average percent of need met:*** 59. ***Average financial aid package:*** $24,378. ***Average need-based loan:*** $4154. ***Average need-based gift aid:*** $9277. ***Average non-need-based aid:*** $10,416. ***Average indebtedness upon graduation:*** $37,228.

APPLYING
Standardized Tests *Required:* SAT or ACT (for admission).

Options: electronic application, early admission, deferred entrance.

Required: high school transcript, minimum 2.0 GPA. ***Required for some:*** essay or personal statement. ***Recommended:*** interview.

Application deadlines: rolling (freshmen), rolling (transfers).

Notification: continuous (freshmen), continuous (transfers).

CONTACT
Barry University, 11300 Northeast Second Avenue, Miami Shores, FL 33161-6695. *Phone:* 305-899-3394. *Toll-free phone:* 800-695-2279.

Beacon College
Leesburg, Florida
http://www.beaconcollege.edu/

- **Independent** 4-year, founded 1989
- **Small-town** 20-acre campus with easy access to Orlando
- **Endowment** $100,811
- **Coed** 416 undergraduate students, 98% full-time, 37% women, 63% men
- **Moderately difficult** entrance level, 51% of applicants were admitted

UNDERGRAD STUDENTS
408 full-time, 8 part-time. Students come from 37 states and territories; 3 other countries; 62% are from out of state; 16% Black or African American, non-Hispanic/Latino; 8% Hispanic/Latino; 5% Asian, non-Hispanic/Latino; 0.2% Native Hawaiian or other Pacific Islander, non-Hispanic/Latino; 2% American Indian or Alaska Native, non-Hispanic/Latino; 3% Two or more races, non-Hispanic/Latino; 1% international; 6% transferred in; 87% live on campus.

Freshmen:
Admission: 286 applied, 145 admitted, 98 enrolled. ***Average high school GPA:*** 3.2.

Retention: 71% of full-time freshmen returned.

FACULTY
Total: 44, 84% full-time, 55% with terminal degrees.

Student/faculty ratio: 11:1.

ACADEMICS
Calendar: semesters. *Degree:* bachelor's.

Special study options: academic remediation for entering students, advanced placement credit, double majors, independent study, internships, part-time degree program, services for LD students, study abroad, summer session for credit.

Computers: 150 computers/terminals and 450 ports are available on campus for general student use. Students can access the following: campus intranet, computer help desk, free student e-mail accounts, online (class) grades, online (class) schedules. Campuswide network is available. 100% of college-owned or -operated housing units are wired for high-speed Internet access. Wireless service is available via entire campus. **Library:** Beacon College Library. *Books:* 11,113 (physical), 346,154 (digital/electronic); *Serial titles:* 40 (physical); *Databases:* 15. Weekly public service hours: 76; students can reserve study rooms.

STUDENT LIFE
Housing options: coed. Campus housing is university owned. Freshman campus housing is guaranteed.

Activities and organizations: drama/theater group, student-run radio station, choral group, Student Government Association, Card Game Club, Equestrian Club, Wrestling Club, Beacon's Got Talent.

Athletics ***Intercollegiate sports:*** basketball M(c), football M(c). ***Intramural sports:*** basketball M(c)/W(c), football M(c)/W(c), soccer M(c)/W(c), softball M(c)/W(c), volleyball M(c)/W(c), weight lifting M(c)/W(c).

Campus security: 24-hour emergency response devices and patrols, student patrols, late-night transport/escort service, controlled dormitory access.

Student services: health clinic, personal/psychological counseling.

COSTS & FINANCIAL AID
Costs (2020–21) ***Comprehensive fee:*** $55,470 includes full-time tuition ($42,600), mandatory fees ($300), and room and board ($12,570). Full-time tuition and fees vary according to course load. Part-time tuition: $1420 per credit hour. Part-time tuition and fees vary according to course load. ***Required fees:*** $300 per year part-time. ***College room only:*** $7590. Room and board charges vary according to board plan and housing facility. ***Payment plan:*** installment. ***Waivers:*** employees or children of employees.

Financial Aid Of all full-time matriculated undergraduates who enrolled in 2018, 359 applied for aid, 323 were judged to have need. 53,000 Federal Work-Study jobs (averaging $53,000). 10,000 state and other part-time jobs (averaging $9000). In 2018, 11 non-need-based awards were made. ***Average financial aid package:*** $15,496. ***Average need-based loan:*** $3783. ***Average need-based gift aid:*** $5000. ***Average non-need-based aid:*** $6000. ***Average indebtedness upon graduation:*** $27,000.

APPLYING
Options: electronic application, early admission, deferred entrance.
Application fee: $50.
Required: high school transcript, 3 letters of recommendation, interview, psycho-educational evaluation showing diagnosed learning disability or ADHD. ***Recommended:*** minimum 2.0 GPA.
Application deadlines: rolling (freshmen), rolling (transfers).
Notification: 8/1 (freshmen), 8/1 (transfers).

CONTACT
Ms. Dale Herold, Vice President of Admissions and Enrollment Management, Beacon College, 105 East Main Street, Leesburg, FL 34748. *Phone:* 352-638-9778. *Fax:* 352-787-0796. *E-mail:* dherold@beaconcollege.edu.

Belhaven University
Orlando, Florida
http://orlando.belhaven.edu/

CONTACT
Jeremy Couch, Director of Admission, Belhaven University, 5200 Vineland Road, Suite 100, Orlando, FL 32811. *Phone:* 407-804-1424. *Toll-free phone:* 877-804-1424. *Fax:* 407-661-1732. *E-mail:* orlando@belhaven.edu.

Bethune-Cookman University
Daytona Beach, Florida
http://www.cookman.edu/

CONTACT
Treran Porter, Director of Recruitment, Bethune-Cookman University, FL. *Phone:* 386-481-2603. *Toll-free phone:* 800-448-0228. *E-mail:* portert@cookman.edu.

Broward College
Fort Lauderdale, Florida
http://www.broward.edu/

CONTACT
Mr. Willie J. Alexander, Associate Vice President for Student Affairs/College Registrar, Broward College, 225 East Las Olas Boulevard, Fort Lauderdale, FL 33301. *Phone:* 954-201-7471. *Fax:* 954-201-7466. *E-mail:* walexand@broward.edu.

Chamberlain College of Nursing - Jacksonville
Jacksonville, Florida
http://www.chamberlain.edu/

CONTACT
Admissions, Chamberlain College of Nursing - Jacksonville, 5200 Belfort Road, Jacksonville, FL 32256. *Phone:* 904-251-8100. *Toll-free phone:* 877-751-5783.

Chamberlain College of Nursing - Miramar
Miramar, Florida
http://www.chamberlain.edu/

CONTACT
Director of Recruitment, Chamberlain College of Nursing - Miramar, 2300 SW 145th Avenue, Miramar, FL 33027. *Phone:* 954-885-3510. *Toll-free phone:* 877-751-5783.

Chipola College
Marianna, Florida
http://www.chipola.edu/

CONTACT
Mrs. Kathy L. Rehberg, Registrar, Chipola College, 3094 Indian Circle, Marianna, FL 32446-3065. *Phone:* 850-718-2233. *Fax:* 850-718-2287. *E-mail:* rehbergk@chipola.edu.

City College
Altamonte Springs, Florida
http://www.citycollege.edu/

- **Independent** primarily 2-year
- **Coed, primarily women**
- **Noncompetitive** entrance level

FACULTY
Student/faculty ratio: 17:1.

ACADEMICS
Calendar: semesters. *Degrees:* diplomas, associate, and bachelor's.

STUDENT LIFE
Housing options: college housing not available.

APPLYING
Standardized Tests *Required:* TABE (for admission).
Application fee: $25.
Required: high school transcript, interview.

CONTACT
Ms. Kimberly Bowden, Director of Admissions, City College, 177 Montgomery Road, Altamonte Springs, FL 32714. *Phone:* 352-335-4000. *Fax:* 352-335-4303. *E-mail:* kbowden@citycollege.edu.

City College
Fort Lauderdale, Florida
http://www.citycollege.edu/

- **Independent** primarily 2-year, founded 1984
- **Coed**
- 91% of applicants were admitted

FACULTY
Student/faculty ratio: 20:1.

ACADEMICS
Calendar: semesters. *Degrees:* certificates, associate, and bachelor's.

STUDENT LIFE
Housing options: college housing not available.

APPLYING
Standardized Tests *Required:* TABE (for admission).
Application fee: $40.
Required: high school transcript, interview.

CONTACT
City College, 2000 West Commercial Boulevard, Suite 200, Fort Lauderdale, FL 33309. *Phone:* 954-492-5353. *Toll-free phone:* 866-314-5681.

City College
Gainesville, Florida
http://www.citycollege.edu/

- **Independent** primarily 2-year, founded 1986
- **Coed**
- 98% of applicants were admitted

FACULTY
Student/faculty ratio: 15:1.

ACADEMICS
Calendar: semesters. *Degrees:* certificates, associate, and bachelor's.

STUDENT LIFE
Housing options: college housing not available.

APPLYING
Standardized Tests *Required:* TABE (for admission).

Application fee: $40.

Required: high school transcript, interview.

CONTACT
Admissions Office, City College, 7001 Northwest 4th Boulevard, Gainesville, FL 32607. *Phone:* 352-335-4000.

City College

Hollywood, Florida

http://www.citycollege.edu/

CONTACT
City College, 6565 Taft Street, Hollywood, FL 33024. *Toll-free phone:* 866-314-5681.

City College

Miami, Florida

http://www.citycollege.edu/

- **Independent** primarily 2-year, founded 1997
- **Coed**
- 62% of applicants were admitted

FACULTY
Student/faculty ratio: 22:1.

ACADEMICS
Calendar: semesters. *Degrees:* certificates, associate, and bachelor's.

STUDENT LIFE
Housing options: college housing not available.

APPLYING
Standardized Tests *Required:* TABE (for admission).

Application fee: $40.

Required: high school transcript, interview.

CONTACT
Admissions Office, City College, 9300 South Dadeland Boulevard, Suite PH, Miami, FL 33156. *Phone:* 305-666-9242. *Fax:* 305-666-9243.

College of Business and Technology–Main Campus

Miami, Florida

http://www.cbt.edu/

CONTACT
College of Business and Technology–Main Campus, 8700 West Flagler Street, Suite 420, Miami, FL 33174. *Phone:* 305-273-4499 Ext. 1100.

College of Business and Technology–Miami Gardens

Miami Gardens, Florida

http://www.cbt.edu/

CONTACT
College of Business and Technology–Miami Gardens, 5190 NW 167 Street, Miami Gardens, FL 33014. *Phone:* 305-273-4499 Ext. 1100.

College of Central Florida

Ocala, Florida

http://www.cf.edu/

- **State and locally supported** primarily 2-year, founded 1957, part of Florida College System
- **Small-town** 139-acre campus
- **Endowment** $65.4 million
- **Coed**
- **Noncompetitive** entrance level

ACADEMICS
Calendar: semesters. *Degrees:* certificates, diplomas, associate, and bachelor's.
Library: Clifford B. Stearns Learning Resources Center. *Books:* 75,935 (physical), 43,910 (digital/electronic); *Databases:* 152. Students can reserve study rooms.

STUDENT LIFE
Housing options: college housing not available.

Activities and organizations: drama/theater group, student-run newspaper, choral group, Inspirational Choir, Model United Nations, Performing Arts, Phi Theta Kappa (PTK), Student Nurses Association.

Athletics Member NJCAA.

Campus security: 24-hour emergency response devices and patrols, student patrols, late-night transport/escort service.

Student services: personal/psychological counseling.

COSTS & FINANCIAL AID
Costs (2019–20) ***Tuition:*** $113 per credit hour part-time; state resident $3388 full-time, $113 per credit part-time; nonresident $13,146 full-time, $438 per credit hour part-time. Full-time tuition and fees vary according to degree level. Part-time tuition and fees vary according to degree level.

Financial Aid Of all full-time matriculated undergraduates who enrolled in 2017, 1,184 applied for aid, 753 were judged to have need, 23 had their need fully met. In 2017, 38 non-need-based awards were made. ***Average percent of need met:*** 55. ***Average financial aid package:*** $1744. ***Average need-based loan:*** $2164. ***Average need-based gift aid:*** $1731. ***Average non-need-based aid:*** $889.

APPLYING
Options: electronic application, early admission.

Application fee: $30.

Required: high school transcript.

CONTACT
Mr. Alton Austin, Director of Enrollment Services/Registrar, College of Central Florida, 3001 SW College Road, Ocala, FL 34474. *Phone:* 352-237-2111 Ext. 1751. *Fax:* 352-873-5882. *E-mail:* austina@cf.edu.

The College of the Florida Keys

Key West, Florida

http://www.fkcc.edu/

CONTACT
The College of the Florida Keys, 5901 College Road, Key West, FL 33040-4397. *Phone:* 305-296-9081 Ext. 237.

Daytona State College

Daytona Beach, Florida

http://www.daytonastate.edu/

- **State-supported** primarily 2-year, founded 1957, part of Florida College System
- **Suburban** 100-acre campus with easy access to Orlando
- **Endowment** $14.1 million
- **Coed** 13,430 undergraduate students, 41% full-time, 61% women, 39% men
- **Noncompetitive** entrance level

UNDERGRAD STUDENTS
5,562 full-time, 7,868 part-time. Students come from 22 other countries; 2% are from out of state; 12% Black or African American, non-Hispanic/Latino; 17% Hispanic/Latino; 2% Asian, non-Hispanic/Latino;

0.2% Native Hawaiian or other Pacific Islander, non-Hispanic/Latino; 0.3% American Indian or Alaska Native, non-Hispanic/Latino; 4% Two or more races, non-Hispanic/Latino; 2% Race/ethnicity unknown; 0.2% international.

Freshmen:
Admission: 1,941 admitted, 1,941 enrolled.

FACULTY
Total: 885, 28% full-time, 16% with terminal degrees.

Student/faculty ratio: 18:1.

ACADEMICS
Calendar: semesters. *Degrees:* certificates, diplomas, associate, bachelor's, and postbachelor's certificates.

Special study options: academic remediation for entering students, adult/continuing education programs, advanced placement credit, cooperative education, distance learning, English as a second language, external degree program, freshman honors college, honors programs, independent study, internships, off-campus study, part-time degree program, services for LD students, study abroad, summer session for credit. ***ROTC:*** Army (c), Air Force (c).

Computers: 3,200 computers/terminals are available on campus for general student use. Students can access the following: campus intranet, computer help desk, free student e-mail accounts, online (class) grades, online (class) registration, online (class) schedules. Campuswide network is available. 100% of college-owned or -operated housing units are wired for high-speed Internet access. Wireless service is available via entire campus.

Library: Daytona State College Library Services plus 1 other. *Books:* 36,740 (physical), 211,462 (digital/electronic); *Serial titles:* 164 (physical); *Databases:* 100. Weekly public service hours: 68; students can reserve study rooms.

STUDENT LIFE
Housing options: college housing not available.

Activities and organizations: drama/theater group, student-run newspaper, choral group, Phi Theta Kappa International Honors Society, Student Government Association, Student Respiratory Therapy Club, Business Club, Student Paralegal Club, national fraternities, national sororities.

Athletics Member NJCAA. ***Intercollegiate sports:*** baseball M(s), basketball M(s)/W(s), cross-country running M(s)/W(s), soccer M(s)/W(s), softball W(s), volleyball W(s). ***Intramural sports:*** basketball M/W, football M/W, golf W, soccer M/W, table tennis M/W, volleyball M/W.

Campus security: 24-hour emergency response devices and patrols, late-night transport/escort service, emergency alert system capable of delivering text messages, voice calls, and email messages to college email accounts.

Student services: personal/psychological counseling, women's center, veterans affairs office.

FINANCIAL AID
Financial Aid Of all full-time matriculated undergraduates who enrolled in 2018, 2,803 applied for aid, 2,799 were judged to have need. 206 Federal Work-Study jobs (averaging $1876). 2 state and other part-time jobs (averaging $1862). In 2018, 81 non-need-based awards were made. ***Average need-based loan:*** $1555. ***Average need-based gift aid:*** $1755. ***Average non-need-based aid:*** $1028. ***Average indebtedness upon graduation:*** $2483.

APPLYING
Options: electronic application, early admission, deferred entrance.

Required: high school transcript.

Application deadlines: rolling (freshmen), rolling (transfers).

Notification: continuous (freshmen), continuous (transfers).

CONTACT
Dr. Karen Sanders, Director of Admissions and Recruitment, Daytona State College, 1200 International Speedway Boulevard, Daytona Beach, FL 32114. *Phone:* 386-506-3050. *E-mail:* karen.sanders@daytonastate.edu.

DeVry University–Jacksonville Campus

Jacksonville, Florida

http://www.devry.edu/

CONTACT
Admissions Office, DeVry University–Jacksonville Campus, 5200 Belfort Road, Suite 175, Jacksonville, FL 32256-6040. *Phone:* 904-367-4942. *Toll-free phone:* 866-338-7934.

DeVry University–Miramar Campus

Miramar, Florida

http://www.devry.edu/

- **Proprietary** comprehensive, founded 2002, part of DeVry University
- **Coed**
- **Minimally difficult** entrance level

FACULTY
Student/faculty ratio: 18:1.

ACADEMICS
Calendar: semesters. *Degrees:* associate, bachelor's, master's, and postbachelor's certificates.

STUDENT LIFE
Housing options: college housing not available.

FINANCIAL AID
Financial Aid Of all full-time matriculated undergraduates who enrolled in 2007, 204 applied for aid, 197 were judged to have need, 2 had their need fully met. In 2007, 35 non-need-based awards were made. ***Average percent of need met:*** 38. ***Average financial aid package:*** $12,172. ***Average need-based loan:*** $7414. ***Average need-based gift aid:*** $7044. ***Average non-need-based aid:*** $12,256. ***Average indebtedness upon graduation:*** $51,131.

APPLYING
Options: deferred entrance.

Application fee: $30.

Required: high school transcript, interview.

CONTACT
DeVry University–Miramar Campus, 2300 Southwest 145th Avenue, Miramar, FL 33027. *Phone:* 954-499-9775. *Toll-free phone:* 866-338-7934.

DeVry University–Orlando Campus

Orlando, Florida

http://www.devry.edu/

CONTACT
DeVry University–Orlando Campus, 7352 Greenbriar Parkway, Orlando, FL 32819. *Phone:* 407-345-2800. *Toll-free phone:* 866-338-7934.

Eastern Florida State College

Cocoa, Florida

http://www.easternflorida.edu/

- **State-supported** primarily 2-year, founded 1960, part of Florida Community College System
- **Suburban** 100-acre campus with easy access to Orlando
- **Coed**
- **Noncompetitive** entrance level

FACULTY
Student/faculty ratio: 23:1.

ACADEMICS
Calendar: semesters. *Degrees:* certificates, associate, and bachelor's.
Library: UCF Library.

STUDENT LIFE
Housing options: college housing not available.

Activities and organizations: drama/theater group, student-run newspaper, television station, choral group, Phi Theta Kappa, The Green Team, African-American Student Union, Student Government Association, Cosmetology in Action.

Athletics Member NJCAA.

Campus security: 24-hour emergency response devices and patrols.

Student services: women's center.

FINANCIAL AID

Financial Aid Of all full-time matriculated undergraduates who enrolled in 2018, 200 Federal Work-Study jobs (averaging $2244), 200 state and other part-time jobs (averaging $2000).

APPLYING

Options: electronic application, early admission.

Application fee: $30.

Required: high school transcript.

CONTACT

Ms. Stephanie Burnette, Registrar, Eastern Florida State College, 1519 Clearlake Road, Cocoa, FL 32922-6597. *Phone:* 321-433-7271. *Fax:* 321-433-7172. *E-mail:* cocoaadmissions@brevardcc.edu.

Eckerd College

St. Petersburg, Florida

http://www.eckerd.edu/

- **Independent Presbyterian** 4-year, founded 1958
- **Suburban** 188-acre campus with easy access to Tampa
- **Endowment** $58.3 million
- **Coed**
- **Moderately difficult** entrance level

FACULTY

Student/faculty ratio: 12:1.

ACADEMICS

Calendar: 4-1-4. *Degree:* bachelor's.
Library: Peter Armacost Library. *Books:* 156,516 (physical), 168,633 (digital/electronic); *Serial titles:* 773 (physical), 182,151 (digital/electronic); *Databases:* 201.

STUDENT LIFE

Housing options: on-campus residence required for freshman year; coed, women-only. Campus housing is university owned. Freshman campus housing is guaranteed.

Activities and organizations: drama/theater group, student-run newspaper, radio and television station, choral group, Marine Science Club, Water Search and Rescue Team, The Current (student newspaper), A cappella Vocal Group, Organization of Students.

Athletics Member NCAA. All Division II except golf (Division I).

Campus security: 24-hour emergency response devices and patrols, student patrols, late-night transport/escort service, controlled dormitory access.

Student services: health clinic, personal/psychological counseling, women's center.

COSTS & FINANCIAL AID

Costs (2019–20) ***Comprehensive fee:*** $59,122 includes full-time tuition ($45,452), mandatory fees ($644), and room and board ($13,026). ***College room only:*** $6814. Room and board charges vary according to board plan and housing facility.

Financial Aid Of all full-time matriculated undergraduates who enrolled in 2018, 1,347 applied for aid, 1,164 were judged to have need, 219 had their need fully met. 956 Federal Work-Study jobs (averaging $2000). In 2018, 763 non-need-based awards were made. ***Average percent of need met:*** 87. ***Average financial aid package:*** $38,458. ***Average need-based loan:*** $3764. ***Average need-based gift aid:*** $26,850. ***Average non-need-based aid:*** $17,765. ***Average indebtedness upon graduation:*** $37,896.

APPLYING

Standardized Tests *Required:* SAT or ACT (for admission). *Recommended:* SAT Subject Tests (for admission).

Options: electronic application, early action, deferred entrance.

Application fee: $40.

Required: essay or personal statement, high school transcript. ***Recommended:*** interview.

CONTACT

Ms. Lucille Lopez, Campus Visit Coordinator, Eckerd College, 4200 54th Avenue South, St. Petersburg, FL 33711. *Phone:* 727-864-8331. *Toll-free phone:* 800-456-9009. *Fax:* 727-866-2304. *E-mail:* admissions@eckerd.edu.

Edward Waters College

Jacksonville, Florida

http://www.ewc.edu/

- **Independent African Methodist Episcopal** 4-year, founded 1866
- **Urban** 50-acre campus
- **Coed**
- **Noncompetitive** entrance level

FACULTY

Student/faculty ratio: 9:1.

ACADEMICS

Calendar: semesters. *Degree:* bachelor's.
Library: Centennial Library.

STUDENT LIFE

Housing options: coed. Campus housing is university owned.

Activities and organizations: drama/theater group, choral group, marching band, national fraternities, national sororities.

Athletics Member NAIA.

Campus security: 24-hour emergency response devices and patrols, student patrols, late-night transport/escort service, controlled dormitory access.

Student services: health clinic, personal/psychological counseling.

FINANCIAL AID

Financial Aid Of all full-time matriculated undergraduates who enrolled in 2001, 1,242 applied for aid, 1,242 were judged to have need, 11 had their need fully met. 318 Federal Work-Study jobs (averaging $851). In 2001, 262 non-need-based awards were made. ***Average percent of need met:*** 61. ***Average financial aid package:*** $4835. ***Average need-based loan:*** $2625. ***Average need-based gift aid:*** $4835. ***Average non-need-based aid:*** $1488. ***Average indebtedness upon graduation:*** $9000.

APPLYING

Standardized Tests *Required:* SAT or ACT (for admission).

Options: electronic application.

Application fee: $25.

Required: high school transcript, 2 letters of recommendation, medical forms.

CONTACT

Edward Waters College, 1658 Kings Road, Jacksonville, FL 32209-6199. *Phone:* 904-470-8202. *Toll-free phone:* 888-898-3191.

Embry-Riddle Aeronautical University–Daytona

Daytona Beach, Florida

http://www.daytonabeach.erau.edu/

- **Independent** university, founded 1926
- **Suburban** 289-acre campus with easy access to Orlando
- **Endowment** $90.4 million
- **Coed**
- **Moderately difficult** entrance level

FACULTY

Student/faculty ratio: 15:1.

ACADEMICS

Calendar: semesters. *Degrees:* associate, bachelor's, master's, doctoral, and postbachelor's certificates.
Library: Jack R. Hunt Memorial Library. *Books:* 53,116 (physical), 122,788 (digital/electronic); *Serial titles:* 456 (physical), 78,964 (digital/electronic); *Databases:* 172. Students can reserve study rooms.

STUDENT LIFE

Housing options: on-campus residence required for freshman year; coed. Campus housing is university owned. Freshman campus housing is guaranteed.

Activities and organizations: drama/theater group, student-run newspaper, radio station, choral group, Eagle Wing, Future Professional Pilots Association, African Student Association, Caribbean Student Association, Sigma Gamma Tau, national fraternities, national sororities.

Athletics Member NCAA, NAIA. All NCAA Division II except men's and women's golf (Division I).

Campus security: 24-hour emergency response devices and patrols, student patrols, late-night transport/escort service, controlled dormitory access.

Student services: health clinic, personal/psychological counseling, women's center, veterans affairs office.

COSTS & FINANCIAL AID

Costs (2019–20) ***One-time required fee:*** $150. ***Comprehensive fee:*** $48,614 includes full-time tuition ($35,424), mandatory fees ($1444), and room and board ($11,746). Part-time tuition: $1476 per credit hour. ***Required fees:*** $722 per term part time. ***College room only:*** $7080.

Financial Aid Of all full-time matriculated undergraduates who enrolled in 2018, 3,868 applied for aid, 3,392 were judged to have need. In 2018, 1267 non-need-based awards were made. ***Average financial aid package:*** $18,528. ***Average need-based loan:*** $4229. ***Average need-based gift aid:*** $14,779. ***Average non-need-based aid:*** $11,104.

APPLYING

Standardized Tests *Recommended:* SAT or ACT (for admission).

Options: electronic application, deferred entrance.

Application fee: $50.

Required: high school transcript, minimum 2.0 GPA. ***Required for some:*** medical examination for flight students. ***Recommended:*** essay or personal statement, 2 letters of recommendation.

CONTACT

Mr. Pablo A Alvarez, Director, Daytona Beach Admissions, Embry-Riddle Aeronautical University–Daytona, 600 South Clyde Morris Boulevard, Daytona Beach, FL 32114-3900. *Phone:* 386-226-6100. *Toll-free phone:* 800-862-2416. *Fax:* 386-226-7070. *E-mail:* dbadmit@erau.edu.

Embry-Riddle Aeronautical University–Worldwide

Daytona Beach, Florida

http://www.worldwide.erau.edu/

- **Independent** comprehensive, founded 1970
- **Endowment** $3.6 million
- **Coed**
- **Minimally difficult** entrance level

ACADEMICS

Calendar: 5 9-week terms with monthly starts. *Degrees:* certificates, associate, bachelor's, master's, doctoral, and postbachelor's certificates (programs offered at 100 military bases worldwide).

Library: Jack R. Hunt Memorial Library located in Daytona Beach. *Books:* 53,116 (physical), 122,788 (digital/electronic); *Serial titles:* 456 (physical), 78,964 (digital/electronic); *Databases:* 172.

STUDENT LIFE

Student services: veterans affairs office.

COSTS & FINANCIAL AID

Costs (2019–20) ***Tuition:*** $413 per credit hour part-time.

Financial Aid Of all full-time matriculated undergraduates who enrolled in 2017, 1,166 applied for aid, 1,116 were judged to have need. ***Average financial aid package:*** $5326. ***Average need-based loan:*** $4402. ***Average need-based gift aid:*** $4534.

APPLYING

Standardized Tests *Required for some:* SAT or ACT (for admission).

Options: electronic application, deferred entrance.

Application fee: $50.

Required: minimum 2.0 GPA. ***Required for some:*** high school transcript, 2 letters of recommendation.

CONTACT

Ms. Valerie Kisseloff, Director of Admissions, Embry-Riddle Aeronautical University–Worldwide, 600 South Clyde Morris Boulevard, Daytona Beach, FL 32114-3900. *Phone:* 800-522-6787. *Toll-free phone:* 800-522-6787. *Fax:* 386-226-6984. *E-mail:* worldwide@erau.edu.

Everglades University

Boca Raton, Florida

http://www.evergladesuniversity.edu/

CONTACT

Everglades University, 5002 T-Rex Avenue, Suite 100, Boca Raton, FL 33431. *Phone:* 561-912-1211. *Toll-free phone:* 888-772-6077.

Everglades University

Maitland, Florida

http://www.evergladesuniversity.edu/

CONTACT

Everglades University, 850 Trafalgar Court, Suite 100, Maitland, FL 32751. *Phone:* 407-277-0311. *Toll-free phone:* 866-289-1078.

Everglades University

Sarasota, Florida

http://www.evergladesuniversity.edu/

CONTACT

Everglades University, 6001 Lake Osprey Drive #110, Sarasota, FL 34240. *Phone:* 866-289-1078. *Toll-free phone:* 888-854-8308.

Flagler College

St. Augustine, Florida

http://www.flagler.edu/

- **Independent** comprehensive, founded 1968
- **Suburban** 47-acre campus with easy access to Jacksonville, FL
- **Coed** 2,889 undergraduate students, 98% full-time, 67% women, 33% men
- 65% of applicants were admitted

UNDERGRAD STUDENTS

2,819 full-time, 70 part-time. Students come from 47 states and territories; 55 other countries; 59% are from out of state; 5% Black or African American, non-Hispanic/Latino; 10% Hispanic/Latino; 1% Asian, non-Hispanic/Latino; 0.1% Native Hawaiian or other Pacific Islander, non-Hispanic/Latino; 0.2% American Indian or Alaska Native, non-Hispanic/Latino; 3% Two or more races, non-Hispanic/Latino; 4% Race/ethnicity unknown; 3% international; 45% live on campus.

Freshmen:

Admission: 4,569 applied, 2,959 admitted, 641 enrolled. ***Average high school GPA:*** 3.5. ***Test scores:*** SAT evidence-based reading and writing scores over 500: 90%; SAT math scores over 500: 79%; ACT scores over 18: 96%; SAT evidence-based reading and writing scores over 600: 42%; SAT math scores over 600: 21%; ACT scores over 24: 50%; SAT evidence-based reading and writing scores over 700: 3%; SAT math scores over 700: 3%; ACT scores over 30: 8%.

Retention: 74% of full-time freshmen returned.

FACULTY

Total: 317, 40% full-time, 32% with terminal degrees.

Student/faculty ratio: 15:1.

ACADEMICS

Calendar: semesters. *Degrees:* bachelor's and master's.

Special study options: academic remediation for entering students, accelerated degree program, advanced placement credit, cooperative education, distance learning, double majors, honors programs, independent study, internships, services for LD students, study abroad, summer session for credit.

Computers: Campuswide network is available. 100% of college-owned or -operated housing units are wired for high-speed Internet access. Wireless service is available via entire campus.
Library: Proctor Library. *Books:* 93,031 (physical), 252,378 (digital/electronic); *Serial titles:* 76 (physical), 47,031 (digital/electronic); *Databases:* 49. Weekly public service hours: 96; students can reserve study rooms.

STUDENT LIFE
Housing options: on-campus residence required for freshman year; coed, men-only, women-only. Campus housing is university owned. Freshman campus housing is guaranteed.

Activities and organizations: drama/theater group, student-run newspaper, radio station, choral group, Student Government Association, Phi Alpha Omega (local), Campus Activities Board, Flagler College Volunteers, national fraternities.

Athletics Member NCAA. All Division II. ***Intercollegiate sports:*** baseball M(s), basketball M(s)/W(s), cheerleading W(c), cross-country running M(s)/W(s), golf M(s)/W(s), soccer M(s)/W(s), softball W(s), tennis M(s)/W(s), track and field M(s)/W(s), volleyball W(s). ***Intramural sports:*** lacrosse M(c).

Campus security: 24-hour patrols, late-night transport/escort service, controlled dormitory access.

Student services: health clinic, personal/psychological counseling.

COSTS & FINANCIAL AID
Costs (2020–21) ***Tuition:*** $682 per credit hour part-time. Full-time tuition and fees vary according to location and program. Part-time tuition and fees vary according to location and program. ***Room only:*** Room and board charges vary according to board plan and housing facility. ***Payment plan:*** installment. ***Waivers:*** employees or children of employees.

Financial Aid Of all full-time matriculated undergraduates who enrolled in 2017, 2,074 applied for aid, 1,679 were judged to have need, 233 had their need fully met. In 2017, 551 non-need-based awards were made. ***Average percent of need met:*** 59. ***Average financial aid package:*** $13,564. ***Average need-based loan:*** $4316. ***Average need-based gift aid:*** $9579. ***Average non-need-based aid:*** $2785. ***Average indebtedness upon graduation:*** $29,705.

APPLYING
Standardized Tests *Required for some:* SAT or ACT (for admission).

Options: electronic application, early admission, early decision, deferred entrance.

Application fee: $50.

Required: essay or personal statement. ***Required for some:*** high school transcript.

CONTACT
Steven Albano, Director of First Year Admissions, Flagler College, 74 King Street, St. Augustine, FL 32084. *Phone:* 904-819-6495. *Toll-free phone:* 800-304-4208. *E-mail:* salbano@flagler.edu.

Flagler College–Tallahassee
Tallahassee, Florida
http://www.flagler.edu/

- **Independent** 4-year, founded 2000
- **Coed**
- 57% of applicants were admitted

FACULTY
Student/faculty ratio: 16:1.

ACADEMICS
Degree: bachelor's.

STUDENT LIFE
Housing options: men-only, women-only.

APPLYING
Options: early decision.

CONTACT
Flagler College–Tallahassee, 444 Appleyard Drive, Tallahassee, FL 32304.

Florida Agricultural and Mechanical University
Tallahassee, Florida
http://www.famu.edu/

- **State-supported** university, founded 1887, part of State University System of Florida
- **Urban** 419-acre campus with easy access to Jacksonville
- **Endowment** $96.4 million
- **Coed** 7,818 undergraduate students, 87% full time, 65% women, 35% men
- **Moderately difficult** entrance level, 36% of applicants were admitted

UNDERGRAD STUDENTS
6,802 full-time, 1,016 part-time. 15% are from out of state; 88% Black or African American, non-Hispanic/Latino; 4% Hispanic/Latino; 0.5% Asian, non-Hispanic/Latino; 3% Two or more races, non-Hispanic/Latino; 0.4% international; 6% transferred in.

Freshmen:
Admission: 10,269 applied, 3,665 admitted, 1,340 enrolled. ***Average high school GPA:*** 3.5. ***Test scores:*** SAT evidence-based reading and writing scores over 500: 91%; SAT math scores over 500: 83%; ACT scores over 18: 89%; SAT evidence-based reading and writing scores over 600: 23%; SAT math scores over 600: 16%; ACT scores over 24: 22%; SAT evidence-based reading and writing scores over 700: 1%; SAT math scores over 700: 2%; ACT scores over 30: 2%.

Retention: 80% of full-time freshmen returned.

FACULTY
Total: 704, 78% full-time, 57% with terminal degrees.

Student/faculty ratio: 15:1.

ACADEMICS
Calendar: semesters. *Degrees:* bachelor's, master's, doctoral, and post-master's certificates.

Special study options: academic remediation for entering students, accelerated degree program, adult/continuing education programs, advanced placement credit, cooperative education, distance learning, double majors, honors programs, independent study, internships, off-campus study, part-time degree program, services for LD students, study abroad, summer session for credit. ***ROTC:*** Army (b), Navy (b), Air Force (c).

Unusual degree programs: 3-2 business administration; occupational therapy, architecture.

Computers: 4,000 computers/terminals and 8,000 ports are available on campus for general student use. Students can access the following: campus intranet, computer help desk, free student e-mail accounts, online (class) grades, online (class) registration, online (class) schedules. Campuswide network is available. 100% of college-owned or -operated housing units are wired for high-speed Internet access. Wireless service is available via classrooms, computer centers, computer labs, dorm rooms, learning centers, libraries, student centers.
Library: Samuel H. Coleman Memorial Library plus 4 others. *Books:* 1.1 million (physical), 468,561 (digital/electronic); *Serial titles:* 17,167 (physical), 240,002 (digital/electronic); *Databases:* 314. Weekly public service hours: 135; study areas open 24 hours, 5–7 days a week; students can reserve study rooms.

STUDENT LIFE
Housing options: on-campus residence required for freshman year; coed, men-only, women-only, special housing for students with disabilities. Campus housing is university owned. Freshman applicants given priority for college housing.

Activities and organizations: drama/theater group, student-run newspaper, radio and television station, choral group, marching band, National Council of Negro Women, FAMU Chapter, American Society of Mechanical Engineers, Psi Chi International Honor Society, Caribbean Student Association, Academy of Student Pharmacists/Student National Pharmaceutical Association, national fraternities, national sororities.

Athletics Member NCAA. All Division I except football (Division I-AA). ***Intercollegiate sports:*** baseball M(s), basketball M(s)/W(s), bowling W(s), cheerleading M/W, cross-country running M(s)/W(s), golf M(s)/W(s)(c), softball W(s), swimming and diving M(s)/W(s), tennis

M(s)/W(s), track and field M(s)/W(s), volleyball W(s). ***Intramural sports:*** badminton M/W, basketball M/W, bowling M/W, cheerleading W, football M, golf M/W, gymnastics M/W, racquetball M/W, skiing (downhill) M/W, soccer M/W, softball M/W, swimming and diving M/W, table tennis M/W, tennis M/W, track and field M/W, ultimate Frisbee M/W, volleyball M/W, weight lifting M/W, wrestling M/W.

Campus security: 24-hour emergency response devices and patrols, late-night transport/escort service, controlled dormitory access.

Student services: health clinic, personal/psychological counseling.

COSTS & FINANCIAL AID

Costs (2020–21) ***Tuition:*** area resident $5645 full-time, $188 per credit hour part-time; state resident $5645 full-time, $188 per credit hour part-time; nonresident $17,585 full-time, $586 per credit hour part-time. ***Required fees:*** $140 full-time. ***Room and board:*** $10,986; room only: $6012. ***Payment plan:*** tuition prepayment.

Financial Aid Of all full-time matriculated undergraduates who enrolled in 2018, 6,602 applied for aid, 6,122 were judged to have need, 598 had their need fully met. In 2018, 161 non-need-based awards were made. ***Average percent of need met:*** 60. ***Average financial aid package:*** $13,284. ***Average need-based loan:*** $4043. ***Average need-based gift aid:*** $6660. ***Average non-need-based aid:*** $9223. ***Average indebtedness upon graduation:*** $28,284.

APPLYING

Standardized Tests *Required:* SAT or ACT (for admission).

Options: electronic application.

Application fee: $35.

Required: essay or personal statement, high school transcript, minimum 2.5 GPA, 3 letters of recommendation. ***Required for some:*** interview, audition for music major applicants. ***Recommended:*** minimum 3.0 GPA.

Notification: continuous (freshmen), continuous (transfers).

CONTACT

Ms. Chestr Hood, Director, Admissions, Florida Agricultural and Mechanical University, Office of Admissions, Tallahassee, FL 32307. *Phone:* 850-599-3796. *Toll-free phone:* 866-642-1198. *Fax:* 850-599-3069. *E-mail:* ugrdadmissions@famu.edu.

Florida Atlantic University

Boca Raton, Florida

http://www.fau.edu/

- **State-supported** university, founded 1961, part of State University System of Florida
- **Suburban** 850-acre campus with easy access to Miami, Fort Lauderdale, West Palm Beach
- **Endowment** $295.0 million
- **Coed** 24,842 undergraduate students, 67% full-time, 57% women, 43% men
- **Moderately difficult** entrance level, 63% of applicants were admitted

UNDERGRAD STUDENTS

16,679 full-time, 8,163 part-time. Students come from 48 states and territories; 110 other countries; 6% are from out of state; 20% Black or African American, non-Hispanic/Latino; 28% Hispanic/Latino; 4% Asian, non-Hispanic/Latino; 0.1% Native Hawaiian or other Pacific Islander, non-Hispanic/Latino; 0.1% American Indian or Alaska Native, non-Hispanic/Latino; 4% Two or more races, non-Hispanic/Latino; 0.9% Race/ethnicity unknown; 3% international; 10% transferred in; 18% live on campus.

Freshmen:

Admission: 18,854 applied, 11,930 admitted, 3,247 enrolled. ***Average high school GPA:*** 3.7. ***Test scores:*** SAT evidence-based reading and writing scores over 500: 96%; SAT math scores over 500: 93%; ACT scores over 18: 98%; SAT evidence-based reading and writing scores over 600: 42%; SAT math scores over 600: 33%; ACT scores over 24: 50%; SAT evidence-based reading and writing scores over 700: 5%; SAT math scores over 700: 6%; ACT scores over 30: 9%.

Retention: 82% of full-time freshmen returned.

FACULTY

Total: 1,483, 618% full-time, 70% with terminal degrees.

Student/faculty ratio: 24:1.

ACADEMICS

Calendar: semesters. *Degrees:* certificates, associate, bachelor's, master's, doctoral, and post-master's certificates.

Special study options: accelerated degree program, adult/continuing education programs, advanced placement credit, cooperative education, distance learning, double majors, English as a second language, freshman honors college, honors programs, independent study, internships, off-campus study, part-time degree program, services for LD students, study abroad, summer session for credit. ***ROTC:*** Army (b), Air Force (c).

Unusual degree programs: 3-2 business administration; engineering; nursing; social work; architecture, mathematics.

Computers: 1,350 computers/terminals are available on campus for general student use. Students can access the following: campus intranet, computer help desk, free student e-mail accounts, online (class) grades, online (class) registration, online (class) schedules. Campuswide network is available. 100% of college-owned or -operated housing units are wired for high-speed Internet access. Wireless service is available via entire campus.

Library: S. E. Wimberly Library plus 2 others. *Books:* 1.0 million (physical), 1.3 million (digital/electronic); *Serial titles:* 29,365 (physical), 104,949 (digital/electronic); *Databases:* 487. Weekly public service hours: 134; study areas open 24 hours, 5–7 days a week.

STUDENT LIFE

Housing options: on-campus residence required for freshman year; coed. Campus housing is university owned. Freshman campus housing is guaranteed.

Activities and organizations: drama/theater group, student-run newspaper, radio and television station, choral group, marching band, American Society of Civil Engineers, Dive Club, Pre-Law Society, Submarine Club, American Criminal Justice Society, national fraternities, national sororities.

Athletics Member NCAA. All Division I. ***Intercollegiate sports:*** baseball M(s), basketball M(s)/W(s), cheerleading M/W, cross-country running M/W, football M(s), golf M(s)/W(s)(c), soccer M/W, softball W(s), swimming and diving M/W, tennis M/W, track and field W, volleyball W(s). ***Intramural sports:*** baseball M/W, bowling M/W, football M, ice hockey M(c)/W(c), lacrosse M(c), rock climbing M(c)/W(c), rugby M(c)/W(c), sailing M(c)/W(c), soccer M/W, softball W, table tennis M/W, ultimate Frisbee M/W, volleyball M/W, weight lifting M(c), wrestling M(c).

Campus security: 24-hour emergency response devices and patrols, student patrols, late-night transport/escort service, controlled dormitory access.

Student services: health clinic, personal/psychological counseling, women's center, veterans affairs office.

COSTS & FINANCIAL AID

Costs (2020–21) ***Tuition:*** state resident $6099 full-time, $105 per credit hour part-time; nonresident $21,655 full-time, $599 per credit hour part-time. Full-time tuition and fees vary according to course load and location. Part-time tuition and fees vary according to course load and location. ***Required fees:*** $98 part-time. ***Room and board:*** $12,030; room only: $8320. Room and board charges vary according to board plan and housing facility. ***Payment plans:*** installment, deferred payment. ***Waivers:*** senior citizens and employees or children of employees.

Financial Aid Of all full-time matriculated undergraduates who enrolled in 2018, 11,785 applied for aid, 9,954 were judged to have need, 625 had their need fully met. 334 Federal Work-Study jobs (averaging $2376). 9 state and other part-time jobs (averaging $2066). In 2018, 170 non-need-based awards were made. ***Average percent of need met:*** 56. ***Average financial aid package:*** $14,639. ***Average need-based loan:*** $7131. ***Average need-based gift aid:*** $8103. ***Average non-need-based aid:*** $3609. ***Average indebtedness upon graduation:*** $23,439.

APPLYING

Standardized Tests *Required:* SAT or ACT (for admission).

Options: electronic application, early admission, deferred entrance.

Application fee: $30.

Required: high school transcript.

Notification: continuous (freshmen), continuous (transfers).

CONTACT
Florida Atlantic University, 777 Glades Road, Boca Raton, FL 33431-0991. *Phone:* 561-297-3040.

Florida College
Temple Terrace, Florida
http://www.floridacollege.edu/

- **Independent** 4-year, founded 1944
- **Suburban** 95-acre campus with easy access to Tampa
- **Endowment** $16.5 million
- **Coed**
- **Moderately difficult** entrance level

FACULTY
Student/faculty ratio: 13:1.

ACADEMICS
Calendar: semesters. *Degrees:* associate and bachelor's.
Library: Chatlos Library.

STUDENT LIFE
Housing options: on-campus residence required through sophomore year; men-only, women-only. Campus housing is university owned. Freshman campus housing is guaranteed.

Activities and organizations: drama/theater group, choral group, Co-ed Societies, ROTARACT CLUB, NAFME, SBGA, Footlighters.

Athletics Member NAIA, USCAA.

Campus security: controlled dormitory access.

Student services: health clinic, personal/psychological counseling.

COSTS & FINANCIAL AID
Costs (2019–20) ***Comprehensive fee:*** $25,990 includes full-time tuition ($16,300), mandatory fees ($1000), and room and board ($8690). Part-time tuition: $643 per credit hour. Part-time tuition and fees vary according to course load. ***Required fees:*** $200 per term part-time. ***College room only:*** $5000. Room and board charges vary according to board plan and housing facility.

Financial Aid Of all full-time matriculated undergraduates who enrolled in 2015, 434 applied for aid, 372 were judged to have need, 41 had their need fully met. 35 Federal Work-Study jobs (averaging $665). In 2015, 75 non-need-based awards were made. ***Average percent of need met:*** 56. ***Average financial aid package:*** $10,644. ***Average need-based loan:*** $4113. ***Average need-based gift aid:*** $7068. ***Average non-need-based aid:*** $4048.

APPLYING
Standardized Tests *Required:* SAT or ACT (for admission).

Options: electronic application.

Application fee: $40.

Required: high school transcript, minimum 2.0 GPA, 2 letters of recommendation. ***Required for some:*** essay for international students.

CONTACT
Mrs. Colleen Engel, Assistant Director of Admissions, Florida College, 119 North Glen Arven Avenue, Temple Terrace, FL 33617. *Phone:* 813-988-5131 Ext. 152. *Fax:* 813-899-1799. *E-mail:* admissions@floridacollege.edu.

Florida Gateway College
Lake City, Florida
http://www.fgc.edu/

CONTACT
Admissions, Florida Gateway College, 149 SE College Place, Lake City, FL 32025-8703. *Phone:* 386-755-4236. *E-mail:* admissions@fgc.edu.

Florida Gulf Coast University
Fort Myers, Florida
http://www.fgcu.edu/

- **State-supported** comprehensive, founded 1991, part of State University System of Florida
- **Suburban** 760-acre campus
- **Endowment** $94.5 million
- **Coed** 13,699 undergraduate students, 82% full-time, 56% women, 44% men
- **Moderately difficult** entrance level, 67% of applicants were admitted

UNDERGRAD STUDENTS
11,194 full-time, 2,505 part-time. Students come from 48 states and territories; 85 other countries; 8% are from out of state; 7% Black or African American, non-Hispanic/Latino; 23% Hispanic/Latino; 2% Asian, non-Hispanic/Latino; 0.1% Native Hawaiian or other Pacific Islander, non-Hispanic/Latino; 0.3% American Indian or Alaska Native, non-Hispanic/Latino; 3% Two or more races, non-Hispanic/Latino; 1% Race/ethnicity unknown; 2% international; 8% transferred in; 35% live on campus.

Freshmen:
Admission: 13,735 applied, 9,157 admitted, 2,779 enrolled. ***Average high school GPA:*** 3.9. ***Test scores:*** SAT evidence-based reading and writing scores over 500: 97%; SAT math scores over 500: 91%; ACT scores over 18: 97%; SAT evidence-based reading and writing scores over 600: 37%; SAT math scores over 600: 23%; ACT scores over 24: 40%; SAT evidence-based reading and writing scores over 700: 3%; SAT math scores over 700: 2%; ACT scores over 30: 4%.

Retention: 80% of full-time freshmen returned.

FACULTY
Total: 799, 63% full-time, 47% with terminal degrees.

Student/faculty ratio: 21:1.

ACADEMICS
Calendar: semesters. *Degrees:* certificates, associate, bachelor's, master's, doctoral, and post-master's certificates.

Special study options: academic remediation for entering students, accelerated degree program, advanced placement credit, cooperative education, distance learning, double majors, honors programs, independent study, internships, off-campus study, part-time degree program, services for LD students, study abroad, summer session for credit.

Computers: 1,029 computers/terminals are available on campus for general student use. Students can access the following: computer help desk, free student e-mail accounts, online (class) registration, online (class) schedules, online admissions and advising. Campuswide network is available. 100% of college-owned or -operated housing units are wired for high-speed Internet access. Wireless service is available via entire campus.
Library: Library Services plus 1 other. *Books:* 242,131 (physical), 126,942 (digital/electronic); *Serial titles:* 128,865 (digital/electronic); *Databases:* 389. Students can reserve study rooms.

STUDENT LIFE
Housing options: coed. Campus housing is university owned.

Activities and organizations: drama/theater group, student-run newspaper, Student Government, Ignite (Religious Organization), International Club, Martial Arts Club, Physical Therapy Association, national fraternities, national sororities.

Athletics Member NCAA. All Division I. ***Intercollegiate sports:*** baseball M(s), basketball M(s)/W(s), cheerleading W, cross-country running M(s)/W(s), golf M(s)/W(s), soccer M(s)/W(s), softball W(s), swimming and diving W(s), tennis M(s)/W(s), volleyball W(s). ***Intramural sports:*** basketball M/W, cross-country running M(c)/W(c), fencing M(c)/W(c), football M/W, ice hockey M(c), lacrosse M(c)/W(c), sailing M(c)/W(c), skiing (downhill) M(c)/W(c), soccer M/W, softball M/W, swimming and diving M(c)/W(c), table tennis M/W, tennis M(c)/W(c), ultimate Frisbee M/W, volleyball M/W, water polo M/W, weight lifting M(c)/W(c), wrestling M(c)/W(c).

Campus security: 24-hour emergency response devices and patrols, late-night transport/escort service.

Student services: health clinic, personal/psychological counseling.

COSTS & FINANCIAL AID
Costs (2019–20) ***Tuition:*** area resident $4191 full-time; state resident $4191 full-time; nonresident $22,328 full-time. Full-time tuition and fees vary according to course load. Part-time tuition and fees vary according to course load. ***Required fees:*** $1979 full-time. ***Room and board:*** $8580; room only: $4820. Room and board charges vary according to board plan.

Financial Aid Of all full-time matriculated undergraduates who enrolled in 2018, 7,727 applied for aid, 5,172 were judged to have need, 466 had their need fully met. 242 Federal Work-Study jobs (averaging $1878). In 2018, 437 non-need-based awards were made. ***Average percent of need met:*** 62. ***Average financial aid package:*** $10,750. ***Average need-based loan:*** $7064. ***Average need-based gift aid:*** $6557. ***Average non-need-based aid:*** $3244. ***Average indebtedness upon graduation:*** $28,581. ***Financial aid deadline:*** 6/30.

APPLYING
Standardized Tests *Required:* SAT or ACT (for admission).

Options: electronic application, deferred entrance.

Application fee: $30.

Required: high school transcript, minimum 2.5 GPA.

Application deadlines: 3/1 (freshmen), 7/1 (transfers).

Notification: continuous (freshmen), continuous (transfers).

CONTACT
Florida Gulf Coast University, 10501 FGCU Boulevard South, Fort Myers, FL 33965-6565. *Phone:* 239-745-4597. *Toll-free phone:* 888-889-1095.

Florida Institute of Technology
Melbourne, Florida
http://www.fit.edu/

- **Independent** university, founded 1958
- **Suburban** 130-acre campus with easy access to Orlando
- **Endowment** $87.8 million
- **Coed** 3,565 undergraduate students, 89% full-time, 29% women, 71% men
- **Moderately difficult** entrance level, 66% of applicants were admitted

UNDERGRAD STUDENTS
3,169 full-time, 396 part-time. Students come from 54 states and territories; 92 other countries; 46% are from out of state; 6% Black or African American, non-Hispanic/Latino; 10% Hispanic/Latino; 2% Asian, non-Hispanic/Latino; 0.2% Native Hawaiian or other Pacific Islander, non-Hispanic/Latino; 0.3% American Indian or Alaska Native, non-Hispanic/Latino; 3% Two or more races, non-Hispanic/Latino; 2% Race/ethnicity unknown; 24% international; 6% transferred in; 48% live on campus.

Freshmen:
Admission: 9,743 applied, 6,406 admitted, 668 enrolled. ***Average high school GPA:*** 3.7. ***Test scores:*** SAT evidence-based reading and writing scores over 500: 98%; SAT math scores over 500: 98%; ACT scores over 18: 99%; SAT evidence-based reading and writing scores over 600: 64%; SAT math scores over 600: 68%; ACT scores over 24: 76%; SAT evidence-based reading and writing scores over 700: 14%; SAT math scores over 700: 22%; ACT scores over 30: 31%.

Retention: 79% of full-time freshmen returned.

FACULTY
Total: 476, 61% full-time, 82% with terminal degrees.

Student/faculty ratio: 14:1.

ACADEMICS
Calendar: semesters. *Degrees:* certificates, associate, bachelor's, master's, doctoral, post-master's, and postbachelor's certificates.

Special study options: academic remediation for entering students, accelerated degree program, adult/continuing education programs, advanced placement credit, cooperative education, distance learning, double majors, English as a second language, freshman honors college, honors programs, independent study, internships, part-time degree program, services for LD students, student-designed majors, study abroad, summer session for credit. ***ROTC:*** Army (b).

Computers: 254 computers/terminals and 100 ports are available on campus for general student use. Students can access the following: campus intranet, computer help desk, free student e-mail accounts, online (class) grades, online (class) registration, online (class) schedules. Campuswide network is available. 100% of college-owned or -operated housing units are wired for high-speed Internet access. Wireless service is available via entire campus.

Library: Evans Library. *Books:* 130,809 (physical), 755,673 (digital/electronic); *Serial titles:* 1,501 (physical), 68,741 (digital/electronic); *Databases:* 228. Weekly public service hours: 96; students can reserve study rooms.

STUDENT LIFE
Housing options: on-campus residence required through sophomore year; coed. Campus housing is university owned. Freshman campus housing is guaranteed.

Activities and organizations: drama/theater group, student-run newspaper, radio station, choral group, Phi Eta Sigma Honor Society, American Institute of Aeronautics & Astronautics, Student Government Association (SGA), India Student Association, Student Rocket Society, national fraternities, national sororities.

Athletics Member NCAA. All Division II. ***Intercollegiate sports:*** baseball M(s), basketball M(s)/W(s), crew M(s)/W(s), football M(s), golf M(s), lacrosse M(s)/W(s), rowing M/W, soccer M(s)/W(s), softball W(s), swimming and diving M(s)/W(s), track and field M(s)/W(s), volleyball W(s). ***Intramural sports:*** badminton M(c)/W(c), baseball M(c), basketball M/W, bowling M/W, ice hockey M(c)/W(c), sailing M(c)/W(c), soccer M/W, swimming and diving M(c)/W(c), ultimate Frisbee M(c)/W(c), volleyball M(c)/W(c).

Campus security: 24-hour emergency response devices and patrols, controlled dormitory access.

Student services: health clinic, personal/psychological counseling, veterans affairs office.

COSTS & FINANCIAL AID
Costs (2019–20) ***Comprehensive fee:*** $55,350 includes full-time tuition ($41,720), mandatory fees ($750), and room and board ($12,880). Full-time tuition and fees vary according to course load and program. Part-time tuition: $1170 per credit hour. ***College room only:*** $7000. Room and board charges vary according to board plan and housing facility. ***Payment plan:*** installment. ***Waivers:*** senior citizens and employees or children of employees.

Financial Aid Of all full-time matriculated undergraduates who enrolled in 2019, 2,062 applied for aid, 1,811 were judged to have need, 610 had their need fully met. 390 Federal Work-Study jobs (averaging $2000). 522 state and other part-time jobs (averaging $2361). In 2019, 842 non-need-based awards were made. ***Average percent of need met:*** 83. ***Average financial aid package:*** $36,489. ***Average need-based loan:*** $4379. ***Average need-based gift aid:*** $27,213. ***Average non-need-based aid:*** $15,620. ***Average indebtedness upon graduation:*** $38,943.

APPLYING
Standardized Tests *Required:* SAT or ACT (for admission).

Options: electronic application, deferred entrance.

Required: essay or personal statement, high school transcript, 1 letter of recommendation. ***Recommended:*** interview.

Application deadlines: rolling (freshmen), rolling (out-of-state freshmen), rolling (transfers).

Notification: continuous (freshmen), continuous (transfers).

CONTACT
Mike Perry, Interim Exec. Director of Admissions, Florida Institute of Technology, 150 W. University Blvd, Melbourne, FL 32901. *Phone:* 321-674-8030. *Toll-free phone:* 800-888-4348. *E-mail:* admission@fit.edu.

Florida International University

Miami, Florida

http://www.fiu.edu/

- **State-supported** university, founded 1965, part of State University System of Florida
- **Urban** 576-acre campus with easy access to Miami
- **Endowment** $196.3 million
- **Coed**
- **Moderately difficult** entrance level

FACULTY
Student/faculty ratio: 24:1.

ACADEMICS
Calendar: semesters. *Degrees:* bachelor's, master's, doctoral, and postbachelor's certificates.
Library: Steven and Dorothea Green Library plus 4 others. *Books:* 1.5 million (physical), 443,863 (digital/electronic); *Serial titles:* 63,945 (physical), 111,662 (digital/electronic); *Databases:* 808. Weekly public service hours: 112; students can reserve study rooms.

STUDENT LIFE
Housing options: coed. Campus housing is university owned.

Activities and organizations: drama/theater group, student-run newspaper, radio station, choral group, marching band, Students for Community Service, Black Student Leadership Council, Hospitality Management Student Club, Hispanic Students Association, Haitian Students Organization, national fraternities, national sororities.

Athletics Member NCAA. All Division I.

Campus security: 24-hour emergency response devices and patrols, late-night transport/escort service, controlled dormitory access.

Student services: health clinic, personal/psychological counseling, women's center.

COSTS & FINANCIAL AID
Costs (2019–20) ***Tuition:*** area resident $6168 full-time, $206 per credit hour part-time; state resident $6168 full-time, $206 per credit hour part-time; nonresident $18,566 full-time, $619 per credit hour part-time. ***Required fees:*** $398 full-time. ***Room and board:*** $11,136; room only: $7536.

Financial Aid Of all full-time matriculated undergraduates who enrolled in 2018, 19,110 applied for aid, 18,834 were judged to have need, 1,867 had their need fully met. In 2018, 1269 non-need-based awards were made. ***Average percent of need met:*** 39. ***Average financial aid package:*** $9847. ***Average need-based loan:*** $4485. ***Average need-based gift aid:*** $7256. ***Average non-need-based aid:*** $2163. ***Average indebtedness upon graduation:*** $19,705. ***Financial aid deadline:*** 5/15.

APPLYING
Standardized Tests *Required:* SAT or ACT (for admission). *Required for some:* TOEFL for applicants whose native language is not English.

Options: electronic application.

Application fee: $30.

Required: high school transcript. ***Required for some:*** portfolio or audition.

CONTACT
Ms. Jody Glassman, Director of Admissions, Florida International University, 11200 SW Eighth Street, PC 140, Miami, FL 33199. *Phone:* 305-348-3662. *E-mail:* admiss@fiu.edu.

Florida Memorial University

Miami-Dade, Florida

http://www.fmuniv.edu/

- **Independent** comprehensive, founded 1879, affiliated with Baptist Church
- **Suburban** 77-acre campus
- **Endowment** $6.7 million
- **Coed**
- **Noncompetitive** entrance level

FACULTY
Student/faculty ratio: 12:1.

ACADEMICS
Calendar: semesters. *Degrees:* bachelor's and master's.
Library: Florida Memorial College Library.

STUDENT LIFE
Housing options: coed. Freshman applicants given priority for college housing.

Activities and organizations: drama/theater group, student-run newspaper, national fraternities, national sororities.

Athletics Member NAIA.

Student services: health clinic.

FINANCIAL AID
Financial Aid Of all full-time matriculated undergraduates who enrolled in 2003, 2,074 applied for aid, 1,763 were judged to have need, 284 had their need fully met. 350 Federal Work-Study jobs (averaging $1600). 18 state and other part-time jobs (averaging $1200). ***Average percent of need met:*** 62. ***Average financial aid package:*** $10,950. ***Average need-based loan:*** $3500. ***Average need-based gift aid:*** $3000. ***Average indebtedness upon graduation:*** $3500. ***Financial aid deadline:*** 4/15.

APPLYING
Standardized Tests *Recommended:* SAT or ACT (for admission).

Options: electronic application.

Application fee: $15.

Required: essay or personal statement, high school transcript, minimum 2.2 GPA, 2 letters of recommendation.

CONTACT
Mrs. Peggy Murray Martin, Director of Admissions and International Student Advisor, Florida Memorial University, 15800 NW 42nd Avenue, Miami-Dade, FL 33054. *Phone:* 305-626-3147. *Toll-free phone:* 800-822-1362.

Florida National University

Hialeah, Florida

http://www.fnu.edu/

- **Proprietary** comprehensive, founded 1982
- **Urban** 1-acre campus with easy access to Miami
- **Coed** 3,708 undergraduate students, 71% full-time, 71% women, 37% men
- **Moderately difficult** entrance level, 98% of applicants were admitted

UNDERGRAD STUDENTS
2,622 full-time, 1,386 part-time. Students come from 24 states and territories; 39 other countries; 2% are from out of state; 4% Black or African American, non-Hispanic/Latino; 77% Hispanic/Latino; 0.4% Asian, non-Hispanic/Latino; 0.1% American Indian or Alaska Native, non-Hispanic/Latino; 0.1% Race/ethnicity unknown; 17% international; 6% transferred in.

Freshmen:
Admission: 1,557 applied, 1,527 admitted, 937 enrolled.
Retention: 83% of full-time freshmen returned.

FACULTY
Total: 190, 56% full-time, 12% with terminal degrees.
Student/faculty ratio: 22:1.

ACADEMICS
Calendar: semesters. *Degrees:* certificates, diplomas, associate, bachelor's, master's, post-master's, and postbachelor's certificates.

Special study options: academic remediation for entering students, accelerated degree program, adult/continuing education programs, advanced placement credit, cooperative education, distance learning, English as a second language, independent study, internships, part-time degree program, services for LD students, summer session for credit.

Computers: 356 computers/terminals are available on campus for general student use. Students can access the following: computer help desk, free student e-mail accounts, online (class) grades, online (class) registration, online (class) schedules. Campuswide network is available. Wireless service is available via entire campus.
Library: Hialeah Campus Library plus 1 other. *Books:* 2,479 (physical), 171,052 (digital/electronic); *Serial titles:* 19 (physical), 1,900

(digital/electronic); *Databases:* 32. Weekly public service hours: 78; students can reserve study rooms.

STUDENT LIFE
Housing options: college housing not available.

Activities and organizations: student-run newspaper, Student Government Association, Bible Club, Salsa Club, W.I.C.S (Women Community Service), Criminal Justice Society, national fraternities.

Athletics Member NAIA, USCAA. ***Intercollegiate sports:*** baseball M(s), basketball M(s)/W(s), cross-country running M(s)/W(s), soccer M(s)/W(s), softball W(s), tennis M(s)/W(s), volleyball W(s).

Campus security: 24-hour emergency response devices.

COSTS & FINANCIAL AID
Costs (2020–21) ***Tuition:*** $13,200 full-time, $550 per credit hour part-time. No tuition increase for student's term of enrollment. ***Required fees:*** $488 full-time. ***Payment plans:*** tuition prepayment, installment. ***Waivers:*** employees or children of employees.

Financial Aid Of all full-time matriculated undergraduates who enrolled in 2018, 2,490 applied for aid, 2,365 were judged to have need. 39 Federal Work-Study jobs (averaging $3962). ***Average indebtedness upon graduation:*** $11,700.

APPLYING
Standardized Tests *Required:* SAT or ACT (for admission).

Options: electronic application, deferred entrance.

Required: high school transcript, interview.

Application deadlines: rolling (freshmen), rolling (transfers).

Notification: continuous (freshmen), continuous (transfers).

CONTACT
Mr. Robert Lopez, Director of Admissions, Florida National University, 4425 W. Jose Regueiro (20th) Avenue, Hialeah, FL 33012. *Phone:* 305-821-3333. *Fax:* 305-362-0595. *E-mail:* rlopez@fnu.edu.

Florida Polytechnic University
Lakeland, Florida
http://www.floridapoly.edu/

- **State-supported** comprehensive, part of State University System of Florida
- **Suburban** 171-acre campus with easy access to Tampa Bay
- **Endowment** $840,663
- **Coed** 1,294 undergraduate students, 88% full-time, 14% women, 86% men
- **Moderately difficult** entrance level, 56% of applicants were admitted

UNDERGRAD STUDENTS
1,141 full-time, 153 part-time. Students come from 23 states and territories; 9 other countries; 2% are from out of state; 6% Black or African American, non-Hispanic/Latino; 20% Hispanic/Latino; 4% Asian, non-Hispanic/Latino; 0.3% Native Hawaiian or other Pacific Islander, non-Hispanic/Latino; 0.5% American Indian or Alaska Native, non-Hispanic/Latino; 3% Two or more races, non-Hispanic/Latino; 1% Race/ethnicity unknown; 1% international; 5% transferred in; 44% live on campus.

Freshmen:
Admission: 1,207 applied, 672 admitted, 277 enrolled. ***Average high school GPA:*** 4.0. ***Test scores:*** SAT evidence-based reading and writing scores over 500: 97%; SAT math scores over 500: 100%; ACT scores over 18: 86%; SAT evidence-based reading and writing scores over 600: 68%; SAT math scores over 600: 77%; ACT scores over 24: 81%; SAT evidence-based reading and writing scores over 700: 13%; SAT math scores over 700: 24%; ACT scores over 30: 41%.

Retention: 69% of full-time freshmen returned.

FACULTY
Total: 90, 83% full-time, 87% with terminal degrees.

Student/faculty ratio: 15:1.

ACADEMICS
Calendar: semesters. *Degrees:* bachelor's and master's.

Special study options: accelerated degree program, independent study, internships, study abroad.

Computers: 240 computers/terminals are available on campus for general student use. Students can access the following: campus intranet, computer help desk, free student e-mail accounts, online (class) grades, online (class) registration, online (class) schedules. Campuswide network is available. 100% of college-owned or -operated housing units are wired for high-speed Internet access. Wireless service is available via entire campus.

Library: Main Library plus 1 other. *Books:* 8,300 (physical), 157,000 (digital/electronic); *Serial titles:* 56 (physical); *Databases:* 28,635. Study areas open 24 hours, 5–7 days a week.

STUDENT LIFE
Housing options: coed. Campus housing is university owned.

Activities and organizations: student-run newspaper.

Athletics ***Intramural sports:*** basketball M/W, soccer M/W.

Campus security: 24-hour emergency response devices and patrols, controlled dormitory access.

Student services: health clinic, personal/psychological counseling.

COSTS
Costs (2020–21) ***Tuition:*** state resident $4940 full-time; nonresident $21,005 full-time. ***Room and board:*** $11,430. Room and board charges vary according to board plan and housing facility. ***Payment plan:*** deferred payment. ***Waivers:*** senior citizens and employees or children of employees.

APPLYING
Standardized Tests *Required:* SAT or ACT (for admission).

Options: electronic application, early admission, deferred entrance.

Application fee: $30.

Required: high school transcript. ***Recommended:*** essay or personal statement, letters of recommendation.

Notification: continuous until 9/1 (freshmen).

CONTACT
Ms. Michelle Powell, Senior Associate Director, Florida Polytechnic University, 4700 Research Way, Lakeland, FL 33805. *Phone:* 863-874-8634. *E-mail:* mpowell@floridapoly.edu.

Florida Southern College
Lakeland, Florida
http://www.flsouthern.edu/

- **Independent** comprehensive, founded 1885, affiliated with United Methodist Church
- **Suburban** 113-acre campus with easy access to Tampa, Orlando
- **Endowment** $91.5 million
- **Coed** 2,755 undergraduate students, 92% full-time, 63% women, 37% men
- **Moderately difficult** entrance level, 71% of applicants were admitted

UNDERGRAD STUDENTS
2,537 full-time, 218 part-time. Students come from 48 states and territories; 37 other countries; 32% are from out of state; 7% Black or African American, non-Hispanic/Latino; 13% Hispanic/Latino; 3% Asian, non-Hispanic/Latino; 0.2% Native Hawaiian or other Pacific Islander, non-Hispanic/Latino; 1% American Indian or Alaska Native, non-Hispanic/Latino; 0.5% Two or more races, non-Hispanic/Latino; 1% Race/ethnicity unknown; 3% international; 4% transferred in; 80% live on campus.

Freshmen:
Admission: 5,914 applied, 4,171 admitted, 685 enrolled. ***Average high school GPA:*** 3.7. ***Test scores:*** SAT evidence-based reading and writing scores over 500: 99%; SAT math scores over 500: 97%; ACT scores over 18: 100%; SAT evidence-based reading and writing scores over 600: 56%; SAT math scores over 600: 42%; ACT scores over 24: 76%; SAT evidence-based reading and writing scores over 700: 9%; SAT math scores over 700: 8%; ACT scores over 30: 22%.

Retention: 82% of full-time freshmen returned.

FACULTY
Total: 335, 47% full-time, 62% with terminal degrees.

Student/faculty ratio: 14:1.

ACADEMICS
Calendar: semesters. *Degrees:* bachelor's, master's, and doctoral.

Special study options: accelerated degree program, adult/continuing education programs, advanced placement credit, distance learning, double majors, external degree program, honors programs, independent study, internships, off-campus study, part-time degree program, student-designed majors, study abroad, summer session for credit. ***ROTC:*** Army (b), Air Force (c).

Unusual degree programs: 3-2 business administration; engineering with Washington University in St. Louis; Environmental science with Duke University, Medicine with Lake Erie College of Osteopathic Medicine, 4+1 Master of Arts in Teaching with Florida Southern College Accounting/Master of Accountancy with Florida Southern College.

Computers: 490 computers/terminals and 65 ports are available on campus for general student use. Students can access the following: campus intranet, computer help desk, free student e-mail accounts, online (class) grades, online (class) registration, online (class) schedules, campus portal. Campuswide network is available. 100% of college-owned or -operated housing units are wired for high-speed Internet access. Wireless service is available via entire campus.
Library: Roux Library plus 1 other. *Books:* 160,667 (physical), 167,731 (digital/electronic); *Serial titles:* 22 (physical), 97,772 (digital/electronic); *Databases:* 118. Weekly public service hours: 104; study areas open 24 hours, 5–7 days a week; students can reserve study rooms.

STUDENT LIFE
Housing options: on-campus residence required through senior year; coed, men-only, women-only, special housing for students with disabilities. Campus housing is university owned. Freshman campus housing is guaranteed.

Activities and organizations: drama/theater group, student-run newspaper, radio and television station, choral group, Astronomy Club, FLoSoCo, Beyond (Campus Ministry), ACE, Garden Club, national fraternities, national sororities.

Athletics Member NCAA. All Division II. ***Intercollegiate sports:*** baseball M(s), basketball M(s)/W(s), cheerleading M(c)/W(c), cross-country running M(s)/W(s), equestrian sports W(c), golf M(s)/W(s), ice hockey M(c), lacrosse M(s)/W(s), sand volleyball W(s), soccer M(s)/W(s), softball W(s), swimming and diving M(s)/W(s), tennis M(s)/W(s), track and field M(s)/W(s), volleyball W(s). ***Intramural sports:*** basketball M/W, bowling M/W, football M/W, soccer M/W, softball M/W, swimming and diving M/W, tennis M/W, ultimate Frisbee M/W, volleyball M/W.

Campus security: 24-hour emergency response devices and patrols, student patrols, late-night transport/escort service, controlled dormitory access.

Student services: health clinic, personal/psychological counseling.

COSTS & FINANCIAL AID
Costs (2019–20) ***One-time required fee:*** $100. ***Comprehensive fee:*** $49,520 includes full-time tuition ($36,860), mandatory fees ($780), and room and board ($11,880). Part-time tuition: $998 per credit hour. Part-time tuition and fees vary according to class time and course load. ***College room only:*** $7170. Room and board charges vary according to board plan and housing facility. ***Payment plan:*** installment. ***Waivers:*** employees or children of employees.

Financial Aid Of all full-time matriculated undergraduates who enrolled in 2018, 1,920 applied for aid, 1,653 were judged to have need, 455 had their need fully met. 172 Federal Work-Study jobs (averaging $2260). In 2018, 771 non-need-based awards were made. ***Average percent of need met:*** 77. ***Average financial aid package:*** $31,099. ***Average need-based loan:*** $5293. ***Average need-based gift aid:*** $24,633. ***Average non-need-based aid:*** $24,106. ***Average indebtedness upon graduation:*** $28,974. ***Financial aid deadline:*** 7/1.

APPLYING
Standardized Tests *Required:* SAT or ACT (for admission).

Options: electronic application, early admission, early decision, deferred entrance.

Required: high school transcript, minimum 2.0 GPA, 1 letter of recommendation. ***Recommended:*** essay or personal statement, interview.

Application deadlines: 5/1 (freshmen), 5/1 (out-of-state freshmen), rolling (transfers).

Early decision deadline: 11/1.

Notification: continuous (freshmen), continuous (out-of-state freshmen), continuous (transfers), 12/1 (early decision).

CONTACT
Florida Southern College, 111 Lake Hollingsworth Drive, Lakeland, FL 33801-5698. *Phone:* 863-680-4131. *Toll-free phone:* 800-274-4131.

Florida SouthWestern State College

Fort Myers, Florida

http://www.fsw.edu/

- **State and locally supported** primarily 2-year, founded 1962, part of Florida College System
- **Urban** 413-acre campus with easy access to Fort Myers / Cape Coral
- **Endowment** $19.0 million
- **Coed** 16,672 undergraduate students, 38% full-time, 64% women, 36% men
- **Noncompetitive** entrance level, 79% of applicants were admitted

UNDERGRAD STUDENTS
6,337 full-time, 10,335 part-time. Students come from 44 states and territories; 33 other countries; 2% are from out of state; 12% Black or African American, non-Hispanic/Latino; 34% Hispanic/Latino; 2% Asian, non-Hispanic/Latino; 0.2% Native Hawaiian or other Pacific Islander, non-Hispanic/Latino; 0.4% American Indian or Alaska Native, non-Hispanic/Latino; 2% Two or more races, non-Hispanic/Latino; 6% Race/ethnicity unknown; 2% international; 3% transferred in; 2% live on campus.

Freshmen:
Admission: 6,397 applied, 5,084 admitted, 2,809 enrolled. ***Average high school GPA:*** 2.9.

Retention: 63% of full-time freshmen returned.

FACULTY
Total: 605, 36% full-time, 36% with terminal degrees.

Student/faculty ratio: 28:1.

ACADEMICS
Calendar: semesters. *Degrees:* certificates, associate, and bachelor's.

Special study options: academic remediation for entering students, accelerated degree program, advanced placement credit, distance learning, double majors, English as a second language, honors programs, independent study, internships, off-campus study, part-time degree program, services for LD students, study abroad, summer session for credit.

Computers: 2,548 computers/terminals are available on campus for general student use. Students can access the following: computer help desk, free student e-mail accounts, online (class) grades, online (class) registration, online (class) schedules. Campuswide network is available. 100% of college-owned or -operated housing units are wired for high-speed Internet access. Wireless service is available via entire campus.
Library: Richard H. Rush Library. *Books:* 37,233 (physical), 35,669 (digital/electronic); *Databases:* 120. Weekly public service hours: 79.

STUDENT LIFE
Housing options: coed. Campus housing is university owned.

Activities and organizations: drama/theater group, student-run newspaper, choral group.

Athletics Member NJCAA. ***Intercollegiate sports:*** baseball M(s), basketball M(s)/W(s), softball W(s), volleyball W(s). ***Intramural sports:*** basketball M/W, soccer M/W, volleyball W.

Campus security: 24-hour emergency response devices and patrols, late-night transport/escort service, controlled dormitory access, Rave Guardian app for students, faculty, and staff.

Student services: personal/psychological counseling, veterans affairs office.

COSTS & FINANCIAL AID
Costs (2019–20) ***Tuition:*** state resident $2436 full-time, $81 per credit hour part-time; nonresident $9750 full-time, $325 per credit hour part-time. Full-time tuition and fees vary according to degree level. Part-time tuition and fees vary according to degree level. ***Required fees:*** $965 full-time, $32 per credit hour part-time. ***Room and board:*** $10,500; room

only: $6000. ***Payment plan:*** installment. ***Waivers:*** employees or children of employees.

Financial Aid Of all full-time matriculated undergraduates who enrolled in 2014, 3,887 applied for aid, 3,311 were judged to have need, 68 had their need fully met. In 2014, 166 non-need-based awards were made. ***Average percent of need met:*** 47. ***Average financial aid package:*** $6172. ***Average need-based loan:*** $3461. ***Average need-based gift aid:*** $5119. ***Average non-need-based aid:*** $2588.

APPLYING

Options: electronic application, early admission, deferred entrance.

Application fee: $30.

Required: high school transcript.

Application deadlines: 7/31 (freshmen), 7/31 (transfers).

Notification: continuous (freshmen), continuous (transfers).

CONTACT

FSW Admissions, Florida SouthWestern State College, 8099 College Parkway, Fort Myers, FL 33919. *Phone:* 239-489-9054. *Fax:* 239-489-9094. *E-mail:* admissions@fsw.edu.

Florida State College at Jacksonville

Jacksonville, Florida

http://www.fscj.edu/

CONTACT

Dr. Peter Biegel, Registrar, Florida State College at Jacksonville, 501 West State Street, Jacksonville, FL 32202. *Phone:* 904-632-5112. *Toll-free phone:* 888-873-1145. *E-mail:* pbiegel@fscj.edu.

Florida State University

Tallahassee, Florida

http://www.fsu.edu/

- **State-supported** university, founded 1851, part of State University System of Florida
- **Suburban** 486-acre campus
- **Endowment** $750.2 million
- **Coed** 33,038 undergraduate students, 90% full-time, 57% women, 43% men
- **Very difficult** entrance level, 36% of applicants were admitted

UNDERGRAD STUDENTS

29,647 full-time, 3,391 part-time. Students come from 51 states and territories; 102 other countries; 11% are from out of state; 9% Black or African American, non-Hispanic/Latino; 22% Hispanic/Latino; 3% Asian, non-Hispanic/Latino; 0.1% Native Hawaiian or other Pacific Islander, non-Hispanic/Latino; 0.1% American Indian or Alaska Native, non-Hispanic/Latino; 4% Two or more races, non-Hispanic/Latino; 1% Race/ethnicity unknown; 2% international; 6% transferred in; 20% live on campus.

Freshmen:

Admission: 58,921 applied, 21,197 admitted, 6,874 enrolled. ***Average high school GPA:*** 4.1. ***Test scores:*** SAT evidence-based reading and writing scores over 500: 99%; SAT math scores over 500: 99%; ACT scores over 18: 100%; SAT evidence-based reading and writing scores over 600: 86%; SAT math scores over 600: 73%; ACT scores over 24: 96%; SAT evidence-based reading and writing scores over 700: 15%; SAT math scores over 700: 14%; ACT scores over 30: 36%.

Retention: 93% of full-time freshmen returned.

FACULTY

Total: 1,928, 83% full-time, 91% with terminal degrees.

Student/faculty ratio: 21:1.

ACADEMICS

Calendar: semesters. *Degrees:* certificates, associate, bachelor's, master's, doctoral, post-master's, and postbachelor's certificates.

Special study options: accelerated degree program, advanced placement credit, cooperative education, distance learning, double majors, English as a second language, honors programs, independent study, internships, off-campus study, part-time degree program, services for LD students, study abroad, summer session for credit. ***ROTC:*** Army (b), Navy (c), Air Force (b).

Unusual degree programs: 3-2 engineering; education, criminology, mathematics, computer science, statistics, law.

Computers: 1,100 computers/terminals are available on campus for general student use. Students can access the following: computer help desk, free student e-mail accounts, online (class) grades, online (class) registration, online (class) schedules, course home pages, course search, online fee payment. Campuswide network is available. 100% of college-owned or -operated housing units are wired for high-speed Internet access. Wireless service is available via entire campus.

Library: Robert Manning Strozier Library plus 8 others. *Books:* 2.1 million (physical), 1.9 million (digital/electronic); *Serial titles:* 334,556 (digital/electronic); *Databases:* 659. Weekly public service hours: 134; study areas open 24 hours, 5–7 days a week; students can reserve study rooms.

STUDENT LIFE

Housing options: coed, special housing for students with disabilities. Campus housing is university owned. Freshman applicants given priority for college housing.

Activities and organizations: drama/theater group, student-run newspaper, radio and television station, choral group, marching band, Student Government, Honors Program, Golden Key Honor Society, Marching Chiefs, Intramural Sports, national fraternities, national sororities.

Athletics Member NCAA. All Division I except football (Division I-A). ***Intercollegiate sports:*** baseball M(s), basketball M(s)/W(s), bowling M(c)/W(c), cheerleading M/W, cross-country running M(s)/W(s), golf M(s)/W(s), rugby M(c)/W(c), sand volleyball W(s), soccer M(c)/W(s), softball W(s), swimming and diving M(s)/W(s), table tennis M(c)/W(c), tennis M(s)/W(s), track and field M(s)/W(s), volleyball M(c)/W(s). ***Intramural sports:*** badminton M(c)/W(c), baseball M(c), basketball M/W, bowling M/W, cheerleading W(c), crew M(c)/W(c), equestrian sports M(c)/W(c), fencing M(c)/W(c), field hockey M(c)/W(c), football M/W, golf M/W, gymnastics M(c)/W(c), ice hockey M(c)/W(c), lacrosse M(c)/W(c), racquetball M/W, sailing M(c)/W(c), sand volleyball M/W, soccer M/W, softball M/W(c), swimming and diving M(c)/W(c), table tennis M/W, tennis M/W, track and field M/W, ultimate Frisbee M(c)/W(c), volleyball M(c)/W(c), water polo M(c)/W(c), weight lifting M/W, wrestling M/W.

Campus security: 24-hour emergency response devices and patrols, late-night transport/escort service, controlled dormitory access.

Student services: health clinic, personal/psychological counseling, women's center, legal services, veterans affairs office.

COSTS & FINANCIAL AID

Costs (2019–20) ***Tuition:*** area resident $4640 full-time, $216 per credit hour part-time; state resident $4640 full-time, $216 per credit hour part-time; nonresident $19,806 full-time, $721 per credit hour part-time. Full-time tuition and fees vary according to course load, degree level, and location. Part-time tuition and fees vary according to course load, degree level, and location. ***Required fees:*** $1877 full-time. ***Room and board:*** $10,780; room only: $6540. Room and board charges vary according to board plan and housing facility. ***Payment plans:*** tuition prepayment, installment. ***Waivers:*** senior citizens and employees or children of employees.

Financial Aid Of all full-time matriculated undergraduates who enrolled in 2016, 20,291 applied for aid, 14,299 were judged to have need, 1,545 had their need fully met. 855 Federal Work-Study jobs (averaging $2400). 21 state and other part-time jobs (averaging $2400). In 2016, 4466 non-need-based awards were made. ***Average percent of need met:*** 65. ***Average financial aid package:*** $13,013. ***Average need-based loan:*** $4450. ***Average need-based gift aid:*** $10,859. ***Average non-need-based aid:*** $4987. ***Average indebtedness upon graduation:*** $23,679.

APPLYING

Standardized Tests *Required:* SAT or ACT (for admission).

Options: electronic application, early admission.

Application fee: $30.

Required: high school transcript. ***Recommended:*** essay or personal statement.

Application deadlines: 3/1 (freshmen), 6/1 (transfers).

Notification: 1/27 (freshmen), continuous (transfers).

CONTACT
Florida State University, 600 West College Avenue, Tallahassee, FL 32306. *Phone:* 850-644-1389.

Fortis College

Cutler Bay, Florida

http://www.fortis.edu/

CONTACT
Fortis College, 19600 South Dixie Highway, Suite B, Cutler Bay, FL 33157. *Toll-free phone:* 855-4-FORTIS.

Full Sail University

Winter Park, Florida

http://www.fullsail.edu/

CONTACT
Ms. Mary Beth Plank, Director of Admissions, Full Sail University, 3300 University Boulevard, Winter Park, FL 32792-7437. *Phone:* 407-679-6333. *Toll-free phone:* 800-226-7625. *E-mail:* admissions@fullsail.com.

Gulf Coast State College

Panama City, Florida

http://www.gulfcoast.edu/

- **State-supported** primarily 2-year, founded 1957, part of Florida College System
- **Urban** 80-acre campus
- **Coed** 4,797 undergraduate students, 34% full-time, 63% women, 37% men
- **Noncompetitive** entrance level

UNDERGRAD STUDENTS
1,625 full-time, 3,172 part-time. Students come from 15 states and territories; 3% are from out of state; 11% Black or African American, non-Hispanic/Latino; 7% Hispanic/Latino; 3% Asian, non-Hispanic/Latino; 0.1% Native Hawaiian or other Pacific Islander, non-Hispanic/Latino; 0.6% American Indian or Alaska Native, non-Hispanic/Latino; 4% Two or more races, non-Hispanic/Latino; 4% Race/ethnicity unknown; 0.6% international; 3% transferred in.

Freshmen:
Admission: 855 enrolled.

FACULTY
Total: 282, 47% full-time.

Student/faculty ratio: 19:1.

ACADEMICS
Calendar: semesters. *Degrees:* certificates, associate, and bachelor's.

Special study options: academic remediation for entering students, accelerated degree program, adult/continuing education programs, advanced placement credit, cooperative education, distance learning, double majors, English as a second language, external degree program, honors programs, independent study, off-campus study, part-time degree program, services for LD students, study abroad, summer session for credit.

Computers: 1,000 computers/terminals are available on campus for general student use. Students can access the following: computer help desk, free student e-mail accounts, online (class) grades, online (class) registration, online (class) schedules. Campuswide network is available. Wireless service is available via entire campus.
Library: Gulf Coast State College Library. *Books:* 29,718 (physical), 84,826 (digital/electronic); *Serial titles:* 44 (physical), 42,430 (digital/electronic); *Databases:* 133.

STUDENT LIFE
Housing options: college housing not available.

Activities and organizations: drama/theater group, student-run newspaper, radio and television station, choral group, Student Government Association, TRiO Society, Visionaries Ink, Student Veteran's Association.

Athletics Member NJCAA. ***Intercollegiate sports:*** baseball M(s), basketball M(s)/W(s), softball W(s), volleyball W(s).

Campus security: 24-hour patrols, late-night transport/escort service, patrols by trained security personnel during campus hours.

Student services: personal/psychological counseling, veterans affairs office.

COSTS & FINANCIAL AID
Costs (2019–20) ***Tuition:*** state resident $2370 full-time, $99 per credit hour part-time; nonresident $8633 full-time, $360 per credit hour part-time. Full-time tuition and fees vary according to degree level. Part-time tuition and fees vary according to degree level. ***Required fees:*** $620 full-time, $26 per credit hour part-time.

Financial Aid Of all full-time matriculated undergraduates who enrolled in 2018, 145 Federal Work-Study jobs (averaging $3200). 60 state and other part-time jobs (averaging $2600).

APPLYING
Options: electronic application, early admission, deferred entrance.

Application fee: $20.

Required: high school transcript.

Application deadlines: rolling (freshmen), rolling (transfers).

Notification: continuous (freshmen).

CONTACT
Ms. Shelby Antolchick, Application Process Specialist, Gulf Coast State College, 5230 West U.S. Highway 98, Panama City, FL 32401. *Phone:* 850-769-1551 Ext. 2936. *Fax:* 850-913-3308. *E-mail:* santolchi@gulfcoast.edu.

Herzing University

Winter Park, Florida

http://www.herzing.edu/orlando

CONTACT
Herzing University, 1865 SR 436, Winter Park, FL 32792. *Toll-free phone:* 800-596-0724.

Hobe Sound Bible College

Hobe Sound, Florida

http://www.hsbc.edu/

CONTACT
Mrs. Elizabeth McMillan, Director of Admissions, Hobe Sound Bible College, PO Box 1065, Hobe Sound, FL 33475-1065. *Phone:* 772-545-1400 Ext. 1019. *E-mail:* elizabethmcmillan@hsbc.edu.

Hodges University

Naples, Florida

http://www.hodges.edu/

CONTACT
Hodges University, 2655 Northbrooke Drive, Naples, FL 34119. *Phone:* 239-513-1122 Ext. 6104. *Toll-free phone:* 800-466-8017.

Indian River State College

Fort Pierce, Florida

http://www.irsc.edu/

CONTACT
Mr. Eileen Storck, Dean of Educational Services, Indian River State College, 3209 Virginia Avenue, Fort Pierce, FL 34981-5596. *Phone:* 772-462-7361. *Toll-free phone:* 866-792-4772. *E-mail:* estrock@irsc.edu.

Jacksonville University

Jacksonville, Florida

http://www.ju.edu/

- **Independent** comprehensive, founded 1934
- **Suburban** 260-acre campus with easy access to Jacksonville, Saint Augustine
- **Endowment** $44.7 million
- **Coed** 2,928 undergraduate students, 82% full-time, 59% women, 41% men
- **Moderately difficult** entrance level, 92% of applicants were admitted

UNDERGRAD STUDENTS

2,391 full-time, 537 part-time. Students come from 48 states and territories; 45 other countries; 33% are from out of state; 20% Black or African American, non-Hispanic/Latino; 12% Hispanic/Latino; 2% Asian, non-Hispanic/Latino; 0.5% Native Hawaiian or other Pacific Islander, non-Hispanic/Latino; 0.5% American Indian or Alaska Native, non-Hispanic/Latino; 3% Two or more races, non-Hispanic/Latino; 3% Race/ethnicity unknown; 7% international; 12% transferred in; 58% live on campus.

Freshmen:

Admission: 5,139 applied, 4,712 admitted, 657 enrolled. ***Average high school GPA:*** 3.5. ***Test scores:*** SAT evidence-based reading and writing scores over 500: 56%; SAT math scores over 500: 56%; ACT scores over 18: 81%; SAT evidence-based reading and writing scores over 600: 25%; SAT math scores over 600: 13%; ACT scores over 24: 36%; SAT math scores over 700: 6%; ACT scores over 30: 6%.

Retention: 74% of full-time freshmen returned.

FACULTY

Total: 429, 56% full-time, 56% with terminal degrees.

Student/faculty ratio: 11:1.

ACADEMICS

Calendar: semesters. *Degrees:* bachelor's, master's, doctoral, post-master's, and postbachelor's certificates.

Special study options: academic remediation for entering students, accelerated degree program, adult/continuing education programs, advanced placement credit, cooperative education, distance learning, double majors, English as a second language, freshman honors college, honors programs, independent study, internships, off-campus study, part-time degree program, services for LD students, student-designed majors, study abroad, summer session for credit. ***ROTC:*** Army (b), Navy (b).

Computers: 400 computers/terminals and 1,205 ports are available on campus for general student use. Students can access the following: campus intranet, computer help desk, free student e-mail accounts, online (class) grades, online (class) registration, online (class) schedules, learning management systems. Campuswide network is available. 100% of college-owned or -operated housing units are wired for high-speed Internet access. Wireless service is available via entire campus.
Library: Carl S. Swisher Library. *Books:* 187,294 (physical), 268,187 (digital/electronic); *Serial titles:* 7,434 (physical), 55,516 (digital/electronic); *Databases:* 69. Weekly public service hours: 88; students can reserve study rooms.

STUDENT LIFE

Housing options: on-campus residence required through junior year; coed, special housing for students with disabilities. Campus housing is university owned. Freshman campus housing is guaranteed.

Activities and organizations: drama/theater group, student-run newspaper, radio and television station, choral group, marching band, Campus Connection, Outing Club, International Students Association, Colleges Against Cancer, Medical Professionals Society, national fraternities, national sororities.

Athletics Member NCAA. All Division I. ***Intercollegiate sports:*** baseball M(s), basketball M(s)/W(s), crew M(s)/W(s), cross-country running M/W(s), golf M(s)/W(s)(c), lacrosse M(s)/W(s), rowing M/W, sand volleyball W, soccer M(s)/W(s), softball W(s), track and field W(s), volleyball W(s). ***Intramural sports:*** basketball M/W, cheerleading M(c)/W(c), football M/W, riflery M(c)/W(c), sailing M(c)/W(c), sand volleyball M/W, soccer M/W, softball M/W, ultimate Frisbee M/W, volleyball M/W.

Campus security: 24-hour emergency response devices and patrols, student patrols, late-night transport/escort service, controlled dormitory access, trained security patrols during evening hours.

Student services: health clinic, personal/psychological counseling, veterans affairs office.

COSTS & FINANCIAL AID

Costs (2020–21) ***Comprehensive fee:*** $54,710 includes full-time tuition ($39,900) and room and board ($14,810). Full-time tuition and fees vary according to degree level and program. Part-time tuition: $1335 per credit hour. Part-time tuition and fees vary according to degree level and program. ***Required fees:*** $28 per credit hour part-time. ***College room only:*** $9500. Room and board charges vary according to board plan. ***Payment plan:*** installment. ***Waivers:*** employees or children of employees.

Financial Aid Of all full-time matriculated undergraduates who enrolled in 2019, 1,900 applied for aid, 1,708 were judged to have need, 296 had their need fully met. 293 Federal Work-Study jobs (averaging $856). 254 state and other part-time jobs (averaging $1031). In 2019, 529 non-need-based awards were made. ***Average percent of need met:*** 67. ***Average financial aid package:*** $29,666. ***Average need-based loan:*** $4095. ***Average need-based gift aid:*** $21,262. ***Average non-need-based aid:*** $18,450. ***Average indebtedness upon graduation:*** $44,279.

APPLYING

Options: electronic application, early admission, deferred entrance.

Application fee: $30.

Required: high school transcript, minimum 2.0 GPA. ***Required for some:*** essay or personal statement, 2 letters of recommendation, audition for music, dance, and theater majors; portfolio for art, computer art, and design majors; interview for the Honors Program. ***Recommended:*** interview.

Application deadlines: rolling (freshmen), rolling (out-of-state freshmen), rolling (transfers).

Notification: continuous (freshmen), continuous (out-of-state freshmen), continuous (transfers).

CONTACT

Jacksonville University, 2800 University Boulevard North, Jacksonville, FL 32211. *Phone:* 904-256-7005. *Toll-free phone:* 800-225-2027.

Johnson & Wales University

North Miami, Florida

http://www.jwu.edu/northmiami/

CONTACT

Jeff Greenip, Director of Admissions, Johnson & Wales University, 1701 Northeast 127th Street, North Miami, FL 33181. *Phone:* 305-892-7600. *Toll-free phone:* 866-598-3567. *Fax:* 305-892-7020. *E-mail:* mia@admissions.jwu.edu.

Johnson University Florida

Kissimmee, Florida

http://www.johnsonu.edu/

- **Independent** comprehensive, founded 1976, affiliated with Christian Churches and Churches of Christ
- **Small-town** 40-acre campus with easy access to Orlando
- **Coed** 182 undergraduate students, 93% full-time, 43% women, 57% men
- **Minimally difficult** entrance level, 31% of applicants were admitted

UNDERGRAD STUDENTS

170 full-time, 12 part-time. 12% are from out of state; 20% Black or African American, non-Hispanic/Latino; 20% Hispanic/Latino; 0.5% Asian, non-Hispanic/Latino; 0.5% Native Hawaiian or other Pacific Islander, non-Hispanic/Latino; 3% Two or more races, non-Hispanic/Latino; 4% Race/ethnicity unknown; 5% international; 9% transferred in; 69% live on campus.

Freshmen:

Admission: 371 applied, 114 admitted, 56 enrolled. ***Average high school GPA:*** 3.2. ***Test scores:*** SAT evidence-based reading and writing scores over 500: 49%; SAT math scores over 500: 45%; ACT scores over 18: 63%; SAT evidence-based reading and writing scores over 600: 23%; SAT math scores over 600: 10%; ACT scores over 24: 5%; SAT evidence-based reading and writing scores over 700: 5%.

Retention: 46% of full-time freshmen returned.

FACULTY

Total: 37, 35% full-time, 57% with terminal degrees.

Student/faculty ratio: 8:1.

ACADEMICS

Calendar: semesters. *Degrees:* certificates, associate, bachelor's, and master's.

Special study options: adult/continuing education programs, advanced placement credit, distance learning, double majors, independent study, internships, part-time degree program, summer session for credit.

Computers: 16 computers/terminals are available on campus for general student use. Students can access the following: campus intranet, computer help desk, free student e-mail accounts, online (class) grades, online (class) registration, online (class) schedules. Campuswide network is available. 100% of college-owned or -operated housing units are wired for high-speed Internet access. Wireless service is available via entire campus.

Library: Library. *Books:* 35,023 (physical), 345,536 (digital/electronic); *Serial titles:* 120 (physical), 44,275 (digital/electronic); *Databases:* 2,145.

STUDENT LIFE

Housing options: men-only, women-only. Campus housing is university owned.

Activities and organizations: choral group, Student Government Association, Harvesters (Missions), Timothy club (preachers), Ultimate Frisbee.

Athletics Member NCCAA. ***Intercollegiate sports:*** basketball M/W, soccer M, volleyball W. ***Intramural sports:*** sand volleyball M/W, ultimate Frisbee M.

Campus security: controlled dormitory access.

Student services: personal/psychological counseling.

COSTS & FINANCIAL AID

Costs (2020–21) ***Tuition:*** $16,400 full-time. ***Required fees:*** $1230 full-time. ***Room only:*** $3600. Room and board charges vary according to board plan. ***Payment plan:*** installment. ***Waivers:*** employees or children of employees.

Financial Aid Of all full-time matriculated undergraduates who enrolled in 2017, 162 applied for aid, 151 were judged to have need, 19 had their need fully met. In 2017, 11 non-need-based awards were made. ***Average percent of need met:*** 66. ***Average financial aid package:*** $12,008. ***Average need-based loan:*** $3660. ***Average need-based gift aid:*** $9040. ***Average non-need-based aid:*** $4961. ***Average indebtedness upon graduation:*** $28,906.

APPLYING

Standardized Tests *Required:* SAT or ACT (for admission).

Options: electronic application, early admission, deferred entrance.

Application fee: $35.

Required: essay or personal statement, high school transcript, minimum 2.5 GPA, 3 letters of recommendation. ***Required for some:*** interview.

Application deadlines: 7/15 (freshmen), 7/15 (out-of-state freshmen), 7/15 (transfers).

Notification: continuous until 8/15 (freshmen), continuous until 8/15 (transfers).

CONTACT

Mr. Doug Johnson, Director of Admissions, Johnson University Florida, 1011 Bill Beck Boulevard, Kissimmee, FL 34744. *Phone:* 407-569-1380. *Toll-free phone:* 888-468-6322. *Fax:* 321-206-2007. *E-mail:* djohnson@johnsonu.edu.

Jose Maria Vargas University

Pembroke Pines, Florida

http://www.jmvu.edu/

CONTACT

Jose Maria Vargas University, 10131 Pines Boulevard, Pembroke Pines, FL 33026.

Keiser University

Fort Lauderdale, Florida

http://www.keiseruniversity.edu/

- **Independent** university, founded 1977
- **Urban** campus
- **Coed** 17,530 undergraduate students, 60% full-time, 70% women, 30% men
- 99% of applicants were admitted

UNDERGRAD STUDENTS

10,487 full-time, 7,043 part-time. Students come from 34 states and territories; 12% are from out of state; 19% Black or African American, non-Hispanic/Latino; 29% Hispanic/Latino; 3% Asian, non-Hispanic/Latino; 0.3% Native Hawaiian or other Pacific Islander, non-Hispanic/Latino; 0.8% American Indian or Alaska Native, non-Hispanic/Latino; 2% Two or more races, non-Hispanic/Latino; 15% Race/ethnicity unknown; 0.9% international; 3% transferred in.

Freshmen:

Admission: 5,971 applied, 5,923 admitted, 6,267 enrolled.

Retention: 81% of full-time freshmen returned.

FACULTY

Total: 1,802, 66% full-time, 34% with terminal degrees.

Student/faculty ratio: 14:1.

ACADEMICS

Calendar: 3 semesters per year. *Degrees:* associate, bachelor's, master's, doctoral, and post-master's certificates (profile includes data from campuses located in Daytona Beach, Fort Lauderdale, Fort Myers, Jacksonville, Lakeland, Melbourne, Miami, Orlando, Pembroke Pines, Port St. Lucie, Sarasota, Tallahassee, Tampa, and West Palm Beach; not all programs offered at all locations, but many classes offered 100% online).

Special study options: advanced placement credit, distance learning, English as a second language, internships, part-time degree program, study abroad, summer session for credit.

Computers: Students can access the following: free student e-mail accounts, online (class) grades, online (class) registration, online (class) schedules. Campuswide network is available. Wireless service is available via entire campus.

Library: Keiser University Library. *Books:* 118,140 (physical), 159,000 (digital/electronic); *Serial titles:* 155 (physical), 67 (digital/electronic); *Databases:* 238.

STUDENT LIFE

Activities and organizations: Student Government Association, Phi Theta Kappa, Student Veterans of America, Alpha Phi Sigma National Honor Society, Student Nurses Association.

Athletics Member NAIA. ***Intercollegiate sports:*** baseball M, basketball M/W, cross-country running M/W, football M, golf M/W, lacrosse M/W, soccer M/W, softball W, swimming and diving M/W, tennis M/W, track and field M/W, volleyball W.

Campus security: 24-hour patrols, late-night transport/escort service, AlertNow Rapid Communications Service, Campus Response Teams.

Student services: veterans affairs office.

COSTS & FINANCIAL AID

Costs (2020–21) ***Comprehensive fee:*** $46,954 includes full-time tuition ($30,768), mandatory fees ($2100), and room and board ($14,086). Full-time tuition and fees vary according to location and program. Part-time tuition: $1282 per credit hour. Part-time tuition and fees vary according to location and program. ***Payment plan:*** installment. ***Waivers:*** employees or children of employees.

Financial Aid Of all full-time matriculated undergraduates who enrolled in 2018, 9,488 applied for aid, 9,488 were judged to have need, 9,488 had their need fully met. 28 Federal Work-Study jobs (averaging $3856). In 2018, 7911 non-need-based awards were made. ***Average percent of need met:*** 88. ***Average financial aid package:*** $6254. ***Average need-based loan:*** $14,105. ***Average need-based gift aid:*** $6254. ***Average non-need-based aid:*** $3329.

APPLYING

Standardized Tests *Required:* SAT or ACT or Wonderlic aptitude test (for admission).

Options: electronic application.

Application fee: $55.

Required: high school transcript.

Application deadlines: rolling (freshmen), rolling (transfers).

Notification: continuous (freshmen), continuous (transfers).

CONTACT

Keiser University, 1500 NW 49th Street, Fort Lauderdale, FL 33309. *Phone:* 954-776-4476. *Toll-free phone:* 888-534-7379.

Lynn University

Boca Raton, Florida

http://www.lynn.edu/

- **Independent** comprehensive, founded 1962
- **Suburban** 123-acre campus with easy access to Fort Lauderdale
- **Endowment** $27.6 million
- **Coed** 2,422 undergraduate students, 92% full-time, 50% women, 50% men
- **Moderately difficult** entrance level, 74% of applicants were admitted

UNDERGRAD STUDENTS

2,218 full-time, 204 part-time. Students come from 45 states and territories; 90 other countries; 48% are from out of state; 10% Black or African American, non-Hispanic/Latino; 18% Hispanic/Latino; 1% Asian, non-Hispanic/Latino; 0.2% Native Hawaiian or other Pacific Islander, non-Hispanic/Latino; 0.4% American Indian or Alaska Native, non-Hispanic/Latino; 2% Two or more races, non-Hispanic/Latino; 5% Race/ethnicity unknown; 16% international; 7% transferred in; 72% live on campus.

Freshmen:

Admission: 7,387 applied, 5,483 admitted, 739 enrolled. ***Average high school GPA:*** 3.2. ***Test scores:*** SAT evidence-based reading and writing scores over 500: 79%; SAT math scores over 500: 69%; ACT scores over 18: 94%; SAT evidence-based reading and writing scores over 600: 23%; SAT math scores over 600: 18%; ACT scores over 24: 42%; SAT evidence-based reading and writing scores over 700: 3%; SAT math scores over 700: 4%; ACT scores over 30: 5%.

Retention: 71% of full-time freshmen returned.

FACULTY

Total: 222, 59% full-time, 42% with terminal degrees.

Student/faculty ratio: 18:1.

ACADEMICS

Calendar: semesters plus 3 summer sessions. *Degrees:* certificates, associate, bachelor's, master's, doctoral, post-master's, and postbachelor's certificates.

Special study options: academic remediation for entering students, accelerated degree program, advanced placement credit, cooperative education, distance learning, double majors, English as a second language, independent study, internships, part-time degree program, services for LD students, student-designed majors, study abroad, summer session for credit. ***ROTC:*** Air Force (c).

Computers: 150 computers/terminals are available on campus for general student use. Students can access the following: campus intranet, computer help desk, free student e-mail accounts, online (class) grades, online (class) registration, online (class) schedules. Campuswide network is available. 100% of college-owned or -operated housing units are wired for high-speed Internet access. Wireless service is available via entire campus.

Library: Eugene M. and Christine E. Lynn Library. *Books:* 47,403 (physical), 406,452 (digital/electronic); *Serial titles:* 1,603 (physical), 71,094 (digital/electronic); *Databases:* 125. Weekly public service hours: 96; students can reserve study rooms.

STUDENT LIFE

Housing options: on-campus residence required through sophomore year; coed, special housing for students with disabilities. Campus housing is university owned. Freshman campus housing is guaranteed.

Activities and organizations: drama/theater group, student-run newspaper, radio and television station, Theta Phi Alpha, Sigma Alpha Epsilon, Sigma Sigma Sigma, Game Club, Student Activities Board, national fraternities, national sororities.

Athletics Member NCAA. All Division II. ***Intercollegiate sports:*** baseball M(s), basketball M(s)/W(s), cross-country running M(s)/W(s), golf M(s)/W(s), lacrosse M(s), soccer M(s)/W(s), softball W(s), swimming and diving W(s), tennis M(s)/W(s), track and field W(s), volleyball W(s). ***Intramural sports:*** basketball M/W, soccer M/W, tennis M/W, ultimate Frisbee M/W, volleyball M/W.

Campus security: 24-hour emergency response devices and patrols, late-night transport/escort service, controlled dormitory access, video monitor at residence entrances.

Student services: health clinic, personal/psychological counseling, women's center.

COSTS & FINANCIAL AID

Costs (2020–21) ***One-time required fee:*** $1000. ***Comprehensive fee:*** $52,320 includes full-time tuition ($37,600), mandatory fees ($2250), and room and board ($12,470). Full-time tuition and fees vary according to program. Part-time tuition: $1080 per credit hour. Part-time tuition and fees vary according to course load and program. ***Room and board:*** Room and board charges vary according to board plan and housing facility. ***Payment plans:*** installment, deferred payment. ***Waivers:*** children of alumni and employees or children of employees.

Financial Aid Of all full-time matriculated undergraduates who enrolled in 2019, 2,102 applied for aid, 1,054 were judged to have need, 1,049 had their need fully met. 157 Federal Work-Study jobs (averaging $1630). 6 state and other part-time jobs (averaging $1229). In 2019, 815 non-need-based awards were made. ***Average percent of need met:*** 55. ***Average financial aid package:*** $24,022. ***Average need-based loan:*** $4597. ***Average need-based gift aid:*** $9593. ***Average non-need-based aid:*** $12,395. ***Average indebtedness upon graduation:*** $3451.

APPLYING

Standardized Tests *Recommended:* SAT or ACT (for admission).

Options: electronic application, early admission, early action, deferred entrance.

Required: essay or personal statement, high school transcript. ***Required for some:*** audition for Conservatory of Music. ***Recommended:*** interview.

Application deadlines: 8/1 (freshmen), rolling (transfers), 11/15 (early action).

Notification: continuous until 9/1 (freshmen), continuous (transfers), 12/15 (early action).

CONTACT

Stefano Papaleo, Director of Undergraduate Admission, Lynn University, Admission, 3601 North Military Trail, Boca Raton, FL 33431. *Phone:* 561-237-7831. *Toll-free phone:* 800-888-5966. *Fax:* 561-237-7100. *E-mail:* spapaleo@lynn.edu.

Marconi International University

Miami, Florida

http://www.miuniversity.edu/

CONTACT

Admissions, Marconi International University, 141 NE 3rd Avenue 7th Floor, Miami, FL 33132. *Phone:* 954-374-4701. *E-mail:* info@marconiinternational.org.

Miami Dade College

Miami, Florida

http://www.mdc.edu/

- **State and locally supported** primarily 2-year, founded 1960, part of Florida College System
- **Urban** campus
- **Endowment** $137.1 million
- **Coed** 56,001 undergraduate students, 42% full-time, 57% women, 43% men
- **Noncompetitive** entrance level, 100% of applicants were admitted

UNDERGRAD STUDENTS
23,589 full-time, 32,412 part-time. Students come from 37 states and territories; 165 other countries; 0.4% are from out of state; 14% Black or African American, non-Hispanic/Latino; 70% Hispanic/Latino; 1% Asian, non-Hispanic/Latino; 0.1% Native Hawaiian or other Pacific Islander, non-Hispanic/Latino; 0.1% American Indian or Alaska Native, non-Hispanic/Latino; 0.6% Two or more races, non-Hispanic/Latino; 2% Race/ethnicity unknown; 6% international; 0.1% transferred in.

Freshmen:
Admission: 44,910 applied, 44,910 admitted, 12,173 enrolled.

FACULTY
Total: 2,355, 30% full-time, 25% with terminal degrees.

Student/faculty ratio: 26:1.

ACADEMICS
Calendar: 16-16-6-6. *Degrees:* certificates, associate, bachelor's, and postbachelor's certificates.

Special study options: academic remediation for entering students, accelerated degree program, adult/continuing education programs, advanced placement credit, cooperative education, distance learning, English as a second language, freshman honors college, honors programs, independent study, internships, off-campus study, part-time degree program, services for LD students, study abroad, summer session for credit. ***ROTC:*** Army (b), Air Force (c).

Computers: 9,655 computers/terminals and 1,500 ports are available on campus for general student use. Students can access the following: campus intranet, computer help desk, free student e-mail accounts, online (class) grades, online (class) registration, online (class) schedules, admissions, student feedback of faculty, financial aid. Campuswide network is available. Wireless service is available via entire campus.
Library: Miami Dade College Learning Resources plus 9 others. *Books:* 185,820 (physical), 60,221 (digital/electronic); *Serial titles:* 708 (physical), 46,482 (digital/electronic); *Databases:* 126. Weekly public service hours: 69; students can reserve study rooms.

STUDENT LIFE
Housing options: college housing not available.

Activities and organizations: drama/theater group, student-run newspaper, radio and television station, choral group, Student Government Association, Phi Theta Kappa, Phi Beta Lambda (business), Future Educators of America Professional, Kappa Delta Pi Honor Society (education).

Athletics Member NCAA, NJCAA. All NCAA Division I.
Intercollegiate sports: baseball M(s), basketball M(s)/W(s), softball W(s), volleyball W(s).

Campus security: 24-hour emergency response devices and patrols, student patrols, late-night transport/escort service, Emergency Mass Notification System (EMNS), campus public address systems, LiveSafe mobile safety App for students/employees.

Student services: health clinic, personal/psychological counseling, veterans affairs office.

COSTS & FINANCIAL AID
Costs (2019–20) ***One-time required fee:*** $30. ***Tuition:*** state resident $1987 full-time, $83 per credit hour part-time; nonresident $7947 full-time, $331 per credit hour part-time. Full-time tuition and fees vary according to course load, degree level, and program. Part-time tuition and fees vary according to course load, degree level, and program. ***Required fees:*** $851 full-time, $35 per semester hour part-time. ***Payment plan:*** installment. ***Waivers:*** employees or children of employees.

Financial Aid Of all full-time matriculated undergraduates who enrolled in 2018, 800 Federal Work-Study jobs (averaging $5000). 125 state and other part-time jobs (averaging $5000).

APPLYING
Options: electronic application, early admission.

Application fee: $30.

Required: high school transcript.

Application deadlines: rolling (freshmen), rolling (transfers).

Notification: continuous (freshmen), continuous (transfers).

CONTACT
Ms. Elisabet Vizoso, Interim College Registrar, Miami Dade College, 11011 SW 104th Street, Miami, FL 33176. *Phone:* 305-237-2206. *Fax:* 305-237-2532. *E-mail:* evizoso@mdc.edu.

Miami International University of Art & Design

Miami, Florida

http://www.artinstitutes.edu/miami/

CONTACT
Miami International University of Art & Design, 1501 Biscayne Boulevard, Suite 100, Miami, FL 33132-1418. *Phone:* 305-428-5700. *Toll-free phone:* 800-225-9023.

Miami Regional University

Miami Springs, Florida

http://www.mru.edu/

CONTACT
Miami Regional University, 700 South Royal Poinciana Boulevard, Miami Springs, FL 33166.

Millennia Atlantic University

Doral, Florida

http://www.maufl.edu/

- **Proprietary** comprehensive
- **Coed**

FACULTY
Student/faculty ratio: 20:1.

ACADEMICS
Calendar: semesters. *Degrees:* associate, bachelor's, and master's.

FINANCIAL AID
Financial Aid Of all full-time matriculated undergraduates who enrolled in 2019, 1 applied for aid, 1 were judged to have need. ***Average percent of need met:*** 100. ***Average financial aid package:*** $3197. ***Average need-based gift aid:*** $5567.

APPLYING
Application fee: $50.

CONTACT
Millennia Atlantic University, 3801 NW 97th Avenue, Doral, FL 33178.

New College of Florida

Sarasota, Florida

http://www.ncf.edu/

- **State-supported** comprehensive, founded 1960, part of State University System of Florida
- **Suburban** 110-acre campus with easy access to Tampa-St. Petersburg
- **Endowment** $41.7 million
- **Coed** 702 undergraduate students, 100% full-time, 63% women, 37% men
- **Very difficult** entrance level, 73% of applicants were admitted

UNDERGRAD STUDENTS
702 full-time. Students come from 36 states and territories; 14 other countries; 17% are from out of state; 3% Black or African American, non-Hispanic/Latino; 18% Hispanic/Latino; 3% Asian, non-Hispanic/Latino; 4% Two or more races, non-Hispanic/Latino; 0.7% Race/ethnicity unknown; 2% international; 4% transferred in; 80% live on campus.

Freshmen:
Admission: 1,226 applied, 896 admitted, 147 enrolled. ***Average high school GPA:*** 3.9. ***Test scores:*** SAT evidence-based reading and writing scores over 500: 98%; SAT math scores over 500: 95%; ACT scores over 18: 100%; SAT evidence-based reading and writing scores over 600: 80%; SAT math scores over 600: 50%; ACT scores over 24: 88%; SAT evidence-based reading and writing scores over 700: 29%; SAT math scores over 700: 10%; ACT scores over 30: 41%.

Retention: 86% of full-time freshmen returned.

FACULTY
Total: 135, 73% full-time, 87% with terminal degrees.

Student/faculty ratio: 7:1.

ACADEMICS
Calendar: 4-1-4. *Degrees:* bachelor's and master's.

Special study options: accelerated degree program, advanced placement credit, double majors, freshman honors college, honors programs, independent study, internships, off-campus study, services for LD students, student-designed majors, study abroad, summer session for credit.

Computers: 105 computers/terminals and 1,356 ports are available on campus for general student use. Students can access the following: campus intranet, computer help desk, free student e-mail accounts, online (class) grades, online (class) registration, online (class) schedules. Campuswide network is available. 100% of college-owned or -operated housing units are wired for high-speed Internet access. Wireless service is available via classrooms, computer labs, dorm rooms, learning centers, libraries, student centers.

Library: Jane Bancroft Cook Library. *Books:* 220,873 (physical), 2,172 (digital/electronic); *Serial titles:* 49 (physical), 2,663 (digital/electronic); *Databases:* 210. Weekly public service hours: 96; students can reserve study rooms.

STUDENT LIFE
Housing options: on-campus residence required through senior year; coed, special housing for students with disabilities. Campus housing is university owned. Freshman campus housing is guaranteed.

Activities and organizations: drama/theater group, student-run newspaper, radio station, choral group, Association for Computing Machinery, Volleyball Club, Swim Club, Psychology Club, Council for Green Affairs.

Athletics ***Intercollegiate sports:*** sailing M/W. ***Intramural sports:*** basketball M(c)/W(c), golf M(c)/W(c), racquetball M(c)/W(c), sailing M(c)/W(c), sand volleyball M(c)/W(c), soccer M(c)/W(c), softball M(c)/W(c), swimming and diving M(c)/W(c), table tennis M(c)/W(c), tennis M(c)/W(c), ultimate Frisbee M(c)/W(c), weight lifting M(c)/W(c).

Campus security: 24-hour emergency response devices and patrols, student patrols, late-night transport/escort service, controlled dormitory access, campus police are state certified police officers and available 24/7.

Student services: health clinic, personal/psychological counseling.

COSTS & FINANCIAL AID
Costs (2020–21) ***Tuition:*** state resident $6916 full-time, $192 per credit hour part-time; nonresident $29,944 full-time, $832 per credit hour part-time. ***Room and board:*** Room and board charges vary according to board plan and housing facility. ***Payment plan:*** installment.

Financial Aid Of all full-time matriculated undergraduates who enrolled in 2018, 623 applied for aid, 430 were judged to have need, 119 had their need fully met. 33 Federal Work-Study jobs (averaging $910). In 2018, 298 non-need-based awards were made. ***Average percent of need met:*** 88. ***Average financial aid package:*** $14,877. ***Average need-based loan:*** $3692. ***Average need-based gift aid:*** $9987. ***Average non-need-based aid:*** $2557. ***Average indebtedness upon graduation:*** $17,466.

APPLYING
Standardized Tests *Required:* SAT or ACT (for admission).

Options: electronic application, early admission, early decision, early action, deferred entrance.

Application fee: $30.

Required: 1 letter of recommendation. ***Required for some:*** high school transcript. ***Recommended:*** minimum 3.0 GPA.

Application deadlines: 4/15 (freshmen), 7/1 (transfers).

Notification: 4/25 (freshmen), 7/31 (transfers).

CONTACT
New College of Florida, 5800 Bay Shore Road, Sarasota, FL 34243.
Phone: 941-487-5000.

See below for display ad and page 1088 for the College Close-Up.

New World School of the Arts

Miami, Florida

http://www.mdc.edu/nwsa/

CONTACT

Eloisa Ferrer, Recruitment and Admissions Coordinator, New World School of the Arts, 300 NE 2nd Avenue, Miami, FL 33132. *Phone:* 305-237-7408. *Fax:* 305-237-3794. *E-mail:* eferrer2@mdc.edu.

Northwest Florida State College

Niceville, Florida

http://www.nwfsc.edu/

CONTACT

Ms. Karen Cooper, Director of Admissions, Northwest Florida State College, 100 College Boulevard, Niceville, FL 32578. *Phone:* 850-729-4901. *Fax:* 850-729-5206. *E-mail:* cooperk@nwfsc.edu.

Nova Southeastern University

Fort Lauderdale, Florida

http://www.nova.edu/

- **Independent** university, founded 1964
- **Suburban** 314-acre campus
- **Endowment** $117.8 million
- **Coed** 5,666 undergraduate students, 82% full-time, 71% women, 29% men
- **Moderately difficult** entrance level, 58% of applicants were admitted

UNDERGRAD STUDENTS

4,619 full-time, 1,047 part-time. Students come from 47 states and territories; 67 other countries; 25% are from out of state; 14% Black or African American, non-Hispanic/Latino; 36% Hispanic/Latino; 11% Asian, non-Hispanic/Latino; 0.1% Native Hawaiian or other Pacific Islander, non-Hispanic/Latino; 0.3% American Indian or Alaska Native, non-Hispanic/Latino; 3% Two or more races, non-Hispanic/Latino; 4% Race/ethnicity unknown; 5% international; 10% transferred in; 37% live on campus.

Freshmen:

Admission: 7,779 applied, 4,525 admitted, 1,526 enrolled. ***Average high school GPA:*** 4.0. ***Test scores:*** SAT evidence-based reading and writing scores over 500: 96%; SAT math scores over 500: 90%; ACT scores over 18: 98%; SAT evidence-based reading and writing scores over 600: 51%; SAT math scores over 600: 43%; ACT scores over 24: 68%; SAT evidence-based reading and writing scores over 700: 6%; SAT math scores over 700: 7%; ACT scores over 30: 17%.

Retention: 81% of full-time freshmen returned.

FACULTY

Total: 1,521, 53% full-time, 71% with terminal degrees.

Student/faculty ratio: 17:1.

ACADEMICS

Calendar: trimesters. *Degrees:* certificates, associate, bachelor's, master's, doctoral, post-master's, and postbachelor's certificates.

Special study options: academic remediation for entering students, adult/continuing education programs, advanced placement credit, distance learning, double majors, external degree program, freshman honors college, honors programs, independent study, internships, off-campus study, part-time degree program, services for LD students, study abroad, summer session for credit. ***ROTC:*** Army (b).

Unusual degree programs: 3-2 business administration; computer science, criminal justice, humanities and social sciences.

Computers: 3,000 computers/terminals and 6,000 ports are available on campus for general student use. Students can access the following: campus intranet, computer help desk, free student e-mail accounts, online (class) grades, online (class) registration, online (class) schedules. Campuswide network is available. 100% of college-owned or -operated housing units are wired for high-speed Internet access. Wireless service is available via entire campus.

Library: Alvin Sherman Library, Research, and Information Technology Center plus 4 others. *Books:* 498,823 (physical), 379,928 (digital/electronic); *Serial titles:* 6,035 (physical), 20,738 (digital/electronic); *Databases:* 577. Study areas open 24 hours, 5–7 days a week; students can reserve study rooms.

STUDENT LIFE

Housing options: on-campus residence required through sophomore year; coed, special housing for students with disabilities. Campus housing is university owned. Freshman campus housing is guaranteed.

Activities and organizations: drama/theater group, student-run newspaper, radio and television station, choral group, HOSA: Future Health Professionals, Make-a Meal Service Organization, Student Government Association, Delta Epsilon Iota, Pre Med, national fraternities, national sororities.

Athletics Member NCAA. All Division II. ***Intercollegiate sports:*** baseball M(s), basketball M(s)/W(s), cheerleading W, crew W(s), cross-country running M(s)/W(s), golf M(s)/W(s), soccer M(s)/W(s), softball W(s), swimming and diving M(s)/W(s), tennis W(s), track and field M(s)/W(s), volleyball W(s). ***Intramural sports:*** badminton M/W, basketball M/W, equestrian sports M/W, racquetball M/W, rowing W, soccer M/W, softball W, table tennis M/W, tennis W, ultimate Frisbee M/W, volleyball M/W.

Campus security: 24-hour emergency response devices and patrols, late-night transport/escort service, controlled dormitory access, shuttle bus service.

Student services: health clinic, personal/psychological counseling, veterans affairs office.

COSTS & FINANCIAL AID

Costs (2020–21) ***Comprehensive fee:*** $47,086 includes full-time tuition ($32,370), mandatory fees ($1060), and room and board ($13,656). Full-time tuition and fees vary according to program. Part-time tuition: $1079 per credit hour. Part-time tuition and fees vary according to course load and program. ***Required fees:*** $1079 per credit hour part-time. ***College room only:*** $10,466. Room and board charges vary according to board plan and housing facility. ***Payment plans:*** installment, deferred payment. ***Waivers:*** employees or children of employees.

Financial Aid Of all full-time matriculated undergraduates who enrolled in 2018, 3,008 applied for aid, 2,670 were judged to have need, 395 had their need fully met. 1,427 Federal Work-Study jobs (averaging $4912). 538 state and other part-time jobs (averaging $1260). In 2018, 856 non-need-based awards were made. ***Average percent of need met:*** 77. ***Average financial aid package:*** $32,151. ***Average need-based loan:*** $2936. ***Average need-based gift aid:*** $20,726. ***Average non-need-based aid:*** $13,369. ***Average indebtedness upon graduation:*** $31,438.

APPLYING

Standardized Tests *Required:* SAT or ACT (for admission).

Options: electronic application, early admission, early decision, early action, deferred entrance.

Application fee: $50.

Required: minimum 3.0 GPA. ***Required for some:*** essay or personal statement, high school transcript.

Application deadlines: 2/1 (freshmen), 4/1 (transfers), 11/1 (early action).

Early decision deadline: 11/1.

Notification: continuous (freshmen), 10/16 (early decision), rolling (early action).

CONTACT

Nova Southeastern University, 3301 College Avenue, Fort Lauderdale, FL 33314-7796. *Toll-free phone:* 800-541-NOVA.

Palm Beach Atlantic University

West Palm Beach, Florida

http://www.pba.edu/

- **Independent nondenominational** comprehensive, founded 1968
- **Urban** 100-acre campus with easy access to Miami-Dade County and Broward County
- **Endowment** $81.2 million
- **Coed** 2,883 undergraduate students, 79% full-time, 63% women, 37% men
- **Moderately difficult** entrance level, 95% of applicants were admitted

UNDERGRAD STUDENTS
2,264 full-time, 619 part-time. 35% are from out of state; 10% Black or African American, non-Hispanic/Latino; 15% Hispanic/Latino; 2% Asian, non-Hispanic/Latino; 0.3% Native Hawaiian or other Pacific Islander, non-Hispanic/Latino; 0.2% American Indian or Alaska Native, non-Hispanic/Latino; 4% Two or more races, non-Hispanic/Latino; 5% Race/ethnicity unknown; 4% international; 8% transferred in; 49% live on campus.

Freshmen:
Admission: 1,534 applied, 1,464 admitted, 520 enrolled.
Retention: 76% of full-time freshmen returned.

FACULTY
Total: 371, 48% full-time, 77% with terminal degrees.
Student/faculty ratio: 12:1.

ACADEMICS
Calendar: semesters. *Degrees:* bachelor's, master's, and doctoral.
Special study options: academic remediation for entering students, accelerated degree program, adult/continuing education programs, advanced placement credit, distance learning, double majors, external degree program, honors programs, independent study, internships, off campus study, part-time degree program, services for LD students, student-designed majors, study abroad, summer session for credit. ***ROTC:*** Army (c).
Unusual degree programs: 3-2 nursing; Divinity.
Computers: 340 computers/terminals are available on campus for general student use. Students can access the following: campus intranet, computer help desk, free student e-mail accounts, online (class) grades, online (class) registration, online (class) schedules, Center for Writing Excellence; Academic Tutoring. Campuswide network is available. 100% of college-owned or -operated housing units are wired for high-speed Internet access. Wireless service is available via entire campus.
Library: Warren Library plus 1 other. *Books:* 143,334 (physical), 126,921 (digital/electronic); *Serial titles:* 114 (physical), 121,795 (digital/electronic); *Databases:* 143. Weekly public service hours: 100; students can reserve study rooms.

STUDENT LIFE
Housing options: on-campus residence required through senior year; coed, men-only. Campus housing is university owned. Freshman campus housing is guaranteed.
Activities and organizations: drama/theater group, student-run newspaper, choral group, Impact Leadership Team, Nursing Student Association, Nurses Christian Fellowship, Student Government, Sigma Alpha Omega.
Athletics Member NCAA. All Division II. ***Intercollegiate sports:*** baseball M(s)/W, basketball M(s)/W(s), cheerleading M(c)/W(c), crew M(c)/W(c), cross-country running M(s)/W(s), golf M(s)/W(s), lacrosse M(s)/W(s), sand volleyball W(s), soccer M(s)/W(s), softball W(s), tennis M(s)/W(s), track and field M(s)/W(s), volleyball W(s). ***Intramural sports:*** basketball M/W, sand volleyball M/W, soccer M/W, softball M/W, ultimate Frisbee M/W, volleyball M/W.
Campus security: 24-hour emergency response devices and patrols, late-night transport/escort service, controlled dormitory access.
Student services: health clinic, personal/psychological counseling.

COSTS & FINANCIAL AID
Costs (2020–21) ***Tuition:*** $32,880 full-time, $790 per credit hour part-time. Full-time tuition and fees vary according to location and program. Part-time tuition and fees vary according to location and program. ***Required fees:*** $595 full-time. ***Room only:*** $5696. Room and board charges vary according to board plan and housing facility. ***Payment plan:*** installment. ***Waivers:*** employees or children of employees.
Financial Aid Of all full-time matriculated undergraduates who enrolled in 2019, 1,872 applied for aid, 1,640 were judged to have need, 217 had their need fully met. In 2019, 560 non-need-based awards were made. ***Average percent of need met:*** 62. ***Average financial aid package:*** $23,772. ***Average need-based loan:*** $3783. ***Average need-based gift aid:*** $21,190. ***Average non-need-based aid:*** $13,581. ***Average indebtedness upon graduation:*** $27,530.

APPLYING
Options: electronic application, early admission, early action, deferred entrance.
Application fee: $50.
Required: essay or personal statement, high school transcript. ***Required for some:*** interview.
Application deadlines: rolling (freshmen), rolling (transfers), 5/1 (early action).
Notification: continuous (freshmen), continuous (transfers), 6/1 (early action).

CONTACT
Mr. Tim Worley, Vice President for Admissions, Palm Beach Atlantic University, 901 South Flagler Drive, PO Box 24708, West Palm Beach, FL 33416-4708. *Phone:* 561-803-2102. *Toll-free phone:* 888-GO-TO-PBA. *Fax:* 561-803-2115. *E-mail:* admit@pba.edu.

Palm Beach State College
Lake Worth, Florida
http://www.palmbeachstate.edu/

CONTACT
Palm Beach State College, 4200 Congress Avenue, Lake Worth, FL 33461-4796.

Pasco-Hernando State College
New Port Richey, Florida
http://www.phsc.edu/

CONTACT
Ms. Estela Carrion, Director of Admissions and Student Records, Pasco-Hernando State College, 10230 Ridge Road, New Port Richey, FL 34654-5199. *Phone:* 727-816-3261. *Toll-free phone:* 877-TRY-PHSC. *Fax:* 727-816-3389. *E-mail:* carrioe@phsc.edu.

Pensacola Christian College
Pensacola, Florida
http://www.pcci.edu/

CONTACT
Pensacola Christian College, 250 Brent Lane, Pensacola, FL 32503-2267. *Toll-free phone:* 800-722-4636.

Pensacola State College
Pensacola, Florida
http://www.pensacolastate.edu/

- **State-supported** primarily 2-year, founded 1948, part of Florida College System
- **Urban** 130-acre campus with easy access to Mobile, Alabama
- **Endowment** $11.3 million
- **Coed** 10,661 undergraduate students, 32% full-time, 46% women, 27% men
- **Noncompetitive** entrance level, 100% of applicants were admitted

UNDERGRAD STUDENTS
3,410 full-time, 4,361 part-time. Students come from 25 states and territories; 5% are from out of state; 15% Black or African American, non-Hispanic/Latino; 7% Hispanic/Latino; 3% Asian, non-Hispanic/Latino; 0.4% Native Hawaiian or other Pacific Islander, non-Hispanic/Latino; 0.7% American Indian or Alaska Native, non-Hispanic/Latino; 6% Two or more races, non-Hispanic/Latino; 2% Race/ethnicity unknown; 0.4% international; 3% transferred in.

Freshmen:
Admission: 3,410 applied, 3,410 admitted, 1,376 enrolled. ***Average high school GPA:*** 2.5.

FACULTY
Student/faculty ratio: 19:1.

ACADEMICS
Calendar: semesters. *Degrees:* certificates, diplomas, associate, and bachelor's.

Special study options: academic remediation for entering students, adult/continuing education programs, advanced placement credit, cooperative education, distance learning, double majors, English as a second language, external degree program, honors programs, independent study, internships, part-time degree program, services for LD students, summer session for credit. ***ROTC:*** Army (b).

Computers: 1,700 computers/terminals are available on campus for general student use. Students can access the following: campus intranet, computer help desk, free student e-mail accounts, online (class) grades, online (class) registration, online (class) schedules. Campuswide network is available. Wireless service is available via entire campus.
Library: Edward M. Chadbourne Library plus 3 others. Students can reserve study rooms.

STUDENT LIFE
Activities and organizations: drama/theater group, student-run newspaper, choral group, Student Government Association, Health Occupations Students of America (HOSA), SkillsUSA, African-American Student Association, Forestry Club.

Athletics Member NJCAA. ***Intercollegiate sports:*** baseball M(s), basketball M(s)/W(s), softball W(s), volleyball W(s). ***Intramural sports:*** archery M/W, badminton M/W, basketball M/W, bowling M/W, racquetball M/W, soccer M/W, softball W, tennis M/W, volleyball M/W.

Campus security: 24-hour emergency response devices and patrols, late-night transport/escort service.

Student services: personal/psychological counseling, veterans affairs office.

COSTS & FINANCIAL AID
Costs (2020–21) ***One-time required fee:*** $30. ***Tuition:*** state resident $2572 full-time, $105 per credit hour part-time; nonresident $10,289 full-time, $420 per credit hour part-time. Full-time tuition and fees vary according to course level and degree level. Part-time tuition and fees vary according to course level and degree level. ***Room and board:*** $7650. ***Payment plans:*** installment, deferred payment. ***Waivers:*** employees or children of employees.

Financial Aid Of all full-time matriculated undergraduates who enrolled in 2018, 120 Federal Work-Study jobs (averaging $3000).

APPLYING
Options: electronic application, early admission.

Application fee: $30.

Required: high school transcript.

Application deadlines: 8/30 (freshmen), 8/30 (transfers).

Notification: continuous until 8/30 (freshmen), continuous until 8/30 (transfers).

CONTACT
Ms. Kathy Dutremble, Registrar, Pensacola State College, 1000 College Boulevard, Pensacola, FL 32504. *Phone:* 850-484-2076. *Fax:* 850-484-1020. *E-mail:* kdutremble@pensacolastate.edu.

Polk State College
Winter Haven, Florida
http://www.polk.edu/

- **State-supported** 4-year, founded 1964, part of Florida College System
- **Suburban** 98-acre campus with easy access to Orlando, Tampa
- **Coed** 10,827 undergraduate students, 36% full-time, 65% women, 35% men
- **Noncompetitive** entrance level

UNDERGRAD STUDENTS
3,866 full-time, 6,961 part-time. Students come from 7 states and territories; 5 other countries; 1% are from out of state; 18% Black or African American, non-Hispanic/Latino; 27% Hispanic/Latino; 2% Asian, non-Hispanic/Latino; 0.2% Native Hawaiian or other Pacific Islander, non-Hispanic/Latino; 0.4% American Indian or Alaska Native, non-Hispanic/Latino; 4% Two or more races, non-Hispanic/Latino; 1% Race/ethnicity unknown; 1% international; 5% transferred in.

Freshmen:
Admission: 1,529 enrolled.
Retention: 62% of full-time freshmen returned.

FACULTY
Total: 368, 43% full-time, 25% with terminal degrees.

Student/faculty ratio: 27:1.

ACADEMICS
Calendar: semesters 16-16-6-6. *Degrees:* certificates, diplomas, associate, and bachelor's.

Special study options: academic remediation for entering students, accelerated degree program, adult/continuing education programs, advanced placement credit, distance learning, double majors, English as a second language, honors programs, independent study, internships, off-campus study, part-time degree program, services for LD students, study abroad, summer session for credit. ***ROTC:*** Army (c), Air Force (c).

Computers: 800 computers/terminals are available on campus for general student use. Students can access the following: computer help desk, free student e-mail accounts, online (class) grades, online (class) registration, online (class) schedules. Campuswide network is available. Wireless service is available via entire campus.
Library: Polk State College Libraries plus 1 other. *Books:* 82,640 (physical), 110,114 (digital/electronic).

STUDENT LIFE
Activities and organizations: drama/theater group, choral group, Florida Student Nursing Association, Honors Program Student Council, Phi Theta Kappa (PTK), Student Government Association, SALO (Student Activities and Leadership Office).

Athletics Member NJCAA. ***Intercollegiate sports:*** baseball M(s), basketball M(s), soccer W(s), softball W(s), volleyball W(s). ***Intramural sports:*** basketball M/W, bowling M/W, cheerleading M/W, football M/W, sand volleyball M/W, table tennis M/W, volleyball W.

Campus security: 24-hour emergency response devices and patrols.

Student services: personal/psychological counseling, legal services, veterans affairs office.

COSTS
Costs (2020–21) ***Tuition:*** state resident $3367 full-time, $112 per credit hour part-time; nonresident $12,272 full-time, $409 per credit hour part-time. Full-time tuition and fees vary according to course level, course load, and degree level. Part-time tuition and fees vary according to course level, course load, and degree level. ***Room and board:*** $8080. ***Waivers:*** employees or children of employees.

APPLYING
Options: electronic application, early admission, deferred entrance.

Required: high school transcript.

Application deadlines: rolling (freshmen), rolling (transfers).

Notification: continuous (freshmen), continuous (transfers).

CONTACT
Polk State College, 999 Avenue H, NE, Winter Haven, FL 33881-4299. *Phone:* 863-297-1021.

Polytechnic University of Puerto Rico, Miami Campus
Miami, Florida
http://www.pupr.edu/miami/

- **Independent** comprehensive
- **Urban** campus with easy access to Miami-Dade
- **Coed**

FACULTY
Student/faculty ratio: 7:1.

ACADEMICS
Degrees: bachelor's and master's.

STUDENT LIFE
Housing options: college housing not available.

APPLYING
Options: electronic application.

Application fee: $30.

CONTACT
Polytechnic University of Puerto Rico, Miami Campus, 8180 Northwest 36th Street, Suite 401, Miami, FL 33166. *Phone:* 305-418-8000. *Toll-free phone:* 888-729-7659.

Polytechnic University of Puerto Rico, Orlando Campus

Orlando, Florida

http://www.pupr.edu/orlando/

- **Independent** comprehensive
- **Coed**
- 89% of applicants were admitted

FACULTY
Student/faculty ratio: 5:1.

ACADEMICS
Degrees: bachelor's and master's.

STUDENT LIFE
Housing options: college housing not available.

FINANCIAL AID
Financial Aid Of all full-time matriculated undergraduates who enrolled in 2012, 24 applied for aid, 24 were judged to have need. 2 Federal Work-Study jobs (averaging $5220). ***Average percent of need met:*** 55. ***Average financial aid package:*** $7315. ***Average need-based loan:*** $4454. ***Average need-based gift aid:*** $5021.

APPLYING
Application fee: $30.

CONTACT
Teresa Cardona, Director of Recruitment and Admission, Polytechnic University of Puerto Rico, Orlando Campus, 550 North Econlockhatchee Trail, Orlando, FL 32825. *Phone:* 407-677-7000. *Toll-free phone:* 888-577-POLY. *Fax:* 407-677-5082.

Rasmussen College Fort Myers

Fort Myers, Florida

http://www.rasmussen.edu/

- **Proprietary** 4-year, part of Rasmussen College System
- **Suburban** campus
- **Coed** 705 undergraduate students, 47% full-time, 85% women, 15% men
- 100% of applicants were admitted

UNDERGRAD STUDENTS
333 full-time, 372 part-time. Students come from 51 states and territories; 27% are from out of state; 15% Black or African American, non-Hispanic/Latino; 27% Hispanic/Latino; 2% Asian, non-Hispanic/Latino; 0.1% Native Hawaiian or other Pacific Islander, non-Hispanic/Latino; 2% Two or more races, non-Hispanic/Latino; 19% Race/ethnicity unknown.

Freshmen:
Admission: 189 applied, 189 admitted, 77 enrolled.

ACADEMICS
Calendar: quarters. *Degrees:* certificates, diplomas, associate, and bachelor's.

Special study options: academic remediation for entering students, accelerated degree program, adult/continuing education programs, distance learning, double majors, internships, part-time degree program, summer session for credit.

Computers: 129 computers/terminals are available on campus for general student use. Students can access the following: computer help desk, free student e-mail accounts, online (class) grades, online (class) schedules. Campuswide network is available. Wireless service is available via entire campus.
Library: Rasmussen College Library - Fort Myers.

STUDENT LIFE
Housing options: college housing not available.

APPLYING
Options: early admission, deferred entrance.

Required: high school transcript, minimum 2.0 GPA. ***Required for some:*** interview.

Application deadlines: rolling (freshmen), rolling (transfers).

CONTACT
Ms. Susan Hammerstrom, Director of Admissions, Rasmussen College Fort Myers, 9160 Forum Corporate Parkway, Suite 100, Fort Myers, FL 33905. *Phone:* 239-477-2100. *Toll-free phone:* 888-549-6755. *E-mail:* susan.hammerstrom@rasmussen.edu.

Rasmussen College Land O' Lakes

Land O' Lakes, Florida

http://www.rasmussen.edu/

- **Proprietary** 4-year, part of Rasmussen College System
- **Suburban** campus
- **Coed** 443 undergraduate students, 56% full-time, 85% women, 15% men
- 100% of applicants were admitted

UNDERGRAD STUDENTS
250 full-time, 193 part-time. Students come from 51 states and territories; 27% are from out of state; 11% Black or African American, non-Hispanic/Latino; 17% Hispanic/Latino; 2% Asian, non-Hispanic/Latino; 0.5% American Indian or Alaska Native, non-Hispanic/Latino; 3% Two or more races, non-Hispanic/Latino; 30% Race/ethnicity unknown.

Freshmen:
Admission: 104 applied, 104 admitted, 77 enrolled.

ACADEMICS
Calendar: quarters. *Degrees:* certificates, diplomas, associate, and bachelor's.

Special study options: academic remediation for entering students, accelerated degree program, adult/continuing education programs, distance learning, double majors, internships, part-time degree program, summer session for credit.

Computers: 61 computers/terminals are available on campus for general student use. Students can access the following: computer help desk, free student e-mail accounts, online (class) grades, online (class) schedules. Campuswide network is available. Wireless service is available via entire campus.
Library: Rasmussen College Library - Land O' Lakes.

STUDENT LIFE
Housing options: college housing not available.

COSTS
Costs (2019–20) ***Tuition:*** $13,371 full-time, $10,618 per year part-time. Full-time tuition and fees vary according to course level, course load, degree level, location, and program. Part-time tuition and fees vary according to course level, course load, degree level, location, and program. No tuition increase for student's term of enrollment. ***Required fees:*** $3869 full-time, $2154 per year part-time. ***Payment plans:*** installment, deferred payment. ***Waivers:*** employees or children of employees.

APPLYING
Options: early admission, deferred entrance.

Required: high school transcript, minimum 2.0 GPA. ***Required for some:*** interview.

Application deadlines: rolling (freshmen), rolling (transfers).

CONTACT
Ms. Susan Hammerstrom, Director of Admissions, Rasmussen College Land O' Lakes, 18600 Fernview Street, Land O' Lakes, FL 34638. *Phone:* 813-435-3601. *Toll-free phone:* 888-549-6755. *E-mail:* susan.hammerstrom@rasmussen.edu.

Rasmussen College New Port Richey

New Port Richey, Florida

http://www.rasmussen.edu/

- **Proprietary** 4-year, part of Rasmussen College System
- **Suburban** campus
- **Coed** 644 undergraduate students, 53% full-time, 86% women, 14% men
- 100% of applicants were admitted

UNDERGRAD STUDENTS
340 full-time, 304 part-time. Students come from 51 states and territories; 27% are from out of state; 5% Black or African American, non-Hispanic/Latino; 17% Hispanic/Latino; 1% Asian, non-Hispanic/Latino; 0.3% Native Hawaiian or other Pacific Islander, non-Hispanic/Latino; 0.2% American Indian or Alaska Native, non-Hispanic/Latino; 1% Two or more races, non-Hispanic/Latino; 22% Race/ethnicity unknown.

Freshmen:
Admission: 147 applied, 147 admitted, 102 enrolled.

ACADEMICS
Calendar: quarters. *Degrees:* certificates, diplomas, associate, bachelor's, and postbachelor's certificates.

Special study options: academic remediation for entering students, accelerated degree program, adult/continuing education programs, distance learning, double majors, internships, part-time degree program, summer session for credit.

Computers: 118 computers/terminals are available on campus for general student use. Students can access the following: computer help desk, free student e-mail accounts, online (class) grades, online (class) schedules. Campuswide network is available. Wireless service is available via entire campus.
Library: Rasmussen College Library - New Port Richey.

STUDENT LIFE
Housing options: college housing not available.

FINANCIAL AID
Financial Aid Of all full-time matriculated undergraduates who enrolled in 2018, 6 Federal Work-Study jobs.

APPLYING
Options: early admission, deferred entrance.

Required: high school transcript, minimum 2.0 GPA. ***Required for some:*** interview.

Application deadlines: rolling (freshmen), rolling (transfers).

CONTACT
Dwayne Bertotto, Vice President of Admissions and Student Experience, Rasmussen College New Port Richey, 8300 Norman Center Drive, Suite 300, Bloomington, MN 55437. *Phone:* 952-806-3958. *Toll-free phone:* 888-549-6755. *E-mail:* dwayne.bertotto@rasmussen.edu.

Rasmussen College Ocala

Ocala, Florida

http://www.rasmussen.edu/

- **Proprietary** 4-year, founded 1984, part of Rasmussen College System
- **Suburban** campus with easy access to Orlando
- **Coed** 1,356 undergraduate students, 54% full-time, 88% women, 12% men
- 100% of applicants were admitted

UNDERGRAD STUDENTS
737 full-time, 619 part-time. Students come from 51 states and territories; 27% are from out of state; 21% Black or African American, non-Hispanic/Latino; 14% Hispanic/Latino; 3% Asian, non-Hispanic/Latino; 0.1% Native Hawaiian or other Pacific Islander, non-Hispanic/Latino; 0.1% American Indian or Alaska Native, non-Hispanic/Latino; 3% Two or more races, non-Hispanic/Latino; 15% Race/ethnicity unknown.

Freshmen:
Admission: 313 applied, 313 admitted, 203 enrolled.

ACADEMICS
Calendar: quarters. *Degrees:* certificates, diplomas, associate, and bachelor's.

Special study options: academic remediation for entering students, accelerated degree program, adult/continuing education programs, distance learning, double majors, internships, part-time degree program, summer session for credit.

Computers: 124 computers/terminals are available on campus for general student use. Students can access the following: computer help desk, free student e-mail accounts, online (class) grades, online (class) schedules. Campuswide network is available. Wireless service is available via entire campus.
Library: Rasmussen College Library - Ocala.

STUDENT LIFE
Housing options: college housing not available.

APPLYING
Options: early admission, deferred entrance.

Required: high school transcript, minimum 2.0 GPA. ***Required for some:*** interview.

Application deadlines: rolling (freshmen), rolling (transfers).

CONTACT
Dwayne Bertotto, Vice President of Admissions and Student Experience, Rasmussen College Ocala, 8300 Norman Center Drive, Suite 300, Bloomington, MN 55437. *Phone:* 952-806-3958. *Toll-free phone:* 888-549-6755. *E-mail:* dwayne.bertotto@rasmussen.edu.

Rasmussen College Ocala School of Nursing

Ocala, Florida

http://www.rasmussen.edu/

- **Proprietary** 4-year, part of Rasmussen College System
- **Suburban** campus
- **Coed** 185 undergraduate students, 48% full-time, 87% women, 13% men
- **Minimally difficult** entrance level, 100% of applicants were admitted

UNDERGRAD STUDENTS
88 full-time, 97 part-time. Students come from 51 states and territories; 27% are from out of state; 29% Black or African American, non-Hispanic/Latino; 19% Hispanic/Latino; 1% Asian, non-Hispanic/Latino; 0.5% American Indian or Alaska Native, non-Hispanic/Latino; 3% Two or more races, non-Hispanic/Latino; 22% Race/ethnicity unknown.

Freshmen:
Admission: 78 applied, 78 admitted, 24 enrolled.

ACADEMICS
Calendar: quarters. *Degrees:* associate and bachelor's.

Special study options: academic remediation for entering students, accelerated degree program, adult/continuing education programs, distance learning, double majors, internships, part-time degree program, summer session for credit.

Computers: Students can access the following: computer help desk, free student e-mail accounts, online (class) grades, online (class) schedules. Campuswide network is available. Wireless service is available via entire campus.
Library: Rasmussen College Library - Ocala.

STUDENT LIFE
Housing options: college housing not available.

COSTS
Costs (2019–20) ***Tuition:*** $12,417 full-time, $10,256 per year part-time. Full-time tuition and fees vary according to course level, course load, degree level, location, and program. Part-time tuition and fees vary according to course level, course load, degree level, location, and program. No tuition increase for student's term of enrollment. ***Required fees:*** $2874 full-time, $2003 per year part-time. ***Payment plans:*** installment, deferred payment. ***Waivers:*** employees or children of employees.

APPLYING
Standardized Tests *Required:* institutional exam (for admission).

Options: electronic application, early admission, deferred entrance.

Required: high school transcript, minimum 2.0 GPA. ***Required for some:*** interview.

Application deadlines: rolling (freshmen), rolling (transfers).

CONTACT
Ms. Susan Hammerstrom, Director of Admissions, Rasmussen College Ocala School of Nursing, 2100 SW 22nd Place, Ocala, FL 34471. *Phone:* 352-291-8560. *Toll-free phone:* 888-549-6755. *E-mail:* susan.hammerstrom@rasmussen.edu.

Rasmussen College Tampa/Brandon

Tampa, Florida

http://www.rasmussen.edu/

- **Proprietary** 4-year, part of Rasmussen College System
- **Suburban** campus
- **Coed** 1,020 undergraduate students, 50% full-time, 86% women, 14% men
- 100% of applicants were admitted

UNDERGRAD STUDENTS
508 full-time, 512 part-time. Students come from 51 states and territories; 27% are from out of state; 26% Black or African American, non-Hispanic/Latino; 19% Hispanic/Latino; 4% Asian, non-Hispanic/Latino; 0.6% Native Hawaiian or other Pacific Islander, non Hispanic/Latino; 0.6% American Indian or Alaska Native, non-Hispanic/Latino; 2% Two or more races, non-Hispanic/Latino; 20% Race/ethnicity unknown.

Freshmen:
Admission: 261 applied, 261 admitted, 122 enrolled.

ACADEMICS
Calendar: quarters. *Degrees:* certificates, diplomas, associate, and bachelor's.

Special study options: academic remediation for entering students, accelerated degree program, adult/continuing education programs, distance learning, double majors, internships, part-time degree program, summer session for credit.

Computers: 47 computers/terminals are available on campus for general student use. Students can access the following: computer help desk, free student e-mail accounts, online (class) grades, online (class) schedules. Campuswide network is available. Wireless service is available via entire campus.
Library: Rasmussen College Library - Tampa.

STUDENT LIFE
Housing options: college housing not available.

COSTS
Costs (2019–20) ***Tuition:*** $13,988 full-time, $12,291 per year part-time. Full-time tuition and fees vary according to course level, course load, degree level, location, and program. Part-time tuition and fees vary according to course level, course load, degree level, location, and program. No tuition increase for student's term of enrollment. ***Required fees:*** $3541 full-time, $2564 per year part-time. ***Payment plans:*** installment, deferred payment. ***Waivers:*** employees or children of employees.

APPLYING
Options: early admission, deferred entrance.

Required: high school transcript, minimum 2.0 GPA. ***Required for some:*** interview.

Application deadlines: rolling (freshmen), rolling (transfers).

CONTACT
Ms. Susan Hammerstrom, Director of Admissions, Rasmussen College Tampa/Brandon, 4042 Park Oaks Boulevard, Suite 100, Tampa, FL 33610. *Phone:* 813-246-7600. *Toll-free phone:* 888-549-6755. *E-mail:* susan.hammerstrom@rasmussen.edu.

Ringling College of Art and Design

Sarasota, Florida

http://www.ringling.edu/

- **Independent** 4-year, founded 1931
- **Urban** 49-acre campus with easy access to Tampa-St. Petersburg
- **Endowment** $47.5 million
- **Coed**
- **Moderately difficult** entrance level

FACULTY
Student/faculty ratio: 11:1.

ACADEMICS
Calendar: semesters. *Degree:* bachelor's.
Library: Alfred R. Goldstein Library. *Books:* 51,891 (physical), 133,879 (digital/electronic); *Serial titles:* 12,169 (physical); *Databases:* 28. Weekly public service hours: 84; study areas open 24 hours, 5–7 days a week; students can reserve study rooms.

STUDENT LIFE
Housing options: coed, men-only, women-only. Campus housing is university owned. Freshman applicants given priority for college housing.

Activities and organizations: drama/theater group, student-run television station, choral group, Student Government Association, Digital Painting Sketch Club, Resident Student Association, MOSAIC, Quidditch Team.

Campus security: 24-hour emergency response devices and patrols, late-night transport/escort service, controlled dormitory access, lighted campus.

Student services: health clinic, personal/psychological counseling, legal services.

COSTS & FINANCIAL AID
Costs (2019–20) ***Comprehensive fee:*** $63,550 includes full-time tuition ($43,710), mandatory fees ($4260), and room and board ($15,580). Full-time tuition and fees vary according to course load, program, and student level. Part-time tuition: $2035 per credit hour. Part-time tuition and fees vary according to program and student level. ***Room and board:*** Room and board charges vary according to board plan and housing facility.

Financial Aid Of all full-time matriculated undergraduates who enrolled in 2019, 1,097 applied for aid, 979 were judged to have need, 63 had their need fully met. In 2019, 553 non-need-based awards were made. ***Average percent of need met:*** 51. ***Average financial aid package:*** $27,804. ***Average need-based loan:*** $9468. ***Average need-based gift aid:*** $17,829. ***Average non-need-based aid:*** $12,114. ***Average indebtedness upon graduation:*** $46,947.

APPLYING
Options: electronic application, early action, deferred entrance.

Application fee: $70.

Required: essay or personal statement, high school transcript, minimum 2.0 GPA, 2 letters of recommendation, portfolio, resume. ***Recommended:*** interview.

CONTACT
Ringling College of Art and Design, 2700 North Tamiami Trail, Sarasota, FL 34234-5895. *Phone:* 941-359-7523. *Toll-free phone:* 800-255-7695. *E-mail:* admissions@ringling.edu.

Rollins College

Winter Park, Florida

http://www.rollins.edu/

- **Independent** comprehensive, founded 1885
- **Suburban** 80-acre campus with easy access to Orlando
- **Endowment** $354.8 million
- **Coed** 2,135 undergraduate students, 100% full-time, 60% women, 40% men
- **Moderately difficult** entrance level, 58% of applicants were admitted

UNDERGRAD STUDENTS
2,129 full-time, 6 part-time. Students come from 48 states and territories; 66 other countries; 45% are from out of state; 4% Black or African American, non-Hispanic/Latino; 18% Hispanic/Latino; 3% Asian, non-Hispanic/Latino; 0.1% American Indian or Alaska Native, non-Hispanic/Latino; 5% Two or more races, non-Hispanic/Latino; 2%

Race/ethnicity unknown; 10% international; 4% transferred in; 57% live on campus.

Freshmen:
Admission: 6,167 applied, 3,598 admitted, 556 enrolled. ***Average high school GPA:*** 3.3. ***Test scores:*** SAT evidence-based reading and writing scores over 500: 98%; SAT math scores over 500: 95%; ACT scores over 18: 99%; SAT evidence-based reading and writing scores over 600: 77%; SAT math scores over 600: 58%; ACT scores over 24: 82%; SAT evidence-based reading and writing scores over 700: 18%; SAT math scores over 700: 13%; ACT scores over 30: 27%.

Retention: 87% of full-time freshmen returned.

FACULTY
Total: 225, 100% full-time, 92% with terminal degrees.

Student/faculty ratio: 11:1.

ACADEMICS
Calendar: semesters. *Degrees:* bachelor's, master's, and doctoral.

Special study options: academic remediation for entering students, accelerated degree program, adult/continuing education programs, advanced placement credit, double majors, honors programs, independent study, internships, off-campus study, part-time degree program, services for LD students, student-designed majors, study abroad, summer session for credit.

Unusual degree programs: 3-2 business administration with Rollins College, Crummer Graduate School of Business; engineering with Columbia University, Washington University in St. Louis, Auburn University; environmental management with Duke University.

Computers: 254 computers/terminals are available on campus for general student use. Students can access the following: campus intranet, computer help desk, free student e-mail accounts, online (class) grades, online (class) registration, online (class) schedules. Campuswide network is available. 100% of college-owned or -operated housing units are wired for high-speed Internet access. Wireless service is available via entire campus.

Library: Olin Library. *Books:* 204,677 (physical), 236,421 (digital/electronic); *Serial titles:* 117 (physical), 104,688 (digital/electronic); *Databases:* 107. Weekly public service hours: 96; study areas open 24 hours, 5–7 days a week; students can reserve study rooms.

STUDENT LIFE
Housing options: on-campus residence required through sophomore year; coed, men-only, women-only, special housing for students with disabilities. Campus housing is university owned. Freshman campus housing is guaranteed.

Activities and organizations: drama/theater group, student-run newspaper, radio and television station, choral group, Black Student Union, Student Government Association, Eco-Rollins, Spectrum, WPRK 91.5, national fraternities, national sororities.

Athletics Member NCAA. All Division II except golf (Division I). ***Intercollegiate sports:*** baseball M(s), basketball M(s)/W(s), crew M/W, cross-country running M/W, golf M(s)/W(s), lacrosse M/W, sailing M/W, skiing (downhill) W, soccer M(s)/W(s), softball W(s), swimming and diving M/W, tennis M(s)/W(s), volleyball W(s). ***Intramural sports:*** baseball M, basketball M/W, bowling M/W, equestrian sports W(c), ice hockey M(c), soccer M/W, softball M/W, table tennis M/W, tennis M/W, ultimate Frisbee M/W, volleyball M/W.

Campus security: 24-hour emergency response devices and patrols, late-night transport/escort service, controlled dormitory access.

Student services: health clinic, personal/psychological counseling, women's center.

COSTS & FINANCIAL AID
Costs (2020–21) ***Comprehensive fee:*** $68,916 includes full-time tuition ($53,716) and room and board ($15,200). ***College room only:*** $9250. Room and board charges vary according to board plan and housing facility. ***Payment plan:*** installment. ***Waivers:*** employees or children of employees.

Financial Aid Of all full-time matriculated undergraduates who enrolled in 2019, 1,333 applied for aid, 1,141 were judged to have need, 382 had their need fully met. 392 Federal Work-Study jobs (averaging $2500). In 2019, 725 non-need-based awards were made. ***Average percent of need met:*** 88. ***Average financial aid package:*** $42,681. ***Average need-based loan:*** $4501. ***Average need-based gift aid:*** $35,944. ***Average non-need-based aid:*** $23,812. ***Average indebtedness upon graduation:*** $31,992.

APPLYING
Standardized Tests *Required:* Selection of Test Score Waived Option (TSWO) or official SAT/ACT scores (for admission). *Required for some:* SAT or ACT (for admission). *Recommended:* SAT or ACT (for admission), Selection of Test Score Waived Option (TSWO) or official SAT/ACT scores.

Options: electronic application, early admission, early decision, deferred entrance.

Application fee: $50.

Required: essay or personal statement, high school transcript, 1 letter of recommendation. ***Recommended:*** minimum 2.0 GPA, interview.

Application deadlines: 2/1 (freshmen), 4/15 (transfers).

Early decision deadline: 11/15.

Notification: 4/1 (freshmen), continuous (transfers).

CONTACT
Dr. Faye Tydlaska, Vice President of Enrollment Management and Marketing, Rollins College, 1000 Holt Avenue, Campus Box 2720, Winter Park, FL 32789. *Phone:* 407-646-2000 Ext. 2161. *E-mail:* admissions@rollins.edu.

St. John Vianney College Seminary

Miami, Florida

http://www.sjvcs.edu/

CONTACT
Br. Edward Van Merrienboer, Academic Dean, St. John Vianney College Seminary, 2900 Southwest 87th Avenue, Miami, FL 33165-3244. *Phone:* 305-223-4561 Ext. 13.

Saint Leo University

Saint Leo, Florida

http://www.saintleo.edu/

- **Independent Roman Catholic** comprehensive, founded 1889
- **Rural** 280-acre campus with easy access to Tampa, Orlando
- **Endowment** $69.6 million
- **Coed** 2,282 undergraduate students, 97% full-time, 58% women, 42% men
- **Moderately difficult** entrance level, 72% of applicants were admitted

UNDERGRAD STUDENTS
2,223 full-time, 59 part-time. Students come from 43 states and territories; 79 other countries; 26% are from out of state; 14% Black or African American, non-Hispanic/Latino; 21% Hispanic/Latino; 1% Asian, non-Hispanic/Latino; 0.4% American Indian or Alaska Native, non-Hispanic/Latino; 2% Two or more races, non-Hispanic/Latino; 10% Race/ethnicity unknown; 14% international; 8% transferred in; 68% live on campus.

Freshmen:
Admission: 5,195 applied, 3,745 admitted, 782 enrolled. ***Average high school GPA:*** 3.1. ***Test scores:*** SAT evidence-based reading and writing scores over 500: 90%; SAT math scores over 500: 82%; ACT scores over 18: 96%; SAT evidence-based reading and writing scores over 600: 25%; SAT math scores over 600: 24%; ACT scores over 24: 52%; SAT evidence-based reading and writing scores over 700: 6%; SAT math scores over 700: 2%; ACT scores over 30: 9%.

Retention: 69% of full-time freshmen returned.

FACULTY
Total: 168, 60% full-time, 64% with terminal degrees.

Student/faculty ratio: 18:1.

ACADEMICS
Calendar: semesters. *Degrees:* certificates, associate, bachelor's, master's, doctoral, and postbachelor's certificates.

Special study options: academic remediation for entering students, accelerated degree program, adult/continuing education programs, advanced placement credit, distance learning, double majors, English as a second language, honors programs, independent study, internships, part-time degree program, services for LD students, study abroad, summer session for credit. ***ROTC:*** Army (b), Air Force (c).

Unusual degree programs: 3-2 business administration; engineering; social work.

Computers: 150 computers/terminals are available on campus for general student use. Students can access the following: campus intranet, computer help desk, free student e-mail accounts, online (class) grades, online (class) registration, online (class) schedules. Campuswide network is available. 100% of college-owned or -operated housing units are wired for high-speed Internet access. Wireless service is available via entire campus.

Library: Cannon Memorial Library plus 1 other. *Books:* 91,413 (physical), 403,690 (digital/electronic); *Serial titles:* 8,106 (physical), 570,461 (digital/electronic); *Databases:* 121. Weekly public service hours: 112.

STUDENT LIFE

Housing options: on-campus residence required through junior year; coed, men-only, women-only, special housing for students with disabilities. Campus housing is university owned. Freshman applicants given priority for college housing.

Activities and organizations: drama/theater group, student-run newspaper, radio station, choral group, Caribbean Student Association, Alpha Phi Omega, Intercultural Student Association, Leo for St. Jude, American Marketing Association, national fraternities, national sororities.

Athletics Member NCAA. All Division II except golf (Division I). ***Intercollegiate sports:*** baseball M(s), basketball M(s)/W(s), cross-country running M(s)/W(s), golf M(s)/W(s), lacrosse M(s)/W(s), soccer M(s)/W(s), softball W(s), swimming and diving M(s)/W(s), tennis M(s)/W(s), track and field M(s)/W(s), volleyball W(s). ***Intramural sports:*** basketball M/W, bowling M/W, fencing W, field hockey M, football M/W, sand volleyball M/W, soccer M/W, ultimate Frisbee M/W.

Campus security: 24-hour emergency response devices and patrols, late-night transport/escort service, controlled dormitory access.

Student services: health clinic, personal/psychological counseling, veterans affairs office.

COSTS & FINANCIAL AID

Costs (2020–21) ***One-time required fee:*** $310. ***Comprehensive fee:*** $38,140 includes full-time tuition ($23,990), mandatory fees ($650), and room and board ($13,500). ***College room only:*** $8100. Room and board charges vary according to board plan, housing facility, and location. ***Payment plans:*** installment, deferred payment. ***Waivers:*** employees or children of employees.

Financial Aid Of all full-time matriculated undergraduates who enrolled in 2019, 1,781 applied for aid, 1,543 were judged to have need, 359 had their need fully met. 808 Federal Work-Study jobs (averaging $4905). 4 state and other part-time jobs (averaging $5400). In 2019, 638 non-need-based awards were made. ***Average percent of need met:*** 81. ***Average financial aid package:*** $25,819. ***Average need-based loan:*** $4031. ***Average need-based gift aid:*** $19,225. ***Average non-need-based aid:*** $10,278. ***Average indebtedness upon graduation:*** $27,813.

APPLYING

Options: electronic application, deferred entrance.

Required: high school transcript, 1 letter of recommendation. ***Recommended:*** interview.

Application deadlines: rolling (freshmen), rolling (transfers).

Notification: continuous (freshmen), continuous (transfers).

CONTACT

Mr. Nicholas Macchio, University Enrollment Manager, Saint Leo University, MC 2008, PO Box 6665, Saint Leo, FL 33574-6665. *Phone:* 800-334-5532. *Toll-free phone:* 800-334-5532. *Fax:* 352-588-8257. *E-mail:* admissions@saintleo.edu.

St. Petersburg College

St. Petersburg, Florida

http://www.spcollege.edu/

- **State and locally supported** 4-year, founded 1927
- **Suburban** 410-acre campus with easy access to Tampa
- **Coed** 28,853 undergraduate students, 31% full-time, 62% women, 38% men
- **Noncompetitive** entrance level

UNDERGRAD STUDENTS

8,841 full-time, 20,012 part-time. 1% are from out of state; 14% Black or African American, non-Hispanic/Latino; 16% Hispanic/Latino; 4% Asian, non-Hispanic/Latino; 0.3% Native Hawaiian or other Pacific Islander, non-Hispanic/Latino; 0.3% American Indian or Alaska Native, non-Hispanic/Latino; 4% Two or more races, non-Hispanic/Latino; 2% Race/ethnicity unknown; 0.8% international.

Freshmen:
Admission: 2,805 enrolled.

FACULTY

Total: 1,475, 23% full-time, 11% with terminal degrees.

Student/faculty ratio: 22:1.

ACADEMICS

Calendar: semesters. *Degrees:* certificates, diplomas, associate, and bachelor's.

Special study options: academic remediation for entering students, accelerated degree program, adult/continuing education programs, advanced placement credit, cooperative education, distance learning, English as a second language, external degree program, freshman honors college, honors programs, internships, off-campus study, part-time degree program, services for LD students, study abroad, summer session for credit. ***ROTC:*** Army (c).

Computers: Students can access the following: campus intranet, computer help desk, free student e-mail accounts, online (class) grades, online (class) registration, online (class) schedules. Campuswide network is available. Wireless service is available via entire campus.

Library: M. M. Bennett Library.

STUDENT LIFE

Housing options: college housing not available.

Activities and organizations: drama/theater group, student-run newspaper, choral group.

Athletics Member NJCAA. ***Intercollegiate sports:*** baseball M(s), basketball M(s)/W(s), softball W(s), tennis W(s), volleyball W(s).

Campus security: late-night transport/escort service.

Student services: women's center.

FINANCIAL AID

Financial Aid Of all full-time matriculated undergraduates who enrolled in 2018, 5,304 applied for aid, 4,941 were judged to have need, 167 had their need fully met. In 2018, 64 non-need-based awards were made. ***Average percent of need met:*** 49. ***Average financial aid package:*** $7402. ***Average need-based loan:*** $3240. ***Average need-based gift aid:*** $5989. ***Average non-need-based aid:*** $1659. ***Average indebtedness upon graduation:*** $29,008.

APPLYING

Standardized Tests *Required:* SAT or ACT (for admission).

Options: electronic application, early admission, deferred entrance.

Application fee: $40.

Required: high school transcript.

Notification: continuous (freshmen).

CONTACT

Ms. Eva Christensen, Director of Admissions and Records, St. Petersburg College, PO Box 13489, St. Petersburg, FL 33733-3489. *Phone:* 727-341-3166. *E-mail:* information@spcollege.edu.

St. Thomas University - Florida

Miami Gardens, Florida

http://www.stu.edu/

- **Independent Roman Catholic** university, founded 1961
- **Suburban** 140-acre campus with easy access to Miami, FL
- **Endowment** $25.6 million
- **Coed** 3,100 undergraduate students, 40% full-time, 53% women, 47% men
- **Moderately difficult** entrance level, 55% of applicants were admitted

UNDERGRAD STUDENTS
1,246 full-time, 1,854 part-time. Students come from 27 states and territories; 48 other countries; 11% are from out of state; 34% Black or African American, non-Hispanic/Latino; 39% Hispanic/Latino; 0.4% Asian, non-Hispanic/Latino; 0.1% Native Hawaiian or other Pacific Islander, non-Hispanic/Latino; 0.2% American Indian or Alaska Native, non-Hispanic/Latino; 3% Two or more races, non-Hispanic/Latino; 6% Race/ethnicity unknown; 11% international; 6% transferred in; 40% live on campus.

Freshmen:
Admission: 5,062 applied, 2,785 admitted, 468 enrolled. ***Average high school GPA:*** 3.2. ***Test scores:*** SAT evidence-based reading and writing scores over 500: 53%; SAT math scores over 500: 49%; SAT evidence-based reading and writing scores over 600: 10%; SAT math scores over 600: 11%; SAT evidence-based reading and writing scores over 700: 1%; SAT math scores over 700: 1%.

Retention: 72% of full-time freshmen returned.

FACULTY
Total: 145, 68% full-time, 14% with terminal degrees.

Student/faculty ratio: 12:1.

ACADEMICS
Calendar: semesters. *Degrees:* certificates, diplomas, bachelor's, master's, doctoral, post-master's, and postbachelor's certificates.

Special study options: academic remediation for entering students, accelerated degree program, adult/continuing education programs, advanced placement credit, distance learning, double majors, English as a second language, external degree program, honors programs, independent study, internships, part-time degree program, services for LD students, study abroad, summer session for credit.

Computers: 100 computers/terminals and 20 ports are available on campus for general student use. Students can access the following: campus intranet, computer help desk, free student e-mail accounts, online (class) grades, online (class) registration, online (class) schedules. Campuswide network is available. 100% of college-owned or -operated housing units are wired for high-speed Internet access. Wireless service is available via entire campus.
Library: St. Thomas University Library plus 1 other. *Books:* 555,242 (physical), 479,232 (digital/electronic); *Serial titles:* 146,423 (physical), 146,423 (digital/electronic); *Databases:* 410. Weekly public service hours: 101; students can reserve study rooms.

STUDENT LIFE
Housing options: coed. Campus housing is university owned.

Activities and organizations: choral group, marching band, Psychology Club, Nursing Students Association, Criminal Justice, Caribbean Students Association, Future Teachers of America.

Athletics Member NAIA. ***Intercollegiate sports:*** baseball M(s), basketball M(s)/W(s), cheerleading W(s), cross-country running M(s)/W(s), football M, golf M(s)/W, sand volleyball W(s), soccer M(s)/W(s), softball W(s), swimming and diving M/W, tennis M(s)/W(s), track and field M(s)/W(s), volleyball W(s), wrestling M/W. ***Intramural sports:*** badminton M/W, baseball M, basketball M/W, cross-country running M/W, football M/W, golf M/W, racquetball M/W, sand volleyball M/W, soccer M/W, softball M/W, table tennis M/W, tennis M/W, volleyball M/W.

Campus security: 24-hour emergency response devices and patrols, late-night transport/escort service, controlled dormitory access.

Student services: health clinic, personal/psychological counseling.

COSTS
Costs (2020–21) ***Comprehensive fee:*** $45,400 includes full-time tuition ($31,800), mandatory fees ($2280), and room and board ($11,320). Full-time tuition and fees vary according to course load and program. Part-time tuition: $795 per credit hour. Part-time tuition and fees vary according to course load and program. ***College room only:*** $6690. Room and board charges vary according to board plan and housing facility. ***Payment plans:*** installment, deferred payment. ***Waivers:*** employees or children of employees.

APPLYING
Standardized Tests *Required for some:* SAT or ACT (for admission).

Options: electronic application, deferred entrance.

Required: high school transcript, minimum 2.5 GPA. ***Recommended:*** essay or personal statement.

Notification: continuous (freshmen).

CONTACT
Mr. Otis L. Miller, Director University Admissions, St. Thomas University - Florida, 16401 Northwest 37th Avenue, Miami Gardens, FL 33054-6459. *Phone:* 305-628-6753. *Toll-free phone:* 800-367-9010. *E-mail:* omiller@stu.edu.

San Ignacio University

Doral, Florida

http://www.sanignaciouniversity.edu/

CONTACT
San Ignacio University, 10395 NW 41st Street, Suite 125, Doral, FL 33178.

Santa Fe College

Gainesville, Florida

http://www.sfcollege.edu/

CONTACT
Santa Fe College, 3000 Northwest 83rd Street, Gainesville, FL 32606. *Phone:* 352-395-4177.

Schiller International University - Tampa

Largo, Florida

http://www.schiller.edu/

CONTACT
Admissions Officer, Schiller International University - Tampa, Largo, FL 33770. *Toll-free phone:* 800-261-9571 (in-state); 800-261-9751 (out-of-state). *Fax:* 727-738-6376. *E-mail:* admissions@schiller.edu.

Seminole State College of Florida

Sanford, Florida

http://www.seminolestate.edu/

- **State and locally supported** primarily 2-year, founded 1966, part of Florida College System
- **Small-town** 200-acre campus with easy access to Orlando
- **Endowment** $24.6 million
- **Coed**
- **Noncompetitive** entrance level

FACULTY
Student/faculty ratio: 26:1.

ACADEMICS
Calendar: semesters. *Degrees:* certificates, diplomas, associate, bachelor's, and postbachelor's certificates.
Library: Seminole State Library at Sanford Lake Mary plus 3 others. *Books:* 67,023 (physical), 145,374 (digital/electronic); *Serial titles:* 520 (physical), 18,003 (digital/electronic); *Databases:* 130. Weekly public service hours: 60; students can reserve study rooms.

STUDENT LIFE
Housing options: college housing not available.

Activities and organizations: drama/theater group, student-run newspaper, choral group, Phi Beta Lambda, Phi Theta Kappa, Student Government Association, Sigma Phi Gamma, Hispanic Student Association.

Athletics Member NJCAA.

Campus security: 24-hour emergency response devices and patrols, late-night transport/escort service.

Student services: personal/psychological counseling, veterans affairs office.

APPLYING
Options: electronic application, early admission, deferred entrance.

Required: high school transcript, minimum 2.0 GPA.

CONTACT
Seminole State College of Florida, 100 Weldon Boulevard, Sanford, FL 32773-6199.

Southeastern University

Lakeland, Florida

http://www.seu.edu/

- **Independent** comprehensive, founded 1935, affiliated with Assemblies of God
- **Suburban** 87-acre campus with easy access to Tampa, Orlando
- **Endowment** $9.3 million
- **Coed** 7,708 undergraduate students, 64% full-time, 57% women, 43% men
- **Minimally difficult** entrance level, 48% of applicants were admitted

UNDERGRAD STUDENTS
4,909 full-time, 2,799 part-time. 49% are from out of state; 12% transferred in; 31% live on campus.

Freshmen:
Admission: 4,996 applied, 2,405 admitted, 1,460 enrolled. ***Average high school GPA:*** 3.5.

Retention: 68% of full-time freshmen returned.

ACADEMICS
Calendar: semesters. *Degrees:* certificates, associate, bachelor's, master's, doctoral, post-master's, and postbachelor's certificates.

Special study options: academic remediation for entering students, adult/continuing education programs, advanced placement credit, cooperative education, distance learning, double majors, honors programs, independent study, internships, off-campus study, part-time degree program, services for LD students, study abroad, summer session for credit. ***ROTC:*** Army (c).

Computers: 220 computers/terminals are available on campus for general student use. Students can access the following: campus intranet, computer help desk, free student e-mail accounts, online (class) grades, online (class) registration, online (class) schedules, network programs. Campuswide network is available. 100% of college-owned or -operated housing units are wired for high-speed Internet access. Wireless service is available via entire campus.
Library: Steelman Library.

STUDENT LIFE
Housing options: on-campus residence required through sophomore year; men-only, women-only. Campus housing is university owned. Freshman campus housing is guaranteed.

Activities and organizations: drama/theater group, student-run newspaper, radio and television station, choral group.

Athletics ***Intercollegiate sports:*** baseball M(s), basketball M(s)/W(s), cheerleading M/W, cross-country running M(s)/W(s), football M(s), golf M(s), soccer M(s)/W(s), softball W(s), tennis M(s)/W(s), volleyball W(s), wrestling M(s). ***Intramural sports:*** basketball M/W, football M/W, soccer M/W, softball M/W, ultimate Frisbee M/W, volleyball M/W.

Campus security: 24-hour emergency response devices and patrols, late-night transport/escort service, controlled dormitory access.

Student services: health clinic, personal/psychological counseling.

COSTS & FINANCIAL AID
Costs (2019–20) ***Comprehensive fee:*** $36,650 includes full-time tuition ($25,620), mandatory fees ($1000), and room and board ($10,030). Full-time tuition and fees vary according to class time, degree level, location, and reciprocity agreements. Part-time tuition: $1068 per credit hour. Part-time tuition and fees vary according to class time, course load, degree level, location, and reciprocity agreements. ***Required fees:*** $200 per term part-time. ***Room and board:*** Room and board charges vary according to board plan and housing facility. ***Payment plan:*** installment. ***Waivers:*** employees or children of employees.

Financial Aid Of all full-time matriculated undergraduates who enrolled in 2019, 4,323 applied for aid, 3,784 were judged to have need, 376 had their need fully met. 101 Federal Work-Study jobs (averaging $2045). In 2019, 976 non-need-based awards were made. ***Average percent of need met:*** 52. ***Average financial aid package:*** $15,978. ***Average need-based loan:*** $4169. ***Average need-based gift aid:*** $5543. ***Average non-need-based aid:*** $10,319. ***Average indebtedness upon graduation:*** $30,027.

APPLYING
Standardized Tests *Required:* SAT or ACT (for admission).

Options: electronic application, early admission, deferred entrance.

Application fee: $40.

Required: essay or personal statement, high school transcript, 1 letter of recommendation. ***Required for some:*** interview.

Notification: 6/1 (freshmen), continuous (transfers).

CONTACT
Ms. Sarah Clark, Executive Director of Admission, Southeastern University, 1000 Longfellow Boulevard, Lakeland, FL 33801. *Phone:* 863-667-5018. *Toll-free phone:* 800-500-8760. *E-mail:* admission@seu.edu.

Southern Technical College

Fort Myers, Florida

http://www.southerntech.edu/locations/ft-myers/

CONTACT
Ms. Tiffany Quinlan, Director of Admissions, Southern Technical College, 1685 Medical Lane, Fort Myers, FL 33907. *Phone:* 239-939-4766. *Toll-free phone:* 877-347-5492. *Fax:* 239-936-4040. *E-mail:* tquinlan@southerntech.edu.

Southern Technical College

Tampa, Florida

http://www.southerntech.edu/locations/tampa/

CONTACT
Admissions, Southern Technical College, 3910 Riga Boulevard, Tampa, FL 33619. *Phone:* 813-630-4401. *Toll-free phone:* 877-347-5492.

South Florida Bible College and Theological Seminary

Deerfield Beach, Florida

http://www.sfbc.edu/

CONTACT
South Florida Bible College and Theological Seminary, 2200 SW 10th Street, Deerfield Beach, FL 33442.

South Florida State College

Avon Park, Florida

http://www.southflorida.edu/

CONTACT
Ms. Brenda Desantiago, Admissions, South Florida State College, 600 West College Drive, Avon Park, FL 33825. *Phone:* 863-784-7416.

South University - Tampa

Tampa, Florida

http://www.southuniversity.edu/tampa/

CONTACT
South University - Tampa, 4401 North Himes Avenue, Suite 175, Tampa, FL 33614. *Phone:* 813-393-3800. *Toll-free phone:* 800-846-1472.

South University - West Palm Beach

Royal Palm Beach, Florida

http://www.southuniversity.edu/west-palm-beach/

CONTACT
South University - West Palm Beach, University Centre, 9801 Belvedere Road, Royal Palm Beach, FL 33411. *Phone:* 561-273-6500. *Toll-free phone:* 866-629-2902.

State College of Florida Manatee-Sarasota

Bradenton, Florida

http://www.scf.edu/

- **State-supported** 4-year, founded 1957, part of Florida Community College System
- **Suburban** 100-acre campus with easy access to Tampa-St. Petersburg
- **Coed**
- **Noncompetitive** entrance level

ACADEMICS
Calendar: semesters. *Degrees:* certificates, associate, and bachelor's.
Library: Sara Harlee Library. *Books:* 129,690 (physical), 731,905 (digital/electronic); *Databases:* 140.

STUDENT LIFE
Housing options: college housing not available.

Activities and organizations: drama/theater group, student-run newspaper, choral group, Student Government Association, Phi Theta Kappa, American Chemical Society Student Affiliate, Campus Ministry, Medical Community Club.

Athletics Member NJCAA.

Campus security: 24-hour emergency response devices and patrols, late-night transport/escort service.

Student services: veterans affairs office.

FINANCIAL AID
Financial Aid Of all full-time matriculated undergraduates who enrolled in 2018, 82 Federal Work-Study jobs (averaging $2800). ***Financial aid deadline:*** 8/15.

APPLYING
Options: electronic application, early admission.

Required: high school transcript.

CONTACT
Ms. MariLynn Lewy, Assistant Vice President of Student Services, State College of Florida Manatee-Sarasota, Bradenton, FL 34206. *Phone:* 941-752-5384. *Fax:* 941-727-6380. *E-mail:* lewym@scf.edu.

Stetson University

DeLand, Florida

http://www.stetson.edu/

- **Independent** comprehensive, founded 1883
- **Small-town** 185-acre campus with easy access to Orlando
- **Endowment** $255.4 million
- **Coed** 3,183 undergraduate students, 98% full-time, 57% women, 43% men
- **Moderately difficult** entrance level, 72% of applicants were admitted

UNDERGRAD STUDENTS
3,133 full-time, 50 part-time. Students come from 49 states and territories; 63 other countries; 25% are from out of state; 8% Black or African American, non-Hispanic/Latino; 18% Hispanic/Latino; 2% Asian, non-Hispanic/Latino; 0.1% Native Hawaiian or other Pacific Islander, non-Hispanic/Latino; 0.1% American Indian or Alaska Native, non-Hispanic/Latino; 5% Two or more races, non-Hispanic/Latino; 1% Race/ethnicity unknown; 6% international; 4% transferred in; 65% live on campus.

Freshmen:
Admission: 13,005 applied, 9,410 admitted, 934 enrolled. ***Average high school GPA:*** 3.9. ***Test scores:*** SAT evidence-based reading and writing scores over 500: 97%; SAT math scores over 500: 93%; ACT scores over 18: 100%; SAT evidence-based reading and writing scores over 600: 62%; SAT math scores over 600: 46%; ACT scores over 24: 69%; SAT evidence-based reading and writing scores over 700: 10%; SAT math scores over 700: 8%; ACT scores over 30: 22%.

Retention: 77% of full-time freshmen returned.

FACULTY
Total: 432, 62% full-time, 81% with terminal degrees.

Student/faculty ratio: 13:1.

ACADEMICS
Calendar: semesters. *Degrees:* bachelor's, master's, doctoral, and post-master's certificates.

Special study options: accelerated degree program, advanced placement credit, distance learning, double majors, honors programs, independent study, internships, off-campus study, part-time degree program, services for LD students, student-designed majors, study abroad, summer session for credit. ***ROTC:*** Army (c), Air Force (c).

Unusual degree programs: 3-2 engineering; forestry with Duke University; environmental management with Duke University, public administration with American University.

Computers: 600 computers/terminals are available on campus for general student use. Students can access the following: campus intranet, computer help desk, free student e-mail accounts, online (class) grades, online (class) registration, online (class) schedules. Campuswide network is available. 100% of college-owned or -operated housing units are wired for high-speed Internet access. Wireless service is available via entire campus.
Library: duPont-Ball Library plus 1 other. *Books:* 219,200 (physical), 166,549 (digital/electronic); *Serial titles:* 228 (physical), 186,552 (digital/electronic); *Databases:* 247. Weekly public service hours: 104; study areas open 24 hours, 5–7 days a week; students can reserve study rooms.

STUDENT LIFE
Housing options: on-campus residence required through junior year; coed, men-only, women-only. Campus housing is university owned. Freshman campus housing is guaranteed.

Activities and organizations: drama/theater group, student-run newspaper, radio station, choral group, Caribbean Student Association, Fellowship of Christian Athletes, Kaleidoscope (promotes inclusivity), Black Student Association, Hatter Productions, national fraternities, national sororities.

Athletics Member NCAA. All Division I. ***Intercollegiate sports:*** baseball M(s), basketball M(s)/W(s), crew M(s)/W(s), cross-country running M(s)/W(s), football M, golf M(s)/W(s)(c), lacrosse W(s), soccer M(s)/W(s), softball W(s), tennis M(s)/W(s), volleyball W(s). ***Intramural sports:*** baseball M(c)/W(c), basketball M/W, equestrian sports M(c)/W(c), riflery M(c)/W(c), sand volleyball M/W, soccer M(c)/W(c), softball M(c)/W(c), tennis M/W, ultimate Frisbee M(c)/W(c), volleyball M/W(c).

Campus security: 24-hour emergency response devices and patrols, student patrols, late-night transport/escort service, controlled dormitory access.

Student services: health clinic, personal/psychological counseling, veterans affairs office.

COSTS & FINANCIAL AID
Costs (2020–21) ***Comprehensive fee:*** $64,040 includes full-time tuition ($49,140), mandatory fees ($360), and room and board ($14,540). Part-time tuition: $1238 per credit hour. ***College room only:*** $8640. Room and board charges vary according to board plan. ***Payment plan:*** installment. ***Waivers:*** employees or children of employees.

Financial Aid Of all full-time matriculated undergraduates who enrolled in 2019, 2,291 applied for aid, 2,063 were judged to have need, 470 had their need fully met. 930 Federal Work-Study jobs (averaging $2184). 69

state and other part-time jobs (averaging $3940). In 2019, 830 non-need-based awards were made. ***Average percent of need met:*** 78. ***Average financial aid package:*** $40,976. ***Average need-based loan:*** $4322. ***Average need-based gift aid:*** $33,564. ***Average non-need-based aid:*** $26,807. ***Average indebtedness upon graduation:*** $32,601.

APPLYING

Standardized Tests *Required for some:* SAT or ACT (for admission).

Options: electronic application, early action, deferred entrance.

Application fee: $50.

Required: essay or personal statement, high school transcript, 1 letter of recommendation. ***Recommended:*** interview.

Application deadlines: rolling (freshmen), rolling (transfers).

Notification: continuous (freshmen), continuous (transfers).

CONTACT

Ms. Dana Simmons, Director of Enrollment Operations and Communications, Stetson University, 421 N. Woodland Boulevard, Unit 8378, DeLand, FL 32723. *Phone:* 386-822-7100. *Toll-free phone:* 800-688-0101. *Fax:* 386-822-7112. *E-mail:* admissions@stetson.edu.

Strayer University - Baymeadows

Jacksonville, Florida

http://www.strayer.edu/florida/baymeadows/

CONTACT

Strayer University - Baymeadows, 8375 Dix Ellis Trail, Suite 200, Jacksonville, FL 32256. *Toll-free phone:* 888-311-0355.

Strayer University–Fort Lauderdale Campus

Fort Lauderdale, Florida

http://www.strayer.edu/florida/fort-lauderdale/

CONTACT

Strayer University–Fort Lauderdale Campus, 2307 West Broward Boulevard, Suite 100, Fort Lauderdale, FL 33312. *Toll-free phone:* 888-311-0355.

Strayer University–Maitland Campus

Maitland, Florida

http://www.strayer.edu/florida/maitland/

CONTACT

Strayer University–Maitland Campus, 901 North Lake Destiny Road, Suite 370, Maitland, FL 32751. *Toll-free phone:* 888-311-0355.

Strayer University–Miramar Campus

Hollywood, Florida

http://www.strayer.edu/florida/miramar/

CONTACT

Strayer University–Miramar Campus, 15620 Southwest 29th Street, Hollywood, FL 33027. *Toll-free phone:* 888-311-0355.

Strayer University–Orlando East Campus

Orlando, Florida

http://www.strayer.edu/florida/orlando-east/

CONTACT

Strayer University–Orlando East Campus, 2200 North Alafaya Trail, Suite 500, Orlando, FL 32826. *Toll-free phone:* 888-311-0355.

Strayer University–Palm Beach Gardens Campus

West Palm Beach, Florida

http://www.strayer.edu/florida/palm-beach-gardens/

CONTACT

Strayer University–Palm Beach Gardens Campus, 11025 RCA Center Drive, Suite 200, West Palm Beach, FL 33410. *Toll-free phone:* 888-311-0355.

Strayer University–Sand Lake Campus

Orlando, Florida

http://www.strayer.edu/florida/sand-lake/

CONTACT

Strayer University–Sand Lake Campus, 8529 South Park Circle, Orlando, FL 32819. *Toll-free phone:* 888-311-0355.

Strayer University–Tampa East Campus

Tampa, Florida

http://www.strayer.edu/florida/tampa-east/

CONTACT

Strayer University–Tampa East Campus, 5650 Breckenridge Park Drive, Suite 300, Tampa, FL 33610. *Toll-free phone:* 888-311-0355.

Tallahassee Community College

Tallahassee, Florida

http://www.tcc.fl.edu/

CONTACT

Student Success Center, Tallahassee Community College, 444 Appleyard Drive, Tallahassee, FL 32304-2895. *Phone:* 850-201-8555. *E-mail:* admissions@tcc.fl.edu.

Talmudic University

Miami Beach, Florida

http://www.talmudicu.edu/

CONTACT

Rabbi Yeshaya Greenberg, Dean of Students, Talmudic University, 4000 Alton Road, Miami Beach, FL 33140. *Phone:* 305-534-7050. *Fax:* 305-534-8444. *E-mail:* yandtg@gmail.com.

Trinity Baptist College

Jacksonville, Florida

http://www.tbc.edu/

CONTACT

Melissa Gibson, Trinity Baptist College, 800 Hammond Boulevard, Jacksonville, FL 32219. *Phone:* 904-596-2307. *Toll-free phone:* 800-786-2206. *E-mail:* mgibson@tbc.edu.

Trinity College of Florida

Trinity, Florida

http://www.trinitycollege.edu/

- **Independent nondenominational** 4-year, founded 1932
- **Small-town** 40-acre campus with easy access to Tampa
- **Endowment** $784,846
- **Coed** 220 undergraduate students, 83% full-time, 52% women, 48% men
- **Noncompetitive** entrance level, 86% of applicants were admitted

UNDERGRAD STUDENTS

182 full-time, 38 part-time. Students come from 18 states and territories; 3 other countries; 10% are from out of state; 25% Black or African American, non-Hispanic/Latino; 19% Hispanic/Latino; 2% Asian, non-

Hispanic/Latino; 1% American Indian or Alaska Native, non-Hispanic/Latino; 9% Race/ethnicity unknown; 2% international; 16% transferred in; 57% live on campus.

Freshmen:
Admission: 113 applied, 97 admitted, 34 enrolled. ***Average high school GPA:*** 3.1. ***Test scores:*** SAT evidence-based reading and writing scores over 500: 35%; SAT math scores over 500: 27%; ACT scores over 18: 57%; SAT math scores over 600: 4%.

Retention: 55% of full-time freshmen returned.

FACULTY
Total: 23, 39% full-time, 30% with terminal degrees.

Student/faculty ratio: 9:1.

ACADEMICS
Calendar: semesters. *Degrees:* certificates, associate, and bachelor's.

Special study options: academic remediation for entering students, accelerated degree program, adult/continuing education programs, advanced placement credit, cooperative education, distance learning, double majors, honors programs, independent study, part-time degree program, services for LD students, summer session for credit.

Computers: 17 computers/terminals and 144 ports are available on campus for general student use. Students can access the following: campus intranet, computer help desk, free student e-mail accounts, online (class) grades, online (class) registration, online (class) schedules. Campuswide network is available. 100% of college-owned or -operated housing units are wired for high-speed Internet access. Wireless service is available via entire campus.
Library: Raymond H. Center, M.D. Library. *Books:* 26,725 (physical), 165,300 (digital/electronic); *Serial titles:* 38 (physical); *Databases:* 8. Weekly public service hours: 60.

STUDENT LIFE
Housing options: men-only, women-only, special housing for students with disabilities. Campus housing is university owned. Freshman applicants given priority for college housing.

Activities and organizations: choral group, Student Government Association, Great Commission Missionary Fellowship, Speaking Truth, Trinity Against Trafficking.

Athletics Member NCCAA. ***Intercollegiate sports:*** basketball M/W, soccer M, volleyball W.

Campus security: 24-hour emergency response devices, controlled dormitory access, security cameras; security guards 4:30 PM to 4:30 AM.

Student services: personal/psychological counseling.

COSTS & FINANCIAL AID
Costs (2020–21) ***Comprehensive fee:*** $23,900 includes full-time tuition ($15,200), mandatory fees ($1100), and room and board ($7600). Full-time tuition and fees vary according to course load and program. Part-time tuition: $510 per credit hour. Part-time tuition and fees vary according to course load and program. ***Required fees:*** $550 per term part-time. ***College room only:*** $5400. ***Payment plan:*** installment. ***Waivers:*** senior citizens and employees or children of employees.

Financial Aid Of all full-time matriculated undergraduates who enrolled in 2019, 167 applied for aid, 146 were judged to have need, 26 had their need fully met. 13 Federal Work-Study jobs (averaging $4335). 1 state and other part-time job (averaging $5250). In 2019, 18 non-need-based awards were made. ***Average percent of need met:*** 83. ***Average financial aid package:*** $14,489. ***Average need-based loan:*** $7243. ***Average need-based gift aid:*** $8210. ***Average non-need-based aid:*** $6391. ***Average indebtedness upon graduation:*** $26,617.

APPLYING
Standardized Tests *Required:* SAT or ACT (for admission).

Options: electronic application, deferred entrance.

Application fee: $35.

Required: essay or personal statement, high school transcript, 2 letters of recommendation. ***Required for some:*** interview. ***Recommended:*** minimum 2.2 GPA.

Application deadlines: 7/31 (freshmen), 7/31 (transfers).

Notification: continuous (freshmen), continuous (out-of-state freshmen), continuous (transfers).

CONTACT
Mrs. Rachel Noble, Director of Admissions and Marketing Coordinator, Trinity College of Florida, 2430 Welbilt Boulevard, Trinity, FL 34655. *Phone:* 727-569-1410. *Toll-free phone:* 800-388-0869. *Fax:* 727-569-1410. *E-mail:* rachel.noble@trinitycollege.edu.

Unilatina International College

Miramar, Florida

http://www.unilatina.edu/

CONTACT
Unilatina International College, 3130 Commerce Parkway, Miramar, FL 33025.

University of Central Florida

Orlando, Florida

http://www.ucf.edu/

- **State-supported** university, founded 1963, part of State University System of Florida
- **Suburban** 1415-acre campus with easy access to Orlando
- **Endowment** $162.8 million
- **Coed** 59,483 undergraduate students, 71% full-time, 55% women, 45% men
- **Moderately difficult** entrance level, 44% of applicants were admitted

UNDERGRAD STUDENTS
42,468 full-time, 17,015 part-time. Students come from 50 states and territories; 136 other countries; 7% are from out of state; 11% Black or African American, non-Hispanic/Latino; 28% Hispanic/Latino; 6% Asian, non-Hispanic/Latino; 0.2% Native Hawaiian or other Pacific Islander, non-Hispanic/Latino; 0.2% American Indian or Alaska Native, non-Hispanic/Latino; 4% Two or more races, non-Hispanic/Latino; 0.7% Race/ethnicity unknown; 3% international; 11% transferred in; 18% live on campus.

Freshmen:
Admission: 45,118 applied, 20,016 admitted, 7,323 enrolled. ***Average high school GPA:*** 4.1. ***Test scores:*** SAT evidence-based reading and writing scores over 500: 99%; SAT math scores over 500: 98%; ACT scores over 18: 100%; SAT evidence-based reading and writing scores over 600: 75%; SAT math scores over 600: 64%; ACT scores over 24: 85%; SAT evidence-based reading and writing scores over 700: 14%; SAT math scores over 700: 16%; ACT scores over 30: 28%.

Retention: 92% of full-time freshmen returned.

FACULTY
Total: 2,159, 77% full-time, 75% with terminal degrees.

Student/faculty ratio: 30:1.

ACADEMICS
Calendar: semesters. *Degrees:* certificates, associate, bachelor's, master's, doctoral, post-master's, and postbachelor's certificates.

Special study options: accelerated degree program, adult/continuing education programs, advanced placement credit, cooperative education, distance learning, double majors, English as a second language, freshman honors college, honors programs, independent study, internships, part-time degree program, services for LD students, study abroad, summer session for credit. ***ROTC:*** Army (b), Air Force (b).

Unusual degree programs: 3-2 engineering; nursing; history, communicative sciences and disorders, computer science, law.

Computers: 4,233 computers/terminals and 500 ports are available on campus for general student use. Students can access the following: campus intranet, computer help desk, free student e-mail accounts, online (class) grades, online (class) registration, online (class) schedules. Campuswide network is available. 100% of college-owned or -operated housing units are wired for high-speed Internet access. Wireless service is available via entire campus.
Library: University Libraries plus 3 others. *Books:* 1.6 million (physical), 221,333 (digital/electronic); *Serial titles:* 646 (physical), 53,148 (digital/electronic); *Databases:* 508. Weekly public service hours: 105; students can reserve study rooms.

STUDENT LIFE
Housing options: coed. Campus housing is university owned. Freshman applicants given priority for college housing.

Activities and organizations: drama/theater group, student-run radio and television station, choral group, marching band, Volunteer UCF, RWC Intramural Sports, Fraternity and Sorority Life, Multicultural Student Center and Organizations, Knight-thon Dance Marathon, national fraternities, national sororities.

Athletics Member NCAA. All Division I except football (Division I-A). ***Intercollegiate sports:*** baseball M(s), basketball M(s)/W(s), cheerleading W(s), crew W(s), cross-country running W(s), golf M(s)/W(s)(c), soccer M(s)/W(s), softball W(s), tennis M(s)/W(s), track and field W(s), volleyball W(s). ***Intramural sports:*** badminton M/W, baseball M, basketball M/W, bowling M(c)/W(c), crew M(c)/W, equestrian sports M(c)/W(c), fencing M(c), golf M/W, ice hockey M(c), lacrosse M(c)/W(c), racquetball M/W, rock climbing M(c)/W(c), rugby M(c)/W(c), sailing M(c)/W(c), sand volleyball M/W, soccer M/W, softball M/W, swimming and diving M(c)/W(c), table tennis M(c)/W(c), tennis M/W, triathlon M(c)/W(c), ultimate Frisbee M(c)/W(c), volleyball M/W, water polo M(c)/W(c), wrestling M(c)/W(c).

Campus security: 24-hour emergency response devices and patrols, late-night transport/escort service, controlled dormitory access.

Student services: health clinic, personal/psychological counseling, women's center, legal services, veterans affairs office.

COSTS & FINANCIAL AID
Costs (2019–20) ***Tuition:*** area resident $6368 full-time; state resident $6368 full-time, $212 per credit hour part-time; nonresident $22,467 full-time, $749 per credit hour part-time. Full-time tuition and fees vary according to course load. Part-time tuition and fees vary according to course load. ***Room and board:*** $9580; room only: $5400. Room and board charges vary according to board plan and housing facility. ***Payment plans:*** tuition prepayment, deferred payment. ***Waivers:*** senior citizens and employees or children of employees.

Financial Aid Of all full-time matriculated undergraduates who enrolled in 2018, 32,519 applied for aid, 25,219 were judged to have need, 3,777 had their need fully met. 1,014 Federal Work-Study jobs (averaging $3460). In 2018, 2904 non-need-based awards were made. ***Average percent of need met:*** 64. ***Average financial aid package:*** $10,852. ***Average need-based loan:*** $4588. ***Average need-based gift aid:*** $7160. ***Average non-need-based aid:*** $3659. ***Average indebtedness upon graduation:*** $22,561. ***Financial aid deadline:*** 6/30.

APPLYING
Standardized Tests *Required:* SAT or ACT (for admission).

Options: electronic application, early admission.

Application fee: $30.

Required: minimum 2.5 GPA. ***Required for some:*** high school transcript.

Application deadlines: 5/1 (freshmen), 7/1 (transfers).

Notification: continuous (freshmen), continuous (transfers).

CONTACT
Dr. Gordon Chavis Jr., Associate Vice President, Undergraduate Admissions, Student Financial Assistance and Outreach Programs, University of Central Florida, PO Box 160111, Orlando, FL 32816-0111. *Phone:* 407-823-3000. *Fax:* 407-823-5625. *E-mail:* admission@ucf.edu.

University of Florida

Gainesville, Florida

http://www.ufl.edu/

- **State-supported** university, founded 1853, part of Board of Trustees
- **Suburban** 2000-acre campus with easy access to Jacksonville
- **Endowment** $1.7 million
- **Coed**
- **Very difficult** entrance level

ACADEMICS
Calendar: semesters. *Degrees:* certificates, associate, bachelor's, master's, doctoral, post-master's, and postbachelor's certificates.

Library: George A. Smathers Libraries plus 7 others. *Books:* 5.8 million (physical), 1.5 million (digital/electronic); *Serial titles:* 2,716 (physical), 125,667 (digital/electronic); *Databases:* 1,092. Weekly public service hours: 168; study areas open 24 hours, 5–7 days a week; students can reserve study rooms.

STUDENT LIFE
Housing options: coed, special housing for students with disabilities. Campus housing is university owned and is provided by a third party.

Activities and organizations: drama/theater group, student-run newspaper, radio and television station, choral group, marching band, Student Government, Hispanic Student Association, Black Student Union, Inter-Residence Hall Association, Asian American Student Union, national fraternities, national sororities.

Athletics Member NCAA. All Division I.

Campus security: 24-hour emergency response devices and patrols, student patrols, late-night transport/escort service, controlled dormitory access, crime and rape prevention programs.

Student services: health clinic, personal/psychological counseling, women's center, legal services, veterans affairs office.

COSTS & FINANCIAL AID
Costs (2019–20) ***Tuition:*** area resident $4477 full-time; state resident $4477 full-time; nonresident $25,694 full-time. ***Required fees:*** $1904 full-time. ***Room and board:*** $10,220; room only: $5750. Room and board charges vary according to board plan and housing facility.

Financial Aid Of all full-time matriculated undergraduates who enrolled in 2017, 22,536 applied for aid, 16,548 were judged to have need, 3,960 had their need fully met. 1,066 Federal Work-Study jobs (averaging $2283). 5,369 state and other part-time jobs (averaging $3545). In 2017, 1929 non-need-based awards were made. ***Average percent of need met:*** 98. ***Average financial aid package:*** $14,611. ***Average need-based loan:*** $4397. ***Average need-based gift aid:*** $8476. ***Average non-need-based aid:*** $2814. ***Average indebtedness upon graduation:*** $21,800.

APPLYING
Standardized Tests *Required:* SAT or ACT (for admission). *Required for some:* SAT Subject Tests (for admission).

Options: electronic application.

Application fee: $30.

Required: essay or personal statement. ***Required for some:*** high school transcript.

CONTACT
Dr. Zina Evans, Vice President for Enrollment Management and Associate Provost, University of Florida, Gainesville, FL 32611. *Phone:* 352-392-1365. *E-mail:* zevans@ufl.edu.

University of Fort Lauderdale

Lauderhill, Florida

http://uftl.edu/

CONTACT
University of Fort Lauderdale, 4093 NW 16th Street, Lauderhill, FL 33313.

University of Miami

Coral Gables, Florida

http://www.miami.edu/

- **Independent** university, founded 1925
- **Suburban** 239-acre campus with easy access to Miami
- **Endowment** $997.4 million
- **Coed** 11,307 undergraduate students, 95% full-time, 54% women, 46% men
- **Very difficult** entrance level, 27% of applicants were admitted

UNDERGRAD STUDENTS
10,701 full-time, 606 part-time. Students come from 51 states and territories; 104 other countries; 61% are from out of state; 9% Black or African American, non-Hispanic/Latino; 22% Hispanic/Latino; 4% Asian, non-Hispanic/Latino; 0.2% Native Hawaiian or other Pacific Islander, non-Hispanic/Latino; 0.1% American Indian or Alaska Native, non-Hispanic/Latino; 3% Two or more races, non-Hispanic/Latino; 4% Race/ethnicity unknown; 14% international; 6% transferred in; 37% live on campus.

Freshmen:
Admission: 38,919 applied, 10,557 admitted, 2,203 enrolled. ***Average high school GPA:*** 3.6. ***Test scores:*** SAT evidence-based reading and writing scores over 500: 98%; SAT math scores over 500: 99%; ACT scores over 18: 100%; SAT evidence-based reading and writing scores over 600: 87%; SAT math scores over 600: 90%; ACT scores over 24: 97%; SAT evidence-based reading and writing scores over 700: 29%; SAT math scores over 700: 47%; ACT scores over 30: 68%.

Retention: 93% of full-time freshmen returned.

FACULTY
Total: 1,694, 67% full-time, 78% with terminal degrees.

Student/faculty ratio: 12:1.

ACADEMICS
Calendar: semesters. *Degrees:* certificates, bachelor's, master's, doctoral, post-master's, and postbachelor's certificates.

Special study options: academic remediation for entering students, accelerated degree program, adult/continuing education programs, advanced placement credit, cooperative education, distance learning, double majors, English as a second language, honors programs, independent study, internships, off-campus study, part-time degree program, services for LD students, student-designed majors, study abroad, summer session for credit. ***ROTC:*** Army (b), Air Force (b).

Unusual degree programs: 3-2 business administration; engineering; nursing; law, medicine.

STUDENT LIFE
Housing options: on-campus residence required for freshman year; coed, special housing for students with disabilities. Campus housing is university owned. Freshman campus housing is guaranteed.

Activities and organizations: drama/theater group, student-run newspaper, radio and television station, choral group, marching band, Hurricane Productions, Federation of Club Sports, Association of Greek Letter Organizations, Panhellenic Council, Scuba Club, national fraternities, national sororities.

Campus security: 24-hour emergency response devices and patrols, student patrols, late-night transport/escort service, controlled dormitory access, programs, seminars, activities, classes and publications are available to students, faculty, staff, parents and friends.

Student services: health clinic, personal/psychological counseling, veterans affairs office.

COSTS & FINANCIAL AID
Costs (2020–21) ***Comprehensive fee:*** $69,152 includes full-time tuition ($52,080), mandatory fees ($1602), and room and board ($15,470). Part-time tuition: $2170 per credit hour. ***Required fees:*** $570 part-time, $285 part-time. ***College room only:*** $8900. Room and board charges vary according to board plan and housing facility. ***Payment plan:*** installment. ***Waivers:*** employees or children of employees.

Financial Aid Of all full-time matriculated undergraduates who enrolled in 2019, 5,894 applied for aid, 4,618 were judged to have need, 3,621 had their need fully met. 2,132 Federal Work-Study jobs (averaging $2926). 172 state and other part-time jobs (averaging $2977). In 2019, 2659 non-need-based awards were made. ***Average percent of need met:*** 97. ***Average financial aid package:*** $41,057. ***Average need-based loan:*** $4460. ***Average need-based gift aid:*** $35,768. ***Average non-need-based aid:*** $22,986. ***Average indebtedness upon graduation:*** $21,000. ***Financial aid deadline:*** 4/15.

APPLYING
Standardized Tests *Required:* SAT or ACT (for admission). *Required for some:* SAT and SAT Subject Tests or ACT (for admission).

Options: electronic application, early admission, early decision, early action, deferred entrance.

Application fee: $70.

Required: essay or personal statement, high school transcript, 2 letters of recommendation. ***Required for some:*** college transcript(s) and statement of good standing from prior institution(s), auditions for selected academic programs.

Application deadlines: 1/1 (freshmen), 11/1 (early action).

Early decision deadline: 11/1 (for plan 1), 1/1 (for plan 2).

Notification: 4/1 (freshmen), 1/1 (early decision plan 1), 3/1 (early decision plan 2), 2/1 (early action).

CONTACT
University of Miami, PO Box 248025, Coral Gables, FL 33124.

University of North Florida

Jacksonville, Florida

http://www.unf.edu/

- **State-supported** comprehensive, founded 1965, part of State University System of Florida
- **Urban** 1300-acre campus with easy access to Jacksonville, FL
- **Endowment** $107.1 million
- **Coed** 14,734 undergraduate students, 73% full-time, 57% women, 43% men
- **Moderately difficult** entrance level, 72% of applicants were admitted

UNDERGRAD STUDENTS
10,757 full-time, 3,977 part-time. Students come from 48 states and territories; 72 other countries; 4% are from out of state; 9% Black or African American, non-Hispanic/Latino; 14% Hispanic/Latino; 5% Asian, non-Hispanic/Latino; 0.1% Native Hawaiian or other Pacific Islander, non-Hispanic/Latino; 0.2% American Indian or Alaska Native, non-Hispanic/Latino; 5% Two or more races, non-Hispanic/Latino; 0.4% Race/ethnicity unknown; 2% international; 9% transferred in; 22% live on campus.

Freshmen:
Admission: 16,305 applied, 11,786 admitted, 2,641 enrolled. ***Average high school GPA:*** 3.9. ***Test scores:*** SAT evidence-based reading and writing scores over 500: 94%; SAT math scores over 500: 90%; ACT scores over 18: 91%; SAT evidence-based reading and writing scores over 600: 57%; SAT math scores over 600: 39%; ACT scores over 24: 36%; SAT evidence-based reading and writing scores over 700: 8%; SAT math scores over 700: 4%; ACT scores over 30: 4%.

Retention: 83% of full-time freshmen returned.

FACULTY
Total: 995, 56% full-time, 59% with terminal degrees.

Student/faculty ratio: 19:1.

ACADEMICS
Calendar: semesters. *Degrees:* associate, bachelor's, master's, doctoral, post-master's, and postbachelor's certificates (doctoral degree in education only).

Special study options: accelerated degree program, adult/continuing education programs, advanced placement credit, cooperative education, distance learning, double majors, English as a second language, honors programs, independent study, internships, off-campus study, part-time degree program, services for LD students, study abroad, summer session for credit. ***ROTC:*** Army (b), Navy (c).

Unusual degree programs: 3-2 computer science.

Computers: 700 computers/terminals are available on campus for general student use. Students can access the following: campus intranet, computer help desk, free student e-mail accounts, online (class) grades, online (class) registration, online (class) schedules, reduced prices for students on certain business and design software. Campuswide network is available. 100% of college-owned or -operated housing units are wired for high-speed Internet access. Wireless service is available via entire campus.

Library: Thomas G. Carpenter Library. *Books:* 568,299 (physical), 543,121 (digital/electronic); *Serial titles:* 12,479 (physical), 211,959 (digital/electronic); *Databases:* 284. Students can reserve study rooms.

STUDENT LIFE
Housing options: coed, special housing for students with disabilities. Campus housing is university owned. Freshman campus housing is guaranteed.

Activities and organizations: drama/theater group, student-run newspaper, radio and television station, choral group, Student Government Association, African American Student Association, International Student Association, Filipino Student Association, National Education Association, national fraternities, national sororities.

Athletics Member NCAA. All Division I. ***Intercollegiate sports:*** baseball M(s), basketball M(s)/W(s), cross-country running M(s)/W(s), golf M(s)/W(c), soccer M(s)/W(s), softball W(s), swimming and diving W(s), tennis M(s)/W(s), track and field M(s)/W(s), volleyball W(s). ***Intramural***

sports: badminton M/W, basketball M/W, bowling M/W, fencing M(c), field hockey W(c), football M/W, golf M/W, lacrosse M(c)/W(c), racquetball M(c)/W(c), rugby M(c), sailing M(c)/W(c), soccer M/W, swimming and diving M/W, table tennis M/W, track and field M/W, ultimate Frisbee M(c)/W(c), volleyball M(c)/W(c).

Campus security: 24-hour emergency response devices and patrols, late-night transport/escort service, controlled dormitory access, electronic parking lot security.

Student services: health clinic, personal/psychological counseling, women's center.

COSTS & FINANCIAL AID

Costs (2019–20) ***Tuition:*** state resident $4281 full-time, $143 per credit hour part-time; nonresident $17,999 full-time, $600 per credit hour part-time. Full-time tuition and fees vary according to course load. Part-time tuition and fees vary according to course load. ***Required fees:*** $2108 full-time, $70 per credit hour part-time. ***Room and board:*** $9921; room only: $5772. Room and board charges vary according to board plan and housing facility. ***Payment plan:*** installment. ***Waivers:*** senior citizens and employees or children of employees.

Financial Aid Of all full-time matriculated undergraduates who enrolled in 2018, 7,220 applied for aid, 5,403 were judged to have need, 391 had their need fully met. 163 Federal Work-Study jobs (averaging $2916). In 2018, 1259 non-need-based awards were made. ***Average percent of need met:*** 90. ***Average financial aid package:*** $10,079. ***Average need-based loan:*** $4132. ***Average need-based gift aid:*** $7436. ***Average non-need-based aid:*** $3024. ***Average indebtedness upon graduation:*** $19,290.

APPLYING

Standardized Tests *Required:* SAT or ACT (for admission).

Options: electronic application, deferred entrance.

Application fee: $30.

Required: high school transcript, minimum 2.5 GPA. ***Required for some:*** essay or personal statement. ***Recommended:*** minimum 3.0 GPA.

Application deadlines: rolling (freshmen), 5/10 (transfers).

Notification: continuous (freshmen), continuous (transfers).

CONTACT

Ms. Karen Lucas, Director of Admissions, University of North Florida, 1 UNF Drive, Jacksonville, FL 32224. *Phone:* 904-620-5252. *Fax:* 904-620-2014. *E-mail:* admissions@unf.edu.

University of South Florida

Tampa, Florida

http://www.usf.edu/

- **State-supported** university, founded 1956, part of State University System of Florida
- **Urban** 1562-acre campus
- **Endowment** $480.4 million
- **Coed** 32,681 undergraduate students, 78% full-time, 55% women, 45% men
- 48% of applicants were admitted

UNDERGRAD STUDENTS

25,457 full-time, 7,224 part-time. 6% are from out of state; 10% Black or African American, non-Hispanic/Latino; 22% Hispanic/Latino; 7% Asian, non-Hispanic/Latino; 0.2% Native Hawaiian or other Pacific Islander, non-Hispanic/Latino; 0.1% American Indian or Alaska Native, non-Hispanic/Latino; 4% Two or more races, non-Hispanic/Latino; 4% Race/ethnicity unknown; 7% international; 10% transferred in; 15% live on campus.

Freshmen:

Admission: 36,986 applied, 17,627 admitted, 5,113 enrolled. ***Average high school GPA:*** 4.0. ***Test scores:*** SAT evidence-based reading and writing scores over 500: 99%; SAT math scores over 500: 99%; ACT scores over 18: 100%; SAT evidence-based reading and writing scores over 600: 71%; SAT math scores over 600: 63%; ACT scores over 24: 90%; SAT evidence-based reading and writing scores over 700: 10%; SAT math scores over 700: 14%; ACT scores over 30: 28%.

Retention: 91% of full-time freshmen returned.

FACULTY

Total: 1,946, 67% full-time, 70% with terminal degrees.

Student/faculty ratio: 23:1.

ACADEMICS

Calendar: semesters. *Degrees:* bachelor's, master's, and doctoral.

Special study options: academic remediation for entering students, accelerated degree program, adult/continuing education programs, advanced placement credit, cooperative education, distance learning, double majors, English as a second language, freshman honors college, honors programs, independent study, internships, off-campus study, part-time degree program, services for LD students, study abroad, summer session for credit. ***ROTC:*** Army (b), Navy (b), Air Force (b).

Computers: 825 computers/terminals and 2,000 ports are available on campus for general student use. Students can access the following: campus intranet, computer help desk, free student e-mail accounts, online (class) grades, online (class) registration, online (class) schedules. Campuswide network is available. 100% of college-owned or -operated housing units are wired for high-speed Internet access. Wireless service is available via entire campus.

Library: Tampa Campus Library plus 3 others. *Books:* 1.8 million (physical), 652,513 (digital/electronic); *Serial titles:* 537 (physical), 58,975 (digital/electronic); *Databases:* 939. Weekly public service hours: 116; study areas open 24 hours, 5–7 days a week; students can reserve study rooms.

STUDENT LIFE

Housing options: coed, men-only, women-only, special housing for students with disabilities. Campus housing is university owned.

Activities and organizations: drama/theater group, student-run radio and television station, choral group, marching band, Student Government, Campus Activities Board, USF Ambassadors, Student Admissions Representatives, national fraternities, national sororities.

Athletics Member NCAA. All Division I except football (Division I-A). ***Intercollegiate sports:*** badminton M(c)/W(c), baseball M(s), basketball W(s), bowling M(c)/W(c), crew M(c)/W(c), cross-country running M(s)/W(s), fencing M(c)/W(c), golf M(s)/W(s)(c), gymnastics M(c)/W(c), rugby M(c)/W(c), soccer M(s)/W(s), softball W(s), tennis M(s)/W(s), track and field M(s)/W(s), volleyball M(c)/W(s). ***Intramural sports:*** badminton M/W, basketball M/W, bowling M/W, football M, golf M/W, racquetball M/W, soccer M/W, swimming and diving M/W, tennis M/W, track and field M/W, volleyball M/W, weight lifting M.

Campus security: 24-hour emergency response devices and patrols, student patrols, late-night transport/escort service, controlled dormitory access.

Student services: health clinic, personal/psychological counseling, women's center, legal services.

COSTS & FINANCIAL AID

Costs (2020–21) ***Tuition:*** area resident $4559 full-time, $152 per credit hour part-time; state resident $152 per credit hour part-time; nonresident $15,473 full-time, $516 per credit hour part-time. ***Required fees:*** $1851 full-time. ***Room and board:*** $11,836; room only: $7878.

Financial Aid Of all full-time matriculated undergraduates who enrolled in 2018, 18,254 applied for aid, 15,110 were judged to have need, 1,829 had their need fully met. 785 Federal Work-Study jobs (averaging $3294). 243 state and other part-time jobs (averaging $1670). In 2018, 2418 non-need-based awards were made. ***Average percent of need met:*** 64. ***Average financial aid package:*** $12,978. ***Average need-based loan:*** $6085. ***Average need-based gift aid:*** $9911. ***Average non-need-based aid:*** $3125. ***Average indebtedness upon graduation:*** $21,463.

APPLYING

Standardized Tests *Required:* SAT or ACT (for admission).

Options: electronic application, early admission, deferred entrance.

Application fee: $30.

CONTACT

University of South Florida, 4202 East Fowler Avenue, Tampa, FL 33620-9951. *Phone:* 813-974-3350.

University of South Florida, St. Petersburg

St. Petersburg, Florida

http://www.usfsp.edu/

- **State-supported** comprehensive, founded 1965, part of University of South Florida System
- **Urban** 48-acre campus with easy access to Tampa
- **Endowment** $22.0 million
- **Coed** 4,334 undergraduate students, 65% full-time, 63% women, 37% men
- 40% of applicants were admitted

UNDERGRAD STUDENTS
2,837 full-time, 1,497 part-time. 4% are from out of state; 8% Black or African American, non-Hispanic/Latino; 17% Hispanic/Latino; 3% Asian, non-Hispanic/Latino; 0.1% Native Hawaiian or other Pacific Islander, non-Hispanic/Latino; 0.3% American Indian or Alaska Native, non-Hispanic/Latino; 4% Two or more races, non-Hispanic/Latino; 3% Race/ethnicity unknown; 0.7% international; 13% transferred in; 17% live on campus.

Freshmen:
Admission: 5,575 applied, 2,226 admitted, 645 enrolled. ***Average high school GPA:*** 3.7.

ACADEMICS
Calendar: semesters. *Degrees:* certificates, bachelor's, and master's.

Special study options: distance learning, double majors, freshman honors college, honors programs, independent study, internships, services for LD students, study abroad, summer session for credit. ***ROTC:*** Army (b).

Computers: 125 computers/terminals and 350 ports are available on campus for general student use. Students can access the following: computer help desk, free student e-mail accounts, online (class) grades, online (class) registration, online (class) schedules. Campuswide network is available. 100% of college-owned or -operated housing units are wired for high-speed Internet access. Wireless service is available via entire campus.
Library: Nelson Poynter Memorial Library. Weekly public service hours: 79; students can reserve study rooms.

STUDENT LIFE
Housing options: on-campus residence required for freshman year; coed. Campus housing is university owned. Freshman applicants given priority for college housing.

Activities and organizations: drama/theater group, student-run newspaper, radio station, Student Government, Harborside Activities Board, Delta Sigma Pi, Multicultural Activities Council, HERD Step Team.

Athletics *Intercollegiate sports:* baseball M(c), sailing W(c). ***Intramural sports:*** basketball M/W, football M/W, sailing M/W, soccer M/W, volleyball M/W.

Campus security: 24-hour emergency response devices and patrols, late-night transport/escort service, controlled dormitory access.

Student services: health clinic, personal/psychological counseling, veterans affairs office.

COSTS
Costs (2020–21) *Tuition:* area resident $4206 full-time; state resident $4206 full-time; nonresident $15,473 full-time. ***Required fees:*** $1615 full-time. ***Room and board:*** $11,836; room only: $7878.

APPLYING
Standardized Tests *Required:* SAT or ACT (for admission).

Options: early admission, early action.

Application fee: $30.

CONTACT
University of South Florida, St. Petersburg, 140 Seventh Avenue South, St. Petersburg, FL 33701. *Phone:* 727-873-4142. *Fax:* 727-873-4525. *E-mail:* admissions@usfsp.edu.

University of South Florida Sarasota-Manatee

Sarasota, Florida

http://www.usfsm.edu/

- **State-supported** comprehensive, founded 1956, part of University of South Florida System
- **Urban** 31-acre campus with easy access to Tampa
- **Endowment** $10.8 million
- **Coed**
- **Moderately difficult** entrance level

FACULTY
Student/faculty ratio: 14:1.

ACADEMICS
Calendar: semesters. *Degrees:* certificates, associate, bachelor's, master's, and post-master's certificates.
Library: USF Libraries. *Books:* 1,231 (physical), 721,020 (digital/electronic); *Serial titles:* 65,050 (digital/electronic); *Databases:* 941. Weekly public service hours: 96; students can reserve study rooms.

STUDENT LIFE
Housing options: college housing not available.

Activities and organizations: Box Office Bulls, The Adventure Club, Gamers' Club, Student Veteran Society, The Criminology Club.

Campus security: 24-hour emergency response devices and patrols, late-night transport/escort service.

Student services: health clinic, personal/psychological counseling, veterans affairs office.

COSTS
Costs (2019–20) *Tuition:* state resident $4206 full-time, $140 per credit hour part-time; nonresident $15,120 full-time, $504 per credit hour part-time. Full-time tuition and fees vary according to course load and program. Part-time tuition and fees vary according to course load and program. ***Required fees:*** $1381 full-time, $46 per credit hour part-time, $10 per term part-time.

APPLYING
Standardized Tests *Required:* SAT or ACT (for admission). *Recommended:* SAT Subject Tests (for admission).

Options: electronic application, deferred entrance.

Application fee: $30.

Required: high school transcript, minimum 3.3 GPA. ***Required for some:*** minimum 3.3 GPA, interview. ***Recommended:*** essay or personal statement, minimum 3.3 GPA, 2 letters of recommendation.

CONTACT
Mr. Brandon Avery, Interim Director, Admissions, University of South Florida Sarasota-Manatee, 8350 N. Tamiami Trail, C107, Sarasota, FL 34232. *Phone:* 941-359-4330. *Fax:* 941-359-4264. *E-mail:* bavery@sar.usf.edu.

The University of Tampa

Tampa, Florida

http://www.ut.edu/

- **Independent** comprehensive, founded 1931
- **Urban** 110-acre campus with easy access to Tampa-St. Petersburg, Clearwater
- **Coed** 8,697 undergraduate students, 97% full-time, 58% women, 42% men
- **Moderately difficult** entrance level, 44% of applicants were admitted

UNDERGRAD STUDENTS
8,441 full-time, 256 part-time. Students come from 50 states and territories; 140 other countries; 69% are from out of state; 4% Black or African American, non-Hispanic/Latino; 12% Hispanic/Latino; 2% Asian, non-Hispanic/Latino; 0.1% Native Hawaiian or other Pacific Islander, non-Hispanic/Latino; 0.1% American Indian or Alaska Native, non-Hispanic/Latino; 3% Two or more races, non-Hispanic/Latino; 9% Race/ethnicity unknown; 8% international; 5% transferred in; 49% live on campus.

Freshmen:

Admission: 23,341 applied, 10,231 admitted, 2,184 enrolled. ***Average high school GPA:*** 3.4. ***Test scores:*** SAT evidence-based reading and writing scores over 500: 97%; SAT math scores over 500: 95%; ACT scores over 18: 98%; SAT evidence-based reading and writing scores over 600: 47%; SAT math scores over 600: 42%; ACT scores over 24: 66%; SAT evidence-based reading and writing scores over 700: 4%; SAT math scores over 700: 4%; ACT scores over 30: 11%.

Retention: 78% of full-time freshmen returned.

FACULTY

Total: 815, 48% full-time, 59% with terminal degrees.

Student/faculty ratio: 17:1.

ACADEMICS

Calendar: semesters. *Degrees:* certificates, bachelor's, master's, doctoral, and post-master's certificates.

Special study options: academic remediation for entering students, adult/continuing education programs, advanced placement credit, cooperative education, double majors, English as a second language, honors programs, independent study, internships, part-time degree program, services for LD students, study abroad, summer session for credit. ***ROTC:*** Army (b), Navy (c), Air Force (c).

Unusual degree programs: 3-2 chemistry/business administration.

Computers: 791 computers/terminals and 8,000 ports are available on campus for general student use. Students can access the following: campus intranet, computer help desk, free student e-mail accounts, online (class) grades, online (class) registration, online (class) schedules. Campuswide network is available. 100% of college-owned or -operated housing units are wired for high-speed Internet access. Wireless service is available via entire campus.

Library: Macdonald Kelce Library. *Books:* 237,771 (physical), 111,179 (digital/electronic); *Serial titles:* 1,142 (physical), 124,474 (digital/electronic); *Databases:* 278. Weekly public service hours: 100; students can reserve study rooms.

STUDENT LIFE

Housing options: coed, special housing for students with disabilities. Campus housing is university owned. Freshman applicants given priority for college housing.

Activities and organizations: drama/theater group, student-run newspaper, radio and television station, choral group, Greek Life, student government, PEACE (volunteer organization), Student Productions, Minaret, national fraternities, national sororities.

Athletics Member NCAA. All Division II except golf (Division I), lacrosse (Division I), track and field (Division I). ***Intercollegiate sports:*** baseball M(s), basketball M(s)/W(s), crew W(s), cross-country running M(s)/W(s), golf M(s)/W(s), lacrosse M(s)/W(s), soccer M(s)/W(s), softball W(s), swimming and diving M(s)/W(s), tennis W(s), track and field M(s)/W(s), volleyball W(s). ***Intramural sports:*** basketball M/W, cheerleading W(c), crew M(c), equestrian sports W(c), fencing W(c), field hockey M(c), football M/W, golf M/W, ice hockey M(c), soccer M/W, softball M/W, swimming and diving M/W, tennis M(c)/W(c), ultimate Frisbee M/W, volleyball M/W.

Campus security: 24-hour emergency response devices and patrols, student patrols, late-night transport/escort service, controlled dormitory access.

Student services: health clinic, personal/psychological counseling, women's center.

COSTS & FINANCIAL AID

Costs (2020–21) ***Comprehensive fee:*** $42,410 includes full-time tuition ($28,802), mandatory fees ($2082), and room and board ($11,526). Full-time tuition and fees vary according to class time, course load, and program. Part-time tuition: $613 per credit hour. Part-time tuition and fees vary according to class time, course load, and program. ***Required fees:*** $40 per term part-time. ***College room only:*** $6084. Room and board charges vary according to board plan and housing facility. ***Payment plan:*** installment. ***Waivers:*** employees or children of employees.

Financial Aid Of all full-time matriculated undergraduates who enrolled in 2019, 6,067 applied for aid, 4,818 were judged to have need, 542 had their need fully met. 733 Federal Work-Study jobs (averaging $2000). 4 state and other part-time jobs (averaging $2000). In 2019, 2968 non-need-based awards were made. ***Average percent of need met:*** 62. ***Average financial aid package:*** $18,061. ***Average need-based loan:*** $4301. ***Average need-based gift aid:*** $14,254. ***Average non-need-based aid:*** $8582. ***Average indebtedness upon graduation:*** $335,034.

APPLYING

Standardized Tests *Required:* SAT or ACT (for admission).

Options: electronic application, early admission, early action, deferred entrance.

Application fee: $40.

Required: essay or personal statement, high school transcript, minimum 2.0 GPA. ***Required for some:*** 1 letter of recommendation. ***Recommended:*** interview.

Application deadlines: rolling (freshmen), rolling (transfers), 11/15 (early action).

Notification: continuous until 10/1 (freshmen), continuous (transfers).

CONTACT

Mr. Dennis Nostrand, Vice President for Enrollment, The University of Tampa, 401 West Kennedy Boulevard, Tampa, FL 33606-1480. *Phone:* 813-257-1808. *Toll-free phone:* 888-646-2738 (in-state); 888-MINARET (out-of-state). *Fax:* 813-258-7398. *E-mail:* admissions@ut.edu.

University of West Florida

Pensacola, Florida

http://www.uwf.edu/

- **State-supported** comprehensive, founded 1963, part of State University System of Florida
- **Suburban** 1600-acre campus
- **Endowment** $62.8 million
- **Coed** 9,531 undergraduate students, 69% full-time, 57% women, 43% men
- **Moderately difficult** entrance level, 31% of applicants were admitted

UNDERGRAD STUDENTS

6,601 full-time, 2,930 part-time. 11% are from out of state; 11% Black or African American, non-Hispanic/Latino; 10% Hispanic/Latino; 3% Asian, non-Hispanic/Latino; 0.3% Native Hawaiian or other Pacific Islander, non-Hispanic/Latino; 0.6% American Indian or Alaska Native, non-Hispanic/Latino; 6% Two or more races, non-Hispanic/Latino; 1% Race/ethnicity unknown; 2% international; 12% transferred in; 15% live on campus.

Freshmen:

Admission: 7,194 applied, 2,230 admitted, 998 enrolled. ***Average high school GPA:*** 3.8. ***Test scores:*** SAT evidence-based reading and writing scores over 500: 93%; SAT math scores over 500: 90%; ACT scores over 18: 98%; SAT evidence-based reading and writing scores over 600: 42%; SAT math scores over 600: 29%; ACT scores over 24: 58%; SAT evidence-based reading and writing scores over 700: 4%; SAT math scores over 700: 3%; ACT scores over 30: 9%.

Retention: 82% of full-time freshmen returned.

FACULTY

Total: 620, 57% full-time.

Student/faculty ratio: 20:1.

ACADEMICS

Calendar: semesters. *Degrees:* certificates, associate, bachelor's, master's, doctoral, and post-master's certificates.

Special study options: accelerated degree program, advanced placement credit, cooperative education, distance learning, double majors, English as a second language, external degree program, honors programs, independent study, internships, off-campus study, part-time degree program, services for LD students, study abroad, summer session for credit. ***ROTC:*** Army (b), Air Force (b).

Unusual degree programs: 3-2 business administration.

Computers: 1,228 computers/terminals and 30 ports are available on campus for general student use. Students can access the following: campus intranet, computer help desk, free student e-mail accounts, online (class) grades, online (class) registration, online (class) schedules. Campuswide network is available. 100% of college-owned or -operated housing units are wired for high-speed Internet access. Wireless service is available via entire campus.

Library: John C. Pace Library plus 2 others. *Books:* 834,298 (physical), 163,625 (digital/electronic); *Serial titles:* 288 (physical), 80,370 (digital/electronic); *Databases:* 167. Weekly public service hours: 107.

STUDENT LIFE

Housing options: coed. Campus housing is university owned.

Activities and organizations: drama/theater group, student-run newspaper, radio and television station, choral group, National Society of Leadership and Service, Baptist Collegiate Ministries, Alpha Chi Omega, Alpha Delta Pi, Student Alumni Association, national fraternities, national sororities.

Athletics Member NCAA. All Division II. ***Intercollegiate sports:*** baseball M(s), basketball M(s)/W(s), cross-country running M(s)/W(s), golf M(s)/W(s), soccer M(s)/W(s), softball W(s), swimming and diving W(s), tennis M(s)/W(s), volleyball W(s). ***Intramural sports:*** basketball M/W, bowling M/W, cheerleading W, fencing M/W, football M/W, sailing M/W, soccer M/W, softball W, swimming and diving M/W, tennis M/W, volleyball M/W.

Campus security: 24-hour emergency response devices and patrols, student patrols, late-night transport/escort service, controlled dormitory access.

Student services: health clinic, personal/psychological counseling.

COSTS & FINANCIAL AID

Costs (2019–20) ***Tuition:*** area resident $4319 full-time; state resident $16,587 full-time; nonresident $16,587 full-time. ***Required fees:*** $2041 full-time. ***Room and board:*** $10,248; room only: $5880.

Financial Aid Of all full-time matriculated undergraduates who enrolled in 2016, 5,297 applied for aid, 2,381 were judged to have need, 304 had their need fully met. In 2016, 910 non-need-based awards were made. ***Average percent of need met:*** 64. ***Average financial aid package:*** $10,166. ***Average need-based loan:*** $4092. ***Average need-based gift aid:*** $7347. ***Average non-need-based aid:*** $1722.

APPLYING

Standardized Tests *Required:* SAT or ACT (for admission).

Options: electronic application, early admission, deferred entrance.

Application fee: $30.

Required: high school transcript, minimum 2.5 GPA.

Application deadlines: 6/1 (freshmen), 6/1 (transfers).

Notification: continuous (freshmen), continuous (transfers).

CONTACT

Katie Condon, Director of Admissions, University of West Florida, Admissions, 11000 University Parkway, Pensacola, FL 32514. *Phone:* 850-474-2230. *Toll-free phone:* 800-263-1074. *Fax:* 850-474-3460. *E-mail:* admissions@uwf.edu.

Valencia College

Orlando, Florida

http://valenciacollege.edu/

- **State-supported** 4-year, founded 1967, part of Florida College System
- **Urban** 654-acre campus with easy access to Orlando
- **Endowment** $70.3 million
- **Coed** 47,940 undergraduate students, 35% full-time, 58% women, 42% men
- 93% of applicants were admitted

UNDERGRAD STUDENTS

16,689 full-time, 31,251 part-time. 3% are from out of state; 17% Black or African American, non-Hispanic/Latino; 40% Hispanic/Latino; 4% Asian, non-Hispanic/Latino; 0.3% Native Hawaiian or other Pacific Islander, non-Hispanic/Latino; 0.3% American Indian or Alaska Native, non-Hispanic/Latino; 3% Two or more races, non-Hispanic/Latino; 6% Race/ethnicity unknown; 5% international; 11% transferred in.

Freshmen:

Admission: 16,145 applied, 14,980 admitted, 9,066 enrolled.

ACADEMICS

Calendar: semesters. *Degrees:* certificates, diplomas, associate, and bachelor's.

Special study options: academic remediation for entering students, accelerated degree program, adult/continuing education programs, advanced placement credit, cooperative education, distance learning, double majors, English as a second language, freshman honors college, honors programs, independent study, internships, part-time degree program, services for LD students, student-designed majors, study abroad, summer session for credit. ***ROTC:*** Army (c), Air Force (c).

Computers: Students can access the following: campus intranet, computer help desk, free student e-mail accounts, online (class) grades, online (class) registration, online (class) schedules, education plans, 'what if analysis' degree audit, degree plan, view and print unofficial transcripts, order official transcripts, career exploration. Campuswide network is available. Wireless service is available via entire campus.

Library: Library plus 4 others. *Books:* 153,869 (physical), 180,848 (digital/electronic); *Serial titles:* 261 (physical), 52,262 (digital/electronic); *Databases:* 188. Weekly public service hours: 87; students can reserve study rooms.

STUDENT LIFE

Housing options: college housing not available.

Activities and organizations: drama/theater group, student-run newspaper, radio station, choral group, National Society for Leadership and Success, PTK, Honors, Gay-Straight Alliance, Valencia Hospitality.

Athletics ***Intramural sports:*** basketball M/W, soccer M/W, volleyball M/W.

Campus security: 24-hour emergency response devices and patrols, late-night transport/escort service, video monitoring for certain areas.

Student services: personal/psychological counseling, veterans affairs office.

FINANCIAL AID

Financial Aid Of all full-time matriculated undergraduates who enrolled in 2017, 10,723 applied for aid, 9,098 were judged to have need, 88 had their need fully met. 244 Federal Work-Study jobs (averaging $3019). 114 state and other part-time jobs (averaging $4275). In 2017, 126 non-need-based awards were made. ***Average percent of need met:*** 41. ***Average financial aid package:*** $6373. ***Average need-based loan:*** $2810. ***Average need-based gift aid:*** $5687. ***Average non-need-based aid:*** $1486. ***Average indebtedness upon graduation:*** $20,951.

APPLYING

Options: electronic application, early admission, deferred entrance.

Application fee: $35.

Required for some: high school transcript, professional license for some allied health bachelors programs. ***Recommended:*** high school transcript.

Application deadlines: rolling (freshmen), rolling (out-of-state freshmen), rolling (transfers).

CONTACT

Dr. Linda K. Herlocker, Assistant Vice President of Admissions and Records, Valencia College, West Campus, MC 4-8, 1800 S. Kirkman Road, SSB 104-D, Orlando, FL 32811-2302. *Phone:* 407-582-1511. *Fax:* 407-582-1866. *E-mail:* lherlocker@valenciacollege.edu.

Warner University

Lake Wales, Florida

http://www.warner.edu/

CONTACT

Mr. Jason Roe, Director of Admissions, Warner University, Warner Southern Center, 13895 Highway 27, Lake Wales, FL 33859. *Phone:* 863-638-7212 Ext. 7213. *Toll-free phone:* 800-309-9563. *Fax:* 863-638-1472. *E-mail:* admissions@warner.edu.

Webber International University

Babson Park, Florida

http://www.webber.edu/

- **Independent** comprehensive, founded 1927
- **Small-town** 110-acre campus with easy access to Orlando
- **Coed** 665 undergraduate students, 97% full-time, 31% women, 69% men
- **Minimally difficult** entrance level, 42% of applicants were admitted

UNDERGRAD STUDENTS

642 full-time, 23 part-time. Students come from 30 states and territories; 33 other countries; 5% are from out of state; 31% Black or African

American, non-Hispanic/Latino; 12% Hispanic/Latino; 0.3% Asian, non-Hispanic/Latino; 0.9% Native Hawaiian or other Pacific Islander, non-Hispanic/Latino; 1% American Indian or Alaska Native, non-Hispanic/Latino; 2% Two or more races, non-Hispanic/Latino; 14% international; 14% transferred in; 46% live on campus.

Freshmen:
Admission: 1,690 applied, 714 admitted, 203 enrolled. ***Average high school GPA:*** 3.0. ***Test scores:*** ACT scores over 18: 73%; ACT scores over 24: 7%.

Retention: 553% of full-time freshmen returned.

FACULTY
Total: 41, 51% full-time, 41% with terminal degrees.

Student/faculty ratio: 23:1.

ACADEMICS
Calendar: semesters. *Degrees:* associate, bachelor's, and master's.

Special study options: academic remediation for entering students, accelerated degree program, adult/continuing education programs, advanced placement credit, cooperative education, distance learning, double majors, freshman honors college, honors programs, internships, part-time degree program, services for LD students, study abroad, summer session for credit.

Computers: 92 computers/terminals are available on campus for general student use. Students can access the following: campus intranet, computer help desk, free student e-mail accounts, online (class) grades, online (class) registration, online (class) schedules. Campuswide network is available. 100% of college-owned or -operated housing units are wired for high-speed Internet access. Wireless service is available via entire campus.

Library: Grace and Roger Babson Library. *Books:* 1,041 (physical); *Databases:* 127. Weekly public service hours: 70; students can reserve study rooms.

STUDENT LIFE
Housing options: on-campus residence required through sophomore year; men-only, women-only. Campus housing is university owned.

Activities and organizations: student-run newspaper, Student Leadership Association, Phi Beta Lambda, Society of International Students, Fellowship of Christian Athletes, Rotaract.

Athletics Member NAIA. ***Intercollegiate sports:*** baseball M(s), basketball M(s)/W(s), bowling M(s)/W(s), cheerleading W(s), cross-country running M(s)/W(s), football M(s), golf M(s)/W(s), lacrosse M(s)/W(s), sand volleyball M(s)/W(s), soccer M(s)/W(s), softball W(s), tennis M(s)/W(s), track and field M(s)/W(s), triathlon M(s)/W(s), volleyball M(s)/W(s).

Campus security: 24-hour emergency response devices and patrols, late-night transport/escort service.

Student services: health clinic, personal/psychological counseling, veterans affairs office.

COSTS & FINANCIAL AID
Costs (2020–21) ***Comprehensive fee:*** $38,438 includes full-time tuition ($25,526), mandatory fees ($2972), and room and board ($9940). Full-time tuition and fees vary according to program and reciprocity agreements. Part-time tuition: $377 per semester hour. Part-time tuition and fees vary according to course load, program, and reciprocity agreements. ***Room and board:*** Room and board charges vary according to board plan and housing facility. ***Payment plan:*** installment. ***Waivers:*** children of alumni, adult students, senior citizens, and employees or children of employees.

Financial Aid Of all full-time matriculated undergraduates who enrolled in 2018, 468 applied for aid, 442 were judged to have need, 33 had their need fully met. In 2018, 116 non-need-based awards were made. ***Average percent of need met:*** 60. ***Average financial aid package:*** $20,114. ***Average need-based loan:*** $3807. ***Average need-based gift aid:*** $16,727. ***Average non-need-based aid:*** $6240. ***Average indebtedness upon graduation:*** $27,083.

APPLYING
Standardized Tests *Required for some:* SAT or ACT (for admission).

Options: electronic application, deferred entrance.

Required: high school transcript, minimum 2.0 GPA. ***Required for some:*** letters of recommendation, interview. ***Recommended:*** essay or personal statement.

Application deadlines: 8/1 (freshmen), 8/1 (out-of-state freshmen), 8/1 (transfers).

Notification: continuous (freshmen), continuous (out-of-state freshmen), continuous (transfers).

CONTACT
Office of Admissions, Webber International University, PO Box 96, Babson Park, FL 33827. *Phone:* 863-638-2910. *Toll-free phone:* 800-741-1844. *Fax:* 863-638-1591. *E-mail:* admissions@webber.edu.

West Coast University
Doral, Florida
http://westcoastuniversity.edu/

CONTACT
West Coast University, 9250 NW 36th Street, Doral, FL 33178.

Yeshiva Gedolah Rabbinical College
Miami Beach, Florida

CONTACT
Yeshiva Gedolah Rabbinical College, 1140 Alton Road, Miami Beach, FL 33139.

GEORGIA

Abraham Baldwin Agricultural College
Tifton, Georgia
http://www.abac.edu/

- **State-supported** 4-year, founded 1933, part of University System of Georgia
- **Small-town** 421-acre campus
- **Coed**
- **Minimally difficult** entrance level

FACULTY
Student/faculty ratio: 24:1.

ACADEMICS
Calendar: semesters. *Degrees:* certificates, associate, and bachelor's.
Library: Baldwin Library.

STUDENT LIFE
Housing options: on-campus residence required for freshman year; coed, special housing for students with disabilities. Campus housing is university owned. Freshman applicants given priority for college housing.

Activities and organizations: drama/theater group, student-run newspaper, radio station, choral group, Campus Activities Board, Baptist Collegiate Ministry, Forestry/Wildlife Club, Agriculture Engineering Technology, Residence Hall Association, national fraternities, national sororities.

Athletics Member NJCAA.

Campus security: 24-hour emergency response devices and patrols, controlled dormitory access.

Student services: health clinic, personal/psychological counseling.

FINANCIAL AID
Financial Aid Of all full-time matriculated undergraduates who enrolled in 2013, 133 Federal Work-Study jobs (averaging $1539). ***Financial aid deadline:*** 7/1.

APPLYING
Standardized Tests *Required:* SAT or ACT (for admission).

Options: electronic application, early admission, deferred entrance.

Application fee: $20.

Required: high school transcript. ***Required for some:*** minimum high school GPA of 2.0 for College Prep Diploma and 2.2 for Tech Prep Diploma.

CONTACT
Mrs. Donna Webb, Director of Enrollment Services, Abraham Baldwin Agricultural College, Box 4, 2802 Moore Highway, Tifton, GA 31793-2601. *Phone:* 229-391-5004. *Toll-free phone:* 800-733-3653. *Fax:* 229-391-5002. *E-mail:* dwebb@abac.edu.

Agnes Scott College
Decatur, Georgia
http://www.agnesscott.edu/

- **Independent** comprehensive, founded 1889, affiliated with Presbyterian Church (U.S.A.)
- **Urban** 100-acre campus with easy access to Atlanta
- **Endowment** $217.1 million
- **Women only** 1,005 undergraduate students, 99% full-time
- **Moderately difficult** entrance level, 65% of applicants were admitted

UNDERGRAD STUDENTS
990 full-time, 15 part-time. Students come from 44 states and territories; 22 other countries; 40% are from out of state; 32% Black or African American, non-Hispanic/Latino; 14% Hispanic/Latino; 8% Asian, non-Hispanic/Latino; 0.3% Native Hawaiian or other Pacific Islander, non-Hispanic/Latino; 0.2% American Indian or Alaska Native, non-Hispanic/Latino; 6% Two or more races, non-Hispanic/Latino; 3% Race/ethnicity unknown; 6% international; 1% transferred in; 82% live on campus.

Freshmen:
Admission: 1,751 applied, 1,135 admitted, 299 enrolled. ***Average high school GPA:*** 3.8. ***Test scores:*** SAT evidence-based reading and writing scores over 500: 99%; SAT math scores over 500: 95%; ACT scores over 18: 99%; SAT evidence-based reading and writing scores over 600: 75%; SAT math scores over 600: 45%; ACT scores over 24: 76%; SAT evidence-based reading and writing scores over 700: 24%; SAT math scores over 700: 15%; ACT scores over 30: 28%.

Retention: 85% of full-time freshmen returned.

FACULTY
Total: 133, 69% full-time, 80% with terminal degrees.

Student/faculty ratio: 10:1.

ACADEMICS
Calendar: semesters. *Degrees:* bachelor's, master's, and postbachelor's certificates.

Special study options: accelerated degree program, adult/continuing education programs, advanced placement credit, distance learning, double majors, independent study, internships, off-campus study, part-time degree program, services for LD students, student-designed majors, study abroad, summer session for credit. ***ROTC:*** Army (c), Air Force (c).

Unusual degree programs: 3-2 engineering with Georgia Institute of Technology; nursing with Emory University; computer science with Emory University.

Computers: 450 computers/terminals are available on campus for general student use. Students can access the following: campus intranet, computer help desk, free student e-mail accounts, online (class) grades, online (class) registration, online (class) schedules. Campuswide network is available. 100% of college-owned or -operated housing units are wired for high-speed Internet access. Wireless service is available via entire campus.

Library: McCain Library. *Books:* 207,088 (physical), 276,823 (digital/electronic); *Databases:* 416. Study areas open 24 hours, 5–7 days a week.

STUDENT LIFE
Housing options: on-campus residence required through senior year; women-only. Campus housing is university owned. Freshman campus housing is guaranteed.

Activities and organizations: drama/theater group, student-run newspaper, radio station, choral group, marching band.

Athletics Member NCAA. All Division III. ***Intercollegiate sports:*** basketball W, cross-country running W, soccer W, softball W, tennis W, volleyball W. ***Intramural sports:*** archery W, badminton W, cheerleading W(c), lacrosse W(c), swimming and diving W(c), tennis W.

Campus security: 24-hour emergency response devices and patrols, late-night transport/escort service, controlled dormitory access.

Student services: health clinic, personal/psychological counseling.

COSTS & FINANCIAL AID
Costs (2020–21) ***One-time required fee:*** $200. ***Comprehensive fee:*** $57,300 includes full-time tuition ($43,920), mandatory fees ($330), and room and board ($13,050). Part-time tuition: $1830 per credit hour. ***Room and board:*** Room and board charges vary according to board plan and housing facility. ***Payment plan:*** installment. ***Waivers:*** employees or children of employees.

Financial Aid Of all full-time matriculated undergraduates who enrolled in 2019, 829 applied for aid, 749 were judged to have need, 162 had their need fully met. In 2019, 215 non-need-based awards were made. ***Average percent of need met:*** 85. ***Average financial aid package:*** $38,618. ***Average need-based loan:*** $4433. ***Average need-based gift aid:*** $31,975. ***Average non-need-based aid:*** $30,458. ***Average indebtedness upon graduation:*** $31,271.

APPLYING
Standardized Tests *Required for some:* SAT or ACT (for admission).

Options: electronic application, early admission, early decision, early action, deferred entrance.

Required: essay or personal statement, high school transcript. ***Recommended:*** interview.

Application deadlines: 6/1 (transfers), 11/15 (early action).

Early decision deadline: 11/1.

Notification: 4/15 (freshmen), continuous (transfers), 12/1 (early decision), 1/15 (early action).

CONTACT
Agnes Scott College, 141 East College Avenue, Decatur, GA 30030-3797. *Phone:* 404-471-6285. *Toll-free phone:* 800-868-8602.

Albany State University
Albany, Georgia
http://www.asurams.edu/

- **State-supported** comprehensive, founded 1903, part of University System of Georgia
- **Urban** 232-acre campus
- **Endowment** $1.8 million
- **Coed**
- **Minimally difficult** entrance level

FACULTY
Student/faculty ratio: 15:1.

ACADEMICS
Calendar: semesters. *Degrees:* bachelor's, master's, and post-master's certificates.
Library: James Pendergrast Memorial Library.

STUDENT LIFE
Housing options: on-campus residence required for freshman year; men-only, women-only. Campus housing is university owned. Freshman applicants given priority for college housing.

Activities and organizations: drama/theater group, student-run newspaper, radio and television station, choral group, marching band, ASU Anointed Gospel Choir, ASU Pan-Hellenic Council (Greeks), Peer Educators, SIFE (Students In Free Enterprise), Student Government Association, national fraternities, national sororities.

Athletics Member NCAA. All Division II.

Campus security: 24-hour emergency response devices and patrols, late-night transport/escort service, controlled dormitory access, ConnectED Emergency E-mail, Emergency sirens, Active Shooter Team, Certified Police Officers.

Student services: health clinic, personal/psychological counseling, veterans affairs office.

FINANCIAL AID
Financial Aid Of all full-time matriculated undergraduates who enrolled in 2017, 3,660 applied for aid, 3,287 were judged to have need, 397 had

their need fully met. In 2017, 30 non-need-based awards were made. ***Average percent of need met:*** 72. ***Average financial aid package:*** $4720. ***Average need-based loan:*** $2020. ***Average need-based gift aid:*** $2716. ***Average non-need-based aid:*** $970. ***Financial aid deadline:*** 7/1.

APPLYING
Standardized Tests *Required:* SAT or ACT (for admission). *Required for some:* SAT and SAT Subject Tests or ACT (for admission).

Options: electronic application, early admission, deferred entrance.

Application fee: $20.

Required: high school transcript, minimum 2.2 GPA.

CONTACT
Interim Director, Enrollment Services, Albany State University, 504 College Drive, Albany, GA 31705-2717. *Phone:* 229-430-4646. *Toll-free phone:* 800-822-7267. *Fax:* 229-430-4105. *E-mail:* enrollmentservices@asurams.edu.

American InterContinental University Atlanta

Atlanta, Georgia

http://www.aiuniv.edu/

CONTACT
American InterContinental University Atlanta, 6600 Peachtree-Dunwoody Road, 500 Embassy Row, Atlanta, GA 30328. *Phone:* 877-564-6248. *Toll-free phone:* 800-353-1744. *Fax:* 877-564-6248.

Argosy University, Atlanta

Atlanta, Georgia

http://www.argosy.edu/locations/atlanta/

CONTACT
Argosy University, Atlanta, 980 Hammond Drive, Suite 100, Atlanta, GA 30328. *Phone:* 770-671-1200. *Toll-free phone:* 888-671-4777.

The Art Institute of Atlanta

Atlanta, Georgia

http://www.artinstitutes.edu/atlanta/

CONTACT
The Art Institute of Atlanta, 6600 Peachtree Dunwoody Road, NE, 100 Embassy Row, Atlanta, GA 30328. *Phone:* 770-394-8300. *Toll-free phone:* 800-275-4242.

Ashworth College

Norcross, Georgia

http://www.ashworthcollege.edu/

CONTACT
Mr. Eric Ryall, Registrar, Ashworth College, 6625 The Corners Parkway, Suite 500, Norcross, GA 30092. *Phone:* 770-729-8400 Ext. 5297. *Toll-free phone:* 800-957-5412.

Augusta University

Augusta, Georgia

http://www.augusta.edu/

- **State-supported** university, founded 1828, part of University System of Georgia
- **Urban** 670-acre campus
- **Endowment** $9.4 million
- **Coed**
- 11% of applicants were admitted

ACADEMICS
Calendar: semesters. *Degrees:* associate, bachelor's, master's, doctoral, post-master's, and postbachelor's certificates.
Library: Main Library plus 2 others.

STUDENT LIFE
Housing options: coed. Campus housing is university owned.

Activities and organizations: drama/theater group, student-run newspaper, choral group, national fraternities, national sororities.

Athletics Member NCAA. All Division II except men's and women's golf (Division I).

Campus security: 24-hour emergency response devices and patrols, late-night transport/escort service.

Student services: health clinic, personal/psychological counseling, veterans affairs office.

FINANCIAL AID
Financial Aid Of all full-time matriculated undergraduates who enrolled in 2016, 3,070 applied for aid, 2,452 were judged to have need, 167 had their need fully met. 169 Federal Work-Study jobs (averaging $2931). In 2016, 42 non-need-based awards were made. ***Average financial aid package:*** $2390. ***Average need-based loan:*** $2159. ***Average need-based gift aid:*** $2216. ***Average non-need-based aid:*** $1421. ***Financial aid deadline:*** 3/1.

APPLYING
Standardized Tests *Required:* SAT or ACT (for admission).

Options: electronic application, early action.

Application fee: $50.

Required: Freshman Index (FI). ***Required for some:*** high school transcript.

CONTACT
Augusta University, 1120 15th Street, Augusta, GA 30912. *Phone:* 706-737-1632. *Toll-free phone:* 800-519-3388.

Berry College

Mount Berry, Georgia

http://www.berry.edu/

- **Independent interdenominational** comprehensive, founded 1902
- **Suburban** 27,000-acre campus with easy access to Atlanta
- **Endowment** $1.1 billion
- **Coed** 1,943 undergraduate students, 98% full-time, 61% women, 39% men
- **Moderately difficult** entrance level, 71% of applicants were admitted

UNDERGRAD STUDENTS
1,911 full-time, 32 part-time. Students come from 35 states and territories; 18 other countries; 30% are from out of state; 7% Black or African American, non-Hispanic/Latino; 7% Hispanic/Latino; 2% Asian, non-Hispanic/Latino; 0.4% American Indian or Alaska Native, non-Hispanic/Latino; 4% Two or more races, non-Hispanic/Latino; 0.5% Race/ethnicity unknown; 1% international; 2% transferred in; 89% live on campus.

Freshmen:
Admission: 4,328 applied, 3,055 admitted, 577 enrolled. ***Average high school GPA:*** 3.7. ***Test scores:*** SAT evidence-based reading and writing scores over 500: 96%; SAT math scores over 500: 92%; ACT scores over 18: 99%; SAT evidence-based reading and writing scores over 600: 60%; SAT math scores over 600: 46%; ACT scores over 24: 80%; SAT evidence-based reading and writing scores over 700: 15%; SAT math scores over 700: 9%; ACT scores over 30: 29%.

Retention: 83% of full-time freshmen returned.

FACULTY
Total: 227, 72% full-time, 80% with terminal degrees.

Student/faculty ratio: 11:1.

ACADEMICS
Calendar: semesters. *Degrees:* bachelor's and master's.

Special study options: adult/continuing education programs, advanced placement credit, double majors, honors programs, independent study, internships, part-time degree program, services for LD students, student-designed majors, study abroad, summer session for credit.

Unusual degree programs: 3-2 engineering with Georgia Institute of Technology, Kennesaw State University; University of Hawaii at Hilo, Dual-Degree Astronomy.

Computers: 200 computers/terminals and 80 ports are available on campus for general student use. Students can access the following: computer help desk, free student e-mail accounts, online (class) grades,

online (class) registration, online (class) schedules. Campuswide network is available. 100% of college-owned or -operated housing units are wired for high-speed Internet access. Wireless service is available via classrooms, computer centers, computer labs, dorm rooms, learning centers, libraries, student centers.
Library: Memorial Library plus 1 other. *Books:* 229,531 (physical), 1.1 million (digital/electronic); *Serial titles:* 6,932 (physical), 86,384 (digital/electronic); *Databases:* 223. Weekly public service hours: 100; students can reserve study rooms.

STUDENT LIFE
Housing options: on-campus residence required through senior year; coed, men-only, women-only, special housing for students with disabilities. Campus housing is university owned. Freshman campus housing is guaranteed.

Activities and organizations: drama/theater group, student-run newspaper, choral group, Student Government Association, Campus Outreach, Block-n-Bridle, Allied Health, Athletes Bettering the Community.

Athletics Member NCAA. All Division III. ***Intercollegiate sports:*** baseball M, basketball M/W, cross-country running M/W, equestrian sports W, football M, golf M/W, lacrosse M/W, soccer M/W, softball W, swimming and diving M/W, tennis M/W, track and field M/W, volleyball W. ***Intramural sports:*** basketball M/W, cheerleading M(c)/W(c), crew M(c)/W(c), football M/W, golf M/W, racquetball M/W, rowing M(c)/W(c), sand volleyball M/W, soccer M/W, softball M/W, swimming and diving M/W, tennis M/W, ultimate Frisbee M/W, volleyball M/W.

Campus security: 24-hour patrols, controlled dormitory access, lighted pathways, gated campus, mobile police patrols, identification of valuables, limited access to campus, on-campus police officers.

Student services: health clinic, personal/psychological counseling.

COSTS & FINANCIAL AID
Costs (2019–20) ***Comprehensive fee:*** $50,316 includes full-time tuition ($37,020), mandatory fees ($226), and room and board ($13,070). Part-time tuition: $1234 per credit hour. ***College room only:*** $7360. Room and board charges vary according to board plan and housing facility. ***Payment plan:*** installment. ***Waivers:*** senior citizens and employees or children of employees.

Financial Aid Of all full-time matriculated undergraduates who enrolled in 2019, 1,663 applied for aid, 1,330 were judged to have need, 393 had their need fully met. In 2019, 571 non-need-based awards were made. ***Average percent of need met:*** 85. ***Average financial aid package:*** $31,911. ***Average need-based loan:*** $4665. ***Average need-based gift aid:*** $27,857. ***Average non-need-based aid:*** $18,274. ***Average indebtedness upon graduation:*** $31,336.

APPLYING
Standardized Tests *Required:* SAT or ACT (for admission).

Options: electronic application, early decision, early action.

Required: high school transcript, 1 letter of recommendation. ***Required for some:*** 2 letters of recommendation. ***Recommended:*** interview.

Application deadlines: 7/24 (freshmen), 7/20 (transfers).

Notification: continuous (freshmen), continuous (transfers).

CONTACT
Mr. Glenn Getchell, Director of Admissions and Enrollment Management, Berry College, PO Box 490159, 2277 Martha Berry Highway, NW, Mount Berry, GA 30149-0159. *Phone:* 706-236-2215. *Toll-free phone:* 800-237-7942. *E-mail:* admissions@berry.edu.

Beulah Heights University

Atlanta, Georgia

http://www.beulah.edu/

CONTACT
Mrs. Bianca Phillips, Admissions Coordinator, Beulah Heights University, 892 Berne Street, SE, Atlanta, GA 30316. *Phone:* 404-627-2681 Ext. 117. *Toll-free phone:* 888-777-BHBC. *E-mail:* bianca.phillips@beulah.edu.

Brenau University

Gainesville, Georgia

http://www.brenau.edu/

- **Independent** comprehensive, founded 1878
- **Suburban** 57-acre campus with easy access to Atlanta
- **Endowment** $49.5 million
- **Coed, primarily women** 1,756 undergraduate students, 63% full-time, 90% women, 10% men
- **Moderately difficult** entrance level, 64% of applicants were admitted

UNDERGRAD STUDENTS
1,108 full-time, 648 part-time. Students come from 25 states and territories; 15 other countries; 5% are from out of state; 29% Black or African American, non-Hispanic/Latino; 11% Hispanic/Latino; 2% Asian, non-Hispanic/Latino; 0.5% American Indian or Alaska Native, non-Hispanic/Latino; 2% Two or more races, non-Hispanic/Latino; 4% Race/ethnicity unknown; 7% international; 18% transferred in; 19% live on campus.

Freshmen:
Admission: 1,912 applied, 1,219 admitted, 156 enrolled. ***Average high school GPA:*** 3.5.

Retention: 55% of full-time freshmen returned.

FACULTY
Total: 108, 63% full-time, 69% with terminal degrees.

Student/faculty ratio: 9:1.

ACADEMICS
Calendar: semesters. *Degrees:* certificates, associate, bachelor's, master's, doctoral, post-master's, and postbachelor's certificates (also offers coed evening and weekend programs with significant enrollment not reflected in profile).

Special study options: academic remediation for entering students, accelerated degree program, advanced placement credit, distance learning, double majors, honors programs, independent study, internships, part-time degree program, services for LD students, study abroad, summer session for credit.

Computers: 157 computers/terminals and 190 ports are available on campus for general student use. Students can access the following: campus intranet, computer help desk, free student e-mail accounts, online (class) grades, online (class) registration, online (class) schedules. Campuswide network is available. 100% of college-owned or -operated housing units are wired for high-speed Internet access. Wireless service is available via entire campus.
Library: Brenau Trustee Library. *Books:* 82,519 (physical), 647,881 (digital/electronic); *Serial titles:* 178 (physical), 87,285 (digital/electronic); *Databases:* 167. Weekly public service hours: 76; students can reserve study rooms.

STUDENT LIFE
Housing options: on-campus residence required through junior year; men-only, women-only, special housing for students with disabilities. Campus housing is university owned. Freshman campus housing is guaranteed.

Activities and organizations: drama/theater group, student-run newspaper, radio station, choral group, Student Activities Board, Student Government Association, Black Student Association, International Student Association, Her Campus, national sororities.

Athletics Member NAIA. ***Intercollegiate sports:*** basketball W(s), cheerleading W(s), crew W(c), cross-country running W(s), golf W(s), lacrosse W(s), soccer W(s), softball W(s), swimming and diving W(s), tennis W(s), track and field W(s), volleyball W(s).

Campus security: 24-hour emergency response devices and patrols, late-night transport/escort service.

Student services: health clinic, personal/psychological counseling, women's center, veterans affairs office.

COSTS & FINANCIAL AID
Costs (2020–21) ***Comprehensive fee:*** $44,220 includes full-time tuition ($30,000), mandatory fees ($1720), and room and board ($12,500). Full-time tuition and fees vary according to class time, degree level, location, and program. Part-time tuition: $1000 per semester hour. Part-time tuition and fees vary according to class time, degree level, location, and program.

Required fees: $279 part-time. ***Payment plans:*** installment, deferred payment. ***Waivers:*** employees or children of employees.

Financial Aid Of all full-time matriculated undergraduates who enrolled in 2017, 958 applied for aid, 904 were judged to have need, 94 had their need fully met. 115 Federal Work-Study jobs (averaging $1854). 107 state and other part-time jobs (averaging $1303). In 2017, 33 non-need-based awards were made. ***Average percent of need met:*** 57. ***Average financial aid package:*** $19,551. ***Average need-based loan:*** $5136. ***Average need-based gift aid:*** $14,503. ***Average non-need-based aid:*** $11,907. ***Average indebtedness upon graduation:*** $35,719.

APPLYING

Options: electronic application, deferred entrance.

Required for some: essay or personal statement, high school transcript, minimum 2.0 GPA, interview.

Application deadlines: rolling (freshmen), rolling (out-of-state freshmen), rolling (transfers).

Notification: continuous (freshmen), continuous (out-of-state freshmen), continuous (transfers).

CONTACT

Ms. Sahara Outler, Brenau University, Admissions, 500 Washington Street, SE, Gainesville, GA 30501. *Phone:* 770-534-6100. *Toll-free phone:* 800-252-5119. *Fax:* 770-538-4701. *E-mail:* soutler1@brenau.edu.

Brewton-Parker College

Mt. Vernon, Georgia

http://www.bpc.edu/

CONTACT

Ms. Tiffany Quarterman, Admissions Office Manager, Brewton-Parker College, PO Box 197, Mount Vernon, GA 30445. *Phone:* 912-583-3250. *Toll-free phone:* 800-342-1087. *Fax:* 912-583-3598. *E-mail:* admissions@bpc.edu.

Carver College

Atlanta, Georgia

http://www.carver.edu/

CONTACT

Bertha Mack, Admissions Officer, Carver College, 3870 Cascade Road SW, Atlanta, GA 30331. *Phone:* 404-527-4520 Ext. 209. *Fax:* 404-527-4524. *E-mail:* info@carver.edu.

Chamberlain College of Nursing - Atlanta

Atlanta, Georgia

http://www.chamberlain.edu/

CONTACT

Chamberlain College of Nursing - Atlanta, 5775 Peachtree Dunwoody Road NE, Suite A-100, Atlanta, GA 30342. *Toll-free phone:* 877-751-5783.

Clark Atlanta University

Atlanta, Georgia

http://www.cau.edu/

- **Independent United Methodist** university, founded 1865
- **Urban** 126-acre campus
- **Endowment** $72.5 million
- **Coed** 3,318 undergraduate students, 98% full-time, 76% women, 24% men
- **Moderately difficult** entrance level, 55% of applicants were admitted

UNDERGRAD STUDENTS

3,255 full-time, 63 part-time. Students come from 40 states and territories; 10 other countries; 66% are from out of state; 92% Black or African American, non-Hispanic/Latino; 0.2% Hispanic/Latino; 0.1% Asian, non-Hispanic/Latino; 0.2% American Indian or Alaska Native, non-Hispanic/Latino; 5% Race/ethnicity unknown; 3% international; 4% transferred in; 58% live on campus.

Freshmen:

Admission: 16,483 applied, 9,036 admitted, 814 enrolled. ***Average high school GPA:*** 3.3. ***Test scores:*** SAT evidence-based reading and writing scores over 500: 66%; SAT math scores over 500: 52%; ACT scores over 18: 75%; SAT evidence-based reading and writing scores over 600: 9%; SAT math scores over 600: 5%; ACT scores over 24: 5%.

Retention: 74% of full-time freshmen returned.

FACULTY

Total: 305, 59% full-time, 73% with terminal degrees.

Student/faculty ratio: 19:1.

ACADEMICS

Calendar: semesters. *Degrees:* bachelor's, master's, doctoral, post-master's, and postbachelor's certificates.

Special study options: academic remediation for entering students, accelerated degree program, adult/continuing education programs, advanced placement credit, cooperative education, double majors, honors programs, independent study, internships, off-campus study, part-time degree program, services for LD students, study abroad, summer session for credit. ***ROTC:*** Army (c), Navy (c).

Unusual degree programs: 3-2 engineering with Georgia Institute of Technology, Boston University, North Carolina Agricultural and Technical State University.

Computers: 741 computers/terminals and 2,000 ports are available on campus for general student use. Students can access the following: computer help desk, free student e-mail accounts, online (class) grades, online (class) registration, online (class) schedules. Campuswide network is available. 100% of college-owned or -operated housing units are wired for high-speed Internet access. Wireless service is available via entire campus.

Library: Robert W. Woodruff Library. *Books:* 491,098 (physical), 238,454 (digital/electronic); *Serial titles:* 929 (physical), 158,194 (digital/electronic); *Databases:* 360.

STUDENT LIFE

Housing options: on-campus residence required through sophomore year; coed, men-only, women-only. Campus housing is university owned. Freshman applicants given priority for college housing.

Activities and organizations: drama/theater group, student-run newspaper, radio and television station, choral group, marching band, Spirit Boosters, Pre-Alumni Council, Campus Activities Board, Orientation Guides, National Association for the Advancement of Colored People, national fraternities, national sororities.

Athletics Member NCAA. All Division II. ***Intercollegiate sports:*** baseball M(s), basketball M(s)/W(s), cross-country running M(s)/W(s), football M(s), softball W(s), tennis W(s), track and field M(s)/W(s), volleyball W(s). ***Intramural sports:*** basketball M/W, football M, softball W, tennis W, track and field M/W, volleyball M/W.

Campus security: 24-hour emergency response devices and patrols, late-night transport/escort service, controlled dormitory access.

Student services: health clinic, personal/psychological counseling.

COSTS & FINANCIAL AID

Costs (2020–21) ***Comprehensive fee:*** $36,413 includes full-time tuition ($21,098), mandatory fees ($3809), and room and board ($11,506). Part-time tuition: $879 per credit hour. ***Room and board:*** Room and board charges vary according to board plan and location.

Financial Aid Of all full-time matriculated undergraduates who enrolled in 2016, 2,780 applied for aid, 2,638 were judged to have need, 1,261 had their need fully met. 201 Federal Work-Study jobs (averaging $1740). ***Average percent of need met:*** 45. ***Average financial aid package:*** $7324. ***Average need-based loan:*** $2453. ***Average need-based gift aid:*** $5425. ***Average indebtedness upon graduation:*** $40,393.

APPLYING

Standardized Tests *Required:* SAT or ACT (for admission).

Options: electronic application, early admission, deferred entrance.

Application fee: $35.

Required: essay or personal statement, high school transcript, minimum 2.5 GPA, 2 letters of recommendation. ***Required for some:*** interview.

Application deadlines: 6/1 (freshmen), 6/1 (transfers).

Notification: continuous (freshmen), continuous (transfers).

CONTACT

Ms. Lorri Rice, Director of Recruitment and Admissions, Clark Atlanta University, 223 James P. Brawley Drive, SW, Atlanta, GA 30314. *Phone:* 404-880-8043. *Toll-free phone:* 800-688-3228. *Fax:* 404-880-6174. *E-mail:* cauadmissions@cau.edu.

Clayton State University

Morrow, Georgia

http://www.clayton.edu/

- **State-supported** comprehensive, founded 1969, part of University System of Georgia
- **Suburban** 163-acre campus with easy access to Atlanta
- **Coed** 6,368 undergraduate students, 60% full-time, 69% women, 31% men
- **Minimally difficult** entrance level, 51% of applicants were admitted

UNDERGRAD STUDENTS

3,837 full-time, 2,531 part-time. 4% are from out of state; 66% Black or African American, non-Hispanic/Latino; 8% Hispanic/Latino; 6% Asian, non-Hispanic/Latino; 0.1% Native Hawaiian or other Pacific Islander, non-Hispanic/Latino; 0.1% American Indian or Alaska Native, non-Hispanic/Latino; 3% Two or more races, non-Hispanic/Latino; 2% Race/ethnicity unknown; 2% international; 10% transferred in; 18% live on campus.

Freshmen:

Admission: 1,938 applied, 991 admitted, 597 enrolled. ***Average high school GPA:*** 3.1. ***Test scores:*** SAT evidence-based reading and writing scores over 500: 50%; SAT math scores over 500: 26%; ACT scores over 18: 78%; SAT evidence-based reading and writing scores over 600: 5%; SAT math scores over 600: 4%; ACT scores over 24: 9%; SAT evidence-based reading and writing scores over 700: 1%; ACT scores over 30: 1%.

Retention: 71% of full-time freshmen returned.

FACULTY

Total: 328, 67% full-time, 67% with terminal degrees.

Student/faculty ratio: 19:1.

ACADEMICS

Calendar: semesters. *Degrees:* certificates, associate, bachelor's, and master's.

Special study options: academic remediation for entering students, adult/continuing education programs, advanced placement credit, cooperative education, distance learning, double majors, honors programs, independent study, internships, off-campus study, part-time degree program, services for LD students, student-designed majors, study abroad, summer session for credit. ***ROTC:*** Army (c), Navy (c), Air Force (c).

Computers: 3,500 computers/terminals are available on campus for general student use. Students can access the following: computer help desk, free student e-mail accounts, online (class) grades, online (class) registration, online (class) schedules. Campuswide network is available. 100% of college-owned or -operated housing units are wired for high-speed Internet access. Wireless service is available via entire campus. **Library:** Clayton State University Library. Students can reserve study rooms.

STUDENT LIFE

Housing options: on-campus residence required for freshman year; coed. Campus housing is university owned. Freshman applicants given priority for college housing.

Activities and organizations: drama/theater group, student-run newspaper, radio station, choral group, national fraternities, national sororities.

Athletics Member NCAA. All Division II. ***Intercollegiate sports:*** basketball M(s)/W(s), cheerleading W(s)(c), cross-country running M(s)/W(s), golf M(s), soccer M(s)/W(s), tennis W(s), track and field M(s)/W(s). ***Intramural sports:*** bowling M/W, softball M/W, table tennis M/W, volleyball M/W.

Campus security: 24-hour emergency response devices and patrols, late-night transport/escort service, controlled dormitory access, lighted pathways.

Student services: health clinic, personal/psychological counseling, veterans affairs office.

COSTS & FINANCIAL AID

Costs (2020–21) ***Tuition:*** area resident $5080 full-time, $169 per credit hour part-time; state resident $5080 full-time, $169 per credit hour part-time; nonresident $18,482 full-time, $516 per credit hour part-time. ***Required fees:*** $1474 full-time, $737 per term part-time. ***Room and board:*** $10,397.

Financial Aid Of all full-time matriculated undergraduates who enrolled in 2017, 3,251 applied for aid, 3,029 were judged to have need, 86 had their need fully met. 67 Federal Work-Study jobs (averaging $4556). In 2017, 25 non-need-based awards were made. ***Average percent of need met:*** 47. ***Average financial aid package:*** $10,024. ***Average need-based loan:*** $4067. ***Average need-based gift aid:*** $7108. ***Average non-need-based aid:*** $2045. ***Average indebtedness upon graduation:*** $30,423.

APPLYING

Standardized Tests *Required:* SAT or ACT (for admission).

Options: electronic application, early admission, deferred entrance.

Application fee: $40.

Required: high school transcript, proof of immunization.

Notification: continuous (freshmen), continuous (transfers).

CONTACT

Admissions, Clayton State University, 2000 Clayton State Boulevard, Morrow, GA 30260-0285. *Phone:* 678-466-4115. *Fax:* 678-466-4149. *E-mail:* csc-info@clayton.edu.

College of Coastal Georgia

Brunswick, Georgia

http://www.ccga.edu/

- **State-supported** 4-year, founded 1961, part of University System of Georgia
- **Small-town** 193-acre campus with easy access to Jacksonville
- **Endowment** $8.8 million
- **Coed**
- **Minimally difficult** entrance level

FACULTY

Student/faculty ratio: 19:1.

ACADEMICS

Calendar: semesters. *Degrees:* associate and bachelor's.

Library: Clara Wood Gould Memorial Library. *Books:* 54,662 (physical), 150,476 (digital/electronic); *Serial titles:* 109 (physical), 168,333 (digital/electronic); *Databases:* 338. Weekly public service hours: 77; students can reserve study rooms.

STUDENT LIFE

Housing options: on-campus residence required for freshman year; coed. Campus housing is university owned, leased by the school and is provided by a third party. Freshman campus housing is guaranteed.

Activities and organizations: student-run newspaper, International Association, Coastal Georgia Association of Nursing Students, Urban Gaming Club, Association of Coastal Educators, CCGA Biology Club.

Athletics Member NAIA.

Campus security: 24-hour emergency response devices and patrols, late-night transport/escort service, controlled dormitory access.

Student services: health clinic, personal/psychological counseling, veterans affairs office.

COSTS & FINANCIAL AID

Costs (2019–20) ***One-time required fee:*** $25. ***Tuition:*** state resident $3204 full-time, $107 per credit hour part-time; nonresident $11,836 full-time, $395 per credit hour part-time. Full-time tuition and fees vary according to course load. Part-time tuition and fees vary according to course load. ***Required fees:*** $1570 full-time, $425 per term part-time. ***Room and board:*** $10,328; room only: $6608. Room and board charges vary according to board plan, housing facility, and location.

Financial Aid Of all full-time matriculated undergraduates who enrolled in 2017, 1,716 applied for aid, 1,267 were judged to have need, 44 had their need fully met. 8 Federal Work-Study jobs (averaging $363). In 2017, 100 non-need-based awards were made. ***Average percent of need met:*** 61. ***Average financial aid package:*** $10,843. ***Average need-based loan:*** $3443. ***Average need-based gift aid:*** $6428. ***Average non-need-***

based aid: $1883. ***Average indebtedness upon graduation:*** $19,554. ***Financial aid deadline:*** 6/1.

APPLYING

Standardized Tests *Required:* SAT or ACT (for admission).

Options: electronic application, early admission, deferred entrance.

Application fee: $25.

Required: high school transcript, minimum 2.0 GPA, immunization records, proof of residency.

CONTACT

Dr. Amy Clines, AVP Recruitment and Admissions, College of Coastal Georgia, One College Drive, Brunswick, GA 31520. *Phone:* 912-279-5775. *Toll-free phone:* 800-675-7235. *Fax:* 912-262-3072. *E-mail:* admiss@ccga.edu.

Columbus State University

Columbus, Georgia

http://www.columbusstate.edu/

- **State-supported** comprehensive, founded 1958, part of University System of Georgia
- **Suburban** 132-acre campus with easy access to Atlanta
- **Coed**
- **Minimally difficult** entrance level

FACULTY

Student/faculty ratio: 17:1.

ACADEMICS

Calendar: semesters. *Degrees:* certificates, associate, bachelor's, master's, doctoral, post-master's, and postbachelor's certificates.
Library: Simon Schwob Memorial Library plus 1 other. *Books:* 379,660 (physical); *Serial titles:* 1,103 (physical).

STUDENT LIFE

Housing options: on-campus residence required for freshman year; coed, men-only, women-only, special housing for students with disabilities. Campus housing is university owned. Freshman applicants given priority for college housing.

Activities and organizations: drama/theater group, student-run newspaper, choral group, Student Government Association, Student Activities Council, Campus Ministry Association, African Students Association, SABER Student Newspaper, national fraternities, national sororities.

Athletics Member NCAA. All Division II.

Campus security: 24-hour emergency response devices and patrols, late-night transport/escort service, controlled dormitory access.

Student services: health clinic, personal/psychological counseling, veterans affairs office.

COSTS & FINANCIAL AID

Costs (2019–20) ***Tuition:*** area resident $5330 full-time, $178 per credit hour part-time; state resident $5330 full-time, $178 per credit hour part-time; nonresident $18,812 full-time, $627 per credit hour part-time. ***Required fees:*** $1870 full-time. ***Room and board:*** $9380; room only: $5830.

Financial Aid Of all full-time matriculated undergraduates who enrolled in 2019, 3,965 applied for aid, 3,188 were judged to have need, 110 had their need fully met. In 2019, 238 non-need-based awards were made. ***Average percent of need met:*** 62. ***Average financial aid package:*** $10,142. ***Average need-based loan:*** $4318. ***Average need-based gift aid:*** $5165. ***Average non-need-based aid:*** $1880. ***Average indebtedness upon graduation:*** $32,587.

APPLYING

Standardized Tests *Required:* SAT or ACT (for admission).

Options: electronic application, early admission, deferred entrance.

Application fee: $40.

Required: high school transcript, minimum 2.5 GPA, proof of immunization.

CONTACT

Columbus State University, 4225 University Avenue, Columbus, GA 31907-5645. *Phone:* 706-507-8827. *Toll-free phone:* 866-264-2035.

Covenant College

Lookout Mountain, Georgia

http://www.covenant.edu/

- **Independent** comprehensive, founded 1955, affiliated with Presbyterian Church in America
- **Suburban** 350-acre campus
- **Coed** 946 undergraduate students, 94% full-time, 53% women, 47% men
- **Moderately difficult** entrance level, 98% of applicants were admitted

UNDERGRAD STUDENTS

887 full-time, 59 part-time. 71% are from out of state; 3% Black or African American, non-Hispanic/Latino; 1% Hispanic/Latino; 1% Asian, non-Hispanic/Latino; 0.1% Native Hawaiian or other Pacific Islander, non-Hispanic/Latino; 0.8% American Indian or Alaska Native, non-Hispanic/Latino; 5% Two or more races, non-Hispanic/Latino; 1% Race/ethnicity unknown; 3% international; 2% transferred in; 82% live on campus.

Freshmen:

Admission: 561 applied, 551 admitted, 219 enrolled. ***Average high school GPA:*** 3.7. ***Test scores:*** SAT evidence-based reading and writing scores over 500: 98%; SAT math scores over 500: 89%; ACT scores over 18: 99%; SAT evidence-based reading and writing scores over 600: 63%; SAT math scores over 600: 49%; ACT scores over 24: 71%; SAT evidence-based reading and writing scores over 700: 22%; SAT math scores over 700: 11%; ACT scores over 30: 24%.

Retention: 84% of full-time freshmen returned.

FACULTY

Total: 101, 61% full-time, 70% with terminal degrees.

Student/faculty ratio: 12:1.

ACADEMICS

Calendar: semesters. *Degrees:* bachelor's and master's (master's degree in education only).

Special study options: academic remediation for entering students, adult/continuing education programs, advanced placement credit, double majors, English as a second language, independent study, internships, off-campus study, part-time degree program, services for LD students, student-designed majors, study abroad, summer session for credit. ***ROTC:*** Army (c).

Computers: Students can access the following: computer help desk, free student e-mail accounts, online (class) registration, online student information system. Campuswide network is available. 100% of college-owned or -operated housing units are wired for high-speed Internet access. Wireless service is available via classrooms, computer labs, dorm rooms, libraries.
Library: Kresge Memorial Library.

STUDENT LIFE

Housing options: on-campus residence required through junior year; coed. Campus housing is university owned. Freshman campus housing is guaranteed.

Activities and organizations: drama/theater group, student-run newspaper, radio station, choral group.

Athletics Member NCAA, NAIA, NCCAA. All NCAA Division III. ***Intercollegiate sports:*** baseball M, basketball M/W, cross-country running M/W, golf M, soccer M/W, softball W, tennis M/W, volleyball W. ***Intramural sports:*** badminton M/W, basketball M/W, football M, soccer M/W, volleyball M/W.

Campus security: controlled dormitory access, night security guards.

Student services: health clinic, personal/psychological counseling, women's center.

COSTS & FINANCIAL AID

Costs (2020–21) ***Comprehensive fee:*** $47,680 includes full-time tuition ($35,670), mandatory fees ($1040), and room and board ($10,970). Part-time tuition: $1530 per credit hour.

Financial Aid Of all full-time matriculated undergraduates who enrolled in 2018, 770 applied for aid, 653 were judged to have need, 232 had their need fully met. In 2018, 302 non-need-based awards were made. ***Average percent of need met:*** 80. ***Average financial aid package:*** $29,745. ***Average need-based loan:*** $6273. ***Average need-based gift aid:*** $24,148.

COLLEGES AT-A-GLANCE

Average non-need-based aid: $17,545. ***Average indebtedness upon graduation:*** $23,723.

APPLYING
Standardized Tests *Required:* SAT or ACT (for admission).

Options: electronic application, early admission, early action, deferred entrance.

Application fee: $35.

Required: essay or personal statement, high school transcript, minimum 2.5 GPA, 2 letters of recommendation, interview.

Notification: 12/1 (early action).

CONTACT
Mr. Philip Howlett, Assistant Director of Admissions, Covenant College, 14049 Scenic Highway, Lookout Mountain, GA 30750. *Phone:* 706-419-1145. *Toll-free phone:* 888-451-2683. *Fax:* 706-820-0893. *E-mail:* admissions@covenant.edu.

Dalton State College

Dalton, Georgia

http://www.daltonstate.edu/

CONTACT
Katherine Logan, Director of Admissions, Dalton State College, 650 College Drive, Dalton, GA 30720-3797. *Phone:* 706-272-4524. *Toll-free phone:* 800-829-4436. *Fax:* 706-272-2530. *E-mail:* klogan@daltonstate.edu.

DeVry University–Alpharetta Campus

Alpharetta, Georgia

http://www.devry.edu/

CONTACT
Admissions Office, DeVry University–Alpharetta Campus, 2555 Northwinds Parkway, Alpharetta, GA 30009. *Phone:* 770-619-3600. *Toll-free phone:* 866-338-7934.

DeVry University–Decatur Campus

Decatur, Georgia

http://www.devry.edu/

- **Proprietary** comprehensive, founded 1969, part of DeVry University
- **Suburban** campus
- **Coed**
- **Minimally difficult** entrance level

FACULTY
Student/faculty ratio: 21:1.

ACADEMICS
Calendar: semesters. *Degrees:* associate, bachelor's, master's, and postbachelor's certificates.
Library: Learning Resource Center.

STUDENT LIFE
Housing options: college housing not available.

APPLYING
Options: deferred entrance.

Application fee: $30.

Required: high school transcript, interview.

CONTACT
DeVry University–Decatur Campus, 1 West Court Square, Suite 100, Decatur, GA 30030. *Phone:* 404-270-2700. *Toll-free phone:* 866-338-7934.

East Georgia State College

Swainsboro, Georgia

http://www.ega.edu/

- **State-supported** primarily 2-year, founded 1973, part of University System of Georgia
- **Rural** 207-acre campus
- **Coed**
- **Minimally difficult** entrance level

FACULTY
Student/faculty ratio: 26:1.

ACADEMICS
Calendar: semesters. *Degrees:* certificates, associate, and bachelor's.
Library: East Georgia College Library. Students can reserve study rooms.

STUDENT LIFE
Housing options: coed. Campus housing is provided by a third party.

Activities and organizations: drama/theater group, student-run newspaper, choral group.

Athletics Member NJCAA.

Campus security: 24-hour patrols, late-night transport/escort service, controlled dormitory access.

Student services: health clinic, personal/psychological counseling, veterans affairs office.

FINANCIAL AID
Financial Aid Of all full-time matriculated undergraduates who enrolled in 2018, 43 Federal Work-Study jobs (averaging $1560).

APPLYING
Options: early admission, deferred entrance.

Application fee: $20.

Required: high school transcript.

CONTACT
East Georgia State College, 131 College Circle, Swainsboro, GA 30401-2699. *Phone:* 478-289-2112.

Emmanuel College

Franklin Springs, Georgia

http://www.ec.edu/

- **Independent** 4-year, founded 1919, affiliated with Pentecostal Holiness Church
- **Rural** 90-acre campus with easy access to Atlanta, GA
- **Endowment** $1.6 million
- **Coed** 958 undergraduate students, 87% full-time, 47% women, 53% men
- **Minimally difficult** entrance level, 46% of applicants were admitted

UNDERGRAD STUDENTS
829 full-time, 129 part-time. Students come from 35 states and territories; 20 other countries; 31% are from out of state; 15% Black or African American, non-Hispanic/Latino; 7% Hispanic/Latino; 1% Asian, non-Hispanic/Latino; 0.6% Native Hawaiian or other Pacific Islander, non-Hispanic/Latino; 0.6% American Indian or Alaska Native, non-Hispanic/Latino; 4% Two or more races, non-Hispanic/Latino; 8% international; 6% transferred in; 63% live on campus.

Freshmen:
Admission: 767 applied, 354 admitted, 248 enrolled. ***Average high school GPA:*** 3.3.

Retention: 68% of full-time freshmen returned.

FACULTY
Total: 87, 53% full-time, 52% with terminal degrees.

Student/faculty ratio: 15:1.

ACADEMICS
Calendar: semesters. *Degrees:* associate and bachelor's.

Special study options: academic remediation for entering students, advanced placement credit, distance learning, honors programs, independent study, internships, part-time degree program, services for LD students, study abroad, summer session for credit.

Unusual degree programs: 3-2 psychology with Richmont University.

Computers: 80 computers/terminals are available on campus for general student use. Students can access the following: campus intranet, computer help desk, free student e-mail accounts, online (class) grades, online (class) registration, online (class) schedules. Campuswide network is available. 100% of college-owned or -operated housing units are wired for high-speed Internet access. Wireless service is available via entire campus.
Library: Shaw-Leslie Library plus 1 other. *Books:* 37,501 (physical), 51,628 (digital/electronic); *Serial titles:* 85 (physical), 2,435 (digital/electronic); *Databases:* 125. Weekly public service hours: 84; students can reserve study rooms.

STUDENT LIFE
Housing options: on-campus residence required through sophomore year; men-only, women-only. Campus housing is university owned. Freshman campus housing is guaranteed.

Activities and organizations: drama/theater group, choral group, Students in Free Enterprise (SIFE), Fellowship of Christian Athletes, SOS, BSU, International Students Club.

Athletics Member NCAA, NCCAA. All NCAA Division II. *Intercollegiate sports:* archery M(s)/W(s), baseball M(s), basketball M(s)/W(s), bowling M(s)/W(s), cross-country running M(s)/W(s), golf M(s), lacrosse M(s)/W(s), riflery M(s)/W(s), soccer M(s)/W(s), softball W(s), swimming and diving M(s)/W(s), tennis M(s)/W(s), track and field M(s)/W(s), volleyball M(s)/W(s), wrestling M(s)/W(s). *Intramural sports:* basketball M/W, football M/W, golf M/W, soccer M/W, tennis M/W, track and field M/W, volleyball M/W, weight lifting M/W.

Student services: personal/psychological counseling, veterans affairs office.

COSTS & FINANCIAL AID
Costs (2020–21) ***Comprehensive fee:*** $29,282 includes full-time tuition ($20,760), mandatory fees ($460), and room and board ($8062). Full-time tuition and fees vary according to location. Part-time tuition: $873 per credit hour. ***Required fees:*** $115 per term part-time. ***Room and board:*** Room and board charges vary according to housing facility. ***Waivers:*** senior citizens and employees or children of employees.

Financial Aid Of all full-time matriculated undergraduates who enrolled in 2019, 681 applied for aid, 600 were judged to have need, 123 had their need fully met. 100 Federal Work-Study jobs (averaging $1038). 91 state and other part-time jobs (averaging $1281). In 2019, 134 non-need-based awards were made. ***Average percent of need met:*** 71. ***Average financial aid package:*** $16,881. ***Average need-based loan:*** $3842. ***Average need-based gift aid:*** $13,074. ***Average non-need-based aid:*** $4764. ***Average indebtedness upon graduation:*** $24,028. ***Financial aid deadline:*** 6/15.

APPLYING
Standardized Tests *Required:* SAT or ACT (for admission).

Options: electronic application, early admission, deferred entrance.

Application fee: $25.

Required: essay or personal statement, high school transcript. ***Required for some:*** interview.

Notification: continuous until 8/1 (freshmen), continuous until 8/1 (transfers).

CONTACT
Ms. Kelley Garrett, Director of Admissions, Emmanuel College, PO Box 129, 181 Spring Street, Franklin Springs, GA 30639-0129. *Phone:* 706-245-7226 Ext. 2814. *Toll-free phone:* 800-860-8800. *E-mail:* admissions@ec.edu.

Emory University

Atlanta, Georgia

http://www.emory.edu/

- **Independent Methodist** university, founded 1836
- **Suburban** 631-acre campus with easy access to Atlanta
- **Endowment** $8.6 billion
- **Coed** 7,118 undergraduate students, 99% full-time, 60% women, 40% men
- **Most difficult** entrance level, 16% of applicants were admitted

UNDERGRAD STUDENTS
7,012 full-time, 106 part-time. Students come from 55 states and territories; 69 other countries; 80% are from out of state; 8% Black or African American, non-Hispanic/Latino; 11% Hispanic/Latino; 22% Asian, non-Hispanic/Latino; 0.1% Native Hawaiian or other Pacific Islander, non-Hispanic/Latino; 0.1% American Indian or Alaska Native, non-Hispanic/Latino; 4% Two or more races, non-Hispanic/Latino; 0.9% Race/ethnicity unknown; 15% international; 1% transferred in; 63% live on campus.

Freshmen:
Admission: 30,017 applied, 4,682 admitted, 1,374 enrolled. ***Average high school GPA:*** 3.8. ***Test scores:*** SAT evidence-based reading and writing scores over 500: 100%; SAT math scores over 500: 100%; ACT scores over 18: 100%; SAT evidence-based reading and writing scores over 600: 98%; SAT math scores over 600: 97%; ACT scores over 24: 100%; SAT evidence-based reading and writing scores over 700: 61%; SAT math scores over 700: 75%; ACT scores over 30: 85%.

Retention: 95% of full-time freshmen returned.

FACULTY
Total: 1,247, 88% full-time, 94% with terminal degrees.

Student/faculty ratio: 9:1.

ACADEMICS
Calendar: semesters. *Degrees:* bachelor's, master's, doctoral, post-master's, and postbachelor's certificates (enrollment figures include Emory University, Oxford College; application data for main campus only).

Special study options: advanced placement credit, cooperative education, double majors, English as a second language, external degree program, honors programs, independent study, internships, off-campus study, services for LD students, study abroad, summer session for credit. ***ROTC:*** Army (c), Navy (c), Air Force (c).

Unusual degree programs: 3-2 business administration; engineering with Georgia Institute of Technology; nursing.

Computers: Students can access the following: campus intranet, computer help desk, free student e-mail accounts, online (class) grades, online (class) registration, online (class) schedules, computer repair system. Campuswide network is available. 100% of college-owned or -operated housing units are wired for high-speed Internet access. Wireless service is available via entire campus.
Library: Robert W. Woodruff Library plus 8 others. *Books:* 2.4 million (physical), 1.3 million (digital/electronic); *Serial titles:* 68,803 (physical), 374,653 (digital/electronic); *Databases:* 1,048.

STUDENT LIFE
Housing options: on-campus residence required through sophomore year; coed. Campus housing is university owned. Freshman campus housing is guaranteed.

Activities and organizations: drama/theater group, student-run newspaper, radio and television station, choral group, national fraternities, national sororities.

Athletics Member NCAA. All Division III. *Intercollegiate sports:* badminton M(c)/W(c), baseball M, basketball M/W, cheerleading M(c)/W(c), crew M(c)/W(c), cross-country running M/W, equestrian sports M(c)/W(c), fencing M(c)/W(c), field hockey M(c)/W(c), golf M/W, gymnastics W(c), lacrosse M(c)/W(c), rock climbing M(c)/W(c), rugby M(c)/W(c), soccer M/W, softball W, squash M(c)/W(c), swimming and diving M/W, tennis M/W, track and field M/W, ultimate Frisbee W(c), volleyball W, water polo M(c), weight lifting M(c)/W(c). *Intramural sports:* basketball M/W, soccer M/W, softball W, swimming and diving M/W, table tennis M/W, tennis M/W, volleyball M/W.

Campus security: 24-hour emergency response devices and patrols, student patrols, late-night transport/escort service, controlled dormitory access.

Student services: health clinic, personal/psychological counseling, women's center, legal services, veterans affairs office.

COSTS & FINANCIAL AID
Costs (2020–21) ***Comprehensive fee:*** $71,570 includes full-time tuition ($55,200), mandatory fees ($798), and room and board ($15,572). Part-time tuition: $2300 per credit hour. ***College room only:*** $8984. Room and board charges vary according to board plan and housing facility. ***Payment plan:*** installment. ***Waivers:*** employees or children of employees.

Financial Aid Of all full-time matriculated undergraduates who enrolled in 2019, 3,743 applied for aid, 3,277 were judged to have need, 3,199 had their need fully met. In 2019, 343 non-need-based awards were made. ***Average percent of need met:*** 100. ***Average financial aid package:*** $47,223. ***Average need-based loan:*** $6151. ***Average need-based gift aid:*** $43,659. ***Average non-need-based aid:*** $28,668. ***Average indebtedness upon graduation:*** $24,889. ***Financial aid deadline:*** 3/1.

APPLYING

Standardized Tests *Required:* SAT or ACT (for admission).

Options: electronic application, early admission, early decision, deferred entrance.

Application fee: $75.

Required: essay or personal statement, high school transcript, 2 letters of recommendation.

Application deadlines: 1/1 (freshmen), 3/15 (transfers).

Early decision deadline: 11/1 (for plan 1), 1/1 (for plan 2).

Notification: 4/1 (freshmen), 4/30 (transfers), 12/15 (early decision plan 1), 2/15 (early decision plan 2).

CONTACT

Emory University, 1390 Oxford Road NE, 3rd Floor, Atlanta, GA 30322. *Phone:* 404-727-6036. *Toll-free phone:* 800-727-6036. *E-mail:* admiss@emory.edu.

Fort Valley State University

Fort Valley, Georgia

http://www.fvsu.edu/

- **State-supported** comprehensive, founded 1895, part of University System of Georgia
- **Small-town** 1365-acre campus
- **Coed**
- **Moderately difficult** entrance level

FACULTY

Student/faculty ratio: 21:1.

ACADEMICS

Calendar: semesters. *Degrees:* bachelor's, master's, and post-master's certificates.

Library: Henry A. Hunt Memorial Library.

STUDENT LIFE

Housing options: men-only, women-only. Campus housing is university owned and leased by the school.

Activities and organizations: drama/theater group, student-run newspaper, radio and television station, choral group, marching band, Drama Group, Christian Student Organization, Habitat for Humanity, Debate Club, national fraternities, national sororities.

Athletics Member NCAA. All Division II.

Campus security: 24-hour emergency response devices and patrols, student patrols, late-night transport/escort service.

Student services: health clinic, personal/psychological counseling.

FINANCIAL AID

Financial Aid Of all full-time matriculated undergraduates who enrolled in 2015, 1,950 applied for aid, 1,950 were judged to have need, 1,784 had their need fully met. ***Average percent of need met:*** 92. ***Average financial aid package:*** $7367. ***Average need-based loan:*** $2874. ***Average need-based gift aid:*** $4960.

APPLYING

Standardized Tests *Required:* SAT or ACT (for admission).

Options: electronic application, early admission, deferred entrance.

Application fee: $20.

Required: high school transcript.

CONTACT

Mr. Donald Moore, Director of Admissions and Recruitment, Fort Valley State University, 1005 State University Drive, Fort Valley, GA 31030. *Phone:* 478-825-6307. *Toll-free phone:* 877-462-3878. *Fax:* 478-825-6169. *E-mail:* admissap@fvsu.edu.

Georgia College & State University

Milledgeville, Georgia

http://www.gcsu.edu/

- **State-supported** comprehensive, founded 1889, part of University System of Georgia
- **Small-town** 680-acre campus
- **Endowment** $45.3 million
- **Coed** 5,844 undergraduate students, 92% full-time, 64% women, 36% men
- **Moderately difficult** entrance level, 79% of applicants were admitted

UNDERGRAD STUDENTS

5,364 full-time, 480 part-time. Students come from 20 states and territories; 27 other countries; 1% are from out of state; 5% Black or African American, non-Hispanic/Latino; 6% Hispanic/Latino; 1% Asian, non-Hispanic/Latino; 0.2% American Indian or Alaska Native, non-Hispanic/Latino; 3% Two or more races, non-Hispanic/Latino; 0.3% Race/ethnicity unknown; 0.5% international; 4% transferred in; 36% live on campus.

Freshmen:

Admission: 4,401 applied, 3,495 admitted, 1,481 enrolled. ***Average high school GPA:*** 3.5. ***Test scores:*** SAT evidence-based reading and writing scores over 500: 98%; SAT math scores over 500: 96%; ACT scores over 18: 100%; SAT evidence-based reading and writing scores over 600: 57%; SAT math scores over 600: 41%; ACT scores over 24: 66%; SAT evidence-based reading and writing scores over 700: 7%; SAT math scores over 700: 4%; ACT scores over 30: 9%.

Retention: 86% of full-time freshmen returned.

FACULTY

Total: 416, 80% full-time, 72% with terminal degrees.

Student/faculty ratio: 17:1.

ACADEMICS

Calendar: semesters. *Degrees:* certificates, bachelor's, master's, doctoral, and post-master's certificates.

Special study options: accelerated degree program, advanced placement credit, distance learning, double majors, English as a second language, external degree program, freshman honors college, honors programs, independent study, internships, part-time degree program, services for LD students, student-designed majors, study abroad, summer session for credit. ***ROTC:*** Army (c).

Unusual degree programs: 3-2 Georgia Institute of Technology.

Computers: 900 computers/terminals and 6,295 ports are available on campus for general student use. Students can access the following: campus intranet, computer help desk, free student e-mail accounts, online (class) grades, online (class) registration, online (class) schedules. Campuswide network is available. 100% of college-owned or -operated housing units are wired for high-speed Internet access. Wireless service is available via entire campus.

Library: Ina Dillard Russell Library plus 1 other. *Books:* 168,723 (physical), 720,251 (digital/electronic); *Serial titles:* 4,076 (physical), 170,730 (digital/electronic); *Databases:* 360. Weekly public service hours: 102; students can reserve study rooms.

STUDENT LIFE

Housing options: on-campus residence required for freshman year; coed, cooperative, special housing for students with disabilities. Campus housing is university owned. Freshman campus housing is guaranteed.

Activities and organizations: drama/theater group, student-run newspaper, radio station, choral group, Georgia College Miracle, Alpha Delta Pi, Zeta Tau Alpha, Swipe out Hunger, Wesley Foundation of Campus Ministries, national fraternities, national sororities.

Athletics Member NCAA. All Division II. ***Intercollegiate sports:*** baseball M(s), basketball M(s)/W(s), cheerleading M/W, cross-country running M(s)/W(s), golf M(s), soccer W(s), softball W(s), tennis M(s)/W(s), volleyball W(s). ***Intramural sports:*** baseball M(c), basketball M/W, equestrian sports W(c), football M/W, golf M(c), ice hockey M(c), lacrosse M(c)/W(c), rugby M(c)/W(c), soccer M(c)/W(c), softball M(c)/W(c), swimming and diving W(c), tennis M(c)/W(c), ultimate Frisbee M(c)/W(c), volleyball M/W(c).

Campus security: 24-hour emergency response devices and patrols, student patrols, late-night transport/escort service, controlled dormitory access.

Student services: health clinic, personal/psychological counseling, women's center.

COSTS & FINANCIAL AID

Costs (2020–21) ***Tuition:*** state resident $3754 full-time; nonresident $13,344 full-time. Full-time tuition and fees vary according to course load and program. Part-time tuition and fees vary according to course load and program. ***Required fees:*** $2016 full-time. ***Room and board:*** Room and board charges vary according to board plan, housing facility, and location. ***Payment plan:*** installment. ***Waivers:*** employees or children of employees.

Financial Aid Of all full-time matriculated undergraduates who enrolled in 2019, 4,151 applied for aid, 2,570 were judged to have need, 517 had their need fully met. In 2019, 227 non-need-based awards were made. ***Average percent of need met:*** 59. ***Average financial aid package:*** $11,322. ***Average need-based loan:*** $4627. ***Average need-based gift aid:*** $4650. ***Average non-need-based aid:*** $2064. ***Average indebtedness upon graduation:*** $33,124.

APPLYING

Standardized Tests *Required:* SAT or ACT (for admission). *Required for some:* SAT Subject Tests (for admission).

Options: electronic application, early admission, early action, deferred entrance.

Application fee: $40.

Required: proof of immunization. ***Required for some:*** essay or personal statement, high school transcript.

Application deadlines: rolling (out-of-state freshmen), 7/1 (transfers), 10/15 (early action).

Notification: continuous (freshmen), continuous (out-of-state freshmen), continuous (transfers), 12/15 (early action).

CONTACT

Gwen Chretien, Executive Director of Admissions, Georgia College & State University, CPO Box 023, Milledgeville, GA 31061. *Phone:* 478-445-1283. *Toll-free phone:* 800-342-0471. *Fax:* 478-445-3653. *E-mail:* admissions@gcsu.edu.

Georgia Gwinnett College

Lawrenceville, Georgia

http://www.ggc.edu/

- **State-supported** 4-year, part of University System of Georgia
- **Suburban** 260-acre campus with easy access to Atlanta
- **Coed** 12,831 undergraduate students, 67% full-time, 57% women, 43% men
- **Minimally difficult** entrance level, 94% of applicants were admitted

UNDERGRAD STUDENTS

8,556 full-time, 4,275 part-time. Students come from 30 states and territories; 130 other countries; 1% are from out of state; 33% Black or African American, non-Hispanic/Latino; 23% Hispanic/Latino; 10% Asian, non-Hispanic/Latino; 0.2% Native Hawaiian or other Pacific Islander, non-Hispanic/Latino; 0.1% American Indian or Alaska Native, non-Hispanic/Latino; 4% Two or more races, non-Hispanic/Latino; 0.8% Race/ethnicity unknown; 2% international; 6% transferred in; 7% live on campus.

Freshmen:

Admission: 4,853 applied, 4,559 admitted, 2,800 enrolled. ***Average high school GPA:*** 2.9. ***Test scores:*** SAT evidence-based reading and writing scores over 500: 55%; SAT math scores over 500: 51%; ACT scores over 18: 59%; SAT evidence-based reading and writing scores over 600: 14%; SAT math scores over 600: 9%; ACT scores over 24: 14%; SAT evidence-based reading and writing scores over 700: 1%; SAT math scores over 700: 1%; ACT scores over 30: 1%.

Retention: 67% of full-time freshmen returned.

FACULTY

Total: 709, 64% full-time, 62% with terminal degrees.

Student/faculty ratio: 19:1.

ACADEMICS

Calendar: semesters. *Degrees:* associate and bachelor's.

Special study options: academic remediation for entering students, advanced placement credit, double majors, English as a second language, honors programs, internships, part-time degree program, services for LD students, study abroad, summer session for credit. ***ROTC:*** Army (b).

Computers: 243 computers/terminals are available on campus for general student use. Students can access the following: campus intranet, computer help desk, free student e-mail accounts, online (class) grades, online (class) registration, online (class) schedules. Campuswide network is available. 100% of college-owned or -operated housing units are wired for high-speed Internet access. Wireless service is available via entire campus.

Library: Daniel J. Kaufman Library and Learning Center. *Books:* 78,814 (physical), 362,131 (digital/electronic); *Serial titles:* 450 (physical), 79,612 (digital/electronic); *Databases:* 164. Weekly public service hours: 79; students can reserve study rooms.

STUDENT LIFE

Housing options: coed, men-only, women-only, special housing for students with disabilities. Campus housing is university owned. Freshman campus housing is guaranteed.

Activities and organizations: drama/theater group, student-run newspaper.

Athletics Member NAIA. ***Intercollegiate sports:*** baseball M(s)/W(s), soccer M(s)/W(s), softball W, tennis M(s)/W(s). ***Intramural sports:*** baseball M/W, basketball M/W, football M/W, golf M/W, racquetball M/W, sand volleyball M/W, soccer M/W, softball W, tennis M/W, track and field M/W, volleyball M/W, water polo M/W.

Campus security: 24-hour emergency response devices and patrols, student patrols, late-night transport/escort service, controlled dormitory access.

Student services: health clinic, personal/psychological counseling, legal services, veterans affairs office.

COSTS

Costs (2020–21) ***Tuition:*** area resident $4018 full-time, $134 per credit hour part-time; state resident $4018 full-time, $134 per credit hour part-time; nonresident $15,000 full-time, $500 per credit hour part-time. Full-time tuition and fees vary according to course load. Part-time tuition and fees vary according to course load. ***Required fees:*** $1734 full-time, $495 per term part-time. ***Room and board:*** Room and board charges vary according to board plan and housing facility. ***Payment plans:*** installment, deferred payment. ***Waivers:*** senior citizens and employees or children of employees.

APPLYING

Standardized Tests *Required:* SAT or ACT (for admission).

Options: electronic application, deferred entrance.

Application fee: $20.

Required: high school transcript, minimum 2.0 GPA.

Application deadlines: 6/1 (freshmen), rolling (transfers).

CONTACT

Ms. Susan Meltzer, Director of Admissions, Georgia Gwinnett College, 1000 University Center Lane, Lawrenceville, GA 30043. *Phone:* 678-407-5716. *Toll-free phone:* 877-704-4422. *E-mail:* ggcadmissions@ggc.edu.

Georgia Highlands College

Rome, Georgia

http://www.highlands.edu/

- **State-supported** primarily 2-year, founded 1970, part of University System of Georgia
- **Suburban** 226-acre campus with easy access to Atlanta
- **Endowment** $40,227
- **Coed**
- **Noncompetitive** entrance level

FACULTY

Student/faculty ratio: 21:1.

ACADEMICS

Calendar: semesters. *Degrees:* associate and bachelor's.

Library: Georgia Highlands College Library–Floyd Campus plus 4 others. *Books:* 79,592 (physical), 178,561 (digital/electronic); *Serial titles:* 48 (physical), 4,380 (digital/electronic); *Databases:* 382. Weekly public service hours: 58; students can reserve study rooms.

STUDENT LIFE

Housing options: college housing not available.

Activities and organizations: student-run newspaper, Association of Nursing Students, Green Highlands, Brother 2 Brother, Student Government Association, Phi Theta Kappa.

Athletics Member NJCAA.

Campus security: 24-hour emergency response devices and patrols, emergency phone/email alert system.

Student services: personal/psychological counseling, veterans affairs office.

FINANCIAL AID

Financial Aid Of all full-time matriculated undergraduates who enrolled in 2018, 50 Federal Work-Study jobs (averaging $3500).

APPLYING

Standardized Tests *Required for some:* COMPASS. *Recommended:* SAT or ACT (for admission).

Options: electronic application, deferred entrance.

Application fee: $30.

Required: high school transcript, minimum 2.0 GPA.

CONTACT

Charlene Graham, Assistant Director of Admissions, Georgia Highlands College, 3175 Cedartown Highway, Rome, GA 30161. *Phone:* 706-295-6339. *Toll-free phone:* 800-332-2406. *Fax:* 706-295-6341. *E-mail:* cgraham@highlands.edu.

Georgia Institute of Technology

Atlanta, Georgia

http://www.gatech.edu/

- **State-supported** university, founded 1885, part of University System of Georgia
- **Urban** 400-acre campus
- **Endowment** $2.0 billion
- **Coed** 16,159 undergraduate students, 90% full-time, 39% women, 61% men
- 21% of applicants were admitted

UNDERGRAD STUDENTS

14,503 full-time, 1,656 part-time. 30% are from out of state; 7% Black or African American, non-Hispanic/Latino; 7% Hispanic/Latino; 23% Asian, non-Hispanic/Latino; 4% Two or more races, non-Hispanic/Latino; 3% Race/ethnicity unknown; 10% international; 4% transferred in; 50% live on campus.

Freshmen:

Admission: 36,856 applied, 7,584 admitted, 3,076 enrolled. ***Average high school GPA:*** 4.1. ***Test scores:*** SAT evidence-based reading and writing scores over 500: 100%; SAT math scores over 500: 100%; ACT scores over 18: 100%; SAT evidence-based reading and writing scores over 600: 95%; SAT math scores over 600: 96%; ACT scores over 24: 97%; SAT evidence-based reading and writing scores over 700: 58%; SAT math scores over 700: 77%; ACT scores over 30: 83%.

Retention: 97% of full-time freshmen returned.

FACULTY

Total: 1,222, 86% full-time, 82% with terminal degrees.

Student/faculty ratio: 19:1.

ACADEMICS

Calendar: semesters. *Degrees:* bachelor's, master's, and doctoral.

Special study options: academic remediation for entering students, accelerated degree program, advanced placement credit, cooperative education, distance learning, double majors, English as a second language, honors programs, independent study, internships, off-campus study, part-time degree program, services for LD students, student-designed majors, study abroad, summer session for credit. ***ROTC:*** Army (b), Navy (b), Air Force (b).

Unusual degree programs: 3-2 engineering with Georgia Institute of Technology.

Computers: 2,500 computers/terminals and 22,981 ports are available on campus for general student use. Students can access the following: campus intranet, computer help desk, free student e-mail accounts, online (class) grades, online (class) registration, online (class) schedules, access to a virtual lab environment from a personal device or GT computer. Campuswide network is available. 100% of college-owned or -operated housing units are wired for high-speed Internet access. Wireless service is available via entire campus.

Library: Georgia Institute of Technology Library plus 1 other. *Books:* 909,730 (physical), 1.0 million (digital/electronic); *Serial titles:* 12,999 (physical), 29,621 (digital/electronic); *Databases:* 336. Weekly public service hours: 168; study areas open 24 hours, 5–7 days a week; students can reserve study rooms.

STUDENT LIFE

Housing options: coed, men-only, women-only, special housing for students with disabilities. Campus housing is university owned. Freshman campus housing is guaranteed.

Activities and organizations: drama/theater group, student-run newspaper, radio and television station, choral group, marching band, national fraternities, national sororities.

Athletics Member NCAA. All Division I. ***Intercollegiate sports:*** baseball M(s), basketball M(s)/W(s), cheerleading M(s)/W(s), cross-country running M(s)/W(s), football M(s), golf M(s), softball W(s), swimming and diving M(s)/W(s), tennis M(s)/W(s), track and field M(s)/W(s), volleyball W(s). ***Intramural sports:*** archery M(c)/W(c), badminton M(c)/W(c), baseball M(c)/W(c), basketball M/W, bowling M/W, crew M(c)/W(c), equestrian sports M(c)/W(c), fencing M(c)/W(c), field hockey M(c)/W(c), golf M(c)/W(c), gymnastics M(c)/W(c), ice hockey M(c)/W(c), lacrosse M(c)/W(c), racquetball M/W, rowing M(c)/W(c), rugby M(c)/W(c), sailing M(c)/W(c), soccer M/W, softball M, squash M(c)/W(c), swimming and diving M(c)/W(c), tennis M(c)/W(c), triathlon M(c)/W(c), ultimate Frisbee M(c)/W(c), volleyball M/W, water polo M(c)/W(c), weight lifting M(c), wrestling M(c).

Campus security: 24-hour emergency response devices and patrols, late-night transport/escort service, controlled dormitory access, lighted pathways/sidewalks, emergency notification system, self-defense education, emergency telephones, shuttle buses, video cameras.

Student services: health clinic, personal/psychological counseling, women's center, legal services, veterans affairs office.

COSTS & FINANCIAL AID

Costs (2020–21) ***Tuition:*** area resident $10,258 full-time, $3048 per credit hour part-time; state resident $10,258 full-time, $3048 per credit hour part-time; nonresident $31,370 full-time, $9308 per credit hour part-time. Part-time tuition and fees vary according to course load. ***Required fees:*** $2424 full-time. ***Room and board:*** $14,830; room only: $9658. Room and board charges vary according to board plan, housing facility, and student level. ***Payment plan:*** deferred payment. ***Waivers:*** senior citizens and employees or children of employees.

Financial Aid Of all full-time matriculated undergraduates who enrolled in 2018, 6,961 applied for aid, 4,469 were judged to have need, 1,144 had their need fully met. In 2018, 3137 non-need-based awards were made. ***Average percent of need met:*** 57. ***Average financial aid package:*** $14,292. ***Average need-based loan:*** $10,553. ***Average need-based gift aid:*** $12,474. ***Average non-need-based aid:*** $9794. ***Average indebtedness upon graduation:*** $31,545. ***Financial aid deadline:*** 7/1.

APPLYING

Standardized Tests *Required:* SAT or ACT (for admission).

Options: electronic application, early admission, early action, deferred entrance.

Application fee: $75.

CONTACT

Mr. Rick A. Clark Jr., Director of Undergraduate Admissions, Georgia Institute of Technology, Office of Undergraduate Admission, Atlanta, GA 30332-0320. *Phone:* 404-894-4154. *Fax:* 404-894-9511. *E-mail:* admission@gatech.edu.

Georgia Military College

Milledgeville, Georgia

http://www.gmc.edu/

CONTACT
Georgia Military College, 201 East Greene Street, Old Capitol Building, Milledgeville, GA 31061-3398. *Phone:* 478-387-4890. *Toll-free phone:* 800-342-0413.

Georgia Southern University

Statesboro, Georgia

http://www.georgiasouthern.edu/

- **State-supported** university, founded 1906, part of University System of Georgia
- **Small-town** 900-acre campus
- **Endowment** $47.7 million
- **Coed** 22,715 undergraduate students, 84% full-time, 56% women, 44% men
- **Moderately difficult** entrance level, 54% of applicants were admitted

UNDERGRAD STUDENTS
19,156 full-time, 3,559 part-time. Students come from 50 states and territories; 84 other countries; 7% are from out of state; 25% Black or African American, non-Hispanic/Latino; 7% Hispanic/Latino; 2% Asian, non-Hispanic/Latino; 0.1% Native Hawaiian or other Pacific Islander, non-Hispanic/Latino; 0.4% American Indian or Alaska Native, non-Hispanic/Latino; 4% Two or more races, non-Hispanic/Latino; 0.5% Race/ethnicity unknown; 1% international; 6% transferred in; 25% live on campus.

Freshmen:
Admission: 13,858 applied, 7,549 admitted, 4,260 enrolled. ***Average high school GPA:*** 3.4. ***Test scores:*** SAT evidence-based reading and writing scores over 500: 94%; SAT math scores over 500: 87%; ACT scores over 18: 97%; SAT evidence-based reading and writing scores over 600: 34%; SAT math scores over 600: 21%; ACT scores over 24: 37%; SAT evidence-based reading and writing scores over 700: 3%; SAT math scores over 700: 2%; ACT scores over 30: 5%.

Retention: 78% of full-time freshmen returned.

FACULTY
Total: 1,298, 81% full-time, 71% with terminal degrees.

Student/faculty ratio: 20:1.

ACADEMICS
Calendar: semesters. *Degrees:* certificates, bachelor's, master's, doctoral, post-master's, and postbachelor's certificates.

Special study options: academic remediation for entering students, accelerated degree program, adult/continuing education programs, advanced placement credit, cooperative education, distance learning, double majors, English as a second language, honors programs, independent study, internships, off-campus study, part-time degree program, services for LD students, student-designed majors, study abroad, summer session for credit. ***ROTC:*** Army (b).

Unusual degree programs: 3-2 engineering with Georgia Institute of Technology.

Computers: 3,743 computers/terminals and 5,200 ports are available on campus for general student use. Students can access the following: campus intranet, computer help desk, free student e-mail accounts, online (class) grades, online (class) registration, online (class) schedules, online degree audit, online career services, and online healthcare. Campuswide network is available. 100% of college-owned or -operated housing units are wired for high-speed Internet access. Wireless service is available via entire campus.

Library: Henderson Library. *Books:* 649,104 (physical), 656,518 (digital/electronic); *Serial titles:* 15,006 (physical), 104,711 (digital/electronic); *Databases:* 325. Weekly public service hours: 143; study areas open 24 hours, 5–7 days a week; students can reserve study rooms.

STUDENT LIFE
Housing options: on-campus residence required for freshman year; coed, special housing for students with disabilities. Campus housing is university owned. Freshman applicants given priority for college housing.

Activities and organizations: drama/theater group, student-run newspaper, radio station, choral group, marching band, Campus Crusade for Christ, Sigma Alpha Pi, Phi Eta Sigma, Gay-Straight Alliance, Geeks 'n' Gamers, national fraternities, national sororities.

Athletics Member NCAA. All Division I. ***Intercollegiate sports:*** baseball M(s), basketball M(s)/W(s), cheerleading M/W, cross-country running W(s), football M(s), golf M(s)/W(s)(c), riflery W(s), soccer M(s)/W(s), softball W(s), swimming and diving W(s), tennis M(s)/W(s), track and field W(s), volleyball W(s). ***Intramural sports:*** archery M/W, baseball M(c), basketball M/W, bowling M/W, cheerleading M(c)/W(c), cross-country running M(c)/W(c), equestrian sports M(c)/W(c), fencing M(c), field hockey W(c), football M/W, golf M/W, lacrosse M(c)/W(c), riflery M(c)/W(c), rugby M(c)/W(c), soccer M/W, softball M/W, swimming and diving M(c)/W(c), tennis M/W, track and field M(c)/W(c), ultimate Frisbee M/W, volleyball M/W, water polo M(c)/W(c), wrestling M(c).

Campus security: 24-hour emergency response devices and patrols, student patrols, late night transport/escort service, controlled dormitory access.

Student services: health clinic, personal/psychological counseling, women's center, legal services, veterans affairs office.

COSTS & FINANCIAL AID
Costs (2019–20) ***Tuition:*** state resident $5464 full-time, $182 per credit hour part-time; nonresident $19,282 full-time, $643 per credit hour part-time. Full-time tuition and fees vary according to course load, degree level, location, and program. Part-time tuition and fees vary according to course load, degree level, location, and program. ***Required fees:*** $2092 full-time, $1046 per term part-time. ***Room and board:*** $10,070; room only: $6320. Room and board charges vary according to board plan, housing facility, and location. ***Payment plan:*** installment. ***Waivers:*** senior citizens and employees or children of employees.

Financial Aid Of all full-time matriculated undergraduates who enrolled in 2017, 14,174 applied for aid, 10,074 were judged to have need, 1,205 had their need fully met. 214 Federal Work-Study jobs (averaging $1650). In 2017, 423 non-need-based awards were made. ***Average percent of need met:*** 57. ***Average financial aid package:*** $10,873. ***Average need-based loan:*** $5435. ***Average need-based gift aid:*** $7680. ***Average non-need-based aid:*** $1907. ***Average indebtedness upon graduation:*** $29,030.

APPLYING
Standardized Tests *Required:* SAT or ACT (for admission).

Options: electronic application, early admission, deferred entrance.

Application fee: $30.

Required: minimum 2.5 GPA. ***Required for some:*** high school transcript.

Application deadlines: 5/1 (freshmen), 5/1 (out-of-state freshmen), 8/1 (transfers).

Notification: continuous (freshmen), continuous (out-of-state freshmen), continuous (transfers).

CONTACT
Dr. Amy Clines, Director - Undergraduate Admissions, Georgia Southern University, PO Box 8024, Statesboro, GA 30460. *Phone:* 912-478-5391. *Fax:* 912-478-7240. *E-mail:* admissions@georgiasouthern.edu.

Georgia Southern University–Armstrong Campus

Savannah, Georgia

http://www.georgiasouthern.edu/

CONTACT
Amy Smither, Director of Admissions, Georgia Southern University–Armstrong Campus, 11935 Abercorn Street, Savannah, GA 31419. *Phone:* 912-478-5391. *Toll-free phone:* 800-633-2349. *Fax:* 912-344-3417. *E-mail:* amysmith@georgiasouthern.com.

Georgia Southwestern State University

Americus, Georgia

http://www.gsw.edu/

CONTACT

Mr. David Jenkins, Assistant Director of Admissions, Georgia Southwestern State University, Americus, GA 31709. *Phone:* 229-928-1273. *Toll-free phone:* 800-338-0082. *Fax:* 229-931-2983. *E-mail:* admissions@gsw.edu.

Georgia State University

Atlanta, Georgia

http://www.gsu.edu/

- **State-supported** university, founded 1913, part of University System of Georgia
- **Urban** 109-acre campus with easy access to Atlanta
- **Endowment** $178.8 million
- **Coed** 27,969 undergraduate students, 79% full-time, 59% women, 41% men
- **Moderately difficult** entrance level, 57% of applicants were admitted

UNDERGRAD STUDENTS

21,978 full-time, 5,991 part-time. Students come from 53 states and territories; 144 other countries; 5% are from out of state; 41% Black or African American, non-Hispanic/Latino; 12% Hispanic/Latino; 15% Asian, non-Hispanic/Latino; 0.1% Native Hawaiian or other Pacific Islander, non-Hispanic/Latino; 0.1% American Indian or Alaska Native, non-Hispanic/Latino; 6% Two or more races, non-Hispanic/Latino; 0.6% Race/ethnicity unknown; 3% international; 6% transferred in; 21% live on campus.

Freshmen:

Admission: 20,949 applied, 12,028 admitted, 5,018 enrolled. ***Average high school GPA:*** 3.5. ***Test scores:*** SAT evidence-based reading and writing scores over 500: 81%; SAT math scores over 500: 69%; ACT scores over 18: 94%; SAT evidence-based reading and writing scores over 600: 21%; SAT math scores over 600: 26%; ACT scores over 24: 46%; SAT evidence-based reading and writing scores over 700: 3%; SAT math scores over 700: 5%; ACT scores over 30: 10%.

Retention: 80% of full-time freshmen returned.

FACULTY

Total: 1,608, 73% full-time, 82% with terminal degrees.

Student/faculty ratio: 26:1.

ACADEMICS

Calendar: semesters. *Degrees:* certificates, associate, bachelor's, master's, doctoral, post-master's, and postbachelor's certificates.

Special study options: advanced placement credit, cooperative education, distance learning, double majors, English as a second language, honors programs, independent study, internships, part-time degree program, services for LD students, study abroad, summer session for credit. ***ROTC:*** Army (b), Navy (c), Air Force (c).

Computers: 2,059 computers/terminals and 25,443 ports are available on campus for general student use. Students can access the following: computer help desk, free student e-mail accounts, online (class) grades, online (class) registration, online (class) schedules. Campuswide network is available. 100% of college-owned or -operated housing units are wired for high-speed Internet access. Wireless service is available via entire campus.

Library: University Library plus 6 others. *Books:* 1.9 million (physical), 1.3 million (digital/electronic); *Serial titles:* 36,191 (physical), 246,459 (digital/electronic). Students can reserve study rooms.

STUDENT LIFE

Housing options: coed, special housing for students with disabilities. Campus housing is university owned. Freshman applicants given priority for college housing.

Activities and organizations: drama/theater group, student-run newspaper, radio and television station, choral group, marching band, Spotlight Programs Board, Fraternities/Sororities, Service Organizations, Academic Organizations, Sports Clubs, national fraternities, national sororities.

Athletics Member NCAA. All Division I. ***Intercollegiate sports:*** baseball M(s), basketball M(s)/W(s), cross-country running W(s), football M(s), golf M(s)/W(s)(c), sand volleyball W(s), soccer M(s)/W(s), softball W(s), table tennis M(c)/W(c), tennis M(s)/W(s), track and field W(s), ultimate Frisbee M(c)/W(c), volleyball M(c)/W(s). ***Intramural sports:*** badminton M(c)/W(c), basketball M/W, bowling M/W, crew M(c)/W(c), equestrian sports M(c)/W(c), fencing M(c)/W(c), football M/W, golf M/W, ice hockey M(c)/W(c), lacrosse M(c)/W(c), racquetball M/W, rock climbing M(c)/W(c), rowing M(c)/W(c), rugby M(c), sand volleyball M/W, soccer M/W, softball M/W, swimming and diving M(c)/W(c), table tennis M/W, tennis M(c)/W(c), ultimate Frisbee M/W, volleyball M/W, wrestling M(c)/W(c).

Campus security: 24-hour emergency response devices and patrols, late-night transport/escort service, controlled dormitory access.

Student services: health clinic, personal/psychological counseling.

COSTS & FINANCIAL AID

Costs (2020–21) ***Tuition:*** area resident $8948 full-time, $298 per credit hour part-time; state resident $8948 full-time, $298 per credit hour part-time; nonresident $27,986 full-time, $933 per credit hour part-time. Part-time tuition and fees vary according to course load. ***Required fees:*** $1064 per term part-time. ***Room and board:*** $14,958; room only: $11,090. Room and board charges vary according to board plan and housing facility. ***Waivers:*** senior citizens and employees or children of employees.

Financial Aid Of all full-time matriculated undergraduates who enrolled in 2018, 24,784 applied for aid, 21,049 were judged to have need, 1,123 had their need fully met. ***Average percent of need met:*** 55. ***Average financial aid package:*** $10,976. ***Average need-based gift aid:*** $5607. ***Average indebtedness upon graduation:*** $28,864.

APPLYING

Standardized Tests *Required:* SAT or ACT (for admission).

Options: electronic application, early admission, early action, deferred entrance.

Application fee: $60.

Required: high school transcript, minimum 2.8 GPA, college preparatory curriculum as specified by the University System of Georgia Board of Regents, combined SAT of 830, minimum Freshman Index of 2500. ***Recommended:*** essay or personal statement, 1 letter of recommendation.

Application deadlines: 3/1 (freshmen), 3/1 (out-of-state freshmen), 8/1 (transfers), 11/15 (early action).

Notification: 4/15 (freshmen), 4/15 (out-of-state freshmen), continuous (transfers), 12/15 (early action).

CONTACT

Scott Burke, Assistant Vice President for Undergraduate Admissions, Georgia State University, PO Box 4009, Atlanta, GA 30302-4009. *Phone:* 404-413-2500. *Fax:* 404-413-2002. *E-mail:* onestopshop@gsu.edu.

Gordon State College

Barnesville, Georgia

http://www.gordonstate.edu/

CONTACT

Gordon State College, 419 College Drive, Barnesville, GA 30204-1762. *Phone:* 678-359-5021. *Toll-free phone:* 800-282-6504.

Herzing University

Atlanta, Georgia

http://www.herzing.edu/atlanta/

CONTACT

Herzing University, 3393 Peachtree Road, NE, Suite 1003, Atlanta, GA 30326. *Toll-free phone:* 800-596-0724.

Kennesaw State University

Kennesaw, Georgia

http://www.kennesaw.edu/

- **State-supported** comprehensive, founded 1963, part of University System of Georgia
- **Suburban** 602-acre campus with easy access to Atlanta
- **Endowment** $40.3 million
- **Coed** 34,499 undergraduate students, 75% full-time, 48% women, 52% men
- **Moderately difficult** entrance level, 75% of applicants were admitted

UNDERGRAD STUDENTS

25,745 full-time, 8,754 part-time. 22% Black or African American, non-Hispanic/Latino; 12% Hispanic/Latino; 5% Asian, non-Hispanic/Latino; 0.1% Native Hawaiian or other Pacific Islander, non-Hispanic/Latino; 0.1% American Indian or Alaska Native, non-Hispanic/Latino; 5% Two or more races, non-Hispanic/Latino; 2% Race/ethnicity unknown; 2% international; 7% transferred in; 15% live on campus.

Freshmen:

Admission: 15,691 applied, 11,803 admitted, 6,533 enrolled. ***Average high school GPA:*** 3.4. ***Test scores:*** SAT evidence-based reading and writing scores over 500: 92%; SAT math scores over 500: 87%; ACT scores over 18: 95%; SAT evidence-based reading and writing scores over 600: 39%; SAT math scores over 600: 30%; ACT scores over 24: 43%; SAT evidence-based reading and writing scores over 700: 4%; SAT math scores over 700: 5%; ACT scores over 30: 8%.

Retention: 80% of full-time freshmen returned.

FACULTY

Total: 1,942, 63% full-time, 65% with terminal degrees.

Student/faculty ratio: 21:1.

ACADEMICS

Calendar: semesters. *Degrees:* certificates, bachelor's, master's, doctoral, post-master's, and postbachelor's certificates.

Special study options: adult/continuing education programs, advanced placement credit, cooperative education, distance learning, double majors, English as a second language, freshman honors college, honors programs, internships, off-campus study, part-time degree program, services for LD students, study abroad, summer session for credit. ***ROTC:*** Army (c), Navy (c), Air Force (c).

Computers: 4,500 computers/terminals and 38,000 ports are available on campus for general student use. Students can access the following: campus intranet, computer help desk, free student e-mail accounts, online (class) grades, online (class) registration, online (class) schedules. Campuswide network is available. 100% of college-owned or -operated housing units are wired for high-speed Internet access. Wireless service is available via classrooms, computer centers, computer labs, dorm rooms, learning centers, libraries, student centers.

Library: Kennesaw State University Library System plus 2 others. *Books:* 378,276 (physical), 656,005 (digital/electronic); *Serial titles:* 1,273 (physical), 115,672 (digital/electronic); *Databases:* 476. Students can reserve study rooms.

STUDENT LIFE

Housing options: Campus housing is university owned. Freshman applicants given priority for college housing.

Activities and organizations: drama/theater group, student-run newspaper, radio station, choral group, marching band, Kennesaw Activities Board, African American Student Alliance, International Student Association, KSU eSports Organization, IEEE Computer Society, national fraternities, national sororities.

Athletics Member NCAA. All Division I. ***Intercollegiate sports:*** baseball M(s), basketball M(s)/W(s), cross-country running M(s)/W(s), football M(s), golf M(s)/W(s), lacrosse W(s), soccer W(s), softball W(s), tennis M(s)/W(s), track and field M(s)/W(s), volleyball W(s). ***Intramural sports:*** archery M(c)/W(c), badminton M, baseball M(c), basketball M/W, bowling M/W, cross-country running M(c)/W(c), equestrian sports W(c), fencing M(c)/W(c), field hockey W(c), football M/W, golf M/W, gymnastics M(c)/W(c), ice hockey M(c), lacrosse M(c)/W(c), racquetball M/W, rugby M(c)/W(c), sand volleyball M/W, soccer M/W, softball M/W, swimming and diving M(c)/W(c), table tennis M(c)/W(c), tennis M/W, ultimate Frisbee M(c)/W(c), volleyball M(c)/W(c), water polo M(c)/W(c).

Campus security: 24-hour emergency response devices and patrols, student patrols, late-night transport/escort service, controlled dormitory access.

Student services: health clinic, personal/psychological counseling, veterans affairs office.

FINANCIAL AID

Financial Aid Of all full-time matriculated undergraduates who enrolled in 2019, 21,393 applied for aid, 17,991 were judged to have need, 916 had their need fully met. In 2019, 97 non-need-based awards were made. ***Average percent of need met:*** 42. ***Average financial aid package:*** $11,585. ***Average need-based loan:*** $4050. ***Average need-based gift aid:*** $7250. ***Average non-need-based aid:*** $1608. ***Average indebtedness upon graduation:*** $26,009. ***Financial aid deadline:*** 6/1.

APPLYING

Standardized Tests *Required:* SAT or ACT (for admission), (for admission).

Options: electronic application, deferred entrance.

Application fee: $40.

Required: high school transcript, minimum 2.5 GPA.

Application deadlines: 5/3 (freshmen), 5/3 (out-of-state freshmen), 6/14 (transfers).

Notification: continuous until 12/1 (freshmen), 12/1 (out-of-state freshmen).

CONTACT

Kennesaw State University, 1000 Chastain Road, Kennesaw, GA 30144. *Phone:* 770-578-2548.

LaGrange College

LaGrange, Georgia

http://www.lagrange.edu/

- **Independent United Methodist** comprehensive, founded 1831
- **Small-town** 120-acre campus with easy access to Atlanta
- **Endowment** $53.0 million
- **Coed** 872 undergraduate students, 97% full-time, 49% women, 51% men
- **Moderately difficult** entrance level, 49% of applicants were admitted

UNDERGRAD STUDENTS

847 full-time, 25 part-time. Students come from 17 states and territories; 6 other countries; 17% are from out of state; 22% Black or African American, non-Hispanic/Latino; 2% Hispanic/Latino; 1% Asian, non-Hispanic/Latino; 0.6% American Indian or Alaska Native, non-Hispanic/Latino; 2% Two or more races, non-Hispanic/Latino; 0.2% Race/ethnicity unknown; 0.8% international; 8% transferred in; 63% live on campus.

Freshmen:

Admission: 1,686 applied, 823 admitted, 200 enrolled. ***Average high school GPA:*** 3.5. ***Test scores:*** SAT evidence-based reading and writing scores over 500: 79%; SAT math scores over 500: 77%; ACT scores over 18: 94%; SAT evidence-based reading and writing scores over 600: 19%; SAT math scores over 600: 18%; ACT scores over 24: 23%; SAT evidence-based reading and writing scores over 700: 3%; SAT math scores over 700: 1%; ACT scores over 30: 2%.

Retention: 70% of full-time freshmen returned.

FACULTY

Total: 112, 67% full-time, 62% with terminal degrees.

Student/faculty ratio: 11:1.

ACADEMICS

Calendar: 4-1-4. *Degrees:* bachelor's and master's.

Special study options: accelerated degree program, adult/continuing education programs, advanced placement credit, distance learning, double majors, independent study, internships, part-time degree program, services for LD students, student-designed majors, study abroad, summer session for credit.

Unusual degree programs: 3-2 engineering with Georgia Institute of Technology, Auburn University.

Computers: 116 computers/terminals and 960 ports are available on campus for general student use. Students can access the following: campus intranet, free student e-mail accounts, online (class) grades, online

(class) registration, online (class) schedules. Campuswide network is available. 100% of college-owned or -operated housing units are wired for high-speed Internet access. Wireless service is available via entire campus.
Library: Frank and Laura Lewis Library. *Books:* 84,237 (physical), 420,923 (digital/electronic); *Serial titles:* 21 (physical), 24 (digital/electronic); *Databases:* 302. Weekly public service hours: 80; study areas open 24 hours, 5–7 days a week; students can reserve study rooms.

STUDENT LIFE

Housing options: on-campus residence required through senior year; coed, men-only, women-only, special housing for students with disabilities. Campus housing is university owned. Freshman campus housing is guaranteed.

Activities and organizations: drama/theater group, student-run newspaper, choral group, marching band, Campus Circle, LC Miracle, Panhellenic (Sorority Leadership), Black Student Union, Student Government, national fraternities, national sororities.

Athletics Member NCAA. All Division III. ***Intercollegiate sports:*** baseball M, basketball M/W, cheerleading W, cross-country running M/W, football M, golf M, lacrosse M/W, sand volleyball W, soccer M/W, softball W, swimming and diving M/W, tennis M/W, volleyball W. ***Intramural sports:*** basketball M/W, softball M/W, table tennis M/W, water polo M/W.

Campus security: 24-hour patrols, controlled dormitory access, mass notification system (e2Campus) to send emergency messages to students and employees.

Student services: health clinic, personal/psychological counseling.

COSTS & FINANCIAL AID

Costs (2019–20) ***One-time required fee:*** $150. ***Comprehensive fee:*** $43,510 includes full-time tuition ($31,200), mandatory fees ($340), and room and board ($11,970). Full-time tuition and fees vary according to class time, course load, degree level, and program. Part-time tuition: $1285 per semester hour. Part-time tuition and fees vary according to class time, course load, degree level, and program. ***College room only:*** $6430. Room and board charges vary according to board plan and housing facility. ***Payment plan:*** installment. ***Waivers:*** senior citizens and employees or children of employees.

Financial Aid Of all full-time matriculated undergraduates who enrolled in 2019, 819 applied for aid, 752 were judged to have need, 117 had their need fully met. In 2019, 79 non-need-based awards were made. ***Average percent of need met:*** 81. ***Average financial aid package:*** $27,550. ***Average need-based loan:*** $4136. ***Average need-based gift aid:*** $5785. ***Average non-need-based aid:*** $12,870. ***Average indebtedness upon graduation:*** $37,680. ***Financial aid deadline:*** 5/1.

APPLYING

Standardized Tests *Required:* SAT or ACT (for admission). *Required for some:* SAT (for admission), ACT (for admission).

Options: electronic application, deferred entrance.

Required: essay or personal statement, high school transcript. ***Required for some:*** minimum 2.5 GPA, 3 letters of recommendation, interview.

Application deadlines: rolling (freshmen), rolling (transfers).

Notification: continuous (freshmen), continuous (transfers).

CONTACT

Ms. Holly Phillips, Administrative Coordinator, LaGrange College, 601 Broad Street, LaGrange, GA 30240-2999. *Phone:* 706-880-8005. *Toll-free phone:* 800-593-2885. *Fax:* 706-880-8010. *E-mail:* hphillips@lagrange.edu.

Life University

Marietta, Georgia

http://www.life.edu/

- **Independent** comprehensive, founded 1974
- **Suburban** 96-acre campus with easy access to Atlanta Metro
- **Coed** 880 undergraduate students, 83% full-time, 54% women, 46% men
- **Minimally difficult** entrance level, 96% of applicants were admitted

UNDERGRAD STUDENTS

730 full-time, 150 part-time. 69% are from out of state; 27% Black or African American, non-Hispanic/Latino; 13% Hispanic/Latino; 3% Asian, non-Hispanic/Latino; 1% American Indian or Alaska Native, non-Hispanic/Latino; 3% Race/ethnicity unknown; 11% international; 14% transferred in; 23% live on campus.

Freshmen:
Admission: 364 applied, 348 admitted, 136 enrolled. ***Average high school GPA:*** 3.1. ***Test scores:*** SAT evidence-based reading and writing scores over 500: 57%; SAT math scores over 500: 52%; ACT scores over 18: 53%; SAT evidence-based reading and writing scores over 600: 11%; SAT math scores over 600: 12%; ACT scores over 24: 23%; SAT math scores over 700: 1%; ACT scores over 30: 1%.

Retention: 65% of full-time freshmen returned.

FACULTY

Total: 94, 44% full-time, 56% with terminal degrees.

Student/faculty ratio: 13:1.

ACADEMICS

Calendar: quarters. *Degrees:* certificates, associate, bachelor's, master's, and doctoral.

Special study options: academic remediation for entering students, accelerated degree program, advanced placement credit, cooperative education, distance learning, double majors, English as a second language, independent study, internships, off-campus study, part-time degree program, services for LD students, student-designed majors, study abroad, summer session for credit.

Computers: Students can access the following: campus intranet, computer help desk, free student e-mail accounts, online (class) grades, online (class) registration. Campuswide network is available. 100% of college-owned or -operated housing units are wired for high-speed Internet access. Wireless service is available via entire campus.
Library: Library & Learning Services. *Books:* 33,771 (physical), 39,225 (digital/electronic); *Serial titles:* 66 (physical), 31,104 (digital/electronic); *Databases:* 25. Weekly public service hours: 98; students can reserve study rooms.

STUDENT LIFE

Housing options: coed. Campus housing is university owned.

Activities and organizations: student-run newspaper, Student Ambassadors, Campus Activities Board, League of Chiropractic Women, Functional Neurology Club, Hispanic Club.

Athletics Member NAIA. ***Intercollegiate sports:*** basketball M(s)/W(s), bowling M(s)/W, cheerleading M/W, cross-country running W(s), ice hockey M(s), lacrosse W(s), rugby M(s)/W(s), soccer M(s)/W(s), swimming and diving W(s), track and field W(s), volleyball W(s), wrestling M(s)/W(s). ***Intramural sports:*** basketball M/W, cross-country running M/W, rugby M/W, soccer M, softball M/W, table tennis M, tennis M/W, volleyball M/W, weight lifting M/W.

Campus security: 24-hour emergency response devices and patrols, controlled dormitory access.

Student services: health clinic, personal/psychological counseling.

COSTS & FINANCIAL AID

Costs (2019–20) ***Comprehensive fee:*** $27,501 includes full-time tuition ($11,610), mandatory fees ($1491), and room and board ($14,400). Full-time tuition and fees vary according to course load. Part-time tuition: $295 per credit hour. ***Room and board:*** Room and board charges vary according to housing facility. ***Payment plan:*** installment. ***Waivers:*** employees or children of employees.

Financial Aid Of all full-time matriculated undergraduates who enrolled in 2019, 569 applied for aid, 526 were judged to have need, 3 had their need fully met. In 2019, 2 non-need-based awards were made. ***Average percent of need met:*** 36. ***Average financial aid package:*** $12,500. ***Average need-based loan:*** $4250. ***Average need-based gift aid:*** $5800. ***Average non-need-based aid:*** $3750. ***Average indebtedness upon graduation:*** $26,000.

APPLYING

Standardized Tests *Required:* SAT or ACT (for admission).

Options: electronic application, deferred entrance.

Application fee: $50.

Required: high school transcript, minimum 2.0 GPA.

Notification: continuous (freshmen), continuous (transfers).

CONTACT

Cynthia Boyd, Vice President Enrollment Management and Marketing, Life University, 1269 Barclay Circle, Marietta, GA 30060. *Phone:* 770-426-2756. *Toll-free phone:* 800-543-3202. *Fax:* 770-426-2895.

Luther Rice College & Seminary

Lithonia, Georgia

http://www.lutherrice.edu/

CONTACT

Laura Powell, Admissions Associate, Luther Rice College & Seminary, 3038 Evans Mill Road, Lithonia, GA 30038. *Phone:* 770-484-1204 Ext. 5278. *Toll-free phone:* 800-442-1577. *Fax:* 770-484-1155. *E-mail:* admissions@lutherrice.edu.

Mercer University

Macon, Georgia

http://www.mercer.edu/

- **Independent Baptist** university, founded 1833
- **Urban** 150-acre campus
- **Coed** 3,949 undergraduate students, 98% full-time, 61% women, 39% men
- **Very difficult** entrance level, 74% of applicants were admitted

UNDERGRAD STUDENTS

3,882 full-time, 67 part-time. Students come from 38 states and territories; 33 other countries; 16% are from out of state; 20% Black or African American, non-Hispanic/Latino; 7% Hispanic/Latino; 10% Asian, non-Hispanic/Latino; 0.2% American Indian or Alaska Native, non-Hispanic/Latino; 4% Two or more races, non-Hispanic/Latino; 3% Race/ethnicity unknown; 2% international; 2% transferred in; 78% live on campus.

Freshmen:

Admission: 5,034 applied, 3,736 admitted, 900 enrolled. ***Average high school GPA:*** 3.9. ***Test scores:*** SAT evidence-based reading and writing scores over 500: 99%; SAT math scores over 500: 99%; ACT scores over 18: 100%; SAT evidence-based reading and writing scores over 600: 72%; SAT math scores over 600: 64%; ACT scores over 24: 85%; SAT evidence-based reading and writing scores over 700: 17%; SAT math scores over 700: 17%; ACT scores over 30: 30%.

Retention: 86% of full-time freshmen returned.

FACULTY

Total: 782, 51% full-time, 77% with terminal degrees.

Student/faculty ratio: 13:1.

ACADEMICS

Calendar: semesters. *Degrees:* certificates, bachelor's, master's, doctoral, post-master's, and postbachelor's certificates.

Special study options: accelerated degree program, adult/continuing education programs, advanced placement credit, cooperative education, distance learning, double majors, English as a second language, honors programs, independent study, internships, off-campus study, part-time degree program, services for LD students, student-designed majors, study abroad, summer session for credit. ***ROTC:*** Army (b).

Unusual degree programs: 3-2 engineering; nursing; pharmacy, physical therapy, physicians assistant.

Computers: Students can access the following: campus intranet, computer help desk, free student e-mail accounts, online (class) grades, online (class) registration, online (class) schedules. Campuswide network is available. 100% of college-owned or -operated housing units are wired for high-speed Internet access. Wireless service is available via entire campus.

Library: Jack Tarver Library plus 3 others. Study areas open 24 hours, 5–7 days a week; students can reserve study rooms.

STUDENT LIFE

Housing options: on-campus residence required through junior year; coed, men-only, women-only, special housing for students with disabilities. Campus housing is university owned. Freshman campus housing is guaranteed.

Activities and organizations: drama/theater group, student-run newspaper, choral group, marching band, national fraternities, national sororities.

Athletics Member NCAA. All Division I. ***Intercollegiate sports:*** baseball M(s), basketball M(s)/W(s), cross-country running M(s)/W(s), football M(s), golf M(s)/W(s), lacrosse M(s)/W(s), sand volleyball W(s), soccer M(s)/W(s), softball W(s), tennis M(s)/W(s), track and field W(s), volleyball W(s). ***Intramural sports:*** baseball M, cheerleading M/W, fencing M/W, golf M/W, lacrosse M(c), soccer M(c)/W(c), swimming and diving M(c)/W(c), table tennis M/W, tennis M/W.

Campus security: 24-hour emergency response devices and patrols, student patrols, late-night transport/escort service, controlled dormitory access.

Student services: health clinic, personal/psychological counseling.

FINANCIAL AID

Financial Aid Of all full-time matriculated undergraduates who enrolled in 2019, 2,783 applied for aid, 2,247 were judged to have need, 924 had their need fully met. In 2019, 1029 non-need-based awards were made. ***Average percent of need met.*** 05. ***Average financial aid package:*** $37,583. ***Average need-based loan:*** $10,951. ***Average need-based gift aid:*** $26,745. ***Average non-need-based aid:*** $20,027. ***Average indebtedness upon graduation:*** $27,949.

APPLYING

Standardized Tests *Required:* SAT or ACT (for admission).

Options: electronic application, early action, deferred entrance.

Application fee: $50.

Required: essay or personal statement, high school transcript, minimum 3.3 GPA, 1 letter of recommendation. ***Recommended:*** interview.

Application deadlines: 7/1 (freshmen), rolling (transfers), 2/1 (early action).

Notification: continuous (freshmen), continuous (transfers), rolling (early action).

CONTACT

Jena Palmer, Interim Director of Freshman Admissions, Mercer University, 1501 Mercer University Drive, Macon, GA 31207-0003. *Phone:* 478-301-2316. *Toll-free phone:* 800-MERCER-U. *Fax:* 478-301-2828. *E-mail:* palmer_jc@mercer.edu.

Middle Georgia State University

Macon, Georgia

http://www.mga.edu/

- **State-supported** comprehensive, founded 2015, part of University System of Georgia
- **Urban** 419-acre campus with easy access to Atlanta
- **Endowment** $874,853
- **Coed**
- **Minimally difficult** entrance level

FACULTY

Student/faculty ratio: 19:1.

ACADEMICS

Calendar: semesters. *Degrees:* certificates, associate, bachelor's, master's, and postbachelor's certificates.

Library: Macon State University Library. *Books:* 125,996 (physical), 246,646 (digital/electronic); *Serial titles:* 85 (physical), 51,575 (digital/electronic); *Databases:* 138. Weekly public service hours: 23; students can reserve study rooms.

STUDENT LIFE

Housing options: on-campus residence required for freshman year; coed. Campus housing is university owned.

Activities and organizations: drama/theater group, student-run newspaper, television station, choral group, marching band, Brothers of Leadership and Distinction (BOLD), Middle Georgia State Association of Nursing Students (MGSANS), Black Student Unification (BSU), Student Government Association (SGA), International Students and Studies Association (ISSA), national fraternities, national sororities.

Athletics Member NAIA.

Campus security: 24-hour emergency response devices and patrols, late-night transport/escort service.

Student services: health clinic, personal/psychological counseling, veterans affairs office.

COSTS

Costs (2019–20) ***One-time required fee:*** $25. ***Tuition:*** state resident $2725 full-time, $114 per credit hour part-time; nonresident $10,075 full-time, $420 per credit hour part-time. Full-time tuition and fees vary according to location and program. Part-time tuition and fees vary according to location and program. ***Required fees:*** $1314 full-time, $414 per credit hour part-time. ***Room and board:*** $8260; room only: $4910. Room and board charges vary according to board plan, housing facility, and location.

APPLYING

Standardized Tests *Required:* SAT or ACT (for admission).

Options: electronic application, early admission.

Application fee: $30.

Required: high school transcript, minimum 2.0 GPA.

CONTACT

Middle Georgia State University, 100 University Parkway, Macon, GA 31206. *Toll-free phone:* 877-238-8664.

Morehouse College

Atlanta, Georgia

http://www.morehouse.edu/

- **Independent** 4-year, founded 1867
- **Urban** 66-acre campus with easy access to Atlanta, Georgia
- **Men only**
- **Moderately difficult** entrance level

FACULTY

Student/faculty ratio: 14:1.

ACADEMICS

Calendar: semesters. *Degree:* bachelor's.
Library: Atlanta University Center Robert R. Woodruff Library. Students can reserve study rooms.

STUDENT LIFE

Housing options: on-campus residence required through junior year; men-only. Campus housing is university owned. Freshman campus housing is guaranteed.

Activities and organizations: drama/theater group, student-run newspaper, choral group, marching band, Morehouse College Glee Club, Morehouse Business Association, SGA, Morehouse Public Health Association, Pre-Law Society, national fraternities.

Athletics Member NCAA. All Division II.

Campus security: 24-hour patrols, late-night transport/escort service, controlled dormitory access, emergency call boxes, safety tips and awareness training.

Student services: health clinic, personal/psychological counseling.

FINANCIAL AID

Financial Aid Of all full-time matriculated undergraduates who enrolled in 2017, 1,956 applied for aid, 1,712 were judged to have need. In 2017, 24 non-need-based awards were made. ***Average financial aid package:*** $23,565. ***Average need-based loan:*** $4349. ***Average need-based gift aid:*** $20,851. ***Average non-need-based aid:*** $28,810. ***Average indebtedness upon graduation:*** $31,833. ***Financial aid deadline:*** 4/1.

APPLYING

Standardized Tests *Required:* SAT or ACT (for admission). *Recommended:* SAT and SAT Subject Tests or ACT (for admission).

Options: electronic application, early admission, deferred entrance.

Application fee: $50.

Required: essay or personal statement, high school transcript, interview. ***Recommended:*** minimum 3.0 GPA.

CONTACT

Morehouse College, 830 Westview Drive, SW, Atlanta, GA 30314. *Phone:* 470-639-0391. *Toll-free phone:* 800-851-1254.

Oglethorpe University

Atlanta, Georgia

http://www.oglethorpe.edu/

- **Independent** 4-year, founded 1835
- **Suburban** 102-acre campus with easy access to Atlanta
- **Endowment** $34.3 million
- **Coed** 1,385 undergraduate students, 96% full-time, 59% women, 41% men
- **Very difficult** entrance level, 68% of applicants were admitted

UNDERGRAD STUDENTS

1,329 full-time, 56 part-time. 27% are from out of state; 24% Black or African American, non-Hispanic/Latino; 13% Hispanic/Latino; 5% Asian, non-Hispanic/Latino; 0.8% American Indian or Alaska Native, non-Hispanic/Latino; 0.7% Two or more races, non-Hispanic/Latino; 4% Race/ethnicity unknown; 9% international; 4% transferred in; 55% live on campus.

Freshmen:

Admission: 2,327 applied, 1,572 admitted, 400 enrolled. ***Average high school GPA:*** 3.7. ***Test scores:*** SAT evidence-based reading and writing scores over 500: 98%; SAT math scores over 500: 96%; ACT scores over 18: 99%; SAT evidence-based reading and writing scores over 600: 67%; SAT math scores over 600: 39%; ACT scores over 24: 67%; SAT evidence-based reading and writing scores over 700: 11%; SAT math scores over 700: 8%; ACT scores over 30: 17%.

Retention: 80% of full-time freshmen returned.

FACULTY

Total: 119, 61% full-time, 82% with terminal degrees.

Student/faculty ratio: 15:1.

ACADEMICS

Calendar: semesters. *Degree:* bachelor's.

Special study options: accelerated degree program, adult/continuing education programs, advanced placement credit, cooperative education, double majors, honors programs, independent study, internships, off-campus study, part-time degree program, services for LD students, student-designed majors, study abroad, summer session for credit. ***ROTC:*** Army (c), Navy (c), Air Force (c).

Unusual degree programs: 3-2 engineering.

Computers: 65 computers/terminals and 500 ports are available on campus for general student use. Students can access the following: campus intranet, computer help desk, free student e-mail accounts, online (class) grades, online (class) registration, online (class) schedules. Campuswide network is available. Wireless service is available via entire campus.
Library: Philip Weltner Library. *Books:* 129,876 (physical), 936,821 (digital/electronic); *Serial titles:* 278 (physical), 27,589 (digital/electronic); *Databases:* 308. Weekly public service hours: 81; study areas open 24 hours, 5–7 days a week.

STUDENT LIFE

Housing options: on-campus residence required through sophomore year; coed. Campus housing is university owned. Freshman campus housing is guaranteed.

Activities and organizations: drama/theater group, student-run newspaper, choral group, SGA, Oglethorpe South Asian Club (OSAC), Historical Martial Arts (HMA), Oglethorpe Latinx Organization ((H)OLA), mOUthing Off Improv, national fraternities, national sororities.

Athletics Member NCAA. All Division III. ***Intercollegiate sports:*** baseball M, basketball M/W, cross-country running M/W, golf M/W, lacrosse M/W, soccer M/W, tennis M/W, track and field M/W, volleyball W. ***Intramural sports:*** badminton M/W, basketball M/W, football M/W, lacrosse M/W, softball M/W, table tennis M/W, tennis M/W, volleyball M/W.

Campus security: 24-hour emergency response devices and patrols, late-night transport/escort service, controlled dormitory access.

Student services: health clinic, personal/psychological counseling.

COSTS & FINANCIAL AID

Costs (2020–21) ***Comprehensive fee:*** $55,210 includes full-time tuition ($41,130), mandatory fees ($280), and room and board ($13,800). Part-

time tuition: $1713 per credit hour. ***Room and board:*** Room and board charges vary according to housing facility. ***Payment plan:*** installment. ***Waivers:*** employees or children of employees.

Financial Aid Of all full-time matriculated undergraduates who enrolled in 2019, 1,050 applied for aid, 941 were judged to have need, 172 had their need fully met. In 2019, 387 non-need-based awards were made. ***Average percent of need met:*** 77. ***Average financial aid package:*** $34,660. ***Average need-based loan:*** $4052. ***Average need-based gift aid:*** $29,759. ***Average non-need-based aid:*** $24,292. ***Average indebtedness upon graduation:*** $35,732.

APPLYING
Standardized Tests *Required:* SAT or ACT (for admission).

Options: electronic application, early decision, early action, deferred entrance.

Application fee: $50.

Required: essay or personal statement, high school transcript, 1 letter of recommendation. ***Recommended:*** minimum 2.5 GPA, interview.

Application deadlines: rolling (freshmen), rolling (out-of-state freshmen), rolling (transfers), 11/15 (early action).

Notification: continuous (freshmen), continuous (transfers), rolling (early action).

CONTACT
Lucy Leusch, Vice President for Enrollment and Financial Aid, Oglethorpe University, 4484 Peachtree Road NE, Atlanta, GA 30319. *Phone:* 404-3648309. *Toll-free phone:* 800-428-4484. *E-mail:* lleusch@oglethorpe.edu.

Paine College

Augusta, Georgia

http://www.paine.edu/

CONTACT
Mr. R. Wayne Woodson, Dean of Students, Paine College, 1235 15th Street, Augusta, GA 30901-3182. *Phone:* 706-821-8320. *Toll-free phone:* 800-476-7703. *Fax:* 706-821-8691. *E-mail:* rwoodson@paine.edu.

Piedmont College

Demorest, Georgia

http://www.piedmont.edu/

- **Independent** comprehensive, founded 1897, affiliated with United Church of Christ
- **Rural** 186-acre campus with easy access to Atlanta
- **Endowment** $53.0 million
- **Coed**
- **Moderately difficult** entrance level

FACULTY
Student/faculty ratio: 10:1.

ACADEMICS
Calendar: semesters. *Degrees:* certificates, bachelor's, master's, doctoral, and post-master's certificates.
Library: Arrendale Library plus 2 others. *Books:* 85,631 (physical), 766,654 (digital/electronic); *Serial titles:* 76 (physical); *Databases:* 197. Students can reserve study rooms.

STUDENT LIFE
Housing options: on-campus residence required through sophomore year; coed, men-only, women-only, special housing for students with disabilities. Campus housing is university owned. Freshman campus housing is guaranteed.

Activities and organizations: drama/theater group, student-run newspaper, radio and television station, choral group, Campus Activity Board, Student Government Association, Team Piedmont, National Society of Leadership and Success, American Marketing Association-Piedmont Chapter.

Athletics Member NCAA. All Division III.

Campus security: 24-hour emergency response devices and patrols, late-night transport/escort service.

Student services: personal/psychological counseling, veterans affairs office.

COSTS & FINANCIAL AID
Costs (2019–20) ***Comprehensive fee:*** $37,216 includes full-time tuition ($26,492), mandatory fees ($200), and room and board ($10,524). Full-time tuition and fees vary according to location. Part-time tuition: $1011 per credit hour. Part-time tuition and fees vary according to course load and location. ***Required fees:*** $100 per term part-time. ***Room and board:*** Room and board charges vary according to board plan.

Financial Aid Of all full-time matriculated undergraduates who enrolled in 2019, 1,076 applied for aid, 954 were judged to have need, 164 had their need fully met. 142 Federal Work-Study jobs (averaging $2128). 215 state and other part-time jobs (averaging $2536). In 2019, 177 non-need-based awards were made. ***Average percent of need met:*** 71. ***Average financial aid package:*** $21,690. ***Average need-based loan:*** $4237. ***Average need-based gift aid:*** $17,050. ***Average non-need-based aid:*** $12,174. ***Average indebtedness upon graduation:*** $30,559.

APPLYING
Standardized Tests *Required:* SAT or ACT (for admission).

Options: electronic application, early admission, deferred entrance.

Required: high school transcript. ***Required for some:*** interview. ***Recommended:*** essay or personal statement.

CONTACT
Ms. Brenda Boonstra, Director of Undergraduate Admissions, Piedmont College, PO Box 10, 165 Central Avenue, Demorest, GA 30535. *Phone:* 706-776-0103 Ext. 1188. *Toll-free phone:* 800-277-7020. *Fax:* 706-776-6635. *E-mail:* bboonstra@piedmont.edu.

Point University

West Point, Georgia

http://point.edu/

- **Independent Christian** comprehensive, founded 1937
- **Small-town** campus with easy access to Atlanta, GA and Montgomery, AL
- **Coed**
- **Moderately difficult** entrance level

FACULTY
Student/faculty ratio: 15:1.

ACADEMICS
Calendar: semesters. *Degrees:* certificates, associate, bachelor's, and master's.
Library: Point University Library plus 1 other.

STUDENT LIFE
Housing options: on-campus residence required through sophomore year; men-only, women-only. Campus housing is leased by the school. Freshman campus housing is guaranteed.

Activities and organizations: choral group, marching band, Student Government Association, Community Concert Band, Campus Life Ministers, Campus Activities Board, Fellowship of Christian Athletes (FCA).

Athletics Member NAIA.

Campus security: 24-hour patrols.

Student services: personal/psychological counseling.

COSTS
Costs (2019–20) ***Comprehensive fee:*** $29,285 includes full-time tuition ($20,085), mandatory fees ($1200), and room and board ($8000). Part-time tuition: $650 per credit hour. ***College room only:*** $4000.

APPLYING
Options: electronic application, deferred entrance.

Required: high school transcript, minimum 2.0 GPA, 1 letter of recommendation. ***Required for some:*** essay or personal statement, college transcript if applicable.

CONTACT
Rusty Hassell, Executive Director of Enrollment, Point University, 507 West 10th Street, West Point, GA 31833. *Phone:* 706-385-1000. *Toll-free phone:* 855-37-POINT. *Fax:* 706-645-9473. *E-mail:* admissions@point.edu.

Reformed University
Lawrenceville, Georgia

CONTACT
Reformed University, 1724 Atkinson Road, Lawrenceville, GA 30043.

Reinhardt University
Waleska, Georgia
http://www.reinhardt.edu/

- **Independent** comprehensive, founded 1883, affiliated with United Methodist Church
- **Rural** 600-acre campus with easy access to Atlanta
- **Coed**
- **Moderately difficult** entrance level

FACULTY
Student/faculty ratio: 12:1.

ACADEMICS
Calendar: semesters. *Degrees:* associate, bachelor's, and master's.
Library: Hill Freeman Library/Spruill Learning Center plus 1 other. *Books:* 61,496 (physical), 183,453 (digital/electronic); *Serial titles:* 52 (physical), 27,855 (digital/electronic); *Databases:* 167.

STUDENT LIFE
Housing options: on-campus residence required for freshman year; men-only, women-only, special housing for students with disabilities. Campus housing is university owned. Freshman campus housing is guaranteed.

Activities and organizations: drama/theater group, student-run newspaper, television station, choral group.

Athletics Member NAIA.

Campus security: 24-hour emergency response devices and patrols, late-night transport/escort service, controlled dormitory access.

Student services: health clinic, personal/psychological counseling.

COSTS & FINANCIAL AID
Costs (2019–20) ***Comprehensive fee:*** $34,800 includes full-time tuition ($23,300), mandatory fees ($1000), and room and board ($10,500). Full-time tuition and fees vary according to course load, location, and program. Part-time tuition: $792 per credit hour. Part-time tuition and fees vary according to course load, location, and program. ***Room and board:*** Room and board charges vary according to board plan and housing facility.

Financial Aid Of all full-time matriculated undergraduates who enrolled in 2017, 1,110 applied for aid, 984 were judged to have need, 133 had their need fully met. 122 Federal Work-Study jobs (averaging $613). 162 state and other part-time jobs (averaging $513). In 2017, 182 non-need-based awards were made. ***Average percent of need met:*** 61. ***Average financial aid package:*** $15,618. ***Average need-based loan:*** $4064. ***Average need-based gift aid:*** $12,576. ***Average non-need-based aid:*** $6376. ***Average indebtedness upon graduation:*** $27,532.

APPLYING
Standardized Tests *Required:* SAT or ACT (for admission).

Options: electronic application, early admission, deferred entrance.

Required: high school transcript, minimum 2.0 GPA.

CONTACT
Ms. Lacey L. Satterfield, Director of Admissions, Reinhardt University, 7300 Reinhardt Circle, Waleska, GA 30183-0128. *Phone:* 770-720-5620. *E-mail:* lls@reinhardt.edu.

Savannah College of Art and Design
Savannah, Georgia
http://www.scad.edu/

- **Independent** comprehensive, founded 1978
- **Urban** campus
- **Coed**
- **Moderately difficult** entrance level

FACULTY
Student/faculty ratio: 20:1.

ACADEMICS
Calendar: quarters. *Degrees:* certificates, bachelor's, and master's.
Library: Jen Library plus 4 others. *Books:* 264,695 (physical), 215,544 (digital/electronic); *Serial titles:* 901 (physical), 50,630 (digital/electronic); *Databases:* 81. Weekly public service hours: 106; students can reserve study rooms.

STUDENT LIFE
Housing options: coed, special housing for students with disabilities. Campus housing is university owned and leased by the school. Freshman applicants given priority for college housing.

Activities and organizations: drama/theater group, student-run newspaper, radio station, choral group.

Athletics Member NAIA.

Campus security: 24-hour emergency response devices and patrols, late-night transport/escort service, controlled dormitory access.

Student services: health clinic, personal/psychological counseling.

COSTS & FINANCIAL AID
Costs (2019–20) ***One-time required fee:*** $500. ***Comprehensive fee:*** $52,737 includes full-time tuition ($37,575) and room and board ($15,162). Full-time tuition and fees vary according to course load and degree level. Part-time tuition: $4175 per course. Part-time tuition and fees vary according to course load and degree level. ***College room only:*** $10,224. Room and board charges vary according to board plan, housing facility, and location.

Financial Aid Of all full-time matriculated undergraduates who enrolled in 2017, 5,574 applied for aid, 4,721 were judged to have need, 332 had their need fully met. 395 Federal Work-Study jobs (averaging $1186). 770 state and other part-time jobs (averaging $1279). In 2017, 4067 non-need-based awards were made. ***Average percent of need met:*** 41. ***Average financial aid package:*** $16,982. ***Average need-based loan:*** $4144. ***Average need-based gift aid:*** $13,217. ***Average non-need-based aid:*** $10,093. ***Average indebtedness upon graduation:*** $39,328.

APPLYING
Standardized Tests *Required:* SAT or ACT (for admission), TOEFL scores are required for International students (for admission).

Options: electronic application, early admission, deferred entrance.

Application fee: $40.

Required for some: essay or personal statement, high school transcript, interview, portfolio/audition for performing arts, riding, writing, or visual arts. ***Recommended:*** essay or personal statement, interview.

CONTACT
Ms. Jenny Jaquillard, Executive Director of Admissions Recruitment, Savannah College of Art and Design, 342 Bull Street, PO Box 3146, Savannah, GA 31402-3146. *Phone:* 912-525-5100. *Toll-free phone:* 800-869-7223. *E-mail:* admission@scad.edu.

Savannah State University
Savannah, Georgia
http://www.savannahstate.edu/

- **State-supported** comprehensive, founded 1890, part of University System of Georgia
- **Suburban** 173-acre campus
- **Endowment** $5.4 million
- **Coed**
- **Minimally difficult** entrance level

FACULTY
Student/faculty ratio: 21:1.

ACADEMICS
Calendar: semesters. *Degrees:* certificates, associate, bachelor's, master's, and postbachelor's certificates.
Library: Asa H. Gordon Library. *Books:* 108,766 (physical), 185,056 (digital/electronic); *Serial titles:* 217 (physical), 2,000 (digital/electronic); *Databases:* 298. Weekly public service hours: 84.

STUDENT LIFE
Housing options: coed, men-only, women-only. Campus housing is university owned.

Activities and organizations: drama/theater group, student-run newspaper, radio and television station, choral group, marching band, Marching band, Wesleyan Gospel Choir, Residence Hall Association, Student Government Association, Tiger Ambassadors, national fraternities, national sororities.

Athletics Member NCAA. All Division I.

Campus security: 24-hour emergency response devices and patrols, late-night transport/escort service, controlled dormitory access.

Student services: health clinic, personal/psychological counseling, women's center, veterans affairs office.

COSTS & FINANCIAL AID

Costs (2019–20) ***Tuition:*** area resident $5080 full-time, $165 per credit hour part-time; state resident $5080 full-time, $165 per credit hour part-time; nonresident $18,482 full-time, $601 per credit hour part-time. Full-time tuition and fees vary according to course load, program, and reciprocity agreements. Part-time tuition and fees vary according to course load, program, and reciprocity agreements. ***Required fees:*** $1838 full-time, $751 per term part-time. ***Room and board:*** $10,616; room only: $6586. Room and board charges vary according to board plan and housing facility.

Financial Aid ***Financial aid deadline:*** 7/31.

APPLYING

Standardized Tests *Required:* SAT or ACT (for admission). *Required for some:* SAT Subject Tests (for admission). *Recommended:* SAT (for admission).

Options: electronic application, early admission, deferred entrance.

Required: high school transcript, minimum 2.3 GPA. ***Required for some:*** essay or personal statement, interview.

CONTACT

Mr. Descatur Potier, Assistant Vice President of Academic Affairs for Enrollment Services/Director of Admission, Savannah State University, PO Box 20209, 3219 College Street, Savannah, GA 31404. *Phone:* 912-358-4014. *Toll-free phone:* 800-788-0478. *Fax:* 912-650-8009. *E-mail:* potierd@savannahstate.edu.

Shorter University

Rome, Georgia

http://www.shorter.edu/

CONTACT

Shorter University, 315 Shorter Avenue, Rome, GA 30165. *Phone:* 706-233-7342. *Toll-free phone:* 800-868-6980.

South Georgia State College

Douglas, Georgia

http://www.sgc.edu/

CONTACT

South Georgia State College, 100 West College Park Drive, Douglas, GA 31533-5098. *Phone:* 912-260-4409. *Toll-free phone:* 800-342-6364.

South University - Savannah

Savannah, Georgia

http://www.southuniversity.edu/savannah/

CONTACT

South University - Savannah, 709 Mall Boulevard, Savannah, GA 31406. *Phone:* 912-201-8000. *Toll-free phone:* 866-629-2901.

Spelman College

Atlanta, Georgia

http://www.spelman.edu/

- **Independent** 4-year, founded 1881
- **Urban** 39-acre campus with easy access to Atlanta
- **Endowment** $367.9 million
- **Women only**
- **Very difficult** entrance level

FACULTY

Student/faculty ratio: 11:1.

ACADEMICS

Calendar: semesters. *Degree:* bachelor's.

Library: Robert Woodruff Library plus 1 other. *Books:* 489,081 (physical), 139,636 (digital/electronic); *Serial titles:* 987 (physical), 122,146 (digital/electronic); *Databases:* 317. Weekly public service hours: 95; students can reserve study rooms.

STUDENT LIFE

Housing options: on-campus residence required through sophomore year; women-only. Campus housing is university owned and leased by the school. Freshman applicants given priority for college housing.

Activities and organizations: drama/theater group, student-run newspaper, choral group, Glee Club, Theater Program, Student Government, Honors Program, Religious Groups, national sororities.

Campus security: 24-hour emergency response devices and patrols, late-night transport/escort service, controlled dormitory access, lighted pathways/sidewalks.

Student services: health clinic, personal/psychological counseling, women's center.

FINANCIAL AID

Financial Aid Of all full-time matriculated undergraduates who enrolled in 2018, 1,902 applied for aid, 1,726 were judged to have need, 823 had their need fully met. In 2018, 20 non-need-based awards were made. ***Average percent of need met:*** 34. ***Average financial aid package:*** $17,630. ***Average need-based loan:*** $4812. ***Average need-based gift aid:*** $14,611. ***Average non-need-based aid:*** $16,426. ***Average indebtedness upon graduation:*** $35,582.

APPLYING

Standardized Tests *Required:* SAT or ACT (for admission). *Required for some:* SAT and SAT Subject Tests or ACT (for admission).

Options: electronic application, early admission, early decision, early action, deferred entrance.

Application fee: $40.

Required: essay or personal statement, high school transcript, minimum 2.0 GPA, 2 letters of recommendation.

CONTACT

Ms. Tiffany Nelson, Director of Admissions, Spelman College, 350 Spelman Lane, SW, Atlanta, GA 30314-4399. *Phone:* 800-982-2411. *Toll-free phone:* 800-982-2411. *Fax:* 404-270-5201. *E-mail:* admiss@spelman.edu.

Strayer University - Augusta

Augusta, Georgia

http://www.strayer.edu/georgia/augusta/

CONTACT

Strayer University - Augusta, 1330 Augusta West Parkway, Augusta, GA 30909. *Toll-free phone:* 888-311-0355.

Strayer University–Chamblee Campus

Atlanta, Georgia

http://www.strayer.edu/georgia/chamblee/

CONTACT

Strayer University–Chamblee Campus, 3355 Northeast Expressway, Suite 100, Atlanta, GA 30341. *Toll-free phone:* 888-311-0355.

Strayer University–Cobb County Campus

Atlanta, Georgia

http://www.strayer.edu/georgia/cobb-county/

CONTACT

Strayer University–Cobb County Campus, 3101 Towercreek Parkway, SE, Suite 700, Atlanta, GA 30339. *Toll-free phone:* 888-311-0355.

Strayer University–Columbus Campus

Columbus, Georgia

http://www.strayer.edu/georgia/columbus/

CONTACT
Strayer University–Columbus Campus, 408 12th Street, Suite 102, Columbus, GA 31901. *Toll-free phone:* 888-311-0355.

Strayer University–Douglasville Campus

Douglasville, Georgia

http://www.strayer.edu/georgia/douglasville/

CONTACT
Strayer University–Douglasville Campus, 4655 Timber Ridge Drive, Douglasville, GA 30135. *Toll-free phone:* 888-311-0355.

Strayer University–Lithonia Campus

Lithonia, Georgia

http://www.strayer.edu/georgia/lithonia/

CONTACT
Strayer University–Lithonia Campus, 3120 Stonecrest Boulevard, Suite 200, Lithonia, GA 30038. *Toll-free phone:* 888-311-0355.

Strayer University–Morrow Campus

Morrow, Georgia

http://www.strayer.edu/georgia/morrow/

CONTACT
Strayer University–Morrow Campus, 3000 Corporate Center Drive, Suite 100, Morrow, GA 30260. *Toll-free phone:* 888-311-0355.

Strayer University–Savannah Campus

Savannah, Georgia

http://www.strayer.edu/georgia/savannah/

CONTACT
Strayer University–Savannah Campus, 8001 Chatham Center Drive, Suite 300, Savannah, GA 31405. *Toll-free phone:* 888-311-0355.

Thomas University

Thomasville, Georgia

http://www.thomasu.edu/

CONTACT
Mrs. Rita Gagliano, Office of Admission, Thomas University, 1501 Millpond Road, Thomasville, GA 31792. *Phone:* 229-227-6942. *Toll-free phone:* 800-538-9784. *Fax:* 229-227-6919. *E-mail:* rgagliano@thomasu.edu.

Toccoa Falls College

Toccoa Falls, Georgia

http://www.tfc.edu/

- **Independent interdenominational** 4-year, founded 1907
- **Small-town** 1100-acre campus with easy access to Atlanta, GA metro area
- **Endowment** $3.2 million
- **Coed** 1,833 undergraduate students, 50% full-time, 60% women, 40% men
- **Moderately difficult** entrance level, 60% of applicants were admitted

UNDERGRAD STUDENTS
911 full-time, 922 part-time. Students come from 33 states and territories; 3 other countries; 30% are from out of state; 11% Black or African American, non-Hispanic/Latino; 6% Hispanic/Latino; 5% Asian, non-Hispanic/Latino; 0.2% Native Hawaiian or other Pacific Islander, non-Hispanic/Latino; 0.5% American Indian or Alaska Native, non-Hispanic/Latino; 3% Two or more races, non-Hispanic/Latino; 1% Race/ethnicity unknown; 0.3% international; 3% transferred in; 52% live on campus.

Freshmen:
Admission: 1,176 applied, 703 admitted, 218 enrolled. ***Average high school GPA:*** 3.4. ***Test scores:*** SAT evidence-based reading and writing scores over 500: 61%; SAT math scores over 500: 54%; ACT scores over 18: 61%; SAT evidence-based reading and writing scores over 600: 26%; SAT math scores over 600: 11%; ACT scores over 24: 20%; SAT evidence-based reading and writing scores over 700: 3%; SAT math scores over 700: 1%; ACT scores over 30: 4%.

Retention: 64% of full-time freshmen returned.

FACULTY
Total: 139, 34% full-time, 42% with terminal degrees.

Student/faculty ratio: 16:1.

ACADEMICS
Calendar: 4-1-4. *Degrees:* certificates, associate, and bachelor's.

Special study options: advanced placement credit, distance learning, double majors, independent study, internships, part-time degree program, services for LD students, study abroad, summer session for credit.

Computers: 50 computers/terminals are available on campus for general student use. Students can access the following: campus intranet, computer help desk, free student e-mail accounts, online (class) grades, online (class) registration, online (class) schedules. Campuswide network is available. 95% of college-owned or -operated housing units are wired for high-speed Internet access. Wireless service is available via entire campus.
Library: Seby Jones Library plus 1 other. *Books:* 53,407 (physical), 719,708 (digital/electronic); *Serial titles:* 33 (physical), 73,000 (digital/electronic); *Databases:* 282. Weekly public service hours: 74; students can reserve study rooms.

STUDENT LIFE
Housing options: on-campus residence required through junior year; men-only, women-only, special housing for students with disabilities. Campus housing is university owned. Freshman campus housing is guaranteed.

Activities and organizations: drama/theater group, student-run newspaper, radio station, choral group, Hmong Student Fellowship, Theatrical Society, Student Missions Fellowship (SMF), Adventure Bound, Clarkston Refugee Ministry.

Athletics Member NCCAA. ***Intercollegiate sports:*** baseball M, basketball M/W, soccer M/W, volleyball W. ***Intramural sports:*** basketball M/W, football M/W, soccer M/W, softball M/W, ultimate Frisbee M/W, volleyball M/W.

Campus security: student patrols.

Student services: personal/psychological counseling.

COSTS & FINANCIAL AID
Costs (2020–21) ***Comprehensive fee:*** $29,620 includes full-time tuition ($21,120) and room and board ($8500). Part-time tuition: $880 per credit hour. ***Payment plan:*** installment. ***Waivers:*** employees or children of employees.

Financial Aid Of all full-time matriculated undergraduates who enrolled in 2019, 634 applied for aid, 574 were judged to have need, 87 had their need fully met. In 2019, 71 non-need-based awards were made. ***Average percent of need met:*** 69. ***Average financial aid package:*** $20,208. ***Average need-based loan:*** $3885. ***Average need-based gift aid:*** $16,076. ***Average non-need-based aid:*** $11,253.

APPLYING
Standardized Tests *Required:* SAT or ACT (for admission).

Options: electronic application, early admission, deferred entrance.

Application fee: $30.

Required: essay or personal statement, high school transcript, minimum 2.0 GPA, 1 letter of recommendation. ***Required for some:*** interview.

Application deadlines: rolling (freshmen), rolling (transfers).

Notification: continuous (freshmen), continuous (transfers).

CONTACT
Mr. Ronnie Stewart, Toccoa Falls College, 107 Kincaid Drive, MSC 899, Toccoa Falls, GA 30598. *Phone:* 706-886-6831 Ext. 5378. *Toll-free phone:* 888-785-5624. *Fax:* 706-282-6012. *E-mail:* rstewart@tfc.edu.

Truett McConnell University

Cleveland, Georgia

http://www.truett.edu/

- **Independent Baptist** comprehensive, founded 1946
- **Small-town** 240-acre campus with easy access to Atlanta
- **Coed** 2,983 undergraduate students, 29% full-time, 56% women, 44% men
- **Noncompetitive** entrance level, 94% of applicants were admitted

UNDERGRAD STUDENTS
852 full-time, 2,132 part-time. Students come from 25 states and territories; 15 other countries; 11% are from out of state; 6% Black or African American, non-Hispanic/Latino; 4% Hispanic/Latino; 0.4% Asian, non-Hispanic/Latino; 0.5% American Indian or Alaska Native, non-Hispanic/Latino; 7% Race/ethnicity unknown; 3% international; 1% transferred in.

Freshmen:
Admission: 611 applied, 575 admitted, 215 enrolled. ***Average high school GPA:*** 3.5. ***Test scores:*** SAT evidence-based reading and writing scores over 500: 67%; SAT math scores over 500: 55%; ACT scores over 18: 69%; SAT evidence-based reading and writing scores over 600: 24%; SAT math scores over 600: 17%; ACT scores over 24: 23%; SAT evidence-based reading and writing scores over 700: 2%; SAT math scores over 700: 1%; ACT scores over 30: 1%.

Retention: 63% of full-time freshmen returned.

FACULTY
Student/faculty ratio: 18:1.

ACADEMICS
Calendar: semesters. *Degrees:* bachelor's, master's, and postbachelor's certificates.

Special study options: academic remediation for entering students, advanced placement credit, distance learning, double majors, services for LD students, summer session for credit.

Computers: 40 computers/terminals are available on campus for general student use. Students can access the following: computer help desk, free student e-mail accounts, online (class) grades, online (class) registration, online (class) schedules. Campuswide network is available. 100% of college-owned or -operated housing units are wired for high-speed Internet access. Wireless service is available via entire campus.
Library: Cofer Library.

STUDENT LIFE
Housing options: on-campus residence required through senior year; men-only, women-only. Campus housing is university owned.

Activities and organizations: choral group.

Athletics Member NAIA. ***Intercollegiate sports:*** baseball M(s), basketball M(s)/W(s), cross-country running M(s)/W(s), golf M(s)/W(s), lacrosse W(s), soccer M(s)/W(s), softball W(s), track and field M(s)/W(s), volleyball W(s), wrestling M(s).

Campus security: 24-hour weekday patrols, 10-hour weekend patrols by trained security personnel.

COSTS & FINANCIAL AID
Costs (2020–21) ***Comprehensive fee:*** $30,098 includes full-time tuition ($20,928), mandatory fees ($1010), and room and board ($8160). Full-time tuition and fees vary according to course load, degree level, location, and program. Part-time tuition: $872 per credit hour. Part-time tuition and fees vary according to course load, degree level, location, and program. ***Required fees:*** $1010 per year part-time. ***Room and board:*** Room and board charges vary according to housing facility. ***Payment plan:*** installment. ***Waivers:*** employees or children of employees.

Financial Aid Of all full-time matriculated undergraduates who enrolled in 2019, 700 applied for aid, 602 were judged to have need, 145 had their need fully met. 33 Federal Work-Study jobs (averaging $1644). In 2019, 152 non-need-based awards were made. ***Average percent of need met:*** 73. ***Average financial aid package:*** $16,161. ***Average need-based loan:*** $4609. ***Average need-based gift aid:*** $13,232. ***Average non-need-based aid:*** $7198. ***Average indebtedness upon graduation:*** $29,610.

APPLYING
Standardized Tests *Required:* SAT or ACT (for admission).

Options: electronic application, deferred entrance.

Required: high school transcript, minimum 2.0 GPA. ***Required for some:*** essay or personal statement, 1 letter of recommendation.

Application deadlines: 8/1 (freshmen), 8/1 (transfers).

Notification: continuous (freshmen), continuous (transfers).

CONTACT
Truett McConnell University, 100 Alumni Drive, Cleveland, GA 30528. *Phone:* 706-865-2134 Ext. 4301. *Toll-free phone:* 800-226-8621.

University of Georgia

Athens, Georgia

http://www.uga.edu/

- **State-supported** university, founded 1785, part of University System of Georgia
- **Suburban** 767-acre campus with easy access to Atlanta
- **Endowment** $1.3 billion
- **Coed**
- **Moderately difficult** entrance level

FACULTY
Student/faculty ratio: 17:1.

ACADEMICS
Calendar: semesters. *Degrees:* certificates, bachelor's, master's, doctoral, post-master's, and postbachelor's certificates.
Library: Ilah Dunlap Little Memorial Library plus 4 others. *Books:* 5.3 million (digital/electronic). Students can reserve study rooms.

STUDENT LIFE
Housing options: on-campus residence required for freshman year; coed, women-only, special housing for students with disabilities. Campus housing is university owned. Freshman campus housing is guaranteed.

Activities and organizations: drama/theater group, student-run newspaper, radio station, choral group, marching band, Intramural Sports, Recreational sports program, Tate Movie Screening, University Union, Red Coat Band, national fraternities, national sororities.

Athletics Member NCAA. All Division I except football (Division I-A).

Campus security: 24-hour emergency response devices and patrols, late-night transport/escort service, controlled dormitory access.

Student services: health clinic, personal/psychological counseling, women's center, legal services, veterans affairs office.

COSTS & FINANCIAL AID
Costs (2019–20) ***Tuition:*** state resident $9790 full-time; nonresident $28,830 full-time. Full-time tuition and fees vary according to course load, location, and program. Part-time tuition and fees vary according to course load, location, and program. ***Required fees:*** $2290 full-time. ***Room and board:*** $10,314; room only: $6278. Room and board charges vary according to board plan and housing facility.

Financial Aid Of all full-time matriculated undergraduates who enrolled in 2019, 20,166 applied for aid, 11,661 were judged to have need, 3,112 had their need fully met. 453 Federal Work-Study jobs (averaging $3201). In 2019, 992 non-need-based awards were made. ***Average percent of need met:*** 74. ***Average financial aid package:*** $12,934. ***Average need-based loan:*** $4238. ***Average need-based gift aid:*** $10,009. ***Average non-need-based aid:*** $3073. ***Average indebtedness upon graduation:*** $22,918.

APPLYING
Standardized Tests *Required:* SAT or ACT (for admission).

Options: electronic application, early admission, early action, deferred entrance.

Application fee: $70.

Required: high school transcript, counselor evaluation. ***Recommended:*** essay or personal statement, minimum 2.0 GPA.

CONTACT
Mr. Charles Carabello, Associate Director for Enrollment Management, University of Georgia, Terrell Hall, Athens, GA 30602. *Phone:* 706-542-8776. *Fax:* 706-542-1466. *E-mail:* admproc@uga.edu.

University of North Georgia

Dahlonega, Georgia

http://www.ung.edu/

- **State-supported** comprehensive, founded 1873, part of University System of Georgia
- **Small-town** 1077-acre campus with easy access to Atlanta
- **Endowment** $58.4 million
- **Coed**
- **Moderately difficult** entrance level

FACULTY
Student/faculty ratio: 20:1.

ACADEMICS
Calendar: semesters. *Degrees:* certificates, associate, bachelor's, master's, doctoral, post-master's, and postbachelor's certificates.
Library: Library Technology Center plus 4 others. *Books:* 195,525 (physical), 433,929 (digital/electronic); *Serial titles:* 168 (physical); *Databases:* 298. Weekly public service hours: 94; students can reserve study rooms.

STUDENT LIFE
Housing options: on-campus residence required through sophomore year; coed, men-only, women-only, special housing for students with disabilities. Campus housing is university owned. Freshman applicants given priority for college housing.

Activities and organizations: drama/theater group, student-run newspaper, radio station, choral group, marching band, Student Government Association, Commuter Council, Graduate Student Senate, Student Activities Board, Greek organizations, national fraternities, national sororities.

Athletics Member NCAA. All Division II.

Campus security: 24-hour emergency response devices and patrols, late-night transport/escort service, controlled dormitory access.

Student services: health clinic, personal/psychological counseling, veterans affairs office.

FINANCIAL AID
Financial Aid Of all full-time matriculated undergraduates who enrolled in 2017, 9,980 applied for aid, 7,603 were judged to have need, 4,401 had their need fully met. 178 Federal Work-Study jobs (averaging $1195). In 2017, 562 non-need-based awards were made. ***Average percent of need met:*** 63. ***Average financial aid package:*** $14,234. ***Average need-based loan:*** $5230. ***Average need-based gift aid:*** $5948. ***Average non-need-based aid:*** $1349. ***Average indebtedness upon graduation:*** $12,345.

APPLYING
Standardized Tests *Required:* SAT or ACT (for admission).

Options: electronic application, early admission.

Application fee: $30.

Required: high school transcript, minimum 2.0 GPA, proof of immunization.

CONTACT
Molly Potts, Director of Admissions, University of North Georgia, Admissions Center, 3820 Mundy Mill Road, Oakwood, GA 30566. *Phone:* 678-717-3849. *Toll-free phone:* 800-498-9581. *E-mail:* molly.potts@ung.edu.

University of West Georgia

Carrollton, Georgia

http://www.westga.edu/

- **State-supported** comprehensive, founded 1933, part of University System of Georgia
- **Small-town** 645-acre campus with easy access to Atlanta
- **Endowment** $34.3 million
- **Coed** 10,411 undergraduate students, 78% full-time, 64% women, 36% men
- **Moderately difficult** entrance level, 59% of applicants were admitted

UNDERGRAD STUDENTS
8,090 full-time, 2,321 part-time. Students come from 31 states and territories; 30 other countries; 5% are from out of state; 37% Black or African American, non-Hispanic/Latino; 8% Hispanic/Latino; 1% Asian, non-Hispanic/Latino; 0.1% Native Hawaiian or other Pacific Islander, non-Hispanic/Latino; 0.2% American Indian or Alaska Native, non-Hispanic/Latino; 4% Two or more races, non-Hispanic/Latino; 1% Race/ethnicity unknown; 1% international; 6% transferred in; 25% live on campus.

Freshmen:
Admission: 7,124 applied, 4,236 admitted, 1,852 enrolled. ***Average high school GPA:*** 3.2. ***Test scores:*** SAT math scores over 500: 34%; ACT scores over 18: 80%; SAT math scores over 600: 4%; ACT scores over 24: 16%; ACT scores over 30: 2%.

Retention: 69% of full-time freshmen returned.

FACULTY
Total: 723, 64% full-time, 65% with terminal degrees.

Student/faculty ratio: 18:1.

ACADEMICS
Calendar: semesters. *Degrees:* bachelor's, master's, doctoral, post-master's, and postbachelor's certificates.

Special study options: accelerated degree program, advanced placement credit, cooperative education, distance learning, double majors, external degree program, freshman honors college, honors programs, independent study, internships, off-campus study, part-time degree program, services for LD students, study abroad, summer session for credit. ***ROTC:*** Air Force (c).

Computers: 1,200 computers/terminals are available on campus for general student use. Students can access the following: campus intranet, computer help desk, free student e-mail accounts, online (class) grades, online (class) registration, online (class) schedules. Campuswide network is available. 100% of college-owned or -operated housing units are wired for high-speed Internet access. Wireless service is available via entire campus.
Library: Irvine Sullivan Ingram Library plus 1 other. Weekly public service hours: 110; students can reserve study rooms.

STUDENT LIFE
Housing options: on-campus residence required for freshman year; coed, women-only, special housing for students with disabilities. Campus housing is university owned. Freshman campus housing is guaranteed.

Activities and organizations: drama/theater group, student-run newspaper, radio and television station, choral group, marching band, Black Student Alliance, Student Activities Council, Baptist Collegiate Ministries, Campus Outreach, United Voices Gospel Choir, national fraternities, national sororities.

Athletics Member NCAA. All Division II. ***Intercollegiate sports:*** baseball M(s), basketball M(s)/W(s), cheerleading W(s), cross-country running M(s)/W(s), football M(s), golf M(s)/W(s), soccer W(s), softball W(s), tennis W(s), track and field W(s), volleyball W(s). ***Intramural sports:*** baseball M(c), basketball M(c)/W(c), equestrian sports W(c), golf M/W, lacrosse M(c), rock climbing M(c)/W(c), soccer M(c), ultimate Frisbee M/W, weight lifting M/W, wrestling M(c).

Campus security: 24-hour emergency response devices and patrols, student patrols, late-night transport/escort service, controlled dormitory access.

Student services: health clinic, personal/psychological counseling, veterans affairs office.

COSTS & FINANCIAL AID
Costs (2020–21) ***Tuition:*** state resident $5464 full-time, $182 per semester hour part-time; nonresident $19,282 full-time, $643 per semester hour part-time. Full-time tuition and fees vary according to course load, degree level, location, and program. Part-time tuition and fees vary according to course load, degree level, location, and program. ***Required fees:*** $2024 full-time. ***Room and board:*** $10,340; room only: $5740. Room and board charges vary according to board plan and housing facility. ***Payment plan:*** installment. ***Waivers:*** senior citizens and employees or children of employees.

Financial Aid Of all full-time matriculated undergraduates who enrolled in 2019, 7,286 applied for aid, 5,800 were judged to have need, 3,566 had their need fully met. In 2019, 439 non-need-based awards were made. ***Average percent of need met:*** 49. ***Average financial aid package:*** $8186. ***Average need-based loan:*** $4005. ***Average need-based gift aid:*** $5041. ***Average non-need-based aid:*** $2552. ***Average indebtedness upon graduation:*** $26,376.

APPLYING
Standardized Tests *Required:* SAT or ACT (for admission).

Options: electronic application, early admission, deferred entrance.

Application fee: $40.

Required: minimum 2.5 GPA, proof of immunization. ***Required for some:*** high school transcript.

Application deadlines: rolling (freshmen), rolling (transfers).

Notification: continuous (freshmen), continuous (transfers).

CONTACT
University of West Georgia, 1601 Maple Street, Carrollton, GA 30118. *Phone:* 678-839-5600.

Valdosta State University

Valdosta, Georgia

http://www.valdosta.edu/

- **State-supported** university, founded 1906, part of University System of Georgia
- **Small-town** 180-acre campus
- **Endowment** $7.5 million
- **Coed** 8,590 undergraduate students, 79% full-time, 64% women, 36% men
- **Moderately difficult** entrance level, 57% of applicants were admitted

UNDERGRAD STUDENTS
6,797 full-time, 1,793 part-time. Students come from 49 states and territories; 45 other countries; 18% are from out of state; 39% Black or African American, non-Hispanic/Latino; 7% Hispanic/Latino; 1% Asian, non-Hispanic/Latino; 0.1% Native Hawaiian or other Pacific Islander, non-Hispanic/Latino; 0.2% American Indian or Alaska Native, non-Hispanic/Latino; 4% Two or more races, non-Hispanic/Latino; 0.4% Race/ethnicity unknown; 1% international; 7% transferred in; 30% live on campus.

Freshmen:
Admission: 7,563 applied, 4,324 admitted, 1,657 enrolled. ***Average high school GPA:*** 3.4. ***Test scores:*** SAT evidence-based reading and writing scores over 500: 82%; SAT math scores over 500: 68%; ACT scores over 18: 88%; SAT evidence-based reading and writing scores over 600: 22%; SAT math scores over 600: 10%; ACT scores over 24: 20%; SAT evidence-based reading and writing scores over 700: 2%; SAT math scores over 700: 1%; ACT scores over 30: 3%.

Retention: 70% of full-time freshmen returned.

FACULTY
Total: 565, 72% full-time, 68% with terminal degrees.

Student/faculty ratio: 20:1.

ACADEMICS
Calendar: semesters. *Degrees:* certificates, associate, bachelor's, master's, doctoral, post-master's, and postbachelor's certificates.

Special study options: accelerated degree program, adult/continuing education programs, advanced placement credit, cooperative education, distance learning, double majors, English as a second language, external degree program, honors programs, independent study, internships, off-campus study, part-time degree program, services for LD students, study abroad, summer session for credit. ***ROTC:*** Air Force (b).

Unusual degree programs: 3-2 engineering with Georgia Institute of Technology.

Computers: 1,756 computers/terminals are available on campus for general student use. Students can access the following: campus intranet, computer help desk, free student e-mail accounts, online (class) grades, online (class) registration, online (class) schedules. Campuswide network is available. 100% of college-owned or -operated housing units are wired for high-speed Internet access. Wireless service is available via entire campus.

Library: Odum Library. *Books:* 476,976 (physical), 629,983 (digital/electronic); *Serial titles:* 5,131 (physical), 137,536 (digital/electronic); *Databases:* 236. Students can reserve study rooms.

STUDENT LIFE
Housing options: on-campus residence required for freshman year; coed, men-only, cooperative, special housing for students with disabilities. Campus housing is university owned. Freshman applicants given priority for college housing.

Activities and organizations: drama/theater group, student-run newspaper, radio and television station, choral group, marching band, Psychology CLub, ENACTUS, Honors Student Association, Student Government Association, Anime/Manga Club/National Council of Negro Women, national fraternities, national sororities.

Athletics Member NCAA. All Division II. ***Intercollegiate sports:*** baseball M(s), basketball M(s)/W(s), cheerleading M/W, cross-country running M(s)/W(s), football M(s), golf M(s), soccer W(s), softball W(s), tennis M(s)/W(s), volleyball W(s). ***Intramural sports:*** basketball M/W, bowling M/W, football M/W, golf M/W, lacrosse M(c), rugby M(c), soccer M/W, softball M/W, table tennis M/W, tennis M/W, ultimate Frisbee M/W, volleyball M/W.

Campus security: 24-hour emergency response devices and patrols, late-night transport/escort service, controlled dormitory access, bicycle patrols, security cameras, mobile security app.

Student services: health clinic, personal/psychological counseling, veterans affairs office.

COSTS & FINANCIAL AID
Costs (2020–21) ***Tuition:*** area resident $4371 full-time, $182 per credit hour part-time; state resident $4371 full-time, $182 per credit hour part-time; nonresident $15,426 full-time, $643 per credit hour part-time. Full-time tuition and fees vary according to course load, degree level, location, program, and reciprocity agreements. Part-time tuition and fees vary according to course load, degree level, location, program, and reciprocity agreements. ***Required fees:*** $2212 full-time, $1106 per term part-time. ***Room and board:*** $8332; room only: $4330. Room and board charges vary according to board plan. ***Waivers:*** employees or children of employees.

Financial Aid Of all full-time matriculated undergraduates who enrolled in 2017, 6,202 applied for aid, 5,481 were judged to have need, 620 had their need fully met. In 2017, 135 non-need-based awards were made. ***Average percent of need met:*** 89. ***Average financial aid package:*** $16,121. ***Average need-based loan:*** $4006. ***Average need-based gift aid:*** $6419. ***Average non-need-based aid:*** $2368. ***Average indebtedness upon graduation:*** $27,233.

APPLYING
Standardized Tests *Required:* SAT or ACT (for admission).

Options: electronic application, deferred entrance.

Application fee: $40.

Required: high school transcript.

Application deadlines: 6/15 (freshmen), rolling (out-of-state freshmen), 6/15 (transfers).

Notification: continuous until 9/1 (freshmen), continuous until 8/1 (out-of-state freshmen), continuous until 8/1 (transfers).

CONTACT
Mr. Ryan M. Hogan, Director of Admissions, Valdosta State University, Office of Admissions, 1500 North Patterson Street, Valdosta, GA 31698. *Phone:* 229-333-5791. *Toll-free phone:* 800-618-1878. *Fax:* 229-333-5482. *E-mail:* admissions@valdosta.edu.

Wesleyan College

Macon, Georgia

http://www.wesleyancollege.edu/

- **Independent United Methodist** comprehensive, founded 1836
- **Suburban** 200-acre campus with easy access to Atlanta
- **Endowment** $56.5 million
- **Undergraduate: women only; graduate: coed** 754 undergraduate students, 63% full-time, 92% women, 8% men
- **Moderately difficult** entrance level, 44% of applicants were admitted

UNDERGRAD STUDENTS

476 full-time, 278 part-time. Students come from 11 states and territories; 20 other countries; 7% are from out of state; 37% Black or African American, non-Hispanic/Latino; 5% Hispanic/Latino; 0.9% Asian, non-Hispanic/Latino; 0.3% American Indian or Alaska Native, non-Hispanic/Latino; 4% Two or more races, non-Hispanic/Latino; 2% Race/ethnicity unknown; 7% international; 6% transferred in; 55% live on campus.

Freshmen:

Admission: 737 applied, 323 admitted, 135 enrolled. ***Average high school GPA:*** 3.4. ***Test scores:*** SAT evidence-based reading and writing scores over 500: 66%; SAT math scores over 500: 55%; ACT scores over 18: 71%; SAT evidence-based reading and writing scores over 600: 16%; SAT math scores over 600: 8%; ACT scores over 24: 17%; SAT evidence-based reading and writing scores over 700: 2%; SAT math scores over 700: 2%; ACT scores over 30: 2%.

Retention: 68% of full-time freshmen returned.

FACULTY

Total: 100, 53% full-time, 49% with terminal degrees.

Student/faculty ratio: 8:1.

ACADEMICS

Calendar: semesters. *Degrees:* bachelor's and master's.

Special study options: adult/continuing education programs, advanced placement credit, cooperative education, distance learning, double majors, honors programs, independent study, internships, off-campus study, part-time degree program, services for LD students, student-designed majors, study abroad, summer session for credit. ***ROTC:*** Army (c).

Unusual degree programs: 3-2 engineering with Georgia Institute of Technology, Auburn University, Mercer University; Dual-degree J.D. program with Mercer University.

Computers: 93 computers/terminals are available on campus for general student use. Students can access the following: campus intranet, computer help desk, free student e-mail accounts, online (class) grades, online (class) registration, online (class) schedules, online payment. Campuswide network is available. 100% of college-owned or -operated housing units are wired for high-speed Internet access. Wireless service is available via entire campus.

Library: Willet Memorial Library. *Books:* 66,200 (physical), 427,245 (digital/electronic); *Serial titles:* 635 (physical), 65,438 (digital/electronic); *Databases:* 281. Study areas open 24 hours, 5–7 days a week; students can reserve study rooms.

STUDENT LIFE

Housing options: women-only, special housing for students with disabilities. Campus housing is university owned. Freshman campus housing is guaranteed.

Activities and organizations: drama/theater group, student-run newspaper, choral group, Student Government Association (SGA), Black Student Alliance (BSA), A.X.I.S. (Association of eXemplary International Students), GLBAL (Gay, Lesbian, Bi-sexual Alliance), Campus Activities Board (CAB).

Athletics Member NCAA. All Division III. ***Intercollegiate sports:*** basketball W, cross-country running W, equestrian sports W, soccer W, softball W, tennis W, volleyball W.

Campus security: 24-hour emergency response devices and patrols, late-night transport/escort service, controlled dormitory access.

Student services: health clinic, personal/psychological counseling, women's center.

COSTS & FINANCIAL AID

Costs (2020–21) ***One-time required fee:*** $200. ***Comprehensive fee:*** $35,555 includes full-time tuition ($23,990), mandatory fees ($1200), and room and board ($10,365). Full-time tuition and fees vary according to course load, program, and reciprocity agreements. Part-time tuition: $570 per semester hour. Part-time tuition and fees vary according to course load, program, and reciprocity agreements. ***Required fees:*** $48 per semester hour part-time. ***Room and board:*** Room and board charges vary according to housing facility. ***Waivers:*** employees or children of employees.

Financial Aid Of all full-time matriculated undergraduates who enrolled in 2019, 412 applied for aid, 379 were judged to have need, 72 had their need fully met. In 2019, 78 non-need-based awards were made. ***Average percent of need met:*** 78. ***Average financial aid package:*** $22,597. ***Average need-based loan:*** $4439. ***Average need-based gift aid:*** $19,303. ***Average non-need-based aid:*** $13,643. ***Average indebtedness upon graduation:*** $28,882.

APPLYING

Standardized Tests *Required:* SAT or ACT (for admission).

Options: electronic application, early admission, deferred entrance.

Required: high school transcript, minimum 2.0 GPA.

Application deadlines: rolling (freshmen), rolling (out-of-state freshmen), rolling (transfers).

Notification: continuous (freshmen), continuous (out-of-state freshmen), continuous (transfers).

CONTACT

Clint Hobbs, Vice President of Enrollment, Wesleyan College, 4760 Forsyth Road, Macon, GA 31210-4462. *Phone:* 478-757-5206. *Toll-free phone:* 800-447-6610. *Fax:* 478-757-4030. *E-mail:* admissions@wesleyancollege.edu.

Young Harris College

Young Harris, Georgia

http://www.yhc.edu/

- **Independent United Methodist** 4-year, founded 1886
- **Small-town** 800-acre campus
- **Endowment** $93.7 million
- **Coed**
- **Moderately difficult** entrance level

FACULTY

Student/faculty ratio: 11:1.

ACADEMICS

Calendar: semesters. *Degree:* bachelor's.

Library: Duckworth Library. *Databases:* 72. Study areas open 24 hours, 5–7 days a week.

STUDENT LIFE

Housing options: on-campus residence required through senior year; coed, men-only, women-only, special housing for students with disabilities. Campus housing is university owned. Freshman campus housing is guaranteed.

Activities and organizations: drama/theater group, student-run newspaper, choral group, Greek life, religious organizations/Bible study, intramural sports, Student Government Association, Campus Activities Board, national fraternities, national sororities.

Athletics Member NCAA. All Division II.

Campus security: 24-hour emergency response devices and patrols, student patrols, late-night transport/escort service, controlled dormitory access.

Student services: health clinic, personal/psychological counseling.

FINANCIAL AID

Financial Aid Of all full-time matriculated undergraduates who enrolled in 2017, 851 applied for aid, 755 were judged to have need, 144 had their need fully met. 132 Federal Work-Study jobs (averaging $904). 313 state and other part-time jobs (averaging $949). In 2017, 244 non-need-based awards were made. ***Average percent of need met:*** 76. ***Average financial aid package:*** $25,610. ***Average need-based loan:*** $3950. ***Average need-based gift aid:*** $22,408. ***Average non-need-based aid:*** $14,483. ***Average indebtedness upon graduation:*** $27,123.

APPLYING
Standardized Tests *Required:* SAT or ACT (for admission).
Options: electronic application.
Required: high school transcript.

CONTACT
Mr. Clinton G. Hobbs, Vice President for Enrollment Management, Young Harris College, PO Box 116, Young Harris, GA 30582-0098. *Phone:* 706-379-3111. *Toll-free phone:* 800-241-3754. *Fax:* 706-379-3108. *E-mail:* admissions@yhc.edu.

HAWAII

Argosy University, Hawai`i
Honolulu, Hawaii
http://www.argosy.edu/locations/hawaii/

CONTACT
Argosy University, Hawai`i, 1001 Bishop Street, Suite 400, Honolulu, HI 96813. *Phone:* 808-536-5555. *Toll-free phone:* 888-323-2777.

Brigham Young University–Hawaii
Laie, Hawaii
http://www.byuh.edu/

CONTACT
Mr. Arapata P. Meha, Brigham Young University–Hawaii, 55-220 Kulanui Street, Laie, HI 96762-1294. *Phone:* 808-675-3731. *Fax:* 808-675-3741. *E-mail:* admissions@byuh.edu.

Chaminade University of Honolulu
Honolulu, Hawaii
http://www.chaminade.edu/

- **Independent Roman Catholic** comprehensive, founded 1955
- **Urban** 62-acre campus with easy access to Honolulu
- **Endowment** $21.9 million
- **Coed** 1,099 undergraduate students, 97% full-time, 75% women, 25% men
- **Moderately difficult** entrance level, 94% of applicants were admitted

UNDERGRAD STUDENTS
1,063 full-time, 36 part-time. Students come from 35 states and territories; 10 other countries; 26% are from out of state; 3% Black or African American, non-Hispanic/Latino; 4% Hispanic/Latino; 37% Asian, non-Hispanic/Latino; 30% Native Hawaiian or other Pacific Islander, non-Hispanic/Latino; 0.6% American Indian or Alaska Native, non-Hispanic/Latino; 8% Two or more races, non-Hispanic/Latino; 4% Race/ethnicity unknown; 2% international; 10% transferred in; 23% live on campus.

Freshmen:
Admission: 1,490 applied, 1,405 admitted, 196 enrolled. ***Average high school GPA:*** 3.5. ***Test scores:*** SAT evidence-based reading and writing scores over 500: 74%; SAT math scores over 500: 69%; ACT scores over 18: 88%; SAT evidence-based reading and writing scores over 600: 18%; SAT math scores over 600: 12%; ACT scores over 24: 18%; SAT math scores over 700: 2%; ACT scores over 30: 3%.
Retention: 86% of full-time freshmen returned.

FACULTY
Total: 130, 68% full-time.
Student/faculty ratio: 11:1.

ACADEMICS
Calendar: semesters. *Degrees:* associate, bachelor's, master's, doctoral, post-master's, and postbachelor's certificates.
Special study options: academic remediation for entering students, accelerated degree program, adult/continuing education programs, advanced placement credit, distance learning, double majors, independent study, internships, off-campus study, part-time degree program, study abroad, summer session for credit. ***ROTC:*** Army (c), Air Force (c).
Computers: 200 computers/terminals are available on campus for general student use. Students can access the following: computer help desk, free student e-mail accounts, online (class) grades, online (class) registration, online (class) schedules. Campuswide network is available. 100% of college-owned or -operated housing units are wired for high-speed Internet access. Wireless service is available via entire campus.
Library: Sullivan Library. *Books:* 49,737 (physical), 149,162 (digital/electronic); *Serial titles:* 112 (physical), 27,423 (digital/electronic); *Databases:* 97.

STUDENT LIFE
Housing options: coed, women-only, special housing for students with disabilities. Campus housing is university owned.
Activities and organizations: drama/theater group, student-run newspaper, radio station, choral group, Lumana O Samoa (Samoan Club), Kaimi Lalakea (Hawaiian Club), Rotaract, Residence Hall Association, Chaminade Student Government Association.
Athletics Member NCAA. All Division II. ***Intercollegiate sports:*** basketball M(s)/W(s), cross-country running M(s)/W(s), golf M(s), soccer M(s)/W(s), softball W(s), tennis W(s), volleyball W(s). ***Intramural sports:*** basketball M/W.
Campus security: 24-hour emergency response devices and patrols, late-night transport/escort service, controlled dormitory access.
Student services: personal/psychological counseling.

COSTS & FINANCIAL AID
Costs (2020–21) ***One-time required fee:*** $180. ***Comprehensive fee:*** $41,524 includes full-time tuition ($26,800), mandatory fees ($114), and room and board ($14,610). Full-time tuition and fees vary according to course load, location, and program. Part-time tuition: $893 per credit. Part-time tuition and fees vary according to course load, location, and program. ***Room and board:*** Room and board charges vary according to board plan and housing facility. ***Payment plan:*** installment. ***Waivers:*** employees or children of employees.
Financial Aid Of all full-time matriculated undergraduates who enrolled in 2018, 846 applied for aid, 686 were judged to have need, 73 had their need fully met. In 2018, 340 non-need-based awards were made. ***Average percent of need met:*** 66. ***Average financial aid package:*** $22,052. ***Average need-based loan:*** $4280. ***Average need-based gift aid:*** $4624. ***Average non-need-based aid:*** $13,182. ***Average indebtedness upon graduation:*** $22,158.

APPLYING
Standardized Tests *Required:* SAT or ACT (for admission), TOEFL for international students (for admission).
Options: electronic application, early admission, deferred entrance.
Application fee: $50.
Required: essay or personal statement, high school transcript, minimum 2.5 GPA. ***Required for some:*** minimum 2.8 GPA, 2 letters of recommendation, interview. ***Recommended:*** minimum 3.0 GPA.
Application deadlines: rolling (freshmen), rolling (transfers).
Notification: continuous (freshmen), continuous (transfers).

CONTACT
Office of Admissions, Chaminade University of Honolulu, 3140 Waialae Avenue, Honolulu, HI 96816-1578. *Phone:* 808-735-8340. *Toll-free phone:* 800-735-3733. *Fax:* 808-739-4647. *E-mail:* admissions@chaminade.edu.

Hawai`i Pacific University
Honolulu, Hawaii
http://www.hpu.edu/

CONTACT
Marissa Bratton, Director of Admissions, Hawai`i Pacific University, 1 Aloha Tower Drive, Honolulu, HI 96813. *Phone:* 808-544-0238. *Toll-free phone:* 866-225-5478. *Fax:* 808-544-1136. *E-mail:* admissions@hpu.edu.

Pacific Rim Christian University

Honolulu, Hawaii

http://www.pacrim.edu/

- **Independent Christian** comprehensive
- **Coed**
- 70% of applicants were admitted

FACULTY
Student/faculty ratio: 13:1.

ACADEMICS
Degrees: associate, bachelor's, and master's.

CONTACT
Pacific Rim Christian University, 2223 Ho'one'e Place, Honolulu, HI 96819.

Remington College–Honolulu Campus

Honolulu, Hawaii

http://www.remingtoncollege.edu/

CONTACT
Louis LaMair, Director of Recruitment, Remington College–Honolulu Campus, 1111 Bishop Street, Suite 400, Honolulu, HI 96813. *Phone:* 808-942-1000. *Toll-free phone:* 800-323-8122. *Fax:* 808-533-3064. *E-mail:* louis.lamair@remingtoncollege.edu.

University of Hawaii at Hilo

Hilo, Hawaii

http://hilo.hawaii.edu/

CONTACT
University of Hawaii at Hilo, Admissions, 200 W. Kawili Street, Hilo, HI 96720. *Phone:* 808-932-7446. *Toll-free phone:* 800-897-4456. *Fax:* 808-932-7459. *E-mail:* uhhadm@hawaii.edu.

University of Hawaii at Manoa

Honolulu, Hawaii

http://manoa.hawaii.edu/

- **State-supported** university, founded 1907, part of University of Hawaii System
- **Urban** 320-acre campus with easy access to Honolulu
- **Coed** 12,631 undergraduate students, 84% full-time, 58% women, 42% men
- **Moderately difficult** entrance level, 58% of applicants were admitted

UNDERGRAD STUDENTS
10,560 full-time, 2,071 part-time. Students come from 51 states and territories; 55 other countries; 30% are from out of state; 2% Black or African American, non-Hispanic/Latino; 2% Hispanic/Latino; 39% Asian, non-Hispanic/Latino; 17% Native Hawaiian or other Pacific Islander, non-Hispanic/Latino; 0.4% American Indian or Alaska Native, non-Hispanic/Latino; 16% Two or more races, non-Hispanic/Latino; 0.3% Race/ethnicity unknown; 3% international; 11% transferred in; 23% live on campus.

Freshmen:
Admission: 16,244 applied, 9,493 admitted, 2,020 enrolled. ***Average high school GPA:*** 3.7. ***Test scores:*** SAT evidence-based reading and writing scores over 500: 94%; SAT math scores over 500: 94%; ACT scores over 18: 96%; SAT evidence-based reading and writing scores over 600: 45%; SAT math scores over 600: 42%; ACT scores over 24: 47%; SAT evidence-based reading and writing scores over 700: 6%; SAT math scores over 700: 9%; ACT scores over 30: 8%.

Retention: 81% of full-time freshmen returned.

FACULTY
Total: 1,413, 82% full-time, 88% with terminal degrees.
Student/faculty ratio: 10:1.

ACADEMICS
Calendar: semesters. *Degrees:* bachelor's, master's, doctoral, and postbachelor's certificates.

Special study options: advanced placement credit, cooperative education, distance learning, double majors, English as a second language, honors programs, independent study, internships, off-campus study, part-time degree program, services for LD students, student-designed majors, study abroad, summer session for credit. ***ROTC:*** Army (b), Air Force (b).

Computers: 117 computers/terminals and 6 ports are available on campus for general student use. Students can access the following: campus intranet, computer help desk, free student e-mail accounts, online (class) grades, online (class) registration, online (class) schedules. Campuswide network is available. 100% of college-owned or -operated housing units are wired for high-speed Internet access. Wireless service is available via entire campus.

Library: Hamilton Library plus 6 others. *Books:* 2.3 million (physical), 242,278 (digital/electronic); *Serial titles:* 86,153 (physical), 81,547 (digital/electronic); *Databases:* 304. Weekly public service hours: 89; study areas open 24 hours, 5–7 days a week; students can reserve study rooms.

STUDENT LIFE
Housing options: coed, special housing for students with disabilities. Campus housing is university owned. Freshman applicants given priority for college housing.

Activities and organizations: drama/theater group, student-run newspaper, radio station, choral group, marching band, Biology Club, Pre-Medical Association, International Student Association, Katipunan, Timpuyog, national fraternities, national sororities.

Athletics Member NCAA. All Division I except football (Division I-A). ***Intercollegiate sports:*** archery M, baseball M(s), basketball M(s)/W(s), cheerleading M(s)/W(s), cross-country running W(s), golf M(s)/W(s)(c), sailing M/W, sand volleyball W(s), soccer W(s), softball W(s), swimming and diving M(s)/W(s), tennis M(s)/W(s), track and field W(s), volleyball M(s)/W(s), water polo W(s). ***Intramural sports:*** badminton M/W, basketball M/W, crew M/W, cross-country running M/W, golf M/W, rugby M, sailing M/W, soccer M, softball M, swimming and diving M/W, table tennis M/W, tennis M/W, track and field M/W, ultimate Frisbee M/W, volleyball M/W, weight lifting M/W, wrestling M/W.

Campus security: 24-hour emergency response devices and patrols, student patrols, late-night transport/escort service, controlled dormitory access.

Student services: health clinic, personal/psychological counseling, women's center.

COSTS & FINANCIAL AID
Costs (2020–21) ***Tuition:*** area resident $11,304 full-time, $471 per credit hour part-time; state resident $11,304 full-time, $471 per credit hour part-time; nonresident $33,336 full-time, $1389 per credit hour part-time. ***Required fees:*** $882 full-time, $436 per term part-time. ***Room and board:*** $13,366; room only: $9239.

Financial Aid Of all full-time matriculated undergraduates who enrolled in 2018, 9,033 applied for aid, 6,112 were judged to have need, 1,695 had their need fully met. In 2018, 2664 non-need-based awards were made. ***Average percent of need met:*** 69. ***Average financial aid package:*** $15,223. ***Average need-based loan:*** $4558. ***Average need-based gift aid:*** $10,488. ***Average non-need-based aid:*** $13,390. ***Average indebtedness upon graduation:*** $24,223.

APPLYING
Standardized Tests *Required:* SAT or ACT (for admission). *Recommended:* SAT (for admission), ACT (for admission).

Options: electronic application.

Application fee: $70.

Required: high school transcript, minimum 2.8 GPA.

Notification: continuous (freshmen), continuous (transfers).

CONTACT
Ms. Lisa Buto, Student Services Specialist, University of Hawaii at Manoa, 2600 Campus Road, Room 001, Honolulu, HI 96822. *Phone:* 808-956-8975. *Toll-free phone:* 800-823-9771. *Fax:* 808-956-4148. *E-mail:* uhmanoa.admissions@hawaii.edu.

University of Hawaii Maui College

Kahului, Hawaii

http://maui.hawaii.edu/

CONTACT

Mr. Stephen Kameda, Director of Admissions and Records, University of Hawaii Maui College, 310 Kaahumanu Avenue, Kahului, HI 96732. *Phone:* 808-984-3267. *Toll-free phone:* 800-479-6692. *Fax:* 808-984-3872. *E-mail:* skameda@hawaii.edu.

University of Hawaii–West Oahu

Kapolei, Hawaii

http://www.uhwo.hawaii.edu/

- **State-supported** 4-year, founded 1976, part of University of Hawaii System
- **Small-town** 300-acre campus with easy access to Honolulu
- **Coed** 3,049 undergraduate students, 55% full-time, 67% women, 33% men
- **Moderately difficult** entrance level, 84% of applicants were admitted

UNDERGRAD STUDENTS

1,683 full-time, 1,366 part-time. Students come from 18 states and territories; 6 other countries; 3% are from out of state; 2% Black or African American, non-Hispanic/Latino; 1% Hispanic/Latino; 40% Asian, non-Hispanic/Latino; 30% Native Hawaiian or other Pacific Islander, non-Hispanic/Latino; 0.5% American Indian or Alaska Native, non-Hispanic/Latino; 15% Two or more races, non-Hispanic/Latino; 0.1% Race/ethnicity unknown; 0.3% international; 17% transferred in.

Freshmen:

Admission: 673 applied, 565 admitted, 217 enrolled. ***Average high school GPA:*** 3.4. ***Test scores:*** SAT evidence-based reading and writing scores over 500: 53%; SAT math scores over 500: 61%; ACT scores over 18: 57%; SAT evidence-based reading and writing scores over 600: 14%; SAT math scores over 600: 10%; ACT scores over 24: 12%; SAT math scores over 700: 1%; ACT scores over 30: 2%.

Retention: 76% of full-time freshmen returned.

FACULTY

Total: 85.

Student/faculty ratio: 25:1.

ACADEMICS

Calendar: semesters. *Degree:* certificates and bachelor's.

Special study options: distance learning, double majors, internships, part-time degree program, services for LD students, summer session for credit. ***ROTC:*** Army (c), Air Force (c).

Computers: 59 computers/terminals are available on campus for general student use. Students can access the following: computer help desk, free student e-mail accounts, online (class) grades, online (class) registration, online (class) schedules. Campuswide network is available. Wireless service is available via entire campus.

Library: University of Hawaii-West Oahu Library. *Books:* 54,136 (digital/electronic); *Serial titles:* 39 (physical). Students can reserve study rooms.

STUDENT LIFE

Housing options: college housing not available.

Activities and organizations: student-run newspaper.

Athletics ***Intramural sports:*** badminton M/W, basketball M/W, bowling M/W, golf M/W, soccer M/W, softball M/W, tennis M(c)/W(c), ultimate Frisbee M/W, volleyball M/W.

Campus security: 24-hour emergency response devices and patrols, late-night transport/escort service, Security Assessments.

Student services: personal/psychological counseling.

COSTS & FINANCIAL AID

Costs (2020–21) ***Tuition:*** area resident $7344 full-time, $306 per credit part-time; state resident $7344 full-time, $306 per credit part-time; nonresident $20,304 full-time, $846 per credit part-time. ***Required fees:*** $240 full-time. ***Payment plan:*** installment. ***Waivers:*** employees or children of employees.

Financial Aid Of all full-time matriculated undergraduates who enrolled in 2018, 929 applied for aid, 829 were judged to have need. In 2018, 5 non-need-based awards were made. ***Average financial aid package:*** $7097. ***Average need-based loan:*** $4136. ***Average need-based gift aid:*** $2640. ***Average non-need-based aid:*** $1498. ***Average indebtedness upon graduation:*** $17,079. ***Financial aid deadline:*** 4/1.

APPLYING

Standardized Tests *Required for some:* SAT (for admission), ACT (for admission), SAT or ACT (for admission).

Options: deferred entrance.

Application fee: $50.

Required: minimum 2.7 GPA. ***Required for some:*** high school transcript, 2 letters of recommendation, college transcripts.

Application deadlines: 7/1 (freshmen), 7/1 (transfers).

Notification: continuous until 12/15 (freshmen), continuous until 12/15 (transfers).

CONTACT

Michelle Cohen, University of Hawaii–West Oahu, HI. *Phone:* 808-689-2916. *Toll-free phone:* 866-299-8656. *E-mail:* uhwo.admissions@hawaii.edu.

University of Phoenix–Hawaii Campus

Honolulu, Hawaii

http://www.phoenix.edu/

CONTACT

Marc Booker, Senior Director, Office of Admissions and Evaluation, University of Phoenix–Hawaii Campus, 4035 South Riverpoint Parkway, Mail Stop CF-L101, Phoenix, AZ 85040. *Phone:* 602-557-4609. *Toll-free phone:* 866-766-0766. *Fax:* 480-643-1156.

IDAHO

Boise Bible College

Boise, Idaho

http://www.boisebible.edu/

- **Independent nondenominational** 4-year, founded 1945
- **Suburban** 17-acre campus
- **Coed** 121 undergraduate students
- **Minimally difficult** entrance level, 40% of applicants were admitted

UNDERGRAD STUDENTS

Students come from 12 states and territories; 7 other countries; 56% are from out of state.

Freshmen:

Admission: 121 applied, 48 admitted.

Retention: 68% of full-time freshmen returned.

FACULTY

Total: 15, 67% full-time, 40% with terminal degrees.

Student/faculty ratio: 15:1.

ACADEMICS

Calendar: semesters. *Degrees:* certificates, associate, and bachelor's.

Special study options: academic remediation for entering students, accelerated degree program, adult/continuing education programs, advanced placement credit, double majors, freshman honors college, honors programs, independent study, internships, part-time degree program, services for LD students, student-designed majors.

Computers: Students can access the following: campus intranet, computer help desk, free student e-mail accounts, online (class) grades, online (class) registration, online (class) schedules. Campuswide network is available. 100% of college-owned or -operated housing units are wired for high-speed Internet access. Wireless service is available via entire campus.

Library: Boise Bible College Library.

STUDENT LIFE
Housing options: on-campus residence required through sophomore year; men-only, women-only, special housing for students with disabilities. Campus housing is university owned. Freshman campus housing is guaranteed.

Activities and organizations: drama/theater group, student-run newspaper, choral group.

Athletics ***Intramural sports:*** basketball M/W, football M/W, rock climbing M/W, skiing (cross-country) M/W, skiing (downhill) M/W, soccer M/W, softball M/W, ultimate Frisbee M/W, volleyball M/W.

Campus security: controlled dormitory access, patrols by police officers.

Student services: personal/psychological counseling.

COSTS & FINANCIAL AID
Costs (2020–21) ***Tuition:*** $415 per credit hour part-time. ***Required fees:*** $650 full-time. ***Room only:*** Room and board charges vary according to board plan and housing facility. ***Payment plan:*** installment. ***Waivers:*** employees or children of employees.

Financial Aid Of all full-time matriculated undergraduates who enrolled in 2018, 82 applied for aid, 58 were judged to have need. In 2018, 15 non-need-based awards were made. ***Average percent of need met:*** 63. ***Average financial aid package:*** $14,791. ***Average need-based loan:*** $3211. ***Average need-based gift aid:*** $7909. ***Average non-need-based aid:*** $6259. ***Average indebtedness upon graduation:*** $13,828.

APPLYING
Standardized Tests *Required:* SAT or ACT (for admission).

Options: electronic application, deferred entrance.

Application fee: $25.

Required: essay or personal statement, high school transcript, minimum 2.5 GPA.

Application deadlines: 8/1 (freshmen), 8/1 (transfers).

Notification: continuous (freshmen), continuous (transfers).

CONTACT
Russell Grove, Director of Admissions, Boise Bible College, 8695 West Marigold Street, Boise, ID 83714-1220. *Phone:* 208-376-7731. *Toll-free phone:* 800-893-7755. *Fax:* 208-376-7743. *E-mail:* rgrove@boisebible.edu.

Boise State University

Boise, Idaho

http://www.boisestate.edu/

- **State-supported** university, founded 1932, part of Idaho System of Higher Education
- **Urban** 287-acre campus
- **Coed** 22,939 undergraduate students, 57% full-time, 57% women, 43% men
- **Moderately difficult** entrance level, 77% of applicants were admitted

UNDERGRAD STUDENTS
13,104 full-time, 9,835 part-time. 34% are from out of state; 2% Black or African American, non-Hispanic/Latino; 14% Hispanic/Latino; 3% Asian, non-Hispanic/Latino; 0.5% Native Hawaiian or other Pacific Islander, non-Hispanic/Latino; 0.3% American Indian or Alaska Native, non-Hispanic/Latino; 5% Two or more races, non-Hispanic/Latino; 1% Race/ethnicity unknown; 1% international; 6% transferred in.

Freshmen:
Admission: 15,029 applied, 11,637 admitted, 3,023 enrolled. ***Average high school GPA:*** 3.5. ***Test scores:*** SAT evidence-based reading and writing scores over 500: 81%; SAT math scores over 500: 77%; ACT scores over 18: 87%; SAT evidence-based reading and writing scores over 600: 38%; SAT math scores over 600: 32%; ACT scores over 24: 45%; SAT evidence-based reading and writing scores over 700: 6%; SAT math scores over 700: 6%; ACT scores over 30: 10%.

Retention: 80% of full-time freshmen returned.

ACADEMICS
Calendar: semesters. *Degrees:* certificates, associate, bachelor's, master's, doctoral, post-master's, and postbachelor's certificates.

Special study options: academic remediation for entering students, adult/continuing education programs, advanced placement credit, distance learning, double majors, freshman honors college, honors programs, independent study, internships, off-campus study, part-time degree program, services for LD students, student-designed majors, study abroad, summer session for credit. ***ROTC:*** Army (b).

Computers: 900 computers/terminals are available on campus for general student use. Students can access the following: campus intranet, computer help desk, free student e-mail accounts, online (class) grades, online (class) registration, online (class) schedules. Campuswide network is available. 100% of college-owned or -operated housing units are wired for high-speed Internet access. Wireless service is available via classrooms, computer centers, computer labs, dorm rooms, learning centers, libraries, student centers.

Library: Albertson's Library plus 1 other. *Books:* 644,899 (physical), 60,977 (digital/electronic); *Serial titles:* 112,213 (digital/electronic); *Databases:* 303. Weekly public service hours: 115; study areas open 24 hours, 5–7 days a week; students can reserve study rooms.

STUDENT LIFE
Housing options: coed. Campus housing is university owned. Freshman applicants given priority for college housing.

Activities and organizations: drama/theater group, student-run newspaper, radio station, choral group, marching band, national fraternities, national sororities.

Athletics Member NCAA. All Division I except football (Division I-A). ***Intercollegiate sports:*** basketball M(s)/W(s), cross-country running M(s)/W(s), golf M(s)/W(s), gymnastics W(s), soccer W(s), softball W(s), swimming and diving W(s), tennis M(s)/W(s), track and field M(s)/W(s), volleyball W(s). ***Intramural sports:*** baseball M, basketball M/W, golf M/W, lacrosse M(c)/W(c), rugby M(c)/W(c), soccer M(c)/W(c), softball W(c), swimming and diving M/W, track and field M/W, triathlon M/W, ultimate Frisbee M(c)/W(c), volleyball M(c)/W(c), water polo M/W.

Campus security: 24-hour emergency response devices and patrols, late-night transport/escort service, controlled dormitory access.

Student services: health clinic, personal/psychological counseling, women's center, legal services, veterans affairs office.

COSTS & FINANCIAL AID
Costs (2019–20) ***Tuition:*** state resident $5532 full-time, $252 per credit hour part-time; nonresident $22,452 full-time, $609 per credit hour part-time. Full-time tuition and fees vary according to course load, location, and reciprocity agreements. Part-time tuition and fees vary according to course load and location. ***Required fees:*** $2536 full-time, $115 per term part-time. ***Room and board:*** $9760; room only: $6652. Room and board charges vary according to board plan, housing facility, and student level. ***Payment plan:*** installment. ***Waivers:*** senior citizens and employees or children of employees.

Financial Aid Of all full-time matriculated undergraduates who enrolled in 2018, 7,540 applied for aid, 7,427 were judged to have need, 1,032 had their need fully met. In 2018, 237 non-need-based awards were made. ***Average percent of need met:*** 58. ***Average financial aid package:*** $10,384. ***Average need-based loan:*** $4106. ***Average need-based gift aid:*** $6166. ***Average non-need-based aid:*** $2739. ***Average indebtedness upon graduation:*** $27,052.

APPLYING
Standardized Tests *Required for some:* SAT or ACT (for admission).

Options: electronic application, deferred entrance.

Application fee: $50.

CONTACT
Ms. Kelly Talbert, Director/Admissions, Boise State University, 1910 University Drive, Boise, ID 83725. *Phone:* 208-426-3844. *Toll-free phone:* 800-824-7017. *E-mail:* bsuinfo@boisestate.edu.

Brigham Young University–Idaho

Rexburg, Idaho

http://www.byui.edu/

CONTACT
Brigham Young University–Idaho, 525 South Center Street, Rexburg, ID 83460. *Phone:* 208-496-1310.

The College of Idaho

Caldwell, Idaho

http://www.collegeofidaho.edu/

- **Independent** comprehensive, founded 1891
- **Suburban** 50-acre campus
- **Coed** 1,077 undergraduate students, 98% full-time, 51% women, 49% men
- **Moderately difficult** entrance level, 49% of applicants were admitted

UNDERGRAD STUDENTS
1,051 full-time, 26 part-time. 32% are from out of state; 2% Black or African American, non-Hispanic/Latino; 13% Hispanic/Latino; 2% Asian, non-Hispanic/Latino; 0.6% Native Hawaiian or other Pacific Islander, non-Hispanic/Latino; 0.6% American Indian or Alaska Native, non-Hispanic/Latino; 5% Two or more races, non-Hispanic/Latino; 2% Race/ethnicity unknown; 18% international; 4% transferred in; 65% live on campus.

Freshmen:
Admission: 2,399 applied, 1,166 admitted, 361 enrolled. ***Average high school GPA:*** 3.6. ***Test scores:*** SAT evidence-based reading and writing scores over 500: 83%; SAT math scores over 500: 84%; ACT scores over 18: 97%; SAT evidence-based reading and writing scores over 600: 40%; SAT math scores over 600: 28%; ACT scores over 24: 54%; SAT evidence-based reading and writing scores over 700: 7%; SAT math scores over 700: 3%; ACT scores over 30: 13%.

Retention: 78% of full-time freshmen returned.

FACULTY
Total: 138, 54% full-time, 56% with terminal degrees.

Student/faculty ratio: 11:1.

ACADEMICS
Calendar: 12-6-12 week calendar. *Degrees:* bachelor's and master's.

Special study options: academic remediation for entering students, advanced placement credit, cooperative education, double majors, English as a second language, honors programs, independent study, internships, off-campus study, part-time degree program, services for LD students, study abroad, summer session for credit. ***ROTC:*** Army (c).

Unusual degree programs: 3-2 engineering with Washington University in St. Louis, Columbia University; nursing with Idaho State University.

Computers: 100 computers/terminals are available on campus for general student use. Students can access the following: campus intranet, computer help desk, free student e-mail accounts, online (class) grades, online (class) registration, online (class) schedules, online course syllabi, course assignments, course discussion. Campuswide network is available. 100% of college-owned or -operated housing units are wired for high-speed Internet access. Wireless service is available via entire campus.
Library: Cruzen-Murray.

STUDENT LIFE
Housing options: on-campus residence required through junior year; coed, special housing for students with disabilities. Campus housing is university owned. Freshman campus housing is guaranteed.

Activities and organizations: drama/theater group, student-run newspaper, choral group, marching band, national fraternities, national sororities.

Athletics Member NAIA. ***Intercollegiate sports:*** baseball M(s), basketball M(s)/W(s), cross-country running M(s)/W(s), golf M(s), lacrosse M(c)/W(c), skiing (cross-country) M/W, skiing (downhill) W(s), soccer M(s)/W(s), softball W(s), swimming and diving M(s)/W(s), tennis W(s), track and field M(s)/W(s), volleyball W(s). ***Intramural sports:*** badminton M/W, basketball M/W, football M/W, soccer M/W, softball M/W, ultimate Frisbee M/W, volleyball M/W.

Campus security: 24-hour emergency response devices and patrols, student patrols, late-night transport/escort service, controlled dormitory access.

Student services: health clinic, personal/psychological counseling, women's center, veterans affairs office.

COSTS & FINANCIAL AID
Costs (2020–21) ***Comprehensive fee:*** $43,455 includes full-time tuition ($32,100), mandatory fees ($755), and room and board ($10,600). Part-time tuition: $1330 per credit.

Financial Aid Of all full-time matriculated undergraduates who enrolled in 2019, 727 applied for aid, 625 were judged to have need, 174 had their need fully met. In 2019, 418 non-need-based awards were made. ***Average percent of need met:*** 28. ***Average financial aid package:*** $23,045. ***Average need-based loan:*** $4205. ***Average need-based gift aid:*** $6156. ***Average non-need-based aid:*** $24,348. ***Average indebtedness upon graduation:*** $29,130.

APPLYING
Standardized Tests *Required for some:* SAT or ACT (for admission).

Options: electronic application, early action, deferred entrance.

Required: essay or personal statement, high school transcript, 1 letter of recommendation. ***Recommended:*** interview, class rank, extracurricular resumé.

Application deadlines: 2/16 (freshmen), 8/1 (transfers), 11/15 (early action).

Notification: continuous (freshmen), continuous (transfers), 12/21 (early action).

CONTACT
Brian Bava, Vice President of Enrollment Management, The College of Idaho, 2112 Cleveland Boulevard, Caldwell, ID 83605-4432. *Phone:* 208-459-5319. *Toll-free phone:* 800-244-3246. *E-mail:* admission@collegeofidaho.edu.

Idaho State University

Pocatello, Idaho

http://www.isu.edu/

- **State-supported** university, founded 1901
- **Urban** 1100-acre campus
- **Coed**
- **Minimally difficult** entrance level

FACULTY
Student/faculty ratio: 14:1.

ACADEMICS
Calendar: semesters. *Degrees:* certificates, bachelor's, master's, doctoral, post-master's, and postbachelor's certificates.
Library: Eli M. Oboler Library. *Books:* 620,925 (physical), 211,589 (digital/electronic); *Serial titles:* 150,874 (physical), 15,214 (digital/electronic); *Databases:* 173. Weekly public service hours: 103; students can reserve study rooms.

STUDENT LIFE
Housing options: coed, men-only, women-only, special housing for students with disabilities. Campus housing is university owned.

Activities and organizations: drama/theater group, student-run newspaper, radio and television station, choral group, marching band, national fraternities, national sororities.

Athletics Member NCAA. All Division I except football (Division I-AA).

Campus security: 24-hour emergency response devices and patrols, late-night transport/escort service, controlled dormitory access.

Student services: health clinic, personal/psychological counseling, women's center, veterans affairs office.

FINANCIAL AID
Financial Aid Of all full-time matriculated undergraduates who enrolled in 2018, 4,917 applied for aid, 4,181 were judged to have need, 236 had their need fully met. In 2018, 599 non-need-based awards were made. ***Average percent of need met:*** 48. ***Average financial aid package:*** $9154. ***Average need-based loan:*** $3775. ***Average need-based gift aid:*** $5339. ***Average non-need-based aid:*** $2438. ***Average indebtedness upon graduation:*** $27,056.

APPLYING
Standardized Tests *Required:* SAT or ACT (for admission). *Recommended:* ACT (for admission).

Options: electronic application, early admission, deferred entrance.

Application fee: $50.

Required: high school transcript, minimum 2.0 GPA.

CONTACT
Ms. Nicole Joseph, Director of Admissions, Idaho State University, 921 South 8th Avenue, Pocatello, ID 83209. *Phone:* 208-282-2475. *Fax:* 208-282-4511. *E-mail:* admiss@isu.edu.

Lewis-Clark State College

Lewiston, Idaho

http://www.lcsc.edu/

- **State-supported** 4-year, founded 1893
- **Small-town** 44-acre campus
- **Coed** 3,684 undergraduate students, 60% full-time, 63% women, 37% men
- **Minimally difficult** entrance level, 100% of applicants were admitted

UNDERGRAD STUDENTS
2,209 full-time, 1,475 part-time. 18% are from out of state; 0.9% Black or African American, non-Hispanic/Latino; 8% Hispanic/Latino; 1% Asian, non-Hispanic/Latino; 0.2% Native Hawaiian or other Pacific Islander, non-Hispanic/Latino; 2% American Indian or Alaska Native, non-Hispanic/Latino; 4% Two or more races, non-Hispanic/Latino; 2% Race/ethnicity unknown; 2% international; 8% transferred in; 15% live on campus.

Freshmen:
Admission: 1,867 applied, 1,865 admitted, 509 enrolled. ***Average high school GPA:*** 3.1. ***Test scores:*** SAT evidence-based reading and writing scores over 500: 56%; SAT math scores over 500: 51%; ACT scores over 18: 67%; SAT evidence-based reading and writing scores over 600: 13%; SAT math scores over 600: 11%; ACT scores over 24: 15%; SAT math scores over 700: 1%; ACT scores over 30: 1%.

Retention: 63% of full-time freshmen returned.

FACULTY
Total: 267, 73% full-time.

Student/faculty ratio: 12:1.

ACADEMICS
Calendar: semesters. *Degrees:* certificates, associate, and bachelor's.

Special study options: accelerated degree program, adult/continuing education programs, cooperative education, distance learning, double majors, independent study, internships, part-time degree program, student-designed majors, study abroad. ***ROTC:*** Army (c), Navy (c), Air Force (c).

Computers: Students can access the following: online (class) registration. Campuswide network is available.
Library: Lewis-Clark State College Library.

STUDENT LIFE
Housing options: coed. Campus housing is university owned.

Activities and organizations: drama/theater group, student-run newspaper, radio station.

Athletics Member NAIA. ***Intercollegiate sports:*** baseball M(s), basketball M(s)/W(s), cross-country running M(s)/W(s), golf M(s)/W(s), tennis M(s)/W(s), volleyball W(s). ***Intramural sports:*** badminton M/W, baseball M/W, basketball M/W, bowling M/W, field hockey M/W, football M/W, golf M/W, lacrosse M/W, rock climbing M/W, rugby M/W, skiing (cross-country) M/W, skiing (downhill) M/W, soccer M/W, softball M/W, table tennis M/W, tennis M/W, track and field M/W, volleyball M/W, weight lifting M/W.

Campus security: 24-hour emergency response devices and patrols, student patrols, late-night transport/escort service.

COSTS & FINANCIAL AID
Costs (2020–21) ***Tuition:*** area resident $10,552 full-time, $338 per credit hour part-time; state resident $6618 full-time, $338 per credit hour part-time; nonresident $19,236 full-time, $338 per credit hour part-time. ***Room and board:*** $6650; room only: $3200.

Financial Aid Of all full-time matriculated undergraduates who enrolled in 2018, 2,319 applied for aid, 1,271 were judged to have need, 119 had their need fully met. In 2018, 240 non-need-based awards were made. ***Average percent of need met:*** 71. ***Average financial aid package:*** $8632. ***Average need-based loan:*** $3816. ***Average need-based gift aid:*** $4729. ***Average non-need-based aid:*** $2898. ***Average indebtedness upon graduation:*** $25,473.

APPLYING
Standardized Tests *Required for some:* SAT or ACT (for admission).

Options: electronic application.

Required: high school transcript, minimum 2.0 GPA. ***Required for some:*** interview.

CONTACT
Soo Lee Bruce-Smith, Coordinator of New Student Recruitment, Lewis-Clark State College, 500 Eighth Avenue, Lewiston, ID 83501-2698. *Phone:* 208-792-2210. *Toll-free phone:* 800-933-5272. *Fax:* 208-792-2876. *E-mail:* admissions@lcsc.edu.

New Saint Andrews College

Moscow, Idaho

http://www.nsa.edu/

- **Independent Christian** comprehensive, founded 1993
- **Small-town** campus
- **Coed** 140 undergraduate students, 91% full-time, 58% women, 42% men
- **Moderately difficult** entrance level, 93% of applicants were admitted

UNDERGRAD STUDENTS
128 full-time, 12 part-time. Students come from 28 states and territories; 5 other countries; 93% are from out of state; 4% Hispanic/Latino; 2% Asian, non-Hispanic/Latino; 0.8% American Indian or Alaska Native, non-Hispanic/Latino; 0.8% Two or more races, non-Hispanic/Latino; 8% Race/ethnicity unknown; 7% international.

Freshmen:
Admission: 68 applied, 63 admitted, 31 enrolled.

Retention: 76% of full-time freshmen returned.

ACADEMICS
Calendar: 4 8-week terms. *Degrees:* associate, bachelor's, master's, and postbachelor's certificates.

Special study options: advanced placement credit, independent study, part-time degree program, summer session for credit.

Computers: 4 computers/terminals are available on campus for general student use. Students can access the following: campus intranet, free student e-mail accounts, online (class) grades, online (class) registration, online (class) schedules. Campuswide network is available. Wireless service is available via entire campus.
Library: Tyndale Library plus 1 other. Students can reserve study rooms.

STUDENT LIFE
Housing options: college housing not available.

Activities and organizations: drama/theater group, choral group, Students for the Relief of the Oppressed, Nursing Home Visits and Elderly Assistance (snow and leaf removal, firewood distribution), Blood Drives, Fall Carnival, St. Andrews Day Food Bank Drive.

Athletics ***Intramural sports:*** rugby M(c), soccer M(c), volleyball W(c).

Campus security: 24-hour emergency response devices.

Student services: personal/psychological counseling.

COSTS
Costs (2019–20) ***Tuition:*** $550 per credit hour part-time. Full-time tuition and fees vary according to course load and program. Part-time tuition and fees vary according to program. ***Payment plans:*** tuition prepayment, installment. ***Waivers:*** children of alumni and employees or children of employees.

APPLYING
Standardized Tests *Required:* SAT or ACT (for admission).

Options: electronic application, deferred entrance.

Application fee: $40.

Required: essay or personal statement, high school transcript, 2 letters of recommendation. ***Required for some:*** interview.

Application deadlines: 2/15 (freshmen), 2/15 (transfers).

Notification: 3/15 (freshmen), 3/15 (transfers).

CONTACT
Mr. John Sawyer, Director of Student Recruitment, New Saint Andrews College, PO Box 9025, Moscow, ID 83843. *Phone:* 208-882-1566 Ext. 100. *Fax:* 208-882-4293. *E-mail:* info@nsa.edu.

Northwest Nazarene University

Nampa, Idaho

http://www.nnu.edu/

- **Independent** comprehensive, founded 1913, affiliated with Church of the Nazarene
- **Small-town** 85-acre campus with easy access to Boise
- **Coed** 1,225 undergraduate students, 87% full-time, 60% women, 40% men
- **Moderately difficult** entrance level, 86% of applicants were admitted

UNDERGRAD STUDENTS
1,066 full-time, 159 part-time. 43% are from out of state; 2% Black or African American, non-Hispanic/Latino; 13% Hispanic/Latino; 2% Asian, non-Hispanic/Latino; 0.4% Native Hawaiian or other Pacific Islander, non-Hispanic/Latino; 0.3% American Indian or Alaska Native, non-Hispanic/Latino; 3% Two or more races, non-Hispanic/Latino; 1% Race/ethnicity unknown; 2% international; 5% transferred in; 66% live on campus.

Freshmen:
Admission: 1,666 applied, 1,425 admitted, 279 enrolled. ***Average high school GPA:*** 3.6. ***Test scores:*** ACT scores over 18: 93%; ACT scores over 24: 45%; ACT scores over 30: 5%.

FACULTY
Total: 112, 99% full-time, 66% with terminal degrees.
Student/faculty ratio: 17:1.

ACADEMICS
Calendar: semesters. *Degrees:* associate, bachelor's, master's, doctoral, and post-master's certificates.
Special study options: academic remediation for entering students, accelerated degree program, adult/continuing education programs, advanced placement credit, cooperative education, distance learning, double majors, English as a second language, external degree program, freshman honors college, honors programs, independent study, internships, off-campus study, part-time degree program, services for LD students, student-designed majors, study abroad, summer session for credit. ***ROTC:*** Army (b).
Computers: Students can access the following: campus intranet, computer help desk, free student e-mail accounts, online (class) grades, online (class) registration, online (class) schedules. Campuswide network is available. 99% of college-owned or -operated housing units are wired for high-speed Internet access. Wireless service is available via entire campus.
Library: John E. Riley Library.

STUDENT LIFE
Housing options: on-campus residence required through sophomore year; men-only, women-only, special housing for students with disabilities. Campus housing is university owned. Freshman campus housing is guaranteed.
Activities and organizations: drama/theater group, choral group, Students in Free Enterprise (SIFE), Student Government Association, Fellowship of Christian Athletes, The Crusader newspaper, The Oasis yearbook.
Athletics Member NCAA. All Division II. ***Intercollegiate sports:*** baseball M(s), basketball M(s)/W(s), cheerleading W(c), cross-country running M(s)/W(s), golf M(s)/W(s), soccer M/W(s), softball W(s), track and field M(s)/W(s), volleyball W(s). ***Intramural sports:*** basketball M/W, cross-country running M/W, football M/W, lacrosse W, softball M/W, table tennis M/W, tennis M/W, ultimate Frisbee M/W, volleyball M/W.
Campus security: 24-hour emergency response devices and patrols, student patrols, late-night transport/escort service, controlled dormitory access, residence hall check-in system, on-campus police hub.
Student services: health clinic, personal/psychological counseling.

COSTS & FINANCIAL AID
Costs (2020–21) ***Comprehensive fee:*** $41,430 includes full-time tuition ($32,130), mandatory fees ($500), and room and board ($8800). Part-time tuition: $1275 per credit hour. ***College room only:*** $4200.
Financial Aid Of all full-time matriculated undergraduates who enrolled in 2018, 881 applied for aid, 788 were judged to have need, 167 had their need fully met. In 2018, 131 non-need-based awards were made. ***Average percent of need met:*** 72. ***Average financial aid package:*** $28,871. ***Average need-based loan:*** $4022. ***Average need-based gift aid:*** $17,607. ***Average non-need-based aid:*** $13,474. ***Average indebtedness upon graduation:*** $27,339.

APPLYING
Standardized Tests *Required:* SAT or ACT (for admission).
Options: electronic application, early action, deferred entrance.
Required: essay or personal statement, high school transcript, minimum 2.5 GPA, 2 letters of recommendation. ***Required for some:*** interview.
Application deadlines: 8/15 (freshmen), 8/15 (transfers), 12/15 (early action).
Notification: continuous (freshmen), continuous (transfers), 12/15 (early action).

CONTACT
Northwest Nazarene University, 623 S. University Boulevard, Nampa, ID 83686-5897. *Phone:* 208-467-8950. *Toll-free phone:* 877-668-4968.

Stevens-Henager College

Boise, Idaho

http://www.stevenshenager.edu/

CONTACT
David Breck, Director of Admission, Stevens-Henager College, 1444 South Entertainment Avenue, Boise, ID 83709. *Phone:* 208-383-4540. *Toll-free phone:* 800-622-2640. *Fax:* 208-345-6999.

Stevens-Henager College

Idaho Falls, Idaho

http://www.stevenshenager.edu/

CONTACT
Stevens-Henager College, 901 Pier View Drive, Suite 105, Idaho Falls, ID 83402. *Toll-free phone:* 800-622-2640.

University of Idaho

Moscow, Idaho

http://www.uidaho.edu/

- **State-supported** university, founded 1889
- **Small-town** 810-acre campus
- **Endowment** $291.9 million
- **Coed** 9,392 undergraduate students, 72% full-time, 51% women, 49% men
- **Moderately difficult** entrance level, 78% of applicants were admitted

UNDERGRAD STUDENTS
6,788 full-time, 2,604 part-time. Students come from 51 states and territories; 45 other countries; 23% are from out of state; 1% Black or African American, non-Hispanic/Latino; 11% Hispanic/Latino; 2% Asian, non-Hispanic/Latino; 0.3% Native Hawaiian or other Pacific Islander, non-Hispanic/Latino; 0.7% American Indian or Alaska Native, non-Hispanic/Latino; 4% Two or more races, non-Hispanic/Latino; 2% Race/ethnicity unknown; 4% international; 6% transferred in; 39% live on campus.

Freshmen:
Admission: 8,071 applied, 6,276 admitted, 1,475 enrolled. ***Average high school GPA:*** 3.5. ***Test scores:*** SAT evidence-based reading and writing scores over 500: 81%; SAT math scores over 500: 76%; ACT scores over 18: 90%; SAT evidence-based reading and writing scores over 600: 39%; SAT math scores over 600: 30%; ACT scores over 24: 50%; SAT evidence-based reading and writing scores over 700: 6%; SAT math scores over 700: 6%; ACT scores over 30: 11%.
Retention: 77% of full-time freshmen returned.

FACULTY
Total: 684, 86% full-time, 80% with terminal degrees.
Student/faculty ratio: 16:1.

ACADEMICS
Calendar: semesters. *Degrees:* certificates, bachelor's, master's, doctoral, post-master's, and postbachelor's certificates.

Special study options: academic remediation for entering students, accelerated degree program, adult/continuing education programs, advanced placement credit, cooperative education, distance learning, double majors, English as a second language, honors programs, independent study, internships, off-campus study, part-time degree program, services for LD students, study abroad, summer session for credit. ***ROTC:*** Army (b), Navy (b), Air Force (c).

Computers: 510 computers/terminals are available on campus for general student use. Students can access the following: campus intranet, computer help desk, free student e-mail accounts, online (class) grades, online (class) registration, online (class) schedules. Campuswide network is available. 100% of college-owned or -operated housing units are wired for high-speed Internet access. Wireless service is available via entire campus.

Library: University of Idaho Library plus 1 other. *Books:* 1.6 million (physical), 817,592 (digital/electronic); *Serial titles:* 127,212 (physical), 173,681 (digital/electronic).

STUDENT LIFE

Housing options: on-campus residence required for freshman year; coed, men-only, women-only, cooperative, special housing for students with disabilities. Campus housing is university owned. Freshman campus housing is guaranteed.

Activities and organizations: drama/theater group, student-run newspaper, radio and television station, choral group, marching band, Student Alumni Relations Board (SARB), Associate Students University of Idaho (ASUI), Vandal Volunteers Club, Earth Club, Gender and Sexuality Alliance, national fraternities, national sororities.

Athletics Member NCAA. All Division I except football (Division I-A). ***Intercollegiate sports:*** basketball M(s)/W(s), cross-country running M(s)/W(s), golf M(s)/W(s), soccer W(s), swimming and diving W(s), tennis M(s)/W(s), track and field M(s)/W(s), volleyball W(s). ***Intramural sports:*** badminton M/W, baseball M(c), basketball M/W, equestrian sports M(c)/W(c), football M, golf W, ice hockey M(c)/W(c), lacrosse M(c)/W(c), racquetball M/W, rock climbing M/W, rugby M(c)/W(c), sand volleyball M/W, skiing (cross-country) M/W, skiing (downhill) M(c)/W(c), soccer M(c)/W(c), softball W(c), swimming and diving W, table tennis M/W, tennis M/W, track and field M/W, ultimate Frisbee M(c)/W(c), volleyball M(c)/W(c), water polo M(c)/W(c), weight lifting M/W.

Campus security: 24-hour emergency response devices and patrols, late-night transport/escort service, controlled dormitory access.

Student services: health clinic, personal/psychological counseling, women's center, veterans affairs office.

COSTS & FINANCIAL AID

Costs (2019–20) ***Tuition:*** state resident $6182 full-time, $368 per credit hour part-time; nonresident $25,418 full-time, $1330 per credit hour part-time. Full-time tuition and fees vary according to course load, program, and reciprocity agreements. Part-time tuition and fees vary according to program and reciprocity agreements. ***Required fees:*** $2122 full-time, $47 per credit hour part-time. ***Room and board:*** $9080. Room and board charges vary according to board plan and housing facility. ***Payment plan:*** installment. ***Waivers:*** employees or children of employees.

Financial Aid Of all full-time matriculated undergraduates who enrolled in 2018, 5,808 applied for aid, 4,650 were judged to have need, 1,512 had their need fully met. In 2018, 1751 non-need-based awards were made. ***Average percent of need met:*** 76. ***Average financial aid package:*** $13,613. ***Average need-based loan:*** $6248. ***Average need-based gift aid:*** $5069. ***Average non-need-based aid:*** $5342. ***Average indebtedness upon graduation:*** $23,105.

APPLYING

Standardized Tests *Required:* SAT or ACT (for admission). *Required for some:* SAT and SAT Subject Tests or ACT (for admission).

Options: electronic application, deferred entrance.

Application fee: $60.

Required: high school transcript, minimum 2.2 GPA. ***Required for some:*** essay or personal statement.

Application deadlines: 8/1 (freshmen), rolling (transfers).

Notification: continuous (freshmen), continuous (transfers).

CONTACT

Ms. Melissa Goodwin, Associate Director, Admissions, University of Idaho, 875 Perimeter Drive, MS 4264, Moscow, ID 83844-4264. *Phone:* 208-885-9030. *Toll-free phone:* 888-884-3246. *Fax:* 208-885-9119. *E-mail:* admissions@uidaho.edu.

ILLINOIS

Ambria College of Nursing

Hoffman Estates, Illinois

http://www.ambria.edu/

CONTACT

Ambria College of Nursing, 5210 Trillium Boulevard, Hoffman Estates, IL 60192.

American Academy of Art

Chicago, Illinois

http://www.aaart.edu/

- **Independent** 4-year, founded 1923
- **Urban** campus with easy access to Chicago
- **Coed** 260 undergraduate students, 74% full-time, 62% women, 38% men
- **Moderately difficult** entrance level

UNDERGRAD STUDENTS

193 full-time, 67 part-time. Students come from 7 states and territories; 18% are from out of state; 10% Black or African American, non-Hispanic/Latino; 36% Hispanic/Latino; 4% Asian, non-Hispanic/Latino; 0.8% Native Hawaiian or other Pacific Islander, non-Hispanic/Latino; 0.4% American Indian or Alaska Native, non-Hispanic/Latino; 5% Two or more races, non-Hispanic/Latino; 2% transferred in.

Freshmen:

Admission: 56 enrolled.

Retention: 75% of full-time freshmen returned.

FACULTY

Total: 26, 100% full-time, 4% with terminal degrees.

Student/faculty ratio: 14:1.

ACADEMICS

Calendar: semesters. *Degree:* bachelor's.

Special study options: academic remediation for entering students, accelerated degree program, adult/continuing education programs, independent study, internships, part-time degree program, study abroad, summer session for credit.

Library: Irving Shapiro Library.

STUDENT LIFE

Housing options: Campus housing is university owned.

Campus security: 24-hour emergency response devices.

FINANCIAL AID

Financial Aid ***Average percent of need met:*** 70.

APPLYING

Options: electronic application.

Application fee: $25.

Required: high school transcript, interview.

Application deadlines: rolling (freshmen), rolling (transfers).

CONTACT

Mr. Stuart Rosenbloom, Director of Admissions, American Academy of Art, 332 South Michigan Avenue, Suite 300, Chicago, IL 60604-4302. *Phone:* 312-461-0600 Ext. 129. *Toll-free phone:* 888-461-0600. *E-mail:* srosenbloom@aaart.edu.

American InterContinental University Online

Schaumburg, Illinois

http://www.aiuniv.edu/

CONTACT

Jennifer Ziegenmier, Senior Vice President of Admissions and Marketing, American InterContinental University Online, 231 N. Martingale Road, 6th Floor, Schaumburg, IL 60173. *Phone:* 877-564-6248. *Toll-free phone:* 877-701-3800. *E-mail:* jziegenmier@aiuonline.edu.

Argosy University, Chicago

Chicago, Illinois

http://www.argosy.edu/chicago-illinois/default.aspx

CONTACT

Argosy University, Chicago, 225 North Michigan Avenue, Suite 1300, Chicago, IL 60601. *Phone:* 312-777-7600. *Toll-free phone:* 800-626-4123.

Augustana College

Rock Island, Illinois

http://www.augustana.edu/

- **Independent** 4-year, founded 1860, affiliated with Evangelical Lutheran Church in America
- **Suburban** 115-acre campus
- **Endowment** $168.8 million
- **Coed** 2,546 undergraduate students, 100% full-time, 56% women, 44% men
- **Moderately difficult** entrance level, 57% of applicants were admitted

UNDERGRAD STUDENTS

2,534 full-time, 12 part-time. Students come from 30 states and territories; 44 other countries; 16% are from out of state; 4% Black or African American, non-Hispanic/Latino; 11% Hispanic/Latino; 3% Asian, non-Hispanic/Latino; 0.1% Native Hawaiian or other Pacific Islander, non-Hispanic/Latino; 0.1% American Indian or Alaska Native, non-Hispanic/Latino; 4% Two or more races, non-Hispanic/Latino; 1% Race/ethnicity unknown; 12% international; 2% transferred in; 70% live on campus.

Freshmen:

Admission: 6,757 applied, 3,826 admitted, 678 enrolled. ***Average high school GPA:*** 3.4. ***Test scores:*** SAT evidence-based reading and writing scores over 500: 91%; SAT math scores over 500: 86%; ACT scores over 18: 95%; SAT evidence-based reading and writing scores over 600: 45%; SAT math scores over 600: 45%; ACT scores over 24: 65%; SAT evidence-based reading and writing scores over 700: 7%; SAT math scores over 700: 10%; ACT scores over 30: 20%.

Retention: 83% of full-time freshmen returned.

FACULTY

Total: 260, 77% full-time, 78% with terminal degrees.

Student/faculty ratio: 11:1.

ACADEMICS

Calendar: quarters. *Degree:* bachelor's.

Special study options: advanced placement credit, double majors, English as a second language, honors programs, independent study, internships, off-campus study, part-time degree program, services for LD students, student-designed majors, study abroad, summer session for credit.

Unusual degree programs: 3-2 engineering with Washington University in St. Louis, Northern Illinois University; forestry with Duke University; nursing with Trinity College; accounting with Wake Forest University, occupational therapy and/or physical therapy with Washington University in St. Louis, landscape architecture and veterinary medicine with University of Illinois, optometry with Illinois College of Optometry, pre-Law with Capital University.

Computers: 600 computers/terminals and 1,800 ports are available on campus for general student use. Students can access the following: campus intranet, computer help desk, free student e-mail accounts, online (class) grades, online (class) registration, online (class) schedules. Campuswide network is available. 100% of college-owned or -operated housing units are wired for high-speed Internet access. Wireless service is available via entire campus.

Library: Thomas Tredway Library plus 1 other. *Books:* 128,238 (physical), 4,470 (digital/electronic); *Serial titles:* 233 (physical), 120,219 (digital/electronic); *Databases:* 106. Weekly public service hours: 100.

STUDENT LIFE

Housing options: on-campus residence required through junior year; coed. Campus housing is university owned. Freshman campus housing is guaranteed.

Activities and organizations: drama/theater group, student-run newspaper, radio station, choral group, College Union Board of Managers, Student Government Association, student newspaper, student radio station, service organizations (APO, Dance Marathon committee).

Athletics Member NCAA. All Division III. ***Intercollegiate sports:*** baseball M, basketball M/W, cheerleading W(c), crew M(c)/W(c), cross-country running M/W, equestrian sports M(c)/W(c), fencing M(c)/W(c), football M, golf M/W, ice hockey M(c), lacrosse M/W, soccer M/W, softball W, swimming and diving M/W, tennis M/W, track and field M/W, ultimate Frisbee M(c)/W(c), volleyball M(c)/W, water polo M(c)/W(c), wrestling M. ***Intramural sports:*** badminton M/W, basketball M/W, bowling M/W, cross-country running M/W, football M/W, golf M/W, racquetball M/W, rugby M, skiing (cross-country) M/W, skiing (downhill) M/W, soccer M/W, softball M/W, swimming and diving M/W, table tennis M/W, tennis M/W, track and field M/W, ultimate Frisbee M/W, volleyball M/W, wrestling M.

Campus security: 24-hour emergency response devices and patrols, late-night transport/escort service, controlled dormitory access.

Student services: personal/psychological counseling.

COSTS & FINANCIAL AID

Costs (2020–21) ***Comprehensive fee:*** $56,352 includes full-time tuition ($45,136) and room and board ($11,216). Part-time tuition: $1882 per credit hour. ***College room only:*** $5538.

Financial Aid ***Average indebtedness upon graduation:*** $34,964.

APPLYING

Options: electronic application, early admission, early decision, early action, deferred entrance.

Required: high school transcript. ***Required for some:*** essay or personal statement, interview. ***Recommended:*** essay or personal statement, 1 letter of recommendation, interview.

Application deadlines: rolling (freshmen), rolling (transfers), 11/1 (early action).

Early decision deadline: 11/1.

Notification: continuous (freshmen), continuous (transfers), 11/15 (early decision), 12/1 (early action).

CONTACT

W. Kent Barnds, Vice President of Enrollment Management, Augustana College, 639 38th Street, Rock Island, IL 61201. *Phone:* 309-794-7662. *Toll-free phone:* 800-798-8100. *Fax:* 309-794-8797. *E-mail:* admissions@augustana.edu.

Aurora University

Aurora, Illinois

http://www.aurora.edu/

- **Independent** comprehensive, founded 1893
- **Suburban** 70-acre campus with easy access to Chicago
- **Endowment** $41.2 million
- **Coed** 4,104 undergraduate students, 90% full-time, 66% women, 34% men
- **Moderately difficult** entrance level, 87% of applicants were admitted

UNDERGRAD STUDENTS

3,679 full-time, 425 part-time. Students come from 38 states and territories; 3 other countries; 11% are from out of state; 7% Black or African American, non-Hispanic/Latino; 34% Hispanic/Latino; 3% Asian, non-Hispanic/Latino; 0.2% Native Hawaiian or other Pacific Islander, non-Hispanic/Latino; 0.3% American Indian or Alaska Native, non-Hispanic/Latino; 3% Two or more races, non-Hispanic/Latino; 6%

Race/ethnicity unknown; 0.5% international; 14% transferred in; 17% live on campus.

Freshmen:

Admission: 2,902 applied, 2,517 admitted, 814 enrolled. ***Average high school GPA:*** 3.4. ***Test scores:*** SAT evidence-based reading and writing scores over 500: 70%; SAT math scores over 500: 68%; ACT scores over 18: 82%; SAT evidence-based reading and writing scores over 600: 15%; SAT math scores over 600: 15%; ACT scores over 24: 25%; SAT evidence-based reading and writing scores over 700: 1%; SAT math scores over 700: 2%; ACT scores over 30: 3%.

Retention: 74% of full-time freshmen returned.

FACULTY

Total: 521, 27% full-time.

Student/faculty ratio: 17:1.

ACADEMICS

Calendar: semesters. *Degrees:* bachelor's, master's, doctoral, and post-master's certificates.

Special study options: academic remediation for entering students, accelerated degree program, adult/continuing education programs, advanced placement credit, distance learning, double majors, independent study, internships, off-campus study, part-time degree program, services for LD students, student-designed majors, study abroad, summer session for credit. ***ROTC:*** Army (c).

Computers: 193 computers/terminals are available on campus for general student use. Students can access the following: campus intranet, computer help desk, free student e-mail accounts, online (class) grades, online (class) registration, online (class) schedules, learning management system. Campuswide network is available. 100% of college-owned or -operated housing units are wired for high-speed Internet access. Wireless service is available via classrooms, computer labs, dorm rooms, learning centers, libraries, student centers.

Library: Charles B. Phillips Library plus 1 other. *Books:* 24,587 (physical), 197,381 (digital/electronic); *Serial titles:* 2 (physical), 55,369 (digital/electronic); *Databases:* 63. Weekly public service hours: 99; students can reserve study rooms.

STUDENT LIFE

Housing options: coed. Campus housing is university owned. Freshman applicants given priority for college housing.

Activities and organizations: drama/theater group, student-run newspaper, radio and television station, choral group, Latin American Student Organization, American Marketing Association, Student Nursing Association, Phi Eta Sigma, Spartan Athletic Training Student Organization, national fraternities, national sororities.

Athletics Member NCAA. All Division III. ***Intercollegiate sports:*** baseball M, basketball M/W, bowling W, cross-country running M/W, football M, golf M/W, ice hockey M/W, lacrosse M/W, soccer M/W, softball W, track and field M/W, volleyball M/W. ***Intramural sports:*** badminton M/W, basketball M/W, cheerleading M(c)/W(c), football M/W, ice hockey M(c), soccer M/W, softball M/W, ultimate Frisbee M/W, volleyball M/W.

Campus security: 24-hour emergency response devices and patrols, late-night transport/escort service, controlled dormitory access.

Student services: health clinic, personal/psychological counseling.

COSTS & FINANCIAL AID

Costs (2020–21) ***Comprehensive fee:*** $37,980 includes full-time tuition ($25,600), mandatory fees ($360), and room and board ($12,020). Full-time tuition and fees vary according to course load, location, and program. Part-time tuition: $735 per semester hour. Part-time tuition and fees vary according to course load, location, and program. ***College room only:*** $6690. Room and board charges vary according to board plan, housing facility, and location. ***Payment plans:*** installment, deferred payment. ***Waivers:*** employees or children of employees.

Financial Aid Of all full-time matriculated undergraduates who enrolled in 2019, 3,230 applied for aid, 2,942 were judged to have need, 324 had their need fully met. In 2019, 648 non-need-based awards were made. ***Average percent of need met:*** 80. ***Average financial aid package:*** $21,920. ***Average need-based loan:*** $3222. ***Average need-based gift aid:*** $16,342. ***Average non-need-based aid:*** $11,200. ***Average indebtedness upon graduation:*** $27,851.

APPLYING

Standardized Tests *Required:* SAT or ACT (for admission).

Options: electronic application, early action, deferred entrance.

Required: high school transcript, minimum 2.0 GPA. ***Required for some:*** essay or personal statement, 2 letters of recommendation, interview.

Application deadlines: rolling (freshmen), rolling (transfers).

Notification: continuous (freshmen), continuous (transfers).

CONTACT

Mr. Joel Ortega, Director of Freshman Enrollment, Aurora University, 347 South Gladstone Avenue, Aurora, IL 60506-4892. *Phone:* 630-844-5533. *Toll-free phone:* 800-742-5281. *Fax:* 630-844-5535. *E-mail:* admission@aurora.edu.

Benedictine University

Lisle, Illinois

http://www.ben.edu/

- **Independent Roman Catholic** comprehensive, founded 1887
- **Suburban** 108-acre campus with easy access to Chicago
- **Endowment** $36.4 million
- **Coed** 2,493 undergraduate students, 85% full-time, 54% women, 46% men
- **Moderately difficult** entrance level, 42% of applicants were admitted

UNDERGRAD STUDENTS

2,131 full-time, 362 part-time. 12% are from out of state; 9% Black or African American, non-Hispanic/Latino; 18% Hispanic/Latino; 16% Asian, non-Hispanic/Latino; 0.5% Native Hawaiian or other Pacific Islander, non-Hispanic/Latino; 1% American Indian or Alaska Native, non-Hispanic/Latino; 11% Race/ethnicity unknown; 2% international; 12% transferred in; 78% live on campus.

Freshmen:

Admission: 4,850 applied, 2,023 admitted, 347 enrolled. ***Average high school GPA:*** 3.3. ***Test scores:*** SAT evidence-based reading and writing scores over 500: 65%; SAT math scores over 500: 81%; ACT scores over 18: 83%; SAT evidence-based reading and writing scores over 600: 16%; SAT math scores over 600: 28%; ACT scores over 24: 37%; SAT evidence-based reading and writing scores over 700: 2%; SAT math scores over 700: 5%; ACT scores over 30: 6%.

Retention: 69% of full-time freshmen returned.

FACULTY

Total: 401, 35% full-time, 55% with terminal degrees.

Student/faculty ratio: 14:1.

ACADEMICS

Calendar: semesters. *Degrees:* certificates, bachelor's, master's, doctoral, and postbachelor's certificates.

Special study options: academic remediation for entering students, accelerated degree program, adult/continuing education programs, advanced placement credit, distance learning, double majors, English as a second language, honors programs, independent study, internships, off-campus study, part-time degree program, services for LD students, study abroad, summer session for credit. ***ROTC:*** Army (c).

Unusual degree programs: 3-2 engineering with Illinois Institute of Technology; nursing.

Computers: 275 computers/terminals and 275 ports are available on campus for general student use. Students can access the following: computer help desk, free student e-mail accounts, online (class) grades, online (class) registration, online (class) schedules. Campuswide network is available. 100% of college-owned or -operated housing units are wired for high-speed Internet access. Wireless service is available via entire campus.

Library: Benedictine Library. *Books:* 90,762 (physical), 187,960 (digital/electronic); *Serial titles:* 1,498 (physical), 51,758 (digital/electronic); *Databases:* 61. Students can reserve study rooms.

STUDENT LIFE

Housing options: coed, men-only, women-only, special housing for students with disabilities. Campus housing is university owned. Freshman campus housing is guaranteed.

Activities and organizations: drama/theater group, student-run newspaper, television station, choral group, Student Senate, MSA-Muslim Student Association, AMSA-American Medical Student Association, The Candor-Student Newspaper, Programming Board.

Athletics Member NCAA, NAIA. All NCAA Division III except golf (Division II). ***Intercollegiate sports:*** baseball M, basketball M/W, cross-country running M/W, football M, golf M/W, lacrosse M/W, soccer M/W, softball W, track and field M/W, volleyball M/W. ***Intramural sports:*** basketball M/W, bowling M/W, cheerleading W(c), football M, lacrosse M(c), softball M/W, table tennis M/W, volleyball M/W.

Campus security: 24-hour emergency response devices and patrols, late-night transport/escort service, controlled dormitory access.

Student services: health clinic, personal/psychological counseling.

COSTS & FINANCIAL AID

Costs (2020–21) ***Comprehensive fee:*** $32,700 includes full-time tuition ($32,700), mandatory fees ($1590), and room and board ($4960). Part-time tuition: $1090 per credit hour. ***College room only:*** $3250. Room and board charges vary according to board plan, housing facility, and location.

Financial Aid Of all full-time matriculated undergraduates who enrolled in 2019, 1,764 applied for aid, 1,634 were judged to have need. In 2019, 403 non-need-based awards were made. ***Average financial aid package:*** $25,511. ***Average need-based loan:*** $4285. ***Average need-based gift aid:*** $9674. ***Average non-need-based aid:*** $14,352. ***Average indebtedness upon graduation:*** $26,447.

APPLYING

Standardized Tests *Required:* SAT or ACT (for admission).

Options: electronic application, deferred entrance.

Application fee: $40.

Required: essay or personal statement, high school transcript. ***Required for some:*** interview. ***Recommended:*** rank in upper 50% of high school class.

Application deadlines: rolling (freshmen), rolling (transfers).

Notification: continuous (freshmen), continuous (transfers).

CONTACT

Ms. Karen Campana, Chief Retention Officer, Benedictine University, 5700 College Road, Lisle, IL 60532-0900. *Toll-free phone:* 888-829-6363. *E-mail:* admissions@ben.edu.

Blackburn College

Carlinville, Illinois

http://www.blackburn.edu/

- **Independent Presbyterian** 4-year, founded 1837
- **Small-town** 80-acre campus with easy access to St. Louis
- **Endowment** $23.4 million
- **Coed**
- **Moderately difficult** entrance level

FACULTY

Student/faculty ratio: 13:1.

ACADEMICS

Calendar: semesters. *Degree:* bachelor's.

Library: Lumpkin Learning Commons. *Books:* 62,000 (physical); *Serial titles:* 40 (physical); *Databases:* 21. Weekly public service hours: 80; students can reserve study rooms.

STUDENT LIFE

Housing options: on-campus residence required through junior year; coed, men-only, women-only. Campus housing is university owned. Freshman campus housing is guaranteed.

Activities and organizations: drama/theater group, student-run newspaper, radio station, choral group, Habitat for Humanity, Pre-Health Professions, Running Club, Trading Card Games, Spectrum.

Athletics Member NCAA. All Division III.

Campus security: student patrols, late-night transport/escort service.

Student services: personal/psychological counseling.

COSTS & FINANCIAL AID

Costs (2019–20) ***Comprehensive fee:*** $31,610 includes full-time tuition ($23,510) and room and board ($8100). Full-time tuition and fees vary according to student level. Part-time tuition: $765 per credit hour. Part-time tuition and fees vary according to student level. ***College room only:*** $4800.

Financial Aid Of all full-time matriculated undergraduates who enrolled in 2018, 532 applied for aid, 495 were judged to have need, 432 had their need fully met. In 2018, 39 non-need-based awards were made. ***Average percent of need met:*** 87. ***Average financial aid package:*** $19,123. ***Average need-based loan:*** $3677. ***Average need-based gift aid:*** $19,123. ***Average non-need-based aid:*** $4607. ***Average indebtedness upon graduation:*** $30,677.

APPLYING

Standardized Tests *Required:* SAT or ACT (for admission).

Options: electronic application, deferred entrance.

Required: high school transcript, minimum 2.0 GPA. ***Required for some:*** essay or personal statement, 3 letters of recommendation, interview. ***Recommended:*** minimum 2.5 GPA.

CONTACT

Mr. Justin Norwood, Director of Admissions, Blackburn College, 700 College Avenue, Carlinville, IL 62626. *Phone:* 217-854-5559. *Toll-free phone:* 800-233-3550. *E-mail:* justin.norwood@blackburn.edu.

Blessing-Rieman College of Nursing & Health Sciences

Quincy, Illinois

http://www.brcn.edu/

CONTACT

Ms. Heather Mutter, Admissions Counselor, Blessing-Rieman College of Nursing & Health Sciences, Broadway at 11th Street, POB 7005, Quincy, IL 62305-7005. *Phone:* 217-228-5520 Ext. 6979. *Toll-free phone:* 800-877-9140. *Fax:* 217-223-4661. *E-mail:* admissions@brcn.edu.

Bradley University

Peoria, Illinois

http://www.bradley.edu/

- **Independent** comprehensive, founded 1897
- **Suburban** 85-acre campus
- **Endowment** $312.5 million
- **Coed** 4,606 undergraduate students, 97% full-time, 51% women, 49% men
- **Moderately difficult** entrance level, 67% of applicants were admitted

UNDERGRAD STUDENTS

4,462 full-time, 144 part-time. Students come from 47 states and territories; 42 other countries; 18% are from out of state; 7% Black or African American, non-Hispanic/Latino; 10% Hispanic/Latino; 3% Asian, non-Hispanic/Latino; 3% Two or more races, non-Hispanic/Latino; 2% Race/ethnicity unknown; 2% international; 4% transferred in; 67% live on campus.

Freshmen:

Admission: 11,209 applied, 7,489 admitted, 1,090 enrolled. ***Average high school GPA:*** 3.8.

Retention: 82% of full-time freshmen returned.

ACADEMICS

Calendar: semesters. *Degrees:* bachelor's, master's, doctoral, post-master's, and postbachelor's certificates.

Special study options: accelerated degree program, advanced placement credit, cooperative education, distance learning, double majors, honors programs, independent study, internships, off-campus study, part-time degree program, services for LD students, student-designed majors, study abroad, summer session for credit. ***ROTC:*** Army (b).

Computers: 80 computers/terminals and 3,123 ports are available on campus for general student use. Students can access the following: campus intranet, computer help desk, free student e-mail accounts, online (class) grades, online (class) registration, online (class) schedules, Online directory, catalog, library materials and other resources. Campuswide network is available. 100% of college-owned or -operated housing units are wired for high-speed Internet access. Wireless service is available via entire campus.

Library: Cullom-Davis Library. Weekly public service hours: 129; students can reserve study rooms.

STUDENT LIFE

Housing options: on-campus residence required through sophomore year; coed. Campus housing is university owned. Freshman campus housing is guaranteed.

Activities and organizations: drama/theater group, student-run newspaper, radio and television station, choral group, Activities Council of Bradley University, CRU (Campus Christian group), Fraternity/Sorority Life, Service on Saturday, Alpha Phi Omega (Coed Service), national fraternities, national sororities.

Athletics ***Intercollegiate sports:*** baseball M(s), basketball M(s)/W(s), cheerleading M/W, cross-country running M(s)/W(s), golf M(s)/W(s)(c), soccer M(s), softball W(s), table tennis M(c), tennis W(s), track and field M(s)/W(s), volleyball M(c)/W(s), wrestling M(c). ***Intramural sports:*** badminton M/W, baseball M(c), basketball M/W, bowling M/W, fencing M(c), field hockey W(c), football M/W, golf M/W, ice hockey M(c), lacrosse M(c)/W(c), racquetball M/W, rock climbing M(c)/W(c), soccer M(c)/W(c), softball M/W(c), swimming and diving M/W, table tennis M/W, tennis M/W, triathlon M(c)/W(c), ultimate Frisbee M(c)/W(c), volleyball M/W, water polo M(c)/W(c), wrestling M/W.

Campus security: 24-hour emergency response devices and patrols, student patrols, late-night transport/escort service, controlled dormitory access, emergency text messaging, mass notification/emergency communication system in 20 academic buildings.

Student services: health clinic, personal/psychological counseling.

COSTS & FINANCIAL AID

Costs (2020–21) ***One-time required fee:*** $200. ***Comprehensive fee:*** $46,760 includes full-time tuition ($35,060), mandatory fees ($420), and room and board ($11,280). Full-time tuition and fees vary according to course load and program. Part-time tuition: $930 per credit hour. Part-time tuition and fees vary according to course load and program. ***Required fees:*** $420 per year part-time. ***College room only:*** $6520. Room and board charges vary according to board plan and housing facility. ***Payment plans:*** installment, deferred payment. ***Waivers:*** senior citizens and employees or children of employees.

Financial Aid Of all full-time matriculated undergraduates who enrolled in 2019, 3,837 applied for aid, 3,265 were judged to have need, 566 had their need fully met. 345 Federal Work-Study jobs (averaging $1200). In 2019, 1183 non-need-based awards were made. ***Average percent of need met:*** 75. ***Average financial aid package:*** $25,827. ***Average need-based loan:*** $6072. ***Average need-based gift aid:*** $20,854. ***Average non-need-based aid:*** $12,925. ***Average indebtedness upon graduation:*** $31,111.

APPLYING

Standardized Tests *Required:* SAT or ACT (for admission).

Options: electronic application, deferred entrance.

Required: essay or personal statement, high school transcript. ***Required for some:*** audition required of music majors and recommended for theatre majors, portfolio recommended for art majors. ***Recommended:*** minimum 2.8 GPA, 1 letter of recommendation, interview.

Application deadlines: rolling (freshmen), rolling (transfers).

Notification: continuous (freshmen), continuous (transfers).

CONTACT

Dr. Justin Ball, Vice President for Enrollment Management, Bradley University, 1501 W. Bradley Avenue, Peoria, IL 61625. *Phone:* 309-677-1000. *Toll-free phone:* 800-447-6460. *Fax:* 309-677-2797. *E-mail:* admissions@bradley.edu.

Chamberlain College of Nursing - Addison

Addison, Illinois

http://www.chamberlain.edu/

CONTACT

Admissions, Chamberlain College of Nursing - Addison, 1221 North Swift Road, Addison, IL 60101. *Phone:* 630-953-3680. *Toll-free phone:* 877-751-5783.

Chamberlain College of Nursing - Chicago

Chicago, Illinois

http://www.chamberlain.edu/

CONTACT

Admissions, Chamberlain College of Nursing - Chicago, 3300 North Campbell Avenue, Chicago, IL 60618. *Phone:* 773-961-3000. *Toll-free phone:* 877-751-5783.

Chamberlain College of Nursing - Tinley Park

Tinley Park, Illinois

http://www.chamberlain.edu/

CONTACT

Chamberlain College of Nursing - Tinley Park, 18624 West Creek Drive, Tinley Park, IL 60477. *Toll-free phone:* 877-751-5783.

Chicago State University

Chicago, Illinois

http://www.csu.edu/

- **State-supported** comprehensive, founded 1867
- **Urban** 161-acre campus
- **Coed**
- **Minimally difficult** entrance level

FACULTY

Student/faculty ratio: 13:1.

ACADEMICS

Calendar: semesters. *Degrees:* bachelor's, master's, doctoral, and postbachelor's certificates.

Library: New Academic Library.

STUDENT LIFE

Housing options: coed. Campus housing is university owned.

Activities and organizations: drama/theater group, student-run newspaper, radio station, choral group, national fraternities, national sororities.

Athletics Member NCAA. All Division I.

Campus security: 24-hour emergency response devices and patrols, student patrols, late-night transport/escort service, controlled dormitory access.

Student services: health clinic, personal/psychological counseling, women's center.

FINANCIAL AID

Financial Aid Of all full-time matriculated undergraduates who enrolled in 2013, 2,703 applied for aid, 2,701 were judged to have need. In 2013, 22 non-need-based awards were made. ***Average percent of need met:*** 40. ***Average financial aid package:*** $11,606. ***Average need-based loan:*** $4343. ***Average need-based gift aid:*** $7724. ***Average non-need-based aid:*** $5931. ***Average indebtedness upon graduation:*** $29,731. ***Financial aid deadline:*** 6/30.

APPLYING

Standardized Tests *Required:* SAT or ACT (for admission).

Options: electronic application.

Application fee: $25.

Required: high school transcript, minimum 2.5 GPA. ***Required for some:*** essay or personal statement, interview.

CONTACT

Mr. John Martinez, Associate Director of Admissions, Chicago State University, 95th Street at King Drive, ADM 200, Chicago, IL 60628. *Phone:* 773-995-3578. *Fax:* 773-995-3820. *E-mail:* jmarti21@csu.edu.

Columbia College Chicago

Chicago, Illinois

http://www.colum.edu/

- **Independent** comprehensive, founded 1890
- **Urban** campus with easy access to Chicago
- **Coed** 6,708 undergraduate students, 93% full-time, 58% women, 42% men
- **Minimally difficult** entrance level, 90% of applicants were admitted

UNDERGRAD STUDENTS
6,252 full-time, 456 part-time. Students come from 52 states and territories; 55 other countries; 43% are from out of state; 14% Black or African American, non-Hispanic/Latino; 19% Hispanic/Latino; 4% Asian, non-Hispanic/Latino; 0.2% Native Hawaiian or other Pacific Islander, non-Hispanic/Latino; 0.2% American Indian or Alaska Native, non-Hispanic/Latino; 5% Two or more races, non-Hispanic/Latino; 2% Race/ethnicity unknown; 4% international; 10% transferred in; 35% live on campus.

Freshmen:
Admission: 7,130 applied, 6,703 admitted, 1,718 enrolled. ***Average high school GPA:*** 3.4. ***Test scores:*** SAT evidence-based reading and writing scores over 500: 73%; SAT math scores over 500: 66%; ACT scores over 18: 90%; SAT evidence-based reading and writing scores over 600: 33%; SAT math scores over 600: 20%; ACT scores over 24: 53%; SAT evidence-based reading and writing scores over 700: 5%; SAT math scores over 700: 4%; ACT scores over 30: 12%.

Retention: 71% of full-time freshmen returned.

FACULTY
Total: 856, 30% full-time, 18% with terminal degrees.

Student/faculty ratio: 14:1.

ACADEMICS
Calendar: semesters. *Degrees:* bachelor's, master's, and postbachelor's certificates.

Special study options: academic remediation for entering students, cooperative education, distance learning, double majors, English as a second language, honors programs, independent study, internships, off-campus study, part-time degree program, services for LD students, study abroad, summer session for credit. ***ROTC:*** Army (c), Navy (c), Air Force (c).

Computers: Students can access the following: campus intranet, computer help desk, free student e-mail accounts, online (class) grades, online (class) registration, online (class) schedules. Campuswide network is available. Wireless service is available via classrooms, computer centers, computer labs, learning centers, libraries, student centers.
Library: Columbia College Chicago Library. *Books:* 207,635 (physical), 131,083 (digital/electronic); *Serial titles:* 274 (physical); *Databases:* 138. Students can reserve study rooms.

STUDENT LIFE
Housing options: coed, special housing for students with disabilities. Campus housing is university owned.

Activities and organizations: drama/theater group, student-run newspaper, radio and television station, choral group, marching band, Black Student Union, Student Government Association, Asian Student Organization, Columbia Pride, Latino Alliance.

Athletics ***Intramural sports:*** basketball M/W, football M/W, soccer M/W, ultimate Frisbee M/W, volleyball M/W.

Campus security: 24-hour emergency response devices and patrols, late-night transport/escort service, controlled dormitory access, Marked security vehicle, segways and bicycles to provide rapid response to incidents.

Student services: health clinic, personal/psychological counseling, veterans affairs office.

COSTS & FINANCIAL AID
Costs (2020–21) ***Comprehensive fee:*** $44,774 includes full-time tuition ($27,142), mandatory fees ($1176), and room and board ($16,456). Part-time tuition: $937 per credit hour. ***Room and board:*** Room and board charges vary according to housing facility. ***Payment plan:*** deferred payment. ***Waivers:*** employees or children of employees.

Financial Aid Of all full-time matriculated undergraduates who enrolled in 2019, 5,169 applied for aid, 3,988 were judged to have need, 1,525 had their need fully met. 139 Federal Work-Study jobs (averaging $4609). In 2019, 42 non-need-based awards were made. ***Average percent of need met:*** 47. ***Average financial aid package:*** $14,717. ***Average need-based loan:*** $4070. ***Average need-based gift aid:*** $14,998. ***Average non-need-based aid:*** $18,959. ***Average indebtedness upon graduation:*** $34,328. ***Financial aid deadline:*** 6/30.

APPLYING
Options: electronic application, deferred entrance.

Application fee: $25.

Required: high school transcript. ***Required for some:*** interview, ACT or SAT scores, AP scores, IB exam results, portfolio or audition for BFA or BMus program, proof of English language proficiency for international students.

Application deadlines: 8/15 (freshmen), 8/15 (out-of-state freshmen), rolling (transfers).

Notification: continuous until 11/1 (freshmen), continuous until 11/1 (out-of-state freshmen), continuous (transfers).

CONTACT
Derek Brinkley, Assistant Vice President Undergraduate Admissions, Columbia College Chicago, 600 South Michigan Avenue, Chicago, IL 60605-1996. *Phone:* 312-369-7493. *E-mail:* dbrinkley@colum.edu.

Concordia University Chicago

River Forest, Illinois

http://www.cuchicago.edu/

- **Independent** comprehensive, founded 1864, affiliated with Lutheran Church–Missouri Synod, part of Concordia University System
- **Suburban** 40-acre campus with easy access to Chicago
- **Coed** 1,515 undergraduate students, 91% full-time, 58% women, 42% men
- **Moderately difficult** entrance level, 75% of applicants were admitted

UNDERGRAD STUDENTS
1,376 full-time, 139 part-time. 29% are from out of state; 11% Black or African American, non-Hispanic/Latino; 31% Hispanic/Latino; 2% Asian, non-Hispanic/Latino; 0.2% Native Hawaiian or other Pacific Islander, non-Hispanic/Latino; 4% Two or more races, non-Hispanic/Latino; 0.9% Race/ethnicity unknown; 3% international; 6% transferred in; 38% live on campus.

Freshmen:
Admission: 4,498 applied, 3,361 admitted, 351 enrolled. ***Average high school GPA:*** 3.1. ***Test scores:*** SAT evidence-based reading and writing scores over 500: 79%; SAT math scores over 500: 82%; ACT scores over 18: 94%; SAT evidence-based reading and writing scores over 600: 23%; SAT math scores over 600: 21%; ACT scores over 24: 45%; SAT evidence-based reading and writing scores over 700: 2%; SAT math scores over 700: 2%; ACT scores over 30: 11%.

Retention: 62% of full-time freshmen returned.

FACULTY
Total: 492, 30% full-time, 57% with terminal degrees.

Student/faculty ratio: 12:1.

ACADEMICS
Calendar: semesters. *Degrees:* certificates, associate, bachelor's, master's, doctoral, and post-master's certificates.

Special study options: accelerated degree program, adult/continuing education programs, distance learning, double majors, honors programs, independent study, internships, part-time degree program, student-designed majors, study abroad.

Computers: Students can access the following: campus intranet, computer help desk, free student e-mail accounts, online (class) grades, online (class) registration, online (class) schedules. Campuswide network is available. 100% of college-owned or -operated housing units are wired for high-speed Internet access. Wireless service is available via entire campus.
Library: Klinck Memorial Library. *Books:* 160,000 (physical); *Databases:* 80. Weekly public service hours: 89; students can reserve study rooms.

STUDENT LIFE

Housing options: coed. Campus housing is university owned. Freshman campus housing is guaranteed.

Activities and organizations: drama/theater group, student-run newspaper, radio and television station, choral group, Campus Ministry, College Life, Student Government Association, Campus Activities Board, Art Club.

Athletics Member NCAA. All Division III. ***Intercollegiate sports:*** basketball M/W, cheerleading W, cross-country running M/W, football M, lacrosse M/W, soccer M/W, tennis M/W, track and field M/W, volleyball W. ***Intramural sports:*** baseball M(c), basketball M(c)/W(c), soccer M(c)/W(c), softball W(c), ultimate Frisbee M(c)/W(c), volleyball M(c)/W(c).

Campus security: 24-hour emergency response devices and patrols, student patrols, late-night transport/escort service, controlled dormitory access, emergency call boxes.

Student services: health clinic, personal/psychological counseling.

COSTS & FINANCIAL AID

Costs (2020–21) ***Comprehensive fee:*** $43,862 includes full-time tuition ($32,660), mandatory fees ($976), and room and board ($10,226). Part-time tuition: $978 per credit hour. ***College room only:*** $6424. Room and board charges vary according to board plan and housing facility. ***Payment plan:*** installment. ***Waivers:*** children of alumni and employees or children of employees.

Financial Aid Of all full-time matriculated undergraduates who enrolled in 2018, 1,232 applied for aid, 1,152 were judged to have need, 202 had their need fully met. In 2018, 181 non-need-based awards were made. ***Average percent of need met:*** 79. ***Average financial aid package:*** $24,637. ***Average need-based loan:*** $3962. ***Average need-based gift aid:*** $20,666. ***Average non-need-based aid:*** $15,698. ***Average indebtedness upon graduation:*** $28,122. ***Financial aid deadline:*** 6/1.

APPLYING

Standardized Tests *Required:* SAT or ACT (for admission).

Options: electronic application, early admission, deferred entrance.

Required: high school transcript, minimum 2.0 GPA, 1 letter of recommendation, general college preparatory program for degree seeking students. ***Required for some:*** essay or personal statement, interview.

Application deadlines: rolling (freshmen), rolling (transfers).

CONTACT

Ms. Gwen Kanelos, Director of Admission, Concordia University Chicago, 7400 Augusta Street, River Forest, IL 60305. *Phone:* 708-209-3101. *Toll-free phone:* 800-285-2668. *Fax:* 708-209-3473. *E-mail:* gwen.kanelos@cuchicago.edu.

DePaul University

Chicago, Illinois

http://www.depaul.edu/

- **Independent Roman Catholic** university, founded 1898
- **Urban** 38-acre campus with easy access to Chicago
- **Endowment** $696.5 million
- **Coed** 14,214 undergraduate students, 90% full-time, 53% women, 47% men
- **Moderately difficult** entrance level, 68% of applicants were admitted

UNDERGRAD STUDENTS

12,784 full-time, 1,430 part-time. Students come from 54 states and territories; 113 other countries; 25% are from out of state; 8% Black or African American, non-Hispanic/Latino; 20% Hispanic/Latino; 11% Asian, non-Hispanic/Latino; 0.2% Native Hawaiian or other Pacific Islander, non-Hispanic/Latino; 0.2% American Indian or Alaska Native, non-Hispanic/Latino; 4% Two or more races, non-Hispanic/Latino; 2% Race/ethnicity unknown; 3% international; 8% transferred in; 19% live on campus.

Freshmen:

Admission: 26,895 applied, 18,348 admitted, 2,627 enrolled. ***Average high school GPA:*** 3.7. ***Test scores:*** SAT evidence-based reading and writing scores over 500: 88%; SAT math scores over 500: 89%; SAT evidence-based reading and writing scores over 600: 50%; SAT math scores over 600: 46%; SAT evidence-based reading and writing scores over 700: 11%; SAT math scores over 700: 10%.

Retention: 85% of full-time freshmen returned.

FACULTY

Total: 1,832, 47% full-time, 52% with terminal degrees.

Student/faculty ratio: 16:1.

ACADEMICS

Calendar: quarters College of Law on semester system. *Degrees:* certificates, bachelor's, master's, doctoral, post-master's, and postbachelor's certificates.

Special study options: academic remediation for entering students, accelerated degree program, adult/continuing education programs, advanced placement credit, distance learning, double majors, English as a second language, freshman honors college, honors programs, independent study, internships, off-campus study, part-time degree program, services for LD students, study abroad, summer session for credit. ***ROTC:*** Army (b).

Unusual degree programs: 3-2 engineering with Chemical Engineering combined degree program with the Illinois Institute of Technology (IIT); visit https://www.depaul.edu/academics/undergraduate/Pages/combined-degrees.aspx for combined degree programs.

Computers: 1,500 computers/terminals are available on campus for general student use. Students can access the following: campus intranet, computer help desk, free student e-mail accounts, online (class) grades, online (class) registration, online (class) schedules, tuition payments, degree progress, financial aid, transcript requests, housing services, student employment information. Campuswide network is available. 100% of college-owned or -operated housing units are wired for high-speed Internet access. Wireless service is available via entire campus.

Library: John T. Richardson Library plus 2 others. *Books:* 572,388 (physical), 661,170 (digital/electronic); *Serial titles:* 20,007 (physical), 99,267 (digital/electronic). Students can reserve study rooms.

STUDENT LIFE

Housing options: coed, special housing for students with disabilities. Campus housing is university owned. Freshman campus housing is guaranteed.

Activities and organizations: drama/theater group, student-run newspaper, radio station, choral group, DePaul Community Service Association (DCSA), Black Student Union, DemonTHON, Panhellenic Council, DePaul Activities Board, national fraternities, national sororities.

Athletics Member NCAA. All Division I. ***Intercollegiate sports:*** basketball M(s)/W(s), cross-country running M(s)/W(s), golf M(s), soccer M(s)/W(s), softball W(s), tennis M(s)/W(s), track and field M(s)/W(s), volleyball W(s). ***Intramural sports:*** badminton M/W, baseball M(c)/W(c), basketball M/W(c), crew M(c)/W(c), fencing M(c)/W(c), golf M(c)/W(c), ice hockey M(c)/W(c), lacrosse M(c)/W(c), rock climbing M(c)/W(c), rowing M(c)/W(c), rugby M(c)/W(c), skiing (downhill) M(c)/W(c), soccer M(c)/W(c), softball M/W, swimming and diving M(c)/W(c), table tennis M/W, tennis M(c)/W(c), ultimate Frisbee M(c)/W(c), volleyball M(c)/W(c), water polo M(c)/W(c).

Campus security: 24-hour emergency response devices and patrols, late-night transport/escort service, controlled dormitory access, security lighting, prevention/awareness programs, on-campus public safety officers, video cameras, smoke detectors in residence halls.

Student services: health clinic, personal/psychological counseling, women's center, legal services, veterans affairs office.

COSTS & FINANCIAL AID

Costs (2019–20) ***Comprehensive fee:*** $55,938 includes full-time tuition ($40,551), mandatory fees ($651), and room and board ($14,736). Full-time tuition and fees vary according to course load, program, and student level. Part-time tuition: $655 per credit hour. Part-time tuition and fees vary according to course load, program, and student level. ***College room only:*** $10,428. Room and board charges vary according to board plan, housing facility, and location. ***Payment plans:*** installment, deferred payment. ***Waivers:*** employees or children of employees.

Financial Aid Of all full-time matriculated undergraduates who enrolled in 2018, 10,371 applied for aid, 9,093 were judged to have need, 767 had their need fully met. 679 Federal Work-Study jobs (averaging $4308). In 2018, 2450 non-need-based awards were made. ***Average percent of need met:*** 65. ***Average financial aid package:*** $25,548. ***Average need-based***

loan: $4116. ***Average need-based gift aid:*** $21,739. ***Average non-need-based aid:*** $14,886. ***Average indebtedness upon graduation:*** $29,621.

APPLYING
Standardized Tests *Recommended:* SAT or ACT (for admission).

Options: electronic application, early action, deferred entrance.

Required: high school transcript, minimum 2.3 GPA, 1 letter of recommendation. ***Required for some:*** minimum 3.0 GPA, interview, audition/interviews required for School of Music and Theatre School applicants, portfolio and creative statement required for animation majors. ***Recommended:*** essay or personal statement, minimum 2.8 GPA.

Application deadlines: 2/1 (freshmen), rolling (transfers), 11/15 (early action).

Notification: 3/15 (freshmen), continuous (transfers), 1/15 (early action).

CONTACT
Carlene Klaas, Dean of Undergraduate Admission, DePaul University, 1 East Jackson Boulevard, Suite 900, Chicago, IL 60604. *Phone:* 312-362-8300. *Toll-free phone:* 800-4DE-PAUL. *E-mail:* admission@depaul.edu.

DeVry University–Addison Campus
Addison, Illinois
http://www.devry.edu/

CONTACT
Admissions Office, DeVry University–Addison Campus, 1221 North Swift Road, Addison, IL 60101-6106. *Phone:* 630-953-1300. *Toll-free phone:* 866-338-7934.

DeVry University–Chicago Campus
Chicago, Illinois
http://www.devry.edu/

- **Proprietary** comprehensive, founded 1931, part of DeVry University
- **Urban** campus
- **Coed**
- **Minimally difficult** entrance level

FACULTY
Student/faculty ratio: 16:1.

ACADEMICS
Calendar: semesters. *Degrees:* associate, bachelor's, master's, and postbachelor's certificates.
Library: Learning Resource Center.

STUDENT LIFE
Housing options: college housing not available.

FINANCIAL AID
Financial Aid Of all full-time matriculated undergraduates who enrolled in 2007, 479 applied for aid, 467 were judged to have need, 5 had their need fully met. In 2007, 14 non-need-based awards were made. ***Average percent of need met:*** 48. ***Average financial aid package:*** $16,145. ***Average need-based loan:*** $8033. ***Average need-based gift aid:*** $8371. ***Average non-need-based aid:*** $11,220. ***Average indebtedness upon graduation:*** $49,157.

APPLYING
Application fee: $30.

Required: high school transcript, interview.

CONTACT
DeVry University–Chicago Campus, 3300 North Campbell Avenue, Chicago, IL 60618. *Phone:* 773-929-8500. *Toll-free phone:* 866-338-7934.

DeVry University Online
Addison, Illinois
http://www.devry.edu/

CONTACT
DeVry University Online, 1221 North Swift Road, Addison, IL 60101. *Phone:* 877-496-9050. *Toll-free phone:* 866-338-7934.

DeVry University–Tinley Park Campus
Tinley Park, Illinois
http://www.devry.edu/

CONTACT
Admissions Office, DeVry University–Tinley Park Campus, 18624 West Creek Drive, Tinley Park, IL 60477 . *Phone:* 708-342-3300. *Toll-free phone:* 866-338-7934.

Dominican University
River Forest, Illinois
http://www.dom.edu/

- **Independent Roman Catholic** comprehensive, founded 1901
- **Suburban** 30-acre campus with easy access to Chicago
- **Endowment** $38.1 million
- **Coed** 2,151 undergraduate students, 93% full-time, 68% women, 32% men
- **Moderately difficult** entrance level, 64% of applicants were admitted

UNDERGRAD STUDENTS
2,011 full-time, 140 part-time. Students come from 32 states and territories; 9 other countries; 8% are from out of state; 6% Black or African American, non-Hispanic/Latino; 55% Hispanic/Latino; 4% Asian, non-Hispanic/Latino; 0.1% Native Hawaiian or other Pacific Islander, non-Hispanic/Latino; 0.3% American Indian or Alaska Native, non-Hispanic/Latino; 1% Two or more races, non-Hispanic/Latino; 4% Race/ethnicity unknown; 2% international; 10% transferred in; 23% live on campus.

Freshmen:
Admission: 5,188 applied, 3,338 admitted, 419 enrolled. ***Average high school GPA:*** 3.8. ***Test scores:*** SAT evidence-based reading and writing scores over 500: 77%; SAT math scores over 500: 80%; ACT scores over 18: 95%; SAT evidence-based reading and writing scores over 600: 25%; SAT math scores over 600: 27%; ACT scores over 24: 37%; SAT evidence-based reading and writing scores over 700: 2%; SAT math scores over 700: 3%; ACT scores over 30: 7%.

Retention: 77% of full-time freshmen returned.

FACULTY
Total: 428, 36% full-time, 57% with terminal degrees.

Student/faculty ratio: 10:1.

ACADEMICS
Calendar: semesters. *Degrees:* bachelor's, master's, doctoral, post-master's, and postbachelor's certificates.

Special study options: academic remediation for entering students, accelerated degree program, adult/continuing education programs, advanced placement credit, distance learning, double majors, English as a second language, honors programs, independent study, internships, off-campus study, part-time degree program, services for LD students, student-designed majors, study abroad, summer session for credit.

Unusual degree programs: 3-2 business administration; engineering with Illinois Institute of Technology; nursing; social work; library science, pharmacy with Midwestern University.

Computers: 550 computers/terminals and 4,000 ports are available on campus for general student use. Students can access the following: campus intranet, computer help desk, free student e-mail accounts, online (class) grades, online (class) registration, online (class) schedules. Campuswide network is available. 100% of college-owned or -operated housing units are wired for high-speed Internet access. Wireless service is available via entire campus.
Library: Rebecca Crown Library. *Books:* 208,632 (physical), 24,977 (digital/electronic); *Serial titles:* 1,339 (physical), 62,595 (digital/electronic); *Databases:* 129. Weekly public service hours: 100; students can reserve study rooms.

STUDENT LIFE
Housing options: coed, women-only, special housing for students with disabilities. Campus housing is university owned. Freshman applicants given priority for college housing.

Activities and organizations: drama/theater group, student-run newspaper, choral group, Polish Club, Commuter Student Association, Nutrition Club, Organization of Latin American Students, Fashion Club.

Athletics Member NCAA. All Division III. ***Intercollegiate sports:*** baseball M, basketball M/W, bowling W, cross-country running M/W, golf M, soccer M/W, softball W, tennis M/W, volleyball M/W. ***Intramural sports:*** basketball M/W, bowling M/W, football M/W, racquetball M/W, soccer M/W, ultimate Frisbee M/W, volleyball M/W.

Campus security: 24-hour emergency response devices and patrols, student patrols, late-night transport/escort service, controlled dormitory access.

Student services: health clinic, personal/psychological counseling.

COSTS & FINANCIAL AID

Costs (2020–21) ***One-time required fee:*** $150. ***Comprehensive fee:*** $46,285 includes full-time tuition ($34,950), mandatory fees ($470), and room and board ($10,865). Full-time tuition and fees vary according to program. Part-time tuition: $1167 per credit hour. Part-time tuition and fees vary according to program. ***Required fees:*** $90 per term part-time. ***Room and board:*** Room and board charges vary according to housing facility. ***Payment plan:*** installment. ***Waivers:*** employees or children of employees.

Financial Aid Of all full-time matriculated undergraduates who enrolled in 2018, 1,680 applied for aid, 1,605 were judged to have need, 144 had their need fully met. In 2018, 278 non-need-based awards were made. ***Average percent of need met:*** 73. ***Average financial aid package:*** $26,129. ***Average need-based loan:*** $4392. ***Average need-based gift aid:*** $21,905. ***Average non-need-based aid:*** $18,782. ***Average indebtedness upon graduation:*** $28,387.

APPLYING

Standardized Tests *Required:* SAT or ACT (for admission).

Options: electronic application, deferred entrance.

Application fee: $25.

Required: high school transcript. ***Required for some:*** interview. ***Recommended:*** essay or personal statement, minimum 2.5 GPA.

Application deadlines: rolling (freshmen), rolling (out-of-state freshmen), rolling (transfers).

Notification: continuous (freshmen), continuous (out-of-state freshmen), continuous (transfers).

CONTACT

Mr. Glenn Hamilton, Assistant Vice President, Enrollment Management, Dominican University, 7900 West Division Street, River Forest, IL 60305. *Phone:* 708-524-6800. *Toll-free phone:* 800-828-8475. *Fax:* 708-524-6864. *E-mail:* domadmis@dom.edu.

Eastern Illinois University

Charleston, Illinois

http://www.eiu.edu/

- **State-supported** comprehensive, founded 1895
- **Small-town** 320-acre campus
- **Endowment** $87.0 million
- **Coed** 6,229 undergraduate students, 64% full-time, 57% women, 43% men
- **Moderately difficult** entrance level, 53% of applicants were admitted

UNDERGRAD STUDENTS

3,990 full-time, 2,239 part-time. Students come from 38 states and territories; 46 other countries; 7% are from out of state; 22% Black or African American, non-Hispanic/Latino; 9% Hispanic/Latino; 1% Asian, non-Hispanic/Latino; 0.1% Native Hawaiian or other Pacific Islander, non-Hispanic/Latino; 0.3% American Indian or Alaska Native, non-Hispanic/Latino; 3% Two or more races, non-Hispanic/Latino; 3% Race/ethnicity unknown; 3% international; 35% transferred in; 32% live on campus.

Freshmen:

Admission: 8,859 applied, 4,651 admitted, 925 enrolled. ***Average high school GPA:*** 3.2. ***Test scores:*** SAT evidence-based reading and writing scores over 500: 62%; SAT math scores over 500: 60%; ACT scores over 18: 79%; SAT evidence-based reading and writing scores over 600: 16%; SAT math scores over 600: 12%; ACT scores over 24: 21%; SAT evidence-based reading and writing scores over 700: 2%; SAT math scores over 700: 1%; ACT scores over 30: 2%.

Retention: 73% of full-time freshmen returned.

FACULTY

Total: 493, 75% full-time, 55% with terminal degrees.

Student/faculty ratio: 14:1.

ACADEMICS

Calendar: semesters. *Degrees:* bachelor's, master's, post-master's, and postbachelor's certificates.

Special study options: academic remediation for entering students, accelerated degree program, adult/continuing education programs, advanced placement credit, distance learning, double majors, English as a second language, freshman honors college, honors programs, independent study, internships, off-campus study, part-time degree program, services for LD students, study abroad, summer session for credit. ***ROTC:*** Army (b).

Unusual degree programs: 3-2 engineering with University of Illinois at Urbana–Champaign, Southern Illinois University at Carbondale.

Computers: 900 computers/terminals and 10,000 ports are available on campus for general student use. Students can access the following: computer help desk, free student e-mail accounts, online (class) grades, online (class) registration, online (class) schedules. Campuswide network is available. 100% of college-owned or -operated housing units are wired for high-speed Internet access. Wireless service is available via classrooms, computer centers, computer labs, dorm rooms, learning centers, libraries, student centers.

Library: Booth Library. *Books:* 932,870 (physical), 1.3 million (digital/electronic); *Databases:* 251. Weekly public service hours: 93.

STUDENT LIFE

Housing options: on-campus residence required for freshman year; coed, men-only, women-only. Campus housing is university owned. Freshman campus housing is guaranteed.

Activities and organizations: drama/theater group, student-run newspaper, radio and television station, choral group, marching band, Greek Organizations, Registered Student Organizations, Intramural Sports, University Board, Civic Engagement & Volunteerism, national fraternities, national sororities.

Athletics Member NCAA. All Division I except football (Division I-AA). ***Intercollegiate sports:*** baseball M(s), basketball M(s)/W(s), cross-country running M(s)/W(s), golf M(s)/W(s), soccer M(s)/W(s), softball W(s), swimming and diving M(s)/W(s), tennis M(s)/W(s), track and field M(s)/W(s), volleyball W(s). ***Intramural sports:*** badminton M(c)/W(c), baseball M(c)/W(c), basketball M/W, bowling M/W, equestrian sports M(c)/W(c), ice hockey M(c)/W(c), racquetball M(c)/W(c), soccer M(c)/W(c), softball M(c)/W(c), table tennis M/W, tennis M/W, triathlon M(c)/W(c), ultimate Frisbee M(c)/W(c), volleyball M/W(c), weight lifting M/W.

Campus security: 24-hour emergency response devices and patrols, student patrols, controlled dormitory access, Alert EIU and warning sirens.

Student services: health clinic, personal/psychological counseling, women's center, legal services, veterans affairs office.

COSTS & FINANCIAL AID

Costs (2019–20) ***Tuition:*** state resident $9060 full-time, $302 per credit hour part-time; nonresident $11,340 full-time, $378 per credit hour part-time. Full-time tuition and fees vary according to course load and program. Part-time tuition and fees vary according to course load and program. No tuition increase for student's term of enrollment. ***Required fees:*** $2929 full-time, $116 per credit hour part-time. ***Room and board:*** $10,030. Room and board charges vary according to board plan and housing facility. ***Payment plan:*** installment. ***Waivers:*** senior citizens and employees or children of employees.

Financial Aid Of all full-time matriculated undergraduates who enrolled in 2019, 3,485 applied for aid, 2,895 were judged to have need, 262 had their need fully met. 157 Federal Work-Study jobs (averaging $786). 1,106 state and other part-time jobs (averaging $1249). In 2019, 494 non-need-based awards were made. ***Average percent of need met:*** 58. ***Average financial aid package:*** $14,088. ***Average need-based loan:*** $4233. ***Average need-based gift aid:*** $9705. ***Average non-need-based aid:*** $4211. ***Average indebtedness upon graduation:*** $30,695.

APPLYING

Standardized Tests *Required:* SAT or ACT (for admission). *Required for some:* SAT and SAT Subject Tests or ACT (for admission), SAT Subject Tests (for admission). *Recommended:* SAT and SAT Subject Tests or ACT (for admission), SAT Subject Tests (for admission).

Options: electronic application, deferred entrance.

Application fee: $30.

Required: high school transcript, minimum 2.5 GPA. ***Required for some:*** essay or personal statement, letters of recommendation, audition for music program.

Application deadlines: rolling (freshmen), rolling (out-of-state freshmen), rolling (transfers).

CONTACT

Kelly Miller, Director of Admissions, Eastern Illinois University, 600 Lincoln Avenue, Charleston, IL 61920. *Phone:* 217-581-2233. *Toll-free phone:* 877-581-2348. *Fax:* 217-581-7060. *E-mail:* admissions@eiu.edu.

East-West University

Chicago, Illinois

http://www.eastwest.edu/

- **Independent** 4-year, founded 1978
- **Urban** 1-acre campus with easy access to Chicago
- **Endowment** $56.1 million
- **Coed**
- **Minimally difficult** entrance level

FACULTY

Student/faculty ratio: 15:1.

ACADEMICS

Calendar: quarters. *Degrees:* certificates, associate, and bachelor's.
Library: East-West University Library.

STUDENT LIFE

Activities and organizations: drama/theater group, student-run newspaper, choral group, Student Government, performing arts, Black Student Union, Latino Student Association, Multicultural Student Association.

Student services: personal/psychological counseling.

FINANCIAL AID

Financial Aid Of all full-time matriculated undergraduates who enrolled in 2012, 42 Federal Work-Study jobs (averaging $1600). ***Average indebtedness upon graduation:*** $4100.

APPLYING

Standardized Tests *Required:* ACT (for admission).

Options: electronic application, early decision.

Application fee: $40.

Required: essay or personal statement, high school transcript, minimum 2.0 GPA, interview. ***Required for some:*** 1 letter of recommendation.

CONTACT

Bryan Lambert, Director of Enrollment, East-West University, 816 South Michigan Avenue, Chicago, IL 60605-2103. *Phone:* 312-939-0112 Ext. 1701.

Elmhurst College

Elmhurst, Illinois

http://www.elmhurst.edu/

CONTACT

Christine Grenier, Senior Director of First-Year Admission, Elmhurst College, Admission Office, 190 South Prospect Avenue, Elmhurst, IL 60126-3296. *Phone:* 630-617-3071. *Toll-free phone:* 800-697-1871. *E-mail:* cgrenier@elmhurst.edu.

Eureka College

Eureka, Illinois

http://www.eureka.edu/

CONTACT

Mr. Mike Murtagh, Vice President of Institutional Advancement, Eureka College, 300 East College Avenue, Eureka, IL 61530. *Phone:* 309-467-6315. *Toll-free phone:* 888-4-EUREKA. *E-mail:* mmurtagh@eureka.edu.

Governors State University

University Park, Illinois

http://www.govst.edu/

- **State-supported** university, founded 1969
- **Suburban** 742-acre campus with easy access to Chicago
- **Endowment** $2.1 million
- **Coed** 3,232 undergraduate students, 60% full-time, 63% women, 37% men
- **Moderately difficult** entrance level, 46% of applicants were admitted

UNDERGRAD STUDENTS

1,926 full-time, 1,306 part-time. Students come from 14 states and territories; 25 other countries; 2% are from out of state; 40% Black or African American, non-Hispanic/Latino; 15% Hispanic/Latino; 2% Asian, non-Hispanic/Latino; 0.1% Native Hawaiian or other Pacific Islander, non-Hispanic/Latino; 3% Two or more races, non-Hispanic/Latino; 9% Race/ethnicity unknown; 1% international; 22% transferred in; 7% live on campus.

Freshmen:

Admission: 1,434 applied, 654 admitted, 240 enrolled. ***Average high school GPA:*** 3.0. ***Test scores:*** SAT evidence-based reading and writing scores over 500: 38%; SAT math scores over 500: 34%; ACT scores over 18: 70%; SAT evidence-based reading and writing scores over 600: 6%; SAT math scores over 600: 4%; ACT scores over 24: 11%; SAT evidence-based reading and writing scores over 700: 1%; ACT scores over 30: 2%.

Retention: 52% of full-time freshmen returned.

FACULTY

Total: 520, 43% full-time, 55% with terminal degrees.

Student/faculty ratio: 12:1.

ACADEMICS

Calendar: semesters. *Degrees:* certificates, bachelor's, master's, doctoral, post-master's, and postbachelor's certificates.

Special study options: adult/continuing education programs, advanced placement credit, distance learning, double majors, English as a second language, honors programs, independent study, internships, off-campus study, part-time degree program, services for LD students, student-designed majors, study abroad, summer session for credit. ***ROTC:*** Army (c), Air Force (c).

Computers: 670 computers/terminals are available on campus for general student use. Students can access the following: campus intranet, computer help desk, free student e-mail accounts, online (class) grades, online (class) registration, online (class) schedules, student portal. Campuswide network is available. 100% of college-owned or -operated housing units are wired for high-speed Internet access. Wireless service is available via entire campus.

Library: Governors State University Library. *Books:* 260,817 (physical), 388,203 (digital/electronic); *Serial titles:* 9,808 (physical), 11,430 (digital/electronic); *Databases:* 170. Weekly public service hours: 75; students can reserve study rooms.

STUDENT LIFE

Housing options: coed. Campus housing is university owned. Freshman campus housing is guaranteed.

Activities and organizations: student-run newspaper, choral group.

Athletics Member NAIA. ***Intercollegiate sports:*** basketball M(s)/W(s), cross-country running M(s)/W(s), golf M(s)/W(s), soccer M/W, volleyball M(s)/W(s). ***Intramural sports:*** basketball M/W, table tennis M/W.

Campus security: 24-hour emergency response devices and patrols, late-night transport/escort service, controlled dormitory access.

Student services: health clinic, personal/psychological counseling, veterans affairs office.

COSTS & FINANCIAL AID
Costs (2020–21) ***Tuition:*** state resident $9390 full-time, $313 per credit hour part-time; nonresident $18,780 full-time, $626 per credit hour part-time. Full-time tuition and fees vary according to course load, program, and reciprocity agreements. Part-time tuition and fees vary according to course level, course load, program, and reciprocity agreements. No tuition increase for student's term of enrollment. ***Required fees:*** $3226 full-time, $105 per credit hour part-time, $38 per term part-time. ***Room and board:*** $8102; room only: $6102. Room and board charges vary according to board plan and housing facility. ***Payment plan:*** installment. ***Waivers:*** senior citizens and employees or children of employees.

Financial Aid Of all full-time matriculated undergraduates who enrolled in 2018, 1,576 applied for aid, 1,466 were judged to have need, 1,021 had their need fully met. 134 Federal Work-Study jobs (averaging $2455). In 2018, 2 non-need-based awards were made. ***Average percent of need met:*** 70. ***Average financial aid package:*** $12,133. ***Average need-based loan:*** $4377. ***Average need-based gift aid:*** $9763. ***Average non-need-based aid:*** $6819. ***Financial aid deadline:*** 10/1.

APPLYING
Standardized Tests *Required:* SAT and SAT Subject Tests or ACT (for admission).

Options: electronic application, early admission, early decision, deferred entrance.

Application fee: $25.

Required: high school transcript, minimum 2.8 GPA. ***Required for some:*** essay or personal statement, interview.

Early decision deadline: 11/15.

Notification: continuous (transfers), 12/15 (early decision).

CONTACT
Mr. Paul McGuinness, Associate Vice President Enrollment Management, Governors State University, One University Parkway, University Park, IL 60484. *Phone:* 708-235-7308 Ext. 7308. *Toll-free phone:* 800-478-8478. *E-mail:* pmcguinness@govst.edu.

Greenville University

Greenville, Illinois

http://www.greenville.edu/

- **Independent Free Methodist** comprehensive, founded 1892
- **Small-town** 50-acre campus with easy access to St. Louis
- **Endowment** $16.3 million
- **Coed**
- **Moderately difficult** entrance level

FACULTY
Student/faculty ratio: 13:1.

ACADEMICS
Calendar: 4-1-4. *Degrees:* bachelor's and master's.
Library: Ruby E. Dare Library. *Books:* 131,047 (physical), 7,408 (digital/electronic). Students can reserve study rooms.

STUDENT LIFE
Housing options: on-campus residence required through senior year; men-only, women-only. Campus housing is university owned. Freshman campus housing is guaranteed.

Activities and organizations: drama/theater group, student-run newspaper, radio station, choral group, marching band, Campus Activity Board, Panther Corps Marching Band, Greenville College Student Association, Habitat for Humanity, Music and Entertainment Industry Student Association.

Athletics Member NCAA, NCCAA. All NCAA Division III.

Campus security: 24-hour emergency response devices and patrols, late-night transport/escort service, controlled dormitory access.

Student services: personal/psychological counseling.

COSTS & FINANCIAL AID
Costs (2019–20) ***Comprehensive fee:*** $37,458 includes full-time tuition ($27,580), mandatory fees ($330), and room and board ($9548). Part-time tuition: $434 per credit hour. ***College room only:*** $4698.

Financial Aid Of all full-time matriculated undergraduates who enrolled in 2019, 690 applied for aid, 632 were judged to have need, 90 had their need fully met. 117 Federal Work-Study jobs (averaging $1213). In 2019, 107 non-need-based awards were made. ***Average percent of need met:*** 74. ***Average financial aid package:*** $22,943. ***Average need-based loan:*** $4061. ***Average need-based gift aid:*** $19,123. ***Average non-need-based aid:*** $13,738. ***Average indebtedness upon graduation:*** $28,759.

APPLYING
Standardized Tests *Required:* SAT or ACT (for admission).

Options: electronic application, early admission, deferred entrance.

Required: essay or personal statement, high school transcript, minimum 2.3 GPA, agreement to lifestyle statement. ***Required for some:*** interview.

CONTACT
Mr. Colin McLaughlin, Director of Traditional Admissions, Greenville University, 315 East College Avenue, Greenville, IL 62246. *Phone:* 618-664-7100. *Toll-free phone:* 800-345-4440. *Fax:* 618-664-9841. *E-mail:* admissions@greenville.edu.

Hebrew Theological College

Skokie, Illinois

http://www.htc.edu/

CONTACT
Rabbi Berish Cardash, Hebrew Theological College, 7135 North Carpenter Road, Skokie, IL 60077-3263. *Phone:* 847-982-2500.

Illinois College

Jacksonville, Illinois

http://www.ic.edu/

- **Independent interdenominational** comprehensive, founded 1829
- **Small-town** 62-acre campus with easy access to St. Louis
- **Coed** 1,057 undergraduate students, 99% full-time, 52% women, 48% men
- **Moderately difficult** entrance level, 78% of applicants were admitted

UNDERGRAD STUDENTS
1,046 full-time, 11 part-time. 10% are from out of state; 11% Black or African American, non-Hispanic/Latino; 7% Hispanic/Latino; 0.8% Asian, non-Hispanic/Latino; 0.1% American Indian or Alaska Native, non-Hispanic/Latino; 3% Two or more races, non-Hispanic/Latino; 0.3% Race/ethnicity unknown; 5% international; 5% transferred in; 87% live on campus.

Freshmen:
Admission: 3,735 applied, 2,905 admitted, 323 enrolled. ***Average high school GPA:*** 3.6. ***Test scores:*** SAT evidence-based reading and writing scores over 500: 70%; SAT math scores over 500: 71%; ACT scores over 18: 92%; SAT evidence-based reading and writing scores over 600: 22%; SAT math scores over 600: 22%; ACT scores over 24: 35%; SAT evidence-based reading and writing scores over 700: 1%; SAT math scores over 700: 3%; ACT scores over 30: 3%.

Retention: 78% of full-time freshmen returned.

FACULTY
Total: 94, 77% full-time, 64% with terminal degrees.

Student/faculty ratio: 13:1.

ACADEMICS
Calendar: semesters. *Degrees:* bachelor's and master's.

Computers: Students can access the following: computer help desk, free student e-mail accounts, online (class) grades, online (class) registration, online (class) schedules. Campuswide network is available. Wireless service is available via entire campus.
Library: Schewe Library.

STUDENT LIFE
Housing options: on-campus residence required through junior year; coed, men-only, women-only. Campus housing is university owned. Freshman campus housing is guaranteed.

Athletics Member NCAA. All Division III except golf (Division II). ***Intercollegiate sports:*** baseball M, cheerleading W, cross-country running M/W, football M, golf M/W, soccer M/W, softball W, swimming and diving M/W, tennis M/W, track and field M/W, volleyball W. ***Intramural sports:*** badminton M/W, basketball M/W, fencing M, field hockey W, football M, racquetball M/W, softball M/W, swimming and diving M/W, volleyball M/W, water polo M/W, weight lifting M/W.

Campus security: 24-hour emergency response devices and patrols, late-night transport/escort service, controlled dormitory access.

FINANCIAL AID

Financial Aid Of all full-time matriculated undergraduates who enrolled in 2018, 869 applied for aid, 819 were judged to have need, 191 had their need fully met. In 2018, 49 non-need-based awards were made. ***Average percent of need met:*** 86. ***Average financial aid package:*** $29,989. ***Average need-based loan:*** $4080. ***Average need-based gift aid:*** $25,593. ***Average non-need-based aid:*** $18,669. ***Average indebtedness upon graduation:*** $30,990.

APPLYING

Options: electronic application, early action, deferred entrance.

Required: essay or personal statement, high school transcript. ***Required for some:*** essay or personal statement, 1 letter of recommendation. ***Recommended:*** minimum 2.5 GPA.

Notification: continuous until 9/1 (freshmen), continuous until 9/1 (out-of-state freshmen), continuous until 9/1 (transfers), 12/23 (early action).

CONTACT

Mr. Rick Bystry, Associate Director of Admission, Illinois College, 1101 West College, Jacksonville, IL 62650. *Phone:* 217-245-3030. *Toll-free phone:* 866-464-5265. *Fax:* 217-245-3034. *E-mail:* admissions@ic.edu.

Illinois Institute of Technology

Chicago, Illinois

http://www.iit.edu/

- **Independent** university, founded 1890
- **Urban** 120-acre campus with easy access to Chicago
- **Endowment** $235.5 million
- **Coed** 3,144 undergraduate students, 92% full-time, 32% women, 68% men
- **Moderately difficult** entrance level, 60% of applicants were admitted

UNDERGRAD STUDENTS

2,882 full-time, 262 part-time. 23% are from out of state; 5% Black or African American, non-Hispanic/Latino; 17% Hispanic/Latino; 16% Asian, non-Hispanic/Latino; 0.1% American Indian or Alaska Native, non-Hispanic/Latino; 4% Two or more races, non-Hispanic/Latino; 3% Race/ethnicity unknown; 18% international; 6% transferred in; 43% live on campus.

Freshmen:

Admission: 5,049 applied, 3,041 admitted, 583 enrolled. ***Test scores:*** SAT evidence-based reading and writing scores over 500: 97%; SAT math scores over 500: 100%; ACT scores over 18: 100%; SAT evidence-based reading and writing scores over 600: 66%; SAT math scores over 600: 89%; ACT scores over 24: 90%; SAT evidence-based reading and writing scores over 700: 15%; SAT math scores over 700: 40%; ACT scores over 30: 42%.

Retention: 88% of full-time freshmen returned.

FACULTY

Total: 347, 96% full-time, 71% with terminal degrees.

Student/faculty ratio: 12:1.

ACADEMICS

Calendar: semesters. *Degrees:* bachelor's, master's, and doctoral.

Special study options: advanced placement credit, cooperative education, distance learning, double majors, English as a second language, independent study, internships, off-campus study, part-time degree program, services for LD students, study abroad, summer session for credit. ***ROTC:*** Army (b), Navy (b), Air Force (b).

Unusual degree programs: 3-2 business administration; engineering; applied math; architecture/construction engineering and management; biology; computer science/ applied math, data science, intellectual property management and marketing; physics/health physics.

Computers: 586 computers/terminals are available on campus for general student use. Students can access the following: campus intranet, computer help desk, free student e-mail accounts, online (class) grades, online (class) registration, online (class) schedules. Campuswide network is available. 100% of college-owned or -operated housing units are wired for high-speed Internet access. Wireless service is available via classrooms, computer centers, computer labs, dorm rooms, learning centers, libraries, student centers.

Library: Paul V. Galvin Library plus 5 others. *Books:* 1.7 million (physical), 99,658 (digital/electronic); *Serial titles:* 895 (physical); *Databases:* 464. Study areas open 24 hours, 5–7 days a week; students can reserve study rooms.

STUDENT LIFE

Housing options: on-campus residence required for freshman year; coed. Campus housing is university owned. Freshman applicants given priority for college housing.

Activities and organizations: drama/theater group, student-run newspaper, radio station, choral group, Union Board, International Students Association, Student Government Association, Greek Council, Commuter Student Associate, national fraternities, national sororities.

Athletics Member NCAA. All Division III. ***Intercollegiate sports:*** badminton M(c)/W(c), baseball M(s), basketball M/W, bowling M(c)/W(c), cross-country running M(s)/W(s), lacrosse M(c)/W, rugby M(c)/W(c), soccer M(s)/W(s), swimming and diving M(s)/W(s), track and field M/W, ultimate Frisbee M(c)/W(c), volleyball M(c)/W(s). ***Intramural sports:*** badminton M/W, basketball M/W, bowling M/W, field hockey M/W, football M/W, racquetball M/W, soccer M/W, softball M/W, squash M/W, table tennis M/W, tennis M(c)/W(c), track and field M(c)/W(c), ultimate Frisbee M/W, volleyball M/W.

Campus security: 24-hour emergency response devices and patrols, late-night transport/escort service, controlled dormitory access.

Student services: health clinic, personal/psychological counseling, women's center, legal services.

FINANCIAL AID

Financial Aid Of all full-time matriculated undergraduates who enrolled in 2018, 1,915 applied for aid, 1,813 were judged to have need, 218 had their need fully met. In 2018, 894 non-need-based awards were made. ***Average percent of need met:*** 79. ***Average financial aid package:*** $41,568. ***Average need-based loan:*** $4570. ***Average need-based gift aid:*** $36,218. ***Average non-need-based aid:*** $26,201. ***Average indebtedness upon graduation:*** $29,594.

APPLYING

Standardized Tests *Required:* SAT or ACT (for admission).

Options: electronic application, deferred entrance.

Required: essay or personal statement, high school transcript, 1 letter of recommendation. ***Recommended:*** interview.

Application deadlines: 8/1 (freshmen), 6/1 (transfers).

Notification: continuous (freshmen), continuous (transfers).

CONTACT

Ms. Toni Riley, Director, Undergraduate Admissions Office, Illinois Institute of Technology, Office of Undergraduate Admission, Perlstein 101, 10 West 33rd Street, Chicago, IL 60616. *Phone:* 312-567-5239. *Toll-free phone:* 800-448-2329. *E-mail:* admission@iit.edu.

Illinois State University

Normal, Illinois

http://www.illinoisstate.edu/

- **State-supported** university, founded 1857
- **Suburban** 1111-acre campus
- **Endowment** $112.7 million
- **Coed** 18,250 undergraduate students, 94% full-time, 55% women, 45% men
- **Minimally difficult** entrance level, 82% of applicants were admitted

UNDERGRAD STUDENTS

17,092 full-time, 1,158 part-time. Students come from 49 states and territories; 71 other countries; 2% are from out of state; 9% Black or African American, non-Hispanic/Latino; 12% Hispanic/Latino; 2% Asian, non-Hispanic/Latino; 0.1% Native Hawaiian or other Pacific Islander, non-Hispanic/Latino; 0.1% American Indian or Alaska Native, non-Hispanic/Latino; 3% Two or more races, non-Hispanic/Latino; 0.4% Race/ethnicity unknown; 0.6% international; 10% transferred in; 31% live on campus.

Freshmen:

Admission: 16,151 applied, 13,234 admitted, 3,860 enrolled. ***Average high school GPA:*** 3.5. ***Test scores:*** SAT evidence-based reading and writing scores over 500: 83%; SAT math scores over 500: 83%; ACT scores over 18: 97%; SAT evidence-based reading and writing scores over 600: 31%; SAT math scores over 600: 29%; ACT scores over 24: 43%; SAT evidence-based reading and writing scores over 700: 4%; SAT math scores over 700: 6%; ACT scores over 30: 9%.

Retention: 79% of full-time freshmen returned.

FACULTY

Total. 1,372, 66% full-time, 65% with terminal degrees.

Student/faculty ratio: 19:1.

ACADEMICS

Calendar: semesters. *Degrees:* certificates, bachelor's, master's, doctoral, post-master's, and postbachelor's certificates.

Special study options: academic remediation for entering students, accelerated degree program, adult/continuing education programs, advanced placement credit, cooperative education, distance learning, double majors, English as a second language, honors programs, independent study, internships, off-campus study, part-time degree program, services for LD students, student-designed majors, study abroad, summer session for credit. ***ROTC:*** Army (b).

Unusual degree programs: 3-2 engineering with University of Illinois, Bradley University.

Computers: 2,500 computers/terminals and 2,500 ports are available on campus for general student use. Students can access the following: computer help desk, free student e-mail accounts, online (class) grades, online (class) registration, online (class) schedules. Campuswide network is available. 100% of college-owned or -operated housing units are wired for high-speed Internet access. Wireless service is available via entire campus.

Library: Milner Library. *Books:* 1.4 million (physical), 190,817 (digital/electronic); *Serial titles:* 141,304 (digital/electronic); *Databases:* 284. Students can reserve study rooms.

STUDENT LIFE

Housing options: on-campus residence required through sophomore year; coed, women-only, special housing for students with disabilities. Campus housing is university owned. Freshman campus housing is guaranteed.

Activities and organizations: drama/theater group, student-run newspaper, radio and television station, choral group, marching band, national fraternities, national sororities.

Athletics Member NCAA. All Division I except football (Division I-AA). ***Intercollegiate sports:*** baseball M(s), basketball M(s)/W(s), cross-country running M(s)/W(s), golf M(s)/W(s), gymnastics W(s), soccer W(s), softball W(s), swimming and diving W(s), tennis M(s)/W(s), track and field M(s)/W(s), volleyball W(s). ***Intramural sports:*** badminton M(c)/W(c), baseball M(c), basketball M/W(c), cheerleading W(c), cross-country running M(c)/W(c), equestrian sports M(c)/W(c), fencing M(c)/W(c), golf M(c)/W(c), ice hockey M(c), lacrosse M(c)/W(c), rugby M(c)/W(c), soccer M(c)/W(c), softball M(c)/W(c), table tennis M(c)/W(c), tennis M(c)/W(c), triathlon M(c)/W(c), ultimate Frisbee M(c)/W(c), volleyball M(c)/W(c), water polo M(c)/W(c), wrestling M(c)/W(c).

Campus security: 24-hour emergency response devices and patrols, student patrols, late-night transport/escort service, controlled dormitory access.

Student services: health clinic, personal/psychological counseling, women's center, legal services, veterans affairs office.

COSTS & FINANCIAL AID

Costs (2020–21) ***Tuition:*** state resident $11,524 full-time, $384 per credit hour part-time; nonresident $23,524 full-time, $768 per credit hour part-time. Full-time tuition and fees vary according to degree level. Part-time tuition and fees vary according to degree level. No tuition increase for student's term of enrollment. ***Required fees:*** $3308 full-time, $92 per credit hour part-time. ***Room and board:*** $9850; room only: $5334. Room and board charges vary according to board plan and housing facility. ***Payment plan:*** installment. ***Waivers:*** minority students, senior citizens, and employees or children of employees.

Financial Aid Of all full-time matriculated undergraduates who enrolled in 2018, 13,626 applied for aid, 10,656 were judged to have need, 891 had their need fully met. 592 Federal Work-Study jobs (averaging $1713). In 2018, 1884 non-need-based awards were made. ***Average percent of need met:*** 56. ***Average financial aid package:*** $12,087. ***Average need-based loan:*** $4190. ***Average need-based gift aid:*** $9984. ***Average non-need-based aid:*** $3514. ***Average indebtedness upon graduation:*** $31,687.

APPLYING

Standardized Tests *Required:* SAT or ACT (for admission). *Required for some:* SAT and SAT Subject Tests or ACT (for admission).

Options: electronic application.

Application fee: $50.

Required for some: interview. ***Recommended:*** essay or personal statement, high school transcript.

Application deadlines: 4/1 (freshmen), rolling (transfers).

Notification: continuous (freshmen), continuous (out-of-state freshmen), continuous (transfers).

CONTACT

Mr. Jeff Mavros, Director of Admissions, Illinois State University, Campus Box 2200, Normal, IL 61790-2200. *Phone:* 309-438-2181. *Toll-free phone:* 800-366-2478. *Fax:* 309-438-3932. *E-mail:* admissions@ilstu.edu.

Illinois Wesleyan University

Bloomington, Illinois

http://www.iwu.edu/

- **Independent** 4-year, founded 1850
- **Suburban** 85-acre campus
- **Coed** 1,629 undergraduate students, 99% full-time, 52% women, 48% men
- **Very difficult** entrance level, 61% of applicants were admitted

UNDERGRAD STUDENTS

1,616 full-time, 13 part-time. Students come from 34 states and territories; 23 other countries; 21% are from out of state; 7% Black or African American, non-Hispanic/Latino; 9% Hispanic/Latino; 7% Asian, non-Hispanic/Latino; 0.1% Native Hawaiian or other Pacific Islander, non-Hispanic/Latino; 2% Two or more races, non-Hispanic/Latino; 1% Race/ethnicity unknown; 5% international; 2% transferred in; 99% live on campus.

Freshmen:

Admission: 3,719 applied, 2,261 admitted, 409 enrolled. ***Average high school GPA:*** 3.8. ***Test scores:*** SAT evidence-based reading and writing scores over 500: 98%; SAT math scores over 500: 98%; ACT scores over 18: 100%; SAT evidence-based reading and writing scores over 600: 56%; SAT math scores over 600: 57%; ACT scores over 24: 78%; SAT evidence-based reading and writing scores over 700: 8%; SAT math scores over 700: 18%; ACT scores over 30: 22%.

Retention: 84% of full-time freshmen returned.

FACULTY

Total: 189, 68% full-time, 82% with terminal degrees.

Student/faculty ratio: 11:1.

ACADEMICS

Calendar: 4-4-1. *Degree:* bachelor's.

Special study options: advanced placement credit, distance learning, double majors, English as a second language, honors programs, independent study, internships, off-campus study, services for LD students, student-designed majors, study abroad. ***ROTC:*** Army (c).

Unusual degree programs: 3-2 engineering with Case Western Reserve University, Northwestern University, Washington University in St. Louis, Dartmouth College, University of Illinois; forestry with Duke University; occupational therapy.

Computers: 400 computers/terminals are available on campus for general student use. Students can access the following: campus intranet, computer help desk, free student e-mail accounts, online (class) grades, online (class) registration, online (class) schedules. Campuswide network is available. 100% of college-owned or -operated housing units are wired for high-speed Internet access. Wireless service is available via entire campus.

Library: The Ames Library. *Books:* 193,789 (physical), 35,089 (digital/electronic); *Serial titles:* 2,056 (physical), 80,933 (digital/electronic); *Databases:* 181. Students can reserve study rooms.

STUDENT LIFE
Housing options: on-campus residence required through junior year; coed, special housing for students with disabilities. Campus housing is university owned. Freshman campus housing is guaranteed.

Activities and organizations: drama/theater group, student-run newspaper, radio and television station, choral group, national fraternities, national sororities.

Athletics Member NCAA. All Division III. ***Intercollegiate sports:*** baseball M, basketball M/W, cheerleading M(c)/W(c), cross-country running M/W, football M, golf M/W, lacrosse M/W, soccer M/W, softball W, swimming and diving M/W, tennis M/W, track and field M/W, ultimate Frisbee M(c)/W(c), volleyball M(c)/W, water polo M(c). ***Intramural sports:*** badminton M/W, basketball M/W, football M/W, golf M/W, racquetball M/W, soccer M/W, softball M/W, tennis M/W, volleyball M/W.

Campus security: 24-hour emergency response devices and patrols, late-night transport/escort service, controlled dormitory access, emergency response team.

Student services: health clinic, personal/psychological counseling.

COSTS & FINANCIAL AID
Costs (2020–21) ***Comprehensive fee:*** $63,176 includes full-time tuition ($51,132), mandatory fees ($204), and room and board ($11,840). Part-time tuition: $1598 per credit hour. ***College room only:*** $7414. Room and board charges vary according to housing facility. ***Payment plan:*** installment. ***Waivers:*** employees or children of employees.

Financial Aid Of all full-time matriculated undergraduates who enrolled in 2019, 1,350 applied for aid, 1,172 were judged to have need, 221 had their need fully met. In 2019, 430 non-need-based awards were made. ***Average percent of need met:*** 83. ***Average financial aid package:*** $37,608. ***Average need-based loan:*** $5587. ***Average need-based gift aid:*** $31,078. ***Average non-need-based aid:*** $23,610. ***Average indebtedness upon graduation:*** $34,268.

APPLYING
Standardized Tests *Required:* SAT or ACT (for admission).

Options: electronic application, early admission, early action, deferred entrance.

Required: essay or personal statement, high school transcript, minimum 2.0 GPA, 1 letter of recommendation. ***Recommended:*** minimum 3.0 GPA, 2 letters of recommendation, interview.

Notification: 12/15 (early action).

CONTACT
Mr. Greg King, Associate Vice President for Enrollment Management, Illinois Wesleyan University, PO Box 2900, Bloomington, IL 61702-2900. *Phone:* 309-556-3031. *Toll-free phone:* 800-332-2498. *Fax:* 309-556-3820. *E-mail:* iwuadmit@iwu.edu.

Judson University

Elgin, Illinois

http://www.judsonu.edu/

- **Independent Baptist** comprehensive, founded 1963
- **Suburban** 90-acre campus with easy access to Chicago
- **Endowment** $11.2 million
- **Coed**
- **Moderately difficult** entrance level

FACULTY
Student/faculty ratio: 10:1.

ACADEMICS
Calendar: semesters. *Degrees:* certificates, associate, bachelor's, master's, doctoral, and postbachelor's certificates.
Library: Benjamin P. Browne Library. *Books:* 120,765 (physical), 6,280 (digital/electronic); *Serial titles:* 158 (physical), 48,401 (digital/electronic); *Databases:* 53. Weekly public service hours: 76; students can reserve study rooms.

STUDENT LIFE
Housing options: on-campus residence required through senior year; coed, men-only, women-only, special housing for students with disabilities. Campus housing is university owned. Freshman campus housing is guaranteed.

Activities and organizations: drama/theater group, choral group, Judson Student Organization, University Ministries, Judson Choir, Fellowship of Christian Athletes, Judson Business Society.

Athletics Member NAIA, NCCAA.

Campus security: 24-hour emergency response devices and patrols, controlled dormitory access.

Student services: health clinic, personal/psychological counseling.

COSTS & FINANCIAL AID
Costs (2019–20) ***One-time required fee:*** $100. ***Comprehensive fee:*** $40,660 includes full-time tuition ($28,840), mandatory fees ($1030), and room and board ($10,790). Full-time tuition and fees vary according to degree level, program, and reciprocity agreements. Part-time tuition: $1185 per credit hour. Part-time tuition and fees vary according to course load, degree level, program, and reciprocity agreements. ***Room and board:*** Room and board charges vary according to board plan.

Financial Aid Of all full-time matriculated undergraduates who enrolled in 2019, 771 applied for aid, 518 were judged to have need, 133 had their need fully met. 162 Federal Work-Study jobs (averaging $1547). In 2019, 159 non-need-based awards were made. ***Average percent of need met:*** 60. ***Average financial aid package:*** $20,982. ***Average need-based loan:*** $4153. ***Average need-based gift aid:*** $8328. ***Average non-need-based aid:*** $17,564. ***Average indebtedness upon graduation:*** $24,736. ***Financial aid deadline:*** 5/1.

APPLYING
Standardized Tests *Required:* SAT or ACT (for admission).

Options: electronic application.

Application fee: $50.

Required: high school transcript, minimum 2.0 GPA, minimum ACT score of 21, lifestyle statement. ***Required for some:*** essay or personal statement. ***Recommended:*** essay or personal statement.

CONTACT
Mrs. Molly Smith, Director of Admissions, Judson University, 1151 North State Street, Elgin, IL 60123. *Phone:* 847-628-2521. *Toll-free phone:* 800-879-5376. *Fax:* 847-628-2526. *E-mail:* molly.smith@judsonu.edu.

Kendall College at National Louis University

Chicago, Illinois

http://www.kendall.edu/

CONTACT
Ms. Angela Batchelor, Manager of Enrollment, Kendall College at National Louis University, 900 North Branch Street, Chicago, IL 60642. *Toll-free phone:* 888-90-KENDALL. *E-mail:* info@kendall.edu.

Knox College

Galesburg, Illinois

http://www.knox.edu/

- **Independent** 4-year, founded 1837
- **Small-town** 82-acre campus with easy access to Peoria, Quad Cities
- **Endowment** $170.2 million
- **Coed** 1,258 undergraduate students, 97% full-time, 57% women, 43% men
- **Very difficult** entrance level, 68% of applicants were admitted

UNDERGRAD STUDENTS
1,222 full-time, 36 part-time. Students come from 45 states and territories; 49 other countries; 46% are from out of state; 8% Black or African American, non-Hispanic/Latino; 14% Hispanic/Latino; 5% Asian, non-Hispanic/Latino; 0.2% Native Hawaiian or other Pacific Islander, non-Hispanic/Latino; 0.1% American Indian or Alaska Native, non-Hispanic/Latino; 6% Two or more races, non-Hispanic/Latino; 2% Race/ethnicity unknown; 19% international; 2% transferred in; 82% live on campus.

Freshmen:
Admission: 3,397 applied, 2,321 admitted, 320 enrolled. ***Test scores:*** SAT evidence-based reading and writing scores over 500: 94%; SAT math scores over 500: 94%; ACT scores over 18: 98%; SAT evidence-based reading and writing scores over 600: 62%; SAT math scores over 600: 62%; ACT scores over 24: 75%; SAT evidence-based reading and writing scores over 700: 19%; SAT math scores over 700: 27%; ACT scores over 30: 31%.

Retention: 81% of full-time freshmen returned.

FACULTY
Total: 144, 75% full-time, 84% with terminal degrees.

Student/faculty ratio: 10:1.

ACADEMICS
Calendar: trimesters. *Degree:* bachelor's.

Special study options: advanced placement credit, double majors, English as a second language, honors programs, independent study, internships, off-campus study, part-time degree program, services for LD students, student-designed majors, study abroad.

Unusual degree programs: 3-2 engineering with University of Illinois at Urbana–Champaign, Washington University in St. Louis, Columbia University, Rensselaer Polytechnic Institute; forestry with Duke University; nursing with Rush University.

Computers: 275 computers/terminals are available on campus for general student use. Students can access the following: campus intranet, computer help desk, free student e-mail accounts, online (class) grades, online (class) registration, online (class) schedules, transcripts, learning management system, streaming video, print billing. Campuswide network is available. 100% of college-owned or -operated housing units are wired for high-speed Internet access. Wireless service is available via entire campus.

Library: Henry M. Seymour Library plus 1 other. *Books:* 213,122 (physical), 18,063 (digital/electronic); *Serial titles:* 142 (physical), 85,202 (digital/electronic); *Databases:* 57. Weekly public service hours: 106.

STUDENT LIFE
Housing options: on-campus residence required through junior year; coed, men-only, women-only, special housing for students with disabilities. Campus housing is university owned. Freshman campus housing is guaranteed.

Activities and organizations: drama/theater group, student-run newspaper, radio station, choral group, International Club, Best Buddies (Assistance and Friendship for Individuals with Intellectual Disabilities), Blessings in a Backpack, Alpha Phi Omega (APO, Co-ed Service Fraternity), Improv Club, national fraternities, national sororities.

Athletics Member NCAA. All Division III except golf (Division II). ***Intercollegiate sports:*** baseball M, basketball M/W, cross-country running M/W, football M, golf M/W, soccer M/W, softball W, swimming and diving M/W, track and field M/W, volleyball W. ***Intramural sports:*** basketball M/W, equestrian sports M(c)/W(c), soccer M/W, ultimate Frisbee M(c)/W(c), volleyball M/W, water polo M(c)/W(c).

Campus security: 24-hour emergency response devices and patrols, late-night transport/escort service.

Student services: health clinic, personal/psychological counseling.

COSTS & FINANCIAL AID
Costs (2020–21) ***Comprehensive fee:*** $60,144 includes full-time tuition ($49,185), mandatory fees ($789), and room and board ($10,170). Full-time tuition and fees vary according to course load. Part-time tuition: $5465 per credit. Part-time tuition and fees vary according to course load. ***College room only:*** $5040. Room and board charges vary according to housing facility. ***Payment plan:*** installment. ***Waivers:*** employees or children of employees.

Financial Aid Of all full-time matriculated undergraduates who enrolled in 2018, 1,147 applied for aid, 947 were judged to have need, 216 had their need fully met. 648 Federal Work-Study jobs (averaging $2200). In 2018, 320 non-need-based awards were made. ***Average percent of need met:*** 89. ***Average financial aid package:*** $38,817. ***Average need-based loan:*** $3604. ***Average need-based gift aid:*** $31,428. ***Average non-need-based aid:*** $22,708. ***Average indebtedness upon graduation:*** $32,212.

APPLYING
Standardized Tests *Required for some:* SAT or ACT (for admission).

Options: electronic application, early admission, early decision, early action, deferred entrance.

Application fee: $50.

Required: essay or personal statement, high school transcript, 2 letters of recommendation. ***Recommended:*** interview.

Application deadlines: 1/15 (freshmen), 4/1 (transfers), 11/1 (early action).

Early decision deadline: 11/1.

Notification: 3/15 (freshmen), 5/1 (transfers), 11/15 (early decision), 12/15 (early action).

CONTACT
Mr. Paul Steenis, Vice President for Enrollment & Dean of Admission, Knox College, 2 East South Street, Campus Box148, Galesburg, IL 61401. *Phone:* 309-341-7100. *Toll-free phone:* 800-678-KNOX. *Fax:* 309-341-7070. *E-mail:* admission@knox.edu.

Lake Forest College

Lake Forest, Illinois

http://www.lakeforest.edu/

- **Independent** comprehensive, founded 1857
- **Suburban** 107-acre campus with easy access to Chicago
- **Endowment** $90.6 million
- **Coed** 1,492 undergraduate students, 99% full-time, 57% women, 43% men
- **Moderately difficult** entrance level, 58% of applicants were admitted

UNDERGRAD STUDENTS
1,472 full-time, 20 part-time. Students come from 41 states and territories; 77 other countries; 38% are from out of state; 5% Black or African American, non-Hispanic/Latino; 14% Hispanic/Latino; 5% Asian, non-Hispanic/Latino; 0.1% Native Hawaiian or other Pacific Islander, non-Hispanic/Latino; 0.3% American Indian or Alaska Native, non-Hispanic/Latino; 4% Two or more races, non-Hispanic/Latino; 4% Race/ethnicity unknown; 11% international; 5% transferred in; 78% live on campus.

Freshmen:
Admission: 4,147 applied, 2,402 admitted, 392 enrolled. ***Average high school GPA:*** 3.6.

Retention: 83% of full-time freshmen returned.

FACULTY
Total: 178, 57% full-time, 73% with terminal degrees.

Student/faculty ratio: 12:1.

ACADEMICS
Calendar: semesters. *Degrees:* bachelor's, master's, and postbachelor's certificates.

Special study options: accelerated degree program, advanced placement credit, double majors, honors programs, independent study, internships, off-campus study, part-time degree program, services for LD students, student-designed majors, study abroad, summer session for credit.

Unusual degree programs: 3-2 engineering with Washington University in St. Louis.

Computers: 400 computers/terminals and 2,000 ports are available on campus for general student use. Students can access the following: campus intranet, computer help desk, free student e-mail accounts, online (class) grades, online (class) registration, online (class) schedules, file storage. Campuswide network is available. 100% of college-owned or -operated housing units are wired for high-speed Internet access. Wireless service is available via entire campus.

Library: Donnelley and Lee Library. *Books:* 199,540 (physical), 213,024 (digital/electronic); *Serial titles:* 86,824 (physical). Study areas open 24 hours, 5–7 days a week; students can reserve study rooms.

STUDENT LIFE
Housing options: on-campus residence required through junior year; coed. Campus housing is university owned. Freshman applicants given priority for college housing.

Activities and organizations: drama/theater group, student-run newspaper, radio station, choral group, Athletic Council, Student

Government, United Black Association, PRIDE, Alpha Tau Omega, national fraternities, national sororities.

Athletics Member NCAA. All Division III. ***Intercollegiate sports:*** archery M(c)/W(c), basketball M/W, cheerleading M(c)/W(c), cross-country running M/W, equestrian sports M(c)/W(c), fencing M(c)/W(c), football M, golf M/W, ice hockey M/W, lacrosse M(c)/W(c), rugby M(c)/W(c), sailing M(c)/W(c), soccer M/W, softball W, swimming and diving M/W, tennis M/W, track and field M/W, ultimate Frisbee M(c)/W(c), volleyball W, water polo M(c)/W(c). ***Intramural sports:*** badminton M/W, basketball M/W, ice hockey M/W, soccer M/W, table tennis M/W, volleyball M/W.

Campus security: 24-hour emergency response devices and patrols, student patrols, late-night transport/escort service, controlled dormitory access.

Student services: health clinic, personal/psychological counseling.

COSTS & FINANCIAL AID

Costs (2020–21) ***Comprehensive fee:*** $60,776 includes full-time tuition ($48,920), mandatory fees ($902), and room and board ($10,954). Part-time tuition: $5960 per course. ***College room only:*** $5274. ***Payment plan:*** installment.

Financial Aid Of all full-time matriculated undergraduates who enrolled in 2019, 1,288 applied for aid, 1,100 were judged to have need, 331 had their need fully met. In 2019, 408 non-need-based awards were made. ***Average percent of need met:*** 86. ***Average financial aid package:*** $43,010. ***Average need-based loan:*** $4500. ***Average need-based gift aid:*** $38,560. ***Average non-need-based aid:*** $24,740. ***Average indebtedness upon graduation:*** $34,587. ***Financial aid deadline:*** 5/1.

APPLYING

Standardized Tests *Recommended:* SAT or ACT (for admission).

Options: electronic application, early decision, early action, deferred entrance.

Required: essay or personal statement, high school transcript, 1 letter of recommendation. ***Recommended:*** interview.

Application deadlines: 2/15 (freshmen), 1/1 (transfers), 11/15 (early action).

Early decision deadline: 11/15.

Notification: continuous until 3/10 (freshmen), 12/15 (early decision).

CONTACT

Christopher Ellertson, Vice President for Enrollment, Lake Forest College, 555 North Sheridan Road, Lake Forest, IL 60045-2338. *Phone:* 847-735-5000. *Toll-free phone:* 800-828-4751. *Fax:* 847-735-6271. *E-mail:* admissions@lakeforest.edu.

Lakeview College of Nursing

Danville, Illinois

http://www.lakeviewcol.edu/

- **Independent** upper-level, founded 1987
- **Small-town** 1-acre campus
- **Coed, primarily women** 148 undergraduate students, 90% full-time, 82% women, 18% men
- **Moderately difficult** entrance level

UNDERGRAD STUDENTS

133 full-time, 15 part-time. Students come from 7 states and territories; 10% Black or African American, non-Hispanic/Latino; 3% Hispanic/Latino; 8% Asian, non-Hispanic/Latino; 1% American Indian or Alaska Native, non-Hispanic/Latino; 3% Two or more races, non-Hispanic/Latino; 0.7% Race/ethnicity unknown; 33% transferred in.

FACULTY

Total: 16, 94% full-time.

Student/faculty ratio: 8:1.

ACADEMICS

Calendar: semesters. *Degree:* bachelor's.

Special study options: academic remediation for entering students, accelerated degree program, off-campus study, part-time degree program, services for LD students, summer session for credit. ***ROTC:*** Army (c), Air Force (c).

Computers: 61 computers/terminals are available on campus for general student use. Students can access the following: free student e-mail accounts, online (class) grades, online (class) schedules. Campuswide network is available. Wireless service is available via classrooms, computer centers, computer labs, libraries, student centers.

Library: Lakeview College of Nursing Library plus 1 other.

STUDENT LIFE

Housing options: college housing not available.

Campus security: 24-hour emergency response devices and patrols.

COSTS & FINANCIAL AID

Costs (2020–21) ***Tuition:*** $450 per credit hour part-time. ***Required fees:*** $65 per credit hour part-time.

Financial Aid Of all full-time matriculated undergraduates who enrolled in 2017, 384 applied for aid, 371 were judged to have need. ***Average percent of need met:*** 82. ***Average financial aid package:*** $22,950. ***Average need-based loan:*** $5500. ***Average need-based gift aid:*** $5750. ***Financial aid deadline:*** 10/1.

APPLYING

Options: early admission, early decision.

Application fee: $30.

CONTACT

Admissions Office, Lakeview College of Nursing, 903 North Logan Avenue, Danville, IL 61832. *Phone:* 217-709-0920. *Fax:* 217-709-0953. *E-mail:* admission@lakeviewcol.edu.

Lewis University

Romeoville, Illinois

http://www.lewisu.edu/

- **Independent** comprehensive, founded 1932, affiliated with Roman Catholic Church
- **Suburban** 410-acre campus with easy access to Chicago
- **Endowment** $79.8 million
- **Coed** 4,274 undergraduate students, 83% full-time, 50% women, 50% men
- **Moderately difficult** entrance level, 64% of applicants were admitted

UNDERGRAD STUDENTS

3,542 full-time, 732 part-time. Students come from 35 states and territories; 39 other countries; 8% are from out of state; 6% Black or African American, non-Hispanic/Latino; 22% Hispanic/Latino; 5% Asian, non-Hispanic/Latino; 0.2% Native Hawaiian or other Pacific Islander, non-Hispanic/Latino; 0.1% American Indian or Alaska Native, non-Hispanic/Latino; 2% Two or more races, non-Hispanic/Latino; 3% Race/ethnicity unknown; 2% international; 14% transferred in; 26% live on campus.

Freshmen:

Admission: 6,674 applied, 4,265 admitted, 639 enrolled. ***Average high school GPA:*** 3.5. ***Test scores:*** SAT evidence-based reading and writing scores over 500: 79%; SAT math scores over 500: 82%; ACT scores over 18: 98%; SAT evidence-based reading and writing scores over 600: 26%; SAT math scores over 600: 29%; ACT scores over 24: 49%; SAT evidence-based reading and writing scores over 700: 2%; SAT math scores over 700: 5%; ACT scores over 30: 7%.

Retention: 84% of full-time freshmen returned.

FACULTY

Total: 642, 37% full-time, 33% with terminal degrees.

Student/faculty ratio: 13:1.

ACADEMICS

Calendar: semesters. *Degrees:* certificates, associate, bachelor's, master's, doctoral, post-master's, and postbachelor's certificates.

Special study options: academic remediation for entering students, accelerated degree program, adult/continuing education programs, advanced placement credit, distance learning, double majors, English as a second language, honors programs, independent study, internships, off-campus study, part-time degree program, services for LD students, student-designed majors, study abroad, summer session for credit. ***ROTC:*** Army (c), Air Force (c).

Computers: Students can access the following: campus intranet, computer help desk, free student e-mail accounts, online (class) grades, online (class) registration, online (class) schedules, online help desk, online billing, online financial aid, online payments, online admission application, online housing application, online application for graduation, online Blackboard course management system, online tutoring. Campuswide network is available. 100% of college-owned or -operated housing units are wired for high-speed Internet access. Wireless service is available via entire campus.
Library: Lewis University Library. *Books:* 91,369 (physical), 267,351 (digital/electronic); *Serial titles:* 1,143 (physical), 117,860 (digital/electronic); *Databases:* 76. Weekly public service hours: 98; students can reserve study rooms.

STUDENT LIFE
Housing options: on-campus residence required through sophomore year; coed. Campus housing is university owned. Freshman campus housing is guaranteed.

Activities and organizations: drama/theater group, student-run newspaper, radio and television station, choral group, Student Governing Board, Student Nurses Association, Latin American Student Organization, national fraternities, national sororities.

Athletics Member NCAA. All Division II except volleyball (Division I). ***Intercollegiate sports:*** badminton M(c)/W(c), baseball M(s), basketball M(s)/W(s), bowling M(s)/W(s), cheerleading W(s), cross-country running M(s)/W(s), golf M(s)/W(s), ice hockey M(c), lacrosse M(s)/W(s), sand volleyball M(c)/W(c), soccer M(s)/W(s), softball W(s), swimming and diving M(s)/W(s), tennis M(s)/W(s), track and field M(s)/W(s), ultimate Frisbee M(c)/W(c), volleyball M(s)/W(s), water polo M(c)/W(c). ***Intramural sports:*** archery M(c)/W(c), badminton M/W, baseball M(c), basketball M(c)/W, bowling M/W, football M/W, golf M(c)/W(c), rugby M(c)/W(c), sand volleyball M/W, soccer M(c)/W, softball M/W, table tennis M/W, tennis M/W, ultimate Frisbee M/W, volleyball M(c)/W(c), water polo M/W, weight lifting M(c)/W(c).

Campus security: 24-hour emergency response devices and patrols, late-night transport/escort service, controlled dormitory access, Emergency notification system.

Student services: health clinic, personal/psychological counseling, veterans affairs office.

COSTS & FINANCIAL AID
Costs (2020–21) ***Comprehensive fee:*** $45,528 includes full-time tuition ($34,268), mandatory fees ($210), and room and board ($11,050). Full-time tuition and fees vary according to course load, location, and program. Part-time tuition: $996 per credit hour. Part-time tuition and fees vary according to course load, location, and program. ***Required fees:*** $100 per term part-time. ***Room and board:*** Room and board charges vary according to board plan and housing facility. ***Payment plan:*** installment. ***Waivers:*** children of alumni and employees or children of employees.

Financial Aid Of all full-time matriculated undergraduates who enrolled in 2019, 2,954 applied for aid, 2,653 were judged to have need, 648 had their need fully met. In 2019, 687 non-need-based awards were made. ***Average percent of need met:*** 91. ***Average financial aid package:*** $28,523. ***Average need-based loan:*** $4456. ***Average need-based gift aid:*** $18,996. ***Average non-need-based aid:*** $13,503. ***Average indebtedness upon graduation:*** $36,653. ***Financial aid deadline:*** 5/1.

APPLYING
Standardized Tests *Required:* SAT or ACT (for admission).

Options: electronic application, deferred entrance.

Application fee: $40.

Required: high school transcript, minimum 2.0 GPA. ***Required for some:*** interview. ***Recommended:*** essay or personal statement.

Application deadlines: rolling (freshmen), rolling (transfers).

Notification: continuous (freshmen), continuous (transfers).

CONTACT
Mr. Ryan Cockerill, Director of Admission, Lewis University, Unit #297, 1 University Parkway, Romeoville, IL 60446. *Phone:* 815-836-5237. *Toll-free phone:* 800-897-9000. *Fax:* 815-836-5002. *E-mail:* cockerry@lewisu.edu.

Lincoln Christian University

Lincoln, Illinois

http://www.lincolnchristian.edu/

- **Independent** comprehensive, founded 1944, affiliated with Christian Churches and Churches of Christ
- **Small-town** 100-acre campus
- **Endowment** $5.2 million
- **Coed**
- **Moderately difficult** entrance level

FACULTY
Student/faculty ratio: 12:1.

ACADEMICS
Calendar: semesters. *Degrees:* associate, bachelor's, master's, and doctoral.
Library: Jessie Eury Library. *Books:* 92,813 (physical), 55,082 (digital/electronic); *Serial titles:* 719 (physical), 15,442 (digital/electronic); *Databases:* 52. Weekly public service hours: 82; students can reserve study rooms.

STUDENT LIFE
Housing options: on-campus residence required through senior year; men-only, women-only. Campus housing is university owned. Freshman campus housing is guaranteed.

Activities and organizations: drama/theater group, choral group, Chorale, Student Cabinet, American Association of Christian Counselors (AACC) - Student Chapter, Cheerleading.

Athletics Member NAIA, NCCAA.

Campus security: 24-hour emergency response devices, student patrols, controlled dormitory access.

Student services: personal/psychological counseling, veterans affairs office.

FINANCIAL AID
Financial Aid Of all full-time matriculated undergraduates who enrolled in 2017, 348 applied for aid, 289 were judged to have need, 18 had their need fully met. In 2017, 53 non-need-based awards were made. ***Average percent of need met:*** 56. ***Average financial aid package:*** $13,404. ***Average need-based loan:*** $3881. ***Average need-based gift aid:*** $7987. ***Average non-need-based aid:*** $2600. ***Average indebtedness upon graduation:*** $26,654.

APPLYING
Standardized Tests *Required:* SAT or ACT (for admission).

Options: electronic application, deferred entrance.

Required: essay or personal statement, 3 letters of recommendation. ***Required for some:*** high school transcript, interview.

CONTACT
Mrs. Mary K. Davis, Admissions Office Manager, Lincoln Christian University, 100 Campus View Drive, Lincoln, IL 62656. *Phone:* 217-732-3168 Ext. 2251. *Toll-free phone:* 888-522-5228. *Fax:* 217-732-4199. *E-mail:* enroll@lincolnchristian.edu.

Lincoln College

Lincoln, Illinois

http://www.lincolncollege.edu/

CONTACT
Lincoln College, 300 Keokuk Street, Lincoln, IL 62656-1699. *Phone:* 217-735-7251 Ext. 7251. *Toll-free phone:* 800-569-0558.

Loyola University Chicago

Chicago, Illinois

http://www.luc.edu/

- **Independent Roman Catholic (Jesuit)** university, founded 1870
- **Urban** 105-acre campus
- **Endowment** $640.3 million
- **Coed** 12,240 undergraduate students, 95% full-time, 67% women, 33% men
- **Moderately difficult** entrance level, 67% of applicants were admitted

UNDERGRAD STUDENTS
11,622 full-time, 618 part-time. Students come from 52 states and territories; 102 other countries; 39% are from out of state; 5% Black or African American, non-Hispanic/Latino; 17% Hispanic/Latino; 12% Asian, non-Hispanic/Latino; 0.2% Native Hawaiian or other Pacific Islander, non-Hispanic/Latino; 0.1% American Indian or Alaska Native, non-Hispanic/Latino; 4% Two or more races, non-Hispanic/Latino; 1% Race/ethnicity unknown; 4% international; 4% transferred in; 38% live on campus.

Freshmen:
Admission: 25,583 applied, 17,198 admitted, 2,630 enrolled. ***Average high school GPA:*** 3.7. ***Test scores:*** SAT evidence-based reading and writing scores over 500: 98%; SAT math scores over 500: 96%; ACT scores over 18: 99%; SAT evidence-based reading and writing scores over 600: 62%; SAT math scores over 600: 55%; ACT scores over 24: 84%; SAT evidence-based reading and writing scores over 700: 12%; SAT math scores over 700: 13%; ACT scores over 30: 33%.

Retention: 86% of full-time freshmen returned.

FACULTY
Total: 1,660, 50% full-time, 46% with terminal degrees.
Student/faculty ratio: 14:1.

ACADEMICS
Calendar: semesters. *Degrees:* certificates, associate, bachelor's, master's, doctoral, post-master's, and postbachelor's certificates (also offers adult part-time program with significant enrollment not reflected in profile).

Special study options: accelerated degree program, adult/continuing education programs, advanced placement credit, distance learning, double majors, English as a second language, freshman honors college, honors programs, independent study, internships, off-campus study, part-time degree program, services for LD students, study abroad, summer session for credit. ***ROTC:*** Army (b), Navy (c), Air Force (c).

Unusual degree programs: 3-2 business administration; engineering; social work; political science, sociology, psychology/applied social psychology, computers, biology, accounting, information technology, criminal justice and criminology.

Computers: 1,300 computers/terminals are available on campus for general student use. Students can access the following: campus intranet, computer help desk, free student e-mail accounts, online (class) grades, online (class) registration, online (class) schedules. Campuswide network is available. 100% of college-owned or -operated housing units are wired for high-speed Internet access. Wireless service is available via entire campus.

Library: Cudahy Library plus 7 others. *Books:* 916,582 (physical), 810,385 (digital/electronic); *Serial titles:* 2,078 (physical), 97,083 (digital/electronic); *Databases:* 553. Weekly public service hours: 144; study areas open 24 hours, 5–7 days a week; students can reserve study rooms.

STUDENT LIFE
Housing options: on-campus residence required through sophomore year; coed, special housing for students with disabilities. Campus housing is university owned. Freshman campus housing is guaranteed.

Activities and organizations: drama/theater group, student-run newspaper, radio station, choral group, Panhellenic Council, National Society of Collegiate Scholars, Vegetarian and Vegan Society, Interfraternity Council, American Medical Student Association, national fraternities, national sororities.

Athletics Member NCAA. All Division I. ***Intercollegiate sports:*** basketball M(s)/W(s), cross-country running M(s)/W(s), golf M(s)/W(s)(c), soccer M(s)/W(s), softball W(s), track and field M(s)/W(s), volleyball M(s)/W(s). ***Intramural sports:*** baseball M(c), basketball M/W, cross-country running M(c)/W(c), field hockey M(c)/W(c), football M(c), golf M(c)/W(c), ice hockey M(c)/W(c), lacrosse M(c)/W(c), rugby M(c)/W(c), soccer M(c)/W(c), softball W(c), swimming and diving M(c)/W(c), table tennis M(c)/W(c), tennis M(c)/W(c), ultimate Frisbee M(c)/W(c), volleyball M(c)/W(c), water polo M(c)/W(c).

Campus security: 24-hour emergency response devices, late-night transport/escort service, controlled dormitory access.

Student services: health clinic, personal/psychological counseling, women's center, veterans affairs office.

COSTS & FINANCIAL AID
Costs (2020–21) ***Comprehensive fee:*** $61,918 includes full-time tuition ($45,500), mandatory fees ($1398), and room and board ($15,020). Full-time tuition and fees vary according to degree level. Part-time tuition: $840 per credit hour. Part-time tuition and fees vary according to degree level. ***College room only:*** $9400. ***Waivers:*** employees or children of employees.

Financial Aid Of all full-time matriculated undergraduates who enrolled in 2019, 8,535 applied for aid, 7,241 were judged to have need, 1,153 had their need fully met. 5,111 Federal Work-Study jobs (averaging $2764). In 2019, 3808 non-need-based awards were made. ***Average percent of need met:*** 84. ***Average financial aid package:*** $35,786. ***Average need-based loan:*** $4349. ***Average need-based gift aid:*** $22,915. ***Average non-need-based aid:*** $18,001. ***Average indebtedness upon graduation:*** $35,030.

APPLYING
Standardized Tests *Required:* SAT or ACT (for admission).

Options: electronic application.

Required: high school transcript, minimum 3.7 GPA, 1 letter of recommendation. ***Recommended:*** essay or personal statement, interview.

Application deadlines: rolling (freshmen), rolling (out-of-state freshmen), rolling (transfers).

Notification: continuous (freshmen), continuous (out-of-state freshmen), continuous (transfers).

CONTACT
Ms. Erin Moriarty, Assoc VP of Undergraduate Admissions, Loyola University Chicago, 1032 West Sheridan Road, Chicago, IL 60660. *Phone:* 773-508-3079. *Toll-free phone:* 800-262-2373. *E-mail:* admission@luc.edu.

McKendree University

Lebanon, Illinois

http://www.mckendree.edu/

- **Independent** university, founded 1828, affiliated with United Methodist Church
- **Suburban** 235-acre campus with easy access to St. Louis, MO; Belleville, IL
- **Coed** 1,788 undergraduate students, 83% full-time, 52% women, 48% men
- **Moderately difficult** entrance level, 63% of applicants were admitted

UNDERGRAD STUDENTS
1,484 full-time, 304 part-time. 32% are from out of state; 12% Black or African American, non-Hispanic/Latino; 5% Hispanic/Latino; 0.7% Asian, non-Hispanic/Latino; 0.1% Native Hawaiian or other Pacific Islander, non-Hispanic/Latino; 0.2% American Indian or Alaska Native, non-Hispanic/Latino; 4% Two or more races, non-Hispanic/Latino; 11% Race/ethnicity unknown; 5% international; 4% transferred in; 73% live on campus.

Freshmen:
Admission: 1,997 applied, 1,265 admitted, 332 enrolled. ***Average high school GPA:*** 3.4. ***Test scores:*** SAT evidence-based reading and writing scores over 500: 70%; SAT math scores over 500: 72%; ACT scores over 18: 100%; SAT evidence-based reading and writing scores over 600: 27%; SAT math scores over 600: 21%; ACT scores over 24: 39%; SAT evidence-based reading and writing scores over 700: 2%; SAT math scores over 700: 2%; ACT scores over 30: 6%.

Retention: 75% of full-time freshmen returned.

FACULTY
Total: 219, 42% full-time, 55% with terminal degrees.
Student/faculty ratio: 14:1.

ACADEMICS
Calendar: semesters. *Degrees:* associate, bachelor's, master's, doctoral, and post-master's certificates.

Special study options: academic remediation for entering students, accelerated degree program, adult/continuing education programs, advanced placement credit, cooperative education, distance learning, double majors, external degree program, freshman honors college, honors programs, independent study, internships, off-campus study, part-time degree program, services for LD students, student-designed majors, study abroad, summer session for credit. ***ROTC:*** Army (c), Air Force (c).

Unusual degree programs: 3-2 occupational therapy with Washington University in St. Louis.

Computers: 380 computers/terminals are available on campus for general student use. Students can access the following: campus intranet, computer help desk, free student e-mail accounts, online (class) grades, online (class) registration, online (class) schedules. Campuswide network is available. 100% of college-owned or -operated housing units are wired for high-speed Internet access. Wireless service is available via entire campus.

Library: Holman Library. *Books:* 76,806 (physical), 11,853 (digital/electronic); *Serial titles:* 5,099 (physical), 7,229 (digital/electronic); *Databases:* 59. Students can reserve study rooms.

STUDENT LIFE

Housing options: on-campus residence required through junior year; coed, special housing for students with disabilities. Campus housing is university owned. Freshman campus housing is guaranteed.

Activities and organizations: drama/theater group, student-run newspaper, radio station, choral group, marching band, Center for Public Service, Wonders of Wellness, Campus Ministries, APO, Debate, national fraternities, national sororities.

Athletics Member NCAA. All Division II except volleyball (Division I). ***Intercollegiate sports:*** baseball M(s), basketball M(s)/W(s), bowling M(c)/W(s), cheerleading M(s)(c)/W(s)(c), cross-country running M(s)/W(s), fencing M(c)/W(c), football M(s), golf M(s)/W(s), ice hockey M(c)/W(c), lacrosse W(s), soccer M(s)/W(s), softball W(s), swimming and diving M(s)/W(s), tennis M(s)/W(s), track and field M(s)/W(s), volleyball M(s)/W(s), water polo M(s)/W(s), weight lifting M(c)/W(c), wrestling M(s)/W(s)(c). ***Intramural sports:*** basketball M/W, football M/W, softball M/W, ultimate Frisbee M/W, volleyball M/W.

Campus security: 24-hour emergency response devices and patrols, student patrols, late-night transport/escort service, controlled dormitory access.

Student services: health clinic, personal/psychological counseling.

COSTS & FINANCIAL AID

Costs (2019–20) ***One-time required fee:*** $400. ***Comprehensive fee:*** $41,560 includes full-time tuition ($30,540), mandatory fees ($1100), and room and board ($9920). Full-time tuition and fees vary according to course load, degree level, and location. Part-time tuition: $990 per credit hour. Part-time tuition and fees vary according to course load, degree level, and location. ***College room only:*** $5370. Room and board charges vary according to board plan and housing facility. ***Payment plans:*** installment, deferred payment. ***Waivers:*** children of alumni and employees or children of employees.

Financial Aid Of all full-time matriculated undergraduates who enrolled in 2018, 1,312 applied for aid, 1,201 were judged to have need, 230 had their need fully met. 265 Federal Work-Study jobs (averaging $871). 75 state and other part-time jobs (averaging $1178). In 2018, 272 non-need-based awards were made. ***Average percent of need met:*** 72. ***Average financial aid package:*** $22,125. ***Average need-based loan:*** $4550. ***Average need-based gift aid:*** $19,062. ***Average non-need-based aid:*** $13,412. ***Average indebtedness upon graduation:*** $28,754.

APPLYING

Standardized Tests *Required for some:* SAT or ACT (for admission).

Options: electronic application, deferred entrance.

Required: essay or personal statement, high school transcript, minimum 2.5 GPA, 1 letter of recommendation, rank in upper 50% of high school class, minimum ACT score of 20. ***Required for some:*** interview.

Application deadlines: rolling (freshmen), rolling (transfers).

Notification: continuous (freshmen), continuous (transfers).

CONTACT

Mrs. Josie Blasdel, Director of Undergraduate Admission, McKendree University, 701 College Road, Lebanon, IL 62254. *Phone:* 618-537-6836. *Toll-free phone:* 800-232-7228. *E-mail:* jlblasdel@mckendree.edu.

Methodist College

Peoria, Illinois

http://www.methodistcol.edu/

CONTACT

Methodist College, 415 St. Mark Court, Peoria, IL 61603.

Millikin University

Decatur, Illinois

http://www.millikin.edu/

- **Independent** comprehensive, founded 1901, affiliated with Presbyterian Church (U.S.A.)
- **Suburban** 75-acre campus
- **Endowment** $106.9 million
- **Coed** 1,995 undergraduate students, 96% full-time, 55% women, 45% men
- **Moderately difficult** entrance level, 71% of applicants were admitted

UNDERGRAD STUDENTS

1,918 full-time, 77 part-time. Students come from 40 states and territories; 33 other countries; 22% are from out of state; 14% Black or African American, non-Hispanic/Latino; 5% Hispanic/Latino; 2% Asian, non-Hispanic/Latino; 0.1% Native Hawaiian or other Pacific Islander, non-Hispanic/Latino; 0.2% American Indian or Alaska Native, non-Hispanic/Latino; 4% Two or more races, non-Hispanic/Latino; 3% Race/ethnicity unknown; 4% international; 5% transferred in; 60% live on campus.

Freshmen:

Admission: 3,520 applied, 2,509 admitted, 486 enrolled. ***Average high school GPA:*** 3.4. ***Test scores:*** SAT evidence-based reading and writing scores over 500: 73%; SAT math scores over 500: 70%; ACT scores over 18: 90%; SAT evidence-based reading and writing scores over 600: 31%; SAT math scores over 600: 24%; ACT scores over 24: 46%; SAT evidence-based reading and writing scores over 700: 6%; SAT math scores over 700: 4%; ACT scores over 30: 12%.

Retention: 75% of full-time freshmen returned.

FACULTY

Total: 287, 53% full-time, 49% with terminal degrees.

Student/faculty ratio: 10:1.

ACADEMICS

Calendar: semesters. *Degrees:* certificates, bachelor's, master's, doctoral, and postbachelor's certificates.

Special study options: academic remediation for entering students, adult/continuing education programs, advanced placement credit, distance learning, double majors, English as a second language, honors programs, independent study, internships, off-campus study, part-time degree program, services for LD students, student-designed majors, study abroad, summer session for credit.

Unusual degree programs: 3-2 engineering with Washington University in St. Louis, University of Missouri in Kansas City; occupational therapy with Washington University, pharmacy with Midwestern University.

Computers: 135 computers/terminals and 300 ports are available on campus for general student use. Students can access the following: computer help desk, free student e-mail accounts, online (class) grades, online (class) registration, online (class) schedules, online degree audit, online financials (view and pay bills, financial aid). Campuswide network is available. 100% of college-owned or -operated housing units are wired for high-speed Internet access. Wireless service is available via entire campus.

Library: Staley Library. *Books:* 125,046 (physical), 29,809 (digital/electronic); *Serial titles:* 543 (physical), 45 (digital/electronic); *Databases:* 50. Weekly public service hours: 87; students can reserve study rooms.

STUDENT LIFE

Housing options: on-campus residence required through junior year; coed, men-only, women-only, special housing for students with disabilities. Campus housing is university owned. Freshman campus housing is guaranteed.

Activities and organizations: drama/theater group, student-run newspaper, radio station, choral group, University Center Board, Multicultural Student Council, Student Housing Council, Panhellenic Council, Interfraternity Council, national fraternities, national sororities.

Athletics Member NCAA. All Division III except golf (Division II). ***Intercollegiate sports:*** baseball M, basketball M/W, cross-country running M/W, football M, golf M/W, soccer M/W, softball W, swimming and diving M/W, tennis M/W, track and field M/W, triathlon W, volleyball M/W, wrestling M. ***Intramural sports:*** basketball M/W, cheerleading M(c)/W(c), football M/W, soccer M/W, softball M/W, ultimate Frisbee M/W, volleyball M/W.

Campus security: 24-hour emergency response devices and patrols, late-night transport/escort service, controlled dormitory access.

Student services: health clinic, personal/psychological counseling, women's center.

COSTS & FINANCIAL AID

Costs (2020–21) ***Comprehensive fee:*** $51,042 includes full-time tuition ($38,800), mandatory fees ($792), and room and board ($11,450). Part-time tuition: $499 per credit hour. ***Required fees:*** $22 per credit hour part-time. ***College room only:*** $9400. Room and board charges vary according to board plan. ***Payment plan:*** installment. ***Waivers:*** employees or children of employees.

Financial Aid Of all full-time matriculated undergraduates who enrolled in 2018, 1,667 applied for aid, 1,531 were judged to have need, 505 had their need fully met. 472 Federal Work-Study jobs (averaging $1067). 410 state and other part-time jobs (averaging $815). In 2018, 128 non-need-based awards were made. ***Average percent of need met:*** 83. ***Average financial aid package:*** $27,736. ***Average need-based loan:*** $4237. ***Average need-based gift aid:*** $9635. ***Average non-need-based aid:*** $18,472. ***Average indebtedness upon graduation:*** $35,596.

APPLYING

Standardized Tests *Required:* SAT or ACT (for admission).

Options: electronic application, deferred entrance.

Required: high school transcript, minimum 2.0 GPA, 2 letters of recommendation. ***Required for some:*** audition for music/theatre, art portfolio review. ***Recommended:*** interview.

Application deadlines: rolling (freshmen), rolling (transfers).

Notification: continuous (freshmen), continuous (transfers).

CONTACT

Mr. Kyle Taylor, Director of Admission, Millikin University, 1184 West Main Street, Decatur, IL 62522-2084. *Phone:* 217-424-6210. *Toll-free phone:* 800-373-7733. *Fax:* 217-425-4669. *E-mail:* admis@millikin.edu.

Monmouth College

Monmouth, Illinois

http://www.monmouthcollege.edu/

CONTACT

Mr. Trent Gilbert, Vice President for Enrollment Management, Monmouth College, 700 East Broadway, Monmouth, IL 61462-1988. *Phone:* 309-457-2131. *Toll-free phone:* 800-747-2687. *Fax:* 309-457-2141. *E-mail:* admissions@monmouthcollege.edu.

Moody Bible Institute

Chicago, Illinois

http://www.moody.edu/

CONTACT

Ms. Jacqueline Holman, Admissions Office, Moody Bible Institute, 820 North LaSalle Boulevard, Chicago, IL 60610. *Phone:* 312-329-4307. *Toll-free phone:* 800-967-4MBI. *Fax:* 312-329-8987. *E-mail:* admissions@moody.edu.

National Louis University

Chicago, Illinois

http://www.nl.edu/

CONTACT

National Louis University, 1000 Capitol Drive, Wheeling, IL 60090. *Phone:* 888-NLU-TODAY. *Toll-free phone:* 888-658-8632.

North Central College

Naperville, Illinois

http://www.northcentralcollege.edu/

CONTACT

Ms. Martha Stolze, Dean of Admission, North Central College, 30 North Brainard Street, PO Box 3063, Naperville, IL 60566-7063. *Phone:* 630-637-5800. *Toll-free phone:* 800-411-1861. *Fax:* 630-637-5819. *E-mail:* admissions@noctrl.edu.

Northeastern Illinois University

Chicago, Illinois

http://www.neiu.edu/

- **State-supported** comprehensive, founded 1961
- **Urban** 67-acre campus with easy access to Chicago
- **Endowment** $768,031
- **Coed** 5,705 undergraduate students, 58% full-time, 57% women, 43% men
- **Minimally difficult** entrance level, 58% of applicants were admitted

UNDERGRAD STUDENTS

3,299 full-time, 2,406 part-time. 0.6% are from out of state; 11% Black or African American, non-Hispanic/Latino; 40% Hispanic/Latino; 9% Asian, non-Hispanic/Latino; 0.3% Native Hawaiian or other Pacific Islander, non-Hispanic/Latino; 0.2% American Indian or Alaska Native, non-Hispanic/Latino; 2% Two or more races, non-Hispanic/Latino; 10% Race/ethnicity unknown; 2% international; 16% transferred in; 3% live on campus.

Freshmen:

Admission: 4,711 applied, 2,755 admitted, 457 enrolled. ***Average high school GPA:*** 3.0. ***Test scores:*** ACT scores over 18: 57%; ACT scores over 24: 11%; ACT scores over 30: 2%.

Retention: 59% of full-time freshmen returned.

FACULTY

Total: 563, 53% full-time, 60% with terminal degrees.

Student/faculty ratio: 13:1.

ACADEMICS

Calendar: semesters. *Degrees:* certificates, bachelor's, and master's.

Special study options: academic remediation for entering students, adult/continuing education programs, advanced placement credit, cooperative education, distance learning, double majors, English as a second language, honors programs, independent study, internships, off-campus study, part-time degree program, services for LD students, study abroad, summer session for credit. ***ROTC:*** Army (c), Air Force (c).

Computers: Students can access the following: computer help desk, free student e-mail accounts, online (class) grades, online (class) registration, online (class) schedules, productivity software. Campuswide network is available. Wireless service is available via classrooms, computer centers, computer labs, learning centers, libraries, student centers.

Library: Ronald Williams Library plus 3 others. *Books:* 688,147 (physical), 156,705 (digital/electronic); *Serial titles:* 742 (physical), 86,898 (digital/electronic); *Databases:* 188. Weekly public service hours: 92.

STUDENT LIFE

Housing options: coed, special housing for students with disabilities. Campus housing is university owned.

Activities and organizations: drama/theater group, student-run newspaper, radio station, choral group, Student Government Association, United Greek Council, ASSW - Association of Student Social Workers, Accounting Associates, Computer Science Society, national fraternities, national sororities.

Athletics ***Intramural sports:*** badminton M/W, baseball M(c), basketball M(c)/W(c), crew M/W, cross-country running M/W, football M/W, ice hockey M/W, racquetball M/W, rock climbing M/W, soccer M(c)/W(c), softball M/W, table tennis M/W, tennis M/W, volleyball M(c)/W(c), weight lifting M/W.

Campus security: 24-hour emergency response devices and patrols, late-night transport/escort service, controlled dormitory access.

Student services: health clinic, personal/psychological counseling, women's center, veterans affairs office.

COSTS & FINANCIAL AID

Costs (2020–21) ***Tuition:*** area resident $11,582 full-time, $412 per credit hour part-time; nonresident $23,165 full-time, $824 per credit hour part-time. ***Required fees:*** $2416 full-time. ***Room only:*** $8426.

Financial Aid Of all full-time matriculated undergraduates who enrolled in 2019, 2,687 applied for aid, 2,400 were judged to have need, 167 had their need fully met. In 2019, 124 non-need-based awards were made. ***Average percent of need met:*** 19. ***Average financial aid package:*** $11,090. ***Average need-based loan:*** $3375. ***Average need-based gift aid:*** $8262. ***Average non-need-based aid:*** $5945. ***Average indebtedness upon graduation:*** $11,355.

APPLYING

Standardized Tests *Required:* SAT or ACT (for admission).

Options: electronic application, deferred entrance.

Application fee: $30.

Required: high school transcript.

Notification: continuous (transfers).

CONTACT

Ms. Zarrin Kerwell, Admissions Counselor, Northeastern Illinois University, 5500 North St. Louis Avenue, Chicago, IL 60625. *Phone:* 773-442-4026. *Fax:* 773-794-6243. *E-mail:* admrec@neiu.edu.

Northern Illinois University

De Kalb, Illinois

http://www.niu.edu/

- **State-supported** university, founded 1895
- **Small-town** 650-acre campus with easy access to Chicago
- **Endowment** $8.1 million
- **Coed** 12,131 undergraduate students, 87% full-time, 51% women, 49% men
- **Moderately difficult** entrance level, 48% of applicants were admitted

UNDERGRAD STUDENTS

10,567 full-time, 1,564 part-time. Students come from 36 states and territories; 49 other countries; 3% are from out of state; 17% Black or African American, non-Hispanic/Latino; 19% Hispanic/Latino; 6% Asian, non-Hispanic/Latino; 0.1% Native Hawaiian or other Pacific Islander, non-Hispanic/Latino; 0.1% American Indian or Alaska Native, non-Hispanic/Latino; 4% Two or more races, non-Hispanic/Latino; 0.2% Race/ethnicity unknown; 2% international; 13% transferred in; 30% live on campus.

Freshmen:

Admission: 15,687 applied, 7,587 admitted, 1,897 enrolled. ***Average high school GPA:*** 3.4.

Retention: 73% of full-time freshmen returned.

FACULTY

Total: 1,055, 76% full-time, 73% with terminal degrees.

Student/faculty ratio: 13:1.

ACADEMICS

Calendar: semesters. *Degrees:* bachelor's, master's, and doctoral.

Special study options: accelerated degree program, adult/continuing education programs, advanced placement credit, cooperative education, double majors, honors programs, independent study, internships, off-campus study, part-time degree program, services for LD students, student-designed majors, study abroad, summer session for credit. ***ROTC:*** Army (b), Air Force (c).

Computers: 1,500 computers/terminals are available on campus for general student use. Students can access the following: computer help desk, free student e-mail accounts, online (class) grades, online (class) registration, online (class) schedules. Campuswide network is available. 100% of college-owned or -operated housing units are wired for high-speed Internet access. Wireless service is available via entire campus.

Library: Founders Memorial Library plus 4 others. *Books:* 1.8 million (physical), 750,000 (digital/electronic); *Serial titles:* 1,227 (physical), 83,137 (digital/electronic); *Databases:* 314. Weekly public service hours: 100; students can reserve study rooms.

STUDENT LIFE

Housing options: on-campus residence required for freshman year; coed. Campus housing is university owned. Freshman applicants given priority for college housing.

Activities and organizations: drama/theater group, student-run newspaper, radio station, choral group, marching band, American Marketing Association, Delta Sigma Pi, Pi Sigma Epsilon, Black Choir, Student Volunteer Choir, national fraternities, national sororities.

Athletics Member NCAA. All Division I except football (Division I-A). ***Intercollegiate sports:*** baseball M(s), basketball M(s)/W(s), cross-country running W, golf M(s)/W(s)(c), gymnastics W(s), soccer M(s)/W(s), softball W(s), swimming and diving M(s)/W(s), tennis M(s)/W(s), volleyball W(s), wrestling M(s). ***Intramural sports:*** archery M(c)/W(c), badminton M/W, basketball M/W, bowling M(c)/W(c), cross-country running W, football M/W, golf M/W, ice hockey M(c)/W(c), lacrosse M(c)/W(c), racquetball M/W, rugby M(c)/W(c), skiing (downhill) M(c)/W(c), soccer M/W, softball M/W, table tennis M/W, tennis M/W, track and field M(c)/W(c), volleyball M/W, water polo M(c)/W(c), weight lifting M(c)/W(c).

Campus security: 24-hour emergency response devices and patrols, student patrols, late-night transport/escort service, controlled dormitory access.

Student services: health clinic, personal/psychological counseling, women's center, legal services.

COSTS & FINANCIAL AID

Costs (2020–21) ***Tuition:*** area resident $9466 full-time, $349 per credit hour part-time; state resident $9466 full-time, $349 per credit hour part-time; nonresident $9466 full-time, $349 per credit hour part-time. Full-time tuition and fees vary according to program. Part-time tuition and fees vary according to program. No tuition increase for student's term of enrollment. ***Required fees:*** $2795 full-time, $92 per credit hour part-time, $125 per term part-time. ***Room and board:*** $10,880. Room and board charges vary according to housing facility. ***Payment plan:*** installment. ***Waivers:*** children of alumni and employees or children of employees.

Financial Aid Of all full-time matriculated undergraduates who enrolled in 2018, 9,690 applied for aid, 8,494 were judged to have need, 702 had their need fully met. 3,099 Federal Work-Study jobs (averaging $2695). In 2018, 1382 non-need-based awards were made. ***Average percent of need met:*** 61. ***Average financial aid package:*** $12,587. ***Average need-based loan:*** $4375. ***Average need-based gift aid:*** $8611. ***Average non-need-based aid:*** $3976. ***Average indebtedness upon graduation:*** $33,915.

APPLYING

Options: electronic application.

Application fee: $40.

Required: high school transcript, high school class rank.

Notification: continuous (freshmen), continuous (transfers).

CONTACT

Quinten Clay, Director of Admissions, Northern Illinois University, Student Affairs & Enrollment Management, DeKalb, IL 60115-2857. *Phone:* 815-753-0446. *Toll-free phone:* 800-892-3050. *E-mail:* admissions@niu.edu.

North Park University

Chicago, Illinois

http://www.northpark.edu/

- **Independent** comprehensive, founded 1891, affiliated with Evangelical Covenant Church
- **Urban** 30-acre campus
- **Coed**
- **Moderately difficult** entrance level

FACULTY

Student/faculty ratio: 12:1.

ACADEMICS
Calendar: semesters. *Degrees:* bachelor's, master's, doctoral, and post-master's certificates.
Library: Brandel Library.

STUDENT LIFE
Housing options: on-campus residence required through junior year; men-only, women-only. Campus housing is university owned. Freshman campus housing is guaranteed.

Activities and organizations: drama/theater group, student-run newspaper, choral group.

Athletics Member NCAA. All Division III.

Campus security: 24-hour emergency response devices and patrols, late-night transport/escort service, controlled dormitory access.

Student services: health clinic, personal/psychological counseling.

FINANCIAL AID
Financial Aid Of all full-time matriculated undergraduates who enrolled in 2008, 158 Federal Work-Study jobs (averaging $1500).

APPLYING
Standardized Tests *Required:* SAT or ACT (for admission).

Options: electronic application, early admission.

Application fee: $40.

Required: essay or personal statement, high school transcript, minimum 2.8 GPA, 2 letters of recommendation. ***Required for some:*** interview. ***Recommended:*** minimum 3.0 GPA.

CONTACT
Office of Admissions, North Park University, 3225 West Foster Avenue, Chicago, IL 60625-4895. *Phone:* 773-244-5500. *Toll-free phone:* 800-888-NPC8. *Fax:* 773-583-0858. *E-mail:* afao@northpark.edu.

Northwestern University

Evanston, Illinois

http://www.northwestern.edu/

- **Independent** university, founded 1851
- **Suburban** 250-acre campus with easy access to Chicago
- **Coed** 8,327 undergraduate students, 98% full-time, 51% women, 49% men
- **Most difficult** entrance level, 9% of applicants were admitted

UNDERGRAD STUDENTS
8,186 full-time, 141 part-time. 69% are from out of state; 6% Black or African American, non-Hispanic/Latino; 12% Hispanic/Latino; 18% Asian, non-Hispanic/Latino; 0.1% American Indian or Alaska Native, non-Hispanic/Latino; 6% Two or more races, non-Hispanic/Latino; 3% Race/ethnicity unknown; 10% international; 3% transferred in; 60% live on campus.

Freshmen:
Admission: 40,585 applied, 3,673 admitted, 2,006 enrolled. ***Test scores:*** SAT evidence-based reading and writing scores over 500: 100%; SAT math scores over 500: 100%; ACT scores over 18: 100%; SAT evidence-based reading and writing scores over 600: 98%; SAT math scores over 600: 98%; ACT scores over 24: 99%; SAT evidence-based reading and writing scores over 700: 78%; SAT math scores over 700: 85%; ACT scores over 30: 91%.

Retention: 98% of full-time freshmen returned.

FACULTY
Total: 1,753, 87% full-time, 100% with terminal degrees.

Student/faculty ratio: 6:1.

ACADEMICS
Calendar: quarters. *Degrees:* certificates, bachelor's, master's, doctoral, post-master's, and postbachelor's certificates.

Special study options: accelerated degree program, adult/continuing education programs, advanced placement credit, cooperative education, double majors, honors programs, independent study, internships, part-time degree program, services for LD students, student-designed majors, study abroad, summer session for credit. ***ROTC:*** Army (c), Navy (b), Air Force (c).

Computers: Students can access the following: campus intranet, computer help desk, free student e-mail accounts, online (class) grades, online (class) registration, online (class) schedules. Campuswide network is available. 100% of college-owned or -operated housing units are wired for high-speed Internet access. Wireless service is available via entire campus.
Library: University Library plus 6 others.

STUDENT LIFE
Housing options: coed, men-only, women-only. Campus housing is university owned. Freshman campus housing is guaranteed.

Activities and organizations: drama/theater group, student-run newspaper, radio and television station, choral group, marching band, national fraternities, national sororities.

Athletics Member NCAA. All Division I.

Campus security: 24-hour emergency response devices and patrols, late-night transport/escort service, controlled dormitory access.

Student services: health clinic, personal/psychological counseling, women's center, veterans affairs office.

COSTS & FINANCIAL AID
Costs (2019–20) ***Comprehensive fee:*** $73,710 includes full-time tuition ($56,232), mandatory fees ($459), and room and board ($17,019). ***Room and board:*** Room and board charges vary according to board plan and housing facility. ***Payment plan:*** installment.

Financial Aid Of all full-time matriculated undergraduates who enrolled in 2019, 4,310 applied for aid, 3,803 were judged to have need, 3,803 had their need fully met. In 2019, 381 non-need-based awards were made. ***Average percent of need met:*** 100. ***Average financial aid package:*** $54,473. ***Average need-based loan:*** $3669. ***Average need-based gift aid:*** $52,629. ***Average non-need-based aid:*** $6014. ***Average indebtedness upon graduation:*** $36,350. ***Financial aid deadline:*** 3/1.

APPLYING
Standardized Tests *Required:* SAT or ACT (for admission).

Options: electronic application, early decision, deferred entrance.

Application fee: $75.

Required: essay or personal statement, high school transcript, 1 letter of recommendation. ***Required for some:*** audition for music program.

Application deadlines: 1/1 (freshmen), 3/15 (transfers).

Early decision deadline: 11/1.

Notification: 4/1 (freshmen), continuous (transfers).

CONTACT
Mr. Christopher Watson, Dean of Undergraduate Enrollment and Assistant Vice President for Student Outreach, Northwestern University, 1801 Hinman Avenue, PO Box 3060, Evanston, IL 60208. *Phone:* 847-491-7271. *E-mail:* ug-admission@northwestern.edu.

Olivet Nazarene University

Bourbonnais, Illinois

http://www.olivet.edu/

- **Independent** comprehensive, founded 1907, affiliated with Church of the Nazarene
- **Small-town** 275-acre campus with easy access to Chicago
- **Endowment** $42.3 million
- **Coed** 3,110 undergraduate students, 92% full-time, 59% women, 41% men
- **Moderately difficult** entrance level, 67% of applicants were admitted

UNDERGRAD STUDENTS
2,855 full-time, 255 part-time. 9% Black or African American, non-Hispanic/Latino; 10% Hispanic/Latino; 2% Asian, non-Hispanic/Latino; 0.1% Native Hawaiian or other Pacific Islander, non-Hispanic/Latino; 0.1% American Indian or Alaska Native, non-Hispanic/Latino; 3% Two or more races, non-Hispanic/Latino; 2% Race/ethnicity unknown; 1% international.

Freshmen:
Admission: 4,207 applied, 2,833 admitted, 696 enrolled.
Retention: 77% of full-time freshmen returned.

FACULTY
Total: 125.

Student/faculty ratio: 14:1.

ACADEMICS
Calendar: semesters. *Degrees:* bachelor's, master's, and doctoral.

Special study options: academic remediation for entering students, adult/continuing education programs, advanced placement credit, cooperative education, distance learning, double majors, honors programs, independent study, internships, off-campus study, part-time degree program, services for LD students, student-designed majors, study abroad, summer session for credit. ***ROTC:*** Army (b).

Computers: Students can access the following: campus intranet, computer help desk, free student e-mail accounts, online (class) grades, online (class) registration, online (class) schedules. Campuswide network is available. 100% of college-owned or -operated housing units are wired for high-speed Internet access. Wireless service is available via entire campus.

Library: Benner Library. *Books:* 124,780 (physical), 239,619 (digital/electronic); *Serial titles:* 724 (physical), 75,635 (digital/electronic); *Databases:* 177. Students can reserve study rooms.

STUDENT LIFE
Housing options: on-campus residence required through senior year; men-only, women-only. Campus housing is university owned. Freshman campus housing is guaranteed.

Activities and organizations: drama/theater group, student-run newspaper, radio station, choral group, marching band, Fellowship of Christian Athletes, C.A.U.S.E. (College and University Serving and Enabling), Diakonia, Student Education Association, Women's Residence Association.

Athletics Member NAIA, NCCAA. ***Intercollegiate sports:*** baseball M(s), basketball M(s)/W(s), cheerleading M(s)/W(s), cross-country running M(s)/W(s), football M(s), golf M(s), soccer M(s)/W(s), softball W(s), tennis M(s)/W(s), track and field M(s)/W(s), volleyball M(s)/W(s). ***Intramural sports:*** baseball M, basketball M/W, football M/W, golf M/W, racquetball M/W, soccer M/W, softball M/W, table tennis M/W, tennis M/W, track and field M/W, volleyball M/W.

Campus security: 24-hour patrols, late-night transport/escort service.

Student services: health clinic, personal/psychological counseling.

COSTS & FINANCIAL AID
Costs (2020–21) ***Comprehensive fee:*** $45,940 includes full-time tuition ($35,960), mandatory fees ($990), and room and board ($8990). Part-time tuition: $1500 per semester hour. Part-time tuition and fees vary according to course load. ***Room and board:*** Room and board charges vary according to board plan. ***Payment plan:*** installment. ***Waivers:*** employees or children of employees.

Financial Aid Of all full-time matriculated undergraduates who enrolled in 2019, 2,477 applied for aid, 2,247 were judged to have need, 566 had their need fully met. In 2019, 483 non-need-based awards were made. ***Average percent of need met:*** 85. ***Average financial aid package:*** $31,466. ***Average need-based loan:*** $4237. ***Average need-based gift aid:*** $26,205. ***Average non-need-based aid:*** $17,587. ***Average indebtedness upon graduation:*** $31,640.

APPLYING
Standardized Tests *Required:* SAT or ACT (for admission).

Options: electronic application, deferred entrance.

Application fee: $25.

Required: high school transcript, minimum 2.0 GPA. ***Required for some:*** 2 letters of recommendation. ***Recommended:*** essay or personal statement, interview.

Application deadlines: rolling (freshmen), rolling (transfers).

Notification: continuous (freshmen), continuous (transfers).

CONTACT
Olivet Nazarene University, One University Avenue, Bourbonnais, IL 60914. *Phone:* 815-928-5768. *Toll-free phone:* 800-648-1463.

Principia College

Elsah, Illinois

http://www.principiacollege.edu/

CONTACT
Ms. Tami Gavaletz, Director of Admissions and Financial Aid, Principia College, 1 Maybeck Place, Elsah, IL 62028. *Phone:* 618-374-5187. *Toll-free phone:* 800-277-4648 Ext. 2804.

Quincy University

Quincy, Illinois

http://www.quincy.edu/

- **Independent Roman Catholic** comprehensive, founded 1860
- **Small-town** 70-acre campus
- **Endowment** $18.1 million
- **Coed**
- **Moderately difficult** entrance level

FACULTY
Student/faculty ratio: 15:1.

ACADEMICS
Calendar: semesters. *Degrees:* associate, bachelor's, and master's.
Library: Brenner Library.

STUDENT LIFE
Housing options: on-campus residence required through junior year; coed, special housing for students with disabilities. Campus housing is university owned. Freshman campus housing is guaranteed.

Activities and organizations: drama/theater group, student-run newspaper, choral group, marching band, Student Senate, Kappa Kappa Psi, Student Programming Board, Minority Student Association, Students in Free Enterprise (SIFE), national fraternities, national sororities.

Athletics Member NCAA. All Division II except volleyball (Division I).

Campus security: 24-hour emergency response devices and patrols, student patrols, late-night transport/escort service, controlled dormitory access, self-defense education, shuttle buses, lighted pathways/sidewalks.

Student services: health clinic, personal/psychological counseling.

FINANCIAL AID
Financial Aid Of all full-time matriculated undergraduates who enrolled in 2015, 938 applied for aid, 851 were judged to have need, 232 had their need fully met. 250 Federal Work-Study jobs (averaging $1794). 107 state and other part-time jobs (averaging $1580). In 2015, 97 non-need-based awards were made. ***Average percent of need met:*** 88. ***Average financial aid package:*** $24,970. ***Average need-based loan:*** $5820. ***Average need-based gift aid:*** $17,839. ***Average non-need-based aid:*** $11,165. ***Average indebtedness upon graduation:*** $28,607.

APPLYING
Standardized Tests *Required:* SAT or ACT (for admission).

Options: electronic application, deferred entrance.

Application fee: $25.

Required: essay or personal statement, high school transcript, minimum 2.5 GPA. ***Required for some:*** 1 letter of recommendation, audition for music majors, portfolio recommended for art majors. ***Recommended:*** interview.

CONTACT
Ms. Abby Wayman, Associate Director, Admissions, Quincy University, Admissions Office, 1800 College Avenue, Quincy, IL 62301-2699. *Phone:* 217-228-5432 Ext. 3414. *Toll-free phone:* 800-688-4295. *E-mail:* admissions@quincy.edu.

Rasmussen College Aurora

Aurora, Illinois

http://www.rasmussen.edu/

- **Proprietary** 4-year, part of Rasmussen College System
- **Suburban** campus
- **Coed** 369 undergraduate students, 55% full-time, 89% women, 11% men
- 100% of applicants were admitted

UNDERGRAD STUDENTS
202 full-time, 167 part-time. Students come from 51 states and territories; 27% are from out of state; 27% Black or African American, non-Hispanic/Latino; 20% Hispanic/Latino; 5% Asian, non-Hispanic/Latino; 0.5% Native Hawaiian or other Pacific Islander, non-Hispanic/Latino; 0.5% American Indian or Alaska Native, non-Hispanic/Latino; 2% Two or more races, non-Hispanic/Latino; 18% Race/ethnicity unknown.

Freshmen:
Admission: 129 applied, 129 admitted, 82 enrolled.

ACADEMICS
Calendar: quarters. *Degrees:* certificates, diplomas, associate, and bachelor's.

Special study options: academic remediation for entering students, accelerated degree program, adult/continuing education programs, distance learning, double majors, internships, part-time degree program, summer session for credit.

Computers: 87 computers/terminals are available on campus for general student use. Students can access the following: computer help desk, free student e-mail accounts, online (class) grades, online (class) schedules. Campuswide network is available. Wireless service is available via entire campus.
Library: Rasmussen College Library - Aurora.

STUDENT LIFE
Housing options: college housing not available.

APPLYING
Options: early admission, deferred entrance.

Required: high school transcript, minimum 2.0 GPA. ***Required for some:*** interview.

Application deadlines: rolling (freshmen), rolling (transfers).

CONTACT
Ms. Susan Hammerstrom, Director of Admissions, Rasmussen College Aurora, 2363 Sequoia Drive, Aurora, IL 60506. *Phone:* 630-888-3500. *Toll-free phone:* 888-549-6755. *E-mail:* susan.hammerstrom@rasmussen.edu.

Rasmussen College Mokena/Tinley Park

Mokena, Illinois

http://www.rasmussen.edu/

- **Proprietary** 4-year, part of Rasmussen College System
- **Suburban** campus
- **Coed** 469 undergraduate students, 70% full-time, 94% women, 6% men
- 100% of applicants were admitted

UNDERGRAD STUDENTS
328 full-time, 141 part-time. Students come from 51 states and territories; 27% are from out of state; 53% Black or African American, non-Hispanic/Latino; 8% Hispanic/Latino; 0.4% Asian, non-Hispanic/Latino; 0.6% American Indian or Alaska Native, non-Hispanic/Latino; 2% Two or more races, non-Hispanic/Latino; 22% Race/ethnicity unknown.

Freshmen:
Admission: 211 applied, 211 admitted, 66 enrolled.

ACADEMICS
Calendar: quarters. *Degrees:* certificates, diplomas, associate, and bachelor's.

Computers: 73 computers/terminals are available on campus for general student use. Students can access the following: computer help desk, free student e-mail accounts, online (class) grades, online (class) schedules. Campuswide network is available. Wireless service is available via entire campus.
Library: Rasmussen College Library - Mokena.

STUDENT LIFE
Housing options: college housing not available.

COSTS
Costs (2019–20) ***Tuition:*** $10,967 full-time, $9848 per year part-time. Full-time tuition and fees vary according to course level, course load, degree level, location, and program. Part-time tuition and fees vary according to course level, course load, degree level, location, and program. No tuition increase for student's term of enrollment. ***Required fees:*** $2245 full-time, $1776 per year part-time. ***Payment plans:*** installment, deferred payment. ***Waivers:*** employees or children of employees.

APPLYING
Options: early admission, deferred entrance.

Required: high school transcript, minimum 2.0 GPA. ***Required for some:*** interview.

Application deadlines: rolling (freshmen), rolling (transfers).

CONTACT
Ms. Susan Hammerstrom, Director of Admissions, Rasmussen College Mokena/Tinley Park, 8650 West Spring Lake Road, Mokena, IL 60448. *Phone:* 815-534-3300. *Toll-free phone:* 888-549-6755.

Rasmussen College Rockford

Rockford, Illinois

http://www.rasmussen.edu/

- **Proprietary** 4-year, part of Rasmussen College System
- **Suburban** campus
- **Coed** 571 undergraduate students, 51% full-time, 90% women, 10% men
- 100% of applicants were admitted

UNDERGRAD STUDENTS
293 full-time, 278 part-time. Students come from 51 states and territories; 27% are from out of state; 15% Black or African American, non-Hispanic/Latino; 14% Hispanic/Latino; 1% Asian, non-Hispanic/Latino; 0.2% Native Hawaiian or other Pacific Islander, non-Hispanic/Latino; 0.2% American Indian or Alaska Native, non-Hispanic/Latino; 4% Two or more races, non-Hispanic/Latino; 15% Race/ethnicity unknown.

Freshmen:
Admission: 164 applied, 164 admitted, 82 enrolled.

ACADEMICS
Calendar: quarters. *Degrees:* certificates, diplomas, associate, and bachelor's.

Special study options: academic remediation for entering students, accelerated degree program, adult/continuing education programs, distance learning, double majors, internships, part-time degree program, summer session for credit.

Computers: 103 computers/terminals are available on campus for general student use. Students can access the following: computer help desk, free student e-mail accounts, online (class) grades, online (class) schedules. Campuswide network is available. Wireless service is available via entire campus.
Library: Rasmussen College Library - Rockford.

STUDENT LIFE
Housing options: college housing not available.

APPLYING
Options: early admission, deferred entrance.

Required: high school transcript, minimum 2.0 GPA. ***Required for some:*** interview.

Application deadlines: rolling (freshmen), rolling (transfers).

CONTACT
Dwayne Bertotto, Vice President of Admissions and Student Experience, Rasmussen College Rockford, 8300 Norman Center Drive, Suite 300, Bloomington, MN 55437. *Phone:* 952-806-3958. *Toll-free phone:* 888-549-6755. *E-mail:* dwayne.bertotto@rasmussen.edu.

Rasmussen College Romeoville/Joliet

Romeoville, Illinois

http://www.rasmussen.edu/

- **Proprietary** 4-year, part of Rasmussen College System
- **Suburban** campus
- **Coed** 692 undergraduate students, 48% full-time, 89% women, 11% men
- **Minimally difficult** entrance level, 100% of applicants were admitted

UNDERGRAD STUDENTS
333 full-time, 359 part-time. Students come from 51 states and territories; 27% are from out of state; 30% Black or African American, non-Hispanic/Latino; 23% Hispanic/Latino; 6% Asian, non-Hispanic/Latino; 0.1% American Indian or Alaska Native, non-Hispanic/Latino; 2% Two or more races, non-Hispanic/Latino; 15% Race/ethnicity unknown.

Freshmen:
Admission: 160 applied, 160 admitted, 71 enrolled.

ACADEMICS
Calendar: quarters. *Degrees:* certificates, diplomas, associate, and bachelor's.

Special study options: academic remediation for entering students, accelerated degree program, adult/continuing education programs, distance learning, double majors, internships, part-time degree program, summer session for credit.

Computers: 87 computers/terminals are available on campus for general student use. Students can access the following: computer help desk, free student e-mail accounts, online (class) grades, online (class) schedules. Campuswide network is available. Wireless service is available via entire campus.
Library: Rasmussen College Library - Romeoville.

STUDENT LIFE
Housing options: college housing not available.

COSTS
Costs (2019–20) ***Tuition:*** $13,803 full-time, $13,018 per year part-time. Full-time tuition and fees vary according to course level, course load, degree level, location, and program. Part-time tuition and fees vary according to course level, course load, degree level, location, and program. No tuition increase for student's term of enrollment. ***Required fees:*** $3088 full-time, $2820 per year part-time. ***Payment plans:*** installment, deferred payment. ***Waivers:*** employees or children of employees.

APPLYING
Standardized Tests *Required:* institutional exam (for admission).

Options: electronic application, early admission, deferred entrance.

Required: high school transcript, minimum 2.0 GPA. ***Required for some:*** interview.

Application deadlines: rolling (freshmen), rolling (transfers).

CONTACT
Ms. Susan Hammerstrom, Director of Admissions, Rasmussen College Romeoville/Joliet, 1400 West Normantown Road, Romeoville, IL 60446. *Phone:* 815-306-2600. *Toll-free phone:* 888-549-6755. *E-mail:* susan.hammerstrom@rasmussen.edu.

Resurrection University

Chicago, Illinois

http://www.resu.edu/

CONTACT
Resurrection University, 1431 N. Claremont Avenue, Chicago, IL 60622. *Phone:* 773-252-5307.

Robert Morris University Illinois

Chicago, Illinois

http://www.robertmorris.edu/

CONTACT
Admissions Office, Robert Morris University Illinois, 401 South State Street, Chicago, IL 60605. *Phone:* 800-762-5960. *Toll-free phone:* 800-762-5960. *Fax:* 312-935-4440. *E-mail:* enroll@robertmorris.edu.

Rockford University

Rockford, Illinois

http://www.rockford.edu/

- **Independent** comprehensive, founded 1847
- **Suburban** 150-acre campus with easy access to Chicago
- **Coed**
- **Minimally difficult** entrance level

FACULTY
Student/faculty ratio: 10:1.

ACADEMICS
Calendar: semesters. *Degrees:* bachelor's, master's, and postbachelor's certificates.
Library: Howard Colman Library. *Books:* 134,831 (physical), 140,140 (digital/electronic); *Serial titles:* 157 (physical), 23,000 (digital/electronic); *Databases:* 27. Weekly public service hours: 85; students can reserve study rooms.

STUDENT LIFE
Housing options: coed, special housing for students with disabilities. Campus housing is university owned.

Activities and organizations: drama/theater group, student-run newspaper, radio station, choral group, Campus Activities Board, Multicultural Club, Student Government Association, Nursing Student Organization, Alpha Helix.

Athletics Member NCAA. All Division III.

Campus security: 24-hour emergency response devices and patrols, student patrols, late-night transport/escort service, controlled dormitory access.

Student services: health clinic, personal/psychological counseling.

FINANCIAL AID
Financial Aid Of all full-time matriculated undergraduates who enrolled in 2018, 766 applied for aid, 732 were judged to have need, 74 had their need fully met. 127 Federal Work-Study jobs (averaging $712). 193 state and other part-time jobs (averaging $754). In 2018, 74 non-need-based awards were made. ***Average percent of need met:*** 63. ***Average financial aid package:*** $21,100. ***Average need-based loan:*** $4631. ***Average need-based gift aid:*** $16,964. ***Average non-need-based aid:*** $13,048. ***Average indebtedness upon graduation:*** $36,476.

APPLYING
Standardized Tests *Required:* SAT or ACT (for admission).

Options: electronic application, early admission.

Required: high school transcript. ***Required for some:*** essay or personal statement, minimum 2.7 GPA, 2 letters of recommendation. ***Recommended:*** minimum 2.7 GPA.

CONTACT
Ms. Jennifer Nordstrom, Associate Vice President for Undergraduate Admission, Rockford University, 5050 East State Street, Rockford, IL 61108-2393. *Phone:* 815-226-4050. *Toll-free phone:* 800-892-2984. *Fax:* 815-226-2822. *E-mail:* admissions@rockford.edu.

Roosevelt University

Chicago, Illinois

http://www.roosevelt.edu/

CONTACT
Mr. Al Nunez, Director of Admission, Roosevelt University, 430 S. Michigan Avenue, Chicago, IL 60605. *Phone:* 312-341-2187. *Toll-free phone:* 877-APPLYRU. *E-mail:* anunez13@roosevelt.edu.

Rush University

Chicago, Illinois

http://www.rushu.rush.edu/

CONTACT
Rush University, 600 South Paulina, Chicago, IL 60612-3832. *Phone:* 312-942-7100.

Saint Anthony College of Nursing

Rockford, Illinois

http://www.sacn.edu/

CONTACT

Ms. April Lipnitzky, Enrollment Management Coordinator, Saint Anthony College of Nursing, 5658 East State Street, Rockford, IL 61108-2468. *Phone:* 815-227-2141. *Fax:* 815-227-2730. *E-mail:* admissions@sacn.edu.

St. Augustine College

Chicago, Illinois

http://www.staugustine.edu/

CONTACT

Ms. Gloria Quiroz, Director of Admissions, St. Augustine College, 1333-1345 West Argyle, Chicago, IL 60640-3501. *Phone:* 773-878-3256. *Fax:* 773-878-0937. *E-mail:* info@staugustine.edu.

Saint Francis Medical Center College of Nursing

Peoria, Illinois

http://www.sfmccon.edu/

- **Independent Roman Catholic** upper-level, founded 1986
- **Urban** campus
- **Coed, primarily women** 320 undergraduate students, 80% full-time, 87% women, 13% men
- 96% of applicants were admitted

UNDERGRAD STUDENTS

257 full-time, 63 part-time. Students come from 3 states and territories; 1 other country; 1% are from out of state; 5% Black or African American, non-Hispanic/Latino; 3% Hispanic/Latino; 3% Asian, non-Hispanic/Latino; 4% Two or more races, non-Hispanic/Latino; 0.3% Race/ethnicity unknown; 0.3% international; 23% transferred in; 20% live on campus.

Freshmen:

Admission: 152 applied, 146 admitted.

FACULTY

Total: 57, 70% full-time, 28% with terminal degrees.

Student/faculty ratio: 9:1.

ACADEMICS

Calendar: semesters. *Degrees:* bachelor's, master's, doctoral, and post-master's certificates.

Special study options: academic remediation for entering students, accelerated degree program, adult/continuing education programs, advanced placement credit, distance learning, independent study, part-time degree program, summer session for credit.

Computers: 62 computers/terminals and 53 ports are available on campus for general student use. Students can access the following: computer help desk, online (class) grades, online (class) registration, online (class) schedules. Campuswide network is available. 100% of college-owned or -operated housing units are wired for high-speed Internet access. Wireless service is available via entire campus.

Library: Sister Mary Ludgera Pieperbeck Learning and Resource Center plus 1 other. *Books:* 3,884 (physical), 392 (digital/electronic); *Serial titles:* 61 (physical); *Databases:* 64. Students can reserve study rooms.

STUDENT LIFE

Housing options: coed. Campus housing is university owned.

Activities and organizations: Student Senate, SNAI, Minority Student Association, Tau Omicron.

Campus security: 24-hour emergency response devices and patrols, late-night transport/escort service, controlled dormitory access.

Student services: health clinic, personal/psychological counseling.

COSTS & FINANCIAL AID

Costs (2020–21) ***Tuition:*** $655 per semester hour part-time. Full-time tuition and fees vary according to course load, degree level, program, and student level. Part-time tuition and fees vary according to course load, degree level, program, and student level. ***Required fees:*** $1550 full-time, $225 per term part-time. ***Room only:*** $1950. ***Payment plan:*** installment.

Financial Aid Of all full-time matriculated undergraduates who enrolled in 2019, 210 applied for aid, 175 were judged to have need, 11 had their need fully met. In 2019, 24 non-need-based awards were made. ***Average percent of need met:*** 46. ***Average financial aid package:*** $11,004. ***Average need-based loan:*** $5181. ***Average need-based gift aid:*** $7635. ***Average non-need-based aid:*** $2956.

APPLYING

Options: deferred entrance.

Application fee: $50.

Notification: 10/15 (transfers).

CONTACT

Saint Francis Medical Center College of Nursing, 511 Northeast Greenleaf Street, Peoria, IL 61603-3783. *Phone:* 309-624-8980.

St. John's College

Springfield, Illinois

http://www.sjcs.edu/

CONTACT

St. John's College, 729 East Carpenter Street, Springfield, IL 62702. *Phone:* 217-525-5628.

Saint Xavier University

Chicago, Illinois

http://www.sxu.edu/

- **Independent Roman Catholic** comprehensive, founded 1847
- **Urban** 70-acre campus
- **Endowment** $7.1 million
- **Coed**
- **Moderately difficult** entrance level

FACULTY

Student/faculty ratio: 15:1.

ACADEMICS

Calendar: semesters. *Degrees:* certificates, bachelor's, master's, post-master's, and postbachelor's certificates.

Library: Byrne Memorial Library.

STUDENT LIFE

Housing options: coed. Campus housing is university owned.

Activities and organizations: drama/theater group, student-run newspaper, radio station, choral group, marching band, Student Activities Board, Black Student Union, UNIDOS (Hispanic Organization), Student Nurses Association, Business Students Association.

Athletics Member NAIA.

Campus security: 24-hour emergency response devices and patrols, late-night transport/escort service.

Student services: health clinic, personal/psychological counseling, women's center.

FINANCIAL AID

Financial Aid Of all full-time matriculated undergraduates who enrolled in 2015, 2,434 applied for aid, 2,315 were judged to have need, 334 had their need fully met. In 2015, 300 non-need-based awards were made. ***Average percent of need met:*** 77. ***Average financial aid package:*** $24,699. ***Average need-based loan:*** $4078. ***Average need-based gift aid:*** $20,004. ***Average non-need-based aid:*** $15,202. ***Average indebtedness upon graduation:*** $34,094.

APPLYING

Standardized Tests *Required:* SAT or ACT (for admission).

Options: electronic application, deferred entrance.

Application fee: $25.

Required: high school transcript. ***Recommended:*** essay or personal statement, minimum 2.5 GPA, interview.

CONTACT
Dr. Kathleen Carlson, Vice President, Saint Xavier University, 3700 West 103rd Street, Chicago, IL 60655-3105. *Phone:* 773-298-3305. *Toll-free phone:* 800-462-9288. *E-mail:* carlson@sxu.edu.

School of the Art Institute of Chicago

Chicago, Illinois

http://www.saic.edu/

- **Independent** comprehensive, founded 1866
- **Urban** 1-acre campus with easy access to Chicago
- **Coed**
- **Very difficult** entrance level

FACULTY
Student/faculty ratio: 11:1.

ACADEMICS
Calendar: semesters. *Degrees:* bachelor's, master's, and postbachelor's certificates.
Library: The John M. Flaxman Library plus 1 other. *Books:* 110,287 (physical), 203,725 (digital/electronic); *Serial titles:* 19,541 (physical), 204,634 (digital/electronic); *Databases:* 177.

STUDENT LIFE
Housing options: coed, special housing for students with disabilities. Campus housing is university owned.

Activities and organizations: drama/theater group, student-run newspaper, radio and television station, Student Association/Student Union Galleries, Korean Student Association, InterVarsity, Curatorial Community, Good 'Ol Futbol.

Campus security: 24-hour emergency response devices and patrols, late-night transport/escort service, controlled dormitory access.

Student services: health clinic, personal/psychological counseling.

COSTS
Costs (2019–20) ***Comprehensive fee:*** $67,230 includes full-time tuition ($49,980), mandatory fees ($940), and room and board ($16,310). Full-time tuition and fees vary according to course load, degree level, and program. Part-time tuition: $1666 per credit hour. Part-time tuition and fees vary according to course load, degree level, and program. ***Required fees:*** $315 per term part-time. ***College room only:*** $12,670. Room and board charges vary according to board plan and housing facility.

APPLYING
Standardized Tests *Required:* SAT or ACT (for admission).

Options: electronic application, early action, deferred entrance.

Application fee: $65.

Required: essay or personal statement, high school transcript. ***Recommended:*** interview.

CONTACT
Ms. Asia Mitchell, Director, Undergraduate Admissions, School of the Art Institute of Chicago, 36 South Wabash, Chicago, IL 60603. *Phone:* 312-629-6100. *Toll-free phone:* 800-232-SAIC. *Fax:* 312-629-6101. *E-mail:* ugadmiss@saic.edu.

Southern Illinois University Carbondale

Carbondale, Illinois

http://www.siu.edu/

- **State-supported** university, founded 1869, part of Southern Illinois University
- **Rural** 1136-acre campus with easy access to St. Louis
- **Coed** 9,512 undergraduate students, 85% full-time, 46% women, 54% men
- **Moderately difficult** entrance level, 72% of applicants were admitted

UNDERGRAD STUDENTS
8,070 full-time, 1,442 part-time. 20% are from out of state; 13% transferred in; 22% live on campus.

Freshmen:
Admission: 6,219 applied, 4,475 admitted, 1,133 enrolled. ***Average high school GPA:*** 3.2.

Retention: 71% of full-time freshmen returned.

ACADEMICS
Calendar: semesters plus 8-week summer session. *Degrees:* certificates, associate, bachelor's, master's, doctoral, and postbachelor's certificates.

Special study options: academic remediation for entering students, accelerated degree program, adult/continuing education programs, advanced placement credit, cooperative education, distance learning, double majors, English as a second language, honors programs, independent study, internships, off-campus study, part-time degree program, services for LD students, student-designed majors, study abroad, summer session for credit. ***ROTC:*** Army (b), Air Force (b).

Computers: 1,900 computers/terminals are available on campus for general student use. Students can access the following: computer help desk, free student e-mail accounts, online (class) grades, online (class) registration, online (class) schedules. Campuswide network is available. 100% of college-owned or -operated housing units are wired for high-speed Internet access. Wireless service is available via classrooms, computer centers, computer labs, dorm rooms, learning centers, libraries, student centers.
Library: Morris Library plus 1 other. Weekly public service hours: 100; students can reserve study rooms.

STUDENT LIFE
Housing options: on-campus residence required for freshman year; coed, men-only, women-only, special housing for students with disabilities. Campus housing is university owned. Freshman campus housing is guaranteed.

Activities and organizations: drama/theater group, student-run newspaper, radio and television station, choral group, marching band, Undergraduate Student Government, Greek Councils, International Student Council, Black Affairs Council, Dawg Pound, national fraternities, national sororities.

Athletics ***Intercollegiate sports:*** baseball M(s), basketball M(s)/W(s), cheerleading M/W, cross-country running M(s)/W(s), golf M(s)/W(s), soccer M(c)/W(s), softball W(s), swimming and diving M(s)/W(s), track and field M(s)/W(s), volleyball W(s). ***Intramural sports:*** archery M(c)/W(c), badminton M(c)/W(c), baseball M(c), basketball M/W, bowling M(c)/W(c), equestrian sports M(c)/W(c), fencing M(c), field hockey W(c), gymnastics M(c)/W(c), lacrosse M(c), racquetball M/W, rock climbing M(c)/W(c), rugby M(c)/W(c), sailing M(c)/W(c), soccer M(c)/W(c), softball W(c), swimming and diving W, table tennis M(c)/W(c), tennis M(c)/W(c), triathlon M(c)/W(c), ultimate Frisbee M(c)/W(c), volleyball M(c)/W(c), water polo M(c)/W(c), weight lifting M(c)/W(c), wrestling M(c)/W(c).

Campus security: 24-hour emergency response devices and patrols, student patrols, late-night transport/escort service, controlled dormitory access, well-lit pathways, night safety vans, student transit system and extensive video security camera system.

Student services: health clinic, personal/psychological counseling, women's center, legal services, veterans affairs office.

COSTS & FINANCIAL AID
Costs (2019–20) ***Tuition:*** state resident $9638 full-time; nonresident $9638 full-time. Full-time tuition and fees vary according to course load, location, program, reciprocity agreements, and student level. Part-time tuition and fees vary according to course load, location, program, reciprocity agreements, and student level. No tuition increase for student's term of enrollment. ***Required fees:*** $5226 full-time. ***Room and board:*** $10,622. Room and board charges vary according to board plan and housing facility. ***Payment plan:*** installment. ***Waivers:*** children of alumni, senior citizens, and employees or children of employees.

Financial Aid Of all full-time matriculated undergraduates who enrolled in 2019, 4,365 applied for aid, 4,886 were judged to have need, 555 had their need fully met. 1,048 Federal Work-Study jobs (averaging $1751). In 2019, 505 non-need-based awards were made. ***Average percent of need met:*** 57. ***Average financial aid package:*** $16,031. ***Average need-based loan:*** $4548. ***Average need-based gift aid:*** $8636. ***Average non-need-based aid:*** $8270. ***Average indebtedness upon graduation:*** $30,292.

APPLYING

Standardized Tests *Required:* SAT or ACT (for admission).

Options: electronic application, deferred entrance.

Application fee: $40.

Application deadlines: rolling (freshmen), rolling (transfers).

Notification: continuous (freshmen), continuous (transfers).

CONTACT

Tamora Workman, Director of the Registrar's Office, Southern Illinois University Carbondale, Office of Registrar, 1263 Lincoln Drive, MC 4701, Carbondale, IL 62901. *Phone:* 618-453-2963. *Fax:* 618-453-2915. *E-mail:* regstrar@siu.edu.

Southern Illinois University Edwardsville

Edwardsville, Illinois

http://www.siue.edu/

- **State-supported** university, founded 1957, part of Southern Illinois University
- **Suburban** 2660-acre campus with easy access to St. Louis
- **Endowment** $23.1 million
- **Coed** 10,400 undergraduate students, 83% full-time, 54% women, 46% men
- **Moderately difficult** entrance level, 86% of applicants were admitted

UNDERGRAD STUDENTS

8,615 full-time, 1,785 part-time. Students come from 38 states and territories; 40 other countries; 14% are from out of state; 14% Black or African American, non-Hispanic/Latino; 5% Hispanic/Latino; 2% Asian, non-Hispanic/Latino; 0.1% Native Hawaiian or other Pacific Islander, non-Hispanic/Latino; 0.2% American Indian or Alaska Native, non-Hispanic/Latino; 4% Two or more races, non-Hispanic/Latino; 1% Race/ethnicity unknown; 1% international; 11% transferred in; 25% live on campus.

Freshmen:

Admission: 7,306 applied, 6,259 admitted, 1,667 enrolled. ***Average high school GPA:*** 3.5. ***Test scores:*** SAT evidence-based reading and writing scores over 500: 84%; SAT math scores over 500: 82%; ACT scores over 18: 94%; SAT evidence-based reading and writing scores over 600: 31%; SAT math scores over 600: 31%; ACT scores over 24: 48%; SAT evidence-based reading and writing scores over 700: 3%; SAT math scores over 700: 7%; ACT scores over 30: 8%.

Retention: 79% of full-time freshmen returned.

FACULTY

Total: 881, 69% full-time, 67% with terminal degrees.

Student/faculty ratio: 15:1.

ACADEMICS

Calendar: semesters. *Degrees:* bachelor's, master's, doctoral, post-master's, and postbachelor's certificates.

Special study options: academic remediation for entering students, accelerated degree program, advanced placement credit, cooperative education, distance learning, double majors, English as a second language, external degree program, honors programs, independent study, internships, off-campus study, part-time degree program, services for LD students, student-designed majors, study abroad, summer session for credit. ***ROTC:*** Army (b), Air Force (c).

Unusual degree programs: 3-2 engineering.

Computers: 315 computers/terminals are available on campus for general student use. Students can access the following: campus intranet, computer help desk, free student e-mail accounts, online (class) grades, online (class) registration, online (class) schedules, online job finder. Campuswide network is available. 100% of college-owned or -operated housing units are wired for high-speed Internet access. Wireless service is available via entire campus.

Library: Lovejoy Library. *Books:* 522,502 (physical), 91,353 (digital/electronic); *Serial titles:* 35,778 (physical), 35,637 (digital/electronic). Students can reserve study rooms.

STUDENT LIFE

Housing options: coed, special housing for students with disabilities. Campus housing is university owned. Freshman applicants given priority for college housing.

Activities and organizations: drama/theater group, student-run newspaper, radio station, choral group, Fraternity and Sorority Life, Campus Activities Board, Sports Clubs/Intramurals, Dance Marathon, Student Government, national fraternities, national sororities.

Athletics Member NCAA. All Division I. ***Intercollegiate sports:*** baseball M(s), basketball M(s)/W(s), cross-country running M(s)/W(s), golf M(s), soccer M(s)/W(s), softball W(s), tennis W(s), track and field M(s)/W(s), volleyball W(s), wrestling M(s). ***Intramural sports:*** archery M(c)/W(c), badminton M/W, baseball M(c), basketball M/W, bowling M/W, cheerleading M(c)/W(c), equestrian sports M(c)/W(c), fencing M(c)/W(c), football M(c), golf M(c)/W(c), ice hockey M(c), racquetball M/W, rock climbing M(c)/W(c), sand volleyball M/W, soccer M/W, softball M/W, swimming and diving M(c)/W(c), table tennis M/W, tennis M/W, ultimate Frisbee M(c)/W(c), volleyball M(c)/W(c), water polo W(c).

Campus security: 24-hour emergency response devices and patrols, late-night transport/escort service, controlled dormitory access.

Student services: health clinic, personal/psychological counseling, veterans affairs office.

COSTS & FINANCIAL AID

Costs (2020–21) ***Tuition:*** state resident $9123 full-time. Full-time tuition and fees vary according to course load, program, and reciprocity agreements. Part-time tuition and fees vary according to course load, program, and reciprocity agreements. No tuition increase for student's term of enrollment. ***Required fees:*** $3096 full-time. ***Room and board:*** $10,701; room only: $7110. Room and board charges vary according to board plan and housing facility. ***Payment plans:*** installment, deferred payment. ***Waivers:*** employees or children of employees.

Financial Aid Of all full-time matriculated undergraduates who enrolled in 2018, 7,175 applied for aid, 5,932 were judged to have need, 1,978 had their need fully met. In 2018, 625 non-need-based awards were made. ***Average percent of need met:*** 63. ***Average financial aid package:*** $12,552. ***Average need-based loan:*** $4460. ***Average need-based gift aid:*** $8991. ***Average non-need-based aid:*** $6891. ***Average indebtedness upon graduation:*** $22,610.

APPLYING

Standardized Tests *Required:* SAT or ACT (for admission).

Options: electronic application, early admission, deferred entrance.

Application fee: $40.

Required: high school transcript, minimum 2.0 GPA, college transcript(s). ***Required for some:*** essay or personal statement.

Application deadlines: 5/1 (freshmen), 5/1 (out-of-state freshmen), 7/24 (transfers).

Notification: continuous until 9/1 (freshmen), continuous until 9/1 (transfers).

CONTACT

Mr. Todd Burrell, Director of Undergraduate Admissions, Southern Illinois University Edwardsville, Campus Box 1600, Rendleman Hall, Edwardsville, IL 62026-1600. *Phone:* 618-650-3705. *Toll-free phone:* 800-447-SIUE. *Fax:* 618-650-5013. *E-mail:* admissions@siue.edu.

Telshe Yeshiva–Chicago

Chicago, Illinois

CONTACT

Rosh Hayeshiva, Telshe Yeshiva–Chicago, 3535 West Foster Avenue, Chicago, IL 60625-5598. *Phone:* 773-463-7738.

Trinity Christian College

Palos Heights, Illinois

http://www.trnty.edu/

- **Independent Christian Reformed** comprehensive, founded 1959
- **Suburban** 53-acre campus with easy access to Chicago
- **Endowment** $10.8 million
- **Coed**
- **Moderately difficult** entrance level

FACULTY
Student/faculty ratio: 10:1.

ACADEMICS
Calendar: semesters plus 2 week interim term. *Degrees:* bachelor's and master's.
Library: Jennie Huizenga Memorial Library plus 1 other. *Books:* 60,951 (physical), 6,449 (digital/electronic); *Serial titles:* 20 (physical), 45,797 (digital/electronic); *Databases:* 61. Weekly public service hours: 84; students can reserve study rooms.

STUDENT LIFE
Housing options: coed. Campus housing is university owned. Freshman campus housing is guaranteed.

Activities and organizations: drama/theater group, student-run newspaper, choral group, Student Association, Student ministries, Campus newspaper, Pro-Life Task Force, PACE (prison tutoring program).

Athletics Member NAIA, NCCAA.

Campus security: 24-hour emergency response devices and patrols, student patrols, late-night transport/escort service, controlled dormitory access, security cameras, Code Blue Emergency Phones.

Student services: personal/psychological counseling.

COSTS & FINANCIAL AID
Costs (2019–20) ***One-time required fee:*** $225. ***Comprehensive fee:*** $40,900 includes full-time tuition ($30,700), mandatory fees ($250), and room and board ($9950). Part-time tuition: $992 per credit hour.

Financial Aid Of all full-time matriculated undergraduates who enrolled in 2017, 770 applied for aid, 697 were judged to have need, 115 had their need fully met. In 2017, 99 non-need-based awards were made. ***Average percent of need met:*** 73. ***Average financial aid package:*** $20,865. ***Average need-based loan:*** $4589. ***Average need-based gift aid:*** $16,760. ***Average non-need-based aid:*** $10,560. ***Average indebtedness upon graduation:*** $29,978.

APPLYING
Standardized Tests *Required:* SAT or ACT (for admission).

Options: electronic application, deferred entrance.

Required: essay or personal statement, high school transcript, minimum 2.5 GPA, interview. ***Required for some:*** 1 letter of recommendation, ACT Composite score of 19 or combined SAT score of 980.

CONTACT
Brittany Minnesma, Assistant Director of Admissions, Trinity Christian College, 6601 West College Drive, Palos Heights, IL 60463. *Phone:* 708-239-4808. *Toll-free phone:* 866-TRIN-4-ME. *Fax:* 708-239-4826. *E-mail:* brittany.minnesma@trnty.edu.

Trinity College of Nursing and Health Sciences

Rock Island, Illinois

http://www.trinitycollegeqc.edu/

CONTACT
Ms. Lori Perez, Admissions Representative, Trinity College of Nursing and Health Sciences, 2122 25th Avenue, Rock Island, IL 61201. *Phone:* 309-779-7700. *Fax:* 309-779-7748. *E-mail:* perezlj@ihs.org.

Trinity International University

Deerfield, Illinois

http://www.tiu.edu/

CONTACT
Mr. Aaron Mahl, Director of Undergraduate Admissions, Trinity International University, 2065 Half Day Road, Deerfield, IL 60015-1284. *Phone:* 847-317-7000. *Toll-free phone:* 800-822-3225. *Fax:* 847-317-8097. *E-mail:* tcadmissions@tiu.edu.

University of Chicago

Chicago, Illinois

http://www.uchicago.edu/

- **Independent** university, founded 1890
- **Urban** 217-acre campus with easy access to Chicago
- **Coed**
- **Most difficult** entrance level

FACULTY
Student/faculty ratio: 5:1.

ACADEMICS
Calendar: quarters. *Degrees:* bachelor's, master's, doctoral, and postbachelor's certificates.
Library: Joseph Regenstein Library plus 5 others. Students can reserve study rooms.

STUDENT LIFE
Housing options: on-campus residence required for freshman year; coed, special housing for students with disabilities. Campus housing is university owned. Freshman campus housing is guaranteed.

Activities and organizations: drama/theater group, student-run newspaper, radio station, choral group, University Theatre, Model United Nations, Council on University Programming, South Asian Students Association, Splash, national fraternities, national sororities.

Athletics Member NCAA. All Division III.

Campus security: 24-hour emergency response devices and patrols, student patrols, late-night transport/escort service, controlled dormitory access.

Student services: health clinic, personal/psychological counseling, women's center.

FINANCIAL AID
Financial Aid Of all full-time matriculated undergraduates who enrolled in 2019, 3,134 applied for aid, 2,695 were judged to have need, 2,673 had their need fully met. ***Average percent of need met:*** 100. ***Average financial aid package:*** $57,464. ***Average need-based loan:*** $3776. ***Average need-based gift aid:*** $52,471. ***Average indebtedness upon graduation:*** $26,619.

APPLYING
Options: electronic application, early admission, early decision, early action, deferred entrance.

Application fee: $75.

Required: essay or personal statement, high school transcript, 2 letters of recommendation.

CONTACT
Mr. James G. Nondorf, Vice President for Enrollment and Student Advancement and Dean of Admissions and Financial Aid, University of Chicago, Rosenwald Hall, 1101 East 58th Street, Suite 105, Chicago, IL 60637. *Phone:* 773-702-8650. *Fax:* 773-702-4199. *E-mail:* collegeadmissions@uchicago.edu.

University of Illinois at Chicago

Chicago, Illinois

http://www.uic.edu/

- **State-supported** university, founded 1946, part of University of Illinois System
- **Urban** 240-acre campus with easy access to Chicago
- **Endowment** $321.6 million
- **Coed** 21,641 undergraduate students, 93% full-time, 52% women, 48% men
- **Moderately difficult** entrance level, 73% of applicants were admitted

UNDERGRAD STUDENTS
20,195 full-time, 1,446 part-time. 3% are from out of state; 8% Black or African American, non-Hispanic/Latino; 34% Hispanic/Latino; 21% Asian, non-Hispanic/Latino; 3% Two or more races, non-Hispanic/Latino; 2% Race/ethnicity unknown; 6% international; 10% transferred in; 14% live on campus.

Freshmen:
Admission: 22,696 applied, 16,501 admitted, 4,407 enrolled. ***Average high school GPA:*** 3.4. ***Test scores:*** SAT evidence-based reading and writing scores over 500: 82%; SAT math scores over 500: 87%; ACT scores over 18: 96%; SAT evidence-based reading and writing scores over 600: 33%; SAT math scores over 600: 38%; ACT scores over 24: 55%; SAT evidence-based reading and writing scores over 700: 5%; SAT math scores over 700: 10%; ACT scores over 30: 20%.

Retention: 79% of full-time freshmen returned.

FACULTY
Total: 1,742, 75% full-time, 81% with terminal degrees.

Student/faculty ratio: 18:1.

ACADEMICS
Calendar: semesters. *Degrees:* bachelor's, master's, doctoral, post-master's, and postbachelor's certificates.

Special study options: academic remediation for entering students, accelerated degree program, advanced placement credit, cooperative education, distance learning, double majors, freshman honors college, honors programs, independent study, internships, off-campus study, part-time degree program, services for LD students, student-designed majors, study abroad, summer session for credit. ***ROTC:*** Army (b), Navy (c), Air Force (c).

Computers: 1,052 computers/terminals are available on campus for general student use. Students can access the following: campus intranet, computer help desk, free student e-mail accounts, online (class) grades, online (class) registration, online (class) schedules. Campuswide network is available. 100% of college-owned or -operated housing units are wired for high-speed Internet access. Wireless service is available via entire campus.

Library: Richard J. Daley Library plus 2 others. *Books:* 1.6 million (physical), 617,614 (digital/electronic); *Serial titles:* 61,000 (digital/electronic); *Databases:* 100. Weekly public service hours: 140; study areas open 24 hours, 5–7 days a week; students can reserve study rooms.

STUDENT LIFE
Housing options: coed, special housing for students with disabilities. Campus housing is university owned.

Activities and organizations: drama/theater group, student-run newspaper, radio station, choral group, Muslim Student Association, Alternative Spring Break, Filipinos in Alliance, Society of Future Physicians, Ski and Snowboard Club, national fraternities, national sororities.

Athletics Member NCAA. All Division I. ***Intercollegiate sports:*** baseball M(s), basketball M(s)/W(s), cross-country running M(s)/W(s), gymnastics M(s)/W(s), soccer M(s), softball W(s), swimming and diving M(s)/W(s), tennis M(s)/W(s), track and field M(s)/W(s), volleyball W(s). ***Intramural sports:*** badminton M/W, basketball M/W, bowling M/W, fencing M(c)/W(c), field hockey W, football M/W, golf M/W, racquetball M/W, rugby M(c)/W(c), soccer M/W, softball M/W, squash M/W, table tennis M/W, tennis M/W, volleyball M(c)/W, water polo M(c)/W(c), wrestling M.

Campus security: 24-hour emergency response devices and patrols, student patrols, late-night transport/escort service, controlled dormitory access, housing ID stickers, guest escort policy, 24-hour closed circuit videos for exits and entrances, security screen for first floor.

Student services: health clinic, personal/psychological counseling, women's center, legal services, veterans affairs office.

COSTS & FINANCIAL AID
Costs (2019–20) ***Tuition:*** area resident $10,584 full-time, $464 per credit hour part-time; state resident $10,584 full-time, $464 per credit hour part-time; nonresident $24,276 full-time, $808 per credit hour part-time. Full-time tuition and fees vary according to program. Part-time tuition and fees vary according to program. No tuition increase for student's term of enrollment. ***Required fees:*** $3290 full-time. ***Room and board:*** $12,479; room only: $8082. Room and board charges vary according to board plan and housing facility. ***Payment plan:*** installment.

Financial Aid Of all full-time matriculated undergraduates who enrolled in 2018, 15,677 applied for aid, 14,050 were judged to have need, 1,145 had their need fully met. 943 Federal Work-Study jobs (averaging $3000). 3,287 state and other part-time jobs (averaging $2500). In 2018, 622 non-need-based awards were made. ***Average percent of need met:*** 63. ***Average financial aid package:*** $15,209. ***Average need-based loan:*** $4297. ***Average need-based gift aid:*** $12,978. ***Average non-need-based aid:*** $5100. ***Average indebtedness upon graduation:*** $21,931.

APPLYING
Standardized Tests *Required:* SAT or ACT (for admission).

Options: electronic application, early action.

Application fee: $60.

Required: essay or personal statement, high school transcript. ***Required for some:*** audition for music and theater majors, portfolio for art majors.

Application deadlines: 1/15 (freshmen), 3/31 (transfers), 11/1 (early action).

Notification: continuous until 11/30 (freshmen), continuous (transfers), 12/1 (early action).

CONTACT
Ms. Maureen Woods, Associate Director, Admissions Undergraduate, University of Illinois at Chicago, Chicago. *Phone:* 312-996-4111. *Fax:* 312-413-7628. *E-mail:* uic.admit@uic.edu.

University of Illinois at Springfield

Springfield, Illinois

http://www.uis.edu/

- **State-supported** comprehensive, founded 1969, part of University of Illinois System
- **Suburban** 746-acre campus
- **Endowment** $19.4 million
- **Coed** 2,674 undergraduate students, 69% full-time, 51% women, 49% men
- **Moderately difficult** entrance level, 77% of applicants were admitted

UNDERGRAD STUDENTS
1,853 full-time, 821 part-time. Students come from 44 states and territories; 31 other countries; 12% are from out of state; 15% Black or African American, non-Hispanic/Latino; 11% Hispanic/Latino; 4% Asian, non-Hispanic/Latino; 0.1% Native Hawaiian or other Pacific Islander, non-Hispanic/Latino; 0.2% American Indian or Alaska Native, non-Hispanic/Latino; 4% Two or more races, non-Hispanic/Latino; 1% Race/ethnicity unknown; 3% international; 18% transferred in; 35% live on campus.

Freshmen:
Admission: 2,117 applied, 1,626 admitted, 373 enrolled. ***Average high school GPA:*** 3.7. ***Test scores:*** SAT evidence-based reading and writing scores over 500: 76%; SAT math scores over 500: 75%; ACT scores over 18: 95%; SAT evidence-based reading and writing scores over 600: 32%; SAT math scores over 600: 29%; ACT scores over 24: 43%; SAT evidence-based reading and writing scores over 700: 6%; SAT math scores over 700: 7%; ACT scores over 30: 11%.

Retention: 79% of full-time freshmen returned.

FACULTY
Total: 344, 60% full-time, 64% with terminal degrees.

Student/faculty ratio: 13:1.

ACADEMICS
Calendar: semesters. *Degrees:* bachelor's, master's, doctoral, post-master's, and postbachelor's certificates.

Special study options: academic remediation for entering students, advanced placement credit, cooperative education, distance learning, English as a second language, honors programs, independent study, internships, off-campus study, part-time degree program, services for LD students, study abroad, summer session for credit.

Computers: 560 computers/terminals are available on campus for general student use. Students can access the following: campus intranet, computer help desk, free student e-mail accounts, online (class) grades, online (class) registration, online (class) schedules. Campuswide network is available. 100% of college-owned or -operated housing units are wired for high-speed Internet access. Wireless service is available via entire campus.
Library: Norris L Brookens Library plus 1 other. *Books:* 342,013 (physical), 240,597 (digital/electronic); *Serial titles:* 8,456 (physical), 18,139 (digital/electronic); *Databases:* 179. Weekly public service hours: 90; students can reserve study rooms.

STUDENT LIFE
Housing options: on-campus residence required for freshman year; coed, special housing for students with disabilities. Campus housing is university owned. Freshman campus housing is guaranteed.

Activities and organizations: drama/theater group, student-run newspaper, radio station, choral group, Christian Student Fellowship, Sigma Sigma Sigma, Delta Kappa Epsilon, International Student Organization, Alternative Spring Break, national fraternities, national sororities.

Athletics Member NCAA. All Division II. ***Intercollegiate sports:*** baseball M(s), basketball M(s)/W(s), cheerleading M(s)/W(s), cross-country running M(s)/W(s), golf M(s)/W(s), soccer M(s)/W(s), softball W(s), tennis M(s)/W(s), track and field M(s)/W(s), volleyball W(s). ***Intramural sports:*** badminton M/W, basketball M/W, football M/W, racquetball M/W, sand volleyball M/W, soccer W, softball M/W, table tennis M/W, tennis M/W, volleyball M(c)/W(c).

Campus security: 24-hour emergency response devices and patrols, late-night transport/escort service, controlled dormitory access.

Student services: health clinic, personal/psychological counseling, women's center, veterans affairs office.

COSTS & FINANCIAL AID
Costs (2019–20) ***Tuition:*** state resident $9405 full-time, $314 per credit hour part-time; nonresident $18,930 full-time, $631 per credit hour part-time. No tuition increase for student's term of enrollment. ***Required fees:*** $2408 full-time. ***Room and board:*** $11,660; room only: $7460. Room and board charges vary according to board plan and housing facility. ***Payment plan:*** installment. ***Waivers:*** senior citizens and employees or children of employees.

Financial Aid Of all full-time matriculated undergraduates who enrolled in 2018, 1,493 applied for aid, 1,225 were judged to have need, 178 had their need fully met. In 2018, 273 non-need-based awards were made. ***Average percent of need met:*** 71. ***Average financial aid package:*** $14,275. ***Average need-based loan:*** $4267. ***Average need-based gift aid:*** $11,731. ***Average non-need-based aid:*** $8281. ***Average indebtedness upon graduation:*** $22,248. ***Financial aid deadline:*** 11/15.

APPLYING
Standardized Tests *Required:* SAT or ACT (for admission). *Recommended:* SAT and SAT Subject Tests or ACT (for admission).

Options: electronic application, deferred entrance.

Required: high school transcript.

Application deadlines: rolling (freshmen), rolling (transfers).

Notification: continuous (transfers).

CONTACT
Kathryn Kleeman, Interim Director of Admissions, University of Illinois at Springfield, One University Plaza, MS UHB 1080, Springfield, IL 62703-5407. *Phone:* 217-206-4847. *Toll-free phone:* 888-977-4847. *E-mail:* admissions@uis.edu.

University of Illinois at Urbana-Champaign

Champaign, Illinois

http://www.illinois.edu/

- **State-supported** university, founded 1867, part of University of Illinois System
- **Urban** 1783-acre campus
- **Coed**
- **Very difficult** entrance level

FACULTY
Student/faculty ratio: 20:1.

ACADEMICS
Calendar: semesters. *Degrees:* certificates, bachelor's, master's, doctoral, post-master's, and postbachelor's certificates.
Library: University Library plus 20 others.

STUDENT LIFE
Housing options: on-campus residence required for freshman year; coed, men-only, women-only, cooperative, special housing for students with disabilities. Campus housing is university owned and is provided by a third party. Freshman campus housing is guaranteed.

Activities and organizations: drama/theater group, student-run newspaper, radio and television station, choral group, marching band, Volunteer Illini Project, October Lovers, Illini Pride Student Board, National Society of Collegiate Scholars, Phi Eta Sigma Freshman Honor Society, national fraternities, national sororities.

Athletics Member NCAA. All Division I except football (Division I-A).

Campus security: 24-hour emergency response devices and patrols, student patrols, late-night transport/escort service, controlled dormitory access, safety training classes, ID cards with safety numbers.

Student services: health clinic, personal/psychological counseling, women's center, legal services.

COSTS & FINANCIAL AID
Costs (2019–20) ***Tuition:*** area resident $12,036 full-time; state resident $12,036 full-time; nonresident $29,178 full-time. Full-time tuition and fees vary according to program and student level. No tuition increase for student's term of enrollment. ***Required fees:*** $4174 full-time. ***Room and board:*** $11,672; room only: $5470. Room and board charges vary according to board plan, housing facility, and student level.

Financial Aid Of all full-time matriculated undergraduates who enrolled in 2018, 20,086 applied for aid, 15,257 were judged to have need, 1,617 had their need fully met. In 2018, 3517 non-need-based awards were made. ***Average percent of need met:*** 67. ***Average financial aid package:*** $18,024. ***Average need-based loan:*** $4360. ***Average need-based gift aid:*** $16,498. ***Average non-need-based aid:*** $5276. ***Average indebtedness upon graduation:*** $24,655.

APPLYING
Standardized Tests *Required:* SAT or ACT (for admission).

Options: electronic application, early admission, deferred entrance.

Application fee: $50.

Required: essay or personal statement, high school transcript. ***Required for some:*** audition or portfolio.

CONTACT
Stacey Kostell, Director of Admissions, University of Illinois at Urbana-Champaign, 901 West Illinois, Urbana, IL 61801. *Phone:* 217-333-0302. *Fax:* 217-244-4614. *E-mail:* ugradadmissions@uiuc.edu.

University of St. Francis

Joliet, Illinois

http://www.stfrancis.edu/

- **Independent Roman Catholic** comprehensive, founded 1920
- **Suburban** 24-acre campus with easy access to Chicago
- **Endowment** $21.8 million
- **Coed** 1,746 undergraduate students, 82% full-time, 66% women, 34% men
- **Moderately difficult** entrance level, 46% of applicants were admitted

UNDERGRAD STUDENTS
1,427 full-time, 319 part-time. Students come from 33 states and territories; 14 other countries; 9% are from out of state; 9% Black or African American, non-Hispanic/Latino; 22% Hispanic/Latino; 3% Asian, non-Hispanic/Latino; 0.1% Native Hawaiian or other Pacific Islander, non-Hispanic/Latino; 0.1% American Indian or Alaska Native, non-Hispanic/Latino; 3% Two or more races, non-Hispanic/Latino; 1% Race/ethnicity unknown; 3% international; 14% transferred in; 23% live on campus.

Freshmen:
Admission: 2,273 applied, 1,037 admitted, 236 enrolled. ***Average high school GPA:*** 3.6. ***Test scores:*** SAT evidence-based reading and writing scores over 500: 82%; SAT math scores over 500: 85%; ACT scores over 18: 97%; SAT evidence-based reading and writing scores over 600: 35%; SAT math scores over 600: 25%; ACT scores over 24: 47%; SAT evidence-based reading and writing scores over 700: 6%; SAT math scores over 700: 5%; ACT scores over 30: 8%.

Retention: 81% of full-time freshmen returned.

FACULTY
Total: 303, 33% full-time, 46% with terminal degrees.
Student/faculty ratio: 13:1.

ACADEMICS
Calendar: semesters. *Degrees:* certificates, bachelor's, master's, doctoral, post-master's, and postbachelor's certificates.

Special study options: academic remediation for entering students, accelerated degree program, adult/continuing education programs, advanced placement credit, distance learning, double majors, English as a second language, honors programs, independent study, internships, off-campus study, part-time degree program, services for LD students, student-designed majors, study abroad, summer session for credit. ***ROTC:*** Army (c).

Computers: 560 computers/terminals and 2,300 ports are available on campus for general student use. Students can access the following: campus intranet, computer help desk, free student e-mail accounts, online (class) grades, online (class) registration, online (class) schedules, billing/payment. Campuswide network is available. 100% of college-owned or -operated housing units are wired for high-speed Internet access. Wireless service is available via entire campus.
Library: Brown Library. *Books:* 88,389 (physical), 16,299 (digital/electronic); *Serial titles:* 1,942 (physical), 109 (digital/electronic); *Databases:* 128. Weekly public service hours: 74; study areas open 24 hours, 5–7 days a week; students can reserve study rooms.

STUDENT LIFE
Housing options: coed, special housing for students with disabilities. Campus housing is university owned. Freshman campus housing is guaranteed.

Activities and organizations: drama/theater group, student-run newspaper, radio and television station, choral group, Justice League, International Club, Alpha Phi, Black Student Association (BSA), Unidos Vamos a Alcanzar (UVA), national fraternities, national sororities.

Athletics Member NAIA. ***Intercollegiate sports:*** baseball M(s), basketball M(s)/W(s), bowling M(s)/W(s), cheerleading M(s)/W(s), cross-country running M(s)/W(s), football M(s), golf M(s)/W(s), soccer M(s)/W(s), softball W(s), tennis M(s)/W(s), track and field M(s)/W(s), volleyball W(s). ***Intramural sports:*** basketball M/W, bowling M/W, table tennis M/W, volleyball M/W.

Campus security: 24-hour emergency response devices and patrols, student patrols, late-night transport/escort service, controlled dormitory access, First Response trained security personnel.

Student services: health clinic, personal/psychological counseling.

COSTS & FINANCIAL AID
Costs (2020–21) ***Comprehensive fee:*** $45,210 includes full-time tuition ($35,000) and room and board ($10,210). Full-time tuition and fees vary according to degree level, location, and program. Part-time tuition: $875 per credit hour. Part-time tuition and fees vary according to degree level and program. ***Required fees:*** $75 per term part-time. ***Room and board:*** Room and board charges vary according to housing facility. ***Payment plans:*** installment, deferred payment. ***Waivers:*** children of alumni and employees or children of employees.

Financial Aid Of all full-time matriculated undergraduates who enrolled in 2019, 1,272 applied for aid, 1,149 were judged to have need, 336 had their need fully met. 168 Federal Work-Study jobs (averaging $2602). 300 state and other part-time jobs (averaging $2500). In 2019, 224 non-need-based awards were made. ***Average percent of need met:*** 75. ***Average financial aid package:*** $26,685. ***Average need-based loan:*** $4522. ***Average need-based gift aid:*** $22,898. ***Average non-need-based aid:*** $13,846. ***Average indebtedness upon graduation:*** $30,274.

APPLYING
Standardized Tests *Required:* SAT or ACT (for admission).

Options: electronic application, deferred entrance.

Required: high school transcript, minimum 2.5 GPA. ***Required for some:*** essay or personal statement, 2 letters of recommendation, interview.

Notification: continuous (freshmen), continuous (transfers).

CONTACT
Mr. Eric Ruiz, Director of Freshman Admissions, University of St. Francis, 500 North Wilcox Street, Joliet, IL 60435-6188. *Phone:* 800-735-7500. *Toll-free phone:* 800-735-7500. *Fax:* 815-740-5070. *E-mail:* eruiz@stfrancis.edu.

VanderCook College of Music
Chicago, Illinois
http://www.vandercook.edu/

- **Independent** comprehensive, founded 1909
- **Urban** 1-acre campus with easy access to Chicago
- **Endowment** $514,572
- **Coed** 107 undergraduate students, 65% full-time, 40% women, 60% men
- **Moderately difficult** entrance level, 89% of applicants were admitted

UNDERGRAD STUDENTS
70 full-time, 37 part-time. 8% are from out of state; 11% Black or African American, non-Hispanic/Latino; 31% Hispanic/Latino; 3% Asian, non-Hispanic/Latino; 7% Two or more races, non-Hispanic/Latino; 1% international; 5% transferred in; 10% live on campus.

Freshmen:
Admission: 27 applied, 24 admitted, 18 enrolled. ***Average high school GPA:*** 3.1.

Retention: 94% of full-time freshmen returned.

FACULTY
Total: 29, 34% full-time, 34% with terminal degrees.
Student/faculty ratio: 4:1.

ACADEMICS
Calendar: semesters. *Degrees:* bachelor's and master's.

Special study options: academic remediation for entering students, advanced placement credit.

Computers: 21 computers/terminals are available on campus for general student use. Students can access the following: free student e-mail accounts, Dedicated WiFi network. Campuswide network is available. 100% of college-owned or -operated housing units are wired for high-speed Internet access. Wireless service is available via entire campus.
Library: Harry Ruppel Memorial Library plus 1 other. *Books:* 16,985 (physical), 6,827 (digital/electronic); *Serial titles:* 200 (physical), 100 (digital/electronic); *Databases:* 28. Weekly public service hours: 54; students can reserve study rooms.

STUDENT LIFE
Housing options: coed. Campus housing is university owned.

Activities and organizations: student-run newspaper, radio station, NAfME (National Association for Music Education), ACDA (American Choral Directors Association), NBA (National Band Association), ASTA (American String Teachers Association), national fraternities, national sororities.

Campus security: 24-hour emergency response devices and patrols, late-night transport/escort service, controlled dormitory access.

Student services: health clinic, personal/psychological counseling.

FINANCIAL AID
Financial Aid Of all full-time matriculated undergraduates who enrolled in 2019, 55 applied for aid, 53 were judged to have need. In 2019, 12 non-

need-based awards were made. ***Average financial aid package:*** $17,617. ***Average need-based loan:*** $4198. ***Average need-based gift aid:*** $2175. ***Average non-need-based aid:*** $8100. ***Average indebtedness upon graduation:*** $46,917.

APPLYING
Standardized Tests *Required:* SAT or ACT (for admission).

Options: electronic application, deferred entrance.

Application fee: $35.

Required: essay or personal statement, high school transcript, 3 letters of recommendation, interview, audition on the applicant's primary instrument or voice. ***Required for some:*** minimum 3.0 GPA. ***Recommended:*** minimum 3.0 GPA.

Application deadlines: 4/1 (freshmen), 4/1 (out-of-state freshmen).

Notification: continuous (freshmen), continuous (out-of-state freshmen), continuous (transfers).

CONTACT
Ms. Cindy Tovar, Director of Admissions and Alumni Relations, VanderCook College of Music, 3140 South Federal Street, Chicago, IL 60616. *Phone:* 312-788-1120 Ext. 230. *Fax:* 312-225-5211. *E-mail:* admissions@vandercook.edu.

Western Illinois University

Macomb, Illinois

http://www.wiu.edu/

- **State-supported** comprehensive, founded 1899
- **Small-town** 1050-acre campus with easy access to Quad Cities; Peoria, IL; Springfield, IL
- **Endowment** $55.8 million
- **Coed**
- **Moderately difficult** entrance level

FACULTY
Student/faculty ratio: 14:1.

ACADEMICS
Calendar: semesters. *Degrees:* bachelor's, master's, doctoral, post-master's, and postbachelor's certificates.
Library: Leslie Malpass Library plus 4 others. *Books:* 765,987 (physical), 149,419 (digital/electronic); *Serial titles:* 154,171 (physical), 77,503 (digital/electronic); *Databases:* 116.

STUDENT LIFE
Housing options: on-campus residence required through sophomore year; coed, men-only, women-only, special housing for students with disabilities. Campus housing is university owned. Freshman campus housing is guaranteed.

Activities and organizations: drama/theater group, student-run newspaper, radio and television station, choral group, marching band, Student Government Association, Black Student Association, University Union Board, Western's All Volunteer Effort (WAVE), Inter Hall Council, national fraternities, national sororities.

Athletics Member NCAA. All Division I except football (Division I-AA).

Campus security: 24-hour emergency response devices and patrols, student patrols, late-night transport/escort service, controlled dormitory access.

Student services: health clinic, personal/psychological counseling, women's center, legal services, veterans affairs office.

COSTS & FINANCIAL AID
Costs (2019–20) ***One-time required fee:*** $210. ***Tuition:*** state resident $8883 full-time, $296 per credit hour part-time; nonresident $8883 full-time, $296 per credit hour part-time. Full-time tuition and fees vary according to course load, location, and student level. Part-time tuition and fees vary according to course load, location, and student level. No tuition increase for student's term of enrollment. ***Required fees:*** $2783 full-time, $93 per credit hour part-time. ***Room and board:*** $9800; room only: $6000. Room and board charges vary according to board plan, housing facility, and student level.

Financial Aid Of all full-time matriculated undergraduates who enrolled in 2019, 4,531 applied for aid, 3,905 were judged to have need, 1,090 had their need fully met. 221 Federal Work-Study jobs (averaging $2240). 1,118 state and other part-time jobs (averaging $1713). In 2019, 566 non-need-based awards were made. ***Average percent of need met:*** 66. ***Average financial aid package:*** $13,378. ***Average need-based loan:*** $4302. ***Average need-based gift aid:*** $10,481. ***Average non-need-based aid:*** $3722. ***Average indebtedness upon graduation:*** $30,522.

APPLYING
Standardized Tests *Required:* SAT or ACT (for admission).

Options: electronic application, deferred entrance.

Application fee: $30.

Required: high school transcript, minimum 2.5 GPA.

CONTACT
Ms. Kassandra Daly, Interim Director of Admissions, Western Illinois University, 1 University Circle, Macomb, IL 61455-1390. *Phone:* 309-298-3157. *Toll-free phone:* 877-742-5948. *Fax:* 309-298-3111. *E-mail:* kj-daly@wiu.edu.

Wheaton College

Wheaton, Illinois

http://www.wheaton.edu/

- **Independent nondenominational** comprehensive, founded 1860
- **Suburban** 80-acre campus with easy access to Chicago
- **Endowment** $503.4 million
- **Coed** 2,395 undergraduate students, 97% full-time, 54% women, 46% men
- **Very difficult** entrance level, 85% of applicants were admitted

UNDERGRAD STUDENTS
2,328 full-time, 67 part-time. Students come from 51 states and territories; 41 other countries; 73% are from out of state; 3% Black or African American, non-Hispanic/Latino; 7% Hispanic/Latino; 10% Asian, non-Hispanic/Latino; 0.1% Native Hawaiian or other Pacific Islander, non-Hispanic/Latino; 0.1% American Indian or Alaska Native, non-Hispanic/Latino; 5% Two or more races, non-Hispanic/Latino; 0.3% Race/ethnicity unknown; 4% international; 2% transferred in; 91% live on campus.

Freshmen:
Admission: 1,889 applied, 1,602 admitted, 614 enrolled. ***Average high school GPA:*** 3.7. ***Test scores:*** SAT evidence-based reading and writing scores over 500: 99%; SAT math scores over 500: 98%; ACT scores over 18: 100%; SAT evidence-based reading and writing scores over 600: 85%; SAT math scores over 600: 77%; ACT scores over 24: 90%; SAT evidence-based reading and writing scores over 700: 37%; SAT math scores over 700: 34%; ACT scores over 30: 52%.

Retention: 93% of full-time freshmen returned.

FACULTY
Total: 343, 64% full-time, 74% with terminal degrees.

Student/faculty ratio: 10:1.

ACADEMICS
Calendar: semesters. *Degrees:* bachelor's, master's, doctoral, and postbachelor's certificates.

Special study options: advanced placement credit, double majors, independent study, internships, off-campus study, services for LD students, student-designed majors, study abroad, summer session for credit. ***ROTC:*** Army (b), Air Force (c).

Unusual degree programs: 3-2 engineering with Illinois Institute of Technology; nursing with Elmhurst College, Emory University, Indiana Wesleyan University.

Computers: 325 computers/terminals and 3,500 ports are available on campus for general student use. Students can access the following: campus intranet, computer help desk, free student e-mail accounts, online (class) grades, online (class) registration, online (class) schedules, financial information, degree requirements evaluation. Campuswide network is available. 100% of college-owned or -operated housing units are wired for high-speed Internet access. Wireless service is available via entire campus.

Library: Buswell Memorial Library. *Books:* 359,725 (physical), 167,199 (digital/electronic); *Serial titles:* 352 (physical), 6,146 (digital/electronic); *Databases:* 170. Weekly public service hours: 94; students can reserve study rooms.

STUDENT LIFE

Housing options: on-campus residence required through senior year; coed, men-only, women-only, cooperative, special housing for students with disabilities. Campus housing is university owned. Freshman campus housing is guaranteed.

Activities and organizations: drama/theater group, student-run newspaper, choral group, Discipleship small groups, intramurals, Club Sports, Christian Service Council, New Student Orientation.

Athletics Member NCAA. All Division III except golf (Division II). ***Intercollegiate sports:*** baseball M, basketball M/W, cheerleading W(c), crew M(c)/W(c), cross-country running M/W, football M, golf M/W, ice hockey M(c), lacrosse M(c)/W(c), rowing M(c)/W, soccer M/W, softball W, swimming and diving M/W, tennis M/W, track and field M/W, volleyball W, wrestling M. ***Intramural sports:*** badminton M/W, basketball M/W, football M, golf M/W, soccer M/W, softball M, ultimate Frisbee M/W, volleyball M/W, water polo M/W.

Campus security: 24-hour emergency response devices and patrols, student patrols, late-night transport/escort service, controlled dormitory access.

Student services: health clinic, personal/psychological counseling.

COSTS & FINANCIAL AID

Costs (2020–21) ***Comprehensive fee:*** $50,090 includes full-time tuition ($39,100) and room and board ($10,990). Full-time tuition and fees vary according to program. Part-time tuition: $1629 per credit hour. Part-time tuition and fees vary according to course load and program. ***College room only:*** $6500. Room and board charges vary according to board plan, housing facility, and location. ***Payment plan:*** installment.

Financial Aid Of all full-time matriculated undergraduates who enrolled in 2019, 1,725 applied for aid, 1,433 were judged to have need, 148 had their need fully met. 226 Federal Work-Study jobs (averaging $1282). In 2019, 496 non-need-based awards were made. ***Average percent of need met:*** 71. ***Average financial aid package:*** $25,684. ***Average need-based loan:*** $4370. ***Average need-based gift aid:*** $22,583. ***Average non-need-based aid:*** $11,440. ***Average indebtedness upon graduation:*** $29,555.

APPLYING

Standardized Tests *Required:* SAT or ACT (for admission).

Options: electronic application, early action, deferred entrance.

Application fee: $50.

Required: essay or personal statement, high school transcript, 2 letters of recommendation. ***Recommended:*** interview.

Application deadlines: 1/10 (freshmen), 3/1 (transfers), 11/1 (early action).

Notification: 4/1 (freshmen), continuous until 3/1 (transfers), 12/31 (early action).

CONTACT

Jason Kircher, Director of Admissions, Wheaton College, 501 College Avenue, Wheaton, IL 60187-5593. *Phone:* 630-752-5011. *Toll-free phone:* 800-222-2419. *Fax:* 630-752-5285. *E-mail:* admissions@wheaton.edu.

See below for display ad and page 1138 for the College Close-Up.

INDIANA

Anderson University

Anderson, Indiana

http://www.anderson.edu/

- **Independent** comprehensive, founded 1917, affiliated with Church of God
- **Suburban** 163-acre campus with easy access to Indianapolis
- **Endowment** $33.7 million
- **Coed** 1,311 undergraduate students, 93% full-time, 58% women, 42% men

UNDERGRAD STUDENTS

1,213 full-time, 98 part-time. Students come from 27 states and territories; 8 other countries; 21% are from out of state; 7% Black or African American, non-Hispanic/Latino; 5% Hispanic/Latino; 0.5% Asian, non-Hispanic/Latino; 0.1% Native Hawaiian or other Pacific Islander, non-Hispanic/Latino; 0.2% American Indian or Alaska Native, non-

Hispanic/Latino; 5% Two or more races, non-Hispanic/Latino; 0.8% Race/ethnicity unknown; 1% international; 4% transferred in.

Freshmen:

Admission: 330 enrolled. ***Average high school GPA:*** 3.4.

Retention: 69% of full-time freshmen returned.

ACADEMICS

Calendar: semesters. *Degrees:* associate, bachelor's, master's, and doctoral.

COSTS & FINANCIAL AID

Costs (2019–20) ***Comprehensive fee:*** $41,240 includes full-time tuition ($30,700), mandatory fees ($500), and room and board ($10,040). Part-time tuition: $1280 per semester hour. ***College room only:*** $6240.

Financial Aid Of all full-time matriculated undergraduates who enrolled in 2014, 1,549 applied for aid, 1,410 were judged to have need, 604 had their need fully met. In 2014, 307 non-need-based awards were made. ***Average percent of need met:*** 88. ***Average financial aid package:*** $23,905. ***Average need-based loan:*** $10,011. ***Average need-based gift aid:*** $15,932. ***Average non-need-based aid:*** $14,313.

CONTACT

Ms. Kynan Simison, Director of Admissions, Anderson University, 1100 East 5th Street, Anderson, IN 46012-3495. *Phone:* 765-641-4076. *Toll-free phone:* 800-428-6414. *Fax:* 765-641-3851. *E-mail:* info@anderson.edu.

Ball State University

Muncie, Indiana

http://www.bsu.edu/

- **State-supported** university, founded 1918
- **Suburban** 1140-acre campus with easy access to Indianapolis
- **Endowment** $201.8 million
- **Coed** 16,702 undergraduate students, 88% full-time, 60% women, 40% men
- 77% of applicants were admitted

UNDERGRAD STUDENTS

14,713 full-time, 1,989 part-time. 15% are from out of state; 8% Black or African American, non-Hispanic/Latino; 6% Hispanic/Latino; 1% Asian, non-Hispanic/Latino; 0.1% Native Hawaiian or other Pacific Islander, non-Hispanic/Latino; 4% Two or more races, non-Hispanic/Latino; 1% Race/ethnicity unknown; 1% international; 4% transferred in; 37% live on campus.

Freshmen:

Admission: 23,305 applied, 17,878 admitted, 4,003 enrolled. ***Average high school GPA:*** 3.5.

Retention: 75% of full-time freshmen returned.

FACULTY

Total: 1,766, 60% full-time, 48% with terminal degrees.

Student/faculty ratio: 14:1.

ACADEMICS

Calendar: semesters. *Degrees:* certificates, bachelor's, master's, doctoral, post-master's, and postbachelor's certificates.

Special study options: accelerated degree program, adult/continuing education programs, advanced placement credit, cooperative education, distance learning, double majors, English as a second language, freshman honors college, honors programs, independent study, internships, part-time degree program, services for LD students, student-designed majors, study abroad, summer session for credit. ***ROTC:*** Army (b).

Computers: 578 computers/terminals and 9,337 ports are available on campus for general student use. Students can access the following: campus intranet, computer help desk, free student e-mail accounts, online (class) grades, online (class) registration, online (class) schedules, room reservations, testing and test results, manage and pay tuition, order/buy textbooks, request room repairs, order transcripts, manage meal plan, manage and prepay long distance service, undergraduate degree progress report. Campuswide network is available. 100% of college-owned or -operated housing units are wired for high-speed Internet access. Wireless service is available via entire campus.

Library: Bracken Library plus 2 others. *Books:* 822,983 (physical), 15,244 (digital/electronic); *Serial titles:* 13,599 (physical), 103,640 (digital/electronic); *Databases:* 296. Weekly public service hours: 123; students can reserve study rooms.

STUDENT LIFE

Housing options: on-campus residence required for freshman year; coed, special housing for students with disabilities. Campus housing is university owned. Freshman campus housing is guaranteed.

Activities and organizations: drama/theater group, student-run newspaper, radio and television station, choral group, marching band, Student Voluntary Services, National Society of Collegiate Scholars, Dance Marathon, Cardinal Catholic, National Society of Leadership and Success, national fraternities, national sororities.

Athletics Member NCAA. All Division I except football (Division I-A). ***Intercollegiate sports:*** baseball M(s)/W(c), basketball M(s)/W(s), bowling M(c)/W(c), cheerleading M/W, cross-country running W(s), equestrian sports M(c)/W(c), fencing M(c)/W(c), field hockey W(s), golf M(s)/W(s), gymnastics W(s), lacrosse M(c)/W(c), racquetball M(c)/W(c), rock climbing M(c)/W(c), rugby M(c)/W(c), soccer M(c)/W(s), softball W(s), swimming and diving M(s)/W(s), tennis M(s)/W(s), track and field W(s), triathlon M(c)/W(c), ultimate Frisbee M(c)/W(c), volleyball M(s)/W(s), water polo M(c)/W(c), wrestling M(c). ***Intramural sports:*** archery M(c)/W(c), badminton M/W, basketball M/W, bowling M/W, golf M/W, gymnastics W(c), ice hockey M(c), racquetball M/W, soccer M/W, softball M/W, swimming and diving M/W, table tennis M/W, tennis M/W, track and field M/W, ultimate Frisbee M/W, volleyball M/W.

Campus security: 24-hour emergency response devices and patrols, late-night transport/escort service, controlled dormitory access.

Student services: health clinic, personal/psychological counseling, women's center, legal services, veterans affairs office.

COSTS & FINANCIAL AID

Costs (2020–21) ***Tuition:*** area resident $9358 full-time; state resident $9358 full-time; nonresident $26,138 full-time. Full-time tuition and fees vary according to program and reciprocity agreements. Part-time tuition and fees vary according to course load, program, and reciprocity agreements. ***Required fees:*** $662 full-time. ***Room and board:*** $10,870; room only: $4742. Room and board charges vary according to board plan and housing facility. ***Payment plan:*** installment. ***Waivers:*** senior citizens and employees or children of employees.

Financial Aid Of all full-time matriculated undergraduates who enrolled in 2019, 12,684 applied for aid, 9,927 were judged to have need, 4,760 had their need fully met. In 2019, 2151 non-need-based awards were made. ***Average percent of need met:*** 74. ***Average financial aid package:*** $14,335. ***Average need-based loan:*** $4121. ***Average need-based gift aid:*** $6715. ***Average non-need-based aid:*** $8040. ***Average indebtedness upon graduation:*** $28,603.

APPLYING

Options: early action.

Application fee: $60.

Notification: 5/1 (early action).

CONTACT

Ball State University, 2000 West University Avenue, Muncie, IN 47306. *Phone:* 765-285-8300. *Toll-free phone:* 800-482-4BSU.

Bethel University

Mishawaka, Indiana

http://betheluniversity.edu

- **Independent** comprehensive, founded 1947, affiliated with Missionary Church
- **Suburban** 80-acre campus
- **Endowment** $9.9 million
- **Coed** 1,220 undergraduate students, 83% full-time, 62% women, 38% men
- **Minimally difficult** entrance level, 94% of applicants were admitted

UNDERGRAD STUDENTS

1,015 full-time, 205 part-time. Students come from 29 states and territories; 21 other countries; 27% are from out of state; 10% Black or African American, non-Hispanic/Latino; 11% Hispanic/Latino; 1% Asian, non-Hispanic/Latino; 0.2% American Indian or Alaska Native, non-

Hispanic/Latino; 7% Two or more races, non-Hispanic/Latino; 1% Race/ethnicity unknown; 3% international; 6% transferred in; 54% live on campus.

Freshmen:
Admission: 1,359 applied, 1,274 admitted, 307 enrolled. ***Average high school GPA:*** 3.4. ***Test scores:*** SAT evidence-based reading and writing scores over 500: 69%; SAT math scores over 500: 68%; ACT scores over 18: 82%; SAT evidence-based reading and writing scores over 600: 23%; SAT math scores over 600: 18%; ACT scores over 24: 30%; SAT evidence-based reading and writing scores over 700: 3%; SAT math scores over 700: 3%; ACT scores over 30: 7%.

Retention: 64% of full-time freshmen returned.

FACULTY
Total: 193, 32% full-time, 37% with terminal degrees.

Student/faculty ratio: 11:1.

ACADEMICS
Calendar: semesters. *Degrees:* associate, bachelor's, and master's.

Special study options: academic remediation for entering students, accelerated degree program, adult/continuing education programs, advanced placement credit, distance learning, double majors, external degree program, honors programs, independent study, internships, off-campus study, part-time degree program, services for LD students, student-designed majors, study abroad, summer session for credit. ***ROTC:*** Army (c), Air Force (c).

Unusual degree programs: 3-2 engineering with University of Notre Dame, Trine University.

Computers: 132 computers/terminals and 440 ports are available on campus for general student use. Students can access the following: campus intranet, computer help desk, free student e-mail accounts, online (class) grades, online (class) schedules. Campuswide network is available. 100% of college-owned or -operated housing units are wired for high-speed Internet access. Wireless service is available via entire campus.
Library: Otis and Elizabeth Bowen Library. *Books:* 112,075 (physical), 238,744 (digital/electronic); *Serial titles:* 1,304 (physical), 38,336 (digital/electronic); *Databases:* 98. Weekly public service hours: 79.

STUDENT LIFE
Housing options: on-campus residence required through sophomore year; men-only, women-only. Campus housing is university owned.

Activities and organizations: drama/theater group, student-run newspaper, choral group, Student Government, Psychology Club, Campus Activities Board, Theatre Club.

Athletics Member NAIA, NCCAA. ***Intercollegiate sports:*** baseball M(s), basketball M(s)/W(s), bowling M(s)/W(s), cheerleading M(s)/W(s), cross-country running M(s)/W(s), golf M(s)/W(s), lacrosse W(s), rugby M(s), soccer M(s)/W(s), softball W(s), swimming and diving M(s)/W(s), tennis M(s)/W(s), track and field M(s)/W(s), volleyball W(s). ***Intramural sports:*** basketball M/W, volleyball M/W.

Campus security: 24-hour emergency response devices and patrols, late-night transport/escort service, controlled dormitory access.

Student services: health clinic, personal/psychological counseling.

COSTS & FINANCIAL AID
Costs (2020–21) ***Comprehensive fee:*** $39,100 includes full-time tuition ($29,250), mandatory fees ($540), and room and board ($9310). Full-time tuition and fees vary according to program. Part-time tuition: $930 per credit hour. Part-time tuition and fees vary according to course load and program. ***Required fees:*** $310 per year part-time. ***College room only:*** $4430. Room and board charges vary according to board plan and housing facility. ***Payment plan:*** installment. ***Waivers:*** employees or children of employees.

Financial Aid Of all full-time matriculated undergraduates who enrolled in 2019, 84 Federal Work-Study jobs (averaging $721). In 2019, 154 non-need-based awards were made. ***Average non-need-based aid:*** $17,110. ***Average indebtedness upon graduation:*** $30,797.

APPLYING
Standardized Tests *Required:* SAT or ACT (for admission).

Options: electronic application, early admission, deferred entrance.

Required: high school transcript, minimum 2.0 GPA. ***Recommended:*** essay or personal statement, minimum 2.5 GPA, interview.

Application deadlines: 8/15 (freshmen), 8/15 (transfers).

Notification: continuous (freshmen), continuous (transfers).

CONTACT
Stephanie Hochstetler, Director of Admission, Bethel University, 1001 Bethel Circle, Mishawaka, IN 46545. *Phone:* 574-807-7600. *Toll-free phone:* 800-422-4101. *Fax:* 574-807-7650. *E-mail:* admissions@betheluniversity.edu.

Butler University

Indianapolis, Indiana

http://www.butler.edu/

- **Independent** comprehensive, founded 1855
- **Suburban** 301-acre campus with easy access to Indianapolis
- **Endowment** $206.0 million
- **Coed** 4,685 undergraduate students, 96% full-time, 60% women, 40% men
- **Moderately difficult** entrance level, 73% of applicants were admitted

UNDERGRAD STUDENTS
4,509 full-time, 176 part-time. 55% are from out of state; 4% Black or African American, non-Hispanic/Latino; 5% Hispanic/Latino; 3% Asian, non-Hispanic/Latino; 0.2% American Indian or Alaska Native, non-Hispanic/Latino; 4% Two or more races, non-Hispanic/Latino; 0.8% Race/ethnicity unknown; 0.7% international; 2% transferred in; 67% live on campus.

Freshmen:
Admission: 14,891 applied, 10,896 admitted, 1,116 enrolled. ***Average high school GPA:*** 3.9. ***Test scores:*** SAT evidence-based reading and writing scores over 500: 98%; SAT math scores over 500: 98%; ACT scores over 18: 100%; SAT evidence-based reading and writing scores over 600: 68%; SAT math scores over 600: 60%; ACT scores over 24: 82%; SAT evidence-based reading and writing scores over 700: 10%; SAT math scores over 700: 15%; ACT scores over 30: 30%.

Retention: 88% of full-time freshmen returned.

FACULTY
Total: 645, 59% full-time.

Student/faculty ratio: 11:1.

ACADEMICS
Calendar: semesters. *Degrees:* associate, bachelor's, master's, doctoral, and postbachelor's certificates.

Special study options: accelerated degree program, advanced placement credit, cooperative education, distance learning, double majors, English as a second language, honors programs, independent study, internships, off-campus study, services for LD students, student-designed majors, study abroad, summer session for credit. ***ROTC:*** Army (c), Air Force (c).

Unusual degree programs: 3-2 engineering with Indiana University–Purdue University Indianapolis.

Computers: 490 computers/terminals are available on campus for general student use. Students can access the following: campus intranet, computer help desk, free student e-mail accounts, online (class) grades, online (class) registration, online (class) schedules. Campuswide network is available. 100% of college-owned or -operated housing units are wired for high-speed Internet access. Wireless service is available via entire campus.
Library: Irwin Library plus 2 others. *Books:* 175,278 (physical), 540,672 (digital/electronic); *Serial titles:* 5,310 (physical), 94,125 (digital/electronic); *Databases:* 338. Weekly public service hours: 106; students can reserve study rooms.

STUDENT LIFE
Housing options: on-campus residence required through junior year; coed, women-only. Campus housing is university owned. Freshman campus housing is guaranteed.

Activities and organizations: drama/theater group, student-run newspaper, choral group, marching band, Pre-Pharmacy Club, American Chemical Society Students Affiliate, Answers for Autism (Butler University Chapter), Delta Delta Delta, Kappa Psi Pharmaceutical Fraternity, national fraternities, national sororities.

Athletics Member NCAA. All Division I except football (Division I-AA). ***Intercollegiate sports:*** baseball M(s), basketball M(s)/W(s), crew

M(c)/W(c), cross-country running M(s)/W(s), equestrian sports W(c), golf M(s)/W(s), ice hockey M(c), lacrosse M(c)/W(s), rugby M(c), soccer M(s)/W(s), softball W(s), swimming and diving M(c)/W, tennis M(s)/W(s), track and field M(s)/W(s), ultimate Frisbee M(c)/W(c), volleyball M(c)/W(s). ***Intramural sports:*** badminton M/W, baseball M, basketball M/W, bowling M/W, cheerleading M(c)/W(c), football M, soccer M/W, softball M/W, swimming and diving M/W, table tennis M/W, tennis M/W, track and field M/W, volleyball M/W, weight lifting M/W.

Campus security: 24-hour emergency response devices and patrols, late-night transport/escort service, controlled dormitory access.

Student services: health clinic, personal/psychological counseling.

COSTS & FINANCIAL AID

Costs (2020–21) ***Comprehensive fee:*** $57,780 includes full-time tuition ($42,410), mandatory fees ($990), and room and board ($14,380). Part-time tuition: $1760 per credit hour. ***College room only:*** $6950. Room and board charges vary according to board plan and housing facility. ***Waivers:*** employees or children of employees.

Financial Aid Of all full-time matriculated undergraduates who enrolled in 2019, 4,509 applied for aid, 2,508 were judged to have need, 303 had their need fully met. 276 Federal Work-Study jobs (averaging $960). In 2019, 1967 non-need-based awards were made. ***Average percent of need met:*** 65. ***Average financial aid package:*** $25,549. ***Average need-based loan:*** $4497. ***Average need-based gift aid:*** $21,703. ***Average non-need-based aid:*** $16,546. ***Average indebtedness upon graduation:*** $36,695.

APPLYING

Standardized Tests *Required:* SAT or ACT (for admission).

Options: electronic application, early action, deferred entrance.

Required: essay or personal statement, high school transcript. ***Recommended:*** letters of recommendation.

Application deadlines: rolling (freshmen), 8/15 (transfers), 11/1 (early action).

Notification: continuous (freshmen), continuous (transfers).

CONTACT

Jerome Dueweke, Interim Director of Admission, Butler University, 4600 Sunset Avenue, Indianapolis, IN 46208-3485. *Phone:* 317-940-8100. *Toll-free phone:* 888-940-8100. *Fax:* 317-940-8150. *E-mail:* admission@butler.edu.

Calumet College of Saint Joseph

Whiting, Indiana

http://www.ccsj.edu/

- **Independent Roman Catholic** comprehensive, founded 1951
- **Urban** 25-acre campus with easy access to Chicago
- **Endowment** $4.4 million
- **Coed** 549 undergraduate students, 69% full-time, 46% women, 54% men
- **Noncompetitive** entrance level, 31% of applicants were admitted

UNDERGRAD STUDENTS

380 full-time, 169 part-time. Students come from 22 states and territories; 9 other countries; 49% are from out of state; 28% Black or African American, non-Hispanic/Latino; 31% Hispanic/Latino; 1% Asian, non-Hispanic/Latino; 0.2% Native Hawaiian or other Pacific Islander, non-Hispanic/Latino; 0.4% American Indian or Alaska Native, non-Hispanic/Latino; 3% Two or more races, non-Hispanic/Latino; 17% transferred in.

Freshmen:

Admission: 661 applied, 207 admitted, 135 enrolled. ***Average high school GPA:*** 2.8. ***Test scores:*** ACT scores over 18: 10%; ACT scores over 24: 2%.

Retention: 50% of full-time freshmen returned.

FACULTY

Total: 83, 28% full-time, 47% with terminal degrees.

Student/faculty ratio: 11:1.

ACADEMICS

Calendar: semesters. *Degrees:* certificates, associate, bachelor's, and master's.

Special study options: academic remediation for entering students, accelerated degree program, adult/continuing education programs, advanced placement credit, cooperative education, distance learning, double majors, external degree program, honors programs, independent study, internships, part-time degree program, services for LD students, summer session for credit.

Computers: 241 computers/terminals are available on campus for general student use. Students can access the following: computer help desk, free student e-mail accounts, online (class) grades, online (class) schedules. Campuswide network is available. Wireless service is available via entire campus.

Library: Mary Gorman Specker Memorial Library. *Books:* 100,000 (physical), 7,100 (digital/electronic); *Serial titles:* 2 (physical); *Databases:* 65. Weekly public service hours: 58.

STUDENT LIFE

Activities and organizations: drama/theater group, student-run newspaper, Student Government, Los Amigos Hispanic Club, Criminal Justice Club, Drama Club, GIVE.

Athletics Member NAIA. ***Intercollegiate sports:*** baseball M(s), basketball M(s)/W(s), bowling M(s)/W(s), cheerleading W(s), cross-country running M(s)/W(s), golf M(s), soccer M(s)/W(s), softball W(s), tennis M(s)/W(s), track and field M(s)/W(s), volleyball M(s)/W(s), wrestling M(s).

Student services: personal/psychological counseling, veterans affairs office.

COSTS & FINANCIAL AID

Costs (2020–21) ***Tuition:*** $19,900 full-time, $635 per credit hour part-time. ***Required fees:*** $1070 full-time, $135 per term part-time. ***Room only:*** $6000. ***Payment plan:*** installment. ***Waivers:*** employees or children of employees.

Financial Aid Of all full-time matriculated undergraduates who enrolled in 2018, 323 applied for aid, 300 were judged to have need. 32 Federal Work-Study jobs (averaging $1256). In 2018, 7 non-need-based awards were made. ***Average percent of need met:*** 36. ***Average financial aid package:*** $10,920. ***Average need-based loan:*** $3700. ***Average need-based gift aid:*** $7219. ***Average non-need-based aid:*** $4807. ***Average indebtedness upon graduation:*** $24,431.

APPLYING

Standardized Tests *Required:* ACCUPLACER (for admission). *Recommended:* SAT or ACT (for admission).

Options: electronic application, deferred entrance.

Required: high school transcript. ***Required for some:*** essay or personal statement, 1 letter of recommendation. ***Recommended:*** minimum 2.0 GPA, interview.

Application deadlines: rolling (freshmen), rolling (transfers).

Notification: continuous (freshmen), continuous (transfers).

CONTACT

Mr. Andy Marks, Director of Enrollment, Calumet College of Saint Joseph, 2400 New York Avenue, Whiting, IN 46394. *Phone:* 219-473-4295. *Toll-free phone:* 877-700-9100. *Fax:* 219-473-4336. *E-mail:* admissions@ccsj.edu.

Chamberlain College of Nursing - Indianapolis

Indianapolis, Indiana

http://www.chamberlain.edu/

CONTACT

Chamberlain College of Nursing - Indianapolis, 9100 Keystone Crossing, Indianapolis, IN 46240. *Toll-free phone:* 877-751-5783.

Crossroads Bible College

Indianapolis, Indiana

http://www.crossroads.edu/

CONTACT

Michael Garrison, Admissions Counselor, Crossroads Bible College, 601 North Shortridge Road, Indianapolis, IN 46219. *Phone:* 317-789-8266. *Toll-free phone:* 800-822-3119. *E-mail:* admissions@crossroads.edu.

DePauw University

Greencastle, Indiana

http://www.depauw.edu/

- **Independent** 4-year, founded 1837, affiliated with United Methodist Church
- **Small-town** 655-acre campus with easy access to Indianapolis
- **Endowment** $614.6 million
- **Coed** 1,972 undergraduate students, 99% full-time, 52% women, 48% men
- **Moderately difficult** entrance level, 64% of applicants were admitted

UNDERGRAD STUDENTS
1,943 full-time, 29 part-time. 6% Black or African American, non-Hispanic/Latino; 10% Hispanic/Latino; 3% Asian, non-Hispanic/Latino; 0.2% American Indian or Alaska Native, non-Hispanic/Latino; 3% Two or more races, non-Hispanic/Latino; 1% Race/ethnicity unknown; 14% international; 0.6% transferred in; 96% live on campus.

Freshmen:
Admission: 4,935 applied, 3,176 admitted, 423 enrolled. ***Average high school GPA:*** 3.9. ***Test scores:*** SAT evidence-based reading and writing scores over 500: 95%; SAT math scores over 500: 98%; ACT scores over 18: 100%; SAT evidence-based reading and writing scores over 600: 59%; SAT math scores over 600: 65%; ACT scores over 24: 74%; SAT evidence-based reading and writing scores over 700: 11%; SAT math scores over 700: 27%; ACT scores over 30: 25%.

Retention: 86% of full-time freshmen returned.

FACULTY
Total: 255, 87% full-time, 94% with terminal degrees.

Student/faculty ratio: 8:1.

ACADEMICS
Calendar: 4-1-4. *Degree:* bachelor's.

Special study options: advanced placement credit, cooperative education, double majors, English as a second language, honors programs, independent study, internships, off-campus study, part-time degree program, services for LD students, student-designed majors, study abroad. ***ROTC:*** Army (c), Air Force (c).

Unusual degree programs: 3-2 engineering with Columbia University, Washington University in St. Louis.

Computers: Students can access the following: campus intranet, computer help desk, free student e-mail accounts, online (class) grades, online (class) registration, online (class) schedules. Campuswide network is available. 100% of college-owned or -operated housing units are wired for high-speed Internet access. Wireless service is available via entire campus.
Library: Roy O. West Library plus 2 others. Study areas open 24 hours, 5–7 days a week; students can reserve study rooms.

STUDENT LIFE
Housing options: on-campus residence required through senior year; coed, special housing for students with disabilities. Campus housing is university owned. Freshman campus housing is guaranteed.

Activities and organizations: drama/theater group, student-run newspaper, radio and television station, choral group, national fraternities, national sororities.

Athletics Member NCAA. All Division III. ***Intercollegiate sports:*** baseball M, basketball M/W, cheerleading M(c)/W(c), crew M(c)/W(c), cross-country running M/W, field hockey W, football M, golf M/W, lacrosse M/W, rugby M(c), soccer M/W, softball W, swimming and diving M/W, tennis M/W, track and field M/W, volleyball W. ***Intramural sports:*** badminton M/W, basketball M/W, bowling M/W, football M/W, golf M, racquetball M/W, soccer M/W, softball M/W, table tennis M/W, tennis M/W, ultimate Frisbee M/W, volleyball M/W.

Campus security: 24-hour emergency response devices and patrols, student patrols, late-night transport/escort service, controlled dormitory access.

Student services: health clinic, personal/psychological counseling, women's center.

COSTS & FINANCIAL AID
Costs (2020–21) ***Comprehensive fee:*** $66,498 includes full-time tuition ($52,710) and room and board ($13,788). Part-time tuition: $1617 per credit hour. ***Room and board:*** Room and board charges vary according to board plan. ***Payment plan:*** installment. ***Waivers:*** employees or children of employees.

Financial Aid Of all full-time matriculated undergraduates who enrolled in 2019, 1,325 applied for aid, 1,154 were judged to have need, 318 had their need fully met. In 2019, 729 non-need-based awards were made. ***Average percent of need met:*** 89. ***Average financial aid package:*** $44,766. ***Average need-based loan:*** $4439. ***Average need-based gift aid:*** $40,242. ***Average non-need-based aid:*** $25,101. ***Average indebtedness upon graduation:*** $25,904. ***Financial aid deadline:*** 2/1.

APPLYING
Standardized Tests *Required:* SAT or ACT (for admission).

Options: electronic application, early decision, early action, deferred entrance.

Required: essay or personal statement, high school transcript, 1 letter of recommendation. ***Recommended:*** interview.

Application deadlines: 2/1 (freshmen), 3/1 (transfers), 12/1 (early action).

Early decision deadline: 11/15 (for plan 1), 1/15 (for plan 2).

Notification: continuous until 12/1 (freshmen), continuous (out-of-state freshmen), 4/1 (transfers), 12/1 (early decision plan 1), 2/1 (early decision plan 2), 1/15 (early action).

CONTACT
Ms. Rachel Schmidtke, Director of Recruitment, DePauw University, 204 East Seminary Street, Greencastle, IN 46135. *Phone:* 765-658-4104. *Toll-free phone:* 800-447-2495. *Fax:* 765-658-4007. *E-mail:* rachelschmidtke@depauw.edu.

Earlham College

Richmond, Indiana

http://www.earlham.edu/

- **Independent** comprehensive, founded 1847, affiliated with Society of Friends
- **Small-town** 800-acre campus with easy access to Cincinnati, Indianapolis, Dayton
- **Endowment** $425.4 million
- **Coed** 957 undergraduate students, 99% full-time, 57% women, 43% men
- **Very difficult** entrance level, 63% of applicants were admitted

UNDERGRAD STUDENTS
948 full-time, 9 part-time. 90% are from out of state; 7% Black or African American, non-Hispanic/Latino; 8% Hispanic/Latino; 4% Asian, non-Hispanic/Latino; 5% Two or more races, non-Hispanic/Latino; 2% Race/ethnicity unknown; 23% international; 0.9% transferred in; 95% live on campus.

Freshmen:
Admission: 2,070 applied, 1,313 admitted, 172 enrolled. ***Average high school GPA:*** 3.6. ***Test scores:*** SAT evidence-based reading and writing scores over 500: 89%; SAT math scores over 500: 95%; ACT scores over 18: 97%; SAT evidence-based reading and writing scores over 600: 56%; SAT math scores over 600: 58%; ACT scores over 24: 69%; SAT evidence-based reading and writing scores over 700: 21%; SAT math scores over 700: 16%; ACT scores over 30: 26%.

Retention: 80% of full-time freshmen returned.

FACULTY
Total: 105, 90% full-time, 91% with terminal degrees.

Student/faculty ratio: 10:1.

ACADEMICS
Calendar: semesters. *Degrees:* bachelor's, master's, and postbachelor's certificates.

Special study options: double majors, English as a second language, honors programs, independent study, internships, off-campus study, services for LD students, student-designed majors, study abroad.

Unusual degree programs: 3-2 engineering with Columbia University, University of Minnesota, Rensselaer Polytechnic Institute.

Computers: 266 computers/terminals are available on campus for general student use. Students can access the following: campus intranet, computer help desk, free student e-mail accounts, online (class) grades, online (class) registration, online (class) schedules. Campuswide network is available. 100% of college-owned or -operated housing units are wired for high-speed Internet access. Wireless service is available via entire campus.

Library: Lilly Library plus 1 other. *Books:* 329,649 (physical), 1.9 million (digital/electronic); *Databases:* 169. Students can reserve study rooms.

STUDENT LIFE

Housing options: on-campus residence required through senior year; coed, men-only, women-only, cooperative, special housing for students with disabilities. Campus housing is university owned. Freshman campus housing is guaranteed.

Activities and organizations: drama/theater group, student-run newspaper, radio station, choral group, Gospel Revelations Chorus, Dance Alloy, club sports, Student Government, Black Student Union.

Athletics Member NCAA, NAIA. All NCAA Division III. ***Intercollegiate sports:*** baseball M, basketball M/W, cross-country running W, equestrian sports M(c), field hockey W, golf M, lacrosse M/W, soccer M/W, tennis M/W, track and field M/W, volleyball W. ***Intramural sports:*** basketball M, bowling M, cross-country running M(c), equestrian sports W, racquetball M, rock climbing M/W, rugby M/W, soccer M, ultimate Frisbee M/W, volleyball M.

Campus security: 24-hour emergency response devices and patrols, student patrols, late-night transport/escort service, controlled dormitory access.

Student services: health clinic, personal/psychological counseling, women's center.

COSTS & FINANCIAL AID

Costs (2020–21) ***Tuition:*** $47,106 full-time. ***Required fees:*** $985 full-time. ***Room only:*** $6020. Room and board charges vary according to board plan. ***Payment plans:*** installment, deferred payment. ***Waivers:*** employees or children of employees.

Financial Aid Of all full-time matriculated undergraduates who enrolled in 2018, 941 applied for aid, 896 were judged to have need, 462 had their need fully met. In 2018, 125 non-need-based awards were made. ***Average percent of need met:*** 93. ***Average financial aid package:*** $40,435. ***Average need-based loan:*** $4275. ***Average need-based gift aid:*** $34,312. ***Average non-need-based aid:*** $24,726. ***Average indebtedness upon graduation:*** $26,103.

APPLYING

Standardized Tests *Required for some:* SAT or ACT (for admission).

Options: electronic application, early action, deferred entrance.

Required: essay or personal statement, high school transcript, 2 letters of recommendation. ***Recommended:*** minimum 3.0 GPA, interview.

Application deadlines: 2/15 (freshmen), 4/1 (transfers), 1/1 (early action).

Early decision deadline: 11/15.

Notification: 4/1 (freshmen), continuous until 5/1 (transfers), 12/15 (early decision), 2/1 (early action).

CONTACT

Susan Hillmann de Castaneda, Director of Admissions, Earlham College, 801 National Road West, Richmond, IN 47374. *Phone:* 765-983-1600. *Toll-free phone:* 800-327-5426. *Fax:* 765-983-1560. *E-mail:* admission@earlham.edu.

Franklin College

Franklin, Indiana

http://www.franklincollege.edu/

- **Independent** comprehensive, founded 1834, affiliated with American Baptist Churches in the U.S.A.
- **Suburban** 207-acre campus with easy access to Indianapolis
- **Endowment** $84.6 million
- **Coed** 1,016 undergraduate students, 95% full-time, 52% women, 48% men
- **Moderately difficult** entrance level, 62% of applicants were admitted

UNDERGRAD STUDENTS

962 full-time, 54 part-time. Students come from 17 states and territories; 3 other countries; 7% are from out of state; 3% transferred in; 69% live on campus.

Freshmen:

Admission: 2,301 applied, 1,418 admitted, 267 enrolled. ***Average high school GPA:*** 3.5.

Retention: 76% of full-time freshmen returned.

ACADEMICS

Calendar: 4-1-4. *Degrees:* bachelor's and master's.

Special study options: academic remediation for entering students, advanced placement credit, cooperative education, double majors, English as a second language, independent study, internships, off-campus study, part-time degree program, services for LD students, student-designed majors, study abroad, summer session for credit. ***ROTC:*** Army (c).

Unusual degree programs: 3-2 engineering with Indiana University–Purdue University Indianapolis; athletic training with Franklin College, public health with Indiana University-Purdue University Indianapolis.

Computers: 150 computers/terminals are available on campus for general student use. Students can access the following: campus intranet, computer help desk, free student e-mail accounts, online (class) grades, online (class) registration, online (class) schedules. Campuswide network is available. 100% of college-owned or -operated housing units are wired for high-speed Internet access. Wireless service is available via classrooms, computer centers, computer labs, dorm rooms, learning centers, libraries, student centers.

Library: Hamilton Library. Weekly public service hours: 83; students can reserve study rooms.

STUDENT LIFE

Housing options: on-campus residence required through junior year; coed, men-only, women-only, special housing for students with disabilities. Campus housing is university owned. Freshman campus housing is guaranteed.

Activities and organizations: drama/theater group, student-run newspaper, radio station, choral group, Student Entertainment Board, Student Congress, FC Volunteers, national fraternities, national sororities.

Athletics ***Intercollegiate sports:*** baseball M, basketball M/W, cheerleading W(c), cross-country running M/W, football M, golf M/W, lacrosse W, soccer M/W, softball W, swimming and diving M/W, tennis M/W, track and field M/W, volleyball W. ***Intramural sports:*** basketball M/W.

Campus security: 24-hour emergency response devices and patrols, student patrols, late-night transport/escort service, controlled dormitory access.

Student services: health clinic, personal/psychological counseling.

COSTS & FINANCIAL AID

Costs (2020–21) ***Comprehensive fee:*** $44,500 includes full-time tuition ($33,754), mandatory fees ($200), and room and board ($10,546). Full-time tuition and fees vary according to course load and degree level. Part-time tuition: $485 per credit hour. Part-time tuition and fees vary according to course load and degree level. ***Required fees:*** $7 per credit hour part-time. ***College room only:*** $6026. Room and board charges vary according to board plan. ***Payment plan:*** installment. ***Waivers:*** senior citizens and employees or children of employees.

Financial Aid Of all full-time matriculated undergraduates who enrolled in 2018, 859 applied for aid, 765 were judged to have need, 110 had their need fully met. In 2018, 140 non-need-based awards were made. ***Average percent of need met:*** 73. ***Average financial aid package:*** $24,966. ***Average need-based loan:*** $3797. ***Average need-based gift aid:*** $22,097. ***Average non-need-based aid:*** $15,277. ***Average indebtedness upon graduation:*** $38,057.

APPLYING

Standardized Tests *Required:* SAT or ACT (for admission).

Options: electronic application, deferred entrance.

Application fee: $40.

Required: high school transcript. ***Required for some:*** interview. ***Recommended:*** essay or personal statement.

Application deadlines: rolling (freshmen), rolling (transfers).

Notification: continuous (freshmen), continuous (transfers).

CONTACT
Ms. Tara Evans, Director of Admissions, Franklin College, 101 Branigin Boulevard, Franklin, IN 46131-2623. *Phone:* 317-738-8075. *Toll-free phone:* 800-852-0232. *Fax:* 317-738-8075. *E-mail:* admissions@franklincollege.edu.

Goshen College

Goshen, Indiana

http://www.goshen.edu/

- **Independent Mennonite** comprehensive, founded 1894
- **Small-town** 135-acre campus
- **Endowment** $113.6 million
- **Coed** 826 undergraduate students, 91% full-time, 62% women, 38% men
- **Moderately difficult** entrance level, 65% of applicants were admitted

UNDERGRAD STUDENTS
751 full-time, 75 part-time. Students come from 37 states and territories; 25 other countries; 36% are from out of state; 4% Black or African American, non-Hispanic/Latino; 24% Hispanic/Latino; 2% Asian, non-Hispanic/Latino; 0.2% Native Hawaiian or other Pacific Islander, non Hispanic/Latino; 2% Two or more races, non-Hispanic/Latino; 2% Race/ethnicity unknown; 7% international; 8% transferred in; 57% live on campus.

Freshmen:
Admission: 1,278 applied, 827 admitted, 160 enrolled. ***Average high school GPA:*** 3.6. ***Test scores:*** SAT evidence-based reading and writing scores over 500: 76%; SAT math scores over 500: 80%; ACT scores over 18: 100%; SAT evidence-based reading and writing scores over 600: 28%; SAT math scores over 600: 30%; ACT scores over 24: 56%; SAT evidence-based reading and writing scores over 700: 11%; SAT math scores over 700: 7%; ACT scores over 30: 24%.

Retention: 76% of full-time freshmen returned.

FACULTY
Total: 110, 55% full-time, 47% with terminal degrees.

Student/faculty ratio: 10:1.

ACADEMICS
Calendar: semesters. *Degrees:* bachelor's, master's, and doctoral.

Special study options: academic remediation for entering students, accelerated degree program, adult/continuing education programs, advanced placement credit, distance learning, double majors, independent study, internships, off-campus study, part-time degree program, services for LD students, student-designed majors, study abroad, summer session for credit.

Unusual degree programs: 3-2 engineering with Case Western Reserve University, University of Illinois at Urbana–Champaign, University of Notre Dame, Washington University in St. Louis.

Computers: 160 computers/terminals and 2,000 ports are available on campus for general student use. Students can access the following: campus intranet, computer help desk, free student e-mail accounts, online (class) grades, online (class) registration, online (class) schedules. Campuswide network is available. 100% of college-owned or -operated housing units are wired for high-speed Internet access. Wireless service is available via entire campus.

Library: The Harold and Wilma Good Library plus 1 other. *Books:* 188,371 (physical), 243,626 (digital/electronic); *Serial titles:* 3,196 (physical), 13,072 (digital/electronic); *Databases:* 72. Weekly public service hours: 89; students can reserve study rooms.

STUDENT LIFE
Housing options: on-campus residence required through junior year; coed, men-only, women-only, special housing for students with disabilities. Campus housing is university owned. Freshman campus housing is guaranteed.

Activities and organizations: drama/theater group, student-run newspaper, radio and television station, choral group, International Student Club, Latino Student Union, PAX - Peace Club, Goshen Student Women's Organization, Business Club.

Athletics *Intercollegiate sports:* baseball M(s), basketball M(s)/W(s), cross-country running M(s)/W(s), golf M(s), soccer M(s)/W(s), softball W(s), tennis M(s)/W(s), track and field M(s)/W(s), volleyball M(s)/W(s). ***Intramural sports:*** badminton M/W, basketball M/W, racquetball M/W, soccer M/W, softball W, table tennis M/W, tennis M/W, ultimate Frisbee M/W, volleyball M/W.

Campus security: 24-hour emergency response devices and patrols, late-night transport/escort service, controlled dormitory access.

Student services: health clinic, personal/psychological counseling.

COSTS & FINANCIAL AID
Costs (2020–21) *Comprehensive fee:* $46,100 includes full-time tuition ($35,230) and room and board ($10,870). Part-time tuition: $1425 per credit hour. ***College room only:*** $5870. Room and board charges vary according to board plan and housing facility. ***Payment plan:*** installment. ***Waivers:*** employees or children of employees.

Financial Aid Of all full-time matriculated undergraduates who enrolled in 2019, 624 applied for aid, 572 were judged to have need, 114 had their need fully met. 351 Federal Work-Study jobs (averaging $1124). 52 state and other part-time jobs (averaging $1725). In 2019, 176 non-need-based awards were made. ***Average percent of need met:*** 82. ***Average financial aid package:*** $29,993. ***Average need-based loan:*** $4915. ***Average need-based gift aid:*** $25,573. ***Average non-need-based aid:*** $16,789. ***Average indebtedness upon graduation:*** $28,693.

APPLYING
Standardized Tests *Required:* SAT or ACT (for admission).

Options: electronic application, deferred entrance.

Required: minimum 2.0 GPA. ***Required for some:*** essay or personal statement, high school transcript. ***Recommended:*** minimum 2.8 GPA, 1 letter of recommendation, interview.

Application deadlines: 7/15 (freshmen), 8/15 (transfers).

Notification: continuous (freshmen), continuous (transfers).

CONTACT
Ms. Linda VandenBosch, Director of Admissions, Goshen College, 1700 S Main St, Goshen, IN 46526. *Phone:* 574-5357535. *Toll-free phone:* 800-348-7422. *E-mail:* admissions@goshen.edu.

Grace College

Winona Lake, Indiana

http://www.grace.edu/

CONTACT
Mrs. Nikki Sproul, Admissions Office, Grace College, 200 Seminary Drive, Winona Lake, IN 46590. *Phone:* 574-372-5100 Ext. 6008. *Toll-free phone:* 800-54-GRACE. *Fax:* 574-372-5120. *E-mail:* enroll@grace.edu.

Hanover College

Hanover, Indiana

http://www.hanover.edu/

- **Independent Presbyterian** 4-year, founded 1827
- **Rural** 630-acre campus with easy access to Louisville
- **Endowment** $146.1 million
- **Coed** 1,070 undergraduate students, 100% full-time, 56% women, 44% men
- **Moderately difficult** entrance level, 65% of applicants were admitted

UNDERGRAD STUDENTS
1,065 full-time, 5 part-time. Students come from 19 states and territories; 14 other countries; 33% are from out of state; 5% Black or African American, non-Hispanic/Latino; 3% Hispanic/Latino; 0.7% Asian, non-Hispanic/Latino; 0.3% Native Hawaiian or other Pacific Islander, non-Hispanic/Latino; 0.4% American Indian or Alaska Native, non-Hispanic/Latino; 3% Two or more races, non-Hispanic/Latino; 10% Race/ethnicity unknown; 3% international; 1% transferred in; 93% live on campus.

Freshmen:
Admission: 3,127 applied, 2,027 admitted, 290 enrolled. ***Average high school GPA:*** 3.7. ***Test scores:*** SAT evidence-based reading and writing scores over 500: 84%; SAT math scores over 500: 81%; ACT scores over 18: 92%; SAT evidence-based reading and writing scores over 600: 36%; SAT math scores over 600: 36%; ACT scores over 24: 50%; SAT

evidence-based reading and writing scores over 700: 6%; SAT math scores over 700: 5%; ACT scores over 30: 9%.

Retention: 79% of full-time freshmen returned.

FACULTY

Total: 98, 86% full-time, 90% with terminal degrees.

Student/faculty ratio: 12:1.

ACADEMICS

Calendar: 4-4-1. *Degree:* bachelor's.

Special study options: advanced placement credit, cooperative education, distance learning, double majors, independent study, internships, off campus study, services for LD students, student-designed majors, study abroad, summer session for credit.

Unusual degree programs: 3-2 nursing.

Computers: 120 computers/terminals and 1,550 ports are available on campus for general student use. Students can access the following: campus intranet, computer help desk, free student e-mail accounts, online (class) grades, online (class) registration, online (class) schedules. Campuswide network is available. 100% of college-owned or -operated housing units are wired for high-speed Internet access. Wireless service is available via entire campus.

Library: Duggan Library. *Books:* 196,284 (physical), 213,376 (digital/electronic); *Serial titles:* 6,584 (physical), 183,744 (digital/electronic); *Databases:* 117. Students can reserve study rooms.

STUDENT LIFE

Housing options: on-campus residence required through senior year; coed, men-only, women-only. Campus housing is university owned. Freshman campus housing is guaranteed.

Activities and organizations: drama/theater group, student-run newspaper, radio and television station, choral group, marching band, Delight Ministries, Alpha Lambda Delta, Love Out Loud, Art Club, International Club, national fraternities, national sororities.

Athletics Member NCAA. All Division III. ***Intercollegiate sports:*** baseball M, basketball M/W, cross-country running M/W, football M, golf M/W, lacrosse M/W, soccer M/W, softball W, swimming and diving M/W, tennis M/W, track and field M/W, volleyball W. ***Intramural sports:*** archery W(c), basketball M/W, football M/W, rugby M(c)/W(c), soccer M/W, softball M/W, ultimate Frisbee M(c), volleyball M/W.

Campus security: 24-hour emergency response devices and patrols, late-night transport/escort service, controlled dormitory access.

Student services: health clinic, personal/psychological counseling.

COSTS & FINANCIAL AID

Costs (2020–21) ***One-time required fee:*** $350. ***Comprehensive fee:*** $51,950 includes full-time tuition ($38,880), mandatory fees ($770), and room and board ($12,300). Part-time tuition: $1080 per credit hour. ***College room only:*** $6125. ***Waivers:*** senior citizens and employees or children of employees.

Financial Aid Of all full-time matriculated undergraduates who enrolled in 2018, 943 applied for aid, 852 were judged to have need, 256 had their need fully met. 378 Federal Work-Study jobs (averaging $1914). In 2018, 238 non-need-based awards were made. ***Average percent of need met:*** 83. ***Average financial aid package:*** $32,942. ***Average need-based loan:*** $4270. ***Average need-based gift aid:*** $28,617. ***Average non-need-based aid:*** $23,696. ***Average indebtedness upon graduation:*** $29,190.

APPLYING

Standardized Tests *Required for some:* SAT or ACT (for admission).

Options: electronic application, early action, deferred entrance.

Required: essay or personal statement, high school transcript, 1 letter of recommendation. ***Recommended:*** interview.

Application deadlines: rolling (freshmen), rolling (transfers).

Notification: continuous until 9/1 (freshmen), continuous (transfers).

CONTACT

Ms. Angela Jackinowski, Application Specialist, Hanover College, 517 Ball Drive, Hanover, IN 47243. *Phone:* 812-866-7023. *Toll-free phone:* 800-213-2178. *Fax:* 812-866-7098. *E-mail:* admission@hanover.edu.

Holy Cross College

Notre Dame, Indiana

http://www.hcc-nd.edu/

CONTACT

Holy Cross College, 54515 SR 933 N., PO Box 308, Notre Dame, IN 46556. *Phone:* 574-239-8338. *E-mail:* admissions@hcc-nd.edu.

Horizon University

Indianapolis, Indiana

http://www.horizonuniversity.edu/

CONTACT

Horizon University, 7700 Indian Lake Road, Indianapolis, IN 46236. *Toll-free phone:* 800-553-HORIZON.

Huntington University

Huntington, Indiana

http://www.huntington.edu/

CONTACT

Huntington University, 2303 College Avenue, Huntington, IN 46750-1299. *Phone:* 260-356-6000. *Toll-free phone:* 800-642-6493.

Indiana State University

Terre Haute, Indiana

http://www.indstate.edu/

- **State-supported** university, founded 1865
- **Small-town** 435-acre campus with easy access to Indianapolis
- **Endowment** $46.9 million
- **Coed** 10,216 undergraduate students, 79% full-time, 56% women, 44% men
- **Moderately difficult** entrance level, 90% of applicants were admitted

UNDERGRAD STUDENTS

8,105 full-time, 2,111 part-time. Students come from 51 states and territories; 52 other countries; 28% are from out of state; 18% Black or African American, non-Hispanic/Latino; 5% Hispanic/Latino; 1% Asian, non-Hispanic/Latino; 0.1% Native Hawaiian or other Pacific Islander, non-Hispanic/Latino; 0.3% American Indian or Alaska Native, non-Hispanic/Latino; 4% Two or more races, non-Hispanic/Latino; 0.5% Race/ethnicity unknown; 2% international; 8% transferred in; 30% live on campus.

Freshmen:

Admission: 10,008 applied, 8,964 admitted, 1,893 enrolled. ***Average high school GPA:*** 3.2.

Retention: 65% of full-time freshmen returned.

FACULTY

Total: 692, 68% full-time, 64% with terminal degrees.

Student/faculty ratio: 18:1.

ACADEMICS

Calendar: semesters. *Degrees:* certificates, bachelor's, master's, doctoral, post-master's, and postbachelor's certificates.

Special study options: academic remediation for entering students, accelerated degree program, adult/continuing education programs, advanced placement credit, cooperative education, distance learning, double majors, English as a second language, freshman honors college, honors programs, independent study, internships, off-campus study, part-time degree program, services for LD students, study abroad, summer session for credit. ***ROTC:*** Army (b), Air Force (b).

Computers: 170 computers/terminals are available on campus for general student use. Students can access the following: campus intranet, computer help desk, free student e-mail accounts, online (class) grades, online (class) registration, online (class) schedules. Campuswide network is available. 100% of college-owned or -operated housing units are wired for high-speed Internet access. Wireless service is available via entire campus.

Library: Cunningham Memorial Library plus 1 other. *Books:* 1.1 million (physical), 818,526 (digital/electronic); *Serial titles:* 66,830 (physical),

95,614 (digital/electronic); *Databases:* 362. Weekly public service hours: 132; study areas open 24 hours, 5–7 days a week; students can reserve study rooms.

STUDENT LIFE

Housing options: on-campus residence required for freshman year; coed, special housing for students with disabilities. Campus housing is university owned. Freshman campus housing is guaranteed.

Activities and organizations: drama/theater group, student-run newspaper, radio station, choral group, marching band, Student Government Association, Interfraternity Council (fraternities), Panhellenic Association (sororities), Residence Hall Association, Union Board, national fraternities, national sororities.

Athletics Member NCAA. All Division I except football (Division I-AA). ***Intercollegiate sports:*** baseball M(s), basketball M(s)/W(s), cross-country running M(s)/W(s), golf W(s), soccer W(s), softball W(s), swimming and diving W(s), track and field M(s)/W(s), volleyball W(s). ***Intramural sports:*** badminton M/W, basketball M/W, bowling M(c)/W(c), rugby M(c), sand volleyball M/W, soccer M/W, softball M/W, swimming and diving M(c)/W(c), tennis M/W, ultimate Frisbee M/W, volleyball M/W, weight lifting M(c)/W(c), wrestling M(c)/W(c).

Campus security: 24-hour emergency response devices and patrols, student patrols, late-night transport/escort service, RAVE Campus Alert Emails/Texts; Workshops and Video Training; Motorist Assistance; Other Education Opportunities;.

Student services: health clinic, personal/psychological counseling, women's center, veterans affairs office.

COSTS & FINANCIAL AID

Costs (2020–21) ***Tuition:*** area resident $9186 full-time, $332 per credit hour part-time; state resident $9186 full-time, $332 per credit hour part-time; nonresident $20,290 full-time, $717 per credit hour part-time. Full-time tuition and fees vary according to reciprocity agreements. Part-time tuition and fees vary according to course load and reciprocity agreements. ***Required fees:*** $280 full-time, $140 per term part-time. ***Room and board:*** $11,016; room only: $7237. Room and board charges vary according to board plan, housing facility, and student level. ***Payment plans:*** installment, deferred payment. ***Waivers:*** senior citizens and employees or children of employees.

Financial Aid Of all full-time matriculated undergraduates who enrolled in 2018, 7,836 applied for aid, 6,717 were judged to have need, 647 had their need fully met. 1,086 Federal Work-Study jobs (averaging $2110). In 2018, 773 non-need-based awards were made. ***Average percent of need met:*** 80. ***Average financial aid package:*** $11,089. ***Average need-based loan:*** $3797. ***Average need-based gift aid:*** $6554. ***Average non-need-based aid:*** $5205. ***Average indebtedness upon graduation:*** $26,223.

APPLYING

Options: electronic application, deferred entrance.

Application fee: $25.

Required: high school transcript. ***Required for some:*** interview. ***Recommended:*** minimum 2.5 GPA.

Application deadlines: rolling (freshmen), rolling (out-of-state freshmen), rolling (transfers).

Notification: continuous (freshmen), continuous (transfers).

CONTACT

Mr. Richard Toomey, Assistant Vice President of Enrollment Management, Indiana State University, 318 North Sixth Street, John W. Moore Welcome Center, Terre Haute, IN 47809-9989. *Phone:* 812-237-2121. *Toll-free phone:* 800-468-6478. *Fax:* 812-237-8023. *E-mail:* admissions@indstate.edu.

Indiana Tech

Fort Wayne, Indiana

http://www.indianatech.edu/

CONTACT

Mr. Robert Confer, Director of Admissions, Indiana Tech, 1600 East Washington Boulevard, Fort Wayne, IN 46803. *Phone:* 260-422-5561 Ext. 2424. *Toll-free phone:* 800-937-2448. *Fax:* 260-422-7696. *E-mail:* admissions@indianatech.edu.

Indiana University Bloomington

Bloomington, Indiana

http://www.iub.edu/

- **State-supported** university, founded 1820, part of Indiana University System
- **Small-town** 1939-acre campus with easy access to Indianapolis
- **Endowment** $1.4 billion
- **Coed** 33,084 undergraduate students, 97% full-time, 49% women, 51% men
- **Moderately difficult** entrance level, 78% of applicants were admitted

UNDERGRAD STUDENTS

31,981 full-time, 1,103 part-time. Students come from 54 states and territories; 140 other countries; 36% are from out of state; 5% Black or African American, non-Hispanic/Latino; 7% Hispanic/Latino; 6% Asian, non-Hispanic/Latino; 0.1% American Indian or Alaska Native, non-Hispanic/Latino; 5% Two or more races, non-Hispanic/Latino; 0.3% Race/ethnicity unknown; 8% international; 2% transferred in; 33% live on campus.

Freshmen:

Admission: 12,902 applied, 33,125 admitted, 8,291 enrolled. ***Average high school GPA:*** 3.7. ***Test scores:*** SAT evidence-based reading and writing scores over 500: 96%; SAT math scores over 500: 97%; ACT scores over 18: 98%; SAT evidence-based reading and writing scores over 600: 65%; SAT math scores over 600: 65%; ACT scores over 24: 79%; SAT evidence-based reading and writing scores over 700: 15%; SAT math scores over 700: 24%; ACT scores over 30: 39%.

Retention: 90% of full-time freshmen returned.

FACULTY

Total: 2,495, 86% full-time, 81% with terminal degrees.

Student/faculty ratio: 17:1.

ACADEMICS

Calendar: semesters plus summer sessions. *Degrees:* certificates, diplomas, associate, bachelor's, master's, doctoral, post-master's, and postbachelor's certificates.

Special study options: academic remediation for entering students, accelerated degree program, adult/continuing education programs, advanced placement credit, cooperative education, distance learning, double majors, English as a second language, external degree program, freshman honors college, honors programs, independent study, internships, off-campus study, part-time degree program, services for LD students, student-designed majors, study abroad, summer session for credit. ***ROTC:*** Army (b), Air Force (b).

Unusual degree programs: 3-2 business administration.

Computers: 2,150 computers/terminals are available on campus for general student use. Students can access the following: campus intranet, computer help desk, free student e-mail accounts, online (class) grades, online (class) registration, online (class) schedules. Campuswide network is available. 95% of college-owned or -operated housing units are wired for high-speed Internet access. Wireless service is available via entire campus.

Library: Indiana University Library plus 16 others. *Books:* 4.7 million (physical), 2.2 million (digital/electronic); *Serial titles:* 153,391 (physical), 220,794 (digital/electronic); *Databases:* 1,962. Study areas open 24 hours, 5–7 days a week; students can reserve study rooms.

STUDENT LIFE

Housing options: on-campus residence required for freshman year; coed, men-only, women-only, cooperative, special housing for students with disabilities. Campus housing is university owned. Freshman campus housing is guaranteed.

Activities and organizations: drama/theater group, student-run newspaper, radio and television station, choral group, marching band, Union Board, Student Association, Student Foundation, Habitat for Humanity, Student Athletic Board, national fraternities, national sororities.

Athletics Member NCAA. All Division I. ***Intercollegiate sports:*** baseball M(s), basketball M(s)/W(s), cross-country running M(s)/W(s), field hockey W, football M(s), golf M(s)/W(s), rowing W(s), soccer M(s)/W(s), softball W(s), swimming and diving M(s)/W(s), tennis M(s)/W(s), track and field M(s)/W(s), volleyball W(s), water polo W(s), wrestling M(s).

Intramural sports: badminton M(c)/W(c), baseball M(c)/W(c), basketball M/W, equestrian sports M(c)/W(c), fencing M(c)/W(c), field hockey M(c)/W(c), gymnastics M(c)/W(c), ice hockey M(c)/W(c), lacrosse M(c)/W(c), racquetball M/W, rugby M(c)/W(c), sailing M(c)/W(c), soccer M/W, softball M/W, swimming and diving M(c)/W(c), table tennis M/W, tennis M/W, track and field M/W, ultimate Frisbee M/W, volleyball M/W, water polo M(c).

Campus security: 24-hour emergency response devices and patrols, late-night transport/escort service.

Student services: health clinic, personal/psychological counseling, women's center, legal services, veterans affairs office.

COSTS & FINANCIAL AID

Costs (2020–21) ***Tuition:*** area resident $9575 full-time, $299 per credit hour part-time; state resident $9575 full-time, $299 per credit hour part-time; nonresident $35,140 full-time, $1098 per credit hour part-time. Full-time tuition and fees vary according to program. Part-time tuition and fees vary according to course load and program. ***Required fees:*** $1372 full-time. ***Room and board:*** $10,830. Room and board charges vary according to board plan and housing facility. ***Payment plans:*** installment, deferred payment. ***Waivers:*** senior citizens and employees or children of employees.

Financial Aid Of all full-time matriculated undergraduates who enrolled in 2018, 19,207 applied for aid, 13,106 were judged to have need, 3,755 had their need fully met. 633 Federal Work-Study jobs (averaging $1863). In 2018, 8968 non-need-based awards were made. ***Average percent of need met:*** 71. ***Average financial aid package:*** $14,196. ***Average need-based loan:*** $3934. ***Average need-based gift aid:*** $12,679. ***Average non-need-based aid:*** $7761. ***Average indebtedness upon graduation:*** $27,555.

APPLYING

Standardized Tests *Required:* SAT or ACT (for admission). *Recommended:* SAT Subject Tests (for admission).

Options: electronic application, early action, deferred entrance.

Application fee: $65.

Required: essay or personal statement, high school transcript.

Application deadlines: rolling (freshmen), rolling (transfers), 11/1 (early action).

Notification: continuous until 1/15 (freshmen), continuous (transfers), 1/15 (early action).

CONTACT

Ms. Sacha Thieme, Executive Director of Admissions, Indiana University Bloomington, 940 E. Seventh Street, Bloomington, IN 47405. *Phone:* 812-855-0661. *Fax:* 812-855-5102. *E-mail:* iuadmit@indiana.edu.

Indiana University East

Richmond, Indiana

http://www.iue.edu/

- **State-supported** comprehensive, founded 1971, part of Indiana University System
- **Small-town** 182-acre campus with easy access to Indianapolis
- **Endowment** $5.7 million
- **Coed** 3,500 undergraduate students, 58% full-time, 64% women, 36% men
- **Moderately difficult** entrance level, 63% of applicants were admitted

UNDERGRAD STUDENTS

2,031 full-time, 1,469 part-time. Students come from 51 states and territories; 54 other countries; 28% are from out of state; 5% Black or African American, non-Hispanic/Latino; 4% Hispanic/Latino; 1% Asian, non-Hispanic/Latino; 0.1% Native Hawaiian or other Pacific Islander, non-Hispanic/Latino; 0.2% American Indian or Alaska Native, non-Hispanic/Latino; 4% Two or more races, non-Hispanic/Latino; 8% Race/ethnicity unknown; 2% international; 12% transferred in.

Freshmen:

Admission: 2,316 applied, 1,448 admitted, 451 enrolled. ***Average high school GPA:*** 3.3. ***Test scores:*** SAT evidence-based reading and writing scores over 500: 68%; SAT math scores over 500: 61%; ACT scores over 18: 74%; SAT evidence-based reading and writing scores over 600: 17%; SAT math scores over 600: 13%; ACT scores over 24: 20%; SAT evidence-based reading and writing scores over 700: 2%; SAT math scores over 700: 2%; ACT scores over 30: 2%.

Retention: 63% of full-time freshmen returned.

FACULTY

Total: 287, 39% full-time, 48% with terminal degrees.

Student/faculty ratio: 15:1.

ACADEMICS

Calendar: semesters. *Degrees:* certificates, bachelor's, master's, and postbachelor's certificates.

Special study options: academic remediation for entering students, accelerated degree program, adult/continuing education programs, advanced placement credit, cooperative education, distance learning, double majors, external degree program, honors programs, independent study, internships, off-campus study, part-time degree program, services for LD students, study abroad, summer session for credit.

Computers: 196 computers/terminals are available on campus for general student use. Students can access the following: free student e-mail accounts, online (class) grades, online (class) registration, online (class) schedules. Campuswide network is available. Wireless service is available via entire campus.

Library: IU East Campus Library. *Books:* 20,114 (physical), 195,430 (digital/electronic); *Serial titles:* 2 (physical), 114,075 (digital/electronic); *Databases:* 564. Students can reserve study rooms.

STUDENT LIFE

Housing options: college housing not available.

Activities and organizations: drama/theater group, student-run newspaper, television station, choral group, Student Government Association.

Athletics Member NAIA. ***Intercollegiate sports:*** basketball M/W, cross-country running M/W, golf M/W, soccer M/W, tennis M/W, track and field M/W, volleyball W.

Campus security: 24-hour emergency response devices, late-night transport/escort service.

Student services: personal/psychological counseling, veterans affairs office.

COSTS & FINANCIAL AID

Costs (2020–21) ***Tuition:*** state resident $6895 full-time, $230 per credit hour part-time; nonresident $19,346 full-time, $645 per credit hour part-time. Full-time tuition and fees vary according to program and reciprocity agreements. Part-time tuition and fees vary according to course load, program, and reciprocity agreements. ***Required fees:*** $632 full-time. ***Payment plans:*** installment, deferred payment. ***Waivers:*** senior citizens and employees or children of employees.

Financial Aid Of all full-time matriculated undergraduates who enrolled in 2018, 1,730 applied for aid, 1,472 were judged to have need, 271 had their need fully met. 52 Federal Work-Study jobs (averaging $2059). In 2018, 140 non-need-based awards were made. ***Average percent of need met:*** 69. ***Average financial aid package:*** $9366. ***Average need-based loan:*** $3660. ***Average need-based gift aid:*** $7837. ***Average non-need-based aid:*** $2485. ***Average indebtedness upon graduation:*** $22,513.

APPLYING

Standardized Tests *Required for some:* SAT or ACT (for admission).

Options: electronic application, early admission, deferred entrance.

Application fee: $35.

Required: high school transcript. ***Required for some:*** 1 letter of recommendation.

Application deadlines: rolling (freshmen), rolling (transfers).

Notification: continuous (freshmen), continuous (transfers).

CONTACT

Ms. Molly Vanderpool, Executive Director, Recruitment and Transitions, Admissions, Indiana University East, 2325 Chester Boulevard, Whitewater Hall 151, Richmond, IN 47374-1289. *Phone:* 765-973-8208. *Toll-free phone:* 800-959-EAST. *Fax:* 765-973-8209. *E-mail:* applynow@iue.edu.

Indiana University Kokomo

Kokomo, Indiana

http://www.iuk.edu/

- **State-supported** comprehensive, founded 1945, part of Indiana University System
- **Small-town** 51-acre campus with easy access to Indianapolis
- **Endowment** $6.6 million
- **Coed** 2,912 undergraduate students, 78% full-time, 64% women, 36% men
- **Minimally difficult** entrance level, 80% of applicants were admitted

UNDERGRAD STUDENTS
2,259 full-time, 653 part-time. Students come from 17 states and territories; 25 other countries; 2% are from out of state; 9% transferred in.

Freshmen:
Admission: 2,499 applied, 1,999 admitted, 639 enrolled. ***Average high school GPA:*** 3.3.

Retention: 60% of full-time freshmen returned.

ACADEMICS
Calendar: semesters. *Degrees:* certificates, associate, bachelor's, master's, and postbachelor's certificates.

Special study options: academic remediation for entering students, accelerated degree program, adult/continuing education programs, advanced placement credit, distance learning, double majors, English as a second language, external degree program, freshman honors college, honors programs, independent study, internships, part-time degree program, services for LD students, study abroad, summer session for credit.

Computers: 325 computers/terminals are available on campus for general student use. Students can access the following: campus intranet, computer help desk, free student e-mail accounts, online (class) grades, online (class) registration, online (class) schedules. Campuswide network is available. Wireless service is available via entire campus.
Library: IU Kokomo Library. Students can reserve study rooms.

STUDENT LIFE
Housing options: college housing not available.

Activities and organizations: drama/theater group, student-run newspaper, choral group, national sororities.

Athletics ***Intercollegiate sports:*** baseball M, basketball M/W, cross-country running M/W, golf M/W, soccer W, tennis W, track and field M/W, volleyball W.

Campus security: late-night transport/escort service.

Student services: personal/psychological counseling.

COSTS & FINANCIAL AID
Costs (2020–21) ***Tuition:*** state resident $6895 full-time, $230 per credit hour part-time; nonresident $19,346 full-time, $645 per credit hour part-time. Full-time tuition and fees vary according to program and reciprocity agreements. Part-time tuition and fees vary according to course load, program, and reciprocity agreements. ***Required fees:*** $632 full-time. ***Payment plans:*** installment, deferred payment. ***Waivers:*** senior citizens and employees or children of employees.

Financial Aid Of all full-time matriculated undergraduates who enrolled in 2018, 1,958 applied for aid, 1,553 were judged to have need, 235 had their need fully met. 69 Federal Work-Study jobs (averaging $1563). In 2018, 158 non-need-based awards were made. ***Average percent of need met:*** 67. ***Average financial aid package:*** $8934. ***Average need-based loan:*** $3519. ***Average need-based gift aid:*** $8061. ***Average non-need-based aid:*** $2336. ***Average indebtedness upon graduation:*** $23,518.

APPLYING
Standardized Tests *Required for some:* SAT or ACT (for admission).

Options: electronic application, deferred entrance.

Application fee: $35.

Notification: continuous (freshmen), continuous (transfers).

CONTACT
Ms. Angie Siders, Director of Admissions, Indiana University Kokomo, Kelley Student Center, Room 230, 2300 South Washington Street, Kokomo, IN 46904-9003. *Phone:* 765-455-9217. *Toll-free phone:* 888-875-4485. *Fax:* 765-455-9537. *E-mail:* iuadmis@iuk.edu.

Indiana University Northwest

Gary, Indiana

http://www.iun.edu/

- **State-supported** comprehensive, founded 1959, part of Indiana University System
- **Suburban** 43-acre campus with easy access to Chicago
- **Endowment** $10.3 million
- **Coed** 3,534 undergraduate students, 71% full-time, 70% women, 30% men
- **Minimally difficult** entrance level, 80% of applicants were admitted

UNDERGRAD STUDENTS
2,515 full-time, 1,019 part-time. Students come from 12 states and territories; 34 other countries; 3% are from out of state; 8% transferred in.

Freshmen:
Admission: 2,182 applied, 1,737 admitted, 674 enrolled. ***Average high school GPA:*** 3.0.

Retention: 66% of full-time freshmen returned.

ACADEMICS
Calendar: semesters. *Degrees:* certificates, associate, bachelor's, master's, and postbachelor's certificates.

Special study options: academic remediation for entering students, accelerated degree program, adult/continuing education programs, advanced placement credit, cooperative education, distance learning, double majors, external degree program, honors programs, independent study, internships, off-campus study, part-time degree program, services for LD students, student-designed majors, study abroad, summer session for credit. ***ROTC:*** Army (b).

Computers: 682 computers/terminals are available on campus for general student use. Students can access the following: campus intranet, computer help desk, free student e-mail accounts, online (class) grades, online (class) registration, online (class) schedules. Campuswide network is available. Wireless service is available via entire campus.
Library: John W. Anderson Library. Students can reserve study rooms.

STUDENT LIFE
Housing options: college housing not available.

Activities and organizations: drama/theater group, student-run newspaper, radio station, Student Government Association, Student Ambassadors, Art Club, Modern Languages Club, national fraternities, national sororities.

Athletics ***Intercollegiate sports:*** basketball M(s)/W(s), cross-country running M(s)/W(s), golf M(s)/W(s), soccer M, tennis M/W, volleyball W(s). ***Intramural sports:*** basketball M/W, cheerleading M(c)/W(c), cross-country running M(c)/W(c), football M(c)/W(c), ice hockey M(c)/W(c), soccer M(c)/W(c), softball M(c)/W(c), volleyball M/W.

Campus security: 24-hour emergency response devices and patrols, late-night transport/escort service.

Student services: health clinic, personal/psychological counseling, veterans affairs office.

COSTS & FINANCIAL AID
Costs (2020–21) ***Tuition:*** state resident $6895 full-time, $230 per credit hour part-time; nonresident $19,346 full-time, $645 per credit hour part-time. Full-time tuition and fees vary according to program and reciprocity agreements. Part-time tuition and fees vary according to course load, program, and reciprocity agreements. ***Required fees:*** $632 full-time. ***Payment plans:*** installment, deferred payment. ***Waivers:*** senior citizens and employees or children of employees.

Financial Aid Of all full-time matriculated undergraduates who enrolled in 2018, 2,150 applied for aid, 1,735 were judged to have need, 280 had their need fully met. 72 Federal Work-Study jobs (averaging $1562). In 2018, 163 non-need-based awards were made. ***Average percent of need met:*** 68. ***Average financial aid package:*** $8847. ***Average need-based loan:*** $3589. ***Average need-based gift aid:*** $7850. ***Average non-need-based aid:*** $4053. ***Average indebtedness upon graduation:*** $26,940.

APPLYING
Standardized Tests *Required:* SAT or ACT (for admission).

Options: electronic application, deferred entrance.

Application fee: $35.

Application deadlines: rolling (freshmen), rolling (transfers).

Notification: continuous (freshmen), continuous (transfers).

CONTACT

Indiana University Northwest, 3400 Broadway, Gary, IN 46408-1197. *Phone:* 219-980-6994. *Toll-free phone:* 800-968-7486.

Indiana University-Purdue University Indianapolis

Indianapolis, Indiana

http://www.iupui.edu/

- **State-supported** university, founded 1969, part of Indiana University System
- **Urban** 536-acre campus with easy access to Indianapolis
- **Endowment** $1.0 billion
- **Coed** 21,246 undergraduate students, 83% full-time, 58% women, 42% men
- **Moderately difficult** entrance level, 81% of applicants were admitted

UNDERGRAD STUDENTS

17,555 full-time, 3,691 part-time. Students come from 46 states and territories; 135 other countries; 5% are from out of state; 6% transferred in; 12% live on campus.

Freshmen:

Admission: 13,339 applied, 10,820 admitted, 4,103 enrolled. ***Average high school GPA:*** 3.5.

Retention: 72% of full-time freshmen returned.

ACADEMICS

Calendar: semesters. *Degrees:* certificates, associate, bachelor's, master's, doctoral, post-master's, and postbachelor's certificates.

Special study options: academic remediation for entering students, accelerated degree program, adult/continuing education programs, advanced placement credit, cooperative education, distance learning, double majors, English as a second language, external degree program, freshman honors college, honors programs, independent study, internships, off-campus study, part-time degree program, services for LD students, student-designed majors, study abroad, summer session for credit. ***ROTC:*** Army (b), Air Force (c).

Computers: 1,158 computers/terminals are available on campus for general student use. Students can access the following: campus intranet, computer help desk, free student e-mail accounts, online (class) grades, online (class) registration, online (class) schedules. Campuswide network is available. 100% of college-owned or -operated housing units are wired for high-speed Internet access. Wireless service is available via entire campus.

Library: University Library plus 4 others. Study areas open 24 hours, 5–7 days a week; students can reserve study rooms.

STUDENT LIFE

Housing options: coed, special housing for students with disabilities. Campus housing is university owned.

Activities and organizations: drama/theater group, student-run newspaper, choral group, national fraternities, national sororities.

Athletics *Intercollegiate sports:* basketball M(s)/W(s), cheerleading M/W, cross-country running M(s)/W(s), golf M(s)/W(s), soccer M(s)/W(s), softball W(s), swimming and diving M(s)/W(s), tennis M(s)/W(s), track and field M(s)/W(s), volleyball W(s). ***Intramural sports:*** badminton M(c)/W(c), baseball M(c)/W(c), basketball M/W, cross-country running M(c)/W(c), equestrian sports M(c)/W(c), fencing M(c)/W(c), football M/W, golf M(c)/W(c), ice hockey M(c)/W(c), rowing M(c)/W(c), rugby M(c)/W(c), soccer M/W, tennis M(c)/W(c), track and field M(c)/W(c), ultimate Frisbee M/W, volleyball M/W.

Campus security: 24-hour emergency response devices and patrols, late-night transport/escort service, controlled dormitory access.

Student services: health clinic, personal/psychological counseling, women's center, veterans affairs office.

COSTS & FINANCIAL AID

Costs (2020–21) *Tuition:* state resident $8580 full-time, $286 per credit hour part-time; nonresident $29,589 full-time, $986 per credit hour part-time. Full-time tuition and fees vary according to location, program, and reciprocity agreements. Part-time tuition and fees vary according to course load, location, program, and reciprocity agreements. ***Required fees:*** $1121 full-time. ***Room and board:*** $10,000. Room and board charges vary according to board plan and housing facility. ***Payment plans:*** installment, deferred payment. ***Waivers:*** senior citizens and employees or children of employees.

Financial Aid Of all full-time matriculated undergraduates who enrolled in 2018, 14,346 applied for aid, 11,552 were judged to have need, 2,438 had their need fully met. 801 Federal Work-Study jobs (averaging $2340). In 2018, 1854 non-need-based awards were made. ***Average percent of need met:*** 69. ***Average financial aid package:*** $11,849. ***Average need-based loan:*** $3860. ***Average need-based gift aid:*** $10,573. ***Average non-need-based aid:*** $6878. ***Average indebtedness upon graduation:*** $27,022.

APPLYING

Standardized Tests *Required:* SAT or ACT (for admission).

Options: electronic application.

Application fee: $65.

Required: essay or personal statement, high school transcript. ***Required for some:*** portfolio for art program.

Notification: continuous (freshmen), continuous (transfers).

CONTACT

Indiana University-Purdue University Indianapolis, 420 University Boulevard, Indianapolis, IN 46202.

Indiana University South Bend

South Bend, Indiana

http://www.iusb.edu/

- **State-supported** comprehensive, founded 1922, part of Indiana University System
- **Suburban** 105-acre campus with easy access to Chicago
- **Endowment** $19.1 million
- **Coed** 4,707 undergraduate students, 77% full-time, 63% women, 37% men
- **Moderately difficult** entrance level, 82% of applicants were admitted

UNDERGRAD STUDENTS

3,614 full-time, 1,093 part-time. Students come from 16 states and territories; 26 other countries; 5% are from out of state; 7% transferred in; 8% live on campus.

Freshmen:

Admission: 3,011 applied, 2,466 admitted, 929 enrolled. ***Average high school GPA:*** 3.2.

Retention: 63% of full-time freshmen returned.

ACADEMICS

Calendar: semesters. *Degrees:* certificates, diplomas, associate, bachelor's, master's, and postbachelor's certificates.

Special study options: accelerated degree program, adult/continuing education programs, advanced placement credit, distance learning, double majors, English as a second language, external degree program, freshman honors college, honors programs, independent study, internships, off-campus study, part-time degree program, services for LD students, study abroad, summer session for credit. ***ROTC:*** Army (c), Air Force (c).

Computers: 730 computers/terminals are available on campus for general student use. Students can access the following: computer help desk, free student e-mail accounts, online (class) grades, online (class) registration, online (class) schedules. Campuswide network is available. 100% of college-owned or -operated housing units are wired for high-speed Internet access. Wireless service is available via entire campus.

Library: Franklin D. Schurz Library plus 1 other. Students can reserve study rooms.

STUDENT LIFE

Housing options: coed. Campus housing is university owned.

Activities and organizations: drama/theater group, student-run newspaper, choral group, national fraternities, national sororities.

Athletics *Intercollegiate sports:* baseball M(s), basketball M(s)/W(s), cross-country running M(s)/W(s), golf M(s)/W(s), soccer W(s), softball W(s), tennis M(s)/W(s), volleyball W(s). ***Intramural sports:*** cheerleading

M(c)/W(c), equestrian sports M(c)/W(c), golf M(c)/W(c), soccer M(c), volleyball W(c).

Campus security: 24-hour emergency response devices and patrols, late-night transport/escort service.

Student services: health clinic, personal/psychological counseling, women's center, veterans affairs office.

COSTS & FINANCIAL AID
Costs (2020–21) ***Tuition:*** state resident $6895 full-time, $230 per credit hour part-time; nonresident $19,346 full-time, $645 per credit hour part-time. Full-time tuition and fees vary according to program and reciprocity agreements. Part-time tuition and fees vary according to course load, program, and reciprocity agreements. ***Required fees:*** $632 full-time. ***Room only:*** $7346. Room and board charges vary according to housing facility. ***Payment plans:*** installment, deferred payment. ***Waivers:*** senior citizens and employees or children of employees.

Financial Aid Of all full-time matriculated undergraduates who enrolled in 2018, 3,104 applied for aid, 2,594 were judged to have need, 329 had their need fully met. 243 Federal Work-Study jobs (averaging $1950). In 2018, 320 non-need-based awards were made. ***Average percent of need met:*** 66. ***Average financial aid package:*** $9343. ***Average need-based loan:*** $3540. ***Average need-based gift aid:*** $7990. ***Average non-need-based aid:*** $2520. ***Average indebtedness upon graduation:*** $24,879.

APPLYING
Standardized Tests *Required:* SAT or ACT (for admission).

Options: electronic application, deferred entrance.

Application fee: $35.

Application deadlines: rolling (freshmen), rolling (transfers).

Notification: continuous (freshmen), continuous (transfers).

CONTACT
Ms. Constance Peterson-Miller, Director of Admissions and International Student Services, Indiana University South Bend, 1700 Mishawaka Avenue, PO Box 7111, South Bend, IN 46634-7111. *Phone:* 574-520-4839. *Toll-free phone:* 877-GO-2-IUSB. *Fax:* 574-520-4834. *E-mail:* admissions@iusb.edu.

Indiana University Southeast

New Albany, Indiana

http://www.ius.edu/

- **State-supported** comprehensive, founded 1941, part of Indiana University System
- **Suburban** 179-acre campus with easy access to Louisville
- **Endowment** $17.0 million
- **Coed** 4,461 undergraduate students, 71% full-time, 61% women, 39% men
- **Minimally difficult** entrance level, 82% of applicants were admitted

UNDERGRAD STUDENTS
3,158 full-time, 1,303 part-time. Students come from 17 states and territories; 48 other countries; 29% are from out of state; 7% Black or African American, non-Hispanic/Latino; 5% Hispanic/Latino; 2% Asian, non-Hispanic/Latino; 0.1% Native Hawaiian or other Pacific Islander, non-Hispanic/Latino; 0.1% American Indian or Alaska Native, non-Hispanic/Latino; 4% Two or more races, non-Hispanic/Latino; 0.6% Race/ethnicity unknown; 0.6% international; 7% transferred in; 8% live on campus.

Freshmen:
Admission: 2,831 applied, 2,319 admitted, 1,012 enrolled. ***Average high school GPA:*** 3.2. ***Test scores:*** SAT evidence-based reading and writing scores over 500: 64%; SAT math scores over 500: 57%; ACT scores over 18: 70%; SAT evidence-based reading and writing scores over 600: 19%; SAT math scores over 600: 12%; ACT scores over 24: 21%; SAT evidence-based reading and writing scores over 700: 1%; SAT math scores over 700: 1%; ACT scores over 30: 2%.

Retention: 62% of full-time freshmen returned.

FACULTY
Total: 440, 48% full-time, 57% with terminal degrees.
Student/faculty ratio: 13:1.

ACADEMICS
Calendar: semesters. *Degrees:* certificates, bachelor's, master's, and postbachelor's certificates.

Special study options: academic remediation for entering students, accelerated degree program, adult/continuing education programs, advanced placement credit, distance learning, double majors, English as a second language, external degree program, honors programs, independent study, internships, off-campus study, part-time degree program, services for LD students, student-designed majors, study abroad, summer session for credit. ***ROTC:*** Army (c), Air Force (c).

Computers: 890 computers/terminals are available on campus for general student use. Students can access the following: computer help desk, free student e-mail accounts, online (class) grades, online (class) registration, online (class) schedules. Campuswide network is available. 100% of college-owned or -operated housing units are wired for high-speed Internet access. Wireless service is available via entire campus.
Library: IU Southeast Library. *Books:* 351,274 (physical), 972,075 (digital/electronic); *Serial titles:* 199 (physical), 162,610 (digital/electronic); *Databases:* 370. Students can reserve study rooms.

STUDENT LIFE
Housing options: Campus housing is university owned.

Activities and organizations: drama/theater group, student-run newspaper, choral group, national fraternities, national sororities.

Athletics Member NAIA. ***Intercollegiate sports:*** baseball M(s), basketball M(s)/W(s), softball W(s), tennis M(s)/W(s), volleyball W(s).

Campus security: 24-hour emergency response devices and patrols, late-night transport/escort service.

Student services: personal/psychological counseling, veterans affairs office.

COSTS & FINANCIAL AID
Costs (2020–21) ***Tuition:*** state resident $6290 full-time, $230 per credit hour part-time; nonresident $19,346 full-time, $645 per credit hour part-time. Full-time tuition and fees vary according to program and reciprocity agreements. Part-time tuition and fees vary according to course load, program, and reciprocity agreements. ***Required fees:*** $632 full-time. ***Room only:*** $6290. Room and board charges vary according to board plan and housing facility. ***Payment plans:*** installment, deferred payment. ***Waivers:*** senior citizens and employees or children of employees.

Financial Aid Of all full-time matriculated undergraduates who enrolled in 2018, 2,678 applied for aid, 2,114 were judged to have need, 210 had their need fully met. 119 Federal Work-Study jobs (averaging $1682). In 2018, 238 non-need-based awards were made. ***Average percent of need met:*** 63. ***Average financial aid package:*** $8724. ***Average need-based loan:*** $3650. ***Average need-based gift aid:*** $7297. ***Average non-need-based aid:*** $2571. ***Average indebtedness upon graduation:*** $21,460.

APPLYING
Standardized Tests *Required:* SAT or ACT (for admission).

Options: electronic application, early admission, deferred entrance.

Application fee: $35.

Required: high school transcript.

Application deadlines: rolling (freshmen), rolling (transfers).

Notification: continuous (freshmen), continuous (transfers).

CONTACT
Mr. Christopher Crews, Director of Recruitment and Admission, Indiana University Southeast, University Center South Room 102, 4201 Grant Line Road, New Albany, IN 47150-6405. *Phone:* 812-941-2212. *Toll-free phone:* 800-852-8835. *Fax:* 812-941-2595. *E-mail:* admissions@ius.edu.

Indiana Wesleyan University

Marion, Indiana

http://www.indwes.edu/

CONTACT
Mr. Adam Farmer, Director of Admissions, Indiana Wesleyan University, 4201 South Washington Street, Marion, IN 46953. *Phone:* 866-468-6498 Ext. 2138. *Toll-free phone:* 866-468-6498. *E-mail:* admissions@indwes.edu.

International Business College

Fort Wayne, Indiana

http://www.ibcfortwayne.edu/

CONTACT

Admissions Office, International Business College, 5699 Coventry Lane, Fort Wayne, IN 46804. *Phone:* 260-459-4500. *Toll-free phone:* 800-589-6363.

Manchester University

North Manchester, Indiana

http://www.manchester.edu/

- **Independent** comprehensive, founded 1889, affiliated with Church of the Brethren
- **Small-town** 125-acre campus
- **Endowment** $60.2 million
- **Coed**
- **Moderately difficult** entrance level

FACULTY

Student/faculty ratio: 14:1.

ACADEMICS

Calendar: 4-1-4. *Degrees:* associate, bachelor's, master's, and doctoral.
Library: Funderburg Library. Study areas open 24 hours, 5–7 days a week.

STUDENT LIFE

Housing options: on-campus residence required through junior year; coed, special housing for students with disabilities. Campus housing is university owned. Freshman campus housing is guaranteed.

Activities and organizations: drama/theater group, student-run newspaper, radio station, choral group, College of Business Club, Fellowship of Christian Athletes, Student Education Association, African Student Association, Asian Awareness Association.

Athletics Member NCAA. All Division III except golf (Division II).

Campus security: 24-hour patrols, student patrols, late-night transport/escort service.

Student services: health clinic, personal/psychological counseling.

COSTS & FINANCIAL AID

Costs (2019–20) ***One-time required fee:*** $250. ***Comprehensive fee:*** $43,674 includes full-time tuition ($32,366), mandatory fees ($1258), and room and board ($10,050). Part-time tuition: $745 per credit hour. ***Required fees:*** $35 per credit hour part-time. ***College room only:*** $5350.

Financial Aid Of all full-time matriculated undergraduates who enrolled in 2018, 1,078 applied for aid, 981 were judged to have need, 220 had their need fully met. In 2018, 168 non-need-based awards were made. ***Average percent of need met:*** 85. ***Average financial aid package:*** $30,801. ***Average need-based loan:*** $4084. ***Average need-based gift aid:*** $25,397. ***Average non-need-based aid:*** $19,168. ***Average indebtedness upon graduation:*** $33,838.

APPLYING

Options: electronic application, deferred entrance.

Application fee: $25.

Required: high school transcript, 1 letter of recommendation, rank in upper 50% of high school class. ***Required for some:*** minimum 3.0 GPA. ***Recommended:*** minimum 2.3 GPA.

CONTACT

Ms. Brandi Chauncey, Director of Admissions, Manchester University, 604 East College Avenue, North Manchester, IN 46962. *Phone:* 260-982-5232. *Toll-free phone:* 800-852-3648. *E-mail:* bcchauncey@manchester.edu.

Marian University

Indianapolis, Indiana

http://www.marian.edu/

- **Independent Roman Catholic** comprehensive, founded 1851
- **Suburban** 114-acre campus with easy access to Indianapolis
- **Endowment** $69.3 million
- **Coed** 2,405 undergraduate students, 85% full-time, 63% women, 37% men
- **Moderately difficult** entrance level, 62% of applicants were admitted

UNDERGRAD STUDENTS

2,040 full-time, 365 part-time. Students come from 39 states and territories; 27 other countries; 18% are from out of state; 12% Black or African American, non-Hispanic/Latino; 7% Hispanic/Latino; 3% Asian, non-Hispanic/Latino; 4% Two or more races, non-Hispanic/Latino; 2% Race/ethnicity unknown; 2% international; 2% transferred in; 47% live on campus.

Freshmen:

Admission: 2,525 applied, 1,554 admitted, 385 enrolled. ***Average high school GPA:*** 3.6. ***Test scores:*** SAT evidence-based reading and writing scores over 500: 74%; SAT math scores over 500: 71%; ACT scores over 18: 84%; SAT evidence-based reading and writing scores over 600: 25%; SAT math scores over 600: 24%; ACT scores over 24: 36%; SAT evidence-based reading and writing scores over 700: 2%; SAT math scores over 700: 3%; ACT scores over 30: 10%.

Retention: 83% of full-time freshmen returned.

FACULTY

Total: 326, 53% full-time, 45% with terminal degrees.

Student/faculty ratio: 13:1.

ACADEMICS

Calendar: semesters. *Degrees:* associate, bachelor's, master's, and doctoral.

Special study options: academic remediation for entering students, accelerated degree program, adult/continuing education programs, advanced placement credit, cooperative education, distance learning, double majors, honors programs, independent study, internships, off-campus study, part-time degree program, services for LD students, study abroad, summer session for credit. ***ROTC:*** Army (c).

Computers: 201 computers/terminals are available on campus for general student use. Students can access the following: computer help desk, free student e-mail accounts, online (class) grades, online (class) registration, online (class) schedules. Campuswide network is available. 100% of college-owned or -operated housing units are wired for high-speed Internet access. Wireless service is available via entire campus.
Library: Mother Theresa Hackelmeier Memorial Library. *Books:* 724,949 (physical), 354,307 (digital/electronic); *Serial titles:* 1,301 (physical), 58,444 (digital/electronic).

STUDENT LIFE

Housing options: on-campus residence required through junior year; coed. Campus housing is university owned. Freshman campus housing is guaranteed.

Activities and organizations: drama/theater group, student-run newspaper, choral group, marching band, Student Government Association, College Mentors for Kids, Best Buddies, Knight Nation, Sophia Club.

Athletics Member NAIA. ***Intercollegiate sports:*** baseball M(s), basketball M(s)/W(s), bowling M(s)/W(s), cheerleading M(s)(c)/W(s)(c), cross-country running M(s)/W(s), football M(s), golf M(s)/W(s), lacrosse W(s), soccer M(s)/W(s), softball W(s), tennis M(s)/W(s), track and field M(s)/W(s), volleyball W(s), weight lifting M(s)/W(s), wrestling M(s). ***Intramural sports:*** football M/W, ultimate Frisbee M/W, volleyball M/W.

Campus security: 24-hour emergency response devices and patrols, student patrols, late-night transport/escort service, controlled dormitory access.

Student services: health clinic, personal/psychological counseling.

COSTS & FINANCIAL AID

Costs (2020–21) ***Comprehensive fee:*** $47,320 includes full-time tuition ($36,000) and room and board ($11,320). Full-time tuition and fees vary according to degree level and location. Part-time tuition: $1600 per credit hour. Part-time tuition and fees vary according to degree level and location. ***Room and board:*** Room and board charges vary according to board plan and housing facility. ***Payment plan:*** installment. ***Waivers:*** employees or children of employees.

Financial Aid Of all full-time matriculated undergraduates who enrolled in 2017, 1,418 applied for aid, 1,154 were judged to have need, 201 had their need fully met. 148 Federal Work-Study jobs (averaging $1500). In 2017, 227 non-need-based awards were made. ***Average percent of need met:*** 77. ***Average financial aid package:*** $27,762. ***Average need-based loan:*** $4194. ***Average need-based gift aid:*** $24,294. ***Average non-need-based aid:*** $13,310. ***Average indebtedness upon graduation:*** $34,435.

APPLYING

Standardized Tests *Required:* SAT or ACT (for admission).

Options: electronic application, deferred entrance.

Required: high school transcript, college transcripts for transfer students. ***Required for some:*** essay or personal statement, 1 letter of recommendation, interview.

Notification: continuous (freshmen), continuous (transfers).

CONTACT

Ms. Luann Brames, Director of Freshmen Admission, Marian University, 3200 Cold Spring Road, Indianapolis, IN 46222. *Phone:* 317-955-6300. *Toll-free phone:* 800-772-7264. *Fax:* 317-955-6401. *E-mail:* admissions@marian.edu.

Martin University

Indianapolis, Indiana

http://www.martin.edu/

CONTACT

Ms. Brenda Shaheed, Director of Enrollment Management, Martin University, 2171 Avondale Place, PO Box 18567, Indianapolis, IN 46218-3867. *Phone:* 317-543-3237. *Fax:* 317-543-4790.

Mid-America College of Funeral Service

Jeffersonville, Indiana

http://www.mid-america.edu/

CONTACT

Mr. Richard Nelson, Dean of Students, Mid-America College of Funeral Service, 3111 Hamburg Pike, Jeffersonville, IN 47130-9630. *Phone:* 812-288-8878. *Toll-free phone:* 800-221-6158. *Fax:* 812-288-5942. *E-mail:* macfs@mindspring.com.

National American University

Indianapolis, Indiana

http://www.national.edu/

CONTACT

Dr. Rhonda Parker, Campus Director, National American University, 3600 Woodview Trace, Suite 200, Indianapolis, IN 46268. *Phone:* 317-578-7353. *Toll-free phone:* 800-609-1430.

Oakland City University

Oakland City, Indiana

http://www.oak.edu/

- **Independent General Baptist** comprehensive, founded 1885
- **Rural** 34-acre campus
- **Endowment** $5.5 million
- **Coed** 1,231 undergraduate students, 48% full-time, 53% women, 47% men
- **Minimally difficult** entrance level, 50% of applicants were admitted

UNDERGRAD STUDENTS

597 full-time, 634 part-time. Students come from 17 states and territories; 12 other countries; 19% are from out of state; 7% Black or African American, non-Hispanic/Latino; 4% Hispanic/Latino; 0.2% Asian, non-Hispanic/Latino; 0.5% American Indian or Alaska Native, non-Hispanic/Latino; 3% Two or more races, non-Hispanic/Latino; 7% Race/ethnicity unknown; 3% international; 5% transferred in; 61% live on campus.

Freshmen:

Admission: 1,010 applied, 502 admitted, 140 enrolled. ***Average high school GPA:*** 3.3. ***Test scores:*** SAT evidence-based reading and writing scores over 500: 55%; SAT math scores over 500: 62%; ACT scores over 18: 60%; SAT evidence-based reading and writing scores over 600: 9%; SAT math scores over 600: 8%; ACT scores over 24: 12%; SAT evidence-based reading and writing scores over 700: 4%; ACT scores over 30: 2%.

Retention: 62% of full-time freshmen returned.

FACULTY

Total: 155, 23% full-time.

Student/faculty ratio: 12:1.

ACADEMICS

Calendar: semesters. *Degrees:* certificates, associate, bachelor's, master's, and doctoral.

Special study options: academic remediation for entering students, accelerated degree program, adult/continuing education programs, advanced placement credit, distance learning, external degree program, part-time degree program, services for LD students, summer session for credit.

Computers: 200 computers/terminals are available on campus for general student use. Students can access the following: campus intranet, computer help desk, free student e-mail accounts, online (class) grades, online (class) registration, online (class) schedules. Campuswide network is available. 100% of college-owned or -operated housing units are wired for high-speed Internet access. Wireless service is available via entire campus.

Library: Barger-Richardson Library. *Books:* 84,412 (physical), 17,690 (digital/electronic); *Serial titles:* 79 (physical), 50,255 (digital/electronic); *Databases:* 52.

STUDENT LIFE

Housing options: men-only, women-only. Campus housing is university owned. Freshman campus housing is guaranteed.

Activities and organizations: drama/theater group, student-run newspaper, choral group, Student Government Association, Good News Players, Art Guild, FOCUS, intramural sports.

Athletics Member NCAA, NCCAA. All NCAA Division II except golf (Division I). ***Intercollegiate sports:*** baseball M(s), basketball M(s)/W(s), cheerleading W(s), cross-country running M(s)/W(s), golf M(s)/W(s), soccer M(s)/W(s), softball W(s), tennis M(s)/W(s), volleyball W(s). ***Intramural sports:*** basketball M/W, bowling M/W, football M/W, softball M/W, table tennis M/W, tennis M/W, volleyball M/W.

Campus security: 24-hour patrols, student patrols.

Student services: personal/psychological counseling.

COSTS & FINANCIAL AID

Costs (2020–21) ***Comprehensive fee:*** $35,390 includes full-time tuition ($24,990) and room and board ($10,400). Full-time tuition and fees vary according to location. Part-time tuition: $833 per credit hour. Part-time tuition and fees vary according to location. ***College room only:*** $3600. ***Payment plan:*** installment. ***Waivers:*** employees or children of employees.

Financial Aid Of all full-time matriculated undergraduates who enrolled in 2017, 411 applied for aid, 411 were judged to have need. ***Average percent of need met:*** 35. ***Average financial aid package:*** $13,420. ***Average need-based gift aid:*** $11,594.

APPLYING

Standardized Tests *Required for some:* SAT or ACT (for admission).

Options: electronic application, early admission, deferred entrance.

Application fee: $35.

Required: high school transcript, minimum 2.0 GPA. ***Recommended:*** essay or personal statement, interview.

CONTACT

Miss Jennifer Cates, Assistant Director of Admissions, Oakland City University, 138 North Lucretia Street, Oakland City, IN 47660. *Phone:* 812-749-1220. *Toll-free phone:* 800-737-5125. *E-mail:* jcates@oak.edu.

Purdue University

West Lafayette, Indiana

http://www.purdue.edu/

- **State-supported** university, founded 1869, part of Purdue University System
- **Suburban** 2660-acre campus with easy access to Indianapolis
- **Endowment** $2.5 billion
- **Coed**
- **Moderately difficult** entrance level

FACULTY
Student/faculty ratio: 13:1.

ACADEMICS
Calendar: semesters. *Degrees:* certificates, associate, bachelor's, master's, doctoral, post-master's, and postbachelor's certificates. **Library:** Purdue University Libraries plus 9 others. *Books:* 946,376 (physical), 2.5 million (digital/electronic); *Serial titles:* 44,788 (physical), 136,167 (digital/electronic); *Databases:* 580. Weekly public service hours: 168; study areas open 24 hours, 5–7 days a week; students can reserve study rooms.

STUDENT LIFE
Housing options: coed, men-only, women-only, cooperative, special housing for students with disabilities. Campus housing is university owned. Freshman applicants given priority for college housing.

Activities and organizations: drama/theater group, student-run newspaper, radio station, choral group, marching band, Purdue Student Government, FSCL Councils, RHA, Purdue Engineering Student Council, AG Council, national fraternities, national sororities.

Athletics Member NCAA. All Division I except football (Division I-A).

Campus security: 24-hour emergency response devices and patrols, student patrols, late-night transport/escort service, controlled dormitory access.

Student services: health clinic, personal/psychological counseling, women's center, legal services, veterans affairs office.

COSTS & FINANCIAL AID
Costs (2019–20) ***Tuition:*** state resident $9208 full-time, $330 per credit hour part-time; nonresident $28,010 full-time, $930 per credit hour part-time. Full-time tuition and fees vary according to course load and program. Part-time tuition and fees vary according to course load. ***Required fees:*** $784 full-time, $18 per credit hour part-time. ***Room and board:*** $10,030; room only: $4860. Room and board charges vary according to board plan and housing facility.

Financial Aid Of all full-time matriculated undergraduates who enrolled in 2018, 19,383 applied for aid, 12,919 were judged to have need, 5,162 had their need fully met. In 2018, 4202 non-need-based awards were made. ***Average percent of need met:*** 80. ***Average financial aid package:*** $14,258. ***Average need-based loan:*** $4930. ***Average need-based gift aid:*** $12,029. ***Average non-need-based aid:*** $5536. ***Average indebtedness upon graduation:*** $27,673.

APPLYING
Standardized Tests *Required:* SAT or ACT (for admission).

Options: electronic application, early admission, early action, deferred entrance.

Application fee: $60.

Required: essay or personal statement, high school transcript.

CONTACT
Ms. Kristina M. Wong Davis, Vice Provost for Enrollment Management, Purdue University, 475 Stadium Mall Drive, Schleman Hall, West Lafayette, IN 47907-2050. *Phone:* 765-494-9116. *Fax:* 765-494-0544. *E-mail:* admissions@purdue.edu.

Purdue University Fort Wayne

Fort Wayne, Indiana

http://www.pfw.edu/

- **State-supported** comprehensive, founded 1917, part of Purdue University System
- **Urban** 683-acre campus
- **Endowment** $60.3 million
- **Coed** 9,697 undergraduate students, 55% full-time, 54% women, 46% men
- **Minimally difficult** entrance level, 83% of applicants were admitted

UNDERGRAD STUDENTS
5,370 full-time, 4,327 part-time. Students come from 32 states and territories; 45 other countries; 8% are from out of state; 5% Black or African American, non-Hispanic/Latino; 5% Hispanic/Latino; 2% Asian, non-Hispanic/Latino; 0.1% Native Hawaiian or other Pacific Islander, non-Hispanic/Latino; 0.1% American Indian or Alaska Native, non-Hispanic/Latino; 3% Two or more races, non-Hispanic/Latino; 0.2% Race/ethnicity unknown; 2% international; 4% transferred in; 10% live on campus.

Freshmen:
Admission: 6,287 applied, 5,192 admitted, 1,609 enrolled. ***Average high school GPA:*** 3.2. ***Test scores:*** SAT evidence-based reading and writing scores over 500: 70%; SAT math scores over 500: 70%; ACT scores over 18: 84%; SAT evidence-based reading and writing scores over 600: 26%; SAT math scores over 600: 21%; ACT scores over 24: 32%; SAT evidence-based reading and writing scores over 700: 2%; SAT math scores over 700: 3%; ACT scores over 30: 8%.

Retention: 57% of full-time freshmen returned.

FACULTY
Total: 733, 57% full-time, 43% with terminal degrees.

Student/faculty ratio: 14:1.

ACADEMICS
Calendar: semesters. *Degrees:* certificates, associate, bachelor's, master's, and postbachelor's certificates.

Special study options: academic remediation for entering students, accelerated degree program, adult/continuing education programs, advanced placement credit, cooperative education, distance learning, double majors, English as a second language, honors programs, independent study, internships, off-campus study, part-time degree program, services for LD students, student-designed majors, study abroad, summer session for credit. ***ROTC:*** Army (b).

Computers: 642 computers/terminals are available on campus for general student use. Students can access the following: computer help desk, free student e-mail accounts, online (class) grades, online (class) registration, online (class) schedules, student academic records. Campuswide network is available. 100% of college-owned or -operated housing units are wired for high-speed Internet access. Wireless service is available via entire campus.
Library: Helmke Library. *Books:* 218,195 (physical), 761,303 (digital/electronic); *Serial titles:* 4,124 (physical), 117,571 (digital/electronic); *Databases:* 295. Students can reserve study rooms.

STUDENT LIFE
Housing options: coed. Campus housing is university owned.

Activities and organizations: drama/theater group, student-run newspaper, television station, choral group, Live Action Combat Club, Active Minds, InterVarsity Christian Fellowship, Student Athlete Leadership Team, League of Legends (LOL).

Athletics Member NCAA. All Division I. ***Intercollegiate sports:*** baseball M(s), basketball M(s)/W(s), cross-country running M(s)/W(s), golf M(s)/W(s), soccer M(s)/W(s), softball W(s), tennis M(s)/W(s), track and field W(s), volleyball M(s)/W(s). ***Intramural sports:*** basketball M/W, football M/W, golf M/W, gymnastics W(c), ice hockey M(c), racquetball M/W, rugby M(c)/W(c), soccer M/W, softball W, tennis M/W, ultimate Frisbee M/W, volleyball M/W, wrestling W(c).

Campus security: 24-hour emergency response devices and patrols, late-night transport/escort service, controlled dormitory access.

Student services: health clinic, personal/psychological counseling, women's center.

COSTS & FINANCIAL AID
Costs (2020–21) ***Tuition:*** $286 per credit hour part-time; state resident $8589 full-time, $286 per credit hour part-time; nonresident $20,622 full-time, $687 per credit hour part-time. ***Required fees:*** $1119 full-time. ***Room and board:*** $9620; room only: $6108.

Financial Aid Of all full-time matriculated undergraduates who enrolled in 2018, 4,770 applied for aid, 3,850 were judged to have need, 402 had their need fully met. In 2018, 502 non-need-based awards were made. ***Average percent of need met:*** 60. ***Average financial aid package:*** $10,606. ***Average need-based loan:*** $3458. ***Average need-based gift aid:*** $6249. ***Average non-need-based aid:*** $2650. ***Average indebtedness upon graduation:*** $22,354.

APPLYING
Standardized Tests *Required:* SAT or ACT (for admission).

Options: electronic application, deferred entrance.

Application fee: $50.

Required: high school transcript, minimum 2.8 GPA. ***Recommended:*** rank in upper 50% of high school class.

Application deadlines: 8/1 (freshmen), 8/1 (transfers).

Notification: continuous (freshmen), continuous (out-of-state freshmen), continuous (transfers).

CONTACT
Belinda Johnson, Undergraduate Admissions Specialist, Purdue University Fort Wayne, 2101 East Coliseum Boulevard, Fort Wayne, IN 46805-1499. *Phone:* 260-481-0348. *Toll-free phone:* 800-324-4739. *Fax:* 260-481-6880. *E-mail:* johnsob@pfw.edu.

Purdue University Global

Indianapolis, Indiana

http://www.purdueglobal.edu/

CONTACT
Purdue University Global, 9000 Keystone Crossing, Suite 800, Indianapolis, IN 46240.

Purdue University Northwest

Hammond, Indiana

http://www.pnw.edu/

- **State-supported** comprehensive, founded 2016, part of Purdue University System
- **Urban** 454-acre campus with easy access to Chicago
- **Endowment** $30.0 million
- **Coed** 7,717 undergraduate students, 72% full-time, 55% women, 45% men
- **Moderately difficult** entrance level, 29% of applicants were admitted

UNDERGRAD STUDENTS
5,558 full-time, 2,159 part-time. Students come from 32 states and territories; 47 other countries; 10% are from out of state; 10% Black or African American, non-Hispanic/Latino; 21% Hispanic/Latino; 3% Asian, non-Hispanic/Latino; 0.1% Native Hawaiian or other Pacific Islander, non-Hispanic/Latino; 0.2% American Indian or Alaska Native, non-Hispanic/Latino; 3% Two or more races, non-Hispanic/Latino; 1% Race/ethnicity unknown; 2% international; 8% transferred in; 7% live on campus.

Freshmen:
Admission: 5,670 applied, 1,620 admitted, 1,235 enrolled. ***Average high school GPA:*** 3.2. ***Test scores:*** SAT evidence-based reading and writing scores over 500: 73%; SAT math scores over 500: 73%; ACT scores over 18: 85%; SAT evidence-based reading and writing scores over 600: 21%; SAT math scores over 600: 19%; ACT scores over 24: 32%; SAT evidence-based reading and writing scores over 700: 1%; SAT math scores over 700: 3%; ACT scores over 30: 5%.

Retention: 68% of full-time freshmen returned.

FACULTY
Total: 692, 63% full-time, 40% with terminal degrees.

Student/faculty ratio: 12:1.

ACADEMICS
Calendar: semesters. *Degrees:* certificates, bachelor's, master's, doctoral, post-master's, and postbachelor's certificates.

Special study options: academic remediation for entering students, accelerated degree program, adult/continuing education programs, advanced placement credit, cooperative education, distance learning, double majors, English as a second language, freshman honors college, honors programs, independent study, internships, part-time degree program, services for LD students, study abroad, summer session for credit. ***ROTC:*** Army (b).

Computers: 1,700 computers/terminals and 1,700 ports are available on campus for general student use. Students can access the following: campus intranet, computer help desk, free student e-mail accounts, online (class) grades, online (class) registration, online (class) schedules. Campuswide network is available. 100% of college-owned or -operated housing units are wired for high-speed Internet access. Wireless service is available via entire campus.

Library: Purdue University Northwest Libraries plus 2 others. *Books:* 203,808 (physical), 398,124 (digital/electronic); *Serial titles:* 1,673 (physical), 129,852 (digital/electronic); *Databases:* 177. Weekly public service hours: 138.

STUDENT LIFE
Housing options: coed. Campus housing is university owned.

Activities and organizations: drama/theater group, student-run newspaper, choral group, Black Student Union, Women in Business, National Society of Black Engineers, American Sign Language Club, Student Athlete Advisory Committee, national fraternities, national sororities.

Athletics Member NCAA, NAIA. All NCAA Division II. ***Intercollegiate sports:*** baseball M(s), basketball M(s)/W(s), cross-country running M(s)/W(s), golf M(s), ice hockey M(c), soccer M(s)/W(s), softball W(s), tennis M(s)/W(s), volleyball W(s). ***Intramural sports:*** basketball M/W, bowling M/W, football M/W, golf M/W, racquetball M/W, sand volleyball M/W, soccer M/W, table tennis M/W, ultimate Frisbee M/W, volleyball M/W.

Campus security: 24-hour emergency response devices and patrols, late-night transport/escort service, controlled dormitory access.

Student services: health clinic, personal/psychological counseling, veterans affairs office.

COSTS & FINANCIAL AID
Costs (2020–21) ***Tuition:*** state resident $7942 full-time, $235 per credit hour part-time; nonresident $11,523 full-time, $352 per credit hour part-time. Full-time tuition and fees vary according to program. Part-time tuition and fees vary according to program. ***Required fees:*** $26 per credit hour part-time. ***Room and board:*** $7821. ***Payment plans:*** installment, deferred payment. ***Waivers:*** senior citizens and employees or children of employees.

Financial Aid Of all full-time matriculated undergraduates who enrolled in 2018, 5,755 applied for aid, 3,967 were judged to have need, 475 had their need fully met. In 2018, 4 non-need-based awards were made. ***Average percent of need met:*** 11. ***Average financial aid package:*** $13,393. ***Average need-based loan:*** $2085. ***Average need-based gift aid:*** $4097. ***Average non-need-based aid:*** $1875. ***Average indebtedness upon graduation:*** $12,568.

APPLYING
Standardized Tests *Required:* SAT or ACT (for admission).

Options: electronic application.

Application fee: $25.

Required: high school transcript, minimum 2.0 GPA.

Application deadlines: 8/1 (freshmen), 8/1 (out-of-state freshmen), 8/1 (transfers).

Notification: continuous (freshmen), continuous (out-of-state freshmen), continuous (transfers).

CONTACT
Purdue University Northwest, 2200 169th Street, Hammond, IN 46323-2094. *Phone:* 219-989-2768. *Toll-free phone:* 800-447-8738.

Radiological Technologies University VT

South Bend, Indiana

http://www.rtuvt.edu/

CONTACT
Radiological Technologies University VT, 100 East Wayne Street, Suite 140, South Bend, IN 46601.

Rose-Hulman Institute of Technology

Terre Haute, Indiana

http://www.rose-hulman.edu/

- **Independent** comprehensive, founded 1874
- **Suburban** 1300-acre campus with easy access to Indianapolis
- **Endowment** $218.2 million
- **Coed, primarily men** 2,000 undergraduate students, 99% full-time, 24% women, 76% men
- **Very difficult** entrance level, 74% of applicants were admitted

UNDERGRAD STUDENTS
1,980 full-time, 20 part-time. Students come from 43 states and territories; 15 other countries; 65% are from out of state; 4% Black or African American, non-Hispanic/Latino; 5% Hispanic/Latino; 6% Asian, non-Hispanic/Latino; 0.1% Native Hawaiian or other Pacific Islander, non-Hispanic/Latino; 0.2% American Indian or Alaska Native, non-Hispanic/Latino; 5% Two or more races, non-Hispanic/Latino; 2% Race/ethnicity unknown; 14% international; 0.7% transferred in; 56% live on campus.

Freshmen:
Admission: 4,350 applied, 3,228 admitted, 496 enrolled. ***Average high school GPA:*** 4.0. ***Test scores:*** SAT evidence-based reading and writing scores over 500: 100%; SAT math scores over 500: 100%; ACT scores over 18: 100%; SAT evidence-based reading and writing scores over 600: 78%; SAT math scores over 600: 89%; ACT scores over 24: 94%; SAT evidence-based reading and writing scores over 700: 25%; SAT math scores over 700: 52%; ACT scores over 30: 58%.

Retention: 90% of full-time freshmen returned.

FACULTY
Total: 196, 95% full-time, 97% with terminal degrees.

Student/faculty ratio: 11:1.

ACADEMICS
Calendar: quarters. *Degrees:* bachelor's and master's.

Special study options: accelerated degree program, adult/continuing education programs, advanced placement credit, cooperative education, double majors, English as a second language, independent study, off-campus study, services for LD students, study abroad, summer session for credit. ***ROTC:*** Army (b), Air Force (b).

Computers: 15 computers/terminals and 8,000 ports are available on campus for general student use. Students can access the following: campus intranet, computer help desk, free student e-mail accounts, online (class) grades, online (class) registration, online (class) schedules. Campuswide network is available. 100% of college-owned or -operated housing units are wired for high-speed Internet access. Wireless service is available via entire campus.

Library: John A. Logan Library. *Books:* 28,477 (physical), 552,296 (digital/electronic); *Serial titles:* 26 (physical), 87,425 (digital/electronic); *Databases:* 37. Weekly public service hours: 101; students can reserve study rooms.

STUDENT LIFE
Housing options: on-campus residence required for freshman year; coed, men-only. Campus housing is university owned. Freshman applicants given priority for college housing.

Activities and organizations: drama/theater group, student-run newspaper, radio station, choral group, Residence Hall Association, Student Activities Board, Branam Innovation Center competition teams, Drama Club, Diversity organizations, national fraternities, national sororities.

Athletics Member NCAA. All Division III. ***Intercollegiate sports:*** baseball M, basketball M/W, cross-country running M/W, football M, golf M/W, soccer M/W, softball W, swimming and diving M/W, tennis M/W, track and field M/W, volleyball W. ***Intramural sports:*** badminton M/W, basketball M/W, bowling M/W, cross-country running M/W, golf M/W, lacrosse W(c), racquetball M/W, skiing (downhill) M(c)/W(c), soccer M/W, softball M/W, swimming and diving M/W, table tennis M/W, tennis M/W, track and field M/W, ultimate Frisbee M/W, volleyball M/W.

Campus security: 24-hour emergency response devices and patrols, late-night transport/escort service, controlled dormitory access.

Student services: health clinic, personal/psychological counseling.

COSTS & FINANCIAL AID
Costs (2019–20) ***One-time required fee:*** $2400. ***Comprehensive fee:*** $64,941 includes full-time tuition ($48,507), mandatory fees ($1020), and room and board ($15,414). Full-time tuition and fees vary according to course load. Part-time tuition: $1415 per credit hour. Part-time tuition and fees vary according to course load. ***College room only:*** $9348. Room and board charges vary according to board plan. ***Payment plans:*** tuition prepayment, installment. ***Waivers:*** employees or children of employees.

Financial Aid Of all full-time matriculated undergraduates who enrolled in 2019, 1,334 applied for aid, 1,125 were judged to have need, 205 had their need fully met. 622 Federal Work-Study jobs (averaging $1275). In 2019, 837 non-need-based awards were made. ***Average percent of need met:*** 64. ***Average financial aid package:*** $32,356. ***Average need-based loan:*** $4420. ***Average need-based gift aid:*** $30,680. ***Average non-need-based aid:*** $14,175. ***Average indebtedness upon graduation:*** $47,953.

APPLYING
Standardized Tests *Required:* SAT or ACT (for admission).

Options: electronic application, early action, deferred entrance.

Application fee: $50.

Required: essay or personal statement, high school transcript, 1 letter of recommendation, curricular prerequisites.

Application deadlines: 2/1 (freshmen), 11/1 (early action).

Notification: 3/15 (freshmen), continuous (transfers), 12/16 (early action).

CONTACT
Mrs. Lisa Norton, Dean of Admissions, Rose-Hulman Institute of Technology, 5500 Wabash Avenue, CM 1, Terre Haute, IN 47803-3920. *Phone:* 812-877-8213. *Toll-free phone:* 800-248-7448. *Fax:* 812-877-8941. *E-mail:* admissions@rose-hulman.edu.

Saint Mary-of-the-Woods College

Saint Mary of the Woods, Indiana

http://www.smwc.edu/

- **Independent Roman Catholic** comprehensive, founded 1840
- **Rural** 227-acre campus with easy access to Indianapolis
- **Coed, primarily women** 767 undergraduate students, 82% full-time, 86% women, 14% men
- **Minimally difficult** entrance level, 67% of applicants were admitted

UNDERGRAD STUDENTS
629 full-time, 138 part-time. Students come from 21 states and territories; 4 other countries; 14% are from out of state; 5% Black or African American, non-Hispanic/Latino; 3% Hispanic/Latino; 0.5% Asian, non-Hispanic/Latino; 0.1% Native Hawaiian or other Pacific Islander, non-Hispanic/Latino; 12% Two or more races, non-Hispanic/Latino; 4% Race/ethnicity unknown; 0.7% international; 11% transferred in; 46% live on campus.

Freshmen:
Admission: 714 applied, 480 admitted, 146 enrolled. ***Average high school GPA:*** 3.3. ***Test scores:*** SAT evidence-based reading and writing scores over 500: 62%; SAT math scores over 500: 56%; ACT scores over 18: 72%; SAT evidence-based reading and writing scores over 600: 16%; SAT math scores over 600: 8%; ACT scores over 24: 8%; SAT evidence-based reading and writing scores over 700: 1%; SAT math scores over 700: 1%.

Retention: 66% of full-time freshmen returned.

FACULTY
Total: 151, 36% full-time, 39% with terminal degrees.

Student/faculty ratio: 10:1.

ACADEMICS

Calendar: semesters. *Degrees:* associate, bachelor's, master's, and postbachelor's certificates (also offers external degree program with significant enrollment not reflected in profile).

Special study options: academic remediation for entering students, accelerated degree program, advanced placement credit, distance learning, double majors, external degree program, honors programs, independent study, internships, off-campus study, part-time degree program, services for LD students, student-designed majors, study abroad, summer session for credit. ***ROTC:*** Army (c), Navy (c), Air Force (c).

Unusual degree programs: 3-2 business administration.

Computers: Students can access the following: campus intranet, computer help desk, free student e-mail accounts, online (class) grades, online (class) schedules. Campuswide network is available. 100% of college-owned or -operated housing units are wired for high-speed Internet access. Wireless service is available via entire campus.
Library: Rooney Library.

STUDENT LIFE

Housing options: coed, special housing for students with disabilities. Campus housing is university owned. Freshman campus housing is guaranteed.

Activities and organizations: drama/theater group, student-run newspaper, choral group.

Athletics Member USCAA. ***Intercollegiate sports:*** basketball W(s), cross-country running M(s)/W(s), equestrian sports W(s), golf M(s)/W(s), soccer M(s)/W(s), softball W(s), track and field M(s)/W(s), volleyball W(s). ***Intramural sports:*** rowing M(c)/W(c).

Campus security: 24-hour emergency response devices and patrols, late-night transport/escort service, controlled dormitory access, Resident Assistants (RAs) patrol the residence hall 3-4 times per night.

Student services: health clinic, personal/psychological counseling.

COSTS & FINANCIAL AID

Costs (2020–21) ***Comprehensive fee:*** $41,740 includes full-time tuition ($29,950), mandatory fees ($550), and room and board ($11,240). Full-time tuition and fees vary according to course load and program. Part-time tuition: $496 per credit hour. Part-time tuition and fees vary according to course load and program. No tuition increase for student's term of enrollment. ***College room only:*** $4440. Room and board charges vary according to board plan and housing facility. ***Waivers:*** employees or children of employees.

Financial Aid Of all full-time matriculated undergraduates who enrolled in 2017, 481 applied for aid, 481 were judged to have need. ***Average financial aid package:*** $26,216. ***Average need-based loan:*** $3844. ***Average need-based gift aid:*** $21,230. ***Financial aid deadline:*** 3/10.

APPLYING

Options: electronic application, early admission, deferred entrance.

Required: high school transcript, minimum 2.0 GPA. ***Required for some:*** essay or personal statement, minimum 1.0 GPA, official transcripts from all previous institutions for transfers; proof of RN license, valid driver's license, and background check for RN-to-BSN program; background check and Praxis II scores for teacher licensure. ***Recommended:*** essay or personal statement.

CONTACT

Crystal Cox, Associate Director of Admissions, Saint Mary-of-the-Woods College, Rooney Library, 1 St. Mary of the Woods College, St Mary of the Woods, IN 47876. *Phone:* 812-535-5263. *Toll-free phone:* 800-926-SMWC. *Fax:* 812-535-5010. *E-mail:* Crystal.Cox@smwc.edu.

Saint Mary's College

Notre Dame, Indiana

http://www.saintmarys.edu/

- **Independent Roman Catholic** comprehensive, founded 1844
- **Suburban** 100-acre campus
- **Endowment** $201.1 million
- **Women only** 1,452 undergraduate students, 98% full-time
- **Moderately difficult** entrance level, 81% of applicants were admitted

UNDERGRAD STUDENTS

1,421 full-time, 31 part-time. Students come from 44 states and territories; 9 other countries; 68% are from out of state; 2% Black or African American, non-Hispanic/Latino; 15% Hispanic/Latino; 2% Asian, non-Hispanic/Latino; 0.1% Native Hawaiian or other Pacific Islander, non-Hispanic/Latino; 0.1% American Indian or Alaska Native, non-Hispanic/Latino; 3% Two or more races, non-Hispanic/Latino; 2% Race/ethnicity unknown; 0.9% international; 1% transferred in; 84% live on campus.

Freshmen:

Admission: 2,033 applied, 1,651 admitted, 374 enrolled. ***Average high school GPA:*** 3.8. ***Test scores:*** SAT evidence-based reading and writing scores over 500: 92%; SAT math scores over 500: 90%; ACT scores over 18: 99%; SAT evidence-based reading and writing scores over 600: 49%; SAT math scores over 600: 32%; ACT scores over 24: 75%; SAT evidence-based reading and writing scores over 700: 7%; SAT math scores over 700: 6%; ACT scores over 30: 16%.

Retention: 82% of full-time freshmen returned.

FACULTY

Total: 168, 80% full-time, 76% with terminal degrees.
Student/faculty ratio: 10:1.

ACADEMICS

Calendar: semesters. *Degrees:* bachelor's, master's, and doctoral.

Special study options: advanced placement credit, distance learning, double majors, independent study, internships, off-campus study, part-time degree program, services for LD students, student-designed majors, study abroad, summer session for credit. ***ROTC:*** Army (c), Navy (c), Air Force (c).

Computers: 284 computers/terminals are available on campus for general student use. Students can access the following: campus intranet, computer help desk, free student e-mail accounts, online (class) grades, online (class) registration, online (class) schedules. Campuswide network is available. 100% of college-owned or -operated housing units are wired for high-speed Internet access. Wireless service is available via classrooms, computer centers, computer labs, dorm rooms, learning centers, libraries, student centers.
Library: Cushwa-Leighton Library. *Books:* 154,790 (physical), 170,212 (digital/electronic); *Serial titles:* 3,122 (physical), 66,162 (digital/electronic); *Databases:* 99. Weekly public service hours: 54; study areas open 24 hours, 5–7 days a week; students can reserve study rooms.

STUDENT LIFE

Housing options: on-campus residence required through junior year; women-only, special housing for students with disabilities. Campus housing is university owned. Freshman campus housing is guaranteed.

Activities and organizations: drama/theater group, student-run newspaper, radio and television station, choral group, marching band, Student Government Association, Dance Marathon, Class Boards, Residence Hall Association, Student Diversity Board.

Athletics Member NCAA. All Division III. ***Intercollegiate sports:*** basketball W, cross-country running W, golf W, lacrosse W, soccer W, softball W, tennis W, volleyball W. ***Intramural sports:*** cheerleading W(c), field hockey W(c), volleyball W(c).

Campus security: 24-hour emergency response devices and patrols, late-night transport/escort service, controlled dormitory access.

Student services: health clinic, personal/psychological counseling, women's center.

COSTS & FINANCIAL AID

Costs (2020–21) ***One-time required fee:*** $150. ***Comprehensive fee:*** $59,190 includes full-time tuition ($44,760), mandatory fees ($960), and room and board ($13,470). Full-time tuition and fees vary according to course load. Part-time tuition: $1780 per credit hour. ***College room only:*** $8350. Room and board charges vary according to board plan and housing facility. ***Payment plan:*** installment. ***Waivers:*** employees or children of employees.

Financial Aid Of all full-time matriculated undergraduates who enrolled in 2019, 1,188 applied for aid, 1,043 were judged to have need, 194 had their need fully met. In 2019, 362 non-need-based awards were made. ***Average percent of need met:*** 88. ***Average financial aid package:*** $38,653. ***Average need-based loan:*** $4370. ***Average need-based gift aid:***

$34,049. ***Average non-need-based aid:*** $18,870. ***Average indebtedness upon graduation:*** $47,977. ***Financial aid deadline:*** 3/1.

APPLYING

Standardized Tests *Required for some:* SAT or ACT (for admission). *Recommended:* SAT or ACT (for admission).

Options: electronic application, early admission, early decision, deferred entrance.

Required: essay or personal statement, high school transcript, 1 letter of recommendation, 16 high school academic units, minimum two years of study of the same foreign language.

Application deadlines: 2/15 (freshmen), 4/15 (transfers).

Early decision deadline: 11/15.

Notification: continuous (freshmen), continuous (transfers), 12/15 (early decision).

CONTACT

Sarah Dvorak, Director of Admission, Saint Mary's College, Notre Dame, IN 46556. *Phone:* 574-284-4587. *Toll-free phone:* 800-551-7621. *Fax:* 574-284-4841. *E-mail:* sdvorak@saintmarys.edu.

See below for display ad and page 1108 for the College Close-Up.

Taylor University

Upland, Indiana

http://www.taylor.edu/

- **Independent interdenominational** comprehensive, founded 1846
- **Rural** 950-acre campus with easy access to Indianapolis
- **Endowment** $95.5 million
- **Coed** 2,148 undergraduate students, 84% full-time, 55% women, 45% men
- **Moderately difficult** entrance level, 68% of applicants were admitted

UNDERGRAD STUDENTS

1,799 full-time, 349 part-time. Students come from 43 states and territories; 31 other countries; 45% are from out of state; 3% Black or African American, non-Hispanic/Latino; 4% Hispanic/Latino; 3% Asian, non-Hispanic/Latino; 0.3% Native Hawaiian or other Pacific Islander, non-Hispanic/Latino; 0.3% American Indian or Alaska Native, non-Hispanic/Latino; 1% Two or more races, non-Hispanic/Latino; 5% international; 2% transferred in; 90% live on campus.

Freshmen:

Admission: 2,341 applied, 1,595 admitted, 490 enrolled. ***Average high school GPA:*** 3.8. ***Test scores:*** SAT evidence-based reading and writing scores over 500: 89%; SAT math scores over 500: 89%; ACT scores over 18: 94%; SAT evidence-based reading and writing scores over 600: 51%; SAT math scores over 600: 48%; ACT scores over 24: 62%; SAT evidence-based reading and writing scores over 700: 11%; SAT math scores over 700: 12%; ACT scores over 30: 18%.

Retention: 85% of full-time freshmen returned.

FACULTY

Total: 207, 65% full-time, 73% with terminal degrees.

Student/faculty ratio: 13:1.

ACADEMICS

Calendar: 4-1-4. *Degrees:* diplomas, bachelor's, and master's.

Special study options: academic remediation for entering students, advanced placement credit, cooperative education, distance learning, double majors, English as a second language, honors programs, independent study, internships, off-campus study, part-time degree program, services for LD students, student-designed majors, study abroad, summer session for credit.

Computers: 375 computers/terminals are available on campus for general student use. Students can access the following: campus intranet, computer help desk, free student e-mail accounts, online (class) grades, online (class) registration, online (class) schedules. Campuswide network is available. 100% of college-owned or -operated housing units are wired for high-speed Internet access. Wireless service is available via entire campus.

Library: Zondervan Library. *Books:* 128,733 (physical), 228,315 (digital/electronic); *Serial titles:* 631 (physical); *Databases:* 115. Weekly public service hours: 96; study areas open 24 hours, 5–7 days a week.

STUDENT LIFE
Housing options: on-campus residence required through junior year; coed, men-only, women-only. Campus housing is university owned. Freshman campus housing is guaranteed.

Activities and organizations: drama/theater group, student-run newspaper, radio and television station, choral group, Spring Break Missions, Lighthouse, Alpha Pi Lota, Encounter, Kappa Delta Pi.

Athletics Member NAIA. ***Intercollegiate sports:*** baseball M(s), basketball M(s)/W(s), cross-country running M(s)/W(s), football M(s), golf M(s), lacrosse M, soccer M(s)/W(s), softball W(s), tennis M(s)/W(s), track and field M(s)/W(s), volleyball W(s). ***Intramural sports:*** badminton M/W, basketball M/W, equestrian sports W(c), lacrosse M(c)/W(c), racquetball M/W, soccer M/W, softball M/W, tennis M/W, ultimate Frisbee M/W, volleyball M/W.

Campus security: 24-hour patrols, student patrols, late-night transport/escort service, controlled dormitory access.

Student services: health clinic, personal/psychological counseling.

COSTS & FINANCIAL AID
Costs (2019–20) ***Comprehensive fee:*** $45,255 includes full-time tuition ($35,050), mandatory fees ($255), and room and board ($9950). Full-time tuition and fees vary according to course load and reciprocity agreements. Part-time tuition: $1235 per credit hour. ***Required fees:*** $45 per term part-time. ***College room only:*** $5230. ***Payment plan:*** installment. ***Waivers:*** senior citizens and employees or children of employees.

Financial Aid Of all full-time matriculated undergraduates who enrolled in 2019, 1,354 applied for aid, 1,145 were judged to have need, 344 had their need fully met. 800 Federal Work-Study jobs (averaging $638). In 2019, 515 non-need-based awards were made. ***Average percent of need met:*** 80. ***Average financial aid package:*** $26,360. ***Average need-based loan:*** $4280. ***Average need-based gift aid:*** $22,545. ***Average non-need-based aid:*** $15,322. ***Average indebtedness upon graduation:*** $26,009.

APPLYING
Standardized Tests *Required:* SAT or ACT (for admission).

Options: electronic application, early action, deferred entrance.

Application fee: $25.

Required: essay or personal statement, high school transcript, 2 letters of recommendation. ***Recommended:*** minimum 2.8 GPA, interview.

Application deadlines: rolling (freshmen), rolling (transfers).

Notification: continuous (freshmen), continuous (transfers).

CONTACT
Jesslyn Ridge, Visit Coordinator, Taylor University, 236 West Reade Avenue, Upland, IN 46989-1001. *Phone:* 765-998-5511. *Toll-free phone:* 800-882-3456. *Fax:* 765-998-4925. *E-mail:* admissions@taylor.edu.

Trine University

Angola, Indiana

http://www.trine.edu/

- **Independent** comprehensive, founded 1884
- **Small-town** 400-acre campus
- **Endowment** $32.0 million
- **Coed** 3,808 undergraduate students, 56% full-time, 47% women, 53% men
- **Moderately difficult** entrance level, 82% of applicants were admitted

UNDERGRAD STUDENTS
2,125 full-time, 1,683 part-time. 4% Black or African American, non-Hispanic/Latino; 5% Hispanic/Latino; 2% Asian, non-Hispanic/Latino; 0.2% American Indian or Alaska Native, non-Hispanic/Latino; 3% Two or more races, non-Hispanic/Latino; 1% Race/ethnicity unknown; 4% international; 70% live on campus.

Freshmen:
Admission: 4,063 applied, 3,312 admitted, 618 enrolled. ***Average high school GPA:*** 3.6. ***Test scores:*** SAT evidence-based reading and writing scores over 500: 82%; SAT math scores over 500: 87%; ACT scores over 18: 94%; SAT evidence-based reading and writing scores over 600: 38%; SAT math scores over 600: 42%; ACT scores over 24: 58%; SAT evidence-based reading and writing scores over 700: 6%; SAT math scores over 700: 11%; ACT scores over 30: 14%.

Retention: 76% of full-time freshmen returned.

FACULTY
Total: 124, 99% full-time, 85% with terminal degrees.

Student/faculty ratio: 15:1.

ACADEMICS
Calendar: semesters. *Degrees:* associate, bachelor's, master's, and doctoral.

Special study options: academic remediation for entering students, accelerated degree program, adult/continuing education programs, advanced placement credit, cooperative education, distance learning, double majors, honors programs, independent study, internships, part-time degree program, services for LD students, student-designed majors, study abroad, summer session for credit. ***ROTC:*** Air Force (c).

Unusual degree programs: 3-2 engineering.

Computers: 400 computers/terminals and 1,100 ports are available on campus for general student use. Students can access the following: computer help desk, free student e-mail accounts, online (class) grades, online (class) registration, online (class) schedules, online campus billing accounts, course management system. Campuswide network is available. 100% of college-owned or -operated housing units are wired for high-speed Internet access. Wireless service is available via entire campus.

Library: Sponsel Library plus 1 other. *Books:* 23,523 (physical), 225,584 (digital/electronic); *Serial titles:* 19 (physical), 21,141 (digital/electronic); *Databases:* 87.

STUDENT LIFE
Housing options: on-campus residence required through senior year; coed, men-only, women-only, special housing for students with disabilities. Campus housing is university owned. Freshman campus housing is guaranteed.

Activities and organizations: drama/theater group, student-run radio station, choral group, marching band, Campus Christian House, Society of Women Engineers, Multicultural Student Organization, SPEAK, Trine Disc Golf Collective, national fraternities, national sororities.

Athletics Member NCAA. All Division III. ***Intercollegiate sports:*** baseball M, basketball M/W, bowling M(c)/W(c), cross-country running M/W, field hockey W, football M, golf M/W, ice hockey M/W, lacrosse M/W, soccer M/W, softball W, tennis M/W, track and field M/W, triathlon W, volleyball M/W, wrestling M. ***Intramural sports:*** basketball M/W, football M, golf M/W, sand volleyball M/W, skiing (downhill) M(c)/W(c), table tennis M(c)/W(c), ultimate Frisbee M(c)/W(c), volleyball M/W.

Campus security: 24-hour emergency response devices and patrols, late-night transport/escort service, controlled dormitory access.

Student services: health clinic, personal/psychological counseling.

COSTS & FINANCIAL AID
Costs (2020–21) ***Tuition:*** $32,990 full-time, $1060 per credit hour part-time. ***Required fees:*** $500 full-time. ***Room only:*** $6700.

Financial Aid Of all full-time matriculated undergraduates who enrolled in 2019, 1,961 applied for aid, 1,730 were judged to have need, 401 had their need fully met. In 2019, 313 non-need-based awards were made. ***Average percent of need met:*** 78. ***Average financial aid package:*** $26,469. ***Average need-based loan:*** $3753. ***Average need-based gift aid:*** $22,274. ***Average non-need-based aid:*** $15,293. ***Average indebtedness upon graduation:*** $33,933.

APPLYING
Standardized Tests *Required:* SAT or ACT (for admission).

Options: electronic application, deferred entrance.

Required: high school transcript, minimum 2.5 GPA. ***Recommended:*** essay or personal statement, 2 letters of recommendation, interview.

Application deadlines: 8/1 (freshmen), 8/1 (transfers).

Notification: 8/15 (freshmen), continuous until 8/15 (transfers).

CONTACT
Ms. Theresa Knight, Admission Coordinator, Trine University, 1 University Avenue, Angola, IN 46703. *Phone:* 260-665-4132. *Toll-free phone:* 800-347-4878. *E-mail:* admit@trine.edu.

University of Evansville

Evansville, Indiana

http://www.evansville.edu/

CONTACT

Kenton Hargis, Director of Admission, University of Evansville, 1800 Lincoln Avenue, Evansville, IN 47722. *Phone:* 812-488-2142. *Toll-free phone:* 800-423-8633 Ext. 2468. *E-mail:* kh88@evansville.edu.

University of Indianapolis

Indianapolis, Indiana

http://www.uindy.edu/

CONTACT

Mr. Ronald Wilks, Associate Vice President of Admissions, University of Indianapolis, 1400 East Hanna Avenue, Indianapolis, IN 46227-3697. *Phone:* 317-788-3216. *Toll-free phone:* 800-232-8634 Ext. 3216. *Fax:* 317-788-3300. *E-mail:* admissions@uindy.edu.

University of Notre Dame

Notre Dame, Indiana

http://www.nd.edu/

- **Independent Roman Catholic** university, founded 1842
- **Suburban** 1250-acre campus
- **Endowment** $14.0 billion
- **Coed** 8,731 undergraduate students, 100% full-time, 48% women, 52% men
- **Most difficult** entrance level, 16% of applicants were admitted

UNDERGRAD STUDENTS

8,707 full-time, 24 part-time. Students come from 54 states and territories; 71 other countries; 91% are from out of state; 4% Black or African American, non-Hispanic/Latino; 11% Hispanic/Latino; 5% Asian, non-Hispanic/Latino; 0.1% Native Hawaiian or other Pacific Islander, non-Hispanic/Latino; 0.2% American Indian or Alaska Native, non-Hispanic/Latino; 5% Two or more races, non-Hispanic/Latino; 1% Race/ethnicity unknown; 7% international; 2% transferred in; 78% live on campus.

Freshmen:

Admission: 22,200 applied, 3,515 admitted, 2,051 enrolled. ***Test scores:*** SAT evidence-based reading and writing scores over 500: 100%; SAT math scores over 500: 100%; ACT scores over 18: 99%; SAT evidence-based reading and writing scores over 600: 98%; SAT math scores over 600: 98%; ACT scores over 24: 98%; SAT evidence-based reading and writing scores over 700: 70%; SAT math scores over 700: 80%; ACT scores over 30: 89%.

Retention: 98% of full-time freshmen returned.

FACULTY

Total: 1,396, 88% full-time, 86% with terminal degrees.

Student/faculty ratio: 10:1.

ACADEMICS

Calendar: semesters. *Degrees:* bachelor's, master's, and doctoral.

Special study options: advanced placement credit, distance learning, double majors, honors programs, independent study, internships, off-campus study, services for LD students, student-designed majors, study abroad, summer session for credit. ***ROTC:*** Army (b), Navy (b), Air Force (b).

Computers: 782 computers/terminals and 14,887 ports are available on campus for general student use. Students can access the following: computer help desk, free student e-mail accounts, online (class) grades, online (class) registration, online (class) schedules. Campuswide network is available. Wireless service is available via entire campus.
Library: Hesburgh Library plus 11 others.

STUDENT LIFE

Housing options: on-campus residence required for freshman year; men-only, women-only. Campus housing is university owned. Freshman campus housing is guaranteed.

Activities and organizations: drama/theater group, student-run newspaper, radio station, choral group, marching band, marching band, Circle K, Finance Club, Notre Dame/St. Mary's Right to Life.

Athletics Member NCAA. All Division I except football (Division I-A). ***Intercollegiate sports:*** baseball M(s), basketball M(s)/W(s), crew W(s), cross-country running M(s)/W(s), fencing M(s)/W(s), golf M(s)/W(s)(c), ice hockey M(s), lacrosse M(s)/W(s), soccer M(s)/W(s), softball W(s), swimming and diving M(s)/W(s), tennis M(s)/W(s), track and field M(s)/W(s), volleyball W(s). ***Intramural sports:*** badminton M/W, baseball M, basketball M/W, bowling M(c)/W(c), crew M(c), equestrian sports M(c)/W(c), fencing W(c), football M/W, golf M/W, gymnastics M(c)/W(c), ice hockey M/W(c), lacrosse M/W, racquetball M/W, rugby M(c)/W(c), sailing M(c)/W(c), skiing (cross-country) M(c)/W(c), skiing (downhill) M(c)/W(c), soccer M/W, softball M/W, squash M(c)/W(c), table tennis M/W, tennis M/W, ultimate Frisbee M/W, volleyball M(c)/W(c), water polo M(c)/W(c), wrestling M(c).

Campus security: 24-hour emergency response devices and patrols, student patrols, late-night transport/escort service, controlled dormitory access.

Student services: health clinic, personal/psychological counseling, women's center.

COSTS & FINANCIAL AID

Costs (2020–21) ***Comprehensive fee:*** $73,683 includes full-time tuition ($57,192), mandatory fees ($507), and room and board ($15,984). Part-time tuition: $2383 per credit hour. ***Payment plan:*** installment. ***Waivers:*** employees or children of employees.

Financial Aid Of all full-time matriculated undergraduates who enrolled in 2019, 5,098 applied for aid, 4,142 were judged to have need, 4,129 had their need fully met. 1,409 Federal Work-Study jobs (averaging $2627). 3,394 state and other part-time jobs (averaging $3414). In 2019, 437 non-need-based awards were made. ***Average percent of need met:*** 100. ***Average financial aid package:*** $52,593. ***Average need-based loan:*** $5245. ***Average need-based gift aid:*** $42,382. ***Average non-need-based aid:*** $12,648. ***Average indebtedness upon graduation:*** $27,460.

APPLYING

Standardized Tests *Required:* SAT or ACT (for admission). *Required for some:* SAT Subject Tests (for admission).

Options: electronic application, early action, deferred entrance.

Application fee: $80.

Required: essay or personal statement, high school transcript, 1 letter of recommendation.

Application deadlines: 12/1 (freshmen), 3/15 (transfers), 11/1 (early action).

Notification: 4/10 (freshmen).

CONTACT

University of Notre Dame, Notre Dame, IN 46556. *Phone:* 574-631-7505.

University of Saint Francis

Fort Wayne, Indiana

http://www.sf.edu/

- **Independent Roman Catholic** comprehensive, founded 1890
- **Urban** 100-acre campus
- **Endowment** $31.2 million
- **Coed** 1,745 undergraduate students, 86% full-time, 70% women, 30% men
- **Noncompetitive** entrance level, 96% of applicants were admitted

UNDERGRAD STUDENTS

1,497 full-time, 248 part-time. Students come from 21 states and territories; 8 other countries; 11% are from out of state; 9% Black or African American, non-Hispanic/Latino; 10% Hispanic/Latino; 2% Asian, non-Hispanic/Latino; 0.1% American Indian or Alaska Native, non-Hispanic/Latino; 3% Two or more races, non-Hispanic/Latino; 1% Race/ethnicity unknown; 1% international; 8% transferred in; 22% live on campus.

Freshmen:

Admission: 1,587 applied, 1,527 admitted, 394 enrolled. ***Average high school GPA:*** 3.4. ***Test scores:*** SAT evidence-based reading and writing scores over 500: 66%; SAT math scores over 500: 67%; ACT scores over

18: 79%; SAT evidence-based reading and writing scores over 600: 23%; SAT math scores over 600: 16%; ACT scores over 24: 30%; SAT evidence-based reading and writing scores over 700: 1%; SAT math scores over 700: 1%; ACT scores over 30: 3%.

Retention: 69% of full-time freshmen returned.

FACULTY

Total: 298, 43% full-time, 30% with terminal degrees.

Student/faculty ratio: 11:1.

ACADEMICS

Calendar: semesters. *Degrees:* certificates, associate, bachelor's, master's, doctoral, and post-master's certificates.

Special study options: academic remediation for entering students, advanced placement credit, cooperative education, distance learning, double majors, honors programs, independent study, internships, off-campus study, part-time degree program, services for LD students, student-designed majors, summer session for credit. ***ROTC:*** Army (c).

Computers: 105 computers/terminals are available on campus for general student use. Students can access the following: campus intranet, computer help desk, free student e-mail accounts, online (class) grades, online (class) registration, online (class) schedules. Campuswide network is available. 100% of college-owned or -operated housing units are wired for high-speed Internet access. Wireless service is available via entire campus.

Library: Lee and Jim Vann Library. *Books:* 64,995 (physical), 239,068 (digital/electronic); *Serial titles:* 799 (physical), 36,336 (digital/electronic); *Databases:* 111. Weekly public service hours: 86; students can reserve study rooms.

STUDENT LIFE

Housing options: on-campus residence required through junior year; coed, men-only, women-only, special housing for students with disabilities. Campus housing is university owned. Freshman applicants given priority for college housing.

Activities and organizations: drama/theater group, choral group, marching band, Student Activities Council, Student Government Association, Intramural Sports, Residence Hall Association, Kinesiology and Nutrition Club.

Athletics Member NAIA. ***Intercollegiate sports:*** baseball M(s), basketball M(s)/W(s), cheerleading M(s)/W(s), cross-country running M(s)/W(s), football M(s), golf M(s)/W(s), soccer M(s)/W(s), softball W(s), tennis M(s)/W(s), track and field M(s)/W(s), volleyball W(s). ***Intramural sports:*** basketball M/W, bowling M/W, football M/W, skiing (downhill) M/W, ultimate Frisbee M(c)/W(c), volleyball M/W.

Campus security: 24-hour emergency response devices and patrols, late-night transport/escort service, controlled dormitory access.

Student services: personal/psychological counseling.

COSTS & FINANCIAL AID

Costs (2020–21) ***One-time required fee:*** $195. ***Comprehensive fee:*** $42,910 includes full-time tuition ($31,290), mandatory fees ($1130), and room and board ($10,490). Full-time tuition and fees vary according to course load and location. Part-time tuition: $995 per semester hour. Part-time tuition and fees vary according to course load and location. ***Required fees:*** $30 per semester hour part-time, $160 per term part-time. ***Payment plan:*** installment. ***Waivers:*** employees or children of employees.

Financial Aid Of all full-time matriculated undergraduates who enrolled in 2019, 1,402 applied for aid, 1,269 were judged to have need, 221 had their need fully met. In 2019, 147 non-need-based awards were made. ***Average percent of need met:*** 73. ***Average financial aid package:*** $23,587. ***Average need-based loan:*** $3715. ***Average need-based gift aid:*** $20,164. ***Average non-need-based aid:*** $10,539. ***Average indebtedness upon graduation:*** $42,336.

APPLYING

Standardized Tests *Required:* SAT or ACT (for admission).

Options: electronic application, deferred entrance.

Required: high school transcript, minimum 2.3 GPA. ***Required for some:*** essay or personal statement, 2 letters of recommendation, interview.

Application deadlines: rolling (freshmen), rolling (out-of-state freshmen), rolling (transfers).

Notification: continuous (freshmen), continuous (out-of-state freshmen), continuous (transfers).

CONTACT

Mrs. Michelle Kuhlhorst, Executive Director of Enrollment Management, University of Saint Francis, 2701 Spring Street, Fort Wayne, IN 46808. *Phone:* 260-399-7700 Ext. 6307. *Toll-free phone:* 800-729-4732. *E-mail:* admis@sf.edu.

University of Southern Indiana

Evansville, Indiana

http://www.usi.edu/

- **State-supported** comprehensive, founded 1965, part of Indiana Commission for Higher Education
- **Suburban** 1400-acre campus
- **Coed** 7,094 undergraduate students, 86% full-time, 63% women, 37% men
- **Moderately difficult** entrance level, 93% of applicants were admitted

UNDERGRAD STUDENTS

6,125 full-time, 969 part-time. 16% are from out of state; 4% Black or African American, non-Hispanic/Latino; 4% Hispanic/Latino; 1% Asian, non-Hispanic/Latino; 0.1% Native Hawaiian or other Pacific Islander, non-Hispanic/Latino; 0.1% American Indian or Alaska Native, non-Hispanic/Latino; 3% Two or more races, non-Hispanic/Latino; 0.1% Race/ethnicity unknown; 2% international; 7% transferred in; 35% live on campus.

Freshmen:

Admission: 4,614 applied, 4,306 admitted, 1,585 enrolled. ***Average high school GPA:*** 3.5. ***Test scores:*** SAT evidence-based reading and writing scores over 500: 73%; SAT math scores over 500: 73%; ACT scores over 18: 91%; SAT evidence-based reading and writing scores over 600: 23%; SAT math scores over 600: 20%; ACT scores over 24: 36%; SAT evidence-based reading and writing scores over 700: 2%; SAT math scores over 700: 2%; ACT scores over 30: 5%.

Retention: 67% of full-time freshmen returned.

FACULTY

Total: 650, 56% full-time, 53% with terminal degrees.

Student/faculty ratio: 17:1.

ACADEMICS

Calendar: semesters. *Degrees:* certificates, associate, bachelor's, master's, doctoral, post-master's, and postbachelor's certificates.

Special study options: academic remediation for entering students, accelerated degree program, adult/continuing education programs, advanced placement credit, cooperative education, distance learning, double majors, English as a second language, external degree program, honors programs, independent study, internships, part-time degree program, services for LD students, study abroad, summer session for credit. ***ROTC:*** Army (b).

Computers: 1,165 computers/terminals are available on campus for general student use. Students can access the following: campus intranet, computer help desk, free student e-mail accounts, online (class) grades, online (class) registration, online (class) schedules. Campuswide network is available. 100% of college-owned or -operated housing units are wired for high-speed Internet access. Wireless service is available via entire campus.

Library: David L. Rice Library. *Books:* 241,710 (physical), 230,844 (digital/electronic); *Serial titles:* 1,075 (physical), 141,229 (digital/electronic); *Databases:* 168. Weekly public service hours: 114; students can reserve study rooms.

STUDENT LIFE

Housing options: coed, special housing for students with disabilities. Campus housing is university owned.

Activities and organizations: drama/theater group, student-run newspaper, radio and television station, choral group, Sororities, Fraternities, Riley Dance Marathon, Activities Programming Board, Student Government Association, national fraternities, national sororities.

Athletics Member NCAA. All Division II except golf (Division I). ***Intercollegiate sports:*** baseball M(s), basketball M(s)/W(s), cheerleading M(c)/W(c), cross-country running M(s)/W(s), golf M(s)/W(s), soccer M(s)/W(s), softball W(s), tennis M(s)/W(s), track and field M(s)/W(s), volleyball W(s). ***Intramural sports:*** badminton M/W, basketball M/W, bowling M/W, football M/W, golf M/W, rugby M(c)/W(c), sand volleyball

M/W, soccer M/W, softball M/W, table tennis M/W, tennis M/W, ultimate Frisbee M(c)/W(c), volleyball M/W, wrestling M(c).

Campus security: 24-hour emergency response devices and patrols, student patrols, late-night transport/escort service, controlled dormitory access.

Student services: health clinic, personal/psychological counseling, veterans affairs office.

FINANCIAL AID

Financial Aid Of all full-time matriculated undergraduates who enrolled in 2019, 5,665 applied for aid, 3,844 were judged to have need, 1,240 had their need fully met. In 2019, 1298 non-need-based awards were made. ***Average percent of need met:*** 86. ***Average financial aid package:*** $10,422. ***Average need-based loan:*** $4027. ***Average need-based gift aid:*** $10,588. ***Average non-need-based aid:*** $4830. ***Average indebtedness upon graduation:*** $24,427.

APPLYING

Standardized Tests *Required:* SAT or ACT (for admission).

Options: electronic application.

Application fee: $40.

Required: high school transcript. ***Required for some:*** interview. ***Recommended:*** minimum 2.5 GPA.

Notification: continuous (freshmen).

CONTACT

Mr. Rashad Smith, Director of Undergraduate Admissions, University of Southern Indiana, 8600 University Boulevard, Evansville, IN 47712-3590. *Phone:* 812-464-1765. *Toll-free phone:* 800-467-1965. *Fax:* 812-465-7154. *E-mail:* enroll@usi.edu.

Valparaiso University

Valparaiso, Indiana

http://www.valpo.edu/

- **Independent** comprehensive, founded 1859, affiliated with Lutheran Church
- **Small-town** 350-acre campus with easy access to Chicago
- **Endowment** $259.0 million
- **Coed** 3,009 undergraduate students, 98% full-time, 56% women, 44% men
- **Moderately difficult** entrance level, 86% of applicants were admitted

UNDERGRAD STUDENTS

2,956 full-time, 53 part-time. Students come from 49 states and territories; 38 other countries; 54% are from out of state; 5% Black or African American, non-Hispanic/Latino; 11% Hispanic/Latino; 2% Asian, non-Hispanic/Latino; 0.1% American Indian or Alaska Native, non-Hispanic/Latino; 3% Two or more races, non-Hispanic/Latino; 3% Race/ethnicity unknown; 3% international; 5% transferred in; 60% live on campus.

Freshmen:

Admission: 5,491 applied, 4,705 admitted, 647 enrolled. ***Average high school GPA:*** 3.8. ***Test scores:*** SAT evidence-based reading and writing scores over 500: 91%; SAT math scores over 500: 92%; ACT scores over 18: 98%; SAT evidence-based reading and writing scores over 600: 45%; SAT math scores over 600: 44%; ACT scores over 24: 64%; SAT evidence-based reading and writing scores over 700: 8%; SAT math scores over 700: 13%; ACT scores over 30: 22%.

Retention: 84% of full-time freshmen returned.

FACULTY

Total: 396, 73% full-time.

Student/faculty ratio: 10:1.

ACADEMICS

Calendar: semesters. *Degrees:* certificates, associate, bachelor's, master's, doctoral, post-master's, and postbachelor's certificates.

Special study options: accelerated degree program, adult/continuing education programs, advanced placement credit, cooperative education, distance learning, double majors, English as a second language, freshman honors college, honors programs, independent study, internships, off-campus study, part-time degree program, services for LD students, student-designed majors, study abroad, summer session for credit. ***ROTC:*** Army (c), Air Force (c).

Unusual degree programs: 3-2 physician assistant.

Computers: 500 computers/terminals are available on campus for general student use. Students can access the following: campus intranet, computer help desk, free student e-mail accounts, online (class) grades, online (class) registration, online (class) schedules, Web Academic Information, Degree Audit, Online Course Evaluations, Online Bills, Online Financial Award. Campuswide network is available. 100% of college-owned or -operated housing units are wired for high-speed Internet access. Wireless service is available via entire campus.

Library: Christopher Center for Library and Information Resources. *Books:* 321,605 (physical), 181,183 (digital/electronic); *Serial titles:* 85 (physical), 311,264 (digital/electronic); *Databases:* 201. Weekly public service hours: 113.

STUDENT LIFE

Housing options: on-campus residence required through junior year; coed, women-only, special housing for students with disabilities. Campus housing is university owned. Freshman campus housing is guaranteed.

Activities and organizations: drama/theater group, student-run newspaper, radio station, choral group, Student Government, Student Volunteer Organization, Chapel Programs, Union Board, national fraternities, national sororities.

Athletics Member NCAA. All Division I except football (Division I-AA). ***Intercollegiate sports:*** baseball M(s), basketball M(s)/W(s), bowling W(s), cross-country running M(s)/W(s), golf M(s)/W(s), soccer M(s)/W(s), softball W(s), swimming and diving M(s)/W(s), tennis M(s)/W(s), track and field M(s)/W(s), volleyball W(s). ***Intramural sports:*** badminton M/W, basketball M/W, bowling M/W, cheerleading M/W, football M/W, golf M/W, racquetball M/W, soccer M(c)/W(c), softball W(c), table tennis M/W, tennis M(c)/W(c), triathlon M/W, ultimate Frisbee M(c)/W(c), volleyball M/W.

Campus security: 24-hour emergency response devices and patrols, late-night transport/escort service, controlled dormitory access.

Student services: health clinic, personal/psychological counseling, legal services, veterans affairs office.

COSTS & FINANCIAL AID

Costs (2020–21) ***Comprehensive fee:*** $55,906 includes full-time tuition ($41,940), mandatory fees ($1346), and room and board ($12,620). Full-time tuition and fees vary according to course load, program, and student level. Part-time tuition: $1840 per credit hour. Part-time tuition and fees vary according to course load, program, and student level. ***Required fees:*** $130 per term part-time. ***College room only:*** $7800. Room and board charges vary according to board plan, housing facility, and student level. ***Payment plan:*** installment. ***Waivers:*** employees or children of employees.

Financial Aid Of all full-time matriculated undergraduates who enrolled in 2018, 2,654 applied for aid, 2,413 were judged to have need, 1,092 had their need fully met. 640 Federal Work-Study jobs (averaging $2300). 1,248 state and other part-time jobs (averaging $1982). In 2018, 647 non-need-based awards were made. ***Average percent of need met:*** 94. ***Average financial aid package:*** $32,990. ***Average need-based loan:*** $4470. ***Average need-based gift aid:*** $28,935. ***Average non-need-based aid:*** $20,367. ***Average indebtedness upon graduation:*** $35,968.

APPLYING

Standardized Tests *Required:* SAT or ACT (for admission).

Options: electronic application, deferred entrance.

Required: essay or personal statement, high school transcript. ***Recommended:*** 2 letters of recommendation, interview.

Application deadlines: rolling (freshmen), rolling (transfers).

Notification: continuous (freshmen), continuous (transfers).

CONTACT

Mr. Bart Harvey, Executive Director of Undergraduate Admission, Valparaiso University, Duesenberg Welcome Center, 1620 Chapel Drive, Valparaiso, IN 46383-6493. *Phone:* 219-464-5011. *Toll-free phone:* 888-GO-VALPO. *Fax:* 219-464-6898. *E-mail:* undergrad.admission@valpo.edu.

Vincennes University

Vincennes, Indiana

http://www.vinu.edu/

- **State-supported** primarily 2-year, founded 1801
- **Small-town** 160-acre campus
- **Coed** 17,239 undergraduate students, 55% full-time, 76% women, 24% men
- **Noncompetitive** entrance level, 77% of applicants were admitted

UNDERGRAD STUDENTS

9,543 full-time, 7,696 part-time. 14% are from out of state; 8% Black or African American, non-Hispanic/Latino; 13% Hispanic/Latino; 0.8% Asian, non-Hispanic/Latino; 0.2% Native Hawaiian or other Pacific Islander, non-Hispanic/Latino; 0.4% American Indian or Alaska Native, non-Hispanic/Latino; 2% Two or more races, non-Hispanic/Latino; 3% Race/ethnicity unknown; 0.7% international; 0.8% transferred in; 37% live on campus.

Freshmen:

Admission: 4,631 applied, 3,566 admitted, 1,602 enrolled.

Retention: 32% of full-time freshmen returned.

FACULTY

Total: 817, 22% full-time.

Student/faculty ratio: 22:1.

ACADEMICS

Calendar: semesters. *Degrees:* certificates, associate, and bachelor's.

Special study options: academic remediation for entering students, accelerated degree program, adult/continuing education programs, advanced placement credit, distance learning, double majors, English as a second language, external degree program, freshman honors college, honors programs, independent study, internships, off-campus study, part-time degree program, services for LD students, student-designed majors, summer session for credit. ***ROTC:*** Army (c).

Computers: 1,500 computers/terminals are available on campus for general student use. Campuswide network is available.

Library: Shake Learning Resource Center. *Books:* 85,614 (physical), 104,859 (digital/electronic); *Serial titles:* 1,377 (physical); *Databases:* 99.

STUDENT LIFE

Housing options: on-campus residence required for freshman year; coed, men-only, women-only, special housing for students with disabilities. Campus housing is university owned. Freshman campus housing is guaranteed.

Activities and organizations: drama/theater group, student-run newspaper, radio and television station, choral group, national fraternities, national sororities.

Athletics Member NJCAA. ***Intercollegiate sports:*** baseball M, basketball M/W, bowling M, cross-country running M/W, golf M, track and field M/W, volleyball W.

Campus security: 24-hour emergency response devices and patrols, student patrols, late-night transport/escort service, controlled dormitory access.

Student services: health clinic, personal/psychological counseling.

COSTS

Costs (2019–20) ***Tuition:*** area resident $5581 full-time, $186 per credit hour part-time; state resident $5581 full-time, $186 per credit hour part-time; nonresident $13,871 full-time, $462 per credit hour part-time. Full-time tuition and fees vary according to course level, course load, location, program, reciprocity agreements, and student level. Part-time tuition and fees vary according to course level, course load, location, program, reciprocity agreements, and student level. ***Required fees:*** $493 full-time, $7 per credit hour part-time, $270 per year part-time. ***Room and board:*** $10,590. Room and board charges vary according to board plan and housing facility. ***Payment plan:*** installment. ***Waivers:*** senior citizens and employees or children of employees.

APPLYING

Options: electronic application, deferred entrance.

Application fee: $20.

Required: high school transcript. ***Required for some:*** interview.

Application deadlines: rolling (freshmen), rolling (transfers).

Notification: continuous until 8/1 (freshmen), continuous (transfers).

CONTACT

Vincennes University, 1002 North First Street, Vincennes, IN 47591.
Phone: 812-888-4313. *Toll-free phone:* 800-742-9198.

Wabash College

Crawfordsville, Indiana

http://www.wabash.edu/

- **Independent** 4-year, founded 1832
- **Small-town** 94-acre campus with easy access to Indianapolis
- **Endowment** $344.3 million
- **Men only** 867 undergraduate students, 100% full-time
- **Moderately difficult** entrance level, 64% of applicants were admitted

UNDERGRAD STUDENTS

866 full-time, 1 part-time. Students come from 27 states and territories; 20 other countries; 20% are from out of state; 5% Black or African American, non-Hispanic/Latino; 9% Hispanic/Latino; 0.9% Asian, non-Hispanic/Latino, 3% Two or more races, non-Hispanic/Latino, 2% Race/ethnicity unknown; 5% international; 0.7% transferred in; 99% live on campus.

Freshmen:

Admission: 1,307 applied, 839 admitted, 229 enrolled. ***Average high school GPA:*** 3.8. ***Test scores:*** SAT evidence-based reading and writing scores over 500: 97%; SAT math scores over 500: 98%; ACT scores over 18: 97%; SAT evidence-based reading and writing scores over 600: 56%; SAT math scores over 600: 56%; ACT scores over 24: 66%; SAT evidence-based reading and writing scores over 700: 8%; SAT math scores over 700: 18%; ACT scores over 30: 22%.

Retention: 91% of full-time freshmen returned.

FACULTY

Total: 100, 82% full-time, 95% with terminal degrees.

Student/faculty ratio: 10:1.

ACADEMICS

Calendar: semesters. *Degree:* bachelor's.

Special study options: advanced placement credit, double majors, independent study, internships, off-campus study, services for LD students, student-designed majors, study abroad. ***ROTC:*** Army (c).

Unusual degree programs: 3-2 engineering with Purdue University, Columbia University, Washington University in St. Louis.

Computers: 314 computers/terminals and 2,600 ports are available on campus for general student use. Students can access the following: campus intranet, computer help desk, free student e-mail accounts, online (class) grades, online (class) registration, online (class) schedules, online course management, degree audit, expenses. Campuswide network is available. 100% of college-owned or -operated housing units are wired for high-speed Internet access. Wireless service is available via entire campus.

Library: Lilly Library. *Books:* 243,187 (physical), 503,668 (digital/electronic); *Serial titles:* 15 (physical), 87,778 (digital/electronic); *Databases:* 113. Weekly public service hours: 105.

STUDENT LIFE

Housing options: on-campus residence required through senior year; men-only. Campus housing is university owned. Freshman campus housing is guaranteed.

Activities and organizations: drama/theater group, student-run newspaper, radio station, choral group, Inter-Fraternity Council, Malcolm X Institute for Black Studies, Sphinx Club, Student Government, Independent Men's Association, national fraternities.

Athletics Member NCAA. All Division III. ***Intercollegiate sports:*** baseball M, basketball M, cross-country running M, football M, golf M, lacrosse M, soccer M, swimming and diving M, tennis M, track and field M, wrestling M. ***Intramural sports:*** basketball M, football M, soccer M, softball M.

Campus security: 24-hour emergency response devices and patrols.

Student services: health clinic, personal/psychological counseling.

COSTS & FINANCIAL AID
Costs (2020–21) ***Comprehensive fee:*** $56,750 includes full-time tuition ($45,000), mandatory fees ($850), and room and board ($10,900). Part-time tuition: $7500 per course. Part-time tuition and fees vary according to course load. ***College room only:*** $5900. Room and board charges vary according to board plan, housing facility, and student level. ***Payment plans:*** tuition prepayment, installment. ***Waivers:*** employees or children of employees.

Financial Aid Of all full-time matriculated undergraduates who enrolled in 2019, 785 applied for aid, 660 were judged to have need, 516 had their need fully met. 223 Federal Work-Study jobs (averaging $2896). 328 state and other part-time jobs (averaging $2925). In 2019, 202 non-need-based awards were made. ***Average percent of need met:*** 93. ***Average financial aid package:*** $42,236. ***Average need-based loan:*** $4436. ***Average need-based gift aid:*** $34,377. ***Average non-need-based aid:*** $27,499. ***Average indebtedness upon graduation:*** $35,273.

APPLYING
Standardized Tests *Required:* SAT or ACT (for admission).

Options: electronic application, early decision, early action, deferred entrance.

Application fee: $50.

Required: high school transcript, 1 letter of recommendation, general college-preparatory program. ***Required for some:*** essay or personal statement, interview.

Application deadlines: 7/1 (freshmen), 7/1 (out-of-state freshmen), rolling (transfers), 12/1 (early action).

Early decision deadline: 11/1.

Notification: continuous until 1/28 (freshmen), continuous until 1/28 (out-of-state freshmen), continuous (transfers), 12/5 (early decision), 12/31 (early action).

CONTACT
Mr. Charles M Timmons, Director of Admissions and Dean for Enrollment Management, Wabash College, PO Box 362, 410 West Wabash Avenue, Crawfordsville, IN 47933-0352. *Phone:* 765-361-6054. *Toll-free phone:* 800-345-5385. *Fax:* 765-361-6437. *E-mail:* timmonsc@wabash.edu.

IOWA

Allen College
Waterloo, Iowa
http://www.allencollege.edu/

- **Independent** comprehensive, founded 1989
- **Suburban** 20-acre campus
- **Endowment** $8.1 million
- **Coed, primarily women** 338 undergraduate students, 90% full-time, 91% women, 9% men
- **Moderately difficult** entrance level

UNDERGRAD STUDENTS
305 full-time, 33 part-time. Students come from 8 states and territories; 4% are from out of state; 2% Black or African American, non-Hispanic/Latino; 2% Hispanic/Latino; 1% Asian, non-Hispanic/Latino; 2% Two or more races, non-Hispanic/Latino; 8% Race/ethnicity unknown; 55% transferred in.

FACULTY
Total: 58, 78% full-time, 64% with terminal degrees.

ACADEMICS
Calendar: semesters. *Degrees:* certificates, associate, bachelor's, master's, doctoral, and post-master's certificates (liberal arts and general education courses offered at either University of North Iowa or Wartburg College).

Special study options: accelerated degree program, advanced placement credit, cooperative education, distance learning, honors programs, independent study, internships, off-campus study. ***ROTC:*** Army (c).

Unusual degree programs: 3-2 nursing with Wartburg College, Loras College, Central College, Simpson College.

Computers: 32 computers/terminals are available on campus for general student use. Students can access the following: campus intranet, computer help desk, free student e-mail accounts, online (class) grades, online (class) schedules, online proctoring exams. Campuswide network is available. 100% of college-owned or -operated housing units are wired for high-speed Internet access. Wireless service is available via entire campus.

Library: Barrett Library plus 1 other. *Books:* 13,280 (physical), 9,138 (digital/electronic); *Serial titles:* 208 (physical), 3,610 (digital/electronic); *Databases:* 47. Weekly public service hours: 50; study areas open 24 hours, 5–7 days a week; students can reserve study rooms.

STUDENT LIFE
Activities and organizations: choral group, Allen Student Nurse's Association, Nurse's Christian Fellowship.

Campus security: 24-hour patrols, late-night transport/escort service, controlled dormitory access.

Student services: health clinic, personal/psychological counseling.

COSTS & FINANCIAL AID
Costs (2020–21) ***Comprehensive fee:*** $26,792 includes full-time tuition ($17,864), mandatory fees ($1648), and room and board ($7280). Part-time tuition: $638 per credit hour. ***Required fees:*** $87 per credit hour part-time. ***College room only:*** $3640. ***Payment plan:*** deferred payment.

Financial Aid Of all full-time matriculated undergraduates who enrolled in 2018, 275 applied for aid, 230 were judged to have need, 16 had their need fully met. 14 Federal Work-Study jobs (averaging $3744). In 2018, 39 non-need-based awards were made. ***Average need-based loan:*** $4245. ***Average need-based gift aid:*** $8238. ***Average non-need-based aid:*** $1576.

APPLYING
Options: electronic application.

Application fee: $50.

Required for some: essay or personal statement, high school transcript, 1 letter of recommendation, interview.

Application deadlines: 2/1 (freshmen), 2/1 (transfers).

Notification: continuous until 3/1 (freshmen), continuous until 3/1 (transfers).

CONTACT
Jamie Jordan, Administrative Assistant, Student Services, Allen College, Barrett Forum, 1825 Logan Avenue, Waterloo, IA 50703. *Phone:* 319-226-2014. *Fax:* 319-226-2010. *E-mail:* admissions@allencollege.edu.

Briar Cliff University
Sioux City, Iowa
http://www.briarcliff.edu/

CONTACT
Mr. Brian Eben, Assistant Vice President for Enrollment Management, Briar Cliff University, 3303 Rebecca Street, Sioux City, IA 51104. *Phone:* 712-279-5200. *Toll-free phone:* 800-662-3303. *Fax:* 712-279-1632. *E-mail:* admissions@briarcliff.edu.

Buena Vista University
Storm Lake, Iowa
http://www.bvu.edu/

- **Independent** comprehensive, founded 1891, affiliated with Presbyterian Church (U.S.A.)
- **Small-town** 60-acre campus
- **Endowment** $138.1 million
- **Coed**
- **Moderately difficult** entrance level

FACULTY
Student/faculty ratio: 9:1.

ACADEMICS
Calendar: 4-1-4. *Degrees:* bachelor's and master's.

Library: BVU Library. *Books:* 107,288 (physical), 164,907 (digital/electronic); *Serial titles:* 842 (physical), 23,059 (digital/electronic); *Databases:* 104. Weekly public service hours: 94; students can reserve study rooms.

STUDENT LIFE

Housing options: on-campus residence required through senior year; coed, special housing for students with disabilities. Campus housing is university owned. Freshman campus housing is guaranteed.

Activities and organizations: drama/theater group, student-run newspaper, radio and television station, choral group, Student Activities Board, Orientation Team, Esprit De Corps, Student Senate, Student Mobilizing Outreach and Volunteer Efforts.

Athletics Member NCAA. All Division III except golf (Division II).

Campus security: 24-hour emergency response devices, late-night transport/escort service, controlled dormitory access, night security patrols.

Student services: health clinic, personal/psychological counseling.

COSTS & FINANCIAL AID

Costs (2019–20) ***Comprehensive fee:*** $45,066 includes full-time tuition ($35,194) and room and board ($9872). Part-time tuition: $1184 per credit hour. ***College room only:*** $4941. Room and board charges vary according to housing facility.

Financial Aid Of all full-time matriculated undergraduates who enrolled in 2018, 651 applied for aid, 605 were judged to have need, 114 had their need fully met. In 2018, 98 non-need-based awards were made. ***Average percent of need met:*** 80. ***Average financial aid package:*** $30,158. ***Average need-based loan:*** $4713. ***Average need-based gift aid:*** $25,206. ***Average non-need-based aid:*** $18,570. ***Average indebtedness upon graduation:*** $38,938.

APPLYING

Standardized Tests *Required:* SAT or ACT (for admission). *Recommended:* ACT (for admission).

Options: electronic application, deferred entrance.

Required: high school transcript. ***Required for some:*** essay or personal statement, interview. ***Recommended:*** minimum 3.0 GPA.

CONTACT

Nick Boone, Director of Admissions, Buena Vista University, 610 West Fourth Street, Storm Lake, IA 50588. *Phone:* 712-749-2078. *Toll-free phone:* 800-383-9600. *E-mail:* BooneN@bvu.edu.

Central College

Pella, Iowa

http://www.central.edu/

- **Independent** 4-year, founded 1853, affiliated with Reformed Church in America
- **Small-town** 169-acre campus with easy access to Des Moines
- **Endowment** $79.9 million
- **Coed** 1,274 undergraduate students, 97% full-time, 53% women, 47% men
- **Moderately difficult** entrance level, 64% of applicants were admitted

UNDERGRAD STUDENTS

1,230 full-time, 44 part-time. Students come from 27 states and territories; 3 other countries; 27% are from out of state; 2% Black or African American, non-Hispanic/Latino; 4% Hispanic/Latino; 1% Asian, non-Hispanic/Latino; 0.1% Native Hawaiian or other Pacific Islander, non-Hispanic/Latino; 0.2% American Indian or Alaska Native, non-Hispanic/Latino; 1% Two or more races, non-Hispanic/Latino; 3% Race/ethnicity unknown; 1% international; 3% transferred in; 91% live on campus.

Freshmen:

Admission: 3,071 applied, 1,974 admitted, 317 enrolled. ***Average high school GPA:*** 3.6.

Retention: 78% of full-time freshmen returned.

ACADEMICS

Calendar: semesters. *Degree:* bachelor's.

Special study options: advanced placement credit, cooperative education, double majors, honors programs, independent study, internships, off-campus study, part-time degree program, services for LD students, student-designed majors, study abroad, summer session for credit.

Unusual degree programs: 3-2 nursing with Allen College; chiropractic with Palmer College of Chiropractic.

Computers: 200 computers/terminals and 1,600 ports are available on campus for general student use. Students can access the following: campus intranet, computer help desk, free student e-mail accounts, online (class) grades, online (class) registration, online (class) schedules. Campuswide network is available. 100% of college-owned or -operated housing units are wired for high-speed Internet access. Wireless service is available via entire campus.

Library: Geisler Library plus 2 others. Students can reserve study rooms.

STUDENT LIFE

Housing options: on-campus residence required through senior year; coed, men-only, women-only, special housing for students with disabilities. Campus housing is university owned. Freshman campus housing is guaranteed.

Activities and organizations: drama/theater group, choral group, Academic Honorary Associations and Health Professions Club, Music Ensembles, Campus Ministries, Student Senate, Students Concerned About the Environment (SCATE).

Athletics ***Intercollegiate sports:*** baseball M, basketball M/W, cross-country running M/W, football M, golf M/W, soccer M/W, softball W, tennis M/W, track and field M/W, volleyball W, wrestling M. ***Intramural sports:*** basketball M/W, football M, racquetball M/W, rugby M, soccer M/W, softball M/W, volleyball M/W.

Campus security: 24-hour emergency response devices and patrols, late-night transport/escort service, controlled dormitory access.

Student services: personal/psychological counseling.

COSTS & FINANCIAL AID

Costs (2020–21) ***Comprehensive fee:*** $28,880 includes full-time tuition ($18,600) and room and board ($10,280). Part-time tuition: $775 per credit hour. Part-time tuition and fees vary according to course load. ***Required fees:*** $775 per credit hour part-time. ***College room only:*** $4892. Room and board charges vary according to board plan. ***Payment plan:*** installment. ***Waivers:*** employees or children of employees.

Financial Aid Of all full-time matriculated undergraduates who enrolled in 2019, 1,002 applied for aid, 904 were judged to have need, 206 had their need fully met. In 2019, 202 non-need-based awards were made. ***Average percent of need met:*** 84. ***Average financial aid package:*** $33,653. ***Average need-based loan:*** $3191. ***Average need-based gift aid:*** $26,453. ***Average non-need-based aid:*** $23,884. ***Average indebtedness upon graduation:*** $37,983.

APPLYING

Standardized Tests *Required:* SAT or ACT (for admission).

Options: electronic application, deferred entrance.

Application fee: $25.

Required: high school transcript. ***Required for some:*** essay or personal statement, 3 letters of recommendation, interview. ***Recommended:*** minimum 2.7 GPA.

Application deadlines: 8/15 (freshmen), rolling (transfers).

Notification: continuous (freshmen), continuous (transfers).

CONTACT

Chevy Freiburger, Director of Admission, Central College, 812 University, Pella, IA 50112. *Phone:* 641-628-7637. *Toll-free phone:* 877-462-3687. *Fax:* 641-628-5983. *E-mail:* freiburgerc@central.edu.

Clarke University

Dubuque, Iowa

http://www.clarke.edu/

- **Independent Roman Catholic** comprehensive, founded 1843
- **Urban** 55-acre campus
- **Endowment** $31.3 million
- **Coed**
- **Moderately difficult** entrance level

FACULTY

Student/faculty ratio: 9:1.

ACADEMICS

Calendar: semesters. *Degrees:* associate, bachelor's, master's, and doctoral.

Library: Nicholas J. Schrupp Library. *Books:* 76,525 (physical), 136,800 (digital/electronic); *Serial titles:* 150 (physical), 53,000 (digital/electronic); *Databases:* 60. Weekly public service hours: 90.

STUDENT LIFE

Housing options: on-campus residence required through sophomore year; coed, men-only, women-only. Campus housing is university owned. Freshman campus housing is guaranteed.

Activities and organizations: drama/theater group, choral group, Admissions Student Team, Student Multicultural Organization, Concert Choir, Campus Ministry, Student Government.

Athletics Member NAIA.

Campus security: 24-hour emergency response devices and patrols, late-night transport/escort service, controlled dormitory access.

Student services: health clinic, personal/psychological counseling.

COSTS & FINANCIAL AID

Costs (2019–20) ***Tuition:*** $33,350 full-time.

Financial Aid Of all full-time matriculated undergraduates who enrolled in 2018, 417 applied for aid, 386 were judged to have need, 99 had their need fully met. In 2018, 117 non-need-based awards were made. ***Average percent of need met:*** 81. ***Average financial aid package:*** $30,781. ***Average need-based loan:*** $4055. ***Average need-based gift aid:*** $25,738. ***Average non-need-based aid:*** $28,892. ***Average indebtedness upon graduation:*** $11,079.

APPLYING

Standardized Tests *Required:* SAT or ACT (for admission).

Options: electronic application, deferred entrance.

Application fee: $25.

Required: high school transcript, minimum 2.0 GPA.

CONTACT

Mrs. Alicia Schmitt, Associate Director of Admissions, Clarke University, 1550 Clarke Drive, Dubuque, IA 52001-3198. *Phone:* 563-588-6373. *Toll-free phone:* 800-383-2345. *E-mail:* admissions@clarke.edu.

Coe College

Cedar Rapids, Iowa

http://www.coe.edu/

- **Independent** 4-year, founded 1851, affiliated with Presbyterian Church
- **Urban** 53-acre campus
- **Endowment** $85.6 million
- **Coed** 1,428 undergraduate students, 97% full-time, 55% women, 45% men
- **Moderately difficult** entrance level, 63% of applicants were admitted

UNDERGRAD STUDENTS

1,380 full-time, 48 part-time. Students come from 39 states and territories; 22 other countries; 54% are from out of state; 7% Black or African American, non-Hispanic/Latino; 12% Hispanic/Latino; 5% Asian, non-Hispanic/Latino; 0.1% Native Hawaiian or other Pacific Islander, non-Hispanic/Latino; 0.4% American Indian or Alaska Native, non-Hispanic/Latino; 3% Two or more races, non-Hispanic/Latino; 4% Race/ethnicity unknown; 1% international; 3% transferred in; 86% live on campus.

Freshmen:

Admission: 7,431 applied, 4,706 admitted, 379 enrolled. ***Average high school GPA:*** 3.7. ***Test scores:*** SAT evidence-based reading and writing scores over 500: 94%; SAT math scores over 500: 90%; ACT scores over 18: 98%; SAT evidence-based reading and writing scores over 600: 48%; SAT math scores over 600: 33%; ACT scores over 24: 50%; SAT evidence-based reading and writing scores over 700: 7%; SAT math scores over 700: 7%; ACT scores over 30: 16%.

Retention: 80% of full-time freshmen returned.

FACULTY

Total: 158, 63% full-time, 77% with terminal degrees.

Student/faculty ratio: 12:1.

ACADEMICS

Calendar: 4-4-1. *Degree:* bachelor's.

Special study options: advanced placement credit, double majors, English as a second language, honors programs, independent study, internships, off-campus study, part-time degree program, services for LD students, student-designed majors, study abroad, summer session for credit. ***ROTC:*** Army (b), Air Force (c).

Unusual degree programs: 3-2 engineering; public health with University of Iowa; law with University of Iowa.

Computers: 450 computers/terminals and 2,000 ports are available on campus for general student use. Students can access the following: campus intranet, computer help desk, free student e-mail accounts, online (class) grades, online (class) registration, online (class) schedules. Campuswide network is available. 100% of college-owned or -operated housing units are wired for high-speed Internet access. Wireless service is available via entire campus.

Library: Stewart Memorial Library plus 1 other. *Books:* 229,047 (physical), 293,070 (digital/electronic); *Serial titles:* 751 (physical), 3,630 (digital/electronic); *Databases:* 140. Weekly public service hours: 106.

STUDENT LIFE

Housing options: on-campus residence required through senior year; coed, men-only, women-only, special housing for students with disabilities. Campus housing is university owned. Freshman campus housing is guaranteed.

Activities and organizations: drama/theater group, student-run newspaper, radio station, choral group, Multicultural Fusion, Coe Alliance, Student Senate, Habitat for Humanity, International Club, national fraternities, national sororities.

Athletics Member NCAA. All Division III. ***Intercollegiate sports:*** baseball M, basketball M/W, cross-country running M/W, football M, golf M/W, soccer M/W, softball W, swimming and diving M/W, tennis M/W, track and field M/W, volleyball W, wrestling M. ***Intramural sports:*** lacrosse M/W, rock climbing M/W, soccer M/W, ultimate Frisbee M(c)/W(c), volleyball W.

Campus security: 24-hour emergency response devices and patrols, late-night transport/escort service, controlled dormitory access.

Student services: health clinic, personal/psychological counseling.

COSTS & FINANCIAL AID

Costs (2020–21) ***Comprehensive fee:*** $57,354 includes full-time tuition ($46,870), mandatory fees ($350), and room and board ($10,134). Part-time tuition: $1465 per semester hour. Part-time tuition and fees vary according to course load. ***Room and board:*** Room and board charges vary according to board plan and housing facility. ***Payment plan:*** installment. ***Waivers:*** employees or children of employees.

Financial Aid Of all full-time matriculated undergraduates who enrolled in 2019, 1,224 applied for aid, 1,144 were judged to have need, 232 had their need fully met. 668 Federal Work-Study jobs (averaging $1743). 327 state and other part-time jobs (averaging $1629). In 2019, 219 non-need-based awards were made. ***Average percent of need met:*** 84. ***Average financial aid package:*** $39,070. ***Average need-based loan:*** $4213. ***Average need-based gift aid:*** $34,609. ***Average non-need-based aid:*** $27,713. ***Average indebtedness upon graduation:*** $35,012.

APPLYING

Standardized Tests *Required:* SAT or ACT (for admission).

Options: electronic application, early action, deferred entrance.

Application fee: $30.

Required: essay or personal statement, high school transcript, 1 letter of recommendation. ***Recommended:*** minimum 3.0 GPA, interview.

Application deadlines: 3/1 (freshmen), rolling (transfers), 12/10 (early action).

Notification: 3/15 (freshmen), continuous (transfers).

CONTACT

Julie Staker, Vice President for Admission and Marketing, Coe College, 1220 1st Avenue NE, Cedar Rapids, IA 52402-5070. *Phone:* 319-399-8500. *Toll-free phone:* 877-225-5263. *Fax:* 319-399-8816. *E-mail:* admission@coe.edu.

Cornell College

Mount Vernon, Iowa

http://www.cornellcollege.edu/

- **Independent Methodist** 4-year, founded 1853
- **Coed**

ACADEMICS
Calendar: 8 3.5 week terms.

COSTS & FINANCIAL AID
Costs (2019–20) ***Comprehensive fee:*** $53,856 includes full-time tuition ($43,550), mandatory fees ($546), and room and board ($9760). Part-time tuition: $3266 per course. ***Required fees:*** $160 per year part-time. ***College room only:*** $4500.

Financial Aid Of all full-time matriculated undergraduates who enrolled in 2019, 795 applied for aid, 699 were judged to have need, 165 had their need fully met. In 2019, 291 non-need-based awards were made. ***Average percent of need met:*** 82. ***Average financial aid package:*** $33,307. ***Average need-based loan:*** $4446. ***Average need-based gift aid:*** $30,116. ***Average non-need-based aid:*** $23,751. ***Average indebtedness upon graduation:*** $38,215.

CONTACT
Cornell College, 600 First Street South West, Mount Vernon, IA 52314-1098. *Toll-free phone:* 800-747-1112.

Divine Word College

Epworth, Iowa

http://www.dwci.edu/

CONTACT
Divine Word College, 102 Jacoby Drive SW, Epworth, IA 52045-0380. *Phone:* 563-876-3353. *Toll-free phone:* 800-553-3321.

Dordt University

Sioux Center, Iowa

http://www.dordt.edu/

CONTACT
Mr. Howard Wislon, Vice President for Enrollment, Dordt University, 498 4th Avenue, NE, Sioux Center, IA 51250-1697. *Phone:* 712-722-6080. *Toll-free phone:* 800-343-6738. *Fax:* 712-722-6035. *E-mail:* admissions@dordt.edu.

Drake University

Des Moines, Iowa

http://www.drake.edu/

- **Independent** university, founded 1881
- **Urban** 120-acre campus
- **Endowment** $226.2 million
- **Coed** 2,954 undergraduate students, 96% full-time, 59% women, 41% men
- **Moderately difficult** entrance level, 68% of applicants were admitted

UNDERGRAD STUDENTS
2,830 full-time, 124 part-time. Students come from 44 states and territories; 25 other countries; 61% are from out of state; 6% Black or African American, non-Hispanic/Latino; 7% Hispanic/Latino; 5% Asian, non-Hispanic/Latino; 3% Two or more races, non-Hispanic/Latino; 0.2% Race/ethnicity unknown; 4% international; 4% transferred in; 70% live on campus.

Freshmen:
Admission: 6,944 applied, 4,697 admitted, 782 enrolled. ***Average high school GPA:*** 3.7. ***Test scores:*** SAT evidence-based reading and writing scores over 500: 94%; SAT math scores over 500: 92%; ACT scores over 18: 98%; SAT evidence-based reading and writing scores over 600: 63%; SAT math scores over 600: 62%; ACT scores over 24: 76%; SAT evidence-based reading and writing scores over 700: 22%; SAT math scores over 700: 22%; ACT scores over 30: 31%.

Retention: 84% of full-time freshmen returned.

FACULTY
Total: 474, 66% full-time, 72% with terminal degrees.

Student/faculty ratio: 10:1.

ACADEMICS
Calendar: semesters. *Degrees:* bachelor's, master's, doctoral, post-master's, and postbachelor's certificates.

Special study options: accelerated degree program, advanced placement credit, cooperative education, distance learning, double majors, English as a second language, honors programs, independent study, internships, off-campus study, part-time degree program, services for LD students, student-designed majors, study abroad, summer session for credit. ***ROTC:*** Army (c), Air Force (c).

Unusual degree programs: 3-2 journalism and law, arts and sciences and law, accounting.

Computers: Students can access the following: campus intranet, computer help desk, free student e-mail accounts, online (class) grades, online (class) registration, online (class) schedules. Campuswide network is available. 100% of college-owned or -operated housing units are wired for high-speed Internet access. Wireless service is available via entire campus.

Library: Cowles Library plus 1 other. Study areas open 24 hours, 5–7 days a week; students can reserve study rooms.

STUDENT LIFE
Housing options: on-campus residence required through sophomore year; coed, special housing for students with disabilities. Campus housing is university owned. Freshman campus housing is guaranteed.

Activities and organizations: drama/theater group, student-run newspaper, radio and television station, choral group, marching band, Student Activities Board, Drake Magazine, Dog Pound Pep Squad, Alpha Phi Omega, Residence Hall Association, national fraternities, national sororities.

Athletics Member NCAA. All Division I except football (Division I-AA). ***Intercollegiate sports:*** basketball M(s)/W(s), cheerleading M(s)/W(s), crew W, cross-country running M(s)/W(s), golf M(s), soccer M(s)/W(s), softball W(s), tennis M(s)/W(s), track and field M(s)/W(s), volleyball W(s). ***Intramural sports:*** badminton M/W, basketball M/W, football M/W, golf M/W, racquetball M/W, soccer M(c)/W, softball M/W, swimming and diving M/W, tennis M/W, volleyball M/W(c).

Campus security: 24-hour emergency response devices and patrols, late-night transport/escort service, controlled dormitory access.

Student services: health clinic, personal/psychological counseling, legal services, veterans affairs office.

COSTS & FINANCIAL AID
Costs (2020–21) ***Comprehensive fee:*** $55,486 includes full-time tuition ($44,188), mandatory fees ($146), and room and board ($11,152). Full-time tuition and fees vary according to course load, degree level, program, and student level. Part-time tuition: $1133 per credit hour. Part-time tuition and fees vary according to class time, degree level, and program. No tuition increase for student's term of enrollment. ***College room only:*** $6084. Room and board charges vary according to board plan and housing facility. ***Payment plan:*** installment. ***Waivers:*** children of alumni, senior citizens, and employees or children of employees.

Financial Aid Of all full-time matriculated undergraduates who enrolled in 2019, 2,127 applied for aid, 1,792 were judged to have need, 495 had their need fully met. 1,354 Federal Work-Study jobs (averaging $1900). In 2019, 844 non-need-based awards were made. ***Average percent of need met:*** 77. ***Average financial aid package:*** $30,942. ***Average need-based loan:*** $3976. ***Average need-based gift aid:*** $24,256. ***Average non-need-based aid:*** $20,058. ***Average indebtedness upon graduation:*** $34,492.

APPLYING
Standardized Tests *Required for some:* SAT or ACT (for admission).

Options: electronic application, early admission, deferred entrance.

Required: high school transcript. ***Recommended:*** essay or personal statement, letters of recommendation, interview.

Application deadlines: 3/1 (freshmen), rolling (transfers).

Notification: continuous (freshmen), continuous (transfers).

CONTACT
Drake University, 2507 University Avenue, Des Moines, IA 50311-4516. *Phone:* 515-271-3182. *Toll-free phone:* 800-44-DRAKE Ext. 3181.

Emmaus Bible College

Dubuque, Iowa

http://www.emmaus.edu/

- **Independent nondenominational** 4-year, founded 1941
- **Small-town** 22-acre campus
- **Coed** 215 undergraduate students, 87% full-time, 57% women, 43% men
- **Noncompetitive** entrance level, 94% of applicants were admitted

UNDERGRAD STUDENTS

186 full-time, 29 part-time. 60% are from out of state; 4% Black or African American, non-Hispanic/Latino, 7% Hispanic/Latino; 4% Asian, non-Hispanic/Latino; 2% American Indian or Alaska Native, non-Hispanic/Latino; 3% Two or more races, non-Hispanic/Latino; 2% Race/ethnicity unknown; 3% international; 5% transferred in; 78% live on campus.

Freshmen:

Admission: 113 applied, 106 admitted, 52 enrolled. ***Average high school GPA:*** 3.6. ***Test scores:*** SAT evidence-based reading and writing scores over 500: 56%; SAT math scores over 500: 62%; ACT scores over 18: 79%; SAT evidence-based reading and writing scores over 600: 44%; SAT math scores over 600: 31%; ACT scores over 24: 46%; SAT evidence-based reading and writing scores over 700: 25%; SAT math scores over 700: 6%; ACT scores over 30: 15%.

Retention: 77% of full-time freshmen returned.

FACULTY

Total: 36, 58% full-time, 25% with terminal degrees.

Student/faculty ratio: 8:1.

ACADEMICS

Calendar: semesters. *Degrees:* certificates, associate, bachelor's, and postbachelor's certificates.

Special study options: advanced placement credit, distance learning, double majors, independent study, internships, off-campus study, part-time degree program, services for LD students, summer session for credit.

Computers: Students can access the following: campus intranet, computer help desk, free student e-mail accounts, online (class) grades, online (class) registration, online (class) schedules. Campuswide network is available. Wireless service is available via entire campus.

Library: The Emmaus Bible College Library plus 1 other. Weekly public service hours: 130.

STUDENT LIFE

Housing options: on-campus residence required through senior yearCampus housing is university owned. Freshman campus housing is guaranteed.

Athletics Member NCCAA. ***Intercollegiate sports:*** basketball M/W, soccer M, volleyball W. ***Intramural sports:*** badminton M/W, basketball M/W, golf M/W, racquetball M/W, soccer M/W, softball M/W, table tennis M/W, tennis M/W, ultimate Frisbee M/W, volleyball M/W.

Campus security: 24-hour emergency response devices, student patrols, controlled dormitory access.

Student services: personal/psychological counseling, veterans affairs office.

COSTS

Costs (2020–21) ***Comprehensive fee:*** $28,100 includes full-time tuition ($19,250) and room and board ($8850). Part-time tuition: $802 per credit hour.

APPLYING

Standardized Tests *Required:* SAT or ACT (for admission).

Options: electronic application, deferred entrance.

Required: essay or personal statement, high school transcript, minimum 2.0 GPA, 1 letter of recommendation.

Application deadlines: 8/1 (freshmen), 8/1 (transfers).

Notification: continuous (freshmen), continuous (transfers).

CONTACT

Emmaus Bible College, 2570 Asbury Road, Dubuque, IA 52001-3097. *Toll-free phone:* 800-397-2425.

Faith Baptist Bible College and Theological Seminary

Ankeny, Iowa

http://www.faith.edu/

CONTACT

Miss Mary Tubbs, Admissions Coordinator, Faith Baptist Bible College and Theological Seminary, 1900 NW 4th Street, Ankeny, IA 50023. *Phone:* 515-964-0601. *Toll-free phone:* 888-FAITH 4U. *Fax:* 515-964-1638. *E-mail:* admissions@faith.edu.

Graceland University

Lamoni, Iowa

http://www.graceland.edu/

- **Independent Community of Christ** comprehensive, founded 1895
- **Rural** 170-acre campus with easy access to Des Moines
- **Endowment** $53.3 million
- **Coed** 1,038 undergraduate students, 87% full-time, 56% women, 44% men
- **Moderately difficult** entrance level, 58% of applicants were admitted

UNDERGRAD STUDENTS

898 full-time, 140 part-time. Students come from 40 states and territories; 20 other countries; 72% are from out of state; 9% Black or African American, non-Hispanic/Latino; 10% Hispanic/Latino; 1% Asian, non-Hispanic/Latino; 2% Native Hawaiian or other Pacific Islander, non-Hispanic/Latino; 0.5% American Indian or Alaska Native, non-Hispanic/Latino; 4% Two or more races, non-Hispanic/Latino; 8% Race/ethnicity unknown; 6% international; 9% transferred in; 78% live on campus.

Freshmen:

Admission: 3,004 applied, 1,744 admitted, 193 enrolled. ***Average high school GPA:*** 3.4. ***Test scores:*** SAT evidence-based reading and writing scores over 500: 62%; SAT math scores over 500: 61%; ACT scores over 18: 81%; SAT evidence-based reading and writing scores over 600: 13%; SAT math scores over 600: 12%; ACT scores over 24: 17%; ACT scores over 30: 4%.

Retention: 66% of full-time freshmen returned.

FACULTY

Total: 158, 47% full-time, 59% with terminal degrees.

Student/faculty ratio: 14:1.

ACADEMICS

Calendar: 4-1-4. *Degrees:* certificates, bachelor's, master's, doctoral, and post-master's certificates.

Special study options: academic remediation for entering students, accelerated degree program, adult/continuing education programs, advanced placement credit, cooperative education, distance learning, double majors, freshman honors college, honors programs, independent study, internships, part-time degree program, services for LD students, student-designed majors, study abroad, summer session for credit.

Computers: 178 computers/terminals are available on campus for general student use. Students can access the following: campus intranet, computer help desk, free student e-mail accounts, online (class) grades, online (class) registration, online (class) schedules. Campuswide network is available. 100% of college-owned or -operated housing units are wired for high-speed Internet access. Wireless service is available via classrooms, computer centers, computer labs, dorm rooms, learning centers, libraries, student centers.

Library: F. M. Smith Library. *Books:* 80,000 (physical), 350,000 (digital/electronic); *Serial titles:* 130 (physical), 60 (digital/electronic); *Databases:* 50. Weekly public service hours: 80; students can reserve study rooms.

STUDENT LIFE

Housing options: on-campus residence required through senior year; men-only, women-only. Campus housing is university owned. Freshman campus housing is guaranteed.

Activities and organizations: drama/theater group, student-run newspaper, radio station, choral group, marching band, Black Student

Union, Latin Club, Enactus, Social Equality Alliance, Communication Club.

Athletics Member NAIA. ***Intercollegiate sports:*** baseball M(s), basketball M(s)/W(s), cheerleading M(s)/W(s), cross-country running M(s)/W(s), football M(s), golf M(s)/W(s), soccer M(s)/W(s), softball W(s), track and field M(s)/W(s), volleyball M(s)/W(s), wrestling M(s). ***Intramural sports:*** basketball M/W, football M/W, soccer M/W, softball M/W, table tennis M/W, ultimate Frisbee M/W, volleyball M/W.

Campus security: 24-hour emergency response devices, controlled dormitory access.

Student services: health clinic, personal/psychological counseling.

COSTS & FINANCIAL AID

Costs (2020–21) ***Comprehensive fee:*** $40,760 includes full-time tuition ($30,650), mandatory fees ($670), and room and board ($9440). Full-time tuition and fees vary according to course load, degree level, location, and program. Part-time tuition: $950 per semester hour. Part-time tuition and fees vary according to course load, degree level, location, and program. ***College room only:*** $3630. Room and board charges vary according to housing facility and location. ***Payment plan:*** installment. ***Waivers:*** senior citizens and employees or children of employees.

Financial Aid Of all full-time matriculated undergraduates who enrolled in 2019, 805 applied for aid, 747 were judged to have need, 92 had their need fully met. In 2019, 51 non-need-based awards were made. ***Average percent of need met:*** 65. ***Average financial aid package:*** $22,852. ***Average need-based gift aid:*** $21,904. ***Average non-need-based aid:*** $16,502. ***Average indebtedness upon graduation:*** $44,984.

APPLYING

Standardized Tests *Required:* SAT or ACT (for admission), TOEFL or IELTS for all students whose first language is not English (for admission).

Options: electronic application.

Required: high school transcript, 2 of the following: minimum high school GPA of 2.5, rank in top half of class, or minimum SAT score of 960/ACT of 21. ***Required for some:*** essay or personal statement, 2 letters of recommendation, interview.

Application deadlines: rolling (freshmen), rolling (transfers).

Notification: continuous (freshmen), continuous (transfers).

CONTACT

Mr. Kevin Brown, Director of Admissions, Graceland University, 1 University Place, Lamoni, IA 50140. *Phone:* 641-784-5149. *Toll-free phone:* 866-GRACELAND. *Fax:* 641-784-5480. *E-mail:* admissions@graceland.edu.

Grand View University

Des Moines, Iowa

http://www.grandview.edu/

CONTACT

Mr. Ryan Thompson, Director of Admissions, Grand View University, 1200 Grandview Avenue, Des Moines, IA 50316-1599. *Phone:* 515-263-2810. *Toll-free phone:* 800-444-6083. *Fax:* 515-263-2974. *E-mail:* admissions@grandview.edu.

See below for display ad and page 1062 for the College Close-Up.

Grinnell College

Grinnell, Iowa

http://www.grinnell.edu/

- **Independent** 4-year, founded 1846
- **Small-town** 120-acre campus
- **Endowment** $2.1 billion
- **Coed** 1,733 undergraduate students, 98% full-time, 53% women, 47% men
- **Very difficult** entrance level, 23% of applicants were admitted

UNDERGRAD STUDENTS

1,700 full-time, 33 part-time. Students come from 52 states and territories; 45 other countries; 91% are from out of state; 0.5% Black or African American, non-Hispanic/Latino; 8% Hispanic/Latino; 8% Asian, non-Hispanic/Latino; 4% Two or more races, non-Hispanic/Latino; 4% Race/ethnicity unknown; 20% international; 0.1% transferred in; 88% live on campus.

Freshmen:

Admission: 8,004 applied, 1,847 admitted, 459 enrolled. ***Test scores:*** SAT evidence-based reading and writing scores over 500: 100%; SAT math scores over 500: 100%; ACT scores over 18: 100%; SAT evidence-based reading and writing scores over 600: 96%; SAT math scores over 600: 99%; ACT scores over 24: 100%; SAT evidence-based reading and writing scores over 700: 60%; SAT math scores over 700: 78%; ACT scores over 30: 84%.

Retention: 94% of full-time freshmen returned.

FACULTY

Total: 218, 80% full-time, 89% with terminal degrees.

Student/faculty ratio: 9:1.

ACADEMICS

Calendar: semesters. *Degree:* bachelor's.

Special study options: accelerated degree program, advanced placement credit, double majors, independent study, internships, off-campus study, services for LD students, student-designed majors, study abroad.

Unusual degree programs: 3-2 engineering with Columbia University, California Institute of Technology, Rensselaer Polytechnic Institute, Washington University in St. Louis; architecture with Washington University in St. Louis, law with Columbia University.

Computers: 200 computers/terminals are available on campus for general student use. Students can access the following: campus intranet, computer help desk, free student e-mail accounts, online (class) grades, online (class) registration, online (class) schedules. Campuswide network is available. 100% of college-owned or -operated housing units are wired for high-speed Internet access. Wireless service is available via entire campus.

Library: Burling Library plus 2 others. *Books:* 670,228 (physical), 1.0 million (digital/electronic); *Serial titles:* 5,030 (physical), 76,834 (digital/electronic); *Databases:* 263. Weekly public service hours: 109.

STUDENT LIFE

Housing options: on-campus residence required through sophomore year; coed, cooperative, special housing for students with disabilities. Campus housing is university owned. Freshman campus housing is guaranteed.

Activities and organizations: drama/theater group, student-run newspaper, radio station, choral group, Concerned Black Students, International Student Organization, Student Organization of Latinas/Latinos, Campus Democrats, Ultimate Frisbee.

Athletics Member NCAA. All Division III. ***Intercollegiate sports:*** baseball M, basketball M/W, cross-country running M/W, football M, golf M/W, soccer M/W, softball W, swimming and diving M/W, tennis M/W, track and field M/W, volleyball W. ***Intramural sports:*** ultimate Frisbee M/W, water polo M/W.

Campus security: 24-hour emergency response devices and patrols, student patrols, late-night transport/escort service, controlled dormitory access.

Student services: health clinic, personal/psychological counseling.

COSTS & FINANCIAL AID

Costs (2020–21) ***Comprehensive fee:*** $70,544 includes full-time tuition ($56,188), mandatory fees ($492), and room and board ($13,864). Part-time tuition: $1684 per credit hour. ***Required fees:*** $1684 per credit hour part-time. ***College room only:*** $6548. Room and board charges vary according to board plan and housing facility. ***Payment plan:*** installment. ***Waivers:*** employees or children of employees.

Financial Aid Of all full-time matriculated undergraduates who enrolled in 2019, 1,218 applied for aid, 1,108 were judged to have need, 1,108 had their need fully met. In 2019, 354 non-need-based awards were made. ***Average percent of need met:*** 100. ***Average financial aid package:*** $51,571. ***Average need-based loan:*** $3866. ***Average need-based gift aid:*** $45,482. ***Average non-need-based aid:*** $19,505. ***Average indebtedness upon graduation:*** $20,093. ***Financial aid deadline:*** 1/15.

APPLYING

Standardized Tests *Required:* SAT or ACT (for admission).

Options: electronic application, early admission, early decision, deferred entrance.

Required: essay or personal statement, high school transcript, 3 letters of recommendation. ***Recommended:*** interview.

Application deadlines: 1/15 (freshmen), 4/1 (transfers).

Early decision deadline: 11/15 (for plan 1), 1/1 (for plan 2).

Notification: 4/1 (freshmen), 5/20 (transfers), 12/15 (early decision plan 1), 2/1 (early decision plan 2).

CONTACT

Ms. Sarah Fischer, Director of Admission, Grinnell College, 1103 Park Street, Grinnell, IA 50112. *Phone:* 641-269-3600. *Toll-free phone:* 800-247-0113. *Fax:* 641-269-4800. *E-mail:* askgrin@grinnell.edu.

Hamilton Technical College

Davenport, Iowa

http://www.hamiltontechcollege.edu/

CONTACT

Hamilton Technical College, 1011 East 53rd Street, Davenport, IA 52807-2653. *Phone:* 563-386-3570. *Toll-free phone:* 866-966-4825.

INSTE Bible College

Ankeny, Iowa

http://www.inste.edu/

CONTACT

Admissions, INSTE Bible College, 2302 SW 3rd Street, Ankeny, IA 50023. *Phone:* 515-289-9200. *Fax:* 515-289-9201. *E-mail:* inste@inste.edu.

Iowa State University of Science and Technology

Ames, Iowa

http://www.iastate.edu/

- **State-supported** university, founded 1858
- **Suburban** 1795-acre campus with easy access to Des Moines
- **Endowment** $838.9 million
- **Coed** 29,621 undergraduate students, 94% full-time, 42% women, 58% men
- **Moderately difficult** entrance level, 92% of applicants were admitted

UNDERGRAD STUDENTS

27,929 full-time, 1,692 part-time. Students come from 52 states and territories; 123 other countries; 37% are from out of state; 3% Black or African American, non-Hispanic/Latino; 6% Hispanic/Latino; 3% Asian, non-Hispanic/Latino; 0.1% Native Hawaiian or other Pacific Islander, non-Hispanic/Latino; 0.2% American Indian or Alaska Native, non-Hispanic/Latino; 2% Two or more races, non-Hispanic/Latino; 5% Race/ethnicity unknown; 6% international; 5% transferred in; 39% live on campus.

Freshmen:

Admission: 18,246 applied, 16,796 admitted, 6,047 enrolled. ***Average high school GPA:*** 3.6. ***Test scores:*** SAT evidence-based reading and writing scores over 500: 90%; SAT math scores over 500: 92%; ACT scores over 18: 96%; SAT evidence-based reading and writing scores over 600: 55%; SAT math scores over 600: 59%; ACT scores over 24: 59%; SAT evidence-based reading and writing scores over 700: 12%; SAT math scores over 700: 23%; ACT scores over 30: 18%.

Retention: 88% of full-time freshmen returned.

FACULTY

Total: 1,892, 84% full-time, 86% with terminal degrees.

Student/faculty ratio: 18:1.

ACADEMICS

Calendar: semesters. *Degrees:* bachelor's, master's, doctoral, post-master's, and postbachelor's certificates.

Special study options: academic remediation for entering students, accelerated degree program, adult/continuing education programs, advanced placement credit, cooperative education, distance learning, double majors, English as a second language, external degree program, freshman honors college, honors programs, independent study, internships, off-campus study, part-time degree program, services for LD students, student-designed majors, study abroad, summer session for credit. ***ROTC:*** Army (b), Navy (b), Air Force (b).

Unusual degree programs: 3-2 engineering with William Penn College.

Computers: 2,557 computers/terminals are available on campus for general student use. Students can access the following: campus intranet, computer help desk, free student e-mail accounts, online (class) grades, online (class) registration, online (class) schedules, network services. Campuswide network is available. 100% of college-owned or -operated housing units are wired for high-speed Internet access. Wireless service is available via entire campus.

Library: Parks Library (University Library) plus 1 other. *Books:* 2.8 million (physical), 460,516 (digital/electronic); *Serial titles:* 32,462 (physical), 110,162 (digital/electronic); *Databases:* 287. Weekly public service hours: 113; students can reserve study rooms.

STUDENT LIFE

Housing options: coed, men-only, women-only, special housing for students with disabilities. Campus housing is university owned.

Activities and organizations: drama/theater group, student-run newspaper, radio and television station, choral group, marching band, Greek Life, Intramural Sports Activities, Club Sports, national fraternities, national sororities.

Athletics Member NCAA. All Division I except football (Division I-A). ***Intercollegiate sports:*** basketball M(s)/W(s), cross country running M(s)/W(s), golf M(s)/W(s), gymnastics W(s), soccer W(s), softball W(s), swimming and diving W(s), tennis W(s), track and field M(s)/W(s), volleyball W(s), wrestling M(s). ***Intramural sports:*** archery M(c)/W(c), badminton M(c)/W(c), baseball M(c)/W(c), basketball M/W, bowling M(c)/W(c), crew M(c)/W(c), equestrian sports M(c)/W(c), fencing M(c)/W(c), field hockey M(c)/W(c), football M/W, golf M/W, gymnastics W, ice hockey M/W, lacrosse M(c)/W(c), racquetball M(c)/W(c), riflery M(c)/W(c), rock climbing M(c)/W(c), rugby M(c)/W(c), skiing (downhill) M(c)/W(c), soccer M/W, softball W(c), swimming and diving M(c)/W(c), table tennis M(c)/W(c), tennis M/W, track and field M/W, ultimate Frisbee M/W, volleyball M/W, water polo M(c)/W(c), weight lifting M(c)/W(c), wrestling M/W.

Campus security: 24-hour emergency response devices and patrols, late-night transport/escort service, controlled dormitory access.

Student services: health clinic, personal/psychological counseling, women's center, legal services, veterans affairs office.

COSTS & FINANCIAL AID

Costs (2019–20) ***Tuition:*** state resident $8042 full-time, $336 per credit hour part-time; nonresident $23,230 full-time, $968 per credit hour part-time. Full-time tuition and fees vary according to class time, course level, degree level, program, and student level. Part-time tuition and fees vary according to class time, course level, course load, degree level, program, and student level. ***Required fees:*** $1278 full-time. ***Room and board:*** $9149; room only: $4783. Room and board charges vary according to board plan and housing facility. ***Payment plans:*** installment, deferred payment.

Financial Aid Of all full-time matriculated undergraduates who enrolled in 2017, 21,524 applied for aid, 14,775 were judged to have need, 3,087 had their need fully met. 1,596 Federal Work-Study jobs (averaging $841). 11,694 state and other part-time jobs (averaging $2092). In 2017, 9495 non-need-based awards were made. ***Average percent of need met:*** 78. ***Average financial aid package:*** $13,006. ***Average need-based loan:*** $4362. ***Average need-based gift aid:*** $8066. ***Average non-need-based aid:*** $3738. ***Average indebtedness upon graduation:*** $28,701.

APPLYING

Standardized Tests *Required:* SAT or ACT (for admission).

Options: electronic application, deferred entrance.

Application fee: $40.

Required: high school transcript, minimum Regent Admission Index (RAI) of245, high school course requirements.

Application deadlines: rolling (freshmen), rolling (transfers).

Notification: continuous (freshmen), continuous (transfers).

CONTACT

Phillip B. Caffrey, Associate Director for Admissions, Iowa State University of Science and Technology, 100 Enrollment Services, 2433 Union Drive, Ames, IA 50011-2042. *Phone:* 515-294-5836. *Toll-free phone:* 800-262-3810. *Fax:* 515-294-2592. *E-mail:* pbcaffr@iastate.edu.

Iowa Wesleyan University

Mount Pleasant, Iowa

http://www.iw.edu/

CONTACT

Julie Duplessis, Director of Enrollment, Iowa Wesleyan University, 601 N. Main Street, Mount Pleasant, IA 52641. *Phone:* 319-385-6208. *Toll-free phone:* 800-582-2383. *Fax:* 319-385-6240. *E-mail:* julie.duplessis@iw.edu.

Loras College

Dubuque, Iowa

http://www.loras.edu/

- **Independent Roman Catholic** comprehensive, founded 1839
- **Suburban** 64-acre campus
- **Endowment** $42.7 million
- **Coed** 1,317 undergraduate students, 96% full-time, 43% women, 57% men
- **Moderately difficult** entrance level, 75% of applicants were admitted

UNDERGRAD STUDENTS

1,264 full-time, 53 part-time. Students come from 27 states and territories; 9 other countries; 59% are from out of state; 3% Black or African American, non-Hispanic/Latino; 9% Hispanic/Latino; 0.7% Asian, non-Hispanic/Latino; 0.2% Native Hawaiian or other Pacific Islander, non-Hispanic/Latino; 2% Two or more races, non-Hispanic/Latino; 4% Race/ethnicity unknown; 2% international; 3% transferred in; 61% live on campus.

Freshmen:

Admission: 1,491 applied, 1,123 admitted, 326 enrolled. ***Average high school GPA:*** 3.5. ***Test scores:*** SAT evidence-based reading and writing scores over 500: 66%; SAT math scores over 500: 73%; ACT scores over 18: 89%; SAT evidence-based reading and writing scores over 600: 19%; SAT math scores over 600: 19%; ACT scores over 24: 38%; SAT evidence-based reading and writing scores over 700: 5%; SAT math scores over 700: 3%; ACT scores over 30: 8%.

Retention: 76% of full-time freshmen returned.

FACULTY

Total: 143, 73% full-time, 72% with terminal degrees.

Student/faculty ratio: 12:1.

ACADEMICS

Calendar: semesters plus January term. *Degrees:* bachelor's and master's.

Special study options: academic remediation for entering students, advanced placement credit, cooperative education, distance learning, double majors, honors programs, independent study, internships, off-campus study, part-time degree program, services for LD students, student-designed majors, study abroad, summer session for credit. ***ROTC:*** Army (c).

Unusual degree programs: 3-2 business administration; nursing with Allen College; athletic training.

Computers: 5 computers/terminals and 991 ports are available on campus for general student use. Students can access the following: campus intranet, computer help desk, free student e-mail accounts, online (class) grades, online (class) registration, online (class) schedules. Campuswide network is available. 100% of college-owned or -operated housing units are wired for high-speed Internet access. Wireless service is available via entire campus.

Library: Loras College Library. *Books:* 184,328 (physical), 212,123 (digital/electronic); *Serial titles:* 12 (physical), 43,245 (digital/electronic); *Databases:* 120. Weekly public service hours: 91; students can reserve study rooms.

STUDENT LIFE

Housing options: on-campus residence required through junior year; coed, men-only, women-only. Campus housing is university owned. Freshman campus housing is guaranteed.

Activities and organizations: drama/theater group, student-run newspaper, radio and television station, choral group, Dance Marathon,

The Lorian, DuBuddies, Education Club, American Chemical Society, national fraternities, national sororities.

Athletics Member NCAA. All Division III except golf (Division II). ***Intercollegiate sports:*** baseball M, basketball M/W, cheerleading M(c)/W(c), cross-country running M/W, football M, golf M/W, ice hockey M(c)/W(c), lacrosse W, rugby M(c)/W(c), soccer M/W, softball W, swimming and diving M/W, tennis M/W, track and field M/W, ultimate Frisbee M(c)/W(c), volleyball M/W, wrestling M. ***Intramural sports:*** basketball M/W, racquetball M/W, soccer M/W, softball M/W, volleyball M/W.

Campus security: 24-hour emergency response devices and patrols, late night transport/escort service, controlled dormitory access.

Student services: health clinic, personal/psychological counseling.

COSTS & FINANCIAL AID

Costs (2020–21) ***Comprehensive fee:*** $43,818 includes full-time tuition ($33,500), mandatory fees ($1718), and room and board ($8600). Full-time tuition and fees vary according to course load and degree level. Part-time tuition: $750 per credit hour. ***Required fees:*** $55 per credit hour part-time. ***College room only:*** $4000. Room and board charges vary according to board plan and housing facility. ***Payment plan:*** installment. ***Waivers:*** employees or children of employees.

Financial Aid Of all full-time matriculated undergraduates who enrolled in 2019, 1,160 applied for aid, 1,018 were judged to have need, 304 had their need fully met. 525 Federal Work-Study jobs (averaging $2794). 4 state and other part-time jobs (averaging $1500). In 2019, 242 non-need-based awards were made. ***Average percent of need met:*** 87. ***Average financial aid package:*** $29,160. ***Average need-based loan:*** $4292. ***Average need-based gift aid:*** $23,110. ***Average non-need-based aid:*** $18,643. ***Average indebtedness upon graduation:*** $28,964.

APPLYING

Standardized Tests *Required:* SAT or ACT (for admission).

Options: electronic application, deferred entrance.

Required: high school transcript, minimum 2.5 GPA. ***Required for some:*** essay or personal statement, 1 letter of recommendation, interview. ***Recommended:*** 1 letter of recommendation.

Application deadlines: rolling (freshmen), rolling (transfers).

Notification: continuous (freshmen), continuous (transfers).

CONTACT

Loras College, 1450 Alta Vista, Dubuque, IA 52004-0178. *Phone:* 563-588-7639. *Toll-free phone:* 800-245-6727.

Luther College

Decorah, Iowa

http://www.luther.edu/

- **Independent** 4-year, founded 1861, affiliated with Evangelical Lutheran Church in America
- **Small-town** 200-acre campus
- **Endowment** $161.8 million
- **Coed**
- **Moderately difficult** entrance level

FACULTY

Student/faculty ratio: 11:1.

ACADEMICS

Calendar: 4-1-4. *Degree:* bachelor's.

Library: Preus Library. *Books:* 202,938 (physical), 292,640 (digital/electronic); *Serial titles:* 17,086 (physical), 17,086 (digital/electronic); *Databases:* 99. Weekly public service hours: 104; students can reserve study rooms.

STUDENT LIFE

Housing options: on-campus residence required through senior year; coed, special housing for students with disabilities. Campus housing is university owned. Freshman campus housing is guaranteed.

Activities and organizations: drama/theater group, student-run newspaper, radio station, choral group, Alpha Phi Omega, college ministries, recreational sports, Student Activities Council, Diversity groups.

Athletics Member NCAA. All Division III.

Campus security: 24-hour emergency response devices and patrols, late-night transport/escort service, controlled dormitory access.

Student services: health clinic, personal/psychological counseling, women's center.

COSTS & FINANCIAL AID

Costs (2019–20) ***Tuition:*** $43,500 full-time, $1554 per credit hour part-time. ***Required fees:*** $570 full-time. ***Room only:*** $4560.

Financial Aid Of all full-time matriculated undergraduates who enrolled in 2018, 1,722 applied for aid, 1,520 were judged to have need, 607 had their need fully met. 749 Federal Work-Study jobs (averaging $2099). 71 state and other part-time jobs (averaging $4713). In 2018, 426 non-need-based awards were made. ***Average percent of need met:*** 90. ***Average financial aid package:*** $37,623. ***Average need-based loan:*** $8070. ***Average need-based gift aid:*** $30,183. ***Average non-need-based aid:*** $22,783. ***Average indebtedness upon graduation:*** $35,809.

APPLYING

Standardized Tests *Required:* SAT or ACT (for admission).

Options: electronic application, deferred entrance.

Required: essay or personal statement, high school transcript, 1 letter of recommendation. ***Recommended:*** interview.

CONTACT

Mr. Derek Hartl, Associate Vice President and Director of Admissions, Luther College, 700 College Drive, Decorah, IA 52101. *Phone:* 563-387-1433. *Toll-free phone:* 800-458-8437. *Fax:* 563-387-2159. *E-mail:* hartde01@luther.edu.

See below for display ad and page 1076 for the College Close-Up.

Maharishi International University

Fairfield, Iowa

http://www.mum.edu/

- **Independent** university, founded 1971
- **Small-town** 242-acre campus
- **Coed**
- **Moderately difficult** entrance level

FACULTY

Student/faculty ratio: 9:1.

ACADEMICS

Calendar: semesters. *Degrees:* certificates, bachelor's, master's, doctoral, and postbachelor's certificates.

Library: Maharishi University of Management Library. Weekly public service hours: 55.

STUDENT LIFE

Housing options: on-campus residence required through senior year; men-only, women-only. Campus housing is university owned. Freshman campus housing is guaranteed.

Campus security: 24-hour emergency response devices and patrols, late-night transport/escort service, controlled dormitory access.

Student services: health clinic, personal/psychological counseling.

COSTS & FINANCIAL AID

Costs (2019–20) ***Comprehensive fee:*** $23,930 includes full-time tuition ($16,000), mandatory fees ($530), and room and board ($7400). Full-time tuition and fees vary according to course load. Part-time tuition: $500 per unit. Part-time tuition and fees vary according to course load.

Financial Aid Of all full-time matriculated undergraduates who enrolled in 2006, 150 applied for aid, 148 were judged to have need, 32 had their need fully met. 120 Federal Work-Study jobs (averaging $1422). 7 state and other part-time jobs (averaging $2729). In 2006, 5 non-need-based awards were made. ***Average percent of need met:*** 89. ***Average financial aid package:*** $23,963. ***Average need-based loan:*** $8281. ***Average need-based gift aid:*** $14,082. ***Average non-need-based aid:*** $9300. ***Average indebtedness upon graduation:*** $22,691.

APPLYING

Options: electronic application, early admission, deferred entrance.

Application fee: $20.

Required: essay or personal statement, high school transcript, minimum 2.5 GPA, 2 letters of recommendation. ***Recommended:*** interview.

CONTACT

June Humphreys, Lead US Admissions Counselor, Maharishi International University, Office of Admissions, Fairfield, IA 52557. *Phone:* 641-472-1110 Ext. 4807. *Toll-free phone:* 800-369-6480. *Fax:* 641-472-1179. *E-mail:* admissions@mum.edu.

Mercy College of Health Sciences

Des Moines, Iowa

http://www.mchs.edu/

CONTACT

Heather Gaumer, Director of Admissions, Mercy College of Health Sciences, 921 Sixth Avenue, Des Moines, IA 50309-1200. *Phone:* 515-643-6604. *Toll-free phone:* 800-637-2994. *Fax:* 515-643-6698. *E-mail:* hgaumer@mercydesmoines.org.

Morningside College

Sioux City, Iowa

http://www.morningside.edu/

- **Independent** comprehensive, founded 1894, affiliated with United Methodist Church
- **Suburban** 69-acre campus with easy access to Omaha, NE
- **Endowment** $47.1 million
- **Coed**
- **Moderately difficult** entrance level

FACULTY

Student/faculty ratio: 14:1.

ACADEMICS

Calendar: semesters. *Degrees:* bachelor's, master's, post-master's, and postbachelor's certificates.

Library: Hickman-Johnson-Furrow Learning Center. *Books:* 40,458 (physical), 325 (digital/electronic); *Serial titles:* 516 (physical), 74 (digital/electronic); *Databases:* 46. Weekly public service hours: 93.

STUDENT LIFE

Housing options: on-campus residence required through junior year; coed. Campus housing is university owned. Freshman campus housing is guaranteed.

Activities and organizations: drama/theater group, student-run newspaper, radio and television station, choral group, marching band, Student Government/Activities Council, Student Ambassadors, Homecoming Committee, national fraternities, national sororities.

Athletics Member NCAA, NAIA. All NCAA Division II.

Campus security: 24-hour emergency response devices and patrols, student patrols, late-night transport/escort service, controlled dormitory access.

Student services: health clinic, personal/psychological counseling, women's center.

COSTS & FINANCIAL AID

Costs (2019–20) ***Comprehensive fee:*** $42,560 includes full-time tuition ($31,220), mandatory fees ($1500), and room and board ($9840). Part-time tuition: $570 per credit hour. Part-time tuition and fees vary according to course load. ***College room only:*** $5320. Room and board charges vary according to housing facility.

Financial Aid Of all full-time matriculated undergraduates who enrolled in 2017, 1,107 applied for aid, 994 were judged to have need, 238 had their need fully met. 542 Federal Work-Study jobs (averaging $1346). 265 state and other part-time jobs (averaging $2000). In 2017, 257 non-need-based awards were made. ***Average percent of need met:*** 74. ***Average financial aid package:*** $24,135. ***Average need-based loan:*** $4635. ***Average need-based gift aid:*** $6366. ***Average non-need-based aid:*** $15,529. ***Average indebtedness upon graduation:*** $36,449.

APPLYING

Standardized Tests *Required:* SAT or ACT (for admission).

Options: electronic application, deferred entrance.

Required: high school transcript, minimum 2.5 GPA, minimum ACT score of 20 or SAT of 1410 and either rank in top half of class or 2.5 GPA. ***Recommended:*** interview.

CONTACT
Mrs. Stephanie Peters, Director of Admissions, Morningside College, 1501 Morningside Avenue, Sioux City, IA 51106. *Phone:* 712-274-5111. *Toll-free phone:* 800-831-0806 Ext. 5111. *Fax:* 712-274-5101. *E-mail:* mscadm@morningside.edu.

Mount Mercy University

Cedar Rapids, Iowa

http://www.mtmercy.edu/

- **Independent Roman Catholic** comprehensive, founded 1928
- **Suburban** 40-acre campus with easy access to Iowa City
- **Endowment** $28.7 million
- **Coed** 1,442 undergraduate students, 74% full-time, 68% women, 32% men
- **Moderately difficult** entrance level, 66% of applicants were admitted

UNDERGRAD STUDENTS
1,070 full-time, 372 part-time. Students come from 33 states and territories; 26 other countries; 13% are from out of state; 9% Black or African American, non-Hispanic/Latino; 0.7% Hispanic/Latino; 2% Asian, non-Hispanic/Latino; 0.6% Native Hawaiian or other Pacific Islander, non-Hispanic/Latino; 0.9% American Indian or Alaska Native, non-Hispanic/Latino; 2% Two or more races, non-Hispanic/Latino; 6% Race/ethnicity unknown; 4% international; 9% transferred in; 43% live on campus.

Freshmen:
Admission: 1,176 applied, 776 admitted, 218 enrolled. ***Average high school GPA:*** 3.4. ***Test scores:*** ACT scores over 18: 79%; ACT scores over 24: 27%; ACT scores over 30: 3%.

Retention: 75% of full-time freshmen returned.

FACULTY
Total: 176, 45% full-time, 39% with terminal degrees.

Student/faculty ratio: 15:1.

ACADEMICS
Calendar: 4-1-4. *Degrees:* bachelor's, master's, and doctoral.

Special study options: academic remediation for entering students, accelerated degree program, adult/continuing education programs, advanced placement credit, double majors, external degree program, honors programs, independent study, internships, off-campus study, part-time degree program, services for LD students, study abroad, summer session for credit.

Computers: 120 computers/terminals and 200 ports are available on campus for general student use. Students can access the following: campus intranet, computer help desk, free student e-mail accounts, online (class) grades, online (class) registration, online (class) schedules. Campuswide network is available. 100% of college-owned or -operated housing units are wired for high-speed Internet access. Wireless service is available via entire campus.
Library: Busse Library. *Books:* 83,046 (physical), 211,399 (digital/electronic); *Serial titles:* 3,956 (physical). Weekly public service hours: 83; students can reserve study rooms.

STUDENT LIFE
Housing options: on-campus residence required through sophomore year; coed, men-only, women-only. Campus housing is university owned. Freshman campus housing is guaranteed.

Activities and organizations: drama/theater group, student-run newspaper, choral group, Student Ambassadors, Mount Mercy University Association of Nursing Students, Cheerleaders, Black Student Union, Student Government Association.

Athletics Member NCAA, NAIA. All NCAA Division III. ***Intercollegiate sports:*** baseball M(s), basketball M(s)/W(s), bowling M(s)/W(s), cheerleading M(s)/W(s), cross-country running M(s)/W(s), golf M(s)/W(s), soccer M(s)/W(s), softball W(s), track and field M(s)/W(s), volleyball M(s)/W(s). ***Intramural sports:*** baseball M, basketball M/W, bowling M/W, cheerleading W, football M/W, racquetball M/W, tennis M/W, volleyball M/W, weight lifting M/W.

Campus security: 24-hour emergency response devices and patrols, student patrols, late-night transport/escort service, controlled dormitory access, Department of Public Safety operational 24-hours a day, 7 days a week.

Student services: health clinic, personal/psychological counseling, veterans affairs office.

COSTS & FINANCIAL AID
Costs (2020–21) ***Comprehensive fee:*** $45,686 includes full-time tuition ($34,506), mandatory fees ($1068), and room and board ($10,112). Full-time tuition and fees vary according to course load, degree level, and location. Part-time tuition: $1046 per credit hour. Part-time tuition and fees vary according to course load, degree level, and location. ***Required fees:*** $600 part-time. ***Room and board:*** Room and board charges vary according to board plan and housing facility. ***Payment plan:*** installment. ***Waivers:*** employees or children of employees.

Financial Aid Of all full-time matriculated undergraduates who enrolled in 2018, 1,017 applied for aid, 928 were judged to have need, 163 had their need fully met. In 2018, 176 non-need-based awards were made. ***Average percent of need met:*** 74. ***Average financial aid package:*** $25,140. ***Average need-based loan:*** $3866. ***Average need-based gift aid:*** $21,468. ***Average non-need-based aid:*** $14,102. ***Average indebtedness upon graduation:*** $25,739.

APPLYING
Standardized Tests *Required:* SAT or ACT (for admission).

Options: electronic application, deferred entrance.

Required: high school transcript, minimum 2.5 GPA. ***Required for some:*** 1 letter of recommendation.

Application deadlines: 8/15 (freshmen), 8/15 (transfers).

Notification: continuous (freshmen), continuous (transfers).

CONTACT
Dr. Teresa Crumley, Dean of Admission, Mount Mercy University, 1330 Elmhurst Drive, NE, Cedar Rapids, IA 52402. *Phone:* 319-368-6460. *Toll-free phone:* 800-248-4504. *Fax:* 319-363-5270. *E-mail:* tcrumley@mtmercy.edu.

Northwestern College

Orange City, Iowa

http://www.nwciowa.edu/

- **Independent** comprehensive, founded 1882, affiliated with Reformed Church in America
- **Small-town** 100-acre campus
- **Endowment** $49.4 million
- **Coed** 1,061 undergraduate students, 94% full-time, 56% women, 43% men
- **Moderately difficult** entrance level, 68% of applicants were admitted

UNDERGRAD STUDENTS
997 full-time, 52 part-time. Students come from 31 states and territories; 20 other countries; 42% are from out of state; 1% transferred in; 92% live on campus.

Freshmen:
Admission: 1,959 applied, 1,334 admitted, 281 enrolled. ***Average high school GPA:*** 3.6.

Retention: 77% of full-time freshmen returned.

ACADEMICS
Calendar: semesters. *Degrees:* bachelor's, master's, and postbachelor's certificates.

Special study options: academic remediation for entering students, advanced placement credit, cooperative education, distance learning, double majors, English as a second language, honors programs, independent study, internships, off-campus study, services for LD students, student-designed majors, study abroad, summer session for credit.

Unusual degree programs: 3-2 engineering with Washington University in St. Louis.

Computers: 250 computers/terminals and 1,200 ports are available on campus for general student use. Students can access the following: campus intranet, computer help desk, free student e-mail accounts, online (class) grades, online (class) registration, online (class) schedules, online degree audits. Campuswide network is available. 100% of college-owned or -operated housing units are wired for high-speed Internet access. Wireless service is available via entire campus.

Library: DeWitt Learning Commons plus 1 other. Weekly public service hours: 98; students can reserve study rooms.

STUDENT LIFE

Housing options: on-campus residence required through senior year; men-only, women-only, special housing for students with disabilities. Campus housing is university owned. Freshman campus housing is guaranteed.

Activities and organizations: drama/theater group, student-run newspaper, choral group, Drama Ministries Ensemble, A cappella Choir, Discipleship Groups, Fellowship of Christian Athletes, International Club.

Athletics ***Intercollegiate sports:*** baseball M(s), basketball M(s)/W(s), cheerleading M(s)/W(s), cross-country running M(s)/W(s), football M(s), golf M(s)/W(s), rugby W(c), soccer M(s)/W(s), softball W(s), tennis M(s)/W(s), track and field M(s)/W(s), volleyball W(s), wrestling M(s). ***Intramural sports:*** badminton M/W, basketball M/W, bowling M/W, football M/W, golf M/W, racquetball M/W, soccer M/W, softball M/W, table tennis M/W, tennis M/W, ultimate Frisbee M/W, volleyball M/W.

Campus security: 24-hour emergency response devices, controlled dormitory access.

Student services: health clinic, personal/psychological counseling.

COSTS & FINANCIAL AID

Costs (2019–20) ***Comprehensive fee:*** $73,710 includes full-time tuition ($56,232), mandatory fees ($459), and room and board ($17,019). Part-time tuition and fees vary according to course load. ***Room and board:*** Room and board charges vary according to board plan and housing facility. ***Payment plans:*** tuition prepayment, installment. ***Waivers:*** employees or children of employees.

Financial Aid Of all full-time matriculated undergraduates who enrolled in 2017, 845 applied for aid, 734 were judged to have need, 444 had their need fully met. 144 Federal Work-Study jobs (averaging $1550). 666 state and other part-time jobs (averaging $1089). In 2017, 253 non-need-based awards were made. ***Average percent of need met:*** 93. ***Average financial aid package:*** $25,672. ***Average need-based loan:*** $4947. ***Average need-based gift aid:*** $7244. ***Average non-need-based aid:*** $12,162. ***Average indebtedness upon graduation:*** $32,164.

APPLYING

Standardized Tests *Required:* SAT or ACT (for admission).

Options: electronic application, early admission, deferred entrance.

Required: essay or personal statement, high school transcript, minimum 2.0 GPA. ***Recommended:*** minimum 2.5 GPA, 1 letter of recommendation, interview.

Application deadlines: rolling (freshmen), rolling (transfers).

Notification: continuous (freshmen), continuous (transfers).

CONTACT

Mrs. Jackie Davis, Director of Admissions, Northwestern College, 101 7th Street SW, Orange City, IA 51041. *Phone:* 712-737-7114. *Toll-free phone:* 800-747-4757. *Fax:* 712-707-7164. *E-mail:* admissions@nwciowa.edu.

Purdue University Global

Cedar Falls, Iowa

http://www.purdueglobal.edu/

CONTACT

Purdue University Global, 7009 Nordic Drive, Cedar Falls, IA 50613. *Phone:* 319-277-0220. *Toll-free phone:* 844-PURDUE-G.

Purdue University Global

Cedar Rapids, Iowa

http://www.purdueglobal.edu/

CONTACT

Purdue University Global, 3165 Edgewood Parkway, SW, Cedar Rapids, IA 52404. *Phone:* 319-363-0481. *Toll-free phone:* 844-PURDUE-G.

Purdue University Global

Davenport, Iowa

http://www.purdueglobal.edu/

CONTACT

Purdue University Global, 1801 East Kimberly Road, Suite 1, Davenport, IA 52807. *Phone:* 563-355-3500. *Toll-free phone:* 844-PURDUE-G.

Purdue University Global

Mason City, Iowa

http://www.purdueglobal.edu/

CONTACT

Purdue University Global, 2570 4th Street, SW, Mason City, IA 50401. *Phone:* 641-423-2530. *Toll-free phone:* 844-PURDUE-G.

Purdue University Global

Urbandale, Iowa

http://www.purdueglobal.edu/

CONTACT

Purdue University Global, 4655 121st Street, Urbandale, IA 50323. *Phone:* 515-727-2100. *Toll-free phone:* 844-PURDUE-G.

St. Ambrose University

Davenport, Iowa

http://www.sau.edu/

- **Independent Roman Catholic** comprehensive, founded 1882
- **Urban** 113-acre campus with easy access to 168 miles from Des Moines, 175 miles from Chicago
- **Endowment** $171.5 million
- **Coed** 2,260 undergraduate students, 94% full-time, 55% women, 45% men
- **Moderately difficult** entrance level, 77% of applicants were admitted

UNDERGRAD STUDENTS

2,122 full-time, 138 part-time. Students come from 33 states and territories; 21 other countries; 66% are from out of state; 5% Black or African American, non-Hispanic/Latino; 9% Hispanic/Latino; 1% Asian, non-Hispanic/Latino; 0.1% Native Hawaiian or other Pacific Islander, non-Hispanic/Latino; 0.1% American Indian or Alaska Native, non-Hispanic/Latino; 3% Two or more races, non-Hispanic/Latino; 4% Race/ethnicity unknown; 4% international; 9% transferred in; 69% live on campus.

Freshmen:

Admission: 4,877 applied, 3,745 admitted, 477 enrolled. ***Average high school GPA:*** 3.4. ***Test scores:*** SAT evidence-based reading and writing scores over 500: 75%; SAT math scores over 500: 85%; ACT scores over 18: 94%; SAT evidence-based reading and writing scores over 600: 22%; SAT math scores over 600: 26%; ACT scores over 24: 39%; SAT evidence-based reading and writing scores over 700: 2%; SAT math scores over 700: 2%; ACT scores over 30: 5%.

Retention: 76% of full-time freshmen returned.

FACULTY

Total: 342, 59% full-time, 60% with terminal degrees.

Student/faculty ratio: 11:1.

ACADEMICS

Calendar: semesters. *Degrees:* bachelor's, master's, doctoral, and post-master's certificates.

Special study options: academic remediation for entering students, accelerated degree program, adult/continuing education programs, advanced placement credit, cooperative education, distance learning, double majors, English as a second language, honors programs, independent study, internships, off-campus study, part-time degree program, services for LD students, student-designed majors, study abroad, summer session for credit.

Unusual degree programs: 3-2 social work; physical therapy, criminal justice.

Computers: 500 computers/terminals and 520 ports are available on campus for general student use. Students can access the following: campus intranet, computer help desk, free student e-mail accounts, online (class) grades, online (class) registration, online (class) schedules, online course syllabi, online payments. Campuswide network is available. 100% of college-owned or -operated housing units are wired for high-speed Internet access. Wireless service is available via entire campus.
Library: SAU Library plus 1 other. *Books:* 175,256 (physical); *Serial titles:* 248 (physical), 322,385 (digital/electronic); *Databases:* 85. Weekly public service hours: 94; students can reserve study rooms.

STUDENT LIFE
Housing options: on-campus residence required through sophomore year; coed, men-only, women-only, special housing for students with disabilities. Campus housing is university owned. Freshman campus housing is guaranteed.

Activities and organizations: drama/theater group, student-run newspaper, radio and television station, choral group, marching band, Dance Marathon, Bridge Bible Fellowship, SPTO - Student Physical Therapy Organization, Kappa Delta Pi Iota Sigma - Education Honors, CAB - Campus Activity Board.

Athletics Member NAIA. ***Intercollegiate sports:*** baseball M(s), basketball M(s)/W(s), bowling M/W, cheerleading M/W, cross-country running M(s)/W(s), football M(s), golf M(s)/W(s), lacrosse M(s), soccer M(s)/W(s), softball W(s), swimming and diving M(s)/W(s), tennis M(s)/W(s), track and field M(s)/W(s), volleyball M(s)/W(s). ***Intramural sports:*** basketball M/W, cross-country running M(c)/W(c), football M/W, racquetball M(c)/W(c), rowing M(c)/W(c), sand volleyball M/W, soccer M/W, softball M/W, table tennis M/W, volleyball M/W.

Campus security: 24-hour emergency response devices and patrols, student patrols, late-night transport/escort service, controlled dormitory access.

Student services: health clinic, personal/psychological counseling, veterans affairs office.

COSTS & FINANCIAL AID
Costs (2020–21) ***Comprehensive fee:*** $44,112 includes full-time tuition ($32,478), mandatory fees ($280), and room and board ($11,354). Full-time tuition and fees vary according to course load. Part-time tuition: $970 per credit hour. Part-time tuition and fees vary according to course load. ***Required fees:*** $140 per term part-time. ***College room only:*** $7020. Room and board charges vary according to board plan and housing facility. ***Payment plans:*** installment, deferred payment. ***Waivers:*** children of alumni and employees or children of employees.

Financial Aid Of all full-time matriculated undergraduates who enrolled in 2019, 1,799 applied for aid, 1,579 were judged to have need, 422 had their need fully met. 1,270 Federal Work-Study jobs (averaging $1850). 295 state and other part-time jobs (averaging $1850). In 2019, 444 non-need-based awards were made. ***Average percent of need met:*** 72. ***Average financial aid package:*** $24,736. ***Average need-based loan:*** $4438. ***Average need-based gift aid:*** $19,287. ***Average non-need-based aid:*** $15,164. ***Average indebtedness upon graduation:*** $38,149.

APPLYING
Standardized Tests *Required:* SAT or ACT (for admission).

Options: electronic application, deferred entrance.

Required: high school transcript, minimum 2.5 GPA. ***Required for some:*** interview. ***Recommended:*** interview.

Application deadlines: rolling (freshmen), rolling (transfers).

Notification: 10/1 (freshmen), continuous (transfers).

CONTACT
Ms. Allison Conklin, Associate Director of First Year Admissions, St. Ambrose University, 518 W. Locust Street, Davenport, IA 52803. *Phone:* 563-333-6300. *Toll-free phone:* 800-383-2627. *Fax:* 563-333-6297. *E-mail:* conklinallisonj@sau.edu.

St. Luke's College
Sioux City, Iowa
http://stlukescollege.edu/

- **Independent** primarily 2-year, founded 1967
- **Rural** 3-acre campus with easy access to Omaha
- **Endowment** $1.2 million
- **Coed** 235 undergraduate students, 52% full-time, 93% women, 7% men
- **Minimally difficult** entrance level, 15% of applicants were admitted

UNDERGRAD STUDENTS
123 full-time, 112 part-time. Students come from 21 states and territories; 39% are from out of state; 2% Black or African American, non-Hispanic/Latino; 8% Hispanic/Latino; 3% Asian, non-Hispanic/Latino; 0.9% Native Hawaiian or other Pacific Islander, non-Hispanic/Latino; 2% American Indian or Alaska Native, non-Hispanic/Latino; 2% Two or more races, non-Hispanic/Latino; 0.4% Race/ethnicity unknown; 23% transferred in.

Freshmen:
Admission: 53 applied, 8 admitted, 6 enrolled. ***Average high school GPA:*** 3.3.

Retention: 100% of full-time freshmen returned.

FACULTY
Total: 41, 61% full-time, 12% with terminal degrees.

Student/faculty ratio: 5:1.

ACADEMICS
Calendar: semesters. *Degrees:* certificates, associate, and bachelor's.

Special study options: advanced placement credit, distance learning, internships, services for LD students, summer session for credit.

Computers: 9 computers/terminals are available on campus for general student use. Students can access the following: campus intranet, computer help desk, free student e-mail accounts, online (class) grades, online (class) registration, online (class) schedules. Campuswide network is available. Wireless service is available via entire campus.
Library: St. Luke's College Library. *Books:* 1,435 (physical), 4,700 (digital/electronic); *Databases:* 5. Weekly public service hours: 56.

STUDENT LIFE
Housing options: college housing not available.

Campus security: 24-hour emergency response devices and patrols, late-night transport/escort service.

Student services: health clinic, personal/psychological counseling.

COSTS & FINANCIAL AID
Costs (2020–21) ***Tuition:*** $19,440 full-time, $540 per credit hour part-time. Full-time tuition and fees vary according to degree level and program. Part-time tuition and fees vary according to degree level and program. ***Required fees:*** $1650 full-time, $1650 per year part-time. ***Payment plan:*** installment.

Financial Aid Of all full-time matriculated undergraduates who enrolled in 2017, 81 applied for aid, 81 were judged to have need. 5 Federal Work-Study jobs (averaging $900). ***Average percent of need met:*** 80. ***Average financial aid package:*** $11,650. ***Average need-based loan:*** $6938. ***Average need-based gift aid:*** $4981. ***Average indebtedness upon graduation:*** $19,465.

APPLYING
Standardized Tests *Required:* SAT or ACT (for admission).

Options: electronic application.

Required: essay or personal statement, high school transcript, minimum 2.5 GPA, interview.

Notification: continuous (freshmen), continuous (out-of-state freshmen), continuous (transfers), rolling (early decision plan 1), rolling (early decision plan 2), rolling (early action).

CONTACT
Ms. Sherry McCarthy, Admissions Coordinator, St. Luke's College, 2720 Stone Park Boulevard, Sioux City, IA 51104. *Phone:* 712-279-3149. *Toll-free phone:* 800-352-4660 Ext. 3149. *Fax:* 712-233-8017. *E-mail:* sherry.mccarthy@stlukescollege.edu.

Shiloh University

Kalona, Iowa

http://www.shilohuniversity.edu/

- **Independent** comprehensive, founded 2007
- **Small-town** 200-acre campus
- **Coed**
- **Noncompetitive** entrance level

FACULTY

Student/faculty ratio: 1:1.

ACADEMICS

Degrees: certificates, associate, bachelor's, master's, doctoral, and postbachelor's certificates.
Library: University e-Library. *Databases:* 2.

COSTS

Costs (2019–20) ***Tuition:*** $4725 full-time, $175 per credit hour part-time.

APPLYING

Options: electronic application, early admission, deferred entrance.
Required: essay or personal statement, high school transcript, minimum 2.0 GPA. ***Required for some:*** 1 letter of recommendation.

CONTACT

Mr. Jeremy Daniel Richardson, Admissions Coordinator, Shiloh University, 100 Shiloh Drive, Kalona, IA 52247. *Phone:* 319-656-2447. *Fax:* 319-656-2448. *E-mail:* admissions@shilohuniversity.edu.

Simpson College

Indianola, Iowa

http://www.simpson.edu/

CONTACT

Simpson College, 701 North C Street, Indianola, IA 50125-1297. *Toll-free phone:* 800-362-2454.

University of Dubuque

Dubuque, Iowa

http://www.dbq.edu/

- **Independent Presbyterian** comprehensive, founded 1852
- **Suburban** 77-acre campus
- **Endowment** $153.3 million
- **Coed** 1,900 undergraduate students, 82% full-time, 45% women, 55% men
- **Moderately difficult** entrance level, 73% of applicants were admitted

UNDERGRAD STUDENTS

1,554 full-time, 346 part-time. Students come from 42 states and territories; 9 other countries; 54% are from out of state; 14% Black or African American, non-Hispanic/Latino; 8% Hispanic/Latino; 1% Asian, non-Hispanic/Latino; 0.4% Native Hawaiian or other Pacific Islander, non-Hispanic/Latino; 0.2% American Indian or Alaska Native, non-Hispanic/Latino; 3% Two or more races, non-Hispanic/Latino; 3% Race/ethnicity unknown; 7% international; 6% transferred in; 42% live on campus.

Freshmen:

Admission: 2,054 applied, 1,493 admitted, 386 enrolled. ***Average high school GPA:*** 3.0. ***Test scores:*** SAT evidence-based reading and writing scores over 500: 41%; SAT math scores over 500: 44%; ACT scores over 18: 68%; SAT evidence-based reading and writing scores over 600: 9%; SAT math scores over 600: 9%; ACT scores over 24: 14%; SAT evidence-based reading and writing scores over 700: 1%; SAT math scores over 700: 1%; ACT scores over 30: 1%.

Retention: 62% of full-time freshmen returned.

FACULTY

Total: 403, 27% full-time, 22% with terminal degrees.

Student/faculty ratio: 18:1.

ACADEMICS

Calendar: 4-1-4. *Degrees:* associate, bachelor's, master's, and doctoral.

Special study options: academic remediation for entering students, accelerated degree program, adult/continuing education programs, advanced placement credit, distance learning, double majors, honors programs, independent study, internships, off-campus study, part-time degree program, services for LD students, student-designed majors, study abroad, summer session for credit. ***ROTC:*** Army (b).

Unusual degree programs: 3-2 business administration; communications, theology.

Computers: 244 computers/terminals are available on campus for general student use. Students can access the following: campus intranet, computer help desk, free student e-mail accounts, online (class) grades, online (class) registration, online (class) schedules. Campuswide network is available. 100% of college-owned or -operated housing units are wired for high-speed Internet access. Wireless service is available via entire campus.
Library: Charles C. Myers Library. *Books:* 120,740 (physical), 229,930 (digital/electronic); *Serial titles:* 155 (physical), 44,709 (digital/electronic); *Databases:* 107. Weekly public service hours: 109.

STUDENT LIFE

Housing options: on-campus residence required through junior year; coed, special housing for students with disabilities. Campus housing is university owned. Freshman campus housing is guaranteed.

Activities and organizations: drama/theater group, student-run newspaper, choral group, Greek Council, Saudi Student Organization, Student Nurses Association, Accounting Club, ROTC.

Athletics Member NCAA. All Division III except golf (Division II). ***Intercollegiate sports:*** baseball M, basketball M/W, cross-country running M/W, football M, golf M/W, soccer M/W, softball W, tennis M/W, track and field M/W, volleyball W, wrestling M. ***Intramural sports:*** badminton M/W, basketball M/W, bowling M/W, cheerleading M(c)/W(c), football M/W, golf M/W, soccer M/W, softball M/W, table tennis M/W, tennis M/W, ultimate Frisbee M/W, volleyball M/W.

Campus security: 24-hour patrols, late-night transport/escort service, controlled dormitory access.

Student services: health clinic, personal/psychological counseling, veterans affairs office.

COSTS & FINANCIAL AID

Costs (2020–21) ***Comprehensive fee:*** $47,110 includes full-time tuition ($35,060), mandatory fees ($1550), and room and board ($10,500). Part-time tuition: $1052 per credit hour. ***Room and board:*** Room and board charges vary according to board plan. ***Waivers:*** employees or children of employees.

Financial Aid Of all full-time matriculated undergraduates who enrolled in 2019, 1,436 applied for aid, 1,320 were judged to have need, 222 had their need fully met. 198 Federal Work-Study jobs (averaging $2000). 178 state and other part-time jobs (averaging $2000). In 2019, 183 non-need-based awards were made. ***Average percent of need met:*** 70. ***Average financial aid package:*** $29,385. ***Average need-based loan:*** $7207. ***Average need-based gift aid:*** $23,456. ***Average non-need-based aid:*** $15,664. ***Average indebtedness upon graduation:*** $33,454.

APPLYING

Standardized Tests *Required:* SAT or ACT (for admission).

Options: electronic application, deferred entrance.

Application fee: $25.

Required: essay or personal statement, high school transcript, 2 letters of recommendation. ***Recommended:*** interview.

Application deadlines: rolling (freshmen), rolling (transfers).

Notification: continuous (freshmen), continuous (transfers).

CONTACT

Mr. Bob Broshous, Director of Admissions, University of Dubuque, 2000 University Avenue, Dubuque, IA 52001-5099. *Phone:* 563-589-3199. *Toll-free phone:* 800-722-5583. *Fax:* 563-589-3690. *E-mail:* admissns@dbq.edu.

The University of Iowa
Iowa City, Iowa
http://www.uiowa.edu/

- **State-supported** university, founded 1847
- **Small-town** 1700-acre campus
- **Endowment** $1.3 billion
- **Coed** 23,483 undergraduate students, 90% full-time, 54% women, 46% men
- **Moderately difficult** entrance level, 83% of applicants were admitted

UNDERGRAD STUDENTS
21,212 full-time, 2,271 part-time. 32% are from out of state; 3% Black or African American, non-Hispanic/Latino; 8% Hispanic/Latino; 4% Asian, non-Hispanic/Latino; 0.1% Native Hawaiian or other Pacific Islander, non-Hispanic/Latino; 0.2% American Indian or Alaska Native, non-Hispanic/Latino; 3% Two or more races, non-Hispanic/Latino; 2% Race/ethnicity unknown; 5% international; 5% transferred in; 28% live on campus.

Freshmen:
Admission: 25,928 applied, 21,404 admitted, 4,986 enrolled. ***Average high school GPA:*** 3.8. ***Test scores:*** SAT evidence-based reading and writing scores over 500: 95%; SAT math scores over 500: 95%; ACT scores over 18: 98%; SAT evidence-based reading and writing scores over 600: 59%; SAT math scores over 600: 62%; ACT scores over 24: 65%; SAT evidence-based reading and writing scores over 700: 12%; SAT math scores over 700: 18%; ACT scores over 30: 21%.

Retention: 86% of full-time freshmen returned.

FACULTY
Total: 1,668, 87% full-time, 86% with terminal degrees.

Student/faculty ratio: 15:1.

ACADEMICS
Calendar: semesters. *Degrees:* bachelor's, master's, doctoral, post-master's, and postbachelor's certificates.

Special study options: accelerated degree program, adult/continuing education programs, advanced placement credit, cooperative education, distance learning, double majors, English as a second language, external degree program, honors programs, independent study, internships, off-campus study, part-time degree program, services for LD students, student-designed majors, study abroad, summer session for credit. ***ROTC:*** Army (b), Air Force (b).

Unusual degree programs: 3-2 engineering; urban and regional planning, education, computer science, public health, law, biochemistry, epidemiology, occupational and environmental health, linguistics, microbiology.

Computers: 1,468 computers/terminals are available on campus for general student use. Students can access the following: computer help desk, free student e-mail accounts, online (class) grades, online (class) registration, online (class) schedules, online degree process, financial aid summary, university bill. Campuswide network is available. 100% of college-owned or -operated housing units are wired for high-speed Internet access. Wireless service is available via classrooms, computer centers, computer labs, dorm rooms, learning centers, libraries, student centers.
Library: Main Library plus 8 others.

STUDENT LIFE
Housing options: coed. Campus housing is university owned.

Activities and organizations: drama/theater group, student-run newspaper, radio and television station, choral group, marching band, Association of Residence Halls, Graduate Student Senate, National Society of Collegiate Scholars, Organization for the Active Support of International Students (OASIS), Dance Marathon, national fraternities, national sororities.

Athletics Member NCAA. All Division I except football (Division I-A). ***Intercollegiate sports:*** baseball M(s), basketball M(s)/W(s), cheerleading M/W, crew M(c)/W(s), cross-country running M(s)/W(s), field hockey W(s), golf M(s)/W(s), gymnastics M(s)/W(s), ice hockey M(c)/W(c), lacrosse M(c)/W(c), rugby M(c)/W(c), sailing M(c)/W(c), soccer M(c)/W(s), softball W(s), swimming and diving M(s)/W(s), table tennis M(c)/W(c), tennis M(s)/W(s), track and field M(s)/W(s), ultimate Frisbee M(c)/W(c), volleyball M(c)/W(s), wrestling M(s). ***Intramural sports:*** archery M(c)/W(c), badminton M/W, basketball M/W, bowling M/W, fencing M(c)/W(c), field hockey W(c), football M/W, golf M/W, racquetball M/W, rugby M(c)/W(c), sailing M(c)/W(c), skiing (cross-country) M(c)/W(c), skiing (downhill) M(c)/W(c), soccer M/W, softball M/W, swimming and diving M/W, table tennis M/W, tennis M/W, track and field M/W, ultimate Frisbee M/W, volleyball M/W, water polo M(c)/W(c), weight lifting M(c)/W(c), wrestling M/W.

Campus security: 24-hour emergency response devices and patrols, late-night transport/escort service, controlled dormitory access.

Student services: health clinic, personal/psychological counseling, women's center, legal services.

FINANCIAL AID
Financial Aid Of all full-time matriculated undergraduates who enrolled in 2018, 14,804 applied for aid, 10,374 were judged to have need, 1,310 had their need fully met. In 2018, 5699 non-need-based awards were made. ***Average percent of need met:*** 52. ***Average financial aid package:*** $12,652. ***Average need-based loan:*** $4041. ***Average need-based gift aid:*** $9095. ***Average non-need-based aid:*** $5677. ***Average indebtedness upon graduation:*** $28,328.

APPLYING
Standardized Tests *Required:* SAT or ACT (for admission).

Options: electronic application, early admission, deferred entrance.

Application fee: $40.

Required: high school transcript, minimum Regent Admission Index (RAI) requirement of 245 for residents, 255 for nonresidents.

Application deadlines: 4/1 (freshmen), 4/1 (transfers).

Notification: continuous (freshmen), continuous (transfers).

CONTACT
Debra Miller, Senior Associate Director, Undergraduate Evaluation, The University of Iowa, 108 Calvin Hall, Iowa City, IA 52242. *Phone:* 319-335-3847. *Toll-free phone:* 800-553-4692. *Fax:* 319-335-1535. *E-mail:* admissions@uiowa.edu.

University of Northern Iowa
Cedar Falls, Iowa
http://www.uni.edu/

- **State-supported** comprehensive, founded 1876, part of Board of Regents, State of Iowa
- **Suburban** 908-acre campus
- **Endowment** $149.1 million
- **Coed** 8,973 undergraduate students, 92% full-time, 59% women, 41% men
- **Moderately difficult** entrance level, 79% of applicants were admitted

UNDERGRAD STUDENTS
8,228 full-time, 745 part-time. Students come from 35 states and territories; 48 other countries; 6% are from out of state; 2% Black or African American, non-Hispanic/Latino; 4% Hispanic/Latino; 1% Asian, non-Hispanic/Latino; 0.1% Native Hawaiian or other Pacific Islander, non-Hispanic/Latino; 0.1% American Indian or Alaska Native, non-Hispanic/Latino; 3% Two or more races, non-Hispanic/Latino; 4% Race/ethnicity unknown; 2% international; 8% transferred in; 31% live on campus.

Freshmen:
Admission: 4,701 applied, 3,716 admitted, 1,465 enrolled. ***Average high school GPA:*** 3.6. ***Test scores:*** ACT scores over 18: 91%; ACT scores over 24: 39%; ACT scores over 30: 6%.

Retention: 83% of full-time freshmen returned.

FACULTY
Total: 639, 81% full-time, 72% with terminal degrees.

Student/faculty ratio: 17:1.

ACADEMICS
Calendar: semesters. *Degrees:* bachelor's, master's, doctoral, and post-master's certificates.

Special study options: academic remediation for entering students, accelerated degree program, adult/continuing education programs, advanced placement credit, cooperative education, distance learning, double majors, English as a second language, external degree program, honors programs, independent study, internships, off-campus study, part-time degree program, services for LD students, student-designed majors, study abroad, summer session for credit. ***ROTC:*** Army (b).

Unusual degree programs: 3-2 nursing with Allen College, University of Iowa; medical technology with University of Iowa Medical School, cytotechnology with Mayo School of Health-Related Sciences and Mercy College of Health Sciences, chiropractic with Logan College of Chiropractic and Palmer College of Chiropractic.

Computers: 1,900 computers/terminals are available on campus for general student use. Students can access the following: campus intranet, computer help desk, free student e-mail accounts, online (class) grades, online (class) registration, online (class) schedules, student account, degree audit, program of study. Campuswide network is available. 100% of college-owned or -operated housing units are wired for high-speed Internet access. Wireless service is available via entire campus.

Library: Rod Library plus 1 other. *Books:* 746,455 (physical), 367,841 (digital/electronic); *Serial titles:* 20,762 (physical), 77,427 (digital/electronic); *Databases:* 217. Weekly public service hours: 97; students can reserve study rooms.

STUDENT LIFE

Housing options: coed, men-only, women-only. Campus housing is university owned. Freshman campus housing is guaranteed.

Activities and organizations: drama/theater group, student-run newspaper, radio station, choral group, marching band, Dance Marathon, Colleges Against Cancer/Relay for Life, Accounting Club, Phi Eta Sigma, Students Today Alumni Tomorrow, national fraternities, national sororities.

Athletics Member NCAA. All Division I except football (Division I-AA). ***Intercollegiate sports:*** basketball M(s)/W(s), cross-country running M(s)/W(s), golf M(s)/W(s)(c), soccer W(s), softball W(s), swimming and diving W(s), tennis W(s), track and field M(s)/W(s), volleyball W(s), wrestling M(s). ***Intramural sports:*** badminton M/W, baseball M(c), basketball M/W, bowling M(c)/W(c), cheerleading M/W, crew M(c)/W(c), cross-country running M(c)/W(c), football M(c), golf M(c)/W(c), ice hockey M(c), racquetball M(c)/W(c), rugby M(c)/W(c), skiing (downhill) M(c)/W(c), soccer M(c)/W(c), softball M(c)/W(c), swimming and diving M(c)/W(c), table tennis M/W, tennis M(c)/W(c), track and field M(c)/W(c), ultimate Frisbee M(c)/W(c), volleyball M/W(c).

Campus security: 24-hour emergency response devices and patrols, student patrols, late-night transport/escort service, controlled dormitory access.

Student services: health clinic, personal/psychological counseling, veterans affairs office.

COSTS & FINANCIAL AID

Costs (2019–20) ***Tuition:*** state resident $7665 full-time, $320 per credit hour part-time; nonresident $18,207 full-time, $759 per credit hour part-time. Full-time tuition and fees vary according to course load and program. Part-time tuition and fees vary according to course load and program. ***Required fees:*** $1273 full-time. ***Room and board:*** $9160; room only: $4699. Room and board charges vary according to board plan and housing facility. ***Payment plan:*** installment.

Financial Aid Of all full-time matriculated undergraduates who enrolled in 2018, 6,829 applied for aid, 5,309 were judged to have need, 828 had their need fully met. In 2018, 1164 non-need-based awards were made. ***Average percent of need met:*** 63. ***Average financial aid package:*** $8442. ***Average need-based loan:*** $4198. ***Average need-based gift aid:*** $4987. ***Average non-need-based aid:*** $3290. ***Average indebtedness upon graduation:*** $23,671.

APPLYING

Standardized Tests *Required:* SAT or ACT (for admission). *Recommended:* SAT (for admission), ACT (for admission).

Options: electronic application, deferred entrance.

Application fee: $40.

Required: high school transcript, 4 years of English; 3 years each of math, science and social studies; 2 or more years of electives, which may include foreign language and fine arts. ***Required for some:*** interview.

Notification: 7/1 (freshmen), 8/1 (transfers).

CONTACT

Amy S. Schipper, Associate Director, Operations & Data, University of Northern Iowa, 002 Gilchrist, Cedar Falls, IA 50614. *Phone:* 319-273-2281. *Toll-free phone:* 800-772-2037. *Fax:* 319-273-2885. *E-mail:* admissions@uni.edu.

Upper Iowa University

Fayette, Iowa

http://www.uiu.edu/

- **Independent** comprehensive, founded 1857
- **Rural** 100-acre campus with easy access to Minneapolis-St. Paul, Chicago
- **Endowment** $18.8 million
- **Coed** 3,680 undergraduate students, 50% full-time, 62% women, 38% men
- **Moderately difficult** entrance level, 56% of applicants were admitted

UNDERGRAD STUDENTS

1,856 full-time, 1,824 part-time. Students come from 50 states and territories; 46 other countries; 121% are from out of state; 19% Black or African American, non-Hispanic/Latino; 5% Hispanic/Latino; 1% Asian, non-Hispanic/Latino; 0.4% Native Hawaiian or other Pacific Islander, non-Hispanic/Latino; 0.2% American Indian or Alaska Native, non-Hispanic/Latino; 2% Two or more races, non-Hispanic/Latino; 5% Race/ethnicity unknown; 5% international; 2% transferred in; 56% live on campus.

Freshmen:

Admission: 1,901 applied, 1,056 admitted, 190 enrolled. ***Average high school GPA:*** 3.2.

Retention: 60% of full-time freshmen returned.

ACADEMICS

Calendar: 6 8-week terms. *Degrees:* certificates, associate, bachelor's, and master's (enrollment figures include extended learning centers and online and distance education programs).

Special study options: academic remediation for entering students, accelerated degree program, adult/continuing education programs, advanced placement credit, cooperative education, distance learning, double majors, English as a second language, external degree program, freshman honors college, honors programs, independent study, internships, off-campus study, part-time degree program, services for LD students, student-designed majors, study abroad, summer session for credit.

Computers: 630 computers/terminals and 630 ports are available on campus for general student use. Students can access the following: campus intranet, computer help desk, free student e-mail accounts, online (class) grades, online (class) registration, online (class) schedules. Campuswide network is available. 100% of college-owned or -operated housing units are wired for high-speed Internet access. Wireless service is available via classrooms, computer centers, computer labs, dorm rooms, learning centers, libraries, student centers.

Library: Henderson Wilder Library. *Books:* 68,870 (physical), 7,450 (digital/electronic); *Serial titles:* 211 (physical), 83,993 (digital/electronic); *Databases:* 40. Weekly public service hours: 85.

STUDENT LIFE

Housing options: on-campus residence required through junior year; coed, men-only, women-only. Campus housing is university owned. Freshman campus housing is guaranteed.

Activities and organizations: drama/theater group, student-run newspaper, choral group, Student Athlete Advisory Committee, Peacock Alumni for Student Traditions, UIU Science and Environment Club, Student Government Association, Peacocks for Progress.

Athletics ***Intercollegiate sports:*** baseball M(s), basketball M(s)/W(s), cross-country running W(s), football M(s), golf M(s)/W(s), soccer M(s)/W(s), softball W(s), tennis W(s), track and field W(s), volleyball W(s), wrestling M(s). ***Intramural sports:*** badminton M/W, basketball M/W, bowling M/W, cheerleading M(c)/W(c), football M, golf M/W, soccer M/W, softball M/W, table tennis M/W, ultimate Frisbee M/W, volleyball M/W.

Campus security: late-night transport/escort service, controlled dormitory access.

Student services: personal/psychological counseling, veterans affairs office.

FINANCIAL AID

Financial Aid Of all full-time matriculated undergraduates who enrolled in 2019, 1,717 applied for aid, 1,621 were judged to have need, 179 had their need fully met. 140 Federal Work-Study jobs (averaging $2598). In 2019, 138 non-need-based awards were made. ***Average percent of need met:*** 57. ***Average financial aid package:*** $17,646. ***Average need-based loan:*** $5327. ***Average need-based gift aid:*** $14,027. ***Average non-need-based aid:*** $18,220. ***Average indebtedness upon graduation:*** $26,664.

APPLYING

Standardized Tests *Required:* SAT or ACT (for admission).

Options: electronic application.

Required: high school transcript, minimum 2.0 GPA.

Application deadlines: rolling (freshmen), rolling (transfers).

CONTACT

Ms. Kathy Franken, Vice President of Enrollment Management, Upper Iowa University, 605 Washington Street, Parker Fox Hall, Fayette, IA 52142. *Phone:* 563-425-5868. *Toll-free phone:* 800-553-4150. *Fax:* 563-425-5323. *E-mail:* frankenk@uiu.edu.

Waldorf University

Forest City, Iowa

http://www.waldorf.edu/

CONTACT

Waldorf University, 106 South 6th Street, Forest City, IA 50436. *Toll-free phone:* 800-292-1903.

Wartburg College

Waverly, Iowa

http://www.wartburg.edu/

- **Independent Lutheran** 4-year, founded 1852
- **Small-town** 170-acre campus
- **Endowment** $76.5 million
- **Coed** 1,501 undergraduate students, 97% full-time, 54% women, 46% men
- **Moderately difficult** entrance level, 75% of applicants were admitted

UNDERGRAD STUDENTS

1,462 full-time, 39 part-time. Students come from 38 states and territories; 59 other countries; 31% are from out of state; 4% Black or African American, non-Hispanic/Latino; 5% Hispanic/Latino; 1% Asian, non-Hispanic/Latino; 0.2% Native Hawaiian or other Pacific Islander, non-Hispanic/Latino; 0.1% American Indian or Alaska Native, non-Hispanic/Latino; 3% Two or more races, non-Hispanic/Latino; 1% Race/ethnicity unknown; 8% international; 2% transferred in; 86% live on campus.

Freshmen:

Admission: 4,018 applied, 3,019 admitted, 398 enrolled. ***Average high school GPA:*** 3.6. ***Test scores:*** SAT evidence-based reading and writing scores over 500: 83%; SAT math scores over 500: 86%; ACT scores over 18: 96%; SAT evidence-based reading and writing scores over 600: 43%; SAT math scores over 600: 32%; ACT scores over 24: 47%; SAT math scores over 700: 3%; ACT scores over 30: 8%.

Retention: 78% of full-time freshmen returned.

FACULTY

Total: 155, 59% full-time, 57% with terminal degrees.

Student/faculty ratio: 11:1.

ACADEMICS

Calendar: 4-4-1. *Degrees:* bachelor's, master's, and postbachelor's certificates.

Special study options: academic remediation for entering students, accelerated degree program, advanced placement credit, distance learning, double majors, honors programs, independent study, internships, off-campus study, part-time degree program, services for LD students, student-designed majors, study abroad, summer session for credit.

Unusual degree programs: 3-2 engineering with Iowa State University; nursing with Allen College; pre-seminary with Wartburg Seminary, clinical laboratory science with Mercy College of Health Sciences, pre-Law with The University of Iowa, museum studies with Western Illinois University.

Computers: 355 computers/terminals are available on campus for general student use. Students can access the following: campus intranet, computer help desk, free student e-mail accounts, online (class) grades, online (class) registration, online (class) schedules, billing. Campuswide network is available. 100% of college-owned or -operated housing units are wired for high-speed Internet access. Wireless service is available via entire campus.

Library: Vogel Library. *Books:* 129,577 (physical), 165,133 (digital/electronic); *Serial titles:* 3,332 (physical), 63,358 (digital/electronic); *Databases:* 170. Weekly public service hours: 91.

STUDENT LIFE

Housing options: on-campus residence required through senior year; coed, men-only, women-only, special housing for students with disabilities. Campus housing is university owned. Freshman campus housing is guaranteed.

Activities and organizations: drama/theater group, student-run newspaper, radio and television station, choral group, Entertainment To Knight (ETK), Student Senate, Wartburg College Dance Marathon (WCDM), Symphonic Band, Wartburg Choir.

Athletics Member NCAA. All Division III except golf (Division II). ***Intercollegiate sports:*** baseball M, basketball M/W, bowling M/W, cross-country running M/W, football M, golf M/W, lacrosse W, soccer M/W, softball W, tennis M/W, track and field M/W, volleyball W, wrestling M. ***Intramural sports:*** basketball M/W, bowling M/W, cheerleading W(c), golf M/W, sand volleyball M/W, soccer M/W, softball M/W.

Campus security: 24-hour emergency response devices and patrols, late-night transport/escort service, controlled dormitory access.

Student services: health clinic, personal/psychological counseling.

COSTS & FINANCIAL AID

Costs (2020–21) ***Comprehensive fee:*** $55,272 includes full-time tuition ($43,500), mandatory fees ($2180), and room and board ($9592). Part-time tuition: $2500 per course. Part-time tuition and fees vary according to course load. ***Required fees:*** $130 per term part-time. ***College room only:*** $5492. Room and board charges vary according to board plan and housing facility. ***Payment plan:*** installment. ***Waivers:*** employees or children of employees.

Financial Aid Of all full-time matriculated undergraduates who enrolled in 2018, 1,270 applied for aid, 1,132 were judged to have need, 304 had their need fully met. 503 Federal Work-Study jobs (averaging $1226). 482 state and other part-time jobs (averaging $1890). In 2018, 303 non-need-based awards were made. ***Average percent of need met:*** 86. ***Average financial aid package:*** $33,037. ***Average need-based loan:*** $5901. ***Average need-based gift aid:*** $28,182. ***Average non-need-based aid:*** $25,743. ***Average indebtedness upon graduation:*** $39,559.

APPLYING

Standardized Tests *Required:* SAT or ACT (for admission).

Options: electronic application, early action, deferred entrance.

Required: high school transcript, minimum 2.5 GPA. ***Recommended:*** secondary school report.

Application deadlines: rolling (freshmen), rolling (transfers).

Notification: continuous (freshmen), continuous (transfers).

CONTACT

Tara Winter, Director of Student Recruitment, Wartburg College, 100 Wartburg Boulevard, PO Box 1003, Waverly, IA 50677-0903. *Phone:* 319-352-8475. *Toll-free phone:* 800-772-2085. *Fax:* 319-352-8579. *E-mail:* admissions@wartburg.edu.

William Penn University

Oskaloosa, Iowa

http://www.wmpenn.edu/

- **Independent** comprehensive, founded 1873, affiliated with Society of Friends
- **Rural** 60-acre campus with easy access to Des Moines
- **Endowment** $6.6 million
- **Coed** 1,197 undergraduate students, 91% full-time, 46% women, 54% men
- **Minimally difficult** entrance level, 58% of applicants were admitted

UNDERGRAD STUDENTS
1,091 full-time, 106 part-time. Students come from 44 states and territories; 20 other countries; 53% are from out of state; 20% Black or African American, non-Hispanic/Latino; 10% Hispanic/Latino; 1% Asian, non-Hispanic/Latino; 0.5% Native Hawaiian or other Pacific Islander, non-Hispanic/Latino; 0.8% American Indian or Alaska Native, non-Hispanic/Latino; 3% Two or more races, non-Hispanic/Latino; 6% Race/ethnicity unknown; 4% international; 16% transferred in; 68% live on campus.

Freshmen:
Admission: 1,632 applied, 952 admitted, 363 enrolled. ***Average high school GPA:*** 3.0. ***Test scores:*** ACT scores over 18: 59%; ACT scores over 24: 7%.

Retention: 56% of full-time freshmen returned.

FACULTY
Total: 153, 30% full-time, 20% with terminal degrees.

Student/faculty ratio: 16:1.

ACADEMICS
Calendar: semesters. *Degrees:* bachelor's and master's.

Special study options: academic remediation for entering students, adult/continuing education programs, advanced placement credit, cooperative education, distance learning, double majors, honors programs, independent study, internships, part-time degree program, services for LD students, study abroad, summer session for credit.

Unusual degree programs: 3-2 engineering with Iowa State University.

Computers: 200 computers/terminals and 665 ports are available on campus for general student use. Students can access the following: computer help desk, free student e-mail accounts, online (class) grades, online (class) schedules. Campuswide network is available. 100% of college-owned or -operated housing units are wired for high-speed Internet access. Wireless service is available via entire campus.
Library: Wilcox Library plus 1 other. *Books:* 62,273 (physical), 174,336 (digital/electronic); *Serial titles:* 50 (physical), 107,717 (digital/electronic); *Databases:* 86. Weekly public service hours: 90; students can reserve study rooms.

STUDENT LIFE
Housing options: on-campus residence required through sophomore year; coed, men-only, women-only. Campus housing is university owned. Freshman campus housing is guaranteed.

Activities and organizations: drama/theater group, student-run newspaper, radio and television station, choral group, marching band, Greek Council, Biology Club, Education Club, Student Government Association, Computer Club.

Athletics Member NAIA. ***Intercollegiate sports:*** baseball M(s), basketball M(s)/W(s), bowling M(s)/W(s), cheerleading M(s)/W(s), cross-country running M(s)/W(s), football M(s), golf M(s)/W(s), lacrosse M(s)/W(s), soccer M(s)/W(s), softball W(s), track and field M(s)/W(s), volleyball M(s)/W(s), wrestling M(s)/W(s). ***Intramural sports:*** badminton M/W, basketball M/W, sand volleyball M/W, soccer M/W, volleyball M/W.

Campus security: 24-hour emergency response devices and patrols, late-night transport/escort service, controlled dormitory access.

Student services: health clinic, personal/psychological counseling.

COSTS & FINANCIAL AID
Costs (2020–21) ***Comprehensive fee:*** $33,776 includes full-time tuition ($26,600) and room and board ($7176). Full-time tuition and fees vary according to class time, course load, location, and program. Part-time tuition: $400 per credit hour. Part-time tuition and fees vary according to class time, course load, location, and program. ***College room only:*** $3206. Room and board charges vary according to board plan and housing facility. ***Payment plan:*** installment. ***Waivers:*** children of alumni, senior citizens, and employees or children of employees.

Financial Aid Of all full-time matriculated undergraduates who enrolled in 2005, 808 applied for aid, 768 were judged to have need, 238 had their need fully met. 511 Federal Work-Study jobs (averaging $1287). 1 state and other part-time job (averaging $1103). In 2005, 2 non-need-based awards were made. ***Average percent of need met:*** 82. ***Average financial aid package:*** $17,782. ***Average need-based loan:*** $4600. ***Average need-based gift aid:*** $11,300. ***Average non-need-based aid:*** $4500. ***Average indebtedness upon graduation:*** $22,169.

APPLYING
Standardized Tests *Required:* SAT or ACT (for admission).

Options: electronic application, deferred entrance.

Required: high school transcript, minimum 2.0 GPA. ***Required for some:*** essay or personal statement, letters of recommendation, interview.

Application deadlines: rolling (freshmen), rolling (out-of-state freshmen), rolling (transfers).

Notification: continuous (freshmen), continuous (out-of-state freshmen), continuous (transfers).

CONTACT
Ms. Madison Steinke, Director of Admissions, William Penn University, 201 Trueblood Avenue, Oskaloosa, IA 52577-1799. *Phone:* 641-673-1012. *Fax:* 641-673-2113. *E-mail:* admissions@wmpenn.edu.

KANSAS

Baker University

Baldwin City, Kansas

http://www.bakeru.edu/

- **Independent United Methodist** comprehensive, founded 1858
- **Small-town** 26-acre campus with easy access to Kansas City
- **Endowment** $38.6 million
- **Coed** 1,214 undergraduate students, 70% full-time, 50% women, 50% men
- **Moderately difficult** entrance level, 88% of applicants were admitted

UNDERGRAD STUDENTS
850 full-time, 364 part-time. Students come from 27 states and territories; 15 other countries; 28% are from out of state; 5% transferred in; 83% live on campus.

Freshmen:
Admission: 804 applied, 704 admitted, 244 enrolled. ***Average high school GPA:*** 3.5.

Retention: 81% of full-time freshmen returned.

ACADEMICS
Calendar: 4-1-4 semesters for nursing program. *Degrees:* bachelor's, master's, and doctoral (profile includes information primarily for undergraduate residential campus in Baldwin City, KS).

Special study options: advanced placement credit, double majors, honors programs, independent study, internships, services for LD students, student-designed majors, study abroad, summer session for credit. ***ROTC:*** Army (c), Air Force (c).

Unusual degree programs: 3-2 engineering with Washington University in St. Louis, University of Kansas, Kansas State University, University of Missouri–Kansas City.

Computers: 140 computers/terminals are available on campus for general student use. Students can access the following: computer help desk, free student e-mail accounts, online (class) grades, online (class) registration, online (class) schedules. Campuswide network is available. 100% of college-owned or -operated housing units are wired for high-speed Internet access. Wireless service is available via entire campus.
Library: Baker University Library. Weekly public service hours: 73; study areas open 24 hours, 5–7 days a week; students can reserve study rooms.

STUDENT LIFE
Housing options: on-campus residence required through senior year; coed, men-only, women-only, special housing for students with disabilities. Campus housing is university owned. Freshman campus housing is guaranteed.

Activities and organizations: drama/theater group, student-run newspaper, radio and television station, choral group, Exercise Science Student Alliance, Baker University Speech Choir, Mungano, Student Senate, Student Activities Council, national fraternities, national sororities.

Athletics ***Intercollegiate sports:*** baseball M(s), basketball M(s)/W(s), bowling M(s)/W(s), cheerleading M(s)/W(s), cross-country running M(s)/W(s), football M(s), golf M(s), soccer M(s)/W(s), softball W(s), tennis M(s)/W(s), track and field M(s)/W(s), volleyball W(s), wrestling M(s)/W(s). ***Intramural sports:*** basketball M/W, football M/W, sand volleyball M/W, softball M/W, table tennis M/W, ultimate Frisbee M/W, volleyball M/W.

Campus security: 24-hour emergency response devices and patrols, controlled dormitory access.

Student services: health clinic, personal/psychological counseling.

COSTS & FINANCIAL AID
Costs (2019–20) ***One-time required fee:*** $100. ***Comprehensive fee:*** $38,230 includes full-time tuition ($29,300), mandatory fees ($580), and room and board ($8350). Part-time tuition: $945 per credit hour. ***Required fees:*** $200 per year part-time. ***College room only:*** $3950. Room and board charges vary according to board plan and housing facility. ***Waivers:*** senior citizens and employees or children of employees.

Financial Aid Of all full-time matriculated undergraduates who enrolled in 2018, 780 applied for aid, 667 were judged to have need. In 2018, 142 non-need-based awards were made. ***Average percent of need met:*** 85. ***Average financial aid package:*** $24,639. ***Average need-based loan:*** $4095. ***Average need-based gift aid:*** $6453. ***Average non-need-based aid:*** $9332. ***Average indebtedness upon graduation:*** $33,046.

APPLYING
Standardized Tests *Required:* SAT or ACT (for admission).

Options: electronic application, deferred entrance.

Required: high school transcript. ***Required for some:*** essay or personal statement, 1 letter of recommendation, interview, ACT or SAT scores.

CONTACT
Mrs. Emma Carter, Director of Admissions, Baker University, PO Box 65, Baldwin City, KS 66006-0065. *Phone:* 785-594-8327. *Toll-free phone:* 800-873-4282. *Fax:* 785-594-8353. *E-mail:* admissions@bakeru.edu.

Barclay College
Haviland, Kansas
http://www.barclaycollege.edu/

CONTACT
Mr. Justin Kendall, Admissions Recruiter, Barclay College, 607 North Kingman, Haviland, KS 67059. *Phone:* 620-862-5252 Ext. 21. *Toll-free phone:* 800-862-0226. *Fax:* 620-862-5242. *E-mail:* jkendall@barclaycollege.edu.

Benedictine College
Atchison, Kansas
http://www.benedictine.edu/

- **Independent Roman Catholic** comprehensive, founded 1859
- **Small-town** 225-acre campus with easy access to Kansas City
- **Endowment** $28.3 million
- **Coed** 2,084 undergraduate students, 93% full-time, 52% women, 48% men
- **Minimally difficult** entrance level, 99% of applicants were admitted

UNDERGRAD STUDENTS
1,935 full-time, 149 part-time. Students come from 49 states and territories; 16 other countries; 77% are from out of state; 3% Black or African American, non-Hispanic/Latino; 9% Hispanic/Latino; 1% Asian, non-Hispanic/Latino; 0.4% Native Hawaiian or other Pacific Islander, non-Hispanic/Latino; 0.6% American Indian or Alaska Native, non-Hispanic/Latino; 4% Two or more races, non-Hispanic/Latino; 1% Race/ethnicity unknown; 2% international; 3% transferred in; 80% live on campus.

Freshmen:
Admission: 2,202 applied, 2,172 admitted, 524 enrolled. ***Average high school GPA:*** 3.6. ***Test scores:*** SAT evidence-based reading and writing scores over 500: 94%; SAT math scores over 500: 84%; ACT scores over 18: 95%; SAT evidence-based reading and writing scores over 600: 62%; SAT math scores over 600: 45%; ACT scores over 24: 63%; SAT evidence-based reading and writing scores over 700: 14%; SAT math scores over 700: 10%; ACT scores over 30: 18%.

Retention: 76% of full-time freshmen returned.

FACULTY
Total: 180, 67% full-time, 54% with terminal degrees.

Student/faculty ratio: 14:1.

ACADEMICS
Calendar: semesters. *Degrees:* certificates, diplomas, associate, bachelor's, master's, and postbachelor's certificates.

Special study options: academic remediation for entering students, advanced placement credit, cooperative education, distance learning, double majors, English as a second language, honors programs, independent study, internships, off-campus study, part-time degree program, services for LD students, student-designed majors, study abroad, summer session for credit. ***ROTC:*** Army (c), Air Force (c).

Computers: 100 computers/terminals and 1,800 ports are available on campus for general student use. Students can access the following: computer help desk, free student e-mail accounts, online (class) grades, online (class) registration, online (class) schedules. Campuswide network is available. 100% of college-owned or -operated housing units are wired for high-speed Internet access. Wireless service is available via entire campus.

Library: Benedictine College Library. *Books:* 170,305 (physical), 157,301 (digital/electronic); *Serial titles:* 43,218 (physical); *Databases:* 61. Weekly public service hours: 85.

STUDENT LIFE
Housing options: on-campus residence required through senior year; men-only, women-only. Campus housing is university owned. Freshman campus housing is guaranteed.

Activities and organizations: drama/theater group, student-run newspaper, choral group, marching band, Student Government, Cray Lab, Knights of Columbus, Concert Chorale/Chamber Singers, Ravens Respect Life.

Athletics Member NAIA. ***Intercollegiate sports:*** baseball M(s), basketball M(s)/W(s), cheerleading W(s), cross-country running M(s)/W(s), football M(s), lacrosse M(s)/W(s), soccer M(s)/W(s), softball W(s), track and field M(s)/W(s), volleyball W(s), wrestling M(s). ***Intramural sports:*** basketball M/W, football M/W, golf M/W, lacrosse M/W, racquetball M/W, rugby M/W, soccer M/W, softball M/W, table tennis M/W, ultimate Frisbee M/W, volleyball M/W.

Campus security: 24-hour emergency response devices and patrols, late-night transport/escort service, controlled dormitory access.

Student services: health clinic, personal/psychological counseling.

COSTS & FINANCIAL AID
Costs (2019–20) ***Comprehensive fee:*** $40,980 includes full-time tuition ($29,730), mandatory fees ($800), and room and board ($10,450). Full-time tuition and fees vary according to course load and degree level. Part-time tuition: $850 per credit hour. Part-time tuition and fees vary according to course load and degree level. ***College room only:*** $5630. Room and board charges vary according to board plan and housing facility. ***Payment plan:*** installment. ***Waivers:*** senior citizens and employees or children of employees.

Financial Aid Of all full-time matriculated undergraduates who enrolled in 2017, 1,441 applied for aid, 1,228 were judged to have need, 295 had their need fully met. 291 Federal Work-Study jobs (averaging $620). In 2017, 571 non-need-based awards were made. ***Average percent of need met:*** 80. ***Average financial aid package:*** $23,698. ***Average need-based loan:*** $4984. ***Average need-based gift aid:*** $15,796. ***Average non-need-based aid:*** $12,748. ***Average indebtedness upon graduation:*** $29,196.

APPLYING
Standardized Tests *Required:* SAT or ACT (for admission).

Options: electronic application, deferred entrance.

Application fee: $50.

Required: high school transcript, minimum 2.0 GPA, 1 letter of recommendation. ***Required for some:*** interview.

Application deadlines: rolling (freshmen), rolling (out-of-state freshmen), rolling (transfers).

Notification: continuous (freshmen), continuous (transfers).

CONTACT

Mr. Pete Helgesen, Dean of Enrollment Management, Benedictine College, 1020 North 2nd Street, Atchison, KS 66002-1499. *Phone:* 913-367-5340 Ext. 2476. *Toll-free phone:* 800-467-5340. *E-mail:* phelgesen@benedictine.edu.

Bethany College

Lindsborg, Kansas

http://www.bethanylb.edu/

- **Independent Lutheran** 4-year, founded 1881
- **Small-town** 80-acre campus
- **Endowment** $24.1 million
- **Coed**
- **Moderately difficult** entrance level

FACULTY

Student/faculty ratio: 12:1.

ACADEMICS

Calendar: 4-1-4. *Degree:* bachelor's.
Library: Wallerstedt Library plus 1 other.

STUDENT LIFE

Housing options: on-campus residence required through junior year; coed, men-only, women-only, special housing for students with disabilities. Campus housing is university owned. Freshman campus housing is guaranteed.

Activities and organizations: drama/theater group, student-run newspaper, choral group, Student Activities Board (SAB), Alpha Theta Chi, Alpha Sigma Nu, Fellowship of Christian Athletes (FCA), Bethany Youth Ministries Team.

Athletics Member NAIA.

Campus security: 24-hour emergency response devices, controlled dormitory access, night patrols by security personnel.

Student services: health clinic, personal/psychological counseling.

FINANCIAL AID

Financial Aid Of all full-time matriculated undergraduates who enrolled in 2011, 541 applied for aid, 466 were judged to have need, 188 had their need fully met. 381 Federal Work-Study jobs (averaging $1342). In 2011, 1 non-need-based awards were made. ***Average percent of need met:*** 91. ***Average financial aid package:*** $22,887. ***Average need-based loan:*** $7529. ***Average need-based gift aid:*** $6935. ***Average non-need-based aid:*** $4800. ***Average indebtedness upon graduation:*** $22,015.

APPLYING

Standardized Tests *Required:* SAT or ACT (for admission).

Options: electronic application, deferred entrance.

Required: high school transcript, minimum 2.0 GPA. ***Required for some:*** essay or personal statement, letters of recommendation.

CONTACT

Katie Laier, Dean of Admissions and Financial Aid, Bethany College, 335 East Swensson Avenue, Lindsborg, KS 67456-1895. *Phone:* 785-227-3311 Ext. 8344. *Toll-free phone:* 800-826-2281. *Fax:* 785-227-8993. *E-mail:* admissions@bethanylb.edu.

Bethel College

North Newton, Kansas

http://www.bethelks.edu/

- **Independent** 4-year, founded 1887, affiliated with Mennonite Church USA
- **Small-town** 90-acre campus with easy access to Wichita
- **Endowment** $18.9 million
- **Coed**
- **Moderately difficult** entrance level

FACULTY

Student/faculty ratio: 10:1.

ACADEMICS

Calendar: 4-1-4. *Degree:* certificates and bachelor's.
Library: Mantz Library plus 1 other. *Books:* 120,875 (physical), 155,552 (digital/electronic); *Serial titles:* 2,990 (physical), 109,552 (digital/electronic); *Databases:* 97. Weekly public service hours: 91; students can reserve study rooms.

STUDENT LIFE

Housing options: on-campus residence required through senior year; coed, special housing for students with disabilities. Campus housing is university owned. Freshman campus housing is guaranteed.

Activities and organizations: drama/theater group, student-run newspaper, radio and television station, choral group, FEMCORE, Fellowship of Christian Athletes, Rock-climbing Club, Social Work Student Organization, We-Belong or Business Club.

Athletics Member NAIA.

Campus security: 24-hour emergency response devices and patrols, controlled dormitory access, SMS Alert System.

Student services: health clinic, personal/psychological counseling.

COSTS & FINANCIAL AID

Costs (2019–20) ***Comprehensive fee:*** $38,370 includes full-time tuition ($29,150), mandatory fees ($240), and room and board ($8980). ***College room only:*** $4340.

Financial Aid Of all full-time matriculated undergraduates who enrolled in 2019, 446 applied for aid, 411 were judged to have need, 107 had their need fully met. 272 Federal Work-Study jobs (averaging $1741). In 2019, 38 non-need-based awards were made. ***Average percent of need met:*** 84. ***Average financial aid package:*** $28,735. ***Average need-based loan:*** $8326. ***Average need-based gift aid:*** $5782. ***Average non-need-based aid:*** $13,648. ***Average indebtedness upon graduation:*** $5633.

APPLYING

Standardized Tests *Required:* SAT or ACT (for admission).

Options: electronic application, deferred entrance.

Required: high school transcript. ***Required for some:*** essay or personal statement, minimum 2.5 GPA, 2 letters of recommendation. ***Recommended:*** interview.

CONTACT

Mr. Andy Johnson, Vice President for Admissions, Bethel College, 300 East 27th Street, North Newton, KS 67117-0531. *Phone:* 316-284-5230. *Toll-free phone:* 800-522-1887 Ext. 230. *Fax:* 316-284-5870. *E-mail:* admissions@bethelks.edu.

Central Christian College of Kansas

McPherson, Kansas

http://www.centralchristian.edu/

- **Independent Free Methodist** 4-year, founded 1884
- **Small-town** 16-acre campus with easy access to Wichita, Kansas
- **Endowment** $6.9 million
- **Coed** 726 undergraduate students, 45% full-time, 31% women, 33% men
- **Minimally difficult** entrance level, 99% of applicants were admitted

UNDERGRAD STUDENTS

328 full-time, 138 part-time. Students come from 26 states and territories; 6 other countries; 72% are from out of state; 29% transferred in; 85% live on campus.

Freshmen:
Admission: 402 applied, 397 admitted, 97 enrolled. ***Average high school GPA:*** 3.3.

Retention: 41% of full-time freshmen returned.

FACULTY
Total: 75, 27% full-time, 8% with terminal degrees.

Student/faculty ratio: 13:1.

ACADEMICS
Calendar: 4-1-4. *Degrees:* certificates, associate, and bachelor's.

Special study options: academic remediation for entering students, accelerated degree program, adult/continuing education programs, advanced placement credit, cooperative education, distance learning, double majors, English as a second language, independent study, internships, off-campus study, part-time degree program, services for LD students, student-designed majors, study abroad, summer session for credit.

Computers: 28 computers/terminals and 28 ports are available on campus for general student use. Students can access the following: computer help desk, free student e-mail accounts, online (class) grades, online (class) registration, online (class) schedules. Campuswide network is available. 100% of college-owned or -operated housing units are wired for high-speed Internet access. Wireless service is available via entire campus.
Library: Briner Library. Students can reserve study rooms.

STUDENT LIFE
Housing options: on-campus residence required through senior year; men-only, women-only, special housing for students with disabilities. Campus housing is university owned. Freshman campus housing is guaranteed.

Activities and organizations: drama/theater group, student-run newspaper, choral group, Student Government, Outreach Central, Student Activities Committee, Social Awareness Board, Phi Beta Lambda Business Club.

Athletics Member NAIA, NCCAA. ***Intercollegiate sports:*** baseball M(s), basketball M(s)/W(s), cheerleading M(s)/W(s), golf M(s)/W(s), soccer M(s)/W(s), softball W(s), tennis M(s)/W(s), volleyball W(s). ***Intramural sports:*** basketball M/W, football M/W, soccer M/W, softball M/W, table tennis M/W, track and field M/W, ultimate Frisbee M/W, volleyball M/W.

Student services: health clinic, personal/psychological counseling.

COSTS & FINANCIAL AID
Costs (2020–21) ***Required fees:*** $450 full-time. ***Room and board:*** $7500; room only: $4250.

Financial Aid Of all full-time matriculated undergraduates who enrolled in 2007, 267 applied for aid, 244 were judged to have need, 57 had their need fully met. 58 Federal Work-Study jobs (averaging $1000). In 2007, 53 non-need-based awards were made. ***Average percent of need met:*** 75. ***Average financial aid package:*** $13,423. ***Average need-based loan:*** $5024. ***Average need-based gift aid:*** $4383. ***Average non-need-based aid:*** $5284. ***Average indebtedness upon graduation:*** $20,000.

APPLYING
Options: electronic application, deferred entrance.

Required: high school transcript, minimum 2.5 GPA. ***Required for some:*** essay or personal statement, 2 letters of recommendation, interview.

Application deadlines: rolling (freshmen), rolling (transfers).

Notification: continuous (freshmen), continuous (transfers).

CONTACT
Central Christian College of Kansas, 1200 South Main, PO Box 1403, McPherson, KS 67460-5799. *Phone:* 620-241-0723 Ext. 121. *Toll-free phone:* 800-835-0078.

Cleveland University–Kansas City

Overland Park, Kansas

http://www.cleveland.edu/

CONTACT
Ms. Melissa Denton, Director of Admissions, Cleveland University–Kansas City, 10850 Lowell Avenue, Overland Park, KS 66210. *Phone:* 913-234-0750. *Toll-free phone:* 800-467-2252. *Fax:* 913-234-0906. *E-mail:* kc.admissions@cleveland.edu.

Donnelly College

Kansas City, Kansas

http://www.donnelly.edu/

- **Independent Roman Catholic** primarily 2-year, founded 1949
- **Urban** 4-acre campus
- **Coed** 303 undergraduate students, 54% full-time, 71% women, 29% men

UNDERGRAD STUDENTS
164 full-time, 139 part-time. Students come from 2 states and territories; 32% are from out of state; 35% Black or African American, non-Hispanic/Latino; 38% Hispanic/Latino; 8% Asian, non-Hispanic/Latino; 0.3% Native Hawaiian or other Pacific Islander, non-Hispanic/Latino; 2% American Indian or Alaska Native, non-Hispanic/Latino; 3% Two or more races, non-Hispanic/Latino; 1% Race/ethnicity unknown; 1% international; 16% transferred in.

Freshmen:
Admission: 59 enrolled.

Retention: 73% of full-time freshmen returned.

FACULTY
Total: 34, 41% full-time.

Student/faculty ratio: 11:1.

ACADEMICS
Calendar: semesters. *Degrees:* certificates, associate, and bachelor's.

Special study options: academic remediation for entering students, advanced placement credit, cooperative education, distance learning, English as a second language, external degree program, honors programs, independent study, internships, part-time degree program, services for LD students, summer session for credit.

Computers: Students can access the following: campus intranet, computer help desk, free student e-mail accounts, online (class) grades, online (class) registration, online (class) schedules. Campuswide network is available. Wireless service is available via entire campus.
Library: Dean-Loyoza Family Academic Resource Center plus 1 other.

STUDENT LIFE
Housing options: college housing not available.

Activities and organizations: Organization of Student Leadership, Student Ambassadors, Healthy Student Task Force, Men's Soccer Club, Women's Soccer Club.

Athletics ***Intramural sports:*** soccer M/W.

Campus security: 24-hour emergency response devices.

Student services: personal/psychological counseling.

APPLYING
Options: electronic application.

Recommended: high school transcript.

Application deadlines: rolling (freshmen), rolling (transfers).

CONTACT
Donnelly College, 608 North 18th Street, Kansas City, KS 66102. *Phone:* 913-621-8762. *Fax:* 913-621-8719. *E-mail:* admissions@donnelly.edu.

Emporia State University

Emporia, Kansas

http://www.emporia.edu/

- **State-supported** comprehensive, founded 1863, part of Kansas State Board of Regents
- **Small-town** 207-acre campus with easy access to Wichita
- **Endowment** $74.4 million
- **Coed** 3,405 undergraduate students, 91% full-time, 63% women, 37% men
- **Noncompetitive** entrance level, 85% of applicants were admitted

UNDERGRAD STUDENTS
3,101 full-time, 304 part-time. 9% are from out of state; 5% Black or African American, non-Hispanic/Latino; 7% Hispanic/Latino; 0.9% Asian, non-Hispanic/Latino; 0.1% Native Hawaiian or other Pacific Islander, non-Hispanic/Latino; 0.4% American Indian or Alaska Native, non-Hispanic/Latino; 10% Two or more races, non-Hispanic/Latino; 2%

Race/ethnicity unknown; 5% international; 9% transferred in; 23% live on campus.

Freshmen:

Admission: 1,670 applied, 1,414 admitted, 680 enrolled. ***Average high school GPA:*** 3.4. ***Test scores:*** SAT evidence-based reading and writing scores over 500: 61%; SAT math scores over 500: 65%; ACT scores over 18: 87%; SAT evidence-based reading and writing scores over 600: 9%; SAT math scores over 600: 13%; ACT scores over 24: 34%; ACT scores over 30: 5%.

Retention: 77% of full-time freshmen returned.

FACULTY

Total: 282, 88% full-time, 78% with terminal degrees.

Student/faculty ratio: 17:1.

ACADEMICS

Calendar: semesters. *Degrees:* bachelor's, master's, doctoral, post-master's, and postbachelor's certificates.

Special study options: academic remediation for entering students, adult/continuing education programs, advanced placement credit, distance learning, double majors, freshman honors college, honors programs, independent study, internships, off-campus study, part-time degree program, services for LD students, student-designed majors, study abroad, summer session for credit.

Unusual degree programs: 3-2 engineering with Kansas State University, University of Kansas, Wichita State University.

Computers: 410 computers/terminals are available on campus for general student use. Students can access the following: campus intranet, computer help desk, free student e-mail accounts, online (class) grades, online (class) registration, online (class) schedules. Campuswide network is available. 100% of college-owned or -operated housing units are wired for high-speed Internet access. Wireless service is available via entire campus.

Library: William Allen White Library plus 1 other. *Books:* 389,595 (physical), 153,016 (digital/electronic); *Serial titles:* 35,153 (physical), 278 (digital/electronic); *Databases:* 97. Weekly public service hours: 79; study areas open 24 hours, 5–7 days a week; students can reserve study rooms.

STUDENT LIFE

Housing options: on-campus residence required for freshman year; coed, cooperative, special housing for students with disabilities. Campus housing is university owned. Freshman campus housing is guaranteed.

Activities and organizations: drama/theater group, student-run newspaper, choral group, marching band, Phi Eta Sigma, Student Chapter of the American Library Association of ESU, TradPlus Student Organization, Arabic Culture Student Organization, Emporia Kansas Association of Nursing Students, national fraternities, national sororities.

Athletics Member NCAA. All Division II. ***Intercollegiate sports:*** baseball M(s), basketball M(s)/W(s), cheerleading M(s)/W(s), cross-country running M(s)/W(s), football M(s), soccer W(s), softball W(s), tennis M(s)/W(s), track and field M(s)/W(s), volleyball W(s). ***Intramural sports:*** badminton M/W, basketball M/W, fencing M(c), field hockey W(c), football M/W, rugby M(c), soccer M(c)/W(c), softball M/W, table tennis M/W, tennis M/W, volleyball M/W.

Campus security: 24-hour emergency response devices and patrols, student patrols, late-night transport/escort service, controlled dormitory access, 24-hour residence hall monitoring, safety and self-awareness programs.

Student services: health clinic, personal/psychological counseling, women's center, legal services.

COSTS & FINANCIAL AID

Costs (2019–20) ***Tuition:*** state resident $5154 full-time, $172 per credit hour part-time; nonresident $19,071 full-time, $636 per credit hour part-time. Full-time tuition and fees vary according to course load, degree level, and location. Part-time tuition and fees vary according to course load, degree level, and location. ***Required fees:*** $1806 full-time, $91 per credit hour part-time. ***Room and board:*** $9408; room only: $6120. Room and board charges vary according to board plan, housing facility, and location. ***Payment plans:*** installment, deferred payment. ***Waivers:*** senior citizens and employees or children of employees.

Financial Aid Of all full-time matriculated undergraduates who enrolled in 2019, 2,418 applied for aid, 1,899 were judged to have need, 328 had their need fully met. 162 Federal Work-Study jobs (averaging $2224). 13 state and other part-time jobs (averaging $2200). In 2019, 505 non-need-based awards were made. ***Average percent of need met:*** 60. ***Average financial aid package:*** $9587. ***Average need-based loan:*** $6164. ***Average need-based gift aid:*** $6173. ***Average non-need-based aid:*** $2886. ***Average indebtedness upon graduation:*** $22,692.

APPLYING

Standardized Tests *Required:* SAT or ACT (for admission).

Options: electronic application, deferred entrance.

Application fee: $30.

Required: high school transcript, minimum ACT score of 21, or rank in the top 1/3 and completed QA core classes with cum 2.0 GPA, 22 Math subscore, or completed 4th year of math. ***Recommended:*** minimum 2.0 GPA.

Application deadlines: rolling (freshmen), rolling (transfers).

Notification: continuous (freshmen), continuous (transfers).

CONTACT

Ms. Roxie Pearson, Associate Director of Data Management, Emporia State University, 1 Kellogg Circle, Campus Box 4034, Emporia, KS 66801-5087. *Phone:* 620-341-5465. *Toll-free phone:* 877-GOTOESU (in-state); 877-468-6378 (out-of-state). *Fax:* 620-341-5599. *E-mail:* go2esu@emporia.edu.

Fort Hays State University

Hays, Kansas

http://www.fhsu.edu/

- **State-supported** comprehensive, founded 1902
- **Small-town** 200-acre campus
- **Coed**

FACULTY

Student/faculty ratio: 14:1.

ACADEMICS

Calendar: semesters. *Degrees:* certificates, associate, bachelor's, master's, and post-master's certificates.

Library: Forsyth Library.

STUDENT LIFE

Housing options: on-campus residence required for freshman year; coed, men-only, women-only. Campus housing is university owned and leased by the school.

Activities and organizations: drama/theater group, student-run newspaper, radio and television station, choral group, marching band, Students for Life, Honors Society, Panhellenic Council, Residents Hall Association, Catholic Disciples.

Campus security: 24-hour emergency response devices and patrols.

Student services: health clinic.

FINANCIAL AID

Financial Aid Of all full-time matriculated undergraduates who enrolled in 2018, 4,758 applied for aid, 4,003 were judged to have need, 426 had their need fully met. In 2018, 628 non-need-based awards were made. ***Average percent of need met:*** 50. ***Average financial aid package:*** $7880. ***Average need-based loan:*** $3754. ***Average need-based gift aid:*** $5755. ***Average non-need-based aid:*** $2387. ***Average indebtedness upon graduation:*** $26,240.

APPLYING

Standardized Tests *Required for some:* SAT or ACT (for admission).

Required: high school transcript.

CONTACT

Tricia Cline, Director, Admissions, Fort Hays State University, 600 Park Street, Hays, KS 67601-4099. *Phone:* 785-628-4091. *Toll-free phone:* 800-628-FHSU. *E-mail:* tcline@fhsu.edu.

Friends University

Wichita, Kansas

http://www.friends.edu/

- **Independent** comprehensive, founded 1898, affiliated with Christian non-denominational
- **Urban** 55-acre campus
- **Endowment** $53.3 million
- **Coed** 1,291 undergraduate students, 67% full-time, 55% women, 45% men
- **Moderately difficult** entrance level, 46% of applicants were admitted

UNDERGRAD STUDENTS

860 full-time, 431 part-time. Students come from 34 states and territories; 12 other countries; 24% are from out of state; 8% Black or African American, non-Hispanic/Latino; 8% Hispanic/Latino; 5% Asian, non-Hispanic/Latino; 0.2% Native Hawaiian or other Pacific Islander, non-Hispanic/Latino; 1% American Indian or Alaska Native, non-Hispanic/Latino; 5% Two or more races, non-Hispanic/Latino; 12% Race/ethnicity unknown; 2% international; 12% transferred in; 33% live on campus.

Freshmen:

Admission: 1,266 applied, 580 admitted, 177 enrolled. ***Average high school GPA:*** 3.5. ***Test scores:*** SAT evidence-based reading and writing scores over 500: 73%; SAT math scores over 500: 68%; ACT scores over 18: 91%; SAT evidence-based reading and writing scores over 600: 17%; SAT math scores over 600: 13%; ACT scores over 24: 32%; SAT evidence-based reading and writing scores over 700: 3%; ACT scores over 30: 4%.

Retention: 69% of full-time freshmen returned.

FACULTY

Total: 190, 32% full-time, 39% with terminal degrees.

Student/faculty ratio: 11:1.

ACADEMICS

Calendar: semesters. *Degrees:* bachelor's and master's.

Special study options: academic remediation for entering students, accelerated degree program, adult/continuing education programs, advanced placement credit, cooperative education, distance learning, double majors, honors programs, independent study, internships, off-campus study, part-time degree program, services for LD students, student-designed majors, study abroad, summer session for credit.

Computers: 360 computers/terminals are available on campus for general student use. Students can access the following: campus intranet, computer help desk, free student e-mail accounts, online (class) grades, online (class) registration, online (class) schedules. Campuswide network is available. 100% of college-owned or -operated housing units are wired for high-speed Internet access. Wireless service is available via entire campus.

Library: Edmund Stanley Library plus 1 other. *Books:* 90,464 (physical), 182,096 (digital/electronic); *Serial titles:* 373 (physical), 161 (digital/electronic); *Databases:* 107.

STUDENT LIFE

Housing options: on-campus residence required for freshman year; coed. Campus housing is university owned.

Activities and organizations: drama/theater group, choral group, Concert Choir, Singing Quakers, Zoo Science Club, Psychology Club, Spanish Club.

Athletics Member NAIA. ***Intercollegiate sports:*** baseball M(s), basketball M(s)/W(s), cheerleading M(s)/W(s), cross-country running M(s)/W(s), football M(s), golf W(s), soccer M(s)/W(s), softball W(s), tennis M(s)/W(s), track and field M(s)/W(s), volleyball W(s), weight lifting M(s)/W(s). ***Intramural sports:*** basketball M/W, bowling M/W, football M/W, racquetball M/W, sand volleyball M/W, soccer M/W, table tennis M/W, tennis M/W, ultimate Frisbee M/W, volleyball M/W, weight lifting M/W.

Campus security: 24-hour emergency response devices and patrols, late-night transport/escort service, controlled dormitory access.

Student services: health clinic, personal/psychological counseling.

COSTS & FINANCIAL AID

Costs (2020–21) ***Comprehensive fee:*** $38,470 includes full-time tuition ($29,670), mandatory fees ($450), and room and board ($8350). Full-time tuition and fees vary according to class time, course load, degree level, and location. Part-time tuition: $989 per credit hour. Part-time tuition and fees vary according to class time, course load, degree level, and location. ***College room only:*** $3914. Room and board charges vary according to board plan and housing facility. ***Payment plan:*** installment. ***Waivers:*** children of alumni and employees or children of employees.

Financial Aid Of all full-time matriculated undergraduates who enrolled in 2015, 905 applied for aid, 805 were judged to have need, 283 had their need fully met. 204 Federal Work-Study jobs (averaging $1091). 252 state and other part-time jobs (averaging $1306). In 2015, 100 non-need-based awards were made. ***Average percent of need met:*** 82. ***Average financial aid package:*** $16,394. ***Average need-based loan:*** $4158. ***Average need-based gift aid:*** $8359. ***Average non-need-based aid:*** $8975. ***Average indebtedness upon graduation:*** $28,175.

APPLYING

Standardized Tests *Required for some:* SAT or ACT (for admission). *Recommended:* ACT (for admission), SAT and SAT Subject Tests or ACT (for admission).

Options: electronic application.

Required for some: high school transcript, minimum 2.0 GPA, interview, audition for music, dance and theater programs; portfolio for art program.

Application deadlines: rolling (freshmen), rolling (transfers).

Notification: continuous (freshmen), continuous (transfers).

CONTACT

Mrs. Jordan Audette, Director of Recruiting, Friends University, 2100 West University Avenue, Wichita, KS 67213. *Phone:* 316-295-5100. *Toll-free phone:* 800-794-6945. *Fax:* 316-295-5101. *E-mail:* learn@friends.edu.

Grantham University

Lenexa, Kansas

http://www.grantham.edu/

CONTACT

Mr. Les Hyde, Vice President Admissions, Grantham University, 16025 W 113th Street Lenexa, KS 66219. *Phone:* 800-955-2527. *Toll-free phone:* 800-955-2527. *Fax:* 816-595-5757. *E-mail:* admissions@grantham.edu.

Haskell Indian Nations University

Lawrence, Kansas

http://www.haskell.edu/

CONTACT

Ms. Patty Grant, Recruitment Officer, Haskell Indian Nations University, 155 Indian Avenue, #5031, Lawrence, KS 66046-4800. *Phone:* 785-749-8437 Ext. 437.

Hesston College

Hesston, Kansas

http://www.hesston.edu/

- **Independent Mennonite** primarily 2-year, founded 1909
- **Small-town** 50-acre campus with easy access to Wichita
- **Endowment** $13.9 million
- **Coed** 378 undergraduate students, 91% full-time, 58% women, 42% men
- **Noncompetitive** entrance level, 52% of applicants were admitted

UNDERGRAD STUDENTS

343 full-time, 35 part-time. Students come from 25 states and territories; 23 other countries; 39% are from out of state; 6% Black or African American, non-Hispanic/Latino; 13% Hispanic/Latino; 2% Asian, non-Hispanic/Latino; 0.8% American Indian or Alaska Native, non-Hispanic/Latino; 2% Two or more races, non-Hispanic/Latino; 0.3% Race/ethnicity unknown; 15% international; 13% transferred in; 69% live on campus.

Freshmen:
Admission: 595 applied, 308 admitted, 130 enrolled. ***Average high school GPA:*** 3.4. ***Test scores:*** SAT evidence-based reading and writing scores over 500: 54%; SAT math scores over 500: 63%; ACT scores over 18: 86%; SAT evidence-based reading and writing scores over 600: 30%; SAT math scores over 600: 30%; ACT scores over 24: 23%; SAT evidence-based reading and writing scores over 700: 3%; SAT math scores over 700: 3%; ACT scores over 30: 1%.

Retention: 86% of full-time freshmen returned.

FACULTY
Total: 52, 69% full-time, 21% with terminal degrees.

Student/faculty ratio: 7:1.

ACADEMICS
Calendar: semesters. *Degrees:* associate and bachelor's.

Special study options: academic remediation for entering students, adult/continuing education programs, advanced placement credit, cooperative education, double majors, English as a second language, independent study, internships, part-time degree program, services for LD students, summer session for credit.

Computers: 115 computers/terminals are available on campus for general student use. Students can access the following: computer help desk, free student e-mail accounts, online (class) grades, online (class) registration, online (class) schedules. Campuswide network is available. 100% of college-owned or -operated housing units are wired for high-speed Internet access. Wireless service is available via classrooms, computer centers, computer labs, dorm rooms, learning centers, libraries, student centers.

Library: Mary Miller Library. *Books:* 28,000 (physical); *Serial titles:* 101 (physical); *Databases:* 88. Weekly public service hours: 87; students can reserve study rooms.

STUDENT LIFE
Housing options: on-campus residence required through sophomore year; men-only, women-only. Campus housing is university owned. Freshman campus housing is guaranteed.

Activities and organizations: drama/theater group, student-run newspaper, choral group, Peace and Service Club, Intramural Sports, Ministry Assistants.

Athletics Member NJCAA. ***Intercollegiate sports:*** baseball M(s), basketball M(s)/W(s), cross-country running M(s)/W(s), golf M(s), soccer M(s)/W(s), softball W(s), track and field M(s)/W(s), volleyball W(s). ***Intramural sports:*** basketball M/W, golf M(c)/W(c), sand volleyball M/W, soccer M/W, ultimate Frisbee M/W, volleyball M/W.

Campus security: 24-hour emergency response devices, controlled dormitory access.

Student services: personal/psychological counseling.

COSTS & FINANCIAL AID
Costs (2020–21) ***Comprehensive fee:*** $37,920 includes full-time tuition ($27,984), mandatory fees ($456), and room and board ($9480). Full-time tuition and fees vary according to course load and program. Part-time tuition: $1166 per credit hour. Part-time tuition and fees vary according to course load and program. ***Required fees:*** $114 per term part-time. ***Room and board:*** Room and board charges vary according to board plan and housing facility. ***Payment plans:*** installment, deferred payment. ***Waivers:*** employees or children of employees.

Financial Aid Of all full-time matriculated undergraduates who enrolled in 2018, 120 Federal Work-Study jobs (averaging $800).

APPLYING
Standardized Tests *Required:* SAT or ACT (for admission).

Options: electronic application, early admission, deferred entrance.

Required: high school transcript. ***Required for some:*** 2 letters of recommendation, interview.

Application deadlines: rolling (freshmen), rolling (transfers).

CONTACT
Del Hershberger, Vice President of Admissions, Hesston College, Hesston, KS 67062. *Phone:* 620-327-8206. *Toll-free phone:* 800-995-2757. *Fax:* 620-327-8300. *E-mail:* admissions@hesston.edu.

Kansas State University

Manhattan, Kansas

http://www.k-state.edu/

- **State-supported** university, founded 1863, part of Kansas Board of Regents
- **Suburban** 668-acre campus
- **Endowment** $506.4 million
- **Coed** 17,210 undergraduate students, 90% full-time, 48% women, 52% men
- **Minimally difficult** entrance level, 96% of applicants were admitted

UNDERGRAD STUDENTS
15,548 full-time, 1,662 part-time. 19% are from out of state; 3% Black or African American, non-Hispanic/Latino; 8% Hispanic/Latino; 2% Asian, non-Hispanic/Latino; 0.1% Native Hawaiian or other Pacific Islander, non-Hispanic/Latino; 0.5% American Indian or Alaska Native, non-Hispanic/Latino; 4% Two or more races, non-Hispanic/Latino; 1% Race/ethnicity unknown; 4% international; 7% transferred in; 23% live on campus.

Freshmen:
Admission: 8,140 applied, 7,788 admitted, 3,202 enrolled. ***Average high school GPA:*** 3.6. ***Test scores:*** ACT scores over 18: 96%; ACT scores over 24: 59%; ACT scores over 30: 18%.

Retention: 86% of full-time freshmen returned.

FACULTY
Total: 1,138, 88% full-time, 75% with terminal degrees.

Student/faculty ratio: 18:1.

ACADEMICS
Calendar: semesters. *Degrees:* certificates, bachelor's, master's, doctoral, and postbachelor's certificates.

Special study options: academic remediation for entering students, adult/continuing education programs, advanced placement credit, cooperative education, distance learning, double majors, English as a second language, freshman honors college, honors programs, independent study, internships, off-campus study, part-time degree program, services for LD students, study abroad, summer session for credit. ***ROTC:*** Army (b), Air Force (b).

Unusual degree programs: 3-2 engineering; biology, kinesiology, horticulture, master of public health, biochemistry, mathematics, human nutrition, hospitality management, agricultural economics, political science/master of public administration, accounting/MBA, architectural engineering, industrial engineering, bio/ag engineering.

Computers: Students can access the following: computer help desk, free student e-mail accounts, online (class) grades, online (class) registration, online (class) schedules. Campuswide network is available. Wireless service is available via entire campus.

Library: Hale Library plus 3 others. *Books:* 1.3 million (physical), 1.5 million (digital/electronic); *Serial titles:* 51,881 (physical), 114,285 (digital/electronic); *Databases:* 278. Weekly public service hours: 80; study areas open 24 hours, 5–7 days a week; students can reserve study rooms.

STUDENT LIFE
Housing options: coed, men-only, women-only, cooperative, special housing for students with disabilities. Campus housing is university owned.

Activities and organizations: drama/theater group, student-run newspaper, radio and television station, choral group, marching band, athletic department groups, marching band, Union Governing Board, theater productions, debate team, national fraternities, national sororities.

Athletics Member NCAA. All Division I except football (Division I-A). ***Intercollegiate sports:*** baseball M(s), basketball M(s)/W(s), crew W(s), cross-country running M(s)/W(s), golf M(s)/W(s), soccer W, tennis W(s), track and field M(s)/W(s), volleyball W(s). ***Intramural sports:*** badminton M/W, basketball M/W, bowling M/W, crew M/W, cross-country running M/W, football M/W, golf M/W, ice hockey M, lacrosse M, racquetball M/W, soccer M/W, softball M/W, table tennis M/W, tennis M/W, track and field M/W, volleyball M/W, water polo M/W, weight lifting M/W, wrestling M.

Campus security: 24-hour emergency response devices and patrols, late-night transport/escort service, controlled dormitory access.

Student services: health clinic, personal/psychological counseling, women's center, legal services.

FINANCIAL AID
Financial Aid Of all full-time matriculated undergraduates who enrolled in 2016, 11,643 applied for aid, 8,771 were judged to have need, 1,667 had their need fully met. In 2016, 1542 non-need-based awards were made. ***Average percent of need met:*** 78. ***Average financial aid package:*** $13,182. ***Average need-based loan:*** $4454. ***Average need-based gift aid:*** $4299. ***Average non-need-based aid:*** $4421. ***Average indebtedness upon graduation:*** $28,318.

APPLYING
Standardized Tests *Required:* SAT or ACT (for admission).

Options: electronic application.

Application fee: $40.

CONTACT
Ms. Molly McGaughey, Associate Director of Admissions, Kansas State University, 119 Anderson Hall, Manhattan, KS 66506. *Phone:* 785-532-6250. *Toll-free phone:* 800-432-8270. *Fax:* 785-532-6393. *E-mail:* k-state@k-state.edu.

Kansas State University Polytechnic Campus

Salina, Kansas

http://www.polytechnic.k-state.edu/

CONTACT
Kansas State University Polytechnic Campus, 2310 Centennial Road, Salina, KS 67401.

Kansas Wesleyan University

Salina, Kansas

http://www.kwu.edu/

- **Independent United Methodist** comprehensive, founded 1886
- **Small-town** 28-acre campus
- **Endowment** $31.2 million
- **Coed** 653 undergraduate students, 93% full-time, 42% women, 58% men
- **Moderately difficult** entrance level, 61% of applicants were admitted

UNDERGRAD STUDENTS
607 full-time, 46 part-time. Students come from 29 states and territories; 8 other countries; 55% are from out of state; 13% Black or African American, non-Hispanic/Latino; 18% Hispanic/Latino; 0.3% Asian, non-Hispanic/Latino; 0.2% Native Hawaiian or other Pacific Islander, non-Hispanic/Latino; 0.6% American Indian or Alaska Native, non-Hispanic/Latino; 3% Two or more races, non-Hispanic/Latino; 1% international; 12% transferred in; 61% live on campus.

Freshmen:
Admission: 1,242 applied, 753 admitted, 141 enrolled. ***Average high school GPA:*** 3.5. ***Test scores:*** SAT evidence-based reading and writing scores over 500: 76%; SAT math scores over 500: 72%; ACT scores over 18: 91%; SAT evidence-based reading and writing scores over 600: 14%; SAT math scores over 600: 6%; ACT scores over 24: 29%; ACT scores over 30: 2%.

Retention: 68% of full-time freshmen returned.

FACULTY
Total: 75, 63% full-time, 53% with terminal degrees.

Student/faculty ratio: 11:1.

ACADEMICS
Calendar: semesters plus summer term. *Degrees:* bachelor's and master's.

Special study options: academic remediation for entering students, accelerated degree program, advanced placement credit, distance learning, double majors, honors programs, independent study, internships, off-campus study, part-time degree program, services for LD students, student-designed majors, study abroad, summer session for credit.

Unusual degree programs: 3-2 engineering with Washington University in St. Louis; Ecospheric Studies with Western Colorado State University Christian Leadership with St. Paul's School of Theology (3+3).

Computers: 215 computers/terminals and 500 ports are available on campus for general student use. Students can access the following: computer help desk, free student e-mail accounts, online (class) grades, online (class) registration, online (class) schedules. Campuswide network is available. 100% of college-owned or -operated housing units are wired for high-speed Internet access. Wireless service is available via entire campus.

Library: Memorial Library. *Books:* 61,859 (physical), 7,272 (digital/electronic); *Serial titles:* 402 (physical); *Databases:* 66. Weekly public service hours: 78; students can reserve study rooms.

STUDENT LIFE
Housing options: on-campus residence required through sophomore year; coed, men-only, women-only. Campus housing is university owned. Freshman campus housing is guaranteed.

Activities and organizations: drama/theater group, student-run newspaper, radio station, choral group, Fellowship of Christian Athletes, Student Government, Wesleyan Chorale, Coyote Gaming Club, Coyote Activities Board.

Athletics Member NAIA. ***Intercollegiate sports:*** baseball M(s), basketball M(s)/W(s), bowling M(s)/W(s), cheerleading M(s)/W(s), cross-country running M(s)/W(s), football M(s)/W, golf M(s)/W(s), soccer M(s)/W(s), softball W(s), tennis M(s)/W(s), track and field M(s)/W(s), volleyball W(s). ***Intramural sports:*** basketball M/W, bowling M/W, football M/W, sand volleyball M/W, softball M/W, table tennis M/W, ultimate Frisbee M/W, volleyball M/W.

Campus security: 24-hour emergency response devices, student patrols, late-night transport/escort service, controlled dormitory access.

Student services: personal/psychological counseling.

COSTS & FINANCIAL AID
Costs (2020–21) ***One-time required fee:*** $200. ***Comprehensive fee:*** $40,570 includes full-time tuition ($30,250), mandatory fees ($320), and room and board ($10,000). Full-time tuition and fees vary according to course load. Part-time tuition: $850 per credit hour. ***Required fees:*** $60 per term part-time. ***Room and board:*** Room and board charges vary according to housing facility. ***Payment plan:*** installment. ***Waivers:*** children of alumni, senior citizens, and employees or children of employees.

Financial Aid Of all full-time matriculated undergraduates who enrolled in 2016, 657 applied for aid, 559 were judged to have need, 105 had their need fully met. 98 Federal Work-Study jobs (averaging $1488). 31 state and other part-time jobs (averaging $828). In 2016, 82 non-need-based awards were made. ***Average percent of need met:*** 68. ***Average financial aid package:*** $21,316. ***Average need-based loan:*** $4294. ***Average need-based gift aid:*** $7695. ***Average non-need-based aid:*** $11,252. ***Average indebtedness upon graduation:*** $34,526.

APPLYING
Standardized Tests *Required:* SAT or ACT (for admission).

Options: electronic application, deferred entrance.

Application fee: $20.

Required: high school transcript, minimum 2.5 GPA. ***Required for some:*** essay or personal statement, interview.

Application deadlines: rolling (freshmen), rolling (transfers).

Notification: continuous (freshmen), continuous (transfers).

CONTACT
Mrs. Claire Massey, Associate Director of Undergraduate Recruiting, Kansas Wesleyan University, 100 East Claflin Avenue, Box 20, Salina, KS 67401. *Phone:* 785-833-4419. *Toll-free phone:* 800-874-1154 Ext. 1285. *Fax:* 785-404-1485. *E-mail:* claire.massey@kwu.edu.

Manhattan Christian College

Manhattan, Kansas

http://www.mccks.edu/

CONTACT
Ms. Connie Hill, Admissions Office Manager, Manhattan Christian College, 1415 Anderson Avenue, Manhattan, KS 66502. *Phone:* 877-246-

4622 Ext. 212. *Toll-free phone:* 877-246-4622. *E-mail:* teka.wilson@mccks.edu.

McPherson College

McPherson, Kansas

http://www.mcpherson.edu/

- **Independent** comprehensive, founded 1887, affiliated with Church of the Brethren
- **Small-town** 26-acre campus
- **Endowment** $39.1 million
- **Coed**
- **Moderately difficult** entrance level

FACULTY
Student/faculty ratio: 13:1.

ACADEMICS
Calendar: 4-1-4. *Degrees:* bachelor's and master's.
Library: Miller Library. *Books:* 42,629 (physical), 164,814 (digital/electronic); *Serial titles:* 681 (physical), 92,937 (digital/electronic); *Databases:* 65. Weekly public service hours: 86; students can reserve study rooms.

STUDENT LIFE
Housing options: coed, men-only, women-only, special housing for students with disabilities. Campus housing is university owned and leased by the school. Freshman campus housing is guaranteed.

Activities and organizations: drama/theater group, student-run newspaper, choral group, Student Activities Board, Student Government Association, CARS Club, Business Club, Multicultural Student Association.

Athletics Member NAIA.

Campus security: student patrols, controlled dormitory access, security cameras.

Student services: health clinic, personal/psychological counseling.

FINANCIAL AID
Financial Aid Of all full-time matriculated undergraduates who enrolled in 2016, 558 applied for aid, 558 were judged to have need, 129 had their need fully met. In 2016, 54 non-need-based awards were made. ***Average percent of need met:*** 82. ***Average financial aid package:*** $24,898. ***Average need-based loan:*** $8592. ***Average need-based gift aid:*** $5722. ***Average non-need-based aid:*** $14,626. ***Average indebtedness upon graduation:*** $28,615.

APPLYING
Standardized Tests *Required:* SAT or ACT (for admission).

Options: electronic application, deferred entrance.

Required: high school transcript, minimum 2.0 GPA.

CONTACT
Ms. Sara Brubaker, Director of Admissions Operations and Financial Aid, McPherson College, 1600 East Euclid, McPherson, KS 67460. *Phone:* 800-365-7402. *Toll-free phone:* 800-365-7402. *E-mail:* admiss@mcpherson.edu.

MidAmerica Nazarene University

Olathe, Kansas

http://www.mnu.edu/

- **Independent** comprehensive, founded 1966, affiliated with Church of the Nazarene
- **Suburban** 105-acre campus with easy access to Kansas City
- **Endowment** $13.6 million
- **Coed** 1,252 undergraduate students, 75% full-time, 59% women, 41% men
- **Minimally difficult** entrance level, 55% of applicants were admitted

UNDERGRAD STUDENTS
938 full-time, 314 part-time. Students come from 35 states and territories; 16 other countries; 39% are from out of state; 13% Black or African American, non-Hispanic/Latino; 3% Hispanic/Latino; 2% Asian, non-Hispanic/Latino; 0.4% Native Hawaiian or other Pacific Islander, non-Hispanic/Latino; 1% American Indian or Alaska Native, non-Hispanic/Latino; 3% Two or more races, non-Hispanic/Latino; 11% Race/ethnicity unknown; 3% international; 6% transferred in; 56% live on campus.

Freshmen:
Admission: 1,197 applied, 654 admitted, 180 enrolled. ***Average high school GPA:*** 3.4. ***Test scores:*** SAT evidence-based reading and writing scores over 500: 58%; SAT math scores over 500: 65%; ACT scores over 18: 81%; SAT evidence-based reading and writing scores over 600: 24%; SAT math scores over 600: 24%; ACT scores over 24: 32%; SAT evidence-based reading and writing scores over 700: 3%; SAT math scores over 700: 3%; ACT scores over 30: 6%.

Retention: 71% of full-time freshmen returned.

FACULTY
Total: 230, 35% full-time, 31% with terminal degrees.
Student/faculty ratio: 13:1.

ACADEMICS
Calendar: semesters. *Degrees:* associate, bachelor's, master's, post-master's, and postbachelor's certificates.

Special study options: academic remediation for entering students, accelerated degree program, adult/continuing education programs, advanced placement credit, cooperative education, distance learning, double majors, English as a second language, freshman honors college, honors programs, independent study, internships, off-campus study, part-time degree program, services for LD students, student-designed majors, study abroad, summer session for credit. ***ROTC:*** Army (c), Air Force (c).

Unusual degree programs: 3-2 nursing.

Computers: 142 computers/terminals and 142 ports are available on campus for general student use. Students can access the following: campus intranet, computer help desk, free student e-mail accounts, online (class) grades, online (class) registration, online (class) schedules. Campuswide network is available. 100% of college-owned or -operated housing units are wired for high-speed Internet access. Wireless service is available via entire campus.
Library: Mabee Library. *Books:* 69,432 (physical), 197,000 (digital/electronic); *Serial titles:* 133 (digital/electronic); *Databases:* 39. Weekly public service hours: 83; study areas open 24 hours, 5–7 days a week; students can reserve study rooms.

STUDENT LIFE
Housing options: on-campus residence required through senior year; men-only, women-only, special housing for students with disabilities. Campus housing is university owned. Freshman campus housing is guaranteed.

Activities and organizations: drama/theater group, student-run newspaper, radio and television station, choral group, LOL - Loving on Littles, S.M.I.L.E. - Students Ministering in the Lives of Elderly, Center for Grace, Freedom Fire, Students for Social Justice.

Athletics Member NAIA. ***Intercollegiate sports:*** baseball M(s), basketball M(s)/W(s), cheerleading M(s)/W(s), cross-country running M(s)/W(s), football M(s), soccer M(s)/W(s), softball W(s), track and field M(s)/W(s), volleyball W(s). ***Intramural sports:*** basketball M/W, football M/W, soccer M/W, softball M/W, tennis M/W, volleyball M/W, weight lifting M.

Campus security: 24-hour emergency response devices and patrols, student patrols, late-night transport/escort service, controlled dormitory access.

Student services: personal/psychological counseling, veterans affairs office.

COSTS & FINANCIAL AID
Costs (2020–21) ***Comprehensive fee:*** $42,154 includes full-time tuition ($32,122), mandatory fees ($750), and room and board ($9282).

Financial Aid Of all full-time matriculated undergraduates who enrolled in 2018, 685 applied for aid, 623 were judged to have need, 71 had their need fully met. In 2018, 146 non-need-based awards were made. ***Average percent of need met:*** 63. ***Average financial aid package:*** $25,849. ***Average need-based loan:*** $4319. ***Average need-based gift aid:*** $21,201. ***Average non-need-based aid:*** $11,814. ***Average indebtedness upon graduation:*** $28,755.

APPLYING
Standardized Tests *Required for some:* SAT or ACT (for admission). *Recommended:* TOEFL for international applicants.

Options: electronic application, deferred entrance.

Required: high school transcript, minimum 2.0 GPA.

Application deadlines: 8/1 (freshmen), 8/1 (transfers).

Notification: continuous (freshmen), continuous (transfers).

CONTACT

Meghan Luoma, MidAmerica Nazarene University, 2030 College Avenue, Olathe, KS 66062. *Phone:* 913-971-3783. *Toll-free phone:* 800-800-8887. *E-mail:* mvluoma@mnu.edu.

National American University

Garden City, Kansas

http://www.national.edu/

CONTACT

National American University, 801 Campus Drive, Garden City, KS 67846.

National American University

Overland Park, Kansas

http://www.national.edu/

CONTACT

Admissions Office, National American University, 10310 Mastin Street, Overland Park, KS 66212. *Toll-free phone:* 866-628-1288.

National American University

Wichita, Kansas

http://www.national.edu/

CONTACT

National American University, 7309 East 21st Street, Suite G40, Wichita, KS 67206. *Toll-free phone:* 877-628-9424.

National American University

Wichita, Kansas

http://www.national.edu/

CONTACT

National American University, 8428 West 13th Street North, Suite 120, Wichita, KS 67212. *Toll-free phone:* 877-628-9424.

Newman University

Wichita, Kansas

http://www.newmanu.edu/

- **Independent Roman Catholic** comprehensive, founded 1933
- **Urban** 61-acre campus with easy access to Sedgwick County
- **Coed** 2,705 undergraduate students, 35% full-time, 62% women, 38% men
- **Minimally difficult** entrance level, 67% of applicants were admitted

UNDERGRAD STUDENTS

944 full-time, 1,761 part-time. 20% are from out of state; 5% Black or African American, non-Hispanic/Latino; 14% Hispanic/Latino; 6% Asian, non-Hispanic/Latino; 0.3% Native Hawaiian or other Pacific Islander, non-Hispanic/Latino; 1% American Indian or Alaska Native, non-Hispanic/Latino; 3% Two or more races, non-Hispanic/Latino; 2% Race/ethnicity unknown; 5% international; 5% transferred in; 21% live on campus.

Freshmen:

Admission: 1,076 applied, 726 admitted, 184 enrolled. ***Average high school GPA:*** 3.6. ***Test scores:*** SAT evidence-based reading and writing scores over 500: 76%; SAT math scores over 500: 76%; ACT scores over 18: 83%; SAT evidence-based reading and writing scores over 600: 23%; SAT math scores over 600: 29%; ACT scores over 24: 33%; ACT scores over 30: 7%.

FACULTY

Total: 162, 48% full-time, 37% with terminal degrees.

Student/faculty ratio: 12:1.

ACADEMICS

Calendar: semesters. *Degrees:* associate, bachelor's, and master's.

Special study options: academic remediation for entering students, accelerated degree program, adult/continuing education programs, advanced placement credit, cooperative education, distance learning, double majors, honors programs, independent study, internships, off-campus study, part-time degree program, services for LD students, student-designed majors, study abroad, summer session for credit.

Unusual degree programs: 3-2 occupational therapy with Washington University in St. Louis.

Computers: Students can access the following: computer help desk, free student e-mail accounts, online (class) grades, online (class) registration, online (class) schedules. Campuswide network is available. 100% of college-owned or -operated housing units are wired for high-speed Internet access. Wireless service is available via entire campus.

Library: Dugan Library. Students can reserve study rooms.

STUDENT LIFE

Housing options: on-campus residence required for freshman year; coed. Campus housing is university owned. Freshman campus housing is guaranteed.

Activities and organizations: drama/theater group, student-run newspaper, choral group, Newman University Medical Professionals Club (NUMPC), National Society of Leadership and Success, Student Athlete Advisory Committee, Swing Dance Club, Hispanic American Leadership Organization (HALO).

Athletics Member NCAA. All Division II. ***Intercollegiate sports:*** baseball M(s), basketball M(s)/W(s), bowling M(s)(c)/W(s)(c), cross-country running M(s)/W(s), golf M(s)/W(s), soccer M(s)/W(s), softball W(s), tennis M(s)/W(s), volleyball W(s), wrestling M(s). ***Intramural sports:*** baseball M, basketball M/W, bowling M/W, football M/W, golf M/W, soccer M/W, softball M/W, table tennis M/W, triathlon M/W, ultimate Frisbee M/W, volleyball M/W, weight lifting M/W.

Campus security: 24-hour emergency response devices and patrols, student patrols, late-night transport/escort service, controlled dormitory access.

Student services: personal/psychological counseling.

FINANCIAL AID

Financial Aid Of all full-time matriculated undergraduates who enrolled in 2019, 770 applied for aid, 728 were judged to have need, 124 had their need fully met. In 2019, 146 non-need-based awards were made. ***Average percent of need met:*** 67. ***Average financial aid package:*** $24,386. ***Average need-based loan:*** $3958. ***Average need-based gift aid:*** $21,356. ***Average non-need-based aid:*** $14,086. ***Average indebtedness upon graduation:*** $30,532.

APPLYING

Standardized Tests *Recommended:* SAT or ACT (for admission).

Options: electronic application, deferred entrance.

Application fee: $25.

Required: high school transcript, minimum 2.0 GPA. ***Recommended:*** interview.

Application deadlines: rolling (freshmen), rolling (transfers).

Notification: continuous (freshmen), continuous (transfers).

CONTACT

Kristen English, Director of Undergraduate Admissions, Newman University, 3100 McCormick Avenue, Wichita, KS 67213. *Phone:* 316-942-4291 Ext. 2146. *Toll-free phone:* 877-NEWMANU. *Fax:* 316-942-4483. *E-mail:* englishk@newmanu.edu.

Ottawa University

Ottawa, Kansas

http://www.ottawa.edu/

- **Independent American Baptist Churches in the USA** comprehensive, founded 1865
- **Small-town** 64-acre campus with easy access to Kansas City
- **Endowment** $16.9 million
- **Coed** 2,418 undergraduate students, 67% full-time, 54% women, 46% men
- **Moderately difficult** entrance level, 26% of applicants were admitted

UNDERGRAD STUDENTS
1,623 full-time, 795 part-time. Students come from 44 states and territories; 19 other countries; 46% are from out of state; 13% Black or African American, non-Hispanic/Latino; 17% Hispanic/Latino; 2% Asian, non-Hispanic/Latino; 0.6% Native Hawaiian or other Pacific Islander, non-Hispanic/Latino; 2% American Indian or Alaska Native, non-Hispanic/Latino; 2% Two or more races, non-Hispanic/Latino; 7% Race/ethnicity unknown; 2% international; 22% transferred in; 67% live on campus.

Freshmen:
Admission: 1,168 applied, 302 admitted, 389 enrolled. ***Average high school GPA:*** 3.1. ***Test scores:*** SAT evidence-based reading and writing scores over 500: 14%; SAT math scores over 500: 12%; ACT scores over 18: 53%; SAT evidence-based reading and writing scores over 600: 5%; SAT math scores over 600: 3%; ACT scores over 24: 14%; ACT scores over 30: 1%.

Retention: 44% of full-time freshmen returned.

FACULTY
Total: 68, 38% full-time, 26% with terminal degrees.

Student/faculty ratio: 18:1.

ACADEMICS
Calendar: semesters. *Degrees:* certificates, bachelor's, and master's (also offers master's, adult, international and on-line education programs with significant enrollment not reflected in profile).

Special study options: advanced placement credit, distance learning, double majors, independent study, internships, part-time degree program, student-designed majors, study abroad, summer session for credit.

Computers: 40 computers/terminals are available on campus for general student use. Students can access the following: campus intranet, computer help desk, free student e-mail accounts, online (class) grades, online (class) registration, online (class) schedules. Campuswide network is available. 100% of college-owned or -operated housing units are wired for high-speed Internet access. Wireless service is available via entire campus.
Library: Gangwish Library. *Books:* 42,485 (digital/electronic); *Databases:* 119. Weekly public service hours: 84; students can reserve study rooms.

STUDENT LIFE
Housing options: on-campus residence required through junior year; coed, women-only. Campus housing is university owned. Freshman campus housing is guaranteed.

Activities and organizations: drama/theater group, student-run newspaper, radio station, choral group, Christian Faith In Action, Student Activities Force, Education Club, Whole Earth Club, Fellowship of Christian Athletes, national fraternities, national sororities.

Athletics Member NAIA. ***Intercollegiate sports:*** baseball M(s), basketball M(s)/W(s), bowling M(s)/W(s), cheerleading M(s)/W(s), cross-country running M(s)/W(s), football M(s), golf M(s)/W(s), lacrosse M(s)/W(s), sand volleyball W(s), soccer M(s)/W(s), softball W(s), tennis M(s)/W(s), track and field M(s)/W(s), volleyball M(s)/W(s), weight lifting M(s)/W(s), wrestling M(s)/W(s). ***Intramural sports:*** basketball M/W, volleyball M/W, weight lifting M/W.

Campus security: 24-hour emergency response devices and patrols, controlled dormitory access.

Student services: health clinic, personal/psychological counseling.

COSTS
Costs (2020–21) ***One-time required fee:*** $270. ***Comprehensive fee:*** $42,780 includes full-time tuition ($29,980), mandatory fees ($1600), and room and board ($11,200). Full-time tuition and fees vary according to course load, program, and reciprocity agreements. Part-time tuition: $1220 per credit hour. Part-time tuition and fees vary according to course load, program, and reciprocity agreements. ***Required fees:*** $835 per year part-time. ***College room only:*** $5700. Room and board charges vary according to board plan, housing facility, and location. ***Payment plan:*** installment. ***Waivers:*** employees or children of employees.

APPLYING
Standardized Tests *Recommended:* SAT or ACT (for admission), SAT and SAT Subject Tests or ACT (for admission).

Options: electronic application.

Application fee: $25.

Required: high school transcript, minimum 2.5 GPA, rank in upper 50% of high school class. ***Required for some:*** essay or personal statement. ***Recommended:*** 2 letters of recommendation, interview.

Application deadlines: rolling (freshmen), rolling (out-of-state freshmen), rolling (transfers).

Notification: continuous (freshmen), continuous (out-of-state freshmen), continuous (transfers).

CONTACT
Andy J. Stiles, andy.stiles@ottawa.edu, Ottawa University, 1001 S. Cedar St., Ottawa, KS 66067. *Phone:* 785-248-2373. *Toll-free phone:* 800-755-5200. *Fax:* 785-229-1008. *E-mail:* andy.stiles@ottawa.edu.

Pittsburg State University

Pittsburg, Kansas

http://www.pittstate.edu/

- **State-supported** comprehensive, founded 1903, part of Kansas State Board of Regents
- **Small-town** 630-acre campus
- **Coed** 5,181 undergraduate students, 90% full-time, 50% women, 50% men
- **Minimally difficult** entrance level, 96% of applicants were admitted

UNDERGRAD STUDENTS
4,650 full-time, 531 part-time. 29% are from out of state; 3% Black or African American, non-Hispanic/Latino; 6% Hispanic/Latino; 0.9% Asian, non-Hispanic/Latino; 0.1% Native Hawaiian or other Pacific Islander, non-Hispanic/Latino; 1% American Indian or Alaska Native, non-Hispanic/Latino; 6% Two or more races, non-Hispanic/Latino; 0.1% Race/ethnicity unknown; 2% international; 11% transferred in.

Freshmen:
Admission: 1,822 applied, 1,741 admitted, 825 enrolled. ***Average high school GPA:*** 3.4. ***Test scores:*** SAT evidence-based reading and writing scores over 500: 61%; SAT math scores over 500: 67%; ACT scores over 18: 82%; SAT evidence-based reading and writing scores over 600: 25%; SAT math scores over 600: 28%; ACT scores over 24: 31%; SAT evidence-based reading and writing scores over 700: 3%; SAT math scores over 700: 6%; ACT scores over 30: 5%.

Retention: 74% of full-time freshmen returned.

FACULTY
Total: 432, 70% full-time, 62% with terminal degrees.

Student/faculty ratio: 16:1.

ACADEMICS
Calendar: semesters. *Degrees:* certificates, associate, bachelor's, master's, doctoral, post-master's, and postbachelor's certificates.

Special study options: accelerated degree program, adult/continuing education programs, distance learning, double majors, freshman honors college, honors programs, independent study, internships, off-campus study, part-time degree program, services for LD students, student-designed majors, study abroad, summer session for credit. ***ROTC:*** Army (b).

Computers: Students can access the following: campus intranet, computer help desk, free student e-mail accounts, online (class) grades, online (class) registration, online (class) schedules. Campuswide network is available. 100% of college-owned or -operated housing units are wired for high-speed Internet access. Wireless service is available via entire campus.
Library: Leonard H. Axe Library plus 2 others.

STUDENT LIFE
Housing options: on-campus residence required for freshman year; coed, special housing for students with disabilities. Campus housing is university owned. Freshman applicants given priority for college housing.

Activities and organizations: drama/theater group, student-run newspaper, radio and television station, choral group, marching band, Student Government Association, student yearbook, student newspaper, Student Activities Council, Students in Free Enterprise (SIFE), national fraternities, national sororities.

Athletics Member NCAA. All Division II. ***Intercollegiate sports:*** baseball M(s), basketball M(s)/W(s), cheerleading M(s)/W(s), cross-country running M(s)/W(s), football M(s), golf M(s), softball W(s), track and field M(s)/W(s), volleyball W(s). ***Intramural sports:*** badminton M/W, basketball M/W, football M/W, lacrosse M(c), racquetball M/W, rugby M(c), soccer M(c)/W(c), softball M/W, table tennis M/W, tennis M/W, ultimate Frisbee M/W, volleyball M/W.

Campus security: 24-hour emergency response devices and patrols, late-night transport/escort service, controlled dormitory access.

Student services: health clinic, personal/psychological counseling, legal services.

FINANCIAL AID

Financial Aid Of all full-time matriculated undergraduates who enrolled in 2018, 2,739 were judged to have need. ***Average financial aid package:*** $8009. ***Average need-based loan:*** $3741. ***Average need-based gift aid:*** $4716. ***Average indebtedness upon graduation:*** $24,533.

APPLYING

Standardized Tests *Recommended:* ACT (for admission).

Options: electronic application, deferred entrance.

Application fee: $30.

Required: high school transcript. ***Required for some:*** minimum 2.0 GPA.

Application deadlines: rolling (freshmen), rolling (transfers).

CONTACT

Director of Admission, Pittsburg State University, 1701 South Broadway, Pittsburg, KS 66762. *Phone:* 620-235-4251. *Toll-free phone:* 800-854-7488. *Fax:* 620-235-6003. *E-mail:* psuadmit@pittstate.edu.

Rasmussen College Kansas City/Overland Park

Overland Park, Kansas

http://www.rasmussen.edu/

- **Proprietary** 4-year, founded 2013, part of Rasmussen College System
- **Suburban** campus
- **Coed** 347 undergraduate students, 54% full-time, 91% women, 9% men
- 100% of applicants were admitted

UNDERGRAD STUDENTS

186 full-time, 161 part-time. Students come from 51 states and territories; 27% are from out of state; 15% Black or African American, non-Hispanic/Latino; 7% Hispanic/Latino; 3% Asian, non-Hispanic/Latino; 1% Native Hawaiian or other Pacific Islander, non-Hispanic/Latino; 0.9% American Indian or Alaska Native, non-Hispanic/Latino; 5% Two or more races, non-Hispanic/Latino; 15% Race/ethnicity unknown.

Freshmen:

Admission: 75 applied, 75 admitted, 39 enrolled.

ACADEMICS

Calendar: quarters. *Degrees:* certificates, diplomas, associate, bachelor's, and postbachelor's certificates.

Special study options: academic remediation for entering students, accelerated degree program, adult/continuing education programs, distance learning, double majors, internships, part-time degree program, summer session for credit.

Computers: Students can access the following: computer help desk, free student e-mail accounts, online (class) grades, online (class) schedules. Campuswide network is available. Wireless service is available via entire campus.

Library: Rasmussen College Library - Kansas City/Overland Park.

STUDENT LIFE

Housing options: college housing not available.

COSTS

Costs (2019–20) ***Tuition:*** $13,799 full-time, $12,648 per year part-time. Full-time tuition and fees vary according to course level, course load, degree level, location, and program. Part-time tuition and fees vary according to course level, course load, degree level, location, and program. No tuition increase for student's term of enrollment. ***Required fees:*** $3183 full-time, $2542 per year part-time. ***Payment plans:*** installment, deferred payment. ***Waivers:*** employees or children of employees.

APPLYING

Options: early admission, deferred entrance.

Required: high school transcript, minimum 2.0 GPA. ***Required for some:*** interview.

Application deadlines: rolling (freshmen), rolling (transfers).

CONTACT

Ms. Susan Hammerstrom, Director of Admissions, Rasmussen College Kansas City/Overland Park, 11600 College Boulevard, Overland Park, KS 66210. *Phone:* 913-491-7870. *Toll-free phone:* 888-549-6755. *E-mail:* susan.hammerstrom@rasmussen.edu.

Rasmussen College Topeka

Topeka, Kansas

http://www.rasmussen.edu/

- **Proprietary** 4-year, founded 2013, part of Rasmussen College System
- **Suburban** campus
- **Coed** 264 undergraduate students, 52% full-time, 90% women, 10% men
- **Minimally difficult** entrance level, 100% of applicants were admitted

UNDERGRAD STUDENTS

138 full-time, 126 part-time. Students come from 51 states and territories; 27% are from out of state; 11% Black or African American, non-Hispanic/Latino; 9% Hispanic/Latino; 0.4% Asian, non-Hispanic/Latino; 2% American Indian or Alaska Native, non-Hispanic/Latino; 7% Two or more races, non-Hispanic/Latino; 14% Race/ethnicity unknown.

Freshmen:

Admission: 53 applied, 53 admitted, 34 enrolled.

ACADEMICS

Calendar: quarters. *Degrees:* certificates, diplomas, associate, bachelor's, and postbachelor's certificates.

Special study options: academic remediation for entering students, accelerated degree program, adult/continuing education programs, distance learning, double majors, internships, part-time degree program, summer session for credit.

Computers: Students can access the following: computer help desk, free student e-mail accounts, online (class) grades, online (class) schedules. Campuswide network is available. Wireless service is available via entire campus.

Library: Rasmussen College Library - Topeka.

STUDENT LIFE

Housing options: college housing not available.

COSTS

Costs (2019–20) ***Tuition:*** $13,657 full-time, $12,659 per year part-time. Full-time tuition and fees vary according to course level, course load, degree level, location, and program. Part-time tuition and fees vary according to course level, course load, degree level, location, and program. No tuition increase for student's term of enrollment. ***Required fees:*** $2931 full-time, $2562 per year part-time. ***Payment plans:*** installment, deferred payment. ***Waivers:*** employees or children of employees.

APPLYING

Standardized Tests *Required:* institutional exam (for admission).

Options: electronic application, early admission, deferred entrance.

Required: high school transcript, minimum 2.0 GPA. ***Required for some:*** interview.

Application deadlines: rolling (freshmen), rolling (transfers).

CONTACT

Ms. Susan Hammerstrom, Director of Admissions, Rasmussen College Topeka, 620 SW Governor View, Topeka, KS 66606. *Phone:* 785-228-7320. *Toll-free phone:* 888-549-6755. *E-mail:* susan.hammerstrom@rasmussen.edu.

Southwestern College
Winfield, Kansas
http://www.sckans.edu/

- **Independent United Methodist** comprehensive, founded 1885
- **Small-town** 70-acre campus with easy access to Wichita
- **Endowment** $27.8 million
- **Coed** 1,360 undergraduate students, 50% full-time, 36% women, 64% men
- **Minimally difficult** entrance level, 51% of applicants were admitted

UNDERGRAD STUDENTS
678 full-time, 682 part-time. Students come from 48 states and territories; 20 other countries; 68% are from out of state; 12% Black or African American, non-Hispanic/Latino; 11% Hispanic/Latino; 2% Asian, non-Hispanic/Latino; 0.5% Native Hawaiian or other Pacific Islander, non-Hispanic/Latino; 0.6% American Indian or Alaska Native, non-Hispanic/Latino; 3% Two or more races, non-Hispanic/Latino; 27% Race/ethnicity unknown; 3% international; 16% transferred in; 66% live on campus.

Freshmen:
Admission: 914 applied, 466 admitted, 149 enrolled. ***Average high school GPA:*** 3.2. ***Test scores:*** SAT evidence-based reading and writing scores over 500: 47%; SAT math scores over 500: 53%; ACT scores over 18: 79%; SAT evidence-based reading and writing scores over 600: 7%; SAT math scores over 600: 5%; ACT scores over 24: 21%; SAT math scores over 700: 2%; ACT scores over 30: 5%.

Retention: 66% of full-time freshmen returned.

FACULTY
Total: 207, 20% full-time, 36% with terminal degrees.

Student/faculty ratio: 10:1.

ACADEMICS
Calendar: semesters. *Degrees:* certificates, bachelor's, master's, doctoral, and postbachelor's certificates.

Special study options: academic remediation for entering students, accelerated degree program, adult/continuing education programs, advanced placement credit, distance learning, double majors, English as a second language, honors programs, independent study, internships, off-campus study, part-time degree program, services for LD students, student-designed majors, study abroad, summer session for credit.

Computers: 45 computers/terminals and 30 ports are available on campus for general student use. Students can access the following: campus intranet, computer help desk, free student e-mail accounts, online (class) grades, online (class) registration, online (class) schedules, everything in Self-Service and BlackBoard. Campuswide network is available. 100% of college-owned or -operated housing units are wired for high-speed Internet access. Wireless service is available via entire campus.
Library: Harold and Mary Ellen Deets Library. *Books:* 44,435 (physical), 847,600 (digital/electronic); *Serial titles:* 3 (physical); *Databases:* 182. Weekly public service hours: 91; students can reserve study rooms.

STUDENT LIFE
Housing options: on-campus residence required through junior year; coed, men-only, women-only. Campus housing is university owned. Freshman campus housing is guaranteed.

Activities and organizations: drama/theater group, student-run newspaper, radio and television station, choral group, Discipleship SC, Leadership SC, Student Foundation, Student Government Association, Gaming Club.

Athletics Member NAIA. ***Intercollegiate sports:*** baseball M(s), basketball M(s)/W(s), cross-country running M(s)/W(s), football M(s), golf M(s)/W(s), soccer M(s)/W(s), softball W(s), tennis M(s)/W(s), track and field M(s)/W(s), volleyball W(s). ***Intramural sports:*** basketball M/W, cheerleading M(c)/W(c).

Campus security: 24-hour emergency response devices and patrols, late-night transport/escort service, controlled dormitory access.

Student services: personal/psychological counseling, veterans affairs office.

COSTS & FINANCIAL AID
Costs (2020–21) ***Comprehensive fee:*** $41,750 includes full-time tuition ($33,100), mandatory fees ($150), and room and board ($8500). Full-time tuition and fees vary according to course load, degree level, location, and program. Part-time tuition: $1380 per credit hour. Part-time tuition and fees vary according to course load, degree level, location, and program. ***College room only:*** $4000. Room and board charges vary according to board plan and housing facility. ***Payment plan:*** installment. ***Waivers:*** senior citizens and employees or children of employees.

Financial Aid Of all full-time matriculated undergraduates who enrolled in 2018, 587 applied for aid, 554 were judged to have need, 64 had their need fully met. 117 Federal Work-Study jobs (averaging $1425). In 2018, 95 non-need-based awards were made. ***Average percent of need met:*** 69. ***Average financial aid package:*** $23,398. ***Average need-based loan:*** $4092. ***Average need-based gift aid:*** $19,270. ***Average non-need-based aid:*** $8792. ***Average indebtedness upon graduation:*** $37,490.

APPLYING
Standardized Tests *Required:* SAT or ACT (for admission).

Options: electronic application.

Application fee: $25.

Required: high school transcript, minimum 2.6 GPA. ***Required for some:*** essay or personal statement, 2 letters of recommendation.

Application deadlines: 8/24 (freshmen), 8/24 (transfers).

Notification: continuous (freshmen), continuous (out-of-state freshmen), continuous (transfers).

CONTACT
Southwestern College, 100 College Street, Winfield, KS 67156-2499. *Phone:* 620-229-6241. *Toll-free phone:* 800-846-1543.

Sterling College
Sterling, Kansas
http://www.sterling.edu/

- **Independent Presbyterian** 4-year, founded 1887
- **Rural** 46-acre campus
- **Endowment** $16.0 million
- **Coed** 643 undergraduate students, 82% full-time, 42% women, 58% men
- **Minimally difficult** entrance level, 40% of applicants were admitted

UNDERGRAD STUDENTS
527 full-time, 116 part-time. 60% are from out of state; 16% Black or African American, non-Hispanic/Latino; 15% Hispanic/Latino; 1% Asian, non-Hispanic/Latino; 2% American Indian or Alaska Native, non-Hispanic/Latino; 4% Two or more races, non-Hispanic/Latino; 1% Race/ethnicity unknown; 4% international; 7% transferred in; 76% live on campus.

Freshmen:
Admission: 1,596 applied, 637 admitted, 139 enrolled. ***Average high school GPA:*** 3.2. ***Test scores:*** SAT evidence-based reading and writing scores over 500: 47%; SAT math scores over 500: 53%; ACT scores over 18: 84%; SAT evidence-based reading and writing scores over 600: 3%; SAT math scores over 600: 1%; ACT scores over 24: 23%; ACT scores over 30: 4%.

Retention: 58% of full-time freshmen returned.

FACULTY
Total: 75, 64% full-time, 31% with terminal degrees.

Student/faculty ratio: 11:1.

ACADEMICS
Calendar: 4-1-4. *Degree:* bachelor's.

Special study options: advanced placement credit, distance learning, double majors, honors programs, independent study, internships, off-campus study, services for LD students, student-designed majors, study abroad, summer session for credit.

Unusual degree programs: 3-2 biology/medical technology with Wichita State University.

Computers: 50 computers/terminals are available on campus for general student use. Students can access the following: campus intranet, computer help desk, free student e-mail accounts, online (class) grades, online (class) registration, online (class) schedules. Campuswide network is available. 100% of college-owned or -operated housing units are wired for high-speed Internet access. Wireless service is available via entire campus.

Library: Mabee Library. *Books:* 50,908 (physical), 80,159 (digital/electronic); *Serial titles:* 74 (physical); *Databases:* 28. Weekly public service hours: 75; students can reserve study rooms.

STUDENT LIFE

Housing options: on-campus residence required through senior year; men-only, women-only. Campus housing is university owned. Freshman campus housing is guaranteed.

Activities and organizations: drama/theater group, student-run newspaper, radio and television station, choral group, Fellowship of Christian Athletes, Student Activities Council, Bible study groups, theatre, Mission teams.

Athletics Member NAIA. ***Intercollegiate sports:*** baseball M(s), basketball M(s)/W(s), cheerleading M(s)/W(s), cross-country running M(s)/W(s), football M(s), golf M(s)/W(s), soccer M(s)/W(s), softball W(s), track and field M(s)/W(s), volleyball W(s). ***Intramural sports:*** basketball M/W, softball M/W, ultimate Frisbee M/W, volleyball M/W.

Campus security: controlled dormitory access, late night security patrol.

Student services: health clinic, personal/psychological counseling.

COSTS & FINANCIAL AID

Costs (2020–21) ***Tuition:*** $26,000 full-time, $484 per credit hour part-time. Full-time tuition and fees vary according to course load and degree level. Part-time tuition and fees vary according to course load and degree level. ***Required fees:*** $1300 full-time. ***Room only:*** $3516. Room and board charges vary according to board plan and housing facility. ***Payment plan:*** installment. ***Waivers:*** senior citizens and employees or children of employees.

Financial Aid Of all full-time matriculated undergraduates who enrolled in 2018, 528 applied for aid, 476 were judged to have need, 112 had their need fully met. In 2018, 60 non-need-based awards were made. ***Average percent of need met:*** 79. ***Average financial aid package:*** $23,594. ***Average need-based loan:*** $6133. ***Average need-based gift aid:*** $10,901. ***Average non-need-based aid:*** $8971. ***Average indebtedness upon graduation:*** $24,843.

APPLYING

Standardized Tests *Required:* SAT or ACT (for admission).

Options: electronic application, deferred entrance.

Required: high school transcript, minimum 2.2 GPA. ***Required for some:*** 2 letters of recommendation. ***Recommended:*** essay or personal statement, interview.

Application deadlines: rolling (freshmen), rolling (transfers).

Notification: continuous (freshmen), continuous (transfers).

CONTACT

Marge Jones, Admissions Office Manager, Sterling College, 125 West Cooper, Sterling, KS 67579. *Phone:* 620-278-4275. *Toll-free phone:* 800-346-1017. *Fax:* 620-278-4416. *E-mail:* admissions@sterling.edu.

Tabor College

Hillsboro, Kansas

http://www.tabor.edu/

- **Independent Mennonite Brethren** comprehensive, founded 1908
- **Small-town** 87-acre campus with easy access to Wichita
- **Endowment** $11.0 million
- **Coed** 574 undergraduate students, 84% full-time, 42% women, 58% men
- **Moderately difficult** entrance level, 56% of applicants were admitted

UNDERGRAD STUDENTS

481 full-time, 93 part-time. Students come from 36 states and territories; 9 other countries; 54% are from out of state; 14% Black or African American, non-Hispanic/Latino; 11% Hispanic/Latino; 0.5% Asian, non-Hispanic/Latino; 0.3% Native Hawaiian or other Pacific Islander, non-Hispanic/Latino; 2% American Indian or Alaska Native, non-Hispanic/Latino; 7% Two or more races, non-Hispanic/Latino; 0.7% Race/ethnicity unknown; 2% international; 11% transferred in; 92% live on campus.

Freshmen:

Admission: 812 applied, 454 admitted, 128 enrolled. ***Average high school GPA:*** 3.2. ***Test scores:*** SAT evidence-based reading and writing scores over 500: 59%; SAT math scores over 500: 68%; ACT scores over 18: 73%; SAT evidence-based reading and writing scores over 600: 18%; SAT math scores over 600: 9%; ACT scores over 24: 20%; ACT scores over 30: 2%.

Retention: 60% of full-time freshmen returned.

FACULTY

Total: 74, 32% full-time, 47% with terminal degrees.

Student/faculty ratio: 13:1.

ACADEMICS

Calendar: 4-1-4 (adult and graduate studies programs run by cohort groups). *Degrees:* associate, bachelor's, and master's.

Special study options: academic remediation for entering students, accelerated degree program, adult/continuing education programs, advanced placement credit, cooperative education, distance learning, double majors, honors programs, independent study, internships, off-campus study, part-time degree program, services for LD students, student-designed majors, study abroad.

Computers: 35 computers/terminals are available on campus for general student use. Students can access the following: computer help desk, free student e-mail accounts, online (class) grades, online (class) registration, online (class) schedules, online registration for Hillsboro undergraduate students. Campuswide network is available. 100% of college-owned or -operated housing units are wired for high-speed Internet access. Wireless service is available via entire campus.

Library: Tabor College Library. *Books:* 61,550 (physical), 225,000 (digital/electronic); *Serial titles:* 148 (physical), 5,000 (digital/electronic); *Databases:* 41. Weekly public service hours: 85; students can reserve study rooms.

STUDENT LIFE

Housing options: on-campus residence required through senior year; men-only, women-only, special housing for students with disabilities. Campus housing is university owned.

Activities and organizations: drama/theater group, student-run newspaper, choral group, Student Activities Board, CHUMS (Challenging, Helping and Understanding through Mentorship), Intramurals, WUMP (Wichita Urban Ministries Plunge), Multi-Cultural Student Union.

Athletics Member NAIA. ***Intercollegiate sports:*** baseball M(s), basketball M(s)/W(s), cheerleading M(s)/W(s), cross-country running M(s)/W(s), football M(s), golf M, soccer M(s)/W(s), softball W(s), swimming and diving M(s)/W(s), tennis M(s)/W(s), track and field M(s)/W(s), volleyball W(s). ***Intramural sports:*** basketball M/W, soccer M/W, softball M/W, volleyball M/W.

Student services: personal/psychological counseling.

COSTS & FINANCIAL AID

Costs (2019–20) ***Comprehensive fee:*** $39,350 includes full-time tuition ($28,400), mandatory fees ($975), and room and board ($9975). Part-time tuition: $570 per hour. ***Required fees:*** $20 per hour part-time. ***Room and board:*** Room and board charges vary according to board plan and housing facility. ***Payment plan:*** installment. ***Waivers:*** employees or children of employees.

Financial Aid Of all full-time matriculated undergraduates who enrolled in 2018, 547 applied for aid, 462 were judged to have need, 75 had their need fully met. In 2018, 86 non-need-based awards were made. ***Average percent of need met:*** 73. ***Average financial aid package:*** $23,387. ***Average need-based loan:*** $7778. ***Average need-based gift aid:*** $3036. ***Average non-need-based aid:*** $11,124. ***Average indebtedness upon graduation:*** $27,126. ***Financial aid deadline:*** 8/15.

APPLYING

Standardized Tests *Required:* SAT or ACT (for admission).

Options: electronic application, deferred entrance.

Application fee: $50.

Required: essay or personal statement, high school transcript, minimum 2.0 GPA, validation of high school graduation date for transfers. ***Recommended:*** interview.

Application deadlines: rolling (freshmen), rolling (transfers).

Notification: continuous (freshmen), continuous (transfers).

CONTACT

Ms. Kelly Dugger, Assistant Director of Admissions, Tabor College, 400 South Jefferson, Hillsboro, KS 67063. *Phone:* 620-947-3121 Ext. 1724.

Toll-free phone: 800-822-6799. *Fax:* 620-947-3789. *E-mail:* kellydugger@tabor.edu.

The University of Kansas

Lawrence, Kansas

http://www.ku.edu/

- **State-supported** university, founded 1866, part of Kansas Board of Regents
- **Suburban** 1000-acre campus with easy access to Kansas City
- **Endowment** $1.8 billion
- **Coed** 19,667 undergraduate students, 88% full-time, 52% women, 48% men
- **Moderately difficult** entrance level, 93% of applicants were admitted

UNDERGRAD STUDENTS

17,257 full-time, 2,410 part-time. Students come from 52 states and territories; 83 other countries; 29% are from out of state; 4% Black or African American, non-Hispanic/Latino; 9% Hispanic/Latino; 5% Asian, non-Hispanic/Latino; 0.1% Native Hawaiian or other Pacific Islander, non-Hispanic/Latino; 0.3% American Indian or Alaska Native, non-Hispanic/Latino; 3% Two or more races, non-Hispanic/Latino; 0.4% Race/ethnicity unknown; 5% international; 5% transferred in; 25% live on campus.

Freshmen:

Admission: 15,093 applied, 14,052 admitted, 4,125 enrolled. ***Average high school GPA:*** 3.6. ***Test scores:*** ACT scores over 18: 97%; ACT scores over 24: 67%; ACT scores over 30: 21%.

Retention: 86% of full-time freshmen returned.

FACULTY

Total: 1,632, 87% full-time, 72% with terminal degrees.

Student/faculty ratio: 17:1.

ACADEMICS

Calendar: semesters. *Degrees:* certificates, bachelor's, master's, doctoral, post-master's, and postbachelor's certificates (University of Kansas is a single institution with academic programs and facilities at two primary locations: Lawrence and Kansas City).

Special study options: academic remediation for entering students, accelerated degree program, adult/continuing education programs, advanced placement credit, cooperative education, distance learning, double majors, English as a second language, freshman honors college, honors programs, independent study, internships, off-campus study, part-time degree program, services for LD students, study abroad, summer session for credit. ***ROTC:*** Army (b), Navy (b), Air Force (b).

Computers: 1,500 computers/terminals are available on campus for general student use. Students can access the following: campus intranet, computer help desk, free student e-mail accounts, online (class) grades, online (class) registration, online (class) schedules, online payments. Campuswide network is available. 100% of college-owned or -operated housing units are wired for high-speed Internet access. Wireless service is available via entire campus.

Library: Watson Library plus 11 others. *Books:* 4.7 million (physical), 1.0 million (digital/electronic). Weekly public service hours: 168; study areas open 24 hours, 5–7 days a week; students can reserve study rooms.

STUDENT LIFE

Housing options: coed, men-only, women-only, cooperative. Campus housing is university owned.

Activities and organizations: drama/theater group, student-run newspaper, radio and television station, choral group, marching band, national fraternities, national sororities.

Athletics Member NCAA. All Division I except football (Division I-A). ***Intercollegiate sports:*** baseball M(s), basketball M(s)/W(s), cheerleading M/W, crew W(s), cross-country running M(s)/W(s), golf M(s)/W(s), rugby M(c), soccer W(s), softball W(s), swimming and diving W(s), tennis W(s), track and field M(s)/W(s), volleyball W(s). ***Intramural sports:*** badminton M(c)/W(c), baseball M(c), basketball M/W, crew M(c)/W(c), cross-country running M(c)/W(c), football M/W, golf M(c)/W(c), gymnastics M(c)/W(c), ice hockey M(c), lacrosse M(c)/W(c), racquetball M/W, rock climbing M(c)/W(c), rugby M(c)/W(c), sailing M(c)/W(c), sand volleyball M/W, soccer M(c)/W(c), softball M/W(c), swimming and diving M(c)/W(c), table tennis M(c)/W(c), tennis M(c)/W(c), track and field M(c)/W(c), ultimate Frisbee M(c)/W(c), volleyball M(c)/W(c), water polo M(c)/W(c).

Campus security: 24-hour emergency response devices and patrols, late-night transport/escort service, controlled dormitory access, University police department.

Student services: health clinic, personal/psychological counseling, women's center, legal services, veterans affairs office.

COSTS & FINANCIAL AID

Costs (2019–20) ***Tuition:*** state resident $10,092 full-time, $336 per credit hour part-time; nonresident $26,960 full-time, $899 per credit hour part-time. Full-time tuition and fees vary according to course load, location, and reciprocity agreements. Part-time tuition and fees vary according to course load, location, and reciprocity agreements. ***Required fees:*** $1074 full-time, $85 per credit hour part-time. ***Room and board:*** $10,350; room only: $6084. Room and board charges vary according to board plan and housing facility. ***Payment plan:*** installment. ***Waivers:*** employees or children of employees.

Financial Aid Of all full-time matriculated undergraduates who enrolled in 2018, 11,320 applied for aid, 8,120 were judged to have need, 3,242 had their need fully met. 784 Federal Work-Study jobs (averaging $1192). 41 state and other part-time jobs (averaging $1668). In 2018, 3787 non-need-based awards were made. ***Average percent of need met:*** 77. ***Average financial aid package:*** $16,795. ***Average need-based loan:*** $4246. ***Average need-based gift aid:*** $8305. ***Average non-need-based aid:*** $6740. ***Average indebtedness upon graduation:*** $28,176.

APPLYING

Standardized Tests *Required:* SAT or ACT (for admission).

Options: electronic application, deferred entrance.

Application fee: $40.

Required: high school transcript, minimum 3.0 GPA, Kansas Qualified Admissions Curriculum with minimum 2.0 GPA for state residents and 2.5 for nonresidents and minimum 3.0 overall GPA and ACT score of 24/SAT of 1160 or minimum 3.25 overall GPA and ACT score of 21/SAT of 1060. ***Required for some:*** essay or personal statement.

Application deadlines: 8/19 (freshmen), 8/19 (transfers).

Notification: continuous (freshmen), continuous (transfers).

CONTACT

Ms. Lisa Pinamonti Kress, Director of Admissions, The University of Kansas, KU Visitor Center, 1502 Iowa Street, Lawrence, KS 66045-7576. *Phone:* 785-864-3911. *Toll-free phone:* 888-686-7323. *Fax:* 785-864-5017. *E-mail:* adm@ku.edu.

University of Saint Mary

Leavenworth, Kansas

http://www.stmary.edu/

- **Independent Roman Catholic** comprehensive, founded 1923
- **Small-town** 240-acre campus with easy access to Kansas City
- **Endowment** $21.8 million
- **Coed** 782 undergraduate students, 91% full-time, 50% women, 50% men
- **Moderately difficult** entrance level, 84% of applicants were admitted

UNDERGRAD STUDENTS

713 full-time, 69 part-time. Students come from 40 states and territories; 5 other countries; 49% are from out of state; 14% Black or African American, non-Hispanic/Latino; 15% Hispanic/Latino; 1% Asian, non-Hispanic/Latino; 2% Native Hawaiian or other Pacific Islander, non-Hispanic/Latino; 1% American Indian or Alaska Native, non-Hispanic/Latino; 5% Two or more races, non-Hispanic/Latino; 16% Race/ethnicity unknown; 0.8% international; 15% transferred in; 39% live on campus.

Freshmen:

Admission: 699 applied, 587 admitted, 149 enrolled. ***Average high school GPA:*** 3.3. ***Test scores:*** SAT evidence-based reading and writing scores over 500: 64%; ACT scores over 18: 86%; SAT evidence-based reading and writing scores over 600: 24%; ACT scores over 24: 25%; ACT scores over 30: 2%.

Retention: 62% of full-time freshmen returned.

FACULTY

Total: 159, 45% full-time, 52% with terminal degrees.

Student/faculty ratio: 11:1.

ACADEMICS

Calendar: semesters. *Degrees:* associate, bachelor's, master's, and doctoral.

Special study options: academic remediation for entering students, accelerated degree program, adult/continuing education programs, advanced placement credit, cooperative education, distance learning, double majors, honors programs, independent study, internships, off-campus study, part-time degree program, services for LD students, study abroad, summer session for credit. ***ROTC:*** Army (c).

Unusual degree programs: 3-2 engineering with University of Missouri - Kansas City; Athletic Training - BS in Health and Sport Science and MS in Athletic Training from the University of Saint Mary.

Computers: 30 computers/terminals are available on campus for general student use. Students can access the following: campus intranet, computer help desk, free student e-mail accounts, online (class) grades, online (class) registration, online (class) schedules. Campuswide network is available. 100% of college-owned or -operated housing units are wired for high-speed Internet access. Wireless service is available via entire campus.

Library: Keleher Learning Commons. *Books:* 45,000 (physical), 10,500 (digital/electronic); *Serial titles:* 15 (physical), 38,459 (digital/electronic); *Databases:* 63. Weekly public service hours: 67; students can reserve study rooms.

STUDENT LIFE

Housing options: on-campus residence required through sophomore year; coed. Campus housing is university owned. Freshman campus housing is guaranteed.

Activities and organizations: drama/theater group, choral group, Campus Activities Board, Spanish Club, Journalism Communication Club, STEM Club, Health Care Careers Club.

Athletics Member NAIA. ***Intercollegiate sports:*** baseball M(s), basketball M(s)/W(s), cheerleading M(s)/W(s), cross-country running M(s)/W(s), football M(s), lacrosse M(s)/W(s), soccer M(s)/W(s), softball W(s), swimming and diving M(s)/W(s), track and field M(s)/W(s), volleyball W(s), wrestling M(s)/W(s).

Campus security: 24-hour patrols, late-night transport/escort service, controlled dormitory access.

Student services: personal/psychological counseling.

COSTS & FINANCIAL AID

Costs (2019–20) ***Comprehensive fee:*** $38,070 includes full-time tuition ($28,860), mandatory fees ($1070), and room and board ($8140). Part-time tuition: $665 per credit hour. ***Room and board:*** Room and board charges vary according to board plan and housing facility. ***Payment plan:*** installment. ***Waivers:*** employees or children of employees.

Financial Aid Of all full-time matriculated undergraduates who enrolled in 2018, 629 applied for aid, 582 were judged to have need, 74 had their need fully met. In 2018, 70 non-need-based awards were made. ***Average percent of need met:*** 67. ***Average financial aid package:*** $22,134. ***Average need-based loan:*** $5255. ***Average need-based gift aid:*** $18,217. ***Average non-need-based aid:*** $13,786. ***Average indebtedness upon graduation:*** $27,409.

APPLYING

Standardized Tests *Required:* SAT or ACT (for admission). *Recommended:* ACT (for admission).

Options: electronic application.

Application fee: $25.

Required: high school transcript, minimum 2.5 GPA.

Application deadlines: rolling (freshmen), rolling (transfers).

Notification: continuous (freshmen), continuous (transfers).

CONTACT

Mr. John Shultz, Vice President of Admissions and Marketing, University of Saint Mary, 4100 South 4th Street, Leavenworth, KS 66048. *Phone:* 913-758-6329. *Toll-free phone:* 800-752-7043. *E-mail:* admiss@stmary.edu.

Washburn University

Topeka, Kansas

http://www.washburn.edu/

- **City-supported** comprehensive, founded 1865
- **Urban** 160-acre campus with easy access to Kansas City
- **Endowment** $172.4 million
- **Coed**
- **Noncompetitive** entrance level

FACULTY

Student/faculty ratio: 14:1.

ACADEMICS

Calendar: semesters. *Degrees:* certificates, associate, bachelor's, master's, doctoral, post-master's, and postbachelor's certificates.

Library: Mabee Library plus 1 other. *Books:* 441,448 (physical), 292,840 (digital/electronic); *Serial titles:* 93,914 (physical); *Databases:* 182. Weekly public service hours: 104; students can reserve study rooms.

STUDENT LIFE

Housing options: coed. Campus housing is university owned.

Activities and organizations: drama/theater group, student-run newspaper, television station, choral group, marching band, national fraternities, national sororities.

Athletics Member NCAA. All Division II.

Campus security: 24-hour emergency response devices and patrols, student patrols, late-night transport/escort service.

Student services: health clinic, personal/psychological counseling, legal services.

FINANCIAL AID

Financial Aid Of all full-time matriculated undergraduates who enrolled in 2016, 3,366 applied for aid, 2,314 were judged to have need, 286 had their need fully met. In 2016, 521 non-need-based awards were made. ***Average percent of need met:*** 37. ***Average financial aid package:*** $9580. ***Average need-based loan:*** $4128. ***Average need-based gift aid:*** $5140. ***Average non-need-based aid:*** $3331. ***Average indebtedness upon graduation:*** $23,552.

APPLYING

Standardized Tests *Required:* ACT (for admission).

Options: electronic application.

Application fee: $20.

Required: high school transcript.

CONTACT

Ms. Kris Klima, Director of Admissions, Washburn University, 1700 SW College, MO 114, Topeka, KS 66621. *Phone:* 785-670-1030. *Toll-free phone:* 800-332-0291. *Fax:* 785-670-1113. *E-mail:* admissions@washburn.edu.

Wichita State University

Wichita, Kansas

http://www.wichita.edu/

- **State-supported** university, founded 1895, part of Kansas Board of Regents
- **Urban** 335-acre campus
- **Endowment** $368.8 million
- **Coed** 13,217 undergraduate students, 68% full-time, 55% women, 45% men
- **Minimally difficult** entrance level, 56% of applicants were admitted

UNDERGRAD STUDENTS

8,994 full-time, 4,223 part-time. Students come from 49 states and territories; 112 other countries; 12% are from out of state; 6% Black or African American, non-Hispanic/Latino; 13% Hispanic/Latino; 7% Asian, non-Hispanic/Latino; 0.1% Native Hawaiian or other Pacific Islander, non-Hispanic/Latino; 0.6% American Indian or Alaska Native, non-Hispanic/Latino; 5% Two or more races, non-Hispanic/Latino; 2% Race/ethnicity unknown; 6% international; 9% transferred in; 13% live on campus.

Freshmen:
Admission: 5,947 applied, 3,342 admitted, 1,655 enrolled. ***Average high school GPA:*** 3.5. ***Test scores:*** SAT evidence-based reading and writing scores over 500: 82%; SAT math scores over 500: 84%; ACT scores over 18: 91%; SAT evidence-based reading and writing scores over 600: 40%; SAT math scores over 600: 42%; ACT scores over 24: 48%; SAT evidence-based reading and writing scores over 700: 8%; SAT math scores over 700: 10%; ACT scores over 30: 11%.

Retention: 71% of full-time freshmen returned.

FACULTY
Total: 826, 67% full-time, 56% with terminal degrees.
Student/faculty ratio: 19:1.

ACADEMICS
Calendar: semesters. *Degrees:* certificates, associate, bachelor's, master's, doctoral, post-master's, and postbachelor's certificates.

Special study options: academic remediation for entering students, accelerated degree program, adult/continuing education programs, advanced placement credit, cooperative education, distance learning, double majors, English as a second language, external degree program, freshman honors college, honors programs, independent study, internships, off-campus study, part-time degree program, services for LD students, study abroad, summer session for credit. ***ROTC:*** Army (b).

Computers: 1,500 computers/terminals are available on campus for general student use. Students can access the following: computer help desk, free student e-mail accounts, online (class) grades, online (class) registration, online (class) schedules, learning management system. Campuswide network is available. 100% of college-owned or -operated housing units are wired for high-speed Internet access. Wireless service is available via entire campus.

Library: Ablah Library plus 2 others. *Books:* 188,268 (physical), 763,530 (digital/electronic); *Serial titles:* 31,502 (physical), 270,605 (digital/electronic); *Databases:* 366. Study areas open 24 hours, 5–7 days a week; students can reserve study rooms.

STUDENT LIFE
Housing options: on-campus residence required for freshman year; coed, special housing for students with disabilities. Campus housing is university owned. Freshman campus housing is guaranteed.

Activities and organizations: drama/theater group, student-run newspaper, radio station, choral group, marching band, national fraternities, national sororities.

Athletics Member NCAA. All Division I. ***Intercollegiate sports:*** baseball M(s), basketball M(s)/W(s), bowling M(s)/W(s), cheerleading M(s)/W(s), cross-country running M(s)/W(s), golf M(s)/W(s), softball W(s), tennis M(s)/W(s), track and field M(s)/W(s), volleyball W(s). ***Intramural sports:*** basketball M/W, bowling M/W, crew M/W, golf M/W, rowing M/W, softball W, tennis M/W, track and field M/W, volleyball W.

Campus security: 24-hour emergency response devices and patrols, student patrols, late-night transport/escort service, controlled dormitory access, bicycle patrols by campus security.

Student services: health clinic, personal/psychological counseling, women's center, veterans affairs office.

COSTS & FINANCIAL AID
Costs (2019–20) ***Tuition:*** state resident $6708 full-time, $224 per credit hour part-time; nonresident $15,890 full-time, $530 per credit hour part-time. Full-time tuition and fees vary according to course level, course load, degree level, and program. Part-time tuition and fees vary according to course level, course load, degree level, and program. ***Required fees:*** $1591 full-time, $8 part-time, $453 part-time. ***Room and board:*** $12,620. Room and board charges vary according to board plan and housing facility. ***Payment plan:*** installment. ***Waivers:*** senior citizens and employees or children of employees.

Financial Aid Of all full-time matriculated undergraduates who enrolled in 2018, 6,583 applied for aid, 5,364 were judged to have need, 905 had their need fully met. 135 Federal Work-Study jobs (averaging $2512). 84 state and other part-time jobs (averaging $1227). In 2018, 1429 non-need-based awards were made. ***Average percent of need met:*** 64. ***Average financial aid package:*** $8155. ***Average need-based loan:*** $2156. ***Average need-based gift aid:*** $5299. ***Average non-need-based aid:*** $1273. ***Average indebtedness upon graduation:*** $24,839.

APPLYING
Standardized Tests *Required for some:* SAT (for admission), ACT (for admission), SAT or ACT (for admission), SAT and SAT Subject Tests or ACT (for admission), SAT Subject Tests (for admission). *Recommended:* SAT (for admission), ACT (for admission), SAT or ACT (for admission), SAT and SAT Subject Tests or ACT (for admission), SAT Subject Tests (for admission).

Options: electronic application, deferred entrance.

Application fee: $30.

Required: high school transcript. ***Required for some:*** minimum 2.5 GPA, rank in upper one-third of high school class or complete the pre-college curriculum with a minimum 2.0 GPA (2.5 GPA for nonresidents).

Application deadlines: rolling (freshmen), rolling (out-of-state freshmen), rolling (transfers).

Notification: continuous (freshmen), continuous (out-of-state freshmen), continuous (transfers).

CONTACT
Wichita State University, 1845 North Fairmount, Wichita, KS 67260. *Phone:* 316-978-3085. *Toll-free phone:* 800-362-2594.

KENTUCKY

Alice Lloyd College
Pippa Passes, Kentucky
http://www.alc.edu/

CONTACT
Mr. J. D. Cornett, Director of Admissions, Alice Lloyd College, 100 Purpose Road, Pippa Passes, KY 41844. *Phone:* 606-368-6134. *Toll-free phone:* 888-280-4252. *Fax:* 606-368-6038. *E-mail:* jdcornett@alc.edu.

American National University - Louisville
Louisville, Kentucky
http://www.an.edu/

- **Proprietary** primarily 2-year, founded 1990, part of National College of Business and Technology
- **Coed**
- **Noncompetitive** entrance level

FACULTY
Student/faculty ratio: 7:1.

ACADEMICS
Calendar: quarters. *Degrees:* diplomas, associate, and bachelor's.

STUDENT LIFE
Housing options: college housing not available.

FINANCIAL AID
Financial Aid Of all full-time matriculated undergraduates who enrolled in 2018, 2 Federal Work-Study jobs.

APPLYING
Options: electronic application.

Required for some: high school transcript. ***Recommended:*** interview.

CONTACT
Vincent C. Tinebra, Campus Director, American National University - Louisville, 4205 Dixie Highway, Louisville, KY 40216. *Phone:* 502-447-7634. *Toll-free phone:* 888-9-JOBREADY.

Asbury University
Wilmore, Kentucky
http://www.asbury.edu/

CONTACT
Mr. Brandon Combs, Director of Undergraduate Admissions, Asbury University, One Macklem Drive, Wilmore, KY 40390. *Phone:* 800-888-1818. *Toll-free phone:* 800-888-1818. *E-mail:* admissions@asbury.edu.

Beckfield College

Florence, Kentucky

http://www.beckfield.edu/

CONTACT

Mrs. Leah Boerger, Director of Admissions, Beckfield College, 16 Spiral Drive, Florence, KY 41042. *Phone:* 859-371-9393. *E-mail:* lboerger@beckfield.edu.

Bellarmine University

Louisville, Kentucky

http://www.bellarmine.edu/

- **Independent Roman Catholic** comprehensive, founded 1950
- **Suburban** 175-acre campus with easy access to Louisville
- **Endowment** $66.9 million
- **Coed**
- **Moderately difficult** entrance level

FACULTY

Student/faculty ratio: 12:1.

ACADEMICS

Calendar: semesters. *Degrees:* certificates, bachelor's, master's, doctoral, and postbachelor's certificates.

Library: W. L. Lyons Brown Library. *Books:* 130,534 (physical), 288,828 (digital/electronic); *Serial titles:* 189 (physical), 88,144 (digital/electronic); *Databases:* 145. Weekly public service hours: 140; study areas open 24 hours, 5–7 days a week.

STUDENT LIFE

Housing options: on-campus residence required through junior year; coed, men-only, women-only, special housing for students with disabilities. Campus housing is university owned. Freshman campus housing is guaranteed.

Activities and organizations: drama/theater group, student-run newspaper, radio station, choral group, Student Government, Bellarmine Activities Council, Knights Nation, Fellowship of Christian Athletes, Delta Sigma Pi, national fraternities, national sororities.

Athletics Member NCAA. All Division II except lacrosse (Division I).

Campus security: 24-hour emergency response devices and patrols, student patrols, late-night transport/escort service, controlled dormitory access, 24-hour locked residence hall entrances, security cameras.

Student services: health clinic, personal/psychological counseling, veterans affairs office.

COSTS & FINANCIAL AID

Costs (2019–20) ***One-time required fee:*** $400. ***Comprehensive fee:*** $51,850 includes full-time tuition ($40,880), mandatory fees ($1550), and room and board ($9420). Part-time tuition: $950 per credit hour. ***College room only:*** $4800.

Financial Aid Of all full-time matriculated undergraduates who enrolled in 2019, 2,162 applied for aid, 1,888 were judged to have need, 529 had their need fully met. In 2019, 466 non-need-based awards were made. ***Average percent of need met:*** 80. ***Average financial aid package:*** $34,671. ***Average need-based loan:*** $4165. ***Average need-based gift aid:*** $26,705. ***Average non-need-based aid:*** $25,373. ***Average indebtedness upon graduation:*** $30,850.

APPLYING

Standardized Tests *Required:* SAT or ACT (for admission).

Options: electronic application, early admission, early action, deferred entrance.

Application fee: $25.

Required: high school transcript, minimum 2.5 GPA, 1 letter of recommendation. ***Required for some:*** essay or personal statement. ***Recommended:*** interview.

CONTACT

Mr. Timothy A. Sturgeon, Dean of Admission, Bellarmine University, 2001 Newburg Road, Louisville, KY 40205-0671. *Phone:* 502-272-8131. *Toll-free phone:* 800-274-4723 Ext. 8131. *E-mail:* admissions@bellarmine.edu.

Berea College

Berea, Kentucky

http://www.berea.edu/

- **Independent** 4-year, founded 1855
- **Small-town** 140-acre campus
- **Endowment** $1.2 billion
- **Coed** 1,688 undergraduate students, 98% full-time, 58% women, 42% men
- **Moderately difficult** entrance level, 30% of applicants were admitted

UNDERGRAD STUDENTS

1,652 full-time, 36 part-time. Students come from 43 states and territories; 76 other countries; 47% are from out of state; 17% Black or African American, non-Hispanic/Latino; 13% Hispanic/Latino; 3% Asian, non-Hispanic/Latino; 0.1% Native Hawaiian or other Pacific Islander, non-Hispanic/Latino; 8% Two or more races, non-Hispanic/Latino; 0.2% Race/ethnicity unknown; 8% international; 3% transferred in; 99% live on campus.

Freshmen:

Admission: 1,965 applied, 595 admitted, 413 enrolled. ***Average high school GPA:*** 3.6. ***Test scores:*** SAT evidence-based reading and writing scores over 500: 98%; SAT math scores over 500: 97%; ACT scores over 18: 100%; SAT evidence-based reading and writing scores over 600: 52%; SAT math scores over 600: 39%; ACT scores over 24: 65%; SAT evidence-based reading and writing scores over 700: 10%; SAT math scores over 700: 10%; ACT scores over 30: 12%.

Retention: 84% of full-time freshmen returned.

FACULTY

Total: 189, 74% full-time, 82% with terminal degrees.

Student/faculty ratio: 10:1.

ACADEMICS

Calendar: semesters. *Degree:* bachelor's.

Special study options: academic remediation for entering students, advanced placement credit, double majors, English as a second language, honors programs, independent study, internships, off-campus study, services for LD students, student-designed majors, study abroad, summer session for credit.

Unusual degree programs: 3-2 engineering with University of Kentucky.

Computers: 7,000 ports are available on campus for general student use. Students can access the following: campus intranet, computer help desk, free student e-mail accounts, online (class) grades, online (class) registration, online (class) schedules. Campuswide network is available. 100% of college-owned or -operated housing units are wired for high-speed Internet access. Wireless service is available via entire campus.

Library: Hutchins Library plus 1 other. *Books:* 343,041 (physical), 245,353 (digital/electronic); *Serial titles:* 99,400 (physical), 30,731 (digital/electronic). Weekly public service hours: 94; students can reserve study rooms.

STUDENT LIFE

Housing options: on-campus residence required through senior year; men-only, women-only. Campus housing is university owned. Freshman campus housing is guaranteed.

Activities and organizations: drama/theater group, student-run newspaper, choral group, Campus Activities Board, Cosmopolitan Club, CELTS (Center for Excellence in Learning through Service), Black Cultural Center, African Student Association.

Athletics Member NCAA. All Division III. ***Intercollegiate sports:*** baseball M, basketball M/W, cross-country running M/W, golf M, soccer M/W, softball W, tennis M/W, track and field M/W, volleyball W. ***Intramural sports:*** basketball M/W, football M/W, racquetball M/W, soccer M/W, softball M/W, ultimate Frisbee M/W, volleyball M/W.

Campus security: 24-hour emergency response devices and patrols, late-night transport/escort service, controlled dormitory access.

Student services: health clinic, personal/psychological counseling, women's center.

COSTS & FINANCIAL AID

Costs (2020–21) ***Tuition:*** Financial aid is provided to all students for tuition costs.

Financial Aid Of all full-time matriculated undergraduates who enrolled in 2018, 1,626 applied for aid, 1,626 were judged to have need, 16 had their need fully met. ***Average percent of need met:*** 94. ***Average financial aid package:*** $46,997. ***Average need-based loan:*** $1349. ***Average need-based gift aid:*** $44,650. ***Average indebtedness upon graduation:*** $5517. ***Financial aid deadline:*** 5/1.

APPLYING

Standardized Tests *Required:* SAT or ACT (for admission).

Options: electronic application.

Required: essay or personal statement, high school transcript. ***Recommended:*** 2 letters of recommendation, interview.

Application deadlines: 3/31 (freshmen), 3/31 (out-of-state freshmen), 3/31 (transfers).

Notification: continuous until 11/1 (freshmen), continuous until 11/1 (out-of-state freshmen), continuous until 4/15 (transfers).

CONTACT

Mr. Luke Hodson, Director of Admissions, Berea College, CPO 2220, Berea, KY 40404. *Phone:* 859-985-3500. *Toll-free phone:* 800-326-5948. *Fax:* 859-985-3512. *E-mail:* admissions@berea.edu.

Brescia University

Owensboro, Kentucky

http://www.brescia.edu/

CONTACT

Brescia University, 717 Frederica Street, Owensboro, KY 42301-3023. *Phone:* 270-686-4241 Ext. 241. *Toll-free phone:* 877-273-7242.

Campbellsville University

Campbellsville, Kentucky

http://www.campbellsville.edu/

- **Independent** comprehensive, founded 1906, affiliated with Kentucky Baptist Convention
- **Small-town** 90-acre campus
- **Endowment** $21.0 million
- **Coed** 6,083 undergraduate students, 41% full-time, 61% women, 39% men
- **Moderately difficult** entrance level, 70% of applicants were admitted

UNDERGRAD STUDENTS

2,481 full-time, 3,602 part-time. Students come from 44 states and territories; 54 other countries; 15% are from out of state; 15% Black or African American, non-Hispanic/Latino; 4% Hispanic/Latino; 0.8% Asian, non-Hispanic/Latino; 0.1% Native Hawaiian or other Pacific Islander, non-Hispanic/Latino; 0.3% American Indian or Alaska Native, non-Hispanic/Latino; 2% Two or more races, non-Hispanic/Latino; 3% Race/ethnicity unknown; 7% international; 5% transferred in; 58% live on campus.

Freshmen:

Admission: 4,146 applied, 2,905 admitted, 662 enrolled. ***Average high school GPA:*** 3.2. ***Test scores:*** SAT evidence-based reading and writing scores over 500: 57%; SAT math scores over 500: 65%; ACT scores over 18: 78%; SAT evidence-based reading and writing scores over 600: 11%; SAT math scores over 600: 20%; ACT scores over 24: 25%; ACT scores over 30: 4%.

Retention: 68% of full-time freshmen returned.

FACULTY

Total: 588, 35% full-time, 29% with terminal degrees.

Student/faculty ratio: 14:1.

ACADEMICS

Calendar: semesters. *Degrees:* certificates, associate, bachelor's, master's, doctoral, post-master's, and postbachelor's certificates.

Special study options: academic remediation for entering students, accelerated degree program, adult/continuing education programs, advanced placement credit, cooperative education, distance learning, double majors, English as a second language, honors programs, independent study, internships, off-campus study, part-time degree program, services for LD students, study abroad, summer session for credit. ***ROTC:*** Army (c).

Computers: 250 computers/terminals are available on campus for general student use. Students can access the following: campus intranet, computer help desk, free student e-mail accounts, online (class) grades, online (class) registration, online (class) schedules. Campuswide network is available. 100% of college-owned or -operated housing units are wired for high-speed Internet access. Wireless service is available via entire campus.

Library: Montgomery Library. *Books:* 128,057 (physical), 1.3 million (digital/electronic); *Serial titles:* 178,330 (digital/electronic); *Databases:* 150. Weekly public service hours: 77; students can reserve study rooms.

STUDENT LIFE

Housing options: on-campus residence required through sophomore year; men-only, women-only. Campus housing is university owned. Freshman campus housing is guaranteed.

Activities and organizations: drama/theater group, student-run newspaper, radio and television station, choral group, marching band, Baptist Campus Ministries, Student Government Association, International Student Association, Black Student Association, KANS (Nursing Society).

Athletics Member NAIA, NCCAA. ***Intercollegiate sports:*** archery M(s)/W(s), baseball M(s), basketball M(s)/W(s), bowling M(s)/W(s), cheerleading M(s)/W(s), cross-country running M(s)/W(s), football M(s), golf M(s)/W(s), soccer M(s)/W(s), softball W(s), swimming and diving M(s)/W(s), tennis M(s)/W(s), track and field M(s)/W(s), volleyball M(s)/W(s), wrestling M(s)/W(s). ***Intramural sports:*** basketball M/W, football M/W, sand volleyball M/W, soccer M/W, softball M/W, table tennis M/W, tennis M/W, ultimate Frisbee M/W, volleyball M/W.

Campus security: 24-hour emergency response devices and patrols, student patrols, late-night transport/escort service, controlled dormitory access.

Student services: health clinic, personal/psychological counseling.

COSTS & FINANCIAL AID

Costs (2020–21) ***Comprehensive fee:*** $33,400 includes full-time tuition ($24,900), mandatory fees ($500), and room and board ($8000). Full-time tuition and fees vary according to location. Part-time tuition: $1038 per credit hour. Part-time tuition and fees vary according to course load and location. ***Required fees:*** $250 per year part-time. ***Room and board:*** Room and board charges vary according to board plan, housing facility, and location. ***Payment plan:*** installment. ***Waivers:*** senior citizens and employees or children of employees.

Financial Aid Of all full-time matriculated undergraduates who enrolled in 2018, 1,929 applied for aid, 1,816 were judged to have need, 228 had their need fully met. In 2018, 148 non-need-based awards were made. ***Average percent of need met:*** 70. ***Average financial aid package:*** $20,458. ***Average need-based loan:*** $3636. ***Average need-based gift aid:*** $18,022. ***Average non-need-based aid:*** $11,408. ***Average indebtedness upon graduation:*** $20,439.

APPLYING

Standardized Tests *Recommended:* SAT or ACT (for admission).

Options: electronic application, deferred entrance.

Required: high school transcript, minimum 2.0 GPA. ***Recommended:*** essay or personal statement, minimum 3.0 GPA, interview.

Application deadlines: rolling (freshmen), rolling (transfers).

Notification: continuous (freshmen), continuous (transfers).

CONTACT

Mrs. Laura Day, Assistant Director of On-Campus Enrollment, Campbellsville University, 1 University Drive, UPO 782, Campbellsville, KY 42718-2799. *Phone:* 270-789-5526. *Toll-free phone:* 800-264-6014. *Fax:* 270-789-5071. *E-mail:* admissions@campbellsville.edu.

Centre College

Danville, Kentucky

http://www.centre.edu/

- **Independent** 4-year, founded 1819, affiliated with Presbyterian Church (U.S.A.)
- **Small-town** 160-acre campus
- **Endowment** $269.4 million
- **Coed** 1,411 undergraduate students, 100% full-time, 52% women, 48% men
- **Very difficult** entrance level, 76% of applicants were admitted

UNDERGRAD STUDENTS

1,410 full-time, 1 part-time. 43% are from out of state; 5% Black or African American, non-Hispanic/Latino; 6% Hispanic/Latino; 4% Asian, non-Hispanic/Latino; 0.1% Native Hawaiian or other Pacific Islander, non-Hispanic/Latino; 0.2% American Indian or Alaska Native, non-Hispanic/Latino; 4% Two or more races, non-Hispanic/Latino; 1% Race/ethnicity unknown; 6% international; 99% live on campus.

Freshmen:

Admission: 2,211 applied, 1,690 admitted, 355 enrolled. ***Average high school GPA:*** 3.6. ***Test scores:*** SAT evidence-based reading and writing scores over 500: 95%; SAT math scores over 500: 93%; ACT scores over 18: 100%; SAT evidence-based reading and writing scores over 600: 57%; SAT math scores over 600: 66%; ACT scores over 24: 91%; SAT evidence-based reading and writing scores over 700: 11%; SAT math scores over 700: 32%; ACT scores over 30: 48%.

Retention: 90% of full-time freshmen returned.

FACULTY

Total: 150, 88% full-time, 92% with terminal degrees.

Student/faculty ratio: 10:1.

ACADEMICS

Calendar: 4-1-4. *Degree:* bachelor's.

Special study options: advanced placement credit, double majors, honors programs, independent study, internships, off-campus study, services for LD students, student-designed majors, study abroad. ***ROTC:*** Army (b), Air Force (c).

Unusual degree programs: 3-2 engineering with Washington University in St. Louis, Vanderbilt University, University of Kentucky.

Computers: 425 computers/terminals and 1,500 ports are available on campus for general student use. Students can access the following: campus intranet, computer help desk, free student e-mail accounts, online (class) grades, online (class) registration, online (class) schedules. Campuswide network is available. 100% of college-owned or -operated housing units are wired for high-speed Internet access. Wireless service is available via entire campus.

Library: Doherty Library. *Books:* 231,820 (physical), 33,042 (digital/electronic); *Serial titles:* 536 (physical), 27,570 (digital/electronic); *Databases:* 530. Weekly public service hours: 113; study areas open 24 hours, 5–7 days a week; students can reserve study rooms.

STUDENT LIFE

Housing options: on-campus residence required through senior year; coed, men-only, women-only, special housing for students with disabilities. Campus housing is university owned. Freshman campus housing is guaranteed.

Activities and organizations: drama/theater group, student-run newspaper, choral group, Student Government Association, Centre Action Reaches Everyone, Student Activities Council, Christian fellowship group, Diversity Student Union, national fraternities, national sororities.

Athletics Member NCAA. All Division III. ***Intercollegiate sports:*** baseball M, basketball M/W, cheerleading W, cross-country running M/W, field hockey W, football M, golf M/W, lacrosse M/W, soccer M/W, softball W, swimming and diving M/W, tennis M/W, track and field M/W, volleyball W. ***Intramural sports:*** basketball M/W, football M/W, golf M/W, soccer M/W, softball M/W, tennis M/W, volleyball M/W.

Campus security: 24-hour emergency response devices and patrols, late-night transport/escort service, controlled dormitory access.

Student services: health clinic, personal/psychological counseling.

COSTS & FINANCIAL AID

Costs (2020–21) ***Comprehensive fee:*** $53,740 includes full-time tuition ($43,000) and room and board ($10,740). Part-time tuition: $1536 per credit hour. ***College room only:*** $5370.

Financial Aid Of all full-time matriculated undergraduates who enrolled in 2019, 1,010 applied for aid, 814 were judged to have need, 259 had their need fully met. In 2019, 553 non-need-based awards were made. ***Average percent of need met:*** 87. ***Average financial aid package:*** $36,841. ***Average need-based loan:*** $4495. ***Average need-based gift aid:*** $33,652. ***Average non-need-based aid:*** $26,542. ***Average indebtedness upon graduation:*** $27,418. ***Financial aid deadline:*** 1/31.

APPLYING

Standardized Tests *Required:* SAT or ACT (for admission).

Options: electronic application, early admission, early decision, early action, deferred entrance.

Required: essay or personal statement, high school transcript, 1 letter of recommendation. ***Recommended:*** interview.

Application deadlines: 1/15 (freshmen), rolling (transfers), 12/1 (early action).

Early decision deadline: 11/15.

Notification: 3/31 (freshmen), 12/15 (early decision), 1/15 (early action).

CONTACT

Mr. Bob Nesmith, Dean of Admission and Student Financial Aid, Centre College, 600 West Walnut Street, Danville, KY 40422-1394. *Phone:* 859-238-5350. *Toll-free phone:* 800-423-6236. *Fax:* 859-238-5373. *E-mail:* admission@centre.edu.

Clear Creek Baptist Bible College

Pineville, Kentucky

http://www.ccbbc.edu/

CONTACT

Mr. Billy Howell, Director of Admissions, Clear Creek Baptist Bible College, 300 Clear Creek Road, Pineville, KY 40977. *Phone:* 606-337-3196 Ext. 103. *Fax:* 606-337-1631. *E-mail:* bhowell@ccbbc.edu.

Eastern Kentucky University

Richmond, Kentucky

http://www.eku.edu/

- **State-supported** comprehensive, founded 1906
- **Small-town** 500-acre campus with easy access to Lexington
- **Endowment** $60.2 million
- **Coed** 12,662 undergraduate students, 78% full-time, 57% women, 43% men
- **Minimally difficult** entrance level, 94% of applicants were admitted

UNDERGRAD STUDENTS

9,908 full-time, 2,754 part-time. 15% are from out of state; 6% Black or African American, non-Hispanic/Latino; 4% Hispanic/Latino; 0.9% Asian, non-Hispanic/Latino; 0.1% Native Hawaiian or other Pacific Islander, non-Hispanic/Latino; 0.2% American Indian or Alaska Native, non-Hispanic/Latino; 3% Two or more races, non-Hispanic/Latino; 1% Race/ethnicity unknown; 1% international; 6% transferred in; 36% live on campus.

Freshmen:

Admission: 8,969 applied, 8,419 admitted, 2,345 enrolled. ***Average high school GPA:*** 3.4. ***Test scores:*** SAT evidence-based reading and writing scores over 500: 72%; SAT math scores over 500: 75%; ACT scores over 18: 89%; SAT evidence-based reading and writing scores over 600: 24%; SAT math scores over 600: 17%; ACT scores over 24: 41%; SAT evidence-based reading and writing scores over 700: 4%; SAT math scores over 700: 2%; ACT scores over 30: 6%.

Retention: 75% of full-time freshmen returned.

FACULTY

Total: 1,054, 56% full-time, 51% with terminal degrees.

Student/faculty ratio: 15:1.

ACADEMICS

Calendar: semesters. *Degrees:* certificates, associate, bachelor's, master's, doctoral, post-master's, and postbachelor's certificates.

Special study options: academic remediation for entering students, adult/continuing education programs, advanced placement credit, cooperative education, distance learning, double majors, English as a second language, external degree program, honors programs, independent study, internships, part-time degree program, services for LD students, student-designed majors, study abroad, summer session for credit. ***ROTC:*** Army (b), Air Force (c).

Unusual degree programs: 3-2 engineering with University of Kentucky, Auburn University.

Computers: 1,800 computers/terminals and 2,000 ports are available on campus for general student use. Students can access the following: campus intranet, computer help desk, free student e-mail accounts, online (class) grades, online (class) registration, online (class) schedules. Campuswide network is available. 90% of college-owned or -operated housing units are wired for high-speed Internet access. Wireless service is available via entire campus.
Library: John Grant Crabbe Library plus 2 others.

STUDENT LIFE

Housing options: on-campus residence required through sophomore yearCampus housing is university owned. Freshman campus housing is guaranteed.

Activities and organizations: drama/theater group, student-run newspaper, radio station, choral group, marching band, Honor Society, Regular Society, national fraternities, national sororities.

Athletics Member NCAA. All Division I. ***Intercollegiate sports:*** baseball M(s), basketball M(s)/W(s), cheerleading M/W, cross-country running M(s)/W(s), football M(s), golf M(s)/W(s), softball W(s), tennis M(s)/W(s), track and field M(s)/W(s), volleyball W(s). ***Intramural sports:*** archery M(c)/W(c), baseball M(c), basketball M/W, bowling M/W, equestrian sports W(c), fencing M(c)/W(c), football M/W, golf M/W, ice hockey M(c), lacrosse M(c), racquetball M/W, riflery M(c)/W(c), rock climbing M(c)/W(c), rugby M(c)/W(c), soccer M(c)/W(c), softball M/W, table tennis M/W, tennis M/W, track and field M/W, ultimate Frisbee M/W, volleyball M/W, water polo M/W, weight lifting M/W.

Campus security: 24-hour emergency response devices and patrols, student patrols, late-night transport/escort service, controlled dormitory access.

Student services: health clinic, personal/psychological counseling, veterans affairs office.

COSTS & FINANCIAL AID

Costs (2020–21) ***Tuition:*** area resident $9266 full-time, $386 per credit hour part-time; state resident $9266 full-time; nonresident $10,173 full-time, $806 per credit hour part-time. ***Required fees:*** $540 full-time. ***Room and board:*** $10,173.

Financial Aid Of all full-time matriculated undergraduates who enrolled in 2019, 8,314 applied for aid, 7,054 were judged to have need, 1,915 had their need fully met. In 2019, 1504 non-need-based awards were made. ***Average percent of need met:*** 76. ***Average financial aid package:*** $12,422. ***Average need-based loan:*** $3974. ***Average need-based gift aid:*** $6427. ***Average non-need-based aid:*** $5968. ***Average indebtedness upon graduation:*** $27,465.

APPLYING

Standardized Tests *Required:* SAT or ACT (for admission).

Options: electronic application, deferred entrance.

Application fee: $35.

Required: high school transcript, minimum 2.0 GPA. ***Recommended:*** minimum 2.5 GPA.

Application deadlines: 8/1 (freshmen), 8/1 (transfers).

Notification: continuous (freshmen), continuous (out-of-state freshmen), continuous (transfers).

CONTACT

Ms. Stephanie Leigh Whaley, Director of Admissions, Eastern Kentucky University, SSB CPO 54, 521 Lancaster Avenue, Richmond, KY 40475-3102. *Phone:* 859-622-2106. *Toll-free phone:* 800-465-9191. *Fax:* 859-622-8024. *E-mail:* admissions@eku.edu.

Galen College of Nursing

Louisville, Kentucky

http://www.galencollege.edu/

CONTACT

Galen College of Nursing, 1031 Zorn Avenue, Suite 400, Louisville, KY 40207. *Toll-free phone:* 877-223-7040.

Georgetown College

Georgetown, Kentucky

http://www.georgetowncollege.edu/

- **Independent** comprehensive, founded 1829, affiliated with Baptist Church
- **Suburban** 104-acre campus with easy access to Cincinnati, OH; Louisville, KY
- **Endowment** $40.8 million
- **Coed** 983 undergraduate students, 95% full-time, 55% women, 45% men
- **Moderately difficult** entrance level, 63% of applicants were admitted

UNDERGRAD STUDENTS

932 full-time, 51 part-time. Students come from 31 states and territories; 10 other countries; 27% are from out of state; 10% Black or African American, non-Hispanic/Latino; 5% Hispanic/Latino; 0.5% Asian, non-Hispanic/Latino; 0.1% American Indian or Alaska Native, non-Hispanic/Latino; 5% Two or more races, non-Hispanic/Latino; 3% Race/ethnicity unknown; 2% international; 4% transferred in; 93% live on campus.

Freshmen:

Admission: 2,791 applied, 1,768 admitted, 314 enrolled. ***Average high school GPA:*** 3.6. ***Test scores:*** SAT evidence-based reading and writing scores over 500: 90%; SAT math scores over 500: 83%; ACT scores over 18: 95%; SAT evidence-based reading and writing scores over 600: 40%; SAT math scores over 600: 48%; ACT scores over 24: 48%; SAT evidence-based reading and writing scores over 700: 3%; SAT math scores over 700: 10%; ACT scores over 30: 9%.

Retention: 71% of full-time freshmen returned.

FACULTY

Total: 156, 53% full-time.

Student/faculty ratio: 11:1.

ACADEMICS

Calendar: semesters. *Degrees:* bachelor's and master's.

Special study options: advanced placement credit, cooperative education, distance learning, double majors, honors programs, independent study, internships, part-time degree program, services for LD students, student-designed majors, study abroad, summer session for credit. ***ROTC:*** Army (c), Air Force (c).

Unusual degree programs: 3-2 engineering with University of Kentucky; nursing with University of Kentucky.

Computers: 120 computers/terminals and 2,000 ports are available on campus for general student use. Students can access the following: campus intranet, computer help desk, free student e-mail accounts, online (class) grades, online (class) registration, online (class) schedules, Library apps for smartphones. Campuswide network is available. 100% of college-owned or -operated housing units are wired for high-speed Internet access. Wireless service is available via entire campus.
Library: Anna Ashcraft Ensor Learning Resource Center. *Books:* 127,775 (physical), 516,956 (digital/electronic); *Serial titles:* 15 (physical), 41,980 (digital/electronic); *Databases:* 134. Weekly public service hours: 92; students can reserve study rooms.

STUDENT LIFE

Housing options: on-campus residence required through senior year; men-only, women-only. Campus housing is university owned. Freshman campus housing is guaranteed.

Activities and organizations: drama/theater group, student-run newspaper, radio station, choral group, national fraternities, national sororities.

Athletics Member NAIA. ***Intercollegiate sports:*** archery M(c)/W(c), baseball M(s), basketball M(s)/W(s), cheerleading M(s)/W(s), cross-country running M(s)/W(s), football M(s), golf M(s)/W(s), gymnastics

W(s), lacrosse W(s), soccer M(s)/W(s), softball W(s), tennis M(s)/W(s), track and field M(s)/W(s), volleyball W(s). ***Intramural sports:*** basketball M/W, football M/W, racquetball M/W, soccer M/W, softball M/W, table tennis M/W, tennis M/W, ultimate Frisbee M/W, volleyball M/W, water polo M/W.

Campus security: 24-hour emergency response devices and patrols, late-night transport/escort service, controlled dormitory access.

Student services: health clinic, personal/psychological counseling.

COSTS & FINANCIAL AID

Costs (2020–21) ***Comprehensive fee:*** $51,470 includes full-time tuition ($39,810), mandatory fees ($990), and room and board ($10,670). Full-time tuition and fees vary according to course load and reciprocity agreements. Part-time tuition: $1230 per credit hour. Part-time tuition and fees vary according to course load and reciprocity agreements. ***College room only:*** $5145. Room and board charges vary according to board plan and housing facility. ***Payment plan:*** installment. ***Waivers:*** employees or children of employees.

Financial Aid Of all full-time matriculated undergraduates who enrolled in 2019, 850 applied for aid, 800 were judged to have need, 263 had their need fully met. In 2019, 50 non-need-based awards were made. ***Average percent of need met:*** 86. ***Average financial aid package:*** $36,964. ***Average need-based loan:*** $2734. ***Average need-based gift aid:*** $22,557. ***Average non-need-based aid:*** $18,431. ***Average indebtedness upon graduation:*** $34,766.

APPLYING

Standardized Tests *Required:* SAT or ACT (for admission).

Options: electronic application, deferred entrance.

Required: high school transcript, minimum 2.0 GPA. ***Required for some:*** essay or personal statement, interview.

Application deadlines: 8/20 (freshmen), 8/20 (out-of-state freshmen), 8/20 (transfers).

Notification: continuous (freshmen), continuous (out-of-state freshmen), continuous (transfers).

CONTACT

Mr. Ticha Chikuni, Director of Admissions, Georgetown College, 400 East College Street, Georgetown, KY 40324. *Phone:* 502-863-8727. *Toll-free phone:* 800-788-9985. *E-mail:* admissions@georgetowncollege.edu.

Kentucky Christian University

Grayson, Kentucky

http://www.kcu.edu/

CONTACT

Ms. Heather Stacy, Director of Admissions, Kentucky Christian University, 100 Academic Parkway, Grayson, KY 41143. *Phone:* 606-474-3284. *Toll-free phone:* 800-522-3181. *Fax:* 606-474-3155. *E-mail:* sgreer@kcu.edu.

Kentucky Mountain Bible College

Jackson, Kentucky

http://www.kmbc.edu/

- **Independent interdenominational** 4-year, founded 1931
- **Rural** 500-acre campus with easy access to Lexington
- **Coed** 72 undergraduate students, 68% full-time, 42% women, 58% men
- **Minimally difficult** entrance level, 48% of applicants were admitted

UNDERGRAD STUDENTS

49 full-time, 23 part-time. Students come from 16 states and territories; 2 other countries; 71% are from out of state; 4% Black or African American, non-Hispanic/Latino; 4% Hispanic/Latino; 1% Asian, non-Hispanic/Latino; 3% international; 11% transferred in; 92% live on campus.

Freshmen:

Admission: 85 applied, 41 admitted, 15 enrolled. ***Average high school GPA:*** 3.2. ***Test scores:*** ACT scores over 18: 72%; ACT scores over 24: 9%.

Retention: 71% of full-time freshmen returned.

FACULTY

Total: 15, 7% with terminal degrees.

Student/faculty ratio: 14:1.

ACADEMICS

Calendar: semesters. *Degrees:* associate and bachelor's.

Special study options: academic remediation for entering students, cooperative education, distance learning, independent study, internships, part-time degree program.

Computers: 4 computers/terminals are available on campus for general student use. Students can access the following: campus intranet, free student e-mail accounts, online (class) grades, online (class) registration, online (class) schedules. Campuswide network is available. 100% of college-owned or -operated housing units are wired for high-speed Internet access. Wireless service is available via entire campus.

Library: Gibson Library plus 1 other. *Books:* 36,704 (physical), 52 (digital/electronic); *Serial titles:* 115 (physical), 250 (digital/electronic). Weekly public service hours: 70.

STUDENT LIFE

Housing options: on-campus residence required through senior year; men-only, women-only. Campus housing is university owned. Freshman campus housing is guaranteed.

Activities and organizations: drama/theater group, student-run newspaper, choral group, Missionary Involvement, Class Organizations.

Athletics ***Intramural sports:*** basketball M, volleyball W.

Campus security: student patrols.

Student services: personal/psychological counseling.

COSTS & FINANCIAL AID

Costs (2019–20) ***Comprehensive fee:*** $15,330 includes full-time tuition ($9280), mandatory fees ($910), and room and board ($5140). Full-time tuition and fees vary according to program. Part-time tuition: $290 per credit hour. Part-time tuition and fees vary according to program. ***Required fees:*** $290 per term part-time. ***College room only:*** $1940. Room and board charges vary according to housing facility. ***Payment plan:*** installment. ***Waivers:*** employees or children of employees.

Financial Aid Of all full-time matriculated undergraduates who enrolled in 2019, 46 applied for aid, 46 were judged to have need. 25,616 Federal Work-Study jobs (averaging $500). 52,438 state and other part-time jobs (averaging $650). In 2019, 8 non-need-based awards were made. ***Average percent of need met:*** 71. ***Average financial aid package:*** $13,059. ***Average need-based loan:*** $4960. ***Average need-based gift aid:*** $4328. ***Average non-need-based aid:*** $3656. ***Average indebtedness upon graduation:*** $7370.

APPLYING

Standardized Tests *Required:* SAT or ACT (for admission).

Application fee: $25.

Required: essay or personal statement, high school transcript, minimum 2.0 GPA, testimony of Christian belief and practice. ***Recommended:*** minimum 2.0 GPA, interview.

Application deadlines: rolling (freshmen), rolling (transfers).

Notification: continuous (freshmen), continuous (transfers).

CONTACT

Mr. David Lorimer, Director of Recruiting, Kentucky Mountain Bible College, PO Box 10, Vancleve, KY 41385. *Phone:* 606-693-5000 Ext. 138. *Toll-free phone:* 800-879-KMBC. *Fax:* 606-693-4884. *E-mail:* dlorimer@kmbc.edu.

Kentucky State University

Frankfort, Kentucky

http://www.kysu.edu/

- **State-related** comprehensive, founded 1886
- **Small-town** 916-acre campus with easy access to Louisville
- **Endowment** $16.6 million
- **Coed**
- 45% of applicants were admitted

FACULTY

Student/faculty ratio: 11:1.

ACADEMICS
Calendar: semesters. *Degrees:* certificates, associate, bachelor's, master's, and doctoral.
Library: Paul G. Blazer Library. *Books:* 170,726 (physical), 23,417 (digital/electronic); *Serial titles:* 1,894 (physical), 38,647 (digital/electronic); *Databases:* 56. Weekly public service hours: 101; study areas open 24 hours, 5–7 days a week.

STUDENT LIFE
Housing options: on-campus residence required through sophomore year; coed, men-only, women-only, special housing for students with disabilities. Campus housing is university owned. Freshman campus housing is guaranteed.

Activities and organizations: drama/theater group, student-run newspaper, choral group, marching band, Collegiate100, Alpha Phi Omega, Drive Our Peer's Education DOPE, Student Ambassador's, Alpha Phi Alpha, national fraternities, national sororities.

Athletics Member NCAA. All Division II.

Campus security: 24-hour emergency response devices and patrols, student patrols, late-night transport/escort service, controlled dormitory access.

Student services: health clinic, personal/psychological counseling, veterans affairs office.

COSTS & FINANCIAL AID
Costs (2019–20) ***Tuition:*** state resident $7406 full-time, $325 per credit hour part-time; nonresident $18,314 full-time, $802 per credit hour part-time. Full-time tuition and fees vary according to course load. Part-time tuition and fees vary according to course load. ***Required fees:*** $390 full-time. ***Room and board:*** $6690. Room and board charges vary according to board plan and housing facility.

Financial Aid Of all full-time matriculated undergraduates who enrolled in 2019, 1,007 applied for aid, 992 were judged to have need, 106 had their need fully met. 169 Federal Work-Study jobs (averaging $1962). 43 state and other part-time jobs (averaging $6048). In 2019, 83 non-need-based awards were made. ***Average percent of need met:*** 70. ***Average financial aid package:*** $13,132. ***Average need-based loan:*** $4000. ***Average need-based gift aid:*** $15,022. ***Average non-need-based aid:*** $5877. ***Average indebtedness upon graduation:*** $28,394.

APPLYING
Standardized Tests *Required:* SAT or ACT (for admission).

Application fee: $30.

Required: high school transcript, minimum 2.5 GPA, minimum ACT score of 18.

CONTACT
Kentucky State University, 320 Hill Student Center, 400 East Main Street, Frankfort, KY 40601. *Phone:* 502-597-6813. *Toll-free phone:* 877-367-5978. *Fax:* 502-597-5814. *E-mail:* admissions@kysu.edu.

Kentucky Wesleyan College
Owensboro, Kentucky
http://www.kwc.edu/

CONTACT
Kentucky Wesleyan College, 3000 Frederica Street, Owensboro, KY 42301. *Phone:* 270-852-3120. *Toll-free phone:* 800-999-0592 (in-state); 800-990-0592 (out-of-state).

Lindsey Wilson College
Columbia, Kentucky
http://www.lindsey.edu/

CONTACT
Mrs. Charity Ferguson, Assistant Director of Admissions, Lindsey Wilson College, 210 Lindsey Wilson Street, Columbia, KY 42728-1298. *Phone:* 270-384-8100. *Toll-free phone:* 800-264-0138. *Fax:* 270-384-8591.

Midway University
Midway, Kentucky
http://www.midway.edu/

- **Independent** comprehensive, founded 1847, affiliated with Christian Church (Disciples of Christ)
- **Rural** 200-acre campus with easy access to Louisville, Lexington
- **Coed** 1,481 undergraduate students, 60% full-time, 68% women, 32% men
- **Minimally difficult** entrance level, 60% of applicants were admitted

UNDERGRAD STUDENTS
887 full-time, 594 part-time. Students come from 39 states and territories; 2 other countries; 19% are from out of state; 6% Black or African American, non-Hispanic/Latino; 5% Hispanic/Latino; 0.5% Asian, non-Hispanic/Latino; 0.1% Native Hawaiian or other Pacific Islander, non-Hispanic/Latino; 0.2% American Indian or Alaska Native, non-Hispanic/Latino; 2% Two or more races, non-Hispanic/Latino; 28% Race/ethnicity unknown; 0.1% international; 10% transferred in; 33% live on campus.

Freshmen:
Admission: 1,162 applied, 693 admitted, 217 enrolled. ***Average high school GPA:*** 3.3. ***Test scores:*** ACT scores over 18: 91%; ACT scores over 24: 20%; ACT scores over 30: 1%.

Retention: 67% of full-time freshmen returned.

FACULTY
Total: 129, 22% full-time.

Student/faculty ratio: 17:1.

ACADEMICS
Calendar: semesters. *Degrees:* associate, bachelor's, and master's.

Special study options: academic remediation for entering students, accelerated degree program, adult/continuing education programs, advanced placement credit, cooperative education, distance learning, double majors, English as a second language, external degree program, internships, off-campus study, part-time degree program, services for LD students, student-designed majors, study abroad, summer session for credit. ***ROTC:*** Army (c), Air Force (c).

Computers: 60 computers/terminals are available on campus for general student use. Students can access the following: campus intranet, computer help desk, free student e-mail accounts, online (class) grades, online (class) registration, online (class) schedules. Wireless service is available via entire campus.
Library: Little Memorial Library. *Books:* 32,749 (physical), 524,649 (digital/electronic); *Serial titles:* 50,380 (digital/electronic); *Databases:* 67. Weekly public service hours: 90; study areas open 24 hours, 5–7 days a week; students can reserve study rooms.

STUDENT LIFE
Housing options: on-campus residence required through sophomore year; coed. Campus housing is university owned.

Activities and organizations: drama/theater group, choral group.

Athletics Member NAIA. ***Intercollegiate sports:*** archery M(s)/W(s), baseball M(s), basketball M(s)/W(s), bowling M(s)/W(s), cheerleading M(s)/W(s), cross-country running M(s)/W(s), equestrian sports M(s)/W(s), golf M(s)/W(s), soccer M(s)/W(s), softball W(s), swimming and diving M(s)/W(s), tennis M(s)/W(s), track and field M(s)/W(s), volleyball M(s)/W(s), wrestling M.

Campus security: 24-hour emergency response devices and patrols, late-night transport/escort service.

Student services: health clinic, personal/psychological counseling, women's center, veterans affairs office.

COSTS
Costs (2020–21) ***Comprehensive fee:*** $33,450 includes full-time tuition ($24,500), mandatory fees ($350), and room and board ($8600). Part-time tuition: $910 per credit hour. ***College room only:*** $4400.

APPLYING
Standardized Tests *Required:* SAT or ACT (for admission).

Options: electronic application, early admission, deferred entrance.

Application fee: $30.

Required: high school transcript, minimum 2.5 GPA.

Application deadlines: rolling (freshmen), rolling (out-of-state freshmen), rolling (transfers).

Notification: continuous (freshmen), continuous (out-of-state freshmen), continuous (transfers).

CONTACT
Ashley Dudgeon, Director of Undergraduate Admissions, Midway University, 512 E. Stephens Street, Midway, KY 40347. *Phone:* 859-8465767. *Toll-free phone:* 800-755-0031. *E-mail:* adudgeon@midway.edu.

Morehead State University

Morehead, Kentucky

http://www.moreheadstate.edu/

- **State-supported** comprehensive, founded 1922
- **Small-town** 1588-acre campus
- **Endowment** $43.5 million
- **Coed** 8,964 undergraduate students, 60% full-time, 61% women, 39% men
- **Minimally difficult** entrance level, 78% of applicants were admitted

UNDERGRAD STUDENTS
5,393 full-time, 3,571 part-time. Students come from 43 states and territories; 14 other countries; 13% are from out of state; 4% Black or African American, non-Hispanic/Latino; 2% Hispanic/Latino; 0.4% Asian, non-Hispanic/Latino; 0.1% Native Hawaiian or other Pacific Islander, non-Hispanic/Latino; 0.1% American Indian or Alaska Native, non-Hispanic/Latino; 3% Two or more races, non-Hispanic/Latino; 0.7% Race/ethnicity unknown; 2% international; 4% transferred in; 44% live on campus.

Freshmen:
Admission: 8,032 applied, 6,233 admitted, 1,204 enrolled. ***Average high school GPA:*** 3.5. ***Test scores:*** SAT evidence-based reading and writing scores over 500: 68%; SAT math scores over 500: 68%; ACT scores over 18: 91%; SAT evidence-based reading and writing scores over 600: 29%; SAT math scores over 600: 29%; ACT scores over 24: 43%; SAT evidence-based reading and writing scores over 700: 5%; SAT math scores over 700: 2%; ACT scores over 30: 7%.

Retention: 73% of full-time freshmen returned.

FACULTY
Total: 416, 74% full-time, 63% with terminal degrees.

Student/faculty ratio: 16:1.

ACADEMICS
Calendar: semesters. *Degrees:* certificates, associate, bachelor's, master's, doctoral, post-master's, and postbachelor's certificates.

Special study options: academic remediation for entering students, accelerated degree program, adult/continuing education programs, advanced placement credit, cooperative education, distance learning, double majors, English as a second language, honors programs, independent study, internships, off-campus study, part-time degree program, services for LD students, student-designed majors, study abroad, summer session for credit. ***ROTC:*** Army (b).

Unusual degree programs: 3-2 engineering with University of Kentucky.

Computers: 950 computers/terminals and 25 ports are available on campus for general student use. Students can access the following: campus intranet, computer help desk, free student e-mail accounts, online (class) grades, online (class) registration, online (class) schedules. Campuswide network is available. 100% of college-owned or -operated housing units are wired for high-speed Internet access. Wireless service is available via entire campus.

Library: Camden Carroll Library. *Books:* 347,507 (physical), 215,552 (digital/electronic); *Serial titles:* 52,680 (physical), 104,203 (digital/electronic); *Databases:* 159. Students can reserve study rooms.

STUDENT LIFE
Housing options: on-campus residence required through sophomore year; coed, special housing for students with disabilities. Campus housing is university owned. Freshman applicants given priority for college housing.

Activities and organizations: drama/theater group, student-run newspaper, radio and television station, choral group, marching band, Chi Omega Sorority, Collegiate FFA, Academic Honors Student Association, Phi Sigma Pi Honors Fraternity, Kappa Delta Sorority, national fraternities, national sororities.

Athletics Member NCAA. All Division I except football (Division I-AA). ***Intercollegiate sports:*** baseball M(s), basketball M(s)/W(s), bowling M(c)/W(c), cheerleading M(s)(c)/W(s)(c), cross-country running M(s)/W(s), equestrian sports M(c)/W(c), golf M(s)/W(s), riflery M(s)/W(s), sand volleyball W(s), soccer W(s), softball W(s), track and field M(s)/W(s), volleyball W(s). ***Intramural sports:*** archery M/W, badminton M/W, basketball M/W, bowling M/W, golf M/W, racquetball M/W, soccer M(c)/W, softball M/W, swimming and diving M/W, table tennis M/W, tennis M/W, track and field M/W, volleyball M/W.

Campus security: 24-hour emergency response devices and patrols, student patrols, late-night transport/escort service, controlled dormitory access, LiveSafe app—a two-way communication safety app between students and University Police.

Student services: health clinic, personal/psychological counseling, veterans affairs office.

COSTS & FINANCIAL AID
Costs (2019–20) ***Tuition:*** state resident $8970 full-time, $374 per credit hour part-time; nonresident $13,556 full-time, $565 per credit hour part-time. Full-time tuition and fees vary according to course load, degree level, location, reciprocity agreements, and student level. Part-time tuition and fees vary according to course load, degree level, location, reciprocity agreements, and student level. ***Required fees:*** $320 full-time, $14 per credit hour part-time. ***Room and board:*** $9490; room only: $5308. Room and board charges vary according to board plan and housing facility. ***Payment plans:*** installment, deferred payment. ***Waivers:*** minority students, children of alumni, senior citizens, and employees or children of employees.

Financial Aid Of all full-time matriculated undergraduates who enrolled in 2019, 4,604 applied for aid, 3,976 were judged to have need, 937 had their need fully met. 414 Federal Work-Study jobs (averaging $2426). 769 state and other part-time jobs (averaging $2886). In 2019, 954 non-need-based awards were made. ***Average percent of need met:*** 64. ***Average financial aid package:*** $12,520. ***Average need-based loan:*** $3647. ***Average need-based gift aid:*** $6219. ***Average non-need-based aid:*** $7576. ***Average indebtedness upon graduation:*** $26,576.

APPLYING
Standardized Tests *Required:* SAT or ACT (for admission).

Options: electronic application, deferred entrance.

Application fee: $30.

Required: high school transcript. ***Required for some:*** essay or personal statement, 1 letter of recommendation, interview.

Application deadlines: rolling (freshmen), rolling (transfers).

Notification: continuous (freshmen), continuous (transfers).

CONTACT
Mr. Tim Rhodes, Assistant Vice President for Enrollment Services, Morehead State University, 407 Enrollment Services Center, Morehead, KY 40351. *Phone:* 606-783-2000. *Toll-free phone:* 800-585-6781. *Fax:* 606-783-5038. *E-mail:* admissions@moreheadstate.edu.

Murray State University

Murray, Kentucky

http://www.murraystate.edu/

- **State-supported** university, founded 1922
- **Small-town** 261-acre campus
- **Coed** 8,215 undergraduate students, 76% full-time, 61% women, 39% men
- **Moderately difficult** entrance level, 83% of applicants were admitted

UNDERGRAD STUDENTS
6,219 full-time, 1,996 part-time. Students come from 44 states and territories; 39 other countries; 29% are from out of state; 6% Black or African American, non-Hispanic/Latino; 2% Hispanic/Latino; 0.7% Asian, non-Hispanic/Latino; 0.1% Native Hawaiian or other Pacific Islander, non-Hispanic/Latino; 0.3% American Indian or Alaska Native, non-Hispanic/Latino; 3% Two or more races, non-Hispanic/Latino; 3% Race/ethnicity unknown; 3% international; 8% transferred in; 33% live on campus.

Freshmen:
Admission: 8,304 applied, 6,861 admitted, 1,421 enrolled. ***Average high school GPA:*** 3.0. ***Test scores:*** ACT scores over 18: 97%; ACT scores over 24: 55%; ACT scores over 30: 15%.

Retention: 76% of full-time freshmen returned.

FACULTY
Total: 578, 78% full-time, 58% with terminal degrees.

Student/faculty ratio: 15:1.

ACADEMICS
Calendar: semesters. *Degrees:* certificates, bachelor's, master's, doctoral, and postbachelor's certificates.

Special study options: academic remediation for entering students, adult/continuing education programs, advanced placement credit, cooperative education, distance learning, double majors, English as a second language, external degree program, freshman honors college, honors programs, independent study, internships, off-campus study, part-time degree program, services for LD students, student-designed majors, study abroad, summer session for credit. ***ROTC:*** Army (b).

Computers: Students can access the following: campus intranet, computer help desk, free student e-mail accounts, online (class) grades, online (class) registration, online (class) schedules, billing accounts, course evaluation forms, receive instant campus alerts, secure on-campus housing, pre-order of food or take-out. Campuswide network is available. 100% of college-owned or -operated housing units are wired for high-speed Internet access. Wireless service is available via entire campus.
Library: Waterfield Library plus 4 others. *Books:* 330,959 (physical), 51,049 (digital/electronic); *Serial titles:* 1,305 (physical), 64,102 (digital/electronic); *Databases:* 127. Weekly public service hours: 107; students can reserve study rooms.

STUDENT LIFE
Housing options: on-campus residence required through sophomore year; coed, women-only, special housing for students with disabilities. Campus housing is university owned. Freshman applicants given priority for college housing.

Activities and organizations: drama/theater group, student-run newspaper, television station, choral group, marching band, Racer Band, Student Government Association, National Panhellenic Council, International Student Organization, MSU Student Ambassadors, national fraternities, national sororities.

Athletics Member NCAA. All Division I except football (Division I-AA). ***Intercollegiate sports:*** baseball M(s), basketball M(s)/W(s), cheerleading M(c)/W(c), crew M(c)/W(c), cross-country running M/W(s), equestrian sports M(c)/W(c), golf M(s)/W(s)(c), riflery M(s)/W(s), rowing M(c)/W(c), soccer W(s), softball W(s), tennis W(s), track and field W(s), volleyball W(s). ***Intramural sports:*** archery M(c)/W(c), basketball M/W, bowling M/W, fencing M(c), field hockey W(c), football M/W, golf M/W, racquetball M(c)/W(c), rugby M(c), soccer M/W, softball M/W, swimming and diving M/W, table tennis M/W, tennis M/W, ultimate Frisbee M/W, volleyball M/W, water polo M/W.

Campus security: 24-hour emergency response devices and patrols, student patrols, late-night transport/escort service, controlled dormitory access.

Student services: health clinic, personal/psychological counseling, women's center, veterans affairs office.

FINANCIAL AID
Financial Aid Of all full-time matriculated undergraduates who enrolled in 2018, 5,497 applied for aid, 4,216 were judged to have need, 994 had their need fully met. In 2018, 846 non-need-based awards were made. ***Average percent of need met:*** 39. ***Average financial aid package:*** $12,987. ***Average need-based loan:*** $6243. ***Average need-based gift aid:*** $7310. ***Average non-need-based aid:*** $6576. ***Average indebtedness upon graduation:*** $28,277.

APPLYING
Standardized Tests *Required:* SAT or ACT (for admission). *Recommended:* ACT (for admission).

Options: electronic application, early admission.

Application fee: $40.

Required: high school transcript, minimum 3.0 GPA, minimum ACT composite score of 18 or SAT score of 870, rank in the top half of high school class or minimum 3.0 GPA; high school curriculum criteria.

Application deadlines: rolling (freshmen), rolling (transfers).

Notification: continuous (freshmen), continuous (transfers).

CONTACT
Ms. Stacy Bell, Assistant Director of Undergraduate Admissions, Murray State University, 102 Curris Center, Murray, KY 42701-0009. *Phone:* 270-809-5044. *Toll-free phone:* 800-272-4678. *E-mail:* msu.admissions@murraystate.edu.

Northern Kentucky University

Highland Heights, Kentucky

http://www.nku.edu/

- **State-supported** comprehensive, founded 1968
- **Suburban** 428-acre campus with easy access to Cincinnati
- **Endowment** $105.5 million
- **Coed** 11,882 undergraduate students, 69% full-time, 59% women, 41% men
- **Moderately difficult** entrance level, 90% of applicants were admitted

UNDERGRAD STUDENTS
8,257 full-time, 3,625 part-time. Students come from 38 states and territories; 57 other countries; 30% are from out of state; 7% Black or African American, non-Hispanic/Latino; 4% Hispanic/Latino; 1% Asian, non-Hispanic/Latino; 0.1% Native Hawaiian or other Pacific Islander, non-Hispanic/Latino; 0.2% American Indian or Alaska Native, non-Hispanic/Latino; 3% Two or more races, non-Hispanic/Latino; 0.7% Race/ethnicity unknown; 3% international; 6% transferred in; 22% live on campus.

Freshmen:
Admission: 6,080 applied, 5,483 admitted, 1,950 enrolled. ***Average high school GPA:*** 3.4. ***Test scores:*** SAT evidence-based reading and writing scores over 500: 85%; SAT math scores over 500: 86%; ACT scores over 18: 95%; SAT evidence-based reading and writing scores over 600: 29%; SAT math scores over 600: 33%; ACT scores over 24: 45%; SAT evidence-based reading and writing scores over 700: 4%; SAT math scores over 700: 15%; ACT scores over 30: 9%.

Retention: 71% of full-time freshmen returned.

FACULTY
Total: 1,082, 56% full-time, 50% with terminal degrees.

Student/faculty ratio: 18:1.

ACADEMICS
Calendar: semesters. *Degrees:* certificates, bachelor's, master's, doctoral, post-master's, and postbachelor's certificates.

Special study options: academic remediation for entering students, accelerated degree program, adult/continuing education programs, advanced placement credit, cooperative education, distance learning, double majors, English as a second language, freshman honors college, honors programs, independent study, internships, off-campus study, part-time degree program, services for LD students, student-designed majors, study abroad, summer session for credit. ***ROTC:*** Army (c), Air Force (c).

Unusual degree programs: 3-2 engineering with University of Louisville, University of Kentucky; nursing with Hanover College.

Computers: 200 computers/terminals and 1,500 ports are available on campus for general student use. Students can access the following: campus intranet, computer help desk, free student e-mail accounts, online (class) grades, online (class) registration, online (class) schedules. Campuswide network is available. 100% of college-owned or -operated housing units are wired for high-speed Internet access. Wireless service is available via entire campus.
Library: W. Frank Steely Library plus 1 other. *Books:* 461,256 (physical), 130,271 (digital/electronic); *Serial titles:* 86,710 (digital/electronic); *Databases:* 108. Weekly public service hours: 102; students can reserve study rooms.

STUDENT LIFE
Housing options: on-campus residence required for freshman year; coed, special housing for students with disabilities. Campus housing is university owned. Freshman applicants given priority for college housing.

Activities and organizations: drama/theater group, student-run newspaper, radio and television station, choral group, Sororities, Fraternities, Freshmen Service Leadership Committee, Student Alumni Association, Activities Programming Board, national fraternities, national sororities.

Athletics Member NCAA. All Division I. ***Intercollegiate sports:*** baseball M(s), basketball M(s)/W(s), cheerleading M(s)/W(s), cross-country running M(s)/W(s), golf M(s)/W(s), soccer M(s)/W(s), softball W(s), tennis M(s)/W(s), track and field M(s)/W(s), volleyball W(s). ***Intramural sports:*** badminton M(c)/W(c), basketball M/W, bowling M(c)/W(c), cross-country running M(c)/W(c), equestrian sports M(c)/W(c), lacrosse M(c)/W(c), rock climbing M(c)/W(c), skiing (downhill) W(c), soccer M(c)/W(c), tennis M/W, ultimate Frisbee M/W, volleyball M/W, water polo M/W, weight lifting M/W, wrestling M(c).

Campus security: 24-hour emergency response devices and patrols, late-night transport/escort service, controlled dormitory access.

Student services: health clinic, personal/psychological counseling, women's center, legal services, veterans affairs office.

FINANCIAL AID

Financial Aid Of all full-time matriculated undergraduates who enrolled in 2018, 6,723 applied for aid, 5,464 were judged to have need, 1,167 had their need fully met. In 2018, 1496 non-need-based awards were made. ***Average percent of need met:*** 68. ***Average financial aid package:*** $12,149. ***Average need-based loan:*** $4311. ***Average need-based gift aid:*** $6099. ***Average non-need-based aid:*** $6326. ***Average indebtedness upon graduation:*** $26,502.

APPLYING

Standardized Tests *Required:* SAT or ACT (for admission).

Options: electronic application.

Application fee: $40.

Required: high school transcript, minimum 2.0 GPA. ***Required for some:*** Some programs require separate applications.

Application deadlines: 8/15 (freshmen), 8/15 (out-of-state freshmen), 8/15 (transfers).

Notification: continuous (freshmen), continuous (out-of-state freshmen), continuous (transfers).

CONTACT

Mrs. Melissa Gorbandt, Office of Admissions, Northern Kentucky University, Lucas Administrative Center, 400 Nunn Drive, Highland Heights, KY 41099. *Phone:* 859-572-5220. *Toll-free phone:* 800-637-9948. *Fax:* 859-572-6665. *E-mail:* beanorse@nku.edu.

Simmons College of Kentucky

Louisville, Kentucky

http://www.simmonscollegeky.edu/

CONTACT

Simmons College of Kentucky, 1018 South 7th Street, Louisville, KY 40203.

The Southern Baptist Theological Seminary

Louisville, Kentucky

http://www.sbts.edu/

CONTACT

Dr. Daniel DeWitt, The Southern Baptist Theological Seminary, 2825 Lexington Road, Louisville, KY 40280-0004. *Phone:* 502-897-4011 Ext. 4617.

Spalding University

Louisville, Kentucky

http://www.spalding.edu/

CONTACT

Mr. Matt Elder, Director, Undergraduate Admissions, Spalding University, 845 South Third Street, Louisville, KY 40203. *Phone:* 502-873-4177. *Toll-free phone:* 800-896-8941. *Fax:* 502-992-2418. *E-mail:* melder@spalding.edu.

Sullivan University

Louisville, Kentucky

http://www.sullivan.edu/

- **Proprietary** comprehensive, founded 1962, part of The Sullivan University System, Inc.
- **Suburban** 15-acre campus
- **Coed** 2,625 undergraduate students, 62% full-time, 64% women, 36% men
- **Minimally difficult** entrance level, 66% of applicants were admitted

UNDERGRAD STUDENTS

1,637 full-time, 988 part-time. Students come from 44 states and territories; 16 other countries; 18% are from out of state; 17% Black or African American, non-Hispanic/Latino; 2% Asian, non-Hispanic/Latino; 0.3% Native Hawaiian or other Pacific Islander, non-Hispanic/Latino; 0.5% American Indian or Alaska Native, non-Hispanic/Latino; 9% Two or more races, non-Hispanic/Latino; 13% Race/ethnicity unknown; 2% transferred in; 6% live on campus.

Freshmen:

Admission: 1,529 applied, 1,006 admitted, 311 enrolled. ***Test scores:*** ACT scores over 18: 85%; ACT scores over 24: 20%; ACT scores over 30: 3%.

FACULTY

Total: 213, 39% full-time.

Student/faculty ratio: 18:1.

ACADEMICS

Calendar: quarters. *Degrees:* certificates, diplomas, associate, bachelor's, master's, doctoral, and postbachelor's certificates.

Special study options: academic remediation for entering students, accelerated degree program, adult/continuing education programs, distance learning, double majors, independent study, internships, part-time degree program, services for LD students, student-designed majors.

Computers: 93 computers/terminals are available on campus for general student use. Students can access the following: campus intranet, computer help desk, free student e-mail accounts, online (class) grades, online (class) registration, online (class) schedules. Campuswide network is available. 100% of college-owned or -operated housing units are wired for high-speed Internet access. Wireless service is available via entire campus.

Library: Sullivan University Libraries. *Books:* 52,600 (physical), 67,908 (digital/electronic); *Serial titles:* 97 (physical), 43,372 (digital/electronic); *Databases:* 83. Weekly public service hours: 82; students can reserve study rooms.

STUDENT LIFE

Housing options: coed, special housing for students with disabilities. Campus housing is university owned. Freshman campus housing is guaranteed.

Activities and organizations: Sexual and Gender Alliance (SAGA), Student Activities Board (SAB), Student Veterans Association (SVA), Creative Writing Club, F.E.E.D. (Dining Club).

Athletics ***Intramural sports:*** basketball M/W, sand volleyball M/W, soccer M/W, softball M/W, volleyball M/W.

Campus security: 24-hour emergency response devices and patrols, late-night transport/escort service, controlled dormitory access.

Student services: personal/psychological counseling.

FINANCIAL AID

Financial Aid Of all full-time matriculated undergraduates who enrolled in 2002, 6,028 applied for aid, 5,247 were judged to have need. 31 Federal Work-Study jobs (averaging $2065). In 2002, 374 non-need-based awards were made. ***Average non-need-based aid:*** $2000. ***Average indebtedness upon graduation:*** $15,000.

APPLYING

Standardized Tests *Recommended:* SAT or ACT (for admission).

Options: electronic application, deferred entrance.

Application fee: $30.

Required for some: essay or personal statement, high school transcript, interview, criminal background check and no felony convictions, drug testing, and immunizations.

Application deadlines: rolling (freshmen), rolling (out-of-state freshmen), rolling (transfers).

Notification: continuous (freshmen), continuous (out-of-state freshmen), continuous (transfers).

CONTACT

Ms. Heather Cunningham, Senior Director of Admissions, Sullivan University, 3101 Bardstown Road, Louisville, KY 40205. *Phone:* 502-456-6505. *Toll-free phone:* 800-844-1354. *Fax:* 502-456-0040. *E-mail:* admissions@sullivan.edu.

Thomas More University

Crestview Hills, Kentucky

http://www.thomasmore.edu/

- **Independent Roman Catholic** comprehensive, founded 1921
- **Suburban** 100-acre campus with easy access to Cincinnati
- **Endowment** $20.7 million
- **Coed**
- **Moderately difficult** entrance level

FACULTY

Student/faculty ratio: 16:1.

ACADEMICS

Calendar: semesters. *Degrees:* certificates, associate, bachelor's, and master's.

Library: Thomas More College Library plus 1 other. *Books:* 87,667 (physical), 3,056 (digital/electronic); *Serial titles:* 329 (physical); *Databases:* 65. Weekly public service hours: 76.

STUDENT LIFE

Housing options: on-campus residence required through sophomore year; men-only, women-only, special housing for students with disabilities. Campus housing is university owned. Freshman campus housing is guaranteed.

Activities and organizations: drama/theater group, choral group, marching band, Student Government Association, Student Activities Board, More Ministry, Outdoors Adventure Club, Education Club, national fraternities, national sororities.

Athletics Member NCAA. All Division III.

Campus security: 24-hour emergency response devices and patrols, late-night transport/escort service, controlled dormitory access.

Student services: health clinic, personal/psychological counseling, veterans affairs office.

FINANCIAL AID

Financial Aid Of all full-time matriculated undergraduates who enrolled in 2019, 1,177 applied for aid, 1,050 were judged to have need, 277 had their need fully met. 179 Federal Work-Study jobs (averaging $937). 255 state and other part-time jobs (averaging $743). In 2019, 224 non-need-based awards were made. ***Average percent of need met:*** 73. ***Average financial aid package:*** $23,793. ***Average need-based loan:*** $3728. ***Average need-based gift aid:*** $19,113. ***Average non-need-based aid:*** $16,564. ***Average indebtedness upon graduation:*** $33,687.

APPLYING

Standardized Tests *Required:* SAT or ACT (for admission).

Options: electronic application, deferred entrance.

Application fee: $25.

Required: high school transcript, minimum 2.5 GPA.

CONTACT

Justin Vogel, Director of Admissions, Thomas More University, 333 Thomas More Parkway, Crestview Hills, KY 41017-3495. *Phone:* 859-344-3307. *Toll-free phone:* 800-825-4557. *Fax:* 859-344-3444. *E-mail:* admissions@thomasmore.edu.

Transylvania University

Lexington, Kentucky

http://www.transy.edu/

- **Independent** 4-year, founded 1780, affiliated with Christian Church (Disciples of Christ)
- **Urban** 40-acre campus with easy access to Cincinnati, Louisville
- **Endowment** $179.2 million
- **Coed** 949 undergraduate students, 100% full-time, 60% women, 40% men
- **Very difficult** entrance level, 89% of applicants were admitted

UNDERGRAD STUDENTS

946 full-time, 3 part-time. 22% are from out of state; 5% Black or African American, non-Hispanic/Latino; 4% Hispanic/Latino; 2% Asian, non-Hispanic/Latino; 0.2% American Indian or Alaska Native, non-Hispanic/Latino; 5% Two or more races, non-Hispanic/Latino; 4% Race/ethnicity unknown; 2% transferred in; 68% live on campus.

Freshmen:

Admission: 1,786 applied, 1,598 admitted, 284 enrolled. ***Average high school GPA:*** 3.7. ***Test scores:*** SAT evidence-based reading and writing scores over 500: 96%; SAT math scores over 500: 96%; ACT scores over 18: 100%; SAT evidence-based reading and writing scores over 600: 57%; SAT math scores over 600: 50%; ACT scores over 24: 71%; SAT evidence-based reading and writing scores over 700: 14%; SAT math scores over 700: 14%; ACT scores over 30: 28%.

Retention: 83% of full-time freshmen returned.

FACULTY

Total: 108, 76% full-time, 83% with terminal degrees.

Student/faculty ratio: 10:1.

ACADEMICS

Calendar: 4-4-1. *Degree:* bachelor's.

Special study options: advanced placement credit, double majors, independent study, internships, off-campus study, part-time degree program, services for LD students, student-designed majors, study abroad, summer session for credit. ***ROTC:*** Army (c), Air Force (c).

Unusual degree programs: 3-2 engineering with University of Kentucky, Vanderbilt University.

Computers: 90 computers/terminals are available on campus for general student use. Students can access the following: campus intranet, computer help desk, free student e-mail accounts, online (class) grades, online (class) registration, online (class) schedules. Campuswide network is available. 100% of college-owned or -operated housing units are wired for high-speed Internet access. Wireless service is available via entire campus.

Library: J. Douglas Gay Jr./Frances Carrick Thomas Library. *Books:* 124,199 (physical), 170,342 (digital/electronic); *Serial titles:* 530 (physical), 23,600 (digital/electronic); *Databases:* 70. Weekly public service hours: 102; students can reserve study rooms.

STUDENT LIFE

Housing options: on-campus residence required through junior year; coed, men-only, women-only. Campus housing is university owned. Freshman campus housing is guaranteed.

Activities and organizations: drama/theater group, student-run newspaper, radio station, choral group, Student Government Association, Delta Sigma Phi, Phi Mu, Delta Delta Delta, Chi Omega, national fraternities, national sororities.

Athletics Member NCAA. All Division III. ***Intercollegiate sports:*** baseball M, basketball M/W, cheerleading M/W, cross-country running M/W, equestrian sports M/W, field hockey W, golf M/W, lacrosse M/W, soccer M/W, softball W, swimming and diving M/W, tennis M/W, track and field M/W, volleyball W. ***Intramural sports:*** badminton M/W, basketball M/W, soccer M/W, softball M/W, table tennis M/W, ultimate Frisbee M/W, volleyball M/W.

Campus security: 24-hour emergency response devices and patrols, late-night transport/escort service, controlled dormitory access.

Student services: health clinic, personal/psychological counseling.

COSTS & FINANCIAL AID

Costs (2020–21) ***Comprehensive fee:*** $52,920 includes full-time tuition ($39,920), mandatory fees ($1690), and room and board ($11,310). Part-

time tuition: $4450 per course. Part-time tuition and fees vary according to course load. ***College room only:*** $6260. Room and board charges vary according to board plan and housing facility. ***Payment plan:*** installment. ***Waivers:*** employees or children of employees.

Financial Aid Of all full-time matriculated undergraduates who enrolled in 2019, 795 applied for aid, 681 were judged to have need, 175 had their need fully met. In 2019, 253 non-need-based awards were made. ***Average percent of need met:*** 78. ***Average financial aid package:*** $30,215. ***Average need-based loan:*** $3975. ***Average need-based gift aid:*** $26,730. ***Average non-need-based aid:*** $18,926. ***Average indebtedness upon graduation:*** $30,826.

APPLYING

Options: electronic application, early action, deferred entrance.

Required: essay or personal statement, high school transcript, minimum 2.8 GPA, 2 letters of recommendation. ***Required for some:*** interview. ***Recommended:*** interview.

Application deadlines: 11/15 (freshmen), rolling (transfers), 10/15 (early action).

Notification: 12/1 (freshmen), 11/1 (early action).

CONTACT

Dr. Holly Sheilley, Vice President for Enrollment and Student Life, Transylvania University, 300 North Broadway, Lexington, KY 40508-1797. *Phone:* 859-233-8242. *Toll-free phone:* 800-872-6798. *Fax:* 859-281-3649. *E-mail:* admissions@transy.edu.

Union College

Barbourville, Kentucky

http://www.unionky.edu/

- **Independent United Methodist** comprehensive, founded 1879
- **Small-town** 100-acre campus
- **Endowment** $22.7 million
- **Coed**
- **Moderately difficult** entrance level

FACULTY

Student/faculty ratio: 12:1.

ACADEMICS

Calendar: semesters. *Degrees:* certificates, bachelor's, master's, post-master's, and postbachelor's certificates.

Library: Weeks-Townsend Memorial Library plus 1 other. *Books:* 121,623 (physical), 386,171 (digital/electronic); *Serial titles:* 42,795 (physical); *Databases:* 124,060.

STUDENT LIFE

Housing options: on-campus residence required through sophomore year; men-only, women-only. Campus housing is university owned. Freshman campus housing is guaranteed.

Activities and organizations: drama/theater group, choral group, Student Ambassadors, Student Government Association, Union Singers, International Club, Spiritual Life Team.

Athletics Member NAIA.

Campus security: 24-hour emergency response devices and patrols, late-night transport/escort service, controlled dormitory access.

Student services: health clinic, personal/psychological counseling.

COSTS & FINANCIAL AID

Costs (2019–20) ***Comprehensive fee:*** $35,450 includes full-time tuition ($26,330), mandatory fees ($1620), and room and board ($7500). Part-time tuition: $345 per credit hour. ***College room only:*** $3300.

Financial Aid Of all full-time matriculated undergraduates who enrolled in 2018, 900 applied for aid, 854 were judged to have need, 87 had their need fully met. In 2018, 121 non-need-based awards were made. ***Average percent of need met:*** 58. ***Average financial aid package:*** $23,525. ***Average need-based loan:*** $3896. ***Average need-based gift aid:*** $20,145. ***Average non-need-based aid:*** $16,452.

APPLYING

Standardized Tests *Required:* SAT or ACT (for admission).

Options: electronic application, deferred entrance.

Required: high school transcript, minimum 2.0 GPA. ***Required for some:*** interview, non-refundable application fee of $100 for international students only.

CONTACT

Mr. Craig Grooms, Vice President for Enrollment and Student Life, Union College, 310 College Street, Barbourville, KY 40906. *Phone:* 606-546-1750. *Toll-free phone:* 800-489-8646. *Fax:* 606-546-1769. *E-mail:* enrollme@unionky.edu.

University of Kentucky

Lexington, Kentucky

http://www.uky.edu/

- **State-supported** university, founded 1865, part of Kentucky does not have a state system.
- **Urban** 813-acre campus with easy access to Cincinnati, Louisville
- **Endowment** $1.3 billion
- **Coed** 22,236 undergraduate students, 93% full-time, 56% women, 44% men
- **Moderately difficult** entrance level, 96% of applicants were admitted

UNDERGRAD STUDENTS

20,622 full-time, 1,614 part-time. 31% are from out of state; 7% Black or African American, non-Hispanic/Latino; 5% Hispanic/Latino; 3% Asian, non-Hispanic/Latino; 0.1% Native Hawaiian or other Pacific Islander, non-Hispanic/Latino; 0.2% American Indian or Alaska Native, non-Hispanic/Latino; 4% Two or more races, non-Hispanic/Latino; 3% Race/ethnicity unknown; 2% international; 5% transferred in; 33% live on campus.

Freshmen:

Admission: 18,759 applied, 17,981 admitted, 5,348 enrolled. ***Average high school GPA:*** 3.5. ***Test scores:*** SAT evidence-based reading and writing scores over 500: 90%; SAT math scores over 500: 88%; ACT scores over 18: 98%; SAT evidence-based reading and writing scores over 600: 51%; SAT math scores over 600: 49%; ACT scores over 24: 66%; SAT evidence-based reading and writing scores over 700: 12%; SAT math scores over 700: 16%; ACT scores over 30: 24%.

Retention: 85% of full-time freshmen returned.

FACULTY

Total: 2,033, 82% full-time, 85% with terminal degrees.

ACADEMICS

Calendar: semesters. *Degrees:* certificates, bachelor's, master's, doctoral, post-master's, and postbachelor's certificates.

Special study options: academic remediation for entering students, accelerated degree program, adult/continuing education programs, advanced placement credit, cooperative education, distance learning, double majors, English as a second language, honors programs, independent study, internships, off-campus study, part-time degree program, services for LD students, student-designed majors, study abroad, summer session for credit. ***ROTC:*** Army (b), Air Force (b).

Unusual degree programs: 3-2 business administration.

Computers: 1,000 computers/terminals are available on campus for general student use. Students can access the following: campus intranet, computer help desk, free student e-mail accounts, online (class) grades, online (class) registration, online (class) schedules. Campuswide network is available. 100% of college-owned or -operated housing units are wired for high-speed Internet access. Wireless service is available via entire campus.

Library: William T. Young Library plus 10 others. *Books:* 2.5 million (physical), 1.7 million (digital/electronic); *Serial titles:* 56,959 (physical), 175,865 (digital/electronic); *Databases:* 435. Study areas open 24 hours, 5–7 days a week; students can reserve study rooms.

STUDENT LIFE

Housing options: coed, men-only, cooperative, special housing for students with disabilities. Campus housing is university owned. Freshman applicants given priority for college housing.

Activities and organizations: drama/theater group, student-run newspaper, radio and television station, choral group, marching band, Student Activities Board, Student Government Association, Campus Progressive Coalition, Ski and Snowboard Club, Society of Women Engineers, national fraternities, national sororities.

COLLEGES AT-A-GLANCE

Athletics Member NCAA. All Division I except football (Division I-A). ***Intercollegiate sports:*** baseball M(s), basketball M(s)/W(s), cheerleading M/W, cross-country running M(s)/W(s), golf M(s)/W(s), gymnastics W(s), riflery M(s)/W(s), soccer M(s)/W(s), softball W(s), swimming and diving M(s)/W(s), tennis M(s)/W(s), track and field M(s)/W(s), volleyball W(s). ***Intramural sports:*** archery M/W, badminton M/W, baseball M(c), basketball M/W, bowling M/W, cheerleading M/W, cross-country running M/W, equestrian sports M(c)/W(c), fencing M/W, field hockey W(c), football M/W, golf M(c)/W, gymnastics M, ice hockey M(c), lacrosse M(c)/W, racquetball M/W, rock climbing M/W, rugby M/W(c), skiing (cross-country) M(c)/W(c), skiing (downhill) M(c)/W(c), soccer M/W, softball M/W(c), squash M/W, swimming and diving M/W, table tennis M/W, tennis M/W, track and field M/W, triathlon M(c)/W(c), ultimate Frisbee M(c)/W(c), volleyball M/W, water polo M(c)/W(c), weight lifting M(c)/W(c), wrestling M/W.

Campus security: 24-hour emergency response devices and patrols, late-night transport/escort service, controlled dormitory access.

Student services: health clinic, personal/psychological counseling, women's center, legal services, veterans affairs office.

COSTS & FINANCIAL AID

Costs (2019–20) ***Tuition:*** area resident $11,011 full-time, $459 per credit hour part-time; state resident $11,011 full-time, $459 per credit hour part-time; nonresident $29,331 full-time, $1223 per credit hour part-time. Full-time tuition and fees vary according to location, program, reciprocity agreements, and student level. Part-time tuition and fees vary according to course load, location, program, reciprocity agreements, and student level. ***Required fees:*** $1349 full-time. ***Room and board:*** $13,210; room only: $8930. Room and board charges vary according to board plan and housing facility. ***Payment plan:*** installment. ***Waivers:*** employees or children of employees.

Financial Aid Of all full-time matriculated undergraduates who enrolled in 2018, 13,593 applied for aid, 10,668 were judged to have need, 1,754 had their need fully met. 195 Federal Work-Study jobs (averaging $406,051). In 2018, 5589 non-need-based awards were made. ***Average percent of need met:*** 54. ***Average financial aid package:*** $13,562. ***Average need-based loan:*** $4083. ***Average need-based gift aid:*** $6037. ***Average non-need-based aid:*** $9501. ***Average indebtedness upon graduation:*** $33,927.

APPLYING

Standardized Tests *Required:* SAT or ACT (for admission).

Options: electronic application, early action, deferred entrance.

Application fee: $50.

Required: essay or personal statement, high school transcript. ***Required for some:*** audition required of music and dance majors.

Application deadlines: 2/15 (freshmen), 2/15 (out-of-state freshmen), 8/1 (transfers), 12/1 (early action).

Notification: continuous until 3/15 (freshmen), continuous until 3/15 (out-of-state freshmen), continuous (transfers), 12/20 (early action).

CONTACT

Scott McDonald, University of Kentucky, 100 W.D. Funkhouser Building, Lexington, KY 40506-0054. *Phone:* 859-257-2000. *Toll-free phone:* 866-900-GO-UK. *Fax:* 859-257-3823. *E-mail:* admission@uky.edu.

University of Louisville

Louisville, Kentucky

http://www.louisville.edu/

- **State-supported** university, founded 1798
- **Urban** 640-acre campus with easy access to Louisville
- **Endowment** $719.8 million
- **Coed** 15,860 undergraduate students, 73% full-time, 54% women, 46% men
- **Moderately difficult** entrance level, 70% of applicants were admitted

UNDERGRAD STUDENTS

11,560 full-time, 4,300 part-time. Students come from 51 states and territories; 65 other countries; 18% are from out of state; 12% Black or African American, non-Hispanic/Latino; 6% Hispanic/Latino; 4% Asian, non-Hispanic/Latino; 0.1% American Indian or Alaska Native, non-Hispanic/Latino; 6% Two or more races, non-Hispanic/Latino; 1% international; 6% transferred in; 23% live on campus.

Freshmen:

Admission: 14,447 applied, 10,076 admitted, 2,803 enrolled. ***Average high school GPA:*** 3.6. ***Test scores:*** ACT scores over 18: 99%; ACT scores over 24: 61%; ACT scores over 30: 24%.

Retention: 80% of full-time freshmen returned.

FACULTY

Total: 1,634, 55% full-time, 64% with terminal degrees.

Student/faculty ratio: 14:1.

ACADEMICS

Calendar: semesters. *Degrees:* certificates, associate, bachelor's, master's, doctoral, post-master's, and postbachelor's certificates.

Special study options: academic remediation for entering students, accelerated degree program, adult/continuing education programs, advanced placement credit, cooperative education, distance learning, double majors, English as a second language, honors programs, independent study, internships, off-campus study, part-time degree program, services for LD students, study abroad, summer session for credit. ***ROTC:*** Army (b), Air Force (b).

Unusual degree programs: 3-2 engineering.

Computers: 400 computers/terminals are available on campus for general student use. Students can access the following: computer help desk, free student e-mail accounts, online (class) grades, online (class) registration, online (class) schedules. Campuswide network is available. 100% of college-owned or -operated housing units are wired for high-speed Internet access. Wireless service is available via entire campus.

Library: William F. Ekstrom Library plus 6 others. *Books:* 1.6 million (physical), 215,864 (digital/electronic); *Serial titles:* 2,158 (physical), 90,689 (digital/electronic); *Databases:* 338. Weekly public service hours: 97; study areas open 24 hours, 5–7 days a week; students can reserve study rooms.

STUDENT LIFE

Housing options: on-campus residence required for freshman year; coed, men-only, special housing for students with disabilities. Campus housing is university owned. Freshman campus housing is guaranteed.

Activities and organizations: drama/theater group, student-run newspaper, choral group, marching band, Baptist Campus Ministry, Society of Porter Scholars, Association of Black Students, Common Ground, Raise Red Dance Marathon, national fraternities, national sororities.

Athletics Member NCAA. All Division I except football (Division I-A). ***Intercollegiate sports:*** baseball M(s), basketball M(s)/W(s), cheerleading M/W, cross-country running M(s)/W(s), field hockey W(s), golf M(s)/W(s), lacrosse W(s), rowing W(s), soccer M(s)/W(s), softball W(s), swimming and diving M(s)/W(s), tennis M(s)/W(s), track and field M(s)/W(s), volleyball W(s). ***Intramural sports:*** badminton M/W, basketball M/W, bowling M/W, cross-country running M/W, equestrian sports W(c), fencing M(c), field hockey W, football M/W, golf M/W, ice hockey M(c), lacrosse M(c)/W(c), racquetball M/W, rugby M(c), soccer M/W, softball W, swimming and diving M/W, table tennis M/W, tennis M/W, track and field M/W, ultimate Frisbee M/W, volleyball M/W, wrestling M(c)/W(c).

Campus security: 24-hour emergency response devices and patrols, late-night transport/escort service, controlled dormitory access.

Student services: health clinic, personal/psychological counseling, women's center, veterans affairs office.

COSTS & FINANCIAL AID

Costs (2019–20) ***Tuition:*** state resident $11,732 full-time, $489 per credit hour part-time; nonresident $27,758 full-time, $1157 per credit hour part-time. Full-time tuition and fees vary according to reciprocity agreements. Part-time tuition and fees vary according to course load and reciprocity agreements. ***Required fees:*** $196 full-time. ***Room and board:*** $9452; room only: $5234. Room and board charges vary according to housing facility. ***Payment plans:*** installment, deferred payment. ***Waivers:*** senior citizens.

Financial Aid Of all full-time matriculated undergraduates who enrolled in 2019, 8,884 applied for aid, 7,195 were judged to have need, 1,204 had their need fully met. 634 Federal Work-Study jobs (averaging $4003). In 2019, 1756 non-need-based awards were made. ***Average percent of need met:*** 59. ***Average financial aid package:*** $13,464. ***Average need-based***

loan: $4116. ***Average need-based gift aid:*** $10,623. ***Average non-need-based aid:*** $8690. ***Average indebtedness upon graduation:*** $24,840.

APPLYING

Standardized Tests *Required:* SAT or ACT (for admission). *Required for some:* TOEFL for students whose primary language is not English.

Options: electronic application, early admission, deferred entrance.

Application fee: $25.

Required: high school transcript, minimum 2.5 GPA.

Application deadlines: 8/1 (freshmen), rolling (transfers).

Notification: continuous (transfers).

CONTACT

Ms. Jenny L. Sawyer, Executive Director of Admissions, University of Louisville, 2301 South Third Street, Houchens Room 150, Louisville, KY 40292-0001. *Phone:* 502-852-6531. *Toll-free phone:* 800-334-8635. *Fax:* 502-852-4776. *E-mail:* admitme@louisville.edu.

University of Pikeville

Pikeville, Kentucky

http://www.upike.edu/

- **Independent** comprehensive, founded 1889, affiliated with Presbyterian Church (U.S.A.)
- **Small-town** 25-acre campus
- **Endowment** $23.4 million
- **Coed** 1,404 undergraduate students, 77% full-time, 51% women, 49% men
- **Noncompetitive** entrance level, 100% of applicants were admitted

UNDERGRAD STUDENTS

1,075 full-time, 329 part-time. Students come from 31 states and territories; 13 other countries; 21% are from out of state; 12% Black or African American, non-Hispanic/Latino; 1% Hispanic/Latino; 0.5% Asian, non-Hispanic/Latino; 0.1% Native Hawaiian or other Pacific Islander, non-Hispanic/Latino; 0.6% American Indian or Alaska Native, non-Hispanic/Latino; 2% international; 6% transferred in; 53% live on campus.

Freshmen:

Admission: 1,925 applied, 1,925 admitted, 328 enrolled. ***Average high school GPA:*** 3.3. ***Test scores:*** SAT evidence-based reading and writing scores over 500: 58%; SAT math scores over 500: 61%; ACT scores over 18: 77%; SAT evidence-based reading and writing scores over 600: 24%; SAT math scores over 600: 16%; ACT scores over 24: 26%; SAT evidence-based reading and writing scores over 700: 3%; ACT scores over 30: 2%.

Retention: 63% of full-time freshmen returned.

FACULTY

Total: 100, 61% full-time, 50% with terminal degrees.

Student/faculty ratio: 15:1.

ACADEMICS

Calendar: semesters. *Degrees:* associate, bachelor's, master's, doctoral, and postbachelor's certificates.

Special study options: academic remediation for entering students, advanced placement credit, distance learning, double majors, English as a second language, honors programs, internships, part-time degree program, services for LD students, student-designed majors, study abroad, summer session for credit. ***ROTC:*** Army (b).

Computers: 308 computers/terminals are available on campus for general student use. Students can access the following: computer help desk, free student e-mail accounts, online (class) grades, online (class) schedules. Campuswide network is available. 100% of college-owned or -operated housing units are wired for high-speed Internet access. Wireless service is available via entire campus.

Library: Allara Library plus 2 others. *Books:* 63,935 (physical), 294,261 (digital/electronic); *Serial titles:* 115 (physical), 86,810 (digital/electronic); *Databases:* 124. Weekly public service hours: 105; students can reserve study rooms.

STUDENT LIFE

Housing options: coed, men-only, women-only. Campus housing is university owned.

Activities and organizations: drama/theater group, student-run newspaper, choral group, marching band, Student Government, Phi Beta Lambda, Lambda Sigma, Concert Choir, Student Nurses at UPIKE.

Athletics Member NAIA. ***Intercollegiate sports:*** archery M(s)/W(s), baseball M(s), basketball M(s)/W(s), bowling M(s)/W(s), cheerleading M(s)/W(s), cross-country running M(s)/W(s), football M(s), golf M(s)/W(s), soccer M(s)/W(s), softball W(s), tennis M(s)/W(s), track and field M(s)/W(s), volleyball W(s). ***Intramural sports:*** basketball M/W, football M.

Campus security: 24-hour patrols, controlled dormitory access.

Student services: health clinic, personal/psychological counseling, veterans affairs office.

COSTS & FINANCIAL AID

Costs (2020–21) ***Comprehensive fee:*** $30,100 includes full-time tuition ($21,900), mandatory fees ($150), and room and board ($8050). Full-time tuition and fees vary according to course load. Part-time tuition: $915 per credit hour. Part-time tuition and fees vary according to course load. ***Room and board:*** Room and board charges vary according to housing facility. ***Payment plan:*** installment. ***Waivers:*** senior citizens and employees or children of employees.

Financial Aid Of all full-time matriculated undergraduates who enrolled in 2019, 1,059 applied for aid, 1,059 were judged to have need, 443 had their need fully met. 400 Federal Work-Study jobs (averaging $1933). ***Average percent of need met:*** 82. ***Average financial aid package:*** $22,417. ***Average need-based loan:*** $3962. ***Average need-based gift aid:*** $15,556. ***Average indebtedness upon graduation:*** $24,825.

APPLYING

Standardized Tests *Required:* SAT or ACT (for admission).

Options: electronic application, deferred entrance.

Required: high school transcript.

Application deadlines: 8/15 (freshmen), 8/15 (transfers).

Notification: continuous (freshmen), continuous (transfers).

CONTACT

Mr. Corey Gannon, Assistant Director of Admissions, University of Pikeville, 147 Sycamore Street, Pikeville, KY 41501. *Phone:* 606-218-5251. *Toll-free phone:* 866-232-7700. *Fax:* 606-218-5255. *E-mail:* wewantyou@pc.edu.

University of the Cumberlands

Williamsburg, Kentucky

http://www.ucumberlands.edu/

CONTACT

Mrs. Erica Harris, Director of Admissions, University of the Cumberlands, 6178 College Station Drive, Williamsburg, KY 40769. *Phone:* 606-539-4241. *Toll-free phone:* 800-343-1609. *Fax:* 606-539-4303. *E-mail:* admiss@ucumberlands.edu.

Western Kentucky University

Bowling Green, Kentucky

http://www.wku.edu/

- **State-supported** comprehensive, founded 1906
- **Suburban** 235-acre campus with easy access to Nashville
- **Endowment** $184.9 million
- **Coed** 15,895 undergraduate students, 74% full-time, 60% women, 40% men
- **Minimally difficult** entrance level, 97% of applicants were admitted

UNDERGRAD STUDENTS

11,815 full-time, 4,080 part-time. Students come from 45 states and territories; 55 other countries; 24% are from out of state; 8% Black or African American, non-Hispanic/Latino; 4% Hispanic/Latino; 2% Asian, non-Hispanic/Latino; 0.1% Native Hawaiian or other Pacific Islander, non-Hispanic/Latino; 0.2% American Indian or Alaska Native, non-Hispanic/Latino; 3% Two or more races, non-Hispanic/Latino; 0.5% Race/ethnicity unknown; 2% international; 5% transferred in; 35% live on campus.

Freshmen:
Admission: 8,245 applied, 8,019 admitted, 2,714 enrolled. ***Average high school GPA:*** 3.4. ***Test scores:*** SAT evidence-based reading and writing scores over 500: 77%; SAT math scores over 500: 73%; ACT scores over 18: 87%; SAT evidence-based reading and writing scores over 600: 34%; SAT math scores over 600: 26%; ACT scores over 24: 45%; SAT evidence-based reading and writing scores over 700: 5%; SAT math scores over 700: 3%; ACT scores over 30: 10%.

Retention: 73% of full-time freshmen returned.

FACULTY
Total: 1,044, 65% full-time, 62% with terminal degrees.

Student/faculty ratio: 18:1.

ACADEMICS
Calendar: semesters. *Degrees:* certificates, associate, bachelor's, master's, doctoral, post-master's, and postbachelor's certificates.

Special study options: academic remediation for entering students, accelerated degree program, adult/continuing education programs, advanced placement credit, cooperative education, distance learning, double majors, English as a second language, freshman honors college, honors programs, independent study, internships, off-campus study, part-time degree program, services for LD students, student-designed majors, study abroad, summer session for credit. ***ROTC:*** Army (b), Air Force (c).

Unusual degree programs: 3-2 physics, applied sciences, engineering.

Computers: 272 computers/terminals are available on campus for general student use. Students can access the following: campus intranet, computer help desk, free student e-mail accounts, online (class) grades, online (class) registration, online (class) schedules. Campuswide network is available. 100% of college-owned or -operated housing units are wired for high-speed Internet access. Wireless service is available via entire campus.

Library: Helm-Cravens Library plus 2 others. *Books:* 682,383 (physical), 109,404 (digital/electronic); *Serial titles:* 10,101 (physical), 49,031 (digital/electronic); *Databases:* 179. Weekly public service hours: 94; students can reserve study rooms.

STUDENT LIFE
Housing options: on-campus residence required through sophomore year; coed, men-only, women-only. Campus housing is university owned. Freshman applicants given priority for college housing.

Activities and organizations: drama/theater group, student-run newspaper, radio and television station, choral group, marching band, Student Government Association, Campus Activities Board, National Pan-Hellenic Council, Campus Ministries, Residence Hall Association, national fraternities, national sororities.

Athletics Member NCAA. All Division I except football (Division I-A). ***Intercollegiate sports:*** baseball M(s), basketball M(s)/W(s), cross-country running M(s)/W(s), golf M(s)/W(s), soccer W, softball W(s), tennis W(s), track and field M(s)/W(s), volleyball W(s). ***Intramural sports:*** badminton M(c)/W(c), basketball M/W, fencing M(c)/W(c), golf M/W, lacrosse M(c)/W(c), rugby M(c)/W(c), soccer M/W, softball M/W, swimming and diving M(c)/W(c), tennis M(c)/W(c), ultimate Frisbee M/W, volleyball M/W, wrestling M(c)/W(c).

Campus security: 24-hour emergency response devices and patrols, student patrols, late-night transport/escort service, controlled dormitory access.

Student services: health clinic, personal/psychological counseling, women's center, legal services, veterans affairs office.

COSTS & FINANCIAL AID
Costs (2020–21) ***Tuition:*** area resident $10,802 full-time, $450 per credit hour part-time; state resident $10,802 full-time, $450 per credit hour part-time; nonresident $26,496 full-time, $1104 per credit hour part-time. Full-time tuition and fees vary according to reciprocity agreements. Part-time tuition and fees vary according to reciprocity agreements. ***Room and board:*** $8432; room only: $4678. Room and board charges vary according to board plan and housing facility. ***Payment plan:*** installment. ***Waivers:*** senior citizens and employees or children of employees.

Financial Aid Of all full-time matriculated undergraduates who enrolled in 2018, 9,938 applied for aid, 7,833 were judged to have need, 1,378 had their need fully met. 791 Federal Work-Study jobs (averaging $2182). 1,707 state and other part-time jobs (averaging $2404). In 2018, 2089 non-need-based awards were made. ***Average percent of need met:*** 18. ***Average financial aid package:*** $15,349. ***Average need-based loan:*** $3857. ***Average need-based gift aid:*** $5702. ***Average non-need-based aid:*** $6102. ***Average indebtedness upon graduation:*** $26,803.

APPLYING
Standardized Tests *Required:* SAT or ACT (for admission).

Options: electronic application, deferred entrance.

Application fee: $45.

Required: high school transcript, minimum of 2.0 unweighted high school GPA, Composite Admission Index (CAI) score of at least 60.

Application deadlines: 8/1 (freshmen), 8/1 (transfers).

Notification: continuous (freshmen), continuous (transfers).

CONTACT
Western Kentucky University, 1906 College Heights Boulevard, Bowling Green, KY 42101. *Phone:* 270-745-2551. *Toll-free phone:* 800-495-8463.

LOUISIANA

Centenary College of Louisiana
Shreveport, Louisiana
http://www.centenary.edu/

- **Independent United Methodist** comprehensive, founded 1825
- **Urban** 65-acre campus with easy access to Shreveport
- **Coed**
- **Moderately difficult** entrance level

FACULTY
Student/faculty ratio: 9:1.

ACADEMICS
Calendar: 4-4-1. *Degrees:* bachelor's and master's.
Library: Magale Library plus 1 other. Students can reserve study rooms.

STUDENT LIFE
Housing options: on-campus residence required through senior year; coed. Campus housing is university owned. Freshman campus housing is guaranteed.

Activities and organizations: drama/theater group, student-run newspaper, radio station, choral group, Intramural sports, Residence Life (Centenary Activities Board), Fellowship of Christian Athletes, Christian Leadership Center, Media Group, national fraternities, national sororities.

Athletics Member NCAA. All Division III.

Campus security: 24-hour emergency response devices and patrols, late-night transport/escort service, controlled dormitory access.

Student services: health clinic, personal/psychological counseling.

COSTS & FINANCIAL AID
Costs (2019–20) ***One-time required fee:*** $250. ***Comprehensive fee:*** $50,980 includes full-time tuition ($37,310) and room and board ($13,670). Part-time tuition: $1554 per credit hour.

Financial Aid Of all full-time matriculated undergraduates who enrolled in 2019, 470 applied for aid, 425 were judged to have need, 108 had their need fully met. 203 Federal Work-Study jobs (averaging $2346). 47 state and other part-time jobs (averaging $1921). In 2019, 105 non-need-based awards were made. ***Average percent of need met:*** 75. ***Average financial aid package:*** $32,543. ***Average need-based loan:*** $4070. ***Average need-based gift aid:*** $28,770. ***Average non-need-based aid:*** $24,820. ***Average indebtedness upon graduation:*** $25,363.

APPLYING
Standardized Tests *Required:* SAT or ACT (for admission).

Options: electronic application, early admission, early action, deferred entrance.

CONTACT
Ms. Lauren Carlton Hawkins, Associate Director of Admission, Recruitment, Centenary College of Louisiana, Office of Admission, 2911 Centenary Boulevard, Shreveport, LA 71104. *Phone:* 318-869-5131. *Toll-free phone:* 800-234-4448. *Fax:* 318-869-5005. *E-mail:* lcarlton@centenary.edu.

Dillard University
New Orleans, Louisiana
http://www.dillard.edu/

- **Independent interdenominational** 4-year, founded 1869
- **Urban** 55-acre campus
- **Endowment** $58.4 million
- **Coed** 1,235 undergraduate students, 94% full-time, 75% women, 25% men
- **Moderately difficult** entrance level, 39% of applicants were admitted

UNDERGRAD STUDENTS
1,164 full-time, 71 part-time. 46% are from out of state; 71% Black or African American, non-Hispanic/Latino; 2% Hispanic/Latino; 0.1% Native Hawaiian or other Pacific Islander, non-Hispanic/Latino; 0.2% American Indian or Alaska Native, non-Hispanic/Latino; 2% Two or more races, non-Hispanic/Latino; 24% Race/ethnicity unknown; 0.4% international; 5% transferred in; 65% live on campus.

Freshmen:
Admission: 9,203 applied, 3,572 admitted, 319 enrolled. ***Average high school GPA:*** 3.2. ***Test scores:*** SAT evidence-based reading and writing scores over 500: 79%; SAT math scores over 500: 63%; ACT scores over 18: 94%; SAT evidence-based reading and writing scores over 600: 16%; SAT math scores over 600: 7%; ACT scores over 24: 21%; SAT evidence-based reading and writing scores over 700: 2%; SAT math scores over 700: 2%; ACT scores over 30: 2%.

FACULTY
Total: 125, 57% full-time, 44% with terminal degrees.
Student/faculty ratio: 13:1.

ACADEMICS
Calendar: semesters. *Degree:* bachelor's.
Special study options: academic remediation for entering students, advanced placement credit, double majors, honors programs, part-time degree program, services for LD students, summer session for credit. ***ROTC:*** Army (c), Navy (c), Air Force (c).
Unusual degree programs: 3-2 engineering with Columbia University, Tulane University, University of New Orleans, Georgia Institute of Technology; biology with Boston University, Meharry Medical College, New York College of Podiatric Medicine, Ohio College of Medicine; public health with Louisiana State University, Tulane University.
Computers: 75 computers/terminals and 300 ports are available on campus for general student use. Students can access the following: free student e-mail accounts, online (class) grades, online (class) registration, online (class) schedules. Campuswide network is available. 100% of college-owned or -operated housing units are wired for high-speed Internet access. Wireless service is available via dorm rooms, student centers.
Library: Will W. Alexander Library plus 1 other.

STUDENT LIFE
Housing options: on-campus residence required for freshman year; men-only, women-only, special housing for students with disabilities. Campus housing is university owned. Freshman campus housing is guaranteed.
Activities and organizations: drama/theater group, student-run newspaper, radio station, choral group, Student Government Association, Student Activities Board, National Pan-Hellenic Council, Collegiate 100, Class Councils, national fraternities, national sororities.
Athletics Member NAIA. ***Intercollegiate sports:*** basketball M(s)/W(s), cross-country running M(s)/W(s), track and field M(s)/W(s), volleyball W(s). ***Intramural sports:*** basketball M/W, football M/W, tennis M/W, volleyball M/W, weight lifting M/W.
Campus security: 24-hour emergency response devices and patrols, late-night transport/escort service, controlled dormitory access.
Student services: health clinic, personal/psychological counseling, legal services.

COSTS & FINANCIAL AID
Costs (2020–21) ***Tuition:*** $17,410 full-time, $726 per credit hour part-time. ***Required fees:*** $1871 full-time. ***Room only:*** $6156.
Financial Aid Of all full-time matriculated undergraduates who enrolled in 2018, 1,223 applied for aid, 1,181 were judged to have need, 84 had their need fully met. In 2018, 42 non-need-based awards were made. ***Average percent of need met:*** 58. ***Average financial aid package:*** $17,207. ***Average need-based loan:*** $4044. ***Average need-based gift aid:*** $13,644. ***Average non-need-based aid:*** $8283.

APPLYING
Standardized Tests *Required:* SAT or ACT (for admission), minimum SAT score of 870 (math and verbal) or minimum ACT composite score of 18 (for admission).
Options: electronic application, early admission, deferred entrance.
Application fee: $36.
Required: high school transcript, minimum 2.5 GPA. ***Required for some:*** essay or personal statement, 2 letters of recommendation.
Application deadlines: rolling (freshmen), rolling (transfers).
Notification: continuous (freshmen), continuous (transfers).

CONTACT
Ms. Monica White, Director for Recruitment, Admissions and Programming, Dillard University, 2601 Gentilly Boulevard, New Orleans, LA 70122-3097. *Phone:* 504-816-4374. *Toll-free phone:* 800-216-8094. *Fax:* 504-816-4895. *E-mail:* acyprian@dillard.edu.

Franciscan Missionaries of Our Lady University
Baton Rouge, Louisiana
http://www.franu.edu/

CONTACT
Franciscan Missionaries of Our Lady University, LA. *Phone:* 225-768-1718. *E-mail:* admissions@franu.edu.

Grambling State University
Grambling, Louisiana
http://www.gram.edu/

- **State-supported** university, founded 1901, part of University of Louisiana System
- **Small-town** 590-acre campus with easy access to Shreveport
- **Endowment** $6.8 million
- **Coed** 4,153 undergraduate students, 92% full-time, 62% women, 38% men
- **Noncompetitive** entrance level, 97% of applicants were admitted

UNDERGRAD STUDENTS
3,813 full-time, 340 part-time. 93% Black or African American, non-Hispanic/Latino; 0.8% Hispanic/Latino; 0.2% Asian, non-Hispanic/Latino; 0.1% American Indian or Alaska Native, non-Hispanic/Latino; 0.9% Race/ethnicity unknown; 5% international.

Freshmen:
Admission: 3,109 applied, 3,023 admitted, 857 enrolled. ***Average high school GPA:*** 3.0. ***Test scores:*** SAT evidence-based reading and writing scores over 500: 57%; SAT math scores over 500: 54%; ACT scores over 18: 54%; SAT evidence-based reading and writing scores over 600: 6%; SAT math scores over 600: 4%; ACT scores over 24: 5%.

FACULTY
Total: 188, 85% full-time, 29% with terminal degrees.

ACADEMICS
Calendar: semesters. *Degrees:* bachelor's, master's, doctoral, and post-master's certificates.
Special study options: academic remediation for entering students, adult/continuing education programs, advanced placement credit, distance learning, double majors, honors programs, independent study, internships, off-campus study, part-time degree program, services for LD students, summer session for credit. ***ROTC:*** Army (b), Air Force (c).
Computers: 500 computers/terminals and 500 ports are available on campus for general student use. Students can access the following: campus intranet, computer help desk, free student e-mail accounts, online (class) grades, online (class) registration, online (class) schedules. Campuswide network is available. 100% of college-owned or -operated housing units are wired for high-speed Internet access. Wireless service is available via entire campus.

Library: A. C. Lewis Memorial Library. *Books:* 127,508 (physical), 205,483 (digital/electronic); *Serial titles:* 835 (physical), 51,728 (digital/electronic); *Databases:* 101. Weekly public service hours: 49; students can reserve study rooms.

STUDENT LIFE

Housing options: on-campus residence required through sophomore year; coed, men-only, women-only, special housing for students with disabilities. Campus housing is university owned. Freshman applicants given priority for college housing.

Activities and organizations: drama/theater group, student-run newspaper, radio and television station, choral group, marching band, Tiger Marching Band, Black Dynasty Modeling Troupe, Academic and Professional Clubs, sororities, fraternities, national fraternities, national sororities.

Athletics Member NCAA. All Division I except football (Division I-AA). ***Intercollegiate sports:*** baseball M(s), basketball M(s)/W(s), bowling W(s), cross-country running M/W, soccer W, softball W(s), tennis W(s), track and field M(s)/W(s), volleyball W(s). ***Intramural sports:*** badminton M(c)/W(c), basketball M/W, bowling M(c)/W(c), racquetball M(c)/W(c), soccer M(c)/W(c), softball W, table tennis M/W, tennis M(c)/W(c), volleyball M(c)/W(c), weight lifting M/W.

Campus security: 24-hour emergency response devices and patrols, student patrols, late-night transport/escort service, controlled dormitory access.

Student services: health clinic, personal/psychological counseling, veterans affairs office.

COSTS & FINANCIAL AID

Costs (2020–21) ***Tuition:*** area resident $5140 full-time, $215 per credit hour part-time; state resident $5140 full-time; nonresident $5140 full-time, $215 per credit hour part-time. ***Required fees:*** $11,566 full-time. ***Room only:*** $5572.

Financial Aid Of all full-time matriculated undergraduates who enrolled in 2019, 3,577 applied for aid, 3,011 were judged to have need. In 2019, 259 non-need-based awards were made. ***Average financial aid package:*** $10,595. ***Average need-based loan:*** $4055. ***Average need-based gift aid:*** $5841. ***Average non-need-based aid:*** $2658. ***Average indebtedness upon graduation:*** $42,963. ***Financial aid deadline:*** 6/1.

APPLYING

Standardized Tests *Required:* SAT or ACT (for admission).

Options: electronic application, early action, deferred entrance.

Application fee: $20.

Required: high school transcript, minimum 2.0 GPA, 19 units from Required Core 4 Curriculum including no more than one developmental course.

Application deadlines: 8/15 (freshmen), 7/15 (transfers), 8/23 (early action).

Notification: 4/1 (freshmen), continuous until 6/15 (transfers), 8/23 (early action).

CONTACT

DeVaria Hudson, Director of Admissions and Recruitment, Grambling State University, GSU Box 4200, Grambling, LA 71245. *Phone:* 318-274-6100. *Toll-free phone:* 800-569-4714. *Fax:* 318-274-3292. *E-mail:* hudsond@gram.edu.

Herzing University

Kenner, Louisiana

http://www.herzing.edu/new-orleans

CONTACT

Herzing University, 2500 Williams Boulevard, Kenner, LA 70062. *Toll-free phone:* 800-596-0724.

Louisiana College

Pineville, Louisiana

http://www.lacollege.edu/

- **Independent Southern Baptist** comprehensive, founded 1906
- **Small-town** 81-acre campus
- **Endowment** $37.9 million
- **Coed**
- **Moderately difficult** entrance level

FACULTY

Student/faculty ratio: 12:1.

ACADEMICS

Calendar: semesters. *Degrees:* certificates, associate, bachelor's, and master's.

Library: Richard W. Norton Memorial Library. *Books:* 81,432 (physical), 301,231 (digital/electronic); *Serial titles:* 84 (physical), 86,957 (digital/electronic); *Databases:* 138. Weekly public service hours: 70; students can reserve study rooms.

STUDENT LIFE

Housing options: on-campus residence required through sophomore year; men-only, women-only. Campus housing is university owned. Freshman campus housing is guaranteed.

Activities and organizations: drama/theater group, student-run radio and television station, choral group, marching band, Baptist Collegiate Ministry, Delta Xi Omega, Student Government Association, Union Board, Lambda Chi Beta.

Athletics Member NCAA. All Division III.

Campus security: 24-hour emergency response devices and patrols, student patrols, late-night transport/escort service, controlled dormitory access.

Student services: health clinic, personal/psychological counseling.

COSTS & FINANCIAL AID

Costs (2019–20) ***Comprehensive fee:*** $23,146 includes full-time tuition ($17,500) and room and board ($5646). Full-time tuition and fees vary according to course load. Part-time tuition: $547 per credit hour. Part-time tuition and fees vary according to course load. ***College room only:*** $2282. Room and board charges vary according to board plan and housing facility.

Financial Aid Of all full-time matriculated undergraduates who enrolled in 2018, 842 applied for aid, 719 were judged to have need, 157 had their need fully met. In 2018, 137 non-need-based awards were made. ***Average percent of need met:*** 64. ***Average financial aid package:*** $14,478. ***Average need-based loan:*** $3441. ***Average need-based gift aid:*** $12,150. ***Average non-need-based aid:*** $7780. ***Average indebtedness upon graduation:*** $25,885.

APPLYING

Standardized Tests *Required:* SAT or ACT (for admission). *Recommended:* ACT (for admission).

Options: electronic application, early action.

Application fee: $25.

Required: high school transcript, minimum 2.0 GPA. ***Required for some:*** essay or personal statement.

CONTACT

Ms. Renee Melder, Director of Admissions, Louisiana College, LC Box 566, Pineville, LA 71359. *Phone:* 318-487-7439. *Toll-free phone:* 800-487-1906. *E-mail:* admissions@lacollege.edu.

Louisiana Culinary Institute

Baton Rouge, Louisiana

http://www.lci.edu/

CONTACT

Louisiana Culinary Institute, 10550 Airline Highway, Baton Rouge, LA 70816. *Toll-free phone:* 877-533-3198.

Louisiana State University and Agricultural & Mechanical College

Baton Rouge, Louisiana

http://www.lsu.edu/

- **State-supported** university, founded 1860, part of Louisiana State University System
- **Urban** 2000-acre campus with easy access to New Orleans
- **Endowment** $457.7 million
- **Coed** 25,361 undergraduate students, 88% full-time, 53% women, 47% men
- **Moderately difficult** entrance level, 74% of applicants were admitted

UNDERGRAD STUDENTS
22,433 full-time, 2,928 part-time. Students come from 52 states and territories; 71 other countries; 18% are from out of state; 3% transferred in; 30% live on campus.

Freshmen:
Admission: 24,280 applied, 18,024 admitted, 5,812 enrolled. ***Average high school GPA:*** 3.4.

Retention: 84% of full-time freshmen returned.

ACADEMICS
Calendar: semesters. *Degrees:* certificates, bachelor's, master's, doctoral, post-master's, and postbachelor's certificates.

Special study options: accelerated degree program, adult/continuing education programs, advanced placement credit, cooperative education, distance learning, double majors, English as a second language, freshman honors college, honors programs, independent study, internships, off-campus study, part-time degree program, services for LD students, student-designed majors, study abroad, summer session for credit. ***ROTC:*** Army (b), Navy (c), Air Force (b).

Computers: 1,314 computers/terminals and 15,000 ports are available on campus for general student use. Students can access the following: computer help desk, free student e-mail accounts, online (class) grades, online (class) registration, online (class) schedules, free software for download, storage, discounts on hardware, virtual computer lab. Campuswide network is available. 100% of college-owned or -operated housing units are wired for high-speed Internet access. Wireless service is available via entire campus.
Library: Troy H. Middleton Library plus 4 others. Study areas open 24 hours, 5–7 days a week; students can reserve study rooms.

STUDENT LIFE
Housing options: on-campus residence required for freshman year; coed, men-only, women-only, special housing for students with disabilities. Campus housing is university owned. Freshman campus housing is guaranteed.

Activities and organizations: drama/theater group, student-run newspaper, radio and television station, choral group, marching band, intramural athletics, student political organizations, student professional organizations, religious organizations, cultural organizations, national fraternities, national sororities.

Athletics ***Intercollegiate sports:*** baseball M(s), basketball M(s)/W(s), cheerleading M/W, cross-country running M(s)/W(s), golf M(s)/W(s)(c), gymnastics W(s), soccer W(s), softball W(s), swimming and diving M(s)/W(s), tennis M(s)/W(s), track and field M(s)/W(s), volleyball W(s). ***Intramural sports:*** badminton M/W, baseball M(c), basketball M(c)/W, cross-country running M(c)/W(c), equestrian sports W(c), football M/W, golf M/W, ice hockey M(c)/W(c), lacrosse M(c)/W(c), racquetball M/W, rock climbing M/W, rowing M(c)/W(c), rugby M(c)/W(c), sand volleyball M/W, soccer M(c)/W(c), softball M/W, table tennis M(c)/W(c), tennis M(c)/W(c), triathlon M(c)/W(c), ultimate Frisbee M(c)/W(c), volleyball M(c)/W(c), water polo M(c)/W(c), weight lifting M(c)/W(c).

Campus security: 24-hour emergency response devices and patrols, late-night transport/escort service, controlled dormitory access.

Student services: health clinic, personal/psychological counseling, women's center, legal services, veterans affairs office.

COSTS & FINANCIAL AID
Costs (2019–20) ***Tuition:*** state resident $8038 full-time; nonresident $24,715 full-time. Full-time tuition and fees vary according to course load. Part-time tuition and fees vary according to course load. ***Required fees:*** $3924 full-time. ***Room and board:*** $12,276; room only: $8030. Room and board charges vary according to board plan and housing facility. ***Payment plan:*** deferred payment. ***Waivers:*** employees or children of employees.

Financial Aid Of all full-time matriculated undergraduates who enrolled in 2018, 14,349 applied for aid, 11,155 were judged to have need, 1,506 had their need fully met. In 2018, 3837 non-need-based awards were made. ***Average percent of need met:*** 61. ***Average financial aid package:*** $15,620. ***Average need-based loan:*** $4198. ***Average need-based gift aid:*** $12,782. ***Average non-need-based aid:*** $5912. ***Average indebtedness upon graduation:*** $24,851

APPLYING
Standardized Tests *Required:* SAT or ACT (for admission).

Options: electronic application, early admission, deferred entrance.

Application fee: $50.

Required: high school transcript, minimum 3.0 GPA, 1 letter of recommendation, ACT Composite score of 22 (18 in English and 19 in Math) or SAT Total Score of 1100 (500 in English and 510 in Math). ***Required for some:*** essay or personal statement.

CONTACT
Mr. Emmett Brown, Associate Director, Undergraduate Admissions, Louisiana State University and Agricultural & Mechanical College, 1146 Pleasant Hall, Baton Rouge, LA 70803. *Phone:* 225-578-1175. *Fax:* 225-578-4433. *E-mail:* cbrow63@lsu.edu.

Louisiana State University at Alexandria

Alexandria, Louisiana

http://www.lsua.edu/

CONTACT
Ms. Shelly Kieffer, Director of Enrollment Management, Louisiana State University at Alexandria, 8100 Highway 71 South, Alexandria, LA 71302-9121. *Phone:* 318-473-6424. *Toll-free phone:* 888-473-6417. *Fax:* 318-473-6418. *E-mail:* admissions@lsua.edu.

Louisiana State University Health Sciences Center

New Orleans, Louisiana

http://www.lsuhsc.edu/

- **State-supported** university, founded 1931, part of Louisiana State University System
- **Urban** 80-acre campus with easy access to New Orleans
- **Endowment** $120.1 million
- **Coed** 921 undergraduate students, 90% full-time, 85% women, 15% men

UNDERGRAD STUDENTS
831 full-time, 90 part-time. Students come from 19 states and territories; 10 other countries; 6% are from out of state; 11% Black or African American, non-Hispanic/Latino; 7% Hispanic/Latino; 5% Asian, non-Hispanic/Latino; 0.1% American Indian or Alaska Native, non-Hispanic/Latino; 2% Two or more races, non-Hispanic/Latino; 0.4% Race/ethnicity unknown; 0.1% international; 24% transferred in; 10% live on campus.

FACULTY
Total: 897, 76% full-time, 86% with terminal degrees.

Student/faculty ratio: 4:1.

ACADEMICS
Calendar: varies by academic program. *Degrees:* associate, bachelor's, master's, and doctoral.

Special study options: academic remediation for entering students, accelerated degree program, adult/continuing education programs, advanced placement credit, cooperative education, distance learning, double majors, independent study, internships, services for LD students, summer session for credit. ***ROTC:*** Army (c), Navy (c), Air Force (c).

Computers: 120 computers/terminals and 3,800 ports are available on campus for general student use. Students can access the following: campus intranet, computer help desk, free student e-mail accounts, online (class) grades, online (class) registration, online (class) schedules. Campuswide network is available. 100% of college-owned or -operated housing units are wired for high-speed Internet access. Wireless service is available via entire campus.

Library: John P. Ische Library plus 2 others. *Books:* 61,199 (physical); *Serial titles:* 4,968 (physical), 3,068 (digital/electronic); *Databases:* 204. Weekly public service hours: 97; study areas open 24 hours, 5–7 days a week.

STUDENT LIFE

Housing options: coed, special housing for students with disabilities. Campus housing is university owned.

Campus security: 24-hour emergency response devices and patrols, late-night transport/escort service, controlled dormitory access.

Student services: health clinic, personal/psychological counseling, veterans affairs office.

COSTS

Costs (2020–21) ***Tuition:*** state resident $5612 full-time, $357 per credit hour part-time; nonresident $12,394 full-time, $781 per credit hour part-time. Full-time tuition and fees vary according to degree level, program, and reciprocity agreements. Part-time tuition and fees vary according to course load, degree level, program, and reciprocity agreements. ***Required fees:*** $2696 full-time, $158 per credit hour part-time. ***Room only:*** $5598. Room and board charges vary according to housing facility.

APPLYING

Options: electronic application.

Application fee: $50.

Notification: 8/1 (transfers).

CONTACT

Louisiana State University Health Sciences Center, 433 Bolivar Street, New Orleans, LA 70112-2223.

Louisiana State University in Shreveport

Shreveport, Louisiana

http://www.lsus.edu/

- **State-supported** comprehensive, founded 1965, part of Louisiana State University System
- **Urban** 250-acre campus
- **Endowment** $26.3 million
- **Coed** 2,577 undergraduate students, 67% full-time, 61% women, 39% men
- 84% of applicants were admitted

UNDERGRAD STUDENTS

1,728 full-time, 849 part-time. Students come from 32 states and territories; 41 other countries; 9% are from out of state; 21% Black or African American, non-Hispanic/Latino; 5% Hispanic/Latino; 2% Asian, non-Hispanic/Latino; 0.1% Native Hawaiian or other Pacific Islander, non-Hispanic/Latino; 0.3% American Indian or Alaska Native, non-Hispanic/Latino; 5% Two or more races, non-Hispanic/Latino; 11% Race/ethnicity unknown; 4% international; 15% transferred in.

Freshmen:

Admission: 812 applied, 683 admitted, 338 enrolled. ***Average high school GPA:*** 3.3. ***Test scores:*** SAT evidence-based reading and writing scores over 500: 75%; SAT math scores over 500: 74%; ACT scores over 18: 96%; SAT evidence-based reading and writing scores over 600: 17%; SAT math scores over 600: 16%; ACT scores over 24: 36%; SAT math scores over 700: 8%; ACT scores over 30: 6%.

Retention: 65% of full-time freshmen returned.

FACULTY

Total: 246, 58% full-time, 54% with terminal degrees.

Student/faculty ratio: 27:1.

ACADEMICS

Calendar: semesters plus 8-week and two 4-week summer terms. *Degrees:* certificates, bachelor's, master's, doctoral, and post-master's certificates.

Special study options: accelerated degree program, advanced placement credit, distance learning, double majors, independent study, internships, part-time degree program, services for LD students, summer session for credit. ***ROTC:*** Army (c).

Computers: 250 computers/terminals are available on campus for general student use. Students can access the following: computer help desk, free student e-mail accounts, online (class) grades, online (class) registration, online (class) schedules. Campuswide network is available. Wireless service is available via entire campus.

Library: Noel Memorial Library. *Books:* 320,049 (physical), 308,035 (digital/electronic); *Serial titles:* 3,352 (physical), 95,807 (digital/electronic); *Databases:* 130. Weekly public service hours: 71; students can reserve study rooms.

STUDENT LIFE

Housing options: college housing not available.

Activities and organizations: drama/theater group, student-run newspaper, national fraternities, national sororities.

Athletics Member NAIA. ***Intercollegiate sports:*** baseball M(s), basketball M(s)/W(s), soccer M(s)/W(s), tennis W(s). ***Intramural sports:*** basketball M/W, football M/W, soccer M/W, softball M/W, volleyball M/W.

Campus security: 24-hour emergency response devices and patrols.

Student services: personal/psychological counseling, veterans affairs office.

APPLYING

Standardized Tests *Required:* SAT or ACT (for admission).

Options: electronic application.

Application fee: $20.

Required: high school transcript, minimum 2.0 GPA.

Application deadlines: rolling (freshmen), rolling (out-of-state freshmen), rolling (transfers).

Notification: continuous (freshmen), continuous (out-of-state freshmen), continuous (transfers).

CONTACT

Louisiana State University in Shreveport, 1 University Place, Shreveport, LA 71115-2399. *Phone:* 318-797-5061. *Toll-free phone:* 800-229-5957.

Louisiana Tech University

Ruston, Louisiana

http://www.latech.edu/

- **State-supported** university, founded 1894, part of University of Louisiana System
- **Small-town** 247-acre campus
- **Coed** 11,185 undergraduate students, 73% full-time, 48% women, 52% men
- **Moderately difficult** entrance level, 63% of applicants were admitted

UNDERGRAD STUDENTS

8,147 full-time, 3,038 part-time. 10% are from out of state; 2% transferred in; 15% live on campus.

Freshmen:

Admission: 7,297 applied, 4,602 admitted, 2,186 enrolled. ***Average high school GPA:*** 3.5.

Retention: 79% of full-time freshmen returned.

ACADEMICS

Calendar: quarters. *Degrees:* associate, bachelor's, master's, doctoral, post-master's, and postbachelor's certificates.

Special study options: academic remediation for entering students, adult/continuing education programs, advanced placement credit, distance learning, double majors, honors programs, independent study, internships, off-campus study, part-time degree program, study abroad, summer session for credit. ***ROTC:*** Army (c), Air Force (b).

Computers: Campuswide network is available.

Library: Prescott Memorial Library.

STUDENT LIFE
Housing options: on-campus residence required through sophomore year; men-only, women-only, special housing for students with disabilities. Campus housing is university owned.

Activities and organizations: drama/theater group, student-run newspaper, radio and television station, choral group, marching band, Student Government Association, Association of Women's Studies, Union Board, national fraternities, national sororities.

Athletics ***Intercollegiate sports:*** baseball M(s), basketball M(s)/W(s), cross-country running M(s)/W(s), golf M(s), softball W(s), tennis W(s), track and field M(s)/W(s), volleyball W(s), weight lifting M/W. ***Intramural sports:*** basketball M/W, bowling M/W, cross-country running M/W, football M/W, golf M, racquetball M/W, soccer M, softball M/W, tennis M/W, track and field M/W, volleyball M/W.

Campus security: 24-hour emergency response devices and patrols, student patrols, late-night transport/escort service, controlled dormitory access.

Student services: health clinic, personal/psychological counseling, legal services.

FINANCIAL AID
Financial Aid Of all full-time matriculated undergraduates who enrolled in 2017, 6,434 applied for aid, 4,569 were judged to have need, 1,034 had their need fully met. In 2017, 1752 non-need-based awards were made. ***Average percent of need met:*** 72. ***Average financial aid package:*** $11,449. ***Average need-based loan:*** $3647. ***Average need-based gift aid:*** $9779. ***Average non-need-based aid:*** $4512. ***Average indebtedness upon graduation:*** $23,659.

APPLYING
Standardized Tests *Required:* SAT or ACT (for admission). *Recommended:* ACT (for admission).

Options: early admission.

Application fee: $20.

CONTACT
Mrs. Jan B. Albritton, Director of Admissions, Louisiana Tech University, PO Box 3168, Ruston, LA 71272. *Phone:* 318-257-3036. *Toll-free phone:* 800-528-3241. *Fax:* 318-257-2499. *E-mail:* bulldog@latech.edu.

Loyola University New Orleans

New Orleans, Louisiana

http://www.loyno.edu/

- **Independent Roman Catholic (Jesuit)** comprehensive, founded 1912
- **Suburban** 26-acre campus with easy access to New Orleans
- **Endowment** $234.0 million
- **Coed** 3,188 undergraduate students, 91% full-time, 66% women, 34% men
- **Moderately difficult** entrance level, 75% of applicants were admitted

UNDERGRAD STUDENTS
2,886 full-time, 302 part-time. Students come from 53 states and territories; 41 other countries; 57% are from out of state; 17% Black or African American, non-Hispanic/Latino; 19% Hispanic/Latino; 3% Asian, non-Hispanic/Latino; 0.2% Native Hawaiian or other Pacific Islander, non-Hispanic/Latino; 0.5% American Indian or Alaska Native, non-Hispanic/Latino; 5% Two or more races, non-Hispanic/Latino; 6% Race/ethnicity unknown; 3% international; 6% transferred in; 54% live on campus.

Freshmen:
Admission: 5,857 applied, 4,394 admitted, 826 enrolled. ***Average high school GPA:*** 3.5. ***Test scores:*** SAT evidence-based reading and writing scores over 500: 89%; SAT math scores over 500: 582%; ACT scores over 18: 97%; SAT evidence-based reading and writing scores over 600: 50%; SAT math scores over 600: 31%; ACT scores over 24: 59%; SAT evidence-based reading and writing scores over 700: 6%; SAT math scores over 700: 4%; ACT scores over 30: 15%.

Retention: 79% of full-time freshmen returned.

FACULTY
Total: 447, 53% full-time, 76% with terminal degrees.

Student/faculty ratio: 12:1.

ACADEMICS
Calendar: semesters. *Degrees:* bachelor's, master's, doctoral, post-master's, and postbachelor's certificates.

Special study options: accelerated degree program, adult/continuing education programs, advanced placement credit, cooperative education, distance learning, double majors, English as a second language, external degree program, honors programs, independent study, internships, off-campus study, part-time degree program, services for LD students, student-designed majors, study abroad, summer session for credit. ***ROTC:*** Army (c), Navy (c), Air Force (c).

Unusual degree programs: 3-2 engineering with University of New Orleans, The Catholic University of America.

Computers: 525 computers/terminals and 2,500 ports are available on campus for general student use. Students can access the following: campus intranet, computer help desk, free student e-mail accounts, online (class) grades, online (class) registration, online (class) schedules. Campuswide network is available. 100% of college-owned or -operated housing units are wired for high-speed Internet access. Wireless service is available via entire campus.

Library: Monroe Library plus 1 other. *Books:* 363,298 (physical), 59,595 (digital/electronic); *Serial titles:* 1,385 (physical), 277,557 (digital/electronic); *Databases:* 129. Weekly public service hours: 114; students can reserve study rooms.

STUDENT LIFE
Housing options: on-campus residence required through sophomore year; coed, special housing for students with disabilities. Campus housing is university owned. Freshman campus housing is guaranteed.

Activities and organizations: drama/theater group, student-run newspaper, radio station, choral group, Panhellenic Council, Black Student Union, Honor Student Association, International Student Association, Interfraternity Council, national fraternities, national sororities.

Athletics Member NAIA. ***Intercollegiate sports:*** baseball M(s), basketball M(s)/W(s), cheerleading M(s)/W(s), cross-country running M(s)/W(s), golf M(s)/W(s), swimming and diving M(s)/W(s), tennis M(s)/W(s), track and field M(s)/W(s), volleyball W(s). ***Intramural sports:*** basketball M/W, football M/W, rugby M(c), sailing M(c)/W(c), soccer M/W, softball M/W, table tennis M/W, volleyball M/W, water polo M(c)/W(c).

Campus security: 24-hour emergency response devices and patrols, student patrols, late-night transport/escort service, controlled dormitory access.

Student services: health clinic, personal/psychological counseling, women's center.

COSTS & FINANCIAL AID
Costs (2020–21) ***One-time required fee:*** $250. ***Comprehensive fee:*** $55,636 includes full-time tuition ($40,288), mandatory fees ($1742), and room and board ($13,606). Part-time tuition: $1094 per credit hour. ***Required fees:*** $426 part-time. ***College room only:*** $7688. Room and board charges vary according to board plan. ***Waivers:*** senior citizens and employees or children of employees.

Financial Aid Of all full-time matriculated undergraduates who enrolled in 2019, 2,330 applied for aid, 2,079 were judged to have need, 344 had their need fully met. In 2019, 611 non-need-based awards were made. ***Average percent of need met:*** 76. ***Average financial aid package:*** $33,885. ***Average need-based loan:*** $4009. ***Average need-based gift aid:*** $30,629. ***Average non-need-based aid:*** $19,707. ***Average indebtedness upon graduation:*** $27,049.

APPLYING
Standardized Tests *Required:* SAT or ACT (for admission).

Options: electronic application, early admission, early action.

Required: essay or personal statement, high school transcript, 1 letter of recommendation. ***Recommended:*** interview.

Application deadlines: rolling (freshmen), rolling (out-of-state freshmen), rolling (transfers).

Notification: continuous (freshmen), continuous (out-of-state freshmen), continuous (transfers).

CONTACT
Mr. Nathan E Ament, Director of Admissions, Loyola University New Orleans, 6363 St. Charles Avenue, Campus Box 18, New Orleans, LA

70118. *Phone:* 504-865-3240. *Toll-free phone:* 800-4-LOYOLA. *Fax:* 504-865-3383. *E-mail:* nament@loyno.edu.

McNeese State University

Lake Charles, Louisiana

http://www.mcneese.edu/

- **State-supported** comprehensive, founded 1939, part of University of Louisiana System
- **Suburban** 1560-acre campus
- **Coed** 6,693 undergraduate students, 20% full-time, 12% women, 9% men
- 81% of applicants were admitted

UNDERGRAD STUDENTS
1,354 full-time, 19 part-time. Students come from 36 states and territories; 52 other countries; 7% are from out of state; 16% Black or African American, non-Hispanic/Latino; 4% Hispanic/Latino; 2% Asian, non-Hispanic/Latino; 0.1% Native Hawaiian or other Pacific Islander, non-Hispanic/Latino; 0.5% American Indian or Alaska Native, non-Hispanic/Latino; 3% Two or more races, non-Hispanic/Latino; 0.3% Race/ethnicity unknown; 7% international; 23% transferred in.

Freshmen:
Admission: 2,352 applied, 1,899 admitted, 1,373 enrolled. ***Average high school GPA:*** 3.5.

Retention: 70% of full-time freshmen returned.

FACULTY
Total: 427, 62% full-time.

Student/faculty ratio: 20:1.

ACADEMICS
Calendar: semesters. *Degrees:* associate, bachelor's, master's, post-master's, and postbachelor's certificates.

Special study options: academic remediation for entering students, accelerated degree program, advanced placement credit, cooperative education, distance learning, double majors, English as a second language, freshman honors college, honors programs, independent study, internships, off-campus study, part-time degree program, services for LD students, study abroad, summer session for credit.

Computers: Students can access the following: computer help desk, free student e-mail accounts, online (class) grades, online (class) registration, online (class) schedules. Campuswide network is available. 100% of college-owned or -operated housing units are wired for high-speed Internet access. Wireless service is available via entire campus.
Library: Frazar Memorial Library. *Books:* 492,782 (physical), 201,584 (digital/electronic); *Serial titles:* 48,291 (physical), 130,906 (digital/electronic); *Databases:* 122. Students can reserve study rooms.

STUDENT LIFE
Housing options: coed. Campus housing is university owned.

Activities and organizations: drama/theater group, student-run newspaper, choral group, marching band, Student Government Association, International Students Association, national fraternities, national sororities.

Athletics Member NCAA. All Division I except football (Division I-AA). ***Intercollegiate sports:*** baseball M(s), basketball M(s)/W(s), cross-country running M(s)/W(s), golf M(s)/W(s), soccer W(s), softball W(s), tennis W(s), track and field M(s)/W(s), volleyball W(s). ***Intramural sports:*** basketball M/W, football M/W, sand volleyball M/W, softball M/W, table tennis M/W, tennis M/W, ultimate Frisbee M/W.

Campus security: 24-hour emergency response devices and patrols, late-night transport/escort service, controlled dormitory access.

Student services: health clinic, personal/psychological counseling, women's center.

COSTS & FINANCIAL AID
Costs (2020–21) ***Tuition:*** state resident $5147 full-time; nonresident $13,185 full-time. Full-time tuition and fees vary according to course load. Part-time tuition and fees vary according to course load. ***Required fees:*** $2955 full-time. ***Room and board:*** $8624. Room and board charges vary according to board plan and housing facility. ***Payment plan:*** installment. ***Waivers:*** senior citizens and employees or children of employees.

Financial Aid Of all full-time matriculated undergraduates who enrolled in 2014, 4,704 applied for aid, 3,627 were judged to have need, 408 had their need fully met. ***Average percent of need met:*** 61. ***Average financial aid package:*** $9508. ***Average need-based loan:*** $3711. ***Average need-based gift aid:*** $4838.

APPLYING
Standardized Tests *Required:* SAT or ACT (for admission).

Options: electronic application, early admission, deferred entrance.

Application fee: $20.

Required: high school transcript, minimum 2.4 GPA, Louisiana Board of Regents high school Core 4 curriculum.

Application deadlines: rolling (freshmen), rolling (out-of-state freshmen), rolling (transfers).

Notification: continuous (freshmen), continuous (out-of-state freshmen), continuous (transfers).

CONTACT
Ms. Kourtney Istre, Director of Admissions and Recruiting, McNeese State University, Box 91740, Lake Charles, LA 70609. *Phone:* 337-475-5505. *Toll-free phone:* 800-622-3352. *Fax:* 337-475-5978. *E-mail:* kistre@mcneese.edu.

New Orleans Baptist Theological Seminary

New Orleans, Louisiana

http://www.nobts.edu/

CONTACT
Dr. Paul E. Gregoire Jr., Registrar/Director of Admissions, New Orleans Baptist Theological Seminary, 3939 Gentilly Boulevard, New Orleans, LA 70126-4858. *Phone:* 504-282-4455 Ext. 3337. *Toll-free phone:* 800-662-8701.

Nicholls State University

Thibodaux, Louisiana

http://www.nicholls.edu/

- **State-supported** comprehensive, founded 1948, part of University of Louisiana System
- **Small-town** 210-acre campus with easy access to New Orleans
- **Coed**
- **Noncompetitive** entrance level

FACULTY
Student/faculty ratio: 19:1.

ACADEMICS
Calendar: semesters. *Degrees:* certificates, associate, bachelor's, master's, post-master's, and postbachelor's certificates.
Library: Allen J. Ellender Memorial Library plus 3 others.

STUDENT LIFE
Housing options: on-campus residence required for freshman year; coed. Campus housing is university owned. Freshman campus housing is guaranteed.

Activities and organizations: drama/theater group, student-run newspaper, radio and television station, choral group, marching band, Student Government Association, Student Programming Association, Residence Hall Association, Food Advisory Association, national fraternities, national sororities.

Athletics Member NCAA. All Division I except football (Division I-AA).

Campus security: 24-hour emergency response devices and patrols, student patrols, late-night transport/escort service.

Student services: health clinic, personal/psychological counseling, women's center, legal services.

COSTS & FINANCIAL AID
Costs (2019–20) ***One-time required fee:*** $72. ***Tuition:*** area resident $4922 full-time, $4512 per year part-time; state resident $4922 full-time, $4512 per year part-time; nonresident $6015 full-time, $5514 per year part-time. Full-time tuition and fees vary according to location and program. Part-time tuition and fees vary according to course load, location, and program. ***Required fees:*** $2976 full-time, $3809 per year

part-time. ***Room and board:*** $9818; room only: $6580. Room and board charges vary according to board plan, housing facility, and location. ***Payment plans:*** installment, deferred payment.

Financial Aid Of all full-time matriculated undergraduates who enrolled in 2018, 4,312 applied for aid, 3,260 were judged to have need, 353 had their need fully met. ***Average percent of need met:*** 52. ***Average financial aid package:*** $8444. ***Average need-based loan:*** $2658. ***Average need-based gift aid:*** $6814. ***Financial aid deadline:*** 6/30.

APPLYING

Standardized Tests *Required:* SAT or ACT (for admission).

Options: electronic application, early admission, deferred entrance.

Application fee: $20.

Required: high school transcript, minimum 2.0 GPA, minimum state core curriculum (19 units), minimum overall GPA of 2.0.

CONTACT

Mrs. Becky L. Durocher, Director of Admissions, Nicholls State University, PO Box 2004-NSU, Thibodaux, LA 70310. *Phone:* 985-448-4507. *Toll-free phone:* 877-NICHOLLS. *Fax:* 985-448-4929. *E-mail:* nicholls@nicholls.edu.

Northwestern State University of Louisiana

Natchitoches, Louisiana

http://www.nsula.edu/

- **State-supported** comprehensive, founded 1884, part of University of Louisiana System
- **Small-town** 916-acre campus
- **Endowment** $15.4 million
- **Coed** 9,833 undergraduate students, 64% full-time, 71% women, 29% men
- **Moderately difficult** entrance level, 64% of applicants were admitted

UNDERGRAD STUDENTS

6,340 full-time, 3,493 part-time. 32% Black or African American, non-Hispanic/Latino; 7% Hispanic/Latino; 0.8% Asian, non-Hispanic/Latino; 0.1% Native Hawaiian or other Pacific Islander, non-Hispanic/Latino; 1% American Indian or Alaska Native, non-Hispanic/Latino; 5% Two or more races, non-Hispanic/Latino; 1% Race/ethnicity unknown; 1% international; 6% transferred in; 16% live on campus.

Freshmen:

Admission: 5,089 applied, 3,236 admitted, 1,515 enrolled. ***Average high school GPA:*** 3.4. ***Test scores:*** SAT evidence-based reading and writing scores over 500: 77%; SAT math scores over 500: 81%; ACT scores over 18: 86%; SAT evidence-based reading and writing scores over 600: 35%; SAT math scores over 600: 27%; ACT scores over 24: 25%; SAT evidence-based reading and writing scores over 700: 1%; SAT math scores over 700: 6%; ACT scores over 30: 3%.

Retention: 70% of full-time freshmen returned.

FACULTY

Total: 563, 59% full-time.

Student/faculty ratio: 20:1.

ACADEMICS

Calendar: semesters. *Degrees:* associate, bachelor's, master's, doctoral, post-master's, and postbachelor's certificates.

Special study options: adult/continuing education programs, advanced placement credit, cooperative education, distance learning, double majors, freshman honors college, honors programs, independent study, internships, part-time degree program, services for LD students, study abroad, summer session for credit. ***ROTC:*** Army (b).

Computers: 1,500 computers/terminals and 1,500 ports are available on campus for general student use. Students can access the following: computer help desk, free student e-mail accounts, online (class) grades, online (class) registration, online (class) schedules. Campuswide network is available. 100% of college-owned or -operated housing units are wired for high-speed Internet access. Wireless service is available via classrooms, computer centers, computer labs, dorm rooms, learning centers, libraries, student centers.

Library: Eugene P. Watson Memorial Library plus 1 other. *Books:* 310,849 (physical), 38,166 (digital/electronic); *Serial titles:* 329 (physical), 230 (digital/electronic); *Databases:* 111. Weekly public service hours: 87; students can reserve study rooms.

STUDENT LIFE

Housing options: coed, special housing for students with disabilities. Campus housing is university owned. Freshman applicants given priority for college housing.

Activities and organizations: drama/theater group, student-run newspaper, radio and television station, choral group, marching band, Student Activities Board, Student Government Associate, College Panhellenic Council, national fraternities, national sororities.

Athletics Member NCAA. All Division I except football (Division I-AA). ***Intercollegiate sports:*** baseball M(s), basketball M(s)/W(s), cheerleading M(s)/W(s), cross-country running M(s)/W(s), soccer W(s), softball W(s), tennis W(s), track and field M(s)/W(s), volleyball W(s). ***Intramural sports:*** archery M(c)/W(c), badminton M/W, basketball M/W, bowling M/W, crew M(c)/W(c), fencing M(c)/W(c), football M/W, racquetball M/W, softball M/W, swimming and diving M/W, table tennis M/W, tennis M/W, volleyball M/W.

Campus security: 24-hour emergency response devices and patrols, student patrols, late-night transport/escort service, controlled dormitory access.

Student services: health clinic, personal/psychological counseling, veterans affairs office.

COSTS & FINANCIAL AID

Costs (2019–20) ***Tuition:*** state resident $5180 full-time; nonresident $15,968 full-time. Full-time tuition and fees vary according to course load and location. Part-time tuition and fees vary according to course load and location. ***Required fees:*** $3588 full-time. ***Room and board:*** $9244; room only: $5404. Room and board charges vary according to board plan and housing facility. ***Payment plan:*** installment. ***Waivers:*** senior citizens and employees or children of employees.

Financial Aid Of all full-time matriculated undergraduates who enrolled in 2018, 5,833 applied for aid, 5,210 were judged to have need, 846 had their need fully met. In 2018, 360 non-need-based awards were made. ***Average percent of need met:*** 62. ***Average financial aid package:*** $14,859. ***Average need-based loan:*** $7240. ***Average need-based gift aid:*** $7944. ***Average non-need-based aid:*** $4420. ***Average indebtedness upon graduation:*** $29,793.

APPLYING

Standardized Tests *Required:* SAT or ACT (for admission).

Options: electronic application, deferred entrance.

Application fee: $20.

Required: high school transcript, minimum 2.4 GPA, college preparatory curriculum.

Application deadlines: 7/6 (freshmen), 7/6 (transfers).

Notification: continuous (freshmen), continuous (out-of-state freshmen), continuous (transfers).

CONTACT

Ms. Jana Lucky, Director of University Recruiting, Northwestern State University of Louisiana, 175 Sam Sibley Drive, Recruiting Office, Student Services Center, 1st Floor, Natchitoches, LA 71497. *Phone:* 318-357-4503. *Toll-free phone:* 800-327-1903. *Fax:* 318-357-5567. *E-mail:* recruiting@nsula.edu.

Saint Joseph Seminary College

Saint Benedict, Louisiana

http://www.sjasc.edu/

CONTACT

Saint Joseph Seminary College, 75376 River Road, St. Benedict, LA 70457. *Phone:* 985-867-2273. *Fax:* 985-327-1085. *E-mail:* registrar@sjasc.edu.

Southeastern Louisiana University

Hammond, Louisiana

http://www.southeastern.edu/

- **State-supported** comprehensive, founded 1925, part of University of Louisiana System
- **Small-town** 375-acre campus with easy access to New Orleans
- **Endowment** $55.0 million
- **Coed** 13,296 undergraduate students, 70% full-time, 62% women, 38% men
- **Moderately difficult** entrance level, 91% of applicants were admitted

UNDERGRAD STUDENTS
9,248 full-time, 4,048 part-time. Students come from 44 states and territories; 55 other countries; 4% are from out of state; 20% Black or African American, non-Hispanic/Latino; 7% Hispanic/Latino; 1% Asian, non-Hispanic/Latino; 0.1% Native Hawaiian or other Pacific Islander, non-Hispanic/Latino; 0.2% American Indian or Alaska Native, non-Hispanic/Latino; 4% Two or more races, non-Hispanic/Latino; 3% Race/ethnicity unknown; 1% international; 5% transferred in; 23% live on campus.

Freshmen:
Admission: 4,325 applied, 3,925 admitted, 2,733 enrolled. ***Average high school GPA:*** 3.4. ***Test scores:*** ACT scores over 18: 95%; ACT scores over 24: 40%; ACT scores over 30: 4%.

Retention: 68% of full-time freshmen returned.

FACULTY
Total: 624, 82% full-time, 61% with terminal degrees.

Student/faculty ratio: 19:1.

ACADEMICS
Calendar: semesters. *Degrees:* certificates, associate, bachelor's, master's, doctoral, post-master's, and postbachelor's certificates.

Special study options: academic remediation for entering students, accelerated degree program, adult/continuing education programs, advanced placement credit, distance learning, double majors, English as a second language, honors programs, independent study, internships, off-campus study, part-time degree program, services for LD students, study abroad, summer session for credit. ***ROTC:*** Army (b).

Computers: 1,123 computers/terminals and 600 ports are available on campus for general student use. Students can access the following: campus intranet, computer help desk, free student e-mail accounts, online (class) grades, online (class) registration, online (class) schedules, campus Webmail, student newspaper, transcripts, bookstore. Campuswide network is available. 100% of college-owned or -operated housing units are wired for high-speed Internet access. Wireless service is available via entire campus.

Library: Linus A. Sims Memorial Library plus 1 other. *Books:* 1.3 million (physical), 513,005 (digital/electronic); *Serial titles:* 499 (physical), 56,076 (digital/electronic). Students can reserve study rooms.

STUDENT LIFE
Housing options: coed, women-only, special housing for students with disabilities. Campus housing is university owned.

Activities and organizations: drama/theater group, student-run newspaper, radio and television station, choral group, marching band, Student Government Association, Honors Club, Catholic Student Association, Fellowship of Christian Athletes, National Association for the Advancement of Colored People, national fraternities, national sororities.

Athletics Member NCAA. All Division I except football (Division I-AA). ***Intercollegiate sports:*** baseball M(s), basketball M(s)/W(s), cross-country running M(s)/W(s), golf M(s), sand volleyball W, soccer W(s), softball W(s), tennis W(s), track and field M(s)/W(s), volleyball W(s). ***Intramural sports:*** badminton M/W, basketball M/W, cross-country running M(c)/W(c), football M/W, racquetball M/W, rugby M(c), soccer M/W, softball M/W, tennis M/W, volleyball M/W.

Campus security: 24-hour emergency response devices and patrols, student patrols, late-night transport/escort service, controlled dormitory access.

Student services: health clinic, personal/psychological counseling, veterans affairs office.

COSTS & FINANCIAL AID
Costs (2019–20) ***Tuition:*** state resident $5777 full-time, $347 per credit hour part-time; nonresident $18,255 full-time, $867 per credit hour part-time. Full-time tuition and fees vary according to course load. Part-time tuition and fees vary according to course load. ***Required fees:*** $2552 full-time. ***Room and board:*** $8600; room only: $5050. Room and board charges vary according to board plan and housing facility. ***Payment plan:*** installment. ***Waivers:*** employees or children of employees.

Financial Aid Of all full-time matriculated undergraduates who enrolled in 2018, 7,685 applied for aid, 6,720 were judged to have need, 581 had their need fully met. 159 Federal Work-Study jobs (averaging $2242). 814 state and other part-time jobs (averaging $1935). In 2018, 653 non-need-based awards were made. ***Average need-based loan:*** $3614. ***Average need-based gift aid:*** $5487. ***Average non-need-based aid:*** $1875. ***Average indebtedness upon graduation:*** $19,356.

APPLYING
Standardized Tests *Required:* SAT or ACT (for admission).

Options: electronic application.

Application fee: $20.

Required: high school transcript, minimum 2.4 GPA, proof of immunization; Regents Core Curriculum(English-4, Math-4, Science-4, Social Studies-4, Foreign Language-2, Art-1); no more than one developmental course requirement; either have ACT composite 21 or Regents Core GPA 2.0; college transcripts and statement of good standing required for some.

Application deadlines: 8/1 (freshmen), 8/1 (transfers).

Notification: continuous until 9/15 (freshmen), continuous until 9/15 (transfers).

CONTACT
Southeastern Louisiana University, 548 Ned McGehee Drive, Hammond, LA 70402. *Phone:* 985-549-3329. *Toll-free phone:* 800-222-7358.

Southern University and Agricultural and Mechanical College

Baton Rouge, Louisiana

http://www.subr.edu/

- **State-supported** university, founded 1880, part of Southern University System
- **Suburban** 964-acre campus
- **Endowment** $12.9 million
- **Coed**
- **Moderately difficult** entrance level

FACULTY
Student/faculty ratio: 16:1.

ACADEMICS
Calendar: semesters. *Degrees:* bachelor's, master's, doctoral, and post-master's certificates.
Library: John B. Cade Library plus 2 others.

STUDENT LIFE
Housing options: on-campus residence required for freshman year; men-only, women-only. Campus housing is university owned. Freshman applicants given priority for college housing.

Activities and organizations: drama/theater group, student-run newspaper, choral group, marching band, Student Government Association, Association for Women Students, Men's Federation, Collegiate 100 Black Men, Southern University Pan Hellenic Council, national fraternities, national sororities.

Athletics Member NCAA. All Division I except football (Division I-AA).

Campus security: 24-hour emergency response devices and patrols, late-night transport/escort service, controlled dormitory access.

Student services: health clinic, personal/psychological counseling, women's center, legal services.

FINANCIAL AID
Financial Aid Of all full-time matriculated undergraduates who enrolled in 2006, 6,032 applied for aid, 5,642 were judged to have need, 85 had their need fully met. 900 Federal Work-Study jobs (averaging $1800). 300 state and other part-time jobs (averaging $2500). ***Average percent of need***

met: 85. ***Average financial aid package:*** $7444. ***Average need-based loan:*** $3738. ***Average need-based gift aid:*** $3436. ***Average non-need-based aid:*** $3151. ***Average indebtedness upon graduation:*** $23,000.

APPLYING
Standardized Tests *Required:* SAT or ACT (for admission).

Options: electronic application, early admission.

Application fee: $20.

Required: high school transcript, minimum 2.0 GPA, Louisiana Board of Regents Core curriculum of 16.5 units of selected courses.

CONTACT
Dr. Manicia Finch, Director of Admissions, Southern University and Agricultural and Mechanical College, PO Box 9901, Baton Rouge, LA 70813. *Phone:* 225-771-2430. *Fax:* 225-771-2500. *E-mail:* manicia_finch@subr.edu.

Southern University at New Orleans

New Orleans, Louisiana

http://www.suno.edu/

CONTACT
Southern University at New Orleans, 6400 Press Drive, New Orleans, LA 70126-1009. *Phone:* 504-286-5033.

Southwest University

Kenner, Louisiana

http://www.southwest.edu/

CONTACT
Admissions Office, Southwest University, 2200 Veterans Memorial Boulevard, Kenner, LA 70062. *Phone:* 504-468-2900. *Toll-free phone:* 800-433-5923. *Fax:* 504-468-3213. *E-mail:* admissions@southwest.edu.

Tulane University

New Orleans, Louisiana

http://www.tulane.edu/

- **Independent** university, founded 1834
- **Urban** 110-acre campus
- **Endowment** $1.7 billion
- **Coed** 6,968 undergraduate students, 100% full-time, 59% women, 41% men
- **Very difficult** entrance level, 13% of applicants were admitted

UNDERGRAD STUDENTS
6,934 full-time, 34 part-time. Students come from 53 states and territories; 62 other countries; 80% are from out of state; 5% Black or African American, non-Hispanic/Latino; 7% Hispanic/Latino; 6% Asian, non-Hispanic/Latino; 0.1% Native Hawaiian or other Pacific Islander, non-Hispanic/Latino; 0.1% American Indian or Alaska Native, non-Hispanic/Latino; 4% Two or more races, non-Hispanic/Latino; 1% Race/ethnicity unknown; 5% international; 2% transferred in; 46% live on campus.

Freshmen:
Admission: 42,185 applied, 5,431 admitted, 1,821 enrolled. ***Average high school GPA:*** 3.6. ***Test scores:*** SAT evidence-based reading and writing scores over 500: 100%; SAT math scores over 500: 100%; ACT scores over 18: 100%; SAT evidence-based reading and writing scores over 600: 94%; SAT math scores over 600: 95%; ACT scores over 24: 99%; SAT evidence-based reading and writing scores over 700: 52%; SAT math scores over 700: 75%; ACT scores over 30: 88%.

Retention: 93% of full-time freshmen returned.

FACULTY
Total: 1,269, 63% full-time, 79% with terminal degrees.

Student/faculty ratio: 8:1.

ACADEMICS
Calendar: semesters plus 3 summer sessions. *Degrees:* certificates, bachelor's, master's, doctoral, and postbachelor's certificates.

Special study options: accelerated degree program, adult/continuing education programs, advanced placement credit, cooperative education, distance learning, double majors, English as a second language, freshman honors college, honors programs, independent study, internships, off-campus study, part-time degree program, services for LD students, student-designed majors, study abroad, summer session for credit. ***ROTC:*** Army (b), Navy (b), Air Force (b).

Unusual degree programs: 3-2 business administration; public health tropical medicine, science and engineering.

Computers: 556 computers/terminals are available on campus for general student use. Students can access the following: campus intranet, computer help desk, free student e-mail accounts, online (class) grades, online (class) registration, online (class) schedules. Campuswide network is available. 100% of college-owned or -operated housing units are wired for high-speed Internet access. Wireless service is available via entire campus.

Library: Howard Tilton Memorial Library plus 8 others. *Books:* 4.6 million (physical); *Serial titles:* 66,832 (physical). Study areas open 24 hours, 5–7 days a week; students can reserve study rooms.

STUDENT LIFE
Housing options: on-campus residence required through sophomore year; coed, women-only, special housing for students with disabilities. Campus housing is university owned. Freshman campus housing is guaranteed.

Activities and organizations: drama/theater group, student-run newspaper, radio and television station, choral group, marching band, Community Action Council of Tulane Students (CACTUS), Associated Student Body, Tulane University Campus Programming (TUCP), Association of Club Sports (ACS), National Pan-Hellenic Council, national fraternities, national sororities.

Athletics Member NCAA. All Division I except football (Division I-A). ***Intercollegiate sports:*** baseball M(s), basketball M(s)/W(s), crew M(c)/W(c), cross-country running M(s)/W(s), golf W(s)(c), gymnastics M(c)/W(c), ice hockey M(c)/W(c), lacrosse M(c)/W(c), rugby M(c), sailing M(c)/W(c), soccer M(c)/W(s), swimming and diving M(c)/W(s), tennis M(s)/W(s), track and field M(c)/W(s), volleyball M(c)/W(s), water polo M(c)/W(c). ***Intramural sports:*** baseball M(c), cheerleading M(c)/W(c), crew M(c)/W(c), cross-country running M(c), fencing M(c)/W(c), field hockey M(c)/W(c), gymnastics M(c)/W(c), ice hockey M(c), lacrosse M(c)/W(c), racquetball M(c)/W(c), rock climbing M(c)/W(c), rugby M(c), sailing M(c)/W(c), soccer M(c)/W(c), swimming and diving M(c)/W(c), tennis M(c)/W(c), track and field M(c)/W, ultimate Frisbee M(c)/W(c), volleyball M(c)/W(c), water polo M(c)/W(c).

Campus security: 24-hour emergency response devices and patrols, student patrols, late-night transport/escort service, controlled dormitory access, on and off-campus shuttle service, crime prevention programs, lighted pathways, TUPD patrols 24 hrs a day 365 days a year, virtual.

Student services: health clinic, personal/psychological counseling, women's center, legal services, veterans affairs office.

COSTS & FINANCIAL AID
Costs (2019–20) ***Comprehensive fee:*** $72,574 includes full-time tuition ($52,760), mandatory fees ($4040), and room and board ($15,774). ***College room only:*** $9010. Room and board charges vary according to board plan and housing facility. ***Payment plan:*** tuition prepayment. ***Waivers:*** employees or children of employees.

Financial Aid Of all full-time matriculated undergraduates who enrolled in 2019, 3,267 applied for aid, 2,294 were judged to have need, 1,101 had their need fully met. In 2019, 3144 non-need-based awards were made. ***Average percent of need met:*** 93. ***Average financial aid package:*** $47,419. ***Average need-based loan:*** $4372. ***Average need-based gift aid:*** $37,297. ***Average non-need-based aid:*** $24,189. ***Average indebtedness upon graduation:*** $31,306.

APPLYING
Standardized Tests *Required:* SAT or ACT (for admission).

Options: electronic application, early decision, early action, deferred entrance.

Required: essay or personal statement, high school transcript, 1 letter of recommendation.

Application deadlines: 11/15 (freshmen), 11/15 (early action).

Early decision deadline: 11/1 (for plan 1), 1/6 (for plan 2).

Notification: 12/15 (early decision plan 1), 1/31 (early decision plan 2), 1/15 (early action).

COLLEGES AT-A-GLANCE

CONTACT

Satyajit Dattagupta, Vice President for Enrollment Management and Dean of Admissions, Tulane University, Office of Admissions, 210 Gibson Hall, New Orleans, LA 70118. *Phone:* 504-865-5731. *Toll-free phone:* 800-873-9283. *Fax:* 504-862-8715. *E-mail:* undergrad.admission@tulane.edu.

University of Holy Cross

New Orleans, Louisiana

http://www.uhcno.edu/

CONTACT

Donna Kennedy, Director of Admissions and Financial Aid, University of Holy Cross, 4123 Woodland Drive, New Orleans, LA 70131-7399. *Phone:* 504-398-2175. *Toll-free phone:* 800-259-7744. *E-mail:* dkennedy@olhcc.edu.

University of Louisiana at Lafayette

Lafayette, Louisiana

http://www.louisiana.edu/

- **State-supported** university, founded 1898, part of University of Louisiana System
- **Urban** 1375-acre campus
- **Endowment** $132.9 million
- **Coed** 14,603 undergraduate students, 82% full-time, 57% women, 43% men
- **Moderately difficult** entrance level, 68% of applicants were admitted

UNDERGRAD STUDENTS

11,929 full-time, 2,674 part-time. Students come from 44 states and territories; 57 other countries; 6% are from out of state; 21% Black or African American, non-Hispanic/Latino; 6% Hispanic/Latino; 3% Asian, non-Hispanic/Latino; 0.1% Native Hawaiian or other Pacific Islander, non-Hispanic/Latino; 0.3% American Indian or Alaska Native, non-Hispanic/Latino; 3% Two or more races, non-Hispanic/Latino; 3% Race/ethnicity unknown; 1% international; 5% transferred in; 24% live on campus.

Freshmen:

Admission: 9,138 applied, 6,206 admitted, 2,387 enrolled. ***Average high school GPA:*** 3.4. ***Test scores:*** SAT evidence-based reading and writing scores over 500: 82%; SAT math scores over 500: 81%; ACT scores over 18: 97%; SAT evidence-based reading and writing scores over 600: 46%; SAT math scores over 600: 34%; ACT scores over 24: 45%; SAT evidence-based reading and writing scores over 700: 11%; SAT math scores over 700: 11%; ACT scores over 30: 9%.

Retention: 76% of full-time freshmen returned.

FACULTY

Total: 848, 78% full-time, 59% with terminal degrees.

Student/faculty ratio: 20:1.

ACADEMICS

Calendar: semesters. *Degrees:* bachelor's, master's, doctoral, post-master's, and postbachelor's certificates.

Special study options: academic remediation for entering students, accelerated degree program, adult/continuing education programs, advanced placement credit, cooperative education, distance learning, double majors, honors programs, independent study, internships, part-time degree program, services for LD students, student-designed majors, study abroad, summer session for credit. ***ROTC:*** Army (b).

Computers: 413 computers/terminals and 800 ports are available on campus for general student use. Students can access the following: campus intranet, computer help desk, free student e-mail accounts, online (class) grades, online (class) registration, online (class) schedules. Campuswide network is available. 98% of college-owned or -operated housing units are wired for high-speed Internet access. Wireless service is available via entire campus.

Library: Edith Garland Dupre Library. *Books:* 1.5 million (physical), 529,730 (digital/electronic); *Serial titles:* 26,860 (physical), 171,673 (digital/electronic); *Databases:* 232. Students can reserve study rooms.

STUDENT LIFE

Housing options: on-campus residence required for freshman year; coed, men-only, women-only. Campus housing is university owned. Freshman campus housing is guaranteed.

Activities and organizations: drama/theater group, student-run newspaper, radio station, choral group, marching band, Union Program Council, Chi Alpha, Student Government Association, Greek Council, Newman Club, national fraternities, national sororities.

Athletics Member NCAA. All Division I. ***Intercollegiate sports:*** baseball M(s), basketball M(s)/W(s), cross-country running M(s)/W(s), football M(s), golf M(s), soccer W, softball W(s), tennis M(s)/W(s), track and field M(s)/W(s), volleyball W(s). ***Intramural sports:*** badminton M/W, baseball M, basketball M/W, bowling M/W, football M/W, ice hockey M, lacrosse M, racquetball M/W, rugby M, soccer M, softball M/W, tennis M/W, ultimate Frisbee M/W, volleyball M/W, weight lifting M/W.

Campus security: 24-hour emergency response devices and patrols, late-night transport/escort service, controlled dormitory access.

Student services: health clinic, personal/psychological counseling, women's center, legal services.

COSTS & FINANCIAL AID

Costs (2019–20) ***Tuition:*** area resident $5407 full-time, $433 per credit hour part-time; state resident $5407 full-time, $433 per credit hour part-time; nonresident $19,135 full-time, $1005 per credit hour part-time. ***Required fees:*** $4975 full-time. ***Room and board:*** $10,708; room only: $6590. Room and board charges vary according to board plan and housing facility. ***Waivers:*** children of alumni and employees or children of employees.

Financial Aid Of all full-time matriculated undergraduates who enrolled in 2018, 10,499 applied for aid, 8,096 were judged to have need, 901 had their need fully met. 471 Federal Work-Study jobs (averaging $1420). In 2018, 1513 non-need-based awards were made. ***Average percent of need met:*** 64. ***Average financial aid package:*** $9018. ***Average need-based loan:*** $3895. ***Average need-based gift aid:*** $5905. ***Average non-need-based aid:*** $4704.

APPLYING

Standardized Tests *Required:* SAT or ACT (for admission).

Options: electronic application, early admission, deferred entrance.

Application fee: $25.

Required: high school transcript, minimum 2.0 GPA, core requirements.

Application deadlines: rolling (freshmen), rolling (transfers).

CONTACT

Ms. Amy DesOrmeaux, Director of Undergraduate Admissions, University of Louisiana at Lafayette, PO Drawer 41210, Lafayette, LA 70504. *Phone:* 337-482-1325. *Toll-free phone:* 800-752-6553. *Fax:* 337-482-1317. *E-mail:* admissions@louisiana.edu.

University of Louisiana at Monroe

Monroe, Louisiana

http://www.ulm.edu/

- **State-supported** university, founded 1931, part of University of Louisiana System
- **Urban** 238-acre campus
- **Endowment** $32.7 million
- **Coed** 6,876 undergraduate students, 82% full-time, 77% women, 36% men
- **Moderately difficult** entrance level, 79% of applicants were admitted

UNDERGRAD STUDENTS

5,660 full-time, 2,116 part-time. Students come from 42 states and territories; 46 other countries; 12% are from out of state; 24% Black or African American, non-Hispanic/Latino; 3% Hispanic/Latino; 2% Asian, non-Hispanic/Latino; 0.3% American Indian or Alaska Native, non-Hispanic/Latino; 3% Two or more races, non-Hispanic/Latino; 3% Race/ethnicity unknown; 5% international; 5% transferred in; 30% live on campus.

Freshmen:

Admission: 4,036 applied, 3,203 admitted, 1,143 enrolled. ***Average high school GPA:*** 3.5. ***Test scores:*** ACT scores over 18: 91%; ACT scores over 24: 31%; ACT scores over 30: 4%.

Retention: 73% of full-time freshmen returned.

FACULTY
Total: 441, 73% full-time.

Student/faculty ratio: 18:1.

ACADEMICS
Calendar: semesters. *Degrees:* associate, bachelor's, master's, doctoral, post-master's, and postbachelor's certificates.

Special study options: academic remediation for entering students, accelerated degree program, adult/continuing education programs, advanced placement credit, cooperative education, distance learning, double majors, English as a second language, external degree program, honors programs, independent study, internships, off-campus study, part-time degree program, services for LD students, study abroad, summer session for credit. ***ROTC:*** Army (c).

Computers: Students can access the following: campus intranet, computer help desk, free student e-mail accounts, online (class) grades, online (class) registration, online (class) schedules. Campuswide network is available. 100% of college-owned or -operated housing units are wired for high-speed Internet access. Wireless service is available via entire campus.
Library: University Library. *Books:* 218,492 (physical), 293,246 (digital/electronic); *Serial titles:* 245 (physical), 198,009 (digital/electronic); *Databases:* 104. Students can reserve study rooms.

STUDENT LIFE
Housing options: coed, men-only, women-only. Campus housing is university owned. Freshman applicants given priority for college housing.

Activities and organizations: drama/theater group, student-run newspaper, radio and television station, choral group, marching band, Maroon Platoon, Alpha Lambda Delta, Louisiana Pharmacist Alliance, Association for Students in Kinesiology, Pre-Pharmacy Organization/Sound of Today, national fraternities, national sororities.

Athletics Member NCAA. All Division I except football (Division I-A). ***Intercollegiate sports:*** baseball M(s), basketball M(s)/W(s), cross-country running M(s)/W(s), golf M(s)/W(s), sand volleyball W(s), soccer W(s), softball W(s), tennis W(s), track and field M(s)/W(s), volleyball W(s).

Campus security: 24-hour emergency response devices and patrols, student patrols, late-night transport/escort service, controlled dormitory access.

Student services: health clinic, personal/psychological counseling.

FINANCIAL AID
Financial Aid Of all full-time matriculated undergraduates who enrolled in 2019, 4,263 applied for aid, 3,390 were judged to have need, 313 had their need fully met. 363 Federal Work-Study jobs (averaging $2455). In 2019, 1084 non-need-based awards were made. ***Average percent of need met:*** 69. ***Average financial aid package:*** $12,356. ***Average need-based loan:*** $3822. ***Average need-based gift aid:*** $5002. ***Average non-need-based aid:*** $9036.

APPLYING
Standardized Tests *Required:* SAT or ACT (for admission).

Options: electronic application, early admission.

Application fee: $20.

Required: high school transcript, minimum 2.4 GPA.

Application deadlines: rolling (freshmen), rolling (transfers).

Notification: continuous (freshmen), continuous (transfers).

CONTACT
University of Louisiana at Monroe, 700 University Avenue, Monroe, LA 71209-0001. *Phone:* 318-342-5259. *Toll-free phone:* 800-372-5127.

University of New Orleans

New Orleans, Louisiana

http://www.uno.edu/

- **State-supported** university, founded 1958, part of University of Louisiana System
- **Urban** 345-acre campus
- **Coed**
- 57% of applicants were admitted

FACULTY
Student/faculty ratio: 22:1.

ACADEMICS
Calendar: semesters. *Degrees:* bachelor's, master's, doctoral, and postbachelor's certificates.
Library: Earl K. Long Library. *Books:* 1.0 million (physical), 220,863 (digital/electronic); *Serial titles:* 25,831 (physical), 55,551 (digital/electronic); *Databases:* 154. Students can reserve study rooms.

STUDENT LIFE
Housing options: coed. Campus housing is university owned and is provided by a third party. Freshman applicants given priority for college housing.

Activities and organizations: drama/theater group, student-run newspaper, choral group, Student Activities Council, Student Government, International Student Organization, Vietnamese American Student Association, Greek Life, national fraternities, national sororities.

Athletics Member NCAA. All Division I.

Campus security: 24-hour emergency response devices and patrols, late-night transport/escort service, controlled dormitory access.

Student services: health clinic, personal/psychological counseling, women's center, legal services, veterans affairs office.

FINANCIAL AID
Financial Aid Of all full-time matriculated undergraduates who enrolled in 2016, 3,680 applied for aid, 3,094 were judged to have need, 386 had their need fully met. In 2016, 325 non-need-based awards were made. ***Average percent of need met:*** 64. ***Average financial aid package:*** $9587. ***Average need-based loan:*** $3813. ***Average need-based gift aid:*** $5126. ***Average non-need-based aid:*** $2605. ***Average indebtedness upon graduation:*** $20,723. ***Financial aid deadline:*** 6/30.

APPLYING
Standardized Tests *Required:* SAT or ACT (for admission).

Options: electronic application, deferred entrance.

Application fee: $25.

Required: high school transcript.

CONTACT
Mr. Brett Hornsby, Director, Enrollment Operations, University of New Orleans, Privateer Enrollment Center, 105 Earl K. Long Library, New Orleans, LA 70148. *Phone:* 504-280-7394. *Toll-free phone:* 888-514-4275. *Fax:* 504-280-3973. *E-mail:* bjhornsb@uno.edu.

Xavier University of Louisiana

New Orleans, Louisiana

http://www.xula.edu/

- **Independent Roman Catholic** comprehensive, founded 1925
- **Urban** 23-acre campus
- **Coed** 2,530 undergraduate students, 96% full-time, 76% women, 24% men
- **Moderately difficult** entrance level, 60% of applicants were admitted

UNDERGRAD STUDENTS
2,424 full-time, 106 part-time. 62% are from out of state; 79% Black or African American, non-Hispanic/Latino; 5% Hispanic/Latino; 4% Asian, non-Hispanic/Latino; 0.1% American Indian or Alaska Native, non-Hispanic/Latino; 4% Two or more races, non-Hispanic/Latino; 5% Race/ethnicity unknown; 2% international; 3% transferred in; 62% live on campus.

Freshmen:
Admission: 9,291 applied, 5,573 admitted, 832 enrolled. ***Average high school GPA:*** 3.7. ***Test scores:*** SAT evidence-based reading and writing scores over 500: 89%; SAT math scores over 500: 70%; ACT scores over 18: 93%; SAT evidence-based reading and writing scores over 600: 13%; SAT math scores over 600: 20%; ACT scores over 24: 42%; SAT math scores over 700: 3%; ACT scores over 30: 9%.

Retention: 70% of full-time freshmen returned.

FACULTY
Total: 272, 86% full-time, 88% with terminal degrees.

Student/faculty ratio: 15:1.

ACADEMICS

Calendar: semesters. *Degrees:* bachelor's, master's, and doctoral.

Special study options: academic remediation for entering students, accelerated degree program, adult/continuing education programs, advanced placement credit, cooperative education, distance learning, double majors, freshman honors college, honors programs, independent study, internships, off-campus study, part-time degree program, services for LD students, study abroad, summer session for credit. ***ROTC:*** Army (c), Navy (c), Air Force (c).

Unusual degree programs: 3-2 business administration with Tulane University; engineering with Tulane University, University of Maryland, University of New Orleans, Georgia Institute of Technology, University of Wisconsin–Madison, Morgan State University, Southern University and Agricultural and Mechanical College; biostatistics with Louisiana State University Medical Center.

Computers: Students can access the following: computer help desk, free student e-mail accounts, online (class) grades, online (class) registration, online (class) schedules. Campuswide network is available. 100% of college-owned or -operated housing units are wired for high-speed Internet access. Wireless service is available via entire campus.

Library: Xavier Library.

STUDENT LIFE

Housing options: coed, men-only, women-only. Campus housing is university owned. Freshman applicants given priority for college housing.

Activities and organizations: drama/theater group, student-run newspaper, television station, choral group, national fraternities, national sororities.

Athletics Member NAIA. ***Intercollegiate sports:*** basketball M(s)/W(s), cross-country running M/W, tennis M(s)/W(s). ***Intramural sports:*** badminton M/W, basketball M/W, football M/W, golf M/W, softball M/W, swimming and diving M/W, table tennis M/W, tennis M/W, track and field M/W, volleyball M/W.

Campus security: 24-hour emergency response devices and patrols, student patrols, bicycle patrols.

Student services: health clinic, personal/psychological counseling.

COSTS & FINANCIAL AID

Costs (2019–20) ***One-time required fee:*** $150. ***Comprehensive fee:*** $35,185 includes full-time tuition ($22,503), mandatory fees ($2682), and room and board ($10,000). Full-time tuition and fees vary according to course load. Part-time tuition: $938 per credit hour. Part-time tuition and fees vary according to course load. ***Required fees:*** $275 per term part-time. ***Room and board:*** Room and board charges vary according to board plan and housing facility. ***Payment plan:*** installment. ***Waivers:*** employees or children of employees.

Financial Aid Of all full-time matriculated undergraduates who enrolled in 2017, 2,161 applied for aid, 1,734 were judged to have need, 869 had their need fully met. ***Average percent of need met:*** 72. ***Average financial aid package:*** $9897. ***Average need-based loan:*** $1550. ***Average need-based gift aid:*** $8330. ***Average indebtedness upon graduation:*** $21,821.

APPLYING

Standardized Tests *Required:* SAT or ACT (for admission).

Options: electronic application, deferred entrance.

Required: high school transcript, minimum 2.0 GPA, 1 letter of recommendation. ***Required for some:*** interview.

Notification: continuous (freshmen).

CONTACT

Mr. Winston Brown, Dean of Admissions, Xavier University of Louisiana, 7325 Palmetto Street, New Orleans, LA 70125. *Phone:* 504-520-7388. *Toll-free phone:* 877-XAVIERU. *Fax:* 504-520-7941. *E-mail:* apply@xula.edu.

MAINE

Bates College

Lewiston, Maine

http://www.bates.edu/

- **Independent** 4-year, founded 1855
- **Small-town** 133-acre campus
- **Endowment** $293.8 million
- **Coed** 1,820 undergraduate students, 100% full-time, 50% women, 50% men
- **Very difficult** entrance level, 12% of applicants were admitted

UNDERGRAD STUDENTS

1,820 full-time. 90% are from out of state; 6% Black or African American, non-Hispanic/Latino; 8% Hispanic/Latino; 5% Asian, non-Hispanic/Latino; 0.1% Native Hawaiian or other Pacific Islander, non-Hispanic/Latino; 0.1% American Indian or Alaska Native, non-Hispanic/Latino; 6% Two or more races, non-Hispanic/Latino; 0.5% Race/ethnicity unknown; 8% international; 0.3% transferred in.

Freshmen:

Admission: 8,222 applied, 998 admitted, 499 enrolled. ***Test scores:*** SAT evidence-based reading and writing scores over 500: 99%; SAT math scores over 500: 99%; ACT scores over 18: 100%; SAT evidence-based reading and writing scores over 600: 87%; SAT math scores over 600: 89%; ACT scores over 24: 94%; SAT evidence-based reading and writing scores over 700: 51%; SAT math scores over 700: 44%; ACT scores over 30: 71%.

Retention: 94% of full-time freshmen returned.

FACULTY

Total: 199, 88% full-time, 95% with terminal degrees.

Student/faculty ratio: 10:1.

ACADEMICS

Calendar: 4-4-1. *Degree:* bachelor's.

Special study options: accelerated degree program, advanced placement credit, double majors, honors programs, independent study, internships, off-campus study, services for LD students, student-designed majors, study abroad.

Unusual degree programs: 3-2 engineering with Columbia University, Rensselaer Polytechnic Institute, Case Western Reserve University, Washington University in St. Louis, Dartmouth College.

Computers: 400 computers/terminals and 2,075 ports are available on campus for general student use. Students can access the following: computer help desk, free student e-mail accounts, online (class) grades, online (class) registration, online (class) schedules, course Web pages; course management system; software applications for learning, teaching and research; online course evaluation, transcripts, major declaration, degree audit, financial records. Campuswide network is available. 100% of college-owned or -operated housing units are wired for high-speed Internet access. Wireless service is available via classrooms, computer labs, dorm rooms, learning centers, libraries, student centers.

Library: Ladd Library plus 1 other. *Books:* 602,011 (physical), 725,335 (digital/electronic); *Databases:* 371.

STUDENT LIFE

Housing options: on-campus residence required through senior year; coed, men-only, women-only. Campus housing is university owned. Freshman campus housing is guaranteed.

Activities and organizations: drama/theater group, student-run newspaper, radio station, choral group, Outing Club (outdoor recreation), International Club, Chase Hall Committee (student activities planning), Representative Assembly, WRBC (student radio station).

Athletics Member NCAA. All Division III. ***Intercollegiate sports:*** baseball M, basketball M/W, crew M/W, cross-country running M/W, equestrian sports M(c)/W(c), fencing M(c)/W(c), field hockey W, football M, golf M/W, ice hockey M(c)/W(c), lacrosse M/W, rugby M(c)/W(c), sailing M(c)/W(c), skiing (cross-country) M/W, skiing (downhill) M/W, soccer M/W, softball W, squash M/W, swimming and diving M/W, tennis M/W, track and field M/W, ultimate Frisbee M(c)/W(c), volleyball M(c)/W, water polo M(c)/W(c). ***Intramural sports:*** basketball M/W, bowling M/W, ice hockey M/W, racquetball M/W, soccer M/W, softball M/W, squash M/W, tennis M/W, volleyball M/W.

Campus security: 24-hour emergency response devices and patrols, student patrols, late-night transport/escort service, controlled dormitory access, emergency contact/notification system.

Student services: health clinic, personal/psychological counseling, women's center.

COSTS & FINANCIAL AID

Costs (2019–20) ***Comprehensive fee:*** $71,388 includes full-time tuition ($55,683) and room and board ($15,705). ***Payment plans:*** tuition prepayment, installment. ***Waivers:*** employees or children of employees.

Financial Aid Of all full-time matriculated undergraduates who enrolled in 2019, 806 applied for aid, 785 were judged to have need, 785 had their need fully met. ***Average percent of need met:*** 100. ***Average financial aid package:*** $51,099. ***Average need-based loan:*** $2935. ***Average need-based gift aid:*** $47,069. ***Average indebtedness upon graduation:*** $23,383. ***Financial aid deadline:*** 1/1.

APPLYING

Options: electronic application, early decision, deferred entrance.

Application fee: $60.

Required: essay or personal statement, high school transcript, 3 letters of recommendation. ***Recommended:*** interview.

Application deadlines: 1/1 (freshmen), 3/1 (transfers).

Early decision deadline: 11/15 (for plan 1), 1/1 (for plan 2).

Notification: 4/1 (freshmen), 4/30 (transfers), 12/20 (early decision plan 1), 2/15 (early decision plan 2).

CONTACT

Leigh Weisenburger, Dean of Admission and Financial Aid, Bates College, 23 Campus Avenue, Lindholm House, Lewiston, ME 04240-6028. *Phone:* 855-228-3755. *Toll-free phone:* 855-228-3755. *Fax:* 207-786-6025. *E-mail:* admission@bates.edu.

Bowdoin College

Brunswick, Maine

http://www.bowdoin.edu/

- **Independent** 4-year, founded 1794
- **Small-town** 207-acre campus with easy access to Portland
- **Endowment** $1.7 billion
- **Coed** 1,835 undergraduate students, 100% full-time, 51% women, 49% men
- **Most difficult** entrance level, 9% of applicants were admitted

UNDERGRAD STUDENTS

1,834 full-time, 1 part-time. Students come from 51 states and territories; 44 other countries; 89% are from out of state; 8% Black or African American, non-Hispanic/Latino; 11% Hispanic/Latino; 7% Asian, non-Hispanic/Latino; 0.2% Native Hawaiian or other Pacific Islander, non-Hispanic/Latino; 0.3% American Indian or Alaska Native, non-Hispanic/Latino; 7% Two or more races, non-Hispanic/Latino; 0.5% Race/ethnicity unknown; 7% international; 0.2% transferred in; 92% live on campus.

Freshmen:

Admission: 9,332 applied, 845 admitted, 498 enrolled. ***Test scores:*** SAT evidence-based reading and writing scores over 500: 100%; SAT math scores over 500: 100%; ACT scores over 18: 100%; SAT evidence-based reading and writing scores over 600: 96%; SAT math scores over 600: 92%; ACT scores over 24: 97%; SAT evidence-based reading and writing scores over 700: 58%; SAT math scores over 700: 66%; ACT scores over 30: 85%.

Retention: 98% of full-time freshmen returned.

FACULTY

Total: 229, 88% full-time, 98% with terminal degrees.

Student/faculty ratio: 9:1.

ACADEMICS

Calendar: semesters. *Degree:* bachelor's.

Special study options: accelerated degree program, advanced placement credit, double majors, independent study, off-campus study, services for LD students, student-designed majors, study abroad.

Unusual degree programs: 3-2 engineering with California Institute of Technology, Columbia University, Dartmouth College, University of Maine Orono; law with Columbia University.

Computers: 500 computers/terminals and 600 ports are available on campus for general student use. Students can access the following: campus intranet, computer help desk, free student e-mail accounts, online (class) grades, online (class) registration, online (class) schedules, computer repair; training classes; 24/7 software support; free equipment loaner pool: laptops, video and digital cameras, sound and lighting systems, iPads; movie streaming service; free office software; digital media lab. Campuswide network is available. 100% of college-owned or -operated housing units are wired for high-speed Internet access. Wireless service is available via entire campus.

Library: Hawthorne-Longfellow Library plus 3 others. *Books:* 1.1 million (physical), 847,639 (digital/electronic); *Serial titles:* 10,874 (physical), 160,878 (digital/electronic); *Databases:* 459. Weekly public service hours: 112; students can reserve study rooms.

STUDENT LIFE

Housing options: on-campus residence required through sophomore year; coed, special housing for students with disabilities. Campus housing is university owned. Freshman campus housing is guaranteed.

Activities and organizations: drama/theater group, student-run newspaper, radio station, choral group, Outing Club, Intramural sports, Community Service Volunteer Programs, WBOR 91.1 FM Radio, Bowdoin Orient Student Newspaper.

Athletics Member NCAA. All Division III except men's and women's sailing (Division I), men's and women's skiing (cross-country) (Division I), men's and women's squash (Division I). ***Intercollegiate sports:*** baseball M, basketball M/W, crew M(c)/W(c), cross-country running M/W, equestrian sports M(c)/W(c), fencing M(c)/W(c), field hockey W, football M, golf M/W, ice hockey M/W, lacrosse M/W, rugby M(c)/W, sailing M/W, skiing (cross-country) M/W, soccer M/W, softball W, squash M/W, swimming and diving M/W, tennis M/W, track and field M/W, ultimate Frisbee M(c)/W(c), volleyball M(c)/W, water polo M(c)/W(c). ***Intramural sports:*** badminton M/W, basketball M/W, cheerleading M(c)/W(c), field hockey M/W, ice hockey M/W, skiing (downhill) M(c)/W(c), soccer M/W, softball M/W, tennis M(c)/W(c).

Campus security: 24-hour emergency response devices and patrols, late-night transport/escort service, controlled dormitory access, self-defense education, safe ride service, emergency notification system.

Student services: health clinic, personal/psychological counseling, women's center.

COSTS & FINANCIAL AID

Costs (2019–20) ***Comprehensive fee:*** $71,710 includes full-time tuition ($55,822), mandatory fees ($528), and room and board ($15,360). Part-time tuition: $1090 per credit hour. ***College room only:*** $7372. Room and board charges vary according to board plan. ***Payment plan:*** installment. ***Waivers:*** employees or children of employees.

Financial Aid Of all full-time matriculated undergraduates who enrolled in 2019, 998 applied for aid, 891 were judged to have need, 891 had their need fully met. 570 Federal Work-Study jobs (averaging $1969). 314 state and other part-time jobs (averaging $1986). In 2019, 36 non-need-based awards were made. ***Average percent of need met:*** 100. ***Average financial aid package:*** $51,107. ***Average need-based gift aid:*** $49,124. ***Average non-need-based aid:*** $1000. ***Average indebtedness upon graduation:*** $26,775. ***Financial aid deadline:*** 2/1.

APPLYING

Options: electronic application, early admission, early decision, deferred entrance.

Application fee: $65.

Required: essay or personal statement, high school transcript, 3 letters of recommendation. ***Recommended:*** interview.

Application deadlines: 1/1 (freshmen), 3/1 (transfers).

Early decision deadline: 11/15 (for plan 1), 1/1 (for plan 2).

Notification: 3/20 (freshmen), 5/1 (transfers), 12/15 (early decision plan 1), 2/15 (early decision plan 2).

CONTACT

Claudia Marroquin, Director of Admissions, Bowdoin College, 255 Maine Street, Brunswick, ME 04011. *Phone:* 207-725-3100. *Fax:* 207-725-3101. *E-mail:* admissions@bowdoin.edu.

Colby College

Waterville, Maine

http://www.colby.edu/

- **Independent** 4-year, founded 1813
- **Small-town** 714-acre campus with easy access to Portland, ME
- **Coed** 2,003 undergraduate students, 100% full-time, 54% women, 46% men
- 10% of applicants were admitted

UNDERGRAD STUDENTS
2,003 full-time. 91% are from out of state; 5% Black or African American, non-Hispanic/Latino; 8% Hispanic/Latino; 8% Asian, non-Hispanic/Latino; 0.2% Native Hawaiian or other Pacific Islander, non-Hispanic/Latino; 0.3% American Indian or Alaska Native, non-Hispanic/Latino; 5% Two or more races, non-Hispanic/Latino; 2% Race/ethnicity unknown; 10% international; 0.1% transferred in; 96% live on campus.

Freshmen:
Admission: 13,584 applied, 1,314 admitted, 522 enrolled. ***Test scores:*** SAT evidence-based reading and writing scores over 500: 100%; SAT math scores over 500: 100%; ACT scores over 18: 100%; SAT evidence-based reading and writing scores over 600: 96%; SAT math scores over 600: 96%; ACT scores over 24: 99%; SAT evidence-based reading and writing scores over 700: 58%; SAT math scores over 700: 77%; ACT scores over 30: 92%.

Retention: 93% of full-time freshmen returned.

FACULTY
Total: 223, 94% full-time, 99% with terminal degrees.

Student/faculty ratio: 9:1.

ACADEMICS
Calendar: 4-1-4. *Degree:* bachelor's.

Special study options: advanced placement credit, double majors, independent study, internships, off-campus study, services for LD students, student-designed majors, study abroad. ***ROTC:*** Army (c).

Unusual degree programs: 3-2 engineering with Dartmouth College, Columbia University.

Computers: 158 computers/terminals and 3,000 ports are available on campus for general student use. Students can access the following: campus intranet, computer help desk, free student e-mail accounts, online (class) grades, online (class) registration, online (class) schedules, software license for every student computer, unlimited technology training, video editing lab, high performance natural science research computing, GIS lab. Campuswide network is available. 100% of college-owned or -operated housing units are wired for high-speed Internet access. Wireless service is available via entire campus.
Library: Miller Library plus 3 others. *Books:* 527,596 (physical), 881,578 (digital/electronic); *Serial titles:* 2,787 (physical), 108,706 (digital/electronic); *Databases:* 789. Study areas open 24 hours, 5–7 days a week.

STUDENT LIFE
Housing options: on-campus residence required through senior year; coed, cooperative, special housing for students with disabilities. Campus housing is university owned. Freshman campus housing is guaranteed.

Activities and organizations: drama/theater group, student-run newspaper, radio station, choral group, Outing Club, Student Government Association, Student Athlete Advisory Committee, Student Programming Board, Pugh Community Board.

Athletics Member NCAA. All Division III except men's and women's skiing (cross-country) (Division I), men's and women's skiing (downhill) (Division I). ***Intercollegiate sports:*** baseball M, basketball M/W, crew M/W, cross-country running M/W, fencing M(c)/W(c), field hockey W, football M, golf M/W, ice hockey M/W, lacrosse M/W, rugby M(c)/W(c), sailing M(c)/W(c), skiing (cross-country) M/W, skiing (downhill) M/W, soccer M/W, softball W, squash M/W, swimming and diving M/W, tennis M/W, track and field M/W, ultimate Frisbee M(c)/W(c), volleyball M(c)/W, water polo M(c)/W(c). ***Intramural sports:*** basketball M/W, field hockey M/W, football M/W, soccer M/W, softball M/W, tennis M/W.

Campus security: 24-hour emergency response devices and patrols, student patrols, late-night transport/escort service, controlled dormitory access, campus lighting, student emergency response team, self-defense class, property ID program, party monitors.

Student services: health clinic, personal/psychological counseling, women's center.

COSTS & FINANCIAL AID
Costs (2019–20) ***Comprehensive fee:*** $72,000 includes full-time tuition ($54,870), mandatory fees ($2410), and room and board ($14,720). Part-time tuition: $2100 per credit hour. Part-time tuition and fees vary according to course load. ***Payment plan:*** installment. ***Waivers:*** employees or children of employees.

Financial Aid Of all full-time matriculated undergraduates who enrolled in 2019, 1,051 applied for aid, 830 were judged to have need, 830 had their need fully met. ***Average percent of need met:*** 100. ***Average financial aid package:*** $50,475. ***Average need-based gift aid:*** $51,617. ***Average indebtedness upon graduation:*** $24,380. ***Financial aid deadline:*** 2/1.

APPLYING
Options: electronic application, early decision, deferred entrance.

Required: essay or personal statement, high school transcript, 3 letters of recommendation.

Application deadlines: 1/1 (freshmen), 4/1 (transfers).

Early decision deadline: 11/15 (for plan 1), 1/1 (for plan 2).

Notification: 4/1 (freshmen), 4/1 (out-of-state freshmen), 5/15 (transfers), 12/15 (early decision plan 1), 2/15 (early decision plan 2).

CONTACT
Colby College, 4000 Mayflower Hill, Waterville, ME 04901-8840.
Phone: 207-859-4802. *Toll-free phone:* 800-723-3032.

College of the Atlantic

Bar Harbor, Maine

http://www.coa.edu/

- **Independent** comprehensive, founded 1969
- **Small-town** 35-acre campus
- **Endowment** $53.0 million
- **Coed**
- **Very difficult** entrance level

FACULTY
Student/faculty ratio: 10:1.

ACADEMICS
Calendar: trimesters. *Degrees:* bachelor's and master's.
Library: Thorndike Library. *Books:* 45,700 (physical), 15,500 (digital/electronic); *Serial titles:* 400 (physical), 62,600 (digital/electronic); *Databases:* 76. Weekly public service hours: 101; students can reserve study rooms.

STUDENT LIFE
Housing options: on-campus residence required for freshman year; coed. Campus housing is university owned. Freshman campus housing is guaranteed.

Activities and organizations: drama/theater group, student-run newspaper, choral group, Earth in Brackets [earth], Outing Club, Campus Committee for Sustainability, Spectrum (LGBTQ+), Futbol (soccer) Club.

Campus security: 24-hour emergency response devices and patrols, late-night transport/escort service.

Student services: health clinic, personal/psychological counseling.

COSTS & FINANCIAL AID
Costs (2019–20) ***Comprehensive fee:*** $53,289 includes full-time tuition ($42,993), mandatory fees ($549), and room and board ($9747). Full-time tuition and fees vary according to course load and degree level. Part-time tuition: $4777 per credit. Part-time tuition and fees vary according to course load and degree level. ***Required fees:*** $183 per term part-time. ***College room only:*** $6210. Room and board charges vary according to board plan.

Financial Aid Of all full-time matriculated undergraduates who enrolled in 2018, 284 applied for aid, 263 were judged to have need, 102 had their need fully met. 159 Federal Work-Study jobs (averaging $2875). 85 state and other part-time jobs (averaging $2973). In 2018, 41 non-need-based awards were made. ***Average percent of need met:*** 94. ***Average financial aid package:*** $41,564. ***Average need-based loan:*** $4625. ***Average need-***

based gift aid: $36,091. *Average non-need-based aid:* $15,100. *Average indebtedness upon graduation:* $24,496. *Financial aid deadline:* 2/1.

APPLYING
Options: electronic application, early admission, early decision, deferred entrance.

Application fee: $50.

Required: essay or personal statement, high school transcript, 3 letters of recommendation. ***Recommended:*** minimum 3.0 GPA, interview.

CONTACT
Ms. Heather Albert-Knopp, Dean of Admission, College of the Atlantic, 105 Eden Street, Bar Harbor, ME 04609-1198. *Phone:* 207-288-5015. *Toll-free phone:* 800-528-0025. *Fax:* 207-288-4126. *E-mail:* inquiry@coa.edu.

Husson University

Bangor, Maine

http://www.husson.edu/

- **Independent** comprehensive, founded 1898
- **Suburban** 208-acre campus
- **Endowment** $20.0 million
- **Coed** 2,866 undergraduate students, 84% full-time, 58% women, 42% men
- **Moderately difficult** entrance level, 82% of applicants were admitted

UNDERGRAD STUDENTS
2,407 full-time, 459 part-time. Students come from 44 states and territories; 24 other countries; 25% are from out of state; 4% Black or African American, non-Hispanic/Latino; 1% Hispanic/Latino; 1% Asian, non-Hispanic/Latino; 0.1% Native Hawaiian or other Pacific Islander, non-Hispanic/Latino; 0.4% American Indian or Alaska Native, non-Hispanic/Latino; 3% Two or more races, non-Hispanic/Latino; 5% Race/ethnicity unknown; 2% international; 4% transferred in; 33% live on campus.

Freshmen:
Admission: 2,619 applied, 2,139 admitted, 568 enrolled. *Average high school GPA:* 3.3. *Test scores:* SAT evidence-based reading and writing scores over 500: 69%; SAT math scores over 500: 69%; ACT scores over 18: 84%; SAT evidence-based reading and writing scores over 600: 19%; SAT math scores over 600: 14%; ACT scores over 24: 23%; SAT evidence-based reading and writing scores over 700: 1%; SAT math scores over 700: 1%; ACT scores over 30: 2%.

Retention: 74% of full-time freshmen returned.

FACULTY
Total: 435, 31% full-time, 38% with terminal degrees.

Student/faculty ratio: 13:1.

ACADEMICS
Calendar: semesters. *Degrees:* certificates, associate, bachelor's, master's, doctoral, post-master's, and postbachelor's certificates.

Special study options: academic remediation for entering students, adult/continuing education programs, advanced placement credit, cooperative education, distance learning, double majors, English as a second language, honors programs, independent study, internships, off-campus study, part-time degree program, services for LD students, student-designed majors, study abroad, summer session for credit. ***ROTC:*** Army (b), Navy (c).

Unusual degree programs: 3-2 business administration; nursing; occupational therapy, criminal justice administration.

Computers: 131 computers/terminals and 131 ports are available on campus for general student use. Students can access the following: campus intranet, computer help desk, free student e-mail accounts, online (class) grades, online (class) registration, online (class) schedules. Campuswide network is available. 100% of college-owned or -operated housing units are wired for high-speed Internet access. Wireless service is available via entire campus.

Library: Sawyer Library. *Books:* 41,659 (physical), 5,539 (digital/electronic); *Serial titles:* 74 (physical), 151 (digital/electronic); *Databases:* 91. Weekly public service hours: 98; study areas open 24 hours, 5–7 days a week; students can reserve study rooms.

STUDENT LIFE
Housing options: on-campus residence required through sophomore year; coed. Campus housing is university owned. Freshman campus housing is guaranteed.

Activities and organizations: drama/theater group, student-run radio station, choral group, Organization of Student Nurses, Organization of Physical Therapy Students, Outdoors Club, International Student Association, Habitat for Humanity, national fraternities, national sororities.

Athletics Member NCAA. All Division III. ***Intercollegiate sports:*** baseball M, basketball M/W, cross-country running M/W, field hockey W, football M, golf M/W, lacrosse M/W, soccer M/W, softball W, swimming and diving M/W, tennis W, track and field M/W, volleyball W. ***Intramural sports:*** basketball M/W, cheerleading M(c)/W(c), football M/W, ice hockey M(c), soccer M/W, softball M/W, volleyball M/W, wrestling M(c).

Campus security: 24-hour emergency response devices and patrols, late-night transport/escort service, controlled dormitory access.

Student services: health clinic, personal/psychological counseling, veterans affairs office.

COSTS & FINANCIAL AID
Costs (2020–21) ***Comprehensive fee:*** $30,404 includes full-time tuition ($18,972), mandatory fees ($800), and room and board ($10,632). Part-time tuition: $612 per credit hour. ***Required fees:*** $96 part-time. ***College room only:*** $5354. Room and board charges vary according to housing facility. ***Payment plan:*** installment.

Financial Aid Of all full-time matriculated undergraduates who enrolled in 2018, 2,466 applied for aid, 2,102 were judged to have need, 217 had their need fully met. 1,266 Federal Work-Study jobs (averaging $1885). In 2018, 209 non-need-based awards were made. ***Average percent of need met:*** 69. ***Average financial aid package:*** $15,034. ***Average need-based loan:*** $4259. ***Average need-based gift aid:*** $9582. ***Average non-need-based aid:*** $3652. ***Average indebtedness upon graduation:*** $35,681. ***Financial aid deadline:*** 4/15.

APPLYING
Standardized Tests *Required:* SAT or ACT (for admission). *Recommended:* SAT Subject Tests (for admission).

Options: electronic application, deferred entrance.

Application fee: $40.

Required: essay or personal statement, high school transcript, 1 letter of recommendation. ***Recommended:*** minimum 3.0 GPA, interview.

Application deadlines: 8/15 (freshmen), 8/15 (transfers).

Notification: continuous (freshmen), continuous (transfers).

CONTACT
Ms. Melissa Rosenburg, Vice President Enrollment Management, Husson University, 1 College Circle, Bangor, ME 04401-2999. *Phone:* 207-941-7175. *Toll-free phone:* 800-4-HUSSON. *E-mail:* rosenburgm@husson.edu.

Maine College of Art

Portland, Maine

http://www.meca.edu/

CONTACT
Maine College of Art, 522 Congress Street, Portland, ME 04101. *Phone:* 207-699-5023. *Toll-free phone:* 800-699-1509.

Maine College of Health Professions

Lewiston, Maine

http://www.mchp.edu/

CONTACT
Ms. Erica Watson, Admissions Director, Maine College of Health Professions, 70 Middle Street, Lewiston, ME 04240. *Phone:* 207-795-2843. *Fax:* 207-795-2849. *E-mail:* watsoner@mchp.edu.

Maine Maritime Academy

Castine, Maine

http://www.mainemaritime.edu/

CONTACT

Maine Maritime Academy, 1 Pleasant Street, Castine, ME 04420. *Phone:* 207-326-2215. *Toll-free phone:* 800-464-6565 (in-state); 800-227-8465 (out-of-state).

Purdue University Global

Augusta, Maine

http://www.purdueglobal.edu/

CONTACT

Purdue University Global, 14 Marketplace Drive, Augusta, ME 04330. *Toll-free phone:* 844-PURDUE-G.

Purdue University Global

Lewiston, Maine

http://www.purdueglobal.edu/

CONTACT

Purdue University Global, 475 Lisbon Street, Lewiston, ME 04240. *Phone:* 207-333-3300. *Toll-free phone:* 844-PURDUE-G.

Saint Joseph's College of Maine

Standish, Maine

http://www.sjcme.edu/

CONTACT

Kathleen Davis, Vice President for Enrollment Management, Saint Joseph's College of Maine, 278 Whites Bridge Road, Standish, ME 04084-5263. *Phone:* 207-893-7746. *Toll-free phone:* 800-338-7057. *Fax:* 207-893-7862. *E-mail:* admission@sjcme.edu.

Thomas College

Waterville, Maine

http://www.thomas.edu/

CONTACT

Ms. Angela Stinchfield, Director of Admissions, Thomas College, 180 West River Road, Waterville, ME 04901. *Phone:* 207-859-1101. *Toll-free phone:* 800-339-7001. *Fax:* 207-859-1114. *E-mail:* admiss@thomas.edu.

Unity College

Unity, Maine

http://www.unity.edu/

CONTACT

Mr. Joe Saltalamachia, Director of Admissions, Unity College, 90 Quaker Hill Road, Unity, ME 04988. *Phone:* 207-509-7205. *E-mail:* jsalty@unity.edu.

University of Maine

Orono, Maine

http://www.umaine.edu/

- **State-supported** university, founded 1865, part of University of Maine System
- **Small-town** 660-acre campus
- **Endowment** $333.7 million
- **Coed** 9,430 undergraduate students, 85% full-time, 47% women, 53% men
- **Moderately difficult** entrance level, 90% of applicants were admitted

UNDERGRAD STUDENTS

8,060 full-time, 1,370 part-time. Students come from 50 states and territories; 59 other countries; 33% are from out of state; 2% Black or African American, non-Hispanic/Latino; 4% Hispanic/Latino; 2% Asian, non-Hispanic/Latino; 0.9% American Indian or Alaska Native, non-Hispanic/Latino; 4% Two or more races, non-Hispanic/Latino; 2%

Race/ethnicity unknown; 2% international; 5% transferred in; 38% live on campus.

Freshmen:
Admission: 13,118 applied, 11,838 admitted, 2,140 enrolled. ***Average high school GPA:*** 3.3. ***Test scores:*** SAT evidence-based reading and writing scores over 500: 88%; SAT math scores over 500: 87%; ACT scores over 18: 96%; SAT evidence-based reading and writing scores over 600: 43%; SAT math scores over 600: 37%; ACT scores over 24: 48%; SAT evidence-based reading and writing scores over 700: 7%; SAT math scores over 700: 8%; ACT scores over 30: 11%.

Retention: 74% of full-time freshmen returned.

FACULTY
Total: 866, 62% full-time, 64% with terminal degrees.

Student/faculty ratio: 15:1.

ACADEMICS
Calendar: semesters. *Degrees:* bachelor's, master's, doctoral, post-master's, and postbachelor's certificates.

Special study options: accelerated degree program, advanced placement credit, cooperative education, distance learning, double majors, English as a second language, external degree program, freshman honors college, honors programs, independent study, internships, off-campus study, part-time degree program, services for LD students, study abroad, summer session for credit. ***ROTC:*** Army (b), Navy (b).

Computers: 600 computers/terminals are available on campus for general student use. Students can access the following: campus intranet, computer help desk, free student e-mail accounts, online (class) grades, online (class) registration, online (class) schedules, online housing and financial aid information. Campuswide network is available. 100% of college-owned or -operated housing units are wired for high-speed Internet access. Wireless service is available via entire campus.

Library: Fogler Library. *Books:* 1.6 million (physical), 1.2 million (digital/electronic); *Serial titles:* 53,449 (physical), 143,082 (digital/electronic); *Databases:* 360. Weekly public service hours: 101; students can reserve study rooms.

STUDENT LIFE
Housing options: on-campus residence required for freshman year; coed, special housing for students with disabilities. Campus housing is university owned. Freshman campus housing is guaranteed.

Activities and organizations: drama/theater group, student-run newspaper, radio station, choral group, marching band, Fraternity and Sorority Life, Alternative Breaks, UMaine Student Government, Campus Activities Board, Wilde Stein, national fraternities, national sororities.

Athletics Member NCAA. All Division I except football (Division I-AA). ***Intercollegiate sports:*** baseball M(s), basketball M(s)/W(s), cheerleading M(c)/W(c), cross-country running M(s)/W(s), field hockey W(s), ice hockey M(s)/W(s), soccer M(c)/W(s), softball W(s), swimming and diving M/W(s), tennis M(c)/W(c), track and field M(s)/W(s). ***Intramural sports:*** badminton M/W, baseball M(c), basketball M/W, crew M(c)/W(c), equestrian sports M(c)/W(c), fencing M(c)/W(c), field hockey M(c)/W(c), football M(c), golf M(c)/W(c), ice hockey M(c)/W(c), lacrosse M(c)/W(c), racquetball M/W, rock climbing M(c)/W(c), rugby M(c)/W(c), skiing (cross-country) M/W, skiing (downhill) M(c)/W(c), soccer M/W, softball M/W, swimming and diving M/W, table tennis M/W, tennis M/W, track and field M/W, ultimate Frisbee M(c)/W(c), volleyball M(c)/W(c), water polo M/W, wrestling M(c).

Campus security: 24-hour emergency response devices and patrols, late-night transport/escort service, controlled dormitory access, area emergency text and email message system.

Student services: health clinic, personal/psychological counseling, women's center, legal services, veterans affairs office.

COSTS & FINANCIAL AID
Costs (2019–20) ***Tuition:*** area resident $9000 full-time, $300 per credit hour part-time; state resident $9000 full-time, $300 per credit hour part-time; nonresident $29,310 full-time, $977 per credit hour part-time. Full-time tuition and fees vary according to course load. Part-time tuition and fees vary according to course load. ***Required fees:*** $2438 full-time. ***Room and board:*** $10,966. Room and board charges vary according to board plan and housing facility. ***Payment plan:*** installment. ***Waivers:*** senior citizens and employees or children of employees.

Financial Aid Of all full-time matriculated undergraduates who enrolled in 2019, 6,693 applied for aid, 5,157 were judged to have need, 923 had their need fully met. In 2019, 2352 non-need-based awards were made. ***Average percent of need met:*** 68. ***Average financial aid package:*** $14,450. ***Average need-based loan:*** $4111. ***Average need-based gift aid:*** $9614. ***Average non-need-based aid:*** $7136. ***Average indebtedness upon graduation:*** $34,703. ***Financial aid deadline:*** 4/15.

APPLYING
Standardized Tests *Required:* SAT or ACT (for admission).

Options: electronic application, early admission, early action, deferred entrance.

Required: essay or personal statement, high school transcript, 1 letter of recommendation.

Application deadlines: 2/1 (freshmen), 2/1 (out-of-state freshmen), rolling (transfers), 12/1 (early action).

Notification: continuous (freshmen), continuous (out-of-state freshmen), continuous (transfers), 1/15 (early action).

CONTACT
Lateef O'Connor, Senior Associate Director of Admissions, University of Maine, 5713 Chadbourne Hall, Orono, ME 04469-5713. *Phone:* 207-581-1561. *Toll-free phone:* 877-486-2364. *Fax:* 207-581-1213. *E-mail:* um-admit@maine.edu.

See below for display ad and page 1126 for the College Close-Up.

University of Maine at Augusta

Augusta, Maine

http://www.uma.edu/

- **State-supported** 4-year, founded 1965, part of University of Maine System
- **Small-town** 159-acre campus
- **Endowment** $7.3 million
- **Coed**
- **Noncompetitive** entrance level

FACULTY
Student/faculty ratio: 16:1.

ACADEMICS
Calendar: semesters. *Degrees:* certificates, associate, and bachelor's (also offers some graduate courses and continuing education programs with significant enrollment not reflected in profile).
Library: The Bennett D. Katz Library.

STUDENT LIFE
Housing options: college housing not available.

Activities and organizations: drama/theater group, student-run newspaper, Honors Program Student Association, Arts and Architecture Students of UMA, Student Nurse Association, Student American Dental Hygiene Association, International Student Club.

Athletics Member USCAA.

Campus security: 24-hour emergency response devices, late-night transport/escort service.

Student services: personal/psychological counseling.

COSTS & FINANCIAL AID
Costs (2019–20) ***Tuition:*** state resident $7170 full-time, $239 per credit hour part-time; nonresident $17,340 full-time, $578 per credit hour part-time. Full-time tuition and fees vary according to course load, location, program, and reciprocity agreements. Part-time tuition and fees vary according to course load, location, program, and reciprocity agreements. ***Required fees:*** $998 full-time, $33 per credit hour part-time.

Financial Aid Of all full-time matriculated undergraduates who enrolled in 2016, 1,364 applied for aid, 1,279 were judged to have need, 51 had their need fully met. In 2016, 6 non-need-based awards were made. ***Average percent of need met:*** 55. ***Average financial aid package:*** $9316. ***Average need-based loan:*** $7529. ***Average need-based gift aid:*** $6242. ***Average non-need-based aid:*** $839. ***Average indebtedness upon graduation:*** $30,457.

APPLYING
Options: electronic application, early admission, deferred entrance.

Application fee: $40.

Required for some: high school transcript, interview, music audition. ***Recommended:*** essay or personal statement.

CONTACT
Pamela Proulx-Curry, Interim Dean of Enrollment Services, University of Maine at Augusta, 46 University Drive, Robinson Hall, Augusta, ME 04330. *Phone:* 207-621-3465. *Toll-free phone:* 877-862-1234 Ext. 3185 (in-state); 877-862-1234 (out-of-state). *Fax:* 207-621-3333. *E-mail:* umaadm@maine.edu.

University of Maine at Farmington

Farmington, Maine

http://www.umf.maine.edu/

- **State-supported** comprehensive, founded 1863, part of University of Maine System
- **Small-town** 55-acre campus
- **Endowment** $13.1 million
- **Coed**
- **Moderately difficult** entrance level

FACULTY
Student/faculty ratio: 13:1.

ACADEMICS
Calendar: semesters 3 summer sessions: one of 5 weeks and two of 4 weeks each. *Degrees:* certificates, bachelor's, master's, and postbachelor's certificates.
Library: Mantor Library plus 1 other. Weekly public service hours: 88; students can reserve study rooms.

STUDENT LIFE
Housing options: on-campus residence required for freshman year; coed, women-only, cooperative, special housing for students with disabilities. Campus housing is university owned. Freshman campus housing is guaranteed.

Activities and organizations: drama/theater group, student-run newspaper, radio station, choral group, Bust-A-Move Beavers, Commuter Council, Intervarsity Christian Fellowship, Student Senate, Campus Residence Council.

Athletics Member NCAA. All Division III.

Campus security: 24-hour emergency response devices and patrols, student patrols, late-night transport/escort service, controlled dormitory access, safety whistles, security cameras.

Student services: health clinic, personal/psychological counseling.

COSTS & FINANCIAL AID
Costs (2019–20) ***Tuition:*** state resident $8429 full-time, $281 per credit hour part-time; nonresident $18,599 full-time, $620 per credit hour part-time. Full-time tuition and fees vary according to course load and reciprocity agreements. Part-time tuition and fees vary according to course load and reciprocity agreements. ***Required fees:*** $915 full-time. ***Room and board:*** $9902; room only: $5356. Room and board charges vary according to board plan and housing facility.

Financial Aid Of all full-time matriculated undergraduates who enrolled in 2018, 1,410 applied for aid, 1,219 were judged to have need, 504 had their need fully met. In 2018, 118 non-need-based awards were made. ***Average percent of need met:*** 82. ***Average financial aid package:*** $14,619. ***Average need-based loan:*** $6471. ***Average need-based gift aid:*** $8093. ***Average non-need-based aid:*** $2614. ***Average indebtedness upon graduation:*** $30,315.

APPLYING
Options: electronic application, early admission, early action, deferred entrance.

Required: high school transcript, 1 letter of recommendation. ***Required for some:*** essay or personal statement, minimum 2.75 GPA for College of Education transfers, 2.5 for Health and Rehabilitation, 2.0 for all others. ***Recommended:*** interview.

CONTACT
Lisa Ellrich, Associate Director of Admissions, University of Maine at Farmington, 246 Main Street, Farmington, ME 04938-1994. *Phone:* 207-778-7050. *E-mail:* ellrich@maine.edu.

University of Maine at Fort Kent

Fort Kent, Maine

http://www.umfk.maine.edu/

CONTACT
University of Maine at Fort Kent, 23 University Drive, Fort Kent, ME 04743-1292. *Phone:* 207-834-7600. *Toll-free phone:* 888-TRY-UMFK.

University of Maine at Machias

Machias, Maine

http://www.machias.edu/

- **State-supported** 4-year, founded 1909, part of University of Maine System
- **Rural** 42-acre campus
- **Endowment** $2.5 million
- **Coed**
- **Moderately difficult** entrance level

FACULTY
Student/faculty ratio: 12:1.

ACADEMICS
Calendar: semesters. *Degrees:* certificates, associate, and bachelor's.
Library: Merrill Library.

STUDENT LIFE
Housing options: on-campus residence required through sophomore year; coed, special housing for students with disabilities. Campus housing is university owned.

Athletics Member NAIA.

COSTS & FINANCIAL AID
Costs (2019–20) ***Tuition:*** area resident $7170 full-time, $239 per credit hour part-time; state resident $7170 full-time, $239 per credit hour part-time; nonresident $14,250 full-time, $475 per credit hour part-time. Full-time tuition and fees vary according to course load. Part-time tuition and fees vary according to course load. ***Required fees:*** $866 full-time. ***Room and board:*** $9180. Room and board charges vary according to housing facility.

Financial Aid Of all full-time matriculated undergraduates who enrolled in 2016, 394 applied for aid, 354 were judged to have need, 217 had their need fully met. In 2016, 2 non-need-based awards were made. ***Average percent of need met:*** 83. ***Average financial aid package:*** $14,175. ***Average need-based loan:*** $6053. ***Average need-based gift aid:*** $8858. ***Average non-need-based aid:*** $750. ***Average indebtedness upon graduation:*** $25,702.

APPLYING
Options: electronic application, early admission, early action, deferred entrance.

Application fee: $40.

Required: essay or personal statement, high school transcript, 1 letter of recommendation. ***Required for some:*** minimum 2.0 GPA. ***Recommended:*** minimum 2.5 GPA, 2 letters of recommendation, interview.

CONTACT
Lizzie Wahab, Vice President for Enrollment Management, University of Maine at Machias, 116 O'Brien Avenue, Machias, ME 04654. *Phone:* 207-255-1318. *Toll-free phone:* 888-GOTOUMM (in-state); 888-468-6866 (out-of-state). *E-mail:* ummadmissions@maine.edu.

University of Maine at Presque Isle

Presque Isle, Maine

http://www.umpi.edu/

- **State-supported** 4-year, founded 1903, part of University of Maine System
- **Small-town** 150-acre campus
- **Endowment** $1.3 million
- **Coed** 1,554 undergraduate students, 43% full-time, 61% women, 39% men
- **Minimally difficult** entrance level, 92% of applicants were admitted

UNDERGRAD STUDENTS
673 full-time, 881 part-time. Students come from 32 states and territories; 8 other countries; 14% are from out of state; 3% Black or African American, non-Hispanic/Latino; 2% Hispanic/Latino; 0.8% Asian, non-Hispanic/Latino; 0.1% Native Hawaiian or other Pacific Islander, non-Hispanic/Latino; 2% American Indian or Alaska Native, non-Hispanic/Latino; 2% Two or more races, non-Hispanic/Latino; 11% Race/ethnicity unknown; 2% international; 7% transferred in; 34% live on campus.

Freshmen:
Admission: 801 applied, 734 admitted, 168 enrolled. ***Average high school GPA:*** 3.0. ***Test scores:*** SAT evidence-based reading and writing scores over 500: 56%; SAT math scores over 500: 53%; ACT scores over 18: 66%; SAT evidence-based reading and writing scores over 600: 19%; SAT math scores over 600: 9%; ACT scores over 24: 22%; SAT math scores over 700: 1%.

Retention: 62% of full-time freshmen returned.

FACULTY
Total: 95, 35% full-time.

Student/faculty ratio: 13:1.

ACADEMICS
Calendar: semesters. *Degrees:* certificates, associate, and bachelor's.

Special study options: academic remediation for entering students, accelerated degree program, adult/continuing education programs, advanced placement credit, cooperative education, distance learning, double majors, honors programs, independent study, internships, off-campus study, part-time degree program, services for LD students, student-designed majors, study abroad, summer session for credit.

Computers: Students can access the following: campus intranet, computer help desk, free student e-mail accounts, online (class) grades, online (class) registration, online (class) schedules. Campuswide network is available. 100% of college-owned or -operated housing units are wired for high-speed Internet access. Wireless service is available via entire campus.

Library: Center for Innovative Learning plus 1 other. *Books:* 63,527 (physical), 159,418 (digital/electronic); *Serial titles:* 8 (physical), 75,843 (digital/electronic); *Databases:* 153. Weekly public service hours: 72.

STUDENT LIFE
Housing options: coed, special housing for students with disabilities. Campus housing is university owned. Freshman applicants given priority for college housing.

Activities and organizations: student-run newspaper, radio station, national fraternities, national sororities.

Athletics Member NCAA. All Division III. ***Intercollegiate sports:*** baseball M, basketball M/W, cross-country running M/W, golf M, skiing (cross-country) M/W, soccer M/W, softball W, volleyball W. ***Intramural sports:*** basketball M/W, cross-country running M/W, ice hockey M(c)/W(c), skiing (cross-country) M/W, skiing (downhill) M/W, soccer M/W, softball M/W, tennis M, track and field W, volleyball M/W.

Campus security: student patrols, late-night transport/escort service, controlled dormitory access.

Student services: health clinic, personal/psychological counseling, veterans affairs office.

COSTS & FINANCIAL AID
Costs (2020–21) ***Tuition:*** state resident $7350 full-time, $245 per credit hour part-time; nonresident $11,760 full-time, $392 per credit hour part-time. ***Required fees:*** $1224 full-time, $25 per credit hour part-time, $54 per term part-time. ***Room and board:*** $8738; room only: $4850. Room and board charges vary according to board plan. ***Waivers:*** minority students, senior citizens, and employees or children of employees.

Financial Aid Of all full-time matriculated undergraduates who enrolled in 2019, 509 applied for aid, 427 were judged to have need, 261 had their need fully met. In 2019, 32 non-need-based awards were made. ***Average percent of need met:*** 87. ***Average financial aid package:*** $12,438. ***Average need-based loan:*** $4985. ***Average need-based gift aid:*** $7644. ***Average non-need-based aid:*** $2718. ***Average indebtedness upon graduation:*** $22,205.

APPLYING
Options: electronic application, early admission, deferred entrance.

Application fee: $40.

Required: essay or personal statement, high school transcript, 1 letter of recommendation. ***Required for some:*** interview. ***Recommended:*** minimum 2.0 GPA.

Application deadlines: rolling (freshmen), rolling (out-of-state freshmen), rolling (transfers), rolling (early action).

Early decision deadline: rolling (for plan 1), rolling (for plan 2).

Notification: continuous (freshmen), continuous (out-of-state freshmen), continuous (transfers), rolling (early decision plan 1), rolling (early decision plan 2), rolling (early action).

CONTACT
Susan White, Director of Admission, University of Maine at Presque Isle, 181 Main Street, Presque Isle, ME 04769. *Phone:* 207-768-9533. *E-mail:* susan.r.white@umpi.edu.

University of New England

Biddeford, Maine

http://www.une.edu/

- **Independent** comprehensive, founded 1831
- **Small-town** 540-acre campus
- **Endowment** $35.5 million
- **Coed** 4,275 undergraduate students, 57% full-time, 70% women, 30% men
- **Moderately difficult** entrance level, 84% of applicants were admitted

UNDERGRAD STUDENTS
2,425 full-time, 1,850 part-time. Students come from 40 states and territories; 9 other countries; 73% are from out of state; 2% Black or African American, non-Hispanic/Latino; 0.3% Hispanic/Latino; 3% Asian, non-Hispanic/Latino; 0.2% American Indian or Alaska Native, non-Hispanic/Latino; 2% Two or more races, non-Hispanic/Latino; 3% Race/ethnicity unknown; 0.5% international; 2% transferred in; 62% live on campus.

Freshmen:
Admission: 5,175 applied, 4,367 admitted, 712 enrolled. ***Average high school GPA:*** 3.4. ***Test scores:*** SAT evidence-based reading and writing scores over 500: 85%; SAT math scores over 500: 85%; ACT scores over 18: 95%; SAT evidence-based reading and writing scores over 600: 37%; SAT math scores over 600: 34%; ACT scores over 24: 49%; SAT evidence-based reading and writing scores over 700: 4%; SAT math scores over 700: 4%; ACT scores over 30: 10%.

Retention: 82% of full-time freshmen returned.

FACULTY
Total: 528, 57% full-time.

Student/faculty ratio: 13:1.

ACADEMICS
Calendar: semesters. *Degrees:* bachelor's, master's, doctoral, post-master's, and postbachelor's certificates.

Special study options: academic remediation for entering students, accelerated degree program, adult/continuing education programs, advanced placement credit, cooperative education, distance learning, double majors, honors programs, independent study, internships, off-campus study, part-time degree program, services for LD students, study abroad, summer session for credit. ***ROTC:*** Army (c).

Unusual degree programs: 3-2 physician assistant.

Computers: 91 computers/terminals are available on campus for general student use. Students can access the following: campus intranet, computer help desk, free student e-mail accounts, online (class) grades, online (class) registration, online (class) schedules. Campuswide network is available. 100% of college-owned or -operated housing units are wired for high-speed Internet access. Wireless service is available via entire campus.

Library: Jack S. Ketchum Library plus 1 other. *Books:* 135,000 (physical), 1.2 million (digital/electronic); *Serial titles:* 140,000 (digital/electronic); *Databases:* 200. Weekly public service hours: 146; study areas open 24 hours, 5–7 days a week; students can reserve study rooms.

STUDENT LIFE

Housing options: on-campus residence required through junior year; coed, women-only, special housing for students with disabilities. Campus housing is university owned. Freshman campus housing is guaranteed.

Activities and organizations: drama/theater group, student-run newspaper, choral group, Student Government, Outing Club, Campus Programming Board, Earth's Eco, Dance Team.

Athletics Member NCAA. All Division III. ***Intercollegiate sports:*** basketball M/W, cross-country running M/W, field hockey W, football M, golf M, ice hockey M/W, lacrosse M/W, rugby W, soccer M/W, softball W, swimming and diving W, volleyball W. ***Intramural sports:*** baseball M(c), basketball M/W, cheerleading M(c)/W(c), equestrian sports M(c)/W(c), gymnastics M(c)/W(c), ice hockey M(c)/W(c), racquetball M/W, rugby M(c)/W(c), sailing M(c)/W(c), soccer M/W, softball M/W, swimming and diving M(c), table tennis M/W, tennis M(c)/W(c), track and field M(c)/W(c), ultimate Frisbee M/W, volleyball M(c)/W(c), water polo W(c).

Campus security: 24-hour emergency response devices and patrols, late-night transport/escort service, controlled dormitory access.

Student services: health clinic, personal/psychological counseling.

COSTS & FINANCIAL AID

Costs (2019–20) ***Comprehensive fee:*** $53,160 includes full-time tuition ($37,390), mandatory fees ($1360), and room and board ($14,410). Full-time tuition and fees vary according to course load and program. Part-time tuition: $1320 per credit hour. Part-time tuition and fees vary according to course load and program. ***Required fees:*** $1360 per year part-time. ***Room and board:*** Room and board charges vary according to board plan and housing facility. ***Payment plan:*** installment. ***Waivers:*** children of alumni and employees or children of employees.

Financial Aid Of all full-time matriculated undergraduates who enrolled in 2018, 2,055 applied for aid, 1,876 were judged to have need. ***Average financial aid package:*** $24,047. ***Average need-based loan:*** $3961. ***Average need-based gift aid:*** $7290. ***Average indebtedness upon graduation:*** $40,683.

APPLYING

Standardized Tests *Required for some:* SAT or ACT (for admission).

Options: electronic application, early admission, early action, deferred entrance.

Application fee: $40.

Required: essay or personal statement, high school transcript. ***Recommended:*** 1 letter of recommendation.

Application deadlines: 2/15 (freshmen), rolling (transfers), 12/1 (early action).

Notification: continuous (freshmen), continuous (transfers), rolling (early action).

CONTACT

Office of Undergraduate Admissions, University of New England, 11 Hills Beach Road, Biddeford, ME 04005-9526. *Phone:* 800-477-4863. *Toll-free phone:* 800-477-4863. *Fax:* 207-602-5900. *E-mail:* admissions@une.edu.

University of Southern Maine

Portland, Maine

http://www.usm.maine.edu/

- **State-supported** comprehensive, founded 1878, part of University of Maine System
- **Urban** 144-acre campus
- **Coed** 6,675 undergraduate students, 61% full-time, 57% women, 43% men
- **Moderately difficult** entrance level, 81% of applicants were admitted

UNDERGRAD STUDENTS

4,062 full-time, 2,613 part-time. Students come from 38 states and territories; 23 other countries; 15% are from out of state; 7% Black or African American, non-Hispanic/Latino; 3% Hispanic/Latino; 2% Asian, non-Hispanic/Latino; 0.7% American Indian or Alaska Native, non-Hispanic/Latino; 4% Two or more races, non-Hispanic/Latino; 3% Race/ethnicity unknown; 1% international; 9% transferred in; 26% live on campus.

Freshmen:

Admission: 4,996 applied, 4,042 admitted, 893 enrolled. ***Average high school GPA:*** 3.3. ***Test scores:*** SAT evidence-based reading and writing scores over 500: 68%; SAT math scores over 500: 64%; ACT scores over 18: 87%; SAT evidence-based reading and writing scores over 600: 23%; SAT math scores over 600: 15%; ACT scores over 24: 31%; SAT evidence-based reading and writing scores over 700: 2%; SAT math scores over 700: 2%; ACT scores over 30: 13%.

Retention: 69% of full-time freshmen returned.

FACULTY

Total: 824, 36% full-time, 39% with terminal degrees.

Student/faculty ratio: 13:1.

ACADEMICS

Calendar: semesters. *Degrees:* certificates, bachelor's, master's, doctoral, post-master's, and postbachelor's certificates.

Special study options: academic remediation for entering students, accelerated degree program, adult/continuing education programs, advanced placement credit, cooperative education, distance learning, double majors, English as a second language, honors programs, independent study, internships, off-campus study, part-time degree program, services for LD students, student-designed majors, study abroad, summer session for credit. ***ROTC:*** Army (c), Air Force (c).

Unusual degree programs: 3-2 business administration.

Computers: 219 computers/terminals are available on campus for general student use. Students can access the following: campus intranet, computer help desk, free student e-mail accounts, online (class) grades, online (class) registration, online (class) schedules. Campuswide network is available. 100% of college-owned or -operated housing units are wired for high-speed Internet access. Wireless service is available via entire campus.

Library: Glickman Library plus 3 others.

STUDENT LIFE

Housing options: coed, special housing for students with disabilities. Campus housing is university owned. Freshman applicants given priority for college housing.

Activities and organizations: drama/theater group, student-run newspaper, radio station, choral group, Outing and Ski Clubs, Gorham Events Board, Commuter Student Group, Circle K, national fraternities, national sororities.

Athletics Member NCAA. All Division III except golf (Division II). ***Intercollegiate sports:*** baseball M, basketball M/W, cross-country running M/W, fencing M/W(c), field hockey W, golf M/W, ice hockey M/W, lacrosse M/W, sailing M/W, soccer M/W, softball W, tennis M/W, track and field M/W, volleyball W, wrestling M. ***Intramural sports:*** baseball M, basketball M/W, cheerleading M(c)/W(c), football M/W, ice hockey M/W, lacrosse M(c)/W(c), racquetball M/W, rugby M(c)/W(c), skiing (downhill) M(c)/W(c), soccer M/W, softball M/W, squash M/W, table tennis M/W, tennis M/W, ultimate Frisbee M/W, volleyball M/W, weight lifting M/W.

Campus security: 24-hour emergency response devices and patrols, late-night transport/escort service, controlled dormitory access, security lighting, preventive programs within residence halls.

Student services: health clinic, personal/psychological counseling, women's center, legal services, veterans affairs office.

COSTS & FINANCIAL AID

Costs (2019–20) ***Tuition:*** $281 per credit hour part-time; state resident $8430 full-time, $281 per credit hour part-time; nonresident $22,170 full-time, $739 per credit hour part-time. Full-time tuition and fees vary according to course load, degree level, and reciprocity agreements. Part-time tuition and fees vary according to course load, degree level, and reciprocity agreements. ***Required fees:*** $1420 full-time, $31 per credit hour part-time. ***Room and board:*** $9826; room only: $5200. Room and board charges vary according to board plan and housing facility. ***Payment plan:*** installment. ***Waivers:*** employees or children of employees.

Financial Aid Of all full-time matriculated undergraduates who enrolled in 2018, 3,447 applied for aid, 2,901 were judged to have need, 1,449 had their need fully met. In 2018, 348 non-need-based awards were made. ***Average percent of need met:*** 80. ***Average financial aid package:*** $14,271. ***Average need-based loan:*** $6338. ***Average need-based gift aid:*** $9530. ***Average non-need-based aid:*** $4226.

APPLYING

Standardized Tests *Required for some:* SAT (for admission), ACT (for admission), SAT or ACT (for admission), SAT and SAT Subject Tests or ACT (for admission), SAT Subject Tests (for admission).

Options: electronic application, early admission, deferred entrance.

Required: essay or personal statement, high school transcript. ***Required for some:*** interview, audition for music majors. ***Recommended:*** 1 letter of recommendation, interview.

Notification: continuous (freshmen), continuous (transfers).

CONTACT

Admissions, University of Southern Maine, Portland, ME 04104-9300. *Phone:* 207-780-5670. *Toll-free phone:* 800-800-4USM Ext. 5670. *E-mail:* admitusm@maine.edu.

MARYLAND

Bais HaMedrash and Mesivta of Baltimore

Baltimore, Maryland

http://www.bhmb.edu/

CONTACT

Bais HaMedrash and Mesivta of Baltimore, 6823 Old Pimlico Road, Baltimore, MD 21209.

Bowie State University

Bowie, Maryland

http://www.bowiestate.edu/

- **State-supported** comprehensive, founded 1865, part of University System of Maryland
- **Small-town** 295-acre campus with easy access to Baltimore and Washington, DC
- **Coed**
- **Minimally difficult** entrance level

FACULTY

Student/faculty ratio: 16:1.

ACADEMICS

Calendar: semesters. *Degrees:* certificates, bachelor's, master's, doctoral, and postbachelor's certificates.

Library: Thurgood Marshall Library. Students can reserve study rooms.

STUDENT LIFE

Housing options: coed, men-only, women-only. Campus housing is university owned and is provided by a third party. Freshman applicants given priority for college housing.

Activities and organizations: drama/theater group, student-run newspaper, radio and television station, choral group, marching band, Honda Campus All-Star Challenge, national fraternities, national sororities.

Athletics Member NCAA. All Division II.

Campus security: 24-hour emergency response devices and patrols, student patrols, late-night transport/escort service, controlled dormitory access.

Student services: health clinic, personal/psychological counseling.

COSTS & FINANCIAL AID

Costs (2019–20) ***Tuition:*** state resident $5647 full-time, $248 per credit hour part-time; nonresident $16,338 full-time, $687 per credit hour part-time. ***Required fees:*** $2798 full-time, $124 per credit hour part-time. ***Room and board:*** $9916. Room and board charges vary according to board plan and housing facility. ***Payment plans:*** installment, deferred payment.

Financial Aid Of all full-time matriculated undergraduates who enrolled in 2018, 3,183 applied for aid, 3,178 were judged to have need, 568 had their need fully met. In 2018, 58 non-need-based awards were made. ***Average percent of need met:*** 41. ***Average financial aid package:*** $8916. ***Average need-based loan:*** $3892. ***Average need-based gift aid:*** $7535. ***Average non-need-based aid:*** $112. ***Average indebtedness upon graduation:*** $28,807.

APPLYING

Standardized Tests *Required:* SAT or ACT (for admission).

Options: electronic application.

Application fee: $40.

Required: high school transcript, minimum 2.5 GPA.

CONTACT

Mrs. Shirley Holt, Assistant Director of Admissions, Bowie State University, Administration Building, 1st Floor. *Phone:* 301-860-3415. *Toll-free phone:* 877-772-6943. *Fax:* 301-860-3438. *E-mail:* sholt@bowiestate.edu.

Capitol Technology University

Laurel, Maryland

http://www.captechu.edu/

CONTACT

Capitol Technology University, 11301 Springfield Road, Laurel, MD 20708-9759. *Phone:* 301-953-3200 Ext. 3033. *Toll-free phone:* 800-950-1992.

Cecil College

North East, Maryland

http://www.cecil.edu/

CONTACT

Dr. Christy Dryer, Cecil College, One Seahawk Drive, North East, MD 21901-1999. *Phone:* 410-287-6060. *Fax:* 410-287-1001. *E-mail:* cdryer@cecil.edu.

Coppin State University

Baltimore, Maryland

http://www.coppin.edu/

- **State-supported** comprehensive, founded 1900, part of University System of Maryland
- **Urban** 33-acre campus
- **Coed**
- **Moderately difficult** entrance level

FACULTY

Student/faculty ratio: 15:1.

ACADEMICS

Calendar: semesters. *Degrees:* bachelor's, master's, and postbachelor's certificates.

Library: Parlett L. Moore Library.

STUDENT LIFE

Housing options: coed. Campus housing is university owned.

Activities and organizations: drama/theater group, student-run newspaper, choral group, national fraternities, national sororities.

Athletics Member NCAA. All Division I.

Campus security: 24-hour emergency response devices and patrols, late-night transport/escort service, controlled dormitory access.

Student services: health clinic, personal/psychological counseling.

FINANCIAL AID

Financial Aid Of all full-time matriculated undergraduates who enrolled in 2013, 1,889 applied for aid, 1,877 were judged to have need, 178 had their need fully met. In 2013, 16 non-need-based awards were made. ***Average percent of need met:*** 70. ***Average financial aid package:*** $11,871. ***Average need-based loan:*** $4242. ***Average need-based gift aid:*** $7744. ***Average non-need-based aid:*** $2999.

APPLYING

Standardized Tests *Required:* SAT or ACT (for admission).

Options: electronic application, early admission, deferred entrance.

Application fee: $35.

Required: high school transcript. ***Required for some:*** 2 letters of recommendation. ***Recommended:*** minimum 2.5 GPA, interview.

CONTACT
Ms. Michelle Gross, Director of Admissions, Coppin State University, 2500 West North Avenue, Baltimore, MD 21216-3698. *Phone:* 410-951-3600. *Toll-free phone:* 800-635-3674. *Fax:* 410-523-7351. *E-mail:* mgross@coppin.edu.

Faith Theological Seminary

Baltimore, Maryland

http://www.fts.edu/

CONTACT
Faith Theological Seminary, 529 Walker Avenue, Baltimore, MD 21212. *Phone:* 410-323-6211.

Frostburg State University

Frostburg, Maryland

http://www.frostburg.edu/

- **State-supported** comprehensive, founded 1898, part of University System of Maryland
- **Small-town** 260-acre campus with easy access to Baltimore and Washington, DC
- **Endowment** $25.1 million
- **Coed**
- **Moderately difficult** entrance level

FACULTY
Student/faculty ratio: 16:1.

ACADEMICS
Calendar: semesters. *Degrees:* bachelor's, master's, and doctoral. **Library:** Lewis J. Ort Library.

STUDENT LIFE
Housing options: coed, men-only, women-only. Campus housing is university owned and is provided by a third party.

Activities and organizations: drama/theater group, student-run newspaper, radio and television station, choral group, marching band, Student Government Association, Black Student Association, Campus Activities Board, Residence Hall Association, University Programming Council, national fraternities, national sororities.

Athletics Member NCAA. All Division III.

Campus security: 24-hour emergency response devices and patrols, student patrols, late-night transport/escort service, controlled dormitory access, bicycle patrols.

Student services: health clinic, personal/psychological counseling, women's center.

COSTS & FINANCIAL AID
Costs (2019–20) ***Tuition:*** area resident $6700 full-time, $437 per credit hour part-time; state resident $6700 full-time, $437 per credit hour part-time; nonresident $20,800 full-time, $560 per credit hour part-time. Full-time tuition and fees vary according to location. Part-time tuition and fees vary according to course load and location. ***Required fees:*** $2710 full-time, $135 per credit hour part-time, $25 per term part-time. ***Room and board:*** $5274; room only: $4676. Room and board charges vary according to board plan.

Financial Aid Of all full-time matriculated undergraduates who enrolled in 2017, 3,480 applied for aid, 2,669 were judged to have need, 386 had their need fully met. 130 Federal Work-Study jobs (averaging $674). In 2017, 853 non-need-based awards were made. ***Average percent of need met:*** 59. ***Average financial aid package:*** $9993. ***Average need-based loan:*** $3932. ***Average need-based gift aid:*** $7651. ***Average non-need-based aid:*** $3427. ***Average indebtedness upon graduation:*** $29,802.

APPLYING
Standardized Tests *Required:* SAT or ACT (for admission).

Options: electronic application, early admission.

Application fee: $30.

Required: high school transcript, minimum 2.0 GPA. ***Required for some:*** essay or personal statement. ***Recommended:*** interview.

CONTACT
Frostburg State University, 101 Braddock Road, Frostburg, MD 21532-1099. *Phone:* 301-687-4201.

Goucher College

Baltimore, Maryland

http://www.goucher.edu/

- **Independent** comprehensive, founded 1885
- **Suburban** 287-acre campus with easy access to Baltimore and Washington, DC
- **Endowment** $201.5 million
- **Coed** 1,449 undergraduate students, 91% full-time, 67% women, 33% men
- **Moderately difficult** entrance level, 81% of applicants were admitted

UNDERGRAD STUDENTS
1,325 full-time, 124 part-time. Students come from 46 states and territories; 26 other countries; 40% are from out of state; 18% Black or African American, non-Hispanic/Latino; 10% Hispanic/Latino; 4% Asian, non-Hispanic/Latino; 0.3% Native Hawaiian or other Pacific Islander, non-Hispanic/Latino; 4% Two or more races, non Hispanic/Latino; 7% Race/ethnicity unknown; 3% international; 3% transferred in; 85% live on campus.

Freshmen:
Admission: 2,610 applied, 2,122 admitted, 340 enrolled. ***Average high school GPA:*** 3.2. ***Test scores:*** SAT evidence-based reading and writing scores over 500: 88%; SAT math scores over 500: 79%; ACT scores over 18: 93%; SAT evidence-based reading and writing scores over 600: 51%; SAT math scores over 600: 36%; ACT scores over 24: 63%; SAT evidence-based reading and writing scores over 700: 14%; SAT math scores over 700: 6%; ACT scores over 30: 20%.

Retention: 77% of full-time freshmen returned.

FACULTY
Total: 175, 75% full-time, 80% with terminal degrees.

Student/faculty ratio: 10:1.

ACADEMICS
Calendar: semesters. *Degrees:* bachelor's, master's, and postbachelor's certificates.

Special study options: accelerated degree program, adult/continuing education programs, advanced placement credit, distance learning, double majors, independent study, internships, off-campus study, part-time degree program, services for LD students, student-designed majors, study abroad, summer session for credit. ***ROTC:*** Army (c), Air Force (c).

Unusual degree programs: 3-2 engineering with Johns Hopkins University, Columbia University.

Computers: 130 computers/terminals are available on campus for general student use. Students can access the following: campus intranet, computer help desk, free student e-mail accounts, online (class) grades, online (class) registration, online (class) schedules, transcripts, financial aid information, billing, ePortfolios, academic progress reports, study abroad plans. Campuswide network is available. 100% of college-owned or -operated housing units are wired for high-speed Internet access. Wireless service is available via entire campus.
Library: Goucher College Library plus 1 other. *Books:* 250,000 (physical), 300,000 (digital/electronic); *Serial titles:* 96,000 (digital/electronic); *Databases:* 120. Weekly public service hours: 168; study areas open 24 hours, 5–7 days a week.

STUDENT LIFE
Housing options: on-campus residence required through senior year; coed, men-only, women-only, special housing for students with disabilities. Campus housing is university owned. Freshman applicants given priority for college housing.

Activities and organizations: drama/theater group, student-run newspaper, radio station, choral group, Ultimate Frisbee, Yoga Club, Hip Hop Team, Umoja: The Black Student Union, Model Senate.

Athletics Member NCAA. All Division III. ***Intercollegiate sports:*** basketball M/W, cross-country running M/W, equestrian sports M/W, field hockey W, golf M/W, lacrosse M/W, soccer M/W, swimming and diving M/W, tennis M/W, track and field M/W, volleyball W. ***Intramural sports:***

basketball M/W, fencing M(c)/W(c), soccer M/W, ultimate Frisbee M(c)/W(c).

Campus security: 24-hour emergency response devices and patrols, late-night transport/escort service, controlled dormitory access, E2 campus alerts.

Student services: health clinic, personal/psychological counseling.

COSTS & FINANCIAL AID
Costs (2020–21) ***Comprehensive fee:*** $61,182 includes full-time tuition ($47,100), mandatory fees ($200), and room and board ($13,882). Part-time tuition: $1570 per credit hour. ***College room only:*** $7688. Room and board charges vary according to board plan and housing facility. ***Payment plan:*** installment. ***Waivers:*** minority students and employees or children of employees.

Financial Aid Of all full-time matriculated undergraduates who enrolled in 2019, 1,077 applied for aid, 958 were judged to have need, 200 had their need fully met. In 2019, 337 non-need-based awards were made. ***Average percent of need met:*** 82. ***Average financial aid package:*** $40,413. ***Average need-based loan:*** $3862. ***Average need-based gift aid:*** $36,594. ***Average non-need-based aid:*** $21,434. ***Average indebtedness upon graduation:*** $28,145.

APPLYING
Options: electronic application, early admission, early decision, early action, deferred entrance.

Required: essay or personal statement, a short video, digital application, signed statement of academic integrity, two works from high school career (one of which must be a graded writing assignment) for Goucher Video Application. ***Required for some:*** high school transcript. ***Recommended:*** 3 letters of recommendation, interview.

Application deadlines: 1/15 (freshmen), 5/1 (transfers), 12/1 (early action).

Early decision deadline: 12/1.

Notification: 4/1 (freshmen), 5/1 (transfers), 2/1 (early decision), 2/1 (early action).

CONTACT
Mr. Christopher Wild, Associate Director of Admissions, Goucher College, 1021 Dulaney Valley Road, Baltimore, MD 21204. *Phone:* 410-337-6363. *Toll-free phone:* 800-468-2437. *E-mail:* admissions@goucher.edu.

Hood College

Frederick, Maryland

http://www.hood.edu/

- **Independent** comprehensive, founded 1893
- **Suburban** 50-acre campus with easy access to Baltimore and Washington, DC
- **Endowment** $99.7 million
- **Coed**
- **Moderately difficult** entrance level

FACULTY
Student/faculty ratio: 10:1.

ACADEMICS
Calendar: semesters. *Degrees:* certificates, bachelor's, master's, doctoral, and postbachelor's certificates (also offers adult program with significant enrollment not reflected in profile).

Library: Beneficial-Hodson Library and Information Technology Center plus 1 other. *Books:* 113,587 (physical), 367,563 (digital/electronic); *Serial titles:* 1,546 (physical), 2,440 (digital/electronic); *Databases:* 148. Students can reserve study rooms.

STUDENT LIFE
Housing options: on-campus residence required through junior year; coed. Campus housing is university owned. Freshman campus housing is guaranteed.

Activities and organizations: drama/theater group, student-run newspaper, radio station, choral group, Black Student Union (BSU), Campus Activities Board (CAB), La Comunidad, Queer Student Union (QSU), Enactus.

Athletics Member NCAA. All Division III.

Campus security: 24-hour emergency response devices and patrols, late-night transport/escort service, controlled dormitory access.

Student services: health clinic, personal/psychological counseling.

COSTS & FINANCIAL AID
Costs (2019–20) ***Comprehensive fee:*** $53,940 includes full-time tuition ($40,460), mandatory fees ($600), and room and board ($12,880). Part-time tuition: $1180 per credit hour. ***Required fees:*** $195 per term part-time. ***College room only:*** $6600. Room and board charges vary according to board plan.

Financial Aid Of all full-time matriculated undergraduates who enrolled in 2018, 905 applied for aid, 824 were judged to have need, 134 had their need fully met. In 2018, 162 non-need-based awards were made. ***Average percent of need met:*** 74. ***Average financial aid package:*** $31,926. ***Average need-based loan:*** $4095. ***Average need-based gift aid:*** $28,296. ***Average non-need-based aid:*** $18,840. ***Average indebtedness upon graduation:*** $35,237.

APPLYING
Options: electronic application.

Required: essay or personal statement, high school transcript, minimum 2.0 GPA. ***Recommended:*** 2 letters of recommendation, interview.

CONTACT
Mr. William Brown, Vice President for Enrollment Management, Hood College, 401 Rosemont Avenue, Frederick, MD 21701. *Phone:* 301-696-3400. *Toll-free phone:* 800-922-1599. *Fax:* 301-696-3819. *E-mail:* admission@hood.edu.

Johns Hopkins University

Baltimore, Maryland

http://www.jhu.edu/

- **Independent** university, founded 1876
- **Urban** 140-acre campus with easy access to Baltimore and Washington, DC
- **Endowment** $6.3 billion
- **Coed** 5,534 undergraduate students, 98% full-time, 52% women, 48% men
- **Most difficult** entrance level, 10% of applicants were admitted

UNDERGRAD STUDENTS
5,444 full-time, 90 part-time. Students come from 57 states and territories; 53 other countries; 89% are from out of state; 8% Black or African American, non-Hispanic/Latino; 16% Hispanic/Latino; 27% Asian, non-Hispanic/Latino; 0.2% Native Hawaiian or other Pacific Islander, non-Hispanic/Latino; 0.1% American Indian or Alaska Native, non-Hispanic/Latino; 6% Two or more races, non-Hispanic/Latino; 5% Race/ethnicity unknown; 11% international; 2% transferred in; 51% live on campus.

Freshmen:
Admission: 30,164 applied, 2,937 admitted, 1,355 enrolled. ***Average high school GPA:*** 3.9. ***Test scores:*** SAT evidence-based reading and writing scores over 500: 100%; SAT math scores over 500: 100%; ACT scores over 18: 100%; SAT evidence-based reading and writing scores over 600: 99%; SAT math scores over 600: 99%; ACT scores over 24: 100%; SAT evidence-based reading and writing scores over 700: 87%; SAT math scores over 700: 94%; ACT scores over 30: 97%.

Retention: 98% of full-time freshmen returned.

FACULTY
Total: 757, 97% full-time, 96% with terminal degrees.

Student/faculty ratio: 7:1.

ACADEMICS
Calendar: 4-1-4. *Degrees:* certificates, diplomas, bachelor's, master's, doctoral, and postbachelor's certificates.

Special study options: advanced placement credit, double majors, independent study, internships, off-campus study, services for LD students, student-designed majors, study abroad, summer session for credit. ***ROTC:*** Army (b), Air Force (c).

Unusual degree programs: 3-2 engineering; biology, classics, German, history, international studies, mathematics, molecular and cellular biology,

APPLY.JHU.EDU

neuroscience, public health studies; Peabody Double Degree Program: Bachelor of Music or Fine Arts and BA or BS from JHU.

Computers: 200 computers/terminals and 4,000 ports are available on campus for general student use. Students can access the following: campus intranet, computer help desk, free student e-mail accounts, online (class) grades, online (class) registration, online (class) schedules. Campuswide network is available. 100% of college-owned or -operated housing units are wired for high-speed Internet access. Wireless service is available via entire campus.

Library: The Sheridan Libraries plus 2 others. *Books:* 2.4 million (physical), 1.8 million (digital/electronic); *Serial titles:* 52,559 (physical), 171,703 (digital/electronic); *Databases:* 836. Study areas open 24 hours, 5–7 days a week; students can reserve study rooms.

STUDENT LIFE

Housing options: on-campus residence required through sophomore year; coed, special housing for students with disabilities. Campus housing is university owned. Freshman campus housing is guaranteed.

Activities and organizations: drama/theater group, student-run newspaper, radio station, choral group, national fraternities, national sororities.

Athletics Member NCAA. All Division III except men's and women's lacrosse (Division I). ***Intercollegiate sports:*** baseball M, basketball M/W, cross-country running M/W, fencing M/W, field hockey W, football M, lacrosse M(s)/W(s), soccer M/W, swimming and diving M/W, tennis M/W, track and field M/W, volleyball W, water polo M, wrestling M. ***Intramural sports:*** badminton M(c)/W(c), baseball M(c), basketball M/W, cheerleading W(c), equestrian sports M(c)/W(c), fencing W(c), football M/W, golf M(c)/W(c), ice hockey M(c), lacrosse M(c)/W(c), racquetball M(c)/W(c), riflery M(c)/W(c), rock climbing M/W, rugby M(c)/W(c), soccer M/W, softball W(c), squash M(c)/W(c), swimming and diving M(c)/W(c), table tennis M(c)/W(c), tennis M(c)/W(c), track and field M(c)/W(c), triathlon M(c)/W(c), ultimate Frisbee M(c)/W(c), volleyball M(c)/W(c), water polo M(c)/W(c), wrestling M(c).

Campus security: 24-hour emergency response devices and patrols, student patrols, late-night transport/escort service, controlled dormitory access, CCTV monitoring of public areas.

Student services: health clinic, personal/psychological counseling, women's center.

COSTS & FINANCIAL AID

Costs (2019–20) ***One-time required fee:*** $500. ***Comprehensive fee:*** $71,660 includes full-time tuition ($55,350) and room and board ($16,310). Part-time tuition: $1845 per credit hour. Part-time tuition and fees vary according to course load. ***College room only:*** $9452. Room and board charges vary according to board plan and housing facility. ***Payment plan:*** installment. ***Waivers:*** employees or children of employees.

Financial Aid Of all full-time matriculated undergraduates who enrolled in 2018, 3,194 applied for aid, 2,793 were judged to have need, 2,772 had their need fully met. 2,175 Federal Work-Study jobs (averaging $2282). In 2018, 155 non-need-based awards were made. ***Average percent of need met:*** 100. ***Average financial aid package:*** $44,147. ***Average need-based loan:*** $1534. ***Average need-based gift aid:*** $41,904. ***Average non-need-based aid:*** $25,181. ***Average indebtedness upon graduation:*** $25,697. ***Financial aid deadline:*** 1/15.

APPLYING

Standardized Tests *Required:* SAT or ACT (for admission).

Options: electronic application, early decision, deferred entrance.

Application fee: $70.

Required: essay or personal statement, high school transcript, 2 letters of recommendation.

Application deadlines: 1/1 (freshmen), 3/1 (transfers).

Early decision deadline: 11/1.

Notification: 3/15 (freshmen), 5/15 (transfers), 12/15 (early decision).

CONTACT

Johns Hopkins University, 3400 North Charles Street, Baltimore, MD 21218.

See below for display ad and page 1070 for the College Close-Up.

Loyola University Maryland

Baltimore, Maryland

http://www.loyola.edu/

- **Independent Roman Catholic (Jesuit)** university, founded 1852
- **Urban** 89-acre campus with easy access to Washington, DC
- **Endowment** $193.8 million
- **Coed** 3,879 undergraduate students, 99% full-time, 58% women, 42% men
- **Moderately difficult** entrance level, 79% of applicants were admitted

UNDERGRAD STUDENTS

3,833 full-time, 46 part-time. 80% are from out of state; 6% Black or African American, non-Hispanic/Latino; 10% Hispanic/Latino; 4% Asian, non-Hispanic/Latino; 0.2% American Indian or Alaska Native, non-Hispanic/Latino; 3% Two or more races, non-Hispanic/Latino; 0.1% Race/ethnicity unknown; 0.7% international; 1% transferred in; 82% live on campus.

Freshmen:

Admission: 10,251 applied, 8,072 admitted, 1,069 enrolled. ***Average high school GPA:*** 3.5. ***Test scores:*** SAT evidence-based reading and writing scores over 500: 98%; SAT math scores over 500: 97%; ACT scores over 18: 100%; SAT evidence-based reading and writing scores over 600: 69%; SAT math scores over 600: 58%; ACT scores over 24: 84%; SAT evidence-based reading and writing scores over 700: 11%; SAT math scores over 700: 13%; ACT scores over 30: 31%.

Retention: 88% of full-time freshmen returned.

FACULTY

Total: 490, 73% full-time, 64% with terminal degrees.

Student/faculty ratio: 12:1.

ACADEMICS

Calendar: semesters. *Degrees:* bachelor's, master's, doctoral, post-master's, and postbachelor's certificates.

Special study options: accelerated degree program, advanced placement credit, cooperative education, double majors, honors programs, independent study, internships, off-campus study, part-time degree program, services for LD students, study abroad, summer session for credit. ***ROTC:*** Army (b), Air Force (c).

Unusual degree programs: 3-2 nursing with Johns Hopkins University.

Computers: 690 computers/terminals and 50 ports are available on campus for general student use. Students can access the following: campus intranet, computer help desk, free student e-mail accounts, online (class) grades, online (class) registration, online (class) schedules. Campuswide network is available. 100% of college-owned or -operated housing units are wired for high-speed Internet access. Wireless service is available via entire campus.

Library: Loyola/Notre Dame Library plus 1 other.

STUDENT LIFE

Housing options: coed, cooperative. Campus housing is university owned. Freshman campus housing is guaranteed.

Activities and organizations: drama/theater group, student-run newspaper, radio and television station, choral group, Student Government Association, Resident Affairs Council (RAC), Relay for Life, Resident Assistants (RA), The Evergreens.

Athletics Member NCAA. All Division I. ***Intercollegiate sports:*** basketball M(s)/W(s), crew M(s)/W(s), cross-country running M(s)/W(s), golf M(s), lacrosse M(s)/W(s), soccer M(s)/W(s), swimming and diving M(s)/W(s), tennis M(s)/W(s), track and field W(s), volleyball W(s). ***Intramural sports:*** badminton M(c)/W(c), baseball M(c), basketball M(c)/W(c), field hockey W(c), ice hockey M(c), lacrosse M(c)/W(c), riflery M(c)/W(c), rugby M(c), sailing M(c)/W(c), soccer M(c)/W(c), softball W(c), swimming and diving M(c)/W(c), tennis M(c)/W(c), ultimate Frisbee M(c)/W(c), volleyball M(c)/W(c), water polo M(c)/W(c).

Campus security: 24-hour emergency response devices and patrols, late-night transport/escort service, controlled dormitory access.

Student services: health clinic, personal/psychological counseling, women's center.

COSTS & FINANCIAL AID

Costs (2019–20) ***Comprehensive fee:*** $64,975 includes full-time tuition ($48,700), mandatory fees ($1565), and room and board ($14,710). Full-time tuition and fees vary according to course load. Part-time tuition: $785 per credit. Part-time tuition and fees vary according to course load. ***Room***

and board: Room and board charges vary according to board plan and housing facility. ***Payment plan:*** installment. ***Waivers:*** employees or children of employees.

Financial Aid Of all full-time matriculated undergraduates who enrolled in 2018, 2,604 applied for aid, 2,057 were judged to have need, 149 had their need fully met. 458 Federal Work-Study jobs (averaging $3595). 206 state and other part-time jobs (averaging $5791). In 2018, 1265 non-need-based awards were made. ***Average percent of need met:*** 88. ***Average financial aid package:*** $31,909. ***Average need-based loan:*** $4640. ***Average need-based gift aid:*** $19,256. ***Average non-need-based aid:*** $19,753. ***Average indebtedness upon graduation:*** $41,443. ***Financial aid deadline:*** 1/15.

APPLYING

Options: electronic application, early admission, early action, deferred entrance.

Application fee: $60.

Required: essay or personal statement, high school transcript.

Application deadlines: 1/15 (freshmen), 7/15 (transfers), 11/15 (early action).

Early decision deadline: 11/1.

Notification: 4/1 (freshmen), 4/1 (out-of-state freshmen), continuous (transfers), 1/15 (early action).

CONTACT

Loyola University Maryland, 4501 North Charles Street, Baltimore, MD 21210-2699. *Phone:* 410-617-2000. *Toll-free phone:* 800-221-9107.

See below for display ad and page 1074 for the College Close-Up.

Maple Springs Baptist Bible College and Seminary

Capitol Heights, Maryland

http://www.msbbcs.edu/

CONTACT

Ms. Jeannie Bowman, Assistant Director of Admissions and Records, Maple Springs Baptist Bible College and Seminary, 4130 Belt Road, Capitol Heights, MD 20743. *Phone:* 301-736-3631. *Fax:* 301-735-6507.

Maryland Institute College of Art

Baltimore, Maryland

http://www.mica.edu/

- **Independent** comprehensive, founded 1826
- **Urban** 16-acre campus with easy access to Washington, DC
- **Endowment** $90.8 million
- **Coed**
- **Very difficult** entrance level

FACULTY

Student/faculty ratio: 8:1.

ACADEMICS

Calendar: semesters. *Degrees:* bachelor's, master's, and postbachelor's certificates.

Library: Decker Library. *Books:* 76,337 (physical), 191,873 (digital/electronic); *Serial titles:* 407 (physical); *Databases:* 41. Weekly public service hours: 70; students can reserve study rooms.

STUDENT LIFE

Housing options: on-campus residence required through sophomore year; coed, special housing for students with disabilities. Campus housing is university owned. Freshman campus housing is guaranteed.

Activities and organizations: drama/theater group, student-run radio station, choral group, Haunted House, Urban Gaming Club, Oy , Korean International Student Association, MICA Design League.

Campus security: 24-hour emergency response devices and patrols, student patrols, late-night transport/escort service, controlled dormitory access, self-defense education, 24-hour building security, safety awareness programs, campus patrols by city police, Rave Guardian mobile app.

Student services: health clinic, personal/psychological counseling.

FINANCIAL AID

Financial Aid *Average indebtedness upon graduation:* $17,472.

APPLYING

Standardized Tests *Required:* SAT or ACT (for admission).

Options: electronic application, early admission, early decision, early action, deferred entrance.

Application fee: $70.

Required: essay or personal statement, high school transcript, 3 letters of recommendation, art portfolio, test scores, and a list of activities and interests. ***Recommended:*** interview.

CONTACT

Kelly Teeling, Maryland Institute College of Art, 1300 Mount Royal Avenue, Baltimore, MD 21217. *Phone:* 410-225-2222. *E-mail:* admissions@mica.edu.

McDaniel College

Westminster, Maryland

http://www.mcdaniel.edu/

- **Independent** comprehensive, founded 1867
- **Suburban** 160-acre campus with easy access to Baltimore and Washington, DC
- **Endowment** $132.0 million
- **Coed** 1,680 undergraduate students, 98% full-time, 52% women, 48% men
- **Moderately difficult** entrance level, 92% of applicants were admitted

UNDERGRAD STUDENTS

1,653 full-time, 27 part-time. 32% are from out of state; 21% Black or African American, non-Hispanic/Latino; 6% Hispanic/Latino; 2% Asian, non-Hispanic/Latino; 0.3% American Indian or Alaska Native, non-Hispanic/Latino; 3% Two or more races, non-Hispanic/Latino; 7% Race/ethnicity unknown; 3% international; 3% transferred in; 86% live on campus.

Freshmen:

Admission: 3,761 applied, 3,454 admitted, 575 enrolled. ***Average high school GPA:*** 3.5.

Retention: 77% of full-time freshmen returned.

FACULTY

Total: 583, 22% full-time, 44% with terminal degrees.

Student/faculty ratio: 12:1.

ACADEMICS

Calendar: 4-1-4. *Degrees:* bachelor's, master's, and postbachelor's certificates.

Special study options: academic remediation for entering students, adult/continuing education programs, advanced placement credit, distance learning, double majors, honors programs, independent study, internships, off-campus study, part-time degree program, services for LD students, student-designed majors, study abroad, summer session for credit. ***ROTC:*** Army (b), Air Force (c).

Unusual degree programs: 3-2 gerontology, human services management, music education, secondary education, special education.

Computers: 138 computers/terminals and 1,500 ports are available on campus for general student use. Students can access the following: campus intranet, computer help desk, free student e-mail accounts, online (class) grades, online (class) registration, online (class) schedules, online billing summaries, financial aid letter, tax information. Campuswide network is available. 100% of college-owned or -operated housing units are wired for high-speed Internet access. Wireless service is available via entire campus.

Library: Hoover Library. *Books:* 181,489 (physical), 193,549 (digital/electronic); *Serial titles:* 1,440 (physical), 83,076 (digital/electronic); *Databases:* 87. Weekly public service hours: 103; study areas open 24 hours, 5–7 days a week; students can reserve study rooms.

STUDENT LIFE

Housing options: on-campus residence required through junior year; coed, special housing for students with disabilities. Campus housing is university owned. Freshman campus housing is guaranteed.

Activities and organizations: drama/theater group, student-run newspaper, radio and television station, choral group, Student Government Association, Black Student Union, International Club, Maryland State Legislature, McDaniel Allies, national fraternities, national sororities.

Athletics Member NCAA. All Division III except golf (Division II). ***Intercollegiate sports:*** baseball M, basketball M/W, cross-country running M/W, field hockey W, football M, golf M/W, lacrosse M/W, soccer M/W, softball W, swimming and diving M/W, tennis M/W, track and field M/W, volleyball W, wrestling M. ***Intramural sports:*** basketball M/W, cheerleading M(c)/W(c), football M/W, golf M/W, soccer M/W, softball M/W, ultimate Frisbee M/W, volleyball M/W.

Campus security: 24-hour emergency response devices and patrols, late-night transport/escort service.

Student services: health clinic, personal/psychological counseling.

COSTS & FINANCIAL AID

Costs (2019–20) ***Comprehensive fee:*** $56,312 includes full-time tuition ($44,540) and room and board ($11,772). Full-time tuition and fees vary according to course load. Part-time tuition: $1392 per credit hour. Part-time tuition and fees vary according to course load. ***College room only:*** $5408. Room and board charges vary according to board plan and housing facility. ***Payment plan:*** installment. ***Waivers:*** children of alumni and employees or children of employees.

Financial Aid Of all full-time matriculated undergraduates who enrolled in 2019, 1,448 applied for aid, 1,345 were judged to have need, 285 had their need fully met. In 2019, 318 non-need-based awards were made. ***Average percent of need met:*** 84. ***Average financial aid package:*** $39,063. ***Average need-based loan:*** $2825. ***Average need-based gift aid:*** $36,238. ***Average non-need-based aid:*** $22,609. ***Average indebtedness upon graduation:*** $16,622.

APPLYING

Options: electronic application, early admission, early decision, early action, deferred entrance.

Required: essay or personal statement, high school transcript, minimum 2.5 GPA, 2 letters of recommendation. ***Recommended:*** interview.

Application deadlines: rolling (freshmen), rolling (out-of-state freshmen), 8/15 (transfers), 12/15 (early action).

Early decision deadline: 11/1 (for plan 1), 1/15 (for plan 2).

Notification: continuous (freshmen), continuous (out-of-state freshmen), continuous (transfers), 12/1 (early decision plan 1), 2/1 (early decision plan 2), 1/15 (early action).

CONTACT

Mrs. Janelle Holmboe, Vice President for Enrollment Management and Dean of Admissions, McDaniel College, 2 College Hill, Westminster, MD 21157-4390. *Phone:* 410-857-2230. *Toll-free phone:* 800-638-5005. *Fax:* 410-857-2757. *E-mail:* admissions@mcdaniel.edu.

Morgan State University

Baltimore, Maryland

http://www.morgan.edu/

- **State-supported** university, founded 1867
- **Urban** 143-acre campus with easy access to Washington, DC
- **Coed**
- **Moderately difficult** entrance level

FACULTY

Student/faculty ratio: 13:1.

ACADEMICS

Calendar: semesters. *Degrees:* bachelor's, master's, and doctoral.
Library: Soper Library.

STUDENT LIFE

Housing options: on-campus residence required for freshman year; coed, men-only, women-only. Campus housing is university owned. Freshman applicants given priority for college housing.

Activities and organizations: drama/theater group, student-run newspaper, radio station, choral group, marching band, Student Government Association, Greek Life, choir, band, cultural organizations, national fraternities, national sororities.

Athletics Member NCAA. All Division I except football (Division I-AA).

Campus security: 24-hour emergency response devices and patrols, late-night transport/escort service, controlled dormitory access.

Student services: health clinic, personal/psychological counseling.

FINANCIAL AID

Financial Aid Of all full-time matriculated undergraduates who enrolled in 2018, 4,921 applied for aid, 4,498 were judged to have need, 366 had their need fully met. 247 Federal Work-Study jobs (averaging $2220). In 2018, 152 non-need-based awards were made. ***Average percent of need met:*** 47. ***Average financial aid package:*** $11,510. ***Average need-based loan:*** $4911. ***Average need-based gift aid:*** $7869. ***Average non-need-based aid:*** $6016. ***Average indebtedness upon graduation:*** $46,194.

APPLYING

Standardized Tests *Required:* SAT or ACT (for admission). *Required for some:* SAT Subject Tests (for admission).

Options: electronic application, early admission, deferred entrance.

Application fee: $35.

Required: high school transcript, minimum 2.0 GPA. ***Required for some:*** 2 letters of recommendation, interview. ***Recommended:*** essay or personal statement.

CONTACT

Ms. Shonda Gray, Acting Director of Admissions and Recruitment, Morgan State University, 1700 East Cold Spring Lane, Baltimore, MD 21251. *Phone:* 443-885-3000. *Toll-free phone:* 800-332-6674. *E-mail:* shantell.saunders@morgan.edu.

Mount St. Mary's University

Emmitsburg, Maryland

http://www.msmary.edu/

- **Independent Roman Catholic** comprehensive, founded 1808
- **Rural** 1500-acre campus with easy access to Baltimore and Washington, DC
- **Endowment** $52.3 million
- **Coed** 1,898 undergraduate students, 93% full-time, 50% women, 50% men
- **Moderately difficult** entrance level, 75% of applicants were admitted

UNDERGRAD STUDENTS

1,762 full-time, 136 part-time. Students come from 44 states and territories; 14 other countries; 43% are from out of state; 17% Black or African American, non-Hispanic/Latino; 13% Hispanic/Latino; 3% Asian, non-Hispanic/Latino; 0.7% Native Hawaiian or other Pacific Islander, non-Hispanic/Latino; 0.5% American Indian or Alaska Native, non-Hispanic/Latino; 5% Two or more races, non-Hispanic/Latino; 1% Race/ethnicity unknown; 1% international; 4% transferred in; 68% live on campus.

Freshmen:

Admission: 4,716 applied, 3,527 admitted, 513 enrolled. ***Average high school GPA:*** 3.5. ***Test scores:*** SAT evidence-based reading and writing scores over 500: 76%; SAT math scores over 500: 71%; ACT scores over 18: 85%; SAT evidence-based reading and writing scores over 600: 33%; SAT math scores over 600: 23%; ACT scores over 24: 31%; SAT evidence-based reading and writing scores over 700: 4%; SAT math scores over 700: 4%; ACT scores over 30: 5%.

Retention: 79% of full-time freshmen returned.

FACULTY

Total: 256, 52% full-time, 44% with terminal degrees.

Student/faculty ratio: 12:1.

ACADEMICS

Calendar: semesters. *Degrees:* bachelor's, master's, post-master's, and postbachelor's certificates.

Special study options: academic remediation for entering students, accelerated degree program, adult/continuing education programs, advanced placement credit, double majors, honors programs, independent study, internships, off-campus study, part-time degree program, services for LD students, student-designed majors, study abroad, summer session for credit. ***ROTC:*** Army (c).

Unusual degree programs: 3-2 nursing with University of Maryland, Shenandoah University.

Computers: 80 computers/terminals are available on campus for general student use. Students can access the following: campus intranet, computer help desk, free student e-mail accounts, online (class) grades, online (class) registration, online (class) schedules, tuition payment, course management system. Campuswide network is available. 100% of college-owned or -operated housing units are wired for high-speed Internet access. Wireless service is available via entire campus.
Library: Phillips Library. *Books:* 149,042 (physical), 3.0 million (digital/electronic); *Serial titles:* 170 (physical), 21,747 (digital/electronic); *Databases:* 133.

STUDENT LIFE
Housing options: coed, special housing for students with disabilities. Campus housing is university owned. Freshman campus housing is guaranteed.

Activities and organizations: drama/theater group, student-run newspaper, radio station, choral group.

Athletics Member NCAA. All Division I. ***Intercollegiate sports:*** baseball M(s), basketball M(s)/W(s), bowling W(s), cross-country running M(s)/W(s), equestrian sports M(c)/W(c), field hockey W(c), golf M(s)/W(s), gymnastics M(s)/W(s), ice hockey M(c), lacrosse M(s)/W(s), rugby M(c)/W(s), soccer M(s)/W(s), softball W(s), swimming and diving M(s)/W(s), tennis M(s)/W(s), track and field M(s)/W(s), ultimate Frisbee M(c)/W(c), volleyball W(c). ***Intramural sports:*** baseball M(c), basketball M/W, field hockey W, racquetball M/W, sand volleyball M/W, soccer M(c), softball W(c), tennis M/W.

Campus security: 24-hour emergency response devices and patrols, late-night transport/escort service, controlled dormitory access.

Student services: health clinic, personal/psychological counseling.

COSTS & FINANCIAL AID
Costs (2020–21) ***Tuition:*** $42,200 full-time, $1370 per credit hour part-time. ***Required fees:*** $1450 full-time. ***Room only:*** $6940.

Financial Aid Of all full-time matriculated undergraduates who enrolled in 2019, 1,393 applied for aid, 1,248 were judged to have need, 346 had their need fully met. In 2019, 419 non-need-based awards were made. ***Average percent of need met:*** 75. ***Average financial aid package:*** $31,489. ***Average need-based loan:*** $3793. ***Average need-based gift aid:*** $27,781. ***Average non-need-based aid:*** $21,106. ***Average indebtedness upon graduation:*** $38,998. ***Financial aid deadline:*** 3/1.

APPLYING
Standardized Tests *Recommended:* SAT or ACT (for admission).

Options: electronic application, early action, deferred entrance.

Application fee: $45.

Required: high school transcript, minimum 2.0 GPA, 1 letter of recommendation. ***Recommended:*** essay or personal statement, minimum 3.0 GPA, interview.

Application deadlines: 3/1 (freshmen), 6/1 (transfers), 12/1 (early action).

Notification: continuous (freshmen), continuous (transfers), 12/25 (early action).

CONTACT
Mr. Eric M. Danielson, Director of Admissions, Mount St. Mary's University, 16300 Old Emmitsburg Road, Emmitsburg, MD 21727. *Phone:* 301-447-5505. *Toll-free phone:* 800-448-4347. *Fax:* 301-447-5818. *E-mail:* admissions@msmary.edu.

Ner Israel Rabbinical College

Baltimore, Maryland

CONTACT
Ner Israel Rabbinical College, 400 Mount Wilson Lane, Baltimore, MD 21208. *Phone:* 410-484-7200.

Notre Dame of Maryland University

Baltimore, Maryland

http://www.ndm.edu/

CONTACT
Angela Baumler, Director of Admissions (Women's College), Notre Dame of Maryland University, 4701 North Charles Street, Baltimore, MD 21210. *Phone:* 410-532-5330. *Toll-free phone:* 800-435-0200. *E-mail:* abaumler@ndm.edu.

Peabody Conservatory of The Johns Hopkins University

Baltimore, Maryland

http://www.peabody.jhu.edu/

CONTACT
Mr. David Lane, Director of Admissions, Peabody Conservatory of The Johns Hopkins University, Peabody Conservatory Admissions Office, One East Mount Vernon Place, Baltimore, MD 21202-2397. *Phone:* 410-234-4848. *Toll-free phone:* 800-368-2521.

Purdue University Global

Hagerstown, Maryland

http://www.purdueglobal.edu/

CONTACT
Purdue University Global, 18618 Crestwood Drive, Hagerstown, MD 21742. *Phone:* 301-739-2680 Ext. 217. *Toll-free phone:* 844-PURDUE-G.

St. John's College

Annapolis, Maryland

http://www.sjc.edu/

- **Independent** comprehensive, founded 1696
- **Small-town** 36-acre campus with easy access to Washington, D.C. and Baltimore, MD
- **Endowment** $120.9 million
- **Coed**
- **Very difficult** entrance level

FACULTY
Student/faculty ratio: 7:1.

ACADEMICS
Calendar: semesters. *Degrees:* bachelor's and master's.
Library: Greenfield Library plus 1 other. *Books:* 111,240 (physical), 538 (digital/electronic); *Serial titles:* 128 (physical), 2,410 (digital/electronic); *Databases:* 14. Weekly public service hours: 94; students can reserve study rooms.

STUDENT LIFE
Housing options: on-campus residence required for freshman year; coed, special housing for students with disabilities. Campus housing is university owned. Freshman campus housing is guaranteed.

Activities and organizations: drama/theater group, student-run newspaper, choral group, King William's Players (drama), Reality (social), Delegate Council (student government), Waltz (social), Student Committee on Instruction (advisory).

Athletics Member USCAA.

Campus security: 24-hour emergency response devices and patrols, late-night transport/escort service, controlled dormitory access.

Student services: health clinic, personal/psychological counseling.

COSTS & FINANCIAL AID
Costs (2019–20) ***One-time required fee:*** $100. ***Comprehensive fee:*** $49,271 includes full-time tuition ($35,000), mandatory fees ($635), and room and board ($13,636). ***College room only:*** $7000. Room and board charges vary according to board plan and housing facility.

Financial Aid Of all full-time matriculated undergraduates who enrolled in 2019, 381 applied for aid, 326 were judged to have need, 43 had their need fully met. 90 Federal Work-Study jobs (averaging $3000). 115 state and other part-time jobs (averaging $3000). In 2019, 123 non-need-based awards were made. ***Average percent of need met:*** 78. ***Average financial aid package:*** $29,906. ***Average need-based loan:*** $3929. ***Average need-based gift aid:*** $25,523. ***Average non-need-based aid:*** $8461. ***Average indebtedness upon graduation:*** $20,067.

APPLYING
Standardized Tests *Required for some:* SAT or ACT (for admission). *Recommended:* SAT/ACT, TOEFL/IELTS or interview for international

applicants; SAT/ACT/CLT for homeschooled students and applicants who have not and will not graduate high school.

Options: electronic application, early admission, early action, deferred entrance.

Required: essay or personal statement, high school transcript, 2 letters of recommendation. ***Required for some:*** outline of curriculum for homeschooled applicants. ***Recommended:*** interview.

CONTACT

Mr. Benjamin Baum, Director of Admissions, St. John's College, 60 College Avenue, Annapolis, MD 21401. *Phone:* 410-626-2522. *Toll-free phone:* 800-727-9238. *Fax:* 410-269-7916. *E-mail:* annapolis.admissions@sjc.edu.

St. Mary's College of Maryland

St. Mary's City, Maryland

http://www.smcm.edu/

- **State-supported** comprehensive, founded 1840
- **Rural** 361-acre campus
- **Endowment** $37.1 million
- **Coed** 1,491 undergraduate students, 96% full-time, 59% women, 41% men
- **Moderately difficult** entrance level, 84% of applicants were admitted

UNDERGRAD STUDENTS

1,435 full-time, 56 part-time. Students come from 23 states and territories; 5 other countries; 5% are from out of state; 10% Black or African American, non-Hispanic/Latino; 7% Hispanic/Latino; 4% Asian, non-Hispanic/Latino; 0.1% Native Hawaiian or other Pacific Islander, non-Hispanic/Latino; 0.1% American Indian or Alaska Native, non-Hispanic/Latino; 6% Two or more races, non-Hispanic/Latino; 2% Race/ethnicity unknown; 0.5% international; 6% transferred in; 80% live on campus.

Freshmen:

Admission: 1,621 applied, 1,366 admitted, 320 enrolled. ***Average high school GPA:*** 3.4. ***Test scores:*** SAT evidence-based reading and writing scores over 500: 89%; SAT math scores over 500: 83%; ACT scores over 18: 90%; SAT evidence-based reading and writing scores over 600: 53%; SAT math scores over 600: 41%; ACT scores over 24: 66%; SAT evidence-based reading and writing scores over 700: 10%; SAT math scores over 700: 8%; ACT scores over 30: 19%.

Retention: 85% of full-time freshmen returned.

FACULTY

Total: 210, 62% full-time, 71% with terminal degrees.

Student/faculty ratio: 9:1.

ACADEMICS

Calendar: semesters. *Degrees:* bachelor's and master's.

Special study options: advanced placement credit, cooperative education, double majors, freshman honors college, independent study, internships, part-time degree program, services for LD students, student-designed majors, study abroad, summer session for credit.

Computers: 317 computers/terminals are available on campus for general student use. Students can access the following: campus intranet, computer help desk, free student e-mail accounts, online (class) grades, online (class) registration, online (class) schedules, learning management system. Campuswide network is available. 100% of college-owned or -operated housing units are wired for high-speed Internet access. Wireless service is available via entire campus.

Library: Library, Archives, and Media Center. *Books:* 118,066 (physical), 12,955 (digital/electronic); *Serial titles:* 1,077 (physical), 111,374 (digital/electronic); *Databases:* 108. Weekly public service hours: 96; study areas open 24 hours, 5–7 days a week; students can reserve study rooms.

STUDENT LIFE

Housing options: coed, men-only, women-only, special housing for students with disabilities. Campus housing is university owned. Freshman campus housing is guaranteed.

Activities and organizations: drama/theater group, student-run newspaper, radio station, choral group, Dance Club, Humans vs. Zombies, InterVarsity Christian Fellowship, Habitat for Humanity, Club Sports.

Athletics Member NCAA. All Division III. ***Intercollegiate sports:*** baseball M, basketball M/W, crew M/W, cross-country running M/W, equestrian sports M(c)/W(c), fencing M(c)/W(c), field hockey W, lacrosse M/W, rock climbing M(c)/W(c), rowing M/W, rugby M(c)/W(c), sailing M/W, soccer M/W, softball W(c), swimming and diving M/W, tennis M/W, ultimate Frisbee M(c)/W(c), volleyball W. ***Intramural sports:*** badminton M/W, basketball M/W, soccer M/W, volleyball M/W.

Campus security: 24-hour emergency response devices and patrols, late-night transport/escort service, controlled dormitory access.

Student services: health clinic, personal/psychological counseling.

FINANCIAL AID

Financial Aid Of all full-time matriculated undergraduates who enrolled in 2018, 1,145 applied for aid, 827 were judged to have need, 32 had their need fully met. 101 Federal Work-Study jobs (averaging $934). In 2018, 479 non-need-based awards were made. ***Average percent of need met:*** 68. ***Average financial aid package:*** $20,476. ***Average need-based loan:*** $4246. ***Average need-based gift aid:*** $9406. ***Average non-need-based aid:*** $3914. ***Average indebtedness upon graduation:*** $25,579.

APPLYING

Standardized Tests *Required for some:* SAT (for admission).

Options: electronic application, early decision, early action, deferred entrance.

Application fee: $50.

Required: essay or personal statement, high school transcript, 2 letters of recommendation, Common Application. ***Recommended:*** interview.

Application deadlines: 1/15 (freshmen), 1/15 (out-of-state freshmen), 8/1 (transfers), 11/1 (early action).

Early decision deadline: 11/1.

Notification: continuous until 4/1 (freshmen), continuous until 4/1 (out-of-state freshmen), continuous until 5/1 (transfers), 12/1 (early decision), 1/1 (early action).

CONTACT

Dr. Bhargavi Bandi, Director of Enrollment Operations, St. Mary's College of Maryland, 47645 College Drive, St. Mary's City, MD 20686-3001. *Phone:* 240-895-2011. *Toll-free phone:* 800-492-7181. *Fax:* 240-895-5001. *E-mail:* admissions@smcm.edu.

Salisbury University

Salisbury, Maryland

http://www.salisbury.edu/

- **State-supported** comprehensive, founded 1925, part of University System of Maryland
- **Small-town** 201-acre campus
- **Endowment** $72.9 million
- **Coed** 7,686 undergraduate students, 92% full-time, 56% women, 44% men
- **Moderately difficult** entrance level, 74% of applicants were admitted

UNDERGRAD STUDENTS

7,090 full-time, 596 part-time. Students come from 32 states and territories; 33 other countries; 13% are from out of state; 14% Black or African American, non-Hispanic/Latino; 5% Hispanic/Latino; 4% Asian, non-Hispanic/Latino; 0.1% Native Hawaiian or other Pacific Islander, non-Hispanic/Latino; 0.8% American Indian or Alaska Native, non-Hispanic/Latino; 2% Two or more races, non-Hispanic/Latino; 3% Race/ethnicity unknown; 1% international; 9% transferred in; 31% live on campus.

Freshmen:

Admission: 8,421 applied, 6,190 admitted, 1,470 enrolled. ***Average high school GPA:*** 3.7. ***Test scores:*** SAT evidence-based reading and writing scores over 500: 96%; SAT math scores over 500: 95%; ACT scores over 18: 91%; SAT evidence-based reading and writing scores over 600: 59%; SAT math scores over 600: 49%; ACT scores over 24: 25%; SAT evidence-based reading and writing scores over 700: 6%; SAT math scores over 700: 5%; ACT scores over 30: 4%.

Retention: 81% of full-time freshmen returned.

FACULTY

Total: 670, 67% full-time, 60% with terminal degrees.

Student/faculty ratio: 15:1.

ACADEMICS
Calendar: 4-1-4. *Degrees:* certificates, bachelor's, master's, doctoral, post-master's, and postbachelor's certificates.

Special study options: accelerated degree program, advanced placement credit, cooperative education, distance learning, double majors, English as a second language, freshman honors college, honors programs, independent study, internships, off-campus study, part-time degree program, services for LD students, student-designed majors, study abroad, summer session for credit. ***ROTC:*** Army (b), Air Force (c).

Unusual degree programs: 3-2 engineering with University of Maryland, College Park; Old Dominion University; Widener University; social work with University of Maryland Eastern Shore; biology and environmental marine science with University of Maryland Eastern Shore.

Computers: 1,000 computers/terminals and 3,552 ports are available on campus for general student use. Students can access the following: campus intranet, computer help desk, free student e-mail accounts, online (class) grades, online (class) registration, online (class) schedules, student web hosting, computer repair service, discounted computer hardware and software. Campuswide network is available. 100% of college-owned or -operated housing units are wired for high-speed Internet access. Wireless service is available via entire campus.

Library: SU Libraries plus 2 others. *Books:* 273,282 (physical), 426 (digital/electronic); *Serial titles:* 652 (physical), 152 (digital/electronic); *Databases:* 122. Weekly public service hours: 108; students can reserve study rooms.

STUDENT LIFE
Housing options: on-campus residence required through sophomore year; coed, special housing for students with disabilities. Campus housing is university owned. Freshman applicants given priority for college housing.

Activities and organizations: drama/theater group, student-run newspaper, radio and television station, choral group, Student Government Association, Radio (WXSU) / SU TV / The Flyer Newspaper, Student Organization for Activity Planning (SOAP), Campus Crusade for Christ, Black Student Union, national fraternities, national sororities.

Athletics Member NCAA. All Division III. ***Intercollegiate sports:*** baseball M, basketball M/W, cross-country running M/W, field hockey W, football M, lacrosse M/W, soccer M/W, softball W, swimming and diving M/W, tennis M/W, track and field M/W, volleyball W. ***Intramural sports:*** basketball M/W, cheerleading M(c)/W(c), equestrian sports M(c)/W(c), field hockey M(c)/W(c), golf M/W, gymnastics M(c)/W(c), ice hockey M(c)/W(c), lacrosse M(c)/W(c), rock climbing M/W, rugby M(c)/W(c), sailing M(c)/W(c), soccer M/W, softball M/W, ultimate Frisbee M(c)/W(c), volleyball M/W, weight lifting M(c)/W(c).

Campus security: 24-hour emergency response devices and patrols, student patrols, late-night transport/escort service, controlled dormitory access.

Student services: health clinic, personal/psychological counseling, veterans affairs office.

COSTS & FINANCIAL AID
Costs (2019–20) ***Tuition:*** state resident $7264 full-time, $297 per credit hour part-time; nonresident $17,330 full-time, $716 per credit hour part-time. Full-time tuition and fees vary according to location. Part-time tuition and fees vary according to location. ***Required fees:*** $2780 full-time, $108 per credit hour part-time. ***Room and board:*** $12,360; room only: $7160. Room and board charges vary according to board plan and housing facility. ***Payment plan:*** installment. ***Waivers:*** senior citizens and employees or children of employees.

Financial Aid Of all full-time matriculated undergraduates who enrolled in 2018, 5,384 applied for aid, 3,875 were judged to have need, 365 had their need fully met. In 2018, 1416 non-need-based awards were made. ***Average percent of need met:*** 53. ***Average financial aid package:*** $8767. ***Average need-based loan:*** $4154. ***Average need-based gift aid:*** $7098. ***Average non-need-based aid:*** $2616. ***Average indebtedness upon graduation:*** $27,355.

APPLYING
Standardized Tests *Required for some:* SAT (for admission), ACT (for admission), SAT or ACT (for admission).

Options: electronic application, early admission, early decision, early action, deferred entrance.

Application fee: $50.

Required: essay or personal statement, high school transcript, minimum 2.0 GPA, 1 letter of recommendation. ***Required for some:*** SAT or ACT test scores are required for applicants with a weighted cumulative GPA below 3.5.

Application deadlines: 1/15 (freshmen), 1/15 (out-of-state freshmen), rolling (transfers), 12/1 (early action).

Early decision deadline: 11/15.

Notification: 3/15 (freshmen), 3/15 (out-of-state freshmen), continuous (transfers), 12/15 (early decision), 1/15 (early action).

CONTACT
Elizabeth Skoglund, Director of Admissions, Salisbury University, Salisbury University - Admissions House, 1101 Camden Avenue, Salisbury, MD 21801. *Phone:* 410-543-6161. *Toll-free phone:* 888-543-0148. *Fax:* 410-546-6016. *E-mail:* admissions@salisbury.edu.

Stevenson University
Stevenson, Maryland
http://www.stevenson.edu/

- **Independent** comprehensive, founded 1952
- **Suburban** 163-acre campus with easy access to Baltimore
- **Endowment** $98.3 million
- **Coed** 3,107 undergraduate students, 88% full-time, 64% women, 36% men
- **Moderately difficult** entrance level, 81% of applicants were admitted

UNDERGRAD STUDENTS
2,724 full-time, 383 part-time. Students come from 43 states and territories; 15 other countries; 22% are from out of state; 26% Black or African American, non-Hispanic/Latino; 7% Hispanic/Latino; 4% Asian, non-Hispanic/Latino; 0.1% Native Hawaiian or other Pacific Islander, non-Hispanic/Latino; 0.3% American Indian or Alaska Native, non-Hispanic/Latino; 5% Two or more races, non-Hispanic/Latino; 3% Race/ethnicity unknown; 0.7% international; 4% transferred in; 54% live on campus.

Freshmen:

Admission: 4,413 applied, 3,565 admitted, 694 enrolled. ***Average high school GPA:*** 3.1. ***Test scores:*** SAT evidence-based reading and writing scores over 500: 81%; SAT math scores over 500: 76%; ACT scores over 18: 83%; SAT evidence-based reading and writing scores over 600: 29%; SAT math scores over 600: 22%; ACT scores over 24: 29%; SAT evidence-based reading and writing scores over 700: 3%; SAT math scores over 700: 2%; ACT scores over 30: 4%.

Retention: 82% of full-time freshmen returned.

FACULTY
Total: 380, 33% full-time, 56% with terminal degrees.

Student/faculty ratio: 15:1.

ACADEMICS
Calendar: semesters. *Degrees:* bachelor's, master's, and postbachelor's certificates.

Special study options: academic remediation for entering students, accelerated degree program, adult/continuing education programs, advanced placement credit, cooperative education, distance learning, double majors, honors programs, independent study, internships, off-campus study, part-time degree program, services for LD students, student-designed majors, study abroad, summer session for credit. ***ROTC:*** Army (c), Air Force (c).

Computers: 552 computers/terminals and 3,000 ports are available on campus for general student use. Students can access the following: campus intranet, computer help desk, free student e-mail accounts, online (class) grades, online (class) registration, online (class) schedules. Campuswide network is available. 100% of college-owned or -operated housing units are wired for high-speed Internet access. Wireless service is available via entire campus.

Library: Stevenson University Learning Resource Center-Greenspring Campus plus 2 others. *Books:* 60,915 (physical), 383,563 (digital/electronic); *Serial titles:* 240 (physical), 34,695

(digital/electronic); *Databases:* 86. Weekly public service hours: 136; students can reserve study rooms.

STUDENT LIFE

Housing options: coed. Campus housing is university owned. Freshman applicants given priority for college housing.

Activities and organizations: drama/theater group, student-run newspaper, radio station, choral group, marching band, Relay for Life, Mustang Activities Programming, Black Student Union, American Chemical Society, Phi Sigma Sigma, national fraternities, national sororities.

Athletics Member NCAA. All Division III. ***Intercollegiate sports:*** baseball M, basketball M/W, cheerleading M/W, cross-country running M/W, field hockey W, football M, golf M/W, ice hockey M/W, lacrosse M/W, soccer M/W, softball W, tennis M/W, track and field M/W, volleyball M/W. ***Intramural sports:*** badminton M, baseball M, basketball M/W, field hockey W, football M/W, ice hockey M, soccer M/W, softball W, tennis M/W, volleyball M/W.

Campus security: 24-hour emergency response devices and patrols, late-night transport/escort service, controlled dormitory access, patrols by trained security personnel during campus hours.

Student services: health clinic, personal/psychological counseling.

COSTS & FINANCIAL AID

Costs (2019–20) ***Comprehensive fee:*** $50,766 includes full-time tuition ($34,528), mandatory fees ($2614), and room and board ($13,624). Full-time tuition and fees vary according to course load and degree level. Part-time tuition: $870 per credit. Part-time tuition and fees vary according to degree level. ***Required fees:*** $75 per term part-time. ***College room only:*** $8656. Room and board charges vary according to board plan and housing facility. ***Payment plan:*** installment. ***Waivers:*** employees or children of employees.

Financial Aid Of all full-time matriculated undergraduates who enrolled in 2019, 2,346 applied for aid, 2,086 were judged to have need, 375 had their need fully met. 243 Federal Work-Study jobs (averaging $2258). In 2019, 559 non-need-based awards were made. ***Average percent of need met:*** 71. ***Average financial aid package:*** $26,376. ***Average need-based loan:*** $4287. ***Average need-based gift aid:*** $23,624. ***Average non-need-based aid:*** $18,981. ***Average indebtedness upon graduation:*** $37,112.

APPLYING

Standardized Tests *Required:* SAT or ACT (for admission).

Options: electronic application, early admission, deferred entrance.

Application fee: $40.

Required: essay or personal statement, high school transcript, letters of recommendation. ***Required for some:*** interview.

Application deadlines: rolling (freshmen), rolling (transfers).

Notification: continuous (freshmen), continuous (transfers).

CONTACT

Mr. Mark Hergan, Vice President, Enrollment Management, Stevenson University, 1525 Greenspring Valley Road, Stevenson, MD 21153. *Phone:* 410-486-7000. *Toll-free phone:* 877-468-6852 (in-state); 877-468-3852 (out-of-state). *Fax:* 410-352-4440. *E-mail:* admissions@stevenson.edu.

Stratford University

Baltimore, Maryland

http://www.stratford.edu/

CONTACT

Admissions, Stratford University, 210 South Central Avenue, Baltimore, MD 21202. *Phone:* 410-752-4710. *Toll-free phone:* 800-624-9926 (in-state); 800-624-9926 Ext. 120 (out-of-state). *E-mail:* baadmissions@stratford.edu.

Strayer University - Anne Arundel

Millersville, Maryland

http://www.strayer.edu/maryland/anne-arundel/

CONTACT

Strayer University - Anne Arundel, 1520 Jabez Run, Suite 100, Millersville, MD 21108. *Toll-free phone:* 888-311-0355.

Strayer University–Owings Mills Campus

Owings Mills, Maryland

http://www.strayer.edu/maryland/owings-mills/

CONTACT

Strayer University–Owings Mills Campus, 500 Redland Court, Suite 100, Owings Mills, MD 21117. *Toll-free phone:* 888-311-0355.

Strayer University–Prince George's Campus

Suitland, Maryland

http://www.strayer.edu/maryland/prince-georges/

CONTACT

Strayer University–Prince George's Campus, 5110 Auth Way, Suitland, MD 20746. *Toll-free phone:* 888-311-0355.

Strayer University–Rockville Campus

Rockville, Maryland

http://www.strayer.edu/maryland/rockville/

CONTACT

Strayer University–Rockville Campus, 1803 Research Boulevard, Suite 110, Rockville, MD 20850. *Toll-free phone:* 888-311-0355.

Strayer University–White Marsh Campus

Baltimore, Maryland

http://www.strayer.edu/maryland/white-marsh/

CONTACT

Strayer University–White Marsh Campus, 9920 Franklin Square Drive, Suite 200, Baltimore, MD 21236. *Toll-free phone:* 888-311-0355.

Towson University

Towson, Maryland

http://www.towson.edu/

- **State-supported** university, founded 1866, part of University System of Maryland
- **Suburban** 329-acre campus with easy access to Baltimore and Washington, DC
- **Endowment** $87.8 million
- **Coed** 19,619 undergraduate students, 88% full-time, 59% women, 41% men
- **Moderately difficult** entrance level, 76% of applicants were admitted

UNDERGRAD STUDENTS

17,209 full-time, 2,410 part-time. Students come from 46 states and territories; 75 other countries; 11% are from out of state; 24% Black or African American, non-Hispanic/Latino; 9% Hispanic/Latino; 7% Asian, non-Hispanic/Latino; 0.1% Native Hawaiian or other Pacific Islander, non-Hispanic/Latino; 0.1% American Indian or Alaska Native, non-Hispanic/Latino; 5% Two or more races, non-Hispanic/Latino; 1% Race/ethnicity unknown; 2% international; 11% transferred in; 34% live on campus.

Freshmen:

Admission: 12,678 applied, 9,674 admitted, 2,795 enrolled. ***Average high school GPA:*** 3.7. ***Test scores:*** SAT evidence-based reading and writing scores over 500: 93%; SAT math scores over 500: 88%; ACT scores over 18: 94%; SAT evidence-based reading and writing scores over 600: 37%; SAT math scores over 600: 28%; ACT scores over 24: 37%; SAT evidence-based reading and writing scores over 700: 4%; SAT math scores over 700: 3%; ACT scores over 30: 6%.

Retention: 86% of full-time freshmen returned.

FACULTY

Total: 1,764, 52% full-time, 53% with terminal degrees.

Student/faculty ratio: 16:1.

ACADEMICS
Calendar: semesters. *Degrees:* bachelor's, master's, doctoral, post-master's, and postbachelor's certificates.

Special study options: academic remediation for entering students, adult/continuing education programs, advanced placement credit, cooperative education, distance learning, double majors, English as a second language, freshman honors college, honors programs, independent study, internships, off-campus study, part-time degree program, services for LD students, student-designed majors, study abroad, summer session for credit. ***ROTC:*** Army (c), Air Force (c).

Unusual degree programs: 3-2 engineering with University of Maryland, College Park; law with University of Baltimore School of Law.

Computers: 4,157 computers/terminals and 10,310 ports are available on campus for general student use. Students can access the following: campus intranet, computer help desk, free student e-mail accounts, online (class) grades, online (class) registration, online (class) schedules. Campuswide network is available. 100% of college-owned or -operated housing units are wired for high-speed Internet access. Wireless service is available via entire campus.

Library: Cook Library. *Books:* 384,697 (physical), 516,920 (digital/electronic); *Serial titles:* 22,544 (physical), 79,916 (digital/electronic); *Databases:* 308. Weekly public service hours: 108; study areas open 24 hours, 5–7 days a week; students can reserve study rooms.

STUDENT LIFE
Housing options: coed, special housing for students with disabilities. Campus housing is university owned. Freshman campus housing is guaranteed.

Activities and organizations: drama/theater group, student-run newspaper, radio and television station, choral group, marching band, University Residence Government, Latin American Student Organization, Black Student Union, Hillel, African Diaspora Club, national fraternities, national sororities.

Athletics Member NCAA. All Division I. ***Intercollegiate sports:*** baseball M(s), basketball M(s)/W(s), cross-country running W(s), field hockey W(s), football M(s), golf M(s)/W(s), gymnastics W(s), lacrosse M(s)/W(s), soccer W(s), softball W(s), swimming and diving M(s)/W(s), tennis W(s), track and field W(s), ultimate Frisbee W(s), volleyball W(s). ***Intramural sports:*** badminton M/W, baseball M(c), basketball M/W, cheerleading M(c)/W(c), cross-country running M(c)/W(c), equestrian sports M(c)/W(c), field hockey M(c)/W(c), golf M(c)/W(c), gymnastics M(c)/W(c), ice hockey M(c)/W(c), lacrosse M(c)/W(c), rugby M(c)/W(c), soccer M/W, softball M/W, swimming and diving M(c)/W(c), table tennis M/W, tennis M(c)/W(c), track and field M(c)/W(c), ultimate Frisbee M/W, volleyball M/W, water polo M(c)/W(c), wrestling M(c)/W(c).

Campus security: 24-hour emergency response devices and patrols, late-night transport/escort service, controlled dormitory access.

Student services: health clinic, personal/psychological counseling, women's center, veterans affairs office.

COSTS & FINANCIAL AID
Costs (2019–20) ***Tuition:*** state resident $6962 full-time, $299 per credit hour part-time; nonresident $21,098 full-time, $888 per credit hour part-time. Full-time tuition and fees vary according to course load and location. Part-time tuition and fees vary according to course load and location. ***Required fees:*** $3236 full-time, $147 per credit hour part-time. ***Room and board:*** $13,446; room only: $7446. Room and board charges vary according to board plan and housing facility. ***Waivers:*** senior citizens and employees or children of employees.

Financial Aid Of all full-time matriculated undergraduates who enrolled in 2019, 13,094 applied for aid, 9,844 were judged to have need, 889 had their need fully met. 824 Federal Work-Study jobs (averaging $2596). In 2019, 1137 non-need-based awards were made. ***Average percent of need met:*** 59. ***Average financial aid package:*** $11,275. ***Average need-based loan:*** $4200. ***Average need-based gift aid:*** $9793. ***Average non-need-based aid:*** $5038. ***Average indebtedness upon graduation:*** $27,610.

APPLYING
Standardized Tests *Required:* SAT or ACT (for admission).

Options: electronic application, early admission, early action, deferred entrance.

Application fee: $45.

Required: essay or personal statement, high school transcript. ***Required for some:*** interview. ***Recommended:*** minimum 3.0 GPA, 2 letters of recommendation, resume or activity list.

Application deadlines: rolling (transfers), 12/1 (early action).

Notification: continuous (freshmen), continuous (transfers), 12/31 (early action).

CONTACT
Mr. David Fedorchak, Director of University Admissions, Towson University, 8000 York Road, Towson, MD 21252. *Phone:* 410-704-2113. *Fax:* 410-704-3030. *E-mail:* admissions@towson.edu.

United States Naval Academy

Annapolis, Maryland

http://www.usna.edu/

- **Federally supported** 4-year, founded 1845
- **Small-town** 338-acre campus with easy access to Baltimore and Washington, DC
- **Endowment** $223.3 million
- **Coed**
- **Very difficult** entrance level

FACULTY
Student/faculty ratio: 8:1.

ACADEMICS
Calendar: semesters. *Degree:* bachelor's.
Library: Nimitz Library. *Books:* 580,342 (physical), 425,564 (digital/electronic); *Serial titles:* 4,594 (physical), 71,757 (digital/electronic); *Databases:* 170. Weekly public service hours: 100.

STUDENT LIFE
Housing options: on-campus residence required through senior year; coed. Campus housing is university owned. Freshman campus housing is guaranteed.

Activities and organizations: drama/theater group, student-run radio station, choral group, marching band, Mountaineering Club, Semper Fi, Black Studies Club, Midshipmen Action Club, Martial Arts Club.

Athletics Member NCAA. All Division I except football (Division I-A).

Campus security: 24-hour emergency response devices and patrols, campus gate security.

Student services: health clinic, personal/psychological counseling, women's center, legal services.

COSTS
Costs (2019–20) ***Tuition:*** area resident $0 full-time; state resident $0 full-time; nonresident $0 full-time. No tuition increase for student's term of enrollment. The Navy pays for the tuition, room and board, medical and dental care of Naval Academy midshipmen.

APPLYING
Standardized Tests *Required:* SAT or ACT (for admission).

Options: electronic application, early action.

Required: essay or personal statement, high school transcript, 2 letters of recommendation, interview, age 17-22, medical exam, authorized nomination, candidate fitness test.

CONTACT
Capt. Ann Kubera, Director of Admissions, United States Naval Academy, 52 King George Street, Annapolis, MD 21402. *Phone:* 410-293-4361. *Toll-free phone:* 888-249-7707. *Fax:* 410-293-4348. *E-mail:* webmail@usna.edu.

University of Baltimore

Baltimore, Maryland

http://www.ubalt.edu/

CONTACT
David Waggoner, Associate Vice President of Admission, University of Baltimore, 1420 North Charles Street, Baltimore, MD 21201. *Phone:* 410-837-4777. *Fax:* 410-837-4793. *E-mail:* admission@ubalt.edu.

University of Maryland, Baltimore County

Baltimore, Maryland

http://www.umbc.edu/

- **State-supported** university, founded 1963, part of University System of Maryland
- **Suburban** 530-acre campus with easy access to Washington, DC
- **Endowment** $111.6 million
- **Coed** 11,060 undergraduate students, 85% full-time, 45% women, 55% men
- **Moderately difficult** entrance level, 61% of applicants were admitted

UNDERGRAD STUDENTS

9,436 full-time, 1,624 part-time. Students come from 45 states and territories; 85 other countries; 5% are from out of state; 19% Black or African American, non-Hispanic/Latino; 8% Hispanic/Latino; 22% Asian, non-Hispanic/Latino; 0.1% Native Hawaiian or other Pacific Islander, non-Hispanic/Latino; 0.1% American Indian or Alaska Native, non-Hispanic/Latino; 5% Two or more races, non-Hispanic/Latino; 2% Race/ethnicity unknown; 4% international; 10% transferred in; 36% live on campus.

Freshmen:

Admission: 11,842 applied, 7,227 admitted, 1,701 enrolled. ***Average high school GPA:*** 3.9. ***Test scores:*** SAT evidence-based reading and writing scores over 500: 99%; SAT math scores over 500: 98%; ACT scores over 18: 97%; SAT evidence-based reading and writing scores over 600: 74%; SAT math scores over 600: 71%; ACT scores over 24: 76%; SAT evidence-based reading and writing scores over 700: 16%; SAT math scores over 700: 24%; ACT scores over 30: 23%.

Retention: 87% of full-time freshmen returned.

FACULTY

Total: 931, 60% full-time, 67% with terminal degrees.

Student/faculty ratio: 17:1.

ACADEMICS

Calendar: 4-1-4. *Degrees:* certificates, bachelor's, master's, doctoral, and postbachelor's certificates.

Special study options: academic remediation for entering students, adult/continuing education programs, advanced placement credit, cooperative education, distance learning, double majors, English as a second language, external degree program, freshman honors college, honors programs, independent study, internships, off-campus study, part-time degree program, services for LD students, student-designed majors, study abroad, summer session for credit. ***ROTC:*** Army (c), Navy (b), Air Force (c).

Computers: 1,065 computers/terminals and 4,000 ports are available on campus for general student use. Students can access the following: campus intranet, computer help desk, free student e-mail accounts, online (class) grades, online (class) registration, online (class) schedules, billing, housing, parking, degree audit and advising. Campuswide network is available. 100% of college-owned or -operated housing units are wired for high-speed Internet access. Wireless service is available via entire campus.

Library: Albin O. Kuhn Library and Gallery. *Books:* 1.3 million (physical), 172,520 (digital/electronic); *Serial titles:* 27,505 (physical), 185,984 (digital/electronic); *Databases:* 388. Weekly public service hours: 94; study areas open 24 hours, 5–7 days a week; students can reserve study rooms.

STUDENT LIFE

Housing options: coed, special housing for students with disabilities. Campus housing is university owned. Freshman campus housing is guaranteed.

Activities and organizations: drama/theater group, student-run newspaper, radio station, choral group, Student Government Association, Student Events Board, Retriever Weekly, Resident Student Association, WMBC, Campus Radio, national fraternities, national sororities.

Athletics Member NCAA. All Division I. ***Intercollegiate sports:*** baseball M(s), basketball M(s)/W(s), crew M(c)/W(c), cross-country running M(s)/W(s), equestrian sports M(c)/W(c), fencing M(c)/W(c), ice hockey M(c), lacrosse M(s)/W(s), rugby M(c)/W(c), sailing M(c)/W(c), soccer M(s)/W(s), softball W(s), swimming and diving M(s)/W(s), tennis M(c)/W(c), track and field M(s)/W(s), ultimate Frisbee M(c)/W(c), volleyball M(c)/W(s), wrestling M(c)/W(c). ***Intramural sports:*** basketball M/W, cross-country running M(c)/W(c), football M/W, lacrosse M(c)/W(c), sand volleyball M/W, soccer M/W, softball M/W, track and field M(c)/W(c), volleyball M/W(c).

Campus security: 24-hour emergency response devices and patrols, late-night transport/escort service.

Student services: health clinic, personal/psychological counseling, women's center, veterans affairs office.

COSTS & FINANCIAL AID

Costs (2019–20) ***One-time required fee:*** $225. ***Tuition:*** state resident $8704 full-time, $361 per credit hour part-time; nonresident $24,338 full-time, $1010 per credit hour part-time. Full-time tuition and fees vary according to location and program. Part-time tuition and fees vary according to location and program. ***Required fees:*** $3324 full-time, $144 per credit hour part-time. ***Room and board:*** $12,000; room only: $7234. Room and board charges vary according to board plan and housing facility. ***Payment plan:*** installment. ***Waivers:*** senior citizens and employees or children of employees.

Financial Aid Of all full-time matriculated undergraduates who enrolled in 2019, 6,503 applied for aid, 5,037 were judged to have need, 545 had their need fully met. 123 Federal Work-Study jobs (averaging $3118). 118 state and other part-time jobs (averaging $10,976). In 2019, 1679 non-need-based awards were made. ***Average percent of need met:*** 56. ***Average financial aid package:*** $11,738. ***Average need-based loan:*** $4228. ***Average need-based gift aid:*** $10,368. ***Average non-need-based aid:*** $7661. ***Average indebtedness upon graduation:*** $26,359.

APPLYING

Standardized Tests *Required:* SAT (for admission), ACT (for admission), SAT or ACT (for admission).

Options: electronic application, early admission, early action, deferred entrance.

Application fee: $75.

Required: essay or personal statement, high school transcript. ***Recommended:*** minimum 3.0 GPA, 2 letters of recommendation.

Application deadlines: 2/1 (freshmen), 12/15 (transfers), 11/1 (early action).

Notification: continuous (freshmen), continuous (transfers), 12/15 (early action).

CONTACT

Mr. Dale Bittinger, Director of Admissions, University of Maryland, Baltimore County, 1000 Hilltop Circle, Baltimore, MD 21250. *Phone:* 410-455-2291. *Toll-free phone:* 800-UMBC-4U2 (in-state); 800-862-2402 (out-of-state). *Fax:* 410-455-1094. *E-mail:* admissions@umbc.edu.

University of Maryland, College Park

College Park, Maryland

http://www.umd.edu/

- **State-supported** university, founded 1856, part of University System of Maryland
- **Suburban** 1335-acre campus with easy access to Baltimore and Washington, DC
- **Endowment** $531.2 million
- **Coed**
- **Moderately difficult** entrance level

FACULTY

Student/faculty ratio: 18:1.

ACADEMICS

Calendar: semesters. *Degrees:* certificates, bachelor's, master's, doctoral, post-master's, and postbachelor's certificates.

Library: McKeldin Library plus 6 others. *Books:* 2.1 million (physical), 2.8 million (digital/electronic); *Serial titles:* 2,759 (physical), 63,891 (digital/electronic); *Databases:* 164. Weekly public service hours: 140; study areas open 24 hours, 5–7 days a week; students can reserve study rooms.

STUDENT LIFE
Housing options: coed, women-only, cooperative, special housing for students with disabilities. Campus housing is university owned and is provided by a third party. Freshman applicants given priority for college housing.

Activities and organizations: drama/theater group, student-run newspaper, radio and television station, choral group, marching band, Student Government Association, Residence Hall Association, Black Student Union, Asian-American Student Union/Jewish Student Union, Commuter Students Association, national fraternities, national sororities.

Athletics Member NCAA. All Division I.

Campus security: 24-hour emergency response devices and patrols, student patrols, late-night transport/escort service, controlled dormitory access.

Student services: health clinic, personal/psychological counseling, women's center, legal services, veterans affairs office.

COSTS & FINANCIAL AID
Costs (2019–20) ***Tuition:*** state resident $8824 full-time, $367 per credit hour part-time; nonresident $36,891 full-time, $1456 per credit hour part-time. Full time tuition and fees vary according to location, program, and student level. Part-time tuition and fees vary according to course load, location, program, and student level. ***Required fees:*** $1955 full-time, $455 per term part-time. ***Room and board:*** $12,935; room only: $7755. Room and board charges vary according to board plan and housing facility. ***Payment plans:*** installment, deferred payment.

Financial Aid Of all full-time matriculated undergraduates who enrolled in 2018, 17,137 applied for aid, 11,675 were judged to have need, 1,702 had their need fully met. In 2018, 3723 non-need-based awards were made. ***Average percent of need met:*** 60. ***Average financial aid package:*** $12,448. ***Average need-based loan:*** $4349. ***Average need-based gift aid:*** $10,577. ***Average non-need-based aid:*** $7032. ***Average indebtedness upon graduation:*** $29,133.

APPLYING
Standardized Tests *Required:* SAT or ACT (for admission).

Options: electronic application, early admission, early action, deferred entrance.

Application fee: $75.

Required: essay or personal statement, high school transcript. ***Required for some:*** resume of activities, audition for music applicants, drawing requirement for architecture applicants. ***Recommended:*** 2 letters of recommendation.

CONTACT
Ms. Shannon Gundy, Director, Office of Undergraduate Admissions, University of Maryland, College Park, Clarence Mitchell Building, 7999 Regents Drive, College Park, MD 20742. *Phone:* 301-314-8385. *Toll-free phone:* 800-422-5867. *Fax:* 301-314-9693. *E-mail:* ApplyMaryland@umd.edu.

University of Maryland Eastern Shore

Princess Anne, Maryland

http://www.umes.edu/

- **State-supported** university, founded 1886, part of University System of Maryland
- **Rural** 745-acre campus
- **Endowment** $27.9 million
- **Coed**
- **Moderately difficult** entrance level

FACULTY
Student/faculty ratio: 13:1.

ACADEMICS
Calendar: semesters. *Degrees:* certificates, bachelor's, master's, and doctoral.

Library: Frederick Douglass Library. *Books:* 131,714 (physical), 28,157 (digital/electronic); *Serial titles:* 170 (physical), 1,152 (digital/electronic); *Databases:* 149. Study areas open 24 hours, 5–7 days a week; students can reserve study rooms.

STUDENT LIFE
Housing options: coed, men-only, women-only. Campus housing is university owned and leased by the school.

Athletics Member NCAA. All Division I.

Campus security: 24-hour emergency response devices and patrols, student patrols, late-night transport/escort service, controlled dormitory access.

COSTS & FINANCIAL AID
Costs (2019–20) ***Tuition:*** area resident $5418 full-time, $224 per credit hour part-time; state resident $5418 full-time, $224 per credit hour part-time; nonresident $15,828 full-time, $583 per credit hour part-time. ***Required fees:*** $3140 full-time, $84 per credit hour part-time. ***Room and board:*** $11,189; room only: $6730.

Financial Aid Of all full-time matriculated undergraduates who enrolled in 2015, 3,133 applied for aid, 2,697 were judged to have need, 21 had their need fully met. 88 Federal Work-Study jobs (averaging $2955). In 2015, 92 non-need-based awards were made. ***Average percent of need met:*** 34. ***Average financial aid package:*** $4416. ***Average need-based loan:*** $3996. ***Average need-based gift aid:*** $3337. ***Average non-need-based aid:*** $4545. ***Average indebtedness upon graduation:*** $9861.

APPLYING
Standardized Tests *Required:* SAT or ACT (for admission).

Options: electronic application, deferred entrance.

Application fee: $35.

Required: essay or personal statement, high school transcript, minimum 2.5 GPA, 3 letters of recommendation. ***Required for some:*** interview.

CONTACT
Dr. Eric V. Hilton, Director of Admissions and Recruitment, University of Maryland Eastern Shore, 11868 Academic Oval, Princess Anne, MD 21853. *Phone:* 410-651-6410 Ext. 6410. *Fax:* 410-651-7922 Ext. 7922. *E-mail:* evhilton@umes.edu.

University of Maryland Global Campus

Adelphi, Maryland

http://www.umuc.edu/

- **State-supported** comprehensive, founded 1947, part of University System of Maryland
- **Suburban** campus with easy access to Washington, DC
- **Coed** 46,162 undergraduate students, 21% full-time, 45% women, 55% men
- **Noncompetitive** entrance level, 100% of applicants were admitted

UNDERGRAD STUDENTS
9,472 full-time, 36,690 part-time. Students come from 56 states and territories; 52 other countries; 63% are from out of state; 27% Black or African American, non-Hispanic/Latino; 15% Hispanic/Latino; 5% Asian, non-Hispanic/Latino; 0.7% Native Hawaiian or other Pacific Islander, non-Hispanic/Latino; 0.5% American Indian or Alaska Native, non-Hispanic/Latino; 5% Two or more races, non-Hispanic/Latino; 9% Race/ethnicity unknown; 1% international; 23% transferred in.

Freshmen:
Admission: 3,165 applied, 3,165 admitted, 646 enrolled.

FACULTY
Total: 3,745, 6% full-time, 56% with terminal degrees.

Student/faculty ratio: 19:1.

ACADEMICS
Calendar: semesters. *Degrees:* certificates, associate, bachelor's, master's, doctoral, and postbachelor's certificates (offers primarily part-time evening and weekend degree programs at more than 30 off-campus locations in Maryland and the Washington, DC area, and more than 180 military communities in Europe and Asia with military enrollment not reflected in this profile; associate of arts program available to military students only).

Special study options: academic remediation for entering students, accelerated degree program, advanced placement credit, cooperative education, distance learning, double majors, external degree program, independent study, internships, off-campus study, part-time degree program, services for LD students, summer session for credit.

Computers: 510 computers/terminals are available on campus for general student use. Students can access the following: campus intranet, computer help desk, free student e-mail accounts, online (class) grades, online (class) registration, online (class) schedules. Campuswide network is available. Wireless service is available via entire campus.
Library: Library plus 1 other. *Books:* 1,234 (physical), 94,961 (digital/electronic); *Serial titles:* 207,528 (digital/electronic); *Databases:* 127. Weekly public service hours: 77.

STUDENT LIFE
Housing options: college housing not available.

Campus security: 24-hour emergency response devices and patrols, late-night transport/escort service.

COSTS & FINANCIAL AID
Costs (2020–21) ***Tuition:*** state resident $7200 full-time; nonresident $11,976 full-time. ***Required fees:*** $360 full-time. ***Payment plan:*** installment. ***Waivers:*** senior citizens and employees or children of employees.

Financial Aid Of all full-time matriculated undergraduates who enrolled in 2018, 5,927 applied for aid, 5,686 were judged to have need, 41 had their need fully met. ***Average percent of need met:*** 29. ***Average financial aid package:*** $7858. ***Average need-based loan:*** $4433. ***Average need-based gift aid:*** $5620.

APPLYING
Options: electronic application, early admission, deferred entrance.

Application fee: $50.

Required: high school transcript.

Application deadlines: rolling (freshmen), rolling (transfers).

Notification: continuous (freshmen), continuous (transfers).

CONTACT
University of Maryland Global Campus, 3501 University Boulevard East, Adelphi, MD 20783. *Phone:* 800-888-UMUC. *Toll-free phone:* 800-888-8682.

Washington Adventist University
Takoma Park, Maryland
http://www.wau.edu/

CONTACT
Elaine Oliver, Associate Vice President, Enrollment Services, Washington Adventist University, 7600 Flower Avenue, Takoma Park, MD 20912. *Phone:* 301-891-4502. *Toll-free phone:* 800-835-4212. *Fax:* 301-971-4230. *E-mail:* enroll@cuc.edu.

Washington College
Chestertown, Maryland
http://www.washcoll.edu/

- **Independent** 4-year, founded 1782
- **Small-town** 140-acre campus with easy access to Baltimore and Washington, DC
- **Endowment** $229.1 million
- **Coed** 1,342 undergraduate students, 98% full-time, 61% women, 39% men
- **Moderately difficult** entrance level, 92% of applicants were admitted

UNDERGRAD STUDENTS
1,319 full-time, 23 part-time. Students come from 37 states and territories; 21 other countries; 56% are from out of state; 11% Black or African American, non-Hispanic/Latino; 6% Hispanic/Latino; 3% Asian, non-Hispanic/Latino; 0.2% Native Hawaiian or other Pacific Islander, non-Hispanic/Latino; 0.4% American Indian or Alaska Native, non-Hispanic/Latino; 0.1% Two or more races, non-Hispanic/Latino; 5% Race/ethnicity unknown; 5% international; 1% transferred in; 80% live on campus.

Freshmen:
Admission: 2,225 applied, 2,055 admitted, 325 enrolled. ***Average high school GPA:*** 3.6. ***Test scores:*** SAT evidence-based reading and writing scores over 500: 90%; SAT math scores over 500: 89%; ACT scores over 18: 91%; SAT evidence-based reading and writing scores over 600: 56%; SAT math scores over 600: 44%; ACT scores over 24: 62%; SAT evidence-based reading and writing scores over 700: 12%; SAT math scores over 700: 10%; ACT scores over 30: 24%.

Retention: 81% of full-time freshmen returned.

FACULTY
Total: 158, 66% full-time, 64% with terminal degrees.

Student/faculty ratio: 10:1.

ACADEMICS
Calendar: semesters. *Degree:* bachelor's.

Special study options: accelerated degree program, double majors, English as a second language, honors programs, independent study, internships, off-campus study, part-time degree program, services for LD students, student-designed majors, study abroad, summer session for credit.

Unusual degree programs: 3-2 engineering with Columbia University; nursing with University of Maryland; pharmacy with University of Maryland.

Computers: 100 computers/terminals and 1,450 ports are available on campus for general student use. Students can access the following: campus intranet, computer help desk, free student e-mail accounts, online (class) grades, online (class) registration, online (class) schedules. Campuswide network is available. 100% of college-owned or -operated housing units are wired for high-speed Internet access. Wireless service is available via entire campus.
Library: Clifton M. Miller Library.

STUDENT LIFE
Housing options: on-campus residence required through sophomore year; coed, men-only, women-only, special housing for students with disabilities. Campus housing is university owned. Freshman campus housing is guaranteed.

Activities and organizations: drama/theater group, student-run newspaper, radio station, choral group, Student environmental alliance, Student Government association, Sorority and fraternity life, National Society of Leadership and Success, E-sports, national fraternities, national sororities.

Athletics Member NCAA. All Division III. ***Intercollegiate sports:*** baseball M, basketball M/W, cheerleading W(c), crew M/W, equestrian sports M(c)/W(c), field hockey W, ice hockey M(c), lacrosse M/W, rugby M(c)/W(c), sailing M/W, soccer M/W, softball W, swimming and diving M/W, tennis M/W, volleyball W, water polo M(c)/W(c). ***Intramural sports:*** badminton M/W, basketball M/W, football M/W, lacrosse M(c), racquetball M/W, rugby M/W, sailing M/W, soccer M/W, squash M/W, table tennis M/W, tennis M/W, ultimate Frisbee M/W, volleyball M/W.

Campus security: 24-hour emergency response devices and patrols, student patrols, late-night transport/escort service, controlled dormitory access, LiveSafe mobile app.

Student services: health clinic, personal/psychological counseling.

COSTS & FINANCIAL AID
Costs (2020–21) ***Comprehensive fee:*** $62,490 includes full-time tuition ($48,678), mandatory fees ($1090), and room and board ($12,722). Part-time tuition: $2028 per credit hour. Part-time tuition and fees vary according to course load. ***College room only:*** $6673. Room and board charges vary according to board plan, housing facility, and location. ***Payment plan:*** installment. ***Waivers:*** employees or children of employees.

Financial Aid Of all full-time matriculated undergraduates who enrolled in 2019, 1,014 applied for aid, 869 were judged to have need, 147 had their need fully met. 162 Federal Work-Study jobs (averaging $1959). In 2019, 340 non-need-based awards were made. ***Average percent of need met:*** 85. ***Average financial aid package:*** $36,163. ***Average need-based loan:*** $4091. ***Average need-based gift aid:*** $36,365. ***Average non-need-based aid:*** $22,636. ***Average indebtedness upon graduation:*** $34,903.

APPLYING
Standardized Tests *Required:* SAT or ACT (for admission).

Options: electronic application, early admission, early decision, early action, deferred entrance.

Required: essay or personal statement, high school transcript, 1 letter of recommendation. ***Required for some:*** interview. ***Recommended:*** interview.

Application deadlines: 2/15 (freshmen), rolling (transfers), 12/1 (early action).

Early decision deadline: 11/15 (for plan 1), 12/15 (for plan 2).

Notification: continuous (freshmen), continuous (transfers), 12/15 (early decision plan 1), 1/15 (early decision plan 2), 1/15 (early action).

CONTACT
Washington College, 300 Washington Avenue, Chestertown, MD 21620. *Phone:* 410-778-7700. *Toll-free phone:* 800-422-1782. *Fax:* 410-778-7287. *E-mail:* wc_admissions@washcoll.edu.

Yeshiva College of the Nation's Capital

Silver Spring, Maryland

http://www.yeshiva.edu/

CONTACT
Yeshiva College of the Nation's Capital, 1216 Arcola Avenue, Silver Spring, MD 20902.

MASSACHUSETTS

American International College

Springfield, Massachusetts

http://www.aic.edu/

CONTACT
Mr. Jonathan Scully, Director of Undergraduate Admissions, American International College, 1000 State Street, Springfield, MA 01109-3189. *Phone:* 413-205-3270. *Toll-free phone:* 800-242-3142. *Fax:* 413-205-3051. *E-mail:* jonathan.scully@aic.edu.

Amherst College

Amherst, Massachusetts

http://www.amherst.edu/

- **Independent** 4-year, founded 1821
- **Small-town** 1020-acre campus
- **Coed** 1,839 undergraduate students, 100% full-time, 50% women, 50% men
- **Most difficult** entrance level, 11% of applicants were admitted

UNDERGRAD STUDENTS
1,839 full-time. Students come from 49 states and territories; 61 other countries; 86% are from out of state; 10% Black or African American, non-Hispanic/Latino; 13% Hispanic/Latino; 15% Asian, non-Hispanic/Latino; 0.1% Native Hawaiian or other Pacific Islander, non-Hispanic/Latino; 0.5% American Indian or Alaska Native, non-Hispanic/Latino; 7% Two or more races, non-Hispanic/Latino; 3% Race/ethnicity unknown; 9% international; 0.8% transferred in; 98% live on campus.

Freshmen:
Admission: 10,569 applied, 1,195 admitted, 470 enrolled. ***Test scores:*** SAT evidence-based reading and writing scores over 500: 100%; SAT math scores over 500: 100%; ACT scores over 18: 100%; SAT evidence-based reading and writing scores over 600: 100%; SAT math scores over 600: 100%; ACT scores over 24: 100%; SAT evidence-based reading and writing scores over 700: 74%; SAT math scores over 700: 83%; ACT scores over 30: 91%.

Retention: 97% of full-time freshmen returned.

FACULTY
Total: 292, 79% full-time, 93% with terminal degrees.

Student/faculty ratio: 7:1.

ACADEMICS
Calendar: semesters. *Degree:* bachelor's.

Special study options: double majors, independent study, internships, off-campus study, services for LD students, student-designed majors, study abroad. ***ROTC:*** Army (c), Air Force (c).

Computers: Students can access the following: campus intranet, computer help desk, free student e-mail accounts, online (class) grades, online (class) registration, online (class) schedules. Campuswide network is available. 100% of college-owned or -operated housing units are wired for high-speed Internet access. Wireless service is available via entire campus.

Library: Robert Frost Library plus 3 others.

STUDENT LIFE
Housing options: on-campus residence required for freshman year; coed, women-only, cooperative, special housing for students with disabilities. Campus housing is university owned. Freshman campus housing is guaranteed.

Activities and organizations: drama/theater group, student-run newspaper, radio station, choral group, Association of Amherst Students, Black Students Union, Student Publications (e.g., Amherst Student, Indicator), A Capella Groups (e.g., Zumbye's, Bluestockings), Amherst Dance.

Athletics Member NCAA. All Division III. ***Intercollegiate sports:*** baseball M, basketball M/W, cheerleading W(c), crew M(c)/W(c), cross-country running M/W, equestrian sports M(c)/W(c), fencing M(c)/W(c), field hockey W, football M, golf M/W, ice hockey M/W, lacrosse M/W, rugby M(c)/W(c), sailing M(c)/W(c), skiing (downhill) M(c)/W(c), soccer M/W, softball W, squash M/W, swimming and diving M/W, tennis M/W, track and field M/W, ultimate Frisbee M(c)/W(c), volleyball M(c)/W, water polo M(c)/W(c), wrestling M(c)/W(c). ***Intramural sports:*** badminton M/W, basketball M/W, golf M/W, ice hockey M/W, rock climbing M/W, soccer M/W, softball M/W, squash M/W, tennis M/W, track and field M/W, volleyball M/W.

Campus security: 24-hour emergency response devices and patrols, late-night transport/escort service, controlled dormitory access.

Student services: health clinic, personal/psychological counseling, women's center.

COSTS & FINANCIAL AID
Costs (2020–21) ***Comprehensive fee:*** $76,800 includes full-time tuition ($59,890), mandatory fees ($1000), and room and board ($15,910). ***College room only:*** $8630. ***Payment plan:*** installment.

Financial Aid Of all full-time matriculated undergraduates who enrolled in 2019, 1,234 applied for aid, 1,099 were judged to have need, 1,099 had their need fully met. 866 Federal Work-Study jobs (averaging $1564). 223 state and other part-time jobs (averaging $1724). ***Average percent of need met:*** 100. ***Average financial aid package:*** $58,806. ***Average need-based loan:*** $389. ***Average need-based gift aid:*** $57,760. ***Average indebtedness upon graduation:*** $22,629.

APPLYING
Standardized Tests *Required:* SAT or ACT (for admission).

Options: electronic application, early admission, early decision, deferred entrance.

Application fee: $65.

Required: essay or personal statement, high school transcript, 3 letters of recommendation, Amherst College Supplement.

Application deadlines: 1/1 (freshmen), 3/1 (transfers).

Early decision deadline: 11/1.

Notification: 4/1 (freshmen), 4/15 (transfers), 12/15 (early decision).

CONTACT
Matthew L. McGann, Dean of Admission and Financial Aid, Amherst College, PO Box 5000, Amherst, MA 01002-5000. *Phone:* 413-542-2328. *Fax:* 413-542-2040. *E-mail:* admission@amherst.edu.

Anna Maria College

Paxton, Massachusetts

http://www.annamaria.edu/

- **Independent Roman Catholic** comprehensive, founded 1946
- **Rural** 192-acre campus with easy access to Boston
- **Endowment** $4.3 million
- **Coed**
- **Minimally difficult** entrance level

FACULTY

Student/faculty ratio: 12:1.

ACADEMICS

Calendar: semesters. *Degrees:* certificates, bachelor's, master's, doctoral, post-master's, and postbachelor's certificates.
Library: Mondor-Eagen Library. *Books:* 59,659 (physical), 132,939 (digital/electronic); *Databases:* 98.

STUDENT LIFE

Housing options: coed, special housing for students with disabilities. Campus housing is university owned. Freshman campus housing is guaranteed.

Activities and organizations: drama/theater group, choral group, marching band, Habitat for Humanity, Social Action Group, Chorus Club, Alana, Programming Board - AMCAB.

Athletics Member NCAA. All Division III.

Campus security: 24-hour emergency response devices and patrols, late-night transport/escort service, controlled dormitory access.

Student services: health clinic, personal/psychological counseling.

FINANCIAL AID

Financial Aid Of all full-time matriculated undergraduates who enrolled in 2016, 681 applied for aid, 675 were judged to have need, 98 had their need fully met. In 2016, 34 non-need-based awards were made. ***Average financial aid package:*** $28,771. ***Average need-based loan:*** $4425. ***Average need-based gift aid:*** $7830. ***Average non-need-based aid:*** $13,175.

APPLYING

Options: electronic application, deferred entrance.

Application fee: $25.

Required: high school transcript, minimum 2.0 GPA. ***Required for some:*** essay or personal statement, audition for music programs, portfolio for art programs. ***Recommended:*** 1 letter of recommendation, interview.

CONTACT

Mr. Peter Miller, Dean of Admissions and Financial Aid, Anna Maria College, 50 Sunset Lane, Paxton, MA 01612. *Phone:* 508-849-3586. *Fax:* 508-849-3362. *E-mail:* admissions@annamaria.edu.

Assumption College

Worcester, Massachusetts

http://www.assumption.edu/

- **Independent Roman Catholic** comprehensive, founded 1904
- **Suburban** 180-acre campus with easy access to Boston
- **Endowment** $107.1 million
- **Coed** 1,982 undergraduate students, 98% full-time, 56% women, 44% men
- **Moderately difficult** entrance level, 81% of applicants were admitted

UNDERGRAD STUDENTS

1,946 full-time, 36 part-time. 34% are from out of state; 5% Black or African American, non-Hispanic/Latino; 7% Hispanic/Latino; 3% Asian, non-Hispanic/Latino; 0.1% Native Hawaiian or other Pacific Islander, non-Hispanic/Latino; 0.1% American Indian or Alaska Native, non-Hispanic/Latino; 3% Two or more races, non-Hispanic/Latino; 4% Race/ethnicity unknown; 1% international; 2% transferred in; 85% live on campus.

Freshmen:

Admission: 4,465 applied, 3,620 admitted, 563 enrolled. ***Average high school GPA:*** 3.4. ***Test scores:*** SAT evidence-based reading and writing scores over 500: 92%; SAT math scores over 500: 92%; ACT scores over 18: 97%; SAT evidence-based reading and writing scores over 600: 44%; SAT math scores over 600: 38%; ACT scores over 24: 69%; SAT evidence-based reading and writing scores over 700: 6%; SAT math scores over 700: 4%; ACT scores over 30: 17%.

Retention: 85% of full-time freshmen returned.

FACULTY

Total: 222, 62% full-time, 80% with terminal degrees.

Student/faculty ratio: 12:1.

ACADEMICS

Calendar: semesters. *Degrees:* bachelor's, master's, post-master's, and postbachelor's certificates.

Special study options: advanced placement credit, double majors, honors programs, independent study, internships, services for LD students, student-designed majors, study abroad, summer session for credit. ***ROTC:*** Army (c), Air Force (c).

Unusual degree programs: 3-2 business administration with accounting; engineering with University of Notre Dame; Washington University at St. Louis; forestry with Duke University.

Computers: 361 computers/terminals and 2,476 ports are available on campus for general student use. Students can access the following: campus intranet, computer help desk, free student e-mail accounts, online (class) grades, online (class) registration, online (class) schedules. Campuswide network is available. 100% of college-owned or -operated housing units are wired for high-speed Internet access. Wireless service is available via entire campus.
Library: Emmanuel d'Alzon Library. *Books:* 127,617 (physical), 171,058 (digital/electronic); *Serial titles:* 1,830 (physical), 43,143 (digital/electronic); *Databases:* 75. Weekly public service hours: 102; students can reserve study rooms.

STUDENT LIFE

Housing options: coed, women-only, special housing for students with disabilities. Campus housing is university owned. Freshman campus housing is guaranteed.

Activities and organizations: drama/theater group, student-run newspaper, television station, choral group, Volunteer center, Campus Activities Board, Student Government, Campus Ministry, intramural sports.

Athletics Member NCAA. All Division II. ***Intercollegiate sports:*** baseball M, basketball M(s)/W(s), cheerleading M(c)/W(c), cross-country running M/W, equestrian sports M(c)/W(c), field hockey W, football M, golf M, ice hockey M/W(c), lacrosse M/W, rowing W, soccer M/W, softball W, swimming and diving M(c)/W, tennis M/W, track and field M/W, ultimate Frisbee M(c)/W(c), volleyball M(c)/W. ***Intramural sports:*** basketball M/W, football M/W, sand volleyball M/W, soccer M/W, softball M/W, swimming and diving M/W, table tennis M/W, volleyball M/W.

Campus security: 24-hour emergency response devices and patrols, student patrols, late-night transport/escort service, controlled dormitory access, front gate security, well-lit pathways.

Student services: health clinic, personal/psychological counseling.

COSTS & FINANCIAL AID

Costs (2019–20) ***Comprehensive fee:*** $55,444 includes full-time tuition ($41,516), mandatory fees ($800), and room and board ($13,128). Full-time tuition and fees vary according to course load, reciprocity agreements, and student level. Part-time tuition: $1384 per credit hour. Part-time tuition and fees vary according to course load. ***College room only:*** $8310. Room and board charges vary according to board plan and housing facility. ***Waivers:*** employees or children of employees.

Financial Aid Of all full-time matriculated undergraduates who enrolled in 2019, 1,669 applied for aid, 1,467 were judged to have need, 443 had their need fully met. 439 Federal Work-Study jobs (averaging $1547). In 2019, 433 non-need-based awards were made. ***Average percent of need met:*** 79. ***Average financial aid package:*** $30,845. ***Average need-based loan:*** $4370. ***Average need-based gift aid:*** $25,250. ***Average non-need-based aid:*** $18,304. ***Financial aid deadline:*** 2/15.

APPLYING

Options: electronic application, early decision, early action, deferred entrance.

Application fee: $50.

Required: essay or personal statement, high school transcript, 1 letter of recommendation. ***Recommended:*** interview.

Application deadlines: 2/15 (freshmen), 7/1 (transfers), 11/1 (early action).

Early decision deadline: 11/1.

Notification: continuous (freshmen), continuous (transfers), 12/1 (early decision), 12/15 (early action).

CONTACT

Assumption College, 500 Salisbury Street, Worcester, MA 01609-1296. *Phone:* 508-767-7286. *Toll-free phone:* 866-477-7776.

Babson College

Wellesley, Massachusetts

http://www.babson.edu/

- **Independent** comprehensive, founded 1919
- **Suburban** 370-acre campus with easy access to Boston
- **Endowment** $348.6 million
- **Coed** 2,386 undergraduate students, 98% full-time, 46% women, 53% men
- **Very difficult** entrance level, 26% of applicants were admitted

UNDERGRAD STUDENTS

2,347 full-time. Students come from 49 states and territories; 80 other countries; 75% are from out of state; 4% Black or African American, non-Hispanic/Latino; 12% Hispanic/Latino; 10% Asian, non-Hispanic/Latino; 0.1% American Indian or Alaska Native, non-Hispanic/Latino; 2% Two or more races, non-Hispanic/Latino; 8% Race/ethnicity unknown; 30% international; 3% transferred in; 79% live on campus.

Freshmen:

Admission: 6,362 applied, 1,680 admitted, 600 enrolled. ***Test scores:*** SAT evidence-based reading and writing scores over 500: 100%; SAT math scores over 500: 100%; ACT scores over 18: 100%; SAT evidence-based reading and writing scores over 600: 87%; SAT math scores over 600: 92%; ACT scores over 24: 95%; SAT evidence-based reading and writing scores over 700: 24%; SAT math scores over 700: 54%; ACT scores over 30: 55%.

Retention: 95% of full-time freshmen returned.

FACULTY

Total: 267, 72% full-time, 67% with terminal degrees.

Student/faculty ratio: 14:1.

ACADEMICS

Calendar: semesters. *Degrees:* bachelor's, master's, and postbachelor's certificates.

Special study options: advanced placement credit, freshman honors college, honors programs, independent study, internships, off-campus study, services for LD students, student-designed majors, study abroad, summer session for credit. ***ROTC:*** Army (c).

Computers: Students can access the following: campus intranet, computer help desk, free student e-mail accounts, online (class) grades, online (class) registration, online (class) schedules. Campuswide network is available. Wireless service is available via entire campus.

Library: Horn Library plus 1 other.

STUDENT LIFE

Housing options: on-campus residence required for freshman year; coed, men-only, special housing for students with disabilities. Campus housing is university owned. Freshman campus housing is guaranteed.

Activities and organizations: drama/theater group, student-run newspaper, radio station, choral group, national fraternities, national sororities.

Athletics Member NCAA. All Division III except skiing (downhill) (Division II). ***Intercollegiate sports:*** baseball M, basketball M/W, cheerleading W(c), cross-country running M/W, field hockey W, golf M, ice hockey M/W(c), lacrosse M/W, rugby M(c)/W(c), skiing (downhill) M/W, soccer M/W, softball W, swimming and diving M/W, tennis M/W, track and field M/W, volleyball W. ***Intramural sports:*** basketball M/W, football M, ice hockey M/W, racquetball M/W, soccer M/W, softball M/W, squash M/W, tennis M/W, ultimate Frisbee M/W, volleyball M/W, wrestling M(c).

Campus security: 24-hour emergency response devices and patrols, late-night transport/escort service, controlled dormitory access.

Student services: health clinic, personal/psychological counseling, women's center.

COSTS & FINANCIAL AID

Costs (2020–21) ***Comprehensive fee:*** $71,810 includes full-time tuition ($54,144) and room and board ($17,666).

Financial Aid Of all full-time matriculated undergraduates who enrolled in 2018, 1,043 applied for aid, 970 were judged to have need, 610 had their need fully met. In 2018, 155 non-need-based awards were made. ***Average percent of need met:*** 99. ***Average financial aid package:*** $44,121. ***Average need-based loan:*** $4586. ***Average need-based gift aid:*** $41,446. ***Average non-need-based aid:*** $15,826. ***Average indebtedness upon graduation:*** $37,866. ***Financial aid deadline:*** 2/1.

APPLYING

Standardized Tests *Required:* SAT or ACT (for admission). *Recommended:* TOEFL or IELTS for non-native English speakers.

Options: electronic application, early decision, early action, deferred entrance.

Application fee: $75.

Required: essay or personal statement, high school transcript, 2 letters of recommendation. ***Recommended:*** interview.

Application deadlines: 1/2 (freshmen), 3/15 (transfers).

Early decision deadline: 11/1 (for plan 1), 1/2 (for plan 2).

Notification: 4/1 (freshmen), 5/15 (transfers), 12/15 (early decision).

CONTACT

Mrs. Christina Hamilton, Associate Director of Undergraduate Admission, Babson College, Lunder Undergraduate Admission Center, Babson Park, MA 02457-0310. *Phone:* 781-239-5522. *Toll-free phone:* 800-488-3696. *Fax:* 781-239-4135. *E-mail:* ugradadmission@babson.edu.

Bard College at Simon's Rock

Great Barrington, Massachusetts

http://www.simons-rock.edu/

- **Independent** 4-year, founded 1964
- **Small-town** 210-acre campus with easy access to Boston, New York City
- **Coed**
- **Moderately difficult** entrance level

FACULTY

Student/faculty ratio: 6:1.

ACADEMICS

Calendar: semesters. *Degrees:* associate and bachelor's.

Library: Alumni Library. *Books:* 68,511 (physical), 3,850 (digital/electronic); *Serial titles:* 120 (physical), 41,033 (digital/electronic); *Databases:* 22. Weekly public service hours: 106.

STUDENT LIFE

Housing options: on-campus residence required through senior year; coed, men-only, women-only. Campus housing is university owned. Freshman campus housing is guaranteed.

Activities and organizations: drama/theater group, student-run newspaper, choral group, Black Student Union, QueerSA, Student Action Service Learning, U.S.O. (Untitled Student Organization), Boffing.

Campus security: 24-hour emergency response devices and patrols, controlled dormitory access, security escorts, late night transport.

Student services: health clinic, personal/psychological counseling, women's center.

APPLYING

Options: electronic application.

Application fee: $50.

Required: essay or personal statement, high school transcript, 3 letters of recommendation, interview, school report, parent supplement.

CONTACT

Chandra Joos deKoven, Director of Admissions, Bard College at Simon's Rock, 84 Alford Road, Great Barrington, MA 01230-9702. *Phone:* 800-

235-7186. *Toll-free phone:* 800-235-7186. *Fax:* 413-541-0081. *E-mail:* admit@simons-rock.edu.

Bay Path University

Longmeadow, Massachusetts

http://www.baypath.edu/

CONTACT

Dawn Bryden, Dean of Traditional Undergraduate Enrollment and Admissions, Bay Path University, 588 Longmeadow Street, Longmeadow, MA 01106-2292. *Phone:* 413-565-1235. *Toll-free phone:* 800-782-7284 Ext. 1331. *E-mail:* dbryden@baypath.edu.

Bay State College

Boston, Massachusetts

http://www.baystate.edu/

CONTACT

Kimberly Odusami, Director of Admissions, Bay State College, 122 Commonwealth Avenue, Boston, MA 02116. *Phone:* 617-217-9186. *Toll-free phone:* 800-81-LEARN. *E-mail:* admissions@baystate.edu.

Becker College

Worcester, Massachusetts

http://www.becker.edu/

- **Independent** comprehensive, founded 1784
- **Urban** 60-acre campus with easy access to Boston, MA; Providence, RI; Hartford, CT
- **Endowment** $5.1 million
- **Coed** 1,672 undergraduate students, 79% full-time, 59% women, 41% men
- **Moderately difficult** entrance level, 70% of applicants were admitted

UNDERGRAD STUDENTS

1,321 full-time, 351 part-time. Students come from 35 states and territories; 15 other countries; 34% are from out of state; 8% Black or African American, non-Hispanic/Latino; 10% Hispanic/Latino; 3% Asian, non-Hispanic/Latino; 0.2% Native Hawaiian or other Pacific Islander, non-Hispanic/Latino; 0.3% American Indian or Alaska Native, non-Hispanic/Latino; 3% Two or more races, non-Hispanic/Latino; 12% Race/ethnicity unknown; 0.8% international; 8% transferred in; 41% live on campus.

Freshmen:

Admission: 2,902 applied, 2,036 admitted, 259 enrolled. ***Average high school GPA:*** 3.2. ***Test scores:*** SAT evidence-based reading and writing scores over 500: 67%; SAT math scores over 500: 65%; ACT scores over 18: 67%; SAT evidence-based reading and writing scores over 600: 24%; SAT math scores over 600: 19%; ACT scores over 24: 40%; SAT evidence-based reading and writing scores over 700: 3%; SAT math scores over 700: 4%; ACT scores over 30: 13%.

Retention: 78% of full-time freshmen returned.

FACULTY

Total: 247, 20% full-time, 25% with terminal degrees.

Student/faculty ratio: 12:1.

ACADEMICS

Calendar: semesters. *Degrees:* certificates, associate, bachelor's, and master's (also includes Leicester, MA small town campus).

Special study options: academic remediation for entering students, accelerated degree program, adult/continuing education programs, advanced placement credit, cooperative education, distance learning, double majors, independent study, internships, off-campus study, part-time degree program, services for LD students, study abroad, summer session for credit. ***ROTC:*** Army (c), Navy (c), Air Force (c).

Unusual degree programs: 3-2 business administration; nursing; mental health counseling, veterinary science, veterinary technology, computer science, esports management, graphic design, interactive media design, forensic science, exercise science, health science, legal studies, criminal justice.

Computers: 404 computers/terminals and 370 ports are available on campus for general student use. Students can access the following: campus intranet, computer help desk, free student e-mail accounts, online (class) grades, online (class) registration, online (class) schedules, Portal, 24X7 Library Chat, 24X7 online Tutoring. Campuswide network is available. 100% of college-owned or -operated housing units are wired for high-speed Internet access. Wireless service is available via entire campus.

Library: Ruska Library plus 1 other. *Books:* 14,679 (physical), 224,889 (digital/electronic); *Serial titles:* 17 (physical), 28,239 (digital/electronic); *Databases:* 78. Weekly public service hours: 168; study areas open 24 hours, 5–7 days a week; students can reserve study rooms.

STUDENT LIFE

Housing options: coed, special housing for students with disabilities. Campus housing is university owned.

Activities and organizations: drama/theater group, Campus Activities Board (CAB), Animal Health Club/Pre-Veterinary Club, International Game Developers Association (IGDA), Dance Club, Marine Wildlife Conversation Club.

Athletics *Intercollegiate sports:* baseball M, basketball M/W, cheerleading M(c)/W(c), equestrian sports M/W, field hockey W, football M, golf M, ice hockey M/W, lacrosse M/W, soccer M/W, softball W, tennis M/W, ultimate Frisbee M(c)/W(c), volleyball W.

Campus security: 24-hour emergency response devices and patrols, late-night transport/escort service, controlled dormitory access.

Student services: health clinic, personal/psychological counseling.

COSTS & FINANCIAL AID

Costs (2020–21) *Comprehensive fee:* $53,950 includes full-time tuition ($36,300), mandatory fees ($3850), and room and board ($13,800). Full-time tuition and fees vary according to class time, course load, and program. Part-time tuition: $1515 per credit hour. Part-time tuition and fees vary according to class time, course load, and program. ***Room and board:*** Room and board charges vary according to housing facility. ***Payment plan:*** installment. ***Waivers:*** employees or children of employees.

Financial Aid Of all full-time matriculated undergraduates who enrolled in 2018, 1,297 applied for aid, 999 were judged to have need, 195 had their need fully met. In 2018, 162 non-need-based awards were made. ***Average percent of need met:*** 55. ***Average financial aid package:*** $21,586. ***Average need-based loan:*** $4135. ***Average need-based gift aid:*** $17,856. ***Average non-need-based aid:*** $14,481.

APPLYING

Standardized Tests *Required for some:* SAT or ACT (for admission).

Options: electronic application, early decision, early action.

Required: high school transcript, minimum 2.0 GPA. ***Recommended:*** essay or personal statement, letters of recommendation, interview.

Application deadlines: rolling (freshmen), rolling (transfers), 11/15 (early action).

Notification: continuous (freshmen), continuous (transfers), 12/15 (early action).

CONTACT

Mr. Michael Perron, Dean of Admissions, Becker College, 61 Sever Street, Worcester, MA 01609. *Phone:* 508-373-9400. *Toll-free phone:* 877-5BECKER. *Fax:* 508-890-1500. *E-mail:* admissions@becker.edu.

Benjamin Franklin Institute of Technology

Boston, Massachusetts

http://www.bfit.edu/

- **Independent** primarily 2-year, founded 1908
- **Urban** 3-acre campus
- **Coed** 597 undergraduate students, 78% full-time, 15% women, 85% men
- **Minimally difficult** entrance level, 71% of applicants were admitted

UNDERGRAD STUDENTS

466 full-time, 131 part-time. 3% are from out of state; 36% Black or African American, non-Hispanic/Latino; 28% Hispanic/Latino; 6% Asian, non-Hispanic/Latino; 0.4% Native Hawaiian or other Pacific Islander, non-Hispanic/Latino; 1% American Indian or Alaska Native, non-

Hispanic/Latino; 2% Two or more races, non-Hispanic/Latino; 8% Race/ethnicity unknown; 2% international; 11% transferred in.

Freshmen:
Admission: 725 applied, 514 admitted, 208 enrolled. ***Average high school GPA:*** 2.3.

ACADEMICS
Calendar: semesters. *Degrees:* certificates, associate, and bachelor's.

Special study options: academic remediation for entering students, accelerated degree program, adult/continuing education programs, advanced placement credit, independent study, internships, off-campus study, part-time degree program, services for LD students, summer session for credit.

Computers: Students can access the following: free student e-mail accounts, online (class) grades, online (class) schedules, online payments. Campuswide network is available. 100% of college-owned or -operated housing units are wired for high-speed Internet access. Wireless service is available via classrooms, computer labs, dorm rooms, learning centers, libraries, student centers.
Library: Lufkin Memorial Library.

STUDENT LIFE
Housing options: college housing not available.

Activities and organizations: Phi Theta Kappa, Student Government and Leadership, yearbook and video club, Green Technology Club, Women's Forum.

Athletics Member NJCAA. ***Intercollegiate sports:*** soccer M. ***Intramural sports:*** basketball M/W, table tennis M/W.

Campus security: 24-hour emergency response devices.

Student services: personal/psychological counseling.

FINANCIAL AID
Financial Aid ***Average percent of need met:*** 45. ***Average financial aid package:*** $11,677. ***Average need-based gift aid:*** $8581.

APPLYING
Options: electronic application, early action, deferred entrance.

Application fee: $25.

Required: high school transcript. ***Recommended:*** essay or personal statement, minimum 2.0 GPA, interview.

Notification: 12/21 (early action).

CONTACT
Ms. Brittainy Johnson, Associate Director of Admissions, Benjamin Franklin Institute of Technology, Boston, MA 02116. *Phone:* 617-423-4630 Ext. 122. *Toll-free phone:* 877-400-BFIT. *Fax:* 617-482-3706. *E-mail:* bjohnson@bfit.edu.

Bentley University

Waltham, Massachusetts

http://www.bentley.edu/

- **Independent** comprehensive, founded 1917
- **Suburban** 163-acre campus with easy access to Boston
- **Endowment** $286.1 million
- **Coed** 4,228 undergraduate students, 99% full-time, 41% women, 59% men
- **Very difficult** entrance level, 47% of applicants were admitted

UNDERGRAD STUDENTS
4,177 full-time, 51 part-time. Students come from 44 states and territories; 69 other countries; 58% are from out of state; 4% Black or African American, non-Hispanic/Latino; 7% Hispanic/Latino; 9% Asian, non-Hispanic/Latino; 3% Two or more races, non-Hispanic/Latino; 4% Race/ethnicity unknown; 15% international; 2% transferred in; 78% live on campus.

Freshmen:
Admission: 9,017 applied, 4,213 admitted, 944 enrolled. ***Test scores:*** SAT evidence-based reading and writing scores over 500: 99%; SAT math scores over 500: 99%; ACT scores over 18: 100%; SAT evidence-based reading and writing scores over 600: 79%; SAT math scores over 600: 85%; ACT scores over 24: 92%; SAT evidence-based reading and writing scores over 700: 17%; SAT math scores over 700: 40%; ACT scores over 30: 43%.

Retention: 92% of full-time freshmen returned.

FACULTY
Total: 513, 57% full-time, 69% with terminal degrees.

Student/faculty ratio: 11:1.

ACADEMICS
Calendar: semesters. *Degrees:* bachelor's, master's, doctoral, post-master's, and postbachelor's certificates.

Special study options: advanced placement credit, double majors, English as a second language, honors programs, independent study, internships, off-campus study, services for LD students, study abroad, summer session for credit. ***ROTC:*** Army (c), Air Force (c).

Computers: 3,730 computers/terminals and 10,752 ports are available on campus for general student use. Students can access the following: campus intranet, computer help desk, free student e-mail accounts, online (class) grades, online (class) registration, online (class) schedules, grade checking; online admission; blackboard; resume review; student employment; interlibary loan; free software. Campuswide network is available. 100% of college owned or operated housing units are wired for high-speed Internet access. Wireless service is available via entire campus.
Library: Bentley Library. *Books:* 153,308 (physical), 238,717 (digital/electronic); *Serial titles:* 2,442 (physical), 115,861 (digital/electronic); *Databases:* 108. Weekly public service hours: 110; students can reserve study rooms.

STUDENT LIFE
Housing options: coed, special housing for students with disabilities. Campus housing is university owned. Freshman campus housing is guaranteed.

Activities and organizations: drama/theater group, student-run newspaper, radio station, choral group, Bentley Investing Group, Campus Activities Board, South Asian Student Association, Bentley Association of Chinese Students, Delta Sigma Pi, national fraternities, national sororities.

Athletics Member NCAA. All Division II except ice hockey (Division I). ***Intercollegiate sports:*** baseball M, basketball M(s)/W(s), cross-country running M/W, field hockey W, football M, golf M, ice hockey M(s), lacrosse M/W, soccer M/W, softball W, swimming and diving M/W, tennis M/W, track and field M/W, volleyball W. ***Intramural sports:*** basketball M/W, cheerleading M(c)/W(c), equestrian sports M(c)/W(c), golf M(c)/W(c), ice hockey M(c)/W(c), rugby M(c)/W(c), sailing M(c)/W(c), soccer M/W, softball M/W, triathlon M(c)/W(c), ultimate Frisbee M/W, volleyball M/W.

Campus security: 24-hour emergency response devices and patrols, late-night transport/escort service, controlled dormitory access, CCTV security cameras; Community Policing team; Rape Aggression Defense classes; CPR, AED and first-aid training.

Student services: health clinic, personal/psychological counseling, women's center.

COSTS & FINANCIAL AID
Costs (2019–20) ***Comprehensive fee:*** $68,790 includes full-time tuition ($50,060), mandatory fees ($1770), and room and board ($16,960). Part-time tuition and fees vary according to course load. ***College room only:*** $10,290. Room and board charges vary according to board plan and housing facility. ***Payment plan:*** installment. ***Waivers:*** employees or children of employees.

Financial Aid Of all full-time matriculated undergraduates who enrolled in 2018, 2,456 applied for aid, 1,794 were judged to have need, 641 had their need fully met. 813 Federal Work-Study jobs (averaging $2181). 829 state and other part-time jobs (averaging $1807). In 2018, 1024 non-need-based awards were made. ***Average percent of need met:*** 92. ***Average financial aid package:*** $39,159. ***Average need-based loan:*** $4631. ***Average need-based gift aid:*** $34,395. ***Average non-need-based aid:*** $19,768. ***Average indebtedness upon graduation:*** $35,187. ***Financial aid deadline:*** 1/7.

APPLYING
Standardized Tests *Required:* TOEFL or IELTS is required for non-native English speakers (for admission).

Options: electronic application, early admission, early decision, deferred entrance.

Application fee: $75.

Required: essay or personal statement, high school transcript, 2 letters of recommendation. ***Recommended:*** interview.

Application deadlines: 1/7 (freshmen), 1/7 (out-of-state freshmen).

Early decision deadline: 11/15 (for plan 1), 1/7 (for plan 2).

Notification: 3/31 (freshmen), 3/31 (out-of-state freshmen), continuous (transfers), 12/21 (early decision plan 1), 2/1 (early decision plan 2).

CONTACT

Office of Undergraduate Admissions, Bentley University, 175 Forest St., Waltham, MA 02452. *Phone:* 781-891-2244. *Toll-free phone:* 800-523-2354. *E-mail:* ugadmission@bentley.edu.

Berklee College of Music

Boston, Massachusetts

http://www.berklee.edu/

- **Independent** comprehensive, founded 1945
- **Urban** campus
- **Coed** 6,439 undergraduate students, 78% full-time, 41% women, 59% men
- **Moderately difficult** entrance level, 51% of applicants were admitted

UNDERGRAD STUDENTS

5,041 full-time, 1,398 part-time. 88% are from out of state; 7% Black or African American, non-Hispanic/Latino; 10% Hispanic/Latino; 5% Asian, non-Hispanic/Latino; 0.1% Native Hawaiian or other Pacific Islander, non-Hispanic/Latino; 0.2% American Indian or Alaska Native, non-Hispanic/Latino; 5% Two or more races, non-Hispanic/Latino; 3% Race/ethnicity unknown; 28% international; 7% transferred in; 30% live on campus.

Freshmen:

Admission: 6,763 applied, 3,479 admitted, 1,311 enrolled.

Retention: 86% of full-time freshmen returned.

FACULTY

Total: 986, 36% full-time.

Student/faculty ratio: 10:1.

ACADEMICS

Calendar: semesters. *Degrees:* diplomas, bachelor's, master's, post-master's, and postbachelor's certificates.

Special study options: accelerated degree program, cooperative education, distance learning, double majors, English as a second language, independent study, internships, student-designed majors, study abroad. ***ROTC:*** Army (c).

Computers: Students can access the following: free student e-mail accounts, online (class) grades, online (class) registration, online (class) schedules. Campuswide network is available. Wireless service is available via entire campus.

Library: The Stan Getz Media Center and Library.

STUDENT LIFE

Housing options: coed, special housing for students with disabilities. Campus housing is university owned. Freshman applicants given priority for college housing.

Activities and organizations: drama/theater group, student-run newspaper, radio station, choral group, marching band.

Athletics ***Intramural sports:*** ice hockey M/W, rock climbing M/W, soccer M/W, table tennis M/W.

Campus security: 24-hour patrols.

COSTS & FINANCIAL AID

Costs (2020–21) ***Comprehensive fee:*** $66,060 includes full-time tuition ($45,890), mandatory fees ($1340), and room and board ($18,830). Part-time tuition: $1670 per credit hour.

Financial Aid Of all full-time matriculated undergraduates who enrolled in 2019, 2,351 applied for aid, 1,977 were judged to have need, 184 had their need fully met. In 2019, 1333 non-need-based awards were made. ***Average percent of need met:*** 65. ***Average financial aid package:*** $24,330. ***Average need-based loan:*** $3424. ***Average need-based gift aid:*** $7229. ***Average non-need-based aid:*** $20,521. ***Average indebtedness upon graduation:*** $43,826.

APPLYING

Options: electronic application, early action, deferred entrance.

Application fee: $150.

Required: essay or personal statement, high school transcript, 2 letters of recommendation, interview, 2 years of formal music study, audition.

Application deadlines: 1/15 (freshmen), 1/15 (transfers), 11/1 (early action).

Notification: 3/31 (freshmen), 3/31 (transfers), 1/31 (early action).

CONTACT

Mr. Damien Bracken, Director of Admissions, Berklee College of Music, 1140 Boylston Street, Boston, MA 02215-3693. *Phone:* 617-747-2222. *Toll-free phone:* 800-BERKLEE. *Fax:* 617-747-2047. *E-mail:* admissions@berklee.edu.

Boston Architectural College

Boston, Massachusetts

http://www.the-bac.edu/

- **Independent** comprehensive, founded 1889
- **Urban** 1-acre campus with easy access to Boston
- **Endowment** $10.1 million
- **Coed** 472 undergraduate students, 75% full-time, 42% women, 58% men
- **Noncompetitive** entrance level, 15% of applicants were admitted

UNDERGRAD STUDENTS

354 full-time, 118 part-time. Students come from 40 other countries; 6% Black or African American, non-Hispanic/Latino; 17% Hispanic/Latino; 9% Asian, non-Hispanic/Latino; 0.3% Native Hawaiian or other Pacific Islander, non-Hispanic/Latino; 0.3% American Indian or Alaska Native, non-Hispanic/Latino; 4% Two or more races, non-Hispanic/Latino; 8% Race/ethnicity unknown; 5% international.

Freshmen:

Admission: 178 applied, 26 admitted, 24 enrolled.

Retention: 75% of full-time freshmen returned.

FACULTY

Total: 264, 10% full-time, 100% with terminal degrees.

Student/faculty ratio: 4:1.

ACADEMICS

Calendar: semesters. *Degrees:* certificates, bachelor's, and master's.

Special study options: adult/continuing education programs, advanced placement credit, distance learning, independent study, internships, off-campus study, services for LD students, summer session for credit.

Computers: 84 computers/terminals are available on campus for general student use. Students can access the following: campus intranet, computer help desk, free student e-mail accounts, online (class) grades, online (class) registration, online (class) schedules. Campuswide network is available. Wireless service is available via entire campus.

Library: Shaw and Stone Library. *Books:* 42,224 (physical), 117,108 (digital/electronic); *Serial titles:* 613 (physical), 313,728 (digital/electronic); *Databases:* 73. Weekly public service hours: 71.

STUDENT LIFE

Housing options: college housing not available.

Activities and organizations: Student Government Association, Student American Society of Landscape Architects, BAC Interior Design Society (IIDA and ASID), National Organization of Minority Architecture Students (NOMAS), American Institute of Architectural Students.

Campus security: 24-hour emergency response devices and patrols, late-night transport/escort service, electronically operated building access, closed-circuit TV systems.

Student services: personal/psychological counseling, legal services.

COSTS & FINANCIAL AID

Costs (2020–21) ***One-time required fee:*** $150. ***Tuition:*** $25,753 full-time, $1762 per credit hour part-time. ***Required fees:*** $750 full-time, $150 per term part-time. ***Payment plan:*** installment. ***Waivers:*** employees or children of employees.

Financial Aid Of all full-time matriculated undergraduates who enrolled in 2019, 86 applied for aid, 85 were judged to have need, 2 had their need fully met. 17 Federal Work-Study jobs (averaging $2935). In 2019, 1 non-need-based awards were made. ***Average percent of need met:*** 36. ***Average financial aid package:*** $12,871. ***Average need-based loan:*** $5975. ***Average need-based gift aid:*** $8807. ***Average non-need-based aid:*** $1012.

APPLYING
Options: electronic application.

Required: essay or personal statement, high school transcript, resumé and creative exercise. ***Recommended:*** interview.

CONTACT
Ms. Meredith Spinnato, Director of Admission Office, Boston Architectural College, 320 Newbury Street, Boston, MA 02115-2795. *Phone:* 617-585-0123. *Fax:* 617-585-0121. *E-mail:* admissions@the-bac.edu.

Boston Baptist College
Boston, Massachusetts
http://www.boston.edu/

CONTACT
Mrs. Kim Melton, Director of Admissions, Boston Baptist College, 950 Metropolitan Avenue, Boston, MA 02136. *Phone:* 617-364-3510 Ext. 233. *Toll-free phone:* 888-235-2014. *Fax:* 617-399-8220. *E-mail:* kmelton@boston.edu.

Boston College
Chestnut Hill, Massachusetts
http://www.bc.edu/

- **Independent Roman Catholic (Jesuit)** university, founded 1863
- **Suburban** 228-acre campus with easy access to Boston
- **Endowment** $2.5 billion
- **Coed** 9,370 undergraduate students, 100% full-time, 53% women, 47% men
- **Very difficult** entrance level, 27% of applicants were admitted

UNDERGRAD STUDENTS
9,370 full-time. Students come from 52 states and territories; 66 other countries; 73% are from out of state; 4% Black or African American, non-Hispanic/Latino; 12% Hispanic/Latino; 11% Asian, non-Hispanic/Latino; 4% Two or more races, non-Hispanic/Latino; 4% Race/ethnicity unknown; 8% international; 1% transferred in; 84% live on campus.

Freshmen:
Admission: 35,552 applied, 9,679 admitted, 2,297 enrolled. ***Test scores:*** SAT evidence-based reading and writing scores over 500: 99%; SAT math scores over 500: 99%; ACT scores over 18: 100%; SAT evidence-based reading and writing scores over 600: 94%; SAT math scores over 600: 94%; ACT scores over 24: 98%; SAT evidence-based reading and writing scores over 700: 54%; SAT math scores over 700: 69%; ACT scores over 30: 88%.

Retention: 95% of full-time freshmen returned.

FACULTY
Total: 1,386, 62% full-time, 95% with terminal degrees.

Student/faculty ratio: 11:1.

ACADEMICS
Calendar: semesters. *Degrees:* certificates, bachelor's, master's, doctoral, and post-master's certificates (also offers continuing education program with significant enrollment not reflected in profile).

Special study options: accelerated degree program, advanced placement credit, double majors, honors programs, independent study, internships, off-campus study, part-time degree program, services for LD students, student-designed majors, study abroad, summer session for credit. ***ROTC:*** Army (c), Navy (c), Air Force (c).

Computers: 1,000 computers/terminals are available on campus for general student use. Students can access the following: campus intranet, computer help desk, free student e-mail accounts, online (class) grades, online (class) registration, online (class) schedules. Campuswide network is available. 100% of college-owned or -operated housing units are wired for high-speed Internet access. Wireless service is available via entire campus.

Library: O'Neill Library plus 8 others. *Books:* 3.3 million (physical), 1.0 million (digital/electronic); *Serial titles:* 3,424 (physical), 42,082 (digital/electronic). Study areas open 24 hours, 5–7 days a week; students can reserve study rooms.

STUDENT LIFE
Housing options: coed, women-only. Campus housing is university owned. Freshman campus housing is guaranteed.

Activities and organizations: drama/theater group, student-run newspaper, radio and television station, choral group, marching band, UGBC and individual School Senates, Asian Caucus, Appalachia Volunteers, Dance Marathon, 4Boston.

Athletics Member NCAA. All Division I except football (Division I-A). ***Intercollegiate sports:*** baseball M(s), basketball M(s)/W(s), cheerleading M(c)/W(c), crew W(s), cross-country running M(s)/W(s), fencing M/W, field hockey W(s), golf M(s)/W(s)(c), ice hockey M(s)/W(s), lacrosse W(s), sailing M/W, skiing (downhill) M(c)/W, soccer M(s)/W(s), softball W(s), swimming and diving M(s)/W(s), tennis M(s)/W(s), track and field M(s)/W(s), volleyball W(s). ***Intramural sports:*** badminton M/W, basketball M(c)/W(c), crew M(c), cross-country running M(c)/W(c), equestrian sports M(c)/W(c), fencing W(c), golf M(c)/W(c), ice hockey M/W, lacrosse M(c)/W(c), racquetball M/W, rugby M(c)/W(c), soccer M(c)/W(c), softball M/W, squash M/W, tennis M/W, track and field M(c)/W(c), ultimate Frisbee M(c)/W(c), volleyball M(c)/W, water polo M(c)/W(c).

Campus security: 24-hour emergency response devices and patrols, late-night transport/escort service, controlled dormitory access.

Student services: health clinic, personal/psychological counseling, women's center.

COSTS & FINANCIAL AID
Costs (2019–20) ***Comprehensive fee:*** $71,606 includes full-time tuition ($56,780) and room and board ($14,826). ***College room only:*** $9300. Room and board charges vary according to board plan and housing facility. ***Payment plan:*** installment. ***Waivers:*** employees or children of employees.

Financial Aid Of all full-time matriculated undergraduates who enrolled in 2019, 4,459 applied for aid, 3,955 were judged to have need, 3,955 had their need fully met. In 2019, 200 non-need-based awards were made. ***Average percent of need met:*** 100. ***Average financial aid package:*** $47,647. ***Average need-based loan:*** $4010. ***Average need-based gift aid:*** $44,424. ***Average non-need-based aid:*** $23,898. ***Average indebtedness upon graduation:*** $23,136.

APPLYING
Standardized Tests *Required:* SAT or ACT (for admission).

Options: electronic application, early admission, early decision, deferred entrance.

Application fee: $80.

Required: essay or personal statement, high school transcript, 2 letters of recommendation.

Application deadlines: 1/1 (freshmen), 3/15 (transfers).

Early decision deadline: 11/1 (for plan 1), 1/1 (for plan 2).

Notification: 4/1 (freshmen), 6/15 (transfers), 12/15 (early decision plan 1), 2/15 (early decision plan 2).

CONTACT
Office of Undergraduate Admission, Boston College, 140 Commonwealth Avenue, Chestnut Hill, MA 02467-3800. *Phone:* -617-552-3100. *Toll-free phone:* 800-360-2522. *E-mail:* admission@bc.edu.

See page 1044 for the College Close-Up.

Boston University
Boston, Massachusetts
http://www.bu.edu/

- **Independent** university, founded 1839
- **Urban** 169-acre campus with easy access to Boston
- **Endowment** $2.2 billion
- **Coed**
- **Very difficult** entrance level

FACULTY
Student/faculty ratio: 10:1.

ACADEMICS
Calendar: semesters. *Degrees:* certificates, bachelor's, master's, doctoral, post-master's, and postbachelor's certificates.
Library: Mugar Memorial Library plus 20 others. *Books:* 1.2 million (physical), 2.1 million (digital/electronic); *Serial titles:* 248,885 (physical), 111,406 (digital/electronic); *Databases:* 721. Weekly public service hours: 123; students can reserve study rooms.

STUDENT LIFE
Housing options: on-campus residence required for freshman year; coed, women-only, cooperative, special housing for students with disabilities. Campus housing is university owned. Freshman campus housing is guaranteed.

Activities and organizations: drama/theater group, student-run newspaper, radio and television station, choral group, marching band, performing and Acappella groups, cultural organizations, service organizations, Student Government, residence hall associations, national fraternities, national sororities.

Athletics Member NCAA. All Division I.

Campus security: 24-hour emergency response devices and patrols, late-night transport/escort service, controlled dormitory access.

Student services: health clinic, personal/psychological counseling, women's center, veterans affairs office.

COSTS & FINANCIAL AID
Costs (2019–20) ***Comprehensive fee:*** $72,052 includes full-time tuition ($54,720), mandatory fees ($1172), and room and board ($16,160). Full-time tuition and fees vary according to class time and course load. Part-time tuition: $1710 per credit. Part-time tuition and fees vary according to class time, course level, and course load. ***Required fees:*** $60 per term part-time. ***College room only:*** $10,680. Room and board charges vary according to board plan, housing facility, and location. ***Payment plans:*** tuition prepayment, installment.

Financial Aid Of all full-time matriculated undergraduates who enrolled in 2019, 8,138 applied for aid, 6,906 were judged to have need, 1,750 had their need fully met. 2,847 Federal Work-Study jobs (averaging $2279). In 2019, 885 non-need-based awards were made. ***Average percent of need met:*** 85. ***Average financial aid package:*** $46,252. ***Average need-based loan:*** $3294. ***Average need-based gift aid:*** $40,969. ***Average non-need-based aid:*** $23,596. ***Average indebtedness upon graduation:*** $40,349. ***Financial aid deadline:*** 1/6.

APPLYING
Standardized Tests *Required for some:* SAT or ACT (for admission), SAT Subject Tests (for admission).

Options: electronic application, early admission, early decision, deferred entrance.

Application fee: $80.

Required: essay or personal statement, high school transcript, 2 letters of recommendation. ***Required for some:*** interview, audition, portfolio.

CONTACT
Ms. Kelly A. Walter, Associate Vice President for Enrollment and Dean of Admissions, Boston University, 233 Bay State Road, Boston, MA 02215. *Phone:* 617-353-2300. *E-mail:* admissions@bu.edu.

See below for display ad and page 1046 for the College Close-Up.

Brandeis University
Waltham, Massachusetts
http://www.brandeis.edu/

- **Independent** university, founded 1948
- **Suburban** 235-acre campus with easy access to Boston
- **Endowment** $1.1 billion
- **Coed** 3,688 undergraduate students, 100% full-time, 61% women, 39% men
- **Most difficult** entrance level, 30% of applicants were admitted

UNDERGRAD STUDENTS
3,673 full-time, 15 part-time. Students come from 50 states and territories; 67 other countries; 70% are from out of state; 5% Black or African American, non-Hispanic/Latino; 8% Hispanic/Latino; 14% Asian, non-

Hispanic/Latino; 0.2% Native Hawaiian or other Pacific Islander, non-Hispanic/Latino; 0.1% American Indian or Alaska Native, non-Hispanic/Latino; 4% Two or more races, non-Hispanic/Latino; 2% Race/ethnicity unknown; 20% international; 1% transferred in; 76% live on campus.

Freshmen:

Admission: 11,343 applied, 3,391 admitted, 863 enrolled. ***Average high school GPA:*** 3.8. ***Test scores:*** SAT evidence-based reading and writing scores over 500: 99%; SAT math scores over 500: 100%; ACT scores over 18: 100%; SAT evidence-based reading and writing scores over 600: 95%; SAT math scores over 600: 95%; ACT scores over 24: 99%; SAT evidence-based reading and writing scores over 700: 48%; SAT math scores over 700: 74%; ACT scores over 30: 86%.

Retention: 93% of full-time freshmen returned.

FACULTY

Total: 550, 69% full-time, 83% with terminal degrees.

Student/faculty ratio: 10:1.

ACADEMICS

Calendar: semesters. *Degrees:* bachelor's, master's, doctoral, and post-master's certificates.

Special study options: advanced placement credit, double majors, independent study, internships, off-campus study, services for LD students, student-designed majors, study abroad, summer session for credit. ***ROTC:*** Army (c), Air Force (c).

Unusual degree programs: 3-2 engineering with Columbia University.

Computers: 130 computers/terminals are available on campus for general student use. Students can access the following: computer help desk, free student e-mail accounts, online (class) grades, online (class) registration, online (class) schedules, educational software. Campuswide network is available. 100% of college-owned or -operated housing units are wired for high-speed Internet access. Wireless service is available via entire campus.

Library: Brandeis Library plus 1 other. *Books:* 1.0 million (physical), 1.1 million (digital/electronic); *Serial titles:* 11,942 (physical), 49,626 (digital/electronic); *Databases:* 641. Students can reserve study rooms.

STUDENT LIFE

Housing options: on-campus residence required for freshman year; coed, special housing for students with disabilities. Campus housing is university owned. Freshman campus housing is guaranteed.

Activities and organizations: drama/theater group, student-run newspaper, radio station, choral group, Waltham Group, Undergraduate Theater Collective, Mountain Club, Student Union, BEMCo - student EMTs.

Athletics Member NCAA. All Division III. ***Intercollegiate sports:*** baseball M, basketball M/W, cross-country running M/W, fencing M/W, soccer M/W, softball W, swimming and diving M/W, tennis M/W, track and field M/W, volleyball W. ***Intramural sports:*** archery M(c)/W(c), badminton M/W, basketball M/W, cheerleading M(c)/W(c), crew M(c)/W(c), equestrian sports M(c)/W(c), fencing M(c)/W(c), gymnastics M(c)/W(c), rock climbing M(c)/W(c), rowing M(c)/W(c), rugby M(c)/W(c), sailing M(c)/W(c), skiing (cross-country) M(c)/W(c), skiing (downhill) M(c)/W(c), soccer M/W, softball M/W, squash M/W, table tennis M/W, tennis M/W, ultimate Frisbee M(c)/W(c), volleyball M/W.

Campus security: 24-hour emergency response devices and patrols, late-night transport/escort service, controlled dormitory access.

Student services: health clinic, personal/psychological counseling, women's center.

COSTS & FINANCIAL AID

Costs (2019–20) ***Comprehensive fee:*** $73,641 includes full-time tuition ($55,340), mandatory fees ($2221), and room and board ($16,080). Part-time tuition: $1729 per credit hour. ***Required fees:*** $2221 per year part-time. ***College room only:*** $9060.

Financial Aid Of all full-time matriculated undergraduates who enrolled in 2018, 1,946 applied for aid, 1,695 were judged to have need, 1,587 had their need fully met. 1,395 Federal Work-Study jobs (averaging $2470). 69 state and other part-time jobs (averaging $2810). In 2018, 495 non-need-based awards were made. ***Average percent of need met:*** 97. ***Average financial aid package:*** $46,990. ***Average need-based loan:*** $4606. ***Average need-based gift aid:*** $42,876. ***Average non-need-based aid:*** $14,481. ***Average indebtedness upon graduation:*** $32,158. ***Financial aid deadline:*** 1/1.

APPLYING

Standardized Tests *Required:* SAT or ACT (for admission). *Required for some:* SAT Subject Tests (for admission).

Options: electronic application, early decision, deferred entrance.

Application fee: $80.

Required: essay or personal statement, high school transcript, 1 letter of recommendation. ***Recommended:*** interview.

Application deadlines: 1/1 (freshmen), 3/15 (transfers).

Early decision deadline: 11/1 (for plan 1), 1/1 (for plan 2).

Notification: 4/1 (freshmen), 5/25 (transfers), 12/15 (early decision plan 1), 2/1 (early decision plan 2).

CONTACT

Jennifer Walker, Dean of Admissions & Financial Aid, Brandeis University, 415 South Street, PO Box 549110, Waltham, MA 02454-9110. *Phone:* 781-736-3500. *Toll-free phone:* 800-622-0622. *Fax:* 781-736-3536. *E-mail:* admissions@brandeis.edu.

Bridgewater State University

Bridgewater, Massachusetts

http://www.bridgew.edu/

- **State-supported** comprehensive, founded 1840, part of Massachusetts Department of Higher Education
- **Suburban** 278-acre campus with easy access to Boston
- **Endowment** $45.0 million
- **Coed** 9,463 undergraduate students, 81% full-time, 59% women, 41% men
- **Moderately difficult** entrance level, 88% of applicants were admitted

UNDERGRAD STUDENTS

7,681 full-time, 1,782 part-time. Students come from 25 states and territories; 26 other countries; 4% are from out of state; 12% Black or African American, non-Hispanic/Latino; 8% Hispanic/Latino; 2% Asian, non-Hispanic/Latino; 0.1% Native Hawaiian or other Pacific Islander, non-Hispanic/Latino; 0.2% American Indian or Alaska Native, non-Hispanic/Latino; 5% Two or more races, non-Hispanic/Latino; 1% Race/ethnicity unknown; 0.4% international; 10% transferred in; 41% live on campus.

Freshmen:

Admission: 9,800 applied, 8,591 admitted, 1,611 enrolled. ***Average high school GPA:*** 3.2. ***Test scores:*** SAT evidence-based reading and writing scores over 500: 71%; SAT math scores over 500: 70%; SAT evidence-based reading and writing scores over 600: 19%; SAT math scores over 600: 15%; SAT evidence-based reading and writing scores over 700: 2%; SAT math scores over 700: 2%.

Retention: 77% of full-time freshmen returned.

FACULTY

Total: 799, 45% full-time, 60% with terminal degrees.

Student/faculty ratio: 18:1.

ACADEMICS

Calendar: semesters. *Degrees:* bachelor's, master's, post-master's, and postbachelor's certificates.

Special study options: academic remediation for entering students, accelerated degree program, adult/continuing education programs, advanced placement credit, distance learning, double majors, English as a second language, honors programs, independent study, internships, off-campus study, part-time degree program, services for LD students, study abroad, summer session for credit. ***ROTC:*** Army (c), Air Force (c).

Computers: 780 computers/terminals and 20 ports are available on campus for general student use. Students can access the following: campus intranet, computer help desk, free student e-mail accounts, online (class) grades, online (class) registration, online (class) schedules, student account information, application software. Campuswide network is available. 100% of college-owned or -operated housing units are wired for high-speed Internet access. Wireless service is available via entire campus.

Library: Clement C. Maxwell Library. *Books:* 238,401 (physical), 59,015 (digital/electronic); *Serial titles:* 1,744 (physical), 29,106 (digital/electronic); *Databases:* 208. Weekly public service hours: 94; students can reserve study rooms.

STUDENT LIFE
Housing options: coed, special housing for students with disabilities. Campus housing is university owned. Freshman applicants given priority for college housing.

Activities and organizations: drama/theater group, student-run newspaper, radio and television station, choral group, Best Buddies, Panhellenic Council, Residence Hall Association, Program Council, Fellowship of Military Scholars, national fraternities, national sororities.

Athletics Member NCAA. All Division III. ***Intercollegiate sports:*** baseball M, basketball M/W, cross-country running M/W, field hockey W, football M, lacrosse W, soccer M/W, softball W, swimming and diving M/W, tennis M/W, track and field M/W, volleyball W, wrestling M. ***Intramural sports:*** basketball M/W, cheerleading W(c), equestrian sports W(c), football M/W, ice hockey M(c), lacrosse M(c), rugby W(c), soccer M/W, softball M/W, ultimate Frisbee M(c)/W(c), volleyball M/W.

Campus security: 24-hour emergency response devices and patrols, late-night transport/escort service, controlled dormitory access.

Student services: health clinic, personal/psychological counseling, veterans affairs office.

COSTS & FINANCIAL AID
Costs (2020–21) ***Tuition:*** state resident $38 per credit hour part-time; nonresident $294 per credit hour part-time. ***Room and board:*** Room and board charges vary according to board plan and housing facility. ***Payment plan:*** installment. ***Waivers:*** minority students and employees or children of employees.

Financial Aid Of all full-time matriculated undergraduates who enrolled in 2018, 7,098 applied for aid, 5,589 were judged to have need, 741 had their need fully met. In 2018, 42 non-need-based awards were made. ***Average percent of need met:*** 69. ***Average financial aid package:*** $8521. ***Average need-based loan:*** $3721. ***Average need-based gift aid:*** $6010. ***Average non-need-based aid:*** $3666. ***Average indebtedness upon graduation:*** $33,367.

APPLYING
Options: electronic application, early action, deferred entrance.

Application fee: $50.

Required: high school transcript. ***Recommended:*** essay or personal statement.

Application deadlines: 2/15 (freshmen), 2/15 (transfers), 11/15 (early action).

Notification: continuous until 4/15 (freshmen), continuous until 4/15 (transfers), 12/15 (early action).

CONTACT
Mr. Gregg Meyer, Dean of University Admissions, Bridgewater State University, Undergraduate Admissions Welcome Center, 45 Plymouth St, Bridgewater, MA 02325. *Phone:* 508-531-1237. *Fax:* 508-531-1746. *E-mail:* admission@bridgew.edu.

Cambridge College

Boston, Massachusetts

http://www.cambridgecollege.edu/

- **Independent** comprehensive, founded 1971
- **Urban** campus with easy access to Boston
- **Endowment** $11.4 million
- **Coed**
- **Noncompetitive** entrance level

FACULTY
Student/faculty ratio: 11:1.

ACADEMICS
Calendar: trimesters. *Degrees:* certificates, bachelor's, master's, doctoral, and post-master's certificates.
Library: Cambridge College Online Library.

STUDENT LIFE
Housing options: college housing not available.

FINANCIAL AID
Financial Aid ***Financial aid deadline:*** 10/1.

APPLYING
Options: electronic application, deferred entrance.

Application fee: $50.

Required: essay or personal statement, high school transcript, 1 letter of recommendation, resumé, health insurance, immunizations form, application form. ***Recommended:*** interview.

CONTACT
Denise Haile, Director of Admissions, Cambridge College, 1000 Massachusetts Avenue, Cambridge, MA 02138-5304. *Phone:* 800-877-4725. *Toll-free phone:* 800-877-4723. *Fax:* 617-349-3561. *E-mail:* denise.haile@cambridgecollege.edu.

Clark University

Worcester, Massachusetts

http://www.clarku.edu/

- **Independent** university, founded 1887
- **Urban** 50-acre campus with easy access to Boston
- **Endowment** $436.9 million
- **Coed** 2,304 undergraduate students, 98% full-time, 61% women, 39% men
- **Moderately difficult** entrance level, 59% of applicants were admitted

UNDERGRAD STUDENTS
2,263 full-time, 41 part-time. Students come from 43 states and territories; 56 other countries; 61% are from out of state; 4% Black or African American, non-Hispanic/Latino; 9% Hispanic/Latino; 8% Asian, non-Hispanic/Latino; 3% Two or more races, non-Hispanic/Latino; 6% Race/ethnicity unknown; 12% international; 2% transferred in; 66% live on campus.

Freshmen:
Admission: 7,687 applied, 4,565 admitted, 582 enrolled. ***Average high school GPA:*** 3.7.

Retention: 87% of full-time freshmen returned.

ACADEMICS
Calendar: semesters. *Degrees:* bachelor's, master's, doctoral, and post-master's certificates.

Special study options: accelerated degree program, adult/continuing education programs, advanced placement credit, distance learning, double majors, English as a second language, honors programs, independent study, internships, off-campus study, part-time degree program, services for LD students, student-designed majors, study abroad, summer session for credit. ***ROTC:*** Army (c), Air Force (c).

Unusual degree programs: 3-2 business administration; engineering with Columbia University; environmental studies, international development, community planning, biology, biochemistry, chemistry, physics, economics, history, communications, public administration, geographic information systems.

Computers: Students can access the following: campus intranet, computer help desk, free student e-mail accounts, online (class) grades, online (class) registration, online (class) schedules, online course support. Campuswide network is available. 100% of college-owned or -operated housing units are wired for high-speed Internet access. Wireless service is available via entire campus.
Library: Robert Hutchings Goddard Library plus 8 others. Students can reserve study rooms.

STUDENT LIFE
Housing options: on-campus residence required through sophomore year; coed, women-only, special housing for students with disabilities. Campus housing is university owned. Freshman campus housing is guaranteed.

Activities and organizations: drama/theater group, student-run newspaper, radio and television station, choral group, marching band, International Students Association, Science Fiction People of Clark, Outing Club, Hillel, Clark Musical Theater.

Athletics Member NCAA, NAIA. All NCAA Division III. ***Intercollegiate sports:*** baseball M, basketball M/W, crew M/W, cross-country running M/W, field hockey W, lacrosse M/W, soccer M/W, softball W, swimming and diving M/W, tennis M/W, volleyball W. ***Intramural sports:*** basketball

M/W, equestrian sports W(c), ice hockey M(c), lacrosse W(c), racquetball M/W, soccer M(c)/W, softball M/W, tennis M(c)/W(c), ultimate Frisbee M(c)/W(c), volleyball M(c)/W(c), water polo M/W.

Campus security: 24-hour emergency response devices and patrols, student patrols, late-night transport/escort service, controlled dormitory access.

Student services: health clinic, personal/psychological counseling, women's center.

COSTS & FINANCIAL AID

Costs (2019–20) ***Comprehensive fee:*** $56,680 includes full-time tuition ($46,850), mandatory fees ($350), and room and board ($9480). Part-time tuition: $1464 per unit. ***Room and board:*** Room and board charges vary according to board plan and housing facility. ***Payment plan:*** tuition prepayment. ***Waivers:*** employees or children of employees.

Financial Aid Of all full-time matriculated undergraduates who enrolled in 2019, 1,885 applied for aid, 1,452 were judged to have need, 409 had their need fully met. In 2019, 646 non-need-based awards were made. ***Average percent of need met:*** 90. ***Average financial aid package:*** $34,421. ***Average need-based loan:*** $4336. ***Average need-based gift aid:*** $30,669. ***Average non-need-based aid:*** $17,319. ***Average indebtedness upon graduation:*** $34,390. ***Financial aid deadline:*** 2/1.

APPLYING

Options: electronic application, early admission, early decision, early action, deferred entrance.

Application fee: $60.

Required: essay or personal statement, high school transcript, 2 letters of recommendation. ***Recommended:*** interview.

Application deadlines: 1/15 (freshmen), 5/1 (transfers), 11/1 (early action).

Early decision deadline: 11/1 (for plan 1), 1/15 (for plan 2).

Notification: 4/1 (freshmen), 6/1 (transfers), 12/15 (early decision plan 1), 2/15 (early decision plan 2), 1/15 (early action).

CONTACT

Ms. Meredith Twombly, Vice President of Admissions and Financial Aid, Clark University, Admissions House, 950 Main Street, Worcester, MA 01610. *Phone:* 508-793-7431. *Toll-free phone:* 800-GO-CLARK. *Fax:* 508-793-8821. *E-mail:* admissions@clarku.edu.

College of the Holy Cross

Worcester, Massachusetts

http://www.holycross.edu/

- **Independent Roman Catholic (Jesuit)** 4-year, founded 1843
- **Suburban** 174-acre campus with easy access to Boston
- **Endowment** $785.9 million
- **Coed** 3,174 undergraduate students, 99% full-time, 53% women, 47% men
- **Very difficult** entrance level, 34% of applicants were admitted

UNDERGRAD STUDENTS

3,142 full-time, 32 part-time. Students come from 47 states and territories; 22 other countries; 60% are from out of state; 5% Black or African American, non-Hispanic/Latino; 11% Hispanic/Latino; 4% Asian, non-Hispanic/Latino; 0.1% Native Hawaiian or other Pacific Islander, non-Hispanic/Latino; 3% Two or more races, non-Hispanic/Latino; 3% Race/ethnicity unknown; 3% international; 0.2% transferred in; 90% live on campus.

Freshmen:

Admission: 7,200 applied, 2,464 admitted, 829 enrolled. ***Test scores:*** SAT evidence-based reading and writing scores over 500: 100%; SAT math scores over 500: 100%; ACT scores over 18: 100%; SAT evidence-based reading and writing scores over 600: 86%; SAT math scores over 600: 86%; ACT scores over 24: 97%; SAT evidence-based reading and writing scores over 700: 29%; SAT math scores over 700: 38%; ACT scores over 30: 50%.

Retention: 93% of full-time freshmen returned.

FACULTY

Total: 336, 89% full-time, 90% with terminal degrees.

Student/faculty ratio: 10:1.

ACADEMICS

Calendar: semesters. *Degree:* bachelor's.

Special study options: accelerated degree program, advanced placement credit, double majors, honors programs, independent study, internships, off-campus study, services for LD students, student-designed majors, study abroad, summer session for credit. ***ROTC:*** Army (c), Navy (b), Air Force (c).

Unusual degree programs: 3-2 engineering with Columbia University; Data Science / University of Notre Dame.

Computers: 298 computers/terminals are available on campus for general student use. Students can access the following: computer help desk, free student e-mail accounts, online (class) grades, online (class) registration. Campuswide network is available. 100% of college-owned or -operated housing units are wired for high-speed Internet access. Wireless service is available via entire campus.

Library: Dinand Library plus 4 others. *Books:* 648,546 (physical), 301,957 (digital/electronic); *Serial titles:* 369 (physical), 28,658 (digital/electronic); *Databases:* 325. Study areas open 24 hours, 5–7 days a week, students can reserve study rooms.

STUDENT LIFE

Housing options: on-campus residence required through sophomore year; coed, special housing for students with disabilities. Campus housing is university owned. Freshman campus housing is guaranteed.

Activities and organizations: drama/theater group, student-run newspaper, radio station, choral group, marching band, SPUD (community service organization), choral and music groups, Campus Activities Board, Student Government Association, Purple Key Society.

Athletics Member NCAA. All Division I except football (Division I-AA). ***Intercollegiate sports:*** baseball M, basketball M(s)/W(s), crew M/W(s), cross-country running M/W(s), field hockey W(s), golf M/W, ice hockey M(s)/W(s), lacrosse M(s)/W(s), soccer M(s)/W(s), softball W(s), swimming and diving M/W(s), tennis M/W, track and field M/W(s), volleyball W(s). ***Intramural sports:*** baseball M(c), basketball M(c)/W(c), equestrian sports M(c)/W(c), fencing W(c), field hockey W(c), football M/W, golf M(c)/W(c), ice hockey M(c)/W(c), lacrosse M(c)/W(c), rugby M(c)/W(c), sailing M(c)/W(c), skiing (downhill) M(c)/W(c), soccer M(c)/W(c), softball M/W, swimming and diving M(c)/W(c), tennis M(c)/W(c), ultimate Frisbee M(c)/W(c), volleyball M(c)/W(c), water polo M/W.

Campus security: 24-hour emergency response devices and patrols, late-night transport/escort service, controlled dormitory access.

Student services: health clinic, personal/psychological counseling.

COSTS & FINANCIAL AID

Costs (2020–21) ***Comprehensive fee:*** $72,080 includes full-time tuition ($55,800), mandatory fees ($720), and room and board ($15,560). ***College room only:*** $8520.

Financial Aid Of all full-time matriculated undergraduates who enrolled in 2019, 2,083 applied for aid, 1,684 were judged to have need, 1,684 had their need fully met. In 2019, 160 non-need-based awards were made. ***Average percent of need met:*** 100. ***Average financial aid package:*** $41,584. ***Average need-based loan:*** $4484. ***Average need-based gift aid:*** $40,064. ***Average non-need-based aid:*** $20,393. ***Average indebtedness upon graduation:*** $26,258.

APPLYING

Options: electronic application, early admission, early decision, deferred entrance.

Application fee: $60.

Required: essay or personal statement, high school transcript, 2 letters of recommendation. ***Recommended:*** interview.

Application deadlines: 1/15 (freshmen), 4/1 (transfers).

Early decision deadline: 12/15 (for plan 1), 1/15 (for plan 2).

Notification: 4/1 (freshmen), 6/1 (transfers), rolling (early decision plan 1), rolling (early decision plan 2).

CONTACT

College of the Holy Cross, 1 College Street, Worcester, MA 01610-2395. *Phone:* 508-793-2443. *Toll-free phone:* 800-442-2421.

Curry College

Milton, Massachusetts

http://www.curry.edu/

- **Independent** comprehensive, founded 1879
- **Suburban** 131-acre campus with easy access to Boston
- **Endowment** $99.4 million
- **Coed**
- **Moderately difficult** entrance level

FACULTY

Student/faculty ratio: 13:1.

ACADEMICS

Calendar: semesters. *Degrees:* bachelor's, master's, and post-master's certificates.

Library: Levin Library. *Books:* 71,564 (physical), 141,518 (digital/electronic); *Serial titles:* 66 (physical), 109,694 (digital/electronic); *Databases:* 101. Weekly public service hours: 98; students can reserve study rooms.

STUDENT LIFE

Housing options: coed, men-only, women-only. Campus housing is university owned.

Activities and organizations: drama/theater group, student-run newspaper, radio and television station, choral group, Students Entertainment and Events (SEE), Black Student Union (BSU), Latino Student Union (LSU), Multicultural Student Union (MSU), Student Government Association (SGA).

Athletics Member NCAA. All Division III.

Campus security: 24-hour emergency response devices and patrols, late-night transport/escort service, controlled dormitory access, campus safety office.

Student services: health clinic, personal/psychological counseling.

COSTS & FINANCIAL AID

Costs (2019–20) ***One-time required fee:*** $360. ***Comprehensive fee:*** $57,210 includes full-time tuition ($38,950), mandatory fees ($1920), and room and board ($16,340). Full-time tuition and fees vary according to class time, course load, location, and program. Part-time tuition: $1298 per credit. Part-time tuition and fees vary according to class time, course load, location, and program. ***Required fees:*** $440 per year part-time. ***College room only:*** $8780. Room and board charges vary according to board plan and housing facility.

Financial Aid Of all full-time matriculated undergraduates who enrolled in 2017, 1,632 applied for aid, 1,586 were judged to have need, 185 had their need fully met. 923 Federal Work-Study jobs (averaging $2338). In 2017, 379 non-need-based awards were made. ***Average percent of need met:*** 69. ***Average financial aid package:*** $28,668. ***Average need-based loan:*** $4394. ***Average need-based gift aid:*** $24,285. ***Average non-need-based aid:*** $16,232. ***Average indebtedness upon graduation:*** $45,947.

APPLYING

Standardized Tests *Required for some:* SAT or ACT (for admission), TOEFL for international applicants whose native language is not English.

Options: electronic application, early admission, early action, deferred entrance.

Application fee: $50.

Required: essay or personal statement, high school transcript, minimum 2.0 GPA, 1 letter of recommendation, Common Application Supplement and Program for Advancement of Learning (PAL), Cognitive and Achievement Testing for PAL. ***Required for some:*** interview.

CONTACT

Mr. Keith Robichaud, Associate Vice President and Dean of Admission, Curry College, 1071 Blue Hill Avenue, Milton, MA 02186. *Phone:* 617-333-2210. *Toll-free phone:* 800-669-0686. *Fax:* 617-333-2114. *E-mail:* curryadm@curry.edu.

Dean College

Franklin, Massachusetts

http://www.dean.edu/

- **Independent** 4-year, founded 1865
- **Suburban** 100-acre campus with easy access to Boston, MA and Providence, RI
- **Endowment** $48.6 million
- **Coed** 1,320 undergraduate students, 90% full-time, 52% women, 48% men
- **Moderately difficult** entrance level, 69% of applicants were admitted

UNDERGRAD STUDENTS

1,184 full-time, 136 part-time. Students come from 37 states and territories; 14 other countries; 46% are from out of state; 14% Black or African American, non-Hispanic/Latino; 9% Hispanic/Latino; 2% Asian, non-Hispanic/Latino; 0.2% Native Hawaiian or other Pacific Islander, non-Hispanic/Latino; 0.3% American Indian or Alaska Native, non-Hispanic/Latino; 4% Two or more races, non-Hispanic/Latino; 9% Race/ethnicity unknown; 4% international; 3% transferred in; 88% live on campus.

Freshmen:

Admission: 6,241 applied, 4,293 admitted, 442 enrolled. ***Average high school GPA:*** 2.8. ***Test scores:*** SAT evidence-based reading and writing scores over 500: 58%; SAT math scores over 500: 53%; ACT scores over 18: 58%; SAT evidence-based reading and writing scores over 600: 17%; SAT math scores over 600: 8%; ACT scores over 24: 20%; SAT evidence-based reading and writing scores over 700: 1%; ACT scores over 30: 8%.

Retention: 70% of full-time freshmen returned.

FACULTY

Total: 150, 21% full-time, 41% with terminal degrees.

Student/faculty ratio: 17:1.

ACADEMICS

Calendar: semesters. *Degrees:* certificates, associate, and bachelor's.

Special study options: accelerated degree program, adult/continuing education programs, advanced placement credit, distance learning, double majors, honors programs, independent study, internships, off-campus study, part-time degree program, services for LD students, student-designed majors, study abroad, summer session for credit.

Computers: 36 computers/terminals are available on campus for general student use. Students can access the following: campus intranet, computer help desk, free student e-mail accounts, online (class) grades, online (class) registration, online (class) schedules, Wireless network. Campuswide network is available. Wireless service is available via entire campus.

Library: E. Ross Anderson Library. *Books:* 31,727 (physical), 60,278 (digital/electronic); *Databases:* 53. Weekly public service hours: 77; study areas open 24 hours, 5–7 days a week.

STUDENT LIFE

Housing options: on-campus residence required through senior year; coed, men-only, women-only. Campus housing is university owned. Freshman campus housing is guaranteed.

Activities and organizations: drama/theater group, student-run newspaper, radio and television station, choral group, National Society of Leadership and Success, Student Activities Committee, Residence Hall Association, International Student Association, Dean Community Outreach.

Athletics Member NCAA. All Division III. ***Intercollegiate sports:*** baseball M, basketball M/W, cross-country running M/W, field hockey W, football M, golf M/W, lacrosse M/W, soccer M/W, softball W, volleyball M/W. ***Intramural sports:*** badminton M/W, basketball M/W, rock climbing M/W, sand volleyball M/W, soccer M/W, softball M/W, table tennis M/W, volleyball M/W.

Campus security: 24-hour emergency response devices and patrols, student patrols, late-night transport/escort service, controlled dormitory access.

Student services: health clinic, personal/psychological counseling.

COSTS & FINANCIAL AID

Costs (2020–21) ***One-time required fee:*** $300. ***Comprehensive fee:*** $58,966 includes full-time tuition ($41,118), mandatory fees ($200), and room and board ($17,648). Full-time tuition and fees vary according to class time and course load. Part-time tuition: $365 per credit hour. Part-time tuition and fees vary according to class time and course load. ***Required fees:*** $25 per term part-time. ***Room and board:*** Room and board charges vary according to housing facility. ***Payment plan:*** installment. ***Waivers:*** employees or children of employees.

Financial Aid Of all full-time matriculated undergraduates who enrolled in 2019, 993 applied for aid, 921 were judged to have need, 135 had their need fully met. In 2019, 263 non-need-based awards were made. ***Average percent of need met:*** 69. ***Average financial aid package:*** $31,567. ***Average need-based loan:*** $3393. ***Average need-based gift aid:*** $27,872. ***Average non-need-based aid:*** $19,314.

APPLYING

Options: electronic application, early admission, early action, deferred entrance.

Required: high school transcript. ***Required for some:*** students applying to a performing arts major must complete an audition or portfolio review, students applying to the Arch Learning Community are required to interview. ***Recommended:*** essay or personal statement, minimum 2.0 GPA, 1 letter of recommendation, interview.

Application deadlines: rolling (freshmen), rolling (transfers), 12/1 (early action).

Notification: continuous (freshmen), 1/15 (early action).

CONTACT

Ms. Iris P. Godes, Associate Vice President of Enrollment/Dean of Admissions, Dean College, 99 Main Street, Franklin, MA 02038. *Phone:* 508-541-1508. *Toll-free phone:* 877-TRY-DEAN. *Fax:* 508-541-8726. *E-mail:* igodes@dean.edu.

See below for display ad and page 1052 for the College Close-Up.

Eastern Nazarene College

Quincy, Massachusetts

http://www.enc.edu/

CONTACT

Ms. Ashley Rudeen, Assistant Director of Admission/International DSO, Eastern Nazarene College, 23 East Elm Avenue, Quincy, MA 02170. *Phone:* 617-745-3861. *Toll-free phone:* 800-88-ENC88. *Fax:* 617-745-3992. *E-mail:* ashley.rudeen@enc.edu.

Elms College

Chicopee, Massachusetts

http://www.elms.edu/

- **Independent Roman Catholic** comprehensive, founded 1928
- **Suburban** 32-acre campus
- **Endowment** $13.2 million
- **Coed** 1,123 undergraduate students, 89% full-time, 76% women, 24% men
- **Moderately difficult** entrance level, 75% of applicants were admitted

UNDERGRAD STUDENTS

997 full-time, 126 part-time. Students come from 27 states and territories; 11 other countries; 28% are from out of state; 8% Black or African American, non-Hispanic/Latino; 14% Hispanic/Latino; 2% Asian, non-Hispanic/Latino; 0.1% Native Hawaiian or other Pacific Islander, non-Hispanic/Latino; 0.3% American Indian or Alaska Native, non-Hispanic/Latino; 2% Two or more races, non-Hispanic/Latino; 23% Race/ethnicity unknown; 0.5% international; 23% transferred in; 32% live on campus.

Freshmen:

Admission: 875 applied, 657 admitted, 180 enrolled. ***Average high school GPA:*** 3.5. ***Test scores:*** SAT evidence-based reading and writing scores over 500: 74%; SAT math scores over 500: 66%; ACT scores over 18: 86%; SAT evidence-based reading and writing scores over 600: 20%; SAT math scores over 600: 12%; ACT scores over 24: 29%; SAT math scores over 700: 1%.

Retention: 82% of full-time freshmen returned.

FACULTY
Total: 200, 31% full-time, 64% with terminal degrees.
Student/faculty ratio: 11:1.

ACADEMICS
Calendar: semesters. *Degrees:* certificates, associate, bachelor's, master's, doctoral, post-master's, and postbachelor's certificates.

Special study options: accelerated degree program, adult/continuing education programs, advanced placement credit, cooperative education, distance learning, double majors, English as a second language, honors programs, independent study, internships, off-campus study, part-time degree program, services for LD students, study abroad, summer session for credit. ***ROTC:*** Army (c), Air Force (c).

Computers: 175 computers/terminals are available on campus for general student use. Students can access the following: computer help desk, free student e-mail accounts, online (class) grades, online (class) registration, online (class) schedules. Campuswide network is available. 100% of college-owned or -operated housing units are wired for high-speed Internet access. Wireless service is available via entire campus.
Library: Alumnae Library plus 1 other. *Books:* 30,603 (physical), 293,001 (digital/electronic); *Serial titles:* 150 (physical), 163,547 (digital/electronic); *Databases:* 141. Students can reserve study rooms.

STUDENT LIFE
Housing options: coed. Campus housing is university owned. Freshman campus housing is guaranteed.

Activities and organizations: choral group.

Athletics Member NCAA. All Division III. ***Intercollegiate sports:*** baseball M, basketball M/W, cross-country running M/W, field hockey W, golf M, lacrosse W, soccer M/W, softball W, swimming and diving M/W, track and field M/W, volleyball M/W. ***Intramural sports:*** basketball M/W, cross-country running M/W, field hockey W, lacrosse W, soccer M/W, softball W, swimming and diving M/W, volleyball M/W, weight lifting W.

Campus security: 24-hour emergency response devices and patrols, controlled dormitory access.

Student services: health clinic, personal/psychological counseling.

COSTS & FINANCIAL AID
Costs (2020–21) ***Comprehensive fee:*** $52,401 includes full-time tuition ($36,596), mandatory fees ($1795), and room and board ($14,010). Part-time tuition: $742 per credit hour. Part-time tuition and fees vary according to location and program. ***Room and board:*** Room and board charges vary according to board plan. ***Payment plan:*** installment. ***Waivers:*** senior citizens and employees or children of employees.

Financial Aid Of all full-time matriculated undergraduates who enrolled in 2019, 926 applied for aid, 874 were judged to have need, 61 had their need fully met. 121 Federal Work-Study jobs (averaging $1123). In 2019, 52 non-need-based awards were made. ***Average percent of need met:*** 61. ***Average financial aid package:*** $22,908. ***Average need-based loan:*** $4580. ***Average need-based gift aid:*** $19,543. ***Average non-need-based aid:*** $16,182. ***Average indebtedness upon graduation:*** $49,156.

APPLYING
Options: early admission, deferred entrance.

Required: essay or personal statement, high school transcript, 2 letters of recommendation. ***Recommended:*** interview.

Application deadlines: rolling (freshmen), rolling (transfers).

Notification: continuous (freshmen), continuous (transfers).

CONTACT
Jenna Stolarik, Director of Admissions, Elms College, Chicopee, MA 01013-2839. *Phone:* 413-592-3189. *Toll-free phone:* 800-255-ELMS. *Fax:* 413-594-2781. *E-mail:* admissions@elms.edu.

Emerson College

Boston, Massachusetts

http://www.emerson.edu/

- **Independent** comprehensive, founded 1880
- **Urban** campus with easy access to Boston, MA
- **Endowment** $171.6 million
- **Coed**
- **Very difficult** entrance level

FACULTY
Student/faculty ratio: 13:1.

ACADEMICS
Calendar: semesters. *Degrees:* certificates, bachelor's, master's, and doctoral.
Library: Iwasaki Library plus 1 other. *Books:* 336,669 (physical), 2,484 (digital/electronic); *Serial titles:* 67,760 (digital/electronic); *Databases:* 125. Weekly public service hours: 93; students can reserve study rooms.

STUDENT LIFE
Housing options: on-campus residence required through junior year; coed. Campus housing is university owned. Freshman campus housing is guaranteed.

Activities and organizations: drama/theater group, student-run newspaper, radio and television station, choral group, EIV (Emerson Independent Video), National Broadcasting Society (student chapter), SPEC (Screenwriting), Entertainment Monthly (entertainment news), Emerson International (international student group), national fraternities, national sororities.

Athletics Member NCAA. All Division III.

Campus security: 24-hour emergency response devices and patrols, late-night transport/escort service, controlled dormitory access.

Student services: health clinic, personal/psychological counseling.

COSTS & FINANCIAL AID
Costs (2019–20) ***Comprehensive fee:*** $67,128 includes full-time tuition ($47,856), mandatory fees ($872), and room and board ($18,400).

Financial Aid Of all full-time matriculated undergraduates who enrolled in 2018, 2,428 applied for aid, 2,050 were judged to have need, 161 had their need fully met. In 2018, 593 non-need-based awards were made. ***Average percent of need met:*** 49. ***Average financial aid package:*** $23,479. ***Average need-based loan:*** $4551. ***Average need-based gift aid:*** $20,114. ***Average non-need-based aid:*** $13,850. ***Average indebtedness upon graduation:*** $23,653. ***Financial aid deadline:*** 2/1.

APPLYING
Options: electronic application, early admission, early action, deferred entrance.

Application fee: $65.

Required: essay or personal statement, high school transcript, 1 letter of recommendation. ***Required for some:*** interview.

CONTACT
Mr. Michael Lynch, Director of Undergraduate Admission, Emerson College, 120 Boylston Street, Boston, MA 02116-4624. *Phone:* 617-824-8600. *Fax:* 617-824-8609. *E-mail:* admission@emerson.edu.

See below for display ad and page 1058 for the College Close-Up.

Emmanuel College

Boston, Massachusetts

http://www.emmanuel.edu/

- **Independent Roman Catholic** comprehensive, founded 1919
- **Urban** 17-acre campus
- **Endowment** $151.7 million
- **Coed** 2,112 undergraduate students, 92% full-time, 76% women, 24% men
- 78% of applicants were admitted

UNDERGRAD STUDENTS
1,953 full-time, 159 part-time. Students come from 39 states and territories; 42 other countries; 40% are from out of state; 7% Black or African American, non-Hispanic/Latino; 11% Hispanic/Latino; 5% Asian,

non-Hispanic/Latino; 0.1% Native Hawaiian or other Pacific Islander, non-Hispanic/Latino; 0.2% American Indian or Alaska Native, non-Hispanic/Latino; 3% Two or more races, non-Hispanic/Latino; 4% Race/ethnicity unknown; 1% international; 3% transferred in; 74% live on campus.

Freshmen:
Admission: 5,832 applied, 4,557 admitted, 582 enrolled. ***Average high school GPA:*** 3.7. ***Test scores:*** SAT evidence-based reading and writing scores over 500: 93%; SAT math scores over 500: 92%; ACT scores over 18: 98%; SAT evidence-based reading and writing scores over 600: 53%; SAT math scores over 600: 37%; ACT scores over 24: 56%; SAT evidence-based reading and writing scores over 700: 5%; SAT math scores over 700: 4%; ACT scores over 30: 12%.

Retention: 79% of full-time freshmen returned.

FACULTY
Total: 205, 49% full-time, 66% with terminal degrees.

Student/faculty ratio: 13:1.

ACADEMICS
Calendar: semesters. *Degrees:* bachelor's, master's, post-master's, and postbachelor's certificates.

Special study options: advanced placement credit, distance learning, double majors, honors programs, independent study, internships, off-campus study, part-time degree program, services for LD students, student-designed majors, study abroad, summer session for credit. ***ROTC:*** Army (c).

Computers: 284 computers/terminals are available on campus for general student use. Students can access the following: campus intranet, computer help desk, free student e-mail accounts, online (class) registration, online (class) schedules, Online learning management system (Canvas). Online Office productivity tools (Office 365). Campuswide network is available. 100% of college-owned or -operated housing units are wired for high-speed Internet access. Wireless service is available via entire campus.
Library: Cardinal Cushing Library/Learning Commons. *Books:* 63,625 (physical), 265,865 (digital/electronic); *Serial titles:* 70 (physical), 83,504 (digital/electronic); *Databases:* 61. Weekly public service hours: 108; students can reserve study rooms.

STUDENT LIFE
Housing options: coed. Campus housing is university owned. Freshman campus housing is guaranteed.

Activities and organizations: drama/theater group, student-run newspaper, choral group, Student Government Association, Biology Club, Black Student Union, HUELLAS (LatinX Society), Emmanuel College Community Outreach.

Athletics Member NCAA. All Division III. ***Intercollegiate sports:*** basketball M/W, cross-country running M/W, golf M, lacrosse M/W, soccer M/W, softball W, track and field M/W, volleyball M/W. ***Intramural sports:*** baseball M(c), field hockey M(c)/W(c), table tennis M(c)/W(c), tennis M(c)/W(c), ultimate Frisbee M(c)/W(c).

Campus security: 24-hour emergency response devices and patrols, student patrols, late-night transport/escort service, controlled dormitory access.

Student services: health clinic, personal/psychological counseling.

COSTS & FINANCIAL AID
Costs (2020–21) ***One-time required fee:*** $350. ***Comprehensive fee:*** $58,362 includes full-time tuition ($42,096), mandatory fees ($420), and room and board ($15,846). Full-time tuition and fees vary according to course load. Part-time tuition: $1316 per credit hour. Part-time tuition and fees vary according to course load. ***Room and board:*** Room and board charges vary according to board plan and housing facility. ***Payment plan:*** installment. ***Waivers:*** employees or children of employees.

Financial Aid Of all full-time matriculated undergraduates who enrolled in 2018, 1,695 applied for aid, 1,563 were judged to have need, 625 had their need fully met. 456 Federal Work-Study jobs (averaging $2005). In 2018, 388 non-need-based awards were made. ***Average percent of need met:*** 74. ***Average financial aid package:*** $30,737. ***Average need-based loan:*** $4438. ***Average need-based gift aid:*** $26,831. ***Average non-need-based aid:*** $23,488.

APPLYING

Options: electronic application, early admission, early action, deferred entrance.

Application fee: $60.

Required: essay or personal statement, high school transcript, 2 letters of recommendation. ***Recommended:*** interview.

Application deadlines: 2/15 (freshmen), 4/1 (transfers), 11/1 (early action).

Notification: continuous until 1/15 (freshmen), 5/1 (transfers), 12/15 (early action).

CONTACT

Ms. Sandra Robbins, Dean for Enrollment, Emmanuel College, Admission Office, 400 The Fenway, Boston, MA 02115. *Phone:* 617-735-9715. *Fax:* 617-735-9801. *E-mail:* enroll@emmanuel.edu.

Endicott College

Beverly, Massachusetts

http://www.endicott.edu/

- **Independent** comprehensive, founded 1939
- **Suburban** 235-acre campus with easy access to Boston
- **Endowment** $95.7 million
- **Coed** 3,322 undergraduate students, 92% full-time, 62% women, 38% men
- **Moderately difficult** entrance level, 69% of applicants were admitted

UNDERGRAD STUDENTS

3,063 full-time, 259 part-time. Students come from 30 states and territories; 38 other countries; 52% are from out of state; 2% Black or African American, non-Hispanic/Latino; 4% Hispanic/Latino; 2% Asian, non-Hispanic/Latino; 0.1% American Indian or Alaska Native, non-Hispanic/Latino; 3% Two or more races, non-Hispanic/Latino; 7% Race/ethnicity unknown; 2% international; 2% transferred in; 93% live on campus.

Freshmen:

Admission: 5,031 applied, 3,487 admitted, 842 enrolled. ***Average high school GPA:*** 3.5. ***Test scores:*** SAT evidence-based reading and writing scores over 500: 95%; SAT math scores over 500: 94%; ACT scores over 18: 95%; SAT evidence-based reading and writing scores over 600: 47%; SAT math scores over 600: 36%; ACT scores over 24: 38%; SAT evidence-based reading and writing scores over 700: 6%; SAT math scores over 700: 3%; ACT scores over 30: 2%.

Retention: 86% of full-time freshmen returned.

FACULTY

Total: 590, 19% full-time, 40% with terminal degrees.

Student/faculty ratio: 13:1.

ACADEMICS

Calendar: semesters. *Degrees:* certificates, associate, bachelor's, master's, doctoral, post-master's, and postbachelor's certificates.

Special study options: accelerated degree program, adult/continuing education programs, advanced placement credit, cooperative education, distance learning, double majors, English as a second language, honors programs, independent study, internships, off-campus study, part-time degree program, services for LD students, student-designed majors, study abroad, summer session for credit. ***ROTC:*** Army (c).

Computers: 350 computers/terminals are available on campus for general student use. Students can access the following: campus intranet, computer help desk, free student e-mail accounts, online (class) grades, online (class) registration, online (class) schedules. Campuswide network is available. 100% of college-owned or -operated housing units are wired for high-speed Internet access. Wireless service is available via entire campus.

Library: Diane M. Halle Library. *Books:* 112,262 (physical), 189,985 (digital/electronic); *Serial titles:* 26 (physical), 145,447 (digital/electronic); *Databases:* 152. Weekly public service hours: 97; students can reserve study rooms.

STUDENT LIFE

Housing options: coed, women-only, special housing for students with disabilities. Campus housing is university owned. Freshman campus housing is guaranteed.

Activities and organizations: drama/theater group, student-run newspaper, radio and television station, choral group.

Athletics Member NCAA. All Division III. ***Intercollegiate sports:*** baseball M, basketball M/W, cheerleading W(c), crew M(c)/W(c), cross-country running M/W, equestrian sports M/W, field hockey W, football M, golf M, ice hockey M/W, lacrosse M/W, rowing M(c)/W(c), rugby M(c)/W(c), soccer M/W, softball W, tennis M/W, track and field W, volleyball M/W. ***Intramural sports:*** basketball M/W, football M/W, ice hockey M/W, soccer M/W, softball M/W, ultimate Frisbee M/W, volleyball M/W.

Campus security: 24-hour emergency response devices and patrols, student patrols, late-night transport/escort service, controlled dormitory access, crime prevention programs, rape awareness defense, property identification, front gate.

Student services: health clinic, personal/psychological counseling, veterans affairs office.

COSTS & FINANCIAL AID

Costs (2020–21) ***Comprehensive fee:*** $51,450 includes full-time tuition ($34,470), mandatory fees ($850), and room and board ($16,130). Full-time tuition and fees vary according to location. Part-time tuition: $1060 per credit hour. Part-time tuition and fees vary according to location. ***College room only:*** $11,118. Room and board charges vary according to board plan and housing facility. ***Payment plans:*** tuition prepayment, installment. ***Waivers:*** employees or children of employees.

Financial Aid Of all full-time matriculated undergraduates who enrolled in 2019, 2,296 applied for aid, 1,850 were judged to have need, 202 had their need fully met. 796 state and other part-time jobs (averaging $2000). In 2019, 837 non-need-based awards were made. ***Average percent of need met:*** 65. ***Average financial aid package:*** $22,560. ***Average need-based loan:*** $4459. ***Average need-based gift aid:*** $17,391. ***Average non-need-based aid:*** $10,823. ***Average indebtedness upon graduation:*** $44,178.

APPLYING

Standardized Tests *Required for some:* SAT or ACT (for admission).

Options: electronic application, early admission, early decision, early action, deferred entrance.

Application fee: $50.

Required: essay or personal statement, high school transcript, minimum 2.5 GPA, 1 letter of recommendation. ***Recommended:*** interview.

Application deadlines: 2/15 (freshmen), 3/15 (transfers), 11/1 (early action).

Early decision deadline: 11/1.

Notification: continuous (freshmen), continuous (transfers), 12/15 (early decision), 1/15 (early action).

CONTACT

Mr. Evan Lipp, Vice President of Admission and Financial Aid, Endicott College, 376 Hale Street, Beverly, MA 01915. *Phone:* 978-232-2005. *Toll-free phone:* 800-325-1114. *Fax:* 978-232-2520. *E-mail:* admissio@endicott.edu.

Fisher College

Boston, Massachusetts

http://www.fisher.edu/

- **Independent** comprehensive, founded 1903
- **Urban** 1-acre campus with easy access to Boston
- **Endowment** $34.0 million
- **Coed** 1,551 undergraduate students, 42% full-time, 72% women, 28% men
- 69% of applicants were admitted

UNDERGRAD STUDENTS

648 full-time, 903 part-time. 33% are from out of state; 12% Black or African American, non-Hispanic/Latino; 13% Hispanic/Latino; 1% Asian, non-Hispanic/Latino; 0.4% American Indian or Alaska Native, non-Hispanic/Latino; 3% Two or more races, non-Hispanic/Latino; 33% Race/ethnicity unknown; 11% international; 6% transferred in; 52% live on campus.

Freshmen:

Admission: 2,068 applied, 1,433 admitted, 157 enrolled. ***Average high school GPA:*** 2.6. ***Test scores:*** SAT evidence-based reading and writing

scores over 500: 33%; SAT math scores over 500: 33%; ACT scores over 18: 50%; SAT evidence-based reading and writing scores over 600: 6%; SAT math scores over 600: 5%; ACT scores over 24: 25%; SAT evidence-based reading and writing scores over 700: 1%; SAT math scores over 700: 1%.

Retention: 62% of full-time freshmen returned.

FACULTY
Total: 141, 26% full-time, 43% with terminal degrees.

Student/faculty ratio: 14:1.

ACADEMICS
Calendar: semesters. *Degrees:* certificates, associate, bachelor's, and master's.

Special study options: academic remediation for entering students, accelerated degree program, adult/continuing education programs, advanced placement credit, distance learning, English as a second language, honors programs, independent study, internships, off-campus study, part-time degree program, services for LD students, study abroad, summer session for credit. ***ROTC:*** Army (c).

Computers: 208 computers/terminals are available on campus for general student use. Students can access the following: campus intranet, computer help desk, free student e-mail accounts, online (class) grades, online (class) registration, online (class) schedules. Campuswide network is available. 100% of college-owned or -operated housing units are wired for high-speed Internet access. Wireless service is available via entire campus.

Library: Fisher College Library. *Books:* 23,902 (physical), 105,119 (digital/electronic); *Serial titles:* 40 (physical); *Databases:* 104. Weekly public service hours: 72; study areas open 24 hours, 5–7 days a week; students can reserve study rooms.

STUDENT LIFE
Housing options: coed, women-only. Campus housing is university owned.

Activities and organizations: drama/theater group, choral group, National Society of Leadership and Success (NSLS), Psychology Club, Criminal Justice Club, Fashion Club, Multi-Cultural Club.

Athletics Member NAIA. ***Intercollegiate sports:*** baseball M, basketball M/W, soccer M/W, softball W.

Campus security: 24-hour emergency response devices and patrols, student patrols, controlled dormitory access.

Student services: health clinic, personal/psychological counseling, women's center.

COSTS & FINANCIAL AID
Costs (2020–21) ***Comprehensive fee:*** $49,269 includes full-time tuition ($31,700), mandatory fees ($1000), and room and board ($16,569). Part-time tuition: $1057 per course. Part-time tuition and fees vary according to class time and course load. ***Room and board:*** Room and board charges vary according to housing facility. ***Payment plan:*** installment. ***Waivers:*** employees or children of employees.

Financial Aid Of all full-time matriculated undergraduates who enrolled in 2019, 518 applied for aid, 471 were judged to have need. In 2019, 128 non-need-based awards were made. ***Average financial aid package:*** $27,992. ***Average need-based loan:*** $3964. ***Average need-based gift aid:*** $11,621. ***Average non-need-based aid:*** $11,451. ***Average indebtedness upon graduation:*** $32,551. ***Financial aid deadline:*** 3/15.

APPLYING
Standardized Tests *Required for some:* SAT or ACT (for admission).

Options: electronic application, deferred entrance.

Application fee: $50.

Required: high school transcript. ***Required for some:*** essay or personal statement, interview. ***Recommended:*** minimum 2.0 GPA.

CONTACT
Mr. Robert Melaragni, Vice President of Enrollment Management, Fisher College, Boston, MA 02116. *Phone:* 617-236-8818. *Fax:* 617-236-5473. *E-mail:* admissions@fisher.edu.

Fitchburg State University

Fitchburg, Massachusetts

http://www.fitchburgstate.edu/

- **State-supported** comprehensive, founded 1894, part of Massachusetts Public Higher Education System
- **Suburban** 78-acre campus with easy access to Boston
- **Endowment** $19.9 million
- **Coed** 4,044 undergraduate students, 78% full-time, 53% women, 47% men
- **Minimally difficult** entrance level, 88% of applicants were admitted

UNDERGRAD STUDENTS
3,164 full-time, 880 part-time. Students come from 36 states and territories; 8 other countries; 8% are from out of state; 11% Black or African American, non-Hispanic/Latino; 13% Hispanic/Latino; 3% Asian, non-Hispanic/Latino; 0.1% American Indian or Alaska Native, non-Hispanic/Latino; 4% Two or more races, non-Hispanic/Latino; 0.6% Race/ethnicity unknown; 0.6% international; 8% transferred in; 36% live on campus.

Freshmen:
Admission: 2,902 applied, 2,564 admitted, 674 enrolled. ***Average high school GPA:*** 3.0. ***Test scores:*** SAT evidence-based reading and writing scores over 500: 73%; SAT math scores over 500: 75%; ACT scores over 18: 96%; SAT evidence-based reading and writing scores over 600: 19%; SAT math scores over 600: 16%; ACT scores over 24: 38%; SAT evidence-based reading and writing scores over 700: 1%; SAT math scores over 700: 3%; ACT scores over 30: 4%.

Retention: 74% of full-time freshmen returned.

FACULTY
Total: 336, 61% full-time.

Student/faculty ratio: 13:1.

ACADEMICS
Calendar: semesters. *Degrees:* certificates, bachelor's, master's, post-master's, and postbachelor's certificates.

Special study options: academic remediation for entering students, accelerated degree program, adult/continuing education programs, advanced placement credit, distance learning, double majors, honors programs, independent study, internships, off-campus study, part-time degree program, services for LD students, student-designed majors, study abroad, summer session for credit. ***ROTC:*** Army (b).

Computers: 261 computers/terminals are available on campus for general student use. Students can access the following: campus intranet, computer help desk, free student e-mail accounts, online (class) grades, online (class) registration, online (class) schedules. Campuswide network is available. 100% of college-owned or -operated housing units are wired for high-speed Internet access. Wireless service is available via entire campus.

Library: Amelia V. Galucci-Cirio Library. *Books:* 182,715 (physical), 219,732 (digital/electronic); *Serial titles:* 1,393 (physical), 109,220 (digital/electronic); *Databases:* 168. Weekly public service hours: 91; students can reserve study rooms.

STUDENT LIFE
Housing options: coed, special housing for students with disabilities. Campus housing is university owned. Freshman campus housing is guaranteed.

Activities and organizations: drama/theater group, student-run newspaper, radio station, choral group, Student Government Association, Dance Club, Activities Board, Greek Council, MASSPIRG, national fraternities, national sororities.

Athletics Member NCAA. All Division III. ***Intercollegiate sports:*** baseball M, basketball M/W, cross-country running M/W, field hockey W, football M, ice hockey M, lacrosse W, soccer M/W, softball W, track and field M/W. ***Intramural sports:*** basketball M/W, cheerleading W(c), racquetball M/W, sand volleyball M/W, soccer M/W, softball M/W, ultimate Frisbee M/W, volleyball M/W, water polo M/W.

Campus security: 24-hour emergency response devices and patrols, student patrols, late-night transport/escort service, controlled dormitory access.

Student services: health clinic, personal/psychological counseling.

COSTS & FINANCIAL AID
Costs (2019–20) ***One-time required fee:*** $50. ***Tuition:*** state resident $970 full-time, $40 per credit part-time; nonresident $7050 full-time, $294 per credit part-time. Full-time tuition and fees vary according to class time and reciprocity agreements. Part-time tuition and fees vary according to class time and reciprocity agreements. ***Required fees:*** $9535 full-time, $397 per credit part-time. ***Room and board:*** $11,261; room only: $7731. Room and board charges vary according to board plan and housing facility. ***Payment plan:*** installment. ***Waivers:*** senior citizens and employees or children of employees.

Financial Aid Of all full-time matriculated undergraduates who enrolled in 2018, 2,879 applied for aid, 2,312 were judged to have need. 182 Federal Work-Study jobs (averaging $1639). In 2018, 177 non-need-based awards were made. ***Average percent of need met:*** 75. ***Average financial aid package:*** $10,072. ***Average need-based loan:*** $4550. ***Average need-based gift aid:*** $7110. ***Average non-need-based aid:*** $1427. ***Average indebtedness upon graduation:*** $26,543.

APPLYING
Standardized Tests *Required for some:* SAT or ACT (for admission).

Options: electronic application, deferred entrance.

Application fee: $50.

Required: essay or personal statement, high school transcript, minimum 2.0 GPA, 17 core courses.

Application deadlines: rolling (freshmen), rolling (transfers).

Notification: continuous (freshmen), continuous (transfers).

CONTACT
Ms. Jinawa McNeil, Director of Admissions, Fitchburg State University, 160 Pearl Street, Fitchburg, MA 01420-2697. *Phone:* 978-665-3140. *Toll-free phone:* 800-705-9692. *Fax:* 978-665-4540. *E-mail:* admissions@fitchburgstate.edu.

Framingham State University

Framingham, Massachusetts

http://www.framingham.edu/

- **State-supported** comprehensive, founded 1839, part of Massachusetts Public Higher Education System
- **Suburban** 77-acre campus with easy access to Boston
- **Endowment** $45.6 million
- **Coed** 3,857 undergraduate students, 88% full-time, 56% women, 44% men
- **Moderately difficult** entrance level, 74% of applicants were admitted

UNDERGRAD STUDENTS
3,376 full-time, 481 part-time. Students come from 30 states and territories; 12 other countries; 5% are from out of state; 14% Black or African American, non-Hispanic/Latino; 17% Hispanic/Latino; 3% Asian, non-Hispanic/Latino; 0.1% American Indian or Alaska Native, non-Hispanic/Latino; 4% Two or more races, non-Hispanic/Latino; 2% Race/ethnicity unknown; 0.4% international; 10% transferred in; 47% live on campus.

Freshmen:
Admission: 5,942 applied, 4,417 admitted, 776 enrolled. ***Average high school GPA:*** 3.1. ***Test scores:*** SAT evidence-based reading and writing scores over 500: 68%; SAT math scores over 500: 69%; ACT scores over 18: 95%; SAT evidence-based reading and writing scores over 600: 18%; SAT math scores over 600: 13%; ACT scores over 24: 65%; SAT evidence-based reading and writing scores over 700: 2%; SAT math scores over 700: 2%; ACT scores over 30: 5%.

Retention: 74% of full-time freshmen returned.

FACULTY
Total: 325, 61% full-time, 74% with terminal degrees.

Student/faculty ratio: 13:1.

ACADEMICS
Calendar: semesters. *Degrees:* bachelor's, master's, and postbachelor's certificates.

Special study options: advanced placement credit, cooperative education, distance learning, double majors, English as a second language, honors programs, independent study, internships, off-campus study, part-time degree program, services for LD students, student-designed majors, study abroad, summer session for credit.

Computers: 216 computers/terminals and 3,500 ports are available on campus for general student use. Students can access the following: campus intranet, computer help desk, free student e-mail accounts, online (class) grades, online (class) registration, online (class) schedules. Campuswide network is available. 100% of college-owned or -operated housing units are wired for high-speed Internet access. Wireless service is available via entire campus.

Library: Henry Whittemore Library. *Books:* 151,567 (physical), 11 (digital/electronic); *Serial titles:* 90 (physical); *Databases:* 51. Weekly public service hours: 99.

STUDENT LIFE
Housing options: coed, women-only, special housing for students with disabilities. Campus housing is university owned. Freshman applicants given priority for college housing.

Activities and organizations: drama/theater group, student-run newspaper, radio station, choral group, Dance Club, Student Union Activities Board, Gatepost (student newspaper), Student Government Association, Hilltop Players (theater group).

Athletics Member NCAA. All Division III. ***Intercollegiate sports:*** baseball M, basketball M/W, cross-country running M/W, field hockey W, football M, ice hockey M, lacrosse W, soccer M/W, softball W, track and field W, volleyball W. ***Intramural sports:*** basketball M/W, cheerleading W(c), football M/W, golf M/W, lacrosse M(c), rugby M(c)/W(c), soccer M/W, volleyball M/W, weight lifting M/W.

Campus security: 24-hour emergency response devices and patrols, student patrols, late-night transport/escort service, controlled dormitory access.

Student services: health clinic, personal/psychological counseling, legal services, veterans affairs office.

COSTS & FINANCIAL AID
Costs (2020–21) ***Tuition:*** state resident $970 full-time, $162 per course part-time; nonresident $7050 full-time, $1175 per course part-time. ***Required fees:*** $10,130 full-time, $1561 per course part-time. ***Room and board:*** $12,604. ***Payment plan:*** tuition prepayment.

Financial Aid Of all full-time matriculated undergraduates who enrolled in 2018, 2,872 applied for aid, 2,351 were judged to have need, 168 had their need fully met. In 2018, 191 non-need-based awards were made. ***Average percent of need met:*** 55. ***Average financial aid package:*** $10,051. ***Average need-based loan:*** $5117. ***Average need-based gift aid:*** $6317. ***Average non-need-based aid:*** $1218. ***Average indebtedness upon graduation:*** $31,465.

APPLYING
Standardized Tests *Required:* SAT or ACT (for admission).

Options: electronic application, early action, deferred entrance.

Application fee: $50.

Required: high school transcript, minimum 2.0 GPA, minimum of 16 college preparatory courses in specified areas. ***Recommended:*** minimum 3.0 GPA.

Application deadlines: 2/15 (freshmen), 11/15 (early action).

Notification: continuous (freshmen), continuous (transfers).

CONTACT
Ms. Shayna Eddy, Associate Dean of Admissions, Framingham State University, 100 State Street, PO Box 9101, Framingham, MA 01701-9101. *Phone:* 508-626-4500. *Fax:* 508-626-4017. *E-mail:* admissions@framingham.edu.

Franklin W. Olin College of Engineering

Needham, Massachusetts

http://www.olin.edu/

- **Independent** 4-year, founded 1997
- **Suburban** 75-acre campus with easy access to Boston
- **Endowment** $384.0 million
- **Coed** 386 undergraduate students, 90% full-time, 53% women, 47% men
- **Most difficult** entrance level, 16% of applicants were admitted

UNDERGRAD STUDENTS
347 full-time, 39 part-time. Students come from 43 states and territories; 10 other countries; 88% are from out of state; 3% Black or African American, non-Hispanic/Latino; 12% Hispanic/Latino; 16% Asian, non-Hispanic/Latino; 9% Two or more races, non-Hispanic/Latino; 6% Race/ethnicity unknown; 8% international; 0.5% transferred in; 100% live on campus.

Freshmen:
Admission: 905 applied, 142 admitted, 85 enrolled. ***Average high school GPA:*** 3.9. ***Test scores:*** SAT evidence-based reading and writing scores over 500: 100%; SAT math scores over 500: 100%; ACT scores over 18: 100%; SAT evidence-based reading and writing scores over 600: 100%; SAT math scores over 600: 100%; ACT scores over 24: 97%; SAT evidence-based reading and writing scores over 700: 79%; SAT math scores over 700: 97%; ACT scores over 30: 92%.

Retention: 99% of full-time freshmen returned.

FACULTY
Total: 58, 72% full-time, 81% with terminal degrees.

Student/faculty ratio: 8:1.

ACADEMICS
Calendar: semesters. *Degree:* bachelor's.

Special study options: independent study, internships, off-campus study, services for LD students, student-designed majors, study abroad.

Computers: 2,364 ports are available on campus for general student use. Students can access the following: campus intranet, computer help desk, free student e-mail accounts, online (class) grades, online (class) registration, online (class) schedules. Campuswide network is available. 100% of college-owned or -operated housing units are wired for high-speed Internet access. Wireless service is available via entire campus.
Library: Franklin W. Olin Library. *Books:* 15,514 (physical), 3.1 million (digital/electronic); *Serial titles:* 20 (physical), 159,148 (digital/electronic); *Databases:* 31. Study areas open 24 hours, 5–7 days a week; students can reserve study rooms.

STUDENT LIFE
Housing options: on-campus residence required through senior year; coed, special housing for students with disabilities. Campus housing is university owned. Freshman campus housing is guaranteed.

Activities and organizations: drama/theater group, student-run newspaper, choral group, Council of Olin Representatives, Stay Late and Create, Support, Encourage and Recognize Volunteerism (SERV), Mini Baja, Olin Fire Arts Club.

Athletics ***Intercollegiate sports:*** soccer M(c)/W(c), ultimate Frisbee M(c)/W(c). ***Intramural sports:*** basketball M/W, softball M/W, volleyball M/W.

Campus security: 24-hour emergency response devices and patrols, controlled dormitory access.

Student services: health clinic, personal/psychological counseling.

COSTS & FINANCIAL AID
Costs (2020–21) ***One-time required fee:*** $2656. ***Comprehensive fee:*** $72,160 includes full-time tuition ($53,990), mandatory fees ($710), and room and board ($17,460). Part-time tuition: $1688 per credit. ***Payment plan:*** installment.

Financial Aid Of all full-time matriculated undergraduates who enrolled in 2019, 196 applied for aid, 166 were judged to have need, 165 had their need fully met. In 2019, 186 non-need-based awards were made. ***Average percent of need met:*** 99. ***Average financial aid package:*** $50,583. ***Average need-based loan:*** $3174. ***Average need-based gift aid:*** $48,901. ***Average non-need-based aid:*** $25,480. ***Average indebtedness upon graduation:*** $13,480.

APPLYING
Standardized Tests *Required:* SAT or ACT (for admission).

Options: electronic application, deferred entrance.

Application fee: $85.

Required: essay or personal statement, high school transcript, 3 letters of recommendation, interview.

Notification: 4/1 (freshmen).

CONTACT
Franklin W. Olin College of Engineering, 1000 Olin Way, Needham, MA 02492-1200. *Phone:* 781-292-2222.

Gordon College

Wenham, Massachusetts

http://www.gordon.edu/

- **Independent nondenominational** comprehensive, founded 1889, part of Private (nonprofit)
- **Suburban** 485-acre campus with easy access to Boston
- **Endowment** $56.8 million
- **Coed** 1,507 undergraduate students, 96% full-time, 62% women, 38% men
- **Moderately difficult** entrance level, 74% of applicants were admitted

UNDERGRAD STUDENTS
1,440 full-time, 67 part-time. Students come from 44 states and territories; 52 other countries; 66% are from out of state; 4% Black or African American, non-Hispanic/Latino; 10% Hispanic/Latino; 4% Asian, non-Hispanic/Latino; 0.3% Native Hawaiian or other Pacific Islander, non-Hispanic/Latino; 3% Two or more races, non Hispanic/Latino; 0.7% Race/ethnicity unknown; 10% international; 2% transferred in; 88% live on campus.

Freshmen:
Admission: 2,624 applied, 1,943 admitted, 358 enrolled. ***Average high school GPA:*** 3.6. ***Test scores:*** SAT evidence-based reading and writing scores over 500: 87%; SAT math scores over 500: 84%; ACT scores over 18: 95%; SAT evidence-based reading and writing scores over 600: 52%; SAT math scores over 600: 40%; ACT scores over 24: 64%; SAT evidence-based reading and writing scores over 700: 11%; SAT math scores over 700: 13%; ACT scores over 30: 26%.

Retention: 83% of full-time freshmen returned.

FACULTY
Total: 251, 34% full-time, 30% with terminal degrees.

Student/faculty ratio: 10:1.

ACADEMICS
Calendar: semesters. *Degrees:* bachelor's and master's.

Special study options: advanced placement credit, cooperative education, double majors, honors programs, independent study, internships, off-campus study, part-time degree program, services for LD students, student-designed majors, study abroad, summer session for credit. ***ROTC:*** Army (c), Air Force (c).

Unusual degree programs: 3-2 engineering with University of Southern California; nursing with Curry College.

Computers: 100 computers/terminals and 10 ports are available on campus for general student use. Students can access the following: campus intranet, computer help desk, free student e-mail accounts, online (class) grades, online (class) registration, online (class) schedules, Rental equipment. Campuswide network is available. 100% of college-owned or -operated housing units are wired for high-speed Internet access. Wireless service is available via entire campus.
Library: Jenks Learning Resource Center. *Books:* 133,328 (physical), 223,065 (digital/electronic); *Serial titles:* 126 (physical). Weekly public service hours: 103; students can reserve study rooms.

STUDENT LIFE
Housing options: on-campus residence required through senior year; coed, men-only, women-only, special housing for students with disabilities. Campus housing is university owned. Freshman campus housing is guaranteed.

Activities and organizations: drama/theater group, student-run newspaper, radio station, choral group, Student Government Association, Student ministries and volunteer programs, Diverse music ensembles, Intramural sports, Short-term missions.

Athletics Member NCAA. All Division III. ***Intercollegiate sports:*** baseball M, basketball M/W, cross-country running M/W, field hockey W, lacrosse M/W, soccer M/W, softball W, swimming and diving M/W, tennis M/W, track and field M/W, volleyball W. ***Intramural sports:*** badminton M/W, basketball M/W, football M/W, golf M, racquetball M/W, rowing M(c)/W(c), soccer M/W, triathlon M/W, volleyball M/W, water polo M/W.

Campus security: 24-hour emergency response devices and patrols, late-night transport/escort service, controlled dormitory access, Gates entrance.

Student services: health clinic, personal/psychological counseling, women's center.

COSTS & FINANCIAL AID

Costs (2020–21) ***Comprehensive fee:*** $50,650 includes full-time tuition ($37,560), mandatory fees ($1670), and room and board ($11,420). Full-time tuition and fees vary according to course load and program. Part-time tuition: $939 per credit hour. Part-time tuition and fees vary according to course load and program. ***College room only:*** $7210. Room and board charges vary according to board plan and housing facility. ***Payment plan:*** installment. ***Waivers:*** employees or children of employees.

Financial Aid Of all full-time matriculated undergraduates who enrolled in 2019, 1,147 applied for aid, 978 were judged to have need, 185 had their need fully met. 592 Federal Work-Study jobs (averaging $422). In 2019, 453 non-need-based awards were made. ***Average percent of need met:*** 73. ***Average financial aid package:*** $27,240. ***Average need-based loan:*** $4149. ***Average need-based gift aid:*** $23,073. ***Average non-need-based aid:*** $17,771. ***Average indebtedness upon graduation:*** $35,210.

APPLYING

Standardized Tests *Required:* SAT or ACT (for admission), TOEFL (in place of SAT/ACT) (for admission).

Options: electronic application, early action, deferred entrance.

Application fee: $50.

Required: essay or personal statement, high school transcript, 1 letter of recommendation, Finance form for international students. ***Recommended:*** minimum 3.0 GPA, interview.

Application deadlines: 8/1 (freshmen), 3/1 (out-of-state freshmen), 11/1 (transfers), 12/1 (early action).

Notification: continuous until 8/15 (freshmen), continuous (out-of-state freshmen), continuous until 11/15 (transfers), 12/15 (early action).

CONTACT

Miss June Bodoni, Associate Vice President for Enrollment, Gordon College, 255 Grapevine Road, Wenham, MA 01984. *Phone:* 978-867-4218. *Toll-free phone:* 866-464-6736. *Fax:* 978-867-4682. *E-mail:* admissions@gordon.edu.

Hampshire College

Amherst, Massachusetts

http://www.hampshire.edu/

- **Independent** 4-year, founded 1965
- **Small-town** 800-acre campus
- **Endowment** $48.5 million
- **Coed** 745 undergraduate students, 100% full-time, 61% women, 39% men
- **Moderately difficult** entrance level, 2% of applicants were admitted

UNDERGRAD STUDENTS

745 full-time. 78% are from out of state; 8% Black or African American, non-Hispanic/Latino; 12% Hispanic/Latino; 3% Asian, non-Hispanic/Latino; 0.1% American Indian or Alaska Native, non-Hispanic/Latino; 5% Two or more races, non-Hispanic/Latino; 6% Race/ethnicity unknown; 6% international; 82% live on campus.

Freshmen:

Admission: 2,485 applied, 49 admitted, 19 enrolled.

Retention: 67% of full-time freshmen returned.

FACULTY

Total: 83, 51% full-time.

Student/faculty ratio: 13:1.

ACADEMICS

Calendar: semesters. *Degree:* bachelor's.

Special study options: advanced placement credit, independent study, internships, off-campus study, services for LD students, student-designed majors, study abroad. ***ROTC:*** Army (c).

Computers: 205 computers/terminals are available on campus for general student use. Students can access the following: campus intranet, computer help desk, free student e-mail accounts, online (class) grades, online (class) registration, online (class) schedules. Campuswide network is available. 100% of college-owned or -operated housing units are wired for high-speed Internet access. Wireless service is available via entire campus.

Library: Harold F. Johnson Library. *Books:* 125,971 (physical), 194,919 (digital/electronic); *Serial titles:* 753 (physical), 37,716 (digital/electronic); *Databases:* 133. Weekly public service hours: 102; study areas open 24 hours, 5–7 days a week; students can reserve study rooms.

STUDENT LIFE

Housing options: on-campus residence required through senior year; coed, men-only, women-only, cooperative, special housing for students with disabilities. Campus housing is university owned. Freshman campus housing is guaranteed.

Activities and organizations: drama/theater group, student-run newspaper, radio station, choral group, Red Scare Frisbee, Queer Community Alliance, Excalibur (fantasy/role playing), Sports Coop, Circus Folks Unite.

Athletics Member USCAA. ***Intercollegiate sports:*** basketball M(c)/W(c), cross-country running M/W, equestrian sports M(c)/W(c), fencing M/W, soccer M/W, ultimate Frisbee M/W. ***Intramural sports:*** basketball M/W, equestrian sports M(c)/W(c), rock climbing M(c)/W(c), soccer M/W, table tennis M(c)/W(c), ultimate Frisbee M/W.

Campus security: 24-hour emergency response devices and patrols.

Student services: health clinic, personal/psychological counseling, women's center.

COSTS & FINANCIAL AID

Costs (2020–21) ***Comprehensive fee:*** $66,188 includes full-time tuition ($50,030), mandatory fees ($2038), and room and board ($14,120). ***College room only:*** $8520.

Financial Aid Of all full-time matriculated undergraduates who enrolled in 2019, 577 applied for aid, 520 were judged to have need, 36 had their need fully met. In 2019, 193 non-need-based awards were made. ***Average percent of need met:*** 82. ***Average financial aid package:*** $41,778. ***Average need-based loan:*** $4114. ***Average need-based gift aid:*** $36,044. ***Average non-need-based aid:*** $12,995. ***Average indebtedness upon graduation:*** $29,499. ***Financial aid deadline:*** 1/15.

APPLYING

Options: electronic application, early admission, early decision, early action, deferred entrance.

Required: essay or personal statement, high school transcript, 1 letter of recommendation. ***Recommended:*** interview.

Application deadlines: 1/15 (freshmen), 3/15 (transfers), 12/1 (early action).

Early decision deadline: 11/15 (for plan 1), 1/1 (for plan 2).

Notification: 4/1 (freshmen), 4/15 (transfers), 12/15 (early decision plan 1), 2/1 (early decision plan 2), 2/15 (early action).

CONTACT

Hampshire College, 893 West Street, Amherst, MA 01002. *Phone:* 413-559-5752. *Toll-free phone:* 877-937-4267. *E-mail:* admissions@hampshire.edu.

Harvard University

Cambridge, Massachusetts

http://www.harvard.edu/

- **Independent** university, founded 1636
- **Urban** 380-acre campus with easy access to Boston
- **Endowment** $40.9 billion
- **Coed** 6,755 undergraduate students, 100% full-time, 49% women, 51% men
- **Most difficult** entrance level, 5% of applicants were admitted

UNDERGRAD STUDENTS

6,740 full-time, 15 part-time. Students come from 56 states and territories; 109 other countries; 84% are from out of state; 9% Black or African American, non-Hispanic/Latino; 11% Hispanic/Latino; 21% Asian, non-Hispanic/Latino; 0.2% American Indian or Alaska Native, non-Hispanic/Latino; 8% Two or more races, non-Hispanic/Latino; 1%

Race/ethnicity unknown; 12% international; 0.2% transferred in; 98% live on campus.

Freshmen:

Admission: 43,330 applied, 2,009 admitted, 1,644 enrolled. ***Average high school GPA:*** 4.2. ***Test scores:*** SAT evidence-based reading and writing scores over 500: 100%; SAT math scores over 500: 100%; ACT scores over 18: 100%; SAT evidence-based reading and writing scores over 600: 99%; SAT math scores over 600: 99%; ACT scores over 24: 100%; SAT evidence-based reading and writing scores over 700: 83%; SAT math scores over 700: 89%; ACT scores over 30: 94%.

Retention: 97% of full-time freshmen returned.

FACULTY

Total: 1,153, 88% full-time, 85% with terminal degrees.

Student/faculty ratio: 6:1.

ACADEMICS

Calendar: semesters. *Degrees:* bachelor's, master's, and doctoral.

Special study options: accelerated degree program, advanced placement credit, double majors, honors programs, independent study, internships, off-campus study, services for LD students, student-designed majors, study abroad, summer session for credit. ***ROTC:*** Army (b), Navy (b), Air Force (b).

Computers: 605 computers/terminals are available on campus for general student use. Students can access the following: computer help desk, free student e-mail accounts, online (class) grades, online (class) registration, online (class) schedules. Campuswide network is available. 100% of college-owned or -operated housing units are wired for high-speed Internet access. Wireless service is available via entire campus.

Library: Widener Library.

STUDENT LIFE

Housing options: on-campus residence required for freshman year; coed, cooperative, special housing for students with disabilities. Campus housing is university owned. Freshman campus housing is guaranteed.

Activities and organizations: drama/theater group, student-run newspaper, radio and television station, choral group, marching band, Phillips Brooks House Association, Asian-American Association, International Relations Council, Harvard Crimson (newspaper), Harvard/Radcliffe Chorus.

Athletics Member NCAA. All Division I except football (Division I-AA). ***Intercollegiate sports:*** baseball M, basketball M/W, crew M/W, cross-country running M/W, fencing M/W, field hockey W, golf M/W(c), ice hockey M/W, lacrosse M/W, rugby W, sailing M/W, skiing (cross-country) M/W, skiing (downhill) M(c)/W, soccer M/W, softball W, squash M/W, swimming and diving M/W, tennis M/W, track and field M/W, volleyball M/W, water polo M/W, wrestling M. ***Intramural sports:*** archery M(c)/W(c), badminton M(c)/W(c), baseball M(c), basketball M/W, bowling M(c)/W(c), cheerleading M(c)/W(c), cross-country running M/W, fencing M/W(c), field hockey W, golf M(c)/W(c), gymnastics M(c)/W(c), ice hockey M/W, lacrosse M(c)/W(c), rugby M(c), skiing (cross-country) M(c)/W(c), skiing (downhill) M(c)/W(c), soccer M/W, squash M/W, swimming and diving M/W, table tennis M/W, tennis M/W, ultimate Frisbee M/W, volleyball M/W, water polo M(c)/W(c), weight lifting M(c)/W(c), wrestling M(c)/W(c).

Campus security: 24-hour emergency response devices and patrols, late-night transport/escort service, controlled dormitory access, required and optional safety courses.

Student services: health clinic, personal/psychological counseling, women's center.

COSTS & FINANCIAL AID

Costs (2019–20) ***Comprehensive fee:*** $69,607 includes full-time tuition ($47,730), mandatory fees ($4195), and room and board ($17,682). ***College room only:*** $10,927. ***Payment plans:*** tuition prepayment, installment.

Financial Aid Of all full-time matriculated undergraduates who enrolled in 2017, 3,973 applied for aid, 3,661 were judged to have need, 3,661 had their need fully met. 919 Federal Work-Study jobs (averaging $2805). 2,136 state and other part-time jobs (averaging $2871). In 2017, 13 non-need-based awards were made. ***Average percent of need met:*** 100. ***Average financial aid package:*** $56,820. ***Average need-based loan:*** $4406. ***Average need-based gift aid:*** $54,001. ***Average non-need-based aid:*** $15,730. ***Average indebtedness upon graduation:*** $13,372.

APPLYING

Standardized Tests *Required:* SAT or ACT (for admission), SAT Subject Tests (for admission).

Options: electronic application, early admission, early action, deferred entrance.

Application fee: $75.

Required: essay or personal statement, high school transcript. ***Recommended:*** 2 letters of recommendation, interview.

Application deadlines: 1/1 (freshmen), 3/1 (transfers).

Notification: 4/1 (freshmen), 6/15 (transfers).

CONTACT

Harvard University, Cambridge, MA 02138. *Phone:* 617-495-1551.

Hellenic College

Brookline, Massachusetts

http://www.hchc.edu/

CONTACT

Mr. Gregory Floor, Director of Admissions, Hellenic College, 50 Goddard Avenue, Brookline, MA 02445-7496. *Phone:* 617-850-1285. *Toll-free phone:* 866-424-2338. *Fax:* 617-850-1460. *E-mail:* admissions@hchc.edu.

Hult International Business School

Cambridge, Massachusetts

http://www.hult.edu/

CONTACT

Hult International Business School, 1 Education Street, Cambridge, MA 02141.

Lasell College

Newton, Massachusetts

http://www.lasell.edu/

- **Independent** comprehensive, founded 1851
- **Suburban** 54-acre campus with easy access to Boston
- **Endowment** $43.2 million
- **Coed** 1,639 undergraduate students, 98% full-time, 64% women, 36% men
- **Moderately difficult** entrance level, 84% of applicants were admitted

UNDERGRAD STUDENTS

1,604 full-time, 35 part-time. Students come from 26 states and territories; 16 other countries; 39% are from out of state; 9% Black or African American, non-Hispanic/Latino; 10% Hispanic/Latino; 3% Asian, non-Hispanic/Latino; 0.1% Native Hawaiian or other Pacific Islander, non-Hispanic/Latino; 0.1% American Indian or Alaska Native, non-Hispanic/Latino; 2% Two or more races, non-Hispanic/Latino; 5% Race/ethnicity unknown; 5% international; 7% transferred in; 75% live on campus.

Freshmen:

Admission: 2,489 applied, 2,082 admitted, 454 enrolled. ***Average high school GPA:*** 3.0. ***Test scores:*** SAT evidence-based reading and writing scores over 500: 74%; SAT math scores over 500: 70%; ACT scores over 18: 80%; SAT evidence-based reading and writing scores over 600: 24%; SAT math scores over 600: 16%; ACT scores over 24: 32%; SAT evidence-based reading and writing scores over 700: 1%; ACT scores over 30: 4%.

Retention: 74% of full-time freshmen returned.

FACULTY

Total: 288, 29% full-time, 46% with terminal degrees.

Student/faculty ratio: 14:1.

ACADEMICS

Calendar: semesters. *Degrees:* bachelor's and master's.

Special study options: accelerated degree program, advanced placement credit, cooperative education, distance learning, double majors, English as a second language, honors programs, independent study, internships, off-campus study, part-time degree program, services for LD students, student-designed majors, study abroad, summer session for credit.

Unusual degree programs: 3-2 business administration; communication, sport management.

Computers: 219 computers/terminals are available on campus for general student use. Students can access the following: campus intranet, computer help desk, free student e-mail accounts, online (class) grades, online (class) registration, online (class) schedules, online tutoring. Campuswide network is available. 100% of college-owned or -operated housing units are wired for high-speed Internet access. Wireless service is available via entire campus.

Library: Brennan Library. *Books:* 34,031 (physical), 70,716 (digital/electronic); *Serial titles:* 60 (physical), 83,985 (digital/electronic); *Databases:* 107. Weekly public service hours: 83; students can reserve study rooms.

STUDENT LIFE

Housing options: coed, women-only, special housing for students with disabilities. Campus housing is university owned. Freshman campus housing is guaranteed.

Activities and organizations: drama/theater group, student-run newspaper, radio station, choral group, 19851 Chronicle, Campus Activities Board, Hope for Humanity, Lasell College Drama Club, Lasell College Radio (Marathon Monday).

Athletics Member NCAA. All Division III. ***Intercollegiate sports:*** baseball M, basketball M/W, cross-country running M/W, field hockey W, lacrosse M/W, soccer M/W, softball W, track and field M/W, volleyball M/W. ***Intramural sports:*** basketball M/W, cheerleading M(c)/W(c), crew M(c)/W(c), rugby M(c)/W(c), skiing (downhill) M(c)/W(c), tennis M(c)/W(c), ultimate Frisbee M(c).

Campus security: 24-hour emergency response devices and patrols, late-night transport/escort service, controlled dormitory access.

Student services: health clinic, personal/psychological counseling.

COSTS & FINANCIAL AID

Costs (2020–21) ***Comprehensive fee:*** $55,000 includes full-time tuition ($37,500), mandatory fees ($1500), and room and board ($16,000). Part-time tuition: $1250 per credit hour. Part-time tuition and fees vary according to course load. ***Required fees:*** $325 per term part-time. ***Room and board:*** Room and board charges vary according to housing facility. ***Payment plan:*** installment. ***Waivers:*** children of alumni and employees or children of employees.

Financial Aid Of all full-time matriculated undergraduates who enrolled in 2019, 1,394 applied for aid, 1,282 were judged to have need, 314 had their need fully met. In 2019, 269 non-need-based awards were made. ***Average percent of need met:*** 67. ***Average financial aid package:*** $23,383. ***Average need-based loan:*** $4389. ***Average need-based gift aid:*** $24,911. ***Average non-need-based aid:*** $16,992. ***Average indebtedness upon graduation:*** $40,580.

APPLYING

Standardized Tests *Required for some:* SAT or ACT (for admission).

Options: electronic application, early action, deferred entrance.

Required: essay or personal statement, high school transcript, 2 letters of recommendation, college preparatory program. ***Recommended:*** interview.

Application deadlines: rolling (freshmen), rolling (transfers), 11/15 (early action).

Notification: continuous until 3/15 (freshmen), continuous (transfers).

CONTACT

Mr. Yavuz Kiremit, Director of Undergraduate Admission, Lasell College, 1844 Commonwealth Avenue, Newton, MA 02466. *Phone:* 617-243-2225. *Toll-free phone:* 888-LASELL-4. *Fax:* 617-243-2380. *E-mail:* info@lasell.edu.

Lesley University

Cambridge, Massachusetts

http://www.lesley.edu/

- **Independent** comprehensive, founded 1909
- **Urban** campus with easy access to Boston
- **Coed, primarily women** 2,128 undergraduate students, 75% full-time, 77% women, 23% men
- 75% of applicants were admitted

UNDERGRAD STUDENTS

1,599 full-time, 529 part-time. 33% are from out of state; 9% Black or African American, non-Hispanic/Latino; 16% Hispanic/Latino; 5% Asian, non-Hispanic/Latino; 0.2% Native Hawaiian or other Pacific Islander, non-Hispanic/Latino; 0.3% American Indian or Alaska Native, non-Hispanic/Latino; 3% Two or more races, non-Hispanic/Latino; 5% Race/ethnicity unknown; 5% international; 5% transferred in; 43% live on campus.

Freshmen:

Admission: 3,049 applied, 2,277 admitted, 320 enrolled. ***Average high school GPA:*** 3.3. ***Test scores:*** SAT evidence-based reading and writing scores over 500: 80%; SAT math scores over 500: 75%; ACT scores over 18: 91%; SAT evidence-based reading and writing scores over 600: 34%; SAT math scores over 600: 21%; ACT scores over 24: 48%; SAT evidence-based reading and writing scores over 700: 7%; SAT math scores over 700: 3%; ACT scores over 30: 22%.

Retention: 81% of full-time freshmen returned.

FACULTY

Total: 571, 26% full-time, 42% with terminal degrees.

Student/faculty ratio: 8:1.

ACADEMICS

Calendar: semesters. *Degrees:* certificates, associate, bachelor's, master's, doctoral, post-master's, and postbachelor's certificates.

Special study options: academic remediation for entering students, accelerated degree program, adult/continuing education programs, advanced placement credit, distance learning, double majors, freshman honors college, honors programs, independent study, internships, off-campus study, part-time degree program, services for LD students, student-designed majors, study abroad, summer session for credit.

Computers: Students can access the following: free student e-mail accounts, online (class) registration. Campuswide network is available. Wireless service is available via classrooms, student centers.

Library: Sherrill Library.

STUDENT LIFE

Housing options: coed, women-only. Campus housing is university owned. Freshman applicants given priority for college housing.

Activities and organizations: drama/theater group, student-run newspaper, choral group.

Athletics Member NCAA. All Division III except baseball (Division II). ***Intercollegiate sports:*** baseball M, basketball M/W, cross-country running M/W, soccer M/W, softball W, volleyball M/W. ***Intramural sports:*** swimming and diving M/W, tennis M.

Campus security: 24-hour emergency response devices and patrols, late-night transport/escort service, controlled dormitory access.

Student services: health clinic, personal/psychological counseling.

COSTS & FINANCIAL AID

Costs (2020–21) ***Comprehensive fee:*** $47,080 includes full-time tuition ($29,200), mandatory fees ($250), and room and board ($17,630). Part-time tuition: $973 per credit hour. ***College room only:*** $10,060.

Financial Aid Of all full-time matriculated undergraduates who enrolled in 2018, 1,243 applied for aid, 1,064 were judged to have need, 64 had their need fully met. In 2018, 496 non-need-based awards were made. ***Average percent of need met:*** 60. ***Average financial aid package:*** $17,787. ***Average need-based loan:*** $3668. ***Average need-based gift aid:*** $13,789. ***Average non-need-based aid:*** $10,716. ***Average indebtedness upon graduation:*** $22,371.

APPLYING

Standardized Tests *Required for some:* SAT or ACT (for admission).

Options: electronic application, early action, deferred entrance.

Required: essay or personal statement, high school transcript. ***Recommended:*** interview.

Application deadlines: rolling (transfers), 12/1 (early action).

Notification: continuous until 1/15 (freshmen), continuous (transfers), 12/23 (early action).

CONTACT

Lesley University, 29 Everett Street, Cambridge, MA 02138-2790. *Phone:* 617-349-8800. *Toll-free phone:* 800-999-1959 Ext. 8800.

Massachusetts College of Art and Design

Boston, Massachusetts

http://www.massart.edu/

- **State-supported** comprehensive, founded 1873, part of Massachusetts Public Higher Education System
- **Urban** 5-acre campus
- **Endowment** $16.0 million
- **Coed** 1,931 undergraduate students, 86% full-time, 70% women, 30% men
- **Moderately difficult** entrance level, 71% of applicants were admitted

UNDERGRAD STUDENTS

1,662 full-time, 269 part-time. Students come from 32 states and territories; 45 other countries; 32% are from out of state; 6% transferred in; 41% live on campus.

Freshmen:

Admission: 2,386 applied, 1,686 admitted, 424 enrolled. ***Average high school GPA:*** 3.5.

Retention: 87% of full-time freshmen returned.

ACADEMICS

Calendar: semesters. *Degrees:* certificates, bachelor's, master's, and postbachelor's certificates.

Special study options: double majors, independent study, internships, off-campus study, part-time degree program, student-designed majors, study abroad, summer session for credit.

Computers: 370 computers/terminals are available on campus for general student use. Students can access the following: campus intranet, computer help desk, free student e-mail accounts, online (class) grades, online (class) registration, online (class) schedules. Campuswide network is available. 100% of college-owned or -operated housing units are wired for high-speed Internet access. Wireless service is available via entire campus.

Library: Morton R. Godine Library.

STUDENT LIFE

Housing options: coed. Campus housing is university owned. Freshman campus housing is guaranteed.

Activities and organizations: drama/theater group, student-run newspaper, radio and television station, choral group, International Students' Club, Design Research Unit, Spectrum, film society, Event Works.

Athletics ***Intramural sports:*** basketball M/W, cross-country running M/W, field hockey M/W, ice hockey M/W, soccer M/W, softball M/W, table tennis M/W, tennis M/W, volleyball M/W.

Campus security: 24-hour emergency response devices and patrols, late-night transport/escort service, controlled dormitory access, security lighting, self-defense workshops.

Student services: health clinic, personal/psychological counseling, women's center.

COSTS & FINANCIAL AID

Costs (2019–20) ***Tuition:*** $340 per credit part-time; state resident $13,700 full-time, $340 per credit part-time; nonresident $38,400 full-time, $340 per credit part-time. ***Room and board:*** Room and board charges vary according to board plan and housing facility.

Financial Aid Of all full-time matriculated undergraduates who enrolled in 2019, 1,321 applied for aid, 1,063 were judged to have need, 87 had their need fully met. In 2019, 180 non-need-based awards were made. ***Average percent of need met:*** 59. ***Average financial aid package:*** $12,403. ***Average need-based loan:*** $4454. ***Average need-based gift aid:*** $7181. ***Average non-need-based aid:*** $2757. ***Average indebtedness upon graduation:*** $26,720.

APPLYING

Options: electronic application, early action, deferred entrance.

Application fee: $70.

Required: essay or personal statement, high school transcript, 2 letters of recommendation, portfolio of 15-20 pieces of artwork completed in the last 2 years. ***Recommended:*** minimum 3.0 GPA.

Application deadlines: 2/1 (freshmen), 2/1 (transfers), 12/1 (early action).

Notification: 1/5 (early action).

CONTACT

Lauren Wilshusen, Massachusetts College of Art and Design, 621 Huntington Avenue, Boston, MA 02115. *Phone:* 617-879-7222. *Fax:* 617-879-7250. *E-mail:* admissions@massart.edu.

Massachusetts College of Liberal Arts

North Adams, Massachusetts

http://www.mcla.edu/

- **State-supported** comprehensive, founded 1894, part of Massachusetts State University System
- **Small-town** 105-acre campus with easy access to Albany-Schenectady-Troy New York Metro Area
- **Coed**
- **Moderately difficult** entrance level

FACULTY

Student/faculty ratio: 12:1.

ACADEMICS

Calendar: semesters. *Degrees:* certificates, bachelor's, master's, post-master's, and postbachelor's certificates.

Library: Eugene L. Freel Library. *Books:* 125,000 (physical), 229,000 (digital/electronic); *Serial titles:* 1,000 (physical), 43,000 (digital/electronic); *Databases:* 82.

STUDENT LIFE

Housing options: on-campus residence required through junior year; coed, special housing for students with disabilities. Campus housing is university owned. Freshman campus housing is guaranteed.

Activities and organizations: drama/theater group, student-run newspaper, radio and television station, choral group, Student Activities Council, Student Government Association, The Beacon (Student Newspaper), Harlequin-Musical Theatre Company, Dance Company.

Athletics Member NCAA. All Division III.

Campus security: 24-hour emergency response devices and patrols, late-night transport/escort service, controlled dormitory access.

Student services: health clinic, personal/psychological counseling, women's center, veterans affairs office.

COSTS & FINANCIAL AID

Costs (2019–20) ***Tuition:*** state resident $1030 full-time, $43 per credit part-time; nonresident $9975 full-time, $416 per credit part-time. Full-time tuition and fees vary according to reciprocity agreements. Part-time tuition and fees vary according to course load and reciprocity agreements. ***Required fees:*** $9900 full-time, $417 per credit part-time. ***Room and board:*** $11,430. Room and board charges vary according to board plan and housing facility.

Financial Aid Of all full-time matriculated undergraduates who enrolled in 2019, 1,095 applied for aid, 873 were judged to have need, 666 had their need fully met. In 2019, 157 non-need-based awards were made. ***Average percent of need met:*** 80. ***Average financial aid package:*** $16,911. ***Average need-based loan:*** $3719. ***Average need-based gift aid:*** $7894. ***Average non-need-based aid:*** $3295. ***Average indebtedness upon graduation:*** $29,416.

APPLYING

Standardized Tests *Required:* SAT or ACT (for admission).

Options: electronic application, early admission, early action, deferred entrance.

Required: essay or personal statement, high school transcript, minimum 3.0 GPA, 1 letter of recommendation. ***Required for some:*** interview, sliding scale applies (GPA and SAT) if below 3.0.

CONTACT

Ms. Kayla Hollins, Associate Director of Admission, Massachusetts College of Liberal Arts, 375 Church Street, North Adams, MA 01247. *Phone:* 413-662-5410. *Toll-free phone:* 800-989-MCLA. *E-mail:* kayla.kollins@mcla.edu.

Massachusetts Institute of Technology

Cambridge, Massachusetts

http://www.mit.edu/

- **Independent** university, founded 1861
- **Urban** 166-acre campus with easy access to Boston
- **Endowment** $16.4 billion
- **Coed**
- **Most difficult** entrance level

FACULTY

Student/faculty ratio: 3:1.

ACADEMICS

Calendar: 4-1-4. *Degrees:* bachelor's, master's, and doctoral.
Library: MIT Libraries plus 5 others. *Books:* 1.3 million (physical), 758,981 (digital/electronic); *Serial titles:* 50,139 (physical), 58,996 (digital/electronic); *Databases:* 336. Weekly public service hours: 95; study areas open 24 hours, 5–7 days a week; students can reserve study rooms.

STUDENT LIFE

Housing options: on-campus residence required for freshman year; coed, women-only, cooperative, special housing for students with disabilities. Campus housing is university owned. Freshman campus housing is guaranteed.

Activities and organizations: drama/theater group, student-run newspaper, radio and television station, choral group, marching band, Educational Studies Program, Dance Troupe, Science Fiction Society, The Tech (student newspaper), Anime Club, national fraternities, national sororities.

Athletics Member NCAA. All Division III except men's and women's crew (Division I), men's and women's rowing (Division I).

Campus security: 24-hour emergency response devices and patrols, late-night transport/escort service, controlled dormitory access.

Student services: health clinic, personal/psychological counseling.

COSTS & FINANCIAL AID

Costs (2019–20) ***Comprehensive fee:*** $70,180 includes full-time tuition ($53,450), mandatory fees ($340), and room and board ($16,390). Part-time tuition and fees vary according to course load. ***Required fees:*** $830 per credit hour part-time. ***College room only:*** $10,430. Room and board charges vary according to housing facility.

Financial Aid Of all full-time matriculated undergraduates who enrolled in 2017, 2,947 applied for aid, 2,652 were judged to have need, 2,650 had their need fully met. 436 Federal Work-Study jobs (averaging $2957). 1,437 state and other part-time jobs (averaging $2835). ***Average percent of need met:*** 100. ***Average financial aid package:*** $50,292. ***Average need-based loan:*** $2959. ***Average need-based gift aid:*** $48,562. ***Average indebtedness upon graduation:*** $22,696. ***Financial aid deadline:*** 2/15.

APPLYING

Standardized Tests *Required:* SAT or ACT (for admission), SAT Subject Tests (for admission).

Options: electronic application, early admission, early action, deferred entrance.

Application fee: $75.

Required: essay or personal statement, high school transcript, 2 letters of recommendation. ***Recommended:*** interview.

CONTACT

Stuart Schmill, Dean of Admissions, Massachusetts Institute of Technology, 77 Massachusetts Avenue, Cambridge, MA 02139-4307. *Phone:* 617-253-3400. *Fax:* 617-258-8304. *E-mail:* admissions@mit.edu.

Massachusetts Maritime Academy

Buzzards Bay, Massachusetts

http://www.maritime.edu/

- **State-supported** comprehensive, founded 1891, part of Massachusetts State University System
- **Small-town** 54-acre campus with easy access to Boston, Providence
- **Endowment** $44.7 million
- **Coed** 1,695 undergraduate students, 95% full-time, 13% women, 87% men
- **Moderately difficult** entrance level, 91% of applicants were admitted

UNDERGRAD STUDENTS

1,616 full-time, 79 part-time. Students come from 34 states and territories; 20% are from out of state; 1% Black or African American, non-Hispanic/Latino; 4% Hispanic/Latino; 1% Asian, non-Hispanic/Latino; 0.2% American Indian or Alaska Native, non-Hispanic/Latino; 3% Two or more races, non-Hispanic/Latino; 5% Race/ethnicity unknown; 0.6% international; 2% transferred in; 96% live on campus.

Freshmen:

Admission: 773 applied, 707 admitted, 404 enrolled. ***Average high school GPA:*** 3.1. ***Test scores:*** SAT evidence-based reading and writing scores over 500: 82%; SAT math scores over 500: 84%; ACT scores over 18: 82%; SAT evidence-based reading and writing scores over 600: 20%; SAT math scores over 600: 24%; ACT scores over 24: 25%; SAT evidence-based reading and writing scores over 700: 2%; SAT math scores over 700: 2%; ACT scores over 30: 11%.

Retention: 87% of full-time freshmen returned.

FACULTY

Total: 149, 59% full-time, 46% with terminal degrees.

Student/faculty ratio: 15:1.

ACADEMICS

Calendar: 4-1-4 plus sea term. *Degrees:* bachelor's and master's.

Special study options: advanced placement credit, cooperative education, distance learning, double majors, independent study, internships, off-campus study, part-time degree program, services for LD students, study abroad, summer session for credit. ***ROTC:*** Army (c).

Computers: 130 computers/terminals and 1,800 ports are available on campus for general student use. Students can access the following: computer help desk, free student e-mail accounts, online (class) grades, online (class) registration, online (class) schedules, course-supported e-learning. Campuswide network is available. 100% of college-owned or -operated housing units are wired for high-speed Internet access. Wireless service is available via entire campus.
Library: American Bureau of Shipping Information Commons. *Books:* 29,740 (physical), 265,738 (digital/electronic); *Serial titles:* 104 (physical), 63,941 (digital/electronic); *Databases:* 134.

STUDENT LIFE

Housing options: on-campus residence required through senior year; coed. Campus housing is university owned. Freshman campus housing is guaranteed.

Activities and organizations: drama/theater group, marching band, Student Government, Intramurals, Regimental Leadership, Band/Honor Guard, NCAA Division 3 Athletics.

Athletics Member NCAA. All Division III. ***Intercollegiate sports:*** baseball M, crew M/W, cross-country running M/W, football M, lacrosse M/W, sailing M/W, soccer M/W, softball W, track and field M/W, volleyball W. ***Intramural sports:*** basketball M/W, equestrian sports M(c)/W(c), football M/W, golf M(c)/W(c), ice hockey M(c)/W(c), lacrosse M(c)/W(c), rock climbing M(c)/W(c), soccer M/W, softball M/W, swimming and diving M(c)/W(c), volleyball M(c)/W(c), wrestling M(c)/W(c).

Campus security: 24-hour emergency response devices and patrols, late-night transport/escort service, controlled dormitory access.

Student services: health clinic, personal/psychological counseling, women's center, veterans affairs office.

COSTS & FINANCIAL AID

Costs (2020–21) ***Tuition:*** state resident $1890 full-time, $79 per credit hour part-time; nonresident $17,010 full-time, $709 per credit hour part-time. Full-time tuition and fees vary according to reciprocity agreements.

Part-time tuition and fees vary according to course load and reciprocity agreements. ***Required fees:*** $8424 full-time, $340 per credit hour part-time, $264 per year part-time. ***Room and board:*** $13,352; room only: $8004. ***Payment plan:*** installment. ***Waivers:*** employees or children of employees.

Financial Aid Of all full-time matriculated undergraduates who enrolled in 2019, 931 applied for aid, 931 were judged to have need, 350 had their need fully met. 410 Federal Work-Study jobs (averaging $1500). In 2019, 146 non-need-based awards were made. ***Average percent of need met:*** 68. ***Average financial aid package:*** $14,285. ***Average need-based loan:*** $4300. ***Average need-based gift aid:*** $12,774. ***Average non-need-based aid:*** $5236. ***Average indebtedness upon graduation:*** $37,414.

APPLYING

Standardized Tests *Required:* SAT or ACT (for admission).

Options: electronic application, early action, deferred entrance.

Application fee: $50.

Required: essay or personal statement, high school transcript, minimum 2.0 GPA, 2 letters of recommendation, minimum college GPA 2.5 if transferring 12-23 credits, minimum college GPA 2.0 for more than 24 transferable credits. ***Recommended:*** interview.

Application deadlines: 4/15 (freshmen), 4/15 (out-of-state freshmen), rolling (transfers), 11/15 (early action).

Notification: continuous (freshmen), continuous (out-of-state freshmen), continuous (transfers), 12/7 (early action).

CONTACT

Mr. Joshua Tefft, Director of Admissions, Massachusetts Maritime Academy, 101 Academy Drive, Flanagan Hall, Buzzards Bay, MA 02532. *Phone:* 508-830-6687. *Toll-free phone:* 800-544-3411. *E-mail:* jtefft@maritime.edu.

MCPHS University

Boston, Massachusetts

http://www.mcphs.edu/

- **Independent** university, founded 1823
- **Urban** 3-acre campus
- **Endowment** $847.8 million
- **Coed**
- 84% of applicants were admitted

ACADEMICS

Calendar: semesters. *Degrees:* certificates, bachelor's, master's, doctoral, post-master's, and postbachelor's certificates.

Library: Henrietta DeBenedictis Library plus 2 others.

STUDENT LIFE

Housing options: coed, special housing for students with disabilities. Campus housing is university owned, leased by the school and is provided by a third party. Freshman campus housing is guaranteed.

Activities and organizations: drama/theater group, student-run newspaper, choral group, Residence Hall Council, Vietnamese Student Association, Student Government Association, Campus Activities Board, Student Indian Organization, national fraternities.

Campus security: 24-hour emergency response devices and patrols, late-night transport/escort service, controlled dormitory access, electronically operated academic area entrances, security guards at entrance.

Student services: health clinic, personal/psychological counseling.

FINANCIAL AID

Financial Aid Of all full-time matriculated undergraduates who enrolled in 2017, 2,640 applied for aid, 2,467 were judged to have need, 834 had their need fully met. In 2017, 885 non-need-based awards were made. ***Average percent of need met:*** 21. ***Average financial aid package:*** $8116. ***Average need-based loan:*** $2941. ***Average need-based gift aid:*** $5748. ***Average non-need-based aid:*** $6122. ***Average indebtedness upon graduation:*** $58,012.

APPLYING

Standardized Tests *Required:* SAT or ACT (for admission).

Options: electronic application, early action, deferred entrance.

Required: essay or personal statement, 1 letter of recommendation. ***Required for some:*** high school transcript, interview.

CONTACT

Giselle Colon, Visit Concierge, MCPHS University, 179 Longwood Avenue, Boston, MA 02115. *Phone:* 617-732-2744. *Fax:* 617-732-2118. *E-mail:* admissions@mcphs.edu.

Merrimack College

North Andover, Massachusetts

http://www.merrimack.edu/

- **Independent Roman Catholic** comprehensive, founded 1947
- **Suburban** 220-acre campus with easy access to Boston
- **Coed** 4,015 undergraduate students, 97% full-time, 52% women, 48% men
- **Moderately difficult** entrance level, 82% of applicants were admitted

UNDERGRAD STUDENTS

3,898 full-time, 117 part-time. Students come from 31 states and territories; 27 other countries; 29% are from out of state; 4% Black or African American, non-Hispanic/Latino; 7% Hispanic/Latino; 2% Asian, non-Hispanic/Latino; 0.1% American Indian or Alaska Native, non-Hispanic/Latino; 2% Two or more races, non-Hispanic/Latino; 6% Race/ethnicity unknown, 2% international, 2% transferred in, 71% live on campus.

Freshmen:

Admission: 9,747 applied, 7,983 admitted, 1,179 enrolled. ***Average high school GPA:*** 3.2.

Retention: 83% of full-time freshmen returned.

FACULTY

Total: 492, 41% full-time.

Student/faculty ratio: 15:1.

ACADEMICS

Calendar: semesters. *Degrees:* bachelor's, master's, post-master's, and postbachelor's certificates.

Special study options: academic remediation for entering students, accelerated degree program, adult/continuing education programs, advanced placement credit, cooperative education, distance learning, double majors, honors programs, independent study, internships, off-campus study, part-time degree program, services for LD students, student-designed majors, study abroad, summer session for credit. ***ROTC:*** Air Force (c).

Computers: Students can access the following: campus intranet, computer help desk, free student e-mail accounts, online (class) grades, online (class) registration, online (class) schedules. Campuswide network is available. 100% of college-owned or -operated housing units are wired for high-speed Internet access. Wireless service is available via entire campus.

Library: McQuade Library. *Books:* 90,794 (physical), 203,605 (digital/electronic); *Serial titles:* 56 (physical), 147,800 (digital/electronic); *Databases:* 233.

STUDENT LIFE

Housing options: coed, special housing for students with disabilities. Campus housing is university owned. Freshman campus housing is guaranteed.

Activities and organizations: drama/theater group, student-run newspaper, radio and television station, choral group, Onstagers, Live to Give (Relay for Life), Zeta Tau Alpha, WMCK, Young Athletes Program/Special Olympics, national fraternities, national sororities.

Athletics Member NCAA. All Division I. ***Intercollegiate sports:*** baseball M(s), basketball M(s)/W(s), crew W(s), cross-country running M(s)/W(s), field hockey W(s), football M(s), golf W(s), ice hockey M(s)/W(s), lacrosse M(s)/W(s), rowing W(s), soccer M(s)/W(s), softball W(s), swimming and diving W(s), tennis M(s)/W(s), track and field M(s)/W(s), volleyball W(s). ***Intramural sports:*** badminton M/W, baseball M(c), basketball M(c)/W, cheerleading W(c), field hockey M(c)/W(c), golf M(c), gymnastics W(c), ice hockey M(c)/W(c), lacrosse M(c)/W(c), rugby M(c)/W(c), soccer M(c)/W, softball M/W(c), ultimate Frisbee M(c)/W(c), volleyball M/W(c).

Campus security: 24-hour emergency response devices and patrols, late-night transport/escort service, controlled dormitory access.

Student services: health clinic, personal/psychological counseling.

FINANCIAL AID
Financial Aid Of all full-time matriculated undergraduates who enrolled in 2019, 3,175 applied for aid, 2,769 were judged to have need, 404 had their need fully met. In 2019, 913 non-need-based awards were made. ***Average percent of need met:*** 67. ***Average financial aid package:*** $26,574. ***Average need-based loan:*** $4341. ***Average need-based gift aid:*** $23,021. ***Average non-need-based aid:*** $15,918.

APPLYING
Options: electronic application, early admission, early decision, early action, deferred entrance.

Required: essay or personal statement, high school transcript, 1 letter of recommendation, first quarter senior grades. ***Recommended:*** interview.

Application deadlines: 2/15 (freshmen), 8/25 (transfers), 1/15 (early action).

Early decision deadline: 11/15.

Notification: continuous until 3/16 (freshmen), continuous (transfers), 12/15 (early decision), 2/15 (early action).

CONTACT
Merrimack College, 315 Turnpike Street, North Andover, MA 01845-5800. *Phone:* 978-837-5154.

Montserrat College of Art

Beverly, Massachusetts

http://www.montserrat.edu/

CONTACT
Mr. Jeffrey Newell, Director of Admissions, Montserrat College of Art, 23 Essex Street, Beverly, MA 01915. *Phone:* 978-921-4242 Ext. 1152. *Toll-free phone:* 800-836-0487. *Fax:* 978-921-4241. *E-mail:* jeffrey.newell@montserrat.edu.

Mount Holyoke College

South Hadley, Massachusetts

http://www.mtholyoke.edu/

- **Independent** comprehensive, founded 1837
- **Small-town** 800-acre campus with easy access to Springfield
- **Endowment** $729.4 million
- **Women only** 2,208 undergraduate students, 99% full-time
- **Very difficult** entrance level, 51% of applicants were admitted

UNDERGRAD STUDENTS
2,177 full-time, 31 part-time. Students come from 46 states and territories; 57 other countries; 73% are from out of state; 2% transferred in; 96% live on campus.

Freshmen:
Admission: 3,699 applied, 1,883 admitted, 628 enrolled. ***Average high school GPA:*** 3.8.
Retention: 92% of full-time freshmen returned.

ACADEMICS
Calendar: semesters. *Degrees:* bachelor's and master's.

Special study options: adult/continuing education programs, advanced placement credit, distance learning, double majors, independent study, internships, off-campus study, part-time degree program, services for LD students, student-designed majors, study abroad, summer session for credit. ***ROTC:*** Army (c), Air Force (c).

Unusual degree programs: 3-2 engineering with Dartmouth College, University of Massachusetts, California Institute of Technology.

Computers: 392 computers/terminals and 3,000 ports are available on campus for general student use. Students can access the following: campus intranet, computer help desk, free student e-mail accounts, online (class) grades, online (class) registration, online (class) schedules, personal Web pages. Campuswide network is available. 100% of college-owned or -operated housing units are wired for high-speed Internet access. Wireless service is available via classrooms, computer centers, computer labs, dorm rooms, learning centers, libraries, student centers.
Library: Williston Memorial Library plus 2 others. Weekly public service hours: 115; students can reserve study rooms.

STUDENT LIFE
Housing options: on-campus residence required through senior year; women-only, special housing for students with disabilities. Campus housing is university owned. Freshman campus housing is guaranteed.

Activities and organizations: drama/theater group, student-run newspaper, radio station, choral group, Student Government Association, C.A.U.S.E. (Creating Awareness and Unity for Social Equality), MHC Outing Club, Mount Holyoke Symphony Orchestra, Mount Holyoke News.

Athletics ***Intercollegiate sports:*** basketball W, crew W, cross-country running W, equestrian sports W, field hockey W, golf W, lacrosse W, soccer W, squash W, swimming and diving W, tennis W, track and field W, volleyball W. ***Intramural sports:*** equestrian sports W(c), fencing W(c), ice hockey W(c), rugby W(c), ultimate Frisbee W(c).

Campus security: 24-hour emergency response devices and patrols, student patrols, late-night transport/escort service, controlled dormitory access, police officers on-campus.

Student services: health clinic, personal/psychological counseling.

COSTS & FINANCIAL AID
Costs (2019–20) ***Comprehensive fee:*** $67,578 includes full-time tuition ($52,040), mandatory fees ($218), and room and board ($15,320). Part-time tuition: $1630 per credit hour. ***College room only:*** $7504. ***Payment plan:*** installment. ***Waivers:*** employees or children of employees.

Financial Aid Of all full-time matriculated undergraduates who enrolled in 2019, 1,470 applied for aid, 1,312 were judged to have need, 1,312 had their need fully met. 813 Federal Work-Study jobs (averaging $2217). 224 state and other part-time jobs (averaging $2158). In 2019, 287 non-need-based awards were made. ***Average percent of need met:*** 100. ***Average financial aid package:*** $42,565. ***Average need-based loan:*** $4238. ***Average need-based gift aid:*** $37,322. ***Average non-need-based aid:*** $22,429. ***Average indebtedness upon graduation:*** $25,811. ***Financial aid deadline:*** 2/1.

APPLYING
Options: electronic application, early admission, early decision, deferred entrance.

Application fee: $60.

Required: essay or personal statement, high school transcript, 2 letters of recommendation. ***Recommended:*** interview.

Application deadlines: 1/15 (freshmen), 3/1 (transfers).

Early decision deadline: 11/15 (for plan 1), 1/1 (for plan 2).

Notification: 4/1 (freshmen), continuous until 4/15 (transfers), 1/1 (early decision plan 1), 2/1 (early decision plan 2).

CONTACT
Ms. Gail Berson, Vice President of Enrollment and Dean of Admission, Mount Holyoke College, Office of Admission, South Hadley, MA 01075. *Phone:* 413-538-2023. *Fax:* 413-538-2409. *E-mail:* admission@mtholyoke.edu.

New England College of Business and Finance

Boston, Massachusetts

http://necb.edu/

CONTACT
New England College of Business and Finance, 10 High Street, Suite 204, Boston, MA 02111-2645. *Phone:* 617-951-2350 Ext. 6912. *Toll-free phone:* 800-997-1673.

New England Conservatory of Music

Boston, Massachusetts

http://necmusic.edu/

CONTACT
New England Conservatory of Music, 290 Huntington Avenue, Boston, MA 02115-5000. *Phone:* 617-585-1103.

Nichols College

Dudley, Massachusetts

http://www.nichols.edu/

- **Independent** comprehensive, founded 1815
- **Small-town** 250-acre campus with easy access to Boston
- **Endowment** $15.4 million
- **Coed** 1,326 undergraduate students, 92% full-time, 37% women, 63% men
- **Minimally difficult** entrance level, 80% of applicants were admitted

UNDERGRAD STUDENTS

1,218 full-time, 108 part-time. 39% are from out of state; 6% Black or African American, non-Hispanic/Latino; 9% Hispanic/Latino; 1% Asian, non-Hispanic/Latino; 0.2% Native Hawaiian or other Pacific Islander, non-Hispanic/Latino; 0.4% American Indian or Alaska Native, non-Hispanic/Latino; 4% Two or more races, non-Hispanic/Latino; 0.3% Race/ethnicity unknown; 2% international; 3% transferred in; 74% live on campus.

Freshmen:
Admission: 2,488 applied, 1,984 admitted, 344 enrolled. ***Average high school GPA:*** 2.9. ***Test scores:*** SAT evidence-based reading and writing scores over 500: 66%; SAT math scores over 500: 66%; ACT scores over 18: 89%; SAT evidence-based reading and writing scores over 600: 14%; SAT math scores over 600: 15%; ACT scores over 24: 34%; SAT evidence-based reading and writing scores over 700: 1%; SAT math scores over 700: 3%; ACT scores over 30: 6%.

Retention: 76% of full-time freshmen returned.

FACULTY

Total: 140, 37% full-time, 27% with terminal degrees.

Student/faculty ratio: 16:1.

ACADEMICS

Calendar: semesters. *Degrees:* bachelor's and master's.

Special study options: accelerated degree program, adult/continuing education programs, advanced placement credit, cooperative education, distance learning, double majors, honors programs, independent study, internships, off-campus study, part-time degree program, services for LD students, study abroad, summer session for credit.

Unusual degree programs: 3-2 business administration.

Computers: 154 computers/terminals are available on campus for general student use. Students can access the following: campus intranet, computer help desk, free student e-mail accounts, online (class) grades, online (class) registration, online (class) schedules. Campuswide network is available. 100% of college-owned or -operated housing units are wired for high-speed Internet access. Wireless service is available via entire campus.

Library: Conant Library. *Books:* 27,627 (physical), 150,177 (digital/electronic); *Serial titles:* 42 (physical); *Databases:* 35. Weekly public service hours: 102; study areas open 24 hours, 5–7 days a week; students can reserve study rooms.

STUDENT LIFE

Housing options: coed, men-only, women-only, special housing for students with disabilities. Campus housing is university owned. Freshman campus housing is guaranteed.

Activities and organizations: student-run radio station, Campus Activities Board, Institute for Women's Leadership, Student Government Association, Student Athletic Advisory Council, Student Alumni Association.

Athletics Member NCAA. All Division III. ***Intercollegiate sports:*** baseball M, basketball M/W, cheerleading M(c)/W(c), cross-country running M/W, field hockey W, football M, golf M, ice hockey M/W, lacrosse M/W, rugby M(c)/W(c), soccer M/W, softball W, tennis M/W, track and field M/W, volleyball M/W. ***Intramural sports:*** baseball M, basketball M/W, bowling M/W, football M/W, ice hockey M(c)/W(c), racquetball M(c)/W(c), rock climbing M/W, sand volleyball M/W, skiing (downhill) M/W, soccer M/W, volleyball M/W.

Campus security: 24-hour emergency response devices and patrols, student patrols, late-night transport/escort service, controlled dormitory access.

Student services: health clinic, personal/psychological counseling, women's center.

COSTS & FINANCIAL AID

Costs (2020–21) ***Comprehensive fee:*** $50,490 includes full-time tuition ($35,290), mandatory fees ($1250), and room and board ($13,950). Full-time tuition and fees vary according to class time and location. Part-time tuition: $1000 per credit hour. Part-time tuition and fees vary according to class time and location. ***College room only:*** $8000. Room and board charges vary according to housing facility. ***Payment plan:*** installment. ***Waivers:*** employees or children of employees.

Financial Aid Of all full-time matriculated undergraduates who enrolled in 2018, 1,066 applied for aid, 974 were judged to have need, 183 had their need fully met. 224 Federal Work-Study jobs (averaging $2436). In 2018, 240 non-need-based awards were made. ***Average percent of need met:*** 78. ***Average financial aid package:*** $26,857. ***Average need-based loan:*** $3765. ***Average need-based gift aid:*** $18,861. ***Average non-need-based aid:*** $18,916. ***Average indebtedness upon graduation:*** $34,873.

APPLYING

Standardized Tests *Required for some:* SAT or ACT (for admission).

Options: electronic application, early action, deferred entrance.

Required: essay or personal statement, high school transcript, 1 letter of recommendation. ***Required for some:*** interview. ***Recommended:*** 2 letters of recommendation.

Application deadlines: rolling (freshmen), rolling (out-of-state freshmen), rolling (transfers), 12/1 (early action).

Notification: continuous (out-of-state freshmen), continuous (transfers), 12/1 (early action).

CONTACT

Mr. Paul Brower, Assistant Dean for Enrollment, Nichols College, 129 Center Road, Dudley, MA 01571. *Phone:* 508-213-2371. *Toll-free phone:* 800-470-3379. *E-mail:* paul.brower@nichols.edu.

Northeastern University

Boston, Massachusetts

http://www.northeastern.edu/

- **Independent** university, founded 1898
- **Urban** 73-acre campus
- **Coed**
- **Very difficult** entrance level

FACULTY

Student/faculty ratio: 14:1.

ACADEMICS

Calendar: semesters. *Degrees:* bachelor's, master's, doctoral, and post-master's certificates.

Library: Snell Library plus 3 others. *Books:* 530,566 (physical), 589,334 (digital/electronic). Study areas open 24 hours, 5–7 days a week; students can reserve study rooms.

STUDENT LIFE

Housing options: on-campus residence required through sophomore year; coed. Campus housing is university owned and leased by the school. Freshman campus housing is guaranteed.

Activities and organizations: drama/theater group, student-run newspaper, radio and television station, choral group, Student Government Association, Council for University Programs, Resident Student Association, Downhillers Ski and Snowboard Club, Northeastern University Huskiers and Outing Club, national fraternities, national sororities.

Athletics Member NCAA. All Division I.

Campus security: 24-hour emergency response devices and patrols, student patrols, late-night transport/escort service, controlled dormitory access, public safety website.

Student services: health clinic, personal/psychological counseling, veterans affairs office.

COSTS & FINANCIAL AID

Costs (2019–20) ***Comprehensive fee:*** $70,436 includes full-time tuition ($52,420), mandatory fees ($1086), and room and board ($16,930).

College room only: $9250. Room and board charges vary according to board plan and housing facility.

Financial Aid Of all full-time matriculated undergraduates who enrolled in 2019, 1,425 applied for aid, 1,161 were judged to have need, 243 had their need fully met. In 2019, 738 non-need-based awards were made. ***Average percent of need met:*** 85. ***Average financial aid package:*** $38,819. ***Average need-based loan:*** $6473. ***Average need-based gift aid:*** $27,705. ***Average non-need-based aid:*** $18,120. ***Average indebtedness upon graduation:*** $33,661.

APPLYING

Standardized Tests *Required:* SAT or ACT (for admission).

Options: electronic application, early admission, early decision, early action, deferred entrance.

Application fee: $75.

CONTACT

Northeastern University, 360 Huntington Avenue, Boston, MA 02115. *Phone:* 617-373-2200. *E-mail:* admissions@northeastern.edu.

See below for display ad and page 1090 for the College Close-Up.

Northpoint Bible College

Haverhill, Massachusetts

http://northpoint.edu/

CONTACT

Helen Brouillette, Admissions Director, Northpoint Bible College, 320 South Main Street, Haverhill, MA 01835. *Phone:* 800-356-4014. *Toll-free phone:* 800-356-4014. *E-mail:* admissions@zbc.edu.

Pine Manor College

Chestnut Hill, Massachusetts

http://www.pmc.edu/

CONTACT

Pine Manor College, 400 Heath Street, Chestnut Hill, MA 02467. *Phone:* 617-731-7107. *Toll-free phone:* 800-762-1357.

Regis College

Weston, Massachusetts

http://www.regiscollege.edu/

- **Independent Roman Catholic** comprehensive, founded 1927
- **Suburban** 131-acre campus with easy access to Boston
- **Coed** 1,353 undergraduate students, 83% full-time, 82% women, 18% men
- **Moderately difficult** entrance level, 79% of applicants were admitted

UNDERGRAD STUDENTS

1,124 full-time, 229 part-time. Students come from 11 states and territories; 2 other countries; 19% are from out of state; 11% Black or African American, non-Hispanic/Latino; 14% Hispanic/Latino; 3% Asian, non-Hispanic/Latino; 1% Two or more races, non-Hispanic/Latino; 27% Race/ethnicity unknown; 0.8% international; 4% transferred in; 50% live on campus.

Freshmen:

Admission: 2,256 applied, 1,788 admitted, 212 enrolled.

Retention: 89% of full-time freshmen returned.

FACULTY

Total: 401, 31% full-time.

ACADEMICS

Calendar: semesters. *Degrees:* certificates, associate, bachelor's, master's, doctoral, post-master's, and postbachelor's certificates.

Special study options: academic remediation for entering students, accelerated degree program, adult/continuing education programs, advanced placement credit, distance learning, double majors, honors programs, independent study, internships, off-campus study, part-time degree program, services for LD students, student-designed majors, study abroad, summer session for credit. ***ROTC:*** Army (c).

Unusual degree programs: 3-2 business administration; nursing; social work.

Computers: 196 computers/terminals are available on campus for general student use. Students can access the following: campus intranet, computer help desk, free student e-mail accounts, online (class) grades, online (class) registration, online (class) schedules, online bills, financial aid award letters and check-in requirements. Campuswide network is available. 100% of college-owned or -operated housing units are wired for high-speed Internet access. Wireless service is available via entire campus.

Library: Regis College Library. *Books:* 48,867 (physical), 381,876 (digital/electronic); *Serial titles:* 51 (physical), 1,106 (digital/electronic); *Databases:* 62. Weekly public service hours: 108.

STUDENT LIFE

Housing options: coed, special housing for students with disabilities. Campus housing is university owned. Freshman campus housing is guaranteed.

Activities and organizations: drama/theater group, choral group, Campus Ministry, SGA-Student Government Association, Asian American Student Organization, Dynasty Step Squad, Black Student Organization.

Athletics Member NCAA. All Division III. ***Intercollegiate sports:*** basketball M/W, cross-country running M/W, field hockey W, lacrosse M/W, soccer M/W, softball W, swimming and diving M/W, tennis M/W, track and field M/W, volleyball M/W. ***Intramural sports:*** basketball M/W, soccer M/W, volleyball M/W.

Campus security: 24-hour emergency response devices and patrols, late-night transport/escort service, controlled dormitory access.

Student services: health clinic, personal/psychological counseling, veterans affairs office.

COSTS & FINANCIAL AID

Costs (2020–21) ***Comprehensive fee:*** $58,440 includes full-time tuition ($42,650) and room and board ($15,790). Part-time tuition: $1422 per credit hour. ***Room and board:*** Room and board charges vary according to housing facility. ***Payment plan:*** installment. ***Waivers:*** children of alumni and employees or children of employees.

Financial Aid ***Average indebtedness upon graduation:*** $24,178.

APPLYING

Standardized Tests *Required for some:* SAT or ACT (for admission).

Options: electronic application, early admission, early action, deferred entrance.

Application fee: $50.

Required: essay or personal statement, high school transcript, minimum 2.0 GPA, 2 letters of recommendation. ***Required for some:*** interview. ***Recommended:*** minimum 3.0 GPA, interview, rank in upper 50% of high school class.

CONTACT

Dr. Laura Bertonazzi, Dean of Undergraduate Enrollment and Retention, Regis College, 235 Wellesley Street, Weston, MA 02493. *Phone:* 781-768-7060. *Toll-free phone:* 866-438-7344. *Fax:* 781-768-7060. *E-mail:* admission@regiscollege.edu.

Salem State University

Salem, Massachusetts

http://www.salemstate.edu/

- **State-supported** comprehensive, founded 1854, part of Massachusetts Public Higher Education System
- **Urban** 62-acre campus with easy access to Boston
- **Coed** 6,273 undergraduate students, 80% full-time, 62% women, 38% men
- **Minimally difficult** entrance level, 86% of applicants were admitted

UNDERGRAD STUDENTS

4,997 full-time, 1,276 part-time. 4% are from out of state; 9% Black or African American, non-Hispanic/Latino; 19% Hispanic/Latino; 3% Asian, non-Hispanic/Latino; 0.1% Native Hawaiian or other Pacific Islander, non-Hispanic/Latino; 0.2% American Indian or Alaska Native, non-Hispanic/Latino; 3% Two or more races, non-Hispanic/Latino; 2% Race/ethnicity unknown; 3% international; 8% transferred in; 31% live on campus.

Freshmen:

Admission: 5,825 applied, 4,985 admitted, 1,011 enrolled. ***Average high school GPA:*** 3.2. ***Test scores:*** SAT evidence-based reading and writing scores over 500: 71%; SAT math scores over 500: 70%; SAT evidence-based reading and writing scores over 600: 20%; SAT math scores over 600: 13%; SAT evidence-based reading and writing scores over 700: 2%; SAT math scores over 700: 1%.

Retention: 73% of full-time freshmen returned.

FACULTY

Total: 757, 42% full-time.

Student/faculty ratio: 13:1.

ACADEMICS

Calendar: semesters. *Degrees:* bachelor's, master's, post-master's, and postbachelor's certificates.

Special study options: academic remediation for entering students, accelerated degree program, adult/continuing education programs, advanced placement credit, distance learning, double majors, English as a second language, external degree program, honors programs, independent study, internships, off-campus study, part-time degree program, services for LD students, student-designed majors, study abroad, summer session for credit. ***ROTC:*** Army (c), Air Force (c).

Computers: 255 computers/terminals are available on campus for general student use. Students can access the following: campus intranet, computer help desk, free student e-mail accounts, online (class) grades, online (class) registration, online (class) schedules. Campuswide network is available. 100% of college-owned or -operated housing units are wired for high-speed Internet access. Wireless service is available via entire campus.

Library: Salem State University Library.

STUDENT LIFE

Housing options: coed, men-only, women-only, cooperative, special housing for students with disabilities. Campus housing is university owned. Freshman applicants given priority for college housing.

Activities and organizations: drama/theater group, student-run radio station, choral group, Student Government Association, Program Council, Residence Hall Association, Multicultural Student Association, International Student Association, national fraternities, national sororities.

Athletics Member NCAA. All Division III. ***Intercollegiate sports:*** baseball M, basketball M/W, cross-country running M/W, field hockey W, golf M, ice hockey M/W(c), lacrosse M/W, soccer M/W, softball W, tennis M/W, volleyball W. ***Intramural sports:*** cheerleading M/W, football M/W, rugby M/W, ultimate Frisbee M/W, volleyball M/W.

Campus security: 24-hour emergency response devices and patrols, late-night transport/escort service, controlled dormitory access.

Student services: health clinic, personal/psychological counseling, women's center, legal services.

FINANCIAL AID

Financial Aid Of all full-time matriculated undergraduates who enrolled in 2018, 4,580 applied for aid, 3,903 were judged to have need, 317 had their need fully met. In 2018, 213 non-need-based awards were made. ***Average percent of need met:*** 58. ***Average financial aid package:*** $10,189. ***Average need-based loan:*** $4323. ***Average need-based gift aid:*** $6297. ***Average non-need-based aid:*** $1771. ***Average indebtedness upon graduation:*** $26,204.

APPLYING

Standardized Tests *Required for some:* SAT or ACT (for admission).

Options: electronic application, early action, deferred entrance.

Application fee: $50.

Required: high school transcript. ***Required for some:*** interview.

Application deadlines: 5/1 (freshmen), rolling (transfers), 11/15 (early action).

Notification: continuous (freshmen), continuous (transfers), 1/1 (early action).

CONTACT

Dr. Mary Dunn, Assistant Dean for Undergraduate Admissions, Salem State University, 352 Lafayette Street, Salem, MA 01970. *Phone:* 978-542-6202. *Fax:* 978-542-6893. *E-mail:* admissions@salemstate.edu.

Simmons University

Boston, Massachusetts

http://www.simmons.edu/

- **Independent** university, founded 1899
- **Urban** 12-acre campus with easy access to Boston
- **Endowment** $195.7 million
- **Undergraduate: women only; graduate: coed** 1,777 undergraduate students, 90% full-time, 100% women, 0% men
- **Moderately difficult** entrance level, 73% of applicants were admitted

UNDERGRAD STUDENTS

1,607 full-time, 170 part-time. Students come from 50 states and territories; 11 other countries; 38% are from out of state; 7% Black or African American, non-Hispanic/Latino; 8% Hispanic/Latino; 11% Asian, non-Hispanic/Latino; 5% Two or more races, non-Hispanic/Latino; 3% Race/ethnicity unknown; 5% international; 2% transferred in; 61% live on campus.

Freshmen:

Admission: 2,933 applied, 2,145 admitted, 433 enrolled. ***Average high school GPA:*** 3.9. ***Test scores:*** SAT evidence-based reading and writing scores over 500: 98%; SAT math scores over 500: 98%; ACT scores over 18: 95%; SAT evidence-based reading and writing scores over 600: 61%; SAT math scores over 600: 43%; ACT scores over 24: 71%; SAT evidence-based reading and writing scores over 700: 10%; SAT math scores over 700: 6%; ACT scores over 30: 24%.

Retention: 83% of full-time freshmen returned.

FACULTY

Total: 970, 24% full-time, 15% with terminal degrees.

Student/faculty ratio: 8:1.

ACADEMICS

Calendar: semesters. *Degrees:* bachelor's, master's, doctoral, and post-master's certificates.

Special study options: accelerated degree program, adult/continuing education programs, advanced placement credit, distance learning, double majors, external degree program, honors programs, independent study, internships, off-campus study, part-time degree program, services for LD students, student-designed majors, study abroad, summer session for credit. ***ROTC:*** Army (c).

Unusual degree programs: 3-2 business administration; nursing; social work.

Computers: 570 computers/terminals are available on campus for general student use. Students can access the following: campus intranet, computer help desk, free student e-mail accounts, online (class) grades, online (class) registration, online (class) schedules. Campuswide network is available. 100% of college-owned or -operated housing units are wired for high-speed Internet access. Wireless service is available via entire campus.

Library: Beatley Library. *Books:* 147,693 (physical), 38,799 (digital/electronic); *Serial titles:* 50,977 (digital/electronic); *Databases:* 123. Weekly public service hours: 105; study areas open 24 hours, 5–7 days a week; students can reserve study rooms.

STUDENT LIFE

Housing options: on-campus residence required for freshman year; coed, women-only. Campus housing is university owned. Freshman applicants given priority for college housing.

Activities and organizations: drama/theater group, student-run newspaper, radio station, choral group, Simmons College Dance Company, Student Government Association, Simmons Student Nursing Association, Sexuality Women and Gender (SWAG), Class Councils.

Athletics Member NCAA. All Division III. ***Intercollegiate sports:*** basketball W, crew W, cross-country running W, field hockey W, lacrosse W, soccer W, softball W, swimming and diving W, tennis W, volleyball W. ***Intramural sports:*** basketball M/W, rugby W(c), soccer M/W, softball M/W, tennis M/W, volleyball M/W.

Campus security: 24-hour emergency response devices and patrols, late-night transport/escort service, controlled dormitory access.

Student services: health clinic, personal/psychological counseling, women's center.

COSTS & FINANCIAL AID

Costs (2020–21) ***Comprehensive fee:*** $58,990 includes full-time tuition ($42,080), mandatory fees ($1250), and room and board ($15,660). Full-time tuition and fees vary according to course load and program. Part-time tuition: $1315 per credit hour. Part-time tuition and fees vary according to course load and program. ***Required fees:*** $260 per term part-time. ***Room and board:*** Room and board charges vary according to board plan and location. ***Payment plan:*** installment. ***Waivers:*** employees or children of employees.

Financial Aid Of all full-time matriculated undergraduates who enrolled in 2019, 1,329 applied for aid, 1,213 were judged to have need, 247 had their need fully met. 887 Federal Work-Study jobs (averaging $2523). In 2019, 359 non-need-based awards were made. ***Average percent of need met:*** 79. ***Average financial aid package:*** $34,674. ***Average need-based loan:*** $4054. ***Average need-based gift aid:*** $30,651. ***Average non-need-based aid:*** $22,538. ***Average indebtedness upon graduation:*** $37,935.

APPLYING

Standardized Tests *Required:* SAT or ACT (for admission).

Options: electronic application, early action, deferred entrance.

Application fee: $55.

Required: essay or personal statement, high school transcript, 2 letters of recommendation. ***Recommended:*** minimum 3.0 GPA, interview.

Application deadlines: 2/1 (freshmen), 4/1 (transfers), 12/1 (early action).

Notification: continuous until 3/15 (freshmen), 3/15 (out-of-state freshmen), 1/15 (early action).

CONTACT

Danielle Navarro, Director of Enrollment Reporting Operations, Simmons University, 300 The Fenway, Boston, MA 02115. *Phone:* 617-521-2512. *Toll-free phone:* 800-345-8468. *Fax:* 617-521-3190. *E-mail:* danielle.navarro@simmons.edu.

Smith College

Northampton, Massachusetts

http://www.smith.edu/

- **Independent** comprehensive, founded 1871
- **Small-town** 147-acre campus with easy access to Hartford
- **Undergraduate: women only; graduate: coed** 2,531 undergraduate students, 100% full-time, 100% women, 0% men
- **Very difficult** entrance level, 32% of applicants were admitted

UNDERGRAD STUDENTS

2,519 full-time, 12 part-time. 81% are from out of state; 6% Black or African American, non-Hispanic/Latino; 12% Hispanic/Latino; 10% Asian, non-Hispanic/Latino; 0.1% Native Hawaiian or other Pacific Islander, non-Hispanic/Latino; 5% Two or more races, non-Hispanic/Latino; 4% Race/ethnicity unknown; 14% international; 2% transferred in; 94% live on campus.

Freshmen:

Admission: 5,597 applied, 1,817 admitted, 633 enrolled. ***Average high school GPA:*** 4.0. ***Test scores:*** SAT evidence-based reading and writing scores over 500: 100%; SAT math scores over 500: 100%; ACT scores over 18: 100%; SAT evidence-based reading and writing scores over 600: 98%; SAT math scores over 600: 90%; ACT scores over 24: 100%; SAT evidence-based reading and writing scores over 700: 62%; SAT math scores over 700: 62%; ACT scores over 30: 82%.

Retention: 94% of full-time freshmen returned.

FACULTY

Total: 307, 94% full-time, 96% with terminal degrees.

Student/faculty ratio: 9:1.

ACADEMICS

Calendar: semesters. *Degrees:* bachelor's, master's, doctoral, post-master's, and postbachelor's certificates.

Special study options: accelerated degree program, adult/continuing education programs, double majors, honors programs, independent study, internships, part-time degree program, student-designed majors, study abroad. ***ROTC:*** Army (c), Air Force (c).

Computers: Students can access the following: campus intranet, computer help desk, free student e-mail accounts, online (class) grades, online (class) registration, online (class) schedules. Campuswide network is available. 100% of college-owned or -operated housing units are wired for high-speed Internet access. Wireless service is available via classrooms, computer centers, computer labs, dorm rooms, learning centers, libraries, student centers.
Library: Neilson Library.

STUDENT LIFE
Housing options: on-campus residence required through senior year; women-only, cooperative. Campus housing is university owned. Freshman campus housing is guaranteed.

Activities and organizations: drama/theater group, student-run newspaper, radio and television station, choral group.

Athletics Member NCAA. All Division III. ***Intercollegiate sports:*** basketball W, crew W, cross-country running W, equestrian sports W, field hockey W, lacrosse W, soccer W, softball W, squash W, swimming and diving W, tennis W, track and field W, volleyball W. ***Intramural sports:*** badminton W(c), cheerleading W(c), crew W, equestrian sports W(c), fencing W(c), golf W(c), ice hockey W(c), rock climbing W, rugby W(c), soccer W, squash W, ultimate Frisbee W(c).

Campus security: 24-hour emergency response devices and patrols, late-night transport/escort service, self-defense workshops, emergency telephones, programs in crime and sexual assault prevention.

COSTS & FINANCIAL AID
Costs (2020–21) ***Comprehensive fee:*** $74,874 includes full-time tuition ($55,830), mandatory fees ($284), and room and board ($18,760). Part-time tuition: $1740 per credit. ***College room only:*** $9400. ***Payment plans:*** tuition prepayment, installment. ***Waivers:*** employees or children of employees.

Financial Aid Of all full-time matriculated undergraduates who enrolled in 2019, 1,688 applied for aid, 1,515 were judged to have need, 1,515 had their need fully met. In 2019, 221 non-need-based awards were made. ***Average percent of need met:*** 100. ***Average financial aid package:*** $56,230. ***Average need-based loan:*** $4111. ***Average need-based gift aid:*** $51,099. ***Average non-need-based aid:*** $16,497. ***Average indebtedness upon graduation:*** $21,460.

APPLYING
Standardized Tests *Required for some:* SAT or ACT (for admission).

Options: electronic application, early admission, early decision, deferred entrance.

Required: essay or personal statement, high school transcript, 3 letters of recommendation. ***Recommended:*** interview.

Early decision deadline: 11/15 (for plan 1), 1/1 (for plan 2).

Notification: 12/15 (early decision).

CONTACT
Ms. Debra Shaver, Dean of Admissions, Smith College, 7 College Lane, Northampton, MA 01063. *Phone:* 413-585-2500. *Toll-free phone:* 800-383-3232. *Fax:* 413-585-2527. *E-mail:* admission@smith.edu.

Springfield College
Springfield, Massachusetts
http://www.springfield.edu/

- **Independent** comprehensive, founded 1885
- **Suburban** 150-acre campus
- **Coed** 2,175 undergraduate students, 99% full-time, 50% women, 50% men
- **Moderately difficult** entrance level, 68% of applicants were admitted

UNDERGRAD STUDENTS
2,158 full-time, 17 part-time. 62% are from out of state; 5% Black or African American, non-Hispanic/Latino; 8% Hispanic/Latino; 2% Asian, non-Hispanic/Latino; 0.3% American Indian or Alaska Native, non-Hispanic/Latino; 3% Two or more races, non-Hispanic/Latino; 4% Race/ethnicity unknown; 4% international; 4% transferred in; 87% live on campus.

Freshmen:
Admission: 3,616 applied, 2,461 admitted, 596 enrolled. ***Average high school GPA:*** 3.4. ***Test scores:*** SAT evidence-based reading and writing scores over 500: 82%; SAT math scores over 500: 82%; ACT scores over 18: 91%; SAT evidence-based reading and writing scores over 600: 34%; SAT math scores over 600: 31%; ACT scores over 24: 52%; SAT evidence-based reading and writing scores over 700: 4%; SAT math scores over 700: 4%; ACT scores over 30: 8%.

Retention: 86% of full-time freshmen returned.

FACULTY
Total: 398, 49% full-time, 58% with terminal degrees.

ACADEMICS
Calendar: semesters. *Degrees:* bachelor's, master's, doctoral, and post-master's certificates.

Special study options: adult/continuing education programs, advanced placement credit, double majors, English as a second language, external degree program, honors programs, independent study, internships, off-campus study, part-time degree program, services for LD students, student-designed majors, study abroad, summer session for credit. ***ROTC:*** Army (c), Air Force (c).

Unusual degree programs: 3-2 physical therapy, physician assistant, occupational therapy.

Computers: Campuswide network is available.
Library: Babson Library.

STUDENT LIFE
Housing options: on-campus residence required through junior year; coed, special housing for students with disabilities. Campus housing is university owned. Freshman campus housing is guaranteed.

Activities and organizations: drama/theater group, student-run newspaper, radio and television station, choral group.

Athletics Member NCAA. All Division III. ***Intercollegiate sports:*** baseball M, basketball M/W, cross-country running M/W, field hockey W, football M, golf M, gymnastics M/W, lacrosse M/W, soccer M/W, softball W, swimming and diving M/W, tennis M/W, track and field M/W, volleyball M/W, wrestling M.

Student services: health clinic, personal/psychological counseling.

COSTS & FINANCIAL AID
Costs (2020–21) ***Comprehensive fee:*** $51,495 includes full-time tuition ($38,030), mandatory fees ($535), and room and board ($12,930). Full-time tuition and fees vary according to class time, course load, location, and program. Part-time tuition: $1142 per credit hour. Part-time tuition and fees vary according to class time, course load, location, and program. ***College room only:*** $7040. Room and board charges vary according to board plan and housing facility. ***Payment plan:*** installment. ***Waivers:*** employees or children of employees.

Financial Aid Of all full-time matriculated undergraduates who enrolled in 2019, 1,920 applied for aid, 1,717 were judged to have need, 246 had their need fully met. In 2019, 374 non-need-based awards were made. ***Average percent of need met:*** 64. ***Average financial aid package:*** $28,667. ***Average need-based loan:*** $4019. ***Average need-based gift aid:*** $23,983. ***Average non-need-based aid:*** $18,399. ***Average indebtedness upon graduation:*** $43,821.

APPLYING
Standardized Tests *Required for some:* SAT or ACT (for admission).

Options: electronic application, early decision, deferred entrance.

Application fee: $50.

Required: high school transcript, 1 letter of recommendation. ***Required for some:*** portfolio. ***Recommended:*** interview.

Application deadlines: 4/1 (freshmen), 8/1 (transfers).

Early decision deadline: 12/1 (for plan 1), 1/15 (for plan 2).

Notification: continuous (freshmen), continuous (transfers), 2/1 (early decision plan 1), 3/1 (early decision plan 2).

CONTACT
Richard K. Veres, Director of Undergraduate Admissions, Springfield College, 263 Alden Street, Springfield, MA 01109. *Phone:* 413-748-3136. *Toll-free phone:* 800-343-1257. *Fax:* 413-748-3694. *E-mail:* admissions@spfldcol.edu.

Stonehill College

Easton, Massachusetts

http://www.stonehill.edu/

- **Independent Roman Catholic** comprehensive, founded 1948
- **Suburban** 384-acre campus with easy access to Boston
- **Endowment** $211.4 million
- **Coed**
- **Very difficult** entrance level

FACULTY
Student/faculty ratio: 12:1.

ACADEMICS
Calendar: semesters. *Degrees:* bachelor's and master's.
Library: MacPhaidin Library plus 2 others. *Books:* 163,838 (physical), 302,839 (digital/electronic); *Serial titles:* 3,788 (physical), 79,489 (digital/electronic); *Databases:* 67. Weekly public service hours: 110; students can reserve study rooms.

STUDENT LIFE
Housing options: coed, women-only, special housing for students with disabilities. Campus housing is university owned.

Activities and organizations: drama/theater group, student-run newspaper, radio station, choral group, Community Engagement, Recreation/Intramural Sports Teams, Dance Club, Student Government Association, Financial Management Association.

Athletics Member NCAA. All Division II except golf (Division I).

Campus security: 24-hour emergency response devices and patrols, late-night transport/escort service, controlled dormitory access, restricted access on weekends.

Student services: health clinic, personal/psychological counseling.

COSTS & FINANCIAL AID
Costs (2019–20) ***Comprehensive fee:*** $61,040 includes full-time tuition ($44,420) and room and board ($16,620). Part-time tuition: $1481 per credit hour. Part-time tuition and fees vary according to course load. ***College room only:*** $10,379. ***Payment plans:*** tuition prepayment, installment.

Financial Aid Of all full-time matriculated undergraduates who enrolled in 2019, 1,894 applied for aid, 1,546 were judged to have need, 806 had their need fully met. In 2019, 866 non-need-based awards were made. ***Average percent of need met:*** 90. ***Average financial aid package:*** $31,521. ***Average need-based loan:*** $4365. ***Average need-based gift aid:*** $26,331. ***Average non-need-based aid:*** $20,340. ***Average indebtedness upon graduation:*** $38,359. ***Financial aid deadline:*** 2/1.

APPLYING
Options: electronic application, early decision, early action, deferred entrance.

Application fee: $60.

Required: essay or personal statement, high school transcript, 2 letters of recommendation. ***Recommended:*** interview.

CONTACT
Mr. Joseph P. Dacey, Dean of Admission, Stonehill College, 320 Washington Street, Easton, MA 02357. *Phone:* 508-565-1373. *Fax:* 508-565-1545. *E-mail:* admission@stonehill.edu.

Suffolk University

Boston, Massachusetts

http://www.suffolk.edu/

- **Independent** comprehensive, founded 1906
- **Urban** 4-acre campus with easy access to Boston, MA
- **Endowment** $256.3 million
- **Coed** 4,983 undergraduate students, 96% full-time, 56% women, 44% men
- **Moderately difficult** entrance level, 84% of applicants were admitted

UNDERGRAD STUDENTS
4,783 full-time, 200 part-time. Students come from 45 states and territories; 100 other countries; 32% are from out of state; 5% Black or African American, non-Hispanic/Latino; 13% Hispanic/Latino; 7% Asian, non-Hispanic/Latino; 0.1% Native Hawaiian or other Pacific Islander, non-Hispanic/Latino; 0.2% American Indian or Alaska Native, non-Hispanic/Latino; 3% Two or more races, non-Hispanic/Latino; 4% Race/ethnicity unknown; 20% international; 7% transferred in; 31% live on campus.

Freshmen:
Admission: 8,362 applied, 7,001 admitted, 1,118 enrolled. ***Average high school GPA:*** 3.3. ***Test scores:*** SAT evidence-based reading and writing scores over 500: 83%; SAT math scores over 500: 81%; ACT scores over 18: 91%; SAT evidence-based reading and writing scores over 600: 35%; SAT math scores over 600: 28%; ACT scores over 24: 49%; SAT evidence-based reading and writing scores over 700: 3%; SAT math scores over 700: 3%; ACT scores over 30: 10%.

Retention: 77% of full-time freshmen returned.

FACULTY
Total: 650, 59% full-time, 50% with terminal degrees.
Student/faculty ratio: 15:1.

ACADEMICS
Calendar: semesters. *Degrees:* certificates, diplomas, associate, bachelor's, master's, doctoral, post-master's, and postbachelor's certificates (doctoral degree in law).

Special study options: academic remediation for entering students, accelerated degree program, adult/continuing education programs, advanced placement credit, distance learning, double majors, English as a second language, honors programs, independent study, internships, part-time degree program, services for LD students, student-designed majors, study abroad, summer session for credit. ***ROTC:*** Army (c).

Computers: 675 computers/terminals and 8,000 ports are available on campus for general student use. Students can access the following: campus intranet, computer help desk, free student e-mail accounts, online (class) grades, online (class) registration, online (class) schedules. Campuswide network is available. 100% of college-owned or -operated housing units are wired for high-speed Internet access. Wireless service is available via entire campus.
Library: Mildred Sawyer Library plus 2 others. *Books:* 128,945 (physical), 296,604 (digital/electronic); *Serial titles:* 307 (physical), 76,045 (digital/electronic); *Databases:* 144. Weekly public service hours: 103; students can reserve study rooms.

STUDENT LIFE
Housing options: coed, special housing for students with disabilities. Campus housing is university owned. Freshman campus housing is guaranteed.

Activities and organizations: drama/theater group, student-run newspaper, radio and television station, choral group, Student Government Association, Program Council, Caribbean Student Network, Black Student Union, Asian American Association, national fraternities, national sororities.

Athletics Member NCAA. All Division III. ***Intercollegiate sports:*** baseball M, basketball M/W, cross-country running M/W, golf M/W, ice hockey M/W, soccer M/W, softball W, tennis M/W, track and field M/W, volleyball W. ***Intramural sports:*** cheerleading M(c)/W(c), soccer M(c)/W(c).

Campus security: 24-hour emergency response devices, late-night transport/escort service, controlled dormitory access.

Student services: health clinic, personal/psychological counseling.

COSTS & FINANCIAL AID
Costs (2020–21) ***One-time required fee:*** $260. ***Comprehensive fee:*** $60,042 includes full-time tuition ($41,242), mandatory fees ($666), and room and board ($18,134). Full-time tuition and fees vary according to location and reciprocity agreements. Part-time tuition: $1213 per credit hour. Part-time tuition and fees vary according to course load, location, and reciprocity agreements. ***Required fees:*** $70 per term part-time. ***College room only:*** $14,560. Room and board charges vary according to board plan, housing facility, and location. ***Payment plans:*** installment, deferred payment. ***Waivers:*** children of alumni, senior citizens, and employees or children of employees.

Financial Aid Of all full-time matriculated undergraduates who enrolled in 2019, 3,161 applied for aid, 2,896 were judged to have need, 330 had their need fully met. 711 Federal Work-Study jobs (averaging $2443). 533 state and other part-time jobs (averaging $2566). In 2019, 1417 non-need-based awards were made. ***Average percent of need met:*** 68. ***Average financial aid package:*** $28,833. ***Average need-based loan:*** $4519.

Average need-based gift aid: $10,563. ***Average non-need-based aid:*** $14,264. ***Average indebtedness upon graduation:*** $28,582. ***Financial aid deadline:*** 6/30.

APPLYING
Standardized Tests *Required for some:* SAT or ACT (for admission).

Options: electronic application, early action, deferred entrance.

Application fee: $50.

Required: essay or personal statement, high school transcript, 1 letter of recommendation. ***Required for some:*** interview.

Application deadlines: 2/15 (freshmen), 6/30 (transfers), 11/15 (early action).

Notification: continuous (freshmen), continuous (transfers).

CONTACT
Ms. Donna Grand Pre, Vice President for Admissions and Financial Aid, Suffolk University, 8 Ashburton Place, Boston, MA 02108-2770. *Phone:* 617-573-8460. *Toll-free phone:* 800-6-SUFFOLK. *Fax:* 617-742-4291. *E-mail:* admission@suffolk.edu.

Thomas Aquinas College - New England

Northfield, Massachusetts

http://www.thomasaquinas.edu/

CONTACT
Thomas Aquinas College - New England, 231 Main Street, Northfield, MA 01360.

Tufts University

Medford, Massachusetts

http://www.tufts.edu/

- **Independent** university, founded 1852
- **Suburban** 150-acre campus with easy access to Boston
- **Coed**
- **Most difficult** entrance level

FACULTY
Student/faculty ratio: 9:1.

ACADEMICS
Calendar: semesters. *Degrees:* certificates, bachelor's, master's, doctoral, post-master's, and postbachelor's certificates.
Library: Tisch Library plus 3 others. *Books:* 1.3 million (physical), 432,877 (digital/electronic); *Serial titles:* 1,012 (physical); *Databases:* 83,216. Weekly public service hours: 110; students can reserve study rooms.

STUDENT LIFE
Housing options: on-campus residence required through sophomore year; coed, women-only, special housing for students with disabilities. Campus housing is university owned. Freshman campus housing is guaranteed.

Activities and organizations: drama/theater group, student-run newspaper, radio and television station, choral group, Leonard Carmichael Society (community service), Tufts Dance Collective, intramural sports, Tufts Daily (newspaper), Tufts Mountain Club, national fraternities, national sororities.

Athletics Member NCAA. All Division III.

Campus security: 24-hour emergency response devices and patrols, late-night transport/escort service, controlled dormitory access, security lighting, call boxes to campus police.

Student services: health clinic, personal/psychological counseling, women's center, legal services.

COSTS & FINANCIAL AID
Costs (2019–20) ***Comprehensive fee:*** $73,664 includes full-time tuition ($57,324), mandatory fees ($1254), and room and board ($15,086). Part-time tuition: $2389 per credit hour. ***Room and board:*** Room and board charges vary according to board plan. ***Payment plans:*** tuition prepayment, installment.

Financial Aid Of all full-time matriculated undergraduates who enrolled in 2019, 2,480 applied for aid, 2,113 were judged to have need, 2,078 had their need fully met. 1,609 Federal Work-Study jobs (averaging $2015). 181 state and other part-time jobs (averaging $2080). In 2019, 90 non-need-based awards were made. ***Average percent of need met:*** 98. ***Average financial aid package:*** $49,215. ***Average need-based loan:*** $2910. ***Average need-based gift aid:*** $47,554. ***Average non-need-based aid:*** $4572. ***Average indebtedness upon graduation:*** $27,006.

APPLYING
Standardized Tests *Required:* SAT or ACT (for admission). *Required for some:* art portfolio in lieu of Subject Tests for applicants to the School of Museum of Fine Arts.

Options: electronic application, early admission, early decision, deferred entrance.

Application fee: $75.

Required: essay or personal statement, high school transcript, 2 letters of recommendation, Common Application or Coalition Application or QuestBridge Application, the Tufts Supplement. ***Recommended:*** interview.

CONTACT
Office of Undergraduate Admissions, Tufts University, Bendetson Hall, Medford, MA 02155. *Phone:* 617-627-3170. *Fax:* 617-627-3860. *E-mail:* undergraduate.admissions@tufts.edu.

University of Massachusetts Amherst

Amherst, Massachusetts

http://www.umass.edu/

- **State-supported** university, founded 1863, part of University of Massachusetts
- **Small-town** 1463-acre campus with easy access to Springfield, MA and Hartford, CT
- **Endowment** $362.6 million
- **Coed** 24,209 undergraduate students, 93% full-time, 50% women, 50% men
- **Moderately difficult** entrance level, 64% of applicants were admitted

UNDERGRAD STUDENTS
22,491 full-time, 1,718 part-time. Students come from 49 states and territories; 86 other countries; 17% are from out of state; 5% Black or African American, non-Hispanic/Latino; 8% Hispanic/Latino; 11% Asian, non-Hispanic/Latino; 0.1% Native Hawaiian or other Pacific Islander, non-Hispanic/Latino; 0.1% American Indian or Alaska Native, non-Hispanic/Latino; 3% Two or more races, non-Hispanic/Latino; 5% Race/ethnicity unknown; 7% international; 6% transferred in; 62% live on campus.

Freshmen:
Admission: 42,157 applied, 26,895 admitted, 5,766 enrolled. ***Average high school GPA:*** 3.9. ***Test scores:*** SAT evidence-based reading and writing scores over 500: 99%; SAT math scores over 500: 99%; ACT scores over 18: 100%; SAT evidence-based reading and writing scores over 600: 75%; SAT math scores over 600: 77%; ACT scores over 24: 91%; SAT evidence-based reading and writing scores over 700: 18%; SAT math scores over 700: 30%; ACT scores over 30: 46%.

Retention: 91% of full-time freshmen returned.

FACULTY
Total: 1,787, 82% full-time, 88% with terminal degrees.

Student/faculty ratio: 17:1.

ACADEMICS
Calendar: semesters. *Degrees:* certificates, associate, bachelor's, master's, doctoral, post-master's, and postbachelor's certificates.

Special study options: accelerated degree program, adult/continuing education programs, advanced placement credit, cooperative education, distance learning, double majors, English as a second language, freshman honors college, honors programs, independent study, internships, off-campus study, part-time degree program, services for LD students, student-designed majors, study abroad, summer session for credit. ***ROTC:*** Army (b), Air Force (b).

Computers: 539 computers/terminals and 430 ports are available on campus for general student use. Students can access the following: computer help desk, free student e-mail accounts, online (class) grades, online (class) registration, online (class) schedules, online housing

assignments, bill payment, Learning Management System, file storage, Web hosting, blogs. Campuswide network is available. 100% of college-owned or -operated housing units are wired for high-speed Internet access. Wireless service is available via entire campus.
Library: W. E. B. Du Bois Library plus 1 other. *Books:* 2.8 million (physical), 1.8 million (digital/electronic); *Serial titles:* 71,479 (physical), 168,025 (digital/electronic); *Databases:* 578. Weekly public service hours: 142; study areas open 24 hours, 5–7 days a week; students can reserve study rooms.

STUDENT LIFE
Housing options: on-campus residence required for freshman year; coed, special housing for students with disabilities. Campus housing is university owned. Freshman campus housing is guaranteed.

Activities and organizations: drama/theater group, student-run newspaper, radio and television station, choral group, marching band, Minutemen Marching Band, Ski and Board Club, Outing Club, University Programming Council, Student Government Association, national fraternities, national sororities.

Athletics Member NCAA. All Division I except football (Division I-A). ***Intercollegiate sports:*** baseball M(s), basketball M(s)/W(s), cheerleading W, crew W(s), cross-country running M(s)/W(s), field hockey W(s), ice hockey M(s), lacrosse M(s)/W(s), soccer M(s)/W(s), softball W(s), swimming and diving M(s)/W(s), tennis W(s), track and field M(s)/W(s). ***Intramural sports:*** badminton M/W, baseball M(c), basketball M/W, crew M(c), equestrian sports M(c)/W(c), fencing M(c)/W(c), field hockey W(c), football M/W, golf M(c)/W(c), gymnastics W(c), ice hockey M(c)/W(c), lacrosse M(c)/W(c), racquetball M/W, rugby M(c)/W(c), sailing M(c)/W(c), sand volleyball M/W, skiing (downhill) M(c)/W(c), soccer M(c)/W(c), softball W(c), swimming and diving M(c)/W(c), table tennis M(c)/W, tennis M(c)/W(c), triathlon M(c)/W(c), ultimate Frisbee M(c)/W(c), volleyball M(c)/W(c), water polo M(c)/W(c), wrestling M(c)/W(c).

Campus security: 24-hour emergency response devices and patrols, student patrols, late-night transport/escort service, controlled dormitory access.

Student services: health clinic, personal/psychological counseling, women's center, legal services, veterans affairs office.

COSTS & FINANCIAL AID
Costs (2019–20) ***One-time required fee:*** $485. ***Tuition:*** state resident $15,791 full-time, $658 per credit part-time; nonresident $35,112 full-time, $1463 per credit part-time. Full-time tuition and fees vary according to class time, location, program, reciprocity agreements, and student level. Part-time tuition and fees vary according to class time, course load, location, program, reciprocity agreements, and student level. ***Required fees:*** $598 full-time, $299 per term part-time. ***Room and board:*** $13,598; room only: $7280. Room and board charges vary according to board plan and housing facility. ***Payment plan:*** installment. ***Waivers:*** senior citizens and employees or children of employees.

Financial Aid Of all full-time matriculated undergraduates who enrolled in 2018, 16,826 applied for aid, 12,065 were judged to have need, 1,566 had their need fully met. 3,327 Federal Work-Study jobs (averaging $1918). In 2018, 5345 non-need-based awards were made. ***Average percent of need met:*** 82. ***Average financial aid package:*** $18,623. ***Average need-based loan:*** $4366. ***Average need-based gift aid:*** $11,180. ***Average non-need-based aid:*** $5595. ***Average indebtedness upon graduation:*** $31,755.

APPLYING
Standardized Tests *Required:* SAT or ACT (for admission).

Options: electronic application, early action, deferred entrance.

Application fee: $80.

Required: essay or personal statement, high school transcript, 1 letter of recommendation.

Application deadlines: 1/15 (freshmen), 4/15 (transfers), 11/1 (early action).

Notification: continuous (freshmen), continuous (transfers), 12/15 (early action).

CONTACT
Dr. James Roche, Vice Provost of Enrollment Management, University of Massachusetts Amherst, 255 Whitmore, Amherst, MA 01003. *Phone:* 413-545-0222. *Fax:* 413-545-4312. *E-mail:* mail@admissions.umass.edu.

University of Massachusetts Boston
Boston, Massachusetts
http://www.umb.edu/

- **State-supported** university, founded 1964, part of University of Massachusetts
- **Urban** 120-acre campus
- **Endowment** $88.6 million
- **Coed** 12,595 undergraduate students, 79% full-time, 55% women, 45% men
- **Moderately difficult** entrance level, 76% of applicants were admitted

UNDERGRAD STUDENTS
9,995 full-time, 2,600 part-time. Students come from 129 states and territories; 41 other countries; 5% are from out of state; 17% Black or African American, non-Hispanic/Latino; 17% Hispanic/Latino; 14% Asian, non-Hispanic/Latino; 0.2% American Indian or Alaska Native, non-Hispanic/Latino; 3% Two or more races, non-Hispanic/Latino; 5% Race/ethnicity unknown; 10% international; 11% transferred in; 9% live on campus.

Freshmen:
Admission: 13,649 applied, 10,393 admitted, 2,123 enrolled. ***Average high school GPA:*** 3.4. ***Test scores:*** SAT evidence-based reading and writing scores over 500: 87%; SAT math scores over 500: 82%; ACT scores over 18: 93%; SAT evidence-based reading and writing scores over 600: 41%; SAT math scores over 600: 31%; ACT scores over 24: 49%; SAT evidence-based reading and writing scores over 700: 3%; SAT math scores over 700: 5%; ACT scores over 30: 11%.

Retention: 75% of full-time freshmen returned.

FACULTY
Total: 1,135, 61% full-time, 66% with terminal degrees.

Student/faculty ratio: 16:1.

ACADEMICS
Calendar: semesters. *Degrees:* certificates, bachelor's, master's, doctoral, post-master's, and postbachelor's certificates.

Special study options: academic remediation for entering students, accelerated degree program, adult/continuing education programs, advanced placement credit, cooperative education, distance learning, double majors, English as a second language, freshman honors college, honors programs, independent study, internships, off-campus study, part-time degree program, services for LD students, student-designed majors, study abroad, summer session for credit. ***ROTC:*** Army (c), Navy (c), Air Force (c).

Computers: 350 computers/terminals are available on campus for general student use. Students can access the following: computer help desk, free student e-mail accounts, online (class) grades, online (class) registration, online (class) schedules. Campuswide network is available. Wireless service is available via entire campus.
Library: Joseph P. Healey Library. *Books:* 384,946 (physical), 607,630 (digital/electronic); *Serial titles:* 8,312 (physical), 101,013 (digital/electronic); *Databases:* 180.

STUDENT LIFE
Housing options: coed. Campus housing is university owned.

Activities and organizations: drama/theater group, student-run newspaper, radio station, choral group, Student Arts and Events Council, Haitian Student Association, Golden Key Honor Society, Campus Kitchens, Mass Media.

Athletics Member NCAA. All Division III. ***Intercollegiate sports:*** baseball M, basketball M/W, cross-country running M/W, ice hockey M/W, lacrosse M, soccer M/W, softball W, tennis M/W, track and field M/W, volleyball W. ***Intramural sports:*** basketball M/W, bowling M/W, football M, golf M/W, racquetball M/W, soccer M/W, softball M/W, volleyball M/W.

Campus security: 24-hour emergency response devices and patrols, late-night transport/escort service, crime prevention program, bicycle patrols.

Student services: health clinic, personal/psychological counseling, women's center, veterans affairs office.

COSTS & FINANCIAL AID
Costs (2019–20) ***Tuition:*** state resident $14,187 full-time, $591 per credit hour part-time; nonresident $34,649 full-time, $1444 per credit hour part-

time. Full-time tuition and fees vary according to program. Part-time tuition and fees vary according to program. ***Required fees:*** $426 full-time, $18 per credit hour part-time. ***Room and board:*** $16,902; room only: $11,352.

Financial Aid Of all full-time matriculated undergraduates who enrolled in 2018, 7,618 applied for aid, 6,834 were judged to have need, 1,273 had their need fully met. In 2018, 711 non-need-based awards were made. ***Average percent of need met:*** 83. ***Average financial aid package:*** $17,239. ***Average need-based loan:*** $4593. ***Average need-based gift aid:*** $10,586. ***Average non-need-based aid:*** $7929. ***Average indebtedness upon graduation:*** $25,645.

APPLYING

Standardized Tests *Required for some:* SAT or ACT (for admission).

Options: electronic application, early admission, early action, deferred entrance.

Application fee: $60.

Required: high school transcript, minimum 2.5 GPA, 1 letter of recommendation. ***Required for some:*** essay or personal statement, minimum 2.8 GPA.

Application deadlines: 3/1 (freshmen), 11/1 (early action).

Notification: continuous (freshmen).

CONTACT

Mr. Corey Ford, Director of Undergraduate Admissions, University of Massachusetts Boston, 100 Morrissey Boulevard, Boston, MA 02125-3393. *Phone:* 617-287-6100. *Fax:* 617-287-5999. *E-mail:* enrollment.info@umb.edu.

University of Massachusetts Dartmouth

North Dartmouth, Massachusetts

http://www.umassd.edu/

- **State-supported** university, founded 1895, part of University of Massachusetts
- **Suburban** 710-acre campus with easy access to Boston, Providence
- **Endowment** $58.2 million
- **Coed** 6,405 undergraduate students, 85% full-time, 50% women, 50% men
- **Moderately difficult** entrance level, 75% of applicants were admitted

UNDERGRAD STUDENTS

5,465 full-time, 940 part-time. Students come from 38 states and territories; 31 other countries; 9% are from out of state; 17% Black or African American, non-Hispanic/Latino; 10% Hispanic/Latino; 4% Asian, non-Hispanic/Latino; 0.1% American Indian or Alaska Native, non-Hispanic/Latino; 4% Two or more races, non-Hispanic/Latino; 4% Race/ethnicity unknown; 2% international; 8% transferred in; 49% live on campus.

Freshmen:

Admission: 8,623 applied, 6,453 admitted, 1,320 enrolled. ***Average high school GPA:*** 3.3. ***Test scores:*** SAT evidence-based reading and writing scores over 500: 74%; SAT math scores over 500: 78%; ACT scores over 18: 81%; SAT evidence-based reading and writing scores over 600: 27%; SAT math scores over 600: 24%; ACT scores over 24: 31%; SAT evidence-based reading and writing scores over 700: 3%; SAT math scores over 700: 3%; ACT scores over 30: 6%.

Retention: 70% of full-time freshmen returned.

FACULTY

Total: 599, 66% full-time, 686% with terminal degrees.

Student/faculty ratio: 16:1.

ACADEMICS

Calendar: semesters. *Degrees:* certificates, bachelor's, master's, doctoral, post-master's, and postbachelor's certificates.

Special study options: academic remediation for entering students, accelerated degree program, advanced placement credit, cooperative education, distance learning, double majors, English as a second language, honors programs, independent study, internships, off-campus study, part-time degree program, services for LD students, student-designed majors, study abroad, summer session for credit. ***ROTC:*** Army (c).

Unusual degree programs: 3-2 engineering; nursing.

Computers: 400 computers/terminals and 27,000 ports are available on campus for general student use. Students can access the following: campus intranet, computer help desk, free student e-mail accounts, online (class) grades, online (class) registration, online (class) schedules. Campuswide network is available. 100% of college-owned or -operated housing units are wired for high-speed Internet access. Wireless service is available via entire campus.

Library: Claire T. Carney Library. *Books:* 179,835 (physical), 97,780 (digital/electronic); *Serial titles:* 1,336 (physical), 130,988 (digital/electronic); *Databases:* 140. Students can reserve study rooms.

STUDENT LIFE

Housing options: coed, special housing for students with disabilities. Campus housing is university owned.

Activities and organizations: drama/theater group, student-run newspaper, radio station, choral group, Outdoor Club, Ski and Snowboard Club, 20 Cent Fiction, Relay for Life, American Red Cross, national fraternities, national sororities.

Athletics Member NCAA. All Division III. ***Intercollegiate sports:*** baseball M, basketball M/W, cross-country running M/W, equestrian sports W, field hockey W, football M, golf M, ice hockey M, lacrosse M/W, sailing W, soccer M/W, softball W, swimming and diving M/W, tennis M/W, track and field M/W, volleyball W. ***Intramural sports:*** badminton M/W, basketball M/W, football M/W, rugby M(c)/W(c), skiing (downhill) M(c)/W(c), soccer M/W, triathlon M/W, ultimate Frisbee M/W, volleyball M/W, water polo M/W.

Campus security: 24-hour emergency response devices and patrols, student patrols, late-night transport/escort service, controlled dormitory access.

Student services: health clinic, personal/psychological counseling, women's center.

COSTS & FINANCIAL AID

Costs (2019–20) ***One-time required fee:*** $100. ***Tuition:*** state resident $13,833 full-time, $576 per credit part-time; nonresident $29,578 full-time, $1232 per credit part-time. Full-time tuition and fees vary according to class time, program, and reciprocity agreements. Part-time tuition and fees vary according to class time, course load, program, and reciprocity agreements. ***Required fees:*** $525 full-time, $31 per credit part-time. ***Room and board:*** $14,064; room only: $5034. Room and board charges vary according to board plan and housing facility. ***Payment plan:*** installment. ***Waivers:*** senior citizens and employees or children of employees.

Financial Aid Of all full-time matriculated undergraduates who enrolled in 2018, 5,201 applied for aid, 4,398 were judged to have need, 855 had their need fully met. 2,042 Federal Work-Study jobs (averaging $1370). In 2018, 670 non-need-based awards were made. ***Average percent of need met:*** 83. ***Average financial aid package:*** $17,717. ***Average need-based loan:*** $4083. ***Average need-based gift aid:*** $10,854. ***Average non-need-based aid:*** $5927. ***Average indebtedness upon graduation:*** $34,824. ***Financial aid deadline:*** 6/30.

APPLYING

Standardized Tests *Required:* SAT or ACT (for admission).

Options: electronic application, early action, deferred entrance.

Application fee: $60.

Required: high school transcript, minimum 2.0 GPA. ***Recommended:*** essay or personal statement, 1 letter of recommendation.

Application deadlines: rolling (freshmen), rolling (out-of-state freshmen), rolling (transfers), rolling (early action).

Notification: continuous (freshmen), continuous (out-of-state freshmen), continuous (transfers), rolling (early action).

CONTACT

University of Massachusetts Dartmouth, 285 Old Westport Road, North Dartmouth, MA 02747-2300. *Phone:* 508-999-8605.

University of Massachusetts Lowell

Lowell, Massachusetts

http://www.uml.edu/

- **State-supported** university, founded 1894, part of University of Massachusetts
- **Urban** 100-acre campus with easy access to Boston
- **Endowment** $91.7 million
- **Coed** 14,155 undergraduate students, 77% full-time, 40% women, 60% men
- **Moderately difficult** entrance level, 73% of applicants were admitted

UNDERGRAD STUDENTS
10,862 full-time, 3,293 part-time. 8% are from out of state; 7% Black or African American, non-Hispanic/Latino; 12% Hispanic/Latino; 12% Asian, non-Hispanic/Latino; 0.1% American Indian or Alaska Native, non-Hispanic/Latino; 3% Two or more races, non-Hispanic/Latino; 4% Race/ethnicity unknown; 3% international; 7% transferred in; 39% live on campus.

Freshmen:
Admission: 12,586 applied, 9,215 admitted, 2,354 enrolled. ***Average high school GPA:*** 3.6. ***Test scores:*** SAT evidence-based reading and writing scores over 500: 98%; SAT math scores over 500: 99%; ACT scores over 18: 99%; SAT evidence-based reading and writing scores over 600: 57%; SAT math scores over 600: 63%; ACT scores over 24: 76%; SAT evidence-based reading and writing scores over 700: 8%; SAT math scores over 700: 14%; ACT scores over 30: 23%.

Retention: 83% of full-time freshmen returned.

FACULTY
Total: 1,136, 57% full-time, 71% with terminal degrees.

Student/faculty ratio: 17:1.

ACADEMICS
Calendar: semesters. *Degrees:* certificates, associate, bachelor's, master's, doctoral, post-master's, and postbachelor's certificates.

Special study options: accelerated degree program, adult/continuing education programs, advanced placement credit, cooperative education, distance learning, double majors, honors programs, independent study, internships, off-campus study, part-time degree program, services for LD students, study abroad, summer session for credit. ***ROTC:*** Army (b), Air Force (b).

Computers: 2,145 computers/terminals and 4,100 ports are available on campus for general student use. Students can access the following: campus intranet, computer help desk, free student e-mail accounts, online (class) grades, online (class) registration, online (class) schedules. Campuswide network is available. 100% of college-owned or -operated housing units are wired for high-speed Internet access. Wireless service is available via entire campus.
Library: O'Leary Library and Learning Commons plus 2 others. *Books:* 224,700 (physical), 192,900 (digital/electronic); *Serial titles:* 5,641 (physical), 127,540 (digital/electronic); *Databases:* 180. Weekly public service hours: 118; students can reserve study rooms.

STUDENT LIFE
Housing options: coed. Campus housing is university owned.

Activities and organizations: drama/theater group, student-run newspaper, radio station, choral group, marching band, Student Government Association, Recreational Sports Clubs, Association of Students of African Origin, WUML (radio station), Campus Activities Programming Association, national fraternities, national sororities.

Athletics Member NCAA. All Division I. ***Intercollegiate sports:*** baseball M(s), basketball M(s)/W(s), cross-country running M(s)/W(s), field hockey W(s), ice hockey M(s), lacrosse M(s)/W(s), soccer M(s)/W(s), softball W(s), track and field M(s)/W(s). ***Intramural sports:*** badminton M/W, baseball M(c), basketball M/W, cheerleading M(c)/W(c), cross-country running M/W, fencing W(c), football M/W, golf M(c)/W(c), ice hockey M/W, lacrosse M(c)/W(c), racquetball M/W, rowing M(c)/W(c), rugby M(c)/W(c), skiing (cross-country) M(c)/W(c), skiing (downhill) M(c)/W(c), soccer M/W, softball M/W, squash M/W, swimming and diving M(c)/W(c), table tennis M/W, tennis M/W, track and field M(c)/W(c), triathlon M/W, ultimate Frisbee M/W, volleyball M/W.

Campus security: 24-hour emergency response devices and patrols, controlled dormitory access, police and security patrols.

Student services: health clinic, personal/psychological counseling, veterans affairs office.

FINANCIAL AID
Financial Aid Of all full-time matriculated undergraduates who enrolled in 2018, 8,600 applied for aid, 6,641 were judged to have need, 1,707 had their need fully met. In 2018, 1633 non-need-based awards were made. ***Average percent of need met:*** 88. ***Average financial aid package:*** $16,864. ***Average need-based loan:*** $4210. ***Average need-based gift aid:*** $10,141. ***Average non-need-based aid:*** $7164. ***Average indebtedness upon graduation:*** $32,317.

APPLYING
Standardized Tests *Required:* SAT or ACT (for admission). *Required for some:* short answer questions for No Test option.

Options: electronic application, early action, deferred entrance.

Application fee: $60.

Notification: continuous (transfers), 12/10 (early action).

CONTACT
University of Massachusetts Lowell, 1 University Avenue, Lowell, MA 01854. *Phone:* 978-934-3948.

Wellesley College

Wellesley, Massachusetts

http://www.wellesley.edu/

- **Independent** 4-year, founded 1870
- **Suburban** 500-acre campus with easy access to Boston
- **Endowment** $1.9 billion
- **Women only**
- **Most difficult** entrance level

FACULTY
Student/faculty ratio: 8:1.

ACADEMICS
Calendar: semesters. *Degrees:* bachelor's (double bachelor's degree with Massachusetts Institute of Technology).
Library: Margaret Clapp Library plus 5 others. *Books:* 717,924 (physical), 770,553 (digital/electronic); *Serial titles:* 319,932 (physical), 94,450 (digital/electronic). Students can reserve study rooms.

STUDENT LIFE
Housing options: women-only, cooperative. Campus housing is university owned. Freshman campus housing is guaranteed.

Activities and organizations: drama/theater group, student-run newspaper, radio and television station, choral group, Student Government, community service organizations, cultural clubs, societies, theater groups.

Athletics Member NCAA. All Division III.

Campus security: 24-hour emergency response devices and patrols, late-night transport/escort service, controlled dormitory access.

Student services: health clinic, personal/psychological counseling, women's center.

COSTS & FINANCIAL AID
Costs (2019–20) ***Comprehensive fee:*** $73,148 includes full-time tuition ($55,728), mandatory fees ($324), and room and board ($17,096). Part-time tuition: $6966 per credit hour. ***College room only:*** $8824.

Financial Aid Of all full-time matriculated undergraduates who enrolled in 2018, 1,501 applied for aid, 1,335 were judged to have need, 1,335 had their need fully met. ***Average percent of need met:*** 100. ***Average financial aid package:*** $53,776. ***Average need-based loan:*** $2416. ***Average need-based gift aid:*** $50,752. ***Average indebtedness upon graduation:*** $16,122.

APPLYING
Standardized Tests *Required:* SAT or ACT (for admission).

Options: electronic application, early admission, early decision, deferred entrance.

Application fee: $50.

Required: essay or personal statement, high school transcript, 3 letters of recommendation, first senior marking period grades and mid-year report. ***Required for some:*** interview. ***Recommended:*** interview.

CONTACT
Ms. Grace Cheng, Director of Admission, Wellesley College, 106 Central Street, Wellesley, MA 02481. *Phone:* 781-283-2270. *Fax:* 781-283-3678. *E-mail:* admission@wellesley.edu.

Wentworth Institute of Technology

Boston, Massachusetts

http://www.wit.edu/

- **Independent** comprehensive, founded 1904
- **Urban** 31-acre campus with easy access to Boston, MA
- **Endowment** $112.6 million
- **Coed** 4,307 undergraduate students, 91% full-time, 22% women, 78% men
- **Moderately difficult** entrance level, 69% of applicants were admitted

UNDERGRAD STUDENTS
3,904 full-time, 403 part-time. 32% are from out of state; 6% Black or African American, non-Hispanic/Latino; 8% Hispanic/Latino; 9% Asian, non-Hispanic/Latino; 0.1% Native Hawaiian or other Pacific Islander, non-Hispanic/Latino; 3% Two or more races, non-Hispanic/Latino; 5% Race/ethnicity unknown; 7% international; 3% transferred in; 48% live on campus.

Freshmen:
Admission: 7,311 applied, 5,012 admitted, 968 enrolled. ***Average high school GPA:*** 3.1. ***Test scores:*** SAT evidence-based reading and writing scores over 500: 82%; SAT math scores over 500: 92%; ACT scores over 18: 96%; SAT evidence-based reading and writing scores over 600: 39%; SAT math scores over 600: 46%; ACT scores over 24: 61%; SAT evidence-based reading and writing scores over 700: 5%; SAT math scores over 700: 9%; ACT scores over 30: 18%.
Retention: 83% of full-time freshmen returned.

FACULTY
Total: 381, 42% full-time.
Student/faculty ratio: 18:1.

ACADEMICS
Calendar: semesters for freshmen and sophomores, trimesters for juniors and seniors. *Degrees:* certificates, associate, bachelor's, and master's.
Special study options: academic remediation for entering students, advanced placement credit, cooperative education, distance learning, double majors, English as a second language, external degree program, independent study, internships, off-campus study, part-time degree program, services for LD students, study abroad, summer session for credit. ***ROTC:*** Army (c), Air Force (c).
Computers: 320 computers/terminals and 200 ports are available on campus for general student use. Students can access the following: campus intranet, computer help desk, free student e-mail accounts, online (class) grades, online (class) registration, online (class) schedules. Campuswide network is available. 100% of college-owned or -operated housing units are wired for high-speed Internet access. Wireless service is available via entire campus.
Library: Douglas D. Schumann Library & Learning Commons plus 1 other. *Books:* 39,690 (physical), 341,758 (digital/electronic); *Serial titles:* 316 (physical), 160,788 (digital/electronic); *Databases:* 94. Weekly public service hours: 100.

STUDENT LIFE
Housing options: on-campus residence required through sophomore year; coed, special housing for students with disabilities. Campus housing is university owned. Freshman campus housing is guaranteed.
Activities and organizations: drama/theater group, student-run radio station, choral group, Intramural Sports, Wentworth Events Board, Multicultural Student Association, Phi Sigma Pi, Major Particular Professional Student Associations.
Athletics Member NCAA. All Division III. ***Intercollegiate sports:*** baseball M, basketball M/W, crew M, cross-country running M, golf M, ice hockey M, lacrosse M/W, rugby M(c)/W(c), soccer M/W, softball W, tennis M/W, track and field M/W, ultimate Frisbee M(c)/W(c), volleyball M/W. ***Intramural sports:*** basketball M(c)/W(c), bowling M(c)/W(c), soccer M(c)/W(c), volleyball M(c)/W(c).
Campus security: 24-hour emergency response devices and patrols, student patrols, late-night transport/escort service, controlled dormitory access.
Student services: health clinic, personal/psychological counseling, women's center.

COSTS & FINANCIAL AID
Costs (2020–21) ***Comprehensive fee:*** $49,160 includes full-time tuition ($34,970) and room and board ($14,190). Full-time tuition and fees vary according to class time, course load, and program. Part-time tuition: $1095 per credit. Part-time tuition and fees vary according to class time, course load, and program. ***College room only:*** $11,090. Room and board charges vary according to board plan and housing facility. ***Payment plan:*** installment. ***Waivers:*** employees or children of employees.
Financial Aid Of all full-time matriculated undergraduates who enrolled in 2019, 2,590 applied for aid, 2,559 were judged to have need, 168 had their need fully met. In 2019, 998 non-need-based awards were made. ***Average percent of need met:*** 61. ***Average financial aid package:*** $2780. ***Average need-based loan:*** $2738. ***Average need-based gift aid:*** $3108. ***Average non-need-based aid:*** $9655. ***Average indebtedness upon graduation:*** $58,867.

APPLYING
Standardized Tests *Required for some:* SAT or ACT (for admission).
Options: electronic application, deferred entrance.
Required: essay or personal statement, high school transcript, 1 letter of recommendation. ***Recommended:*** minimum 2.0 GPA, interview.
Application deadlines: 2/15 (freshmen), 2/15 (out-of-state freshmen), 5/1 (transfers).
Notification: continuous (freshmen), continuous (transfers).

CONTACT
Maureen Dischino, Assistant Vice President of Enrollment Management/ Director of Admissions, Wentworth Institute of Technology, 550 Huntington Avenue, Boston, MA 02115. *Phone:* 617-989-4000. *Toll-free phone:* 800-556-0610. *E-mail:* admissions@wit.edu.

Western New England University

Springfield, Massachusetts

http://www.wne.edu/

- **Independent** university, founded 1919
- **Suburban** 215-acre campus
- **Endowment** $66.9 million
- **Coed** 2,698 undergraduate students, 96% full-time, 39% women, 61% men
- **Moderately difficult** entrance level, 85% of applicants were admitted

UNDERGRAD STUDENTS
2,580 full-time, 118 part-time. Students come from 31 states and territories; 15 other countries; 48% are from out of state; 4% Black or African American, non-Hispanic/Latino; 9% Hispanic/Latino; 3% Asian, non-Hispanic/Latino; 0.1% Native Hawaiian or other Pacific Islander, non-Hispanic/Latino; 0.2% American Indian or Alaska Native, non-Hispanic/Latino; 3% Two or more races, non-Hispanic/Latino; 3% Race/ethnicity unknown; 3% international; 4% transferred in; 56% live on campus.

Freshmen:
Admission: 6,862 applied, 5,845 admitted, 691 enrolled. ***Average high school GPA:*** 3.6. ***Test scores:*** SAT evidence-based reading and writing scores over 500: 92%; SAT math scores over 500: 93%; ACT scores over 18: 100%; SAT evidence-based reading and writing scores over 600: 38%; SAT math scores over 600: 43%; ACT scores over 24: 71%; SAT evidence-based reading and writing scores over 700: 2%; SAT math scores over 700: 6%; ACT scores over 30: 9%.
Retention: 76% of full-time freshmen returned.

FACULTY
Total: 338, 67% full-time, 59% with terminal degrees.
Student/faculty ratio: 13:1.

ACADEMICS
Calendar: semesters. *Degrees:* certificates, associate, bachelor's, master's, doctoral, and postbachelor's certificates.

Special study options: accelerated degree program, adult/continuing education programs, advanced placement credit, distance learning, double majors, honors programs, independent study, internships, off-campus study, part-time degree program, services for LD students, study abroad, summer session for credit. ***ROTC:*** Army (b), Air Force (c).

Unusual degree programs: 3-2 business administration; engineering.

Computers: 914 computers/terminals are available on campus for general student use. Students can access the following: campus intranet, computer help desk, free student e-mail accounts, online (class) grades, online (class) registration, online (class) schedules. Campuswide network is available. 100% of college-owned or -operated housing units are wired for high-speed Internet access. Wireless service is available via entire campus.

Library: D'Amour Library plus 1 other. *Books:* 119,005 (physical), 41,490 (digital/electronic); *Serial titles:* 1,124 (physical), 84,778 (digital/electronic); *Databases:* 107. Weekly public service hours: 94; study areas open 24 hours, 5–7 days a week.

STUDENT LIFE

Housing options: on-campus residence required through sophomore year; coed, special housing for students with disabilities. Campus housing is university owned. Freshman campus housing is guaranteed.

Activities and organizations: drama/theater group, student-run newspaper, radio and television station, choral group, Student Senate, Residence Hall Association, Campus Activities Board, student radio station, The Westerner (student newspaper).

Athletics Member NCAA. All Division III. ***Intercollegiate sports:*** baseball M, basketball M/W, cross-country running M/W, field hockey W, football M, golf M, ice hockey M/W, lacrosse M/W, soccer M/W, softball W, swimming and diving W, tennis M/W, volleyball W, wrestling M. ***Intramural sports:*** basketball M/W, bowling M/W, football M/W, racquetball M/W, rugby M(c), soccer M/W, softball M/W, table tennis M/W, volleyball M/W, water polo M/W.

Campus security: 24-hour emergency response devices and patrols, student patrols, late-night transport/escort service, controlled dormitory access, security cameras.

Student services: health clinic, personal/psychological counseling.

COSTS & FINANCIAL AID

Costs (2020–21) ***Comprehensive fee:*** $53,470 includes full-time tuition ($36,606), mandatory fees ($2620), and room and board ($14,244). Full-time tuition and fees vary according to course load and program. Part-time tuition: $980 per credit. Part-time tuition and fees vary according to course load and program. ***Room and board:*** Room and board charges vary according to board plan and housing facility. ***Payment plans:*** tuition prepayment, installment. ***Waivers:*** employees or children of employees.

Financial Aid Of all full-time matriculated undergraduates who enrolled in 2019, 2,228 applied for aid, 2,010 were judged to have need, 314 had their need fully met. 1,050 Federal Work-Study jobs (averaging $1800). In 2019, 568 non-need-based awards were made. ***Average percent of need met:*** 74. ***Average financial aid package:*** $27,353. ***Average need-based loan:*** $3758. ***Average need-based gift aid:*** $22,537. ***Average non-need-based aid:*** $14,913. ***Average indebtedness upon graduation:*** $43,980.

APPLYING

Standardized Tests *Required for some:* SAT or ACT (for admission).

Options: electronic application, early admission, deferred entrance.

Application fee: $40.

Required: high school transcript, 1 letter of recommendation. ***Recommended:*** essay or personal statement, interview.

Application deadlines: rolling (freshmen), rolling (transfers).

Notification: continuous (freshmen), continuous (transfers).

CONTACT

Mr. Bryan Gross, Vice President for Enrollment Management, Western New England University, 1215 Wilbraham Road, Springfield, MA 01119. *Phone:* 413-782-1321. *Toll-free phone:* 800-325-1122 Ext. 1321. *Fax:* 413-782-1777. *E-mail:* learn@wne.edu.

Westfield State University

Westfield, Massachusetts

http://www.westfield.ma.edu/

- **State-supported** comprehensive, founded 1839, part of Massachusetts Public Higher Education System
- **Suburban** 256-acre campus
- **Endowment** $7.3 million
- **Coed** 5,084 undergraduate students, 84% full-time, 55% women, 45% men
- **Moderately difficult** entrance level, 87% of applicants were admitted

UNDERGRAD STUDENTS

4,268 full-time, 816 part-time. Students come from 27 states and territories; 12 other countries; 8% are from out of state; 5% Black or African American, non-Hispanic/Latino; 11% Hispanic/Latino; 2% Asian, non-Hispanic/Latino; 0.3% American Indian or Alaska Native, non-Hispanic/Latino; 3% Two or more races, non-Hispanic/Latino; 4% Race/ethnicity unknown; 0.4% international; 8% transferred in; 48% live on campus.

Freshmen:

Admission: 4,455 applied, 3,883 admitted, 1,042 enrolled. ***Average high school GPA:*** 3.2. ***Test scores:*** SAT evidence-based reading and writing scores over 500: 73%; SAT math scores over 500: 70%; ACT scores over 18: 83%; SAT evidence-based reading and writing scores over 600: 19%; SAT math scores over 600: 16%; ACT scores over 24: 33%; SAT evidence-based reading and writing scores over 700: 1%; SAT math scores over 700: 1%; ACT scores over 30: 8%.

Retention: 72% of full-time freshmen returned.

FACULTY

Total: 528, 45% full-time, 55% with terminal degrees.

Student/faculty ratio: 15:1.

ACADEMICS

Calendar: semesters. *Degrees:* bachelor's, master's, and postbachelor's certificates.

Special study options: adult/continuing education programs, advanced placement credit, distance learning, double majors, honors programs, independent study, internships, off-campus study, part-time degree program, services for LD students, student-designed majors, study abroad, summer session for credit. ***ROTC:*** Army (c), Air Force (c).

Unusual degree programs: 3-2 law (3+3) with University of Massachusetts, Dartmouth; education (bachelors and masters) with Westfield State University.

Computers: 814 computers/terminals are available on campus for general student use. Students can access the following: computer help desk, free student e-mail accounts, online (class) grades, online (class) registration, online (class) schedules, online transcripts and billing information, Web portal. Campuswide network is available. 100% of college-owned or -operated housing units are wired for high-speed Internet access. Wireless service is available via entire campus.

Library: Governor Joseph B. Ely Library. *Books:* 130,426 (physical), 162,253 (digital/electronic); *Serial titles:* 745 (physical), 26,032 (digital/electronic); *Databases:* 143. Weekly public service hours: 92; students can reserve study rooms.

STUDENT LIFE

Housing options: coed, special housing for students with disabilities. Campus housing is university owned. Freshman applicants given priority for college housing.

Activities and organizations: drama/theater group, student-run newspaper, radio and television station, choral group, Student National Education Association, Student Government Association, Campus Activities Board, The Dance Company, Multicultural Student Association.

Athletics Member NCAA. All Division III. ***Intercollegiate sports:*** baseball M, basketball M/W, cross-country running M/W, field hockey W, football M, golf M/W, ice hockey M, lacrosse W, soccer M/W, softball W, swimming and diving W, track and field M/W, volleyball W. ***Intramural sports:*** basketball M, equestrian sports M(c)/W(c), football M, ice hockey M(c)/W(c), lacrosse M(c), rock climbing M(c)/W(c), rugby M(c)/W(c), skiing (downhill) M(c)/W(c), soccer M/W, softball M/W, ultimate Frisbee M(c)/W(c), volleyball M/W, weight lifting M(c)/W(c).

Campus security: 24-hour emergency response devices and patrols, student patrols, late-night transport/escort service, controlled dormitory access.

Student services: health clinic, personal/psychological counseling, legal services, veterans affairs office.

COSTS & FINANCIAL AID

Costs (2019–20) ***Tuition:*** state resident $970 full-time, $85 per credit hour part-time; nonresident $7050 full-time, $85 per credit hour part-time. Full-time tuition and fees vary according to program and reciprocity agreements. Part-time tuition and fees vary according to course load. ***Required fees:*** $9879 full-time, $235 per credit hour part-time, $75 per term part-time. ***Room and board:*** $11,453. Room and board charges vary according to board plan and housing facility. ***Payment plan:*** installment. ***Waivers:*** senior citizens and employees or children of employees.

Financial Aid Of all full-time matriculated undergraduates who enrolled in 2017, 4,205 applied for aid, 3,138 were judged to have need, 283 had their need fully met. 278 Federal Work-Study jobs (averaging $1754). In 2017, 67 non-need-based awards were made. ***Average percent of need met:*** 59. ***Average financial aid package:*** $9008. ***Average need-based loan:*** $4216. ***Average need-based gift aid:*** $8379. ***Average non-need-based aid:*** $3303. ***Average indebtedness upon graduation:*** $29,050.

APPLYING

Standardized Tests *Required:* SAT or ACT (for admission).

Options: electronic application, deferred entrance.

Application fee: $50.

Required: high school transcript, minimum 3.0 GPA. ***Required for some:*** interview, audition for music majors, portfolio for art majors, essay and interview for nursing majors, sliding scale minimum high school GPA using SAT/ACT scores for GPAs between 2.0 and 3.0.

Application deadlines: 3/1 (freshmen), 3/1 (transfers).

Notification: continuous until 3/15 (freshmen), continuous until 3/15 (transfers).

CONTACT

Dr. Kelly Hart, Director of Admissions, Westfield State University, 333 Western Avenue, Westfield, MA 01002. *Phone:* 413-572-5218. *Fax:* 413-572-0520. *E-mail:* admission@westfield.ma.edu.

Wheaton College

Norton, Massachusetts

http://www.wheatoncollege.edu/

- **Independent** 4-year, founded 1834
- **Suburban** 478-acre campus with easy access to Boston, MA
- **Endowment** $213.0 million
- **Coed** 1,774 undergraduate students, 99% full-time, 60% women, 40% men
- **Very difficult** entrance level, 74% of applicants were admitted

UNDERGRAD STUDENTS

1,764 full-time, 10 part-time. 63% are from out of state; 6% Black or African American, non-Hispanic/Latino; 9% Hispanic/Latino; 4% Asian, non-Hispanic/Latino; 0.1% American Indian or Alaska Native, non-Hispanic/Latino; 5% Two or more races, non-Hispanic/Latino; 2% Race/ethnicity unknown; 8% international; 0.9% transferred in; 96% live on campus.

Freshmen:

Admission: 3,460 applied, 2,556 admitted, 451 enrolled. ***Average high school GPA:*** 3.4. ***Test scores:*** SAT evidence-based reading and writing scores over 500: 99%; SAT math scores over 500: 98%; ACT scores over 18: 100%; SAT evidence-based reading and writing scores over 600: 76%; SAT math scores over 600: 61%; ACT scores over 24: 92%; SAT evidence-based reading and writing scores over 700: 18%; SAT math scores over 700: 14%; ACT scores over 30: 34%.

Retention: 83% of full-time freshmen returned.

FACULTY

Total: 187, 76% full-time, 82% with terminal degrees.

Student/faculty ratio: 11:1.

ACADEMICS

Calendar: semesters. *Degree:* bachelor's.

Special study options: accelerated degree program, advanced placement credit, cooperative education, double majors, honors programs, independent study, internships, off-campus study, services for LD students, student-designed majors, study abroad, summer session for credit. ***ROTC:*** Army (c).

Computers: 196 computers/terminals are available on campus for general student use. Students can access the following: campus intranet, computer help desk, free student e-mail accounts, online (class) grades, online (class) registration, online (class) schedules, assistive technology, online software training, media equipment loan program. Campuswide network is available. 100% of college-owned or -operated housing units are wired for high-speed Internet access. Wireless service is available via entire campus.

Library: Madeleine Clark Wallace Library. *Books:* 297,992 (physical), 167,919 (digital/electronic); *Serial titles:* 4,504 (physical), 33,166 (digital/electronic); *Databases:* 157. Weekly public service hours: 114; students can reserve study rooms.

STUDENT LIFE

Housing options: coed, women-only, special housing for students with disabilities. Campus housing is university owned. Freshman campus housing is guaranteed.

Activities and organizations: drama/theater group, student-run newspaper, radio station, choral group, Student Government Association, Performance Groups (a capella, dance and improv), Black Student Association (BSA), Programming Activities Council, Feminist Association of Wheaton (FAW).

Athletics Member NCAA. All Division III. ***Intercollegiate sports:*** baseball M, basketball M/W, cross-country running M/W, field hockey W, lacrosse M/W, soccer M/W, softball W, swimming and diving M/W, tennis M/W, track and field M/W, volleyball W. ***Intramural sports:*** archery M(c)/W(c), basketball M/W, cheerleading M(c)/W(c), equestrian sports M(c)/W(c), fencing M(c)/W(c), football M/W, golf M/W, ice hockey M(c)/W(c), rugby M(c)/W(c), soccer M/W, tennis M(c)/W(c), ultimate Frisbee M(c)/W(c), volleyball M/W.

Campus security: 24-hour emergency response devices and patrols, student patrols, late-night transport/escort service, controlled dormitory access.

Student services: health clinic, personal/psychological counseling.

COSTS & FINANCIAL AID

Costs (2020–21) ***Comprehensive fee:*** $70,744 includes full-time tuition ($55,904), mandatory fees ($462), and room and board ($14,378). Full-time tuition and fees vary according to course load. Part-time tuition: $1747 per credit hour. Part-time tuition and fees vary according to course load. ***College room only:*** $7764. ***Payment plan:*** installment. ***Waivers:*** employees or children of employees.

Financial Aid Of all full-time matriculated undergraduates who enrolled in 2019, 1,351 applied for aid, 1,237 were judged to have need, 320 had their need fully met. 642 Federal Work-Study jobs (averaging $1868). 338 state and other part-time jobs (averaging $1896). In 2019, 379 non-need-based awards were made. ***Average percent of need met:*** 93. ***Average financial aid package:*** $46,154. ***Average need-based loan:*** $3754. ***Average need-based gift aid:*** $41,648. ***Average non-need-based aid:*** $23,547. ***Average indebtedness upon graduation:*** $34,530. ***Financial aid deadline:*** 2/1.

APPLYING

Options: electronic application, early decision, early action, deferred entrance.

Application fee: $60.

Required: essay or personal statement, high school transcript, 2 letters of recommendation. ***Recommended:*** interview.

Application deadlines: 1/1 (freshmen), 1/1 (out-of-state freshmen), 5/1 (transfers), 11/15 (early action).

Early decision deadline: 11/15 (for plan 1), 1/15 (for plan 2).

Notification: 3/31 (freshmen), 3/31 (out-of-state freshmen), continuous (transfers), 12/20 (early decision plan 1), 2/1 (early decision plan 2), 12/20 (early action).

CONTACT

Chris Hooker-Haring, Interim Vice President of Enrollment, Wheaton College, 26 East Main Street, Norton, MA 02766. *Phone:* 508-286-8251.

Toll-free phone: 800-394-6003. *Fax:* 508-286-8271. *E-mail:* admission@wheatoncollege.edu.

William James College

Newton, Massachusetts

http://www.williamjames.edu/

- **Independent** upper-level, founded 1974
- **Suburban** campus with easy access to Boston, MA
- **Coed, primarily women**

ACADEMICS

Calendar: semesters. *Degrees:* certificates, bachelor's, master's, doctoral, and post-master's certificates.

CONTACT

Mario Murga, Director of Admissions, William James College, One Wells Avenue, Newton, MA 02459. *Phone:* 617-564-9376. *Toll-free phone:* 888-664-MSPP. *E-mail:* admissions@williamjames.edu.

Williams College

Williamstown, Massachusetts

http://www.williams.edu/

- **Independent** comprehensive, founded 1793
- **Small-town** 450-acre campus with easy access to Albany NY
- **Endowment** $2.9 billion
- **Coed** 2,078 undergraduate students, 98% full-time, 50% women, 50% men
- **Most difficult** entrance level, 13% of applicants were admitted

UNDERGRAD STUDENTS

2,027 full-time, 51 part-time. Students come from 51 states and territories; 67 other countries; 84% are from out of state; 7% Black or African American, non-Hispanic/Latino; 13% Hispanic/Latino; 12% Asian, non-Hispanic/Latino; 0.0% Native Hawaiian or other Pacific Islander, non-Hispanic/Latino; 0.1% American Indian or Alaska Native, non-Hispanic/Latino; 6% Two or more races, non-Hispanic/Latino; 4% Race/ethnicity unknown; 9% international; 0.4% transferred in; 93% live on campus.

Freshmen:

Admission: 9,715 applied, 1,224 admitted, 546 enrolled. ***Test scores:*** SAT evidence-based reading and writing scores over 500: 100%; SAT math scores over 500: 100%; ACT scores over 18: 100%; SAT evidence-based reading and writing scores over 600: 100%; SAT math scores over 600: 98%; ACT scores over 24: 100%; SAT evidence-based reading and writing scores over 700: 77%; SAT math scores over 700: 82%; ACT scores over 30: 91%.

Retention: 97% of full-time freshmen returned.

FACULTY

Total: 363, 82% full-time, 94% with terminal degrees.

Student/faculty ratio: 7:1.

ACADEMICS

Calendar: 4-1-4. *Degrees:* bachelor's and master's.

Special study options: double majors, independent study, internships, off-campus study, services for LD students, student-designed majors, study abroad. ***ROTC:*** Air Force (c).

Unusual degree programs: 3-2 engineering with Columbia University, Dartmouth College.

Computers: 1,000 computers/terminals are available on campus for general student use. Students can access the following: computer help desk, free student e-mail accounts, online (class) grades, online (class) registration, online (class) schedules. Campuswide network is available. 100% of college-owned or -operated housing units are wired for high-speed Internet access. Wireless service is available via entire campus.
Library: Sawyer Library plus 2 others. *Books:* 1.0 million (physical); *Serial titles:* 272 (physical), 126,699 (digital/electronic). Weekly public service hours: 118; study areas open 24 hours, 5–7 days a week; students can reserve study rooms.

STUDENT LIFE

Housing options: on-campus residence required through junior year; coed, cooperative, special housing for students with disabilities. Campus housing is university owned. Freshman campus housing is guaranteed.

Activities and organizations: drama/theater group, student-run newspaper, radio station, choral group, marching band.

Athletics Member NCAA. All Division III except golf (Division II), men's and women's skiing (cross-country) (Division I), skiing (downhill) (Division I). ***Intercollegiate sports:*** badminton M(c)/W(c), baseball M, basketball M/W, crew M(c)/W, cross-country running M/W, equestrian sports M(c)/W(c), fencing M(c)/W(c), field hockey W, football M, golf M/W, ice hockey M/W, lacrosse M/W, rugby M(c)/W(c), sailing M(c)/W(c), skiing (cross-country) M/W, skiing (downhill) M/W, soccer M/W, softball W, squash M/W, swimming and diving M/W, tennis M/W, track and field M/W, ultimate Frisbee M(c)/W(c), volleyball M(c)/W, water polo M(c)/W(c), wrestling M. ***Intramural sports:*** basketball M/W, bowling M/W, gymnastics M/W, ice hockey M/W, skiing (cross-country) M/W, skiing (downhill) M/W, soccer M/W, softball M/W, tennis M(c)/W(c), ultimate Frisbee M/W, volleyball M/W, water polo M/W.

Campus security: 24-hour emergency response devices and patrols, student patrols, late-night transport/escort service, controlled dormitory access.

Student services: health clinic, personal/psychological counseling.

COSTS & FINANCIAL AID

Costs (2020–21) ***Comprehensive fee:*** $74,660 includes full-time tuition ($59,350), mandatory fees ($310), and room and board ($15,000). ***College room only:*** $7625. Room and board charges vary according to board plan. ***Payment plan:*** installment.

Financial Aid Of all full-time matriculated undergraduates who enrolled in 2019, 1,167 applied for aid, 1,060 were judged to have need, 1,060 had their need fully met. 385 Federal Work-Study jobs (averaging $2448). 543 state and other part-time jobs (averaging $2427). ***Average percent of need met:*** 100. ***Average financial aid package:*** $59,941. ***Average need-based loan:*** $2925. ***Average need-based gift aid:*** $56,788. ***Average indebtedness upon graduation:*** $15,911. ***Financial aid deadline:*** 1/15.

APPLYING

Standardized Tests *Required:* SAT or ACT (for admission).

Options: electronic application, early admission, early decision, deferred entrance.

Application fee: $65.

Required: essay or personal statement, high school transcript, 2 letters of recommendation.

Application deadlines: 1/1 (freshmen), 3/1 (transfers).

Early decision deadline: 11/15.

Notification: 4/7 (freshmen), 4/15 (transfers), 12/15 (early decision).

CONTACT

Sulgi Lim, Director of Admission, Williams College, 995 Main Street, Williamstown, MA 01267. *Phone:* 413-597-2211. *Fax:* 413-597-4052. *E-mail:* admission@williams.edu.

Worcester Polytechnic Institute

Worcester, Massachusetts

http://www.wpi.edu/

- **Independent** university, founded 1865
- **Suburban** 95-acre campus with easy access to Boston
- **Endowment** $528.3 million
- **Coed** 4,761 undergraduate students, 98% full-time, 40% women, 60% men
- **Very difficult** entrance level, 49% of applicants were admitted

UNDERGRAD STUDENTS

4,642 full-time, 119 part-time. Students come from 45 states and territories; 62 other countries; 55% are from out of state; 3% Black or African American, non-Hispanic/Latino; 9% Hispanic/Latino; 6% Asian, non-Hispanic/Latino; 0.2% American Indian or Alaska Native, non-Hispanic/Latino; 3% Two or more races, non-Hispanic/Latino; 8% Race/ethnicity unknown; 9% international; 0.8% transferred in; 60% live on campus.

Freshmen:
Admission: 10,645 applied, 5,255 admitted, 1,199 enrolled. *Average high school GPA:* 3.9. *Test scores:* SAT evidence-based reading and writing scores over 500: 100%; SAT math scores over 500: 100%; ACT scores over 18: 100%; SAT evidence-based reading and writing scores over 600: 90%; SAT math scores over 600: 97%; ACT scores over 24: 98%; SAT evidence-based reading and writing scores over 700: 33%; SAT math scores over 700: 63%; ACT scores over 30: 69%.

Retention: 95% of full-time freshmen returned.

FACULTY
Total: 502, 83% full-time, 82% with terminal degrees.

Student/faculty ratio: 14:1.

ACADEMICS
Calendar: 4 7-week terms. *Degrees:* bachelor's, master's, doctoral, and postbachelor's certificates.

Special study options: accelerated degree program, advanced placement credit, cooperative education, distance learning, double majors, English as a second language, independent study, internships, off-campus study, part-time degree program, services for LD students, student-designed majors, study abroad, summer session for credit. *ROTC:* Army (b), Navy (c), Air Force (b).

Computers: 860 computers/terminals and 800 ports are available on campus for general student use. Students can access the following: campus intranet, computer help desk, free student e-mail accounts, online (class) grades, online (class) registration, online (class) schedules, online course content. Campuswide network is available. 100% of college-owned or -operated housing units are wired for high-speed Internet access. Wireless service is available via entire campus.

Library: George C. Gordon Library. *Books:* 180,101 (physical), 756,454 (digital/electronic); *Serial titles:* 5,491 (physical), 159,716 (digital/electronic); *Databases:* 252. Weekly public service hours: 107; students can reserve study rooms.

STUDENT LIFE
Housing options: on-campus residence required for freshman year; coed, special housing for students with disabilities. Campus housing is university owned. Freshman campus housing is guaranteed.

Activities and organizations: drama/theater group, student-run newspaper, radio station, choral group, Student Government Association, Panhellenic, Interfraternity Council, Intramural and Club Sports, Music Association, national fraternities, national sororities.

Athletics Member NCAA. All Division III. *Intercollegiate sports:* baseball M, basketball M/W, crew M/W, cross-country running M/W, field hockey W, football M, soccer M/W, softball W, swimming and diving M/W, track and field M/W, volleyball W, wrestling M. *Intramural sports:* badminton M(c)/W(c), basketball M/W, cheerleading M(c)/W(c), fencing M(c)/W(c), football M, golf M(c)/W(c), ice hockey M(c)/W(c), lacrosse M(c)/W(c), rugby M(c)/W(c), sailing M(c)/W(c), skiing (downhill) M(c)/W(c), soccer M/W, squash M(c)/W(c), table tennis M(c)/W(c), tennis M(c)/W(c), ultimate Frisbee M(c)/W(c), volleyball M/W, water polo M(c)/W(c), wrestling M(c).

Campus security: 24-hour emergency response devices and patrols, student patrols, late-night transport/escort service, controlled dormitory access.

Student services: health clinic, personal/psychological counseling.

COSTS & FINANCIAL AID
Costs (2020–21) *One-time required fee:* $200. *Comprehensive fee:* $69,984 includes full-time tuition ($53,410), mandatory fees ($736), and room and board ($15,838). Part-time tuition: $1484 per credit hour. Part-time tuition and fees vary according to course load. *College room only:* $9042. Room and board charges vary according to board plan and housing facility. *Payment plans:* tuition prepayment, installment. *Waivers:* employees or children of employees.

Financial Aid Of all full-time matriculated undergraduates who enrolled in 2018, 3,245 applied for aid, 2,712 were judged to have need, 1,278 had their need fully met. 444 Federal Work-Study jobs (averaging $1747). In 2018, 1694 non-need-based awards were made. *Average percent of need met:* 80. *Average financial aid package:* $38,719. *Average need-based loan:* $2274. *Average need-based gift aid:* $25,304. *Average non-need-based aid:* $17,418.

APPLYING
Standardized Tests *Required for some:* IELTS or TOEFL.

Options: electronic application, early admission, early decision, early action, deferred entrance.

Application fee: $65.

Required: essay or personal statement, high school transcript, 2 letters of recommendation. *Required for some:* interview.

Application deadlines: 1/15 (freshmen), 5/15 (transfers), 11/1 (early action).

Early decision deadline: 11/1 (for plan 1), 1/15 (for plan 2).

Notification: 3/15 (freshmen), continuous (transfers), 12/15 (early decision plan 1), 2/15 (early decision plan 2), 1/15 (early action).

CONTACT
Jennifer Cluett, Director of Undergraduate Admissions, Worcester Polytechnic Institute, 100 Institute Road, Worcester, MA 01609-2280. *Phone:* 508-831-5286. *Fax:* 508-831-5875. *E-mail:* admissions@wpi.edu.

Worcester State University

Worcester, Massachusetts

http://www.worcester.edu/

- **State-supported** comprehensive, founded 1874, part of Massachusetts Public Higher Education System
- **Urban** 58-acre campus with easy access to Boston
- **Endowment** $18.0 million
- **Coed** 5,332 undergraduate students, 76% full-time, 62% women, 38% men
- **Moderately difficult** entrance level, 81% of applicants were admitted

UNDERGRAD STUDENTS
4,078 full-time, 1,254 part-time. Students come from 28 states and territories; 7 other countries; 4% are from out of state; 9% Black or African American, non-Hispanic/Latino; 13% Hispanic/Latino; 5% Asian, non-Hispanic/Latino; 0.3% American Indian or Alaska Native, non-Hispanic/Latino; 3% Two or more races, non-Hispanic/Latino; 4% Race/ethnicity unknown; 1% international; 9% transferred in; 31% live on campus.

Freshmen:
Admission: 3,896 applied, 3,145 admitted, 886 enrolled. *Average high school GPA:* 3.4. *Test scores:* SAT evidence-based reading and writing scores over 500: 78%; SAT math scores over 500: 80%; ACT scores over 18: 97%; SAT evidence-based reading and writing scores over 600: 29%; SAT math scores over 600: 22%; ACT scores over 24: 53%; SAT evidence-based reading and writing scores over 700: 2%; SAT math scores over 700: 2%; ACT scores over 30: 9%.

Retention: 79% of full-time freshmen returned.

FACULTY
Total: 444, 47% full-time, 56% with terminal degrees.

Student/faculty ratio: 17:1.

ACADEMICS
Calendar: semesters. *Degrees:* bachelor's, master's, post-master's, and postbachelor's certificates.

Special study options: academic remediation for entering students, accelerated degree program, adult/continuing education programs, advanced placement credit, distance learning, double majors, English as a second language, honors programs, independent study, internships, off-campus study, part-time degree program, services for LD students, student-designed majors, study abroad, summer session for credit. *ROTC:* Army (c), Navy (c), Air Force (c).

Computers: Students can access the following: campus intranet, computer help desk, free student e-mail accounts, online (class) grades, online (class) registration, online (class) schedules. Campuswide network is available. 100% of college-owned or -operated housing units are wired for high-speed Internet access. Wireless service is available via entire campus.

Library: Learning Resource Center. *Books:* 129,248 (physical), 173,109 (digital/electronic); *Serial titles:* 202 (physical), 151,915 (digital/electronic); *Databases:* 287. Weekly public service hours: 100.

STUDENT LIFE

Housing options: coed, men-only, women-only, special housing for students with disabilities. Campus housing is university owned.

Activities and organizations: drama/theater group, student-run radio and television station, choral group, DC (Dance Company/Club), SS (Student Senate), TWA (Third World Alliance), Eanuctus, SEC (Student Events Committee).

Athletics Member NCAA. All Division III except golf (Division II). ***Intercollegiate sports:*** baseball M, basketball M/W, cross-country running M/W, field hockey W, football M, golf M/W, ice hockey M, lacrosse W, soccer M/W, softball W, tennis W, track and field M/W, volleyball W. ***Intramural sports:*** basketball M/W, cheerleading M/W, equestrian sports M/W, lacrosse M/W.

Campus security: 24-hour emergency response devices and patrols, late-night transport/escort service, controlled dormitory access, well-lit campus, limited access to campus at night.

Student services: health clinic, personal/psychological counseling, veterans affairs office.

COSTS & FINANCIAL AID

Costs (2019–20) ***Tuition:*** state resident $970 full-time, $40 per credit hour part-time; nonresident $7050 full-time, $294 per credit hour part-time. Full-time tuition and fees vary according to class time, course load, degree level, and reciprocity agreements. Part-time tuition and fees vary according to class time, course load, degree level, and reciprocity agreements. ***Required fees:*** $9191 full-time, $383 per credit hour part-time, $4596 per term part-time. ***Room and board:*** $12,360; room only: $8428. Room and board charges vary according to board plan and housing facility. ***Payment plan:*** installment. ***Waivers:*** senior citizens and employees or children of employees.

Financial Aid Of all full-time matriculated undergraduates who enrolled in 2018, 3,541 applied for aid, 2,635 were judged to have need, 912 had their need fully met. In 2018, 125 non-need-based awards were made. ***Average percent of need met:*** 77. ***Average financial aid package:*** $15,384. ***Average need-based loan:*** $3022. ***Average need-based gift aid:*** $5191. ***Average non-need-based aid:*** $2886. ***Average indebtedness upon graduation:*** $30,629. ***Financial aid deadline:*** 5/1.

APPLYING

Standardized Tests *Required for some:* SAT or ACT (for admission).

Options: electronic application, early action, deferred entrance.

Application fee: $50.

Required: high school transcript, minimum 2.0 GPA. ***Required for some:*** essay or personal statement.

Application deadlines: rolling (transfers), 11/15 (early action).

Notification: 1/2 (freshmen), continuous (transfers).

CONTACT

Worcester State University, 486 Chandler Street, Worcester, MA 01602-2597. *Phone:* 508-929-8040.

MICHIGAN

Adrian College

Adrian, Michigan

http://www.adrian.edu/

CONTACT

Mr. Frank Hribar, Vice President for Enrollment, Adrian College, 110 S. Madison Street, Adrian, MI 49221. *Phone:* 800-877-2246. *Toll-free phone:* 800-877-2246. *Fax:* 517-264-3331. *E-mail:* admissions@adrian.edu.

Albion College

Albion, Michigan

http://www.albion.edu/

- **Independent Methodist** 4-year, founded 1835
- **Small-town** 574-acre campus with easy access to Detroit
- **Endowment** $170.1 million
- **Coed** 1,475 undergraduate students, 99% full-time, 54% women, 46% men
- **Moderately difficult** entrance level, 69% of applicants were admitted

UNDERGRAD STUDENTS

1,455 full-time, 20 part-time. Students come from 33 states and territories; 14 other countries; 28% are from out of state; 16% Black or African American, non-Hispanic/Latino; 12% Hispanic/Latino; 2% Asian, non-Hispanic/Latino; 0.3% American Indian or Alaska Native, non-Hispanic/Latino; 3% Two or more races, non-Hispanic/Latino; 6% Race/ethnicity unknown; 2% international; 2% transferred in; 93% live on campus.

Freshmen:

Admission: 4,043 applied, 2,780 admitted, 401 enrolled. ***Average high school GPA:*** 3.5. ***Test scores:*** SAT evidence-based reading and writing scores over 500: 74%; SAT math scores over 500: 73%; ACT scores over 18: 94%; SAT evidence-based reading and writing scores over 600: 28%; SAT math scores over 600: 20%; ACT scores over 24: 49%; SAT evidence-based reading and writing scores over 700: 3%; SAT math scores over 700: 3%; ACT scores over 30: 11%.

Retention: 80% of full-time freshmen returned.

FACULTY

Total: 156, 73% full-time, 83% with terminal degrees.

Student/faculty ratio: 11:1.

ACADEMICS

Calendar: semesters. *Degree:* bachelor's.

Special study options: advanced placement credit, distance learning, double majors, honors programs, independent study, internships, off-campus study, part-time degree program, services for LD students, student-designed majors, study abroad, summer session for credit. ***ROTC:*** Army (c).

Unusual degree programs: 3-2 engineering with Columbia University, University of Michigan, Case Western Reserve University, Michigan Technological University; forestry with Duke University School of the Environment; nursing with Oakland University.

Computers: 250 computers/terminals and 1,217 ports are available on campus for general student use. Students can access the following: computer help desk, free student e-mail accounts, online (class) grades, online (class) registration, online (class) schedules, online student account and financial aid. Campuswide network is available. 100% of college-owned or -operated housing units are wired for high-speed Internet access. Wireless service is available via entire campus.

Library: Stockwell Mudd Libraries. *Books:* 297,083 (physical), 438,170 (digital/electronic); *Serial titles:* 125 (physical), 73,022 (digital/electronic); *Databases:* 207. Weekly public service hours: 110.

STUDENT LIFE

Housing options: on-campus residence required through senior year; coed, women-only, cooperative, special housing for students with disabilities. Campus housing is university owned. Freshman campus housing is guaranteed.

Activities and organizations: drama/theater group, student-run newspaper, radio station, choral group, marching band, Greek Life (Fraternities and Sororities), Student Senate (Student Government), Union Board (programming Board), Student Volunteer Bureau, Umbrella, national fraternities, national sororities.

Athletics Member NCAA. All Division III. ***Intercollegiate sports:*** baseball M, basketball M/W, cross-country running M/W, equestrian sports M/W, football M, golf M/W, lacrosse M/W, soccer M/W, softball W, swimming and diving M/W, tennis M/W, track and field M/W, volleyball W. ***Intramural sports:*** basketball M/W, cheerleading M(c)/W(c), equestrian sports M(c)/W(c), football M/W, ice hockey M(c)/W(c), racquetball M/W, skiing (downhill) M(c)/W(c), soccer M/W, softball M/W, tennis M/W, ultimate Frisbee M/W, volleyball M/W.

Campus security: 24-hour emergency response devices and patrols, late-night transport/escort service, controlled dormitory access.

Student services: personal/psychological counseling, women's center.

COSTS & FINANCIAL AID

Costs (2020–21) ***One-time required fee:*** $185. ***Comprehensive fee:*** $62,970 includes full-time tuition ($50,070), mandatory fees ($520), and room and board ($12,380). Part-time tuition: $2080 per semester hour. Part-time tuition and fees vary according to course load. ***Required fees:*** $520 per year part-time. ***College room only:*** $6080. Room and board charges vary according to board plan and housing facility. ***Payment plan:*** installment. ***Waivers:*** employees or children of employees.

Financial Aid Of all full-time matriculated undergraduates who enrolled in 2019, 1,251 applied for aid, 1,158 were judged to have need, 254 had their need fully met. 424 Federal Work-Study jobs (averaging $1724). 103 state and other part-time jobs (averaging $1343). In 2019, 291 non-need-based awards were made. ***Average percent of need met:*** 89. ***Average financial aid package:*** $45,275. ***Average need-based loan:*** $4524. ***Average need-based gift aid:*** $40,700. ***Average non-need-based aid:*** $29,727. ***Average indebtedness upon graduation:*** $35,529.

APPLYING

Standardized Tests *Required:* SAT or ACT (for admission).

Options: electronic application, early admission, early action, deferred entrance.

Required: high school transcript, 1 letter of recommendation. ***Recommended:*** essay or personal statement, interview.

Application deadlines: rolling (freshmen), 8/15 (transfers), 12/1 (early action).

Notification: continuous until 10/15 (freshmen), continuous until 8/15 (transfers), rolling (early action).

CONTACT

Shar Sanders, Admissions Assistant, Albion College, 611 E. Porter Street, Albion, MI 49224. *Phone:* 517-629-0466. *Toll-free phone:* 800-858-6770. *Fax:* 517-629-0569. *E-mail:* ssanders@albion.edu.

Alma College

Alma, Michigan

http://www.alma.edu/

- **Independent Presbyterian** 4-year, founded 1886
- **Small-town** 128-acre campus with easy access to Lansing
- **Endowment** $120.2 million
- **Coed**
- **Moderately difficult** entrance level

FACULTY

Student/faculty ratio: 12:1.

ACADEMICS

Calendar: 4-4-1. *Degree:* bachelor's.

Library: Kerhl Building-Monteith Library. *Books:* 245,135 (physical), 150,135 (digital/electronic); *Serial titles:* 1,000 (physical). Weekly public service hours: 100; students can reserve study rooms.

STUDENT LIFE

Housing options: on-campus residence required through senior year; coed, special housing for students with disabilities. Campus housing is university owned. Freshman campus housing is guaranteed.

Activities and organizations: drama/theater group, student-run newspaper, choral group, marching band, Alma Ambassadors, Alma College Union Board, Alma College Otaku Gamers (ACOG), Student Congress, Alpha Phi Omega, national fraternities, national sororities.

Athletics Member NCAA. All Division III.

Campus security: 24-hour emergency response devices, late-night transport/escort service, controlled dormitory access.

Student services: health clinic, personal/psychological counseling.

COSTS & FINANCIAL AID

Costs (2019–20) ***Comprehensive fee:*** $52,782 includes full-time tuition ($41,138), mandatory fees ($260), and room and board ($11,384). Part-time tuition: $1285 per credit hour. Part-time tuition and fees vary according to course load. ***Room and board:*** Room and board charges vary according to board plan and housing facility. ***Payment plans:*** installment, deferred payment.

Financial Aid Of all full-time matriculated undergraduates who enrolled in 2019, 1,277 applied for aid, 1,161 were judged to have need, 180 had their need fully met. 600 Federal Work-Study jobs (averaging $1200). In 2019, 206 non-need-based awards were made. ***Average percent of need met:*** 72. ***Average financial aid package:*** $30,408. ***Average need-based loan:*** $4634. ***Average need-based gift aid:*** $29,259. ***Average non-need-based aid:*** $25,269. ***Average indebtedness upon graduation:*** $40,387.

APPLYING

Standardized Tests *Required:* SAT or ACT (for admission).

Options: electronic application.

Application fee: $25.

Required: essay or personal statement, high school transcript. ***Required for some:*** interview.

CONTACT

Craig Aimar, Director of Admissions, Alma College, 614 W. Superior Street, Alma, MI 48801-1599. *Phone:* 800-321-2562. *Toll-free phone:* 800-321-ALMA. *E-mail:* admissions@alma.edu.

Andrews University

Berrien Springs, Michigan

http://www.andrews.edu/

- **Independent Seventh-day Adventist** university, founded 1874
- **Small-town** 1650-acre campus
- **Endowment** $55.6 million
- **Coed** 1,708 undergraduate students, 79% full-time, 54% women, 46% men
- **Moderately difficult** entrance level, 67% of applicants were admitted

UNDERGRAD STUDENTS

1,352 full-time, 356 part-time. Students come from 47 states and territories; 63 other countries; 64% are from out of state; 20% Black or African American, non-Hispanic/Latino; 16% Hispanic/Latino; 13% Asian, non-Hispanic/Latino; 0.3% Native Hawaiian or other Pacific Islander, non-Hispanic/Latino; 0.3% American Indian or Alaska Native, non-Hispanic/Latino; 6% Two or more races, non-Hispanic/Latino; 2% Race/ethnicity unknown; 17% international; 4% transferred in; 60% live on campus.

Freshmen:

Admission: 1,438 applied, 964 admitted, 283 enrolled. ***Average high school GPA:*** 3.6. ***Test scores:*** SAT evidence-based reading and writing scores over 500: 90%; SAT math scores over 500: 82%; ACT scores over 18: 95%; SAT evidence-based reading and writing scores over 600: 60%; SAT math scores over 600: 43%; ACT scores over 24: 59%; SAT evidence-based reading and writing scores over 700: 19%; SAT math scores over 700: 19%; ACT scores over 30: 23%.

Retention: 87% of full-time freshmen returned.

FACULTY

Total: 317, 69% full-time, 63% with terminal degrees.

Student/faculty ratio: 11:1.

ACADEMICS

Calendar: semesters. *Degrees:* certificates, associate, bachelor's, master's, doctoral, post-master's, and postbachelor's certificates.

Special study options: academic remediation for entering students, accelerated degree program, adult/continuing education programs, advanced placement credit, cooperative education, distance learning, double majors, English as a second language, freshman honors college, honors programs, internships, off-campus study, part-time degree program, student-designed majors, study abroad, summer session for credit.

Unusual degree programs: 3-2 physical therapy and architecture.

Computers: 100 computers/terminals are available on campus for general student use. Students can access the following: campus intranet, computer help desk, free student e-mail accounts, online (class) grades, online (class) registration, online (class) schedules, degree audit. Campuswide network is available. 99% of college-owned or -operated housing units are wired for high-speed Internet access. Wireless service is available via entire campus.

Library: James White Library plus 2 others. *Books:* 882,326 (physical), 743,147 (digital/electronic); *Serial titles:* 218,638 (physical), 198,545 (digital/electronic); *Databases:* 216.

STUDENT LIFE

Housing options: on-campus residence required through senior year; men-only, women-only. Campus housing is university owned. Freshman campus housing is guaranteed.

Activities and organizations: drama/theater group, student-run newspaper, radio station, choral group.

Athletics ***Intramural sports:*** basketball M/W, football M/W, golf M/W, gymnastics M/W, racquetball M/W, soccer M/W, softball M/W, volleyball M/W, water polo M/W.

Campus security: 24-hour emergency response devices and patrols, controlled dormitory access.

Student services: health clinic, personal/psychological counseling.

COSTS & FINANCIAL AID

Costs (2020–21) ***Comprehensive fee:*** $40,548 includes full-time tuition ($29,808), mandatory fees ($1200), and room and board ($9540). Full-time tuition and fees vary according to course load. Part-time tuition: $1242 per credit hour. Part-time tuition and fees vary according to course load. ***Required fees:*** $140 part-time. ***College room only:*** $5040. Room and board charges vary according to board plan. ***Payment plan:*** installment. ***Waivers:*** senior citizens and employees or children of employees.

Financial Aid Of all full-time matriculated undergraduates who enrolled in 2019, 834 applied for aid, 751 were judged to have need, 165 had their need fully met. 478 Federal Work-Study jobs (averaging $932). In 2019, 543 non-need-based awards were made. ***Average percent of need met:*** 88. ***Average financial aid package:*** $32,665. ***Average need-based loan:*** $4196. ***Average need-based gift aid:*** $7072. ***Average non-need-based aid:*** $14,359. ***Average indebtedness upon graduation:*** $33,335.

APPLYING

Standardized Tests *Required:* SAT or ACT (for admission).

Options: electronic application, deferred entrance.

Application fee: $30.

Required: high school transcript, minimum 2.3 GPA, 2 letters of recommendation.

Application deadlines: rolling (freshmen), rolling (transfers).

Notification: continuous (freshmen), continuous (transfers).

CONTACT

Elivette Diaz, Undergraduate Admissions Coordinator, Andrews University, Berrien Springs, MI 49104. *Phone:* 800-253-2874. *Toll-free phone:* 800-253-2874. *Fax:* 269-471-3228. *E-mail:* enroll@andrews.edu.

Aquinas College

Grand Rapids, Michigan

http://www.aquinas.edu/

- **Independent Roman Catholic** comprehensive, founded 1886
- **Suburban** 117-acre campus with easy access to Grand Rapids
- **Endowment** $40.8 million
- **Coed** 1,456 undergraduate students, 82% full-time, 57% women, 43% men
- **Moderately difficult** entrance level, 69% of applicants were admitted

UNDERGRAD STUDENTS

1,196 full-time, 260 part-time. 9% are from out of state; 5% Black or African American, non-Hispanic/Latino; 8% Hispanic/Latino; 1% Asian, non-Hispanic/Latino; 0.1% Native Hawaiian or other Pacific Islander, non-Hispanic/Latino; 0.4% American Indian or Alaska Native, non-Hispanic/Latino; 2% Two or more races, non-Hispanic/Latino; 15% Race/ethnicity unknown; 3% international; 5% transferred in; 46% live on campus.

Freshmen:

Admission: 1,883 applied, 1,305 admitted, 262 enrolled. ***Average high school GPA:*** 3.5. ***Test scores:*** SAT evidence-based reading and writing scores over 500: 80%; SAT math scores over 500: 74%; ACT scores over 18: 89%; SAT evidence-based reading and writing scores over 600: 31%; SAT math scores over 600: 27%; ACT scores over 24: 48%; SAT evidence-based reading and writing scores over 700: 4%; SAT math scores over 700: 4%; ACT scores over 30: 11%.

Retention: 78% of full-time freshmen returned.

FACULTY

Total: 200, 45% full-time, 50% with terminal degrees.

Student/faculty ratio: 10:1.

ACADEMICS

Calendar: semesters. *Degrees:* associate, bachelor's, and master's.

Special study options: academic remediation for entering students, adult/continuing education programs, advanced placement credit, cooperative education, distance learning, double majors, English as a second language, honors programs, independent study, internships, off-campus study, part-time degree program, services for LD students, student-designed majors, study abroad, summer session for credit.

Computers: 210 computers/terminals are available on campus for general student use. Students can access the following: campus intranet, computer help desk, free student e-mail accounts, online (class) grades, online (class) registration, online (class) schedules. Campuswide network is available. 100% of college-owned or -operated housing units are wired for high-speed Internet access. Wireless service is available via entire campus.

Library: Grace Hauenstein Library plus 1 other. *Books:* 85,348 (physical), 196,003 (digital/electronic); *Serial titles:* 231 (physical); *Databases:* 85. Weekly public service hours: 90; students can reserve study rooms.

STUDENT LIFE

Housing options: on-campus residence required through junior year; coed. Campus housing is university owned. Freshman campus housing is guaranteed.

Activities and organizations: drama/theater group, student-run newspaper, radio station, choral group, Community Senate Programming Board, The Saint (newspaper), Insignis Honors Group, Community Action Volunteers of Aquinas (CAVA), Residence Hall Association.

Athletics Member NAIA. ***Intercollegiate sports:*** baseball M(s), basketball M(s)/W(s), bowling M(s)/W(s), cheerleading M(s)/W(s), cross-country running M(s)/W(s), golf M(s)/W(s), ice hockey M/W, lacrosse M(s)/W(s), soccer M(s)/W(s), softball W(s), tennis M(s)/W(s), track and field M(s)/W(s), volleyball W(s). ***Intramural sports:*** basketball M/W, football M/W, golf M, skiing (cross-country) M/W, skiing (downhill) M/W, soccer M/W, softball M/W, tennis M/W, volleyball M/W.

Campus security: 24-hour emergency response devices and patrols, student patrols, late-night transport/escort service, controlled dormitory access.

Student services: health clinic, personal/psychological counseling, women's center, veterans affairs office.

COSTS & FINANCIAL AID

Costs (2020–21) ***Comprehensive fee:*** $44,962 includes full-time tuition ($34,386), mandatory fees ($700), and room and board ($9876). Full-time tuition and fees vary according to course load. Part-time tuition: $536 per credit hour. Part-time tuition and fees vary according to course load. ***College room only:*** $4630. Room and board charges vary according to board plan and housing facility. ***Payment plans:*** installment, deferred payment. ***Waivers:*** employees or children of employees.

Financial Aid Of all full-time matriculated undergraduates who enrolled in 2019, 998 applied for aid, 883 were judged to have need, 250 had their need fully met. 92 Federal Work-Study jobs (averaging $1327). In 2019, 165 non-need-based awards were made. ***Average percent of need met:*** 79. ***Average financial aid package:*** $26,667. ***Average need-based loan:*** $2350. ***Average need-based gift aid:*** $24,317. ***Average non-need-based aid:*** $17,280. ***Average indebtedness upon graduation:*** $30,158.

APPLYING

Standardized Tests *Required:* SAT or ACT (for admission).

Options: electronic application, deferred entrance.

Required: high school transcript, minimum 2.5 GPA. ***Required for some:*** essay or personal statement, interview.

Application deadlines: rolling (freshmen), rolling (transfers).

CONTACT

Ms. Rebecca Roberts, Assistant Director of CRM Systems, Aquinas College, 1700 Fulton Street E., Grand Rapids, MI 49506-1801. *Phone:*

616-632-2900. *Toll-free phone:* 800-678-9593. *Fax:* 616-732-4469. *E-mail:* rrr001@aquinas.edu.

Baker College

Flint, Michigan

http://www.baker.edu/

CONTACT
Mr. Mark Heaton, System Marketing/Admission, Baker College, 1050 West Bristol Road, Flint, MI 48507-5508. *Phone:* 810-766-4280. *Toll-free phone:* 800-964-4299. *Fax:* 810-766-4279. *E-mail:* mark.heaton@baker.edu.

Calvin College

Grand Rapids, Michigan

http://www.calvin.edu/

- **Independent Christian Reformed** comprehensive, founded 1876
- **Suburban** 400-acre campus with easy access to Grand Rapids, MI
- **Endowment** $176.5 million
- **Coed** 3,467 undergraduate students, 93% full-time, 49% women, 51% men
- **Moderately difficult** entrance level, 77% of applicants were admitted

UNDERGRAD STUDENTS
3,234 full-time, 233 part-time. Students come from 47 states and territories; 64 other countries; 42% are from out of state; 3% Black or African American, non-Hispanic/Latino; 5% Hispanic/Latino; 5% Asian, non-Hispanic/Latino; 0.1% American Indian or Alaska Native, non-Hispanic/Latino; 3% Two or more races, non-Hispanic/Latino; 1% Race/ethnicity unknown; 13% international; 2% transferred in; 59% live on campus.

Freshmen:
Admission: 3,401 applied, 2,616 admitted, 779 enrolled. ***Average high school GPA:*** 3.8. ***Test scores:*** SAT evidence-based reading and writing scores over 500: 94%; SAT math scores over 500: 92%; ACT scores over 18: 99%; SAT evidence-based reading and writing scores over 600: 64%; SAT math scores over 600: 61%; ACT scores over 24: 76%; SAT evidence-based reading and writing scores over 700: 16%; SAT math scores over 700: 20%; ACT scores over 30: 32%.

Retention: 85% of full-time freshmen returned.

FACULTY
Total: 332, 67% full-time, 70% with terminal degrees.

Student/faculty ratio: 13:1.

ACADEMICS
Calendar: 4-1-4. *Degrees:* certificates, associate, bachelor's, and master's.

Special study options: academic remediation for entering students, accelerated degree program, advanced placement credit, distance learning, double majors, honors programs, independent study, internships, off-campus study, part-time degree program, services for LD students, student-designed majors, study abroad, summer session for credit. ***ROTC:*** Army (c).

Unusual degree programs: 3-2 occupational therapy with Washington University in St. Louis, speech pathology with Calvin.

Computers: 1,025 computers/terminals and 2,656 ports are available on campus for general student use. Students can access the following: campus intranet, computer help desk, free student e-mail accounts, online (class) grades, online (class) registration, online (class) schedules. Campuswide network is available. 100% of college-owned or -operated housing units are wired for high-speed Internet access. Wireless service is available via classrooms, computer centers, computer labs, dorm rooms, learning centers, libraries, student centers.

Library: Hekman Library. *Books:* 528,095 (physical), 552,442 (digital/electronic); *Serial titles:* 6,111 (physical), 40,919 (digital/electronic); *Databases:* 119. Weekly public service hours: 90; students can reserve study rooms.

STUDENT LIFE
Housing options: on-campus residence required through sophomore year; men-only, women-only. Campus housing is university owned. Freshman campus housing is guaranteed.

Activities and organizations: drama/theater group, student-run newspaper, choral group, Dance Guild, Pre-Health Professionals, Calvin Outdoor Recreation, National Student Speech, Language, and Hearing Association, African Students Association.

Athletics Member NCAA. All Division III except ice hockey (Division I). ***Intercollegiate sports:*** baseball M, basketball M/W, cross-country running M/W, equestrian sports M(c)/W(c), golf M/W, ice hockey M, lacrosse M/W, rugby M(c)/W(c), soccer M/W, softball W, swimming and diving M/W, tennis M/W, track and field M/W, triathlon W, ultimate Frisbee M(c)/W(c), volleyball M(c)/W. ***Intramural sports:*** badminton M/W, basketball M/W, cross-country running M/W, football M/W, golf M/W, racquetball M/W, rock climbing M/W, rowing M(c)/W(c), sand volleyball M/W, skiing (downhill) M/W, soccer M/W, softball M/W, swimming and diving M/W, table tennis M/W, tennis M/W, track and field M/W, volleyball M/W, water polo M/W.

Campus security: 24-hour emergency response devices and patrols, student patrols, late-night transport/escort service, controlled dormitory access.

Student services: health clinic, personal/psychological counseling.

COSTS & FINANCIAL AID
Costs (2020–21) ***Comprehensive fee:*** $48,606 includes full-time tuition ($37,600), mandatory fees ($206), and room and board ($10,800). Full-time tuition and fees vary according to course load, program, and student level. Part-time tuition: $904 per credit hour. ***Room and board:*** Room and board charges vary according to board plan and housing facility. ***Payment plan:*** installment. ***Waivers:*** employees or children of employees.

Financial Aid Of all full-time matriculated undergraduates who enrolled in 2019, 2,563 applied for aid, 1,837 were judged to have need, 428 had their need fully met. 1,401 Federal Work-Study jobs (averaging $6130). In 2019, 1311 non-need-based awards were made. ***Average percent of need met:*** 75. ***Average financial aid package:*** $25,974. ***Average need-based loan:*** $5753. ***Average need-based gift aid:*** $20,082. ***Average non-need-based aid:*** $14,747. ***Average indebtedness upon graduation:*** $25,888.

APPLYING
Standardized Tests *Required:* SAT or ACT (for admission), or CLT (for admission).

Options: electronic application, deferred entrance.

Application fee: $35.

Required: essay or personal statement, high school transcript, 1 letter of recommendation. ***Recommended:*** interview.

Application deadlines: 8/15 (freshmen), 8/15 (out-of-state freshmen), rolling (transfers).

Notification: continuous (freshmen).

CONTACT
Ms. Robin Wait, Associate Director of Admissions, Calvin College, 3201 Burton Street, SE, Grand Rapids, MI 49546. *Phone:* 616-526-6106. *Toll-free phone:* 800-688-0122. *Fax:* 616-526-6777. *E-mail:* admissions@calvin.edu.

Central Michigan University

Mount Pleasant, Michigan

http://www.cmich.edu/

- **State-supported** university, founded 1892
- **Small-town** 854-acre campus
- **Endowment** $189.3 million
- **Coed** 14,672 undergraduate students, 87% full-time, 59% women, 41% men
- **Moderately difficult** entrance level, 70% of applicants were admitted

UNDERGRAD STUDENTS
12,800 full-time, 1,872 part-time. Students come from 52 states and territories; 46 other countries; 10% are from out of state; 10% Black or African American, non-Hispanic/Latino; 5% Hispanic/Latino; 1% Asian, non-Hispanic/Latino; 0.1% Native Hawaiian or other Pacific Islander, non-Hispanic/Latino; 0.8% American Indian or Alaska Native, non-Hispanic/Latino; 4% Two or more races, non-Hispanic/Latino; 1%

Race/ethnicity unknown; 2% international; 7% transferred in; 33% live on campus.

Freshmen:
Admission: 16,411 applied, 11,408 admitted, 2,473 enrolled. ***Average high school GPA:*** 3.4. ***Test scores:*** SAT evidence-based reading and writing scores over 500: 76%; SAT math scores over 500: 73%; ACT scores over 18: 90%; SAT evidence-based reading and writing scores over 600: 30%; SAT math scores over 600: 25%; ACT scores over 24: 38%; SAT evidence-based reading and writing scores over 700: 3%; SAT math scores over 700: 5%; ACT scores over 30: 9%.
Retention: 74% of full-time freshmen returned.

FACULTY
Total: 1,134, 64% full-time, 68% with terminal degrees.

Student/faculty ratio: 19:1.

ACADEMICS
Calendar: semesters. *Degrees:* bachelor's, master's, doctoral, post-master's, and postbachelor's certificates.

Special study options: academic remediation for entering students, accelerated degree program, advanced placement credit, distance learning, double majors, English as a second language, honors programs, independent study, off-campus study, part-time degree program, services for LD students, student-designed majors, study abroad, summer session for credit. ***ROTC:*** Army (b), Air Force (c).

Computers: 490 computers/terminals and 26,902 ports are available on campus for general student use. Students can access the following: campus intranet, computer help desk, free student e-mail accounts, online (class) grades, online (class) registration, online (class) schedules, learning management system. Campuswide network is available. 100% of college-owned or -operated housing units are wired for high-speed Internet access. Wireless service is available via entire campus.
Library: Charles V. Park Library. *Books:* 895,460 (physical), 709,885 (digital/electronic); *Serial titles:* 2,156 (physical), 114,678 (digital/electronic); *Databases:* 336. Weekly public service hours: 101; students can reserve study rooms.

STUDENT LIFE
Housing options: on-campus residence required for freshman year; coed, special housing for students with disabilities. Campus housing is university owned. Freshman campus housing is guaranteed.

Activities and organizations: drama/theater group, student-run newspaper, radio and television station, choral group, marching band, national fraternities, national sororities.

Athletics Member NCAA. All Division I except football (Division I-A). ***Intercollegiate sports:*** baseball M(s), basketball M(s)/W(s), cross-country running M(s)/W(s), field hockey W(s), golf W(s), gymnastics W(s), lacrosse W(s), soccer W(s), softball W(s), track and field M(s)/W(s), volleyball W(s), wrestling M(s). ***Intramural sports:*** baseball M(c), basketball M/W, bowling M/W, cross-country running M(c)/W(c), equestrian sports M(c)/W(c), football M/W, golf M(c)/W(c), ice hockey M(c)/W(c), lacrosse M(c)/W(c), racquetball M/W, rugby M(c)/W(c), skiing (downhill) M(c)/W(c), soccer M/W, softball M/W, swimming and diving M(c)/W(c), table tennis M/W, tennis M/W, track and field M(c)/W(c), triathlon M(c)/W(c), ultimate Frisbee M(c)/W(c), volleyball M/W, water polo M(c)/W(c), weight lifting M/W, wrestling M/W.

Campus security: 24-hour emergency response devices and patrols, late-night transport/escort service, controlled dormitory access.

Student services: health clinic, personal/psychological counseling, veterans affairs office.

COSTS & FINANCIAL AID
Costs (2019–20) ***Tuition:*** state resident $12,810 full-time, $427 per credit hour part-time; nonresident $12,810 full-time, $427 per credit hour part-time. Full-time tuition and fees vary according to student level. Part-time tuition and fees vary according to student level. ***Required fees:*** $450 full-time, $225 per term part-time. ***Room and board:*** $10,328; room only: $5164. Room and board charges vary according to board plan and housing facility. ***Payment plan:*** installment. ***Waivers:*** children of alumni, senior citizens, and employees or children of employees.

Financial Aid Of all full-time matriculated undergraduates who enrolled in 2018, 11,028 applied for aid, 8,729 were judged to have need, 8,536 had their need fully met. 573 Federal Work-Study jobs (averaging $2262). 342 state and other part-time jobs (averaging $2014). In 2018, 2217 non-need-based awards were made. ***Average percent of need met:*** 80. ***Average financial aid package:*** $14,640. ***Average need-based loan:*** $5952. ***Average need-based gift aid:*** $10,146. ***Average non-need-based aid:*** $6299. ***Average indebtedness upon graduation:*** $31,683.

APPLYING
Standardized Tests *Required:* SAT or ACT (for admission).

Options: electronic application, deferred entrance.

Application fee: $40.

Required: high school transcript. ***Required for some:*** essay or personal statement, interview.

Application deadlines: rolling (freshmen), rolling (out-of-state freshmen), rolling (transfers).

Notification: continuous (freshmen), continuous (out-of-state freshmen), continuous (transfers).

CONTACT
Central Michigan University, 1200 South Franklin Street, Mount Pleasant, MI 48859. *Phone:* 989-774-2446. *Toll-free phone:* 888-292-5366.

Chamberlain College of Nursing - Troy

Troy, Michigan

http://www.chamberlain.edu/

CONTACT
Chamberlain College of Nursing - Troy, 200 Kirts Boulevard, Troy, MI 48084. *Toll-free phone:* 877-751-5783.

Cleary University

Howell, Michigan

http://www.cleary.edu/

- **Independent** comprehensive, founded 1883
- **Suburban** 32-acre campus with easy access to Detroit, Ann Arbor
- **Endowment** $998,704
- **Coed**
- **Moderately difficult** entrance level

FACULTY
Student/faculty ratio: 15:1.

ACADEMICS
Calendar: semesters. *Degrees:* certificates, associate, bachelor's, and master's.
Library: Cleary Online Library.

STUDENT LIFE
Housing options: on-campus residence required for freshman year; coed. Campus housing is university owned. Freshman applicants given priority for college housing.

Activities and organizations: Cleary Professional Accounting Associates, Human Resources and Organizational Leadership Association, Event and Meeting Planning Student Association, Veterans Club, Accounting/Fraud Examiners Club.

Athletics Member USCAA.

Campus security: 24-hour emergency response devices, access to facilities limited to authorized persons.

Student services: personal/psychological counseling.

FINANCIAL AID
Financial Aid Of all full-time matriculated undergraduates who enrolled in 2015, 11 Federal Work-Study jobs (averaging $3209).

APPLYING
Standardized Tests *Required:* SAT or ACT (for admission). *Required for some:* SAT Subject Tests (for admission).

Options: electronic application, early admission, deferred entrance.

Application fee: $35.

Required: high school transcript, minimum 2.5 GPA. ***Required for some:*** essay or personal statement, minimum ACT score of 19 for freshmen, minimum high school GPA of 2.0 for non-traditional and transfer students. ***Recommended:*** interview.

CONTACT
Eric Brown, Director of Admissions, Cleary University, 3750 Cleary Drive, Howell, MI 48843. *Phone:* 800-686-1883. *Toll-free phone:* 800-686-1883. *Fax:* 517-338-5075. *E-mail:* admissions@cleary.edu.

College for Creative Studies

Detroit, Michigan

http://www.collegeforcreativestudies.edu/

CONTACT
Office of Admissions, College for Creative Studies, 201 East Kirby, Detroit, MI 48202-4034. *Phone:* 800-952-2787. *Toll-free phone:* 800-952-ARTS. *Fax:* 313-872-2739. *E-mail:* admissions@collegeforcreativestudies.edu.

Compass College of Cinematic Arts

Grand Rapids, Michigan

http://www.compass.edu/

- **Independent** 4-year
- **Urban** campus
- **Coed**
- **Minimally difficult** entrance level

ACADEMICS
Degrees: associate and bachelor's.

APPLYING
Standardized Tests *Recommended:* SAT or ACT (for admission).

Required: essay or personal statement, high school transcript, minimum 2.0 GPA, 2 letters of recommendation, interview, Portfolio of 2 film pieces and 2 non-film pieces.

CONTACT
Compass College of Cinematic Arts, 41 Sheldon Boulevard SE, Grand Rapids, MI 49503.

Concordia University Ann Arbor

Ann Arbor, Michigan

http://www.cuaa.edu/

- **Independent** comprehensive, founded 1963, affiliated with Lutheran Church–Missouri Synod, part of Concordia University System
- **Suburban** 187-acre campus with easy access to Detroit
- **Endowment** $7.6 million
- **Coed**
- **Moderately difficult** entrance level

FACULTY
Student/faculty ratio: 10:1.

ACADEMICS
Calendar: semesters. *Degrees:* associate, bachelor's, master's, and postbachelor's certificates.
Library: Zimmerman Library.

STUDENT LIFE
Housing options: on-campus residence required through sophomore year; men-only, women-only. Campus housing is university owned. Freshman campus housing is guaranteed.

Activities and organizations: drama/theater group, choral group, Student Activities Committee, Athletes in Action, Student Senate, Spiritual Life Committee, Off-campus ministries.

Athletics Member NAIA.

Campus security: 24-hour emergency response devices and patrols, late-night transport/escort service, controlled dormitory access.

Student services: personal/psychological counseling.

COSTS & FINANCIAL AID
Costs (2019–20) ***Comprehensive fee:*** $42,070 includes full-time tuition ($29,180), mandatory fees ($270), and room and board ($12,620). Part-time tuition: $1200 per credit hour. ***College room only:*** $5870.

Financial Aid Of all full-time matriculated undergraduates who enrolled in 2016, 712 applied for aid, 654 were judged to have need, 146 had their need fully met. In 2016, 41 non-need-based awards were made. ***Average percent of need met:*** 70. ***Average financial aid package:*** $22,110. ***Average need-based loan:*** $6765. ***Average need-based gift aid:*** $14,781. ***Average non-need-based aid:*** $10,354. ***Average indebtedness upon graduation:*** $20,641.

APPLYING
Standardized Tests *Required:* SAT or ACT (for admission). *Recommended:* ACT (for admission).

Options: electronic application, deferred entrance.

Application fee: $25.

Required: high school transcript. ***Required for some:*** essay or personal statement, 1 letter of recommendation, interview. ***Recommended:*** minimum 2.5 GPA.

CONTACT
Mr. Ben Limback, Director of Admissions, Concordia University Ann Arbor, 4090 Geddes Road, Ann Arbor, MI 48105-2797. *Phone:* 734-995-7311. *Toll-free phone:* 877-995-7520 (in-state); 877-955-7520 (out-of-state). *Fax:* 734-995-4610. *E-mail:* admissions@cuaa.edu.

Cornerstone University

Grand Rapids, Michigan

http://www.cornerstone.edu/

CONTACT
Mrs. Lisa Link, Office of Admissions, Cornerstone University, 1001 East Beltline Avenue, NE, Grand Rapids, MI 49525. *Phone:* 616-222-1426. *Toll-free phone:* 800-787-9778. *Fax:* 616-222-1418. *E-mail:* admissions@cornerstone.edu.

Davenport University

Grand Rapids, Michigan

http://www.davenport.edu/

- **Independent** comprehensive, founded 1866
- **Suburban** 77-acre campus with easy access to Grand Rapids
- **Endowment** $26.5 million
- **Coed** 5,078 undergraduate students, 49% full-time, 55% women, 45% men
- **Minimally difficult** entrance level, 82% of applicants were admitted

UNDERGRAD STUDENTS
2,467 full-time, 2,611 part-time. Students come from 38 states and territories; 20 other countries; 2% are from out of state; 12% Black or African American, non-Hispanic/Latino; 5% Hispanic/Latino; 2% Asian, non-Hispanic/Latino; 0.2% Native Hawaiian or other Pacific Islander, non-Hispanic/Latino; 0.7% American Indian or Alaska Native, non-Hispanic/Latino; 3% Two or more races, non-Hispanic/Latino; 5% Race/ethnicity unknown; 3% international; 12% transferred in; 6% live on campus.

Freshmen:
Admission: 2,568 applied, 2,104 admitted, 616 enrolled. ***Average high school GPA:*** 3.2.

Retention: 76% of full-time freshmen returned.

FACULTY
Total: 610, 22% full-time, 30% with terminal degrees.

Student/faculty ratio: 12:1.

ACADEMICS
Calendar: semesters. *Degrees:* certificates, diplomas, associate, bachelor's, master's, post-master's, and postbachelor's certificates.

Special study options: academic remediation for entering students, accelerated degree program, adult/continuing education programs, advanced placement credit, cooperative education, distance learning, English as a second language, independent study, internships, part-time degree program, services for LD students, study abroad, summer session for credit. ***ROTC:*** Army (c).

Computers: 3,098 computers/terminals and 315 ports are available on campus for general student use. Students can access the following: campus intranet, computer help desk, free student e-mail accounts, online (class) grades, online (class) registration, online (class) schedules. Campuswide network is available. 100% of college-owned or -operated housing units are wired for high-speed Internet access. Wireless service is available via entire campus.

Library: Margaret D. Sneden Library Information Commons plus 3 others. Students can reserve study rooms.

STUDENT LIFE

Housing options: coed. Campus housing is university owned. Freshman applicants given priority for college housing.

Activities and organizations: marching band, Business Professionals of America, Delta Epsilon Chi, Student Government, Health Occupations Students of America, Connect.

Athletics Member NCAA, NAIA. All NCAA Division III. ***Intercollegiate sports:*** baseball M(s), basketball M(s)/W(s), bowling M(s)/W(s), cheerleading W(s), cross-country running M(s)/W(s), football M(s), golf M(s)/W(s), ice hockey M(s)/W(s), lacrosse M(s)/W(s), rugby M(s)/W(s), soccer M(s)/W(s), softball M(s)/W(s), swimming and diving M(s)/W(s), tennis M(s)/W(s), track and field M(s)/W(s), volleyball W(s), water polo M(s)/W(s), wrestling M(s).

Campus security: 24-hour emergency response devices and patrols, late-night transport/escort service, controlled dormitory access.

Student services: personal/psychological counseling.

COSTS

Costs (2020–21) ***Tuition:*** $24,150 full-time, $805 per credit hour part-time. Full-time tuition and fees vary according to location and program. Part-time tuition and fees vary according to location and program. ***Required fees:*** $445 per term part-time. ***Room only:*** Room and board charges vary according to board plan and housing facility. ***Payment plan:*** installment. ***Waivers:*** employees or children of employees.

APPLYING

Standardized Tests *Recommended:* SAT (for admission), ACT (for admission).

Options: electronic application, deferred entrance.

Application fee: $25.

Required: high school transcript. ***Recommended:*** interview.

Application deadlines: rolling (freshmen), rolling (transfers).

Notification: continuous (freshmen), continuous (transfers).

CONTACT

Ms. David Lawrence, Executive Director of Admissions, Davenport University, 6191 Kraft Avenue SE, Grand Rapids, MI 49512. *Phone:* 616-451-3511. *Toll-free phone:* 800-686-1600 (in-state); 866-686-1600 (out-of-state). *Fax:* 616-732-1145. *E-mail:* david.lawrence@davenport.edu.

Eastern Michigan University

Ypsilanti, Michigan

http://www.emich.edu/

- **State-supported** comprehensive, founded 1849
- **Suburban** 460-acre campus with easy access to Detroit
- **Endowment** $67.2 million
- **Coed** 15,725 undergraduate students, 73% full-time, 60% women, 40% men
- **Moderately difficult** entrance level, 76% of applicants were admitted

UNDERGRAD STUDENTS

11,403 full-time, 4,322 part-time. 10% are from out of state; 18% Black or African American, non-Hispanic/Latino; 5% Hispanic/Latino; 3% Asian, non-Hispanic/Latino; 0.1% Native Hawaiian or other Pacific Islander, non-Hispanic/Latino; 0.3% American Indian or Alaska Native, non-Hispanic/Latino; 4% Two or more races, non-Hispanic/Latino; 5% Race/ethnicity unknown; 2% international; 9% transferred in; 21% live on campus.

Freshmen:

Admission: 14,461 applied, 10,995 admitted, 2,404 enrolled. ***Average high school GPA:*** 3.3.

Retention: 71% of full-time freshmen returned.

FACULTY

Total: 1,261, 58% full-time, 57% with terminal degrees.

Student/faculty ratio: 14:1.

ACADEMICS

Calendar: semesters. *Degrees:* bachelor's, master's, doctoral, post-master's, and postbachelor's certificates.

Special study options: academic remediation for entering students, accelerated degree program, advanced placement credit, cooperative education, distance learning, double majors, English as a second language, external degree program, honors programs, independent study, internships, part-time degree program, services for LD students, student-designed majors, study abroad, summer session for credit. ***ROTC:*** Army (b), Navy (c), Air Force (c).

Unusual degree programs: 3-2 accounting, occupational therapy.

Computers: 1,600 computers/terminals and 200 ports are available on campus for general student use. Students can access the following: campus intranet, computer help desk, free student e-mail accounts, online (class) grades, online (class) registration, online (class) schedules. Campuswide network is available. 100% of college-owned or -operated housing units are wired for high-speed Internet access. Wireless service is available via entire campus.

Library: Bruce T. Halle Library.

STUDENT LIFE

Housing options: on-campus residence required through sophomore year; coed, cooperative, special housing for students with disabilities. Campus housing is university owned.

Activities and organizations: drama/theater group, student-run newspaper, radio and television station, choral group, marching band, International Student Association, Golden Key International Honor Society, Psychology Club, Indian Student Association, GREEN (Gathering Resources to Educate about our Environment and Nature), national fraternities, national sororities.

Athletics Member NCAA. All Division I except football (Division I-A). ***Intercollegiate sports:*** baseball M(s), basketball M(s)/W(s), crew W(s), cross-country running M(s)/W(s), golf M(s)/W(s), gymnastics W(s), soccer W(s), softball W(s), swimming and diving M(s)/W(s), tennis W(s), track and field M(s)/W(s), volleyball W(s), wrestling M(s). ***Intramural sports:*** badminton M/W, basketball M/W, bowling M/W, cross-country running M/W, golf M/W, racquetball M/W, rock climbing M/W, soccer M/W, softball M/W, swimming and diving M/W, table tennis M/W, track and field M/W, ultimate Frisbee M/W, volleyball M/W, weight lifting M/W.

Campus security: 24-hour emergency response devices and patrols, student patrols, late-night transport/escort service, controlled dormitory access, bicycle patrols, local police in dormitories, self-defense education, lighted pathways, bike lock lease program.

Student services: health clinic, personal/psychological counseling, women's center, legal services.

COSTS & FINANCIAL AID

Costs (2019–20) ***Tuition:*** area resident $11,128 full-time, $414 per credit hour part-time; state resident $11,128 full-time, $414 per credit hour part-time; nonresident $27,170 full-time, $414 per credit hour part-time. ***Room and board:*** $10,248; room only: $4434.

Financial Aid Of all full-time matriculated undergraduates who enrolled in 2018, 9,206 applied for aid, 7,786 were judged to have need, 361 had their need fully met. 505 Federal Work-Study jobs (averaging $2289). In 2018, 2148 non-need-based awards were made. ***Average percent of need met:*** 42. ***Average financial aid package:*** $10,477. ***Average need-based loan:*** $4066. ***Average need-based gift aid:*** $6191. ***Average non-need-based aid:*** $5399. ***Average indebtedness upon graduation:*** $27,475.

APPLYING

Standardized Tests *Required:* SAT or ACT (for admission).

Options: electronic application, deferred entrance.

Application fee: $35.

Required: high school transcript, minimum 2.0 GPA. ***Required for some:*** 1 letter of recommendation, interview.

Application deadlines: rolling (freshmen), rolling (transfers).

Notification: continuous (freshmen), continuous (transfers).

CONTACT

Eastern Michigan University, Ypsilanti, MI 48197. *Phone:* 734-487-3060. *Toll-free phone:* 800-GO TO EMU.

Ferris State University

Big Rapids, Michigan

http://www.ferris.edu/

- **State-supported** comprehensive, founded 1884
- **Small-town** 930-acre campus with easy access to Grand Rapids
- **Endowment** $87.2 million
- **Coed** 11,184 undergraduate students, 70% full-time, 53% women, 47% men
- **Minimally difficult** entrance level, 87% of applicants were admitted

UNDERGRAD STUDENTS

7,779 full-time, 3,405 part-time. Students come from 44 states and territories; 39 other countries; 5% are from out of state; 8% Black or African American, non-Hispanic/Latino; 6% Hispanic/Latino; 1% Asian, non-Hispanic/Latino; 0.1% Native Hawaiian or other Pacific Islander, non-Hispanic/Latino; 0.5% American Indian or Alaska Native, non-Hispanic/Latino; 4% Two or more races, non-Hispanic/Latino; 0.7% Race/ethnicity unknown; 1% international; 9% transferred in; 30% live on campus.

Freshmen:

Admission: 9,175 applied, 7,949 admitted, 1,892 enrolled. ***Average high school GPA:*** 3.3. ***Test scores:*** SAT evidence-based reading and writing scores over 500: 63%; SAT math scores over 500: 63%; ACT scores over 18: 82%; SAT evidence-based reading and writing scores over 600: 22%; SAT math scores over 600: 20%; ACT scores over 24: 36%; SAT evidence-based reading and writing scores over 700: 3%; SAT math scores over 700: 3%; ACT scores over 30: 7%.

Retention: 76% of full-time freshmen returned.

FACULTY

Total: 876, 65% full-time, 36% with terminal degrees.

Student/faculty ratio: 16:1.

ACADEMICS

Calendar: semesters. *Degrees:* certificates, associate, bachelor's, master's, doctoral, and postbachelor's certificates.

Special study options: academic remediation for entering students, accelerated degree program, adult/continuing education programs, advanced placement credit, cooperative education, distance learning, double majors, English as a second language, external degree program, freshman honors college, honors programs, independent study, internships, off-campus study, part-time degree program, services for LD students, student-designed majors, study abroad, summer session for credit. ***ROTC:*** Army (c).

Computers: 1,751 computers/terminals are available on campus for general student use. Students can access the following: computer help desk, free student e-mail accounts, online (class) grades, online (class) registration, online (class) schedules. Campuswide network is available. 100% of college-owned or -operated housing units are wired for high-speed Internet access. Wireless service is available via entire campus.

Library: Ferris Library for Information, Technology and Education. *Books:* 181,270 (physical), 483,402 (digital/electronic); *Serial titles:* 5,430 (physical), 325,776 (digital/electronic); *Databases:* 170. Weekly public service hours: 93; students can reserve study rooms.

STUDENT LIFE

Housing options: on-campus residence required for freshman year; coed, special housing for students with disabilities. Campus housing is university owned. Freshman campus housing is guaranteed.

Activities and organizations: drama/theater group, student-run newspaper, radio and television station, choral group, Student American Dental Hygiene Association, Pre-Pharm D, American Pharmacist Association, Student Nurses Association, American Marketing Association, national fraternities, national sororities.

Athletics Member NCAA. All Division II. ***Intercollegiate sports:*** basketball M(s)/W(s), cross-country running M(s)/W(s), football M(s), golf M(s)/W(s), ice hockey M(s), soccer W(s), softball W(s), tennis M(s)/W(s), track and field M(s)/W(s), volleyball W(s). ***Intramural sports:*** archery M(c)/W(c), badminton M/W, baseball M(c), basketball M/W, bowling M/W, cheerleading M(c)/W(c), equestrian sports W(c), football M/W, golf M(c)/W(c), ice hockey M, lacrosse M(c)/W(c), rugby M(c)/W(c), soccer M(c)/W(c), softball W, swimming and diving M(c)/W(c), table tennis M(c)/W(c), tennis M/W, ultimate Frisbee M/W, volleyball M/W, weight lifting M(c)/W(c), wrestling M(c).

Campus security: 24-hour emergency response devices, student patrols, late-night transport/escort service, controlled dormitory access.

Student services: health clinic, personal/psychological counseling, veterans affairs office.

COSTS & FINANCIAL AID

Costs (2019–20) ***Tuition:*** $431 per credit hour part-time; state resident $12,930 full-time, $431 per credit hour part-time; nonresident $12,930 full-time, $431 per credit hour part-time. Full-time tuition and fees vary according to location, program, and student level. Part-time tuition and fees vary according to location and student level. ***Room and board:*** $10,044. Room and board charges vary according to board plan and housing facility. ***Payment plan:*** installment. ***Waivers:*** employees or children of employees.

Financial Aid Of all full-time matriculated undergraduates who enrolled in 2019, 7,500 applied for aid, 5,600 were judged to have need, 992 had their need fully met. 394 Federal Work-Study jobs (averaging $2580). 173 state and other part-time jobs (averaging $1950). In 2019, 1212 non-need-based awards were made. ***Average percent of need met:*** 68. ***Average financial aid package:*** $12,300. ***Average need-based loan:*** $4110. ***Average need-based gift aid:*** $5440. ***Average non-need-based aid:*** $4460. ***Average indebtedness upon graduation:*** $34,590.

APPLYING

Standardized Tests *Required for some:* SAT or ACT (for admission).

Options: electronic application, deferred entrance.

Required: minimum 2.5 GPA. ***Required for some:*** essay or personal statement, high school transcript, interview.

Application deadlines: 8/1 (freshmen), 7/1 (transfers).

Notification: continuous (freshmen), continuous (transfers).

CONTACT

Mr. Jason Daday, Associate Director of Admissions, Ferris State University, 1201 South State Street, CSS 201, Big Rapids, MI 49307-2742. *Phone:* 231-591-3106. *Toll-free phone:* 800-433-7747. *Fax:* 231-591-2242. *E-mail:* dadayja@ferris.edu.

Finlandia University

Hancock, Michigan

http://www.finlandia.edu/

- **Independent** 4-year, founded 1896, affiliated with Evangelical Lutheran Church in America
- **Small-town** 25-acre campus
- **Endowment** $2.5 million
- **Coed**
- **Minimally difficult** entrance level

FACULTY

Student/faculty ratio: 9:1.

ACADEMICS

Calendar: semesters. *Degrees:* associate and bachelor's.

Library: Sulo and Aileen Maki Library.

STUDENT LIFE

Housing options: on-campus residence required through sophomore year; coed, special housing for students with disabilities. Campus housing is university owned.

Activities and organizations: drama/theater group, student-run newspaper, choral group, Student Senate, Campus Ministry, student newspaper, International Club, Artists Coalition.

Campus security: 24-hour emergency response devices, student patrols.

APPLYING

Standardized Tests *Recommended:* SAT or ACT (for admission).

Options: electronic application, early admission.

Application fee: $30.

Required: essay or personal statement, high school transcript, minimum 2.0 GPA. ***Required for some:*** interview.

CONTACT
Martin Kinard, Finlandia University, 601 Quincy Street, Hancock, MI 49930. *Phone:* 906-487-7352. *Toll-free phone:* 877-202-5491. *Fax:* 906-487-7383. *E-mail:* admissions@finlandia.edu.

Grace Bible College

Grand Rapids, Michigan

http://www.gbcol.edu/

CONTACT
Mr. Kevin Gilliam, Director of Enrollment, Grace Bible College, 1101 Aldon Street, SW, PO Box 910, Grand Rapids, MI 49509. *Phone:* 616-538-2330 Ext. 239. *Toll-free phone:* 800-968-1887. *Fax:* 616-538-0599. *E-mail:* gbc@gbcol.edu.

Grand Valley State University

Allendale, Michigan

http://www.gvsu.edu/

- **State-supported** comprehensive, founded 1960
- **Small-town** 1391-acre campus with easy access to Grand Rapids, MI
- **Endowment** $130.3 million
- **Coed** 21,112 undergraduate students, 89% full-time, 60% women, 40% men
- **Moderately difficult** entrance level, 83% of applicants were admitted

UNDERGRAD STUDENTS
18,810 full-time, 2,302 part-time. Students come from 49 states and territories; 70 other countries; 8% are from out of state; 4% Black or African American, non-Hispanic/Latino; 6% Hispanic/Latino; 2% Asian, non-Hispanic/Latino; 0.1% Native Hawaiian or other Pacific Islander, non-Hispanic/Latino; 0.3% American Indian or Alaska Native, non-Hispanic/Latino; 4% Two or more races, non-Hispanic/Latino; 0.3% Race/ethnicity unknown; 1% international; 6% transferred in; 28% live on campus.

Freshmen:
Admission: 16,478 applied, 13,691 admitted, 3,863 enrolled. ***Average high school GPA:*** 3.7. ***Test scores:*** SAT evidence-based reading and writing scores over 500: 88%; SAT math scores over 500: 86%; ACT scores over 18: 97%; SAT evidence-based reading and writing scores over 600: 39%; SAT math scores over 600: 35%; ACT scores over 24: 53%; SAT evidence-based reading and writing scores over 700: 4%; SAT math scores over 700: 5%; ACT scores over 30: 10%.

Retention: 85% of full-time freshmen returned.

FACULTY
Total: 1,774, 66% full-time, 57% with terminal degrees.

Student/faculty ratio: 16:1.

ACADEMICS
Calendar: semesters. *Degrees:* certificates, bachelor's, master's, doctoral, post-master's, and postbachelor's certificates.

Special study options: academic remediation for entering students, accelerated degree program, adult/continuing education programs, advanced placement credit, cooperative education, distance learning, double majors, English as a second language, freshman honors college, honors programs, independent study, internships, part-time degree program, services for LD students, student-designed majors, study abroad, summer session for credit. ***ROTC:*** Army (c), Air Force (c).

Computers: 2,600 computers/terminals are available on campus for general student use. Students can access the following: campus intranet, computer help desk, free student e-mail accounts, online (class) grades, online (class) registration, online (class) schedules, transcript, degree audit, credit card payments. Campuswide network is available. 100% of college-owned or -operated housing units are wired for high-speed Internet access. Wireless service is available via entire campus.

Library: Mary Idema Pew Library Learning and Information Commons plus 5 others. *Books:* 527,588 (physical), 1.0 million (digital/electronic). Students can reserve study rooms.

STUDENT LIFE
Housing options: coed. Campus housing is university owned. Freshman campus housing is guaranteed.

Activities and organizations: drama/theater group, student-run newspaper, radio and television station, choral group, marching band, Habitat for Humanity, Alternative Breaks, Hospitality and tourism Management Club, Dance Troupe, Colleges Against Cancer, national fraternities, national sororities.

Athletics Member NCAA. All Division II except golf (Division I). ***Intercollegiate sports:*** baseball M(s), basketball M(s)/W(s), cheerleading M(c)/W(c), crew M(c)/W(c), cross-country running M(s)/W(s), football M(s), golf M(s)/W(s), ice hockey M/W, lacrosse M(c)/W, rowing M/W, rugby M(c)/W(c), sailing M(c)/W(c), skiing (downhill) W(c), soccer M(c)/W(s), softball W(s), swimming and diving M(s)/W(s), tennis M(s)/W(s), track and field M(s)/W(s), volleyball M(c)/W(s), water polo M(c)/W(c), wrestling M(c). ***Intramural sports:*** archery M/W, basketball M/W, bowling M/W, cheerleading M/W, crew M/W, cross-country running M/W, fencing M/W, field hockey M/W, football M, golf M/W, gymnastics M/W, lacrosse M/W, racquetball M/W, skiing (cross-country) M/W, skiing (downhill) M/W, soccer M/W, softball M/W, squash M/W, swimming and diving M/W, tennis M/W, volleyball M/W, water polo M/W, weight lifting M/W, wrestling M.

Campus security: 24-hour emergency response devices and patrols, student patrols, late-night transport/escort service, controlled dormitory access.

Student services: health clinic, personal/psychological counseling, women's center.

COSTS & FINANCIAL AID
Costs (2019–20) ***Tuition:*** state resident $12,860 full-time, $540 per credit hour part-time; nonresident $18,296 full-time, $768 per credit hour part-time. Full-time tuition and fees vary according to course level, course load, program, and student level. Part-time tuition and fees vary according to course level, course load, program, and student level. ***Room and board:*** $8820; room only: $5570. Room and board charges vary according to board plan and housing facility. ***Payment plans:*** installment, deferred payment. ***Waivers:*** employees or children of employees.

Financial Aid Of all full-time matriculated undergraduates who enrolled in 2019, 15,320 applied for aid, 10,504 were judged to have need, 2,096 had their need fully met. In 2019, 3873 non-need-based awards were made. ***Average percent of need met:*** 67. ***Average financial aid package:*** $10,716. ***Average need-based loan:*** $4204. ***Average need-based gift aid:*** $8221. ***Average non-need-based aid:*** $4425. ***Average indebtedness upon graduation:*** $28,131.

APPLYING
Standardized Tests *Required:* SAT or ACT (for admission).

Options: electronic application.

Application fee: $30.

Required: high school transcript. ***Required for some:*** essay or personal statement, interview.

Notification: 5/1 (freshmen), continuous (transfers).

CONTACT
Ms. Jodi Chycinski, Director of Admissions, Grand Valley State University, 1 Campus Drive, Allendale, MI 49401. *Phone:* 616-331-2025. *Toll-free phone:* 800-748-0246. *Fax:* 616-331-2000. *E-mail:* go2gvsu@gvsu.edu.

Great Lakes Christian College

Lansing, Michigan

http://www.glcc.edu/

CONTACT
Marie Riggs, Administrative Secretary, Great Lakes Christian College, 6211 West Willow Highway, Lansing, MI 48917-1299. *Phone:* 517-321-0242. *Toll-free phone:* 800-YES-GLCC. *Fax:* 517-321-5902. *E-mail:* mriggs@glcc.edu.

COLLEGES AT-A-GLANCE

Hillsdale College
Hillsdale, Michigan
http://www.hillsdale.edu/

- **Independent** comprehensive, founded 1844
- **Small-town** 400-acre campus
- **Endowment** $710.3 million
- **Coed** 1,468 undergraduate students, 97% full-time, 48% women, 52% men
- **Most difficult** entrance level, 48% of applicants were admitted

UNDERGRAD STUDENTS
1,431 full-time, 37 part-time. Students come from 51 states and territories; 9 other countries; 69% are from out of state; 100% Race/ethnicity unknown; 2% transferred in; 74% live on campus.

Freshmen:
Admission: 1,593 applied, 769 admitted, 343 enrolled. ***Average high school GPA:*** 3.9. ***Test scores:*** SAT evidence-based reading and writing scores over 500: 100%; SAT math scores over 500: 100%; ACT scores over 18: 100%; SAT evidence-based reading and writing scores over 600: 91%; SAT math scores over 600: 93%; ACT scores over 24: 99%; SAT evidence-based reading and writing scores over 700: 53%; SAT math scores over 700: 43%; ACT scores over 30: 68%.

Retention: 96% of full-time freshmen returned.

FACULTY
Total: 211, 69% full-time, 75% with terminal degrees.

Student/faculty ratio: 9:1.

ACADEMICS
Calendar: semesters. *Degrees:* bachelor's, master's, and doctoral.

Special study options: advanced placement credit, double majors, honors programs, independent study, internships, off-campus study, part-time degree program, student-designed majors, study abroad, summer session for credit.

Unusual degree programs: 3-2 engineering.

Computers: 345 computers/terminals and 1 port are available on campus for general student use. Students can access the following: campus intranet, computer help desk, free student e-mail accounts, online (class) grades, online (class) registration, online (class) schedules. Campuswide network is available. 100% of college-owned or -operated housing units are wired for high-speed Internet access. Wireless service is available via entire campus.

Library: Michael Alex Mossey Library. *Books:* 227,424 (physical), 868,409 (digital/electronic); *Serial titles:* 172 (physical), 154,317 (digital/electronic); *Databases:* 122.

STUDENT LIFE
Housing options: on-campus residence required through sophomore year; men-only, women-only, cooperative. Campus housing is university owned. Freshman campus housing is guaranteed.

Activities and organizations: drama/theater group, student-run newspaper, radio station, choral group, InterVarsity, College Republicans, Hillsdale College for Life, Young Americans for Freedom, 1844 Society, national fraternities, national sororities.

Athletics Member NCAA. All Division II. ***Intercollegiate sports:*** archery M(c)/W(c), baseball M(s), basketball M(s)/W(s), cheerleading W(c), crew M(c)/W(c), cross-country running M(s)/W(s), equestrian sports M(c)/W(c), football M(s), golf M(s), riflery M(c)/W(c), rugby M(c), sailing M(c)/W(c), soccer M(c)/W(c), softball W(s), swimming and diving W(s), tennis M(s)/W(s), track and field M(s)/W(s), volleyball M(c)/W(s). ***Intramural sports:*** basketball M/W, football M/W, golf M/W, rock climbing M/W, soccer M/W, table tennis M/W, volleyball M/W, water polo M/W.

Campus security: 24-hour emergency response devices and patrols, student patrols, late-night transport/escort service, controlled dormitory access.

Student services: health clinic, personal/psychological counseling.

COSTS & FINANCIAL AID
Costs (2020–21) ***One-time required fee:*** $300. ***Comprehensive fee:*** $41,392 includes full-time tuition ($28,170), mandatory fees ($1312), and room and board ($11,910). Full-time tuition and fees vary according to degree level. Part-time tuition: $1120 per credit hour. Part-time tuition and fees vary according to degree level. ***Required fees:*** $85 per credit hour part-time, $1312 per year part-time. ***College room only:*** $5900. Room and

board charges vary according to board plan and housing facility. ***Payment plan:*** installment. ***Waivers:*** children of alumni and employees or children of employees.

Financial Aid Of all full-time matriculated undergraduates who enrolled in 2019, 748 applied for aid, 725 were judged to have need, 294 had their need fully met. In 2019, 623 non-need-based awards were made. ***Average percent of need met:*** 60. ***Average financial aid package:*** $20,665. ***Average need-based loan:*** $5778. ***Average need-based gift aid:*** $8184. ***Average non-need-based aid:*** $19,427. ***Average indebtedness upon graduation:*** $32,198.

APPLYING

Standardized Tests *Required:* SAT or ACT (for admission), CLT also accepted in place of SAT/ACT (for admission).

Options: electronic application, early admission, early decision.

Application fee: $35.

Required: essay or personal statement, high school transcript, 2 letters of recommendation. ***Recommended:*** minimum 3.5 GPA, interview, campus visit, college prep courses.

Application deadlines: 4/1 (freshmen), 4/1 (out-of-state freshmen), 4/1 (transfers).

Early decision deadline: 11/1.

Notification: continuous (freshmen), continuous (out-of-state freshmen), continuous (transfers), 12/1 (early decision).

CONTACT

Mr. Douglas Banbury, Vice President Admissions, Hillsdale College, 33 East College Street, Hillsdale, MI 49242-1298. *Phone:* 517-607-2327. *Fax:* 517-607-2223. *E-mail:* admissions@hillsdale.edu.

See below for display ad and page 1064 for the College Close-Up.

Hope College

Holland, Michigan

http://www.hope.edu/

- **Independent** 4-year, founded 1866, affiliated with Reformed Church in America
- **Suburban** 91-acre campus with easy access to Grand Rapids
- **Endowment** $208.0 million
- **Coed** 3,056 undergraduate students, 95% full-time, 62% women, 38% men
- **Moderately difficult** entrance level, 86% of applicants were admitted

UNDERGRAD STUDENTS

2,917 full-time, 139 part-time. Students come from 36 states and territories; 35 other countries; 29% are from out of state; 2% Black or African American, non-Hispanic/Latino; 8% Hispanic/Latino; 2% Asian, non-Hispanic/Latino; 3% Two or more races, non-Hispanic/Latino; 0.3% Race/ethnicity unknown; 2% international; 1% transferred in; 78% live on campus.

Freshmen:

Admission: 3,748 applied, 3,211 admitted, 686 enrolled. ***Average high school GPA:*** 3.9. ***Test scores:*** SAT evidence-based reading and writing scores over 500: 94%; SAT math scores over 500: 94%; ACT scores over 18: 100%; SAT evidence-based reading and writing scores over 600: 64%; SAT math scores over 600: 57%; ACT scores over 24: 75%; SAT evidence-based reading and writing scores over 700: 12%; SAT math scores over 700: 16%; ACT scores over 30: 24%.

Retention: 92% of full-time freshmen returned.

FACULTY

Total: 328, 70% full-time.

Student/faculty ratio: 11:1.

ACADEMICS

Calendar: semesters. *Degree:* bachelor's.

Special study options: advanced placement credit, double majors, English as a second language, independent study, internships, off-campus study, part-time degree program, services for LD students, student-designed majors, study abroad, summer session for credit. ***ROTC:*** Army (c).

Computers: 300 computers/terminals and 5,000 ports are available on campus for general student use. Students can access the following: campus intranet, computer help desk, free student e-mail accounts, online (class) grades, online (class) registration, online (class) schedules. Campuswide network is available. 100% of college-owned or -operated housing units are wired for high-speed Internet access. Wireless service is available via entire campus.

Library: Van Wylen Library plus 2 others. *Books:* 247,002 (physical), 242,414 (digital/electronic); *Serial titles:* 2,530 (physical), 41,509 (digital/electronic); *Databases:* 166. Weekly public service hours: 96.

STUDENT LIFE

Housing options: on-campus residence required through junior year; coed, men-only, women-only, special housing for students with disabilities. Campus housing is university owned. Freshman campus housing is guaranteed.

Activities and organizations: drama/theater group, student-run newspaper, radio station, choral group, Social Activities Committee, Greek Life, Dance Marathon, Hockey Club, Relay for Life, national fraternities, national sororities.

Athletics Member NCAA. All Division III. ***Intercollegiate sports:*** baseball M, basketball M/W, cheerleading M/W, cross-country running M/W, football M, golf M/W, ice hockey M(c), lacrosse M/W, sailing M(c)/W(c), soccer M/W, softball W, swimming and diving M/W, tennis M/W, track and field M/W, volleyball W. ***Intramural sports:*** badminton M/W, basketball M/W, football M/W, ice hockey M(c), rugby M(c), sailing M(c)/W(c), soccer M/W, softball M/W, tennis M/W, ultimate Frisbee M/W, volleyball M/W, water polo M/W.

Campus security: 24-hour emergency response devices and patrols, late-night transport/escort service, controlled dormitory access.

Student services: health clinic, personal/psychological counseling.

COSTS & FINANCIAL AID

Costs (2019–20) ***Comprehensive fee:*** $45,960 includes full-time tuition ($34,990), mandatory fees ($340), and room and board ($10,630). Part-time tuition and fees vary according to course load and program. ***College room only:*** $4880. Room and board charges vary according to board plan. ***Payment plan:*** installment. ***Waivers:*** employees or children of employees.

Financial Aid Of all full-time matriculated undergraduates who enrolled in 2019, 2,087 applied for aid, 1,657 were judged to have need, 458 had their need fully met. 148 Federal Work-Study jobs (averaging $2521). 486 state and other part-time jobs (averaging $1178). In 2019, 902 non-need-based awards were made. ***Average percent of need met:*** 80. ***Average financial aid package:*** $28,350. ***Average need-based loan:*** $4422. ***Average need-based gift aid:*** $22,335. ***Average non-need-based aid:*** $9993. ***Average indebtedness upon graduation:*** $33,856.

APPLYING

Standardized Tests *Required:* SAT or ACT (for admission).

Options: electronic application, early admission, early action, deferred entrance.

Application fee: $35.

Required: essay or personal statement, high school transcript. ***Required for some:*** 1 letter of recommendation. ***Recommended:*** interview.

Application deadlines: rolling (freshmen), rolling (transfers), 11/1 (early action).

Notification: continuous (freshmen), continuous (transfers), 11/24 (early action).

CONTACT

Admissions Office, Hope College, 69 East 10th Street, PO Box 9000, Holland, MI 49422-9000. *Phone:* 616-395-7850. *Toll-free phone:* 800-968-7850. *E-mail:* admissions@hope.edu.

Kalamazoo College

Kalamazoo, Michigan

http://www.kzoo.edu/

- **Independent** 4-year, founded 1833, affiliated with American Baptist Churches in the U.S.A.
- **Urban** 60-acre campus with easy access to Grand Rapids
- **Endowment** $227.0 million
- **Coed** 1,286 undergraduate students, 99% full-time, 56% women, 44% men
- **Very difficult** entrance level, 76% of applicants were admitted

UNDERGRAD STUDENTS
1,275 full-time, 11 part-time. 33% are from out of state; 7% Black or African American, non-Hispanic/Latino; 15% Hispanic/Latino; 7% Asian, non-Hispanic/Latino; 0.1% Native Hawaiian or other Pacific Islander, non-Hispanic/Latino; 0.2% American Indian or Alaska Native, non-Hispanic/Latino; 5% Two or more races, non-Hispanic/Latino; 2% Race/ethnicity unknown; 7% international; 0.7% transferred in; 53% live on campus.

Freshmen:
Admission: 3,576 applied, 2,716 admitted, 395 enrolled. ***Average high school GPA:*** 3.9. ***Test scores:*** SAT evidence-based reading and writing scores over 500: 96%; SAT math scores over 500: 97%; ACT scores over 18: 100%; SAT evidence-based reading and writing scores over 600: 72%; SAT math scores over 600: 67%; ACT scores over 24: 82%; SAT evidence-based reading and writing scores over 700: 25%; SAT math scores over 700: 16%; ACT scores over 30: 34%.

Retention: 88% of full-time freshmen returned.

FACULTY
Total: 141, 74% full-time, 86% with terminal degrees.

Student/faculty ratio: 11:1.

ACADEMICS
Calendar: quarters. *Degree:* bachelor's.

Special study options: accelerated degree program, advanced placement credit, double majors, English as a second language, independent study, internships, off-campus study, services for LD students, student-designed majors, study abroad. ***ROTC:*** Army (c).

Unusual degree programs: 3-2 engineering with University of Michigan, Washington University in St. Louis.

Computers: 250 computers/terminals are available on campus for general student use. Students can access the following: campus intranet, computer help desk, free student e-mail accounts, online (class) grades, online (class) registration, online (class) schedules, residential computer consultant. Campuswide network is available. 100% of college-owned or -operated housing units are wired for high-speed Internet access. Wireless service is available via entire campus.

Library: Upjohn Library Commons. *Books:* 272,425 (physical), 162,857 (digital/electronic); *Serial titles:* 2,660 (physical), 176,641 (digital/electronic); *Databases:* 517. Weekly public service hours: 114.

STUDENT LIFE
Housing options: on-campus residence required through junior year; coed. Campus housing is university owned. Freshman campus housing is guaranteed.

Activities and organizations: drama/theater group, student-run newspaper, radio and television station, choral group, Cirque du K, A cappella groups, Food Recovery Network, Women of Color, Swing Club.

Athletics Member NCAA. All Division III. ***Intercollegiate sports:*** baseball M, basketball M/W, cross-country running M/W, football M, golf M/W, lacrosse M/W, soccer M/W, softball W, swimming and diving M/W, tennis M/W, volleyball W. ***Intramural sports:*** badminton M/W, basketball M/W, cheerleading M(c)/W(c), lacrosse M(c)/W(c), racquetball M/W, soccer M/W, softball M/W, table tennis M/W, tennis M/W, ultimate Frisbee M(c)/W(c), volleyball M/W.

Campus security: 24-hour emergency response devices and patrols, late-night transport/escort service, controlled dormitory access.

Student services: health clinic, personal/psychological counseling.

COSTS & FINANCIAL AID
Costs (2020–21) ***Comprehensive fee:*** $63,060 includes full-time tuition ($51,999), mandatory fees ($531), and room and board ($10,530). ***College room only:*** $5121. ***Payment plan:*** installment.

Financial Aid Of all full-time matriculated undergraduates who enrolled in 2019, 1,198 applied for aid, 1,059 were judged to have need, 394 had their need fully met. In 2019, 373 non-need-based awards were made. ***Average percent of need met:*** 92. ***Average financial aid package:*** $44,311. ***Average need-based loan:*** $4373. ***Average need-based gift aid:*** $36,997. ***Average non-need-based aid:*** $27,315. ***Average indebtedness upon graduation:*** $34,179. ***Financial aid deadline:*** 3/1.

APPLYING
Options: electronic application, early decision, early action, deferred entrance.

Required: essay or personal statement, high school transcript, 2 letters of recommendation. ***Recommended:*** minimum 3.0 GPA, interview.

Application deadlines: 1/15 (freshmen), 5/1 (transfers), 11/1 (early action).

Early decision deadline: 11/1 (for plan 1), 2/1 (for plan 2).

Notification: 4/1 (freshmen), 5/15 (transfers), 12/1 (early decision plan 1), 2/15 (early decision plan 2), 12/20 (early action).

CONTACT
Gabriela Lovell, Records Assistant, Kalamazoo College, 1200 Academy Street, Kalamazoo, MI 49006. *Phone:* 269-337-5759. *Toll-free phone:* 800-253-3602. *Fax:* 269-552-5083. *E-mail:* gabriela.lovell@kzoo.edu.

Kettering University

Flint, Michigan

http://www.kettering.edu/

- **Independent** comprehensive, founded 1919
- **Urban** 90-acre campus with easy access to Detroit
- **Endowment** $90.4 million
- **Coed** 1,799 undergraduate students, 96% full-time, 21% women, 79% men
- **Very difficult** entrance level, 73% of applicants were admitted

UNDERGRAD STUDENTS
1,720 full-time, 79 part-time. Students come from 31 states and territories; 16 other countries; 13% are from out of state; 2% Black or African American, non-Hispanic/Latino; 5% Hispanic/Latino; 6% Asian, non-Hispanic/Latino; 0.2% American Indian or Alaska Native, non-Hispanic/Latino; 4% Two or more races, non-Hispanic/Latino; 4% Race/ethnicity unknown; 4% international; 2% transferred in.

Freshmen:
Admission: 2,262 applied, 1,651 admitted, 346 enrolled. ***Average high school GPA:*** 3.8. ***Test scores:*** SAT evidence-based reading and writing scores over 500: 97%; SAT math scores over 500: 100%; ACT scores over 18: 99%; SAT evidence-based reading and writing scores over 600: 70%; SAT math scores over 600: 83%; ACT scores over 24: 85%; SAT evidence-based reading and writing scores over 700: 10%; SAT math scores over 700: 26%; ACT scores over 30: 28%.

Retention: 90% of full-time freshmen returned.

FACULTY
Total: 152, 72% full-time, 64% with terminal degrees.

Student/faculty ratio: 14:1.

ACADEMICS
Calendar: semesters (11 weeks of full-time study plus 12 weeks of paid co-op experience per semester). *Degrees:* bachelor's and master's.

Special study options: advanced placement credit, cooperative education, English as a second language, honors programs, independent study, internships, services for LD students, study abroad, summer session for credit.

Computers: 100 computers/terminals are available on campus for general student use. Students can access the following: campus intranet, computer help desk, free student e-mail accounts, online (class) grades, online (class) registration, online (class) schedules. Campuswide network is available. 100% of college-owned or -operated housing units are wired for high-speed Internet access. Wireless service is available via entire campus.

Library: Kettering University Library. *Books:* 164,180 (physical), 33,150 (digital/electronic); *Serial titles:* 400 (physical); *Databases:* 104.

STUDENT LIFE
Housing options: on-campus residence required for freshman year; coed, men-only, women-only, special housing for students with disabilities. Campus housing is university owned. Freshman campus housing is guaranteed.

Activities and organizations: student-run newspaper, radio station, Asian American Association, International Club, Firebirds, Gamers Club, Physics Club, national fraternities, national sororities.

Athletics ***Intramural sports:*** badminton M/W, basketball M/W, golf M(c)/W(c), ice hockey M(c)/W(c), rock climbing M(c)/W(c), skiing (downhill) M(c)/W(c), soccer M(c)/W(c), softball M/W, swimming and diving M(c)/W(c), table tennis M/W, ultimate Frisbee M(c)/W(c), volleyball M/W, water polo M/W, weight lifting M/W.

Campus security: 24-hour emergency response devices and patrols, late-night transport/escort service, controlled dormitory access, security card access to all campus buildings 24/7 except the campus center main entrance which is secure 11pm-7am.

Student services: health clinic, personal/psychological counseling, women's center.

COSTS & FINANCIAL AID
Costs (2019–20) ***Comprehensive fee:*** $52,780 includes full-time tuition ($44,380) and room and board ($8400). No tuition increase for student's term of enrollment. ***College room only:*** $5100. ***Payment plan:*** installment. ***Waivers:*** employees or children of employees.

Financial Aid Of all full-time matriculated undergraduates who enrolled in 2018, 1,423 applied for aid, 1,297 were judged to have need, 138 had their need fully met. In 2018, 490 non-need-based awards were made. ***Average percent of need met:*** 63. ***Average financial aid package:*** $22,631. ***Average need-based loan:*** $4517. ***Average need-based gift aid:*** $18,588. ***Average non-need-based aid:*** $16,048.

APPLYING
Standardized Tests *Required:* SAT or ACT (for admission).

Options: electronic application, early action, deferred entrance.

Required: high school transcript. ***Required for some:*** essay or personal statement. ***Recommended:*** minimum 3.0 GPA, interview.

Application deadlines: rolling (freshmen), rolling (transfers), 11/15 (early action).

Notification: continuous (freshmen), continuous (transfers), 12/15 (early action).

CONTACT
Mr. Kip Darcy, Vice President of Enrollment Management and Marketing, Kettering University, 1700 University Avenue, Flint, MI 48504-6214. *Phone:* 810-762-9511. *Toll-free phone:* 800-955-4464 Ext. 7865 (in-state); 800-955-4464 (out-of-state). *Fax:* 810-762-9837. *E-mail:* kdarcy@kettering.edu.

Kuyper College

Grand Rapids, Michigan

http://www.kuyper.edu/

- **Independent Christian** 4-year, founded 1939
- **Suburban** 34-acre campus with easy access to Grand Rapids
- **Coed**
- **Moderately difficult** entrance level

FACULTY
Student/faculty ratio: 12:1.

ACADEMICS
Calendar: semesters. *Degrees:* certificates, associate, bachelor's, and master's.
Library: Zondervan Library plus 1 other. *Books:* 78,702 (physical), 14,199 (digital/electronic); *Databases:* 101. Weekly public service hours: 72; students can reserve study rooms.

STUDENT LIFE
Housing options: on-campus residence required through sophomore year; coed. Campus housing is university owned. Freshman campus housing is guaranteed.

Activities and organizations: drama/theater group, choral group, intramurals, Student Activities Club, Helping and Nurturing During Service, Yearbook, Roots.

Campus security: 24-hour emergency response devices, student patrols, late-night transport/escort service, controlled dormitory access.

Student services: health clinic, personal/psychological counseling.

FINANCIAL AID
Financial Aid Of all full-time matriculated undergraduates who enrolled in 2019, 97 applied for aid, 91 were judged to have need, 10 had their need fully met. 16 Federal Work-Study jobs (averaging $2498). In 2019, 6 non-need-based awards were made. ***Average percent of need met:*** 67. ***Average financial aid package:*** $17,289. ***Average need-based loan:*** $3940. ***Average need-based gift aid:*** $14,597. ***Average non-need-based aid:*** $2000. ***Average indebtedness upon graduation:*** $22,674.

APPLYING
Standardized Tests *Required:* SAT or ACT (for admission).

Options: electronic application, deferred entrance.

Required: essay or personal statement, high school transcript, minimum 2.3 GPA. ***Recommended:*** interview.

CONTACT
Ken Capisciolto, Vice President of Development, Kuyper College, 3333 East Beltline, NE, Grand Rapids, MI 49525-9749. *Phone:* 616-988-3676. *Fax:* 616-222-3045. *E-mail:* admissions@kuyper.edu.

Lake Superior State University

Sault Sainte Marie, Michigan

http://www.lssu.edu/

- **State-supported** comprehensive, founded 1946
- **Small-town** 115-acre campus
- **Endowment** $9.0 million
- **Coed**
- **Moderately difficult** entrance level

FACULTY
Student/faculty ratio: 16:1.

ACADEMICS
Calendar: semesters. *Degrees:* certificates, associate, bachelor's, master's, and postbachelor's certificates.
Library: Kenneth Shouldice Library.

STUDENT LIFE
Housing options: on-campus residence required through sophomore year; coed, men-only, women-only. Campus housing is university owned. Freshman campus housing is guaranteed.

Activities and organizations: drama/theater group, student-run newspaper, radio station, choral group, Activities Board, SAILS - Student Alumni Involved in Lake State, Fisheries and Wildlife, Enactus (Formally known as SIFE), Chemistry and Environmental Science Club, national fraternities, national sororities.

Athletics Member NCAA. All Division II except ice hockey (Division I).

Campus security: 24-hour emergency response devices and patrols, student patrols, late-night transport/escort service.

Student services: health clinic, personal/psychological counseling.

COSTS & FINANCIAL AID
Costs (2019–20) ***Tuition:*** state resident $12,000 full-time, $500 per credit hour part-time; nonresident $12,000 full-time. ***Required fees:*** $190 full-time. ***Room and board:*** $10,230.

Financial Aid Of all full-time matriculated undergraduates who enrolled in 2017, 1,400 applied for aid, 1,167 were judged to have need, 337 had their need fully met. In 2017, 209 non-need-based awards were made. ***Average percent of need met:*** 47. ***Average financial aid package:*** $11,745. ***Average need-based loan:*** $4566. ***Average need-based gift aid:*** $8802. ***Average non-need-based aid:*** $4634. ***Average indebtedness upon graduation:*** $28,075.

APPLYING
Standardized Tests *Required:* SAT or ACT (for admission).

Options: electronic application, deferred entrance.

Application fee: $25.

Required: high school transcript.

CONTACT
Lake Superior State University, 650 West Easterday Avenue, Sault Sainte Marie, MI 49783. *Phone:* 906-635-2231. *Toll-free phone:* 888-800-LSSU Ext. 2231.

Lawrence Technological University

Southfield, Michigan

http://www.ltu.edu/

- **Independent** university, founded 1932
- **Suburban** 107-acre campus with easy access to Detroit
- **Endowment** $50.2 million
- **Coed** 2,136 undergraduate students, 79% full-time, 29% women, 71% men
- **Moderately difficult** entrance level, 79% of applicants were admitted

UNDERGRAD STUDENTS

1,677 full-time, 459 part-time. Students come from 33 states and territories; 38 other countries; 9% are from out of state; 8% Black or African American, non-Hispanic/Latino; 3% Hispanic/Latino; 3% Asian, non-Hispanic/Latino; 0.1% American Indian or Alaska Native, non-Hispanic/Latino; 2% Two or more races, non-Hispanic/Latino; 11% Race/ethnicity unknown; 10% international; 7% transferred in; 41% live on campus.

Freshmen:

Admission: 2,390 applied, 1,901 admitted, 361 enrolled. ***Average high school GPA:*** 3.5. ***Test scores:*** SAT evidence-based reading and writing scores over 500: 79%; SAT math scores over 500: 81%; ACT scores over 18: 92%; SAT evidence-based reading and writing scores over 600: 34%; SAT math scores over 600: 43%; ACT scores over 24: 56%; SAT evidence-based reading and writing scores over 700: 4%; SAT math scores over 700: 9%; ACT scores over 30: 11%.

Retention: 74% of full-time freshmen returned.

FACULTY

Total: 337, 35% full-time, 48% with terminal degrees.

Student/faculty ratio: 11:1.

ACADEMICS

Calendar: semesters. *Degrees:* certificates, associate, bachelor's, master's, doctoral, and postbachelor's certificates.

Special study options: academic remediation for entering students, accelerated degree program, adult/continuing education programs, advanced placement credit, cooperative education, distance learning, double majors, English as a second language, honors programs, independent study, internships, off-campus study, part-time degree program, services for LD students, study abroad, summer session for credit. ***ROTC:*** Army (c), Air Force (c).

Computers: 52 computers/terminals and 3,993 ports are available on campus for general student use. Students can access the following: campus intranet, computer help desk, free student e-mail accounts, online (class) grades, online (class) registration, online (class) schedules, degree audit, Canvas/Blackboard, Banner (student information), personal websites, document collection, Handshake, Placement, Mapworks advising. Campuswide network is available. 100% of college-owned or -operated housing units are wired for high-speed Internet access. Wireless service is available via entire campus.

Library: Lawrence Technological University Library plus 1 other. *Books:* 119,278 (physical), 597,667 (digital/electronic); *Serial titles:* 85,850 (digital/electronic); *Databases:* 171. Weekly public service hours: 73; students can reserve study rooms.

STUDENT LIFE

Housing options: coed, special housing for students with disabilities. Campus housing is university owned. Freshman applicants given priority for college housing.

Activities and organizations: drama/theater group, marching band, American Institute of Architecture Students, American Society of Mechanical Engineers, Sigma Phi Epsilon, American Society of Civil Engineers, Student Government, national fraternities, national sororities.

Athletics Member NAIA. ***Intercollegiate sports:*** baseball M(s), basketball M(s)/W(s), bowling M(s)/W(s), cross-country running M(s)/W(s), football M(s), golf M(s), ice hockey M, lacrosse M(s)/W(s), soccer M(s)/W(s), softball W(s), tennis M(s)/W(s), track and field M(s)/W(s), volleyball M(s)/W(s). ***Intramural sports:*** badminton M/W, basketball M/W, ice hockey M(c), racquetball M/W, soccer M/W, softball M/W, table tennis M/W, tennis M/W, track and field M(c)/W(c), ultimate Frisbee M(c)/W(c), volleyball M/W.

Campus security: 24-hour emergency response devices and patrols, late-night transport/escort service, controlled dormitory access.

Student services: personal/psychological counseling, veterans affairs office.

COSTS & FINANCIAL AID

Costs (2020–21) ***Comprehensive fee:*** $47,530 includes full-time tuition ($35,430), mandatory fees ($1200), and room and board ($10,900). Full-time tuition and fees vary according to course level, degree level, location, program, and student level. Part-time tuition: $1181 per credit hour. Part-time tuition and fees vary according to course level, degree level, location, program, and student level. ***College room only:*** $7300. Room and board charges vary according to board plan and housing facility. ***Payment plan:*** installment. ***Waivers:*** employees or children of employees.

Financial Aid Of all full-time matriculated undergraduates who enrolled in 2018, 1,418 applied for aid, 1,056 were judged to have need, 164 had their need fully met. In 2018, 318 non-need-based awards were made. ***Average percent of need met:*** 70. ***Average financial aid package:*** $25,476. ***Average need-based loan:*** $6940. ***Average need-based gift aid:*** $15,285. ***Average non-need-based aid:*** $15,496. ***Average indebtedness upon graduation:*** $32,735.

APPLYING

Standardized Tests *Required:* SAT or ACT (for admission).

Options: electronic application.

Application fee: $30.

Required: essay or personal statement, high school transcript, minimum 2.5 GPA. ***Required for some:*** minimum 2.8 GPA, interview.

Application deadlines: rolling (freshmen), rolling (transfers).

Notification: continuous (freshmen), continuous (transfers).

CONTACT

Jane Rohrback, Director of Admissions, Lawrence Technological University, 21000 West Ten Mile Road, Southfield, MI 48075. *Phone:* 248-204-3160. *Toll-free phone:* 800-225-5588. *Fax:* 248-204-2228. *E-mail:* admissions@ltu.edu.

Madonna University

Livonia, Michigan

http://www.madonna.edu/

- **Independent Roman Catholic** comprehensive, founded 1947
- **Suburban** 85-acre campus with easy access to Detroit
- **Endowment** $41.1 million
- **Coed** 2,440 undergraduate students, 59% full-time, 65% women, 35% men
- **Moderately difficult** entrance level, 78% of applicants were admitted

UNDERGRAD STUDENTS

1,431 full-time, 1,009 part-time. Students come from 20 states and territories; 5 other countries; 2% are from out of state; 20% transferred in; 12% live on campus.

Freshmen:

Admission: 985 applied, 771 admitted, 220 enrolled. ***Average high school GPA:*** 3.3.

Retention: 76% of full-time freshmen returned.

ACADEMICS

Calendar: semesters. *Degrees:* certificates, associate, bachelor's, master's, doctoral, post-master's, and postbachelor's certificates.

Special study options: accelerated degree program, adult/continuing education programs, advanced placement credit, cooperative education, distance learning, double majors, English as a second language, independent study, internships, off-campus study, part-time degree program, services for LD students, student-designed majors, study abroad, summer session for credit. ***ROTC:*** Army (c).

Computers: 205 computers/terminals and 205 ports are available on campus for general student use. Students can access the following: campus intranet, computer help desk, free student e-mail accounts, online (class) grades, online (class) registration, online (class) schedules, online payments, online statements, online unofficial transcripts. Campuswide network is available. 100% of college-owned or -operated housing units are wired for high-speed Internet access. Wireless service is available via classrooms, computer labs, dorm rooms, learning centers, libraries, student centers.

Library: Madonna University Library. *Books:* 71,562 (physical), 181,927 (digital/electronic); *Serial titles:* 190 (physical), 70,781 (digital/electronic); *Databases:* 130. Weekly public service hours: 100; students can reserve study rooms.

STUDENT LIFE

Housing options: men-only, women-only. Campus housing is university owned. Freshman campus housing is guaranteed.

Activities and organizations: drama/theater group, student-run newspaper, radio and television station, choral group, Campus Ministry, Madonna University Nursing Student Association, Broadcast and Film Club, Society of Future Teachers, Michigan Blood Club.

Athletics ***Intercollegiate sports:*** baseball M(s), basketball M(s)/W(s), bowling M(s)/W(s), cross-country running M(s)/W(s), football M(s), golf M(s)/W(s), lacrosse M(s)/W(s), soccer M(s)/W(s), softball W(s), track and field M(s)/W(s), volleyball W(s). ***Intramural sports:*** basketball M/W.

Campus security: 24-hour emergency response devices and patrols, late-night transport/escort service, controlled dormitory access.

Student services: personal/psychological counseling.

COSTS & FINANCIAL AID

Costs (2019–20) ***Comprehensive fee:*** $34,550 includes full-time tuition ($23,100) and room and board ($11,450). Full-time tuition and fees vary according to course load, location, and program. Part-time tuition: $770 per credit hour. Part-time tuition and fees vary according to location and program. ***College room only:*** $5500. Room and board charges vary according to board plan and housing facility. ***Payment plan:*** deferred payment. ***Waivers:*** senior citizens and employees or children of employees.

Financial Aid Of all full-time matriculated undergraduates who enrolled in 2007, 862 applied for aid, 698 were judged to have need, 122 had their need fully met. In 2007, 172 non-need-based awards were made. ***Average percent of need met:*** 56. ***Average financial aid package:*** $7396. ***Average need-based loan:*** $3862. ***Average need-based gift aid:*** $4508. ***Average non-need-based aid:*** $2427.

APPLYING

Standardized Tests *Required:* SAT or ACT (for admission).

Options: electronic application, early decision, deferred entrance.

Required for some: essay or personal statement, high school transcript, 2 letters of recommendation, music performance and dance majors require auditions before selection to the program. ***Recommended:*** minimum 2.8 GPA.

Application deadlines: rolling (freshmen), rolling (out-of-state freshmen), rolling (transfers).

Early decision deadline: 12/1.

Notification: continuous (freshmen), continuous (out-of-state freshmen), continuous (transfers), 1/15 (early decision).

CONTACT

Mr. Mark A. Schroeder, Director of Undergraduate Admissions, Madonna University, 36600 Schoolcraft Road, Livonia, MI 48150-1173. *Phone:* 734-432-5339. *Toll-free phone:* 800-852-4951. *Fax:* 734-432-5424. *E-mail:* mschroeder@madonna.edu.

Michigan State University

East Lansing, Michigan

http://www.msu.edu/

- **State-supported** university, founded 1855
- **Suburban** 5192-acre campus with easy access to Detroit
- **Endowment** $3.3 billion
- **Coed** 39,176 undergraduate students, 91% full-time, 51% women, 49% men
- **Moderately difficult** entrance level, 71% of applicants were admitted

UNDERGRAD STUDENTS

35,722 full-time, 3,454 part-time. 14% are from out of state; 7% Black or African American, non-Hispanic/Latino; 5% Hispanic/Latino; 6% Asian, non-Hispanic/Latino; 0.1% Native Hawaiian or other Pacific Islander, non-Hispanic/Latino; 0.2% American Indian or Alaska Native, non-Hispanic/Latino; 3% Two or more races, non-Hispanic/Latino; 0.9% Race/ethnicity unknown; 9% international; 3% transferred in; 39% live on campus.

Freshmen:

Admission: 44,322 applied, 31,522 admitted, 8,801 enrolled. ***Average high school GPA:*** 3.8. ***Test scores:*** SAT evidence-based reading and writing scores over 500: 94%; SAT math scores over 500: 94%; ACT scores over 18: 98%; SAT evidence-based reading and writing scores over 600: 54%; SAT math scores over 600: 56%; ACT scores over 24: 72%; SAT evidence-based reading and writing scores over 700: 10%; SAT math scores over 700: 18%; ACT scores over 30: 24%.

Retention: 92% of full-time freshmen returned.

FACULTY

Total: 2,900, 88% full-time, 86% with terminal degrees.

Student/faculty ratio: 16:1.

ACADEMICS

Calendar: semesters. *Degrees:* certificates, bachelor's, master's, doctoral, post-master's, and postbachelor's certificates.

Special study options: academic remediation for entering students, accelerated degree program, adult/continuing education programs, advanced placement credit, cooperative education, distance learning, double majors, English as a second language, freshman honors college, honors programs, independent study, internships, off-campus study, part-time degree program, services for LD students, student-designed majors, study abroad, summer session for credit. ***ROTC:*** Army (b), Air Force (b).

Unusual degree programs: 3-2 engineering.

Computers: Students can access the following: campus intranet, computer help desk, free student e-mail accounts, online (class) grades, online (class) registration, online (class) schedules. Campuswide network is available. 100% of college-owned or -operated housing units are wired for high-speed Internet access. Wireless service is available via classrooms, computer centers, computer labs, dorm rooms, learning centers, libraries, student centers.

Library: Main Library plus 2 others. *Books:* 3.6 million (physical), 3.0 million (digital/electronic); *Serial titles:* 136,425 (physical), 194,857 (digital/electronic). Weekly public service hours: 142.

STUDENT LIFE

Housing options: on-campus residence required for freshman year; coed, women-only, cooperative, special housing for students with disabilities. Campus housing is university owned. Freshman campus housing is guaranteed.

Activities and organizations: drama/theater group, student-run newspaper, radio and television station, choral group, marching band, national fraternities, national sororities.

Athletics Member NCAA. All Division I except football (Division I-A). ***Intercollegiate sports:*** baseball M(s), basketball M(s)/W(s), cheerleading M/W, crew M(c)/W(s), cross-country running M(s)/W(s), equestrian sports M(c)/W(c), fencing M(c)/W(c), field hockey W(s), golf M(s)/W(s)(c), gymnastics W(s), ice hockey M(s)/W(c), lacrosse M(c)/W(c), rowing M(c)/W(s), rugby M(c)/W(c), sailing M(c)/W(c), soccer M(s)/W(s), softball W(s), swimming and diving M(s)/W(s), table tennis M(c)/W(c), tennis M(s)/W(s), track and field M(s)/W(s), volleyball M(c)/W(s), water polo M(c)/W(c), wrestling M(s). ***Intramural sports:*** baseball M(c), basketball M/W, cheerleading W(c), crew M(c)/W(c), football M/W, ice hockey M/W, racquetball M/W, riflery M/W, rowing M(c)/W(c), rugby M(c)/W(c), sand volleyball M/W, soccer M(c)/W(c), softball M/W, squash M/W, table tennis M/W, tennis M/W, ultimate Frisbee M(c)/W(c), volleyball M/W, water polo M/W.

Campus security: 24-hour emergency response devices and patrols, late-night transport/escort service, controlled dormitory access.

Student services: health clinic, personal/psychological counseling, women's center, legal services, veterans affairs office.

COSTS & FINANCIAL AID

Costs (2019–20) ***Tuition:*** state resident $14,460 full-time, $482 per credit part-time; nonresident $39,766 full-time, $1326 per credit part-time. Full-time tuition and fees vary according to course load, program, and student level. Part-time tuition and fees vary according to course load, program, and student level. ***Room and board:*** $10,522; room only: $4374. Room and board charges vary according to board plan and housing facility. ***Payment plan:*** deferred payment. ***Waivers:*** employees or children of employees.

Financial Aid Of all full-time matriculated undergraduates who enrolled in 2019, 22,597 applied for aid, 16,637 were judged to have need, 1,751 had their need fully met. 1,653 Federal Work-Study jobs (averaging $2166). In 2019, 3903 non-need-based awards were made. ***Average percent of need met:*** 53. ***Average financial aid package:*** $16,389. ***Average need-based loan:*** $4077. ***Average need-based gift aid:*** $11,628. ***Average non-need-based aid:*** $8977. ***Average indebtedness upon graduation:*** $31,393.

APPLYING

Standardized Tests *Required:* SAT or ACT (for admission). *Recommended:* SAT (for admission), ACT (for admission).

Options: electronic application, early action, deferred entrance.

Application fee: $65.

Notification: continuous (freshmen), continuous (out-of-state freshmen), continuous (transfers), 1/15 (early action).

CONTACT

John M Ambrose, Senior Associate Director of Admissions, Michigan State University, 250 Administration Building, East Lansing, MI 48824. *Phone:* 517-355-8332. *Fax:* 517-353-1647. *E-mail:* admis@msu.edu.

Michigan Technological University

Houghton, Michigan

http://www.mtu.edu/

- **State-supported** university, founded 1885
- **Small-town** 925-acre campus
- **Endowment** $113.6 million
- **Coed** 5,764 undergraduate students, 94% full-time, 29% women, 71% men
- **Moderately difficult** entrance level, 74% of applicants were admitted

UNDERGRAD STUDENTS

5,393 full-time, 371 part-time. Students come from 41 states and territories; 30 other countries; 22% are from out of state; 1% Black or African American, non-Hispanic/Latino; 2% Hispanic/Latino; 2% Asian, non-Hispanic/Latino; 0.3% American Indian or Alaska Native, non-Hispanic/Latino; 4% Two or more races, non-Hispanic/Latino; 1% Race/ethnicity unknown; 2% international; 3% transferred in; 46% live on campus.

Freshmen:

Admission: 5,978 applied, 4,442 admitted, 1,301 enrolled. ***Average high school GPA:*** 3.8. ***Test scores:*** SAT evidence-based reading and writing scores over 500: 96%; SAT math scores over 500: 99%; ACT scores over 18: 101%; SAT evidence-based reading and writing scores over 600: 68%; SAT math scores over 600: 71%; ACT scores over 24: 88%; SAT evidence-based reading and writing scores over 700: 17%; SAT math scores over 700: 23%; ACT scores over 30: 31%.

Retention: 84% of full-time freshmen returned.

FACULTY

Total: 438, 93% full-time, 85% with terminal degrees.

Student/faculty ratio: 12:1.

ACADEMICS

Calendar: semesters. *Degrees:* certificates, associate, bachelor's, master's, doctoral, and postbachelor's certificates.

Special study options: accelerated degree program, advanced placement credit, cooperative education, distance learning, double majors, English as a second language, honors programs, independent study, internships, off-campus study, part-time degree program, services for LD students, study abroad, summer session for credit. ***ROTC:*** Army (b), Air Force (b).

Computers: 1,079 computers/terminals and 6,082 ports are available on campus for general student use. Students can access the following: campus intranet, computer help desk, free student e-mail accounts, online (class) grades, online (class) registration, online (class) schedules. Campuswide network is available. 100% of college-owned or -operated housing units are wired for high-speed Internet access. Wireless service is available via entire campus.

Library: J. R. Van Pelt and John and Ruanne Opie Library. *Books:* 372,479 (physical), 295,187 (digital/electronic); *Serial titles:* 14,193 (physical), 74,714 (digital/electronic); *Databases:* 183. Weekly public service hours: 105; study areas open 24 hours, 5–7 days a week; students can reserve study rooms.

STUDENT LIFE

Housing options: on-campus residence required for freshman year; coed, special housing for students with disabilities. Campus housing is university owned. Freshman campus housing is guaranteed.

Activities and organizations: drama/theater group, student-run newspaper, radio station, choral group, Indian Students Associate, Ski and Snowboard Club of Michigan Tech, Mitch's Misfits, Fishing Club, Huskies Pep Band, national fraternities, national sororities.

Athletics Member NCAA. All Division II except ice hockey (Division I). ***Intercollegiate sports:*** archery M(c)/W(c), badminton M(c)/W(c), baseball M(c), basketball M(s)/W(s), cheerleading M(c)/W(c), crew M(c)/W(c), cross-country running M(s)/W(s), fencing M(c)/W(c), football M(s), golf M(c)/W(c), gymnastics M(c)/W(c), ice hockey M(s)/W(c), lacrosse M(c)/W(c), racquetball M(c)/W(c), riflery M(c)/W(c), rugby M(c)/W(c), sailing M(c)/W(c), skiing (cross-country) M(s)/W(s), skiing (downhill) M(c)/W(c), soccer M(c)/W(s), softball W(c), tennis M(s)/W(s), track and field M(s)/W(s), ultimate Frisbee M(c)/W(c), volleyball M(c)/W(s), water polo M(c)/W(c). ***Intramural sports:*** badminton M/W, basketball M/W, bowling M/W, golf M/W, ice hockey M/W, racquetball M/W, riflery M/W, sand volleyball M/W, soccer M/W, softball M/W, swimming and diving M/W, table tennis M/W, tennis M/W, ultimate Frisbee M/W, volleyball M/W, water polo M/W, weight lifting M(c)/W(c).

Campus security: 24-hour emergency response devices and patrols, late-night transport/escort service, controlled dormitory access.

Student services: health clinic, personal/psychological counseling, women's center, veterans affairs office.

COSTS & FINANCIAL AID

Costs (2019–20) ***Tuition:*** state resident $15,660 full-time, $591 per credit hour part-time; nonresident $34,896 full-time, $1292 per credit hour part-time. Full-time tuition and fees vary according to program and student level. Part-time tuition and fees vary according to course load, program, and student level. ***Required fees:*** $300 full-time, $150 per term part-time. ***Room and board:*** $11,004; room only: $6137. Room and board charges vary according to board plan and housing facility. ***Payment plans:*** installment, deferred payment. ***Waivers:*** children of alumni, senior citizens, and employees or children of employees.

Financial Aid Of all full-time matriculated undergraduates who enrolled in 2019, 4,331 applied for aid, 3,395 were judged to have need, 665 had their need fully met. 136 Federal Work-Study jobs (averaging $1544). In 2019, 1438 non-need-based awards were made. ***Average percent of need met:*** 72. ***Average financial aid package:*** $16,038. ***Average need-based loan:*** $4159. ***Average need-based gift aid:*** $8088. ***Average non-need-based aid:*** $6086. ***Average indebtedness upon graduation:*** $37,903.

APPLYING

Standardized Tests *Required:* SAT or ACT (for admission).

Options: electronic application.

Required: high school transcript. ***Required for some:*** essay or personal statement, examples of creative work for some majors in Visual and Performing Arts Department. ***Recommended:*** minimum 2.8 GPA.

Application deadlines: rolling (freshmen), rolling (transfers).

Notification: continuous (freshmen), continuous (transfers).

CONTACT

Ms. Allison Carter, Director of Admissions, Michigan Technological University, 1400 Townsend Drive, Houghton, MI 49931-1295. *Phone:* 888-688-1885. *Toll-free phone:* 888-MTU-1885. *Fax:* 906-487-2125. *E-mail:* mtu4u@mtu.edu.

Northern Michigan University

Marquette, Michigan

http://www.nmu.edu/

- **State-supported** comprehensive, founded 1899
- **Small-town** 360-acre campus
- **Coed**
- 66% of applicants were admitted

FACULTY
Student/faculty ratio: 20:1.

ACADEMICS
Calendar: semesters. *Degrees:* certificates, associate, bachelor's, master's, doctoral, post-master's, and postbachelor's certificates.
Library: Lydia M. Olson Library.

STUDENT LIFE
Housing options: on-campus residence required through sophomore year; coed, men-only, women-only, special housing for students with disabilities. Campus housing is university owned. Freshman campus housing is guaranteed.

Activities and organizations: drama/theater group, student-run newspaper, radio and television station, choral group, marching band, national fraternities, national sororities.

Athletics Member NCAA. All Division II.

Campus security: 24-hour emergency response devices and patrols, student patrols, late-night transport/escort service, controlled dormitory access.

Student services: health clinic, personal/psychological counseling, veterans affairs office.

COSTS & FINANCIAL AID
Costs (2019–20) ***One-time required fee:*** $265. ***Tuition:*** state resident $10,758 full-time, $448 per credit hour part-time; nonresident $16,380 full-time, $683 per credit hour part-time. Full-time tuition and fees vary according to student level. Part-time tuition and fees vary according to student level. ***Required fees:*** $767 full-time, $121 per term part-time. ***Room and board:*** $10,774; room only: $5874. Room and board charges vary according to board plan, housing facility, and student level. ***Payment plans:*** installment, deferred payment.

Financial Aid Of all full-time matriculated undergraduates who enrolled in 2017, 5,028 applied for aid, 4,249 were judged to have need, 531 had their need fully met. 589 Federal Work-Study jobs (averaging $1799). In 2017, 474 non-need-based awards were made. ***Average percent of need met:*** 61. ***Average financial aid package:*** $11,189. ***Average need-based loan:*** $4288. ***Average need-based gift aid:*** $4786. ***Average non-need-based aid:*** $3097. ***Average indebtedness upon graduation:*** $30,459.

APPLYING
Standardized Tests *Required:* SAT or ACT (for admission).

Options: electronic application, deferred entrance.

Application fee: $35.

Required: high school transcript.

CONTACT
Ms. Gerri Daniels, Director of Admissions, Northern Michigan University, 1401 Presque Isle Avenue, Marquette, MI 49855. *Phone:* 906-227-2650. *Toll-free phone:* 800-682-9797. *Fax:* 906-227-1747. *E-mail:* admissions@nmu.edu.

Northwestern Michigan College

Traverse City, Michigan

http://www.nmc.edu/

CONTACT
Catheryn Claerhout, Director of Admissions, Northwestern Michigan College, 1701 E. Front Street, Traverse City, MI 49686. *Phone:* 231-995-1034. *Toll-free phone:* 800-748-0566. *E-mail:* c.claerhout@nmc.edu.

Northwood University, Michigan Campus

Midland, Michigan

http://www.northwood.edu/

- **Independent** comprehensive, founded 1959
- **Small-town** 468-acre campus
- **Endowment** $99.5 million
- **Coed**
- **Moderately difficult** entrance level

FACULTY
Student/faculty ratio: 20:1.

ACADEMICS
Calendar: semesters. *Degrees:* associate, bachelor's, and master's.
Library: Strosacker Library. *Books:* 30,504 (physical); *Databases:* 26. Weekly public service hours: 89; students can reserve study rooms.

STUDENT LIFE
Housing options: on-campus residence required for freshman year; coed, men-only, women-only, special housing for students with disabilities. Campus housing is university owned. Freshman campus housing is guaranteed.

Activities and organizations: drama/theater group, student-run newspaper, Student Government Association, intramural sports/club sports, United Way, Northwood University International Auto Show (NUTAS), Student Alumni Network, national fraternities, national sororities.

Athletics Member NCAA. All Division II.

Campus security: 24-hour emergency response devices and patrols, late-night transport/escort service, controlled dormitory access.

Student services: health clinic, personal/psychological counseling.

COSTS & FINANCIAL AID
Costs (2019–20) ***Comprehensive fee:*** $38,870 includes full-time tuition ($26,690), mandatory fees ($1390), and room and board ($10,790). Full-time tuition and fees vary according to course load and location. Part-time tuition: $1027 per credit hour. Part-time tuition and fees vary according to course load and location. ***College room only:*** $5620. Room and board charges vary according to board plan.

Financial Aid Of all full-time matriculated undergraduates who enrolled in 2017, 950 applied for aid, 831 were judged to have need, 178 had their need fully met. 136 Federal Work-Study jobs (averaging $1531). In 2017, 241 non-need-based awards were made. ***Average percent of need met:*** 63. ***Average financial aid package:*** $18,932. ***Average need-based loan:*** $4422. ***Average need-based gift aid:*** $6001. ***Average non-need-based aid:*** $7541. ***Average indebtedness upon graduation:*** $31,992.

APPLYING
Standardized Tests *Required:* SAT or ACT (for admission).

Options: electronic application, early admission, deferred entrance.

Application fee: $30.

Required: essay or personal statement, high school transcript, minimum 2.0 GPA. ***Recommended:*** 1 letter of recommendation, interview.

CONTACT
Miss Heidi Schall, Director of Admissions, Northwood University, Michigan Campus, 4000 Whiting Drive, Midland, MI 48640. *Phone:* 989-837-4342. *Toll-free phone:* 800-457-7878. *Fax:* 989-837-4490. *E-mail:* miadmit@northwood.edu.

Oakland University

Rochester, Michigan

http://www.oakland.edu/

- **State-supported** university, founded 1957
- **Suburban** 1444-acre campus with easy access to Detroit
- **Endowment** $99.1 million
- **Coed** 15,543 undergraduate students, 80% full-time, 57% women, 43% men
- **Moderately difficult** entrance level, 83% of applicants were admitted

UNDERGRAD STUDENTS
12,454 full-time, 3,089 part-time. Students come from 38 states and territories; 48 other countries; 2% are from out of state; 8% Black or African American, non-Hispanic/Latino; 4% Hispanic/Latino; 5% Asian, non-Hispanic/Latino; 0.1% Native Hawaiian or other Pacific Islander, non-Hispanic/Latino; 0.3% American Indian or Alaska Native, non-Hispanic/Latino; 3% Two or more races, non-Hispanic/Latino; 4% Race/ethnicity unknown; 2% international; 9% transferred in; 19% live on campus.

Freshmen:
Admission: 12,443 applied, 10,334 admitted, 2,667 enrolled. ***Average high school GPA:*** 3.6. ***Test scores:*** SAT evidence-based reading and writing scores over 500: 81%; SAT math scores over 500: 80%; ACT scores over 18: 91%; SAT evidence-based reading and writing scores over 600: 35%; SAT math scores over 600: 32%; ACT scores over 24: 48%;

SAT evidence-based reading and writing scores over 700: 6%; SAT math scores over 700: 8%; ACT scores over 30: 14%.

Retention: 76% of full-time freshmen returned.

FACULTY

Total: 1,236, 49% full-time, 62% with terminal degrees.

Student/faculty ratio: 19:1.

ACADEMICS

Calendar: semesters. *Degrees:* bachelor's, master's, doctoral, post-master's, and postbachelor's certificates.

Special study options: academic remediation for entering students, accelerated degree program, adult/continuing education programs, advanced placement credit, cooperative education, distance learning, double majors, English as a second language, freshman honors college, honors programs, independent study, internships, off-campus study, part-time degree program, services for LD students, student-designed majors, study abroad, summer session for credit. ***ROTC:*** Air Force (c).

Computers: Students can access the following: computer help desk, free student e-mail accounts, online (class) grades, online (class) registration, online (class) schedules. Campuswide network is available. 100% of college-owned or -operated housing units are wired for high speed Internet access. Wireless service is available via entire campus.

Library: Kresge Library plus 1 other. *Books:* 512,415 (physical), 682,722 (digital/electronic); *Serial titles:* 3,568 (physical), 71,808 (digital/electronic); *Databases:* 240. Weekly public service hours: 168; study areas open 24 hours, 5–7 days a week; students can reserve study rooms.

STUDENT LIFE

Housing options: coed, cooperative, special housing for students with disabilities. Campus housing is university owned. Freshman applicants given priority for college housing.

Activities and organizations: drama/theater group, student-run newspaper, radio and television station, choral group, Grizz Gang, Student program Board, Collegiate DECA, Alternative Spring Break, Beta Alpha Psi, national fraternities, national sororities.

Athletics Member NCAA. All Division I. ***Intercollegiate sports:*** baseball M(s), basketball M(s)/W(s), cheerleading M(c)/W(c), cross-country running M(s)/W(s), football M(c), golf M(s)/W(s), ice hockey M(c), soccer M(s)/W(s), softball W(s), swimming and diving M(s)/W(s), tennis W(s), track and field M(s)/W(s), volleyball W(s). ***Intramural sports:*** badminton M(c)/W(c), baseball M(c), basketball M/W, cross-country running M(c)/W(c), equestrian sports M(c)/W(c), fencing M(c)/W(c), football M(c), golf M(c)/W(c), ice hockey M(c), lacrosse M(c)/W(c), rugby M(c)/W(c), sand volleyball M/W, soccer M(c)/W(c), softball M(c)/W(c), swimming and diving M(c)/W(c), table tennis M/W, tennis M(c)/W(c), ultimate Frisbee M(c)/W(c), volleyball M/W(c), water polo M(c)/W(c).

Campus security: 24-hour emergency response devices and patrols, student patrols, late-night transport/escort service, controlled dormitory access, state certified police officers, security lighting, extensive camera system, self-defense/alcohol abuse classes.

Student services: health clinic, personal/psychological counseling, veterans affairs office.

COSTS & FINANCIAL AID

Costs (2019–20) ***Tuition:*** area resident $13,346 full-time, $449 per credit part-time; state resident $13,346 full-time, $449 per credit part-time; nonresident $24,710 full-time, $796 per credit part-time. Full-time tuition and fees vary according to course level and program. Part-time tuition and fees vary according to course level and program. ***Room and board:*** $10,430. Room and board charges vary according to housing facility. ***Payment plans:*** installment, deferred payment. ***Waivers:*** senior citizens and employees or children of employees.

Financial Aid Of all full-time matriculated undergraduates who enrolled in 2018, 9,597 applied for aid, 7,946 were judged to have need, 760 had their need fully met. 438 Federal Work-Study jobs (averaging $1833). In 2018, 2258 non-need-based awards were made. ***Average percent of need met:*** 47. ***Average financial aid package:*** $10,262. ***Average need-based loan:*** $3931. ***Average need-based gift aid:*** $7082. ***Average non-need-based aid:*** $5164. ***Average indebtedness upon graduation:*** $27,095.

APPLYING

Standardized Tests *Required:* SAT or ACT (for admission).

Options: electronic application, deferred entrance.

Required: high school transcript, minimum 2.5 GPA. ***Required for some:*** interview, audition for music, theatre, and dance.

Application deadlines: rolling (freshmen), rolling (transfers).

Notification: continuous until 9/1 (freshmen), continuous (transfers).

CONTACT

Oakland University, 201 Meadow Brook Road, Rochester, MI 48309-4401. *Phone:* 248-3704431. *Toll-free phone:* 800-OAK-UNIV.

Olivet College

Olivet, Michigan

http://www.olivetcollege.edu/

- **Independent** comprehensive, founded 1844, affiliated with Congregational Christian Church
- **Small-town** 92-acre campus with easy access to Lansing, Battle Creek
- **Endowment** $16.8 million
- **Coed**
- **Minimally difficult** entrance level

FACULTY

Student/faculty ratio: 16:1.

ACADEMICS

Calendar: 4-4-1. *Degrees:* bachelor's and master's.

Library: Burrage Library plus 1 other. *Books:* 61,268 (physical); *Serial titles:* 211 (physical), 68,401 (digital/electronic); *Databases:* 14. Students can reserve study rooms.

STUDENT LIFE

Housing options: on-campus residence required through junior year; coed, men-only, women-only. Campus housing is university owned. Freshman campus housing is guaranteed.

Activities and organizations: student-run newspaper, radio station, choral group, marching band, Minority Association of Premedical Students, Gay-Straight Alliance, Mathletes, OC Association Computing Machinery, Black Student Union.

Athletics Member NCAA. All Division III.

Campus security: 24-hour patrols, late-night transport/escort service, security cameras in all dorms and campus surveillance.

Student services: women's center.

COSTS & FINANCIAL AID

Costs (2019–20) ***Comprehensive fee:*** $38,792 includes full-time tuition ($27,700), mandatory fees ($992), and room and board ($10,100).

Financial Aid Of all full-time matriculated undergraduates who enrolled in 2018, 984 applied for aid, 873 were judged to have need, 154 had their need fully met. 184 Federal Work-Study jobs (averaging $967). In 2018, 98 non-need-based awards were made. ***Average percent of need met:*** 80. ***Average financial aid package:*** $19,240. ***Average need-based loan:*** $5342. ***Average need-based gift aid:*** $15,700. ***Average non-need-based aid:*** $14,225. ***Average indebtedness upon graduation:*** $26,872.

APPLYING

Standardized Tests *Required:* SAT or ACT (for admission).

Options: electronic application, deferred entrance.

Application fee: $25.

Required: high school transcript. ***Required for some:*** essay or personal statement, interview. ***Recommended:*** minimum 2.6 GPA.

CONTACT

Admissions, Olivet College, 320 S. Main Street, Olivet, MI 49076. *Phone:* 800-456-7189. *Toll-free phone:* 800-456-7189. *E-mail:* admissions@olivetcollege.edu.

Rochester University

Rochester Hills, Michigan

http://www.rc.edu/

- **Independent** comprehensive, founded 1959, affiliated with Church of Christ
- **Suburban** 81-acre campus with easy access to Detroit
- **Coed** 1,044 undergraduate students, 63% full-time, 64% women, 36% men
- **Minimally difficult** entrance level, 100% of applicants were admitted

UNDERGRAD STUDENTS

658 full-time, 386 part-time. Students come from 20 states and territories; 11 other countries; 3% are from out of state; 20% Black or African American, non-Hispanic/Latino; 2% Hispanic/Latino; 1% Asian, non-Hispanic/Latino; 0.5% American Indian or Alaska Native, non-Hispanic/Latino; 3% Two or more races, non-Hispanic/Latino; 1% Race/ethnicity unknown; 3% international; 9% transferred in; 26% live on campus.

Freshmen:

Admission: 432 applied, 432 admitted, 142 enrolled.

Retention: 61% of full-time freshmen returned.

FACULTY

Total: 138, 29% full-time, 37% with terminal degrees.

Student/faculty ratio: 9:1.

ACADEMICS

Calendar: semesters. *Degrees:* associate, bachelor's, and master's.

Special study options: academic remediation for entering students, accelerated degree program, adult/continuing education programs, advanced placement credit, distance learning, double majors, external degree program, honors programs, independent study, internships, off-campus study, part-time degree program, services for LD students, study abroad, summer session for credit.

Computers: 40 computers/terminals and 40 ports are available on campus for general student use. Students can access the following: campus intranet, computer help desk, free student e-mail accounts, online (class) grades, online (class) registration, online (class) schedules. Campuswide network is available. 100% of college-owned or -operated housing units are wired for high-speed Internet access. Wireless service is available via entire campus.

Library: Ennis and Nancy Ham Library. *Books:* 46,582 (physical), 9,514 (digital/electronic); *Serial titles:* 27 (physical), 37,060 (digital/electronic); *Databases:* 87. Weekly public service hours: 69; students can reserve study rooms.

STUDENT LIFE

Housing options: on-campus residence required through sophomore year; men-only, women-only, special housing for students with disabilities. Campus housing is university owned. Freshman campus housing is guaranteed.

Activities and organizations: drama/theater group, student-run newspaper, choral group, Theatre, Shield Magazine and Shield Online, Emerging and Fellowship Leaders, Campus Ministry.

Athletics Member NAIA. ***Intercollegiate sports:*** baseball M(s), basketball M(s)/W(s), bowling M(s)/W(s), cheerleading M(s)/W(s), cross-country running M(s)/W(s), golf M(s)/W(s), ice hockey M, lacrosse W(s), soccer M(s)/W(s), softball W(s), track and field M(s)/W(s), volleyball W(s), wrestling M(s).

Campus security: 24-hour emergency response devices, late-night transport/escort service, controlled dormitory access.

Student services: personal/psychological counseling.

COSTS

Costs (2020–21) ***Comprehensive fee:*** $33,560 includes full-time tuition ($24,720) and room and board ($8840). Full-time tuition and fees vary according to class time and location. Part-time tuition: $752 per semester hour. Part-time tuition and fees vary according to class time and location. ***Room and board:*** Room and board charges vary according to board plan. ***Payment plan:*** installment. ***Waivers:*** children of alumni and employees or children of employees.

APPLYING

Standardized Tests *Required:* SAT or ACT (for admission). *Recommended:* SAT (for admission).

Options: electronic application, early admission, deferred entrance.

Required: high school transcript, minimum 2.3 GPA. ***Required for some:*** essay or personal statement, interview.

Application deadlines: rolling (freshmen), rolling (out-of-state freshmen), rolling (transfers).

Notification: continuous (freshmen), continuous (out-of-state freshmen), continuous (transfers).

CONTACT

Mr. Scott Samuels, Vice President, Rochester University, 800 West Avon Road, Rochester Hills, MI 48307. *Phone:* 248-218-2123. *Toll-free phone:* 800-521-6010. *E-mail:* ssamuels@rc.edu.

Sacred Heart Major Seminary

Detroit, Michigan

http://www.shms.edu/

CONTACT

Fr. Michael Byrnes, Vice Rector, Sacred Heart Major Seminary, 2701 Chicago Boulevard, Detroit, MI 48206. *Phone:* 313-883-8552. *Fax:* 313-868-6400.

Saginaw Valley State University

University Center, Michigan

http://www.svsu.edu/

- **State-supported** comprehensive, founded 1963
- **Small-town** 782-acre campus
- **Endowment** $79.8 million
- **Coed** 7,490 undergraduate students, 85% full-time, 62% women, 38% men
- **Moderately difficult** entrance level, 73% of applicants were admitted

UNDERGRAD STUDENTS

6,359 full-time, 1,131 part-time. 2% are from out of state; 8% Black or African American, non-Hispanic/Latino; 5% Hispanic/Latino; 0.8% Asian, non-Hispanic/Latino; 0.3% American Indian or Alaska Native, non-Hispanic/Latino; 4% Two or more races, non-Hispanic/Latino; 2% Race/ethnicity unknown; 5% international; 6% transferred in; 33% live on campus.

Freshmen:

Admission: 7,149 applied, 5,227 admitted, 1,470 enrolled. ***Average high school GPA:*** 3.5. ***Test scores:*** SAT evidence-based reading and writing scores over 500: 74%; SAT math scores over 500: 71%; ACT scores over 18: 90%; SAT evidence-based reading and writing scores over 600: 27%; SAT math scores over 600: 21%; ACT scores over 24: 35%; SAT evidence-based reading and writing scores over 700: 2%; SAT math scores over 700: 1%; ACT scores over 30: 5%.

Retention: 74% of full-time freshmen returned.

FACULTY

Total: 286.

Student/faculty ratio: 17:1.

ACADEMICS

Calendar: semesters plus summer session. *Degrees:* bachelor's, master's, doctoral, and post-master's certificates.

Special study options: academic remediation for entering students, accelerated degree program, adult/continuing education programs, advanced placement credit, cooperative education, distance learning, double majors, English as a second language, external degree program, honors programs, independent study, internships, part-time degree program, services for LD students, study abroad, summer session for credit.

Computers: 424 computers/terminals are available on campus for general student use. Students can access the following: computer help desk, free student e-mail accounts, online (class) grades, online (class) registration, online (class) schedules. Campuswide network is available. 100% of college-owned or -operated housing units are wired for high-speed Internet access. Wireless service is available via entire campus.

Library: Zahnow Library. *Books:* 217,900 (physical), 107,479 (digital/electronic); *Serial titles:* 127 (physical), 50,164 (digital/electronic); *Databases:* 63. Weekly public service hours: 92.

STUDENT LIFE

Housing options: coed, special housing for students with disabilities. Campus housing is university owned. Freshman applicants given priority for college housing.

Activities and organizations: drama/theater group, student-run newspaper, radio station, choral group, marching band, His House Christian Fellowship, Criminal Justice Society, Delta Sigma Pi, Alpha Phi Omega, International Students Club, national fraternities, national sororities.

Athletics Member NCAA. All Division II. ***Intercollegiate sports:*** baseball M(s), basketball M(s)/W(s), bowling M(c)/W(c), cheerleading M(c)/W(c), cross-country running M(s)/W(s), equestrian sports M(c)/W(c), football M(s), golf M(s), gymnastics M(c)/W(c), ice hockey M(c)/W(c), lacrosse M(c)/W(c), rugby M(c)/W(c), soccer M(s)/W(s), softball W(s), swimming and diving M(s)/W(s), tennis M(c)/W(s), track and field M(s)/W(s), volleyball W(s), wrestling M(c). ***Intramural sports:*** badminton M/W, basketball M/W, football M/W, golf M/W, ice hockey M/W, racquetball M/W, soccer M/W, softball M/W, table tennis M/W, tennis M/W, volleyball M/W, water polo M/W.

Campus security: 24-hour emergency response devices and patrols, student patrols, late-night transport/escort service, controlled dormitory access, Sexual Assault Prevention Program.

Student services: health clinic, personal/psychological counseling, veterans affairs office.

COSTS & FINANCIAL AID

Costs (2019–20) ***Tuition:*** state resident $10,376 full-time, $346 per credit hour part-time; nonresident $24,963 full-time, $832 per credit hour part-time. Full-time tuition and fees vary according to course level, degree level, location, and program. Part-time tuition and fees vary according to course level, degree level, location, and program. ***Required fees:*** $438 full-time, $15 per credit hour part-time. ***Room and board:*** $10,440; room only: $4430. Room and board charges vary according to board plan and housing facility. ***Payment plan:*** installment. ***Waivers:*** employees or children of employees.

Financial Aid Of all full-time matriculated undergraduates who enrolled in 2019, 5,084 applied for aid, 4,255 were judged to have need, 361 had their need fully met. In 2019, 1211 non-need-based awards were made. ***Average percent of need met:*** 63. ***Average financial aid package:*** $10,187. ***Average need-based loan:*** $3842. ***Average need-based gift aid:*** $7677. ***Average non-need-based aid:*** $8109. ***Average indebtedness upon graduation:*** $31,353.

APPLYING

Standardized Tests *Required:* SAT or ACT (for admission).

Options: electronic application, deferred entrance.

Application fee: $30.

Required: high school transcript, minimum 2.5 GPA.

Application deadlines: rolling (freshmen), rolling (transfers).

Notification: continuous (freshmen), continuous (transfers).

CONTACT

Jennifer Pahl, Director of Admissions, Saginaw Valley State University, 7400 Bay Road, University Center, MI 48710-0001. *Phone:* 989-964-4200. *Toll-free phone:* 800-968-9500. *Fax:* 989-790-0180. *E-mail:* admissions@svsu.edu.

Schoolcraft College

Livonia, Michigan

http://www.schoolcraft.edu/

- **District-supported** primarily 2-year, founded 1961, part of Michigan Department of Education
- **Suburban** campus with easy access to Detroit
- **Coed** 9,230 undergraduate students, 24% full-time, 54% women, 46% men
- **Noncompetitive** entrance level

UNDERGRAD STUDENTS

2,240 full-time, 6,990 part-time. 14% Black or African American, non-Hispanic/Latino; 5% Hispanic/Latino; 5% Asian, non-Hispanic/Latino; 0.1% Native Hawaiian or other Pacific Islander, non-Hispanic/Latino; 0.4% American Indian or Alaska Native, non-Hispanic/Latino; 3% Two or more races, non-Hispanic/Latino; 6% Race/ethnicity unknown; 2% international; 9% transferred in.

Freshmen:

Admission: 1,744 enrolled. ***Average high school GPA:*** 2.8.

Retention: 66% of full-time freshmen returned.

FACULTY

Total: 482, 18% full-time.

Student/faculty ratio: 20:1.

ACADEMICS

Calendar: semesters. *Degrees:* certificates, associate, and bachelor's.

Special study options: academic remediation for entering students, advanced placement credit, distance learning, English as a second language, honors programs, independent study, internships, part-time degree program, services for LD students, study abroad, summer session for credit.

Computers: Students can access the following: campus intranet, computer help desk, free student e-mail accounts, online (class) grades, online (class) registration, online (class) schedules. Campuswide network is available. Wireless service is available via entire campus.

Library: Bradner Library plus 1 other. *Books:* 64,514 (physical), 319,132 (digital/electronic); *Serial titles:* 351 (physical); *Databases:* 142. Students can reserve study rooms.

STUDENT LIFE

Housing options: college housing not available.

Activities and organizations: drama/theater group, student-run newspaper, Phi Theta Kappa, Early Childhood/Special Education Student Educators, Health Information Technology Club, Otaku Anime Japanese Animation Club, Student Nurse Association.

Athletics Member NJCAA. ***Intercollegiate sports:*** baseball M, basketball M(s)/W(s), bowling M/W, soccer M/W, softball W, volleyball W.

Campus security: 24-hour emergency response devices and patrols, late-night transport/escort service.

Student services: health clinic, personal/psychological counseling, women's center, veterans affairs office.

COSTS & FINANCIAL AID

Costs (2020–21) ***Tuition:*** area resident $3198 full-time, $123 per credit hour part-time; state resident $4602 full-time, $177 per credit hour part-time; nonresident $6760 full-time, $260 per credit hour part-time. ***Required fees:*** $26 per credit hour part-time, $43 per term part-time. ***Payment plan:*** installment. ***Waivers:*** senior citizens and employees or children of employees.

Financial Aid Of all full-time matriculated undergraduates who enrolled in 2017, 124 Federal Work-Study jobs (averaging $4000).

APPLYING

Options: electronic application, early admission, deferred entrance.

Required for some: high school transcript. ***Recommended:*** high school transcript.

Application deadlines: rolling (freshmen), rolling (transfers).

CONTACT

Ms. Lisa Bushaw, Director of Admissions, Schoolcraft College, 18600 Haggerty Road, Livonia, MI 48152-2696. *Phone:* 734-462-4683. *E-mail:* admissions@schoolcraft.edu.

Siena Heights University

Adrian, Michigan

http://www.sienaheights.edu/

- **Independent Roman Catholic** comprehensive, founded 1919
- **Small-town** 140-acre campus with easy access to Detroit, Toledo
- **Coed** 2,130 undergraduate students, 59% full-time, 58% women, 42% men
- **Moderately difficult** entrance level, 73% of applicants were admitted

UNDERGRAD STUDENTS
1,257 full-time, 873 part-time. Students come from 43 states and territories; 23 other countries; 16% are from out of state; 11% Black or African American, non-Hispanic/Latino; 7% Hispanic/Latino; 1% Asian, non-Hispanic/Latino; 0.1% Native Hawaiian or other Pacific Islander, non-Hispanic/Latino; 0.4% American Indian or Alaska Native, non-Hispanic/Latino; 4% Two or more races, non-Hispanic/Latino; 10% Race/ethnicity unknown; 2% international; 14% transferred in; 25% live on campus.

Freshmen:
Admission: 1,722 applied, 1,264 admitted, 327 enrolled. ***Average high school GPA:*** 3.0.

Retention: 68% of full-time freshmen returned.

FACULTY
Total: 220, 41% full-time.

Student/faculty ratio: 10:1.

ACADEMICS
Calendar: semesters. *Degrees:* certificates, associate, bachelor's, and master's.

Special study options: academic remediation for entering students, accelerated degree program, adult/continuing education programs, advanced placement credit, cooperative education, distance learning, double majors, English as a second language, independent study, internships, off-campus study, part-time degree program, services for LD students, student-designed majors, study abroad, summer session for credit.

Computers: 180 computers/terminals are available on campus for general student use. Students can access the following: campus intranet, computer help desk, free student e-mail accounts, online (class) grades, online (class) registration, online (class) schedules. Campuswide network is available. 100% of college-owned or -operated housing units are wired for high-speed Internet access. Wireless service is available via entire campus.

Library: Siena Heights University Library plus 1 other. *Books:* 98,000 (physical), 155,630 (digital/electronic); *Serial titles:* 85 (physical), 3,898 (digital/electronic); *Databases:* 122. Weekly public service hours: 78.

STUDENT LIFE
Housing options: on-campus residence required through junior year; coed, special housing for students with disabilities. Campus housing is university owned. Freshman campus housing is guaranteed.

Activities and organizations: drama/theater group, student-run newspaper, choral group, marching band, Student Athletic Leadership Team (SALT), Criminal Justice Club, Social Work Student Association, Psychology Club, Black Student Union.

Athletics Member NAIA. ***Intercollegiate sports:*** baseball M(s), basketball M(s)/W(s), bowling M(s)/W(s), cheerleading M/W, cross-country running M(s)/W(s), football M(s), golf M(s)/W(s), lacrosse M(s)/W(s), soccer M(s)/W(s), softball W(s), track and field M(s)/W(s), volleyball M(s)/W(s). ***Intramural sports:*** basketball M/W, softball M/W, volleyball M/W.

Campus security: 24-hour emergency response devices and patrols, student patrols, late-night transport/escort service.

Student services: health clinic, personal/psychological counseling.

COSTS & FINANCIAL AID
Costs (2020–21) ***Comprehensive fee:*** $38,142 includes full-time tuition ($26,558), mandatory fees ($594), and room and board ($10,990). Full-time tuition and fees vary according to degree level, location, and reciprocity agreements. Part-time tuition: $530 per credit hour. Part-time tuition and fees vary according to degree level, location, and reciprocity agreements. ***Required fees:*** $58 per term part-time. ***Waivers:*** employees or children of employees.

Financial Aid In 2002, 166 non-need-based awards were made. ***Average percent of need met:*** 66. ***Average financial aid package:*** $12,200. ***Average indebtedness upon graduation:*** $13,500.

APPLYING
Options: electronic application, deferred entrance.

Required: high school transcript.

Application deadlines: rolling (freshmen), rolling (transfers).

CONTACT
Ms. Trudy Mohre, Director of Admissions, Siena Heights University, 1247 East Siena Heights Drive, Adrian, MI 49221. *Phone:* 517-264-7185. *Toll-free phone:* 800-521-0009. *E-mail:* tmohre@sienaheights.edu.

Spring Arbor University
Spring Arbor, Michigan
http://www.arbor.edu/

- **Independent Free Methodist** comprehensive, founded 1873
- **Rural** 100-acre campus
- **Endowment** $13.3 million
- **Coed** 1,614 undergraduate students, 70% full-time, 67% women, 33% men
- **Moderately difficult** entrance level, 66% of applicants were admitted

UNDERGRAD STUDENTS
1,134 full-time, 480 part-time. Students come from 21 states and territories; 10 other countries; 13% are from out of state; 9% Black or African American, non-Hispanic/Latino; 4% Hispanic/Latino; 1% Asian, non-Hispanic/Latino; 0.5% American Indian or Alaska Native, non-Hispanic/Latino; 3% Two or more races, non-Hispanic/Latino; 12% Race/ethnicity unknown; 0.1% international; 3% transferred in; 71% live on campus.

Freshmen:
Admission: 1,448 applied, 958 admitted, 216 enrolled. ***Average high school GPA:*** 3.6. ***Test scores:*** SAT evidence-based reading and writing scores over 500: 180%; SAT math scores over 500: 125%; ACT scores over 18: 40%; SAT evidence-based reading and writing scores over 600: 101%; SAT math scores over 600: 55%; ACT scores over 24: 25%; SAT evidence-based reading and writing scores over 700: 60%; SAT math scores over 700: 4%; ACT scores over 30: 7%.

Retention: 78% of full-time freshmen returned.

FACULTY
Total: 116, 59% full-time.

Student/faculty ratio: 12:1.

ACADEMICS
Calendar: 4-1-4. *Degrees:* associate, bachelor's, master's, and postbachelor's certificates.

Special study options: academic remediation for entering students, accelerated degree program, adult/continuing education programs, advanced placement credit, distance learning, double majors, English as a second language, honors programs, independent study, internships, off-campus study, part-time degree program, services for LD students, student-designed majors, study abroad, summer session for credit. ***ROTC:*** Army (c), Air Force (c).

Unusual degree programs: 3-2 engineering with University of Michigan.

Computers: 80 computers/terminals and 1,120 ports are available on campus for general student use. Students can access the following: campus intranet, computer help desk, free student e-mail accounts, online (class) grades, online (class) registration, online (class) schedules. Campuswide network is available. 100% of college-owned or -operated housing units are wired for high-speed Internet access. Wireless service is available via entire campus.

Library: Hugh A. White Library. *Books:* 98,490 (physical), 195,812 (digital/electronic); *Serial titles:* 1,055 (physical), 65,932 (digital/electronic); *Databases:* 113. Weekly public service hours: 69; students can reserve study rooms.

STUDENT LIFE
Housing options: on-campus residence required through senior year; men-only, women-only, special housing for students with disabilities. Campus housing is university owned. Freshman campus housing is guaranteed.

Activities and organizations: drama/theater group, student-run newspaper, radio station, choral group, Inter-faith Shelter Ministries, Band of Brothers, Action Jackson, Circle of Sisters, Heartside Homeless.

Athletics Member NAIA, NCCAA. ***Intercollegiate sports:*** baseball M(s), basketball M(s)/W(s), cross-country running M(s)/W(s), golf M(s)/W(s), soccer M(s)/W(s), softball W(s), tennis M(s)/W(s), track and field M(s)/W(s), volleyball W(s). ***Intramural sports:*** basketball M/W, field hockey M, football M/W, soccer M/W, softball M/W, table tennis M/W, tennis M/W, ultimate Frisbee M/W, volleyball M/W.

Campus security: 24-hour emergency response devices, student patrols, late-night transport/escort service, controlled dormitory access.

Student services: health clinic, personal/psychological counseling.

FINANCIAL AID

Financial Aid Of all full-time matriculated undergraduates who enrolled in 2016, 1,106 applied for aid, 1,009 were judged to have need, 216 had their need fully met. In 2016, 4 non-need-based awards were made. ***Average percent of need met:*** 79. ***Average financial aid package:*** $23,256. ***Average need-based loan:*** $4845. ***Average need-based gift aid:*** $15,712. ***Average non-need-based aid:*** $4578. ***Average indebtedness upon graduation:*** $32,602.

APPLYING

Standardized Tests *Required:* SAT or ACT (for admission). *Recommended:* ACT (for admission).

Options: electronic application, early admission, deferred entrance.

Application fee: $30.

Required: high school transcript. ***Required for some:*** essay or personal statement, interview. ***Recommended:*** minimum 2.6 GPA, guidance counselor's form, minimum ACT score of 20 or SAT score of 930.

Application deadlines: 8/1 (freshmen), rolling (transfers).

Notification: continuous (freshmen), continuous (out-of-state freshmen), continuous (transfers).

CONTACT

Office of Admissions, Spring Arbor University, 106 East Main Street, Spring Arbor, MI 49283-9799. *Phone:* 517-750-1200 Ext. 1468. *Toll-free phone:* 800-968-0011. *Fax:* 517-750-6620. *E-mail:* admissions@arbor.edu.

University of Detroit Mercy

Detroit, Michigan

http://www.udmercy.edu/

- **Independent Roman Catholic (Jesuit)** university, founded 1877
- **Urban** 70-acre campus with easy access to Detroit, MI
- **Endowment** $43.9 million
- **Coed** 2,745 undergraduate students, 86% full-time, 62% women, 38% men
- **Moderately difficult** entrance level, 77% of applicants were admitted

UNDERGRAD STUDENTS

2,350 full-time, 395 part-time. 6% are from out of state; 13% Black or African American, non-Hispanic/Latino; 6% Hispanic/Latino; 6% Asian, non-Hispanic/Latino; 0.2% Native Hawaiian or other Pacific Islander, non-Hispanic/Latino; 0.3% American Indian or Alaska Native, non-Hispanic/Latino; 2% Two or more races, non-Hispanic/Latino; 5% Race/ethnicity unknown; 7% international; 6% transferred in; 31% live on campus.

Freshmen:

Admission: 4,358 applied, 3,377 admitted, 530 enrolled. ***Average high school GPA:*** 3.6. ***Test scores:*** SAT evidence-based reading and writing scores over 500: 88%; SAT math scores over 500: 89%; ACT scores over 18: 99%; SAT evidence-based reading and writing scores over 600: 37%; SAT math scores over 600: 36%; ACT scores over 24: 57%; SAT evidence-based reading and writing scores over 700: 6%; SAT math scores over 700: 9%; ACT scores over 30: 17%.

Retention: 82% of full-time freshmen returned.

FACULTY

Total: 770, 44% full-time, 74% with terminal degrees.

Student/faculty ratio: 11:1.

ACADEMICS

Calendar: semesters. *Degrees:* certificates, diplomas, bachelor's, master's, doctoral, post-master's, and postbachelor's certificates.

Special study options: academic remediation for entering students, accelerated degree program, advanced placement credit, cooperative education, distance learning, double majors, English as a second language, honors programs, independent study, internships, off-campus study, part-time degree program, services for LD students, study abroad, summer session for credit.

Computers: 157 computers/terminals are available on campus for general student use. Students can access the following: campus intranet, computer help desk, free student e-mail accounts, online (class) grades, online (class) registration, online (class) schedules. Campuswide network is available. 100% of college-owned or -operated housing units are wired for high-speed Internet access. Wireless service is available via entire campus.

Library: McNichols Campus Library. *Books:* 468,257 (physical), 175,312 (digital/electronic); *Serial titles:* 107,735 (digital/electronic); *Databases:* 84. Weekly public service hours: 80.

STUDENT LIFE

Housing options: coed. Campus housing is university owned. Freshman campus housing is guaranteed.

Activities and organizations: drama/theater group, student-run newspaper, radio station, choral group, Alpha Phi Omega, Biology Club, Chemistry Club, Pre-Dentistry Club, Greek Organizations - NPC, NIC, and NPHC, national fraternities, national sororities.

Athletics Member NCAA. All Division I. ***Intercollegiate sports:*** basketball M(s)/W(s), cross-country running M(s)/W(s), fencing M(s)/W(s), golf M(s)/W(s)(c), lacrosse M(s)/W(s), soccer M(s)/W(s), softball W(s), tennis M(s)/W(s), track and field M(s)/W(s). ***Intramural sports:*** basketball M/W, cheerleading M/W, soccer M/W, table tennis M/W, volleyball M/W.

Campus security: 24-hour emergency response devices and patrols, student patrols, late-night transport/escort service.

Student services: health clinic, personal/psychological counseling.

COSTS & FINANCIAL AID

Costs (2020–21) ***Comprehensive fee:*** $39,606 includes full-time tuition ($29,416) and room and board ($10,190). Full-time tuition and fees vary according to location and program. Part-time tuition: $1102 per credit hour. Part-time tuition and fees vary according to location and program. ***Room and board:*** Room and board charges vary according to board plan and housing facility. ***Payment plan:*** installment. ***Waivers:*** children of alumni, senior citizens, and employees or children of employees.

Financial Aid Of all full-time matriculated undergraduates who enrolled in 2018, 2,013 applied for aid, 1,605 were judged to have need, 151 had their need fully met. In 2018, 750 non-need-based awards were made. ***Average percent of need met:*** 66. ***Average financial aid package:*** $21,954. ***Average need-based loan:*** $3832. ***Average need-based gift aid:*** $16,938. ***Average non-need-based aid:*** $11,184. ***Average indebtedness upon graduation:*** $44,180.

APPLYING

Standardized Tests *Required:* SAT or ACT (for admission).

Options: electronic application, early admission, early decision, deferred entrance.

Required: essay or personal statement, high school transcript, minimum 2.5 GPA. ***Recommended:*** 1 letter of recommendation, interview.

Application deadlines: rolling (freshmen), rolling (transfers).

Early decision deadline: 11/1 (for plan 1), 1/15 (for plan 2).

Notification: continuous (freshmen), continuous (transfers), 12/1 (early decision plan 1), 3/15 (early decision plan 2).

CONTACT

University of Detroit Mercy, 4001 West McNichols Road, Detroit, MI 48221. *Phone:* 313-993-1245. *Toll-free phone:* 800-635-5020.

University of Michigan

Ann Arbor, Michigan

http://www.umich.edu/

- **State-supported** university, founded 1817
- **Urban** 3207-acre campus with easy access to Detroit
- **Endowment** $12.3 billion
- **Coed** 31,266 undergraduate students, 97% full-time, 50% women, 50% men
- **Very difficult** entrance level, 23% of applicants were admitted

UNDERGRAD STUDENTS
30,204 full-time, 1,062 part-time. Students come from 54 states and territories; 92 other countries; 41% are from out of state; 4% Black or African American, non-Hispanic/Latino; 7% Hispanic/Latino; 16% Asian, non-Hispanic/Latino; 0.1% American Indian or Alaska Native, non-Hispanic/Latino; 5% Two or more races, non-Hispanic/Latino; 5% Race/ethnicity unknown; 7% international; 4% transferred in; 31% live on campus.

Freshmen:
Admission: 64,972 applied, 14,883 admitted, 6,830 enrolled. ***Average high school GPA:*** 3.9. ***Test scores:*** SAT evidence-based reading and writing scores over 500: 100%; SAT math scores over 500: 100%; ACT scores over 18: 100%; SAT evidence-based reading and writing scores over 600: 94%; SAT math scores over 600: 94%; ACT scores over 24: 97%; SAT evidence-based reading and writing scores over 700: 56%; SAT math scores over 700: 71%; ACT scores over 30: 85%.

Retention: 97% of full-time freshmen returned.

FACULTY
Total: 3,562, 82% full-time, 89% with terminal degrees.

Student/faculty ratio: 15:1.

ACADEMICS
Calendar: trimesters. *Degrees:* bachelor's, master's, doctoral, post-master's, and postbachelor's certificates.

Special study options: accelerated degree program, adult/continuing education programs, advanced placement credit, cooperative education, distance learning, double majors, English as a second language, external degree program, honors programs, independent study, internships, off-campus study, part-time degree program, services for LD students, student-designed majors, study abroad, summer session for credit. ***ROTC:*** Army (b), Navy (b), Air Force (b).

Unusual degree programs: 3-2 business administration; engineering.

Computers: 4,000 computers/terminals are available on campus for general student use. Students can access the following: campus intranet, computer help desk, free student e-mail accounts, online (class) grades, online (class) registration, online (class) schedules, file storage, personal Web pages, printing. Campuswide network is available. 100% of college-owned or -operated housing units are wired for high-speed Internet access. Wireless service is available via entire campus.

Library: Shapiro Undergraduate Library plus 9 others. *Books:* 5.1 million (physical), 3.1 million (digital/electronic); *Serial titles:* 356,309 (physical), 291,791 (digital/electronic); *Databases:* 2,774. Weekly public service hours: 168; study areas open 24 hours, 5–7 days a week; students can reserve study rooms.

STUDENT LIFE
Housing options: coed, women-only, cooperative. Campus housing is university owned. Freshman campus housing is guaranteed.

Activities and organizations: drama/theater group, student-run newspaper, radio and television station, choral group, marching band, Hillel Society, K-Grams, M-Powered Entrepreneurial Club, Dance Marathon, Alternative Spring Break, national fraternities, national sororities.

Athletics Member NCAA. All Division I except football (Division I-AA). ***Intercollegiate sports:*** baseball M(s), basketball M(s)/W(s), cheerleading M(s)(c)/W(s)(c), crew M(c)/W(s), cross-country running M(s)/W(s), fencing M(c)/W(c), field hockey W(s), golf M(s)/W(s), gymnastics M(s)/W(s), ice hockey M(s)/W(c), lacrosse M(s)/W(s), riflery M(c)/W(c), rowing M(c), rugby M(c)/W(c), sailing M(c)/W(c), soccer M(s)/W(s), softball W(s), swimming and diving M(s)/W(s), table tennis M(c)/W(c), tennis M(s)/W(s), track and field M(s)/W(s), triathlon M(c), ultimate Frisbee M(c)/W(c), volleyball M(c)/W(s), water polo M(c)/W(s), wrestling M(s). ***Intramural sports:*** badminton M/W, baseball M(c), basketball M/W, cross-country running M(c)/W(c), fencing W, field hockey M, gymnastics W(c), ice hockey M(c)/W(c), lacrosse W(c), racquetball M/W, sand volleyball M/W, soccer M(c)/W(c), softball W(c), squash M/W, swimming and diving M/W(c), table tennis M/W, tennis M(c)/W(c), track and field M/W, ultimate Frisbee M/W, volleyball M/W, wrestling M(c).

Campus security: 24-hour emergency response devices and patrols, student patrols, late-night transport/escort service, controlled dormitory access, SafeRide (no-cost night-time ride service).

Student services: health clinic, personal/psychological counseling, women's center, legal services, veterans affairs office.

COSTS & FINANCIAL AID
Costs (2019–20) ***Tuition:*** state resident $15,230 full-time, $611 per credit hour part-time; nonresident $50,872 full-time, $2088 per credit hour part-time. Full-time tuition and fees vary according to course load, degree level, program, and student level. Part-time tuition and fees vary according to course load, degree level, program, and student level. ***Required fees:*** $328 full-time, $164 per term part-time, $164 per term part-time. ***Room and board:*** $11,996. Room and board charges vary according to board plan and housing facility. ***Payment plan:*** installment.

Financial Aid Of all full-time matriculated undergraduates who enrolled in 2018, 15,973 applied for aid, 11,706 were judged to have need, 8,637 had their need fully met. In 2018, 3156 non-need-based awards were made. ***Average percent of need met:*** 92. ***Average financial aid package:*** $28,711. ***Average need-based loan:*** $4301. ***Average need-based gift aid:*** $21,665. ***Average non-need-based aid:*** $5853. ***Average indebtedness upon graduation:*** $25,777. ***Financial aid deadline:*** 3/31.

APPLYING
Standardized Tests *Required:* SAT or ACT (for admission). *Required for some:* SAT Subject Tests (for admission).

Options: electronic application, early action, deferred entrance.

Application fee: $75.

Required: essay or personal statement, high school transcript, 1 letter of recommendation. ***Required for some:*** interview, audition for School of Music, Theatre and Dance; portfolio for School of Art and Design.

Application deadlines: 2/1 (freshmen), 2/1 (out-of-state freshmen), 2/1 (transfers), 11/1 (early action).

Notification: continuous (transfers), 12/24 (early action).

CONTACT
University of Michigan, Ann Arbor, MI 48109. *Phone:* 734-764-7433.

University of Michigan–Dearborn

Dearborn, Michigan

http://www.umdearborn.edu/

- **State-supported** comprehensive, founded 1959, part of University of Michigan
- **Suburban** 202-acre campus with easy access to Detroit
- **Endowment** $57.7 million
- **Coed** 6,914 undergraduate students, 73% full-time, 46% women, 54% men
- **Moderately difficult** entrance level, 62% of applicants were admitted

UNDERGRAD STUDENTS
5,051 full-time, 1,863 part-time. Students come from 20 states and territories; 34 other countries; 3% are from out of state; 8% Black or African American, non-Hispanic/Latino; 6% Hispanic/Latino; 9% Asian, non-Hispanic/Latino; 0.1% Native Hawaiian or other Pacific Islander, non-Hispanic/Latino; 0.3% American Indian or Alaska Native, non-Hispanic/Latino; 4% Two or more races, non-Hispanic/Latino; 2% Race/ethnicity unknown; 2% international; 9% transferred in.

Freshmen:
Admission: 6,447 applied, 3,993 admitted, 1,014 enrolled. ***Average high school GPA:*** 3.7. ***Test scores:*** SAT evidence-based reading and writing scores over 500: 92%; SAT math scores over 500: 93%; ACT scores over 18: 98%; SAT evidence-based reading and writing scores over 600: 46%; SAT math scores over 600: 49%; ACT scores over 24: 60%; SAT evidence-based reading and writing scores over 700: 8%; SAT math scores over 700: 16%; ACT scores over 30: 20%.

Retention: 83% of full-time freshmen returned.

FACULTY
Total: 549, 68% full-time, 68% with terminal degrees.

Student/faculty ratio: 16:1.

ACADEMICS
Calendar: semesters. *Degrees:* bachelor's, master's, doctoral, post-master's, and postbachelor's certificates.

Special study options: academic remediation for entering students, adult/continuing education programs, advanced placement credit, cooperative education, distance learning, double majors, English as a second language, honors programs, independent study, internships, off-campus study, part-time degree program, services for LD students, student-designed majors, study abroad, summer session for credit. ***ROTC:*** Navy (c), Air Force (c).

Computers: 750 computers/terminals are available on campus for general student use. Students can access the following: computer help desk, free student e-mail accounts, online (class) grades, online (class) registration, online (class) schedules, tuition and application payments accepted online. Campuswide network is available. Wireless service is available via entire campus.

Library: Mardigian Library. *Books:* 189,535 (physical), 705,108 (digital/electronic); *Serial titles:* 310 (physical), 116,547 (digital/electronic); *Databases:* 847. Weekly public service hours: 95; students can reserve study rooms.

STUDENT LIFE

Activities and organizations: student-run newspaper, radio station, national fraternities, national sororities.

Athletics Member NAIA. ***Intercollegiate sports:*** baseball M(s), basketball M(s)/W(s), bowling M(s)/W(s), cross-country running M(s)/W(s), golf M(s)/W(s), ice hockey M(c)/W(c), lacrosse M(s), soccer M(s)/W(s), softball W(s), volleyball W(s). ***Intramural sports:*** basketball M/W, tennis M(c)/W(c), volleyball M/W, wrestling M(c)/W(c).

Campus security: 24-hour emergency response devices and patrols, late-night transport/escort service.

Student services: personal/psychological counseling, women's center, veterans affairs office.

COSTS & FINANCIAL AID

Costs (2020–21) ***One-time required fee:*** $75. ***Tuition:*** state resident $13,836 full-time, $529 per credit hour part-time; nonresident $27,476 full-time, $1068 per credit hour part-time. Full-time tuition and fees vary according to program and student level. Part-time tuition and fees vary according to program and student level. ***Required fees:*** $400 full-time, $200 per term part-time. ***Room and board:*** $2262. ***Payment plan:*** installment. ***Waivers:*** senior citizens and employees or children of employees.

Financial Aid Of all full-time matriculated undergraduates who enrolled in 2018, 4,010 applied for aid, 3,409 were judged to have need, 302 had their need fully met. 220 Federal Work-Study jobs (averaging $2080). 584 state and other part-time jobs (averaging $2862). In 2018, 843 non-need-based awards were made. ***Average percent of need met:*** 69. ***Average financial aid package:*** $13,486. ***Average need-based loan:*** $4857. ***Average need-based gift aid:*** $7787. ***Average non-need-based aid:*** $5332. ***Average indebtedness upon graduation:*** $25,268.

APPLYING

Standardized Tests *Required:* SAT or ACT (for admission).

Options: electronic application, deferred entrance.

Required: high school transcript. ***Recommended:*** minimum 2.5 GPA.

Application deadlines: rolling (freshmen), rolling (transfers).

Notification: continuous (freshmen), continuous (transfers).

CONTACT

Ms. Deb Peffer, Director of Admissions, University of Michigan–Dearborn, 4901 Evergreen Road, Room 1145 UC, Dearborn, MI 48128-1491. *Phone:* 313-593-5661. *Fax:* 313-436-9167. *E-mail:* umd-admissions@umich.edu.

University of Michigan–Flint

Flint, Michigan

http://www.umflint.edu/

- **State-supported** comprehensive, founded 1956, part of University of Michigan System
- **Urban** 76-acre campus with easy access to Detroit, Lansing
- **Endowment** $117.3 million
- **Coed** 5,862 undergraduate students, 62% full-time, 62% women, 38% men
- **Moderately difficult** entrance level, 66% of applicants were admitted

UNDERGRAD STUDENTS

3,633 full-time, 2,229 part-time. Students come from 23 states and territories; 35 other countries; 2% are from out of state; 13% Black or African American, non-Hispanic/Latino; 6% Hispanic/Latino; 2% Asian, non-Hispanic/Latino; 0.1% Native Hawaiian or other Pacific Islander, non-Hispanic/Latino; 0.7% American Indian or Alaska Native, non-Hispanic/Latino; 4% Two or more races, non-Hispanic/Latino; 3% Race/ethnicity unknown; 3% international; 10% transferred in; 6% live on campus.

Freshmen:

Admission: 4,254 applied, 2,806 admitted, 604 enrolled. ***Average high school GPA:*** 3.5. ***Test scores:*** SAT evidence-based reading and writing scores over 500: 75%; SAT math scores over 500: 67%; ACT scores over 18: 83%; SAT evidence-based reading and writing scores over 600: 33%; SAT math scores over 600: 25%; ACT scores over 24: 49%; SAT evidence-based reading and writing scores over 700: 5%; SAT math scores over 700: 4%; ACT scores over 30: 13%.

Retention: 74% of full-time freshmen returned.

FACULTY

Total: 550, 55% full-time, 61% with terminal degrees.

Student/faculty ratio: 14:1.

ACADEMICS

Calendar: semesters. *Degrees:* bachelor's, master's, doctoral, post-master's, and postbachelor's certificates.

Special study options: academic remediation for entering students, accelerated degree program, adult/continuing education programs, advanced placement credit, cooperative education, distance learning, double majors, English as a second language, honors programs, independent study, internships, off-campus study, part-time degree program, services for LD students, student-designed majors, study abroad, summer session for credit. ***ROTC:*** Army (c), Navy (c), Air Force (c).

Unusual degree programs: 3-2 engineering with University of Michigan (Ann Arbor).

Computers: 502 computers/terminals are available on campus for general student use. Students can access the following: campus intranet, computer help desk, free student e-mail accounts, online (class) grades, online (class) registration, online (class) schedules. Campuswide network is available. 100% of college-owned or -operated housing units are wired for high-speed Internet access. Wireless service is available via entire campus.

Library: Frances Willson Thompson Library plus 1 other. *Books:* 228,601 (physical), 195,382 (digital/electronic); *Serial titles:* 1,862 (physical), 238,105 (digital/electronic); *Databases:* 1,849. Weekly public service hours: 96; students can reserve study rooms.

STUDENT LIFE

Housing options: coed. Campus housing is university owned.

Activities and organizations: drama/theater group, student-run newspaper, choral group, Fraternity and Sorority Life, National Society for Leadership and Success, Psychology Club, Baccalaureate Student Nurses Organization, Student Nurse Practitioner Association, national fraternities, national sororities.

Athletics ***Intramural sports:*** badminton M/W, basketball M/W, cheerleading M(c)/W(c), football M(c), ice hockey M(c), soccer M/W, volleyball M/W.

Campus security: 24-hour emergency response devices and patrols, student patrols, late-night transport/escort service, controlled dormitory access.

Student services: personal/psychological counseling, women's center, veterans affairs office.

COSTS & FINANCIAL AID

Costs (2019–20) ***Tuition:*** state resident $11,952 full-time, $472 per credit hour part-time; nonresident $23,238 full-time, $939 per credit hour part-time. Full-time tuition and fees vary according to course level, course load, degree level, program, and student level. Part-time tuition and fees vary according to course level, course load, degree level, program, and student level. ***Required fees:*** $454 full-time, $227 per term part-time. ***Room and board:*** $9116; room only: $5994. Room and board charges vary according to housing facility. ***Payment plan:*** installment. ***Waivers:*** senior citizens.

Financial Aid Of all full-time matriculated undergraduates who enrolled in 2018, 3,003 applied for aid, 2,630 were judged to have need, 169 had their need fully met. 215 Federal Work-Study jobs (averaging $1840). In 2018, 169 non-need-based awards were made. ***Average percent of need met:*** 63. ***Average financial aid package:*** $12,802. ***Average need-based loan:*** $4041. ***Average need-based gift aid:*** $7124. ***Average non-need-based aid:*** $4312. ***Average indebtedness upon graduation:*** $29,645.

APPLYING

Standardized Tests *Required:* SAT or ACT (for admission).

Options: electronic application, deferred entrance.

Application fee: $30.

Required: high school transcript, minimum 2.7 GPA.

Application deadlines: 8/22 (freshmen), 8/20 (transfers).

Notification: continuous (freshmen), continuous (transfers).

CONTACT

Ms. Karen Cuzydlo, Admissions Senior Associate Director, University of Michigan–Flint, 303 East Kearsley Street, 245 University Pavilion, Flint, MI 48502. *Phone:* 810-762-3300. *Toll-free phone:* 800-942-5636. *Fax:* 810-762-3272. *E-mail:* admissions@umflint.edu.

Walsh College of Accountancy and Business Administration

Troy, Michigan

http://www.walshcollege.edu/

CONTACT

Walsh College of Accountancy and Business Administration, 3838 Livernois Road, Troy, MI 48083. *Phone:* 248-823-1610. *Toll-free phone:* 800-925-7401.

Wayne State University

Detroit, Michigan

http://www.wayne.edu/

- **State-supported** university, founded 1868
- **Urban** 195-acre campus with easy access to Detroit
- **Endowment** $366.7 million
- **Coed** 17,663 undergraduate students, 74% full-time, 57% women, 43% men
- **Moderately difficult** entrance level, 73% of applicants were admitted

UNDERGRAD STUDENTS

13,107 full-time, 4,556 part-time. 2% are from out of state; 15% Black or African American, non-Hispanic/Latino; 6% Hispanic/Latino; 11% Asian, non-Hispanic/Latino; 0.1% Native Hawaiian or other Pacific Islander, non-Hispanic/Latino; 0.2% American Indian or Alaska Native, non-Hispanic/Latino; 5% Two or more races, non-Hispanic/Latino; 3% Race/ethnicity unknown; 2% international; 10% transferred in; 15% live on campus.

Freshmen:

Admission: 15,716 applied, 11,495 admitted, 2,968 enrolled. ***Average high school GPA:*** 3.4. ***Test scores:*** SAT evidence-based reading and writing scores over 500: 83%; SAT math scores over 500: 79%; ACT scores over 18: 94%; SAT evidence-based reading and writing scores over 600: 35%; SAT math scores over 600: 31%; ACT scores over 24: 53%; SAT evidence-based reading and writing scores over 700: 5%; SAT math scores over 700: 7%; ACT scores over 30: 14%.

Retention: 79% of full-time freshmen returned.

FACULTY

Total: 1,763, 59% full-time.

Student/faculty ratio: 16:1.

ACADEMICS

Calendar: semesters. *Degrees:* certificates, bachelor's, master's, doctoral, post-master's, and postbachelor's certificates.

Special study options: academic remediation for entering students, accelerated degree program, advanced placement credit, cooperative education, distance learning, double majors, English as a second language, external degree program, freshman honors college, honors programs, independent study, internships, off-campus study, part-time degree program, services for LD students, study abroad, summer session for credit. ***ROTC:*** Army (c), Air Force (c).

Unusual degree programs: 3-2 business administration with Northwest University of Politics and Law (NWUPL); engineering.

Computers: Students can access the following: computer help desk, free student e-mail accounts, online (class) grades, online (class) registration, online (class) schedules. Campuswide network is available. 100% of college-owned or -operated housing units are wired for high-speed Internet access. Wireless service is available via entire campus.

Library: David Adamany Undergraduate Library plus 5 others. *Books:* 1.7 million (physical), 1.1 million (digital/electronic); *Serial titles:* 60,832 (physical), 112,521 (digital/electronic); *Databases:* 700. Weekly public service hours: 138; study areas open 24 hours, 5–7 days a week.

STUDENT LIFE

Housing options: coed. Campus housing is university owned. Freshman applicants given priority for college housing.

Activities and organizations: drama/theater group, student-run newspaper, radio station, choral group, marching band, national fraternities, national sororities.

Athletics Member NCAA. All Division II. ***Intercollegiate sports:*** baseball M(s), basketball M(s)/W(s), cross-country running M(s)/W(s), fencing M(s)/W(s), football M(s), golf M(s)/W(s), lacrosse M(c), soccer M(c)/W(c), softball W(s), swimming and diving M(s)/W(s), tennis M(s)/W(s), track and field W(s), volleyball M(c)/W(s). ***Intramural sports:*** badminton M/W, basketball M/W(c), football M/W, rock climbing M/W, soccer M/W, softball M/W, table tennis M/W, tennis M/W, ultimate Frisbee M/W, volleyball M/W(c).

Campus security: 24-hour emergency response devices and patrols, late-night transport/escort service, controlled dormitory access, VIN etching, bike patrol, safety and defense classes, K-9 unit, victim assistance, confidential tip line.

Student services: health clinic, personal/psychological counseling, legal services, veterans affairs office.

FINANCIAL AID

Financial Aid Of all full-time matriculated undergraduates who enrolled in 2018, 10,619 applied for aid, 9,263 were judged to have need, 396 had their need fully met. In 2018, 2443 non-need-based awards were made. ***Average percent of need met:*** 52. ***Average financial aid package:*** $11,603. ***Average need-based loan:*** $4002. ***Average need-based gift aid:*** $7132. ***Average non-need-based aid:*** $4996. ***Average indebtedness upon graduation:*** $25,095. ***Financial aid deadline:*** 6/30.

APPLYING

Standardized Tests *Required:* SAT or ACT (for admission).

Options: electronic application, early decision, early action.

Application fee: $25.

Required: high school transcript.

Application deadlines: 8/1 (freshmen), 8/15 (transfers), 12/15 (early action).

Notification: 2/15 (early action).

CONTACT

Ms. Ericka M. Jackson, Director of Undergraduate Admissions, Wayne State University, 42 West Warren, Office of Undergraduate Admissions, Detroit 48202. *Phone:* 313-577-2100. *Toll-free phone:* 877-WSU-INFO. *E-mail:* admissions@wayne.edu.

Western Michigan University

Kalamazoo, Michigan

http://www.wmich.edu/

- **State-supported** university, founded 1903
- **Urban** 1289-acre campus
- **Endowment** $386.6 million
- **Coed** 17,760 undergraduate students, 84% full-time, 49% women, 51% men
- **Moderately difficult** entrance level, 81% of applicants were admitted

UNDERGRAD STUDENTS

14,983 full-time, 2,777 part-time. Students come from 43 states and territories; 57 other countries; 13% are from out of state; 12% Black or African American, non-Hispanic/Latino; 7% Hispanic/Latino; 2% Asian, non-Hispanic/Latino; 0.1% Native Hawaiian or other Pacific Islander, non-Hispanic/Latino; 0.5% American Indian or Alaska Native, non-Hispanic/Latino; 4% Two or more races, non-Hispanic/Latino; 1% Race/ethnicity unknown; 5% international; 9% transferred in; 27% live on campus.

Freshmen:
Admission: 17,051 applied, 13,829 admitted, 3,023 enrolled. ***Average high school GPA:*** 3.4. ***Test scores:*** SAT evidence-based reading and writing scores over 500: 78%; SAT math scores over 500: 74%; ACT scores over 18: 97%; SAT evidence-based reading and writing scores over 600: 29%; SAT math scores over 600: 24%; ACT scores over 24: 44%; SAT evidence-based reading and writing scores over 700: 3%; SAT math scores over 700: 4%; ACT scores over 30: 9%.

Retention: 80% of full-time freshmen returned.

FACULTY
Total: 1,463, 65% full-time, 56% with terminal degrees.

Student/faculty ratio: 16:1.

ACADEMICS
Calendar: semesters. *Degrees:* certificates, bachelor's, master's, doctoral, post-master's, and postbachelor's certificates.

Special study options: academic remediation for entering students, accelerated degree program, adult/continuing education programs, advanced placement credit, cooperative education, distance learning, double majors, English as a second language, freshman honors college, honors programs, independent study, internships, off-campus study, part-time degree program, services for LD students, student-designed majors, study abroad, summer session for credit. ***ROTC:*** Army (b).

Computers: 2,250 computers/terminals and 100 ports are available on campus for general student use. Students can access the following: computer help desk, free student e-mail accounts, online (class) grades, online (class) registration, online (class) schedules. Campuswide network is available. 100% of college-owned or -operated housing units are wired for high-speed Internet access. Wireless service is available via entire campus.

Library: Waldo Library plus 4 others. *Books:* 1.8 million (physical), 661,724 (digital/electronic); *Serial titles:* 936 (physical), 80,141 (digital/electronic); *Databases:* 638. Weekly public service hours: 106; students can reserve study rooms.

STUDENT LIFE
Housing options: coed, men-only, women-only, special housing for students with disabilities. Campus housing is university owned. Freshman campus housing is guaranteed.

Activities and organizations: drama/theater group, student-run newspaper, radio station, choral group, marching band, Campus Activities Board, Western Student Association, Young Black Male Support Network, Drive Safe Kalamazoo, Alternative Spring Break, national fraternities, national sororities.

Athletics Member NCAA. All Division I except football (Division I-A). ***Intercollegiate sports:*** baseball M(s), basketball M(s)/W(s), cross-country running W(s), equestrian sports W(c), golf M(c)/W(s), gymnastics W(s), ice hockey M(s), lacrosse M(c)/W(c), racquetball M/W, rock climbing M(c)/W(c), rugby M(c)/W(c), sailing M(c)/W(c), skiing (downhill) M(c)/W(c), soccer M(s)/W(s), softball W(s), swimming and diving M(c)/W(c), tennis M(s)/W(s), track and field W(s), ultimate Frisbee M(c), volleyball M(c)/W(s), water polo M(c)/W(c). ***Intramural sports:*** badminton M/W, basketball M/W, golf M/W, ice hockey M/W, racquetball M/W, rock climbing M/W, sand volleyball M/W, soccer M/W, softball M/W, table tennis M/W, tennis M/W, ultimate Frisbee M/W, volleyball M/W.

Campus security: 24-hour emergency response devices and patrols, student patrols, late-night transport/escort service, controlled dormitory access, residence hall security system, engravers for identification of items, free bicycle registration.

Student services: health clinic, personal/psychological counseling, women's center, veterans affairs office.

COSTS & FINANCIAL AID
Costs (2019–20) ***Tuition:*** state resident $12,094 full-time, $504 per credit hour part-time; nonresident $15,118 full-time, $630 per credit hour part-time. Full-time tuition and fees vary according to course load, location, program, reciprocity agreements, and student level. Part-time tuition and fees vary according to course load, location, program, reciprocity agreements, and student level. ***Required fees:*** $923 full-time, $259 per term part-time. ***Room and board:*** $10,567; room only: $5395. Room and board charges vary according to board plan and housing facility. ***Payment plan:*** installment. ***Waivers:*** senior citizens and employees or children of employees.

Financial Aid Of all full-time matriculated undergraduates who enrolled in 2018, 11,186 applied for aid, 8,915 were judged to have need, 838 had their need fully met. 544 Federal Work-Study jobs (averaging $1876). In 2018, 1401 non-need-based awards were made. ***Average percent of need met:*** 56. ***Average financial aid package:*** $11,650. ***Average need-based loan:*** $4266. ***Average need-based gift aid:*** $9216. ***Average non-need-based aid:*** $5324. ***Average indebtedness upon graduation:*** $35,204.

APPLYING
Standardized Tests *Required:* SAT or ACT (for admission).

Options: electronic application.

Application fee: $40.

Required: high school transcript, minimum 2.5 GPA.

Application deadlines: rolling (freshmen), rolling (transfers).

Notification: continuous (freshmen), continuous (transfers).

CONTACT
Western Michigan University, 1903 West Michigan Avenue, Kalamazoo, MI 49008. *Phone:* 269-387-2000. *E-mail:* ask-wmu@wmich.edu.

Yeshiva Beth Yehuda–Yeshiva Gedolah of Greater Detroit

Oak Park, Michigan

CONTACT
Rabbi P. Rushnawitz, Director, Yeshiva Beth Yehuda–Yeshiva Gedolah of Greater Detroit, 24600 Greenfield, Oak Park, MI 48237-1544.

MINNESOTA

Academy College

Bloomington, Minnesota

http://www.academycollege.edu/

CONTACT
Mr. Andrew Scoblionko, Director of Admissions, Academy College, 1600 W. 82nd Street, Suite 100, Bloomington, MN 55431. *Phone:* 952-851-0066. *Toll-free phone:* 800-292-9149. *Fax:* 952-851-0094. *E-mail:* admissions@academycollege.edu.

Argosy University, Twin Cities

Eagan, Minnesota

http://www.argosy.edu/locations/twin-cities/

CONTACT
Argosy University, Twin Cities, 1515 Central Parkway, Eagan, MN 55121. *Phone:* 651-846-2882. *Toll-free phone:* 888-844-2004.

Augsburg University

Minneapolis, Minnesota

http://www.augsburg.edu/

- **Independent Lutheran** comprehensive, founded 1869
- **Urban** 23-acre campus with easy access to Minneapolis-St. Paul
- **Coed** 2,512 undergraduate students, 87% full-time, 56% women, 44% men
- **Moderately difficult** entrance level, 59% of applicants were admitted

UNDERGRAD STUDENTS
2,178 full-time, 334 part-time. 9% are from out of state; 19% Black or African American, non-Hispanic/Latino; 12% Hispanic/Latino; 10% Asian, non-Hispanic/Latino; 0.1% Native Hawaiian or other Pacific Islander, non-Hispanic/Latino; 0.7% American Indian or Alaska Native,

non-Hispanic/Latino; 6% Two or more races, non-Hispanic/Latino; 6% Race/ethnicity unknown; 3% international; 10% transferred in; 38% live on campus.

Freshmen:
Admission: 3,435 applied, 2,014 admitted, 636 enrolled. ***Average high school GPA:*** 3.2. ***Test scores:*** SAT evidence-based reading and writing scores over 500: 89%; SAT math scores over 500: 89%; ACT scores over 18: 75%; SAT evidence-based reading and writing scores over 600: 56%; SAT math scores over 600: 44%; ACT scores over 24: 24%; SAT math scores over 700: 11%; ACT scores over 30: 4%.

Retention: 72% of full-time freshmen returned.

FACULTY
Total: 399, 44% full-time, 61% with terminal degrees.

Student/faculty ratio: 12:1.

ACADEMICS
Calendar: semesters for undergraduate programs; trimesters for graduate programs and weekend college. *Degrees:* certificates, bachelor's, master's, doctoral, and postbachelor's certificates.

Special study options: academic remediation for entering students, adult/continuing education programs, advanced placement credit, cooperative education, double majors, English as a second language, freshman honors college, honors programs, independent study, internships, off-campus study, part-time degree program, services for LD students, student-designed majors, study abroad, summer session for credit. ***ROTC:*** Army (c), Air Force (c).

Unusual degree programs: 3-2 engineering with Michigan Technological University.

Computers: Students can access the following: campus intranet, computer help desk, free student e-mail accounts, online (class) grades, online (class) registration, online (class) schedules. Campuswide network is available. 100% of college-owned or -operated housing units are wired for high-speed Internet access. Wireless service is available via entire campus.

Library: James G. Lindell Library. Students can reserve study rooms.

STUDENT LIFE
Housing options: coed, special housing for students with disabilities. Campus housing is university owned. Freshman applicants given priority for college housing.

Activities and organizations: drama/theater group, student-run newspaper, radio station, choral group, Pan-Afrikan Student Union, Augsburg Business Organization, Queer Pride Alliance, Students for Racial Justice, Augsburg Asian Student Association.

Athletics Member NCAA. All Division III. ***Intercollegiate sports:*** baseball M, basketball M/W, cross-country running M/W, football M, golf M/W, ice hockey M/W, lacrosse W, soccer M/W, softball W, swimming and diving W, track and field M/W, volleyball W, wrestling M/W. ***Intramural sports:*** basketball M/W, football M, skiing (cross-country) M(c)/W(c), skiing (downhill) M(c)/W(c), softball M/W, volleyball M/W, wrestling M.

Campus security: 24-hour emergency response devices and patrols, student patrols, late-night transport/escort service, controlled dormitory access.

Student services: health clinic, personal/psychological counseling, women's center, veterans affairs office.

COSTS & FINANCIAL AID
Costs (2020–21) ***Comprehensive fee:*** $51,971 includes full-time tuition ($40,376), mandatory fees ($710), and room and board ($10,885). Full-time tuition and fees vary according to class time and location. Part-time tuition: $1228 per credit hour. Part-time tuition and fees vary according to class time and location. ***College room only:*** $5740. Room and board charges vary according to board plan and housing facility. ***Payment plan:*** installment. ***Waivers:*** employees or children of employees.

Financial Aid Of all full-time matriculated undergraduates who enrolled in 2018, 1,719 applied for aid, 1,620 were judged to have need, 180 had their need fully met. In 2018, 341 non-need-based awards were made. ***Average percent of need met:*** 74. ***Average financial aid package:*** $32,507. ***Average need-based loan:*** $4154. ***Average need-based gift aid:*** $26,902. ***Average non-need-based aid:*** $17,864. ***Average indebtedness upon graduation:*** $40,574.

APPLYING
Options: electronic application, deferred entrance.

Required: essay or personal statement, high school transcript, 1 letter of recommendation, letter of recommendation from an academic teacher. ***Recommended:*** minimum 2.8 GPA, interview.

Application deadlines: 8/1 (freshmen), 8/1 (transfers).

Notification: continuous (freshmen), continuous (transfers).

CONTACT
Mr. Devon Ross, Director of Undergraduate and International Admission, Augsburg University, 2211 Riverside Avenue, Minneapolis, MN 55454-1351. *Phone:* 612-330-1001. *Toll-free phone:* 800-788-5678. *E-mail:* ross@augsburg.edu.

Bemidji State University

Bemidji, Minnesota

http://www.bemidjistate.edu/

- **State-supported** comprehensive, founded 1919, part of Minnesota State Colleges and Universities System
- **Small-town** 89-acre campus
- **Coed** 4,476 undergraduate students, 68% full-time, 57% women, 43% men
- **Moderately difficult** entrance level, 65% of applicants were admitted

UNDERGRAD STUDENTS
3,065 full-time, 1,411 part-time. Students come from 45 states and territories; 35 other countries; 11% are from out of state; 3% Black or African American, non-Hispanic/Latino; 3% Hispanic/Latino; 1% Asian, non-Hispanic/Latino; 0.1% Native Hawaiian or other Pacific Islander, non-Hispanic/Latino; 3% American Indian or Alaska Native, non-Hispanic/Latino; 4% Two or more races, non-Hispanic/Latino; 0.9% Race/ethnicity unknown; 2% international; 12% transferred in; 28% live on campus.

Freshmen:
Admission: 3,027 applied, 1,968 admitted, 631 enrolled. ***Average high school GPA:*** 3.3. ***Test scores:*** ACT scores over 18: 87%; ACT scores over 24: 24%; ACT scores over 30: 3%.

Retention: 71% of full-time freshmen returned.

FACULTY
Total: 246, 64% full-time, 53% with terminal degrees.

Student/faculty ratio: 19:1.

ACADEMICS
Calendar: semesters. *Degrees:* certificates, associate, bachelor's, master's, and postbachelor's certificates.

Special study options: academic remediation for entering students, accelerated degree program, adult/continuing education programs, advanced placement credit, cooperative education, distance learning, double majors, English as a second language, external degree program, honors programs, independent study, internships, off-campus study, part-time degree program, services for LD students, student-designed majors, study abroad, summer session for credit.

Computers: Students can access the following: computer help desk, free student e-mail accounts, online (class) grades, online (class) registration, online (class) schedules. Campuswide network is available. Wireless service is available via entire campus.

Library: A. C. Clark Library. Weekly public service hours: 64; students can reserve study rooms.

STUDENT LIFE
Housing options: on-campus residence required for freshman year; coed, special housing for students with disabilities. Campus housing is university owned. Freshman campus housing is guaranteed.

Activities and organizations: student-run newspaper, radio station, choral group.

Athletics Member NCAA. All Division II except men's and women's ice hockey (Division I). ***Intercollegiate sports:*** baseball M(s), basketball M(s)/W(s), cross-country running W(s), football M(s), golf M(s)/W(s), ice hockey M(s)/W(s), soccer W(s), softball W(s), tennis W(s), track and field W(s), volleyball W(s). ***Intramural sports:*** basketball M/W, football M, ice hockey M/W, soccer M/W, softball M/W, volleyball M/W.

Campus security: 24-hour emergency response devices and patrols, late-night transport/escort service, controlled dormitory access.

Student services: health clinic, personal/psychological counseling, veterans affairs office.

COSTS & FINANCIAL AID

Costs (2020–21) ***Tuition:*** area resident $3929 full-time, $274 per credit part-time; state resident $3929 full-time, $274 per credit part-time; nonresident $3929 full-time, $274 per credit part-time. ***Required fees:*** $370 full-time. ***Room and board:*** $8660.

Financial Aid Of all full-time matriculated undergraduates who enrolled in 2018, 2,684 applied for aid, 2,028 were judged to have need, 331 had their need fully met. 233 Federal Work-Study jobs (averaging $1680). 249 state and other part-time jobs (averaging $1705). In 2018, 595 non-need-based awards were made. ***Average percent of need met:*** 60. ***Average financial aid package:*** $9725. ***Average need-based loan:*** $3779. ***Average need-based gift aid:*** $6082. ***Average non-need-based aid:*** $10,333.

APPLYING

Standardized Tests *Required:* SAT or ACT (for admission).

Options: electronic application, early action, deferred entrance.

Application fee: $20.

Required: high school transcript. ***Required for some:*** essay or personal statement, interview.

CONTACT

Bemidji State University, 1500 Birchmont Drive, NE, Bemidji, MN 56601-2699. *Phone:* 218-755-2175. *Toll-free phone:* 800-475-2001.

Bethany Global University

Bloomington, Minnesota

http://www.bethanygu.edu/

- **Independent Christian** comprehensive, founded 1948
- **Suburban** 32-acre campus with easy access to Minneapolis, MN
- **Coed** 317 undergraduate students, 97% full-time, 75% women, 25% men
- **Moderately difficult** entrance level, 92% of applicants were admitted

UNDERGRAD STUDENTS

306 full-time, 11 part-time. Students come from 41 states and territories; 5 other countries; 90% are from out of state; 3% Black or African American, non-Hispanic/Latino; 0.3% Hispanic/Latino; 0.3% Asian, non-Hispanic/Latino; 4% Two or more races, non-Hispanic/Latino; 9% Race/ethnicity unknown; 3% international; 20% transferred in; 71% live on campus.

Freshmen:

Admission: 209 applied, 192 admitted, 71 enrolled. ***Average high school GPA:*** 3.4.

Retention: 72% of full-time freshmen returned.

ACADEMICS

Degrees: certificates, associate, bachelor's, and master's.

Computers: Students can access the following: free student e-mail accounts, online (class) grades, online (class) registration, online (class) schedules. Campuswide network is available.

STUDENT LIFE

Housing options: on-campus residence required through sophomore year; men-only, women-only. Campus housing is university owned. Freshman campus housing is guaranteed.

COSTS

Costs (2020–21) ***One-time required fee:*** $350. ***Comprehensive fee:*** $23,700 includes full-time tuition ($13,500), mandatory fees ($1950), and room and board ($8250). Full-time tuition and fees vary according to student level. Part-time tuition and fees vary according to student level. ***College room only:*** $6910. ***Payment plan:*** installment. ***Waivers:*** employees or children of employees.

APPLYING

Options: electronic application.

Required: essay or personal statement, high school transcript, minimum 2.0 GPA, Personal History, Pastoral reference, & Personal Reference.

Application deadlines: 7/31 (freshmen), 7/31 (out-of-state freshmen), 7/31 (transfers).

Notification: continuous (freshmen), continuous (out-of-state freshmen), continuous (transfers).

CONTACT

Ms. Malaina Kirschner, Associate Director of Recruitment, Bethany Global University, 6820 Auto Club Road Suite C, Bloomington, MN 55438. *Phone:* 952-918-1893. *Toll-free phone:* 800-323-3417. *Fax:* 952-829-2765. *E-mail:* malaina.kirschner@bethanygu.edu.

Bethany Lutheran College

Mankato, Minnesota

http://www.blc.edu/

- **Independent Lutheran** 4-year, founded 1927
- **Small-town** 50-acre campus with easy access to Minneapolis-St. Paul
- **Endowment** $44.1 million
- **Coed** 741 undergraduate students, 80% full-time, 55% women, 45% men
- **Moderately difficult** entrance level, 73% of applicants were admitted

UNDERGRAD STUDENTS

591 full-time, 150 part-time. Students come from 23 states and territories; 21 other countries; 27% are from out of state; 3% Black or African American, non-Hispanic/Latino; 5% Hispanic/Latino; 2% Asian, non-Hispanic/Latino; 0.2% Native Hawaiian or other Pacific Islander, non-Hispanic/Latino; 0.3% American Indian or Alaska Native, non-Hispanic/Latino; 3% Two or more races, non-Hispanic/Latino; 1% Race/ethnicity unknown; 14% international; 5% transferred in; 71% live on campus.

Freshmen:

Admission: 636 applied, 462 admitted, 179 enrolled. ***Average high school GPA:*** 3.4. ***Test scores:*** SAT evidence-based reading and writing scores over 500: 74%; SAT math scores over 500: 74%; ACT scores over 18: 96%; SAT evidence-based reading and writing scores over 600: 16%; SAT math scores over 600: 16%; ACT scores over 24: 47%; SAT math scores over 700: 5%; ACT scores over 30: 10%.

Retention: 71% of full-time freshmen returned.

FACULTY

Total: 68, 62% full-time, 32% with terminal degrees.

Student/faculty ratio: 11:1.

ACADEMICS

Calendar: semesters. *Degree:* certificates and bachelor's.

Special study options: academic remediation for entering students, adult/continuing education programs, advanced placement credit, cooperative education, distance learning, double majors, English as a second language, independent study, services for LD students, study abroad, summer session for credit. ***ROTC:*** Army (c).

Computers: 100 computers/terminals and 400 ports are available on campus for general student use. Students can access the following: campus intranet, computer help desk, free student e-mail accounts, online (class) grades, online (class) registration, online (class) schedules. Campuswide network is available. 100% of college-owned or -operated housing units are wired for high-speed Internet access. Wireless service is available via entire campus.

Library: Memorial Library plus 1 other. *Books:* 66,250 (physical), 28,121 (digital/electronic); *Serial titles:* 651 (physical), 30,000 (digital/electronic); *Databases:* 89. Weekly public service hours: 88.

STUDENT LIFE

Housing options: on-campus residence required through sophomore year; men-only, women-only. Campus housing is university owned. Freshman campus housing is guaranteed.

Activities and organizations: drama/theater group, student-run newspaper, choral group, Bethany Activities Committee, Student Senate, Scholastic Leadership Society, PAMA (Promoting Awareness, spurring Motivation, and encouraging Action), Bethany Society of Royal Scientists.

Athletics Member NCAA. All Division III except golf (Division II). ***Intercollegiate sports:*** baseball M, basketball M/W, cross-country running M/W, golf M/W, soccer M/W, softball W, tennis M/W, track and field M/W, volleyball W. ***Intramural sports:*** basketball M/W, football M/W, racquetball M/W, sand volleyball M/W, soccer M/W, volleyball M/W.

Campus security: 24-hour emergency response devices and patrols, late-night transport/escort service, controlled dormitory access.

Student services: health clinic, personal/psychological counseling.

COSTS & FINANCIAL AID

Costs (2020–21) ***One-time required fee:*** $130. ***Comprehensive fee:*** $36,530 includes full-time tuition ($27,700), mandatory fees ($680), and room and board ($8150). Full-time tuition and fees vary according to course load. Part-time tuition: $1170 per credit hour. Part-time tuition and fees vary according to course load. ***Required fees:*** $340 per term part-time. ***Room and board:*** Room and board charges vary according to board plan and housing facility. ***Payment plan:*** installment. ***Waivers:*** senior citizens and employees or children of employees.

Financial Aid Of all full-time matriculated undergraduates who enrolled in 2018, 485 applied for aid, 445 were judged to have need, 96 had their need fully met. 29 Federal Work-Study jobs (averaging $1632). 299 state and other part-time jobs (averaging $1162). In 2018, 79 non-need-based awards were made. ***Average percent of need met:*** 85. ***Average financial aid package:*** $23,183. ***Average need-based loan:*** $4522. ***Average need-based gift aid:*** $19,208. ***Average non-need-based aid:*** $10,584. ***Average indebtedness upon graduation:*** $32,152.

APPLYING

Standardized Tests *Required:* SAT or ACT (for admission).

Options: electronic application, deferred entrance.

Required: high school transcript, minimum 2.4 GPA. ***Required for some:*** letters of recommendation, interview. ***Recommended:*** essay or personal statement, minimum 3.2 GPA, interview.

Application deadlines: 7/1 (freshmen), 7/1 (out-of-state freshmen), 7/1 (transfers).

Notification: continuous (freshmen), continuous (out-of-state freshmen), continuous (transfers).

CONTACT

Mr. Jeffrey Lemke, Vice President of Admissions and Enrollment Management, Bethany Lutheran College, 700 Luther Drive, Mankato, MN 56001. *Phone:* 507-344-7000 Ext. 373. *Toll-free phone:* 800-944-3066. *Fax:* 507-344-7376. *E-mail:* jeff.lemke@blc.edu.

Bethel University

St. Paul, Minnesota

http://www.bethel.edu/

- **Independent** comprehensive, founded 1871, affiliated with Baptist General Conference
- **Suburban** 289-acre campus with easy access to Minneapolis-St. Paul
- **Endowment** $50.7 million
- **Coed** 2,799 undergraduate students, 83% full-time, 63% women, 37% men
- **Moderately difficult** entrance level, 79% of applicants were admitted

UNDERGRAD STUDENTS

2,327 full-time, 472 part-time. Students come from 36 states and territories; 10 other countries; 19% are from out of state; 4% Black or African American, non-Hispanic/Latino; 5% Hispanic/Latino; 5% Asian, non-Hispanic/Latino; 0.1% Native Hawaiian or other Pacific Islander, non-Hispanic/Latino; 0.4% American Indian or Alaska Native, non-Hispanic/Latino; 4% Two or more races, non-Hispanic/Latino; 2% Race/ethnicity unknown; 0.5% international; 3% transferred in; 66% live on campus.

Freshmen:

Admission: 2,435 applied, 1,912 admitted, 590 enrolled. ***Average high school GPA:*** 3.6. ***Test scores:*** ACT scores over 18: 96%; ACT scores over 24: 53%; ACT scores over 30: 13%.

Retention: 83% of full-time freshmen returned.

FACULTY

Total: 291, 57% full-time, 64% with terminal degrees.

Student/faculty ratio: 11:1.

ACADEMICS

Calendar: 4-1-4. *Degrees:* associate, bachelor's, master's, doctoral, post-master's, and postbachelor's certificates.

Special study options: academic remediation for entering students, adult/continuing education programs, advanced placement credit, distance learning, double majors, honors programs, independent study, internships, off-campus study, part-time degree program, services for LD students, student-designed majors, study abroad, summer session for credit. ***ROTC:*** Army (c), Air Force (c).

Computers: 203 computers/terminals are available on campus for general student use. Students can access the following: campus intranet, computer help desk, free student e-mail accounts, online (class) grades, online (class) registration, online (class) schedules. Campuswide network is available. 100% of college owned or operated housing units are wired for high-speed Internet access. Wireless service is available via entire campus.

Library: Bethel University Library plus 1 other. *Books:* 191,618 (physical), 227,695 (digital/electronic); *Serial titles:* 568 (physical), 55,194 (digital/electronic); *Databases:* 126. Weekly public service hours: 96; students can reserve study rooms.

STUDENT LIFE

Housing options: on-campus residence required through sophomore year; special housing for students with disabilities. Campus housing is university owned. Freshman campus housing is guaranteed.

Activities and organizations: drama/theater group, student-run newspaper, radio station, choral group, Bethel Student Government, Bethel Business and Economics Association, Bethel Rec Sports, Welcome Week.

Athletics Member NCAA. All Division III. ***Intercollegiate sports:*** baseball M, basketball M/W, cross-country running M/W, football M, golf M/W, ice hockey M/W, soccer M/W, softball W, tennis M/W, track and field M/W, volleyball M(c)/W. ***Intramural sports:*** basketball M/W, football M, lacrosse M(c)/W(c), rugby M(c), volleyball M(c)/W.

Campus security: 24-hour emergency response devices and patrols, student patrols, late-night transport/escort service, controlled dormitory access, video surveillance for residence halls, academic buildings, and parking lots.

Student services: health clinic, personal/psychological counseling.

COSTS & FINANCIAL AID

Costs (2020–21) ***Comprehensive fee:*** $49,990 includes full-time tuition ($38,870), mandatory fees ($160), and room and board ($10,960). Part-time tuition: $1620 per credit. ***College room only:*** $5900. Room and board charges vary according to board plan. ***Payment plan:*** tuition prepayment. ***Waivers:*** employees or children of employees.

Financial Aid Of all full-time matriculated undergraduates who enrolled in 2018, 1,978 applied for aid, 1,699 were judged to have need, 361 had their need fully met. In 2018, 519 non-need-based awards were made. ***Average percent of need met:*** 83. ***Average financial aid package:*** $30,734. ***Average need-based loan:*** $3909. ***Average need-based gift aid:*** $24,362. ***Average non-need-based aid:*** $15,382. ***Average indebtedness upon graduation:*** $37,883.

APPLYING

Standardized Tests *Required:* SAT or ACT (for admission).

Options: electronic application, early admission.

Required: essay or personal statement, high school transcript, rank in upper 50% of high school class. ***Required for some:*** 2 letters of recommendation. ***Recommended:*** minimum 2.5 GPA, interview.

Application deadlines: rolling (freshmen), rolling (transfers).

Notification: continuous (freshmen), continuous (transfers).

CONTACT

Bethel University, 3900 Bethel Drive, St. Paul, MN 55112-6999. *Phone:* 651-638-6242. *Toll-free phone:* 800-255-8706 Ext. 6242.

Bethlehem College & Seminary

Minneapolis, Minnesota

http://www.bcsmn.edu/

CONTACT

Bethlehem College & Seminary, 720 13th Avenue South, Minneapolis, MN 55415.

Capella University
Minneapolis, Minnesota
http://www.capella.edu/

- **Proprietary** upper-level, founded 1993
- **Urban** campus
- **Coed**
- **Minimally difficult** entrance level

ACADEMICS
Calendar: quarters. *Degrees:* certificates, bachelor's, master's, doctoral, post-master's, and postbachelor's certificates (offers only distance learning degree programs).
Library: Capella University Library.

FINANCIAL AID
Financial Aid ***Average percent of need met:*** 90. ***Average financial aid package:*** $10,500. ***Average indebtedness upon graduation:*** $8000.

APPLYING
Options: electronic application.

Application fee: $50.

CONTACT
Enrollment Services, Capella University, 225 South Sixth Street, Capella Tower, 9th Floor, Minneapolis, MN 55402. *Phone:* 866-283-7921. *Toll-free phone:* 866-283-7921. *Fax:* 612-977-5060. *E-mail:* info@capella.edu.

Carleton College
Northfield, Minnesota
http://www.carleton.edu/

- **Independent** 4-year, founded 1866
- **Small-town** 955-acre campus with easy access to Minneapolis-St. Paul
- **Endowment** $828.2 million
- **Coed** 2,097 undergraduate students, 99% full-time, 50% women, 50% men
- **Very difficult** entrance level, 20% of applicants were admitted

UNDERGRAD STUDENTS
2,077 full-time, 20 part-time. Students come from 50 states and territories; 42 other countries; 84% are from out of state; 0.4% transferred in; 96% live on campus.

Freshmen:
Admission: 7,092 applied, 1,407 admitted, 529 enrolled.

Retention: 97% of full-time freshmen returned.

ACADEMICS
Calendar: 3 courses for each of three terms. *Degree:* bachelor's.

Special study options: accelerated degree program, advanced placement credit, double majors, independent study, internships, off-campus study, services for LD students, student-designed majors, study abroad.

Unusual degree programs: 3-2 engineering with Columbia University.

Computers: 250 computers/terminals and 220 ports are available on campus for general student use. Students can access the following: campus intranet, computer help desk, free student e-mail accounts, online (class) grades, online (class) registration, online (class) schedules. Campuswide network is available. 100% of college-owned or -operated housing units are wired for high-speed Internet access. Wireless service is available via entire campus.
Library: Laurence McKinley Gould Library plus 1 other. Weekly public service hours: 118.

STUDENT LIFE
Housing options: on-campus residence required through senior year; coed, cooperative, special housing for students with disabilities. Campus housing is university owned. Freshman campus housing is guaranteed.

Activities and organizations: drama/theater group, student-run newspaper, radio station, choral group, CANOE (Carleton Association of Nature and Outdoor Enthusiasts), Farm Club, Ebony II, WHIMS (Women in Math and Science), Amnesty International.

Athletics ***Intercollegiate sports:*** badminton M(c)/W(c), baseball M, basketball M/W, cross-country running M/W, equestrian sports M(c)/W(c), fencing M(c)/W(c), field hockey W(c), football M, golf M/W, ice hockey M(c)/W(c), lacrosse M(c)/W(c), rugby M(c)/W(c), sailing M(c)/W(c), skiing (cross-country) M(c)/W(c), skiing (downhill) M(c)/W(c), soccer M/W, softball W, swimming and diving M/W, table tennis M(c)/W(c), tennis M/W, track and field M/W, ultimate Frisbee M(c)/W(c), volleyball M(c)/W, water polo M(c)/W(c). ***Intramural sports:*** badminton M/W, basketball M/W, soccer M/W, softball M/W, table tennis M/W, tennis M/W, ultimate Frisbee M/W, volleyball M/W.

Campus security: 24-hour emergency response devices and patrols, student patrols, late-night transport/escort service, controlled dormitory access, Emergency Notification Service (cell phone text and email alerts).

Student services: health clinic, personal/psychological counseling, women's center.

COSTS & FINANCIAL AID
Costs (2019–20) ***Comprehensive fee:*** $71,769 includes full-time tuition ($56,778), mandatory fees ($333), and room and board ($14,658). ***College room only:*** $7704.

Financial Aid Of all full-time matriculated undergraduates who enrolled in 2018, 1,266 applied for aid, 1,152 were judged to have need, 1,152 had their need fully met. 418 Federal Work-Study jobs (averaging $2697). 1,308 state and other part-time jobs (averaging $2723). In 2018, 73 non-need based awards were made. ***Average percent of need met:*** 100. ***Average financial aid package:*** $51,761. ***Average need-based loan:*** $5257. ***Average need-based gift aid:*** $44,774. ***Average non-need-based aid:*** $3104. ***Average indebtedness upon graduation:*** $19,405.

APPLYING
Standardized Tests *Required:* SAT or ACT (for admission). *Recommended:* SAT Subject Tests (for admission).

Options: electronic application, early admission, early decision, deferred entrance.

Application fee: $30.

Required: essay or personal statement, high school transcript, 2 letters of recommendation, Common Application Supplement. ***Recommended:*** interview.

Application deadlines: 1/15 (freshmen), 3/31 (transfers).

Early decision deadline: 11/15 (for plan 1), 1/15 (for plan 2).

Notification: 3/31 (freshmen), 5/15 (transfers), 12/15 (early decision plan 1), 2/15 (early decision plan 2).

CONTACT
Carleton College, One North College Street, Northfield, MN 55057-4001. *Phone:* 507-222-4190. *Toll-free phone:* 800-995-2275.

College of Saint Benedict
Saint Joseph, Minnesota
http://www.csbsju.edu/

- **Independent Roman Catholic** 4-year, founded 1913
- **Small-town** 300-acre campus with easy access to Minneapolis-St. Paul
- **Endowment** $83.5 million
- **Women only** 1,748 undergraduate students, 99% full-time
- **Moderately difficult** entrance level, 80% of applicants were admitted

UNDERGRAD STUDENTS
1,731 full-time, 17 part-time. Students come from 31 states and territories; 10 other countries; 16% are from out of state; 3% Black or African American, non-Hispanic/Latino; 9% Hispanic/Latino; 5% Asian, non-Hispanic/Latino; 0.1% Native Hawaiian or other Pacific Islander, non-Hispanic/Latino; 0.7% American Indian or Alaska Native, non-Hispanic/Latino; 3% international; 0.9% transferred in; 93% live on campus.

Freshmen:
Admission: 2,052 applied, 1,651 admitted, 439 enrolled. ***Average high school GPA:*** 3.6. ***Test scores:*** SAT evidence-based reading and writing scores over 500: 81%; SAT math scores over 500: 65%; ACT scores over 18: 98%; SAT evidence-based reading and writing scores over 600: 24%; SAT math scores over 600: 21%; ACT scores over 24: 60%; SAT math scores over 700: 2%; ACT scores over 30: 16%.

Retention: 85% of full-time freshmen returned.

FACULTY
Total: 169, 84% full-time, 78% with terminal degrees.

Student/faculty ratio: 11:1.

ACADEMICS

Calendar: semesters. *Degrees:* bachelor's (coordinate with Saint John's University for men).

Special study options: advanced placement credit, double majors, English as a second language, honors programs, independent study, internships, off-campus study, services for LD students, student-designed majors, study abroad. ***ROTC:*** Army (c).

Computers: 248 computers/terminals and 4,600 ports are available on campus for general student use. Students can access the following: campus intranet, computer help desk, free student e-mail accounts, online (class) grades, online (class) registration, online (class) schedules, online student accounts. Campuswide network is available. 100% of college-owned or -operated housing units are wired for high-speed Internet access. Wireless service is available via entire campus.

Library: Clemens Library plus 2 others. *Books:* 527,784 (physical), 1.1 million (digital/electronic); *Serial titles:* 737 (physical), 49,092 (digital/electronic); *Databases:* 211. Weekly public service hours: 104; students can reserve study rooms.

STUDENT LIFE

Housing options: on-campus residence required through senior year; women-only, special housing for students with disabilities. Campus housing is university owned. Freshman campus housing is guaranteed.

Activities and organizations: drama/theater group, student-run newspaper, radio and television station, choral group, Joint Events Council, Outdoor Leadership Center, Magis Ministries, Enactus, Archipelago Caribbean Association.

Athletics Member NCAA. All Division III. ***Intercollegiate sports:*** basketball W, crew W(c), cross-country running W, golf W, ice hockey W, lacrosse W(c), rugby W(c), skiing (cross-country) W(c), soccer W, softball W, swimming and diving W, tennis W, track and field W, ultimate Frisbee W(c), volleyball W. ***Intramural sports:*** badminton W, basketball W, football W, racquetball W, soccer W, softball W, tennis W, volleyball W.

Campus security: 24-hour emergency response devices and patrols, student patrols, late-night transport/escort service, controlled dormitory access.

Student services: health clinic, personal/psychological counseling, women's center.

COSTS & FINANCIAL AID

Costs (2020–21) ***Comprehensive fee:*** $59,788 includes full-time tuition ($47,330), mandatory fees ($1112), and room and board ($11,346). Part-time tuition: $1905 per credit hour. Part-time tuition and fees vary according to course load. ***College room only:*** $5630. Room and board charges vary according to board plan and housing facility. ***Payment plans:*** tuition prepayment, installment. ***Waivers:*** employees or children of employees.

Financial Aid Of all full-time matriculated undergraduates who enrolled in 2019, 1,441 applied for aid, 1,258 were judged to have need, 424 had their need fully met. 273 Federal Work-Study jobs (averaging $2827). 1,023 state and other part-time jobs (averaging $2959). In 2019, 442 non-need-based awards were made. ***Average percent of need met:*** 89. ***Average financial aid package:*** $38,360. ***Average need-based loan:*** $4446. ***Average need-based gift aid:*** $32,636. ***Average non-need-based aid:*** $21,784. ***Average indebtedness upon graduation:*** $43,615.

APPLYING

Standardized Tests *Required:* SAT or ACT (for admission).

Options: electronic application, early action, deferred entrance.

Required: high school transcript, college preparatory program. ***Recommended:*** minimum 3.0 GPA.

Application deadlines: rolling (transfers), 12/15 (early action).

Notification: continuous until 10/1 (freshmen), continuous (transfers), 1/15 (early action).

CONTACT

Ms. Karen Backes, Dean of Admissions, College of Saint Benedict, PO Box 7155, Collegeville, MN 56321-7155. *Phone:* 320-363-5055. *Toll-free phone:* 800-544-1489. *Fax:* 320-363-5650. *E-mail:* admissions@csbsju.edu.

The College of St. Scholastica

Duluth, Minnesota

http://www.css.edu/

- **Independent** comprehensive, founded 1912, affiliated with Roman Catholic Church
- **Suburban** 186-acre campus
- **Endowment** $92.6 million
- **Coed** 2,482 undergraduate students, 83% full-time, 71% women, 29% men
- **Moderately difficult** entrance level, 76% of applicants were admitted

UNDERGRAD STUDENTS

2,062 full-time, 420 part-time. Students come from 37 states and territories; 19 other countries; 12% are from out of state; 3% Black or African American, non-Hispanic/Latino; 4% Hispanic/Latino; 3% Asian, non-Hispanic/Latino; 1% American Indian or Alaska Native, non-Hispanic/Latino; 3% Two or more races, non-Hispanic/Latino; 0.7% Race/ethnicity unknown; 2% international; 17% transferred in; 49% live on campus.

Freshmen:

Admission: 1,956 applied, 1,494 admitted, 450 enrolled. ***Average high school GPA:*** 3.5. ***Test scores:*** ACT scores over 18: 99%; ACT scores over 24: 60%; ACT scores over 30: 10%.

Retention: 81% of full-time freshmen returned.

FACULTY

Total: 403, 53% full-time, 51% with terminal degrees.

Student/faculty ratio: 14:1.

ACADEMICS

Calendar: semesters. *Degrees:* certificates, bachelor's, master's, doctoral, post-master's, and postbachelor's certificates.

Special study options: accelerated degree program, adult/continuing education programs, advanced placement credit, distance learning, double majors, honors programs, independent study, internships, off-campus study, part-time degree program, services for LD students, student-designed majors, study abroad, summer session for credit. ***ROTC:*** Air Force (c).

Unusual degree programs: 3-2 occupational therapy.

Computers: 614 computers/terminals are available on campus for general student use. Students can access the following: campus intranet, computer help desk, free student e-mail accounts, online (class) grades, online (class) registration, online (class) schedules, student account information, transcripts. Campuswide network is available. 100% of college-owned or -operated housing units are wired for high-speed Internet access. Wireless service is available via entire campus.

Library: College of St. Scholastica Library. *Books:* 111,707 (physical), 10,470 (digital/electronic); *Serial titles:* 112 (physical), 211 (digital/electronic); *Databases:* 173. Weekly public service hours: 91; students can reserve study rooms.

STUDENT LIFE

Housing options: on-campus residence required through sophomore year; coed, special housing for students with disabilities. Campus housing is university owned. Freshman applicants given priority for college housing.

Activities and organizations: drama/theater group, student-run newspaper, choral group, Campus Activity Board, Inter-Varsity, Habitat for Humanity, SHIMA, Volunteers Involved Through Action.

Athletics Member NCAA. All Division III except golf (Division II). ***Intercollegiate sports:*** baseball M, basketball M/W, cross-country running M/W, football M, golf M/W, ice hockey M/W, skiing (cross-country) M/W, soccer M/W, softball W, tennis M/W, track and field M/W, volleyball W. ***Intramural sports:*** badminton M/W, basketball M/W, bowling M/W, cheerleading W(c), football M/W, rugby M(c)/W(c), skiing (cross-country) M(c)/W(c), soccer M/W, softball M/W, swimming and diving M(c)/W(c), tennis M/W, volleyball M/W.

Campus security: 24-hour emergency response devices and patrols, late-night transport/escort service, controlled dormitory access, student door monitor at night.

Student services: health clinic, personal/psychological counseling, veterans affairs office.

COSTS & FINANCIAL AID
Costs (2020–21) ***Comprehensive fee:*** $49,750 includes full-time tuition ($38,750), mandatory fees ($660), and room and board ($10,340). Part-time tuition: $1215 per credit. ***College room only:*** $5742. Room and board charges vary according to housing facility. ***Payment plan:*** installment.

Financial Aid Of all full-time matriculated undergraduates who enrolled in 2019, 1,822 applied for aid, 1,635 were judged to have need, 397 had their need fully met. In 2019, 365 non-need-based awards were made. ***Average percent of need met:*** 73. ***Average financial aid package:*** $27,478. ***Average need-based loan:*** $4452. ***Average need-based gift aid:*** $7826. ***Average non-need-based aid:*** $20,311. ***Average indebtedness upon graduation:*** $41,577.

APPLYING
Options: electronic application, early action, deferred entrance.

Required: high school transcript. ***Required for some:*** essay or personal statement.

Application deadlines: rolling (freshmen), rolling (transfers).

Notification: continuous (freshmen), continuous (transfers).

CONTACT
Brenda Panger, Associate Director, The College of St. Scholastica, 1200 Kenwood Avenue, Duluth, MN 55811-4199. *Phone:* 218-723-6067. *Toll-free phone:* 800-249-6412. *E-mail:* bpanger@css.edu.

Concordia College

Moorhead, Minnesota

http://www.concordiacollege.edu/

- **Independent** comprehensive, founded 1891, affiliated with Evangelical Lutheran Church in America
- **Suburban** 113-acre campus
- **Endowment** $129.0 million
- **Coed** 2,010 undergraduate students, 97% full-time, 58% women, 42% men
- **Moderately difficult** entrance level, 68% of applicants were admitted

UNDERGRAD STUDENTS
1,956 full-time, 54 part-time. Students come from 27 states and territories; 34 other countries; 29% are from out of state; 3% Black or African American, non-Hispanic/Latino; 3% Hispanic/Latino; 2% Asian, non-Hispanic/Latino; 0.1% Native Hawaiian or other Pacific Islander, non-Hispanic/Latino; 0.6% American Indian or Alaska Native, non-Hispanic/Latino; 2% Two or more races, non-Hispanic/Latino; 4% Race/ethnicity unknown; 4% international; 1% transferred in; 57% live on campus.

Freshmen:
Admission: 3,395 applied, 2,321 admitted, 517 enrolled. ***Average high school GPA:*** 3.6. ***Test scores:*** SAT evidence-based reading and writing scores over 500: 72%; SAT math scores over 500: 72%; ACT scores over 18: 93%; SAT evidence-based reading and writing scores over 600: 39%; SAT math scores over 600: 44%; ACT scores over 24: 53%; SAT evidence-based reading and writing scores over 700: 11%; SAT math scores over 700: 22%; ACT scores over 30: 11%.

Retention: 80% of full-time freshmen returned.

FACULTY
Total: 210, 77% full-time, 76% with terminal degrees.

Student/faculty ratio: 11:1.

ACADEMICS
Calendar: semesters. *Degrees:* bachelor's and master's.

Special study options: accelerated degree program, advanced placement credit, cooperative education, distance learning, double majors, English as a second language, independent study, internships, off-campus study, services for LD students, student-designed majors, study abroad, summer session for credit. ***ROTC:*** Army (c), Air Force (c).

Computers: 506 computers/terminals and 87 ports are available on campus for general student use. Students can access the following: campus intranet, computer help desk, free student e-mail accounts, online (class) grades, online (class) registration, online (class) schedules, online degree audit. Campuswide network is available. 100% of college-owned or -operated housing units are wired for high-speed Internet access. Wireless service is available via entire campus.

Library: Carl B. Ylvisaker Library. *Books:* 230,778 (physical), 221,444 (digital/electronic); *Serial titles:* 1,306 (physical), 60,025 (digital/electronic); *Databases:* 145. Weekly public service hours: 93; students can reserve study rooms.

STUDENT LIFE
Housing options: on-campus residence required through sophomore year; coed. Campus housing is university owned. Freshman campus housing is guaranteed.

Activities and organizations: drama/theater group, student-run newspaper, radio and television station, choral group, Campus Entertainment Commission, Habitat for Humanity, Dance Marathon, Student Government Association, Campus Ministry Commission.

Athletics Member NCAA. All Division III. ***Intercollegiate sports:*** baseball M, basketball M/W, cross-country running M/W, football M, golf M/W, ice hockey M/W, soccer M/W, softball W, swimming and diving W, tennis M/W, track and field M/W, volleyball W, wrestling M. ***Intramural sports:*** basketball M/W, cheerleading M(c)/W(c), ice hockey M(c)/W(c), lacrosse M/W(c), rugby W(c), skiing (cross-country) M(c)/W(c), skiing (downhill) M(c)/W(c), soccer M(c)/W(c), ultimate Frisbee M(c)/W(c), volleyball M/W.

Campus security: 24-hour emergency response devices and patrols, controlled dormitory access, well-lighted campus; outdoor campus emergency phones.

Student services: personal/psychological counseling.

COSTS & FINANCIAL AID
Costs (2020–21) ***Comprehensive fee:*** $50,176 includes full-time tuition ($41,150), mandatory fees ($416), and room and board ($8610). Full-time tuition and fees vary according to course load. Part-time tuition: $1545 per credit hour. ***College room only:*** $3740. Room and board charges vary according to board plan and housing facility. ***Payment plan:*** installment. ***Waivers:*** employees or children of employees.

Financial Aid Of all full-time matriculated undergraduates who enrolled in 2018, 1,707 applied for aid, 1,497 were judged to have need, 337 had their need fully met. In 2018, 496 non-need-based awards were made. ***Average percent of need met:*** 89. ***Average financial aid package:*** $32,140. ***Average need-based loan:*** $4239. ***Average need-based gift aid:*** $25,284. ***Average non-need-based aid:*** $18,683.

APPLYING
Standardized Tests *Required:* SAT or ACT (for admission).

Options: electronic application, deferred entrance.

Required: high school transcript. ***Required for some:*** Test scores ACT/SAT. ***Recommended:*** Test scores ACT/SAT.

Application deadlines: rolling (freshmen), rolling (out-of-state freshmen), rolling (transfers).

Notification: continuous (freshmen), continuous (out-of-state freshmen), continuous (transfers).

CONTACT
Mr. Mike Vandenberg, Director of Recruitment, Concordia College, 901 8th Street South, Moorhead, MN 56562. *Phone:* 218-299-3004. *Toll-free phone:* 800-699-9897. *Fax:* 218-299-4720. *E-mail:* mikev@cord.edu.

Concordia University, St. Paul

St. Paul, Minnesota

http://www.csp.edu/

- **Independent** comprehensive, founded 1893, affiliated with Lutheran Church–Missouri Synod
- **Urban** 37-acre campus with easy access to Minneapolis-St. Paul
- **Endowment** $49.9 million
- **Coed** 3,127 undergraduate students, 57% full-time, 62% women, 38% men
- **Minimally difficult** entrance level, 98% of applicants were admitted

UNDERGRAD STUDENTS
1,786 full-time, 1,341 part-time. Students come from 49 states and territories; 18 other countries; 21% are from out of state; 12% Black or African American, non-Hispanic/Latino; 7% Hispanic/Latino; 10% Asian, non-Hispanic/Latino; 0.3% Native Hawaiian or other Pacific Islander,

non-Hispanic/Latino; 0.4% American Indian or Alaska Native, non-Hispanic/Latino; 4% Two or more races, non-Hispanic/Latino; 3% Race/ethnicity unknown; 4% international; 18% transferred in; 16% live on campus.

Freshmen:
Admission: 1,323 applied, 1,297 admitted, 351 enrolled. ***Average high school GPA:*** 3.2.

Retention: 64% of full-time freshmen returned.

FACULTY
Total: 439, 23% full-time, 37% with terminal degrees.

Student/faculty ratio: 18:1.

ACADEMICS
Calendar: semesters. *Degrees:* certificates, associate, bachelor's, master's, doctoral, post-master's, and postbachelor's certificates.

Special study options: academic remediation for entering students, accelerated degree program, adult/continuing education programs, advanced placement credit, distance learning, double majors, independent study, internships, off-campus study, part-time degree program, services for LD students, student-designed majors, study abroad, summer session for credit. ***ROTC:*** Army (c), Air Force (c).

Unusual degree programs: 3-2 exercise science.

Computers: 10 computers/terminals and 180 ports are available on campus for general student use. Students can access the following: campus intranet, computer help desk, free student e-mail accounts, online (class) grades, online (class) registration, online (class) schedules. Campuswide network is available. 100% of college-owned or -operated housing units are wired for high-speed Internet access. Wireless service is available via entire campus.

Library: Library Technology Center. *Books:* 84,956 (physical), 218,505 (digital/electronic); *Serial titles:* 622 (physical), 40,440 (digital/electronic); *Databases:* 160. Weekly public service hours: 74; students can reserve study rooms.

STUDENT LIFE
Housing options: coed, men-only, women-only, special housing for students with disabilities. Campus housing is university owned. Freshman campus housing is guaranteed.

Activities and organizations: drama/theater group, student-run newspaper, choral group, Southeast Asian Student Organization, United Minds of Joint Action.

Athletics Member NCAA. All Division II. ***Intercollegiate sports:*** baseball M(s), basketball M(s)/W(s), cross-country running M(s)/W(s), football M(s), golf M(s)/W(s), lacrosse W(s), soccer W(s), softball W(s), swimming and diving W(s), track and field M(s)/W(s), volleyball W(s). ***Intramural sports:*** basketball M/W, football M/W, soccer M/W, volleyball M/W.

Campus security: 24-hour emergency response devices and patrols, late-night transport/escort service, controlled dormitory access.

Student services: personal/psychological counseling, veterans affairs office.

COSTS & FINANCIAL AID
Costs (2020–21) ***Comprehensive fee:*** $33,000 includes full-time tuition ($23,400) and room and board ($9600). Full-time tuition and fees vary according to degree level and program. Part-time tuition: $420 per credit. Part-time tuition and fees vary according to course load, degree level, and program. ***Room and board:*** Room and board charges vary according to board plan and housing facility. ***Payment plan:*** installment. ***Waivers:*** employees or children of employees.

Financial Aid Of all full-time matriculated undergraduates who enrolled in 2019, 1,431 applied for aid, 1,229 were judged to have need, 130 had their need fully met. 148 Federal Work-Study jobs (averaging $2384). 520 state and other part-time jobs (averaging $2464). In 2019, 165 non-need-based awards were made. ***Average percent of need met:*** 62. ***Average financial aid package:*** $16,836. ***Average need-based loan:*** $4369. ***Average need-based gift aid:*** $12,501. ***Average non-need-based aid:*** $5128. ***Average indebtedness upon graduation:*** $32,815.

APPLYING
Options: electronic application, early admission, deferred entrance.

Required: high school transcript. ***Required for some:*** essay or personal statement. ***Recommended:*** minimum 2.0 GPA, 2 letters of recommendation.

Application deadlines: 8/1 (freshmen), 8/1 (transfers).

Notification: continuous (freshmen), continuous (transfers).

CONTACT
Ms. Leah Martin, Director of Traditional Admission, Concordia University, St. Paul, 1282 Concordia Avenue, St. Paul, MN 55104-5494. *Phone:* 651-641-8230. *Toll-free phone:* 800-333-4705. *Fax:* 651-603-6320. *E-mail:* admission@csp.edu.

Crown College

St. Bonifacius, Minnesota

http://www.crown.edu/

CONTACT
Mr. Bret Hyder, Assistant Director of Admissions, Crown College, 8700 College View Drive, St. Bonifacius, MN 55375-9001. *Phone:* 952-446-4142. *Toll-free phone:* 800-68-CROWN. *Fax:* 952-446-4149. *E-mail:* admissions@crown.edu.

Dunwoody College of Technology

Minneapolis, Minnesota

http://www.dunwoody.edu/

- **Independent** primarily 2-year, founded 1914
- **Urban** 11-acre campus with easy access to Minneapolis-St. Paul
- **Endowment** $23.3 million
- **Coed, primarily men** 1,358 undergraduate students, 82% full-time, 18% women, 82% men
- **Minimally difficult** entrance level, 65% of applicants were admitted

UNDERGRAD STUDENTS
1,109 full-time, 249 part-time. Students come from 3 other countries; 3% are from out of state; 4% Black or African American, non-Hispanic/Latino; 3% Hispanic/Latino; 5% Asian, non-Hispanic/Latino; 0.1% Native Hawaiian or other Pacific Islander, non-Hispanic/Latino; 0.7% American Indian or Alaska Native, non-Hispanic/Latino; 5% Two or more races, non-Hispanic/Latino; 15% Race/ethnicity unknown; 0.2% international; 16% transferred in; 1% live on campus.

Freshmen:
Admission: 672 applied, 434 admitted, 237 enrolled. ***Average high school GPA:*** 2.8.

Retention: 86% of full-time freshmen returned.

FACULTY
Total: 161, 55% full-time, 24% with terminal degrees.

Student/faculty ratio: 11:1.

ACADEMICS
Calendar: semesters. *Degrees:* certificates, associate, and bachelor's.

Special study options: academic remediation for entering students, adult/continuing education programs, cooperative education, distance learning, double majors, independent study, internships, study abroad, summer session for credit.

Computers: 300 computers/terminals and 1,000 ports are available on campus for general student use. Students can access the following: campus intranet, computer help desk, free student e-mail accounts, online (class) grades, online (class) registration, online (class) schedules. Campuswide network is available. Wireless service is available via entire campus.

Library: Learning Resource Center plus 1 other. *Books:* 8,000 (physical), 188,153 (digital/electronic); *Serial titles:* 136 (physical); *Databases:* 26. Weekly public service hours: 55.

STUDENT LIFE
Housing options: coed. Campus housing is university owned.

Activities and organizations: Phi Theta Kappa, Historic Green, Dunwoody Motorsports Club, Architectural Institute of America Student Chapter, Professional Association for Design.

Campus security: 24-hour emergency response devices, late-night transport/escort service.

Student services: women's center.

COSTS & FINANCIAL AID

Costs (2020–21) ***Tuition:*** $21,941 full-time, $815 per credit hour part-time. Full-time tuition and fees vary according to course load and program. Part-time tuition and fees vary according to course load and program. ***Required fees:*** $1729 full-time. ***Room only:*** $1100. ***Payment plan:*** installment.

Financial Aid Of all full-time matriculated undergraduates who enrolled in 2018, 1,186 applied for aid, 985 were judged to have need, 32 had their need fully met. 17 Federal Work-Study jobs (averaging $6029). 26 state and other part-time jobs (averaging $6611). In 2018, 24 non-need-based awards were made. ***Average percent of need met:*** 34. ***Average financial aid package:*** $12,031. ***Average need-based loan:*** $3562. ***Average need-based gift aid:*** $10,271. ***Average non-need-based aid:*** $4541. ***Average indebtedness upon graduation:*** $16,342.

APPLYING

Standardized Tests *Required for some:* SAT or ACT (for admission).

Options: electronic application, deferred entrance.

Application fee: $50.

Required: essay or personal statement, high school transcript, interview. ***Required for some:*** 1 letter of recommendation, ACT scores and Resumes. ***Recommended:*** minimum 2.5 GPA, interview.

Application deadlines: rolling (freshmen), rolling (transfers).

Notification: continuous (freshmen), continuous (transfers).

CONTACT

Kelly O'Brien, Director of Admissions, Dunwoody College of Technology, 818 Dunwoody Boulevard, Minneapolis, MN 55403. *Phone:* 612-381-3302. *Toll-free phone:* 800-292-4625. *Fax:* 612-677-3131. *E-mail:* kobrien@dunwoody.edu.

Gustavus Adolphus College

St. Peter, Minnesota

http://www.gustavus.edu/

- **Independent** 4-year, founded 1862, affiliated with Evangelical Lutheran Church in America
- **Small-town** 340-acre campus with easy access to Minneapolis-St. Paul
- **Endowment** $166.8 million
- **Coed** 2,235 undergraduate students, 99% full-time, 59% women, 41% men
- **Very difficult** entrance level, 69% of applicants were admitted

UNDERGRAD STUDENTS

2,213 full-time, 22 part-time. 17% are from out of state; 3% Black or African American, non-Hispanic/Latino; 5% Hispanic/Latino; 5% Asian, non-Hispanic/Latino; 0.1% Native Hawaiian or other Pacific Islander, non-Hispanic/Latino; 0.1% American Indian or Alaska Native, non-Hispanic/Latino; 4% Two or more races, non-Hispanic/Latino; 0.5% Race/ethnicity unknown; 3% international; 1% transferred in; 92% live on campus.

Freshmen:

Admission: 4,957 applied, 3,432 admitted, 642 enrolled. ***Average high school GPA:*** 3.7. ***Test scores:*** ACT scores over 18: 100%; ACT scores over 24: 85%; ACT scores over 30: 33%.

Retention: 88% of full-time freshmen returned.

FACULTY

Total: 213, 84% full-time, 83% with terminal degrees.

Student/faculty ratio: 12:1.

ACADEMICS

Calendar: 4-1-4. *Degree:* bachelor's.

Special study options: advanced placement credit, double majors, honors programs, independent study, internships, off-campus study, services for LD students, student-designed majors, study abroad. ***ROTC:*** Army (c).

Unusual degree programs: engineering with Minnesota State University, Mankato; University of Minnesota; social work; occupational therapy with Washington University in St. Louis.

Computers: 400 computers/terminals are available on campus for general student use. Students can access the following: computer help desk, free student e-mail accounts, online (class) grades, online (class) registration, online (class) schedules. Campuswide network is available. 100% of college-owned or -operated housing units are wired for high-speed Internet access. Wireless service is available via entire campus.

Library: Folke Bernadotte Memorial Library. *Books:* 326,681 (physical), 53,368 (digital/electronic); *Serial titles:* 1,126 (physical); *Databases:* 108. Students can reserve study rooms.

STUDENT LIFE

Housing options: on-campus residence required through senior year; coed, special housing for students with disabilities. Campus housing is university owned. Freshman campus housing is guaranteed.

Activities and organizations: drama/theater group, student-run newspaper, radio station, choral group, Proclaim, Big Partner/Little Partner, Study Buddies, I am...We are, Pound Pals, national fraternities, national sororities.

Athletics Member NCAA. All Division III. ***Intercollegiate sports:*** baseball M, basketball M/W, cross-country running M/W, football M, golf M/W, gymnastics W, ice hockey M/W, lacrosse M(c), rugby M(c)/W(c), skiing (cross-country) M/W, soccer M/W, softball W, swimming and diving M/W, tennis M/W, track and field M/W, ultimate Frisbee M(c)/W(c), volleyball M(c)/W. ***Intramural sports:*** badminton M/W, basketball M/W, golf M/W, ice hockey M/W, racquetball M/W, rugby M/W, skiing (cross-country) M/W, skiing (downhill) M/W, soccer M/W, softball M/W, swimming and diving M/W, tennis M/W, track and field M/W, ultimate Frisbee M/W, volleyball M/W, water polo M/W, weight lifting M/W.

Campus security: 24-hour emergency response devices and patrols, late-night transport/escort service, controlled dormitory access.

Student services: health clinic, personal/psychological counseling, women's center.

COSTS & FINANCIAL AID

Costs (2020–21) ***Comprehensive fee:*** $58,890 includes full-time tuition ($48,250), mandatory fees ($210), and room and board ($10,430). Part-time tuition: $8300 per credit hour. ***College room only:*** $6600. Room and board charges vary according to housing facility. ***Payment plan:*** installment.

Financial Aid Of all full-time matriculated undergraduates who enrolled in 2019, 1,817 applied for aid, 1,616 were judged to have need, 596 had their need fully met. In 2019, 563 non-need-based awards were made. ***Average percent of need met:*** 92. ***Average financial aid package:*** $44,800. ***Average need-based loan:*** $4480. ***Average need-based gift aid:*** $37,560. ***Average non-need-based aid:*** $26,171. ***Average indebtedness upon graduation:*** $35,145. ***Financial aid deadline:*** 4/15.

APPLYING

Options: electronic application, early admission, early action, deferred entrance.

Required: essay or personal statement, high school transcript, 1 letter of recommendation. ***Recommended:*** interview.

Application deadlines: 4/1 (freshmen), rolling (transfers), 11/1 (early action).

Notification: continuous (freshmen), continuous (transfers), 11/15 (early action).

CONTACT

Mr. Richard Aune, Vice President for Enrollment Management, Gustavus Adolphus College, 800 West College Avenue, St. Peter, MN 56082-1498. *Phone:* 507-933-7676. *Toll-free phone:* 800-GUSTAVU(S). *Fax:* 507-933-7474. *E-mail:* admission@gac.edu.

Hamline University

St. Paul, Minnesota

http://www.hamline.edu/

- **Independent** comprehensive, founded 1854, affiliated with United Methodist Church
- **Urban** 60-acre campus with easy access to Minneapolis-St. Paul
- **Endowment** $95.7 million
- **Coed** 2,088 undergraduate students, 96% full-time, 63% women, 37% men
- **Moderately difficult** entrance level, 68% of applicants were admitted

UNDERGRAD STUDENTS
2,008 full-time, 80 part-time. Students come from 39 states and territories; 39 other countries; 18% are from out of state; 10% Black or African American, non-Hispanic/Latino; 10% Hispanic/Latino; 9% Asian, non-Hispanic/Latino; 0.2% American Indian or Alaska Native, non-Hispanic/Latino; 6% Two or more races, non-Hispanic/Latino; 2% Race/ethnicity unknown; 0.7% international; 6% transferred in; 34% live on campus.

Freshmen:
Admission: 4,602 applied, 3,117 admitted, 547 enrolled. ***Average high school GPA:*** 3.5. ***Test scores:*** SAT evidence-based reading and writing scores over 500: 76%; SAT math scores over 500: 75%; ACT scores over 18: 88%; SAT evidence-based reading and writing scores over 600: 40%; SAT math scores over 600: 47%; ACT scores over 24: 41%; SAT evidence-based reading and writing scores over 700: 4%; SAT math scores over 700: 9%; ACT scores over 30: 8%.

Retention: 78% of full-time freshmen returned.

FACULTY
Total: 272, 55% full-time, 64% with terminal degrees.

Student/faculty ratio: 13:1.

ACADEMICS
Calendar: 4-1-4. *Degrees:* certificates, bachelor's, master's, doctoral, post-master's, and postbachelor's certificates.

Special study options: advanced placement credit, cooperative education, distance learning, double majors, honors programs, independent study, internships, off-campus study, part-time degree program, services for LD students, student-designed majors, study abroad, summer session for credit. ***ROTC:*** Army (c), Air Force (c).

Computers: 300 computers/terminals are available on campus for general student use. Students can access the following: campus intranet, computer help desk, free student e-mail accounts, online (class) grades, online (class) registration, online (class) schedules. Campuswide network is available. 99% of college-owned or -operated housing units are wired for high-speed Internet access. Wireless service is available via entire campus.

Library: Bush Library. *Books:* 128,360 (physical), 528,521 (digital/electronic); *Serial titles:* 756 (physical), 71,196 (digital/electronic); *Databases:* 127. Weekly public service hours: 103; students can reserve study rooms.

STUDENT LIFE
Housing options: coed, special housing for students with disabilities. Campus housing is university owned. Freshman campus housing is guaranteed.

Activities and organizations: drama/theater group, student-run newspaper, radio and television station, choral group, Hamline Undergraduate Student Congress (HUSC), Hamline University Programming Board (HUPB), Black Student Collective (BSC), Student Athlete Advisory Coalition (SAAC), Asian Pacific American Coalition (APAC), national fraternities, national sororities.

Athletics Member NCAA. All Division III. ***Intercollegiate sports:*** baseball M, basketball M/W, cross-country running M/W, football M, gymnastics W, ice hockey M/W, lacrosse W, soccer M/W, softball W, swimming and diving M/W, tennis M/W, track and field M/W, volleyball W. ***Intramural sports:*** badminton M/W, basketball M/W, football M/W, rock climbing M(c)/W(c), soccer M/W, volleyball M/W.

Campus security: 24-hour emergency response devices and patrols, student patrols, late-night transport/escort service, controlled dormitory access.

Student services: health clinic, personal/psychological counseling, women's center, veterans affairs office.

COSTS & FINANCIAL AID
Costs (2020–21) ***Comprehensive fee:*** $55,040 includes full-time tuition ($43,154), mandatory fees ($1076), and room and board ($10,810). Part-time tuition: $1349 per credit hour. Part-time tuition and fees vary according to course load. ***Required fees:*** $827 per year part-time. ***College room only:*** $5150. Room and board charges vary according to housing facility. ***Payment plan:*** installment. ***Waivers:*** employees or children of employees.

Financial Aid Of all full-time matriculated undergraduates who enrolled in 2018, 1,845 applied for aid, 1,716 were judged to have need, 285 had their need fully met. In 2018, 278 non-need-based awards were made. ***Average percent of need met:*** 79. ***Average financial aid package:*** $31,667. ***Average need-based loan:*** $4344. ***Average need-based gift aid:*** $25,922. ***Average non-need-based aid:*** $18,781. ***Average indebtedness upon graduation:*** $36,676.

APPLYING
Standardized Tests *Required for some:* SAT or ACT (for admission).

Options: electronic application, early admission, early decision, early action, deferred entrance.

Required: essay or personal statement, high school transcript, 1 letter of recommendation. ***Recommended:*** interview.

Application deadlines: rolling (freshmen), rolling (out-of-state freshmen), rolling (transfers), 12/1 (early action).

Early decision deadline: 11/1.

Notification: continuous (freshmen), continuous (out-of-state freshmen), continuous (transfers), 11/15 (early decision), rolling (early action).

CONTACT
Hamline University, 1536 Hewitt Avenue, St. Paul, MN 55104-1284. *Phone:* 651-523-2207. *Toll-free phone:* 800-753-9753.

Herzing University

Minneapolis, Minnesota

http://www.herzing.edu/minneapolis

CONTACT
Ms. Shelly Larson, Director of Admissions, Herzing University, 5700 West Broadway, Minneapolis, MN 55428. *Phone:* 763-231-3155. *Toll-free phone:* 800-596-0724. *Fax:* 763-535-9205. *E-mail:* info@mpls.herzing.edu.

Macalester College

St. Paul, Minnesota

http://www.macalester.edu/

- **Independent** 4-year, founded 1874
- **Urban** 53-acre campus
- **Endowment** $767.5 million
- **Coed**
- **Very difficult** entrance level

FACULTY
Student/faculty ratio: 10:1.

ACADEMICS
Calendar: semesters. *Degree:* bachelor's.
Library: DeWitt Wallace Library. *Books:* 326,620 (physical), 179,946 (digital/electronic); *Serial titles:* 2,412 (physical), 76,659 (digital/electronic); *Databases:* 202. Weekly public service hours: 109; study areas open 24 hours, 5–7 days a week; students can reserve study rooms.

STUDENT LIFE
Housing options: on-campus residence required through sophomore year; coed, men-only, women-only, cooperative. Campus housing is university owned. Freshman campus housing is guaranteed.

Activities and organizations: drama/theater group, student-run newspaper, radio station, choral group, Program Board, WMCN - Macalester College Radio, The Mac Weekly, Outing Club, Climbing Club.

Athletics Member NCAA. All Division III.

Campus security: 24-hour emergency response devices and patrols, late-night transport/escort service, controlled dormitory access.

Student services: health clinic, personal/psychological counseling.

COSTS & FINANCIAL AID
Costs (2019–20) ***Comprehensive fee:*** $68,884 includes full-time tuition ($56,062), mandatory fees ($230), and room and board ($12,592). Full-time tuition and fees vary according to course load. Part-time tuition: $1751 per credit. Part-time tuition and fees vary according to course load. ***Required fees:*** $1751 per credit part-time. ***College room only:*** $6762. Room and board charges vary according to housing facility.

Financial Aid Of all full-time matriculated undergraduates who enrolled in 2019, 1,500 applied for aid, 1,366 were judged to have need, 881 had their need fully met. In 2019, 328 non-need-based awards were made. ***Average percent of need met:*** 100. ***Average financial aid package:*** $49,693. ***Average need-based loan:*** $5071. ***Average need-based gift aid:*** $42,774. ***Average non-need-based aid:*** $15,182. ***Average indebtedness upon graduation:*** $23,060.

APPLYING
Standardized Tests *Required:* SAT or ACT (for admission).

Options: electronic application, early admission, early decision, deferred entrance.

Application fee: $40.

Required: essay or personal statement, high school transcript, 2 letters of recommendation. ***Recommended:*** interview.

CONTACT
Mr. Jeff Allen, Vice President of Admissions and Financial Aid, Macalester College, 1600 Grand Avenue, St. Paul, MN 55105-1899. *Phone:* 651-696-6357. *Toll-free phone:* 800-231-7974. *Fax:* 651-696-6724. *E-mail:* admissions@macalester.edu.

Martin Luther College

New Ulm, Minnesota

http://www.mlc-wels.edu/

- **Independent** comprehensive, founded 1995, affiliated with Wisconsin Evangelical Lutheran Synod
- **Small-town** 50-acre campus
- **Coed** 910 undergraduate students, 78% full-time, 55% women, 45% men
- **Moderately difficult** entrance level, 84% of applicants were admitted

UNDERGRAD STUDENTS
707 full-time, 203 part-time. 83% are from out of state; 1% Black or African American, non-Hispanic/Latino; 2% Hispanic/Latino; 1% Asian, non-Hispanic/Latino; 0.1% Native Hawaiian or other Pacific Islander, non-Hispanic/Latino; 0.1% American Indian or Alaska Native, non-Hispanic/Latino; 1% Two or more races, non-Hispanic/Latino; 0.1% Race/ethnicity unknown; 2% international; 1% transferred in; 91% live on campus.

Freshmen:
Admission: 266 applied, 223 admitted, 168 enrolled. ***Average high school GPA:*** 3.6. ***Test scores:*** SAT evidence-based reading and writing scores over 500: 75%; SAT math scores over 500: 90%; ACT scores over 18: 98%; SAT evidence-based reading and writing scores over 600: 63%; SAT math scores over 600: 38%; ACT scores over 24: 63%; SAT evidence-based reading and writing scores over 700: 13%; SAT math scores over 700: 13%; ACT scores over 30: 18%.

Retention: 81% of full-time freshmen returned.

FACULTY
Total: 78, 72% full-time, 35% with terminal degrees.

Student/faculty ratio: 12:1.

ACADEMICS
Calendar: semesters. *Degrees:* certificates, diplomas, bachelor's, and master's.

Special study options: advanced placement credit, distance learning, double majors, summer session for credit.

Computers: Campuswide network is available.
Library: Martin Luther College Library.

STUDENT LIFE
Housing options: on-campus residence required for freshman year; men-only, women-only, special housing for students with disabilities. Campus housing is university owned. Freshman campus housing is guaranteed.

Activities and organizations: drama/theater group, choral group.

Athletics Member NCAA, NAIA. All NCAA Division III except golf (Division II). ***Intercollegiate sports:*** baseball M, basketball M/W, cross-country running M/W, football M, golf M/W, soccer M/W, softball W, tennis M/W, track and field M/W, volleyball W. ***Intramural sports:*** badminton M/W, basketball M/W, bowling M/W, football M, soccer M/W, softball M/W, tennis M/W, volleyball M/W.

Student services: health clinic, personal/psychological counseling.

COSTS & FINANCIAL AID
Costs (2020–21) ***Comprehensive fee:*** $22,900 includes full-time tuition ($16,420) and room and board ($6480).

Financial Aid Of all full-time matriculated undergraduates who enrolled in 2018, 631 applied for aid, 576 were judged to have need, 70 had their need fully met. In 2018, 82 non-need-based awards were made. ***Average percent of need met:*** 66. ***Average financial aid package:*** $12,243. ***Average need-based loan:*** $3973. ***Average need-based gift aid:*** $9268. ***Average non-need-based aid:*** $3224. ***Average indebtedness upon graduation:*** $26,791. ***Financial aid deadline:*** 4/15.

APPLYING
Standardized Tests *Required:* SAT or ACT (for admission).

Options: deferred entrance.

Required: high school transcript, minimum 2.0 GPA.

CONTACT
Mark Stein, Director of Admissions, Martin Luther College, 1995 Luther Court, New Ulm, MN 56073. *Phone:* 507-354-8221 Ext. 360. *Toll-free phone:* 877-MLC-1995. *Fax:* 507-354-8225. *E-mail:* steinma@mlc-wels.edu.

Metropolitan State University

St. Paul, Minnesota

http://www.metrostate.edu/

CONTACT
Mr. Daryl Johnson, Director, Metropolitan State University, 700 East 7th Street, St. Paul, MN 55106. *Phone:* 651-793-1227. *Fax:* 651-793-1546. *E-mail:* daryl.johnson@metrostate.edu.

Minneapolis College of Art and Design

Minneapolis, Minnesota

http://www.mcad.edu/

- **Independent** comprehensive, founded 1886
- **Urban** 3-acre campus
- **Endowment** $56.7 million
- **Coed** 709 undergraduate students, 98% full-time, 70% women, 30% men
- **Moderately difficult** entrance level, 59% of applicants were admitted

UNDERGRAD STUDENTS
698 full-time, 11 part-time. Students come from 14 other countries; 43% are from out of state; 5% Black or African American, non-Hispanic/Latino; 9% Hispanic/Latino; 9% Asian, non-Hispanic/Latino; 0.4% Native Hawaiian or other Pacific Islander, non-Hispanic/Latino; 2% American Indian or Alaska Native, non-Hispanic/Latino; 3% Two or more races, non-Hispanic/Latino; 3% Race/ethnicity unknown; 2% international; 5% transferred in; 38% live on campus.

Freshmen:
Admission: 747 applied, 437 admitted, 178 enrolled. ***Average high school GPA:*** 3.2. ***Test scores:*** SAT evidence-based reading and writing scores over 500: 88%; SAT math scores over 500: 69%; ACT scores over 18: 95%; SAT evidence-based reading and writing scores over 600: 51%; SAT math scores over 600: 24%; ACT scores over 24: 43%; SAT evidence-based reading and writing scores over 700: 10%; SAT math scores over 700: 2%; ACT scores over 30: 8%.

Retention: 72% of full-time freshmen returned.

FACULTY
Total: 139, 24% full-time, 70% with terminal degrees.

Student/faculty ratio: 10:1.

ACADEMICS
Calendar: semesters. *Degrees:* bachelor's and master's.

Special study options: adult/continuing education programs, advanced placement credit, cooperative education, distance learning, independent study, internships, off-campus study, part-time degree program, services for LD students, study abroad, summer session for credit.

Computers: Students can access the following: campus intranet, computer help desk, free student e-mail accounts, online (class) grades, online (class) registration, online (class) schedules. Campuswide network is available. 100% of college-owned or -operated housing units are wired for high-speed Internet access. Wireless service is available via entire campus.

Library: MCAD Library. *Books:* 50,000 (physical), 145,000 (digital/electronic); *Serial titles:* 329 (physical); *Databases:* 8.

STUDENT LIFE

Housing options: coed. Campus housing is university owned. Freshman applicants given priority for college housing.

Activities and organizations: Peoples Library, Black Artist Student Union, Animation Study Group, Comic Club, Kinda Midnight Movies Club.

Athletics ***Intramural sports:*** soccer M(c)/W(c), softball M(c)/W(c).

Campus security: 24-hour emergency response devices and patrols, late-night transport/escort service, controlled dormitory access.

Student services: personal/psychological counseling.

COSTS & FINANCIAL AID

Costs (2020–21) ***Comprehensive fee:*** $62,104 includes full-time tuition ($55,674), mandatory fees ($450), and room and board ($5980). Part-time tuition: $1723 per credit hour. ***College room only:*** $5980.

Financial Aid Of all full-time matriculated undergraduates who enrolled in 2019, 619 applied for aid, 557 were judged to have need, 47 had their need fully met. In 2019, 129 non-need-based awards were made. ***Average percent of need met:*** 71. ***Average financial aid package:*** $28,894. ***Average need-based loan:*** $4569. ***Average need-based gift aid:*** $23,424. ***Average non-need-based aid:*** $13,907. ***Average indebtedness upon graduation:*** $37,788. ***Financial aid deadline:*** 4/1.

APPLYING

Standardized Tests *Required for some:* SAT or ACT (for admission).

Options: electronic application, early action.

Application fee: $50.

Required: essay or personal statement, high school transcript. ***Recommended:*** interview.

Application deadlines: 5/1 (freshmen), 5/1 (transfers), 12/1 (early action).

Notification: continuous (freshmen), continuous (transfers), 12/15 (early action).

CONTACT

Minneapolis College of Art and Design, 2501 Stevens Avenue, Minneapolis, MN 55404-4347. *Phone:* 612-874-3764. *Toll-free phone:* 800-874-6223.

Minnesota State University Mankato

Mankato, Minnesota

http://mankato.mnsu.edu/

- **State-supported** university, founded 1868, part of Minnesota State Colleges and Universities System
- **Small-town** 303-acre campus with easy access to Minneapolis-St. Paul
- **Coed** 12,450 undergraduate students
- 63% of applicants were admitted

UNDERGRAD STUDENTS

17% are from out of state; 5% Black or African American, non-Hispanic/Latino; 5% Hispanic/Latino; 4% Asian, non-Hispanic/Latino; 0.1% Native Hawaiian or other Pacific Islander, non-Hispanic/Latino; 0.3% American Indian or Alaska Native, non-Hispanic/Latino; 4% Two or more races, non-Hispanic/Latino; 0.6% Race/ethnicity unknown; 9% international; 23% live on campus.

Freshmen:

Admission: 10,349 applied, 6,490 admitted. ***Average high school GPA:*** 3.4. ***Test scores:*** ACT scores over 18: 89%; ACT scores over 24: 28%; ACT scores over 30: 2%.

Retention: 77% of full-time freshmen returned.

FACULTY

Student/faculty ratio: 22:1.

ACADEMICS

Calendar: semesters. *Degrees:* certificates, associate, bachelor's, master's, doctoral, post-master's, and postbachelor's certificates.

Special study options: academic remediation for entering students, adult/continuing education programs, advanced placement credit, distance learning, double majors, English as a second language, external degree program, honors programs, independent study, internships, off-campus study, part-time degree program, services for LD students, study abroad, summer session for credit. ***ROTC:*** Army (b).

Computers: 900 computers/terminals are available on campus for general student use. Students can access the following: campus intranet, computer help desk, free student e-mail accounts, online (class) grades, online (class) registration, online (class) schedules. Campuswide network is available. Wireless service is available via entire campus.

Library: Memorial Library.

STUDENT LIFE

Housing options: coed, special housing for students with disabilities. Campus housing is university owned. Freshman applicants given priority for college housing.

Activities and organizations: drama/theater group, student-run newspaper, radio station, choral group, marching band, national fraternities, national sororities.

Athletics Member NCAA. All Division II except men's and women's ice hockey (Division I). ***Intercollegiate sports:*** baseball M(s), basketball M(s)/W(s), bowling W, cheerleading M/W, cross-country running M(s)/W(s), football M(s), golf M(s)/W(s), ice hockey M(s)/W(s), soccer W(s), softball W(s), swimming and diving W(s), tennis M(s)/W(s), track and field M(s)/W(s), volleyball W(s), wrestling M(s). ***Intramural sports:*** archery M/W, basketball M/W, bowling M/W, fencing M/W, football M/W, golf M/W, ice hockey M/W, lacrosse M/W, racquetball M/W, rock climbing M/W, rugby M(c)/W(c), sailing M/W, skiing (downhill) M/W, soccer M/W, softball M/W, swimming and diving W, table tennis M/W, tennis M/W, track and field M/W, volleyball M/W, wrestling M.

Campus security: 24-hour emergency response devices and patrols, student patrols, late-night transport/escort service, controlled dormitory access, Night Owl security program in residence halls, closed circuit cameras in parking lots.

Student services: health clinic, personal/psychological counseling, women's center, legal services, veterans affairs office.

COSTS & FINANCIAL AID

Costs (2020–21) ***Tuition:*** $289 per credit hour part-time; state resident $289 per credit hour part-time; nonresident $622 per credit hour part-time.

Financial Aid Of all full-time matriculated undergraduates who enrolled in 2019, 7,931 applied for aid, 5,151 were judged to have need, 1,161 had their need fully met. 474 Federal Work-Study jobs (averaging $3657). 511 state and other part-time jobs (averaging $3646). In 2019, 1328 non-need-based awards were made. ***Average percent of need met:*** 74. ***Average financial aid package:*** $9901. ***Average need-based loan:*** $3974. ***Average need-based gift aid:*** $6236. ***Average non-need-based aid:*** $5533. ***Average indebtedness upon graduation:*** $30,482.

APPLYING

Standardized Tests *Required:* ACT (for admission).

Options: deferred entrance.

Application fee: $20.

Required: high school transcript. ***Required for some:*** essay or personal statement, 1 letter of recommendation, personal statement, letter and senior grades.

CONTACT

Office of Admissions, Minnesota State University Mankato, 122 Taylor Center, Mankato, MN 56001. *Phone:* 507-389-1822. *Toll-free phone:* 800-722-0544. *Fax:* 507-389-1511. *E-mail:* admissions@mnsu.edu.

Minnesota State University Moorhead

Moorhead, Minnesota

http://www.mnstate.edu/

- **State-supported** comprehensive, founded 1885, part of Minnesota State Colleges and Universities System
- **Urban** 119-acre campus
- **Endowment** $24.5 million
- **Coed**
- **Moderately difficult** entrance level

FACULTY
Student/faculty ratio: 19:1.

ACADEMICS
Calendar: semesters. *Degrees:* certificates, bachelor's, master's, doctoral, post-master's, and postbachelor's certificates.
Library: Livingston Lord Library plus 1 other. *Books:* 326,187 (physical), 20,401 (digital/electronic); *Serial titles:* 1,634 (physical), 18,041 (digital/electronic); *Databases:* 84. Weekly public service hours: 79.

STUDENT LIFE
Housing options: coed, special housing for students with disabilities. Campus housing is university owned. Freshman campus housing is guaranteed.

Activities and organizations: drama/theater group, student-run newspaper, radio and television station, choral group, NSSLHA / Collegiate SERTOMA, Cinethusiasts, Student Council for Exceptional Children, Education Minnesota Student Program, National Society of Leadership and Success, national fraternities, national sororities.

Athletics Member NCAA. All Division II except golf (Division I).

Campus security: 24-hour emergency response devices and patrols, student patrols, late-night transport/escort service, controlled dormitory access.

Student services: health clinic, personal/psychological counseling, women's center, veterans affairs office.

FINANCIAL AID
Financial Aid Of all full-time matriculated undergraduates who enrolled in 2019, 3,082 applied for aid, 2,345 were judged to have need. 210 Federal Work-Study jobs (averaging $2763). 180 state and other part-time jobs (averaging $2760). ***Average financial aid package:*** $3392. ***Average need-based loan:*** $4058. ***Average need-based gift aid:*** $3035. ***Average indebtedness upon graduation:*** $31,205.

APPLYING
Standardized Tests *Required:* SAT or ACT (for admission). *Recommended:* ACT (for admission).

Options: electronic application, deferred entrance.

Application fee: $20.

Required: high school transcript.

CONTACT
Ms. Brenda Amenson-Hill, Vice President of Enrollment Management & Student Affairs, Minnesota State University Moorhead, 1104 7th Avenue South, Moorhead, MN 56563. *Phone:* 218-477-2200. *Toll-free phone:* 800-593-7246. *E-mail:* brenda.amensonhill@mnstate.edu.

National American University
Bloomington, Minnesota
http://www.national.edu/

CONTACT
Ms. Jennifer Michaelson, Admissions Assistant, National American University, 321 Kansas City Street, Rapid City, SD 57201. *Phone:* 605-394-4827. *Toll-free phone:* 866-628-6387. *E-mail:* jmichaelson@national.edu.

National American University
Brooklyn Center, Minnesota
http://www.national.edu/

CONTACT
Admissions Office, National American University, 6200 Shingle Creek Parkway, Suite 130, Brooklyn Center, MN 55430. *Toll-free phone:* 866-628-6387.

National American University
Burnsville, Minnesota
http://www.national.edu/

CONTACT
National American University, 513 West Travelers Trail, Burnsville, MN 55337. *Toll-free phone:* 866-628-6387.

National American University
Roseville, Minnesota
http://www.national.edu/

CONTACT
Mr. Steve Grunlan, Director of Admissions, National American University, 1550 West Highway 36, Roseville, MN 55113. *Phone:* 651-644-1265. *Toll-free phone:* 866-628-6387.

North Central University
Minneapolis, Minnesota
http://www.northcentral.edu/

- **Independent** 4-year, founded 1930, affiliated with Assemblies of God
- **Urban** 9-acre campus
- **Coed** 1,085 undergraduate students, 89% full-time, 58% women, 42% men
- **Noncompetitive** entrance level, 90% of applicants were admitted

UNDERGRAD STUDENTS
967 full-time, 118 part-time. Students come from 42 states and territories; 6 other countries; 6% Black or African American, non-Hispanic/Latino; 10% Hispanic/Latino; 4% Asian, non-Hispanic/Latino; 0.4% Native Hawaiian or other Pacific Islander, non-Hispanic/Latino; 0.5% American Indian or Alaska Native, non-Hispanic/Latino; 5% Two or more races, non-Hispanic/Latino; 5% Race/ethnicity unknown; 6% transferred in; 78% live on campus.

Freshmen:
Admission: 620 applied, 560 admitted, 245 enrolled. ***Average high school GPA:*** 3.4. ***Test scores:*** SAT evidence-based reading and writing scores over 500: 71%; SAT math scores over 500: 54%; ACT scores over 18: 81%; SAT evidence-based reading and writing scores over 600: 23%; SAT math scores over 600: 17%; ACT scores over 24: 28%; SAT evidence-based reading and writing scores over 700: 3%; ACT scores over 30: 3%.
Retention: 80% of full-time freshmen returned.

FACULTY
Total: 107, 39% full-time, 37% with terminal degrees.
Student/faculty ratio: 16:1.

ACADEMICS
Calendar: semesters plus January and May terms. *Degrees:* certificates, diplomas, associate, and bachelor's.

Special study options: academic remediation for entering students, advanced placement credit, cooperative education, double majors, independent study, internships, off-campus study, part-time degree program, services for LD students, student-designed majors, summer session for credit.

Computers: 40 computers/terminals and 40 ports are available on campus for general student use. Students can access the following: campus intranet, computer help desk, free student e-mail accounts, online (class) grades, online (class) registration. Campuswide network is available. 100% of college-owned or -operated housing units are wired for high-speed Internet access. Wireless service is available via classrooms, libraries.
Library: T. J. Jones Information Resource Center.

STUDENT LIFE
Housing options: on-campus residence required through senior year; coed, men-only, women-only, special housing for students with disabilities. Campus housing is university owned. Freshman campus housing is guaranteed.

Activities and organizations: drama/theater group, student-run newspaper, radio station, choral group, Residence Life, Discipleship

Leaders, Orientation Leaders, Student Ministries Board, Student Activities Committee.

Athletics Member NCAA, NCCAA. All NCAA Division III. ***Intercollegiate sports:*** baseball M, basketball M/W, cross-country running M/W, golf M, soccer M/W, softball W, tennis M/W, track and field M/W, volleyball W. ***Intramural sports:*** baseball M(c), football M/W, golf M(c), softball W(c), table tennis M/W, volleyball M/W.

Campus security: 24-hour emergency response devices and patrols, late-night transport/escort service, controlled dormitory access.

Student services: personal/psychological counseling.

COSTS & FINANCIAL AID

Costs (2020–21) ***Comprehensive fee:*** $34,460 includes full-time tuition ($25,430), mandatory fees ($850), and room and board ($8180). Part-time tuition: $1005 per credit hour. ***College room only:*** $4560.

Financial Aid Of all full-time matriculated undergraduates who enrolled in 2003, 1,020 were judged to have need. 80 Federal Work-Study jobs (averaging $1738). 38 state and other part-time jobs (averaging $1257). ***Average indebtedness upon graduation:*** $21,965.

APPLYING

Standardized Tests *Required:* SAT or ACT (for admission).

Options: electronic application, deferred entrance.

Application fee: $25.

Required: essay or personal statement, high school transcript, minimum 2.2 GPA, Christian testimony. ***Required for some:*** interview.

Application deadlines: 6/1 (freshmen), 6/1 (transfers).

Notification: 6/15 (freshmen), 6/15 (transfers).

CONTACT

Ms. Sigi Shawa, Assistant Director, North Central University, 910 Elliot Avenue, Minneapolis, MN 55404-1322. *Phone:* 612-343-4460. *Toll-free phone:* 800-289-6222. *Fax:* 612-343-4146. *E-mail:* admissions@northcentral.edu.

Oak Hills Christian College

Bemidji, Minnesota

http://www.oakhills.edu/

CONTACT

Shelly Fast, Assistant Director of Admissions, Oak Hills Christian College, 1600 Oak Hills Road SW, Bemidji, MN 56601. *Phone:* 218-751-8670 Ext. 1285. *Toll-free phone:* 888-751-8670 Ext. 1285. *Fax:* 218-751-8825. *E-mail:* admissions@oakhills.edu.

Rasmussen College Blaine

Blaine, Minnesota

http://www.rasmussen.edu/

- **Proprietary** 4-year, part of Rasmussen College System
- **Suburban** campus with easy access to Minneapolis-St. Paul
- **Coed** 476 undergraduate students, 41% full-time, 86% women, 14% men

UNDERGRAD STUDENTS

197 full-time, 279 part-time. Students come from 51 states and territories; 27% are from out of state; 22% Black or African American, non-Hispanic/Latino; 2% Hispanic/Latino; 3% Asian, non-Hispanic/Latino; 0.2% Native Hawaiian or other Pacific Islander, non-Hispanic/Latino; 0.6% American Indian or Alaska Native, non-Hispanic/Latino; 3% Two or more races, non-Hispanic/Latino; 22% Race/ethnicity unknown.

Freshmen:

Admission: 36 enrolled.

ACADEMICS

Calendar: quarters. *Degrees:* certificates, diplomas, associate, and bachelor's.

Special study options: academic remediation for entering students, accelerated degree program, adult/continuing education programs, distance learning, double majors, internships, part-time degree program, summer session for credit.

Computers: 81 computers/terminals are available on campus for general student use. Students can access the following: computer help desk, free student e-mail accounts, online (class) grades, online (class) schedules. Campuswide network is available. Wireless service is available via entire campus.

Library: Rasmussen College Library - Blaine.

STUDENT LIFE

Housing options: college housing not available.

COSTS

Costs (2019–20) ***Tuition:*** $14,062 full-time, $13,353 per year part-time. Full-time tuition and fees vary according to course level, course load, degree level, location, and program. Part-time tuition and fees vary according to course level, course load, degree level, location, and program. No tuition increase for student's term of enrollment. ***Required fees:*** $3083 full-time, $2838 per year part-time. ***Payment plans:*** installment, deferred payment. ***Waivers:*** employees or children of employees.

CONTACT

Ms. Susan Hammerstrom, Director of Admissions, Rasmussen College Blaine, 3629 95th Avenue NE, Blaine, MN 55014. *Phone:* 763-795-4720. *Toll-free phone:* 888-549-6755. *E-mail:* susan.hammerstrom@rasmussen.edu.

Rasmussen College Bloomington

Bloomington, Minnesota

http://www.rasmussen.edu/

- **Proprietary** 4-year, founded 1904, part of Rasmussen College System
- **Suburban** campus with easy access to Minneapolis-St. Paul
- **Coed** 1,129 undergraduate students, 45% full-time, 85% women, 15% men
- 100% of applicants were admitted

UNDERGRAD STUDENTS

510 full-time, 619 part-time. Students come from 51 states and territories; 27% are from out of state; 26% Black or African American, non-Hispanic/Latino; 5% Hispanic/Latino; 5% Asian, non-Hispanic/Latino; 0.2% Native Hawaiian or other Pacific Islander, non-Hispanic/Latino; 0.3% American Indian or Alaska Native, non-Hispanic/Latino; 3% Two or more races, non-Hispanic/Latino; 18% Race/ethnicity unknown.

Freshmen:

Admission: 251 applied, 251 admitted, 39 enrolled.

ACADEMICS

Calendar: quarters. *Degrees:* certificates, diplomas, associate, bachelor's, and postbachelor's certificates.

Special study options: academic remediation for entering students, accelerated degree program, adult/continuing education programs, distance learning, double majors, internships, part-time degree program, summer session for credit.

Computers: 68 computers/terminals are available on campus for general student use. Students can access the following: computer help desk, free student e-mail accounts, online (class) grades, online (class) schedules. Campuswide network is available. Wireless service is available via entire campus.

Library: Rasmussen College Library - Bloomington.

STUDENT LIFE

Housing options: college housing not available.

FINANCIAL AID

Financial Aid Of all full-time matriculated undergraduates who enrolled in 2018, 3 state and other part-time jobs (averaging $4338).

APPLYING

Options: early admission, deferred entrance.

Required: high school transcript, minimum 2.0 GPA. ***Required for some:*** interview.

Application deadlines: rolling (freshmen), rolling (transfers).

CONTACT

Dwayne Bertotto, Vice President of Admissions and Student Experience, Rasmussen College Bloomington, 8300 Norman Center Drive, Suite 300, Bloomington, MN 55437. *Phone:* 952-806-3958. *Toll-free phone:* 888-549-6755. *E-mail:* dwayne.bertotto@rasmussen.edu.

Rasmussen College Brooklyn Park

Brooklyn Park, Minnesota

http://www.rasmussen.edu/

- **Proprietary** 4-year, part of Rasmussen College System
- **Suburban** campus with easy access to Minneapolis-St. Paul
- **Coed** 437 undergraduate students, 44% full-time, 80% women, 20% men
- **Minimally difficult** entrance level, 100% of applicants were admitted

UNDERGRAD STUDENTS

194 full-time, 243 part-time. Students come from 51 states and territories; 27% are from out of state; 28% Black or African American, non-Hispanic/Latino; 5% Hispanic/Latino; 4% Asian, non-Hispanic/Latino; 0.5% American Indian or Alaska Native, non-Hispanic/Latino; 4% Two or more races, non-Hispanic/Latino; 22% Race/ethnicity unknown.

Freshmen:
Admission: 123 applied, 123 admitted, 82 enrolled.

ACADEMICS

Calendar: quarters. *Degrees:* certificates, diplomas, associate, and bachelor's.

Special study options: academic remediation for entering students, accelerated degree program, adult/continuing education programs, distance learning, double majors, internships, part-time degree program, summer session for credit.

Computers: 80 computers/terminals are available on campus for general student use. Students can access the following: computer help desk, free student e-mail accounts, online (class) grades, online (class) schedules. Campuswide network is available. Wireless service is available via entire campus.
Library: Rasmussen College Library - Brooklyn Park.

STUDENT LIFE

Housing options: college housing not available.

APPLYING

Standardized Tests *Required:* institutional exam (for admission).

Options: electronic application, early admission, deferred entrance.

Required: high school transcript, minimum 2.0 GPA. ***Required for some:*** interview.

Application deadlines: rolling (freshmen), rolling (transfers).

CONTACT

Dwayne Bertotto, Vice President of Admissions and Student Experience, Rasmussen College Brooklyn Park, 8300 Norman Center Drive, Suite 300, Bloomington, MN 55437. *Phone:* 952-806-3958. *Toll-free phone:* 888-549-6755. *E-mail:* dwayne.bertotto@rasmussen.edu.

Rasmussen College Eagan

Eagan, Minnesota

http://www.rasmussen.edu/

- **Proprietary** 4-year, founded 1904, part of Rasmussen College System
- **Suburban** campus with easy access to Minneapolis-St. Paul
- **Coed** 415 undergraduate students, 54% full-time, 81% women, 24% men
- 100% of applicants were admitted

UNDERGRAD STUDENTS

225 full-time, 210 part-time. Students come from 51 states and territories; 27% are from out of state; 21% Black or African American, non-Hispanic/Latino; 10% Hispanic/Latino; 5% Asian, non-Hispanic/Latino; 0.2% American Indian or Alaska Native, non-Hispanic/Latino; 2% Two or more races, non-Hispanic/Latino; 16% Race/ethnicity unknown.

Freshmen:
Admission: 109 applied, 109 admitted, 87 enrolled.

ACADEMICS

Calendar: quarters. *Degrees:* certificates, diplomas, associate, bachelor's, and postbachelor's certificates.

Special study options: academic remediation for entering students, accelerated degree program, adult/continuing education programs, distance learning, double majors, internships, part-time degree program, summer session for credit.

Computers: 93 computers/terminals are available on campus for general student use. Students can access the following: computer help desk, free student e-mail accounts, online (class) grades, online (class) schedules. Campuswide network is available. Wireless service is available via entire campus.
Library: Rasmussen College Library - Eagan.

STUDENT LIFE

Housing options: college housing not available.

APPLYING

Options: early admission, deferred entrance.

Required: high school transcript, minimum 2.0 GPA. ***Required for some:*** interview.

Application deadlines: rolling (freshmen), rolling (transfers).

CONTACT

Mr. Dwayne Bertotto, Vice President of Admissions and Student Experience, Rasmussen College Eagan, 8300 Norman Center Drive, Suite 300, Bloomington, MN 55437. *Phone:* 952-806-3958. *Toll-free phone:* 888-549-6755. *E-mail:* dwayne.bertotto@rasmussen.edu.

Rasmussen College Lake Elmo/Woodbury

Lake Elmo, Minnesota

http://www.rasmussen.edu/

- **Proprietary** 4-year, part of Rasmussen College System
- **Suburban** campus with easy access to Minneapolis-St. Paul
- **Coed** 305 undergraduate students, 57% full-time, 84% women, 16% men
- 100% of applicants were admitted

UNDERGRAD STUDENTS

175 full-time, 130 part-time. Students come from 51 states and territories; 27% are from out of state; 10% Black or African American, non-Hispanic/Latino; 5% Hispanic/Latino; 11% Asian, non-Hispanic/Latino; 0.7% American Indian or Alaska Native, non-Hispanic/Latino; 2% Two or more races, non-Hispanic/Latino; 25% Race/ethnicity unknown.

Freshmen:
Admission: 90 applied, 90 admitted, 62 enrolled.

ACADEMICS

Calendar: quarters. *Degrees:* certificates, diplomas, associate, and bachelor's.

Special study options: academic remediation for entering students, accelerated degree program, adult/continuing education programs, distance learning, double majors, internships, part-time degree program, summer session for credit.

Computers: 85 computers/terminals are available on campus for general student use. Students can access the following: computer help desk, free student e-mail accounts, online (class) grades, online (class) schedules. Campuswide network is available. Wireless service is available via entire campus.
Library: Rasmussen College Library - Lake Elmo.

STUDENT LIFE

Housing options: college housing not available.

APPLYING

Options: early admission, deferred entrance.

Required: high school transcript, minimum 2.0 GPA. ***Required for some:*** interview.

Application deadlines: rolling (freshmen), rolling (transfers).

CONTACT

Ms. Susan Hammerstrom, Director of Admissions, Rasmussen College Lake Elmo/Woodbury, 8565 Eagle Point Circle, Lake Elmo, MN 55042. *Phone:* 651-259-6600. *Toll-free phone:* 888-549-6755. *E-mail:* susan.hammerstrom@rasmussen.edu.

Rasmussen College Mankato

Mankato, Minnesota

http://www.rasmussen.edu/

- **Proprietary** 4-year, founded 1904, part of Rasmussen College System
- **Suburban** campus with easy access to Minneapolis-St. Paul
- **Coed** 575 undergraduate students, 56% full-time, 89% women, 11% men
- 100% of applicants were admitted

UNDERGRAD STUDENTS
322 full-time, 253 part-time. Students come from 51 states and territories; 27% are from out of state; 2% Black or African American, non-Hispanic/Latino; 7% Hispanic/Latino; 2% Asian, non-Hispanic/Latino; 0.3% Native Hawaiian or other Pacific Islander, non-Hispanic/Latino; 0.2% American Indian or Alaska Native, non-Hispanic/Latino; 2% Two or more races, non-Hispanic/Latino; 16% Race/ethnicity unknown.

Freshmen:
Admission: 132 applied, 132 admitted, 56 enrolled.

ACADEMICS
Calendar: quarters. *Degrees:* certificates, diplomas, associate, bachelor's, and postbachelor's certificates.

Special study options: academic remediation for entering students, accelerated degree program, adult/continuing education programs, distance learning, double majors, internships, part-time degree program, summer session for credit.

Computers: 116 computers/terminals are available on campus for general student use. Students can access the following: computer help desk, free student e-mail accounts, online (class) grades, online (class) schedules. Campuswide network is available. Wireless service is available via entire campus.
Library: Rasmussen College Library - Mankato.

STUDENT LIFE
Housing options: college housing not available.

FINANCIAL AID
Financial Aid Of all full-time matriculated undergraduates who enrolled in 2018, 15 Federal Work-Study jobs (averaging $4000). 13 state and other part-time jobs (averaging $4000).

APPLYING
Options: early admission, deferred entrance.

Required: high school transcript, minimum 2.0 GPA. ***Required for some:*** interview.

Application deadlines: rolling (freshmen), rolling (transfers).

CONTACT
Mr. Dwayne Bertotto, Vice President of Admissions and Student Experience, Rasmussen College Mankato, 1400 Madison Avenue, Mankato, MN 56001. *Phone:* 952-806-3958. *Toll-free phone:* 888-549-6755. *E-mail:* dwayne.bertto@rasmussen.edu.

Rasmussen College Moorhead

Moorhead, Minnesota

http://www.rasmussen.edu/

- **Proprietary** 4-year, part of Rasmussen College System
- **Suburban** campus
- **Coed** 417 undergraduate students, 59% full-time, 86% women, 14% men
- 100% of applicants were admitted

UNDERGRAD STUDENTS
244 full-time, 173 part-time. Students come from 51 states and territories; 27% are from out of state; 13% Black or African American, non-Hispanic/Latino; 5% Hispanic/Latino; 3% Asian, non-Hispanic/Latino; 2% American Indian or Alaska Native, non-Hispanic/Latino; 4% Two or more races, non-Hispanic/Latino; 19% Race/ethnicity unknown.

Freshmen:
Admission: 114 applied, 114 admitted, 27 enrolled.

ACADEMICS
Calendar: quarters. *Degrees:* certificates, diplomas, associate, and bachelor's.

Special study options: academic remediation for entering students, accelerated degree program, adult/continuing education programs, distance learning, double majors, internships, part-time degree program, summer session for credit.

Computers: 31 computers/terminals are available on campus for general student use. Students can access the following: computer help desk, free student e-mail accounts, online (class) grades, online (class) schedules. Campuswide network is available. Wireless service is available via entire campus.
Library: Rasmussen College Library - Moorhead.

STUDENT LIFE
Housing options: college housing not available.

APPLYING
Options: early admission, deferred entrance.

Required: high school transcript, minimum 2.0 GPA. ***Required for some:*** interview.

Application deadlines: rolling (freshmen), rolling (transfers).

CONTACT
Ms. Susan Hammerstrom, Director of Admissions, Rasmussen College Moorhead, 1250 29th Avenue South, Moorhead, MN 56560. *Phone:* 218-304-6200. *Toll-free phone:* 888-549-6755. *E-mail:* susan.hammerstrom@rasmussen.edu.

Rasmussen College St. Cloud

St. Cloud, Minnesota

http://www.rasmussen.edu/

- **Proprietary** 4-year, founded 1904, part of Rasmussen College System
- **Suburban** campus
- **Coed** 551 undergraduate students, 51% full-time, 89% women, 11% men
- 100% of applicants were admitted

UNDERGRAD STUDENTS
280 full-time, 271 part-time. Students come from 51 states and territories; 27% are from out of state; 4% Black or African American, non-Hispanic/Latino; 4% Hispanic/Latino; 1% Asian, non-Hispanic/Latino; 0.2% Native Hawaiian or other Pacific Islander, non-Hispanic/Latino; 1% American Indian or Alaska Native, non-Hispanic/Latino; 2% Two or more races, non-Hispanic/Latino; 26% Race/ethnicity unknown.

Freshmen:
Admission: 148 applied, 148 admitted, 70 enrolled.

ACADEMICS
Calendar: quarters. *Degrees:* certificates, diplomas, associate, bachelor's, and postbachelor's certificates.

Special study options: academic remediation for entering students, accelerated degree program, adult/continuing education programs, distance learning, double majors, internships, part-time degree program, summer session for credit.

Computers: 91 computers/terminals are available on campus for general student use. Students can access the following: computer help desk, free student e-mail accounts, online (class) grades, online (class) schedules. Campuswide network is available. Wireless service is available via entire campus.
Library: Rasmussen College Library - St. Cloud.

STUDENT LIFE
Housing options: college housing not available.

FINANCIAL AID
Financial Aid Of all full-time matriculated undergraduates who enrolled in 2018, 34 Federal Work-Study jobs (averaging $866). 51 state and other part-time jobs (averaging $700).

APPLYING
Options: early admission, deferred entrance.

Required: high school transcript, minimum 2.0 GPA. ***Required for some:*** interview.

Application deadlines: rolling (freshmen), rolling (transfers).

CONTACT
Dwayne Bertotto, Vice President of Admissions and Student Experience, Rasmussen College St. Cloud, 8300 Norman Center Drive, Suite 300,

Bloomington, MN 55437. *Phone:* 952-806-3958. *Toll-free phone:* 888-549-6755. *E-mail:* dwayne.bertotto@rasmussen.edu.

St. Catherine University

St. Paul, Minnesota

http://www.stkate.edu/

- **Independent Roman Catholic** comprehensive, founded 1905
- **Urban** 110-acre campus with easy access to Minneapolis-St. Paul
- **Undergraduate: women only; graduate: coed** 3,153 undergraduate students, 64% full-time, 95% women, 5% men
- **Moderately difficult** entrance level, 67% of applicants were admitted

UNDERGRAD STUDENTS

2,004 full-time, 1,149 part-time. 26% are from out of state; 10% Black or African American, non-Hispanic/Latino; 11% Hispanic/Latino; 12% Asian, non-Hispanic/Latino; 0.3% Native Hawaiian or other Pacific Islander, non-Hispanic/Latino; 0.1% American Indian or Alaska Native, non-Hispanic/Latino; 4% Two or more races, non-Hispanic/Latino; 2% Race/ethnicity unknown; 0.6% international; 12% transferred in; 39% live on campus.

Freshmen:

Admission: 2,443 applied, 1,645 admitted, 335 enrolled. ***Average high school GPA:*** 3.7. ***Test scores:*** SAT evidence-based reading and writing scores over 500: 94%; SAT math scores over 500: 438%; ACT scores over 18: 88%; SAT evidence-based reading and writing scores over 600: 56%; SAT math scores over 600: 394%; ACT scores over 24: 37%; SAT evidence-based reading and writing scores over 700: 6%; SAT math scores over 700: 6%; ACT scores over 30: 7%.

Retention: 80% of full-time freshmen returned.

FACULTY

Total: 509, 54% full-time, 41% with terminal degrees.

Student/faculty ratio: 11:1.

ACADEMICS

Calendar: 4-1-4. *Degrees:* certificates, associate, bachelor's, master's, doctoral, and postbachelor's certificates.

Special study options: adult/continuing education programs, distance learning, double majors, honors programs, independent study, internships, part-time degree program, student-designed majors, study abroad. ***ROTC:*** Army (c), Air Force (c).

Computers: Students can access the following: campus intranet, computer help desk, free student e-mail accounts, online (class) grades, online (class) registration, online (class) schedules, transcript. Campuswide network is available. Wireless service is available via entire campus.

Library: St. Catherine Library.

STUDENT LIFE

Housing options: women-only. Campus housing is university owned. Freshman campus housing is guaranteed.

Activities and organizations: drama/theater group, student-run newspaper, radio station, choral group.

Athletics Member NCAA. All Division III. ***Intercollegiate sports:*** basketball W, cross-country running W, ice hockey W, soccer W, softball W, swimming and diving W, tennis W, track and field W, volleyball W. ***Intramural sports:*** basketball W, cheerleading W, cross-country running W, football W, golf W, lacrosse W, racquetball W, soccer W, softball W, swimming and diving W, tennis W, track and field W, volleyball W.

Campus security: 24-hour emergency response devices and patrols, student patrols, late-night transport/escort service, controlled dormitory access.

FINANCIAL AID

Financial Aid Of all full-time matriculated undergraduates who enrolled in 2019, 1,596 applied for aid, 1,340 were judged to have need, 575 had their need fully met. In 2019, 256 non-need-based awards were made. ***Average percent of need met:*** 91. ***Average financial aid package:*** $38,266. ***Average need-based loan:*** $4594. ***Average need-based gift aid:*** $9534. ***Average non-need-based aid:*** $21,890. ***Average indebtedness upon graduation:*** $33,587.

APPLYING

Standardized Tests *Required:* SAT or ACT (for admission).

Required: high school transcript, 1 letter of recommendation. ***Required for some:*** essay or personal statement, interview. ***Recommended:*** interview.

CONTACT

Associate Director of Admission and Financial Aid, St. Catherine University, 2004 Randolph Avenue, St. Paul, MN 55105. *Phone:* 651-690-6047. *Toll-free phone:* 800-945-4599. *E-mail:* stkate@stkate.edu.

St. Cloud State University

St. Cloud, Minnesota

http://www.stcloudstate.edu/

- **State-supported** comprehensive, founded 1869, part of Minnesota State Colleges and Universities System
- **Suburban** 100-acre campus with easy access to Minneapolis-St. Paul
- **Endowment** $24.7 million
- **Coed** 10,914 undergraduate students, 64% full-time, 53% women, 47% men
- **Moderately difficult** entrance level, 90% of applicants were admitted

UNDERGRAD STUDENTS

6,952 full-time, 3,962 part-time. 11% are from out of state; 9% Black or African American, non-Hispanic/Latino; 4% Hispanic/Latino; 7% Asian, non-Hispanic/Latino; 0.1% Native Hawaiian or other Pacific Islander, non-Hispanic/Latino; 0.2% American Indian or Alaska Native, non-Hispanic/Latino; 4% Two or more races, non-Hispanic/Latino; 0.4% Race/ethnicity unknown; 11% international; 7% transferred in; 19% live on campus.

Freshmen:

Admission: 5,171 applied, 4,656 admitted, 1,237 enrolled. ***Average high school GPA:*** 3.3. ***Test scores:*** SAT evidence-based reading and writing scores over 500: 68%; SAT math scores over 500: 62%; ACT scores over 18: 80%; SAT evidence-based reading and writing scores over 600: 19%; SAT math scores over 600: 28%; ACT scores over 24: 28%; SAT evidence-based reading and writing scores over 700: 2%; SAT math scores over 700: 8%; ACT scores over 30: 3%.

Retention: 67% of full-time freshmen returned.

FACULTY

Total: 656, 71% full-time, 67% with terminal degrees.

Student/faculty ratio: 17:1.

ACADEMICS

Calendar: semesters. *Degrees:* certificates, associate, bachelor's, master's, doctoral, and postbachelor's certificates.

Special study options: academic remediation for entering students, adult/continuing education programs, advanced placement credit, distance learning, double majors, English as a second language, external degree program, honors programs, independent study, internships, off-campus study, part-time degree program, services for LD students, student-designed majors, study abroad, summer session for credit. ***ROTC:*** Army (c).

Unusual degree programs: 3-2 economics.

Computers: Students can access the following: campus intranet, computer help desk, free student e-mail accounts, online (class) grades, online (class) registration, online (class) schedules. Campuswide network is available. 100% of college-owned or -operated housing units are wired for high-speed Internet access. Wireless service is available via entire campus.

Library: James W. Miller Learning Resources Center.

STUDENT LIFE

Housing options: coed. Campus housing is university owned. Freshman applicants given priority for college housing.

Activities and organizations: drama/theater group, student-run newspaper, radio and television station, choral group, Nepalese Student Association, Residence Hall Association, International Student Association, College Panhellenic Council, KVSC - Campus Radio Station, national fraternities, national sororities.

Athletics Member NCAA. All Division II except men's and women's ice hockey (Division I). ***Intercollegiate sports:*** baseball M(s), basketball M(s)/W(s), bowling M(c)/W(c), cheerleading M(c)/W(c), crew M(c)/W(c), cross-country running W(s), equestrian sports M(c)/W(c), football M(s), golf M(s)/W(s), ice hockey M(s)/W(s), rock climbing M(c)/W(c), skiing (cross-country) M(c)/W(s), skiing (downhill) M(c)/W(c), soccer M(c)/W(s), softball W(s), swimming and diving M(s)/W(s), tennis W(s), track and field W(s), ultimate Frisbee M(c)/W(c), volleyball M(c)/W(s), wrestling M(s). ***Intramural sports:*** archery M(c)/W(c), badminton M/W, basketball M/W, bowling M/W, crew M/W, equestrian sports M(c)/W(c), field hockey M/W, football M/W, golf M/W, ice hockey M(c), lacrosse M(c)/W(c), racquetball M/W, rock climbing M/W, rugby M(c)/W(c), skiing (downhill) M(c)/W(c), soccer M/W, softball M/W, squash M/W, tennis M/W, ultimate Frisbee M(c)/W(c), volleyball M/W, wrestling M.

Campus security: 24-hour emergency response devices and patrols, student patrols, late-night transport/escort service.

Student services: health clinic, personal/psychological counseling, women's center, legal services, veterans affairs office.

FINANCIAL AID

Financial Aid Of all full-time matriculated undergraduates who enrolled in 2019, 4,993 applied for aid, 3,886 were judged to have need, 1,027 had their need fully met. In 2019, 425 non-need-based awards were made. ***Average percent of need met:*** 72. ***Average financial aid package:*** $12,336. ***Average need-based loan:*** $4360. ***Average need-based gift aid:*** $6823. ***Average non-need-based aid:*** $3091. ***Average indebtedness upon graduation:*** $29,580.

APPLYING

Standardized Tests *Required:* SAT or ACT (for admission).

Options: electronic application, deferred entrance.

Application fee: $20.

Required: high school transcript.

Application deadlines: 8/1 (freshmen), 8/1 (transfers).

Notification: continuous (freshmen), continuous (out-of-state freshmen), continuous (transfers).

CONTACT

Ms. Amber Schultz, Assistant Vice President for Admissions, Marketing, and Recruitment, St. Cloud State University, 720 4th Avenue South, AS 115, St. Cloud, MN 56301-4498. *Phone:* 320-308-3870. *Toll-free phone:* 877-654-7278. *Fax:* 320-308-2243. *E-mail:* scsu4u@stcloudstate.edu.

Saint John's University

Collegeville, Minnesota

http://www.csbsju.edu/

- **Independent Roman Catholic** comprehensive, founded 1857
- **Rural** 2500-acre campus with easy access to Minneapolis-St. Paul
- **Endowment** $208.7 million
- **Undergraduate: men only; graduate: coed** 1,625 undergraduate students, 99% full-time, 100% men
- **Moderately difficult** entrance level, 78% of applicants were admitted

UNDERGRAD STUDENTS

1,608 full-time, 17 part-time. Students come from 44 states and territories; 10 other countries; 20% are from out of state; 4% Black or African American, non-Hispanic/Latino; 8% Hispanic/Latino; 4% Asian, non-Hispanic/Latino; 0.3% Native Hawaiian or other Pacific Islander, non-Hispanic/Latino; 0.7% American Indian or Alaska Native, non-Hispanic/Latino; 0.1% Two or more races, non-Hispanic/Latino; 5% international; 1% transferred in; 89% live on campus.

Freshmen:

Admission: 1,746 applied, 1,367 admitted, 414 enrolled. ***Average high school GPA:*** 3.6. ***Test scores:*** SAT evidence-based reading and writing scores over 500: 86%; SAT math scores over 500: 82%; ACT scores over 18: 99%; SAT evidence-based reading and writing scores over 600: 32%; SAT math scores over 600: 39%; ACT scores over 24: 61%; SAT evidence-based reading and writing scores over 700: 15%; SAT math scores over 700: 9%; ACT scores over 30: 14%.

Retention: 85% of full-time freshmen returned.

FACULTY

Total: 165, 84% full-time, 76% with terminal degrees.

Student/faculty ratio: 11:1.

ACADEMICS

Calendar: semesters. *Degrees:* bachelor's and master's (coordinate with College of Saint Benedict for women).

Special study options: advanced placement credit, distance learning, double majors, English as a second language, honors programs, independent study, internships, off-campus study, services for LD students, student-designed majors, study abroad. ***ROTC:*** Army (b).

Computers: 248 computers/terminals and 4,600 ports are available on campus for general student use. Students can access the following: campus intranet, computer help desk, free student e-mail accounts, online (class) grades, online (class) registration, online (class) schedules, online student accounts. Campuswide network is available. 100% of college-owned or -operated housing units are wired for high-speed Internet access. Wireless service is available via entire campus.

Library: Alcuin Library plus 2 others. *Books:* 527,784 (physical), 1.1 million (digital/electronic); *Serial titles:* 737 (physical), 49,092 (digital/electronic); *Databases:* 211. Weekly public service hours: 104; students can reserve study rooms.

STUDENT LIFE

Housing options: on-campus residence required through senior year; men-only, special housing for students with disabilities. Campus housing is university owned. Freshman campus housing is guaranteed.

Activities and organizations: drama/theater group, student-run newspaper, radio and television station, choral group, Joint Events Council, Outdoor Leadership Center, Magis Ministries, Enactus, Archipelago Caribbean Association.

Athletics Member NCAA. All Division III. ***Intercollegiate sports:*** baseball M, basketball M, crew M(c), cross-country running M, football M, golf M, ice hockey M, lacrosse M(c), riflery M(c), rugby M(c), skiing (cross-country) M(c), soccer M, swimming and diving M, tennis M, track and field M, ultimate Frisbee M(c), volleyball M(c), water polo M(c), wrestling M. ***Intramural sports:*** basketball M, football M, racquetball M, soccer M, softball M, ultimate Frisbee M, volleyball M.

Campus security: 24-hour emergency response devices and patrols, student patrols, late-night transport/escort service, controlled dormitory access.

Student services: health clinic, personal/psychological counseling.

COSTS & FINANCIAL AID

Costs (2020–21) ***Comprehensive fee:*** $60,362 includes full-time tuition ($48,166), mandatory fees ($834), and room and board ($11,362). Part-time tuition: $1905 per credit hour. Part-time tuition and fees vary according to course load. ***College room only:*** $5436. Room and board charges vary according to board plan and housing facility. ***Payment plan:*** installment. ***Waivers:*** employees or children of employees.

Financial Aid Of all full-time matriculated undergraduates who enrolled in 2019, 1,255 applied for aid, 1,081 were judged to have need, 375 had their need fully met. 161 Federal Work-Study jobs (averaging $3450). 820 state and other part-time jobs (averaging $3450). In 2019, 405 non-need-based awards were made. ***Average percent of need met:*** 89. ***Average financial aid package:*** $36,512. ***Average need-based loan:*** $4422. ***Average need-based gift aid:*** $32,212. ***Average non-need-based aid:*** $18,670. ***Average indebtedness upon graduation:*** $38,642.

APPLYING

Standardized Tests *Required:* SAT or ACT (for admission).

Options: electronic application, early action, deferred entrance.

Required: high school transcript, college preparatory program. ***Recommended:*** minimum 3.0 GPA.

Application deadlines: rolling (transfers), 12/15 (early action).

Notification: continuous (transfers), 1/15 (early action).

CONTACT

Mr. Matt Beirne, Director of Admission, Saint John's University, PO Box 7155, Collegeville, MN 56321-7155. *Phone:* 320-363-5060. *Toll-free phone:* 800-544-1489. *Fax:* 320-363-3206. *E-mail:* admissions@ csbsju.edu.

Saint Mary's University of Minnesota

Winona, Minnesota

http://www.smumn.edu/

- **Independent Roman Catholic** comprehensive, founded 1912
- **Small-town** 350-acre campus
- **Coed** 1,467 undergraduate students, 77% full-time, 56% women, 44% men
- **Moderately difficult** entrance level, 92% of applicants were admitted

UNDERGRAD STUDENTS
1,132 full-time, 335 part-time. Students come from 30 states and territories; 19 other countries; 46% are from out of state; 9% Black or African American, non-Hispanic/Latino; 8% Hispanic/Latino; 3% Asian, non-Hispanic/Latino; 0.1% Native Hawaiian or other Pacific Islander, non-Hispanic/Latino; 0.6% American Indian or Alaska Native, non-Hispanic/Latino; 0.5% Two or more races, non-Hispanic/Latino; 5% Race/ethnicity unknown; 3% international; 9% transferred in; 85% live on campus.

Freshmen:
Admission: 1,498 applied, 1,378 admitted, 301 enrolled. ***Average high school GPA:*** 3.6. ***Test scores:*** SAT evidence-based reading and writing scores over 500: 84%; SAT math scores over 500: 79%; ACT scores over 18: 91%; SAT evidence-based reading and writing scores over 600: 34%; SAT math scores over 600: 24%; ACT scores over 24: 50%; SAT evidence-based reading and writing scores over 700: 3%; SAT math scores over 700: 5%; ACT scores over 30: 7%.

Retention: 84% of full-time freshmen returned.

FACULTY
Total: 528, 20% full-time, 49% with terminal degrees.

Student/faculty ratio: 18:1.

ACADEMICS
Calendar: semesters. *Degrees:* bachelor's, master's, doctoral, post-master's, and postbachelor's certificates.

Special study options: academic remediation for entering students, accelerated degree program, adult/continuing education programs, advanced placement credit, cooperative education, distance learning, double majors, English as a second language, honors programs, independent study, internships, off-campus study, part-time degree program, services for LD students, student-designed majors, study abroad, summer session for credit. ***ROTC:*** Army (c).

Computers: 200 computers/terminals and 50 ports are available on campus for general student use. Students can access the following: campus intranet, computer help desk, free student e-mail accounts, online (class) grades, online (class) registration, online (class) schedules. Campuswide network is available. 100% of college-owned or -operated housing units are wired for high-speed Internet access. Wireless service is available via computer centers, computer labs, dorm rooms, libraries, student centers.

Library: Fitzgerald Library plus 1 other. *Books:* 155,417 (physical), 423,045 (digital/electronic); *Serial titles:* 1,120 (physical), 165,670 (digital/electronic); *Databases:* 93. Weekly public service hours: 97; students can reserve study rooms.

STUDENT LIFE
Housing options: on-campus residence required through sophomore year; coed, men-only, women-only, special housing for students with disabilities. Campus housing is university owned. Freshman campus housing is guaranteed.

Activities and organizations: drama/theater group, student-run newspaper, radio station, choral group, Student Activity Committee, PR Business Club, Serving Others United in Love (Soul) - Mission Trips, Colleges Against Cancer, Club Hockey, national fraternities, national sororities.

Athletics Member NCAA. All Division III. ***Intercollegiate sports:*** baseball M, basketball M/W, cross-country running M/W, ice hockey M/W, soccer M/W, softball W, tennis M/W, track and field M/W, volleyball W. ***Intramural sports:*** basketball M/W, bowling M/W, cheerleading W(c), fencing M(c)/W, field hockey M/W(c), football M/W, ice hockey M/W, lacrosse M(c)/W(c), racquetball M/W, rugby M(c), skiing (downhill) M(c)/W(c), soccer M/W, softball M/W, tennis M/W, ultimate Frisbee M/W, volleyball M/W, water polo M(c)/W(c), weight lifting M/W.

Campus security: 24-hour emergency response devices and patrols, late-night transport/escort service, controlled dormitory access.

Student services: health clinic, personal/psychological counseling.

COSTS & FINANCIAL AID
Costs (2020–21) ***Comprehensive fee:*** $47,910 includes full-time tuition ($37,650), mandatory fees ($630), and room and board ($9630). Full-time tuition and fees vary according to course load and location. Part-time tuition: $1250 per credit. Part-time tuition and fees vary according to course load and location. ***College room only:*** $5390. Room and board charges vary according to board plan and housing facility. ***Payment plan:*** installment. ***Waivers:*** employees or children of employees.

Financial Aid Of all full-time matriculated undergraduates who enrolled in 2018, 885 applied for aid, 804 were judged to have need, 182 had their need fully met. In 2018, 266 non-need-based awards were made. ***Average percent of need met:*** 73. ***Average financial aid package:*** $27,072. ***Average need-based loan:*** $3595. ***Average need-based gift aid:*** $24,428. ***Average non-need-based aid:*** $20,068. ***Average indebtedness upon graduation:*** $34,917.

APPLYING
Standardized Tests *Required:* SAT or ACT (for admission).

Options: electronic application, early admission, deferred entrance.

Application fee: $25.

Required: essay or personal statement, high school transcript, minimum 2.5 GPA. ***Required for some:*** interview. ***Recommended:*** 2 letters of recommendation.

Application deadlines: 5/1 (freshmen), rolling (transfers).

Notification: continuous (freshmen), continuous (transfers).

CONTACT
Kristina Lemmer, Director of Admission - College, Saint Mary's University of Minnesota, 700 Terrace Heights, Winona, MN 55987. *Phone:* 507-457-1700. *Toll-free phone:* 800-635-5987. *Fax:* 507-457-1722. *E-mail:* klemmer@smumn.edu.

St. Olaf College

Northfield, Minnesota

http://www.stolaf.edu/

- **Independent Lutheran** 4-year, founded 1874
- **Small-town** 300-acre campus with easy access to Minneapolis-St. Paul
- **Endowment** $540.1 million
- **Coed** 3,072 undergraduate students, 99% full-time, 58% women, 42% men
- **Very difficult** entrance level, 48% of applicants were admitted

UNDERGRAD STUDENTS
3,050 full-time, 22 part-time. Students come from 49 states and territories; 89 other countries; 52% are from out of state; 3% Black or African American, non-Hispanic/Latino; 7% Hispanic/Latino; 7% Asian, non-Hispanic/Latino; 4% Two or more races, non-Hispanic/Latino; 0.5% Race/ethnicity unknown; 10% international; 0.7% transferred in; 95% live on campus.

Freshmen:
Admission: 5,694 applied, 2,705 admitted, 806 enrolled. ***Average high school GPA:*** 3.7. ***Test scores:*** SAT evidence-based reading and writing scores over 500: 95%; SAT math scores over 500: 97%; ACT scores over 18: 99%; SAT evidence-based reading and writing scores over 600: 75%; SAT math scores over 600: 77%; ACT scores over 24: 85%; SAT evidence-based reading and writing scores over 700: 32%; SAT math scores over 700: 35%; ACT scores over 30: 49%.

Retention: 91% of full-time freshmen returned.

FACULTY
Total: 326, 65% full-time, 80% with terminal degrees.

Student/faculty ratio: 12:1.

ACADEMICS
Calendar: 4-1-4. *Degree:* bachelor's.

Special study options: advanced placement credit, double majors, English as a second language, independent study, internships, off-campus study, part-time degree program, services for LD students, student-designed majors, study abroad, summer session for credit.

Computers: 500 computers/terminals and 3,300 ports are available on campus for general student use. Students can access the following: campus intranet, computer help desk, free student e-mail accounts, online (class) grades, online (class) registration, online (class) schedules. Campuswide network is available. 100% of college-owned or -operated housing units are wired for high-speed Internet access. Wireless service is available via entire campus.

Library: Rolvaag Memorial Library plus 3 others. *Books:* 326,790 (physical), 962,800 (digital/electronic); *Serial titles:* 3,007 (physical), 127,162 (digital/electronic); *Databases:* 358. Weekly public service hours: 112.

STUDENT LIFE

Housing options: on-campus residence required through senior year; coed, special housing for students with disabilities. Campus housing is university owned. Freshman campus housing is guaranteed.

Activities and organizations: drama/theater group, student-run newspaper, radio station, choral group, Student Government Association, Ultimate Frisbee Teams, Ole Spring Relief, Alpha Phi Omega, SARN: Sexual Assault Resource Network.

Athletics Member NCAA. All Division III except golf (Division II), skiing (downhill) (Division II). ***Intercollegiate sports:*** baseball M, basketball M/W, cross-country running M/W, football M, golf M/W, ice hockey M/W, skiing (cross-country) M/W, skiing (downhill) M/W, soccer M/W, softball W, swimming and diving M/W, tennis M/W, track and field M/W, volleyball W, wrestling M. ***Intramural sports:*** badminton M(c)/W(c), basketball M/W, crew M(c)/W(c), equestrian sports M(c)/W(c), football M/W, gymnastics M/W, ice hockey M(c), lacrosse M(c)/W(c), rowing M(c)/W(c), rugby M(c)/W(c), sand volleyball M/W, soccer M/W, softball M/W, swimming and diving M/W, table tennis M/W, tennis M/W, triathlon M/W, ultimate Frisbee M/W, volleyball M(c)/W, water polo M/W, weight lifting M/W.

Campus security: 24-hour emergency response devices and patrols, late-night transport/escort service, controlled dormitory access.

Student services: health clinic, personal/psychological counseling.

COSTS & FINANCIAL AID

Costs (2020–21) ***Comprehensive fee:*** $63,110 includes full-time tuition ($51,450) and room and board ($11,660). Part-time tuition: $1610 per credit hour. Part-time tuition and fees vary according to course load. ***College room only:*** $5590. Room and board charges vary according to board plan. ***Payment plan:*** installment. ***Waivers:*** senior citizens and employees or children of employees.

Financial Aid Of all full-time matriculated undergraduates who enrolled in 2019, 2,472 applied for aid, 2,326 were judged to have need, 1,862 had their need fully met. 428 Federal Work-Study jobs (averaging $2594). 1,953 state and other part-time jobs (averaging $2371). In 2019, 618 non-need-based awards were made. ***Average percent of need met:*** 96. ***Average financial aid package:*** $44,181. ***Average need-based loan:*** $4298. ***Average need-based gift aid:*** $37,646. ***Average non-need-based aid:*** $17,508. ***Average indebtedness upon graduation:*** $28,950.

APPLYING

Standardized Tests *Required:* SAT or ACT (for admission).

Options: electronic application, early decision, deferred entrance.

Required: essay or personal statement, high school transcript, 1 letter of recommendation. ***Recommended:*** 2 letters of recommendation, interview.

Application deadlines: 1/15 (freshmen), 4/1 (transfers).

Early decision deadline: 11/15 (for plan 1), 1/8 (for plan 2).

Notification: 3/20 (freshmen), 5/1 (transfers), 12/15 (early decision plan 1), 2/20 (early decision plan 2).

CONTACT

Dave Wagner, Director of Admissions, St. Olaf College, 1520 St. Olaf Avenue, Northfield, MN 55057. *Phone:* 507-786-3025. *Toll-free phone:* 800-800-3025. *Fax:* 507-786-3832. *E-mail:* admissions@stolaf.edu.

Southwest Minnesota State University

Marshall, Minnesota

http://www.smsu.edu/

- **State-supported** comprehensive, founded 1963, part of Minnesota State Colleges and Universities System
- **Small-town** 216-acre campus
- **Coed**
- **Minimally difficult** entrance level

FACULTY

Student/faculty ratio: 15:1.

ACADEMICS

Calendar: semesters. *Degrees:* associate, bachelor's, master's, and postbachelor's certificates.

Library: Southwest Minnesota State University.

STUDENT LIFE

Housing options: on-campus residence required for freshman year; coed, men-only, women-only, special housing for students with disabilities. Campus housing is university owned.

Activities and organizations: drama/theater group, student-run newspaper, radio and television station, choral group, marching band, Students in Free Enterprise (SIFE), Society of Leadership and Success, Family and Child Educators (FACE), Habitat for Humanity, Education Minnesota Student Program.

Athletics Member NCAA. All Division II.

Campus security: 24-hour emergency response devices and patrols, student patrols, late-night transport/escort service, controlled dormitory access.

Student services: health clinic, personal/psychological counseling, women's center.

FINANCIAL AID

Financial Aid Of all full-time matriculated undergraduates who enrolled in 2015, 1,608 applied for aid, 1,243 were judged to have need, 219 had their need fully met. 112 Federal Work-Study jobs (averaging $2258). 141 state and other part-time jobs (averaging $2262). In 2015, 342 non-need-based awards were made. ***Average percent of need met:*** 49. ***Average financial aid package:*** $8732. ***Average need-based loan:*** $3873. ***Average need-based gift aid:*** $5081. ***Average non-need-based aid:*** $2741. ***Average indebtedness upon graduation:*** $20,234.

APPLYING

Standardized Tests *Required:* SAT or ACT (for admission). *Recommended:* ACT (for admission).

Options: electronic application, early admission, deferred entrance.

Application fee: $20.

Required: high school transcript, minimum 3.0 GPA, top half of graduating class or 21 ACT. ***Required for some:*** interview.

CONTACT

Mr. Andrew Hlubeck, Director of Admissions, Southwest Minnesota State University, 1501 State Street, Marshall, MN 56258. *Phone:* 507-537-6286. *Toll-free phone:* 800-642-0684. *Fax:* 507-537-7145. *E-mail:* andrew.hlubek@smsu.edu.

University of Minnesota, Crookston

Crookston, Minnesota

http://www.umcrookston.edu/

- **State-supported** 4-year, founded 1966, part of University of Minnesota System
- **Rural** 237-acre campus
- **Endowment** $15.2 million
- **Coed**
- **Minimally difficult** entrance level

FACULTY

Student/faculty ratio: 16:1.

ACADEMICS

Calendar: semesters. *Degree:* bachelor's.

Library: UMC Library. *Books:* 47,423 (physical), 336,375 (digital/electronic); *Serial titles:* 412 (physical), 8,500 (digital/electronic); *Databases:* 152. Weekly public service hours: 76.

STUDENT LIFE
Housing options: coed, special housing for students with disabilities. Campus housing is university owned. Freshman applicants given priority for college housing.

Activities and organizations: drama/theater group, choral group, National Society for Leadership and Success, Archery Club, Crookston Futbol Club, Choir, Student Athletic Advisory Council, national fraternities.

Athletics Member NCAA. All Division II.

Campus security: 24-hour emergency response devices, student patrols, controlled dormitory access.

Student services: health clinic, personal/psychological counseling, women's center.

COSTS & FINANCIAL AID
Costs (2019–20) ***Tuition:*** area resident $10,438 full-time, $402 per credit hour part-time; state resident $10,438 full-time, $402 per credit hour part-time; nonresident $10,438 full-time, $402 per credit hour part-time. Full-time tuition and fees vary according to program. Part-time tuition and fees vary according to program. ***Required fees:*** $1678 full-time. ***Room and board:*** $9020; room only: $6520. Room and board charges vary according to board plan and housing facility.

Financial Aid Of all full-time matriculated undergraduates who enrolled in 2019, 964 applied for aid, 793 were judged to have need, 170 had their need fully met. In 2019, 110 non-need-based awards were made. ***Average percent of need met:*** 74. ***Average financial aid package:*** $12,382. ***Average need-based loan:*** $4026. ***Average need-based gift aid:*** $9614. ***Average non-need-based aid:*** $2201. ***Average indebtedness upon graduation:*** $26,107.

APPLYING
Standardized Tests *Required:* SAT or ACT (for admission). *Recommended:* ACT (for admission).

Options: electronic application, deferred entrance.

Application fee: $30.

Required: high school transcript, minimum 2.0 GPA, minimum ACT composite score of 21 or SAT of 980.

CONTACT
Michelle Christopherson, Director of Admissions, University of Minnesota, Crookston, 2900 University Avenue, Crookston, MN 56716-5001. *Phone:* 218-281-8679. *Toll-free phone:* 800-862-6466. *E-mail:* mchristo@crk.umn.edu.

University of Minnesota, Duluth

Duluth, Minnesota

http://www.d.umn.edu/

- **State-supported** comprehensive, founded 1947, part of University of Minnesota System
- **Suburban** 250-acre campus
- **Endowment** $182.8 million
- **Coed** 9,847 undergraduate students, 87% full-time, 48% women, 52% men
- **Moderately difficult** entrance level, 76% of applicants were admitted

UNDERGRAD STUDENTS
8,535 full-time, 1,312 part-time. Students come from 37 states and territories; 26 other countries; 12% are from out of state; 2% Black or African American, non-Hispanic/Latino; 3% Hispanic/Latino; 4% Asian, non-Hispanic/Latino; 0.1% Native Hawaiian or other Pacific Islander, non-Hispanic/Latino; 0.6% American Indian or Alaska Native, non-Hispanic/Latino; 3% Two or more races, non-Hispanic/Latino; 1% Race/ethnicity unknown; 1% international; 4% transferred in; 33% live on campus.

Freshmen:
Admission: 8,601 applied, 6,521 admitted, 2,043 enrolled. ***Average high school GPA:*** 3.6. ***Test scores:*** SAT evidence-based reading and writing scores over 500: 87%; SAT math scores over 500: 97%; ACT scores over 18: 97%; SAT evidence-based reading and writing scores over 600: 56%; SAT math scores over 600: 56%; ACT scores over 24: 53%; SAT evidence-based reading and writing scores over 700: 15%; SAT math scores over 700: 27%; ACT scores over 30: 9%.

Retention: 80% of full-time freshmen returned.

FACULTY
Total: 592, 82% full-time, 67% with terminal degrees.

Student/faculty ratio: 17:1.

ACADEMICS
Calendar: semesters. *Degrees:* certificates, bachelor's, master's, doctoral, and postbachelor's certificates.

Special study options: academic remediation for entering students, adult/continuing education programs, advanced placement credit, distance learning, double majors, English as a second language, honors programs, independent study, internships, off-campus study, part-time degree program, services for LD students, student-designed majors, study abroad, summer session for credit. ***ROTC:*** Air Force (b).

Computers: 567 computers/terminals are available on campus for general student use. Students can access the following: campus intranet, computer help desk, free student e-mail accounts, online (class) grades, online (class) registration, online (class) schedules. Campuswide network is available. 100% of college-owned or -operated housing units are wired for high-speed Internet access. Wireless service is available via entire campus.

Library: Kathryn A. Martin Library. *Books:* 276,038 (physical), 642,394 (digital/electronic); *Serial titles:* 3,254 (physical), 164,241 (digital/electronic); *Databases:* 237. Weekly public service hours: 94.

STUDENT LIFE
Housing options: coed, men-only, women-only, special housing for students with disabilities. Campus housing is university owned. Freshman applicants given priority for college housing.

Activities and organizations: drama/theater group, student-run newspaper, choral group, marching band, Gamma Sigma Sigma, Phi Sigma Sigma, UMD Badminton Club, UMD North Shore Climbing Club, S.E.R.V.E., national fraternities, national sororities.

Athletics Member NCAA. All Division II except men's and women's ice hockey (Division I). ***Intercollegiate sports:*** badminton M(c)/W(c), baseball M(s), basketball M(s)/W(s), cheerleading W(c), cross-country running M(s)/W(s), football M(s), ice hockey M(s)/W(s), lacrosse M(s)(c)/W(s)(c), rugby M(c)/W(c), skiing (downhill) W(c), soccer M(c)/W(s), softball W(s), tennis W(s), track and field M/W, volleyball M(c)/W(s), water polo W. ***Intramural sports:*** badminton M/W, basketball M/W, bowling M/W, football M/W, golf M/W, ice hockey M/W, rock climbing M(c)/W(c), rowing M(c)/W(c), soccer M/W, softball M/W, swimming and diving M(c)/W(c), table tennis M(c)/W(c), tennis W, ultimate Frisbee M(c)/W(c), volleyball M/W, water polo M(c)/W(c), wrestling M(c).

Campus security: 24-hour emergency response devices and patrols, late-night transport/escort service.

Student services: health clinic, personal/psychological counseling, women's center.

COSTS & FINANCIAL AID
Costs (2019–20) ***Tuition:*** state resident $12,194 full-time, $469 per credit hour part-time; nonresident $17,394 full-time, $669 per credit hour part-time. Full-time tuition and fees vary according to course load, program, and reciprocity agreements. Part-time tuition and fees vary according to course load, program, and reciprocity agreements. ***Required fees:*** $1487 full-time. ***Room and board:*** $8374; room only: $5366. Room and board charges vary according to board plan and housing facility. ***Payment plan:*** installment. ***Waivers:*** children of alumni and employees or children of employees.

Financial Aid Of all full-time matriculated undergraduates who enrolled in 2018, 7,057 applied for aid, 5,023 were judged to have need, 1,522 had their need fully met. 580 Federal Work-Study jobs (averaging $1461). 1,611 state and other part-time jobs (averaging $615). In 2018, 1389 non-need-based awards were made. ***Average percent of need met:*** 73. ***Average financial aid package:*** $13,203. ***Average need-based loan:*** $6638. ***Average need-based gift aid:*** $8578. ***Average non-need-based aid:*** $2149. ***Average indebtedness upon graduation:*** $30,687.

APPLYING
Standardized Tests *Required:* SAT or ACT (for admission).

Options: electronic application.

Application fee: $40.

Required: high school transcript. ***Required for some:*** interview. ***Recommended:*** essay or personal statement.

Application deadlines: 8/1 (freshmen), 8/1 (out-of-state freshmen), 8/1 (transfers).

Notification: continuous until 9/15 (freshmen), continuous until 9/15 (out-of-state freshmen), continuous (transfers).

CONTACT

University of Minnesota, Duluth, 1049 University Drive, Duluth, MN 55812-2496. *Phone:* 218-726-7171. *Toll-free phone:* 800-232-1339.

University of Minnesota, Morris

Morris, Minnesota

http://www.morris.umn.edu/

- **State-supported** 4-year, founded 1959, part of University of Minnesota System
- **Rural** 130-acre campus
- **Endowment** $16.7 million
- **Coed** 1,499 undergraduate students, 91% full-time, 58% women, 42% men
- **Moderately difficult** entrance level, 57% of applicants were admitted

UNDERGRAD STUDENTS

1,368 full-time, 131 part-time. Students come from 34 states and territories; 20 other countries; 18% are from out of state; 3% Black or African American, non-Hispanic/Latino; 6% Hispanic/Latino; 2% Asian, non-Hispanic/Latino; 8% American Indian or Alaska Native, non-Hispanic/Latino; 15% Two or more races, non-Hispanic/Latino; 2% Race/ethnicity unknown; 7% international; 6% transferred in; 50% live on campus.

Freshmen:

Admission: 3,257 applied, 1,852 admitted, 322 enrolled. ***Average high school GPA:*** 3.6. ***Test scores:*** SAT evidence-based reading and writing scores over 500: 88%; SAT math scores over 500: 91%; ACT scores over 18: 96%; SAT evidence-based reading and writing scores over 600: 58%; SAT math scores over 600: 30%; ACT scores over 24: 55%; SAT evidence-based reading and writing scores over 700: 21%; SAT math scores over 700: 9%; ACT scores over 30: 15%.

Retention: 79% of full-time freshmen returned.

FACULTY

Total: 155, 76% full-time, 84% with terminal degrees.

Student/faculty ratio: 11:1.

ACADEMICS

Calendar: semesters. *Degree:* bachelor's.

Special study options: advanced placement credit, distance learning, double majors, English as a second language, external degree program, honors programs, independent study, internships, off-campus study, part-time degree program, services for LD students, student-designed majors, study abroad, summer session for credit.

Unusual degree programs: 3-2 engineering with University of Minnesota, Twin Cities Campus.

Computers: 350 computers/terminals and 545 ports are available on campus for general student use. Students can access the following: campus intranet, computer help desk, free student e-mail accounts, online (class) grades, online (class) registration, online (class) schedules. Campuswide network is available. 100% of college-owned or -operated housing units are wired for high-speed Internet access. Wireless service is available via classrooms, computer labs, dorm rooms, learning centers, libraries, student centers.

Library: Rodney A. Briggs Library plus 1 other. *Books:* 232,131 (physical), 764,113 (digital/electronic); *Serial titles:* 137 (physical), 122,201 (digital/electronic); *Databases:* 139. Weekly public service hours: 99.

STUDENT LIFE

Housing options: coed, special housing for students with disabilities. Campus housing is university owned. Freshman campus housing is guaranteed.

Activities and organizations: drama/theater group, student-run newspaper, radio station, choral group, Student Radio Station, Inter-Varsity Christian Fellowship, Dance Ensemble, Big Friend, Little Friend, Jazz Ensemble/Concert Choir.

Athletics Member NCAA. All Division III. ***Intercollegiate sports:*** baseball M, basketball M/W, cross-country running M/W, football M, golf M/W, soccer M/W, softball W, swimming and diving W, tennis M/W, track and field M/W, volleyball W. ***Intramural sports:*** badminton M/W, baseball M/W, basketball M/W, cheerleading M(c)/W(c), equestrian sports M(c)/W(c), fencing M(c), field hockey W(c), football M/W, racquetball M(c)/W(c), rugby M(c)/W(c), sand volleyball M/W, skiing (cross country) M/W, soccer M(c)/W(c), softball M/W, swimming and diving M(c)/W(c), table tennis M/W, triathlon M(c)/W(c), ultimate Frisbee M/W, volleyball W, weight lifting M(c)/W(c).

Campus security: 24-hour emergency response devices and patrols, late-night transport/escort service, controlled dormitory access.

Student services: health clinic, personal/psychological counseling, women's center, legal services, veterans affairs office.

COSTS & FINANCIAL AID

Costs (2019–20) ***Tuition:*** state resident $12,324 full-time, $474 per credit hour part-time; nonresident $14,378 full-time, $553 per credit hour part-time. Full-time tuition and fees vary according to reciprocity agreements. Part-time tuition and fees vary according to course load and reciprocity agreements. ***Required fees:*** $1254 full-time. ***Room and board:*** $8632; room only: $4100. Room and board charges vary according to board plan and housing facility. ***Payment plan:*** installment. ***Waivers:*** minority students, senior citizens, and employees or children of employees.

Financial Aid Of all full-time matriculated undergraduates who enrolled in 2016, 1,256 applied for aid, 1,019 were judged to have need, 257 had their need fully met. 307 Federal Work-Study jobs (averaging $1317). 96 state and other part-time jobs (averaging $1515). In 2016, 188 non-need-based awards were made. ***Average percent of need met:*** 75. ***Average financial aid package:*** $12,633. ***Average need-based loan:*** $3730. ***Average need-based gift aid:*** $10,095. ***Average non-need-based aid:*** $4187. ***Average indebtedness upon graduation:*** $25,732.

APPLYING

Standardized Tests *Required:* SAT or ACT (for admission).

Options: electronic application, deferred entrance.

Application fee: $25.

Required: high school transcript. ***Required for some:*** essay or personal statement, 1 letter of recommendation, interview.

Application deadlines: 8/1 (freshmen), 5/1 (transfers).

Notification: continuous (freshmen), continuous (transfers).

CONTACT

University of Minnesota, Morris, 600 East 4th Street, Morris, MN 56267-2134. *Phone:* 320-589-6017 Ext. 6017. *Toll-free phone:* 888-866-3382.

University of Minnesota Rochester

Rochester, Minnesota

http://www.r.umn.edu/

CONTACT

University of Minnesota Rochester, 111 South Broadway, Suite 300, Rochester, MN 55904.

University of Minnesota, Twin Cities Campus

Minneapolis, Minnesota

http://www.twin-cities.umn.edu/

- **State-supported** university, founded 1851, part of University of Minnesota System
- **Urban** 2000-acre campus with easy access to Minneapolis-St. Paul
- **Coed** 35,165 undergraduate students, 85% full-time, 54% women, 46% men
- **Moderately difficult** entrance level, 57% of applicants were admitted

UNDERGRAD STUDENTS

29,939 full-time, 5,226 part-time. Students come from 51 states and territories; 108 other countries; 27% are from out of state; 5% Black or

African American, non-Hispanic/Latino; 5% Hispanic/Latino; 10% Asian, non-Hispanic/Latino; 0.1% Native Hawaiian or other Pacific Islander, non-Hispanic/Latino; 0.2% American Indian or Alaska Native, non-Hispanic/Latino; 4% Two or more races, non-Hispanic/Latino; 2% Race/ethnicity unknown; 8% international; 5% transferred in; 23% live on campus.

Freshmen:
Admission: 40,673 applied, 23,076 admitted, 6,278 enrolled. ***Test scores:*** SAT evidence-based reading and writing scores over 500: 97%; SAT math scores over 500: 99%; ACT scores over 18: 99%; SAT evidence-based reading and writing scores over 600: 75%; SAT math scores over 600: 90%; ACT scores over 24: 89%; SAT evidence-based reading and writing scores over 700: 30%; SAT math scores over 700: 59%; ACT scores over 30: 40%.
Retention: 93% of full-time freshmen returned.

FACULTY
Total: 3,828, 70% full-time, 68% with terminal degrees.
Student/faculty ratio: 17:1.

ACADEMICS
Calendar: semesters. *Degrees:* certificates, diplomas, bachelor's, master's, doctoral, post-master's, and postbachelor's certificates.
Special study options: academic remediation for entering students, accelerated degree program, adult/continuing education programs, advanced placement credit, cooperative education, distance learning, double majors, English as a second language, external degree program, freshman honors college, honors programs, independent study, internships, off-campus study, part-time degree program, services for LD students, student-designed majors, study abroad, summer session for credit. ***ROTC:*** Army (b), Navy (b), Air Force (b).
Computers: Students can access the following: computer help desk, free student e-mail accounts, online (class) grades, online (class) registration, online (class) schedules. Campuswide network is available. Wireless service is available via entire campus.
Library: Wilson Library plus 17 others. *Books:* 4.1 million (physical), 1.3 million (digital/electronic); *Serial titles:* 153,623 (physical), 285,695 (digital/electronic); *Databases:* 896. Students can reserve study rooms.

STUDENT LIFE
Housing options: coed, cooperative, special housing for students with disabilities. Campus housing is university owned. Freshman campus housing is guaranteed.
Activities and organizations: drama/theater group, student-run newspaper, radio and television station, choral group, marching band, Student Government, national fraternities, national sororities.
Athletics Member NCAA. All Division I except football (Division I-A). ***Intercollegiate sports:*** baseball M(s), basketball M(s)/W(s), cross-country running M(s)/W(s), golf M(s)/W(s)(c), gymnastics M(s)/W(s), ice hockey M(s)/W(s), soccer W(s), softball W(s), swimming and diving M(s)/W(s), tennis M(s)/W(s), track and field M(s)/W(s), volleyball W(s), wrestling M(s). ***Intramural sports:*** baseball M/W, basketball M/W, bowling M/W, crew M/W, football M/W, golf M/W, ice hockey M/W, rugby M/W, skiing (cross-country) M/W, skiing (downhill) M/W, soccer M/W, softball M/W, tennis M/W, volleyball M/W, water polo M/W, wrestling M/W.
Campus security: 24-hour emergency response devices and patrols, student patrols, late-night transport/escort service, controlled dormitory access.
Student services: health clinic, personal/psychological counseling, women's center, legal services, veterans affairs office.

COSTS & FINANCIAL AID
Costs (2019–20) ***Tuition:*** state resident $13,318 full-time, $512 per credit part-time; nonresident $31,616 full-time, $984 per credit part-time. Full-time tuition and fees vary according to program and reciprocity agreements. Part-time tuition and fees vary according to course load, program, and reciprocity agreements. ***Required fees:*** $1709 full-time. ***Room and board:*** $10,768; room only: $6278. Room and board charges vary according to board plan, housing facility, and location. ***Payment plan:*** installment. ***Waivers:*** senior citizens.
Financial Aid Of all full-time matriculated undergraduates who enrolled in 2019, 19,844 applied for aid, 13,501 were judged to have need, 3,335 had their need fully met. In 2019, 2778 non-need-based awards were made. ***Average percent of need met:*** 74. ***Average financial aid package:*** $14,347. ***Average need-based loan:*** $4288. ***Average need-based gift aid:*** $11,235. ***Average non-need-based aid:*** $5200. ***Average indebtedness upon graduation:*** $27,077.

APPLYING
Standardized Tests *Required:* SAT or ACT (for admission).
Options: electronic application, deferred entrance.
Application fee: $55.
Required: high school transcript. ***Recommended:*** minimum 2.0 GPA.
Application deadlines: rolling (freshmen), rolling (out-of-state freshmen), rolling (transfers).
Notification: continuous (freshmen), continuous (out-of-state freshmen), continuous (transfers).

CONTACT
Heidi Meyer, Executive Director of Admissions, University of Minnesota, Twin Cities Campus, 240 Williamson, Minneapolis, MN 55455-0213. *Phone:* 612-625-2008. *Toll-free phone:* 800-752-1000. *Fax:* 612-626-1693. *E-mail:* admissions@tc.umn.edu.

University of Northwestern–St. Paul

St. Paul, Minnesota

http://www.unwsp.edu/

- **Independent nondenominational** comprehensive, founded 1902
- **Suburban** 107-acre campus with easy access to Minneapolis-St. Paul
- **Endowment** $18.7 million
- **Coed** 3,376 undergraduate students, 61% full-time, 63% women, 37% men
- **Moderately difficult** entrance level, 92% of applicants were admitted

UNDERGRAD STUDENTS
2,073 full-time, 1,303 part-time. Students come from 29 states and territories; 10 other countries; 22% are from out of state; 3% Black or African American, non-Hispanic/Latino; 5% Hispanic/Latino; 3% Asian, non-Hispanic/Latino; 0.3% American Indian or Alaska Native, non-Hispanic/Latino; 4% Two or more races, non-Hispanic/Latino; 2% Race/ethnicity unknown; 1% international; 4% transferred in; 59% live on campus.

Freshmen:
Admission: 1,243 applied, 1,141 admitted, 246 enrolled. ***Average high school GPA:*** 3.5. ***Test scores:*** SAT evidence-based reading and writing scores over 500: 94%; SAT math scores over 500: 97%; ACT scores over 18: 94%; SAT evidence-based reading and writing scores over 600: 48%; SAT math scores over 600: 42%; ACT scores over 24: 53%; SAT evidence-based reading and writing scores over 700: 9%; SAT math scores over 700: 21%; ACT scores over 30: 16%.
Retention: 85% of full-time freshmen returned.

FACULTY
Total: 292, 26% full-time, 41% with terminal degrees.
Student/faculty ratio: 17:1.

ACADEMICS
Calendar: semesters. *Degrees:* certificates, associate, bachelor's, master's, and postbachelor's certificates.
Special study options: academic remediation for entering students, accelerated degree program, adult/continuing education programs, advanced placement credit, distance learning, double majors, honors programs, independent study, internships, off-campus study, part-time degree program, services for LD students, student-designed majors, study abroad, summer session for credit. ***ROTC:*** Army (c), Air Force (c).
Unusual degree programs: 3-2 business administration; BA/MDiv in Pastoral Ministry, BA/MAML in Ministry Leadership.
Computers: 200 computers/terminals and 1,350 ports are available on campus for general student use. Students can access the following: campus intranet, computer help desk, free student e-mail accounts, online (class) grades, online (class) registration, online (class) schedules, network file space, personal website, integrated student portal, b/w and color printing, virtual labs. Campuswide network is available. 100% of college-owned or -operated housing units are wired for high-speed Internet access. Wireless service is available via classrooms, computer

centers, computer labs, dorm rooms, learning centers, libraries, student centers.
Library: Berntsen Resource Center. *Books:* 86,024 (physical), 363,470 (digital/electronic); *Serial titles:* 627 (physical), 52,723 (digital/electronic); *Databases:* 106. Students can reserve study rooms.

STUDENT LIFE
Housing options: on-campus residence required through junior year; coed, men-only, women-only, special housing for students with disabilities. Campus housing is university owned. Freshman campus housing is guaranteed.

Activities and organizations: drama/theater group, student-run newspaper, radio and television station, choral group, Northwestern Student Association (student government), The Gathering (religious group), Student Missions Fellowship, Guardian Angels, Outreach Ministries.

Athletics Member NCAA, NCCAA. All NCAA Division III. ***Intercollegiate sports:*** baseball M, basketball M/W, cross-country running M/W, football M, golf M/W, ice hockey M(c), lacrosse M/W, soccer M/W, softball W, tennis M/W, track and field M/W, volleyball M(c)/W. ***Intramural sports:*** basketball M/W, football M/W, softball M/W, table tennis M/W, tennis M/W, ultimate Frisbee M/W, volleyball M/W.

Campus security: 24-hour emergency response devices and patrols, late-night transport/escort service, controlled dormitory access.

Student services: health clinic, personal/psychological counseling, veterans affairs office.

COSTS & FINANCIAL AID
Costs (2020–21) ***Comprehensive fee:*** $43,200 includes full-time tuition ($32,490), mandatory fees ($710), and room and board ($10,000). Full-time tuition and fees vary according to class time and program. Part-time tuition: $1390 per credit. Part-time tuition and fees vary according to class time and program. ***College room only:*** $5920. Room and board charges vary according to board plan and student level. ***Payment plan:*** installment. ***Waivers:*** employees or children of employees.

Financial Aid Of all full-time matriculated undergraduates who enrolled in 2018, 1,430 applied for aid, 1,269 were judged to have need, 124 had their need fully met. 213 Federal Work-Study jobs (averaging $1291). 275 state and other part-time jobs (averaging $2163). In 2018, 302 non-need-based awards were made. ***Average percent of need met:*** 71. ***Average financial aid package:*** $22,931. ***Average need-based loan:*** $4359. ***Average need-based gift aid:*** $18,391. ***Average non-need-based aid:*** $10,883. ***Average indebtedness upon graduation:*** $44,561. ***Financial aid deadline:*** 8/1.

APPLYING
Standardized Tests *Required:* SAT or ACT (for admission).

Options: electronic application, early action, deferred entrance.

Application fee: $25.

Required: essay or personal statement, high school transcript, minimum 2.0 GPA, 2 letters of recommendation, lifestyle agreement, statement of Christian faith. ***Required for some:*** interview. ***Recommended:*** minimum 3.0 GPA.

Application deadlines: 8/1 (freshmen), 8/1 (out-of-state freshmen), 8/1 (transfers), 11/15 (early action).

Notification: continuous (freshmen), continuous (out-of-state freshmen), continuous (transfers), 12/1 (early action).

CONTACT
University of Northwestern–St. Paul, 3003 Snelling Avenue North, St. Paul, MN 55113-1598. *Phone:* 651-631-5141. *Toll-free phone:* 800-827-6827.

University of St. Thomas

St. Paul, Minnesota

http://www.stthomas.edu/

- **Independent Roman Catholic** university, founded 1885
- **Urban** 78-acre campus with easy access to Minneapolis-St. Paul
- **Endowment** $494.0 million
- **Coed**
- **Moderately difficult** entrance level

FACULTY
Student/faculty ratio: 14:1.

ACADEMICS
Calendar: 4-1-4. *Degrees:* certificates, associate, bachelor's, master's, doctoral, post-master's, and postbachelor's certificates.
Library: O'Shaughnessy-Frey Library plus 7 others. *Books:* 399,594 (physical), 1.2 million (digital/electronic); *Serial titles:* 1,701 (physical), 76,726 (digital/electronic); *Databases:* 308. Students can reserve study rooms.

STUDENT LIFE
Housing options: coed, men-only, women-only, special housing for students with disabilities. Campus housing is university owned. Freshman applicants given priority for college housing.

Activities and organizations: drama/theater group, student-run newspaper, radio and television station, choral group.

Athletics Member NCAA. All Division III except golf (Division II).

Campus security: 24-hour emergency response devices and patrols, late-night transport/escort service, controlled dormitory access.

Student services: health clinic, personal/psychological counseling, women's center, veterans affairs office.

COSTS & FINANCIAL AID
Costs (2019–20) ***Comprehensive fee:*** $56,942 includes full-time tuition ($44,780), mandatory fees ($1000), and room and board ($11,162). ***College room only:*** $6812.

Financial Aid Of all full-time matriculated undergraduates who enrolled in 2018, 4,323 applied for aid, 3,475 were judged to have need, 302 had their need fully met. 1,048 Federal Work-Study jobs (averaging $3119). 867 state and other part-time jobs (averaging $3087). In 2018, 752 non-need-based awards were made. ***Average percent of need met:*** 86. ***Average financial aid package:*** $29,751. ***Average need-based loan:*** $8238. ***Average need-based gift aid:*** $23,085. ***Average non-need-based aid:*** $21,057. ***Average indebtedness upon graduation:*** $40,983.

APPLYING
Standardized Tests *Required:* SAT or ACT (for admission).

Options: electronic application, early action, deferred entrance.

Required: essay or personal statement, high school transcript. ***Recommended:*** interview.

CONTACT
University of St. Thomas, 2115 Summit Avenue, St. Paul, MN 55105-1096. *Toll-free phone:* 800-328-6819.

Walden University

Minneapolis, Minnesota

http://www.waldenu.edu/

CONTACT
Walden University, 100 Washington South, Suite 900, Minneapolis, MN 55401. *Toll-free phone:* 866-492-5336.

Winona State University

Winona, Minnesota

http://www.winona.edu/

CONTACT
Brian Jicinsky, Director of Admissions, Winona State University, 175 West Mark Street, Winona, MN 55987. *Phone:* 507-457-5100. *Toll-free phone:* 800-DIAL WSU. *Fax:* 507-457-5620. *E-mail:* admissions@winona.edu.

MISSISSIPPI

Alcorn State University

Lorman, Mississippi

http://www.alcorn.edu/

CONTACT

Mrs. Kantangelia Tenner, Director of Admissions, Alcorn State University, 1000 ASU Drive, #300, Alcorn State, MS 39096-7500. *Phone:* 601-877-6147. *Toll-free phone:* 800-222-6790. *Fax:* 601-877-6347. *E-mail:* ksampson@alcorn.edu.

Belhaven University

Jackson, Mississippi

http://www.belhaven.edu/

- **Independent Presbyterian** comprehensive, founded 1883
- **Urban** 46-acre campus
- **Endowment** $5.6 million
- **Coed** 2,393 undergraduate students, 50% full-time, 64% women, 35% men
- **Moderately difficult** entrance level, 52% of applicants were admitted

UNDERGRAD STUDENTS

1,199 full-time, 1,171 part-time. Students come from 40 states and territories; 7 other countries; 41% are from out of state; 38% Black or African American, non-Hispanic/Latino; 5% Hispanic/Latino; 1% Asian, non-Hispanic/Latino; 0.3% American Indian or Alaska Native, non-Hispanic/Latino; 2% Two or more races, non-Hispanic/Latino; 8% Race/ethnicity unknown; 1% international; 16% transferred in; 22% live on campus.

Freshmen:

Admission: 1,961 applied, 1,012 admitted, 198 enrolled. ***Average high school GPA:*** 3.4. ***Test scores:*** SAT evidence-based reading and writing scores over 500: 89%; SAT math scores over 500: 79%; ACT scores over 18: 93%; SAT evidence-based reading and writing scores over 600: 43%; SAT math scores over 600: 18%; ACT scores over 24: 36%; SAT evidence-based reading and writing scores over 700: 11%; ACT scores over 30: 5%.

Retention: 67% of full-time freshmen returned.

FACULTY

Total: 429, 27% full-time, 26% with terminal degrees.

Student/faculty ratio: 10:1.

ACADEMICS

Calendar: semesters. *Degrees:* certificates, associate, bachelor's, master's, doctoral, and postbachelor's certificates.

Special study options: academic remediation for entering students, accelerated degree program, adult/continuing education programs, advanced placement credit, distance learning, double majors, English as a second language, honors programs, independent study, internships, off-campus study, part-time degree program, student-designed majors, study abroad, summer session for credit. ***ROTC:*** Army (c), Air Force (c).

Unusual degree programs: 3-2 business administration; engineering with University of Mississippi; nursing; social work.

Computers: 36 computers/terminals are available on campus for general student use. Students can access the following: campus intranet, computer help desk, free student e-mail accounts, online (class) grades, online (class) registration, online (class) schedules. Campuswide network is available. 100% of college-owned or -operated housing units are wired for high-speed Internet access. Wireless service is available via classrooms, computer centers, computer labs, dorm rooms, learning centers, libraries, student centers.

Library: Warren A. Hood Library plus 1 other. *Books:* 42,425 (physical), 106,114 (digital/electronic); *Serial titles:* 160 (physical), 75,718 (digital/electronic); *Databases:* 96. Weekly public service hours: 104; students can reserve study rooms.

STUDENT LIFE

Housing options: men-only, women-only. Campus housing is university owned. Freshman campus housing is guaranteed.

Activities and organizations: drama/theater group, student-run newspaper, choral group, marching band, Belhaven Activities Team, Fellowship of Christian Athletes, Reformed University Fellowship, Phi Beta Lambda, Belhaven University New Music Society.

Athletics Member NCAA. All Division III. ***Intercollegiate sports:*** baseball M, basketball M/W, cheerleading W, cross-country running M/W, football M, golf M/W, soccer M/W, softball W, tennis M/W, volleyball W. ***Intramural sports:*** basketball M/W, football M/W, soccer M/W, softball M/W, volleyball M/W.

Campus security: 24-hour emergency response devices and patrols, late-night transport/escort service, controlled dormitory access.

COSTS & FINANCIAL AID

Costs (2020–21) ***Comprehensive fee:*** $35,825 includes full-time tuition ($26,650), mandatory fees ($375), and room and board ($8800). Full-time tuition and fees vary according to location and program. Part-time tuition: $485 per credit hour. Part-time tuition and fees vary according to course load, location, and program. ***Required fees:*** $25 per credit hour part-time. ***Room and board:*** Room and board charges vary according to housing facility. ***Payment plan:*** installment. ***Waivers:*** employees or children of employees.

Financial Aid Of all full-time matriculated undergraduates who enrolled in 2018, 893 applied for aid, 776 were judged to have need, 82 had their need fully met. In 2018, 206 non-need-based awards were made. ***Average percent of need met:*** 65. ***Average financial aid package:*** $18,628. ***Average need-based loan:*** $4317. ***Average need-based gift aid:*** $13,913. ***Average non-need-based aid:*** $12,541.

APPLYING

Standardized Tests *Required for some:* SAT or ACT (for admission).

Options: electronic application, early admission, deferred entrance.

Application fee: $25.

Required: high school transcript, minimum 2.0 GPA, 1 letter of recommendation. ***Required for some:*** essay or personal statement, interview.

Application deadlines: rolling (freshmen), rolling (transfers).

Notification: continuous (freshmen), continuous (transfers).

CONTACT

Ms. Suzanne T. Sullivan, Assistant Vice President for Traditional and Online Admissions, Belhaven University, 1500 Peachtree Street, Jackson, MS 39202. *Phone:* 601-968-5940. *Toll-free phone:* 800-960-5940. *Fax:* 601-968-8946. *E-mail:* admission@belhaven.edu.

Blue Mountain College

Blue Mountain, Mississippi

http://www.bmc.edu/

CONTACT

Mr. Lynn Gibson, Vice President for Enrollment Services, Blue Mountain College, PO Box 160, Blue Mountain, MS 38610-0160. *Phone:* 662-685-4771 Ext. 176. *Toll-free phone:* 800-235-0136. *Fax:* 662-685-4776. *E-mail:* lgibson@bmc.edu.

Delta State University

Cleveland, Mississippi

http://www.deltastate.edu/

- **State-supported** comprehensive, founded 1924, part of Mississippi Institutions of Higher Learning
- **Small-town** 332-acre campus
- **Endowment** $36.8 million
- **Coed**

UNDERGRAD STUDENTS

27% live on campus.

ACADEMICS

Calendar: semesters. *Degrees:* certificates, bachelor's, master's, doctoral, and post-master's certificates.

STUDENT LIFE

Housing options: on-campus residence required through sophomore year; men-only, women-only, special housing for students with disabilities.

Campus housing is university owned. Freshman campus housing is guaranteed.

Activities and organizations: drama/theater group, student-run newspaper, choral group, marching band, Student Government Association, Baptist Student Union, Union Program Council, Wesley Foundation, Kappa Delta Sorority, national fraternities, national sororities.

Athletics Member NCAA. All Division II. ***Intercollegiate sports:*** baseball M(s), basketball M(s)/W(s), cross-country running W(s), football M(s), golf M(s), soccer M(s)/W(s), softball W(s), swimming and diving M(s)/W(s), tennis M(s)/W(s). ***Intramural sports:*** archery M/W, badminton M/W, basketball M/W, bowling M/W, football M/W, golf M/W, softball M/W, table tennis M/W, tennis M/W, track and field M/W, ultimate Frisbee M/W, volleyball M/W.

Campus security: 24-hour emergency response devices and patrols, late-night transport/escort service, controlled dormitory access.

Student services: health clinic, personal/psychological counseling, veterans affairs office.

COSTS & FINANCIAL AID

Costs (2019–20) ***Tuition:*** area resident $7501 full-time, $313 per credit hour part-time; state resident $7501 full-time, $313 per credit hour part-time; nonresident $7501 full-time, $313 per credit hour part-time. Full-time tuition and fees vary according to course load. Part-time tuition and fees vary according to course load. ***Required fees:*** $170 full-time, $7 per credit hour part-time. ***Room and board:*** $7908; room only: $4530. Room and board charges vary according to board plan and housing facility. ***Payment plan:*** installment. ***Waivers:*** senior citizens and employees or children of employees.

Financial Aid Of all full-time matriculated undergraduates who enrolled in 2018, 1,629 applied for aid, 1,160 were judged to have need. 244 Federal Work-Study jobs (averaging $1956). In 2018, 345 non-need-based awards were made. ***Average financial aid package:*** $10,887. ***Average need-based loan:*** $4155. ***Average need-based gift aid:*** $5622. ***Average non-need-based aid:*** $4801.

CONTACT

Delta State University, Highway 8 West, Cleveland, MS 38733-0001. *Toll-free phone:* 800-468-6378.

Jackson State University

Jackson, Mississippi

http://www.jsums.edu/

- **State-supported** university, founded 1877, part of Mississippi Institutions of Higher Learning
- **Urban** 250-acre campus
- **Coed**
- **Minimally difficult** entrance level

FACULTY

Student/faculty ratio: 17:1.

ACADEMICS

Calendar: semesters. *Degrees:* bachelor's, master's, doctoral, and post-master's certificates.

Library: H. T. Sampson Library plus 4 others. *Books:* 374,387 (digital/electronic); *Serial titles:* 317,232 (digital/electronic); *Databases:* 70.

STUDENT LIFE

Housing options: coed, men-only, women-only, special housing for students with disabilities. Campus housing is university owned and leased by the school. Freshman applicants given priority for college housing.

Activities and organizations: drama/theater group, student-run newspaper, choral group, marching band, Student Government Association, Sonic Boom of the South, MADDRAMA, Interfaith, NAACP, national fraternities, national sororities.

Athletics Member NCAA. All Division I except football (Division I-AA).

Campus security: 24-hour emergency response devices and patrols, controlled dormitory access.

Student services: health clinic, personal/psychological counseling, veterans affairs office.

FINANCIAL AID

Financial Aid Of all full-time matriculated undergraduates who enrolled in 2017, 5,548 applied for aid, 5,036 were judged to have need, 453 had their need fully met. 1,104 Federal Work-Study jobs (averaging $2097). In 2017, 141 non-need-based awards were made. ***Average percent of need met:*** 51. ***Average financial aid package:*** $11,286. ***Average need-based loan:*** $4200. ***Average need-based gift aid:*** $5179. ***Average non-need-based aid:*** $9903. ***Average indebtedness upon graduation:*** $29,864.

APPLYING

Standardized Tests *Required:* SAT or ACT (for admission).

Options: electronic application.

Required: high school transcript, immunization record, minimum ACT Composite score of 16.

CONTACT

Ms. Keiona Miller, Assistant Director of Undergraduate Recruitment, Jackson State University, PO Box 18389, 1400 John R. Lynch Street, Jackson, MS 39217. *Phone:* 601-979-2914. *Toll-free phone:* 800-848-6817. *Fax:* 601-979-2914. *E-mail:* keiona.miller@jsums.edu.

Millsaps College

Jackson, Mississippi

http://www.millsaps.edu/

- **Independent United Methodist** comprehensive, founded 1890
- **Urban** 100-acre campus
- **Endowment** $100.8 million
- **Coed**
- **Moderately difficult** entrance level

FACULTY

Student/faculty ratio: 9:1.

ACADEMICS

Calendar: semesters. *Degrees:* bachelor's and master's.

Library: Millsaps-Wilson Library.

STUDENT LIFE

Housing options: on-campus residence required through sophomore year; coed, men-only, women-only, special housing for students with disabilities. Campus housing is university owned. Freshman campus housing is guaranteed.

Activities and organizations: drama/theater group, student-run newspaper, choral group, Campus Ministry Team, Student Body Association, SAPS (Campus Programming Board), Inter-fraternity/Panhellenic Councils, intramural sports, national fraternities, national sororities.

Athletics Member NCAA. All Division III except golf (Division II).

Campus security: 24-hour emergency response devices and patrols, student patrols, late-night transport/escort service, controlled dormitory access.

Student services: health clinic, personal/psychological counseling.

COSTS & FINANCIAL AID

Costs (2019–20) ***Comprehensive fee:*** $55,524 includes full-time tuition ($38,600), mandatory fees ($2714), and room and board ($14,210). Part-time tuition: $1190 per semester hour. ***College room only:*** $7950.

Financial Aid Of all full-time matriculated undergraduates who enrolled in 2017, 625 applied for aid, 552 were judged to have need, 125 had their need fully met. In 2017, 231 non-need-based awards were made. ***Average percent of need met:*** 78. ***Average financial aid package:*** $35,745. ***Average need-based loan:*** $4434. ***Average need-based gift aid:*** $29,435. ***Average non-need-based aid:*** $25,900. ***Average indebtedness upon graduation:*** $34,619.

APPLYING

Standardized Tests *Required:* SAT or ACT (for admission).

Options: electronic application, early admission, early action, deferred entrance.

Required: essay or personal statement, high school transcript, minimum 2.5 GPA, 1 letter of recommendation, secondary school report. ***Required for some:*** interview.

CONTACT
Dr. Robert Alexander, Vice President of Enrollment and Communications, Millsaps College, 1701 North State Street, Jackson, MS 39210-0001. *Phone:* 601-974-1050. *Toll-free phone:* 800-352-1050. *Fax:* 601-974-1059. *E-mail:* admissions@millsaps.edu.

Mississippi College
Clinton, Mississippi
http://www.mc.edu/

- **Independent Southern Baptist** comprehensive, founded 1826, part of Mississippi Baptist Convention
- **Suburban** 140-acre campus with easy access to Jackson
- **Endowment** $72.5 million
- **Coed**
- **Moderately difficult** entrance level

FACULTY
Student/faculty ratio: 14:1.

ACADEMICS
Calendar: semesters. *Degrees:* bachelor's, master's, doctoral, post-master's, and postbachelor's certificates.
Library: Leland Speed Library plus 1 other. *Books:* 252,127 (physical), 1,634 (digital/electronic); *Serial titles:* 9,071 (physical), 21 (digital/electronic); *Databases:* 55.

STUDENT LIFE
Housing options: on-campus residence required through junior year; men-only, women-only, special housing for students with disabilities. Campus housing is university owned. Freshman applicants given priority for college housing.

Activities and organizations: drama/theater group, student-run newspaper, radio station, choral group, marching band, Baptist Student Union, Nenamoosha Social Tribe, Laguna Social Tribe, Civitan Service Club, Shawreth Service Club.

Athletics Member NCAA. All Division II.

Campus security: 24-hour emergency response devices and patrols, late-night transport/escort service, controlled dormitory access.

Student services: health clinic, personal/psychological counseling.

COSTS & FINANCIAL AID
Costs (2019–20) ***Comprehensive fee:*** $29,220 includes full-time tuition ($17,550), mandatory fees ($1060), and room and board ($10,610). Full-time tuition and fees vary according to course load. Part-time tuition: $550 per credit hour. ***Room and board:*** Room and board charges vary according to housing facility.

Financial Aid Of all full-time matriculated undergraduates who enrolled in 2017, 2,134 applied for aid, 1,444 were judged to have need, 208 had their need fully met. In 2017, 1041 non-need-based awards were made. ***Average percent of need met:*** 70. ***Average financial aid package:*** $16,941. ***Average need-based loan:*** $7007. ***Average need-based gift aid:*** $12,232. ***Average non-need-based aid:*** $8457. ***Average indebtedness upon graduation:*** $28,123.

APPLYING
Standardized Tests *Required:* SAT or ACT (for admission).

Options: electronic application, early admission, deferred entrance.

Application fee: $25.

Required: high school transcript. ***Required for some:*** 2 letters of recommendation. ***Recommended:*** minimum 2.0 GPA, interview.

CONTACT
Mr. William Kyle Brantley, Director of Admissions, Mississippi College, Box 4026, 200 South Capitol Street, Clinton, MS 39058-0001. *Phone:* 601-925-7634. *Toll-free phone:* 800-738-1236. *Fax:* 601-925-3950. *E-mail:* enrollment-services@mc.edu.

Mississippi State University
Mississippi State, Mississippi
http://www.msstate.edu/

- **State-supported** university, founded 1878, part of Mississippi Institutions of Higher Learning
- **Small-town** 4200-acre campus
- **Endowment** $528.7 million
- **Coed** 18,792 undergraduate students, 91% full-time, 49% women, 51% men
- **Moderately difficult** entrance level, 66% of applicants were admitted

UNDERGRAD STUDENTS
17,113 full-time, 1,679 part-time. Students come from 54 states and territories; 59 other countries; 32% are from out of state; 18% Black or African American, non-Hispanic/Latino; 3% Hispanic/Latino; 1% Asian, non-Hispanic/Latino; 0.1% Native Hawaiian or other Pacific Islander, non-Hispanic/Latino; 0.6% American Indian or Alaska Native, non-Hispanic/Latino; 2% Two or more races, non-Hispanic/Latino; 0.3% Race/ethnicity unknown; 1% international; 10% transferred in; 28% live on campus.

Freshmen:
Admission: 18,269 applied, 12,113 admitted, 3,500 enrolled. ***Average high school GPA:*** 3.5. ***Test scores:*** SAT evidence-based reading and writing scores over 500: 91%; SAT math scores over 500: 86%; ACT scores over 18: 97%; SAT evidence-based reading and writing scores over 600: 47%; SAT math scores over 600: 45%; ACT scores over 24: 67%; SAT evidence-based reading and writing scores over 700: 8%; SAT math scores over 700: 14%; ACT scores over 30: 29%.

Retention: 81% of full-time freshmen returned.

FACULTY
Total: 1,365, 76% full-time, 73% with terminal degrees.
Student/faculty ratio: 17:1.

ACADEMICS
Calendar: semesters. *Degrees:* associate, bachelor's, master's, doctoral, and post-master's certificates.

Special study options: academic remediation for entering students, accelerated degree program, adult/continuing education programs, advanced placement credit, cooperative education, distance learning, double majors, English as a second language, freshman honors college, honors programs, independent study, internships, off-campus study, part-time degree program, services for LD students, student-designed majors, study abroad, summer session for credit. ***ROTC:*** Army (b), Air Force (b).

Computers: Students can access the following: campus intranet, computer help desk, free student e-mail accounts, online (class) grades, online (class) registration, online (class) schedules. Campuswide network is available. 100% of college-owned or -operated housing units are wired for high-speed Internet access. Wireless service is available via entire campus.

Library: Mitchell Memorial Library plus 2 others. *Books:* 2.8 million (physical), 73,631 (digital/electronic); *Serial titles:* 1,509 (physical), 295,495 (digital/electronic); *Databases:* 393. Weekly public service hours: 110; students can reserve study rooms.

STUDENT LIFE
Housing options: on-campus residence required for freshman year; coed, men-only, women-only, special housing for students with disabilities. Campus housing is university owned. Freshman applicants given priority for college housing.

Activities and organizations: drama/theater group, student-run newspaper, radio and television station, choral group, marching band, Student Association, Black Student Alliance, Residence Hall Association, Fashion Board, Campus Activities Board, national fraternities, national sororities.

Athletics Member NCAA. All Division I except football (Division I-A). ***Intercollegiate sports:*** baseball M(s), basketball M(s)/W(s), cheerleading M(s)/W(s), cross-country running M/W(s), golf M(s)/W(s), soccer W(s), softball W(s), tennis M(s)/W(s), track and field M(s)/W(s), volleyball W(s). ***Intramural sports:*** archery M(c)/W(c), badminton M(c)/W(c), basketball M/W, bowling M/W, cross-country running W(c), equestrian sports M/W, fencing M(c)/W(c), football M/W, golf M/W, ice hockey M(c)/W(c), lacrosse M(c)/W(c), racquetball M/W, riflery M/W, rugby

M(c), soccer M(c)/W(c), softball M(c)/W(c), swimming and diving M(c)/W(c), table tennis M(c)/W(c), tennis M(c)/W(c), ultimate Frisbee M/W, volleyball M(c)/W(c), water polo M/W, weight lifting M/W.

Campus security: 24-hour emergency response devices and patrols, late-night transport/escort service, controlled dormitory access, bicycle patrols, crime prevention program, RAD program, general law enforcement services.

Student services: health clinic, personal/psychological counseling, veterans affairs office.

COSTS & FINANCIAL AID

Costs (2019–20) ***One-time required fee:*** $110. ***Tuition:*** state resident $8800 full-time, $371 per credit hour part-time; nonresident $23,840 full-time, $998 per credit hour part-time. Full-time tuition and fees vary according to degree level, location, and reciprocity agreements. Part-time tuition and fees vary according to course load, degree level, location, and reciprocity agreements. ***Required fees:*** $110 full-time. ***Room and board:*** $10,436; room only: $6440. Room and board charges vary according to board plan, housing facility, and student level. ***Payment plans:*** tuition prepayment, installment. ***Waivers:*** children of alumni, senior citizens, and employees or children of employees.

Financial Aid Of all full-time matriculated undergraduates who enrolled in 2018, 12,632 applied for aid, 11,042 were judged to have need, 2,277 had their need fully met. 459 Federal Work-Study jobs (averaging $3611). In 2018, 2349 non-need-based awards were made. ***Average percent of need met:*** 56. ***Average financial aid package:*** $15,082. ***Average need-based loan:*** $3710. ***Average need-based gift aid:*** $6973. ***Average non-need-based aid:*** $4751. ***Average indebtedness upon graduation:*** $31,060.

APPLYING

Standardized Tests *Required:* SAT or ACT (for admission).

Options: electronic application.

Application fee: $40.

Required: high school transcript, minimum 2.0 GPA.

Application deadlines: 8/1 (freshmen), 8/1 (transfers).

Notification: continuous (freshmen), continuous (transfers).

CONTACT

Ms. Lori Ball, Director of Undergraduate Admissions, Mississippi State University, PO Box 6334, Mississippi State, MS 39762. *Phone:* 662-325-2224. *Fax:* 662-325-1MSU. *E-mail:* admit@msstate.edu.

Mississippi University for Women

Columbus, Mississippi

http://www.muw.edu/

- **State-supported** comprehensive, founded 1884, part of Mississippi Institutions of Higher Learning
- **Small-town** 110-acre campus
- **Endowment** $50.3 million
- **Coed**
- **Moderately difficult** entrance level

FACULTY

Student/faculty ratio: 13:1.

ACADEMICS

Calendar: semesters. *Degrees:* associate, bachelor's, master's, doctoral, and post-master's certificates.

Library: John Clayton Fant Memorial Library plus 2 others. *Books:* 197,660 (physical); *Serial titles:* 4,889 (physical), 1,560 (digital/electronic); *Databases:* 74. Weekly public service hours: 76; students can reserve study rooms.

STUDENT LIFE

Housing options: men-only, women-only, special housing for students with disabilities. Campus housing is university owned. Freshman campus housing is guaranteed.

Activities and organizations: drama/theater group, student-run newspaper, radio station, choral group, Student Government Association, Wesley Foundation, International Student Association, Baptist Student Union, International Justice Mission, national fraternities, national sororities.

Campus security: 24-hour emergency response devices and patrols, late-night transport/escort service, controlled dormitory access, tornado and voice-over sirens, voice mail and text messaging emergency notification system.

Student services: health clinic, personal/psychological counseling, women's center.

FINANCIAL AID

Financial Aid Of all full-time matriculated undergraduates who enrolled in 2014, 1,783 applied for aid, 1,640 were judged to have need, 472 had their need fully met. 75 Federal Work-Study jobs (averaging $2042). 247 state and other part-time jobs (averaging $1739). In 2014, 292 non-need-based awards were made. ***Average percent of need met:*** 50. ***Average financial aid package:*** $8948. ***Average need-based loan:*** $5223. ***Average need-based gift aid:*** $5487. ***Average non-need-based aid:*** $5548. ***Average indebtedness upon graduation:*** $31,851.

APPLYING

Standardized Tests *Required for some:* SAT or ACT (for admission). *Recommended:* SAT or ACT (for admission).

Options: electronic application, early admission.

Required: high school transcript. ***Required for some:*** minimum 2.0 GPA, rank in upper 50% of high school class.

CONTACT

Mississippi University for Women, 1100 College Street, MUW-1600, Columbus, MS 39701-9998. *Phone:* 662-329-7106. *Toll-free phone:* 877-GO 2 THE W.

Mississippi Valley State University

Itta Bena, Mississippi

http://www.mvsu.edu/

- **State-supported** comprehensive, founded 1946, part of Mississippi Institutions of Higher Learning
- **Small-town** 450-acre campus
- **Endowment** $1.6 million
- **Coed**
- **Minimally difficult** entrance level

FACULTY

Student/faculty ratio: 15:1.

ACADEMICS

Calendar: semesters. *Degrees:* bachelor's and master's.

Library: James Herbert White Library. *Books:* 127,541 (physical), 53,358 (digital/electronic); *Databases:* 62. Weekly public service hours: 84; students can reserve study rooms.

STUDENT LIFE

Housing options: men-only, women-only. Campus housing is university owned.

Activities and organizations: drama/theater group, student-run newspaper, radio and television station, choral group, marching band, Student Government Association, Baptist Student Union, Black Student Fellowship, National Education Association, national fraternities, national sororities.

Athletics Member NCAA. All Division I except football (Division I-AA).

Campus security: 24-hour emergency response devices and patrols, controlled dormitory access.

Student services: health clinic, personal/psychological counseling.

APPLYING

Standardized Tests *Required:* SAT or ACT (for admission).

Options: deferred entrance.

Required: high school transcript. ***Required for some:*** 2.5 letters of recommendation. ***Recommended:*** interview.

CONTACT

Mississippi Valley State University, 14000 Highway 82 West, Itta Bena, MS 38941-1400. *Phone:* 662-254-3345. *Toll-free phone:* 800-844-6885.

Rust College

Holly Springs, Mississippi

http://www.rustcollege.edu/

CONTACT

Mr. Braque Talley, Dean of Enrollment, Rust College, 150 Rust Avenue, Holly Springs, MS 38635-2328. *Phone:* 601-252-8000 Ext. 4059. *Toll-free phone:* 888-886-8492 Ext. 4065. *Fax:* 662-252-8895. *E-mail:* btalley@rustcollege.edu.

Southeastern Baptist College

Laurel, Mississippi

http://www.southeasternbaptist.edu/

CONTACT

Mrs. Emma Bond, Director of Admissions, Southeastern Baptist College, 4229 Highway 15 North, Laurel, MS 39440-1096. *Phone:* 601-426-6346.

Strayer University–Jackson Campus

Jackson, Mississippi

http://www.strayer.edu/mississippi/jackson/

CONTACT

Strayer University–Jackson Campus, 460 Briarwood Drive, Suite 200, Jackson, MS 39206. *Toll-free phone:* 888-311-0355.

Tougaloo College

Tougaloo, Mississippi

http://www.tougaloo.edu/

- **Independent** 4-year, founded 1869, affiliated with United Church of Christ
- **Suburban** 500-acre campus
- **Endowment** $4.7 million
- **Coed**
- **Minimally difficult** entrance level

FACULTY

Student/faculty ratio: 13:1.

ACADEMICS

Calendar: semesters. *Degrees:* associate and bachelor's.
Library: L. Zenobiz Coleman Library.

STUDENT LIFE

Housing options: men-only, women-only. Campus housing is university owned.

Activities and organizations: drama/theater group, student-run newspaper, choral group, concert choir, Student Government Association, gospel choir, NAACP, Pre-Alumni Club, national fraternities, national sororities.

Athletics Member NAIA.

Campus security: 24-hour emergency response devices and patrols.

Student services: health clinic, personal/psychological counseling.

COSTS & FINANCIAL AID

Costs (2019–20) ***Comprehensive fee:*** $28,488 includes full-time tuition ($11,044), mandatory fees ($11,044), and room and board ($6400). Full-time tuition and fees vary according to course load and degree level. Part-time tuition: $4763 per term. Part-time tuition and fees vary according to course load and degree level. No tuition increase for student's term of enrollment. ***Required fees:*** $433 per term part-time, $235 part-time. ***Room and board:*** Room and board charges vary according to gender, housing facility, and student level. ***Payment plans:*** tuition prepayment, installment.

Financial Aid In 2002, 110 non-need-based awards were made. ***Average percent of need met:*** 80. ***Average financial aid package:*** $10,500. ***Average indebtedness upon graduation:*** $25,000.

APPLYING

Standardized Tests *Required:* SAT or ACT (for admission).

Options: early admission.

Application fee: $25.

Required: high school transcript, minimum 2.0 GPA.

CONTACT

Dr. Juno Jacobs, Director of Admissions, Tougaloo College, 500 West County Line Road, Tougaloo, MS 39174. *Phone:* 601-977-7765. *Toll-free phone:* 888-42GALOO. *Fax:* 601-977-4501. *E-mail:* jjacobs@tougaloo.edu.

University of Mississippi

Oxford, Mississippi

http://www.olemiss.edu/

CONTACT

Ms. Martina Brewer, Associate Director of Admissions, University of Mississippi, 128 Martindale Student Services Center, University, MS 38677. *Phone:* 662-915-7226. *Toll-free phone:* 800-653-6477. *Fax:* 662-915-5869. *E-mail:* admissions@olemiss.edu.

University of Mississippi Medical Center

Jackson, Mississippi

http://www.umc.edu/

CONTACT

Ms. Barbara Westerfield, Director of Student Records and Registrar, University of Mississippi Medical Center, 2500 North State Street, Jackson, MS 39216-4505. *Phone:* 601-984-1080. *Fax:* 601-984-1079.

University of Southern Mississippi

Hattiesburg, Mississippi

http://www.usm.edu/

- **State-supported** university, founded 1910, part of Mississippi Institutions of Higher Learning
- **Suburban** 1090-acre campus
- **Coed** 11,594 undergraduate students, 83% full-time, 63% women, 37% men
- **Moderately difficult** entrance level, 97% of applicants were admitted

UNDERGRAD STUDENTS

9,654 full-time, 1,940 part-time. 21% are from out of state; 27% Black or African American, non-Hispanic/Latino; 3% Hispanic/Latino; 1% Asian, non-Hispanic/Latino; 0.1% Native Hawaiian or other Pacific Islander, non-Hispanic/Latino; 0.4% American Indian or Alaska Native, non-Hispanic/Latino; 3% Two or more races, non-Hispanic/Latino; 6% Race/ethnicity unknown; 2% international; 14% transferred in.

Freshmen:

Admission: 9,217 applied, 8,935 admitted, 1,888 enrolled. ***Average high school GPA:*** 3.4. ***Test scores:*** ACT scores over 18: 87%; ACT scores over 24: 39%; ACT scores over 30: 11%.

Retention: 68% of full-time freshmen returned.

FACULTY

Total: 871, 77% full-time, 73% with terminal degrees.

Student/faculty ratio: 17:1.

ACADEMICS

Calendar: semesters. *Degrees:* certificates, bachelor's, master's, doctoral, post-master's, and postbachelor's certificates.

Special study options: academic remediation for entering students, adult/continuing education programs, advanced placement credit, distance learning, double majors, English as a second language, honors programs, internships, off-campus study, part-time degree program, services for LD students, study abroad, summer session for credit. ***ROTC:*** Army (b), Air Force (b).

Computers: 436 computers/terminals are available on campus for general student use. Students can access the following: campus intranet, computer help desk, free student e-mail accounts, online (class) grades, online (class) registration, online (class) schedules. Campuswide network is available. 100% of college-owned or -operated housing units are wired for high-speed Internet access. Wireless service is available via entire campus.

Library: Cook Memorial Library plus 4 others. *Books:* 1.4 million (physical), 331,932 (digital/electronic); *Serial titles:* 27,243 (physical), 118,798 (digital/electronic); *Databases:* 200. Weekly public service hours: 117; students can reserve study rooms.

STUDENT LIFE
Housing options: college housing not available.

Activities and organizations: drama/theater group, student-run newspaper, radio station, choral group, marching band, national fraternities, national sororities.

Athletics Member NCAA. All Division I. ***Intercollegiate sports:*** baseball M(s), basketball M(s)/W(s), cheerleading M/W, cross-country running W(s), football M(s), golf M(s)/W(s), soccer W(s), softball W(s), tennis M(s)/W(s), track and field M(s)/W(s), volleyball W(s). ***Intramural sports:*** badminton M/W, basketball M/W, bowling M/W, racquetball M/W, rugby M, soccer M/W, softball W, tennis M/W, track and field M/W, ultimate Frisbee M/W, volleyball M/W.

Campus security: 24-hour emergency response devices and patrols, late-night transport/escort service, controlled dormitory access.

Student services: health clinic, personal/psychological counseling, women's center, legal services, veterans affairs office.

FINANCIAL AID
Financial Aid Of all full-time matriculated undergraduates who enrolled in 2018, 8,475 applied for aid, 7,331 were judged to have need, 1,608 had their need fully met. In 2018, 809 non-need-based awards were made. ***Average percent of need met:*** 67. ***Average financial aid package:*** $10,833. ***Average need-based loan:*** $11,696. ***Average need-based gift aid:*** $6025. ***Average non-need-based aid:*** $6036. ***Average indebtedness upon graduation:*** $28,003.

APPLYING
Standardized Tests *Required:* SAT or ACT (for admission).

Options: electronic application, early admission.

Application fee: $40.

Required: minimum 2.0 GPA. ***Required for some:*** high school transcript, statement of good standing from prior institutions, college transcripts.

Application deadlines: 6/30 (freshmen), 8/19 (transfers).

CONTACT
University of Southern Mississippi, 118 College Drive, Hattiesburg, MS 39406-0001. *Phone:* 601-266-5000.

William Carey University

Hattiesburg, Mississippi

http://www.wmcarey.edu/

CONTACT
Mr. William N. Curry, Dean of Enrollment Management, William Carey University, 710 William Carey Parkway, Hattiesburg, MS 39401. *Phone:* 601-318-6051. *Toll-free phone:* 800-962-5991. *Fax:* 601-318-6154. *E-mail:* admissions@wmcarey.edu.

MISSOURI

American Business & Technology University

Saint Joseph, Missouri

http://www.abtu.edu/

CONTACT
Richard Lingle, Lead Admission Coordinator, American Business & Technology University, 1018 West St.Maartens Drive, Saint Joseph, MO 64506. *Phone:* 800-908-9329 Ext. 13. *Toll-free phone:* 800-804-1388. *E-mail:* ricahrd@acot.edu.

Avila University

Kansas City, Missouri

http://www.avila.edu/

- **Independent Roman Catholic** comprehensive, founded 1916
- **Suburban** 50-acre campus
- **Endowment** $10.8 million
- **Coed** 1,154 undergraduate students, 86% full-time, 63% women, 37% men
- **Minimally difficult** entrance level, 41% of applicants were admitted

UNDERGRAD STUDENTS
990 full-time, 164 part-time. Students come from 33 states and territories; 12 other countries; 33% are from out of state; 22% Black or African American, non-Hispanic/Latino; 13% Hispanic/Latino; 2% Asian, non-Hispanic/Latino; 0.4% Native Hawaiian or other Pacific Islander, non-Hispanic/Latino; 0.7% American Indian or Alaska Native, non-Hispanic/Latino; 3% Two or more races, non-Hispanic/Latino; 6% international; 11% transferred in; 25% live on campus.

Freshmen:
Admission: 2,302 applied, 946 admitted, 153 enrolled. ***Average high school GPA:*** 3.2. ***Test scores:*** SAT evidence-based reading and writing scores over 500: 75%; SAT math scores over 500: 87%; ACT scores over 18: 94%; SAT evidence-based reading and writing scores over 600: 8%; SAT math scores over 600: 8%; ACT scores over 24: 23%; ACT scores over 30: 3%.

Retention: 74% of full-time freshmen returned.

FACULTY
Total: 238, 31% full-time, 49% with terminal degrees.

Student/faculty ratio: 13:1.

ACADEMICS
Calendar: semesters. *Degrees:* bachelor's, master's, and postbachelor's certificates.

Special study options: academic remediation for entering students, accelerated degree program, adult/continuing education programs, advanced placement credit, cooperative education, distance learning, double majors, English as a second language, independent study, internships, off-campus study, part-time degree program, services for LD students, study abroad, summer session for credit. ***ROTC:*** Army (c).

Unusual degree programs: 3-2 occupational therapy, physical therapy, law with Rockhurst University, University of Missouri–Kansas City.

Computers: 141 computers/terminals and 225 ports are available on campus for general student use. Students can access the following: campus intranet, computer help desk, free student e-mail accounts, online (class) grades, online (class) registration, online (class) schedules, laptop checkout through library. Campuswide network is available. 100% of college-owned or -operated housing units are wired for high-speed Internet access. Wireless service is available via entire campus.
Library: Hooley-Bundshu Library plus 1 other. *Books:* 39,963 (physical), 309,288 (digital/electronic); *Serial titles:* 205 (physical), 389,497 (digital/electronic); *Databases:* 72. Weekly public service hours: 91; students can reserve study rooms.

STUDENT LIFE
Housing options: on-campus residence required through sophomore year; coed, men-only, women-only. Campus housing is university owned. Freshman campus housing is guaranteed.

Activities and organizations: drama/theater group, student-run newspaper, choral group, Avila Ambassadors, Avila Student Nurses Association, Campus Ministries, Saudi Arabian Student Association, Avila University Theatre Company.

Athletics Member NAIA. ***Intercollegiate sports:*** baseball M(s), basketball M(s)/W(s), cheerleading W(s), cross-country running M(s)/W(s), football M(s), golf M(s), soccer M(s)/W(s), softball W(s), track and field M(s)/W(s), volleyball W(s). ***Intramural sports:*** bowling M/W, table tennis M/W.

Campus security: 24-hour emergency response devices and patrols, student patrols, late-night transport/escort service, controlled dormitory access.

Student services: health clinic, personal/psychological counseling.

COSTS & FINANCIAL AID
Costs (2020–21) ***Comprehensive fee:*** $28,455 includes full-time tuition ($21,115) and room and board ($7340). Part-time tuition: $778 per credit hour. No tuition increase for student's term of enrollment. ***College room only:*** $3450. Room and board charges vary according to board plan and housing facility. ***Waivers:*** employees or children of employees.

Financial Aid Of all full-time matriculated undergraduates who enrolled in 2008, 1,927 applied for aid, 1,852 were judged to have need, 1,846 had their need fully met. 161 Federal Work-Study jobs (averaging $903). 55 state and other part-time jobs (averaging $885). In 2008, 60 non-need-based awards were made. ***Average percent of need met:*** 35. ***Average financial aid package:*** $12,976. ***Average need-based loan:*** $5465. ***Average need-based gift aid:*** $7854. ***Average non-need-based aid:*** $9152. ***Average indebtedness upon graduation:*** $16,508.

APPLYING
Standardized Tests *Required:* SAT or ACT (for admission).

Options: electronic application, early admission.

Required: high school transcript, minimum 2.5 GPA, secondary school report. ***Required for some:*** essay or personal statement. ***Recommended:*** interview.

Notification: 8/15 (freshmen), 8/15 (transfers).

CONTACT
Josh Parisse, Director of Undergraduate Admissions, Avila University, 11901 Wornall Road, Kansas City, MO 64145. *Phone:* 816-501-2400. *Toll-free phone:* 800-GO-AVILA. *Fax:* 816-501-2453. *E-mail:* josh.parisse@avila.edu.

Baptist Bible College
Springfield, Missouri
http://www.gobbc.edu/

CONTACT
Mr. Terry Allcorn, Director of Admissions, Baptist Bible College, 628 East Kearney Street, Springfield, MO 65803-3498. *Phone:* 417-268-6000. *Toll-free phone:* 800-228-5754. *Fax:* 417-268-6694.

Bryan University
Springfield, Missouri
http://www.bryanu.edu/

CONTACT
Bryan University, 4255 South Nature Center Way, Springfield, MO 65804. *Toll-free phone:* 855-566-0650.

Calvary University
Kansas City, Missouri
http://www.calvary.edu/

- **Independent nondenominational** comprehensive, founded 1932
- **Suburban** 55-acre campus with easy access to Kansas City
- **Endowment** $1.2 million
- **Coed**
- **Noncompetitive** entrance level

FACULTY
Student/faculty ratio: 12:1.

ACADEMICS
Calendar: semesters. *Degrees:* certificates, associate, bachelor's, and master's.
Library: Hilda Kroeker Library. *Books:* 41,841 (physical), 420 (digital/electronic); *Serial titles:* 268 (physical); *Databases:* 4.

STUDENT LIFE
Housing options: men-only, women-only. Campus housing is university owned. Freshman campus housing is guaranteed.

Activities and organizations: drama/theater group, choral group, Missions Encounter, Masterworks (Fine Arts).

Athletics Member NCCAA.

Campus security: 24-hour emergency response devices and patrols, late-night transport/escort service, controlled dormitory access, night patrols by trained security personnel, monitored closed circuit cameras.

Student services: personal/psychological counseling.

COSTS & FINANCIAL AID
Costs (2019–20) ***Comprehensive fee:*** $19,654 includes full-time tuition ($10,276), mandatory fees ($888), and room and board ($8490). Full-time tuition and fees vary according to location and program. Part-time tuition and fees vary according to location and program. ***College room only:*** $4020. Room and board charges vary according to board plan and housing facility.

Financial Aid Of all full-time matriculated undergraduates who enrolled in 2016, 101 applied for aid, 95 were judged to have need, 7 had their need fully met. 8 Federal Work-Study jobs (averaging $1687). In 2016, 4 non-need-based awards were made. ***Average percent of need met:*** 66. ***Average financial aid package:*** $12,774. ***Average need-based loan:*** $4265. ***Average need-based gift aid:*** $5694. ***Average non-need-based aid:*** $2543. ***Average indebtedness upon graduation:*** $19,246.

APPLYING
Standardized Tests *Required:* SAT or ACT (for admission).

Options: electronic application.

Required: essay or personal statement, minimum 2.0 GPA, 2 letters of recommendation. ***Required for some:*** high school transcript ***Recommended:*** interview.

CONTACT
Ms. Ann Rogers, Admissions Secretary, Calvary University, 15800 Calvary Road, Kansas City, MO 64147-1341. *Phone:* 816-322-0110 Ext. 1323. *Toll-free phone:* 800-326-3960. *Fax:* 816-331-4474. *E-mail:* ann.rogers@cavalry.edu.

Central Christian College of the Bible
Moberly, Missouri
http://www.cccb.edu/

CONTACT
Mr. Aaron Merritt, Director of Admissions, Central Christian College of the Bible, 911 Urbandale Drive East, Moberly, MO 65270-1997. *Phone:* 660-263-3900. *Toll-free phone:* 888-263-3900. *Fax:* 660-263-3936. *E-mail:* admissions@cccb.edu.

Central Methodist University
Fayette, Missouri
http://www.centralmethodist.edu/

- **Independent Methodist** comprehensive, founded 1854
- **Small-town** 80-acre campus
- **Endowment** $45.5 million
- **Coed** 1,145 undergraduate students, 97% full-time, 51% women, 49% men
- **Moderately difficult** entrance level, 94% of applicants were admitted

UNDERGRAD STUDENTS
1,114 full-time, 31 part-time. 31% are from out of state; 10% Black or African American, non-Hispanic/Latino; 9% Hispanic/Latino; 1% Asian, non-Hispanic/Latino; 0.3% American Indian or Alaska Native, non-Hispanic/Latino; 3% Two or more races, non-Hispanic/Latino; 2% Race/ethnicity unknown; 6% international; 9% transferred in; 68% live on campus.

Freshmen:
Admission: 1,486 applied, 1,397 admitted, 321 enrolled. ***Average high school GPA:*** 3.5. ***Test scores:*** SAT evidence-based reading and writing scores over 500: 54%; SAT math scores over 500: 54%; ACT scores over 18: 87%; SAT evidence-based reading and writing scores over 600: 10%; SAT math scores over 600: 7%; ACT scores over 24: 31%; ACT scores over 30: 5%.

Retention: 68% of full-time freshmen returned.

FACULTY
Total: 125, 62% full-time.

Student/faculty ratio: 12:1.

ACADEMICS
Calendar: semesters. *Degrees:* associate, bachelor's, and master's.

Special study options: academic remediation for entering students, advanced placement credit, distance learning, double majors, honors programs, independent study, internships, part-time degree program, services for LD students, student-designed majors, study abroad, summer session for credit. ***ROTC:*** Army (c), Air Force (c).

Unusual degree programs: 3-2 engineering with Missouri University of Science and Technology.

Computers: 100 computers/terminals and 816 ports are available on campus for general student use. Students can access the following: computer help desk, free student e-mail accounts, online (class) grades, online (class) registration, online (class) schedules. Campuswide network is available. 100% of college-owned or -operated housing units are wired for high-speed Internet access. Wireless service is available via entire campus.
Library: Smiley Library. *Books:* 67,581 (physical), 127,545 (digital/electronic); *Serial titles:* 96 (physical), 38,528 (digital/electronic); *Databases:* 35. Students can reserve study rooms.

STUDENT LIFE
Housing options: on-campus residence required through senior year; coed, men-only, women-only. Campus housing is university owned. Freshman applicants given priority for college housing.

Activities and organizations: drama/theater group, student-run newspaper, radio station, choral group, marching band, Student Government Association, Enactus, Alpha Phi Omega, Beta Beta Beta, Campus Ministries, national fraternities, national sororities.

Athletics Member NAIA. ***Intercollegiate sports:*** baseball M(s), basketball M(s)/W(s), cheerleading M(s)/W(s), cross-country running M(s)/W(s), football M(s), soccer M(s)/W(s), softball W(s), track and field M(s)/W(s), volleyball W(s). ***Intramural sports:*** basketball M/W, football M/W, racquetball M/W, soccer M/W, softball M/W, tennis M/W, track and field M/W, volleyball M/W, water polo M/W.

Campus security: 24-hour emergency response devices, late-night transport/escort service, controlled dormitory access.

Student services: health clinic, personal/psychological counseling.

COSTS & FINANCIAL AID
Costs (2020–21) ***Comprehensive fee:*** $34,170 includes full-time tuition ($25,000), mandatory fees ($770), and room and board ($8400). Part-time tuition: $220 per credit hour. ***College room only:*** $4110.

Financial Aid Of all full-time matriculated undergraduates who enrolled in 2019, 967 applied for aid, 902 were judged to have need, 182 had their need fully met. In 2019, 80 non-need-based awards were made. ***Average percent of need met:*** 72. ***Average financial aid package:*** $22,115. ***Average need-based loan:*** $3483. ***Average need-based gift aid:*** $4673. ***Average non-need-based aid:*** $14,123. ***Average indebtedness upon graduation:*** $31,118.

APPLYING
Standardized Tests *Required:* SAT or ACT (for admission).

Options: electronic application, deferred entrance.

Required: high school transcript, minimum 2.5 GPA. ***Required for some:*** 2 letters of recommendation.

Application deadlines: rolling (freshmen), rolling (transfers).

Notification: continuous (freshmen), continuous (transfers).

CONTACT
Central Methodist University, 411 Central Methodist Square, Fayette, MO 65248-1198. *Toll-free phone:* 888-CMU-1854 (in-state); 877-CMU-1854 (out-of-state).

Chamberlain College of Nursing - St. Louis

St. Louis, Missouri

http://www.chamberlain.edu/

CONTACT
Admissions, Chamberlain College of Nursing - St. Louis, 11830 Westline Industrial Drive, Suite 106, St. Louis, MO 63146. *Phone:* 314-991-6200. *Toll-free phone:* 877-751-5783.

City Vision University

Kansas City, Missouri

http://www.cityvision.edu/

CONTACT
Mrs. Nancy Young, Director of Admissions, City Vision University, 3101 Troost Avenue, Suite 200, Kansas City, MO 64109-1845. *Phone:* 816-960-2008 Ext. 3. *Fax:* 816-256-8471. *E-mail:* newstudents@cityvision.edu.

College of the Ozarks

Point Lookout, Missouri

http://www.cofo.edu/

- **Independent Presbyterian** 4-year, founded 1906
- **Rural** 1000-acre campus
- **Endowment** $476.6 million
- **Coed** 1,546 undergraduate students, 97% full-time, 55% women, 45% men
- **Moderately difficult** entrance level, 10% of applicants were admitted

UNDERGRAD STUDENTS
1,504 full-time, 42 part-time. Students come from 33 states and territories; 20 other countries; 29% are from out of state; 1% Black or African American, non-Hispanic/Latino; 3% Hispanic/Latino; 0.9% Asian, non-Hispanic/Latino; 0.1% Native Hawaiian or other Pacific Islander, non-Hispanic/Latino; 0.6% American Indian or Alaska Native, non-Hispanic/Latino; 3% Two or more races, non-Hispanic/Latino; 3% Race/ethnicity unknown; 2% international; 2% transferred in; 90% live on campus.

Freshmen:
Admission: 2,720 applied, 279 admitted, 255 enrolled. ***Average high school GPA:*** 3.7. ***Test scores:*** SAT evidence-based reading and writing scores over 500: 78%; SAT math scores over 500: 61%; ACT scores over 18: 96%; SAT evidence-based reading and writing scores over 600: 39%; SAT math scores over 600: 28%; ACT scores over 24: 45%; SAT evidence-based reading and writing scores over 700: 6%; ACT scores over 30: 7%.

Retention: 82% of full-time freshmen returned.

FACULTY
Total: 142, 65% full-time, 43% with terminal degrees.

Student/faculty ratio: 14:1.

ACADEMICS
Calendar: semesters. *Degree:* bachelor's.

Special study options: academic remediation for entering students, advanced placement credit, double majors, English as a second language, independent study, internships, off-campus study, services for LD students, student-designed majors, summer session for credit.

Computers: 402 computers/terminals and 1,771 ports are available on campus for general student use. Students can access the following: campus intranet, computer help desk, free student e-mail accounts, online (class) grades, online (class) registration, online (class) schedules. Campuswide network is available. 100% of college-owned or -operated housing units are wired for high-speed Internet access. Wireless service is available via classrooms, dorm rooms, libraries, student centers.
Library: Lyons Memorial Library. *Books:* 93,527 (physical), 660,502 (digital/electronic); *Serial titles:* 42 (physical), 52,500 (digital/electronic); *Databases:* 50. Weekly public service hours: 80.

STUDENT LIFE
Housing options: on-campus residence required through senior year; men-only, women-only. Campus housing is university owned.

Activities and organizations: drama/theater group, student-run newspaper, radio station, choral group, Baptist Student Union, Chi Alpha, The Student's Union, Agriculture Club, FCA.

Athletics Member NCAA, NAIA, NCCAA. All NCAA Division II. ***Intercollegiate sports:*** baseball M(s), basketball M(s)/W(s), cross-country running M/W, golf M/W, track and field M/W, volleyball W(s). ***Intramural sports:*** basketball M/W, football M/W, racquetball M/W, softball M/W, volleyball M/W.

Campus security: 24-hour emergency response devices and patrols, student patrols, late-night transport/escort service, controlled dormitory access, front gate closed 6 pm to 5 am, security checks cars for proper credentials for entry.

Student services: health clinic, personal/psychological counseling.

COSTS & FINANCIAL AID

Costs (2020–21) ***Tuition:*** $310 per credit hour part-time. ***Required fees:*** $460 full-time, $230 per term part-time.

Financial Aid Of all full-time matriculated undergraduates who enrolled in 2016, 1,531 applied for aid, 1,366 were judged to have need. ***Average percent of need met:*** 83. ***Average financial aid package:*** $18,500. ***Average need-based gift aid:*** $14,188. ***Average non-need-based aid:*** $14,346.

APPLYING

Standardized Tests *Required:* SAT or ACT (for admission). *Recommended:* ACT (for admission).

Options: electronic application.

Required: high school transcript, minimum 3.0 GPA, 2 letters of recommendation, interview, financial statement.

Application deadlines: 12/31 (freshmen), 12/31 (out-of-state freshmen), 12/31 (transfers).

Notification: continuous (freshmen), 1/15 (out-of-state freshmen), continuous (transfers).

CONTACT

Mrs. Kim Williams, Admissions Manager, College of the Ozarks, PO Box 17, Point Lookout, MO 65726. *Phone:* 417-690-2636. *Toll-free phone:* 800-222-0525. *Fax:* 417-335-2618. *E-mail:* admissions@cofo.edu.

Columbia College

Columbia, Missouri

http://www.ccis.edu/

- **Independent** comprehensive, founded 1851, affiliated with Christian Church (Disciples of Christ)
- **Urban** 33-acre campus with easy access to St. Louis and Kansas City
- **Endowment** $171.7 million
- **Coed** 1,023 undergraduate students, 85% full-time, 56% women, 44% men
- **Minimally difficult** entrance level, 48% of applicants were admitted

UNDERGRAD STUDENTS

865 full-time, 158 part-time. Students come from 28 states and territories; 30 other countries; 12% are from out of state; 12% transferred in; 40% live on campus.

Freshmen:

Admission: 1,796 applied, 870 admitted, 146 enrolled. ***Average high school GPA:*** 3.6.

Retention: 71% of full-time freshmen returned.

ACADEMICS

Calendar: semesters. *Degrees:* certificates, associate, bachelor's, and master's (offers continuing education program with significant enrollment not reflected in profile).

Special study options: adult/continuing education programs, advanced placement credit, cooperative education, distance learning, double majors, English as a second language, honors programs, independent study, internships, off-campus study, part-time degree program, services for LD students, student-designed majors, study abroad, summer session for credit. ***ROTC:*** Army (c), Navy (c), Air Force (c).

Unusual degree programs: 3-2 nursing; education.

Computers: 220 computers/terminals and 1,000 ports are available on campus for general student use. Students can access the following: campus intranet, computer help desk, free student e-mail accounts, online (class) grades, online (class) registration, online (class) schedules. Campuswide network is available. 100% of college-owned or -operated housing units are wired for high-speed Internet access. Wireless service is available via entire campus.

Library: J. W. and Lois Stafford Library. *Books:* 61,551 (physical), 246,591 (digital/electronic); *Serial titles:* 84 (physical), 16,729 (digital/electronic); *Databases:* 74. Weekly public service hours: 94; students can reserve study rooms.

STUDENT LIFE

Housing options: on-campus residence required through sophomore year; coed, women-only, special housing for students with disabilities. Campus housing is university owned. Freshman campus housing is guaranteed.

Activities and organizations: drama/theater group, choral group, Student Government Association, Black Student Coalition, Computer Science Club, International Club, IMPACT.

Athletics Member NAIA. ***Intercollegiate sports:*** baseball M(s), basketball M(s)/W(s), bowling W(s), cross-country running M(s)/W(s), golf M(s)/W(s), lacrosse M(s), soccer M(s)/W(s), softball W(s), track and field M(s)/W(s), volleyball W(s). ***Intramural sports:*** badminton M/W, basketball M/W, football M/W, sand volleyball M/W, soccer M/W, softball M/W, table tennis M(c)/W(c), volleyball M/W.

Campus security: 24-hour emergency response devices and patrols, late-night transport/escort service, controlled dormitory access, building monitor patrols off-campus site.

Student services: health clinic, personal/psychological counseling, veterans affairs office.

COSTS & FINANCIAL AID

Costs (2019–20) ***Comprehensive fee:*** $31,898 includes full-time tuition ($23,498) and room and board ($8400). Full-time tuition and fees vary according to class time, course load, program, reciprocity agreements, and student level. Part-time tuition: $504 per credit hour. Part-time tuition and fees vary according to class time, course load, location, and reciprocity agreements. No tuition increase for student's term of enrollment. ***College room only:*** $4900. Room and board charges vary according to board plan and housing facility. ***Payment plans:*** installment, deferred payment. ***Waivers:*** children of alumni, senior citizens, and employees or children of employees.

Financial Aid Of all full-time matriculated undergraduates who enrolled in 2018, 692 applied for aid, 631 were judged to have need, 103 had their need fully met. In 2018, 100 non-need-based awards were made. ***Average percent of need met:*** 62. ***Average financial aid package:*** $16,846. ***Average need-based loan:*** $3576. ***Average need-based gift aid:*** $5600. ***Average non-need-based aid:*** $252. ***Average indebtedness upon graduation:*** $23,979.

APPLYING

Standardized Tests *Required:* SAT or ACT (for admission).

Options: electronic application, deferred entrance.

Required: high school transcript, minimum 2.5 GPA. ***Required for some:*** essay or personal statement, interview.

CONTACT

Columbia College, 1001 Rogers Street, Columbia, MO 65216-0002. *Phone:* 573-875-7352. *Toll-free phone:* 800-231-2391.

Conception Seminary College

Conception, Missouri

http://www.conception.edu/

CONTACT

Mrs. Jeanette Schieber, Director of Admissions, Conception Seminary College, 37174 State Highway VV, Conception, MO 64433. *Phone:* 660-944-2886. *Fax:* 660-944-2829. *E-mail:* admissions@conception.edu.

Cottey College

Nevada, Missouri

http://www.cottey.edu/

- **Independent** primarily 2-year, founded 1884
- **Small-town** 51-acre campus
- **Endowment** $108.8 million
- **Women only**
- **Moderately difficult** entrance level

FACULTY

Student/faculty ratio: 7:1.

ACADEMICS

Calendar: semesters. *Degrees:* associate and bachelor's.

Library: Blanche Skiff Ross Memorial Library plus 1 other. Weekly public service hours: 88.

STUDENT LIFE
Housing options: women-only. Campus housing is university owned.

Activities and organizations: drama/theater group, choral group, Inter-Society, Golden Key, French Club, Student Government, Global Citizens.

Athletics Member NJCAA.

Campus security: 24-hour emergency response devices and patrols, late-night transport/escort service, controlled dormitory access.

Student services: health clinic, personal/psychological counseling.

COSTS & FINANCIAL AID
Costs (2019–20) ***Comprehensive fee:*** $29,910 includes full-time tuition ($20,500), mandatory fees ($1360), and room and board ($8050). Part-time tuition: $550 per credit hour. Part-time tuition and fees vary according to course load. ***College room only:*** $4300. Room and board charges vary according to housing facility.

Financial Aid Of all full-time matriculated undergraduates who enrolled in 2019, 223 applied for aid, 191 were judged to have need, 64 had their need fully met. In 2019, 59 non-need-based awards were made. ***Average percent of need met:*** 87. ***Average financial aid package:*** $23,100. ***Average need-based loan:*** $2594. ***Average need-based gift aid:*** $19,804. ***Average non-need-based aid:*** $13,741. ***Average indebtedness upon graduation:*** $20,406.

APPLYING
Standardized Tests *Required:* SAT or ACT (for admission). *Required for some:* TOEFL, IELTS.

Options: electronic application, early admission, deferred entrance.

Application fee: $20.

Required: essay or personal statement, high school transcript, 1 letter of recommendation. ***Recommended:*** minimum 2.6 GPA, interview.

CONTACT
Mrs. Angela Moore, Enrollment Office, Cottey College, 1000 West Austin Boulevard, Nevada, MO 64772. *Phone:* 417-667-8181. *Toll-free phone:* 888-526-8839. *Fax:* 417-667-8103. *E-mail:* amoore@cottey.edu.

Cox College

Springfield, Missouri

http://www.coxcollege.edu/

CONTACT
Cox College, 1423 North Jefferson, Springfield, MO 65802. *Phone:* 417-269-3083. *Toll-free phone:* 866-898-5355.

Culver-Stockton College

Canton, Missouri

http://www.culver.edu/

- **Independent** comprehensive, founded 1853, affiliated with Christian Church (Disciples of Christ)
- **Rural** 143-acre campus
- **Endowment** $29.7 million
- **Coed** 971 undergraduate students, 91% full-time, 49% women, 51% men
- **Moderately difficult** entrance level, 52% of applicants were admitted

UNDERGRAD STUDENTS
880 full-time, 91 part-time. Students come from 38 states and territories; 20 other countries; 51% are from out of state; 13% Black or African American, non-Hispanic/Latino; 7% Hispanic/Latino; 0.9% Asian, non-Hispanic/Latino; 0.3% Native Hawaiian or other Pacific Islander, non-Hispanic/Latino; 0.5% American Indian or Alaska Native, non-Hispanic/Latino; 5% Two or more races, non-Hispanic/Latino; 5% international; 6% transferred in; 75% live on campus.

Freshmen:
Admission: 3,277 applied, 1,710 admitted, 254 enrolled. ***Average high school GPA:*** 3.2. ***Test scores:*** SAT evidence-based reading and writing scores over 500: 53%; SAT math scores over 500: 58%; ACT scores over 18: 88%; SAT evidence-based reading and writing scores over 600: 10%; SAT math scores over 600: 11%; ACT scores over 24: 17%.

Retention: 58% of full-time freshmen returned.

FACULTY
Total: 100, 51% full-time, 35% with terminal degrees.

Student/faculty ratio: 14:1.

ACADEMICS
Calendar: semesters. *Degrees:* bachelor's and master's.

Special study options: academic remediation for entering students, accelerated degree program, advanced placement credit, distance learning, double majors, honors programs, independent study, internships, part-time degree program, services for LD students, student-designed majors, study abroad, summer session for credit.

Unusual degree programs: 3-2 business administration; occupational therapy with Washington University in St. Louis, Athletic Training.

Computers: 100 computers/terminals and 50 ports are available on campus for general student use. Students can access the following: campus intranet, computer help desk, free student e-mail accounts, online (class) grades, online (class) registration, online (class) schedules. Campuswide network is available. 100% of college-owned or -operated housing units are wired for high-speed Internet access. Wireless service is available via entire campus.

Library: Carl Johann Memorial Library. *Books:* 107,080 (physical), 317,701 (digital/electronic); *Serial titles:* 755 (physical), 74,422 (digital/electronic); *Databases:* 28. Weekly public service hours: 65; students can reserve study rooms.

STUDENT LIFE
Housing options: on-campus residence required through senior year; coed, men-only, women-only. Campus housing is university owned. Freshman campus housing is guaranteed.

Activities and organizations: drama/theater group, student-run newspaper, radio and television station, choral group, marching band, Campus Programming Council (CPC), The Black Student Union (BSU), Student Government Association (SGA), Health Outreach Peer Educators (HOPE), Institute of Management Accountants (IMA), national fraternities, national sororities.

Athletics Member NAIA. ***Intercollegiate sports:*** baseball M(s), basketball M(s)/W(s), bowling M(s)/W(s), cheerleading M(s)/W(s), cross-country running M(s)/W(s), football M(s), golf M(s)/W(s), lacrosse W(s), soccer M(s)/W(s), softball W(s), track and field M(s)/W(s), volleyball M(s)/W(s). ***Intramural sports:*** baseball M/W, basketball M/W, football M/W, soccer M/W, softball M/W, volleyball M/W.

Campus security: 24-hour emergency response devices and patrols, late-night transport/escort service, controlled dormitory access.

Student services: personal/psychological counseling.

COSTS & FINANCIAL AID
Costs (2020–21) ***One-time required fee:*** $225. ***Comprehensive fee:*** $36,605 includes full-time tuition ($27,315), mandatory fees ($425), and room and board ($8865). Part-time tuition: $620 per credit hour. ***Required fees:*** $18 per credit hour part-time. ***College room only:*** $3970. Room and board charges vary according to board plan and housing facility. ***Payment plan:*** installment. ***Waivers:*** senior citizens and employees or children of employees.

Financial Aid Of all full-time matriculated undergraduates who enrolled in 2017, 851 applied for aid, 789 were judged to have need, 130 had their need fully met. 72 Federal Work-Study jobs (averaging $1146). 383 state and other part-time jobs (averaging $1117). In 2017, 153 non-need-based awards were made. ***Average percent of need met:*** 72. ***Average financial aid package:*** $21,033. ***Average need-based loan:*** $4259. ***Average need-based gift aid:*** $17,185. ***Average non-need-based aid:*** $9964. ***Average indebtedness upon graduation:*** $29,105. ***Financial aid deadline:*** 6/1.

APPLYING
Standardized Tests *Required:* SAT or ACT (for admission).

Options: electronic application, deferred entrance.

Required: high school transcript, minimum 2.0 GPA. ***Recommended:*** essay or personal statement, 1 letter of recommendation, interview.

Application deadlines: rolling (freshmen), rolling (transfers).

Notification: continuous (freshmen), continuous (transfers).

CONTACT
Mr. Eric Kniel, Associate Director of Admission, Culver-Stockton College, One College Hill, Canton, MO 63435-1299. *Phone:* 573-288-

6331. *Toll-free phone:* 800-537-1883. *Fax:* 573-288-6618. *E-mail:* admission@culver.edu.

DeVry University–Kansas City Campus

Kansas City, Missouri

http://www.devry.edu/

- **Proprietary** comprehensive, founded 1931, part of DeVry University
- **Urban** campus
- **Coed**
- **Minimally difficult** entrance level

FACULTY
Student/faculty ratio: 14:1.

ACADEMICS
Calendar: semesters. *Degrees:* associate, bachelor's, master's, and postbachelor's certificates.

FINANCIAL AID
Financial Aid Of all full-time matriculated undergraduates who enrolled in 2007, 294 applied for aid, 281 were judged to have need, 12 had their need fully met. In 2007, 30 non-need-based awards were made. ***Average percent of need met:*** 40. ***Average financial aid package:*** $11,948. ***Average need-based loan:*** $8396. ***Average need-based gift aid:*** $5419. ***Average non-need-based aid:*** $13,609. ***Average indebtedness upon graduation:*** $8969.

APPLYING
Options: deferred entrance.

Application fee: $30.

CONTACT
Admissions Office, DeVry University–Kansas City Campus, 11224 Holmes Road, Kansas City, MO 64131. *Phone:* 816-943-7300. *Toll-free phone:* 866-338-7934.

Drury University

Springfield, Missouri

http://www.drury.edu/

- **Independent** comprehensive, founded 1873
- **Urban** 90-acre campus
- **Endowment** $97.5 million
- **Coed** 1,478 undergraduate students, 98% full-time, 58% women, 42% men
- **Moderately difficult** entrance level, 64% of applicants were admitted

UNDERGRAD STUDENTS
1,443 full-time, 35 part-time. 20% are from out of state; 3% Black or African American, non-Hispanic/Latino; 2% Hispanic/Latino; 0.9% Asian, non-Hispanic/Latino; 0.4% Native Hawaiian or other Pacific Islander, non-Hispanic/Latino; 1% American Indian or Alaska Native, non-Hispanic/Latino; 3% Two or more races, non-Hispanic/Latino; 2% Race/ethnicity unknown; 6% international; 6% transferred in; 63% live on campus.

Freshmen:
Admission: 1,664 applied, 1,072 admitted, 343 enrolled. ***Average high school GPA:*** 3.8. ***Test scores:*** SAT evidence-based reading and writing scores over 500: 88%; ACT scores over 18: 97%; SAT evidence-based reading and writing scores over 600: 37%; ACT scores over 24: 60%; SAT evidence-based reading and writing scores over 700: 5%; ACT scores over 30: 18%.

Retention: 79% of full-time freshmen returned.

FACULTY
Total: 140, 79% full-time, 76% with terminal degrees.

Student/faculty ratio: 13:1.

ACADEMICS
Calendar: semesters. *Degrees:* bachelor's, master's, and postbachelor's certificates (also offers evening program with significant enrollment not reflected in profile).

Special study options: academic remediation for entering students, adult/continuing education programs, advanced placement credit, double majors, English as a second language, freshman honors college, honors programs, independent study, internships, off-campus study, part-time degree program, services for LD students, student-designed majors, study abroad, summer session for credit.

Unusual degree programs: 3-2 engineering with Washington University in St. Louis; international management with American Graduate School of International Management, occupational therapy with Washington University in St. Louis.

Computers: 385 computers/terminals are available on campus for general student use. Students can access the following: campus intranet, computer help desk, free student e-mail accounts, online (class) grades, online (class) registration, online (class) schedules, digital imaging lab, online bill payment/student information. Campuswide network is available. 100% of college-owned or -operated housing units are wired for high-speed Internet access. Wireless service is available via entire campus.

Library: F. W. Olin Library plus 1 other. *Books:* 154,247 (physical), 234,110 (digital/electronic); *Serial titles:* 354 (digital/electronic); *Databases:* 44. Weekly public service hours: 92; students can reserve study rooms.

STUDENT LIFE
Housing options: on-campus residence required through junior year; coed. Campus housing is university owned. Freshman campus housing is guaranteed.

Activities and organizations: drama/theater group, student-run newspaper, radio and television station, choral group, Drury Volunteer Corps (DVC), International Student Association, Fanthers, Drury Allies, Commuter Student Association, national fraternities, national sororities.

Athletics Member NCAA. All Division II. ***Intercollegiate sports:*** baseball M(s), basketball M(s)/W(s), cheerleading M(s)/W(s), cross-country running M(s)/W(s), golf M(s)/W(s), riflery M/W, soccer M(s)/W(s), softball W(s), swimming and diving M(s)/W(s), tennis M(s)/W(s), track and field M(s)/W(s), triathlon W(s), volleyball W(s), wrestling M(s). ***Intramural sports:*** basketball M/W, bowling M(c)/W(c), football M/W, ice hockey M(c), soccer M/W, softball M/W, ultimate Frisbee M(c)/W(c), volleyball M/W.

Campus security: 24-hour emergency response devices and patrols, student patrols, late-night transport/escort service, controlled dormitory access.

Student services: health clinic, personal/psychological counseling, veterans affairs office.

COSTS & FINANCIAL AID
Costs (2020–21) ***Comprehensive fee:*** $40,087 includes full-time tuition ($29,900), mandatory fees ($1015), and room and board ($9172). Full-time tuition and fees vary according to degree level. Part-time tuition: $959 per credit hour. Part-time tuition and fees vary according to degree level. ***College room only:*** $5860. Room and board charges vary according to board plan and housing facility. ***Payment plan:*** installment. ***Waivers:*** employees or children of employees.

Financial Aid Of all full-time matriculated undergraduates who enrolled in 2019, 1,134 applied for aid, 975 were judged to have need, 241 had their need fully met. In 2019, 450 non-need-based awards were made. ***Average percent of need met:*** 76. ***Average financial aid package:*** $23,426. ***Average need-based loan:*** $4015. ***Average need-based gift aid:*** $20,513. ***Average non-need-based aid:*** $12,543. ***Average indebtedness upon graduation:*** $37,144.

APPLYING
Standardized Tests *Required:* SAT or ACT (for admission).

Options: electronic application, deferred entrance.

Required: essay or personal statement, high school transcript, minimum 2.7 GPA, 1 letter of recommendation. ***Recommended:*** interview.

Application deadlines: rolling (freshmen), rolling (transfers).

Notification: continuous (freshmen), continuous (transfers).

CONTACT
Mr. Kevin Kropf, Executive Vice President for Enrollment Management, Drury University, 900 North Benton Avenue, Springfield, MO 65802. *Phone:* 417-873-7205. *Toll-free phone:* 800-922-2274. *Fax:* 417-866-3873. *E-mail:* druryad@drury.edu.

Evangel University

Springfield, Missouri

http://www.evangel.edu/

- **Independent** comprehensive, founded 1955, affiliated with Assemblies of God
- **Urban** 80-acre campus
- **Coed** 1,793 undergraduate students, 86% full-time, 56% women, 44% men
- **Moderately difficult** entrance level, 74% of applicants were admitted

UNDERGRAD STUDENTS
1,539 full-time, 254 part-time. 4% Black or African American, non-Hispanic/Latino; 7% Hispanic/Latino; 1% Asian, non-Hispanic/Latino; 0.1% Native Hawaiian or other Pacific Islander, non-Hispanic/Latino; 0.8% American Indian or Alaska Native, non-Hispanic/Latino; 4% Two or more races, non-Hispanic/Latino; 2% Race/ethnicity unknown; 1% international; 4% transferred in.

Freshmen:
Admission: 1,249 applied, 920 admitted, 443 enrolled. ***Test scores:*** SAT math scores over 700: 2%.

Retention: 80% of full-time freshmen returned.

ACADEMICS
Calendar: semesters. *Degrees:* associate, bachelor's, master's, and doctoral.

ROTC: Army (c).

Computers: Students can access the following: computer help desk, free student e-mail accounts, online (class) grades, online (class) registration, online (class) schedules, online payment. Campuswide network is available. Wireless service is available via classrooms, computer labs, learning centers, libraries, student centers.
Library: Claude Kendrick Library.

STUDENT LIFE
Housing options: on-campus residence required through senior year; coed, men-only, women-only. Campus housing is university owned.

Activities and organizations: drama/theater group, student-run newspaper, radio and television station, choral group, marching band, Activities Board, student government, CrossWalk Student Ministries, Honor Societies, Music Ensembles.

Athletics Member NAIA. ***Intercollegiate sports:*** baseball M(s), basketball M(s)/W(s), cross-country running M(s)/W(s), football M(s), golf M(s)/W(s), softball W(s), tennis M(s)/W(s), track and field M(s)/W(s), volleyball W(s). ***Intramural sports:*** baseball M, basketball M/W, football M, golf M/W, soccer M/W, softball W, tennis M/W, volleyball W.

Campus security: 24-hour emergency response devices and patrols, student patrols, late-night transport/escort service, controlled dormitory access.

Student services: health clinic, personal/psychological counseling.

COSTS & FINANCIAL AID
Costs (2019–20) ***Comprehensive fee:*** $32,849 includes full-time tuition ($23,032), mandatory fees ($1295), and room and board ($8522). Full-time tuition and fees vary according to course load. Part-time tuition: $960 per credit hour. Part-time tuition and fees vary according to course load. ***College room only:*** $4304. Room and board charges vary according to board plan. ***Payment plan:*** installment. ***Waivers:*** employees or children of employees.

Financial Aid Of all full-time matriculated undergraduates who enrolled in 2018, 1,379 applied for aid, 1,203 were judged to have need, 161 had their need fully met. 965 Federal Work-Study jobs (averaging $1821). In 2018, 206 non-need-based awards were made. ***Average percent of need met:*** 70. ***Average financial aid package:*** $18,783. ***Average need-based loan:*** $3667. ***Average need-based gift aid:*** $14,846. ***Average non-need-based aid:*** $9479. ***Average indebtedness upon graduation:*** $31,560.

APPLYING
Options: electronic application, deferred entrance.

Required: essay or personal statement, high school transcript, interview. ***Recommended:*** minimum 2.0 GPA.

CONTACT
Evangel University, 1111 North Glenstone, Springfield, MO 65802. *Phone:* 417-865-2811 Ext. 7205. *Toll-free phone:* 800-382-6435. *Fax:* 417-865-9599. *E-mail:* admissions@evangel.edu.

Fontbonne University

St. Louis, Missouri

http://www.fontbonne.edu/

CONTACT
Mr. Michelle Palumbo, Associate Vice President of Undergraduate Admissions, Fontbonne University, 6800 Wydown Boulevard, St. Louis, MO 63105. *Phone:* 314-889-1400. *Toll-free phone:* 800-205-5862. *Fax:* 314-889-1451. *E-mail:* fbyou@fontbonne.edu.

Global University

Springfield, Missouri

http://www.globaluniversity.edu/

CONTACT
Rev. Todd Waggoner, Enrollment and International Student Services Director, Global University, 1211 South Glenstone Avenue, Springfield, MO 65804. *Phone:* 417-862-9533 Ext. 2335. *Toll-free phone:* 800-443-1083. *Fax:* 417-863-9621. *E-mail:* twaggoner@globaluniversity.edu.

Goldfarb School of Nursing at Barnes-Jewish College

St. Louis, Missouri

http://www.barnesjewishcollege.edu/

CONTACT
Goldfarb School of Nursing at Barnes-Jewish College, 4483 Duncan Avenue, St. Louis, MO 63110. *Phone:* 314-362-9155. *Toll-free phone:* 800-832-9009.

Graceland University

Independence, Missouri

http://www.graceland.edu/

- **Independent Community of Christ** comprehensive
- **Coed**

ACADEMICS
Calendar: 4-1-4. *Degrees:* bachelor's, master's, and post-master's certificates.

COSTS & FINANCIAL AID
Costs (2019–20) ***Comprehensive fee:*** $39,520 includes full-time tuition ($29,750), mandatory fees ($670), and room and board ($9100). Part-time tuition: $800 per credit hour. ***College room only:*** $3490.

Financial Aid Of all full-time matriculated undergraduates who enrolled in 2009, 1,000 applied for aid, 917 were judged to have need, 168 had their need fully met. 383 Federal Work-Study jobs (averaging $1382). 303 state and other part-time jobs (averaging $1708). In 2009, 230 non-need-based awards were made. ***Average percent of need met:*** 78. ***Average financial aid package:*** $18,566. ***Average need-based loan:*** $5397. ***Average need-based gift aid:*** $13,960. ***Average non-need-based aid:*** $10,029. ***Average indebtedness upon graduation:*** $29,934.

CONTACT
Admissions, Graceland University, 1401 West Truman Road, Independence, MO 64050-3434. *Phone:* 816-833-0524. *Toll-free phone:* 866-GRACELAND. *E-mail:* gic@graceland.edu.

Hannibal-LaGrange University

Hannibal, Missouri

http://www.hlg.edu/

CONTACT
Dr. Ray Carty, Vice President for Enrollment Management, Hannibal-LaGrange University, 2800 Palmyra Road, Hannibal, MO 63401-1999.

Phone: 573-629-3094. *Toll-free phone:* 800-HLG-1119. *E-mail:* admissions@hlg.edu.

Harris-Stowe State University

St. Louis, Missouri

http://www.hssu.edu/

- **State-supported** 4-year, founded 1857, part of Missouri Coordinating Board for Higher Education
- **Urban** 22-acre campus with easy access to St. Louis
- **Coed** 1,630 undergraduate students, 84% full-time, 69% women, 31% men
- **Noncompetitive** entrance level, 52% of applicants were admitted

UNDERGRAD STUDENTS

1,370 full-time, 260 part-time. 37% are from out of state; 84% Black or African American, non-Hispanic/Latino; 3% Hispanic/Latino; 0.4% Asian, non-Hispanic/Latino; 0.2% American Indian or Alaska Native, non-Hispanic/Latino; 3% Two or more races, non-Hispanic/Latino; 4% Race/ethnicity unknown; 2% international; 14% transferred in; 37% live on campus.

Freshmen:

Admission: 6,669 applied, 3,500 admitted, 381 enrolled. ***Average high school GPA:*** 2.9. ***Test scores:*** ACT scores over 18: 49%; ACT scores over 24: 7%.

Retention: 55% of full-time freshmen returned.

FACULTY

Total: 180, 20% full-time, 33% with terminal degrees.

Student/faculty ratio: 19:1.

ACADEMICS

Calendar: semesters. *Degree:* certificates and bachelor's.

Special study options: academic remediation for entering students, accelerated degree program, advanced placement credit, cooperative education, distance learning, honors programs, internships, off-campus study, part-time degree program, services for LD students, student-designed majors, study abroad, summer session for credit. ***ROTC:*** Army (c).

Unusual degree programs: 3-2 engineering with Saint Louis University.

Computers: Students can access the following: computer help desk, free student e-mail accounts, online (class) grades, online (class) registration, online (class) schedules. Campuswide network is available. 100% of college-owned or -operated housing units are wired for high-speed Internet access. Wireless service is available via entire campus.

Library: AT&T Library and Technology Center plus 1 other.

STUDENT LIFE

Housing options: coed. Campus housing is university owned. Freshman applicants given priority for college housing.

Activities and organizations: drama/theater group, choral group, Drama Club, Concert chorale, Student Government Association, Multicultural Council, Student Ambassadors, national fraternities, national sororities.

Athletics Member NAIA. ***Intercollegiate sports:*** baseball M(s), basketball M(s)/W(s), cheerleading M(s)/W(s), soccer M(s)/W(s), softball W(s), volleyball W(s). ***Intramural sports:*** basketball M/W, sand volleyball M/W.

Campus security: 24-hour emergency response devices and patrols, late-night transport/escort service, controlled dormitory access.

Student services: health clinic, personal/psychological counseling.

COSTS & FINANCIAL AID

Costs (2020–21) ***Tuition:*** area resident $5040 full-time, $210 per credit hour part-time; state resident $5040 full-time, $210 per credit hour part-time; nonresident $9672 full-time, $304 per credit hour part-time. Full-time tuition and fees vary according to course load. ***Required fees:*** $444 full-time. ***Room and board:*** $9491; room only: $6741. Room and board charges vary according to housing facility. ***Payment plan:*** installment. ***Waivers:*** employees or children of employees.

Financial Aid ***Average financial aid package:*** $7027.

APPLYING

Standardized Tests *Required:* SAT or ACT (for admission).

Options: electronic application, deferred entrance.

Application fee: $20.

Required: high school transcript.

Notification: continuous (freshmen), continuous (transfers).

CONTACT

Dr. Chauvette McElmurry-Green, Registrar, Harris-Stowe State University, 3026 Laclede Avenue, St. Louis, MO 63103. *Phone:* 314-340-3300. *Fax:* 314-340-3555. *E-mail:* admissions@hssu.edu.

Kansas City Art Institute

Kansas City, Missouri

http://www.kcai.edu/

- **Independent** 4-year, founded 1885
- **Urban** 18-acre campus with easy access to Kansas City, MO
- **Coed**
- **Moderately difficult** entrance level

FACULTY

Student/faculty ratio: 9:1.

ACADEMICS

Calendar: semesters. *Degree:* certificates and bachelor's.

Library: Jannes Library. Weekly public service hours: 84; students can reserve study rooms.

STUDENT LIFE

Housing options: on-campus residence required for freshman year; coed. Campus housing is university owned. Freshman applicants given priority for college housing.

Activities and organizations: student-run radio station.

Campus security: 24-hour emergency response devices and patrols, late-night transport/escort service, controlled dormitory access.

Student services: personal/psychological counseling.

COSTS & FINANCIAL AID

Costs (2019–20) ***Tuition:*** $38,700 full-time, $1510 per credit hour part-time. Full-time tuition and fees vary according to reciprocity agreements. Part-time tuition and fees vary according to reciprocity agreements. ***Required fees:*** $500 full-time. ***Room only:*** $8200. Room and board charges vary according to board plan.

Financial Aid Of all full-time matriculated undergraduates who enrolled in 2019, 632 applied for aid, 575 were judged to have need, 93 had their need fully met. In 2019, 118 non-need-based awards were made. ***Average percent of need met:*** 68. ***Average financial aid package:*** $27,588. ***Average need-based loan:*** $4216. ***Average need-based gift aid:*** $23,834. ***Average non-need-based aid:*** $18,649. ***Average indebtedness upon graduation:*** $32,607.

APPLYING

Standardized Tests *Required:* SAT or ACT (for admission). *Required for some:* TOEFL.

Options: electronic application, early admission, deferred entrance.

Application fee: $45.

Required: essay or personal statement, high school transcript, 1 letter of recommendation, portfolio. ***Recommended:*** minimum 2.5 GPA, interview.

CONTACT

Mr. Gerald Valet, Director of Admission Technology, Kansas City Art Institute, 4415 Warwick Boulevard, Kansas City, MO 64111-1874. *Phone:* 816-474-5224. *Toll-free phone:* 800-522-5224. *Fax:* 816-802-3309. *E-mail:* admiss@kcai.edu.

Lincoln University

Jefferson City, Missouri

http://www.lincolnu.edu/

- **State-supported** comprehensive, founded 1866
- **Small-town** 174-acre campus
- **Endowment** $1.6 million
- **Coed** 2,323 undergraduate students, 69% full-time, 59% women, 41% men
- **Noncompetitive** entrance level, 53% of applicants were admitted

UNDERGRAD STUDENTS
1,593 full-time, 730 part-time. Students come from 28 states and territories; 14 other countries; 30% are from out of state; 57% Black or African American, non-Hispanic/Latino; 2% Hispanic/Latino; 0.7% Asian, non-Hispanic/Latino; 0.1% Native Hawaiian or other Pacific Islander, non-Hispanic/Latino; 0.3% American Indian or Alaska Native, non-Hispanic/Latino; 3% Two or more races, non-Hispanic/Latino; 5% Race/ethnicity unknown; 3% international; 6% transferred in; 49% live on campus.

Freshmen:
Admission: 4,295 applied, 2,281 admitted, 397 enrolled. ***Average high school GPA:*** 2.7. ***Test scores:*** SAT evidence-based reading and writing scores over 500: 17%; SAT math scores over 500: 13%; ACT scores over 18: 35%; ACT scores over 24: 5%.

Retention: 54% of full-time freshmen returned.

FACULTY
Total: 160, 66% full-time, 48% with terminal degrees.

Student/faculty ratio: 15:1.

ACADEMICS
Calendar: semesters. *Degrees:* associate, bachelor's, master's, post-master's, and postbachelor's certificates.

Special study options: accelerated degree program, adult/continuing education programs, advanced placement credit, cooperative education, distance learning, double majors, freshman honors college, honors programs, independent study, internships, off-campus study, part-time degree program, services for LD students, study abroad, summer session for credit. ***ROTC:*** Army (b).

Computers: 365 computers/terminals and 1,100 ports are available on campus for general student use. Students can access the following: campus intranet, computer help desk, free student e-mail accounts, online (class) grades, online (class) registration, online (class) schedules. Campuswide network is available. 100% of college-owned or -operated housing units are wired for high-speed Internet access. Wireless service is available via entire campus.
Library: Inman E. Page Library. *Books:* 117,765 (physical), 225,904 (digital/electronic); *Serial titles:* 1,301 (physical), 19,000 (digital/electronic); *Databases:* 50. Weekly public service hours: 84.

STUDENT LIFE
Housing options: on-campus residence required through sophomore year; coed, men-only, women-only. Campus housing is university owned.

Activities and organizations: student-run newspaper, choral group, marching band, Student Government Association (SGA), Lincoln University Band, Alpha Kappa Mu, Army ROTC, International Student Association, national fraternities, national sororities.

Athletics Member NCAA. All Division II except golf (Division I). ***Intercollegiate sports:*** basketball M(s)/W(s), bowling W(s), cross-country running W(s), football M(s), golf M(s)/W(s), softball W(s), track and field M(s)/W(s). ***Intramural sports:*** basketball M(c)/W(c), cheerleading W(c), volleyball M/W.

Campus security: 24-hour emergency response devices and patrols, student patrols, late-night transport/escort service, controlled dormitory access, Rape Aggression Defense class upon request, Operation ID, timely warnings, text message safety alerts, Webpage with helpful tips.

Student services: health clinic, personal/psychological counseling, women's center, veterans affairs office.

COSTS & FINANCIAL AID
Costs (2019–20) ***Tuition:*** state resident $6548 full-time, $218 per credit hour part-time; nonresident $13,350 full-time, $445 per credit hour part-time. Full-time tuition and fees vary according to course load, location, and reciprocity agreements. Part-time tuition and fees vary according to course load, location, and reciprocity agreements. ***Required fees:*** $1362 full-time, $10 per credit hour part-time, $381 per term part-time. ***Room and board:*** $7282; room only: $3728. Room and board charges vary according to board plan and housing facility. ***Payment plans:*** installment, deferred payment. ***Waivers:*** senior citizens and employees or children of employees.

Financial Aid Of all full-time matriculated undergraduates who enrolled in 2018, 1,039 applied for aid, 920 were judged to have need, 48 had their need fully met. 207 Federal Work-Study jobs (averaging $1006). 47 state and other part-time jobs (averaging $2581). In 2018, 8 non-need-based awards were made. ***Average percent of need met:*** 71. ***Average financial aid package:*** $9953. ***Average need-based loan:*** $4375. ***Average need-based gift aid:*** $6155. ***Average non-need-based aid:*** $3276. ***Average indebtedness upon graduation:*** $30,827.

APPLYING
Standardized Tests *Required:* SAT or ACT (for admission).

Options: electronic application, deferred entrance.

Required: high school transcript. ***Required for some:*** minimum 2.0 GPA.

Application deadlines: rolling (freshmen), rolling (transfers).

Notification: continuous (freshmen), continuous (transfers).

CONTACT
Sonja Jackson, Director of Admissions and Undergraduate Recruitment, Lincoln University, Office of Admissions, 820 Chestnut Street, B-7 Young Hall, Jefferson City, MO 65101. *Phone:* 573-681-5102. *Fax:* 573-681-5889. *E-mail:* admissions@lincolnu.edu.

Lindenwood University

St. Charles, Missouri

http://www.lindenwood.edu/

- **Independent Presbyterian** comprehensive, founded 1827
- **Suburban** 285-acre campus with easy access to St. Louis
- **Endowment** $168.3 million
- **Coed** 5,668 undergraduate students, 88% full-time, 55% women, 45% men
- **Moderately difficult** entrance level, 88% of applicants were admitted

UNDERGRAD STUDENTS
5,014 full-time, 654 part-time. Students come from 50 states and territories; 74 other countries; 37% are from out of state; 13% Black or African American, non-Hispanic/Latino; 5% Hispanic/Latino; 1% Asian, non-Hispanic/Latino; 0.6% Native Hawaiian or other Pacific Islander, non-Hispanic/Latino; 0.5% American Indian or Alaska Native, non-Hispanic/Latino; 3% Two or more races, non-Hispanic/Latino; 9% Race/ethnicity unknown; 11% international; 13% transferred in; 51% live on campus.

Freshmen:
Admission: 3,899 applied, 3,414 admitted, 798 enrolled. ***Average high school GPA:*** 3.4. ***Test scores:*** SAT evidence-based reading and writing scores over 500: 68%; SAT math scores over 500: 74%; ACT scores over 18: 90%; SAT evidence-based reading and writing scores over 600: 17%; SAT math scores over 600: 21%; ACT scores over 24: 34%; SAT evidence-based reading and writing scores over 700: 1%; SAT math scores over 700: 2%; ACT scores over 30: 4%.

Retention: 68% of full-time freshmen returned.

FACULTY
Total: 1,174, 22% full-time, 52% with terminal degrees.

Student/faculty ratio: 12:1.

ACADEMICS
Calendar: 4-1-4 for daytime programs; quarters and trimesters for evening programs. *Degrees:* bachelor's, master's, doctoral, post-master's, and postbachelor's certificates.

Special study options: academic remediation for entering students, accelerated degree program, adult/continuing education programs, advanced placement credit, distance learning, double majors, English as a second language, external degree program, freshman honors college, honors programs, independent study, internships, off-campus study, part-time degree program, services for LD students, student-designed majors, study abroad, summer session for credit. ***ROTC:*** Army (c), Air Force (c).

Unusual degree programs: 3-2 engineering with University of Missouri–Columbia, University of Missouri–St. Louis, Washington University in St. Louis; nursing with Golfarb School of Nursing at Barnes-Jewish College.

Computers: 231 computers/terminals are available on campus for general student use. Students can access the following: campus intranet, computer help desk, free student e-mail accounts, online (class) grades, online (class) registration, online (class) schedules. Campuswide network is available. 100% of college-owned or -operated housing units are wired for high-speed Internet access. Wireless service is available via classrooms, computer centers, computer labs, dorm rooms, learning centers, libraries, student centers.

Library: Library and Academic Resource Center plus 1 other. *Books:* 74,272 (physical), 268,719 (digital/electronic); *Serial titles:* 132 (physical), 102 (digital/electronic); *Databases:* 141. Students can reserve study rooms.

STUDENT LIFE

Housing options: coed, men-only, women-only, special housing for students with disabilities. Campus housing is university owned. Freshman applicants given priority for college housing.

Activities and organizations: drama/theater group, student-run newspaper, radio and television station, choral group, marching band, Kappa Delta Pi, Athletes in Action, Black Student Union, Lindenwood Gender Sexualities Alliance, Psychology Interest Club, national fraternities, national sororities.

Athletics Member NCAA, NAIA, USCAA. All NCAA Division II except golf (Division I). ***Intercollegiate sports:*** baseball M(s), basketball M(s)/W(s), bowling M(s)/W(s), cheerleading M(s)/W(s), cross-country running M(s)/W(s), field hockey W(s), football M(s), golf M(s)/W(s), gymnastics W(s), ice hockey M(s)/W(s), lacrosse M(s)/W(s), riflery M(s)/W(s), rugby M(s)/W(s), soccer M(s)/W(s), softball W(s), swimming and diving M(s)/W(s), tennis M(s)/W(s), track and field M(s)/W(s), volleyball M(s)/W(s), water polo M(s)/W(s), weight lifting M(s)/W(s), wrestling M(s)/W(s). ***Intramural sports:*** basketball M/W, sand volleyball M/W, soccer M/W, softball M/W, volleyball M/W.

Campus security: 24-hour emergency response devices and patrols, late-night transport/escort service, controlled dormitory access.

Student services: health clinic, personal/psychological counseling, veterans affairs office.

COSTS & FINANCIAL AID

Costs (2020–21) ***Comprehensive fee:*** $27,900 includes full-time tuition ($18,500), mandatory fees ($100), and room and board ($9300). Full-time tuition and fees vary according to class time. Part-time tuition: $450 per credit hour. Part-time tuition and fees vary according to class time. ***Required fees:*** $75 per term part-time. ***Room and board:*** Room and board charges vary according to board plan.

Financial Aid Of all full-time matriculated undergraduates who enrolled in 2019, 4,080 applied for aid, 3,426 were judged to have need, 799 had their need fully met. 189 Federal Work-Study jobs (averaging $2850). In 2019, 654 non-need-based awards were made. ***Average percent of need met:*** 57. ***Average financial aid package:*** $14,875. ***Average need-based loan:*** $4220. ***Average need-based gift aid:*** $9940. ***Average non-need-based aid:*** $8439. ***Average indebtedness upon graduation:*** $33,365.

APPLYING

Options: electronic application, deferred entrance.

Required: minimum 2.5 GPA, personal resumé indicating community service, youth leadership, clubs, organizations, and non-academic experience. ***Required for some:*** essay or personal statement, high school transcript. ***Recommended:*** 3 letters of recommendation, interview.

Application deadlines: rolling (freshmen), rolling (transfers).

Notification: continuous (freshmen), continuous (transfers).

CONTACT

Kara Schilli, Director, University Admissions, Lindenwood University, 209 South Kings Highway, St. Charles, MO 63301. *Phone:* 636-949-4369. *Fax:* 636-949-4989. *E-mail:* KSchilli@lindenwood.edu.

Logan University

Chesterfield, Missouri

http://www.logan.edu/

CONTACT

Ms. Natach Douglas, Director of Admissions, Logan University, 1851 Schoettler Road, Chesterfield, MO 63017. *Phone:* 636-227-2100 Ext. 1718. *Toll-free phone:* 800-533-9210. *Fax:* 636-207-2425. *E-mail:* admissions@logan.edu.

Maryville University of Saint Louis

St. Louis, Missouri

http://www.maryville.edu/

- **Independent** university, founded 1872
- **Suburban** 130-acre campus with easy access to St. Louis
- **Endowment** $56.3 million
- **Coed** 4,454 undergraduate students, 67% full-time, 66% women, 34% men
- **Moderately difficult** entrance level, 83% of applicants were admitted

UNDERGRAD STUDENTS

2,990 full-time, 1,464 part-time. Students come from 50 states and territories; 49 other countries; 38% are from out of state; 12% Black or African American, non-Hispanic/Latino; 6% Hispanic/Latino; 3% Asian, non-Hispanic/Latino; 0.4% American Indian or Alaska Native, non-Hispanic/Latino; 4% Two or more races, non-Hispanic/Latino; 4% Race/ethnicity unknown; 4% international; 16% transferred in; 16% live on campus.

Freshmen:

Admission: 2,901 applied, 2,405 admitted, 683 enrolled. ***Average high school GPA:*** 3.6. ***Test scores:*** SAT evidence-based reading and writing scores over 500: 81%; SAT math scores over 500: 85%; ACT scores over 18: 91%; SAT evidence-based reading and writing scores over 600: 32%; SAT math scores over 600: 35%; ACT scores over 24: 50%; SAT evidence-based reading and writing scores over 700: 2%; SAT math scores over 700: 4%; ACT scores over 30: 12%.

Retention: 83% of full-time freshmen returned.

FACULTY

Total: 953, 18% full-time, 39% with terminal degrees.

Student/faculty ratio: 14:1.

ACADEMICS

Calendar: semesters. *Degrees:* bachelor's, master's, doctoral, post-master's, and postbachelor's certificates.

Special study options: accelerated degree program, adult/continuing education programs, advanced placement credit, cooperative education, distance learning, double majors, English as a second language, external degree program, honors programs, independent study, internships, off-campus study, part-time degree program, services for LD students, study abroad, summer session for credit. ***ROTC:*** Army (c).

Unusual degree programs: 3-2 business administration; engineering with Washington University in St. Louis; social work with Saint Louis University; education.

Computers: 570 computers/terminals are available on campus for general student use. Students can access the following: campus intranet, computer help desk, free student e-mail accounts, online (class) grades, online (class) registration, online (class) schedules, specialized software, university catalog. Campuswide network is available. 100% of college-owned or -operated housing units are wired for high-speed Internet access. Wireless service is available via entire campus.

Library: University Library. *Books:* 59,710 (physical), 290,347 (digital/electronic); *Serial titles:* 189 (physical), 70,563 (digital/electronic); *Databases:* 141. Weekly public service hours: 105; study areas open 24 hours, 5–7 days a week.

STUDENT LIFE

Housing options: coed. Campus housing is university owned.

Activities and organizations: drama/theater group, student-run newspaper, choral group, Campus Activities Board, Physical Therapy Club, Student Nurses Association, Community Service Club, Green Maryville Student Association.

Athletics Member NCAA. All Division II. ***Intercollegiate sports:*** baseball M(s), basketball M(s)/W(s), bowling W(s), cross-country running M(s)/W(s), golf M(s)/W(s), ice hockey M(c)/W(c), lacrosse M(s)/W(s), soccer M(s)/W(s), softball W(s), swimming and diving M(s)/W(s), tennis M(s)/W(s), track and field M(s)/W(s), volleyball M(c)/W(s), wrestling M(s). ***Intramural sports:*** basketball M/W, cheerleading M/W, lacrosse M/W, rugby M, soccer M/W, softball W, table tennis M/W, tennis M/W, ultimate Frisbee M/W, volleyball M/W.

Campus security: 24-hour emergency response devices and patrols, late-night transport/escort service, controlled dormitory access, video security system in residence halls, self-defense and education programs.

Student services: health clinic, personal/psychological counseling.

COSTS & FINANCIAL AID

Costs (2020–21) ***Comprehensive fee:*** $38,770 includes full-time tuition ($26,070), mandatory fees ($2400), and room and board ($10,300). Full-time tuition and fees vary according to course load and program. Part-time tuition: $781 per credit hour. Part-time tuition and fees vary according to class time, course load, and program. ***Required fees:*** $375 per year part-time. ***Room and board:*** Room and board charges vary according to board plan and housing facility. ***Payment plans:*** installment, deferred payment. ***Waivers:*** senior citizens and employees or children of employees.

Financial Aid Of all full-time matriculated undergraduates who enrolled in 2019, 2,275 applied for aid, 2,016 were judged to have need, 212 had their need fully met. 525 Federal Work-Study jobs (averaging $949). 118 state and other part-time jobs (averaging $3855). In 2019, 813 non-need-based awards were made. ***Average percent of need met:*** 60. ***Average financial aid package:*** $20,367. ***Average need-based loan:*** $4323. ***Average need-based gift aid:*** $15,586. ***Average non-need-based aid:*** $13,960. ***Average indebtedness upon graduation:*** $30,657.

APPLYING

Options: electronic application, deferred entrance.

Required: high school transcript, minimum 2.5 GPA. ***Required for some:*** essay or personal statement, interview, audition, portfolio.

Application deadlines: rolling (freshmen), rolling (out-of-state freshmen), rolling (transfers).

Notification: continuous (freshmen), continuous (out-of-state freshmen), continuous (transfers).

CONTACT

Ms. Shani Lenore-Jenkins, Vice President of Enrollment, Maryville University of Saint Louis, 650 Maryville University Drive, St. Louis, MO 63141-7299. *Phone:* 314-529-9350. *Toll-free phone:* 800-627-9855. *Fax:* 314-529-9927. *E-mail:* admissions@maryville.edu.

Midwest University

Wentzville, Missouri

http://www.midwest.edu/

CONTACT

Jeoung H. Ham, Registrar/Director of Admissions, Midwest University, 851 Parr Road, Wentzville, MO 63385. *Phone:* 636-327-4645. *Fax:* 636-327-4715. *E-mail:* usa@midwest.edu.

Missouri Baptist University

St. Louis, Missouri

http://www.mobap.edu/

- **Independent Southern Baptist** comprehensive, founded 1964
- **Suburban** 65-acre campus with easy access to St. Louis
- **Coed**
- **Moderately difficult** entrance level

FACULTY

Student/faculty ratio: 19:1.

ACADEMICS

Calendar: semesters. *Degrees:* certificates, associate, bachelor's, master's, doctoral, post-master's, and postbachelor's certificates.

Library: Jung-Kellogg Library. *Books:* 48,169 (physical), 222,044 (digital/electronic); *Serial titles:* 512 (physical), 104 (digital/electronic); *Databases:* 92. Weekly public service hours: 76.

STUDENT LIFE

Housing options: men-only, women-only, special housing for students with disabilities. Campus housing is university owned. Freshman applicants given priority for college housing.

Activities and organizations: drama/theater group, student-run radio station, choral group, Enactus: Students in Free Enterprise, Amp Ministries, Student Missouri State Teacher's Association, Gamma Delta Sigma, Ministerial Alliance, national fraternities, national sororities.

Athletics Member NAIA.

Campus security: 24-hour emergency response devices and patrols, late-night transport/escort service, controlled dormitory access.

Student services: health clinic, personal/psychological counseling.

COSTS & FINANCIAL AID

Costs (2019–20) ***Comprehensive fee:*** $37,290 includes full-time tuition ($26,860), mandatory fees ($1360), and room and board ($9070). Full-time tuition and fees vary according to course load, location, and program. Part-time tuition: $929 per credit hour. Part-time tuition and fees vary according to course load, location, and program. ***Required fees:*** $29 per credit hour part-time. ***Room and board:*** Room and board charges vary according to board plan and housing facility.

Financial Aid Of all full-time matriculated undergraduates who enrolled in 2019, 1,276 applied for aid, 1,120 were judged to have need, 401 had their need fully met. 573 Federal Work-Study jobs (averaging $1976). In 2019, 70 non-need-based awards were made. ***Average financial aid package:*** $20,499. ***Average need-based loan:*** $4801. ***Average need-based gift aid:*** $5459. ***Average non-need-based aid:*** $9443. ***Average indebtedness upon graduation:*** $25,674.

APPLYING

Standardized Tests *Required:* SAT or ACT (for admission).

Options: electronic application.

Application fee: $35.

Required: high school transcript, minimum 2.0 GPA, 1 letter of recommendation.

CONTACT

Mrs. Cynthia Sutton, Director of Admissions, Missouri Baptist University, One College Park Drive, St. Louis, MO 63141-8660. *Phone:* 877-434-1115. *Toll-free phone:* 877-434-1115 Ext. 2290. *Fax:* 314-434-7596. *E-mail:* admissions@mobap.edu.

Missouri Southern State University

Joplin, Missouri

http://www.mssu.edu/

- **State-supported** comprehensive, founded 1937
- **Small-town** 365-acre campus
- **Coed** 5,475 undergraduate students, 70% full-time, 61% women, 39% men
- **Moderately difficult** entrance level, 134% of applicants were admitted

UNDERGRAD STUDENTS

3,844 full-time, 1,631 part-time. 23% are from out of state; 6% Black or African American, non-Hispanic/Latino; 8% Hispanic/Latino; 3% Asian, non-Hispanic/Latino; 0.4% Native Hawaiian or other Pacific Islander, non-Hispanic/Latino; 3% American Indian or Alaska Native, non-Hispanic/Latino; 2% Two or more races, non-Hispanic/Latino; 2% Race/ethnicity unknown; 2% international; 15% live on campus.

Freshmen:

Admission: 311 applied, 418 admitted, 729 enrolled. ***Average high school GPA:*** 3.4. ***Test scores:*** SAT evidence-based reading and writing scores over 500: 43%; SAT math scores over 500: 41%; ACT scores over 18: 80%; SAT evidence-based reading and writing scores over 600: 20%; SAT math scores over 600: 14%; ACT scores over 24: 28%; SAT evidence-based reading and writing scores over 700: 4%; SAT math scores over 700: 4%; ACT scores over 30: 6%.

Retention: 65% of full-time freshmen returned.

FACULTY

Student/faculty ratio: 17:1.

ACADEMICS

Calendar: semesters. *Degrees:* certificates, associate, bachelor's, master's, and postbachelor's certificates.

Special study options: academic remediation for entering students, accelerated degree program, adult/continuing education programs, advanced placement credit, cooperative education, distance learning, double majors, English as a second language, external degree program, honors programs, independent study, internships, off-campus study, part-time degree program, services for LD students, study abroad, summer session for credit. ***ROTC:*** Army (b).

Computers: 550 computers/terminals are available on campus for general student use. Students can access the following: campus intranet, computer help desk, free student e-mail accounts, online (class) grades, online (class) registration, online (class) schedules. Campuswide network is available. 100% of college-owned or -operated housing units are wired for high-speed Internet access. Wireless service is available via entire campus.

Library: George A. Spiva Library. *Books:* 262,310 (physical), 362,170 (digital/electronic); *Serial titles:* 6,081 (physical); *Databases:* 221.

STUDENT LIFE

Housing options: on-campus residence required for freshman year; coed, men-only, women-only. Campus housing is university owned. Freshman campus housing is guaranteed.

Activities and organizations: drama/theater group, student-run newspaper, radio and television station, choral group, marching band, national fraternities, national sororities.

Athletics Member NCAA. All Division II. ***Intercollegiate sports:*** baseball M(s), basketball M(s)/W(s), cross-country running M(s)/W(s), football M(s), golf M(s), soccer M(s)/W(s), softball W(s), tennis W(s), track and field M(s)/W(s), volleyball W(s). ***Intramural sports:*** basketball M/W, football M/W, golf M/W, soccer M/W, softball M/W, tennis M/W, volleyball M/W.

Campus security: 24-hour emergency response devices and patrols, late-night transport/escort service, controlled dormitory access, security at campus events, emergency vehicle assistance, safety awareness information to students.

Student services: health clinic, personal/psychological counseling.

FINANCIAL AID

Financial Aid Of all full-time matriculated undergraduates who enrolled in 2019, 3,591 applied for aid, 2,889 were judged to have need, 489 had their need fully met. In 2019, 452 non-need-based awards were made. ***Average percent of need met:*** 43. ***Average financial aid package:*** $9838. ***Average need-based loan:*** $3603. ***Average need-based gift aid:*** $5230. ***Average non-need-based aid:*** $2548. ***Average indebtedness upon graduation:*** $22,514.

APPLYING

Standardized Tests *Required:* SAT or ACT (for admission), SAT and SAT Subject Tests or ACT (for admission). *Recommended:* ACT (for admission).

Options: electronic application, deferred entrance.

Application fee: $30.

Required: high school transcript, minimum 2.3 GPA, class rank of at least 50%, minimum recommended ACT score of at 21. ***Required for some:*** 2 letters of recommendation.

Application deadlines: rolling (freshmen), rolling (transfers).

Notification: continuous until 9/1 (freshmen), continuous until 9/1 (transfers).

CONTACT

Mr. Derek Skaggs, Director of Enrollment Services, Missouri Southern State University, 3950 East Newman Road, Hearnes 106B, Joplin, MO 64801-1595. *Phone:* 417-625-9537. *Toll-free phone:* 866-818-MSSU. *Fax:* 417-659-4429. *E-mail:* admissions@mssu.edu.

Missouri State University

Springfield, Missouri

http://www.missouristate.edu/

- **State-supported** comprehensive, founded 1905
- **Suburban** 225-acre campus
- **Coed** 19,801 undergraduate students, 71% full-time, 59% women, 41% men
- **Moderately difficult** entrance level, 88% of applicants were admitted

UNDERGRAD STUDENTS

14,005 full-time, 5,796 part-time. 10% are from out of state; 4% Black or African American, non-Hispanic/Latino; 4% Hispanic/Latino; 1% Asian, non-Hispanic/Latino; 0.1% Native Hawaiian or other Pacific Islander, non-Hispanic/Latino; 0.5% American Indian or Alaska Native, non-Hispanic/Latino; 4% Two or more races, non-Hispanic/Latino; 0.6% Race/ethnicity unknown; 3% international; 7% transferred in; 24% live on campus.

Freshmen:

Admission: 7,581 applied, 6,667 admitted, 2,679 enrolled. ***Average high school GPA:*** 3.7. ***Test scores:*** SAT evidence-based reading and writing scores over 500: 85%; SAT math scores over 500: 89%; ACT scores over 18: 97%; SAT evidence-based reading and writing scores over 600: 35%; SAT math scores over 600: 35%; ACT scores over 24: 48%; SAT evidence-based reading and writing scores over 700: 5%; SAT math scores over 700: 4%; ACT scores over 30: 9%.

Retention: 78% of full-time freshmen returned.

FACULTY

Total: 1,142, 67% full-time, 61% with terminal degrees.

Student/faculty ratio: 20:1.

ACADEMICS

Calendar: semesters. *Degrees:* certificates, bachelor's, master's, doctoral, post-master's, and postbachelor's certificates.

Special study options: accelerated degree program, advanced placement credit, cooperative education, distance learning, double majors, English as a second language, freshman honors college, honors programs, independent study, internships, off-campus study, part-time degree program, services for LD students, student-designed majors, study abroad, summer session for credit. ***ROTC:*** Army (b).

Computers: Students can access the following: campus intranet, computer help desk, free student e-mail accounts, online (class) grades, online (class) registration, online (class) schedules. Campuswide network is available. 100% of college-owned or -operated housing units are wired for high-speed Internet access. Wireless service is available via classrooms, computer centers, computer labs, learning centers, libraries, student centers.

Library: Meyer Library. Students can reserve study rooms.

STUDENT LIFE

Housing options: on-campus residence required for freshman year; coed, special housing for students with disabilities. Campus housing is university owned. Freshman campus housing is guaranteed.

Activities and organizations: drama/theater group, student-run newspaper, radio and television station, choral group, marching band, Residence Hall Association, Campus Ministries, Fraternity and Sorority Life, Student Government Association, Student Activities Council, national fraternities, national sororities.

Athletics Member NCAA. All Division I except football (Division I-AA). ***Intercollegiate sports:*** baseball M(s), basketball M(s)/W(s), bowling M(c)/W(c), cross-country running W(s), equestrian sports M(c)/W(c), field hockey W(s), golf M(s)/W(s), ice hockey M(c), lacrosse M(c), racquetball M(c)/W(c), soccer M(s)/W(s), softball W(s), swimming and diving M(s)/W(s), track and field W(s), ultimate Frisbee M(c)/W(c), volleyball M(c)/W(s), wrestling M(c). ***Intramural sports:*** basketball M/W, bowling M/W, football M/W, golf M/W, racquetball M/W, soccer M/W, softball M/W, table tennis M/W, tennis M/W, track and field W, ultimate Frisbee M/W, volleyball M/W, weight lifting M/W.

Campus security: 24-hour emergency response devices and patrols, late-night transport/escort service, controlled dormitory access, on-campus police substation.

Student services: health clinic, personal/psychological counseling, legal services.

COSTS & FINANCIAL AID

Costs (2019–20) ***Tuition:*** state resident $6540 full-time, $218 per credit hour part-time; nonresident $14,850 full-time, $495 per credit hour part-time. Full-time tuition and fees vary according to course level, course load, and program. Part-time tuition and fees vary according to course level, course load, and program. ***Required fees:*** $1048 full-time, $182 per credit hour part-time, $524 per term part-time. ***Room and board:*** $9128; room only: $6486. Room and board charges vary according to board plan, housing facility, and location. ***Payment plan:*** deferred payment. ***Waivers:*** children of alumni, senior citizens, and employees or children of employees.

Financial Aid Of all full-time matriculated undergraduates who enrolled in 2019, 10,935 applied for aid, 8,067 were judged to have need, 1,276 had their need fully met. In 2019, 2042 non-need-based awards were made. ***Average percent of need met:*** 68. ***Average financial aid package:*** $11,542. ***Average need-based loan:*** $4150. ***Average need-based gift aid:*** $6152. ***Average non-need-based aid:*** $3283. ***Average indebtedness upon graduation:*** $26,446.

APPLYING

Standardized Tests *Required:* SAT or ACT (for admission).

Options: electronic application, deferred entrance.

Required: high school transcript. ***Required for some:*** essay or personal statement, interview.

CONTACT
Mr. Benjamin Metzger, Associate Director of Admissions, Missouri State University, 901 South National Avenue, Springfield, MO 65897. *Phone:* 417-836-5517. *Toll-free phone:* 800-492-7900. *Fax:* 417-836-5137. *E-mail:* info@missouristate.edu.

Missouri University of Science and Technology

Rolla, Missouri

http://www.mst.edu/

- **State-supported** university, founded 1870, part of University of Missouri System
- **Small-town** 284-acre campus
- **Endowment** $160.2 million
- **Coed** 6,462 undergraduate students, 88% full-time, 24% women, 76% men
- **Very difficult** entrance level, 79% of applicants were admitted

UNDERGRAD STUDENTS
5,692 full-time, 770 part-time. 16% are from out of state; 3% Black or African American, non-Hispanic/Latino; 4% Hispanic/Latino; 4% Asian, non-Hispanic/Latino; 0.3% American Indian or Alaska Native, non-Hispanic/Latino; 3% Two or more races, non-Hispanic/Latino; 1% Race/ethnicity unknown; 3% international; 4% transferred in; 45% live on campus.

Freshmen:
Admission: 5,107 applied, 4,046 admitted, 1,145 enrolled. ***Average high school GPA:*** 4.0. ***Test scores:*** SAT evidence-based reading and writing scores over 500: 98%; SAT math scores over 500: 100%; ACT scores over 18: 100%; SAT evidence-based reading and writing scores over 600: 76%; SAT math scores over 600: 72%; ACT scores over 24: 92%; SAT evidence-based reading and writing scores over 700: 26%; SAT math scores over 700: 40%; ACT scores over 30: 45%.

Retention: 82% of full-time freshmen returned.

FACULTY
Total: 430, 81% full-time, 86% with terminal degrees.

Student/faculty ratio: 19:1.

ACADEMICS
Calendar: semesters. *Degrees:* certificates, bachelor's, master's, doctoral, and postbachelor's certificates.

Special study options: accelerated degree program, adult/continuing education programs, advanced placement credit, cooperative education, distance learning, double majors, English as a second language, freshman honors college, honors programs, independent study, internships, off-campus study, part-time degree program, services for LD students, student-designed majors, study abroad, summer session for credit. ***ROTC:*** Army (b), Air Force (b).

Computers: 980 computers/terminals and 5,720 ports are available on campus for general student use. Students can access the following: campus intranet, computer help desk, free student e-mail accounts, online (class) grades, online (class) registration, online (class) schedules. Campuswide network is available. 100% of college-owned or -operated housing units are wired for high-speed Internet access. Wireless service is available via entire campus.

Library: Curtis Laws Wilson Library. *Books:* 305,834 (physical), 447,868 (digital/electronic); *Serial titles:* 14,178 (physical), 79,586 (digital/electronic); *Databases:* 180. Weekly public service hours: 112; students can reserve study rooms.

STUDENT LIFE
Housing options: on-campus residence required through sophomore year; coed, special housing for students with disabilities. Campus housing is university owned. Freshman campus housing is guaranteed.

Activities and organizations: drama/theater group, student-run newspaper, radio station, choral group, marching band, Academic Organizations, Honor Society, Special Interest Group, Greek Organizations, Recreational and Sports Club, national fraternities, national sororities.

Athletics Member NCAA. All Division II. ***Intercollegiate sports:*** baseball M(s), basketball M(s)/W(s), cross-country running M(s)/W(s), football M(s), soccer M(s)/W(s), softball W(s), swimming and diving M(s), track and field M(s)/W(s), volleyball W(s). ***Intramural sports:*** badminton M/W, basketball M/W, bowling M/W, football M/W, golf M/W, racquetball M/W, soccer M/W, softball M/W, swimming and diving M/W, table tennis M/W, tennis M/W, track and field M/W, ultimate Frisbee M/W, volleyball M/W, water polo M/W, weight lifting M/W.

Campus security: 24-hour emergency response devices and patrols, student patrols, late-night transport/escort service, controlled dormitory access, crime prevention programs.

Student services: health clinic, personal/psychological counseling, women's center, veterans affairs office.

COSTS & FINANCIAL AID
Costs (2019–20) ***Tuition:*** area resident $8973 full-time; state resident $8973 full-time; nonresident $27,921 full-time. Full-time tuition and fees vary according to course load, degree level, program, and student level. Part-time tuition and fees vary according to course load, degree level, program, and student level. ***Required fees:*** $1680 full-time. ***Room and board:*** $10,402; room only: $6855. Room and board charges vary according to board plan, housing facility, and location. ***Payment plan:*** installment. ***Waivers:*** employees or children of employees.

Financial Aid Of all full-time matriculated undergraduates who enrolled in 2019, 4,311 applied for aid, 3,154 were judged to have need, 1,155 had their need fully met. In 2019, 1782 non-need-based awards were made. ***Average percent of need met:*** 77. ***Average financial aid package:*** $14,487. ***Average need-based loan:*** $5608. ***Average need-based gift aid:*** $9070. ***Average non-need-based aid:*** $6666. ***Average indebtedness upon graduation:*** $30,168.

APPLYING
Standardized Tests *Required:* SAT or ACT (for admission). *Recommended:* ACT (for admission).

Options: electronic application, deferred entrance.

Application fee: $50.

Notification: continuous (freshmen), continuous (out-of-state freshmen), continuous (transfers).

CONTACT
Ms. Lynn Stichnote, Admissions Office, Missouri University of Science and Technology, 300 West 13th Street, 106 Parker Hall, Rolla, MO 65409. *Phone:* 573-341-4075. *Toll-free phone:* 800-522-0938. *Fax:* 573-341-4082. *E-mail:* admissions@mst.edu.

Missouri Valley College

Marshall, Missouri

http://www.moval.edu/

- **Independent** comprehensive, founded 1889, affiliated with Presbyterian Church
- **Small-town** 140-acre campus with easy access to Kansas City
- **Coed** 1,740 undergraduate students, 77% full-time, 47% women, 53% men
- **Minimally difficult** entrance level, 54% of applicants were admitted

UNDERGRAD STUDENTS
1,348 full-time, 392 part-time. 50% are from out of state; 18% Black or African American, non-Hispanic/Latino; 10% Hispanic/Latino; 0.9% Asian, non-Hispanic/Latino; 1% Native Hawaiian or other Pacific Islander, non-Hispanic/Latino; 0.7% American Indian or Alaska Native, non-Hispanic/Latino; 4% Two or more races, non-Hispanic/Latino; 2% Race/ethnicity unknown; 18% international; 8% transferred in; 71% live on campus.

Freshmen:
Admission: 2,327 applied, 1,257 admitted, 436 enrolled. ***Average high school GPA:*** 3.0. ***Test scores:*** SAT evidence-based reading and writing scores over 500: 32%; SAT math scores over 500: 42%; ACT scores over 18: 60%; SAT evidence-based reading and writing scores over 600: 8%; SAT math scores over 600: 14%; ACT scores over 24: 12%; SAT evidence-based reading and writing scores over 700: 2%; SAT math scores over 700: 2%.

Retention: 42% of full-time freshmen returned.

FACULTY
Total: 153, 52% full-time, 25% with terminal degrees.

Student/faculty ratio: 13:1.

ACADEMICS
Calendar: semesters plus 2 summer sessions. *Degrees:* associate, bachelor's, and master's.

Special study options: academic remediation for entering students, adult/continuing education programs, advanced placement credit, cooperative education, distance learning, double majors, English as a second language, honors programs, independent study, internships, part-time degree program, services for LD students, student-designed majors, study abroad, summer session for credit. ***ROTC:*** Army (b).

Computers: 300 computers/terminals are available on campus for general student use. Students can access the following: campus intranet, computer help desk, free student e-mail accounts, online (class) grades, online (class) registration, online (class) schedules. Campuswide network is available. 100% of college-owned or -operated housing units are wired for high-speed Internet access. Wireless service is available via entire campus.

Library: Murrell Memorial Library plus 1 other. *Databases:* 37.

STUDENT LIFE
Housing options: men-only, women-only. Campus housing is university owned. Freshman campus housing is guaranteed.

Activities and organizations: drama/theater group, student-run newspaper, radio and television station, choral group, national fraternities, national sororities.

Athletics Member NAIA. ***Intercollegiate sports:*** baseball M(s), basketball M(s)/W(s), cheerleading M(s)/W(s), cross-country running M(s)/W(s), football M(s), golf M(s)/W(s), lacrosse M(s)/W(s), soccer M(s)/W(s), softball W(s), tennis M(s)/W(s), track and field M(s)/W(s), volleyball M(s)/W(s), wrestling M(s)/W(s). ***Intramural sports:*** badminton M/W, baseball M, basketball M/W, bowling M/W, football M/W, soccer M/W, softball M/W, table tennis M/W, tennis M/W, volleyball M/W.

Campus security: 24-hour emergency response devices, student patrols, late-night transport/escort service, evening to 4 am patrol by trained security personnel.

Student services: health clinic, personal/psychological counseling.

COSTS & FINANCIAL AID
Costs (2019–20) ***Comprehensive fee:*** $30,500 includes full-time tuition ($19,700), mandatory fees ($1400), and room and board ($9400). Full-time tuition and fees vary according to program. Part-time tuition: $350 per credit hour. Part-time tuition and fees vary according to program. ***College room only:*** $5000. Room and board charges vary according to board plan, gender, housing facility, location, and student level. ***Payment plans:*** tuition prepayment, installment. ***Waivers:*** children of alumni and employees or children of employees.

Financial Aid Of all full-time matriculated undergraduates who enrolled in 2018, 815 applied for aid, 706 were judged to have need, 58 had their need fully met. In 2018, 283 non-need-based awards were made. ***Average percent of need met:*** 64. ***Average financial aid package:*** $17,190. ***Average need-based loan:*** $3845. ***Average need-based gift aid:*** $7513. ***Average non-need-based aid:*** $14,034. ***Average indebtedness upon graduation:*** $37,801.

APPLYING
Standardized Tests *Required for some:* SAT (for admission), ACT (for admission), SAT or ACT (for admission).

Options: electronic application, deferred entrance.

Required: high school transcript. ***Required for some:*** essay or personal statement, 3 letters of recommendation, interview. ***Recommended:*** minimum 2.0 GPA, interview.

Application deadlines: 9/1 (freshmen), rolling (transfers).

Notification: continuous (freshmen), continuous (transfers).

CONTACT
Ms. Jessica Green, Admissions and Student Visit Coordinator, Missouri Valley College, 500 East College, Marshall, MO 65340-3197. *Phone:* 660-831-4114. *Fax:* 660-831-4233. *E-mail:* admissions@moval.edu.

Missouri Western State University

St. Joseph, Missouri

http://www.missouriwestern.edu/

- **State-supported** comprehensive, founded 1915
- **Suburban** 744-acre campus with easy access to Kansas City
- **Coed**
- **Noncompetitive** entrance level

FACULTY
Student/faculty ratio: 17:1.

ACADEMICS
Calendar: semesters. *Degrees:* certificates, associate, bachelor's, master's, and postbachelor's certificates.
Library: Missouri Western State University Library. *Books:* 166,649 (physical), 215,083 (digital/electronic); *Serial titles:* 1,585 (physical), 57,298 (digital/electronic); *Databases:* 65.

STUDENT LIFE
Housing options: on-campus residence required for freshman year; coed, special housing for students with disabilities. Campus housing is university owned.

Activities and organizations: drama/theater group, student-run newspaper, television station, choral group, marching band, national fraternities, national sororities.

Athletics Member NCAA. All Division II.

Campus security: 24-hour patrols, student patrols, late-night transport/escort service, controlled dormitory access.

Student services: health clinic, personal/psychological counseling, women's center.

FINANCIAL AID
Financial Aid Of all full-time matriculated undergraduates who enrolled in 2018, 285 Federal Work-Study jobs (averaging $1632). 629 state and other part-time jobs (averaging $1722).

APPLYING
Standardized Tests *Required:* SAT or ACT (for admission).

Options: electronic application.

Required: high school transcript.

CONTACT
Mrs. Jamie Sweiger, Assistant Director of Admissions, Missouri Western State University, 4525 Downs Drive, St. Joseph, MO 64507-2294. *Phone:* 816-271-4183. *Toll-free phone:* 800-662-7041. *E-mail:* admission@missouriwestern.edu.

National American University

Independence, Missouri

http://www.national.edu/

CONTACT
National American University, 3620 Arowhead Avenue, Independence, MO 64057. *Toll-free phone:* 866-628-1288.

National American University

Kansas City, Missouri

http://www.national.edu/

CONTACT
Admissions Office, National American University, 7490 Northwest 87th Street, Kansas City, MO 64153. *Phone:* 816-412-5500. *Toll-free phone:* 866-628-1288. *E-mail:* zradmissions@national.edu.

National American University

Lee's Summit, Missouri

http://www.national.edu/

CONTACT
National American University, 401 NW Murray Road, Lee's Summit, MO 64081. *Toll-free phone:* 866-628-1288.

Northwest Missouri State University

Maryville, Missouri

http://www.nwmissouri.edu/

- **State-supported** comprehensive, founded 1905, part of Missouri Coordinating Board for Higher Education
- **Small-town** 370-acre campus with easy access to Kansas City
- **Endowment** $29.8 million
- **Coed** 5,710 undergraduate students, 87% full-time, 58% women, 42% men
- **Moderately difficult** entrance level, 74% of applicants were admitted

UNDERGRAD STUDENTS

4,954 full-time, 756 part-time. Students come from 32 states and territories; 36 other countries; 30% are from out of state; 5% Black or African American, non-Hispanic/Latino; 4% Hispanic/Latino; 0.8% Asian, non-Hispanic/Latino; 0.2% Native Hawaiian or other Pacific Islander, non-Hispanic/Latino; 0.2% American Indian or Alaska Native, non-Hispanic/Latino; 4% Two or more races, non-Hispanic/Latino; 1% Race/ethnicity unknown; 3% international; 6% transferred in; 39% live on campus.

Freshmen:

Admission: 8,770 applied, 6,482 admitted, 1,335 enrolled. ***Average high school GPA:*** 3.4. ***Test scores:*** SAT evidence-based reading and writing scores over 500: 76%; SAT math scores over 500: 78%; ACT scores over 18: 88%; SAT evidence-based reading and writing scores over 600: 34%; SAT math scores over 600: 34%; ACT scores over 24: 33%; SAT evidence-based reading and writing scores over 700: 4%; SAT math scores over 700: 4%; ACT scores over 30: 5%.

Retention: 76% of full-time freshmen returned.

ACADEMICS

Calendar: trimesters. *Degrees:* certificates, bachelor's, master's, post-master's, and postbachelor's certificates.

Computers: 260 computers/terminals and 1,145 ports are available on campus for general student use. Students can access the following: campus intranet, computer help desk, free student e-mail accounts, online (class) grades, online (class) registration, online (class) schedules, online courses with library and databases. Campuswide network is available. 100% of college-owned or -operated housing units are wired for high-speed Internet access. Wireless service is available via classrooms, computer centers, computer labs, dorm rooms, learning centers, libraries, student centers.

Library: Owens Library. *Books:* 96,983 (physical), 243,090 (digital/electronic); *Serial titles:* 5 (physical), 53,342 (digital/electronic); *Databases:* 137. Weekly public service hours: 95; students can reserve study rooms.

STUDENT LIFE

Housing options: on-campus residence required for freshman year; coed, cooperative, special housing for students with disabilities. Campus housing is university owned. Freshman campus housing is guaranteed.

Activities and organizations: drama/theater group, student-run newspaper, radio and television station, choral group, marching band, National Society of Leadership and Success, Sigma Society, Indian Student Association, Sigma Kappa, Sigma Sigma Sigma, national fraternities, national sororities.

Athletics Member NCAA. All Division II. ***Intercollegiate sports:*** baseball M, basketball M(s)/W(s), cheerleading M(s)/W(s), cross-country running M/W, football M(s), golf W, soccer W, softball W, tennis M(s)/W(s), track and field M(s)/W(s), volleyball W(s). ***Intramural sports:*** badminton M/W, basketball M/W, cross-country running M/W, football M, golf M/W, racquetball M/W, riflery M(c)/W(c), sand volleyball M/W, soccer M(c)/W(c), softball W, table tennis M/W, tennis M/W, track and field M/W, ultimate Frisbee M(c)/W(c), volleyball M/W, weight lifting M(c)/W(c), wrestling M(c).

Campus security: 24-hour emergency response devices and patrols, student patrols, late-night transport/escort service, controlled dormitory access, Crisis Manager Mobile App; Safe Ride Shuttle & Taxi.

Student services: health clinic, personal/psychological counseling, women's center, veterans affairs office.

COSTS & FINANCIAL AID

Costs (2019–20) ***Tuition:*** state resident $6195 full-time, $207 per credit hour part-time; nonresident $13,422 full-time, $447 per credit hour part-time. Full-time tuition and fees vary according to course load, location, program, and reciprocity agreements. Part-time tuition and fees vary according to course load and location. ***Required fees:*** $4103 full-time, $137 per credit hour part-time. ***Room and board:*** $10,106; room only: $6356. Room and board charges vary according to board plan and housing facility. ***Payment plans:*** installment, deferred payment. ***Waivers:*** senior citizens and employees or children of employees.

Financial Aid Of all full-time matriculated undergraduates who enrolled in 2018, 4,150 applied for aid, 3,341 were judged to have need, 1,357 had their need fully met. 382 Federal Work-Study jobs (averaging $1277). 1,101 state and other part-time jobs (averaging $1800). In 2018, 474 non-need-based awards were made. ***Average percent of need met:*** 60. ***Average financial aid package:*** $10,112. ***Average need-based loan:*** $3803. ***Average need-based gift aid:*** $6402. ***Average non-need-based aid:*** $3043. ***Average indebtedness upon graduation:*** $35,920.

APPLYING

Standardized Tests *Required:* SAT or ACT (for admission).

Options: electronic application, deferred entrance.

Application fee: $25.

Required: high school transcript, minimum 2.0 GPA, minimum SAT score of 980 or ACT Composite of 21. ***Required for some:*** interview.

Application deadlines: rolling (freshmen), rolling (transfers).

Notification: continuous (freshmen), continuous (transfers).

CONTACT

Mrs. Tammi Grow, Associate Director of Admissions, Northwest Missouri State University, 800 University Drive, Maryville, MO 64468-6001. *Phone:* 660-562-1146. *Toll-free phone:* 800-633-1175. *Fax:* 660-562-1337. *E-mail:* admissions@nwmissouri.edu.

Ozark Christian College

Joplin, Missouri

http://www.occ.edu/

- **Independent Christian** 4-year, founded 1942
- **Small-town** 110-acre campus
- **Coed**
- **Noncompetitive** entrance level

FACULTY

Student/faculty ratio: 15:1.

ACADEMICS

Calendar: semesters. *Degrees:* certificates, associate, and bachelor's.
Library: Seth Wilson Library.

STUDENT LIFE

Housing options: on-campus residence required through senior year; men-only, women-only. Campus housing is university owned. Freshman campus housing is guaranteed.

Activities and organizations: drama/theater group, student-run radio station, choral group, Family Outreach Group, God's Spokesman, Imagine.

Athletics Member NCCAA.

Campus security: 24-hour emergency response devices, controlled dormitory access, 12-hour patrols by trained security personnel.

Student services: health clinic, personal/psychological counseling.

FINANCIAL AID

Financial Aid Of all full-time matriculated undergraduates who enrolled in 2016, 22 Federal Work-Study jobs (averaging $1606).

APPLYING

Standardized Tests *Required:* SAT or ACT (for admission).

Options: electronic application.

Application fee: $30.

Required: essay or personal statement, high school transcript, 2 letters of recommendation. ***Required for some:*** interview.

CONTACT
Mr. Bob Witte, Executive Director of Admissions, Ozark Christian College, 1111 North Main Street, Joplin, MO 64801-4804. *Phone:* 417-624-2518. *Toll-free phone:* 800-299-4622. *Fax:* 417-624-0090. *E-mail:* occadmin@occ.edu.

Park University
Parkville, Missouri
http://www.park.edu/

CONTACT
Mr. Eric Blair, Director of Undergraduate Admissions, Park University, 8700 NW River Park Drive, Campus Box 1, Parkville, MO 64152. *Phone:* 816-584-6858. *Toll-free phone:* 800-745-7275. *Fax:* 816-741-4462. *E-mail:* admissions@mail.park.edu.

Purdue University Global
St. Louis, Missouri
http://www.purdueglobal.edu/

CONTACT
Purdue University Global, 1807 Park 270 Drive, St. Louis, MO 63146.

Ranken Technical College
St. Louis, Missouri
http://www.ranken.edu/

CONTACT
Ranken Technical College, 4431 Finney Avenue, St. Louis, MO 63113. *Phone:* 314-371-0233 Ext. 4811. *Toll-free phone:* 866-4-RANKEN.

Rockhurst University
Kansas City, Missouri
http://www.rockhurst.edu/

CONTACT
Kyle Johnson, Director of Freshman Admissions, Rockhurst University, 1100 Rockhurst Road, Kansas City, MO 64110-2561. *Phone:* 816-501-4100. *Toll-free phone:* 800-842-6776. *Fax:* 816-501-4142. *E-mail:* admission@rockhurst.edu.

Saint Louis Christian College
Florissant, Missouri
http://www.stlchristian.edu/

CONTACT
Bob Farrar, Admissions Director, Saint Louis Christian College, 1360 Grandview Drive, Florissant, MO 63033. *Phone:* 314-837-6777 Ext. 1314. *Toll-free phone:* 800-887-SLCC. *E-mail:* bfarrar@stlchristian.edu.

St. Louis College of Health Careers
Fenton, Missouri
http://www.slchc.com/

CONTACT
St. Louis College of Health Careers, 1297 North Highway Drive, Fenton, MO 63026. *Toll-free phone:* 866-529-2070.

St. Louis College of Pharmacy
St. Louis, Missouri
http://www.stlcop.edu/

CONTACT
Mrs. Connie Horrall, Admissions Processing Coordinator, St. Louis College of Pharmacy, 4588 Parkview Place, St. Louis, MO 63110-1088. *Phone:* 314-446-8328. *Toll-free phone:* 800-278-5267. *Fax:* 314-446-8310. *E-mail:* connie.horrall@stlcop.edu.

Saint Louis University
St. Louis, Missouri
http://www.slu.edu/

- **Independent Roman Catholic (Jesuit)** university, founded 1818
- **Urban** 282-acre campus
- **Coed** 7,217 undergraduate students, 93% full-time, 60% women, 40% men
- **Very difficult** entrance level, 58% of applicants were admitted

UNDERGRAD STUDENTS
6,732 full-time, 485 part-time. 61% are from out of state; 6% Black or African American, non-Hispanic/Latino; 7% Hispanic/Latino; 11% Asian, non-Hispanic/Latino; 0.1% American Indian or Alaska Native, non-Hispanic/Latino; 4% Two or more races, non-Hispanic/Latino; 0.7% Race/ethnicity unknown; 5% international; 4% transferred in; 55% live on campus.

Freshmen:
Admission: 15,573 applied, 9,076 admitted, 1,902 enrolled. ***Average high school GPA:*** 3.9. ***Test scores:*** SAT evidence-based reading and writing scores over 500: 97%; SAT math scores over 500: 96%; ACT scores over 18: 100%; SAT evidence-based reading and writing scores over 600: 72%; SAT math scores over 600: 67%; ACT scores over 24: 84%; SAT evidence-based reading and writing scores over 700: 15%; SAT math scores over 700: 27%; ACT scores over 30: 34%.

Retention: 91% of full-time freshmen returned.

FACULTY
Total: 1,094, 64% full-time, 69% with terminal degrees.

Student/faculty ratio: 9:1.

ACADEMICS
Calendar: semesters. *Degrees:* certificates, bachelor's, master's, doctoral, post-master's, and postbachelor's certificates.

Special study options: academic remediation for entering students, accelerated degree program, adult/continuing education programs, advanced placement credit, cooperative education, distance learning, double majors, English as a second language, honors programs, independent study, internships, part-time degree program, services for LD students, student-designed majors, study abroad, summer session for credit. ***ROTC:*** Army (c), Air Force (b).

Computers: Students can access the following: campus intranet, computer help desk, free student e-mail accounts, online (class) grades, online (class) registration, online (class) schedules. Campuswide network is available. 100% of college-owned or -operated housing units are wired for high-speed Internet access. Wireless service is available via entire campus.

Library: Pius XII Memorial Library plus 2 others. Study areas open 24 hours, 5–7 days a week; students can reserve study rooms.

STUDENT LIFE
Housing options: on-campus residence required through sophomore year; coed, special housing for students with disabilities. Campus housing is university owned. Freshman campus housing is guaranteed.

Activities and organizations: drama/theater group, student-run newspaper, radio and television station, choral group, national fraternities, national sororities.

Athletics Member NCAA. All Division I. ***Intercollegiate sports:*** baseball M(s), basketball M(s)/W(s), cross-country running M(s)/W(s), field hockey W(s), soccer M(s)/W(s), softball W(s), swimming and diving M(s)/W(s), tennis M(s)/W(s), track and field M(s)/W(s), volleyball W(s).

Campus security: 24-hour emergency response devices and patrols, late-night transport/escort service, controlled dormitory access.

Student services: health clinic, personal/psychological counseling, veterans affairs office.

COSTS & FINANCIAL AID
Costs (2019–20) ***One-time required fee:*** $200. ***Comprehensive fee:*** $58,024 includes full-time tuition ($44,700), mandatory fees ($724), and room and board ($12,600). Full-time tuition and fees vary according to course level, course load, degree level, location, and program. Part-time tuition: $1560 per credit. Part-time tuition and fees vary according to course level, course load, degree level, location, and program. ***Required fees:*** $240 part-time. ***Room and board:*** Room and board charges vary

according to board plan, housing facility, and location. ***Payment plans:*** installment, deferred payment. ***Waivers:*** employees or children of employees.

Financial Aid Of all full-time matriculated undergraduates who enrolled in 2018, 4,493 applied for aid, 3,852 were judged to have need, 880 had their need fully met. In 2018, 2153 non-need-based awards were made. ***Average percent of need met:*** 77. ***Average financial aid package:*** $34,131. ***Average need-based loan:*** $4349. ***Average need-based gift aid:*** $26,797. ***Average non-need-based aid:*** $19,213. ***Average indebtedness upon graduation:*** $34,188.

APPLYING

Standardized Tests *Required:* SAT or ACT (for admission).

Options: electronic application, early admission, deferred entrance.

Required: essay or personal statement, high school transcript. ***Recommended:*** 2 letters of recommendation, interview.

Application deadlines: rolling (freshmen), rolling (out-of-state freshmen), rolling (transfers).

Notification: continuous (freshmen), continuous (out-of-state freshmen), continuous (transfers).

CONTACT

Jean M. Cox, Assistant Vice President and Dean of Admissions, Saint Louis University, One N. Grand Boulevard, DuBourg Hall, St. Louis, MO 63103. *Phone:* 314-977-2500. *Toll-free phone:* 800-758-3678. *Fax:* 314-977-7136. *E-mail:* admission@slu.edu.

Saint Luke's College of Health Sciences

Kansas City, Missouri

http://www.saintlukescollege.edu/

CONTACT

Mrs. Jennifer Wright, Student Services Associate, Saint Luke's College of Health Sciences, 624 Westport Road, Kansas City, MO 64111. *Phone:* 816-932-8629. *Fax:* 816-932-9064.

Southeast Missouri State University

Cape Girardeau, Missouri

http://www.semo.edu/

- **State-supported** comprehensive, founded 1873, part of Missouri Coordinating Board for Higher Education
- **Small-town** 400-acre campus
- **Endowment** $79.0 million
- **Coed** 9,524 undergraduate students, 75% full-time, 59% women, 41% men
- **Moderately difficult** entrance level, 84% of applicants were admitted

UNDERGRAD STUDENTS

7,152 full-time, 2,372 part-time. 21% are from out of state; 9% Black or African American, non-Hispanic/Latino; 2% Hispanic/Latino; 1% Asian, non-Hispanic/Latino; 0.1% Native Hawaiian or other Pacific Islander, non-Hispanic/Latino; 0.2% American Indian or Alaska Native, non-Hispanic/Latino; 2% Two or more races, non-Hispanic/Latino; 0.7% Race/ethnicity unknown; 4% international; 6% transferred in; 31% live on campus.

Freshmen:

Admission: 4,638 applied, 3,883 admitted, 1,508 enrolled. ***Average high school GPA:*** 3.5. ***Test scores:*** ACT scores over 18: 92%; ACT scores over 24: 34%; ACT scores over 30: 5%.

Retention: 75% of full-time freshmen returned.

FACULTY

Total: 576, 68% full-time, 59% with terminal degrees.

Student/faculty ratio: 19:1.

ACADEMICS

Calendar: semesters. *Degrees:* certificates, associate, bachelor's, master's, post-master's, and postbachelor's certificates.

Special study options: academic remediation for entering students, accelerated degree program, adult/continuing education programs, advanced placement credit, distance learning, double majors, English as a second language, external degree program, honors programs, independent study, internships, off-campus study, part-time degree program, services for LD students, student-designed majors, study abroad, summer session for credit. ***ROTC:*** Air Force (b).

Computers: 1,550 computers/terminals are available on campus for general student use. Students can access the following: campus intranet, computer help desk, free student e-mail accounts, online (class) grades, online (class) registration, online (class) schedules. Campuswide network is available. 100% of college-owned or -operated housing units are wired for high-speed Internet access. Wireless service is available via classrooms, computer centers, computer labs, dorm rooms, learning centers, libraries, student centers.

Library: Kent Library. *Books:* 380,006 (physical), 263,780 (digital/electronic); *Serial titles:* 4,163 (physical), 58,594 (digital/electronic); *Databases:* 159. Weekly public service hours: 92.

STUDENT LIFE

Housing options: on-campus residence required through sophomore year; coed, special housing for students with disabilities. Campus housing is university owned. Freshman campus housing is guaranteed.

Activities and organizations: drama/theater group, student-run newspaper, radio and television station, choral group, marching band, Student Government, Student Activities Council, Greek Life, Residence Hall Association, International Students Association, national fraternities, national sororities.

Athletics Member NCAA. All Division I. ***Intercollegiate sports:*** baseball M(s), basketball M(s)/W(s), cheerleading M(s)/W(s), cross-country running M(s)/W(s), football M(s), gymnastics W(s), soccer W(s), softball W(s), tennis W(s), track and field M(s)/W(s), volleyball W(s). ***Intramural sports:*** archery M, basketball M/W, bowling M/W, equestrian sports M(c)/W(c), fencing M, field hockey W, football M/W, lacrosse M, riflery M/W, rock climbing M/W, rugby M/W, soccer M/W, softball M/W, table tennis M/W, tennis M/W, ultimate Frisbee M/W, volleyball M/W, weight lifting M/W.

Campus security: 24-hour emergency response devices and patrols, late-night transport/escort service, controlled dormitory access.

Student services: health clinic, personal/psychological counseling, veterans affairs office.

COSTS & FINANCIAL AID

Costs (2020–21) ***Tuition:*** state resident $6606 full-time, $220 per credit hour part-time; nonresident $12,636 full-time, $421 per credit hour part-time. Full-time tuition and fees vary according to course level, course load, location, and program. Part-time tuition and fees vary according to course level, course load, location, and program. ***Required fees:*** $1194 full-time, $40 per credit hour part-time. ***Room and board:*** $9279; room only: $6327. Room and board charges vary according to board plan and housing facility. ***Payment plan:*** installment. ***Waivers:*** senior citizens and employees or children of employees.

Financial Aid Of all full-time matriculated undergraduates who enrolled in 2018, 5,736 applied for aid, 4,538 were judged to have need, 649 had their need fully met. In 2018, 1355 non-need-based awards were made. ***Average percent of need met:*** 59. ***Average financial aid package:*** $9873. ***Average need-based loan:*** $3965. ***Average need-based gift aid:*** $7001. ***Average non-need-based aid:*** $5077. ***Average indebtedness upon graduation:*** $25,380.

APPLYING

Standardized Tests *Recommended:* SAT or ACT (for admission).

Options: electronic application, deferred entrance.

Application fee: $30.

Required: high school transcript, minimum 2.0 GPA.

Application deadlines: 7/1 (freshmen), rolling (out-of-state freshmen), 7/1 (transfers).

Notification: 9/1 (freshmen), continuous until 9/1 (transfers).

CONTACT

Southeast Missouri State University, One University Plaza, Cape Girardeau, MO 63701-4799. *Phone:* 573-651-2539.

Southwest Baptist University

Bolivar, Missouri

http://www.sbuniv.edu/

- **Independent Southern Baptist** comprehensive, founded 1878
- **Small-town** 152-acre campus
- **Endowment** $26.4 million
- **Coed** 2,588 undergraduate students, 66% full-time, 64% women, 36% men
- **Moderately difficult** entrance level, 71% of applicants were admitted

UNDERGRAD STUDENTS
1,701 full-time, 887 part-time. Students come from 34 states and territories; 18 other countries; 19% are from out of state; 5% Black or African American, non-Hispanic/Latino; 3% Hispanic/Latino; 1% Asian, non-Hispanic/Latino; 0.3% Native Hawaiian or other Pacific Islander, non-Hispanic/Latino; 0.7% American Indian or Alaska Native, non-Hispanic/Latino; 2% Two or more races, non-Hispanic/Latino; 7% Race/ethnicity unknown; 1% international; 9% transferred in; 70% live on campus.

Freshmen:
Admission: 1,973 applied, 1,401 admitted, 438 enrolled. ***Average high school GPA:*** 3.5. ***Test scores:*** SAT evidence-based reading and writing scores over 500: 59%; SAT math scores over 500: 51%; ACT scores over 18: 83%; SAT evidence-based reading and writing scores over 600: 26%; SAT math scores over 600: 18%; ACT scores over 24: 35%; SAT evidence-based reading and writing scores over 700: 3%; SAT math scores over 700: 3%; ACT scores over 30: 7%.

Retention: 69% of full-time freshmen returned.

FACULTY
Total: 337, 45% full-time, 30% with terminal degrees.

Student/faculty ratio: 11:1.

ACADEMICS
Calendar: 4-1-4. *Degrees:* associate, bachelor's, master's, doctoral, and post-master's certificates.

Special study options: academic remediation for entering students, advanced placement credit, cooperative education, distance learning, double majors, honors programs, independent study, internships, off-campus study, part-time degree program, services for LD students, student-designed majors, study abroad, summer session for credit. ***ROTC:*** Army (c).

Unusual degree programs: 3-2 engineering with Missouri University of Science and Technology.

Computers: 351 computers/terminals are available on campus for general student use. Students can access the following: campus intranet, computer help desk, free student e-mail accounts, online (class) grades, online (class) registration, online (class) schedules. Campuswide network is available. 100% of college-owned or -operated housing units are wired for high-speed Internet access. Wireless service is available via entire campus.

Library: Harriett K. Hutchens Library. Weekly public service hours: 85; students can reserve study rooms.

STUDENT LIFE
Housing options: on-campus residence required through junior year; men-only, women-only, special housing for students with disabilities. Campus housing is university owned. Freshman campus housing is guaranteed.

Activities and organizations: drama/theater group, student-run newspaper, choral group, Enactus, Student Government Association, Fellowship of Christian Athletes, Student Missouri State Teachers Association, PSY CHI.

Athletics Member NCAA. All Division II except golf (Division I). ***Intercollegiate sports:*** baseball M(s), basketball M(s)/W(s), cheerleading M(s)/W(s), cross-country running M(s)/W(s), football M(s), golf W(s), soccer M(s)/W(s), softball W(s), tennis M(s)/W(s), track and field M(s)/W(s), volleyball W(s). ***Intramural sports:*** basketball M/W, fencing M/W, football M/W, racquetball M/W, rock climbing M/W, sand volleyball M/W, soccer M/W, softball M/W, table tennis M/W, volleyball M/W.

Campus security: 24-hour emergency response devices and patrols, controlled dormitory access.

Student services: health clinic, personal/psychological counseling.

COSTS & FINANCIAL AID
Costs (2020–21) ***Comprehensive fee:*** $33,480 includes full-time tuition ($24,500), mandatory fees ($940), and room and board ($8040). Full-time tuition and fees vary according to course load, degree level, and location. Part-time tuition: $865 per credit hour. Part-time tuition and fees vary according to course load and location. ***Required fees:*** $190 per term part-time. ***College room only:*** $3400. Room and board charges vary according to board plan and housing facility. ***Payment plan:*** installment. ***Waivers:*** employees or children of employees.

Financial Aid Of all full-time matriculated undergraduates who enrolled in 2019, 1,529 applied for aid, 1,371 were judged to have need, 336 had their need fully met. 323 Federal Work-Study jobs (averaging $1820). In 2019, 216 non-need-based awards were made. ***Average percent of need met:*** 68. ***Average financial aid package:*** $22,411. ***Average need-based loan:*** $3837. ***Average need-based gift aid:*** $12,669. ***Average non-need-based aid:*** $3997. ***Average indebtedness upon graduation:*** $25,880.

APPLYING
Standardized Tests *Required:* SAT or ACT (for admission).

Options: electronic application.

Application fee: $30.

Required: high school transcript, minimum 2.5 GPA. ***Required for some:*** 3 letters of recommendation. ***Recommended:*** essay or personal statement, interview.

Application deadlines: rolling (freshmen), rolling (transfers).

Notification: continuous (freshmen), continuous (transfers).

CONTACT
Mrs. Becky Van Stavern, Director of Admissions, Southwest Baptist University, 1600 University Avenue, Bolivar, MO 65613-2597. *Phone:* 417-328-1815. *Toll-free phone:* 800-526-5859. *Fax:* 417-328-1808. *E-mail:* bvanstavern@sbuniv.edu.

Stephens College

Columbia, Missouri

http://www.stephens.edu/

- **Independent** comprehensive, founded 1833
- **Urban** 48-acre campus
- **Endowment** $46.8 million
- **Undergraduate: women only; graduate: coed**
- **Moderately difficult** entrance level

FACULTY
Student/faculty ratio: 8:1.

ACADEMICS
Calendar: semesters. *Degrees:* certificates, associate, bachelor's, master's, post-master's, and postbachelor's certificates.
Library: Hugh Stephens Library.

STUDENT LIFE
Housing options: on-campus residence required through senior year; women-only. Campus housing is university owned and is provided by a third party. Freshman campus housing is guaranteed.

Activities and organizations: drama/theater group, student-run newspaper, television station, choral group, Innovative Fashion Association, Warehouse Theatre, Student Government Association, American Marketing Association (AMA), national sororities.

Athletics Member NAIA.

Campus security: 24-hour emergency response devices and patrols, student patrols, late-night transport/escort service, controlled dormitory access.

Student services: health clinic, personal/psychological counseling.

FINANCIAL AID
Financial Aid Of all full-time matriculated undergraduates who enrolled in 2019, 226 applied for aid, 219 were judged to have need, 48 had their need fully met. 58 Federal Work-Study jobs (averaging $1451). 77 state and other part-time jobs (averaging $1523). In 2019, 98 non-need-based awards were made. ***Average percent of need met:*** 50. ***Average financial aid package:*** $22,396. ***Average need-based loan:*** $3938. ***Average need-based gift aid:*** $2577. ***Average non-need-based aid:*** $18,121.

APPLYING
Standardized Tests *Required:* SAT or ACT (for admission).

Options: electronic application, deferred entrance.

Application fee: $25.

Required: essay or personal statement, high school transcript, minimum 2.0 GPA. ***Required for some:*** 1 letter of recommendation, audition for dance, audition recommended for theater. ***Recommended:*** minimum 2.5 GPA, interview.

CONTACT
Tiffany Goalder, Director of Undergraduate Admissions, Stephens College, 1200 East Broadway, Box 2121, Columbia, MO 65215-0002. *Phone:* 573-876-7239. *Toll-free phone:* 800-876-7207. *Fax:* 573-876-7237. *E-mail:* apply@stephens.edu.

Stevens–The Institute of Business & Arts

St. Louis, Missouri

http://www.siba.edu/

CONTACT
Sara Dorn, Director of Admissions, Stevens–The Institute of Business & Arts, 1521 Washington Avenue, St. Louis, MO 63103. *Phone:* 314-421-0949 Ext. 1118. *Toll-free phone:* 800-871-0949. *Fax:* 314-421-0304. *E-mail:* admission@siba.edu.

Truman State University

Kirksville, Missouri

http://www.truman.edu/

- **State-supported** comprehensive, founded 1867
- **Small-town** 140-acre campus
- **Endowment** $50.6 million
- **Coed** 4,939 undergraduate students, 86% full-time, 59% women, 41% men
- **Moderately difficult** entrance level, 63% of applicants were admitted

UNDERGRAD STUDENTS
4,269 full-time, 670 part-time. Students come from 37 states and territories; 48 other countries; 15% are from out of state; 4% Black or African American, non-Hispanic/Latino; 3% Hispanic/Latino; 2% Asian, non-Hispanic/Latino; 0.3% American Indian or Alaska Native, non-Hispanic/Latino; 4% Two or more races, non-Hispanic/Latino; 1% Race/ethnicity unknown; 8% international; 2% transferred in; 37% live on campus.

Freshmen:
Admission: 4,595 applied, 2,877 admitted, 898 enrolled. ***Average high school GPA:*** 3.8. ***Test scores:*** SAT evidence-based reading and writing scores over 500: 95%; SAT math scores over 500: 93%; ACT scores over 18: 100%; SAT evidence-based reading and writing scores over 600: 70%; SAT math scores over 600: 61%; ACT scores over 24: 81%; SAT evidence-based reading and writing scores over 700: 22%; SAT math scores over 700: 13%; ACT scores over 30: 32%.

Retention: 84% of full-time freshmen returned.

FACULTY
Total: 344, 86% full-time, 79% with terminal degrees.

Student/faculty ratio: 15:1.

ACADEMICS
Calendar: semesters. *Degrees:* bachelor's and master's.

Special study options: accelerated degree program, advanced placement credit, cooperative education, double majors, honors programs, independent study, internships, off-campus study, part-time degree program, services for LD students, student-designed majors, study abroad, summer session for credit. ***ROTC:*** Army (b).

Unusual degree programs: 3-2 engineering with Missouri University of Science and Technology; University of Missouri, Columbia; chiropractic with Logan University.

Computers: 1,056 computers/terminals and 3,690 ports are available on campus for general student use. Students can access the following: campus intranet, computer help desk, free student e-mail accounts, online (class) grades, online (class) registration, online (class) schedules. Campuswide network is available. 100% of college-owned or -operated housing units are wired for high-speed Internet access. Wireless service is available via entire campus.

Library: Pickler Memorial Library. *Books:* 491,954 (physical), 403,847 (digital/electronic); *Serial titles:* 300 (physical), 2,465 (digital/electronic); *Databases:* 107. Weekly public service hours: 105; students can reserve study rooms.

STUDENT LIFE
Housing options: on-campus residence required for freshman year; coed, special housing for students with disabilities. Campus housing is university owned. Freshman campus housing is guaranteed.

Activities and organizations: drama/theater group, student-run newspaper, radio and television station, choral group, marching band, Nursing Student Association, Alpha Sigma Gamma (service sorority), Sigma Kappa (social sorority), Delta Zeta (social sorority), Sigma Sigma Sigma (social sorority), national fraternities, national sororities.

Athletics Member NCAA. All Division II. ***Intercollegiate sports:*** baseball M(s), basketball M(s)/W(s), cheerleading M(c)/W(c), cross-country running M(s)/W(s), equestrian sports M(c)/W(c), football M(s), golf W(s), soccer M(s)/W(s), softball W(s), swimming and diving M(s)/W(s), tennis W(s), track and field M(s)/W(s), ultimate Frisbee M(c)/W(c), volleyball M(c)/W(s). ***Intramural sports:*** badminton M(c)/W(c), basketball M/W, bowling M(c)/W(c), cross-country running M/W, football M/W, golf M(c)/W(c), lacrosse W(c), rugby M(c)/W(c), soccer M/W, softball M/W, swimming and diving M/W, table tennis M/W, tennis M/W, track and field M/W, ultimate Frisbee M/W, volleyball M/W, weight lifting M(c)/W(c).

Campus security: 24-hour emergency response devices and patrols, student patrols, late-night transport/escort service, controlled dormitory access, patrols by commissioned officers, perimeter access system, dual 911 call center for campus/community, emergency text messaging system.

Student services: health clinic, personal/psychological counseling, women's center.

COSTS & FINANCIAL AID
Costs (2019–20) ***One-time required fee:*** $350. ***Tuition:*** state resident $7796 full-time, $325 per credit hour part-time; nonresident $14,990 full-time, $625 per credit hour part-time. ***Required fees:*** $324 full-time, $324 per year part-time. ***Room and board:*** $9012; room only: $5848. Room and board charges vary according to board plan and housing facility. ***Payment plan:*** installment. ***Waivers:*** senior citizens and employees or children of employees.

Financial Aid Of all full-time matriculated undergraduates who enrolled in 2018, 3,421 applied for aid, 2,471 were judged to have need, 868 had their need fully met. 410 Federal Work-Study jobs (averaging $1807). 1,241 state and other part-time jobs (averaging $1211). In 2018, 1837 non-need-based awards were made. ***Average percent of need met:*** 83. ***Average financial aid package:*** $12,674. ***Average need-based loan:*** $4073. ***Average need-based gift aid:*** $8083. ***Average non-need-based aid:*** $6087. ***Average indebtedness upon graduation:*** $25,660.

APPLYING
Options: electronic application, deferred entrance.

Required: essay or personal statement, high school transcript. ***Recommended:*** minimum 3.0 GPA, interview, activities list/resume.

Application deadlines: rolling (freshmen), rolling (transfers).

Notification: continuous (freshmen), continuous (transfers).

CONTACT
Tara Hart, Director of Admission, Truman State University, Ruth Towne Museum and Visitors Center, 100 East Normal Avenue, Kirksville, MO 63501-4221. *Phone:* 660-785-4114. *Toll-free phone:* 800-892-7792. *Fax:* 660-785-7456. *E-mail:* thart@truman.edu.

University of Central Missouri

Warrensburg, Missouri

http://www.ucmo.edu/

- **State-supported** comprehensive, founded 1871
- **Small-town** 1561-acre campus with easy access to Kansas City
- **Coed**
- **Moderately difficult** entrance level

FACULTY
Student/faculty ratio: 16:1.

ACADEMICS
Calendar: semesters. *Degrees:* certificates, bachelor's, master's, post-master's, and postbachelor's certificates.
Library: James C. Kirkpatrick Library plus 1 other. *Books:* 499,982 (physical), 268,431 (digital/electronic); *Serial titles:* 1,579 (physical), 89,008 (digital/electronic); *Databases:* 97. Weekly public service hours: 96; students can reserve study rooms.

STUDENT LIFE
Housing options: on-campus residence required through sophomore year; coed, men-only, women-only, special housing for students with disabilities. Campus housing is university owned. Freshman campus housing is guaranteed.

Activities and organizations: drama/theater group, student-run newspaper, radio and television station, choral group, marching band, Roaring Red (Student Booster Club), Greek Organization, Campus Christian House, BSU (Baptist Student Union), International Student Organization, national fraternities, national sororities.

Athletics Member NCAA. All Division II.

Campus security: 24-hour emergency response devices and patrols, student patrols, late-night transport/escort service, controlled dormitory access, canine patrol.

Student services: health clinic, personal/psychological counseling, women's center, veterans affairs office.

COSTS & FINANCIAL AID
Costs (2019–20) ***Tuition:*** state resident $7128 full-time, $238 per credit hour part-time; nonresident $14,256 full-time, $475 per credit hour part-time. Full-time tuition and fees vary according to course load and location. Part-time tuition and fees vary according to location. ***Required fees:*** $915 full-time, $31 per credit hour part-time. ***Room and board:*** $8962; room only: $5612. Room and board charges vary according to board plan, housing facility, and student level. ***Payment plans:*** installment, deferred payment.

Financial Aid Of all full-time matriculated undergraduates who enrolled in 2016, 4,949 applied for aid, 3,701 were judged to have need, 355 had their need fully met. 87 Federal Work-Study jobs (averaging $1522). 1,690 state and other part-time jobs (averaging $1931). In 2016, 1728 non-need-based awards were made. ***Average percent of need met:*** 62. ***Average financial aid package:*** $8622. ***Average need-based gift aid:*** $2833. ***Average non-need-based aid:*** $3474. ***Average indebtedness upon graduation:*** $27,481.

APPLYING
Standardized Tests *Required:* SAT or ACT (for admission).

Options: electronic application, deferred entrance.

Application fee: $30.

Required: high school transcript, rank in upper two-thirds of high school class.

CONTACT
Mr. J. D. Gragg, Director of Admissions, University of Central Missouri, 1400 Ward Edwards, Warrensburg, MO 64093. *Phone:* 660-543-4290. *Toll-free phone:* 800-729-8266. *Fax:* 660-543-8517. *E-mail:* admit@ucmo.edu.

University of Missouri

Columbia, Missouri

http://www.missouri.edu/

- **State-supported** university, founded 1839, part of University of Missouri System
- **Suburban** 1262-acre campus
- **Endowment** $1.0 billion
- **Coed**
- **Moderately difficult** entrance level

FACULTY
Student/faculty ratio: 18:1.

ACADEMICS
Calendar: semesters. *Degrees:* bachelor's, master's, doctoral, post-master's, and postbachelor's certificates.
Library: Ellis Library plus 9 others. *Books:* 2.1 million (physical), 953,740 (digital/electronic); *Serial titles:* 87,432 (physical), 94,920 (digital/electronic); *Databases:* 60. Students can reserve study rooms.

STUDENT LIFE
Housing options: on-campus residence required for freshman year; coed, men-only, women-only, special housing for students with disabilities. Campus housing is university owned. Freshman campus housing is guaranteed.

Activities and organizations: drama/theater group, student-run newspaper, radio and television station, choral group, marching band, Alpha Kappa Psi Professional Business Fraternity (Academic), Pre-Medical Society (Academic), Alpha Phi Omega (Service), Mizzou Global Medical Training (Service), UM Investment Group (Academic), national fraternities, national sororities.

Athletics Member NCAA. All Division I except football (Division I-A).

Campus security: 24-hour emergency response devices and patrols, late-night transport/escort service, controlled dormitory access.

Student services: health clinic, personal/psychological counseling, women's center, legal services, veterans affairs office.

COSTS & FINANCIAL AID
Costs (2019–20) ***Tuition:*** state resident $9120 full-time, $304 per credit hour part-time; nonresident $26,991 full-time, $900 per credit hour part-time. Full-time tuition and fees vary according to course load, degree level, and program. Part-time tuition and fees vary according to course load, degree level, and program. ***Required fees:*** $1357 full-time, $33 per credit hour part-time. ***Room and board:*** $10,310; room only: $6550. Room and board charges vary according to board plan and housing facility.

Financial Aid Of all full-time matriculated undergraduates who enrolled in 2017, 14,461 applied for aid, 10,634 were judged to have need, 1,448 had their need fully met. In 2017, 4050 non-need-based awards were made. ***Average percent of need met:*** 60. ***Average financial aid package:*** $12,070. ***Average need-based loan:*** $5091. ***Average need-based gift aid:*** $10,146. ***Average non-need-based aid:*** $6338. ***Average indebtedness upon graduation:*** $27,364.

APPLYING
Standardized Tests *Required:* SAT or ACT (for admission). *Recommended:* SAT (for admission), ACT (for admission).

Options: electronic application, deferred entrance.

Application fee: $55.

Required: high school transcript, specific high school curriculum.

CONTACT
Mr. Charles May, Director of Admissions, University of Missouri, 230 Jesse Hall, Columbia, MO 65211. *Phone:* 573-882-7786. *Toll-free phone:* 800-225-6075. *Fax:* 573-882-7887. *E-mail:* mu4u@missouri.edu.

University of Missouri–Kansas City

Kansas City, Missouri

http://www.umkc.edu/

- **State-supported** university, founded 1929, part of University of Missouri System
- **Urban** 191-acre campus with easy access to Kansas City
- **Endowment** $305.8 million
- **Coed**
- **Moderately difficult** entrance level

FACULTY
Student/faculty ratio: 15:1.

ACADEMICS
Calendar: semesters. *Degrees:* bachelor's, master's, doctoral, and post-master's certificates.
Library: Miller-Nichols Library plus 3 others. Students can reserve study rooms.

STUDENT LIFE
Housing options: coed, special housing for students with disabilities. Campus housing is university owned.

Activities and organizations: drama/theater group, student-run newspaper, radio station, choral group, Union Programming Board,

International Student Council, Alpha Phi Omega, Omicron Delta Kappa, Greek Organizations, national fraternities, national sororities.

Athletics Member NCAA. All Division I.

Campus security: 24-hour emergency response devices and patrols, late-night transport/escort service, controlled dormitory access.

Student services: health clinic, personal/psychological counseling, women's center, legal services.

FINANCIAL AID

Financial Aid Of all full-time matriculated undergraduates who enrolled in 2017, 5,144 applied for aid, 4,288 were judged to have need, 394 had their need fully met. In 2017, 1044 non-need-based awards were made. ***Average percent of need met:*** 56. ***Average financial aid package:*** $10,778. ***Average need-based loan:*** $7886. ***Average need-based gift aid:*** $7948. ***Average non-need-based aid:*** $5868. ***Average indebtedness upon graduation:*** $25,438.

APPLYING

Standardized Tests *Required:* SAT or ACT (for admission).

Options: electronic application, deferred entrance.

Application fee: $45.

Required: high school transcript. ***Required for some:*** essay or personal statement, interview.

CONTACT

Ms. Tamera Byland, Director of Admissions, University of Missouri–Kansas City, Office of Admissions, 5100 Rockhill Road, Kansas City, MO 64110-2499. *Phone:* 816-235-1111. *Toll-free phone:* 800-775-8652. *Fax:* 816-235-5544. *E-mail:* admit@umkc.edu.

University of Missouri–St. Louis

St. Louis, Missouri

http://www.umsl.edu/

- **State-supported** university, founded 1963, part of University of Missouri System
- **Suburban** 344-acre campus with easy access to St. Louis
- **Endowment** $89.9 million
- **Coed** 13,045 undergraduate students, 39% full-time, 57% women, 43% men
- **Moderately difficult** entrance level, 73% of applicants were admitted

UNDERGRAD STUDENTS

5,098 full-time, 7,947 part-time. Students come from 39 states and territories; 45 other countries; 11% are from out of state; 15% Black or African American, non-Hispanic/Latino; 3% Hispanic/Latino; 5% Asian, non-Hispanic/Latino; 0.1% Native Hawaiian or other Pacific Islander, non-Hispanic/Latino; 0.3% American Indian or Alaska Native, non-Hispanic/Latino; 4% Two or more races, non-Hispanic/Latino; 9% Race/ethnicity unknown; 3% international; 9% transferred in; 11% live on campus.

Freshmen:

Admission: 2,452 applied, 1,790 admitted, 447 enrolled. ***Average high school GPA:*** 3.5. ***Test scores:*** SAT evidence-based reading and writing scores over 500: 81%; SAT math scores over 500: 86%; ACT scores over 18: 97%; SAT evidence-based reading and writing scores over 600: 32%; SAT math scores over 600: 38%; ACT scores over 24: 61%; SAT evidence-based reading and writing scores over 700: 4%; SAT math scores over 700: 5%; ACT scores over 30: 14%.

Retention: 77% of full-time freshmen returned.

FACULTY

Total: 743, 52% full-time, 59% with terminal degrees.

Student/faculty ratio: 19:1.

ACADEMICS

Calendar: semesters. *Degrees:* certificates, bachelor's, master's, doctoral, post-master's, and postbachelor's certificates.

Special study options: accelerated degree program, adult/continuing education programs, advanced placement credit, cooperative education, distance learning, double majors, English as a second language, external degree program, freshman honors college, honors programs, independent study, internships, off-campus study, part-time degree program, services for LD students, student-designed majors, study abroad, summer session for credit. ***ROTC:*** Army (c), Air Force (c).

Unusual degree programs: 3-2 engineering with Washington University in St. Louis; economics, history, philosophy, political science, sociology.

Computers: 1,752 computers/terminals and 1,752 ports are available on campus for general student use. Students can access the following: campus intranet, computer help desk, free student e-mail accounts, online (class) grades, online (class) registration, online (class) schedules. Campuswide network is available. 100% of college-owned or -operated housing units are wired for high-speed Internet access. Wireless service is available via classrooms, computer centers, computer labs, dorm rooms, learning centers, libraries, student centers.

Library: Thomas Jefferson Library plus 1 other. *Books:* 1.3 million (physical), 211,129 (digital/electronic); *Serial titles:* 20,879 (physical), 190,950 (digital/electronic); *Databases:* 276. Weekly public service hours: 82; students can reserve study rooms.

STUDENT LIFE

Housing options: coed, special housing for students with disabilities. Campus housing is university owned.

Activities and organizations: drama/theater group, student-run newspaper, radio station, choral group, Student Government Association, Associated Black Collegians, Pierre laclede Honors College Student Association, Residence Hall Association, UMSL Radio Station, national fraternities, national sororities.

Athletics Member NCAA. All Division II. ***Intercollegiate sports:*** baseball M(s), basketball M(s)/W(s), cheerleading W, golf M(s)/W(s), ice hockey M(c), soccer M(s)/W(s), softball W(s), swimming and diving M(s)/W(s), tennis M(s)/W(s), volleyball W(s). ***Intramural sports:*** badminton M/W, basketball M/W, football M/W, rock climbing M/W, sand volleyball M/W, soccer M/W, softball M/W, ultimate Frisbee M/W, volleyball M/W, weight lifting M/W.

Campus security: 24-hour emergency response devices and patrols, late-night transport/escort service, controlled dormitory access, criminal investigations.

Student services: health clinic, personal/psychological counseling, women's center, veterans affairs office.

COSTS & FINANCIAL AID

Costs (2019–20) ***Tuition:*** state resident $11,079 full-time; nonresident $29,295 full-time. Full-time tuition and fees vary according to course level, course load, location, program, and reciprocity agreements. Part-time tuition and fees vary according to course level, course load, location, program, and reciprocity agreements. ***Room and board:*** $9550; room only: $5450. Room and board charges vary according to board plan and housing facility. ***Payment plan:*** installment. ***Waivers:*** senior citizens and employees or children of employees.

Financial Aid Of all full-time matriculated undergraduates who enrolled in 2019, 3,925 applied for aid, 3,397 were judged to have need, 350 had their need fully met. 199 Federal Work-Study jobs (averaging $4329). In 2019, 278 non-need-based awards were made. ***Average percent of need met:*** 61. ***Average financial aid package:*** $11,676. ***Average need-based loan:*** $4386. ***Average need-based gift aid:*** $8507. ***Average non-need-based aid:*** $5464. ***Average indebtedness upon graduation:*** $25,110.

APPLYING

Standardized Tests *Required:* SAT or ACT (for admission).

Options: electronic application.

Application fee: $35.

Required: high school transcript, minimum 2.0 GPA, CBHE core requirements. ***Required for some:*** essay or personal statement, 2 letters of recommendation, interview.

Application deadlines: rolling (freshmen), rolling (transfers).

Notification: continuous (freshmen), continuous (transfers).

CONTACT

Ms. Dixie L. Williams, Director of Admissions, University of Missouri–St. Louis, 351 Millennium Student Center, One University Boulevard, St. Louis, MO 63121-4400. *Phone:* 314-516-6941. *Toll-free phone:* 888-GO2-UMSL (in-state); 888-GO2-USML (out-of-state). *Fax:* 314-516-5310. *E-mail:* dixiewilliams@umsl.edu.

Washington University in St. Louis

St. Louis, Missouri

http://www.wustl.edu/

- **Independent** university, founded 1853
- **Urban** 169-acre campus with easy access to St. Louis
- **Endowment** $8.1 billion
- **Coed** 7,822 undergraduate students, 91% full-time, 54% women, 46% men
- **Most difficult** entrance level, 14% of applicants were admitted

UNDERGRAD STUDENTS

7,139 full-time, 683 part-time. Students come from 52 states and territories; 47 other countries; 89% are from out of state; 9% Black or African American, non-Hispanic/Latino; 10% Hispanic/Latino; 16% Asian, non-Hispanic/Latino; 0.1% Native Hawaiian or other Pacific Islander, non-Hispanic/Latino; 0.1% American Indian or Alaska Native, non-Hispanic/Latino; 5% Two or more races, non-Hispanic/Latino; 2% Race/ethnicity unknown; 8% international; 1% transferred in; 72% live on campus.

Freshmen:

Admission: 25,426 applied, 3,522 admitted, 1,732 enrolled. ***Average high school GPA:*** 4.2. ***Test scores:*** SAT evidence-based reading and writing scores over 500: 100%; SAT math scores over 500: 100%; ACT scores over 18: 100%; SAT evidence-based reading and writing scores over 600: 100%; SAT math scores over 600: 100%; ACT scores over 24: 100%; SAT evidence-based reading and writing scores over 700: 86%; SAT math scores over 700: 96%; ACT scores over 30: 96%.

Retention: 97% of full-time freshmen returned.

FACULTY

Total: 1,510, 67% full-time.

Student/faculty ratio: 7:1.

ACADEMICS

Calendar: semesters. *Degrees:* certificates, bachelor's, master's, doctoral, post-master's, and postbachelor's certificates.

Special study options: accelerated degree program, adult/continuing education programs, advanced placement credit, cooperative education, double majors, English as a second language, independent study, internships, off-campus study, part-time degree program, services for LD students, student-designed majors, study abroad, summer session for credit. ***ROTC:*** Army (b), Air Force (c).

Unusual degree programs: 3-2 business administration; engineering; social work; art, occupational therapy, physical therapy.

Computers: 2,500 computers/terminals and 3,500 ports are available on campus for general student use. Students can access the following: campus intranet, computer help desk, free student e-mail accounts, online (class) grades, online (class) registration, online (class) schedules. Campuswide network is available. 95% of college-owned or -operated housing units are wired for high-speed Internet access. Wireless service is available via classrooms, computer centers, computer labs, dorm rooms, learning centers, libraries, student centers.

Library: John M. Olin Library plus 12 others. *Books:* 3.3 million (physical), 2.1 million (digital/electronic); *Serial titles:* 936 (physical), 181,890 (digital/electronic); *Databases:* 965. Weekly public service hours: 168; study areas open 24 hours, 5–7 days a week; students can reserve study rooms.

STUDENT LIFE

Housing options: on-campus residence required for freshman year; coed, men-only, women-only, cooperative, special housing for students with disabilities. Campus housing is university owned. Freshman campus housing is guaranteed.

Activities and organizations: drama/theater group, student-run newspaper, radio and television station, choral group, Campus Kitchen, KWUR - Campus Radio Station, Culinary Arts Society, Association of Latin American Students, Catholic Student Union, national fraternities, national sororities.

Athletics Member NCAA. All Division III except golf (Division II). ***Intercollegiate sports:*** archery M(c)/W(c), badminton M(c)/W(c), baseball M, basketball M/W, cross-country running M/W, equestrian sports M(c)/W(c), fencing M(c)/W(c), field hockey W(c), football M, golf M(c)/W, gymnastics M(c)/W(c), ice hockey M(c), lacrosse M(c)/W(c), rock climbing M(c)/W(c), rowing M(c)/W(c), rugby M(c)/W(c), sailing M(c)/W(c), soccer M/W, softball W, squash M(c)/W(c), swimming and diving M/W, table tennis M(c)/W(c), tennis M/W, track and field M/W, triathlon M(c)/W(c), ultimate Frisbee M(c)/W(c), volleyball M(c)/W, water polo M(c)/W(c), weight lifting M(c)/W(c), wrestling M(c). ***Intramural sports:*** archery M/W, badminton M/W, baseball M(c), basketball M(c)/W(c), bowling M/W, cross-country running M(c)/W(c), football M/W, golf M/W(c), racquetball M/W, sand volleyball M/W, soccer M(c)/W(c), softball M/W(c), squash M/W, swimming and diving M(c)/W(c), table tennis M/W, tennis M(c)/W(c), track and field M/W, ultimate Frisbee M/W, volleyball M/W(c), water polo M/W, weight lifting M/W.

Campus security: 24-hour emergency response devices and patrols, student patrols, late-night transport/escort service, controlled dormitory access, Noonlight safety app for reporting emergencies.

Student services: health clinic, personal/psychological counseling, veterans affairs office.

COSTS & FINANCIAL AID

Costs (2020–21) ***Comprehensive fee:*** $74,788 includes full-time tuition ($56,300), mandatory fees ($1086), and room and board ($17,402). Part-time tuition: $2316 per credit hour. ***College room only:*** $12,000. Room and board charges vary according to board plan and housing facility. ***Payment plans:*** tuition prepayment, installment. ***Waivers:*** employees or children of employees.

Financial Aid Of all full-time matriculated undergraduates who enrolled in 2019, 3,299 applied for aid, 2,993 were judged to have need, 2,973 had their need fully met. 1,412 Federal Work-Study jobs (averaging $2269). In 2019, 561 non-need-based awards were made. ***Average percent of need met:*** 100. ***Average financial aid package:*** $53,500. ***Average need-based loan:*** $4277. ***Average need-based gift aid:*** $50,725. ***Average non-need-based aid:*** $15,068. ***Average indebtedness upon graduation:*** $24,247. ***Financial aid deadline:*** 2/1.

APPLYING

Standardized Tests *Required for some:* SAT or ACT (for admission).

Options: electronic application, early admission, early decision, deferred entrance.

Application fee: $75.

Required: essay or personal statement, high school transcript, 2 letters of recommendation. ***Required for some:*** Portfolio for the College of Art and the College of Architecture. ***Recommended:*** minimum 3.5 GPA.

Application deadlines: 1/2 (freshmen), 3/1 (transfers).

Early decision deadline: 11/1 (for plan 1), 1/2 (for plan 2).

Notification: 4/1 (freshmen), 5/1 (transfers), 12/15 (early decision plan 1), 2/15 (early decision plan 2).

CONTACT

Ms. Emily L. Almas, Assistant Vice Provost & Director of Admissions, Washington University in St. Louis, Campus Box 1089, One Brookings Drive, St. Louis, MO 63130-4899. *Phone:* 314-935-6000. *Toll-free phone:* 800-638-0700. *Fax:* 314-696-0562. *E-mail:* admissions@wustl.edu.

Webster University

St. Louis, Missouri

http://www.webster.edu/

CONTACT

Webster University, 470 East Lockwood Avenue, St. Louis, MO 63119-3194. *Phone:* 314-246-7910. *Toll-free phone:* 800-753-6765.

Westminster College

Fulton, Missouri

http://www.westminster-mo.edu/

- **Independent** 4-year, founded 1851, affiliated with Presbyterian Church
- **Small-town** 80-acre campus
- **Endowment** $56.6 million
- **Coed**
- **Moderately difficult** entrance level

FACULTY

Student/faculty ratio: 11:1.

ACADEMICS
Calendar: semesters. *Degree:* bachelor's.

Library: Reeves Memorial Library plus 1 other. *Books:* 104,327 (physical), 156,300 (digital/electronic); *Databases:* 58. Students can reserve study rooms.

STUDENT LIFE
Housing options: on-campus residence required through junior year; coed, men-only, women-only. Campus housing is university owned. Freshman campus housing is guaranteed.

Activities and organizations: drama/theater group, student-run newspaper, choral group, Student Government Association, Environmentally Concerned Students, International Student Club, Habitat for Humanity, Little Brother/Little Sister, national fraternities, national sororities.

Athletics Member NCAA. All Division III.

Campus security: 24-hour emergency response devices and patrols, late-night transport/escort service, controlled dormitory access, well-lit campus.

Student services: health clinic, personal/psychological counseling, women's center.

FINANCIAL AID
Financial Aid Of all full-time matriculated undergraduates who enrolled in 2018, 592 applied for aid, 488 were judged to have need, 324 had their need fully met. In 2018, 199 non-need-based awards were made. ***Average percent of need met:*** 92. ***Average financial aid package:*** $25,117. ***Average need-based loan:*** $4122. ***Average need-based gift aid:*** $20,138. ***Average non-need-based aid:*** $18,586. ***Average indebtedness upon graduation:*** $29,691.

APPLYING
Standardized Tests *Required:* SAT or ACT (for admission).

Options: electronic application, early admission, deferred entrance.

Required: high school transcript, 1 letter of recommendation. ***Required for some:*** interview. ***Recommended:*** essay or personal statement, minimum 2.5 GPA.

CONTACT
Robert Andrews, Vice President and Dean of Enrollment Management, Westminster College, 501 Westminster Avenue, Fulton, MO 65251-1299. *Phone:* 573-592-5251. *Toll-free phone:* 800-475-3361. *Fax:* 573-592-5255. *E-mail:* admissions@westminster-mo.edu.

William Jewell College
Liberty, Missouri
http://www.jewell.edu/

- **Independent** comprehensive, founded 1849
- **Suburban** 200-acre campus with easy access to Kansas City
- **Endowment** $63.6 million
- **Coed** 734 undergraduate students, 99% full-time, 54% women, 46% men
- **Moderately difficult** entrance level, 46% of applicants were admitted

UNDERGRAD STUDENTS
724 full-time, 10 part-time. Students come from 31 states and territories; 10 other countries; 37% are from out of state; 5% Black or African American, non-Hispanic/Latino; 7% Hispanic/Latino; 1% Asian, non-Hispanic/Latino; 0.4% Native Hawaiian or other Pacific Islander, non-Hispanic/Latino; 0.3% American Indian or Alaska Native, non-Hispanic/Latino; 4% Two or more races, non-Hispanic/Latino; 2% Race/ethnicity unknown; 2% international; 7% transferred in; 85% live on campus.

Freshmen:

Admission: 1,167 applied, 538 admitted, 168 enrolled. ***Average high school GPA:*** 3.6. ***Test scores:*** SAT evidence-based reading and writing scores over 500: 94%; SAT math scores over 500: 94%; ACT scores over 18: 99%; SAT evidence-based reading and writing scores over 600: 45%; SAT math scores over 600: 47%; ACT scores over 24: 60%; SAT evidence-based reading and writing scores over 700: 9%; SAT math scores over 700: 18%; ACT scores over 30: 14%.

Retention: 80% of full-time freshmen returned.

FACULTY
Total: 94, 73% full-time, 71% with terminal degrees.

Student/faculty ratio: 10:1.

ACADEMICS
Calendar: semesters. *Degrees:* bachelor's, master's, and postbachelor's certificates (also offers evening program with significant enrollment not reflected in profile).

Special study options: accelerated degree program, advanced placement credit, cooperative education, distance learning, double majors, English as a second language, honors programs, independent study, internships, off-campus study, services for LD students, student-designed majors, study abroad, summer session for credit. ***ROTC:*** Army (c).

Unusual degree programs: 3-2 engineering with Washington University in St. Louis, University of Kansas, Columbia University, Missouri University of Science and Technology; forestry with Duke University; occupational therapy with Washington University in St. Louis.

Computers: 25 computers/terminals and 900 ports are available on campus for general student use. Students can access the following: campus intranet, computer help desk, free student e-mail accounts, online (class) grades, online (class) registration, online (class) schedules, all students provided with an iPad and support service. Campuswide network is available. 100% of college-owned or -operated housing units are wired for high-speed Internet access. Wireless service is available via entire campus.

Library: Charles F. Curry Library. *Books:* 134,593 (physical), 581,485 (digital/electronic); *Serial titles:* 14 (digital/electronic); *Databases:* 56. Weekly public service hours: 90; study areas open 24 hours, 5–7 days a week; students can reserve study rooms.

STUDENT LIFE
Housing options: on-campus residence required through senior year; coed, men-only, women-only, special housing for students with disabilities. Campus housing is university owned. Freshman campus housing is guaranteed.

Activities and organizations: drama/theater group, student-run newspaper, choral group, marching band, College Union Activities, Student Athlete Advisory Committee, Student Senate, Student Nursing Association, Intramurals, national fraternities, national sororities.

Athletics Member NCAA. All Division II. ***Intercollegiate sports:*** baseball M(s), basketball M(s)/W(s), cheerleading M(s)/W(s), cross-country running M(s)/W(s), football M(s), golf M(s)/W(s), soccer M(s)/W(s), softball W(s), swimming and diving M(s)/W(s), tennis M(s)/W(s), track and field M(s)/W(s), volleyball W(s), weight lifting M(s)/W(s). ***Intramural sports:*** basketball M/W, racquetball M/W, sand volleyball M/W, soccer M/W, softball M/W, tennis M/W, ultimate Frisbee M/W, volleyball M/W.

Campus security: 24-hour emergency response devices and patrols, late-night transport/escort service, controlled dormitory access.

Student services: health clinic, personal/psychological counseling.

COSTS & FINANCIAL AID
Costs (2020–21) ***Comprehensive fee:*** $44,670 includes full-time tuition ($33,500), mandatory fees ($950), and room and board ($10,220). Full-time tuition and fees vary according to program. Part-time tuition: $980 per credit hour. ***Room and board:*** Room and board charges vary according to board plan. ***Payment plan:*** installment. ***Waivers:*** employees or children of employees.

Financial Aid Of all full-time matriculated undergraduates who enrolled in 2018, 597 applied for aid, 503 were judged to have need, 153 had their need fully met. In 2018, 104 non-need-based awards were made. ***Average percent of need met:*** 85. ***Average financial aid package:*** $31,003. ***Average need-based loan:*** $4447. ***Average need-based gift aid:*** $25,967. ***Average non-need-based aid:*** $20,506. ***Average indebtedness upon graduation:*** $32,917.

APPLYING
Standardized Tests *Recommended:* SAT or ACT (for admission).

Options: electronic application, deferred entrance.

Required: essay or personal statement, high school transcript. ***Required for some:*** interview.

Application deadlines: rolling (freshmen), rolling (transfers).

Notification: 9/1 (freshmen), continuous (transfers).

CONTACT
Mr. Brian Haines, Director of Admission Services, William Jewell College, 500 College Hill, Liberty, MO 64068. *Phone:* 816-415-7871. *Toll-free phone:* 888-2JEWELL. *Fax:* 816-415-5040. *E-mail:* hainesb@william.jewell.edu.

William Woods University

Fulton, Missouri

http://www.williamwoods.edu/

CONTACT
Mrs. Ashley Sundin, Admissions Office Coordinator, William Woods University, One University Avenue, Fulton, MO 65251. *Phone:* 573-592-4400. *Toll-free phone:* 800-995-3159 Ext. 4221. *Fax:* 573-592-1146. *E-mail:* ashley.sundin@williamwoods.edu.

MONTANA

Carroll College

Helena, Montana

http://www.carroll.edu/

- **Independent Roman Catholic** 4-year, founded 1909
- **Small-town** 61-acre campus
- **Endowment** $36.0 million
- **Coed**
- **Moderately difficult** entrance level

FACULTY
Student/faculty ratio: 12:1.

ACADEMICS
Calendar: semesters. *Degrees:* certificates, associate, and bachelor's.
Library: Corette Library plus 1 other. *Books:* 76,993 (physical), 230,000 (digital/electronic); *Databases:* 79. Study areas open 24 hours, 5–7 days a week; students can reserve study rooms.

STUDENT LIFE
Housing options: on-campus residence required through sophomore year; coed, special housing for students with disabilities. Campus housing is university owned. Freshman campus housing is guaranteed.

Activities and organizations: drama/theater group, student-run newspaper, radio station, choral group, Student Government, Carroll Outreach Team, Carroll Adventure and Mountaineering Program, Up 'Til Dawn, Engineers Without Borders.

Athletics Member NAIA.

Campus security: 24-hour emergency response devices, late-night transport/escort service, controlled dormitory access.

Student services: health clinic, personal/psychological counseling.

FINANCIAL AID
Financial Aid Of all full-time matriculated undergraduates who enrolled in 2019, 883 applied for aid, 721 were judged to have need, 203 had their need fully met. In 2019, 389 non-need-based awards were made. ***Average percent of need met:*** 80. ***Average financial aid package:*** $29,418. ***Average need-based loan:*** $4090. ***Average need-based gift aid:*** $23,494. ***Average non-need-based aid:*** $17,783. ***Average indebtedness upon graduation:*** $28,667.

APPLYING
Standardized Tests *Required:* SAT or ACT (for admission). *Required for some:* SAT Subject Tests (for admission).

Options: electronic application, early action, deferred entrance.

Application fee: $35.

Required: essay or personal statement, high school transcript. ***Required for some:*** interview. ***Recommended:*** interview.

CONTACT
Director of Admission, Carroll College, 1601 North Benton Avenue, Helena, MT 59625-0002. *Phone:* 406-447-4384. *Toll-free phone:* 800-992-3648. *E-mail:* admission@carroll.edu.

Montana Bible College

Bozeman, Montana

http://www.montanabiblecollege.edu/

CONTACT
Montana Bible College, 3625 South 19th Avenue, Bozeman, MT 59718. *Toll-free phone:* 888-462-2463.

Montana State University

Bozeman, Montana

http://www.montana.edu/

- **State-supported** university, founded 1893, part of Montana University System
- **Small-town** 1850-acre campus
- **Endowment** $126.5 million
- **Coed** 14,817 undergraduate students, 83% full-time, 46% women, 54% men
- **Moderately difficult** entrance level, 82% of applicants were admitted

UNDERGRAD STUDENTS
12,359 full-time, 2,458 part time. 39% are from out of state; 0.4% Black or African American, non-Hispanic/Latino; 5% Hispanic/Latino; 1% Asian, non-Hispanic/Latino; 0.1% Native Hawaiian or other Pacific Islander, non-Hispanic/Latino; 1% American Indian or Alaska Native, non-Hispanic/Latino; 5% Two or more races, non-Hispanic/Latino; 1% Race/ethnicity unknown; 2% international; 5% transferred in; 25% live on campus.

Freshmen:
Admission: 19,142 applied, 15,684 admitted, 3,366 enrolled. ***Average high school GPA:*** 3.5. ***Test scores:*** SAT evidence-based reading and writing scores over 500: 92%; SAT math scores over 500: 91%; ACT scores over 18: 92%; SAT evidence-based reading and writing scores over 600: 57%; SAT math scores over 600: 51%; ACT scores over 24: 53%; SAT evidence-based reading and writing scores over 700: 11%; SAT math scores over 700: 13%; ACT scores over 30: 14%.

Retention: 77% of full-time freshmen returned.

FACULTY
Total: 1,146, 55% full-time, 50% with terminal degrees.

Student/faculty ratio: 18:1.

ACADEMICS
Calendar: semesters. *Degrees:* certificates, associate, bachelor's, master's, doctoral, post-master's, and postbachelor's certificates.

Special study options: academic remediation for entering students, adult/continuing education programs, advanced placement credit, cooperative education, distance learning, double majors, English as a second language, freshman honors college, honors programs, independent study, internships, off-campus study, part-time degree program, services for LD students, student-designed majors, study abroad, summer session for credit. ***ROTC:*** Army (b), Air Force (b).

Computers: Students can access the following: computer help desk, free student e-mail accounts, online (class) grades, online (class) registration, online (class) schedules. Campuswide network is available. 100% of college-owned or -operated housing units are wired for high-speed Internet access. Wireless service is available via entire campus.
Library: Renne Library plus 2 others. Students can reserve study rooms.

STUDENT LIFE
Housing options: on-campus residence required for freshman year; coed, men-only, women-only, cooperative, special housing for students with disabilities. Campus housing is university owned. Freshman campus housing is guaranteed.

Activities and organizations: drama/theater group, student-run newspaper, radio and television station, choral group, marching band, Spurs, Inter-Varsity Christian Fellowship, Campus Crusade for Christ, Fangs, Mortar Board, national fraternities, national sororities.

Athletics Member NCAA. All Division I except football (Division I-AA). ***Intercollegiate sports:*** basketball M(s)/W(s), cheerleading M(s)/W(s), cross-country running M(s)/W(s), golf W(s), skiing (cross-country) M(s)/W(s), skiing (downhill) M(s)/W(s), tennis M(s)/W(s), track and field M(s)/W(s), volleyball W(s). ***Intramural sports:*** archery W, badminton

M/W, baseball M, basketball M/W, bowling M/W, cross-country running M/W, fencing M/W, football M, golf M/W, gymnastics M/W, racquetball M/W, rugby M/W, skiing (cross-country) M/W, skiing (downhill) M/W, soccer M/W, softball M/W, swimming and diving M/W, table tennis M/W, tennis M/W, track and field M/W, ultimate Frisbee M/W, volleyball M/W, water polo M/W, weight lifting M/W, wrestling M.

Campus security: 24-hour emergency response devices and patrols, student patrols, late-night transport/escort service, 24-hour residence hall monitoring.

Student services: health clinic, personal/psychological counseling, women's center, legal services.

COSTS & FINANCIAL AID

Costs (2020–21) ***Tuition:*** area resident $5654 full-time, $236 per credit part-time; state resident $5654 full-time, $236 per credit part-time; nonresident $23,890 full-time, $995 per credit part-time. Full-time tuition and fees vary according to course load, program, and reciprocity agreements. Part-time tuition and fees vary according to course load, program, and reciprocity agreements. ***Required fees:*** $1818 full-time. ***Room and board:*** $10,300. Room and board charges vary according to board plan and housing facility. ***Payment plan:*** deferred payment. ***Waivers:*** adult students and employees or children of employees.

Financial Aid ***Average indebtedness upon graduation:*** $27,764.

APPLYING

Standardized Tests *Required:* SAT or ACT (for admission).

Options: electronic application, early admission, deferred entrance.

Application fee: $38.

Required: high school transcript, minimum 2.5 GPA.

Application deadlines: rolling (freshmen), rolling (out-of-state freshmen), rolling (transfers).

Notification: continuous (freshmen), continuous (out-of-state freshmen), continuous (transfers).

CONTACT

Ms. Ronda Russell, Director of Admissions, Montana State University, PO Box 172190, Bozeman, MT 59717-2190. *Phone:* 406-994-2452. *Toll-free phone:* 888-MSU-CATS. *Fax:* 406-994-1923. *E-mail:* admissions@montana.edu.

Montana State University Billings

Billings, Montana

http://www.msubillings.edu/

- **State-supported** comprehensive, founded 1927, part of Montana University System
- **Urban** 92-acre campus
- **Endowment** $24.7 million
- **Coed**
- **Minimally difficult** entrance level

FACULTY

Student/faculty ratio: 17:1.

ACADEMICS

Calendar: semesters. *Degrees:* certificates, associate, bachelor's, and master's.

Library: Montana State University Billings Library plus 2 others. *Books:* 138,650 (physical), 351,351 (digital/electronic); *Serial titles:* 1,368 (physical), 669,204 (digital/electronic); *Databases:* 170. Weekly public service hours: 82; students can reserve study rooms.

STUDENT LIFE

Housing options: on-campus residence required for freshman year; coed, special housing for students with disabilities. Campus housing is university owned. Freshman applicants given priority for college housing.

Activities and organizations: drama/theater group, student-run newspaper, radio station, choral group, Intervarsity Christian Fellowship, Accounting Club, HEROES, Multicultural Club, Art Student League.

Athletics Member NCAA. All Division II.

Campus security: 24-hour emergency response devices and patrols, late-night transport/escort service, controlled dormitory access.

Student services: health clinic, personal/psychological counseling, women's center, legal services.

FINANCIAL AID

Financial Aid Of all full-time matriculated undergraduates who enrolled in 2018, 1,765 applied for aid, 1,376 were judged to have need, 398 had their need fully met. In 2018, 157 non-need-based awards were made. ***Average percent of need met:*** 72. ***Average financial aid package:*** $10,523. ***Average need-based loan:*** $6173. ***Average need-based gift aid:*** $4942. ***Average non-need-based aid:*** $2008. ***Average indebtedness upon graduation:*** $26,139.

APPLYING

Standardized Tests *Required for some:* SAT or ACT (for admission).

Options: electronic application.

Application fee: $30.

Required: high school transcript.

CONTACT

Ms. Tammi Watson, Associate Director of Admissions, Montana State University Billings, 1500 University Drive, Billings, MT 59101. *Phone:* 406-657-2158. *Toll-free phone:* 800-565-6782. *Fax:* 406-657-2302. *E-mail:* tammi.watson@msubillings.edu.

Montana State University–Northern

Havre, Montana

http://www.msun.edu/

CONTACT

Montana State University–Northern, PO Box 7751, Havre, MT 59501-7751. *Phone:* 406-265-3704. *Toll-free phone:* 800-662-6132.

Montana Technological University

Butte, Montana

http://www.mtech.edu/

- **State-supported** comprehensive, founded 1895, part of Montana University System
- **Small-town** 56-acre campus
- **Endowment** $44.3 million
- **Coed** 2,200 undergraduate students, 77% full-time, 41% women, 59% men
- **Moderately difficult** entrance level, 92% of applicants were admitted

UNDERGRAD STUDENTS

1,697 full-time, 503 part-time. Students come from 34 states and territories; 10 other countries; 17% are from out of state; 0.9% Black or African American, non-Hispanic/Latino; 2% Hispanic/Latino; 1% Asian, non-Hispanic/Latino; 2% American Indian or Alaska Native, non-Hispanic/Latino; 0.4% Two or more races, non-Hispanic/Latino; 7% Race/ethnicity unknown; 6% international; 5% transferred in; 17% live on campus.

Freshmen:

Admission: 1,307 applied, 1,199 admitted, 413 enrolled. ***Average high school GPA:*** 3.6. ***Test scores:*** SAT evidence-based reading and writing scores over 500: 86%; SAT math scores over 500: 91%; ACT scores over 18: 99%; SAT evidence-based reading and writing scores over 600: 35%; SAT math scores over 600: 47%; ACT scores over 24: 51%; SAT evidence-based reading and writing scores over 700: 5%; SAT math scores over 700: 14%; ACT scores over 30: 10%.

Retention: 79% of full-time freshmen returned.

FACULTY

Total: 185, 74% full-time, 45% with terminal degrees.

Student/faculty ratio: 13:1.

ACADEMICS

Calendar: semesters. *Degrees:* certificates, diplomas, associate, bachelor's, master's, doctoral, and postbachelor's certificates.

Special study options: academic remediation for entering students, adult/continuing education programs, advanced placement credit, cooperative education, distance learning, double majors, external degree program, honors programs, independent study, internships, part-time degree program, services for LD students, student-designed majors, summer session for credit.

Computers: 660 computers/terminals are available on campus for general student use. Students can access the following: campus intranet, computer help desk, free student e-mail accounts, online (class) grades, online (class) registration, online (class) schedules. Campuswide network is available. 100% of college-owned or -operated housing units are wired for high-speed Internet access. Wireless service is available via entire campus.

Library: Montana Tech Library. *Books:* 57,343 (physical), 549,676 (digital/electronic); *Serial titles:* 1,862 (physical), 84,127 (digital/electronic); *Databases:* 146. Weekly public service hours: 80; students can reserve study rooms.

STUDENT LIFE

Housing options: on-campus residence required for freshman year; coed, special housing for students with disabilities. Campus housing is university owned. Freshman campus housing is guaranteed.

Activities and organizations: student-run newspaper, choral group, Chi Alpha, Engineers without Borders, Baptist Student union, Swing Dancing Club, NASA Robotics Mining Competition Club.

Athletics Member NAIA. ***Intercollegiate sports:*** basketball M(s)/W(s), cross-country running M(s)/W(s), football M(s), golf M(s)/W(s), volleyball W(s). ***Intramural sports:*** basketball M/W, cheerleading M(c)/W(c), football M/W, ice hockey M(c)/W(c), racquetball M/W, rugby M(c)/W(c), skiing (cross-country) M(c)/W(c), skiing (downhill) M(c)/W(c), softball M/W, volleyball M/W.

Campus security: 24-hour patrols, controlled dormitory access.

Student services: health clinic, personal/psychological counseling.

COSTS & FINANCIAL AID

Costs (2020–21) ***Tuition:*** state resident $5707 full-time, $238 per credit hour part-time; nonresident $20,870 full-time, $866 per credit hour part-time. Full-time tuition and fees vary according to course load, degree level, location, and program. Part-time tuition and fees vary according to course load, degree level, location, and program. ***Required fees:*** $1690 full-time. ***Room and board:*** $10,170. Room and board charges vary according to board plan and housing facility. ***Payment plan:*** installment. ***Waivers:*** minority students, senior citizens, and employees or children of employees.

Financial Aid Of all full-time matriculated undergraduates who enrolled in 2018, 1,271 applied for aid, 957 were judged to have need, 126 had their need fully met. In 2018, 269 non-need-based awards were made. ***Average percent of need met:*** 58. ***Average financial aid package:*** $11,078. ***Average need-based loan:*** $3794. ***Average need-based gift aid:*** $5912. ***Average non-need-based aid:*** $4161. ***Average indebtedness upon graduation:*** $23,632.

APPLYING

Standardized Tests *Required:* SAT or ACT (for admission).

Options: electronic application, deferred entrance.

Application fee: $30.

Required: high school transcript, proof of immunization. ***Required for some:*** minimum 2.5 GPA.

Application deadlines: rolling (freshmen), rolling (transfers).

Notification: continuous (freshmen), continuous (transfers).

CONTACT

Leslie Dickerson, Montana Technological University, 1300 West Park Street, Butte, MT 59701-8997. *Phone:* 406-496-4879. *Toll-free phone:* 800-445-TECH. *E-mail:* ldickerson@mtech.edu.

Rocky Mountain College

Billings, Montana

http://www.rocky.edu/

- **Independent interdenominational** comprehensive, founded 1878
- **Suburban** 60-acre campus
- **Endowment** $32.1 million
- **Coed** 850 undergraduate students, 98% full-time, 49% women, 51% men
- **Moderately difficult** entrance level, 59% of applicants were admitted

UNDERGRAD STUDENTS

829 full-time, 21 part-time. Students come from 43 states and territories; 14 other countries; 49% are from out of state; 2% Black or African American, non-Hispanic/Latino; 7% Hispanic/Latino; 0.4% Asian, non-Hispanic/Latino; 0.8% Native Hawaiian or other Pacific Islander, non-Hispanic/Latino; 3% American Indian or Alaska Native, non-Hispanic/Latino; 7% Two or more races, non-Hispanic/Latino; 1% Race/ethnicity unknown; 3% international; 6% transferred in; 53% live on campus.

Freshmen:

Admission: 1,558 applied, 922 admitted, 245 enrolled. ***Average high school GPA:*** 3.3. ***Test scores:*** SAT evidence-based reading and writing scores over 500: 71%; SAT math scores over 500: 62%; ACT scores over 18: 85%; SAT evidence-based reading and writing scores over 600: 22%; SAT math scores over 600: 16%; ACT scores over 24: 27%; SAT evidence-based reading and writing scores over 700: 4%; SAT math scores over 700: 1%; ACT scores over 30: 1%.

Retention: 70% of full-time freshmen returned.

FACULTY

Total: 109, 60% full-time, 60% with terminal degrees.

Student/faculty ratio: 10:1.

ACADEMICS

Calendar: semesters. *Degrees:* associate, bachelor's, master's, and doctoral.

Special study options: academic remediation for entering students, accelerated degree program, adult/continuing education programs, advanced placement credit, double majors, English as a second language, honors programs, independent study, internships, off-campus study, part-time degree program, services for LD students, student-designed majors, study abroad, summer session for credit. ***ROTC:*** Army (c).

Unusual degree programs: 3-2 accountancy.

Computers: 113 computers/terminals are available on campus for general student use. Students can access the following: campus intranet, free student e-mail accounts, online (class) grades, online (class) registration, online (class) schedules. Campuswide network is available. 100% of college-owned or -operated housing units are wired for high-speed Internet access. Wireless service is available via entire campus.

Library: Paul M. Adams Memorial Library. *Books:* 47,570 (physical), 172,956 (digital/electronic); *Serial titles:* 396 (physical), 51,657 (digital/electronic); *Databases:* 120. Weekly public service hours: 89.

STUDENT LIFE

Housing options: on-campus residence required through sophomore year; coed, special housing for students with disabilities. Campus housing is university owned. Freshman campus housing is guaranteed.

Activities and organizations: drama/theater group, student-run newspaper, choral group, Outdoor Recreation, Enactus, Flight Team/Club, Environmental Club, InterVarsity Christian Fellowship.

Athletics Member NAIA. ***Intercollegiate sports:*** basketball M(s)/W(s), cheerleading M(s)/W(s), cross-country running M(s)/W(s), equestrian sports M(c)/W(c), football M(s), golf M(s)/W(s), skiing (downhill) M(s)/W(s), soccer M(s)/W(s), track and field M(s)/W(s), volleyball W(s). ***Intramural sports:*** basketball M/W, fencing M(c)/W(c), football M/W, golf M/W, ice hockey M(c)/W(c), racquetball M/W, rock climbing M/W, skiing (downhill) M/W, soccer M/W, softball M/W, swimming and diving M/W, table tennis M/W, triathlon M(c)/W(c), ultimate Frisbee M/W, volleyball M/W, weight lifting M(c)/W(c), wrestling M(c)/W(c).

Campus security: 24-hour emergency response devices, student patrols, late-night transport/escort service, controlled dormitory access.

Student services: health clinic, personal/psychological counseling, veterans affairs office.

COSTS & FINANCIAL AID

Costs (2020–21) ***Comprehensive fee:*** $39,182 includes full-time tuition ($29,976), mandatory fees ($610), and room and board ($8596). Full-time tuition and fees vary according to course load, degree level, and program. Part-time tuition: $1249 per credit. Part-time tuition and fees vary according to course load, degree level, and program. ***Required fees:*** $200 per term part-time. ***College room only:*** $4284. Room and board charges vary according to board plan and housing facility. ***Payment plan:*** installment. ***Waivers:*** employees or children of employees.

Financial Aid Of all full-time matriculated undergraduates who enrolled in 2019, 697 applied for aid, 616 were judged to have need, 104 had their need fully met. 298 Federal Work-Study jobs (averaging $415). 147 state and other part-time jobs (averaging $730). In 2019, 38 non-need-based awards were made. ***Average percent of need met:*** 77. ***Average financial aid package:*** $25,766. ***Average need-based loan:*** $4090. ***Average need-based gift aid:*** $20,845. ***Average non-need-based aid:*** $13,702. ***Average indebtedness upon graduation:*** $26,935.

APPLYING
Standardized Tests *Required:* SAT or ACT (for admission).

Options: electronic application, deferred entrance.

Application fee: $35.

Required: high school transcript, minimum 2.5 GPA. ***Required for some:*** essay or personal statement, 2 letters of recommendation, interview.

Application deadlines: rolling (freshmen), rolling (transfers).

Notification: continuous (freshmen), continuous (transfers).

CONTACT
Austin Mapston, Dean for Enrollment Services, Rocky Mountain College, 1511 Poly Drive, Billings, MT 59102. *Phone:* 406-657-1026. *Toll-free phone:* 800-877-6259. *Fax:* 406-259-9751. *E-mail:* admissions@rocky.edu.

Salish Kootenai College

Pablo, Montana

http://www.skc.edu/

CONTACT
Ms. Jackie Moran, Admissions Officer, Salish Kootenai College, PO Box 70, Pablo, MT 59855-0117. *Phone:* 406-275-4866. *Fax:* 406-275-4810. *E-mail:* jackie_moran@skc.edu.

University of Montana

Missoula, Montana

http://www.umt.edu/

- **State-supported** university, founded 1893, part of Montana University System
- **Urban** 220-acre campus
- **Endowment** $166.4 million
- **Coed** 9,323 undergraduate students, 80% full-time, 55% women, 45% men
- **Moderately difficult** entrance level, 93% of applicants were admitted

UNDERGRAD STUDENTS
7,444 full-time, 1,879 part-time. Students come from 56 states and territories; 68 other countries; 28% are from out of state; 1% Black or African American, non-Hispanic/Latino; 5% Hispanic/Latino; 1% Asian, non-Hispanic/Latino; 0.2% Native Hawaiian or other Pacific Islander, non-Hispanic/Latino; 3% American Indian or Alaska Native, non-Hispanic/Latino; 4% Two or more races, non-Hispanic/Latino; 7% Race/ethnicity unknown; 2% international; 9% transferred in; 35% live on campus.

Freshmen:
Admission: 6,182 applied, 5,727 admitted, 1,681 enrolled. ***Average high school GPA:*** 3.6. ***Test scores:*** SAT evidence-based reading and writing scores over 500: 87%; SAT math scores over 500: 85%; ACT scores over 18: 92%; SAT evidence-based reading and writing scores over 600: 48%; SAT math scores over 600: 38%; ACT scores over 24: 50%; SAT evidence-based reading and writing scores over 700: 9%; SAT math scores over 700: 3%; ACT scores over 30: 10%.

Retention: 69% of full-time freshmen returned.

FACULTY
Total: 728, 72% full-time, 69% with terminal degrees.

Student/faculty ratio: 17:1.

ACADEMICS
Calendar: semesters. *Degrees:* certificates, associate, bachelor's, master's, doctoral, post-master's, and postbachelor's certificates.

Special study options: academic remediation for entering students, advanced placement credit, cooperative education, distance learning, double majors, English as a second language, external degree program, freshman honors college, honors programs, independent study, internships, off-campus study, part-time degree program, services for LD students, study abroad, summer session for credit. ***ROTC:*** Army (b).

Computers: Students can access the following: computer help desk, free student e-mail accounts, online (class) registration, online (class) schedules. Campuswide network is available. 100% of college-owned or -operated housing units are wired for high-speed Internet access. Wireless service is available via entire campus.

Library: Maureen and Mike Mansfield Library plus 2 others. *Books:* 139,763 (physical), 602,331 (digital/electronic); *Serial titles:* 15,019 (physical), 62,294 (digital/electronic); *Databases:* 202. Students can reserve study rooms.

STUDENT LIFE
Housing options: on-campus residence required for freshman year; coed, men-only, women-only, special housing for students with disabilities. Campus housing is university owned. Freshman campus housing is guaranteed.

Activities and organizations: drama/theater group, student-run newspaper, radio station, choral group, marching band, Associated Students of University of Montana, Greek Life, Outdoor Program, Intercollegiate Athletics, national fraternities, national sororities.

Athletics Member NCAA. All Division I except football (Division I-AA). ***Intercollegiate sports:*** baseball M(c), basketball M(s)/W(s), crew M(c)/W(c), cross-country running M(s)/W(s), equestrian sports M(c)/W(c), fencing M(c)/W(c), field hockey W(c), golf W(s), gymnastics W(c), ice hockey M(c)/W(c), lacrosse M(c)/W(c), rugby M(c)/W(c), skiing (downhill) M(c)/W(c), soccer W(s), softball W(s), tennis M(s)/W(s), track and field M(s)/W(s), ultimate Frisbee M(c)/W(c), volleyball W(s). ***Intramural sports:*** archery M/W, badminton M/W, baseball M, basketball M/W, bowling M/W, cross-country running M/W, football M/W, ice hockey M, racquetball M/W, rugby M/W, skiing (cross-country) M/W, soccer W, softball M/W, swimming and diving M/W, table tennis M/W, tennis M/W, track and field M/W, volleyball M/W, water polo M/W, weight lifting M/W.

Campus security: 24-hour emergency response devices and patrols, student patrols, late-night transport/escort service, controlled dormitory access.

Student services: health clinic, personal/psychological counseling, women's center, legal services, veterans affairs office.

COSTS & FINANCIAL AID
Costs (2019–20) ***Tuition:*** state resident $5352 full-time, $223 per credit hour part-time; nonresident $24,216 full-time, $1009 per credit hour part-time. Full-time tuition and fees vary according to degree level, location, program, reciprocity agreements, and student level. Part-time tuition and fees vary according to course load, degree level, location, and student level. ***Required fees:*** $2002 full-time, $92 per credit hour part-time. ***Room and board:*** $9966. Room and board charges vary according to board plan and housing facility. ***Payment plan:*** installment. ***Waivers:*** minority students, senior citizens, and employees or children of employees.

Financial Aid Of all full-time matriculated undergraduates who enrolled in 2019, 4,527 applied for aid, 3,595 were judged to have need, 382 had their need fully met. In 2019, 1151 non-need-based awards were made. ***Average percent of need met:*** 61. ***Average financial aid package:*** $11,977. ***Average need-based loan:*** $4250. ***Average need-based gift aid:*** $4991. ***Average non-need-based aid:*** $4708. ***Average indebtedness upon graduation:*** $27,132.

APPLYING
Standardized Tests *Required:* SAT or ACT (for admission).

Options: electronic application, early admission, deferred entrance.

Application fee: $36.

Required: high school transcript, minimum 2.5 GPA.

Application deadlines: rolling (freshmen), rolling (transfers).

CONTACT
University of Montana, Missoula, MT 59812-0002. *Phone:* 406-243-6266. *Toll-free phone:* 800-462-8636. *Fax:* 406-243-5711. *E-mail:* admiss@umontana.edu.

The University of Montana Western

Dillon, Montana

http://www.umwestern.edu/

CONTACT

Mrs. Janet Jones, Admissions Evaluator, The University of Montana Western, 710 South Atlantic, Dillon, MT 59725. *Phone:* 406-683-7331. *Toll-free phone:* 877-683-7331. *E-mail:* janet.jones@umwestern.edu.

University of Providence

Great Falls, Montana

http://www.uprovidence.edu/

- **Independent Roman Catholic** comprehensive, founded 1932
- **Suburban** 40-acre campus
- **Endowment** $10.8 million
- **Coed** 785 undergraduate students, 62% full-time, 67% women, 33% men
- **Noncompetitive** entrance level, 97% of applicants were admitted

UNDERGRAD STUDENTS

484 full-time, 301 part-time. 62% are from out of state; 5% Black or African American, non-Hispanic/Latino; 2% Hispanic/Latino; 4% Asian, non-Hispanic/Latino; 0.9% Native Hawaiian or other Pacific Islander, non-Hispanic/Latino; 1% American Indian or Alaska Native, non-Hispanic/Latino; 7% Race/ethnicity unknown; 2% international; 21% transferred in; 32% live on campus.

Freshmen:

Admission: 316 applied, 308 admitted, 104 enrolled. ***Average high school GPA:*** 3.2. ***Test scores:*** ACT scores over 18: 64%; ACT scores over 24: 18%; ACT scores over 30: 2%.

Retention: 57% of full-time freshmen returned.

FACULTY

Total: 104, 50% full-time, 44% with terminal degrees.

Student/faculty ratio: 9:1.

ACADEMICS

Calendar: semesters. *Degrees:* certificates, associate, bachelor's, and master's.

Special study options: adult/continuing education programs, advanced placement credit, distance learning, double majors, independent study, internships, off-campus study, part-time degree program, services for LD students, summer session for credit.

Computers: Students can access the following: campus intranet, computer help desk, free student e-mail accounts, online (class) grades, online (class) registration, online (class) schedules. Campuswide network is available. 100% of college-owned or -operated housing units are wired for high-speed Internet access. Wireless service is available via entire campus.

Library: University of Providence Library plus 1 other.

STUDENT LIFE

Housing options: on-campus residence required for freshman year; coed. Campus housing is university owned. Freshman campus housing is guaranteed.

Activities and organizations: drama/theater group, student-run newspaper, choral group.

Athletics Member NAIA. ***Intercollegiate sports:*** basketball M(s)/W(s), cheerleading M(s)/W(s), cross-country running M/W, equestrian sports M(s)/W(s), golf M(s), soccer M(s)/W(s), softball W, track and field M(s)/W(s), volleyball W(s), wrestling M(s). ***Intramural sports:*** basketball M/W, equestrian sports M/W(c), football M/W, golf M/W, skiing (downhill) M/W, soccer M/W, softball W, table tennis M/W, track and field M/W, ultimate Frisbee M/W, volleyball M/W, wrestling M.

Campus security: 24-hour emergency response devices and patrols, late-night transport/escort service, controlled dormitory access.

Student services: health clinic, personal/psychological counseling, veterans affairs office.

COSTS & FINANCIAL AID

Costs (2020–21) ***Comprehensive fee:*** $36,832 includes full-time tuition ($26,462), mandatory fees ($200), and room and board ($10,170). Part-time tuition: $862 per credit. Part-time tuition and fees vary according to course load and location. No tuition increase for student's term of enrollment. ***College room only:*** $5510. Room and board charges vary according to board plan. ***Payment plan:*** installment. ***Waivers:*** employees or children of employees.

Financial Aid Of all full-time matriculated undergraduates who enrolled in 2019, 414 applied for aid, 368 were judged to have need, 12 had their need fully met. In 2019, 50 non-need-based awards were made. ***Average percent of need met:*** 63. ***Average financial aid package:*** $20,583. ***Average need-based loan:*** $3533. ***Average need-based gift aid:*** $9851. ***Average non-need-based aid:*** $7101. ***Average indebtedness upon graduation:*** $26,200.

APPLYING

Standardized Tests *Required:* SAT or ACT (for admission). *Recommended:* SAT and SAT Subject Tests or ACT (for admission), SAT Subject Tests (for admission).

Options: electronic application, deferred entrance.

Required: high school transcript. ***Recommended:*** essay or personal statement, interview.

Notification: continuous (freshmen), continuous (transfers).

CONTACT

Katelyn Farrington, Director of Admissions, University of Providence, 1301 20th Street South, Great Falls, MT 59405. *Phone:* 406-791-5202 Ext. 5211. *Toll-free phone:* 800-856-9544. *Fax:* 406-791-5209. *E-mail:* admissions@uprovidence.edu.

Yellowstone Christian College

Billings, Montana

https://yellowstonechristian.edu/

CONTACT

Yellowstone Christian College, 1515 South Shiloh Road, Billings, MT 59106. *Toll-free phone:* 800-487-9950.

NEBRASKA

Bellevue University

Bellevue, Nebraska

http://www.bellevue.edu/

CONTACT

Nick Baker, Director of Undergraduate Enrollment, Bellevue University, 1000 Galvin Road South, Bellevue, NE 68005-3098. *Phone:* 402-557-7250. *Toll-free phone:* 800-756-7920. *E-mail:* nick.baker@bellevue.edu.

Bryan College of Health Sciences

Lincoln, Nebraska

http://www.bryanhealthcollege.edu/

CONTACT

Bryan College of Health Sciences, 1535 South 52nd Street, Lincoln, NE 68506.

Chadron State College

Chadron, Nebraska

http://www.csc.edu/

- **State-supported** comprehensive, founded 1911, part of Nebraska State College System
- **Small-town** 281-acre campus
- **Coed**
- **Noncompetitive** entrance level

FACULTY

Student/faculty ratio: 19:1.

ACADEMICS

Calendar: semesters. *Degrees:* bachelor's and master's.

Library: Reta King Library.

STUDENT LIFE

Housing options: on-campus residence required for freshman year; coed, men-only, women-only. Campus housing is university owned. Freshman campus housing is guaranteed.

Activities and organizations: drama/theater group, student-run newspaper, radio station, choral group.

Athletics Member NCAA. All Division II.

Campus security: 24-hour emergency response devices and patrols, student patrols, late-night transport/escort service.

Student services: health clinic, personal/psychological counseling.

FINANCIAL AID

Financial Aid ***Average financial aid package:*** $2615. ***Average need-based loan:*** $1273. ***Average need-based gift aid:*** $1934. ***Average indebtedness upon graduation:*** $11,000.

APPLYING

Options: electronic application, early admission.

Application fee: $15.

Required: high school transcript, health forms.

CONTACT

Ms. Tena Cook, Director of Admissions, Chadron State College, 1000 Main Street, Chadron, NE 69337-2690. *Phone:* 308-432-6263. *Toll-free phone:* 800-242-3766. *Fax:* 308-432-6229. *E-mail:* inquire@csc.edu.

Clarkson College

Omaha, Nebraska

http://www.clarksoncollege.edu/

CONTACT

Clarkson College, 101 South 42nd Street, Omaha, NE 68131-2739. *Phone:* 402-552-3100. *Toll-free phone:* 800-647-5500.

College of Saint Mary

Omaha, Nebraska

http://www.csm.edu/

- **Independent Roman Catholic** comprehensive, founded 1923
- **Urban** 25-acre campus
- **Endowment** $19.8 million
- **Women only** 861 undergraduate students, 92% full-time
- **Minimally difficult** entrance level, 52% of applicants were admitted

UNDERGRAD STUDENTS

794 full-time, 67 part-time. Students come from 34 states and territories; 11 other countries; 24% are from out of state; 17% transferred in; 25% live on campus.

Freshmen:

Admission: 428 applied, 223 admitted, 119 enrolled. ***Average high school GPA:*** 3.5.

Retention: 78% of full-time freshmen returned.

ACADEMICS

Calendar: semesters. *Degrees:* certificates, associate, bachelor's, master's, doctoral, and postbachelor's certificates.

Special study options: academic remediation for entering students, accelerated degree program, advanced placement credit, distance learning, double majors, honors programs, independent study, internships, part-time degree program, services for LD students, study abroad, summer session for credit. ***ROTC:*** Army (c), Air Force (c).

Computers: 215 computers/terminals and 320 ports are available on campus for general student use. Students can access the following: campus intranet, computer help desk, free student e-mail accounts, online (class) grades, online (class) registration, online (class) schedules. Campuswide network is available. 100% of college-owned or -operated housing units are wired for high-speed Internet access. Wireless service is available via entire campus.

Library: College of Saint Mary Library. Weekly public service hours: 81; study areas open 24 hours, 5–7 days a week.

STUDENT LIFE

Housing options: on-campus residence required through sophomore year; women-only. Campus housing is university owned. Freshman campus housing is guaranteed.

Activities and organizations: drama/theater group, choral group, Residence Hall Council, Campus Activities Board, Student Education Association of Nebraska, Student Occupational Therapy Club, Student Nurses Association.

Athletics Member NAIA. ***Intercollegiate sports:*** basketball W(s), bowling W(s), cross-country running W(s), golf W(s), soccer W(s), softball W(s), swimming and diving W(s), tennis W(s), track and field W(s), volleyball W(s). ***Intramural sports:*** soccer W.

Campus security: 24-hour emergency response devices and patrols, late-night transport/escort service, controlled dormitory access.

Student services: health clinic, personal/psychological counseling.

COSTS & FINANCIAL AID

Costs (2019–20) ***Comprehensive fee:*** $28,600 includes full-time tuition ($20,750) and room and board ($7850). Part-time tuition: $765 per credit. ***Payment plans:*** installment, deferred payment. ***Waivers:*** employees or children of employees.

Financial Aid Of all full-time matriculated undergraduates who enrolled in 2019, 636 applied for aid, 569 were judged to have need, 72 had their need fully met. 130 Federal Work-Study jobs (averaging $2576). 13 state and other part-time jobs (averaging $6642). In 2019, 139 non-need-based awards were made. ***Average percent of need met:*** 62. ***Average financial aid package:*** $16,679. ***Average need-based loan:*** $4408. ***Average need-based gift aid:*** $12,017. ***Average non-need-based aid:*** $10,341. ***Average indebtedness upon graduation:*** $30,516.

APPLYING

Standardized Tests *Required:* SAT or ACT (for admission). *Required for some:* ACT (for admission).

Options: electronic application.

Application fee: $30.

Required: high school transcript, minimum 2.0 GPA. ***Required for some:*** essay or personal statement, 3 letters of recommendation, interview.

Application deadlines: rolling (freshmen), rolling (transfers).

Notification: continuous (freshmen), continuous (transfers).

CONTACT

College of Saint Mary, 7000 Mercy Road, Omaha, NE 68106. *Phone:* 402-399-2350. *Toll-free phone:* 800-926-5534.

Concordia University, Nebraska

Seward, Nebraska

http://www.cune.edu/

CONTACT

Mr. Aaron W. Roberts, Director of Undergraduate Admissions, Concordia University, Nebraska, 800 North Columbia Avenue, Seward, NE 68434-1556. *Phone:* 800-535-5494 Ext. 7233. *Toll-free phone:* 800-535-5494. *Fax:* 402-643-4073. *E-mail:* admiss@cune.edu.

Creative Center

Omaha, Nebraska

http://www.creativecenter.edu/

- **Proprietary** 4-year, founded 1993
- **Urban** 2-acre campus with easy access to Omaha
- **Coed** 40 undergraduate students, 98% full-time, 73% women, 28% men

UNDERGRAD STUDENTS

39 full-time, 1 part-time.

Freshmen:

Admission: 11 enrolled.

FACULTY

Total: 12, 17% full-time, 17% with terminal degrees.

Student/faculty ratio: 8:1.

ACADEMICS

Calendar: semesters. *Degrees:* associate and bachelor's.

Special study options: accelerated degree program, advanced placement credit, part-time degree program, services for LD students.

Computers: 8 computers/terminals are available on campus for general student use. Students can access the following: campus intranet, computer help desk, all students own a laptop computer as part of tuition and fees. Campuswide network is available. Wireless service is available via entire campus.

Library: Student Library plus 1 other. *Books:* 512 (physical), 4 (digital/electronic); *Databases:* 13.

STUDENT LIFE

Housing options: college housing not available.

COSTS

Costs (2020–21) ***One-time required fee:*** $2800. ***Tuition:*** $25,600 full-time, $2560 per course part-time. Full-time tuition and fees vary according to course load, degree level, program, and student level. Part-time tuition and fees vary according to course load, degree level, program, and student level. ***Required fees:*** $2055 full-time, $200 per course part-time.

APPLYING

Application fee: $100.

Required: essay or personal statement, high school transcript, 1 letter of recommendation, interview, portfolio. ***Recommended:*** minimum 2.0 GPA.

Application deadlines: rolling (freshmen), rolling (out-of-state freshmen), rolling (transfers).

Notification: continuous (freshmen), continuous (out-of-state freshmen), continuous (transfers).

CONTACT

Ms. Kathleen Broderick, Director of Admissions, Creative Center, 10850 Emmet Street, Omaha, NE 68164. *Phone:* 402-898-1000 Ext. 216. *Toll-free phone:* 888-898-1789. *Fax:* 402-898-1301. *E-mail:* kathleen_b@creativecenter.edu.

Creighton University

Omaha, Nebraska

http://www.creighton.edu/

- **Independent Roman Catholic (Jesuit)** university, founded 1878
- **Urban** 139-acre campus with easy access to Omaha
- **Endowment** $587.0 million
- **Coed** 4,472 undergraduate students, 97% full-time, 58% women, 42% men
- **Moderately difficult** entrance level, 74% of applicants were admitted

UNDERGRAD STUDENTS

4,325 full-time, 147 part-time. Students come from 50 states and territories; 20 other countries; 78% are from out of state; 2% Black or African American, non-Hispanic/Latino; 8% Hispanic/Latino; 9% Asian, non-Hispanic/Latino; 0.3% Native Hawaiian or other Pacific Islander, non-Hispanic/Latino; 0.3% American Indian or Alaska Native, non-Hispanic/Latino; 5% Two or more races, non-Hispanic/Latino; 1% Race/ethnicity unknown; 2% international; 0.8% transferred in; 53% live on campus.

Freshmen:

Admission: 9,381 applied, 6,915 admitted, 1,076 enrolled. ***Average high school GPA:*** 3.8. ***Test scores:*** SAT evidence-based reading and writing scores over 500: 98%; SAT math scores over 500: 97%; ACT scores over 18: 100%; SAT evidence-based reading and writing scores over 600: 70%; SAT math scores over 600: 66%; ACT scores over 24: 80%; SAT evidence-based reading and writing scores over 700: 14%; SAT math scores over 700: 17%; ACT scores over 30: 26%.

Retention: 90% of full-time freshmen returned.

FACULTY

Total: 1,028, 61% full-time, 68% with terminal degrees.

Student/faculty ratio: 11:1.

ACADEMICS

Calendar: semesters. *Degrees:* certificates, associate, bachelor's, master's, doctoral, post-master's, and postbachelor's certificates.

Special study options: accelerated degree program, adult/continuing education programs, advanced placement credit, distance learning, double majors, English as a second language, honors programs, independent study, internships, off-campus study, part-time degree program, services for LD students, study abroad, summer session for credit. ***ROTC:*** Army (b), Air Force (c).

Computers: 565 computers/terminals are available on campus for general student use. Students can access the following: campus intranet, computer help desk, free student e-mail accounts, online (class) grades, online (class) registration, online (class) schedules, financial aid information. Campuswide network is available. 100% of college-owned or -operated housing units are wired for high-speed Internet access. Wireless service is available via entire campus.

Library: Reinert Alumni Memorial Library plus 2 others. *Books:* 345,198 (physical), 515,607 (digital/electronic); *Serial titles:* 4,297 (physical), 69,034 (digital/electronic); *Databases:* 380. Weekly public service hours: 112; study areas open 24 hours, 5–7 days a week.

STUDENT LIFE

Housing options: on-campus residence required through sophomore year; coed, special housing for students with disabilities. Campus housing is university owned. Freshman campus housing is guaranteed.

Activities and organizations: drama/theater group, student-run newspaper, radio station, choral group, Birdcage, Hui O Hawaii, Pre-Med Society, Partners Against Cancer, American Pharmacists Association Academy of Student Pharmacist, national fraternities, national sororities.

Athletics Member NCAA. All Division I. ***Intercollegiate sports:*** baseball M(s), basketball M(s)/W(s), crew W(s), cross-country running M(s)/W(s), golf M(s)/W(s)(c), soccer M(s)/W(s), softball W(s), tennis M(s)/W(s), volleyball W(s). ***Intramural sports:*** archery M/W, badminton M(c)/W(c), basketball M/W, crew M(c), football M/W, golf M/W, ice hockey M(c), lacrosse M(c)/W(c), racquetball M/W, rugby M(c), skiing (downhill) M(c)/W(c), soccer M/W, softball M/W, table tennis M/W, tennis M/W, ultimate Frisbee M/W, volleyball M/W.

Campus security: 24-hour emergency response devices and patrols, student patrols, late-night transport/escort service, controlled dormitory access.

Student services: health clinic, personal/psychological counseling, women's center, veterans affairs office.

COSTS & FINANCIAL AID

Costs (2020–21) ***One-time required fee:*** $160. ***Comprehensive fee:*** $54,618 includes full-time tuition ($41,176), mandatory fees ($1842), and room and board ($11,600). Part-time tuition: $1288 per credit hour. ***Required fees:*** $182 per term part-time. ***Room and board:*** Room and board charges vary according to board plan, housing facility, and location. ***Payment plan:*** installment. ***Waivers:*** employees or children of employees.

Financial Aid Of all full-time matriculated undergraduates who enrolled in 2018, 2,882 applied for aid, 2,286 were judged to have need, 618 had their need fully met. 855 Federal Work-Study jobs (averaging $2175). In 2018, 1734 non-need-based awards were made. ***Average percent of need met:*** 78. ***Average financial aid package:*** $28,830. ***Average need-based loan:*** $6014. ***Average need-based gift aid:*** $22,423. ***Average non-need-based aid:*** $17,229. ***Average indebtedness upon graduation:*** $37,973.

APPLYING

Standardized Tests *Required for some:* SAT or ACT (for admission).

Options: electronic application, early action, deferred entrance.

Application fee: $40.

Required: essay or personal statement, high school transcript, 1 letter of recommendation. ***Recommended:*** minimum 3.0 GPA.

Application deadlines: rolling (freshmen), 8/1 (transfers), 11/1 (early action).

Notification: continuous (freshmen), continuous (transfers), rolling (early action).

CONTACT

Ms. Sarah Richardson, Director of Admissions and Scholarships, Creighton University, 2500 California Plaza, Omaha, NE 68178-0001. *Phone:* 402-280-2703. *Toll-free phone:* 800-282-5835. *Fax:* 402-280-2685. *E-mail:* admissions@creighton.edu.

Doane University

Crete, Nebraska

http://www.doane.edu/

- **Independent** comprehensive, founded 1872, affiliated with United Church of Christ
- **Small-town** 300-acre campus with easy access to Omaha
- **Endowment** $114.6 million
- **Coed** 1,002 undergraduate students, 99% full-time, 47% women, 53% men
- 71% of applicants were admitted

UNDERGRAD STUDENTS

996 full-time, 6 part-time. Students come from 32 states and territories; 13 other countries; 28% are from out of state; 3% Black or African American, non-Hispanic/Latino; 10% Hispanic/Latino; 2% Asian, non-Hispanic/Latino; 0.4% Native Hawaiian or other Pacific Islander, non-Hispanic/Latino; 0.1% American Indian or Alaska Native, non-Hispanic/Latino; 4% Two or more races, non-Hispanic/Latino; 0.8% Race/ethnicity unknown; 2% international; 5% transferred in; 82% live on campus.

Freshmen:

Admission: 2,116 applied, 1,511 admitted, 314 enrolled. ***Average high school GPA:*** 3.5. ***Test scores:*** ACT scores over 18: 89%; ACT scores over 24: 36%; ACT scores over 30: 5%.

Retention: 71% of full-time freshmen returned.

FACULTY

Total: 125, 63% full-time, 74% with terminal degrees.

Student/faculty ratio: 11:1.

ACADEMICS

Calendar: 4-1-4. *Degrees:* bachelor's, master's, doctoral, and post-master's certificates (non-traditional undergraduate programs and graduate programs offered at Lincoln campus).

Special study options: advanced placement credit, cooperative education, double majors, English as a second language, honors programs, independent study, internships, off-campus study, student-designed majors, study abroad, summer session for credit. ***ROTC:*** Army (c), Air Force (c).

Unusual degree programs: 3-2 engineering with Columbia University, Washington University in St. Louis; forestry with Duke University; environmental studies with Duke University.

Computers: 250 computers/terminals and 1,000 ports are available on campus for general student use. Students can access the following: campus intranet, computer help desk, free student e-mail accounts, online (class) grades, online (class) registration, online (class) schedules. Campuswide network is available. 100% of college-owned or -operated housing units are wired for high-speed Internet access. Wireless service is available via entire campus.

Library: Perkins Library plus 1 other. Study areas open 24 hours, 5–7 days a week; students can reserve study rooms.

STUDENT LIFE

Housing options: on-campus residence required through senior year; coed, women-only. Campus housing is university owned. Freshman campus housing is guaranteed.

Activities and organizations: drama/theater group, student-run newspaper, radio and television station, choral group, marching band, Student Activities Council, Hansen Leadership Program, band/choir, Doane Ambassadors, Doane Art League.

Athletics Member NAIA. ***Intercollegiate sports:*** baseball M(s), basketball M(s)/W(s), cross-country running M(s)/W(s), football M(s), golf M(s)/W(s), soccer M(s)/W(s), softball W(s), tennis M/W, track and field M(s)/W(s), volleyball W(s). ***Intramural sports:*** baseball M(c)/W(c), basketball M/W, bowling M/W, football M/W, golf M/W, ice hockey M, racquetball M(c)/W(c), softball M/W, swimming and diving M/W, table tennis M(c)/W(c), tennis M/W, volleyball M/W, water polo M/W.

Campus security: 24-hour emergency response devices and patrols, student patrols, late-night transport/escort service, controlled dormitory access, evening patrols by trained security personnel.

Student services: health clinic, personal/psychological counseling.

COSTS & FINANCIAL AID

Costs (2020–21) ***Tuition:*** $1150 per credit hour part-time. Full-time tuition and fees vary according to location. Part-time tuition and fees vary according to course load and location. ***Room only:*** Room and board charges vary according to board plan, housing facility, and location. ***Payment plan:*** installment. ***Waivers:*** senior citizens and employees or children of employees.

Financial Aid Of all full-time matriculated undergraduates who enrolled in 2019, 829 applied for aid, 734 were judged to have need, 255 had their need fully met. In 2019, 70 non-need-based awards were made. ***Average percent of need met:*** 89. ***Average financial aid package:*** $27,876. ***Average need-based loan:*** $4278. ***Average need-based gift aid:*** $24,668. ***Average non-need-based aid:*** $20,742. ***Average indebtedness upon graduation:*** $28,490.

APPLYING

Standardized Tests *Required:* SAT or ACT (for admission).

Options: electronic application.

Required: high school transcript, 2 letters of recommendation. ***Required for some:*** interview. ***Recommended:*** minimum 2.0 GPA.

CONTACT

Mr. Kyle McMurray, Director of Admission, Doane University, 1014 Boswell Avenue, Crete, NE 68333. *Phone:* 402-826-8222. *Toll-free phone:* 800-333-6263. *E-mail:* kyle.mcmurray@doane.edu.

Hastings College

Hastings, Nebraska

http://www.hastings.edu/

CONTACT

Mr. Chris Schukei, Director of Admissions, Hastings College, 710 North Turner Avenue, Hastings, NE 68901-7621. *Phone:* 402-461-7341. *Toll-free phone:* 800-532-7642. *Fax:* 402-461-7490. *E-mail:* cschukei@hastings.edu.

Midland University

Fremont, Nebraska

http://www.midlandu.edu/

- **Independent Lutheran** 4-year, founded 1883
- **Small-town** 27-acre campus with easy access to Omaha
- **Endowment** $21.0 million
- **Coed**
- **Moderately difficult** entrance level

FACULTY

Student/faculty ratio: 16:1.

ACADEMICS

Calendar: 4-1-4. *Degrees:* associate and bachelor's.

Library: Luther Library.

STUDENT LIFE

Housing options: on-campus residence required through sophomore year; coed, men-only, women-only. Campus housing is university owned.

Activities and organizations: drama/theater group, student-run newspaper, choral group, marching band, Student Nurses Association, Student Education Association, Phi Beta Lambda, Fellowship of Christian Athletes, Circle K.

Athletics Member NAIA.

Campus security: 24-hour emergency response devices, student patrols, late-night transport/escort service, controlled dormitory access.

Student services: health clinic, personal/psychological counseling.

FINANCIAL AID

Financial Aid Of all full-time matriculated undergraduates who enrolled in 2008, 699 applied for aid, 622 were judged to have need, 332 had their need fully met. 169 Federal Work-Study jobs (averaging $1350). 121 state and other part-time jobs (averaging $1425). In 2008, 55 non-need-based awards were made. ***Average percent of need met:*** 89. ***Average financial aid package:*** $17,904. ***Average need-based loan:*** $4898. ***Average need-based gift aid:*** $11,881. ***Average non-need-based aid:*** $12,840. ***Average indebtedness upon graduation:*** $23,000.

APPLYING
Standardized Tests *Required:* SAT or ACT (for admission).

Options: electronic application, early admission.

Application fee: $30.

Required: high school transcript. ***Required for some:*** interview. ***Recommended:*** essay or personal statement, minimum 3.0 GPA.

CONTACT
Danielle Oliver, Associate Director of Admissions, Midland University, Fremont, NE 68025-4200. *Phone:* 402-941-6501. *Toll-free phone:* 800-642-8382 Ext. 6501. *E-mail:* oliver@midlandu.edu.

National American University

Bellevue, Nebraska

http://www.national.edu/

CONTACT
National American University, 3604 Summit Plaza Drive, Bellevue, NE 68123.

Nebraska Methodist College

Omaha, Nebraska

http://www.methodistcollege.edu/

- **Independent** comprehensive, founded 1891, affiliated with United Methodist Church
- **Urban** 8-acre campus
- **Coed** 766 undergraduate students, 57% full-time, 90% women, 10% men
- **Moderately difficult** entrance level, 97% of applicants were admitted

UNDERGRAD STUDENTS
433 full-time, 333 part-time. Students come from 17 states and territories; 5 other countries; 14% are from out of state; 3% Black or African American, non-Hispanic/Latino; 7% Hispanic/Latino; 2% Asian, non-Hispanic/Latino; 0.1% Native Hawaiian or other Pacific Islander, non-Hispanic/Latino; 0.3% American Indian or Alaska Native, non-Hispanic/Latino; 3% Two or more races, non-Hispanic/Latino; 2% Race/ethnicity unknown; 0.3% international; 19% transferred in; 9% live on campus.

Freshmen:
Admission: 78 applied, 76 admitted, 49 enrolled. ***Average high school GPA:*** 3.6. ***Test scores:*** ACT scores over 18: 98%; ACT scores over 24: 32%; ACT scores over 30: 2%.

Retention: 67% of full-time freshmen returned.

FACULTY
Total: 68, 93% full-time, 28% with terminal degrees.

Student/faculty ratio: 13:1.

ACADEMICS
Calendar: semesters. *Degrees:* certificates, associate, bachelor's, master's, doctoral, post-master's, and postbachelor's certificates.

Special study options: academic remediation for entering students, accelerated degree program, adult/continuing education programs, advanced placement credit, cooperative education, distance learning, external degree program, independent study, services for LD students, summer session for credit. ***ROTC:*** Air Force (c).

Computers: 50 computers/terminals and 25 ports are available on campus for general student use. Students can access the following: campus intranet, computer help desk, online (class) grades, online (class) registration, online (class) schedules. Campuswide network is available. 100% of college-owned or -operated housing units are wired for high-speed Internet access. Wireless service is available via entire campus.

Library: John Moritz Library. *Books:* 1,489 (physical), 13 (digital/electronic); *Serial titles:* 56 (physical), 12,818 (digital/electronic); *Databases:* 23. Weekly public service hours: 65.

STUDENT LIFE
Housing options: coed. Campus housing is university owned.

Activities and organizations: Student Nurses Association, Methodist Allied Health Student Association, Student Government, Student Ambassadors, Residence Hall Council.

Campus security: 24-hour emergency response devices and patrols, late-night transport/escort service, controlled dormitory access.

Student services: health clinic, personal/psychological counseling, veterans affairs office.

COSTS & FINANCIAL AID
Costs (2019–20) ***Comprehensive fee:*** $25,894 includes full-time tuition ($15,660), mandatory fees ($648), and room and board ($9586). Part-time tuition: $580 per credit hour.

Financial Aid Of all full-time matriculated undergraduates who enrolled in 2018, 396 applied for aid, 347 were judged to have need, 10 had their need fully met. In 2018, 48 non-need-based awards were made. ***Average percent of need met:*** 37. ***Average financial aid package:*** $10,624. ***Average need-based loan:*** $4681. ***Average need-based gift aid:*** $7056. ***Average non-need-based aid:*** $4459. ***Average indebtedness upon graduation:*** $30,407.

APPLYING
Standardized Tests *Required:* SAT or ACT (for admission).

Options: electronic application, deferred entrance.

Application fee: $25.

Required: essay or personal statement, high school transcript, minimum 2.5 GPA.

Application deadlines: rolling (freshmen), rolling (transfers).

CONTACT
Ms. Megan Kokenge, Director of Enrollment Services, Nebraska Methodist College, 720 North 87th Street, Omaha, NE 68114. *Phone:* 402-354-7111. *Toll-free phone:* 800-335-5510. *Fax:* 402-354-7020. *E-mail:* megan.maryott@methodistcollege.edu.

Nebraska Wesleyan University

Lincoln, Nebraska

http://www.nebrwesleyan.edu/

- **Independent United Methodist** comprehensive, founded 1887
- **Suburban** 50-acre campus with easy access to Omaha
- **Endowment** $60.5 million
- **Coed** 1,842 undergraduate students, 93% full-time, 59% women, 41% men
- **Moderately difficult** entrance level, 68% of applicants were admitted

UNDERGRAD STUDENTS
1,705 full-time, 137 part-time. Students come from 25 states and territories; 19 other countries; 15% are from out of state; 3% Black or African American, non-Hispanic/Latino; 7% Hispanic/Latino; 2% Asian, non-Hispanic/Latino; 0.1% Native Hawaiian or other Pacific Islander, non-Hispanic/Latino; 0.2% American Indian or Alaska Native, non-Hispanic/Latino; 3% Two or more races, non-Hispanic/Latino; 3% Race/ethnicity unknown; 2% international; 4% transferred in; 58% live on campus.

Freshmen:
Admission: 2,405 applied, 1,630 admitted, 487 enrolled. ***Average high school GPA:*** 3.7. ***Test scores:*** SAT evidence-based reading and writing scores over 500: 91%; SAT math scores over 500: 90%; ACT scores over 18: 98%; SAT evidence-based reading and writing scores over 600: 45%; SAT math scores over 600: 40%; ACT scores over 24: 60%; SAT evidence-based reading and writing scores over 700: 9%; SAT math scores over 700: 4%; ACT scores over 30: 15%.

Retention: 83% of full-time freshmen returned.

FACULTY
Total: 280, 41% full-time, 44% with terminal degrees.

Student/faculty ratio: 10:1.

ACADEMICS
Calendar: semesters. *Degrees:* certificates, bachelor's, master's, post-master's, and postbachelor's certificates.

Special study options: accelerated degree program, adult/continuing education programs, advanced placement credit, double majors, independent study, internships, off-campus study, part-time degree program, services for LD students, student-designed majors, study abroad, summer session for credit. ***ROTC:*** Army (c), Navy (c), Air Force (c).

Unusual degree programs: 3-2 engineering with Washington University in St. Louis, Columbia University, University of Nebraska–Lincoln.

Computers: 360 computers/terminals are available on campus for general student use. Students can access the following: computer help desk, free student e-mail accounts, online (class) grades, online (class) registration, online (class) schedules. Campuswide network is available. 100% of college-owned or -operated housing units are wired for high-speed Internet access. Wireless service is available via entire campus.
Library: Cochrane Woods Library. *Books:* 148,110 (physical), 191,524 (digital/electronic); *Serial titles:* 1,573 (physical), 18,736 (digital/electronic); *Databases:* 48. Weekly public service hours: 98; students can reserve study rooms.

STUDENT LIFE
Housing options: on-campus residence required through junior year; coed, women-only. Campus housing is university owned. Freshman campus housing is guaranteed.

Activities and organizations: drama/theater group, student-run newspaper, radio station, choral group, marching band, national fraternities, national sororities.

Athletics Member NCAA. All Division III. ***Intercollegiate sports:*** baseball M, basketball M/W, cheerleading W, cross-country running M/W, football M, golf M/W, soccer M/W, softball W, swimming and diving M/W, tennis M/W, track and field M/W, volleyball W, wrestling M. ***Intramural sports:*** basketball M/W, football M/W, racquetball M/W, sand volleyball M/W, soccer M/W, ultimate Frisbee M/W, volleyball M/W.

Campus security: 24-hour emergency response devices and patrols, late-night transport/escort service, controlled dormitory access.

Student services: health clinic, personal/psychological counseling, women's center.

COSTS & FINANCIAL AID
Costs (2020–21) ***Comprehensive fee:*** $45,736 includes full-time tuition ($34,582), mandatory fees ($982), and room and board ($10,172). Part-time tuition: $1236 per credit hour. Part-time tuition and fees vary according to class time, degree level, location, and program. ***College room only:*** $5804. Room and board charges vary according to board plan and housing facility. ***Payment plan:*** installment. ***Waivers:*** senior citizens and employees or children of employees.

Financial Aid Of all full-time matriculated undergraduates who enrolled in 2018, 1,381 applied for aid, 1,256 were judged to have need, 203 had their need fully met. 111 Federal Work-Study jobs (averaging $1438). 643 state and other part-time jobs (averaging $1268). In 2018, 361 non-need-based awards were made. ***Average percent of need met:*** 74. ***Average financial aid package:*** $24,765. ***Average need-based loan:*** $4297. ***Average need-based gift aid:*** $20,303. ***Average non-need-based aid:*** $16,557. ***Average indebtedness upon graduation:*** $31,715.

APPLYING
Standardized Tests *Required:* SAT or ACT (for admission).

Options: electronic application, early action, deferred entrance.

Required: high school transcript. ***Required for some:*** essay or personal statement.

Application deadlines: 8/15 (freshmen), 8/15 (transfers), 10/15 (early action).

Notification: continuous (freshmen), continuous (transfers).

CONTACT
Mr. Gordie Coffin, Director of Admissions, Nebraska Wesleyan University, 5000 Saint Paul Avenue, Lincoln, NE 68504. *Phone:* 402-465-2218. *Toll-free phone:* 800-541-3818. *Fax:* 402-465-2177. *E-mail:* admissions@nebrwesleyan.edu.

Peru State College

Peru, Nebraska

http://www.peru.edu/

- **State-supported** comprehensive, founded 1867, part of Nebraska State College System
- **Rural** 104-acre campus
- **Coed**
- **Noncompetitive** entrance level

FACULTY
Student/faculty ratio: 24:1.

ACADEMICS
Calendar: semesters. *Degrees:* bachelor's and master's.
Library: Peru State College Library.

STUDENT LIFE
Housing options: on-campus residence required through sophomore year; coed, men-only, women-only. Campus housing is university owned. Freshman campus housing is guaranteed.

Activities and organizations: drama/theater group, student-run newspaper, choral group, marching band, Campus Activities Board, Black Student Union, Peru Student Education Association (PSEA), Phi Beta Lambda (PBL), Pilot Club.

Athletics Member NAIA.

Campus security: 24-hour emergency response devices and patrols, late-night transport/escort service.

Student services: health clinic.

COSTS
Costs (2019–20) ***One-time required fee:*** $15. ***Tuition:*** state resident $5445 full-time, $182 per credit hour part-time; nonresident $5445 full-time, $182 per credit hour part-time. Full-time tuition and fees vary according to course level, course load, and location. Part-time tuition and fees vary according to course level, course load, and location. ***Required fees:*** $2156 full-time, $72 per credit hour part-time. ***Room and board:*** $9060; room only: $4674. Room and board charges vary according to board plan and housing facility.

APPLYING
Standardized Tests *Required for some:* SAT or ACT (for admission).

Options: electronic application.

Required: high school transcript.

CONTACT
Ms. Micki Willis, Vice President for Enrollment Management and Student Affairs, Peru State College, PO Box 10, Peru, NE 68421. *Phone:* 402-872-2221. *Toll-free phone:* 800-742-4412 (in-state); 800-741-4412 (out-of-state). *Fax:* 402-872-2296. *E-mail:* mwillis@peru.edu.

Purdue University Global

Lincoln, Nebraska

http://www.purdueglobal.edu/

CONTACT
Purdue University Global, 1821 K Street, Lincoln, NE 68508. *Phone:* 402-474-5315. *Toll-free phone:* 844-PURDUE-G.

Purdue University Global

Omaha, Nebraska

http://www.purdueglobal.edu/

CONTACT
Purdue University Global, 5425 North 103rd Street, Omaha, NE 68134. *Phone:* 402-572-8500. *Toll-free phone:* 844-PURDUE-G.

St. Gregory the Great Seminary

Seward, Nebraska

http://www.sggs.edu/

CONTACT
Rev. Peter M. Mitchell, Dean of Men, St. Gregory the Great Seminary, 800 Fletcher Road, Seward, NE 68434. *Phone:* 402-643-4052. *Fax:* 402-643-6964. *E-mail:* sggs@stgregoryseminary.edu.

Union College

Lincoln, Nebraska

http://www.ucollege.edu/

- **Independent Seventh-day Adventist** comprehensive, founded 1891
- **Suburban** 26-acre campus with easy access to Omaha
- **Coed**
- **Moderately difficult** entrance level

FACULTY

Student/faculty ratio: 10:1.

ACADEMICS

Calendar: semesters. *Degrees:* associate, bachelor's, and master's.
Library: Ella Johnson Crandall Library. *Books:* 143,808 (physical), 187,159 (digital/electronic); *Serial titles:* 136 (physical), 136 (digital/electronic); *Databases:* 61. Students can reserve study rooms.

STUDENT LIFE

Housing options: on-campus residence required through junior year; coed, men-only, women-only, special housing for students with disabilities. Campus housing is university owned. Freshman campus housing is guaranteed.

Activities and organizations: drama/theater group, student-run newspaper, choral group, Business and Computer Science Club, Math and Science Club, Nursing Club, Amnesty International, International Club.
Campus security: 24-hour emergency response devices, student patrols, late-night transport/escort service.

Student services: health clinic, personal/psychological counseling.

FINANCIAL AID

Financial Aid Of all full-time matriculated undergraduates who enrolled in 2018, 561 applied for aid, 506 were judged to have need, 82 had their need fully met. 94 Federal Work-Study jobs (averaging $1814). In 2018, 161 non-need-based awards were made. ***Average percent of need met:*** 62. ***Average financial aid package:*** $17,701. ***Average need-based loan:*** $4426. ***Average need-based gift aid:*** $13,696. ***Average non-need-based aid:*** $10,352. ***Average indebtedness upon graduation:*** $32,103.

APPLYING

Standardized Tests *Required:* SAT or ACT (for admission).

Options: electronic application, early decision.

Required: high school transcript, minimum 2.5 GPA, 3 letters of recommendation. ***Required for some:*** essay or personal statement, interview.

CONTACT

Kristina Hammer, Assistant Director of Admissions, Union College, 3800 South 48th Street, Lincoln, NE 68506. *Phone:* 402-486-2969 Ext. 2052. *Toll-free phone:* 800-228-4600. *Fax:* 402-486-2895. *E-mail:* enroll@ucollege.edu.

University of Nebraska at Kearney

Kearney, Nebraska

http://www.unk.edu/

- **State-supported** comprehensive, founded 1903, part of University of Nebraska System
- **Small-town** 235-acre campus
- **Coed** 4,429 undergraduate students, 86% full-time, 60% women, 40% men
- **Moderately difficult** entrance level, 85% of applicants were admitted

UNDERGRAD STUDENTS

3,827 full-time, 602 part-time. 8% are from out of state; 2% Black or African American, non-Hispanic/Latino; 12% Hispanic/Latino; 0.8% Asian, non-Hispanic/Latino; 0.1% Native Hawaiian or other Pacific Islander, non-Hispanic/Latino; 0.1% American Indian or Alaska Native, non-Hispanic/Latino; 2% Two or more races, non-Hispanic/Latino; 0.5% Race/ethnicity unknown; 5% international; 8% transferred in; 35% live on campus.

Freshmen:

Admission: 5,324 applied, 4,535 admitted, 863 enrolled. ***Average high school GPA:*** 3.5. ***Test scores:*** SAT evidence-based reading and writing scores over 500: 62%; SAT math scores over 500: 76%; ACT scores over 18: 91%; SAT evidence-based reading and writing scores over 600: 19%; SAT math scores over 600: 24%; ACT scores over 24: 42%; SAT evidence-based reading and writing scores over 700: 5%; ACT scores over 30: 12%.

Retention: 80% of full-time freshmen returned.

FACULTY

Total: 454, 733% full-time, 61% with terminal degrees.

Student/faculty ratio: 13:1.

ACADEMICS

Calendar: semesters. *Degrees:* certificates, bachelor's, master's, and post-master's certificates.

Special study options: distance learning, double majors, honors programs, independent study, internships, part-time degree program, services for LD students, study abroad. ***ROTC:*** Army (b).

Computers: Students can access the following: computer help desk, free student e-mail accounts, online (class) grades, online (class) registration, online (class) schedules, online degree audit, online personal information update, online bill viewing and payment, online financial aid awards and acceptance. Campuswide network is available. Wireless service is available via entire campus.
Library: Calvin T. Ryan Library.

STUDENT LIFE

Housing options: on-campus residence required for freshman year; coed. Campus housing is university owned. Freshman campus housing is guaranteed.

Activities and organizations: drama/theater group, student-run newspaper, radio and television station, marching band, national fraternities, national sororities.

Athletics Member NCAA. All Division II. ***Intercollegiate sports:*** baseball M(s), basketball M(s)/W(s), cross-country running M(s)/W(s), football M(s), golf M(s)/W(s), soccer W(s), softball W(s), swimming and diving W(s), tennis M(s)/W(s), track and field M(s)/W(s), volleyball W(s), wrestling M(s). ***Intramural sports:*** badminton M/W, basketball M/W, cross-country running M/W, football M/W, golf M/W, racquetball M/W, soccer M/W, softball M/W, tennis M/W, volleyball M/W, water polo M/W, wrestling M/W.

Campus security: 24-hour emergency response devices and patrols, late-night transport/escort service.

Student services: health clinic, personal/psychological counseling.

COSTS & FINANCIAL AID

Costs (2019–20) ***Tuition:*** state resident $6090 full-time, $203 per credit hour part-time; nonresident $13,290 full-time, $443 per credit hour part-time. Full-time tuition and fees vary according to course level, course load, degree level, location, and program. Part-time tuition and fees vary according to course level, course load, degree level, location, and program. ***Required fees:*** $1611 full-time. ***Room and board:*** $9942; room only: $5156. Room and board charges vary according to board plan and housing facility. ***Payment plan:*** installment. ***Waivers:*** employees or children of employees.

Financial Aid Of all full-time matriculated undergraduates who enrolled in 2018, 3,124 applied for aid, 2,655 were judged to have need, 533 had their need fully met. In 2018, 620 non-need-based awards were made. ***Average percent of need met:*** 67. ***Average financial aid package:*** $11,820. ***Average need-based loan:*** $3715. ***Average need-based gift aid:*** $9165. ***Average non-need-based aid:*** $5427. ***Average indebtedness upon graduation:*** $20,774.

APPLYING

Standardized Tests *Required:* SAT or ACT (for admission).

Options: electronic application.

Application fee: $45.

Required: high school transcript, rank in upper 50% of high school class.

Notification: continuous until 9/1 (freshmen), continuous (transfers).

CONTACT

Mr. Dusty Newton, Director of Admissions, University of Nebraska at Kearney, 905 West 25th Street, Kearney, NE 68849-0001. *Phone:* 308-865-8702. *Toll-free phone:* 800-532-7639. *Fax:* 308-865-8987. *E-mail:* admissionsug@unk.edu.

University of Nebraska at Omaha

Omaha, Nebraska

http://www.unomaha.edu/

CONTACT

University of Nebraska at Omaha, 6001 Dodge Street, Omaha, NE 68182. *Phone:* 402-554-3520. *Toll-free phone:* 800-858-8648.

University of Nebraska–Lincoln

Lincoln, Nebraska

http://www.unl.edu/

- **State-supported** university, founded 1869, part of University of Nebraska System
- **Urban** 856-acre campus with easy access to Omaha
- **Endowment** $211.1 million
- **Coed** 20,478 undergraduate students, 93% full-time, 47% women, 53% men
- **Moderately difficult** entrance level, 78% of applicants were admitted

UNDERGRAD STUDENTS

19,132 full-time, 1,346 part-time. Students come from 51 states and territories; 100 other countries; 25% are from out of state; 3% Black or African American, non-Hispanic/Latino; 7% Hispanic/Latino; 3% Asian, non-Hispanic/Latino; 0.0% Native Hawaiian or other Pacific Islander, non-Hispanic/Latino; 0.2% American Indian or Alaska Native, non-Hispanic/Latino; 3% Two or more races, non-Hispanic/Latino; 0.9% Race/ethnicity unknown; 8% international; 4% transferred in; 41% live on campus.

Freshmen:

Admission: 16,829 applied, 13,165 admitted, 4,775 enrolled. ***Average high school GPA:*** 3.6. ***Test scores:*** SAT evidence-based reading and writing scores over 500: 93%; SAT math scores over 500: 93%; ACT scores over 18: 97%; SAT evidence-based reading and writing scores over 600: 59%; SAT math scores over 600: 63%; ACT scores over 24: 63%; SAT evidence-based reading and writing scores over 700: 18%; SAT math scores over 700: 25%; ACT scores over 30: 23%.

Retention: 81% of full-time freshmen returned.

FACULTY

Total: 1,405, 93% full-time, 75% with terminal degrees.

Student/faculty ratio: 17:1.

ACADEMICS

Calendar: semesters. *Degrees:* bachelor's, master's, doctoral, post-master's, and postbachelor's certificates.

Special study options: accelerated degree program, adult/continuing education programs, advanced placement credit, cooperative education, distance learning, double majors, English as a second language, honors programs, independent study, internships, off-campus study, part-time degree program, services for LD students, student-designed majors, study abroad, summer session for credit. ***ROTC:*** Army (b), Navy (b), Air Force (b).

Unusual degree programs: 3-2 design/architecture with University of Nebraska–Lincoln, animal science/veterinary science with Iowa State University.

Computers: 425 computers/terminals are available on campus for general student use. Students can access the following: campus intranet, computer help desk, free student e-mail accounts, online (class) grades, online (class) registration, online (class) schedules, Computer repair service, discounted software, discounted hardware. Campuswide network is available. 100% of college-owned or -operated housing units are wired for high-speed Internet access. Wireless service is available via entire campus.

Library: Love Memorial Library plus 7 others. *Books:* 1.8 million (physical), 705,484 (digital/electronic); *Serial titles:* 98,432 (physical), 84,072 (digital/electronic); *Databases:* 475. Weekly public service hours: 130; students can reserve study rooms.

STUDENT LIFE

Housing options: on-campus residence required for freshman year; coed, women-only, cooperative, special housing for students with disabilities. Campus housing is university owned. Freshman campus housing is guaranteed.

Activities and organizations: drama/theater group, student-run newspaper, radio station, choral group, marching band, Student Alumni Association, Mexican American Student Association, University Program Council Nebraska, eSAB (Engineering Student Advisory Board), ASUN (Association of Students of the University of Nebraska, student body government), national fraternities, national sororities.

Athletics Member NCAA. All Division I except football (Division I-A). ***Intercollegiate sports:*** badminton M(c)/W(c), baseball M(s), basketball M(s)/W(s), bowling W(s), cheerleading M/W, cross-country running M(s)/W(s), golf M(s)/W(s), gymnastics M(s)/W(s), riflery W(s), sand volleyball W(s), soccer W(s), softball W(s), swimming and diving W(s), table tennis M/W, tennis M(s)/W(s), track and field M(s)/W(s), ultimate Frisbee M/W, volleyball W(s), wrestling M(s). ***Intramural sports:*** badminton M/W, baseball M(c)/W, basketball M/W, bowling M/W, crew M(c)/W(c), equestrian sports M(c)/W(c), golf M/W, ice hockey M(c)/W(c), lacrosse M(c)/W(c), racquetball M/W, riflery M(c)/W(c), rock climbing M(c)/W(c), rowing M(c)/W(c), rugby M(c), sailing M(c)/W(c), sand volleyball M/W, soccer M(c)/W(c), softball M/W, swimming and diving M(c)/W(c), table tennis M(c)/W(c), tennis M(c)/W(c), track and field M/W, ultimate Frisbee M(c)/W(c), volleyball M/W, water polo M(c)/W(c), weight lifting M(c)/W(c), wrestling M/W.

Campus security: 24-hour emergency response devices and patrols, late-night transport/escort service, controlled dormitory access, emergency notification system, CCTV surveillance, and public weapons storage for students/faculty/staff.

Student services: health clinic, personal/psychological counseling, women's center, legal services, veterans affairs office.

COSTS & FINANCIAL AID

Costs (2019–20) ***Tuition:*** state resident $7560 full-time, $252 per credit hour part-time; nonresident $24,000 full-time, $800 per credit hour part-time. Full-time tuition and fees vary according to course load, location, program, and reciprocity agreements. Part-time tuition and fees vary according to course load, location, program, and reciprocity agreements. ***Required fees:*** $1806 full-time, $17 per credit hour part-time, $398 per term part-time. ***Room and board:*** $11,830. Room and board charges vary according to board plan and housing facility. ***Payment plan:*** installment. ***Waivers:*** employees or children of employees.

Financial Aid Of all full-time matriculated undergraduates who enrolled in 2018, 14,397 applied for aid, 9,059 were judged to have need, 1,471 had their need fully met. In 2018, 1686 non-need-based awards were made. ***Average percent of need met:*** 71. ***Average financial aid package:*** $14,935. ***Average need-based loan:*** $4156. ***Average need-based gift aid:*** $8304. ***Average non-need-based aid:*** $8044. ***Average indebtedness upon graduation:*** $22,290.

APPLYING

Standardized Tests *Required:* SAT or ACT (for admission). *Recommended:* ACT (for admission).

Options: electronic application.

Application fee: $45.

Required: high school transcript, minimum ACT score of 20 or combined total of 1030 or higher on the SAT Evidence-Based Reading and Writing and SAT Math sections or rank in upper 50% of high school class, or a HS GPA of 3.0 or higher.

Application deadlines: 5/1 (freshmen), 5/1 (out-of-state freshmen), 5/1 (transfers).

Notification: continuous (freshmen), continuous (out-of-state freshmen), continuous (transfers).

CONTACT

Ms. Abby Freeman, Director of Admissions, University of Nebraska–Lincoln, 1410 Q Street, Lincoln, NE 68588-0417. *Phone:* 402-472-2023. *Toll-free phone:* 800-742-8800. *Fax:* 402-472-0670. *E-mail:* admissions@unl.edu.

University of Nebraska Medical Center

Omaha, Nebraska

http://www.unmc.edu/

CONTACT
University of Nebraska Medical Center, Nebraska Medical Center, Omaha, NE 68198. *Toll-free phone:* 800-626-8431 Ext. 6468.

Wayne State College

Wayne, Nebraska

http://www.wsc.edu/

- **State-supported** comprehensive, founded 1910, part of Nebraska State College System
- **Small-town** 128-acre campus
- **Endowment** $25.1 million
- **Coed** 3,148 undergraduate students, 84% full-time, 58% women, 42% men
- **Noncompetitive** entrance level, 100% of applicants were admitted

UNDERGRAD STUDENTS
2,635 full-time, 513 part-time. Students come from 30 states and territories; 31 other countries; 16% are from out of state; 3% Black or African American, non-Hispanic/Latino; 10% Hispanic/Latino; 0.8% Asian, non-Hispanic/Latino; 1% American Indian or Alaska Native, non-Hispanic/Latino; 3% Two or more races, non-Hispanic/Latino; 0.8% Race/ethnicity unknown; 3% international; 7% transferred in; 44% live on campus.

Freshmen:
Admission: 2,060 applied, 2,060 admitted, 730 enrolled. ***Average high school GPA:*** 3.3.

Retention: 69% of full-time freshmen returned.

FACULTY
Total: 215, 56% full-time, 57% with terminal degrees.

Student/faculty ratio: 21:1.

ACADEMICS
Calendar: semesters. *Degrees:* bachelor's, master's, and post-master's certificates.

Special study options: adult/continuing education programs, advanced placement credit, cooperative education, distance learning, double majors, honors programs, independent study, internships, off-campus study, part-time degree program, services for LD students, student-designed majors, study abroad, summer session for credit. ***ROTC:*** Army (c).

Computers: 365 computers/terminals are available on campus for general student use. Students can access the following: campus intranet, computer help desk, free student e-mail accounts, online (class) grades, online (class) registration, online (class) schedules. Campuswide network is available. 100% of college-owned or -operated housing units are wired for high-speed Internet access. Wireless service is available via entire campus.

Library: U. S. Conn Library. *Books:* 156,068 (physical), 190,290 (digital/electronic); *Serial titles:* 816 (physical), 43 (digital/electronic); *Databases:* 53.

STUDENT LIFE
Housing options: on-campus residence required for freshman year; coed. Campus housing is university owned. Freshman campus housing is guaranteed.

Activities and organizations: drama/theater group, student-run newspaper, radio and television station, choral group, marching band, national fraternities, national sororities.

Athletics Member NCAA. All Division II. ***Intercollegiate sports:*** baseball M(s), basketball M(s)/W(s), cheerleading M(c)/W(c), cross-country running M(s)/W(s), football M(s), golf W(s), rugby M(c)/W(c), sand volleyball W(s), soccer M(c)/W(s), softball W(s), track and field M(s)/W(s), volleyball W(s), wrestling M(c). ***Intramural sports:*** archery M/W, badminton M/W, basketball M/W, bowling M/W, football M/W, golf M/W, racquetball M/W, softball M/W, swimming and diving M/W, table tennis M/W, tennis M/W, track and field M/W, volleyball M/W, weight lifting M/W, wrestling M.

Campus security: 24-hour emergency response devices and patrols, student patrols, late-night transport/escort service, controlled dormitory access.

Student services: health clinic, personal/psychological counseling.

FINANCIAL AID
Financial Aid Of all full-time matriculated undergraduates who enrolled in 2019, 2,286 applied for aid, 1,798 were judged to have need, 1,146 had their need fully met. In 2019, 107 non-need-based awards were made. ***Average percent of need met:*** 58. ***Average financial aid package:*** $9764. ***Average need-based loan:*** $3763. ***Average need-based gift aid:*** $6095. ***Average non-need-based aid:*** $2984.

APPLYING
Options: electronic application, deferred entrance.

Required: high school transcript.

Application deadlines: rolling (freshmen), rolling (transfers).

Notification: continuous (freshmen), continuous (transfers).

CONTACT
Mr. Kevin Halle, Director of Admissions, Wayne State College, 1111 Main Street, Wayne, NE 68787. *Phone:* 402-375-7234. *Toll-free phone:* 866-WSC-CATS. *Fax:* 402-375-7204. *E-mail:* admit1@wsc.edu.

York College

York, Nebraska

http://www.york.edu/

CONTACT
Ms. Janae Parsons, York College, 1125 East 8th Street, York, NE 68467-2699. *Phone:* 402-363-5627. *Toll-free phone:* 800-950-9675. *Fax:* 402-363-5623. *E-mail:* enroll@york.edu.

NEVADA

Arizona College–Las Vegas

Las Vegas, Nevada

http://www.arizonacollege.edu/

CONTACT
Arizona College–Las Vegas, 2320 South Rancho Drive, Las Vegas, NV 89102.

The Art Institute of Las Vegas

Henderson, Nevada

http://www.artinstitutes.edu/lasvegas/

CONTACT
The Art Institute of Las Vegas, 2350 Corporate Circle Drive, Henderson, NV 89074. *Phone:* 702-369-9944. *Toll-free phone:* 800-833-2678.

Chamberlain College of Nursing - Las Vegas

Las Vegas, Nevada

http://www.chamberlain.edu/

CONTACT
Chamberlain College of Nursing - Las Vegas, 9901 Covington Cross Drive, Las Vegas, NV 89144. *Toll-free phone:* 877-751-5783.

College of Southern Nevada

Las Vegas, Nevada

http://www.csn.edu/

- **State-supported** primarily 2-year, founded 1971, part of University and Community College System of Nevada
- **Suburban** 89-acre campus with easy access to Las Vegas
- **Coed**
- **Noncompetitive** entrance level

ACADEMICS
Calendar: semesters. *Degrees:* certificates, associate, and bachelor's.
Library: Learning Assistance Center.

STUDENT LIFE
Housing options: college housing not available.

Activities and organizations: drama/theater group, student-run newspaper, choral group.

Athletics Member NJCAA.

Campus security: 24-hour emergency response devices and patrols.

Student services: health clinic, personal/psychological counseling, women's center, legal services.

FINANCIAL AID
Financial Aid Of all full-time matriculated undergraduates who enrolled in 2018, 199 Federal Work-Study jobs (averaging $1753). 170 state and other part-time jobs (averaging $2154).

APPLYING
Options: early admission.

Required: student data form.

CONTACT
Admissions and Records, College of Southern Nevada, 6375 West Charleston Boulevard, Las Vegas, NV 89146. *Phone:* 702-651-4060.

DeVry University–Henderson Campus
Henderson, Nevada
http://www.devry.edu/

- **Proprietary** comprehensive
- **Coed**

ACADEMICS
Calendar: semesters. *Degrees:* associate, bachelor's, and master's.

STUDENT LIFE
Housing options: college housing not available.

FINANCIAL AID
Financial Aid Of all full-time matriculated undergraduates who enrolled in 2007, 32 applied for aid, 32 were judged to have need, 1 had their need fully met. ***Average percent of need met:*** 36. ***Average financial aid package:*** $10,877. ***Average need-based loan:*** $8938. ***Average need-based gift aid:*** $5641. ***Average indebtedness upon graduation:*** $62,400.

CONTACT
Admissions Office, DeVry University–Henderson Campus, 2490 Paseo Verde Parkway, Suite 150, Henderson, NV 89074-7120. *Phone:* 702-933-9700. *Toll-free phone:* 866-338-7934.

Great Basin College
Elko, Nevada
http://www.gbcnv.edu/

CONTACT
Ms. Jan King, Director of Admissions and Registrar, Great Basin College, 1500 College Parkway, Elko, NV 89801. *Phone:* 775-753-2102. *E-mail:* jan.king@gbcnv.edu.

Nevada State College
Henderson, Nevada
http://www.nsc.edu/

CONTACT
Adelfa Sullivan, Registrar, Nevada State College, Office of Admissions and Records, 1300 Nevada State Drive, Henderson, NV 89002. *Phone:* 702-992-2115. *Fax:* 702-992-2111. *E-mail:* admissions@nsc.edu.

Pima Medical Institute - Las Vegas
Las Vegas, Nevada
http://www.pmi.edu/

CONTACT
Admissions Office, Pima Medical Institute - Las Vegas, 3333 East Flamingo Road, Las Vegas, NV 89121. *Phone:* 702-458-9650 Ext. 202. *Toll-free phone:* 800-477-PIMA.

Sierra Nevada College
Incline Village, Nevada
http://www.sierranevada.edu/

- **Independent** comprehensive, founded 1969
- **Small-town** 20-acre campus with easy access to Reno
- **Endowment** $4.3 million
- **Coed** 350 undergraduate students, 95% full-time, 48% women, 52% men
- **Moderately difficult** entrance level, 64% of applicants were admitted

UNDERGRAD STUDENTS
331 full-time, 19 part-time. Students come from 28 states and territories; 9 other countries; 75% are from out of state; 4% Black or African American, non-Hispanic/Latino; 2% Hispanic/Latino; 2% Asian, non-Hispanic/Latino; 0.9% Native Hawaiian or other Pacific Islander, non-Hispanic/Latino; 3% American Indian or Alaska Native, non-Hispanic/Latino; 13% Race/ethnicity unknown; 8% transferred in; 39% live on campus.

Freshmen:
Admission: 830 applied, 528 admitted, 59 enrolled. ***Average high school GPA:*** 3.3. ***Test scores:*** SAT evidence-based reading and writing scores over 500: 64%; SAT math scores over 500: 67%; ACT scores over 18: 83%; SAT evidence-based reading and writing scores over 600: 17%; SAT math scores over 600: 10%; ACT scores over 24: 8%.

Retention: 56% of full-time freshmen returned.

FACULTY
Total: 108, 34% full-time, 39% with terminal degrees.

Student/faculty ratio: 13:1.

ACADEMICS
Calendar: semesters. *Degrees:* certificates, diplomas, bachelor's, and master's.

Special study options: academic remediation for entering students, accelerated degree program, adult/continuing education programs, advanced placement credit, cooperative education, distance learning, double majors, English as a second language, external degree program, honors programs, independent study, internships, part-time degree program, services for LD students, student-designed majors, study abroad, summer session for credit.

Unusual degree programs: 3-2 education.

Computers: 50 computers/terminals are available on campus for general student use. Students can access the following: campus intranet, computer help desk, free student e-mail accounts, online (class) grades, online (class) schedules. Campuswide network is available. 100% of college-owned or -operated housing units are wired for high-speed Internet access. Wireless service is available via entire campus.
Library: Prim Library. *Books:* 27,716 (physical), 7,520 (digital/electronic); *Serial titles:* 1,106 (physical); *Databases:* 35. Weekly public service hours: 40.

STUDENT LIFE
Housing options: on-campus residence required through sophomore year; coed, special housing for students with disabilities. Campus housing is university owned. Freshman campus housing is guaranteed.

Activities and organizations: student-run newspaper, choral group, Film Club, International Club, Sustainability Club, Rock Climbing Club, First Generation Club.

Athletics Member NAIA. ***Intercollegiate sports:*** cross-country running M(s)/W(s), golf M(s)/W(s), lacrosse M(s)/W(s), rock climbing M/W, skiing (downhill) M(s)/W(s), soccer M(s)/W(s). ***Intramural sports:*** rock climbing M/W, skiing (downhill) M/W, soccer M/W, softball M/W, volleyball M/W.

Campus security: 24-hour emergency response devices and patrols, student patrols, controlled dormitory access.

Student services: personal/psychological counseling.

COSTS

Costs (2020–21) ***Comprehensive fee:*** $49,333 includes full-time tuition ($34,319), mandatory fees ($1189), and room and board ($13,825). Full-time tuition and fees vary according to course load, degree level, location, program, and reciprocity agreements. Part-time tuition: $1410 per credit hour. Part-time tuition and fees vary according to course load, degree level, location, program, and reciprocity agreements. ***College room only:*** $6946. Room and board charges vary according to board plan. ***Payment plan:*** installment. ***Waivers:*** employees or children of employees.

APPLYING

Standardized Tests *Required:* SAT or ACT (for admission).

Options: electronic application, deferred entrance.

Required: minimum 2.6 GPA. ***Required for some:*** high school transcript. ***Recommended:*** essay or personal statement, interview.

Application deadlines: rolling (freshmen), rolling (transfers).

CONTACT

Ms. Julie Hernandez, Sierra Nevada College, 999 Tahoe Boulevard, Incline Village, NV 89451. *Phone:* 866-412-4636. *Fax:* 775-831-6223. *E-mail:* admissions@sierranevada.edu.

Truckee Meadows Community College

Reno, Nevada

http://www.tmcc.edu/

- **State-supported** primarily 2-year, founded 1971, part of Nevada System of Higher Education
- **Suburban** 63-acre campus
- **Endowment** $11.2 million
- **Coed** 11,316 undergraduate students, 27% full-time, 46% women, 54% men
- **Noncompetitive** entrance level, 100% of applicants were admitted

UNDERGRAD STUDENTS

3,065 full-time, 8,251 part-time. Students come from 27 states and territories; 18 other countries; 6% are from out of state; 3% Black or African American, non-Hispanic/Latino; 33% Hispanic/Latino; 6% Asian, non-Hispanic/Latino; 0.1% Native Hawaiian or other Pacific Islander, non-Hispanic/Latino; 1% American Indian or Alaska Native, non-Hispanic/Latino; 4% Two or more races, non-Hispanic/Latino; 2% Race/ethnicity unknown; 0.3% international; 5% transferred in.

Freshmen:

Admission: 3,265 applied, 3,265 admitted, 1,638 enrolled.

Retention: 66% of full-time freshmen returned.

FACULTY

Total: 640, 26% full-time.

Student/faculty ratio: 19:1.

ACADEMICS

Calendar: semesters. *Degrees:* certificates, associate, and bachelor's.

Special study options: academic remediation for entering students, accelerated degree program, adult/continuing education programs, advanced placement credit, cooperative education, distance learning, double majors, English as a second language, independent study, internships, part-time degree program, services for LD students, summer session for credit. ***ROTC:*** Army (c).

Computers: 1,442 computers/terminals are available on campus for general student use. Students can access the following: computer help desk, free student e-mail accounts, online (class) grades, online (class) registration, online (class) schedules. Campuswide network is available. Wireless service is available via entire campus.

Library: Elizabeth Sturm Library plus 3 others. *Books:* 49,012 (physical); *Serial titles:* 32 (digital/electronic); *Databases:* 93. Weekly public service hours: 143; students can reserve study rooms.

STUDENT LIFE

Housing options: college housing not available.

Activities and organizations: drama/theater group, student-run newspaper, Entrepreneurship Club, International Club, Phi Theta Kappa, Student Government Association, Student Media and Broadcasting Club.

Athletics Member NJCAA. ***Intercollegiate sports:*** soccer M/W.

Campus security: 24-hour emergency response devices and patrols, late-night transport/escort service.

Student services: personal/psychological counseling, veterans affairs office.

COSTS

Costs (2019–20) ***Tuition:*** state resident $2466 full-time, $103 per credit part-time; nonresident $9656 full-time, $113 per credit part-time. Full-time tuition and fees vary according to course level, course load, degree level, and program. Part-time tuition and fees vary according to course level, course load, degree level, and program. ***Required fees:*** $300 full-time, $13 per credit part-time. ***Payment plan:*** installment. ***Waivers:*** employees or children of employees.

APPLYING

Options: electronic application, early admission.

Application fee: $20.

Application deadlines: rolling (freshmen), rolling (transfers).

Notification: continuous (freshmen), continuous (transfers).

CONTACT

Truckee Meadows Community College, 7000 Dandini Boulevard, Reno, NV 89512-3901. *Phone:* 775-673-7240.

University of Nevada, Las Vegas

Las Vegas, Nevada

http://www.unlv.edu/

- **State-supported** university, founded 1957, part of Nevada System of Higher Education
- **Urban** 332-acre campus with easy access to Las Vegas
- **Endowment** $55.4 million
- **Coed** 25,282 undergraduate students, 74% full-time, 56% women, 44% men
- **Moderately difficult** entrance level, 82% of applicants were admitted

UNDERGRAD STUDENTS

18,764 full-time, 6,518 part-time. 12% are from out of state; 8% Black or African American, non-Hispanic/Latino; 30% Hispanic/Latino; 16% Asian, non-Hispanic/Latino; 0.9% Native Hawaiian or other Pacific Islander, non-Hispanic/Latino; 0.3% American Indian or Alaska Native, non-Hispanic/Latino; 11% Two or more races, non-Hispanic/Latino; 0.9% Race/ethnicity unknown; 3% international; 10% transferred in.

Freshmen:

Admission: 11,613 applied, 9,527 admitted, 3,964 enrolled. ***Average high school GPA:*** 3.4.

Retention: 76% of full-time freshmen returned.

FACULTY

Total: 1,820, 55% full-time.

Student/faculty ratio: 21:1.

ACADEMICS

Calendar: semesters. *Degrees:* certificates, bachelor's, master's, doctoral, post-master's, and postbachelor's certificates.

Special study options: academic remediation for entering students, adult/continuing education programs, advanced placement credit, cooperative education, distance learning, double majors, English as a second language, honors programs, independent study, internships, part-time degree program, services for LD students, study abroad, summer session for credit. ***ROTC:*** Army (b), Air Force (b).

Computers: 2,100 computers/terminals and 25,000 ports are available on campus for general student use. Students can access the following: campus intranet, computer help desk, free student e-mail accounts, online (class) grades, online (class) registration, online (class) schedules. Campuswide network is available. 100% of college-owned or -operated housing units are wired for high-speed Internet access. Wireless service is available via entire campus.

Library: Lied Library plus 4 others. Weekly public service hours: 101; students can reserve study rooms.

STUDENT LIFE
Housing options: coed, special housing for students with disabilities. Campus housing is university owned. Freshman applicants given priority for college housing.

Activities and organizations: drama/theater group, student-run newspaper, radio and television station, choral group, marching band, Social Fraternities and Sororities, Psychology Club, Honors Student Council, Association of Pre-Health Professionals, UNLV Student Nurses Association, national fraternities, national sororities.

Athletics ***Intercollegiate sports:*** baseball M(s), basketball M(s)/W(s), cheerleading M(s)/W(s), cross-country running W(s), golf M(s)/W(s), soccer M(s)/W(s), softball W(s), swimming and diving M(s)/W(s), tennis M(s)/W(s), track and field W(s), volleyball W(s). ***Intramural sports:*** badminton M/W, basketball M/W, bowling M/W, football M/W, golf M/W, ice hockey M(c), lacrosse M(c)/W(c), racquetball M/W, soccer M/W, softball M/W, swimming and diving M/W, tennis M/W, volleyball M/W, wrestling M(c).

Campus security: 24-hour emergency response devices and patrols, late-night transport/escort service, controlled dormitory access.

Student services: health clinic, personal/psychological counseling, women's center, legal services, veterans affairs office.

COSTS & FINANCIAL AID
Costs (2020–21) ***One-time required fee:*** $120. ***Tuition:*** state resident $7268 full-time, $242 per credit hour part-time; nonresident $22,920 full-time, $509 per credit hour part-time. Full-time tuition and fees vary according to course level, program, and reciprocity agreements. Part-time tuition and fees vary according to course level, program, and reciprocity agreements. ***Required fees:*** $718 full-time, $16 per credit hour part-time, $361 per term part-time. ***Room and board:*** $10,924; room only: $5892. Room and board charges vary according to board plan and housing facility. ***Payment plans:*** installment, deferred payment. ***Waivers:*** employees or children of employees.

Financial Aid Of all full-time matriculated undergraduates who enrolled in 2017, 14,430 applied for aid, 11,747 were judged to have need, 1,867 had their need fully met. In 2017, 1481 non-need-based awards were made. ***Average percent of need met:*** 67. ***Average financial aid package:*** $8852. ***Average need-based loan:*** $4189. ***Average need-based gift aid:*** $6697. ***Average non-need-based aid:*** $4158. ***Average indebtedness upon graduation:*** $21,333.

APPLYING
Standardized Tests *Required:* SAT or ACT (for admission).

Options: electronic application, early admission, deferred entrance.

Application fee: $60.

Required: high school transcript, minimum 3.0 GPA.

Notification: continuous (freshmen), continuous (transfers).

CONTACT
Kristine Shay, Executive Director of Undergraduate Admissions, University of Nevada, Las Vegas, 4505 S. Maryland Parkway, Box 451021, Las Vegas, NV 89154-1021. *Phone:* 702-774-2922. *E-mail:* kristine.shay@unlv.edu.

University of Nevada, Reno

Reno, Nevada

http://www.unr.edu/

- **State-supported** university, founded 1874, part of Nevada System of Higher Education
- **Urban** 200-acre campus
- **Endowment** $377.4 million
- **Coed** 17,307 undergraduate students, 85% full-time, 53% women, 47% men
- **Moderately difficult** entrance level, 86% of applicants were admitted

UNDERGRAD STUDENTS
14,788 full-time, 2,519 part-time. Students come from 42 states and territories; 39 other countries; 26% are from out of state; 3% Black or African American, non-Hispanic/Latino; 22% Hispanic/Latino; 8% Asian, non-Hispanic/Latino; 0.5% Native Hawaiian or other Pacific Islander, non-Hispanic/Latino; 0.7% American Indian or Alaska Native, non-Hispanic/Latino; 7% Two or more races, non-Hispanic/Latino; 2% Race/ethnicity unknown; 0.8% international; 6% transferred in; 16% live on campus.

Freshmen:
Admission: 11,043 applied, 9,483 admitted, 3,144 enrolled. ***Average high school GPA:*** 3.4. ***Test scores:*** SAT evidence-based reading and writing scores over 500: 90%; SAT math scores over 500: 90%; ACT scores over 18: 92%; SAT evidence-based reading and writing scores over 600: 46%; SAT math scores over 600: 46%; ACT scores over 24: 47%; SAT evidence-based reading and writing scores over 700: 7%; SAT math scores over 700: 11%; ACT scores over 30: 11%.

Retention: 81% of full-time freshmen returned.

FACULTY
Total: 1,318, 59% full-time, 60% with terminal degrees.

Student/faculty ratio: 18:1.

ACADEMICS
Calendar: semesters. *Degrees:* certificates, bachelor's, master's, doctoral, post-master's, and postbachelor's certificates.

Special study options: academic remediation for entering students, adult/continuing education programs, advanced placement credit, distance learning, double majors, English as a second language, honors programs, independent study, internships, off-campus study, part-time degree program, services for LD students, study abroad, summer session for credit. ***ROTC:*** Army (b).

Computers: Students can access the following: computer help desk, free student e-mail accounts, online (class) grades, online (class) registration, online (class) schedules. Campuswide network is available. 100% of college-owned or -operated housing units are wired for high-speed Internet access. Wireless service is available via entire campus.
Library: Mathewson-IGT Knowledge Center plus 2 others. *Books:* 902,306 (physical), 1.4 million (digital/electronic); *Serial titles:* 29,721 (physical), 126,333 (digital/electronic); *Databases:* 380. Students can reserve study rooms.

STUDENT LIFE
Housing options: coed, special housing for students with disabilities. Campus housing is university owned. Freshman applicants given priority for college housing.

Activities and organizations: drama/theater group, student-run newspaper, radio station, choral group, marching band, Intervarsity Christian Fellowship, Student Ambassadors, Young Democrats, Asian American Association, Blue Crew, national fraternities, national sororities.

Athletics Member NCAA. All Division I except football (Division I-A). ***Intercollegiate sports:*** baseball M(s), basketball M(s)/W(s), cheerleading M(c)/W(c), cross-country running W(s), golf M(s)/W(s)(c), riflery M(s)/W(s), soccer W(s), softball W(s), swimming and diving W(s), tennis M(s)/W(s), track and field W(s), volleyball W(s). ***Intramural sports:*** basketball M/W, bowling M/W, cross-country running M/W, equestrian sports M/W, football M, golf M/W, racquetball M/W, rock climbing M/W, rugby M/W, skiing (cross-country) M/W, skiing (downhill) M/W, soccer M/W, softball M/W, swimming and diving M/W, table tennis M/W, tennis M/W, track and field M/W, ultimate Frisbee M/W, volleyball M/W, water polo M/W.

Campus security: 24-hour emergency response devices and patrols, late-night transport/escort service, controlled dormitory access.

Student services: health clinic, personal/psychological counseling, women's center, legal services, veterans affairs office.

COSTS & FINANCIAL AID
Costs (2020–21) ***Tuition:*** state resident $7688 full-time, $256 per credit hour part-time; nonresident $23,341 full-time, $780 per credit hour part-time. Full-time tuition and fees vary according to course level, course load, degree level, and program. Part-time tuition and fees vary according to course level, course load, degree level, and program. ***Required fees:*** $764 full-time, $282 per term part-time. ***Room and board:*** $10,686; room only: $6100. Room and board charges vary according to board plan and housing facility. ***Payment plan:*** installment. ***Waivers:*** senior citizens and employees or children of employees.

Financial Aid Of all full-time matriculated undergraduates who enrolled in 2018, 10,036 applied for aid, 7,690 were judged to have need, 860 had their need fully met. In 2018, 1676 non-need-based awards were made. ***Average percent of need met:*** 55. ***Average financial aid package:*** $9500.

Average need-based loan: $4155. *Average need-based gift aid:* $7750. *Average non-need-based aid:* $3310. *Average indebtedness upon graduation:* $22,418.

APPLYING
Standardized Tests *Required:* SAT or ACT (for admission).

Options: electronic application, early admission, early action, deferred entrance.

Application fee: $60.

Required: high school transcript, minimum 3.0 GPA.

Notification: continuous (freshmen), continuous (out-of-state freshmen), continuous (transfers), rolling (early action).

CONTACT
Dr. Steve Maples, Director of Undergraduate Admissions, University of Nevada, Reno, Mail Stop 120, Reno, NV 89557. *Phone:* 775-784-4700. *Toll-free phone:* 866-263-8232. *Fax:* 775-784-4283. *E-mail:* asknevada@unr.edu.

University of Phoenix–Las Vegas Campus

Las Vegas, Nevada

http://www.phoenix.edu/

CONTACT
Marc Booker, Senior Director, Office of Admissions and Evaluation, University of Phoenix–Las Vegas Campus, 4305 South Riverpoint Parkway, Mail Stop CF-L101, Phoenix, AZ 85040. *Phone:* 602-557-4609. *Toll-free phone:* 866-766-0766. *Fax:* 480-643-1156.

Western Nevada College

Carson City, Nevada

http://www.wnc.edu/

- **State-supported** primarily 2-year, founded 1971, part of Nevada System of Higher Education
- **Small-town** 200-acre campus
- **Endowment** $250,000
- **Coed** 3,702 undergraduate students, 33% full-time, 58% women, 42% men
- **Noncompetitive** entrance level, 100% of applicants were admitted

UNDERGRAD STUDENTS
1,227 full-time, 2,475 part-time. Students come from 10 states and territories; 20 other countries; 4% are from out of state; 2% Black or African American, non-Hispanic/Latino; 25% Hispanic/Latino; 2% Asian, non-Hispanic/Latino; 0.3% Native Hawaiian or other Pacific Islander, non-Hispanic/Latino; 2% American Indian or Alaska Native, non-Hispanic/Latino; 4% Two or more races, non-Hispanic/Latino; 6% Race/ethnicity unknown; 5% transferred in.

Freshmen:
Admission: 612 applied, 612 admitted, 613 enrolled.

FACULTY
Total: 246, 22% full-time.

Student/faculty ratio: 18:1.

ACADEMICS
Calendar: semesters. *Degrees:* certificates, associate, and bachelor's.

Special study options: academic remediation for entering students, adult/continuing education programs, advanced placement credit, cooperative education, distance learning, double majors, English as a second language, independent study, internships, part-time degree program, services for LD students, summer session for credit.

Computers: 669 computers/terminals and 25 ports are available on campus for general student use. Students can access the following: computer help desk, online (class) grades, online (class) registration, online (class) schedules. Campuswide network is available. Wireless service is available via entire campus.

Library: Western Nevada College Library and Media Services plus 1 other. *Books:* 35,923 (physical), 4,544 (digital/electronic); *Serial titles:* 2,725 (physical); *Databases:* 33. Weekly public service hours: 61; students can reserve study rooms.

STUDENT LIFE
Housing options: college housing not available.

Activities and organizations: drama/theater group, choral group, Associated Students of Western Nevada, Soccer Club, Veterans Club, National Student Nurses Association, American Sign Language Club.

Athletics ***Intramural sports:*** soccer M(c)/W(c).

Campus security: late-night transport/escort service.

Student services: personal/psychological counseling, veterans affairs office.

COSTS & FINANCIAL AID
Costs (2019–20) ***Tuition:*** state resident $3428 full-time; nonresident $10,618 full-time. Full-time tuition and fees vary according to course level. Part-time tuition and fees vary according to course level. ***Payment plans:*** tuition prepayment, installment. ***Waivers:*** employees or children of employees.

Financial Aid Of all full-time matriculated undergraduates who enrolled in 2017, 412 applied for aid, 386 were judged to have need, 21 had their need fully met. In 2017, 41 non-need-based awards were made. ***Average financial aid package:*** $2460. ***Average need-based loan:*** $3302. ***Average need-based gift aid:*** $2681.

APPLYING
Options: electronic application, early admission.

Application fee: $15.

Required for some: high school transcript. ***Recommended:*** high school transcript.

Application deadlines: rolling (freshmen), rolling (out-of-state freshmen), rolling (transfers).

Notification: continuous (freshmen), continuous (out-of-state freshmen), continuous (transfers).

CONTACT
Admissions and Records, Western Nevada College, 2201 West College Parkway, Carson City, NV 89703. *Phone:* 775-445-2377. *Fax:* 775-445-3147. *E-mail:* wncc_aro@wncc.edu.

NEW HAMPSHIRE

Colby-Sawyer College

New London, New Hampshire

http://www.colby-sawyer.edu/

- **Independent** 4-year, founded 1837
- **Small-town** 200-acre campus
- **Endowment** $36.0 million
- **Coed** 851 undergraduate students, 94% full-time, 71% women, 29% men
- **Moderately difficult** entrance level, 90% of applicants were admitted

UNDERGRAD STUDENTS
803 full-time, 48 part-time. Students come from 33 states and territories; 8 other countries; 60% are from out of state; 5% Black or African American, non-Hispanic/Latino; 2% Hispanic/Latino; 3% Asian, non-Hispanic/Latino; 0.9% American Indian or Alaska Native, non-Hispanic/Latino; 9% Race/ethnicity unknown; 2% international; 9% transferred in; 87% live on campus.

Freshmen:
Admission: 2,676 applied, 2,398 admitted, 264 enrolled.
Retention: 167% of full-time freshmen returned.

FACULTY
Total: 98, 53% full-time, 50% with terminal degrees.

Student/faculty ratio: 14:1.

ACADEMICS
Calendar: semesters. *Degrees:* certificates, associate, and bachelor's.

Special study options: accelerated degree program, adult/continuing education programs, advanced placement credit, distance learning, double majors, honors programs, independent study, internships, off-campus study, part-time degree program, services for LD students, student-designed majors, study abroad, summer session for credit. ***ROTC:*** Army (c), Air Force (c).

Unusual degree programs: 3-2 business administration; nursing; social work; law with Vermont Law School.

Computers: 180 computers/terminals and 1,200 ports are available on campus for general student use. Students can access the following: campus intranet, computer help desk, free student e-mail accounts, online (class) grades, online (class) registration, online (class) schedules, online bill payment, SmartCard (for use on campus and with selected local vendors), learning management systems, tutoring, reference librarians via chat, e-databases/e-journals, disk storage space. Campuswide network is available. 100% of college-owned or -operated housing units are wired for high-speed Internet access. Wireless service is available via entire campus.

Library: Susan Colgate Cleveland Library Learning Center. *Books:* 83,409 (physical), 144,473 (digital/electronic); *Serial titles:* 486 (physical); *Databases:* 119. Weekly public service hours: 100; students can reserve study rooms.

STUDENT LIFE

Housing options: on-campus residence required through sophomore year; coed, women-only. Campus housing is university owned. Freshman campus housing is guaranteed.

Activities and organizations: drama/theater group, student-run newspaper, choral group, Campus Activities Board, Student Government Association, Dance Club, Colby-Sawyer Players (Theater), Student Nurses Association.

Athletics Member NCAA. All Division III. ***Intercollegiate sports:*** baseball M, basketball M/W, cross-country running M/W, equestrian sports M/W, field hockey W, golf M(c)/W(c), ice hockey M(c)/W(c), lacrosse W, rugby M(c)/W(c), skiing (downhill) M/W, soccer M/W, softball W(c), swimming and diving M/W, tennis M/W, track and field M/W, volleyball W. ***Intramural sports:*** basketball M/W, cheerleading W(c), football M/W, golf M/W, lacrosse M(c), racquetball M/W, volleyball M/W.

Campus security: 24-hour emergency response devices and patrols, late-night transport/escort service, controlled dormitory access, awareness seminars.

Student services: health clinic, personal/psychological counseling.

COSTS & FINANCIAL AID

Costs (2020–21) ***Comprehensive fee:*** $60,358 includes full-time tuition ($44,130), mandatory fees ($800), and room and board ($15,428). Part-time tuition: $1471 per credit hour. ***Required fees:*** $10 per credit part-time. ***Payment plan:*** installment. ***Waivers:*** employees or children of employees.

Financial Aid Of all full-time matriculated undergraduates who enrolled in 2019, 646 applied for aid, 598 were judged to have need, 147 had their need fully met. In 2019, 135 non-need-based awards were made. ***Average percent of need met:*** 84. ***Average financial aid package:*** $37,574. ***Average need-based loan:*** $3763. ***Average need-based gift aid:*** $33,305. ***Average non-need-based aid:*** $28,330. ***Average indebtedness upon graduation:*** $40,767. ***Financial aid deadline:*** 3/1.

APPLYING

Options: electronic application, early admission, early action, deferred entrance.

Application fee: $45.

Required: essay or personal statement, high school transcript, minimum 2.5 GPA, college preparatory courses: 4 years of English, 3 years of math, 3 years of lab science, 3 years of social science and 2 years of the same language. ***Recommended:*** 1 letter of recommendation, interview.

Application deadlines: 4/1 (freshmen), 8/1 (transfers), 12/1 (early action).

Notification: continuous until 1/1 (freshmen), continuous until 1/1 (transfers).

CONTACT

Ms. Jaimee Hofstetter, Director of Enrollment Operations, Colby-Sawyer College, 541 Main Street, New London, NH 03257-4648. *Phone:* 603-526-3887. *Toll-free phone:* 800-272-1015. *Fax:* 603-526-3452. *E-mail:* admissions@colby-sawyer.edu.

Dartmouth College

Hanover, New Hampshire

http://www.dartmouth.edu/

- **Independent** university, founded 1769
- **Small-town** 269-acre campus
- **Endowment** $5.7 billion
- **Coed** 4,459 undergraduate students, 99% full-time, 49% women, 51% men
- **Most difficult** entrance level, 8% of applicants were admitted

UNDERGRAD STUDENTS

4,401 full-time, 58 part-time. Students come from 45 states and territories; 96 other countries; 97% are from out of state; 6% Black or African American, non-Hispanic/Latino; 11% Hispanic/Latino; 15% Asian, non-Hispanic/Latino; 0.2% Native Hawaiian or other Pacific Islander, non-Hispanic/Latino; 1% American Indian or Alaska Native, non-Hispanic/Latino; 6% Two or more races, non-Hispanic/Latino; 1% Race/ethnicity unknown; 10% international; 0.2% transferred in; 85% live on campus.

Freshmen:

Admission: 23,650 applied, 1,875 admitted, 1,190 enrolled. ***Test scores:*** SAT evidence-based reading and writing scores over 500: 100%; SAT math scores over 500: 100%; ACT scores over 18: 100%; SAT evidence-based reading and writing scores over 600: 98%; SAT math scores over 600: 99%; ACT scores over 24: 98%; SAT evidence-based reading and writing scores over 700: 79%; SAT math scores over 700: 85%; ACT scores over 30: 84%.

Retention: 97% of full-time freshmen returned.

FACULTY

Total: 791, 78% full-time, 92% with terminal degrees.

Student/faculty ratio: 7:1.

ACADEMICS

Calendar: quarters. *Degrees:* bachelor's, master's, and doctoral.

Special study options: advanced placement credit, double majors, honors programs, independent study, internships, off-campus study, services for LD students, student-designed majors, study abroad, summer session for credit. ***ROTC:*** Army (c).

Unusual degree programs: 3-2 engineering.

Computers: 105 computers/terminals are available on campus for general student use. Students can access the following: campus intranet, computer help desk, free student e-mail accounts, online (class) grades, online (class) registration, online (class) schedules. Campuswide network is available. 100% of college-owned or -operated housing units are wired for high-speed Internet access. Wireless service is available via entire campus.

Library: Baker-Berry Library plus 8 others. *Books:* 2.2 million (physical), 1.1 million (digital/electronic); *Serial titles:* 43,919 (physical). Study areas open 24 hours, 5–7 days a week; students can reserve study rooms.

STUDENT LIFE

Housing options: on-campus residence required for freshman year; coed, cooperative. Campus housing is university owned. Freshman campus housing is guaranteed.

Activities and organizations: drama/theater group, student-run newspaper, radio and television station, choral group, marching band, Dartmouth Student Assembly, Dartmouth Outing Club, Collis After Dark, Green Key Society, GLOS - Greek Letter Organizations and Societies, national fraternities, national sororities.

Athletics Member NCAA. All Division I except football (Division I-AA). ***Intercollegiate sports:*** badminton M(c)/W(c), baseball M, basketball M/W, cheerleading M(c)/W(c), crew M/W, cross-country running M/W, equestrian sports M/W, fencing M(c)/W(c), field hockey W, golf M/W, gymnastics M(c)/W(c), ice hockey M/W, lacrosse M/W, rowing M/W, rugby M(c)/W, sailing M/W, skiing (cross-country) M/W, skiing (downhill) M(c)/W, soccer M/W, softball W, squash M/W, swimming and diving M/W, table tennis M(c)/W(c), tennis M/W, track and field M/W, ultimate Frisbee M(c)/W(c), volleyball M(c)/W, water polo M(c)/W(c), wrestling M(c). ***Intramural sports:*** baseball M, basketball M/W, cross-country running M/W, football M/W, golf M/W, ice hockey M/W, lacrosse M/W, rugby M/W, skiing (cross-country) M/W, skiing (downhill) M/W, soccer M/W, softball M/W, squash M/W, swimming and diving M/W, table tennis M/W, tennis M/W, track and field M/W, volleyball M/W, water polo M/W, weight lifting M/W, wrestling M.

Campus security: 24-hour emergency response devices and patrols, late-night transport/escort service, controlled dormitory access.

Student services: health clinic, personal/psychological counseling, women's center.

COSTS & FINANCIAL AID

Costs (2019–20) ***One-time required fee:*** $418. ***Comprehensive fee:*** $73,578 includes full-time tuition ($55,605), mandatory fees ($1599), and room and board ($16,374). ***College room only:*** $9879. Room and board charges vary according to board plan. ***Payment plans:*** tuition prepayment, installment.

Financial Aid Of all full-time matriculated undergraduates who enrolled in 2018, 2,503 applied for aid, 2,215 were judged to have need, 2,215 had their need fully met. 1,381 Federal Work-Study jobs (averaging $2234). 598 state and other part-time jobs (averaging $2477). ***Average percent of need met:*** 100. ***Average financial aid package:*** $52,357. ***Average need-based loan:*** $4036. ***Average need-based gift aid:*** $51,118. ***Average indebtedness upon graduation:*** $18,903. ***Financial aid deadline:*** 2/1.

APPLYING

Standardized Tests *Required:* SAT or ACT (for admission), SAT and SAT Subject Tests or ACT (for admission).

Options: electronic application, early admission, early decision, deferred entrance.

Application fee: $80.

Required: essay or personal statement, high school transcript, 3 letters of recommendation, peer evaluation. ***Recommended:*** interview.

Application deadlines: 1/2 (freshmen), 3/1 (transfers).

Early decision deadline: 11/1.

Notification: 4/1 (freshmen), 5/15 (transfers), 12/15 (early decision).

CONTACT

Paul Sunde, Director of Admissions, Dartmouth College, 6016 McNutt Hall, Hanover, NH 03755. *Phone:* 603-646-2875. *E-mail:* admissions.reply@dartmouth.edu.

Franklin Pierce University

Rindge, New Hampshire

http://www.franklinpierce.edu/

- **Independent** comprehensive, founded 1962
- **Rural** 1200-acre campus
- **Endowment** $13.2 million
- **Coed**
- **Minimally difficult** entrance level

FACULTY

Student/faculty ratio: 13:1.

ACADEMICS

Calendar: differs by branch and program. *Degrees:* certificates, associate, bachelor's, master's, doctoral, and postbachelor's certificates (profile does not reflect significant enrollment at 6 continuing education sites; master's degree is only offered at these sites).

Library: Frank S. DiPietro Library plus 1 other. *Books:* 105,736 (physical), 246,080 (digital/electronic); *Serial titles:* 72 (physical), 70,000 (digital/electronic); *Databases:* 70. Weekly public service hours: 95.

STUDENT LIFE

Housing options: on-campus residence required for freshman year; coed. Campus housing is university owned. Freshman campus housing is guaranteed.

Activities and organizations: drama/theater group, student-run newspaper, radio and television station, choral group, Peer Leadership, Health Sciences Club, Student Government, Honors Program, Hope Happens Here.

Athletics Member NCAA. All Division II.

Campus security: 24-hour emergency response devices and patrols, student patrols, late-night transport/escort service, controlled dormitory access.

Student services: health clinic, personal/psychological counseling, veterans affairs office.

COSTS & FINANCIAL AID

Costs (2019–20) ***Comprehensive fee:*** $52,100 includes full-time tuition ($34,900), mandatory fees ($3300), and room and board ($13,900). Part-time tuition: $1197 per credit hour. ***College room only:*** $8100.

Financial Aid Of all full-time matriculated undergraduates who enrolled in 2018, 1,196 applied for aid, 1,076 were judged to have need, 261 had their need fully met. In 2018, 298 non-need-based awards were made. ***Average percent of need met:*** 72. ***Average financial aid package:*** $26,363. ***Average need-based loan:*** $4038. ***Average need-based gift aid:*** $23,014. ***Average non-need-based aid:*** $12,148. ***Average indebtedness upon graduation:*** $41,661.

APPLYING

Standardized Tests *Required for some:* SAT or ACT (for admission).

Options: electronic application, early admission, deferred entrance.

Application fee: $40.

Required: essay or personal statement, high school transcript, 1 letter of recommendation. ***Required for some:*** minimum 2.0 GPA. ***Recommended:*** minimum 2.2 GPA, interview.

CONTACT

Ms. Linda Quimby, Vice President for Enrollment, Franklin Pierce University, 40 University Drive, Rindge, NH 03461-0060. *Phone:* 603-899-4050. *Toll-free phone:* 800-437-0048. *E-mail:* admissions@fpc.edu.

Granite State College

Concord, New Hampshire

http://www.granite.edu/

- **State and locally supported** comprehensive, founded 1972, part of University System of New Hampshire
- **Suburban** campus
- **Endowment** $8.0 million
- **Coed** 1,729 undergraduate students, 48% full-time, 69% women, 31% men
- **Noncompetitive** entrance level, 100% of applicants were admitted

UNDERGRAD STUDENTS

827 full-time, 902 part-time. Students come from 48 states and territories; 1 other country; 21% are from out of state; 4% Black or African American, non-Hispanic/Latino; 5% Hispanic/Latino; 1% Asian, non-Hispanic/Latino; 0.3% Native Hawaiian or other Pacific Islander, non-Hispanic/Latino; 0.3% American Indian or Alaska Native, non-Hispanic/Latino; 2% Two or more races, non-Hispanic/Latino; 5% Race/ethnicity unknown; 23% transferred in.

Freshmen:

Admission: 263 applied, 263 admitted, 79 enrolled.

Retention: 48% of full-time freshmen returned.

FACULTY

Total: 182, 7% full-time, 22% with terminal degrees.

Student/faculty ratio: 17:1.

ACADEMICS

Calendar: trimesters. *Degrees:* associate, bachelor's, master's, and postbachelor's certificates (offers primarily part-time degree programs; courses offered at 50 locations in New Hampshire).

Special study options: academic remediation for entering students, accelerated degree program, adult/continuing education programs, advanced placement credit, cooperative education, distance learning, double majors, independent study, internships, off-campus study, part-time degree program, services for LD students, student-designed majors, summer session for credit.

Computers: 120 computers/terminals are available on campus for general student use. Students can access the following: campus intranet, computer help desk, free student e-mail accounts, online (class) grades, online (class) registration, online (class) schedules. Campuswide network is available. Wireless service is available via entire campus.

Library: GSC Library and Information Commons. *Books:* 400,000 (digital/electronic); *Serial titles:* 900 (digital/electronic); *Databases:* 22. Weekly public service hours: 160.

STUDENT LIFE
Activities and organizations: Alumni Advisory Board, Student Advisory Board.

Student services: personal/psychological counseling.

COSTS
Costs (2020–21) ***Tuition:*** area resident $7536 full-time, $314 per credit part-time; state resident $7536 full-time, $314 per credit part-time; nonresident $8760 full-time, $365 per credit part-time. ***Required fees:*** $225 full-time, $255 per term part-time. ***Payment plans:*** installment, deferred payment. ***Waivers:*** senior citizens and employees or children of employees.

APPLYING
Options: electronic application.

Required for some: high school transcript, associate degree for some BS programs.

Application deadlines: rolling (freshmen), rolling (transfers).

Notification: continuous (freshmen), continuous (transfers).

CONTACT
Ms. Christine Williams, Assistant Vice President of Enrollment Operations, Granite State College, 25 Hall Street, Concord, NH 03301. *Phone:* 603-228-3000. *Toll-free phone:* 888-228-3000. *Fax:* 603-513-1386. *E-mail:* gsc.admissions@granite.edu.

Hellenic American University
Nashua, New Hampshire
http://www.hauniv.edu/

CONTACT
Hellenic American University, 505 Amherst Street, Nashua, NH 03063.

Keene State College
Keene, New Hampshire
http://www.keene.edu/

- **State-supported** comprehensive, founded 1909, part of University System of New Hampshire
- **Small-town** 150-acre campus
- **Coed**
- **Moderately difficult** entrance level

ACADEMICS
Calendar: semesters. *Degrees:* certificates, bachelor's, master's, post-master's, and postbachelor's certificates.
Library: Mason Library. *Books:* 247,720 (physical), 319,081 (digital/electronic); *Serial titles:* 142 (physical), 73,114 (digital/electronic); *Databases:* 92. Weekly public service hours: 102; students can reserve study rooms.

STUDENT LIFE
Housing options: on-campus residence required through sophomore year; coed, women-only. Campus housing is university owned. Freshman campus housing is guaranteed.

Activities and organizations: drama/theater group, student-run newspaper, radio and television station, choral group, Environmental Outing Club, Social Activities Council, Student Government, Chock Full O Notes, The Equinox student newspaper, national fraternities, national sororities.

Athletics Member NCAA. All Division III.

Campus security: 24-hour emergency response devices and patrols, late-night transport/escort service, controlled dormitory access, Emergency Notification System.

Student services: health clinic, personal/psychological counseling, women's center, veterans affairs office.

COSTS & FINANCIAL AID
Costs (2019–20) ***Tuition:*** state resident $11,754 full-time, $490 per credit part-time; nonresident $20,942 full-time, $874 per credit part-time. Part-time tuition and fees vary according to course load. ***Required fees:*** $2814 full-time, $114 per credit part-time. ***Room and board:*** $11,560. Room and board charges vary according to board plan and housing facility.

Financial Aid Of all full-time matriculated undergraduates who enrolled in 2018, 2,893 applied for aid, 2,324 were judged to have need, 354 had their need fully met. 985 Federal Work-Study jobs (averaging $2326). 466 state and other part-time jobs (averaging $1303). In 2018, 680 non-need-based awards were made. ***Average percent of need met:*** 68. ***Average financial aid package:*** $13,647. ***Average need-based loan:*** $4158. ***Average need-based gift aid:*** $6803. ***Average non-need-based aid:*** $5774. ***Average indebtedness upon graduation:*** $40,125.

APPLYING
Options: electronic application, deferred entrance.

Application fee: $50.

Required: essay or personal statement, high school transcript. ***Recommended:*** 1 letter of recommendation.

CONTACT
Ms. Peggy Richmond, Director of Admissions, Keene State College, 229 Main Street, Keene, NH 03435-2604. *Phone:* 603-358-2273. *Toll-free phone:* 800-KSC-1909. *Fax:* 603-358-2767. *E-mail:* mrichmon@keene.edu.

Magdalen College of the Liberal Arts
Warner, New Hampshire
http://www.magdalen.edu/

CONTACT
Admissions Director, Magdalen College of the Liberal Arts, 511 Kearsarge Mountain Road, Warner, NH 03278. *Phone:* 603-456-2656. *Toll-free phone:* 877-498-1723. *Fax:* 603-456-2660. *E-mail:* admissions@magdalen.edu.

New England College
Henniker, New Hampshire
http://www.nec.edu/

- **Independent** comprehensive, founded 1946
- **Small-town** 225-acre campus with easy access to Boston
- **Endowment** $11.9 million
- **Coed** 1,869 undergraduate students, 97% full-time, 59% women, 41% men
- **Minimally difficult** entrance level, 100% of applicants were admitted

UNDERGRAD STUDENTS
1,820 full-time, 49 part-time. Students come from 52 states and territories; 5 other countries; 54% are from out of state; 20% Black or African American, non-Hispanic/Latino; 10% Hispanic/Latino; 1% Asian, non-Hispanic/Latino; 0.2% Native Hawaiian or other Pacific Islander, non-Hispanic/Latino; 0.4% American Indian or Alaska Native, non-Hispanic/Latino; 4% Two or more races, non-Hispanic/Latino; 13% Race/ethnicity unknown; 3% international; 10% transferred in; 41% live on campus.

Freshmen:

Admission: 10,183 applied, 10,179 admitted, 483 enrolled. ***Average high school GPA:*** 2.6.

Retention: 59% of full-time freshmen returned.

FACULTY
Total: 328, 19% full-time, 51% with terminal degrees.

Student/faculty ratio: 15:1.

ACADEMICS
Calendar: semesters for residential undergraduates; 7-week terms for online undergraduate and graduate programs. *Degrees:* associate, bachelor's, master's, doctoral, and postbachelor's certificates.

Special study options: academic remediation for entering students, accelerated degree program, adult/continuing education programs, advanced placement credit, distance learning, double majors, English as a second language, external degree program, freshman honors college, honors programs, independent study, internships, off-campus study, part-time degree program, services for LD students, student-designed majors, study abroad, summer session for credit. ***ROTC:*** Army (c), Air Force (c).

Computers: 212 computers/terminals and 350 ports are available on campus for general student use. Students can access the following: campus intranet, computer help desk, free student e-mail accounts, online (class) grades, online (class) registration, online (class) schedules, financial aid, billing, advising, degree audit. Campuswide network is available. 100% of college-owned or -operated housing units are wired for high-speed Internet access. Wireless service is available via entire campus.

Library: Danforth Library plus 1 other. *Books:* 116,235 (physical), 208,126 (digital/electronic); *Serial titles:* 75 (physical); *Databases:* 50. Weekly public service hours: 126; study areas open 24 hours, 5–7 days a week; students can reserve study rooms.

STUDENT LIFE

Housing options: on-campus residence required through junior year; coed. Campus housing is university owned. Freshman campus housing is guaranteed.

Activities and organizations: drama/theater group, student-run newspaper, radio station, Student Senate, Campus Activities Board, Criminal Justice Club, International Student Association, Political Science Club.

Athletics Member NCAA. All Division III. ***Intercollegiate sports:*** baseball M, basketball M/W, cross-country running M/W, field hockey W, ice hockey M/W, lacrosse M/W, rugby M(c)/W(c), skiing (downhill) M/W, soccer M/W, softball W, volleyball W, wrestling M. ***Intramural sports:*** basketball M/W, cheerleading W, golf M/W, ice hockey M/W, lacrosse M/W, soccer M/W, softball W, table tennis M/W, tennis M/W, ultimate Frisbee M/W, volleyball M/W.

Campus security: 24-hour emergency response devices and patrols, student patrols, late-night transport/escort service, controlled dormitory access, emergency text system.

Student services: health clinic, personal/psychological counseling, women's center, veterans affairs office.

COSTS & FINANCIAL AID

Costs (2020–21) ***Comprehensive fee:*** $51,660 includes full-time tuition ($37,490) and room and board ($14,170). Full-time tuition and fees vary according to location. Part-time tuition: $450 per credit hour. Part-time tuition and fees vary according to location. ***Required fees:*** $214 per term part-time. ***College room only:*** $7610. Room and board charges vary according to board plan, housing facility, and location. ***Payment plan:*** installment. ***Waivers:*** children of alumni, adult students, and employees or children of employees.

Financial Aid Of all full-time matriculated undergraduates who enrolled in 2018, 1,546 applied for aid, 1,485 were judged to have need, 97 had their need fully met. 397 Federal Work-Study jobs (averaging $1887). 29 state and other part-time jobs (averaging $1096). In 2018, 158 non-need-based awards were made. ***Average percent of need met:*** 52. ***Average financial aid package:*** $20,100. ***Average need-based loan:*** $4030. ***Average need-based gift aid:*** $18,672. ***Average non-need-based aid:*** $20,490. ***Average indebtedness upon graduation:*** $37,747.

APPLYING

Options: electronic application, deferred entrance.

Required: high school transcript. ***Recommended:*** essay or personal statement, interview.

Application deadlines: rolling (freshmen), rolling (out-of-state freshmen), 9/5 (transfers).

Notification: continuous (freshmen), continuous (out-of-state freshmen), continuous (transfers).

CONTACT

Emily Lorentsen, Senior Assistant Director of Admission, New England College, 102 Bridge Street, Henniker, NH 03242. *Phone:* 603-428-2392. *Toll-free phone:* 800-521-7642. *Fax:* 603-428-3155. *E-mail:* elorentsen@nec.edu.

New Hampshire Institute of Art

Manchester, New Hampshire

http://www.nhia.edu/

CONTACT

Mr. Scott Ramon, Director of Student Recruitment, New Hampshire Institute of Art, 148 Concord Street, Manchester, NH 03104-4158. *Phone:* 603-836-2148. *Toll-free phone:* 866-241-4918. *E-mail:* admissions@nhia.edu.

Plymouth State University

Plymouth, New Hampshire

http://www.plymouth.edu/

- **State-supported** comprehensive, founded 1871, part of University System of New Hampshire
- **Small-town** 170-acre campus with easy access to Manchester
- **Endowment** $19.3 million
- **Coed**
- **Moderately difficult** entrance level

FACULTY

Student/faculty ratio: 17:1.

ACADEMICS

Calendar: semesters. *Degrees:* certificates, bachelor's, master's, doctoral, post-master's, and postbachelor's certificates.

Library: Lamson Learning Commons. *Books:* 344,605 (physical), 155,000 (digital/electronic); *Serial titles:* 790 (physical), 1,500 (digital/electronic); *Databases:* 87. Weekly public service hours: 94.

STUDENT LIFE

Housing options: on-campus residence required through sophomore year; coed, cooperative, special housing for students with disabilities. Campus housing is university owned. Freshman campus housing is guaranteed.

Activities and organizations: drama/theater group, student-run newspaper, radio station, choral group, Pre Medical Professional Society, Student Nurse Association, Marketing Association of Plymouth State, Gaming Club, Programing Activities in a Campus Environment, national sororities.

Athletics Member NCAA. All Division III.

Campus security: 24-hour emergency response devices and patrols, late-night transport/escort service, controlled dormitory access, shuttle bus service, crime prevention programs, self-defense education.

Student services: health clinic, personal/psychological counseling, women's center, veterans affairs office.

FINANCIAL AID

Financial Aid Of all full-time matriculated undergraduates who enrolled in 2018, 2,805 were judged to have need, 422 had their need fully met. In 2018, 944 non-need-based awards were made. ***Average percent of need met:*** 59. ***Average financial aid package:*** $13,058. ***Average need-based loan:*** $3937. ***Average need-based gift aid:*** $8341. ***Average non-need-based aid:*** $4794. ***Average indebtedness upon graduation:*** $40,809.

APPLYING

Options: electronic application, deferred entrance.

Application fee: $50.

Required: essay or personal statement, 1 letter of recommendation. ***Required for some:*** high school transcript, interview. ***Recommended:*** minimum 2.5 GPA.

CONTACT

Mr. Tony Trodella, Director of Undergraduate Recruitment, Plymouth State University, Plymouth, NH 03264-1595. *Phone:* 603-535-2237. *Toll-free phone:* 800-842-6900. *Fax:* 603-535-2714. *E-mail:* admissions@plymouth.edu.

Rivier University

Nashua, New Hampshire

http://www.rivier.edu/

CONTACT

Valerie Leclair, Executive Director of Undergraduate and Graduate Admissions, Rivier University, 420 South Main Street, Nashua, NH 03060. *Phone:* 603-897-8515. *Toll-free phone:* 800-44RIVIER. *Fax:* 603-891-1799. *E-mail:* rivadmit@rivier.edu.

See below for display ad and page 1104 for the College Close-Up.

Saint Anselm College

Manchester, New Hampshire

http://www.anselm.edu/

- **Independent Roman Catholic** 4-year, founded 1889
- **Suburban** 380-acre campus with easy access to Boston
- **Endowment** $134.6 million
- **Coed**
- **Moderately difficult** entrance level

FACULTY

Student/faculty ratio: 11:1.

ACADEMICS

Calendar: semesters. *Degree:* bachelor's.

Library: Geisel Library plus 2 others. Students can reserve study rooms.

STUDENT LIFE

Housing options: coed, men-only, women-only, special housing for students with disabilities. Campus housing is university owned. Freshman campus housing is guaranteed.

Activities and organizations: drama/theater group, student-run newspaper, choral group, Meelia Center for Community Engagement, Anselmian Abbey Players, Club Sports, Service and Solidarity Mission Trips, Saint Anselm College Crier (School Newspaper).

Athletics Member NCAA. All Division II.

Campus security: 24-hour emergency response devices and patrols, student patrols, late-night transport/escort service, controlled dormitory access.

Student services: health clinic, personal/psychological counseling.

COSTS & FINANCIAL AID

Costs (2019–20) ***Comprehensive fee:*** $56,550 includes full-time tuition ($40,500), mandatory fees ($1300), and room and board ($14,750). Full-time tuition and fees vary according to program. Part-time tuition: $1000 per credit. Part-time tuition and fees vary according to course load. ***Required fees:*** $1000 per credit hour part-time, $600 per term part-time. ***College room only:*** $8850. Room and board charges vary according to board plan and housing facility.

Financial Aid Of all full-time matriculated undergraduates who enrolled in 2019, 1,620 applied for aid, 1,375 were judged to have need, 412 had their need fully met. In 2019, 567 non-need-based awards were made. ***Average percent of need met:*** 82. ***Average financial aid package:*** $31,666. ***Average need-based loan:*** $3659. ***Average need-based gift aid:*** $27,299. ***Average non-need-based aid:*** $18,945. ***Average indebtedness upon graduation:*** $32,769. ***Financial aid deadline:*** 2/15.

APPLYING

Standardized Tests *Required for some:* SAT or ACT (for admission).

Options: electronic application, early admission, early decision, early action, deferred entrance.

Application fee: $50.

Required: essay or personal statement, high school transcript, 2 letters of recommendation. ***Recommended:*** interview.

CONTACT

Mr. Eric Nichols, Vice President for Enrollment and Dean of Admission, Saint Anselm College, 100 Saint Anselm Drive, Manchester, NH 03102-1310. *Phone:* 603-641-7500. *Toll-free phone:* 888-4ANSELM. *E-mail:* admission@anselm.edu.

Southern New Hampshire University

Manchester, New Hampshire

http://www.snhu.edu/

- **Independent** university, founded 1932
- **Suburban** 317-acre campus with easy access to Boston
- **Coed**
- **Moderately difficult** entrance level

FACULTY

Student/faculty ratio: 13:1.

ACADEMICS

Calendar: semesters. *Degrees:* certificates, associate, bachelor's, master's, doctoral, post-master's, and postbachelor's certificates.

Library: Shapiro Library and Learning Commons. Students can reserve study rooms.

STUDENT LIFE

Housing options: coed, special housing for students with disabilities. Campus housing is university owned.

Activities and organizations: drama/theater group, student-run newspaper, radio and television station, choral group, Coordinators of Activities and Programming Events (CAPE), Psychology Club, Economics/Finance Association, Gaming Club, Outing Club, national fraternities, national sororities.

Athletics Member NCAA. All Division II.

Campus security: 24-hour emergency response devices and patrols, student patrols, late-night transport/escort service, controlled dormitory access.

Student services: health clinic, women's center, veterans affairs office.

FINANCIAL AID

Financial Aid Of all full-time matriculated undergraduates who enrolled in 2018, 2,366 applied for aid, 2,140 were judged to have need, 338 had their need fully met. In 2018, 624 non-need-based awards were made. ***Average percent of need met:*** 62. ***Average financial aid package:*** $22,854. ***Average need-based loan:*** $4064. ***Average need-based gift aid:*** $6894. ***Average non-need-based aid:*** $13,243. ***Average indebtedness upon graduation:*** $43,106.

APPLYING

Options: electronic application, early action, deferred entrance.

Required: essay or personal statement, high school transcript, minimum 2.0 GPA, 1 letter of recommendation. ***Recommended:*** interview.

CONTACT

Mr. Tim Whittum, Director of Freshman Admission, Southern New Hampshire University, 2500 North River Road, Manchester, NH 03106-1045. *Phone:* 603-645-9611. *Toll-free phone:* 888-327-7648. *Fax:* 603-645-9693. *E-mail:* t.whittum@snhu.edu.

Thomas More College of Liberal Arts

Merrimack, New Hampshire

http://www.thomasmorecollege.edu/

CONTACT

Mr. Jonathan Rensch, Director of Admissions, Thomas More College of Liberal Arts, 6 Manchester Street, Merrimack, NH 03054-4818. *Phone:* 603-880-8308 Ext. 14. *Toll-free phone:* 800-880-8308. *Fax:* 603-546-0034. *E-mail:* jrensch@thomasmorecollege.edu.

University of New Hampshire

Durham, New Hampshire

http://www.unh.edu/

- **State-supported** university, founded 1866, part of University System of New Hampshire
- **Small-town** 2600-acre campus with easy access to Boston
- **Endowment** $389.5 million
- **Coed** 12,202 undergraduate students, 98% full-time, 56% women, 44% men
- **Moderately difficult** entrance level, 84% of applicants were admitted

UNDERGRAD STUDENTS

11,931 full-time, 271 part-time. Students come from 49 states and territories; 35 other countries; 52% are from out of state; 1% Black or African American, non-Hispanic/Latino; 4% Hispanic/Latino; 3% Asian, non-Hispanic/Latino; 0.1% American Indian or Alaska Native, non-Hispanic/Latino; 2% Two or more races, non-Hispanic/Latino; 4% Race/ethnicity unknown; 3% international; 4% transferred in; 55% live on campus.

Freshmen:

Admission: 18,040 applied, 15,159 admitted, 2,731 enrolled. ***Average high school GPA:*** 3.5. ***Test scores:*** SAT evidence-based reading and writing scores over 500: 92%; SAT math scores over 500: 92%; ACT scores over 18: 97%; SAT evidence-based reading and writing scores over 600: 47%; SAT math scores over 600: 42%; ACT scores over 24: 63%; SAT evidence-based reading and writing scores over 700: 6%; SAT math scores over 700: 7%; ACT scores over 30: 15%.

Retention: 86% of full-time freshmen returned.

FACULTY

Total: 997, 75% full-time, 65% with terminal degrees.

Student/faculty ratio: 17:1.

ACADEMICS

Calendar: semesters. *Degrees:* associate, bachelor's, master's, doctoral, and postbachelor's certificates.

Special study options: accelerated degree program, advanced placement credit, distance learning, double majors, English as a second language, honors programs, independent study, internships, off-campus study, part-time degree program, services for LD students, student-designed majors, study abroad, summer session for credit. ***ROTC:*** Army (b), Air Force (b).

Unusual degree programs: 3-2 business administration; social work; occupational therapy.

Computers: 320 computers/terminals are available on campus for general student use. Students can access the following: campus intranet, computer help desk, free student e-mail accounts, online (class) grades, online (class) registration, online (class) schedules. Campuswide network is available. 100% of college-owned or -operated housing units are wired for high-speed Internet access. Wireless service is available via entire campus.

Library: Dimond Library plus 4 others. *Books:* 1.6 million (physical), 889,664 (digital/electronic); *Serial titles:* 749 (physical), 84,556 (digital/electronic); *Databases:* 430. Weekly public service hours: 117; students can reserve study rooms.

STUDENT LIFE

Housing options: coed, special housing for students with disabilities. Campus housing is university owned. Freshman campus housing is guaranteed.

Activities and organizations: drama/theater group, student-run newspaper, radio station, choral group, marching band, Campus Activity Board, The Outing Club, Resident Hall Association, Alpha Phi Omega, Memorial Union Student Organization, national fraternities, national sororities.

Athletics Member NCAA. All Division I except football (Division I-AA). ***Intercollegiate sports:*** archery M(c)/W(c), baseball M(c), basketball M(s)/W(s), crew M(c)/W(c), cross-country running M(s)/W(s), fencing M(c)/W(c), field hockey W(s), golf M(c)/W(c), gymnastics W(s), ice hockey M(s)/W(s), lacrosse M(c)/W(s), riflery M(c)/W(c), rock climbing M(c)/W(c), rugby M(c)/W(c), sailing M(c)/W(c), skiing (cross-country) M(s)/W(s), skiing (downhill) M(s)/W(s), soccer M(s)/W(s), softball W(c), swimming and diving W(s), tennis M(c)/W(c), track and field M(s)/W(s), ultimate Frisbee M(c)/W(c), volleyball M(c)/W(s), wrestling M(c)/W(c). ***Intramural sports:*** basketball M/W, football M/W, ice hockey M/W, sand volleyball M/W, soccer M/W, softball M/W, table tennis M/W, tennis M/W, ultimate Frisbee M/W, volleyball M/W.

Campus security: 24-hour emergency response devices, late-night transport/escort service, controlled dormitory access, nationally accredited police department that provides 24 hour coverage to the campus, emergency blue phones.

Student services: health clinic, personal/psychological counseling, women's center, veterans affairs office.

COSTS & FINANCIAL AID

Costs (2020–21) ***Tuition:*** area resident $15,520 full-time, $645 per credit hour part-time; state resident $15,520 full-time, $645 per credit hour part-time; nonresident $32,860 full-time, $1368 per credit hour part-time. Full-time tuition and fees vary according to program. Part-time tuition and fees vary according to course load and program. ***Required fees:*** $3418 full-time. ***Room and board:*** $12,242; room only: $7660. Room and board charges vary according to board plan and housing facility. ***Payment plan:*** installment. ***Waivers:*** employees or children of employees.

Financial Aid Of all full-time matriculated undergraduates who enrolled in 2018, 9,743 applied for aid, 8,116 were judged to have need, 1,284 had their need fully met. In 2018, 2067 non-need-based awards were made. ***Average percent of need met:*** 75. ***Average financial aid package:*** $24,851. ***Average need-based loan:*** $3467. ***Average need-based gift aid:*** $6230. ***Average non-need-based aid:*** $6654. ***Average indebtedness upon graduation:*** $42,246.

APPLYING
Options: electronic application, early action, deferred entrance.

Application fee: $50.

Required: high school transcript, 1 letter of recommendation, Common Application, audition for some majors in music and theater, portfolio for art studio majors. ***Recommended:*** minimum 3.0 GPA.

Application deadlines: 2/1 (freshmen), 2/1 (out-of-state freshmen), 4/1 (transfers), 11/15 (early action).

Notification: continuous until 12/1 (freshmen), continuous (out-of-state freshmen), continuous until 4/15 (transfers).

CONTACT
University of New Hampshire, Durham, NH 03824. *Phone:* 603-862-5292.

University of New Hampshire at Manchester

Manchester, New Hampshire

http://manchester.unh.edu/

CONTACT
Erika Couture, Senior Associate Director of Admission, University of New Hampshire at Manchester, 88 Commerical Street, Manchester, NH 03101. *Phone:* 603-641-4150. *E-mail:* erika.couture@unh.edu.

NEW JERSEY

Bais Medrash Mayan Hatorah

Lakewood, New Jersey

http://www.baismedrashmayanhatorah.com/

CONTACT
Bais Medrash Mayan Hatorah, 101 Milton Street, Lakewood, NJ 08701.

Bais Medrash Toras Chesed

Lakewood, New Jersey

http://www.bmtc.edu/

CONTACT
Bais Medrash Toras Chesed, 910 Monmouth Avenue, Lakewood, NJ 08701.

Berkeley College–Woodland Park Campus

Woodland Park, New Jersey

http://www.berkeleycollege.edu/

- **Proprietary** comprehensive, founded 1931
- **Suburban** 25-acre campus with easy access to New York City
- **Coed**
- **Minimally difficult** entrance level

FACULTY
Student/faculty ratio: 14:1.

ACADEMICS
Calendar: semesters. *Degrees:* certificates, associate, bachelor's, and master's.
Library: Walter A. Brower Library. *Books:* 52,322 (physical), 168,797 (digital/electronic); *Serial titles:* 152 (physical), 72,544 (digital/electronic); *Databases:* 84. Students can reserve study rooms.

STUDENT LIFE
Activities and organizations: student-run newspaper, Student Veterans of America, Latino/Hispanic Club, Sister-2-Sister Group, Multicultural Club, Law and Justice Studies Club.

Athletics Member USCAA.

Campus security: 24-hour emergency response devices and patrols.

Student services: personal/psychological counseling, veterans affairs office.

COSTS
Costs (2019–20) ***One-time required fee:*** $100. ***Tuition:*** $24,800 full-time, $855 per credit part-time. No tuition increase for student's term of enrollment. ***Required fees:*** $1700 full-time, $425 per term part-time.

APPLYING
Options: electronic application, deferred entrance.

Application fee: $50.

Required: essay or personal statement, high school transcript. ***Recommended:*** interview.

CONTACT
Carol J. Covino, Associate Vice President, High School Admissions, Berkeley College–Woodland Park Campus, 44 Rifle Camp Road, Woodland Park, NJ 07424. *Phone:* 973-278-5400. *Toll-free phone:* 800-446-5400. *E-mail:* info@berkeleycollege.edu.

Beth Medrash Govoha

Lakewood, New Jersey

CONTACT
Beth Medrash Govoha, 617 Sixth Street, Lakewood, NJ 08701-2797. *Phone:* 732-367-1060 Ext. 4224.

Bloomfield College

Bloomfield, New Jersey

http://www.bloomfield.edu/

CONTACT
Ms. Nicole Cibelli, Director of Admissions, Bloomfield College, Office of Enrollment Management and Admission, Bloomfield, NJ 07003-9981. *Phone:* 973-748-9000 Ext. 1390. *Toll-free phone:* 800-848-4555 Ext. 230. *Fax:* 973-748-0916. *E-mail:* nicole_cibelli@bloomfield.edu.

Caldwell University

Caldwell, New Jersey

http://www.caldwell.edu/

- **Independent Roman Catholic** comprehensive, founded 1939
- **Suburban** 70-acre campus with easy access to New York City
- **Endowment** $4.7 million
- **Coed** 1,704 undergraduate students, 94% full-time, 64% women, 36% men
- **Moderately difficult** entrance level, 93% of applicants were admitted

UNDERGRAD STUDENTS
1,608 full-time, 96 part-time. Students come from 22 states and territories; 35 other countries; 8% are from out of state; 15% Black or African American, non-Hispanic/Latino; 31% Hispanic/Latino; 3% Asian, non-Hispanic/Latino; 0.1% Native Hawaiian or other Pacific Islander, non-Hispanic/Latino; 0.1% American Indian or Alaska Native, non-Hispanic/Latino; 0.8% Two or more races, non-Hispanic/Latino; 6% Race/ethnicity unknown; 11% international; 2% transferred in; 36% live on campus.

Freshmen:
Admission: 3,527 applied, 3,289 admitted, 445 enrolled. ***Average high school GPA:*** 3.3. ***Test scores:*** SAT evidence-based reading and writing scores over 500: 63%; SAT math scores over 500: 66%; ACT scores over 18: 74%; SAT evidence-based reading and writing scores over 600: 17%; SAT math scores over 600: 19%; ACT scores over 24: 17%; SAT evidence-based reading and writing scores over 700: 1%; SAT math scores over 700: 6%; ACT scores over 30: 2%.

Retention: 79% of full-time freshmen returned.

FACULTY
Total: 308, 28% full-time, 50% with terminal degrees.

Student/faculty ratio: 13:1.

ACADEMICS
Calendar: semesters. *Degrees:* bachelor's, master's, doctoral, post-master's, and postbachelor's certificates.

Special study options: academic remediation for entering students, accelerated degree program, adult/continuing education programs, advanced placement credit, distance learning, double majors, English as a second language, honors programs, independent study, internships, part-time degree program, services for LD students, student-designed majors, study abroad, summer session for credit. ***ROTC:*** Army (c).

Unusual degree programs: 3-2 business administration; social work with Rutgers University; biology or psychology/occupational therapy with Columbia University, biology/athletic training with Seton Hall University, psychology/counseling psychology, psychology/applied behavior analysis, education/curriculum and instruction.

Computers: 52 computers/terminals and 796 ports are available on campus for general student use. Students can access the following: campus intranet, computer help desk, free student e-mail accounts, online (class) grades, online (class) registration, online (class) schedules. Campuswide network is available. 100% of college-owned or -operated housing units are wired for high-speed Internet access. Wireless service is available via entire campus.

Library: Jennings Library. *Books:* 145,000 (physical), 210,323 (digital/electronic); *Serial titles:* 120 (physical), 78,630 (digital/electronic); *Databases:* 67. Students can reserve study rooms.

STUDENT LIFE

Housing options: coed. Campus housing is university owned. Freshman applicants given priority for college housing.

Activities and organizations: drama/theater group, student-run newspaper, television station, choral group, marching band, International Student Organization (ISO), Latino American Student Organization (LASO), Filipino Organization Rooted in Caldwell's Excellence (FORCE), Health Professions Club (HPC), Dance Team, national fraternities, national sororities.

Athletics Member NCAA. All Division II. ***Intercollegiate sports:*** baseball M(s), basketball M(s)/W(s), bowling W(s), cross-country running M(s)/W(s), football M(c), lacrosse M(s)/W(s), soccer M(s)/W(s), softball W(s), tennis W(s), track and field M(s)/W(s), volleyball W(s).

Campus security: 24-hour emergency response devices and patrols, late-night transport/escort service, controlled dormitory access.

Student services: health clinic, personal/psychological counseling, veterans affairs office.

COSTS & FINANCIAL AID

Costs (2020–21) ***Comprehensive fee:*** $49,660 includes full-time tuition ($34,900), mandatory fees ($2000), and room and board ($12,760). Full-time tuition and fees vary according to course load, location, and program. Part-time tuition: $950 per credit hour. Part-time tuition and fees vary according to course load, location, and program. ***Required fees:*** $235 per term part-time. ***College room only:*** $6690. Room and board charges vary according to board plan and housing facility. ***Payment plan:*** installment. ***Waivers:*** children of alumni, adult students, senior citizens, and employees or children of employees.

Financial Aid Of all full-time matriculated undergraduates who enrolled in 2019, 1,335 applied for aid, 1,270 were judged to have need, 167 had their need fully met. In 2019, 289 non-need-based awards were made. ***Average percent of need met:*** 78. ***Average financial aid package:*** $32,209. ***Average need-based loan:*** $3980. ***Average need-based gift aid:*** $28,747. ***Average non-need-based aid:*** $22,254. ***Average indebtedness upon graduation:*** $26,962.

APPLYING

Options: electronic application, early action, deferred entrance.

Application fee: $50.

Required: essay or personal statement, high school transcript, 2 letters of recommendation. ***Recommended:*** minimum 3.0 GPA, interview, 16 units of college preparatory coursework.

Application deadlines: 4/1 (freshmen), 4/1 (out-of-state freshmen), rolling (transfers), 12/1 (early action).

Notification: 4/15 (freshmen), continuous (transfers), 12/31 (early action).

CONTACT

Mr. Jan Marco Jiras, Director of Admissions, Caldwell University, 120 Bloomfield Avenue, Caldwell, NJ 07006. *Phone:* 973-618-3620. *Fax:* 973-618-3600. *E-mail:* JJiras@caldwell.edu.

Centenary University

Hackettstown, New Jersey

http://www.centenaryuniversity.edu/

CONTACT

Jenna Yount, Director of Admissions, Centenary University, 400 Jefferson Street, Hackettstown, NJ 07840. *Phone:* 908-852-1400 Ext. 2082. *Toll-free phone:* 800-236-8679. *E-mail:* yountj@centenaryuniversity.edu.

Chamberlain College of Nursing - North Brunswick

North Brunswick, New Jersey

http://www.chamberlain.edu/

CONTACT

Chamberlain College of Nursing - North Brunswick, 630 U.S. Highway 1, North Brunswick, NJ 08902. *Toll-free phone:* 877-751-5783.

The College of New Jersey

Ewing, New Jersey

http://www.tcnj.edu/

- **State-supported** comprehensive, founded 1855
- **Suburban** 255-acre campus with easy access to Philadelphia
- **Coed**
- **Very difficult** entrance level

FACULTY

Student/faculty ratio: 13:1.

ACADEMICS

Calendar: semesters. *Degrees:* certificates, bachelor's, master's, post-master's, and postbachelor's certificates.

Library: The College of New Jersey Library. *Books:* 694,461 (physical), 6,455 (digital/electronic); *Serial titles:* 44,898 (physical), 8,859 (digital/electronic); *Databases:* 114. Weekly public service hours: 98; students can reserve study rooms.

STUDENT LIFE

Housing options: on-campus residence required for freshman year; coed, women-only, special housing for students with disabilities. Campus housing is university owned. Freshman campus housing is guaranteed.

Activities and organizations: drama/theater group, student-run newspaper, radio and television station, choral group, Student Government Association, College Union Board, Inter-Greek Council, The Signal, national fraternities, national sororities.

Athletics Member NCAA. All Division III.

Campus security: 24-hour emergency response devices and patrols, student patrols, late-night transport/escort service, controlled dormitory access.

Student services: health clinic, personal/psychological counseling, women's center, legal services, veterans affairs office.

COSTS & FINANCIAL AID

Costs (2019–20) ***Tuition:*** state resident $13,239 full-time, $470 per credit hour part-time; nonresident $25,217 full-time, $893 per credit hour part-time. Full-time tuition and fees vary according to course load. Part-time tuition and fees vary according to course load. ***Required fees:*** $3684 full-time, $153 per credit hour part-time. ***Room and board:*** $14,048; room only: $4532. Room and board charges vary according to board plan.

Financial Aid Of all full-time matriculated undergraduates who enrolled in 2018, 4,866 applied for aid, 3,523 were judged to have need, 373 had their need fully met. In 2018, 549 non-need-based awards were made. ***Average percent of need met:*** 43. ***Average financial aid package:*** $11,321. ***Average need-based loan:*** $4264. ***Average need-based gift aid:*** $11,609. ***Average non-need-based aid:*** $4983. ***Average indebtedness upon graduation:*** $38,937. ***Financial aid deadline:*** 10/1.

APPLYING

Standardized Tests *Required:* SAT or ACT (for admission).

Options: electronic application, early decision, deferred entrance.

Application fee: $75.

Required: essay or personal statement, high school transcript. ***Required for some:*** interview, art portfolio or music audition. ***Recommended:*** minimum 2.5 GPA, 3 letters of recommendation.

CONTACT

The College of New Jersey, 2000 Pennington Road, PO Box 7718, Ewing, NJ 08628.

College of Saint Elizabeth

Morristown, New Jersey

http://www.cse.edu/

- **Independent Roman Catholic** comprehensive, founded 1899
- **Suburban** 200-acre campus with easy access to New York City
- **Endowment** $19.5 million
- **Coed** 828 undergraduate students, 76% full-time, 70% women, 30% men
- **Minimally difficult** entrance level, 73% of applicants were admitted

UNDERGRAD STUDENTS

628 full-time, 200 part-time. Students come from 8 states and territories; 34 other countries; 5% are from out of state; 33% Black or African American, non-Hispanic/Latino; 27% Hispanic/Latino; 3% Asian, non-Hispanic/Latino; 0.6% Native Hawaiian or other Pacific Islander, non-Hispanic/Latino; 0.3% American Indian or Alaska Native, non-Hispanic/Latino; 1% Two or more races, non-Hispanic/Latino; 10% Race/ethnicity unknown; 2% international; 5% transferred in; 49% live on campus.

Freshmen:

Admission: 1,674 applied, 1,229 admitted, 169 enrolled. ***Average high school GPA:*** 2.9.

Retention: 69% of full-time freshmen returned.

FACULTY

Total: 199, 29% full-time.

Student/faculty ratio: 9:1.

ACADEMICS

Calendar: semesters. *Degrees:* certificates, bachelor's, master's, doctoral, and postbachelor's certificates (also offers coed adult undergraduate degree program and coed graduate programs).

Special study options: academic remediation for entering students, adult/continuing education programs, advanced placement credit, distance learning, double majors, English as a second language, external degree program, honors programs, independent study, internships, off-campus study, part-time degree program, services for LD students, student-designed majors, study abroad, summer session for credit.

Unusual degree programs: 3-2 business administration; Religious Studies/Theology, Criminal Justice/Justice Administration and Public Service, Foods and Nutrition/Nutrition, Psychology/Counseling Psychology, Elementary Education/Education.

Computers: 127 computers/terminals and 668 ports are available on campus for general student use. Students can access the following: computer help desk, free student e-mail accounts, online (class) grades, online (class) registration, online (class) schedules, online course evaluations; online system for registering for student activities, clubs, and events. Campuswide network is available. 100% of college-owned or -operated housing units are wired for high-speed Internet access. Wireless service is available via entire campus.

Library: Mahoney Library. *Books:* 109,450 (physical), 194,996 (digital/electronic); *Serial titles:* 135 (physical), 157,849 (digital/electronic); *Databases:* 124. Weekly public service hours: 75.

STUDENT LIFE

Housing options: coed, women-only, special housing for students with disabilities. Campus housing is university owned. Freshman campus housing is guaranteed.

Activities and organizations: choral group, Student Government Association (SGA), Students Take Action Committee (STAC) Volunteer Organization, International/Intercultural Clubs, College Activities Board (CAB), Campus Ministry.

Athletics Member NCAA. All Division III. ***Intercollegiate sports:*** baseball M, basketball M/W, cross-country running M/W, soccer M/W, softball W, tennis M/W, volleyball M/W.

Campus security: 24-hour emergency response devices and patrols, controlled dormitory access, security will walk students to and from buildings at night if needed.

Student services: health clinic, personal/psychological counseling.

COSTS & FINANCIAL AID

Costs (2020–21) ***One-time required fee:*** $175. ***Comprehensive fee:*** $47,615 includes full-time tuition ($32,895), mandatory fees ($1976), and room and board ($12,744). Full-time tuition and fees vary according to course load. Part-time tuition: $914 per credit hour. Part-time tuition and fees vary according to course load. ***Room and board:*** Room and board charges vary according to housing facility. ***Payment plans:*** installment, deferred payment. ***Waivers:*** senior citizens and employees or children of employees.

Financial Aid Of all full-time matriculated undergraduates who enrolled in 2018, 566 applied for aid, 546 were judged to have need, 40 had their need fully met. In 2018, 34 non-need-based awards were made. ***Average percent of need met:*** 75. ***Average financial aid package:*** $30,405. ***Average need-based loan:*** $7130. ***Average need-based gift aid:*** $27,408. ***Average non-need-based aid:*** $14,486. ***Average indebtedness upon graduation:*** $29,315.

APPLYING

Options: electronic application, deferred entrance.

Required: essay or personal statement, high school transcript, minimum 2.0 GPA, 2 letters of recommendation.

Application deadlines: rolling (freshmen), rolling (transfers).

Notification: continuous (freshmen), continuous (transfers).

CONTACT

Ms. Nadine Hawkins, Director of Undergraduate Admissions, College of Saint Elizabeth, 2 Convent Road, Morristown, NJ 07960-6989. *Phone:* 973-290-4700. *Toll-free phone:* 800-210-7900. *Fax:* 973-290-4710. *E-mail:* apply@cse.edu.

DeVry University–North Brunswick Campus

North Brunswick, New Jersey

http://www.devry.edu/

- **Proprietary** comprehensive, founded 1969, part of DeVry University
- **Urban** campus
- **Coed**
- **Minimally difficult** entrance level

FACULTY

Student/faculty ratio: 14:1.

ACADEMICS

Calendar: semesters. *Degrees:* associate, bachelor's, and master's.

Library: Learning Resource Center.

STUDENT LIFE

Housing options: college housing not available.

APPLYING

Options: deferred entrance.

Application fee: $30.

Required: high school transcript, interview.

CONTACT

DeVry University–North Brunswick Campus, 630 US Highway 1, North Brunswick, NJ 08902. *Phone:* 732-729-3532. *Toll-free phone:* 866-338-7934.

Drew University

Madison, New Jersey

http://www.drew.edu/

- **Independent** university, founded 1867, affiliated with United Methodist Church
- **Suburban** 186-acre campus with easy access to New York City
- **Coed** 1,712 undergraduate students, 99% full-time, 58% women, 42% men
- **Moderately difficult** entrance level, 71% of applicants were admitted

UNDERGRAD STUDENTS
1,688 full-time, 24 part-time. Students come from 34 states and territories; 52 other countries; 33% are from out of state; 8% Black or African American, non-Hispanic/Latino; 17% Hispanic/Latino; 5% Asian, non-Hispanic/Latino; 0.1% American Indian or Alaska Native, non-Hispanic/Latino; 3% Two or more races, non-Hispanic/Latino; 4% Race/ethnicity unknown; 12% international; 6% transferred in; 80% live on campus.

Freshmen:
Admission: 3,928 applied, 2,805 admitted, 400 enrolled. ***Average high school GPA:*** 3.5. ***Test scores:*** SAT evidence-based reading and writing scores over 500: 95%; SAT math scores over 500: 90%; ACT scores over 18: 100%; SAT evidence-based reading and writing scores over 600: 55%; SAT math scores over 600: 42%; ACT scores over 24: 70%; SAT evidence-based reading and writing scores over 700: 12%; SAT math scores over 700: 10%; ACT scores over 30: 21%.

Retention: 85% of full-time freshmen returned.

FACULTY
Total: 265, 52% full-time.

Student/faculty ratio: 12:1.

ACADEMICS
Calendar: semesters. *Degrees:* bachelor's, master's, doctoral, post-master's, and postbachelor's certificates.

Special study options: accelerated degree program, adult/continuing education programs, advanced placement credit, double majors, English as a second language, freshman honors college, honors programs, independent study, internships, off-campus study, part-time degree program, services for LD students, student-designed majors, study abroad, summer session for credit. ***ROTC:*** Army (c).

Unusual degree programs: 3-2 engineering with Columbia University, Stevens Institute of Technology, Washington University (St Louis); forestry with Duke University; nursing with Drexel University; Business Management with Wake Forest University, Environment Management with Duke University, Forestry with Duke University, Law School with NYU or Seton Hall, MD with Rutgers New Jersey Medical School, dual degree program in Nutrition/Dietetics (BA/MS) with Drexel University.

Computers: 95 computers/terminals are available on campus for general student use. Students can access the following: campus intranet, computer help desk, free student e-mail accounts, online (class) grades, online (class) registration, online (class) schedules. Campuswide network is available. 100% of college-owned or -operated housing units are wired for high-speed Internet access. Wireless service is available via entire campus.

Library: Rose Memorial Library plus 1 other. *Books:* 448,828 (physical), 279,468 (digital/electronic); *Serial titles:* 6,550 (physical), 138,582 (digital/electronic); *Databases:* 207. Weekly public service hours: 108; students can reserve study rooms.

STUDENT LIFE
Housing options: coed, special housing for students with disabilities. Campus housing is university owned. Freshman campus housing is guaranteed.

Activities and organizations: drama/theater group, student-run newspaper, radio station, choral group, Drew Organization of Gaming, International Student Association, ARIEL Latin Culture Society, Drew Unversity Chemistry Society, Drew African Students Association.

Athletics Member NCAA. All Division III except golf (Division II). ***Intercollegiate sports:*** baseball M, basketball M/W, cross-country running M/W, equestrian sports W, fencing M/W, field hockey W, golf M/W, lacrosse M/W, rugby M(c)/W(c), soccer M/W, softball W, swimming and diving M/W, tennis M/W, track and field M/W, volleyball M/W. ***Intramural sports:*** badminton M/W, basketball M/W, football M, racquetball M/W, soccer M/W, squash M/W, table tennis M/W, volleyball M/W.

Campus security: 24-hour emergency response devices and patrols, late-night transport/escort service, controlled dormitory access.

Student services: health clinic, personal/psychological counseling.

COSTS & FINANCIAL AID
Costs (2019–20) ***Comprehensive fee:*** $55,332 includes full-time tuition ($39,828), mandatory fees ($832), and room and board ($14,672). Part-time tuition: $1660 per credit. Part-time tuition and fees vary according to course load. ***College room only:*** $9264. Room and board charges vary according to board plan and housing facility. ***Payment plans:*** tuition prepayment, installment, deferred payment. ***Waivers:*** employees or children of employees.

Financial Aid Of all full-time matriculated undergraduates who enrolled in 2019, 1,161 applied for aid, 1,060 were judged to have need, 160 had their need fully met. 752 Federal Work-Study jobs (averaging $2000). In 2019, 423 non-need-based awards were made. ***Average percent of need met:*** 83. ***Average financial aid package:*** $37,235. ***Average need-based loan:*** $4418. ***Average need-based gift aid:*** $31,510. ***Average non-need-based aid:*** $15,394. ***Average indebtedness upon graduation:*** $25,049.

APPLYING
Options: electronic application, early admission, early decision, early action, deferred entrance.

Application fee: $40.

Required: essay or personal statement, high school transcript, 2 letters of recommendation. ***Recommended:*** interview.

Application deadlines: 2/1 (freshmen), 12/15 (transfers).

Early decision deadline: 11/15.

Notification: 3/18 (freshmen), continuous (transfers), 12/15 (early decision).

CONTACT
Drew University, 36 Madison Avenue, Madison, NJ 07940-1493. *Phone:* 973-408-DREW.

Eastern International College

Belleville, New Jersey
http://www.eicollege.edu/

- **Proprietary** primarily 2-year
- **Urban** campus with easy access to Manhattan, New York
- **Coed**

ACADEMICS
Degrees: associate and bachelor's.

CONTACT
Eastern International College, 251 Washington Avenue, Belleville, NJ 07109.

Eastern International College

Jersey City, New Jersey
http://www.eicollege.edu/

CONTACT
Eastern International College, 684 Newark Avenue, Jersey City, NJ 07306.

Eastwick College

Ramsey, New Jersey
http://www.eastwickcollege.edu/

CONTACT
Eastwick College, 10 South Franklin Turnpike, Ramsey, NJ 07446.

Fairleigh Dickinson University

Teaneck, New Jersey
http://www.fdu.edu/

- **Independent** university, founded 1942
- **Suburban** 88-acre campus with easy access to New York City
- **Coed** 8,934 undergraduate students, 52% full-time, 58% women, 42% men
- 93% of applicants were admitted

UNDERGRAD STUDENTS
4,633 full-time, 4,301 part-time. Students come from 37 states and territories; 63 other countries; 13% are from out of state; 9% Black or African American, non-Hispanic/Latino; 32% Hispanic/Latino; 5% Asian, non-Hispanic/Latino; 0.1% Native Hawaiian or other Pacific Islander, non-Hispanic/Latino; 0.1% American Indian or Alaska Native, non-

Hispanic/Latino; 2% Two or more races, non-Hispanic/Latino; 10% Race/ethnicity unknown; 3% international; 4% transferred in; 39% live on campus.

Freshmen:

Admission: 5,762 applied, 5,361 admitted, 1,134 enrolled. ***Average high school GPA:*** 3.5.

Retention: 81% of full-time freshmen returned.

FACULTY

Total: 1,222, 27% full-time.

Student/faculty ratio: 14:1.

ACADEMICS

Degrees: certificates, diplomas, associate, bachelor's, master's, doctoral, post-master's, and postbachelor's certificates.

Special study options: academic remediation for entering students, adult/continuing education programs, distance learning, double majors, external degree program, honors programs, independent study, part-time degree program, services for LD students, study abroad, summer session for credit. ***ROTC:*** Army (c), Air Force (c).

Unusual degree programs: 3-2 business administration; engineering; nursing.

Computers: 600 computers/terminals are available on campus for general student use. Students can access the following: campus intranet, computer help desk, free student e-mail accounts, online (class) grades, online (class) registration, online (class) schedules. Campuswide network is available. 100% of college-owned or -operated housing units are wired for high-speed Internet access. Wireless service is available via entire campus.

Library: Fairleigh Dickinson University Library plus 3 others. *Books:* 355,184 (physical), 210,703 (digital/electronic); *Serial titles:* 11,727 (physical), 56,135 (digital/electronic); *Databases:* 194. Weekly public service hours: 86; students can reserve study rooms.

STUDENT LIFE

Housing options: coed, men-only, women-only, special housing for students with disabilities. Campus housing is university owned. Freshman campus housing is guaranteed.

Activities and organizations: drama/theater group, student-run newspaper, radio station, national fraternities, national sororities.

Athletics Member NCAA. All Division I. ***Intercollegiate sports:*** baseball M(s), basketball M(s)/W(s), bowling W(s), cheerleading W(s), cross-country running M(s)/W(s), fencing W(s), golf M(s)/W(s), soccer M(s)/W(s), softball W(s), tennis M(s)/W(s), track and field M(s)/W(s), volleyball W(s). ***Intramural sports:*** badminton M/W, basketball M/W.

Student services: health clinic, personal/psychological counseling, veterans affairs office.

COSTS

Costs (2020–21) ***Comprehensive fee:*** $57,129 includes full-time tuition ($42,404), mandatory fees ($1064), and room and board ($13,661). Full-time tuition and fees vary according to location. ***Room and board:*** Room and board charges vary according to location.

APPLYING

Options: electronic application, early decision, deferred entrance.

Required: high school transcript. ***Required for some:*** essay or personal statement, interview.

Application deadlines: rolling (freshmen), rolling (out-of-state freshmen), rolling (transfers).

Early decision deadline: rolling.

CONTACT

Fairleigh Dickinson University, 1000 River Road, Teaneck, NJ 07666. *Phone:* 201-692-7308.

Fairleigh Dickinson University, Florham Campus

Madison, New Jersey

http://www.fdu.edu/

CONTACT

Fairleigh Dickinson University, Florham Campus, 285 Madison Avenue, Madison, NJ 07940-1099. *Toll-free phone:* 800-338-8803.

Fairleigh Dickinson University, Metropolitan Campus

Teaneck, New Jersey

http://www.fdu.edu/

CONTACT

Fairleigh Dickinson University, Metropolitan Campus, 1000 River Road, Teaneck, NJ 07666-1914. *Toll-free phone:* 800-338-8803.

Felician University

Lodi, New Jersey

http://www.felician.edu/

- **Independent Roman Catholic** comprehensive, founded 1942
- **Suburban** 37-acre campus with easy access to New York City
- **Endowment** $7.0 million
- **Coed** 1,852 undergraduate students, 89% full-time, 72% women, 28% men
- **Moderately difficult** entrance level, 86% of applicants were admitted

UNDERGRAD STUDENTS

1,640 full-time, 212 part-time. Students come from 19 states and territories; 10 other countries; 7% are from out of state; 20% Black or African American, non-Hispanic/Latino; 32% Hispanic/Latino; 5% Asian, non-Hispanic/Latino; 0.5% Native Hawaiian or other Pacific Islander, non-Hispanic/Latino; 0.2% American Indian or Alaska Native, non-Hispanic/Latino; 0.7% Two or more races, non-Hispanic/Latino; 12% Race/ethnicity unknown; 4% international; 12% transferred in; 28% live on campus.

Freshmen:

Admission: 2,545 applied, 2,191 admitted, 382 enrolled. ***Average high school GPA:*** 3.0. ***Test scores:*** SAT evidence-based reading and writing scores over 500: 50%; SAT math scores over 500: 51%; ACT scores over 18: 42%; SAT evidence-based reading and writing scores over 600: 8%; SAT math scores over 600: 4%; ACT scores over 24: 8%; SAT math scores over 700: 1%.

Retention: 78% of full-time freshmen returned.

FACULTY

Total: 236, 35% full-time, 42% with terminal degrees.

Student/faculty ratio: 14:1.

ACADEMICS

Calendar: semesters. *Degrees:* certificates, associate, bachelor's, master's, doctoral, post-master's, and postbachelor's certificates.

Special study options: academic remediation for entering students, accelerated degree program, adult/continuing education programs, advanced placement credit, cooperative education, distance learning, double majors, English as a second language, external degree program, honors programs, independent study, internships, off-campus study, part-time degree program, services for LD students, student-designed majors, study abroad, summer session for credit. ***ROTC:*** Army (c), Air Force (c).

Unusual degree programs: 3-2 business administration; psychology/counseling, computer science.

Computers: 190 computers/terminals and 50 ports are available on campus for general student use. Students can access the following: computer help desk, free student e-mail accounts, online (class) grades, online (class) registration, online (class) schedules. Campuswide network is available. 100% of college-owned or -operated housing units are wired for high-speed Internet access. Wireless service is available via entire campus.

Library: Felician University Library plus 1 other. *Books:* 58,346 (physical), 178,572 (digital/electronic); *Serial titles:* 91,102 (digital/electronic); *Databases:* 61. Weekly public service hours: 142; students can reserve study rooms.

STUDENT LIFE

Housing options: men-only, women-only, special housing for students with disabilities. Campus housing is university owned. Freshman applicants given priority for college housing.

Activities and organizations: drama/theater group, student-run radio station, choral group, Student Nurses Association, Campus Activity Board, Black Student Union, National Society of Leadership & Success, Young Entrepreneur Club.

Athletics Member NCAA. All Division II. ***Intercollegiate sports:*** baseball M(s), basketball M(s)/W(s), bowling W(s), cross-country running M(s)/W(s), golf M(s), lacrosse M/W, soccer M(s)/W(s), softball W(s), track and field M/W, volleyball W(s). ***Intramural sports:*** cheerleading W(c), soccer M/W, softball W, volleyball M/W, weight lifting M/W.

Campus security: 24-hour patrols, student patrols, late-night transport/escort service.

Student services: health clinic, personal/psychological counseling, veterans affairs office.

COSTS & FINANCIAL AID

Costs (2020–21) ***Comprehensive fee:*** $48,140 includes full-time tuition ($32,550), mandatory fees ($2450), and room and board ($13,140). Full-time tuition and fees vary according to program. Part-time tuition: $1075 per credit hour. Part-time tuition and fees vary according to course load and program. ***Required fees:*** $485 per term part-time. ***Room and board:*** Room and board charges vary according to housing facility. ***Payment plan:*** installment. ***Waivers:*** employees or children of employees.

Financial Aid Of all full-time matriculated undergraduates who enrolled in 2018, 1,370 applied for aid, 1,325 were judged to have need, 102 had their need fully met. 71 Federal Work-Study jobs (averaging $2355). In 2018, 42 non-need-based awards were made. ***Average percent of need met:*** 68. ***Average financial aid package:*** $29,168. ***Average need-based loan:*** $4263. ***Average need-based gift aid:*** $14,534. ***Average non-need-based aid:*** $17,998.

APPLYING

Standardized Tests *Required:* SAT or ACT (for admission). *Required for some:* SAT (for admission), ACT (for admission), SAT Subject Tests (for admission). *Recommended:* SAT and SAT Subject Tests or ACT (for admission).

Options: early action, deferred entrance.

Application fee: $30.

Required: essay or personal statement, high school transcript, minimum 2.0 GPA, letters of recommendation. ***Required for some:*** interview.

Application deadlines: 6/1 (freshmen), 2/15 (out-of-state freshmen), rolling (transfers).

Notification: continuous (freshmen), continuous (out-of-state freshmen), continuous (transfers).

CONTACT

Camille Braker-Balkum, Executive Director of Admissions, Felician University, 262 South Main Street, Lodi, NJ 07644-2117. *Phone:* 201-355-1465. *E-mail:* brakerc@felician.edu.

Georgian Court University

Lakewood, New Jersey

http://www.georgian.edu/

- **Independent Roman Catholic** comprehensive, founded 1908
- **Suburban** 156-acre campus with easy access to New York City, Philadelphia
- **Endowment** $54.9 million
- **Coed** 1,793 undergraduate students, 79% full-time, 72% women, 28% men
- **Moderately difficult** entrance level, 71% of applicants were admitted

UNDERGRAD STUDENTS

1,417 full-time, 376 part-time. Students come from 27 states and territories; 21 other countries; 7% are from out of state; 10% Black or African American, non-Hispanic/Latino; 15% Hispanic/Latino; 3% Asian, non-Hispanic/Latino; 0.1% Native Hawaiian or other Pacific Islander, non-Hispanic/Latino; 0.6% American Indian or Alaska Native, non-Hispanic/Latino; 1% Two or more races, non-Hispanic/Latino; 5% Race/ethnicity unknown; 2% international; 12% transferred in; 25% live on campus.

Freshmen:

Admission: 1,934 applied, 1,377 admitted, 197 enrolled. ***Average high school GPA:*** 3.5. ***Test scores:*** SAT evidence-based reading and writing scores over 500: 71%; SAT math scores over 500: 69%; ACT scores over 18: 90%; SAT evidence-based reading and writing scores over 600: 19%; SAT math scores over 600: 19%; ACT scores over 24: 30%; SAT evidence-based reading and writing scores over 700: 1%; SAT math scores over 700: 1%.

Retention: 79% of full-time freshmen returned.

FACULTY

Total: 289, 31% full-time, 53% with terminal degrees.

Student/faculty ratio: 12:1.

ACADEMICS

Calendar: semesters. *Degrees:* certificates, bachelor's, master's, doctoral, post-master's, and postbachelor's certificates.

Special study options: academic remediation for entering students, accelerated degree program, adult/continuing education programs, advanced placement credit, distance learning, double majors, English as a second language, honors programs, independent study, internships, off-campus study, part-time degree program, services for LD students, student-designed majors, study abroad, summer session for credit.

Computers: 228 computers/terminals and 300 ports are available on campus for general student use. Students can access the following: campus intranet, computer help desk, free student e-mail accounts, online (class) grades, online (class) registration, online (class) schedules. Campuswide network is available. 100% of college-owned or -operated housing units are wired for high-speed Internet access. Wireless service is available via entire campus.

Library: The Sister Mary Joseph Cunningham Library. *Books:* 532,946 (physical), 167,764 (digital/electronic); *Serial titles:* 57,032 (physical), 53,706 (digital/electronic); *Databases:* 111. Weekly public service hours: 85; students can reserve study rooms.

STUDENT LIFE

Housing options: coed. Campus housing is university owned. Freshman campus housing is guaranteed.

Activities and organizations: student-run newspaper, Student Government Association, WILD, Black Student Union, Campus Activities Board, Nursing Club.

Athletics Member NCAA. All Division II. ***Intercollegiate sports:*** basketball M(s)/W(s), cross-country running M(s)/W(s), lacrosse M(s)/W(s), soccer M(s)/W(s), softball W(s), track and field M(s)/W(s), volleyball W(s).

Campus security: 24-hour emergency response devices and patrols, late-night transport/escort service, controlled dormitory access.

Student services: health clinic, personal/psychological counseling, veterans affairs office.

COSTS & FINANCIAL AID

Costs (2020–21) ***Comprehensive fee:*** $45,192 includes full-time tuition ($32,050), mandatory fees ($1718), and room and board ($11,424). Full-time tuition and fees vary according to location, program, and reciprocity agreements. Part-time tuition: $747 per credit hour. Part-time tuition and fees vary according to location, program, and reciprocity agreements. ***Required fees:*** $372 per term part-time. ***Payment plan:*** installment. ***Waivers:*** senior citizens and employees or children of employees.

Financial Aid Of all full-time matriculated undergraduates who enrolled in 2019, 1,252 applied for aid, 1,166 were judged to have need, 388 had their need fully met. In 2019, 236 non-need-based awards were made. ***Average percent of need met:*** 77. ***Average financial aid package:*** $29,570. ***Average need-based loan:*** $6414. ***Average need-based gift aid:*** $20,606. ***Average non-need-based aid:*** $14,883. ***Average indebtedness upon graduation:*** $38,183. ***Financial aid deadline:*** 7/1.

APPLYING

Standardized Tests *Required:* SAT or ACT (for admission).

Options: electronic application, early action, deferred entrance.

Application fee: $40.

Required: high school transcript, minimum 2.5 GPA. ***Required for some:*** essay or personal statement, interview.

Application deadlines: 8/1 (freshmen), 8/1 (transfers), 12/1 (early action).

Notification: continuous (transfers).

CONTACT

Priscilla Alicea, Assistant Vice President for Undergraduate Admissions, Georgian Court University, 900 Lakewood Avenue, Lakewood, NJ 08701-2697. *Phone:* 732-987-2745. *Toll-free phone:* 800-458-8422. *Fax:* 732-987-2000. *E-mail:* admissions@georgian.edu.

Kean University

Union, New Jersey

http://www.kean.edu/

- **State-supported** university, founded 1855, part of New Jersey State College System
- **Urban** 240-acre campus with easy access to New York City
- **Endowment** $27.1 million
- **Coed** 12,120 undergraduate students, 81% full-time, 60% women, 40% men
- **Moderately difficult** entrance level, 69% of applicants were admitted

UNDERGRAD STUDENTS

9,817 full-time, 2,303 part-time. Students come from 22 states and territories; 49 other countries; 2% are from out of state; 20% Black or African American, non-Hispanic/Latino; 31% Hispanic/Latino; 6% Asian, non-Hispanic/Latino; 0.3% Native Hawaiian or other Pacific Islander, non-Hispanic/Latino; 0.2% American Indian or Alaska Native, non-Hispanic/Latino; 2% Two or more races, non-Hispanic/Latino; 7% Race/ethnicity unknown; 4% international; 13% transferred in; 15% live on campus.

Freshmen:

Admission: 9,540 applied, 6,541 admitted, 1,770 enrolled. ***Average high school GPA:*** 3.1. ***Test scores:*** SAT evidence-based reading and writing scores over 500: 55%; SAT math scores over 500: 59%; ACT scores over 18: 73%; SAT evidence-based reading and writing scores over 600: 12%; SAT math scores over 600: 11%; ACT scores over 24: 24%; SAT evidence-based reading and writing scores over 700: 1%; SAT math scores over 700: 2%; ACT scores over 30: 3%.

Retention: 74% of full-time freshmen returned.

FACULTY

Total: 1,391, 26% full-time.

Student/faculty ratio: 17:1.

ACADEMICS

Calendar: semesters. *Degrees:* bachelor's, master's, doctoral, and post-master's certificates.

Special study options: academic remediation for entering students, accelerated degree program, adult/continuing education programs, advanced placement credit, cooperative education, distance learning, double majors, English as a second language, external degree program, independent study, internships, off-campus study, part-time degree program, services for LD students, study abroad, summer session for credit. ***ROTC:*** Army (c), Air Force (c).

Computers: 1,700 computers/terminals and 1,500 ports are available on campus for general student use. Students can access the following: free student e-mail accounts, online (class) grades, online (class) registration, online (class) schedules. Campuswide network is available. 100% of college-owned or -operated housing units are wired for high-speed Internet access. Wireless service is available via entire campus.

Library: Nancy Thompson Library. *Books:* 172,411 (physical), 12,565 (digital/electronic); *Serial titles:* 55,488 (digital/electronic); *Databases:* 235. Weekly public service hours: 106; students can reserve study rooms.

STUDENT LIFE

Housing options: coed, special housing for students with disabilities. Campus housing is university owned. Freshman applicants given priority for college housing.

Activities and organizations: drama/theater group, student-run newspaper, radio station, choral group, The National Society of Leadership and Success, American Sign Language Club, Kean University Council for Exceptional Children, Active Minds at Kean University, Kean University Rotaract Action Club, national fraternities, national sororities.

Athletics Member NCAA. All Division III. ***Intercollegiate sports:*** baseball M, basketball M/W, field hockey W, football M, lacrosse M/W, soccer M/W, softball W, swimming and diving W, tennis W, volleyball M/W. ***Intramural sports:*** basketball M/W, sand volleyball M/W, soccer M/W, softball M/W, tennis M/W, ultimate Frisbee M/W, volleyball M/W, weight lifting M/W.

Campus security: 24-hour emergency response devices and patrols, student patrols, late-night transport/escort service, controlled dormitory access.

Student services: health clinic, personal/psychological counseling, veterans affairs office.

COSTS & FINANCIAL AID

Costs (2019–20) ***Tuition:*** state resident $9935 full-time, $389 per credit part-time; nonresident $17,111 full-time, $613 per credit part-time. Part-time tuition and fees vary according to course load. ***Required fees:*** $2660 full-time, $91 per credit part-time. ***Room and board:*** $14,802. Room and board charges vary according to board plan, housing facility, location, and student level. ***Payment plan:*** installment. ***Waivers:*** senior citizens and employees or children of employees.

Financial Aid Of all full-time matriculated undergraduates who enrolled in 2019, 8,036 applied for aid, 6,970 were judged to have need, 92 had their need fully met. 256 Federal Work-Study jobs (averaging $3271). In 2019, 290 non-need-based awards were made. ***Average percent of need met:*** 84. ***Average financial aid package:*** $11,242. ***Average need-based loan:*** $4359. ***Average need-based gift aid:*** $8928. ***Average non-need-based aid:*** $2867. ***Average indebtedness upon graduation:*** $34,275.

APPLYING

Standardized Tests *Required:* SAT or ACT (for admission).

Options: electronic application, early action, deferred entrance.

Application fee: $75.

Required: high school transcript, SAT or ACT. ***Required for some:*** interview. ***Recommended:*** essay or personal statement, 2 letters of recommendation.

Application deadlines: 8/15 (freshmen), 8/1 (transfers), 12/1 (early action).

Notification: continuous until 11/1 (freshmen), continuous (transfers), 1/1 (early action).

CONTACT

Mr. Carlos Nazario, Director of Admissions, Kean University, 1000 Morris Avenue, Office of Admissions - Kean Hall, Union, NJ 07083. *Phone:* 908-737-7100. *Fax:* 908-737-7105. *E-mail:* admitme@kean.edu.

Monmouth University

West Long Branch, New Jersey

http://www.monmouth.edu/

CONTACT

Ms. Victoria Bobik, Director of Undergraduate Admission, Monmouth University, 400 Cedar Avenue, West Long Branch, NJ 07764-1898. *Phone:* 732-571-3456. *Toll-free phone:* 800-543-9671. *Fax:* 732-263-5166. *E-mail:* admission@monmouth.edu.

Montclair State University

Montclair, New Jersey

http://www.montclair.edu/

- **State-supported** university, founded 1908
- **Suburban** 250-acre campus with easy access to New York City
- **Endowment** $83.0 million
- **Coed** 16,988 undergraduate students, 89% full-time, 61% women, 39% men
- **Moderately difficult** entrance level, 71% of applicants were admitted

UNDERGRAD STUDENTS
15,133 full-time, 1,855 part-time. Students come from 44 states and territories; 64 other countries; 3% are from out of state; 13% Black or African American, non-Hispanic/Latino; 29% Hispanic/Latino; 6% Asian, non-Hispanic/Latino; 0.2% Native Hawaiian or other Pacific Islander, non-Hispanic/Latino; 0.1% American Indian or Alaska Native, non-Hispanic/Latino; 3% Two or more races, non-Hispanic/Latino; 6% Race/ethnicity unknown; 2% international; 10% transferred in; 30% live on campus.

Freshmen:
Admission: 14,324 applied, 10,157 admitted, 3,180 enrolled. ***Average high school GPA:*** 3.3.

Retention: 80% of full-time freshmen returned.

FACULTY
Total: 1,855, 34% full-time, 34% with terminal degrees.

Student/faculty ratio: 17:1.

ACADEMICS
Calendar: semesters. *Degrees:* certificates, bachelor's, master's, doctoral, and postbachelor's certificates.

Special study options: academic remediation for entering students, accelerated degree program, adult/continuing education programs, advanced placement credit, cooperative education, double majors, English as a second language, freshman honors college, honors programs, independent study, internships, off-campus study, part-time degree program, services for LD students, study abroad, summer session for credit.

Computers: 800 computers/terminals and 27,000 ports are available on campus for general student use. Students can access the following: campus intranet, computer help desk, free student e-mail accounts, online (class) grades, online (class) registration, online (class) schedules, online storage, online course delivery, online computing lab, student online portal. Campuswide network is available. 100% of college-owned or -operated housing units are wired for high-speed Internet access. Wireless service is available via entire campus.

Library: Sprague Library. *Books:* 432,414 (physical), 157,098 (digital/electronic); *Serial titles:* 9,510 (physical), 62,084 (digital/electronic); *Databases:* 238. Weekly public service hours: 93; students can reserve study rooms.

STUDENT LIFE
Housing options: coed. Campus housing is university owned. Freshman campus housing is guaranteed.

Activities and organizations: drama/theater group, student-run newspaper, radio and television station, choral group, Latin American Student Organization, Campus Recreation, MSU Players, Unified Asian American Student Organization, SLAM (Student Life At Montclair), national fraternities, national sororities.

Athletics Member NCAA. All Division III. ***Intercollegiate sports:*** baseball M, basketball M/W, field hockey W, football M, lacrosse M/W, soccer M/W, softball W, swimming and diving M/W, track and field M/W, volleyball W. ***Intramural sports:*** baseball M(c), basketball M/W, cheerleading W(c), fencing W(c), field hockey M(c), ice hockey M(c)/W(c), lacrosse M(c), racquetball M/W, rugby M(c)/W(c), soccer M/W, softball M/W, table tennis M/W, tennis M/W, track and field M(c)/W(c), volleyball M/W, water polo M/W, wrestling M(c)/W(c).

Campus security: 24-hour emergency response devices and patrols, late-night transport/escort service, controlled dormitory access, video surveillance, student escorts.

Student services: health clinic, personal/psychological counseling, women's center, veterans affairs office.

COSTS & FINANCIAL AID
Costs (2019–20) ***Tuition:*** state resident $12,082 full-time, $403 per credit part-time; nonresident $20,042 full-time, $668 per credit part-time. ***Required fees:*** $991 full-time, $33 per credit part-time. ***Room and board:*** $15,674; room only: $11,084. Room and board charges vary according to board plan and housing facility. ***Payment plan:*** installment. ***Waivers:*** senior citizens and employees or children of employees.

Financial Aid Of all full-time matriculated undergraduates who enrolled in 2019, 12,547 applied for aid, 11,066 were judged to have need, 61 had their need fully met. 596 Federal Work-Study jobs (averaging $724,978). In 2019, 443 non-need-based awards were made. ***Average percent of need met:*** 45. ***Average financial aid package:*** $10,658. ***Average need-based loan:*** $4140. ***Average need-based gift aid:*** $9883. ***Average non-need-based aid:*** $4077. ***Average indebtedness upon graduation:*** $45,354.

APPLYING
Options: electronic application, deferred entrance.

Application fee: $65.

Required: essay or personal statement, high school transcript. ***Required for some:*** interview.

Notification: continuous (freshmen), continuous (transfers).

CONTACT
Jeff Indiveri-Gant, Director of Admissions, Montclair State University, One Normal Avenue, Montclair, NJ 07043-1624. *Phone:* 973-655-3316. *Fax:* 973-655-7700. *E-mail:* undergraduate.admissions@montclair.edu.

New Jersey City University

Jersey City, New Jersey

http://www.njcu.edu/

- **State-supported** comprehensive, founded 1927
- **Urban** 51-acre campus with easy access to New York City
- **Coed**
- **Moderately difficult** entrance level

FACULTY
Student/faculty ratio: 15:1.

ACADEMICS
Calendar: semesters. *Degrees:* bachelor's, master's, doctoral, and post-master's certificates.

Library: Congressman Frank J. Guarini Library. *Books:* 300,000 (physical), 150,000 (digital/electronic); *Serial titles:* 150 (physical), 32,000 (digital/electronic); *Databases:* 152. Weekly public service hours: 82.

STUDENT LIFE
Housing options: coed. Campus housing is university owned.

Activities and organizations: drama/theater group, student-run newspaper, radio station, choral group, national fraternities, national sororities.

Athletics Member NCAA. All Division III.

Campus security: 24-hour emergency response devices and patrols, late-night transport/escort service.

Student services: health clinic, personal/psychological counseling, women's center, legal services.

COSTS & FINANCIAL AID
Costs (2019–20) ***Tuition:*** state resident $12,248 full-time, $397 per credit hour part-time; nonresident $22,054 full-time, $714 per credit hour part-time. Part-time tuition and fees vary according to course load. ***Required fees:*** $166 full-time, $3 per credit hour part-time. ***Room and board:*** $14,574. Room and board charges vary according to board plan and housing facility. ***Payment plans:*** installment, deferred payment.

Financial Aid Of all full-time matriculated undergraduates who enrolled in 2017, 4,766 applied for aid, 4,508 were judged to have need, 119 had their need fully met. In 2017, 122 non-need-based awards were made. ***Average percent of need met:*** 49. ***Average financial aid package:*** $11,241. ***Average need-based loan:*** $4003. ***Average need-based gift aid:*** $9167. ***Average non-need-based aid:*** $7685. ***Average indebtedness upon graduation:*** $28,538.

APPLYING
Standardized Tests *Recommended:* SAT (for admission).

Options: electronic application, deferred entrance.

Application fee: $50.

Required: essay or personal statement, high school transcript, minimum 2.8 GPA. ***Required for some:*** interview. ***Recommended:*** 1 letter of recommendation.

CONTACT
Mr. Jose Balda, Director of Admissions, New Jersey City University, 2039 Kennedy Boulevard, Jersey City, NJ 07305. *Phone:* 201-200-3234. *Toll-free phone:* 888-441-NJCU. *E-mail:* admissions@nicu.edu.

New Jersey Institute of Technology

Newark, New Jersey

http://www.njit.edu/

- **State-supported** university, founded 1881, part of State of New Jersey Department of Education
- **Urban** 48-acre campus with easy access to New York City
- **Endowment** $122.8 million
- **Coed** 8,794 undergraduate students, 78% full-time, 25% women, 75% men
- **Moderately difficult** entrance level, 73% of applicants were admitted

UNDERGRAD STUDENTS

6,878 full-time, 1,916 part-time. Students come from 35 states and territories; 79 other countries; 4% are from out of state; 9% Black or African American, non-Hispanic/Latino; 22% Hispanic/Latino; 23% Asian, non-Hispanic/Latino; 0.1% American Indian or Alaska Native, non-Hispanic/Latino; 3% Two or more races, non-Hispanic/Latino; 3% Race/ethnicity unknown; 6% international; 9% transferred in; 24% live on campus.

Freshmen:

Admission: 8,201 applied, 5,971 admitted, 1,360 enrolled. ***Average high school GPA:*** 3.6. ***Test scores:*** SAT evidence-based reading and writing scores over 500: 99%; SAT math scores over 500: 101%; ACT scores over 18: 100%; SAT evidence-based reading and writing scores over 600: 67%; SAT math scores over 600: 85%; ACT scores over 24: 85%; SAT evidence-based reading and writing scores over 700: 16%; SAT math scores over 700: 34%; ACT scores over 30: 32%.

Retention: 88% of full-time freshmen returned.

FACULTY

Total: 879, 52% full-time, 49% with terminal degrees.

Student/faculty ratio: 16:1.

ACADEMICS

Calendar: semesters. *Degrees:* bachelor's, master's, doctoral, and postbachelor's certificates.

Special study options: academic remediation for entering students, accelerated degree program, adult/continuing education programs, advanced placement credit, cooperative education, distance learning, double majors, English as a second language, freshman honors college, honors programs, independent study, internships, off-campus study, part-time degree program, services for LD students, study abroad, summer session for credit. ***ROTC:*** Army (c), Air Force (b).

Unusual degree programs: 3-2 business administration; engineering.

Computers: 1,938 computers/terminals are available on campus for general student use. Students can access the following: campus intranet, computer help desk, free student e-mail accounts, online (class) grades, online (class) registration, online (class) schedules. Campuswide network is available. 100% of college-owned or -operated housing units are wired for high-speed Internet access. Wireless service is available via entire campus.

Library: Van Houten Library plus 1 other. *Books:* 140,063 (physical), 168,865 (digital/electronic); *Serial titles:* 54 (physical), 60,525 (digital/electronic); *Databases:* 37. Weekly public service hours: 111; students can reserve study rooms.

STUDENT LIFE

Housing options: coed. Campus housing is university owned.

Activities and organizations: drama/theater group, student-run newspaper, radio station, choral group, marching band, Student Senate, Student Activities Council, Vector, Institute of Industrial Engineers, WJTB Geek Radio, national fraternities, national sororities.

Athletics Member NCAA. All Division I. ***Intercollegiate sports:*** baseball M(s), basketball M(s)/W(s), bowling M(c), cross-country running M(s)/W(s), fencing M(s)/W(s), ice hockey M(c), lacrosse M(s), soccer M(s)/W(s), swimming and diving M(s), tennis M(s)/W(s), track and field M(s)/W(s), volleyball M(s)/W(s). ***Intramural sports:*** basketball M/W, cheerleading M(c)/W(c), football M/W, racquetball M/W, soccer M/W, table tennis M/W, volleyball M/W.

Campus security: 24-hour emergency response devices and patrols, student patrols, late-night transport/escort service, controlled dormitory access.

Student services: health clinic, personal/psychological counseling, women's center, veterans affairs office.

COSTS & FINANCIAL AID

Costs (2019–20) ***Tuition:*** state resident $14,448 full-time, $549 per credit part-time; nonresident $30,160 full-time, $1289 per credit part-time. Full-time tuition and fees vary according to course load. Part-time tuition and fees vary according to course load. ***Required fees:*** $3226 full-time, $190 per credit part-time. ***Room and board:*** $13,900. Room and board charges vary according to board plan and housing facility. ***Payment plans:*** installment, deferred payment. ***Waivers:*** employees or children of employees.

Financial Aid Of all full-time matriculated undergraduates who enrolled in 2019, 4,315 applied for aid, 3,862 were judged to have need, 466 had their need fully met. 372 Federal Work-Study jobs (averaging $1501). 1,247 state and other part-time jobs (averaging $2461). In 2019, 649 non-need-based awards were made. ***Average percent of need met:*** 55. ***Average financial aid package:*** $14,353. ***Average need-based loan:*** $4577. ***Average need-based gift aid:*** $11,925. ***Average non-need-based aid:*** $14,680. ***Average indebtedness upon graduation:*** $38,718. ***Financial aid deadline:*** 4/15.

APPLYING

Standardized Tests *Required:* SAT or ACT (for admission).

Options: electronic application, early admission, deferred entrance.

Application fee: $75.

Required: high school transcript, 1 letter of recommendation. ***Required for some:*** essay or personal statement, interview.

Application deadlines: 3/1 (freshmen), 8/1 (transfers).

Notification: continuous (freshmen), continuous (transfers).

CONTACT

Mr. Stephen M. Eck, Executive Director of University Admissions, New Jersey Institute of Technology, University Heights, Newark, NJ 07102. *Phone:* 973-596-3306. *Toll-free phone:* 800-925-NJIT. *Fax:* 973-596-3461. *E-mail:* admissions@njit.edu.

Pillar College

Newark, New Jersey

http://www.pillar.edu/

CONTACT

Ms. Linda Aarni, Senior Admissions Counselor, Pillar College, 60 Park Place, Suite 701, Newark, NJ 07102. *Phone:* 973-803-5000. *Toll-free phone:* 800-234-9305. *Fax:* 732-356-4846. *E-mail:* info@pillar.edu.

Princeton University

Princeton, New Jersey

http://www.princeton.edu/

- **Independent** university, founded 1746
- **Suburban** 600-acre campus with easy access to New York City, Philadelphia
- **Coed** 5,422 undergraduate students, 98% full-time, 50% women, 50% men
- **Most difficult** entrance level, 6% of applicants were admitted

UNDERGRAD STUDENTS

5,328 full-time, 94 part-time. 82% are from out of state; 8% Black or African American, non-Hispanic/Latino; 11% Hispanic/Latino; 22% Asian, non-Hispanic/Latino; 0.1% Native Hawaiian or other Pacific Islander, non-Hispanic/Latino; 0.2% American Indian or Alaska Native, non-Hispanic/Latino; 5% Two or more races, non-Hispanic/Latino; 1% Race/ethnicity unknown; 12% international; 0.2% transferred in; 96% live on campus.

Freshmen:

Admission: 32,804 applied, 1,895 admitted, 1,335 enrolled. ***Average high school GPA:*** 3.9. ***Test scores:*** SAT evidence-based reading and writing scores over 500: 100%; SAT math scores over 500: 100%; ACT scores over 18: 100%; SAT evidence-based reading and writing scores over 600: 98%; SAT math scores over 600: 100%; ACT scores over 24: 100%; SAT evidence-based reading and writing scores over 700: 83%; SAT math scores over 700: 90%; ACT scores over 30: 94%.

Retention: 98% of full-time freshmen returned.

FACULTY
Total: 1,263, 77% full-time, 85% with terminal degrees.

Student/faculty ratio: 5:1.

ACADEMICS
Calendar: semesters. *Degrees:* bachelor's, master's, and doctoral.

Special study options: advanced placement credit, independent study, off-campus study, services for LD students, student-designed majors, study abroad. ***ROTC:*** Army (b), Navy (c), Air Force (c).

Computers: 500 computers/terminals and 17,000 ports are available on campus for general student use. Students can access the following: campus intranet, computer help desk, free student e-mail accounts, online (class) grades, online (class) registration, online (class) schedules, academic applications and courseware, printing, network file space, website hosting, media lab, broadcast center. Campuswide network is available. 100% of college-owned or -operated housing units are wired for high-speed Internet access. Wireless service is available via entire campus.

Library: Harvey S. Firestone Memorial Library plus 9 others. *Books:* 7.3 million (physical), 2.1 million (digital/electronic); *Serial titles:* 150,820 (physical), 291,025 (digital/electronic); *Databases:* 1,899. Weekly public service hours: 105.

STUDENT LIFE
Housing options: on-campus residence required through sophomore year; coed, men-only, women-only, special housing for students with disabilities. Campus housing is university owned. Freshman campus housing is guaranteed.

Activities and organizations: drama/theater group, student-run newspaper, radio and television station, choral group, marching band.

Athletics Member NCAA. All Division I except football (Division I-AA). ***Intercollegiate sports:*** baseball M, basketball M/W, crew M/W, cross-country running M/W, fencing M/W, field hockey W, golf M/W(c), ice hockey M/W, lacrosse M/W, soccer M/W, softball W, squash M/W, swimming and diving M/W, tennis M/W, track and field M/W, volleyball M/W, water polo M/W, wrestling M. ***Intramural sports:*** badminton M(c)/W(c), baseball M(c), basketball M(c)/W(c), cheerleading M(c)/W(c), cross-country running M(c)/W(c), equestrian sports M(c)/W(c), fencing M(c)/W(c), field hockey W(c), ice hockey M(c)/W(c), lacrosse M(c)/W(c), rugby M(c)/W(c), sailing M(c)/W(c), skiing (downhill) M(c)/W(c), soccer M(c)/W(c), softball W(c), squash M(c)/W(c), swimming and diving M(c)/W(c), table tennis M(c)/W(c), tennis M(c)/W(c), ultimate Frisbee M(c)/W(c), volleyball M(c)/W(c).

Campus security: 24-hour emergency response devices and patrols, student patrols, late-night transport/escort service, controlled dormitory access.

Student services: health clinic, personal/psychological counseling, women's center, legal services.

COSTS & FINANCIAL AID
Costs (2019–20) ***Comprehensive fee:*** $66,700 includes full-time tuition ($49,450), mandatory fees ($890), and room and board ($16,360). Part-time tuition: $6166 per year. ***Required fees:*** $25 per term part-time. ***College room only:*** $9520. Room and board charges vary according to board plan. ***Waivers:*** employees or children of employees.

Financial Aid Of all full-time matriculated undergraduates who enrolled in 2019, 3,516 applied for aid, 3,289 were judged to have need, 3,289 had their need fully met. ***Average percent of need met:*** 100. ***Average financial aid package:*** $59,389. ***Average need-based gift aid:*** $57,251. ***Average indebtedness upon graduation:*** $9445.

APPLYING
Standardized Tests *Required:* SAT or ACT (for admission). *Recommended:* SAT Subject Tests (for admission).

Options: electronic application, early action, deferred entrance.

Application fee: $75.

Required: high school transcript, 3 letters of recommendation, graded written paper. ***Recommended:*** interview.

Application deadlines: 1/1 (freshmen), 11/1 (early action).

Notification: 4/1 (freshmen), 4/1 (out-of-state freshmen).

CONTACT
Princeton University, Princeton, NJ 08544-1019. *Phone:* 609-258-3040.

Rabbi Jacob Joseph School
Edison, New Jersey

CONTACT
Rabbi Jacob Joseph School, One Plainfield Ave, Edison, NJ 08817.

Rabbinical College of America
Morristown, New Jersey
http://www.rca.edu/

CONTACT
Shoshana Solomon, Registrar, Rabbinical College of America, 226 Sussex Avenue, PO Box 1996, Morristown, NJ 07962-1996. *Phone:* 973-267-9404. *E-mail:* rca079@aol.com.

Ramapo College of New Jersey
Mahwah, New Jersey
http://www.ramapo.edu/

- **State-supported** comprehensive, founded 1969, part of New Jersey State College System
- **Suburban** 300-acre campus with easy access to New York City
- **Coed** 5,574 undergraduate students, 87% full-time, 56% women, 44% men
- **Moderately difficult** entrance level, 66% of applicants were admitted

UNDERGRAD STUDENTS
4,870 full-time, 704 part-time. Students come from 20 states and territories; 42 other countries; 5% are from out of state; 6% Black or African American, non-Hispanic/Latino; 20% Hispanic/Latino; 8% Asian, non-Hispanic/Latino; 0.6% American Indian or Alaska Native, non-Hispanic/Latino; 0.2% Two or more races, non-Hispanic/Latino; 4% Race/ethnicity unknown; 2% international; 8% transferred in; 45% live on campus.

Freshmen:
Admission: 7,331 applied, 4,808 admitted, 1,003 enrolled. ***Average high school GPA:*** 3.4. ***Test scores:*** SAT evidence-based reading and writing scores over 500: 86%; SAT math scores over 500: 84%; ACT scores over 18: 91%; SAT evidence-based reading and writing scores over 600: 34%; SAT math scores over 600: 31%; ACT scores over 24: 49%; SAT evidence-based reading and writing scores over 700: 4%; SAT math scores over 700: 7%; ACT scores over 30: 9%.

Retention: 88% of full-time freshmen returned.

FACULTY
Total: 522, 42% full-time, 40% with terminal degrees.

Student/faculty ratio: 16:1.

ACADEMICS
Calendar: semesters. *Degrees:* certificates, bachelor's, master's, post-master's, and postbachelor's certificates.

Special study options: academic remediation for entering students, accelerated degree program, adult/continuing education programs, advanced placement credit, cooperative education, distance learning, double majors, external degree program, freshman honors college, honors programs, independent study, internships, off-campus study, part-time degree program, services for LD students, student-designed majors, study abroad, summer session for credit. ***ROTC:*** Army (c), Air Force (c).

Unusual degree programs: 3-2 biology, chemistry with Rutgers, The State University of New Jersey; dentistry with New York University; optometry with SUNY State College of Optometry.

Computers: Students can access the following: campus intranet, computer help desk, free student e-mail accounts, online (class) grades, online (class) registration, online (class) schedules. Campuswide network is available. 100% of college-owned or -operated housing units are wired for high-speed Internet access. Wireless service is available via classrooms, computer centers, computer labs, learning centers, libraries, student centers.

Library: George T. Potter Library.

STUDENT LIFE

Housing options: coed. Campus housing is university owned. Freshman campus housing is guaranteed.

Activities and organizations: drama/theater group, student-run newspaper, radio and television station, choral group, national fraternities, national sororities.

Athletics Member NCAA. All Division III. ***Intercollegiate sports:*** baseball M, basketball M/W, cheerleading M(c)/W(c), cross-country running M/W, field hockey W, ice hockey M(c), lacrosse M(c)/W, soccer M/W, softball W, swimming and diving M/W, tennis M/W, track and field M/W, ultimate Frisbee M(c)/W(c), volleyball M/W. ***Intramural sports:*** baseball W, basketball M, bowling M/W, football M/W, rock climbing M/W, soccer M/W, table tennis M/W, ultimate Frisbee M/W, volleyball M/W.

Campus security: 24-hour emergency response devices and patrols, late-night transport/escort service, controlled dormitory access, surveillance cameras, patrols by trained security personnel.

Student services: health clinic, personal/psychological counseling, women's center, veterans affairs office.

COSTS & FINANCIAL AID

Costs (2019–20) ***Tuition:*** state resident $12,171 full-time, $380 per credit part-time; nonresident $21,722 full-time, $679 per credit part-time. Full-time tuition and fees vary according to reciprocity agreements. Part-time tuition and fees vary according to reciprocity agreements. ***Required fees:*** $2507 full-time, $78 per credit part-time. ***Room and board:*** $12,840; room only: $8850. Room and board charges vary according to board plan and housing facility. ***Payment plan:*** installment. ***Waivers:*** senior citizens and employees or children of employees.

Financial Aid Of all full-time matriculated undergraduates who enrolled in 2018, 3,445 applied for aid, 2,602 were judged to have need, 88 had their need fully met. In 2018, 522 non-need-based awards were made. ***Average percent of need met:*** 53. ***Average financial aid package:*** $11,302. ***Average need-based loan:*** $4244. ***Average need-based gift aid:*** $10,325. ***Average non-need-based aid:*** $10,335. ***Average indebtedness upon graduation:*** $35,658.

APPLYING

Standardized Tests *Required:* SAT or ACT (for admission).

Options: electronic application, early decision, early action, deferred entrance.

Application fee: $65.

Required: essay or personal statement, high school transcript. ***Recommended:*** minimum 2.5 GPA.

Application deadlines: 2/1 (freshmen), 2/1 (out-of-state freshmen), 5/1 (transfers), 12/15 (early action).

Early decision deadline: 11/1.

CONTACT

Ramapo College Office of Admissions, Ramapo College of New Jersey, Office of Admissions, 505 Ramapo Valley Road, Mahwah, NJ 07430-1680. *Phone:* 201-684-7300. *Toll-free phone:* 800-9RAMAPO. *Fax:* 201-684-7964. *E-mail:* admissions@ramapo.edu.

Rider University

Lawrenceville, New Jersey

http://www.rider.edu/

- **Independent** comprehensive, founded 1865
- **Suburban** 280-acre campus with easy access to New York City, Philadelphia
- **Endowment** $64.3 million
- **Coed**
- **Moderately difficult** entrance level

FACULTY

Student/faculty ratio: 11:1.

ACADEMICS

Calendar: semesters. *Degrees:* certificates, associate, bachelor's, master's, doctoral, post-master's, and postbachelor's certificates.

Library: Franklin F. Moore Library plus 1 other. *Books:* 311,713 (physical), 174,115 (digital/electronic); *Serial titles:* 723 (physical), 54,382 (digital/electronic); *Databases:* 171. Study areas open 24 hours, 5–7 days a week; students can reserve study rooms.

STUDENT LIFE

Housing options: coed, women-only, special housing for students with disabilities. Campus housing is university owned. Freshman applicants given priority for college housing.

Activities and organizations: drama/theater group, student-run newspaper, radio and television station, choral group, Student Government Association, Greek Council, Association of Commuter Students, Black Student Union, Residence Hall Association, national fraternities, national sororities.

Athletics Member NCAA. All Division I.

Campus security: 24-hour emergency response devices and patrols, student patrols, late-night transport/escort service, controlled dormitory access.

Student services: health clinic, personal/psychological counseling.

COSTS & FINANCIAL AID

Costs (2019–20) ***Comprehensive fee:*** $58,140 includes full-time tuition ($42,120), mandatory fees ($740), and room and board ($15,280). ***College room only:*** $10,020.

Financial Aid Of all full-time matriculated undergraduates who enrolled in 2018, 3,007 applied for aid, 2,750 were judged to have need, 437 had their need fully met. In 2018, 657 non-need-based awards were made. ***Average percent of need met:*** 76. ***Average financial aid package:*** $32,185. ***Average need-based loan:*** $3284. ***Average need-based gift aid:*** $28,285. ***Average non-need-based aid:*** $19,937. ***Average indebtedness upon graduation:*** $36,499.

APPLYING

Options: electronic application, early admission, early action, deferred entrance.

Application fee: $50.

Required: essay or personal statement, high school transcript, 1 letter of recommendation. ***Required for some:*** interview.

CONTACT

Susan Christian, Dean of Enrollment, Rider University, 2083 Lawrenceville Road, Lawrenceville, NJ 08648. *Phone:* 609-896-5042. *Toll-free phone:* 800-257-9026. *Fax:* 609-895-6645.

See below for display ad and page 1102 for the College Close-Up.

Rowan University

Glassboro, New Jersey

http://www.rowan.edu/

- **State-supported** comprehensive, founded 1923, part of New Jersey State College System
- **Suburban** 921-acre campus with easy access to Philadelphia
- **Endowment** $173.2 million
- **Coed** 16,011 undergraduate students, 88% full-time, 46% women, 54% men
- **Moderately difficult** entrance level, 74% of applicants were admitted

UNDERGRAD STUDENTS

14,055 full-time, 1,956 part-time. Students come from 28 states and territories; 22 other countries; 7% are from out of state; 10% Black or African American, non-Hispanic/Latino; 11% Hispanic/Latino; 5% Asian, non-Hispanic/Latino; 0.1% Native Hawaiian or other Pacific Islander, non-Hispanic/Latino; 0.1% American Indian or Alaska Native, non-Hispanic/Latino; 4% Two or more races, non-Hispanic/Latino; 1% Race/ethnicity unknown; 1% international; 11% transferred in; 4% live on campus.

Freshmen:

Admission: 14,370 applied, 10,676 admitted, 2,606 enrolled. ***Average high school GPA:*** 3.6. ***Test scores:*** SAT evidence-based reading and writing scores over 500: 88%; SAT math scores over 500: 87%; ACT scores over 18: 93%; SAT evidence-based reading and writing scores over 600: 38%; SAT math scores over 600: 38%; ACT scores over 24: 53%; SAT evidence-based reading and writing scores over 700: 5%; SAT math scores over 700: 9%; ACT scores over 30: 13%.

Retention: 83% of full-time freshmen returned.

FACULTY

Total: 1,640, 30% full-time, 28% with terminal degrees.

Student/faculty ratio: 17:1.

ACADEMICS

Calendar: semesters. *Degrees:* certificates, bachelor's, master's, doctoral, post-master's, and postbachelor's certificates.

Special study options: academic remediation for entering students, accelerated degree program, adult/continuing education programs, advanced placement credit, cooperative education, distance learning, double majors, English as a second language, freshman honors college, honors programs, independent study, internships, off-campus study, part-time degree program, services for LD students, study abroad, summer session for credit. ***ROTC:*** Army (c).

Unusual degree programs: 3-2 mathematics and computer science.

Computers: 836 computers/terminals and 2,500 ports are available on campus for general student use. Students can access the following: campus intranet, computer help desk, free student e-mail accounts, online (class) grades, online (class) registration, online (class) schedules. Campuswide network is available. 100% of college-owned or -operated housing units are wired for high-speed Internet access. Wireless service is available via entire campus.

Library: Keith and Shirley Campbell Library plus 4 others. *Books:* 328,891 (physical), 494,739 (digital/electronic); *Serial titles:* 129,972 (digital/electronic); *Databases:* 846. Students can reserve study rooms.

STUDENT LIFE

Housing options: on-campus residence required through sophomore year; coed, special housing for students with disabilities. Campus housing is university owned. Freshman campus housing is guaranteed.

Activities and organizations: drama/theater group, student-run newspaper, radio and television station, choral group, Kappa Delta Pi, Public Relations Student Society of America, Student University Programmes, Rowan Television Network, Elementary Education Club, national fraternities, national sororities.

Athletics Member NCAA. All Division III. ***Intercollegiate sports:*** baseball M, basketball M/W, cross-country running M/W, field hockey W, football M, lacrosse M/W, rugby M/W, soccer M/W, softball W, swimming and diving M/W, track and field M/W, volleyball W. ***Intramural sports:*** basketball M/W, cheerleading M/W(c), field hockey W(c), football M/W, golf M/W, racquetball M/W, rock climbing M(c)/W, skiing (downhill) M(c)/W(c), soccer M/W, softball M/W, table tennis M/W, tennis M(c)/W(c), ultimate Frisbee M(c)/W(c), volleyball M/W, water polo M/W, weight lifting M/W, wrestling M(c).

Campus security: 24-hour emergency response devices and patrols, student patrols, late-night transport/escort service, controlled dormitory access, EMS service including 2 ambulances, security and campus police trained as police officers in NJ.

Student services: health clinic, personal/psychological counseling, legal services, veterans affairs office.

COSTS & FINANCIAL AID

Costs (2020–21) ***Tuition:*** $387 per credit hour part-time; state resident $387 per credit hour part-time; nonresident $728 per credit hour part-time.

Financial Aid Of all full-time matriculated undergraduates who enrolled in 2018, 11,422 applied for aid, 9,587 were judged to have need, 1,060 had their need fully met. In 2018, 574 non-need-based awards were made. ***Average percent of need met:*** 65. ***Average financial aid package:*** $10,346. ***Average need-based loan:*** $4300. ***Average need-based gift aid:*** $8987. ***Average non-need-based aid:*** $7148. ***Average indebtedness upon graduation:*** $34,519.

APPLYING

Standardized Tests *Required:* SAT or ACT (for admission).

Options: electronic application, early admission, deferred entrance.

Application fee: $65.

Required: high school transcript, minimum 2.0 GPA. ***Required for some:*** interview.

Application deadlines: 3/1 (freshmen), 3/1 (transfers).

Notification: continuous (freshmen), continuous (transfers).

CONTACT

Rowan University, 201 Mullica Hill Road, Glassboro, NJ 08028-1701. *Toll-free phone:* 800-447-1165 (in-state); 800-447-1165N (out-of-state).

Rutgers University–Camden

Camden, New Jersey

http://www.camden.rutgers.edu/

- **State-supported** university, founded 1926
- **Urban** 29-acre campus with easy access to Philadelphia
- **Endowment** $1.2 million
- **Coed**
- **Moderately difficult** entrance level

FACULTY

Student/faculty ratio: 15:1.

ACADEMICS

Calendar: semesters. *Degrees:* bachelor's, master's, doctoral, post-master's, and postbachelor's certificates.

Library: Paul Robeson Library plus 1 other. Weekly public service hours: 90; students can reserve study rooms.

STUDENT LIFE

Housing options: coed, special housing for students with disabilities. Campus housing is university owned.

Activities and organizations: drama/theater group, student-run newspaper, radio station, choral group, national fraternities, national sororities.

Athletics Member NCAA. All Division III.

Campus security: 24-hour emergency response devices and patrols, student patrols, late-night transport/escort service, controlled dormitory access.

Student services: health clinic, personal/psychological counseling, women's center, legal services, veterans affairs office.

COSTS & FINANCIAL AID

Costs (2019–20) ***Tuition:*** state resident $12,230 full-time, $394 per credit hour part-time; nonresident $28,466 full-time, $924 per credit hour part-time. Full-time tuition and fees vary according to program. Part-time tuition and fees vary according to course load and program. ***Required fees:*** $3034 full-time, $613 per term part-time. ***Room and board:*** $12,691; room only: $8831. Room and board charges vary according to board plan and housing facility.

Financial Aid Of all full-time matriculated undergraduates who enrolled in 2017, 4,202 applied for aid, 3,917 were judged to have need, 119 had their need fully met. 315 Federal Work-Study jobs (averaging $2539). 617 state and other part-time jobs (averaging $3174). In 2017, 91 non-need-based awards were made. ***Average percent of need met:*** 54. ***Average financial aid package:*** $13,937. ***Average need-based loan:*** $4464. ***Average need-based gift aid:*** $10,656. ***Average non-need-based aid:*** $4688. ***Average indebtedness upon graduation:*** $31,307.

APPLYING

Standardized Tests *Required:* SAT or ACT (for admission).

Options: electronic application, early action, deferred entrance.

Application fee: $70.

Required: essay or personal statement. ***Required for some:*** high school transcript, interview.

CONTACT

Office of Graduate and Undergraduate Admissions, Rutgers University–Camden, 330 Cooper Street, Camden, NJ 08102. *Phone:* 856-225-6104. *E-mail:* admissions@camden.rutgers.edu.

Rutgers University–Newark

Newark, New Jersey

http://www.newark.rutgers.edu/

- **State-supported** university, founded 1908
- **Urban** 40-acre campus with easy access to New York City
- **Endowment** $1.2 million
- **Coed**
- **Moderately difficult** entrance level

FACULTY

Student/faculty ratio: 16:1.

ACADEMICS

Calendar: semesters. *Degrees:* bachelor's, master's, doctoral, post-master's, and postbachelor's certificates.

Library: John Cotton Dana Library plus 4 others. Weekly public service hours: 91; students can reserve study rooms.

STUDENT LIFE

Housing options: coed. Campus housing is university owned.

Activities and organizations: drama/theater group, student-run newspaper, radio station, choral group, marching band, national fraternities, national sororities.

Athletics Member NCAA. All Division III.

Campus security: 24-hour emergency response devices and patrols, student patrols, late-night transport/escort service, controlled dormitory access.

Student services: health clinic, personal/psychological counseling, women's center, legal services, veterans affairs office.

COSTS & FINANCIAL AID

Costs (2019–20) ***Tuition:*** state resident $12,230 full-time, $394 per credit hour part-time; nonresident $29,012 full-time, $942 per credit hour part-time. Full-time tuition and fees vary according to program. Part-time tuition and fees vary according to course load and program. ***Required fees:*** $2596 full-time, $502 per term part-time. ***Room and board:*** $13,929; room only: $8615. Room and board charges vary according to board plan and housing facility.

Financial Aid Of all full-time matriculated undergraduates who enrolled in 2018, 6,380 applied for aid, 6,126 were judged to have need, 85 had their need fully met. In 2018, 54 non-need-based awards were made. ***Average percent of need met:*** 49. ***Average financial aid package:*** $15,125. ***Average need-based loan:*** $4258. ***Average need-based gift aid:*** $12,825. ***Average non-need-based aid:*** $8439. ***Average indebtedness upon graduation:*** $27,343.

APPLYING

Standardized Tests *Required:* SAT or ACT (for admission).

Options: electronic application, early action, deferred entrance.

Application fee: $70.

Required: essay or personal statement. ***Required for some:*** high school transcript.

CONTACT

Office of Undergraduate and Graduate Admissions, Rutgers University–Newark, 190 University Avenue, Room 101, Newark, NJ 07102. *Phone:* 973-353-5205. *E-mail:* newarkadmissions@ugadm.rutgers.edu.

Rutgers University–New Brunswick

Piscataway, New Jersey

http://newbrunswick.rutgers.edu/

- **State-supported** university, founded 1766
- **Urban** 2685-acre campus with easy access to New York City
- **Endowment** $1.2 million
- **Coed**
- **Moderately difficult** entrance level

FACULTY

Student/faculty ratio: 16:1.

ACADEMICS

Calendar: semesters. *Degrees:* certificates, diplomas, associate, bachelor's, master's, doctoral, post-master's, and postbachelor's certificates.

Library: Archibald S. Alexander Library plus 15 others. Study areas open 24 hours, 5–7 days a week; students can reserve study rooms.

STUDENT LIFE

Housing options: coed, men-only, women-only, cooperative, special housing for students with disabilities. Campus housing is university owned.

Activities and organizations: drama/theater group, student-run newspaper, radio and television station, choral group, marching band, national fraternities, national sororities.

Athletics Member NCAA. All Division I except football (Division I-A).

Campus security: 24-hour emergency response devices and patrols, student patrols, late-night transport/escort service, controlled dormitory access.

Student services: health clinic, personal/psychological counseling, women's center, legal services, veterans affairs office.

COSTS & FINANCIAL AID

Costs (2019–20) ***Tuition:*** state resident $12,230 full-time, $394 per credit hour part-time; nonresident $29,012 full-time, $942 per credit hour part-time. Full-time tuition and fees vary according to program. Part-time tuition and fees vary according to course load and program. ***Required fees:*** $3177 full-time, $459 per term part-time. ***Room and board:*** $13,075; room only: $7971. Room and board charges vary according to board plan and housing facility.

Financial Aid Of all full-time matriculated undergraduates who enrolled in 2018, 20,697 applied for aid, 17,686 were judged to have need, 719 had their need fully met. In 2018, 909 non-need-based awards were made. ***Average percent of need met:*** 46. ***Average financial aid package:*** $14,433. ***Average need-based loan:*** $4401. ***Average need-based gift aid:*** $12,215. ***Average non-need-based aid:*** $11,310. ***Average indebtedness upon graduation:*** $30,829.

APPLYING

Standardized Tests *Required:* SAT or ACT (for admission).

Options: electronic application, early action, deferred entrance.

Application fee: $70.

Required: essay or personal statement. ***Required for some:*** high school transcript, interview.

CONTACT

Undergraduate Admissions Office, Rutgers University–New Brunswick, 65 Davidson Road, Room 202, Piscataway, NJ 08854. *Phone:* 732-445-1000. *E-mail:* admissions@ugadm.rutgers.edu.

Saint Peter's University

Jersey City, New Jersey

http://www.saintpeters.edu/

CONTACT

Miss Kacey Tillotson, Director of Undergraduate Admissions, Saint Peter's University, Office of Admission, Lee House, Jersey City 07306. *Phone:* 201-761-7100. *Toll-free phone:* 888-SPC-9933. *E-mail:* ktillotson@saintpeters.edu.

Seton Hall University

South Orange, New Jersey

http://www.shu.edu/

CONTACT

Mary Clare Cullum, Director of Undergraduate Admissions, Seton Hall University, Enrollment Management Office, 400 South Orange Avenue, South Orange, NJ 07079-2697. *Phone:* 973-275-2589. *Toll-free phone:* 800-THE HALL. *Fax:* 973-275-2321. *E-mail:* maryclare.cullum@shu.edu.

See below for display ad and page 1110 for the College Close-Up.

Stevens Institute of Technology

Hoboken, New Jersey

http://www.stevens.edu/

- **Independent** university, founded 1870
- **Urban** 55-acre campus with easy access to New York City
- **Endowment** $224.3 million
- **Coed** 3,659 undergraduate students, 100% full-time, 29% women, 71% men
- **Very difficult** entrance level, 40% of applicants were admitted

UNDERGRAD STUDENTS

3,642 full-time, 17 part-time. Students come from 41 states and territories; 50 other countries; 38% are from out of state; 2% Black or African American, non-Hispanic/Latino; 12% Hispanic/Latino; 17% Asian, non-

Hispanic/Latino; 0.1% American Indian or Alaska Native, non-Hispanic/Latino; 4% Race/ethnicity unknown; 3% international; 0.6% transferred in; 51% live on campus.

Freshmen:
Admission: 10,475 applied, 4,186 admitted, 969 enrolled. ***Average high school GPA:*** 3.8. ***Test scores:*** SAT evidence-based reading and writing scores over 500: 100%; SAT math scores over 500: 100%; ACT scores over 18: 100%; SAT evidence-based reading and writing scores over 600: 93%; SAT math scores over 600: 99%; ACT scores over 24: 100%; SAT evidence-based reading and writing scores over 700: 41%; SAT math scores over 700: 78%; ACT scores over 30: 85%.

Retention: 94% of full-time freshmen returned.

FACULTY
Total: 391, 71% full-time, 80% with terminal degrees.

Student/faculty ratio: 11:1.

ACADEMICS
Calendar: semesters. *Degrees:* bachelor's, master's, doctoral, and postbachelor's certificates.

Special study options: accelerated degree program, advanced placement credit, cooperative education, distance learning, double majors, honors programs, independent study, internships, off-campus study, services for LD students, study abroad, summer session for credit. ***ROTC:*** Army (c), Air Force (c).

Computers: 156 computers/terminals and 1,850 ports are available on campus for general student use. Students can access the following: campus intranet, computer help desk, free student e-mail accounts, online (class) grades, online (class) registration, online (class) schedules, online account information, debit dining program, laundry status. Campuswide network is available. 100% of college-owned or -operated housing units are wired for high-speed Internet access. Wireless service is available via entire campus.

Library: Samuel C. Williams Library. *Books:* 66,492 (physical), 210,243 (digital/electronic); *Serial titles:* 898 (physical), 35,353 (digital/electronic); *Databases:* 71. Students can reserve study rooms.

STUDENT LIFE
Housing options: coed, women-only. Campus housing is university owned. Freshman campus housing is guaranteed.

Activities and organizations: drama/theater group, student-run newspaper, radio and television station, choral group, Society of Women Engineers, Computer and Console Gaming Society, Stevens Poker Club, Sustainability, Activism, Volunteering, & Engineering (SAVE), Stevens Climbing and Mountaineering Club, national fraternities, national sororities.

Athletics Member NCAA. All Division III. ***Intercollegiate sports:*** baseball M, basketball M/W, cross-country running M/W, fencing M/W, field hockey W, golf M, lacrosse M/W, soccer M/W, softball W, swimming and diving M/W, tennis M/W, track and field M/W, volleyball M/W, wrestling M. ***Intramural sports:*** archery M(c)/W(c), baseball M(c), basketball M, bowling M(c)/W(c), crew M(c)/W(c), field hockey M, football M/W(c), ice hockey M(c), lacrosse M(c), sailing M(c)/W(c), skiing (cross-country) M(c)/W(c), skiing (downhill) M(c)/W(c), soccer M(c)/W(c), softball W, squash M, ultimate Frisbee M(c), volleyball M(c)/W(c).

Campus security: 24-hour emergency response devices and patrols, late-night transport/escort service, controlled dormitory access.

Student services: health clinic, personal/psychological counseling, women's center, veterans affairs office.

COSTS & FINANCIAL AID
Costs (2020–21) ***Comprehensive fee:*** $72,196 includes full-time tuition ($53,828), mandatory fees ($2124), and room and board ($16,244). Full-time tuition and fees vary according to course load. Part-time tuition: $1799 per credit. Part-time tuition and fees vary according to course load. ***Required fees:*** $1062 per term part-time. ***Room and board:*** Room and board charges vary according to board plan and housing facility. ***Payment plan:*** installment. ***Waivers:*** employees or children of employees.

Financial Aid Of all full-time matriculated undergraduates who enrolled in 2017, 2,361 applied for aid, 2,000 were judged to have need, 325 had their need fully met. In 2017, 912 non-need-based awards were made. ***Average percent of need met:*** 69. ***Average financial aid package:*** $30,331. ***Average need-based loan:*** $4380. ***Average need-based gift aid:*** $13,203. ***Average non-need-based aid:*** $18,498. ***Average indebtedness upon graduation:*** $40,588.

APPLYING
Standardized Tests *Required for some:* SAT or ACT (for admission), SAT and SAT Subject Tests or ACT (for admission), Applicants to Music and Technology or Visual Arts and Technology may submit a digital portfolio in place of standardized test scores. International applicants may submit 2 SAT II scores, 2 AP scores, or 2 IB scores in place of standardized test scores.

Options: electronic application, early admission, early decision, deferred entrance.

Application fee: $70.

Required: essay or personal statement, high school transcript, 2 letters of recommendation. ***Required for some:*** digital portfolio for music and technology or visual arts and technology programs. ***Recommended:*** interview.

Application deadlines: 1/15 (freshmen), 6/1 (transfers).

Early decision deadline: 11/15 (for plan 1), 1/15 (for plan 2).

Notification: 4/1 (freshmen), continuous until 6/30 (transfers), 12/15 (early decision plan 1), 2/15 (early decision plan 2).

CONTACT
Jackie Williams, Dean of Undergraduate Admissions, Stevens Institute of Technology, Castle Point on Hudson, Hoboken, NJ 07030. *Phone:* 201-216-5207. *Toll-free phone:* 800-458-5323. *E-mail:* jackie.williams@stevens.edu.

Stockton University

Galloway, New Jersey

http://www.stockton.edu/

- **State-supported** comprehensive, founded 1969, part of New Jersey State College System
- **Suburban** 2000-acre campus with easy access to Philadelphia
- **Endowment** $33.3 million
- **Coed** 8,893 undergraduate students, 95% full-time, 59% women, 41% men
- **Very difficult** entrance level, 75% of applicants were admitted

UNDERGRAD STUDENTS
8,459 full-time, 434 part-time. Students come from 33 states and territories; 13 other countries; 3% are from out of state; 9% Black or African American, non-Hispanic/Latino; 15% Hispanic/Latino; 7% Asian, non-Hispanic/Latino; 0.1% Native Hawaiian or other Pacific Islander, non-Hispanic/Latino; 0.2% American Indian or Alaska Native, non-Hispanic/Latino; 3% Two or more races, non-Hispanic/Latino; 1% Race/ethnicity unknown; 0.6% international; 13% transferred in; 37% live on campus.

Freshmen:
Admission: 7,004 applied, 5,277 admitted, 1,537 enrolled. ***Test scores:*** SAT evidence-based reading and writing scores over 500: 83%; SAT math scores over 500: 83%; ACT scores over 18: 90%; SAT evidence-based reading and writing scores over 600: 29%; SAT math scores over 600: 29%; ACT scores over 24: 49%; SAT evidence-based reading and writing scores over 700: 3%; SAT math scores over 700: 5%; ACT scores over 30: 7%.

Retention: 83% of full-time freshmen returned.

FACULTY
Total: 721, 49% full-time, 64% with terminal degrees.

Student/faculty ratio: 17:1.

ACADEMICS
Calendar: semesters. *Degrees:* certificates, bachelor's, master's, doctoral, and postbachelor's certificates.

Special study options: academic remediation for entering students, accelerated degree program, adult/continuing education programs, advanced placement credit, distance learning, double majors, English as a second language, honors programs, independent study, internships, off-campus study, part-time degree program, services for LD students, student-designed majors, study abroad, summer session for credit.

Unusual degree programs: 3-2 business administration; engineering with New Jersey Institute of Technology; Rutgers, The State University of New Jersey; Rowan University; public health with Rutgers University, medical technology with University of Delaware.

Computers: 1,879 computers/terminals are available on campus for general student use. Students can access the following: campus intranet, computer help desk, free student e-mail accounts, online (class) grades, online (class) registration, online (class) schedules. Campuswide network is available. 100% of college-owned or -operated housing units are wired for high-speed Internet access. Wireless service is available via entire campus.

Library: Richard E. Bjork Library. *Books:* 198,696 (physical), 251,566 (digital/electronic); *Serial titles:* 85 (physical), 91,490 (digital/electronic); *Databases:* 188. Weekly public service hours: 116.

STUDENT LIFE

Housing options: coed, special housing for students with disabilities. Campus housing is university owned. Freshman campus housing is guaranteed.

Activities and organizations: drama/theater group, student-run newspaper, radio and television station, choral group, Occupational Therapy Club, Sign Language Club, Animal Friendly Organization, Commuters on the Go, Archery Recreational Club of Stockton, national fraternities, national sororities.

Athletics Member NCAA. All Division III. ***Intercollegiate sports:*** baseball M, basketball M/W, crew W, cross-country running M/W, field hockey W, lacrosse M/W, soccer M/W, softball W, tennis W, track and field M/W, volleyball W. ***Intramural sports:*** basketball M/W, bowling M(c)/W(c), crew M(c), fencing M(c), field hockey W(c), golf M(c)/W(c), ice hockey M(c)/W(c), soccer M/W, softball M/W, table tennis M(c)/W(c), tennis M(c)/W(c), ultimate Frisbee M(c)/W(c), volleyball M(c).

Campus security: 24-hour emergency response devices and patrols, late-night transport/escort service, controlled dormitory access.

Student services: health clinic, personal/psychological counseling, women's center, veterans affairs office.

COSTS & FINANCIAL AID

Costs (2019–20) ***Tuition:*** state resident $12,005 full-time, $462 per credit part-time; nonresident $19,293 full-time, $742 per credit part-time. Part-time tuition and fees vary according to course load. ***Required fees:*** $2043 full-time, $79 per credit part-time, $135 per term part-time. ***Room and board:*** $12,496; room only: $8396. Room and board charges vary according to board plan and housing facility. ***Payment plans:*** installment, deferred payment. ***Waivers:*** senior citizens and employees or children of employees.

Financial Aid Of all full-time matriculated undergraduates who enrolled in 2019, 7,329 applied for aid, 6,116 were judged to have need, 2,578 had their need fully met. 251 Federal Work-Study jobs (averaging $2323). 1,007 state and other part-time jobs (averaging $1871). In 2019, 483 non-need-based awards were made. ***Average percent of need met:*** 77. ***Average financial aid package:*** $17,758. ***Average need-based loan:*** $4387. ***Average need-based gift aid:*** $9301. ***Average non-need-based aid:*** $8103. ***Average indebtedness upon graduation:*** $31,470.

APPLYING

Standardized Tests *Required for some:* SAT or ACT (for admission).

Options: electronic application, early admission, deferred entrance.

Application fee: $50.

Required: high school transcript, minimum 2.0 GPA. ***Recommended:*** essay or personal statement, minimum 3.0 GPA, 3 letters of recommendation.

Application deadlines: 8/15 (freshmen), 8/15 (out-of-state freshmen), 6/1 (transfers).

Notification: 9/1 (freshmen), 9/1 (out-of-state freshmen), continuous until 6/15 (transfers).

CONTACT

Stockton University, 101 Vera King Farris Drive, Galloway, NJ 08205-9441. *Phone:* 609-652-4261.

See below for display ad and page 1114 for the College Close-Up.

Strayer University–Cherry Hill Campus

Cherry Hill, New Jersey

http://www.strayer.edu/new-jersey/cherry-hill/

CONTACT
Strayer University–Cherry Hill Campus, 2370 State Route 70 West, Suite 335, Cherry Hill, NJ 08002. *Toll-free phone:* 888-311-0355.

Strayer University–Piscataway Campus

Piscataway, New Jersey

http://www.strayer.edu/new-jersey/piscataway/

CONTACT
Strayer University–Piscataway Campus, 242 Old New Brunswick Road, Suite 220, Piscataway, NJ 08854. *Toll-free phone:* 888-311-0355.

Strayer University–Willingboro Campus

Willingboro, New Jersey

http://www.strayer.edu/new-jersey/willingboro/

CONTACT
Strayer University–Willingboro Campus, 300 Willingboro Parkway, Willingboro Town Center, Suite 125, Willingboro, NJ 08046. *Toll-free phone:* 888-311-0355.

Talmudical Academy of New Jersey

Adelphia, New Jersey

CONTACT
Director of Admissions, Talmudical Academy of New Jersey, 868 Route 524, Adelphia, NJ 07710. *Phone:* 201-431-1600.

Thomas Edison State University

Trenton, New Jersey

http://www.tesu.edu/

- **State-supported** comprehensive, founded 1972
- **Urban** 2-acre campus with easy access to Philadelphia
- **Coed**
- **Noncompetitive** entrance level

FACULTY
Student/faculty ratio: 15:1.

ACADEMICS
Calendar: continuous. *Degrees:* certificates, associate, bachelor's, master's, doctoral, and postbachelor's certificates (offers only distance learning degree programs).

STUDENT LIFE
Housing options: college housing not available.

Campus security: 24-hour emergency response devices and patrols, late-night transport/escort service, security officer from 7 am to 11 pm, local police patrol.

APPLYING
Options: electronic application.

Application fee: $75.

Required: must be 21 or older and a high school graduate.

CONTACT
Ms. Juliette Punchello, Senior Director, Admissions and Enrollment Services, Thomas Edison State University, 111 West State Street, Trenton, NJ 08608. *Phone:* 888-442-8372. *Toll-free phone:* 888-442-8372. *Fax:* 609-984-8447. *E-mail:* admissions@tesu.edu.

William Paterson University of New Jersey

Wayne, New Jersey

http://www.wpunj.edu/

- **State-supported** comprehensive, founded 1855
- **Suburban** 370-acre campus with easy access to New York City
- **Coed** 8,605 undergraduate students, 83% full-time, 56% women, 44% men
- **Moderately difficult** entrance level, 92% of applicants were admitted

UNDERGRAD STUDENTS
7,164 full-time, 1,419 part-time. 2% are from out of state; 19% Black or African American, non-Hispanic/Latino; 33% Hispanic/Latino; 7% Asian, non-Hispanic/Latino; 0.2% American Indian or Alaska Native, non-Hispanic/Latino; 3% Two or more races, non-Hispanic/Latino; 1% Race/ethnicity unknown; 0.5% international; 9% transferred in; 24% live on campus.

Freshmen:
Admission: 9,336 applied, 8,551 admitted, 1,537 enrolled.
Retention: 69% of full-time freshmen returned.

FACULTY
Total: 1,055, 37% full-time, 49% with terminal degrees.
Student/faculty ratio: 14:1.

ACADEMICS
Calendar: semesters. *Degrees:* certificates, bachelor's, master's, doctoral, post-master's, and postbachelor's certificates.

Special study options: academic remediation for entering students, accelerated degree program, adult/continuing education programs, advanced placement credit, distance learning, double majors, English as a second language, freshman honors college, honors programs, independent study, internships, off-campus study, part-time degree program, services for LD students, study abroad, summer session for credit. ***ROTC:*** Air Force (c).

Computers: 1,271 computers/terminals and 3,000 ports are available on campus for general student use. Students can access the following: campus intranet, computer help desk, free student e-mail accounts, online (class) grades, online (class) registration, online (class) schedules. Campuswide network is available. 100% of college-owned or -operated housing units are wired for high-speed Internet access. Wireless service is available via entire campus.
Library: David and Lorraine Cheng Library. *Books:* 369,216 (physical), 116,597 (digital/electronic); *Serial titles:* 3,772 (physical), 164,249 (digital/electronic); *Databases:* 126. Weekly public service hours: 102; students can reserve study rooms.

STUDENT LIFE
Housing options: coed, special housing for students with disabilities. Campus housing is university owned. Freshman campus housing is guaranteed.

Activities and organizations: drama/theater group, student-run newspaper, radio and television station, choral group, Student Activities Programming Board (SAPB), Students for Awareness Black Leadership and Equality (SABLE), Student Government Association (SGA), The B.A.B.Y. Dolls (Community Service org.), Pioneer Players (drama), national fraternities, national sororities.

Athletics Member NCAA. All Division III. ***Intercollegiate sports:*** baseball M, basketball M/W, field hockey W, football M, golf M, soccer M/W, softball W, swimming and diving M/W, tennis W, volleyball W. ***Intramural sports:*** basketball M/W, bowling M(c), cheerleading M(c)/W(c), equestrian sports M(c)/W(c), field hockey W, ice hockey M(c), racquetball M/W, rugby M(c), soccer W, softball M/W, volleyball M/W.

Campus security: 24-hour emergency response devices and patrols, student patrols, late-night transport/escort service, controlled dormitory access.

Student services: health clinic, personal/psychological counseling, women's center, legal services, veterans affairs office.

COSTS & FINANCIAL AID

Costs (2019–20) ***Tuition:*** area resident $13,246 full-time, $424 per credit part-time; state resident $13,246 full-time, $424 per credit part-time; nonresident $21,644 full-time, $701 per credit part-time. Full-time tuition and fees vary according to course load and location. Part-time tuition and fees vary according to course load and location. ***Required fees:*** $124 full-time. ***Room and board:*** $11,900; room only: $7470. Room and board charges vary according to board plan and housing facility. ***Payment plan:*** installment. ***Waivers:*** senior citizens and employees or children of employees.

Financial Aid Of all full-time matriculated undergraduates who enrolled in 2019, 6,509 applied for aid, 5,408 were judged to have need, 1,477 had their need fully met. In 2019, 377 non-need-based awards were made. ***Average financial aid package:*** $11,939. ***Average need-based loan:*** $4287. ***Average need-based gift aid:*** $9602. ***Average non-need-based aid:*** $6457. ***Average indebtedness upon graduation:*** $30,272.

APPLYING

Standardized Tests *Required for some:* SAT or ACT (for admission).

Options: electronic application, deferred entrance.

Application fee: $50.

Required: high school transcript, minimum 2.0 GPA. ***Required for some:*** essay or personal statement, 1 letter of recommendation, interview, portfolio for art, audition for music.

Application deadlines: 6/1 (freshmen), 8/1 (transfers).

Notification: continuous (freshmen), continuous (transfers).

CONTACT

Mr. Anthony Leckey, Senior Associate Director of Admissions, William Paterson University of New Jersey, Undergraduate Admissions, 300 Pompton Road, Wayne, NJ 07470. *Phone:* 973-720-2900. *Toll-free phone:* 877-WPU-EXCEL. *Fax:* 973-720-2910. *E-mail:* leckeya@wpunj.edu.

Yeshiva Bais Aharon

Lakewood, New Jersey

CONTACT

Yeshiva Bais Aharon, 905 Park Avenue, Lakewood, NJ 08701.

Yeshiva Gedolah Shaarei Shmuel

Lakewood, New Jersey

http://www.yeshivagedolahshaareishmuel.com/

CONTACT

Yeshiva Gedolah Shaarei Shmuel, 511 Ocean Avenue, Lakewood, NJ 08701.

Yeshiva Gedolah Zichron Leyma

Linden, New Jersey

CONTACT

Yeshiva Gedolah Zichron Leyma, 1000 Orchard Terrace, Linden, NJ 07036.

Yeshivas Be'er Yitzchok

Elizabeth, New Jersey

http://www.elizabethkollel.org/

CONTACT

Yeshivas Be'er Yitzchok, 1391 North Avenue, Elizabeth, NJ 07208.

Yeshiva Toras Chaim

Lakewood, New Jersey

CONTACT

Yeshiva Toras Chaim, 999 Ridge Avenue, Lakewood, NJ 08701.

Yeshiva Yesodei HaTorah

Lakewood, New Jersey

CONTACT

Yeshiva Yesodei HaTorah, 2 Yesodei Court, Lakewood, NJ 08701.

NEW MEXICO

Eastern New Mexico University

Portales, New Mexico

http://www.enmu.edu/

- **State-supported** comprehensive, founded 1934
- **Rural** 344-acre campus
- **Endowment** $9.8 million
- **Coed** 4,473 undergraduate students, 54% full-time, 58% women, 42% men
- **Noncompetitive** entrance level, 58% of applicants were admitted

UNDERGRAD STUDENTS

2,400 full-time, 2,073 part-time. Students come from 49 states and territories; 31 other countries; 23% are from out of state; 6% Black or African American, non-Hispanic/Latino; 43% Hispanic/Latino; 0.9% Asian, non-Hispanic/Latino; 0.8% Native Hawaiian or other Pacific Islander, non-Hispanic/Latino; 2% American Indian or Alaska Native, non-Hispanic/Latino; 3% Two or more races, non-Hispanic/Latino; 3% Race/ethnicity unknown; 2% international; 10% transferred in; 16% live on campus.

Freshmen:

Admission: 2,714 applied, 1,581 admitted, 558 enrolled. ***Average high school GPA:*** 3.4. ***Test scores:*** SAT evidence-based reading and writing scores over 500: 58%; SAT math scores over 500: 53%; ACT scores over 18: 65%; SAT evidence-based reading and writing scores over 600: 17%; SAT math scores over 600: 15%; ACT scores over 24: 15%; SAT evidence-based reading and writing scores over 700: 1%; SAT math scores over 700: 1%; ACT scores over 30: 1%.

Retention: 63% of full-time freshmen returned.

FACULTY

Total: 241, 68% full-time.

Student/faculty ratio: 17:1.

ACADEMICS

Calendar: semesters. *Degrees:* certificates, associate, bachelor's, master's, and postbachelor's certificates.

Special study options: academic remediation for entering students, accelerated degree program, adult/continuing education programs, advanced placement credit, cooperative education, distance learning, double majors, English as a second language, independent study, internships, part-time degree program, services for LD students, student-designed majors, summer session for credit.

Unusual degree programs: 3-2 chemistry.

Computers: 453 computers/terminals are available on campus for general student use. Students can access the following: campus intranet, computer help desk, free student e-mail accounts, online (class) grades, online (class) registration, online (class) schedules. Campuswide network is available. 100% of college-owned or -operated housing units are wired for high-speed Internet access. Wireless service is available via entire campus.

Library: Golden Student Success Center plus 1 other.

STUDENT LIFE

Housing options: on-campus residence required for freshman year; coed, women-only, special housing for students with disabilities. Campus housing is university owned. Freshman campus housing is guaranteed.

Activities and organizations: drama/theater group, student-run newspaper, radio and television station, choral group, marching band, Student Government, Student Activities Board, Residence Hall Association, IFC (Inter-Fraternity Council)Panhellenic Council, national fraternities, national sororities.

Athletics Member NCAA. All Division II. ***Intercollegiate sports:*** baseball M(s), basketball M(s)/W(s), cross-country running M(s)/W(s), football M(s), soccer M(s)/W(s), softball W(s), track and field M(s)/W(s), volleyball W(s). ***Intramural sports:*** badminton M/W, basketball M/W, cross-country running M/W, football M/W, racquetball M/W, soccer M/W, softball M/W, tennis M/W, volleyball M/W, water polo M/W.

Campus security: 24-hour emergency response devices and patrols, late-night transport/escort service, controlled dormitory access, University Emergency Notification System, security cameras, security lights.

Student services: health clinic, personal/psychological counseling.

COSTS & FINANCIAL AID

Costs (2020–21) ***One-time required fee:*** $95. ***Tuition:*** state resident $4074 full-time, $272 per credit hour part-time; nonresident $6114 full-time, $357 per credit hour part-time. ***Required fees:*** $2454 full-time, $102 per credit hour part-time. ***Room and board:*** $7526; room only: $3672.

Financial Aid Of all full-time matriculated undergraduates who enrolled in 2018, 2,079 applied for aid, 1,639 were judged to have need, 345 had their need fully met. In 2018, 130 non-need-based awards were made. ***Average percent of need met:*** 80. ***Average financial aid package:*** $12,830. ***Average need-based loan:*** $3592. ***Average need-based gift aid:*** $6418. ***Average non-need-based aid:*** $2379. ***Average indebtedness upon graduation:*** $20,497.

APPLYING

Standardized Tests *Required for some:* SAT (for admission), ACT (for admission).

Options: electronic application.

Required: official transcripts from any post-secondary institution attended, good standing with all previous institutions. ***Required for some:*** high school transcript, minimum 2.5 GPA.

Application deadlines: 8/24 (freshmen), rolling (out-of-state freshmen), 8/24 (transfers).

Notification: continuous until 8/1 (freshmen), continuous until 8/1 (out-of-state freshmen), continuous until 8/1 (transfers).

CONTACT

Eastern New Mexico University, 1500 South Avenue K, Portales, NM 88130. *Toll-free phone:* 800-367-3668.

EC-Council University

Albuquerque, New Mexico

http://www.eccu.edu/

CONTACT

EC-Council University, 101 C Sun Avenue NE, Albuquerque, NM 87109.

Institute of American Indian Arts

Santa Fe, New Mexico

http://www.iaia.edu/

CONTACT

Ms. Mary Silentwalker, Director, Admissions and Recruitment, Institute of American Indian Arts, 83 Avan Nu Po Road, Santa Fe, NM 87508. *Phone:* 505-424-2307. *Fax:* 505-424-0909. *E-mail:* mary.silentwalker@iaia.edu.

National American University

Albuquerque, New Mexico

http://www.national.edu/

CONTACT

Admissions Office, National American University, 10131 Coors Boulevard NW, Suite I-01, Albuquerque, NM 87114. *Toll-free phone:* 800-895-9904.

National American University

Albuquerque, New Mexico

http://www.national.edu/

CONTACT

National American University, 4775 Indian School Road NE, Suite 200, Albuquerque, NM 87110. *Phone:* 505-265-7517. *Toll-free phone:* 800-895-9904.

National College of Midwifery

Taos, New Mexico

http://www.midwiferycollege.org/

CONTACT

Ms. Beth Enson, Dean of Students, National College of Midwifery, 1041 Reed Street, Suite C, Taos, NM 87571. *Phone:* 505-758-8914. *E-mail:* info@midwiferycollege.org.

Navajo Technical University

Crownpoint, New Mexico

http://www.navajotech.edu/

- **Independent** comprehensive, founded 1979
- **Coed**

FACULTY

Student/faculty ratio: 12:1.

ACADEMICS

Calendar: semesters. *Degrees:* certificates, associate, bachelor's, and master's.

FINANCIAL AID

Financial Aid Of all full-time matriculated undergraduates who enrolled in 2014, 1,218 applied for aid, 971 were judged to have need, 451 had their need fully met. In 2014, 1 non-need-based awards were made. ***Average percent of need met:*** 33. ***Average financial aid package:*** $6649. ***Average need-based gift aid:*** $6627. ***Average non-need-based aid:*** $1000.

CONTACT

Director of Admission, Navajo Technical University, PO Box 849, Crownpoint, NM 87313. *Phone:* 505-786-4100.

New Mexico Highlands University

Las Vegas, New Mexico

http://www.nmhu.edu/

- **State-supported** comprehensive, founded 1893
- **Small-town** campus
- **Coed** 1,797 undergraduate students, 66% full-time, 64% women, 36% men
- **Minimally difficult** entrance level, 65% of applicants were admitted

UNDERGRAD STUDENTS

1,191 full-time, 606 part-time. 13% are from out of state; 6% Black or African American, non-Hispanic/Latino; 58% Hispanic/Latino; 0.4% Asian, non-Hispanic/Latino; 0.3% Native Hawaiian or other Pacific Islander, non-Hispanic/Latino; 10% American Indian or Alaska Native, non-Hispanic/Latino; 2% Two or more races, non-Hispanic/Latino; 2% Race/ethnicity unknown; 3% international; 17% transferred in; 26% live on campus.

Freshmen:

Admission: 1,395 applied, 903 admitted, 280 enrolled. ***Average high school GPA:*** 3.2.

FACULTY

Total: 237, 56% full-time.

ACADEMICS

Calendar: semesters. *Degrees:* bachelor's, master's, post-master's, and postbachelor's certificates.

Special study options: academic remediation for entering students, accelerated degree program, adult/continuing education programs, advanced placement credit, cooperative education, distance learning, double majors, honors programs, independent study, internships, off-campus study, part-time degree program, services for LD students, summer session for credit.

Computers: Students can access the following: online (class) registration. Campuswide network is available.

Library: Thomas C. Donnelly Library.

STUDENT LIFE

Housing options: coed, special housing for students with disabilities. Campus housing is university owned.

Activities and organizations: drama/theater group, student-run radio station, choral group, marching band, Vatos Rugby, Fire Escape Club, MeChA, NMHU Cheerleaders, NMHU Student Ambassadors, national fraternities, national sororities.

Athletics Member NCAA. All Division II. ***Intercollegiate sports:*** baseball M(s), basketball M(s)/W(s), cross-country running M(s)/W(s), football M(s), soccer W(s), softball W(s), track and field M/W, volleyball W(s). ***Intramural sports:*** badminton M/W, basketball M/W, football M, golf M/W, racquetball M/W, rugby M, skiing (cross-country) M/W, skiing (downhill) M/W, softball W, swimming and diving M/W, table tennis M/W, tennis M/W, volleyball M/W, weight lifting M/W.

Campus security: 24-hour emergency response devices and patrols, late-night transport/escort service, controlled dormitory access.

Student services: health clinic, personal/psychological counseling, women's center.

COSTS & FINANCIAL AID

Costs (2019–20) ***Tuition:*** area resident $4400 full-time; state resident $4400 full-time; nonresident $8712 full-time. ***Required fees:*** $1878 full-time. ***Room and board:*** $8126; room only: $3966. Room and board charges vary according to board plan and housing facility. ***Payment plan:*** installment. ***Waivers:*** senior citizens and employees or children of employees.

Financial Aid Of all full-time matriculated undergraduates who enrolled in 2017, 1,063 applied for aid, 974 were judged to have need, 23 had their need fully met. In 2017, 129 non-need-based awards were made. ***Average percent of need met:*** 53. ***Average financial aid package:*** $9683. ***Average need-based loan:*** $4127. ***Average need-based gift aid:*** $7868. ***Average non-need-based aid:*** $2520. ***Average indebtedness upon graduation:*** $18,767. ***Financial aid deadline:*** 6/30.

APPLYING

Options: electronic application, early admission, deferred entrance.

Application fee: $25.

Required: high school transcript, minimum 2.0 GPA. ***Required for some:*** 2 letters of recommendation, interview.

CONTACT

Ms. Jessica Jaramillo, Director of Recruitment and Admissions, New Mexico Highlands University, Box 9000, Las Vegas, NM 87701. *Phone:* 505-454-3394. *Toll-free phone:* 800-338-6648. *E-mail:* admissions@nmhu.edu.

New Mexico Institute of Mining and Technology

Socorro, New Mexico

http://www.nmt.edu/

- **State-supported** university, founded 1889
- **Small-town** 320-acre campus with easy access to Albuquerque
- **Endowment** $45.0 million
- **Coed** 1,321 undergraduate students, 89% full-time, 33% women, 67% men
- **Moderately difficult** entrance level, 80% of applicants were admitted

UNDERGRAD STUDENTS

1,175 full-time, 146 part-time. Students come from 10 states and territories; 13 other countries; 10% are from out of state; 1% Black or African American, non-Hispanic/Latino; 32% Hispanic/Latino; 4% Asian, non-Hispanic/Latino; 0.2% Native Hawaiian or other Pacific Islander, non-Hispanic/Latino; 4% American Indian or Alaska Native, non-Hispanic/Latino; 4% Two or more races, non-Hispanic/Latino; 2% Race/ethnicity unknown; 1% international; 0.9% transferred in; 50% live on campus.

Freshmen:

Admission: 1,143 applied, 912 admitted, 250 enrolled. ***Average high school GPA:*** 3.7. ***Test scores:*** SAT evidence-based reading and writing scores over 500: 98%; SAT math scores over 500: 99%; ACT scores over 18: 100%; SAT evidence-based reading and writing scores over 600: 68%; SAT math scores over 600: 69%; ACT scores over 24: 70%; SAT evidence-based reading and writing scores over 700: 24%; SAT math scores over 700: 24%; ACT scores over 30: 21%.

Retention: 75% of full-time freshmen returned.

FACULTY

Total: 162, 79% full-time, 83% with terminal degrees.

Student/faculty ratio: 11:1.

ACADEMICS

Calendar: semesters. *Degrees:* associate, bachelor's, master's, and doctoral.

Special study options: accelerated degree program, advanced placement credit, cooperative education, distance learning, double majors, independent study, internships, services for LD students, student-designed majors, summer session for credit.

Unusual degree programs: 3-2 earth science, biology, math, physics.

Computers: 225 computers/terminals are available on campus for general student use. Students can access the following: computer help desk, free student e-mail accounts, online (class) registration, online (class) schedules. Campuswide network is available. Wireless service is available via entire campus.

Library: The Skeen Library. *Books:* 215,855 (physical), 794,455 (digital/electronic); *Serial titles:* 24,175 (physical), 539,485 (digital/electronic); *Databases:* 283. Students can reserve study rooms.

STUDENT LIFE

Housing options: coed, men-only, women-only. Campus housing is university owned.

Activities and organizations: drama/theater group, student-run newspaper, radio station, choral group.

Athletics ***Intercollegiate sports:*** rugby M(c)/W(c), soccer M(c)/W(c). ***Intramural sports:*** badminton M/W, basketball M/W, soccer M/W, softball M/W, volleyball M/W.

Campus security: 24-hour emergency response devices and patrols, late-night transport/escort service.

Student services: health clinic, personal/psychological counseling, veterans affairs office.

COSTS & FINANCIAL AID

Costs (2019–20) ***Tuition:*** state resident $6826 full-time, $284 per credit hour part-time; nonresident $22,194 full-time, $925 per credit hour part-time. Full-time tuition and fees vary according to reciprocity agreements. Part-time tuition and fees vary according to course load. ***Required fees:*** $1330 full-time, $18 per credit hour part-time, $450 per term part-time. ***Room and board:*** $8624. Room and board charges vary according to board plan and housing facility. ***Payment plan:*** installment. ***Waivers:*** senior citizens and employees or children of employees.

Financial Aid Of all full-time matriculated undergraduates who enrolled in 2019, 1,070 applied for aid, 656 were judged to have need, 152 had their need fully met. In 2019, 364 non-need-based awards were made. ***Average percent of need met:*** 77. ***Average financial aid package:*** $13,367. ***Average need-based loan:*** $3991. ***Average need-based gift aid:*** $5569. ***Average non-need-based aid:*** $6611. ***Average indebtedness upon graduation:*** $20,771.

APPLYING

Standardized Tests *Required:* SAT or ACT (for admission). *Recommended:* ACT (for admission).

Options: electronic application, deferred entrance.

Application fee: $15.

Required: high school transcript, minimum 2.5 GPA.

Notification: continuous (freshmen).

CONTACT

Mr. Anthony Ortiz, Director of Admission, New Mexico Institute of Mining and Technology, 801 Leroy Place, Socorro, NM 87801. *Phone:* 575-835-5424. *Toll-free phone:* 800-428-TECH. *Fax:* 575-835-5989. *E-mail:* admission@nmt.edu.

New Mexico State University

Las Cruces, New Mexico

http://www.nmsu.edu/

CONTACT

Danielle Staley, Interim Director of Admissions, New Mexico State University, Box 30001, MSC 3A, Las Cruces, NM 88003-8001. *Phone:* 575-646-3121. *Toll-free phone:* 800-662-6678. *Fax:* 575-646-6330. *E-mail:* admssions@nmsu.edu.

Northern New Mexico College

Española, New Mexico

http://www.nnmc.edu/

CONTACT

Mr. Mike L. Costello, Registrar, Northern New Mexico College, 921 Paseo de Oñate, Española, NM 87532. *Phone:* 505-747-2193. *Fax:* 505-747-2191. *E-mail:* dms@nnmc.edu.

Pima Medical Institute - Albuquerque

Albuquerque, New Mexico

http://www.pmi.edu/

CONTACT

Admissions Office, Pima Medical Institute - Albuquerque, 4400 Cutler Avenue NE, Albuquerque, NM 87110. *Phone:* 505-881-1234. *Toll-free phone:* 800-477-PIMA. *Fax:* 505-881-5329.

St. John's College

Santa Fe, New Mexico

http://www.sjc.edu/

- **Independent** comprehensive, founded 1964
- **Small-town** 250-acre campus with easy access to Albuquerque, NM
- **Endowment** $63.0 million
- **Coed** 317 undergraduate students, 98% full-time, 47% women, 53% men
- **Very difficult** entrance level, 66% of applicants were admitted

UNDERGRAD STUDENTS

312 full-time, 5 part-time. 83% are from out of state; 0.3% Black or African American, non-Hispanic/Latino; 10% Hispanic/Latino; 2% Asian, non-Hispanic/Latino; 7% Two or more races, non-Hispanic/Latino; 2% Race/ethnicity unknown; 21% international; 4% transferred in; 85% live on campus.

Freshmen:

Admission: 422 applied, 280 admitted, 74 enrolled. ***Average high school GPA:*** 3.7. ***Test scores:*** SAT evidence-based reading and writing scores over 500: 100%; SAT math scores over 500: 97%; ACT scores over 18: 96%; SAT evidence-based reading and writing scores over 600: 92%; SAT math scores over 600: 79%; ACT scores over 24: 84%; SAT evidence-based reading and writing scores over 700: 59%; SAT math scores over 700: 33%; ACT scores over 30: 40%.

Retention: 78% of full-time freshmen returned.

FACULTY

Total: 48, 73% full-time, 90% with terminal degrees.

Student/faculty ratio: 7:1.

ACADEMICS

Calendar: semesters. *Degrees:* bachelor's and master's.

Special study options: internships, off-campus study, services for LD students, summer session for credit.

Computers: 16 computers/terminals and 425 ports are available on campus for general student use. Students can access the following: campus intranet, computer help desk, free student e-mail accounts, free wi-fi access throughout the campus; support for "bring your own"; mobile devices. Campuswide network is available. 100% of college-owned or -operated housing units are wired for high-speed Internet access. Wireless service is available via entire campus.

Library: Meem Library. *Books:* 69,127 (physical); *Serial titles:* 68 (physical); *Databases:* 9. Weekly public service hours: 82; study areas open 24 hours, 5–7 days a week.

STUDENT LIFE

Housing options: on-campus residence required through senior year; coed, men-only, women-only, special housing for students with disabilities. Campus housing is university owned. Freshman campus housing is guaranteed.

Activities and organizations: drama/theater group, student-run newspaper, choral group, Student Government (Polity), Iron Bookworm Workout, Intramural sports, PiYo , International Student Association.

Athletics ***Intramural sports:*** archery M(c)/W(c), basketball M(c)/W(c), fencing M(c)/W, field hockey M/W(c), ice hockey M(c)/W(c), rock climbing M/W, skiing (cross-country) M/W, skiing (downhill) M/W, soccer M(c)/W(c), softball M(c)/W, squash M/W, swimming and diving M/W, table tennis M(c)/W(c), tennis M/W, ultimate Frisbee M/W, volleyball M/W, weight lifting M(c)/W(c).

Campus security: 24-hour emergency response devices and patrols, late-night transport/escort service, controlled dormitory access.

Student services: health clinic, personal/psychological counseling.

COSTS & FINANCIAL AID

Costs (2020–21) ***Comprehensive fee:*** $49,270 includes full-time tuition ($35,000), mandatory fees ($1410), and room and board ($12,860). Full-time tuition and fees vary according to location. Part-time tuition: $1029 per credit hour. ***College room only:*** $7210. Room and board charges vary according to board plan, housing facility, and location. ***Payment plan:*** installment. ***Waivers:*** employees or children of employees.

Financial Aid Of all full-time matriculated undergraduates who enrolled in 2019, 346 applied for aid, 320 were judged to have need, 182 had their need fully met. In 2019, 30 non-need-based awards were made. ***Average percent of need met:*** 94. ***Average financial aid package:*** $28,627. ***Average need-based loan:*** $4750. ***Average need-based gift aid:*** $15,450. ***Average non-need-based aid:*** $12,000. ***Average indebtedness upon graduation:*** $34,000.

APPLYING

Standardized Tests *Required for some:* SAT (for admission), ACT (for admission), SAT or ACT (for admission), SAT/ACT, TOEFL/IELTS or interview for international applicants; SAT/ACT/CLT for homeschooled students and applicants who have not and will not graduate high school.

Options: electronic application, early admission, early action, deferred entrance.

Required: essay or personal statement, high school transcript, 2 letters of recommendation. ***Required for some:*** outline of curriculum for home-schooled applicants. ***Recommended:*** interview.

Application deadlines: rolling (freshmen), rolling (transfers), 11/15 (early action).

Notification: continuous (freshmen), continuous (transfers), 12/15 (early action).

CONTACT

Ms. Yvette Sobky Shaffer, Director of Admissions, St. John's College, 1160 Camino Cruz Blanca, Santa Fe, NM 87505. *Phone:* 505-984-6060. *Toll-free phone:* 800-331-5232. *E-mail:* santafe.admissions@sjc.edu.

University of New Mexico

Albuquerque, New Mexico

http://www.unm.edu/

- **State-supported** university, founded 1889
- **Urban** 769-acre campus
- **Endowment** $400.8 million
- **Coed** 16,662 undergraduate students, 76% full-time, 56% women, 44% men
- **Moderately difficult** entrance level, 49% of applicants were admitted

UNDERGRAD STUDENTS

12,676 full-time, 3,986 part-time. 16% are from out of state; 2% Black or African American, non-Hispanic/Latino; 50% Hispanic/Latino; 4% Asian, non-Hispanic/Latino; 0.2% Native Hawaiian or other Pacific Islander, non-Hispanic/Latino; 5% American Indian or Alaska Native, non-Hispanic/Latino; 4% Two or more races, non-Hispanic/Latino; 1% Race/ethnicity unknown; 3% international; 9% transferred in; 11% live on campus.

Freshmen:
Admission: 12,181 applied, 5,973 admitted, 2,599 enrolled. ***Average high school GPA:*** 3.4. ***Test scores:*** SAT evidence-based reading and writing scores over 500: 83%; SAT math scores over 500: 83%; ACT scores over 18: 83%; SAT evidence-based reading and writing scores over 600: 46%; SAT math scores over 600: 38%; ACT scores over 24: 34%; SAT evidence-based reading and writing scores over 700: 9%; SAT math scores over 700: 10%; ACT scores over 30: 8%.

Retention: 77% of full-time freshmen returned.

FACULTY
Total: 1,406, 74% full-time, 69% with terminal degrees.

Student/faculty ratio: 14:1.

ACADEMICS
Calendar: semesters. *Degrees:* certificates, bachelor's, master's, doctoral, and post-master's certificates.

Special study options: academic remediation for entering students, accelerated degree program, adult/continuing education programs, advanced placement credit, cooperative education, distance learning, double majors, English as a second language, freshman honors college, honors programs, independent study, internships, off-campus study, part-time degree program, services for LD students, student-designed majors, study abroad, summer session for credit. ***ROTC:*** Army (b), Navy (b), Air Force (b).

Unusual degree programs: 3-2 business administration; engineering; Latin American studies, business.

Computers: 990 computers/terminals and 56,000 ports are available on campus for general student use. Students can access the following: campus intranet, computer help desk, free student e-mail accounts, online (class) grades, online (class) registration, online (class) schedules. Campuswide network is available. 100% of college-owned or -operated housing units are wired for high-speed Internet access. Wireless service is available via entire campus.

Library: College of University Libraries and Learning Sciences plus 7 others. Students can reserve study rooms.

STUDENT LIFE
Housing options: coed, special housing for students with disabilities. Campus housing is university owned. Freshman campus housing is guaranteed.

Activities and organizations: drama/theater group, student-run newspaper, radio and television station, choral group, marching band, Associated Students of UNM, Graduate and Professional Students Association, Golden Key National Honor Society, national fraternities, national sororities.

Athletics Member NCAA. All Division I except football (Division I-A). ***Intercollegiate sports:*** baseball M(s), basketball M(s)/W(s), cross-country running M(s)/W(s), golf M(s)/W(s)(c), skiing (cross-country) M(s)/W(s), skiing (downhill) M(s)(c)/W(s), soccer M(s)/W(s), softball W(s), swimming and diving M/W(s), tennis M(s)/W(s), track and field M(s)/W(s), volleyball W(s). ***Intramural sports:*** archery M/W, badminton M/W, basketball M/W, bowling M(c)/W(c), cheerleading M(c)/W(c), fencing M, field hockey W, football M, golf M/W, ice hockey M(c)/W(c), lacrosse M(c)/W(c), racquetball M/W, rugby M(c)/W(c), skiing (cross-country) M/W, skiing (downhill) M/W, soccer M/W, softball M/W, swimming and diving W, table tennis M/W, tennis M/W, ultimate Frisbee M(c)/W(c), volleyball M/W, water polo M/W, wrestling M(c).

Campus security: 24-hour emergency response devices and patrols, student patrols, late-night transport/escort service, controlled dormitory access.

Student services: health clinic, personal/psychological counseling, women's center.

COSTS & FINANCIAL AID
Costs (2019–20) ***Tuition:*** state resident $6299 full-time, $263 per credit hour part-time; nonresident $21,716 full-time, $905 per credit hour part-time. Full-time tuition and fees vary according to course level, degree level, program, and reciprocity agreements. Part-time tuition and fees vary according to course level, course load, degree level, program, and reciprocity agreements. ***Required fees:*** $1576 full-time, $66 per credit hour part-time. ***Room and board:*** $9390. Room and board charges vary according to board plan and housing facility. ***Payment plan:*** installment. ***Waivers:*** senior citizens and employees or children of employees.

Financial Aid Of all full-time matriculated undergraduates who enrolled in 2019, 10,035 applied for aid, 8,180 were judged to have need, 981 had their need fully met. ***Average need-based gift aid:*** $6069. ***Average indebtedness upon graduation:*** $20,532.

APPLYING
Standardized Tests *Required:* SAT or ACT (for admission).

Options: electronic application, early admission, deferred entrance.

Application fee: $25.

Required: high school transcript, minimum 2.5 GPA. ***Required for some:*** essay or personal statement, interview.

Application deadlines: rolling (freshmen), rolling (transfers).

Notification: continuous (freshmen), continuous (transfers).

CONTACT
Mr. Matthew Hulett, Director of Admissions and Recruitment Services, University of New Mexico, Office of Admissions, PO Box 4895, Albuquerque, NM 87196-4895. *Phone:* 505-277-8900. *Toll-free phone:* 800-CALL-UNM. *Fax:* 505-277-6686. *E-mail:* apply@unm.edu.

University of the Southwest

Hobbs, New Mexico

http://www.usw.edu/

CONTACT
Lissete Terrazas, Director of Admissions, University of the Southwest, 6610 North Lovington Highway, Hobbs, NM 88240. *Phone:* 575-492-2122. *Toll-free phone:* 800-530-4400. *Fax:* 575-392-6006. *E-mail:* lterrazas@usw.edu.

Western New Mexico University

Silver City, New Mexico

http://www.wnmu.edu/

- **State-supported** comprehensive, founded 1893
- **Rural** 83-acre campus
- **Endowment** $14.4 million
- **Coed** 2,214 undergraduate students, 50% full-time, 64% women, 36% men
- **Noncompetitive** entrance level, 100% of applicants were admitted

UNDERGRAD STUDENTS
1,102 full-time, 1,112 part-time. Students come from 37 states and territories; 32 other countries; 10% are from out of state; 6% Black or African American, non-Hispanic/Latino; 53% Hispanic/Latino; 1% Asian, non-Hispanic/Latino; 0.7% Native Hawaiian or other Pacific Islander, non-Hispanic/Latino; 3% American Indian or Alaska Native, non-Hispanic/Latino; 2% Two or more races, non-Hispanic/Latino; 3% Race/ethnicity unknown; 4% international; 7% transferred in.

Freshmen:
Admission: 872 applied, 872 admitted, 290 enrolled. ***Average high school GPA:*** 2.5.

Retention: 59% of full-time freshmen returned.

FACULTY
Total: 225, 39% full-time.

Student/faculty ratio: 13:1.

ACADEMICS
Calendar: semesters. *Degrees:* certificates, diplomas, associate, bachelor's, master's, and postbachelor's certificates.

Special study options: academic remediation for entering students, accelerated degree program, adult/continuing education programs, advanced placement credit, cooperative education, internships, part-time degree program, services for LD students, student-designed majors, summer session for credit.

Computers: 85 computers/terminals are available on campus for general student use. Students can access the following: computer help desk, free student e-mail accounts, online (class) grades, online (class) registration, online classes in Spanish. Campuswide network is available. Wireless service is available via classrooms, computer centers, computer labs, dorm rooms, learning centers, libraries, student centers.

Library: Miller Library. *Books:* 275,491 (physical); *Serial titles:* 145 (physical), 100,171 (digital/electronic); *Databases:* 123. Weekly public service hours: 77; students can reserve study rooms.

STUDENT LIFE

Housing options: on-campus residence required for freshman year; coed, men-only, women-only. Campus housing is university owned. Freshman campus housing is guaranteed.

Activities and organizations: student-run newspaper, choral group, Student Government, CKI, MECHa, Native American Club, Student Athletic Club.

Athletics Member NCAA. All Division II. ***Intercollegiate sports:*** basketball M(s)/W(s), cheerleading M/W, cross-country running M(s)/W(s), football M(s), golf M(s)/W(s), softball W(s), tennis M(s)/W(s), volleyball W(s). ***Intramural sports:*** basketball M/W, golf M/W, racquetball M/W, rock climbing M/W(c), soccer M/W, swimming and diving M/W, table tennis M/W, tennis M/W, volleyball M/W.

Campus security: 24-hour emergency response devices and patrols, student patrols, late-night transport/escort service.

Student services: health clinic, personal/psychological counseling, veterans affairs office.

COSTS & FINANCIAL AID

Costs (2020–21) ***One-time required fee:*** $83. ***Tuition:*** state resident $7396 full-time, $6026 per year part-time; nonresident $15,252 full-time, $12,427 per year part-time. Full-time tuition and fees vary according to course load. Part-time tuition and fees vary according to course load. ***Required fees:*** $1213 full-time, $1977 per year part-time. ***Room and board:*** $11,390; room only: $7010. Room and board charges vary according to board plan, housing facility, and location. ***Payment plan:*** installment. ***Waivers:*** senior citizens and employees or children of employees.

Financial Aid Of all full-time matriculated undergraduates who enrolled in 2018, 964 applied for aid, 834 were judged to have need, 102 had their need fully met. In 2018, 83 non-need-based awards were made. ***Average percent of need met:*** 6. ***Average financial aid package:*** $11,512. ***Average need-based loan:*** $2893. ***Average need-based gift aid:*** $5790. ***Average non-need-based aid:*** $3875.

APPLYING

Options: electronic application, early admission, deferred entrance.

Application fee: $30.

Required: high school transcript.

Application deadlines: 8/1 (freshmen), 8/1 (out-of-state freshmen), 8/1 (transfers).

Notification: continuous (freshmen), continuous (transfers).

CONTACT

Mr. Andrew Lunt, Director of Admissions, Western New Mexico University, 1000 W. College Ave., PO Box 680, Silver City, NM 88062. *Phone:* 505-538-6106. *Toll-free phone:* 800-872-WNMU. *Fax:* 505-538-6127. *E-mail:* Andrew.Lunt@wnmu.edu.

NEW YORK

Adelphi University

Garden City, New York

http://www.adelphi.edu/

- **Independent** university, founded 1896
- **Suburban** 75-acre campus with easy access to New York City
- **Endowment** $188.6 million
- **Coed**
- **Moderately difficult** entrance level

FACULTY

Student/faculty ratio: 12:1.

ACADEMICS

Calendar: semesters. *Degrees:* certificates, associate, bachelor's, master's, doctoral, post-master's, and postbachelor's certificates.

Library: Swirbul Library. *Books:* 537,868 (physical), 240,988 (digital/electronic); *Serial titles:* 430 (physical), 87,949 (digital/electronic); *Databases:* 249. Students can reserve study rooms.

STUDENT LIFE

Housing options: coed, special housing for students with disabilities. Campus housing is university owned. Freshman applicants given priority for college housing.

Activities and organizations: drama/theater group, student-run newspaper, radio station, choral group, Student Activities Board, C. A. L. I. B. E. R. (Cause to Achieve Leadership, Intelligence, Brotherhood, Excellence, and Respect), Commuter Student Organization, Christian Fellowship, Circle K International, national fraternities, national sororities.

Athletics Member NCAA. All Division II.

Campus security: 24-hour emergency response devices and patrols, late-night transport/escort service, controlled dormitory access.

Student services: health clinic, personal/psychological counseling.

FINANCIAL AID

Financial Aid Of all full-time matriculated undergraduates who enrolled in 2018, 4,077 applied for aid, 3,440 were judged to have need, 656 had their need fully met. 317 Federal Work-Study jobs (averaging $1873). 1,165 state and other part-time jobs (averaging $2181). In 2018, 988 non-need-based awards were made. ***Average percent of need met:*** 48. ***Average financial aid package:*** $22,900. ***Average need-based loan:*** $3859. ***Average need-based gift aid:*** $16,410. ***Average non-need-based aid:*** $16,235. ***Average indebtedness upon graduation:*** $34,980.

APPLYING

Standardized Tests *Required for some:* SAT or ACT (for admission).

Options: electronic application, early action, deferred entrance.

Application fee: $40.

Required: essay or personal statement, high school transcript. ***Required for some:*** interview, auditions/portfolios for performing and fine arts.

CONTACT

Ms. Stephanie Espina, Director of Freshman Admissions, Adelphi University, Nexus Building, Room 110, 1 South Avenue, PO Box 701, Garden City, NY 11530-0701. *Phone:* 516-877-3056. *Toll-free phone:* 800-ADELPHI. *Fax:* 516-877-3039. *E-mail:* admissions@adelphi.edu.

Albany College of Pharmacy and Health Sciences

Albany, New York

http://www.acphs.edu/

CONTACT

Mr. Matthew Stever, Director of Admissions, Albany College of Pharmacy and Health Sciences, 106 New Scotland Avenue, Albany, NY 12208. *Phone:* 518-694-7221. *Toll-free phone:* 888-203-8010. *Fax:* 518-694-7322. *E-mail:* admissions@acphs.edu.

Alfred University

Alfred, New York

http://www.alfred.edu/

- **Independent** university, founded 1836
- **Rural** 232-acre campus with easy access to Rochester
- **Endowment** $129.3 million
- **Coed** 1,715 undergraduate students, 96% full-time, 48% women, 52% men
- **Moderately difficult** entrance level, 66% of applicants were admitted

UNDERGRAD STUDENTS

1,647 full-time, 68 part-time. Students come from 40 states and territories; 16 other countries; 24% are from out of state; 13% Black or African American, non-Hispanic/Latino; 9% Hispanic/Latino; 2% Asian, non-Hispanic/Latino; 0.1% American Indian or Alaska Native, non-Hispanic/Latino; 3% Two or more races, non-Hispanic/Latino; 8% Race/ethnicity unknown; 7% international; 7% transferred in; 71% live on campus.

Freshmen:
Admission: 4,272 applied, 2,801 admitted, 458 enrolled. ***Average high school GPA:*** 3.1. ***Test scores:*** SAT evidence-based reading and writing scores over 500: 67%; SAT math scores over 500: 69%; ACT scores over 18: 83%; SAT evidence-based reading and writing scores over 600: 23%; SAT math scores over 600: 23%; ACT scores over 24: 37%; SAT evidence-based reading and writing scores over 700: 3%; SAT math scores over 700: 6%; ACT scores over 30: 7%.

Retention: 73% of full-time freshmen returned.

FACULTY
Total: 201, 78% full-time, 87% with terminal degrees.
Student/faculty ratio: 12:1.

ACADEMICS
Calendar: semesters. *Degrees:* bachelor's, master's, doctoral, and post-master's certificates.

Special study options: accelerated degree program, advanced placement credit, cooperative education, double majors, honors programs, independent study, internships, off-campus study, part-time degree program, services for LD students, student-designed majors, study abroad, summer session for credit. ***ROTC:*** Army (c)

Computers: 1,231 computers/terminals and 1,231 ports are available on campus for general student use. Students can access the following: campus intranet, computer help desk, free student e-mail accounts, online (class) grades, online (class) registration, online (class) schedules, online bill pay. Campuswide network is available. 100% of college-owned or -operated housing units are wired for high-speed Internet access. Wireless service is available via entire campus.
Library: Herrick Memorial Library plus 1 other. *Books:* 189,737 (physical), 675,346 (digital/electronic); *Serial titles:* 4,013 (physical), 95,505 (digital/electronic); *Databases:* 211. Study areas open 24 hours, 5–7 days a week; students can reserve study rooms.

STUDENT LIFE
Housing options: on-campus residence required through junior year; coed, men-only, women-only, cooperative, special housing for students with disabilities. Campus housing is university owned. Freshman campus housing is guaranteed.

Activities and organizations: drama/theater group, student-run newspaper, radio station, choral group, Carribean Student Association, Student Activities Board, Art Force 5, Student Senate.

Athletics Member NCAA. All Division III. ***Intercollegiate sports:*** basketball M/W, cheerleading M/W, cross-country running M/W, equestrian sports M/W, football M, lacrosse M/W, skiing (cross-country) M/W, skiing (downhill) M/W, soccer M/W, softball W, swimming and diving M/W, tennis M/W, track and field M/W, volleyball W. ***Intramural sports:*** baseball M(c), basketball M/W.

Campus security: 24-hour emergency response devices, student patrols, late-night transport/escort service, controlled dormitory access.

Student services: health clinic, personal/psychological counseling, women's center, veterans affairs office.

COSTS & FINANCIAL AID
Costs (2020–21) ***Comprehensive fee:*** $49,200 includes full-time tuition ($35,076), mandatory fees ($1200), and room and board ($12,924). Full-time tuition and fees vary according to program. Part-time tuition: $1076 per credit hour. ***Required fees:*** $86 per term part-time. ***College room only:*** $6498. Room and board charges vary according to board plan. ***Waivers:*** employees or children of employees.

Financial Aid Of all full-time matriculated undergraduates who enrolled in 2019, 1,529 applied for aid, 1,390 were judged to have need, 364 had their need fully met. In 2019, 17 non-need-based awards were made. ***Average percent of need met:*** 82. ***Average financial aid package:*** $28,774. ***Average need-based loan:*** $5454. ***Average need-based gift aid:*** $24,438. ***Average non-need-based aid:*** $14,824. ***Average indebtedness upon graduation:*** $33,666. ***Financial aid deadline:*** 3/15.

APPLYING
Standardized Tests *Recommended:* SAT (for admission), SAT or ACT (for admission).

Options: electronic application, early admission, early decision, deferred entrance.

Application fee: $50.

Required: essay or personal statement, high school transcript, 1 letter of recommendation. ***Required for some:*** portfolio for applicants to the School of Art and Design. ***Recommended:*** interview.

Application deadlines: rolling (out-of-state freshmen), 8/1 (transfers).

Early decision deadline: 12/1.

Notification: continuous (freshmen), continuous (out-of-state freshmen), continuous (transfers).

CONTACT
Mr. Jonathan Kent, Director of Admissions, Alfred University, Alumni Hall, Alfred, NY 14802-1205. *Phone:* 607-871-2115. *Toll-free phone:* 800-541-9229. *Fax:* 607-871-2198. *E-mail:* admissions@alfred.edu.

Bard College
Annandale-on-Hudson, New York
http://www.bard.edu/

- **Independent** comprehensive, founded 1860
- **Rural** 1000-acre campus
- **Coed**
- **Moderately difficult** entrance level

FACULTY
Student/faculty ratio: 9:1.

ACADEMICS
Calendar: semesters. *Degrees:* bachelor's, master's, and doctoral.
Library: Stevenson Library plus 3 others. Weekly public service hours: 75; students can reserve study rooms.

STUDENT LIFE
Housing options: on-campus residence required through sophomore year; coed, women-only, cooperative, special housing for students with disabilities. Campus housing is university owned. Freshman campus housing is guaranteed.

Activities and organizations: drama/theater group, student-run newspaper, radio station, choral group.

Athletics Member NCAA, NAIA. All NCAA Division III.

Campus security: 24-hour emergency response devices and patrols, student patrols, late-night transport/escort service, controlled dormitory access.

Student services: health clinic, personal/psychological counseling, legal services.

COSTS & FINANCIAL AID
Costs (2019–20) ***Comprehensive fee:*** $71,912 includes full-time tuition ($55,566), mandatory fees ($470), and room and board ($15,876). Full-time tuition and fees vary according to degree level and location. Part-time tuition: $1730 per credit. Part-time tuition and fees vary according to degree level and location. ***Room and board:*** Room and board charges vary according to location. ***Payment plans:*** tuition prepayment, installment.

Financial Aid Of all full-time matriculated undergraduates who enrolled in 2018, 1,328 applied for aid, 1,272 were judged to have need, 279 had their need fully met. 825 Federal Work-Study jobs (averaging $1694). In 2018, 34 non-need-based awards were made. ***Average percent of need met:*** 79. ***Average financial aid package:*** $48,432. ***Average need-based loan:*** $5519. ***Average need-based gift aid:*** $44,444. ***Average non-need-based aid:*** $23,252. ***Average indebtedness upon graduation:*** $27,726. ***Financial aid deadline:*** 2/15.

APPLYING
Options: electronic application, early admission, early decision, early action, deferred entrance.

Application fee: $50.

Required: essay or personal statement, high school transcript, minimum 3.0 GPA, 3 letters of recommendation.

CONTACT
Ms. Mackie Siebens, Director of Admissions, Bard College, PO Box 5000, 30 Campus Road, Annandale-on-Hudson, NY 12504-5000. *Phone:* 845-758-7472. *Fax:* 845-758-5208. *E-mail:* admission@bard.edu.

Barnard College

New York, New York

http://www.barnard.edu/

- **Independent** 4-year, founded 1889
- **Urban** 4-acre campus with easy access to New York City
- **Endowment** $363.6 million
- **Women only** 2,631 undergraduate students, 98% full-time
- **Most difficult** entrance level, 12% of applicants were admitted

UNDERGRAD STUDENTS

2,584 full-time, 47 part-time. Students come from 52 states and territories; 67 other countries; 71% are from out of state; 5% Black or African American, non-Hispanic/Latino; 11% Hispanic/Latino; 15% Asian, non-Hispanic/Latino; 0.1% Native Hawaiian or other Pacific Islander, non-Hispanic/Latino; 0.1% American Indian or Alaska Native, non-Hispanic/Latino; 6% Two or more races, non-Hispanic/Latino; 0.4% Race/ethnicity unknown; 11% international; 4% transferred in; 91% live on campus.

Freshmen:

Admission: 9,320 applied, 1,097 admitted, 632 enrolled. ***Test scores:*** SAT evidence-based reading and writing scores over 500: 100%; SAT math scores over 500: 100%; ACT scores over 18: 100%; SAT evidence-based reading and writing scores over 600: 97%; SAT math scores over 600: 96%; ACT scores over 24: 99%; SAT evidence-based reading and writing scores over 700: 62%; SAT math scores over 700: 62%; ACT scores over 30: 85%.

Retention: 95% of full-time freshmen returned.

FACULTY

Total: 357, 70% full-time, 98% with terminal degrees.

Student/faculty ratio: 9:1.

ACADEMICS

Calendar: semesters. *Degree:* bachelor's.

Special study options: accelerated degree program, advanced placement credit, double majors, independent study, internships, off-campus study, services for LD students, student-designed majors, study abroad. ***ROTC:*** Army (c), Navy (c), Air Force (c).

Unusual degree programs: 3-2 engineering with Columbia University; international affairs, public administration with Columbia University; music with The Juilliard School; religion with Jewish Theological Seminary; music with Manhattan School of Music; law; dentistry.

Computers: Students can access the following: campus intranet, computer help desk, free student e-mail accounts, online (class) grades, online (class) registration, online (class) schedules. Campuswide network is available. 100% of college-owned or -operated housing units are wired for high-speed Internet access. Wireless service is available via entire campus.

Library: The Cheryl and Philip Milstein Center for Teaching and Learning plus 20 others. Study areas open 24 hours, 5–7 days a week; students can reserve study rooms.

STUDENT LIFE

Housing options: women-only, special housing for students with disabilities. Campus housing is university owned. Freshman campus housing is guaranteed.

Activities and organizations: drama/theater group, student-run newspaper, radio and television station, choral group, marching band, Community Impact (community service), Student Government Association, Take Back the Night, Student Activities Council, Musical Theater Society, national sororities.

Athletics Member NCAA. All Division I. ***Intercollegiate sports:*** archery W, basketball W, crew W, cross-country running W, equestrian sports W(c), fencing W, field hockey W, golf W, ice hockey W(c), lacrosse W, rugby W(c), sailing W(c), skiing (downhill) W(c), soccer W, softball W, squash W, swimming and diving W, tennis W, track and field W, volleyball W, water polo W(c). ***Intramural sports:*** archery W, badminton W, basketball W, equestrian sports W, ice hockey W, rugby W, sailing W, soccer W, squash W, table tennis W, tennis W, volleyball W, water polo W.

Campus security: 24-hour emergency response devices and patrols, late-night transport/escort service, controlled dormitory access, gated campus with permanent security posts.

Student services: health clinic, personal/psychological counseling, women's center.

COSTS & FINANCIAL AID
Costs (2019–20) ***Comprehensive fee:*** $75,524 includes full-time tuition ($55,781), mandatory fees ($1887), and room and board ($17,856). ***College room only:*** $10,826. Room and board charges vary according to board plan and housing facility. ***Payment plans:*** tuition prepayment, installment, deferred payment. ***Waivers:*** employees or children of employees.

Financial Aid Of all full-time matriculated undergraduates who enrolled in 2019, 1,197 applied for aid, 1,007 were judged to have need, 927 had their need fully met. 216 Federal Work-Study jobs (averaging $2655). 252 state and other part-time jobs (averaging $2940). ***Average percent of need met:*** 100. ***Average financial aid package:*** $50,557. ***Average need-based loan:*** $3195. ***Average need-based gift aid:*** $49,096. ***Average indebtedness upon graduation:*** $20,829.

APPLYING
Standardized Tests *Required:* SAT or ACT (for admission).

Options: electronic application, early admission, early decision, deferred entrance.

Application fee: $75.

Required: essay or personal statement, high school transcript, 3 letters of recommendation, Common Application with Barnard Supplement. *Recommended:* interview.

Application deadlines: 1/1 (freshmen), 3/15 (transfers).

Early decision deadline: 11/1.

Notification: 4/1 (freshmen), 5/15 (transfers), 12/15 (early decision).

CONTACT
Ms. Jennifer Gill Fondiller, Vice President for Enrollment, Barnard College, Barnard College, 3009 Broadway, New York, NY 10027. *Phone:* 212-854-2014. *Fax:* 212-854-6220. *E-mail:* admissions@barnard.edu.

See below for display ad and page 1042 for the College Close-Up.

Baruch College of the City University of New York

New York, New York

http://www.baruch.cuny.edu/

- **State and locally supported** comprehensive, founded 1919, part of City University of New York System
- **Urban** 4-acre campus with easy access to New York
- **Coed** 15,482 undergraduate students, 78% full-time, 47% women, 53% men
- **Very difficult** entrance level, 43% of applicants were admitted

UNDERGRAD STUDENTS
12,091 full-time, 3,391 part-time. Students come from 30 states and territories; 3% are from out of state; 9% Black or African American, non-Hispanic/Latino; 26% Hispanic/Latino; 34% Asian, non-Hispanic/Latino; 0.1% Native Hawaiian or other Pacific Islander, non-Hispanic/Latino; 0.1% American Indian or Alaska Native, non-Hispanic/Latino; 2% Two or more races, non-Hispanic/Latino; 10% international; 11% transferred in; 2% live on campus.

Freshmen:
Admission: 20,303 applied, 8,811 admitted, 2,268 enrolled. ***Average high school GPA:*** 3.3. ***Test scores:*** SAT evidence-based reading and writing scores over 500: 94%; SAT math scores over 500: 97%; SAT evidence-based reading and writing scores over 600: 53%; SAT math scores over 600: 69%; SAT evidence-based reading and writing scores over 700: 7%; SAT math scores over 700: 23%.

Retention: 89% of full-time freshmen returned.

FACULTY
Total: 1,089, 45% full-time, 63% with terminal degrees.

Student/faculty ratio: 19:1.

ACADEMICS
Calendar: semesters. *Degrees:* bachelor's, master's, and post-master's certificates.

Special study options: accelerated degree program, adult/continuing education programs, advanced placement credit, distance learning, double majors, English as a second language, freshman honors college, honors programs, independent study, internships, part-time degree program, services for LD students, student-designed majors, study abroad, summer session for credit. ***ROTC:*** Army (c).

Computers: 1,300 computers/terminals are available on campus for general student use. Students can access the following: campus intranet, computer help desk, free student e-mail accounts, online (class) grades, online (class) registration, online (class) schedules. Campuswide network is available. 100% of college-owned or -operated housing units are wired for high-speed Internet access. Wireless service is available via classrooms, computer centers, computer labs, learning centers, libraries, student centers.

Library: The William and Anita Newman Library. *Books:* 330,647 (physical), 515,356 (digital/electronic); *Serial titles:* 117,795 (physical), 117,795 (digital/electronic). Students can reserve study rooms.

STUDENT LIFE
Housing options: coed. Campus housing is university owned.

Activities and organizations: drama/theater group, student-run newspaper, radio station, choral group, Accounting Society, Caribbean Students Association, Association of Latino Professionals in Finance and Accounting, Golden Key International Honor Society, Helpline, national fraternities, national sororities.

Athletics Member NCAA. All Division III. ***Intercollegiate sports:*** baseball M, basketball M/W, cheerleading M/W, cross-country running M/W, soccer M, softball W, swimming and diving M/W, tennis M/W, volleyball M/W. ***Intramural sports:*** archery M(c)/W(c), badminton M/W, basketball M/W, cross-country running M/W, racquetball M/W, swimming and diving M/W, table tennis M/W, volleyball M/W.

Campus security: 24-hour emergency response devices and patrols, late-night transport/escort service.

Student services: health clinic, personal/psychological counseling, legal services.

COSTS
Costs (2019–20) ***Tuition:*** state resident $6930 full-time, $305 per credit hour part-time; nonresident $18,600 full-time, $620 per credit hour part-time. Full-time tuition and fees vary according to course load. Part-time tuition and fees vary according to course load. ***Required fees:*** $531 full-time. ***Room and board:*** Room and board charges vary according to housing facility. ***Payment plans:*** installment, deferred payment. ***Waivers:*** senior citizens and employees or children of employees.

APPLYING
Standardized Tests *Required:* SAT or ACT (for admission).

Options: electronic application, early decision, deferred entrance.

Application fee: $65.

Required: high school transcript, minimum 2.5 GPA, 16 academic units. ***Required for some:*** interview.

Application deadlines: 2/1 (freshmen), 2/1 (transfers).

Notification: 5/15 (freshmen), continuous until 5/1 (transfers).

CONTACT
Baruch College of the City University of New York, 1 Bernard Baruch Way, New York, NY 10010-5585. *Phone:* 646-312-1383.

Be'er Yaakov Talmudic Seminary

Spring Valley, New York

CONTACT
Be'er Yaakov Talmudic Seminary, 12 Jefferson Avenue, Spring Valley, NY 10977.

Beis Medrash Heichal Dovid

Far Rockaway, New York

CONTACT
Beis Medrash Heichal Dovid, 257 Beach 17th Street, Far Rockaway, NY 11691.

Berkeley College–New York City Campus

New York, New York

http://www.berkeleycollege.edu/

- **Proprietary** 4-year, founded 1936
- **Urban** campus with easy access to New York City
- **Coed**
- **Minimally difficult** entrance level

FACULTY

Student/faculty ratio: 11:1.

ACADEMICS

Calendar: semesters. *Degrees:* associate and bachelor's.
Library:*Books:* 31,426 (physical), 168,797 (digital/electronic); *Serial titles:* 134 (physical), 72,544 (digital/electronic); *Databases:* 84.

STUDENT LIFE

Housing options: college housing not available; coed, men-only, women-only.

Activities and organizations: student-run newspaper, International Student, Latino/Hispanic Club, Student Veterans of America, Sista Circle, Business Club.

Athletics Member USCAA.

Campus security: 24-hour emergency response devices.

Student services: personal/psychological counseling, veterans affairs office.

COSTS

Costs (2019–20) ***One-time required fee:*** $100. ***Tuition:*** $24,800 full-time, $855 per credit part-time. No tuition increase for student's term of enrollment. ***Required fees:*** $1700 full-time, $425 per term part-time.

APPLYING

Options: electronic application, early action, deferred entrance.

Application fee: $50.

Required: essay or personal statement, high school transcript.
Recommended: interview.

CONTACT

Michelle Gomez, Senior Director, High School Admissions, Berkeley College–New York City Campus, 3 East 43 Street, New York, NY 1007. *Phone:* 212-986-4343. *Toll-free phone:* 800-446-5400. *E-mail:* info@berkeleycollege.edu.

Berkeley College–White Plains Campus

White Plains, New York

http://www.berkeleycollege.edu/

- **Proprietary** 4-year, founded 1945
- **Suburban** campus with easy access to New York City
- **Coed**
- **Minimally difficult** entrance level

FACULTY

Student/faculty ratio: 23:1.

ACADEMICS

Calendar: semesters. *Degrees:* associate and bachelor's.
Library:*Books:* 168,797 (digital/electronic); *Serial titles:* 72,544 (digital/electronic); *Databases:* 84.

STUDENT LIFE

Housing options: coed. Campus housing is university owned.

Activities and organizations: student-run newspaper.

Athletics Member USCAA.

Campus security: 24-hour emergency response devices, controlled dormitory access.

Student services: personal/psychological counseling, veterans affairs office.

COSTS

Costs (2019–20) ***One-time required fee:*** $100. ***Comprehensive fee:*** $37,900 includes full-time tuition ($24,800), mandatory fees ($1700), and room and board ($11,400). Part-time tuition: $855 per credit. No tuition increase for student's term of enrollment. ***Required fees:*** $425 per term part-time.

APPLYING

Options: electronic application, deferred entrance.

Application fee: $50.

Required: essay or personal statement, high school transcript.
Recommended: interview.

CONTACT

Daniel Lapan, Director of Admissions, Berkeley College–White Plains Campus, 99 Church Street, White Plains, NY 10601. *Phone:* 914-694-1122. *Toll-free phone:* 800-446-5400. *E-mail:* info@berkeleycollege.edu.

Beth HaMedrash Shaarei Yosher Institute

Brooklyn, New York

http://www.bethhamedrashshaareiyosher.com/

CONTACT

Director of Admissions, Beth HaMedrash Shaarei Yosher Institute, 4102-10 Sixteenth Avenue, Brooklyn, NY 11204. *Phone:* 718-854-2290.

Beth Hatalmud Rabbinical College

Brooklyn, New York

CONTACT

Rabbi Osina, Director of Admissions, Beth Hatalmud Rabbinical College, 2127 Eighty-second Street, Brooklyn, NY 11214. *Phone:* 718-259-2525.

Beth Medrash Meor Yitzchok

Monsey, New York

http://www.bethmedrashmeoryitzchok.com/

CONTACT

Beth Medrash Meor Yitzchok, 85 Dykstras Way East, Monsey, NY 10952.

Bet Medrash Gadol Ateret Torah

Brooklyn, New York

http://www.betmedrashgadolaterettorah.com/

CONTACT

Bet Medrash Gadol Ateret Torah, 1750 East Fourth Street, Brooklyn, NY 11223.

Binghamton University, State University of New York

Binghamton, New York

http://www.binghamton.edu/

- **State-supported** university, founded 1946, part of State University of New York System
- **Suburban** 930-acre campus
- **Endowment** $117.3 million
- **Coed** 14,165 undergraduate students, 98% full-time, 50% women, 50% men
- **Very difficult** entrance level, 40% of applicants were admitted

UNDERGRAD STUDENTS

13,845 full-time, 320 part-time. Students come from 37 states and territories; 92 other countries; 6% are from out of state; 5% Black or African American, non-Hispanic/Latino; 12% Hispanic/Latino; 15% Asian, non-Hispanic/Latino; 0.0% American Indian or Alaska Native, non-Hispanic/Latino; 3% Two or more races, non-Hispanic/Latino; 1% Race/ethnicity unknown; 7% international; 6% transferred in; 50% live on campus.

Freshmen:

Admission: 38,755 applied, 15,429 admitted, 2,912 enrolled. ***Average high school GPA:*** 4.0. ***Test scores:*** SAT evidence-based reading and writing scores over 500: 99%; SAT math scores over 500: 99%; ACT scores over 18: 101%; SAT evidence-based reading and writing scores over 600: 92%; SAT math scores over 600: 94%; ACT scores over 24: 98%; SAT evidence-based reading and writing scores over 700: 30%; SAT math scores over 700: 53%; ACT scores over 30: 64%.

Retention: 90% of full-time freshmen returned.

FACULTY

Total: 1,074, 71% full-time, 83% with terminal degrees.

Student/faculty ratio: 19:1.

ACADEMICS

Calendar: semesters. *Degrees:* bachelor's, master's, doctoral, and post-master's certificates.

Special study options: accelerated degree program, adult/continuing education programs, advanced placement credit, distance learning, double majors, English as a second language, honors programs, independent study, internships, off campus study, part time degree program, services for LD students, student-designed majors, study abroad, summer session for credit. ***ROTC:*** Army (c), Air Force (c).

Unusual degree programs: 3-2 business administration; engineering; anthropology; art history; Asian/AsianAmerican studies; biology; chemistry; computer science; economics; education; French; geography; geology; Italian; math; material science; philosophy, politics & law; physics; political science; public administration; sociology; Spanish; systems science; theatre.

Computers: 1,184 computers/terminals and 13,200 ports are available on campus for general student use. Students can access the following: campus intranet, computer help desk, free student e-mail accounts, online (class) registration, online (class) schedules, course management system, personal Web space, wiki, virtual desktop. Campuswide network is available. 100% of college-owned or -operated housing units are wired for high-speed Internet access. Wireless service is available via entire campus.

Library: Glenn G. Bartle Library plus 4 others. *Books:* 1.5 million (physical), 817,118 (digital/electronic); *Serial titles:* 42,649 (physical), 175,748 (digital/electronic); *Databases:* 358. Weekly public service hours: 136; study areas open 24 hours, 5–7 days a week; students can reserve study rooms.

STUDENT LIFE

Housing options: on-campus residence required for freshman year; coed, special housing for students with disabilities. Campus housing is university owned. Freshman campus housing is guaranteed.

Activities and organizations: drama/theater group, student-run newspaper, radio and television station, choral group, Binghamton Transfer Student Association, Binghamton Cheese Club, New York Public Interest Research Group, American Red Cross Club, Paws and Effect, national fraternities, national sororities.

Athletics Member NCAA. All Division I. ***Intercollegiate sports:*** baseball M(s), basketball M(s)/W(s), cross-country running M(s)/W(s), golf M(s), lacrosse M(s)/W(s), soccer M(s)/W(s), softball W(s), swimming and diving M(s)/W(s), tennis M(s)/W(s), track and field M(s)/W(s), volleyball W(s), wrestling M(s). ***Intramural sports:*** badminton M(c)/W(c), baseball M(c), basketball M/W, bowling M/W, crew M(c)/W(c), cross-country running M(c)/W(c), equestrian sports M(c)/W(c), fencing M(c)/W(c), field hockey M(c)/W(c), golf M(c)/W(c), gymnastics M(c)/W(c), ice hockey M(c)/W(c), lacrosse M(c)/W(c), racquetball M/W, rugby M(c)/W(c), skiing (downhill) M(c)/W(c), soccer M/W, softball M/W, swimming and diving M(c)/W(c), table tennis M(c)/W(c), tennis M/W, ultimate Frisbee M(c)/W(c), volleyball M/W, water polo M(c)/W(c).

Campus security: 24-hour emergency response devices and patrols, late-night transport/escort service, controlled dormitory access, only main gate open to traffic 12-5 am, emergency text system, self-defense workshops.

Student services: health clinic, personal/psychological counseling, women's center, legal services, veterans affairs office.

COSTS & FINANCIAL AID

Costs (2020–21) ***Tuition:*** area resident $7270 full-time, $303 per credit hour part-time; state resident $7270 full-time, $303 per credit hour part-time; nonresident $27,043 full-time, $1028 per credit hour part-time. Full-time tuition and fees vary according to program. Part-time tuition and fees vary according to course load and program. ***Required fees:*** $3224 full-time. ***Room and board:*** $16,549. Room and board charges vary according to board plan and housing facility. ***Payment plan:*** installment. ***Waivers:*** employees or children of employees.

Financial Aid Of all full-time matriculated undergraduates who enrolled in 2019, 10,107 applied for aid, 7,105 were judged to have need, 1,371 had their need fully met. 289 Federal Work-Study jobs (averaging $1953). In 2019, 602 non-need-based awards were made. ***Average percent of need met:*** 69. ***Average financial aid package:*** $14,458. ***Average need-based loan:*** $4768. ***Average need-based gift aid:*** $9765. ***Average non-need-based aid:*** $7883. ***Average indebtedness upon graduation:*** $27,679. ***Financial aid deadline:*** 5/1.

APPLYING

Standardized Tests *Required:* SAT or ACT (for admission).

Options: electronic application, early admission, early decision, early action, deferred entrance.

Application fee: $50.

Required: essay or personal statement, high school transcript, 1 letter of recommendation. ***Required for some:*** portfolio, audition.

Application deadlines: rolling (freshmen), rolling (transfers), 11/1 (early action).

Notification: 4/1 (freshmen), continuous (transfers), 1/15 (early action).

CONTACT

Krista Medionte-Phillips, Director of Undergraduate Admissions, Binghamton University, State University of New York, PO Box 6001, Binghamton, NY 13902-6001. *Phone:* 607-777-2171. *Fax:* 607-777-4445. *E-mail:* admit@binghamton.edu.

Boricua College

New York, New York

http://www.boricuacollege.edu/

CONTACT

Mrs. Miriam Pfeffer, Director of Student Services, Boricua College, 186 North 6th Street, Brooklyn, NY 11211. *Phone:* 718-782-2200. *Fax:* 718-782-2025. *E-mail:* mpfeffer@boricuacollege.edu.

Brooklyn College of the City University of New York

Brooklyn, New York

http://www.brooklyn.cuny.edu/

CONTACT

Office of Admissions, Brooklyn College of the City University of New York, 2900 Bedford Avenue, West Quad Building, Room 222, Brooklyn, NY 11210-2889. *Phone:* 718-951-5001. *Fax:* 718-951-4506. *E-mail:* adminqry@brooklyn.cuny.edu.

Bryant & Stratton College–Amherst Campus

Clarence, New York

http://www.bryantstratton.edu/

CONTACT

Mr. Brian K. Dioguardi, Director of Admissions, Bryant & Stratton College–Amherst Campus, Audubon Business Center, 40 Hazelwood Drive, Amherst, NY 14228. *Phone:* 716-691-0012. *Fax:* 716-691-0012. *E-mail:* bkdioguardi@bryantstratton.edu.

Bryant & Stratton College–Buffalo Campus

Buffalo, New York

http://www.bryantstratton.edu/

CONTACT

Mr. Philip J. Struebel, Director of Admissions, Bryant & Stratton College–Buffalo Campus, 465 Main Street, Suite 400, Buffalo, NY 14203. *Phone:* 716-884-9120. *Fax:* 716-884-0091. *E-mail:* pjstruebel@bryantstratton.edu.

Bryant & Stratton College–Orchard Park Campus

Orchard Park, New York

http://www.bryantstratton.edu/

CONTACT

Bryant & Stratton College–Orchard Park Campus, 200 Redtail Road, Orchard Park, NY 14127. *Phone:* 716-677-9500.

Buffalo State College, State University of New York

Buffalo, New York

http://www.buffalostate.edu/

- **State-supported** comprehensive, founded 1867, part of State University of New York System
- **Urban** 115-acre campus
- **Endowment** $42.9 million
- **Coed**
- **Moderately difficult** entrance level

FACULTY

Student/faculty ratio: 15:1.

ACADEMICS

Calendar: semesters. *Degrees:* bachelor's, master's, and post-master's certificates.
Library: E. H. Butler Library plus 1 other.

STUDENT LIFE

Housing options: on-campus residence required through sophomore year; coed. Campus housing is university owned. Freshman campus housing is guaranteed.

Activities and organizations: drama/theater group, student-run newspaper, radio station, choral group, United Student Government, African-American Student Organization, Caribbean Student Organization, The Record, WBNY radio, national fraternities, national sororities.

Athletics Member NCAA. All Division III.

Campus security: 24-hour emergency response devices and patrols, student patrols, late-night transport/escort service, controlled dormitory access.

Student services: health clinic, personal/psychological counseling, women's center, legal services, veterans affairs office.

COSTS & FINANCIAL AID

Costs (2019–20) ***Tuition:*** state resident $7070 full-time, $295 per semester hour part-time; nonresident $16,980 full-time, $708 per semester hour part-time. Part-time tuition and fees vary according to course load. ***Required fees:*** $1402 full-time, $58 per semester hour part-time. ***Room and board:*** $14,380; room only: $8340. Room and board charges vary according to board plan, housing facility, and student level.

Financial Aid ***Average indebtedness upon graduation:*** $26,495. ***Financial aid deadline:*** 5/1.

APPLYING

Standardized Tests *Required:* SAT and SAT Subject Tests or ACT (for admission). *Recommended:* SAT (for admission).

Options: electronic application, early admission, deferred entrance.

Application fee: $50.

Required: high school transcript, minimum 3.0 GPA. ***Required for some:*** essay or personal statement, interview.

CONTACT

Ms. Carmella Thompson, Director of Admissions, Buffalo State College, State University of New York, 110 Moot Hall, Buffalo, NY 14222. *Phone:* 716-878-4017. *Fax:* 716-878-6100. *E-mail:* admissions@buffalostate.edu.

Canisius College

Buffalo, New York

http://www.canisius.edu/

- **Independent Roman Catholic (Jesuit)** comprehensive, founded 1870
- **Urban** 72-acre campus with easy access to Buffalo-Niagara Falls
- **Endowment** $133.9 million
- **Coed**
- **Moderately difficult** entrance level

FACULTY

Student/faculty ratio: 11:1.

ACADEMICS

Calendar: semesters. *Degrees:* associate, bachelor's, master's, post-master's, and postbachelor's certificates.
Library: Andrew L. Bouwhuis Library plus 1 other. *Books:* 222,252 (physical), 1.7 million (digital/electronic); *Serial titles:* 1,143 (physical), 303,210 (digital/electronic); *Databases:* 108. Weekly public service hours: 110; students can reserve study rooms.

STUDENT LIFE

Housing options: on-campus residence required through sophomore year; coed, special housing for students with disabilities. Campus housing is university owned. Freshman applicants given priority for college housing.

Activities and organizations: drama/theater group, student-run newspaper, radio and television station, choral group, Residence Hall Association, UNITY, Afro-American Society, Project Conservation, FUSION Gaming Society, national fraternities, national sororities.

Athletics Member NCAA. All Division I.

Campus security: 24-hour emergency response devices and patrols, late-night transport/escort service, controlled dormitory access.

Student services: health clinic, personal/psychological counseling, veterans affairs office.

COSTS & FINANCIAL AID

Costs (2019–20) ***Comprehensive fee:*** $40,954 includes full-time tuition ($27,940), mandatory fees ($1488), and room and board ($11,526). Part-time tuition: $900 per credit hour. Part-time tuition and fees vary according to course load. ***Required fees:*** $25 per credit hour part-time, $85 per term part-time. ***College room only:*** $5880. Room and board charges vary according to board plan and housing facility. ***Payment plans:*** installment, deferred payment.

Financial Aid Of all full-time matriculated undergraduates who enrolled in 2018, 1,764 applied for aid, 1,550 were judged to have need, 362 had their need fully met. 310 Federal Work-Study jobs (averaging $1905). In 2018, 499 non-need-based awards were made. ***Average percent of need met:*** 75. ***Average financial aid package:*** $22,679. ***Average need-based loan:*** $4388. ***Average need-based gift aid:*** $17,184. ***Average non-need-based aid:*** $11,200. ***Average indebtedness upon graduation:*** $34,561. ***Financial aid deadline:*** 5/1.

APPLYING

Standardized Tests *Required:* SAT or ACT (for admission).

Options: electronic application, early admission, early action, deferred entrance.

Required: high school transcript, minimum 2.0 GPA. ***Recommended:*** essay or personal statement, 1 letter of recommendation, interview.

CONTACT

Mr. Justin P. Rogers, Director of Undergraduate Admissions, Canisius College, 2001 Main Street, Buffalo, NY 14208-1098. *Phone:* 716-888-2200. *Toll-free phone:* 800-843-1517. *Fax:* 716-888-3230. *E-mail:* admissions@canisius.edu.

Cazenovia College

Cazenovia, New York

http://www.cazenovia.edu/

- **Independent** 4-year, founded 1824
- **Small-town** 40-acre campus with easy access to Syracuse
- **Coed** 856 undergraduate students, 81% full-time, 75% women, 25% men
- 94% of applicants were admitted

UNDERGRAD STUDENTS

697 full-time, 163 part-time. Students come from 23 states and territories; 3 other countries; 10% are from out of state; 11% Black or African American, non-Hispanic/Latino; 6% Hispanic/Latino; 0.9% Asian, non-Hispanic/Latino; 0.9% American Indian or Alaska Native, non-Hispanic/Latino; 6% Two or more races, non-Hispanic/Latino; 6% Race/ethnicity unknown; 4% transferred in; 81% live on campus.

Freshmen:

Admission: 2,050 applied, 1,921 admitted, 218 enrolled. ***Average high school GPA:*** 3.1. ***Test scores:*** SAT evidence-based reading and writing scores over 500: 59%; SAT math scores over 500: 58%; ACT scores over 18: 77%; SAT evidence-based reading and writing scores over 600: 21%; SAT math scores over 600: 14%; ACT scores over 24: 36%; SAT evidence-based reading and writing scores over 700: 2%; SAT math scores over 700: 1%.

Retention: 71% of full-time freshmen returned.

FACULTY

Total: 108, 50% full-time, 21% with terminal degrees.

Student/faculty ratio: 12:1.

ACADEMICS

Calendar: semesters. *Degrees:* certificates, associate, bachelor's, and master's.

Special study options: academic remediation for entering students, accelerated degree program, adult/continuing education programs, advanced placement credit, distance learning, double majors, freshman honors college, honors programs, independent study, internships, off-campus study, part-time degree program, services for LD students, study abroad, summer session for credit. ***ROTC:*** Army (c), Air Force (c).

Computers: 400 computers/terminals are available on campus for general student use. Students can access the following: campus intranet, computer help desk, free student e-mail accounts, online (class) grades, online (class) schedules. Campuswide network is available. 100% of college-owned or -operated housing units are wired for high-speed Internet access. Wireless service is available via entire campus.

Library: Witheral Library. *Books:* 57,227 (physical), 5,901 (digital/electronic); *Serial titles:* 492 (physical), 70,775 (digital/electronic); *Databases:* 115. Weekly public service hours: 83; students can reserve study rooms.

STUDENT LIFE

Housing options: on-campus residence required through junior year; coed, men-only, women-only, special housing for students with disabilities. Campus housing is university owned. Freshman campus housing is guaranteed.

Activities and organizations: drama/theater group, student-run newspaper, choral group, Activities Board, Students of Ethnic Diversity, Drama Club, Sports Management Club, Yearbook, national fraternities, national sororities.

Athletics Member NCAA. All Division III. ***Intercollegiate sports:*** baseball M, basketball M/W, cross-country running M/W, lacrosse M/W, soccer M/W, softball W, volleyball W. ***Intramural sports:*** basketball M/W, bowling M/W, cheerleading M(c)/W(c), crew M(c)/W(c), equestrian sports M/W, football M/W, skiing (downhill) M/W, soccer M/W, softball M/W, swimming and diving M/W, tennis M/W, volleyball M(c)/W.

Campus security: 24-hour emergency response devices and patrols, late-night transport/escort service, controlled dormitory access.

Student services: health clinic, personal/psychological counseling, women's center.

COSTS & FINANCIAL AID

Costs (2020–21) ***One-time required fee:*** $642. ***Comprehensive fee:*** $50,769 includes full-time tuition ($36,026) and room and board ($14,743). Part-time tuition: $720 per credit hour. ***College room only:*** $8206. ***Waivers:*** employees or children of employees.

Financial Aid Of all full-time matriculated undergraduates who enrolled in 2018, 645 applied for aid, 596 were judged to have need, 144 had their need fully met. In 2018, 26 non-need-based awards were made. ***Average percent of need met:*** 84. ***Average financial aid package:*** $32,093. ***Average need-based loan:*** $5325. ***Average need-based gift aid:*** $30,089. ***Average non-need-based aid:*** $21,213. ***Average indebtedness upon graduation:*** $35,863.

APPLYING

Standardized Tests *Recommended:* SAT or ACT (for admission).

Options: electronic application.

Required: high school transcript, 1 letter of recommendation. ***Recommended:*** essay or personal statement, minimum 2.0 GPA, interview, portfolio for art and design students.

Notification: continuous until 11/1 (freshmen).

CONTACT

Office of Admission and Enrollment Services, Cazenovia College, 3 Sullivan Street, Cazenovia, NY 13035. *Phone:* 315-655-7208. *Toll-free phone:* 800-654-3210. *Fax:* 315-655-4860. *E-mail:* admission@cazenovia.edu.

Central Yeshiva Beth Joseph

Brooklyn, New York

http://www.centralyeshivabethjoseph.com

CONTACT

Central Yeshiva Beth Joseph, 1502 Avenue N, Brooklyn, NY 11230.

Central Yeshiva Tomchei Tmimim-Lubavitch

Brooklyn, New York

CONTACT

Director of Admissions, Central Yeshiva Tomchei Tmimim-Lubavitch, 841-853 Ocean Parkway, Brooklyn, NY 11230. *Phone:* 718-859-7600.

City College of the City University of New York

New York, New York

http://www.ccny.cuny.edu/

- **State and locally supported** comprehensive, founded 1847, part of City University of New York System
- **Urban** 35-acre campus with easy access to New York City
- **Coed** 13,224 undergraduate students, 77% full-time, 52% women, 48% men
- **Moderately difficult** entrance level, 41% of applicants were admitted

UNDERGRAD STUDENTS

10,201 full-time, 3,023 part-time. 2% are from out of state; 15% Black or African American, non-Hispanic/Latino; 38% Hispanic/Latino; 25% Asian, non-Hispanic/Latino; 0.1% Native Hawaiian or other Pacific Islander, non-Hispanic/Latino; 0.2% American Indian or Alaska Native, non-Hispanic/Latino; 2% Two or more races, non-Hispanic/Latino; 6% international; 9% transferred in; 1% live on campus.

Freshmen:

Admission: 31,420 applied, 12,926 admitted, 2,095 enrolled. ***Average high school GPA:*** 3.4. ***Test scores:*** SAT evidence-based reading and writing scores over 500: 82%; SAT math scores over 500: 87%; ACT scores over 18: 93%; SAT evidence-based reading and writing scores over 600: 29%; SAT math scores over 600: 35%; ACT scores over 24: 68%; SAT evidence-based reading and writing scores over 700: 5%; SAT math scores over 700: 12%; ACT scores over 30: 29%.

FACULTY

Total: 1,755, 36% full-time.

ACADEMICS
Calendar: semesters. *Degrees:* bachelor's, master's, doctoral, post-master's, and postbachelor's certificates.

Special study options: adult/continuing education programs, advanced placement credit, cooperative education, distance learning, double majors, English as a second language, freshman honors college, honors programs, independent study, internships, off-campus study, part-time degree program, services for LD students, student-designed majors, study abroad, summer session for credit. ***ROTC:*** Army (b).

Computers: 3,000 computers/terminals are available on campus for general student use. Students can access the following: campus intranet, computer help desk, free student e-mail accounts, online (class) grades, online (class) registration, online (class) schedules. Campuswide network is available. 100% of college-owned or -operated housing units are wired for high-speed Internet access. Wireless service is available via entire campus.
Library: Morris Raphael Cohen Library plus 8 others. *Books:* 950,000 (physical), 980,000 (digital/electronic); *Serial titles:* 118,000 (digital/electronic); *Databases:* 308. Weekly public service hours: 99; students can reserve study rooms.

STUDENT LIFE
Housing options: Campus housing is university owned.

Activities and organizations: drama/theater group, student-run newspaper, radio and television station, choral group, Latin American Engineering Student Assoc./Society of Hispanic Professional Engineers, National Society of Black Engineers, Bangladesh Student Association, Salsa-Mambo, InterVarsity Christian Fellowship, national fraternities.

Athletics Member NCAA. All Division III. ***Intercollegiate sports:*** baseball M, basketball M/W, cross-country running M/W, fencing W, lacrosse M, soccer M/W, softball W, tennis M/W, track and field M/W, volleyball W. ***Intramural sports:*** basketball M/W, fencing W, soccer M, softball W, tennis M/W, track and field M/W, volleyball W.

Campus security: 24-hour patrols, late-night transport/escort service, controlled dormitory access.

Student services: health clinic, personal/psychological counseling, veterans affairs office.

COSTS & FINANCIAL AID
Costs (2020–21) ***Tuition:*** area resident $13,860 full-time, $13,860 per credit hour part-time; state resident $13,860 full-time, $13,860 per credit hour part-time; nonresident $18,600 full-time, $18,600 per credit hour part-time. ***Required fees:*** $640 full-time. ***Room only:*** $12,123.

Financial Aid Of all full-time matriculated undergraduates who enrolled in 2018, 9,040 applied for aid, 8,899 were judged to have need, 1,200 had their need fully met. In 2018, 1220 non-need-based awards were made. ***Average percent of need met:*** 82. ***Average financial aid package:*** $7273. ***Average need-based loan:*** $7354. ***Average need-based gift aid:*** $6441. ***Average non-need-based aid:*** $195.

APPLYING
Standardized Tests *Required:* SAT or ACT (for admission). *Required for some:* SAT (for admission), ACT (for admission).

Options: deferred entrance.

Application fee: $65.

Required: high school transcript. ***Required for some:*** essay or personal statement, letters of recommendation, creative challenge for architecture, supplemental application for engineering.

Application deadlines: 2/1 (freshmen), 2/1 (transfers).

Notification: continuous until 2/1 (freshmen), continuous until 3/1 (transfers).

CONTACT
City College of the City University of New York, 160 Convent Avenue, New York, NY 10031-9198. *Phone:* 212-650-6977.

Clarkson University

Potsdam, New York

http://www.clarkson.edu/

- **Independent** university, founded 1896
- **Small-town** 640-acre campus
- **Endowment** $201.7 million
- **Coed** 3,081 undergraduate students, 98% full-time, 31% women, 69% men
- **Very difficult** entrance level, 75% of applicants were admitted

UNDERGRAD STUDENTS
3,012 full-time, 69 part-time. Students come from 44 states and territories; 42 other countries; 31% are from out of state; 3% Black or African American, non-Hispanic/Latino; 5% Hispanic/Latino; 4% Asian, non-Hispanic/Latino; 0.1% American Indian or Alaska Native, non-Hispanic/Latino; 4% Two or more races, non-Hispanic/Latino; 2% Race/ethnicity unknown; 3% international; 3% transferred in; 82% live on campus.

Freshmen:
Admission: 6,673 applied, 4,978 admitted, 790 enrolled. ***Average high school GPA:*** 3.7. ***Test scores:*** SAT evidence-based reading and writing scores over 500: 96%; SAT math scores over 500: 79%; ACT scores over 18: 99%; SAT evidence-based reading and writing scores over 600: 59%; SAT math scores over 600: 76%; ACT scores over 24: 72%; SAT evidence-based reading and writing scores over 700: 12%; SAT math scores over 700: 25%; ACT scores over 30: 29%.

Retention: 91% of full-time freshmen returned.

FACULTY
Total: 359, 69% full-time, 75% with terminal degrees.

Student/faculty ratio: 14:1.

ACADEMICS
Calendar: semesters. *Degrees:* bachelor's, master's, doctoral, and postbachelor's certificates.

Special study options: accelerated degree program, advanced placement credit, cooperative education, distance learning, double majors, English as a second language, honors programs, independent study, internships, off-campus study, part-time degree program, services for LD students, student-designed majors, study abroad, summer session for credit. ***ROTC:*** Army (b), Air Force (b).

Unusual degree programs: 3-2 engineering.

Computers: 350 computers/terminals and 6,000 ports are available on campus for general student use. Students can access the following: campus intranet, computer help desk, free student e-mail accounts, online (class) grades, online (class) registration, online (class) schedules. Campuswide network is available. 100% of college-owned or -operated housing units are wired for high-speed Internet access. Wireless service is available via entire campus.
Library: Harriet Call Burnap Memorial Library plus 1 other. *Books:* 119,380 (physical), 246,291 (digital/electronic); *Serial titles:* 7,688 (physical), 48,712 (digital/electronic); *Databases:* 190. Weekly public service hours: 76; study areas open 24 hours, 5–7 days a week.

STUDENT LIFE
Housing options: on-campus residence required through senior year; coed, men-only, women-only, special housing for students with disabilities. Campus housing is university owned. Freshman campus housing is guaranteed.

Activities and organizations: drama/theater group, student-run newspaper, radio and television station, choral group, Outing Club, Ski & Snowboard Club, Pep Band, Institute for Electrical and Electronics Engineers, Spikeball Club, national fraternities, national sororities.

Athletics Member NCAA. All Division III except men's and women's ice hockey (Division I). ***Intercollegiate sports:*** baseball M, basketball M/W, cross-country running M/W, golf M, ice hockey M(s)/W(s), lacrosse M/W, skiing (cross-country) M/W, skiing (downhill) M/W, soccer M/W, softball W, swimming and diving M/W, volleyball W. ***Intramural sports:*** baseball M(c)/W(c), basketball M/W, bowling M(c)/W(c), crew M(c)/W(c), equestrian sports M(c)/W(c), football M(c)/W, golf M(c)/W(c), ice hockey M/W, lacrosse M(c)/W(c), racquetball M(c)/W(c), rowing M(c)/W(c), rugby M(c)/W(c), skiing (cross-country) M(c)/W(c), skiing (downhill) M(c)/W(c), soccer M/W, softball M/W, table tennis M(c)/W(c), tennis

M(c)/W(c), track and field M(c)/W(c), ultimate Frisbee M(c)/W(c), volleyball M/W, wrestling M(c).

Campus security: 24-hour emergency response devices and patrols, controlled dormitory access.

Student services: health clinic, personal/psychological counseling, legal services, veterans affairs office.

COSTS & FINANCIAL AID

Costs (2020–21) ***Comprehensive fee:*** $68,510 includes full-time tuition ($51,454), mandatory fees ($1270), and room and board ($15,786). Full-time tuition and fees vary according to course load. Part-time tuition: $1715 per credit hour. Part-time tuition and fees vary according to course load. ***College room only:*** $8480. Room and board charges vary according to board plan and housing facility. ***Payment plan:*** installment. ***Waivers:*** employees or children of employees.

Financial Aid Of all full-time matriculated undergraduates who enrolled in 2019, 2,620 applied for aid, 2,401 were judged to have need, 570 had their need fully met. 1,403 Federal Work-Study jobs (averaging $1800). 65 state and other part-time jobs (averaging $12,030). In 2019, 482 non-need-based awards were made. ***Average percent of need met:*** 90. ***Average financial aid package:*** $46,636. ***Average need-based loan:*** $4643. ***Average need-based gift aid:*** $34,953. ***Average non-need-based aid:*** $27,576. ***Average indebtedness upon graduation:*** $29,000. ***Financial aid deadline:*** 3/1.

APPLYING

Standardized Tests *Required:* SAT or ACT (for admission). *Recommended:* SAT Subject Tests (for admission).

Options: electronic application, early admission, early decision, deferred entrance.

Application fee: $50.

Required: essay or personal statement, high school transcript, 2 letters of recommendation. ***Recommended:*** interview.

Application deadlines: 1/15 (freshmen), rolling (transfers).

Early decision deadline: 12/1.

Notification: 2/1 (freshmen), continuous (transfers), 1/1 (early decision).

CONTACT

Trish Dobbs, Director of Admissions, Clarkson University, 8 Clarkson Ave, Box 5605, Potsdam, NY 13699. *Phone:* 315-268-6480. *Toll-free phone:* 800-527-6577. *Fax:* 315-268-7647. *E-mail:* admissions@clarkson.edu.

Colgate University

Hamilton, New York

http://www.colgate.edu/

- **Independent** comprehensive, founded 1819
- **Small-town** 575-acre campus with easy access to Syracuse, Utica
- **Coed** 2,980 undergraduate students, 100% full-time, 55% women, 45% men
- **Most difficult** entrance level, 23% of applicants were admitted

UNDERGRAD STUDENTS

2,968 full-time, 12 part-time. 74% are from out of state; 4% Black or African American, non-Hispanic/Latino; 9% Hispanic/Latino; 5% Asian, non-Hispanic/Latino; 0.2% Native Hawaiian or other Pacific Islander, non-Hispanic/Latino; 0.1% American Indian or Alaska Native, non-Hispanic/Latino; 4% Two or more races, non-Hispanic/Latino; 3% Race/ethnicity unknown; 9% international; 0.7% transferred in.

Freshmen:

Admission: 9,951 applied, 2,247 admitted, 786 enrolled. ***Average high school GPA:*** 3.7. ***Test scores:*** SAT evidence-based reading and writing scores over 500: 100%; SAT math scores over 500: 100%; ACT scores over 18: 100%; SAT evidence-based reading and writing scores over 600: 95%; SAT math scores over 600: 95%; ACT scores over 24: 99%; SAT evidence-based reading and writing scores over 700: 53%; SAT math scores over 700: 64%; ACT scores over 30: 83%.

Retention: 95% of full-time freshmen returned.

FACULTY

Total: 360, 94% full-time, 93% with terminal degrees.

Student/faculty ratio: 9:1.

ACADEMICS

Calendar: semesters. *Degrees:* bachelor's and master's.

Special study options: advanced placement credit, double majors, independent study, internships, off-campus study, services for LD students, student-designed majors, study abroad. ***ROTC:*** Army (c).

Unusual degree programs: 3-2 engineering with Columbia University, Rensselaer Polytechnic Institute, Washington University in St. Louis.

Computers: 150 computers/terminals and 12,000 ports are available on campus for general student use. Students can access the following: campus intranet, computer help desk, free student e-mail accounts, online (class) grades, online (class) registration, online (class) schedules, software applications. Campuswide network is available. 100% of college-owned or -operated housing units are wired for high-speed Internet access. Wireless service is available via entire campus.

Library: Case Library and Geyer Center for Information Technology plus 1 other. *Books:* 749,143 (physical), 444,977 (digital/electronic); *Serial titles:* 4,085 (physical), 145,811 (digital/electronic); *Databases:* 305. Study areas open 24 hours, 5–7 days a week; students can reserve study rooms.

STUDENT LIFE

Housing options: on-campus residence required through junior year; coed, cooperative, special housing for students with disabilities. Campus housing is university owned. Freshman campus housing is guaranteed.

Activities and organizations: drama/theater group, student-run newspaper, radio and television station, choral group, COVE (35+ community service groups), Student Government Association, Cultural/ethnic interest groups, Student communications/publications (including WCRU radio station), Club sports/Outdoor Education, national fraternities, national sororities.

Athletics Member NCAA. All Division I. ***Intercollegiate sports:*** badminton M(c)/W(c), baseball M(c), basketball M(s)/W(s), bowling M(c)/W(c), cheerleading M(c)/W(c), cross-country running M/W, equestrian sports M(c)/W(c), fencing M(c)/W(c), field hockey W(s), football M(s), golf M, ice hockey M(s)/W(s), lacrosse M(s)/W(s), rowing M/W, rugby M(c)/W(c), sailing M(c)/W(c), skiing (cross-country) M(c)/W(c), skiing (downhill) M(c)/W(c), soccer M(s)/W(s), softball W(s), squash M(c)/W(c), swimming and diving M/W(s), table tennis M(c)/W(c), tennis M/W, track and field M/W, triathlon M(c)/W(c), ultimate Frisbee M(c)/W(c), volleyball W(s), water polo M(c)/W(c). ***Intramural sports:*** basketball M/W, football M, lacrosse M(c)/W(c), racquetball M/W, rock climbing M(c)/W(c), soccer M(c)/W(c), softball M/W, swimming and diving M(c)/W(c), table tennis M/W, tennis M(c)/W(c), volleyball M(c)/W(c).

Campus security: 24-hour emergency response devices and patrols, student patrols, late-night transport/escort service, controlled dormitory access.

Student services: health clinic, personal/psychological counseling, women's center, legal services.

COSTS & FINANCIAL AID

Costs (2019–20) ***One-time required fee:*** $50. ***Comprehensive fee:*** $72,585 includes full-time tuition ($57,695), mandatory fees ($350), and room and board ($14,540). ***College room only:*** $7020. Room and board charges vary according to board plan. ***Payment plans:*** tuition prepayment, installment.

Financial Aid Of all full-time matriculated undergraduates who enrolled in 2019, 1,086 applied for aid, 965 were judged to have need, 960 had their need fully met. ***Average percent of need met:*** 100. ***Average financial aid package:*** $57,355. ***Average need-based loan:*** $3400. ***Average need-based gift aid:*** $53,556. ***Average indebtedness upon graduation:*** $25,044. ***Financial aid deadline:*** 1/15.

APPLYING

Standardized Tests *Required:* SAT or ACT (for admission).

Options: electronic application, early decision, deferred entrance.

Application fee: $60.

Required: essay or personal statement, high school transcript, 3 letters of recommendation.

Application deadlines: 1/15 (freshmen), 3/15 (transfers).

Early decision deadline: 11/15.

Notification: 4/1 (freshmen), 5/1 (transfers), 12/15 (early decision plan 1), rolling (early decision plan 2).

CONTACT
Ms. Tara E.W. Bubble, Dean of Admission, Colgate University, Colgate Office of Admission, 13 Oak Drive, Hamilton, NY 13346-1383. *Phone:* 315-228-7401. *Fax:* 315-228-7544. *E-mail:* admission@colgate.edu.

College of Mount Saint Vincent

Riverdale, New York

http://www.mountsaintvincent.edu/

CONTACT
College of Mount Saint Vincent, 6301 Riverdale Avenue, Riverdale, NY 10471-1093. *Phone:* 718-405-3268. *Toll-free phone:* 800-665-CMSV.

The College of New Rochelle

New Rochelle, New York

http://www.cnr.edu/

- **Independent** comprehensive, founded 1904
- **Suburban** 20-acre campus with easy access to New York City
- **Endowment** $2.3 million
- **Coed**
- **Moderately difficult** entrance level

FACULTY
Student/faculty ratio: 14:1.

ACADEMICS
Calendar: semesters. *Degrees:* bachelor's, master's, post-master's, and postbachelor's certificates (also offers a non-traditional adult program with significant enrollment not reflected in profile).
Library: Gill Library plus 1 other. *Books:* 93,999 (physical), 153,914 (digital/electronic); *Serial titles:* 886 (physical), 94,336 (digital/electronic); *Databases:* 133. Weekly public service hours: 86; students can reserve study rooms.

STUDENT LIFE
Housing options: coed, special housing for students with disabilities. Campus housing is university owned. Freshman campus housing is guaranteed.

Activities and organizations: choral group, Music Ensembles, CNR Model United Nations, Student Nurses Association, Campus Ministry, Student Government.

Athletics Member NCAA. All Division III except soccer (Division II).

Campus security: 24-hour emergency response devices and patrols, late-night transport/escort service, controlled dormitory access, 24-hour monitored security cameras at residence hall entrances.

Student services: health clinic, personal/psychological counseling.

APPLYING
Standardized Tests *Required:* SAT or ACT (for admission).

Options: electronic application, deferred entrance.

Application fee: $35.

Required: high school transcript. ***Recommended:*** essay or personal statement, 1 letter of recommendation, interview.

CONTACT
Mr. Brian Sondey, Admissions Director, The College of New Rochelle, 29 Castle Place, New Rochelle, NY 10805-2339. *Phone:* 914-654-5921. *Toll-free phone:* 800-933-5923. *Fax:* 914-654-5464. *E-mail:* bsondey@cnr.edu.

The College of Saint Rose

Albany, New York

http://www.strose.edu/

- **Independent** comprehensive, founded 1920
- **Urban** 49-acre campus
- **Coed** 2,433 undergraduate students, 97% full-time, 66% women, 34% men
- **Moderately difficult** entrance level, 87% of applicants were admitted

UNDERGRAD STUDENTS
2,363 full-time, 70 part-time. Students come from 36 states and territories; 56 other countries; 14% are from out of state; 6% Black or African American, non-Hispanic/Latino; 6% Hispanic/Latino; 3% Asian, non-Hispanic/Latino; 0.1% Native Hawaiian or other Pacific Islander, non-Hispanic/Latino; 0.3% American Indian or Alaska Native, non-Hispanic/Latino; 12% Two or more races, non-Hispanic/Latino; 3% Race/ethnicity unknown; 3% international; 7% transferred in; 52% live on campus.

Freshmen:
Admission: 6,576 applied, 5,743 admitted, 640 enrolled. ***Average high school GPA:*** 3.2. ***Test scores:*** SAT evidence-based reading and writing scores over 500: 75%; SAT math scores over 500: 74%; ACT scores over 18: 83%; SAT evidence-based reading and writing scores over 600: 33%; SAT math scores over 600: 26%; ACT scores over 24: 42%; SAT evidence-based reading and writing scores over 700: 3%; SAT math scores over 700: 1%; ACT scores over 30: 6%.

Retention: 70% of full-time freshmen returned.

FACULTY
Total: 341, 50% full-time, 63% with terminal degrees.

Student/faculty ratio: 14:1.

ACADEMICS
Calendar: semesters. *Degrees:* certificates, bachelor's, master's, post-master's, and postbachelor's certificates.

Special study options: academic remediation for entering students, accelerated degree program, advanced placement credit, double majors, English as a second language, independent study, internships, off-campus study, part-time degree program, services for LD students, student-designed majors, study abroad, summer session for credit. ***ROTC:*** Army (b), Air Force (c).

Unusual degree programs: 3-2 engineering with Rensselaer Polytechnic Institute; clinical laboratory science, biology/cytotechnology with Albany College of Pharmacy.

Computers: 822 computers/terminals and 4,661 ports are available on campus for general student use. Students can access the following: computer help desk, free student e-mail accounts, online (class) grades, online (class) registration, online (class) schedules. Campuswide network is available. 100% of college-owned or -operated housing units are wired for high-speed Internet access. Wireless service is available via entire campus.
Library: Neil Hellman Library plus 2 others. *Books:* 241,000 (physical), 225,846 (digital/electronic); *Serial titles:* 1,201 (physical), 10 (digital/electronic); *Databases:* 104. Weekly public service hours: 73; students can reserve study rooms.

STUDENT LIFE
Housing options: on-campus residence required through sophomore year; coed, men-only, women-only, special housing for students with disabilities. Campus housing is university owned. Freshman campus housing is guaranteed.

Activities and organizations: drama/theater group, student-run newspaper, radio and television station, choral group, Student Association, Student Events Board, Spectrum-ALANA Student Union, Colleges Against Cancer, Music and Entertainment Industry Student Association.

Athletics Member NCAA. All Division II. ***Intercollegiate sports:*** baseball M(s), basketball M(s)/W(s), cross-country running M(s)/W(s), golf M(s)/W(s), lacrosse M(s)/W(s), soccer M(s)/W(s), softball W(s), swimming and diving M(s)/W(s), track and field M(s)/W(s), volleyball W(s). ***Intramural sports:*** baseball M(c), basketball M/W, cheerleading M(c)/W(c), soccer M/W, ultimate Frisbee M(c)/W(c), volleyball M/W.

Campus security: 24-hour emergency response devices and patrols, late-night transport/escort service, controlled dormitory access.

Student services: health clinic, personal/psychological counseling, veterans affairs office.

COSTS & FINANCIAL AID
Costs (2020–21) ***One-time required fee:*** $455. ***Comprehensive fee:*** $47,512 includes full-time tuition ($33,152), mandatory fees ($1202), and room and board ($13,158). Full-time tuition and fees vary according to course load. Part-time tuition: $1098 per credit hour. Part-time tuition and fees vary according to course load. ***Required fees:*** $34 per credit hour part-time, $145 per term part-time. ***College room only:*** $6712. Room and board charges vary according to board plan and housing facility. ***Payment plan:*** installment. ***Waivers:*** employees or children of employees.

Financial Aid Of all full-time matriculated undergraduates who enrolled in 2017, 2,193 applied for aid, 2,040 were judged to have need, 324 had their need fully met. In 2017, 232 non-need-based awards were made. ***Average percent of need met:*** 79. ***Average financial aid package:*** $23,717. ***Average need-based loan:*** $4303. ***Average need-based gift aid:*** $8183. ***Average non-need-based aid:*** $14,461. ***Average indebtedness upon graduation:*** $37,506. ***Financial aid deadline:*** 5/1.

APPLYING

Standardized Tests *Required for some:* SAT or ACT (for admission).

Options: electronic application, early action, deferred entrance.

Required: high school transcript, 1 letter of recommendation. ***Required for some:*** interview. ***Recommended:*** essay or personal statement, minimum 2.5 GPA.

Application deadlines: 5/1 (freshmen), 8/1 (transfers), 12/1 (early action).

Notification: continuous (freshmen), continuous (transfers), 12/15 (early action).

CONTACT

Ms. Kathleen Lesko, Assistant Vice President of Undergraduate Admissions, The College of Saint Rose, 1001 Madison Avenue, Albany, NY 12203. *Phone:* 518-454-5154. *Toll-free phone:* 800-637-8556. *Fax:* 518-454-2013. *E-mail:* admit@strose.edu.

College of Staten Island of the City University of New York

Staten Island, New York

http://www.csi.cuny.edu/

- **State and locally supported** comprehensive, founded 1955, part of City University of New York
- **Urban** 204-acre campus with easy access to New York City
- **Endowment** $16.4 million
- **Coed** 11,700 undergraduate students, 78% full-time, 55% women, 45% men
- **Noncompetitive** entrance level, 93% of applicants were admitted

UNDERGRAD STUDENTS

9,124 full-time, 2,576 part-time. Students come from 16 states and territories; 107 other countries; 1% are from out of state; 14% Black or African American, non-Hispanic/Latino; 27% Hispanic/Latino; 11% Asian, non-Hispanic/Latino; 0.1% Native Hawaiian or other Pacific Islander, non-Hispanic/Latino; 0.1% American Indian or Alaska Native, non-Hispanic/Latino; 2% Two or more races, non-Hispanic/Latino; 3% international; 6% transferred in; 3% live on campus.

Freshmen:

Admission: 14,466 applied, 13,440 admitted, 2,361 enrolled. ***Average high school GPA:*** 3.1.

Retention: 75% of full-time freshmen returned.

FACULTY

Total: 1,134, 33% full-time, 52% with terminal degrees.

Student/faculty ratio: 19:1.

ACADEMICS

Calendar: semesters. *Degrees:* associate, bachelor's, master's, doctoral, post-master's, and postbachelor's certificates.

Special study options: academic remediation for entering students, adult/continuing education programs, advanced placement credit, cooperative education, distance learning, double majors, English as a second language, honors programs, independent study, internships, services for LD students, student-designed majors, study abroad, summer session for credit.

Computers: 1,875 computers/terminals and 1,875 ports are available on campus for general student use. Students can access the following: computer help desk, free student e-mail accounts, online (class) registration. Campuswide network is available. 100% of college-owned or -operated housing units are wired for high-speed Internet access. Wireless service is available via classrooms, computer centers, computer labs, learning centers, libraries, student centers.

Library: College of Staten Island Library. *Books:* 203,120 (physical), 569,514 (digital/electronic); *Serial titles:* 1,771 (physical), 121,194 (digital/electronic); *Databases:* 161. Weekly public service hours: 84; students can reserve study rooms.

STUDENT LIFE

Housing options: coed, special housing for students with disabilities. Campus housing is university owned.

Activities and organizations: drama/theater group, student-run newspaper, radio station, choral group, Pre-Med/Pre-PA Society, International Student Club, United African Students in the USA, The CSI Gamers Club, Muslim Student Association.

Athletics Member NCAA. All Division II. ***Intercollegiate sports:*** baseball M, basketball M/W, cross-country running M/W, soccer M/W, softball W, swimming and diving M/W, tennis M/W, track and field M/W. ***Intramural sports:*** badminton M/W, basketball M/W, bowling M(c)/W(c), cheerleading M/W, golf M/W, soccer M/W, swimming and diving M(c)/W(c), table tennis M/W, tennis M(c)/W(c), track and field M/W, ultimate Frisbee M/W, volleyball M/W.

Campus security: 24-hour emergency response devices and patrols, student patrols, late-night transport/escort service, controlled dormitory access, Radar controlled traffic monitoring.

Student services: health clinic, personal/psychological counseling, women's center, veterans affairs office.

COSTS & FINANCIAL AID

Costs (2019–20) ***Tuition:*** $305 per credit hour part-time; state resident $6930 full-time, $305 per credit hour part-time; nonresident $18,600 full-time, $620 per credit hour part-time. ***Required fees:*** $559 full-time, $181 per term part-time. ***Room only:*** $14,745. Room and board charges vary according to housing facility. ***Payment plan:*** installment. ***Waivers:*** senior citizens and employees or children of employees.

Financial Aid Of all full-time matriculated undergraduates who enrolled in 2018, 7,895 applied for aid, 7,096 were judged to have need, 439 had their need fully met. In 2018, 268 non-need-based awards were made. ***Average percent of need met:*** 47. ***Average financial aid package:*** $8645. ***Average need-based loan:*** $9494. ***Average need-based gift aid:*** $8087. ***Average non-need-based aid:*** $4194.

APPLYING

Standardized Tests *Required:* SAT or ACT (for admission).

Options: electronic application, deferred entrance.

Application fee: $65.

Required: high school transcript. ***Required for some:*** essay or personal statement, 2 letters of recommendation, interview.

Application deadlines: rolling (freshmen), rolling (out-of-state freshmen).

Notification: continuous until 2/1 (freshmen), continuous until 2/1 (out-of-state freshmen).

CONTACT

College of Staten Island of the City University of New York, 2800 Victory Blvd, 2A-103, Staten Island, NY 10314. *Phone:* 718-9822010. *Fax:* 718-9822500. *E-mail:* admissions@csi.cuny.edu.

The College of Westchester

White Plains, New York

http://www.cw.edu/

- **Proprietary** primarily 2-year, founded 1915
- **Suburban** campus with easy access to New York City
- **Coed** 906 undergraduate students, 80% full-time, 67% women, 33% men
- **Minimally difficult** entrance level, 97% of applicants were admitted

UNDERGRAD STUDENTS

728 full-time, 178 part-time. Students come from 9 states and territories; 5% are from out of state; 40% Black or African American, non-Hispanic/Latino; 47% Hispanic/Latino; 2% Asian, non-Hispanic/Latino; 0.1% Native Hawaiian or other Pacific Islander, non-Hispanic/Latino; 0.1% American Indian or Alaska Native, non-Hispanic/Latino; 1% Two or more races, non-Hispanic/Latino; 2% Race/ethnicity unknown; 12% transferred in.

Freshmen:

Admission: 824 applied, 796 admitted, 155 enrolled.

Retention: 63% of full-time freshmen returned.

ACADEMICS
Calendar: semesters. *Degrees:* certificates, associate, and bachelor's.

Special study options: academic remediation for entering students, accelerated degree program, adult/continuing education programs, cooperative education, distance learning, double majors, honors programs, internships, part-time degree program, summer session for credit.

Computers: 271 computers/terminals are available on campus for general student use. Students can access the following: campus intranet, computer help desk, free student e-mail accounts, online (class) grades, online (class) schedules. Campuswide network is available.
Library: Dr. William R. Papallo Library.

STUDENT LIFE
Housing options: college housing not available.

Activities and organizations: student-run newspaper.

Student services: personal/psychological counseling, veterans affairs office.

COSTS
Costs (2019–20) ***Tuition:*** $21,060 full-time, $780 per credit part-time. ***Required fees:*** $1350 full-time, $150 per course part-time. ***Payment plan:*** installment. ***Waivers:*** employees or children of employees.

APPLYING
Standardized Tests *Recommended:* SAT (for admission).

Options: electronic application, deferred entrance.

Application fee: $40.

Required: high school transcript, interview. ***Required for some:*** essay or personal statement.

Application deadlines: rolling (freshmen), rolling (transfers).

CONTACT
Mr. Matt Curtis, Vice President, Enrollment Management, The College of Westchester, 325 Central Avenue, PO Box 710, White Plains, NY 10602. *Phone:* 914-948-4442 Ext. 313. *Toll-free phone:* 855-403-7722. *Fax:* 914-948-5441. *E-mail:* admissions@cw.edu.

Columbia University
New York, New York
http://www.columbia.edu/

- **Independent** university, founded 1754
- **Urban** 36-acre campus with easy access to New York City
- **Endowment** $10.9 billion
- **Coed**
- **Most difficult** entrance level

FACULTY
Student/faculty ratio: 6:1.

ACADEMICS
Calendar: semesters. *Degrees:* bachelor's, master's, and doctoral.
Library: Butler plus 18 others. *Books:* 10.7 million (physical), 2.6 million (digital/electronic); *Databases:* 1,587. Weekly public service hours: 86; study areas open 24 hours, 5–7 days a week; students can reserve study rooms.

STUDENT LIFE
Housing options: on-campus residence required for freshman year; coed, cooperative, special housing for students with disabilities. Campus housing is university owned. Freshman campus housing is guaranteed.

Activities and organizations: drama/theater group, student-run newspaper, radio and television station, choral group, marching band, community service, cultural organizations, performing arts, athletics, publications, national fraternities, national sororities.

Athletics Member NCAA. All Division I except football (Division I-AA).

Campus security: 24-hour emergency response devices and patrols, late-night transport/escort service, controlled dormitory access.

Student services: health clinic, personal/psychological counseling, women's center.

COSTS & FINANCIAL AID
Costs (2019–20) ***Comprehensive fee:*** $76,340 includes full-time tuition ($58,920), mandatory fees ($2930), and room and board ($14,490). ***Room and board:*** Room and board charges vary according to board plan. ***Payment plans:*** tuition prepayment, installment.

Financial Aid Of all full-time matriculated undergraduates who enrolled in 2019, 3,302 applied for aid, 3,144 were judged to have need, 2,978 had their need fully met. ***Average percent of need met:*** 100. ***Average financial aid package:*** $63,897. ***Average need-based loan:*** $3661. ***Average need-based gift aid:*** $59,239.

APPLYING
Standardized Tests *Required:* SAT or ACT (for admission).

Options: electronic application, early admission, early decision, deferred entrance.

Application fee: $85.

Required: essay or personal statement, high school transcript, 3 letters of recommendation.

CONTACT
Ms. Jessica Marinaccio, Dean of Undergraduate Admissions and Financial Aid, Columbia University, 116th Street and Broadway, New York, NY 10027. *Phone:* 212-854-1222.

See below for display ad and page 1050 for the College Close-Up.

Columbia University School of General Studies

New York, New York

http://www.gs.columbia.edu/

CONTACT
Mr. Curtis M. Rodgers, Vice Dean, Columbia University School of General Studies, 2970 Broadway, 408 Lewisohn Hall, MC 4101, New York, NY 10027. *Phone:* 212-854-2772. *Toll-free phone:* 800-895-1169. *Fax:* 212-854-6316. *E-mail:* gsdegree@columbia.edu.

Columbia University School of General Studies (Dual and Joint Degree Programs)

New York, New York

http://www.gs.columbia.edu/

CONTACT
Columbia University School of General Studies (Dual and Joint Degree Programs), 2970 Broadway, 408 Lewisohn Hall, MC 4101, New York, NY 10027-6939.

Columbia University School of General Studies (Non Traditional Undergraduate Program)

New York, New York

http://www.gs.columbia.edu/

CONTACT
Columbia University School of General Studies (Non Traditional Undergraduate Program), 2970 Broadway, 408 Lewisohn Hall, MC 4101, New York, NY 10027-6939.

Columbia University School of General Studies (Postbaccalaureate Premedical Program)

New York, New York

http://www.gs.columbia.edu/

CONTACT
Columbia University School of General Studies (Postbaccalaureate Premedical Program), 2970 Broadway, 408 Lewisohn Hall, MC 4101, New York, NY 10027-6939.

Concordia College–New York

Bronxville, New York

http://www.concordia-ny.edu/

- **Independent Lutheran** comprehensive, founded 1881, part of Concordia University System
- **Suburban** 33-acre campus with easy access to New York City
- **Endowment** $6.4 million
- **Coed**
- **Moderately difficult** entrance level

FACULTY
Student/faculty ratio: 11:1.

ACADEMICS
Calendar: semesters. *Degrees:* certificates, diplomas, associate, bachelor's, and master's.
Library: Scheele Memorial Library plus 1 other.

STUDENT LIFE
Housing options: men-only, women-only, special housing for students with disabilities. Campus housing is university owned.
Activities and organizations: drama/theater group, student-run newspaper, choral group, Student Government Association, Choral Groups, Campus Christian Ministries, International and Afro/Latin American Club, Yearbook and newspaper.

Athletics Member NCAA. All Division II.

Campus security: 24-hour emergency response devices and patrols, controlled dormitory access.

Student services: health clinic, personal/psychological counseling.

FINANCIAL AID
Financial Aid Of all full-time matriculated undergraduates who enrolled in 2008, 533 applied for aid, 448 were judged to have need, 89 had their need fully met. In 2008, 100 non-need-based awards were made. ***Average percent of need met:*** 71. ***Average financial aid package:*** $22,309. ***Average need-based loan:*** $4133. ***Average need-based gift aid:*** $11,129. ***Average non-need-based aid:*** $6170. ***Average indebtedness upon graduation:*** $24,153.

APPLYING
Standardized Tests *Required for some:* SAT or ACT (for admission), TOEFL or IELTS for students for whom English is not their first language.

Options: electronic application, early admission, early action, deferred entrance.

Application fee: $60.

Required: essay or personal statement, high school transcript, 2 letters of recommendation. ***Required for some:*** interview. ***Recommended:*** minimum 2.5 GPA.

CONTACT
Ms. Toral Bhatt, Director of Recruitment, Concordia College–New York, 171 White Plains Road, Bronxville, NY 10708. *Phone:* 914-337-9300 Ext. 2124. *Toll-free phone:* 800-YES-COLLEGE. *Fax:* 914-395-4636. *E-mail:* toral.bhatt@concordia-ny.edu.

Cooper Union for the Advancement of Science and Art

New York, New York

http://www.cooper.edu/

CONTACT
Ms. Adrianne Greth, Associate Dean of Admissions, Cooper Union for the Advancement of Science and Art, 30 Cooper Square, New York, NY 10003. *Phone:* 212-353-4121. *Fax:* 212-353-4342. *E-mail:* admissions@cooper.edu.

Cornell University

Ithaca, New York

http://www.cornell.edu/

- **Independent** university, founded 1865, part of State University of New York System
- **Small-town** 745-acre campus with easy access to Syracuse
- **Endowment** $7.0 billion
- **Coed** 15,043 undergraduate students, 100% full-time, 54% women, 46% men
- **Most difficult** entrance level, 11% of applicants were admitted

UNDERGRAD STUDENTS
15,043 full-time. Students come from 90 other countries; 58% are from out of state; 7% Black or African American, non-Hispanic/Latino; 14% Hispanic/Latino; 20% Asian, non-Hispanic/Latino; 0.1% Native Hawaiian or other Pacific Islander, non-Hispanic/Latino; 0.3% American Indian or Alaska Native, non-Hispanic/Latino; 5% Two or more races, non-Hispanic/Latino; 8% Race/ethnicity unknown; 11% international; 4% transferred in; 52% live on campus.

Freshmen:
Admission: 49,114 applied, 5,330 admitted, 3,189 enrolled. ***Test scores:*** SAT evidence-based reading and writing scores over 500: 100%; SAT math scores over 500: 100%; ACT scores over 18: 100%; SAT evidence-based reading and writing scores over 600: 97%; SAT math scores over 600: 98%; ACT scores over 24: 99%; SAT evidence-based reading and writing scores over 700: 69%; SAT math scores over 700: 83%; ACT scores over 30: 91%.

Retention: 97% of full-time freshmen returned.

FACULTY
Total: 2,216, 83% full-time, 87% with terminal degrees.

Student/faculty ratio: 9:1.

ACADEMICS
Calendar: semesters. *Degrees:* bachelor's, master's, and doctoral.

Special study options: academic remediation for entering students, accelerated degree program, advanced placement credit, cooperative education, distance learning, double majors, English as a second language, honors programs, independent study, internships, off-campus study, services for LD students, student-designed majors, study abroad, summer session for credit. ***ROTC:*** Army (b), Navy (b), Air Force (b).

Computers: 1,500 computers/terminals are available on campus for general student use. Students can access the following: campus intranet, computer help desk, free student e-mail accounts, online (class) grades, online (class) registration. Campuswide network is available. 100% of college-owned or -operated housing units are wired for high-speed Internet access. Wireless service is available via entire campus.
Library: Main Library plus 16 others. *Books:* 5.2 million (physical), 1.7 million (digital/electronic); *Serial titles:* 240,369 (physical), 160,209 (digital/electronic); *Databases:* 4,269. Weekly public service hours: 146; study areas open 24 hours, 5–7 days a week; students can reserve study rooms.

STUDENT LIFE
Housing options: coed, women-only, cooperative, special housing for students with disabilities. Campus housing is university owned. Freshman campus housing is guaranteed.

Activities and organizations: drama/theater group, student-run newspaper, radio and television station, choral group, marching band, Class Councils, Cornell Hillel, Interfraternity Council/Panhellenic Association, Outing Club, Student Assembly, national fraternities, national sororities.

Athletics Member NCAA. All Division I. ***Intercollegiate sports:*** baseball M, basketball M/W, crew M/W, cross-country running M/W, equestrian sports W, fencing W, field hockey W, football M, golf M, gymnastics W, ice hockey M/W, lacrosse M/W, sailing W, soccer M/W, softball W, squash M/W, swimming and diving M/W, tennis M/W, track and field M/W, ultimate Frisbee M(c)/W(c), volleyball M(c)/W, water polo M(c)/W(c), wrestling M. ***Intramural sports:*** archery M(c)/W(c), badminton M/W, baseball M(c), basketball M/W, bowling M/W, cheerleading W(c), cross-country running M(c)/W(c), equestrian sports M(c)/W(c), fencing M(c)/W(c), field hockey W(c), football M(c)/W(c), golf M/W, gymnastics M(c)/W(c), ice hockey M(c)/W(c), lacrosse W(c), rugby M(c)/W(c), sailing M(c)/W(c), sand volleyball M(c)/W(c), skiing (cross-country) M(c)/W(c), skiing (downhill) M(c)/W(c), soccer M/W, softball M/W, squash M/W, table tennis M/W, tennis M/W, ultimate Frisbee M/W, volleyball M/W, water polo M/W, wrestling M(c)/W(c).

Campus security: 24-hour emergency response devices and patrols, late-night transport/escort service, controlled dormitory access.

Student services: health clinic, personal/psychological counseling, women's center.

COSTS & FINANCIAL AID
Costs (2019–20) ***Comprehensive fee:*** $72,518 includes full-time tuition ($56,550), mandatory fees ($672), and room and board ($15,296). ***College room only:*** $9152. Room and board charges vary according to board plan and housing facility. ***Payment plan:*** installment. ***Waivers:*** employees or children of employees.

Financial Aid Of all full-time matriculated undergraduates who enrolled in 2019, 7,665 applied for aid, 7,081 were judged to have need, 7,081 had their need fully met. ***Average percent of need met:*** 100. ***Average financial aid package:*** $50,492. ***Average need-based loan:*** $5092. ***Average need-based gift aid:*** $44,026. ***Average indebtedness upon graduation:*** $27,094. ***Financial aid deadline:*** 2/15.

APPLYING
Standardized Tests *Required:* SAT or ACT (for admission). *Required for some:* SAT Subject Tests (for admission).

Options: electronic application, early decision, deferred entrance.

Application fee: $80.

Required: essay or personal statement, high school transcript, 2 letters of recommendation. ***Required for some:*** interview.

Application deadlines: 1/2 (freshmen), 3/15 (transfers).

Early decision deadline: 11/1.

Notification: 3/31 (freshmen), 6/15 (transfers), 12/15 (early decision).

CONTACT
Cornell University, 144 East Avenue, Ithaca, NY 14853. *Phone:* 607-255-5241.

The Culinary Institute of America

Hyde Park, New York

http://www.ciachef.edu/

- **Independent** 4-year, founded 1946
- **Suburban** 170-acre campus
- **Endowment** $138.3 million
- **Coed** 3,007 undergraduate students, 100% full-time, 49% women, 51% men
- **Moderately difficult** entrance level

UNDERGRAD STUDENTS
3,007 full-time. 65% are from out of state; 7% Black or African American, non-Hispanic/Latino; 16% Hispanic/Latino; 7% Asian, non-Hispanic/Latino; 0.3% Native Hawaiian or other Pacific Islander, non-Hispanic/Latino; 0.5% American Indian or Alaska Native, non-Hispanic/Latino; 3% Two or more races, non-Hispanic/Latino; 5% Race/ethnicity unknown; 15% international; 11% transferred in.

Freshmen:
Admission: 610 enrolled. ***Test scores:*** SAT evidence-based reading and writing scores over 500: 77%; SAT math scores over 500: 71%; ACT scores over 18: 79%; SAT evidence-based reading and writing scores over 600: 27%; SAT math scores over 600: 23%; ACT scores over 24: 28%; SAT evidence-based reading and writing scores over 700: 5%; SAT math scores over 700: 5%; ACT scores over 30: 6%.

Retention: 81% of full-time freshmen returned.

FACULTY
Total: 211, 66% full-time.

Student/faculty ratio: 19:1.

ACADEMICS
Calendar: semesters plus 18 or 21 week externship program. *Degrees:* certificates, associate, bachelor's, master's, and postbachelor's certificates.

Special study options: academic remediation for entering students, double majors, internships, off-campus study, services for LD students, study abroad.

Computers: Students can access the following: campus intranet, computer help desk, free student e-mail accounts, online (class) grades, online (class) registration, online (class) schedules, online course guides. Campuswide network is available. Wireless service is available via entire campus.

Library: Conrad N. Hilton Library. Students can reserve study rooms.

STUDENT LIFE

Housing options: Freshman campus housing is guaranteed.

Activities and organizations: student-run newspaper.

Campus security: 24-hour emergency response devices and patrols, late-night transport/escort service, controlled dormitory access, CCTV & Nightly Visitor Screening.

Student services: health clinic, personal/psychological counseling.

COSTS & FINANCIAL AID

Costs (2019–20) ***Comprehensive fee:*** $45,570 includes full-time tuition ($31,080), mandatory fees ($2610), and room and board ($11,880). Full-time tuition and fees vary according to location. Part-time tuition and fees vary according to course load. ***College room only:*** $8080. Room and board charges vary according to board plan, housing facility, and location.

Financial Aid ***Average indebtedness upon graduation:*** $51,200.

APPLYING

Options: electronic application, early action, deferred entrance.

Application fee: $50.

Required: essay or personal statement, high school transcript, 1 letter of recommendation. ***Required for some:*** Affidavit of Support. ***Recommended:*** minimum 2.0 GPA.

Notification: continuous (transfers).

CONTACT

The Culinary Institute of America, 1946 Campus Drive, Hyde Park, NY 12538. *Phone:* 845-451-1459. *Toll-free phone:* 800-CULINARY. *E-mail:* admissions@culinary.edu.

Daemen College

Amherst, New York

http://www.daemen.edu/

- **Independent** comprehensive, founded 1947
- **Suburban** 35-acre campus with easy access to Buffalo
- **Endowment** $14.4 million
- **Coed**
- **Moderately difficult** entrance level

FACULTY

Student/faculty ratio: 12:1.

ACADEMICS

Calendar: semesters. *Degrees:* certificates, bachelor's, master's, doctoral, post-master's, and postbachelor's certificates.

Library: Research and Information Commons. *Books:* 85,205 (physical), 138,085 (digital/electronic); *Serial titles:* 488 (physical); *Databases:* 38. Weekly public service hours: 117; students can reserve study rooms.

STUDENT LIFE

Housing options: on-campus residence required for freshman year; coed, special housing for students with disabilities. Campus housing is university owned and leased by the school. Freshman campus housing is guaranteed.

Activities and organizations: drama/theater group, student-run newspaper, choral group, Game Club, Anime Club, Best Buddies, CRU, Pride Club.

Athletics Member NCAA. All Division II.

Campus security: 24-hour emergency response devices and patrols, late-night transport/escort service, controlled dormitory access, 24-hour security cameras.

Student services: personal/psychological counseling, veterans affairs office.

FINANCIAL AID

Financial Aid Of all full-time matriculated undergraduates who enrolled in 2017, 1,425 applied for aid, 951 were judged to have need, 117 had their need fully met. 612 Federal Work-Study jobs (averaging $2918). 50 state and other part-time jobs (averaging $2040). In 2017, 441 non-need-based awards were made. ***Average percent of need met:*** 82. ***Average financial aid package:*** $28,324. ***Average need-based loan:*** $4630. ***Average need-based gift aid:*** $11,058. ***Average non-need-based aid:*** $11,119. ***Average indebtedness upon graduation:*** $35,530.

APPLYING

Standardized Tests *Required for some:* SAT or ACT (for admission), SAT/ACT or high school course grades, show rigor of courses and teacher recommendations. *Recommended:* SAT or ACT (for admission).

Options: electronic application, early admission, deferred entrance.

Application fee: $25.

Required: essay or personal statement, high school transcript, 1 letter of recommendation. ***Recommended:*** interview.

CONTACT

Ms. Caroline Marciszewski, Associate Director of Undergraduate Admissions, Daemen College, 4380 Main Street, Amherst, NY 14226-3592. *Phone:* 716-566-7856. *Toll-free phone:* 800-462-7652. *Fax:* 716-839-8229. *E-mail:* admissions@daemen.edu.

Davis College

Johnson City, New York

http://www.davisny.edu/

CONTACT

Ms. Hannah Hempstead, Assistant Director of Admissions for Communication, Davis College, 400 Riverside Drive, Johnson City, NY 13790. *Phone:* 607-729-1581 Ext. 341. *Toll-free phone:* 877-949-3248. *Fax:* 607-770-6886. *E-mail:* hhempstead@davisny.edu.

DeVry College of New York–Midtown Manhattan Campus

New York, New York

http://www.devry.edu/

- **Proprietary** comprehensive, founded 1998, part of DeVry University
- **Urban** campus
- **Coed**
- **Minimally difficult** entrance level

FACULTY

Student/faculty ratio: 26:1.

ACADEMICS

Calendar: semesters. *Degrees:* associate, bachelor's, master's, and postbachelor's certificates.

Library: Learning Resource Center.

STUDENT LIFE

Housing options: college housing not available.

FINANCIAL AID

Financial Aid Of all full-time matriculated undergraduates who enrolled in 2007, 387 applied for aid, 371 were judged to have need, 8 had their need fully met. In 2007, 19 non-need-based awards were made. ***Average percent of need met:*** 5. ***Average financial aid package:*** $15,942. ***Average need-based loan:*** $8712. ***Average need-based gift aid:*** $7343. ***Average non-need-based aid:*** $11,806. ***Average indebtedness upon graduation:*** $29,136.

APPLYING

Application fee: $30.

Required: high school transcript, interview.

CONTACT

DeVry College of New York–Midtown Manhattan Campus, 180 Madison Avenue, Suite 900, New York, NY 10016. *Phone:* 212-312-4300. *Toll-free phone:* 866-338-7934.

Dominican College

Orangeburg, New York

http://www.dc.edu/

- **Independent** comprehensive, founded 1952
- **Suburban** 64-acre campus with easy access to New York City
- **Endowment** $6.6 million
- **Coed** 2,754 undergraduate students, 92% full-time, 66% women, 34% men
- **Noncompetitive** entrance level, 78% of applicants were admitted

UNDERGRAD STUDENTS

2,534 full-time, 220 part-time. Students come from 28 states and territories; 12 other countries; 24% are from out of state; 17% Black or African American, non-Hispanic/Latino; 34% Hispanic/Latino; 6% Asian, non-Hispanic/Latino; 0.5% Native Hawaiian or other Pacific Islander, non-Hispanic/Latino; 3% Two or more races, non-Hispanic/Latino; 9% Race/ethnicity unknown; 2% international; 5% transferred in; 48% live on campus.

Freshmen:

Admission: 2,314 applied, 1,800 admitted, 293 enrolled. ***Average high school GPA:*** 3.0.

Retention: 68% of full-time freshmen returned.

FACULTY

Total: 211, 36% full-time, 27% with terminal degrees.

Student/faculty ratio: 15:1.

ACADEMICS

Calendar: semesters. *Degrees:* certificates, diplomas, associate, bachelor's, master's, doctoral, and postbachelor's certificates.

Special study options: academic remediation for entering students, accelerated degree program, adult/continuing education programs, advanced placement credit, cooperative education, distance learning, double majors, honors programs, independent study, internships, off-campus study, part-time degree program, services for LD students, study abroad, summer session for credit.

Unusual degree programs: 3-2 engineering with Manhattan College; occupational therapy.

Computers: 150 computers/terminals are available on campus for general student use. Students can access the following: campus intranet, computer help desk, free student e-mail accounts, online (class) grades, online (class) registration, online (class) schedules, Web portal, learning management system. Campuswide network is available. 100% of college-owned or -operated housing units are wired for high-speed Internet access. Wireless service is available via entire campus.

Library: Sullivan Library plus 1 other. *Books:* 74,226 (physical), 117,187 (digital/electronic); *Serial titles:* 610 (physical), 75,067 (digital/electronic); *Databases:* 85. Weekly public service hours: 89; students can reserve study rooms.

STUDENT LIFE

Housing options: coed. Campus housing is university owned. Freshman campus housing is guaranteed.

Activities and organizations: drama/theater group, student-run radio station, choral group, Student Government Association, Anime and Gaming Club, Aquin Players Drama Society, Verbal Asylum, Student Nursing Association.

Athletics Member NCAA. All Division II except golf (Division III). ***Intercollegiate sports:*** baseball M(s), basketball M(s)/W(s), cross-country running M(s)/W(s), golf M(s)/W(s), lacrosse M(s)/W(s), soccer M(s)/W(s), softball W(s), tennis M(s)/W(s), track and field M(s)/W(s), volleyball W(s). ***Intramural sports:*** basketball M/W, ultimate Frisbee M(c)/W(c), volleyball M/W.

Campus security: 24-hour emergency response devices and patrols, student patrols, late-night transport/escort service, controlled dormitory access.

Student services: health clinic, personal/psychological counseling.

COSTS & FINANCIAL AID

Costs (2020–21) ***Comprehensive fee:*** $43,258 includes full-time tuition ($28,984), mandatory fees ($860), and room and board ($13,414). Part-time tuition: $877 per credit hour. ***Required fees:*** $877 per credit hour part-time. ***Room and board:*** Room and board charges vary according to housing facility. ***Payment plan:*** installment.

Financial Aid Of all full-time matriculated undergraduates who enrolled in 2019, 1,158 applied for aid, 1,046 were judged to have need, 133 had their need fully met. 211 Federal Work-Study jobs (averaging $2000). In 2019, 167 non-need-based awards were made. ***Average percent of need met:*** 66. ***Average financial aid package:*** $23,609. ***Average need-based loan:*** $5259. ***Average need-based gift aid:*** $19,298. ***Average non-need-based aid:*** $11,115. ***Average indebtedness upon graduation:*** $39,347.

APPLYING

Options: electronic application, deferred entrance.

Application fee: $35.

Required: high school transcript. ***Required for some:*** essay or personal statement, interview. ***Recommended:*** interview.

Application deadlines: rolling (freshmen), rolling (transfers).

Notification: continuous (freshmen), continuous (transfers).

CONTACT

Ms. Emma Fortunato, Assistant Director of Freshman Admissions, Dominican College, 470 Western Highway, Orangeburg, NY 10962-1210. *Phone:* 845-359-7906. *Toll-free phone:* 866-432-4636. *Fax:* 845-365-3150. *E-mail:* emma.fortunato@dc.edu.

D'Youville College

Buffalo, New York

http://www.dyc.edu/

- **Independent** comprehensive, founded 1908
- **Urban** 17-acre campus
- **Endowment** $49.6 million
- **Coed** 1,609 undergraduate students, 73% full-time, 75% women, 25% men
- **Moderately difficult** entrance level, 74% of applicants were admitted

UNDERGRAD STUDENTS

1,179 full-time, 430 part-time. Students come from 25 states and territories; 35 other countries; 9% are from out of state; 10% Black or African American, non-Hispanic/Latino; 5% Hispanic/Latino; 6% Asian, non-Hispanic/Latino; 0.6% American Indian or Alaska Native, non-Hispanic/Latino; 2% Two or more races, non-Hispanic/Latino; 5% Race/ethnicity unknown; 2% international; 10% transferred in; 18% live on campus.

Freshmen:

Admission: 1,758 applied, 1,294 admitted, 217 enrolled. ***Average high school GPA:*** 3.7. ***Test scores:*** SAT evidence-based reading and writing scores over 500: 73%; SAT math scores over 500: 84%; ACT scores over 18: 85%; SAT evidence-based reading and writing scores over 600: 24%; SAT math scores over 600: 32%; ACT scores over 24: 31%; SAT evidence-based reading and writing scores over 700: 1%; SAT math scores over 700: 6%; ACT scores over 30: 7%.

Retention: 81% of full-time freshmen returned.

FACULTY

Total: 379, 49% full-time, 39% with terminal degrees.

Student/faculty ratio: 10:1.

ACADEMICS

Calendar: semesters plus summer session. *Degrees:* bachelor's, master's, doctoral, post-master's, and postbachelor's certificates.

Special study options: academic remediation for entering students, accelerated degree program, adult/continuing education programs, advanced placement credit, distance learning, double majors, independent study, internships, off-campus study, part-time degree program, services for LD students, study abroad, summer session for credit. ***ROTC:*** Army (c).

Unusual degree programs: 3-2 nursing; chiropractic, dietetics, occupational therapy, pharmacy, physical therapy, physician assistant.

Computers: 120 computers/terminals are available on campus for general student use. Students can access the following: computer help desk, free student e-mail accounts, online (class) grades, online (class) registration, online (class) schedules. Campuswide network is available. 100% of college-owned or -operated housing units are wired for high-speed Internet access. Wireless service is available via entire campus.

Library: Montante Family Library. *Books:* 51,625 (physical), 5,084 (digital/electronic); *Serial titles:* 500 (physical), 43,469 (digital/electronic); *Databases:* 84. Weekly public service hours: 87; study areas open 24 hours, 5–7 days a week; students can reserve study rooms.

STUDENT LIFE

Housing options: on-campus residence required for freshman year; coed, men-only, women-only, special housing for students with disabilities. Campus housing is university owned. Freshman campus housing is guaranteed.

Activities and organizations: drama/theater group, student-run newspaper, choral group, Student Association, Occupational Therapy Student Association, Physical Therapy Student Association, Student Nurses Association, Black Student Union.

Athletics Member NCAA. All Division III. ***Intercollegiate sports:*** baseball M, basketball M/W, cheerleading W, cross-country running M/W, golf M/W, lacrosse W, soccer M/W, softball W, tennis M/W, volleyball M/W. ***Intramural sports:*** basketball M/W, crew W, volleyball M/W.

Campus security: 24-hour emergency response devices and patrols, late-night transport/escort service, controlled dormitory access.

Student services: health clinic, personal/psychological counseling, veterans affairs office.

COSTS & FINANCIAL AID

Costs (2020–21) ***Required fees:*** $900 full-time. ***Room and board:*** $9500. Room and board charges vary according to housing facility. ***Waivers:*** employees or children of employees.

Financial Aid Of all full-time matriculated undergraduates who enrolled in 2015, 810 applied for aid, 720 were judged to have need, 158 had their need fully met. In 2015, 123 non-need-based awards were made. ***Average percent of need met:*** 73. ***Average financial aid package:*** $19,004. ***Average need-based loan:*** $4353. ***Average need-based gift aid:*** $15,177. ***Average non-need-based aid:*** $8739. ***Average indebtedness upon graduation:*** $34,593.

APPLYING

Standardized Tests *Required:* SAT or ACT (for admission).

Options: electronic application, deferred entrance.

Required: high school transcript, minimum 2.0 GPA. ***Required for some:*** essay or personal statement, minimum 3.0 GPA, interview.

Application deadlines: rolling (freshmen), rolling (transfers).

Notification: continuous (freshmen), continuous (transfers).

CONTACT

Allison Newman, Director of Freshmen Admissions, D'Youville College, 320 Porter Avenue, Buffalo, NY 14201. *Phone:* 716-829-7600. *Toll-free phone:* 800-777-3921. *Fax:* 716-829-7900. *E-mail:* newmana@dyc.edu.

Elmira College

Elmira, New York

http://www.elmira.edu/

CONTACT

Mr. Christopher R. Coons, Vice President of Enrollment Management, Elmira College, 855 College Avenue, Elmira, NY 14901. *Phone:* 607-735-1724. *Toll-free phone:* 800-935-6472. *Fax:* 607-735-1718. *E-mail:* admissions@elmira.edu.

Eugene Lang College of Liberal Arts

New York, New York

http://www.newschool.edu/lang

- **Independent** 4-year, founded 1975, part of The New School
- **Urban** campus with easy access to New York City
- **Endowment** $322.3 million
- **Coed** 1,885 undergraduate students, 96% full-time, 79% women, 21% men
- **Minimally difficult** entrance level, 80% of applicants were admitted

UNDERGRAD STUDENTS

1,817 full-time, 68 part-time. 78% are from out of state; 6% Black or African American, non-Hispanic/Latino; 17% Hispanic/Latino; 7% Asian, non-Hispanic/Latino; 0.1% Native Hawaiian or other Pacific Islander, non-Hispanic/Latino; 0.3% American Indian or Alaska Native, non-Hispanic/Latino; 6% Two or more races, non-Hispanic/Latino; 5% Race/ethnicity unknown; 8% international; 7% transferred in; 10% live on campus.

Freshmen:

Admission: 2,939 applied, 2,344 admitted, 432 enrolled. ***Average high school GPA:*** 3.5. ***Test scores:*** SAT evidence-based reading and writing scores over 500: 97%; SAT math scores over 500: 90%; ACT scores over 18: 98%; SAT evidence-based reading and writing scores over 600: 71%; SAT math scores over 600: 42%; ACT scores over 24: 85%; SAT evidence-based reading and writing scores over 700: 17%; SAT math scores over 700: 6%; ACT scores over 30: 25%.

Retention: 69% of full-time freshmen returned.

FACULTY

Total: 265, 45% full-time, 9% with terminal degrees.

Student/faculty ratio: 11:1.

ACADEMICS

Calendar: semesters. *Degree:* bachelor's.

Special study options: academic remediation for entering students, accelerated degree program, advanced placement credit, cooperative education, distance learning, double majors, English as a second language, independent study, internships, off-campus study, part-time degree program, services for LD students, student-designed majors, study abroad, summer session for credit.

Computers: 717 computers/terminals are available on campus for general student use. Students can access the following: campus intranet, computer help desk, free student e-mail accounts, online (class) grades, online (class) registration, online (class) schedules. Campuswide network is available. 100% of college-owned or -operated housing units are wired for high-speed Internet access. Wireless service is available via entire campus.

Library: New School Libraries & Archives plus 3 others. *Books:* 215,937 (physical), 840,933 (digital/electronic); *Serial titles:* 2,265 (physical), 113,452 (digital/electronic); *Databases:* 376. Weekly public service hours: 155; study areas open 24 hours, 5–7 days a week; students can reserve study rooms.

STUDENT LIFE

Housing options: coed, special housing for students with disabilities. Campus housing is university owned. Freshman applicants given priority for college housing.

Activities and organizations: drama/theater group, student-run newspaper, choral group.

Athletics ***Intramural sports:*** basketball M/W, cross-country running M/W, soccer M/W, tennis M/W.

Campus security: 24-hour emergency response devices, controlled dormitory access, 24-hour desk attendants in residence halls.

Student services: health clinic, personal/psychological counseling, veterans affairs office.

FINANCIAL AID

Financial Aid Of all full-time matriculated undergraduates who enrolled in 2018, 1,093 applied for aid, 1,016 were judged to have need, 60 had their need fully met. In 2018, 645 non-need-based awards were made. ***Average percent of need met:*** 62. ***Average financial aid package:*** $27,199. ***Average need-based loan:*** $3377. ***Average need-based gift aid:*** $14,803. ***Average non-need-based aid:*** $14,743. ***Average indebtedness upon graduation:*** $32,153.

APPLYING

Standardized Tests *Required for some:* TOEFL, IELTS and PTE for some applicants whose first language is not English.

Options: electronic application, early action, deferred entrance.

Application fee: $50.

Required: essay or personal statement, high school transcript, 2 letters of recommendation, online application, 2 supplemental essays, counselor evaluation or teacher evaluation, academic paper (grade preferred). ***Recommended:*** minimum 3.0 GPA.

Application deadlines: 1/15 (freshmen), 4/1 (transfers), 11/1 (early action).

Notification: continuous until 3/15 (freshmen), continuous until 12/20 (transfers), 12/20 (early action).

CONTACT
Ms. Candice MacLusky, Director of Admissions for Lang, Eugene Lang College of Liberal Arts, 65 West 11th Street, New York, NY 10011-8601. *Phone:* 212-229-5155 Ext. 4024. *Toll-free phone:* 800-292-3040. *E-mail:* macluskc@newschool.edu.

Excelsior College

Albany, New York

http://www.excelsior.edu/

- **Independent** comprehensive, founded 1970
- **Suburban** campus with easy access to Albany, NY
- **Coed** 21,056 undergraduate students, 49% women, 51% men

UNDERGRAD STUDENTS
21,056 part-time. Students come from 55 states and territories; 33 other countries; 82% are from out of state; 17% Black or African American, non-Hispanic/Latino; 11% Hispanic/Latino; 3% Asian, non-Hispanic/Latino; 0.6% Native Hawaiian or other Pacific Islander, non-Hispanic/Latino; 0.6% American Indian or Alaska Native, non-Hispanic/Latino; 4% Two or more races, non-Hispanic/Latino; 1% Race/ethnicity unknown; 0.8% international; 10% transferred in.

FACULTY
Total: 1,301, 31% with terminal degrees.

Student/faculty ratio: 8:1.

ACADEMICS
Calendar: continuous. *Degrees:* certificates, associate, bachelor's, master's, and postbachelor's certificates (offers only external degree programs).

Special study options: adult/continuing education programs, distance learning, external degree program, independent study, part-time degree program, services for LD students, student-designed majors.

Unusual degree programs: 3-2 business administration; nursing; nuclear engineering technology, electrical engineering technology, health care management, business, information technology/cybersecurity.

Computers: Students can access the following: computer help desk, online (class) grades, online (class) registration, online (class) schedules. Campuswide network is available.
Library: Excelsior College Library.

STUDENT LIFE
Housing options: college housing not available.

Student services: veterans affairs office.

COSTS
Costs (2020–21) ***Tuition:*** $510 per credit part-time. Part-time tuition and fees vary according to reciprocity agreements. ***Required fees:*** $20 per credit part-time. ***Payment plans:*** installment, deferred payment. ***Waivers:*** employees or children of employees.

APPLYING
Options: electronic application.

Application fee: $50.

Required for some: college transcripts.

Application deadlines: rolling (freshmen), rolling (transfers).

Notification: continuous (freshmen), continuous (transfers).

CONTACT
Excelsior College, 7 Columbia Circle, Albany, NY 12203-5159. *Toll-free phone:* 888-647-2388.

Farmingdale State College

Farmingdale, New York

http://www.farmingdale.edu/

- **State-supported** comprehensive, founded 1912, part of State University of New York System
- **Suburban** 380-acre campus with easy access to New York City
- **Endowment** $5.9 million
- **Coed** 9,939 undergraduate students, 78% full-time, 42% women, 58% men
- **Moderately difficult** entrance level, 55% of applicants were admitted

UNDERGRAD STUDENTS
7,785 full-time, 2,154 part-time. 0.3% are from out of state; 9% Black or African American, non-Hispanic/Latino; 23% Hispanic/Latino; 9% Asian, non-Hispanic/Latino; 0.2% Native Hawaiian or other Pacific Islander, non-Hispanic/Latino; 0.2% American Indian or Alaska Native, non-Hispanic/Latino; 3% Two or more races, non-Hispanic/Latino; 0.4% Race/ethnicity unknown; 2% international; 11% transferred in; 6% live on campus.

Freshmen:
Admission: 6,952 applied, 3,816 admitted, 1,482 enrolled. ***Average high school GPA:*** 3.2. ***Test scores:*** SAT evidence-based reading and writing scores over 500: 72%; SAT math scores over 500: 78%; ACT scores over 18: 86%; SAT evidence-based reading and writing scores over 600: 15%; SAT math scores over 600: 19%; ACT scores over 24: 27%; SAT math scores over 700: 1%; ACT scores over 30: 1%.

Retention: 80% of full-time freshmen returned.

FACULTY
Total: 787, 34% full-time, 26% with terminal degrees.

Student/faculty ratio: 19:1.

ACADEMICS
Calendar: semesters. *Degrees:* certificates, associate, bachelor's, and master's.

Special study options: academic remediation for entering students, advanced placement credit, distance learning, double majors, independent study, internships, part-time degree program, services for LD students, study abroad, summer session for credit. ***ROTC:*** Army (c), Air Force (c).

Computers: 367 computers/terminals are available on campus for general student use. Students can access the following: computer help desk, free student e-mail accounts, online (class) grades, online (class) registration, online (class) schedules. Campuswide network is available. 100% of college-owned or -operated housing units are wired for high-speed Internet access. Wireless service is available via entire campus.
Library: Greenley Library. *Books:* 120,000 (physical), 165,000 (digital/electronic); *Databases:* 102. Weekly public service hours: 86.

STUDENT LIFE
Housing options: coed. Campus housing is university owned.

Activities and organizations: drama/theater group, student-run newspaper, radio station, Student Government Association, Ram Nation Radio, Greek Life, E-Sports, Backstage Theater Company, national fraternities, national sororities.

Athletics Member NCAA. All Division III. ***Intercollegiate sports:*** baseball M, basketball M/W, cheerleading W(c), cross-country running M/W, golf M, ice hockey M(c), lacrosse M/W, skiing (downhill) M(c)/W(c), soccer M/W, softball W, tennis M/W, track and field M/W, volleyball W, wrestling M(c). ***Intramural sports:*** basketball M/W, football M/W, sand volleyball M/W, soccer M/W, softball M/W, ultimate Frisbee M/W, volleyball M/W.

Campus security: 24-hour emergency response devices and patrols, controlled dormitory access.

Student services: health clinic, personal/psychological counseling, veterans affairs office.

COSTS & FINANCIAL AID
Costs (2019–20) ***Tuition:*** state resident $7070 full-time, $295 per credit part-time; nonresident $16,980 full-time, $708 per credit part-time. Full-time tuition and fees vary according to program. Part-time tuition and fees vary according to course load and program. ***Required fees:*** $1468 full-time, $60 per credit part-time, $10 per term part-time. ***Room and board:*** $13,318; room only: $8088. Room and board charges vary according to

board plan and housing facility. ***Payment plan:*** installment. ***Waivers:*** employees or children of employees.

Financial Aid Of all full-time matriculated undergraduates who enrolled in 2018, 5,707 applied for aid, 4,365 were judged to have need, 205 had their need fully met. In 2018, 71 non-need-based awards were made. ***Average percent of need met:*** 58. ***Average financial aid package:*** $8170. ***Average need-based loan:*** $3721. ***Average need-based gift aid:*** $7313. ***Average non-need-based aid:*** $1363. ***Average indebtedness upon graduation:*** $24,531.

APPLYING
Standardized Tests *Required:* SAT or ACT (for admission).

Options: electronic application, deferred entrance.

Application fee: $50.

Required: high school transcript, minimum 3.0 GPA. ***Required for some:*** interview.

Application deadlines: rolling (freshmen), rolling (out-of-state freshmen), rolling (transfers).

Notification: continuous (freshmen), continuous (out-of-state freshmen), continuous (transfers).

CONTACT
Farmingdale State College, 2350 Broadhollow Road, Farmingdale, NY 11735. *Phone:* 631-420-2200.

Fashion Institute of Technology

New York, New York

http://www.fitnyc.edu/

- **State and locally supported** comprehensive, founded 1944, part of State University of New York System
- **Urban** 5-acre campus with easy access to New York City
- **Coed, primarily women** 8,508 undergraduate students, 86% full-time, 82% women, 18% men
- **Moderately difficult** entrance level, 54% of applicants were admitted

UNDERGRAD STUDENTS
7,340 full-time, 1,168 part-time. 32% are from out of state; 9% Black or African American, non-Hispanic/Latino; 22% Hispanic/Latino; 11% Asian, non-Hispanic/Latino; 0.1% Native Hawaiian or other Pacific Islander, non-Hispanic/Latino; 0.1% American Indian or Alaska Native, non-Hispanic/Latino; 4% Two or more races, non-Hispanic/Latino; 0.4% Race/ethnicity unknown; 12% international; 9% transferred in; 20% live on campus.

Freshmen:
Admission: 4,444 applied, 2,395 admitted, 1,403 enrolled. ***Average high school GPA:*** ####.
Retention: 89% of full-time freshmen returned.

FACULTY
Total: 1,011, 23% full-time.
Student/faculty ratio: 16:1.

ACADEMICS
Calendar: semesters. *Degrees:* certificates, associate, bachelor's, and master's.

Special study options: academic remediation for entering students, advanced placement credit, distance learning, English as a second language, honors programs, independent study, internships, part-time degree program, services for LD students, study abroad, summer session for credit.

Computers: Campuswide network is available.
Library: Gladys Marcus Library.

STUDENT LIFE
Housing options: coed, women-only, special housing for students with disabilities. Campus housing is university owned. Freshman applicants given priority for college housing.

Activities and organizations: drama/theater group, student-run newspaper, radio and television station, choral group.

Athletics Member NJCAA. ***Intercollegiate sports:*** cross-country running M/W, soccer W, swimming and diving M/W, table tennis M/W, tennis M/W, track and field M/W, volleyball W.

Campus security: 24-hour emergency response devices and patrols, late-night transport/escort service, controlled dormitory access.

Student services: health clinic, personal/psychological counseling.

COSTS & FINANCIAL AID
Costs (2019–20) ***Tuition:*** state resident $5190 full-time, $216 per credit part-time; nonresident $15,570 full-time, $649 per credit part-time. Full-time tuition and fees vary according to degree level. Part-time tuition and fees vary according to degree level. ***Required fees:*** $920 full-time, $11 per credit part-time, $103 per year part-time. ***Room and board:*** $14,556; room only: $9762. Room and board charges vary according to board plan and housing facility. ***Waivers:*** employees or children of employees.

Financial Aid Of all full-time matriculated undergraduates who enrolled in 2018, 4,674 applied for aid, 3,786 were judged to have need, 1,941 had their need fully met. In 2018, 314 non-need-based awards were made. ***Average percent of need met:*** 66. ***Average financial aid package:*** $11,874. ***Average need-based loan:*** $3101. ***Average need-based gift aid:*** $6757. ***Average non-need-based aid:*** $858. ***Average indebtedness upon graduation:*** $25,832.

APPLYING
Options: electronic application.

Application fee: $50.

Required: essay or personal statement, high school transcript. ***Required for some:*** portfolio for art and design programs.

Application deadlines: 1/1 (freshmen), 1/1 (transfers).

Notification: 4/1 (freshmen), 4/1 (transfers).

CONTACT
Ms. Magda Francois, Director of Admissions and Strategic Recruitment, Fashion Institute of Technology, Seventh Avenue at 27th Street, New York, NY 10001-5992. *E-mail:* fitinfo@fitnyc.edu.

Five Towns College

Dix Hills, New York

http://www.ftc.edu/

CONTACT
Ms. Cynthia Catalano, Admissions, Five Towns College, 305 North Service Road, Dix Hills, NY 11746-6055. *Phone:* 631-424-7000 Ext. 2107. *Fax:* 631-656-2107. *E-mail:* cynthia.catalano@ftc.edu.

Fordham University

New York, New York

http://www.fordham.edu/

- **Independent Roman Catholic (Jesuit)** university, founded 1841
- **Urban** 93-acre campus with easy access to New York City
- **Endowment** $729.2 million
- **Coed** 9,767 undergraduate students, 94% full-time, 57% women, 43% men
- **Very difficult** entrance level, 46% of applicants were admitted

UNDERGRAD STUDENTS
9,229 full-time, 538 part-time. 58% are from out of state; 4% Black or African American, non-Hispanic/Latino; 16% Hispanic/Latino; 11% Asian, non-Hispanic/Latino; 0.1% Native Hawaiian or other Pacific Islander, non-Hispanic/Latino; 4% Two or more races, non-Hispanic/Latino; 1% Race/ethnicity unknown; 8% international; 3% transferred in; 49% live on campus.

Freshmen:
Admission: 47,930 applied, 21,988 admitted, 2,270 enrolled. ***Average high school GPA:*** 3.6. ***Test scores:*** SAT evidence-based reading and writing scores over 500: 100%; SAT math scores over 500: 99%; ACT scores over 18: 100%; SAT evidence-based reading and writing scores over 600: 86%; SAT math scores over 600: 84%; ACT scores over 24: 96%; SAT evidence-based reading and writing scores over 700: 33%; SAT math scores over 700: 42%; ACT scores over 30: 59%.
Retention: 91% of full-time freshmen returned.

FACULTY
Total: 1,889, 40% full-time, 66% with terminal degrees.
Student/faculty ratio: 13:1.

ACADEMICS

Calendar: semesters. *Degrees:* bachelor's, master's, doctoral, post-master's, and postbachelor's certificates (branch locations at Rose Hill and Lincoln Center).

Special study options: accelerated degree program, adult/continuing education programs, advanced placement credit, distance learning, double majors, English as a second language, honors programs, independent study, internships, off-campus study, part-time degree program, services for LD students, student-designed majors, study abroad, summer session for credit. ***ROTC:*** Army (b), Navy (c), Air Force (c).

Unusual degree programs: 3-2 engineering with Columbia University, Case Western Reserve University.

Computers: 2,600 computers/terminals and 2,400 ports are available on campus for general student use. Students can access the following: campus intranet, computer help desk, free student e-mail accounts, online (class) grades, online (class) registration, online (class) schedules, Video Streaming; IP TV Channels; Mobile Apps for University Services; Maker Spaces; University Supplied Software, WebEX Video Conferencing. Campuswide network is available. 100% of college-owned or -operated housing units are wired for high-speed Internet access. Wireless service is available via entire campus.

Library: Walsh Library plus 3 others. *Books:* 1.5 million (physical), 992,000 (digital/electronic); *Serial titles:* 16,353 (physical), 94,307 (digital/electronic); *Databases:* 444. Weekly public service hours: 105; study areas open 24 hours, 5–7 days a week.

STUDENT LIFE

Housing options: coed. Campus housing is university owned.

Activities and organizations: drama/theater group, student-run newspaper, radio and television station, choral group, marching band, United Student Government, Commuting Student Association, Residence Hall Association, Ambassador Program (Admission Department Student Tour Guides), Campus Activities Board.

Athletics Member NCAA. All Division I except football (Division I-AA). ***Intercollegiate sports:*** baseball M(s), basketball M(s)/W(s), cheerleading W, crew M(c)/W(s), cross-country running M(s)/W(s), golf M(s), ice hockey M(c), rowing W(s), sailing M(c)/W(c), soccer M(s)/W(s), softball W(s), squash M(s), swimming and diving M(s)/W(s), tennis M(s)/W(s), track and field M(s)/W(s), volleyball W(s), water polo M(s). ***Intramural sports:*** baseball M(c), basketball M/W, lacrosse M(c)/W(c), rowing M(c), rugby M(c)/W(c), soccer M(c)/W(c), softball W(c), squash W(c), tennis W(c), ultimate Frisbee M(c)/W(c), volleyball M/W.

Campus security: 24-hour emergency response devices and patrols, student patrols, late-night transport/escort service, controlled dormitory access.

Student services: health clinic, personal/psychological counseling, veterans affairs office.

COSTS & FINANCIAL AID

Costs (2020–21) ***Comprehensive fee:*** $74,854 includes full-time tuition ($54,730), mandatory fees ($1058), and room and board ($19,066). Part-time tuition: $1824 per credit hour. Part-time tuition and fees vary according to class time and course load. ***Room and board:*** Room and board charges vary according to board plan, housing facility, and location. ***Payment plan:*** installment. ***Waivers:*** employees or children of employees.

Financial Aid Of all full-time matriculated undergraduates who enrolled in 2019, 7,547 applied for aid, 5,389 were judged to have need, 1,475 had their need fully met. In 2019, 1997 non-need-based awards were made. ***Average percent of need met:*** 76. ***Average financial aid package:*** $38,157. ***Average need-based loan:*** $6016. ***Average need-based gift aid:*** $30,205. ***Average non-need-based aid:*** $20,142. ***Average indebtedness upon graduation:*** $37,283. ***Financial aid deadline:*** 2/1.

APPLYING

Standardized Tests *Required:* SAT or ACT (for admission).

Options: electronic application, early decision, early action, deferred entrance.

Application fee: $70.

Application deadlines: 11/1 (freshmen), 6/1 (transfers), 11/1 (early action).

Early decision deadline: 11/1.

Notification: 4/1 (freshmen), continuous (transfers), 12/20 (early decision), 12/20 (early action).

CONTACT

Dr. Patricia Peek, Dean of Undergraduate Admission, Fordham University, Office of Undergraduate Admission, Duane Library, 441 East Fordham Road, Bronx, NY 10458. *Phone:* 718-817-3706. *Toll-free phone:* 800-FORDHAM. *Fax:* 718-367-9404. *E-mail:* peek@fordham.edu.

Hamilton College

Clinton, New York

http://www.hamilton.edu/

- **Independent** 4-year, founded 1812
- **Small-town** 1300-acre campus
- **Endowment** $964.2 million
- **Coed**
- **Very difficult** entrance level

FACULTY

Student/faculty ratio: 9:1.

ACADEMICS

Calendar: semesters. *Degree:* bachelor's.

Library: Burke Library plus 1 other. *Books:* 491,977 (physical), 630,432 (digital/electronic); *Serial titles:* 5,000 (physical), 150,000 (digital/electronic); *Databases:* 245. Weekly public service hours: 114; study areas open 24 hours, 5–7 days a week; students can reserve study rooms.

STUDENT LIFE

Housing options: on-campus residence required through senior year; coed, cooperative, special housing for students with disabilities. Campus housing is university owned. Freshman campus housing is guaranteed.

Activities and organizations: drama/theater group, student-run newspaper, radio and television station, choral group, WHCL (Hamilton College Radio), Slow Food, Powder Club, Black & Latin Student Union (BLSU), Hamilton College Climbing Club, national fraternities.

Athletics Member NCAA. All Division III except golf (Division II).

Campus security: 24-hour emergency response devices and patrols, late-night transport/escort service, controlled dormitory access, student safety program.

Student services: health clinic, personal/psychological counseling.

COSTS & FINANCIAL AID

Costs (2019–20) ***Comprehensive fee:*** $70,890 includes full-time tuition ($55,970), mandatory fees ($560), and room and board ($14,360). Part-time tuition: $6996 per course. ***College room only:*** $7850.

Financial Aid Of all full-time matriculated undergraduates who enrolled in 2018, 1,032 applied for aid, 995 were judged to have need, 995 had their need fully met. 625 Federal Work-Study jobs (averaging $1831). 45 state and other part-time jobs (averaging $1944). ***Average percent of need met:*** 100. ***Average financial aid package:*** $49,164. ***Average need-based loan:*** $4346. ***Average need-based gift aid:*** $43,434. ***Average indebtedness upon graduation:*** $20,582. ***Financial aid deadline:*** 1/15.

APPLYING

Standardized Tests *Required:* (for admission).

Options: electronic application, early decision, deferred entrance.

Application fee: $60.

Required: essay or personal statement, high school transcript, 1 letter of recommendation. ***Recommended:*** interview.

CONTACT

Ms. T. Peaches Valdes, Dean of Admission, Hamilton College, 198 College Hill Road, Clinton, NY 13323. *Phone:* 800-843-2655. *Toll-free phone:* 800-843-2655. *Fax:* 315-859-4457. *E-mail:* admission@hamilton.edu.

Hartwick College

Oneonta, New York

http://www.hartwick.edu/

- **Independent** 4-year, founded 1797
- **Small-town** 425-acre campus with easy access to Capital District, NY
- **Endowment** $74.3 million
- **Coed**
- **Moderately difficult** entrance level

FACULTY

Student/faculty ratio: 11:1.

ACADEMICS

Calendar: 4-1-4. *Degree:* bachelor's.

Library: Stevens-German Library. *Books:* 209,006 (physical), 4,560 (digital/electronic); *Serial titles:* 1,392 (physical), 38,934 (digital/electronic); *Databases:* 59. Weekly public service hours: 96; students can reserve study rooms.

STUDENT LIFE

Housing options: on-campus residence required through senior year; coed. Campus housing is university owned. Freshman campus housing is guaranteed.

Activities and organizations: drama/theater group, student-run newspaper, radio station, choral group, Student Union, student radio station, Student Senate, Wine to Water, Cardboard Alley Players (theater), national fraternities, national sororities.

Athletics Member NCAA. All Division III.

Campus security: 24-hour emergency response devices and patrols, late-night transport/escort service, controlled dormitory access.

Student services: health clinic, personal/psychological counseling.

COSTS & FINANCIAL AID

Costs (2019–20) ***One-time required fee:*** $400. ***Comprehensive fee:*** $59,760 includes full-time tuition ($45,990), mandatory fees ($936), and room and board ($12,834). Part-time tuition: $1478 per credit hour. ***College room only:*** $6654. Room and board charges vary according to board plan and housing facility.

Financial Aid Of all full-time matriculated undergraduates who enrolled in 2018, 1,019 applied for aid, 952 were judged to have need, 143 had their need fully met. 746 Federal Work-Study jobs (averaging $1869). In 2018, 190 non-need-based awards were made. ***Average percent of need met:*** 80. ***Average financial aid package:*** $38,054. ***Average need-based loan:*** $4415. ***Average need-based gift aid:*** $33,033. ***Average non-need-based aid:*** $28,915. ***Average indebtedness upon graduation:*** $27,653.

APPLYING

Standardized Tests *Required for some:* SAT or ACT (for admission).

Options: electronic application, early admission, early decision, deferred entrance.

Required: high school transcript. ***Required for some:*** audition for music program, portfolio for art majors. ***Recommended:*** minimum 2.5 GPA.

CONTACT

Ms. Lisa Starkey-Wood, Director of Admissions, Hartwick College, PO Box 4022, Oneonta, NY 13820-4022. *Phone:* 607-431-4150. *Toll-free phone:* 888-HARTWICK. *Fax:* 607-431-4102. *E-mail:* admissions@ hartwick.edu.

Helene Fuld College of Nursing

New York, New York

http://www.helenefuld.edu/

CONTACT

Helene Fuld College of Nursing, 24 East 120th Street, New York, NY 10035. *Phone:* 212-616-7271.

Hilbert College

Hamburg, New York

http://www.hilbert.edu/

CONTACT

Mr. Brian Filjones, Director, Admissions, Hilbert College, 5200 South Park Avenue, Hamburg, NY 14075-1597. *Phone:* 716-649-7900 Ext. 210. *Toll-free phone:* 800-649-8003. *Fax:* 716-649-1152. *E-mail:* bfiljones@ hilbert.edu.

Hobart and William Smith Colleges

Geneva, New York

http://www.hws.edu/

- **Independent** comprehensive, founded 1822
- **Small-town** 200-acre campus with easy access to Rochester, Syracuse
- **Endowment** $226.1 million
- **Coed** 2,061 undergraduate students, 99% full-time, 52% women, 48% men
- **Very difficult** entrance level, 66% of applicants were admitted

UNDERGRAD STUDENTS

2,045 full-time, 16 part-time. Students come from 41 states and territories; 28 other countries; 59% are from out of state; 6% Black or African American, non-Hispanic/Latino; 6% Hispanic/Latino; 3% Asian, non-Hispanic/Latino; 0.3% American Indian or Alaska Native, non-Hispanic/Latino; 2% Two or more races, non-Hispanic/Latino; 5% Race/ethnicity unknown; 5% international; 0.4% transferred in; 90% live on campus.

Freshmen:

Admission: 3,439 applied, 2,267 admitted, 458 enrolled. ***Average high school GPA:*** 3.5. ***Test scores:*** SAT evidence-based reading and writing scores over 500: 98%; SAT math scores over 500: 97%; ACT scores over 18: 100%; SAT evidence-based reading and writing scores over 600: 73%; SAT math scores over 600: 73%; ACT scores over 24: 87%; SAT evidence-based reading and writing scores over 700: 15%; SAT math scores over 700: 18%; ACT scores over 30: 39%.

Retention: 88% of full-time freshmen returned.

FACULTY

Total: 220, 92% full-time, 95% with terminal degrees.

Student/faculty ratio: 10:1.

ACADEMICS

Calendar: semesters. *Degrees:* bachelor's and master's.

Special study options: accelerated degree program, adult/continuing education programs, advanced placement credit, double majors, English as a second language, honors programs, independent study, internships, off-campus study, services for LD students, student-designed majors, study abroad. ***ROTC:*** Army (c), Air Force (c).

Unusual degree programs: 3-2 business administration with Clarkson University, Rochester Institute of Technology; engineering with Columbia University, Rensselaer Polytechnic Institute, Dartmouth College; architecture with Washington University in St. Louis.

Computers: 247 computers/terminals and 10,215 ports are available on campus for general student use. Students can access the following: campus intranet, computer help desk, free student e-mail accounts, online (class) grades, online (class) registration, online (class) schedules. Campuswide network is available. 100% of college-owned or -operated housing units are wired for high-speed Internet access. Wireless service is available via entire campus.

Library: Warren Hunting Smith Library plus 1 other. *Books:* 394,418 (physical), 323,922 (digital/electronic); *Serial titles:* 1,515 (physical), 85,666 (digital/electronic); *Databases:* 130. Weekly public service hours: 114; study areas open 24 hours, 5–7 days a week; students can reserve study rooms.

STUDENT LIFE

Housing options: on-campus residence required through junior year; coed, men-only, women-only, cooperative. Campus housing is university owned. Freshman campus housing is guaranteed.

Activities and organizations: drama/theater group, student-run newspaper, radio station, choral group, Student Life and Leadership, student government, campus publications, Service Network, sports clubs, national fraternities, national sororities.

Athletics Member NCAA. All Division III except golf (Division II), lacrosse (Division I). ***Intercollegiate sports:*** basketball M/W, crew M/W, cross-country running M/W, equestrian sports M(c)/W(c), field hockey W, football M, golf M/W, ice hockey M/W, lacrosse M/W, rock climbing M(c)/W(c), rugby M(c)/W(c), sailing M/W, skiing (downhill) W(c), soccer M/W, squash M/W, swimming and diving W, tennis M/W, ultimate Frisbee M(c)/W(c). ***Intramural sports:*** badminton M/W, baseball M, basketball M/W, fencing M, field hockey W, football M, golf M/W, ice hockey M/W, lacrosse M/W, racquetball M/W, skiing (cross-country) M/W, skiing (downhill) M/W, soccer M/W, softball M/W, squash M/W, swimming and diving M/W, table tennis M/W, tennis M/W, track and field M/W, ultimate Frisbee M/W, volleyball M/W, water polo M/W, weight lifting M/W.

Campus security: 24-hour emergency response devices and patrols, late-night transport/escort service, controlled dormitory access.

Student services: health clinic, personal/psychological counseling, women's center.

COSTS & FINANCIAL AID

Costs (2020–21) ***Comprehensive fee:*** $73,740 includes full-time tuition ($57,400), mandatory fees ($1250), and room and board ($15,090). ***Room and board:*** Room and board charges vary according to board plan. ***Payment plans:*** tuition prepayment, installment. ***Waivers:*** employees or children of employees.

Financial Aid Of all full-time matriculated undergraduates who enrolled in 2019, 1,520 applied for aid, 1,287 were judged to have need, 309 had their need fully met. 816 Federal Work-Study jobs (averaging $2055). 542 state and other part-time jobs (averaging $1944). In 2019, 609 non-need-based awards were made. ***Average percent of need met:*** 81. ***Average financial aid package:*** $43,044. ***Average need-based loan:*** $3786. ***Average need-based gift aid:*** $38,920. ***Average non-need-based aid:*** $21,558. ***Average indebtedness upon graduation:*** $34,456. ***Financial aid deadline:*** 2/1.

APPLYING

Standardized Tests *Required for some:* SAT or ACT (for admission).

Options: electronic application, early admission, early decision, deferred entrance.

Required: essay or personal statement, high school transcript, 1 letter of recommendation. ***Recommended:*** interview.

Application deadlines: 2/1 (freshmen), 7/1 (transfers).

Early decision deadline: 11/15 (for plan 1), 1/1 (for plan 2).

Notification: 4/1 (freshmen), continuous (transfers), 12/15 (early decision plan 1), 2/1 (early decision plan 2).

CONTACT

Hobart and William Smith Colleges, 300 Pulteney Street, Geneva, NY 14456. *Phone:* 315-781-3622. *Toll-free phone:* 800-852-2256.

Hofstra University

Hempstead, New York

http://www.hofstra.edu/

- **Independent** university, founded 1935
- **Suburban** 244-acre campus with easy access to New York City
- **Endowment** $624.2 million
- **Coed** 6,498 undergraduate students, 95% full-time, 55% women, 45% men
- **Moderately difficult** entrance level, 68% of applicants were admitted

UNDERGRAD STUDENTS

6,156 full-time, 342 part-time. Students come from 48 states and territories; 77 other countries; 37% are from out of state; 9% Black or African American, non-Hispanic/Latino; 13% Hispanic/Latino; 12% Asian, non-Hispanic/Latino; 0.1% Native Hawaiian or other Pacific Islander, non-Hispanic/Latino; 0.3% American Indian or Alaska Native, non-Hispanic/Latino; 3% Two or more races, non-Hispanic/Latino; 2% Race/ethnicity unknown; 5% international; 4% transferred in; 43% live on campus.

Freshmen:

Admission: 24,425 applied, 16,728 admitted, 1,523 enrolled. ***Average high school GPA:*** 3.7. ***Test scores:*** SAT evidence-based reading and writing scores over 500: 99%; SAT math scores over 500: 99%; ACT scores over 18: 100%; SAT evidence-based reading and writing scores over 600: 68%; SAT math scores over 600: 64%; ACT scores over 24: 85%; SAT evidence-based reading and writing scores over 700: 12%; SAT math scores over 700: 17%; ACT scores over 30: 30%.

Retention: 83% of full-time freshmen returned.

FACULTY

Total: 1,245, 39% full-time, 64% with terminal degrees.

Student/faculty ratio: 13:1.

ACADEMICS

Calendar: semesters. *Degrees:* certificates, bachelor's, master's, doctoral, post-master's, and postbachelor's certificates.

Special study options: accelerated degree program, advanced placement credit, cooperative education, distance learning, double majors, English as a second language, external degree program, freshman honors college, honors programs, independent study, internships, off-campus study, part-time degree program, services for LD students, student-designed majors, study abroad, summer session for credit. ***ROTC:*** Army (b).

Unusual degree programs: 3-2 business administration; MS in physician assistant studies; BA/MS and BS/MS in computer science; BA/JD LEAP program.

Computers: 1,536 computers/terminals and 1,900 ports are available on campus for general student use. Students can access the following: campus intranet, computer help desk, free student e-mail accounts, online (class) grades, online (class) registration, online (class) schedules, Emergency alert system, online course management system, online card services balance update, online e-portfolio, software tutoring, support for specific tech-enhanced assignments, repair and rebuilding-after-virus services, and printing services. Campuswide network is available. 100% of college-owned or -operated housing units are wired for high-speed Internet access. Wireless service is available via entire campus.

Library: Axinn Library plus 2 others. *Books:* 852,704 (physical), 232,970 (digital/electronic); *Serial titles:* 13,004 (physical), 207,565 (digital/electronic); *Databases:* 441. Weekly public service hours: 110; study areas open 24 hours, 5–7 days a week; students can reserve study rooms.

STUDENT LIFE

Housing options: coed, special housing for students with disabilities. Campus housing is university owned. Freshman applicants given priority for college housing.

Activities and organizations: drama/theater group, student-run newspaper, radio and television station, choral group, Masquerade, DanceWorks, Student Government Association, Hillel, Hofstra Chronicle, national fraternities, national sororities.

Athletics Member NCAA. All Division I. ***Intercollegiate sports:*** baseball M(s), basketball M(s)/W(s), cross-country running M(s)/W(s), field hockey W(s), golf M(s)/W(s), lacrosse M(s)/W(s), soccer M(s)/W(s), softball W(s), tennis M(s)/W(s), track and field M(s)/W(s), volleyball W(s), wrestling M(s). ***Intramural sports:*** badminton M(c)/W(c), baseball M(c), basketball M/W, bowling M(c)/W(c), cheerleading M(c)/W(c), cross-country running M(c)/W(c), equestrian sports M(c)/W(c), ice hockey M(c)/W(c), lacrosse M(c)/W(c), rock climbing M(c)/W(c), rugby M(c)/W(c), skiing (downhill) M(c)/W(c), soccer M(c)/W(c), softball M/W, swimming and diving M(c)/W(c), table tennis M(c)/W(c), tennis M(c)/W(c), track and field M(c)/W(c), ultimate Frisbee M(c)/W(c), volleyball M(c)/W(c), weight lifting M(c)/W(c).

Campus security: 24-hour emergency response devices and patrols, student patrols, late-night transport/escort service, controlled dormitory access, Residence hall security cameras, required card access, CCTV, monitored entrance 24/7, bike patrol, motorist assistance program.

Student services: health clinic, personal/psychological counseling.

COSTS & FINANCIAL AID

Costs (2019–20) ***Comprehensive fee:*** $63,938 includes full-time tuition ($46,450), mandatory fees ($1060), and room and board ($16,428). Full-time tuition and fees vary according to course load. Part-time tuition: $1560 per credit hour. Part-time tuition and fees vary according to course load. No tuition increase for student's term of enrollment. ***Required fees:***

$155 per term part-time. ***College room only:*** $10,960. Room and board charges vary according to board plan and housing facility. ***Payment plan:*** installment. ***Waivers:*** employees or children of employees.

Financial Aid Of all full-time matriculated undergraduates who enrolled in 2018, 4,813 applied for aid, 4,050 were judged to have need, 1,026 had their need fully met. 1,514 Federal Work-Study jobs (averaging $3000). 1,489 state and other part-time jobs (averaging $3200). In 2018, 1589 non-need-based awards were made. ***Average percent of need met:*** 68. ***Average financial aid package:*** $32,000. ***Average need-based loan:*** $4000. ***Average need-based gift aid:*** $22,000. ***Average non-need-based aid:*** $20,000.

APPLYING

Standardized Tests *Required for some:* TOEFL for international students.

Options: electronic application, early admission, early action, deferred entrance.

Application fee: $70.

Required: essay or personal statement, high school transcript, 2 letters of recommendation, proof of degree, TOEFL required for international students. ***Required for some:*** interview.

Application deadlines: rolling (freshmen), rolling (transfers), 12/15 (early action).

Notification: continuous (transfers), 1/15 (early action).

CONTACT

Sunil A. Samuel, Assistant Vice President of Admissions, Hofstra University, 100 Hofstra University, Hempstead, NY 11549. *Phone:* 516-463-6700. *Toll-free phone:* 800-HOFSTRA. *Fax:* 516-463-5100. *E-mail:* admission@hofstra.edu.

See below for display ad and page 1066 for the College Close-Up.

Holy Trinity Orthodox Seminary

Jordanville, New York

http://www.hts.edu/

CONTACT

Rev. Fr. Ephraim Willmarth, Assistant Dean and Director of Admissions, Holy Trinity Orthodox Seminary, PO Box 36, Jordanville, NY 13361. *Phone:* 315-858-0945. *Fax:* 315-858-0945. *E-mail:* ejwillmarth@hts.edu.

Houghton College

Houghton, New York

http://www.houghton.edu/

CONTACT

Mr. Ryan Spear, Associate Director of Admission Operations, Houghton College, PO Box 128, Houghton, NY 14744. *Phone:* 585-567-9353. *Toll-free phone:* 800-777-2556. *Fax:* 585-567-9522. *E-mail:* admission@houghton.edu.

Hunter College of the City University of New York

New York, New York

http://www.hunter.cuny.edu/

- **State and locally supported** comprehensive, founded 1870, part of City University of New York System
- **Urban** campus
- **Endowment** $120.0 million
- **Coed**
- **Moderately difficult** entrance level

FACULTY

Student/faculty ratio: 14:1.

ACADEMICS

Calendar: semesters. *Degrees:* bachelor's, master's, doctoral, post-master's, and postbachelor's certificates.

Library: Hunter College Library plus 1 other. *Books:* 438,832 (physical), 602,800 (digital/electronic); *Serial titles:* 3,893 (physical), 105,674 (digital/electronic); *Databases:* 280.

STUDENT LIFE

Housing options: coed.

Activities and organizations: drama/theater group, student-run newspaper, radio and television station, choral group.

Athletics Member NCAA. All Division III.

Campus security: 24-hour emergency response devices and patrols.

Student services: personal/psychological counseling, women's center.

FINANCIAL AID

Financial Aid Of all full-time matriculated undergraduates who enrolled in 2018, 10,929 applied for aid, 9,892 were judged to have need, 5,751 had their need fully met. 254 Federal Work-Study jobs (averaging $2303). In 2018, 417 non-need-based awards were made. ***Average percent of need met:*** 82. ***Average financial aid package:*** $8126. ***Average need-based loan:*** $4123. ***Average need-based gift aid:*** $7950. ***Average non-need-based aid:*** $3450. ***Average indebtedness upon graduation:*** $15,096.

APPLYING

Standardized Tests *Required:* SAT or ACT (for admission).

Options: early admission.

Application fee: $65.

Required: high school transcript.

CONTACT

Ms. Lori Janowski, Associate Director of Undergraduate Admissions, Hunter College of the City University of New York, 695 Park Avenue, New York, NY 10065-5085. *Phone:* 212-772-4490. *Fax:* 212-650-3472. *E-mail:* lori.janowski@hunter.cuny.edu.

Iona College

New Rochelle, New York

http://www.iona.edu/

- **Independent** comprehensive, founded 1940, affiliated with Roman Catholic Church
- **Suburban** 35-acre campus with easy access to New York City
- **Endowment** $16.0 million
- **Coed** 2,981 undergraduate students, 91% full-time, 49% women, 51% men
- **Moderately difficult** entrance level, 84% of applicants were admitted

UNDERGRAD STUDENTS

2,709 full-time, 272 part-time. Students come from 33 states and territories; 37 other countries; 23% are from out of state; 12% Black or African American, non-Hispanic/Latino; 25% Hispanic/Latino; 3% Asian, non-Hispanic/Latino; 0.2% Native Hawaiian or other Pacific Islander, non-Hispanic/Latino; 0.5% American Indian or Alaska Native, non-Hispanic/Latino; 2% Two or more races, non-Hispanic/Latino; 4% Race/ethnicity unknown; 3% international; 3% transferred in; 45% live on campus.

Freshmen:

Admission: 9,965 applied, 8,382 admitted, 641 enrolled. ***Average high school GPA:*** 3.0. ***Test scores:*** SAT evidence-based reading and writing scores over 500: 75%; SAT math scores over 500: 71%; ACT scores over 18: 92%; SAT evidence-based reading and writing scores over 600: 25%; SAT math scores over 600: 20%; ACT scores over 24: 43%; SAT evidence-based reading and writing scores over 700: 2%; SAT math scores over 700: 3%; ACT scores over 30: 9%.

Retention: 72% of full-time freshmen returned.

FACULTY

Total: 319, 53% full-time, 50% with terminal degrees.

Student/faculty ratio: 14:1.

ACADEMICS

Calendar: semesters. *Degrees:* certificates, bachelor's, master's, post-master's, and postbachelor's certificates.

Special study options: accelerated degree program, adult/continuing education programs, advanced placement credit, distance learning, double majors, English as a second language, honors programs, independent study, internships, part-time degree program, services for LD students, study abroad, summer session for credit. ***ROTC:*** Army (c), Air Force (c).

Unusual degree programs: 3-2 business administration.

Computers: 10,000 ports are available on campus for general student use. Students can access the following: campus intranet, computer help desk, free student e-mail accounts, online (class) grades, online (class) registration, online (class) schedules, bill payment. Campuswide network is available. 100% of college-owned or -operated housing units are wired for high-speed Internet access. Wireless service is available via entire campus.

Library: Ryan Library plus 1 other. *Books:* 265,074 (physical), 329,090 (digital/electronic); *Serial titles:* 112 (physical), 347 (digital/electronic); *Databases:* 84. Weekly public service hours: 101; students can reserve study rooms.

STUDENT LIFE

Housing options: coed, special housing for students with disabilities. Campus housing is university owned. Freshman campus housing is guaranteed.

Activities and organizations: drama/theater group, student-run newspaper, radio and television station, choral group, Student Government Association, Gaels Activities Board, Council for Greek Governance, Student Leader Alliance for Multiculturalism, The Ionian - Student Newspaper, national fraternities, national sororities.

Athletics Member NCAA. All Division I. ***Intercollegiate sports:*** baseball M(s), basketball M(s)/W(s), cross-country running M(s)/W(s), golf M(s), lacrosse W(s), rowing M/W, soccer M(s)/W(s), softball W(s), swimming and diving M(s)/W(s), track and field M(s)/W(s), volleyball W(s), water polo M/W(s). ***Intramural sports:*** basketball M/W, cheerleading M(c)/W(c), football M/W, rugby M(c), soccer M/W, table tennis M/W, volleyball M/W.

Campus security: 24-hour emergency response devices and patrols, controlled dormitory access.

Student services: health clinic, personal/psychological counseling.

COSTS & FINANCIAL AID

Costs (2020–21) ***Comprehensive fee:*** $57,788 includes full-time tuition ($39,380), mandatory fees ($2200), and room and board ($16,208). ***Payment plan:*** installment. ***Waivers:*** employees or children of employees.

Financial Aid Of all full-time matriculated undergraduates who enrolled in 2019, 2,673 applied for aid, 2,331 were judged to have need, 454 had their need fully met. In 2019, 334 non-need-based awards were made. ***Average percent of need met:*** 16. ***Average financial aid package:*** $27,937. ***Average need-based loan:*** $3558. ***Average need-based gift aid:*** $6322. ***Average non-need-based aid:*** $22,391. ***Average indebtedness upon graduation:*** $32,948. ***Financial aid deadline:*** 4/15.

APPLYING

Options: electronic application, early action, deferred entrance.

Required: high school transcript. ***Required for some:*** interview. ***Recommended:*** essay or personal statement, 2 letters of recommendation.

Application deadlines: 2/15 (freshmen), 8/15 (transfers).

Notification: continuous (freshmen), continuous (transfers).

CONTACT

Mr. Ryan Depuy, Director of Undergraduate Admissions, Iona College, Admissions, 715 North Avenue, New Rochelle, NY 10801. *Phone:* 914-633-2502. *Toll-free phone:* 800-231-IONA. *Fax:* 914-633-2778. *E-mail:* admissions@iona.edu.

Ithaca College

Ithaca, New York

http://www.ithaca.edu/

- **Independent** comprehensive, founded 1892
- **Small-town** 669-acre campus with easy access to Syracuse
- **Endowment** $334.0 million
- **Coed** 5,852 undergraduate students, 98% full-time, 57% women, 43% men
- **Moderately difficult** entrance level, 73% of applicants were admitted

UNDERGRAD STUDENTS

5,739 full-time, 113 part-time. Students come from 52 states and territories; 43 other countries; 55% are from out of state; 6% Black or African American, non-Hispanic/Latino; 9% Hispanic/Latino; 4% Asian, non-Hispanic/Latino; 0.1% Native Hawaiian or other Pacific Islander, non-Hispanic/Latino; 0.1% American Indian or Alaska Native, non-Hispanic/Latino; 3% Two or more races, non-Hispanic/Latino; 3%

Race/ethnicity unknown; 2% international; 2% transferred in; 73% live on campus.

Freshmen:

Admission: 14,192 applied, 10,326 admitted, 1,509 enrolled. ***Test scores:*** SAT evidence-based reading and writing scores over 500: 97%; SAT math scores over 500: 96%; ACT scores over 18: 99%; SAT evidence-based reading and writing scores over 600: 72%; SAT math scores over 600: 63%; ACT scores over 24: 88%; SAT evidence-based reading and writing scores over 700: 16%; SAT math scores over 700: 15%; ACT scores over 30: 35%.

Retention: 87% of full-time freshmen returned.

FACULTY

Total: 753, 69% full-time, 64% with terminal degrees.

Student/faculty ratio: 10:1.

ACADEMICS

Calendar: semesters. *Degrees:* certificates, bachelor's, master's, and doctoral.

Special study options: adult/continuing education programs, advanced placement credit, distance learning, double majors, honors programs, independent study, internships, off-campus study, services for LD students, student-designed majors, study abroad, summer session for credit. ***ROTC:*** Army (c), Air Force (c).

Unusual degree programs: 3-2 engineering with Cornell University, Rensselaer Polytechnic Institute, Clarkson University, Watson School of Engineering at Binghamton University.

Computers: 700 computers/terminals and 20 ports are available on campus for general student use. Students can access the following: campus intranet, computer help desk, free student e-mail accounts, online (class) grades, online (class) registration, online (class) schedules. Campuswide network is available. 100% of college-owned or -operated housing units are wired for high-speed Internet access. Wireless service is available via entire campus.

Library: Ithaca College Library. *Books:* 303,169 (physical), 194,765 (digital/electronic); *Serial titles:* 577 (physical), 73,113 (digital/electronic); *Databases:* 151. Weekly public service hours: 148; study areas open 24 hours, 5–7 days a week.

STUDENT LIFE

Housing options: on-campus residence required through junior year; coed, special housing for students with disabilities. Campus housing is university owned. Freshman campus housing is guaranteed.

Activities and organizations: drama/theater group, student-run newspaper, radio and television station, choral group, Student Governance Council, Colleges Against Cancer, Brothers 4 Brothers, International Club, Asian American Alliance, national fraternities.

Athletics Member NCAA. All Division III. ***Intercollegiate sports:*** baseball M, basketball M/W, crew M/W, cross-country running M/W, field hockey W, football M, golf W, gymnastics W, lacrosse M/W, soccer M/W, softball W, swimming and diving M/W, tennis M/W, track and field M/W, volleyball W, wrestling M. ***Intramural sports:*** baseball M, basketball M/W, equestrian sports M(c)/W(c), fencing M(c), field hockey W(c), football M, golf M/W, ice hockey M(c), lacrosse M(c)/W(c), rugby M(c)/W(c), skiing (downhill) M(c)/W(c), soccer M/W, softball M/W, squash M(c)/W(c), table tennis M(c)/W(c), tennis M/W, ultimate Frisbee M(c)/W(c), volleyball M/W.

Campus security: 24-hour emergency response devices and patrols, student patrols, late-night transport/escort service, controlled dormitory access.

Student services: health clinic, personal/psychological counseling, veterans affairs office.

COSTS & FINANCIAL AID

Costs (2020–21) ***Comprehensive fee:*** $62,454 includes full-time tuition ($46,610) and room and board ($15,844). Part-time tuition: $1554 per credit hour. ***College room only:*** $8976. Room and board charges vary according to board plan and housing facility. ***Payment plan:*** installment. ***Waivers:*** children of alumni and employees or children of employees.

Financial Aid Of all full-time matriculated undergraduates who enrolled in 2019, 4,626 applied for aid, 3,931 were judged to have need, 1,811 had their need fully met. In 2019, 1503 non-need-based awards were made. ***Average percent of need met:*** 88. ***Average financial aid package:*** $40,304. ***Average need-based loan:*** $5866. ***Average need-based gift aid:*** $29,930. ***Average non-need-based aid:*** $17,179. ***Average indebtedness upon graduation:*** $42,000.

APPLYING

Options: electronic application, early decision, early action, deferred entrance.

Application fee: $60.

Required: essay or personal statement, high school transcript, 1 letter of recommendation. ***Required for some:*** audition for some programs. ***Recommended:*** minimum 3.0 GPA.

Application deadlines: 2/1 (freshmen), 3/1 (transfers), 12/1 (early action).

Early decision deadline: 11/1.

Notification: 4/15 (freshmen), continuous (transfers), 12/15 (early decision), 2/1 (early action).

CONTACT

Ithaca College, 953 Danby Road, Ithaca, NY 14850. *Phone:* 800-429-4274. *Toll-free phone:* 800-429-4274.

Jamestown Business College

Jamestown, New York

http://www.jbc.edu/

CONTACT

Mrs. Brenda Salemme, Director of Admissions, Jamestown Business College, 7 Fairmount Avenue, Box 429, Jamestown, NY 14702-0429. *Phone:* 716-664-5100. *Fax:* 716-664-3144. *E-mail:* brendasalemme@jbc.edu.

The Jewish Theological Seminary

New York, New York

http://www.jtsa.edu/

CONTACT

Mr. Sergio Lineberge, List College Admissions Coordinator, The Jewish Theological Seminary, 3080 Broadway, New York, NY 10027. *Phone:* 212-678-8820. *E-mail:* lcadmissions@jtsa.edu.

John Jay College of Criminal Justice of the City University of New York

New York, New York

http://www.jjay.cuny.edu/

- **State and locally supported** comprehensive, founded 1964, part of City University of New York
- **Urban** campus with easy access to New York City
- **Coed** 13,746 undergraduate students, 81% full-time, 59% women, 41% men
- **Moderately difficult** entrance level, 41% of applicants were admitted

UNDERGRAD STUDENTS

11,200 full-time, 2,546 part-time. Students come from 21 states and territories; 36 other countries; 3% are from out of state; 20% Black or African American, non-Hispanic/Latino; 44% Hispanic/Latino; 13% Asian, non-Hispanic/Latino; 0.4% American Indian or Alaska Native, non-Hispanic/Latino; 3% international; 15% transferred in; 1% live on campus.

Freshmen:

Admission: 20,564 applied, 8,331 admitted, 2,056 enrolled. ***Average high school GPA:*** 3.0. ***Test scores:*** SAT evidence-based reading and writing scores over 500: 66%; SAT math scores over 500: 65%; SAT evidence-based reading and writing scores over 600: 14%; SAT math scores over 600: 12%; SAT evidence-based reading and writing scores over 700: 1%; SAT math scores over 700: 1%.

Retention: 80% of full-time freshmen returned.

ACADEMICS

Calendar: semesters. *Degrees:* certificates, bachelor's, and master's.

Special study options: academic remediation for entering students, advanced placement credit, cooperative education, distance learning, double majors, English as a second language, honors programs, independent study, internships, off-campus study, part-time degree program, services for LD students, study abroad, summer session for credit.

Unusual degree programs: 3-2 social work; public management, law enforcement.

Computers: 2,500 computers/terminals are available on campus for general student use. Students can access the following: campus intranet, computer help desk, free student e-mail accounts, online (class) grades, online (class) registration, online (class) schedules. Campuswide network is available. 100% of college-owned or -operated housing units are wired for high-speed Internet access. Wireless service is available via entire campus.

Library: Lloyd George Sealy Library. *Books:* 216,416 (physical), 992,129 (digital/electronic); *Serial titles:* 7,579 (physical), 153,353 (digital/electronic); *Databases:* 26,247. Weekly public service hours: 77; study areas open 24 hours, 5–7 days a week; students can reserve study rooms.

STUDENT LIFE

Housing options: coed. Campus housing is university owned.

Activities and organizations: drama/theater group, student-run newspaper, radio station, choral group, Auxiliary University Program, Student Athlete Advisory Community Club, Environmental Club, Law Society, Artists United.

Athletics Member NCAA. All Division III. ***Intercollegiate sports:*** baseball M, basketball M/W, cheerleading M/W, cross-country running M/W, riflery M/W, soccer M/W, softball W, swimming and diving W, tennis M/W, volleyball M/W. ***Intramural sports:*** basketball M/W, cheerleading M/W, riflery M/W, soccer M/W, swimming and diving M/W.

Campus security: 24-hour emergency response devices and patrols, controlled dormitory access.

Student services: health clinic, personal/psychological counseling, women's center, legal services.

FINANCIAL AID

Financial Aid Of all full-time matriculated undergraduates who enrolled in 2018, 10,713 applied for aid, 10,316 were judged to have need. ***Average percent of need met:*** 85. ***Average financial aid package:*** $8776. ***Average need-based loan:*** $3979. ***Average need-based gift aid:*** $2745.

APPLYING

Standardized Tests *Required:* SAT or ACT (for admission).

Options: deferred entrance.

Application fee: $65.

Required: high school transcript, minimum 2.0 GPA, minimum SAT score of 1100.

Application deadlines: 5/31 (freshmen), 5/31 (transfers).

Notification: continuous until 2/15 (freshmen), continuous until 2/15 (transfers).

CONTACT

Mr. Vincent Papandrea, Director, John Jay College of Criminal Justice of the City University of New York, 524 West 59th Street, L.64.14NB, New York, NY 10019. *Phone:* 212-237-8864. *Toll-free phone:* 877-JOHNJAY. *E-mail:* vpapandrea@jjay.cuny.edu.

The Juilliard School

New York, New York

http://www.juilliard.edu/

- **Independent** comprehensive, founded 1905
- **Urban** campus with easy access to New York City
- **Coed**
- **Most difficult** entrance level

FACULTY

Student/faculty ratio: 4:1.

ACADEMICS

Calendar: semesters. *Degrees:* diplomas, bachelor's, master's, doctoral, post-master's, and postbachelor's certificates.

Library: Lila Acheson Wallace Library.

STUDENT LIFE

Housing options: on-campus residence required for freshman year; coed. Campus housing is university owned. Freshman campus housing is guaranteed.

Activities and organizations: drama/theater group, student-run newspaper.

Campus security: 24-hour emergency response devices and patrols, controlled dormitory access, electronically operated main building entrances.

Student services: health clinic, personal/psychological counseling.

COSTS & FINANCIAL AID

Costs (2019–20) ***Comprehensive fee:*** $65,440 includes full-time tuition ($47,370), mandatory fees ($100), and room and board ($17,970).

Financial Aid Of all full-time matriculated undergraduates who enrolled in 2019, 424 applied for aid, 353 were judged to have need, 70 had their need fully met. In 2019, 62 non-need-based awards were made. ***Average percent of need met:*** 71. ***Average financial aid package:*** $38,146. ***Average need-based loan:*** $4690. ***Average need-based gift aid:*** $33,483. ***Average non-need-based aid:*** $23,411. ***Average indebtedness upon graduation:*** $26,326. ***Financial aid deadline:*** 3/1.

APPLYING

Standardized Tests *Required for some:* SAT or ACT (for admission).

Options: electronic application.

Application fee: $110.

Required: essay or personal statement, high school transcript, audition.

CONTACT

Ms. Kathy Tesar, Associate Dean for Enrollment Management, The Juilliard School, 60 Lincoln Center Plaza, New York, NY 10023. *Phone:* 212-799-5000 Ext. 223. *Fax:* 212-724-0263. *E-mail:* admissions@juilliard.edu.

Kehilath Yakov Rabbinical Seminary

Ossining, New York

http://kehilathyakov.com/

CONTACT

Admissions Officer, Kehilath Yakov Rabbinical Seminary, 340 Illington Road, Ossining, NY 10562. *Phone:* 718-963-1212.

Keuka College

Keuka Park, New York

http://www.keuka.edu/

- **Independent** comprehensive, founded 1890, affiliated with American Baptist Churches in the U.S.A.
- **Rural** 173-acre campus with easy access to Rochester
- **Endowment** $14.6 million
- **Coed** 1,529 undergraduate students, 84% full-time, 73% women, 27% men
- **Moderately difficult** entrance level, 86% of applicants were admitted

UNDERGRAD STUDENTS

1,285 full-time, 244 part-time. Students come from 26 states and territories; 7 other countries; 9% are from out of state; 7% Black or African American, non-Hispanic/Latino; 6% Hispanic/Latino; 1% Asian, non-Hispanic/Latino; 0.2% Native Hawaiian or other Pacific Islander, non-Hispanic/Latino; 0.6% American Indian or Alaska Native, non-Hispanic/Latino; 3% Two or more races, non-Hispanic/Latino; 5% Race/ethnicity unknown; 1% international; 4% transferred in; 59% live on campus.

Freshmen:

Admission: 2,212 applied, 1,899 admitted, 260 enrolled.

Retention: 79% of full-time freshmen returned.

FACULTY

Total: 200, 43% full-time, 59% with terminal degrees.

Student/faculty ratio: 10:1.

ACADEMICS

Calendar: 4-1-4. *Degrees:* bachelor's, master's, and post-master's certificates.

Special study options: academic remediation for entering students, accelerated degree program, adult/continuing education programs, advanced placement credit, cooperative education, distance learning, double majors, English as a second language, independent study, internships, off-campus study, part-time degree program, services for LD students, student-designed majors, study abroad, summer session for credit.

Computers: 185 computers/terminals and 3,357 ports are available on campus for general student use. Students can access the following: campus intranet, computer help desk, free student e-mail accounts, online (class) grades, online (class) registration, online (class) schedules, phone app for cancellations. Campuswide network is available. 100% of college-owned or -operated housing units are wired for high-speed Internet access. Wireless service is available via entire campus.

Library: Lightner Library plus 1 other. *Books:* 78,791 (physical), 13,006 (digital/electronic); *Serial titles:* 391 (physical), 80 (digital/electronic); *Databases:* 82. Weekly public service hours: 96.

STUDENT LIFE

Housing options: on-campus residence required through senior year; coed, women-only, special housing for students with disabilities. Campus housing is university owned. Freshman campus housing is guaranteed.

Activities and organizations: drama/theater group, student-run newspaper, choral group, Sigma Alpha Pi Honor Society, SOTA, ASL Club, Art Club, KC Chemistry Club.

Athletics Member NCAA. All Division III. ***Intercollegiate sports:*** baseball M, basketball M/W, cheerleading M/W, cross-country running M/W, equestrian sports M/W, field hockey W, golf M/W, lacrosse M/W, soccer M/W, softball W, volleyball M/W. ***Intramural sports:*** badminton M/W, basketball M/W, bowling M/W, football M/W, soccer M/W, softball M/W, table tennis M/W, ultimate Frisbee M/W, volleyball M/W.

Campus security: 24-hour emergency response devices and patrols, late-night transport/escort service, controlled dormitory access.

Student services: health clinic, personal/psychological counseling, women's center.

COSTS & FINANCIAL AID

Costs (2020–21) ***Comprehensive fee:*** $46,176 includes full-time tuition ($32,700), mandatory fees ($1332), and room and board ($12,144). Full-time tuition and fees vary according to course load, degree level, location, program, and reciprocity agreements. Part-time tuition: $1092 per credit hour. Part-time tuition and fees vary according to course load, degree level, location, program, and reciprocity agreements. ***Room and board:*** Room and board charges vary according to board plan and housing facility. ***Payment plan:*** installment. ***Waivers:*** employees or children of employees.

Financial Aid Of all full-time matriculated undergraduates who enrolled in 2018, 1,303 applied for aid, 1,242 were judged to have need, 966 had their need fully met. In 2018, 51 non-need-based awards were made. ***Average percent of need met:*** 65. ***Average financial aid package:*** $33,134. ***Average need-based loan:*** $4369. ***Average need-based gift aid:*** $8114. ***Average non-need-based aid:*** $14,860. ***Average indebtedness upon graduation:*** $44,211. ***Financial aid deadline:*** 11/1.

APPLYING

Options: electronic application, deferred entrance.

Required: high school transcript. ***Required for some:*** interview. ***Recommended:*** minimum 2.8 GPA, 1 letter of recommendation, interview.

Application deadlines: rolling (freshmen), rolling (transfers).

CONTACT

Mrs. Megan Perkins (Ryan), Keuka College, 141 Central Avenue, Keuka Park, NY 14478. *Phone:* 315-279-5254. *Toll-free phone:* 800-33-KEUKA. *Fax:* 315-279-5386. *E-mail:* admissions@keuka.edu.

The King's College

New York, New York

http://www.tkc.edu/

- **Independent nondenominational** 4-year, founded 1939
- **Urban** campus with easy access to New York City
- **Endowment** $488,024
- **Coed** 544 undergraduate students, 96% full-time, 66% women, 34% men
- **Moderately difficult** entrance level, 42% of applicants were admitted

UNDERGRAD STUDENTS

523 full-time, 21 part-time. Students come from 45 states and territories; 10 other countries; 92% are from out of state; 6% Black or African American, non-Hispanic/Latino; 11% Hispanic/Latino; 4% Asian, non-Hispanic/Latino; 2% American Indian or Alaska Native, non-Hispanic/Latino; 7% Race/ethnicity unknown; 3% international; 8% transferred in; 54% live on campus.

Freshmen:

Admission: 2,798 applied, 1,166 admitted, 125 enrolled. ***Average high school GPA:*** 3.7. ***Test scores:*** SAT evidence-based reading and writing scores over 500: 97%; SAT math scores over 500: 85%; ACT scores over 18: 100%; SAT evidence-based reading and writing scores over 600: 73%; SAT math scores over 600: 42%; ACT scores over 24: 71%; SAT evidence-based reading and writing scores over 700: 16%; SAT math scores over 700: 2%; ACT scores over 30: 21%.

Retention: 78% of full-time freshmen returned.

FACULTY

Total: 59, 53% full-time, 76% with terminal degrees.

Student/faculty ratio: 13:1.

ACADEMICS

Calendar: semesters. *Degree:* bachelor's.

Special study options: advanced placement credit, distance learning, double majors, independent study, internships, services for LD students, study abroad, summer session for credit. ***ROTC:*** Army (c).

Computers: 24 computers/terminals are available on campus for general student use. Students can access the following: computer help desk, free student e-mail accounts, online (class) grades, online (class) registration, online (class) schedules. Campuswide network is available. 100% of college-owned or -operated housing units are wired for high-speed Internet access. Wireless service is available via entire campus.

Library: Rosella Battles Library.

STUDENT LIFE

Housing options: men-only, women-only. Campus housing is university owned. Freshman campus housing is guaranteed.

Activities and organizations: drama/theater group, student-run newspaper, choral group, The King's Players, King's Debate Society, Refuge, Empire State Tribune, The Kings of Swing.

Athletics Member NCCAA, USCAA. ***Intercollegiate sports:*** baseball M, basketball M/W, golf M/W, soccer M/W, volleyball W. ***Intramural sports:*** basketball M(c)/W(c), cheerleading W(c), fencing M(c)/W(c), football M(c), rugby M(c), ultimate Frisbee M(c)/W(c).

Campus security: 24-hour emergency response devices, 24-hour security/doormen, fire sprinklers, fire/evacuation emergency plan.

Student services: personal/psychological counseling.

COSTS & FINANCIAL AID

Costs (2020–21) ***Tuition:*** $37,000 full-time, $1590 per credit hour part-time. Part-time tuition and fees vary according to course load. ***Required fees:*** $690 full-time, $250 per term part-time. ***Room only:*** $1440. Room and board charges vary according to location. ***Payment plans:*** installment, deferred payment. ***Waivers:*** employees or children of employees.

Financial Aid Of all full-time matriculated undergraduates who enrolled in 2018, 403 applied for aid, 353 were judged to have need, 70 had their need fully met. In 2018, 165 non-need-based awards were made. ***Average percent of need met:*** 73. ***Average financial aid package:*** $28,575. ***Average need-based loan:*** $3632. ***Average need-based gift aid:*** $22,920. ***Average non-need-based aid:*** $17,725. ***Average indebtedness upon graduation:*** $34,876.

APPLYING

Standardized Tests *Required:* SAT, ACT or CLT (for admission).

Options: electronic application, early action, deferred entrance.

Application fee: $30.

Required: high school transcript. ***Recommended:*** minimum 3.0 GPA, interview.

Application deadlines: rolling (freshmen), rolling (transfers), 11/15 (early action).

Notification: continuous (freshmen), continuous (transfers).

CONTACT

Mr. Noah Hunter, Director of Admissions, The King's College, 56 Broadway, New York, NY 10004. *Phone:* 212-659-3615. *Toll-free phone:* 888-969-7200 Ext. 3610. *Fax:* 212-659-3611. *E-mail:* nhunter@tkc.edu.

Lehman College of the City University of New York

Bronx, New York

http://www.lehman.cuny.edu/

- **State and locally supported** comprehensive, founded 1931, part of City University of New York System
- **Urban** 37-acre campus with easy access to New York City
- **Endowment** $5.2 million
- **Coed** 13,002 undergraduate students, 62% full-time, 68% women, 32% men
- **Moderately difficult** entrance level, 38% of applicants were admitted

UNDERGRAD STUDENTS

8,066 full-time, 4,936 part-time. Students come from 15 states and territories; 99 other countries; 1% are from out of state; 26% Black or African American, non-Hispanic/Latino; 58% Hispanic/Latino; 6% Asian, non-Hispanic/Latino; 0.2% Native Hawaiian or other Pacific Islander, non-Hispanic/Latino; 0.2% American Indian or Alaska Native, non-Hispanic/Latino; 1% Two or more races, non-Hispanic/Latino; 3% international; 17% transferred in.

Freshmen:

Admission: 19,759 applied, 7,462 admitted, 942 enrolled. ***Test scores:*** SAT evidence-based reading and writing scores over 500: 65%; SAT math scores over 500: 64%; SAT evidence-based reading and writing scores over 600: 11%; SAT math scores over 600: 8%.

Retention: 83% of full-time freshmen returned.

FACULTY

Total: 1,020, 37% full-time, 29% with terminal degrees.

Student/faculty ratio: 18:1.

ACADEMICS

Calendar: semesters. *Degrees:* certificates, bachelor's, master's, post-master's, and postbachelor's certificates.

Special study options: adult/continuing education programs, advanced placement credit, cooperative education, distance learning, double majors, English as a second language, freshman honors college, honors programs, independent study, internships, off-campus study, part-time degree program, services for LD students, student-designed majors, study abroad, summer session for credit. ***ROTC:*** Army (c).

Unusual degree programs: 3-2 mathematics.

Computers: 800 computers/terminals are available on campus for general student use. Students can access the following: campus intranet, computer help desk, free student e-mail accounts, online (class) grades, online (class) registration, online (class) schedules. Campuswide network is available. Wireless service is available via entire campus.

Library: Leonard Lief Library plus 1 other. *Books:* 362,674 (physical), 378,426 (digital/electronic); *Serial titles:* 299,414 (physical), 100,000 (digital/electronic). Weekly public service hours: 40; students can reserve study rooms.

STUDENT LIFE

Housing options: Campus housing is university owned.

Activities and organizations: drama/theater group, student-run newspaper, radio and television station, choral group, Club Mac, African Students Association, Dominican Student Association, The Sociology Club, Club Live.

Athletics Member NCAA. All Division III. ***Intercollegiate sports:*** baseball M, basketball M/W, cross-country running M/W, racquetball M/W, soccer M/W, softball M/W, swimming and diving M/W, table tennis M/W, tennis M/W, track and field M/W, volleyball M/W, water polo M, wrestling M. ***Intramural sports:*** badminton M/W, baseball M/W, basketball M/W, cross-country running M/W, racquetball M/W, soccer M, softball M/W, swimming and diving M/W, tennis M/W, volleyball M/W, wrestling M.

Campus security: 24-hour emergency response devices and patrols, student patrols, late-night transport/escort service.

Student services: health clinic, personal/psychological counseling, women's center.

COSTS & FINANCIAL AID

Costs (2020–21) ***Tuition:*** state resident $6930 full-time, $305 per credit hour part-time; nonresident $14,880 full-time, $620 per credit hour part-time. Full-time tuition and fees vary according to course load. Part-time tuition and fees vary according to course load. ***Required fees:*** $480 full-time, $130 per term part-time. ***Waivers:*** employees or children of employees.

Financial Aid Of all full-time matriculated undergraduates who enrolled in 2016, 6,606 applied for aid, 6,407 were judged to have need, 87 had their need fully met. 448 Federal Work-Study jobs (averaging $1846). In 2016, 104 non-need-based awards were made. ***Average percent of need met:*** 54. ***Average financial aid package:*** $9448. ***Average need-based loan:*** $4063. ***Average need-based gift aid:*** $8116. ***Average non-need-based aid:*** $3450. ***Average indebtedness upon graduation:*** $4410.

APPLYING

Standardized Tests *Required:* SAT (for admission), SAT or ACT (for admission).

Options: deferred entrance.

Application fee: $65.

Required: high school transcript, minimum 3.0 GPA. ***Required for some:*** essay or personal statement, interview.

Application deadlines: rolling (freshmen), rolling (transfers).

Notification: continuous (freshmen), continuous (transfers).

CONTACT

Ms. Laurie Austin, Director of Admissions, Lehman College of the City University of New York, 250 Bedford Park Boulevard West, Bronx, NY 10468. *Phone:* 718-960-8706. *Toll-free phone:* 877-LEHMAN1. *Fax:* 718-960-8712. *E-mail:* enroll@lehman.cuny.edu.

Le Moyne College

Syracuse, New York

http://www.lemoyne.edu/

- **Independent Roman Catholic (Jesuit)** comprehensive, founded 1946
- **Suburban** 161-acre campus
- **Endowment** $193.5 million
- **Coed** 2,765 undergraduate students, 87% full-time, 61% women, 39% men
- **Moderately difficult** entrance level, 74% of applicants were admitted

UNDERGRAD STUDENTS

2,392 full-time, 373 part-time. Students come from 28 states and territories; 52 other countries; 7% are from out of state; 6% Black or African American, non-Hispanic/Latino; 7% Hispanic/Latino; 3% Asian, non-Hispanic/Latino; 0.2% American Indian or Alaska Native, non-Hispanic/Latino; 3% Two or more races, non-Hispanic/Latino; 2% Race/ethnicity unknown; 1% international; 5% transferred in; 57% live on campus.

Freshmen:

Admission: 7,323 applied, 5,391 admitted, 654 enrolled. ***Average high school GPA:*** 3.5. ***Test scores:*** SAT evidence-based reading and writing scores over 500: 89%; SAT math scores over 500: 90%; ACT scores over 18: 97%; SAT evidence-based reading and writing scores over 600: 48%; SAT math scores over 600: 48%; ACT scores over 24: 63%; SAT evidence-based reading and writing scores over 700: 6%; SAT math scores over 700: 6%; ACT scores over 30: 13%.

Retention: 87% of full-time freshmen returned.

FACULTY

Total: 360, 49% full-time, 60% with terminal degrees.

Student/faculty ratio: 12:1.

ACADEMICS

Calendar: semesters. *Degrees:* bachelor's, master's, doctoral, post-master's, and postbachelor's certificates.

Special study options: academic remediation for entering students, accelerated degree program, adult/continuing education programs, advanced placement credit, distance learning, double majors, honors programs, independent study, internships, off-campus study, part-time degree program, services for LD students, study abroad, summer session for credit. ***ROTC:*** Army (c), Air Force (c).

Unusual degree programs: 3-2 engineering with Syracuse University.

Computers: 315 computers/terminals and 315 ports are available on campus for general student use. Students can access the following: campus intranet, computer help desk, free student e-mail accounts, online (class) grades, online (class) registration, online (class) schedules, ECHO (campus-wide portal), some virtual access from off campus. Campuswide network is available. 100% of college-owned or -operated housing units are wired for high-speed Internet access. Wireless service is available via entire campus.

Library: Noreen Reale Falcone Library. *Books:* 264,034 (physical), 228,586 (digital/electronic); *Serial titles:* 1,371 (physical), 107,697 (digital/electronic); *Databases:* 251. Weekly public service hours: 110; study areas open 24 hours, 5–7 days a week; students can reserve study rooms.

STUDENT LIFE

Housing options: on-campus residence required through senior year; coed, special housing for students with disabilities. Campus housing is university owned. Freshman campus housing is guaranteed.

Activities and organizations: drama/theater group, student-run newspaper, radio and television station, choral group, Student Programming Board, Outing Club, Performing Arts Groups, Cultural Groups, New Student Orientation Committee.

Athletics Member NCAA. All Division II. ***Intercollegiate sports:*** baseball M(s), basketball M(s)/W(s), cross-country running M(s)/W(s), golf M(s)/W(s), lacrosse M(s)/W(s), soccer M(s)/W(s), softball W(s), swimming and diving M(s)/W(s), tennis M(s)/W(s), track and field M(s)/W(s), volleyball W(s). ***Intramural sports:*** basketball M/W, bowling M(c)/W(c), cheerleading M(c)/W(c), equestrian sports M(c)/W(c), fencing M(c)/W(c), field hockey W(c), football M/W, ice hockey M(c), lacrosse M(c)/W(c), racquetball M/W, rowing M(c)/W(c), rugby M(c)/W(c), sailing M(c)/W(c), soccer M/W, softball M/W, ultimate Frisbee M(c)/W(c), volleyball M/W.

Campus security: 24-hour emergency response devices and patrols, late-night transport/escort service, controlled dormitory access, lighted pathways, closed-circuit security cameras, and emergency code blue phones.

Student services: health clinic, personal/psychological counseling, veterans affairs office.

COSTS & FINANCIAL AID

Costs (2020–21) ***Comprehensive fee:*** $50,380 includes full-time tuition ($34,910), mandatory fees ($1000), and room and board ($14,470). Part-time tuition: $732 per credit hour. Part-time tuition and fees vary according to class time and course load. ***Required fees:*** $70 per year part-time. ***College room only:*** $9020. Room and board charges vary according to board plan and housing facility. ***Payment plans:*** installment, deferred payment. ***Waivers:*** employees or children of employees.

Financial Aid Of all full-time matriculated undergraduates who enrolled in 2018, 2,143 applied for aid, 1,943 were judged to have need, 540 had their need fully met. 399 Federal Work-Study jobs (averaging $1450). 368 state and other part-time jobs (averaging $1650). In 2018, 303 non-need-based awards were made. ***Average percent of need met:*** 79. ***Average financial aid package:*** $27,819. ***Average need-based loan:*** $4229. ***Average need-based gift aid:*** $22,964. ***Average non-need-based aid:*** $16,775. ***Average indebtedness upon graduation:*** $40,522.

APPLYING

Standardized Tests *Required for some:* SAT or ACT (for admission).

Options: electronic application, early admission, early action, deferred entrance.

Required: essay or personal statement, high school transcript, 3 letters of recommendation. ***Recommended:*** interview.

Application deadlines: 2/1 (freshmen), 8/1 (transfers), 11/15 (early action).

Notification: continuous until 1/1 (freshmen), continuous (transfers), 12/15 (early action).

CONTACT

Mrs. Mary M. Chandler, Sr. Director of Admission, Le Moyne College, 1419 Salt Springs Road, Syracuse, NY 13214-1301. *Phone:* 315-445-4300. *Toll-free phone:* 800-333-4733. *Fax:* 315-445-4711. *E-mail:* admission@lemoyne.edu.

LIM College

New York, New York

http://www.limcollege.edu/

- **Proprietary** comprehensive, founded 1939
- **Urban** campus with easy access to New York City
- **Coed, primarily women**
- 83% of applicants were admitted

FACULTY

Student/faculty ratio: 8:1.

ACADEMICS

Calendar: semesters. *Degrees:* certificates, bachelor's, master's, and postbachelor's certificates.

Library: Adrian G. Marcuse Library. *Books:* 15,000 (physical), 700 (digital/electronic); *Serial titles:* 172 (physical); *Databases:* 55. Students can reserve study rooms.

STUDENT LIFE

Housing options: coed. Campus housing is leased by the school.

Activities and organizations: student-run newspaper, Fashion Show Production Club, Lexington Line Magazine, Student Life Activities Board, Dance Team, Black Retail Action Group.

Campus security: 24-hour patrols, controlled dormitory access.

Student services: personal/psychological counseling.

COSTS & FINANCIAL AID

Costs (2019–20) ***Comprehensive fee:*** $48,650 includes full-time tuition ($26,990), mandatory fees ($820), and room and board ($20,840). Part-time tuition: $896 per credit hour. ***College room only:*** $16,840.

Financial Aid ***Average indebtedness upon graduation:*** $40,085.

APPLYING

Options: electronic application, early action.

Application fee: $40.

Required: essay or personal statement, high school transcript, 1 letter of recommendation. ***Required for some:*** interview. ***Recommended:*** minimum 2.0 GPA.

CONTACT

Laura Healy, Associate Director of Admissions Recruitment, LIM College, 12 East 53rd Street, New York, NY 10022. *Phone:* 212-310-0672 Ext. 418. *Toll-free phone:* 800-677-1323. *E-mail:* admissions@limcollege.edu.

Long Island University

New York, New York

http://www.liu.edu/

CONTACT

Long Island University, New York, NY.

Long Island University - Brooklyn

Brooklyn, New York

http://www.liu.edu/

CONTACT

Mr. Luis Santiago, Dean of Enrollment, Long Island University - Brooklyn, 1 University Plaza, Brooklyn, NY 11201. *Phone:* 718-488-1011. *Toll-free phone:* 800-LIU-PLAN. *Fax:* 718-780-6110. *E-mail:* bkln-admissions@liu.edu.

Long Island University - Post

Brookville, New York

http://www.liu.edu/

CONTACT
Ms. Anne Marie Caradonna, Director of Admissions Operations, Long Island University - Post, 720 Northern Boulevard, Brookville, NY 11548-1300. *Phone:* 516-299-2900. *Toll-free phone:* 800-LIU-PLAN. *Fax:* 516-299-2137. *E-mail:* post-enroll@liu.edu.

Machzikei Hadath Rabbinical College

Brooklyn, New York

CONTACT
Rabbi Abraham M. Lezerowitz, Director of Admissions, Machzikei Hadath Rabbinical College, 5407 Sixteenth Avenue, Brooklyn, NY 11204-1805. *Phone:* 718-854-8777.

Manhattan College

Riverdale, New York

http://www.manhattan.edu/

- **Independent** comprehensive, founded 1853, affiliated with Roman Catholic Church
- **Urban** 31-acre campus with easy access to New York City
- **Endowment** $100.6 million
- **Coed** 3,845 undergraduate students, 86% full-time, 39% women, 51% men
- **Moderately difficult** entrance level, 74% of applicants were admitted

UNDERGRAD STUDENTS
3,308 full-time, 177 part-time. 5% Black or African American, non-Hispanic/Latino; 23% Hispanic/Latino; 4% Asian, non-Hispanic/Latino; 0.1% American Indian or Alaska Native, non-Hispanic/Latino; 2% Two or more races, non-Hispanic/Latino; 6% Race/ethnicity unknown; 4% international; 5% transferred in; 67% live on campus.

Freshmen:
Admission: 8,736 applied, 6,434 admitted, 853 enrolled. ***Test scores:*** SAT evidence-based reading and writing scores over 500: 89%; SAT math scores over 500: 88%; ACT scores over 18: 99%; SAT evidence-based reading and writing scores over 600: 43%; SAT math scores over 600: 46%; ACT scores over 24: 64%; SAT evidence-based reading and writing scores over 700: 5%; SAT math scores over 700: 10%; ACT scores over 30: 14%.

Retention: 81% of full-time freshmen returned.

FACULTY
Total: 433, 55% full-time, 71% with terminal degrees.

Student/faculty ratio: 12:1.

ACADEMICS
Calendar: semesters. *Degrees:* bachelor's, master's, post-master's, and postbachelor's certificates.

Special study options: accelerated degree program, adult/continuing education programs, advanced placement credit, cooperative education, distance learning, double majors, English as a second language, honors programs, independent study, internships, off-campus study, part-time degree program, services for LD students, student-designed majors, study abroad, summer session for credit. ***ROTC:*** Army (c), Air Force (b).

Unusual degree programs: 3-2 business administration; engineering; education.

Computers: 450 computers/terminals and 3,000 ports are available on campus for general student use. Students can access the following: campus intranet, computer help desk, free student e-mail accounts, online (class) grades, online (class) registration, online (class) schedules, course management system, degree audit/planning tool, campus card access. Campuswide network is available. 100% of college-owned or -operated housing units are wired for high-speed Internet access. Wireless service is available via entire campus.

Library: Mary Alice and Tom OMalley Library. *Books:* 259,987 (physical), 191,706 (digital/electronic); *Serial titles:* 379 (physical), 186,500 (digital/electronic). Weekly public service hours: 168; study areas open 24 hours, 5–7 days a week.

STUDENT LIFE
Housing options: men-only, women-only, special housing for students with disabilities. Campus housing is university owned. Freshman campus housing is guaranteed.

Activities and organizations: drama/theater group, student-run newspaper, choral group, Society of Hispanic Professional Engineers, Singers, Student Government, Social Life Commission, Manhattan College Players (Theater/Drama group), national fraternities, national sororities.

Athletics Member NCAA. All Division I. ***Intercollegiate sports:*** baseball M(s), basketball M(s)/W(s), cheerleading W, crew M(c)/W, cross-country running M(s)/W(s), golf M(s), lacrosse M(s)/W(s), rugby M(c), soccer M(s)/W(s), softball W(s), swimming and diving M(s)/W(s), track and field M(s)/W(s), volleyball W(s). ***Intramural sports:*** baseball M, basketball M/W, cheerleading M/W, cross-country running M/W, football M/W, soccer M/W, softball M/W, swimming and diving W, track and field M/W, volleyball M/W.

Campus security: 24-hour emergency response devices and patrols, late-night transport/escort service, controlled dormitory access.

Student services: health clinic, personal/psychological counseling, veterans affairs office.

COSTS & FINANCIAL AID
Costs (2019–20) ***Comprehensive fee:*** $61,434 includes full-time tuition ($40,400), mandatory fees ($4164), and room and board ($16,870). Full-time tuition and fees vary according to course load, program, and student level. Part-time tuition: $1040 per credit. Part-time tuition and fees vary according to course load. ***Required fees:*** $982 per term part-time. ***Room and board:*** Room and board charges vary according to board plan. ***Payment plans:*** installment, deferred payment. ***Waivers:*** employees or children of employees.

Financial Aid Of all full-time matriculated undergraduates who enrolled in 2018, 3,001 applied for aid, 2,758 were judged to have need. In 2018, 898 non-need-based awards were made. ***Average percent of need met:*** 41. ***Average financial aid package:*** $19,889. ***Average need-based gift aid:*** $15,550. ***Average non-need-based aid:*** $12,583. ***Average indebtedness upon graduation:*** $11,170. ***Financial aid deadline:*** 4/15.

APPLYING
Standardized Tests *Required:* SAT or ACT (for admission).

Options: electronic application, early admission, early decision, deferred entrance.

Application fee: $75.

Required: essay or personal statement, high school transcript, minimum 2.5 GPA, 1 letter of recommendation. ***Recommended:*** minimum 3.0 GPA, interview.

Application deadlines: rolling (freshmen), 7/1 (transfers).

Early decision deadline: 11/15.

Notification: continuous until 4/15 (freshmen), continuous until 8/15 (transfers), 12/1 (early decision).

CONTACT
Ms. Tara Fay-Reilly, Director of Undergraduate Admissions, Manhattan College, 4513 Manhattan College Parkway, Riverdale, NY 10471. *Phone:* 718-862-7200. *Toll-free phone:* 800-622-9235. *Fax:* 718-862-8019. *E-mail:* admit@manhattan.edu.

See below for display ad and page 1078 for the College Close-Up.

Manhattan School of Music

New York, New York

http://www.msmnyc.edu/

- **Independent** comprehensive, founded 1917
- **Urban** 1-acre campus
- **Endowment** $19.2 million
- **Coed** 389 undergraduate students, 99% full-time, 55% women, 45% men
- **Very difficult** entrance level, 45% of applicants were admitted

UNDERGRAD STUDENTS
385 full-time, 4 part-time. Students come from 32 states and territories; 20 other countries; 61% are from out of state; 2% Black or African American, non-Hispanic/Latino; 7% Hispanic/Latino; 7% Asian, non-Hispanic/Latino; 5% Two or more races, non-Hispanic/Latino; 4% Race/ethnicity unknown; 43% international; 5% transferred in; 67% live on campus.

Freshmen:
Admission: 897 applied, 402 admitted, 113 enrolled. ***Average high school GPA:*** 3.6.

Retention: 81% of full-time freshmen returned.

FACULTY
Total: 299, 91% full-time.

Student/faculty ratio: 6:1.

ACADEMICS
Calendar: semesters. *Degrees:* diplomas, bachelor's, master's, doctoral, and post-master's certificates.

Special study options: academic remediation for entering students, advanced placement credit, cooperative education, distance learning, English as a second language, independent study, off-campus study, services for LD students, study abroad.

Computers: 20 computers/terminals and 20 ports are available on campus for general student use. Students can access the following: campus intranet, computer help desk, free student e-mail accounts, online (class) grades, online (class) registration, online (class) schedules. Campuswide network is available. 100% of college-owned or -operated housing units are wired for high-speed Internet access. Wireless service is available via entire campus.

Library: Peter J. Sharp Library plus 1 other. *Books:* 20,000 (physical), 60,000 (digital/electronic). Weekly public service hours: 75; study areas open 24 hours, 5–7 days a week; students can reserve study rooms.

STUDENT LIFE
Housing options: on-campus residence required through sophomore year; coed. Campus housing is university owned. Freshman campus housing is guaranteed.

Activities and organizations: Student Council, Asian Student Association, Resident Community Council.

Campus security: 24-hour patrols, student patrols, controlled dormitory access.

Student services: health clinic, personal/psychological counseling.

COSTS & FINANCIAL AID
Costs (2020–21) ***Comprehensive fee:*** $65,575 includes full-time tuition ($48,280), mandatory fees ($990), and room and board ($16,305). Part-time tuition: $2150 per credit. Part-time tuition and fees vary according to course load. ***College room only:*** $10,790. Room and board charges vary according to board plan and housing facility. ***Payment plans:*** installment, deferred payment.

Financial Aid ***Financial aid deadline:*** 3/1.

APPLYING
Options: electronic application, deferred entrance.

Application fee: $125.

Required: essay or personal statement, high school transcript, minimum 3.0 GPA, 2-3 letters of recommendation, prescreening, audition. ***Required for some:*** interview. ***Recommended:*** minimum 3.0 GPA.

Application deadlines: 12/1 (freshmen), 12/1 (transfers).

Notification: 4/1 (freshmen), 4/1 (transfers).

CONTACT
Julia Bair, Administrative Assistant, Manhattan School of Music, 120 Claremont Avenue, New York, NY 10027-4698. *Phone:* 917-493-4435. *Fax:* 212-749-3025. *E-mail:* jbair@msmnyc.edu.

Manhattanville College

Purchase, New York

http://www.mville.edu/

- **Independent** comprehensive, founded 1841
- **Suburban** 100-acre campus with easy access to New York City
- **Endowment** $31.2 million
- **Coed** 1,541 undergraduate students, 96% full-time, 58% women, 42% men
- **Minimally difficult** entrance level, 90% of applicants were admitted

UNDERGRAD STUDENTS

1,474 full-time, 67 part-time. Students come from 35 states and territories; 36 other countries; 25% are from out of state; 10% Black or African American, non-Hispanic/Latino; 29% Hispanic/Latino; 2% Asian, non-Hispanic/Latino; 0.2% Native Hawaiian or other Pacific Islander, non-Hispanic/Latino; 0.1% American Indian or Alaska Native, non-Hispanic/Latino; 3% Two or more races, non-Hispanic/Latino; 3% Race/ethnicity unknown; 5% international; 6% transferred in; 59% live on campus.

Freshmen:

Admission: 3,435 applied, 3,100 admitted, 401 enrolled. ***Average high school GPA:*** 3.2. ***Test scores:*** SAT evidence-based reading and writing scores over 500: 71%; SAT math scores over 500: 76%; ACT scores over 18: 97%; SAT evidence-based reading and writing scores over 600: 24%; SAT math scores over 600: 21%; ACT scores over 24: 61%; SAT evidence-based reading and writing scores over 700: 2%; SAT math scores over 700: 3%; ACT scores over 30: 6%.

Retention: 70% of full-time freshmen returned.

FACULTY

Total: 360, 31% full-time, 49% with terminal degrees.

Student/faculty ratio: 11:1.

ACADEMICS

Calendar: semesters. *Degrees:* bachelor's, master's, doctoral, post-master's, and postbachelor's certificates.

Special study options: accelerated degree program, adult/continuing education programs, advanced placement credit, double majors, honors programs, independent study, internships, off-campus study, part-time degree program, services for LD students, student-designed majors, study abroad, summer session for credit.

Computers: 125 computers/terminals are available on campus for general student use. Students can access the following: campus intranet, computer help desk, free student e-mail accounts, online (class) grades, online (class) registration, online (class) schedules, Mobile Apps. Campuswide network is available. 100% of college-owned or -operated housing units are wired for high-speed Internet access. Wireless service is available via entire campus.

Library: Manhattanville College Library. *Books:* 191,679 (physical), 182,461 (digital/electronic); *Serial titles:* 924 (physical), 63,053 (digital/electronic); *Databases:* 119. Weekly public service hours: 109; study areas open 24 hours, 5–7 days a week.

STUDENT LIFE

Housing options: coed, special housing for students with disabilities. Campus housing is university owned. Freshman campus housing is guaranteed.

Activities and organizations: drama/theater group, student-run newspaper, radio station, choral group, National Society for Leadership and Success (NSLC), Paws for a Cause, Student Government Association (SGA), Finance Society, Broadway at Manhattanville (B@M).

Athletics Member NCAA. All Division III. ***Intercollegiate sports:*** baseball M, basketball M/W, cross-country running M/W, field hockey W, golf M/W, ice hockey M/W, lacrosse M/W, rugby W(c), soccer M/W, softball W, tennis M/W, track and field M/W, volleyball W. ***Intramural sports:*** basketball M/W, cheerleading W, soccer M/W, swimming and diving M/W, table tennis M/W, volleyball M/W.

Campus security: 24-hour emergency response devices and patrols, late-night transport/escort service, controlled dormitory access, There is an officer at the main campus gate 24/7, emergency notification system, seminars on campus safety and security practices.

Student services: health clinic, personal/psychological counseling.

COSTS & FINANCIAL AID

Costs (2020–21) ***Comprehensive fee:*** $55,140 includes full-time tuition ($38,880), mandatory fees ($1450), and room and board ($14,810). Part-time tuition: $900 per credit. Part-time tuition and fees vary according to course load and program. ***Required fees:*** $60 per term part-time. ***College room only:*** $8970. Room and board charges vary according to board plan. ***Payment plan:*** installment. ***Waivers:*** children of alumni and employees or children of employees.

Financial Aid Of all full-time matriculated undergraduates who enrolled in 2019, 1,136 applied for aid, 1,012 were judged to have need, 164 had their need fully met. 679 Federal Work-Study jobs (averaging $1810). In 2019, 440 non-need-based awards were made. ***Average percent of need met:*** 73. ***Average financial aid package:*** $29,753. ***Average need-based loan:*** $4340. ***Average need-based gift aid:*** $6116. ***Average non-need-based aid:*** $20,551. ***Average indebtedness upon graduation:*** $35,092.

APPLYING

Standardized Tests *Required for some:* SAT (for admission), ACT (for admission), SAT or ACT (for admission).

Options: electronic application, early action, deferred entrance.

Application fee: $50.

Required: essay or personal statement, high school transcript, minimum 2.8 GPA, 2 letters of recommendation. ***Required for some:*** interview, If a student is applying for dance, theatre, musical theatre or studio art, please visit https://www.mville.edu/admissions/undergraduate-admissions/find-out-more/art-music-dance-theatre-applicants.

Application deadlines: rolling (freshmen), rolling (out-of-state freshmen), rolling (transfers), 12/1 (early action).

Notification: continuous (freshmen), continuous (out-of-state freshmen), continuous (transfers), 1/1 (early action).

CONTACT

Ms. Jessica Tully, Director - Admissions, Manhattanville College, 2900 Purchase Street, Purchase, NY 10577. *Phone:* 914-323-5363. *Toll-free phone:* 800-328-4553. *Fax:* 914-694-1732. *E-mail:* Jessica.Tully@mville.edu.

Maria College

Albany, New York

http://www.mariacollege.edu/

- **Independent** 4-year, founded 1958
- **Urban** 9-acre campus
- **Coed**
- **Minimally difficult** entrance level

FACULTY

Student/faculty ratio: 10:1.

ACADEMICS

Calendar: semesters. *Degrees:* certificates, associate, and bachelor's.

Library: Maria College Library. *Books:* 19,779 (physical), 160,512 (digital/electronic); *Serial titles:* 55 (physical), 230,969 (digital/electronic); *Databases:* 27. Weekly public service hours: 131.

STUDENT LIFE

Housing options: college housing not available.

Campus security: late-night transport/escort service, 8:30 am-10 pm security guard coverage in specified campus buildings.

Student services: personal/psychological counseling.

COSTS & FINANCIAL AID

Costs (2019–20) ***Tuition:*** $7575 full-time, $650 per credit hour part-time. Full-time tuition and fees vary according to course load, program, and reciprocity agreements. Part-time tuition and fees vary according to course load, program, and reciprocity agreements. ***Required fees:*** $460 full-time, $115 per term part-time.

Financial Aid Of all full-time matriculated undergraduates who enrolled in 2018, 282 applied for aid, 251 were judged to have need, 4 had their need fully met. In 2018, 3 non-need-based awards were made. ***Average percent of need met:*** 33. ***Average financial aid package:*** $8758. ***Average need-based loan:*** $3440. ***Average need-based gift aid:*** $6940. ***Average non-need-based aid:*** $6016. ***Average indebtedness upon graduation:*** $18,950.

APPLYING

Standardized Tests *Required for some:* TEAS for AAS in nursing and practical nursing certificate programs. *Recommended:* SAT or ACT (for admission).

Options: electronic application, early admission, deferred entrance.

Application fee: $35.

Required: high school transcript. ***Recommended:*** essay or personal statement, minimum 2.5 GPA, 1 letter of recommendation, interview.

CONTACT
Mr. John Ramoska, Director of Admissions, Maria College, 700 New Scotland Avenue, Albany, NY 12065. *Phone:* 518-861-2519. *Fax:* 518-453-1366. *E-mail:* admissions@mariacollege.edu.

Marist College

Poughkeepsie, New York

http://www.marist.edu/

- **Independent** comprehensive, founded 1929
- **Suburban** 210-acre campus with easy access to Albany, New York City
- **Endowment** $71.2 million
- **Coed**
- **Very difficult** entrance level

FACULTY
Student/faculty ratio: 16:1.

ACADEMICS
Calendar: semesters. *Degrees:* certificates, bachelor's, master's, and postbachelor's certificates.
Library: James A. Cannavino Library. *Books:* 108,161 (physical), 251,090 (digital/electronic); *Serial titles:* 1,085 (physical), 65,765 (digital/electronic); *Databases:* 119. Weekly public service hours: 113; students can reserve study rooms.

STUDENT LIFE
Housing options: coed, special housing for students with disabilities. Campus housing is university owned and is provided by a third party. Freshman campus housing is guaranteed.

Activities and organizations: drama/theater group, student-run newspaper, radio and television station, choral group, marching band, Marist Singers, Dance Club, Student Government, Theater Club, Community Service and Campus Ministry, national fraternities, national sororities.

Athletics Member NCAA. All Division I except football (Division I-AA).

Campus security: 24-hour emergency response devices and patrols, student patrols, late-night transport/escort service, controlled dormitory access, night residence hall monitors.

Student services: health clinic, personal/psychological counseling.

COSTS & FINANCIAL AID
Costs (2019–20) ***One-time required fee:*** $100. ***Comprehensive fee:*** $58,445 includes full-time tuition ($39,925), mandatory fees ($600), and room and board ($17,920). Full-time tuition and fees vary according to location, program, and student level. Part-time tuition: $730 per credit hour. Part-time tuition and fees vary according to course load, location, and program. ***Required fees:*** $40 per term part-time. ***College room only:*** $12,000. Room and board charges vary according to board plan, housing facility, location, and student level.

Financial Aid Of all full-time matriculated undergraduates who enrolled in 2019, 3,618 applied for aid, 2,893 were judged to have need, 539 had their need fully met. 1,436 Federal Work-Study jobs (averaging $2675). 566 state and other part-time jobs (averaging $2006). In 2019, 1636 non-need-based awards were made. ***Average percent of need met:*** 69. ***Average financial aid package:*** $25,803. ***Average need-based loan:*** $3878. ***Average need-based gift aid:*** $20,112. ***Average non-need-based aid:*** $11,108. ***Average indebtedness upon graduation:*** $40,007.

APPLYING
Options: electronic application, early admission, early decision, early action, deferred entrance.

Application fee: $50.

Required: essay or personal statement, high school transcript, 2 letters of recommendation.

CONTACT
Mr. Kent Rinehart, Dean of Undergraduate Admissions, Marist College, 3399 North Road, Poughkeepsie, NY 12601. *Phone:* 845-575-3226. *Toll-free phone:* 800-436-5483. *Fax:* 845-575-3215. *E-mail:* admission@marist.edu.

Marymount Manhattan College

New York, New York

http://www.mmm.edu/

- **Independent** 4-year, founded 1936
- **Urban** campus
- **Endowment** $21.3 million
- **Coed** 1,892 undergraduate students, 88% full-time, 79% women, 21% men
- 80% of applicants were admitted

UNDERGRAD STUDENTS
1,660 full-time, 232 part-time. Students come from 49 states and territories; 45 other countries; 72% are from out of state; 10% Black or African American, non-Hispanic/Latino; 17% Hispanic/Latino; 3% Asian, non-Hispanic/Latino; 0.1% Native Hawaiian or other Pacific Islander, non-Hispanic/Latino; 0.2% American Indian or Alaska Native, non-Hispanic/Latino; 5% Two or more races, non-Hispanic/Latino; 5% Race/ethnicity unknown; 3% international; 4% transferred in; 34% live on campus.

Freshmen
Admission: 5,566 applied, 4,433 admitted, 437 enrolled. ***Average high school GPA:*** 3.4. ***Test scores:*** SAT evidence-based reading and writing scores over 500: 79%; SAT math scores over 500: 68%; ACT scores over 18: 93%; SAT evidence-based reading and writing scores over 600: 37%; SAT math scores over 600: 19%; ACT scores over 24: 52%; SAT evidence-based reading and writing scores over 700: 6%; SAT math scores over 700: 3%; ACT scores over 30: 13%.

Retention: 69% of full-time freshmen returned.

FACULTY
Total: 376, 25% full-time.
Student/faculty ratio: 9:1.

ACADEMICS
Calendar: semesters plus summer and January mini-semesters. *Degree:* bachelor's.

Special study options: academic remediation for entering students, advanced placement credit, distance learning, double majors, freshman honors college, honors programs, independent study, internships, off-campus study, part-time degree program, services for LD students, study abroad, summer session for credit.

Computers: 215 computers/terminals are available on campus for general student use. Students can access the following: campus intranet, computer help desk, free student e-mail accounts, online (class) grades, online (class) registration, online (class) schedules. Campuswide network is available. 100% of college-owned or -operated housing units are wired for high-speed Internet access. Wireless service is available via entire campus.
Library: Thomas J. Shanahan Library. *Books:* 37,334 (physical), 253,240 (digital/electronic); *Serial titles:* 94 (physical), 54,781 (digital/electronic); *Databases:* 81. Students can reserve study rooms.

STUDENT LIFE
Housing options: coed. Campus housing is university owned. Freshman campus housing is guaranteed.

Activities and organizations: drama/theater group, student-run newspaper.

Campus security: 24-hour emergency response devices and patrols.

Student services: health clinic, personal/psychological counseling.

COSTS & FINANCIAL AID
Costs (2020–21) ***Comprehensive fee:*** $55,844 includes full-time tuition ($35,680), mandatory fees ($1730), and room and board ($18,434). Part-time tuition: $1188 per credit hour. ***Required fees:*** $1188 per credit hour part-time, $633 per term part-time. ***College room only:*** $15,734. Room and board charges vary according to board plan. ***Payment plan:*** installment.

Financial Aid Of all full-time matriculated undergraduates who enrolled in 2017, 1,465 applied for aid, 1,296 were judged to have need, 88 had their need fully met. 107 Federal Work-Study jobs (averaging $3372). In 2017, 143 non-need-based awards were made. ***Average percent of need met:*** 54. ***Average financial aid package:*** $18,930. ***Average need-based***

loan: $4190. ***Average need-based gift aid:*** $15,488. ***Average non-need-based aid:*** $9724. ***Average indebtedness upon graduation:*** $36,417.

APPLYING

Options: electronic application, early admission, early decision, early action, deferred entrance.

Application fee: $60.

Required: essay or personal statement, high school transcript, 1 letter of recommendation. ***Required for some:*** interview.

Application deadlines: rolling (freshmen), rolling (out-of-state freshmen), rolling (transfers), 12/1 (early action).

Early decision deadline: 11/1.

Notification: continuous (freshmen), continuous (transfers), 12/1 (early decision), 12/27 (early action).

CONTACT

Paul Kohler, Senior Associate Director of Admission, Marymount Manhattan College, 221 East 71st Street, New York, NY 10021. *Phone:* 212-5170437. *Toll-free phone:* 800-627-9668. *E-mail:* pkohler@mmm.edu.

Mechon L'Hoyroa

Monsey, New York

http://www.mechonlhoyroa.com/

CONTACT

Mechon L'Hoyroa, 168 Maple Avenue, Monsey, NY 10952.

Medaille College

Buffalo, New York

http://www.medaille.edu/

- **Independent** comprehensive, founded 1875
- **Urban** 13-acre campus with easy access to Buffal, Niagara
- **Endowment** $1.2 million
- **Coed**
- **Moderately difficult** entrance level

FACULTY

Student/faculty ratio: 14:1.

ACADEMICS

Calendar: semesters (modular courses available for evening studies and weekend college program). *Degrees:* certificates, associate, bachelor's, master's, doctoral, and post-master's certificates.
Library: Medaille College Library.

STUDENT LIFE

Housing options: coed, men-only, women-only, special housing for students with disabilities. Campus housing is university owned.

Activities and organizations: drama/theater group, student-run newspaper, radio and television station, Student Government, Club Green, Dance Team, WMCB The Lizard (college radio station), ice hockey club.

Athletics Member NCAA. All Division III.

Campus security: 24-hour emergency response devices and patrols, late-night transport/escort service, controlled dormitory access.

Student services: health clinic, personal/psychological counseling.

FINANCIAL AID

Financial Aid Of all full-time matriculated undergraduates who enrolled in 2012, 1,551 applied for aid, 1,496 were judged to have need, 425 had their need fully met. In 2012, 46 non-need-based awards were made. ***Average percent of need met:*** 38. ***Average financial aid package:*** $11,000. ***Average need-based loan:*** $9129. ***Average need-based gift aid:*** $10,908. ***Average non-need-based aid:*** $7622.

APPLYING

Standardized Tests *Required:* SAT or ACT (for admission). *Recommended:* SAT (for admission).

Options: electronic application, early admission, deferred entrance.

Application fee: $25.

Required: high school transcript, interview. ***Required for some:*** essay or personal statement, minimum 2.5 high school GPA for veterinary technology and elementary teacher education majors. ***Recommended:*** essay or personal statement, minimum 2.0 GPA, 1 letter of recommendation.

CONTACT

Christopher LaRusso, Vice President for Enrollment Management and Undergraduate Admissions, Medaille College, Office of Admissions, Buffalo, NY 14214. *Phone:* 716-880-2200. *Toll-free phone:* 800-292-1582. *Fax:* 716-880-2007. *E-mail:* admissionsug@medaille.edu.

Medgar Evers College of the City University of New York

Brooklyn, New York

http://www.mec.cuny.edu/

CONTACT

Dr. Shannon Clarke-Anderson, Director of Admissions, Medgar Evers College of the City University of New York, 1650 Bedford Avenue, Brooklyn, NY 11225. *Phone:* 718-270-5143. *Fax:* 718-270-6411. *E-mail:* shannon@mec.cuny.edu.

Mercy College

Dobbs Ferry, New York

http://www.mercy.edu/

- **Independent** comprehensive, founded 1951, affiliated with Roman Catholic Church
- **Suburban** 66-acre campus with easy access to New York City
- **Endowment** $255.8 million
- **Coed** 7,993 undergraduate students, 78% full-time, 70% women, 30% men
- **Moderately difficult** entrance level, 82% of applicants were admitted

UNDERGRAD STUDENTS

6,223 full-time, 1,770 part-time. Students come from 38 states and territories; 36 other countries; 7% are from out of state; 27% Black or African American, non-Hispanic/Latino; 40% Hispanic/Latino; 4% Asian, non-Hispanic/Latino; 0.2% Native Hawaiian or other Pacific Islander, non-Hispanic/Latino; 0.3% American Indian or Alaska Native, non-Hispanic/Latino; 1% Two or more races, non-Hispanic/Latino; 9% Race/ethnicity unknown; 0.9% international; 24% transferred in; 10% live on campus.

Freshmen:

Admission: 6,720 applied, 5,485 admitted, 999 enrolled. ***Average high school GPA:*** 3.2. ***Test scores:*** SAT evidence-based reading and writing scores over 500: 47%; SAT math scores over 500: 50%; ACT scores over 18: 67%; SAT evidence-based reading and writing scores over 600: 8%; SAT math scores over 600: 8%; ACT scores over 24: 33%; SAT evidence-based reading and writing scores over 700: 1%; SAT math scores over 700: 1%.

Retention: 77% of full-time freshmen returned.

FACULTY

Total: 1,028, 24% full-time.

Student/faculty ratio: 17:1.

ACADEMICS

Calendar: semesters. *Degrees:* certificates, associate, bachelor's, master's, doctoral, post-master's, and postbachelor's certificates.

Special study options: accelerated degree program, adult/continuing education programs, advanced placement credit, cooperative education, distance learning, double majors, freshman honors college, honors programs, independent study, internships, off-campus study, part-time degree program, services for LD students, study abroad, summer session for credit. ***ROTC:*** Army (c), Air Force (c).

Unusual degree programs: 3-2 business administration; education, cybersecurity.

Computers: 1,000 computers/terminals and 600 ports are available on campus for general student use. Students can access the following: campus intranet, computer help desk, free student e-mail accounts, online (class) grades, online (class) registration, online (class) schedules. Campuswide network is available. 100% of college-owned or -operated housing units are wired for high-speed Internet access. Wireless service is available via entire campus.

Library: Mercy College Library plus 3 others. *Books:* 71,778 (physical), 74,320 (digital/electronic); *Serial titles:* 29 (physical), 60,580 (digital/electronic); *Databases:* 43. Students can reserve study rooms.

STUDENT LIFE
Housing options: coed. Campus housing is university owned. Freshman applicants given priority for college housing.

Activities and organizations: drama/theater group, student-run newspaper, choral group, Model United Nations, Honors Club and 17 National Honor Societies, Mercy Gives Back, Maverick Society, ROTARACT Club for Community Volunteer Service.

Athletics Member NCAA. All Division II. ***Intercollegiate sports:*** baseball M(s), basketball M(s)/W(s), field hockey W(s), lacrosse M(s)/W(s), soccer M(s)/W(s), softball W(s), volleyball W(s). ***Intramural sports:*** basketball M/W, cheerleading W, soccer M/W, volleyball M/W.

Campus security: 24-hour emergency response devices and patrols, late-night transport/escort service, controlled dormitory access.

Student services: health clinic, personal/psychological counseling.

COSTS & FINANCIAL AID
Costs (2019–20) ***Comprehensive fee:*** $33,994 includes full-time tuition ($18,934), mandatory fees ($660), and room and board ($14,400). Full-time tuition and fees vary according to course load. Part-time tuition: $796 per credit. Part-time tuition and fees vary according to course load. ***Required fees:*** $166 per term part-time. ***College room only:*** $9750. Room and board charges vary according to board plan and housing facility. ***Payment plans:*** installment, deferred payment. ***Waivers:*** senior citizens and employees or children of employees.

Financial Aid Of all full-time matriculated undergraduates who enrolled in 2018, 4,668 applied for aid, 4,375 were judged to have need, 148 had their need fully met. 297 Federal Work-Study jobs. In 2018, 200 non-need-based awards were made. ***Average percent of need met:*** 53. ***Average financial aid package:*** $15,402. ***Average need-based loan:*** $4110. ***Average need-based gift aid:*** $11,053. ***Average non-need-based aid:*** $5053. ***Average indebtedness upon graduation:*** $23,942.

APPLYING
Standardized Tests *Required for some:* SAT or ACT (for admission).

Options: electronic application, deferred entrance.

Application fee: $40.

Required: high school transcript, minimum 2.0 GPA. ***Required for some:*** essay or personal statement, portfolio required for art program; audition required for music program; RN required for some nursing programs; additional interview with program director required of nursing, occupational therapy, physical therapy, social work, veterinary technology, and computer arts program applicants. ***Recommended:*** 1 letter of recommendation, interview.

Application deadlines: rolling (freshmen), rolling (transfers).

Notification: continuous (freshmen), continuous (transfers).

CONTACT
Mrs. Allison Gurdineer, Executive Director of Admissions, Mercy College, 555 Broadway, Dobbs Ferry, NY 10522-1189. *Phone:* 877-MERCY-GO. *Toll-free phone:* 877-637-2946 (in-state); 877-MERCY-GO (out-of-state). *Fax:* 914-674-7382. *E-mail:* admissions@mercy.edu.

Mesivta of Eastern Parkway–Yeshiva Zichron Meilech
Brooklyn, New York

CONTACT
Mesivta of Eastern Parkway–Yeshiva Zichron Meilech, 510 Dahill Road, Brooklyn, NY 11218-5559. *Phone:* 718-438-1002.

Mesivta Torah Vodaath Rabbinical Seminary
Brooklyn, New York
http://www.torahvodaath.org/

CONTACT
Rabbi Issac Braun, Administrator, Mesivta Torah Vodaath Rabbinical Seminary, 425 East Ninth Street, Brooklyn, NY 11218-5299. *Phone:* 718-941-8000.

Mesivtha Tifereth Jerusalem of America
New York, New York

CONTACT
Rabbi Fishellis, Director of Admissions, Mesivtha Tifereth Jerusalem of America, 145 East Broadway, New York, NY 10002-6301. *Phone:* 212-964-2830.

Metropolitan College of New York
New York, New York
http://www.mcny.edu/

CONTACT
Metropolitan College of New York, 60 West Street, New York, NY 10006. *Phone:* 212-343-1234 Ext. 2700. *Toll-free phone:* 800-33-THINK Ext. 5001. *Fax:* 212-343-8470.

Mirrer Yeshiva Central Institute
Brooklyn, New York

CONTACT
Director of Admissions, Mirrer Yeshiva Central Institute, 1791 Ocean Parkway, Brooklyn, NY 11223-2010. *Phone:* 718-645-0536.

Molloy College
Rockville Centre, New York
http://www.molloy.edu/

- **Independent** comprehensive, founded 1955
- **Suburban** 30-acre campus with easy access to New York City
- **Endowment** $40.8 million
- **Coed** 3,496 undergraduate students, 80% full-time, 73% women, 27% men
- **Moderately difficult** entrance level, 78% of applicants were admitted

UNDERGRAD STUDENTS
2,780 full-time, 716 part-time. Students come from 36 states and territories; 16 other countries; 5% are from out of state; 9% Black or African American, non-Hispanic/Latino; 19% Hispanic/Latino; 8% Asian, non-Hispanic/Latino; 0.2% Native Hawaiian or other Pacific Islander, non-Hispanic/Latino; 0.3% American Indian or Alaska Native, non-Hispanic/Latino; 2% Two or more races, non-Hispanic/Latino; 2% Race/ethnicity unknown; 0.5% international; 9% transferred in; 10% live on campus.

Freshmen:
Admission: 4,624 applied, 3,605 admitted, 581 enrolled. ***Average high school GPA:*** 3.0. ***Test scores:*** SAT evidence-based reading and writing scores over 500: 93%; SAT math scores over 500: 93%; ACT scores over 18: 97%; SAT evidence-based reading and writing scores over 600: 38%; SAT math scores over 600: 36%; ACT scores over 24: 56%; SAT evidence-based reading and writing scores over 700: 2%; SAT math scores over 700: 5%; ACT scores over 30: 14%.

Retention: 84% of full-time freshmen returned.

FACULTY
Total: 725, 26% full-time, 34% with terminal degrees.

Student/faculty ratio: 10:1.

ACADEMICS

Calendar: 4-1-4. *Degrees:* associate, bachelor's, master's, doctoral, post-master's, and postbachelor's certificates.

Special study options: academic remediation for entering students, accelerated degree program, adult/continuing education programs, advanced placement credit, distance learning, double majors, English as a second language, honors programs, independent study, internships, part-time degree program, services for LD students, student-designed majors, study abroad, summer session for credit. ***ROTC:*** Army (c), Navy (c).

Computers: 887 computers/terminals are available on campus for general student use. Students can access the following: computer help desk, free student e-mail accounts, online (class) grades, online (class) registration, online (class) schedules. Campuswide network is available. 100% of college-owned or -operated housing units are wired for high-speed Internet access. Wireless service is available via entire campus.

Library: James Edward Tobin Library plus 1 other. *Books:* 27,612 (physical), 255,591 (digital/electronic); *Serial titles:* 24 (physical), 63,761 (digital/electronic); *Databases:* 206.

STUDENT LIFE

Housing options: coed. Campus housing is university owned. Freshman applicants given priority for college housing.

Activities and organizations: drama/theater group, student-run newspaper, choral group, Molloy Student Government, Molloy Nursing Student Association, Molloy Performing Arts Club, Men's Rugby, MolloyLife Media.

Athletics Member NCAA. All Division II. ***Intercollegiate sports:*** baseball M(s), basketball M(s)/W(s), bowling W(s), cross-country running M(s)/W(s), field hockey W(s), lacrosse M(s)/W(s), rugby W(s), soccer M(s)/W(s), softball W(s), tennis W(s), track and field M(s)/W(s), volleyball W(s). ***Intramural sports:*** cheerleading M(c)/W(c), equestrian sports W(c), rugby M(c), ultimate Frisbee M(c)/W(c).

Campus security: 24-hour emergency response devices and patrols, late-night transport/escort service, controlled dormitory access.

Student services: health clinic, personal/psychological counseling, women's center.

COSTS & FINANCIAL AID

Costs (2019–20) ***Comprehensive fee:*** $48,160 includes full-time tuition ($31,330), mandatory fees ($1270), and room and board ($15,560). Full-time tuition and fees vary according to degree level. Part-time tuition: $1040 per credit hour. Part-time tuition and fees vary according to degree level. ***Room and board:*** Room and board charges vary according to board plan. ***Payment plans:*** installment, deferred payment. ***Waivers:*** senior citizens and employees or children of employees.

Financial Aid Of all full-time matriculated undergraduates who enrolled in 2018, 2,503 applied for aid, 2,199 were judged to have need, 267 had their need fully met. 194 Federal Work-Study jobs (averaging $1695). In 2018, 284 non-need-based awards were made. ***Average percent of need met:*** 47. ***Average financial aid package:*** $17,046. ***Average need-based loan:*** $3826. ***Average need-based gift aid:*** $13,674. ***Average non-need-based aid:*** $10,327. ***Average indebtedness upon graduation:*** $34,553. ***Financial aid deadline:*** 5/1.

APPLYING

Standardized Tests *Required:* SAT or ACT (for admission).

Options: electronic application, early admission, early action, deferred entrance.

Application fee: $40.

Required for some: essay or personal statement, high school transcript, 1 letter of recommendation. ***Recommended:*** interview.

Application deadlines: rolling (freshmen), rolling (transfers), 12/1 (early action).

Notification: continuous (freshmen), continuous (transfers), 12/15 (early action).

CONTACT

Mr. Marc Soevyn, Admissions Counselor, Molloy College, 1000 Hempstead Avenue, PO Box 5002, Rockville Centre, NY 11571-5002. *Phone:* 516-323-4000. *Toll-free phone:* 888-4MOLLOY. *E-mail:* admissions@molloy.edu.

See below for display ad and page 1084 for the College Close-Up.

Monroe College

Bronx, New York

http://www.monroecollege.edu/

CONTACT
Monroe College, 2501 Jerome Avenue, Bronx, NY 10468. *Phone:* 718-933-6700. *Toll-free phone:* 800-55MONROE.

Mount Saint Mary College

Newburgh, New York

http://www.msmc.edu/

- **Independent** comprehensive, founded 1960
- **Suburban** 86-acre campus with easy access to New York City
- **Endowment** $84.2 million
- **Coed** 1,881 undergraduate students, 85% full-time, 72% women, 28% men
- **Moderately difficult** entrance level, 94% of applicants were admitted

UNDERGRAD STUDENTS
1,596 full-time, 285 part-time. Students come from 15 states and territories; 12% are from out of state; 8% Black or African American, non-Hispanic/Latino; 18% Hispanic/Latino; 2% Asian, non-Hispanic/Latino; 0.4% American Indian or Alaska Native, non-Hispanic/Latino; 1% Two or more races, non-Hispanic/Latino; 14% Race/ethnicity unknown; 0.3% international; 8% transferred in; 53% live on campus.

Freshmen:
Admission: 3,249 applied, 3,048 admitted, 339 enrolled. ***Average high school GPA:*** 3.2. ***Test scores:*** SAT evidence-based reading and writing scores over 500: 74%; SAT math scores over 500: 69%; ACT scores over 18: 85%; SAT evidence-based reading and writing scores over 600: 17%; SAT math scores over 600: 16%; ACT scores over 24: 30%; SAT evidence-based reading and writing scores over 700: 1%; SAT math scores over 700: 2%; ACT scores over 30: 2%.

Retention: 80% of full-time freshmen returned.

FACULTY
Total: 251, 34% full-time, 40% with terminal degrees.

Student/faculty ratio: 13:1.

ACADEMICS
Calendar: semesters. *Degrees:* certificates, bachelor's, master's, and post-master's certificates.

Special study options: academic remediation for entering students, accelerated degree program, adult/continuing education programs, advanced placement credit, cooperative education, distance learning, double majors, freshman honors college, honors programs, independent study, internships, off-campus study, part-time degree program, services for LD students, student-designed majors, study abroad, summer session for credit. ***ROTC:*** Army (c).

Unusual degree programs: 3-2 business administration; nursing; publishing, counseling with Pace University.

Computers: 470 computers/terminals are available on campus for general student use. Students can access the following: campus intranet, computer help desk, free student e-mail accounts, online (class) grades, online (class) registration, online (class) schedules. Campuswide network is available. 100% of college-owned or -operated housing units are wired for high-speed Internet access. Wireless service is available via entire campus.

Library: Kaplan Family Library and Learning Center. *Books:* 74,074 (physical), 5,894 (digital/electronic); *Serial titles:* 188 (physical), 78,175 (digital/electronic); *Databases:* 91. Students can reserve study rooms.

STUDENT LIFE
Housing options: on-campus residence required through junior year; coed, men-only, women-only, special housing for students with disabilities. Campus housing is university owned. Freshman campus housing is guaranteed.

Activities and organizations: drama/theater group, student-run newspaper, radio station, choral group, Black Student Union, Student Nurses' Association, Love your Melon, Knight Moves, Habitat for Humanity.

Athletics Member NCAA. All Division III. ***Intercollegiate sports:*** baseball M, basketball M/W, cheerleading W, cross-country running M/W, golf M, lacrosse M/W, soccer M/W, softball W, swimming and diving M/W, tennis M/W, track and field M/W, volleyball W. ***Intramural sports:*** basketball M/W, bowling M/W, football M, soccer M/W, softball M/W, swimming and diving M/W, table tennis M/W, volleyball M/W.

Campus security: 24-hour emergency response devices and patrols, student patrols, late-night transport/escort service, controlled dormitory access, monitored surveillance cameras in all residence halls.

Student services: health clinic, personal/psychological counseling.

COSTS & FINANCIAL AID
Costs (2020–21) ***Comprehensive fee:*** $51,070 includes full-time tuition ($33,126), mandatory fees ($1286), and room and board ($16,658). Full-time tuition and fees vary according to class time, course load, location, and program. Part-time tuition: $1105 per credit. Part-time tuition and fees vary according to class time, course load, location, and program. ***Required fees:*** $190 per year part-time. ***College room only:*** $9650. Room and board charges vary according to board plan and housing facility. ***Payment plan:*** installment. ***Waivers:*** employees or children of employees.

Financial Aid Of all full-time matriculated undergraduates who enrolled in 2019, 1,430 applied for aid, 1,246 were judged to have need, 231 had their need fully met. 295 Federal Work-Study jobs (averaging $1452). In 2019, 267 non-need-based awards were made. ***Average percent of need met:*** 68. ***Average financial aid package:*** $22,634. ***Average need-based loan:*** $5164. ***Average need-based gift aid:*** $17,684. ***Average non-need-based aid:*** $14,095. ***Average indebtedness upon graduation:*** $28,519.

APPLYING
Standardized Tests *Required:* SAT or ACT (for admission).

Options: electronic application, early admission, deferred entrance.

Application fee: $45.

Required: essay or personal statement, high school transcript. ***Required for some:*** 2 letters of recommendation, interview. ***Recommended:*** minimum 3.0 GPA, 2 letters of recommendation.

Application deadlines: 8/15 (freshmen), rolling (transfers).

Notification: continuous (freshmen), continuous (transfers).

CONTACT
Ms. Eileen Bardney, Director of Admissions, Mount Saint Mary College, 330 Powell Avenue, Newburgh, NY 12550. *Phone:* 845-569-3254. *Toll-free phone:* 888-937-6762. *Fax:* 845-569-3438. *E-mail:* eileen.bardney@msmc.edu.

Nazareth College of Rochester

Rochester, New York

http://www.naz.edu/

- **Independent** comprehensive, founded 1924
- **Suburban** 150-acre campus
- **Coed** 2,283 undergraduate students, 95% full-time, 73% women, 27% men
- 64% of applicants were admitted

UNDERGRAD STUDENTS
2,180 full-time, 103 part-time. 12% are from out of state; 5% Black or African American, non-Hispanic/Latino; 6% Hispanic/Latino; 3% Asian, non-Hispanic/Latino; 0.2% American Indian or Alaska Native, non-Hispanic/Latino; 3% Two or more races, non-Hispanic/Latino; 4% Race/ethnicity unknown; 1% international; 54% live on campus.

Freshmen:
Admission: 4,477 applied, 2,887 admitted, 516 enrolled. ***Average high school GPA:*** ####. ***Test scores:*** ACT scores over 18: 98%; ACT scores over 24: 68%; ACT scores over 30: 14%.

FACULTY
Total: 513, 35% full-time, 44% with terminal degrees.

Student/faculty ratio: 9:1.

ACADEMICS
Calendar: semesters. *Degrees:* bachelor's, master's, doctoral, post-master's, and postbachelor's certificates.

Special study options: academic remediation for entering students, advanced placement credit, cooperative education, double majors, English as a second language, honors programs, independent study, internships, off-campus study, part-time degree program, services for LD students, study abroad, summer session for credit. ***ROTC:*** Army (c), Air Force (c).

Computers: Students can access the following: computer help desk, free student e-mail accounts, online (class) grades, online (class) registration, online (class) schedules. Campuswide network is available. Wireless service is available via entire campus.

Library: Lorette Wilmot Library. Students can reserve study rooms.

STUDENT LIFE

Housing options: on-campus residence required through sophomore year; coed, special housing for students with disabilities. Campus housing is university owned. Freshman campus housing is guaranteed.

Activities and organizations: drama/theater group, student-run newspaper, radio station, choral group, Campus Activities Board, Center for Spirituality, Physical Therapy Club, Diversity Council, Intramurals.

Athletics Member NCAA. All Division III except golf (Division II). ***Intercollegiate sports:*** basketball M/W, crew M(c)/W, cross-country running M/W, equestrian sports M/W, field hockey W, golf M/W, ice hockey M/W, lacrosse M/W, rugby M, soccer M/W, softball W, swimming and diving M/W, tennis M/W, track and field M/W, volleyball M/W. ***Intramural sports:*** basketball M/W, rowing M, skiing (downhill) M/W, soccer M/W, ultimate Frisbee M/W, volleyball M/W.

Campus security: 24-hour emergency response devices and patrols, late-night transport/escort service, controlled dormitory access, security beeper, lighted pathways, alert system.

Student services: health clinic, personal/psychological counseling, veterans affairs office.

COSTS & FINANCIAL AID

Costs (2019–20) ***Comprehensive fee:*** $49,646 includes full-time tuition ($33,836), mandatory fees ($1580), and room and board ($14,230). Full-time tuition and fees vary according to course load and program. Part-time tuition: $805 per credit hour. Part-time tuition and fees vary according to course load and program. ***Required fees:*** $25 per term part-time. ***Room and board:*** Room and board charges vary according to board plan and housing facility. ***Payment plan:*** installment. ***Waivers:*** employees or children of employees.

Financial Aid Of all full-time matriculated undergraduates who enrolled in 2019, 2,010 applied for aid, 1,784 were judged to have need, 659 had their need fully met. 1,120 Federal Work-Study jobs (averaging $2061). In 2019, 392 non-need-based awards were made. ***Average percent of need met:*** 82. ***Average financial aid package:*** $28,616. ***Average need-based loan:*** $4389. ***Average need-based gift aid:*** $18,635. ***Average non-need-based aid:*** $19,707. ***Average indebtedness upon graduation:*** $49,827.

APPLYING

Standardized Tests *Required for some:* SAT or ACT (for admission), Student can submit ACT or SAT..

Options: electronic application, early admission, early decision, deferred entrance.

Application fee: $45.

Required: essay or personal statement, high school transcript, 1 letter of recommendation. ***Required for some:*** audition/portfolio review.

Application deadlines: 2/1 (freshmen), rolling (transfers).

Early decision deadline: 11/15 (for plan 1), 1/10 (for plan 2).

Notification: continuous until 3/1 (freshmen), continuous (transfers), 12/15 (early decision plan 1), 1/25 (early decision plan 2).

CONTACT

Nazareth College of Rochester, 4245 East Avenue, Rochester, NY 14618. *Phone:* 585-389-2830. *Toll-free phone:* 800-462-3944.

The New School College of Performing Arts

New York, New York

http://www.newschool.edu/performing-arts/

- **Independent** comprehensive, part of The New School
- **Urban** campus with easy access to New York City
- **Endowment** $322.3 million
- **Coed** 609 undergraduate students, 98% full-time, 48% women, 52% men
- **Moderately difficult** entrance level, 49% of applicants were admitted

UNDERGRAD STUDENTS

597 full-time, 12 part-time. 78% are from out of state; 7% Black or African American, non-Hispanic/Latino; 9% Hispanic/Latino; 5% Asian, non-Hispanic/Latino; 0.2% Native Hawaiian or other Pacific Islander, non-Hispanic/Latino; 5% Two or more races, non-Hispanic/Latino; 5% Race/ethnicity unknown; 29% international; 8% transferred in; 14% live on campus.

Freshmen:

Admission: 1,279 applied, 632 admitted, 135 enrolled. ***Average high school GPA:*** 3.3. ***Test scores:*** SAT evidence-based reading and writing scores over 500: 97%; SAT math scores over 500: 96%; ACT scores over 18: 100%; SAT evidence-based reading and writing scores over 600: 78%; SAT math scores over 600: 52%; ACT scores over 24: 79%; SAT evidence-based reading and writing scores over 700: 37%; SAT math scores over 700: 15%; ACT scores over 30: 43%.

Retention: 76% of full-time freshmen returned.

FACULTY

Total: 373, 4% full-time, 3% with terminal degrees.

Student/faculty ratio: 7:1.

ACADEMICS

Calendar: semesters. *Degrees:* diplomas, bachelor's, and master's.

Special study options: academic remediation for entering students, accelerated degree program, distance learning, double majors, English as a second language, independent study, internships, off-campus study, part-time degree program, services for LD students, student-designed majors, study abroad, summer session for credit.

Computers: 717 computers/terminals are available on campus for general student use. Students can access the following: campus intranet, computer help desk, free student e-mail accounts, online (class) grades, online (class) registration, online (class) schedules. Campuswide network is available. 100% of college-owned or -operated housing units are wired for high-speed Internet access. Wireless service is available via entire campus.

Library: New School Libraries & Archives plus 3 others. *Books:* 215,937 (physical), 840,933 (digital/electronic); *Serial titles:* 2,265 (physical), 113,452 (digital/electronic); *Databases:* 376. Weekly public service hours: 155; study areas open 24 hours, 5–7 days a week; students can reserve study rooms.

STUDENT LIFE

Housing options: coed, special housing for students with disabilities. Campus housing is university owned. Freshman applicants given priority for college housing.

Activities and organizations: drama/theater group, student-run newspaper, choral group.

Athletics ***Intramural sports:*** basketball M/W, cross-country running M/W, soccer M/W, tennis M/W.

Campus security: 24-hour emergency response devices, controlled dormitory access, 24-hour desk attendants in residence halls.

Student services: health clinic, personal/psychological counseling, veterans affairs office.

FINANCIAL AID

Financial Aid Of all full-time matriculated undergraduates who enrolled in 2017, 303 applied for aid, 267 were judged to have need, 21 had their need fully met. 29 Federal Work-Study jobs (averaging $3394). In 2017, 262 non-need-based awards were made. ***Average percent of need met:*** 47. ***Average financial aid package:*** $21,605. ***Average need-based loan:*** $4306. ***Average need-based gift aid:*** $7780. ***Average non-need-based aid:*** $17,827. ***Average indebtedness upon graduation:*** $281,459. ***Financial aid deadline:*** 2/1.

APPLYING

Options: electronic application, early action, deferred entrance.

Application fee: $50.

Required: essay or personal statement, high school transcript, 1 letter of recommendation. ***Required for some:*** interview, prescreening, live audition/interview. ***Recommended:*** minimum 3.0 GPA.

Application deadlines: 1/15 (freshmen), 4/1 (transfers), 11/1 (early action).

Notification: continuous until 3/15 (freshmen), continuous until 3/15 (transfers), 12/20 (early action).

CONTACT

Ms. Amanda Hosking, Director of Admission, The New School College of Performing Arts, 79 Fifth Avenue, New York, NY 10003. *Phone:* 212-229-5150 Ext. 4805. *Toll-free phone:* 800-292-3040. *E-mail:* hoskinga@newschool.edu.

The New School for Public Engagement

New York, New York

http://www.newschool.edu/public-engagement/

CONTACT

Ms. Elizabeth Puleio, Associate Director of Admission, The New School for Public Engagement, 72 Fifth Avenue, New York, NY 10011. *Phone:* 212-229-5150 Ext. 3789. *Toll-free phone:* 800-292-3040. *E-mail:* puleioe@newschool.edu.

New York City College of Technology of the City University of New York

Brooklyn, New York

http://www.citytech.cuny.edu/

- **State and locally supported** 4-year, founded 1946, part of City University of New York System
- **Urban** campus with easy access to New York City
- **Endowment** $17.1 million
- **Coed** 27,236 undergraduate students, 76% full-time, 28% women, 72% men
- **Noncompetitive** entrance level, 88% of applicants were admitted

UNDERGRAD STUDENTS

20,772 full-time, 6,464 part-time. Students come from 10 states and territories; 101 other countries; 3% are from out of state; 28% Black or African American, non-Hispanic/Latino; 35% Hispanic/Latino; 20% Asian, non-Hispanic/Latino; 0.3% Native Hawaiian or other Pacific Islander, non-Hispanic/Latino; 0.4% American Indian or Alaska Native, non-Hispanic/Latino; 2% Two or more races, non-Hispanic/Latino; 4% international.

Freshmen:

Admission: 21,546 applied, 18,896 admitted, 3,466 enrolled.

Retention: 68% of full-time freshmen returned.

FACULTY

Total: 2,375, 27% full-time, 3% with terminal degrees.

ACADEMICS

Calendar: semesters. *Degrees:* certificates, associate, and bachelor's.

Special study options: academic remediation for entering students, accelerated degree program, adult/continuing education programs, advanced placement credit, distance learning, English as a second language, freshman honors college, honors programs, independent study, internships, off-campus study, part-time degree program, services for LD students, student-designed majors, study abroad, summer session for credit.

Computers: Students can access the following: campus intranet, computer help desk, free student e-mail accounts, online (class) grades, online (class) registration, online (class) schedules. Campuswide network is available. Wireless service is available via entire campus.

Library: Ursula C. Schwerin Library. *Books:* 116,667 (physical), 487,902 (digital/electronic); *Serial titles:* 1,650 (physical), 95,329 (digital/electronic); *Databases:* 146. Weekly public service hours: 75; students can reserve study rooms.

STUDENT LIFE

Housing options: college housing not available.

Activities and organizations: drama/theater group, student-run newspaper, Art and Design Club, BMI Club, International Business Organization, SADHA (Dental Hygienists Club), National Society of Collegiate Scholars Club.

Campus security: 24-hour emergency response devices and patrols.

Student services: health clinic, personal/psychological counseling, women's center, veterans affairs office.

COSTS

Costs (2020–21) ***Tuition:*** area resident $6930 full-time, $305 per credit hour part-time; state resident $620 per credit hour part-time; nonresident $14,880 full-time, $620 per credit hour part-time. ***Required fees:*** $390 full-time.

APPLYING

Standardized Tests *Required for some:* SAT (for admission), ACT (for admission), SAT or ACT (for admission).

Options: electronic application, deferred entrance.

Application fee: $65.

Required: high school transcript.

Application deadlines: 2/1 (freshmen), 2/1 (transfers).

Notification: continuous until 2/1 (freshmen), 4/1 (transfers).

CONTACT

Alexis Chaconis, Director of Admissions, New York City College of Technology of the City University of New York, 300 Jay Street, Brooklyn, NY 11201-2983. *Phone:* 718-260-5500. *E-mail:* achaconis@citytech.cuny.edu.

New York College of Health Professions

Syosset, New York

http://www.nycollege.edu/

- **Independent** comprehensive, founded 1981
- **Suburban** campus with easy access to New York City
- **Coed** 801 undergraduate students, 41% full-time, 76% women, 24% men
- **Moderately difficult** entrance level

UNDERGRAD STUDENTS

332 full-time, 469 part-time.

Freshmen:

Admission: 169 enrolled. ***Average high school GPA:*** 2.7.

FACULTY

Total: 93, 18% full-time.

Student/faculty ratio: 19:1.

ACADEMICS

Calendar: trimesters. *Degrees:* associate and master's.

Special study options: academic remediation for entering students, accelerated degree program, adult/continuing education programs, advanced placement credit, cooperative education, double majors, internships, part-time degree program, services for LD students, summer session for credit.

Computers: 3 computers/terminals are available on campus for general student use.

Library: James and Lenore Jacobson Library at the Syosset Campus.

STUDENT LIFE

Housing options: college housing not available.

Campus security: 24-hour emergency response devices and patrols, security guard evening and weekend hours.

Student services: health clinic.

FINANCIAL AID

Financial Aid Of all full-time matriculated undergraduates who enrolled in 2018, 15 Federal Work-Study jobs.

APPLYING

Options: electronic application, deferred entrance.

Application fee: $85.

Required: essay or personal statement, high school transcript, minimum 2.0 GPA, interview.

Application deadlines: rolling (freshmen), rolling (transfers).

Notification: continuous (freshmen), continuous (transfers).

CONTACT
New York College of Health Professions, 6801 Jericho Turnpike, Syosset, NY 11791-4413. *Toll-free phone:* 800-922-7337 Ext. 351.

New York Institute of Technology

Old Westbury, New York

http://www.nyit.edu/

- **Independent** comprehensive, founded 1955
- **Suburban** 215-acre campus with easy access to New York City
- **Endowment** $87.9 million
- **Coed** 3,694 undergraduate students, 91% full-time, 39% women, 61% men
- **Moderately difficult** entrance level, 68% of applicants were admitted

UNDERGRAD STUDENTS
3,357 full-time, 337 part-time. Students come from 39 states and territories; 71 other countries; 14% are from out of state; 10% Black or African American, non-Hispanic/Latino; 19% Hispanic/Latino; 19% Asian, non-Hispanic/Latino; 0.4% Native Hawaiian or other Pacific Islander, non-Hispanic/Latino; 0.3% American Indian or Alaska Native, non-Hispanic/Latino; 5% Two or more races, non-Hispanic/Latino; 6% Race/ethnicity unknown; 15% international; 6% transferred in; 15% live on campus.

Freshmen:
Admission: 11,848 applied, 8,033 admitted, 849 enrolled. ***Average high school GPA:*** 3.5. ***Test scores:*** SAT evidence-based reading and writing scores over 500: 89%; SAT math scores over 500: 94%; ACT scores over 18: 95%; SAT evidence-based reading and writing scores over 600: 42%; SAT math scores over 600: 51%; ACT scores over 24: 66%; SAT evidence-based reading and writing scores over 700: 5%; SAT math scores over 700: 16%; ACT scores over 30: 22%.

Retention: 81% of full-time freshmen returned.

FACULTY
Total: 1,016, 34% full-time, 32% with terminal degrees.

Student/faculty ratio: 12:1.

ACADEMICS
Calendar: semesters. *Degrees:* certificates, diplomas, associate, bachelor's, master's, doctoral, post-master's, and postbachelor's certificates.

Special study options: academic remediation for entering students, accelerated degree program, adult/continuing education programs, advanced placement credit, cooperative education, distance learning, double majors, English as a second language, honors programs, internships, off-campus study, part-time degree program, services for LD students, study abroad, summer session for credit. ***ROTC:*** Army (c), Air Force (c).

Unusual degree programs: 3-2 life sciences/osteopathic medicine, occupational therapy, physical therapy, physician assistant studies.

Computers: Students can access the following: computer help desk, free student e-mail accounts, online (class) grades, online (class) registration, online (class) schedules. Campuswide network is available. 100% of college-owned or -operated housing units are wired for high-speed Internet access. Wireless service is available via entire campus.

Library: George and Gertrude Wisser Memorial Library plus 3 others. *Books:* 75,647 (physical), 83,169 (digital/electronic); *Serial titles:* 2,421 (physical), 93,810 (digital/electronic). Weekly public service hours: 78; students can reserve study rooms.

STUDENT LIFE
Housing options: coed. Campus housing is university owned. Freshman campus housing is guaranteed.

Activities and organizations: student-run newspaper, television station, national fraternities, national sororities.

Athletics Member NCAA. All Division II. ***Intercollegiate sports:*** baseball M(s), basketball M(s)/W(s), cheerleading W(c), cross-country running M(s)/W(s), lacrosse M(s)/W(s), soccer M(s)/W(s), softball W(s). ***Intramural sports:*** basketball M/W, bowling M(c)/W(c), soccer M/W, ultimate Frisbee M(c)/W(c).

Campus security: 24-hour emergency response devices and patrols, late-night transport/escort service, controlled dormitory access.

Student services: health clinic, personal/psychological counseling, veterans affairs office.

COSTS & FINANCIAL AID
Costs (2020–21) ***Comprehensive fee:*** $54,050 includes full-time tuition ($38,060), mandatory fees ($1700), and room and board ($14,290). Full-time tuition and fees vary according to location and program. Part-time tuition: $1290 per credit. Part-time tuition and fees vary according to course load, location, and program. ***Required fees:*** $750 per term part-time. ***College room only:*** $9800. Room and board charges vary according to housing facility and location. ***Payment plan:*** installment. ***Waivers:*** senior citizens and employees or children of employees.

Financial Aid Of all full-time matriculated undergraduates who enrolled in 2018, 2,599 applied for aid, 2,362 were judged to have need. In 2018, 484 non-need-based awards were made. ***Average financial aid package:*** $27,482. ***Average need-based loan:*** $4147. ***Average need-based gift aid:*** $9575. ***Average non-need-based aid:*** $16,545.

APPLYING
Standardized Tests *Required:* SAT or ACT (for admission).

Options: electronic application, deferred entrance.

Application fee: $50.

Required: essay or personal statement, high school transcript, 2 letters of recommendation. ***Required for some:*** interview. ***Recommended:*** minimum 2.7 GPA.

Application deadlines: rolling (freshmen), rolling (transfers).

Notification: continuous (freshmen), continuous (transfers).

CONTACT
Ms. Marcelle Hicks, Senior Director, Undergraduate Admissions, New York Institute of Technology, Old Westbury, NY 11568. *Phone:* 516-686-1020. *Toll-free phone:* 800-345-NYIT. *E-mail:* admissions@nyit.edu.

New York School of Interior Design

New York, New York

http://www.nysid.edu/

CONTACT
Jaspreet Bains, Admissions Associate, New York School of Interior Design, 170 East 70th Street, New York, NY 10021-5110. *Phone:* 212-472-1500 Ext. 212. *Toll-free phone:* 800-336-9743 Ext. 205. *Fax:* 212-472-1867. *E-mail:* admissions@nysid.edu.

New York University

New York, New York

http://www.nyu.edu/

- **Independent** university, founded 1831
- **Urban** 230-acre campus with easy access to New York City
- **Endowment** $4.2 billion
- **Coed** 26,981 undergraduate students, 96% full-time, 58% women, 42% men
- **Very difficult** entrance level, 16% of applicants were admitted

UNDERGRAD STUDENTS
25,872 full-time, 1,109 part-time. Students come from 52 states and territories; 135 other countries; 67% are from out of state; 8% Black or African American, non-Hispanic/Latino; 16% Hispanic/Latino; 19% Asian, non-Hispanic/Latino; 0.1% Native Hawaiian or other Pacific Islander, non-Hispanic/Latino; 0.1% American Indian or Alaska Native, non-Hispanic/Latino; 4% Two or more races, non-Hispanic/Latino; 5% Race/ethnicity unknown; 22% international; 3% transferred in; 42% live on campus.

Freshmen:
Admission: 79,462 applied, 12,873 admitted, 5,752 enrolled. ***Average high school GPA:*** 3.7. ***Test scores:*** SAT evidence-based reading and writing scores over 500: 100%; SAT math scores over 500: 100%; ACT scores over 18: 100%; SAT evidence-based reading and writing scores over 600: 96%; SAT math scores over 600: 94%; ACT scores over 24: 98%; SAT evidence-based reading and writing scores over 700: 54%; SAT math scores over 700: 73%; ACT scores over 30: 80%.

Retention: 94% of full-time freshmen returned.

FACULTY
Total: 6,646, 45% full-time, 75% with terminal degrees.
Student/faculty ratio: 9:1.

ACADEMICS
Calendar: semesters. *Degrees:* certificates, diplomas, associate, bachelor's, master's, doctoral, post-master's, and postbachelor's certificates.

Special study options: accelerated degree program, adult/continuing education programs, advanced placement credit, cooperative education, distance learning, double majors, English as a second language, honors programs, independent study, internships, off-campus study, part-time degree program, services for LD students, student-designed majors, study abroad, summer session for credit. ***ROTC:*** Army (c), Air Force (c).

Unusual degree programs: 3-2 business administration with Stern School of Business; engineering with Tandon School of Engineering and College of Arts and Science; nursing with Rory Meyers College of Nursing; College of Arts and Science, Gallatin School of Individualized Study, Wagner Graduate School of Public Service.

Computers: Students can access the following: computer help desk, free student e-mail accounts, online (class) grades, online (class) registration, online (class) schedules. Campuswide network is available. 100% of college-owned or -operated housing units are wired for high-speed Internet access. Wireless service is available via entire campus.

Library: Elmer H. Bobst Library plus 10 others. *Books:* 351,463 (physical), 207,454 (digital/electronic); *Serial titles:* 51,854 (physical), 233,733 (digital/electronic); *Databases:* 1,269. Study areas open 24 hours, 5–7 days a week; students can reserve study rooms.

STUDENT LIFE
Housing options: coed, special housing for students with disabilities. Campus housing is university owned. Freshman campus housing is guaranteed.

Activities and organizations: drama/theater group, student-run newspaper, radio and television station, choral group, national fraternities, national sororities.

Athletics Member NCAA. All Division III. ***Intercollegiate sports:*** baseball M, basketball M/W, cross-country running M/W, fencing M/W, golf M/W, soccer M/W, softball W, swimming and diving M/W, tennis M/W, track and field M/W, volleyball M/W, wrestling M. ***Intramural sports:*** badminton M(c)/W(c), basketball M/W, bowling M/W, cheerleading M(c)/W(c), equestrian sports M(c)/W(c), football M/W, ice hockey M(c), lacrosse M(c)/W(c), racquetball M(c)/W(c), rowing M(c)/W(c), soccer M/W, softball M/W, squash M(c)/W(c), table tennis M(c)/W(c), triathlon M(c)/W(c), ultimate Frisbee M(c)/W(c), volleyball M/W, water polo M(c)/W(c).

Campus security: 24-hour emergency response devices and patrols, student patrols, late-night transport/escort service, controlled dormitory access.

Student services: health clinic, personal/psychological counseling, women's center, veterans affairs office.

COSTS & FINANCIAL AID
Costs (2019–20) ***Comprehensive fee:*** $71,992 includes full-time tuition ($50,684), mandatory fees ($2624), and room and board ($18,684). Full-time tuition and fees vary according to course load, program, and reciprocity agreements. Part-time tuition: $1493 per credit hour. Part-time tuition and fees vary according to program. ***Required fees:*** $498 per term part-time. ***College room only:*** $13,548. Room and board charges vary according to board plan, housing facility, and location. ***Payment plans:*** tuition prepayment, installment, deferred payment. ***Waivers:*** employees or children of employees.

Financial Aid Of all full-time matriculated undergraduates who enrolled in 2018, 15,301 applied for aid, 11,496 were judged to have need, 1,331 had their need fully met. In 2018, 1078 non-need-based awards were made. ***Average percent of need met:*** 65. ***Average financial aid package:*** $37,841. ***Average need-based loan:*** $4412. ***Average need-based gift aid:*** $32,933. ***Average non-need-based aid:*** $5522. ***Average indebtedness upon graduation:*** $29,242. ***Financial aid deadline:*** 2/15.

APPLYING
Standardized Tests *Required for some:* SAT and SAT Subject Tests or ACT (for admission).

Options: electronic application, early admission, early decision, deferred entrance.

Application fee: $80.

Required: essay or personal statement, high school transcript, 1 letter of recommendation. ***Required for some:*** audition or a portfolio for some specific programs.

Application deadlines: 1/1 (freshmen), 4/1 (transfers).

Early decision deadline: 11/1 (for plan 1), 1/1 (for plan 2).

Notification: 4/1 (freshmen), 5/15 (transfers), 12/15 (early decision plan 1), 2/15 (early decision plan 2).

CONTACT
Kristy Materasso, Undergraduate Admissions Processing Center, New York University, 383 Lafayette Street, New York, NY 10003. *Phone:* 212-998-4500. *Fax:* 212-995-4902. *E-mail:* admissions@nyu.edu.

Niagara University

Niagara Falls, New York

http://www.niagara.edu/

- **Independent comprehensive**, founded 1856, affiliated with Roman Catholic Church
- **Suburban** 160-acre campus with easy access to Buffalo, NY and Toronto, Ontario (Canada)
- **Endowment** $97.2 million
- **Coed** 2,809 undergraduate students, 96% full-time, 64% women, 36% men
- **Moderately difficult** entrance level, 89% of applicants were admitted

UNDERGRAD STUDENTS
2,692 full-time, 117 part-time. Students come from 38 states and territories; 41 other countries; 10% are from out of state; 5% Black or African American, non-Hispanic/Latino; 5% Hispanic/Latino; 1% Asian, non-Hispanic/Latino; 0.1% Native Hawaiian or other Pacific Islander, non-Hispanic/Latino; 0.6% American Indian or Alaska Native, non-Hispanic/Latino; 3% Two or more races, non-Hispanic/Latino; 3% Race/ethnicity unknown; 17% international; 5% transferred in; 42% live on campus.

Freshmen:
Admission: 3,660 applied, 3,265 admitted, 626 enrolled. ***Average high school GPA:*** 3.4. ***Test scores:*** SAT evidence-based reading and writing scores over 500: 79%; SAT math scores over 500: 82%; ACT scores over 18: 90%; SAT evidence-based reading and writing scores over 600: 31%; SAT math scores over 600: 36%; ACT scores over 24: 50%; SAT evidence-based reading and writing scores over 700: 4%; SAT math scores over 700: 5%; ACT scores over 30: 11%.

Retention: 87% of full-time freshmen returned.

FACULTY
Total: 411, 38% full-time, 47% with terminal degrees.
Student/faculty ratio: 11:1.

ACADEMICS
Calendar: semesters. *Degrees:* certificates, associate, bachelor's, master's, doctoral, post-master's, and postbachelor's certificates.

Special study options: academic remediation for entering students, accelerated degree program, advanced placement credit, cooperative education, distance learning, double majors, English as a second language, honors programs, independent study, internships, off-campus study, services for LD students, student-designed majors, study abroad, summer session for credit. ***ROTC:*** Army (b).

Computers: 81 computers/terminals are available on campus for general student use. Students can access the following: campus intranet, computer help desk, free student e-mail accounts, online (class) grades, online (class) registration, online (class) schedules. Campuswide network is available. 100% of college-owned or -operated housing units are wired for high-speed Internet access. Wireless service is available via entire campus.

Library: Our Lady of Angels Library. *Books:* 138,988 (physical), 559,057 (digital/electronic); *Serial titles:* 5 (physical), 40,125 (digital/electronic); *Databases:* 114. Weekly public service hours: 107; study areas open 24 hours, 5–7 days a week; students can reserve study rooms.

STUDENT LIFE

Housing options: on-campus residence required through sophomore year; coed, special housing for students with disabilities. Campus housing is university owned. Freshman campus housing is guaranteed.

Activities and organizations: drama/theater group, student-run newspaper, radio station, choral group, Student Nursing Association, NU Players (theatre), Camp Courage Crew, The Disney Club, Sorority, national fraternities, national sororities.

Athletics Member NCAA. All Division I. ***Intercollegiate sports:*** baseball M(s), basketball M(s)/W(s), cross-country running M(s)/W(s), golf M(s)/W(s), ice hockey M(s), lacrosse W(s), soccer M(s)/W(s), softball W(s), swimming and diving M(s)/W(s), tennis M(s)/W(s), track and field W(s), volleyball W(s). ***Intramural sports:*** badminton M(c)/W(c), baseball M(c), basketball M(c)/W(c), bowling M(c)/W(c), field hockey M(c)/W(c), golf M(c), ice hockey M(c), lacrosse M(c)/W(c), racquetball M/W, rugby M(c)/W(c), soccer M(c)/W(c), softball M/W(c), tennis M/W, volleyball M(c)/W(c), weight lifting M(c)/W(c), wrestling M(c).

Campus security: 24-hour emergency response devices and patrols, late-night transport/escort service, controlled dormitory access, 24-hour escort service, Emergency Notification System.

Student services: health clinic, personal/psychological counseling, veterans affairs office.

COSTS & FINANCIAL AID

Costs (2020–21) ***One-time required fee:*** $200. ***Comprehensive fee:*** $47,090 includes full-time tuition ($33,700), mandatory fees ($1540), and room and board ($11,850). Full-time tuition and fees vary according to program. Part-time tuition: $1125 per credit hour. Part-time tuition and fees vary according to program. ***Room and board:*** Room and board charges vary according to housing facility. ***Payment plans:*** installment, deferred payment. ***Waivers:*** employees or children of employees.

Financial Aid Of all full-time matriculated undergraduates who enrolled in 2019, 2,027 applied for aid, 1,812 were judged to have need, 897 had their need fully met. In 2019, 468 non-need-based awards were made. ***Average percent of need met:*** 82. ***Average financial aid package:*** $28,001. ***Average need-based loan:*** $4384. ***Average need-based gift aid:*** $24,427. ***Average non-need-based aid:*** $16,349. ***Average indebtedness upon graduation:*** $34,046.

APPLYING

Standardized Tests *Required for some:* SAT or ACT (for admission).

Options: electronic application, early action, deferred entrance.

Required: essay or personal statement, high school transcript, 1 letter of recommendation. ***Recommended:*** interview.

Application deadlines: 8/1 (freshmen), 8/15 (transfers).

Notification: continuous (freshmen), continuous (transfers).

CONTACT

Christine McDermott, Director of First Year Enrollment, Niagara University, 5795 Lewiston Road, Gacioch Center, Niagara University, NY 14109. *Phone:* 716-286-8715. *Toll-free phone:* 800-462-2111. *Fax:* 716-286-8733. *E-mail:* admissions@niagara.edu.

Nyack College

New York, New York

http://www.nyack.edu/

- **Independent** comprehensive, founded 1882, affiliated with The Christian and Missionary Alliance
- **Urban** campus with easy access to New York City
- **Coed** 1,028 undergraduate students, 82% full-time, 55% women, 45% men
- **Minimally difficult** entrance level, 98% of applicants were admitted

UNDERGRAD STUDENTS

840 full-time, 188 part-time. Students come from 37 states and territories; 36 other countries; 28% are from out of state; 30% Black or African American, non-Hispanic/Latino; 33% Hispanic/Latino; 6% Asian, non-Hispanic/Latino; 0.3% Native Hawaiian or other Pacific Islander, non-Hispanic/Latino; 0.9% American Indian or Alaska Native, non-Hispanic/Latino; 3% Two or more races, non-Hispanic/Latino; 3% Race/ethnicity unknown; 8% international; 11% transferred in.

Freshmen:

Admission: 223 applied, 218 admitted, 128 enrolled. ***Average high school GPA:*** 2.8. ***Test scores:*** SAT evidence-based reading and writing scores over 500: 48%; SAT math scores over 500: 40%; ACT scores over 18: 56%; SAT evidence-based reading and writing scores over 600: 11%; SAT math scores over 600: 7%; ACT scores over 24: 22%; SAT evidence-based reading and writing scores over 700: 1%; SAT math scores over 700: 3%.

Retention: 64% of full-time freshmen returned.

FACULTY

Total: 221, 28% full-time, 48% with terminal degrees.

Student/faculty ratio: 12:1.

ACADEMICS

Calendar: semesters. *Degrees:* associate, bachelor's, master's, and doctoral.

Special study options: academic remediation for entering students, adult/continuing education programs, advanced placement credit, distance learning, double majors, honors programs, independent study, internships, off-campus study, part-time degree program, services for LD students, student-designed majors, study abroad, summer session for credit.

Unusual degree programs: 3-2 childhood special education.

Computers: 70 computers/terminals are available on campus for general student use. Students can access the following: computer help desk, free student e-mail accounts, online (class) grades, online (class) registration, online (class) schedules, Wireless network throughout the entire campus. Campuswide network is available. 100% of college-owned or -operated housing units are wired for high-speed Internet access. Wireless service is available via entire campus.

Library: Eastman. Students can reserve study rooms.

STUDENT LIFE

Housing options: men-only, women-only. Campus housing is university owned. Freshman campus housing is guaranteed.

Activities and organizations: drama/theater group, choral group, Students Against Hunger, Social Work Organization, Student Worship Teams, Business Club, Psychology Club.

Athletics Member NCAA. All Division II. ***Intercollegiate sports:*** baseball M(s), basketball M(s)/W(s), cross-country running M(s)/W(s), lacrosse W(s), soccer M(s)/W(s), softball W(s), volleyball W(s).

Campus security: 24-hour emergency response devices and patrols.

Student services: personal/psychological counseling.

COSTS & FINANCIAL AID

Costs (2020–21) ***One-time required fee:*** $100. ***Comprehensive fee:*** $35,500 includes full-time tuition ($25,000), mandatory fees ($500), and room and board ($10,000). Part-time tuition: $1040 per credit hour. ***Payment plan:*** installment. ***Waivers:*** employees or children of employees.

Financial Aid Of all full-time matriculated undergraduates who enrolled in 2017, 176 Federal Work-Study jobs (averaging $1028). 239 state and other part-time jobs (averaging $4233). ***Average indebtedness upon graduation:*** $28,926.

APPLYING

Standardized Tests *Required for some:* SAT or ACT (for admission), SAT and SAT Subject Tests or ACT (for admission).

Options: electronic application, deferred entrance.

Application fee: $25.

Required: essay or personal statement, high school transcript, minimum 2.0 GPA, 1 letter of recommendation, signed statement of faith and community life form. ***Required for some:*** interview.

Application deadlines: rolling (freshmen), rolling (transfers).

Notification: continuous (freshmen), continuous (transfers).

CONTACT

Nyack College, 2 Washington Street, New York, NY 10004. *Phone:* 646-378-6101. *Toll-free phone:* 800-33-NYACK. *Fax:* 212-343-2668. *E-mail:* admissions@nyack.edu.

Ohr Hameir Theological Seminary

Cortlandt Manor, New York

http://www.ohrhameir.com/

CONTACT

Director of Admissions, Ohr Hameir Theological Seminary, 141 Furnace Woods Road, Cortlandt Manor, NY 10567. *Phone:* 914-736-1500.

Ohr Somayach/Joseph Tanenbaum Educational Center

Monsey, New York

http://ohr.edu/

CONTACT

Ohr Somayach/Joseph Tanenbaum Educational Center, PO Box 334, 244 Route 306, Monsey, NY 10952-0334. *Phone:* 845-425-1370 Ext. 22.

Pace University

New York, New York

http://www.pace.edu/nyc

- **Independent** university, founded 1906
- **Urban** campus with easy access to New York City
- **Endowment** $169.9 million
- **Coed**
- **Moderately difficult** entrance level

FACULTY

Student/faculty ratio: 16:1.

ACADEMICS

Calendar: semesters. *Degrees:* certificates, associate, bachelor's, master's, doctoral, post-master's, and postbachelor's certificates.

Library: Henry Birnbaum Library. *Books:* 382,858 (physical), 224,418 (digital/electronic); *Serial titles:* 73 (physical), 576,860 (digital/electronic); *Databases:* 172. Weekly public service hours: 93; students can reserve study rooms.

STUDENT LIFE

Housing options: coed, special housing for students with disabilities. Campus housing is university owned and leased by the school. Freshman campus housing is guaranteed.

Activities and organizations: drama/theater group, student-run newspaper, radio and television station, choral group, Kappa Delta, Sigma Delta Tau, Beta Alpha Psi, Profashionals, Programming and Campus Entertainment Board, national fraternities, national sororities.

Athletics Member NCAA. All Division II.

Campus security: 24-hour emergency response devices and patrols, late-night transport/escort service, controlled dormitory access.

Student services: health clinic, personal/psychological counseling, veterans affairs office.

COSTS & FINANCIAL AID

Costs (2019–20) ***Comprehensive fee:*** $63,809 includes full-time tuition ($43,624), mandatory fees ($1656), and room and board ($18,529). Part-time tuition: $1251 per credit hour.

Financial Aid Of all full-time matriculated undergraduates who enrolled in 2018, 3,838 applied for aid, 3,442 were judged to have need, 462 had their need fully met. In 2018, 1533 non-need-based awards were made. ***Average percent of need met:*** 68. ***Average financial aid package:*** $31,957. ***Average need-based loan:*** $4247. ***Average need-based gift aid:*** $27,919. ***Average non-need-based aid:*** $20,951. ***Average indebtedness upon graduation:*** $36,113.

APPLYING

Standardized Tests *Required for some:* SAT or ACT (for admission).

Options: electronic application, early decision, early action, deferred entrance.

Application fee: $50.

Required: essay or personal statement, high school transcript, 2 letters of recommendation. ***Recommended:*** interview.

CONTACT

Mr. Andre Cordon, Dean of Admissions, Pace University, One Pace Plaza, 163 William Street, New York, NY 10038. *Phone:* 212-346-1794. *Toll-*

free phone: 800-874-7223. *Fax:* 212-346-1821. *E-mail:* acordon@pace.edu.

See below for display ad and page 1096 for the College Close-Up.

Pace University, Pleasantville Campus

Pleasantville, New York

http://www.pace.edu/westchester

- **Independent** university, founded 1906
- **Suburban** campus with easy access to New York City
- **Endowment** $169.9 million
- **Coed** 2,606 undergraduate students, 90% full-time, 60% women, 40% men
- **Moderately difficult** entrance level, 79% of applicants were admitted

UNDERGRAD STUDENTS

2,353 full-time, 253 part-time. 27% are from out of state; 13% Black or African American, non-Hispanic/Latino; 17% Hispanic/Latino; 5% Asian, non-Hispanic/Latino; 0.4% American Indian or Alaska Native, non-Hispanic/Latino; 4% Two or more races, non-Hispanic/Latino; 6% Race/ethnicity unknown; 2% international; 6% transferred in; 56% live on campus.

Freshmen:

Admission: 4,579 applied, 3,618 admitted, 522 enrolled. ***Average high school GPA:*** 3.3. ***Test scores:*** SAT evidence-based reading and writing scores over 500: 93%; SAT math scores over 500: 89%; ACT scores over 18: 98%; SAT evidence-based reading and writing scores over 600: 31%; SAT math scores over 600: 30%; ACT scores over 24: 44%; SAT evidence-based reading and writing scores over 700: 2%; SAT math scores over 700: 3%; ACT scores over 30: 4%.

Retention: 85% of full-time freshmen returned.

FACULTY

Total: 467, 33% full-time, 46% with terminal degrees.

Student/faculty ratio: 11:1.

ACADEMICS

Calendar: semesters. *Degrees:* certificates, diplomas, associate, bachelor's, master's, doctoral, post-master's, and postbachelor's certificates.

Special study options: accelerated degree program, adult/continuing education programs, advanced placement credit, cooperative education, distance learning, double majors, English as a second language, freshman honors college, honors programs, independent study, internships, part-time degree program, services for LD students, study abroad, summer session for credit. ***ROTC:*** Army (c), Air Force (c).

Unusual degree programs: 3-2 business administration; engineering with Manhattan College, Rensselaer Polytechnic Institute; occupational therapy with Columbia University, optometry with SUNY College of Optometry, physical therapy with New York Medical College, podiatry with the New York College of Podiatric Medicine.

Computers: 132 computers/terminals are available on campus for general student use. Students can access the following: computer help desk, free student e-mail accounts, online (class) grades, online (class) registration, online (class) schedules, administrative functions (tuition, student records, financial aid, health insurance waiver). Campuswide network is available. 100% of college-owned or -operated housing units are wired for high-speed Internet access. Wireless service is available via entire campus.

Library: Edward and Doris Mortola Library. *Books:* 167,456 (physical), 224,418 (digital/electronic); *Serial titles:* 34 (physical), 576,860 (digital/electronic); *Databases:* 172. Weekly public service hours: 113; students can reserve study rooms.

STUDENT LIFE

Housing options: coed. Campus housing is university owned. Freshman campus housing is guaranteed.

Activities and organizations: drama/theater group, student-run newspaper, radio and television station, choral group, Lubin Business Association, National Student Nurses Association, Future Leaders in Healthcare, Black Student Union, Accounting Society, national fraternities, national sororities.

Athletics Member NCAA. All Division II. ***Intercollegiate sports:*** baseball M(s), basketball M(s)/W(s), cross-country running M(s)/W(s), field hockey W(s), football M(s), lacrosse M(s)/W(s), soccer W(s), softball W(s), swimming and diving M(s)/W(s), volleyball W(s). ***Intramural sports:*** badminton M/W, basketball M/W, soccer M/W, softball M/W, tennis M/W, ultimate Frisbee M/W, volleyball M/W.

Campus security: 24-hour emergency response devices and patrols, late-night transport/escort service, controlled dormitory access.

Student services: health clinic, personal/psychological counseling, veterans affairs office.

FINANCIAL AID

Financial Aid Of all full-time matriculated undergraduates who enrolled in 2018, 2,102 applied for aid, 1,938 were judged to have need, 361 had their need fully met. In 2018, 400 non-need-based awards were made. ***Average percent of need met:*** 78. ***Average financial aid package:*** $36,894. ***Average need-based loan:*** $4296. ***Average need-based gift aid:*** $32,352. ***Average non-need-based aid:*** $23,976. ***Average indebtedness upon graduation:*** $36,302.

APPLYING

Standardized Tests *Required for some:* SAT or ACT (for admission).

Options: electronic application, early decision, early action, deferred entrance.

Application fee: $50.

Required: essay or personal statement, high school transcript, 2 letters of recommendation. ***Recommended:*** interview.

Application deadlines: 2/15 (freshmen), rolling (transfers).

Notification: continuous (freshmen), continuous (transfers).

CONTACT

Mr. Andre Cordon, Dean of Admission, Pace University, Pleasantville Campus, 861 Bedford Road, Pleasantville, NY 10570. *Phone:* 212-346-1794. *Toll-free phone:* 800-874-PACE. *Fax:* 212-346-1821. *E-mail:* acordon@pace.edu.

Parsons School of Design

New York, New York

http://www.newschool.edu/parsons/

- **Independent** comprehensive, founded 1896, part of The New School
- **Urban** campus with easy access to New York City
- **Endowment** $322.3 million
- **Coed** 4,383 undergraduate students, 91% full-time, 79% women, 21% men
- **Moderately difficult** entrance level, 46% of applicants were admitted

UNDERGRAD STUDENTS

4,010 full-time, 373 part-time. 78% are from out of state; 3% Black or African American, non-Hispanic/Latino; 10% Hispanic/Latino; 14% Asian, non-Hispanic/Latino; 0.1% Native Hawaiian or other Pacific Islander, non-Hispanic/Latino; 0.1% American Indian or Alaska Native, non-Hispanic/Latino; 3% Two or more races, non-Hispanic/Latino; 3% Race/ethnicity unknown; 44% international; 5% transferred in; 9% live on campus.

Freshmen:

Admission: 4,959 applied, 2,284 admitted, 889 enrolled. ***Average high school GPA:*** 3.5. ***Test scores:*** SAT evidence-based reading and writing scores over 500: 98%; SAT math scores over 500: 97%; ACT scores over 18: 98%; SAT evidence-based reading and writing scores over 600: 74%; SAT math scores over 600: 75%; ACT scores over 24: 74%; SAT evidence-based reading and writing scores over 700: 14%; SAT math scores over 700: 37%; ACT scores over 30: 14%.

Retention: 90% of full-time freshmen returned.

FACULTY

Total: 1,212, 14% full-time, 10% with terminal degrees.

Student/faculty ratio: 10:1.

ACADEMICS

Calendar: semesters. *Degrees:* associate, bachelor's, master's, and postbachelor's certificates.

Special study options: academic remediation for entering students, accelerated degree program, advanced placement credit, cooperative education, distance learning, double majors, English as a second language, independent study, internships, off-campus study, part-time degree program, services for LD students, student-designed majors, study abroad, summer session for credit.

Computers: 717 computers/terminals are available on campus for general student use. Students can access the following: campus intranet, computer help desk, free student e-mail accounts, online (class) grades, online (class) registration, online (class) schedules. Campuswide network is available. 100% of college-owned or -operated housing units are wired for high-speed Internet access. Wireless service is available via entire campus.

Library: New School Libraries & Archives plus 3 others. *Books:* 215,937 (physical), 840,933 (digital/electronic); *Serial titles:* 2,265 (physical), 113,452 (digital/electronic); *Databases:* 376. Weekly public service hours: 155; study areas open 24 hours, 5–7 days a week; students can reserve study rooms.

STUDENT LIFE

Housing options: coed, special housing for students with disabilities. Campus housing is university owned. Freshman applicants given priority for college housing.

Activities and organizations: drama/theater group, student-run newspaper, choral group.

Athletics ***Intramural sports:*** basketball M/W, cross-country running M/W, soccer M/W, tennis M/W.

Campus security: 24-hour emergency response devices, controlled dormitory access, 24-hour security desk personnel.

Student services: health clinic, personal/psychological counseling, veterans affairs office.

FINANCIAL AID

Financial Aid Of all full-time matriculated undergraduates who enrolled in 2018, 1,441 applied for aid, 1,367 were judged to have need, 49 had their need fully met. 114 Federal Work-Study jobs (averaging $2880). In 2018, 2120 non-need-based awards were made. ***Average percent of need met:*** 80. ***Average financial aid package:*** $26,579. ***Average need-based loan:*** $3177. ***Average need-based gift aid:*** $16,218. ***Average non-need-based aid:*** $9711. ***Average indebtedness upon graduation:*** $32,624.

APPLYING

Standardized Tests *Required for some:* TOEFL/IELTS /PTE for students whose native language is not English.

Options: electronic application, early action, deferred entrance.

Application fee: $50.

Required: essay or personal statement, high school transcript, 2 letters of recommendation, online application, Parsons Challenge portfolio, artist statement. ***Recommended:*** minimum 3.0 GPA.

Application deadlines: 1/15 (freshmen), 4/1 (transfers), 11/1 (early action).

Notification: continuous until 3/15 (freshmen), continuous until 12/20 (transfers), 12/20 (early action).

CONTACT

Ms. Erin Stine, Director of Undergraduate Admissions for Parsons School of Design, Parsons School of Design, 72 Fifth Avenue at 13th Street, New York, NY 10011. *Phone:* 212-229-8989. *Toll-free phone:* 800-292-3040. *E-mail:* stinee@newschool.edu.

Paul Smith's College

Paul Smiths, New York

http://www.paulsmiths.edu/

CONTACT

Admissions Office, Paul Smith's College, Routes 86 and 30, PO Box 265, Paul Smiths, NY 12970. *Phone:* 518-327-6227. *Toll-free phone:* 800-421-2605. *Fax:* 518-327-6016. *E-mail:* admissions@paulsmiths.edu.

Phillips Beth Israel School of Nursing

New York, New York

http://www.mountsinai.org/locations/beth-israel/pson

CONTACT

Mrs. Bernice Pass-Stern, Assistant Dean, Phillips Beth Israel School of Nursing, 776 Sixth Avenue, 4th Floor, New York, NY 10010-6354. *Phone:* 212-614-6176. *Fax:* 212-614-6109. *E-mail:* bstern@chpnet.org.

Plaza College

Forest Hills, New York

http://www.plazacollege.edu/

CONTACT

Dean Vanessa Lopez, Dean of Admissions, Plaza College, 118-33 Queens Boulevard, Forest Hills, NY 11375. *Phone:* 718-779-1430. *E-mail:* info@plazacollege.edu.

Pratt Institute

Brooklyn, New York

http://www.pratt.edu/

- **Independent** comprehensive, founded 1887
- **Urban** 25-acre campus
- **Coed** 3,483 undergraduate students, 97% full-time, 71% women, 29% men
- **Very difficult** entrance level, 49% of applicants were admitted

UNDERGRAD STUDENTS

3,376 full-time, 107 part-time. 74% are from out of state; 3% Black or African American, non-Hispanic/Latino; 9% Hispanic/Latino; 13% Asian, non-Hispanic/Latino; 0.1% Native Hawaiian or other Pacific Islander, non-Hispanic/Latino; 0.1% American Indian or Alaska Native, non-Hispanic/Latino; 3% Two or more races, non-Hispanic/Latino; 1% Race/ethnicity unknown; 34% international; 3% transferred in; 50% live on campus.

Freshmen:

Admission: 7,090 applied, 3,454 admitted, 648 enrolled. ***Average high school GPA:*** 3.9. ***Test scores:*** SAT evidence-based reading and writing scores over 500: 98%; SAT math scores over 500: 98%; ACT scores over 18: 100%; SAT evidence-based reading and writing scores over 600: 75%; SAT math scores over 600: 78%; ACT scores over 24: 87%; SAT evidence-based reading and writing scores over 700: 17%; SAT math scores over 700: 37%; ACT scores over 30: 30%.

Retention: 89% of full-time freshmen returned.

FACULTY

Total: 1,202, 14% full-time, 68% with terminal degrees.

Student/faculty ratio: 9:1.

ACADEMICS

Calendar: semesters plus optional May term and summer session. *Degrees:* associate, bachelor's, master's, and post-master's certificates.

Special study options: part-time degree program. ***ROTC:*** Army (c).

Computers: Students can access the following: online (class) registration. Campuswide network is available.

Library: Pratt Institute Library.

STUDENT LIFE

Housing options: coed, special housing for students with disabilities. Campus housing is university owned. Freshman campus housing is guaranteed.

Athletics Member NCAA. All Division III. ***Intercollegiate sports:*** basketball M, cross-country running M/W, soccer M/W, tennis M/W, track and field M/W, volleyball W. ***Intramural sports:*** badminton M/W, basketball M, field hockey M, football M, golf M, lacrosse M/W, volleyball M, weight lifting M/W.

Campus security: 24-hour emergency response devices and patrols, late-night transport/escort service.

COSTS & FINANCIAL AID
Costs (2020–21) ***Comprehensive fee:*** $69,618 includes full-time tuition ($53,570), mandatory fees ($2060), and room and board ($13,988). Part-time tuition: $1728 per credit hour. ***College room only:*** $10,000.

Financial Aid Of all full-time matriculated undergraduates who enrolled in 2019, 1,550 applied for aid, 1,336 were judged to have need, 159 had their need fully met. In 2019, 1306 non-need-based awards were made. ***Average percent of need met:*** 56. ***Average financial aid package:*** $31,590. ***Average need-based loan:*** $10,139. ***Average need-based gift aid:*** $5636. ***Average non-need-based aid:*** $19,234. ***Average indebtedness upon graduation:*** $41,305. ***Financial aid deadline:*** 3/1.

APPLYING
Standardized Tests *Required:* SAT or ACT (for admission). *Required for some:* SAT Subject Tests (for admission).

Options: electronic application, early action, deferred entrance.

Application fee: $50.

Required: essay or personal statement, high school transcript, 1 letter of recommendation. ***Required for some:*** portfolio. ***Recommended:*** minimum 3.0 GPA.

Notification: 12/22 (early action).

CONTACT
Mr. Adam Ward, Visit Coordinator, Pratt Institute, 200 Willoughby Avenue, DeKalb Hall, Brooklyn, NY 11205. *Phone:* 718-636-3779. *Toll-free phone:* 800-331-0834. *Fax:* 718-636-3670. *E-mail:* visit@pratt.edu.

Purchase College, State University of New York

Purchase, New York

http://www.purchase.edu/

- **State-supported** comprehensive, founded 1967, part of State University of New York System
- **Small-town** 500-acre campus with easy access to New York City
- **Coed** 4,081 undergraduate students, 92% full-time, 58% women, 42% men
- **Moderately difficult** entrance level, 52% of applicants were admitted

UNDERGRAD STUDENTS
3,771 full-time, 310 part-time. Students come from 39 states and territories; 30 other countries; 13% are from out of state; 12% Black or African American, non-Hispanic/Latino; 25% Hispanic/Latino; 4% Asian, non-Hispanic/Latino; 0.2% Native Hawaiian or other Pacific Islander, non-Hispanic/Latino; 0.2% American Indian or Alaska Native, non-Hispanic/Latino; 5% Two or more races, non-Hispanic/Latino; 0.5% Race/ethnicity unknown; 2% international; 10% transferred in; 68% live on campus.

Freshmen:
Admission: 6,486 applied, 3,341 admitted, 798 enrolled. ***Average high school GPA:*** 3.3. ***Test scores:*** SAT evidence-based reading and writing scores over 500: 92%; SAT math scores over 500: 84%; ACT scores over 18: 91%; SAT evidence-based reading and writing scores over 600: 50%; SAT math scores over 600: 36%; ACT scores over 24: 58%; SAT evidence-based reading and writing scores over 700: 11%; SAT math scores over 700: 5%; ACT scores over 30: 12%.

Retention: 81% of full-time freshmen returned.

FACULTY
Total: 469, 40% full-time.

Student/faculty ratio: 14:1.

ACADEMICS
Calendar: semesters. *Degrees:* certificates, bachelor's, master's, post-master's, and postbachelor's certificates.

Special study options: academic remediation for entering students, adult/continuing education programs, advanced placement credit, double majors, English as a second language, independent study, internships, off-campus study, part-time degree program, services for LD students, student-designed majors, study abroad, summer session for credit.

Computers: 600 computers/terminals and 3,500 ports are available on campus for general student use. Students can access the following: campus intranet, computer help desk, free student e-mail accounts, online (class) grades, online (class) registration, online (class) schedules, CNC-routers, 3D printers, laser cutters, vinyl printers, virtual reality lab, fabrication lab, non-liner edit labs for film, music digital audio workstations, 24 and 48" plotters for high-quality photographic output, digital embroidery machine. Campuswide network is available. 100% of college-owned or -operated housing units are wired for high-speed Internet access. Wireless service is available via entire campus. **Library:** Purchase College Library plus 1 other. *Books:* 229,091 (physical), 117,469 (digital/electronic); *Serial titles:* 1,585 (physical), 39 (digital/electronic); *Databases:* 171. Weekly public service hours: 109; students can reserve study rooms.

STUDENT LIFE
Housing options: coed, men-only, women-only, special housing for students with disabilities. Campus housing is university owned. Freshman applicants given priority for college housing.

Activities and organizations: drama/theater group, student-run newspaper, radio and television station, choral group, Latinos Unidos (LU), Students of Caribbean Ancestry (SOCA), Lesbian Gay Bisexual Transgender Questioning Union (LGBTQU), Organization of African People in the Americas (OAPIA), Hillel.

Athletics Member NCAA. All Division III. ***Intercollegiate sports:*** baseball M, basketball M/W, cross-country running M/W, golf M, lacrosse M/W, soccer M/W, softball W, swimming and diving M/W, tennis M/W, volleyball M/W. ***Intramural sports:*** badminton M/W, basketball M/W, bowling M/W, cheerleading M(c)/W(c), cross-country running M/W, fencing M, field hockey W, football M/W, golf M/W, racquetball M/W, skiing (cross-country) M/W, skiing (downhill) M/W, soccer M/W, softball M/W, squash M/W, swimming and diving M/W, table tennis M/W, tennis M/W, volleyball M/W, water polo M/W, weight lifting M/W.

Campus security: 24-hour emergency response devices and patrols, late-night transport/escort service, controlled dormitory access, 24-hour patrols by police officers.

Student services: health clinic, personal/psychological counseling, women's center.

COSTS & FINANCIAL AID
Costs (2019–20) ***One-time required fee:*** $210. ***Tuition:*** state resident $7070 full-time, $295 per credit hour part-time; nonresident $16,980 full-time, $708 per credit hour part-time. Part-time tuition and fees vary according to course load. ***Required fees:*** $1883 full-time, $83 per credit hour part-time. ***Room and board:*** $14,548; room only: $9098. Room and board charges vary according to board plan and housing facility. ***Payment plan:*** installment. ***Waivers:*** employees or children of employees.

Financial Aid Of all full-time matriculated undergraduates who enrolled in 2019, 3,061 applied for aid, 2,443 were judged to have need, 61 had their need fully met. In 2019, 798 non-need-based awards were made. ***Average percent of need met:*** 50. ***Average financial aid package:*** $11,299. ***Average need-based loan:*** $4358. ***Average need-based gift aid:*** $10,870. ***Average non-need-based aid:*** $2479. ***Average indebtedness upon graduation:*** $23,987.

APPLYING
Options: electronic application, early action, deferred entrance.

Application fee: $50.

Required: high school transcript, minimum 3.0 GPA. ***Required for some:*** essay or personal statement, 1 letter of recommendation, interview, audition, portfolio.

Application deadlines: 7/1 (freshmen), 7/1 (out-of-state freshmen), rolling (transfers), 11/15 (early action).

Notification: continuous until 10/1 (freshmen), continuous until 10/1 (out-of-state freshmen), continuous (transfers), rolling (early action).

CONTACT
Caitlin Read, Dean of Enrollment Management, Purchase College, State University of New York, 735 Anderson Hill Road, Purchase, NY 10577-1400. *Phone:* 914-251-6300. *Fax:* 914-251-6314. *E-mail:* admission@purchase.edu.

Queens College of the City University of New York

Queens, New York

http://www.qc.cuny.edu/

- **State and locally supported** comprehensive, founded 1937, part of City University of New York
- **Urban** 80-acre campus with easy access to New York City
- **Endowment** $72.4 million
- **Coed** 16,866 undergraduate students, 74% full-time, 54% women, 46% men
- **Very difficult** entrance level, 49% of applicants were admitted

UNDERGRAD STUDENTS
12,532 full-time, 4,334 part-time. Students come from 33 states and territories; 139 other countries; 1% are from out of state; 9% Black or African American, non-Hispanic/Latino; 30% Hispanic/Latino; 30% Asian, non-Hispanic/Latino; 0.4% Native Hawaiian or other Pacific Islander, non-Hispanic/Latino; 0.3% American Indian or Alaska Native, non-Hispanic/Latino; 2% Two or more races, non-Hispanic/Latino; 5% international; 12% transferred in; 2% live on campus.

Freshmen:
Admission: 24,277 applied, 11,845 admitted, 2,266 enrolled. ***Test scores:*** SAT evidence-based reading and writing scores over 500: 86%; SAT math scores over 500: 93%; SAT evidence-based reading and writing scores over 600: 23%; SAT math scores over 600: 32%; SAT evidence-based reading and writing scores over 700: 3%; SAT math scores over 700: 7%.

Retention: 82% of full-time freshmen returned.

FACULTY
Total: 1,633, 36% full-time, 46% with terminal degrees.

Student/faculty ratio: 16:1.

ACADEMICS
Calendar: semesters. *Degrees:* bachelor's, master's, post-master's, and postbachelor's certificates.

Special study options: accelerated degree program, adult/continuing education programs, advanced placement credit, cooperative education, double majors, English as a second language, honors programs, independent study, internships, off-campus study, part-time degree program, services for LD students, study abroad, summer session for credit. ***ROTC:*** Army (c).

Computers: 2,456 computers/terminals are available on campus for general student use. Students can access the following: campus intranet, computer help desk, free student e-mail accounts, online (class) grades, online (class) registration, online (class) schedules. Campuswide network is available. 100% of college-owned or -operated housing units are wired for high-speed Internet access. Wireless service is available via entire campus.

Library: The Benjamin S. Rosenthal Library plus 1 other. *Books:* 636,993 (physical), 710,396 (digital/electronic); *Serial titles:* 14,700 (physical), 225,715 (digital/electronic); *Databases:* 291. Weekly public service hours: 94; students can reserve study rooms.

STUDENT LIFE
Housing options: coed. Campus housing is university owned.

Activities and organizations: drama/theater group, student-run newspaper, radio station, choral group, Sci-fi/Animation Club, Chabad on Campus, Association of Latino Professionals For America, GLASA, Muslim Student Association, national fraternities, national sororities.

Athletics Member NCAA. All Division II. ***Intercollegiate sports:*** baseball M(s), basketball M(s)/W(s), cross-country running M(s)/W(s), lacrosse W, soccer M(s)/W(s), softball W(s), swimming and diving W(s), tennis M(s)/W(s), track and field M(s)/W(s), volleyball W(s). ***Intramural sports:*** badminton M/W, basketball M/W, cross-country running M/W, football M(c), soccer M/W, swimming and diving M/W, table tennis M/W, tennis M/W, track and field M/W, ultimate Frisbee M/W, volleyball M/W.

Campus security: 24-hour emergency response devices and patrols, controlled dormitory access.

Student services: health clinic, personal/psychological counseling, veterans affairs office.

COSTS & FINANCIAL AID
Costs (2019–20) ***Tuition:*** state resident $305 per credit part-time; nonresident $620 per credit part-time. Full-time tuition and fees vary according to course load. Part-time tuition and fees vary according to course load. ***Required fees:*** $209 per credit part-time. ***Room only:*** $12,752. Room and board charges vary according to board plan and housing facility. ***Payment plan:*** installment. ***Waivers:*** senior citizens and employees or children of employees.

Financial Aid Of all full-time matriculated undergraduates who enrolled in 2018, 9,502 applied for aid, 8,721 were judged to have need, 377 had their need fully met. 249 Federal Work-Study jobs (averaging $3547). In 2018, 133 non-need-based awards were made. ***Average percent of need met:*** 53. ***Average financial aid package:*** $7001. ***Average need-based loan:*** $4249. ***Average need-based gift aid:*** $8244. ***Average non-need-based aid:*** $6260. ***Average indebtedness upon graduation:*** $14,738.

APPLYING
Standardized Tests *Required:* SAT or ACT (for admission). *Required for some:* SAT Subject Tests (for admission).

Options: electronic application, deferred entrance.

Application fee: $65.

Required: high school transcript, minimum 3.0 GPA. ***Required for some:*** essay or personal statement.

Application deadlines: 2/1 (freshmen), 2/1 (transfers).

Notification: 2/1 (freshmen), continuous (transfers).

CONTACT
Ms. Chelsea Lavington, Director of Undergraduate Admissions, Queens College of the City University of New York, 65-30 Kissena Boulevard, Queens, NY 11367. *Phone:* 718-997-5600. *Fax:* 718-997-5617.

Rabbinical Academy Mesivta Rabbi Chaim Berlin

Brooklyn, New York

CONTACT
Executive Administrator, Rabbinical Academy Mesivta Rabbi Chaim Berlin, 1605 Coney Island Avenue, Brooklyn, NY 11230-4715. *Phone:* 718-377-0777. *Fax:* 718-338-5578.

Rabbinical College Beth Shraga

Monsey, New York

CONTACT
Rabbi Sydney Schiff, Director of Admissions, Rabbinical College Beth Shraga, 28 Saddle River Road, Monsey, NY 10952-3035.

Rabbinical College Bobover Yeshiva B'nei Zion

Brooklyn, New York

CONTACT
Director of Admissions, Rabbinical College Bobover Yeshiva B'nei Zion, 1577 Forty-eighth Street, Brooklyn, NY 11219. *Phone:* 718-438-2018.

Rabbinical College of Long Island

Long Beach, New York

CONTACT
Director of Admissions, Rabbinical College of Long Island, 205 West Beech Street, Long Beach, NY 11561-3305. *Phone:* 516-431-7414.

Rabbinical College of Ohr Shimon Yisroel

Brooklyn, New York

CONTACT
Rabbinical College of Ohr Shimon Yisroel, 215-217 Hewes Street, Brooklyn, NY 11211.

Rabbinical College Ohr Yisroel

Brooklyn, New York

http://www.rabbinicalcollegeohryisroel.com/

CONTACT

Rabbinical College Ohr Yisroel, 8800 Seaview Avenue, Brooklyn, NY 11236.

Rabbinical Seminary of America

Flushing, New York

CONTACT

Rabbi Abraham Semmel, Director of Admissions, Rabbinical Seminary of America, 76-01 147th Street, Flushing, NY 11367. *Phone:* 718-268-4700.

Rensselaer Polytechnic Institute

Troy, New York

http://www.rpi.edu/

- **Independent** university, founded 1824
- **Suburban** 284-acre campus with easy access to Albany, NY
- **Endowment** $673.7 million
- **Coed**
- **Very difficult** entrance level

FACULTY

Student/faculty ratio: 13:1.

ACADEMICS

Calendar: semesters. *Degrees:* bachelor's, master's, and doctoral.
Library: Folsom Library plus 2 others. Students can reserve study rooms.

STUDENT LIFE

Housing options: on-campus residence required through sophomore year; coed, special housing for students with disabilities. Campus housing is university owned. Freshman campus housing is guaranteed.

Activities and organizations: drama/theater group, student-run newspaper, radio and television station, choral group, Red Army Spirit Club, Outing Club, Indian Student Association, Chinese American Student Association, pep band, national fraternities, national sororities.

Athletics Member NCAA. All Division III except men's and women's ice hockey (Division I).

Campus security: 24-hour emergency response devices and patrols, late-night transport/escort service, controlled dormitory access, campus foot patrols at night.

Student services: health clinic, personal/psychological counseling, women's center, legal services.

COSTS & FINANCIAL AID

Costs (2019–20) ***Comprehensive fee:*** $70,955 includes full-time tuition ($54,000), mandatory fees ($1375), and room and board ($15,580). Part-time tuition: $2250 per credit hour. ***College room only:*** $8770.

Financial Aid Of all full-time matriculated undergraduates who enrolled in 2019, 3,996 applied for aid, 3,452 were judged to have need, 651 had their need fully met. In 2019, 1707 non-need-based awards were made. ***Average percent of need met:*** 79. ***Average financial aid package:*** $42,951. ***Average need-based loan:*** $4459. ***Average need-based gift aid:*** $38,809. ***Average non-need-based aid:*** $21,732. ***Average indebtedness upon graduation:*** $34,595.

APPLYING

Standardized Tests *Required:* SAT or ACT (for admission). *Required for some:* SAT and SAT Subject Tests or ACT (for admission).

Options: electronic application, early admission, early decision, deferred entrance.

Application fee: $70.

Required for some: essay or personal statement, high school transcript, interview, portfolio for electronic arts. ***Recommended:*** minimum 3.0 GPA, 1 letter of recommendation.

CONTACT

Ms. Karen Long, Director, Undergrad Admissions, Rensselaer Polytechnic Institute, 110 8th Street, Troy, NY 12180. *Phone:* 518-276-6216. *Fax:* 518-276-4072. *E-mail:* admissions@rpi.edu.

Roberts Wesleyan College

Rochester, New York

http://www.roberts.edu/

- **Independent** comprehensive, founded 1866, affiliated with Free Methodist Church of North America
- **Suburban** 188-acre campus with easy access to Rochester
- **Endowment** $24.2 million
- **Coed** 1,293 undergraduate students, 91% full-time, 67% women, 33% men
- **Moderately difficult** entrance level, 69% of applicants were admitted

UNDERGRAD STUDENTS

1,176 full-time, 117 part-time. Students come from 28 states and territories; 32 other countries; 15% are from out of state; 9% Black or African American, non-Hispanic/Latino; 7% Hispanic/Latino; 2% Asian, non-Hispanic/Latino; 0.2% Native Hawaiian or other Pacific Islander, non-Hispanic/Latino; 0.2% American Indian or Alaska Native, non-Hispanic/Latino; 4% Two or more races, non-Hispanic/Latino; 5% international; 4% transferred in; 61% live on campus.

Freshmen:

Admission: 1,330 applied, 916 admitted, 222 enrolled. ***Average high school GPA:*** 3.5. ***Test scores:*** SAT evidence-based reading and writing scores over 500: 88%; SAT math scores over 500: 84%; ACT scores over 18: 98%; SAT evidence-based reading and writing scores over 600: 39%; SAT math scores over 600: 29%; ACT scores over 24: 60%; SAT evidence-based reading and writing scores over 700: 6%; SAT math scores over 700: 5%; ACT scores over 30: 12%.

Retention: 79% of full-time freshmen returned.

FACULTY

Total: 104, 90% full-time, 86% with terminal degrees.

Student/faculty ratio: 12:1.

ACADEMICS

Calendar: semesters. *Degrees:* bachelor's, master's, and doctoral.

Special study options: academic remediation for entering students, accelerated degree program, adult/continuing education programs, advanced placement credit, distance learning, double majors, English as a second language, honors programs, independent study, internships, off-campus study, services for LD students, student-designed majors, study abroad, summer session for credit. ***ROTC:*** Army (c), Air Force (c).

Unusual degree programs: 3-2 engineering with Clarkson University, Rensselaer Polytechnic Institute, Rochester Institute of Technology.

Computers: 140 computers/terminals are available on campus for general student use. Students can access the following: campus intranet, computer help desk, free student e-mail accounts, online (class) grades, online (class) registration, online (class) schedules. Campuswide network is available. 100% of college-owned or -operated housing units are wired for high-speed Internet access. Wireless service is available via entire campus.
Library: B. Thomas Golisano Library. *Books:* 128,708 (physical), 6,200 (digital/electronic); *Databases:* 105. Study areas open 24 hours, 5–7 days a week; students can reserve study rooms.

STUDENT LIFE

Housing options: on-campus residence required through senior year; men-only, women-only, special housing for students with disabilities. Campus housing is university owned. Freshman campus housing is guaranteed.

Activities and organizations: drama/theater group, student-run newspaper, choral group, Intramurals, Foot of the Cross, Fellowship of Christian Athletes, Nursing Club, Drama Club.

Athletics Member NCAA, NCCAA. All NCAA Division II. ***Intercollegiate sports:*** basketball M(s)/W(s), bowling W(s), cheerleading M(c)/W(c), cross-country running M(s)/W(s), golf M(s), lacrosse M(s)/W(s), soccer M(s)/W(s), swimming and diving M(s)/W(s), tennis M(s)/W(s), track and field M(s)/W(s), volleyball W(s). ***Intramural sports:*** basketball M/W, field hockey M/W, football M/W, racquetball M/W, skiing (downhill) M/W, soccer M/W, softball M/W, swimming and diving M/W, table tennis M/W, tennis M/W, ultimate Frisbee M/W, volleyball M/W, water polo M/W.

Campus security: 24-hour emergency response devices and patrols, student patrols, late-night transport/escort service, controlled dormitory access, 24-hour Resident Life staff on-call.

Student services: health clinic, personal/psychological counseling, veterans affairs office.

COSTS & FINANCIAL AID

Costs (2019–20) ***One-time required fee:*** $300. ***Comprehensive fee:*** $43,392 includes full-time tuition ($31,350), mandatory fees ($1144), and room and board ($10,898). Full-time tuition and fees vary according to degree level and program. Part-time tuition and fees vary according to course load, degree level, and program. ***Required fees:*** $1306 per credit hour part-time. ***College room only:*** $6760. Room and board charges vary according to board plan and housing facility. ***Payment plan:*** installment. ***Waivers:*** senior citizens and employees or children of employees.

Financial Aid Of all full-time matriculated undergraduates who enrolled in 2018, 1,020 applied for aid, 959 were judged to have need, 130 had their need fully met. 554 Federal Work-Study jobs (averaging $1975). 62 state and other part-time jobs (averaging $1903). In 2018, 201 non-need-based awards were made. ***Average percent of need met:*** 71. ***Average financial aid package:*** $22,429. ***Average need-based loan:*** $5231. ***Average need-based gift aid:*** $17,644. ***Average non-need-based aid:*** $11,459. ***Average indebtedness upon graduation:*** $34,679.

APPLYING

Standardized Tests *Required:* SAT or ACT (for admission).

Options: electronic application, early admission, early action, deferred entrance.

Required: essay or personal statement, high school transcript. ***Recommended:*** minimum 2.7 GPA, interview.

Application deadlines: 8/20 (freshmen), rolling (transfers), 11/15 (early action).

Notification: continuous until 9/1 (freshmen), continuous (transfers), 12/6 (early action).

CONTACT

Ms. Mary Sasso, Executive Director of Undergraduate Admissions, Roberts Wesleyan College, 2301 Westside Drive, Rochester, NY 14624-1997. *Phone:* 585-594-6400. *Toll-free phone:* 800-777-4RWC. *Fax:* 585-594-6371. *E-mail:* admissions@roberts.edu.

Rochester Institute of Technology

Rochester, New York

http://www.rit.edu/

- **Independent** university, founded 1829
- **Suburban** 1300-acre campus with easy access to Rochester
- **Endowment** $938.2 million
- **Coed**
- **Moderately difficult** entrance level

FACULTY

Student/faculty ratio: 13:1.

ACADEMICS

Calendar: semesters. *Degrees:* certificates, associate, bachelor's, master's, doctoral, and postbachelor's certificates.

Library: Wallace Memorial Library. *Books:* 429,176 (physical), 240,712 (digital/electronic); *Serial titles:* 58,293 (digital/electronic); *Databases:* 113. Weekly public service hours: 147; study areas open 24 hours, 5–7 days a week; students can reserve study rooms.

STUDENT LIFE

Housing options: on-campus residence required for freshman year; coed, men-only, women-only, special housing for students with disabilities. Campus housing is university owned. Freshman campus housing is guaranteed.

Activities and organizations: drama/theater group, student-run newspaper, radio station, choral group, national fraternities, national sororities.

Athletics Member NCAA. All Division III except men's and women's ice hockey (Division I).

Campus security: 24-hour emergency response devices and patrols, student patrols, late-night transport/escort service, controlled dormitory access.

Student services: health clinic, personal/psychological counseling, women's center, legal services, veterans affairs office.

COSTS & FINANCIAL AID

Costs (2019–20) ***Comprehensive fee:*** $59,430 includes full-time tuition ($45,244), mandatory fees ($646), and room and board ($13,540). Full-time tuition and fees vary according to course load and student level. Part-time tuition: $1616 per credit hour. Part-time tuition and fees vary according to class time and course load. ***College room only:*** $7902. Room and board charges vary according to board plan and housing facility. ***Payment plans:*** tuition prepayment, installment, deferred payment.

Financial Aid Of all full-time matriculated undergraduates who enrolled in 2018, 10,239 applied for aid, 9,177 were judged to have need, 7,326 had their need fully met. In 2018, 1560 non-need-based awards were made. ***Average percent of need met:*** 85. ***Average financial aid package:*** $35,000. ***Average need-based loan:*** $5500. ***Average need-based gift aid:*** $30,405. ***Average non-need-based aid:*** $10,700. ***Average indebtedness upon graduation:*** $41,202.

APPLYING

Standardized Tests *Required:* SAT or ACT (for admission).

Options: electronic application, early admission, early decision, deferred entrance.

Application fee: $65.

Required: essay or personal statement, high school transcript. ***Required for some:*** portfolio of original artwork for School of Art, Design and Crafts; interview for BS/MS physician assistant program. ***Recommended:*** minimum 3.4 GPA, 1 letter of recommendation, interview.

CONTACT

Ms. Marian Nicoletti, Director of Admission, Rochester Institute of Technology, 60 Lomb Memorial Drive, Rochester, NY 14623-5604. *Phone:* 585-475-6631. *Fax:* 585-475-7424. *E-mail:* admissions@rit.edu.

The Sage Colleges

Troy, New York

http://www.sage.edu/

- **Independent** comprehensive, founded 1916
- **Urban** 23-acre campus
- **Endowment** $38.9 million
- **Coed** 1,358 undergraduate students, 91% full-time, 78% women, 22% men
- **Moderately difficult** entrance level, 85% of applicants were admitted

UNDERGRAD STUDENTS

1,234 full-time, 124 part-time. Students come from 19 states and territories; 10 other countries; 6% are from out of state; 11% Black or African American, non-Hispanic/Latino; 9% Hispanic/Latino; 5% Asian, non-Hispanic/Latino; 0.4% Native Hawaiian or other Pacific Islander, non-Hispanic/Latino; 0.6% American Indian or Alaska Native, non-Hispanic/Latino; 4% Two or more races, non-Hispanic/Latino; 8% Race/ethnicity unknown; 1% international; 10% transferred in; 46% live on campus.

Freshmen:

Admission: 1,561 applied, 1,327 admitted, 234 enrolled. ***Average high school GPA:*** 3.2. ***Test scores:*** SAT evidence-based reading and writing scores over 500: 53%; SAT math scores over 500: 55%; ACT scores over 18: 67%; SAT evidence-based reading and writing scores over 600: 13%; SAT math scores over 600: 14%; ACT scores over 24: 17%.

Retention: 72% of full-time freshmen returned.

FACULTY

Total: 279, 43% full-time, 52% with terminal degrees.

Student/faculty ratio: 11:1.

ACADEMICS

Calendar: semesters. *Degrees:* bachelor's, master's, doctoral, post-master's, and postbachelor's certificates.

Special study options: accelerated degree program, advanced placement credit, cooperative education, distance learning, double majors, honors programs, independent study, internships, part-time degree program, services for LD students, student-designed majors, study abroad, summer session for credit. ***ROTC:*** Army (c), Air Force (c).

Unusual degree programs: 3-2 business administration with Sage Graduate School; engineering with Rensselaer Polytechnic Institute; nursing with Sage Graduate School; occupational therapy, physical therapy with Sage Graduate School.

Computers: 420 computers/terminals are available on campus for general student use. Students can access the following: campus intranet, computer help desk, free student e-mail accounts, online (class) grades, online (class) registration, online (class) schedules. Campuswide network is available. 100% of college-owned or -operated housing units are wired for high-speed Internet access. Wireless service is available via classrooms, computer labs, learning centers, libraries, student centers.
Library: James Wheelock Clark Library plus 1 other. *Serial titles:* 223 (physical), 67,117 (digital/electronic); *Databases:* 97. Weekly public service hours: 68; students can reserve study rooms.

STUDENT LIFE
Housing options: coed, women-only. Campus housing is university owned. Freshman campus housing is guaranteed.

Activities and organizations: drama/theater group, student-run newspaper, choral group, Dance Ensamble, BLSA (Black & Latin Student Alliance), Circle K (Community Service Organization), Various Academic Clubs, AIGA (Graphic Design).

Athletics Member NCAA. All Division III. ***Intercollegiate sports:*** basketball M/W, cross-country running M/W, field hockey W, golf M, lacrosse M/W, soccer M/W, softball W, tennis M/W, track and field M/W, volleyball M/W. ***Intramural sports:*** football M/W, lacrosse W(c), skiing (downhill) M(c)/W(c).

Campus security: 24-hour emergency response devices and patrols, late-night transport/escort service, controlled dormitory access.

Student services: health clinic, personal/psychological counseling, women's center.

COSTS & FINANCIAL AID
Costs (2019–20) ***Comprehensive fee:*** $44,941 includes full-time tuition ($30,383), mandatory fees ($1500), and room and board ($13,058). Part-time tuition: $1013 per credit hour. ***College room only:*** $6654.

Financial Aid Of all full-time matriculated undergraduates who enrolled in 2018, 1,296 applied for aid, 1,224 were judged to have need. 342 Federal Work-Study jobs (averaging $1930). 31 state and other part-time jobs (averaging $5328). In 2018, 96 non-need-based awards were made. ***Average need-based loan:*** $4202. ***Average need-based gift aid:*** $18,231. ***Average non-need-based aid:*** $14,050. ***Average indebtedness upon graduation:*** $32,497.

APPLYING
Standardized Tests *Required for some:* SAT or ACT (for admission).

Options: electronic application, early admission, deferred entrance.

Required: essay or personal statement, high school transcript, minimum 2.5 GPA, 2 letters of recommendation. ***Required for some:*** portfolio for art and design programs. ***Recommended:*** interview.

Application deadlines: rolling (freshmen), rolling (transfers).

Notification: continuous (freshmen), continuous (transfers).

CONTACT
Ms. Sarah Barrett, Director of Undergraduate Enrollment Management, The Sage Colleges, 65 First Street, Troy, NY 12180. *Phone:* 518-244-2441. *Fax:* 518-292-1912. *E-mail:* barres2@sage.edu.

St. Bonaventure University

St. Bonaventure, New York

http://www.sbu.edu/

- **Independent** comprehensive, founded 1858, affiliated with Roman Catholic Church
- **Small-town** 500-acre campus
- **Endowment** $71.7 million
- **Coed** 1,840 undergraduate students, 96% full-time, 47% women, 53% men
- **Moderately difficult** entrance level, 75% of applicants were admitted

UNDERGRAD STUDENTS
1,767 full-time, 73 part-time. Students come from 22 states and territories; 24 other countries; 25% are from out of state; 6% Black or African American, non-Hispanic/Latino; 7% Hispanic/Latino; 4% Asian, non-Hispanic/Latino; 0.1% Native Hawaiian or other Pacific Islander, non-Hispanic/Latino; 0.5% American Indian or Alaska Native, non-Hispanic/Latino; 2% Two or more races, non-Hispanic/Latino; 4% Race/ethnicity unknown; 3% international; 3% transferred in; 82% live on campus.

Freshmen:
Admission: 3,058 applied, 2,295 admitted, 492 enrolled. ***Average high school GPA:*** 3.3. ***Test scores:*** SAT evidence-based reading and writing scores over 500: 82%; SAT math scores over 500: 85%; ACT scores over 18: 88%; SAT evidence-based reading and writing scores over 600: 34%; SAT math scores over 600: 33%; ACT scores over 24: 43%; SAT evidence-based reading and writing scores over 700: 3%; SAT math scores over 700: 7%; ACT scores over 30: 12%.

Retention: 84% of full-time freshmen returned.

FACULTY
Total: 204, 70% full-time, 63% with terminal degrees.

Student/faculty ratio: 12:1.

ACADEMICS
Calendar: semesters. *Degrees:* associate, bachelor's, master's, post-master's, and postbachelor's certificates.

Special study options: accelerated degree program, advanced placement credit, distance learning, double majors, honors programs, independent study, internships, off-campus study, part-time degree program, services for LD students, student-designed majors, study abroad, summer session for credit. ***ROTC:*** Army (b).

Computers: 320 computers/terminals and 2,500 ports are available on campus for general student use. Students can access the following: campus intranet, computer help desk, free student e-mail accounts, online (class) grades, online (class) registration, online (class) schedules, Moodle. Campuswide network is available. 100% of college-owned or -operated housing units are wired for high-speed Internet access. Wireless service is available via entire campus.
Library: Friedsam Memorial Library. *Books:* 371,691 (physical), 1.6 million (digital/electronic); *Serial titles:* 253 (physical), 269,989 (digital/electronic); *Databases:* 64. Weekly public service hours: 109; students can reserve study rooms.

STUDENT LIFE
Housing options: on-campus residence required through junior year; coed, special housing for students with disabilities. Campus housing is university owned. Freshman campus housing is guaranteed.

Activities and organizations: drama/theater group, student-run newspaper, radio and television station, choral group, Student Government Association, Bona Responds, BV newspaper, Students for the Mountain, Student Ambassadors.

Athletics Member NCAA. All Division I. ***Intercollegiate sports:*** baseball M(s), basketball M(s)/W(s), cross-country running M(s)/W(s), field hockey M(c)/W(c), golf M(s), ice hockey M(c), lacrosse M(s)/W(s), rugby M(c)/W(c), soccer M(s)/W(s), softball W(s), swimming and diving M(s)/W(s), tennis M(s)/W(s), track and field M/W, volleyball M(c)/W(c). ***Intramural sports:*** baseball M(c), basketball M(c)/W(c), football M/W, golf M/W, ice hockey M(c)/W(c), lacrosse M(c)/W(c), skiing (downhill) M(c)/W(c), soccer M(c)/W(c), softball W(c), tennis M/W, track and field M(c)/W(c), ultimate Frisbee M/W, volleyball M/W.

Campus security: 24-hour emergency response devices and patrols, late-night transport/escort service, controlled dormitory access.

Student services: health clinic, personal/psychological counseling, veterans affairs office.

COSTS & FINANCIAL AID
Costs (2020–21) ***Comprehensive fee:*** $50,135 includes full-time tuition ($35,450), mandatory fees ($1065), and room and board ($13,620). Part-time tuition: $1060 per credit hour. Part-time tuition and fees vary according to course load. ***Required fees:*** $40 per credit hour part-time. ***College room only:*** $7490. Room and board charges vary according to board plan and housing facility. ***Waivers:*** senior citizens and employees or children of employees.

Financial Aid Of all full-time matriculated undergraduates who enrolled in 2018, 1,419 applied for aid, 1,257 were judged to have need, 299 had their need fully met. 309 Federal Work-Study jobs (averaging $1405). 322 state and other part-time jobs (averaging $1020). In 2018, 304 non-need-based awards were made. ***Average percent of need met:*** 70. ***Average***

financial aid package: $27,546. ***Average need-based loan:*** $4664. ***Average need-based gift aid:*** $24,215. ***Average non-need-based aid:*** $13,964. ***Average indebtedness upon graduation:*** $34,877.

APPLYING
Standardized Tests *Required for some:* SAT or ACT (for admission), SAT and SAT Subject Tests or ACT (for admission).

Options: electronic application, deferred entrance.

Required: high school transcript, 1 letter of recommendation. ***Required for some:*** essay or personal statement. ***Recommended:*** essay or personal statement, minimum 3.0 GPA, 3 letters of recommendation, interview.

Application deadlines: 7/1 (freshmen), 8/15 (transfers).

Notification: continuous until 10/15 (freshmen), continuous until 10/1 (transfers).

CONTACT
Mr. Doug Brady, Director of Recruitment, St. Bonaventure University, PO Box D, 3261 West State Road, St. Bonaventure, NY 14778. *Phone:* 716-375-2455. *Toll-free phone:* 800-462-5050. *Fax:* 716-375-4005. *E-mail:* dbrady@sbu.edu.

St. Francis College

Brooklyn Heights, New York

http://www.sfc.edu/

CONTACT
Mrs. Lisa Randazzo, Associate Director of Admissions, St. Francis College, 180 Remsen Street, Brooklyn Heights, NY 11201-4398. *Phone:* 718-489-5336. *Fax:* 718-802-0453. *E-mail:* lrandazzo@sfc.edu.

St. John Fisher College

Rochester, New York

http://www.sjfc.edu/

- **Independent** comprehensive, founded 1948, affiliated with Roman Catholic Church
- **Suburban** 154-acre campus
- **Endowment** $93.8 million
- **Coed** 2,752 undergraduate students, 95% full-time, 59% women, 41% men
- **Moderately difficult** entrance level, 64% of applicants were admitted

UNDERGRAD STUDENTS
2,623 full-time, 129 part-time. Students come from 19 states and territories; 3 other countries; 4% are from out of state; 4% Black or African American, non-Hispanic/Latino; 5% Hispanic/Latino; 3% Asian, non-Hispanic/Latino; 0.3% American Indian or Alaska Native, non-Hispanic/Latino; 2% Two or more races, non-Hispanic/Latino; 2% Race/ethnicity unknown; 0.1% international; 6% transferred in; 52% live on campus.

Freshmen:
Admission: 4,594 applied, 2,961 admitted, 601 enrolled. ***Average high school GPA:*** 3.5. ***Test scores:*** SAT evidence-based reading and writing scores over 500: 90%; SAT math scores over 500: 91%; ACT scores over 18: 95%; SAT evidence-based reading and writing scores over 600: 39%; SAT math scores over 600: 42%; ACT scores over 24: 55%; SAT evidence-based reading and writing scores over 700: 2%; SAT math scores over 700: 4%; ACT scores over 30: 7%.

Retention: 87% of full-time freshmen returned.

FACULTY
Total: 449, 51% full-time, 57% with terminal degrees.

Student/faculty ratio: 12:1.

ACADEMICS
Calendar: semesters. *Degrees:* certificates, bachelor's, master's, doctoral, post-master's, and postbachelor's certificates.

Special study options: accelerated degree program, adult/continuing education programs, advanced placement credit, distance learning, double majors, honors programs, independent study, internships, off-campus study, part-time degree program, services for LD students, student-designed majors, study abroad, summer session for credit. ***ROTC:*** Army (c), Navy (c), Air Force (c).

Unusual degree programs: 3-2 engineering with Columbia University, Rensselaer Polytechnic Institute, University of Rochester.

Computers: 550 computers/terminals and 1,875 ports are available on campus for general student use. Students can access the following: campus intranet, computer help desk, free student e-mail accounts, online (class) grades, online (class) registration, online (class) schedules. Campuswide network is available. 100% of college-owned or -operated housing units are wired for high-speed Internet access. Wireless service is available via entire campus.

Library: Charles J. Lavery Library plus 1 other. *Books:* 138,569 (physical), 297,511 (digital/electronic); *Databases:* 156. Students can reserve study rooms.

STUDENT LIFE
Housing options: coed, women-only, special housing for students with disabilities. Campus housing is university owned. Freshman campus housing is guaranteed.

Activities and organizations: drama/theater group, student-run newspaper, television station, choral group, Student Government, Student Activities Board, Commuter Council, Resident Student Association, Teddi Dance for Love.

Athletics Member NCAA. All Division III except golf (Division II). ***Intercollegiate sports:*** baseball M, basketball M/W, crew W, cross-country running M/W, field hockey W, football M, golf M/W, lacrosse M/W, soccer M/W, softball W, tennis M/W, track and field M/W, volleyball M/W. ***Intramural sports:*** basketball M/W, cheerleading W(c), crew M(c), equestrian sports M(c)/W(c), ice hockey M(c)/W(c), rugby M(c)/W(c), soccer M/W, volleyball M.

Campus security: 24-hour emergency response devices and patrols, late-night transport/escort service, controlled dormitory access.

Student services: health clinic, personal/psychological counseling, veterans affairs office.

COSTS & FINANCIAL AID
Costs (2020–21) ***Comprehensive fee:*** $47,800 includes full-time tuition ($34,340), mandatory fees ($810), and room and board ($12,650). Full-time tuition and fees vary according to program. Part-time tuition: $936 per credit hour. Part-time tuition and fees vary according to course load and program. ***Required fees:*** $15 per credit hour part-time. ***College room only:*** $8100. Room and board charges vary according to board plan. ***Payment plans:*** installment, deferred payment. ***Waivers:*** employees or children of employees.

Financial Aid Of all full-time matriculated undergraduates who enrolled in 2019, 2,264 applied for aid, 1,988 were judged to have need, 424 had their need fully met. 1,105 Federal Work-Study jobs (averaging $1500). In 2019, 549 non-need-based awards were made. ***Average percent of need met:*** 70. ***Average financial aid package:*** $23,529. ***Average need-based loan:*** $4414. ***Average need-based gift aid:*** $19,035. ***Average non-need-based aid:*** $14,486. ***Average indebtedness upon graduation:*** $37,064.

APPLYING
Standardized Tests *Required:* SAT or ACT (for admission).

Options: electronic application, early decision, deferred entrance.

Required: essay or personal statement, high school transcript, minimum 3.0 GPA, 1 letter of recommendation. ***Recommended:*** interview.

Application deadlines: rolling (freshmen), rolling (transfers).

Early decision deadline: 12/1.

Notification: continuous until 12/1 (freshmen), continuous until 9/1 (transfers), 12/15 (early decision).

CONTACT
Mrs. Stacy A. Ledermann, Director of Freshmen Admissions, St. John Fisher College, 3690 East Avenue, Rochester, NY 14618. *Phone:* 585-385-8064. *Toll-free phone:* 800-444-4640. *Fax:* 585-385-8386. *E-mail:* admissions@sjfc.edu.

St. John's University

Queens, New York

http://www.stjohns.edu/

- **Independent** university, founded 1870, affiliated with Roman Catholic Church
- **Urban** 102-acre campus with easy access to New York City
- **Endowment** $716.5 million
- **Coed**
- **Moderately difficult** entrance level

FACULTY

Student/faculty ratio: 17:1.

ACADEMICS

Calendar: semesters. *Degrees:* certificates, bachelor's, master's, doctoral, post-master's, and postbachelor's certificates.
Library: St. John's University Library plus 3 others. *Books:* 534,824 (physical), 608,270 (digital/electronic); *Serial titles:* 68,549 (physical), 88,058 (digital/electronic); *Databases:* 226. Weekly public service hours: 92; students can reserve study rooms.

STUDENT LIFE

Housing options: coed, special housing for students with disabilities. Campus housing is university owned and leased by the school.

Activities and organizations: drama/theater group, student-run newspaper, radio and television station, choral group, Student Government, Incorporated, Haraya (Pan-African Students Coalition), American Pharmaceutical Association, Muslim Students, Pare-Philippine- Americans Reaching Everyone, national fraternities, national sororities.

Athletics Member NCAA. All Division I.

Campus security: 24-hour emergency response devices and patrols, late-night transport/escort service, controlled dormitory access, Emergency Notification System, CNS Boards, Public Address System.

Student services: health clinic, personal/psychological counseling, veterans affairs office.

FINANCIAL AID

Financial Aid Of all full-time matriculated undergraduates who enrolled in 2018, 9,522 applied for aid, 8,791 were judged to have need, 1,051 had their need fully met. 753 Federal Work-Study jobs (averaging $2546). In 2018, 705 non-need-based awards were made. ***Average percent of need met:*** 68. ***Average financial aid package:*** $29,457. ***Average need-based loan:*** $4713. ***Average need-based gift aid:*** $8873. ***Average non-need-based aid:*** $19,787. ***Average indebtedness upon graduation:*** $28,264.

APPLYING

Standardized Tests *Required for some:* SAT or ACT (for admission).

Options: electronic application, early admission, early decision, early action, deferred entrance.

Required: high school transcript, minimum 3.0 GPA. ***Required for some:*** essay or personal statement, 2 letters of recommendation, interview. ***Recommended:*** essay or personal statement, 2 letters of recommendation.

CONTACT

St. John's University, 8000 Utopia Parkway, Queens, NY 11439. *Toll-free phone:* 888-9STJOHNS.

St. Joseph's College, Long Island Campus

Patchogue, New York

http://www.sjcny.edu/

- **Independent** comprehensive, founded 1916
- **Suburban** 32-acre campus with easy access to New York City
- **Endowment** $28.5 million
- **Coed**
- **Moderately difficult** entrance level

FACULTY

Student/faculty ratio: 14:1.

ACADEMICS

Calendar: 4-1-4. *Degrees:* certificates, bachelor's, master's, and postbachelor's certificates.
Library: Callahan Library plus 1 other. *Books:* 113,712 (physical), 161,062 (digital/electronic); *Serial titles:* 224 (physical), 59,853 (digital/electronic); *Databases:* 129. Weekly public service hours: 80; students can reserve study rooms.

STUDENT LIFE

Housing options: college housing not available.

Activities and organizations: drama/theater group, student-run newspaper, radio station, choral group, STARS (Students Taking an Active Role in Society), All Greek Life (Alpha Phi Delta and Delta Kappa Epsilon Fraternities), Drama Society, Project Sunshine, SJC Sharps, national fraternities, national sororities.

Athletics Member NCAA. All Division III.

Campus security: 24-hour emergency response devices and patrols, late-night transport/escort service.

Student services: personal/psychological counseling, veterans affairs office.

COSTS & FINANCIAL AID

Costs (2019–20) ***Tuition:*** $28,590 full-time, $925 per credit hour part-time. Full-time tuition and fees vary according to course load, location, and program. Part-time tuition and fees vary according to course load, location, and program. ***Required fees:*** $610 full-time.

Financial Aid Of all full-time matriculated undergraduates who enrolled in 2018, 2,564 applied for aid, 2,077 were judged to have need, 542 had their need fully met. 60 Federal Work-Study jobs (averaging $3518). 82 state and other part-time jobs (averaging $4367). In 2018, 416 non-need-based awards were made. ***Average percent of need met:*** 62. ***Average financial aid package:*** $15,813. ***Average need-based loan:*** $4211. ***Average need-based gift aid:*** $13,299. ***Average non-need-based aid:*** $10,770. ***Average indebtedness upon graduation:*** $31,518.

APPLYING

Standardized Tests *Required:* SAT or ACT (for admission).

Options: electronic application, deferred entrance.

Application fee: $25.

Required: essay or personal statement, high school transcript, minimum 3.0 GPA, 2 letters of recommendation. ***Required for some:*** RN for RN-BSN program. ***Recommended:*** interview.

CONTACT

Ms. Gigi Lamens, Vice President for Enrollment Management, St. Joseph's College, Long Island Campus, 155 West Roe Boulevard, Patchogue, NY 11772. *Phone:* 631-687-4500. *E-mail:* glamens@sjcny.edu.

St. Joseph's College, New York

Brooklyn, New York

http://www.sjcny.edu/

- **Independent** comprehensive, founded 1916
- **Urban** 5-acre campus with easy access to Manhattan
- **Endowment** $8.5 million
- **Coed**
- **Moderately difficult** entrance level

FACULTY

Student/faculty ratio: 11:1.

ACADEMICS

Calendar: semesters. *Degrees:* certificates, bachelor's, master's, and postbachelor's certificates.
Library: McEntegart Hall Library plus 1 other. *Books:* 91,695 (physical), 161,062 (digital/electronic); *Serial titles:* 36 (physical), 59,853 (digital/electronic); *Databases:* 129. Weekly public service hours: 83; students can reserve study rooms.

STUDENT LIFE

Housing options: coed. Campus housing is leased by the school.

Activities and organizations: drama/theater group, Campus Activities Board (C.A.B.), Student Senate, Chapel Players Dramatic Club, Council of Multicultural Organizations, Dance Club, national fraternities.

Athletics Member NCAA. All Division III.

Campus security: 24-hour emergency response devices and patrols, late-night transport/escort service, controlled dormitory access.

Student services: health clinic, personal/psychological counseling, veterans affairs office.

COSTS & FINANCIAL AID

Costs (2019–20) ***Tuition:*** $28,590 full-time, $925 per credit hour part-time. Full-time tuition and fees vary according to course load and program. Part-time tuition and fees vary according to course load and program. ***Required fees:*** $600 full-time. ***Room only:*** $14,800.

Financial Aid Of all full-time matriculated undergraduates who enrolled in 2018, 805 applied for aid, 666 were judged to have need, 107 had their need fully met. 58 Federal Work-Study jobs (averaging $2919). 45 state and other part-time jobs (averaging $2389). In 2018, 120 non-need-based awards were made. ***Average percent of need met:*** 63. ***Average financial aid package:*** $19,484. ***Average need-based loan:*** $3971. ***Average need-based gift aid:*** $16,754. ***Average non-need-based aid:*** $13,996. ***Average indebtedness upon graduation:*** $27,278.

APPLYING

Standardized Tests *Required:* SAT or ACT (for admission).

Options: electronic application, early admission, deferred entrance.

Application fee: $25.

Required: essay or personal statement, high school transcript, minimum 2.5 GPA, 1 letter of recommendation. ***Required for some:*** RN license for the RN to BSN Program. ***Recommended:*** interview.

CONTACT

Ms. Christine Murphy, Vice President for Enrollment Management, St. Joseph's College, New York, 245 Clinton Avenue, Brooklyn, NY 11205. *Phone:* 718-940-5820. *E-mail:* cmurphy@sjcny.edu.

St. Lawrence University

Canton, New York

http://www.stlawu.edu/

- **Independent** 4-year, founded 1856
- **Small-town** 1100-acre campus
- **Endowment** $282.1 million
- **Coed**
- **Moderately difficult** entrance level

FACULTY

Student/faculty ratio: 11:1.

ACADEMICS

Calendar: semesters. *Degrees:* bachelor's, master's, and post-master's certificates.

Library: Owen D. Young Library plus 2 others. *Books:* 602,154 (physical), 303,918 (digital/electronic); *Serial titles:* 98,010 (physical), 123,193 (digital/electronic); *Databases:* 170. Students can reserve study rooms.

STUDENT LIFE

Housing options: on-campus residence required through senior year; coed, women-only, cooperative, special housing for students with disabilities. Campus housing is university owned. Freshman campus housing is guaranteed.

Activities and organizations: drama/theater group, student-run newspaper, radio station, choral group, The Thelomathesian Society (student government), Outing Club, Environmental Action Organization, Association for Campus Entertainment, La Sociedad Hispana, national fraternities, national sororities.

Athletics Member NCAA. All Division III except men's and women's ice hockey (Division I), men's and women's skiing (downhill) (Division I).

Campus security: 24-hour emergency response devices and patrols, student patrols, late-night transport/escort service, controlled dormitory access.

Student services: health clinic, personal/psychological counseling.

COSTS & FINANCIAL AID

Costs (2019–20) ***Comprehensive fee:*** $71,394 includes full-time tuition ($56,360), mandatory fees ($406), and room and board ($14,628). Part-time tuition: $1957 per unit. ***Room and board:*** Room and board charges vary according to board plan. ***Payment plans:*** tuition prepayment, installment.

Financial Aid Of all full-time matriculated undergraduates who enrolled in 2019, 1,771 applied for aid, 1,457 were judged to have need, 490 had their need fully met. In 2019, 688 non-need-based awards were made. ***Average percent of need met:*** 87. ***Average financial aid package:*** $51,110. ***Average need-based loan:*** $4366. ***Average need-based gift aid:*** $40,913. ***Average non-need-based aid:*** $19,173. ***Average indebtedness upon graduation:*** $32,390. ***Financial aid deadline:*** 2/1.

APPLYING

Options: electronic application, early admission, early decision, deferred entrance.

Application fee: $60.

Required: essay or personal statement, high school transcript, 2 letters of recommendation. ***Recommended:*** interview.

CONTACT

Jeremy Freeman, Director of Admissions, St. Lawrence University, 23 Romoda Drive, Canton, NY 13617-1455. *Phone:* 315-229-5261. *Toll-free phone:* 800-285-1856. *Fax:* 315-229-5818. *E-mail:* jfreeman@stlawu.edu.

St. Thomas Aquinas College

Sparkill, New York

http://www.stac.edu/

- **Independent** comprehensive, founded 1952
- **Suburban** 60-acre campus with easy access to New York City
- **Coed** 1,797 undergraduate students, 63% full-time, 50% women, 50% men
- **Moderately difficult** entrance level, 81% of applicants were admitted

UNDERGRAD STUDENTS

1,134 full-time, 663 part-time. Students come from 22 states and territories; 19 other countries; 15% are from out of state; 11% Black or African American, non-Hispanic/Latino; 24% Hispanic/Latino; 3% Asian, non-Hispanic/Latino; 0.2% American Indian or Alaska Native, non-Hispanic/Latino; 1% Two or more races, non-Hispanic/Latino; 5% Race/ethnicity unknown; 6% international; 7% transferred in; 26% live on campus.

Freshmen:

Admission: 1,864 applied, 1,502 admitted, 243 enrolled. ***Average high school GPA:*** 3.0. ***Test scores:*** SAT evidence-based reading and writing scores over 500: 56%; SAT math scores over 500: 59%; ACT scores over 18: 71%; SAT evidence-based reading and writing scores over 600: 20%; SAT math scores over 600: 18%; ACT scores over 24: 21%; SAT math scores over 700: 1%; ACT scores over 30: 6%.

Retention: 71% of full-time freshmen returned.

FACULTY

Total: 160, 31% full-time, 46% with terminal degrees.

Student/faculty ratio: 16:1.

ACADEMICS

Calendar: semesters. *Degrees:* associate, bachelor's, master's, post-master's, and postbachelor's certificates.

Special study options: academic remediation for entering students, accelerated degree program, advanced placement credit, cooperative education, distance learning, double majors, freshman honors college, honors programs, independent study, internships, off-campus study, services for LD students, study abroad, summer session for credit.

Unusual degree programs: 3-2 business administration.

Computers: 200 computers/terminals are available on campus for general student use. Students can access the following: campus intranet, computer help desk, free student e-mail accounts, online (class) grades, online (class) registration, online (class) schedules. Campuswide network is available. 100% of college-owned or -operated housing units are wired for high-speed Internet access. Wireless service is available via entire campus.

Library: ***Books:*** 50,000 (physical); *Serial titles:* 110 (physical), 75,000 (digital/electronic); *Databases:* 68. Weekly public service hours: 83; students can reserve study rooms.

STUDENT LIFE

Housing options: coed. Campus housing is university owned.

Activities and organizations: drama/theater group, student-run newspaper, radio station, choral group, Spartan Volunteers, Campus Activities Board, WSTK Campus Radio, Sports Club, Laetare Players.

Athletics ***Intercollegiate sports:*** baseball M, basketball M/W, bowling W, cross-country running M/W, field hockey W, golf M/W, lacrosse M/W, soccer M/W, softball W, tennis M/W, track and field M/W, triathlon W, volleyball W. ***Intramural sports:*** basketball M/W, ice hockey M(c), volleyball M/W.

Campus security: 24-hour patrols.

Student services: personal/psychological counseling.

COSTS & FINANCIAL AID

Costs (2019–20) ***Comprehensive fee:*** $46,700 includes full-time tuition ($32,250), mandatory fees ($800), and room and board ($13,650). Part-time tuition: $1025 per credit hour. ***Required fees:*** $200 per term part-time. ***College room only:*** $7370. Room and board charges vary according to board plan. ***Payment plan:*** installment.

Financial Aid Of all full-time matriculated undergraduates who enrolled in 2019, 1,029 applied for aid, 795 were judged to have need, 151 had their need fully met. 112 Federal Work-Study jobs (averaging $1331). In 2019, 244 non-need-based awards were made. ***Average percent of need met:*** 40. ***Average financial aid package:*** $18,500. ***Average need-based loan:*** $6800. ***Average need-based gift aid:*** $11,500. ***Average non-need-based aid:*** $15,800. ***Average indebtedness upon graduation:*** $31,000.

APPLYING

Standardized Tests *Required:* SAT or ACT (for admission).

Options: electronic application.

Application fee: $30.

Required: high school transcript, minimum 2.0 GPA. ***Required for some:*** 3 letters of recommendation. ***Recommended:*** essay or personal statement, 2 letters of recommendation, interview.

Application deadlines: 5/1 (freshmen), 5/1 (out-of-state freshmen), 5/1 (transfers).

CONTACT

Mr. Samantha Bazile, Director of Admissions, St. Thomas Aquinas College, 125 Route 340, Sparkill, NY 10976. *Phone:* 845-398-4104. *Fax:* 845-398-4114. *E-mail:* sbazile@stac.edu.

Sarah Lawrence College

Bronxville, New York

http://www.sarahlawrence.edu/

- **Independent** comprehensive, founded 1926
- **Suburban** 44-acre campus with easy access to New York City
- **Endowment** $112.7 million
- **Coed** 1,433 undergraduate students, 99% full-time, 75% women, 25% men
- **Very difficult** entrance level, 53% of applicants were admitted

UNDERGRAD STUDENTS

1,421 full-time, 12 part-time. Students come from 51 states and territories; 38 other countries; 78% are from out of state; 4% Black or African American, non-Hispanic/Latino; 9% Hispanic/Latino; 5% Asian, non-Hispanic/Latino; 0.1% American Indian or Alaska Native, non-Hispanic/Latino; 5% Two or more races, non-Hispanic/Latino; 5% Race/ethnicity unknown; 11% international; 2% transferred in; 84% live on campus.

Freshmen:

Admission: 4,053 applied, 2,152 admitted, 398 enrolled. ***Average high school GPA:*** 3.7. ***Test scores:*** SAT evidence-based reading and writing scores over 500: 100%; SAT math scores over 500: 98%; ACT scores over 18: 100%; SAT evidence-based reading and writing scores over 600: 90%; SAT math scores over 600: 73%; ACT scores over 24: 97%; SAT evidence-based reading and writing scores over 700: 44%; SAT math scores over 700: 30%; ACT scores over 30: 51%.

Retention: 83% of full-time freshmen returned.

FACULTY

Total: 305, 36% full-time, 75% with terminal degrees.

Student/faculty ratio: 9:1.

ACADEMICS

Calendar: semesters. *Degrees:* bachelor's and master's.

Special study options: accelerated degree program, advanced placement credit, double majors, independent study, internships, off-campus study, services for LD students, student-designed majors, study abroad, summer session for credit. ***ROTC:*** Air Force (c).

Unusual degree programs: 3-2 engineering with Columbia University.

Computers: 135 computers/terminals are available on campus for general student use. Students can access the following: campus intranet, computer help desk, free student e-mail accounts, online (class) grades, online (class) schedules. Campuswide network is available. 100% of college-owned or -operated housing units are wired for high-speed Internet access. Wireless service is available via entire campus.

Library: Esther Rauschenbush Library plus 2 others. *Books:* 242,206 (physical), 300,690 (digital/electronic); *Serial titles:* 4,207 (physical), 55,323 (digital/electronic); *Databases:* 146. Weekly public service hours: 109; study areas open 24 hours, 5–7 days a week; students can reserve study rooms.

STUDENT LIFE

Housing options: on-campus residence required for freshman year; coed, men-only, women-only, cooperative, special housing for students with disabilities. Campus housing is university owned. Freshman campus housing is guaranteed.

Activities and organizations: drama/theater group, student-run newspaper, radio station, choral group, Outdoor Adventure Club, VOX: Voices of Planned Parenthood, Rock Climbing Club, Green Rights Organization for the World (GROW), SLC Food & Justice Coalition.

Athletics Member NCAA. All Division III. ***Intercollegiate sports:*** basketball M/W, crew W, cross-country running M/W, equestrian sports M/W, soccer M/W, softball W, swimming and diving M/W, tennis M/W, volleyball M/W. ***Intramural sports:*** basketball M/W, soccer M/W, squash M/W, table tennis M/W, ultimate Frisbee M/W, volleyball M/W.

Campus security: 24-hour emergency response devices and patrols, late-night transport/escort service, controlled dormitory access.

Student services: health clinic, personal/psychological counseling.

COSTS & FINANCIAL AID

Costs (2019–20) ***Comprehensive fee:*** $73,340 includes full-time tuition ($56,020), mandatory fees ($1500), and room and board ($15,820). Full-time tuition and fees vary according to course load. Part-time tuition: $1867 per credit hour. Part-time tuition and fees vary according to course load. ***Required fees:*** $605 per term part-time. ***College room only:*** $10,420. Room and board charges vary according to board plan. ***Payment plan:*** installment. ***Waivers:*** employees or children of employees.

Financial Aid Of all full-time matriculated undergraduates who enrolled in 2019, 927 applied for aid, 777 were judged to have need, 122 had their need fully met. In 2019, 377 non-need-based awards were made. ***Average percent of need met:*** 75. ***Average financial aid package:*** $39,758. ***Average need-based loan:*** $3620. ***Average need-based gift aid:*** $35,692. ***Average non-need-based aid:*** $20,737. ***Average indebtedness upon graduation:*** $26,808. ***Financial aid deadline:*** 1/15.

APPLYING

Options: electronic application, early admission, early decision, early action, deferred entrance.

Application fee: $60.

Required: essay or personal statement, high school transcript, 2 letters of recommendation, counselor recommendation, school report. ***Recommended:*** minimum 3.0 GPA, interview.

Application deadlines: 1/15 (freshmen), 3/1 (transfers), 11/1 (early action).

Early decision deadline: 11/1 (for plan 1), 1/2 (for plan 2).

Notification: 3/15 (freshmen), 6/1 (transfers), 12/15 (early decision plan 1), 2/15 (early decision plan 2), 12/15 (early action).

CONTACT

Ms. Jennifer Gayles, Director of Admission and Multicultural Recruitment, Sarah Lawrence College, 1 Mead Way, Bronxville, NY 10708-5999. *Phone:* 914-395-2510. *Toll-free phone:* 800-888-2858. *Fax:* 914-395-2515. *E-mail:* slcadmit@sarahlawrence.edu.

School of Visual Arts

New York, New York

http://www.sva.edu/

- **Proprietary** comprehensive, founded 1947
- **Urban** 1-acre campus
- **Coed** 3,871 undergraduate students, 98% full-time, 72% women, 28% men
- **Moderately difficult** entrance level, 71% of applicants were admitted

UNDERGRAD STUDENTS
3,783 full-time, 88 part-time. 54% are from out of state; 4% Black or African American, non-Hispanic/Latino; 10% Hispanic/Latino; 14% Asian, non-Hispanic/Latino; 2% Race/ethnicity unknown; 51% international; 6% transferred in; 29% live on campus.

Freshmen:
Admission: 4,261 applied, 3,031 admitted, 896 enrolled. ***Average high school GPA:*** 3.4. ***Test scores:*** SAT evidence-based reading and writing scores over 500: 88%; SAT math scores over 500: 85%; ACT scores over 18: 92%; SAT evidence-based reading and writing scores over 600: 51%; SAT math scores over 600: 58%; ACT scores over 24: 58%; SAT evidence-based reading and writing scores over 700: 9%; SAT math scores over 700: 27%; ACT scores over 30: 18%.

Retention: 87% of full-time freshmen returned.

FACULTY
Total: 1,102, 40% full-time, 18% with terminal degrees.

Student/faculty ratio: 7:1.

ACADEMICS
Calendar: semesters. *Degrees:* bachelor's and master's.

Special study options: academic remediation for entering students, adult/continuing education programs, advanced placement credit, English as a second language, freshman honors college, honors programs, independent study, internships, services for LD students, study abroad, summer session for credit.

Computers: Students can access the following: campus intranet, computer help desk, free student e-mail accounts, online (class) grades, online (class) schedules. Campuswide network is available. Wireless service is available via classrooms, computer centers, computer labs, dorm rooms, libraries, student centers.
Library: School of Visual Arts Library.

STUDENT LIFE
Housing options: coed, women-only. Campus housing is university owned. Freshman applicants given priority for college housing.

Activities and organizations: student-run newspaper, radio station.

Athletics ***Intramural sports:*** baseball M/W, softball M/W.

Campus security: 24-hour patrols.

Student services: health clinic, personal/psychological counseling.

COSTS & FINANCIAL AID
Costs (2020–21) ***Tuition:*** $43,400 full-time, $1450 per credit hour part-time. ***Room only:*** $18,800.

Financial Aid Of all full-time matriculated undergraduates who enrolled in 2019, 1,395 applied for aid, 1,274 were judged to have need, 39 had their need fully met. In 2019, 646 non-need-based awards were made. ***Average percent of need met:*** 28. ***Average financial aid package:*** $20,950. ***Average need-based loan:*** $4408. ***Average need-based gift aid:*** $16,267. ***Average non-need-based aid:*** $12,404. ***Average indebtedness upon graduation:*** $45,588. ***Financial aid deadline:*** 3/1.

APPLYING
Standardized Tests *Required:* SAT or ACT (for admission).

Options: electronic application, early decision, deferred entrance.

Application fee: $50.

Required: essay or personal statement, high school transcript, minimum 2.5 GPA, portfolio. ***Recommended:*** interview.

Application deadlines: rolling (freshmen), rolling (transfers).

Notification: continuous (freshmen), continuous (transfers).

CONTACT
Admissions Office, School of Visual Arts, 209 East 23rd Street, New York, NY 10010. *Phone:* 212-592-2100. *Toll-free phone:* 800-436-4204. *Fax:* 212-592-2116. *E-mail:* admissions@sva.edu.

Sh'or Yoshuv Rabbinical College

Lawrence, New York

CONTACT
Rabbi Moshe Rubin, Registrar, Sh'or Yoshuv Rabbinical College, 1 Cedarlawn Avenue, Lawrence, NY 11559-1714. *Phone:* 516-239-9002 Ext. 124. *Fax:* 516-977-1282. *E-mail:* mrubin@shoryoshuv.org.

Siena College

Loudonville, New York

http://www.siena.edu/

- **Independent Roman Catholic** comprehensive, founded 1937
- **Suburban** 175-acre campus with easy access to Albany-Schenectady-Troy Metro Area, NY
- **Endowment** $137.2 million
- **Coed** 3,191 undergraduate students, 95% full-time, 57% women, 43% men
- 81% of applicants were admitted

UNDERGRAD STUDENTS
3,028 full-time, 163 part-time. Students come from 35 states and territories; 40 other countries; 18% are from out of state; 3% Black or African American, non-Hispanic/Latino; 8% Hispanic/Latino; 5% Asian, non-Hispanic/Latino; 0.2% American Indian or Alaska Native, non-Hispanic/Latino; 3% Two or more races, non-Hispanic/Latino; 0.5% Race/ethnicity unknown; 3% international; 4% transferred in; 75% live on campus.

Freshmen:
Admission: 7,728 applied, 6,269 admitted, 841 enrolled. ***Average high school GPA:*** 3.5. ***Test scores:*** SAT evidence-based reading and writing scores over 500: 88%; SAT math scores over 500: 90%; ACT scores over 18: 95%; SAT evidence-based reading and writing scores over 600: 42%; SAT math scores over 600: 48%; ACT scores over 24: 66%; SAT evidence-based reading and writing scores over 700: 6%; SAT math scores over 700: 8%; ACT scores over 30: 17%.

Retention: 86% of full-time freshmen returned.

FACULTY
Total: 346, 62% full-time, 72% with terminal degrees.

Student/faculty ratio: 12:1.

ACADEMICS
Calendar: semesters. *Degrees:* certificates, bachelor's, master's, and postbachelor's certificates.

Special study options: accelerated degree program, advanced placement credit, double majors, English as a second language, honors programs, independent study, internships, off-campus study, part-time degree program, services for LD students, student-designed majors, study abroad, summer session for credit. ***ROTC:*** Army (b), Air Force (c).

Unusual degree programs: 3-2 engineering with Rensselaer Polytechnic Institute, Clarkson University, SUNY-Binghamton, Western New England College; BS/JD with Albany Law School.

Computers: 520 computers/terminals and 5,341 ports are available on campus for general student use. Students can access the following: campus intranet, computer help desk, free student e-mail accounts, online (class) grades, online (class) registration, online (class) schedules. Campuswide network is available. 100% of college-owned or -operated housing units are wired for high-speed Internet access. Wireless service is available via entire campus.
Library: Standish Library. *Books:* 243,227 (physical), 300,197 (digital/electronic); *Serial titles:* 1,636 (physical), 29,000 (digital/electronic); *Databases:* 167. Weekly public service hours: 102; students can reserve study rooms.

STUDENT LIFE

Housing options: on-campus residence required through senior year; coed, special housing for students with disabilities. Campus housing is university owned. Freshman applicants given priority for college housing.

Activities and organizations: drama/theater group, student-run newspaper, radio and television station, choral group, Habitat for Humanity, Outing Club, Make-a-Wish Wishmakers on Campus, Crossfit, Biology Club.

Athletics Member NCAA. All Division I. ***Intercollegiate sports:*** baseball M(s), basketball M(s)/W(s), cross-country running M(s)/W(s), golf M(s)/W(s), lacrosse M(s)/W(s), soccer M(s)/W(s), softball W(s), swimming and diving W(s), tennis M(s)/W(s), track and field M(s)/W(s), volleyball W(s), water polo W(s). ***Intramural sports:*** baseball M(c), basketball M/W, cheerleading W(c), equestrian sports M(c)/W(c), football M, ice hockey M(c), rugby M(c)/W(c), soccer M/W, softball M/W, squash M(c)/W(c), tennis M(c)/W(c), ultimate Frisbee M(c)/W(c), volleyball M/W.

Campus security: 24-hour emergency response devices and patrols, late-night transport/escort service, controlled dormitory access, gates closed nightly with entrance through welcome booth.

Student services: health clinic, personal/psychological counseling, women's center, veterans affairs office.

COSTS & FINANCIAL AID

Costs (2020–21) ***Comprehensive fee:*** $55,415 includes full-time tuition ($39,200), mandatory fees ($300), and room and board ($15,915). Full-time tuition and fees vary according to course load and student level. Part-time tuition: $675 per credit hour. Part-time tuition and fees vary according to course load and student level. ***Required fees:*** $95 per term part-time. ***College room only:*** $9485. Room and board charges vary according to board plan, housing facility, and student level. ***Payment plan:*** installment. ***Waivers:*** employees or children of employees.

Financial Aid Of all full-time matriculated undergraduates who enrolled in 2018, 2,553 applied for aid, 2,248 were judged to have need, 699 had their need fully met. In 2018, 586 non-need-based awards were made. ***Average percent of need met:*** 80. ***Average financial aid package:*** $31,867. ***Average need-based loan:*** $4342. ***Average need-based gift aid:*** $24,358. ***Average non-need-based aid:*** $13,626. ***Average indebtedness upon graduation:*** $35,057. ***Financial aid deadline:*** 2/15.

APPLYING

Standardized Tests *Required for some:* SAT or ACT (for admission).

Options: electronic application, early admission, early decision, early action, deferred entrance.

Application fee: $50.

Required: high school transcript, 1 letter of recommendation. ***Required for some:*** essay or personal statement. ***Recommended:*** interview.

Application deadlines: 3/1 (freshmen), 8/15 (transfers), 12/1 (early action).

Early decision deadline: 12/1.

Notification: 3/15 (freshmen), continuous (transfers), 1/1 (early decision), 1/7 (early action).

CONTACT

Katie Szalda, Director of Admissions, Siena College, 515 Loudon Road, Loudonville, NY 12211-1462. *Phone:* 518-783-2423. *Toll-free phone:* 888-AT-SIENA. *Fax:* 518-783-2436. *E-mail:* admissions@siena.edu.

Skidmore College

Saratoga Springs, New York

http://www.skidmore.edu/

- **Independent** 4-year, founded 1903
- **Small-town** 890-acre campus with easy access to Albany, NY
- **Endowment** $384.3 million
- **Coed** 2,662 undergraduate students, 98% full-time, 60% women, 40% men
- **Very difficult** entrance level, 30% of applicants were admitted

UNDERGRAD STUDENTS

2,622 full-time, 40 part-time. Students come from 41 states and territories; 65 other countries; 66% are from out of state; 5% Black or African American, non-Hispanic/Latino; 9% Hispanic/Latino; 6% Asian, non-Hispanic/Latino; 5% Two or more races, non-Hispanic/Latino; 2% Race/ethnicity unknown; 11% international; 1% transferred in; 89% live on campus.

Freshmen:

Admission: 11,102 applied, 3,336 admitted, 735 enrolled. ***Test scores:*** SAT evidence-based reading and writing scores over 500: 99%; SAT math scores over 500: 97%; ACT scores over 18: 100%; SAT evidence-based reading and writing scores over 600: 83%; SAT math scores over 600: 80%; ACT scores over 24: 96%; SAT evidence-based reading and writing scores over 700: 27%; SAT math scores over 700: 29%; ACT scores over 30: 59%.

Retention: 91% of full-time freshmen returned.

FACULTY

Total: 399, 72% full-time, 70% with terminal degrees.

Student/faculty ratio: 8:1.

ACADEMICS

Calendar: semesters plus optional 6-week internship period. *Degree:* bachelor's.

Special study options: accelerated degree program, advanced placement credit, double majors, honors programs, independent study, internships, off-campus study, services for LD students, student-designed majors, study abroad, summer session for credit. ***ROTC:*** Army (c), Air Force (c).

Unusual degree programs: 3-2 business administration with Clarkson University, Rochester Institute of Technology, Syracuse University; engineering with Dartmouth College, Clarkson University, Rensselaer Polytechnic Institute; nursing with New York University; finance or accounting with Syracuse University, physical or occupational therapy with Sage Graduate School, accounting with Wake Forest.

Computers: 105 computers/terminals are available on campus for general student use. Students can access the following: campus intranet, computer help desk, free student e-mail accounts, online (class) grades, online (class) registration, online (class) schedules. Campuswide network is available. 100% of college-owned or -operated housing units are wired for high-speed Internet access. Wireless service is available via classrooms, computer centers, computer labs, dorm rooms, learning centers, libraries, student centers.

Library: Scribner Library. *Books:* 358,674 (physical), 134,817 (digital/electronic); *Serial titles:* 1,587 (physical); *Databases:* 416. Weekly public service hours: 109; students can reserve study rooms.

STUDENT LIFE

Housing options: on-campus residence required through sophomore year; coed, women-only, special housing for students with disabilities. Campus housing is university owned. Freshman campus housing is guaranteed.

Activities and organizations: drama/theater group, student-run newspaper, radio and television station, choral group, Student Government Association, Student radio station (WSPN), Benefaction (Student Volunteer), Outing Club, UJIMA.

Athletics Member NCAA. All Division III. ***Intercollegiate sports:*** baseball M, basketball M/W, crew M/W, equestrian sports W, field hockey W, golf M, ice hockey M, lacrosse M/W, soccer M/W, softball W, swimming and diving M/W, tennis M/W, volleyball W. ***Intramural sports:*** basketball M/W, cross-country running M(c)/W(c), ice hockey M(c)/W(c), racquetball M/W, sailing M(c)/W(c), skiing (cross-country) M(c)/W(c), skiing (downhill) M(c)/W(c), soccer M/W, tennis M/W, ultimate Frisbee M(c)/W(c), volleyball M/W.

Campus security: 24-hour emergency response devices and patrols, late-night transport/escort service, controlled dormitory access.

Student services: health clinic, personal/psychological counseling.

COSTS & FINANCIAL AID

Costs (2019–20) ***One-time required fee:*** $150. ***Comprehensive fee:*** $71,172 includes full-time tuition ($55,136), mandatory fees ($1036), and room and board ($15,000). Part-time tuition: $1838 per credit hour. ***Required fees:*** $25 per term part-time. ***College room only:*** $8868.

Financial Aid Of all full-time matriculated undergraduates who enrolled in 2019, 1,318 applied for aid, 1,198 were judged to have need, 1,162 had their need fully met. In 2019, 8 non-need-based awards were made. ***Average percent of need met:*** 99. ***Average financial aid package:*** $53,700. ***Average need-based loan:*** $3100. ***Average need-based gift aid:*** $47,800. ***Average non-need-based aid:*** $16,500. ***Average indebtedness upon graduation:*** $31,381. ***Financial aid deadline:*** 1/15.

APPLYING
Standardized Tests *Required for some:* SAT or ACT (for admission).

Options: electronic application, early admission, early decision, deferred entrance.

Application fee: $65.

Required: essay or personal statement, high school transcript, 2 letters of recommendation. ***Recommended:*** interview.

Application deadlines: 1/15 (freshmen), 4/1 (transfers).

Early decision deadline: 11/15 (for plan 1), 1/15 (for plan 2).

Notification: 4/1 (freshmen), 4/22 (transfers), 12/15 (early decision plan 1), 2/15 (early decision plan 2).

CONTACT
Ms. Mary Lou Bates, Vice President and Dean of Admissions and Financial Aid, Skidmore College, 815 North Broadway, Saratoga Springs, NY 12866-1632. *Phone:* 518-580-5570. *Toll-free phone:* 800-867-6007. *Fax:* 518-580-5584. *E-mail:* admissions@skidmore.edu.

State University of New York at Fredonia

Fredonia, New York

http://www.fredonia.edu/

- **State-supported** comprehensive, founded 1826, part of State University of New York System
- **Small-town** 256-acre campus with easy access to Buffalo
- **Endowment** $39.6 million
- **Coed** 4,226 undergraduate students, 98% full-time, 57% women, 43% men
- **Moderately difficult** entrance level, 71% of applicants were admitted

UNDERGRAD STUDENTS
4,143 full-time, 83 part-time. Students come from 29 states and territories; 13 other countries; 3% are from out of state; 9% Black or African American, non-Hispanic/Latino; 10% Hispanic/Latino; 2% Asian, non-Hispanic/Latino; 0.6% American Indian or Alaska Native, non-Hispanic/Latino; 3% Two or more races, non-Hispanic/Latino; 1% Race/ethnicity unknown; 2% international; 6% transferred in; 55% live on campus.

Freshmen:
Admission: 6,277 applied, 4,464 admitted, 1,007 enrolled. ***Average high school GPA:*** 3.3. ***Test scores:*** SAT evidence-based reading and writing scores over 500: 75%; SAT math scores over 500: 73%; ACT scores over 18: 88%; SAT evidence-based reading and writing scores over 600: 29%; SAT math scores over 600: 24%; ACT scores over 24: 39%; SAT evidence-based reading and writing scores over 700: 2%; SAT math scores over 700: 3%; ACT scores over 30: 4%.

Retention: 70% of full-time freshmen returned.

FACULTY
Total: 433, 57% full-time, 65% with terminal degrees.

Student/faculty ratio: 14:1.

ACADEMICS
Calendar: semesters. *Degrees:* bachelor's, master's, and post-master's certificates.

Special study options: accelerated degree program, adult/continuing education programs, advanced placement credit, distance learning, double majors, English as a second language, honors programs, independent study, internships, off-campus study, part-time degree program, services for LD students, student-designed majors, study abroad, summer session for credit.

Unusual degree programs: 3-2 engineering with Clarkson University, State University of New York at Buffalo, Case Western Reserve, Columbia University, Louisiana Technical University, New York State College of Ceramics at Alfred, Ohio State University.

Computers: 500 computers/terminals are available on campus for general student use. Students can access the following: campus intranet, computer help desk, free student e-mail accounts, online (class) grades, online (class) registration, online (class) schedules. Campuswide network is available. 100% of college-owned or -operated housing units are wired for high-speed Internet access. Wireless service is available via entire campus.

Library: Daniel A. Reed Library. *Books:* 18.0 million (physical); *Serial titles:* 48,000 (physical). Weekly public service hours: 68; students can reserve study rooms.

STUDENT LIFE
Housing options: on-campus residence required through sophomore year; coed, women-only. Campus housing is university owned. Freshman campus housing is guaranteed.

Activities and organizations: drama/theater group, student-run newspaper, radio and television station, choral group, Student Association, Fredonia Radio Systems, Colleges Against Cancer, Applied Communication Association, Spectrum Entertainment Board, national fraternities, national sororities.

Athletics Member NCAA. All Division III. ***Intercollegiate sports:*** baseball M, basketball M/W, cheerleading M/W, cross-country running M/W, field hockey M(c)/W(c), ice hockey M, lacrosse M(c)/W, rugby M(c)/W(c), soccer M/W, softball W, swimming and diving M/W, tennis W, track and field M/W, volleyball W. ***Intramural sports:*** basketball M/W, field hockey W(c), ice hockey M(c), racquetball M/W, rock climbing M/W, sand volleyball M/W, skiing (downhill) M/W, soccer M/W, softball M/W, squash M/W, tennis M/W, ultimate Frisbee M/W, volleyball M/W, water polo M/W.

Campus security: 24-hour emergency response devices and patrols, late-night transport/escort service, controlled dormitory access.

Student services: health clinic, personal/psychological counseling, legal services, veterans affairs office.

COSTS & FINANCIAL AID
Costs (2020–21) ***Tuition:*** state resident $7070 full-time, $295 per credit hour part-time; nonresident $16,980 full-time, $708 per credit hour part-time. ***Required fees:*** $1647 full-time, $68 part-time. ***Room and board:*** $12,830; room only: $7600. Room and board charges vary according to board plan and housing facility. ***Payment plan:*** installment.

Financial Aid Of all full-time matriculated undergraduates who enrolled in 2019, 3,737 applied for aid, 3,018 were judged to have need, 733 had their need fully met. 170 Federal Work-Study jobs (averaging $1840). In 2019, 455 non-need-based awards were made. ***Average percent of need met:*** 66. ***Average financial aid package:*** $12,659. ***Average need-based loan:*** $4218. ***Average need-based gift aid:*** $7251. ***Average non-need-based aid:*** $3558. ***Average indebtedness upon graduation:*** $26,722.

APPLYING
Standardized Tests *Required:* SAT or ACT (for admission).

Options: electronic application, early admission, deferred entrance.

Application fee: $50.

Required: essay or personal statement, high school transcript, 1 letter of recommendation. ***Required for some:*** interview, audition for music, dance and theater programs: portfolio for visual arts and technical theatre programs.

Application deadlines: rolling (freshmen), rolling (transfers).

Notification: continuous (freshmen), continuous (transfers).

CONTACT
Mr. Cory M. Bezek, Executive Director of Enrollment Services, State University of New York at Fredonia, 280 Central Avenue, 6th Floor Maytum Hall, Fredonia, NY 14063. *Phone:* 716-673-3251. *Toll-free phone:* 800-252-1212. *Fax:* 716-673-3249. *E-mail:* admissions@fredonia.edu.

State University of New York at New Paltz

New Paltz, New York

http://www.newpaltz.edu/

- **State-supported** comprehensive, founded 1828, part of State University of New York System
- **Small-town** 216-acre campus
- **Endowment** $26.8 million
- **Coed** 6,807 undergraduate students, 92% full-time, 63% women, 37% men
- **Very difficult** entrance level, 45% of applicants were admitted

UNDERGRAD STUDENTS
6,291 full-time, 516 part-time. Students come from 24 states and territories; 39 other countries; 2% are from out of state; 6% Black or African American, non-Hispanic/Latino; 21% Hispanic/Latino; 5% Asian, non-Hispanic/Latino; 0.1% Native Hawaiian or other Pacific Islander, non-Hispanic/Latino; 0.1% American Indian or Alaska Native, non-Hispanic/Latino; 3% Two or more races, non-Hispanic/Latino; 3% Race/ethnicity unknown; 2% international; 12% transferred in; 45% live on campus.

Freshmen:
Admission: 14,425 applied, 6,517 admitted, 1,125 enrolled. ***Average high school GPA:*** 3.6. ***Test scores:*** SAT evidence-based reading and writing scores over 500: 91%; SAT math scores over 500: 93%; ACT scores over 18: 98%; SAT evidence-based reading and writing scores over 600: 50%; SAT math scores over 600: 44%; ACT scores over 24: 73%; SAT evidence-based reading and writing scores over 700: 6%; SAT math scores over 700: 8%; ACT scores over 30: 12%.

Retention: 85% of full-time freshmen returned.

FACULTY
Total: 667, 52% full-time, 61% with terminal degrees.

Student/faculty ratio: 16:1.

ACADEMICS
Calendar: semesters. *Degrees:* bachelor's, master's, post-master's, and postbachelor's certificates.

Special study options: academic remediation for entering students, advanced placement credit, cooperative education, distance learning, double majors, English as a second language, honors programs, independent study, internships, off-campus study, part-time degree program, services for LD students, student-designed majors, study abroad, summer session for credit.

Unusual degree programs: 3-2 business administration; engineering.

Computers: 800 computers/terminals are available on campus for general student use. Students can access the following: campus intranet, computer help desk, free student e-mail accounts, online (class) grades, online (class) registration, online (class) schedules. Campuswide network is available. 100% of college-owned or -operated housing units are wired for high-speed Internet access. Wireless service is available via entire campus.

Library: Sojourner Truth Library. *Books:* 405,123 (physical), 205,499 (digital/electronic); *Serial titles:* 7,819 (physical), 113,923 (digital/electronic); *Databases:* 98. Weekly public service hours: 103; students can reserve study rooms.

STUDENT LIFE
Housing options: on-campus residence required for freshman year; coed, special housing for students with disabilities. Campus housing is university owned. Freshman campus housing is guaranteed.

Activities and organizations: drama/theater group, student-run newspaper, radio and television station, choral group, Student Association, Residence Hall Student Association, Outing Club, The Oracle Newspaper, United Greek Association, national fraternities, national sororities.

Athletics Member NCAA. All Division III. ***Intercollegiate sports:*** baseball M, basketball M/W, cross-country running M/W, field hockey W, lacrosse W, soccer M/W, swimming and diving M/W, tennis W, volleyball M/W. ***Intramural sports:*** basketball M/W, cheerleading M(c)/W(c), equestrian sports M(c)/W(c), lacrosse M(c)/W(c), racquetball M/W, rugby M(c)/W(c), soccer M/W, swimming and diving M(c)/W(c), table tennis M(c)/W(c), tennis M/W, track and field M(c)/W(c), ultimate Frisbee M(c)/W(c), volleyball M/W, water polo M/W, wrestling M(c).

Campus security: 24-hour emergency response devices and patrols, late-night transport/escort service, controlled dormitory access, safety seminars, RAD Women's Self Defense.

Student services: health clinic, personal/psychological counseling, legal services, veterans affairs office.

COSTS & FINANCIAL AID
Costs (2019–20) ***Tuition:*** state resident $7070 full-time, $295 per credit hour part-time; nonresident $16,980 full-time, $708 per credit hour part-time. ***Required fees:*** $1432 full-time, $42 per credit hour part-time, $210 per term part-time. ***Room and board:*** $13,928; room only: $9128. Room and board charges vary according to board plan. ***Payment plan:*** installment.

Financial Aid Of all full-time matriculated undergraduates who enrolled in 2019, 5,122 applied for aid, 3,948 were judged to have need, 465 had their need fully met. In 2019, 69 non-need-based awards were made. ***Average percent of need met:*** 58. ***Average financial aid package:*** $12,224. ***Average need-based loan:*** $4353. ***Average need-based gift aid:*** $5338. ***Average non-need-based aid:*** $2310. ***Average indebtedness upon graduation:*** $26,771.

APPLYING
Standardized Tests *Required:* SAT or ACT (for admission).

Options: electronic application, early admission, early action.

Application fee: $50.

Required: essay or personal statement, high school transcript, 1 letter of recommendation. ***Required for some:*** portfolio for art program, audition for music and theater programs.

Application deadlines: 5/1 (freshmen), 5/1 (transfers), 11/15 (early action).

Notification: continuous (freshmen), continuous (transfers), rolling (early action).

CONTACT
Ms. Kimberly A. Strano, Director of Freshman Admissions, State University of New York at New Paltz, 1 Hawk Drive, New Paltz, NY 12561-2499. *Phone:* 845-257-3200. *Toll-free phone:* 877-MY-NP-411. *Fax:* 845-257-3209. *E-mail:* admissions@newpaltz.edu.

State University of New York at Oswego

Oswego, New York

http://www.oswego.edu/

- **State-supported** comprehensive, founded 1861, part of State University of New York System
- **Small-town** 696-acre campus with easy access to Syracuse
- **Endowment** $39.4 million
- **Coed** 6,920 undergraduate students, 95% full-time, 51% women, 49% men
- **Moderately difficult** entrance level, 54% of applicants were admitted

UNDERGRAD STUDENTS
6,561 full-time, 359 part-time. Students come from 32 states and territories; 38 other countries; 3% are from out of state; 10% Black or African American, non-Hispanic/Latino; 13% Hispanic/Latino; 2% Asian, non-Hispanic/Latino; 0.4% American Indian or Alaska Native, non-Hispanic/Latino; 3% Two or more races, non-Hispanic/Latino; 3% international; 10% transferred in; 57% live on campus.

Freshmen:
Admission: 12,669 applied, 6,848 admitted, 1,422 enrolled. ***Average high school GPA:*** 3.5. ***Test scores:*** SAT evidence-based reading and writing scores over 500: 88%; SAT math scores over 500: 87%; SAT evidence-based reading and writing scores over 600: 31%; SAT math scores over 600: 30%; SAT evidence-based reading and writing scores over 700: 3%; SAT math scores over 700: 4%.

Retention: 77% of full-time freshmen returned.

FACULTY
Total: 572, 63% full-time, 63% with terminal degrees.

Student/faculty ratio: 17:1.

ACADEMICS
Calendar: semesters. *Degrees:* bachelor's, master's, post-master's, and postbachelor's certificates.

Special study options: accelerated degree program, adult/continuing education programs, advanced placement credit, cooperative education, distance learning, double majors, English as a second language, freshman honors college, honors programs, independent study, internships, off-campus study, part-time degree program, services for LD students, study abroad, summer session for credit. ***ROTC:*** Army (c), Air Force (c).

Unusual degree programs: 3-2 engineering with Clarkson University, Case Western Reserve University, State University of New York at Binghamton.

Computers: 1,250 computers/terminals are available on campus for general student use. Students can access the following: campus intranet, computer help desk, free student e-mail accounts, online (class) grades, online (class) registration, online (class) schedules. Campuswide network is available. 100% of college-owned or -operated housing units are wired for high-speed Internet access. Wireless service is available via entire campus.

Library: Penfield Library. *Books:* 322,252 (physical), 160,131 (digital/electronic); *Serial titles:* 1,916 (physical), 76,526 (digital/electronic); *Databases:* 155. Weekly public service hours: 92; study areas open 24 hours, 5–7 days a week; students can reserve study rooms.

STUDENT LIFE

Housing options: on-campus residence required through sophomore year; coed, special housing for students with disabilities. Campus housing is university owned. Freshman campus housing is guaranteed.

Activities and organizations: drama/theater group, student-run newspaper, radio and television station, choral group, club/intramural sports, student radio/television stations (WNYO and WTOP), Outdoor Club, Dance Organization (Del Sarte), Accounting Society, national fraternities, national sororities.

Athletics Member NCAA. All Division III. ***Intercollegiate sports:*** baseball M, basketball M/W, crew M(c)/W(c), cross-country running M/W, field hockey W, golf M, ice hockey M/W, lacrosse M/W, soccer M/W, softball W, swimming and diving M/W, tennis M/W, track and field M/W, volleyball W, wrestling M. ***Intramural sports:*** badminton M/W, basketball M/W, cheerleading W(c), equestrian sports M(c)/W(c), fencing M(c)/W(c), field hockey W(c), football M/W, golf M/W, gymnastics M(c)/W(c), ice hockey M(c)/W(c), lacrosse M(c), racquetball M/W, rock climbing M(c)/W(c), rugby M(c)/W(c), skiing (cross-country) M(c)/W(c), skiing (downhill) M(c)/W(c), soccer M/W, softball M/W, swimming and diving M/W, table tennis M/W, tennis M/W, ultimate Frisbee M(c)/W(c), volleyball M(c)/W, water polo M/W.

Campus security: 24-hour emergency response devices and patrols, controlled dormitory access, Oswego Guardian.

Student services: health clinic, personal/psychological counseling, women's center, legal services, veterans affairs office.

COSTS & FINANCIAL AID

Costs (2019–20) ***One-time required fee:*** $225. ***Tuition:*** state resident $7070 full-time, $295 per credit hour part-time; nonresident $16,980 full-time, $760 per credit hour part-time. Part-time tuition and fees vary according to course load. ***Required fees:*** $1647 full-time, $68 per credit hour part-time. ***Room and board:*** $14,603; room only: $8790. Room and board charges vary according to board plan and housing facility. ***Payment plan:*** installment.

Financial Aid Of all full-time matriculated undergraduates who enrolled in 2019, 5,678 applied for aid, 4,612 were judged to have need, 1,290 had their need fully met. In 2019, 696 non-need-based awards were made. ***Average percent of need met:*** 61. ***Average financial aid package:*** $11,230. ***Average need-based loan:*** $5246. ***Average need-based gift aid:*** $6185. ***Average non-need-based aid:*** $7604.

APPLYING

Standardized Tests *Required:* SAT or ACT (for admission).

Options: electronic application, early admission, early action, deferred entrance.

Application fee: $50.

Required: essay or personal statement, high school transcript, 1 letter of recommendation. ***Recommended:*** minimum 2.7 GPA, interview.

Application deadlines: rolling (freshmen), rolling (transfers), 11/15 (early action).

Notification: 1/15 (freshmen), 1/15 (out-of-state freshmen), 1/15 (transfers), 12/15 (early action).

CONTACT

Mrs. Victoria Furlong, Interim Director of Admissions, State University of New York at Oswego, 7060 State Route 104, Oswego, NY 13126. *Phone:* 315-312-2250. *Fax:* 315-312-3260. *E-mail:* admiss@oswego.edu.

See below for display ad and page 1112 for the College Close-Up.

State University of New York at Plattsburgh

Plattsburgh, New York

http://www.plattsburgh.edu/

- **State-supported** comprehensive, founded 1889, part of State University of New York System
- **Small-town** 265-acre campus with easy access to Montreal
- **Endowment** $21.1 million
- **Coed**
- **Moderately difficult** entrance level

FACULTY

Student/faculty ratio: 16:1.

ACADEMICS

Calendar: semesters plus 2 5-week summer sessions and 1 winter session. *Degrees:* certificates, bachelor's, master's, and post-master's certificates.

Library: Feinberg Library. *Books:* 249,820 (physical), 54,170 (digital/electronic); *Serial titles:* 95 (physical), 463 (digital/electronic); *Databases:* 119. Weekly public service hours: 100; students can reserve study rooms.

STUDENT LIFE

Housing options: on-campus residence required through sophomore year; coed, special housing for students with disabilities. Campus housing is university owned. Freshman campus housing is guaranteed.

Activities and organizations: drama/theater group, student-run newspaper, radio and television station, choral group, Student Association, Honor Societies, Student Media Organizations, service/leadership organizations, intramural and recreational sports, national fraternities, national sororities.

Athletics Member NCAA. All Division III.

Campus security: 24-hour emergency response devices and patrols, late-night transport/escort service, controlled dormitory access.

Student services: health clinic, personal/psychological counseling, women's center, legal services, veterans affairs office.

COSTS & FINANCIAL AID

Costs (2019–20) ***Tuition:*** state resident $7070 full-time, $295 per credit hour part-time; nonresident $16,980 full-time, $708 per credit hour part-time. ***Required fees:*** $1802 full-time, $75 per credit hour part-time. ***Room and board:*** $13,630; room only: $8740. Room and board charges vary according to board plan.

Financial Aid Of all full-time matriculated undergraduates who enrolled in 2018, 3,998 applied for aid, 3,294 were judged to have need, 592 had their need fully met. 653 Federal Work-Study jobs (averaging $1927). In 2018, 705 non-need-based awards were made. ***Average percent of need met:*** 75. ***Average financial aid package:*** $14,358. ***Average need-based loan:*** $7865. ***Average need-based gift aid:*** $8727. ***Average non-need-based aid:*** $6212. ***Average indebtedness upon graduation:*** $30,919.

APPLYING

Standardized Tests *Required:* SAT or ACT (for admission).

Options: electronic application, early admission, deferred entrance.

Application fee: $50.

Required: essay or personal statement, high school transcript, minimum 2.5 GPA, 1 letter of recommendation. ***Required for some:*** minimum 3.4 GPA. ***Recommended:*** minimum 3.0 GPA, interview.

CONTACT

Mrs. Erin Peters, Assistant Director of Admissions, State University of New York at Plattsburgh, 101 Broad Street, Plattsburgh, NY 12901. *Phone:* 888-673-0012. *Toll-free phone:* 888-673-0012. *Fax:* 518-564-2045. *E-mail:* hamm1417@plattsburgh.edu.

State University of New York College at Cortland

Cortland, New York

http://www.cortland.edu/

- **State-supported** comprehensive, founded 1868, part of State University of New York System
- **Small-town** 191-acre campus with easy access to Syracuse
- **Coed** 6,295 undergraduate students, 98% full-time, 56% women, 44% men
- **Moderately difficult** entrance level, 46% of applicants were admitted

UNDERGRAD STUDENTS

6,170 full-time, 125 part-time. 3% are from out of state; 6% Black or African American, non-Hispanic/Latino; 13% Hispanic/Latino; 1% Asian, non-Hispanic/Latino; 0.2% American Indian or Alaska Native, non-Hispanic/Latino; 2% Two or more races, non-Hispanic/Latino; 4% Race/ethnicity unknown; 0.6% international; 10% transferred in.

Freshmen:

Admission: 12,942 applied, 5,959 admitted, 1,208 enrolled. ***Average high school GPA:*** 3.4. ***Test scores:*** SAT evidence-based reading and writing scores over 500: 88%; SAT math scores over 500: 89%; ACT scores over 18: 97%; SAT evidence-based reading and writing scores over 600: 25%; SAT math scores over 600: 26%; ACT scores over 24: 46%; SAT evidence-based reading and writing scores over 700: 2%; SAT math scores over 700: 2%; ACT scores over 30: 6%.

Retention: 80% of full-time freshmen returned.

FACULTY

Total: 662, 50% full-time, 47% with terminal degrees.

Student/faculty ratio: 15:1.

ACADEMICS

Calendar: semesters. *Degrees:* bachelor's, master's, post-master's, and postbachelor's certificates.

Special study options: adult/continuing education programs, cooperative education, distance learning, double majors, honors programs, independent study, internships, off-campus study, student-designed majors, study abroad. ***ROTC:*** Army (c), Air Force (c).

Unusual degree programs: 3-2 engineering with State University of New York at Buffalo, State University of New York at Stony Brook, Alfred University, Clarkson University, State University of New York at Binghamton, Case Western Reserve University; forestry with Duke University, State University of New York College of Environmental Science and Forestry.

Computers: Campuswide network is available.

Library: Memorial Library.

STUDENT LIFE

Housing options: coed, cooperative, special housing for students with disabilities. Campus housing is university owned.

Activities and organizations: drama/theater group, student-run newspaper, radio and television station, choral group.

Athletics Member NCAA. All Division III except golf (Division II). ***Intercollegiate sports:*** baseball M, basketball M/W, cross-country running M/W, field hockey W, football M/W(c), golf W, gymnastics W, ice hockey M/W(c), lacrosse M/W, racquetball M(c)/W(c), rugby M(c)/W(c), soccer M/W, softball W, swimming and diving M/W, tennis W, track and field M/W, volleyball M(c)/W, wrestling M. ***Intramural sports:*** archery M/W, badminton M/W, baseball M, basketball M/W, bowling M/W, cross-country running M/W, fencing M/W, field hockey W, football M/W, golf M/W, gymnastics W, ice hockey M, lacrosse M/W, racquetball M/W, rugby M/W, skiing (cross-country) M/W, skiing (downhill) M/W, soccer M/W, softball M/W, squash M/W, swimming and diving M/W, table tennis M/W, tennis M/W, track and field M/W, volleyball M/W, weight lifting M/W, wrestling M.

Campus security: 24-hour emergency response devices and patrols, late-night transport/escort service.

COSTS & FINANCIAL AID

Costs (2019–20) ***Tuition:*** state resident $7070 full-time, $295 per credit hour part-time; nonresident $16,980 full-time, $708 per credit hour part-time. Full-time tuition and fees vary according to course load and degree level. Part-time tuition and fees vary according to course load and degree level. ***Required fees:*** $1736 full-time. ***Room and board:*** $13,100; room only: $8060. Room and board charges vary according to board plan and housing facility. ***Payment plan:*** installment. ***Waivers:*** employees or children of employees.

Financial Aid Of all full-time matriculated undergraduates who enrolled in 2018, 5,076 applied for aid, 3,920 were judged to have need, 441 had their need fully met. In 2018, 249 non-need-based awards were made. ***Average percent of need met:*** 68. ***Average financial aid package:*** $15,332. ***Average need-based loan:*** $4070. ***Average need-based gift aid:*** $6024. ***Average non-need-based aid:*** $4577. ***Average indebtedness upon graduation:*** $31,176.

APPLYING

Standardized Tests *Required for some:* SAT or ACT (for admission).

Options: electronic application, early admission, early action, deferred entrance.

Application fee: $50.

Required: essay or personal statement, high school transcript, minimum 2.3 GPA, 1 letter of recommendation. ***Recommended:*** minimum 3.0 GPA, 3 letters of recommendation, interview.

Notification: 1/1 (early action).

CONTACT

Director of Admission, State University of New York College at Cortland, PO Box 2000, Cortland, NY 13045. *Phone:* 607-753-4711. *Fax:* 607-753-5998. *E-mail:* admissions@cortland.edu.

State University of New York College at Geneseo

Geneseo, New York

http://www.geneseo.edu/

- **State-supported** comprehensive, founded 1871, part of State University of New York
- **Small-town** 220-acre campus with easy access to Rochester
- **Endowment** $36.8 million
- **Coed** 5,240 undergraduate students, 97% full-time, 62% women, 38% men
- **Moderately difficult** entrance level, 65% of applicants were admitted

UNDERGRAD STUDENTS

5,099 full-time, 141 part-time. Students come from 24 states and territories; 24 other countries; 1% are from out of state; 3% Black or African American, non-Hispanic/Latino; 8% Hispanic/Latino; 5% Asian, non-Hispanic/Latino; 0.1% Native Hawaiian or other Pacific Islander, non-Hispanic/Latino; 0.1% American Indian or Alaska Native, non-Hispanic/Latino; 2% Two or more races, non-Hispanic/Latino; 3% Race/ethnicity unknown; 1% international; 4% transferred in; 55% live on campus.

Freshmen:

Admission: 10,433 applied, 6,831 admitted, 1,233 enrolled. ***Average high school GPA:*** 3.6. ***Test scores:*** SAT evidence-based reading and writing scores over 500: 96%; SAT math scores over 500: 95%; ACT scores over 18: 97%; SAT evidence-based reading and writing scores over 600: 58%; SAT math scores over 600: 58%; ACT scores over 24: 70%; SAT evidence-based reading and writing scores over 700: 10%; SAT math scores over 700: 11%; ACT scores over 30: 16%.

Retention: 85% of full-time freshmen returned.

FACULTY

Total: 400, 62% full-time, 66% with terminal degrees.

Student/faculty ratio: 17:1.

ACADEMICS

Calendar: semesters. *Degrees:* bachelor's and master's.

Special study options: advanced placement credit, distance learning, double majors, English as a second language, honors programs, independent study, internships, off-campus study, part-time degree program, services for LD students, study abroad, summer session for credit. ***ROTC:*** Army (c), Air Force (c).

Unusual degree programs: 3-2 business administration with Alfred University; Binghamton University, State University of New York; Clarkson University; Rochester Institute of Technology; Union College; engineering with Case Western Reserve; Clarkson University; Columbia University; University at Buffalo, State University of New York; optometry with SUNY College of Optometry, physical therapy with SUNY Upstate Medical University, osteopathy with New York Institute of Technology College of Osteopathic Medicine.

Computers: 273 computers/terminals and 3,000 ports are available on campus for general student use. Students can access the following: campus intranet, computer help desk, free student e-mail accounts, online (class) grades, online (class) registration, online (class) schedules. Campuswide network is available. 100% of college-owned or -operated housing units are wired for high-speed Internet access. Wireless service is available via entire campus.

Library: Milne Library plus 1 other.

STUDENT LIFE

Housing options: on-campus residence required through sophomore year; coed, special housing for students with disabilities. Campus housing is university owned. Freshman campus housing is guaranteed.

Activities and organizations: drama/theater group, student-run newspaper, radio station, choral group, Orchesis, Golden Key, Alpha Phi Omega, Marketing Club, Ultimate Frisbee Club, national fraternities, national sororities.

Athletics Member NCAA. All Division III. ***Intercollegiate sports:*** baseball M(c), basketball M/W, cheerleading M(c)/W(c), crew M(c)/W(c), cross-country running M/W, equestrian sports W, fencing M(c)/W(c), field hockey W, golf W, ice hockey M/W(c), lacrosse M/W, rugby M(c)/W(c), skiing (downhill) M(c)/W(c), soccer M/W, softball W, swimming and diving M/W, tennis M(c)/W, track and field M/W, ultimate Frisbee M(c)/W(c), volleyball M(c)/W, water polo M(c). ***Intramural sports:*** badminton M/W, basketball M/W, ice hockey M(c), racquetball M/W, soccer M/W, softball M/W, table tennis M/W, tennis M/W, volleyball M/W.

Campus security: 24-hour emergency response devices and patrols, student patrols, late-night transport/escort service, controlled dormitory access.

Student services: health clinic, personal/psychological counseling, legal services, veterans affairs office.

COSTS & FINANCIAL AID

Costs (2019–20) ***Tuition:*** state resident $7070 full-time, $295 per credit hour part-time; nonresident $16,980 full-time, $708 per credit hour part-time. Part-time tuition and fees vary according to course load. ***Required fees:*** $1857 full-time, $75 per credit hour part-time. ***Room and board:*** $14,018; room only: $8370. Room and board charges vary according to board plan and housing facility. ***Payment plan:*** installment.

Financial Aid Of all full-time matriculated undergraduates who enrolled in 2019, 3,600 applied for aid, 2,710 were judged to have need, 412 had their need fully met. 444 Federal Work-Study jobs (averaging $1877). In 2019, 366 non-need-based awards were made. ***Average percent of need met:*** 44. ***Average financial aid package:*** $10,463. ***Average need-based loan:*** $4091. ***Average need-based gift aid:*** $6513. ***Average non-need-based aid:*** $4468. ***Average indebtedness upon graduation:*** $23,666.

APPLYING

Standardized Tests *Required:* SAT or ACT (for admission).

Options: electronic application, early admission, early decision, deferred entrance.

Application fee: $50.

Required: high school transcript. ***Recommended:*** essay or personal statement, 1 letter of recommendation.

Application deadlines: 1/1 (freshmen), rolling (transfers).

Early decision deadline: 11/15.

Notification: 3/1 (freshmen), 12/15 (early decision).

CONTACT

Mr. Kevin J. Reed, Assistant Director of Admissions, State University of New York College at Geneseo, Doty Hall 200, Geneseo, NY 14454-1401. *Phone:* 585-245-5571. *Toll-free phone:* 866-245-5211. *Fax:* 585-245-5550. *E-mail:* admissions@geneseo.edu.

State University of New York College at Old Westbury

Old Westbury, New York

http://www.oldwestbury.edu/

- **State-supported** comprehensive, founded 1965, part of State University of New York System
- **Suburban** 604-acre campus with easy access to New York City
- **Coed** 4,242 undergraduate students, 86% full-time, 59% women, 41% men
- **Moderately difficult** entrance level, 69% of applicants were admitted

UNDERGRAD STUDENTS

3,632 full-time, 610 part-time. Students come from 14 states and territories; 11 other countries; 1% are from out of state; 27% Black or African American, non-Hispanic/Latino; 24% Hispanic/Latino; 11% Asian, non-Hispanic/Latino; 0.3% Native Hawaiian or other Pacific Islander, non-Hispanic/Latino; 0.3% American Indian or Alaska Native, non-Hispanic/Latino; 3% Two or more races, non-Hispanic/Latino; 2% Race/ethnicity unknown; 0.1% international; 20% transferred in; 19% live on campus.

Freshmen:

Admission: 3,545 applied, 2,432 admitted, 501 enrolled. ***Average high school GPA:*** 3.1.

Retention: 81% of full-time freshmen returned.

FACULTY

Total: 351, 47% full-time, 57% with terminal degrees.

Student/faculty ratio: 16:1.

ACADEMICS

Calendar: semesters. *Degrees:* certificates, bachelor's, master's, and post-master's certificates.

Special study options: academic remediation for entering students, advanced placement credit, distance learning, double majors, freshman honors college, honors programs, independent study, internships, off-campus study, part-time degree program, services for LD students, study abroad, summer session for credit. ***ROTC:*** Army (c), Air Force (c).

Unusual degree programs: 3-2 engineering with Stony Brook University, State University of New York; biological sciences/osteopathic medicine with New York College of Osteopathic Medicine.

Computers: 480 computers/terminals and 700 ports are available on campus for general student use. Students can access the following: campus intranet, free student e-mail accounts, online (class) grades, online (class) registration, financial aid, billing information. Campuswide network is available. 100% of college-owned or -operated housing units are wired for high-speed Internet access. Wireless service is available via entire campus.

Library: SUNY College at Old Westbury Library plus 1 other. *Books:* 156,872 (physical), 144,263 (digital/electronic); *Databases:* 138. Weekly public service hours: 99.

STUDENT LIFE

Housing options: coed. Campus housing is university owned. Freshman campus housing is guaranteed.

Activities and organizations: drama/theater group, student-run newspaper, radio station, choral group, Student Government Association, Alianza Latina, PRIDE, Step Tunes, Anime Magna Games Club, national fraternities, national sororities.

Athletics Member NCAA. All Division III. ***Intercollegiate sports:*** baseball M, basketball M/W, cross-country running M/W, golf M, lacrosse W, soccer M/W, softball W, swimming and diving M/W, volleyball W. ***Intramural sports:*** badminton M/W, basketball M/W, cheerleading M(c)/W(c), equestrian sports M(c)/W(c), football M/W, racquetball M/W, soccer M/W, softball W, squash M/W, ultimate Frisbee M/W, weight lifting M/W.

Campus security: 24-hour emergency response devices and patrols, student patrols, late-night transport/escort service, controlled dormitory access.

Student services: health clinic, personal/psychological counseling, women's center.

COSTS & FINANCIAL AID

Costs (2019–20) ***Tuition:*** state resident $7070 full-time; nonresident $13,980 full-time. Part-time tuition and fees vary according to course load. ***Required fees:*** $1298 full-time. ***Room and board:*** $11,530; room only: $7660. Room and board charges vary according to housing facility. ***Payment plan:*** installment. ***Waivers:*** senior citizens.

Financial Aid Of all full-time matriculated undergraduates who enrolled in 2015, 2,853 applied for aid, 2,509 were judged to have need, 182 had their need fully met. 245 Federal Work-Study jobs (averaging $975). In 2015, 26 non-need-based awards were made. ***Average percent of need met:*** 60. ***Average financial aid package:*** $10,395. ***Average need-based loan:*** $3960. ***Average need-based gift aid:*** $6876. ***Average non-need-based aid:*** $5636.

APPLYING

Standardized Tests *Required:* SAT or ACT (for admission).

Options: electronic application, early admission, early decision, deferred entrance.

Application fee: $50.

Required: essay or personal statement, high school transcript, 2 letters of recommendation. ***Required for some:*** interview.

Application deadlines: rolling (freshmen), 12/15 (transfers).

Early decision deadline: 11/1.

Notification: continuous (freshmen), continuous (transfers), 12/15 (early decision).

CONTACT

State University of New York College at Old Westbury, PO Box 307, Old Westbury, NY 11568. *Phone:* 516-876-3073. *Fax:* 516-876-3307. *E-mail:* enroll@oldwestbury.edu.

State University of New York College at Oneonta

Oneonta, New York

http://www.oneonta.edu/

- **State-supported** comprehensive, founded 1889, part of State University of New York System
- **Small-town** 250-acre campus
- **Endowment** $49.1 million
- **Coed** 6,064 undergraduate students, 98% full-time, 62% women, 38% men
- **Very difficult** entrance level, 56% of applicants were admitted

UNDERGRAD STUDENTS

5,942 full-time, 122 part-time. 1% are from out of state; 5% Black or African American, non-Hispanic/Latino; 16% Hispanic/Latino; 2% Asian, non-Hispanic/Latino; 0.1% Native Hawaiian or other Pacific Islander, non-Hispanic/Latino; 0.7% American Indian or Alaska Native, non-Hispanic/Latino; 2% Two or more races, non-Hispanic/Latino; 4% Race/ethnicity unknown; 0.5% international; 7% transferred in; 46% live on campus.

Freshmen:

Admission: 12,603 applied, 7,098 admitted, 1,451 enrolled. ***Average high school GPA:*** 3.5. ***Test scores:*** SAT evidence-based reading and writing scores over 500: 89%; SAT math scores over 500: 92%; ACT scores over 18: 96%; SAT evidence-based reading and writing scores over 600: 28%; SAT math scores over 600: 28%; ACT scores over 24: 40%; SAT evidence-based reading and writing scores over 700: 1%; SAT math scores over 700: 2%; ACT scores over 30: 3%.

Retention: 80% of full-time freshmen returned.

FACULTY

Total: 479, 60% full-time, 57% with terminal degrees.

Student/faculty ratio: 17:1.

ACADEMICS

Calendar: semesters. *Degrees:* bachelor's, master's, post-master's, and postbachelor's certificates.

Special study options: academic remediation for entering students, adult/continuing education programs, advanced placement credit, distance learning, double majors, English as a second language, external degree program, independent study, internships, off-campus study, part-time degree program, services for LD students, study abroad, summer session for credit.

Unusual degree programs: 3-2 business administration with State University of New York at Binghamton, Clarkson University, Rochester Institute of Technology, Union College; engineering with University at Buffalo, the State University of New York; Alfred University; Clarkson University; Rensselaer Polytechnic Institute; Syracuse University; accounting at State University of New York at Binghamton, fashion with Fashion Institute of Technology, American Intercontinental University in London.

Computers: 700 computers/terminals are available on campus for general student use. Students can access the following: campus intranet, computer help desk, free student e-mail accounts, online (class) grades, online (class) registration, online (class) schedules, digital video/audio editing suites, presentation rehearsal room using lecture capture software, large format printing, network file storage space. Campuswide network is available. 100% of college-owned or -operated housing units are wired for high-speed Internet access. Wireless service is available via entire campus.

Library: Milne Library. *Books:* 394,015 (physical), 417,737 (digital/electronic); *Serial titles:* 60 (physical), 119,484 (digital/electronic); *Databases:* 251. Students can reserve study rooms.

STUDENT LIFE

Housing options: on-campus residence required through sophomore year; coed, special housing for students with disabilities. Campus housing is university owned. Freshman campus housing is guaranteed.

Activities and organizations: drama/theater group, student-run newspaper, radio and television station, choral group, marching band, Center for Social Responsibility and Community, Music Industry Club, Terpsichorean Dance Company, Student Government, Zombie Defense Corps, national fraternities, national sororities.

Athletics Member NCAA. All Division III. ***Intercollegiate sports:*** baseball M, basketball M/W, cheerleading W(c), cross-country running M/W, fencing M(c)/W(c), field hockey W, ice hockey M(c), lacrosse M/W, rugby W(c), soccer M/W, softball W, swimming and diving M/W, tennis M/W, track and field M/W, volleyball W, wrestling M. ***Intramural sports:*** badminton M(c)/W(c), basketball M/W, equestrian sports M(c)/W(c), football M, racquetball M(c)/W(c), skiing (downhill) M(c)/W(c), soccer M/W, softball M/W, ultimate Frisbee M/W, volleyball M/W.

Campus security: 24-hour emergency response devices and patrols, late-night transport/escort service, controlled dormitory access, Oneonta Emergency Squad: an organization of student volunteers with first responder credential.

Student services: health clinic, personal/psychological counseling, women's center.

COSTS & FINANCIAL AID

Costs (2020–21) ***Tuition:*** area resident $7270 full-time, $303 per credit hour part-time; state resident $7270 full-time, $303 per credit hour part-time; nonresident $17,320 full-time, $722 per credit hour part-time. Part-time tuition and fees vary according to course load. ***Required fees:*** $1652 full-time. ***Room and board:*** Room and board charges vary according to housing facility. ***Payment plan:*** installment. ***Waivers:*** employees or children of employees.

Financial Aid Of all full-time matriculated undergraduates who enrolled in 2019, 4,980 applied for aid, 3,730 were judged to have need, 254 had their need fully met. In 2019, 380 non-need-based awards were made. ***Average percent of need met:*** 64. ***Average financial aid package:*** $15,792. ***Average need-based loan:*** $3181. ***Average need-based gift aid:*** $6889. ***Average non-need-based aid:*** $3681. ***Average indebtedness upon graduation:*** $26,092.

APPLYING

Standardized Tests *Required:* SAT or ACT (for admission).

Options: electronic application, early admission, early action, deferred entrance.

Application fee: $50.

Required: essay or personal statement, high school transcript. ***Recommended:*** minimum 3.0 GPA, 3 letters of recommendation.

Application deadlines: rolling (freshmen), rolling (transfers), 11/15 (early action).

Notification: continuous (freshmen), continuous (transfers), 12/1 (early action).

CONTACT

Ms. Karen Brown, Director of Admissions, State University of New York College at Oneonta, Alumni Hall 116, Oneonta, NY 13820-4015. *Phone:* 607-436-2524. *Toll-free phone:* 800-SUNY-123. *Fax:* 607-436-3074. *E-mail:* admissions@oneonta.edu.

State University of New York College at Potsdam

Potsdam, New York

http://www.potsdam.edu/

- **State-supported** comprehensive, founded 1816, part of State University of New York System
- **Small-town** 240-acre campus
- **Endowment** $36.2 million
- **Coed** 3,063 undergraduate students, 97% full-time, 62% women, 38% men
- **Moderately difficult** entrance level, 68% of applicants were admitted

UNDERGRAD STUDENTS

2,977 full-time, 86 part-time. Students come from 32 states and territories; 6 other countries; 4% are from out of state; 12% Black or African American, non-Hispanic/Latino; 14% Hispanic/Latino; 2% Asian, non-Hispanic/Latino; 0.1% Native Hawaiian or other Pacific Islander, non-Hispanic/Latino; 1% American Indian or Alaska Native, non-Hispanic/Latino; 3% Two or more races, non-Hispanic/Latino; 3% Race/ethnicity unknown; 0.4% international; 7% transferred in; 55% live on campus.

Freshmen:

Admission: 5,079 applied, 3,454 admitted, 622 enrolled. ***Average high school GPA:*** ####. ***Test scores:*** SAT evidence-based reading and writing scores over 500: 82%; SAT math scores over 500: 83%; ACT scores over 18: 91%; SAT evidence-based reading and writing scores over 600: 36%; SAT math scores over 600: 36%; ACT scores over 24: 53%; SAT evidence-based reading and writing scores over 700: 5%; SAT math scores over 700: 6%; ACT scores over 30: 9%.

Retention: 73% of full-time freshmen returned.

FACULTY

Total: 354, 71% full-time, 75% with terminal degrees.

Student/faculty ratio: 11:1.

ACADEMICS

Calendar: semesters. *Degrees:* bachelor's, master's, and post-master's certificates.

Special study options: advanced placement credit, distance learning, double majors, honors programs, independent study, internships, off-campus study, part-time degree program, services for LD students, student-designed majors, study abroad, summer session for credit. ***ROTC:*** Army (c), Air Force (c).

Unusual degree programs: 3-2 business administration with Clarkson University; Alfred University; SUNY Oswego; RIT; Union Graduate College; engineering with Clarkson University; Binghamton University, State University of New York; (4+1) MBA Programs; physics, computer science, chemistry, mathematics with Clarkson University.

Computers: 608 computers/terminals are available on campus for general student use. Students can access the following: campus intranet, computer help desk, free student e-mail accounts, online (class) grades, online (class) registration, online (class) schedules, online access to financial aid status, unofficial transcripts, billing, meal plan and housing sign-up. Campuswide network is available. 100% of college-owned or -operated housing units are wired for high-speed Internet access. Wireless service is available via classrooms, computer centers, computer labs, dorm rooms, learning centers, libraries, student centers.

Library: F. W. Crumb Memorial Library plus 1 other. *Books:* 271,555 (physical), 311,566 (digital/electronic); *Serial titles:* 3,993 (physical), 107,915 (digital/electronic); *Databases:* 148. Weekly public service hours: 99; study areas open 24 hours, 5–7 days a week; students can reserve study rooms.

STUDENT LIFE

Housing options: on-campus residence required through sophomore year; coed, special housing for students with disabilities. Campus housing is university owned. Freshman campus housing is guaranteed.

Activities and organizations: drama/theater group, student-run newspaper, radio station, choral group, Student Government Association, Crane Student Association, Black Student Alliance, SOCO LOCO, Musical Theatre Organization, national fraternities, national sororities.

Athletics Member NCAA. All Division III. ***Intercollegiate sports:*** basketball M/W, cross-country running M/W, ice hockey M/W, lacrosse M/W, soccer M/W, swimming and diving M/W, track and field M/W, volleyball W. ***Intramural sports:*** basketball M/W, bowling M(c)/W(c), cheerleading M(c)/W(c), ice hockey M(c)/W(c), racquetball M/W, rugby M(c)/W(c), skiing (downhill) M(c)/W(c), soccer M/W, softball M/W, ultimate Frisbee M(c)/W(c), volleyball M/W.

Campus security: 24-hour emergency response devices and patrols, late-night transport/escort service, controlled dormitory access, RAVE Guardian, Video Surveillance System, security escort service, self-defense education.

Student services: health clinic, personal/psychological counseling, women's center, legal services.

COSTS & FINANCIAL AID

Costs (2019–20) ***Tuition:*** state resident $7070 full-time, $295 per credit hour part-time; nonresident $16,980 full-time, $708 per credit hour part-time. Full-time tuition and fees vary according to course load. Part-time tuition and fees vary according to course load. ***Required fees:*** $1641 full-time, $58 per credit hour part-time. ***Room and board:*** $13,900; room only: $8150. Room and board charges vary according to board plan and housing facility. ***Payment plan:*** installment.

Financial Aid Of all full-time matriculated undergraduates who enrolled in 2019, 2,880 applied for aid, 2,331 were judged to have need, 313 had their need fully met. 142 Federal Work-Study jobs (averaging $1623). In 2019, 312 non-need-based awards were made. ***Average percent of need met:*** 83. ***Average financial aid package:*** $15,149. ***Average need-based loan:*** $4276. ***Average need-based gift aid:*** $8082. ***Average non-need-based aid:*** $4403. ***Average indebtedness upon graduation:*** $30,057.

APPLYING

Options: electronic application, early admission, deferred entrance.

Application fee: $50.

Required: high school transcript, minimum 2.5 GPA, 1 letter of recommendation. ***Required for some:*** essay or personal statement, minimum 2.0 GPA, DVD audition for music.

Application deadlines: rolling (freshmen), rolling (transfers).

Notification: continuous (freshmen), continuous (transfers).

CONTACT

Mr. Ronald Brown, Interim Vice President of Enrollment, State University of New York College at Potsdam, 44 Pierrepont Avenue, Potsdam, NY 13676. *Phone:* 315-267-2180. *Toll-free phone:* 877-POTSDAM. *Fax:* 315-267-2163. *E-mail:* admissions@potsdam.edu.

State University of New York College of Agriculture and Technology at Cobleskill

Cobleskill, New York

http://www.cobleskill.edu/

- **State-supported** 4-year, founded 1916, part of State University of New York System
- **Rural** 950-acre campus with easy access to Albany, NY
- **Endowment** $3.9 million
- **Coed** 2,208 undergraduate students, 94% full-time, 54% women, 46% men
- **Minimally difficult** entrance level, 54% of applicants were admitted

UNDERGRAD STUDENTS

2,085 full-time, 123 part-time. Students come from 17 states and territories; 4 other countries; 8% are from out of state; 11% Black or African American, non-Hispanic/Latino; 12% Hispanic/Latino; 2% Asian, non-Hispanic/Latino; 0.4% American Indian or Alaska Native, non-Hispanic/Latino; 3% Two or more races, non-Hispanic/Latino; 1% Race/ethnicity unknown; 1% international; 10% transferred in; 50% live on campus.

Freshmen:

Admission: 2,364 applied, 1,270 admitted, 593 enrolled. ***Average high school GPA:*** 2.9. ***Test scores:*** SAT evidence-based reading and writing scores over 500: 51%; SAT math scores over 500: 53%; ACT scores over 18: 70%; SAT evidence-based reading and writing scores over 600: 13%; SAT math scores over 600: 13%; ACT scores over 24: 29%; SAT math scores over 700: 1%; ACT scores over 30: 6%.

Retention: 56% of full-time freshmen returned.

FACULTY

Total: 203, 51% full-time, 28% with terminal degrees.

Student/faculty ratio: 11:1.

ACADEMICS

Calendar: semesters. *Degrees:* certificates, associate, bachelor's, and postbachelor's certificates.

Special study options: academic remediation for entering students, advanced placement credit, cooperative education, distance learning, double majors, English as a second language, honors programs, independent study, internships, off-campus study, part-time degree program, services for LD students, study abroad, summer session for credit.

Computers: 550 computers/terminals and 455 ports are available on campus for general student use. Students can access the following: campus intranet, computer help desk, free student e-mail accounts, online (class) grades, online (class) registration, online (class) schedules, web-based printing services. Campuswide network is available. 100% of college-owned or -operated housing units are wired for high-speed Internet access. Wireless service is available via entire campus.

Library: Jared van Wagenen Library. *Books:* 83,851 (physical), 83,000 (digital/electronic); *Serial titles:* 133 (physical), 110,000 (digital/electronic); *Databases:* 74. Weekly public service hours: 76; study areas open 24 hours, 5–7 days a week; students can reserve study rooms.

STUDENT LIFE

Housing options: on-campus residence required through sophomore year; coed, men-only, women-only, special housing for students with disabilities. Campus housing is university owned. Freshman campus housing is guaranteed.

Activities and organizations: drama/theater group, choral group, dairy cattle club, wildlife society, cobleskill christain fellowship, woodsmens club, american fisheries society, national fraternities, national sororities.

Athletics Member NCAA. All Division III. ***Intercollegiate sports:*** baseball M, basketball M/W, cross-country running M/W, equestrian sports M/W, golf M/W, lacrosse M, soccer M/W, softball W, swimming and diving M/W, track and field M/W, volleyball W. ***Intramural sports:*** badminton M/W, basketball M/W, riflery M/W, soccer M/W, triathlon M/W, volleyball M/W, water polo M/W.

Campus security: 24-hour emergency response devices and patrols, student patrols, late-night transport/escort service, controlled dormitory access, bike and horse-mounted patrols.

Student services: health clinic, personal/psychological counseling, veterans affairs office.

COSTS & FINANCIAL AID

Costs (2020–21) ***One-time required fee:*** $125. ***Comprehensive fee:*** $1564 includes mandatory fees ($1564) and room and board ($13,700). ***Required fees:*** $72 per credit hour part-time. ***College room only:*** $8200. Room and board charges vary according to board plan and housing facility. ***Payment plan:*** installment.

Financial Aid Of all full-time matriculated undergraduates who enrolled in 2016, 2,058 applied for aid, 1,861 were judged to have need, 13 had their need fully met. 97 Federal Work-Study jobs (averaging $1166). 353 state and other part-time jobs (averaging $1506). In 2016, 61 non-need-based awards were made. ***Average percent of need met:*** 60. ***Average financial aid package:*** $7614. ***Average need-based loan:*** $2279. ***Average need-based gift aid:*** $4333. ***Average non-need-based aid:*** $2623. ***Average indebtedness upon graduation:*** $29,645.

APPLYING
Standardized Tests *Required for some:* SAT or ACT (for admission). *Recommended:* SAT (for admission), ACT (for admission), SAT or ACT (for admission).

Options: electronic application, deferred entrance.

Application fee: $50.

Required: high school transcript. ***Required for some:*** letters of recommendation.

Application deadlines: rolling (freshmen), rolling (out-of-state freshmen), rolling (transfers).

Notification: continuous (freshmen), continuous (out-of-state freshmen), continuous (transfers).

CONTACT
Samara Davis, Office Assistant 1, State University of New York College of Agriculture and Technology at Cobleskill, 213 Knapp Hall, Cobleskill, NY 12043. *Phone:* 518-255-5525. *Toll-free phone:* 800-295-8988. *Fax:* 518-255-6769. *E-mail:* admissions@cobleskill.edu.

State University of New York College of Agriculture & Technology at Morrisville

Morrisville, New York

http://www.morrisville.edu/

CONTACT
Ms. Melissa Ward, Assistant Director of Enrollment Marketing, State University of New York College of Agriculture & Technology at Morrisville, PO Box 901, Morrisville, NY 13408. *Phone:* 315-684-6046. *Toll-free phone:* 800-258-0111. *Fax:* 315-684-6427.

State University of New York College of Environmental Science and Forestry

Syracuse, New York

http://www.esf.edu/

- **State-supported** university, founded 1911, part of State University of New York System
- **Urban** 17-acre campus with easy access to Syracuse
- **Endowment** $37.6 million
- **Coed**
- **Very difficult** entrance level

FACULTY
Student/faculty ratio: 13:1.

ACADEMICS
Calendar: semesters. *Degrees:* associate, bachelor's, master's, doctoral, and postbachelor's certificates.
Library: F. Franklin Moon Library plus 1 other. *Books:* 57,565 (physical), 444,963 (digital/electronic); *Serial titles:* 1,568 (physical), 163,166 (digital/electronic); *Databases:* 181. Weekly public service hours: 97.

STUDENT LIFE
Housing options: on-campus residence required for freshman year; coed, special housing for students with disabilities. Campus housing is university owned and is provided by a third party. Freshman campus housing is guaranteed.

Activities and organizations: drama/theater group, student-run newspaper, choral group, marching band, Bob Marshall/Outing Club, Forestry Club, Student Environmental Action Coalition, Student Green Campus Initiative, Alpha Phi Omega (Service).

Athletics Member USCAA.

Campus security: 24-hour emergency response devices and patrols, late-night transport/escort service, controlled dormitory access.

Student services: health clinic, personal/psychological counseling, women's center, legal services.

COSTS & FINANCIAL AID
Costs (2019–20) ***Tuition:*** state resident $7070 full-time, $295 per credit hour part-time; nonresident $16,980 full-time, $708 per credit hour part-time. Full-time tuition and fees vary according to location. Part-time tuition and fees vary according to course load and location. ***Required fees:*** $2045 full-time, $105 per credit hour part-time. ***Room and board:*** $16,270; room only: $8850. Room and board charges vary according to board plan, housing facility, and location.

Financial Aid Of all full-time matriculated undergraduates who enrolled in 2018, 1,464 applied for aid, 1,047 were judged to have need, 354 had their need fully met. 240 Federal Work-Study jobs (averaging $1758). 232 state and other part-time jobs (averaging $940). In 2018, 269 non-need-based awards were made. ***Average percent of need met:*** 63. ***Average financial aid package:*** $10,094. ***Average need-based loan:*** $3973. ***Average need-based gift aid:*** $6955. ***Average non-need-based aid:*** $4064. ***Average indebtedness upon graduation:*** $21,885.

APPLYING
Standardized Tests *Required:* SAT or ACT (for admission).

Options: electronic application, early admission, early decision, deferred entrance.

Application fee: $50.

Required: essay or personal statement, high school transcript, minimum 2.5 GPA. ***Recommended:*** 1 letter of recommendation, interview.

CONTACT
Ms. Susan Sanford, Director of Admissions, State University of New York College of Environmental Science and Forestry, Office of Undergraduate Admissions, Gateway Center 1 Forestry Drive, Syracuse, NY 13210-2779. *Phone:* 315-470-6600. *Fax:* 315-470-6933. *E-mail:* esfinfo@esf.edu.

State University of New York College of Technology at Alfred

Alfred, New York

http://www.alfredstate.edu/

- **State-supported** primarily 2-year, founded 1908, part of State University of New York System
- **Rural** 1084-acre campus with easy access to Rochester
- **Endowment** $5.9 million
- **Coed** 3,780 undergraduate students, 92% full-time, 37% women, 63% men
- **Minimally difficult** entrance level, 67% of applicants were admitted

UNDERGRAD STUDENTS
3,482 full-time, 298 part-time. Students come from 29 states and territories; 7 other countries; 4% are from out of state; 13% Black or African American, non-Hispanic/Latino; 9% Hispanic/Latino; 1% Asian, non-Hispanic/Latino; 0.1% Native Hawaiian or other Pacific Islander, non-Hispanic/Latino; 0.3% American Indian or Alaska Native, non-Hispanic/Latino; 3% Two or more races, non-Hispanic/Latino; 2% Race/ethnicity unknown; 0.3% international; 7% transferred in; 61% live on campus.

Freshmen:
Admission: 6,683 applied, 4,460 admitted, 1,180 enrolled. ***Average high school GPA:*** ####. ***Test scores:*** SAT evidence-based reading and writing scores over 500: 63%; SAT math scores over 500: 67%; ACT scores over 18: 78%; SAT evidence-based reading and writing scores over 600: 19%; SAT math scores over 600: 22%; ACT scores over 24: 36%; SAT evidence-based reading and writing scores over 700: 2%; SAT math scores over 700: 3%; ACT scores over 30: 5%.

Retention: 78% of full-time freshmen returned.

FACULTY
Total: 258, 65% full-time, 32% with terminal degrees.

Student/faculty ratio: 18:1.

ACADEMICS
Calendar: semesters. *Degrees:* certificates, associate, and bachelor's.

Special study options: academic remediation for entering students, accelerated degree program, adult/continuing education programs, advanced placement credit, cooperative education, distance learning, double majors, English as a second language, honors programs, independent study, internships, off-campus study, part-time degree program, services for LD students, student-designed majors, study abroad, summer session for credit. ***ROTC:*** Army (c).

Computers: 108 computers/terminals are available on campus for general student use. Students can access the following: campus intranet, computer help desk, free student e-mail accounts, online (class) grades, online (class) registration, online (class) schedules. Campuswide network is available. 100% of college-owned or -operated housing units are wired for high-speed Internet access. Wireless service is available via entire campus.

Library: Walter C. Hinkle Memorial Library plus 1 other. *Books:* 34,991 (physical), 1,901 (digital/electronic); *Serial titles:* 162 (physical); *Databases:* 228. Weekly public service hours: 88.

STUDENT LIFE

Housing options: coed, men-only, women-only, special housing for students with disabilities. Campus housing is university owned. Freshman campus housing is guaranteed.

Activities and organizations: drama/theater group, student-run newspaper, radio station, choral group, Outdoor Recreation Club, Caribbean Student Association, Alfred Programming Board, Pioneer Woodsmen, Disaster Relief Team.

Athletics Member NCAA, USCAA. All Division III. ***Intercollegiate sports:*** baseball M, basketball M/W, cross-country running M/W, equestrian sports M/W, football M, lacrosse M, soccer M/W, softball W, swimming and diving M/W, track and field M/W, volleyball W, wrestling M. ***Intramural sports:*** archery M(c)/W(c), basketball M/W, cheerleading M(c)/W(c), equestrian sports M(c)/W(c), football M, golf M/W, ice hockey M(c), rock climbing M/W, soccer M/W, softball M/W, swimming and diving M/W, tennis M/W, ultimate Frisbee M/W, volleyball M/W.

Campus security: 24-hour emergency response devices and patrols, late-night transport/escort service, controlled dormitory access, residence hall entrance guards.

Student services: health clinic, personal/psychological counseling, veterans affairs office.

COSTS & FINANCIAL AID

Costs (2019–20) ***One-time required fee:*** $150. ***Tuition:*** area resident $7070 full-time, $295 per credit hour part-time; state resident $7070 full-time, $295 per credit hour part-time; nonresident $16,980 full-time, $460 per credit hour part-time. ***Required fees:*** $1782 full-time, $66 per credit hour part-time, $10 per credit hour part-time. ***Room and board:*** $13,060; room only: $7990. Room and board charges vary according to board plan, housing facility, and location. ***Payment plans:*** installment, deferred payment. ***Waivers:*** employees or children of employees.

Financial Aid Of all full-time matriculated undergraduates who enrolled in 2018, 3,232 applied for aid, 2,864 were judged to have need, 308 had their need fully met. In 2018, 176 non-need-based awards were made. ***Average percent of need met:*** 57. ***Average financial aid package:*** $11,164. ***Average need-based loan:*** $3677. ***Average need-based gift aid:*** $7392. ***Average non-need-based aid:*** $5663. ***Average indebtedness upon graduation:*** $34,177.

APPLYING

Standardized Tests *Required for some:* SAT or ACT (for admission). *Recommended:* SAT or ACT (for admission).

Options: electronic application.

Application fee: $50.

Required: high school transcript, minimum 2.0 GPA, Common Application with essay on supplemental application. ***Recommended:*** essay or personal statement, interview.

Application deadlines: rolling (freshmen), rolling (transfers).

Notification: continuous (freshmen), continuous (transfers).

CONTACT

Ms. Betsy Penrose, Vice President for Enrollment Management, State University of New York College of Technology at Alfred, Huntington Administration Building, 10 Upper College Drive, Alfred, NY 14802. *Phone:* 607-587-3945. *Toll-free phone:* 800-4-ALFRED. *Fax:* 607-587-4299. *E-mail:* admissions@alfredstate.edu.

State University of New York College of Technology at Canton

Canton, New York

http://www.canton.edu/

- **State-supported** 4-year, founded 1906, part of State University of New York System
- **Small-town** 555-acre campus
- **Endowment** $11.9 million
- **Coed** 3,228 undergraduate students, 86% full-time, 56% women, 44% men
- **Minimally difficult** entrance level, 85% of applicants were admitted

UNDERGRAD STUDENTS

2,784 full-time, 444 part-time. Students come from 27 states and territories; 14 other countries; 3% are from out of state; 13% Black or African American, non-Hispanic/Latino; 11% Hispanic/Latino; 1% Asian, non-Hispanic/Latino; 2% American Indian or Alaska Native, non-Hispanic/Latino; 3% Two or more races, non-Hispanic/Latino; 2% Race/ethnicity unknown; 2% international; 10% transferred in; 39% live on campus.

Freshmen:

Admission: 3,809 applied, 3,223 admitted, 707 enrolled. ***Average high school GPA:*** 2.9. ***Test scores:*** SAT evidence-based reading and writing scores over 500: 53%; SAT math scores over 500: 59%; ACT scores over 18: 86%; SAT evidence-based reading and writing scores over 600: 10%; SAT math scores over 600: 13%; ACT scores over 24: 22%; SAT evidence-based reading and writing scores over 700: 1%; SAT math scores over 700: 2%; ACT scores over 30: 2%.

Retention: 70% of full-time freshmen returned.

FACULTY

Total: 232, 53% full-time, 43% with terminal degrees.

Student/faculty ratio: 18:1.

ACADEMICS

Calendar: semesters. *Degrees:* certificates, associate, and bachelor's.

Special study options: academic remediation for entering students, advanced placement credit, cooperative education, distance learning, honors programs, independent study, internships, off-campus study, part-time degree program, services for LD students, study abroad, summer session for credit. ***ROTC:*** Army (c), Air Force (c).

Computers: 907 computers/terminals are available on campus for general student use. Students can access the following: campus intranet, computer help desk, free student e-mail accounts, online (class) grades, online (class) registration, online (class) schedules, online bill payment. Campuswide network is available. 100% of college-owned or -operated housing units are wired for high-speed Internet access. Wireless service is available via entire campus.

Library: Southworth Library. *Books:* 24,866 (physical), 190,079 (digital/electronic); *Serial titles:* 14 (physical), 53,066 (digital/electronic); *Databases:* 84. Weekly public service hours: 125.

STUDENT LIFE

Housing options: on-campus residence required through sophomore year; coed, special housing for students with disabilities. Campus housing is university owned. Freshman applicants given priority for college housing.

Activities and organizations: drama/theater group, choral group, Student Government Alliance, College Activities Board, Greek Council, Brother to Brother, Sister to Sister.

Athletics Member NCAA, USCAA. All Division III. ***Intercollegiate sports:*** baseball M, basketball M/W, cheerleading M/W, cross-country running M/W, golf M/W, ice hockey M/W, lacrosse M/W, soccer M/W, softball W, volleyball W. ***Intramural sports:*** basketball M/W, cheerleading M(c)/W(c), football M/W, soccer M/W, softball M/W, ultimate Frisbee M(c)/W(c), volleyball M/W.

Campus security: 24-hour emergency response devices and patrols, late-night transport/escort service, controlled dormitory access, student EMS group.

Student services: health clinic, personal/psychological counseling, veterans affairs office.

COSTS & FINANCIAL AID

Costs (2019–20) ***One-time required fee:*** $120. ***Tuition:*** state resident $7070 full-time, $295 per credit hour part-time; nonresident $16,980 full-time, $708 per credit hour part-time. Full-time tuition and fees vary according to degree level. Part-time tuition and fees vary according to degree level. ***Required fees:*** $1590 full-time, $64 per credit hour part-time, $5 per term part-time. ***Room and board:*** $13,200; room only: $7950. Room and board charges vary according to board plan and housing facility. ***Payment plans:*** installment, deferred payment. ***Waivers:*** employees or children of employees.

Financial Aid Of all full-time matriculated undergraduates who enrolled in 2018, 2,585 applied for aid, 2,349 were judged to have need, 388 had their need fully met. 103 Federal Work-Study jobs (averaging $1757). In 2018, 61 non-need-based awards were made. ***Average percent of need met:*** 17. ***Average financial aid package:*** $11,039. ***Average need-based loan:*** $3830. ***Average need-based gift aid:*** $8537. ***Average non-need-based aid:*** $2545. ***Average indebtedness upon graduation:*** $31,214.

APPLYING

Standardized Tests *Required for some:* SAT or ACT (for admission).

Options: electronic application, deferred entrance.

Application fee: $50.

Required: high school transcript. ***Required for some:*** essay or personal statement, interview. ***Recommended:*** minimum 2.0 GPA.

Application deadlines: rolling (freshmen), rolling (out-of-state freshmen), rolling (transfers).

Notification: continuous (freshmen), continuous (out-of-state freshmen), continuous (transfers).

CONTACT

Melissa Evans, Director of Admissions, State University of New York College of Technology at Canton, 34 Cornell Drive, Canton, NY 13617. *Phone:* 315-386-7123. *Toll-free phone:* 800-388-7123. *Fax:* 315-386-7929. *E-mail:* admissions@canton.edu.

State University of New York College of Technology at Delhi

Delhi, New York

http://www.delhi.edu/

- **State-supported** comprehensive, founded 1913, part of State University of New York System
- **Rural** 625-acre campus
- **Endowment** $9.1 million
- **Coed** 2,999 undergraduate students, 80% full-time, 54% women, 46% men
- **Moderately difficult** entrance level, 72% of applicants were admitted

UNDERGRAD STUDENTS

2,391 full-time, 608 part-time. Students come from 22 states and territories; 4 other countries; 3% are from out of state; 17% Black or African American, non-Hispanic/Latino; 17% Hispanic/Latino; 2% Asian, non-Hispanic/Latino; 0.5% American Indian or Alaska Native, non-Hispanic/Latino; 3% Two or more races, non-Hispanic/Latino; 3% Race/ethnicity unknown; 0.3% international; 10% transferred in; 53% live on campus.

Freshmen:

Admission: 5,148 applied, 3,708 admitted, 783 enrolled. ***Average high school GPA:*** 2.8.

Retention: 73% of full-time freshmen returned.

FACULTY

Total: 223, 65% full-time, 28% with terminal degrees.

Student/faculty ratio: 16:1.

ACADEMICS

Calendar: semesters. *Degrees:* certificates, associate, bachelor's, and master's.

Special study options: academic remediation for entering students, accelerated degree program, adult/continuing education programs, advanced placement credit, distance learning, double majors, English as a second language, honors programs, independent study, internships, off-campus study, part-time degree program, services for LD students, study abroad, summer session for credit.

Computers: 102 computers/terminals are available on campus for general student use. Students can access the following: computer help desk, free student e-mail accounts, online (class) grades, online (class) registration, online (class) schedules. Campuswide network is available. 100% of college-owned or -operated housing units are wired for high-speed Internet access. Wireless service is available via entire campus.

Library: Resnick Library. *Books:* 34,976 (physical), 180,389 (digital/electronic); *Serial titles:* 98 (physical), 747,277 (digital/electronic); *Databases:* 72. Weekly public service hours: 93; students can reserve study rooms.

STUDENT LIFE

Housing options: on-campus residence required through sophomore year; coed, cooperative, special housing for students with disabilities. Campus housing is university owned. Freshman applicants given priority for college housing.

Activities and organizations: drama/theater group, student-run newspaper, radio and television station, choral group, New York State Association for Veterinary Technicians, National Student Nursing Association, Black Student Union, Bronco's Finest, Equine Club, national fraternities, national sororities.

Athletics Member NCAA. All Division III except golf (Division II). ***Intercollegiate sports:*** basketball M/W, cross-country running M/W, golf M/W, lacrosse M, soccer M/W, softball W, swimming and diving M/W, tennis M/W, track and field M/W, volleyball W. ***Intramural sports:*** badminton M/W, basketball M, bowling M/W, ultimate Frisbee M/W, volleyball M/W.

Campus security: 24-hour emergency response devices and patrols, late-night transport/escort service, controlled dormitory access.

Student services: health clinic, personal/psychological counseling, veterans affairs office.

COSTS & FINANCIAL AID

Costs (2020–21) ***Tuition:*** state resident $7270 full-time, $295 per credit hour part-time; nonresident $10,840 full-time, $452 per credit hour part-time. Full-time tuition and fees vary according to course load, degree level, location, and program. Part-time tuition and fees vary according to course load, degree level, location, and program. ***Required fees:*** $1650 full-time, $88 per credit hour part-time. ***Room and board:*** $12,900; room only: $7500. Room and board charges vary according to board plan, housing facility, and location. ***Payment plan:*** installment. ***Waivers:*** employees or children of employees.

Financial Aid Of all full-time matriculated undergraduates who enrolled in 2018, 2,272 applied for aid, 1,992 were judged to have need, 135 had their need fully met. In 2018, 31 non-need-based awards were made. ***Average percent of need met:*** 61. ***Average financial aid package:*** $11,213. ***Average need-based loan:*** $3705. ***Average need-based gift aid:*** $8329. ***Average non-need-based aid:*** $2174. ***Average indebtedness upon graduation:*** $27,915.

APPLYING

Options: electronic application, deferred entrance.

Application fee: $50.

Required: high school transcript. ***Required for some:*** minimum 2.0 GPA, 2 letters of recommendation, associate degree for some bachelor programs, RN license for BSN program. Letters of recommendation required at the graduate level. ***Recommended:*** interview.

Application deadlines: rolling (freshmen), rolling (out-of-state freshmen), rolling (transfers), 12/1 (early action).

Notification: continuous (freshmen), continuous (out-of-state freshmen), continuous (transfers), 12/15 (early action).

CONTACT

State University of New York College of Technology at Delhi, 454 Delhi Drive, Delhi, NY 13753. *Phone:* 607-746 4550. *Toll-free phone:* 800-96-DELHI. *E-mail:* enroll@delhi.edu.

State University of New York Downstate Medical Center

Brooklyn, New York

http://www.downstate.edu/

CONTACT
Admissions Office, State University of New York Downstate Medical Center, 450 Clarkson Avenue, Brooklyn, NY 11203-2446. *Phone:* 718-270-2446. *Fax:* 718-270-7592. *E-mail:* admissions@downstate.edu.

State University of New York Empire State College

Saratoga Springs, New York

http://www.esc.edu/

- **State-supported** comprehensive, founded 1971, part of State University of New York System
- **Small-town** campus
- **Endowment** $21.3 million
- **Coed** 9,095 undergraduate students, 36% full-time, 63% women, 37% men
- **Noncompetitive** entrance level, 63% of applicants were admitted

UNDERGRAD STUDENTS
3,267 full-time, 5,828 part-time. 5% are from out of state; 16% Black or African American, non-Hispanic/Latino; 14% Hispanic/Latino; 3% Asian, non-Hispanic/Latino; 0.2% Native Hawaiian or other Pacific Islander, non-Hispanic/Latino; 0.3% American Indian or Alaska Native, non-Hispanic/Latino; 3% Two or more races, non-Hispanic/Latino; 8% Race/ethnicity unknown; 0.5% international; 17% transferred in.

Freshmen:
Admission: 538 applied, 340 admitted, 179 enrolled.

FACULTY
Total: 795, 21% full-time.

Student/faculty ratio: 15:1.

ACADEMICS
Calendar: 5 terms. *Degrees:* certificates, associate, bachelor's, master's, and postbachelor's certificates (branch locations at 7 regional centers with 35 auxiliary units).

Special study options: accelerated degree program, adult/continuing education programs, advanced placement credit, distance learning, double majors, external degree program, independent study, off-campus study, part-time degree program, services for LD students, student-designed majors, summer session for credit.

Computers: 300 computers/terminals are available on campus for general student use. Students can access the following: computer help desk, free student e-mail accounts, online (class) grades, online (class) registration, online (class) schedules. Campuswide network is available.
Library:*Books:* 229,000 (digital/electronic); *Databases:* 94.

STUDENT LIFE
Housing options: college housing not available.

Activities and organizations: student-run newspaper.

Student services: veterans affairs office.

COSTS
Costs (2020–21) ***Tuition:*** area resident $7070 full-time; state resident $7070 full-time; nonresident $16,980 full-time. Full-time tuition and fees vary according to program. Part-time tuition and fees vary according to program. ***Required fees:*** $535 full-time. ***Payment plan:*** installment.

APPLYING
Options: electronic application, deferred entrance.

Required: essay or personal statement, high school transcript.

CONTACT
Ms. Jennifer D'Agostino, Senior Director of Admissions, State University of New York Empire State College, Two Union Avenue, Saratoga Springs, NY 12866. *Phone:* 518-587-2100. *Toll-free phone:* 800-847-3000. *E-mail:* admissions@esc.edu.

State University of New York Maritime College

Throggs Neck, New York

http://www.sunymaritime.edu/

- **State-supported** comprehensive, founded 1874, part of State University of New York System
- **Urban** 55-acre campus with easy access to New York City
- **Endowment** $7.7 million
- **Coed** 1,586 undergraduate students, 97% full-time, 12% women, 88% men
- **Very difficult** entrance level, 72% of applicants were admitted

UNDERGRAD STUDENTS
1,542 full-time, 44 part-time. Students come from 33 states and territories; 15 other countries; 23% are from out of state; 5% Black or African American, non-Hispanic/Latino; 14% Hispanic/Latino; 4% Asian, non-Hispanic/Latino; 0.1% American Indian or Alaska Native, non-Hispanic/Latino; 3% Two or more races, non-Hispanic/Latino; 3% Race/ethnicity unknown; 2% international; 6% transferred in; 89% live on campus.

Freshmen:
Admission: 1,355 applied, 971 admitted, 351 enrolled. ***Average high school GPA:*** 3.3. ***Test scores:*** SAT evidence-based reading and writing scores over 500: 91%; SAT math scores over 500: 93%; ACT scores over 18: 99%; SAT evidence-based reading and writing scores over 600: 41%; SAT math scores over 600: 45%; ACT scores over 24: 61%; SAT evidence-based reading and writing scores over 700: 4%; SAT math scores over 700: 5%; ACT scores over 30: 8%.

Retention: 86% of full-time freshmen returned.

FACULTY
Total: 146, 63% full-time, 35% with terminal degrees.

Student/faculty ratio: 15:1.

ACADEMICS
Calendar: semesters plus 2-month summer sea term. *Degrees:* certificates, associate, bachelor's, master's, and postbachelor's certificates.

Special study options: academic remediation for entering students, advanced placement credit, distance learning, double majors, independent study, internships, off-campus study, part-time degree program, services for LD students, study abroad, summer session for credit. ***ROTC:*** Army (c), Navy (b).

Computers: 160 computers/terminals and 650 ports are available on campus for general student use. Students can access the following: computer help desk, free student e-mail accounts, online (class) grades, online (class) registration, online (class) schedules. Campuswide network is available. 100% of college-owned or -operated housing units are wired for high-speed Internet access. Wireless service is available via classrooms, computer centers, computer labs, dorm rooms, learning centers, libraries, student centers.
Library: Stephen B. Luce Library. *Books:* 41,000 (physical), 60,567 (digital/electronic); *Serial titles:* 125 (physical), 323,000 (digital/electronic); *Databases:* 68. Weekly public service hours: 111; students can reserve study rooms.

STUDENT LIFE
Housing options: on-campus residence required through senior year; coed. Campus housing is university owned.

Activities and organizations: choral group, marching band, Student Government, Maritime Activities and Programs, The Cultural Club, Campus Crusade for Christ, The Maritime Divers Association.

Athletics Member NCAA. All Division III. ***Intercollegiate sports:*** baseball M, basketball M, crew M/W, cross-country running M/W, football M, ice hockey M(c), lacrosse M/W, riflery M(c)/W(c), sailing M/W, soccer M/W, swimming and diving M/W, volleyball W. ***Intramural sports:*** basketball M/W, football M/W, soccer M/W, softball M/W, volleyball M/W, water polo M/W.

Campus security: 24-hour emergency response devices and patrols, student patrols, late-night transport/escort service, controlled dormitory access.

Student services: health clinic, personal/psychological counseling, veterans affairs office.

COSTS & FINANCIAL AID

Costs (2019–20) ***Tuition:*** state resident $7070 full-time, $295 per credit hour part-time; nonresident $16,980 full-time, $708 per credit hour part-time. Full-time tuition and fees vary according to course load. Part-time tuition and fees vary according to course load. ***Required fees:*** $1438 full-time. ***Room and board:*** $13,256; room only: $8026. Room and board charges vary according to board plan and housing facility. ***Payment plan:*** installment.

Financial Aid Of all full-time matriculated undergraduates who enrolled in 2018, 1,216 applied for aid, 822 were judged to have need, 69 had their need fully met. In 2018, 112 non-need-based awards were made. ***Average percent of need met:*** 50. ***Average financial aid package:*** $8523. ***Average need-based loan:*** $3678. ***Average need-based gift aid:*** $6723. ***Average non-need-based aid:*** $2829. ***Average indebtedness upon graduation:*** $34,716.

APPLYING

Standardized Tests *Required:* SAT or ACT (for admission).

Options: electronic application, early decision, deferred entrance.

Application fee: $50.

Required: essay or personal statement. ***Recommended:*** high school transcript, interview.

Application deadlines: 1/31 (freshmen), rolling (transfers).

Early decision deadline: 11/1.

Notification: 3/1 (freshmen), continuous (transfers), 12/15 (early decision).

CONTACT

Mr. Rohan Howell, Dean of Admissions, State University of New York Maritime College, 6 Pennyfield Avenue, Throggs Neck, NY 10465. *Phone:* 718-409-2220. *Fax:* 718-409-7465. *E-mail:* rhowell@sunymaritime.edu.

State University of New York Polytechnic Institute

Utica, New York

http://www.sunypoly.edu/

CONTACT

Ms. Gina Liscio, Director of Admissions, State University of New York Polytechnic Institute, 100 Seymour Road, Utica, NY 13502. *Phone:* 315-792-7500. *Toll-free phone:* 866-278-6948. *Fax:* 315-792-7837. *E-mail:* admissions@sunyit.edu.

State University of New York Upstate Medical University

Syracuse, New York

http://www.upstate.edu/

CONTACT

Mrs. Donna L. Vavonese, Associate Director of Admissions, State University of New York Upstate Medical University, Weiskotten Hall, 766 Irving Avenue, Syracuse, NY 13210. *Phone:* 315-464-4570. *Toll-free phone:* 800-736-2171. *Fax:* 315-464-8867. *E-mail:* admiss@upstate.edu.

Stony Brook University, State University of New York

Stony Brook, New York

http://www.stonybrook.edu/

- **State-supported** university, founded 1957, part of State University of New York System
- **Suburban** 1450-acre campus with easy access to New York City
- **Endowment** $265.8 million
- **Coed** 17,909 undergraduate students, 93% full-time, 49% women, 51% men
- **Very difficult** entrance level, 44% of applicants were admitted

UNDERGRAD STUDENTS

16,697 full-time, 1,212 part-time. Students come from 48 states and territories; 89 other countries; 6% are from out of state; 7% Black or African American, non-Hispanic/Latino; 13% Hispanic/Latino; 27% Asian, non-Hispanic/Latino; 0.1% Native Hawaiian or other Pacific Islander, non-Hispanic/Latino; 0.1% American Indian or Alaska Native, non-Hispanic/Latino; 3% Two or more races, non-Hispanic/Latino; 6% Race/ethnicity unknown; 14% international; 9% transferred in; 52% live on campus.

Freshmen:

Admission: 37,079 applied, 16,370 admitted, 3,372 enrolled. ***Average high school GPA:*** 3.8. ***Test scores:*** SAT evidence-based reading and writing scores over 500: 95%; SAT math scores over 500: 100%; ACT scores over 18: 100%; SAT evidence-based reading and writing scores over 600: 74%; SAT math scores over 600: 88%; ACT scores over 24: 87%; SAT evidence-based reading and writing scores over 700: 22%; SAT math scores over 700: 52%; ACT scores over 30: 46%.

Retention: 89% of full-time freshmen returned.

FACULTY

Total: 1,600, 67% full-time, 78% with terminal degrees.

Student/faculty ratio: 19:1.

ACADEMICS

Calendar: semesters. *Degrees:* bachelor's, master's, doctoral, post-master's, and postbachelor's certificates.

Special study options: academic remediation for entering students, accelerated degree program, adult/continuing education programs, advanced placement credit, cooperative education, distance learning, double majors, English as a second language, freshman honors college, honors programs, independent study, internships, off-campus study, part-time degree program, services for LD students, student-designed majors, study abroad, summer session for credit. ***ROTC:*** Army (b), Navy (c), Air Force (c).

Unusual degree programs: 3-2 business administration; engineering; education.

Computers: 1,800 computers/terminals are available on campus for general student use. Students can access the following: campus intranet, computer help desk, free student e-mail accounts, online (class) grades, online (class) registration, online (class) schedules. Campuswide network is available. 100% of college-owned or -operated housing units are wired for high-speed Internet access. Wireless service is available via entire campus.

Library: Frank Melville, Jr. Memorial Library plus 7 others. *Books:* 1.8 million (physical), 354,833 (digital/electronic); *Serial titles:* 1,127 (physical), 170,894 (digital/electronic); *Databases:* 643. Weekly public service hours: 132; study areas open 24 hours, 5–7 days a week; students can reserve study rooms.

STUDENT LIFE

Housing options: coed. Campus housing is university owned. Freshman campus housing is guaranteed.

Activities and organizations: drama/theater group, student-run newspaper, radio and television station, choral group, marching band, Community Service Organization, Residence Hall Association, Commuter Student Association, Asian Students Alliance, Chinese Association at Stony Brook, national fraternities, national sororities.

Athletics Member NCAA. All Division I. ***Intercollegiate sports:*** baseball M(s), basketball M(s)/W(s), cross-country running M(s)/W(s), football M(s), lacrosse M(s)/W(s), soccer M(s)/W(s), softball W(s), swimming and diving W(s), tennis W(s), track and field M(s)/W(s), volleyball W(s). ***Intramural sports:*** archery M(c)/W(c), badminton M(c)/W(c), basketball M/W, bowling M(c)/W(c), cheerleading W, crew M(c)/W(c), cross-country running M(c)/W(c), equestrian sports M(c)/W(c), fencing M(c)/W(c), field hockey W(c), golf M(c)/W(c), ice hockey M(c), lacrosse M(c)/W(c), racquetball M/W, rugby M(c)/W(c), sailing M(c)/W(c), skiing (downhill) M(c)/W(c), soccer M/W, softball M/W, swimming and diving M(c)/W(c), table tennis M(c)/W(c), tennis M(c)/W(c), ultimate Frisbee M(c)/W(c), volleyball M/W, weight lifting M(c)/W(c), wrestling M(c).

Campus security: 24-hour emergency response devices and patrols, late-night transport/escort service, controlled dormitory access.

Student services: health clinic, personal/psychological counseling, women's center, legal services, veterans affairs office.

COSTS & FINANCIAL AID
Costs (2019–20) ***Tuition:*** state resident $7070 full-time, $295 per credit hour part-time; nonresident $24,740 full-time, $1031 per credit hour part-time. Full-time tuition and fees vary according to course load and program. Part-time tuition and fees vary according to course load and program. ***Required fees:*** $3105 full-time, $154 per credit hour part-time. ***Room and board:*** $14,278; room only: $9082. Room and board charges vary according to board plan, housing facility, and location. ***Payment plan:*** installment.

Financial Aid Of all full-time matriculated undergraduates who enrolled in 2018, 11,158 applied for aid, 9,310 were judged to have need, 1,446 had their need fully met. 523 Federal Work-Study jobs (averaging $2728). 2,494 state and other part-time jobs (averaging $4515). In 2018, 1813 non-need-based awards were made. ***Average percent of need met:*** 65. ***Average financial aid package:*** $14,005. ***Average need-based loan:*** $4561. ***Average need-based gift aid:*** $9443. ***Average non-need-based aid:*** $5695. ***Average indebtedness upon graduation:*** $25,678.

APPLYING
Standardized Tests *Required:* SAT or ACT (for admission).

Options: electronic application, deferred entrance.

Application fee: $50.

Required: essay or personal statement, high school transcript, 1 letter of recommendation. ***Required for some:*** interview, audition. ***Recommended:*** minimum 3.5 GPA.

Application deadlines: 1/15 (freshmen), 3/1 (transfers).

Notification: 4/1 (freshmen), continuous until 4/1 (transfers).

CONTACT
Ms. Judith Burke-Berhanan, Dean of Undergraduate Admissions, Stony Brook University, State University of New York, Admissions Office, 118 Administration Building, Stony Brook, NY 11794-1901. *Phone:* 631-632-6868. *Fax:* 631-632-9898. *E-mail:* enroll@stonybrook.edu.

SUNY Brockport

Brockport, New York

http://www.brockport.edu/

- **State-supported** comprehensive, founded 1867, part of State University of New York System
- **Small-town** 464-acre campus with easy access to Rochester
- **Endowment** $14.2 million
- **Coed** 6,673 undergraduate students, 89% full-time, 57% women, 43% men
- **Moderately difficult** entrance level, 55% of applicants were admitted

UNDERGRAD STUDENTS
5,960 full-time, 713 part-time. Students come from 25 states and territories; 21 other countries; 1% are from out of state; 12% Black or African American, non-Hispanic/Latino; 8% Hispanic/Latino; 2% Asian, non-Hispanic/Latino; 0.1% Native Hawaiian or other Pacific Islander, non-Hispanic/Latino; 0.2% American Indian or Alaska Native, non-Hispanic/Latino; 3% Two or more races, non-Hispanic/Latino; 5% Race/ethnicity unknown; 0.8% international; 12% transferred in; 34% live on campus.

Freshmen:
Admission: 9,672 applied, 5,294 admitted, 1,076 enrolled. ***Average high school GPA:*** 3.0. ***Test scores:*** SAT evidence-based reading and writing scores over 500: 80%; SAT math scores over 500: 82%; ACT scores over 18: 87%; SAT evidence-based reading and writing scores over 600: 22%; SAT math scores over 600: 26%; ACT scores over 24: 32%; SAT evidence-based reading and writing scores over 700: 1%; SAT math scores over 700: 2%; ACT scores over 30: 3%.

Retention: 74% of full-time freshmen returned.

FACULTY
Total: 645, 51% full-time, 62% with terminal degrees.

Student/faculty ratio: 17:1.

ACADEMICS
Calendar: semesters. *Degrees:* certificates, bachelor's, master's, post-master's, and postbachelor's certificates.

Special study options: accelerated degree program, advanced placement credit, cooperative education, distance learning, double majors, freshman honors college, honors programs, independent study, internships, off-campus study, part-time degree program, services for LD students, student-designed majors, study abroad, summer session for credit. ***ROTC:*** Army (b), Navy (c), Air Force (c).

Unusual degree programs: 3-2 business administration; nursing; social work; Biology and Pharm-D with University of Buffalo, Doctor of Physical Therapy with SUNY Upstate Medical.

Computers: 1,000 computers/terminals are available on campus for general student use. Students can access the following: campus intranet, computer help desk, free student e-mail accounts, online (class) grades, online (class) registration, online (class) schedules. Campuswide network is available. 100% of college-owned or -operated housing units are wired for high-speed Internet access. Wireless service is available via entire campus.

Library: Drake Memorial Library plus 1 other. *Books:* 395,601 (physical), 376,105 (digital/electronic); *Serial titles:* 7,162 (physical), 114,760 (digital/electronic); *Databases:* 502. Weekly public service hours: 103; students can reserve study rooms.

STUDENT LIFE
Housing options: on-campus residence required through sophomore year; coed, special housing for students with disabilities. Campus housing is university owned. Freshman campus housing is guaranteed.

Activities and organizations: drama/theater group, student-run newspaper, radio and television station, national fraternities, national sororities.

Athletics Member NCAA, NAIA, USCAA. All NCAA Division III. ***Intercollegiate sports:*** baseball M, basketball M/W, cross-country running M/W, field hockey W, football M, gymnastics W, ice hockey M, lacrosse M/W, soccer M/W, softball W, swimming and diving M/W, tennis W, track and field M/W, volleyball W, wrestling M. ***Intramural sports:*** badminton M(c)/W(c), baseball M(c), basketball M(c)/W(c), cheerleading M(c)/W(c), equestrian sports M(c)/W(c), football M(c)/W(c), gymnastics M(c)/W(c), ice hockey M(c)/W(c), lacrosse M(c)/W(c), rugby M(c)/W(c), soccer M(c)/W(c), softball W(c), swimming and diving M(c)/W(c), table tennis M(c)/W(c), tennis M(c)/W(c), ultimate Frisbee M(c)/W(c), volleyball M/W, weight lifting M(c)/W(c).

Campus security: 24-hour emergency response devices and patrols, student patrols, late-night transport/escort service, controlled dormitory access.

Student services: health clinic, personal/psychological counseling, women's center, legal services, veterans affairs office.

COSTS & FINANCIAL AID
Costs (2020–21) ***Tuition:*** area resident $7270 full-time, $303 per credit hour part-time; state resident $7270 full-time, $303 per credit hour part-time; nonresident $17,180 full-time, $716 per credit hour part-time. Part-time tuition and fees vary according to course load. ***Required fees:*** $1656 full-time, $68 per credit hour part-time. ***Room and board:*** $14,160; room only: $8834. Room and board charges vary according to board plan and housing facility. ***Payment plan:*** installment. ***Waivers:*** senior citizens and employees or children of employees.

Financial Aid Of all full-time matriculated undergraduates who enrolled in 2018, 5,653 applied for aid, 4,794 were judged to have need, 521 had their need fully met. In 2018, 266 non-need-based awards were made. ***Average percent of need met:*** 61. ***Average financial aid package:*** $10,576. ***Average need-based loan:*** $4260. ***Average need-based gift aid:*** $7333. ***Average non-need-based aid:*** $4676. ***Average indebtedness upon graduation:*** $31,695.

APPLYING
Standardized Tests *Required:* SAT or ACT (for admission).

Options: electronic application, deferred entrance.

Application fee: $50.

Required: high school transcript, minimum 2.0 GPA, 1 letter of recommendation. ***Required for some:*** interview. ***Recommended:*** essay or personal statement.

Application deadlines: 8/1 (freshmen), 8/1 (out-of-state freshmen), 8/1 (transfers).

Notification: continuous (freshmen), continuous (out-of-state freshmen), continuous (transfers).

CONTACT
SUNY Brockport, 350 New Campus Drive, Brockport, NY 14420-2997. *Phone:* 585-395-2751.

Swedish Institute, College of Health Sciences

New York, New York

http://www.swedishinstitute.edu/

CONTACT
Admissions Advisor, Swedish Institute, College of Health Sciences, 226 West 26th Street, New York, NY 10001. *Phone:* 212-914-5900 Ext. 125. *E-mail:* admissions@swedishinstitute.edu.

Syracuse University

Syracuse, New York

http://www.syracuse.edu/

- **Independent** university, founded 1870
- **Urban** 721 acre campus with easy access to Syracuse, NY
- **Endowment** $1.3 billion
- **Coed**
- **Very difficult** entrance level

FACULTY
Student/faculty ratio: 15:1.

ACADEMICS
Calendar: semesters. *Degrees:* certificates, bachelor's, master's, doctoral, post-master's, and postbachelor's certificates.
Library: E. S. Bird Library plus 4 others. *Books:* 2.6 million (physical), 545,994 (digital/electronic); *Serial titles:* 33,881 (physical), 125,294 (digital/electronic); *Databases:* 586. Weekly public service hours: 146; study areas open 24 hours, 5–7 days a week; students can reserve study rooms.

STUDENT LIFE
Housing options: on-campus residence required through sophomore year; coed, special housing for students with disabilities. Campus housing is university owned. Freshman campus housing is guaranteed.

Activities and organizations: drama/theater group, student-run newspaper, radio and television station, choral group, marching band, Student Association, University Union, Otto, national fraternities, national sororities.

Athletics Member NCAA. All Division I except football (Division I-A).

Campus security: 24-hour emergency response devices and patrols, student patrols, late-night transport/escort service, controlled dormitory access.

Student services: health clinic, personal/psychological counseling, women's center, legal services, veterans affairs office.

COSTS & FINANCIAL AID
Costs (2019–20) ***Comprehensive fee:*** $69,759 includes full-time tuition ($52,210), mandatory fees ($1639), and room and board ($15,910). Full-time tuition and fees vary according to course load. Part-time tuition: $2274 per credit hour. Part-time tuition and fees vary according to course load. ***College room only:*** $8470. Room and board charges vary according to board plan and housing facility. ***Payment plans:*** tuition prepayment, installment.

Financial Aid Of all full-time matriculated undergraduates who enrolled in 2019, 8,395 applied for aid, 5,857 were judged to have need, 3,179 had their need fully met. 4,983 Federal Work-Study jobs (averaging $2926). In 2019, 4653 non-need-based awards were made. ***Average percent of need met:*** 94. ***Average financial aid package:*** $42,550. ***Average need-based loan:*** $4500. ***Average need-based gift aid:*** $34,854. ***Average non-need-based aid:*** $11,060. ***Average indebtedness upon graduation:*** $37,563.

APPLYING
Standardized Tests *Required:* SAT or ACT (for admission).

Options: electronic application, early admission, early decision, deferred entrance.

Application fee: $75.

Required: essay or personal statement, high school transcript, 2 letters of recommendation, visit http://admissions.syr.edu for information on requirements for first-year, transfer, and international applicants. ***Recommended:*** interview.

CONTACT
Mr. Maurice Harris, Dean of Admissions, Syracuse University, 900 South Crouse Avenue, Syracuse, NY 13244. *Phone:* 315-443-3611. *E-mail:* orange@syr.edu.

Talmudical Institute of Upstate New York

Rochester, New York

http://www.tiuny.org/

CONTACT
Rabbi Menachem Davidowitz, Director of Admissions, Talmudical Institute of Upstate New York, 769 Park Avenue, Rochester, NY 14607-3046. *Phone:* 716-473-2810. *E-mail:* yeshiva@tiuny.org.

Talmudical Seminary of Bobov

Brooklyn, New York

CONTACT
Talmudical Seminary of Bobov, 5120 New Utrecht Avenue, Brooklyn, NY 11219.

Talmudical Seminary Oholei Torah

Brooklyn, New York

CONTACT
Rabbi Yisroel Friedman, Director of Academic Affairs, Talmudical Seminary Oholei Torah, 667 Eastern Parkway, Brooklyn, NY 11213-3310. *Phone:* 718-363-2034. *E-mail:* info@oholeitorah.com.

Torah Temimah Talmudical Seminary

Brooklyn, New York

CONTACT
Principal, Torah Temimah Talmudical Seminary, 507 Ocean Parkway, Brooklyn, NY 11218-5913. *Phone:* 718-853-8500.

Touro College

New York, New York

http://www.touro.edu/

- **Independent** comprehensive, founded 1971
- **Urban** campus
- **Coed**
- **Moderately difficult** entrance level

ACADEMICS
Calendar: semesters. *Degrees:* certificates, associate, bachelor's, master's, doctoral, post-master's, and postbachelor's certificates.
Library: Touro College Library plus 14 others.

STUDENT LIFE
Housing options: men-only, women-only. Campus housing is university owned.

Activities and organizations: student-run newspaper.

Campus security: 24-hour emergency response devices and patrols.

Student services: personal/psychological counseling.

COSTS & FINANCIAL AID
Costs (2019–20) ***Comprehensive fee:*** $31,200 includes full-time tuition ($19,750), mandatory fees ($800), and room and board ($10,650). Part-time tuition: $825 per credit hour. ***College room only:*** $7710.

Financial Aid Of all full-time matriculated undergraduates who enrolled in 2017, 3,837 applied for aid, 3,837 were judged to have need, 570 had their need fully met. In 2017, 698 non-need-based awards were made. ***Average percent of need met:*** 68. ***Average financial aid package:***

$11,966. ***Average need-based loan:*** $2251. ***Average need-based gift aid:*** $9031. ***Average non-need-based aid:*** $3109.

APPLYING
Standardized Tests *Recommended:* SAT or ACT (for admission).

Options: early admission, deferred entrance.

Application fee: $50.

Required: high school transcript. ***Required for some:*** minimum 3.0 GPA, 2 letters of recommendation, interview. ***Recommended:*** essay or personal statement, 1 letter of recommendation.

CONTACT
Mr. David Luk, Associate Director of Admissions, Touro College, 27-33 West 23rd Street, New York, NY 10010. *Phone:* 212-463-0400 Ext. 5644. *Fax:* 212-627-9542. *E-mail:* david.luk@touro.edu.

Trocaire College

Buffalo, New York

http://www.trocaire.edu/

CONTACT
Trocaire College, 360 Choate Avenue, Buffalo, NY 14220-2094. *Phone:* 716-826-2558.

Union College

Schenectady, New York

http://www.union.edu/

- **Independent** 4-year, founded 1795
- **Urban** 100-acre campus
- **Endowment** $470.3 million
- **Coed** 2,189 undergraduate students, 99% full-time, 46% women, 54% men
- **Very difficult** entrance level, 43% of applicants were admitted

UNDERGRAD STUDENTS
2,173 full-time, 16 part-time. Students come from 39 states and territories; 48 other countries; 66% are from out of state; 4% Black or African American, non-Hispanic/Latino; 9% Hispanic/Latino; 6% Asian, non-Hispanic/Latino; 3% Two or more races, non-Hispanic/Latino; 0.1% Race/ethnicity unknown; 10% international; 0.8% transferred in; 93% live on campus.

Freshmen:
Admission: 6,086 applied, 2,612 admitted, 550 enrolled. ***Average high school GPA:*** 3.5. ***Test scores:*** SAT evidence-based reading and writing scores over 500: 99%; SAT math scores over 500: 99%; ACT scores over 18: 100%; SAT evidence-based reading and writing scores over 600: 80%; SAT math scores over 600: 84%; ACT scores over 24: 94%; SAT evidence-based reading and writing scores over 700: 19%; SAT math scores over 700: 40%; ACT scores over 30: 58%.

Retention: 93% of full-time freshmen returned.

FACULTY
Total: 242, 86% full-time, 91% with terminal degrees.

Student/faculty ratio: 10:1.

ACADEMICS
Calendar: trimesters. *Degree:* bachelor's.

Special study options: accelerated degree program, advanced placement credit, double majors, honors programs, independent study, internships, off-campus study, student-designed majors, study abroad, summer session for credit. ***ROTC:*** Army (c), Navy (c), Air Force (c).

Computers: 534 computers/terminals and 3,032 ports are available on campus for general student use. Students can access the following: campus intranet, computer help desk, free student e-mail accounts, online (class) grades, online (class) registration, online (class) schedules, Digital Studio and Learning Commons. Campuswide network is available. 100% of college-owned or -operated housing units are wired for high-speed Internet access. Wireless service is available via entire campus.

Library: Schaffer Library. *Books:* 394,288 (physical), 804,669 (digital/electronic); *Serial titles:* 7,473 (physical), 149,863 (digital/electronic); *Databases:* 595. Weekly public service hours: 118; study areas open 24 hours, 5–7 days a week; students can reserve study rooms.

STUDENT LIFE
Housing options: on-campus residence required through junior year; coed. Campus housing is university owned. Freshman campus housing is guaranteed.

Activities and organizations: drama/theater group, student-run newspaper, radio and television station, choral group, U-Program (Programming Board), speaker's forum, student newspaper, Concert Committee, ski club, national fraternities, national sororities.

Athletics Member NCAA. All Division III except golf (Division II), men's and women's ice hockey (Division I). ***Intercollegiate sports:*** baseball M, basketball M/W, cheerleading M(c)/W(c), crew M/W, cross-country running M/W, equestrian sports W, field hockey W, football M, golf W, ice hockey M/W, lacrosse M/W, rugby M(c)/W(c), soccer M/W, softball W, swimming and diving M/W, tennis M/W, track and field M/W, ultimate Frisbee M(c)/W(c), volleyball W. ***Intramural sports:*** badminton M(c)/W(c), basketball M/W, bowling M(c)/W(c), equestrian sports M(c)/W(c), fencing M(c), field hockey W(c), football M/W, golf M(c)/W(c), ice hockey M(c)/W(c), lacrosse M(c)/W, racquetball M/W, rock climbing M(c)/W(c), skiing (downhill) M(c)/W(c), soccer M/W, softball M/W, squash M/W, tennis M/W, volleyball M/W, water polo M/W.

Campus security: 24-hour emergency response devices and patrols, late-night transport/escort service, controlled dormitory access, awareness programs, bicycle patrol, shuttle service.

Student services: health clinic, personal/psychological counseling, women's center.

COSTS & FINANCIAL AID
Costs (2020–21) ***Comprehensive fee:*** $74,010 includes full-time tuition ($58,956), mandatory fees ($471), and room and board ($14,583). Part-time tuition: $6551 per course. ***College room only:*** $7998. ***Payment plan:*** installment. ***Waivers:*** senior citizens and employees or children of employees.

Financial Aid Of all full-time matriculated undergraduates who enrolled in 2019, 1,271 applied for aid, 1,162 were judged to have need, 1,161 had their need fully met. In 2019, 621 non-need-based awards were made. ***Average percent of need met:*** 100. ***Average financial aid package:*** $46,730. ***Average need-based loan:*** $5270. ***Average need-based gift aid:*** $39,940. ***Average non-need-based aid:*** $14,300. ***Average indebtedness upon graduation:*** $36,921. ***Financial aid deadline:*** 1/15.

APPLYING
Standardized Tests *Required for some:* SAT or ACT (for admission), SAT and SAT Subject Tests or ACT (for admission), SAT I and two SAT II tests or ACT for leadership in medicine program, SAT or ACT for law and public policy program.

Options: electronic application, early admission, early decision, deferred entrance.

Required: essay or personal statement, high school transcript, 2 letters of recommendation. ***Recommended:*** interview.

Application deadlines: 1/15 (freshmen), 4/15 (transfers).

Early decision deadline: 11/15 (for plan 1), 1/15 (for plan 2).

Notification: 4/1 (freshmen), continuous (transfers), 12/15 (early decision plan 1), 2/8 (early decision plan 2).

CONTACT
Union College, 807 Union Street, Schenectady, NY 12308-2311. *Phone:* 518-388-6112. *Toll-free phone:* 888-843-6688.

United States Merchant Marine Academy

Kings Point, New York

http://www.usmma.edu/

- **Federally supported** comprehensive, founded 1943
- **Suburban** 82-acre campus with easy access to New York City
- **Coed**
- **Very difficult** entrance level

FACULTY
Student/faculty ratio: 8:1.

ACADEMICS
Calendar: trimesters. *Degrees:* bachelor's and master's.
Library: Schuyler Otis Bland Memorial Library. *Books:* 176,485 (physical), 2,791 (digital/electronic); *Serial titles:* 1,511 (physical), 505 (digital/electronic); *Databases:* 17. Weekly public service hours: 84.

STUDENT LIFE
Housing options: on-campus residence required through senior year; coed. Campus housing is university owned. Freshman campus housing is guaranteed.

Activities and organizations: drama/theater group, student-run newspaper, choral group, marching band, Regimental Band, CFC, Neuman Club, Honor Guard.

Athletics Member NCAA. All Division III.

Campus security: 24-hour emergency response devices and patrols, controlled dormitory access.

Student services: health clinic, personal/psychological counseling.

APPLYING
Standardized Tests *Required:* SAT or ACT (for admission).

Options: electronic application.

Required: essay or personal statement, high school transcript, 3 letters of recommendation. ***Recommended:*** interview.

CONTACT
Lt. Cdr. Keith L. Watson, Assistant Director of Admissions and Financial Aid, United States Merchant Marine Academy, 300 Steamboat Road, Kings Point, NY 11024-1699. *Phone:* 516-726-5642. *Toll-free phone:* 866-546-4778. *Fax:* 516-773-5390. *E-mail:* admissions@usmma.edu.

United States Military Academy

West Point, New York

http://www.usma.edu/

- **Federally supported** 4-year, founded 1802
- **Small-town** 16,080-acre campus with easy access to New York City
- **Endowment** $348.2 million
- **Coed** 4,457 undergraduate students, 100% full-time, 23% women, 77% men
- 10% of applicants were admitted

UNDERGRAD STUDENTS
4,457 full-time. Students come from 56 states and territories; 32 other countries; 94% are from out of state; 12% Black or African American, non-Hispanic/Latino; 10% Hispanic/Latino; 8% Asian, non-Hispanic/Latino; 0.2% Native Hawaiian or other Pacific Islander, non-Hispanic/Latino; 0.8% American Indian or Alaska Native, non-Hispanic/Latino; 3% Two or more races, non-Hispanic/Latino; 1% Race/ethnicity unknown; 1% international; 100% live on campus.

Freshmen:
Admission: 11,675 applied, 1,199 admitted, 1,171 enrolled. ***Average high school GPA:*** 3.9. ***Test scores:*** SAT evidence-based reading and writing scores over 500: 97%; SAT math scores over 500: 98%; ACT scores over 18: 100%; SAT evidence-based reading and writing scores over 600: 57%; SAT math scores over 600: 74%; ACT scores over 24: 100%; SAT evidence-based reading and writing scores over 700: 17%; SAT math scores over 700: 26%; ACT scores over 30: 33%.

Retention: 95% of full-time freshmen returned.

FACULTY
Total: 607, 100% full-time, 48% with terminal degrees.

Student/faculty ratio: 7:1.

ACADEMICS
Calendar: semesters. *Degree:* bachelor's.

Special study options: academic remediation for entering students, advanced placement credit, double majors, honors programs, independent study, off-campus study, student-designed majors, study abroad.

Computers: Students can access the following: campus intranet, computer help desk, free student e-mail accounts, online (class) grades, online (class) registration, online (class) schedules, all cadets will receive a tablet, printer, PDA, and portable memory device; learning management system access. Campuswide network is available. 100% of college-owned or -operated housing units are wired for high-speed Internet access. Wireless service is available via classrooms, dorm rooms, learning centers, libraries, student centers.
Library: United States Military Academy Library at West Point. *Books:* 416,849 (physical), 1.1 million (digital/electronic); *Serial titles:* 169 (physical), 122,080 (digital/electronic); *Databases:* 269. Weekly public service hours: 100.

STUDENT LIFE
Housing options: on-campus residence required through senior year; coed. Campus housing is university owned. Freshman campus housing is guaranteed.

Activities and organizations: drama/theater group, student-run radio station, choral group, Spirit Clubs, Big Brother/Big Sister, Cadet Fine Arts Forum, Film Forum, Philosophy Forum.

Athletics Member NCAA. All Division I except football (Division I-A).
Intercollegiate sports: baseball M, basketball M/W, cheerleading M/W, crew M(c)/W(c), cross-country running M/W, equestrian sports M(c)/W(c), fencing M(c)/W(c), golf M, gymnastics M, ice hockey M, lacrosse M/W, riflery M/W, rugby M/W, soccer M/W, softball W, swimming and diving M/W, tennis M/W, track and field M/W, ultimate Frisbee M(c), volleyball M(c)/W, water polo M(c), wrestling M.
Intramural sports: basketball M/W, bowling M(c)/W(c), crew M(c)/W(c), equestrian sports M(c)/W(c), fencing M(c)/W(c), football M/W, ice hockey M(c), racquetball M(c)/W(c), rock climbing M(c)/W(c), sailing M(c)/W(c), skiing (cross-country) M(c)/W(c), skiing (downhill) M(c)/W(c), soccer M/W, triathlon M(c)/W(c), ultimate Frisbee M/W, volleyball M(c), water polo M(c)/W(c), weight lifting M(c)/W(c), wrestling M/W.

Campus security: 24-hour emergency response devices and patrols, late-night transport/escort service, controlled dormitory access.

Student services: health clinic, personal/psychological counseling, legal services.

COSTS
Costs (2020–21) ***Tuition:*** Cadets receive a full scholarship and an annual salary. There is no tuition charge, but there is a requirement for an initial deposit. Room, board, and medical and dental care are provided by the US Government. A portion of the cadet pay is deposited to a "Cadet Account" to help pay for uniforms, books, a laptop computer, and incidentals. The only cost is a one-time deposit upon admission to defray the initial issue of uniforms, books, supplies, and equipment. If needed, loans of $100 to $2,000 are available for the deposit. Upon graduation, cadets incur a 5-year Active Duty service obligation and 3 years of reserve duty in the US Army.

APPLYING
Standardized Tests *Required:* SAT or ACT (for admission).

Options: electronic application.

Required: essay or personal statement, high school transcript, 4 letters of recommendation, Candidates will be notified if they can compete for admission into West Point after the Service Academies Pre-candidate Questionnaire is submitted to West Pointâ Admission office. ***Recommended:*** interview.

Notification: continuous until 1/15 (freshmen).

CONTACT
United States Military Academy, 600 Thayer Road, West Point, NY 10996. *Phone:* 845-938-5706. *E-mail:* admissions@westpoint.edu.

United Talmudical Seminary

Brooklyn, New York

CONTACT
Director of Admissions, United Talmudical Seminary, 191 Rodney Street, Brooklyn, NY 11211. *Phone:* 718-963-9770.

University at Albany, State University of New York

Albany, New York

http://www.albany.edu/

- **State-supported** university, founded 1844, part of State University of New York System
- **Suburban** 560-acre campus
- **Endowment** $75.1 million
- **Coed** 13,598 undergraduate students, 95% full-time, 51% women, 49% men
- **Very difficult** entrance level, 52% of applicants were admitted

UNDERGRAD STUDENTS

12,899 full-time, 699 part-time. Students come from 36 states and territories; 25 other countries; 4% are from out of state; 19% Black or African American, non-Hispanic/Latino; 18% Hispanic/Latino; 8% Asian, non-Hispanic/Latino; 0.1% Native Hawaiian or other Pacific Islander, non-Hispanic/Latino; 0.2% American Indian or Alaska Native, non-Hispanic/Latino; 3% Two or more races, non-Hispanic/Latino; 3% Race/ethnicity unknown; 5% international; 10% transferred in; 46% live on campus.

Freshmen:

Admission: 27,679 applied, 14,416 admitted, 2,768 enrolled. ***Average high school GPA:*** 3.3. ***Test scores:*** SAT evidence-based reading and writing scores over 500: 95%; SAT math scores over 500: 97%; ACT scores over 18: 100%; SAT evidence-based reading and writing scores over 600: 44%; SAT math scores over 600: 41%; ACT scores over 24: 60%; SAT evidence-based reading and writing scores over 700: 3%; SAT math scores over 700: 6%; ACT scores over 30: 8%.

Retention: 82% of full-time freshmen returned.

FACULTY

Total: 1,210, 56% full-time, 71% with terminal degrees.

Student/faculty ratio: 19:1.

ACADEMICS

Calendar: semesters. *Degrees:* bachelor's, master's, doctoral, post-master's, and postbachelor's certificates.

Special study options: accelerated degree program, advanced placement credit, distance learning, double majors, English as a second language, freshman honors college, honors programs, independent study, internships, off-campus study, part-time degree program, services for LD students, student-designed majors, study abroad, summer session for credit. ***ROTC:*** Army (b), Air Force (c).

Unusual degree programs: 3-2 business administration; engineering.

Computers: 500 computers/terminals are available on campus for general student use. Students can access the following: campus intranet, computer help desk, free student e-mail accounts, online (class) grades, online (class) registration, online (class) schedules. Campuswide network is available. 100% of college-owned or -operated housing units are wired for high-speed Internet access. Wireless service is available via classrooms, computer centers, computer labs, dorm rooms, libraries, student centers.
Library: University Library plus 2 others. *Books:* 2.3 million (physical), 485,479 (digital/electronic); *Serial titles:* 128,734 (physical), 128,734 (digital/electronic); *Databases:* 391. Weekly public service hours: 113; students can reserve study rooms.

STUDENT LIFE

Housing options: on-campus residence required through sophomore year; coed. Campus housing is university owned. Freshman campus housing is guaranteed.

Activities and organizations: drama/theater group, student-run newspaper, radio and television station, choral group, intramural athletics, cultural organizations, political organizations, community service, honor societies, national fraternities, national sororities.

Athletics Member NCAA. All Division I. ***Intercollegiate sports:*** baseball M(s), basketball M(s)/W(s), crew M/W, cross-country running M(s)/W(s), field hockey W(s), football M(s), golf W(s), lacrosse M(s)/W(s), rock climbing M/W, soccer M(s)/W(s), softball W(s), tennis W(s), track and field M(s)/W(s), volleyball W(s). ***Intramural sports:*** badminton M/W, baseball M, basketball M/W, equestrian sports W, fencing M/W, football M/W, ice hockey M, lacrosse M/W, racquetball M/W, rugby M/W, skiing (cross-country) M/W, skiing (downhill) M/W, soccer M/W, softball W, tennis M/W, track and field M/W, ultimate Frisbee M/W, volleyball M/W, wrestling M.

Campus security: 24-hour emergency response devices and patrols, late-night transport/escort service, controlled dormitory access, Five Quad Ambulance Service, on-campus car battery assistance.

Student services: health clinic, personal/psychological counseling, legal services.

COSTS & FINANCIAL AID

Costs (2020–21) ***Tuition:*** area resident $7070 full-time, $286 per credit hour part-time; state resident $7070 full-time, $286 per credit hour part-time; nonresident $24,660 full-time, $988 per credit hour part-time. ***Required fees:*** $2886 full-time. ***Room and board:*** $13,864; room only: $8364. Room and board charges vary according to board plan.

Financial Aid Of all full-time matriculated undergraduates who enrolled in 2019, 10,542 applied for aid, 8,489 were judged to have need, 605 had their need fully met. In 2019, 781 non-need-based awards were made. ***Average percent of need met:*** 58. ***Average financial aid package:*** $11,395. ***Average need-based loan:*** $4217. ***Average need-based gift aid:*** $8608. ***Average non-need-based aid:*** $3716. ***Average indebtedness upon graduation:*** $27,555.

APPLYING

Standardized Tests *Required:* SAT or ACT (for admission).

Options: electronic application, early admission, early action, deferred entrance.

Application fee: $50.

Required: essay or personal statement, high school transcript, 1 letter of recommendation. ***Required for some:*** portfolio, audition.

Application deadlines: 3/16 (freshmen), 7/16 (transfers), 11/1 (early action).

Notification: continuous (freshmen), continuous (transfers), 1/15 (early action).

CONTACT

Herbert Gaige Jr, Assoc Dir of Admissions, University at Albany, State University of New York, Office of Undergraduate Admissions, 1400 Washington Avenue, Albany, NY 12222. *Phone:* 518-442-5435. *Fax:* 518-442-5383. *E-mail:* ugadmissions@albany.edu.

University at Buffalo, the State University of New York

Buffalo, New York

http://www.buffalo.edu/

- **State-supported** university, founded 1846, part of State University of New York System
- **Suburban** 1350-acre campus
- **Endowment** $659.2 million
- **Coed** 21,921 undergraduate students, 93% full-time, 44% women, 56% men
- **Moderately difficult** entrance level, 61% of applicants were admitted

UNDERGRAD STUDENTS

20,401 full-time, 1,520 part-time. 2% are from out of state; 8% Black or African American, non-Hispanic/Latino; 7% Hispanic/Latino; 15% Asian, non-Hispanic/Latino; 0.1% Native Hawaiian or other Pacific Islander, non-Hispanic/Latino; 0.4% American Indian or Alaska Native, non-Hispanic/Latino; 2% Two or more races, non-Hispanic/Latino; 5% Race/ethnicity unknown; 14% international; 8% transferred in; 34% live on campus.

Freshmen:

Admission: 29,900 applied, 18,264 admitted, 4,289 enrolled. ***Average high school GPA:*** ####. ***Test scores:*** SAT evidence-based reading and writing scores over 500: 97%; SAT math scores over 500: 99%; ACT scores over 18: 100%; SAT evidence-based reading and writing scores over 600: 58%; SAT math scores over 600: 70%; ACT scores over 24: 76%; SAT evidence-based reading and writing scores over 700: 9%; SAT math scores over 700: 20%; ACT scores over 30: 22%.

Retention: 86% of full-time freshmen returned.

FACULTY
Total: 1,834, 72% full-time, 91% with terminal degrees.

Student/faculty ratio: 15:1.

ACADEMICS
Calendar: semesters. *Degrees:* certificates, bachelor's, master's, doctoral, and post-master's certificates.

Special study options: academic remediation for entering students, accelerated degree program, advanced placement credit, cooperative education, distance learning, double majors, English as a second language, freshman honors college, honors programs, independent study, internships, off-campus study, part-time degree program, services for LD students, student-designed majors, study abroad, summer session for credit. ***ROTC:*** Army (c).

Unusual degree programs: 3-2 business administration; engineering; nursing; social work; law.

Computers: 3,061 computers/terminals are available on campus for general student use. Students can access the following: campus intranet, computer help desk, free student e-mail accounts, online (class) grades, online (class) registration, online (class) schedules. Campuswide network is available. 100% of college owned or -operated housing units are wired for high-speed Internet access. Wireless service is available via entire campus.
Library: Lockwood Memorial Library plus 11 others. *Books:* 3.4 million (physical), 826,650 (digital/electronic); *Serial titles:* 2,352 (physical), 175,278 (digital/electronic); *Databases:* 383. Weekly public service hours: 168; study areas open 24 hours, 5–7 days a week; students can reserve study rooms.

STUDENT LIFE
Housing options: coed, special housing for students with disabilities. Campus housing is university owned. Freshman campus housing is guaranteed.

Activities and organizations: drama/theater group, student-run newspaper, radio and television station, choral group, marching band, national fraternities, national sororities.

Athletics Member NCAA. All Division I. ***Intercollegiate sports:*** basketball M(s)/W(s), cross-country running M(s)/W(s), football M(s), soccer M, softball W(s), swimming and diving M, tennis M(s)/W(s), track and field M(s)/W(s), volleyball W(s), wrestling M(s). ***Intramural sports:*** baseball M(c), basketball M/W(c), crew M(c)/W(c), cross-country running M(c)/W(c), equestrian sports M(c)/W(c), fencing M(c)/W(c), field hockey M(c)/W(c), golf M(c)/W(c), gymnastics M(c)/W(c), ice hockey M(c)/W(c), lacrosse M(c)/W(c), rugby M(c)/W(c), sailing M(c)/W(c), skiing (downhill) M(c)/W(c), soccer M(c)/W(c), swimming and diving M(c)/W(c), table tennis M(c)/W(c), tennis M(c)/W(c), track and field M(c)/W(c), ultimate Frisbee M(c)/W(c), volleyball M(c)/W(c), water polo M(c)/W(c), wrestling M(c).

Campus security: 24-hour emergency response devices and patrols, student patrols, late-night transport/escort service, controlled dormitory access.

Student services: health clinic, personal/psychological counseling, women's center, legal services, veterans affairs office.

COSTS & FINANCIAL AID
Costs (2019–20) ***Tuition:*** state resident $7070 full-time; nonresident $24,740 full-time. Part-time tuition and fees vary according to course load. ***Required fees:*** $3454 full-time, $148 per credit hour part-time. ***Room and board:*** $14,631; room only: $8521. Room and board charges vary according to board plan and housing facility. ***Payment plan:*** installment. ***Waivers:*** minority students.

Financial Aid Of all full-time matriculated undergraduates who enrolled in 2018, 14,629 applied for aid, 11,754 were judged to have need, 818 had their need fully met. 1,044 Federal Work-Study jobs (averaging $1405). 2,757 state and other part-time jobs (averaging $2552). In 2018, 846 non-need-based awards were made. ***Average percent of need met:*** 52. ***Average financial aid package:*** $11,035. ***Average need-based loan:*** $4245. ***Average need-based gift aid:*** $10,241. ***Average non-need-based aid:*** $3866. ***Average indebtedness upon graduation:*** $25,157.

APPLYING
Standardized Tests *Required:* SAT or ACT (for admission).

Options: electronic application, early admission, early action.

Application fee: $50.

Required: essay or personal statement, high school transcript, letters of recommendation. ***Required for some:*** portfolio for architecture; audition for dance, music theatre, theatre and music.

Notification: continuous (freshmen), continuous (out-of-state freshmen), continuous (transfers), 1/15 (early action).

CONTACT
Mr. Lee Melvin, Vice Provost for Enrollment Management, University at Buffalo, the State University of New York, 1 Capen Hall, North Campus, Buffalo, NY 14260-1660. *Phone:* 716-645-6900. *Toll-free phone:* 888-UB-ADMIT. *E-mail:* ub-admissions@buffalo.edu.

University of Rochester

Rochester, New York

http://www.rochester.edu/

- **Independent** university, founded 1850
- **Suburban** 655-acre campus
- **Endowment** $2.1 billion
- **Coed**
- **Very difficult** entrance level

FACULTY
Student/faculty ratio: 10:1.

ACADEMICS
Calendar: semesters plus optional summer term. *Degrees:* bachelor's, master's, doctoral, post-master's, and postbachelor's certificates.
Library: Rush Rhees Library plus 7 others. Study areas open 24 hours, 5–7 days a week; students can reserve study rooms.

STUDENT LIFE
Housing options: on-campus residence required through sophomore year; coed. Campus housing is university owned and leased by the school. Freshman campus housing is guaranteed.

Activities and organizations: drama/theater group, student-run newspaper, radio and television station, choral group, marching band, Campus Activities Board, Black Students'; Union, Grassroots (environmental group), Women's Caucus, American Sign Language Club, national fraternities, national sororities.

Athletics Member NCAA. All Division III except squash (Division I).

Campus security: 24-hour emergency response devices and patrols, student patrols, late-night transport/escort service, controlled dormitory access.

Student services: health clinic, personal/psychological counseling, women's center, legal services, veterans affairs office.

FINANCIAL AID
Financial Aid Of all full-time matriculated undergraduates who enrolled in 2019, 4,004 applied for aid, 3,414 were judged to have need, 3,103 had their need fully met. 2,126 Federal Work-Study jobs (averaging $3151). 511 state and other part-time jobs (averaging $1216). In 2019, 1607 non-need-based awards were made. ***Average percent of need met:*** 96. ***Average financial aid package:*** $50,665. ***Average need-based loan:*** $3280. ***Average need-based gift aid:*** $46,633. ***Average non-need-based aid:*** $14,575. ***Average indebtedness upon graduation:*** $28,503.

APPLYING
Standardized Tests *Required for some:* SAT and SAT Subject Tests or ACT (for admission). *Recommended:* SAT or ACT (for admission), SAT Subject Tests (for admission).

Options: electronic application, early decision, deferred entrance.

Application fee: $50.

Required: essay or personal statement, high school transcript. ***Required for some:*** audition for Eastman School of Music. ***Recommended:*** 2 letters of recommendation, interview.

CONTACT
Office of Admissions, University of Rochester, PO Box 270251, 300 Wilson Boulevard, Rochester, NY 14627-0251. *Phone:* 585-275-3221. *Toll-free phone:* 888-822-2256. *Fax:* 585-461-4595. *E-mail:* admit@admissions.rochester.edu.

U.T.A. Mesivta of Kiryas Joel

Monroe, New York

CONTACT
U.T.A. Mesivta of Kiryas Joel, 48 Bakertown Road, Suite 501, Monroe, NY 10950.

Utica College

Utica, New York

http://www.utica.edu/

- **Independent** comprehensive, founded 1946
- **Suburban** 128-acre campus
- **Endowment** $25.1 million
- **Coed** 3,488 undergraduate students, 81% full-time, 59% women, 41% men
- **Moderately difficult** entrance level, 87% of applicants were admitted

UNDERGRAD STUDENTS
2,824 full-time, 664 part-time. Students come from 48 states and territories; 28 other countries; 21% are from out of state; 10% Black or African American, non-Hispanic/Latino; 9% Hispanic/Latino; 4% Asian, non-Hispanic/Latino; 0.1% Native Hawaiian or other Pacific Islander, non-Hispanic/Latino; 0.4% American Indian or Alaska Native, non-Hispanic/Latino; 2% Two or more races, non-Hispanic/Latino; 6% Race/ethnicity unknown; 0.8% international; 5% transferred in; 34% live on campus.

Freshmen:
Admission: 3,837 applied, 3,332 admitted, 515 enrolled. ***Average high school GPA:*** 3.3. ***Test scores:*** SAT evidence-based reading and writing scores over 500: 75%; SAT math scores over 500: 80%; ACT scores over 18: 90%; SAT evidence-based reading and writing scores over 600: 27%; SAT math scores over 600: 30%; ACT scores over 24: 46%; SAT evidence-based reading and writing scores over 700: 3%; SAT math scores over 700: 3%; ACT scores over 30: 2%.

Retention: 70% of full-time freshmen returned.

FACULTY
Total: 477, 34% full-time, 41% with terminal degrees.

Student/faculty ratio: 11:1.

ACADEMICS
Calendar: semesters. *Degrees:* certificates, bachelor's, master's, doctoral, and postbachelor's certificates.

Special study options: academic remediation for entering students, accelerated degree program, adult/continuing education programs, advanced placement credit, cooperative education, distance learning, double majors, English as a second language, honors programs, independent study, internships, off-campus study, part-time degree program, services for LD students, study abroad, summer session for credit. ***ROTC:*** Army (b), Air Force (c).

Unusual degree programs: 3-2 engineering with Syracuse University.

Computers: 430 computers/terminals are available on campus for general student use. Students can access the following: computer help desk, free student e-mail accounts, online (class) grades, online (class) registration, online (class) schedules. Campuswide network is available. 100% of college-owned or -operated housing units are wired for high-speed Internet access. Wireless service is available via entire campus.
Library: Frank E. Gannett Memorial Library. *Books:* 307,523 (physical); *Serial titles:* 267,023 (physical). Students can reserve study rooms.

STUDENT LIFE
Housing options: on-campus residence required through sophomore year; coed, special housing for students with disabilities. Campus housing is university owned. Freshman campus housing is guaranteed.

Activities and organizations: drama/theater group, student-run newspaper, radio station, choral group, Physical Therapy Society, Student Nurses Association, Kappa Delta Pi, Student Senate, Utica College Honor Association, national fraternities, national sororities.

Athletics Member NCAA. All Division III except golf (Division II). ***Intercollegiate sports:*** baseball M, basketball M/W, cross-country running M/W, field hockey W, football M, golf M/W, ice hockey M/W, lacrosse M/W, soccer M/W, softball W, swimming and diving M/W, tennis M/W, track and field M/W, volleyball W, water polo W. ***Intramural sports:*** basketball M/W, bowling M/W, cheerleading M(c)/W(c), fencing M(c), field hockey W(c), racquetball M/W, soccer M/W, softball M/W, tennis M/W, volleyball M/W, water polo M/W.

Campus security: 24-hour emergency response devices and patrols, late-night transport/escort service, controlled dormitory access.

Student services: health clinic, personal/psychological counseling, women's center.

COSTS & FINANCIAL AID
Costs (2019–20) ***Comprehensive fee:*** $33,780 includes full-time tuition ($21,560), mandatory fees ($550), and room and board ($11,670). Full-time tuition and fees vary according to course load, degree level, and location. Part-time tuition: $718 per credit hour. Part-time tuition and fees vary according to course load, degree level, and location. ***Required fees:*** $50 per term part-time. ***Room and board:*** Room and board charges vary according to board plan. ***Waivers:*** employees or children of employees.

Financial Aid Of all full-time matriculated undergraduates who enrolled in 2019, 2,590 applied for aid, 2,302 were judged to have need, 198 had their need fully met. In 2019, 284 non-need-based awards were made. ***Average percent of need met:*** 47. ***Average financial aid package:*** $14,855. ***Average need-based loan:*** $4511. ***Average need-based gift aid:*** $5588. ***Average non-need-based aid:*** $4808. ***Average indebtedness upon graduation:*** $30,402.

APPLYING
Standardized Tests *Required for some:* SAT or ACT (for admission).

Options: electronic application, early decision, early action, deferred entrance.

Application fee: $40.

Required: essay or personal statement, high school transcript, minimum 2.0 GPA, 1 letter of recommendation. ***Required for some:*** minimum 3.0 GPA. ***Recommended:*** interview.

Application deadlines: rolling (freshmen), rolling (transfers).

Notification: 9/1 (freshmen), continuous (transfers).

CONTACT
Utica College, 1600 Burrstone Road, Utica, NY 13502-4892. *Phone:* 315-792-3006. *Toll-free phone:* 800-782-8884.

Vassar College

Poughkeepsie, New York

http://www.vassar.edu/

- **Independent** 4-year, founded 1861
- **Suburban** 1000-acre campus with easy access to New York City
- **Endowment** $1.1 billion
- **Coed**
- **Very difficult** entrance level

FACULTY
Student/faculty ratio: 8:1.

ACADEMICS
Calendar: semesters. *Degrees:* bachelor's and master's.
Library: Vassar College Library plus 2 others. *Books:* 1.2 million (physical), 543,272 (digital/electronic); *Serial titles:* 15,914 (physical), 98,004 (digital/electronic); *Databases:* 847. Weekly public service hours: 145; study areas open 24 hours, 5–7 days a week; students can reserve study rooms.

STUDENT LIFE
Housing options: on-campus residence required through senior year; coed, women-only, cooperative, special housing for students with disabilities. Campus housing is university owned. Freshman campus housing is guaranteed.

Activities and organizations: drama/theater group, student-run newspaper, radio station, choral group, Student Association, WVKR radio station, VICE (programming social events), Vassar Greens, Ultimate Frisbee.

Athletics Member NCAA. All Division III except golf (Division II).

Campus security: 24-hour emergency response devices and patrols, student patrols, late-night transport/escort service, controlled dormitory access.

Student services: health clinic, personal/psychological counseling, women's center, veterans affairs office.

COSTS & FINANCIAL AID

Costs (2019–20) ***One-time required fee:*** $80. ***Comprehensive fee:*** $72,990 includes full-time tuition ($57,910), mandatory fees ($860), and room and board ($14,220). Part-time tuition: $6910 per unit. ***College room only:*** $10,030. Room and board charges vary according to housing facility.

Financial Aid Of all full-time matriculated undergraduates who enrolled in 2019, 1,715 applied for aid, 1,478 were judged to have need, 1,469 had their need fully met. ***Average percent of need met:*** 100. ***Average financial aid package:*** $56,765. ***Average need-based loan:*** $3331. ***Average need-based gift aid:*** $50,451. ***Average indebtedness upon graduation:*** $19,474. ***Financial aid deadline:*** 2/1.

APPLYING

Standardized Tests *Required:* SAT or ACT (for admission).

Options: electronic application, early decision, deferred entrance.

Application fee: $65.

Required: essay or personal statement, high school transcript, 2 letters of recommendation.

CONTACT

Dean Art D. Rodriguez, Dean of Admission and Financial Aid, Vassar College, 124 Raymond Avenue, Poughkeepsie, NY 12604. *Phone:* 845-437-7300. *Toll-free phone:* 800-827-7270. *Fax:* 845-437-7063. *E-mail:* admissions@vassar.edu.

Vaughn College of Aeronautics and Technology

Flushing, New York

http://www.vaughn.edu/

- **Independent** comprehensive, founded 1932
- **Urban** 6-acre campus with easy access to New York City
- **Endowment** $24.4 million
- **Coed, primarily men**
- **Moderately difficult** entrance level

FACULTY

Student/faculty ratio: 15:1.

ACADEMICS

Calendar: semesters. *Degrees:* certificates, diplomas, associate, bachelor's, and master's.

Library: Library and Learning Commons. Weekly public service hours: 60.

STUDENT LIFE

Housing options: coed, special housing for students with disabilities. Campus housing is university owned. Freshman applicants given priority for college housing.

Activities and organizations: Robotics Club (2106 Vex World Champions), Society of Women Engineers, Engineers Without Borders, The Unmanned Aerial Vehicle (UAV) Club, SHPE (Society of Hispanic Professional Engineers).

Athletics Member USCAA.

Campus security: 24-hour emergency response devices and patrols, controlled dormitory access.

Student services: personal/psychological counseling, veterans affairs office.

COSTS & FINANCIAL AID

Costs (2019–20) ***One-time required fee:*** $160. ***Comprehensive fee:*** $41,364 includes full-time tuition ($25,680), mandatory fees ($960), and room and board ($14,724). Part-time tuition: $855 per credit. ***Required fees:*** $400 part-time. ***College room only:*** $11,425.

Financial Aid Of all full-time matriculated undergraduates who enrolled in 2018, 1,071 applied for aid, 839 were judged to have need, 247 had their need fully met. In 2018, 70 non-need-based awards were made. ***Average percent of need met:*** 82. ***Average financial aid package:*** $9062. ***Average need-based loan:*** $2063. ***Average need-based gift aid:*** $10,990. ***Average non-need-based aid:*** $2387. ***Average indebtedness upon graduation:*** $37,709.

APPLYING

Standardized Tests *Required:* SAT or ACT (for admission). *Recommended:* SAT and SAT Subject Tests or ACT (for admission).

Options: electronic application.

Application fee: $40.

Required: high school transcript. ***Recommended:*** essay or personal statement, 2 letters of recommendation, interview.

CONTACT

Mr. Celso Alvarez, Associate Vice President of Enrollment for Admissions, Vaughn College of Aeronautics and Technology, 8601 23rd Avenue, Flushing, NY 11369. *Phone:* 718-429-6600 Ext. 117. *Toll-free phone:* 866-6VAUGHN. *Fax:* 718-779-2231. *E-mail:* celso.alvarez@vaughn.edu.

Villa Maria College

Buffalo, New York

http://www.villa.edu/

CONTACT

Mr. Brian Emerson, Vice President for Enrollment and Student Services, Villa Maria College, 240 Pine Ridge Road, Buffalo, NY 14225. *Phone:* 716-896-0700 Ext. 1838. *Fax:* 716-896-0705. *E-mail:* admissions@villa.edu.

Wagner College

Staten Island, New York

http://www.wagner.edu/

- **Independent** comprehensive, founded 1883
- **Urban** 105-acre campus with easy access to New York City
- **Endowment** $88.5 million
- **Coed**
- 70% of applicants were admitted

FACULTY

Student/faculty ratio: 12:1.

ACADEMICS

Calendar: semesters. *Degrees:* bachelor's, master's, doctoral, and post-master's certificates.

Library: August Horrmann Library. *Books:* 70,465 (physical), 180,000 (digital/electronic); *Serial titles:* 79,532 (physical); *Databases:* 61. Weekly public service hours: 120; students can reserve study rooms.

STUDENT LIFE

Housing options: coed. Campus housing is university owned and leased by the school. Freshman campus housing is guaranteed.

Activities and organizations: drama/theater group, student-run newspaper, radio station, choral group, marching band, Student Government Association, Student Activities Board, Wagner College Theatre, Wagner College Choir, student newspaper, national fraternities, national sororities.

Athletics Member NCAA. All Division I except football (Division I-AA).

Campus security: 24-hour emergency response devices and patrols, late-night transport/escort service, controlled dormitory access.

Student services: health clinic, personal/psychological counseling.

FINANCIAL AID

Financial Aid Of all full-time matriculated undergraduates who enrolled in 2016, 1,324 applied for aid, 1,149 were judged to have need, 255 had their need fully met. In 2016, 422 non-need-based awards were made. ***Average percent of need met:*** 70. ***Average financial aid package:*** $29,515. ***Average need-based loan:*** $4937. ***Average need-based gift aid:*** $22,748. ***Average non-need-based aid:*** $17,988.

APPLYING

Standardized Tests *Required for some:* SAT or ACT (for admission).

Options: electronic application, early action, deferred entrance.

Application fee: $60.

Required: essay or personal statement, high school transcript, minimum 2.5 GPA, 2 letters of recommendation. ***Required for some:*** interview. ***Recommended:*** minimum 3.0 GPA, interview.

CONTACT
Mr. James Gibbons, Director of Admissions, Wagner College, One Campus Road, Pape Admissions Building, Staten Island, NY 10301. *Phone:* 718-390-3180. *Toll-free phone:* 800-221-1010. *Fax:* 718-390-3105. *E-mail:* jgibbons@wagner.edu.

Webb Institute

Glen Cove, New York

http://www.webb.edu/

CONTACT
Lauren Carballo, Director of Admissions and Student Services, Webb Institute, 298 Crescent Beach Road, Glen Cove, NY 11542. *Phone:* 516-671-8355. *Fax:* 516-674-9838. *E-mail:* admissions@webb.edu.

Wells College

Aurora, New York

http://www.wells.edu/

CONTACT
Wells College, 170 Main Street, Aurora, NY 13026. *Toll-free phone:* 800-952-9355.

Yeshiva and Kolel Bais Medrash Elyon

Monsey, New York

CONTACT
Yeshiva and Kolel Bais Medrash Elyon, 73 Main Street, Monsey, NY 10952.

Yeshiva and Kollel Harbotzas Torah

Brooklyn, New York

CONTACT
Yeshiva and Kollel Harbotzas Torah, 1049 East 15th Street, Brooklyn, NY 11230.

Yeshiva Derech Chaim

Brooklyn, New York

CONTACT
Yeshiva Derech Chaim, 1573 39th Street, Brooklyn, NY 11218.

Yeshiva D'Monsey Rabbinical College

Monsey, New York

CONTACT
Yeshiva D'Monsey Rabbinical College, 2 Roman Boulevard, Monsey, NY 10952.

Yeshiva Gedolah Imrei Yosef D'Spinka

Brooklyn, New York

CONTACT
Yeshiva Gedolah Imrei Yosef D'Spinka, 1466 56th Street, Brooklyn, NY 11219.

Yeshiva Gedolah Kesser Torah

Monsey, New York

CONTACT
Yeshiva Gedolah Kesser Torah, 28 Cedar Lane, Monsey, NY 10952.

Yeshiva Gedola Ohr Yisrael

Brooklyn, New York

http://www.ohryisroel.org/

CONTACT
Yeshiva Gedola Ohr Yisrael, 2899 Nostrand Avenue, Brooklyn, NY 11229.

Yeshiva Karlin Stolin

Brooklyn, New York

CONTACT
Director of Admissions, Yeshiva Karlin Stolin, 1818 54th Street, Brooklyn, NY 11204. *Phone:* 718-232-7800 Ext. 26.

Yeshiva Kollel Tifereth Elizer

Brooklyn, New York

CONTACT
Yeshiva Kollel Tifereth Elizer, 1227 47th Street, Brooklyn, NY 11219.

Yeshiva of Far Rockaway Derech Ayson Rabbinical Seminary

Far Rockaway, New York

http://www.yofr.org/

CONTACT
Yeshiva of Far Rockaway Derech Ayson Rabbinical Seminary, 802 Hicksville Road, Far Rockaway, NY 11691.

Yeshiva of Machzikai Hadas

Brooklyn, New York

CONTACT
Yeshiva of Machzikai Hadas, 1321 43rd Street, Brooklyn, NY 11219.

Yeshiva of Nitra Rabbinical College

Mount Kisco, New York

CONTACT
Administrator, Yeshiva of Nitra Rabbinical College, Croton Lake Road, Mount Kisco, NY 10549. *Phone:* 718-384-5460. *Fax:* 718-387-9400.

Yeshiva of the Telshe Alumni

Riverdale, New York

CONTACT
Yeshiva of the Telshe Alumni, 4904 Independence Avenue, Riverdale, NY 10471.

Yeshiva Ohr Naftoli

New Windsor, New York

http://www.yeshivaohrnaftoli.com/

CONTACT
Yeshiva Ohr Naftoli, 701 Blooming Grove Turnpike, New Windsor, NY 12553.

Yeshiva Shaarei Torah of Rockland

Suffern, New York

CONTACT
Yeshiva Shaarei Torah of Rockland, 91 West Carlton Road, Suffern, NY 10901.

Yeshiva Shaar Ephraim
Monsey, New York

CONTACT
Yeshiva Shaar Ephraim, 178 Maple Avenue, Monsey, NY 10952.

Yeshiva Shaar Hatorah Talmudic Research Institute
Kew Gardens, New York

CONTACT
Assistant Dean, Yeshiva Shaar Hatorah Talmudic Research Institute, 117-06 84th Avenue, Kew Gardens, NY 11418-1469. *Phone:* 718-846-1940.

Yeshivas Maharit D'Satmar
Monroe, New York
http://www.yeshivasmaharit.com/

CONTACT
Yeshivas Maharit D'Satmar, 475 County Route 105, Monroe, NY 10950.

Yeshivas Novominsk
Brooklyn, New York

CONTACT
Yeshivas Novominsk, 1569 47th Street, Brooklyn, NY 11219.

Yeshivath Viznitz
Monsey, New York

CONTACT
Registrar, Yeshivath Viznitz, 15 Elyon Road, Monsey, NY 10952. *Phone:* 914-356-1010.

Yeshivath Zichron Moshe
South Fallsburg, New York

CONTACT
Rabbi Abba Gorelick, Dean, Yeshivath Zichron Moshe, Laurel Park Road, South Fallsburg, NY 12779. *Phone:* 914-434-5240.

Yeshivat Mikdash Melech
Brooklyn, New York

CONTACT
Rabbi S. Beyda, Director of Admissions, Yeshivat Mikdash Melech, 1326 Ocean Parkway, Brooklyn, NY 11230-5601. *Phone:* 718-339-1090. *E-mail:* mikdashmelech@verizon.net.

Yeshiva University
New York, New York
http://www.yu.edu/

- **Independent** university, founded 1886
- **Urban** campus
- **Endowment** $894.5 million
- **Coed** 2,710 undergraduate students, 98% full-time, 46% women, 54% men
- **Moderately difficult** entrance level, 55% of applicants were admitted

UNDERGRAD STUDENTS
2,643 full-time, 67 part-time. 60% are from out of state; 0.1% Hispanic/Latino; 0.9% Race/ethnicity unknown; 6% international; 1% transferred in; 62% live on campus.

Freshmen:
Admission: 1,660 applied, 919 admitted, 555 enrolled. ***Average high school GPA:*** 3.4. ***Test scores:*** SAT evidence-based reading and writing scores over 500: 100%; SAT math scores over 500: 94%; ACT scores over 18: 100%; SAT evidence-based reading and writing scores over 600: 73%; SAT math scores over 600: 64%; ACT scores over 24: 80%; SAT evidence-based reading and writing scores over 700: 26%; SAT math scores over 700: 24%; ACT scores over 30: 34%.
Retention: 93% of full-time freshmen returned.

FACULTY
Total: 674, 43% full-time, 37% with terminal degrees.
Student/faculty ratio: 7:1.

ACADEMICS
Calendar: semesters. *Degrees:* bachelor's, master's, doctoral, post-master's, and postbachelor's certificates (Yeshiva College and Stern College for Women are coordinate undergraduate colleges of arts and sciences for men and women, respectively. Sy Syms School of Business offers programs at both campuses).
Special study options: advanced placement credit, cooperative education, distance learning, double majors, honors programs, independent study, internships, off-campus study, student-designed majors, study abroad, summer session for credit.
Unusual degree programs: 3-2 engineering with Columbia University, Stonybrook University; nursing with New York University, occupational therapy with Columbia University, physical therapy with Rutgers University, podiatry with New York College of Podiatric Medicine.
Computers: Students can access the following: campus intranet, computer help desk, free student e-mail accounts, online (class) grades, online (class) registration, online (class) schedules. Campuswide network is available. 100% of college-owned or -operated housing units are wired for high-speed Internet access. Wireless service is available via entire campus.
Library: Mendel Gottesman Library. *Books:* 1.1 million (physical), 24,407 (digital/electronic); *Serial titles:* 9,933 (physical); *Databases:* 401.

STUDENT LIFE
Housing options: men-only, women-only, special housing for students with disabilities. Campus housing is university owned.
Activities and organizations: drama/theater group, student-run newspaper, radio station, choral group.
Athletics Member NCAA. All Division III. ***Intercollegiate sports:*** baseball M, basketball M/W, cross-country running M/W, fencing M/W, golf M, soccer M/W, tennis M/W, volleyball M, wrestling M. ***Intramural sports:*** basketball M/W, fencing M/W, swimming and diving M/W, table tennis M, volleyball M/W.
Campus security: 24-hour emergency response devices and patrols, late-night transport/escort service.
Student services: health clinic, personal/psychological counseling.

COSTS & FINANCIAL AID
Costs (2019–20) ***Comprehensive fee:*** $57,400 includes full-time tuition ($42,200), mandatory fees ($2700), and room and board ($12,500). Part-time tuition: $1520 per credit hour. ***College room only:*** $9000.
Financial Aid Of all full-time matriculated undergraduates who enrolled in 2019, 1,877 applied for aid, 1,402 were judged to have need, 425 had their need fully met. In 2019, 728 non-need-based awards were made. ***Average percent of need met:*** 90. ***Average financial aid package:*** $42,654. ***Average need-based loan:*** $7067. ***Average need-based gift aid:*** $31,285. ***Average non-need-based aid:*** $20,577. ***Average indebtedness upon graduation:*** $22,388.

APPLYING
Standardized Tests *Required:* SAT or ACT (for admission).
Options: electronic application, early admission, early decision, deferred entrance.
Application fee: $65.
Required: essay or personal statement, high school transcript, 2 letters of recommendation, interview.
Application deadlines: 2/1 (freshmen), rolling (transfers).
Early decision deadline: 11/1.
Notification: 4/1 (freshmen), 12/15 (early decision).

CONTACT
Yeshiva University, 500 West 185th Street, New York, NY 10033-3201. *Phone:* 212-960-5277.

Yeshiva Zichron Aryeh

Far Rockaway, New York

http://www.yeshivazichronaryeh.com/

CONTACT
Yeshiva Zichron Aryeh, 1213 Bay 25th Street, Far Rockaway, NY 11691.

York College of the City University of New York

Jamaica, New York

http://www.york.cuny.edu/

- **State and locally supported** comprehensive, founded 1967, part of City University of New York System
- **Urban** 50-acre campus with easy access to New York City
- **Endowment** $890,940
- **Coed**
- **Moderately difficult** entrance level

FACULTY
Student/faculty ratio: 23:1.

ACADEMICS
Calendar: semesters. *Degrees:* bachelor's and master's.
Library: Main Library plus 1 other. *Books:* 150,914 (physical), 473,723 (digital/electronic).

STUDENT LIFE
Housing options: college housing not available.

Activities and organizations: drama/theater group, student-run newspaper, television station, choral group, Haitian Students Association, Caribbean Students Association, Haitian Cultural Association, Latin Caucus, Muslim Student Association.

Athletics Member NCAA. All Division III.

Campus security: 24-hour emergency response devices and patrols, late-night transport/escort service.

Student services: health clinic, personal/psychological counseling, women's center.

FINANCIAL AID
Financial Aid Of all full-time matriculated undergraduates who enrolled in 2019, 4,402 applied for aid, 4,295 were judged to have need, 94 had their need fully met. In 2019, 1 non-need-based awards were made. ***Average percent of need met:*** 49. ***Average financial aid package:*** $7189. ***Average need-based loan:*** $4221. ***Average need-based gift aid:*** $7979. ***Average non-need-based aid:*** $4000. ***Average indebtedness upon graduation:*** $5266.

APPLYING
Standardized Tests *Required:* SAT or ACT (for admission).

Options: electronic application, early admission, deferred entrance.

Application fee: $65.

Required: high school transcript, minimum 2.8 GPA. ***Required for some:*** minimum 2.5 GPA. ***Recommended:*** minimum 3.0 GPA.

CONTACT
Dr. La Toro Yates, Director of Admissions, York College of the City University of New York, 94-20 Guy R. Brewer Boulevard, Jamaica, NY 11451. *Phone:* 718-262-2165. *Fax:* 718-262-2601. *E-mail:* lyates@york.cuny.edu.

NORTH CAROLINA

Apex School of Theology

Durham, North Carolina

http://www.apexsot.edu/

CONTACT
Dr. Henry D. Wells Jr., Registrar, Apex School of Theology, 1701 T.W. Alexander Drive, Durham, NC 27703. *Phone:* 919-572-1625. *Fax:* 919-572-1762. *E-mail:* registrar@apexsot.edu.

Appalachian State University

Boone, North Carolina

http://www.appstate.edu/

- **State-supported** comprehensive, founded 1899, part of University of North Carolina System
- **Small-town** 489-acre campus
- **Endowment** $133.2 million
- **Coed** 17,518 undergraduate students, 95% full-time, 56% women, 44% men
- **Moderately difficult** entrance level, 77% of applicants were admitted

UNDERGRAD STUDENTS
16,622 full-time, 896 part-time. Students come from 47 states and territories; 68 other countries; 7% are from out of state; 4% Black or African American, non-Hispanic/Latino; 7% Hispanic/Latino; 2% Asian, non-Hispanic/Latino; 0.3% American Indian or Alaska Native, non-Hispanic/Latino; 4% Two or more races, non-Hispanic/Latino; 0.8% Race/ethnicity unknown; 0.4% international; 8% transferred in; 32% live on campus.

Freshmen:
Admission: 16,664 applied, 12,800 admitted, 3,501 enrolled. ***Average high school GPA:*** 4.3. ***Test scores:*** SAT evidence-based reading and writing scores over 500: 96%; SAT math scores over 500: 95%; ACT scores over 18: 98%; SAT evidence-based reading and writing scores over 600: 58%; SAT math scores over 600: 48%; ACT scores over 24: 65%; SAT evidence-based reading and writing scores over 700: 9%; SAT math scores over 700: 8%; ACT scores over 30: 13%.

Retention: 88% of full-time freshmen returned.

FACULTY
Total: 1,434, 71% full-time, 91% with terminal degrees.

Student/faculty ratio: 16:1.

ACADEMICS
Calendar: semesters. *Degrees:* bachelor's, master's, doctoral, post-master's, and postbachelor's certificates.

Special study options: academic remediation for entering students, adult/continuing education programs, advanced placement credit, distance learning, double majors, English as a second language, honors programs, independent study, internships, off-campus study, part-time degree program, services for LD students, student-designed majors, study abroad, summer session for credit. ***ROTC:*** Army (b).

Unusual degree programs: 3-2 engineering with Auburn University, Clemson University, North Carolina State University.

Computers: 2,280 computers/terminals are available on campus for general student use. Students can access the following: campus intranet, computer help desk, free student e-mail accounts, online (class) grades, online (class) registration, online (class) schedules. Campuswide network is available. 100% of college-owned or -operated housing units are wired for high-speed Internet access. Wireless service is available via entire campus.
Library: Carol Grotnes Belk Library plus 1 other. *Books:* 642,826 (physical), 1.0 million (digital/electronic); *Serial titles:* 12,768 (physical), 178,943 (digital/electronic); *Databases:* 482. Weekly public service hours: 137; study areas open 24 hours, 5–7 days a week; students can reserve study rooms.

STUDENT LIFE
Housing options: on-campus residence required for freshman year; coed, women-only, special housing for students with disabilities. Campus housing is university owned. Freshman campus housing is guaranteed.

Activities and organizations: drama/theater group, student-run newspaper, radio and television station, choral group, marching band, Appalachian Educators, Exercise Science Club, App Sits Meditation Club, The Hiking Club, Gaming Club, national fraternities, national sororities.

Athletics Member NCAA, NAIA. All NCAA Division I except football (Division I-A). ***Intercollegiate sports:*** archery M(c)/W(c), baseball M(s), basketball M(s)/W(s), cross-country running M(s)/W(s), equestrian sports W(c), fencing M(c)/W(c), field hockey W(s), golf M(s)/W(s)(c), ice hockey M(c)/W(c), lacrosse M(c)/W(c), rock climbing M(c)/W(c), rugby M(c)/W(c), skiing (downhill) W(c), soccer M(s)/W(s), softball W(s), swimming and diving M(c)/W(c), tennis M(s)/W(s), track and field

M(s)/W(s), triathlon M(c)/W(c), ultimate Frisbee M(c)/W(c), volleyball M(c)/W(s), wrestling M(s). ***Intramural sports:*** badminton M/W, basketball M/W, bowling M/W, cross-country running M/W, golf M/W, racquetball M/W, soccer M/W, softball M/W, swimming and diving M/W, table tennis M/W, tennis M/W, ultimate Frisbee M/W, volleyball M/W, weight lifting M/W.

Campus security: 24-hour emergency response devices and patrols, late-night transport/escort service, controlled dormitory access.

Student services: health clinic, personal/psychological counseling, women's center, legal services, veterans affairs office.

COSTS & FINANCIAL AID

Costs (2019–20) ***Tuition:*** area resident $4242 full-time; state resident $4242 full-time, $143 per credit hour part-time; nonresident $19,049 full-time, $644 per credit hour part-time. Part-time tuition and fees vary according to course load. No tuition increase for student's term of enrollment. ***Required fees:*** $3168 full-time, $104 per credit hour part-time. ***Room and board:*** $8568; room only: $4620. Room and board charges vary according to board plan and housing facility. ***Payment plan:*** installment. ***Waivers:*** employees or children of employees.

Financial Aid Of all full-time matriculated undergraduates who enrolled in 2019, 11,842 applied for aid, 8,642 were judged to have need, 1,173 had their need fully met. In 2019, 739 non-need-based awards were made. ***Average percent of need met:*** 61. ***Average financial aid package:*** $10,279. ***Average need-based loan:*** $4201. ***Average need-based gift aid:*** $8916. ***Average non-need-based aid:*** $3074. ***Average indebtedness upon graduation:*** $23,105.

APPLYING

Standardized Tests *Required:* SAT or ACT (for admission).

Options: electronic application, early action, deferred entrance.

Application fee: $65.

Required: high school transcript. ***Recommended:*** essay or personal statement.

Application deadlines: 2/1 (freshmen), 2/1 (out-of-state freshmen), rolling (transfers), 11/1 (early action).

Notification: continuous until 1/25 (freshmen), continuous until 1/25 (out-of-state freshmen), continuous (transfers), 1/25 (early action).

CONTACT

Mr. Alexis Pope, Director of Admissions, Appalachian State University, ASU Box 32004, Boone, NC 28608. *Phone:* 828-262-2120. *Fax:* 828-262-3296. *E-mail:* admissions@appstate.edu.

Barton College

Wilson, North Carolina

http://www.barton.edu/

- **Independent** comprehensive, founded 1902, affiliated with Christian Church (Disciples of Christ)
- **Small-town** 76-acre campus with easy access to Raleigh-Durham
- **Endowment** $29.1 million
- **Coed** 976 undergraduate students, 95% full-time, 63% women, 37% men
- **Minimally difficult** entrance level, 40% of applicants were admitted

UNDERGRAD STUDENTS

932 full-time, 44 part-time. Students come from 34 states and territories; 25 other countries; 24% are from out of state; 6% transferred in; 51% live on campus.

Freshmen:

Admission: 3,486 applied, 1,381 admitted, 277 enrolled. ***Average high school GPA:*** 3.2.

Retention: 72% of full-time freshmen returned.

ACADEMICS

Calendar: semesters. *Degrees:* bachelor's and master's.

Special study options: academic remediation for entering students, accelerated degree program, adult/continuing education programs, advanced placement credit, distance learning, double majors, honors programs, independent study, internships, part-time degree program, services for LD students, student-designed majors, study abroad, summer session for credit.

Computers: Students can access the following: campus intranet, computer help desk, free student e-mail accounts, online (class) grades, online (class) registration, online (class) schedules. Campuswide network is available. 100% of college-owned or -operated housing units are wired for high-speed Internet access. Wireless service is available via entire campus.

Library: Willis N. Hackney Library. *Books:* 129,303 (physical), 503,101 (digital/electronic); *Serial titles:* 6 (physical), 888,612 (digital/electronic); *Databases:* 332. Weekly public service hours: 95.

STUDENT LIFE

Housing options: on-campus residence required through sophomore year; coed. Campus housing is university owned. Freshman campus housing is guaranteed.

Activities and organizations: drama/theater group, student-run newspaper, radio and television station, choral group, Student Ambassador Program, Barton College Association of Nursing, Barton College Orientation Team, Barton College Catholic Campus Ministries, Minority Student Association, national fraternities, national sororities.

Athletics Member NCAA. All Division II. ***Intercollegiate sports:*** baseball M(s), basketball M(s)/W(s), cheerleading W(s)(c), cross-country running M(s)/W(s), golf M(s)/W(s), lacrosse M(s)/W(s), soccer M(s)/W(s), softball W(s), swimming and diving M(s)/W(s), tennis M(s)/W(s), track and field M(s)/W(s), volleyball M(s)/W(s). ***Intramural sports:*** basketball M/W, football M/W, soccer M/W, softball M/W, volleyball M/W.

Campus security: 24-hour emergency response devices and patrols, late-night transport/escort service, controlled dormitory access.

Student services: health clinic, personal/psychological counseling, women's center, veterans affairs office.

COSTS & FINANCIAL AID

Costs (2019–20) ***Comprehensive fee:*** $42,154 includes full-time tuition ($31,732) and room and board ($10,422). Part-time tuition: $450 per credit hour. ***College room only:*** $4500. Room and board charges vary according to housing facility. ***Payment plan:*** installment. ***Waivers:*** employees or children of employees.

Financial Aid Of all full-time matriculated undergraduates who enrolled in 2019, 889 applied for aid, 825 were judged to have need, 119 had their need fully met. 122 Federal Work-Study jobs (averaging $1287). In 2019, 151 non-need-based awards were made. ***Average percent of need met:*** 69. ***Average financial aid package:*** $25,681. ***Average need-based loan:*** $3867. ***Average need-based gift aid:*** $21,277. ***Average non-need-based aid:*** $12,163. ***Average indebtedness upon graduation:*** $27,227.

APPLYING

Standardized Tests *Required:* SAT or ACT (for admission).

Options: electronic application.

Required for some: high school transcript.

Application deadlines: rolling (freshmen), rolling (transfers).

Notification: continuous (freshmen), continuous (transfers).

CONTACT

Barton College, PO Box 5000, Wilson, NC 27893-7000. *Phone:* 800-345-4973. *Toll-free phone:* 800-345-4973.

Belmont Abbey College

Belmont, North Carolina

http://www.belmontabbeycollege.edu/

- **Independent Roman Catholic** 4-year, founded 1876
- **Small-town** 150-acre campus with easy access to Charlotte
- **Coed** 1,507 undergraduate students, 92% full-time, 49% women, 51% men
- **Moderately difficult** entrance level, 81% of applicants were admitted

UNDERGRAD STUDENTS

1,388 full-time, 119 part-time. Students come from 45 states and territories; 36 other countries; 43% are from out of state; 13% Black or African American, non-Hispanic/Latino; 2% Hispanic/Latino; 2% Asian, non-Hispanic/Latino; 1% American Indian or Alaska Native, non-Hispanic/Latino; 0.2% Two or more races, non-Hispanic/Latino; 18% Race/ethnicity unknown; 3% international; 6% transferred in; 54% live on campus.

Freshmen:
Admission: 2,134 applied, 1,721 admitted, 368 enrolled. ***Average high school GPA:*** 3.3. ***Test scores:*** SAT evidence-based reading and writing scores over 500: 73%; SAT math scores over 500: 72%; ACT scores over 18: 84%; SAT evidence-based reading and writing scores over 600: 28%; SAT math scores over 600: 29%; ACT scores over 24: 40%; SAT evidence-based reading and writing scores over 700: 4%; SAT math scores over 700: 1%; ACT scores over 30: 9%.

Retention: 62% of full-time freshmen returned.

FACULTY
Total: 124, 61% full-time, 56% with terminal degrees.

Student/faculty ratio: 16:1.

ACADEMICS
Calendar: semesters. *Degree:* bachelor's.

Special study options: advanced placement credit, double majors, freshman honors college, honors programs, independent study, internships, off-campus study, part-time degree program, services for LD students, study abroad, summer session for credit. ***ROTC:*** Army (c), Air Force (c).

Computers: 150 computers/terminals are available on campus for general student use. Students can access the following: campus intranet, computer help desk, free student e-mail accounts, online (class) grades, online (class) registration, online (class) schedules. Campuswide network is available. 100% of college-owned or -operated housing units are wired for high-speed Internet access. Wireless service is available via entire campus.

Library: Abbot Vincent Taylor Library plus 1 other. *Books:* 126,443 (physical), 357,889 (digital/electronic); *Serial titles:* 273 (physical); *Databases:* 119. Students can reserve study rooms.

STUDENT LIFE
Housing options: men-only, women-only. Campus housing is university owned. Freshman campus housing is guaranteed.

Activities and organizations: drama/theater group, student-run newspaper, radio station, choral group, Campus Activities Board, The Crusader (Newspaper Club), Crusaders for Life, Abbey Volunteers, Abbey Players, national fraternities, national sororities.

Athletics Member NCAA. All Division II. ***Intercollegiate sports:*** baseball M(s), basketball M(s)/W(s), bowling M(s)/W(s), cheerleading W(s), cross-country running M(s)/W(s), field hockey W(s), golf M(s)/W(s), lacrosse M(s)/W(s), rugby M(s), soccer M(s)/W(s), softball W(s), tennis M(s)/W(s), track and field M(s)/W(s), volleyball M(s)/W(s), wrestling M(s). ***Intramural sports:*** football M/W, soccer M/W, ultimate Frisbee M/W.

Campus security: 24-hour emergency response devices and patrols.

Student services: health clinic, personal/psychological counseling.

COSTS & FINANCIAL AID
Costs (2020–21) ***Comprehensive fee:*** $28,890 includes full-time tuition ($18,500) and room and board ($10,390). Full-time tuition and fees vary according to course load. Part-time tuition: $617 per credit hour. Part-time tuition and fees vary according to course load. No tuition increase for student's term of enrollment. ***College room only:*** $5826. Room and board charges vary according to board plan and housing facility. ***Waivers:*** employees or children of employees.

Financial Aid Of all full-time matriculated undergraduates who enrolled in 2019, 1,105 applied for aid, 890 were judged to have need, 104 had their need fully met. In 2019, 448 non-need-based awards were made. ***Average percent of need met:*** 56. ***Average financial aid package:*** $13,565. ***Average need-based loan:*** $4349. ***Average need-based gift aid:*** $10,261. ***Average non-need-based aid:*** $5252.

APPLYING
Options: electronic application, early action, deferred entrance.

Required: high school transcript, minimum 2.3 GPA. ***Required for some:*** essay or personal statement. ***Recommended:*** interview.

Application deadlines: 8/15 (transfers), 10/30 (early action).

Notification: continuous (freshmen), continuous (transfers), 11/5 (early action).

CONTACT
Martin Aucoin, Director of Admissions, Belmont Abbey College, 100 Belmont-Mt. Holly Road, Belmont, NC 28012. *Phone:* 704-461-6258. *Toll-free phone:* 888-BAC-0110. *Fax:* 704-461-6220. *E-mail:* MartinAucoin@bac.edu.

Bennett College

Greensboro, North Carolina

http://www.bennett.edu/

- **Independent United Methodist** 4-year, founded 1873
- **Urban** 60-acre campus
- **Endowment** $12.6 million
- **Women only**
- **Minimally difficult** entrance level

FACULTY
Student/faculty ratio: 10:1.

ACADEMICS
Calendar: semesters. *Degree:* bachelor's.
Library: Holgate Library. *Books:* 79,536 (physical), 203,358 (digital/electronic); *Serial titles:* 22 (physical), 22,014 (digital/electronic); *Databases:* 143. Weekly public service hours: 83.

STUDENT LIFE
Housing options: on-campus residence required through sophomore year; women-only. Campus housing is university owned. Freshman campus housing is guaranteed.

Activities and organizations: drama/theater group, choral group, national sororities.

Campus security: 24-hour emergency response devices and patrols, late-night transport/escort service, controlled dormitory access, alerts and educational programs are offered.

Student services: health clinic, personal/psychological counseling.

FINANCIAL AID
Financial Aid Of all full-time matriculated undergraduates who enrolled in 2011, 664 applied for aid, 643 were judged to have need, 22 had their need fully met. In 2011, 7 non-need-based awards were made. ***Average percent of need met:*** 47. ***Average financial aid package:*** $13,092. ***Average need-based loan:*** $4170. ***Average need-based gift aid:*** $9402. ***Average non-need-based aid:*** $4714. ***Financial aid deadline:*** 3/15.

APPLYING
Standardized Tests *Required:* SAT or ACT (for admission).

Options: electronic application, deferred entrance.

Application fee: $35.

Required: high school transcript, minimum 2.5 GPA, 2 letters of recommendation. ***Recommended:*** essay or personal statement.

CONTACT
Mr. James Crawford, Director, Admissions, Bennett College, 900 East Washington Street, Enrollment Management Center, Greensboro, NC 27401. *Phone:* 336-517-1818. *Toll-free phone:* 800-413-5323. *E-mail:* jcrawford@bennett.edu.

Brevard College

Brevard, North Carolina

http://www.brevard.edu/

CONTACT
Mr. David Volrath, Admissions, Brevard College, One Brevard College Drive, Brevard, NC 28712. *Phone:* 828-884-8367. *Toll-free phone:* 800-527-9090. *Fax:* 828-884-3790. *E-mail:* admissions@brevard.edu.

Cabarrus College of Health Sciences

Concord, North Carolina

http://www.cabarruscollege.edu/

- **Independent** comprehensive, founded 1942
- **Suburban** 5-acre campus with easy access to Charlotte
- **Endowment** $2.0 million
- **Coed, primarily women**
- **Moderately difficult** entrance level

ACADEMICS
Calendar: semesters. *Degrees:* certificates, diplomas, associate, bachelor's, and master's.
Library: Cabarrus College Information Resource Center plus 1 other. Study areas open 24 hours, 5–7 days a week.

STUDENT LIFE
Housing options: college housing not available.

Activities and organizations: Rotaract Service Club, Cabarrus College Association of Nursing Students, Student Government Association, Honor Society, Christian Student Union.

Campus security: 24-hour emergency response devices and patrols.

Student services: health clinic, personal/psychological counseling.

APPLYING
Standardized Tests *Required:* SAT or ACT (for admission).

Options: electronic application.

Application fee: $50.

Required: essay or personal statement, high school transcript, minimum 2.0 GPA, 2 letters of recommendation. ***Required for some:*** interview. ***Recommended:*** minimum 3.0 GPA.

CONTACT
McKenzie Allen, Admissions Representative, Cabarrus College of Health Sciences, 401 Medical Park Drive, Concord, NC 28025-2077. *Phone:* 704-403-2589. *Fax:* 704-403-2077. *E-mail:* mckenzie.allen@cabarruscollege.edu.

Campbell University

Buies Creek, North Carolina

http://www.campbell.edu/

CONTACT
Ms. Peggy Mason, Director of Admissions, Campbell University, PO Box 546, 450 Leslie Campbell Avenue, Buies Creek, NC 27506. *Phone:* 910-893-1290. *Toll-free phone:* 800-334-4111. *Fax:* 910-893-1288. *E-mail:* adm@mailcenter.campbell.edu.

Carolina Christian College

Winston-Salem, North Carolina

http://www.carolina.edu/

- **Independent nondenominational** comprehensive, founded 1945
- **Small-town** 2-acre campus
- **Endowment** $250,000
- **Coed** 47 undergraduate students, 100% full-time, 45% women, 55% men
- **Noncompetitive** entrance level, 75% of applicants were admitted

UNDERGRAD STUDENTS
47 full-time. Students come from 5 states and territories; 10% are from out of state; 87% Black or African American, non-Hispanic/Latino; 2% Hispanic/Latino; 2% Two or more races, non-Hispanic/Latino; 9% transferred in; 17% live on campus.

Freshmen:
Admission: 12 applied, 9 admitted, 9 enrolled. ***Average high school GPA:*** 2.6.

Retention: 83% of full-time freshmen returned.

FACULTY
Total: 12, 17% full-time, 8% with terminal degrees.

Student/faculty ratio: 11:1.

ACADEMICS
Calendar: semesters. *Degrees:* associate, bachelor's, master's, and doctoral.

Special study options: accelerated degree program, adult/continuing education programs, external degree program, part-time degree program.

Computers: 8 computers/terminals and 8 ports are available on campus for general student use. Students can access the following: free student e-mail accounts, online (class) registration. Campuswide network is available. 1% of college-owned or -operated housing units are wired for high-speed Internet access. Wireless service is available via entire campus.

Library: Aubrey Payne. *Books:* 14,200 (physical), 3,900 (digital/electronic); *Serial titles:* 1,006 (digital/electronic); *Databases:* 4. Weekly public service hours: 2.

STUDENT LIFE
Housing options: men-only. Campus housing is university owned. Freshman applicants given priority for college housing.

Athletics Member NCCAA. except basketball (Division I-AA)

Campus security: 24-hour emergency response devices.

Student services: personal/psychological counseling.

COSTS & FINANCIAL AID
Costs (2020–21) ***One-time required fee:*** $75. ***Comprehensive fee:*** $10,640 includes full-time tuition ($7600), mandatory fees ($1290), and room and board ($1750). Part-time tuition: $7600 per year. ***Required fees:*** $1290 per year part-time. ***College room only:*** $1600. ***Payment plan:*** installment. ***Waivers:*** employees or children of employees.

Financial Aid Of all full-time matriculated undergraduates who enrolled in 2019, 70 applied for aid, 70 were judged to have need, 56 had their need fully met. ***Average percent of need met:*** 89. ***Average financial aid package:*** $10,590. ***Average need-based gift aid:*** $5300.

APPLYING
Options: electronic application.

Application fee: $50.

Required: essay or personal statement, high school transcript, 2 letters of recommendation, interview.

Application deadlines: rolling (freshmen), rolling (transfers).

Notification: continuous (freshmen), continuous (transfers).

CONTACT
Garriell Lucas, Admission Officer, Carolina Christian College, 4209 Indiana Avenue, Winston-Salem, NC 27105. *Phone:* 336-744-0900.

Carolina College of Biblical Studies

Fayetteville, North Carolina

http://carolinabiblecollege.org/

CONTACT
Carolina College of Biblical Studies, 817 South McPherson Church Road, Fayetteville, NC 28303.

Catawba College

Salisbury, North Carolina

http://www.catawba.edu/

- **Independent** comprehensive, founded 1851, affiliated with United Church of Christ
- **Small-town** 276-acre campus with easy access to Charlotte, NC
- **Endowment** $61.9 million
- **Coed** 1,331 undergraduate students, 92% full-time, 55% women, 45% men
- **Moderately difficult** entrance level, 50% of applicants were admitted

UNDERGRAD STUDENTS
1,229 full-time, 102 part-time. Students come from 31 states and territories; 20% are from out of state; 21% Black or African American, non-Hispanic/Latino; 9% Hispanic/Latino; 0.8% Asian, non-Hispanic/Latino; 0.2% Native Hawaiian or other Pacific Islander, non-Hispanic/Latino; 0.5% American Indian or Alaska Native, non-Hispanic/Latino; 4% Two or more races, non-Hispanic/Latino; 3% Race/ethnicity unknown; 3% international; 5% transferred in; 61% live on campus.

Freshmen:
Admission: 3,335 applied, 1,651 admitted, 347 enrolled. ***Average high school GPA:*** 3.5. ***Test scores:*** SAT evidence-based reading and writing scores over 500: 58%; SAT math scores over 500: 59%; SAT evidence-based reading and writing scores over 600: 14%; SAT math scores over 600: 15%; SAT evidence-based reading and writing scores over 700: 3%; SAT math scores over 700: 1%.

Retention: 72% of full-time freshmen returned.

FACULTY
Total: 147, 56% full-time, 65% with terminal degrees.
Student/faculty ratio: 12:1.

ACADEMICS
Calendar: semesters. *Degrees:* bachelor's and master's.
Special study options: advanced placement credit, double majors, honors programs, independent study, internships, part-time degree program, services for LD students, student-designed majors, study abroad, summer session for credit. ***ROTC:*** Army (c), Air Force (c).
Computers: 175 computers/terminals are available on campus for general student use. Students can access the following: campus intranet, computer help desk, free student e-mail accounts, online (class) grades, online (class) registration, online (class) schedules. Campuswide network is available. 100% of college-owned or -operated housing units are wired for high-speed Internet access. Wireless service is available via entire campus.
Library: Corriher-Linn-Black Memorial Library plus 1 other. *Books:* 134,563 (physical), 249,329 (digital/electronic); *Serial titles:* 12,400 (physical), 114,252 (digital/electronic); *Databases:* 108. Weekly public service hours: 83; students can reserve study rooms.

STUDENT LIFE
Housing options: on-campus residence required for freshman year; coed, men-only, women-only. Campus housing is university owned. Freshman campus housing is guaranteed.
Activities and organizations: drama/theater group, student-run newspaper, radio station, choral group, marching band, Volunteer Catawba, Catawba Ambassadors (admissions guides), Blue Masque (drama), Fellowship of Christian Athletes, Wigwam Productions (student activities board).
Athletics Member NCAA. All Division II. ***Intercollegiate sports:*** baseball M(s), basketball M(s)/W(s), cheerleading M(c)/W(c), cross-country running M(s)/W(s), football M(s), golf M(s)/W(s), lacrosse M(s)/W(s), soccer M(s)/W(s), softball W(s), swimming and diving M(s)/W(s), tennis M(s)/W(s), track and field M/W, volleyball W(s). ***Intramural sports:*** badminton M/W, basketball M/W, bowling M/W, football M, racquetball M/W, soccer M/W, softball M, table tennis M/W, tennis M/W, ultimate Frisbee M/W, volleyball M/W.
Campus security: 24-hour emergency response devices and patrols, late-night transport/escort service, controlled dormitory access.
Student services: health clinic, personal/psychological counseling.

COSTS & FINANCIAL AID
Costs (2020–21) ***Comprehensive fee:*** $89,314 includes full-time tuition ($31,436), mandatory fees ($47,074), and room and board ($10,804). Full-time tuition and fees vary according to class time and course load. Part-time tuition: $898 per credit hour. Part-time tuition and fees vary according to class time and course load. ***College room only:*** $6374. Room and board charges vary according to housing facility. ***Payment plan:*** installment. ***Waivers:*** employees or children of employees.
Financial Aid Of all full-time matriculated undergraduates who enrolled in 2019, 1,075 applied for aid, 1,005 were judged to have need, 284 had their need fully met. 154 Federal Work-Study jobs (averaging $1452). 75 state and other part-time jobs (averaging $1332). In 2019, 198 non-need-based awards were made. ***Average percent of need met:*** 81. ***Average financial aid package:*** $27,292. ***Average need-based loan:*** $3982. ***Average need-based gift aid:*** $8222. ***Average non-need-based aid:*** $17,051. ***Average indebtedness upon graduation:*** $27,806.

APPLYING
Standardized Tests *Required for some:* SAT or ACT (for admission).
Options: electronic application, deferred entrance.
Required: essay or personal statement, high school transcript, minimum 2.0 GPA. ***Recommended:*** 2 letters of recommendation, interview.
Application deadlines: rolling (freshmen), rolling (transfers).
Notification: continuous (freshmen), continuous (transfers).

CONTACT
Catawba College, 2300 West Innes Street, Salisbury, NC 28144-2488. *Phone:* 704-637-4410. *Toll-free phone:* 800-CATAWBA.

Chamberlain College of Nursing - Charlotte

Charlotte, North Carolina

http://www.chamberlain.edu/

CONTACT
Chamberlain College of Nursing - Charlotte, 2015 Ayrsley Town Boulevard, Charlotte, NC 28273.

Charlotte Christian College and Theological Seminary

Charlotte, North Carolina

http://www.charlottechristian.edu/

CONTACT
Mr. George Shears, Director of Admissions, Charlotte Christian College and Theological Seminary, P.O. Box 790106, Charlotte, NC 28206. *Phone:* 704-334-6882 Ext. 115. *Fax:* 704-334-6885. *E-mail:* gshears@charlottechristian.edu.

Chowan University

Murfreesboro, North Carolina

http://www.chowan.edu/

CONTACT
Mr. Scott Parker, Director of Admissions Information, Chowan University, One University Place, Murfreesboro, NC 27855. *Phone:* 252-398-6314. *Toll-free phone:* 888-4-CHOWAN. *Fax:* 252-398-1190. *E-mail:* parkes@chowan.edu.

Davidson College

Davidson, North Carolina

http://www.davidson.edu/

- **Independent Presbyterian** 4-year, founded 1837
- **Suburban** 665-acre campus with easy access to Charlotte
- **Endowment** $881.5 million
- **Coed** 1,837 undergraduate students, 100% full-time, 49% women, 51% men
- 18% of applicants were admitted

UNDERGRAD STUDENTS
1,837 full-time. Students come from 48 states and territories; 46 other countries; 78% are from out of state; 7% Black or African American, non-Hispanic/Latino; 8% Hispanic/Latino; 5% Asian, non-Hispanic/Latino; 0.1% Native Hawaiian or other Pacific Islander, non-Hispanic/Latino; 0.4% American Indian or Alaska Native, non-Hispanic/Latino; 5% Two or more races, non-Hispanic/Latino; 0.8% Race/ethnicity unknown; 7% international; 0.5% transferred in; 95% live on campus.

Freshmen:
Admission: 5,982 applied, 1,080 admitted, 527 enrolled. ***Average high school GPA:*** 3.8. ***Test scores:*** SAT evidence-based reading and writing scores over 500: 100%; SAT math scores over 500: 100%; ACT scores over 18: 100%; SAT evidence-based reading and writing scores over 600: 96%; SAT math scores over 600: 96%; ACT scores over 24: 99%; SAT evidence-based reading and writing scores over 700: 46%; SAT math scores over 700: 54%; ACT scores over 30: 75%.
Retention: 95% of full-time freshmen returned.

FACULTY
Total: 220, 95% full-time, 96% with terminal degrees.
Student/faculty ratio: 9:1.

ACADEMICS
Calendar: semesters. *Degree:* bachelor's.
Special study options: double majors, independent study, off-campus study, services for LD students, student-designed majors, study abroad. ***ROTC:*** Army (b).
Unusual degree programs: 3-2 engineering with Columbia University (NY); Washington University (St. Louis).

Computers: Students can access the following: campus intranet, computer help desk, free student e-mail accounts, online (class) grades, online (class) registration, online (class) schedules. Campuswide network is available. Wireless service is available via entire campus.
Library: E. H. Little Library plus 1 other. *Books:* 479,546 (physical), 856,053 (digital/electronic); *Serial titles:* 8,258 (physical), 152,605 (digital/electronic); *Databases:* 610. Study areas open 24 hours, 5–7 days a week; students can reserve study rooms.

STUDENT LIFE
Housing options: coed, cooperative, special housing for students with disabilities. Campus housing is university owned. Freshman campus housing is guaranteed.

Activities and organizations: drama/theater group, student-run newspaper, choral group, national fraternities, national sororities.

Athletics Member NCAA. All Division I except football (Division I-AA). ***Intercollegiate sports:*** baseball M(s), basketball M(s)/W(s), crew M(c)/W(c), cross-country running M(s)/W(s), fencing M(c)/W(c), field hockey M(c)/W(s), golf M(s), lacrosse M(c)/W(s), rugby M(c), sailing M(c)/W(c), soccer M(s)/W(s), squash M(c), swimming and diving M(s)/W(s), tennis M(s)/W(s), track and field M(s)/W(s), ultimate Frisbee M(c)/W(c), volleyball W(s), wrestling M(s). ***Intramural sports:*** baseball M(c), basketball M(c)/W, field hockey W(c), football M/W, golf M(c), lacrosse W(c), soccer M(c)/W(c), softball M/W, tennis M(c)/W(c), volleyball M/W(c).

Campus security: 24-hour emergency response devices and patrols, late-night transport/escort service, controlled dormitory access.

Student services: health clinic, personal/psychological counseling.

COSTS & FINANCIAL AID
Costs (2020–21) *Comprehensive fee:* $70,285 includes full-time tuition ($54,520), mandatory fees ($540), and room and board ($15,225). ***College room only:*** $7700. Room and board charges vary according to board plan and housing facility. ***Payment plans:*** installment, deferred payment.

Financial Aid Of all full-time matriculated undergraduates who enrolled in 2019, 1,108 applied for aid, 919 were judged to have need, 919 had their need fully met. In 2019, 108 non-need-based awards were made. ***Average percent of need met:*** 100. ***Average financial aid package:*** $51,275. ***Average need-based loan:*** $3551. ***Average need-based gift aid:*** $47,233. ***Average non-need-based aid:*** $24,493. ***Average indebtedness upon graduation:*** $23,535. ***Financial aid deadline:*** 2/15.

APPLYING
Options: electronic application, early decision, deferred entrance.

Application fee: $50.

Required: essay or personal statement, high school transcript, 3 letters of recommendation.

Application deadlines: 1/7 (freshmen), 3/15 (transfers).

Early decision deadline: 11/15 (for plan 1), 1/2 (for plan 2).

Notification: 3/19 (freshmen), 5/25 (transfers), 12/15 (early decision plan 1), 2/1 (early decision plan 2).

CONTACT
https://www.davidson.edu/admission-and-financial-aid/connect-davidson/admission-and-financial-aid-staff, Davidson College, Box 7156 - Admission, Box 7157 - Financial Aid, Davidson, NC 28035. *Phone:* 800-7680380. *Toll-free phone:* 800-768-0380. *E-mail:* admission@davidson.edu.

DeVry University–Charlotte Campus

Charlotte, North Carolina

http://www.devry.edu/

- **Proprietary** comprehensive, part of DeVry University
- **Coed**

ACADEMICS
Calendar: semesters. *Degrees:* associate, bachelor's, and master's.

FINANCIAL AID
Financial Aid Of all full-time matriculated undergraduates who enrolled in 2007, 34 applied for aid, 33 were judged to have need, 1 had their need fully met. In 2007, 2 non-need-based awards were made. ***Average percent of need met:*** 41. ***Average financial aid package:*** $12,613. ***Average need-based loan:*** $9286. ***Average need-based gift aid:*** $8335. ***Average non-need-based aid:*** $7635.

CONTACT
Admissions Office, DeVry University–Charlotte Campus, 2015 Ayrsley Town Boulevard, Suite 109, Charlotte, NC 28273-4068. *Phone:* 704-362-2345. *Toll-free phone:* 866-338-7934.

Duke University

Durham, North Carolina

http://www.duke.edu/

- **Independent** university, founded 1838, affiliated with United Methodist Church
- **Suburban** 8500-acre campus
- **Coed**
- **Most difficult entrance level**

FACULTY
Student/faculty ratio: 6:1.

ACADEMICS
Calendar: semesters. *Degrees:* bachelor's, master's, doctoral, post-master's, and postbachelor's certificates.
Library: Perkins Library.

STUDENT LIFE
Housing options: on-campus residence required through junior year; coed, men-only, women-only. Campus housing is university owned. Freshman campus housing is guaranteed.

Activities and organizations: drama/theater group, student-run newspaper, radio and television station, choral group, marching band, national fraternities, national sororities.

Athletics Member NCAA. All Division I except football (Division I-A).

Campus security: 24-hour emergency response devices and patrols, late-night transport/escort service, controlled dormitory access.

Student services: health clinic, personal/psychological counseling, women's center, legal services.

COSTS & FINANCIAL AID
Costs (2019–20) *Comprehensive fee:* $73,519 includes full-time tuition ($55,880), mandatory fees ($2051), and room and board ($15,588). Part-time tuition: $1746 per credit hour. ***College room only:*** $8924. Room and board charges vary according to board plan and housing facility. ***Payment plans:*** tuition prepayment, installment.

Financial Aid Of all full-time matriculated undergraduates who enrolled in 2019, 3,631 applied for aid, 2,993 were judged to have need, 2,993 had their need fully met. 1,746 Federal Work-Study jobs (averaging $2217). 1,226 state and other part-time jobs (averaging $2024). In 2019, 132 non-need-based awards were made. ***Average percent of need met:*** 100. ***Average financial aid package:*** $57,235. ***Average need-based loan:*** $3207. ***Average need-based gift aid:*** $55,374. ***Average non-need-based aid:*** $74,761. ***Average indebtedness upon graduation:*** $22,369.

APPLYING
Standardized Tests *Required:* SAT and SAT Subject Tests or ACT (for admission).

Options: electronic application, early decision.

Application fee: $85.

Required: essay or personal statement, high school transcript. ***Required for some:*** audition tape for dance, drama, or music; slides of work for art. ***Recommended:*** interview.

CONTACT
Mr. Christoph Guttentag, Director of Admissions, Duke University, Durham, NC 27708. *Phone:* 919-684-3214. *E-mail:* askduke@admiss.duke.edu.

East Carolina University
Greenville, North Carolina
http://www.ecu.edu/

- **State-supported** university, founded 1907, part of University of North Carolina System
- **Urban** 1600-acre campus
- **Endowment** $219.4 million
- **Coed** 23,081 undergraduate students, 83% full-time, 57% women, 43% men
- **Moderately difficult** entrance level, 79% of applicants were admitted

UNDERGRAD STUDENTS
19,204 full-time, 3,877 part-time. 9% are from out of state; 16% Black or African American, non-Hispanic/Latino; 8% Hispanic/Latino; 3% Asian, non-Hispanic/Latino; 0.1% Native Hawaiian or other Pacific Islander, non-Hispanic/Latino; 0.6% American Indian or Alaska Native, non-Hispanic/Latino; 4% Two or more races, non-Hispanic/Latino; 3% Race/ethnicity unknown; 0.5% international; 8% transferred in; 25% live on campus.

Freshmen:
Admission: 19,234 applied, 15,140 admitted, 4,364 enrolled. ***Average high school GPA:*** 3.3. ***Test scores:*** SAT evidence-based reading and writing scores over 500: 87%; SAT math scores over 500: 95%; ACT scores over 18: 93%; SAT evidence-based reading and writing scores over 600: 26%; SAT math scores over 600: 31%; ACT scores over 24: 27%; SAT evidence-based reading and writing scores over 700: 2%; SAT math scores over 700: 2%; ACT scores over 30: 3%.

Retention: 82% of full-time freshmen returned.

FACULTY
Total: 1,519, 82% full-time, 76% with terminal degrees.

Student/faculty ratio: 18:1.

ACADEMICS
Calendar: semesters. *Degrees:* bachelor's, master's, doctoral, post-master's, and postbachelor's certificates.

Special study options: academic remediation for entering students, accelerated degree program, adult/continuing education programs, advanced placement credit, cooperative education, distance learning, double majors, English as a second language, freshman honors college, honors programs, independent study, internships, off-campus study, part-time degree program, services for LD students, student-designed majors, study abroad, summer session for credit. ***ROTC:*** Army (b), Air Force (b).

Unusual degree programs: 3-2 business administration.

Computers: 2,760 computers/terminals and 2,760 ports are available on campus for general student use. Students can access the following: campus intranet, computer help desk, free student e-mail accounts, online (class) grades, online (class) registration, online (class) schedules. Campuswide network is available. 100% of college-owned or -operated housing units are wired for high-speed Internet access. Wireless service is available via entire campus.

Library: Joyner Library plus 2 others. *Books:* 1.0 million (physical), 873,203 (digital/electronic); *Serial titles:* 8,238 (physical), 109,576 (digital/electronic); *Databases:* 456. Weekly public service hours: 142; study areas open 24 hours, 5–7 days a week; students can reserve study rooms.

STUDENT LIFE
Housing options: on-campus residence required for freshman year; coed, women-only, special housing for students with disabilities. Campus housing is university owned. Freshman campus housing is guaranteed.

Activities and organizations: drama/theater group, student-run newspaper, radio and television station, choral group, marching band, Student Government Association, Student Activities Board, Residence Hall Association, Student Pirate Club, Black Student Union, national fraternities, national sororities.

Athletics Member NCAA, CIS. All NCAA Division I. ***Intercollegiate sports:*** baseball M(s), basketball M(s)/W(s), cross-country running M(s)/W(s), football M(s), golf M(s)/W(s)(c), lacrosse W(s), soccer W(s), softball W(s), swimming and diving M(s)/W(s), tennis M(s)/W(s), track and field M(s)/W(s), volleyball W(s). ***Intramural sports:*** badminton M(c)/W(c), baseball M(c), basketball M/W, bowling M/W, cheerleading W(c), cross-country running M(c)/W(c), equestrian sports M(c)/W(c), fencing M(c)/W(c), field hockey M(c)/W(c), football M/W, golf M(c)/W(c), ice hockey M(c), lacrosse M(c)/W(c), racquetball M/W, rock climbing M(c)/W(c), rugby M(c)/W(c), skiing (downhill) M(c)/W(c), soccer M/W, softball M/W, swimming and diving M(c)/W(c), table tennis M/W, tennis M/W, ultimate Frisbee M(c)/W(c), volleyball M/W, weight lifting M(c)/W(c), wrestling M(c)/W(c).

Campus security: 24-hour emergency response devices and patrols, student patrols, late-night transport/escort service, controlled dormitory access.

Student services: health clinic, personal/psychological counseling, women's center, legal services, veterans affairs office.

COSTS & FINANCIAL AID
Costs (2019–20) ***Tuition:*** state resident $4452 full-time, $150 per credit hour part-time; nonresident $20,729 full-time, $700 per credit hour part-time. Full-time tuition and fees vary according to location and program. Part-time tuition and fees vary according to course load, location, and program. No tuition increase for student's term of enrollment. ***Required fees:*** $2787 full-time, $16 per term part-time. ***Room and board:*** $9712; room only: $5520. Room and board charges vary according to board plan and housing facility. ***Payment plans:*** installment, deferred payment. ***Waivers:*** employees or children of employees.

Financial Aid Of all full-time matriculated undergraduates who enrolled in 2019, 13,620 applied for aid, 10,640 were judged to have need, 951 had their need fully met. In 2019, 535 non-need-based awards were made. ***Average percent of need met:*** 62. ***Average financial aid package:*** $10,758. ***Average need-based loan:*** $6877. ***Average need-based gift aid:*** $7918. ***Average non-need-based aid:*** $2770. ***Average indebtedness upon graduation:*** $23,709.

APPLYING
Standardized Tests *Required:* SAT or ACT (for admission).

Options: electronic application, deferred entrance.

Application fee: $75.

Required: high school transcript, minimum 2.5 GPA.

Notification: continuous (freshmen), continuous (transfers).

CONTACT
East Carolina University, East 5th Street, Greenville, NC 27858-4353. *Phone:* 252-328-6444.

Elizabeth City State University
Elizabeth City, North Carolina
http://www.ecsu.edu/

- **State-supported** comprehensive, founded 1891, part of University of North Carolina System
- **Small-town** 200-acre campus with easy access to Norfolk
- **Endowment** $6.0 million
- **Coed**
- **Moderately difficult** entrance level

FACULTY
Student/faculty ratio: 14:1.

ACADEMICS
Calendar: semesters. *Degrees:* bachelor's and master's.
Library: G. R. Little Library plus 1 other. *Books:* 231,406 (physical), 184,579 (digital/electronic); *Serial titles:* 1,923 (physical), 22,828 (digital/electronic); *Databases:* 101. Weekly public service hours: 82.

STUDENT LIFE
Housing options: coed, men-only, women-only. Campus housing is university owned and leased by the school. Freshman campus housing is guaranteed.

Activities and organizations: drama/theater group, student-run newspaper, choral group, marching band, Vans (Vikings Assisting New Students), Student Activities Committee, Vike Nu' Fashion Troupe, Pep Squad, Essence of Praise, national fraternities, national sororities.

Athletics Member NCAA. All Division II.

Campus security: 24-hour emergency response devices and patrols, controlled dormitory access.

Student services: health clinic, personal/psychological counseling.

COSTS & FINANCIAL AID

Costs (2019–20) ***Tuition:*** area resident $500 full-time; state resident $500 full-time, $125 per credit hour part-time; nonresident $2500 full-time, $625 per credit hour part-time. No tuition increase for student's term of enrollment. ***Required fees:*** $3260 full-time, $419 part-time. ***Room and board:*** $9991.

Financial Aid Of all full-time matriculated undergraduates who enrolled in 2017, 1,105 applied for aid, 1,105 were judged to have need. ***Average percent of need met:*** 62. ***Average financial aid package:*** $7742. ***Average need-based gift aid:*** $3884. ***Average indebtedness upon graduation:*** $19,631. ***Financial aid deadline:*** 6/1.

APPLYING

Standardized Tests *Required:* SAT or ACT (for admission).

Options: electronic application, deferred entrance.

Application fee: $30.

Required: high school transcript, minimum 2.3 GPA.

CONTACT

Mr. Darius Eure, Assistant Director, Admissions and Recruitment, Elizabeth City State University, 131 Marion D. Thorpe Administration Building Box 901, 1704 Weeksville Road, Elizabeth City, NC 27909. *Phone:* 252-335-8530. *Toll-free phone:* 800-347-3278. *Fax:* 252-335-3537. *E-mail:* ddeure@ecsu.edu.

Elon University

Elon, North Carolina

http://www.elon.edu/

- **Independent** comprehensive, founded 1889, affiliated with United Church of Christ
- **Suburban** 656-acre campus with easy access to Raleigh
- **Endowment** $269.9 million
- **Coed** 6,475 undergraduate students, 94% full-time, 60% women, 40% men
- **Moderately difficult** entrance level, 76% of applicants were admitted

UNDERGRAD STUDENTS

6,079 full-time, 396 part-time. Students come from 52 states and territories; 47 other countries; 81% are from out of state; 5% Black or African American, non-Hispanic/Latino; 7% Hispanic/Latino; 2% Asian, non-Hispanic/Latino; 0.2% American Indian or Alaska Native, non-Hispanic/Latino; 3% Two or more races, non-Hispanic/Latino; 0.2% Race/ethnicity unknown; 2% international; 1% transferred in; 64% live on campus.

Freshmen:

Admission: 10,500 applied, 7,966 admitted, 1,659 enrolled. ***Average high school GPA:*** 4.0. ***Test scores:*** SAT evidence-based reading and writing scores over 500: 99%; SAT math scores over 500: 98%; ACT scores over 18: 100%; SAT evidence-based reading and writing scores over 600: 70%; SAT math scores over 600: 62%; ACT scores over 24: 84%; SAT evidence-based reading and writing scores over 700: 13%; SAT math scores over 700: 12%; ACT scores over 30: 28%.

Retention: 91% of full-time freshmen returned.

FACULTY

Total: 605, 74% full-time, 77% with terminal degrees.

Student/faculty ratio: 12:1.

ACADEMICS

Calendar: semesters 3-week winter term. *Degrees:* bachelor's, master's, and doctoral.

Special study options: accelerated degree program, advanced placement credit, distance learning, double majors, English as a second language, honors programs, independent study, internships, off-campus study, part-time degree program, services for LD students, student-designed majors, study abroad, summer session for credit. ***ROTC:*** Army (b), Air Force (c).

Unusual degree programs: 3-2 engineering with East Carolina University, North Carolina State University, Georgia Tech, Penn State, Virginia Tech, University of Notre Dame, Columbia University, Washington University in St. Louis, North Carolina A&T State University, University of South Carolina.

Computers: 1,200 computers/terminals and 10,000 ports are available on campus for general student use. Students can access the following: computer help desk, free student e-mail accounts, online (class) grades, online (class) registration, online (class) schedules. Campuswide network is available. 100% of college-owned or -operated housing units are wired for high-speed Internet access. Wireless service is available via entire campus.

Library: Carol Grotnes Belk. *Books:* 195,196 (physical), 1.3 million (digital/electronic); *Serial titles:* 149 (physical), 64,648 (digital/electronic); *Databases:* 272. Weekly public service hours: 143; study areas open 24 hours, 5–7 days a week; students can reserve study rooms.

STUDENT LIFE

Housing options: on-campus residence required through sophomore year; coed, men-only, women-only. Campus housing is university owned. Freshman campus housing is guaranteed.

Activities and organizations: drama/theater group, student-run newspaper, radio and television station, choral group, marching band, Elon Volunteers, Student Media, Intramural Athletics, Religious Life, Habitat for Humanity, national fraternities, national sororities.

Athletics Member NCAA. All Division I except football (Division I-AA). ***Intercollegiate sports:*** baseball M(s), basketball M(s)/W(s), cheerleading M/W, cross-country running M(s)/W(s), equestrian sports M(c)/W(c), field hockey W(c), golf M(s)/W(s), ice hockey M(c), lacrosse M(c)/W(s), rock climbing M(c), rugby M(c)/W(c), soccer M(s)/W(s), softball W(s), swimming and diving M(c)/W(c), tennis M(s)/W(s), track and field W(s), triathlon M(c)/W(c), ultimate Frisbee M(c)/W(c), volleyball M(c)/W(s). ***Intramural sports:*** basketball M/W, bowling M/W, fencing M/W, field hockey W, football M/W, golf M/W, lacrosse M/W, racquetball M/W, rock climbing M/W, sand volleyball M/W, soccer M/W, softball W, squash M/W, table tennis M/W, ultimate Frisbee M/W, volleyball M/W.

Campus security: 24-hour emergency response devices and patrols, late-night transport/escort service, controlled dormitory access, Student Transport Service (Safe Rides).

Student services: health clinic, personal/psychological counseling, women's center.

COSTS & FINANCIAL AID

Costs (2020–21) ***Comprehensive fee:*** $51,052 includes full-time tuition ($37,414), mandatory fees ($507), and room and board ($13,131). Part-time tuition: $1191 per credit hour. ***Required fees:*** $181 per term part-time. ***College room only:*** $6445.

Financial Aid Of all full-time matriculated undergraduates who enrolled in 2019, 2,945 applied for aid, 2,061 were judged to have need, 341 had their need fully met. 1,460 Federal Work-Study jobs (averaging $2374). In 2019, 1604 non-need-based awards were made. ***Average percent of need met:*** 61. ***Average financial aid package:*** $21,162. ***Average need-based loan:*** $4331. ***Average need-based gift aid:*** $16,206. ***Average non-need-based aid:*** $7819. ***Average indebtedness upon graduation:*** $32,028.

APPLYING

Standardized Tests *Required:* SAT or ACT (for admission).

Options: electronic application, early admission, early decision, early action, deferred entrance.

Application fee: $60.

Required: essay or personal statement, high school transcript, counselor evaluation form. ***Required for some:*** interview.

Application deadlines: 1/10 (freshmen), rolling (transfers), 11/1 (early action).

Early decision deadline: 11/1.

Notification: 3/20 (freshmen), continuous (transfers), 12/1 (early decision), 12/20 (early action).

CONTACT

Ms. Melinda Wood, Senior Associate Dean of Admissions, Elon University, 2700 Campus Box, Elon, NC 27244. *Phone:* 336-278-3566. *Toll-free phone:* 800-334-8448. *Fax:* 336-278-7699. *E-mail:* admissions@elon.edu.

Fayetteville State University

Fayetteville, North Carolina

http://www.uncfsu.edu/

- **State-supported** comprehensive, founded 1867, part of University of North Carolina System
- **Urban** 156-acre campus with easy access to Raleigh
- **Endowment** $24.3 million
- **Coed** 5,644 undergraduate students, 72% full-time, 69% women, 31% men
- **Minimally difficult** entrance level, 69% of applicants were admitted

UNDERGRAD STUDENTS

4,071 full-time, 1,573 part-time. Students come from 14 other countries; 6% are from out of state; 60% Black or African American, non-Hispanic/Latino; 9% Hispanic/Latino; 1% Asian, non-Hispanic/Latino; 0.2% Native Hawaiian or other Pacific Islander, non-Hispanic/Latino; 2% American Indian or Alaska Native, non-Hispanic/Latino; 4% Two or more races, non-Hispanic/Latino; 4% Race/ethnicity unknown; 0.6% international; 15% transferred in; 25% live on campus.

Freshmen:

Admission: 4,858 applied, 3,328 admitted, 678 enrolled. ***Average high school GPA:*** 3.3.

Retention: 74% of full-time freshmen returned.

FACULTY

Total: 342, 79% full-time, 71% with terminal degrees.

Student/faculty ratio: 18:1.

ACADEMICS

Calendar: semesters. *Degrees:* bachelor's, master's, doctoral, and postbachelor's certificates.

Special study options: academic remediation for entering students, accelerated degree program, adult/continuing education programs, advanced placement credit, cooperative education, distance learning, double majors, honors programs, independent study, internships, part-time degree program, services for LD students, study abroad, summer session for credit. ***ROTC:*** Army (c), Air Force (b).

Unusual degree programs: 3-2 engineering with North Carolina State University.

Computers: 600 computers/terminals and 2,400 ports are available on campus for general student use. Students can access the following: campus intranet, computer help desk, free student e-mail accounts, online (class) grades, online (class) registration, online (class) schedules. Campuswide network is available. 100% of college-owned or -operated housing units are wired for high-speed Internet access. Wireless service is available via classrooms, computer centers, computer labs, learning centers, libraries, student centers.

Library: Charles W. Chestnut Library. *Books:* 231,506 (physical), 299,552 (digital/electronic); *Serial titles:* 8,727 (physical), 56,051 (digital/electronic); *Databases:* 442. Weekly public service hours: 97; students can reserve study rooms.

STUDENT LIFE

Housing options: coed, men-only, women-only, special housing for students with disabilities. Campus housing is university owned. Freshman applicants given priority for college housing.

Activities and organizations: drama/theater group, student-run newspaper, radio station, choral group, marching band, Student Government Association, Student Activities Council, Pan-Hellenic Council, Residence Hall Association, Illusions and Black Millennium Modeling Clubs, national fraternities, national sororities.

Athletics Member NCAA. All Division II except golf (Division I). ***Intercollegiate sports:*** basketball M(s)/W(s), bowling W, cross-country running M(s)/W(s), football M(s), golf M(s)/W, softball W(s), tennis M/W(s), track and field M/W(s), volleyball W(s). ***Intramural sports:*** baseball M, basketball M/W, bowling M/W, football M, golf M/W, gymnastics M/W, swimming and diving M/W, tennis M, volleyball M/W.

Campus security: 24-hour emergency response devices and patrols, late-night transport/escort service, controlled dormitory access.

Student services: health clinic, personal/psychological counseling, veterans affairs office.

COSTS & FINANCIAL AID

Costs (2019–20) ***Tuition:*** state resident $2982 full-time; nonresident $14,590 full-time. Full-time tuition and fees vary according to course level, course load, degree level, location, and program. Part-time tuition and fees vary according to course level, course load, degree level, location, and program. ***Required fees:*** $1993 full-time. ***Room and board:*** $8616; room only: $4513. Room and board charges vary according to board plan and housing facility. ***Payment plan:*** installment. ***Waivers:*** senior citizens and employees or children of employees.

Financial Aid Of all full-time matriculated undergraduates who enrolled in 2018, 3,572 applied for aid, 3,332 were judged to have need, 285 had their need fully met. In 2018, 4 non-need-based awards were made. ***Average percent of need met:*** 68. ***Average financial aid package:*** $11,162. ***Average need-based loan:*** $4220. ***Average need-based gift aid:*** $8105. ***Average non-need-based aid:*** $2189.

APPLYING

Standardized Tests *Required:* SAT or ACT (for admission).

Options: electronic application, early admission, early decision, early action, deferred entrance.

Application fee: $50.

Required: minimum 2.5 GPA. ***Required for some:*** interview. ***Recommended:*** essay or personal statement, high school transcript.

Application deadlines: 6/30 (freshmen), 6/30 (transfers).

Notification: continuous (freshmen), continuous (transfers).

CONTACT

Mr. Head Michael, Senior Associate Director of Admissions, Fayetteville State University, 1200 Murchison Road, Fayetteville, NC 28301-4298. *Phone:* 910-672-1408. *Toll-free phone:* 800-222-2594. *Fax:* 910-627-1414. *E-mail:* mhead@uncfsu.edu.

Gardner-Webb University

Boiling Springs, North Carolina

http://www.gardner-webb.edu/

- **Independent Baptist** university, founded 1905
- **Small-town** 250-acre campus with easy access to Charlotte
- **Endowment** $51.1 million
- **Coed**
- **Moderately difficult** entrance level

FACULTY

Student/faculty ratio: 13:1.

ACADEMICS

Calendar: semesters. *Degrees:* certificates, associate, bachelor's, master's, and doctoral.

Library: Dover Memorial Library plus 1 other.

STUDENT LIFE

Housing options: on-campus residence required through junior year; men-only, women-only, special housing for students with disabilities. Campus housing is university owned. Freshman campus housing is guaranteed.

Activities and organizations: drama/theater group, student-run newspaper, radio station, choral group, marching band, Campus Ministries United, Student Government Association, Dawg Pound, Honors Student Association, International Club.

Athletics Member NCAA. All Division I except football (Division I-AA).

Campus security: 24-hour emergency response devices and patrols, student patrols, late-night transport/escort service, controlled dormitory access.

Student services: personal/psychological counseling, veterans affairs office.

COSTS & FINANCIAL AID

Costs (2019–20) ***Comprehensive fee:*** $42,030 includes full-time tuition ($31,220), mandatory fees ($420), and room and board ($10,390). ***College room only:*** $5260. Room and board charges vary according to board plan and housing facility.

Financial Aid Of all full-time matriculated undergraduates who enrolled in 2018, 1,134 applied for aid, 1,008 were judged to have need, 126 had their need fully met. 293 Federal Work-Study jobs (averaging $1340). 23

state and other part-time jobs (averaging $1018). In 2018, 322 non-need-based awards were made. ***Average percent of need met:*** 73. ***Average financial aid package:*** $26,016. ***Average need-based loan:*** $4069. ***Average need-based gift aid:*** $8280. ***Average non-need-based aid:*** $12,784. ***Average indebtedness upon graduation:*** $30,808.

APPLYING

Standardized Tests *Required:* SAT or ACT (for admission).

Options: electronic application.

Application fee: $40.

Required: high school transcript, minimum 2.5 GPA. ***Required for some:*** 2 letters of recommendation, interview. ***Recommended:*** essay or personal statement, 2 letters of recommendation.

CONTACT

Associate Vice President of Undergraduate Admissions, Gardner-Webb University, PO Box 817, 110 South Main Street, Boiling Springs, NC 28017. *Phone:* 704-406-4491. *Toll-free phone:* 800-253-6472. *Fax:* 704-406-4488. *E-mail:* admissions@gardner-webb.edu.

Grace College of Divinity

Fayetteville, North Carolina

http://www.gcd.edu/

CONTACT

Grace College of Divinity, 5117 Cliffdale Road, Fayetteville, NC 28314.

Greensboro College

Greensboro, North Carolina

http://www.greensboro.edu/

CONTACT

Greensboro College, 815 West Market Street, Greensboro, NC 27401-1875. *Toll-free phone:* 800-346-8226.

Guilford College

Greensboro, North Carolina

http://www.guilford.edu/

- **Independent** comprehensive, founded 1837, affiliated with Society of Friends
- **Suburban** 351-acre campus with easy access to Raleigh-Durham; Charlotte
- **Endowment** $74.5 million
- **Coed** 1,525 undergraduate students, 90% full-time, 53% women, 47% men
- **Moderately difficult** entrance level, 75% of applicants were admitted

UNDERGRAD STUDENTS

1,373 full-time, 152 part-time. Students come from 40 states and territories; 12 other countries; 26% are from out of state; 24% Black or African American, non-Hispanic/Latino; 12% Hispanic/Latino; 3% Asian, non-Hispanic/Latino; 0.1% Native Hawaiian or other Pacific Islander, non-Hispanic/Latino; 0.2% American Indian or Alaska Native, non-Hispanic/Latino; 4% Two or more races, non-Hispanic/Latino; 2% Race/ethnicity unknown; 1% international; 4% transferred in; 74% live on campus.

Freshmen:

Admission: 3,305 applied, 2,479 admitted, 380 enrolled. ***Average high school GPA:*** 3.4. ***Test scores:*** SAT evidence-based reading and writing scores over 500: 67%; SAT math scores over 500: 66%; ACT scores over 18: 72%; SAT evidence-based reading and writing scores over 600: 28%; SAT math scores over 600: 18%; ACT scores over 24: 27%; SAT evidence-based reading and writing scores over 700: 4%; SAT math scores over 700: 2%; ACT scores over 30: 3%.

Retention: 67% of full-time freshmen returned.

FACULTY

Total: 176, 55% full-time, 58% with terminal degrees.

Student/faculty ratio: 12:1.

ACADEMICS

Calendar: 4-1-4. *Degrees:* bachelor's, master's, and postbachelor's certificates.

Special study options: accelerated degree program, adult/continuing education programs, advanced placement credit, cooperative education, distance learning, double majors, honors programs, independent study, internships, off-campus study, part-time degree program, services for LD students, student-designed majors, study abroad, summer session for credit. ***ROTC:*** Army (c), Air Force (c).

Computers: 275 computers/terminals are available on campus for general student use. Students can access the following: campus intranet, computer help desk, free student e-mail accounts, online (class) grades, online (class) registration, online (class) schedules, network storage. Campuswide network is available. 100% of college-owned or -operated housing units are wired for high-speed Internet access. Wireless service is available via entire campus.

Library: Hege Library. *Books:* 126,217 (physical), 632,861 (digital/electronic); *Serial titles:* 1,315 (physical), 61,103 (digital/electronic); *Databases:* 159. Weekly public service hours: 91; students can reserve study rooms.

STUDENT LIFE

Housing options: on-campus residence required through junior year; coed, women-only, cooperative, special housing for students with disabilities. Campus housing is university owned. Freshman campus housing is guaranteed.

Activities and organizations: drama/theater group, student-run newspaper, radio station, choral group, Student Government, Student Radio Station, Student Newspaper.

Athletics Member NCAA. All Division III. ***Intercollegiate sports:*** baseball M, basketball M/W, cross-country running M/W, football M, golf M, lacrosse M/W, rugby W, soccer M/W, softball W, swimming and diving W, tennis M/W, track and field M/W, volleyball W. ***Intramural sports:*** badminton M(c)/W(c), basketball M(c), football M(c), rugby M(c)/W(c), soccer M(c)/W(c), table tennis M(c)/W(c), tennis M(c)/W(c), ultimate Frisbee M(c)/W(c), volleyball M(c)/W(c).

Campus security: 24-hour emergency response devices and patrols, student patrols, late-night transport/escort service, controlled dormitory access.

Student services: health clinic, personal/psychological counseling.

COSTS & FINANCIAL AID

Costs (2020–21) ***One-time required fee:*** $170. ***Comprehensive fee:*** $52,320 includes full-time tuition ($39,400), mandatory fees ($720), and room and board ($12,200). Full-time tuition and fees vary according to student level. Part-time tuition: $1085 per credit hour. Part-time tuition and fees vary according to student level. No tuition increase for student's term of enrollment. ***Required fees:*** $120 per year part-time. ***College room only:*** $6000. Room and board charges vary according to board plan and housing facility. ***Payment plan:*** installment. ***Waivers:*** employees or children of employees.

Financial Aid Of all full-time matriculated undergraduates who enrolled in 2016, 1,206 applied for aid, 1,073 were judged to have need, 597 had their need fully met. In 2016, 131 non-need-based awards were made. ***Average percent of need met:*** 74. ***Average financial aid package:*** $25,481. ***Average need-based loan:*** $3773. ***Average need-based gift aid:*** $4418. ***Average non-need-based aid:*** $9961. ***Average indebtedness upon graduation:*** $35,392.

APPLYING

Standardized Tests *Recommended:* SAT or ACT (for admission).

Options: electronic application, early admission, early decision, early action, deferred entrance.

Required: essay or personal statement, minimum 2.0 GPA. ***Required for some:*** high school transcript, 1 letter of recommendation. ***Recommended:*** minimum 3.0 GPA, interview.

Application deadlines: rolling (freshmen), rolling (transfers), 12/1 (early action).

Early decision deadline: 11/1.

Notification: continuous (freshmen), continuous (transfers), 11/15 (early decision), 12/15 (early action).

CONTACT
Mr. Kyle Wooden, Director of Admission, Guilford College, 5800 West Friendly Avenue, Greensboro, NC 27410. *Phone:* 336-316-2000. *Toll-free phone:* 800-992-7759. *Fax:* 336-316-2954. *E-mail:* admission@guilford.edu.

Heritage Bible College
Dunn, North Carolina
http://www.heritagebiblecollege.edu/

CONTACT
Ms. Iris Prince, Admissions Director, Heritage Bible College, PO Box 1628, Dunn, NC 28335-1628. *Phone:* 910-892-3178 Ext. 239. *Toll-free phone:* 800-297-6351. *Fax:* 910-891-1660. *E-mail:* iprince@heritagebiblecollege.edu.

High Point University
High Point, North Carolina
http://www.highpoint.edu/

- **Independent United Methodist** university, founded 1924
- **Suburban** 380-acre campus with easy access to Charlotte
- **Endowment** $64.8 million
- **Coed** 4,591 undergraduate students, 99% full-time, 57% women, 43% men
- **Moderately difficult** entrance level, 75% of applicants were admitted

UNDERGRAD STUDENTS
4,557 full-time, 34 part-time. Students come from 47 states and territories; 34 other countries; 74% are from out of state; 5% Black or African American, non-Hispanic/Latino; 6% Hispanic/Latino; 2% Asian, non-Hispanic/Latino; 0.4% American Indian or Alaska Native, non-Hispanic/Latino; 5% Two or more races, non-Hispanic/Latino; 2% Race/ethnicity unknown; 2% international; 1% transferred in; 95% live on campus.

Freshmen:

Admission: 11,298 applied, 8,423 admitted, 1,400 enrolled. ***Average high school GPA:*** 3.3. ***Test scores:*** SAT evidence-based reading and writing scores over 500: 94%; SAT math scores over 500: 92%; ACT scores over 18: 95%; SAT evidence-based reading and writing scores over 600: 46%; SAT math scores over 600: 42%; ACT scores over 24: 64%; SAT evidence-based reading and writing scores over 700: 6%; SAT math scores over 700: 6%; ACT scores over 30: 13%.

Retention: 83% of full-time freshmen returned.

FACULTY
Total: 460, 72% full-time, 69% with terminal degrees.

Student/faculty ratio: 15:1.

ACADEMICS
Calendar: semesters. *Degrees:* bachelor's, master's, doctoral, and postbachelor's certificates.

Special study options: accelerated degree program, advanced placement credit, double majors, English as a second language, honors programs, independent study, internships, services for LD students, student-designed majors, study abroad, summer session for credit. ***ROTC:*** Army (c), Air Force (c).

Unusual degree programs: 3-2 elementary education, strategic communication, athletic training.

Computers: 749 computers/terminals are available on campus for general student use. Students can access the following: campus intranet, computer help desk, free student e-mail accounts, online (class) grades, online (class) registration, online (class) schedules. Campuswide network is available. 100% of college-owned or -operated housing units are wired for high-speed Internet access. Wireless service is available via entire campus.

Library: Smith Library plus 1 other. *Books:* 182,160 (physical), 445,000 (digital/electronic); *Serial titles:* 41,700 (physical), 32,000 (digital/electronic); *Databases:* 192. Weekly public service hours: 168; study areas open 24 hours, 5–7 days a week; students can reserve study rooms.

STUDENT LIFE
Housing options: on-campus residence required through junior year; coed, men-only, women-only, cooperative, special housing for students with disabilities. Campus housing is university owned. Freshman campus housing is guaranteed.

Activities and organizations: drama/theater group, student-run newspaper, radio and television station, choral group, Big Brothers Big Sisters, Campus Activities Team, Purple Reign, Entrepreneurship Club, Volunteer Center, national fraternities, national sororities.

Athletics Member NCAA. All Division I. ***Intercollegiate sports:*** baseball M(s), basketball M(s)/W(s), cheerleading W, cross-country running M(s)/W(s), golf M(s)/W(s)(c), lacrosse M(s)/W(s), soccer M(s)/W(s), track and field M(s)/W(s), volleyball W(s). ***Intramural sports:*** badminton M/W, baseball M(c), basketball M(c)/W(c), bowling M/W, crew M(c)/W(c), cross-country running M(c)/W(c), equestrian sports M(c)/W(c), fencing W(c), football M/W, golf M(c)/W(c), gymnastics M(c)/W(c), ice hockey M(c), lacrosse M(c)/W(c), racquetball M/W, rowing M(c)/W(c), soccer M(c)/W(c), softball W(c), swimming and diving M(c)/W(c), tennis M(c)/W(c), ultimate Frisbee M(c), volleyball M(c)/W(c), water polo M/W, weight lifting M(c)/W(c).

Campus security: 24-hour emergency response devices and patrols, student patrols, late-night transport/escort service, controlled dormitory access.

Student services: health clinic, personal/psychological counseling.

COSTS & FINANCIAL AID
Costs (2019–20) ***Comprehensive fee:*** $50,970 includes full-time tuition ($31,768), mandatory fees ($4500), and room and board ($14,702). Full-time tuition and fees vary according to course load and reciprocity agreements. Part-time tuition: $1026 per credit hour. Part-time tuition and fees vary according to course load and reciprocity agreements. ***Required fees:*** $4500 per term part-time. ***Room and board:*** Room and board charges vary according to board plan and housing facility. ***Payment plan:*** installment. ***Waivers:*** employees or children of employees.

Financial Aid Of all full-time matriculated undergraduates who enrolled in 2018, 2,506 applied for aid, 1,904 were judged to have need, 232 had their need fully met. 252 Federal Work-Study jobs (averaging $1823). In 2018, 1519 non-need-based awards were made. ***Average percent of need met:*** 55. ***Average financial aid package:*** $18,285. ***Average need-based loan:*** $4236. ***Average need-based gift aid:*** $14,388. ***Average non-need-based aid:*** $8440. ***Average indebtedness upon graduation:*** $34,079.

APPLYING
Options: electronic application, early decision, early action, deferred entrance.

Application fee: $50.

Required: essay or personal statement, high school transcript, 1 letter of recommendation. ***Recommended:*** interview.

Application deadlines: 3/1 (freshmen), 7/1 (transfers), 11/15 (early action).

Early decision deadline: 11/1 (for plan 1), 2/1 (for plan 2).

Notification: continuous until 2/1 (freshmen), continuous (transfers), 11/27 (early decision plan 1), 2/1 (early decision plan 2), 12/15 (early action).

CONTACT
Dr. Kerr Ramsay, Associate Vice President of Admissions, High Point University, Office of Undergraduate Admissions, One University Parkway, High Point, NC 27268. *Phone:* 336-841-9176. *Toll-free phone:* 800-345-6993. *Fax:* 336-888-6382. *E-mail:* kramsay@highpoint.edu.

Johnson & Wales University
Charlotte, North Carolina
http://www.jwu.edu/charlotte/

CONTACT
Joseph Campos, Director of Admissions, Johnson & Wales University, 801 West Trade Street, Charlotte, NC 28202. *Phone:* 980-598-1100. *Toll-free phone:* 866-598-2427. *Fax:* 980-598-1111. *E-mail:* clt@admissions.jwu.edu.

Johnson C. Smith University
Charlotte, North Carolina
http://www.jcsu.edu/

- **Independent** comprehensive, founded 1867
- **Urban** 100-acre campus with easy access to Atlanta
- **Endowment** $68.2 million
- **Coed**
- **Moderately difficult** entrance level

FACULTY
Student/faculty ratio: 12:1.

ACADEMICS
Calendar: semesters. *Degrees:* bachelor's and master's.
Library: James B. Duke Library. *Books:* 105,422 (physical), 203,337 (digital/electronic); *Serial titles:* 107 (physical), 23,465 (digital/electronic); *Databases:* 99. Weekly public service hours: 79; study areas open 24 hours, 5–7 days a week; students can reserve study rooms.

STUDENT LIFE
Housing options: coed, men-only, women-only. Campus housing is university owned and leased by the school. Freshman campus housing is guaranteed.

Activities and organizations: drama/theater group, choral group, marching band, national fraternities, national sororities.

Athletics Member NCAA. All Division II.

Campus security: 24-hour emergency response devices and patrols, late-night transport/escort service, controlled dormitory access.

Student services: health clinic, personal/psychological counseling.

COSTS & FINANCIAL AID
Costs (2019–20) ***Comprehensive fee:*** $25,884 includes full-time tuition ($18,784) and room and board ($7100). Full-time tuition and fees vary according to course load. Part-time tuition: $431 per credit hour. Part-time tuition and fees vary according to course load. ***Room and board:*** Room and board charges vary according to board plan and housing facility.

Financial Aid Of all full-time matriculated undergraduates who enrolled in 2018, 1,362 applied for aid, 1,322 were judged to have need, 97 had their need fully met. 192 Federal Work-Study jobs (averaging $3000). In 2018, 46 non-need-based awards were made. ***Average percent of need met:*** 57. ***Average financial aid package:*** $15,432. ***Average need-based loan:*** $3841. ***Average need-based gift aid:*** $11,869. ***Average non-need-based aid:*** $12,845. ***Financial aid deadline:*** 4/1.

APPLYING
Standardized Tests *Required:* SAT or ACT (for admission).

Options: electronic application, deferred entrance.

Application fee: $25.

Required: high school transcript. ***Recommended:*** essay or personal statement, 1 letter of recommendation.

CONTACT
Mr. Vory Billups, Director of Admissions, Johnson C. Smith University, 100 Beatties Ford Road, Charlotte, NC 28216. *Phone:* 704-378-1081. *Toll-free phone:* 800-782-7303. *Fax:* 704-378-1242. *E-mail:* vbillups@jcsu.edu.

Lees-McRae College
Banner Elk, North Carolina
http://www.lmc.edu/

- **Independent** 4-year, founded 1900, affiliated with Presbyterian Church (U.S.A.)
- **Rural** 460-acre campus
- **Endowment** $16.4 million
- **Coed**
- **Minimally difficult** entrance level

FACULTY
Student/faculty ratio: 13:1.

ACADEMICS
Calendar: semesters. *Degree:* bachelor's.
Library: Dotti M. Shelton Learning Commons. *Books:* 70,132 (physical), 200,746 (digital/electronic); *Serial titles:* 225 (physical), 146,361 (digital/electronic); *Databases:* 144. Students can reserve study rooms.

STUDENT LIFE
Housing options: coed, men-only, women-only, special housing for students with disabilities. Campus housing is university owned. Freshman campus housing is guaranteed.

Activities and organizations: drama/theater group, choral group.

Athletics Member NCAA. All Division II.

Campus security: 24-hour emergency response devices and patrols, controlled dormitory access.

Student services: health clinic, personal/psychological counseling.

COSTS & FINANCIAL AID
Costs (2019–20) ***Comprehensive fee:*** $38,391 includes full-time tuition ($25,625), mandatory fees ($1896), and room and board ($10,870). Part-time tuition: $710 per credit hour. No tuition increase for student's term of enrollment. ***College room only:*** $5320.

Financial Aid Of all full-time matriculated undergraduates who enrolled in 2018, 760 applied for aid, 711 were judged to have need, 7 had their need fully met. In 2018, 60 non-need-based awards were made. ***Average percent of need met:*** 72. ***Average financial aid package:*** $23,399. ***Average need-based loan:*** $3694. ***Average need-based gift aid:*** $6473. ***Average non-need-based aid:*** $9688.

APPLYING
Standardized Tests *Required for some:* SAT or ACT (for admission), SAT or ACT scores for prospective intercollegiate athletes and honors program students.

Options: electronic application, early action.

Application fee: $35.

Required: high school transcript, minimum 2.0 GPA. ***Required for some:*** essay or personal statement, interview.

CONTACT
Beverly Hague, Director of Undergraduate and Graduate Admissions, Lees-McRae College, PO Box 128, Banner Elk, NC 28604. *Phone:* 828-898-2417. *Toll-free phone:* 800-280-4562. *Fax:* 828-898-8707. *E-mail:* admissions@lmc.edu.

Lenoir-Rhyne University
Hickory, North Carolina
http://www.lr.edu/

- **Independent Lutheran** comprehensive, founded 1891
- **Small-town** 100-acre campus with easy access to Charlotte
- **Endowment** $114.7 million
- **Coed** 1,846 undergraduate students, 86% full-time, 59% women, 41% men
- **Moderately difficult** entrance level, 78% of applicants were admitted

UNDERGRAD STUDENTS
1,589 full-time, 257 part-time. Students come from 29 states and territories; 25 other countries; 15% are from out of state; 11% Black or African American, non-Hispanic/Latino; 9% Hispanic/Latino; 2% Asian, non-Hispanic/Latino; 0.3% American Indian or Alaska Native, non-Hispanic/Latino; 5% Two or more races, non-Hispanic/Latino; 2% Race/ethnicity unknown; 4% international; 5% transferred in; 54% live on campus.

Freshmen:
Admission: 4,791 applied, 3,734 admitted, 481 enrolled. ***Average high school GPA:*** 3.4. ***Test scores:*** SAT evidence-based reading and writing scores over 500: 71%; SAT math scores over 500: 74%; ACT scores over 18: 82%; SAT evidence-based reading and writing scores over 600: 23%; SAT math scores over 600: 17%; ACT scores over 24: 28%; SAT evidence-based reading and writing scores over 700: 2%; SAT math scores over 700: 1%; ACT scores over 30: 3%.

Retention: 72% of full-time freshmen returned.

FACULTY
Total: 285, 51% full-time, 63% with terminal degrees.
Student/faculty ratio: 12:1.

ACADEMICS
Calendar: semesters. *Degrees:* bachelor's, master's, and doctoral.

Special study options: academic remediation for entering students, accelerated degree program, adult/continuing education programs, advanced placement credit, distance learning, double majors, freshman honors college, honors programs, independent study, internships, off-campus study, part-time degree program, services for LD students, study abroad, summer session for credit.

Unusual degree programs: 3-2 engineering with North Carolina Agricultural and Technical State University, North Carolina State University, University of North Carolina at Charlotte; forestry with Duke University.

Computers: 150 computers/terminals and 150 ports are available on campus for general student use. Students can access the following: campus intranet, computer help desk, free student e-mail accounts, online (class) grades, online (class) registration, online (class) schedules. Campuswide network is available. 100% of college-owned or -operated housing units are wired for high-speed Internet access. Wireless service is available via entire campus.
Library: Carl Rudisill Library. *Books:* 121,005 (physical), 537,443 (digital/electronic); *Serial titles:* 49 (physical), 28,271 (digital/electronic); *Databases:* 135. Weekly public service hours: 89.

STUDENT LIFE
Housing options: on-campus residence required through junior year; coed. Campus housing is university owned. Freshman campus housing is guaranteed.

Activities and organizations: drama/theater group, student-run newspaper, radio station, choral group, marching band, InterVarsity, CAB, Black Student Alliance, Greek Organizations, SEEDS of LRU, national sororities.

Athletics Member NCAA. All Division II. ***Intercollegiate sports:*** baseball M(s), basketball M(s)/W(s), cheerleading M(s)/W(s), cross-country running M(s)/W(s), football M(s), golf M(s)/W(s), lacrosse M(s)/W(s), soccer M(s)/W(s), softball W(s), swimming and diving M(s)/W(s), tennis M(s)/W(s), track and field M(s)/W(s), volleyball W(s). ***Intramural sports:*** archery M/W, basketball M/W, football M/W, sand volleyball M/W.

Campus security: 24-hour emergency response devices and patrols, late-night transport/escort service, controlled dormitory access.

Student services: health clinic, personal/psychological counseling, veterans affairs office.

COSTS & FINANCIAL AID
Costs (2020–21) ***Tuition:*** $1600 per credit hour part-time. ***Payment plan:*** installment. ***Waivers:*** senior citizens and employees or children of employees.

Financial Aid Of all full-time matriculated undergraduates who enrolled in 2018, 1,398 applied for aid, 1,322 were judged to have need, 222 had their need fully met. In 2018, 216 non-need-based awards were made. ***Average percent of need met:*** 75. ***Average financial aid package:*** $31,268. ***Average need-based loan:*** $4207. ***Average need-based gift aid:*** $27,022. ***Average non-need-based aid:*** $20,654. ***Average indebtedness upon graduation:*** $32,622.

APPLYING
Standardized Tests *Required:* SAT or ACT (for admission).

Options: electronic application, early admission, early action, deferred entrance.

Application fee: $35.

Required: high school transcript, minimum 2.5 GPA. ***Recommended:*** letters of recommendation.

Application deadlines: rolling (freshmen), rolling (transfers).

Notification: continuous (freshmen), continuous (transfers), 11/13 (early action).

CONTACT
Lenoir-Rhyne University, 625 7th Avenue NE, Hickory, NC 28601. *Phone:* 828-328-7392. *Toll-free phone:* 800-277-5721.

Living Arts College
Raleigh, North Carolina
http://www.living-arts-college.edu/

CONTACT
Julie Wenta, Director of Admissions, Living Arts College, 3000 Wakefield Crossing Drive, Raleigh, NC 27614. *Phone:* 919-488-5902. *Toll-free phone:* 800-288-7442. *Fax:* 919-488-8490. *E-mail:* jwenta@living-arts-college.edu.

Livingstone College
Salisbury, North Carolina
http://www.livingstone.edu/

CONTACT
Mr. Tony Baldwin, Livingstone College, 701 West Monroe Street, Salisbury, NC 28144. *Phone:* 704-216-6001. *Toll-free phone:* 800-835-3435. *Fax:* 704-216-6215. *E-mail:* admissions@livingstone.edu.

Mars Hill University
Mars Hill, North Carolina
http://www.mhu.edu/

CONTACT
Kristie Vance, Director of Admissions, Mars Hill University, PO Box 370, Mars Hill, NC 28754. *Phone:* 828-689-1201. *Toll-free phone:* 866-648-4968. *Fax:* 828-689-1473. *E-mail:* admissions@mhu.edu.

Meredith College
Raleigh, North Carolina
http://www.meredith.edu/

- **Independent** comprehensive, founded 1891
- **Urban** 225-acre campus
- **Undergraduate: women only; graduate: coed** 1,528 undergraduate students, 96% full-time, 100% women, 0% men
- **Moderately difficult** entrance level, 65% of applicants were admitted

UNDERGRAD STUDENTS
1,464 full-time, 64 part-time. 14% are from out of state; 9% Black or African American, non-Hispanic/Latino; 10% Hispanic/Latino; 4% Asian, non-Hispanic/Latino; 0.1% Native Hawaiian or other Pacific Islander, non-Hispanic/Latino; 0.4% American Indian or Alaska Native, non-Hispanic/Latino; 4% Two or more races, non-Hispanic/Latino; 5% Race/ethnicity unknown; 1% international; 2% transferred in; 53% live on campus.

Freshmen:
Admission: 1,936 applied, 1,253 admitted, 376 enrolled. ***Average high school GPA:*** 3.5. ***Test scores:*** SAT evidence-based reading and writing scores over 500: 84%; SAT math scores over 500: 79%; ACT scores over 18: 84%; SAT evidence-based reading and writing scores over 600: 39%; SAT math scores over 600: 26%; ACT scores over 24: 38%; SAT evidence-based reading and writing scores over 700: 6%; SAT math scores over 700: 4%; ACT scores over 30: 8%.

Retention: 81% of full-time freshmen returned.

FACULTY
Total: 217, 57% full-time, 67% with terminal degrees.

Student/faculty ratio: 11:1.

ACADEMICS
Calendar: semesters. *Degrees:* bachelor's, master's, and postbachelor's certificates.

Special study options: academic remediation for entering students, accelerated degree program, advanced placement credit, cooperative education, double majors, external degree program, honors programs, independent study, internships, off-campus study, part-time degree program, services for LD students, student-designed majors, study abroad, summer session for credit. ***ROTC:*** Army (c), Air Force (c).

Unusual degree programs: 3-2 engineering with North Carolina State University.

Computers: Students can access the following: free student e-mail accounts, online (class) registration. Campuswide network is available. 100% of college-owned or -operated housing units are wired for high-speed Internet access. Wireless service is available via classrooms, computer centers, computer labs, dorm rooms, learning centers, libraries, student centers.
Library: Carlyle Campbell Library.

STUDENT LIFE
Housing options: on-campus residence required through sophomore year; women-only. Campus housing is university owned. Freshman campus housing is guaranteed.

Activities and organizations: drama/theater group, student-run newspaper, choral group, Student Government Association, Entertainment Association, Recreation Association, Class Organizations, choral groups.

Athletics Member NCAA. All Division III. ***Intercollegiate sports:*** basketball W, cross-country running W, lacrosse W, soccer W, softball W, tennis W, track and field W, volleyball W.

Campus security: 24-hour emergency response devices and patrols, late-night transport/escort service, controlled dormitory access.

Student services: health clinic, personal/psychological counseling.

FINANCIAL AID
Financial Aid Of all full-time matriculated undergraduates who enrolled in 2017, 1,274 applied for aid, 1,136 were judged to have need, 201 had their need fully met. In 2017, 124 non-need-based awards were made. ***Average percent of need met:*** 75. ***Average financial aid package:*** $27,707. ***Average need-based loan:*** $4083. ***Average need-based gift aid:*** $23,453. ***Average non-need-based aid:*** $16,687. ***Average indebtedness upon graduation:*** $34,959.

APPLYING
Standardized Tests *Required:* SAT or ACT (for admission).

Options: electronic application, early decision, early action, deferred entrance.

Application fee: $40.

Required: high school transcript, minimum 2.0 GPA, 2 letters of recommendation. ***Required for some:*** essay or personal statement, interview. ***Recommended:*** essay or personal statement.

Application deadlines: 2/15 (freshmen), 11/5 (transfers), 12/1 (early action).

Early decision deadline: 10/30.

Notification: continuous (freshmen), continuous (transfers), 11/15 (early decision), 12/15 (early action).

CONTACT
Shery Boyles, Director of Admissions, Meredith College, 3800 Hillsborough Street, Raleigh, NC 27807-5298. *Phone:* 919-760-8026. *Toll-free phone:* 800-MEREDITH. *Fax:* 919-760-2298. *E-mail:* admissions@meredith.edu.

Methodist University
Fayetteville, North Carolina
http://www.methodist.edu/

- **Independent United Methodist** comprehensive, founded 1956
- **Suburban** 600-acre campus with easy access to Raleigh-Durham
- **Endowment** $13.9 million
- **Coed**
- **Moderately difficult** entrance level

FACULTY
Student/faculty ratio: 11:1.

ACADEMICS
Calendar: semesters. *Degrees:* associate, bachelor's, and master's.
Library: Davis Memorial Library plus 1 other.

STUDENT LIFE
Housing options: on-campus residence required through sophomore year; coed, men-only, women-only. Campus housing is university owned. Freshman campus housing is guaranteed.

Activities and organizations: drama/theater group, student-run newspaper, choral group, marching band, Student Activities Committee, Student Government Association, Student Education Association, Fellowship of Christian Athletes, Residence Hall Association, national fraternities, national sororities.

Athletics Member NCAA. All Division III.

Campus security: 24-hour emergency response devices and patrols, student patrols, late-night transport/escort service, controlled dormitory access, regular patrol by county sheriff department.

Student services: health clinic, personal/psychological counseling.

FINANCIAL AID
Financial Aid Of all full-time matriculated undergraduates who enrolled in 2018, 1,274 applied for aid, 1,203 were judged to have need, 137 had their need fully met. 370 Federal Work-Study jobs (averaging $697). 134 state and other part-time jobs (averaging $1550). In 2018, 281 non-need-based awards were made. ***Average percent of need met:*** 65. ***Average financial aid package:*** $23,452. ***Average need-based loan:*** $5408. ***Average need-based gift aid:*** $19,353. ***Average non-need-based aid:*** $20,717. ***Average indebtedness upon graduation:*** $33,211.

APPLYING
Standardized Tests *Required:* SAT or ACT (for admission).

Options: deferred entrance.

Application fee: $25.

Required: high school transcript. ***Required for some:*** essay or personal statement, interview. ***Recommended:*** interview.

CONTACT
Mr. Jamie Legg, Director of Admissions, Methodist University, 5400 Ramset Street, Fayetteville, NC 28311-1496. *Phone:* 910-630-7027. *Toll-free phone:* 800-488-7110 Ext. 7027. *Fax:* 910-630-7285. *E-mail:* admissions@methodist.edu.

Mid-Atlantic Christian University
Elizabeth City, North Carolina
http://www.macuniversity.edu/

CONTACT
Mid-Atlantic Christian University, 715 North Poindexter Street, Elizabeth City, NC 27909-4054. *Toll-free phone:* 866-996-MACU.

Montreat College
Montreat, North Carolina
http://www.montreat.edu/

CONTACT
Miss Mandi Pike, Senior Admissions Specialist, Montreat College, PO Box 1267, Montreat, NC 28757. *Phone:* 828-669-8012 Ext. 3789. *Toll-free phone:* 800-622-6968. *Fax:* 828-669-0120. *E-mail:* admissions@montreat.edu.

North Carolina Agricultural and Technical State University
Greensboro, North Carolina
http://www.ncat.edu/

- **State-supported** university, founded 1891, part of University of North Carolina System
- **Suburban** 200-acre campus with easy access to Charlotte
- **Coed**
- **Moderately difficult** entrance level

FACULTY
Student/faculty ratio: 18:1.

ACADEMICS
Calendar: semesters. *Degrees:* bachelor's, master's, doctoral, post-master's, and postbachelor's certificates.
Library: F. D. Bluford Library.

STUDENT LIFE
Housing options: coed, men-only, women-only. Campus housing is university owned and is provided by a third party. Freshman applicants given priority for college housing.

Activities and organizations: drama/theater group, student-run newspaper, radio and television station, choral group, marching band, Student Government, national fraternities, national sororities.

Athletics Member NCAA. All Division I.

Campus security: 24-hour emergency response devices and patrols, late-night transport/escort service, controlled dormitory access.

Student services: health clinic, personal/psychological counseling.

COSTS & FINANCIAL AID
Costs (2019–20) ***Tuition:*** area resident $3450 full-time; state resident $3450 full-time, nonresident $17,050 full-time. Full-time tuition and fees vary according to course load, degree level, and program. Part-time tuition and fees vary according to course load, degree level, and program. ***Required fees:*** $3117 full-time. ***Room and board:*** $7930; room only: $4209. Room and board charges vary according to board plan and housing facility.

Financial Aid Of all full-time matriculated undergraduates who enrolled in 2016, 8,221 applied for aid, 7,493 were judged to have need, 489 had their need fully met. In 2016, 179 non-need-based awards were made. ***Average percent of need met:*** 59. ***Average financial aid package:*** $11,092. ***Average need-based loan:*** $4004. ***Average need-based gift aid:*** $8240. ***Average non-need-based aid:*** $5372. ***Average indebtedness upon graduation:*** $34,379.

APPLYING
Standardized Tests *Required:* SAT or ACT (for admission).

Options: early admission, deferred entrance.

Application fee: $55.

Required: high school transcript, minimum 2.0 GPA.

CONTACT
Ms. Cheryl Pollard-Burns, Director of Admissions, North Carolina Agricultural and Technical State University, Webb Hall, 1601 East Market Street, Greensboro, NC 27411. *Phone:* 336-334-7946. *Toll-free phone:* 800-443-8964. *Fax:* 336-334-7478. *E-mail:* uadmit@ncat.edu.

North Carolina Central University

Durham, North Carolina

http://www.nccu.edu/

- **State-supported** comprehensive, founded 1910, part of University of North Carolina System
- **Urban** 115-acre campus with easy access to Raleigh
- **Endowment** $22.9 million
- **Coed** 6,101 undergraduate students, 82% full-time, 68% women, 32% men
- **Minimally difficult** entrance level, 68% of applicants were admitted

UNDERGRAD STUDENTS
5,012 full-time, 1,089 part-time. 16% are from out of state; 81% Black or African American, non-Hispanic/Latino; 6% Hispanic/Latino; 0.9% Asian, non-Hispanic/Latino; 0.3% American Indian or Alaska Native, non-Hispanic/Latino; 5% Two or more races, non-Hispanic/Latino; 1% Race/ethnicity unknown; 0.2% international; 9% transferred in; 43% live on campus.

Freshmen:
Admission: 8,311 applied, 5,650 admitted, 1,027 enrolled. ***Test scores:*** SAT evidence-based reading and writing scores over 500: 41%; SAT math scores over 500: 36%; ACT scores over 18: 44%; SAT evidence-based reading and writing scores over 600: 6%; SAT math scores over 600: 5%; ACT scores over 24: 6%; SAT evidence-based reading and writing scores over 700: 1%; SAT math scores over 700: 1%; ACT scores over 30: 1%.

Retention: 76% of full-time freshmen returned.

FACULTY
Total: 592, 64% full-time, 57% with terminal degrees.

Student/faculty ratio: 16:1.

ACADEMICS
Calendar: semesters. *Degrees:* bachelor's, master's, and doctoral.

Special study options: academic remediation for entering students, accelerated degree program, adult/continuing education programs, advanced placement credit, cooperative education, distance learning, double majors, English as a second language, honors programs, independent study, internships, off-campus study, part-time degree program, services for LD students, study abroad, summer session for credit. ***ROTC:*** Army (b), Air Force (b).

Computers: 1,262 computers/terminals and 3,700 ports are available on campus for general student use. Students can access the following: campus intranet, computer help desk, free student e-mail accounts, online (class) grades, online (class) registration, online (class) schedules. Campuswide network is available. 100% of college-owned or -operated housing units are wired for high-speed Internet access. Wireless service is available via entire campus.

Library: Shepherd Library plus 2 others. Study areas open 24 hours, 5–7 days a week; students can reserve study rooms.

STUDENT LIFE
Housing options: coed, men-only, women-only. Campus housing is university owned. Freshman applicants given priority for college housing.

Activities and organizations: drama/theater group, student-run newspaper, choral group, marching band, national fraternities, national sororities.

Athletics Member NCAA, NAIA. All NCAA Division I. ***Intercollegiate sports:*** baseball M(s), basketball M(s)/W(s), bowling W(s), cross-country running M(s)/W(s), football M(s), golf M(s), softball W(s), tennis M(s)/W(s), track and field M(s)/W(s), volleyball W(s). ***Intramural sports:*** basketball M/W, football M, golf M, soccer M, volleyball W.

Campus security: 24-hour emergency response devices and patrols, student patrols, late-night transport/escort service, controlled dormitory access.

Student services: health clinic, personal/psychological counseling, women's center.

COSTS & FINANCIAL AID
Costs (2020–21) ***Tuition:*** area resident $3728 full-time, $593 per credit hour part-time; state resident $3728 full-time; nonresident $16,435 full-time, $2054 per credit hour part-time. Part-time tuition and fees vary according to course load. No tuition increase for student's term of enrollment. ***Required fees:*** $2806 full-time. ***Room and board:*** $10,227. Room and board charges vary according to board plan, housing facility, and location. ***Payment plan:*** installment. ***Waivers:*** employees or children of employees.

Financial Aid Of all full-time matriculated undergraduates who enrolled in 2017, 5,105 applied for aid, 4,891 were judged to have need, 206 had their need fully met. In 2017, 62 non-need-based awards were made. ***Average percent of need met:*** 57. ***Average financial aid package:*** $14,577. ***Average need-based loan:*** $6701. ***Average need-based gift aid:*** $8826. ***Average non-need-based aid:*** $6217. ***Average indebtedness upon graduation:*** $44,228.

APPLYING
Standardized Tests *Required:* SAT or ACT (for admission). *Recommended:* SAT and SAT Subject Tests or ACT (for admission).

Options: electronic application.

Application fee: $50.

Required: high school transcript, minimum 2.5 GPA, University of North Carolina System minimum course requirements.

Application deadlines: 8/1 (freshmen), 8/1 (transfers).

Notification: continuous until 10/15 (freshmen), continuous until 10/15 (transfers).

CONTACT
North Carolina Central University, 1801 Fayetteville Street, Durham, NC 27707-3129. *Toll-free phone:* 877-667-7533.

North Carolina State University

Raleigh, North Carolina

http://www.ncsu.edu/

- **State-supported** university, founded 1887, part of University of North Carolina System
- **Urban** 2137-acre campus with easy access to Raleigh-Durham
- **Endowment** $1.3 billion
- **Coed**
- **Very difficult** entrance level

FACULTY
Student/faculty ratio: 13:1.

ACADEMICS
Calendar: semesters. *Degrees:* associate, bachelor's, master's, doctoral, and postbachelor's certificates.
Library: D. H. Hill Jr. Library plus 5 others. *Books:* 2.6 million (physical), 1.2 million (digital/electronic); *Serial titles:* 47,189 (physical), 55,481 (digital/electronic); *Databases:* 635. Weekly public service hours: 146; study areas open 24 hours, 5–7 days a week; students can reserve study rooms.

STUDENT LIFE
Housing options: on-campus residence required for freshman year; coed, men-only, women-only, special housing for students with disabilities. Campus housing is university owned. Freshman campus housing is guaranteed.

Activities and organizations: drama/theater group, student-run newspaper, radio and television station, choral group, marching band, Inter-Residence Council, Student Alumni Association, Student Wolfpack Club, College of Education Graduate Advisory Board, American Society of Mechanical Engineers Student Section, national fraternities, national sororities.

Athletics Member NCAA. All Division I.

Campus security: 24-hour emergency response devices and patrols, late-night transport/escort service, controlled dormitory access.

Student services: health clinic, personal/psychological counseling, women's center, legal services, veterans affairs office.

COSTS & FINANCIAL AID
Costs (2019–20) ***Tuition:*** state resident $6535 full-time; nonresident $26,654 full-time. Full-time tuition and fees vary according to course load and program. Part-time tuition and fees vary according to course load and program. No tuition increase for student's term of enrollment. ***Required fees:*** $2566 full-time. ***Room and board:*** $11,359; room only: $6714. Room and board charges vary according to board plan and housing facility.

Financial Aid Of all full-time matriculated undergraduates who enrolled in 2019, 15,791 applied for aid, 10,441 were judged to have need, 2,230 had their need fully met. 1,532 Federal Work-Study jobs (averaging $1750). In 2019, 1163 non-need-based awards were made. ***Average percent of need met:*** 75. ***Average financial aid package:*** $13,488. ***Average need-based loan:*** $3863. ***Average need-based gift aid:*** $10,326. ***Average non-need-based aid:*** $5265. ***Average indebtedness upon graduation:*** $25,893.

APPLYING
Standardized Tests *Required:* SAT (for admission), ACT (for admission), SAT or ACT (for admission).

Options: electronic application, early action, deferred entrance.

Application fee: $85.

Required for some: high school transcript, interview, Students applying for studio-based majors must provide a portfolio. Students applying for Professional Golf Management Students must provide a copy of their GHIN/Handicap scores from their local golf facility and a letter of recommendation from their golf coach or a PGA Professional. ***Recommended:*** essay or personal statement.

CONTACT
Mr. Jon Westover, Associate Vice Provost and Director of Undergraduate Admissions, North Carolina State University, Box 7103, Raleigh, NC 27695. *Phone:* 919-515-2434. *Fax:* 919-515-5039. *E-mail:* undergrad-admissions@ncsu.edu.

North Carolina Wesleyan College

Rocky Mount, North Carolina

http://www.ncwc.edu/

CONTACT
Mr. Ben Lilley, Assistant Director of Admissions, North Carolina Wesleyan College, 3400 North Wesleyan Boulevard, Rocky Mount, NC 27804. *Phone:* 252-985-5113. *Toll-free phone:* 800-488-6292. *Fax:* 252-985-5295. *E-mail:* blilley@ncwc.edu.

Pfeiffer University

Misenheimer, North Carolina

http://www.pfeiffer.edu/

- **Independent United Methodist** comprehensive, founded 1885
- **Rural** 300-acre campus with easy access to Charlotte
- **Endowment** $15.3 million
- **Coed**
- **Moderately difficult** entrance level

FACULTY
Student/faculty ratio: 12:1.

ACADEMICS
Calendar: semesters. *Degrees:* bachelor's, master's, post-master's, and postbachelor's certificates.
Library: Gustavus A. Pfeiffer Library. *Books:* 125,000 (physical).

STUDENT LIFE
Housing options: on-campus residence required through senior year, coed, women-only. Campus housing is university owned. Freshman campus housing is guaranteed.

Activities and organizations: drama/theater group, student-run newspaper, choral group, Student Government Association, Religious Life Council, Commuter Student Association, Programming Activities Council, Residence Hall Association.

Athletics Member NCAA. All Division III.

Campus security: 24-hour emergency response devices and patrols, late-night transport/escort service, controlled dormitory access.

Student services: health clinic, personal/psychological counseling, women's center.

COSTS & FINANCIAL AID
Costs (2019–20) ***Comprehensive fee:*** $42,718 includes full-time tuition ($29,800), mandatory fees ($1260), and room and board ($11,658). Full-time tuition and fees vary according to course load and program. Part-time tuition: $700 per semester hour. Part-time tuition and fees vary according to course load and program. ***Required fees:*** $630 per term part-time. ***College room only:*** $6020. Room and board charges vary according to board plan and housing facility.

Financial Aid Of all full-time matriculated undergraduates who enrolled in 2017, 623 applied for aid, 589 were judged to have need, 96 had their need fully met. In 2017, 75 non-need-based awards were made. ***Average percent of need met:*** 75. ***Average financial aid package:*** $24,502. ***Average need-based loan:*** $3516. ***Average need-based gift aid:*** $21,400. ***Average non-need-based aid:*** $14,609. ***Financial aid deadline:*** 7/1.

APPLYING
Options: electronic application, early admission, deferred entrance.

Required: high school transcript. ***Required for some:*** 2 letters of recommendation. ***Recommended:*** minimum 2.0 GPA, interview.

CONTACT
Emily Carella, Director of Undergraduate Admissions, Pfeiffer University, PO Box 960, Misenheimer, NC 28109. *Phone:* 704-463-3047. *Toll-free phone:* 800-338-2060. *Fax:* 704-463-1363. *E-mail:* emily.carella@pfeiffer.edu.

Piedmont International University

Winston-Salem, North Carolina

http://www.piedmontu.edu/

CONTACT
Mr. Joe Edgerton, Undergraduate Admissions Counselor, Piedmont International University, 420 South Broad Street, Winston-Salem, NC 27101. *Phone:* 336-714-7933. *Toll-free phone:* 800-937-5097. *Fax:* 336-725-5522. *E-mail:* stevensons@piedmontu.edu.

Queens University of Charlotte

Charlotte, North Carolina

http://www.queens.edu/

- **Independent Presbyterian** comprehensive, founded 1857
- **Urban** 95-acre campus with easy access to Charlotte, NC
- **Endowment** $91.2 million
- **Coed** 1,733 undergraduate students, 91% full-time, 67% women, 33% men
- **Moderately difficult** entrance level, 65% of applicants were admitted

UNDERGRAD STUDENTS

1,570 full-time, 163 part-time. 34% are from out of state; 15% Black or African American, non-Hispanic/Latino; 12% Hispanic/Latino; 3% Asian, non-Hispanic/Latino; 0.1% Native Hawaiian or other Pacific Islander, non-Hispanic/Latino; 0.6% American Indian or Alaska Native, non-Hispanic/Latino; 0.5% Two or more races, non-Hispanic/Latino; 4% Race/ethnicity unknown; 9% international; 11% transferred in; 54% live on campus.

Freshmen:

Admission: 3,419 applied, 2,230 admitted, 338 enrolled. ***Test scores:*** SAT evidence-based reading and writing scores over 500: 88%; SAT math scores over 500: 82%; ACT scores over 18: 93%; SAT evidence-based reading and writing scores over 600: 39%; SAT math scores over 600: 29%; ACT scores over 24: 51%; SAT evidence-based reading and writing scores over 700: 7%; SAT math scores over 700: 6%; ACT scores over 30: 13%.

Retention: 75% of full-time freshmen returned.

FACULTY

Total: 312, 43% full-time, 58% with terminal degrees.

Student/faculty ratio: 10:1.

ACADEMICS

Calendar: semesters. *Degrees:* certificates, bachelor's, master's, post-master's, and postbachelor's certificates.

Special study options: accelerated degree program, adult/continuing education programs, advanced placement credit, distance learning, external degree program, honors programs, independent study, internships, off-campus study, part-time degree program, student-designed majors, study abroad, summer session for credit.

Computers: 220 computers/terminals and 100 ports are available on campus for general student use. Students can access the following: campus intranet, computer help desk, free student e-mail accounts, online (class) grades, online (class) registration, online (class) schedules. Campuswide network is available. 100% of college-owned or -operated housing units are wired for high-speed Internet access. Wireless service is available via entire campus.

Library: Everett Library. *Books:* 41,620 (physical), 228,153 (digital/electronic); *Serial titles:* 106 (physical), 19,724 (digital/electronic); *Databases:* 81. Weekly public service hours: 93; students can reserve study rooms.

STUDENT LIFE

Housing options: on-campus residence required through junior year; coed, women-only, special housing for students with disabilities. Campus housing is university owned. Freshman campus housing is guaranteed.

Activities and organizations: drama/theater group, student-run newspaper, choral group, Senate, College Union Board, Royal Ambassadors, Students for Black Awareness, International Club, national fraternities, national sororities.

Athletics Member NCAA. All Division II except golf (Division I). ***Intercollegiate sports:*** basketball M(s)/W(s), cross-country running M(s)/W(s), golf M(s)/W(s), lacrosse M(s)/W(s), soccer M(s)/W(s), softball W(s), swimming and diving M(s)/W(s), tennis M(s)/W(s), track and field M(s)/W(s), volleyball W(s). ***Intramural sports:*** basketball M/W, cheerleading M/W, fencing W(c), soccer M/W, softball M/W, tennis M/W, triathlon M(c)/W(c), volleyball M/W.

Campus security: 24-hour emergency response devices and patrols, late-night transport/escort service, controlled dormitory access, Emergency Alert System.

Student services: health clinic, personal/psychological counseling.

FINANCIAL AID

Financial Aid Of all full-time matriculated undergraduates who enrolled in 2019, 1,173 applied for aid, 1,029 were judged to have need, 212 had their need fully met. In 2019, 457 non-need-based awards were made. ***Average percent of need met:*** 70. ***Average financial aid package:*** $26,200. ***Average need-based loan:*** $4257. ***Average need-based gift aid:*** $20,957. ***Average non-need-based aid:*** $14,304. ***Average indebtedness upon graduation:*** $30,654.

APPLYING

Options: electronic application, early decision, early action, deferred entrance.

Required: essay or personal statement, high school transcript, 1 letter of recommendation. ***Required for some:*** interview.

Application deadlines: rolling (freshmen), rolling (transfers), 12/2 (early action).

Early decision deadline: 11/1.

Notification: continuous (freshmen), continuous (transfers), 12/1 (early decision), 12/31 (early action).

CONTACT

Evan Sprinkle, Director Traditional Undergraduate Admissions, Queens University of Charlotte, 1900 Selwyn Avenue, Harris Welcome Center, MSC 1428, Charlotte, NC 28274. *Phone:* 704-337-2212. *Toll-free phone:* 800-849-0202. *E-mail:* admissions@queens.edu.

St. Andrews University

Laurinburg, North Carolina

http://www.sa.edu/

CONTACT

Erin Balduf, Director of Admissions, St. Andrews University, 1700 Dogwood Mile, Laurinburg, NC 28352. *Phone:* 910-277-5555. *Toll-free phone:* 800-763-0198. *Fax:* 910-277-5087. *E-mail:* admission@sapc.edu.

Saint Augustine's University

Raleigh, North Carolina

http://www.st-aug.edu/

CONTACT

Mr. Chris J. Withers, Director of Admissions, Saint Augustine's University, 1315 Oakwood Avenue, Raleigh, NC 27610-2298. *Phone:* 919-516-4012. *Toll-free phone:* 800-948-1126. *Fax:* 919-516-5804. *E-mail:* jesousa@st-aug.edu.

Salem College

Winston-Salem, North Carolina

http://www.salem.edu/

CONTACT

Dean Katherine Knapp Watts, Dean of Admissions and Financial Aid, Salem College, Single Sisters House, 601 South Church Street, Winston-Salem, NC 27101. *Phone:* 336-721-2621. *Toll-free phone:* 800-327-2536. *Fax:* 336-917-5572. *E-mail:* admissions@salem.edu.

Shaw University

Raleigh, North Carolina

http://www.shawu.edu/

CONTACT

Shaw University, 118 East South Street, Raleigh, NC 27601-2399. *Toll-free phone:* 800-214-6683.

Southeastern Baptist Theological Seminary

Wake Forest, North Carolina

http://www.sebts.edu/

- **Independent Southern Baptist** comprehensive, founded 1950
- **Suburban** 300-acre campus with easy access to Raleigh
- **Coed** 557 undergraduate students, 59% full-time, 30% women, 70% men
- **Noncompetitive** entrance level, 92% of applicants were admitted

UNDERGRAD STUDENTS
327 full-time, 230 part-time. Students come from 52 states and territories; 30 other countries; 55% are from out of state; 10% Black or African American, non-Hispanic/Latino; 6% Hispanic/Latino; 3% Asian, non-Hispanic/Latino; 1% American Indian or Alaska Native, non-Hispanic/Latino; 2% Race/ethnicity unknown; 0.2% international; 5% transferred in.

Freshmen:
Admission: 252 applied, 233 admitted, 129 enrolled.
Retention: 90% of full-time freshmen returned.

FACULTY
Total: 123, 46% full-time, 69% with terminal degrees.
Student/faculty ratio: 25:1.

ACADEMICS
Calendar: semesters. *Degrees:* certificates, associate, bachelor's, master's, and doctoral.
Special study options: academic remediation for entering students, adult/continuing education programs, distance learning, double majors, independent study, internships, off-campus study, part-time degree program, summer session for credit.
Computers: 55 computers/terminals and 1,100 ports are available on campus for general student use. Students can access the following: campus intranet, free student e-mail accounts, online (class) grades, online (class) registration, online (class) schedules. Campuswide network is available. Wireless service is available via classrooms, libraries, student centers.
Library: The Library at Southeastern plus 1 other. *Books:* 154,022 (physical), 461,781 (digital/electronic); *Serial titles:* 2,287 (physical), 516,730 (digital/electronic); *Databases:* 40. Weekly public service hours: 90; students can reserve study rooms.

STUDENT LIFE
Housing options: on-campus residence required for freshman year; men-only, women-only. Campus housing is university owned. Freshman applicants given priority for college housing.
Activities and organizations: drama/theater group, choral group.
Athletics *Intramural sports:* basketball M/W, football M/W, golf M/W, racquetball M/W, table tennis M/W, ultimate Frisbee M/W, volleyball M/W.
Campus security: 24-hour emergency response devices and patrols, late-night transport/escort service.
Student services: health clinic, personal/psychological counseling, women's center.

APPLYING
Standardized Tests *Required:* SAT or ACT (for admission).
Options: electronic application.
Application fee: $40.
Required: essay or personal statement, high school transcript, minimum 2.0 GPA, 3 letters of recommendation.
Application deadlines: 7/20 (freshmen), 7/20 (transfers).
Notification: continuous until 8/20 (freshmen), continuous until 8/20 (transfers).

CONTACT
Jade Marlin, College Admissions Counselor, Southeastern Baptist Theological Seminary, 120 South Wingate Street, Wake Forest, NC 27587. *Phone:* 919-761-2324. *Toll-free phone:* 800-284-6317. *E-mail:* jmarlin@sebts.edu.

Strayer University–Greensboro Campus

Greensboro, North Carolina

http://www.strayer.edu/north-carolina/greensboro/

CONTACT
Strayer University–Greensboro Campus, 4900 Koger Boulevard, Suite 400, Greensboro, NC 27407. *Toll-free phone:* 888-311-0355.

Strayer University–Huntersville Campus

Huntersville, North Carolina

http://www.strayer.edu/north-carolina/huntersville/

CONTACT
Strayer University–Huntersville Campus, 13620 Reese Boulevard, Suite 130, Huntersville, NC 28078. *Toll-free phone:* 888-311-0355.

Strayer University–North Charlotte Campus

Concord, North Carolina

http://www.strayer.edu/north-carolina/north-charlotte/

CONTACT
Strayer University–North Charlotte Campus, 7870 Commons Park Circle NW, Concord, NC 28027. *Toll-free phone:* 888-311-0355.

Strayer University–North Raleigh Campus

Raleigh, North Carolina

http://www.strayer.edu/north-carolina/north-raleigh/

CONTACT
Strayer University–North Raleigh Campus, 8701 Wadford Drive, Raleigh, NC 27616. *Toll-free phone:* 888-311-0355.

Strayer University–Research Triangle Park Campus

Morrisville, North Carolina

http://www.strayer.edu/north-carolina/morrisville

CONTACT
Strayer University–Research Triangle Park Campus, 4 Copley Parkway, Morrisville, NC 27560. *Toll-free phone:* 888-311-0355.

Strayer University–South Charlotte Campus

Charlotte, North Carolina

http://www.strayer.edu/north-carolina/south-charlotte/

CONTACT
Strayer University–South Charlotte Campus, 9101 Kings Parade Boulevard, Suite 200, Charlotte, NC 28273. *Toll-free phone:* 888-311-0355.

Strayer University–South Raleigh Campus

Raleigh, North Carolina

http://www.strayer.edu/north-carolina/south-raleigh/

CONTACT
Strayer University–South Raleigh Campus, 3421 Olympia Drive, Raleigh, NC 27603. *Toll-free phone:* 888-311-0355.

University of Mount Olive

Mount Olive, North Carolina

http://www.umo.edu/

- **Independent Free Will Baptist** comprehensive, founded 1951
- **Small-town** 123-acre campus with easy access to Raleigh
- **Coed**
- **Minimally difficult** entrance level

FACULTY

Student/faculty ratio: 14:1.

ACADEMICS

Calendar: semester or continuous accelerated programs. *Degrees:* associate, bachelor's, and master's.
Library: Moye Library.

STUDENT LIFE

Housing options: on-campus residence required for freshman year; coed, men-only, women-only, special housing for students with disabilities. Campus housing is university owned.

Activities and organizations: choral group, Student Government Association, Phi Beta Lambda, commuters organization, Christian Student Fellowship, English Society.

Athletics Member NCAA. All Division II.

Campus security: overnight security patrols; weekend patrols.

Student services: health clinic, personal/psychological counseling.

FINANCIAL AID

Financial Aid Of all full-time matriculated undergraduates who enrolled in 2016, 1,251 applied for aid, 1,133 were judged to have need, 204 had their need fully met. In 2016, 144 non-need-based awards were made. ***Average percent of need met:*** 67. ***Average financial aid package:*** $14,044. ***Average need-based loan:*** $3897. ***Average need-based gift aid:*** $11,599. ***Average non-need-based aid:*** $5969. ***Average indebtedness upon graduation:*** $32,227.

APPLYING

Standardized Tests *Required for some:* SAT or ACT for those under 21.

Options: electronic application, deferred entrance.

Application fee: $20.

Required: high school transcript. ***Recommended:*** 2 letters of recommendation, interview.

CONTACT

University of Mount Olive, 634 Henderson Street, Mount Olive, NC 28365. *Phone:* 919-658-2502 Ext. 3009. *Toll-free phone:* 800-653-0854.

University of North Carolina Asheville

Asheville, North Carolina

http://www.unca.edu/

- **State-supported** comprehensive, founded 1927, part of University of North Carolina System
- **Urban** 365-acre campus
- **Endowment** $44.2 million
- **Coed**
- **Moderately difficult** entrance level

FACULTY

Student/faculty ratio: 13:1.

ACADEMICS

Calendar: semesters. *Degrees:* bachelor's, master's, and postbachelor's certificates.
Library: Ramsey Library. *Books:* 306,273 (physical), 487,660 (digital/electronic); *Serial titles:* 113 (physical), 82,954 (digital/electronic); *Databases:* 138. Weekly public service hours: 99; students can reserve study rooms.

STUDENT LIFE

Housing options: on-campus residence required for freshman year; coed, special housing for students with disabilities. Campus housing is university owned. Freshman campus housing is guaranteed.

Activities and organizations: drama/theater group, student-run newspaper, radio station, choral group, Student Government Association, Alliance, Black Student Association, Gaming Club, Underdog Productions, national fraternities, national sororities.

Athletics Member NCAA. All Division I.

Campus security: 24-hour emergency response devices and patrols, late-night transport/escort service, controlled dormitory access.

Student services: health clinic, personal/psychological counseling, veterans affairs office.

COSTS & FINANCIAL AID

Costs (2019–20) ***One-time required fee:*** $150. ***Tuition:*** state resident $4122 full-time, $139 per credit hour part-time; nonresident $21,470 full-time, $725 per credit hour part-time. Full-time tuition and fees vary according to course load and degree level. Part-time tuition and fees vary according to course load and degree level. ***Required fees:*** $3109 full-time, $18 per credit hour part-time. ***Room and board:*** $9660; room only: $5446. Room and board charges vary according to board plan and housing facility.

Financial Aid Of all full-time matriculated undergraduates who enrolled in 2018, 2,612 applied for aid, 1,912 were judged to have need, 473 had their need fully met. 60 Federal Work-Study jobs (averaging $2543). 1,870 state and other part-time jobs (averaging $1126). In 2018, 372 non-need-based awards were made. ***Average percent of need met:*** 75. ***Average financial aid package:*** $12,879. ***Average need-based loan:*** $4706. ***Average need-based gift aid:*** $7762. ***Average non-need-based aid:*** $1971. ***Average indebtedness upon graduation:*** $24,476.

APPLYING

Standardized Tests *Required:* SAT or ACT (for admission).

Options: electronic application, deferred entrance.

Application fee: $75.

Required: essay or personal statement, high school transcript, 1 letter of recommendation, minimum course requirement.

CONTACT

Steve McKellips, Senior Director of Admissions and Financial Aid, University of North Carolina Asheville, Brown Hall, CPO # 1320, Asheville, NC 28804-8510. *Phone:* 828-250-3829. *Toll-free phone:* 800-531-9842. *Fax:* 828-251-6482. *E-mail:* admissions@unca.edu.

The University of North Carolina at Chapel Hill

Chapel Hill, North Carolina

http://www.unc.edu/

- **State-supported** university, founded 1789, part of University of North Carolina System
- **Suburban** 729-acre campus with easy access to Raleigh-Durham
- **Endowment** $3.5 billion
- **Coed** 19,546 undergraduate students, 96% full-time, 59% women, 41% men
- **Very difficult** entrance level, 23% of applicants were admitted

UNDERGRAD STUDENTS

18,728 full-time, 818 part-time. Students come from 51 states and territories; 103 other countries; 14% are from out of state; 8% Black or African American, non-Hispanic/Latino; 9% Hispanic/Latino; 11% Asian, non-Hispanic/Latino; 0.1% Native Hawaiian or other Pacific Islander, non-Hispanic/Latino; 0.4% American Indian or Alaska Native, non-Hispanic/Latino; 5% Two or more races, non-Hispanic/Latino; 4% Race/ethnicity unknown; 4% international; 4% transferred in; 52% live on campus.

Freshmen:

Admission: 42,466 applied, 9,608 admitted, 4,182 enrolled. ***Average high school GPA:*** 4.4. ***Test scores:*** SAT evidence-based reading and writing scores over 500: 100%; SAT math scores over 500: 100%; ACT scores over 18: 100%; SAT evidence-based reading and writing scores over 600: 92%; SAT math scores over 600: 90%; ACT scores over 24: 92%; SAT evidence-based reading and writing scores over 700: 47%; SAT math scores over 700: 52%; ACT scores over 30: 58%.

Retention: 96% of full-time freshmen returned.

FACULTY

Total: 2,314, 71% full-time, 75% with terminal degrees.

Student/faculty ratio: 13:1.

ACADEMICS
Calendar: semesters. *Degrees:* certificates, bachelor's, master's, doctoral, post-master's, and postbachelor's certificates.

Special study options: advanced placement credit, distance learning, double majors, honors programs, independent study, internships, off-campus study, part-time degree program, services for LD students, student-designed majors, study abroad, summer session for credit. ***ROTC:*** Army (b), Navy (b), Air Force (b).

Computers: 449 computers/terminals and 10,000 ports are available on campus for general student use. Students can access the following: computer help desk, free student e-mail accounts, online (class) grades, online (class) registration, online (class) schedules. Campuswide network is available. 100% of college-owned or -operated housing units are wired for high-speed Internet access. Wireless service is available via entire campus.

Library: Davis Library plus 12 others. *Books:* 7.5 million (physical), 1.4 million (digital/electronic); *Serial titles:* 224,227 (digital/electronic); *Databases:* 1,285. Weekly public service hours: 140; study areas open 24 hours, 5–7 days a week; students can reserve study rooms.

STUDENT LIFE
Housing options: on-campus residence required for freshman year; coed, men-only, women-only, special housing for students with disabilities. Campus housing is university owned. Freshman campus housing is guaranteed.

Activities and organizations: drama/theater group, student-run newspaper, radio and television station, choral group, marching band, Residence Hall Association, Carolina Fever, Campus Y, UNC-CH Habitat for Humanity, Carolina for the Kids Foundation (Dance Marathon), national fraternities, national sororities.

Athletics Member NCAA. All Division I except football (Division I-A). ***Intercollegiate sports:*** badminton M(c)/W(c), baseball M(s), basketball M(s)/W(s), cheerleading W(c), crew M(c)/W(s), cross-country running M(s)/W(s), equestrian sports M(c)/W(c), fencing M(s)/W(s), field hockey M(c)/W(s), golf M(s)/W(s), gymnastics M(c)/W(s), ice hockey M(c), lacrosse M(s)/W(s), racquetball M(c)/W(c), rugby M(c)/W(c), sailing M(c)/W(c), sand volleyball M(c)/W(c), skiing (downhill) M(c)/W(c), soccer M(s)/W(s), softball W(s), swimming and diving M(s)/W(s), table tennis M(c)/W(c), tennis M(s)/W(s), track and field M(s)/W(s), triathlon M(c)/W(c), ultimate Frisbee M(c)/W(c), volleyball M(c)/W(s), water polo M(c)/W(c), wrestling M(s). ***Intramural sports:*** badminton M/W, baseball M(c), basketball M(c)/W(c), crew W(c), cross-country running M(c)/W(c), golf M(c)/W(c), gymnastics W(c), racquetball M/W, rock climbing M(c)/W(c), sand volleyball M(c)/W(c), soccer M(c)/W(c), softball M/W(c), squash M(c)/W(c), swimming and diving M(c)/W(c), table tennis M/W, tennis M(c)/W(c), track and field M(c)/W(c), ultimate Frisbee M/W, volleyball M/W(c).

Campus security: 24-hour emergency response devices and patrols, late-night transport/escort service, controlled dormitory access, crime prevention initiatives, campus-wide emergency alert system, cell phone/GPS security options.

Student services: health clinic, personal/psychological counseling, women's center, legal services, veterans affairs office.

COSTS & FINANCIAL AID
Costs (2020–21) ***Tuition:*** state resident $7230 full-time; nonresident $35,224 full-time. Part-time tuition and fees vary according to course load. ***Required fees:*** $2002 full-time. ***Room and board:*** $11,740; room only: $6878. Room and board charges vary according to board plan, housing facility, and location. ***Payment plan:*** installment. ***Waivers:*** employees or children of employees.

Financial Aid Of all full-time matriculated undergraduates who enrolled in 2018, 11,091 applied for aid, 8,285 were judged to have need, 6,276 had their need fully met. 2,346 Federal Work-Study jobs (averaging $1735). In 2018, 798 non-need-based awards were made. ***Average percent of need met:*** 100. ***Average financial aid package:*** $19,192. ***Average need-based loan:*** $4922. ***Average need-based gift aid:*** $17,217. ***Average non-need-based aid:*** $7833. ***Average indebtedness upon graduation:*** $22,466.

APPLYING
Standardized Tests *Required:* SAT or ACT (for admission).

Options: electronic application, early action, deferred entrance.

Application fee: $85.

Required: essay or personal statement, high school transcript, 1 letter of recommendation, counselor's statement.

Application deadlines: 1/15 (freshmen), 2/15 (transfers), 10/15 (early action).

Notification: 3/31 (freshmen), 4/15 (transfers), 1/31 (early action).

CONTACT
The University of North Carolina at Chapel Hill, Chapel Hill, NC 27599. *Phone:* 919-966-3932.

The University of North Carolina at Charlotte

Charlotte, North Carolina

http://www.uncc.edu/

- **State-supported** university, founded 1946, part of University of North Carolina System
- **Suburban** 1000-acre campus with easy access to Charlotte
- **Endowment** $84.5 million
- **Coed** 24,070 undergraduate students, 87% full-time, 47% women, 53% men
- **Moderately difficult** entrance level, 65% of applicants were admitted

UNDERGRAD STUDENTS
20,877 full-time, 3,193 part-time. Students come from 45 states and territories; 92 other countries; 5% are from out of state; 16% Black or African American, non-Hispanic/Latino; 11% Hispanic/Latino; 8% Asian, non-Hispanic/Latino; 0.1% Native Hawaiian or other Pacific Islander, non-Hispanic/Latino; 0.3% American Indian or Alaska Native, non-Hispanic/Latino; 5% Two or more races, non-Hispanic/Latino; 2% Race/ethnicity unknown; 2% international; 11% transferred in; 25% live on campus.

Freshmen:
Admission: 21,867 applied, 14,224 admitted, 3,652 enrolled. ***Average high school GPA:*** 3.9. ***Test scores:*** SAT evidence-based reading and writing scores over 500: 98%; SAT math scores over 500: 97%; ACT scores over 18: 98%; SAT evidence-based reading and writing scores over 600: 54%; SAT math scores over 600: 53%; ACT scores over 24: 53%; SAT evidence-based reading and writing scores over 700: 6%; SAT math scores over 700: 9%; ACT scores over 30: 8%.

Retention: 83% of full-time freshmen returned.

FACULTY
Total: 1,637, 70% full-time, 72% with terminal degrees.

Student/faculty ratio: 19:1.

ACADEMICS
Calendar: semesters. *Degrees:* bachelor's, master's, doctoral, post-master's, and postbachelor's certificates.

Special study options: accelerated degree program, adult/continuing education programs, advanced placement credit, cooperative education, distance learning, double majors, English as a second language, freshman honors college, honors programs, independent study, internships, off-campus study, part-time degree program, services for LD students, study abroad, summer session for credit. ***ROTC:*** Army (b), Air Force (b).

Computers: 1,600 computers/terminals are available on campus for general student use. Students can access the following: computer help desk, free student e-mail accounts, online (class) grades, online (class) registration, online (class) schedules. Campuswide network is available. 100% of college-owned or -operated housing units are wired for high-speed Internet access. Wireless service is available via entire campus.

Library: J. Murrey Atkins Library plus 1 other. *Books:* 745,390 (physical), 1.1 million (digital/electronic); *Serial titles:* 23,751 (physical), 132,424 (digital/electronic); *Databases:* 600. Study areas open 24 hours, 5–7 days a week; students can reserve study rooms.

STUDENT LIFE
Housing options: coed, special housing for students with disabilities. Campus housing is university owned.

Activities and organizations: drama/theater group, student-run newspaper, radio station, choral group, marching band, Triveni (Indian Students Association), National Society of Leadership and Success,

Kinesiology Student Organization, Habitat for Humanity, Art & Mindfulness, national fraternities, national sororities.

Athletics Member NCAA. All Division I. ***Intercollegiate sports:*** baseball M(s), basketball M(s)/W(s), cross-country running M(s)/W(s), football M(s), golf M(s)/W(s), soccer M(s)/W(s), softball W(s), tennis M(s)/W(s), track and field M(s)/W(s), volleyball W(s). ***Intramural sports:*** archery M(c)/W(c), badminton M/W, baseball M(c), basketball M/W, bowling M/W, equestrian sports M(c)/W(c), fencing M(c), field hockey M(c)/W(c), football M/W, golf M(c), ice hockey M(c), lacrosse M(c)/W(c), rock climbing M/W, rugby M(c)/W(c), sailing M(c)/W(c), soccer M/W, softball M/W, table tennis M/W, ultimate Frisbee M(c)/W(c), volleyball M/W, water polo M/W, weight lifting M(c)/W(c), wrestling M(c)/W(c).

Campus security: 24-hour emergency response devices and patrols, late-night transport/escort service, controlled dormitory access.

Student services: health clinic, personal/psychological counseling, veterans affairs office.

COSTS & FINANCIAL AID

Costs (2019–20) ***Tuition:*** state resident $3812 full-time; nonresident $17,246 full-time. Full-time tuition and fees vary according to course load and program. Part-time tuition and fees vary according to course load and program. No tuition increase for student's term of enrollment. ***Required fees:*** $3284 full-time. ***Room and board:*** $11,060; room only: $6560. Room and board charges vary according to board plan and housing facility. ***Payment plan:*** installment. ***Waivers:*** senior citizens.

Financial Aid Of all full-time matriculated undergraduates who enrolled in 2019, 16,656 applied for aid, 13,216 were judged to have need, 1,243 had their need fully met. 941 Federal Work-Study jobs (averaging $2830). In 2019, 322 non-need-based awards were made. ***Average percent of need met:*** 54. ***Average financial aid package:*** $9523. ***Average need-based loan:*** $4245. ***Average need-based gift aid:*** $6778. ***Average non-need-based aid:*** $7421. ***Average indebtedness upon graduation:*** $28,316.

APPLYING

Standardized Tests *Required:* SAT or ACT (for admission).

Options: electronic application, early action.

Application fee: $75.

Required: high school transcript, minimum 2.0 GPA.

Application deadlines: 6/1 (freshmen), 6/1 (out-of-state freshmen), 6/1 (transfers), 11/1 (early action).

Notification: continuous until 11/1 (freshmen), continuous until 11/1 (out-of-state freshmen), continuous (transfers), 1/30 (early action).

CONTACT

Ms. Claire Kirby, Director of Admissions, The University of North Carolina at Charlotte, 9201 University City Boulevard, 1st Floor, Cato Hall, Charlotte, NC 28223-0001. *Phone:* 704-687-5507. *Fax:* 704-687-6483. *E-mail:* admissions@uncc.edu.

The University of North Carolina at Greensboro

Greensboro, North Carolina

http://www.uncg.edu/

- **State-supported** university, founded 1891, part of University of North Carolina System
- **Urban** 250-acre campus
- **Endowment** $292.0 million
- **Coed** 16,581 undergraduate students, 84% full-time, 67% women, 33% men
- **Moderately difficult** entrance level, 82% of applicants were admitted

UNDERGRAD STUDENTS

14,007 full-time, 2,574 part-time. 3% are from out of state; 30% Black or African American, non-Hispanic/Latino; 12% Hispanic/Latino; 5% Asian, non-Hispanic/Latino; 0.1% Native Hawaiian or other Pacific Islander, non-Hispanic/Latino; 0.3% American Indian or Alaska Native, non-Hispanic/Latino; 5% Two or more races, non-Hispanic/Latino; 0.8% Race/ethnicity unknown; 1% international; 11% transferred in; 34% live on campus.

Freshmen:

Admission: 9,972 applied, 8,221 admitted, 2,746 enrolled. ***Average high school GPA:*** 3.7. ***Test scores:*** SAT evidence-based reading and writing scores over 500: 79%; SAT math scores over 500: 76%; ACT scores over 18: 89%; SAT evidence-based reading and writing scores over 600: 25%; SAT math scores over 600: 16%; ACT scores over 24: 27%; SAT evidence-based reading and writing scores over 700: 2%; SAT math scores over 700: 2%; ACT scores over 30: 3%.

Retention: 75% of full-time freshmen returned.

FACULTY

Total: 1,146, 75% full-time, 64% with terminal degrees.

Student/faculty ratio: 16:1.

ACADEMICS

Calendar: semesters. *Degrees:* bachelor's, master's, doctoral, post-master's, and postbachelor's certificates.

Special study options: academic remediation for entering students, accelerated degree program, adult/continuing education programs, advanced placement credit, distance learning, double majors, English as a second language, freshman honors college, honors programs, independent study, internships, off-campus study, part-time degree program, services for LD students, student-designed majors, study abroad, summer session for credit. ***ROTC:*** Army (c), Air Force (c).

Unusual degree programs: 3-2 nursing; Applied Economics, English, Communication Studies, Mathematics, Applied Geography, Accounting, Economics, Consumer Apparel and Retail Studies, Information Technology and Management, Computer Science, Recreation and Parks Management, Information Syste.

Computers: 474 computers/terminals are available on campus for general student use. Students can access the following: computer help desk, free student e-mail accounts, online (class) grades, online (class) registration, online (class) schedules, wireless printing services, cloud storage services. Campuswide network is available. 100% of college-owned or -operated housing units are wired for high-speed Internet access. Wireless service is available via entire campus.

Library: Walter Clinton Jackson Library plus 4 others. *Books:* 1.2 million (physical), 1.2 million (digital/electronic); *Serial titles:* 18,527 (physical), 109,122 (digital/electronic); *Databases:* 765. Weekly public service hours: 138; study areas open 24 hours, 5–7 days a week; students can reserve study rooms.

STUDENT LIFE

Housing options: coed, special housing for students with disabilities. Campus housing is university owned.

Activities and organizations: drama/theater group, student-run newspaper, radio station, choral group, Alpha Lamda Delta, Beta Gamma Sigma, Sigma Theta Tau, Gamma Zeta, Golden Key, UNCG Leadership Challenge - Bronze, national fraternities, national sororities.

Athletics Member NCAA. All Division I. ***Intercollegiate sports:*** baseball M(s), basketball M(s)/W(s), cross-country running M(s)/W(s), golf M(s)/W(s)(c), soccer M(s)/W(s), softball W(s), tennis M(s)/W(s), track and field M(s)/W(s), volleyball W(s). ***Intramural sports:*** badminton M/W, basketball M/W, cross-country running M(c)/W(c), equestrian sports M(c)/W(c), fencing M(c)/W, field hockey M/W(c), football M(c)/W(c), lacrosse M(c)/W(c), racquetball M/W, rock climbing M/W, rugby M(c)/W(c), sand volleyball M/W, soccer M/W, softball M(c)/W(c), swimming and diving M(c)/W(c), table tennis M/W, tennis M(c)/W(c), ultimate Frisbee M/W, volleyball M(c)/W(c), water polo M/W.

Campus security: 24-hour emergency response devices and patrols, student patrols, late-night transport/escort service, controlled dormitory access.

Student services: health clinic, personal/psychological counseling, women's center, veterans affairs office.

COSTS & FINANCIAL AID

Costs (2019–20) ***Tuition:*** state resident $4422 full-time, $553 per credit hour part-time; nonresident $19,581 full-time, $2448 per credit hour part-time. Full-time tuition and fees vary according to course load and program. Part-time tuition and fees vary according to course load and program. ***Required fees:*** $2981 full-time, $117 per credit hour part-time. ***Room and board:*** $9264; room only: $5516. Room and board charges vary according to board plan and housing facility. ***Payment plan:***

installment. ***Waivers:*** senior citizens and employees or children of employees.

Financial Aid Of all full-time matriculated undergraduates who enrolled in 2018, 12,135 applied for aid, 10,423 were judged to have need, 1,063 had their need fully met. 717 Federal Work-Study jobs (averaging $2269). In 2018, 373 non-need-based awards were made. ***Average percent of need met:*** 59. ***Average financial aid package:*** $11,491. ***Average need-based loan:*** $3996. ***Average need-based gift aid:*** $8340. ***Average non-need-based aid:*** $3495. ***Average indebtedness upon graduation:*** $23,317. ***Financial aid deadline:*** 12/1.

APPLYING

Standardized Tests *Required:* SAT or ACT (for admission).

Options: electronic application.

Application fee: $65.

Notification: continuous (freshmen), continuous (transfers).

CONTACT

The University of North Carolina at Greensboro, 1400 Spring Garden Street, Greensboro, NC 27412-5001. *Phone:* 336-334-5243.

The University of North Carolina at Pembroke

Pembroke, North Carolina

http://www.uncp.edu/

- **State-supported** comprehensive, founded 1887, part of University of North Carolina System
- **Rural** 264-acre campus
- **Endowment** $20.4 million
- **Coed** 6,353 undergraduate students, 80% full-time, 61% women, 39% men
- **Moderately difficult** entrance level, 85% of applicants were admitted

UNDERGRAD STUDENTS

5,109 full-time, 1,244 part-time. 6% are from out of state; 32% Black or African American, non-Hispanic/Latino; 8% Hispanic/Latino; 1% Asian, non-Hispanic/Latino; 0.1% Native Hawaiian or other Pacific Islander, non-Hispanic/Latino; 14% American Indian or Alaska Native, non-Hispanic/Latino; 6% Two or more races, non-Hispanic/Latino; 2% Race/ethnicity unknown; 1% international; 14% transferred in; 33% live on campus.

Freshmen:

Admission: 5,604 applied, 4,760 admitted, 1,131 enrolled. ***Average high school GPA:*** 3.5. ***Test scores:*** SAT evidence-based reading and writing scores over 500: 52%; SAT math scores over 500: 52%; ACT scores over 18: 71%; SAT evidence-based reading and writing scores over 600: 12%; SAT math scores over 600: 7%; ACT scores over 24: 14%; SAT evidence-based reading and writing scores over 700: 1%; SAT math scores over 700: 1%; ACT scores over 30: 1%.

Retention: 72% of full-time freshmen returned.

FACULTY

Total: 416, 75% full-time, 69% with terminal degrees.

Student/faculty ratio: 18:1.

ACADEMICS

Calendar: semesters. *Degrees:* bachelor's and master's.

Special study options: academic remediation for entering students, accelerated degree program, adult/continuing education programs, advanced placement credit, distance learning, double majors, English as a second language, honors programs, internships, off-campus study, part-time degree program, services for LD students, study abroad, summer session for credit. ***ROTC:*** Army (b), Air Force (b).

Computers: 501 computers/terminals are available on campus for general student use. Students can access the following: campus intranet, computer help desk, free student e-mail accounts, online (class) grades, online (class) registration, online (class) schedules, commuter/off campus connection to network, discounted computer software/hardware. Campuswide network is available. 100% of college-owned or -operated housing units are wired for high-speed Internet access. Wireless service is available via classrooms, computer centers, computer labs, dorm rooms, learning centers, libraries, student centers.

Library: Livermore Library. *Books:* 398,000 (physical), 165,000 (digital/electronic); *Serial titles:* 406 (physical), 54,000 (digital/electronic); *Databases:* 185. Weekly public service hours: 92; students can reserve study rooms.

STUDENT LIFE

Housing options: on-campus residence required for freshman year; coed. Campus housing is university owned. Freshman applicants given priority for college housing.

Activities and organizations: drama/theater group, student-run newspaper, radio and television station, choral group, marching band, Health Careers Club, Spectrum, Graduate Student Organization, Phi Alpha, National Association for the Advancement of Colored People, national fraternities, national sororities.

Athletics Member NCAA. All Division II except golf (Division I). ***Intercollegiate sports:*** baseball M(s), basketball M(s)/W(s), cheerleading M/W, cross-country running M(s)/W(s), football M(s), golf W(s), soccer M(s)/W(s), softball W(s), swimming and diving W, track and field M(s)/W(s), volleyball W(s), wrestling M(s). ***Intramural sports:*** basketball M/W, bowling M/W, cheerleading M/W, football M, golf M, racquetball M/W, rugby M, sand volleyball M/W, soccer M, softball M/W, swimming and diving M/W, tennis M/W, ultimate Frisbee M/W, volleyball M/W, weight lifting M/W, wrestling M.

Campus security: 24-hour emergency response devices and patrols, late-night transport/escort service, controlled dormitory access.

Student services: health clinic, personal/psychological counseling.

COSTS & FINANCIAL AID

Costs (2020–21) ***Tuition:*** area resident $1000 full-time; state resident $1000 full-time; nonresident $5000 full-time. ***Required fees:*** $2490 full-time. ***Room and board:*** $8924. ***Payment plan:*** tuition prepayment.

Financial Aid Of all full-time matriculated undergraduates who enrolled in 2019, 4,499 applied for aid, 3,926 were judged to have need, 301 had their need fully met. 128 Federal Work-Study jobs (averaging $1614). In 2019, 43 non-need-based awards were made. ***Average percent of need met:*** 65. ***Average financial aid package:*** $9010. ***Average need-based loan:*** $4189. ***Average need-based gift aid:*** $5811. ***Average non-need-based aid:*** $1850. ***Average indebtedness upon graduation:*** $27,193.

APPLYING

Standardized Tests *Required:* SAT or ACT (for admission). *Required for some:* TOEFL.

Options: electronic application, deferred entrance.

Application fee: $55.

Required: high school transcript. ***Required for some:*** 1 letter of recommendation, interview. ***Recommended:*** essay or personal statement, minimum 2.0 GPA.

Application deadlines: 6/30 (freshmen), 6/30 (transfers).

Notification: continuous (freshmen), continuous (transfers).

CONTACT

The University of North Carolina at Pembroke, One University Drive, PO Box 1510, Pembroke, NC 28372-1510. *Phone:* 910-522-6464. *Toll-free phone:* 800-949-UNCP.

University of North Carolina School of the Arts

Winston-Salem, North Carolina

http://www.uncsa.edu/

- **State-supported** comprehensive, founded 1963, part of University of North Carolina system
- **Urban** 74-acre campus
- **Endowment** $67.7 million
- **Coed**
- 38% of applicants were admitted

FACULTY

Student/faculty ratio: 6:1.

ACADEMICS

Calendar: semesters. *Degrees:* certificates, bachelor's, master's, and post-master's certificates.

Library: UNCSA Library. *Books:* 101,097 (physical), 37,147 (digital/electronic); *Serial titles:* 1,171 (physical), 73,113 (digital/electronic); *Databases:* 121. Weekly public service hours: 90; students can reserve study rooms.

STUDENT LIFE

Housing options: on-campus residence required through sophomore year; coed. Campus housing is university owned. Freshman campus housing is guaranteed.

Activities and organizations: drama/theater group, student-run newspaper, choral group, A.R.T.S. Club (awareness on social issues through artistic expression), The Artist Underground, Art & Soul, UNCSA Artists of Color.

Campus security: 24-hour emergency response devices and patrols, late-night transport/escort service, controlled dormitory access.

Student services: health clinic, personal/psychological counseling.

COSTS & FINANCIAL AID

Costs (2019–20) ***Tuition:*** state resident $6497 full-time, $266 per credit hour part-time; nonresident $23,040 full-time, $944 per credit hour part-time. No tuition increase for student's term of enrollment. ***Required fees:*** $2861 full-time, $115 per credit hour part-time. ***Room and board:*** $9156; room only: $4654. Room and board charges vary according to housing facility.

Financial Aid Of all full-time matriculated undergraduates who enrolled in 2017, 624 applied for aid, 473 were judged to have need, 61 had their need fully met. 177 Federal Work-Study jobs (averaging $800). In 2017, 49 non-need-based awards were made. ***Average percent of need met:*** 67. ***Average financial aid package:*** $14,145. ***Average need-based loan:*** $4590. ***Average need-based gift aid:*** $9222. ***Average non-need-based aid:*** $3313. ***Average indebtedness upon graduation:*** $28,551.

APPLYING

Standardized Tests *Required:* SAT or ACT (for admission).

Options: deferred entrance.

Application fee: $95.

Required: essay or personal statement, high school transcript, minimum 2.5 GPA, 2 letters of recommendation, interview, audition.

CONTACT

Mr. Paul Razza, Director of Admissions, University of North Carolina School of the Arts, 1533 South Main Street, PO Box 12189, Winston-Salem, NC 27127-2738. *Phone:* 336-770-3290. *Fax:* 336-770-3370. *E-mail:* razzap@uncsa.edu.

The University of North Carolina Wilmington

Wilmington, North Carolina

http://www.uncw.edu/

- **State-supported** comprehensive, founded 1947, part of University of North Carolina System
- **Urban** 661-acre campus
- **Endowment** $104.9 million
- **Coed** 14,785 undergraduate students, 84% full-time, 63% women, 37% men
- **Moderately difficult** entrance level, 65% of applicants were admitted

UNDERGRAD STUDENTS

12,480 full-time, 2,305 part-time. Students come from 56 states and territories; 65 other countries; 12% are from out of state; 4% Black or African American, non-Hispanic/Latino; 7% Hispanic/Latino; 2% Asian, non-Hispanic/Latino; 0.2% Native Hawaiian or other Pacific Islander, non-Hispanic/Latino; 0.4% American Indian or Alaska Native, non-Hispanic/Latino; 4% Two or more races, non-Hispanic/Latino; 2% Race/ethnicity unknown; 1% international; 14% transferred in; 25% live on campus.

Freshmen:

Admission: 13,287 applied, 8,697 admitted, 2,342 enrolled. ***Average high school GPA:*** 4.0. ***Test scores:*** SAT evidence-based reading and writing scores over 500: 100%; SAT math scores over 500: 99%; ACT scores over 18: 100%; SAT evidence-based reading and writing scores over 600: 74%; SAT math scores over 600: 65%; ACT scores over 24: 66%; SAT evidence-based reading and writing scores over 700: 8%; SAT math scores over 700: 10%; ACT scores over 30: 8%.

Retention: 86% of full-time freshmen returned.

FACULTY

Total: 1,110, 62% full-time, 65% with terminal degrees.

Student/faculty ratio: 18:1.

ACADEMICS

Calendar: semesters. *Degrees:* bachelor's, master's, doctoral, post-master's, and postbachelor's certificates.

Special study options: academic remediation for entering students, accelerated degree program, advanced placement credit, cooperative education, distance learning, double majors, English as a second language, honors programs, independent study, internships, off-campus study, services for LD students, study abroad, summer session for credit.

Unusual degree programs: 3-2 Computer Science, English, Exercise Science/Applied Gerontology, Mathematics, Public Health/Applied Gerontology, Recreation Therapy/Applied Gerontology, Secondary Education, Spanish.

Computers: 1,141 computers/terminals and 5,400 ports are available on campus for general student use. Students can access the following: campus intranet, computer help desk, free student e-mail accounts, online (class) grades, online (class) registration, online (class) schedules. Campuswide network is available. 100% of college-owned or -operated housing units are wired for high-speed Internet access. Wireless service is available via entire campus.

Library: William Madison Randall Library. *Books:* 482,109 (physical), 418,670 (digital/electronic); *Serial titles:* 3,636 (physical), 100,047 (digital/electronic); *Databases:* 358. Weekly public service hours: 137; study areas open 24 hours, 5–7 days a week; students can reserve study rooms.

STUDENT LIFE

Housing options: on-campus residence required for freshman year; coed, special housing for students with disabilities. Campus housing is university owned. Freshman applicants given priority for college housing.

Activities and organizations: drama/theater group, student-run newspaper, radio station, choral group, Student Government Association, Association of Campus Entertainment, Residence Hall Association, Sports Club Council, Graduate Student Association, national fraternities, national sororities.

Athletics Member NCAA. All Division I. ***Intercollegiate sports:*** baseball M(s), basketball M(s)/W(s), cheerleading M/W, cross-country running M(s)/W(s), golf M(s)/W(s), soccer M(s)/W(s), softball W(s), swimming and diving M(s)/W(s), tennis M(s)/W(s), track and field M(s)/W(s), volleyball W(s). ***Intramural sports:*** badminton M/W, baseball M(c), basketball M/W, equestrian sports W(c), field hockey W(c), football M/W, golf M(c)/W(c), gymnastics M(c)/W(c), ice hockey M(c), lacrosse M(c)/W(c), rowing M(c)/W(c), rugby M(c)/W(c), sand volleyball M/W, soccer M/W, softball W, swimming and diving M(c)/W(c), table tennis M/W, tennis M(c)/W(c), triathlon M(c)/W(c), ultimate Frisbee M/W, volleyball M(c)/W(c), water polo M(c)/W(c).

Campus security: 24-hour emergency response devices and patrols, late-night transport/escort service, controlled dormitory access.

Student services: health clinic, personal/psychological counseling, women's center, veterans affairs office.

COSTS & FINANCIAL AID

Costs (2019–20) ***Tuition:*** state resident $4443 full-time, $167 per credit hour part-time; nonresident $18,508 full-time, $695 per credit hour part-time. Full-time tuition and fees vary according to course load and location. Part-time tuition and fees vary according to course load and location. ***Required fees:*** $2738 full-time, $82 per credit hour part-time. ***Room and board:*** $10,897; room only: $6790. Room and board charges vary according to board plan and housing facility. ***Payment plan:*** installment. ***Waivers:*** employees or children of employees.

Financial Aid Of all full-time matriculated undergraduates who enrolled in 2018, 8,612 applied for aid, 6,772 were judged to have need, 755 had their need fully met. In 2018, 491 non-need-based awards were made. ***Average percent of need met:*** 42. ***Average financial aid package:*** $9430. ***Average need-based loan:*** $4166. ***Average need-based gift aid:*** $6635. ***Average non-need-based aid:*** $3238. ***Average indebtedness upon graduation:*** $26,568.

APPLYING

Standardized Tests *Required:* SAT or ACT (for admission).

Options: electronic application, early admission, early action, deferred entrance.

Application fee: $80.

Required: essay or personal statement, high school transcript, 1 letter of recommendation.

Application deadlines: 2/1 (freshmen), 3/1 (transfers), 11/1 (early action).

Notification: 3/15 (freshmen), 1/20 (early action).

CONTACT

UNCW Office of Admissions, The University of North Carolina Wilmington, 601 South College Road, Wilmington, NC 28403-3297. *Phone:* 910-962-3243. *Fax:* 910-962-3038. *E-mail:* admissions@uncw.edu.

Wake Forest University

Winston-Salem, North Carolina

http://www.wfu.edu/

- **Independent** university, founded 1834
- **Suburban** 340-acre campus
- **Coed** 5,287 undergraduate students, 99% full-time, 53% women, 47% men
- **Very difficult** entrance level, 30% of applicants were admitted

UNDERGRAD STUDENTS

5,240 full-time, 47 part-time. 78% are from out of state; 6% Black or African American, non-Hispanic/Latino; 7% Hispanic/Latino; 3% Asian, non-Hispanic/Latino; 0.1% American Indian or Alaska Native, non-Hispanic/Latino; 4% Two or more races, non-Hispanic/Latino; 10% international; 0.2% transferred in; 77% live on campus.

Freshmen:

Admission: 12,559 applied, 3,717 admitted, 1,360 enrolled. *Test scores:* SAT evidence-based reading and writing scores over 500: 98%; SAT math scores over 500: 99%; ACT scores over 18: 100%; SAT evidence-based reading and writing scores over 600: 91%; SAT math scores over 600: 89%; ACT scores over 24: 94%; SAT evidence-based reading and writing scores over 700: 44%; SAT math scores over 700: 61%; ACT scores over 30: 76%.

Retention: 94% of full-time freshmen returned.

FACULTY

Total: 824, 75% full-time.

Student/faculty ratio: 10:1.

ACADEMICS

Calendar: semesters. *Degrees:* bachelor's, master's, doctoral, and postbachelor's certificates.

Special study options: advanced placement credit, distance learning, double majors, honors programs, independent study, internships, part-time degree program, services for LD students, study abroad, summer session for credit. *ROTC:* Army (b).

Unusual degree programs: 3-2 engineering.

Computers: Students can access the following: campus intranet, computer help desk, free student e-mail accounts, online (class) grades, online (class) registration, online (class) schedules, financial information online, drop-add, transcript requests. Campuswide network is available. Wireless service is available via entire campus.

Library: Z. Smith Reynolds Library.

STUDENT LIFE

Housing options: on-campus residence required through sophomore year; coed. Campus housing is university owned. Freshman campus housing is guaranteed.

Activities and organizations: drama/theater group, student-run newspaper, radio and television station, choral group, marching band, national fraternities, national sororities.

Athletics Member NCAA. All Division I except football (Division I-A). *Intercollegiate sports:* baseball M(s), basketball M(s)/W(s), cross-country running M(s)/W(s), field hockey W(s), golf M(s)/W(s), soccer M(s)/W(s), tennis M(s)/W(s), track and field M(s)/W(s), volleyball W(s). *Intramural sports:* archery M(c)/W(c), baseball M(c), basketball M/W, bowling M/W, cheerleading M(c)/W(c), crew M(c)/W(c), cross-country running M(c)/W(c), equestrian sports M(c)/W(c), fencing M(c)/W(c), field hockey W(c), football M, golf M(c)/W(c), ice hockey M(c)/W(c), lacrosse M(c)/W(c), racquetball M/W, rugby M(c)/W(c), skiing (cross-country) M(c)/W(c), skiing (downhill) M(c)/W(c), soccer M(c)/W(c), softball M/W(c), swimming and diving M/W, table tennis M/W, tennis M/W, ultimate Frisbee M/W, volleyball M/W, water polo M(c)/W(c), wrestling M(c).

Campus security: 24-hour emergency response devices and patrols, late-night transport/escort service, controlled dormitory access.

Student services: health clinic, personal/psychological counseling.

COSTS & FINANCIAL AID

Costs (2020–21) ***Tuition:*** $56,722 full-time, $2352 per credit hour part-time. ***Required fees:*** $1038 full-time. ***Room only:*** $9848.

Financial Aid Of all full-time matriculated undergraduates who enrolled in 2019, 1,916 applied for aid, 1,508 were judged to have need, 1,508 had their need fully met. In 2019, 486 non-need-based awards were made. ***Average percent of need met:*** 100. ***Average financial aid package:*** $53,115. ***Average need-based loan:*** $4312. ***Average need-based gift aid:*** $50,178. ***Average non-need-based aid:*** $13,288. ***Average indebtedness upon graduation:*** $34,053. ***Financial aid deadline:*** 1/1.

APPLYING

Options: electronic application, early admission, early decision.

Application fee: $65.

Required: essay or personal statement, high school transcript, 1 letter of recommendation. ***Recommended:*** interview.

Early decision deadline: 11/15 (for plan 1), 1/1 (for plan 2).

Notification: continuous (freshmen), rolling (early decision plan 1), 2/15 (early decision plan 2).

CONTACT

Wake Forest University, 1834 Wake Forest Road, PO Box 7373 Reynolda Station, Winston-Salem, NC 27109. *Phone:* 336-758-5201.

Warren Wilson College

Swannanoa, North Carolina

http://www.warren-wilson.edu/

- **Independent** comprehensive, founded 1894, affiliated with Presbyterian Church (U.S.A.)
- **Suburban** 1135-acre campus with easy access to Asheville, North Carolina
- **Endowment** $51.7 million
- **Coed** 706 undergraduate students, 97% full-time, 67% women, 33% men
- **Moderately difficult** entrance level, 85% of applicants were admitted

UNDERGRAD STUDENTS

688 full-time, 18 part-time. 62% are from out of state; 6% transferred in; 88% live on campus.

Freshmen:

Admission: 1,195 applied, 1,011 admitted, 235 enrolled.

Retention: 62% of full-time freshmen returned.

FACULTY

Total: 103, 61% full-time, 81% with terminal degrees.

Student/faculty ratio: 10:1.

ACADEMICS

Calendar: semesters. *Degrees:* bachelor's and master's.

Special study options: advanced placement credit, cooperative education, double majors, English as a second language, honors programs, independent study, internships, off-campus study, part-time degree program, services for LD students, student-designed majors, study abroad, summer session for credit.

Computers: Students can access the following: campus intranet, computer help desk, free student e-mail accounts, online (class) grades, online (class) registration, online (class) schedules, home directory and public html for each user, word processing, GIS, Statistical Analysis. Campuswide network is available. 100% of college-owned or -operated housing units are wired for high-speed Internet access. Wireless service is available via entire campus.

Library: Pew Learning Center and Ellison Library.

STUDENT LIFE

Housing options: on-campus residence required for freshman year; coed, men-only, women-only, cooperative. Campus housing is university owned. Freshman campus housing is guaranteed.

Activities and organizations: drama/theater group, student-run newspaper, choral group, Food Not Bombs, Club Sports: Paddling, Cycling, Cyclocross, Timbersports, Multicultural Student Organizations: Engage, WHOLA, Peace, Social and Environmental Justice Groups, Student Religious Groups: Christian, Jewish, Buddhist, Quaker, Pagan, and Unitarian Universalist.

Athletics Member NCAA, USCAA. All Division III. ***Intercollegiate sports:*** basketball M/W, cross-country running M/W, lacrosse M/W, soccer M/W, swimming and diving M/W, tennis M/W. ***Intramural sports:*** fencing M/W, golf M/W, rock climbing M/W, skiing (downhill) M(c)/W(c), soccer M/W, softball M/W, table tennis M/W, ultimate Frisbee M/W, volleyball M/W, weight lifting M/W.

Campus security: 24-hour emergency response devices and patrols, student patrols, late-night transport/escort service, controlled dormitory access.

Student services: health clinic, personal/psychological counseling.

COSTS & FINANCIAL AID

Costs (2020–21) ***Comprehensive fee:*** $50,100 includes full-time tuition ($37,500), mandatory fees ($850), and room and board ($11,750). Part-time tuition and fees vary according to course load. ***Room and board:*** Room and board charges vary according to board plan. ***Payment plan:*** installment. ***Waivers:*** employees or children of employees.

Financial Aid Of all full-time matriculated undergraduates who enrolled in 2016, 512 applied for aid, 464 were judged to have need, 152 had their need fully met. In 2016, 157 non-need-based awards were made. ***Average percent of need met:*** 84. ***Average financial aid package:*** $30,450. ***Average need-based loan:*** $4047. ***Average need-based gift aid:*** $22,864. ***Average non-need-based aid:*** $10,088. ***Average indebtedness upon graduation:*** $25,740.

APPLYING

Options: electronic application, early admission, early decision, early action, deferred entrance.

Required: essay or personal statement, high school transcript, Common Application, Common Application School Report Form. ***Recommended:*** letters of recommendation, interview.

CONTACT

Monique Cote, Campus Visit Coordinator, Warren Wilson College, PO Box 9000, Asheville, NC 28815-9000. *Phone:* 828-771-2073. *Toll-free phone:* 800-934-3536. *Fax:* 828-298-1440. *E-mail:* admit@warren-wilson.edu.

Western Carolina University

Cullowhee, North Carolina

http://www.wcu.edu/

- **State-supported** university, founded 1889, part of University of North Carolina System
- **Rural** 682-acre campus
- **Coed** 10,469 undergraduate students, 85% full-time, 55% women, 45% men
- **Moderately difficult** entrance level, 43% of applicants were admitted

UNDERGRAD STUDENTS

8,934 full-time, 1,535 part-time. 10% are from out of state; 5% Black or African American, non-Hispanic/Latino; 7% Hispanic/Latino; 1% Asian, non-Hispanic/Latino; 0.8% American Indian or Alaska Native, non-Hispanic/Latino; 4% Two or more races, non-Hispanic/Latino; 1% Race/ethnicity unknown; 2% international; 10% transferred in.

Freshmen:

Admission: 17,766 applied, 7,614 admitted, 2,106 enrolled. ***Average high school GPA:*** 3.8. ***Test scores:*** SAT evidence-based reading and writing scores over 500: 83%; SAT math scores over 500: 84%; ACT scores over 18: 83%; SAT evidence-based reading and writing scores over 600: 32%; SAT math scores over 600: 24%; ACT scores over 24: 32%; SAT evidence-based reading and writing scores over 700: 4%; SAT math scores over 700: 2%; ACT scores over 30: 4%.

Retention: 78% of full-time freshmen returned.

FACULTY

Total: 772, 68% full-time, 66% with terminal degrees.

Student/faculty ratio: 17:1.

ACADEMICS

Calendar: semesters. *Degrees:* bachelor's, master's, doctoral, post-master's, and postbachelor's certificates.

Special study options: advanced placement credit, cooperative education, distance learning, double majors, English as a second language, honors programs, independent study, internships, part-time degree program, services for LD students, student-designed majors, study abroad, summer session for credit.

Computers: Students can access the following: campus intranet, computer help desk, free student e-mail accounts, online (class) grades, online (class) registration, online (class) schedules. Campuswide network is available. 100% of college-owned or -operated housing units are wired for high-speed Internet access. Wireless service is available via entire campus.

Library: Hunter Library. Weekly public service hours: 96; study areas open 24 hours, 5–7 days a week; students can reserve study rooms.

STUDENT LIFE

Housing options: on-campus residence required for freshman year; coed, men-only, women-only, special housing for students with disabilities. Campus housing is university owned. Freshman campus housing is guaranteed.

Activities and organizations: drama/theater group, student-run newspaper, radio and television station, choral group, marching band, national fraternities, national sororities.

Athletics Member NCAA. All Division I except football (Division I-AA). ***Intercollegiate sports:*** baseball M(s), basketball M(s)/W(s), cheerleading M/W, cross-country running M(s)/W(s), equestrian sports M(c)/W(c), fencing M(c)/W(c), golf M(s)/W(s), rock climbing M(c)/W(c), rugby M(c), soccer W(s), softball W(s), swimming and diving M(c)/W(c), tennis M(c)/W(s), track and field M(s)/W(s), ultimate Frisbee M(c)/W(c), volleyball W(s), wrestling M(c). ***Intramural sports:*** badminton M/W, basketball M/W, bowling M/W, cross-country running M/W, racquetball M/W, soccer M/W, softball M/W, swimming and diving M/W, table tennis M/W, tennis M/W, ultimate Frisbee M/W, volleyball M/W, water polo M/W, weight lifting M/W, wrestling M/W.

Campus security: 24-hour emergency response devices and patrols, late-night transport/escort service, controlled dormitory access.

Student services: health clinic, personal/psychological counseling, women's center, veterans affairs office.

COSTS & FINANCIAL AID

Costs (2020–21) ***Tuition:*** state resident $1000 full-time; nonresident $5000 full-time. Full-time tuition and fees vary according to degree level. Part-time tuition and fees vary according to course load and degree level. No tuition increase for student's term of enrollment. ***Room and board:*** Room and board charges vary according to board plan and housing facility. ***Payment plan:*** installment.

Financial Aid Of all full-time matriculated undergraduates who enrolled in 2018, 6,215 applied for aid, 5,085 were judged to have need, 672 had their need fully met. In 2018, 395 non-need-based awards were made. ***Average percent of need met:*** 65. ***Average financial aid package:*** $11,296. ***Average need-based loan:*** $6029. ***Average need-based gift aid:*** $6323. ***Average non-need-based aid:*** $2379. ***Average indebtedness upon graduation:*** $20,123.

APPLYING

Standardized Tests *Required:* SAT or ACT (for admission). *Recommended:* ACT (for admission).

Options: electronic application, early admission, early action.

Application fee: $65.

Required: high school transcript.

CONTACT

Office of Undergraduate Admission, Western Carolina University, 102 Camp Building, Cullowhee, NC 28723. *Phone:* 828-227-7317. *Toll-free phone:* 877-WCU4YOU. *E-mail:* admiss@email.wcu.edu.

William Peace University
Raleigh, North Carolina
http://www.peace.edu/

- **Independent** 4-year, founded 1857, affiliated with Presbyterian Church (U.S.A.)
- **Urban** 21-acre campus with easy access to Raleigh-Cary
- **Endowment** $50.2 million
- **Coed** 889 undergraduate students, 90% full-time, 54% women, 46% men
- **Moderately difficult** entrance level, 46% of applicants were admitted

UNDERGRAD STUDENTS
802 full-time, 87 part-time. Students come from 24 states and territories; 3 other countries; 13% are from out of state; 24% Black or African American, non-Hispanic/Latino; 12% Hispanic/Latino; 2% Asian, non-Hispanic/Latino; 0.1% Native Hawaiian or other Pacific Islander, non-Hispanic/Latino; 0.8% American Indian or Alaska Native, non-Hispanic/Latino; 5% Two or more races, non-Hispanic/Latino; 3% Race/ethnicity unknown; 0.4% international; 11% transferred in; 52% live on campus.

Freshmen:
Admission: 2,129 applied, 978 admitted, 185 enrolled. ***Average high school GPA:*** 3.9. ***Test scores:*** SAT evidence-based reading and writing scores over 500: 59%; SAT math scores over 500: 59%; ACT scores over 18: 77%; SAT evidence-based reading and writing scores over 600: 19%; SAT math scores over 600: 13%; ACT scores over 24: 15%; SAT evidence-based reading and writing scores over 700: 2%; SAT math scores over 700: 2%; ACT scores over 30: 2%.

Retention: 66% of full-time freshmen returned.

FACULTY
Total: 124, 31% full-time, 43% with terminal degrees.

Student/faculty ratio: 12:1.

ACADEMICS
Calendar: semesters. *Degree:* bachelor's.

Special study options: academic remediation for entering students, accelerated degree program, adult/continuing education programs, advanced placement credit, distance learning, double majors, honors programs, independent study, internships, off-campus study, part-time degree program, services for LD students, study abroad, summer session for credit. ***ROTC:*** Army (c), Navy (c), Air Force (c).

Computers: 87 computers/terminals are available on campus for general student use. Students can access the following: campus intranet, computer help desk, free student e-mail accounts, online (class) grades, online (class) registration, online (class) schedules. Campuswide network is available. 100% of college-owned or -operated housing units are wired for high-speed Internet access. Wireless service is available via entire campus.

Library: Lucy Cooper Finch Library. *Books:* 26,903 (physical), 435,204 (digital/electronic); *Serial titles:* 12 (physical), 24,504 (digital/electronic); *Databases:* 96. Weekly public service hours: 90.

STUDENT LIFE
Housing options: on-campus residence required through junior year; coed, special housing for students with disabilities. Campus housing is university owned. Freshman campus housing is guaranteed.

Activities and organizations: drama/theater group, student-run newspaper, choral group, Campus Activities Board, Psychology Club, Black Student Union, 15 Below Student Theatre Company, Political Science Club.

Athletics Member NCAA. All Division III. ***Intercollegiate sports:*** baseball M, basketball M/W, cross-country running M/W, golf M, lacrosse M/W, soccer M/W, softball W, swimming and diving M/W, tennis M/W, track and field M/W, volleyball W. ***Intramural sports:*** basketball M/W, equestrian sports M/W, football M/W, sand volleyball M/W, soccer M/W, volleyball M/W.

Campus security: 24-hour emergency response devices and patrols, late-night transport/escort service, controlled dormitory access.

Student services: health clinic, personal/psychological counseling.

COSTS & FINANCIAL AID
Costs (2020–21) ***Comprehensive fee:*** $44,250 includes full-time tuition ($31,950), mandatory fees ($500), and room and board ($11,800). Full-time tuition and fees vary according to class time, course load, and program. Part-time tuition: $1065 per credit hour. Part-time tuition and fees vary according to class time, course load, and program. ***College room only:*** $7920. Room and board charges vary according to board plan and housing facility. ***Payment plan:*** installment. ***Waivers:*** employees or children of employees.

Financial Aid Of all full-time matriculated undergraduates who enrolled in 2019, 721 applied for aid, 709 were judged to have need, 69 had their need fully met. In 2019, 59 non-need-based awards were made. ***Average financial aid package:*** $23,386. ***Average need-based loan:*** $4108. ***Average need-based gift aid:*** $11,582. ***Average non-need-based aid:*** $7696. ***Average indebtedness upon graduation:*** $26,929.

APPLYING
Standardized Tests *Required:* SAT or ACT (for admission).

Options: electronic application, early admission, deferred entrance.

Application fee: $35.

Required: minimum 2.0 GPA, interview, Dean's Evaluation (transfers). ***Recommended:*** essay or personal statement, 2 letters of recommendation, interview.

Application deadlines: rolling (freshmen), rolling (out-of-state freshmen), rolling (transfers).

Notification: continuous (freshmen), continuous (out-of-state freshmen), continuous (transfers), rolling (early action).

CONTACT
Office of Admissions, William Peace University, 15 East Peace Street, Raleigh, NC 27604. *Phone:* 919-508-2214. *Fax:* 919-508-2326. *E-mail:* admission@peace.edu.

Wingate University
Wingate, North Carolina
http://www.wingate.edu/

- **Independent Baptist** comprehensive, founded 1896
- **Small-town** 400-acre campus with easy access to Charlotte, NC
- **Coed** 2,764 undergraduate students, 98% full-time, 61% women, 39% men
- **Moderately difficult** entrance level, 90% of applicants were admitted

UNDERGRAD STUDENTS
2,706 full-time, 58 part-time. Students come from 39 states and territories; 46 other countries; 27% are from out of state; 20% Black or African American, non-Hispanic/Latino; 2% Hispanic/Latino; 2% Asian, non-Hispanic/Latino; 0.1% Native Hawaiian or other Pacific Islander, non-Hispanic/Latino; 0.2% American Indian or Alaska Native, non-Hispanic/Latino; 8% Two or more races, non-Hispanic/Latino; 9% Race/ethnicity unknown; 4% international; 3% transferred in; 76% live on campus.

Freshmen:
Admission: 17,353 applied, 15,553 admitted, 944 enrolled. ***Average high school GPA:*** 3.3. ***Test scores:*** ACT scores over 18: 94%; ACT scores over 24: 37%; ACT scores over 30: 6%.

Retention: 68% of full-time freshmen returned.

FACULTY
Total: 366, 53% full-time, 61% with terminal degrees.

Student/faculty ratio: 16:1.

ACADEMICS
Calendar: semesters. *Degrees:* bachelor's, master's, doctoral, and post-master's certificates.

Special study options: adult/continuing education programs, advanced placement credit, double majors, honors programs, independent study, internships, off-campus study, part-time degree program, services for LD students, study abroad, summer session for credit. ***ROTC:*** Army (c), Air Force (c).

Computers: Students can access the following: campus intranet, computer help desk, free student e-mail accounts, online (class) grades, online (class) registration, online (class) schedules. Campuswide network is available. 100% of college-owned or -operated housing units are wired for high-speed Internet access. Wireless service is available via entire campus.

Library: Ethel K. Smith Library. Students can reserve study rooms.

STUDENT LIFE
Housing options: on-campus residence required through senior year; coed, men-only, women-only, cooperative, special housing for students with disabilities. Campus housing is university owned. Freshman campus housing is guaranteed.

Activities and organizations: drama/theater group, student-run newspaper, television station, choral group, University and Community Assistance Network (UCAN), Bulldog Activities Resource Committee, Fellowship of Christian Athletes, Student Bulldog Club, Student Government Association, national fraternities, national sororities.

Athletics Member NCAA. All Division II. ***Intercollegiate sports:*** baseball M(s), basketball M(s)/W(s), cross-country running M(s)/W(s), football M(s), golf M(s)/W(s), lacrosse M(s)/W(s), soccer M(s)/W(s), softball W(s), swimming and diving M(s)/W(s), tennis M(s)/W(s), track and field M(s)/W(s), volleyball W(s). ***Intramural sports:*** basketball M/W, bowling M/W, cross-country running M/W, football M/W, golf M/W, racquetball M/W, swimming and diving M/W, table tennis M/W, tennis M/W, track and field M/W, ultimate Frisbee M/W, volleyball M/W, water polo M/W, weight lifting M/W.

Campus security: 24-hour emergency response devices and patrols, late-night transport/escort service, controlled dormitory access.

Student services: health clinic, personal/psychological counseling.

COSTS & FINANCIAL AID
Costs (2020–21) ***One-time required fee:*** $100. ***Comprehensive fee:*** $48,806 includes full-time tuition ($38,796), mandatory fees ($100), and room and board ($9910).

Financial Aid Of all full-time matriculated undergraduates who enrolled in 2019, 2,330 applied for aid, 2,163 were judged to have need, 560 had their need fully met. In 2019, 525 non-need-based awards were made. ***Average percent of need met:*** 83. ***Average financial aid package:*** $31,028. ***Average need-based loan:*** $3179. ***Average need-based gift aid:*** $27,513. ***Average non-need-based aid:*** $23,310. ***Average indebtedness upon graduation:*** $29,823.

APPLYING
Standardized Tests *Required:* SAT or ACT (for admission).

Options: electronic application, deferred entrance.

Required: high school transcript, minimum 2.7 GPA. ***Required for some:*** essay or personal statement. ***Recommended:*** letters of recommendation, interview.

Application deadlines: rolling (freshmen), rolling (transfers).

Notification: continuous (freshmen), continuous (transfers).

CONTACT
Kayla Cherry, Associate Director, First-year Admissions, Wingate University, PO Box 159, Wingate, NC 28174. *Phone:* 704-233-8000. *Toll-free phone:* 800-755-5550. *Fax:* 704-233-8110. *E-mail:* admit@wingate.edu.

Winston-Salem State University
Winston-Salem, North Carolina
http://www.wssu.edu/

- **State-supported** comprehensive, founded 1892, part of University of North Carolina System
- **Urban** 94-acre campus
- **Endowment** $19.5 million
- **Coed**
- **Minimally difficult** entrance level

FACULTY
Student/faculty ratio: 14:1.

ACADEMICS
Calendar: semesters. *Degrees:* certificates, bachelor's, master's, and postbachelor's certificates.
Library: O'Kelly Library.

STUDENT LIFE
Housing options: coed, men-only, women-only. Campus housing is university owned and is provided by a third party. Freshman applicants given priority for college housing.

Activities and organizations: drama/theater group, student-run newspaper, radio station, choral group, marching band, national fraternities, national sororities.

Athletics Member NCAA. All Division I.

Campus security: 24-hour emergency response devices and patrols.

Student services: health clinic, personal/psychological counseling, women's center.

FINANCIAL AID
Financial Aid Of all full-time matriculated undergraduates who enrolled in 2006, 1,611 applied for aid, 1,095 were judged to have need, 354 had their need fully met. 258 Federal Work-Study jobs (averaging $1361). 26 state and other part-time jobs (averaging $2755). In 2006, 54 non-need-based awards were made. ***Average percent of need met:*** 71. ***Average financial aid package:*** $5602. ***Average need-based loan:*** $2926. ***Average need-based gift aid:*** $2350. ***Average non-need-based aid:*** $4414. ***Average indebtedness upon graduation:*** $10,200. ***Financial aid deadline:*** 4/1.

APPLYING
Standardized Tests *Required:* SAT or ACT (for admission).

Options: deferred entrance.

Application fee: $50.

Required: high school transcript. ***Recommended:*** 1 letter of recommendation.

CONTACT
Ms. Tomikia LeGrande, Assistant Vice Chancellor for Enrollment Services, Winston-Salem State University, 601 Martin Luther King, Jr. Drive, Thompson Center, Winston-Salem, NC 27110. *Phone:* 336-750-2070. *Toll-free phone:* 800-257-4052. *Fax:* 336-750-2079. *E-mail:* legrandet@wssu.edu.

NORTH DAKOTA

Bismarck State College
Bismarck, North Dakota
http://www.bismarckstate.edu/

CONTACT
Karen Erickson, Director of Admissions and Enrollment Services, Bismarck State College, PO Box 5587, Bismarck, ND 58506. *Phone:* 701-224-5424. *Toll-free phone:* 800-445-5073. *Fax:* 701-224-5643. *E-mail:* karen.erickson@bismarckstate.edu.

Dickinson State University
Dickinson, North Dakota
http://www.dickinsonstate.edu/

- **State-supported** comprehensive, founded 1918, part of North Dakota University System
- **Small-town** 132-acre campus
- **Coed** 1,321 undergraduate students, 70% full-time, 62% women, 38% men
- **Minimally difficult** entrance level, 100% of applicants were admitted

UNDERGRAD STUDENTS
922 full-time, 399 part-time. Students come from 33 states and territories; 18 other countries; 24% are from out of state; 4% Black or African American, non-Hispanic/Latino; 6% Hispanic/Latino; 1% Asian, non-Hispanic/Latino; 0.3% Native Hawaiian or other Pacific Islander, non-Hispanic/Latino; 2% American Indian or Alaska Native, non-Hispanic/Latino; 3% Two or more races, non-Hispanic/Latino; 1% Race/ethnicity unknown; 4% international; 17% transferred in; 16% live on campus.

Freshmen:
Admission: 376 applied, 375 admitted, 202 enrolled. ***Average high school GPA:*** 3.3. ***Test scores:*** SAT evidence-based reading and writing scores over 500: 63%; SAT math scores over 500: 78%; ACT scores over 18: 76%; SAT evidence-based reading and writing scores over 600: 13%; SAT

math scores over 600: 22%; ACT scores over 24: 19%; ACT scores over 30: 1%.

Retention: 68% of full-time freshmen returned.

FACULTY

Total: 128, 53% full-time, 28% with terminal degrees.

Student/faculty ratio: 12:1.

ACADEMICS

Calendar: semesters. *Degrees:* certificates, associate, bachelor's, and master's.

Special study options: academic remediation for entering students, adult/continuing education programs, advanced placement credit, cooperative education, distance learning, double majors, English as a second language, honors programs, independent study, internships, off-campus study, part-time degree program, services for LD students, study abroad, summer session for credit.

Computers: 274 computers/terminals and 350 ports are available on campus for general student use. Students can access the following: campus intranet, computer help desk, free student e-mail accounts, online (class) grades, online (class) registration, online (class) schedules. Campuswide network is available. 100% of college-owned or -operated housing units are wired for high-speed Internet access. Wireless service is available via entire campus.

Library: Stoxen Library plus 1 other. *Books:* 73,995 (physical), 26,601 (digital/electronic); *Serial titles:* 282 (physical), 126,440 (digital/electronic); *Databases:* 91. Weekly public service hours: 56.

STUDENT LIFE

Housing options: on-campus residence required through sophomore year; coed, men-only, women-only, special housing for students with disabilities. Campus housing is university owned. Freshman campus housing is guaranteed.

Activities and organizations: drama/theater group, choral group, Rodeo Club, chorale, Business Club, Nursing Student Association, Campus Activities Board, national fraternities.

Athletics Member NAIA. ***Intercollegiate sports:*** baseball M(s), basketball M(s)/W(s), cross-country running M(s)/W(s), football M(s), golf M(s)/W(s), softball W(s), track and field M(s)/W(s), volleyball W(s), wrestling M(s). ***Intramural sports:*** basketball M/W, soccer M/W, softball M/W, squash M/W, table tennis M/W, tennis M/W, ultimate Frisbee M/W, volleyball M/W.

Campus security: 24-hour emergency response devices and patrols, late-night transport/escort service, controlled dormitory access, Crisis Manager App. for Phones, Automated Mass Notification System.

Student services: health clinic, veterans affairs office.

COSTS & FINANCIAL AID

Costs (2020–21) ***Tuition:*** area resident $6522 full-time, $251 per credit hour part-time; state resident $6522 full-time, $251 per credit hour part-time; nonresident $9783 full-time, $376 per semester hour part-time. Full-time tuition and fees vary according to course load and reciprocity agreements. Part-time tuition and fees vary according to course load and reciprocity agreements. ***Required fees:*** $1262 full-time, $53 per credit hour part-time, $315 per term part-time. ***Room and board:*** $7686; room only: $3448. Room and board charges vary according to board plan, housing facility, and student level. ***Payment plan:*** installment. ***Waivers:*** employees or children of employees.

Financial Aid Of all full-time matriculated undergraduates who enrolled in 2017, 686 applied for aid, 483 were judged to have need, 176 had their need fully met. In 2017, 66 non-need-based awards were made. ***Average percent of need met:*** 61. ***Average financial aid package:*** $11,224. ***Average need-based loan:*** $6132. ***Average need-based gift aid:*** $5475. ***Average non-need-based aid:*** $1985. ***Average indebtedness upon graduation:*** $21,356.

APPLYING

Standardized Tests *Required for some:* SAT or ACT (for admission).

Options: electronic application, deferred entrance.

Application fee: $35.

Required: high school transcript, minimum 2.0 GPA. ***Required for some:*** essay or personal statement, medical history, proof of measles-rubella shot.

Application deadlines: 8/15 (freshmen), 8/15 (transfers).

Notification: continuous (freshmen), continuous (transfers).

CONTACT

Ms. Megan Robinson, Assistant Director, Dickinson State University, Dickinson, ND 58601. *Phone:* 701-483-2164. *Toll-free phone:* 800-279-4295. *E-mail:* megan.robinson@dickinsonstate.edu.

Mayville State University

Mayville, North Dakota

http://www.mayvillestate.edu/

- **State-supported** 4-year, founded 1889, part of North Dakota University System
- **Rural** 60-acre campus
- **Coed** 1,187 undergraduate students, 50% full-time, 64% women, 36% men
- **Noncompetitive** entrance level

UNDERGRAD STUDENTS

589 full-time, 598 part-time. Students come from 49 states and territories; 7 other countries; 33% are from out of state; 5% Black or African American, non-Hispanic/Latino; 7% Hispanic/Latino; 0.8% Asian, non-Hispanic/Latino; 0.5% Native Hawaiian or other Pacific Islander, non-Hispanic/Latino; 2% American Indian or Alaska Native, non-Hispanic/Latino; 4% Two or more races, non-Hispanic/Latino; 0.6% Race/ethnicity unknown; 4% international; 55% transferred in.

Freshmen:

Admission: 109 enrolled. ***Average high school GPA:*** 3.1. ***Test scores:*** ACT scores over 18: 55%; ACT scores over 24: 14%; ACT scores over 30: 1%.

Retention: 61% of full-time freshmen returned.

FACULTY

Total: 115, 42% full-time, 18% with terminal degrees.

Student/faculty ratio: 13:1.

ACADEMICS

Calendar: semesters. *Degrees:* certificates, associate, bachelor's, and master's.

Special study options: academic remediation for entering students, accelerated degree program, adult/continuing education programs, advanced placement credit, cooperative education, distance learning, double majors, independent study, internships, off-campus study, part-time degree program, services for LD students, student-designed majors, study abroad, summer session for credit. ***ROTC:*** Army (c), Air Force (c).

Computers: Students can access the following: campus intranet, computer help desk, free student e-mail accounts, online (class) grades, online (class) registration, online (class) schedules. Campuswide network is available. 100% of college-owned or -operated housing units are wired for high-speed Internet access. Wireless service is available via entire campus.

Library: Byrnes-Quanbeck Library plus 1 other.

STUDENT LIFE

Housing options: on-campus residence required through sophomore year; coed, men-only, women-only. Campus housing is university owned. Freshman campus housing is guaranteed.

Activities and organizations: drama/theater group, student-run newspaper, radio station, choral group, Student Activities Council, Student Education Association, Health and Physical Education Club, Campus Crusade, Student Ambassadors.

Athletics Member NAIA. ***Intercollegiate sports:*** baseball M(s), basketball M(s)/W(s), football M(s), softball W(s), volleyball W(s). ***Intramural sports:*** basketball M/W, bowling M/W, football M/W, golf M/W, ice hockey M, racquetball M/W, soccer M/W, softball M/W, table tennis M/W, tennis M/W, track and field M/W, volleyball M/W.

Campus security: controlled dormitory access.

Student services: health clinic, personal/psychological counseling.

FINANCIAL AID

Financial Aid Of all full-time matriculated undergraduates who enrolled in 2019, 480 applied for aid, 367 were judged to have need, 118 had their need fully met. 36 Federal Work-Study jobs (averaging $39,218). In 2019, 70 non-need-based awards were made. ***Average percent of need met:*** 72.

Average financial aid package: $11,685. *Average need-based loan:* $6556. *Average need-based gift aid:* $5585. *Average non-need-based aid:* $1388. *Average indebtedness upon graduation:* $31,839.

APPLYING

Standardized Tests *Required:* SAT or ACT (for admission).

Options: electronic application, deferred entrance.

Application fee: $35.

Required: high school transcript.

Application deadlines: rolling (freshmen), rolling (transfers).

Notification: continuous until 1/1 (freshmen), continuous until 1/1 (transfers).

CONTACT

Jim Morowski, Director of Freshmen Enrollment Services, Mayville State University, 330 3rd Street, NE, Mayville, ND 58257-1299. *Phone:* 701-788-4842. *Toll-free phone:* 800-437-4104. *Fax:* 701-788-4748. *E-mail:* james.morowski@mayvillestate.edu.

Minot State University

Minot, North Dakota

http://www.minotstateu.edu/

- **State-supported** comprehensive, founded 1913, part of North Dakota University System
- **Small-town** 103-acre campus
- **Coed** 2,832 undergraduate students, 68% full-time, 61% women, 39% men
- **Moderately difficult** entrance level, 74% of applicants were admitted

UNDERGRAD STUDENTS

1,921 full-time, 911 part-time. 20% are from out of state; 4% Black or African American, non-Hispanic/Latino; 8% Hispanic/Latino; 1% Asian, non-Hispanic/Latino; 0.5% Native Hawaiian or other Pacific Islander, non-Hispanic/Latino; 2% American Indian or Alaska Native, non-Hispanic/Latino; 4% Two or more races, non-Hispanic/Latino; 1% Race/ethnicity unknown; 11% international; 11% transferred in; 14% live on campus.

Freshmen:

Admission: 787 applied, 583 admitted, 399 enrolled. *Average high school GPA:* 3.4. *Test scores:* SAT evidence-based reading and writing scores over 500: 66%; SAT math scores over 500: 61%; ACT scores over 18: 70%; SAT math scores over 600: 11%; ACT scores over 24: 19%; ACT scores over 30: 1%.

Retention: 72% of full-time freshmen returned.

FACULTY

Total: 312, 47% full-time, 29% with terminal degrees.

Student/faculty ratio: 11:1.

ACADEMICS

Calendar: semesters. *Degrees:* certificates, associate, bachelor's, master's, and postbachelor's certificates.

Special study options: academic remediation for entering students, accelerated degree program, advanced placement credit, cooperative education, distance learning, double majors, English as a second language, honors programs, independent study, internships, part-time degree program, services for LD students, student-designed majors, study abroad, summer session for credit.

Computers: Students can access the following: campus intranet, computer help desk, free student e-mail accounts, online (class) grades, online (class) registration, online (class) schedules. Campuswide network is available. Wireless service is available via entire campus.

Library: Gordon B. Olson Library.

STUDENT LIFE

Housing options: on-campus residence required for freshman year; coed, men-only, women-only, special housing for students with disabilities. Campus housing is university owned. Freshman campus housing is guaranteed.

Activities and organizations: drama/theater group, student-run newspaper, radio and television station, choral group, marching band, Residence Hall Association, Student Government Association, Beavers on Business, Student Social Work Organization, National Student Speech and Hearing Association.

Athletics Member NCAA, NAIA, NCCAA. All NCAA Division II. *Intercollegiate sports:* baseball M(s), basketball M(s)/W(s), cheerleading W, cross-country running M(s)/W(s), football M(s), golf M, ice hockey M(c), soccer W, softball W(s), track and field M(s)/W(s), volleyball W(s), wrestling M. *Intramural sports:* basketball M/W, racquetball M/W, softball M/W, volleyball M/W.

Campus security: controlled dormitory access, patrols by trained security personnel.

Student services: health clinic, personal/psychological counseling, women's center.

COSTS & FINANCIAL AID

Costs (2019–20) *Tuition:* state resident $6087 full-time, $254 per credit hour part-time; nonresident $6087 full-time, $254 per credit hour part-time. Full-time tuition and fees vary according to class time, course load, degree level, location, program, and reciprocity agreements. Part-time tuition and fees vary according to class time, course load, degree level, location, program, and reciprocity agreements. *Required fees:* $1503 full-time, $63 per credit hour part-time. *Room and board:* $7315; room only: $2865. Room and board charges vary according to board plan and housing facility. *Payment plan:* installment. *Waivers:* minority students, children of alumni, senior citizens, and employees or children of employees.

Financial Aid Of all full-time matriculated undergraduates who enrolled in 2017, 1,347 applied for aid, 924 were judged to have need, 329 had their need fully met. 89 Federal Work-Study jobs (averaging $1561). In 2017, 313 non-need-based awards were made. *Average percent of need met:* 70. *Average financial aid package:* $10,459. *Average need-based loan:* $6081. *Average need-based gift aid:* $5588. *Average non-need-based aid:* $1438. *Average indebtedness upon graduation:* $23,282.

APPLYING

Standardized Tests *Required:* SAT or ACT (for admission).

Options: electronic application, deferred entrance.

Application fee: $35.

Required: high school transcript. *Required for some:* minimum 2.5 GPA.

CONTACT

Mr. Kevin Harmon, Vice President of Enrollment Management, Minot State University, 500 University Avenue West, Minot, ND 58707-0002. *Phone:* 701-858-3126. *Toll-free phone:* 800-777-0750 Ext. 3350. *Fax:* 701-858-3825. *E-mail:* askmsu@minotstateu.edu.

North Dakota State University

Fargo, North Dakota

http://www.ndsu.edu/

- **State-supported** university, founded 1890, part of North Dakota University System
- **Urban** 2100-acre campus
- **Endowment** $512,215
- **Coed**
- **Moderately difficult** entrance level

FACULTY

Student/faculty ratio: 17:1.

ACADEMICS

Calendar: semesters. *Degrees:* certificates, bachelor's, master's, doctoral, post-master's, and postbachelor's certificates.

Library: North Dakota State University Library plus 6 others. *Books:* 662,884 (physical), 162,977 (digital/electronic); *Serial titles:* 171,924 (physical), 99,565 (digital/electronic); *Databases:* 232. Weekly public service hours: 93; students can reserve study rooms.

STUDENT LIFE

Housing options: on-campus residence required for freshman year; coed, men-only, women-only, special housing for students with disabilities. Campus housing is university owned. Freshman campus housing is guaranteed.

Activities and organizations: drama/theater group, student-run newspaper, radio and television station, choral group, marching band, Saddle and Sirloin, Students Today, Leaders Forever, Chi Alpha Christian

Organization, fraternities/sororities, CRU, national fraternities, national sororities.

Athletics Member NCAA. All Division I.

Campus security: 24-hour emergency response devices and patrols, late-night transport/escort service, controlled dormitory access, Pathlight app.

Student services: health clinic, personal/psychological counseling, veterans affairs office.

COSTS & FINANCIAL AID

Costs (2019–20) ***One-time required fee:*** $135. ***Tuition:*** state resident $8275 full-time, $341 per credit hour part-time; nonresident $12,413 full-time, $511 per credit hour part-time. Full-time tuition and fees vary according to course load, program, and reciprocity agreements. Part-time tuition and fees vary according to course load, program, and reciprocity agreements. ***Required fees:*** $1344 full-time, $56 per credit hour part-time. ***Room and board:*** $8878; room only: $4100. Room and board charges vary according to board plan and housing facility.

Financial Aid Of all full-time matriculated undergraduates who enrolled in 2018, 7,913 applied for aid, 5,288 were judged to have need, 1,794 had their need fully met. 239 Federal Work-Study jobs (averaging $2429). In 2018, 1203 non-need-based awards were made. ***Average percent of need met:*** 66. ***Average financial aid package:*** $12,117. ***Average need-based loan:*** $6977. ***Average need-based gift aid:*** $5640. ***Average non-need-based aid:*** $2508. ***Average indebtedness upon graduation:*** $33,639.

APPLYING

Standardized Tests *Required:* SAT or ACT (for admission).

Options: electronic application.

Application fee: $35.

Required: high school transcript, minimum 2.8 GPA.

CONTACT

Ms. Merideth Sherlin, Director of Admission, North Dakota State University, NDSU Department 2832, PO Box 6050, Fargo, ND 58108-6050. *Phone:* 701-231-8643. *Toll-free phone:* 800-488-6378. *Fax:* 701-231-8802. *E-mail:* ndsu.admission@ndsu.edu.

Rasmussen College Fargo

Fargo, North Dakota

http://www.rasmussen.edu/

- **Proprietary** 4-year, founded 1902, part of Rasmussen College System
- **Suburban** campus
- **Coed** 225 undergraduate students, 69% full-time, 81% women, 19% men
- 100% of applicants were admitted

UNDERGRAD STUDENTS

155 full-time, 70 part-time. Students come from 51 states and territories; 27% are from out of state; 8% Black or African American, non-Hispanic/Latino; 5% Hispanic/Latino; 3% Asian, non-Hispanic/Latino; 3% American Indian or Alaska Native, non-Hispanic/Latino; 2% Two or more races, non-Hispanic/Latino; 12% Race/ethnicity unknown.

Freshmen:

Admission: 66 applied, 66 admitted, 53 enrolled.

ACADEMICS

Calendar: quarters. *Degrees:* certificates, diplomas, associate, and bachelor's.

Special study options: academic remediation for entering students, accelerated degree program, adult/continuing education programs, distance learning, double majors, internships, part-time degree program, summer session for credit.

Computers: 87 computers/terminals are available on campus for general student use. Students can access the following: computer help desk, free student e-mail accounts, online (class) grades, online (class) schedules. Campuswide network is available. Wireless service is available via entire campus.

Library: Rasmussen College Library - Fargo.

STUDENT LIFE

Housing options: college housing not available.

APPLYING

Options: early admission, deferred entrance.

Required: high school transcript, minimum 2.0 GPA. ***Required for some:*** interview.

Application deadlines: rolling (freshmen), rolling (transfers).

CONTACT

Dwayne Bertotto, Vice President of Admissions and Student Experience, Rasmussen College Fargo, 8300 Norman Center Drive, Suite 300, Bloomington, MN 55437. *Phone:* 952-806-3958. *Toll-free phone:* 888-549-6755. *E-mail:* dwayne.bertotto@rasmussen.edu.

Sitting Bull College

Fort Yates, North Dakota

http://www.sittingbull.edu/

CONTACT

Ms. Melody Silk, Director of Registration and Admissions, Sitting Bull College, 1341 92nd Street, Fort Yates, ND 58538-9701. *Phone:* 701-854-3864. *Fax:* 701-854-3403. *E-mail:* melodys@sbcl.edu.

Trinity Bible College and Graduate School

Ellendale, North Dakota

http://www.trinitybiblecollege.edu/

CONTACT

Trinity Bible College and Graduate School, 50 Sixth Avenue South, Ellendale, ND 58436. *Phone:* 701-349-5399. *Toll-free phone:* 800-523-1603. *E-mail:* admissions@trinitybiblecollege.edu.

University of Jamestown

Jamestown, North Dakota

http://www.uj.edu/

- **Independent Presbyterian** comprehensive, founded 1883
- **Small-town** 110-acre campus
- **Endowment** $35.6 million
- **Coed** 914 undergraduate students, 97% full-time, 46% women, 54% men
- **Minimally difficult** entrance level, 69% of applicants were admitted

UNDERGRAD STUDENTS

889 full-time, 25 part-time. 60% are from out of state; 6% Black or African American, non-Hispanic/Latino; 10% Hispanic/Latino; 0.6% Asian, non-Hispanic/Latino; 0.6% Native Hawaiian or other Pacific Islander, non-Hispanic/Latino; 0.1% American Indian or Alaska Native, non-Hispanic/Latino; 3% Two or more races, non-Hispanic/Latino; 9% international; 5% transferred in; 75% live on campus.

Freshmen:

Admission: 1,106 applied, 766 admitted, 256 enrolled. ***Average high school GPA:*** 3.4. ***Test scores:*** SAT evidence-based reading and writing scores over 500: 65%; SAT math scores over 500: 63%; ACT scores over 18: 87%; SAT evidence-based reading and writing scores over 600: 13%; SAT math scores over 600: 15%; ACT scores over 24: 37%; SAT math scores over 700: 2%; ACT scores over 30: 5%.

Retention: 70% of full-time freshmen returned.

FACULTY

Total: 109, 70% full-time, 58% with terminal degrees.

Student/faculty ratio: 10:1.

ACADEMICS

Calendar: semesters. *Degrees:* bachelor's, master's, and doctoral.

Special study options: advanced placement credit, cooperative education, distance learning, double majors, honors programs, independent study, internships, part-time degree program, services for LD students, student-designed majors, study abroad, summer session for credit.

Unusual degree programs: 3-2 engineering with North Dakota State University, University of North Dakota, South Dakota State University, Washington University in St. Louis.

Computers: 200 computers/terminals and 570 ports are available on campus for general student use. Students can access the following: campus intranet, computer help desk, free student e-mail accounts, online (class) grades, online (class) registration, online (class) schedules.

Campuswide network is available. 100% of college-owned or -operated housing units are wired for high-speed Internet access. Wireless service is available via entire campus.

Library: Raugust Library. *Books:* 94,318 (physical), 15,565 (digital/electronic); *Serial titles:* 822 (physical), 343 (digital/electronic); *Databases:* 87. Weekly public service hours: 89; students can reserve study rooms.

STUDENT LIFE

Housing options: on-campus residence required through junior year; coed, special housing for students with disabilities. Campus housing is university owned. Freshman campus housing is guaranteed.

Activities and organizations: drama/theater group, student-run newspaper, choral group, Cru-Ignite, Student Senate, Relay for Life, Habitat for Humanity, Fellowship of Athletes in Christ.

Athletics Member NAIA. ***Intercollegiate sports:*** baseball M(s), basketball M(s)/W(s), cheerleading M(s)/W(s), cross-country running M(s)/W(s), football M(s), golf M(s)/W(s), ice hockey M(c), soccer M(s)/W(s), softball W(s), track and field M(s)/W(s), volleyball W(s), wrestling M(s)/W(s). ***Intramural sports:*** basketball M/W, football M/W, volleyball M/W.

Campus security: 24-hour emergency response devices, late-night transport/escort service, controlled dormitory access, campus security cameras.

Student services: personal/psychological counseling.

COSTS & FINANCIAL AID

Costs (2020–21) ***Comprehensive fee:*** $31,814 includes full-time tuition ($22,718), mandatory fees ($780), and room and board ($8316). Full-time tuition and fees vary according to course load, degree level, and program. Part-time tuition: $435 per credit hour. Part-time tuition and fees vary according to course load, degree level, and program. ***Room and board:*** Room and board charges vary according to housing facility. ***Payment plan:*** installment. ***Waivers:*** employees or children of employees.

Financial Aid Of all full-time matriculated undergraduates who enrolled in 2019, 722 applied for aid, 590 were judged to have need, 142 had their need fully met. 399 Federal Work-Study jobs (averaging $577). 78 state and other part-time jobs (averaging $507). In 2019, 217 non-need-based awards were made. ***Average percent of need met:*** 75. ***Average financial aid package:*** $17,733. ***Average need-based loan:*** $3796. ***Average need-based gift aid:*** $14,544. ***Average non-need-based aid:*** $8053. ***Average indebtedness upon graduation:*** $28,889.

APPLYING

Standardized Tests *Required:* SAT or ACT (for admission).

Options: electronic application, deferred entrance.

Required: high school transcript, minimum 2.5 GPA. ***Required for some:*** interview.

Application deadlines: rolling (freshmen), rolling (transfers).

CONTACT

Mr. Mike Heitkamp, Vice President of Enrollment Management, University of Jamestown, 6081 College Lane, Jamestown, ND 58401. *Phone:* 701-252-3467 Ext. 5512. *Toll-free phone:* 800-336-2554. *Fax:* 701-253-4318. *E-mail:* admissions@uj.edu.

University of Mary

Bismarck, North Dakota

http://www.umary.edu/

CONTACT

Mr. Curtis Ray DeGraw, University of Mary, 7500 University Drive, Bismarck, ND 58504-9652. *Phone:* 701-355-8191. *Toll-free phone:* 800-288-6279. *Fax:* 701-255-7687. *E-mail:* mcheitkamp@umary.edu.

University of North Dakota

Grand Forks, North Dakota

http://www.und.edu/

- **State-supported** university, founded 1883, part of North Dakota University System
- **Urban** 521-acre campus
- **Endowment** $243.5 million
- **Coed** 10,163 undergraduate students, 75% full-time, 43% women, 57% men
- **Minimally difficult** entrance level, 81% of applicants were admitted

UNDERGRAD STUDENTS

7,628 full-time, 2,535 part-time. Students come from 63 states and territories; 78 other countries; 62% are from out of state; 2% Black or African American, non-Hispanic/Latino; 4% Hispanic/Latino; 2% Asian, non-Hispanic/Latino; 0.1% Native Hawaiian or other Pacific Islander, non-Hispanic/Latino; 1% American Indian or Alaska Native, non-Hispanic/Latino; 5% Two or more races, non-Hispanic/Latino; 1% Race/ethnicity unknown; 5% international; 9% transferred in; 25% live on campus.

Freshmen:

Admission: 4,964 applied, 4,027 admitted, 1,673 enrolled. ***Average high school GPA:*** 3.5. ***Test scores:*** SAT evidence-based reading and writing scores over 500: 79%; SAT math scores over 500: 80%; ACT scores over 18: 97%; SAT evidence-based reading and writing scores over 600: 34%; SAT math scores over 600: 37%; ACT scores over 24: 51%; SAT evidence-based reading and writing scores over 700: 2%; SAT math scores over 700: 5%; ACT scores over 30: 9%.

Retention: 78% of full-time freshmen returned.

FACULTY

Total: 760, 94% full-time, 69% with terminal degrees.

Student/faculty ratio: 21:1.

ACADEMICS

Calendar: semesters. *Degrees:* certificates, bachelor's, master's, doctoral, post-master's, and postbachelor's certificates.

Special study options: accelerated degree program, adult/continuing education programs, advanced placement credit, cooperative education, distance learning, double majors, English as a second language, external degree program, honors programs, independent study, internships, off-campus study, part-time degree program, services for LD students, student-designed majors, study abroad, summer session for credit. ***ROTC:*** Army (b), Air Force (b).

Unusual degree programs: 3-2 engineering; applied economics, counseling, chemistry, public administration.

Computers: 50 computers/terminals are available on campus for general student use. Students can access the following: computer help desk, free student e-mail accounts, online (class) grades, online (class) registration, online (class) schedules. Campuswide network is available. 100% of college-owned or -operated housing units are wired for high-speed Internet access. Wireless service is available via classrooms, computer centers, computer labs, dorm rooms, learning centers, libraries, student centers.

Library: Chester Fritz Library plus 2 others. *Books:* 567,782 (physical), 236,566 (digital/electronic); *Serial titles:* 278,683 (physical), 34,878 (digital/electronic); *Databases:* 57. Weekly public service hours: 99.

STUDENT LIFE

Housing options: coed, men-only, women-only, special housing for students with disabilities. Campus housing is university owned.

Activities and organizations: drama/theater group, student-run newspaper, radio and television station, choral group, marching band, Greek Life, Student Aviation Management Association, Cru, Alpha Kappa Psi, Mortar Board, national fraternities, national sororities.

Athletics Member NCAA. All Division I. ***Intercollegiate sports:*** basketball M(s)/W(s), cross-country running M(s)/W(s), football M(s), golf M(s)/W(s), ice hockey M(s), soccer W(s), softball W(s), tennis M(s)/W(s), track and field M(s)/W(s), volleyball W(s). ***Intramural sports:*** basketball M/W.

Campus security: 24-hour emergency response devices and patrols, late-night transport/escort service, controlled dormitory access.

Student services: health clinic, personal/psychological counseling, women's center, legal services, veterans affairs office.

COSTS & FINANCIAL AID
Costs (2019–20) ***Tuition:*** state resident $8213 full-time, $342 per credit hour part-time; nonresident $12,319 full-time, $513 per credit hour part-time. Full-time tuition and fees vary according to degree level, program, and reciprocity agreements. Part-time tuition and fees vary according to course load, degree level, program, and reciprocity agreements. ***Required fees:*** $1524 full-time. ***Room and board:*** $9544. Room and board charges vary according to board plan and housing facility. ***Payment plan:*** deferred payment. ***Waivers:*** minority students and employees or children of employees.

Financial Aid Of all full-time matriculated undergraduates who enrolled in 2018, 5,970 applied for aid, 4,022 were judged to have need, 1,508 had their need fully met. 1,302 Federal Work-Study jobs (averaging $3000). In 2018, 858 non-need-based awards were made. ***Average percent of need met:*** 55. ***Average financial aid package:*** $14,029. ***Average need-based loan:*** $7784. ***Average need-based gift aid:*** $5823. ***Average non-need-based aid:*** $2167.

APPLYING
Standardized Tests *Required:* SAT or ACT (for admission), SAT and SAT Subject Tests or ACT (for admission).

Options: electronic application, deferred entrance.

Application fee: $35.

Required: high school transcript. ***Recommended:*** minimum 2.5 GPA.

Notification: continuous (transfers).

CONTACT
Jennifer Aamodt, University Admissions Director, University of North Dakota, Gorecki Alumni Center, 3501 University Avenue, Stop 8357, Grand Forks, ND 58202. *Phone:* 701-777-3000. *Toll-free phone:* 800-CALL-UND. *Fax:* 701-777-2721. *E-mail:* und.admissions@und.edu.

Valley City State University

Valley City, North Dakota

http://www.vcsu.edu/

- **State-supported** comprehensive, founded 1890, part of North Dakota University System
- **Small-town** 55-acre campus
- **Coed** 1,524 undergraduate students, 59% full-time, 58% women, 42% men
- **Noncompetitive** entrance level, 52% of applicants were admitted

UNDERGRAD STUDENTS
904 full-time, 620 part-time. Students come from 42 states and territories; 10 other countries; 37% are from out of state; 3% Black or African American, non-Hispanic/Latino; 6% Hispanic/Latino; 0.4% Asian, non-Hispanic/Latino; 0.5% Native Hawaiian or other Pacific Islander, non-Hispanic/Latino; 1% American Indian or Alaska Native, non-Hispanic/Latino; 5% Two or more races, non-Hispanic/Latino; 1% Race/ethnicity unknown; 2% international; 8% transferred in; 36% live on campus.

Freshmen:
Admission: 752 applied, 394 admitted, 218 enrolled. ***Average high school GPA:*** 3.3. ***Test scores:*** SAT evidence-based reading and writing scores over 500: 54%; SAT math scores over 500: 61%; ACT scores over 18: 80%; SAT evidence-based reading and writing scores over 600: 11%; ACT scores over 24: 27%; ACT scores over 30: 2%.

Retention: 73% of full-time freshmen returned.

FACULTY
Total: 122, 56% full-time, 44% with terminal degrees.

Student/faculty ratio: 13:1.

ACADEMICS
Calendar: semesters. *Degrees:* bachelor's and master's.

Special study options: academic remediation for entering students, cooperative education, distance learning, double majors, internships, off-campus study, part-time degree program, services for LD students, student-designed majors, study abroad, summer session for credit.

Computers: 1,200 computers/terminals are available on campus for general student use. Students can access the following: campus intranet, computer help desk, free student e-mail accounts, online (class) grades, online (class) registration, online (class) schedules. Campuswide network is available. 100% of college-owned or -operated housing units are wired for high-speed Internet access. Wireless service is available via entire campus.

Library: Allen Memorial Library. *Books:* 77,906 (physical), 140,050 (digital/electronic); *Serial titles:* 1,301 (physical), 29,378 (digital/electronic); *Databases:* 86. Weekly public service hours: 61; students can reserve study rooms.

STUDENT LIFE
Housing options: on-campus residence required for freshman year; coed, men only, women only. Campus housing is university owned. Freshman campus housing is guaranteed.

Activities and organizations: choral group, departmental clubs, Fellowship of Christian Athletes, VCAB, Viking Ambassadors, local fraternities/soroties.

Athletics Member NAIA. ***Intercollegiate sports:*** baseball M(s), basketball M(s)/W(s), cross-country running M(s)/W(s), football M(s), golf M(s), softball W(s), tennis M(c)/W(c), track and field M(s)/W(s), volleyball W(s). ***Intramural sports:*** basketball M/W, bowling M/W, cross-country running M/W, football M/W, golf M/W, ice hockey M/W, racquetball M/W, skiing (cross-country) M/W, soccer M/W, softball M/W, tennis M/W, track and field M/W, volleyball M/W.

Campus security: controlled dormitory access.

Student services: health clinic, personal/psychological counseling.

COSTS & FINANCIAL AID
Costs (2019–20) ***Tuition:*** state resident $5884 full-time, $196 per semester hour part-time; nonresident $10,297 full-time, $343 per semester hour part-time. Full-time tuition and fees vary according to course load and reciprocity agreements. Part-time tuition and fees vary according to course load and reciprocity agreements. ***Required fees:*** $1823 full-time, $76 per semester hour part-time. ***Room and board:*** $6610; room only: $2420. Room and board charges vary according to board plan and housing facility. ***Payment plan:*** installment. ***Waivers:*** minority students, senior citizens, and employees or children of employees.

Financial Aid Of all full-time matriculated undergraduates who enrolled in 2019, 657 applied for aid, 447 were judged to have need, 194 had their need fully met. In 2019, 174 non-need-based awards were made. ***Average percent of need met:*** 78. ***Average financial aid package:*** $12,540. ***Average need-based loan:*** $5425. ***Average need-based gift aid:*** $6727. ***Average non-need-based aid:*** $3128.

APPLYING
Standardized Tests *Required:* SAT or ACT (for admission).

Options: electronic application, deferred entrance.

Application fee: $35.

Required: high school transcript.

Application deadlines: rolling (freshmen), rolling (out-of-state freshmen), rolling (transfers).

Notification: continuous (freshmen), continuous (out-of-state freshmen), continuous (transfers).

CONTACT
Ms. Charlene Stenson, Director of Enrollment Services, Valley City State University, 101 College Street Southwest, Valley City, ND 58072. *Phone:* 701-845-71. *Toll-free phone:* 800-532-8641 Ext. 7101. *Fax:* 701-845-7299. *E-mail:* c.stenson@vcsu.edu.

OHIO

Allegheny Wesleyan College

Salem, Ohio

http://www.awc.edu/

CONTACT

Admissions Office, Allegheny Wesleyan College, 2161 Woodsdale Road, Salem, OH 44460. *Phone:* 330-337-6403. *Toll-free phone:* 800-292-3153. *E-mail:* college@awc.edu.

Antioch College

Yellow Springs, Ohio

http://www.antiochcollege.edu/

- **Independent** 4-year, founded 2011
- **Rural** 1100-acre campus with easy access to Columbus
- **Endowment** $9.2 million
- **Coed**
- **Moderately difficult** entrance level

FACULTY

Student/faculty ratio: 4:1.

ACADEMICS

Calendar: quarters. *Degree:* bachelor's.

Library: Olive Kettering Library. *Books:* 158,578 (physical), 125,344 (digital/electronic); *Serial titles:* 1,402 (physical), 33,099 (digital/electronic); *Databases:* 199. Weekly public service hours: 72.

STUDENT LIFE

Housing options: on-campus residence required through senior year; coed. Campus housing is university owned.

Activities and organizations: drama/theater group, student-run newspaper, radio station, People of Color Group, Queer Center, Outdoors Club, Antioch Creative Collective, ei@A (Entrepreneurs & Innovation @ Antioch).

Campus security: 24-hour emergency response devices and patrols, late-night transport/escort service, controlled dormitory access.

Student services: health clinic, personal/psychological counseling.

COSTS

Costs (2019–20) ***One-time required fee:*** $150. ***Comprehensive fee:*** $44,633 includes full-time tuition ($35,949), mandatory fees ($1044), and room and board ($7640). Part-time tuition: $500 per credit hour. No tuition increase for student's term of enrollment. ***College room only:*** $4622.

APPLYING

Options: electronic application, early admission, early decision, deferred entrance.

Required: essay or personal statement, high school transcript, 2 letters of recommendation. ***Required for some:*** interview.

CONTACT

Office of Admission, Antioch College, 1 Morgan Place, Yellow Springs, OH 45387. *Phone:* 937-319-6082. *E-mail:* admission@antiochcollege.edu.

Art Academy of Cincinnati

Cincinnati, Ohio

http://www.artacademy.edu/

CONTACT

Mr. John J. Wadell, Director of Admissions, Art Academy of Cincinnati, 1212 Jackson Street, Cincinnati, OH 45202-7106. *Phone:* 513-562-8744. *Toll-free phone:* 800-323-5692. *Fax:* 513-562-8778. *E-mail:* admissions@artacademy.edu.

Ashland University

Ashland, Ohio

http://www.ashland.edu/

- **Independent** comprehensive, founded 1878, affiliated with Brethren Church
- **Small-town** 135-acre campus with easy access to Cleveland, Akron
- **Endowment** $36.8 million
- **Coed**
- **Moderately difficult** entrance level

FACULTY

Student/faculty ratio: 16:1.

ACADEMICS

Calendar: semesters. *Degrees:* certificates, diplomas, associate, bachelor's, master's, doctoral, post-master's, and postbachelor's certificates.

Library: Ashland University Library plus 2 others. *Books:* 223,607 (physical), 255,789 (digital/electronic); *Serial titles:* 1,070 (physical), 114,001 (digital/electronic); *Databases:* 200. Weekly public service hours: 102; students can reserve study rooms.

STUDENT LIFE

Housing options: on-campus residence required through junior year; coed, women-only. Campus housing is university owned. Freshman campus housing is guaranteed.

Activities and organizations: drama/theater group, student-run newspaper, radio and television station, choral group, marching band, Campus Activity Board, Fellowship of Christian Athletes, The Well Campus Ministry, intramurals, Sororities, national fraternities, national sororities.

Athletics Member NCAA. All Division II.

Campus security: 24-hour emergency response devices and patrols, student patrols, late-night transport/escort service, controlled dormitory access.

Student services: health clinic, personal/psychological counseling, veterans affairs office.

COSTS & FINANCIAL AID

Costs (2019–20) ***Comprehensive fee:*** $32,170 includes full-time tuition ($20,950), mandatory fees ($1030), and room and board ($10,190). Full-time tuition and fees vary according to class time, course level, course load, degree level, location, program, reciprocity agreements, and student level. Part-time tuition: $940 per credit hour. Part-time tuition and fees vary according to class time, course level, course load, degree level, location, program, reciprocity agreements, and student level. ***College room only:*** $5460. Room and board charges vary according to board plan, housing facility, and location.

Financial Aid Of all full-time matriculated undergraduates who enrolled in 2019, 3,033 applied for aid, 2,736 were judged to have need, 1,254 had their need fully met. In 2019, 368 non-need-based awards were made. ***Average percent of need met:*** 82. ***Average financial aid package:*** $14,785. ***Average need-based loan:*** $4542. ***Average need-based gift aid:*** $11,678. ***Average non-need-based aid:*** $8805.

APPLYING

Standardized Tests *Required:* SAT or ACT (for admission).

Options: electronic application, deferred entrance.

Required: high school transcript, minimum 2.5 GPA, minimum 18 ACT or 860 SAT.

CONTACT

Mr. W. C. Vance, Director of Admissions, Ashland University, 401 College Avenue, Ashland, OH 44805. *Phone:* 419-289-5052. *Toll-free phone:* 800-882-1548. *Fax:* 419-289-5999. *E-mail:* enrollme@ashland.edu.

Aultman College of Nursing and Health Sciences

Canton, Ohio

http://www.aultmancollege.edu/

- **Independent** 4-year, founded 2004
- **Urban** 5-acre campus with easy access to Cleveland
- **Endowment** $2.0 million
- **Coed** 305 undergraduate students, 42% full-time, 90% women, 10% men
- **Moderately difficult** entrance level, 52% of applicants were admitted

UNDERGRAD STUDENTS

128 full-time, 177 part-time. Students come from 1 other state; 4% Black or African American, non-Hispanic/Latino; 2% Hispanic/Latino; 0.7% Asian, non-Hispanic/Latino; 2% American Indian or Alaska Native, non-Hispanic/Latino; 3% Two or more races, non-Hispanic/Latino; 3% Race/ethnicity unknown; 25% transferred in.

Freshmen:

Admission: 91 applied, 47 admitted, 30 enrolled. ***Average high school GPA:*** 3.4. ***Test scores:*** ACT scores over 18: 97%; ACT scores over 24: 16%; ACT scores over 30: 4%.

Retention: 67% of full-time freshmen returned.

FACULTY

Total: 52, 27% full-time, 21% with terminal degrees.

Student/faculty ratio: 6:1.

ACADEMICS

Calendar: semesters. *Degrees:* certificates, associate, and bachelor's.

Special study options: academic remediation for entering students, advanced placement credit, cooperative education, distance learning, double majors, internships, part-time degree program, services for LD students.

Computers: 71 computers/terminals are available on campus for general student use. Students can access the following: campus intranet, computer help desk, free student e-mail accounts, online (class) grades, online (class) registration, online (class) schedules. Campuswide network is available. Wireless service is available via entire campus.

Library: Aultman Health Sciences Library plus 1 other. *Books:* 2,786 (physical), 81,000 (digital/electronic); *Serial titles:* 130 (physical), 10,007 (digital/electronic); *Databases:* 145. Study areas open 24 hours, 5–7 days a week.

STUDENT LIFE

Housing options: college housing not available.

Activities and organizations: Aultman College Student Nurse Association, Radiography Club, Aultman College Campus Ministry, Aultman College Veterans Association, Men in Nursing Association.

Campus security: 24-hour emergency response devices and patrols, late-night transport/escort service.

Student services: health clinic.

COSTS

Costs (2019–20) ***One-time required fee:*** $200. ***Tuition:*** $17,850 full-time, $762 per credit hour part-time. Full-time tuition and fees vary according to course load, degree level, and program. Part-time tuition and fees vary according to course load, degree level, and program. ***Required fees:*** $1100 full-time, $600 per term part-time. ***Room only:*** Room and board charges vary according to housing facility. ***Payment plan:*** installment. ***Waivers:*** employees or children of employees.

APPLYING

Standardized Tests *Required for some:* SAT or ACT (for admission). *Recommended:* SAT or ACT (for admission).

Options: electronic application.

Required: high school transcript. ***Required for some:*** minimum 3.0 GPA, interview.

Notification: continuous until 12/1 (freshmen).

CONTACT

Kellie Blinn, Enrollment Specialist, Aultman College of Nursing and Health Sciences, 2600 6th Street SW, Canton, OH 44710. *Phone:* 330-363-6773. *Fax:* 330-580-6654. *E-mail:* admissions@aultmancollege.edu.

Baldwin Wallace University

Berea, Ohio

http://www.bw.edu/

- **Independent Methodist** comprehensive, founded 1845
- **Suburban** 100-acre campus with easy access to Cleveland
- **Endowment** $174.8 million
- **Coed**
- **Moderately difficult** entrance level

FACULTY

Student/faculty ratio: 11:1.

ACADEMICS

Calendar: semesters. *Degrees:* certificates, bachelor's, master's, and post-master's certificates.

Library: Ritter Library plus 2 others. *Books:* 106,091 (physical), 451,472 (digital/electronic); *Serial titles:* 148 (physical), 86,238 (digital/electronic); *Databases:* 265. Weekly public service hours: 90; study areas open 24 hours, 5–7 days a week; students can reserve study rooms.

STUDENT LIFE

Housing options: on-campus residence required through sophomore year; coed, special housing for students with disabilities. Campus housing is university owned. Freshman applicants given priority for college housing.

Activities and organizations: drama/theater group, student-run newspaper, radio and television station, choral group, marching band, Arts Management Association (AMA), Ohio Collegiate Music Educators Association (OCMEA), Rotaract, Sport Management Club (SMC), Voices of Praise Gospel Choir (VOP), national fraternities, national sororities.

Athletics Member NCAA. All Division III except golf (Division II).

Campus security: 24-hour emergency response devices and patrols, student patrols, late-night transport/escort service, controlled dormitory access.

Student services: health clinic, personal/psychological counseling, veterans affairs office.

COSTS & FINANCIAL AID

Costs (2019–20) ***Comprehensive fee:*** $43,640 includes full-time tuition ($33,530) and room and board ($10,110). Full-time tuition and fees vary according to class time, course level, course load, degree level, program, and reciprocity agreements. Part-time tuition: $1042 per credit hour. Part-time tuition and fees vary according to class time, course level, course load, degree level, program, and reciprocity agreements. ***College room only:*** $5678. Room and board charges vary according to housing facility. ***Payment plans:*** installment, deferred payment.

Financial Aid Of all full-time matriculated undergraduates who enrolled in 2019, 2,428 applied for aid, 2,067 were judged to have need, 865 had their need fully met. 881 Federal Work-Study jobs (averaging $1382). 500 state and other part-time jobs (averaging $1350). In 2019, 672 non-need-based awards were made. ***Average percent of need met:*** 90. ***Average financial aid package:*** $26,293. ***Average need-based loan:*** $4166. ***Average need-based gift aid:*** $21,130. ***Average non-need-based aid:*** $16,759. ***Average indebtedness upon graduation:*** $33,919.

APPLYING

Standardized Tests *Required for some:* SAT or ACT (for admission).

Options: electronic application, deferred entrance.

Application fee: $25.

Required: essay or personal statement, high school transcript. ***Required for some:*** minimum 3.0 cum GPA and recently graded paper in lieu of ACT or SAT scores for Test Optional applicants. ***Recommended:*** minimum 3.0 GPA, 1 letter of recommendation, interview.

CONTACT

Joyce J. Cendroski, Director of First Year RCMT and Admission, Baldwin Wallace University, Durst Welcome Center, 115 Tressel Street, Berea, OH 44017. *Phone:* 440-826-2222. *Toll-free phone:* 877-BW-APPLY. *Fax:* 440-826-3830. *E-mail:* admission@bw.edu.

Bluffton University

Bluffton, Ohio

http://www.bluffton.edu/

- **Independent Mennonite** comprehensive, founded 1899
- **Small-town** 65-acre campus with easy access to Dayton
- **Endowment** $24.2 million
- **Coed** 710 undergraduate students, 89% full-time, 43% women, 57% men
- **Moderately difficult** entrance level, 55% of applicants were admitted

UNDERGRAD STUDENTS

634 full-time, 76 part-time. 13% are from out of state; 11% Black or African American, non-Hispanic/Latino; 3% Hispanic/Latino; 0.4% Asian, non-Hispanic/Latino; 0.6% American Indian or Alaska Native, non-Hispanic/Latino; 3% Two or more races, non-Hispanic/Latino; 4% Race/ethnicity unknown; 3% international; 2% transferred in; 90% live on campus.

Freshmen:

Admission: 1,770 applied, 973 admitted, 231 enrolled. ***Average high school GPA:*** 3.3. ***Test scores:*** SAT evidence-based reading and writing scores over 500: 30%; SAT math scores over 500: 45%; ACT scores over 18: 81%; SAT evidence-based reading and writing scores over 600: 11%; SAT math scores over 600: 6%; ACT scores over 24: 24%; SAT evidence-based reading and writing scores over 700: 2%; ACT scores over 30: 3%.

Retention: 60% of full-time freshmen returned.

FACULTY

Total: 91, 52% full-time, 45% with terminal degrees.

Student/faculty ratio: 11:1.

ACADEMICS

Calendar: semesters. *Degrees:* certificates, bachelor's, and master's.

Special study options: academic remediation for entering students, accelerated degree program, adult/continuing education programs, advanced placement credit, distance learning, double majors, English as a second language, honors programs, independent study, internships, off-campus study, part-time degree program, services for LD students, student-designed majors, study abroad, summer session for credit.

Computers: 175 computers/terminals and 1,600 ports are available on campus for general student use. Students can access the following: campus intranet, computer help desk, free student e-mail accounts, online (class) grades, online (class) registration, online (class) schedules. Campuswide network is available. 100% of college-owned or -operated housing units are wired for high-speed Internet access. Wireless service is available via classrooms, computer centers, computer labs, dorm rooms, libraries, student centers.

Library: Musselman Library plus 1 other. *Books:* 73,648 (physical), 283,031 (digital/electronic); *Serial titles:* 1,001 (physical), 46,672 (digital/electronic); *Databases:* 258. Weekly public service hours: 74; students can reserve study rooms.

STUDENT LIFE

Housing options: on-campus residence required through senior year; coed, men-only, women-only, cooperative, special housing for students with disabilities. Campus housing is university owned. Freshman campus housing is guaranteed.

Activities and organizations: drama/theater group, student-run newspaper, radio station, choral group, Marbeck Center Board, Multicultural Student Organization, Bluffton Education Association, Fellowship of Christian Athletes, Bluffton University Business Leaders.

Athletics Member NCAA. All Division III. ***Intercollegiate sports:*** baseball M, basketball M/W, cross-country running M/W, football M, golf M/W, soccer M/W, softball W, track and field M/W, volleyball W. ***Intramural sports:*** basketball M/W, bowling M/W, football M/W, golf M/W, softball M/W, tennis M/W, ultimate Frisbee M, volleyball M/W.

Campus security: 24-hour emergency response devices, controlled dormitory access, night security guards.

Student services: health clinic, personal/psychological counseling.

COSTS & FINANCIAL AID

Costs (2020–21) ***Comprehensive fee:*** $49,848 includes full-time tuition ($33,952), mandatory fees ($550), and room and board ($11,346). Full-time tuition and fees vary according to course load, degree level, and program. Part-time tuition: $1415 per credit hour. Part-time tuition and fees vary according to course load, degree level, and program. ***College room only:*** $5586. Room and board charges vary according to board plan and housing facility. ***Payment plan:*** installment. ***Waivers:*** employees or children of employees.

Financial Aid Of all full-time matriculated undergraduates who enrolled in 2019, 546 applied for aid, 513 were judged to have need, 81 had their need fully met. In 2019, 103 non-need-based awards were made. ***Average percent of need met:*** 78. ***Average financial aid package:*** $30,037. ***Average need-based loan:*** $4342. ***Average need-based gift aid:*** $25,017. ***Average non-need-based aid:*** $19,669. ***Average indebtedness upon graduation:*** $35,601.

APPLYING

Standardized Tests *Required:* SAT or ACT (for admission).

Options: electronic application, deferred entrance.

Required: high school transcript, minimum 2.3 GPA, 1 letter of recommendation, rank in upper 50% of high school class or minimum ACT score of 19. ***Required for some:*** essay or personal statement. ***Recommended:*** interview.

Application deadlines: rolling (freshmen), rolling (transfers).

Notification: continuous (freshmen), continuous (transfers).

CONTACT

Ms. Emily Warner, Admissions Operation Manager, Bluffton University, 1 University Drive, Bluffton, OH 45817. *Phone:* 419-358-3255. *Toll-free phone:* 800-488-3257. *Fax:* 419-358-3081. *E-mail:* admissions@bluffton.edu.

Bowling Green State University

Bowling Green, Ohio

http://www.bgsu.edu/

- **State-supported** university, founded 1910
- **Small-town** 1338-acre campus with easy access to Toledo
- **Endowment** $175.2 million
- **Coed** 15,103 undergraduate students, 86% full-time, 56% women, 44% men
- **Moderately difficult** entrance level, 72% of applicants were admitted

UNDERGRAD STUDENTS

12,936 full-time, 2,167 part-time. Students come from 54 states and territories; 59 other countries; 11% are from out of state; 8% Black or African American, non-Hispanic/Latino; 4% Hispanic/Latino; 1% Asian, non-Hispanic/Latino; 0.1% Native Hawaiian or other Pacific Islander, non-Hispanic/Latino; 0.2% American Indian or Alaska Native, non-Hispanic/Latino; 3% Two or more races, non-Hispanic/Latino; 2% Race/ethnicity unknown; 2% international; 4% transferred in; 43% live on campus.

Freshmen:

Admission: 17,179 applied, 12,338 admitted, 3,389 enrolled. ***Average high school GPA:*** 3.5. ***Test scores:*** SAT evidence-based reading and writing scores over 500: 78%; SAT math scores over 500: 79%; ACT scores over 18: 94%; SAT evidence-based reading and writing scores over 600: 30%; SAT math scores over 600: 30%; ACT scores over 24: 38%; SAT evidence-based reading and writing scores over 700: 4%; SAT math scores over 700: 4%; ACT scores over 30: 7%.

Retention: 77% of full-time freshmen returned.

FACULTY

Total: 1,176, 65% full-time, 58% with terminal degrees.

Student/faculty ratio: 17:1.

ACADEMICS

Calendar: semesters. *Degrees:* certificates, bachelor's, master's, doctoral, post-master's, and postbachelor's certificates.

Special study options: academic remediation for entering students, accelerated degree program, adult/continuing education programs, advanced placement credit, cooperative education, distance learning, double majors, English as a second language, freshman honors college, honors programs, independent study, internships, off-campus study, part-time degree program, services for LD students, student-designed majors, study abroad, summer session for credit. ***ROTC:*** Army (b), Air Force (b).

Computers: 1,500 computers/terminals and 500 ports are available on campus for general student use. Students can access the following:

campus intranet, computer help desk, free student e-mail accounts, online (class) grades, online (class) registration, online (class) schedules, wireless networking, OneDrive, Bursar billing information and payment, online mid-term grade reporting, view and change personal information, order official and unofficial transcripts, check meal plan balance, apply for graduation, etc. Campuswide network is available. 100% of college-owned or -operated housing units are wired for high-speed Internet access. Wireless service is available via entire campus.
Library: William T. Jerome Library. *Books:* 1.7 million (physical), 242,747 (digital/electronic); *Serial titles:* 471 (physical), 11,958 (digital/electronic); *Databases:* 317. Weekly public service hours: 110; students can reserve study rooms.

STUDENT LIFE
Housing options: on-campus residence required through sophomore year; coed, men-only, women-only, special housing for students with disabilities. Campus housing is university owned. Freshman campus housing is guaranteed.

Activities and organizations: drama/theater group, student-run newspaper, radio and television station, choral group, marching band, Dance Marathon, Undergraduate Student Government, University Activities Organization, Alpha Phi Omega, Athletic Training Student Organization, national fraternities, national sororities.

Athletics Member NCAA. All Division I. ***Intercollegiate sports:*** baseball M(s), basketball M(s)/W(s), cross-country running M(s)/W(s), football M(s), golf M(s)/W(s), gymnastics W(s), ice hockey M(s), soccer M(s)/W(s), softball W(s), swimming and diving W(s), tennis W(s), track and field W(s), volleyball W(s). ***Intramural sports:*** badminton M/W, baseball M(c), basketball M/W, cross-country running M(c)/W(c), fencing M(c)/W(c), gymnastics M(c)/W(c), ice hockey M(c)/W(c), lacrosse M(c)/W(c), rugby M(c)/W(c), soccer M/W, softball W(c), swimming and diving M(c)/W(c), tennis M(c)/W(c), track and field M(c)/W(c), ultimate Frisbee M/W, volleyball M/W, water polo M(c)/W(c).

Campus security: 24-hour emergency response devices and patrols, student patrols, late-night transport/escort service, controlled dormitory access.

Student services: health clinic, personal/psychological counseling, women's center, legal services, veterans affairs office.

COSTS & FINANCIAL AID
Costs (2019–20) ***Tuition:*** state resident $9278 full-time, $387 per credit hour part-time; nonresident $17,267 full-time, $719 per credit hour part-time. Full-time tuition and fees vary according to course load, degree level, location, program, reciprocity agreements, and student level. Part-time tuition and fees vary according to course load, degree level, location, program, reciprocity agreements, and student level. No tuition increase for student's term of enrollment. ***Required fees:*** $2039 full-time, $84 per credit hour part-time. ***Room and board:*** $10,396. Room and board charges vary according to board plan and housing facility. ***Payment plan:*** installment. ***Waivers:*** senior citizens and employees or children of employees.

Financial Aid Of all full-time matriculated undergraduates who enrolled in 2018, 10,726 applied for aid, 8,443 were judged to have need, 1,182 had their need fully met. 391 Federal Work-Study jobs (averaging $1091). In 2018, 2634 non-need-based awards were made. ***Average percent of need met:*** 79. ***Average financial aid package:*** $14,344. ***Average need-based loan:*** $4141. ***Average need-based gift aid:*** $7598. ***Average non-need-based aid:*** $5160. ***Average indebtedness upon graduation:*** $29,958.

APPLYING
Standardized Tests *Required:* SAT or ACT (for admission).

Options: electronic application.

Application fee: $45.

Required: high school transcript. ***Required for some:*** interview.

Application deadlines: 7/15 (freshmen), 7/15 (out-of-state freshmen), 8/1 (transfers).

Notification: continuous until 8/1 (freshmen), continuous until 8/1 (out-of-state freshmen), continuous (transfers).

CONTACT
Ms. Adrea Spoon, Director of Admissions, Bowling Green State University, 200 University Hall, Bowling Green State University, Bowling Green, OH 43403-0085. *Phone:* 419-372-2478. *Fax:* 419-372-6955. *E-mail:* choosebgsu@bgsu.edu.

Bowling Green State University–Firelands College

Huron, Ohio

http://www.firelands.bgsu.edu/

- **State-supported** primarily 2-year, founded 1968, part of Bowling Green State University System
- **Rural** 216-acre campus with easy access to Cleveland, Toledo
- **Coed**
- **Noncompetitive** entrance level

FACULTY
Student/faculty ratio: 20:1.

ACADEMICS
Calendar: semesters. *Degrees:* certificates, associate, and bachelor's (also offers some upper-level and graduate courses).
Library: BGSU Firelands College Library

STUDENT LIFE
Housing options: college housing not available.

Activities and organizations: drama/theater group, choral group, Society of Fandom and Gaming, Student Government, Student Theater Guild, Safe Space, Society of Leadership and Success.

Campus security: 24-hour emergency response devices, late-night transport/escort service, patrols by trained security personnel.

APPLYING
Options: electronic application, early admission, deferred entrance.

Application fee: $45.

Required: high school transcript.

CONTACT
Dr. Megan Zahler, Assistant Dean for Strategic Enrollment Planning, Bowling Green State University–Firelands College, One University Drive, Huron, OH 44839-9791. *Phone:* 419-433-5560. *Toll-free phone:* 800-322-4787. *Fax:* 419-372-0604. *E-mail:* mzahler@bgsu.edu.

Bryant & Stratton College–Akron Campus

Akron, Ohio

http://www.bryantstratton.edu/

CONTACT
Bryant & Stratton College–Akron Campus, 190 Montrose West Avenue, Akron, OH 44321.

Bryant & Stratton College–Cleveland Campus

Cleveland, Ohio

http://www.bryantstratton.edu/

CONTACT
Bryant & Stratton College–Cleveland Campus, Cleveland, OH 44114-3203. *Phone:* 216-771-1700. *Fax:* 216-771-7787.

Bryant & Stratton College–Eastlake Campus

Eastlake, Ohio

http://www.bryantstratton.edu/

CONTACT
Ms. Melanie Pettit, Director of Admissions, Bryant & Stratton College–Eastlake Campus, 35350 Curtis Boulevard, Eastlake, OH 44095. *Phone:* 440-510-1112.

Bryant & Stratton College–Parma Campus

Parma, Ohio

http://www.bryantstratton.edu/

CONTACT
Bryant & Stratton College–Parma Campus, 12955 Snow Road, Parma, OH 44130-1005. *Phone:* 216-265-3151. *Toll-free phone:* 866-948-0571.

Capital University

Columbus, Ohio

http://www.capital.edu/

- **Independent** comprehensive, founded 1830, affiliated with Evangelical Lutheran Church in America
- **Suburban** 48-acre campus with easy access to Columbus
- **Endowment** $106.3 million
- **Coed** 2,504 undergraduate students, 96% full-time, 63% women, 37% men
- **Moderately difficult** entrance level, 72% of applicants were admitted

UNDERGRAD STUDENTS
2,400 full-time, 104 part-time. Students come from 32 states and territories; 23 other countries; 7% are from out of state; 9% Black or African American, non-Hispanic/Latino; 4% Hispanic/Latino; 2% Asian, non-Hispanic/Latino; 0.1% Native Hawaiian or other Pacific Islander, non-Hispanic/Latino; 0.2% American Indian or Alaska Native, non-Hispanic/Latino; 6% Two or more races, non-Hispanic/Latino; 2% Race/ethnicity unknown; 2% international; 3% transferred in; 57% live on campus.

Freshmen:
Admission: 4,794 applied, 3,457 admitted, 723 enrolled. ***Average high school GPA:*** 3.6. ***Test scores:*** SAT evidence-based reading and writing scores over 500: 79%; SAT math scores over 500: 85%; ACT scores over 18: 93%; SAT evidence-based reading and writing scores over 600: 33%; SAT math scores over 600: 30%; ACT scores over 24: 41%; SAT evidence-based reading and writing scores over 700: 2%; SAT math scores over 700: 3%; ACT scores over 30: 8%.

Retention: 78% of full-time freshmen returned.

FACULTY
Total: 398, 41% full-time, 47% with terminal degrees.

Student/faculty ratio: 12:1.

ACADEMICS
Calendar: semesters. *Degrees:* bachelor's, master's, doctoral, and postbachelor's certificates.

Special study options: accelerated degree program, adult/continuing education programs, advanced placement credit, cooperative education, distance learning, double majors, English as a second language, external degree program, honors programs, independent study, internships, off-campus study, part-time degree program, services for LD students, student-designed majors, study abroad, summer session for credit. ***ROTC:*** Army (b), Air Force (c).

Unusual degree programs: 3-2 engineering with Washington University in St. Louis, Case Western Reserve University.

Computers: 457 computers/terminals and 1,400 ports are available on campus for general student use. Students can access the following: campus intranet, computer help desk, free student e-mail accounts, online (class) grades, online (class) registration, online (class) schedules. Campuswide network is available. 100% of college-owned or -operated housing units are wired for high-speed Internet access. Wireless service is available via entire campus.
Library: Blackmore Library plus 2 others. *Books:* 511,520 (physical), 197,883 (digital/electronic); *Serial titles:* 1,304 (physical), 69,224 (digital/electronic); *Databases:* 167.

STUDENT LIFE
Housing options: on-campus residence required through sophomore year; coed, men-only, women-only, special housing for students with disabilities. Campus housing is university owned. Freshman campus housing is guaranteed.

Activities and organizations: drama/theater group, student-run newspaper, radio and television station, choral group, Campus Crusade for Christ, student government, University Programming, College Republicans, American Marketing Association, national fraternities, national sororities.

Athletics Member NCAA. All Division III. ***Intercollegiate sports:*** baseball M, basketball M/W, cross-country running M/W, football M, golf M/W, lacrosse M/W, soccer M/W, softball W, tennis M/W, track and field M/W, volleyball W. ***Intramural sports:*** basketball M/W, cheerleading M(c)/W(c), fencing M(c)/W(c), football M/W, racquetball M/W, ultimate Frisbee M/W, volleyball M/W.

Campus security: 24-hour emergency response devices and patrols, late-night transport/escort service, controlled dormitory access.

Student services: health clinic, personal/psychological counseling, veterans affairs office.

COSTS & FINANCIAL AID
Costs (2020–21) ***Comprehensive fee:*** $49,900 includes full-time tuition ($37,978), mandatory fees ($320), and room and board ($11,602). Part-time tuition: $1266 per credit hour. ***College room only:*** $5710. Room and board charges vary according to board plan and housing facility. ***Payment plan:*** installment. ***Waivers:*** employees or children of employees.

Financial Aid Of all full-time matriculated undergraduates who enrolled in 2018, 1,990 applied for aid, 1,822 were judged to have need, 421 had their need fully met. In 2018, 44 non-need-based awards were made. ***Average percent of need met:*** 80. ***Average financial aid package:*** $30,202. ***Average need-based loan:*** $4448. ***Average need-based gift aid:*** $24,587. ***Average non-need-based aid:*** $21,134. ***Average indebtedness upon graduation:*** $33,461.

APPLYING
Standardized Tests *Required:* SAT or ACT (for admission).

Options: electronic application, deferred entrance.

Application fee: $25.

Required: high school transcript, minimum 2.6 GPA. ***Required for some:*** 1 letter of recommendation, audition for Conservatory of Music. ***Recommended:*** interview.

Application deadlines: 5/1 (freshmen), rolling (transfers).

Notification: 9/30 (freshmen), continuous (transfers).

CONTACT
Mr. Garien Hudson, Director of Admission, Capital University, 1 College and Main, Columbus, OH 43209. *Phone:* 614-236-6232. *Toll-free phone:* 866-544-6175. *Fax:* 614-236-6926. *E-mail:* ghudson@capital.edu.

Case Western Reserve University

Cleveland, Ohio

http://www.case.edu/

CONTACT
Robert McCullough, Director of Undergraduate Admission, Case Western Reserve University, 10900 Euclid Avenue, Cleveland, OH 44106. *Phone:* 216-368-4450. *Fax:* 216-368-5111. *E-mail:* admission@case.edu.

Cedarville University

Cedarville, Ohio

http://www.cedarville.edu/

- **Independent Baptist** comprehensive, founded 1887
- **Small-town** 441-acre campus with easy access to Columbus, Dayton
- **Endowment** $35.4 million
- **Coed** 3,879 undergraduate students, 89% full-time, 54% women, 46% men
- **Moderately difficult** entrance level, 79% of applicants were admitted

UNDERGRAD STUDENTS
3,438 full-time, 441 part-time. Students come from 48 states and territories; 44 other countries; 58% are from out of state; 2% Black or African American, non-Hispanic/Latino; 1% Hispanic/Latino; 3% Asian, non-Hispanic/Latino; 0.2% American Indian or Alaska Native, non-Hispanic/Latino; 3% Two or more races, non-Hispanic/Latino; 1% Race/ethnicity unknown; 2% international; 3% transferred in; 83% live on campus.

Freshmen:
Admission: 3,869 applied, 3,050 admitted, 995 enrolled. ***Average high school GPA:*** 3.9. ***Test scores:*** SAT evidence-based reading and writing scores over 500: 97%; SAT math scores over 500: 93%; ACT scores over 18: 99%; SAT evidence-based reading and writing scores over 600: 69%; SAT math scores over 600: 58%; ACT scores over 24: 70%; SAT evidence-based reading and writing scores over 700: 20%; SAT math scores over 700: 19%; ACT scores over 30: 24%.

Retention: 85% of full-time freshmen returned.

FACULTY
Total: 341, 60% full-time, 64% with terminal degrees.

Student/faculty ratio: 16:1.

ACADEMICS
Calendar: semesters. *Degrees:* certificates, bachelor's, master's, doctoral, post-master's, and postbachelor's certificates.

Special study options: academic remediation for entering students, adult/continuing education programs, advanced placement credit, cooperative education, distance learning, double majors, honors programs, independent study, internships, off-campus study, part-time degree program, services for LD students, student-designed majors, study abroad, summer session for credit. ***ROTC:*** Army (c), Air Force (c).

Computers: 2,300 computers/terminals and 720 ports are available on campus for general student use. Students can access the following: campus intranet, computer help desk, free student e-mail accounts, online (class) grades, online (class) registration, online (class) schedules, over 75 software packages. Campuswide network is available. 100% of college-owned or -operated housing units are wired for high-speed Internet access. Wireless service is available via entire campus.

Library: Centennial Library. *Books:* 185,920 (physical), 154,475 (digital/electronic); *Serial titles:* 619 (physical), 26,884 (digital/electronic); *Databases:* 200. Weekly public service hours: 91; students can reserve study rooms.

STUDENT LIFE
Housing options: on-campus residence required through senior year; men-only, women-only, special housing for students with disabilities. Campus housing is university owned. Freshman campus housing is guaranteed.

Activities and organizations: drama/theater group, student-run newspaper, radio station, choral group, Student Nurses Association, Tau Delta Kappa, Mu Kappa, AYO, MISO (Multicultural International Student Org).

Athletics Member NCAA, NCCAA. All NCAA Division II.
Intercollegiate sports: baseball M(s), basketball M(s)/W(s), cheerleading M/W, cross-country running M(s)/W(s), golf M(s), soccer M(s)/W(s), softball W(s), tennis M(s)/W(s), track and field M(s)/W(s), volleyball W(s). ***Intramural sports:*** badminton M/W, basketball M/W, football M/W, golf M/W, racquetball M/W, riflery M(c)/W(c), rock climbing M/W, rugby M(c)/W(c), soccer M/W, swimming and diving M(c)/W(c), table tennis M/W, tennis M/W, ultimate Frisbee M(c)/W(c), volleyball M/W.

Campus security: 24-hour emergency response devices and patrols, late-night transport/escort service, controlled dormitory access.

Student services: health clinic, personal/psychological counseling.

COSTS & FINANCIAL AID
Costs (2020–21) ***Comprehensive fee:*** $40,486 includes full-time tuition ($32,364), mandatory fees ($200), and room and board ($7922). Full-time tuition and fees vary according to course load. Part-time tuition: $1225 per credit. Part-time tuition and fees vary according to course load. ***Required fees:*** $50 per term part-time. ***College room only:*** $4490. Room and board charges vary according to board plan and housing facility. ***Payment plan:*** installment. ***Waivers:*** adult students, senior citizens, and employees or children of employees.

Financial Aid Of all full-time matriculated undergraduates who enrolled in 2019, 2,854 applied for aid, 2,362 were judged to have need, 1,115 had their need fully met. 211 Federal Work-Study jobs (averaging $2381). 1,533 state and other part-time jobs (averaging $1208). In 2019, 910 non-need-based awards were made. ***Average percent of need met:*** 29. ***Average financial aid package:*** $23,708. ***Average need-based loan:*** $6581. ***Average need-based gift aid:*** $5973. ***Average non-need-based aid:*** $21,293. ***Average indebtedness upon graduation:*** $24,027.

APPLYING
Standardized Tests *Required:* SAT or ACT (for admission), SAT or ACT or CLT (for admission).

Options: electronic application, deferred entrance.

Application fee: $30.

Required: essay or personal statement, high school transcript, minimum 3.0 GPA, 1 letter of recommendation, clear testimony of faith in Jesus Christ and evidence of a consistent Christian lifestyle, minimum ACT score of 22 or SAT score of 1020, minimum 3.0 unweighted, cumulative GPA in college prep course work. ***Required for some:*** interview.

Application deadlines: rolling (freshmen), rolling (out-of-state freshmen), rolling (transfers).

Notification: continuous (freshmen), continuous (out-of-state freshmen), continuous (transfers).

CONTACT
Ms. Rebecca Ferrell, Director of Enrollment Services, Cedarville University, 251 North Main Street, Cedarville, OH 45314-0601. *Phone:* 937-766-7700. *Toll-free phone:* 800-233-2784. *E-mail:* admissions@cedarville.edu.

Central State University

Wilberforce, Ohio

http://www.centralstate.edu/

- **State-supported** 4-year, founded 1887, part of Ohio Board of Regents
- **Rural** 60-acre campus with easy access to Dayton
- **Endowment** $3.9 million
- **Coed** 2,033 undergraduate students, 94% full-time, 61% women, 39% men
- **Minimally difficult** entrance level, 57% of applicants were admitted

UNDERGRAD STUDENTS
1,919 full-time, 114 part-time. Students come from 32 states and territories; 9 other countries; 44% are from out of state; 88% Black or African American, non-Hispanic/Latino; 0.7% Hispanic/Latino; 0.2% Asian, non-Hispanic/Latino; 0.3% American Indian or Alaska Native, non-Hispanic/Latino; 2% Two or more races, non-Hispanic/Latino; 0.1% Race/ethnicity unknown; 5% international; 6% transferred in; 74% live on campus.

Freshmen:
Admission: 13,464 applied, 7,646 admitted, 625 enrolled. ***Average high school GPA:*** 2.7.

Retention: 46% of full-time freshmen returned.

FACULTY
Total: 217, 46% full-time, 43% with terminal degrees.

Student/faculty ratio: 14:1.

ACADEMICS
Calendar: semesters. *Degree:* bachelor's.

Special study options: adult/continuing education programs, cooperative education, double majors, honors programs, independent study, internships, off-campus study, part-time degree program, services for LD students, study abroad, summer session for credit. ***ROTC:*** Army (b).

Computers: 880 computers/terminals and 2,600 ports are available on campus for general student use. Students can access the following: campus intranet, computer help desk, free student e-mail accounts, online (class) grades, online (class) registration, online (class) schedules. Campuswide network is available. 100% of college-owned or -operated housing units are wired for high-speed Internet access. Wireless service is available via entire campus.

Library: Hallie Q. Brown Memorial Library plus 1 other. *Books:* 362,854 (physical), 187,392 (digital/electronic); *Serial titles:* 69 (physical); *Databases:* 277. Weekly public service hours: 77.

STUDENT LIFE
Housing options: on-campus residence required through sophomore year; coed, men-only, women-only. Campus housing is university owned. Freshman campus housing is guaranteed.

Activities and organizations: drama/theater group, student-run newspaper, radio and television station, choral group, marching band, Student Ambassadors, student government, Campus Tour Guides,

Brotherhood of Strong Success, Family Community and Leadership in Action, national fraternities, national sororities.

Athletics Member NCAA. All Division II. ***Intercollegiate sports:*** basketball M(s)/W(s), cheerleading M(s)/W(s), cross-country running M(s)/W(s), football M(s), golf M(s), tennis M(s)/W(s), track and field M(s)/W(s), volleyball W(s). ***Intramural sports:*** basketball M/W, softball M/W, tennis M/W.

Campus security: 24-hour emergency response devices and patrols, controlled dormitory access.

Student services: health clinic, personal/psychological counseling.

COSTS & FINANCIAL AID

Costs (2020–21) ***Tuition:*** area resident $4306 full-time, $290 per credit hour part-time; state resident $4306 full-time, $290 per credit hour part-time; nonresident $6306 full-time, $408 per credit hour part-time. Full-time tuition and fees vary according to course load and reciprocity agreements. Part-time tuition and fees vary according to course load and reciprocity agreements. ***Required fees:*** $2420 full-time. ***Room and board:*** $10,480; room only: $5600. Room and board charges vary according to board plan and housing facility. ***Payment plan:*** installment. ***Waivers:*** senior citizens and employees or children of employees.

Financial Aid Of all full-time matriculated undergraduates who enrolled in 2017, 1,671 applied for aid, 1,668 were judged to have need, 153 had their need fully met. ***Average percent of need met:*** 9. ***Average financial aid package:*** $9695. ***Average need-based loan:*** $3803. ***Average need-based gift aid:*** $7455.

APPLYING

Options: electronic application.

Application fee: $35.

Required: essay or personal statement, high school transcript. ***Required for some:*** minimum 2.2 GPA, 2 letters of recommendation.

Notification: continuous (freshmen), continuous (transfers).

CONTACT

Ms. Isabelle Cayo, Director, Admissions, Central State University, PO Box 1004, 1400 Blush Row Road, Wilberforce, OH 45384. *Phone:* 937-376-6218. *Toll-free phone:* 800-388-CSU1 (in-state); 800-388-2781 (out-of-state). *Fax:* 937-376-6648. *E-mail:* admissions@centralstate.edu.

Chamberlain College of Nursing - Cleveland

Cleveland, Ohio

http://www.chamberlain.edu/

CONTACT

Chamberlain College of Nursing - Cleveland, 6700 Euclid Avenue, Cleveland, OH 44103. *Toll-free phone:* 877-751-5783.

Chamberlain College of Nursing - Columbus

Columbus, Ohio

http://www.chamberlain.edu/

CONTACT

Admissions, Chamberlain College of Nursing - Columbus, 1350 Alum Creek Drive, Columbus, OH 43209. *Phone:* 614-252-8890. *Toll-free phone:* 877-751-5783.

Cincinnati Christian University

Cincinnati, Ohio

http://www.ccuniversity.edu/

- **Independent** comprehensive, founded 1924, affiliated with Church of Christ
- **Urban** 40-acre campus with easy access to Cincinnati
- **Coed**
- **Minimally difficult** entrance level

FACULTY

Student/faculty ratio: 19:1.

ACADEMICS

Calendar: semesters. *Degrees:* associate, bachelor's, and master's.

Library: George Mark Elliot Memorial Library.

STUDENT LIFE

Housing options: on-campus residence required through junior year; men-only, women-only. Campus housing is university owned. Freshman campus housing is guaranteed.

Activities and organizations: drama/theater group, student-run newspaper, choral group.

Athletics Member NAIA.

Campus security: 24-hour emergency response devices and patrols, student patrols, late-night transport/escort service, controlled dormitory access.

Student services: health clinic, personal/psychological counseling.

FINANCIAL AID

Financial Aid Of all full-time matriculated undergraduates who enrolled in 2015, 475 applied for aid, 431 were judged to have need, 37 had their need fully met. In 2015, 57 non-need-based awards were made. ***Average percent of need met:*** 57. ***Average financial aid package:*** $12,945. ***Average need-based loan:*** $3758. ***Average need-based gift aid:*** $9374. ***Average non-need-based aid:*** $6966. ***Average indebtedness upon graduation:*** $25,089.

APPLYING

Standardized Tests *Required:* SAT or ACT (for admission).

Options: electronic application, deferred entrance.

Application fee: $40.

Required: high school transcript, 2 letters of recommendation. ***Required for some:*** essay or personal statement. ***Recommended:*** minimum 2.0 GPA, interview.

CONTACT

Cincinnati Christian University, 2700 Glenway Avenue, PO Box 04320, Cincinnati, OH 45204-3200. *Phone:* 513-244-8110. *Toll-free phone:* 800-949-4228 (in-state); 800-949-4CCU (out-of-state).

Cincinnati College of Mortuary Science

Cincinnati, Ohio

http://www.ccms.edu/

- **Independent** 4-year, founded 1882
- **Urban** 10-acre campus with easy access to Cincinnati
- **Endowment** $80,000
- **Coed** 100 undergraduate students, 100% full-time, 65% women, 35% men

UNDERGRAD STUDENTS

100 full-time. Students come from 9 states and territories; 9% are from out of state; 10% Black or African American, non-Hispanic/Latino; 2% Hispanic/Latino; 86% American Indian or Alaska Native, non-Hispanic/Latino; 2% Two or more races, non-Hispanic/Latino; 45% transferred in.

FACULTY

Total: 10, 40% full-time.

Student/faculty ratio: 15:1.

ACADEMICS

Calendar: semesters. *Degrees:* associate and bachelor's.

Special study options: academic remediation for entering students, adult/continuing education programs, advanced placement credit, services for LD students.

Computers: 10 computers/terminals and 10 ports are available on campus for general student use. Students can access the following: campus intranet, computer help desk, free student e-mail accounts, online (class) grades, online (class) registration, online (class) schedules. Campuswide network is available.

Library: The Cincinnati College of Mortuary Science Library. *Books:* 2,000 (physical); *Serial titles:* 2,000 (physical). Weekly public service hours: 8.

STUDENT LIFE
Housing options: college housing not available.

Activities and organizations: national fraternities, national sororities.

Campus security: 24-hour emergency response devices.

COSTS
Costs (2019–20) ***Tuition:*** $21,405 full-time. Full-time tuition and fees vary according to degree level. No tuition increase for student's term of enrollment. ***Required fees:*** $1595 full-time. ***Payment plans:*** tuition prepayment, installment.

APPLYING
Options: electronic application, deferred entrance.

Application fee: $50.

Notification: continuous (transfers).

CONTACT
Cincinnati College of Mortuary Science, 645 West North Bend Road, Cincinnati, OH 45224-1462. *Phone:* 513-761-2020. *Toll-free phone:* 888-377-8433. *Fax:* 513-761-3333.

Cleveland Institute of Art
Cleveland, Ohio
http://www.cia.edu/

- **Independent** 4-year, founded 1882
- **Urban** 2-acre campus with easy access to Cleveland
- **Endowment** $27.5 million
- **Coed** 632 undergraduate students, 98% full-time, 71% women, 29% men
- **Moderately difficult** entrance level, 70% of applicants were admitted

UNDERGRAD STUDENTS
620 full-time, 12 part-time. Students come from 31 states and territories; 7 other countries; 32% are from out of state; 10% Black or African American, non-Hispanic/Latino; 8% Hispanic/Latino; 3% Asian, non-Hispanic/Latino; 0.2% Native Hawaiian or other Pacific Islander, non-Hispanic/Latino; 0.3% American Indian or Alaska Native, non-Hispanic/Latino; 6% Two or more races, non-Hispanic/Latino; 5% international; 3% transferred in; 48% live on campus.

Freshmen:

Admission: 1,138 applied, 792 admitted, 156 enrolled. ***Average high school GPA:*** 3.3. ***Test scores:*** SAT evidence-based reading and writing scores over 500: 82%; SAT math scores over 500: 69%; ACT scores over 18: 92%; SAT evidence-based reading and writing scores over 600: 53%; SAT math scores over 600: 19%; ACT scores over 24: 36%; SAT evidence-based reading and writing scores over 700: 5%; SAT math scores over 700: 5%; ACT scores over 30: 2%.

Retention: 79% of full-time freshmen returned.

FACULTY
Total: 120, 43% full-time, 49% with terminal degrees.

Student/faculty ratio: 10:1.

ACADEMICS
Calendar: semesters. *Degree:* bachelor's.

Special study options: advanced placement credit, distance learning, double majors, independent study, internships, off-campus study, part-time degree program, services for LD students, study abroad. ***ROTC:*** Army (c), Air Force (c).

Computers: 250 computers/terminals are available on campus for general student use. Students can access the following: campus intranet, computer help desk, free student e-mail accounts, online (class) grades, online (class) registration, online (class) schedules, wireless Internet access available throughout campus. Campuswide network is available. 100% of college-owned or -operated housing units are wired for high-speed Internet access. Wireless service is available via entire campus.

Library: Jessica R Gund Library. *Books:* 48,863 (physical), 347,245 (digital/electronic); *Serial titles:* 412 (physical), 11 (digital/electronic); *Databases:* 200. Weekly public service hours: 74; students can reserve study rooms.

STUDENT LIFE
Housing options: on-campus residence required through sophomore year; coed. Campus housing is university owned. Freshman applicants given priority for college housing.

Activities and organizations: drama/theater group, choral group, marching band, Campus Activities Board, Student Independent Exhibition, International Interior Design Association, Student Leadership Council, Community Outreach Team, national fraternities, national sororities.

Athletics ***Intramural sports:*** basketball M/W, cross-country running M/W, football M/W, golf M/W, racquetball M/W, soccer M/W, softball M/W, swimming and diving M/W, tennis M/W, track and field M/W, ultimate Frisbee M/W, volleyball M/W.

Campus security: 24-hour emergency response devices and patrols, controlled dormitory access.

Student services: health clinic, personal/psychological counseling, women's center.

COSTS & FINANCIAL AID
Costs (2020–21) ***Comprehensive fee:*** $55,975 includes full-time tuition ($41,490), mandatory fees ($2895), and room and board ($11,590). ***Required fees:*** $75 per credit hour part-time, $75 per credit hour part-time. ***College room only:*** $8940. ***Payment plan:*** installment.

Financial Aid Of all full-time matriculated undergraduates who enrolled in 2017, 583 applied for aid, 510 were judged to have need, 52 had their need fully met. 137 Federal Work-Study jobs (averaging $1158). In 2017, 82 non-need-based awards were made. ***Average percent of need met:*** 60. ***Average financial aid package:*** $27,398. ***Average need-based loan:*** $4697. ***Average need-based gift aid:*** $23,073. ***Average non-need-based aid:*** $14,168. ***Average indebtedness upon graduation:*** $41,326.

APPLYING
Options: electronic application, early admission, early action, deferred entrance.

Application fee: $40.

Required: essay or personal statement, high school transcript, minimum 2.0 GPA, 1 letter of recommendation, portfolio. ***Recommended:*** interview.

Notification: continuous (freshmen), continuous (transfers).

CONTACT
Cleveland Institute of Art, 11610 Euclid Avenue, Cleveland, OH 44106. *Toll-free phone:* 800-223-4700.

Cleveland Institute of Music
Cleveland, Ohio
http://www.cim.edu/

- **Independent** comprehensive, founded 1920
- **Urban** 488-acre campus
- **Coed**
- **Very difficult** entrance level

FACULTY
Student/faculty ratio: 7:1.

ACADEMICS
Calendar: semesters. *Degrees:* certificates, bachelor's, master's, and postbachelor's certificates.

Library: Cleveland Institute of Music Library.

STUDENT LIFE
Housing options: on-campus residence required through sophomore year; coed. Campus housing is leased by the school. Freshman campus housing is guaranteed.

Activities and organizations: choral group.

Campus security: 24-hour emergency response devices and patrols, late-night transport/escort service, controlled dormitory access.

Student services: health clinic, personal/psychological counseling.

FINANCIAL AID
Financial Aid Of all full-time matriculated undergraduates who enrolled in 2019, 150 applied for aid, 116 were judged to have need, 30 had their need fully met. 76 Federal Work-Study jobs (averaging $2415). In 2019, 110 non-need-based awards were made. ***Average percent of need met:*** 76. ***Average financial aid package:*** $32,532. ***Average need-based loan:*** $3474. ***Average need-based gift aid:*** $28,766. ***Average non-need-based aid:*** $21,885. ***Average indebtedness upon graduation:*** $22,156.

APPLYING
Standardized Tests *Required for some:* SAT or ACT (for admission).

Options: early admission, deferred entrance.

Application fee: $100.

Required: essay or personal statement, high school transcript, 2 letters of recommendation, audition. ***Recommended:*** interview.

CONTACT
Mr. William Fay, Director of Admission, Cleveland Institute of Music, 11021 East Boulevard, Cleveland, OH 44106-1776. *Phone:* 216-795-3107. *Fax.* 216-791-1530. *E-mail:* william.fay@case.edu.

Cleveland State University
Cleveland, Ohio
http://www.csuohio.edu/

- **State-supported** university, founded 1964, part of University System of Ohio
- **Urban** 85-acre campus with easy access to Cleveland, OH
- **Endowment** $66.2 million
- **Coed**
- **Moderately difficult** entrance level

FACULTY
Student/faculty ratio: 17:1.

ACADEMICS
Calendar: semesters. *Degrees:* bachelor's, master's, doctoral, post-master's, and postbachelor's certificates.
Library: Michael Schwartz Library plus 1 other. *Books:* 524,556 (physical), 228,146 (digital/electronic); *Serial titles:* 6,155 (physical), 194 (digital/electronic); *Databases:* 733. Students can reserve study rooms.

STUDENT LIFE
Housing options: coed, special housing for students with disabilities. Campus housing is university owned. Freshman campus housing is guaranteed.

Activities and organizations: drama/theater group, student-run newspaper, radio station, choral group, Black Student Union, Chinese Students and Scholars Association, Through the Cross Campus Ministries, Student Nurses Association, Joint Engineering Council, national fraternities, national sororities.

Athletics Member NCAA. All Division I.

Campus security: 24-hour emergency response devices and patrols, late-night transport/escort service, controlled dormitory access, Campus Watch, CSU Alert Notification System, Community Emergency and Response Team (CERT).

Student services: health clinic, personal/psychological counseling, women's center, veterans affairs office.

COSTS & FINANCIAL AID
Costs (2019–20) ***Tuition:*** area resident $9636 full-time; state resident $9636 full-time, $433 per credit hour part-time; nonresident $13,711 full-time, $615 per credit hour part-time. Full-time tuition and fees vary according to course load, degree level, location, and program. Part-time tuition and fees vary according to course load, degree level, location, and program. ***Required fees:*** $238 full-time. ***Room and board:*** $14,348; room only: $9388. Room and board charges vary according to board plan and housing facility.

Financial Aid Of all full-time matriculated undergraduates who enrolled in 2019, 7,404 applied for aid, 6,410 were judged to have need, 454 had their need fully met. 348 Federal Work-Study jobs (averaging $3550). In 2019, 874 non-need-based awards were made. ***Average percent of need met:*** 32. ***Average financial aid package:*** $9686. ***Average need-based loan:*** $4072. ***Average need-based gift aid:*** $7790. ***Average non-need-based aid:*** $5229. ***Average indebtedness upon graduation:*** $25,895.

APPLYING
Standardized Tests *Required:* SAT or ACT (for admission).

Options: electronic application, deferred entrance.

Application fee: $40.

Required: high school transcript, minimum 2.3 GPA.

CONTACT
Undergraduate Admissions Office, Cleveland State University, 2121 Euclid Avenue, EC 100, Cleveland, OH 44115. *Phone:* 216-523-7416. *Toll-free phone:* 888-CSU-OHIO. *E-mail:* admissions@csuohio.edu.

The College of Wooster
Wooster, Ohio
http://www.wooster.edu/

- **Independent** 4-year, founded 1866, affiliated with Presbyterian Church (U.S.A.)
- **Small-town** 240-acre campus with easy access to Cleveland
- **Endowment** $280.5 million
- **Coed** 1,947 undergraduate students, 99% full-time, 54% women, 46% men
- **Moderately difficult** entrance level, 55% of applicants were admitted

UNDERGRAD STUDENTS
1,934 full-time, 13 part-time. Students come from 46 states and territories; 58 other countries; 65% are from out of state; 9% Black or African American, non-Hispanic/Latino; 6% Hispanic/Latino; 4% Asian, non-Hispanic/Latino; 0.1% American Indian or Alaska Native, non-Hispanic/Latino; 4% Two or more races, non-Hispanic/Latino; 0.9% Race/ethnicity unknown; 16% international; 0.5% transferred in; 99% live on campus.

Freshmen:
Admission: 6,352 applied, 3,472 admitted, 542 enrolled. ***Average high school GPA:*** 3.6. ***Test scores:*** SAT evidence-based reading and writing scores over 500: 95%; SAT math scores over 500: 95%; ACT scores over 18: 100%; SAT evidence-based reading and writing scores over 600: 67%; SAT math scores over 600: 65%; ACT scores over 24: 75%; SAT evidence-based reading and writing scores over 700: 19%; SAT math scores over 700: 28%; ACT scores over 30: 32%.

Retention: 86% of full-time freshmen returned.

FACULTY
Total: 217, 80% full-time, 90% with terminal degrees.

Student/faculty ratio: 10:1.

ACADEMICS
Calendar: semesters. *Degree:* bachelor's.

Special study options: advanced placement credit, double majors, independent study, internships, off-campus study, services for LD students, student-designed majors, study abroad.

Unusual degree programs: 3-2 engineering with Case Western Reserve University, Washington University in St. Louis, University of Michigan; forestry with Duke University; nursing with Case Western Reserve University; social work with Case Western Reserve University; dentistry with Case Western Reserve University, architecture with Washington University in St. Louis.

Computers: Students can access the following: campus intranet, computer help desk, free student e-mail accounts, online (class) grades, online (class) registration, online (class) schedules, learning management system, campus blogging site, campus wiki site. Campuswide network is available. 100% of college-owned or -operated housing units are wired for high-speed Internet access. Wireless service is available via entire campus.
Library: The College of Wooster Libraries plus 3 others. *Books:* 456,925 (physical), 886,374 (digital/electronic); *Serial titles:* 3,255 (physical), 105,460 (digital/electronic); *Databases:* 379. Weekly public service hours: 114; students can reserve study rooms.

STUDENT LIFE
Housing options: on-campus residence required through senior year; coed, women-only. Campus housing is university owned. Freshman campus housing is guaranteed.

Activities and organizations: drama/theater group, student-run newspaper, radio station, choral group, marching band, Volunteer Network, International Student Association, Inter-Greek Council, Wooster Activities Crew, Women's Athletic and Recreation Association.

Athletics Member NCAA. All Division III. ***Intercollegiate sports:*** baseball M, basketball M/W, cheerleading W(c), cross-country running M/W, field hockey W, football M, golf M/W, lacrosse M/W, rugby W(c), soccer M/W, softball W, swimming and diving M/W, tennis M/W, track and field M/W, volleyball W. ***Intramural sports:*** badminton M/W, equestrian sports M(c)/W(c), fencing M, ice hockey M(c)/W(c), table tennis M(c)/W(c), ultimate Frisbee M(c)/W(c), volleyball M(c).

Campus security: 24-hour emergency response devices and patrols, student patrols, late-night transport/escort service, controlled dormitory access.

Student services: health clinic, personal/psychological counseling, women's center.

COSTS & FINANCIAL AID

Costs (2020–21) ***Comprehensive fee:*** $62,100 includes full-time tuition ($49,810), mandatory fees ($440), and room and board ($11,850). Full-time tuition and fees vary according to course load. Part-time tuition: $1545 per credit hour. Part-time tuition and fees vary according to course load. ***College room only:*** $5750. Room and board charges vary according to board plan and housing facility. ***Payment plan:*** installment. ***Waivers:*** employees or children of employees.

Financial Aid Of all full-time matriculated undergraduates who enrolled in 2019, 1,439 applied for aid, 1,278 were judged to have need, 575 had their need fully met. 719 Federal Work-Study jobs (averaging $2201). 242 state and other part-time jobs (averaging $3585). In 2019, 608 non-need-based awards were made. ***Average percent of need met:*** 93. ***Average financial aid package:*** $47,142. ***Average need-based loan:*** $7084. ***Average need-based gift aid:*** $35,524. ***Average non-need-based aid:*** $26,400. ***Average indebtedness upon graduation:*** $32,194.

APPLYING

Standardized Tests *Required:* SAT or ACT (for admission).

Options: electronic application, early admission, early decision, early action, deferred entrance.

Required: essay or personal statement, high school transcript. ***Recommended:*** letters of recommendation, interview.

Application deadlines: 2/15 (freshmen), 7/15 (transfers), 11/15 (early action).

Early decision deadline: 11/1 (for plan 1), 1/15 (for plan 2).

Notification: 4/1 (freshmen), continuous (transfers), 11/15 (early decision plan 1), 2/1 (early decision plan 2), 12/31 (early action).

CONTACT

Ms. Jennifer Winge, Dean of Admissions, The College of Wooster, 1189 Beall Avenue, Wooster, OH 44691-2363. *Phone:* 330-263-2270. *Toll-free phone:* 800-877-9905. *Fax:* 330-263-2621. *E-mail:* admissions@wooster.edu.

Columbus College of Art & Design

Columbus, Ohio

http://www.ccad.edu/

CONTACT

Columbus College of Art & Design, 60 Cleveland Avenue, Columbus, OH 43215-1758. *Phone:* 614-224-9101. *Toll-free phone:* 877-997-2223. *Fax:* 614-232-8344. *E-mail:* admissions@ccad.edu.

Defiance College

Defiance, Ohio

http://www.defiance.edu/

CONTACT

Mrs. Brenda Averesch, Assistant Dean of Admissions and Financial Aid, Defiance College, 701 North Clinton Street, Defiance, OH 43512. *Phone:* 419-783-2352. *Toll-free phone:* 800-520-4632. *Fax:* 419-783-2468. *E-mail:* baveresch@defiance.edu.

Denison University

Granville, Ohio

http://www.denison.edu/

- **Independent** 4-year, founded 1831
- **Suburban** 931-acre campus with easy access to Columbus
- **Coed**
- **Very difficult** entrance level

FACULTY

Student/faculty ratio: 9:1.

ACADEMICS

Calendar: semesters plus optional May term. *Degree:* bachelor's.

Library: William Howard Doane Library. *Books:* 1.4 million (physical), 912,952 (digital/electronic); *Serial titles:* 540 (physical), 653 (digital/electronic); *Databases:* 464. Weekly public service hours: 104; students can reserve study rooms.

STUDENT LIFE

Housing options: on-campus residence required through senior year; coed, men-only, women-only, cooperative. Campus housing is university owned. Freshman campus housing is guaranteed.

Activities and organizations: drama/theater group, student-run newspaper, radio and television station, choral group, national fraternities, national sororities.

Athletics Member NCAA. All Division III.

Campus security: 24-hour emergency response devices and patrols, student patrols, late-night transport/escort service, controlled dormitory access, security lighting, escort.

Student services: health clinic, personal/psychological counseling, women's center.

FINANCIAL AID

Financial Aid Of all full-time matriculated undergraduates who enrolled in 2019, 1,646 applied for aid, 1,354 were judged to have need, 1,353 had their need fully met. In 2019, 839 non-need-based awards were made. ***Average percent of need met:*** 99. ***Average financial aid package:*** $44,087. ***Average need-based loan:*** $4442. ***Average need-based gift aid:*** $35,428. ***Average non-need-based aid:*** $21,786. ***Average indebtedness upon graduation:*** $33,548.

APPLYING

Options: early admission, early decision, deferred entrance.

Required: essay or personal statement, high school transcript, 2 letters of recommendation. ***Recommended:*** interview.

CONTACT

Mr. Michael S. Hills, Director of Admissions, Denison University, 100 West College Street, Granville, OH 43023. *Phone:* 740-587-6627. *Toll-free phone:* 800-DENISON. *E-mail:* hills@denison.edu.

DeVry University–Columbus Campus

Columbus, Ohio

http://www.devry.edu/

- **Proprietary** comprehensive, founded 1952
- **Urban** campus
- **Coed**
- **Minimally difficult** entrance level

FACULTY

Student/faculty ratio: 35:1.

ACADEMICS

Calendar: semesters. *Degrees:* associate, bachelor's, master's, and postbachelor's certificates.

APPLYING

Application fee: $30.

CONTACT

Admissions Office, DeVry University–Columbus Campus, 1350 Alum Creek Drive, Columbus, OH 43209. *Phone:* 614-253-7291. *Toll-free phone:* 866-338-7934.

DeVry University–Seven Hills Campus

Seven Hills, Ohio

http://www.devry.edu/

CONTACT

Admissions Office, DeVry University–Seven Hills Campus, 4141 Rockside Road, Suite 110, Seven Hills, OH 44131. *Phone:* 216-328-8754. *Toll-free phone:* 866-338-7934.

Franciscan University of Steubenville

Steubenville, Ohio

http://www.franciscan.edu/

- **Independent Roman Catholic** comprehensive, founded 1946
- **Suburban** 235-acre campus with easy access to Pittsburg, PA
- **Endowment** $54.5 million
- **Coed**
- **Moderately difficult** entrance level

FACULTY
Student/faculty ratio: 14:1.

ACADEMICS
Calendar: semesters. *Degrees:* associate, bachelor's, and master's.
Library: St. John Paul II Library. *Books:* 143,662 (physical), 254,496 (digital/electronic); *Serial titles:* 590 (physical), 51,894 (digital/electronic); *Databases:* 131. Weekly public service hours: 93.

STUDENT LIFE
Housing options: on-campus residence required through junior year; men-only, women-only. Campus housing is university owned. Freshman applicants given priority for college housing.

Activities and organizations: drama/theater group, student-run newspaper, radio station, choral group.

Athletics Member NCAA. All Division III.

Campus security: 24-hour emergency response devices and patrols, student patrols, late-night transport/escort service, controlled dormitory access.

Student services: health clinic, personal/psychological counseling.

FINANCIAL AID
Financial Aid Of all full-time matriculated undergraduates who enrolled in 2017, 1,582 applied for aid, 1,281 were judged to have need, 221 had their need fully met. In 2017, 634 non-need-based awards were made. ***Average percent of need met:*** 61. ***Average financial aid package:*** $17,301. ***Average need-based loan:*** $4436. ***Average need-based gift aid:*** $13,194. ***Average non-need-based aid:*** $6928. ***Average indebtedness upon graduation:*** $34,222.

APPLYING
Standardized Tests *Required:* SAT or ACT (for admission).

Options: electronic application, deferred entrance.

Application fee: $20.

Required: high school transcript, minimum 2.4 GPA. ***Required for some:*** essay or personal statement, 3 letters of recommendation. ***Recommended:*** interview.

CONTACT
Miss Victoria Kubicz, Assistant Director of Admissions, Franciscan University of Steubenville, 1235 University Boulevard, Steubenville, OH 43952-1763. *Phone:* 740-284-5863. *Toll-free phone:* 800-783-6220. *Fax:* 740-284-5456. *E-mail:* admissions@franciscan.edu.

Franklin University

Columbus, Ohio

http://www.franklin.edu/

CONTACT
Mrs. Lynne Hull, Director of New Student Enrollment, Franklin University, 201 South Grant Avenue, Columbus, OH 43215. *Phone:* 614-947-6046. *Toll-free phone:* 877-341-6300. *E-mail:* hulll@franklin.edu.

Galen College of Nursing

Cincinnati, Ohio

http://www.galencollege.edu/

CONTACT
Galen College of Nursing, 100 East Business Way, Suite 200, Cincinnati, OH 45241. *Toll-free phone:* 877-223-7040.

God's Bible School and College

Cincinnati, Ohio

http://www.gbs.edu/

CONTACT
Heather Couch, Director of Financial Aid and Admissions, God's Bible School and College, 1810 Young Street, Cincinnati, OH 45202-6838. *Phone:* 513-721-7944 Ext. 1161. *Toll-free phone:* 800-486-4637. *Fax:* 513-763-6649. *E-mail:* hcouch@gbs.edu.

Good Samaritan College of Nursing and Health Science

Cincinnati, Ohio

http://www.gscollege.edu/

CONTACT
Admissions Office, Good Samaritan College of Nursing and Health Science, 375 Dixmyth Avenue, Cincinnati, OH 45220. *Phone:* 513-862-2743. *Fax:* 513-862-3572.

Heidelberg University

Tiffin, Ohio

http://www.heidelberg.edu/

CONTACT
Mr. Mike Brown, Director of Admission, Heidelberg University, 310 East Market Street, Tiffin, OH 44883. *Phone:* 419-448-2507. *Toll-free phone:* 800-434-3352. *Fax:* 419-448-2334. *E-mail:* mbrown@heidelberg.edu.

Herzing University

Akron, Ohio

http://www.herzing.edu/akron

CONTACT
Herzing University, 1600 South Arlington Street, Suite 100, Akron, OH 44306. *Toll-free phone:* 800-596-0724.

Herzing University

Toledo, Ohio

http://www.herzing.edu/toledo

CONTACT
Herzing University, 5212 Hill Avenue, Toledo, OH 43615. *Toll-free phone:* 800-596-0724.

Hiram College

Hiram, Ohio

http://www.hiram.edu/

- **Independent** comprehensive, founded 1850, affiliated with Christian Church (Disciples of Christ)
- **Rural** 110-acre campus with easy access to Cleveland
- **Endowment** $73.4 million
- **Coed**
- **Moderately difficult** entrance level

FACULTY
Student/faculty ratio: 10:1.

ACADEMICS
Calendar: semesters. *Degrees:* bachelor's and master's.
Library: Hiram College Library. *Books:* 177,742 (physical), 168,829 (digital/electronic); *Serial titles:* 85 (physical), 7,340 (digital/electronic); *Databases:* 279. Weekly public service hours: 90.

STUDENT LIFE
Housing options: on-campus residence required through senior year; coed, men-only, women-only, cooperative, special housing for students with disabilities. Campus housing is university owned. Freshman campus housing is guaranteed.

Activities and organizations: drama/theater group, choral group, Black Students United, Intercultural Forum, Terrier Activities Board, Student-Athlete Advisory Committee, Theater Guild.

Athletics Member NCAA. All Division III.

Campus security: 24-hour emergency response devices and patrols, student patrols, late-night transport/escort service, controlled dormitory access.

Student services: health clinic, personal/psychological counseling.

COSTS & FINANCIAL AID

Costs (2019–20) ***Comprehensive fee:*** $48,000 includes full-time tuition ($35,360), mandatory fees ($2350), and room and board ($10,290). Full-time tuition and fees vary according to degree level and location. Part-time tuition: $1179 per credit hour. Part-time tuition and fees vary according to degree level and location. No tuition increase for student's term of enrollment. ***College room only:*** $5150. Room and board charges vary according to board plan and housing facility.

Financial Aid Of all full-time matriculated undergraduates who enrolled in 2019, 765 applied for aid, 732 were judged to have need, 65 had their need fully met. 562 Federal Work-Study jobs (averaging $2128). In 2019, 32 non-need-based awards were made. ***Average percent of need met:*** 75. ***Average financial aid package:*** $29,456. ***Average need-based loan:*** $4176. ***Average need-based gift aid:*** $17,496. ***Average non-need-based aid:*** $13,997. ***Average indebtedness upon graduation:*** $36,500.

APPLYING

Standardized Tests *Required for some:* SAT or ACT (for admission), SAT or ACT for applicants with cumulative GPA below 2.8, nursing or education applicants, or Trustee and/or President's Scholarships applicants.

Options: electronic application, deferred entrance.

Application fee: $25.

Required: essay or personal statement, high school transcript. ***Recommended:*** minimum 2.8 GPA, interview.

CONTACT

Sherman C. Dean II, Director of Admission, Hiram College, PO Box 96, Hiram, OH 44234. *Phone:* 330-569-5169. *Toll-free phone:* 800-362-5280. *Fax:* 330-569-5944. *E-mail:* admission@hiram.edu.

John Carroll University

University Heights, Ohio

http://www.jcu.edu/

- **Independent Roman Catholic (Jesuit)** comprehensive, founded 1886
- **Suburban** 62-acre campus with easy access to Cleveland
- **Endowment** $223.5 million
- **Coed** 3,017 undergraduate students, 97% full-time, 46% women, 54% men
- **Moderately difficult** entrance level, 86% of applicants were admitted

UNDERGRAD STUDENTS

2,925 full-time, 92 part-time. Students come from 34 states and territories; 29 other countries; 34% are from out of state; 4% Black or African American, non-Hispanic/Latino; 4% Hispanic/Latino; 3% Asian, non-Hispanic/Latino; 0.1% American Indian or Alaska Native, non-Hispanic/Latino; 2% Two or more races, non-Hispanic/Latino; 1% Race/ethnicity unknown; 1% international; 2% transferred in; 52% live on campus.

Freshmen:

Admission: 3,782 applied, 3,265 admitted, 725 enrolled. ***Average high school GPA:*** 3.6. ***Test scores:*** SAT evidence-based reading and writing scores over 500: 93%; SAT math scores over 500: 92%; ACT scores over 18: 97%; SAT evidence-based reading and writing scores over 600: 49%; SAT math scores over 600: 48%; ACT scores over 24: 63%; SAT evidence-based reading and writing scores over 700: 7%; SAT math scores over 700: 10%; ACT scores over 30: 16%.

Retention: 89% of full-time freshmen returned.

FACULTY

Total: 378, 48% full-time, 66% with terminal degrees.

Student/faculty ratio: 13:1.

ACADEMICS

Calendar: semesters. *Degrees:* bachelor's, master's, and post-master's certificates.

Special study options: advanced placement credit, distance learning, double majors, honors programs, independent study, internships, off-campus study, part-time degree program, services for LD students, student-designed majors, study abroad, summer session for credit. ***ROTC:*** Army (b).

Unusual degree programs: 3-2 business administration; engineering with Case Western Reserve University; nursing with Ursuline College; social work with Case Western Reserve University.

Computers: 396 computers/terminals are available on campus for general student use. Students can access the following: campus intranet, computer help desk, free student e-mail accounts, online (class) grades, online (class) registration, online (class) schedules, advising system; course management site (Canvas); online financial aid and billing; online housing selection. Campuswide network is available. 100% of college-owned or -operated housing units are wired for high-speed Internet access. Wireless service is available via entire campus.

Library: Grasselli Library. *Books:* 309,993 (physical), 670,707 (digital/electronic); *Serial titles:* 278 (physical), 90,378 (digital/electronic); *Databases:* 308. Weekly public service hours: 111; students can reserve study rooms.

STUDENT LIFE

Housing options: on-campus residence required through sophomore year; coed, women-only, special housing for students with disabilities. Campus housing is university owned. Freshman campus housing is guaranteed.

Activities and organizations: drama/theater group, student-run newspaper, radio and television station, choral group, Cultural Organizations, Student Government, Club Sports, Fraternities and Sororities, Student Union Programming Board, national fraternities, national sororities.

Athletics Member NCAA. All Division III. ***Intercollegiate sports:*** baseball M, basketball M/W, cheerleading M(c)/W(c), cross-country running M/W, football M, golf M/W, ice hockey M(c), lacrosse M/W, rowing M(c)/W(c), rugby M(c), sailing M(c)/W(c), soccer M/W, softball W, swimming and diving M/W, tennis M/W, track and field M/W, ultimate Frisbee M(c)/W(c), volleyball M(c)/W, wrestling M. ***Intramural sports:*** badminton M/W, basketball M/W, football M/W, golf M/W, racquetball M/W, soccer M/W, softball M/W, tennis M/W, volleyball M/W.

Campus security: 24-hour emergency response devices and patrols, late-night transport/escort service, controlled dormitory access, student-led EMS program.

Student services: health clinic, personal/psychological counseling, veterans affairs office.

COSTS & FINANCIAL AID

Costs (2020–21) ***One-time required fee:*** $325. ***Comprehensive fee:*** $56,965 includes full-time tuition ($42,675), mandatory fees ($1730), and room and board ($12,560). Full-time tuition and fees vary according to course load. Part-time tuition: $1415 per credit hour. Part-time tuition and fees vary according to course load. ***College room only:*** $6940. Room and board charges vary according to board plan and housing facility. ***Payment plan:*** installment. ***Waivers:*** employees or children of employees.

Financial Aid Of all full-time matriculated undergraduates who enrolled in 2018, 2,556 applied for aid, 2,143 were judged to have need, 548 had their need fully met. In 2018, 786 non-need-based awards were made. ***Average percent of need met:*** 81. ***Average financial aid package:*** $33,327. ***Average need-based loan:*** $3976. ***Average need-based gift aid:*** $27,317. ***Average non-need-based aid:*** $21,743. ***Average indebtedness upon graduation:*** $32,956.

APPLYING

Standardized Tests *Required:* SAT or ACT (for admission).

Options: electronic application, early admission, early action, deferred entrance.

Required: essay or personal statement, high school transcript, 1 letter of recommendation. ***Required for some:*** interview.

Application deadlines: rolling (freshmen), 8/15 (transfers), 12/1 (early action).

Notification: continuous until 11/1 (freshmen), continuous (transfers), 12/15 (early action).

CONTACT

Mr. Steven P. Vitatoe, Assistant Vice President for Enrollment Operations & Analytics, John Carroll University, 1 John Carroll Boulevard, University Heights, OH 44118. *Phone:* 888-335-6800. *Toll-free phone:* 888-335-6800. *E-mail:* admission@jcu.edu.

Kent State University

Kent, Ohio

http://www.kent.edu/

CONTACT

Mr. Christopher Buttenschon, Senior Assistant Director of Admissions, Kent State University, 161 Michael Schwartz Center, Admissions Office, Kent, OH 44242-0001. *Phone:* 330-672-2444. *Toll-free phone:* 800-988-KENT. *Fax:* 330-672-2499. *E-mail:* cbuttens@kent.edu.

Kent State University at Ashtabula

Ashtabula, Ohio

http://www.ashtabula.kent.edu/

- **State-supported** primarily 2-year, founded 1958, part of Kent State University System
- **Small-town** 83-acre campus with easy access to Cleveland
- **Coed**
- **Noncompetitive** entrance level

FACULTY

Student/faculty ratio: 22:1.

ACADEMICS

Calendar: semesters. *Degrees:* certificates, associate, and bachelor's (also offers some upper-level and graduate courses).
Library: Kent State at Ashtabula Library. Weekly public service hours: 56.

STUDENT LIFE

Housing options: college housing not available.

Activities and organizations: Student Government, Student Veterans Association, Student Nurses Association, Student Occupational Therapy Association, Media Club.

Campus security: 24-hour emergency response devices.

Student services: veterans affairs office.

FINANCIAL AID

Financial Aid Of all full-time matriculated undergraduates who enrolled in 2019, 448 applied for aid, 385 were judged to have need, 9 had their need fully met. 16 Federal Work-Study jobs (averaging $2576). In 2019, 31 non-need-based awards were made. ***Average percent of need met:*** 55. ***Average financial aid package:*** $8076. ***Average need-based loan:*** $3698. ***Average need-based gift aid:*** $5386. ***Average non-need-based aid:*** $1606.

APPLYING

Standardized Tests *Required for some:* SAT or ACT (for admission). *Recommended:* SAT or ACT (for admission).

Options: electronic application, deferred entrance.

Application fee: $40.

Required: high school transcript.

CONTACT

Megan Krippel, Admissions Coordinator, Kent State University at Ashtabula, 3300 Lake Road West, Ashtabula, OH 44004. *Phone:* 440-964-4277. *Fax:* 440-964-4269. *E-mail:* ashtabula_admissions@kent.edu.

Kent State University at East Liverpool

East Liverpool, Ohio

http://www.eliv.kent.edu/

- **State-supported** primarily 2-year, founded 1967, part of Kent State University System
- **Small-town** 3-acre campus with easy access to Pittsburgh, Youngstown
- **Coed**
- **Noncompetitive** entrance level

FACULTY

Student/faculty ratio: 26:1.

ACADEMICS

Calendar: semesters. *Degrees:* certificates, associate, and bachelor's.
Library: Paul Blair Memorial Library. Weekly public service hours: 46.

STUDENT LIFE

Housing options: college housing not available.

Activities and organizations: Undergraduate Student Government, Student Nurses Association, Environmental Club, Student Occupational Therapist Assistants, Physical Therapist Assistant Club.

Campus security: 24-hour emergency response devices, student patrols, late-night transport/escort service.

Student services: personal/psychological counseling, veterans affairs office.

FINANCIAL AID

Financial Aid Of all full-time matriculated undergraduates who enrolled in 2019, 129 applied for aid, 113 were judged to have need, 8 had their need fully met. In 2019, 9 non-need-based awards were made. ***Average percent of need met:*** 59. ***Average financial aid package:*** $7965. ***Average need-based loan:*** $3794. ***Average need-based gift aid:*** $5430. ***Average non-need-based aid:*** $878.

APPLYING

Standardized Tests *Required for some:* SAT or ACT (for admission). *Recommended:* SAT or ACT (for admission).

Options: electronic application, deferred entrance.

Application fee: $40.

Required: high school transcript.

CONTACT

Office of Admissions, Kent State University at East Liverpool, 400 East 4th Street, East Liverpool, OH 43920-3497. *Phone:* 330-385-3805.

Kent State University at Geauga

Burton, Ohio

http://www.geauga.kent.edu/

- **State-supported** comprehensive, founded 1964, part of Kent State University System
- **Rural** 87-acre campus with easy access to Cleveland, Akron, Youngstown
- **Coed**
- **Noncompetitive** entrance level

FACULTY

Student/faculty ratio: 22:1.

ACADEMICS

Calendar: semesters. *Degrees:* certificates, associate, bachelor's, and master's.
Library: Kent State University at Geauga Library. *Books:* 12,083 (physical); *Serial titles:* 43 (physical). Weekly public service hours: 53.

STUDENT LIFE

Housing options: college housing not available.

Activities and organizations: National Student Nurse Association Twinsburg, Geauga Student Nurses Association, Alpha Delta Nu-Gamma Sigma Chapter, Kent State University Geauga College Republicans, Undergraduate Student Government.

Campus security: 24-hour emergency response devices.

Student services: veterans affairs office.

FINANCIAL AID

Financial Aid Of all full-time matriculated undergraduates who enrolled in 2019, 462 applied for aid, 349 were judged to have need, 22 had their need fully met. 10 Federal Work-Study jobs (averaging $2443). In 2019, 26 non-need-based awards were made. ***Average percent of need met:*** 60. ***Average financial aid package:*** $7814. ***Average need-based loan:*** $3638. ***Average need-based gift aid:*** $5273. ***Average non-need-based aid:*** $1096.

APPLYING

Standardized Tests *Recommended:* SAT or ACT (for admission).

Options: electronic application, deferred entrance.

Application fee: $40.

Required: high school transcript.

CONTACT

Kent State University at Geauga, 14111 Claridon-Troy Road, Burton, OH 44021. *Phone:* 440-834-4187. *Fax:* 440-834-3786. *E-mail:* geaugaadmissions@kent.edu.

Kent State University at Salem

Salem, Ohio

http://www.salem.kent.edu/

- **State-supported** primarily 2-year, founded 1966, part of Kent State University System
- **Rural** 100-acre campus with easy access to Youngstown
- **Coed**
- **Noncompetitive** entrance level

FACULTY

Student/faculty ratio: 21:1.

ACADEMICS

Calendar: semesters. *Degrees:* certificates, associate, and bachelor's (also offers some upper-level and graduate courses).

Library: Kent State Salem Library. *Books:* 23,500 (physical); *Serial titles:* 4,500 (physical).

STUDENT LIFE

Housing options: college housing not available.

Campus security: 24-hour emergency response devices, late-night transport/escort service.

Student services: personal/psychological counseling.

FINANCIAL AID

Financial Aid Of all full-time matriculated undergraduates who enrolled in 2019, 543 applied for aid, 420 were judged to have need, 34 had their need fully met. 18 Federal Work-Study jobs (averaging $2425). In 2019, 73 non-need-based awards were made. ***Average percent of need met:*** 60. ***Average financial aid package:*** $7523. ***Average need-based loan:*** $3684. ***Average need-based gift aid:*** $4803. ***Average non-need-based aid:*** $887.

APPLYING

Standardized Tests *Required for some:* SAT or ACT (for admission). *Recommended:* SAT or ACT (for admission).

Options: electronic application, deferred entrance.

Application fee: $40.

Required: high school transcript. ***Required for some:*** essay or personal statement.

CONTACT

Office of Admissions, Kent State University at Salem, 2491 State Route 45 South, Salem, OH 44460-9412. *Phone:* 330-332-0361.

Kent State University at Stark

Canton, Ohio

http://www.stark.kent.edu/

- **State-supported** comprehensive, founded 1946, part of Kent State University System
- **Suburban** 200-acre campus with easy access to Cleveland, Akron, Canton
- **Coed**
- **Noncompetitive** entrance level

FACULTY

Student/faculty ratio: 23:1.

ACADEMICS

Calendar: semesters. *Degrees:* associate, bachelor's, and master's.

Library: Kent State Stark Library. *Serial titles:* 600 (physical). Weekly public service hours: 72; students can reserve study rooms.

STUDENT LIFE

Housing options: college housing not available.

Activities and organizations: drama/theater group, choral group, Music Technology Club, Biology Club, SCRUBS (Nursing Organization), HDFS (Human Development Family Studies), Revive (Faith Based).

Campus security: 24-hour emergency response devices, student patrols, late-night transport/escort service.

Student services: personal/psychological counseling, veterans affairs office.

FINANCIAL AID

Financial Aid Of all full-time matriculated undergraduates who enrolled in 2019, 1,506 applied for aid, 1,151 were judged to have need, 120 had their need fully met. 51 Federal Work-Study jobs (averaging $2317). In 2019, 69 non-need-based awards were made. ***Average percent of need met:*** 62. ***Average financial aid package:*** $7321. ***Average need-based loan:*** $3840. ***Average need-based gift aid:*** $4729. ***Average non-need-based aid:*** $2298.

APPLYING

Standardized Tests *Recommended:* SAT or ACT (for admission).

Options: electronic application, deferred entrance.

Application fee: $40.

Required: high school transcript.

CONTACT

Office of Admissions, Kent State University at Stark, 6000 Frank Avenue NW, North Canton, OH 44720. *Phone:* 330-244-3251. *Fax:* 330-499-0301. *E-mail:* starkadmissions@kent.edu.

Kent State University at Trumbull

Warren, Ohio

http://www.trumbull.kent.edu/

- **State-supported** primarily 2-year, founded 1954, part of Kent State University System
- **Suburban** 438-acre campus with easy access to Akron, Youngstown
- **Coed**
- **Noncompetitive** entrance level

FACULTY

Student/faculty ratio: 25:1.

ACADEMICS

Calendar: semesters. *Degrees:* associate and bachelor's (also offers some upper-level and graduate courses).

Library: Gelbke Library at Kent State Trumbull. *Books:* 40,000 (physical), 100,000 (digital/electronic); *Serial titles:* 40 (physical); *Databases:* 459. Weekly public service hours: 56.

STUDENT LIFE

Housing options: college housing not available.

Activities and organizations: drama/theater group, The National Society for Leadership and Success, Sigma Alpha Pi, Jurisprudence Organization, Student Nurses Association, Pride Alliance, S.E.E.D.S.

Campus security: 24-hour emergency response devices, late-night transport/escort service, patrols by trained security personnel during hours of operation.

Student services: personal/psychological counseling.

FINANCIAL AID

Financial Aid Of all full-time matriculated undergraduates who enrolled in 2019, 606 applied for aid, 516 were judged to have need, 40 had their need fully met. 20 Federal Work-Study jobs (averaging $2989). In 2019, 54 non-need-based awards were made. ***Average percent of need met:*** 60. ***Average financial aid package:*** $8081. ***Average need-based loan:*** $3706. ***Average need-based gift aid:*** $5469. ***Average non-need-based aid:*** $2215.

APPLYING

Standardized Tests *Recommended:* SAT or ACT (for admission).

Options: electronic application, deferred entrance.

Application fee: $40.

Required: high school transcript.

CONTACT
Office of Enrollment Management, Kent State University at Trumbull, 4314 Mahoning Avenue, NW, Warren, OH 44483-1998. *Phone:* 330-675-8860. *E-mail:* trumbullinfo@kent.edu.

Kent State University at Tuscarawas

New Philadelphia, Ohio

http://www.tusc.kent.edu/

- **State-supported** primarily 2-year, founded 1962, part of Kent State University System
- **Small-town** 180-acre campus with easy access to Akron, Canton
- **Coed** 2,168 undergraduate students, 63% full-time, 58% women, 42% men
- **Noncompetitive** entrance level, 100% of applicants were admitted

UNDERGRAD STUDENTS
1,360 full-time, 808 part-time. Students come from 8 states and territories; 3 other countries; 2% are from out of state; 4% Black or African American, non-Hispanic/Latino; 2% Hispanic/Latino; 0.7% Asian, non-Hispanic/Latino; 0.2% American Indian or Alaska Native, non-Hispanic/Latino; 3% Two or more races, non-Hispanic/Latino; 3% Race/ethnicity unknown; 0.9% international; 4% transferred in.

Freshmen:
Admission: 459 applied, 459 admitted, 305 enrolled. ***Average high school GPA:*** 3.1.

Retention: 64% of full-time freshmen returned.

FACULTY
Total: 126, 40% full-time.

Student/faculty ratio: 22:1.

ACADEMICS
Calendar: semesters. *Degrees:* certificates, diplomas, associate, and bachelor's (also offers some upper-level and graduate courses).

Special study options: academic remediation for entering students, accelerated degree program, adult/continuing education programs, advanced placement credit, distance learning, double majors, freshman honors college, honors programs, independent study, internships, part-time degree program, services for LD students, student-designed majors, study abroad, summer session for credit. ***ROTC:*** Army (c), Air Force (c).

Computers: 194 computers/terminals are available on campus for general student use. Students can access the following: computer help desk, free student e-mail accounts, online (class) grades, online (class) registration, online (class) schedules. Campuswide network is available. Wireless service is available via entire campus.
Library: Kent State Tuscarawas Library. *Books:* 52,500 (physical), 12 (digital/electronic); *Serial titles:* 540 (physical).

STUDENT LIFE
Housing options: college housing not available.

Activities and organizations: choral group, Student Nurses Association, Technology Club, Vet Tech Student Chapter, Realms of Roleplay, Vision.

Athletics Member USCAA. ***Intercollegiate sports:*** baseball M, basketball M/W, cross-country running M/W, golf M/W, softball W, track and field M/W, volleyball W, wrestling M.

Campus security: 24-hour emergency response devices.

FINANCIAL AID
Financial Aid Of all full-time matriculated undergraduates who enrolled in 2019, 661 applied for aid, 529 were judged to have need, 66 had their need fully met. 21 Federal Work-Study jobs (averaging $2804). In 2019, 96 non-need-based awards were made. ***Average percent of need met:*** 64. ***Average financial aid package:*** $7265. ***Average need-based loan:*** $3539. ***Average need-based gift aid:*** $4692. ***Average non-need-based aid:*** $1267.

APPLYING
Standardized Tests *Recommended:* SAT or ACT (for admission).

Options: electronic application, deferred entrance.

Application fee: $40.

Required: high school transcript.

Application deadlines: 8/15 (freshmen), 8/15 (transfers).

Notification: continuous (freshmen), continuous (transfers).

CONTACT
Office of Admissions, Kent State University at Tuscarawas, 330 University Drive NE, New Philadelphia, OH 44663-9403. *Phone:* 330-339-3391. *E-mail:* infotusc@kent.edu.

Kenyon College

Gambier, Ohio

http://www.kenyon.edu/

- **Independent** 4-year, founded 1824
- **Rural** 1000-acre campus with easy access to Columbus
- **Endowment** $208.9 million
- **Coed** 1,734 undergraduate students, 99% full-time, 55% women, 45% men
- **Most difficult** entrance level, 36% of applicants were admitted

UNDERGRAD STUDENTS
1,719 full-time, 15 part-time. Students come from 47 states and territories; 46 other countries; 87% are from out of state; 4% Black or African American, non-Hispanic/Latino; 8% Hispanic/Latino; 4% Asian, non-Hispanic/Latino; 5% Two or more races, non-Hispanic/Latino; 3% Race/ethnicity unknown; 7% international; 0.3% transferred in; 99% live on campus.

Freshmen:
Admission: 6,152 applied, 2,204 admitted, 539 enrolled. ***Average high school GPA:*** 3.9. ***Test scores:*** SAT evidence-based reading and writing scores over 500: 100%; SAT math scores over 500: 100%; ACT scores over 18: 100%; SAT evidence-based reading and writing scores over 600: 93%; SAT math scores over 600: 88%; ACT scores over 24: 97%; SAT evidence-based reading and writing scores over 700: 47%; SAT math scores over 700: 48%; ACT scores over 30: 74%.

Retention: 91% of full-time freshmen returned.

FACULTY
Total: 196, 80% full-time, 82% with terminal degrees.

Student/faculty ratio: 10:1.

ACADEMICS
Calendar: semesters. *Degree:* bachelor's.

Special study options: accelerated degree program, advanced placement credit, double majors, honors programs, independent study, internships, off-campus study, services for LD students, student-designed majors, study abroad.

Unusual degree programs: 3-2 engineering with Washington University in St. Louis, Case Western Reserve University, Rensselaer Polytechnic Institute; environmental science with Duke University, education with The Bank Street College of Education.

Computers: 715 computers/terminals are available on campus for general student use. Students can access the following: campus intranet, computer help desk, free student e-mail accounts, online (class) grades, online (class) registration, online (class) schedules, commercial databases. Campuswide network is available. 99% of college-owned or -operated housing units are wired for high-speed Internet access. Wireless service is available via entire campus.
Library: Olin Library plus 1 other. *Books:* 495,501 (physical), 42,965 (digital/electronic); *Serial titles:* 1,670 (physical), 43,534 (digital/electronic); *Databases:* 332. Weekly public service hours: 131; students can reserve study rooms.

STUDENT LIFE
Housing options: on-campus residence required through senior year; coed, men-only, women-only, special housing for students with disabilities. Campus housing is university owned. Freshman campus housing is guaranteed.

Activities and organizations: drama/theater group, student-run newspaper, radio station, choral group, student advisory groups, student radio station, musical groups, intramural sports and clubs, outdoors club, national fraternities, national sororities.

Athletics Member NCAA. All Division III. ***Intercollegiate sports:*** baseball M, basketball M/W, cross-country running M/W, equestrian sports M(c)/W(c), field hockey W, football M, golf M, lacrosse M/W, rugby M(c)/W(c), soccer M/W, softball W, squash M(c)/W(c), swimming and diving M/W, tennis M/W, track and field M/W, ultimate Frisbee M(c)/W(c), volleyball W. ***Intramural sports:*** archery M(c)/W(c), basketball M/W, fencing M(c)/W(c), racquetball M/W, soccer M(c)/W(c), tennis M(c)/W(c), volleyball M/W.

Campus security: 24-hour emergency response devices and patrols, student patrols, late-night transport/escort service, controlled dormitory access.

Student services: health clinic, personal/psychological counseling, women's center.

COSTS & FINANCIAL AID

Costs (2020–21) ***Comprehensive fee:*** $73,930 includes full-time tuition ($60,800), mandatory fees ($300), and room and board ($12,830). Full-time tuition and fees vary according to reciprocity agreements. Part-time tuition and fees vary according to reciprocity agreements. ***College room only:*** $5420. Room and board charges vary according to housing facility and student level. ***Payment plan:*** installment. ***Waivers:*** employees or children of employees.

Financial Aid Of all full-time matriculated undergraduates who enrolled in 2019, 994 applied for aid, 805 were judged to have need, 805 had their need fully met. In 2019, 378 non-need-based awards were made. ***Average percent of need met:*** 100. ***Average financial aid package:*** $46,639. ***Average need-based loan:*** $3160. ***Average need-based gift aid:*** $43,767. ***Average non-need-based aid:*** $14,632. ***Average indebtedness upon graduation:*** $26,865. ***Financial aid deadline:*** 1/15.

APPLYING

Standardized Tests *Required:* SAT or ACT (for admission).

Options: electronic application, early admission, early decision, deferred entrance.

Required: essay or personal statement, high school transcript, counselor recommendation. ***Recommended:*** 2 letters of recommendation, interview.

Application deadlines: 1/15 (freshmen), 4/1 (transfers).

Early decision deadline: 11/15 (for plan 1), 1/15 (for plan 2).

Notification: 4/1 (freshmen), 5/15 (transfers), 12/15 (early decision plan 1), 2/1 (early decision plan 2).

CONTACT

Ms. Diane Anci, Vice President of Enrollment Management and Dean of Admissions and Financial Aid, Kenyon College, Ransom Hall, Gambier, OH 43022. *Phone:* 740-427-5776. *Toll-free phone:* 800-848-2468. *Fax:* 740-427-5770. *E-mail:* admissions@kenyon.edu.

Kettering College

Kettering, Ohio

http://www.kc.edu/

CONTACT

Mrs. Becky McDonald, Director of Enrollment Services, Kettering College, 3737 Southern Boulevard, Kettering, OH 45429-1299. *Phone:* 937-395-8628. *Toll-free phone:* 800-433-5262. *Fax:* 937-296-4238.

Lake Erie College

Painesville, Ohio

http://www.lec.edu/

CONTACT

Mrs. Liz Sellers, Director of Admissions, Lake Erie College, 391 West Washington Street, Painesville, OH 44077-3389. *Phone:* 440-375-7251. *Toll-free phone:* 800-916-0904. *Fax:* 440-375-7058. *E-mail:* admissions@lec.edu.

Lourdes University

Sylvania, Ohio

http://www.lourdes.edu/

CONTACT

Amy Houston, Associate Director of Admissions, Lourdes University, 6832 Convent Boulevard, Sylvania, OH 43560. *Phone:* 419-885-5291. *Toll-free phone:* 800-878-3210.

Malone University

Canton, Ohio

http://www.malone.edu/

- **Independent** comprehensive, founded 1892, affiliated with Evangelical Friends Church–Eastern Region
- **Suburban** 96-acre campus with easy access to Cleveland
- **Endowment** $20.7 million
- **Coed** 1,177 undergraduate students, 78% full-time, 61% women, 39% men
- **Moderately difficult** entrance level, 71% of applicants were admitted

UNDERGRAD STUDENTS

923 full-time, 254 part-time. Students come from 27 states and territories; 10 other countries; 10% are from out of state; 8% Black or African American, non-Hispanic/Latino; 2% Hispanic/Latino; 0.4% Asian, non-Hispanic/Latino; 0.1% American Indian or Alaska Native, non-Hispanic/Latino; 4% Two or more races, non-Hispanic/Latino; 5% Race/ethnicity unknown; 2% international; 3% transferred in; 60% live on campus.

Freshmen:

Admission: 1,899 applied, 1,346 admitted, 244 enrolled. ***Average high school GPA:*** 3.4. ***Test scores:*** SAT evidence-based reading and writing scores over 500: 64%; SAT math scores over 500: 64%; ACT scores over 18: 90%; SAT evidence-based reading and writing scores over 600: 36%; SAT math scores over 600: 21%; ACT scores over 24: 42%; SAT evidence-based reading and writing scores over 700: 2%; SAT math scores over 700: 2%; ACT scores over 30: 5%.

Retention: 60% of full-time freshmen returned.

FACULTY

Total: 163, 46% full-time, 52% with terminal degrees.

Student/faculty ratio: 12:1.

ACADEMICS

Calendar: semesters. *Degrees:* bachelor's, master's, and post-master's certificates.

Special study options: academic remediation for entering students, accelerated degree program, adult/continuing education programs, advanced placement credit, distance learning, double majors, honors programs, independent study, internships, off-campus study, part-time degree program, services for LD students, student-designed majors, study abroad, summer session for credit.

Computers: 220 computers/terminals and 3,900 ports are available on campus for general student use. Students can access the following: campus intranet, free student e-mail accounts, online (class) grades, online (class) registration, online (class) schedules, online advising, online financial aid information, and online credit card payments. Campuswide network is available. 100% of college-owned or -operated housing units are wired for high-speed Internet access. Wireless service is available via entire campus.

Library: Everett L. Cattell Library plus 1 other. *Books:* 169,479 (physical), 312,753 (digital/electronic); *Serial titles:* 2,035 (physical), 39,854 (digital/electronic); *Databases:* 176. Weekly public service hours: 82; study areas open 24 hours, 5–7 days a week.

STUDENT LIFE

Housing options: on-campus residence required through junior year; men-only, women-only, special housing for students with disabilities. Campus housing is university owned. Freshman applicants given priority for college housing.

Activities and organizations: drama/theater group, student-run newspaper, choral group, marching band, Celebration Worship Services (and other Spiritual Formation activities), Student Activities Council, Student Senate, FCA (Fellowship of Christian Athletes), intramural athletics.

Athletics Member NCAA. All Division II. ***Intercollegiate sports:*** baseball M(s), basketball M(s)/W(s), cheerleading M/W, cross-country running M(s)/W(s), golf M(s)/W(s), soccer M(s)/W(s), softball W(s), swimming and diving M(s)/W(s), track and field M(s)/W(s), volleyball W(s). ***Intramural sports:*** basketball M/W, football M/W, soccer M/W, tennis M/W, ultimate Frisbee M/W, volleyball M/W.

Campus security: 24-hour emergency response devices and patrols, late-night transport/escort service, controlled dormitory access.

Student services: health clinic, personal/psychological counseling.

COSTS & FINANCIAL AID
Costs (2020–21) ***Comprehensive fee:*** $42,316 includes full-time tuition ($31,416), mandatory fees ($1000), and room and board ($9900). Part-time tuition: $520 per credit hour. Part-time tuition and fees vary according to course load. ***Required fees:*** $250 per term part-time. ***College room only:*** $4840. Room and board charges vary according to board plan. ***Payment plan:*** installment. ***Waivers:*** senior citizens and employees or children of employees.

Financial Aid Of all full-time matriculated undergraduates who enrolled in 2017, 939 applied for aid, 879 were judged to have need, 145 had their need fully met. 361 Federal Work-Study jobs (averaging $1866). 109 state and other part-time jobs (averaging $1797). In 2017, 144 non-need-based awards were made. ***Average percent of need met:*** 79. ***Average financial aid package:*** $26,785. ***Average need-based loan:*** $4217. ***Average need-based gift aid:*** $23,026. ***Average non-need-based aid:*** $12,874. ***Average indebtedness upon graduation:*** $32,495. ***Financial aid deadline:*** 7/31.

APPLYING
Standardized Tests *Required:* SAT or ACT (for admission).

Options: electronic application, early admission, deferred entrance.

Application fee: $20.

Required: high school transcript, minimum 2.0 GPA. ***Required for some:*** essay or personal statement. ***Recommended:*** interview.

Application deadlines: rolling (freshmen), rolling (out-of-state freshmen), rolling (transfers).

Notification: continuous (freshmen), continuous (out-of-state freshmen), continuous (transfers).

CONTACT
Mrs. Anissa D. Scott, Assistant Director, Admissions, Malone University, 2600 Cleveland Avenue NW, Canton, OH 44709-3308. *Phone:* 330-471-8153. *Toll-free phone:* 800-521-1146. *Fax:* 330-471-8149. *E-mail:* admissions@malone.edu.

Marietta College

Marietta, Ohio

http://www.marietta.edu/

- **Independent** comprehensive, founded 1835
- **Small-town** 90-acre campus
- **Endowment** $70.3 million
- **Coed** 1,065 undergraduate students, 90% full-time, 39% women, 61% men
- **Moderately difficult** entrance level, 93% of applicants were admitted

UNDERGRAD STUDENTS
954 full-time, 111 part-time. Students come from 31 states and territories; 8 other countries; 33% are from out of state; 5% Black or African American, non-Hispanic/Latino; 2% Hispanic/Latino; 0.8% Asian, non-Hispanic/Latino; 0.2% American Indian or Alaska Native, non-Hispanic/Latino; 4% Two or more races, non-Hispanic/Latino; 7% Race/ethnicity unknown; 17% international; 3% transferred in; 70% live on campus.

Freshmen:
Admission: 1,308 applied, 1,217 admitted, 272 enrolled. ***Average high school GPA:*** 3.4. ***Test scores:*** SAT evidence-based reading and writing scores over 500: 73%; SAT math scores over 500: 71%; ACT scores over 18: 93%; SAT evidence-based reading and writing scores over 600: 33%; SAT math scores over 600: 33%; ACT scores over 24: 38%; SAT evidence-based reading and writing scores over 700: 6%; SAT math scores over 700: 8%; ACT scores over 30: 4%.

Retention: 67% of full-time freshmen returned.

FACULTY
Total: 171, 57% full-time, 50% with terminal degrees.

Student/faculty ratio: 9:1.

ACADEMICS
Calendar: semesters. *Degrees:* certificates, associate, bachelor's, and master's.

Special study options: academic remediation for entering students, adult/continuing education programs, advanced placement credit, double majors, English as a second language, honors programs, independent study, internships, off-campus study, part-time degree program, services for LD students, student-designed majors, study abroad, summer session for credit.

Unusual degree programs: 3-2 engineering with Columbia University, Case Western Reserve University, Ohio University; forestry with Duke University.

Computers: 475 computers/terminals and 450 ports are available on campus for general student use. Students can access the following: campus intranet, computer help desk, free student e-mail accounts, online (class) grades, online (class) registration, online (class) schedules. Campuswide network is available. 100% of college-owned or -operated housing units are wired for high-speed Internet access. Wireless service is available via classrooms, computer centers, computer labs, dorm rooms, learning centers, libraries, student centers.
Library: Legacy Library. *Books:* 183,103 (physical), 137,587 (digital/electronic); *Serial titles:* 230 (physical), 15,786 (digital/electronic); *Databases:* 186. Weekly public service hours: 95; students can reserve study rooms.

STUDENT LIFE
Housing options: on-campus residence required through senior year; coed, men-only, women-only, special housing for students with disabilities. Campus housing is university owned. Freshman campus housing is guaranteed.

Activities and organizations: drama/theater group, student-run newspaper, radio and television station, choral group, Pioneer Activities Council, student government, Panhellenic Council, Inter-Varsity Christian Fellowship, Inter Fraternity Council, national fraternities, national sororities.

Athletics Member NCAA. All Division III. ***Intercollegiate sports:*** baseball M, basketball M/W, cheerleading M(c)/W(c), crew M/W, cross-country running M/W, football M, golf M/W, lacrosse M/W, soccer M/W, softball W, tennis M/W, track and field M/W, volleyball W. ***Intramural sports:*** badminton M/W, basketball M/W, bowling M/W, cross-country running M/W, football M/W, golf M/W, racquetball M/W, rock climbing M/W, sand volleyball M/W, soccer M/W, softball M/W, swimming and diving M/W, tennis M/W, ultimate Frisbee M/W, volleyball M/W, weight lifting M/W.

Campus security: 24-hour emergency response devices and patrols, student patrols, late-night transport/escort service, controlled dormitory access.

Student services: health clinic, personal/psychological counseling.

COSTS & FINANCIAL AID
Costs (2020–21) ***One-time required fee:*** $400. ***Comprehensive fee:*** $49,504 includes full-time tuition ($35,732), mandatory fees ($1032), and room and board ($12,740). Full-time tuition and fees vary according to course load. Part-time tuition: $1190 per credit hour. Part-time tuition and fees vary according to course load. ***Room and board:*** Room and board charges vary according to board plan and housing facility. ***Payment plan:*** installment. ***Waivers:*** employees or children of employees.

Financial Aid Of all full-time matriculated undergraduates who enrolled in 2019, 928 applied for aid, 843 were judged to have need, 354 had their need fully met. In 2019, 112 non-need-based awards were made. ***Average percent of need met:*** 100. ***Average financial aid package:*** $36,440. ***Average need-based loan:*** $3520. ***Average need-based gift aid:*** $30,097. ***Average non-need-based aid:*** $19,660.

APPLYING
Standardized Tests *Required:* SAT or ACT (for admission). *Recommended:* SAT Subject Tests (for admission).

Options: electronic application, early admission, deferred entrance.

Required: essay or personal statement, high school transcript, minimum 2.5 GPA. ***Recommended:*** minimum 3.4 GPA, letters of recommendation, interview.

Application deadlines: 7/1 (freshmen), rolling (transfers).

Notification: continuous until 7/1 (freshmen), continuous (transfers).

CONTACT
Mr. Scot Schaeffer, Vice President for Enrollment Management, Marietta College, 215 Fifth Street, Marietta, OH 45750. *Phone:* 740-376-4503. *Toll-free phone:* 800-331-7896. *Fax:* 740-376-8888. *E-mail:* admit@marietta.edu.

Mercy College of Ohio
Toledo, Ohio
http://www.mercycollege.edu/

- **Independent** comprehensive, founded 1993, affiliated with Roman Catholic Church
- **Urban** campus with easy access to Toledo, OH
- **Coed, primarily women** 1,500 undergraduate students, 24% full-time, 87% women, 13% men
- **Moderately difficult** entrance level, 60% of applicants were admitted

UNDERGRAD STUDENTS
365 full-time, 1,135 part-time. Students come from 29 states and territories; 29% are from out of state; 11% Black or African American, non-Hispanic/Latino; 6% Hispanic/Latino; 2% Asian, non-Hispanic/Latino; 0.3% American Indian or Alaska Native, non-Hispanic/Latino; 4% Two or more races, non-Hispanic/Latino; 0.4% Race/ethnicity unknown; 24% transferred in.

Freshmen:
Admission: 449 applied, 270 admitted, 186 enrolled. ***Test scores:*** SAT evidence-based reading and writing scores over 500: 64%; SAT math scores over 500: 64%; ACT scores over 18: 77%; SAT evidence-based reading and writing scores over 600: 21%; ACT scores over 24: 12%; SAT evidence-based reading and writing scores over 700: 7%.

Retention: 92% of full-time freshmen returned.

FACULTY
Total: 204, 29% full-time.

Student/faculty ratio: 7:1.

ACADEMICS
Calendar: semesters. *Degrees:* certificates, associate, bachelor's, master's, and post-master's certificates.

Special study options: accelerated degree program, advanced placement credit, distance learning, double majors, independent study, part-time degree program, services for LD students, summer session for credit.

Computers: 125 computers/terminals and 125 ports are available on campus for general student use. Students can access the following: computer help desk, free student e-mail accounts, online (class) grades, online (class) registration, online (class) schedules. Campuswide network is available. Wireless service is available via classrooms, computer centers, computer labs, learning centers, libraries, student centers.
Library: Mercy College of Ohio Library. *Books:* 7,081 (physical), 98,167 (digital/electronic); *Serial titles:* 334 (physical), 82,313 (digital/electronic); *Databases:* 59. Weekly public service hours: 57; students can reserve study rooms.

STUDENT LIFE
Housing options: college housing not available.

Activities and organizations: American Assembly of Men in Nursing, National Student Nurses Association, Student Government Association.

Campus security: 24-hour emergency response devices and patrols, late-night transport/escort service.

Student services: personal/psychological counseling.

COSTS & FINANCIAL AID
Costs (2020–21) ***One-time required fee:*** $250. ***Tuition:*** $16,200 full-time, $540 per credit hour part-time. ***Required fees:*** $2650 full-time, $65 per credit hour part-time, $350 per term part-time. ***Payment plans:*** installment, deferred payment. ***Waivers:*** employees or children of employees.

Financial Aid Of all full-time matriculated undergraduates who enrolled in 2015, 24 Federal Work-Study jobs (averaging $1744).

APPLYING
Standardized Tests *Required for some:* SAT or ACT (for admission). *Recommended:* SAT or ACT (for admission).

Options: electronic application.

Required: high school transcript, minimum 2.0 GPA.

Application deadlines: rolling (freshmen), rolling (transfers).

Notification: continuous (freshmen), continuous (transfers).

CONTACT
Mercy College of Ohio, 2221 Madison Avenue, Toledo, OH 43604. *Phone:* 419-251-1313. *Toll-free phone:* 888-80-MERCY. *Fax:* 419-251-1462. *E-mail:* admissions@mercycollege.edu.

Miami University
Oxford, Ohio
http://miamioh.edu/

- **State-related** university, founded 1809, part of Miami University System
- **Small-town** 2100-acre campus with easy access to Cincinnati
- **Endowment** $558.6 million
- **Coed** 17,246 undergraduate students, 97% full-time, 50% women, 50% men
- **Moderately difficult** entrance level, 80% of applicants were admitted

UNDERGRAD STUDENTS
16,682 full-time, 564 part-time. Students come from 52 states and territories; 102 other countries; 34% are from out of state; 4% Black or African American, non-Hispanic/Latino; 5% Hispanic/Latino; 2% Asian, non-Hispanic/Latino; 0.1% Native Hawaiian or other Pacific Islander, non-Hispanic/Latino; 0.1% American Indian or Alaska Native, non-Hispanic/Latino; 4% Two or more races, non-Hispanic/Latino; 0.4% Race/ethnicity unknown; 12% international; 1% transferred in; 31% live on campus.

Freshmen:
Admission: 28,920 applied, 23,248 admitted, 4,309 enrolled. ***Average high school GPA:*** 3.8. ***Test scores:*** SAT evidence-based reading and writing scores over 500: 98%; SAT math scores over 500: 99%; ACT scores over 18: 100%; SAT evidence-based reading and writing scores over 600: 76%; SAT math scores over 600: 83%; ACT scores over 24: 90%; SAT evidence-based reading and writing scores over 700: 19%; SAT math scores over 700: 38%; ACT scores over 30: 35%.

Retention: 90% of full-time freshmen returned.

FACULTY
Total: 1,280, 77% full-time, 71% with terminal degrees.

Student/faculty ratio: 17:1.

ACADEMICS
Calendar: semesters. *Degrees:* certificates, associate, bachelor's, master's, doctoral, and post-master's certificates.

Special study options: advanced placement credit, cooperative education, distance learning, double majors, English as a second language, honors programs, independent study, internships, off-campus study, services for LD students, student-designed majors, study abroad, summer session for credit. ***ROTC:*** Army (c), Navy (b), Air Force (b).

Unusual degree programs: 3-2 engineering with Case Western Reserve University, Columbia University.

Computers: 652 computers/terminals are available on campus for general student use. Students can access the following: campus intranet, computer help desk, free student e-mail accounts, online (class) grades, online (class) registration, online (class) schedules. Campuswide network is available. 100% of college-owned or -operated housing units are wired for high-speed Internet access. Wireless service is available via entire campus.
Library: King Library plus 3 others. *Books:* 1.3 million (physical), 586,955 (digital/electronic); *Serial titles:* 43,126 (physical), 197,714 (digital/electronic); *Databases:* 778. Weekly public service hours: 168; study areas open 24 hours, 5–7 days a week; students can reserve study rooms.

STUDENT LIFE
Housing options: on-campus residence required through sophomore year; coed, men-only, women-only, special housing for students with disabilities. Campus housing is university owned. Freshman campus housing is guaranteed.

Activities and organizations: drama/theater group, student-run newspaper, radio and television station, choral group, marching band, CRU (formerly Campus Crusade for Christ), Alpha Phi Omega, College Republicans, 4 Paws for Ability, Best Buddies, national fraternities, national sororities.

Athletics Member NCAA. All Division I except football (Division I-A). ***Intercollegiate sports:*** baseball M(s)/W(c), basketball M(s)/W(s), cross-country running M(s)/W(s), equestrian sports M(c)/W(c), fencing M(c)/W(c), field hockey M(c)/W(s), golf M(s), gymnastics M(c)/W(c), ice hockey M(s)/W(c), lacrosse M(c)/W(c), rugby M(c)/W(c), sailing M(c)/W(c), soccer M(c)/W(s), softball M(c)/W(s), swimming and diving M(s)/W(s), tennis M(c)/W(s), track and field M(s)/W(s), ultimate Frisbee M(c)/W(c), volleyball M(c)/W(s), water polo M(c)/W(c), weight lifting M(c)/W(c), wrestling M(c)/W(c). ***Intramural sports:*** badminton M(c)/W(c), baseball M/W, basketball M/W, golf M(c)/W(c), ice hockey M/W, racquetball M/W, soccer M/W, softball M/W, ultimate Frisbee M/W, volleyball M/W.

Campus security: 24-hour emergency response devices and patrols, student patrols, late-night transport/escort service, controlled dormitory access.

Student services: health clinic, personal/psychological counseling, women's center.

COSTS & FINANCIAL AID

Costs (2019–20) ***Tuition:*** area resident $14,294 full-time; state resident $14,294 full-time; nonresident $33,369 full-time. Full-time tuition and fees vary according to location, program, and student level. Part-time tuition and fees vary according to course load, location, program, and student level. No tuition increase for student's term of enrollment. ***Required fees:*** $938 full-time. ***Room and board:*** $13,397; room only: $8313. Room and board charges vary according to board plan, housing facility, and student level. ***Payment plan:*** installment. ***Waivers:*** employees or children of employees.

Financial Aid Of all full-time matriculated undergraduates who enrolled in 2019, 8,935 applied for aid, 5,666 were judged to have need, 1,150 had their need fully met. 2,805 Federal Work-Study jobs (averaging $902). In 2019, 5755 non-need-based awards were made. ***Average percent of need met:*** 62. ***Average financial aid package:*** $15,916. ***Average need-based loan:*** $4508. ***Average need-based gift aid:*** $12,484. ***Average non-need-based aid:*** $10,859. ***Average indebtedness upon graduation:*** $29,652.

APPLYING

Standardized Tests *Required:* SAT or ACT (for admission).

Options: electronic application, early decision, early action, deferred entrance.

Application fee: $50.

Required: essay or personal statement, high school transcript, 1 letter of recommendation.

Application deadlines: 2/1 (freshmen), 11/1 (early action).

Early decision deadline: 11/1.

Notification: 3/15 (freshmen), continuous (transfers), 12/1 (early decision), 12/15 (early action).

CONTACT

Miami University, Oxford, OH 45056. *Phone:* 513-529-2531.

Miami University Hamilton

Hamilton, Ohio

http://regionals.miamioh.edu/

- **State-supported** comprehensive, founded 1968, part of Miami University System
- **Suburban** 78-acre campus with easy access to Cincinnati
- **Endowment** $7.6 million
- **Coed** 2,539 undergraduate students, 69% full-time, 52% women, 48% men
- **Noncompetitive** entrance level, 100% of applicants were admitted

UNDERGRAD STUDENTS

1,741 full-time, 798 part-time. Students come from 17 states and territories; 19 other countries; 4% are from out of state; 10% Black or African American, non-Hispanic/Latino; 5% Hispanic/Latino; 2% Asian, non-Hispanic/Latino; 0.2% Native Hawaiian or other Pacific Islander, non-Hispanic/Latino; 0.2% American Indian or Alaska Native, non-Hispanic/Latino; 4% Two or more races, non-Hispanic/Latino; 1% Race/ethnicity unknown; 3% international; 7% transferred in.

Freshmen:

Admission: 1,163 applied, 1,163 admitted, 563 enrolled. ***Average high school GPA:*** 3.1.

Retention: 68% of full-time freshmen returned.

FACULTY

Total: 234, 39% full-time, 47% with terminal degrees.

Student/faculty ratio: 14:1.

ACADEMICS

Calendar: semesters plus summer sessions. *Degrees:* certificates, associate, bachelor's, and master's (degrees awarded by Miami University main campus).

Special study options: academic remediation for entering students, adult/continuing education programs, advanced placement credit, cooperative education, distance learning, double majors, English as a second language, honors programs, independent study, internships, part-time degree program, services for LD students, student-designed majors, study abroad, summer session for credit. ***ROTC:*** Navy (c), Air Force (c).

Computers: 300 computers/terminals are available on campus for general student use. Students can access the following: campus intranet, computer help desk, free student e-mail accounts, online (class) grades, online (class) registration, online (class) schedules. Campuswide network is available. Wireless service is available via entire campus.

Library: Rentschler Library. *Books:* 57,132 (physical), 773,916 (digital/electronic); *Serial titles:* 217 (physical), 287,002 (digital/electronic); *Databases:* 757. Weekly public service hours: 69; students can reserve study rooms.

STUDENT LIFE

Housing options: college housing not available.

Activities and organizations: drama/theater group.

Athletics ***Intercollegiate sports:*** baseball M, basketball M/W, cheerleading W, golf M/W, softball W, tennis M/W, volleyball M/W.

Campus security: 24-hour emergency response devices and patrols, late-night transport/escort service.

Student services: personal/psychological counseling, veterans affairs office.

COSTS

Costs (2020–21) ***Tuition:*** area resident $6072 full-time, $267 per credit hour part-time; state resident $6072 full-time, $267 per credit hour part-time; nonresident $16,663 full-time, $692 per credit hour part-time. Full-time tuition and fees vary according to reciprocity agreements. Part-time tuition and fees vary according to course load and reciprocity agreements. No tuition increase for student's term of enrollment. ***Required fees:*** $403 full-time. ***Payment plan:*** installment. ***Waivers:*** employees or children of employees.

APPLYING

Options: electronic application.

Application fee: $35.

Required: high school transcript.

Application deadlines: rolling (freshmen), rolling (transfers).

Notification: continuous (freshmen), continuous (transfers).

CONTACT

Megan Spanel, Director of Admission, Miami University Hamilton, 1601 Peck Boulevard, Hamilton, OH 45011-3399. *Phone:* 513-217-4118. *E-mail:* megan.spanel@miamioh.edu.

Miami University Middletown

Middletown, Ohio

http://regionals.miamioh.edu/

- **State-supported** 4-year, founded 1966, part of Miami University System
- **Suburban** 141-acre campus with easy access to Cincinnati, Dayton
- **Endowment** $4.3 million
- **Coed** 1,842 undergraduate students, 65% full-time, 54% women, 46% men
- **Noncompetitive** entrance level, 100% of applicants were admitted

UNDERGRAD STUDENTS

1,199 full-time, 643 part-time. Students come from 8 states and territories; 8 other countries; 1% are from out of state; 4% Black or African American, non-Hispanic/Latino; 3% Hispanic/Latino; 2% Asian, non-Hispanic/Latino; 0.1% Native Hawaiian or other Pacific Islander, non-Hispanic/Latino; 0.1% American Indian or Alaska Native, non-

Hispanic/Latino; 4% Two or more races, non-Hispanic/Latino; 1% Race/ethnicity unknown; 18% international; 6% transferred in.

Freshmen:

Admission: 637 applied, 637 admitted, 279 enrolled. ***Average high school GPA:*** 3.2.

Retention: 71% of full-time freshmen returned.

FACULTY

Total: 171, 37% full-time, 40% with terminal degrees.

Student/faculty ratio: 14:1.

ACADEMICS

Calendar: semesters. *Degrees:* certificates, diplomas, associate, bachelor's, and master's (also offers up to 2 years of most bachelor's degree programs offered at Miami University main campus).

Special study options: academic remediation for entering students, adult/continuing education programs, advanced placement credit, cooperative education, distance learning, double majors, English as a second language, honors programs, independent study, internships, part-time degree program, services for LD students, student-designed majors, study abroad, summer session for credit. ***ROTC:*** Navy (c), Air Force (c).

Computers: 221 computers/terminals are available on campus for general student use. Students can access the following: campus intranet, computer help desk, free student e-mail accounts, online (class) grades, online (class) registration, online (class) schedules. Campuswide network is available. Wireless service is available via entire campus.

Library: Gardner-Harvey Library. *Books:* 28,733 (physical), 586,955 (digital/electronic); *Serial titles:* 28 (physical), 197,714 (digital/electronic); *Databases:* 756. Weekly public service hours: 65; students can reserve study rooms.

STUDENT LIFE

Housing options: college housing not available.

Activities and organizations: drama/theater group.

Athletics *Intercollegiate sports:* baseball M, basketball M/W, cheerleading W, golf M/W, softball W, tennis M/W, volleyball M/W.

Campus security: 24-hour patrols, student patrols, late-night transport/escort service.

Student services: personal/psychological counseling, veterans affairs office.

COSTS

Costs (2020–21) *Tuition:* area resident $6072 full-time, $267 per credit hour part-time; state resident $6072 full-time, $267 per credit hour part-time; nonresident $16,663 full-time, $692 per credit hour part-time. Full-time tuition and fees vary according to reciprocity agreements. Part-time tuition and fees vary according to course load and reciprocity agreements. No tuition increase for student's term of enrollment. ***Required fees:*** $403 full-time. ***Payment plan:*** installment. ***Waivers:*** employees or children of employees.

APPLYING

Options: electronic application.

Application fee: $35.

Required: high school transcript.

Application deadlines: rolling (freshmen), rolling (transfers).

Notification: continuous (freshmen), continuous (transfers).

CONTACT

Megan Spanel, Director of Admission, Miami University Middletown, 4200 East University Boulevard, Middletown, OH 45042-3497. *Phone:* 513-217-4118. *Toll-free phone:* 866-426-4643. *E-mail:* megan.spanel@miamioh.edu.

Mount Carmel College of Nursing

Columbus, Ohio

http://www.mccn.edu/

- **Independent** comprehensive, founded 1903
- **Urban** campus with easy access to Columbus
- **Endowment** $2.1 million
- **Coed, primarily women** 733 undergraduate students, 75% full-time, 89% women, 11% men
- **Moderately difficult** entrance level, 55% of applicants were admitted

UNDERGRAD STUDENTS

549 full-time, 184 part-time. Students come from 12 states and territories; 3% are from out of state; 13% Black or African American, non-Hispanic/Latino; 1% Hispanic/Latino; 4% Asian, non-Hispanic/Latino; 0.1% Native Hawaiian or other Pacific Islander, non-Hispanic/Latino; 0.4% American Indian or Alaska Native, non-Hispanic/Latino; 4% Two or more races, non-Hispanic/Latino; 0.8% Race/ethnicity unknown; 12% transferred in; 4% live on campus.

Freshmen:

Admission: 179 applied, 98 admitted, 44 enrolled. ***Average high school GPA:*** 3.6. ***Test scores:*** ACT scores over 18: 82%; ACT scores over 24: 11%.

Retention: 60% of full-time freshmen returned.

FACULTY

Total: 123, 42% full-time, 22% with terminal degrees.

Student/faculty ratio: 10:1.

ACADEMICS

Calendar: semesters. *Degrees:* bachelor's, master's, doctoral, and post-master's certificates.

Special study options: accelerated degree program, adult/continuing education programs, advanced placement credit, distance learning, honors programs, off-campus study, summer session for credit. ***ROTC:*** Army (c), Air Force (c).

Computers: 55 computers/terminals are available on campus for general student use. Students can access the following: campus intranet, computer help desk, free student e-mail accounts, online (class) grades, online (class) registration, online (class) schedules. Campuswide network is available. 100% of college-owned or -operated housing units are wired for high-speed Internet access. Wireless service is available via entire campus.

Library: The Mount Carmel Health Sciences Library plus 1 other. *Books:* 8,109 (physical), 400,726 (digital/electronic); *Serial titles:* 682 (physical), 32,726 (digital/electronic); *Databases:* 179. Weekly public service hours: 61; study areas open 24 hours, 5–7 days a week; students can reserve study rooms.

STUDENT LIFE

Housing options: on-campus residence required through sophomore year; coed. Campus housing is university owned. Freshman applicants given priority for college housing.

Activities and organizations: Campus Ministry, Student Nurses Association of Mount Carmel (SNAM), Mount Carmel Rho Omicron Chapter of Sigma Theta Tau International Honor Society, Student Government Association (SGA), Student Ambassador Program.

Athletics *Intramural sports:* basketball W(c), softball W(c), volleyball M(c)/W(c).

Campus security: 24-hour emergency response devices and patrols, late-night transport/escort service, controlled dormitory access.

Student services: health clinic, personal/psychological counseling.

COSTS & FINANCIAL AID

Costs (2019–20) *One-time required fee:* $225. ***Tuition:*** $13,857 full-time, $447 per credit hour part-time. ***Required fees:*** $515 full-time, $515 per year part-time. ***Room only:*** $5000. ***Payment plans:*** installment, deferred payment.

Financial Aid Of all full-time matriculated undergraduates who enrolled in 2019, 442 applied for aid, 394 were judged to have need, 12 had their need fully met. In 2019, 26 non-need-based awards were made. ***Average percent of need met:*** 32. ***Average financial aid package:*** $10,217. ***Average need-based loan:*** $4688. ***Average need-based gift aid:*** $8520. ***Average non-need-based aid:*** $2448. ***Average indebtedness upon graduation:*** $35,781.

APPLYING

Standardized Tests *Required for some:* ACT (for admission).

Options: electronic application.

Application fee: $30.

Required: essay or personal statement, high school transcript, activities/interests resumé. ***Required for some:*** interview. ***Recommended:*** minimum 3.0 GPA.

Notification: continuous (freshmen), continuous (transfers).

CONTACT
Dr. Kim Campbell, Director, Admissions and Recruitment, Mount Carmel College of Nursing, 127 South Davis Avenue, Columbus, OH 43222-1504. *Phone:* 614-234-5144. *Toll-free phone:* 800-556-6942. *Fax:* 614-234-5427. *E-mail:* kcampbell@mccn.edu.

Mount St. Joseph University

Cincinnati, Ohio

http://www.msj.edu/

- **Independent Roman Catholic** comprehensive, founded 1920
- **Suburban** 92-acre campus with easy access to Cincinnati, Ohio
- **Endowment** $39.7 million
- **Coed**
- **Minimally difficult** entrance level

FACULTY

Student/faculty ratio: 11:1.

ACADEMICS

Calendar: semesters. *Degrees:* certificates, associate, bachelor's, master's, doctoral, and postbachelor's certificates.
Library: Archbishop Alter Library. *Books:* 49,354 (physical), 132,008 (digital/electronic); *Serial titles:* 76 (physical), 30,812 (digital/electronic); *Databases:* 143. Weekly public service hours: 82.

STUDENT LIFE

Housing options: on-campus residence required through sophomore year; coed, special housing for students with disabilities. Campus housing is university owned. Freshman applicants given priority for college housing.

Activities and organizations: drama/theater group, student-run newspaper, choral group, marching band, Black Student Union, Campus Activities Board, Student Government Association, Group Fitness, Residence Hall Council, national fraternities.

Athletics Member NCAA. All Division III except golf (Division II).

Campus security: 24-hour emergency response devices and patrols, late-night transport/escort service.

Student services: health clinic, personal/psychological counseling.

COSTS & FINANCIAL AID

Costs (2019–20) ***Comprehensive fee:*** $41,030 includes full-time tuition ($30,100), mandatory fees ($1100), and room and board ($9830). Full-time tuition and fees vary according to course load, location, and reciprocity agreements. Part-time tuition: $555 per credit hour. Part-time tuition and fees vary according to course load, location, and reciprocity agreements. ***Room and board:*** Room and board charges vary according to board plan, housing facility, and location. ***Payment plans:*** installment, deferred payment.

Financial Aid Of all full-time matriculated undergraduates who enrolled in 2017, 914 applied for aid, 826 were judged to have need, 133 had their need fully met. 235 Federal Work-Study jobs (averaging $1488). 138 state and other part-time jobs (averaging $1468). In 2017, 151 non-need-based awards were made. ***Average percent of need met:*** 77. ***Average financial aid package:*** $22,394. ***Average need-based loan:*** $4125. ***Average need-based gift aid:*** $17,776. ***Average non-need-based aid:*** $11,293.

APPLYING

Standardized Tests *Required:* SAT or ACT (for admission).

Options: electronic application, deferred entrance.

Application fee: $25.

Required: high school transcript. ***Recommended:*** minimum 3.0 GPA.

CONTACT

Peggy Minnich, Director of Admission, Mount St. Joseph University, 5701 Delhi Road, Cincinnati, OH 45233-1670. *Phone:* 513-244-4531. *Toll-free phone:* 800-654-9314. *Fax:* 513-244-4629. *E-mail:* admissions@msj.edu.

Mount Vernon Nazarene University

Mount Vernon, Ohio

http://www.mvnu.edu/

- **Independent Nazarene** comprehensive, founded 1968
- **Small-town** 332-acre campus with easy access to Columbus
- **Endowment** $22.6 million
- **Coed** 1,816 undergraduate students, 83% full-time, 61% women, 39% men
- **Moderately difficult** entrance level, 73% of applicants were admitted

UNDERGRAD STUDENTS

1,501 full-time, 315 part-time. 11% are from out of state; 3% Black or African American, non-Hispanic/Latino; 3% Hispanic/Latino; 0.2% Asian, non-Hispanic/Latino; 0.1% Native Hawaiian or other Pacific Islander, non-Hispanic/Latino; 0.4% American Indian or Alaska Native, non-Hispanic/Latino; 3% Two or more races, non-Hispanic/Latino; 3% Race/ethnicity unknown; 0.7% international; 2% transferred in; 55% live on campus.

Freshmen:

Admission: 1,305 applied, 953 admitted, 324 enrolled. ***Average high school GPA:*** 3.6. ***Test scores:*** SAT evidence-based reading and writing scores over 500: 78%; SAT math scores over 500: 69%; ACT scores over 18: 89%; SAT evidence-based reading and writing scores over 600: 25%; SAT math scores over 600: 28%; ACT scores over 24: 37%; SAT evidence-based reading and writing scores over 700: 5%; SAT math scores over 700: 3%; ACT scores over 30: 7%.

Retention: 79% of full-time freshmen returned.

FACULTY

Total: 257, 24% full-time, 42% with terminal degrees.

Student/faculty ratio: 16:1.

ACADEMICS

Calendar: semesters. *Degrees:* associate, bachelor's, and master's.

Special study options: academic remediation for entering students, adult/continuing education programs, advanced placement credit, distance learning, double majors, external degree program, honors programs, independent study, internships, off-campus study, part-time degree program, services for LD students, study abroad, summer session for credit.

Computers: 250 computers/terminals and 915 ports are available on campus for general student use. Students can access the following: campus intranet, computer help desk, free student e-mail accounts, online (class) grades, online (class) registration, online (class) schedules. Campuswide network is available. 100% of college-owned or -operated housing units are wired for high-speed Internet access. Wireless service is available via entire campus.
Library: Thorne Library/Learning Resource Center. *Books:* 100,952 (physical), 790 (digital/electronic); *Serial titles:* 900 (physical), 29,195 (digital/electronic); *Databases:* 242. Weekly public service hours: 93; study areas open 24 hours, 5–7 days a week; students can reserve study rooms.

STUDENT LIFE

Housing options: coed, men-only, women-only. Campus housing is university owned. Freshman campus housing is guaranteed.

Activities and organizations: drama/theater group, student-run newspaper, radio station, choral group, Campus Ministry Groups, Student Government Association, Student Education Association, Drama Club, Music Department Ensembles.

Athletics Member NAIA. ***Intercollegiate sports:*** baseball M(s), basketball M(s)/W(s), cross-country running M(s)/W(s), golf M(s)/W(s), soccer M(s)/W(s), softball W(s), tennis M(s)/W(s), track and field M(s)/W(s), volleyball W(s). ***Intramural sports:*** basketball M/W, cheerleading M(c)/W(c), football M/W, soccer M/W, softball M/W, ultimate Frisbee M/W, volleyball M/W.

Campus security: 24-hour emergency response devices and patrols, late-night transport/escort service, controlled dormitory access.

Student services: health clinic, personal/psychological counseling.

COSTS & FINANCIAL AID

Costs (2020–21) ***Comprehensive fee:*** $40,500 includes full-time tuition ($31,360), mandatory fees ($250), and room and board ($8890). Full-time tuition and fees vary according to program. Part-time tuition: $870 per credit hour. Part-time tuition and fees vary according to course load and program. ***College room only:*** $4938. ***Payment plan:*** installment. ***Waivers:*** senior citizens and employees or children of employees.

Financial Aid Of all full-time matriculated undergraduates who enrolled in 2018, 1,450 applied for aid, 1,378 were judged to have need, 879 had their need fully met. In 2018, 210 non-need-based awards were made. ***Average percent of need met:*** 58. ***Average financial aid package:*** $22,793. ***Average need-based loan:*** $3965. ***Average need-based gift aid:*** $21,647. ***Average non-need-based aid:*** $14,496. ***Average indebtedness upon graduation:*** $22,778.

APPLYING

Standardized Tests *Required:* SAT or ACT (for admission).

Options: electronic application, deferred entrance.

Application fee: $25.

Required: essay or personal statement, high school transcript, minimum 2.5 GPA, 2 letters of recommendation.

Notification: 9/1 (freshmen), continuous (transfers).

CONTACT

Mr. Tracy Waal, Director of Admissions and Student Recruitment, Mount Vernon Nazarene University, 800 Martinsburg Road, Mount Vernon, OH 43050. *Phone:* 740-392-6868 Ext. 4514. *Toll-free phone:* 866-462-6868. *Fax:* 740-393-0511. *E-mail:* admissions@mvnu.edu.

Muskingum University

New Concord, Ohio

http://www.muskingum.edu/

- **Independent** comprehensive, founded 1837, affiliated with Presbyterian Church (U.S.A.)
- **Small-town** 245-acre campus with easy access to Columbus
- **Endowment** $76.3 million
- **Coed** 1,602 undergraduate students, 85% full-time, 56% women, 44% men
- **Moderately difficult** entrance level, 81% of applicants were admitted

UNDERGRAD STUDENTS

1,364 full-time, 238 part-time. Students come from 22 states and territories; 4 other countries; 11% are from out of state; 5% Black or African American, non-Hispanic/Latino; 3% Hispanic/Latino; 1% Asian, non-Hispanic/Latino; 0.3% American Indian or Alaska Native, non-Hispanic/Latino; 3% Two or more races, non-Hispanic/Latino; 4% Race/ethnicity unknown; 2% international; 4% transferred in; 52% live on campus.

Freshmen:

Admission: 2,404 applied, 1,938 admitted, 388 enrolled. ***Average high school GPA:*** 3.4. ***Test scores:*** SAT evidence-based reading and writing scores over 500: 55%; SAT math scores over 500: 53%; ACT scores over 18: 80%; SAT evidence-based reading and writing scores over 600: 12%; SAT math scores over 600: 8%; ACT scores over 24: 24%; SAT math scores over 700: 2%; ACT scores over 30: 3%.

Retention: 72% of full-time freshmen returned.

FACULTY

Total: 107, 94% full-time.

Student/faculty ratio: 13:1.

ACADEMICS

Calendar: semesters. *Degrees:* bachelor's and master's.

Special study options: accelerated degree program, adult/continuing education programs, advanced placement credit, distance learning, double majors, English as a second language, external degree program, independent study, internships, off-campus study, part-time degree program, services for LD students, student-designed majors, study abroad, summer session for credit.

Computers: 303 computers/terminals are available on campus for general student use. Students can access the following: campus intranet, computer help desk, free student e-mail accounts, online (class) grades, online (class) registration, online (class) schedules. Campuswide network is available. 100% of college-owned or -operated housing units are wired for high-speed Internet access. Wireless service is available via entire campus.

Library: Roberta A. Smith Library. *Books:* 101,051 (physical), 412,702 (digital/electronic); *Serial titles:* 1,085 (physical), 72,557 (digital/electronic); *Databases:* 285. Weekly public service hours: 89; students can reserve study rooms.

STUDENT LIFE

Housing options: on-campus residence required through junior year; coed, men-only, women-only. Campus housing is university owned. Freshman campus housing is guaranteed.

Activities and organizations: drama/theater group, student-run newspaper, radio and television station, choral group, marching band, Greek Life, Intramural Sports, Muskingum Programming Board, Multicultural Association:Black Student Union, Game Club, national fraternities, national sororities.

Athletics Member NCAA. All Division III. ***Intercollegiate sports:*** baseball M, basketball M/W, bowling M/W, cheerleading M(c)/W(c), cross-country running M/W, football M, golf M/W, lacrosse M/W, soccer M/W, softball W, tennis M/W, track and field M/W, ultimate Frisbee M(c)/W(c), volleyball W, wrestling M. ***Intramural sports:*** badminton M/W, basketball M/W, cross-country running M/W, football M/W, golf M/W, racquetball M/W, sand volleyball M/W, soccer M/W, softball M/W, swimming and diving M/W, table tennis M/W, tennis M/W, track and field M/W, volleyball M/W, water polo M/W, weight lifting M/W, wrestling M.

Campus security: 24-hour emergency response devices and patrols, late-night transport/escort service, controlled dormitory access.

Student services: health clinic, personal/psychological counseling, women's center.

COSTS & FINANCIAL AID

Costs (2020–21) ***One-time required fee:*** $250. ***Comprehensive fee:*** $41,772 includes full-time tuition ($28,700), mandatory fees ($1040), and room and board ($12,032). Part-time tuition: $625 per credit hour. ***College room only:*** $6130. ***Payment plan:*** installment. ***Waivers:*** employees or children of employees.

Financial Aid Of all full-time matriculated undergraduates who enrolled in 2018, 1,341 applied for aid, 1,276 were judged to have need, 190 had their need fully met. 491 Federal Work-Study jobs (averaging $1087). In 2018, 161 non-need-based awards were made. ***Average percent of need met:*** 68. ***Average financial aid package:*** $23,292. ***Average need-based loan:*** $3921. ***Average need-based gift aid:*** $18,150. ***Average non-need-based aid:*** $14,785. ***Average indebtedness upon graduation:*** $33,026.

APPLYING

Standardized Tests *Required:* SAT or ACT (for admission).

Options: electronic application, early admission, deferred entrance.

Required: high school transcript, minimum 2.0 GPA. ***Recommended:*** essay or personal statement, minimum 3.0 GPA, 1 letter of recommendation, interview.

Application deadlines: rolling (freshmen), rolling (out-of-state freshmen), rolling (transfers).

Notification: continuous (freshmen), continuous (out-of-state freshmen), continuous (transfers).

CONTACT

Mrs. Marcy Ritzert, Director of Admission, Muskingum University, 163 Stormont Street, New Concord, OH 43762. *Phone:* 740-826-8137. *Toll-free phone:* 800-752-6082. *Fax:* 740-826-8100. *E-mail:* adminfo@muskingum.edu.

The North Coast College

Lakewood, Ohio

http://www.thencc.edu/

CONTACT

Regina Reihard, Admissions Representative, The North Coast College, 11724 Detroit Avenue, Lakewood, OH 44107. *Phone:* 216-221-8584 Ext. 113. *E-mail:* rreihard@vmcad.edu.

Notre Dame College

South Euclid, Ohio

http://www.notredamecollege.edu/

- **Independent Roman Catholic** comprehensive, founded 1922
- **Suburban** 53-acre campus with easy access to Cleveland
- **Endowment** $10.0 million
- **Coed** 1,240 undergraduate students, 64% full-time, 66% women, 34% men
- **Moderately difficult** entrance level, 98% of applicants were admitted

UNDERGRAD STUDENTS

793 full-time, 447 part-time. Students come from 17 states and territories; 19 other countries; 11% are from out of state; 33% Black or African American, non-Hispanic/Latino; 6% Hispanic/Latino; 0.7% Asian, non-Hispanic/Latino; 0.2% Native Hawaiian or other Pacific Islander, non-Hispanic/Latino; 0.2% American Indian or Alaska Native, non-Hispanic/Latino; 3% Two or more races, non-Hispanic/Latino; 3% Race/ethnicity unknown; 2% international; 4% transferred in.

Freshmen:

Admission: 2,032 applied, 1,982 admitted, 227 enrolled. ***Average high school GPA:*** 3.1.

Retention: 61% of full-time freshmen returned.

FACULTY

Total: 192, 26% full-time.

Student/faculty ratio: 13:1.

ACADEMICS

Calendar: semesters. *Degrees:* certificates, associate, bachelor's, master's, and postbachelor's certificates.

Special study options: academic remediation for entering students, accelerated degree program, adult/continuing education programs, advanced placement credit, cooperative education, distance learning, double majors, independent study, internships, off-campus study, part-time degree program, services for LD students, student-designed majors, study abroad, summer session for credit. ***ROTC:*** Army (c).

Unusual degree programs: 3-2 engineering with Case Western Reserve University; marine biology, occupational therapy, criminal justice, psychology, mental health counseling, speech language pathology, computer science, education, physical therapy,law program.

Computers: 65 computers/terminals are available on campus for general student use. Students can access the following: campus intranet, computer help desk, free student e-mail accounts, online (class) grades, online (class) registration, online (class) schedules. Campuswide network is available. 100% of college-owned or -operated housing units are wired for high-speed Internet access. Wireless service is available via entire campus.

Library: Clara Fritzsche Library. *Books:* 40,931 (physical), 194,266 (digital/electronic); *Serial titles:* 499 (physical), 32,658 (digital/electronic); *Databases:* 121. Study areas open 24 hours, 5–7 days a week; students can reserve study rooms.

STUDENT LIFE

Housing options: on-campus residence required through sophomore year; coed, men-only, women-only. Campus housing is university owned.

Activities and organizations: drama/theater group, choral group, marching band, Student Athlete Advisory Committee (SAAC), Student Nurses Association, Teacher Education Student Association, Green Team, Japanese Pop Culture Club.

Athletics Member NCAA. All Division II. ***Intercollegiate sports:*** baseball M(s), basketball M(s)/W(s), bowling M(s)(c)/W(s)(c), football M(s), golf M(s)/W(s), lacrosse W(s), rugby M(s)(c)/W(s), soccer M(s)/W(s), softball W(s), swimming and diving M(s)/W(s), tennis W(s), volleyball W(s), wrestling M(s). ***Intramural sports:*** soccer M/W, softball M/W, volleyball M/W.

Campus security: 24-hour emergency response devices and patrols, late-night transport/escort service, controlled dormitory access.

Student services: personal/psychological counseling.

COSTS

Costs (2020–21) ***One-time required fee:*** $100. ***Comprehensive fee:*** $41,000 includes full-time tuition ($30,050), mandatory fees ($700), and room and board ($10,250). Part-time tuition: $580 per credit hour. ***College room only:*** $4850. Room and board charges vary according to board plan and housing facility. ***Payment plan:*** installment.

APPLYING

Standardized Tests *Required:* Students with high school GPAs at or above 2.75 are not required to submit test scores for the purpose of admission. (for admission).

Options: electronic application, deferred entrance.

Application fee: $30.

Required: essay or personal statement, high school transcript, minimum 2.0 GPA, interview. ***Recommended:*** minimum 2.5 GPA.

Application deadlines: rolling (freshmen), rolling (transfers).

Notification: continuous (freshmen), continuous (transfers).

CONTACT

Ms. Beth Ford, Dean of Admissions, Notre Dame College, 4545 Campus Rd, SouthEuclid, OH 44121. *Phone:* 216-373-5355. *Toll-free phone:* 877-NDC-OHIO. *E-mail:* admissinos@ndc.edu.

Oberlin College

Oberlin, Ohio

http://www.oberlin.edu/

- **Independent** comprehensive, founded 1833
- **Small-town** 440-acre campus with easy access to Cleveland
- **Endowment** $820.3 million
- **Coed** 4,884 undergraduate students, 99% full-time, 57% women, 43% men
- **Very difficult** entrance level, 36% of applicants were admitted

UNDERGRAD STUDENTS

4,823 full-time, 61 part-time. Students come from 52 states and territories; 46 other countries; 93% are from out of state; 5% Black or African American, non-Hispanic/Latino; 8% Hispanic/Latino; 4% Asian, non-Hispanic/Latino; 8% Two or more races, non-Hispanic/Latino; 1% Race/ethnicity unknown; 11% international; 0.6% transferred in; 85% live on campus.

Freshmen:

Admission: 7,525 applied, 2,725 admitted, 804 enrolled. ***Average high school GPA:*** 3.6. ***Test scores:*** SAT evidence-based reading and writing scores over 500: 100%; SAT math scores over 500: 98%; ACT scores over 18: 100%; SAT evidence-based reading and writing scores over 600: 94%; SAT math scores over 600: 85%; ACT scores over 24: 97%; SAT evidence-based reading and writing scores over 700: 44%; SAT math scores over 700: 40%; ACT scores over 30: 64%.

Retention: 89% of full-time freshmen returned.

FACULTY

Total: 381.

Student/faculty ratio: 10:1.

ACADEMICS

Calendar: 4-1-4. *Degrees:* diplomas, bachelor's, master's, and postbachelor's certificates.

Special study options: advanced placement credit, double majors, English as a second language, honors programs, independent study, internships, off-campus study, part-time degree program, services for LD students, student-designed majors, study abroad.

Unusual degree programs: 3-2 engineering with Washington University in St. Louis, Case Western Reserve University, California Institute of Technology, Columbia University.

Computers: 250 computers/terminals are available on campus for general student use. Students can access the following: campus intranet, computer help desk, free student e-mail accounts, online (class) grades, online (class) registration, online (class) schedules. Campuswide network is available. 100% of college-owned or -operated housing units are wired for high-speed Internet access. Wireless service is available via entire campus.

Library: Mudd Center Library plus 3 others. *Books:* 1.4 million (physical), 676,883 (digital/electronic); *Serial titles:* 188,472 (physical). Students can reserve study rooms.

STUDENT LIFE

Housing options: on-campus residence required through senior year; coed, women-only, cooperative, special housing for students with disabilities. Campus housing is university owned. Freshman campus housing is guaranteed.

Activities and organizations: drama/theater group, student-run newspaper, radio station, choral group, Experimental College, Community Outreach, Student Government, Student Cooperative Association, student radio station.

Athletics Member NCAA. All Division III. ***Intercollegiate sports:*** badminton M(c)/W(c), baseball M, basketball M/W, bowling M(c)/W(c), cross-country running M/W, equestrian sports M(c)/W(c), fencing M(c)/W(c), field hockey W, football M, golf M(c)/W(c), gymnastics M(c)/W(c), ice hockey M(c)/W(c), lacrosse M/W, rugby M(c)/W(c), soccer M/W, softball W, swimming and diving M/W, table tennis M(c)/W(c), tennis M/W, track and field M/W, ultimate Frisbee M(c)/W(c), volleyball W. ***Intramural sports:*** baseball M/W, basketball M/W, bowling M/W, cross-country running M/W, football M/W, gymnastics M(c)/W(c), racquetball M/W, rock climbing M/W, rugby M, soccer M/W, softball M/W, squash M/W, table tennis M(c)/W, tennis M/W, track and field M/W, volleyball M/W, water polo M/W, weight lifting M/W.

Campus security: 24-hour emergency response devices and patrols, student patrols, late-night transport/escort service, controlled dormitory access, crime prevention programs.

Student services: health clinic, personal/psychological counseling, women's center.

COSTS & FINANCIAL AID

Costs (2019–20) ***Comprehensive fee:*** $73,694 includes full-time tuition ($55,976), mandatory fees ($892), and room and board ($16,826). Part-time tuition: $2334 per credit hour. Part-time tuition and fees vary according to course load. ***College room only:*** $8350. Room and board charges vary according to board plan and housing facility. ***Payment plan:*** installment. ***Waivers:*** employees or children of employees.

Financial Aid Of all full-time matriculated undergraduates who enrolled in 2018, 1,648 applied for aid, 1,412 were judged to have need, 1,412 had their need fully met. In 2018, 1346 non-need-based awards were made. ***Average percent of need met:*** 100. ***Average financial aid package:*** $45,020. ***Average need-based loan:*** $4233. ***Average need-based gift aid:*** $40,459. ***Average non-need-based aid:*** $16,998. ***Average indebtedness upon graduation:*** $27,523. ***Financial aid deadline:*** 2/1.

APPLYING

Standardized Tests *Required:* SAT or ACT (for admission). *Required for some:* SAT and SAT Subject Tests or ACT (for admission).

Options: electronic application, early admission, early decision, deferred entrance.

Required: essay or personal statement, high school transcript, 2 letters of recommendation. ***Required for some:*** interview, audition for the Conservatory of Music, detailed portfolio for homeschooled students. ***Recommended:*** interview.

Application deadlines: 1/15 (freshmen), 3/15 (transfers).

Early decision deadline: 11/15 (for plan 1), 1/2 (for plan 2).

Notification: 4/1 (freshmen), 5/15 (transfers), 12/15 (early decision plan 1), 2/1 (early decision plan 2).

CONTACT

Manuel Carballo, Vice President and Dean of Admissions and Financial Aid, Oberlin College, College of Arts and Sciences Admissions, 38 East College Street, Oberlin, OH 44074. *Phone:* 440-775-8411. *Toll-free phone:* 800-622-OBIE. *Fax:* 440-775-6905. *E-mail:* college.admissions@oberlin.edu.

Ohio Christian University

Circleville, Ohio

http://www.ohiochristian.edu/

- **Independent** comprehensive, founded 1948, affiliated with Churches of Christ in Christian Union
- **Small-town** 40-acre campus with easy access to Columbus
- **Endowment** $4.9 million
- **Coed** 2,531 undergraduate students, 64% full-time, 65% women, 35% men
- **Minimally difficult** entrance level

UNDERGRAD STUDENTS

1,627 full-time, 904 part-time. 38% Black or African American, non-Hispanic/Latino; 4% Hispanic/Latino; 1% Asian, non-Hispanic/Latino; 0.5% American Indian or Alaska Native, non-Hispanic/Latino; 3% Two or more races, non-Hispanic/Latino; 27% Race/ethnicity unknown; 0.4% international; 5% transferred in; 8% live on campus.

Freshmen:

Admission: 224 enrolled.

Retention: 61% of full-time freshmen returned.

FACULTY

Total: 419, 33% full-time.

Student/faculty ratio: 11:1.

ACADEMICS

Calendar: semesters. *Degrees:* associate, bachelor's, and master's.

Special study options: academic remediation for entering students, accelerated degree program, adult/continuing education programs, advanced placement credit, distance learning, double majors, external degree program, honors programs, independent study, internships, off-campus study, part-time degree program, services for LD students, student-designed majors, summer session for credit.

Computers: 30 computers/terminals are available on campus for general student use. Students can access the following: campus intranet, computer help desk, free student e-mail accounts, online (class) grades, online (class) registration, online (class) schedules. Campuswide network is available. 100% of college-owned or -operated housing units are wired for high-speed Internet access. Wireless service is available via entire campus.

Library: Melvin Maxwell Memorial Library. *Books:* 59,755 (physical), 96,276 (digital/electronic); *Serial titles:* 143 (physical), 6,473 (digital/electronic). Weekly public service hours: 88.

STUDENT LIFE

Housing options: men-only, women-only. Campus housing is university owned. Freshman campus housing is guaranteed.

Activities and organizations: drama/theater group, choral group, World Gospel Mission, De-light, Athletics, Choral.

Athletics Member NAIA. ***Intercollegiate sports:*** baseball M(s), basketball M(s)/W(s), cross-country running M/W, golf M/W, soccer M, softball W, tennis M/W, volleyball W. ***Intramural sports:*** basketball M/W, soccer M/W, table tennis M/W, volleyball M/W.

Campus security: controlled dormitory access, security checks after midnight.

Student services: personal/psychological counseling, legal services.

COSTS & FINANCIAL AID

Costs (2019–20) ***Comprehensive fee:*** $29,110 includes full-time tuition ($20,040), mandatory fees ($750), and room and board ($8320). Full-time tuition and fees vary according to class time, course load, degree level, location, and program. Part-time tuition: $391 per credit hour. Part-time tuition and fees vary according to class time, location, and program. ***Required fees:*** $375 per term part-time. ***College room only:*** $4016. Room and board charges vary according to board plan. ***Payment plan:*** installment. ***Waivers:*** senior citizens and employees or children of employees.

Financial Aid In 2018, 3222 non-need-based awards were made. ***Average financial aid package:*** $11,243. ***Average need-based loan:*** $3645. ***Average need-based gift aid:*** $3673. ***Average indebtedness upon graduation:*** $30,000.

APPLYING
Standardized Tests *Required for some:* ACT (for admission).

Options: electronic application, early admission.

Application fee: $25.

Required: essay or personal statement, high school transcript, medical form. ***Required for some:*** interview.

Application deadlines: rolling (freshmen), rolling (transfers).

Notification: continuous (freshmen), continuous (transfers).

CONTACT
Ohio Christian University, 1476 Lancaster Pike, Circleville, OH 43113. *Phone:* 740-477-7741. *Toll-free phone:* 877-762-8669.

Ohio Dominican University

Columbus, Ohio

http://www.ohiodominican.edu/

- **Independent Roman Catholic** comprehensive, founded 1911
- **Urban** 92-acre campus with easy access to Columbus, OH
- **Endowment** $20.0 million
- **Coed** 1,081 undergraduate students, 85% full-time, 54% women, 46% men
- **Moderately difficult** entrance level, 84% of applicants were admitted

UNDERGRAD STUDENTS
920 full-time, 161 part-time. Students come from 14 states and territories; 8 other countries; 5% are from out of state; 26% Black or African American, non-Hispanic/Latino; 5% Hispanic/Latino; 2% Asian, non-Hispanic/Latino; 1% American Indian or Alaska Native, non-Hispanic/Latino; 6% Two or more races, non-Hispanic/Latino; 5% Race/ethnicity unknown; 3% international; 6% transferred in; 48% live on campus.

Freshmen:
Admission: 1,395 applied, 1,171 admitted, 287 enrolled. ***Average high school GPA:*** 3.4. ***Test scores:*** SAT evidence-based reading and writing scores over 500: 78%; SAT math scores over 500: 80%; ACT scores over 18: 94%; SAT evidence-based reading and writing scores over 600: 18%; SAT math scores over 600: 20%; ACT scores over 24: 33%; SAT evidence-based reading and writing scores over 700: 8%; SAT math scores over 700: 3%; ACT scores over 30: 4%.

Retention: 61% of full-time freshmen returned.

FACULTY
Total: 161, 38% full-time, 49% with terminal degrees.

Student/faculty ratio: 13:1.

ACADEMICS
Calendar: semesters. *Degrees:* certificates, associate, bachelor's, master's, and postbachelor's certificates.

Special study options: academic remediation for entering students, accelerated degree program, adult/continuing education programs, advanced placement credit, distance learning, double majors, honors programs, independent study, internships, off-campus study, part-time degree program, services for LD students, student-designed majors, study abroad, summer session for credit. ***ROTC:*** Army (c), Air Force (c).

Unusual degree programs: 3-2 business administration; engineering with University of Dayton; sport management, healthcare administration, English, theology, law with University of Dayton.

Computers: 350 computers/terminals and 2,300 ports are available on campus for general student use. Students can access the following: campus intranet, computer help desk, free student e-mail accounts, online (class) grades, online (class) registration, online (class) schedules. Campuswide network is available. 100% of college-owned or -operated housing units are wired for high-speed Internet access. Wireless service is available via entire campus.

Library: Ohio Dominican Library. *Books:* 79,322 (physical), 123,948 (digital/electronic); *Serial titles:* 416 (physical), 10,463 (digital/electronic); *Databases:* 224. Students can reserve study rooms.

STUDENT LIFE
Housing options: on-campus residence required through sophomore year; coed. Campus housing is university owned. Freshman campus housing is guaranteed.

Activities and organizations: drama/theater group, student-run radio station, choral group, marching band, Panther Activities Council, Student Athletic Advisory Committee, Black Student Union, World Student Club, Panther Players.

Athletics Member NCAA. All Division II. ***Intercollegiate sports:*** baseball M(s), basketball M(s)/W(s), cross-country running M(s)/W(s), football M(s), golf M(s)/W(s), soccer M(s)/W(s), softball W(s), track and field M(s)/W(s), volleyball W(s). ***Intramural sports:*** basketball M/W, cheerleading W(c), sand volleyball M/W, table tennis M/W, ultimate Frisbee M/W.

Campus security: 24-hour emergency response devices and patrols, late-night transport/escort service, controlled dormitory access.

Student services: health clinic, personal/psychological counseling.

COSTS & FINANCIAL AID
Costs (2020–21) ***Comprehensive fee:*** $44,220 includes full-time tuition ($32,300), mandatory fees ($580), and room and board ($11,340). Part-time tuition: $760 per credit hour. Part-time tuition and fees vary according to course load. ***Required fees:*** $175 per term part-time. ***Room and board:*** Room and board charges vary according to board plan and housing facility. ***Payment plan:*** installment. ***Waivers:*** employees or children of employees.

Financial Aid Of all full-time matriculated undergraduates who enrolled in 2018, 200 Federal Work-Study jobs (averaging $2000). ***Average percent of need met:*** 92. ***Average financial aid package:*** $12,467. ***Average indebtedness upon graduation:*** $13,500.

APPLYING
Standardized Tests *Required for some:* SAT or ACT (for admission).

Options: electronic application, deferred entrance.

Required: high school transcript, minimum 2.3 GPA. ***Required for some:*** essay or personal statement. ***Recommended:*** interview.

Application deadlines: rolling (freshmen), rolling (out-of-state freshmen), rolling (transfers).

Notification: continuous (freshmen), continuous (out-of-state freshmen), continuous (transfers).

CONTACT
Ms. Alecia Dennis, Director of Undergraduate Admissions, Ohio Dominican University, 1216 Sunbury Road, Columbus, OH 43219. *Phone:* 614-251-4500. *Toll-free phone:* 800-955-6446. *Fax:* 614-251-0156. *E-mail:* admissions@ohiodominican.edu.

Ohio Northern University

Ada, Ohio

http://www.onu.edu/

- **Independent** comprehensive, founded 1871, affiliated with United Methodist Church
- **Small-town** 342-acre campus
- **Endowment** $162.0 million
- **Coed**
- **Moderately difficult** entrance level

FACULTY
Student/faculty ratio: 11:1.

ACADEMICS
Calendar: semesters. *Degrees:* certificates, bachelor's, master's, doctoral, and postbachelor's certificates.

Library: Heterick Memorial Library plus 1 other. Students can reserve study rooms.

STUDENT LIFE
Housing options: on-campus residence required through junior year; coed, men-only, women-only, special housing for students with disabilities. Campus housing is university owned. Freshman campus housing is guaranteed.

Activities and organizations: drama/theater group, student-run newspaper, radio and television station, choral group, marching band, Habitat for Humanity, Student Planning Committee, Student Senate, Northern Christian Fellowship, Marching Band, national fraternities, national sororities.

Athletics Member NCAA. All Division III.

Campus security: 24-hour emergency response devices and patrols, controlled dormitory access.

Student services: health clinic, personal/psychological counseling, legal services.

COSTS & FINANCIAL AID

Costs (2019–20) ***Comprehensive fee:*** $45,480 includes full-time tuition ($32,500), mandatory fees ($940), and room and board ($12,040). Full-time tuition and fees vary according to course load, degree level, and program. Part-time tuition: $1355 per credit hour. Part-time tuition and fees vary according to course load, degree level, and program. ***Room and board:*** Room and board charges vary according to board plan, housing facility, and student level.

Financial Aid Of all full-time matriculated undergraduates who enrolled in 2018, 1,928 applied for aid, 1,738 were judged to have need, 412 had their need fully met. In 2018, 329 non-need-based awards were made. ***Average percent of need met:*** 24. ***Average financial aid package:*** $27,794. ***Average need-based loan:*** $4530. ***Average need-based gift aid:*** $24,130. ***Average non-need-based aid:*** $15,686. ***Average indebtedness upon graduation:*** $39,221.

APPLYING

Standardized Tests *Required:* SAT or ACT (for admission).

Options: electronic application, deferred entrance.

Required: high school transcript. ***Required for some:*** essay or personal statement, 1 letter of recommendation, interview. ***Recommended:*** essay or personal statement.

CONTACT

Ms. Deborah Miller, Director of Admissions, Ohio Northern University, 525 South Main Street, Ada, OH 45810-1599. *Phone:* 419-772-2260 Ext. 2464. *Toll-free phone:* 888-408-4ONU. *Fax:* 419-772-2821. *E-mail:* admissions-ug@onu.edu.

See below for display ad and page 1094 for the College Close-Up.

The Ohio State University

Columbus, Ohio

http://www.osu.edu/

- **State-supported** university, founded 1870, part of The Ohio State University
- **Urban** 1665-acre campus with easy access to Columbus
- **Endowment** $4.2 billion
- **Coed** 46,818 undergraduate students, 91% full-time, 49% women, 51% men
- **Very difficult** entrance level, 54% of applicants were admitted

UNDERGRAD STUDENTS

42,776 full-time, 4,042 part-time. Students come from 54 states and territories; 71 other countries; 19% are from out of state; 7% Black or African American, non-Hispanic/Latino; 5% Hispanic/Latino; 8% Asian, non-Hispanic/Latino; 0.1% Native Hawaiian or other Pacific Islander, non-Hispanic/Latino; 0.1% American Indian or Alaska Native, non-Hispanic/Latino; 4% Two or more races, non-Hispanic/Latino; 3% Race/ethnicity unknown; 8% international; 5% transferred in; 33% live on campus.

Freshmen:

Admission: 47,703 applied, 25,634 admitted, 7,716 enrolled. ***Test scores:*** SAT evidence-based reading and writing scores over 500: 98%; SAT math scores over 500: 98%; ACT scores over 18: 99%; SAT evidence-based reading and writing scores over 600: 77%; SAT math scores over 600: 88%; ACT scores over 24: 92%; SAT evidence-based reading and writing scores over 700: 24%; SAT math scores over 700: 58%; ACT scores over 30: 55%.

Retention: 94% of full-time freshmen returned.

FACULTY

Total: 5,911, 74% full-time, 88% with terminal degrees.

Student/faculty ratio: 19:1.

ACADEMICS
Calendar: semesters. *Degrees:* certificates, diplomas, associate, bachelor's, master's, doctoral, post-master's, and postbachelor's certificates.

Special study options: academic remediation for entering students, accelerated degree program, adult/continuing education programs, advanced placement credit, cooperative education, distance learning, double majors, English as a second language, freshman honors college, honors programs, independent study, internships, off-campus study, part-time degree program, services for LD students, student-designed majors, study abroad, summer session for credit. ***ROTC:*** Army (b), Navy (b), Air Force (b).

Unusual degree programs: 3-2 business administration.

Computers: Students can access the following: campus intranet, computer help desk, free student e-mail accounts, online (class) grades, online (class) registration, online (class) schedules, admission applications, fee payment. Campuswide network is available. 100% of college-owned or -operated housing units are wired for high-speed Internet access. Wireless service is available via entire campus.
Library: William Oxley Thompson Library plus 10 others. *Books:* 5.0 million (physical), 1.3 million (digital/electronic); *Serial titles:* 664,616 (physical), 55,339 (digital/electronic); *Databases:* 2,046. Study areas open 24 hours, 5–7 days a week; students can reserve study rooms.

STUDENT LIFE
Housing options: on-campus residence required through sophomore year; coed, women-only, cooperative, special housing for students with disabilities. Campus housing is university owned. Freshman campus housing is guaranteed.

Activities and organizations: drama/theater group, student-run newspaper, radio and television station, choral group, marching band, Burritos Club, Vinyl Club, Guitar Club, Artificial Intelligence Club, H20 Students, national fraternities, national sororities.

Athletics Member NCAA. All Division I. ***Intercollegiate sports:*** baseball M(s), basketball M(s)/W(s), cheerleading M(s)/W(s), cross-country running M(s)/W(s), fencing M(s)/W(s), field hockey W(s), football M(s), golf M(s)/W(s), gymnastics M(s)/W(s), ice hockey M(s)/W(s), lacrosse M(s)/W(s), riflery M(s)/W(s), rowing W(s), soccer M(s)/W(s), softball W(s), swimming and diving M(s)/W(s), tennis M(s)/W(s), track and field M(s)/W(s), volleyball M(s)/W(s), wrestling M(s). ***Intramural sports:*** archery M(c)/W(c), badminton M(c)/W(c), baseball M(c), basketball M(c)/W(c), bowling M(c)/W(c), cheerleading W(c), crew M(c)/W(c), equestrian sports M(c)/W(c), fencing M(c)/W(c), field hockey M(c)/W(c), football M(c), golf M(c)/W(c), gymnastics M(c)/W(c), ice hockey M(c)/W(c), lacrosse M(c)/W(c), racquetball M(c)/W(c), riflery M(c)/W(c), rowing M(c)/W(c), rugby M(c)/W(c), sailing M(c)/W(c), sand volleyball M/W, skiing (downhill) M(c)/W(c), soccer M(c)/W(c), softball M/W(c), squash M(c)/W(c), swimming and diving M(c)/W(c), table tennis M/W, tennis M/W, triathlon M(c)/W(c), ultimate Frisbee M(c)/W(c), volleyball M(c)/W(c), water polo M/W(c), weight lifting M/W(c).

Campus security: 24-hour emergency response devices and patrols, student patrols, late-night transport/escort service, controlled dormitory access.

Student services: health clinic, personal/psychological counseling, legal services, veterans affairs office.

COSTS & FINANCIAL AID
Costs (2019–20) ***Tuition:*** state resident $11,084 full-time, $501 per credit hour part-time; nonresident $32,061 full-time, $1375 per credit hour part-time. Full-time tuition and fees vary according to course load, degree level, location, program, reciprocity agreements, and student level. Part-time tuition and fees vary according to course load, degree level, location, program, reciprocity agreements, and student level. No tuition increase for student's term of enrollment. ***Room and board:*** $12,708. Room and board charges vary according to board plan, housing facility, and location. ***Payment plan:*** installment. ***Waivers:*** senior citizens and employees or children of employees.

Financial Aid Of all full-time matriculated undergraduates who enrolled in 2019, 28,401 applied for aid, 19,530 were judged to have need, 4,446 had their need fully met. In 2019, 9160 non-need-based awards were made. ***Average percent of need met:*** 73. ***Average financial aid package:*** $15,392. ***Average need-based loan:*** $4397. ***Average need-based gift aid:*** $12,037. ***Average non-need-based aid:*** $6981. ***Average indebtedness upon graduation:*** $27,242.

APPLYING
Standardized Tests *Required:* SAT or ACT (for admission).

Options: electronic application, early action, deferred entrance.

Application fee: $60.

Required: essay or personal statement, high school transcript.

Application deadlines: 2/1 (freshmen), 2/1 (out-of-state freshmen), 5/1 (transfers), 11/1 (early action).

Notification: 3/31 (freshmen), 3/31 (out-of-state freshmen), continuous (transfers), 1/31 (early action).

CONTACT
The Ohio State University, 281 W. Lane Ave., Student Academic Services Building, Columbus, OH 43210. *Phone:* 614-292-3980.

The Ohio State University at Lima

Lima, Ohio

http://lima.osu.edu/

- **State-supported** comprehensive, founded 1960, part of The Ohio State University
- **Suburban** 562-acre campus
- **Endowment** $5.3 million
- **Coed** 981 undergraduate students, 84% full-time, 57% women, 43% men
- **Noncompetitive** entrance level, 100% of applicants were admitted

UNDERGRAD STUDENTS
824 full-time, 157 part-time. Students come from 4 states and territories; 1 other country; 1% are from out of state; 6% Black or African American, non-Hispanic/Latino; 4% Hispanic/Latino; 2% Asian, non-Hispanic/Latino; 5% Two or more races, non-Hispanic/Latino; 3% Race/ethnicity unknown; 0.2% international; 5% transferred in.

Freshmen:
Admission: 1,669 applied, 1,662 admitted, 363 enrolled. ***Test scores:*** SAT evidence-based reading and writing scores over 500: 61%; SAT math scores over 500: 77%; ACT scores over 18: 88%; SAT evidence-based reading and writing scores over 600: 23%; SAT math scores over 600: 23%; ACT scores over 24: 38%; SAT math scores over 700: 8%; ACT scores over 30: 4%.

Retention: 46% of full-time freshmen returned.

FACULTY
Total: 72, 42% full-time, 68% with terminal degrees.

Student/faculty ratio: 20:1.

ACADEMICS
Calendar: semesters. *Degrees:* associate, bachelor's, and master's.

Special study options: academic remediation for entering students, accelerated degree program, adult/continuing education programs, advanced placement credit, cooperative education, distance learning, double majors, English as a second language, freshman honors college, honors programs, independent study, internships, off-campus study, part-time degree program, services for LD students, student-designed majors, study abroad, summer session for credit.

Computers: Students can access the following: campus intranet, computer help desk, free student e-mail accounts, online (class) grades, online (class) registration, online (class) schedules. Campuswide network is available. Wireless service is available via entire campus.
Library: Lima Campus Library. *Books:* 74,972 (physical), 1.4 million (digital/electronic); *Serial titles:* 34 (physical), 54,576 (digital/electronic); *Databases:* 2,056. Weekly public service hours: 57; students can reserve study rooms.

STUDENT LIFE
Housing options: college housing not available.

Activities and organizations: drama/theater group, choral group, United Way Club, Campus Activities Board, Nert Club, Student Senate, Psych Club.

Athletics ***Intercollegiate sports:*** baseball M, basketball M/W, golf M, volleyball W. ***Intramural sports:*** basketball M/W, football M/W, soccer M/W, softball W, ultimate Frisbee M/W, volleyball M/W.

Campus security: 24-hour emergency response devices and patrols, late-night transport/escort service.

Student services: personal/psychological counseling.

COSTS

Costs (2019–20) ***Tuition:*** state resident $7912 full-time, $330 per credit hour part-time; nonresident $28,889 full-time, $1204 per credit hour part-time. Full-time tuition and fees vary according to course load, degree level, location, program, reciprocity agreements, and student level. Part-time tuition and fees vary according to course load, degree level, location, program, reciprocity agreements, and student level. No tuition increase for student's term of enrollment. ***Payment plan:*** installment. ***Waivers:*** senior citizens and employees or children of employees.

APPLYING

Standardized Tests *Required for some:* SAT or ACT (for admission).

Options: electronic application.

Application fee: $60.

Required: high school transcript.

Application deadlines: 6/1 (freshmen), 6/1 (out-of-state freshmen), 6/1 (transfers).

Notification: continuous (freshmen), continuous (out-of-state freshmen), continuous (transfers).

CONTACT

The Ohio State University at Lima, 4240 Campus Drive, Lima, OH 45804. *Phone:* 567-242-7172.

The Ohio State University at Mansfield

Mansfield, Ohio

http://www.mansfield.osu.edu/

- **State-supported** comprehensive, founded 1958, part of The Ohio State University
- **Small-town** 620-acre campus with easy access to Columbus, Cleveland
- **Endowment** $2.3 million
- **Coed** 1,075 undergraduate students, 84% full-time, 56% women, 44% men
- **Noncompetitive** entrance level, 100% of applicants were admitted

UNDERGRAD STUDENTS

906 full-time, 169 part-time. Students come from 6 states and territories; 2 other countries; 1% are from out of state; 10% Black or African American, non-Hispanic/Latino; 4% Hispanic/Latino; 2% Asian, non-Hispanic/Latino; 0.1% American Indian or Alaska Native, non-Hispanic/Latino; 4% Two or more races, non-Hispanic/Latino; 3% Race/ethnicity unknown; 0.1% international; 5% transferred in; 20% live on campus.

Freshmen:

Admission: 2,721 applied, 2,711 admitted, 429 enrolled. ***Test scores:*** SAT evidence-based reading and writing scores over 500: 60%; SAT math scores over 500: 65%; ACT scores over 18: 83%; SAT evidence-based reading and writing scores over 600: 31%; SAT math scores over 600: 21%; ACT scores over 24: 42%; SAT math scores over 700: 2%; ACT scores over 30: 5%.

Retention: 34% of full-time freshmen returned.

FACULTY

Total: 86, 37% full-time, 56% with terminal degrees.

Student/faculty ratio: 19:1.

ACADEMICS

Calendar: semesters. *Degrees:* associate and bachelor's.

Special study options: academic remediation for entering students, adult/continuing education programs, advanced placement credit, cooperative education, distance learning, double majors, English as a second language, freshman honors college, honors programs, independent study, internships, off-campus study, part-time degree program, services for LD students, student-designed majors, study abroad, summer session for credit.

Computers: Students can access the following: campus intranet, computer help desk, free student e-mail accounts, online (class) grades, online (class) registration, online (class) schedules. Campuswide network is available. 100% of college-owned or -operated housing units are wired for high-speed Internet access. Wireless service is available via entire campus.

Library: Bromfield Library & Information Commons. *Books:* 43,903 (physical), 1.4 million (digital/electronic); *Serial titles:* 126 (physical), 54,781 (digital/electronic); *Databases:* 2,075. Weekly public service hours: 63; students can reserve study rooms.

STUDENT LIFE

Housing options: coed, special housing for students with disabilities. Campus housing is university owned. Freshman applicants given priority for college housing.

Activities and organizations: drama/theater group, choral group, Campus Activities Board, Best Buddies, Awakening, College Democrats, College Republicans.

Athletics ***Intercollegiate sports:*** baseball M(c), basketball M(c)/W(c), volleyball W(c). ***Intramural sports:*** baseball M, basketball M/W, cheerleading M(c)/W(c), football M/W, sand volleyball M/W, soccer M/W, tennis M/W, ultimate Frisbee M/W, volleyball M/W.

Campus security: 24-hour emergency response devices and patrols.

Student services: personal/psychological counseling.

COSTS

Costs (2019–20) ***Tuition:*** state resident $7912 full-time, $330 per credit hour part-time; nonresident $28,889 full-time, $1204 per credit hour part-time. Full-time tuition and fees vary according to course load, degree level, location, program, and student level. Part-time tuition and fees vary according to course load, degree level, location, program, and student level. No tuition increase for student's term of enrollment. ***Room and board:*** $8272; room only: $6564. Room and board charges vary according to board plan, housing facility, and location. ***Payment plan:*** installment. ***Waivers:*** senior citizens and employees or children of employees.

APPLYING

Standardized Tests *Required for some:* SAT or ACT (for admission).

Options: electronic application.

Application fee: $60.

Required: high school transcript.

Application deadlines: 6/1 (freshmen), 6/1 (out-of-state freshmen), 6/1 (transfers).

Notification: continuous (freshmen), continuous (out-of-state freshmen), continuous (transfers).

CONTACT

The Ohio State University at Mansfield, 1680 University Drive, Mansfield, OH 44906-1599. *Phone:* 419-755-4300.

The Ohio State University at Marion

Marion, Ohio

http://osumarion.osu.edu/

- **State-supported** comprehensive, founded 1958, part of The Ohio State University
- **Small-town** 188-acre campus with easy access to Columbus
- **Endowment** $5.6 million
- **Coed** 1,262 undergraduate students, 473% full-time, 439% women, 50% men
- **Noncompetitive** entrance level, 99% of applicants were admitted

UNDERGRAD STUDENTS

5,971 full-time, 191 part-time. Students come from 8 states and territories; 1 other country; 4% Black or African American, non-Hispanic/Latino; 5% Hispanic/Latino; 6% Asian, non-Hispanic/Latino; 0.1% Native Hawaiian or other Pacific Islander, non-Hispanic/Latino; 3% Two or more races, non-Hispanic/Latino; 3% Race/ethnicity unknown; 0.2% international; 4% transferred in.

Freshmen:

Admission: 1,264 applied, 1,254 admitted, 473 enrolled. ***Test scores:*** SAT evidence-based reading and writing scores over 500: 81%; SAT math scores over 500: 90%; ACT scores over 18: 88%; SAT evidence-based reading and writing scores over 600: 33%; SAT math scores over 600: 52%; ACT scores over 24: 42%; SAT evidence-based reading and writing scores over 700: 2%; SAT math scores over 700: 8%; ACT scores over 30: 2%.

Retention: 50% of full-time freshmen returned.

FACULTY

Total: 103, 37% full-time, 66% with terminal degrees.

Student/faculty ratio: 19:1.

ACADEMICS

Calendar: semesters. *Degrees:* associate and bachelor's.

Special study options: academic remediation for entering students, adult/continuing education programs, advanced placement credit, cooperative education, distance learning, double majors, English as a second language, freshman honors college, honors programs, independent study, internships, off-campus study, part-time degree program, services for LD students, student-designed majors, study abroad, summer session for credit.

Computers: Students can access the following: campus intranet, computer help desk, free student e-mail accounts, online (class) grades, online (class) registration, online (class) schedules. Campuswide network is available. Wireless service is available via entire campus.

Library: Marion Campus Library. *Books:* 46,290 (physical), 1.4 million (digital/electronic); *Serial titles:* 54,781 (digital/electronic); *Databases:* 2,056. Weekly public service hours: 57; students can reserve study rooms.

STUDENT LIFE

Housing options: college housing not available.

Activities and organizations: drama/theater group, choral group.

Athletics Member USCAA.

Campus security: 24-hour emergency response devices.

Student services: personal/psychological counseling.

COSTS

Costs (2019–20) ***Tuition:*** state resident $7912 full-time, $330 per credit hour part-time; nonresident $28,889 full-time, $1204 per credit hour part-time. Full-time tuition and fees vary according to course load, location, program, and student level. Part-time tuition and fees vary according to course load, location, program, and student level. No tuition increase for student's term of enrollment. ***Payment plan:*** installment. ***Waivers:*** senior citizens and employees or children of employees.

APPLYING

Standardized Tests *Required for some:* SAT or ACT (for admission).

Options: electronic application.

Application fee: $60.

Required: high school transcript.

Application deadlines: 6/1 (freshmen), 6/1 (out-of-state freshmen), 6/1 (transfers).

Notification: continuous (freshmen), continuous (out-of-state freshmen), continuous (transfers).

CONTACT

The Ohio State University at Marion, 1465 Mount Vernon Avenue, Marion, OH 43302-5695.

The Ohio State University at Newark

Newark, Ohio

http://www.newark.osu.edu/

- **State-supported** comprehensive, founded 1957, part of The Ohio State University
- **Small-town** 111-acre campus with easy access to Columbus
- **Endowment** $4.0 million
- **Coed** 2,939 undergraduate students, 85% full-time, 50% women, 50% men
- **Noncompetitive** entrance level, 100% of applicants were admitted

UNDERGRAD STUDENTS

2,502 full-time, 437 part-time. Students come from 10 states and territories; 1 other country; 17% Black or African American, non-Hispanic/Latino; 5% Hispanic/Latino; 5% Asian, non-Hispanic/Latino; 0.1% American Indian or Alaska Native, non-Hispanic/Latino; 5% Two or more races, non-Hispanic/Latino; 3% Race/ethnicity unknown; 4% transferred in; 11% live on campus.

Freshmen:

Admission: 5,312 applied, 5,289 admitted, 1,557 enrolled. ***Test scores:*** SAT evidence-based reading and writing scores over 500: 67%; SAT math scores over 500: 70%; ACT scores over 18: 82%; SAT evidence-based reading and writing scores over 600: 28%; SAT math scores over 600: 24%; ACT scores over 24: 33%; SAT evidence-based reading and writing scores over 700: 2%; SAT math scores over 700: 5%; ACT scores over 30: 3%.

Retention: 29% of full-time freshmen returned.

FACULTY

Total: 174, 29% full-time, 64% with terminal degrees.

Student/faculty ratio: 29:1.

ACADEMICS

Calendar: semesters. *Degrees:* associate, bachelor's, and master's.

Special study options: academic remediation for entering students, adult/continuing education programs, advanced placement credit, cooperative education, distance learning, double majors, English as a second language, freshman honors college, honors programs, independent study, internships, off-campus study, part-time degree program, services for LD students, student-designed majors, study abroad, summer session for credit. ***ROTC:*** Army (b).

Computers: Students can access the following: campus intranet, computer help desk, free student e-mail accounts, online (class) grades, online (class) registration, online (class) schedules. Campuswide network is available. 100% of college-owned or -operated housing units are wired for high-speed Internet access. Wireless service is available via entire campus.

Library: John L. and Christine Warner Library. *Books:* 52,380 (physical), 1.4 million (digital/electronic); *Serial titles:* 491 (physical), 54,576 (digital/electronic); *Databases:* 2,056. Weekly public service hours: 69; students can reserve study rooms.

STUDENT LIFE

Housing options: coed, special housing for students with disabilities. Campus housing is university owned. Freshman applicants given priority for college housing.

Activities and organizations: drama/theater group, choral group, Campus Activities Board, Ebonye Horizons, Journay Campus Ministry, Collegiate 4 - H, American Sign Language.

Athletics ***Intramural sports:*** badminton M/W, basketball M/W, golf M/W, sand volleyball M/W, soccer M/W, softball M/W, table tennis M/W, ultimate Frisbee M/W, volleyball M/W, weight lifting M/W.

Campus security: 24-hour emergency response devices and patrols, late-night transport/escort service.

Student services: personal/psychological counseling, legal services.

COSTS

Costs (2019–20) ***Tuition:*** state resident $7912 full-time, $330 per credit hour part-time; nonresident $28,889 full-time, $1204 per credit hour part-time. Full-time tuition and fees vary according to course load, degree level, location, program, and student level. Part-time tuition and fees vary according to course load, degree level, location, program, and student level. No tuition increase for student's term of enrollment. ***Room and board:*** $10,860; room only: $8040. Room and board charges vary according to board plan, housing facility, and location. ***Payment plan:*** installment. ***Waivers:*** senior citizens and employees or children of employees.

APPLYING

Standardized Tests *Required for some:* SAT or ACT (for admission).

Options: electronic application.

Application fee: $60.

Required: high school transcript.

Application deadlines: 6/1 (freshmen), 6/1 (out-of-state freshmen), 6/1 (transfers).

Notification: continuous (freshmen), continuous (out-of-state freshmen), continuous (transfers).

CONTACT

Ms. Diane Kanney, Director of Enrollment, The Ohio State University at Newark, 1179 University Drive, Newark, OH 43055. *Phone:* 740-366-9333. *E-mail:* kanney.24@osu.edu.

Ohio University
Athens, Ohio
http://www.ohio.edu/

- **State-supported** university, founded 1804, part of Ohio Board of Regents
- **Small-town** 1800-acre campus
- **Endowment** $568.9 million
- **Coed**
- **Moderately difficult** entrance level

FACULTY
Student/faculty ratio: 17:1.

ACADEMICS
Calendar: semesters. *Degrees:* certificates, associate, bachelor's, master's, doctoral, and postbachelor's certificates.
Library: Alden Library plus 3 others. *Books:* 3.2 million (physical), 1.1 million (digital/electronic); *Serial titles:* 155,515 (physical), 88,338 (digital/electronic); *Databases:* 558. Weekly public service hours: 146; study areas open 24 hours, 5–7 days a week; students can reserve study rooms.

STUDENT LIFE
Housing options: on-campus residence required through sophomore year; coed, women-only, special housing for students with disabilities. Campus housing is university owned. Freshman campus housing is guaranteed.

Activities and organizations: drama/theater group, student-run newspaper, radio and television station, choral group, marching band, Student Senate, Student Alumni Board, International Student Union, University Program Council, Black Student Cultural Programming Board, national fraternities, national sororities.

Athletics Member NCAA. All Division I except football (Division I-A).

Campus security: 24-hour emergency response devices and patrols, student patrols, late-night transport/escort service, controlled dormitory access.

Student services: health clinic, personal/psychological counseling, women's center, legal services, veterans affairs office.

COSTS & FINANCIAL AID
Costs (2019–20) ***Tuition:*** state resident $12,612 full-time, $595 per semester hour part-time; nonresident $22,406 full-time, $1077 per semester hour part-time. Full-time tuition and fees vary according to degree level, location, program, and reciprocity agreements. Part-time tuition and fees vary according to course load, degree level, location, program, and reciprocity agreements. No tuition increase for student's term of enrollment. ***Room and board:*** $12,172; room only: $7308. Room and board charges vary according to board plan.

Financial Aid Of all full-time matriculated undergraduates who enrolled in 2018, 12,027 applied for aid, 9,728 were judged to have need, 720 had their need fully met. 710 Federal Work-Study jobs (averaging $1869). In 2018, 1556 non-need-based awards were made. ***Average percent of need met:*** 49. ***Average financial aid package:*** $8977. ***Average need-based loan:*** $3701. ***Average need-based gift aid:*** $6520. ***Average non-need-based aid:*** $4612. ***Average indebtedness upon graduation:*** $27,993.

APPLYING
Standardized Tests *Required:* SAT or ACT (for admission).

Options: electronic application, early admission, early action, deferred entrance.

Application fee: $50.

Required for some: essay or personal statement, high school transcript, 2 letters of recommendation, Audition required for dance and music programs. Interview required of selected Honors Tutorial College candidates. Portfolio required of visual communication applicants. ***Recommended:*** 2 letters of recommendation.

CONTACT
Ms. Candace Boeninger, Assistant Vice President and Director, Ohio University, Athens, OH 45701-2979. *Phone:* 740-593-4100. *Fax:* 740-593-0560. *E-mail:* admissions@ohio.edu.

Ohio University–Chillicothe
Chillicothe, Ohio
http://www.chillicothe.ohiou.edu/

CONTACT
Neeley Allen, Coordinator, Recruitment, Ohio University–Chillicothe, 101 University Drive, Chillicothe, OH 45601. *Phone:* 740-774-7241. *Toll-free phone:* 877-462-6824. *Fax:* 740-774-7214. *E-mail:* evelandt@ohio.edu.

Ohio University–Eastern
St. Clairsville, Ohio
http://www.eastern.ohiou.edu/

CONTACT
Ms. Lisa Jeffries, Recruitment Coordinator, Ohio University–Eastern, 45425 National Road, St. Clairsville, OH 43950-9724. *Phone:* 740-699-2504. *Toll-free phone:* 800-648-3331. *E-mail:* jeffriee@ohio.edu.

Ohio University–Lancaster
Lancaster, Ohio
http://www.ohiou.edu/lancaster/

- **State-supported** comprehensive, founded 1968, part of Ohio Board of Regents
- **Small-town** 360-acre campus with easy access to Columbus
- **Coed**
- **Noncompetitive** entrance level

FACULTY
Student/faculty ratio: 17:1.

ACADEMICS
Calendar: quarters. *Degrees:* associate, bachelor's, and master's.
Library: Hannah V. McCauley Library.

STUDENT LIFE
Housing options: college housing not available; coed, women-only, special housing for students with disabilities.

Activities and organizations: drama/theater group.

COSTS & FINANCIAL AID
Costs (2019–20) ***Tuition:*** state resident $5674 full-time, $255 per semester hour part-time; nonresident $8666 full-time, $391 per semester hour part-time. Full-time tuition and fees vary according to degree level, location, program, and reciprocity agreements. Part-time tuition and fees vary according to course load, degree level, location, program, and reciprocity agreements. No tuition increase for student's term of enrollment.

Financial Aid Of all full-time matriculated undergraduates who enrolled in 2018, 627 applied for aid, 516 were judged to have need, 16 had their need fully met. 9 Federal Work-Study jobs (averaging $1504). In 2018, 17 non-need-based awards were made. ***Average percent of need met:*** 39. ***Average financial aid package:*** $5377. ***Average need-based loan:*** $2512. ***Average need-based gift aid:*** $4183. ***Average non-need-based aid:*** $2605. ***Average indebtedness upon graduation:*** $27,993.

APPLYING
Options: electronic application, early admission, early action, deferred entrance.

Application fee: $50.

Required: high school transcript. ***Recommended:*** interview.

CONTACT
Pat Fox, Enrollment Manager, Ohio University–Lancaster, 1570 Granville Pike, Lancaster, OH 43130-1097. *Phone:* 740-654-6711 Ext. 215. *Toll-free phone:* 888-446-4468. *E-mail:* fox@ohio.edu.

Ohio University–Southern Campus

Ironton, Ohio

http://www.ohiou.edu/

- **State-supported** comprehensive, founded 1956, part of Ohio Board of Regents
- **Small-town** 9-acre campus
- **Coed**
- **Noncompetitive** entrance level

FACULTY
Student/faculty ratio: 17:1.

ACADEMICS
Calendar: quarters. *Degrees:* associate, bachelor's, and master's.
Library: Ohio University-Southern Campus Library.

STUDENT LIFE
Housing options: college housing not available; coed, women-only, special housing for students with disabilities.

Activities and organizations: choral group.

Student services: legal services.

COSTS & FINANCIAL AID
Costs (2019–20) ***Tuition:*** state resident $5674 full-time, $255 per semester hour part-time; nonresident $8666 full-time, $391 per semester hour part-time. Full-time tuition and fees vary according to degree level, location, program, and reciprocity agreements. Part-time tuition and fees vary according to course load, degree level, location, program, and reciprocity agreements. No tuition increase for student's term of enrollment.

Financial Aid Of all full-time matriculated undergraduates who enrolled in 2018, 656 applied for aid, 591 were judged to have need, 12 had their need fully met. 12 Federal Work-Study jobs (averaging $2060). In 2018, 16 non-need-based awards were made. ***Average percent of need met:*** 42. ***Average financial aid package:*** $5487. ***Average need-based loan:*** $2585. ***Average need-based gift aid:*** $3906. ***Average non-need-based aid:*** $1293. ***Average indebtedness upon graduation:*** $27,993.

APPLYING
Standardized Tests *Required for some:* ACT (for admission).

Options: electronic application, early admission, deferred entrance.

Application fee: $50.

Required for some: high school transcript.

CONTACT
Linda Harlow, Admission, Registration and Records Coordinator, Ohio University–Southern Campus, 1804 Liberty Avenue, Ironton, OH 45638-2214. *Phone:* 740-533-4584. *Toll-free phone:* 800-626-0513. *E-mail:* harlow@ohio.edu.

Ohio University–Zanesville

Zanesville, Ohio

http://www.ohio.edu/zanesville/

- **State-supported** 4-year, founded 1946
- **Rural** 179-acre campus with easy access to Columbus
- **Coed**
- **Noncompetitive** entrance level

FACULTY
Student/faculty ratio: 17:1.

ACADEMICS
Calendar: semesters. *Degrees:* associate and bachelor's (offers first 2 years of most bachelor's degree programs available at the main campus in Athens; also offers several bachelor's degree programs that can be completed at this campus; also offers some graduate courses).
Library: Zanesville Campus Library plus 1 other. Students can reserve study rooms.

STUDENT LIFE
Housing options: college housing not available; coed, women-only, special housing for students with disabilities.

Activities and organizations: student-run radio station, Student Senate, Student Nurses Association, Good Intentions Group, Green Bobcats, Habitat for Humanity Club.

Campus security: student patrols, late-night transport/escort service, night security.

Student services: personal/psychological counseling, legal services, veterans affairs office.

COSTS & FINANCIAL AID
Costs (2019–20) ***Tuition:*** state resident $5674 full-time, $255 per semester hour part-time; nonresident $8666 full-time, $391 per semester hour part-time. Full-time tuition and fees vary according to degree level, location, program, and reciprocity agreements. Part-time tuition and fees vary according to course load, degree level, location, program, and reciprocity agreements. No tuition increase for student's term of enrollment.

Financial Aid Of all full-time matriculated undergraduates who enrolled in 2018, 619 applied for aid, 513 were judged to have need, 21 had their need fully met. 4 Federal Work-Study jobs (averaging $1441). In 2018, 7 non-need-based awards were made. ***Average percent of need met:*** 43. ***Average financial aid package:*** $5620. ***Average need-based loan:*** $2758. ***Average need-based gift aid:*** $4346. ***Average non-need-based aid:*** $1421. ***Average indebtedness upon graduation:*** $27,993.

APPLYING
Standardized Tests *Required for some:* SAT or ACT (for admission).

Options: electronic application, early action.

Application fee: $50.

Required: high school transcript.

CONTACT
Ohio University–Zanesville, Office of Student Services, 1425 Newark Road, Zanesville, OH 43701. *Phone:* 740-588-1440. *Fax:* 740-588-1444. *E-mail:* ouzservices@ohio.edu.

Ohio Wesleyan University

Delaware, Ohio

http://www.owu.edu/

- **Independent United Methodist** 4-year, founded 1842
- **Small-town** 200-acre campus with easy access to Columbus
- **Coed** 1,494 undergraduate students, 100% full-time, 56% women, 44% men
- **Very difficult** entrance level, 67% of applicants were admitted

UNDERGRAD STUDENTS
1,487 full-time, 7 part-time. 38% are from out of state; 8% Black or African American, non-Hispanic/Latino; 6% Hispanic/Latino; 3% Asian, non-Hispanic/Latino; 0.2% Native Hawaiian or other Pacific Islander, non-Hispanic/Latino; 5% Two or more races, non-Hispanic/Latino; 1% Race/ethnicity unknown; 7% international; 2% transferred in; 83% live on campus.

Freshmen:
Admission: 4,281 applied, 2,880 admitted, 389 enrolled. ***Average high school GPA:*** 3.5. ***Test scores:*** SAT evidence-based reading and writing scores over 500: 86%; SAT math scores over 500: 87%; ACT scores over 18: 95%; SAT evidence-based reading and writing scores over 600: 53%; SAT math scores over 600: 55%; ACT scores over 24: 59%; SAT evidence-based reading and writing scores over 700: 13%; SAT math scores over 700: 19%; ACT scores over 30: 14%.

Retention: 78% of full-time freshmen returned.

FACULTY
Total: 193, 64% full-time.

Student/faculty ratio: 10:1.

ACADEMICS
Calendar: semesters. *Degree:* bachelor's.

Special study options: double majors, honors programs, internships, off-campus study, services for LD students, student-designed majors, study abroad, summer session for credit. ***ROTC:*** Army (c), Air Force (c).

Unusual degree programs: 3-2 engineering with Alfred University, California Institute of Technology, Case Western Reserve University,

Polytechnic University, Rensselaer Polytechnic Institute, Washington University in St. Louis.

Computers: Students can access the following: campus intranet, computer help desk, free student e-mail accounts, online (class) grades, online (class) registration, online (class) schedules. Campuswide network is available. 100% of college-owned or -operated housing units are wired for high-speed Internet access. Wireless service is available via entire campus.

Library: L. A. Beeghly Library.

STUDENT LIFE

Housing options: on-campus residence required through senior year; coed, women-only. Campus housing is university owned. Freshman campus housing is guaranteed.

Activities and organizations: drama/theater group, student-run newspaper, radio station, choral group, national fraternities, national sororities.

Athletics Member NCAA. All Division III. ***Intercollegiate sports:*** baseball M, basketball M/W, cheerleading W(c), crew W, cross-country running M/W, equestrian sports M(c)/W(c), field hockey W, football M, golf M/W, ice hockey M(c)/W(c), lacrosse M/W, rowing W, rugby M(c)/W(c), sailing M(c)/W(c), soccer M/W, softball W, swimming and diving M/W, tennis M/W, track and field M/W, ultimate Frisbee M(c)/W(c), volleyball M(c)/W, wrestling M. ***Intramural sports:*** badminton M/W, basketball M/W, football M/W, golf M/W, lacrosse M/W, racquetball M/W, skiing (cross-country) M/W, skiing (downhill) M/W, soccer M/W, softball M/W, squash M/W, swimming and diving M/W, tennis M/W, track and field M/W, volleyball M/W, water polo M/W.

Campus security: 24-hour emergency response devices and patrols, late-night transport/escort service, controlled dormitory access.

Student services: health clinic, personal/psychological counseling, women's center.

COSTS & FINANCIAL AID

Costs (2019–20) ***Comprehensive fee:*** $60,460 includes full-time tuition ($46,870), mandatory fees ($260), and room and board ($13,330). Full-time tuition and fees vary according to course load. Part-time tuition: $5090 per course. Part-time tuition and fees vary according to course load. ***College room only:*** $7000. Room and board charges vary according to board plan and housing facility. ***Payment plan:*** installment. ***Waivers:*** employees or children of employees.

Financial Aid Of all full-time matriculated undergraduates who enrolled in 2018, 1,232 applied for aid, 1,128 were judged to have need, 196 had their need fully met. In 2018, 404 non-need-based awards were made. ***Average percent of need met:*** 81. ***Average financial aid package:*** $38,663. ***Average need-based loan:*** $4259. ***Average need-based gift aid:*** $33,958. ***Average non-need-based aid:*** $24,258. ***Average indebtedness upon graduation:*** $36,680. ***Financial aid deadline:*** 2/15.

APPLYING

Standardized Tests *Required for some:* SAT or ACT (for admission).

Options: electronic application, early decision, early action, deferred entrance.

Required: essay or personal statement, high school transcript, minimum 2.5 GPA, 1 letter of recommendation. ***Recommended:*** 2 letters of recommendation, interview.

Application deadlines: rolling (transfers), 12/1 (early action).

Early decision deadline: 11/15 (for plan 1), 1/15 (for plan 2).

Notification: continuous (freshmen), continuous (out-of-state freshmen), continuous (transfers), 12/15 (early action).

CONTACT

Ms. Alisha Couch, Director of Admission, Ohio Wesleyan University, 61 South Sandusky Street, Delaware, OH 43015. *Phone:* 740-368-3099. *Toll-free phone:* 800-922-8953. *Fax:* 740-368-3314. *E-mail:* amcouch@owu.edu.

Otterbein University

Westerville, Ohio

http://www.otterbein.edu/

CONTACT

Mr. Mark Moffit, Director of Admissions, Otterbein University, 1 South Grove Street, Office of Admission, Westerville, OH 43081-9924. *Phone:* 614-823-1500. *Toll-free phone:* 800-488-8144. *Fax:* 614-823-1200. *E-mail:* uotterb@otterbein.edu.

Pontifical College Josephinum

Columbus, Ohio

http://www.pcj.edu/

CONTACT

Mrs. Arminda Crawford, Secretary for Admissions, Pontifical College Josephinum, 7825 North High Street, Columbus, OH 43235. *Phone:* 614-985-2241. *Toll-free phone:* 888-252-5812. *Fax:* 614-885-2307. *E-mail:* acrawford@pcj.edu.

Rabbinical College of Telshe

Wickliffe, Ohio

CONTACT

Admissions Office, Rabbinical College of Telshe, 28400 Euclid Avenue, Wickliffe, OH 44092-2523. *Phone:* 440-943-5300.

Ross College

Canton, Ohio

http://www.rosseducation.edu/

CONTACT

Ross College, 4300 Munson Street NW, Canton, OH 44718. *Phone:* 330-494-1214. *Toll-free phone:* 866-815-5578.

Shawnee State University

Portsmouth, Ohio

http://www.shawnee.edu/

CONTACT

Amanda Means, Director of Admissions, Shawnee State University, 940 Second Street, Portsmouth, OH 45662. *Phone:* 740-351-3229. *Toll-free phone:* 800-959-2778. *Fax:* 740-351-3111. *E-mail:* ameans@shawnee.edu.

Tiffin University

Tiffin, Ohio

http://www.tiffin.edu/

- **Independent** comprehensive, founded 1888
- **Small-town** 135-acre campus with easy access to Toledo
- **Endowment** $13.1 million
- **Coed** 2,206 undergraduate students, 75% full-time, 50% women, 50% men
- **Moderately difficult** entrance level, 69% of applicants were admitted

UNDERGRAD STUDENTS

1,661 full-time, 545 part-time. Students come from 34 states and territories; 33 other countries; 23% are from out of state; 15% Black or African American, non-Hispanic/Latino; 3% Hispanic/Latino; 1% Asian, non-Hispanic/Latino; 0.1% American Indian or Alaska Native, non-Hispanic/Latino; 2% Two or more races, non-Hispanic/Latino; 16% Race/ethnicity unknown; 9% international; 6% transferred in; 46% live on campus.

Freshmen:

Admission: 4,219 applied, 2,907 admitted, 439 enrolled. ***Average high school GPA:*** 3.0. ***Test scores:*** ACT scores over 18: 71%; ACT scores over 24: 16%; ACT scores over 30: 2%.

Retention: 65% of full-time freshmen returned.

FACULTY
Total: 279, 25% full-time, 48% with terminal degrees.

Student/faculty ratio: 15:1.

ACADEMICS
Calendar: semesters. *Degrees:* certificates, associate, bachelor's, master's, doctoral, post-master's, and postbachelor's certificates.

Special study options: academic remediation for entering students, accelerated degree program, adult/continuing education programs, cooperative education, distance learning, double majors, English as a second language, independent study, internships, off-campus study, part-time degree program, services for LD students, study abroad, summer session for credit. ***ROTC:*** Army (c), Air Force (c).

Unusual degree programs: 3-2 business administration.

Computers: 280 computers/terminals are available on campus for general student use. Students can access the following: campus intranet, computer help desk, free student e-mail accounts, online (class) grades, online (class) registration, online (class) schedules. Campuswide network is available. 100% of college-owned or -operated housing units are wired for high-speed Internet access. Wireless service is available via entire campus.

Library: Pfeiffer Library plus 1 other. *Books:* 43,505 (physical), 317,775 (digital/electronic); *Serial titles:* 331 (physical), 97,873 (digital/electronic); *Databases:* 216. Weekly public service hours: 73.

STUDENT LIFE
Housing options: on-campus residence required through sophomore year; coed, men-only, women-only. Campus housing is university owned. Freshman campus housing is guaranteed.

Activities and organizations: drama/theater group, choral group, marching band, Student Government Association, H2O, International Student Association, Global Affairs Organization, Circle K, national fraternities, national sororities.

Athletics Member NCAA. All Division II. ***Intercollegiate sports:*** baseball M(s), basketball M(s)/W(s), cross-country running M(s)/W(s), equestrian sports M/W, football M(s), golf M(s)/W(s), lacrosse W(s), soccer M(s)/W(s), softball W(s), swimming and diving M(s)/W(s), tennis M(s)/W(s), track and field M(s)/W(s), volleyball W(s), wrestling M(s)/W(s). ***Intramural sports:*** basketball M/W, bowling M/W, cheerleading W(c), equestrian sports M(c)/W(c), football M, rugby M(c), soccer M(c)/W(c), softball W, tennis M/W, volleyball M/W.

Campus security: 24-hour emergency response devices and patrols, student patrols, late-night transport/escort service, controlled dormitory access.

Student services: health clinic, personal/psychological counseling, women's center, veterans affairs office.

COSTS & FINANCIAL AID
Costs (2020–21) ***Comprehensive fee:*** $39,310 includes full-time tuition ($27,210), mandatory fees ($400), and room and board ($11,700). Part-time tuition: $907 per credit hour. ***Required fees:*** $400 per term part-time. ***College room only:*** $6180. Room and board charges vary according to board plan and housing facility. ***Payment plan:*** installment.

Financial Aid Of all full-time matriculated undergraduates who enrolled in 2019, 1,412 applied for aid, 1,289 were judged to have need, 190 had their need fully met. ***Average percent of need met:*** 64. ***Average financial aid package:*** $19,763. ***Average need-based loan:*** $3992. ***Average need-based gift aid:*** $16,402. ***Average indebtedness upon graduation:*** $31,788.

APPLYING
Standardized Tests *Required for some:* SAT (for admission), ACT (for admission), SAT or ACT (for admission).

Options: electronic application.

Application fee: $20.

Required: high school transcript. ***Required for some:*** essay or personal statement, interview. ***Recommended:*** minimum 3.0 GPA.

Application deadlines: rolling (freshmen), rolling (out-of-state freshmen), rolling (transfers).

Notification: continuous (freshmen), continuous (out-of-state freshmen), continuous (transfers).

CONTACT
Mrs. Sarah Johnson, Director of Undergraduate Admissions, Tiffin University, 155 Miami Street, Tiffin, OH 44883. *Phone:* 419-448-3014. *Toll-free phone:* 800-968-6446. *Fax:* 419-443-5006. *E-mail:* depughst@tiffin.edu.

Tri-State Bible College

South Point, Ohio

http://www.tsbc.edu/

CONTACT
Tri-State Bible College, 506 Margaret Street, PO Box 445, South Point, OH 45680-8402. *Phone:* 740-377-2520.

Union Institute & University

Cincinnati, Ohio

http://www.myunion.edu/

CONTACT
Union Institute & University, 440 East McMillan Street, Cincinnati, OH 45206-1925. *Phone:* 513-487-1173. *Toll-free phone:* 800-486-3116.

The University of Akron

Akron, Ohio

http://www.uakron.edu/

- **State-supported** university, founded 1870
- **Urban** 223-acre campus with easy access to Cleveland
- **Endowment** $191.4 million
- **Coed** 14,793 undergraduate students, 79% full-time, 47% women, 53% men
- **Moderately difficult** entrance level, 73% of applicants were admitted

UNDERGRAD STUDENTS
11,641 full-time, 3,152 part-time. 6% are from out of state; 10% Black or African American, non-Hispanic/Latino; 3% Hispanic/Latino; 3% Asian, non-Hispanic/Latino; 0.2% American Indian or Alaska Native, non-Hispanic/Latino; 4% Two or more races, non-Hispanic/Latino; 2% Race/ethnicity unknown; 2% international; 3% transferred in; 20% live on campus.

Freshmen:
Admission: 14,553 applied, 10,629 admitted, 2,739 enrolled. ***Average high school GPA:*** 3.5. ***Test scores:*** SAT evidence-based reading and writing scores over 500: 76%; SAT math scores over 500: 80%; ACT scores over 18: 86%; SAT evidence-based reading and writing scores over 600: 32%; SAT math scores over 600: 35%; ACT scores over 24: 42%; SAT evidence-based reading and writing scores over 700: 3%; SAT math scores over 700: 8%; ACT scores over 30: 7%.

Retention: 72% of full-time freshmen returned.

FACULTY
Total: 1,269, 49% full-time, 49% with terminal degrees.

Student/faculty ratio: 18:1.

ACADEMICS
Calendar: semesters. *Degrees:* certificates, associate, bachelor's, master's, doctoral, post-master's, and postbachelor's certificates.

Special study options: academic remediation for entering students, accelerated degree program, adult/continuing education programs, advanced placement credit, cooperative education, distance learning, double majors, English as a second language, external degree program, freshman honors college, honors programs, independent study, internships, part-time degree program, services for LD students, student-designed majors, study abroad, summer session for credit. ***ROTC:*** Army (b), Air Force (c).

Unusual degree programs: 3-2 business administration; engineering; medicine, polymer chemistry.

Computers: 3,150 computers/terminals and 16,000 ports are available on campus for general student use. Students can access the following: campus intranet, computer help desk, free student e-mail accounts, online (class) grades, online (class) registration, online (class) schedules, library laptops for student checkout. Campuswide network is available. 100% of

college-owned or -operated housing units are wired for high-speed Internet access. Wireless service is available via entire campus.
Library: Bierce Library plus 2 others. *Books:* 1.1 million (physical); *Serial titles:* 25,089 (physical). Study areas open 24 hours, 5–7 days a week; students can reserve study rooms.

STUDENT LIFE
Housing options: on-campus residence required for freshman year; coed. Campus housing is university owned. Freshman applicants given priority for college housing.

Activities and organizations: drama/theater group, student-run newspaper, radio and television station, choral group, marching band, AK-Rowdies, Akron Animation Association, National Society of Leadership and Success, Golden Key International Honor Society, Alpha Phi Omega, national fraternities, national sororities.

Athletics Member NCAA. All Division I except football (Division I-A). ***Intercollegiate sports:*** basketball M(s)/W(s), cheerleading M/W, cross-country running M(s)/W(s), golf M(s)/W(s), riflery M/W(s), soccer M(s)/W(s), softball W(s), swimming and diving W(s), tennis W(s), track and field M(s)/W(s), volleyball W(s). ***Intramural sports:*** badminton M/W, basketball M/W, bowling M/W, cross-country running M/W, golf M/W, racquetball M/W, skiing (cross-country) M/W, skiing (downhill) M/W, soccer M/W, softball M/W, swimming and diving M/W, table tennis M/W, track and field M/W, volleyball W, wrestling M.

Campus security: 24-hour emergency response devices and patrols, student patrols, late-night transport/escort service, controlled dormitory access.

Student services: health clinic, personal/psychological counseling, women's center, legal services.

FINANCIAL AID
Financial Aid Of all full-time matriculated undergraduates who enrolled in 2018, 10,669 applied for aid, 8,087 were judged to have need, 926 had their need fully met. In 2018, 2017 non-need-based awards were made. ***Average percent of need met:*** 55. ***Average financial aid package:*** $7089. ***Average need-based loan:*** $3852. ***Average need-based gift aid:*** $5780. ***Average non-need-based aid:*** $5323. ***Average indebtedness upon graduation:*** $28,643.

APPLYING
Standardized Tests *Required:* SAT or ACT (for admission).

Options: electronic application, early action, deferred entrance.

Application fee: $50.

Required: high school transcript. ***Required for some:*** essay or personal statement, 3 letters of recommendation, interview.

Application deadlines: 8/11 (freshmen), rolling (transfers), 11/1 (early action).

Notification: 9/15 (freshmen), continuous (transfers).

CONTACT
Ms. Kimberley Gentile, Senior Associate Director of Admissions Outreach, The University of Akron, Office of Admissions, Simmons Hall 109N. *Phone:* 330-972-6345. *Toll-free phone:* 800-655-4884. *E-mail:* gentile@uakron.edu.

The University of Akron Wayne College

Orrville, Ohio

http://www.wayne.uakron.edu/

- **State-supported** primarily 2-year, founded 1972, part of The University of Akron
- **Rural** 157-acre campus
- **Coed**
- **Noncompetitive** entrance level

FACULTY
Student/faculty ratio: 20:1.

ACADEMICS
Calendar: semesters. *Degrees:* certificates, associate, and bachelor's.
Library: Wayne College Library.

STUDENT LIFE
Housing options: college housing not available.

Activities and organizations: Associated Student Government (ASG), Campus Crusade for Christ (CRU), Waynessence, Nursing Club, Adult Learner Student Organization (ALSO).

Campus security: 24-hour emergency response devices, late-night transport/escort service.

Student services: personal/psychological counseling.

FINANCIAL AID
Financial Aid Of all full-time matriculated undergraduates who enrolled in 2018, 8 Federal Work-Study jobs (averaging $2200).

APPLYING
Standardized Tests *Required for some:* SAT or ACT (for admission), ACT Compass. *Recommended:* SAT or ACT (for admission), ACT Compass.

Options: electronic application, early admission, deferred entrance.

Application fee: $50.

Required for some: high school transcript.

CONTACT
Ms. Alicia Broadus, Student Services Counselor, The University of Akron Wayne College, Orrville, OH 44667. *Phone:* 800-221-8308 Ext. 8901. *Toll-free phone:* 800-221-8308. *Fax:* 330-684-8989. *E-mail:* wayneadmissions@uakron.edu.

University of Cincinnati

Cincinnati, Ohio

http://www.uc.edu/

- **State-supported** university, founded 1819
- **Urban** 137-acre campus with easy access to Cincinnati
- **Endowment** $1.4 billion
- **Coed** 28,376 undergraduate students, 84% full-time, 50% women, 50% men
- **Moderately difficult** entrance level, 77% of applicants were admitted

UNDERGRAD STUDENTS
23,712 full-time, 4,664 part-time. Students come from 51 states and territories; 138 other countries; 17% are from out of state; 7% Black or African American, non-Hispanic/Latino; 3% Hispanic/Latino; 4% Asian, non-Hispanic/Latino; 0.1% American Indian or Alaska Native, non-Hispanic/Latino; 4% Two or more races, non-Hispanic/Latino; 2% Race/ethnicity unknown; 4% international; 4% transferred in; 24% live on campus.

Freshmen:
Admission: 23,609 applied, 18,102 admitted, 5,480 enrolled. ***Average high school GPA:*** 3.7. ***Test scores:*** SAT evidence-based reading and writing scores over 500: 97%; SAT math scores over 500: 96%; ACT scores over 18: 99%; SAT evidence-based reading and writing scores over 600: 65%; SAT math scores over 600: 67%; ACT scores over 24: 76%; SAT evidence-based reading and writing scores over 700: 17%; SAT math scores over 700: 26%; ACT scores over 30: 21%.

Retention: 88% of full-time freshmen returned.

FACULTY
Total: 3,708, 59% full-time, 67% with terminal degrees.

Student/faculty ratio: 17:1.

ACADEMICS
Calendar: semesters. *Degrees:* certificates, associate, bachelor's, master's, doctoral, post-master's, and postbachelor's certificates.

Special study options: academic remediation for entering students, accelerated degree program, adult/continuing education programs, advanced placement credit, cooperative education, distance learning, double majors, English as a second language, honors programs, independent study, internships, off-campus study, services for LD students, study abroad, summer session for credit. ***ROTC:*** Army (b), Air Force (b).

Computers: 499 computers/terminals are available on campus for general student use. Students can access the following: campus intranet, computer help desk, free student e-mail accounts, online (class) grades, online (class) registration, online (class) schedules. Campuswide network is available. 100% of college-owned or -operated housing units are wired for

high-speed Internet access. Wireless service is available via entire campus.

Library: Walter C. Langsam Library plus 13 others. *Books:* 2.7 million (physical), 1.6 million (digital/electronic); *Serial titles:* 98,491 (physical), 2.1 million (digital/electronic); *Databases:* 1,270. Study areas open 24 hours, 5–7 days a week; students can reserve study rooms.

STUDENT LIFE

Housing options: on-campus residence required for freshman year; coed, men-only, women-only. Campus housing is university owned. Freshman campus housing is guaranteed.

Activities and organizations: drama/theater group, student-run newspaper, radio station, choral group, marching band, Serve Beyond Cincinnati, University of Cincinnati Mountaineering Club, Rally Cats, Engineers Without Borders, UC League of Legends, national fraternities, national sororities.

Athletics Member NCAA. All Division I except football (Division I-A). ***Intercollegiate sports:*** baseball M(s), basketball M(s)/W(s), cheerleading M/W, cross-country running M(s)/W(s), golf M(s)/W(s), lacrosse W(s), soccer M(s)/W(s), swimming and diving M(s)/W(s), tennis W(s), track and field M(s)/W(s), volleyball W(s). ***Intramural sports:*** badminton M(c)/W(c), baseball M(c), basketball M/W, bowling M(c)/W(c), crew M(c)/W(c), cross-country running M(c)/W(c), equestrian sports M(c)/W(c), fencing M(c)/W(c), football M/W, golf M(c)/W(c), gymnastics M(c)/W(c), ice hockey M(c), lacrosse M(c)/W(c), racquetball M(c)/W(c), rugby M(c)/W(c), soccer M(c)/W(c), softball W(c), swimming and diving M(c)/W(c), table tennis M(c)/W(c), tennis M(c)/W(c), triathlon M(c)/W(c), ultimate Frisbee M(c)/W(c), volleyball M(c)/W(c), water polo M(c)/W(c), wrestling M(c).

Campus security: 24-hour emergency response devices and patrols, student patrols, late-night transport/escort service, controlled dormitory access.

Student services: health clinic, personal/psychological counseling, women's center, veterans affairs office.

COSTS & FINANCIAL AID

Costs (2020–21) ***Tuition:*** state resident $9332 full-time, $389 per credit hour part-time; nonresident $24,666 full-time, $1028 per credit hour part-time. Full-time tuition and fees vary according to course load, degree level, location, program, reciprocity agreements, and student level. Part-time tuition and fees vary according to course load, degree level, location, program, reciprocity agreements, and student level. No tuition increase for student's term of enrollment. ***Required fees:*** $1678 full-time. ***Room and board:*** $11,530; room only: $6856. Room and board charges vary according to board plan, housing facility, and student level. ***Payment plan:*** installment. ***Waivers:*** employees or children of employees.

Financial Aid Of all full-time matriculated undergraduates who enrolled in 2018, 15,688 applied for aid, 11,645 were judged to have need, 1,057 had their need fully met. 4,407 Federal Work-Study jobs (averaging $4425). In 2018, 1809 non-need-based awards were made. ***Average percent of need met:*** 36. ***Average financial aid package:*** $5892. ***Average need-based loan:*** $4002. ***Average need-based gift aid:*** $6506. ***Average non-need-based aid:*** $4404. ***Average indebtedness upon graduation:*** $30,350.

APPLYING

Standardized Tests *Required:* SAT or ACT (for admission).

Options: electronic application, deferred entrance.

Application fee: $50.

Required: essay or personal statement, high school transcript. ***Required for some:*** 1 letter of recommendation, audition for performing arts majors.

Application deadlines: 3/1 (freshmen), 7/1 (transfers), 12/1 (early action).

Notification: continuous until 5/1 (freshmen), continuous (transfers), rolling (early action).

CONTACT

Mrs. Tamara Bylabnd, Asst Vice Provost of Admissions, University of Cincinnati, Office of Admissions, PO Box210091, Cincinnati, OH 45221-0091. *Phone:* 513-556-1100. *Fax:* 513-556-1105. *E-mail:* admissions@uc.edu.

University of Cincinnati Blue Ash College

Cincinnati, Ohio

http://www.ucblueash.edu/

CONTACT

University of Cincinnati Blue Ash College, 9555 Plainfield Road, Cincinnati, OH 45236-1007. *Phone:* 513-745-5700.

University of Cincinnati Clermont College

Batavia, Ohio

http://www.ucclermont.edu/

- **State-supported** primarily 2-year, founded 1972, part of University of Cincinnati System
- **Rural** 91-acre campus with easy access to Cincinnati
- **Coed**
- **Noncompetitive** entrance level

FACULTY

Student/faculty ratio: 16:1.

ACADEMICS

Calendar: semesters. *Degrees:* certificates, associate, bachelor's, and postbachelor's certificates.

Library: UC Clermont College Library. Students can reserve study rooms.

STUDENT LIFE

Housing options: college housing not available; coed, men-only, women-only.

Activities and organizations: student-run newspaper, Active Minds, PACE (Professionalism Academics Character Experiences), Phi Theta Kappa, Association of Paralegal Students, Cheerleading.

Athletics Member USCAA.

Campus security: 24-hour emergency response devices and patrols.

Student services: personal/psychological counseling, veterans affairs office.

COSTS & FINANCIAL AID

Costs (2019–20) ***Tuition:*** state resident $4898 full-time, $235 per credit hour part-time; nonresident $12,130 full-time, $536 per credit hour part-time. Full-time tuition and fees vary according to course level, degree level, program, and reciprocity agreements. Part-time tuition and fees vary according to course level, degree level, program, and reciprocity agreements. No tuition increase for student's term of enrollment. ***Required fees:*** $368 full-time.

Financial Aid Of all full-time matriculated undergraduates who enrolled in 2017, 1,129 applied for aid, 941 were judged to have need, 18 had their need fully met. 64 Federal Work-Study jobs (averaging $3002). In 2017, 93 non-need-based awards were made. ***Average percent of need met:*** 35. ***Average financial aid package:*** $6273. ***Average need-based loan:*** $3498. ***Average need-based gift aid:*** $4834. ***Average non-need-based aid:*** $1611.

APPLYING

Options: electronic application, deferred entrance.

Application fee: $50.

Required: high school transcript.

CONTACT

Mrs. Jamie Adkins, University Services Associate, University of Cincinnati Clermont College, 4200 Clermont College Drive, Batavia, OH 45103. *Phone:* 513-732-5294. *Toll-free phone:* 866-446-2822. *Fax:* 513-732-5303. *E-mail:* jamie.adkins@uc.edu.

University of Dayton

Dayton, Ohio

http://www.udayton.edu/

- **Independent Roman Catholic** university, founded 1850
- **Suburban** 388-acre campus with easy access to Cincinnati
- **Coed** 8,483 undergraduate students, 95% full-time, 48% women, 52% men
- **Moderately difficult** entrance level, 72% of applicants were admitted

UNDERGRAD STUDENTS
8,046 full-time, 437 part-time. 50% are from out of state; 3% Black or African American, non-Hispanic/Latino; 7% Hispanic/Latino; 1% Asian, non-Hispanic/Latino; 5% Two or more races, non-Hispanic/Latino; 0.5% Race/ethnicity unknown; 5% international; 2% transferred in; 74% live on campus.

Freshmen:
Admission: 17,462 applied, 12,578 admitted, 2,035 enrolled. ***Average high school GPA:*** 3.7. ***Test scores:*** SAT evidence-based reading and writing scores over 500: 95%; SAT math scores over 500: 94%; ACT scores over 18: 99%; SAT evidence-based reading and writing scores over 600: 58%; SAT math scores over 600: 38%; ACT scores over 24: 71%; SAT evidence-based reading and writing scores over 700: 9%; SAT math scores over 700: 15%; ACT scores over 30: 21%.

Retention: 89% of full-time freshmen returned.

FACULTY
Total: 1,015, 61% full-time, 62% with terminal degrees.

Student/faculty ratio: 14:1.

ACADEMICS
Calendar: semesters plus 2 6-week summer terms. *Degrees:* bachelor's, master's, doctoral, post-master's, and postbachelor's certificates.

Special study options: academic remediation for entering students, accelerated degree program, adult/continuing education programs, advanced placement credit, cooperative education, distance learning, double majors, English as a second language, honors programs, independent study, internships, off-campus study, part-time degree program, services for LD students, student-designed majors, study abroad, summer session for credit. ***ROTC:*** Army (b), Air Force (c).

Unusual degree programs: 3-2 business administration; engineering.

Computers: 7,675 computers/terminals and 19,337 ports are available on campus for general student use. Students can access the following: campus intranet, computer help desk, free student e-mail accounts, online (class) grades, online (class) registration, online (class) schedules, applications, admission/enrollment status, virtual orientation, online digital resources, online courses, assistive technology, learning management system, multimedia labs, payment, cyber cafes, centrally-licensed, downloadable software and training. Campuswide network is available. 100% of college-owned or -operated housing units are wired for high-speed Internet access. Wireless service is available via entire campus.

Library: Roesch Library plus 3 others. *Books:* 881,689 (physical), 972,137 (digital/electronic); *Serial titles:* 2,325 (physical), 96,661 (digital/electronic); *Databases:* 316. Weekly public service hours: 134; students can reserve study rooms.

STUDENT LIFE
Housing options: on-campus residence required through sophomore year; coed, cooperative, special housing for students with disabilities. Campus housing is university owned. Freshman campus housing is guaranteed.

Activities and organizations: drama/theater group, student-run newspaper, radio and television station, choral group, marching band, Student Government Association, Marching Band, Red Scare (basketball student cheering section), Campus Connection, Habitat for Humanity, national fraternities, national sororities.

Athletics Member NCAA. All Division I except football (Division I-AA). ***Intercollegiate sports:*** baseball M(s), basketball M(s)/W(s), cheerleading M/W, crew W, cross-country running M(s)/W(s), golf M(s)/W(c), soccer M(s)/W(s), softball W(s), tennis M(s)/W(s), track and field W(s), volleyball W(s). ***Intramural sports:*** baseball M(c), basketball M(c)/W(c), bowling M/W, crew M(c), cross-country running M(c)/W(c), fencing W(c), field hockey M(c), football M/W, golf M(c)/W(c), gymnastics M(c)/W(c), ice hockey M(c), lacrosse M(c)/W(c), racquetball M(c)/W(c), rugby M(c)/W(c), soccer M(c)/W(c), softball M/W(c), swimming and diving M(c)/W(c), tennis M(c)/W(c), ultimate Frisbee M(c)/W(c), volleyball M(c)/W(c), water polo M(c)/W(c), weight lifting M(c)/W(c), wrestling M(c)/W(c).

Campus security: 24-hour emergency response devices and patrols, student patrols, late-night transport/escort service, controlled dormitory access, approximately 1000 recording video cameras, automated external defibrillators in high density residential facilities and other areas.

Student services: health clinic, personal/psychological counseling, women's center, veterans affairs office.

COSTS & FINANCIAL AID
Costs (2019–20) ***Comprehensive fee:*** $58,150 includes full-time tuition ($44,100) and room and board ($14,050). Part-time tuition: $1610 per credit hour. No tuition increase for student's term of enrollment. ***College room only:*** $8420.

Financial Aid Of all full-time matriculated undergraduates who enrolled in 2019, 6,142 applied for aid, 4,617 were judged to have need, 4,425 had their need fully met. In 2019, 3478 non-need-based awards were made. ***Average percent of need met:*** 84. ***Average financial aid package:*** $34,786. ***Average need-based loan:*** $3128. ***Average need-based gift aid:*** $32,231. ***Average non-need-based aid:*** $21,496. ***Average indebtedness upon graduation:*** $37,533.

APPLYING
Standardized Tests *Required:* SAT or ACT (for admission).

Options: electronic application, early action, deferred entrance.

Notification: 12/15 (early action).

CONTACT
Mr. Robert Durkle, Dean of Admission and Financial Aid, University of Dayton, 300 College Park, Dayton, OH 45469-1310. *Phone:* 937-229-4411. *Toll-free phone:* 800-837-7433. *Fax:* 937-229-4729. *E-mail:* admission@udayton.edu.

The University of Findlay

Findlay, Ohio

http://www.findlay.edu/

- **Independent** comprehensive, founded 1882, affiliated with Church of God
- **Small-town** 390-acre campus
- **Endowment** $35.3 million
- **Coed** 3,527 undergraduate students, 62% full-time, 65% women, 35% men
- **Moderately difficult** entrance level, 77% of applicants were admitted

UNDERGRAD STUDENTS
2,192 full-time, 1,335 part-time. Students come from 45 states and territories; 28 other countries; 19% are from out of state; 3% Black or African American, non-Hispanic/Latino; 3% Hispanic/Latino; 2% Asian, non-Hispanic/Latino; 0.1% Native Hawaiian or other Pacific Islander, non-Hispanic/Latino; 0.1% American Indian or Alaska Native, non-Hispanic/Latino; 2% Two or more races, non-Hispanic/Latino; 17% Race/ethnicity unknown; ####% international; 2% transferred in; 45% live on campus.

Freshmen:
Admission: 3,336 applied, 2,576 admitted, 520 enrolled. ***Average high school GPA:*** 3.6. ***Test scores:*** SAT evidence-based reading and writing scores over 500: 88%; SAT math scores over 500: 86%; ACT scores over 18: 95%; SAT evidence-based reading and writing scores over 600: 43%; SAT math scores over 600: 38%; ACT scores over 24: 48%; SAT evidence-based reading and writing scores over 700: 6%; SAT math scores over 700: 6%; ACT scores over 30: 5%.

Retention: 76% of full-time freshmen returned.

FACULTY
Total: 393, 59% full-time, 39% with terminal degrees.

Student/faculty ratio: 16:1.

ACADEMICS
Calendar: semesters. *Degrees:* certificates, associate, bachelor's, master's, and doctoral.

Special study options: academic remediation for entering students, accelerated degree program, adult/continuing education programs, advanced placement credit, distance learning, double majors, English as a second language, honors programs, independent study, internships, off-campus study, part-time degree program, services for LD students, student-designed majors, study abroad, summer session for credit. ***ROTC:*** Army (c), Air Force (c).

Unusual degree programs: 3-2 athletic training.

Computers: 151 computers/terminals are available on campus for general student use. Students can access the following: campus intranet, computer help desk, free student e-mail accounts, online (class) grades, online (class) registration, online (class) schedules. Campuswide network is available. 100% of college-owned or -operated housing units are wired for high-speed Internet access. Wireless service is available via entire campus.

Library: Shafer Library plus 4 others. *Books:* 82,484 (physical), 428,266 (digital/electronic); *Serial titles:* 356 (physical), 96,301 (digital/electronic); *Databases:* 197. Weekly public service hours: 74.

STUDENT LIFE

Housing options: on-campus residence required through sophomore year; coed, women-only. Campus housing is university owned. Freshman campus housing is guaranteed.

Activities and organizations: drama/theater group, student-run newspaper, radio and television station, choral group, marching band, Habitat for Humanity, Pre-Vet Club, Horse Club, Stride, Black Student Union, national fraternities, national sororities.

Athletics Member NCAA. All Division II. ***Intercollegiate sports:*** baseball M(s), basketball M(s)/W(s), cross-country running M(s)/W(s), football M(s), golf M(s)/W(s), lacrosse W(s), soccer M(s)/W(s), softball W(s), swimming and diving M(s)/W(s), tennis M(s)/W(s), track and field M(s)/W(s), volleyball W(s), wrestling M(s). ***Intramural sports:*** basketball M/W, bowling M/W, soccer M/W, volleyball M/W.

Campus security: 24-hour emergency response devices and patrols, student patrols, late-night transport/escort service, controlled dormitory access, parking lot and building cameras (over 500), campus police.

Student services: health clinic, personal/psychological counseling, women's center.

COSTS & FINANCIAL AID

Costs (2019–20) ***Comprehensive fee:*** $45,610 includes full-time tuition ($34,200), mandatory fees ($1210), and room and board ($10,200). Full-time tuition and fees vary according to program. Part-time tuition: $755 per semester hour. Part-time tuition and fees vary according to course load and program. ***Required fees:*** $45 per semester hour part-time, $75 part-time. ***College room only:*** $5090. Room and board charges vary according to board plan and housing facility. ***Payment plan:*** installment. ***Waivers:*** senior citizens and employees or children of employees.

Financial Aid Of all full-time matriculated undergraduates who enrolled in 2019, 2,027 applied for aid, 1,748 were judged to have need, 481 had their need fully met. In 2019, 912 non-need-based awards were made. ***Average percent of need met:*** 79. ***Average financial aid package:*** $29,297. ***Average need-based loan:*** $4161. ***Average need-based gift aid:*** $25,689. ***Average non-need-based aid:*** $21,677. ***Average indebtedness upon graduation:*** $37,424. ***Financial aid deadline:*** 9/1.

APPLYING

Standardized Tests *Required:* SAT or ACT (for admission).

Options: electronic application, deferred entrance.

Required: high school transcript, minimum 2.5 GPA. ***Required for some:*** essay or personal statement, 1 letter of recommendation. ***Recommended:*** interview.

Application deadlines: rolling (freshmen), rolling (transfers).

Notification: continuous (freshmen), continuous (transfers).

CONTACT

Mr. Shawn Jordan, Assistant Director of Undergraduate Admissions, The University of Findlay, 1000 North Main Street, Findlay, OH 45840-3653. *Phone:* 419-434-4890. *Toll-free phone:* 800-548-0932. *Fax:* 419-434-4898. *E-mail:* jordan@findlay.edu.

University of Mount Union

Alliance, Ohio

http://www.mountunion.edu/

- **Independent United Methodist** comprehensive, founded 1846
- **Suburban** 123-acre campus with easy access to Cleveland
- **Endowment** $141.9 million
- **Coed**
- **Moderately difficult** entrance level

FACULTY

Student/faculty ratio: 13:1.

ACADEMICS

Calendar: semesters. *Degrees:* bachelor's, master's, and doctoral.
Library: University of Mount Union Library plus 1 other. *Books:* 224,248 (physical), 458,288 (digital/electronic); *Serial titles:* 2,492 (physical), 67,046 (digital/electronic); *Databases:* 230. Study areas open 24 hours, 5–7 days a week; students can reserve study rooms.

STUDENT LIFE

Housing options: on-campus residence required through sophomore year; coed, men-only, women-only, special housing for students with disabilities. Campus housing is university owned. Freshman campus housing is guaranteed.

Activities and organizations: drama/theater group, student-run newspaper, radio and television station, choral group, marching band, Alpha Phi Omega, Student Senate, FCA Fellowship of Christian Athletes, Black Student Union, Raider Programming Board, national fraternities, national sororities.

Athletics Member NCAA. All Division III.

Campus security: 24-hour emergency response devices and patrols, late-night transport/escort service, controlled dormitory access.

Student services: health clinic, personal/psychological counseling.

COSTS & FINANCIAL AID

Costs (2019–20) ***Comprehensive fee:*** $42,200 includes full-time tuition ($31,300), mandatory fees ($400), and room and board ($10,500). Part-time tuition: $1330 per credit hour. ***Required fees:*** $100 per term part-time. ***College room only:*** $5200. Room and board charges vary according to board plan and housing facility.

Financial Aid Of all full-time matriculated undergraduates who enrolled in 2018, 1,859 applied for aid, 1,656 were judged to have need, 344 had their need fully met. 207 Federal Work-Study jobs (averaging $970). In 2018, 356 non-need-based awards were made. ***Average percent of need met:*** 76. ***Average financial aid package:*** $23,299. ***Average need-based loan:*** $4258. ***Average need-based gift aid:*** $18,268. ***Average non-need-based aid:*** $14,360. ***Average indebtedness upon graduation:*** $40,112.

APPLYING

Standardized Tests *Required:* SAT or ACT (for admission).

Options: electronic application, early admission, deferred entrance.

Required: essay or personal statement, high school transcript, minimum 2.0 GPA, 1 letter of recommendation. ***Recommended:*** interview.

CONTACT

Mr. Eric Young, Director of Admission, University of Mount Union, 1972 Clark Avenue, Alliance, OH 44601. *Phone:* 330-829-8238. *Toll-free phone:* 800-334-6682. *Fax:* 330-823-5097. *E-mail:* admission@mountunion.edu.

University of Northwestern Ohio

Lima, Ohio

http://www.unoh.edu/

- **Independent** comprehensive, founded 1920
- **Small-town** 200-acre campus with easy access to Dayton, Toledo
- **Coed**
- **Noncompetitive** entrance level

FACULTY

Student/faculty ratio: 20:1.

ACADEMICS

Calendar: quarters. *Degrees:* certificates, diplomas, associate, bachelor's, and master's.

Library: Dr. Cheryl Mueller Library. Students can reserve study rooms.

STUDENT LIFE
Housing options: men-only, women-only, special housing for students with disabilities. Campus housing is university owned and leased by the school. Freshman campus housing is guaranteed.

Activities and organizations: Business Professionals of America, ROTORAC, American Marketing Association, Optimist Club, Drag Club.

Athletics Member NAIA.

Campus security: 24-hour emergency response devices and patrols, late-night transport/escort service.

Student services: personal/psychological counseling, veterans affairs office.

FINANCIAL AID
Financial Aid Of all full-time matriculated undergraduates who enrolled in 2018, 40 Federal Work-Study jobs (averaging $2000).

APPLYING
Options: electronic application, early admission, deferred entrance.

Application fee: $20.

Required: high school transcript.

CONTACT
Mr. Don Lowden, Director of Admissions, University of Northwestern Ohio, 1441 North Cable Road, Lima, OH 45805-1498. *Phone:* 419-998-3120. *E-mail:* dmlowden@unoh.edu.

University of Rio Grande
Rio Grande, Ohio
http://www.rio.edu/

- **Independent** comprehensive, founded 1876
- **Rural** 170-acre campus
- **Endowment** $23.6 million
- **Coed**
- **Noncompetitive** entrance level

FACULTY
Student/faculty ratio: 19:1.

ACADEMICS
Calendar: semesters. *Degrees:* certificates, associate, bachelor's, and master's.
Library: Jeanette Albiez Davis Library.

STUDENT LIFE
Housing options: coed, men-only, women-only. Campus housing is university owned.

Activities and organizations: drama/theater group, student-run newspaper, radio and television station, choral group, Student Government, Honoraries, Bible studies, ENACTA, national fraternities, national sororities.

Athletics Member NAIA.

Campus security: 24-hour emergency response devices and patrols, late-night transport/escort service.

Student services: health clinic, personal/psychological counseling, veterans affairs office.

FINANCIAL AID
Financial Aid Of all full-time matriculated undergraduates who enrolled in 2014, 1,035 applied for aid, 1,035 were judged to have need, 736 had their need fully met. In 2014, 17 non-need-based awards were made. ***Average percent of need met:*** 87. ***Average financial aid package:*** $7030. ***Average need-based loan:*** $3191. ***Average need-based gift aid:*** $3778. ***Average non-need-based aid:*** $11,067. ***Average indebtedness upon graduation:*** $28,617.

APPLYING
Standardized Tests *Recommended:* ACT (for admission).

Options: electronic application.

Application fee: $25.

Required: high school transcript, medical history.

CONTACT
Kristie Russell, Assistant Director of Admissions, University of Rio Grande, PO Box 500, Rio Grande, OH 45674. *Phone:* 740-245-7208. *Toll-free phone:* 800-282-7201. *Fax:* 740-245-7260. *E-mail:* admissions@rio.edu.

The University of Toledo
Toledo, Ohio
http://www.utoledo.edu/

- **State-supported** university, founded 1872
- **Urban** 858-acre campus with easy access to Detroit
- **Endowment** $306.9 million
- **Coed** 15,568 undergraduate students, 81% full-time, 50% women, 50% men
- **Noncompetitive** entrance level, 95% of applicants were admitted

UNDERGRAD STUDENTS
12,548 full-time, 3,020 part-time. 21% are from out of state; 10% Black or African American, non-Hispanic/Latino; 5% Hispanic/Latino; 2% Asian, non-Hispanic/Latino; 0.1% Native Hawaiian or other Pacific Islander, non-Hispanic/Latino; 0.2% American Indian or Alaska Native, non-Hispanic/Latino; 4% Two or more races, non-Hispanic/Latino; 3% Race/ethnicity unknown; 6% international; 5% transferred in; 24% live on campus.

Freshmen:
Admission: 10,228 applied, 9,722 admitted, 3,037 enrolled. ***Average high school GPA:*** 3.5. ***Test scores:*** SAT evidence-based reading and writing scores over 500: 76%; SAT math scores over 500: 79%; ACT scores over 18: 88%; SAT evidence-based reading and writing scores over 600: 32%; SAT math scores over 600: 34%; ACT scores over 24: 45%; SAT evidence-based reading and writing scores over 700: 4%; SAT math scores over 700: 9%; ACT scores over 30: 9%.
Retention: 76% of full-time freshmen returned.

FACULTY
Total: 1,119, 71% full-time, 62% with terminal degrees.

Student/faculty ratio: 20:1.

ACADEMICS
Calendar: semesters. *Degrees:* certificates, diplomas, associate, bachelor's, master's, doctoral, post-master's, and postbachelor's certificates.

Special study options: academic remediation for entering students, accelerated degree program, adult/continuing education programs, advanced placement credit, cooperative education, distance learning, double majors, English as a second language, external degree program, freshman honors college, honors programs, independent study, internships, off-campus study, part-time degree program, services for LD students, student-designed majors, study abroad, summer session for credit. ***ROTC:*** Army (b), Air Force (c).

Unusual degree programs: 3-2 business administration; engineering; nursing; social work; environmental sciences/public health.

Computers: 5,000 computers/terminals and 10,000 ports are available on campus for general student use. Students can access the following: campus intranet, computer help desk, free student e-mail accounts, online (class) grades, online (class) registration, online (class) schedules, online transcripts, student account. Campuswide network is available. 100% of college-owned or -operated housing units are wired for high-speed Internet access. Wireless service is available via entire campus.
Library: Carlson Library plus 3 others. *Books:* 563,687 (physical), 339,697 (digital/electronic); *Serial titles:* 5,602 (physical), 74,382 (digital/electronic); *Databases:* 340. Weekly public service hours: 107; students can reserve study rooms.

STUDENT LIFE
Housing options: on-campus residence required through sophomore year; coed, special housing for students with disabilities. Campus housing is university owned. Freshman campus housing is guaranteed.

Activities and organizations: drama/theater group, student-run newspaper, radio and television station, choral group, marching band, Student Government, University YMCA, Newman Club, International Student Association, Campus Activities and Programming, national fraternities, national sororities.

Athletics Member NCAA. All Division I except football (Division I-A). ***Intercollegiate sports:*** baseball M(s), basketball M(s)/W(s), cross-country running M(s)/W(s), golf M(s)/W(s)(c), soccer W(s), softball W(s), swimming and diving W(s), tennis M(s)/W(s), track and field W(s), volleyball W(s). ***Intramural sports:*** badminton M/W, basketball M/W, bowling M/W, cheerleading W, crew M(c)/W(c), fencing M(c), field hockey W(c), football M/W, golf M/W, lacrosse M/W, racquetball M/W, sailing M(c)/W(c), skiing (cross-country) M(c)/W(c), skiing (downhill) M(c)/W(c), soccer M(c)/W(c), softball M/W, swimming and diving M/W, table tennis M/W, tennis M/W, track and field M/W, volleyball M/W, water polo M/W, weight lifting M/W, wrestling M.

Campus security: 24-hour emergency response devices and patrols, student patrols, late-night transport/escort service, controlled dormitory access, bicycle patrols by security staff, crime prevention officer.

Student services: health clinic, personal/psychological counseling, women's center, legal services, veterans affairs office.

COSTS & FINANCIAL AID

Costs (2020–21) ***Tuition:*** area resident $8582 full-time, $383 per credit hour part-time; state resident $8582 full-time, $383 per credit hour part-time; nonresident $17,942 full-time, $390 per credit hour part-time. Full-time tuition and fees vary according to course load, program, reciprocity agreements, and student level. Part-time tuition and fees vary according to course load, program, reciprocity agreements, and student level. ***Required fees:*** $1957 full-time. ***Room and board:*** $12,285; room only: $8258. Room and board charges vary according to board plan and housing facility. ***Payment plan:*** installment. ***Waivers:*** employees or children of employees.

Financial Aid Of all full-time matriculated undergraduates who enrolled in 2019, 9,991 applied for aid, 7,686 were judged to have need, 1,051 had their need fully met. In 2019, 3374 non-need-based awards were made. ***Average percent of need met:*** 63. ***Average financial aid package:*** $11,699. ***Average need-based loan:*** $3311. ***Average need-based gift aid:*** $9642. ***Average non-need-based aid:*** $5952. ***Average indebtedness upon graduation:*** $27,145.

APPLYING

Standardized Tests *Required:* SAT or ACT (for admission).

Options: electronic application, deferred entrance.

Application fee: $40.

Required: high school transcript. ***Required for some:*** minimum 2.0 GPA, core high school curriculum.

Application deadlines: rolling (freshmen), rolling (transfers).

Notification: continuous (freshmen), continuous (transfers).

CONTACT

William Pierce, Director of Undergraduate Admissions, The University of Toledo, OH. *Phone:* 419-530-5445. *Toll-free phone:* 800-5TOLEDO. *Fax:* 419-530-5713. *E-mail:* william.pierce@utoledo.edu.

Urbana University–A Branch Campus of Franklin University

Urbana, Ohio

http://www.urbana.edu/

CONTACT

Mr. Donnel W. Wiggins, Director of Admissions, Urbana University–A Branch Campus of Franklin University, 579 College Way, Urbana, OH 43078. *Toll-free phone:* 800-7-URBANA. *E-mail:* admiss@urbana.edu.

Ursuline College

Pepper Pike, Ohio

http://www.ursuline.edu/

- **Independent Roman Catholic** comprehensive, founded 1871
- **Suburban** 62-acre campus with easy access to Cleveland
- **Endowment** $23.9 million
- **Coed, primarily women** 651 undergraduate students, 75% full-time, 93% women, 7% men
- **Minimally difficult** entrance level, 85% of applicants were admitted

UNDERGRAD STUDENTS

491 full-time, 160 part-time. Students come from 16 states and territories; 15 other countries; 12% are from out of state; 23% Black or African American, non-Hispanic/Latino; 2% Hispanic/Latino; 3% Asian, non-Hispanic/Latino; 0.3% Native Hawaiian or other Pacific Islander, non-Hispanic/Latino; 5% Two or more races, non-Hispanic/Latino; 4% Race/ethnicity unknown; 3% international; 11% transferred in; 34% live on campus.

Freshmen:

Admission: 543 applied, 463 admitted, 92 enrolled. ***Average high school GPA:*** 3.5. ***Test scores:*** SAT evidence-based reading and writing scores over 500: 86%; ACT scores over 18: 74%; SAT evidence-based reading and writing scores over 600: 43%; ACT scores over 24: 25%; SAT math scores over 700: 3%; ACT scores over 30: 1%.

Retention: 75% of full-time freshmen returned.

FACULTY

Total: 168, 33% full-time, 43% with terminal degrees.

Student/faculty ratio: 7:1.

ACADEMICS

Calendar: semesters. *Degrees:* certificates, bachelor's, master's, doctoral, post-master's, and postbachelor's certificates (applications from men are also accepted).

Special study options: academic remediation for entering students, accelerated degree program, adult/continuing education programs, advanced placement credit, distance learning, double majors, independent study, internships, off-campus study, part-time degree program, services for LD students, student-designed majors, summer session for credit. ***ROTC:*** Army (c), Air Force (c).

Unusual degree programs: 3-2 Biology: Life Science and Medical Technology with Cleveland Clinic.

Computers: 120 computers/terminals are available on campus for general student use. Students can access the following: campus intranet, computer help desk, free student e-mail accounts, online (class) grades, online (class) registration, online (class) schedules. Campuswide network is available. 100% of college-owned or -operated housing units are wired for high-speed Internet access. Wireless service is available via entire campus.

Library: Ralph M. Besse Library. *Books:* 92,462 (physical), 351,238 (digital/electronic); *Serial titles:* 284 (physical), 59,448 (digital/electronic); *Databases:* 162. Weekly public service hours: 94; students can reserve study rooms.

STUDENT LIFE

Housing options: coed, women-only, special housing for students with disabilities. Campus housing is university owned. Freshman campus housing is guaranteed.

Activities and organizations: drama/theater group, Programming Board, Student Nurses of Ursuline College, U-Earth, U-PAW, Ursuline Students of STEM2.

Athletics Member NCAA. All Division II. ***Intercollegiate sports:*** basketball W(s), bowling W(s), cross-country running W(s), golf W(s), lacrosse W(s), soccer W(s), softball W(s), swimming and diving W(s), tennis W(s), track and field W(s), volleyball W(s).

Campus security: 24-hour emergency response devices and patrols, late-night transport/escort service, controlled dormitory access.

Student services: personal/psychological counseling, women's center, veterans affairs office.

COSTS & FINANCIAL AID

Costs (2020–21) ***One-time required fee:*** $100. ***Comprehensive fee:*** $46,144 includes full-time tuition ($34,290), mandatory fees ($340), and room and board ($11,514). Part-time tuition: $1143 per credit hour. ***Required fees:*** $260 part-time. ***Room and board:*** Room and board charges vary according to board plan. ***Payment plan:*** installment. ***Waivers:*** senior citizens and employees or children of employees.

Financial Aid Of all full-time matriculated undergraduates who enrolled in 2019, 430 applied for aid, 410 were judged to have need, 44 had their need fully met. 303 Federal Work-Study jobs (averaging $1000). In 2019, 41 non-need-based awards were made. ***Average percent of need met:*** 68. ***Average financial aid package:*** $24,961. ***Average need-based loan:***

$5621. ***Average need-based gift aid:*** $23,153. ***Average non-need-based aid:*** $11,498. ***Average indebtedness upon graduation:*** $29,220.

APPLYING
Standardized Tests *Required:* SAT or ACT (for admission).

Options: electronic application, deferred entrance.

Required: essay or personal statement, high school transcript, 1 letter of recommendation. ***Recommended:*** minimum 2.5 GPA, interview.

Application deadlines: 2/1 (freshmen), rolling (transfers).

Notification: continuous (freshmen), continuous (out-of-state freshmen), continuous (transfers).

CONTACT
Ms. Emily Haggerty, Director, Admission, Ursuline College, 2550 Lander Road, Pepper Pike, OH 44124. *Phone:* 440-684-6107. *Toll-free phone:* 888-URSULINE. *E-mail:* emily.haggerty@ursuline.edu.

Walsh University

North Canton, Ohio

http://www.walsh.edu/

CONTACT
Ms. Melissa Schoeppner, Campus Visit Coordinator, Walsh University, 2020 East Maple, North Canton, OH 44720. *Phone:* 330-490-7172. *Toll-free phone:* 800-362-9846 (in-state); 800-362-8846 (out-of-state). *Fax:* 330-490-7165. *E-mail:* admissions@walsh.edu.

Wilberforce University

Wilberforce, Ohio

http://www.wilberforce.edu/

CONTACT
Ms. Dadra Driscoll, Director, Office of Admissions, Wilberforce University, 1055 N. Bickett Road, PO Box 1001, Wolfe Administration, Wilberforce, OH 45384. *Phone:* 937-708-5556. *Toll-free phone:* 800-367-8568. *E-mail:* ddriscoll@wilberforce.edu.

Wilmington College

Wilmington, Ohio

http://www.wilmington.edu/

- **Independent Friends** comprehensive, founded 1870
- **Small-town** 100-acre campus with easy access to Cincinnati, Ohio
- **Endowment** $38.3 million
- **Coed** 1,231 undergraduate students, 95% full-time, 53% women, 47% men
- **Moderately difficult** entrance level, 78% of applicants were admitted

UNDERGRAD STUDENTS
1,167 full-time, 64 part-time. Students come from 25 states and territories; 13 other countries; 9% are from out of state; 10% Black or African American, non-Hispanic/Latino; 2% Hispanic/Latino; 0.7% Asian, non-Hispanic/Latino; 0.5% American Indian or Alaska Native, non-Hispanic/Latino; 4% Two or more races, non-Hispanic/Latino; 5% Race/ethnicity unknown; 2% international; 7% transferred in; 70% live on campus.

Freshmen:
Admission: 1,650 applied, 1,290 admitted, 341 enrolled. ***Average high school GPA:*** 3.4. ***Test scores:*** ACT scores over 18: 80%; ACT scores over 24: 24%; ACT scores over 30: 2%.

Retention: 65% of full-time freshmen returned.

FACULTY
Total: 101, 60% full-time, 64% with terminal degrees.

Student/faculty ratio: 15:1.

ACADEMICS
Calendar: semesters. *Degrees:* bachelor's and master's.

Special study options: academic remediation for entering students, accelerated degree program, adult/continuing education programs, advanced placement credit, cooperative education, distance learning, double majors, freshman honors college, honors programs, independent study, internships, part-time degree program, services for LD students, student-designed majors, study abroad, summer session for credit. ***ROTC:*** Army (c).

Unusual degree programs: 3-2 3 + 2 program leading to MSAT: Bachelor's in Exercise Science (3 years) leading to a Master's in Athletic Training (2 years).

Computers: 185 computers/terminals and 310 ports are available on campus for general student use. Students can access the following: campus intranet, computer help desk, free student e-mail accounts, online (class) grades, online (class) registration, online (class) schedules, OhioLink. Campuswide network is available. 100% of college-owned or -operated housing units are wired for high-speed Internet access. Wireless service is available via entire campus.

Library: Watson Library. *Books:* 73,740 (physical), 399,654 (digital/electronic); *Serial titles:* 490 (physical), 85,346 (digital/electronic); *Databases:* 216. Weekly public service hours: 69; students can reserve study rooms.

STUDENT LIFE
Housing options: on-campus residence required through senior year; coed, men-only, women-only. Campus housing is university owned. Freshman campus housing is guaranteed.

Activities and organizations: drama/theater group, student-run newspaper, radio and television station, choral group, marching band, Quaker Thunder Pep Band, Intramural Athletics, Wilmington College Chorale, Black Student Initiative, Wilmington College Science Society, national fraternities, national sororities.

Athletics Member NCAA. All Division III. ***Intercollegiate sports:*** baseball M, basketball M/W, cross-country running M/W, football M, golf M/W, soccer M/W, softball W, swimming and diving M/W, tennis M/W, track and field M/W, volleyball W, wrestling M. ***Intramural sports:*** basketball M/W, football M, racquetball M/W, soccer M/W, softball M/W, squash M/W, swimming and diving M/W, table tennis M/W, volleyball M/W.

Campus security: 24-hour emergency response devices and patrols, late-night transport/escort service, controlled dormitory access.

Student services: health clinic, personal/psychological counseling, veterans affairs office.

COSTS & FINANCIAL AID
Costs (2020–21) ***Tuition:*** $500 per credit hour part-time. Full-time tuition and fees vary according to location. Part-time tuition and fees vary according to course load and location. ***Room only:*** Room and board charges vary according to board plan and housing facility. ***Payment plans:*** tuition prepayment, installment.

Financial Aid Of all full-time matriculated undergraduates who enrolled in 2008, 1,096 applied for aid, 1,021 were judged to have need, 306 had their need fully met. In 2008, 138 non-need-based awards were made. ***Average percent of need met:*** 81. ***Average financial aid package:*** $21,500. ***Average need-based loan:*** $6000. ***Average need-based gift aid:*** $14,300. ***Average non-need-based aid:*** $7300.

APPLYING
Standardized Tests *Required:* SAT or ACT (for admission).

Options: electronic application, deferred entrance.

Required: high school transcript. ***Recommended:*** minimum 2.5 GPA, 1 letter of recommendation, interview.

Application deadlines: 8/1 (freshmen), 8/1 (transfers).

Notification: continuous (freshmen), continuous (transfers).

CONTACT
Adam Lohrey, Director of Admissions, Wilmington College, 1870 Quaker Way, Pyle Box 1325, Wilmington, OH 45177. *Phone:* 937-481-2266. *Toll-free phone:* 800-341-9318. *E-mail:* adam_lohrey@wilmington.edu.

Wittenberg University

Springfield, Ohio

http://www.wittenberg.edu/

- **Independent** comprehensive, founded 1845, affiliated with Evangelical Lutheran Church
- **Suburban** 114-acre campus with easy access to Columbus, Dayton
- **Coed** 1,577 undergraduate students, 95% full-time, 55% women, 45% men
- **Moderately difficult** entrance level, 91% of applicants were admitted

UNDERGRAD STUDENTS
1,504 full-time, 73 part-time. Students come from 38 states and territories; 10 other countries; 23% are from out of state; 9% Black or African American, non-Hispanic/Latino; 4% Hispanic/Latino; 1% Asian, non-Hispanic/Latino; 0.1% American Indian or Alaska Native, non-Hispanic/Latino; 6% Two or more races, non-Hispanic/Latino; 1% Race/ethnicity unknown; 1% international; 2% transferred in; 87% live on campus.

Freshmen:
Admission: 2,392 applied, 2,184 admitted, 344 enrolled. ***Average high school GPA:*** 3.5. ***Test scores:*** SAT evidence-based reading and writing scores over 500: 79%; SAT math scores over 500: 87%; ACT scores over 18: 87%; SAT evidence-based reading and writing scores over 600: 31%; SAT math scores over 600: 21%; ACT scores over 24: 41%; SAT evidence-based reading and writing scores over 700: 7%; SAT math scores over 700: 4%; ACT scores over 30: 7%.

Retention: 70% of full-time freshmen returned.

FACULTY
Total: 189, 62% full-time, 69% with terminal degrees.

Student/faculty ratio: 11:1.

ACADEMICS
Calendar: semesters. *Degrees:* bachelor's and master's.

Special study options: academic remediation for entering students, adult/continuing education programs, advanced placement credit, cooperative education, double majors, freshman honors college, honors programs, independent study, internships, off-campus study, part-time degree program, services for LD students, student-designed majors, study abroad, summer session for credit. ***ROTC:*** Army (c), Air Force (c).

Unusual degree programs: 3-2 engineering with Columbia University; Washington University in St. Louis; Case Western Reserve University; nursing with Case Western Reserve University; social work with Case Western Reserve University; occupational therapy with Washington University in St. Louis, marine science with Duke University.

Computers: 900 computers/terminals and 1,200 ports are available on campus for general student use. Students can access the following: computer help desk, free student e-mail accounts, online (class) grades, online (class) registration, online (class) schedules. Campuswide network is available. 100% of college-owned or -operated housing units are wired for high-speed Internet access. Wireless service is available via entire campus.

Library: Thomas Library plus 1 other. *Books:* 135,595 (digital/electronic); *Serial titles:* 163,369 (digital/electronic); *Databases:* 209. Weekly public service hours: 93.

STUDENT LIFE
Housing options: on-campus residence required through sophomore year; coed, women-only. Campus housing is university owned. Freshman campus housing is guaranteed.

Activities and organizations: drama/theater group, student-run newspaper, radio station, choral group, Student Senate, Union Board, Choirs, Weaver Chapel Association, national fraternities, national sororities.

Athletics Member NCAA. All Division III except golf (Division II). ***Intercollegiate sports:*** baseball M, basketball M/W, crew M(c)/W(c), cross-country running M/W, field hockey W, football M, golf M/W, lacrosse M/W, rugby M(c)/W(c), soccer M/W, softball W, swimming and diving M/W, tennis M/W, track and field M/W, volleyball M/W, water polo W. ***Intramural sports:*** basketball M/W, bowling M(c)/W(c), cheerleading M(c)/W(c), football M, golf M/W, ice hockey M(c)/W(c), sailing M/W, soccer M/W, softball M/W, swimming and diving M/W, tennis M/W, track and field M/W, volleyball M/W.

Campus security: 24-hour emergency response devices and patrols, student patrols, late-night transport/escort service, controlled dormitory access, crime prevention programs.

Student services: health clinic, personal/psychological counseling, women's center.

COSTS & FINANCIAL AID
Costs (2020–21) ***Comprehensive fee:*** $52,306 includes full-time tuition ($40,630), mandatory fees ($846), and room and board ($10,830). Part-time tuition: $1315 per credit hour. Part-time tuition and fees vary according to course load. ***Required fees:*** $415 per term part-time. ***College room only:*** $5530. Room and board charges vary according to board plan and housing facility. ***Payment plan:*** installment. ***Waivers:*** minority students, children of alumni, adult students, senior citizens, and employees or children of employees.

Financial Aid Of all full-time matriculated undergraduates who enrolled in 2019, 1,324 applied for aid, 1,159 were judged to have need, 351 had their need fully met. In 2019, 317 non-need-based awards were made. ***Average percent of need met:*** 82. ***Average financial aid package:*** $34,552. ***Average need-based loan:*** $4472. ***Average need-based gift aid:*** $6944. ***Average non-need-based aid:*** $22,709.

APPLYING
Options: electronic application, early admission, early decision, deferred entrance.

Required: high school transcript, interview. ***Recommended:*** essay or personal statement.

Application deadlines: rolling (transfers), 12/1 (early action).

Early decision deadline: 11/15.

Notification: continuous (freshmen), continuous (transfers), 12/15 (early decision), 1/1 (early action).

CONTACT
Ms. Kelsey Ellis, Director of Admission, Wittenberg University, PO Box 720, Springfield, OH 45501-0720. *Phone:* 877-206-0332 Ext. 6377. *Toll-free phone:* 800-677-7558 Ext. 6314. *Fax:* 937-327-6379. *E-mail:* admission@wittenberg.edu.

Wright State University
Dayton, Ohio
http://www.wright.edu/

- **State-supported** university, founded 1964, part of University System of Ohio
- **Suburban** 557-acre campus with easy access to Dayton, Columbus, Cincinnati
- **Coed** 9,585 undergraduate students, 78% full-time, 53% women, 47% men
- **Minimally difficult** entrance level, 96% of applicants were admitted

UNDERGRAD STUDENTS
7,439 full-time, 2,146 part-time. 2% are from out of state; 11% Black or African American, non-Hispanic/Latino; 4% Hispanic/Latino; 3% Asian, non-Hispanic/Latino; 0.1% Native Hawaiian or other Pacific Islander, non-Hispanic/Latino; 0.2% American Indian or Alaska Native, non-Hispanic/Latino; 5% Two or more races, non-Hispanic/Latino; 0.7% Race/ethnicity unknown; 2% international; 7% transferred in; 19% live on campus.

Freshmen:
Admission: 5,996 applied, 5,738 admitted, 1,511 enrolled. ***Average high school GPA:*** 3.4. ***Test scores:*** SAT evidence-based reading and writing scores over 500: 75%; SAT math scores over 500: 69%; ACT scores over 18: 76%; SAT evidence-based reading and writing scores over 600: 33%; SAT math scores over 600: 28%; ACT scores over 24: 34%; SAT evidence-based reading and writing scores over 700: 6%; SAT math scores over 700: 8%; ACT scores over 30: 6%.

Retention: 62% of full-time freshmen returned.

FACULTY
Student/faculty ratio: 13:1.

ACADEMICS
Calendar: semesters. *Degrees:* certificates, bachelor's, master's, doctoral, post-master's, and postbachelor's certificates.

Special study options: academic remediation for entering students, adult/continuing education programs, advanced placement credit, cooperative education, distance learning, double majors, English as a second language, freshman honors college, honors programs, independent study, internships, off-campus study, part-time degree program, services for LD students, student-designed majors, study abroad, summer session for credit. ***ROTC:*** Army (b), Air Force (b).

Computers: Students can access the following: campus intranet, computer help desk, free student e-mail accounts, online (class) grades, online (class) registration, online (class) schedules, student webpages, Lap tops 2 Go, office software programs. Campuswide network is available.

100% of college-owned or -operated housing units are wired for high-speed Internet access. Wireless service is available via entire campus. **Library:** Paul Laurence Dunbar Library plus 1 other. Students can reserve study rooms.

STUDENT LIFE
Housing options: coed, special housing for students with disabilities. Campus housing is university owned.

Activities and organizations: drama/theater group, student-run newspaper, radio and television station, choral group, national fraternities, national sororities.

Athletics Member NCAA. All Division I. ***Intercollegiate sports:*** baseball M(s), basketball M(s)/W(s), cheerleading M(s)/W(s), cross-country running M(s)/W(s), golf M(s), soccer M(s)/W(s), softball W(s), swimming and diving M(s)/W(s), tennis M(s)/W(s), track and field W(s), volleyball W(s). ***Intramural sports:*** baseball M(c), basketball M, football M(c)/W(c), gymnastics M(c)/W(c), ice hockey M(c), rugby M(c)/W(c), skiing (downhill) M(c)/W(c), soccer M/W, softball M/W, swimming and diving M(c)/W(c), table tennis M, track and field M(c)/W(c), ultimate Frisbee M(c)/W(c), volleyball W, water polo M/W, wrestling M(c).

Campus security: 24-hour emergency response devices and patrols, student patrols, late night transport/escort service, controlled dormitory access.

Student services: health clinic, personal/psychological counseling, women's center, legal services, veterans affairs office.

COSTS & FINANCIAL AID
Costs (2019–20) ***Tuition:*** area resident $9578 full-time, $431 per credit hour part-time; state resident $9578 full-time, $431 per credit hour part-time; nonresident $18,996 full-time, $865 per credit hour part-time. Full-time tuition and fees vary according to course load, location, reciprocity agreements, and student level. Part-time tuition and fees vary according to course load, location, reciprocity agreements, and student level. No tuition increase for student's term of enrollment. ***Room and board:*** $12,084; room only: $6208. Room and board charges vary according to board plan, housing facility, and location. ***Payment plan:*** installment. ***Waivers:*** senior citizens and employees or children of employees.

Financial Aid Of all full-time matriculated undergraduates who enrolled in 2019, 5,688 applied for aid, 4,567 were judged to have need, 781 had their need fully met. In 2019, 1251 non-need-based awards were made. ***Average percent of need met:*** 63. ***Average financial aid package:*** $11,380. ***Average need-based loan:*** $4130. ***Average need-based gift aid:*** $7255. ***Average non-need-based aid:*** $5019. ***Average indebtedness upon graduation:*** $28,607.

APPLYING
Standardized Tests *Required:* SAT or ACT (for admission).

Options: electronic application, deferred entrance.

Application fee: $30.

Required: high school transcript. ***Recommended:*** minimum 2.0 GPA.

Application deadlines: 8/20 (freshmen), rolling (transfers).

Notification: 9/1 (freshmen), continuous (transfers).

CONTACT
Wright State University, 3640 Colonel Glenn Highway, E147 Student Union, Dayton, OH 45435. *Phone:* 937-775-5700. *Toll-free phone:* 800-247-1770. *Fax:* 937-775-5795. *E-mail:* admissions@wright.edu.

Wright State University–Lake Campus

Celina, Ohio

http://www.wright.edu/lake/

- **State-supported** comprehensive, founded 1969
- **Small-town** 211-acre campus
- **Coed** 1,030 undergraduate students, 64% full-time, 57% women, 43% men
- **Minimally difficult** entrance level, 126% of applicants were admitted

UNDERGRAD STUDENTS
664 full-time, 366 part-time. 1% are from out of state; 3% Black or African American, non-Hispanic/Latino; 2% Hispanic/Latino; 0.5% Asian, non-Hispanic/Latino; 0.1% Native Hawaiian or other Pacific Islander, non-Hispanic/Latino; 0.1% American Indian or Alaska Native, non-Hispanic/Latino; 2% Two or more races, non-Hispanic/Latino; 0.5% Race/ethnicity unknown; 4% transferred in; 9% live on campus.

Freshmen:
Admission: 337 applied, 426 admitted, 179 enrolled. ***Average high school GPA:*** 3.3. ***Test scores:*** SAT evidence-based reading and writing scores over 500: 67%; SAT math scores over 500: 33%; ACT scores over 18: 79%; SAT math scores over 600: 33%; ACT scores over 24: 25%; ACT scores over 30: 1%.

Retention: 68% of full-time freshmen returned.

FACULTY
Student/faculty ratio: 14:1.

ACADEMICS
Calendar: semesters. *Degrees:* certificates, associate, and bachelor's.

Special study options: academic remediation for entering students, accelerated degree program, adult/continuing education programs, advanced placement credit, cooperative education, distance learning, double majors, honors programs, independent study, internships, off-campus study, part-time degree program, services for LD students, student-designed majors, study abroad, summer session for credit. ***ROTC:*** Army (c), Air Force (c).

Computers: Students can access the following: campus intranet, computer help desk, free student e-mail accounts, online (class) grades, online (class) registration, online (class) schedules. Campuswide network is available. 100% of college-owned or -operated housing units are wired for high-speed Internet access. Wireless service is available via entire campus.
Library: Lake Campus Library & Technology Center plus 1 other.

STUDENT LIFE
Housing options: Campus housing is university owned.

Athletics Member USCAA. ***Intercollegiate sports:*** baseball M, basketball M/W, softball W, volleyball W.

Campus security: 24-hour emergency response devices, WSU-Police Department presence, 40 hours per week.

Student services: health clinic, personal/psychological counseling, veterans affairs office.

COSTS & FINANCIAL AID
Costs (2019–20) ***Tuition:*** $290 per credit hour part-time; state resident $6410 full-time, $290 per credit hour part-time; nonresident $15,828 full-time, $724 per credit hour part-time. Full-time tuition and fees vary according to course load, location, reciprocity agreements, and student level. Part-time tuition and fees vary according to course load, location, reciprocity agreements, and student level. No tuition increase for student's term of enrollment. ***Room only:*** $5030. Room and board charges vary according to board plan, housing facility, and location. ***Payment plan:*** installment. ***Waivers:*** senior citizens and employees or children of employees.

Financial Aid Of all full-time matriculated undergraduates who enrolled in 2019, 487 applied for aid, 349 were judged to have need, 82 had their need fully met. In 2019, 102 non-need-based awards were made. ***Average percent of need met:*** 70. ***Average financial aid package:*** $9023. ***Average need-based loan:*** $4057. ***Average need-based gift aid:*** $5240. ***Average non-need-based aid:*** $3064. ***Average indebtedness upon graduation:*** $25,975.

APPLYING
Standardized Tests *Required:* SAT or ACT (for admission).

Options: electronic application, deferred entrance.

Application fee: $30.

Required: high school transcript. ***Recommended:*** minimum 2.0 GPA.

Application deadlines: rolling (freshmen), rolling (transfers).

Notification: continuous (freshmen), continuous (transfers).

CONTACT
Ms. Jill Puthoff, Admissions/Communications Coordinator, Wright State University–Lake Campus, 174 Dwyer Hall, Celina, OH 45822. *Phone:* 419-586-0363. *Toll-free phone:* 800-237-1477. *E-mail:* jill.puthoff@wright.edu.

Xavier University
Cincinnati, Ohio
http://www.xavier.edu/

- **Independent Roman Catholic** university, founded 1831
- **Urban** 189-acre campus with easy access to Cincinnati
- **Endowment** $153.5 million
- **Coed** 5,047 undergraduate students, 96% full-time, 54% women, 46% men
- **Moderately difficult** entrance level, 76% of applicants were admitted

UNDERGRAD STUDENTS
4,834 full-time, 213 part-time. 57% are from out of state; 9% Black or African American, non-Hispanic/Latino; 6% Hispanic/Latino; 3% Asian, non-Hispanic/Latino; 0.2% Native Hawaiian or other Pacific Islander, non-Hispanic/Latino; 0.1% American Indian or Alaska Native, non-Hispanic/Latino; 4% Two or more races, non-Hispanic/Latino; 2% Race/ethnicity unknown; 1% international; 0.9% transferred in; 46% live on campus.

Freshmen:
Admission: 14,758 applied, 11,271 admitted, 1,210 enrolled. ***Average high school GPA:*** 3.6. ***Test scores:*** SAT evidence-based reading and writing scores over 500: 91%; SAT math scores over 500: 91%; ACT scores over 18: 98%; SAT evidence-based reading and writing scores over 600: 46%; SAT math scores over 600: 42%; ACT scores over 24: 64%; SAT evidence-based reading and writing scores over 700: 7%; SAT math scores over 700: 9%; ACT scores over 30: 16%.

Retention: 83% of full-time freshmen returned.

FACULTY
Total: 824, 47% full-time, 46% with terminal degrees.

Student/faculty ratio: 11:1.

ACADEMICS
Calendar: semesters. *Degrees:* certificates, associate, bachelor's, master's, doctoral, post-master's, and postbachelor's certificates.

Special study options: academic remediation for entering students, adult/continuing education programs, advanced placement credit, cooperative education, distance learning, double majors, English as a second language, honors programs, independent study, internships, off-campus study, part-time degree program, services for LD students, study abroad, summer session for credit. ***ROTC:*** Army (b), Air Force (c).

Unusual degree programs: 3-2 forestry with Duke University; environmental management, accounting, occupational therapy.

Computers: 450 computers/terminals and 10,128 ports are available on campus for general student use. Students can access the following: campus intranet, computer help desk, free student e-mail accounts, online (class) grades, online (class) registration, online (class) schedules. Campuswide network is available. 100% of college-owned or -operated housing units are wired for high-speed Internet access. Wireless service is available via entire campus.
Library: Xavier University Library plus 1 other.

STUDENT LIFE
Housing options: on-campus residence required through sophomore year; coed, special housing for students with disabilities. Campus housing is university owned. Freshman campus housing is guaranteed.

Activities and organizations: drama/theater group, student-run newspaper, television station, choral group, Student Government Association, Black Student Association, X-treme Fans, Alternative Spring Break, Club Sports.

Athletics Member NCAA. All Division I. ***Intercollegiate sports:*** baseball M(s), basketball M(s)/W(s), cheerleading M(c)/W(c), crew M(c)/W(c), cross-country running M(s)/W(s), equestrian sports M(c)/W(c), fencing M(c)/W(c), golf M(s)/W(s), gymnastics M(c)/W(c), ice hockey M(c)/W(c), lacrosse M(c)/W(c), rugby M(c), soccer M(s)/W(s), softball W(c), swimming and diving M(s)/W(s), tennis M(s)/W(s), track and field M(s)/W(s), ultimate Frisbee M(c), volleyball M(c)/W(s), water polo M(c)/W(c). ***Intramural sports:*** baseball M(c), basketball M/W, bowling M/W, football M/W, golf M(c), racquetball M/W, soccer M(c)/W(c), softball W, swimming and diving M(c)/W(c), tennis M/W, volleyball M/W.

Campus security: 24-hour emergency response devices and patrols, late-night transport/escort service, controlled dormitory access, campus-wide shuttle service.

Student services: health clinic, personal/psychological counseling, women's center, veterans affairs office.

COSTS & FINANCIAL AID
Costs (2020–21) ***Comprehensive fee:*** $55,770 includes full-time tuition ($42,230), mandatory fees ($230), and room and board ($13,310). Full-time tuition and fees vary according to course load, location, and program. Part-time tuition: $873 per credit hour. Part-time tuition and fees vary according to course load, location, and program. ***College room only:*** $7370. Room and board charges vary according to board plan and housing facility. ***Payment plans:*** installment, deferred payment. ***Waivers:*** senior citizens and employees or children of employees.

Financial Aid Of all full-time matriculated undergraduates who enrolled in 2018, 3,391 applied for aid, 2,743 were judged to have need, 163 had their need fully met. In 2018, 633 non-need-based awards were made. ***Average percent of need met:*** 63. ***Average financial aid package:*** $25,338. ***Average need-based loan:*** $3825. ***Average need-based gift aid:*** $23,327. ***Average non-need-based aid:*** $18,163. ***Average indebtedness upon graduation:*** $10,348.

APPLYING
Standardized Tests *Required for some:* SAT or ACT (for admission).

Options: electronic application, deferred entrance.

Application fee: $35.

Required: essay or personal statement, high school transcript, 1 letter of recommendation. ***Required for some:*** minimum 3.0 GPA, interview.

Application deadlines: 2/1 (freshmen), rolling (transfers).

Notification: continuous until 10/15 (freshmen), continuous (transfers).

CONTACT
Xavier University, 3800 Victory Parkway, Cincinnati, OH 45207-5311. *Phone:* 513-745-3301. *Toll-free phone:* 877-XUADMIT. *E-mail:* xuadmit@xavier.edu.

Youngstown State University
Youngstown, Ohio
http://www.ysu.edu/

- **State-supported** comprehensive, founded 1908
- **Urban** 160-acre campus with easy access to Cleveland, Pittsburgh
- **Endowment** $261.2 million
- **Coed** 11,001 undergraduate students, 80% full-time, 54% women, 46% men
- **Minimally difficult** entrance level, 68% of applicants were admitted

UNDERGRAD STUDENTS
8,756 full-time, 2,245 part-time. Students come from 37 states and territories; 58 other countries; 17% are from out of state; 8% Black or African American, non-Hispanic/Latino; 4% Hispanic/Latino; 1% Asian, non-Hispanic/Latino; 0.1% American Indian or Alaska Native, non-Hispanic/Latino; 4% Two or more races, non-Hispanic/Latino; 3% Race/ethnicity unknown; 3% international; 4% transferred in; 21% live on campus.

Freshmen:
Admission: 9,243 applied, 6,246 admitted, 2,010 enrolled. ***Average high school GPA:*** 3.4. ***Test scores:*** SAT evidence-based reading and writing scores over 500: 69%; SAT math scores over 500: 67%; ACT scores over 18: 82%; SAT evidence-based reading and writing scores over 600: 21%; SAT math scores over 600: 23%; ACT scores over 24: 31%; SAT evidence-based reading and writing scores over 700: 3%; SAT math scores over 700: 5%; ACT scores over 30: 4%.

Retention: 74% of full-time freshmen returned.

FACULTY
Total: 989, 40% full-time.

Student/faculty ratio: 22:1.

ACADEMICS
Calendar: semesters. *Degrees:* certificates, diplomas, associate, bachelor's, master's, doctoral, post-master's, and postbachelor's certificates.

Special study options: academic remediation for entering students, accelerated degree program, adult/continuing education programs, advanced placement credit, cooperative education, distance learning, double majors, English as a second language, freshman honors college, honors programs, independent study, internships, off-campus study, part-time degree program, services for LD students, student-designed majors, study abroad, summer session for credit. ***ROTC:*** Army (b), Air Force (c).

Computers: 1,949 computers/terminals are available on campus for general student use. Students can access the following: campus intranet, computer help desk, free student e-mail accounts, online (class) grades, online (class) registration, online (class) schedules. Campuswide network is available. 100% of college-owned or -operated housing units are wired for high-speed Internet access. Wireless service is available via entire campus.

Library: William F. Maag, Jr. Library plus 1 other. *Books:* 606,418 (physical), 203,316 (digital/electronic); *Serial titles:* 8,046 (physical), 104,211 (digital/electronic); *Databases:* 276. Weekly public service hours: 84.

STUDENT LIFE

Housing options: coed, women-only. Campus housing is university owned. Freshman applicants given priority for college housing.

Activities and organizations: drama/theater group, student-run newspaper, radio and television station, choral group, marching band, National Society of Collegiate Scholars, Fraternities/Sororities (IFC, NPHC, Panhellenic), American Society of Mechanical Engineers, Frost Penguins E-Sports, American Medical Student Association, national fraternities, national sororities.

Athletics Member NCAA. All Division I except football (Division I-AA). ***Intercollegiate sports:*** baseball M(s), basketball M(s)/W(s), bowling W, cross-country running M(s)/W(s), golf M(s)/W(s)(c), soccer W(s), softball W(s), swimming and diving W(s), tennis M(s)/W(s), track and field M(s)/W(s), volleyball W(s). ***Intramural sports:*** badminton M/W, basketball M/W, bowling M(c)/W(c), cross-country running M(c)/W(c), equestrian sports M(c)/W(c), fencing M(c)/W(c), football M, lacrosse M(c)/W(c), racquetball M(c)/W(c), rugby W(c), soccer M(c)/W(c), table tennis M/W, track and field M(c)/W(c), ultimate Frisbee M(c)/W(c), volleyball M(c)/W(c), weight lifting M(c)/W(c).

Campus security: 24-hour emergency response devices and patrols, student patrols, late-night transport/escort service, controlled dormitory access.

Student services: health clinic, personal/psychological counseling, veterans affairs office.

COSTS & FINANCIAL AID

Costs (2019–20) ***Tuition:*** state resident $9211 full-time, $384 per credit hour part-time; nonresident $15,211 full-time, $634 per credit hour part-time. Full-time tuition and fees vary according to course load. Part-time tuition and fees vary according to course load. No tuition increase for student's term of enrollment. ***Required fees:*** $68 full-time, $34 per term part-time. ***Room and board:*** $9700. Room and board charges vary according to board plan and housing facility. ***Payment plans:*** installment, deferred payment. ***Waivers:*** senior citizens and employees or children of employees.

Financial Aid Of all full-time matriculated undergraduates who enrolled in 2018, 7,433 applied for aid, 6,142 were judged to have need, 549 had their need fully met. In 2018, 1494 non-need-based awards were made. ***Average percent of need met:*** 35. ***Average financial aid package:*** $9954. ***Average need-based loan:*** $3786. ***Average need-based gift aid:*** $5772. ***Average non-need-based aid:*** $4250. ***Average indebtedness upon graduation:*** $29,360.

APPLYING

Standardized Tests *Required:* SAT or ACT (for admission).

Options: electronic application, early admission, deferred entrance.

Application fee: $45.

Required: high school transcript, minimum 2.0 GPA, minimum ACT composite score of 17 or combined SAT score of 910 from evidence-based writing and reading test and math test.

Application deadlines: 8/1 (freshmen), 8/1 (out-of-state freshmen), 8/1 (transfers).

Notification: continuous (freshmen), continuous (out-of-state freshmen), continuous (transfers).

CONTACT

Ms. Christine Hubert, Acting Director of Undergraduate Admissions, Youngstown State University, One University Plaza, Youngstown, OH 44555-0001. *Phone:* 330-941-2000. *Toll-free phone:* 877-468-6978. *Fax:* 330-941-3674. *E-mail:* enroll@ysu.edu.

OKLAHOMA

Bacone College

Muskogee, Oklahoma

http://www.bacone.edu/

CONTACT

Bacone College, 2299 Old Bacone Road, Muskogee, OK 74403-1597. *Phone:* 918-781-7342. *Toll-free phone:* 888-682-5514 Ext. 7340.

Cameron University

Lawton, Oklahoma

http://www.cameron.edu/

- **State-supported** comprehensive, founded 1908, part of Oklahoma State Regents for Higher Education
- **Small-town** 360-acre campus
- **Endowment** $20.4 million
- **Coed** 3,815 undergraduate students, 67% full-time, 63% women, 37% men
- **Noncompetitive** entrance level, 100% of applicants were admitted

UNDERGRAD STUDENTS

2,562 full-time, 1,253 part-time. Students come from 41 states and territories; 39 other countries; 11% are from out of state; 12% Black or African American, non-Hispanic/Latino; 15% Hispanic/Latino; 2% Asian, non-Hispanic/Latino; 0.4% Native Hawaiian or other Pacific Islander, non-Hispanic/Latino; 6% American Indian or Alaska Native, non-Hispanic/Latino; 10% Two or more races, non-Hispanic/Latino; 4% Race/ethnicity unknown; 3% international; 8% transferred in; 10% live on campus.

Freshmen:

Admission: 994 applied, 993 admitted, 615 enrolled. ***Average high school GPA:*** 3.2. ***Test scores:*** ACT scores over 18: 63%; ACT scores over 24: 15%; ACT scores over 30: 1%.

Retention: 67% of full-time freshmen returned.

FACULTY

Total: 242, 56% full-time, 50% with terminal degrees.

Student/faculty ratio: 19:1.

ACADEMICS

Calendar: semesters. *Degrees:* associate, bachelor's, and master's.

Special study options: academic remediation for entering students, accelerated degree program, adult/continuing education programs, advanced placement credit, distance learning, double majors, honors programs, independent study, internships, off-campus study, part-time degree program, services for LD students, student-designed majors, summer session for credit. ***ROTC:*** Army (b).

Computers: 549 computers/terminals are available on campus for general student use. Students can access the following: computer help desk, free student e-mail accounts, online (class) grades, online (class) registration, online (class) schedules, online courses. Campuswide network is available. 100% of college-owned or -operated housing units are wired for high-speed Internet access. Wireless service is available via classrooms, computer centers, computer labs, dorm rooms, learning centers, libraries, student centers.

Library: Cameron University Library. *Books:* 86,745 (physical), 191,345 (digital/electronic); *Serial titles:* 2,009 (physical), 34,058 (digital/electronic); *Databases:* 74. Weekly public service hours: 94; students can reserve study rooms.

STUDENT LIFE

Housing options: men-only, women-only, special housing for students with disabilities. Campus housing is university owned.

Activities and organizations: drama/theater group, student-run newspaper, television station, choral group, Student Government Association, Phi Eta Sigma Honor Society, Cameron Aggie Club, Military Science Club, Phi Kappa Phi Honor Society, national fraternities, national sororities.

Athletics Member NCAA. All Division II. ***Intercollegiate sports:*** baseball M(s), basketball M(s)/W(s), cross-country running M(s)/W(s), golf M(s)/W(s), softball W(s), tennis M(s)/W(s), track and field M(s)/W(s), volleyball W(s). ***Intramural sports:*** badminton M/W, basketball M/W, bowling M/W, racquetball M/W, soccer M/W, softball M/W, table tennis M/W, tennis M/W, volleyball M/W, weight lifting M/W.

Campus security: 24-hour emergency response devices and patrols, late-night transport/escort service, controlled dormitory access.

Student services: health clinic, personal/psychological counseling, veterans affairs office.

COSTS & FINANCIAL AID

Costs (2019–20) ***Tuition:*** state resident $4740 full-time, $158 per credit hour part-time; nonresident $14,160 full-time, $472 per credit hour part-time. Full-time tuition and fees vary according to course level, course load, location, and program. Part-time tuition and fees vary according to course level, course load, location, and program. ***Required fees:*** $1710 full-time, $57 per credit hour part-time. ***Room and board:*** $5452; room only: $2222. Room and board charges vary according to board plan and housing facility. ***Payment plan:*** installment. ***Waivers:*** children of alumni, senior citizens, and employees or children of employees.

Financial Aid Of all full-time matriculated undergraduates who enrolled in 2018, 2,140 applied for aid, 1,911 were judged to have need, 120 had their need fully met. 53 Federal Work-Study jobs (averaging $2450). 234 state and other part-time jobs (averaging $2353). In 2018, 248 non-need-based awards were made. ***Average percent of need met:*** 57. ***Average financial aid package:*** $9780. ***Average need-based loan:*** $3728. ***Average need-based gift aid:*** $7181. ***Average non-need-based aid:*** $2746. ***Average indebtedness upon graduation:*** $13,890.

APPLYING

Standardized Tests *Required for some:* SAT or ACT (for admission).

Options: electronic application, deferred entrance.

Application fee: $20.

Required for some: high school transcript.

Application deadlines: rolling (freshmen), rolling (out-of-state freshmen), rolling (transfers).

Notification: continuous (freshmen), continuous (out-of-state freshmen), continuous (transfers).

CONTACT

Ms. Brenda Dally, Director of Admissions, Cameron University, Admissions, 2800 West Gore Boulevard, Lawton, OK 73505-6377. *Phone:* 580-581-2289. *Toll-free phone:* 888-454-7600. *Fax:* 580-581-5514. *E-mail:* brendad@cameron.edu.

East Central University

Ada, Oklahoma

http://www.ecok.edu/

- **State-supported** comprehensive, founded 1909, part of RUSO Regional University System of Oklahoma
- **Rural** 144-acre campus
- **Endowment** $33.6 million
- **Coed** 2,981 undergraduate students, 83% full-time, 58% women, 42% men
- 59% of applicants were admitted

UNDERGRAD STUDENTS

2,471 full-time, 510 part-time. Students come from 26 states and territories; 32 other countries; 9% are from out of state; 15% Black or African American, non-Hispanic/Latino; 5% Hispanic/Latino; 0.3% Asian, non-Hispanic/Latino; 56% Native Hawaiian or other Pacific Islander, non-Hispanic/Latino; 5% American Indian or Alaska Native, non-Hispanic/Latino; 4% Two or more races, non-Hispanic/Latino; 3% Race/ethnicity unknown; 10% international; 10% transferred in; 35% live on campus.

Freshmen:

Admission: 1,178 applied, 699 admitted, 494 enrolled. ***Average high school GPA:*** 3.4. ***Test scores:*** SAT evidence-based reading and writing scores over 500: 55%; SAT math scores over 500: 51%; ACT scores over 18: 74%; SAT evidence-based reading and writing scores over 600: 15%; SAT math scores over 600: 16%; ACT scores over 24: 21%; SAT math scores over 700: 2%; ACT scores over 30: 5%.

Retention: 64% of full-time freshmen returned.

FACULTY

Total: 232, 60% full-time, 49% with terminal degrees.

Student/faculty ratio: 18:1.

ACADEMICS

Calendar: semesters. *Degrees:* certificates, bachelor's, master's, and postbachelor's certificates.

Special study options: academic remediation for entering students, accelerated degree program, advanced placement credit, cooperative education, distance learning, double majors, external degree program, honors programs, independent study, off-campus study, part-time degree program, services for LD students, student-designed majors, study abroad, summer session for credit.

Computers: 800 computers/terminals are available on campus for general student use. Students can access the following: campus intranet, computer help desk, free student e-mail accounts, online (class) grades, online (class) registration, online (class) schedules. Campuswide network is available. Wireless service is available via entire campus.

Library: Linscheid Library. *Books:* 113,674 (physical), 41,451 (digital/electronic); *Serial titles:* 51,567 (physical), 2,648 (digital/electronic); *Databases:* 73. Students can reserve study rooms.

STUDENT LIFE

Housing options: on-campus residence required for freshman year; coed. Campus housing is university owned. Freshman applicants given priority for college housing.

Activities and organizations: drama/theater group, choral group, marching band, Campus Activity Board, Greek Life, Student Government Association, national fraternities, national sororities.

Athletics Member NCAA. All Division II. ***Intercollegiate sports:*** baseball M(s), basketball M(s)/W(s), cross-country running M(s)/W(s), football M(s), soccer W(s), softball W(s), track and field M(s)/W(s), volleyball W(s). ***Intramural sports:*** baseball M, basketball M/W, cross-country running M/W, football M, soccer W, softball W, track and field M/W, volleyball W.

Campus security: 24-hour emergency response devices, controlled dormitory access.

Student services: health clinic, personal/psychological counseling, veterans affairs office.

COSTS & FINANCIAL AID

Costs (2019–20) ***Tuition:*** area resident $5648 full-time, $276 per credit hour part-time; state resident $5648 full-time, $276 per credit hour part-time; nonresident $15,008 full-time, $633 per credit hour part-time. No tuition increase for student's term of enrollment. ***Required fees:*** $1404 full-time, $47 per semester hour part-time. ***Room and board:*** $7072; room only: $3662. Room and board charges vary according to board plan. ***Payment plan:*** installment. ***Waivers:*** employees or children of employees.

Financial Aid Of all full-time matriculated undergraduates who enrolled in 2018, 1,958 applied for aid, 1,665 were judged to have need. In 2018, 135 non-need-based awards were made. ***Average financial aid package:*** $6222. ***Average need-based loan:*** $4049. ***Average need-based gift aid:*** $4508. ***Average non-need-based aid:*** $3029. ***Average indebtedness upon graduation:*** $21,665.

APPLYING

Standardized Tests *Required:* ACT (for admission).

Options: electronic application, early admission.

Application fee: $25.

Recommended: high school transcript.

Application deadlines: rolling (freshmen), rolling (out-of-state freshmen), rolling (transfers).

Notification: continuous (freshmen), continuous (out-of-state freshmen), continuous (transfers).

CONTACT
Ms. Kylie Stephens, Assistant Director of Admissions, East Central University, 1100 East 14th Street, PMB R-8, Ada, OK 74820-6999. *Phone:* 580-559-5209. *E-mail:* kstephens@ecok.edu.

Family of Faith Christian University

Shawnee, Oklahoma

http://www.familyoffaith.edu/

CONTACT
Family of Faith Christian University, 30 Kinville, Shawnee, OK 74802.

Langston University

Langston, Oklahoma

http://www.langston.edu/

- **State-supported** comprehensive, founded 1897, part of Oklahoma A&M System
- **Rural** 40-acre campus with easy access to Oklahoma City
- **Endowment** $1.6 million
- **Coed**
- **Moderately difficult** entrance level

FACULTY
Student/faculty ratio: 16:1.

ACADEMICS
Calendar: semesters. *Degrees:* associate, bachelor's, master's, and doctoral.
Library: G. Lamar Harrison Library plus 2 others. *Books:* 44,337 (physical), 189,180 (digital/electronic); *Serial titles:* 111 (physical), 20,763 (digital/electronic); *Databases:* 61. Students can reserve study rooms.

STUDENT LIFE
Housing options: coed, special housing for students with disabilities. Campus housing is university owned and is provided by a third party. Freshman campus housing is guaranteed.

Activities and organizations: drama/theater group, student-run newspaper, radio station, choral group, marching band, Student Government Association, Student Senate, Sorority and Fraternity (Greek Letter), NAACP, Pre- Alumni Council, national fraternities, national sororities.

Athletics Member NAIA.

Campus security: 24-hour emergency response devices and patrols, student patrols, late-night transport/escort service, controlled dormitory access.

Student services: health clinic, personal/psychological counseling, women's center.

FINANCIAL AID
Financial Aid Of all full-time matriculated undergraduates who enrolled in 2015, 1,939 applied for aid, 1,814 were judged to have need, 334 had their need fully met. In 2015, 197 non-need-based awards were made. ***Average percent of need met:*** 54. ***Average financial aid package:*** $10,893. ***Average need-based gift aid:*** $5109. ***Average non-need-based aid:*** $6138. ***Average indebtedness upon graduation:*** $39,681.

APPLYING
Standardized Tests *Required:* SAT or ACT (for admission).

Options: electronic application, deferred entrance.

Required: high school transcript, minimum 2.7 GPA.

CONTACT
Mr. Jeremy Lane, Director of Admissions, Langston University, Box 1550, Langston, OK 73052. *Phone:* 405-466-3428. *Fax:* 405-466-2915. *E-mail:* jlane@langston.edu.

Mid-America Christian University

Oklahoma City, Oklahoma

http://www.macu.edu/

- **Independent** comprehensive, founded 1953, affiliated with Church of God
- **Suburban** 145-acre campus with easy access to Oklahoma City, Oklahoma
- **Endowment** $2.6 million
- **Coed** 1,520 undergraduate students, 71% full-time, 68% women, 32% men
- **Noncompetitive** entrance level

UNDERGRAD STUDENTS
1,072 full-time, 448 part-time. Students come from 38 states and territories; 30 other countries; 20% are from out of state; 13% Black or African American, non-Hispanic/Latino; 29% Hispanic/Latino; 0.7% Asian, non-Hispanic/Latino; 0.1% Native Hawaiian or other Pacific Islander, non-Hispanic/Latino; 5% American Indian or Alaska Native, non-Hispanic/Latino; 1% Two or more races, non-Hispanic/Latino; 7% Race/ethnicity unknown; 4% international; 15% transferred in.

Freshmen:
Admission: 124 enrolled.
Retention: 60% of full-time freshmen returned.

FACULTY
Student/faculty ratio: 7:1.

ACADEMICS
Calendar: semesters. *Degrees:* certificates, associate, bachelor's, master's, post-master's, and postbachelor's certificates.

Special study options: academic remediation for entering students, accelerated degree program, adult/continuing education programs, advanced placement credit, distance learning, double majors, internships, part-time degree program, services for LD students, summer session for credit.

Computers: 24 computers/terminals and 60 ports are available on campus for general student use. Students can access the following: campus intranet, computer help desk, free student e-mail accounts, online (class) grades, online (class) registration, online (class) schedules. Campuswide network is available. 100% of college-owned or -operated housing units are wired for high-speed Internet access. Wireless service is available via entire campus.
Library: Charles Ewing Brown Library plus 1 other. *Books:* 34,757 (physical), 91,107 (digital/electronic); *Serial titles:* 120 (physical), 35,465 (digital/electronic); *Databases:* 77. Weekly public service hours: 70; study areas open 24 hours, 5–7 days a week; students can reserve study rooms.

STUDENT LIFE
Housing options: on-campus residence required through sophomore year; men-only, women-only, special housing for students with disabilities. Campus housing is university owned. Freshman campus housing is guaranteed.

Activities and organizations: choral group.

Athletics Member NAIA. ***Intercollegiate sports:*** baseball M(s), basketball M(s)/W(s), cheerleading M/W, soccer M(s)/W(s), softball W(s), volleyball W(s). ***Intramural sports:*** basketball M/W, soccer M, softball M/W, volleyball M/W.

Campus security: 24-hour patrols, student patrols.

Student services: personal/psychological counseling, veterans affairs office.

COSTS & FINANCIAL AID
Costs (2020–21) ***Comprehensive fee:*** $27,229 includes full-time tuition ($17,568), mandatory fees ($1270), and room and board ($8391). Full-time tuition and fees vary according to class time, course level, course load, location, and program. Part-time tuition and fees vary according to class time, course level, course load, location, and program. ***College room only:*** $4456. Room and board charges vary according to board plan. ***Payment plans:*** installment, deferred payment. ***Waivers:*** employees or children of employees.

Financial Aid Of all full-time matriculated undergraduates who enrolled in 2001, 589 applied for aid, 581 were judged to have need, 68 had their need fully met. In 2001, 41 non-need-based awards were made. ***Average***

percent of need met: 75. ***Average financial aid package:*** $6682. ***Average need-based loan:*** $3617. ***Average need-based gift aid:*** $2734. ***Average non-need-based aid:*** $5214.

APPLYING

Standardized Tests *Recommended:* SAT or ACT (for admission).

Options: early admission.

Required: high school transcript. ***Required for some:*** 2 letters of recommendation, interview.

Application deadlines: rolling (freshmen), rolling (transfers).

CONTACT

Mid-America Christian University, 3500 Southwest 119th Street, Oklahoma City, OK 73170-4504. *Phone:* 405-692-3281. *Toll-free phone:* 888-436-3035.

National American University

Tulsa, Oklahoma

http://www.national.edu/

CONTACT

National American University, 8040 South Sheridan Road, Tulsa, OK 74133. *Toll-free phone:* 800-209-0338.

Northeastern State University

Tahlequah, Oklahoma

http://www.nsuok.edu/

- **State-supported** comprehensive, founded 1846, part of Regional University System of Oklahoma
- **Small-town** 200-acre campus with easy access to Tulsa
- **Endowment** $5.4 million
- **Coed** 6,288 undergraduate students, 69% full-time, 62% women, 38% men
- **Moderately difficult** entrance level, 99% of applicants were admitted

UNDERGRAD STUDENTS

4,352 full-time, 1,936 part-time. Students come from 37 states and territories; 29 other countries; 5% are from out of state; 4% Black or African American, non-Hispanic/Latino; 6% Hispanic/Latino; 2% Asian, non-Hispanic/Latino; 0.1% Native Hawaiian or other Pacific Islander, non-Hispanic/Latino; 19% American Indian or Alaska Native, non-Hispanic/Latino; 18% Two or more races, non-Hispanic/Latino; 0.7% Race/ethnicity unknown; 2% international; 12% transferred in; 19% live on campus.

Freshmen:

Admission: 1,073 applied, 1,067 admitted, 724 enrolled. ***Average high school GPA:*** 3.5. ***Test scores:*** ACT scores over 18: 80%; ACT scores over 24: 26%; ACT scores over 30: 3%.

Retention: 60% of full-time freshmen returned.

FACULTY

Total: 422, 66% full-time, 62% with terminal degrees.

Student/faculty ratio: 19:1.

ACADEMICS

Calendar: semesters. *Degrees:* bachelor's, master's, doctoral, post-master's, and postbachelor's certificates.

Special study options: academic remediation for entering students, adult/continuing education programs, advanced placement credit, cooperative education, distance learning, double majors, honors programs, independent study, internships, part-time degree program, services for LD students, student-designed majors, summer session for credit. ***ROTC:*** Army (b).

Computers: 1,160 computers/terminals and 1,200 ports are available on campus for general student use. Students can access the following: campus intranet, computer help desk, free student e-mail accounts, online (class) grades, online (class) registration, online (class) schedules. Campuswide network is available. 100% of college-owned or -operated housing units are wired for high-speed Internet access. Wireless service is available via entire campus.

Library: John Vaughn Library plus 1 other. *Books:* 344,747 (physical), 71,226 (digital/electronic); *Serial titles:* 11,698 (physical), 34,336 (digital/electronic); *Databases:* 252. Weekly public service hours: 114.

STUDENT LIFE

Housing options: on-campus residence required for freshman year; coed, women-only, special housing for students with disabilities. Campus housing is university owned. Freshman applicants given priority for college housing.

Activities and organizations: drama/theater group, student-run newspaper, television station, choral group, marching band, national fraternities, national sororities.

Athletics Member NCAA. All Division II except golf (Division I). ***Intercollegiate sports:*** baseball M(s), basketball M(s)/W(s), football M(s), golf M(s)/W(s), soccer M(s)/W(s), softball W(s), tennis W(s). ***Intramural sports:*** basketball M/W, football M/W, golf M/W, racquetball M/W, soccer M/W, softball M/W, tennis M/W, volleyball M/W.

Campus security: 24-hour emergency response devices and patrols, late-night transport/escort service, controlled dormitory access.

Student services: health clinic, personal/psychological counseling, veterans affairs office.

COSTS & FINANCIAL AID

Costs (2019–20) ***Tuition:*** area resident $5913 full-time, $197 per credit hour part-time; state resident $5913 full-time, $197 per credit hour part-time; nonresident $14,313 full-time, $477 per credit hour part-time. No tuition increase for student's term of enrollment. ***Required fees:*** $1002 full-time, $33 per credit hour part-time. ***Room and board:*** $7340; room only: $3200. Room and board charges vary according to board plan and housing facility. ***Payment plan:*** installment. ***Waivers:*** employees or children of employees.

Financial Aid Of all full-time matriculated undergraduates who enrolled in 2019, 3,650 applied for aid, 2,916 were judged to have need, 1,733 had their need fully met. 201 Federal Work-Study jobs (averaging $1666). 193 state and other part-time jobs (averaging $1683). In 2019, 184 non-need-based awards were made. ***Average percent of need met:*** 91. ***Average financial aid package:*** $13,932. ***Average need-based loan:*** $7909. ***Average need-based gift aid:*** $7451. ***Average non-need-based aid:*** $2984. ***Average indebtedness upon graduation:*** $20,707.

APPLYING

Standardized Tests *Required:* ACT (for admission).

Options: electronic application, deferred entrance.

Application fee: $25.

Required: high school transcript, minimum 2.7 GPA, upper 50% of class or minimum ACT composite of 20. ***Required for some:*** essay or personal statement, letters of recommendation, interview.

Notification: continuous (freshmen), continuous (transfers).

CONTACT

Ms. Chenoa Worthington, Director, Admissions and Recruitment, Northeastern State University, Case Building Room 220, 701 N. Grand Avenue, Tahlequah, OK 74464. *Phone:* 918-444-4677. *Toll-free phone:* 800-722-9614. *E-mail:* worthi02@nsuok.edu.

Northwestern Oklahoma State University

Alva, Oklahoma

http://www.nwosu.edu/

- **State-supported** comprehensive, founded 1897, part of Oklahoma State Regents for Higher Education
- **Rural** 70-acre campus
- **Endowment** $35.7 million
- **Coed**
- **Moderately difficult** entrance level

FACULTY

Student/faculty ratio: 15:1.

ACADEMICS

Calendar: semesters. *Degrees:* certificates, bachelor's, master's, and doctoral.

Library: J. W. Martin Library. *Books:* 91,123 (physical), 213,917 (digital/electronic); *Serial titles:* 23,390 (physical), 6 (digital/electronic); *Databases:* 45. Weekly public service hours: 84; students can reserve study rooms.

STUDENT LIFE
Housing options: on-campus residence required for freshman year; men-only, women-only. Campus housing is university owned. Freshman campus housing is guaranteed.

Activities and organizations: drama/theater group, student-run newspaper, radio and television station, choral group, marching band, Student Government Association, Aggie Club, Delta Mu Delta, Baptist Student Union, SOEA.

Athletics Member NCAA. All Division II.

Campus security: 24-hour emergency response devices and patrols, late-night transport/escort service.

Student services: personal/psychological counseling, veterans affairs office.

COSTS & FINANCIAL AID
Costs (2019–20) ***Tuition:*** state resident $6593 full-time, $1319 per credit hour part-time; nonresident $13,710 full-time, $2742 per credit hour part-time. Full-time tuition and fees vary according to course load, degree level, location, and program. Part-time tuition and fees vary according to course load, degree level, location, and program. No tuition increase for student's term of enrollment. ***Required fees:*** $653 full-time, $22 per credit hour part-time, $22 per credit hour part-time. ***Room and board:*** $4680; room only: $1880. Room and board charges vary according to board plan.

Financial Aid Of all full-time matriculated undergraduates who enrolled in 2018, 1,170 applied for aid, 856 were judged to have need.

APPLYING
Standardized Tests *Required:* SAT or ACT (for admission).

Options: electronic application, early admission.

Application fee: $15.

Required: high school transcript. ***Required for some:*** essay or personal statement, minimum 2.7 GPA, 3 letters of recommendation.

CONTACT
Ms. Paige Fischer, Director of Recruitment, Northwestern Oklahoma State University, 709 Oklahoma Boulevard, Alva, OK 73717-2799. *Phone:* 580-327-8546. *Fax:* 580-327-8699. *E-mail:* recruit@nwosu.edu.

Oklahoma Baptist University

Shawnee, Oklahoma

http://www.okbu.edu/

- **Independent Southern Baptist** comprehensive, founded 1910
- **Small-town** 125-acre campus with easy access to Oklahoma City
- **Endowment** $116.2 million
- **Coed** 1,759 undergraduate students, 97% full-time, 60% women, 42% men
- **Moderately difficult** entrance level, 57% of applicants were admitted

UNDERGRAD STUDENTS
1,703 full-time, 85 part-time. Students come from 19 states and territories; 9 other countries; 39% are from out of state; 6% Black or African American, non-Hispanic/Latino; 2% Hispanic/Latino; 0.9% Asian, non-Hispanic/Latino; 0.2% Native Hawaiian or other Pacific Islander, non-Hispanic/Latino; 5% American Indian or Alaska Native, non-Hispanic/Latino; 14% Two or more races, non-Hispanic/Latino; 1% Race/ethnicity unknown; 3% international; 4% transferred in; 65% live on campus.

Freshmen:
Admission: 4,292 applied, 2,466 admitted, 448 enrolled. ***Average high school GPA:*** 3.7. ***Test scores:*** ACT scores over 18: 325%; ACT scores over 24: 144%; ACT scores over 30: 26%.

Retention: 78% of full-time freshmen returned.

FACULTY
Total: 153, 75% full-time, 59% with terminal degrees.

Student/faculty ratio: 15:1.

ACADEMICS
Calendar: 4-1-4. *Degrees:* associate, bachelor's, and master's.

Special study options: academic remediation for entering students, advanced placement credit, cooperative education, double majors, honors programs, independent study, internships, off-campus study, part-time degree program, services for LD students, student-designed majors, study abroad, summer session for credit. ***ROTC:*** Air Force (c).

Computers: 175 computers/terminals are available on campus for general student use. Students can access the following: computer help desk, free student e-mail accounts, online (class) grades, online (class) registration, online (class) schedules, campus portal, online course work. Campuswide network is available. 100% of college-owned or -operated housing units are wired for high-speed Internet access. Wireless service is available via entire campus.
Library: Mabee Learning Center. *Books:* 171,809 (physical), 56,378 (digital/electronic); *Serial titles:* 109 (physical); *Databases:* 60. Weekly public service hours: 91; students can reserve study rooms.

STUDENT LIFE
Housing options: on-campus residence required through junior year; men-only, women-only. Campus housing is university owned. Freshman campus housing is guaranteed.

Activities and organizations: drama/theater group, student-run newspaper, television station, choral group, marching band, Campus Activities Board, University Concert Series, Student Foundation, Blitz Week Activities, Canterbury.

Athletics Member NCAA, NCCAA. All NCAA Division II except cross-country running (Division I), golf (Division I), men's and women's swimming and diving (Division I). ***Intercollegiate sports:*** baseball M(s), basketball M(s)/W(s), cross-country running M(s)/W(s), football M(s), golf M(s)/W(s), lacrosse W(s), soccer M(s)/W(s), softball W(s), swimming and diving M(s)/W(s), tennis M(s)/W(s), track and field M(s)/W(s), volleyball W(s). ***Intramural sports:*** archery M/W, basketball M/W, bowling M/W, cheerleading W, football M/W, racquetball M/W, riflery M/W, rock climbing M/W, sand volleyball M/W, soccer M/W, softball M/W, table tennis M/W, tennis M/W, ultimate Frisbee M/W, volleyball M/W.

Campus security: 24-hour emergency response devices and patrols, late-night transport/escort service, controlled dormitory access.

Student services: health clinic, personal/psychological counseling.

COSTS & FINANCIAL AID
Costs (2020–21) ***Comprehensive fee:*** $39,072 includes full-time tuition ($27,912), mandatory fees ($3440), and room and board ($7720). Part-time tuition: $907 per credit hour. Part-time tuition and fees vary according to course load. ***Required fees:*** $3440 per term part-time. ***College room only:*** $3470. Room and board charges vary according to board plan and housing facility. ***Payment plan:*** installment. ***Waivers:*** employees or children of employees.

Financial Aid Of all full-time matriculated undergraduates who enrolled in 2019, 1,390 applied for aid, 1,255 were judged to have need, 49 had their need fully met. 145 Federal Work-Study jobs (averaging $789). In 2019, 398 non-need-based awards were made. ***Average percent of need met:*** 55. ***Average financial aid package:*** $21,528. ***Average need-based loan:*** $4147. ***Average need-based gift aid:*** $9444. ***Average non-need-based aid:*** $9696. ***Average indebtedness upon graduation:*** $25,673.

APPLYING
Standardized Tests *Required:* SAT or ACT (for admission).

Options: electronic application, early admission, deferred entrance.

Required: high school transcript, minimum 3.0 GPA. ***Required for some:*** essay or personal statement, interview.

Application deadlines: rolling (freshmen), 8/1 (transfers).

Notification: continuous (freshmen), continuous until 9/1 (transfers).

CONTACT
Oklahoma Baptist University, 500 West University, Shawnee, OK 74804. *Phone:* 405-585-5120. *Toll-free phone:* 800-654-3285.

Oklahoma Christian University

Oklahoma City, Oklahoma

http://www.oc.edu/

- **Independent** comprehensive, founded 1950, affiliated with Church of Christ
- **Suburban** 200-acre campus with easy access to Oklahoma City
- **Coed**
- **Moderately difficult** entrance level

FACULTY
Student/faculty ratio: 14:1.

ACADEMICS
Calendar: semesters. *Degrees:* certificates, bachelor's, master's, and postbachelor's certificates.
Library: Tom and Ada Beam Library. *Books:* 108,575 (physical), 66,843 (digital/electronic); *Serial titles:* 1,241 (physical), 42,377 (digital/electronic); *Databases:* 76. Weekly public service hours: 82; students can reserve study rooms.

STUDENT LIFE
Housing options: on-campus residence required through senior year; men-only, women-only, special housing for students with disabilities. Campus housing is university owned. Freshman campus housing is guaranteed.

Activities and organizations: drama/theater group, student-run newspaper, radio and television station, choral group, Ethos, Social Service Clubs, Student Government Association, Freshman Class club, Outreach mission organization.

Athletics Member NCAA. All Division II.

Campus security: 24-hour emergency response devices and patrols, late-night transport/escort service, controlled dormitory access.

Student services: health clinic, personal/psychological counseling, veterans affairs office.

COSTS & FINANCIAL AID
Costs (2019–20) ***Comprehensive fee:*** $32,300 includes full-time tuition ($23,450), mandatory fees ($300), and room and board ($8550). Full-time tuition and fees vary according to course load and location. Part-time tuition: $975 per credit hour. Part-time tuition and fees vary according to course load. ***Required fees:*** $10 per credit hour part-time, $75 per term part-time. ***College room only:*** $4550. Room and board charges vary according to board plan, housing facility, and location. ***Payment plans:*** installment, deferred payment.

Financial Aid Of all full-time matriculated undergraduates who enrolled in 2017, 1,455 applied for aid, 1,256 were judged to have need, 493 had their need fully met. In 2017, 505 non-need-based awards were made. ***Average percent of need met:*** 62. ***Average financial aid package:*** $24,125. ***Average need-based loan:*** $2166. ***Average need-based gift aid:*** $3387. ***Average non-need-based aid:*** $7396. ***Average indebtedness upon graduation:*** $30,395.

APPLYING
Standardized Tests *Required:* SAT or ACT (for admission).

Options: electronic application, early admission, deferred entrance.

Application fee: $25.

Required: high school transcript. ***Required for some:*** interview.

CONTACT
Ms. Bonnie Howard, Director of Admissions and International Records, Oklahoma Christian University, Box 11000, Oklahoma City, OK 73136-1100. *Phone:* 405-425-5000. *Toll-free phone:* 800-877-5010. *Fax:* 405-425-5208. *E-mail:* admissions@oc.edu.

Oklahoma City University

Oklahoma City, Oklahoma

http://www.okcu.edu/

CONTACT
Ms. Michelle Cook, Senior Director of Admissions, Oklahoma City University, 2501 North Blackwelder, Oklahoma City, OK 73106. *Phone:* 405-208-5055. *Toll-free phone:* 800-633-7242. *Fax:* 405-208-5916. *E-mail:* michelle.cook@okcu.edu.

Oklahoma Panhandle State University

Goodwell, Oklahoma

http://www.opsu.edu/

- **State-supported** 4-year, founded 1909, part of Oklahoma State Regents for Higher Education
- **Rural** 40-acre campus
- **Coed**
- **Noncompetitive** entrance level

FACULTY
Student/faculty ratio: 16:1.

ACADEMICS
Calendar: semesters. *Degrees:* associate and bachelor's.
Library: McKee Library.

STUDENT LIFE
Housing options: on-campus residence required for freshman year; coed, men-only, women-only. Campus housing is university owned. Freshman campus housing is guaranteed.

Activities and organizations: drama/theater group, student-run newspaper, radio station, choral group, marching band.

Athletics Member NCAA. All Division II.

Campus security: safety bars over door latches.

Student services: health clinic, personal/psychological counseling.

COSTS
Costs (2019–20) ***Tuition:*** area resident $3696 full-time, $154 per credit hour part-time; state resident $3696 full-time, $154 per credit hour part-time; nonresident $3696 full-time, $154 per credit hour part-time. Full-time tuition and fees vary according to location and program. Part-time tuition and fees vary according to location and program. ***Required fees:*** $2520 full-time, $102 per credit hour part-time, $42 per term part-time. ***Room and board:*** $3955; room only: $2400. Room and board charges vary according to board plan and housing facility.

APPLYING
Standardized Tests *Recommended:* SAT or ACT (for admission).

Options: electronic application.

Required: high school transcript.

CONTACT
Mr. Bobby Jenkins, Registrar and Director of Admissions, Oklahoma Panhandle State University, PO Box 430, 323 Eagle Boulevard, Goodwell, OK 73939-0430. *Phone:* 580-349-1376. *Toll-free phone:* 800-664-6778. *Fax:* 580-349-1371. *E-mail:* opsu@opsu.edu.

Oklahoma State University

Stillwater, Oklahoma

http://www.okstate.edu/

- **State-supported** university, founded 1890, part of Oklahoma State University
- **Small-town** 840-acre campus with easy access to Oklahoma City and Tulsa
- **Endowment** $879.5 million
- **Coed** 20,024 undergraduate students, 86% full-time, 50% women, 50% men
- **Moderately difficult** entrance level, 70% of applicants were admitted

UNDERGRAD STUDENTS
17,213 full-time, 2,811 part-time. Students come from 54 states and territories; 55 other countries; 27% are from out of state; 4% Black or African American, non-Hispanic/Latino; 8% Hispanic/Latino; 2% Asian, non-Hispanic/Latino; 0.1% Native Hawaiian or other Pacific Islander, non-Hispanic/Latino; 4% American Indian or Alaska Native, non-Hispanic/Latino; 10% Two or more races, non-Hispanic/Latino; 0.1% Race/ethnicity unknown; 3% international; 7% transferred in; 42% live on campus.

Freshmen:
Admission: 15,277 applied, 10,691 admitted, 4,200 enrolled. ***Average high school GPA:*** 3.6. ***Test scores:*** SAT evidence-based reading and writing scores over 500: 85%; SAT math scores over 500: 82%; ACT scores over 18: 95%; SAT evidence-based reading and writing scores over

600: 45%; SAT math scores over 600: 39%; ACT scores over 24: 56%; SAT evidence-based reading and writing scores over 700: 7%; SAT math scores over 700: 9%; ACT scores over 30: 16%.

Retention: 83% of full-time freshmen returned.

FACULTY
Total: 1,337, 80% full-time, 81% with terminal degrees.

Student/faculty ratio: 18:1.

ACADEMICS
Calendar: semesters. *Degrees:* certificates, bachelor's, master's, doctoral, post-master's, and postbachelor's certificates.

Special study options: accelerated degree program, advanced placement credit, distance learning, double majors, English as a second language, freshman honors college, honors programs, independent study, internships, off-campus study, part-time degree program, services for LD students, student-designed majors, study abroad, summer session for credit. ***ROTC:*** Army (b), Air Force (b).

Unusual degree programs: 3-2 business administration; accounting, special education, biochemistry, early childhood education.

Computers: 177 computers/terminals are available on campus for general student use. Students can access the following: campus intranet, computer help desk, free student e-mail accounts, online (class) grades, online (class) registration, online (class) schedules, Computer labs. Campuswide network is available. 100% of college-owned or -operated housing units are wired for high-speed Internet access. Wireless service is available via entire campus.

Library: Edmon Low Library plus 3 others. *Books:* 1.9 million (physical), 3.2 million (digital/electronic); *Serial titles:* 71,356 (physical), 130,130 (digital/electronic); *Databases:* 54. Weekly public service hours: 146; study areas open 24 hours, 5–7 days a week; students can reserve study rooms.

STUDENT LIFE
Housing options: on-campus residence required for freshman year; coed, men-only, women-only, special housing for students with disabilities. Campus housing is university owned. Freshman applicants given priority for college housing.

Activities and organizations: drama/theater group, student-run newspaper, radio and television station, choral group, marching band, national fraternities, national sororities.

Athletics Member NCAA. All Division I. ***Intercollegiate sports:*** baseball M(s), basketball M(s)/W(s), cheerleading M(s)/W(s), cross-country running M(s)/W(s), equestrian sports W(s), football M(s), golf M(s)/W(s), soccer M(c)/W(s), softball W(s), tennis M(s)/W(s), track and field M(s)/W(s), wrestling M(s). ***Intramural sports:*** archery M(c)/W(c), badminton M(c)/W(c), baseball M(c), basketball M/W, bowling M/W, crew M(c)/W(c), cross-country running M(c)/W(c), football M/W, golf M/W, lacrosse M(c)/W(c), riflery M(c)/W(c), rock climbing M/W, rowing M(c)/W(c), rugby M(c), sailing M(c)/W(c), soccer M/W, softball M/W, swimming and diving M/W, table tennis M/W, tennis M/W, triathlon M(c)/W(c), ultimate Frisbee M/W, volleyball M/W, water polo M/W, weight lifting M/W, wrestling M/W.

Campus security: 24-hour emergency response devices and patrols, student patrols, late-night transport/escort service, controlled dormitory access, Rave Guardian Mobile App.

Student services: health clinic, personal/psychological counseling, legal services, veterans affairs office.

COSTS & FINANCIAL AID
Costs (2019–20) ***One-time required fee:*** $120. ***Tuition:*** state resident $5357 full-time, $179 per credit hour part-time; nonresident $20,877 full-time, $696 per credit hour part-time. Full-time tuition and fees vary according to program. Part-time tuition and fees vary according to course load and program. No tuition increase for student's term of enrollment. ***Required fees:*** $3662 full-time, $122 per credit hour part-time. ***Room and board:*** $9106; room only: $5096. Room and board charges vary according to board plan and housing facility. ***Payment plan:*** installment. ***Waivers:*** children of alumni, senior citizens, and employees or children of employees.

Financial Aid Of all full-time matriculated undergraduates who enrolled in 2018, 12,280 applied for aid, 9,528 were judged to have need, 929 had their need fully met. 363 Federal Work-Study jobs (averaging $2417). 4,827 state and other part-time jobs (averaging $3210). In 2018, 4736 non-need-based awards were made. ***Average percent of need met:*** 72. ***Average financial aid package:*** $15,840. ***Average need-based loan:*** $3945. ***Average need-based gift aid:*** $8146. ***Average non-need-based aid:*** $6615. ***Average indebtedness upon graduation:*** $25,185.

APPLYING
Standardized Tests *Required:* SAT or ACT (for admission).

Options: electronic application, deferred entrance.

Application fee: $40.

Required: high school transcript. ***Required for some:*** essay or personal statement, minimum 3.0 GPA.

Application deadlines: rolling (freshmen), rolling (out-of-state freshmen), rolling (transfers).

Notification: continuous (freshmen), continuous (out-of-state freshmen), continuous (transfers).

CONTACT
Oklahoma State University, Stillwater, OK 74078. *Phone:* 405-744-5358. *Toll-free phone:* 800-233-5019.

Oklahoma State University Institute of Technology

Okmulgee, Oklahoma

http://www.osuit.edu/

- **State-supported** primarily 2-year, founded 1946, part of Oklahoma State University
- **Small-town** 160-acre campus with easy access to Tulsa
- **Endowment** $7.8 million
- **Coed** 2,309 undergraduate students, 63% full-time, 35% women, 65% men
- **Noncompetitive** entrance level, 29% of applicants were admitted

UNDERGRAD STUDENTS
1,464 full-time, 845 part-time. Students come from 26 states and territories; 11 other countries; 9% are from out of state; 3% Black or African American, non-Hispanic/Latino; 7% Hispanic/Latino; 0.6% Asian, non-Hispanic/Latino; 12% American Indian or Alaska Native, non-Hispanic/Latino; 15% Two or more races, non-Hispanic/Latino; 5% Race/ethnicity unknown; 1% international; 9% transferred in; 26% live on campus.

Freshmen:
Admission: 2,518 applied, 734 admitted, 587 enrolled. ***Average high school GPA:*** 3.1. ***Test scores:*** ACT scores over 18: 52%; ACT scores over 24: 8%; ACT scores over 30: 1%.

Retention: 59% of full-time freshmen returned.

FACULTY
Total: 135, 69% full-time, 7% with terminal degrees.

Student/faculty ratio: 16:1.

ACADEMICS
Calendar: trimesters. *Degrees:* associate and bachelor's.

Special study options: academic remediation for entering students, adult/continuing education programs, advanced placement credit, distance learning, double majors, independent study, internships, part-time degree program, services for LD students, summer session for credit.

Computers: 50 computers/terminals are available on campus for general student use. Students can access the following: computer help desk, free student e-mail accounts, online (class) grades, online (class) registration, online (class) schedules. Campuswide network is available. 100% of college-owned or -operated housing units are wired for high-speed Internet access. Wireless service is available via classrooms, computer centers, computer labs, learning centers, libraries, student centers.

Library: Oklahoma State University Institute of Technology Library. *Books:* 11,292 (physical), 152,731 (digital/electronic); *Serial titles:* 107 (physical), 98,630 (digital/electronic); *Databases:* 111. Weekly public service hours: 73; students can reserve study rooms.

STUDENT LIFE
Housing options: on-campus residence required for freshman year; coed, men-only, special housing for students with disabilities. Campus housing

is university owned. Freshman applicants given priority for college housing.

Activities and organizations: Phi Theta Kappa, Visual Communications Collective, Air Conditioning and Refrigeration Club, Future Chefs Association, Association of Information Technology Professionals.

Athletics ***Intramural sports:*** basketball M/W, football M/W, racquetball M/W, soccer M/W, softball M/W, table tennis M/W, volleyball M/W.

Campus security: 24-hour emergency response devices and patrols, late-night transport/escort service, controlled dormitory access.

Student services: health clinic, personal/psychological counseling, veterans affairs office.

COSTS & FINANCIAL AID

Costs (2019–20) ***Tuition:*** state resident $4350 full-time, $145 per credit hour part-time; nonresident $9960 full-time, $332 per credit hour part-time. Full-time tuition and fees vary according to class time, course level, course load, degree level, location, program, and student level. Part-time tuition and fees vary according to class time, course level, course load, degree level, location, program, and student level. ***Required fees:*** $1200 full-time, $40 per credit hour part-time. ***Room and board:*** $7016. Room and board charges vary according to board plan and housing facility. ***Payment plan:*** installment. ***Waivers:*** senior citizens and employees or children of employees.

Financial Aid Of all full-time matriculated undergraduates who enrolled in 2019, 1,201 applied for aid, 1,044 were judged to have need, 14 had their need fully met. In 2019, 19 non-need-based awards were made. ***Average percent of need met:*** 57. ***Average financial aid package:*** $11,363. ***Average need-based loan:*** $3585. ***Average need-based gift aid:*** $7385. ***Average non-need-based aid:*** $2091.

APPLYING

Standardized Tests *Required for some:* SAT or ACT (for admission). *Recommended:* ACT (for admission).

Options: deferred entrance.

Required: high school transcript.

Application deadlines: rolling (freshmen), rolling (out-of-state freshmen), rolling (transfers).

CONTACT

Kyle Gregorio, Assistant Registrar, Oklahoma State University Institute of Technology, 1801 E. 4th Street, Okmulgee, OK 74447. *Phone:* 918-293-5274. *Toll-free phone:* 800-722-4471. *Fax:* 918-293-4643. *E-mail:* kyleg@okstate.edu.

Oklahoma State University–Oklahoma City

Oklahoma City, Oklahoma

http://www.osuokc.edu/

CONTACT

Mr. Kyle Williams, Senior Director of Enrollment Management, Oklahoma State University–Oklahoma City, 900 North Portland Avenue, AD202, Oklahoma City, OK 73107. *Phone:* 405-945-9152. *Toll-free phone:* 800-560-4099. *E-mail:* wilkylw@osuokc.edu.

Oklahoma Wesleyan University

Bartlesville, Oklahoma

http://www.okwu.edu/

CONTACT

Samantha Peterson, Assistant Vice President of Enrollment, Oklahoma Wesleyan University, 2201 Silver Lake Road, Bartlesville, OK 74006. *Phone:* 866-222-8226. *Toll-free phone:* 866-222-8226. *Fax:* 918-335-6229. *E-mail:* admissions@okwu.edu.

Oral Roberts University

Tulsa, Oklahoma

http://www.oru.edu/

- **Independent interdenominational** comprehensive, founded 1963
- **Urban** 263-acre campus
- **Coed** 3,462 undergraduate students, 74% full-time, 59% women, 41% men
- **Moderately difficult** entrance level, 68% of applicants were admitted

UNDERGRAD STUDENTS

2,563 full-time, 897 part-time. 57% are from out of state; 15% Black or African American, non-Hispanic/Latino; 13% Hispanic/Latino; 2% Asian, non-Hispanic/Latino; 3% American Indian or Alaska Native, non-Hispanic/Latino; 5% Two or more races, non-Hispanic/Latino; 5% Race/ethnicity unknown; 14% international; 5% transferred in; 57% live on campus.

Freshmen:

Admission: 3,434 applied, 2,345 admitted, 555 enrolled. ***Average high school GPA:*** 3.6. ***Test scores:*** SAT evidence-based reading and writing scores over 500: 75%; SAT math scores over 500: 75%; ACT scores over 18: 84%; SAT evidence-based reading and writing scores over 600: 35%; SAT math scores over 600: 33%; ACT scores over 24: 30%; SAT evidence-based reading and writing scores over 700: 7%; SAT math scores over 700: 6%; ACT scores over 30: 8%.

Retention: 80% of full-time freshmen returned.

FACULTY

Total: 349, 44% full-time, 54% with terminal degrees.

Student/faculty ratio: 17:1.

ACADEMICS

Calendar: semesters. *Degrees:* certificates, diplomas, bachelor's, master's, and doctoral.

Special study options: adult/continuing education programs, part-time degree program. ***ROTC:*** Air Force (c).

Computers: Students can access the following: free student e-mail accounts, online (class) registration. Campuswide network is available.
Library: John D. Messick Resources Center.

STUDENT LIFE

Housing options: on-campus residence required through senior year; men-only, women-only, special housing for students with disabilities.

Athletics Member NCAA. All Division I. ***Intercollegiate sports:*** baseball M(s), basketball M(s)/W(s), cross-country running M(s)/W(s), golf M(s)/W(s), soccer M(s)/W(s), tennis M(s)/W(s), track and field M(s)/W(s), volleyball W(s), wrestling M. ***Intramural sports:*** badminton M/W, basketball M/W, bowling M/W, cross-country running M/W, football M/W, golf M/W, racquetball M/W, softball M/W, swimming and diving M/W, table tennis M/W, tennis M/W, volleyball M/W.

Campus security: 24-hour emergency response devices and patrols, late-night transport/escort service.

COSTS & FINANCIAL AID

Costs (2020–21) ***Comprehensive fee:*** $39,580 includes full-time tuition ($29,700), mandatory fees ($1230), and room and board ($8650). Part-time tuition: $1237 per credit hour. ***College room only:*** $4050.

Financial Aid Of all full-time matriculated undergraduates who enrolled in 2019, 1,982 applied for aid, 1,775 were judged to have need, 762 had their need fully met. 977 Federal Work-Study jobs (averaging $3000). 704 state and other part-time jobs (averaging $3000). In 2019, 686 non-need-based awards were made. ***Average percent of need met:*** 98. ***Average financial aid package:*** $30,260. ***Average need-based loan:*** $4377. ***Average need-based gift aid:*** $24,869. ***Average non-need-based aid:*** $16,351. ***Average indebtedness upon graduation:*** $35,230.

APPLYING

Standardized Tests *Required:* SAT or ACT (for admission).

Options: deferred entrance.

Application fee: $35.

Required: essay or personal statement, high school transcript, minimum 2.0 GPA, 1 letter of recommendation, proof of immunization. ***Required for some:*** interview. ***Recommended:*** interview.

Notification: continuous until 8/15 (freshmen).

CONTACT
Director of Enrollment, Oral Roberts University, 7777 South Lewis Avenue, Tulsa, OK 74171. *Phone:* 918-495-6529. *Toll-free phone:* 800-678-8876. *Fax:* 918-495-6222. *E-mail:* admissions@oru.edu.

Randall University
Moore, Oklahoma
http://www.ru.edu/

CONTACT
Randall University, PO Box 7208, Moore, OK 73160. *Phone:* 405-912-9007. *Fax:* 405-912-9050. *E-mail:* recruitment@hc.edu.

Rogers State University
Claremore, Oklahoma
http://www.rsu.edu/

- **State-supported** comprehensive, founded 1909, part of Oklahoma State Regents for Higher Education
- **Small-town** 40-acre campus with easy access to Tulsa
- **Endowment** $15.9 million
- **Coed** 3,584 undergraduate students, 64% full-time, 62% women, 38% men
- **Noncompetitive** entrance level, 89% of applicants were admitted

UNDERGRAD STUDENTS
2,281 full-time, 1,303 part-time. Students come from 24 states and territories; 12 other countries; 4% are from out of state; 4% Black or African American, non-Hispanic/Latino; 7% Hispanic/Latino; 3% Asian, non-Hispanic/Latino; 0.2% Native Hawaiian or other Pacific Islander, non-Hispanic/Latino; 13% American Indian or Alaska Native, non-Hispanic/Latino; 16% Two or more races, non-Hispanic/Latino; 1% Race/ethnicity unknown; 9% transferred in; 22% live on campus.

Freshmen:
Admission: 1,263 applied, 1,127 admitted, 503 enrolled. ***Average high school GPA:*** 3.3. ***Test scores:*** ACT scores over 18: 66%; ACT scores over 24: 17%; ACT scores over 30: 1%.

Retention: 62% of full-time freshmen returned.

FACULTY
Total: 228, 43% full-time, 43% with terminal degrees.

Student/faculty ratio: 19:1.

ACADEMICS
Calendar: semesters. *Degrees:* certificates, associate, bachelor's, and master's.

Special study options: academic remediation for entering students, adult/continuing education programs, advanced placement credit, cooperative education, distance learning, double majors, honors programs, independent study, internships, off-campus study, part-time degree program, services for LD students, study abroad, summer session for credit. ***ROTC:*** Air Force (c).

Computers: 251 computers/terminals are available on campus for general student use. Students can access the following: computer help desk, free student e-mail accounts, online (class) grades, online (class) registration, online (class) schedules, software to support courses. Campuswide network is available. 100% of college-owned or -operated housing units are wired for high-speed Internet access. Wireless service is available via entire campus.

Library: Stratton Taylor Library. *Books:* 80,238 (physical), 298,063 (digital/electronic); *Serial titles:* 491 (physical), 67,126 (digital/electronic); *Databases:* 81. Weekly public service hours: 86; students can reserve study rooms.

STUDENT LIFE
Housing options: coed. Campus housing is university owned.

Activities and organizations: drama/theater group, student-run radio station, Student Government Association, Student Nurses Association, President's Leadership Class, Pre-Professional Health Club (Pre-SOMA), Student Athlete Advisory Committee, national sororities.

Athletics Member NCAA. All Division II. ***Intercollegiate sports:*** baseball M(s), basketball M(s)/W(s), cheerleading M(s)/W(s), cross-country running M(s)/W(s), golf M(s)/W(s), soccer M(s)/W(s), softball W(s), track and field M(s)/W(s). ***Intramural sports:*** basketball M/W, soccer M/W, softball M/W, volleyball M/W.

Campus security: 24-hour patrols, student patrols, late-night transport/escort service, controlled dormitory access, state-certified law enforcement officers, comprehensive camera surveillance system.

Student services: health clinic, personal/psychological counseling, veterans affairs office.

COSTS & FINANCIAL AID
Costs (2019–20) ***Tuition:*** state resident $4560 full-time; nonresident $12,900 full-time. ***Required fees:*** $2910 full-time. ***Room and board:*** $8975; room only: $5490. Room and board charges vary according to housing facility. ***Payment plan:*** installment. ***Waivers:*** senior citizens and employees or children of employees.

Financial Aid Of all full-time matriculated undergraduates who enrolled in 2018, 1,864 applied for aid, 1,624 were judged to have need, 112 had their need fully met. 95 Federal Work-Study jobs (averaging $2140). In 2018, 76 non-need-based awards were made. ***Average percent of need met:*** 45. ***Average financial aid package:*** $9350. ***Average need-based loan:*** $3360. ***Average need-based gift aid:*** $7702. ***Average non-need-based aid:*** $6820. ***Average indebtedness upon graduation:*** $13,052.

APPLYING
Standardized Tests *Required:* SAT or ACT (for admission). *Recommended:* ACT (for admission).

Options: electronic application.

Application fee: $20.

Required: high school transcript. ***Required for some:*** minimum 2.7 GPA, minimum ACT composite of 20 or 2.70, GPA and top 50% rank for baccalaureate programs.

Application deadlines: rolling (freshmen), rolling (transfers).

CONTACT
Ms. Joy Lin Hall, Director of Admissions, Rogers State University, 1701 West Will Rogers Boulevard, Claremore, OK 74017. *Phone:* 918-343-7546. *Toll-free phone:* 800-256-7511. *Fax:* 918-343-7595. *E-mail:* admissions@rsu.edu.

Southeastern Oklahoma State University
Durant, Oklahoma
http://www.se.edu/

- **State-supported** comprehensive, founded 1909, part of Oklahoma State Regents for Higher Education
- **Small-town** 276-acre campus
- **Endowment** $23.2 million
- **Coed**
- **Moderately difficult** entrance level

FACULTY
Student/faculty ratio: 18:1.

ACADEMICS
Calendar: semesters. *Degrees:* bachelor's, master's, and post-master's certificates.

Library: Henry G. Bennett Memorial Library plus 1 other. *Books:* 192,351 (physical), 17,845 (digital/electronic); *Serial titles:* 83 (physical), 2,534 (digital/electronic); *Databases:* 108. Weekly public service hours: 79; students can reserve study rooms.

STUDENT LIFE
Housing options: on-campus residence required for freshman year; coed, men-only, women-only, special housing for students with disabilities. Campus housing is university owned. Freshman campus housing is guaranteed.

Activities and organizations: drama/theater group, student-run newspaper, radio station, choral group, marching band, Baptist Collegiate Ministries, Greek Community, Student Government Association, Kappa Kappa Psi, Psychology Club, national fraternities, national sororities.

Athletics Member NCAA. All Division II.

Campus security: 24-hour emergency response devices and patrols, late-night transport/escort service, controlled dormitory access.

Student services: health clinic, personal/psychological counseling.

FINANCIAL AID

Financial Aid Of all full-time matriculated undergraduates who enrolled in 2017, 1,746 applied for aid, 1,577 were judged to have need, 52 had their need fully met. In 2017, 28 non-need-based awards were made. ***Average percent of need met:*** 64. ***Average financial aid package:*** $8802. ***Average need-based loan:*** $2035. ***Average need-based gift aid:*** $2092. ***Average non-need-based aid:*** $835. ***Average indebtedness upon graduation:*** $17,432.

APPLYING

Standardized Tests *Required:* SAT or ACT (for admission).

Options: electronic application.

Application fee: $20.

Required: high school transcript. ***Required for some:*** interview.

CONTACT

Southeastern Oklahoma State University, 1405 North 4th Avenue, Durant, OK 74701-0609. *Toll-free phone:* 800-435-1327.

Southern Nazarene University

Bethany, Oklahoma

http://www.snu.edu/

CONTACT

Dr. Linda Cantwell, Director of Recruitment, Southern Nazarene University, 6729 Northwest 39th Expressway, Bethany, OK 73008. *Phone:* 405-491-6324. *Toll-free phone:* 800-648-9899. *Fax:* 405-491-6320. *E-mail:* admiss@snu.edu.

Southwestern Christian University

Bethany, Oklahoma

http://www.swcu.edu/

CONTACT

Ms. Jessie Burpo, Admissions Counselor, Southwestern Christian University, PO Box 340, Bethany, OK 73008-0340. *Phone:* 405-789-7661 Ext. 3432. *Fax:* 405-495-0078. *E-mail:* admissions@swcu.edu.

Southwestern Oklahoma State University

Weatherford, Oklahoma

http://www.swosu.edu/

- **State-supported** comprehensive, founded 1901
- **Small-town** 73-acre campus with easy access to Oklahoma City
- **Endowment** $22.3 million
- **Coed** 4,092 undergraduate students, 79% full-time, 61% women, 39% men
- **Minimally difficult** entrance level, 91% of applicants were admitted

UNDERGRAD STUDENTS

3,233 full-time, 859 part-time. 8% are from out of state; 4% Black or African American, non-Hispanic/Latino; 12% Hispanic/Latino; 2% Asian, non-Hispanic/Latino; 0.1% Native Hawaiian or other Pacific Islander, non-Hispanic/Latino; 4% American Indian or Alaska Native, non-Hispanic/Latino; 9% Two or more races, non-Hispanic/Latino; 3% Race/ethnicity unknown; 4% international; 9% transferred in; 26% live on campus.

Freshmen:

Admission: 2,220 applied, 2,012 admitted, 855 enrolled. ***Average high school GPA:*** 3.5. ***Test scores:*** ACT scores over 18: 77%; ACT scores over 24: 29%; ACT scores over 30: 6%.

Retention: 61% of full-time freshmen returned.

FACULTY

Total: 295, 68% full-time, 51% with terminal degrees.

Student/faculty ratio: 18:1.

ACADEMICS

Calendar: semesters. *Degrees:* associate, bachelor's, master's, doctoral, and post-master's certificates.

Special study options: academic remediation for entering students, accelerated degree program, adult/continuing education programs, advanced placement credit, distance learning, double majors, external degree program, freshman honors college, honors programs, independent study, internships, part-time degree program, student-designed majors, study abroad, summer session for credit.

Computers: 250 computers/terminals are available on campus for general student use. Students can access the following: computer help desk, free student e-mail accounts, online (class) grades, online (class) registration, online (class) schedules. Campuswide network is available. 100% of college-owned or -operated housing units are wired for high-speed Internet access. Wireless service is available via entire campus.

Library: Al Harris Library plus 1 other. *Books:* 303,978 (physical), 364,203 (digital/electronic); *Serial titles:* 128 (physical), 47,086 (digital/electronic); *Databases:* 99. Weekly public service hours: 84; students can reserve study rooms.

STUDENT LIFE

Housing options: coed, men-only, women-only. Campus housing is university owned.

Activities and organizations: drama/theater group, student-run newspaper, choral group, marching band, Collegiate Activities Board, Southwestern International Student Association, Saudi Arabian Student Organization, SWOSU Computer Club, Kappa Epsilon and Sigma Sigma Chi, national fraternities, national sororities.

Athletics Member NCAA. All Division II. ***Intercollegiate sports:*** baseball M(s), basketball M(s)/W(s), cheerleading M(s)/W(s), cross-country running W(s), equestrian sports M(s)/W(s), football M(s), golf M(s)/W(s), soccer W(s), softball W(s), track and field W, volleyball W(s). ***Intramural sports:*** basketball M/W, football M, soccer M/W, softball M/W, volleyball M/W.

Campus security: late-night transport/escort service, police available 24 hours a day.

Student services: health clinic, personal/psychological counseling, legal services, veterans affairs office.

COSTS & FINANCIAL AID

Costs (2020–21) ***Tuition:*** area resident $6150 full-time, $205 per credit hour part-time; state resident $6150 full-time, $205 per credit hour part-time; nonresident $13,050 full-time, $435 per credit hour part-time. ***Required fees:*** $1545 full-time. ***Room and board:*** $6030; room only: $2700.

Financial Aid Of all full-time matriculated undergraduates who enrolled in 2019, 1,818 applied for aid, 1,586 were judged to have need, 352 had their need fully met. In 2019, 301 non-need-based awards were made. ***Average percent of need met:*** 77. ***Average financial aid package:*** $6292. ***Average need-based loan:*** $2093. ***Average need-based gift aid:*** $2353. ***Average non-need-based aid:*** $1243. ***Average indebtedness upon graduation:*** $23,292. ***Financial aid deadline:*** 3/1.

APPLYING

Standardized Tests *Required:* SAT or ACT (for admission). *Recommended:* ACT (for admission).

Options: electronic application, deferred entrance.

Required: high school transcript. ***Required for some:*** minimum 2.7 GPA, minimum ACT score of 20 (940 SAT) or rank in the upper 50% of high school graduating class or have a high school GPA of 2.7 in the 15-unit core curriculum.

Application deadlines: rolling (freshmen), rolling (out-of-state freshmen), rolling (transfers).

Notification: continuous (freshmen), continuous (out-of-state freshmen), continuous (transfers).

CONTACT

Ms. Cassie Jones, Admissions Coordinator, Southwestern Oklahoma State University, John Hays Administration Building, Room 108-C, Weatherford, OK 73096. *Phone:* 580-774-3009. *Fax:* 580-774-3795. *E-mail:* cassie.jones@swosu.edu.

Spartan College of Aeronautics and Technology

Tulsa, Oklahoma

http://www.spartan.edu/

CONTACT
Mr. Mark Fowler, Vice President of Student Records and Finance, Spartan College of Aeronautics and Technology, 8820 East Pine Street, Tulsa, OK 74115. *Phone:* 918-836-6886. *Toll-free phone:* 800-331-1204.

University of Central Oklahoma

Edmond, Oklahoma

http://www.uco.edu/

CONTACT
Mr. John Stephens, Director of Undergraduate Admissions, University of Central Oklahoma, Office of Undergraduate Admissions, 100 North University Drive, Box 151, Edmond, OK 73034-5209. *Phone:* 405-974-2727. *Fax:* 405-974-3841. *E-mail:* onestop@uco.edu.

University of Oklahoma

Norman, Oklahoma

http://www.ou.edu/

- **State-supported** university, founded 1890
- **Suburban** 3955-acre campus with easy access to Oklahoma City
- **Endowment** $1.1 billion
- **Coed**
- **Moderately difficult** entrance level

FACULTY
Student/faculty ratio: 18:1.

ACADEMICS
Calendar: semesters. *Degrees:* certificates, bachelor's, master's, doctoral, and postbachelor's certificates.
Library: Bizzell Memorial Library plus 5 others. *Books:* 4.4 million (physical), 1.4 million (digital/electronic); *Serial titles:* 71,289 (physical), 128,934 (digital/electronic); *Databases:* 311. Weekly public service hours: 114; students can reserve study rooms.

STUDENT LIFE
Housing options: on-campus residence required for freshman year; coed, men-only, women-only, special housing for students with disabilities. Campus housing is university owned. Freshman campus housing is guaranteed.

Activities and organizations: drama/theater group, student-run newspaper, radio and television station, choral group, marching band, Campus Activities Council Soonerthon, Campus Activities Council Homecoming, Engineers Club, Relay For Life, The Big Event, national fraternities, national sororities.

Athletics Member NCAA. All Division I except football (Division I-A).

Campus security: 24-hour emergency response devices and patrols, late-night transport/escort service, controlled dormitory access, crime prevention programs, police bicycle patrols, self-defense classes, emergency notification system, lighted pathways/sidewalks.

Student services: health clinic, personal/psychological counseling, women's center, legal services, veterans affairs office.

COSTS & FINANCIAL AID
Costs (2019–20) ***Tuition:*** state resident $4788 full-time, $160 per credit hour part-time; nonresident $20,169 full-time, $672 per credit hour part-time. Full-time tuition and fees vary according to course load, degree level, location, and program. Part-time tuition and fees vary according to course load, degree level, location, and program. No tuition increase for student's term of enrollment. ***Required fees:*** $4275 full-time, $134 per credit hour part-time, $127 per term part-time. ***Room and board:*** $10,994; room only: $6378. Room and board charges vary according to board plan and housing facility.

Financial Aid Of all full-time matriculated undergraduates who enrolled in 2018, 11,880 applied for aid, 9,085 were judged to have need, 7,533 had their need fully met. 741 Federal Work-Study jobs (averaging $3726). 114 state and other part-time jobs (averaging $11,083). In 2018, 2004 non-need-based awards were made. ***Average percent of need met:*** 85. ***Average financial aid package:*** $14,330. ***Average need-based loan:*** $4237. ***Average need-based gift aid:*** $6491. ***Average non-need-based aid:*** $2366. ***Average indebtedness upon graduation:*** $30,258.

APPLYING
Standardized Tests *Required:* SAT or ACT (for admission).

Options: electronic application.

Application fee: $40.

Required: essay or personal statement, high school transcript, 15 specified curricular units.

CONTACT
Mr. Jeff Blahnik, Director of Admissions, University of Oklahoma, 1000 Asp Avenue, Room 127, Norman, OK 73019-3032. *Phone:* 405-325-2151. *Toll-free phone:* 800-234-6868. *Fax:* 405-325-7478. *E-mail:* admissions@ou.edu.

University of Science and Arts of Oklahoma

Chickasha, Oklahoma

http://www.usao.edu/

- **State-supported** 4-year, founded 1908, part of Oklahoma State Regents for Higher Education
- **Small-town** 75-acre campus with easy access to Oklahoma City
- **Endowment** $12.8 million
- **Coed** 800 undergraduate students
- **Moderately difficult** entrance level

UNDERGRAD STUDENTS
Students come from 16 states and territories; 22 other countries; 9% are from out of state; 10% Black or African American, non-Hispanic/Latino; 12% Hispanic/Latino; 2% Asian, non-Hispanic/Latino; 0.4% Native Hawaiian or other Pacific Islander, non-Hispanic/Latino; 17% American Indian or Alaska Native, non-Hispanic/Latino; 2% Race/ethnicity unknown; 9% international.

Freshmen:
Average high school GPA: 3.5. ***Test scores:*** ACT scores over 18: 81%; ACT scores over 24: 23%; ACT scores over 30: 4%.
Retention: 52% of full-time freshmen returned.

FACULTY
Total: 50, 100% full-time.
Student/faculty ratio: 12:1.

ACADEMICS
Calendar: trimesters. *Degree:* bachelor's.

Special study options: academic remediation for entering students, accelerated degree program, advanced placement credit, double majors, independent study, internships, off-campus study, part-time degree program, services for LD students, student-designed majors, summer session for credit.

Computers: 185 computers/terminals are available on campus for general student use. Students can access the following: computer help desk, free student e-mail accounts, online (class) schedules. Campuswide network is available. 100% of college-owned or -operated housing units are wired for high-speed Internet access. Wireless service is available via entire campus.
Library: Nash Library plus 1 other. *Books:* 87,603 (physical), 4,798 (digital/electronic); *Serial titles:* 22 (physical), 10,500 (digital/electronic); *Databases:* 60. Weekly public service hours: 81.

STUDENT LIFE
Housing options: on-campus residence required for freshman year; coed. Campus housing is university owned. Freshman campus housing is guaranteed.

Activities and organizations: drama/theater group, student-run newspaper, television station, choral group, Student Activities Board, Volunteer Action Council, Psychology Club, Young Democrats, Young Conservatives, national fraternities.

Athletics Member NAIA. ***Intercollegiate sports:*** baseball M(s), basketball M(s)/W(s), cheerleading M(s)/W(s), cross-country running

M/W, soccer M(s)/W(s), softball W(s), volleyball W. ***Intramural sports:*** basketball M/W, football M/W, golf M/W, softball M/W, volleyball M/W.

Campus security: 24-hour emergency response devices and patrols, controlled dormitory access.

Student services: health clinic, personal/psychological counseling.

FINANCIAL AID

Financial Aid Of all full-time matriculated undergraduates who enrolled in 2019, 569 applied for aid, 493 were judged to have need, 69 had their need fully met. 130 Federal Work-Study jobs (averaging $1412). In 2019, 133 non-need-based awards were made. ***Average percent of need met:*** 67. ***Average financial aid package:*** $13,415. ***Average need-based loan:*** $3187. ***Average need-based gift aid:*** $11,403. ***Average non-need-based aid:*** $4245. ***Average indebtedness upon graduation:*** $23,410.

APPLYING

Standardized Tests *Required:* SAT or ACT (for admission). *Recommended:* SAT (for admission).

Options: electronic application, deferred entrance.

Application fee: $40.

Required for some: high school transcript, minimum 3.0 GPA, minimum ACT score of 24 and 3.0 GPA/top 50% high school class, 3.0 GPA and top 25% high school class, or minimum ACT score of 22 and 3.0 GPA in 15-unit high school core. ***Recommended:*** minimum ACT score of 24 and 3.0 GPA/top 50% high school class, 3.0 GPA and top 25% high school class, or minimum ACT score of 22 and 3.0 GPA in 15-unit high school core.

Application deadlines: 9/2 (freshmen), rolling (out-of-state freshmen), 9/2 (transfers).

Notification: continuous until 1/2 (freshmen), continuous until 1/2 (out-of-state freshmen), continuous (transfers).

CONTACT

Mrs. Laura Coponiti, Dean of Admissions and Financial Aid, University of Science and Arts of Oklahoma, 1727 West Alabama, Chickasha, OK 73018-5322. *Phone:* 405-574-1350. *Toll-free phone:* 800-933-8726. *Fax:* 405-574-1220. *E-mail:* usao-admissions@usao.edu.

The University of Tulsa

Tulsa, Oklahoma

http://www.utulsa.edu/

- **Independent** university, founded 1894, affiliated with Presbyterian Church (U.S.A.)
- **Urban** 209-acre campus with easy access to Tulsa
- **Coed** 3,276 undergraduate students, 97% full-time, 46% women, 54% men
- **Very difficult** entrance level, 36% of applicants were admitted

UNDERGRAD STUDENTS

3,172 full-time, 104 part-time. Students come from 48 states and territories; 65 other countries; 37% are from out of state; 7% Black or African American, non-Hispanic/Latino; 9% Hispanic/Latino; 6% Asian, non-Hispanic/Latino; 0.1% Native Hawaiian or other Pacific Islander, non-Hispanic/Latino; 3% American Indian or Alaska Native, non-Hispanic/Latino; 8% Two or more races, non-Hispanic/Latino; 1% Race/ethnicity unknown; 12% international; 2% transferred in; 72% live on campus.

Freshmen:

Admission: 9,793 applied, 3,510 admitted, 831 enrolled. ***Average high school GPA:*** 4.0. ***Test scores:*** SAT evidence-based reading and writing scores over 500: 91%; SAT math scores over 500: 89%; ACT scores over 18: 99%; SAT evidence-based reading and writing scores over 600: 61%; SAT math scores over 600: 55%; ACT scores over 24: 76%; SAT evidence-based reading and writing scores over 700: 19%; SAT math scores over 700: 22%; ACT scores over 30: 35%.

Retention: 87% of full-time freshmen returned.

FACULTY

Total: 447, 76% full-time, 77% with terminal degrees.

Student/faculty ratio: 11:1.

ACADEMICS

Calendar: semesters. *Degrees:* bachelor's, master's, doctoral, and postbachelor's certificates.

Special study options: accelerated degree program, adult/continuing education programs, advanced placement credit, double majors, English as a second language, honors programs, independent study, internships, part-time degree program, services for LD students, student-designed majors, study abroad, summer session for credit. ***ROTC:*** Air Force (c).

Unusual degree programs: 3-2 business administration; engineering; accountancy, mathematics, athletic training, biochemistry, biology, chemistry, computer science, cyber security, geosciences, geophysics, history, physics, women's and gender studies.

Computers: 710 computers/terminals and 250 ports are available on campus for general student use. Students can access the following: campus intranet, computer help desk, free student e-mail accounts, online (class) grades, online (class) registration, online (class) schedules. Campuswide network is available. 100% of college-owned or -operated housing units are wired for high-speed Internet access. Wireless service is available via entire campus.

Library: McFarlin Library plus 1 other. *Books:* 761,545 (physical), 538,954 (digital/electronic); *Serial titles:* 5,249 (physical), 71,240 (digital/electronic); *Databases:* 226. Weekly public service hours: 89; study areas open 24 hours, 5–7 days a week; students can reserve study rooms.

STUDENT LIFE

Housing options: on-campus residence required through sophomore year; coed, men-only, women-only, special housing for students with disabilities. Campus housing is university owned. Freshman campus housing is guaranteed.

Activities and organizations: drama/theater group, student-run newspaper, radio and television station, choral group, marching band, Student Association, Residence Hall Association, Pre-Professional organizations, intramural sports, Greek life, national fraternities, national sororities.

Athletics Member NCAA. All Division I except football (Division I-A). ***Intercollegiate sports:*** basketball M(s)/W(s), cheerleading M/W, crew W(s), cross-country running M(s)/W(s), golf W(s)(c), soccer M(s)/W(s), softball W(s), tennis M(s)/W(s), track and field M(s)/W(s), volleyball W(s). ***Intramural sports:*** badminton M/W, basketball M/W, bowling M/W, crew M(c), cross-country running M/W, football M/W, golf W, lacrosse M(c), racquetball M/W, rugby M(c), soccer M/W, softball M/W, squash M/W, table tennis M/W, tennis M/W, track and field M/W, volleyball M/W, weight lifting M/W.

Campus security: 24-hour emergency response devices and patrols, late-night transport/escort service, controlled dormitory access.

Student services: health clinic, personal/psychological counseling, legal services, veterans affairs office.

COSTS & FINANCIAL AID

Costs (2020–21) ***One-time required fee:*** $485. ***Comprehensive fee:*** $55,562 includes full-time tuition ($42,950), mandatory fees ($550), and room and board ($12,062). Full-time tuition and fees vary according to course load and program. Part-time tuition: $1542 per credit hour. Part-time tuition and fees vary according to program. ***College room only:*** $6976. Room and board charges vary according to board plan and housing facility. ***Waivers:*** employees or children of employees.

Financial Aid Of all full-time matriculated undergraduates who enrolled in 2018, 1,848 applied for aid, 1,596 were judged to have need, 566 had their need fully met. 500 Federal Work-Study jobs (averaging $2523). In 2018, 939 non-need-based awards were made. ***Average percent of need met:*** 69. ***Average financial aid package:*** $30,423. ***Average need-based loan:*** $4217. ***Average need-based gift aid:*** $28,067. ***Average non-need-based aid:*** $10,689. ***Average indebtedness upon graduation:*** $35,985.

APPLYING

Standardized Tests *Required:* SAT or ACT (for admission).

Options: electronic application, early admission, early action, deferred entrance.

Application fee: $50.

Required: essay or personal statement, high school transcript. *Recommended:* interview.

Application deadlines: rolling (freshmen), rolling (transfers).

Notification: continuous (freshmen), continuous (transfers).

CONTACT

Ms. Patricia DeBolt, Dean of Admission, The University of Tulsa, 800 South Tucker Drive, Tulsa, OK 74104. *Phone:* 918-631-2308. *Toll-free phone:* 800-331-3050. *Fax:* 918-631-5003. *E-mail:* admission@utulsa.edu.

See below for display ad and page 1132 for the College Close-Up.

OREGON

American College of Healthcare Sciences

Portland, Oregon

http://www.achs.edu/

CONTACT

American College of Healthcare Sciences, 5005 SW Macadam Avenue, Portland, OR 97239-3719. *Toll-free phone:* 800-487-8839.

Birthingway College of Midwifery

Portland, Oregon

http://www.birthingway.edu/

CONTACT

Director of Admission, Birthingway College of Midwifery, 12113 SE Foster Road, Portland, OR 97299. *Phone:* 503-760-3131. *E-mail:* info@birthingway.edu.

Corban University

Salem, Oregon

http://www.corban.edu/

CONTACT

Jordan Lindsey, Associate Director of Admissions, Corban University, 5000 Deer Park Drive, SE, Salem, OR 97301-9392. *Phone:* 503-375-7156. *Toll-free phone:* 800-845-3005. *Fax:* 503-585-4316. *E-mail:* admissions@corban.edu.

Eastern Oregon University

La Grande, Oregon

http://www.eou.edu/

- **State-supported** comprehensive, founded 1929
- **Rural** 121-acre campus
- **Endowment** $11.3 million
- **Coed** 2,867 undergraduate students, 57% full-time, 60% women, 40% men
- **Minimally difficult** entrance level, 98% of applicants were admitted

UNDERGRAD STUDENTS

1,639 full-time, 1,228 part-time. 34% are from out of state; 2% Black or African American, non-Hispanic/Latino; 12% Hispanic/Latino; 2% Asian, non-Hispanic/Latino; 4% Native Hawaiian or other Pacific Islander, non-Hispanic/Latino; 2% American Indian or Alaska Native, non-Hispanic/Latino; 6% Two or more races, non-Hispanic/Latino; 2% Race/ethnicity unknown; 2% international; 14% transferred in; 6% live on campus.

Freshmen:

Admission: 890 applied, 872 admitted, 330 enrolled. ***Average high school GPA:*** 3.4. ***Test scores:*** SAT evidence-based reading and writing scores over 500: 62%; SAT math scores over 500: 58%; ACT scores over 18: 72%; SAT evidence-based reading and writing scores over 600: 23%; SAT math scores over 600: 11%; ACT scores over 24: 23%; SAT math scores over 700: 1%; ACT scores over 30: 3%.

Retention: 72% of full-time freshmen returned.

FACULTY

Total: 182, 56% full-time, 59% with terminal degrees.

Student/faculty ratio: 17:1.

ACADEMICS
Calendar: quarters. *Degrees:* certificates, associate, bachelor's, master's, and postbachelor's certificates.

Special study options: academic remediation for entering students, adult/continuing education programs, advanced placement credit, cooperative education, distance learning, double majors, external degree program, honors programs, independent study, internships, off-campus study, part-time degree program, services for LD students, student-designed majors, study abroad, summer session for credit. ***ROTC:*** Army (b).

Computers: Students can access the following: free student e-mail accounts, online (class) grades, online (class) registration, online (class) schedules. Campuswide network is available. 100% of college-owned or -operated housing units are wired for high-speed Internet access. Wireless service is available via entire campus.
Library: Pierce Library. *Books:* 356,951 (physical), 66,379 (digital/electronic); *Serial titles:* 392 (physical), 145 (digital/electronic); *Databases:* 139. Weekly public service hours: 90; students can reserve study rooms.

STUDENT LIFE
Housing options: on-campus residence required for freshman year; coed, special housing for students with disabilities. Campus housing is university owned. Freshman applicants given priority for college housing.

Activities and organizations: drama/theater group, student-run newspaper, radio station, choral group, Outdoor Program, Pre-Professional Health Club, Student Government, International Student Association, Chemistry Club.

Athletics Member NAIA. ***Intercollegiate sports:*** basketball M(s)/W(s), cross-country running M(s)/W(s), football M(s), soccer M(s)/W(s), softball W(s), track and field M(s)/W(s), volleyball W(s), wrestling M(s)/W(s). ***Intramural sports:*** basketball M/W, football M, rock climbing M(c)/W(c), soccer M/W, softball M/W, volleyball M/W.

Campus security: 24-hour emergency response devices, late-night transport/escort service, controlled dormitory access.

Student services: health clinic, personal/psychological counseling, women's center.

FINANCIAL AID
Financial Aid Of all full-time matriculated undergraduates who enrolled in 2018, 1,544 applied for aid, 1,396 were judged to have need, 177 had their need fully met. 165 Federal Work-Study jobs (averaging $2138). In 2018, 165 non-need-based awards were made. ***Average percent of need met:*** 57. ***Average financial aid package:*** $10,357. ***Average need-based loan:*** $4170. ***Average need-based gift aid:*** $8368. ***Average non-need-based aid:*** $2390. ***Average indebtedness upon graduation:*** $25,756.

APPLYING
Standardized Tests *Required:* SAT or ACT (for admission). *Required for some:* SAT and SAT Subject Tests or ACT (for admission).

Options: electronic application, early action, deferred entrance.

Application fee: $50.

Required: high school transcript, minimum 2.8 GPA. ***Required for some:*** essay or personal statement, 2 letters of recommendation.

Application deadlines: 9/1 (freshmen), 9/1 (transfers), 2/1 (early action).

Notification: continuous (freshmen), continuous (transfers), rolling (early action).

CONTACT
Eastern Oregon University, 1 University Boulevard, La Grande, OR 97850-2899. *Phone:* 541-962-3496. *Toll-free phone:* 800-452-8639.

George Fox University

Newberg, Oregon

http://www.georgefox.edu/

- **Independent Friends** university, founded 1891
- **Small-town** 108-acre campus with easy access to Portland
- **Coed** 2,569 undergraduate students, 91% full-time, 56% women, 44% men
- **Moderately difficult** entrance level, 78% of applicants were admitted

UNDERGRAD STUDENTS
2,348 full-time, 221 part-time. 49% are from out of state; 1% transferred in; 55% live on campus.

Freshmen:
Admission: 2,980 applied, 2,334 admitted, 634 enrolled. ***Average high school GPA:*** 3.6.

Retention: 80% of full-time freshmen returned.

ACADEMICS
Calendar: semesters. *Degrees:* bachelor's, master's, doctoral, post-master's, and postbachelor's certificates.

Special study options: academic remediation for entering students, accelerated degree program, adult/continuing education programs, advanced placement credit, distance learning, double majors, English as a second language, honors programs, independent study, internships, off-campus study, part-time degree program, services for LD students, student-designed majors, study abroad, summer session for credit. ***ROTC:*** Air Force (c).

Computers: Students can access the following: campus intranet, computer help desk, free student e-mail accounts, online (class) grades, online (class) registration, online (class) schedules, online acceptance of financial aid. Campuswide network is available. 100% of college-owned or -operated housing units are wired for high-speed Internet access. Wireless service is available via classrooms, computer centers, computer labs, dorm rooms, learning centers, libraries, student centers.
Library: Murdock Learning Resource Center plus 1 other. Weekly public service hours: 93; study areas open 24 hours, 5–7 days a week; students can reserve study rooms.

STUDENT LIFE
Housing options: on-campus residence required through junior year; men-only, women-only, cooperative, special housing for students with disabilities. Campus housing is university owned. Freshman applicants given priority for college housing.

Activities and organizations: drama/theater group, student-run newspaper, radio station, choral group, Student Government, Christian Ministries, Orientation Committee, Outdoor Club and Bruin Ambassadors, Blue Zone.

Athletics ***Intercollegiate sports:*** baseball M, basketball M/W, cross-country running M/W, football M, golf M/W, lacrosse W, soccer M/W, softball W, tennis M/W, track and field M/W, volleyball W. ***Intramural sports:*** badminton M/W, basketball M/W, football M/W, golf M/W, racquetball M/W, rock climbing M/W, soccer M/W, table tennis M/W, tennis M/W, ultimate Frisbee M/W, volleyball M/W.

Campus security: 24-hour emergency response devices and patrols, student patrols, late-night transport/escort service, controlled dormitory access, parking lot cameras, video surveillance of key buildings.

Student services: health clinic, personal/psychological counseling.

COSTS & FINANCIAL AID
Costs (2019–20) ***Comprehensive fee:*** $48,780 includes full-time tuition ($36,750), mandatory fees ($380), and room and board ($11,650). Full-time tuition and fees vary according to reciprocity agreements. Part-time tuition and fees vary according to course load. ***Room and board:*** Room and board charges vary according to board plan. ***Payment plan:*** installment. ***Waivers:*** senior citizens and employees or children of employees.

Financial Aid Of all full-time matriculated undergraduates who enrolled in 2019, 2,033 applied for aid, 1,767 were judged to have need, 733 had their need fully met. 1,255 Federal Work-Study jobs (averaging $2267). In 2019, 595 non-need-based awards were made. ***Average percent of need met:*** 87. ***Average financial aid package:*** $24,325. ***Average need-based loan:*** $4022. ***Average need-based gift aid:*** $20,962. ***Average non-need-based aid:*** $15,013. ***Average indebtedness upon graduation:*** $31,299.

APPLYING
Standardized Tests *Required:* SAT or ACT (for admission).

Options: electronic application, early action, deferred entrance.

Application fee: $40.

Required: essay or personal statement, 1 letter of recommendation. ***Required for some:*** high school transcript. ***Recommended:*** high school transcript.

Application deadlines: rolling (freshmen), 6/1 (transfers), 11/15 (early action).

Notification: continuous until 10/1 (freshmen), continuous (transfers), 12/15 (early action).

CONTACT
Ms. Lindsay Knox, Director of Undergraduate Admissions, George Fox University, 414 North Meridian Street, Newberg, OR 97132. *Phone:* 503-554-2240. *Toll-free phone:* 800-765-4369. *Fax:* 503-554-3110. *E-mail:* admissions@georgefox.edu.

Gutenberg College

Eugene, Oregon

http://www.gutenberg.edu/

- **Independent Christian** 4-year
- **Urban** campus
- **Coed** 14 undergraduate students, 100% full-time, 64% women, 64% men
- **Moderately difficult** entrance level, 100% of applicants were admitted

UNDERGRAD STUDENTS
14 full-time. Students come from 6 states and territories; 2 other countries; 6% are from out of state; 82% live on campus.

Freshmen:
Admission: 10 applied, 10 admitted, 9 enrolled.
Retention: 75% of full-time freshmen returned.

FACULTY
Total: 6, 83% full-time, 67% with terminal degrees.
Student/faculty ratio: 2:1.

ACADEMICS
Degree: bachelor's.

Special study options: study abroad.

Computers: 1 computer/terminal is available on campus for general student use. Students can access the following: free student e-mail accounts. Campuswide network is available. Wireless service is available via entire campus.

STUDENT LIFE
Housing options: coed. Campus housing is university owned. Freshman applicants given priority for college housing.

Student services: personal/psychological counseling, legal services.

COSTS
Costs (2020–21) ***Comprehensive fee:*** $19,500 includes full-time tuition ($14,000), mandatory fees ($500), and room and board ($5000). ***Required fees:*** $400 per credit hour part-time. ***Room and board:*** Room and board charges vary according to housing facility. ***Payment plan:*** installment. ***Waivers:*** employees or children of employees.

APPLYING
Standardized Tests *Required:* SAT or ACT (for admission), CLT (for admission).

Options: electronic application, early admission, early decision.

Application fee: $40.

Required: essay or personal statement, high school transcript, 2 letters of recommendation, interview.

Application deadlines: 3/1 (freshmen), 3/1 (out-of-state freshmen).

Early decision deadline: 1/1.

Notification: continuous (freshmen), continuous (out-of-state freshmen), rolling (early decision).

CONTACT
Dr. Eliot Grasso, Director of Admissions and Development, Gutenberg College, 1883 University St., Eugene, OR 97403. *Phone:* 541-683-5141. *E-mail:* egrasso@gutenberg.edu.

Lewis & Clark College

Portland, Oregon

http://www.lclark.edu/

- **Independent** comprehensive, founded 1867
- **Urban** 137-acre campus with easy access to Portland
- **Endowment** $236.6 million
- **Coed** 1,965 undergraduate students, 98% full-time, 61% women, 39% men
- **Very difficult** entrance level, 72% of applicants were admitted

UNDERGRAD STUDENTS
1,934 full-time, 31 part-time. 88% are from out of state; 3% Black or African American, non-Hispanic/Latino; 13% Hispanic/Latino; 4% Asian, non-Hispanic/Latino; 0.5% Native Hawaiian or other Pacific Islander, non-Hispanic/Latino; 0.4% American Indian or Alaska Native, non-Hispanic/Latino; 7% Two or more races, non-Hispanic/Latino; 2% Race/ethnicity unknown; 4% international; 2% transferred in; 69% live on campus.

Freshmen:
Admission: 5,863 applied, 4,231 admitted, 507 enrolled. ***Average high school GPA:*** 3.9. ***Test scores:*** SAT evidence-based reading and writing scores over 500: 100%; SAT math scores over 500: 99%; ACT scores over 18: 100%; SAT evidence-based reading and writing scores over 600: 87%; SAT math scores over 600: 74%; ACT scores over 24: 95%; SAT evidence-based reading and writing scores over 700: 33%; SAT math scores over 700: 22%; ACT scores over 30: 46%.

FACULTY
Total: 438, 49% full-time, 55% with terminal degrees.
Student/faculty ratio: 11:1.

ACADEMICS
Calendar: semesters. *Degrees:* bachelor's, master's, doctoral, and post-master's certificates.

Special study options: advanced placement credit, double majors, English as a second language, honors programs, independent study, internships, off-campus study, services for LD students, student-designed majors, study abroad, summer session for credit. ***ROTC:*** Army (c).

Unusual degree programs: 3-2 engineering with Columbia University (New York), Washington University in St. Louis, University of Southern California.

Computers: 440 computers/terminals are available on campus for general student use. Students can access the following: campus intranet, computer help desk, free student e-mail accounts, online (class) grades, online (class) registration, online (class) schedules. Campuswide network is available. 100% of college-owned or -operated housing units are wired for high-speed Internet access. Wireless service is available via entire campus.

Library: Aubrey Watzek Library plus 1 other. *Books:* 336,148 (physical), 313,729 (digital/electronic); *Serial titles:* 4,973 (physical), 56,436 (digital/electronic); *Databases:* 304. Weekly public service hours: 141; study areas open 24 hours, 5–7 days a week; students can reserve study rooms.

STUDENT LIFE
Housing options: on-campus residence required through sophomore year; coed, women-only. Campus housing is university owned. Freshman campus housing is guaranteed.

Activities and organizations: drama/theater group, student-run newspaper, radio station, choral group, Bacchus Menâ§ Ultimate Frisbee, Artemis Womenâ§ Ultimate Frisbee, International Affairs Symposium, Hillel, Black Student Union.

Athletics Member NCAA. All Division III except golf (Division II).
Intercollegiate sports: baseball M, basketball M/W, crew M/W, cross-country running M/W, football M, golf M/W, lacrosse W(c), rugby M(c)/W(c), soccer M(c)/W, softball W, swimming and diving M/W, tennis M/W, track and field M/W, ultimate Frisbee M(c)/W(c), volleyball W.
Intramural sports: football M/W, soccer M/W, water polo M/W.

Campus security: 24-hour emergency response devices and patrols, late-night transport/escort service, controlled dormitory access.

Student services: health clinic, personal/psychological counseling, veterans affairs office.

COSTS & FINANCIAL AID

Costs (2019–20) ***Comprehensive fee:*** $65,788 includes full-time tuition ($52,346), mandatory fees ($434), and room and board ($13,008). Part-time tuition: $2617 per credit hour. Part-time tuition and fees vary according to course load. ***Required fees:*** $18 per credit hour part-time. ***College room only:*** $7418. Room and board charges vary according to board plan and housing facility. ***Payment plan:*** installment. ***Waivers:*** employees or children of employees.

Financial Aid Of all full-time matriculated undergraduates who enrolled in 2019, 1,355 applied for aid, 1,089 were judged to have need, 444 had their need fully met. 855 Federal Work-Study jobs (averaging $2817). 136 state and other part-time jobs (averaging $2196). In 2019, 258 non-need-based awards were made. ***Average percent of need met:*** 87. ***Average financial aid package:*** $44,874. ***Average need-based loan:*** $6605. ***Average need-based gift aid:*** $37,401. ***Average non-need-based aid:*** $22,156. ***Average indebtedness upon graduation:*** $30,460.

APPLYING

Standardized Tests *Required:* SAT or ACT scores or Test-Optional Portfolio Path materials (for admission). *Required for some:* SAT or ACT (for admission).

Options: electronic application, early decision, early action, deferred entrance.

Required: essay or personal statement, high school transcript, 1 letter of recommendation. ***Required for some:*** 2 letters of recommendation, graded writing sample, math or science sample, 2 letters of recommendation for Test Optional Portfolio Path. ***Recommended:*** interview.

Application deadlines: 1/15 (freshmen), 4/1 (transfers), 11/1 (early action).

Early decision deadline: 11/1.

Notification: 4/1 (freshmen), continuous (transfers), 12/5 (early decision), 12/31 (early action).

CONTACT

Lewis & Clark College, 0615 Southwest Palatine Hill Road, Portland, OR 97219-7899. *Phone:* 503-768-7040. *Toll-free phone:* 800-444-4111.

Linfield College

McMinnville, Oregon

http://www.linfield.edu/

- **Independent American Baptist Churches in the USA** 4-year, founded 1858, part of Linfield College
- **Small-town** 189-acre campus with easy access to Portland
- **Endowment** $109.1 million
- **Coed** 1,414 undergraduate students, 98% full-time, 62% women, 38% men
- **Moderately difficult** entrance level, 82% of applicants were admitted

UNDERGRAD STUDENTS

1,383 full-time, 31 part-time. Students come from 19 states and territories; 19 other countries; 40% are from out of state; 1% Black or African American, non-Hispanic/Latino; 19% Hispanic/Latino; 5% Asian, non-Hispanic/Latino; 1% Native Hawaiian or other Pacific Islander, non-Hispanic/Latino; 0.7% American Indian or Alaska Native, non-Hispanic/Latino; 7% Two or more races, non-Hispanic/Latino; 2% Race/ethnicity unknown; 2% international; 4% transferred in; 77% live on campus.

Freshmen:

Admission: 2,390 applied, 1,953 admitted, 459 enrolled. ***Average high school GPA:*** 3.6. ***Test scores:*** SAT evidence-based reading and writing scores over 500: 85%; SAT math scores over 500: 86%; ACT scores over 18: 91%; SAT evidence-based reading and writing scores over 600: 38%; SAT math scores over 600: 31%; ACT scores over 24: 47%; SAT evidence-based reading and writing scores over 700: 5%; SAT math scores over 700: 4%; ACT scores over 30: 11%.

Retention: 84% of full-time freshmen returned.

FACULTY

Total: 158, 66% full-time, 77% with terminal degrees.

Student/faculty ratio: 11:1.

ACADEMICS

Calendar: 4-1-4. *Degrees:* bachelor's, master's, and postbachelor's certificates (Linfield College includes the Linfield College McMinnville

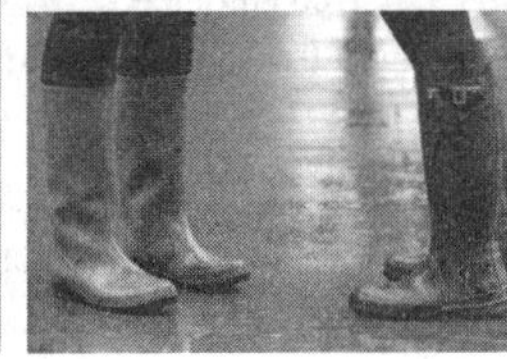

Campus in McMinnville, Oregon; the Linfield-Good Samaritan School of Nursing in Portland, Oregon(Portland Campus) and the Linfield College Adult Degree Program online).

Special study options: accelerated degree program, adult/continuing education programs, advanced placement credit, distance learning, double majors, English as a second language, external degree program, independent study, internships, off-campus study, part-time degree program, services for LD students, student-designed majors, study abroad, summer session for credit. ***ROTC:*** Air Force (c).

Unusual degree programs: 3-2 engineering with Washington State University, Oregon State University, University of Southern California; BA or BS at LInfield in Wine Studies; master's degree ("International Vintage Master") at Ecole Superieure d'Agriculture (Angers, France) and/or any university involved in the consortium of the Vintage Master managed by ESA.

Computers: 80 computers/terminals and 1,500 ports are available on campus for general student use. Students can access the following: computer help desk, free student e-mail accounts, online (class) grades, online (class) registration, online (class) schedules. Campuswide network is available. 100% of college-owned or -operated housing units are wired for high-speed Internet access. Wireless service is available via entire campus.

Library: Jereld R. Nicholson Library. *Books:* 141,289 (physical), 187,425 (digital/electronic); *Serial titles:* 1,420 (physical), 39,302 (digital/electronic); *Databases:* 189. Weekly public service hours: 88.

STUDENT LIFE

Housing options: on-campus residence required through junior year; coed, men-only, women-only, special housing for students with disabilities. Campus housing is university owned. Freshman campus housing is guaranteed.

Activities and organizations: drama/theater group, student-run newspaper, radio station, choral group, marching band, Hawaiian Club, Linfield Ultimate Players Association, Residence Hall Associations, International Club, Outdoor Club, national fraternities, national sororities.

Athletics Member NCAA. All Division III except golf (Division II). ***Intercollegiate sports:*** baseball M, basketball M/W, cross-country running M/W, football M, golf M/W, lacrosse W, soccer M/W, softball W, swimming and diving M/W, tennis M/W, track and field M/W, volleyball W. ***Intramural sports:*** badminton M/W, basketball M/W, football M/W, soccer M/W, softball M/W, ultimate Frisbee M/W, volleyball M/W.

Campus security: 24-hour emergency response devices and patrols, late-night transport/escort service, controlled dormitory access.

Student services: health clinic, personal/psychological counseling.

COSTS & FINANCIAL AID

Costs (2020–21) ***Comprehensive fee:*** $57,992 includes full-time tuition ($44,450), mandatory fees ($612), and room and board ($12,930). Full-time tuition and fees vary according to course load, program, and reciprocity agreements. Part-time tuition: $1390 per semester hour. Part-time tuition and fees vary according to course load, program, and reciprocity agreements. ***Required fees:*** $284 per year part-time. ***College room only:*** $7110. Room and board charges vary according to board plan, housing facility, and location. ***Payment plan:*** installment. ***Waivers:*** adult students, senior citizens, and employees or children of employees.

Financial Aid Of all full-time matriculated undergraduates who enrolled in 2019, 1,214 applied for aid, 1,041 were judged to have need, 366 had their need fully met. 460 Federal Work-Study jobs (averaging $1480). 634 state and other part-time jobs (averaging $2544). In 2019, 293 non-need-based awards were made. ***Average percent of need met:*** 85. ***Average financial aid package:*** $38,507. ***Average need-based loan:*** $4220. ***Average need-based gift aid:*** $31,162. ***Average non-need-based aid:*** $21,126. ***Average indebtedness upon graduation:*** $36,082.

APPLYING

Standardized Tests *Required for some:* SAT or ACT (for admission).

Options: electronic application, early action, deferred entrance.

Required: essay or personal statement, high school transcript, 1 letter of recommendation. ***Recommended:*** interview.

Application deadlines: 2/1 (freshmen), 4/15 (transfers), 11/1 (early action).

Notification: continuous until 4/1 (freshmen), 5/15 (transfers), 1/15 (early action).

CONTACT

Ms. Lisa Knodle-Bragiel, Director of Admission, Linfield College, 900 SE Baker Street, McMinnville, OR 97128. *Phone:* 503-883-2213. *Toll-free phone:* 800-640-2287. *Fax:* 503-883-2472. *E-mail:* admission@ linfield.edu.

See below for display ad and page 1072 for the College Close-Up.

Mount Angel Seminary

Saint Benedict, Oregon

http://www.mountangelabbey.org/seminary/

CONTACT

Registrar/Admissions Officer, Mount Angel Seminary, Saint Benedict, OR 97373. *Phone:* 503-845-3951 Ext. 14. *E-mail:* admissions@ mtangel.edu.

Multnomah University

Portland, Oregon

http://www.multnomah.edu/

- **Independent interdenominational** comprehensive, founded 1936
- **Urban** 25-acre campus with easy access to Portland, OR
- **Endowment** $7.9 million
- **Coed** 365 undergraduate students, 84% full-time, 49% women, 51% men
- **Moderately difficult** entrance level, 54% of applicants were admitted

UNDERGRAD STUDENTS

308 full-time, 57 part-time. Students come from 20 states and territories; 1 other country; 54% are from out of state; 4% Black or African American, non-Hispanic/Latino; 16% Hispanic/Latino; 3% Asian, non-Hispanic/Latino; 1% Native Hawaiian or other Pacific Islander, non-Hispanic/Latino; 0.8% American Indian or Alaska Native, non-Hispanic/Latino; 5% Two or more races, non-Hispanic/Latino; 2% Race/ethnicity unknown; 0.3% international; 16% transferred in; 45% live on campus.

Freshmen:

Admission: 282 applied, 151 admitted, 64 enrolled. ***Average high school GPA:*** 3.3.

Retention: 47% of full-time freshmen returned.

FACULTY

Total: 109, 24% full-time, 60% with terminal degrees.

Student/faculty ratio: 10:1.

ACADEMICS

Calendar: semesters. *Degrees:* bachelor's, master's, doctoral, and postbachelor's certificates.

Special study options: academic remediation for entering students, adult/continuing education programs, advanced placement credit, distance learning, double majors, internships, part-time degree program, services for LD students, study abroad, summer session for credit.

Computers: 20 computers/terminals are available on campus for general student use. Students can access the following: campus intranet, computer help desk, free student e-mail accounts, online (class) grades, online (class) registration, online (class) schedules. Campuswide network is available. 80% of college-owned or -operated housing units are wired for high-speed Internet access. Wireless service is available via entire campus.

Library: John Mitchell Library. *Books:* 108,040 (physical), 156,696 (digital/electronic); *Serial titles:* 316 (physical), 20,000 (digital/electronic); *Databases:* 47. Weekly public service hours: 82.

STUDENT LIFE

Housing options: on-campus residence required through sophomore year; men-only, women-only, special housing for students with disabilities. Campus housing is university owned. Freshman campus housing is guaranteed.

Activities and organizations: Commuter Life, Residence Life, Student Government, Voices Scholars, Spiritual Life.

Athletics Member NAIA. ***Intercollegiate sports:*** basketball M(s)/W(s), cross-country running M(s)/W(s), golf M(s), soccer M(s)/W(s), track and field M(s)/W(s), volleyball W(s). ***Intramural sports:*** basketball M/W, ultimate Frisbee M/W, volleyball M/W.

Campus security: 24-hour emergency response devices and patrols, late-night transport/escort service, controlled dormitory access.

Student services: personal/psychological counseling, veterans affairs office.

COSTS & FINANCIAL AID

Costs (2020–21) ***Comprehensive fee:*** $38,550 includes full-time tuition ($28,030), mandatory fees ($650), and room and board ($9870). Full-time tuition and fees vary according to course load, location, and program. Part-time tuition: $885 per semester hour. Part-time tuition and fees vary according to course load, location, and program. ***Required fees:*** $650 per year part-time. ***Room and board:*** Room and board charges vary according to board plan and housing facility. ***Payment plan:*** installment. ***Waivers:*** employees or children of employees.

Financial Aid Of all full-time matriculated undergraduates who enrolled in 2009, 503 applied for aid, 441 were judged to have need, 11 had their need fully met. 75 Federal Work-Study jobs (averaging $1500). In 2009, 36 non-need-based awards were made. ***Average percent of need met:*** 50. ***Average financial aid package:*** $9211. ***Average need-based loan:*** $4094. ***Average need-based gift aid:*** $5846. ***Average non-need-based aid:*** $1848. ***Average indebtedness upon graduation:*** $21,020.

APPLYING

Options: electronic application, deferred entrance.

Application fee: $40.

Required: essay or personal statement, minimum 2.5 GPA, 1 letter of recommendation. ***Required for some:*** high school transcript.

Application deadlines: rolling (freshmen), rolling (out-of-state freshmen), rolling (transfers).

Notification: continuous (freshmen), continuous (out-of-state freshmen), continuous (transfers).

CONTACT

Ms. Jazmin Miller, Admissions Office Manager, Multnomah University, 8435 Northeast Glisan Street, Portland, OR 97220-5898. *Phone:* 503-251-6485. *Toll-free phone:* 877-251-6560. *Fax:* 503-254-1268. *E-mail:* admiss@multnomah.edu.

New Hope Christian College

Eugene, Oregon

http://www.newhope.edu/

CONTACT

Sarah Slater, Director of Admissions, New Hope Christian College, 2155 Bailey Hill Road, Eugene, OR 97405. *Phone:* 541-485-1780 Ext. 3115. *Toll-free phone:* 800-322-2638. *Fax:* 541-343-5801. *E-mail:* sarahslater@newhope.edu.

Northwest Christian University

Eugene, Oregon

http://www.nwcu.edu/

- **Independent Christian** comprehensive, founded 1895
- **Urban** 8-acre campus with easy access to Portland
- **Endowment** $14.3 million
- **Coed** 593 undergraduate students, 70% full-time, 61% women, 39% men
- **Minimally difficult** entrance level, 62% of applicants were admitted

UNDERGRAD STUDENTS

418 full-time, 175 part-time. Students come from 17 states and territories; 7 other countries; 21% are from out of state; 6% transferred in; 78% live on campus.

Freshmen:

Admission: 479 applied, 299 admitted, 100 enrolled. ***Average high school GPA:*** 3.5.

Retention: 71% of full-time freshmen returned.

ACADEMICS

Calendar: quarters. *Degrees:* associate, bachelor's, master's, and postbachelor's certificates.

Special study options: academic remediation for entering students, accelerated degree program, adult/continuing education programs, advanced placement credit, cooperative education, distance learning, double majors, English as a second language, independent study, internships, part-time degree program, services for LD students, study abroad, summer session for credit. ***ROTC:*** Army (c).

Computers: 16 computers/terminals are available on campus for general student use. Students can access the following: campus intranet, computer help desk, free student e-mail accounts, online (class) grades, online (class) registration, online (class) schedules. Campuswide network is available. Wireless service is available via entire campus.

Library: Edward P. Kellenberger Library. Weekly public service hours: 70.

STUDENT LIFE

Housing options: on-campus residence required through senior year; men-only, women-only. Campus housing is university owned. Freshman campus housing is guaranteed.

Activities and organizations: student-run newspaper, choral group, Embrace the City (community service), FeMystique (Social justice club), Beacon Boards (game board club), History Club, Psychology Club.

Athletics ***Intercollegiate sports:*** basketball M(s)/W(s), cross-country running M(s)/W(s), golf M(s)/W(s), soccer M(s)/W(s), softball W(s), track and field M(s)/W(s), volleyball W(s). ***Intramural sports:*** basketball M/W, volleyball M/W.

Campus security: 24-hour emergency response devices and patrols, late-night transport/escort service, controlled dormitory access.

Student services: personal/psychological counseling.

COSTS & FINANCIAL AID

Costs (2020–21) ***Comprehensive fee:*** $42,370 includes full-time tuition ($32,100), mandatory fees ($220), and room and board ($10,050). Part-time tuition: $1070 per credit hour. ***Required fees:*** $220 per year part-time. ***Room and board:*** Room and board charges vary according to housing facility. ***Payment plan:*** installment. ***Waivers:*** employees or children of employees.

Financial Aid Of all full-time matriculated undergraduates who enrolled in 2019, 392 applied for aid, 356 were judged to have need, 63 had their need fully met. 105 Federal Work-Study jobs (averaging $3250). 3 state and other part-time jobs (averaging $3250). In 2019, 78 non-need-based awards were made. ***Average percent of need met:*** 75. ***Average financial aid package:*** $22,913. ***Average need-based loan:*** $4647. ***Average need-based gift aid:*** $19,408. ***Average non-need-based aid:*** $10,728. ***Average indebtedness upon graduation:*** $25,058.

APPLYING

Standardized Tests *Required:* SAT or ACT (for admission).

Options: electronic application, deferred entrance.

Required: essay or personal statement, minimum 2.5 GPA. ***Required for some:*** high school transcript. ***Recommended:*** interview.

Application deadlines: rolling (freshmen), rolling (transfers).

Notification: continuous (freshmen), continuous (transfers).

CONTACT

Kacie Gerdrum, Dean of Admissions, Northwest Christian University, 828 E. 11th Ave., Eugene, OR 97401-3745. *Phone:* 541-684-7288. *Toll-free phone:* 877-463-6622. *Fax:* 541-684-7317. *E-mail:* kgerdrum@nwcu.edu.

Oregon Health & Science University

Portland, Oregon

http://www.ohsu.edu/

CONTACT

Oregon Health & Science University, 3181 Southwest Sam Jackson Park Road, Portland, OR 97239-3098. *Phone:* 503-494-0954.

Oregon Institute of Technology

Klamath Falls, Oregon

http://www.oit.edu/

- **State-supported** comprehensive, founded 1947
- **Small-town** 190-acre campus
- **Endowment** $7.9 million
- **Coed**
- **Moderately difficult** entrance level

FACULTY
Student/faculty ratio: 16:1.

ACADEMICS
Calendar: quarters. *Degrees:* certificates, associate, bachelor's, master's, and postbachelor's certificates.
Library: ***Books:*** 140,000 (physical); *Databases:* 70. Students can reserve study rooms.

STUDENT LIFE
Housing options: coed, cooperative. Campus housing is university owned.

Activities and organizations: student-run newspaper, radio and television station, choral group, Phi Delta Theta, Christian Fellowship, International Club, Society of Women Engineers, Association of Student Mechanical Engineers, national fraternities.

Athletics Member NAIA.

Campus security: 24-hour emergency response devices and patrols, late-night transport/escort service.

Student services: health clinic, personal/psychological counseling, women's center, veterans affairs office.

COSTS & FINANCIAL AID
Costs (2019–20) ***Tuition:*** state resident $8775 full-time, $195 per credit hour part-time; nonresident $27,929 full-time, $620 per credit hour part-time. Full-time tuition and fees vary according to course load, location, program, and reciprocity agreements. Part-time tuition and fees vary according to course load, location, program, and reciprocity agreements. ***Required fees:*** $1710 full-time, $284 per credit hour part-time, $636 per term part-time. ***Room and board:*** $9133; room only: $5278. Room and board charges vary according to board plan and housing facility.

Financial Aid Of all full-time matriculated undergraduates who enrolled in 2019, 1,313 applied for aid, 1,279 were judged to have need, 79 had their need fully met. In 2019, 184 non-need-based awards were made. ***Average percent of need met:*** 37. ***Average financial aid package:*** $11,256. ***Average need-based loan:*** $4727. ***Average need-based gift aid:*** $7459. ***Average non-need-based aid:*** $2159. ***Average indebtedness upon graduation:*** $27,007.

APPLYING
Standardized Tests *Required:* SAT or ACT (for admission).

Options: electronic application, deferred entrance.

Application fee: $50.

Required: high school transcript, minimum 3.0 GPA.

CONTACT
Oregon Institute of Technology, 3201 Campus Drive, Klamath Falls, OR 97601-8801. *Toll-free phone:* 800-422-2017.

Oregon State University

Corvallis, Oregon

http://www.oregonstate.edu/

- **State-supported** university, founded 1868
- **Small-town** 422-acre campus
- **Endowment** $624.5 million
- **Coed**
- **Moderately difficult** entrance level

FACULTY
Student/faculty ratio: 18:1.

ACADEMICS
Calendar: quarters. *Degrees:* certificates, bachelor's, master's, doctoral, post-master's, and postbachelor's certificates.
Library: Valley Library plus 2 others. *Books:* 1.7 million (physical), 481,665 (digital/electronic); *Serial titles:* 2,376 (physical), 74,203 (digital/electronic); *Databases:* 150. Weekly public service hours: 138; study areas open 24 hours, 5–7 days a week; students can reserve study rooms.

STUDENT LIFE
Housing options: on-campus residence required for freshman year; coed, special housing for students with disabilities. Campus housing is university owned. Freshman applicants given priority for college housing.

Activities and organizations: drama/theater group, student-run newspaper, radio and television station, choral group, marching band, Ballroom Dance Club, Gaming Club, Organic Growers Club, Blood Drive Association, Residence Hall Association, national fraternities, national sororities.

Athletics Member NCAA. All Division I except football (Division I-A).

Campus security: 24-hour emergency response devices and patrols, student patrols, late-night transport/escort service, controlled dormitory access, crime prevention office.

Student services: health clinic, personal/psychological counseling, women's center, legal services.

FINANCIAL AID
Financial Aid Of all full-time matriculated undergraduates who enrolled in 2018, 12,549 applied for aid, 9,540 were judged to have need, 1,163 had their need fully met. In 2018, 3467 non-need-based awards were made. ***Average percent of need met:*** 62. ***Average financial aid package:*** $11,671. ***Average need-based loan:*** $4196. ***Average need-based gift aid:*** $8117. ***Average non-need-based aid:*** $4841. ***Average indebtedness upon graduation:*** $27,392.

APPLYING
Standardized Tests *Required:* SAT or ACT (for admission). *Required for some:* SAT Subject Tests (for admission).

Options: electronic application, early action, deferred entrance.

Application fee: $60.

Required: essay or personal statement, high school transcript, minimum 3.0 GPA.

CONTACT
Oregon State University, Corvallis, OR 97331. *Phone:* 541-737-4411. *Toll-free phone:* 800-291-4192.

Oregon State University–Cascades

Bend, Oregon

http://www.osucascades.edu/

CONTACT
Admissions Department, Oregon State University–Cascades, 2600 Northwest College Way, Bend, OR 97701. *Phone:* 541-322-3150. *E-mail:* cascadeadmit@osucascades.edu.

Pacific Northwest College of Art

Portland, Oregon

http://www.pnca.edu/

- **Independent** comprehensive, founded 1909
- **Urban** 2-acre campus with easy access to Portland
- **Endowment** $12.9 million
- **Coed**
- **Noncompetitive** entrance level

FACULTY
Student/faculty ratio: 9:1.

ACADEMICS
Calendar: semesters. *Degrees:* bachelor's and master's.
Library: Albert Solheim Library. *Books:* 34,806 (physical); *Serial titles:* 270 (physical); *Databases:* 52. Weekly public service hours: 87; students can reserve study rooms.

STUDENT LIFE
Housing options: on-campus residence required for freshman year; coed, men-only, women-only, special housing for students with disabilities. Campus housing is provided by a third party. Freshman campus housing is guaranteed.

Campus security: 24-hour emergency response devices, late-night transport/escort service, controlled dormitory access, entrance security guards and patrols during hours of operation.

Student services: personal/psychological counseling.

FINANCIAL AID
Financial Aid Of all full-time matriculated undergraduates who enrolled in 2006, 264 applied for aid, 238 were judged to have need, 13 had their need fully met. 33 Federal Work-Study jobs (averaging $1200). 33 state

and other part-time jobs (averaging $1200). In 2006, 10 non-need-based awards were made. ***Average percent of need met:*** 54. ***Average financial aid package:*** $11,845. ***Average need-based loan:*** $4040. ***Average need-based gift aid:*** $4699. ***Average non-need-based aid:*** $2442. ***Average indebtedness upon graduation:*** $22,155.

APPLYING
Options: electronic application, early admission, deferred entrance.

Application fee: $45.

Required: essay or personal statement, portfolio of artwork. ***Required for some.*** high school transcript. ***Recommended:*** minimum 2.3 GPA.

CONTACT
Pacific Northwest College of Art, 511 NW Broadway, Portland, OR 97209.

Pacific University

Forest Grove, Oregon

http://www.pacificu.edu/

- **Independent** comprehensive, founded 1849
- **Small-town** 60-acre campus with easy access to Portland
- **Coed** 1,864 undergraduate students, 94% full-time, 64% women, 36% men
- **Moderately difficult** entrance level, 87% of applicants were admitted

UNDERGRAD STUDENTS
1,759 full-time, 105 part-time. Students come from 37 states and territories; 13 other countries; 52% are from out of state; 2% Black or African American, non-Hispanic/Latino; 16% Hispanic/Latino; 12% Asian, non-Hispanic/Latino; 2% Native Hawaiian or other Pacific Islander, non-Hispanic/Latino; 0.7% American Indian or Alaska Native, non-Hispanic/Latino; 13% Two or more races, non-Hispanic/Latino; 6% Race/ethnicity unknown; 1% international; 5% transferred in; 56% live on campus.

Freshmen:
Admission: 2,524 applied, 2,186 admitted, 416 enrolled. ***Average high school GPA:*** 3.7. ***Test scores:*** SAT evidence-based reading and writing scores over 500: 94%; SAT math scores over 500: 90%; ACT scores over 18: 93%; SAT evidence-based reading and writing scores over 600: 43%; SAT math scores over 600: 34%; ACT scores over 24: 52%; SAT evidence-based reading and writing scores over 700: 5%; SAT math scores over 700: 6%; ACT scores over 30: 8%.

Retention: 81% of full-time freshmen returned.

FACULTY
Total: 520, 56% full-time, 55% with terminal degrees.

Student/faculty ratio: 10:1.

ACADEMICS
Calendar: semesters. *Degrees:* bachelor's, master's, doctoral, post-master's, and postbachelor's certificates.

Special study options: accelerated degree program, distance learning, double majors, English as a second language, independent study, internships, part-time degree program, student-designed majors, study abroad, summer session for credit.

Unusual degree programs: 3-2 engineering with Portland State University, Case Western Reserve University.

Computers: Students can access the following: campus intranet, computer help desk, free student e-mail accounts, online (class) grades, online (class) schedules, Web space, printing, student and academic information, learning management system, computer peripherals. Campuswide network is available. 100% of college-owned or -operated housing units are wired for high-speed Internet access. Wireless service is available via entire campus.
Library: Tim & Cathy Tran Library. Study areas open 24 hours, 5–7 days a week; students can reserve study rooms.

STUDENT LIFE
Housing options: on-campus residence required through sophomore year; coed, special housing for students with disabilities. Campus housing is university owned. Freshman campus housing is guaranteed.

Activities and organizations: drama/theater group, student-run newspaper, radio station, choral group.

Athletics Member NCAA, NAIA. All NCAA Division III. ***Intercollegiate sports:*** baseball M, basketball M/W, cross-country running M/W, football M, golf M/W, lacrosse W, soccer M/W, softball W, swimming and diving M/W, tennis M/W, track and field M/W, volleyball W, wrestling M/W. ***Intramural sports:*** basketball M/W, cheerleading M/W, crew M/W, football M/W, racquetball W, softball M/W, volleyball M/W.

Campus security: 24-hour emergency response devices and patrols, late-night transport/escort service, controlled dormitory access.

Student services: health clinic, personal/psychological counseling, women's center.

COSTS & FINANCIAL AID
Costs (2020–21) ***Comprehensive fee:*** $61,680 includes full-time tuition ($47,158), mandatory fees ($1102), and room and board ($13,420). Part-time tuition and fees vary according to course load. ***College room only:*** $7404. Room and board charges vary according to board plan and housing facility. ***Payment plans:*** installment, deferred payment. ***Waivers:*** employees or children of employees.

Financial Aid Of all full-time matriculated undergraduates who enrolled in 2018, 1,561 applied for aid, 1,427 were judged to have need, 242 had their need fully met. In 2018, 305 non-need-based awards were made. ***Average percent of need met:*** 76. ***Average financial aid package:*** $34,684. ***Average need-based loan:*** $3975. ***Average need-based gift aid:*** $28,476. ***Average non-need-based aid:*** $20,267. ***Average indebtedness upon graduation:*** $35,373.

APPLYING
Standardized Tests *Required:* SAT or ACT (for admission).

Options: electronic application, deferred entrance.

Application fee: $40.

Required: essay or personal statement, high school transcript, minimum 3.0 GPA, 1 letter of recommendation.

Application deadlines: 8/15 (freshmen), 8/15 (out-of-state freshmen), 8/15 (transfers).

Notification: continuous until 11/1 (freshmen), continuous until 11/1 (out-of-state freshmen), continuous (transfers).

CONTACT
Ms. Karen Dunston, Asst VP Enrollment Mgmt Undergrad Adm, Pacific University, 2043 College Way, Forest Grove, OR 97116-1797. *Phone:* 503-352-2218. *Toll-free phone:* 877-722-8648. *Fax:* 503-352-2975. *E-mail:* admissions@pacificu.edu.

Pioneer Pacific College

Beaverton, Oregon

http://www.pioneerpacific.edu/

CONTACT
Ms. Juli Lau, Vice President of Admissions, Pioneer Pacific College, 4145 SW Watson Ave Suite 300, Beaverton, OR 97005. *Phone:* 503-682-1862. *Toll-free phone:* 866-PPC-INFO. *Fax:* 503-682-1514. *E-mail:* info@pioneerpacific.edu.

Portland State University

Portland, Oregon

http://www.pdx.edu/

- **State-supported** university, founded 1946
- **Urban** 50-acre campus with easy access to Portland
- **Endowment** $83.5 million
- **Coed** 35,654 undergraduate students, 76% full-time, 54% women, 46% men
- **Minimally difficult** entrance level, 96% of applicants were admitted

UNDERGRAD STUDENTS
27,176 full-time, 8,478 part-time. Students come from 50 states and territories; 70 other countries; 16% are from out of state; 4% Black or African American, non-Hispanic/Latino; 17% Hispanic/Latino; 10% Asian, non-Hispanic/Latino; 0.6% Native Hawaiian or other Pacific Islander, non-Hispanic/Latino; 1% American Indian or Alaska Native, non-Hispanic/Latino; 7% Two or more races, non-Hispanic/Latino; 4% Race/ethnicity unknown; 5% international; 8% transferred in; 9% live on campus.

Freshmen:
Admission: 6,861 applied, 6,573 admitted, 1,569 enrolled. ***Average high school GPA:*** 3.5. ***Test scores:*** SAT evidence-based reading and writing scores over 500: 78%; SAT math scores over 500: 75%; ACT scores over 18: 78%; SAT evidence-based reading and writing scores over 600: 37%; SAT math scores over 600: 24%; ACT scores over 24: 29%; SAT evidence-based reading and writing scores over 700: 6%; SAT math scores over 700: 4%; ACT scores over 30: 5%.

Retention: 73% of full-time freshmen returned.

FACULTY
Total: 1,535, 58% full-time, 55% with terminal degrees.
Student/faculty ratio: 19:1.

ACADEMICS
Calendar: quarters. *Degrees:* certificates, bachelor's, master's, doctoral, and postbachelor's certificates.

Special study options: academic remediation for entering students, accelerated degree program, adult/continuing education programs, advanced placement credit, cooperative education, distance learning, double majors, English as a second language, freshman honors college, honors programs, independent study, internships, off-campus study, part-time degree program, services for LD students, study abroad, summer session for credit. ***ROTC:*** Army (c), Navy (c), Air Force (c).

Computers: Students can access the following: campus intranet, computer help desk, free student e-mail accounts, online (class) grades, online (class) registration, online (class) schedules. Campuswide network is available. 100% of college-owned or -operated housing units are wired for high-speed Internet access. Wireless service is available via entire campus.

Library: Branford P. Millar Library plus 1 other. *Books:* 1.4 million (physical), 1.0 million (digital/electronic); *Serial titles:* 167 (physical), 86,341 (digital/electronic); *Databases:* 390. Students can reserve study rooms.

STUDENT LIFE
Housing options: coed, cooperative, special housing for students with disabilities. Campus housing is university owned. Freshman campus housing is guaranteed.

Activities and organizations: drama/theater group, student-run newspaper, radio station, choral group, national fraternities, national sororities.

Athletics Member NCAA. All Division I except football (Division I-AA). ***Intercollegiate sports:*** badminton M(c)/W(c), baseball M(c)/W(c), basketball M/W, crew M(c)/W(c), cross-country running M/W, fencing M(c)/W(c), golf W(c), ice hockey M(c), lacrosse M(c)/W(c), sailing M(c)/W(c), soccer M(c)/W, softball W, tennis M/W, track and field M/W, volleyball W, wrestling M(c)/W(c).

Campus security: 24-hour emergency response devices and patrols, late-night transport/escort service, controlled dormitory access.

Student services: health clinic, personal/psychological counseling, women's center, legal services, veterans affairs office.

COSTS & FINANCIAL AID
Costs (2020–21) ***Tuition:*** state resident $8078 full-time, $180 per credit hour part-time; nonresident $26,910 full-time, $598 per credit hour part-time. Full-time tuition and fees vary according to program. Part-time tuition and fees vary according to program. ***Required fees:*** $1500 full-time. ***Room and board:*** $11,172; room only: $6780. Room and board charges vary according to board plan, housing facility, and student level. ***Waivers:*** employees or children of employees.

Financial Aid Of all full-time matriculated undergraduates who enrolled in 2019, 10,473 applied for aid, 9,295 were judged to have need, 309 had their need fully met. In 2019, 92 non-need-based awards were made. ***Average percent of need met:*** 53. ***Average financial aid package:*** $10,884. ***Average need-based loan:*** $3922. ***Average need-based gift aid:*** $6380. ***Average non-need-based aid:*** $4516. ***Average indebtedness upon graduation:*** $26,426.

APPLYING
Standardized Tests *Required for some:* SAT or ACT (for admission).

Options: electronic application, deferred entrance.

Application fee: $50.

Required: high school transcript, minimum 3.0 GPA.

Application deadlines: rolling (freshmen), rolling (transfers).

Notification: continuous (freshmen), continuous (transfers).

CONTACT
Portland State University, PO Box 751, Portland, OR 97207-0751. *Toll-free phone:* 800-547-8887.

Reed College

Portland, Oregon

http://www.reed.edu/

- **Independent** comprehensive, founded 1908
- **Urban** 116-acre campus with easy access to Portland
- **Coed**
- **Very difficult** entrance level

FACULTY
Student/faculty ratio: 10:1.

ACADEMICS
Calendar: semesters. *Degrees:* bachelor's and master's.
Library: Eric V. Hauser Memorial Library plus 1 other. Study areas open 24 hours, 5–7 days a week.

STUDENT LIFE
Housing options: coed, women-only, cooperative, special housing for students with disabilities. Campus housing is university owned. Freshman campus housing is guaranteed.

Activities and organizations: drama/theater group, student-run newspaper, radio station, choral group.

Campus security: 24-hour emergency response devices and patrols, student patrols, late-night transport/escort service, controlled dormitory access.

Student services: health clinic, personal/psychological counseling, women's center, legal services.

COSTS & FINANCIAL AID
Costs (2019–20) ***Comprehensive fee:*** $73,060 includes full-time tuition ($58,130), mandatory fees ($310), and room and board ($14,620). Full-time tuition and fees vary according to degree level. Part-time tuition and fees vary according to course load and degree level. ***College room only:*** $7720. Room and board charges vary according to board plan and housing facility.

Financial Aid Of all full-time matriculated undergraduates who enrolled in 2019, 859 applied for aid, 792 were judged to have need, 778 had their need fully met. ***Average percent of need met:*** 100. ***Average financial aid package:*** $43,780. ***Average need-based loan:*** $4262. ***Average need-based gift aid:*** $39,742. ***Average indebtedness upon graduation:*** $25,657. ***Financial aid deadline:*** 1/15.

APPLYING
Standardized Tests *Required:* SAT or ACT (for admission).

Options: electronic application, early admission, early decision, early action, deferred entrance.

Required: essay or personal statement, high school transcript, 2 letters of recommendation. ***Recommended:*** interview.

CONTACT
Office of Admission, Reed College, 3203 Southeast Woodstock Boulevard, Portland, OR 97202-8199. *Phone:* 800-547-4750. *Toll-free phone:* 800-547-4750. *Fax:* 503-777-7553. *E-mail:* admission@reed.edu.

See below for display ad and page 1100 for the College Close-Up.

Southern Oregon University

Ashland, Oregon

http://www.sou.edu/

- **State-supported** comprehensive, founded 1926
- **Small-town** 175-acre campus
- **Endowment** $24.6 million
- **Coed**
- **Moderately difficult** entrance level

FACULTY
Student/faculty ratio: 26:1.

ACADEMICS
Calendar: quarters. *Degrees:* certificates, bachelor's, master's, and postbachelor's certificates.
Library: Lenn and Dixie Hannon Library. *Books:* 340,015 (physical), 135,298 (digital/electronic); *Databases:* 80. Students can reserve study rooms.

STUDENT LIFE
Housing options: on-campus residence required for freshman year; coed, special housing for students with disabilities. Campus housing is university owned. Freshman campus housing is guaranteed.

Activities and organizations: drama/theater group, student-run newspaper, radio and television station, choral group, Native American Student Union, International Student Association, Impact (religious club), Ho`opa`a Hawaii Club, Omicron Delta Kappa.

Athletics Member NAIA.

Campus security: 24-hour emergency response devices and patrols, student patrols, late-night transport/escort service, controlled dormitory access.

Student services: health clinic, personal/psychological counseling, women's center, legal services, veterans affairs office.

FINANCIAL AID
Financial Aid Of all full-time matriculated undergraduates who enrolled in 2018, 2,518 applied for aid, 1,970 were judged to have need, 59 had their need fully met. ***Average percent of need met:*** 98. ***Average financial aid package:*** $10,839. ***Average need-based loan:*** $7263. ***Average need-based gift aid:*** $7050. ***Average indebtedness upon graduation:*** $24,227.

APPLYING
Standardized Tests *Required:* SAT or ACT (for admission). *Required for some:* SAT and SAT Subject Tests or ACT (for admission).

Options: electronic application, early admission, deferred entrance.

Application fee: $60.

Required: high school transcript, minimum 3.0 GPA. ***Required for some:*** essay or personal statement.

CONTACT
Mr. Kelly Moutsatson, Director of Admissions, Southern Oregon University, 1250 Siskiyou Boulevard, Ashland, OR 97520. *Phone:* 541-552-6411. *Toll-free phone:* 855-470-3377. *Fax:* 541-552-6614. *E-mail:* admissions@sou.edu.

University of Oregon

Eugene, Oregon

http://www.uoregon.edu/

- **State-supported** university, founded 1876
- **Suburban** 295-acre campus with easy access to Portland, Oregon
- **Endowment** $912.5 million
- **Coed** 19,101 undergraduate students, 92% full-time, 54% women, 46% men
- **Moderately difficult** entrance level, 83% of applicants were admitted

UNDERGRAD STUDENTS
17,550 full-time, 1,551 part-time. Students come from 53 states and territories; 83 other countries; 42% are from out of state; 6% transferred in; 22% live on campus.

Freshmen:
Admission: 24,474 applied, 20,404 admitted, 4,168 enrolled. ***Average high school GPA:*** 3.6.

Retention: 85% of full-time freshmen returned.

ACADEMICS
Calendar: quarters. *Degrees:* bachelor's, master's, doctoral, post-master's, and postbachelor's certificates.

Special study options: advanced placement credit, cooperative education, distance learning, double majors, English as a second language, honors programs, independent study, internships, off-campus study, part-time degree program, services for LD students, student-designed majors, study abroad, summer session for credit. ***ROTC:*** Army (b), Air Force (c).

Unusual degree programs: 3-2 engineering with Oregon State University.

Computers: 497 computers/terminals are available on campus for general student use. Students can access the following: campus intranet, computer help desk, free student e-mail accounts, online (class) grades, online (class) registration, online (class) schedules. Campuswide network is available. 100% of college-owned or -operated housing units are wired for high-speed Internet access. Wireless service is available via entire campus.

Library: Knight Library plus 6 others. *Books:* 1.7 million (physical), 927,771 (digital/electronic); *Serial titles:* 74,186 (physical), 157,063 (digital/electronic); *Databases:* 514. Weekly public service hours: 124; students can reserve study rooms.

STUDENT LIFE

Housing options: on-campus residence required for freshman year; coed, cooperative. Campus housing is university owned. Freshman applicants given priority for college housing.

Activities and organizations: drama/theater group, student-run newspaper, radio and television station, choral group, marching band, political and environmental action, cultural organizations, major-specific organizations, community service organizations, club sports, national fraternities, national sororities.

Athletics Member NCAA. All Division I except football (Division I-A). ***Intercollegiate sports:*** baseball M(s), basketball M(s)/W(s), cross-country running M(s)/W(s), golf M(s), lacrosse W(s), sand volleyball W(s), soccer W(s), softball W(s), tennis M(s)/W(s), track and field M(s)/W(s), volleyball W(s). ***Intramural sports:*** badminton M(c)/W(c), baseball M(c), basketball M/W, cross-country running M(c)/W(c), equestrian sports M(c)/W(c), fencing M(c), field hockey M/W, football M/W, golf M(c)/W(c), ice hockey M(c)/W(c), lacrosse M(c)/W(c), rock climbing M(c)/W(c), rowing M(c)/W(c), rugby M(c)/W(c), sailing M(c)/W(c), skiing (downhill) M(c)/W(c), soccer M(c)/W(c), softball M(c)/W(c), squash M(c)/W(c), swimming and diving M(c)/W(c), table tennis M(c)/W(c), tennis M(c)/W(c), track and field M/W, triathlon M(c)/W(c), ultimate Frisbee M(c)/W(c), volleyball M(c)/W(c), water polo M(c)/W(c), weight lifting M(c)/W(c).

Campus security: 24-hour emergency response devices and patrols, late-night transport/escort service, controlled dormitory access, Lighted pathways, emergency phones, self-defense classes.

Student services: health clinic, personal/psychological counseling, women's center, legal services, veterans affairs office.

COSTS & FINANCIAL AID

Costs (2020–21) ***One-time required fee:*** $449. ***Tuition:*** state resident $10,755 full-time, $239 per credit hour part-time; nonresident $35,367 full-time, $786 per credit hour part-time. Full-time tuition and fees vary according to course load. Part-time tuition and fees vary according to course load. ***Room and board:*** $12,783. Room and board charges vary according to board plan and housing facility. ***Payment plan:*** installment. ***Waivers:*** employees or children of employees.

Financial Aid Of all full-time matriculated undergraduates who enrolled in 2018, 10,682 applied for aid, 8,056 were judged to have need, 453 had their need fully met. In 2018, 2741 non-need-based awards were made. ***Average percent of need met:*** 55. ***Average financial aid package:*** $11,936. ***Average need-based loan:*** $4358. ***Average need-based gift aid:*** $10,061. ***Average non-need-based aid:*** $6472. ***Average indebtedness upon graduation:*** $26,548.

APPLYING

Standardized Tests *Required:* SAT or ACT (for admission). *Required for some:* SAT and SAT Subject Tests or ACT (for admission).

Options: electronic application, early action, deferred entrance.

Application fee: $65.

Required: essay or personal statement, high school transcript, C+ or better in 15 college preparatory units.

Application deadlines: 1/15 (freshmen), 6/30 (transfers), 11/1 (early action).

Notification: 4/1 (freshmen), 12/15 (early action).

CONTACT

University of Oregon, Eugene, OR 97403. *Phone:* 541-346-3201. *Toll-free phone:* 800-232-3825.

University of Portland

Portland, Oregon

http://www.up.edu/

- **Independent Roman Catholic** comprehensive, founded 1901
- **Urban** 150-acre campus
- **Endowment** $147.0 million
- **Coed** 3,796 undergraduate students, 98% full-time, 61% women, 39% men
- **Moderately difficult** entrance level, 61% of applicants were admitted

UNDERGRAD STUDENTS

3,739 full-time, 57 part-time. 74% are from out of state; 1% Black or African American, non-Hispanic/Latino; 13% Hispanic/Latino; 16% Asian, non-Hispanic/Latino; 2% Native Hawaiian or other Pacific Islander, non-Hispanic/Latino; 0.3% American Indian or Alaska Native, non-Hispanic/Latino; 9% Two or more races, non-Hispanic/Latino; 2% Race/ethnicity unknown; 2% international; 2% transferred in; 56% live on campus.

Freshmen:

Admission: 14,505 applied, 8,919 admitted, 1,003 enrolled. ***Average high school GPA:*** 3.7. ***Test scores:*** SAT evidence-based reading and writing scores over 500: 98%; SAT math scores over 500: 97%; ACT scores over 18: 98%; SAT evidence-based reading and writing scores over 600: 66%; SAT math scores over 600: 61%; ACT scores over 24: 72%; SAT evidence-based reading and writing scores over 700: 12%; SAT math scores over 700: 18%; ACT scores over 30: 22%.

Retention: 90% of full-time freshmen returned.

FACULTY

Total: 480, 53% full-time, 47% with terminal degrees.

Student/faculty ratio: 11:1.

ACADEMICS

Calendar: semesters. *Degrees:* bachelor's, master's, doctoral, and post-master's certificates.

Special study options: adult/continuing education programs, advanced placement credit, distance learning, double majors, honors programs, independent study, internships, off-campus study, part-time degree program, services for LD students, study abroad, summer session for credit. ***ROTC:*** Army (b), Air Force (b).

Computers: 157 computers/terminals and 2,520 ports are available on campus for general student use. Students can access the following: campus intranet, computer help desk, free student e-mail accounts, online (class) grades, online (class) registration, online (class) schedules. Campuswide network is available. 100% of college-owned or -operated housing units are wired for high-speed Internet access. Wireless service is available via entire campus.

Library: Wilson M. Clark Library plus 1 other. *Books:* 191,219 (physical), 138,108 (digital/electronic); *Serial titles:* 1,080 (digital/electronic); *Databases:* 153. Weekly public service hours: 117; students can reserve study rooms.

STUDENT LIFE

Housing options: on-campus residence required for freshman year; coed, men-only, women-only. Campus housing is university owned. Freshman campus housing is guaranteed.

Activities and organizations: drama/theater group, student-run newspaper, radio station, choral group, Hawaii Club, International Club, Student Nurses Association, Feminist Discussion Group, The Bluffoons (Improv Club).

Athletics Member NCAA. All Division I. ***Intercollegiate sports:*** baseball M(s), basketball M(s)/W(s), crew W, cross-country running M(s)/W(s), rugby M(c), soccer M(s)/W(s), tennis M(s)/W(s), track and field M(s)/W(s), volleyball W(s). ***Intramural sports:*** basketball M/W, crew M/W, cross-country running M/W, football M/W, rugby M, skiing (cross-country) M/W, skiing (downhill) M/W, soccer M(c)/W, softball M/W, swimming and diving M/W, tennis M/W, track and field M/W, volleyball M/W, water polo M/W, weight lifting M/W.

Campus security: 24-hour emergency response devices and patrols, student patrols, late-night transport/escort service, controlled dormitory access.

Student services: health clinic, personal/psychological counseling.

COSTS & FINANCIAL AID

Costs (2019–20) ***Comprehensive fee:*** $61,786 includes full-time tuition ($47,478), mandatory fees ($340), and room and board ($13,968). Part-time tuition: $1487 per credit hour.

Financial Aid Of all full-time matriculated undergraduates who enrolled in 2019, 2,664 applied for aid, 2,085 were judged to have need, 138 had their need fully met. In 2019, 1544 non-need-based awards were made. ***Average percent of need met:*** 72. ***Average financial aid package:*** $33,608. ***Average need-based loan:*** $4712. ***Average need-based gift aid:*** $27,321. ***Average non-need-based aid:*** $20,044. ***Average indebtedness upon graduation:*** $32,027.

APPLYING

Standardized Tests *Required:* SAT or ACT (for admission). *Recommended:* SAT (for admission), ACT (for admission).

Options: electronic application, deferred entrance.

Application fee: $50.

Required: essay or personal statement, high school transcript, 1 letter of recommendation.

Application deadlines: 6/1 (freshmen), 6/1 (transfers).

Notification: continuous (freshmen), continuous (transfers).

CONTACT

Mr. Jason McDonald, Dean of Admissions, University of Portland, 5000 North Willamette Boulevard, Portland, OR 97203-5798. *Phone:* 503-943-7147. *Toll-free phone:* 888-627-5601. *Fax:* 503-943-7315. *E-mail:* admissions@up.edu.

Warner Pacific University

Portland, Oregon

http://www.warnerpacific.edu/

CONTACT

Dale Seipp, Vice President for Enrollment Management, Warner Pacific University, 2219 Southeast 68th Avenue, Portland, OR 97215. *Phone:* 503-517-1020. *Toll-free phone:* 800-804-1510. *Fax:* 503-517-1540. *E-mail:* admiss@warnerpacific.edu.

Western Oregon University

Monmouth, Oregon

http://www.wou.edu/

- **State-supported** comprehensive, founded 1856
- **Rural** 157-acre campus with easy access to Portland
- **Coed** 4,426 undergraduate students, 84% full-time, 64% women, 36% men
- **Moderately difficult** entrance level, 85% of applicants were admitted

UNDERGRAD STUDENTS

3,703 full-time, 723 part-time. Students come from 33 states and territories; 22 other countries; 18% are from out of state; 3% Black or African American, non-Hispanic/Latino; 20% Hispanic/Latino; 4% Asian, non-Hispanic/Latino; 2% Native Hawaiian or other Pacific Islander, non-Hispanic/Latino; 1% American Indian or Alaska Native, non-Hispanic/Latino; 4% Two or more races, non-Hispanic/Latino; 3% Race/ethnicity unknown; 4% international; 24% live on campus.

Freshmen:

Admission: 3,069 applied, 2,596 admitted, 789 enrolled. ***Average high school GPA:*** 3.3.

Retention: 74% of full-time freshmen returned.

FACULTY

Total: 379, 78% full-time, 61% with terminal degrees.

Student/faculty ratio: 12:1.

ACADEMICS

Calendar: quarters. *Degrees:* certificates, bachelor's, master's, and postbachelor's certificates.

Special study options: academic remediation for entering students, advanced placement credit, distance learning, double majors, English as a second language, external degree program, freshman honors college, honors programs, independent study, internships, off-campus study, part-time degree program, services for LD students, student-designed majors, study abroad, summer session for credit. ***ROTC:*** Army (c).

Computers: 411 computers/terminals are available on campus for general student use. Students can access the following: computer help desk, free student e-mail accounts, online (class) grades, online (class) registration, online (class) schedules. Campuswide network is available. 100% of college-owned or -operated housing units are wired for high-speed Internet access. Wireless service is available via entire campus.

Library: Wayne and Lynn Hamersly Library. *Books:* 164,610 (physical), 193,700 (digital/electronic); *Serial titles:* 33,400 (physical), 223,223 (digital/electronic); *Databases:* 291. Study areas open 24 hours, 5–7 days a week; students can reserve study rooms.

STUDENT LIFE

Housing options: on-campus residence required for freshman year; coed, men-only, women-only, special housing for students with disabilities. Campus housing is university owned. Freshman campus housing is guaranteed.

Activities and organizations: drama/theater group, student-run newspaper, radio station, choral group, Model United Nations, Multicultural Student Union, Oregon Student Association, Alternative Spring Break (community service), M.E.Ch.A, national fraternities, national sororities.

Athletics Member NCAA. All Division II. ***Intercollegiate sports:*** baseball M(s), basketball M(s)/W(s), cross-country running M(s)/W(s), football M(s), soccer W(s), softball W(s), track and field M(s)/W(s), volleyball W(s). ***Intramural sports:*** badminton M/W, basketball M/W, bowling M/W, cross-country running M(c)/W(c), football M/W, golf M/W, lacrosse M(c), racquetball M(c)/W(c), rugby M(c)/W(c), soccer M(c)/W(c), softball M/W, swimming and diving M(c)/W(c), tennis M/W, track and field M/W, volleyball M(c)/W(c), water polo M(c)/W(c).

Campus security: 24-hour emergency response devices and patrols, late-night transport/escort service, controlled dormitory access.

Student services: health clinic, personal/psychological counseling, women's center, veterans affairs office.

FINANCIAL AID

Financial Aid Of all full-time matriculated undergraduates who enrolled in 2018, 2,988 applied for aid, 2,467 were judged to have need, 283 had their need fully met. 212 Federal Work-Study jobs (averaging $1155). In 2018, 256 non-need-based awards were made. ***Average percent of need met:*** 59. ***Average financial aid package:*** $9800. ***Average need-based loan:*** $3879. ***Average need-based gift aid:*** $7857. ***Average non-need-based aid:*** $3135. ***Average indebtedness upon graduation:*** $6815.

APPLYING

Options: electronic application.

Application fee: $60.

Required: high school transcript, minimum 2.8 GPA, general college preparatory program completion.

Application deadlines: rolling (freshmen), rolling (transfers).

Notification: continuous (freshmen), continuous (transfers).

CONTACT

Mr. David Compton, Assistant Director of Admissions for Recruitment, Western Oregon University, 345 North Monmouth Avenue, Monmouth, OR 97361. *Phone:* 503-838-8211. *Toll-free phone:* 877-877-1593. *Fax:* 503-838-8067. *E-mail:* wolfgram@wou.edu.

Willamette University

Salem, Oregon

http://www.willamette.edu/

- **Independent United Methodist** comprehensive, founded 1842
- **Urban** 72-acre campus with easy access to Portland
- **Endowment** $262.5 million
- **Coed** 1,624 undergraduate students, 96% full-time, 58% women, 42% men
- **Very difficult** entrance level, 78% of applicants were admitted

UNDERGRAD STUDENTS

1,565 full-time, 59 part-time. Students come from 38 states and territories; 8 other countries; 71% are from out of state; 2% Black or African American, non-Hispanic/Latino; 15% Hispanic/Latino; 6% Asian, non-

Hispanic/Latino; 0.3% Native Hawaiian or other Pacific Islander, non-Hispanic/Latino; 0.8% American Indian or Alaska Native, non-Hispanic/Latino; 8% Two or more races, non-Hispanic/Latino; 4% Race/ethnicity unknown; 0.7% international; 2% transferred in; 60% live on campus.

Freshmen:
Admission: 3,972 applied, 3,095 admitted, 371 enrolled. ***Average high school GPA:*** 3.9. ***Test scores:*** SAT evidence-based reading and writing scores over 500: 94%; SAT math scores over 500: 92%; ACT scores over 18: 98%; SAT evidence-based reading and writing scores over 600: 71%; SAT math scores over 600: 55%; ACT scores over 24: 78%; SAT evidence-based reading and writing scores over 700: 16%; SAT math scores over 700: 13%; ACT scores over 30: 36%.

Retention: 84% of full-time freshmen returned.

FACULTY
Total: 255, 70% full-time, 93% with terminal degrees.

Student/faculty ratio: 11:1.

ACADEMICS
Calendar: semesters. *Degrees:* bachelor's, master's, and doctoral.

Special study options: accelerated degree program, advanced placement credit, double majors, independent study, internships, off-campus study, part-time degree program, services for LD students, student-designed majors, study abroad. ***ROTC:*** Army (c), Air Force (c).

Unusual degree programs: 3-2 engineering with University of Southern California, Washington University in St. Louis, Columbia University; forestry with Duke University.

Computers: Students can access the following: computer help desk, free student e-mail accounts, online (class) grades, online (class) registration, online (class) schedules. Campuswide network is available. 100% of college-owned or -operated housing units are wired for high-speed Internet access. Wireless service is available via entire campus.

Library: Mark O. Hatfield Library plus 1 other. Study areas open 24 hours, 5–7 days a week; students can reserve study rooms.

STUDENT LIFE
Housing options: on-campus residence required through sophomore year; coed. Campus housing is university owned. Freshman campus housing is guaranteed.

Activities and organizations: drama/theater group, student-run newspaper, radio station, choral group, national fraternities, national sororities.

Athletics Member NCAA. All Division III except golf (Division II). ***Intercollegiate sports:*** baseball M, basketball M/W, crew M/W, cross-country running M/W, football M, golf M/W, lacrosse M(c), soccer M/W, softball W, swimming and diving M/W, tennis M/W, track and field M/W, volleyball W. ***Intramural sports:*** badminton M/W, basketball M/W, bowling M/W, cross-country running M/W, football M/W, golf M/W, racquetball M/W, skiing (cross-country) M(c)/W(c), skiing (downhill) M(c)/W(c), soccer M/W, softball M/W, table tennis M/W, tennis M/W, ultimate Frisbee M/W, volleyball M/W, water polo M/W, weight lifting M/W.

Campus security: 24-hour emergency response devices and patrols, student patrols, late-night transport/escort service, controlled dormitory access.

Student services: health clinic, personal/psychological counseling, women's center.

COSTS & FINANCIAL AID
Costs (2020–21) ***Comprehensive fee:*** $66,952 includes full-time tuition ($53,300), mandatory fees ($324), and room and board ($13,328). Part-time tuition: $6662 per credit hour. ***Payment plan:*** tuition prepayment.

Financial Aid Of all full-time matriculated undergraduates who enrolled in 2019, 941 applied for aid, 941 were judged to have need, 83 had their need fully met. 378 Federal Work-Study jobs (averaging $2732). In 2019, 150 non-need-based awards were made. ***Average percent of need met:*** 65. ***Average financial aid package:*** $32,918. ***Average need-based loan:*** $4419. ***Average need-based gift aid:*** $28,344. ***Average non-need-based aid:*** $21,261. ***Average indebtedness upon graduation:*** $26,973.

APPLYING
Standardized Tests *Recommended:* SAT and SAT Subject Tests or ACT (for admission).

Options: electronic application, early action, deferred entrance.

Required: essay or personal statement, high school transcript, minimum 2.0 GPA, 1 letter of recommendation. ***Recommended:*** interview.

Application deadlines: 1/15 (freshmen), 2/1 (transfers), 11/15 (early action).

Notification: continuous until 5/1 (freshmen), 3/15 (transfers).

CONTACT
Sue Corner, Senior Associate Director of Admission, Willamette University, 900 State Street, Salem, OR 97301. *Phone:* 503-375-5337. *Toll-free phone:* 877-542-2787. *E-mail:* bearcat@willamette.edu.

PENNSYLVANIA

Albright College

Reading, Pennsylvania

http://www.albright.edu/

- **Independent** comprehensive, founded 1856, affiliated with United Methodist Church
- **Suburban** 118-acre campus with easy access to Philadelphia
- **Endowment** $67.7 million
- **Coed**
- **Moderately difficult** entrance level

FACULTY
Student/faculty ratio: 14:1.

ACADEMICS
Calendar: 4-1-4. *Degrees:* certificates, bachelor's, and master's.
Library: F. W. Gingrich Library plus 1 other. *Databases:* 60. Students can reserve study rooms.

STUDENT LIFE
Housing options: on-campus residence required through senior year; coed, special housing for students with disabilities. Campus housing is university owned and leased by the school. Freshman campus housing is guaranteed.

Activities and organizations: drama/theater group, student-run newspaper, radio and television station, choral group, Greek Organizations (combined), Alpha Phi Omega (service organization), Student Government Association, Albright College Activities Council, Albrightian (newspaper), national fraternities, national sororities.

Athletics Member NCAA. All Division III.

Campus security: 24-hour emergency response devices and patrols, student patrols, late-night transport/escort service, controlled dormitory access.

Student services: health clinic, personal/psychological counseling, women's center, veterans affairs office.

COSTS & FINANCIAL AID
Costs (2019–20) ***Comprehensive fee:*** $38,122 includes full-time tuition ($24,500), mandatory fees ($1142), and room and board ($12,480). ***College room only:*** $6864.

Financial Aid Of all full-time matriculated undergraduates who enrolled in 2018, 1,552 applied for aid, 1,488 were judged to have need, 166 had their need fully met. In 2018, 132 non-need-based awards were made. ***Average percent of need met:*** 81. ***Average financial aid package:*** $39,431. ***Average need-based loan:*** $3964. ***Average need-based gift aid:*** $35,077. ***Average non-need-based aid:*** $24,449. ***Average indebtedness upon graduation:*** $36,422.

APPLYING
Options: electronic application, deferred entrance.

Application fee: $35.

Required: high school transcript, minimum 2.5 GPA. ***Required for some:*** essay or personal statement, 1 letter of recommendation, interview, secondary school report (guidance department), interview for students applying test-optional.

CONTACT
Ms. Jennifer H. Williamson, Director of Admission, Albright College, PO Box 15234, 13th and Bern Streets, Reading, PA 19612-5234. *Phone:* 610-

921-7260. *Toll-free phone:* 800-252-1856. *Fax:* 610-921-7294. *E-mail:* admission@albright.edu.

Allegheny College

Meadville, Pennsylvania

http://www.allegheny.edu/

- **Independent** 4-year, founded 1815
- **Suburban** 566-acre campus
- **Endowment** $230.5 million
- **Coed** 1,775 undergraduate students, 97% full-time, 56% women, 44% men
- **Very difficult** entrance level, 62% of applicants were admitted

UNDERGRAD STUDENTS

1,713 full-time, 62 part-time. Students come from 48 states and territories; 58 other countries; 48% are from out of state; 8% Black or African American, non-Hispanic/Latino; 9% Hispanic/Latino; 4% Asian, non-Hispanic/Latino; 0.3% American Indian or Alaska Native, non-Hispanic/Latino; 4% Two or more races, non-Hispanic/Latino; 3% Race/ethnicity unknown; 3% international; 0.8% transferred in; 94% live on campus.

Freshmen:

Admission: 5,208 applied, 3,237 admitted, 500 enrolled. ***Average high school GPA:*** 3.5.

Retention: 86% of full-time freshmen returned.

FACULTY

Total: 198, 75% full-time, 78% with terminal degrees.

Student/faculty ratio: 11:1.

ACADEMICS

Calendar: semesters. *Degree:* bachelor's.

Special study options: advanced placement credit, double majors, English as a second language, honors programs, independent study, internships, off-campus study, services for LD students, student-designed majors, study abroad. ***ROTC:*** Army (c).

Unusual degree programs: 3-2 engineering with Case Western Reserve University, Washington University, University of Pittsburgh; arts management, public policy and management, health care policy and management, information systems management with Carnegie Mellon University; physician assistant, occupational therapy and psychology with Chatham University.

Computers: 207 computers/terminals and 200 ports are available on campus for general student use. Students can access the following: campus intranet, computer help desk, free student e-mail accounts, online (class) grades, online (class) registration, online (class) schedules, placement testing, course catalog, class lists, transcript review and ordering, billing, payroll time cards, internet kiosks, dataports for laptops, campus organizations, financial aid, room draw, registration, class schedules, grade reports. Campuswide network is available. 100% of college-owned or -operated housing units are wired for high-speed Internet access. Wireless service is available via entire campus.

Library: Lawrence Lee Pelletier Library. *Books:* 313,354 (physical), 676,562 (digital/electronic); *Serial titles:* 48 (physical), 70,618 (digital/electronic). Weekly public service hours: 115; students can reserve study rooms.

STUDENT LIFE

Housing options: on-campus residence required through senior year; coed, men-only, women-only, special housing for students with disabilities. Campus housing is university owned. Freshman campus housing is guaranteed.

Activities and organizations: drama/theater group, student-run newspaper, radio and television station, choral group, Student Government, Gators Activity Programming, Alpha Phi Omega (service fraternity), Outing Club, Fraternity/Sorority Life, national fraternities, national sororities.

Athletics Member NCAA. All Division III except golf (Division II). ***Intercollegiate sports:*** baseball M, basketball M/W, cheerleading M(c)/W(c), cross-country running M/W, equestrian sports M(c)/W(c), fencing M(c)/W(c), field hockey W, football M, golf M/W, ice hockey M(c), lacrosse M/W, rugby M(c)/W(c), soccer M/W, softball W, swimming and diving M/W, tennis M/W, track and field M/W, ultimate Frisbee M(c)/W(c), volleyball W. ***Intramural sports:*** basketball M.

Campus security: 24-hour emergency response devices and patrols, late-night transport/escort service, controlled dormitory access, CCTV system, emergency alert system.

Student services: health clinic, personal/psychological counseling.

COSTS & FINANCIAL AID
Costs (2020–21) ***Comprehensive fee:*** $64,060 includes full-time tuition ($50,480), mandatory fees ($500), and room and board ($13,080). Part-time tuition: $2103 per credit hour. ***Required fees:*** $250 per term part-time. ***College room only:*** $6900. Room and board charges vary according to board plan and housing facility. ***Payment plan:*** installment. ***Waivers:*** employees or children of employees.

Financial Aid Of all full-time matriculated undergraduates who enrolled in 2019, 1,460 applied for aid, 1,311 were judged to have need, 405 had their need fully met. 768 Federal Work-Study jobs (averaging $2470). 123 state and other part-time jobs (averaging $5117). In 2019, 377 non-need-based awards were made. ***Average percent of need met:*** 90. ***Average financial aid package:*** $45,117. ***Average need-based loan:*** $4465. ***Average need-based gift aid:*** $37,471. ***Average non-need-based aid:*** $27,761.

APPLYING
Options: electronic application, early admission, early decision, early action, deferred entrance.

Required: essay or personal statement, high school transcript, 2 letters of recommendation, college preparatory program. ***Recommended:*** interview.

Application deadlines: 2/15 (freshmen), 7/1 (transfers), 12/1 (early action).

Early decision deadline: 11/15 (for plan 1), 2/1 (for plan 2).

Notification: 3/15 (freshmen), 8/1 (transfers), 11/30 (early decision plan 1), 2/15 (early decision plan 2), 1/1 (early action).

CONTACT
Linda Clune, Senior Associate Director of Admissions, Allegheny College, 520 North Main Street, Box 5, Meadville, PA 16335. *Phone:* 814-332-4351. *Toll-free phone:* 800-521-5293. *Fax:* 814-337-0431. *E-mail:* admissions@allegheny.edu.

See below for display ad and page 1040 for the College Close-Up.

Alvernia University

Reading, Pennsylvania

http://www.alvernia.edu/

CONTACT
Mr. Dan Hartzman, Director of Undergraduate Admissions, Alvernia University, 400 Saint Bernardine Street, Reading, PA 19607-1799. *Phone:* 610-568-1530. *Toll-free phone:* 888-ALVERNIA. *Fax:* 610-796-2873. *E-mail:* admissions@alvernia.edu.

Arcadia University

Glenside, Pennsylvania

http://www.arcadia.edu/

- **Independent** comprehensive, founded 1853, affiliated with Presbyterian Church (U.S.A.)
- **Suburban** 76-acre campus with easy access to Philadelphia
- **Coed** 2,151 undergraduate students, 90% full-time, 67% women, 33% men
- **Moderately difficult** entrance level, 66% of applicants were admitted

UNDERGRAD STUDENTS
1,931 full-time, 220 part-time. 37% are from out of state; 10% Black or African American, non-Hispanic/Latino; 10% Hispanic/Latino; 5% Asian, non-Hispanic/Latino; 0.1% Native Hawaiian or other Pacific Islander, non-Hispanic/Latino; 0.4% American Indian or Alaska Native, non-Hispanic/Latino; 5% Two or more races, non-Hispanic/Latino; 4% Race/ethnicity unknown; 3% international; 4% transferred in; 51% live on campus.

Freshmen:
Admission: 10,216 applied, 6,709 admitted, 530 enrolled. ***Average high school GPA:*** 3.7. ***Test scores:*** SAT evidence-based reading and writing scores over 500: 86%; SAT math scores over 500: 81%; ACT scores over 18: 96%; SAT evidence-based reading and writing scores over 600: 44%; SAT math scores over 600: 32%; ACT scores over 24: 59%; SAT evidence-based reading and writing scores over 700: 8%; SAT math scores over 700: 5%; ACT scores over 30: 14%.

Retention: 80% of full-time freshmen returned.

FACULTY
Total: 377, 42% full-time, 59% with terminal degrees.

Student/faculty ratio: 12:1.

ACADEMICS
Calendar: semesters. *Degrees:* certificates, bachelor's, master's, doctoral, post-master's, and postbachelor's certificates.

Special study options: accelerated degree program, advanced placement credit, cooperative education, distance learning, double majors, English as a second language, honors programs, independent study, internships, off-campus study, part-time degree program, services for LD students, student-designed majors, study abroad, summer session for credit.

Unusual degree programs: 3-2 engineering with University of Pittsburgh and Washington University in Saint Louis; forensic science, international peace and conflict resolution.

Computers: Students can access the following: campus intranet, computer help desk, free student e-mail accounts, online (class) grades, online (class) registration, online (class) schedules. Campuswide network is available. 100% of college-owned or -operated housing units are wired for high-speed Internet access. Wireless service is available via entire campus.

Library: Bette E. Landman Library. Students can reserve study rooms.

STUDENT LIFE
Housing options: coed, women-only. Campus housing is university owned. Freshman applicants given priority for college housing.

Activities and organizations: drama/theater group, student-run newspaper, radio station, choral group, Student Program Board, Residence Hall Council, Student Government, Arcadia Christian Fellowship, Student Alumni Association.

Athletics Member NCAA. All Division III. ***Intercollegiate sports:*** baseball M, basketball M/W, cross-country running M/W, field hockey W, golf M/W, ice hockey M/W, lacrosse M/W, soccer M/W, softball W, swimming and diving M/W, tennis M/W, track and field M/W, volleyball M/W. ***Intramural sports:*** basketball M/W, cheerleading M(c)/W(c), equestrian sports M/W, soccer M/W, volleyball M/W.

Campus security: 24-hour emergency response devices and patrols, student patrols, late-night transport/escort service, controlled dormitory access.

Student services: health clinic, personal/psychological counseling.

COSTS & FINANCIAL AID
Costs (2019–20) ***Comprehensive fee:*** $58,340 includes full-time tuition ($43,740), mandatory fees ($700), and room and board ($13,900). Part-time tuition: $730 per credit hour. ***College room only:*** $9000. Room and board charges vary according to board plan and housing facility. ***Payment plan:*** installment. ***Waivers:*** employees or children of employees.

Financial Aid Of all full-time matriculated undergraduates who enrolled in 2016, 2,054 applied for aid, 1,863 were judged to have need, 558 had their need fully met. 140 state and other part-time jobs (averaging $1671). In 2016, 354 non-need-based awards were made. ***Average percent of need met:*** 83. ***Average financial aid package:*** $30,072. ***Average need-based loan:*** $3894. ***Average need-based gift aid:*** $26,516. ***Average non-need-based aid:*** $17,060.

APPLYING
Standardized Tests *Required:* SAT or ACT (for admission).

Options: electronic application, deferred entrance.

Application fee: $30.

Required: essay or personal statement, high school transcript, 2 letters of recommendation. ***Required for some:*** portfolio, audition. ***Recommended:*** minimum 3.0 GPA.

Application deadlines: 3/1 (freshmen), 6/15 (transfers).

Notification: continuous until 9/1 (freshmen), continuous until 9/1 (transfers).

CONTACT
Colleen Pernicello, Interim Vice President of Enrollment Management, Arcadia University, 450 South Easton Road, Glenside, PA 19038. *Phone:*

215-572-2910. *Toll-free phone:* 877-ARCADIA. *Fax:* 215-572-4049. *E-mail:* admiss@arcadia.edu.

The Art Institute of Pittsburgh
Pittsburgh, Pennsylvania
http://www.artinstitutes.edu/pittsburgh/

CONTACT
The Art Institute of Pittsburgh, 420 Boulevard of the Allies, Pittsburgh, PA 15219. *Phone:* 412-263-6600. *Toll-free phone:* 800-275-2470.

Bloomsburg University of Pennsylvania
Bloomsburg, Pennsylvania
http://www.bloomu.edu/

- **State-supported** comprehensive, founded 1839, part of Pennsylvania State System of Higher Education
- **Small-town** 366-acre campus
- **Endowment** $45.0 million
- **Coed**
- **Minimally difficult** entrance level

FACULTY
Student/faculty ratio: 19:1.

ACADEMICS
Calendar: semesters. *Degrees:* certificates, bachelor's, master's, doctoral, and postbachelor's certificates.
Library: Andruss Library. *Books:* 374,393 (physical), 269,435 (digital/electronic); *Serial titles:* 5,838 (physical), 84,065 (digital/electronic); *Databases:* 165. Weekly public service hours: 98; students can reserve study rooms.

STUDENT LIFE
Housing options: on-campus residence required for freshman year; coed. Campus housing is university owned and leased by the school. Freshman campus housing is guaranteed.

Activities and organizations: drama/theater group, student-run newspaper, radio and television station, choral group, marching band, Living and Learning Communities, Band and Music Groups, Greek Organizations, Residence Hall Councils, Club Sports, national fraternities, national sororities.

Athletics Member NCAA. All Division II except wrestling (Division I).

Campus security: 24-hour emergency response devices and patrols, late-night transport/escort service, controlled dormitory access, monitored surveillance cameras.

Student services: health clinic, personal/psychological counseling, women's center, legal services, veterans affairs office.

COSTS & FINANCIAL AID
Costs (2019–20) ***Tuition:*** state resident $7716 full-time, $322 per credit hour part-time; nonresident $19,290 full-time, $805 per credit hour part-time. ***Required fees:*** $3242 full-time. ***Room and board:*** $9686; room only: $6308.

Financial Aid Of all full-time matriculated undergraduates who enrolled in 2019, 6,547 applied for aid, 4,622 were judged to have need, 721 had their need fully met. 1,181 Federal Work-Study jobs (averaging $3847). 1,181 state and other part-time jobs (averaging $3847). In 2019, 424 non-need-based awards were made. ***Average percent of need met:*** 59. ***Average financial aid package:*** $10,181. ***Average need-based loan:*** $4049. ***Average need-based gift aid:*** $5956. ***Average non-need-based aid:*** $3030. ***Average indebtedness upon graduation:*** $38,013.

APPLYING
Standardized Tests *Required:* SAT or ACT (for admission).

Options: electronic application, early admission, early action, deferred entrance.

Application fee: $35.

Required: high school transcript.

CONTACT
Bloomsburg University of Pennsylvania, 400 East Second Street, Bloomsburg, PA 17815-1301.

Bryn Athyn College of the New Church
Bryn Athyn, Pennsylvania
http://www.brynathyn.edu/

- **Independent Christian** comprehensive, founded 1877, affiliated with Church of the New Jerusalem, part of The Academy of the New Church
- **Suburban** 130-acre campus with easy access to Philadelphia
- **Endowment** $58.8 million
- **Coed** 288 undergraduate students, 95% full-time, 52% women, 48% men
- **Minimally difficult** entrance level, 89% of applicants were admitted

UNDERGRAD STUDENTS
273 full-time, 15 part-time. 22% are from out of state; 17% Black or African American, non-Hispanic/Latino; 11% Hispanic/Latino; 2% Asian, non-Hispanic/Latino; 0.4% Native Hawaiian or other Pacific Islander, non-Hispanic/Latino; 0.7% American Indian or Alaska Native, non-Hispanic/Latino; 1% Two or more races, non-Hispanic/Latino; 2% Race/ethnicity unknown; 6% international; 7% transferred in; 44% live on campus.

Freshmen:
Admission: 250 applied, 222 admitted, 81 enrolled. ***Average high school GPA:*** 3.4. ***Test scores:*** SAT evidence-based reading and writing scores over 500: 79%; SAT math scores over 500: 79%; ACT scores over 18: 93%; SAT evidence-based reading and writing scores over 600: 31%; SAT math scores over 600: 25%; ACT scores over 24: 33%; SAT evidence-based reading and writing scores over 700: 6%; SAT math scores over 700: 4%.
Retention: 86% of full-time freshmen returned.

FACULTY
Total: 51, 82% full-time, 96% with terminal degrees.
Student/faculty ratio: 6:1.

ACADEMICS
Calendar: trimesters. *Degrees:* associate, bachelor's, and master's.

Special study options: academic remediation for entering students, accelerated degree program, advanced placement credit, cooperative education, English as a second language, independent study, internships, part-time degree program, services for LD students, student-designed majors, study abroad. ***ROTC:*** Army (c), Air Force (c).

Computers: 18 computers/terminals are available on campus for general student use. Students can access the following: campus intranet, computer help desk, free student e-mail accounts, online (class) grades, online (class) registration, online (class) schedules. Campuswide network is available. 100% of college-owned or -operated housing units are wired for high-speed Internet access. Wireless service is available via entire campus.
Library: Swedenborg Library plus 1 other. *Books:* 70,742 (physical), 252 (digital/electronic); *Serial titles:* 834 (physical), 74 (digital/electronic); *Databases:* 13.

STUDENT LIFE
Housing options: men-only, women-only. Campus housing is university owned. Freshman applicants given priority for college housing.

Activities and organizations: drama/theater group, choral group, C.A.R.E. (Community Service), Student Government, Multicultural Student Organization, Feel Good (Community Service).

Athletics Member NCAA. All Division III. ***Intercollegiate sports:*** basketball M/W, cross-country running M/W, field hockey W, golf M, ice hockey M, lacrosse M/W, soccer M/W, tennis W, volleyball W.

Campus security: 24-hour emergency response devices and patrols, controlled dormitory access.

Student services: health clinic, personal/psychological counseling.

COSTS & FINANCIAL AID
Costs (2020–21) ***Tuition:*** $973 per credit hour part-time. ***Required fees:*** $60 per credit hour part-time. ***Payment plan:*** installment. ***Waivers:*** senior citizens and employees or children of employees.

Financial Aid Of all full-time matriculated undergraduates who enrolled in 2018, 222 applied for aid, 115 were judged to have need, 32 had their need fully met. 15,000 Federal Work-Study jobs. In 2018, 109 non-need-based awards were made. ***Average percent of need met:*** 29. ***Average***

financial aid package: $26,235. ***Average need-based loan:*** $4346. ***Average need-based gift aid:*** $10,257. ***Average non-need-based aid:*** $6457. ***Average indebtedness upon graduation:*** $2825.

APPLYING

Standardized Tests *Required:* SAT or ACT (for admission).

Options: electronic application, deferred entrance.

Required: essay or personal statement, high school transcript, minimum 2.0 GPA, 1 letter of recommendation. ***Required for some:*** interview.

Application deadlines: rolling (freshmen), rolling (transfers).

Notification: continuous (freshmen), continuous (transfers).

CONTACT

Ms. Nicole D'Amico, Director of Admissions Office, Bryn Athyn College of the New Church, 2945 College Drive, Box 717, Bryn Athyn, PA 19009. *Phone:* 267-502-6000. *Toll-free phone:* 800-767-9552. *Fax:* 267-502-2593. *E-mail:* admissions@brynathyn.edu.

Bryn Mawr College

Bryn Mawr, Pennsylvania

http://www.brynmawr.edu/

- **Independent** comprehensive, founded 1885
- **Suburban** 135-acre campus with easy access to Philadelphia
- **Endowment** $852.7 million
- **Undergraduate: women only; graduate: coed**
- **Most difficult** entrance level

FACULTY

Student/faculty ratio: 9:1.

ACADEMICS

Calendar: semesters. *Degrees:* bachelor's, master's, doctoral, and postbachelor's certificates.

Library: Canaday Library plus 2 others. *Books:* 740,887 (physical), 754,968 (digital/electronic); *Serial titles:* 9,146 (physical), 123,010 (digital/electronic); *Databases:* 170. Weekly public service hours: 105; study areas open 24 hours, 5–7 days a week.

STUDENT LIFE

Housing options: on-campus residence required for freshman year; coed, women-only, cooperative. Campus housing is university owned. Freshman campus housing is guaranteed.

Activities and organizations: drama/theater group, student-run newspaper, radio station, choral group, Student Government Association.

Athletics Member NCAA. All Division III.

Campus security: 24-hour emergency response devices and patrols, late-night transport/escort service, controlled dormitory access, shuttle bus service, awareness programs, bicycle registration, security Web site.

Student services: health clinic, personal/psychological counseling, women's center.

COSTS & FINANCIAL AID

Costs (2019–20) ***Comprehensive fee:*** $71,540 includes full-time tuition ($53,180), mandatory fees ($1260), and room and board ($17,100). Part-time tuition: $6650 per course. ***College room only:*** $9760.

Financial Aid Of all full-time matriculated undergraduates who enrolled in 2019, 813 applied for aid, 707 were judged to have need, 707 had their need fully met. In 2019, 264 non-need-based awards were made. ***Average percent of need met:*** 100. ***Average financial aid package:*** $53,763. ***Average need-based loan:*** $5280. ***Average need-based gift aid:*** $46,447. ***Average non-need-based aid:*** $18,972. ***Average indebtedness upon graduation:*** $28,772. ***Financial aid deadline:*** 1/15.

APPLYING

Standardized Tests *Required for some:* SAT and SAT Subject Tests or ACT (for admission).

Options: electronic application, early admission, early decision, deferred entrance.

Application fee: $50.

Required: essay or personal statement, high school transcript, 3 letters of recommendation. ***Recommended:*** interview.

CONTACT

Dr. Cheryl Lynn Horsey, Chief Enrollment Officer, Bryn Mawr College, 101 North Merion Avenue, Bryn Mawr, PA 19010. *Phone:* 610-526-6522.

Toll-free phone: 800-BMC-1885. *Fax:* 610-526-7471. *E-mail:* chorsey@brynmawr.edu.

See below for display ad and page 1048 for the College Close-Up.

Bucknell University
Lewisburg, Pennsylvania
http://www.bucknell.edu/

- **Independent** comprehensive, founded 1846
- **Small-town** 446-acre campus
- **Endowment** $866.8 million
- **Coed** 3,627 undergraduate students, 99% full-time, 51% women, 49% men
- **Most difficult** entrance level, 34% of applicants were admitted

UNDERGRAD STUDENTS
3,606 full-time, 21 part-time. Students come from 41 states and territories; 51 other countries; 79% are from out of state; 3% Black or African American, non-Hispanic/Latino; 7% Hispanic/Latino; 5% Asian, non-Hispanic/Latino; 0.1% American Indian or Alaska Native, non-Hispanic/Latino; 4% Two or more races, non-Hispanic/Latino; 0.1% Race/ethnicity unknown; 6% international; 0.7% transferred in; 91% live on campus.

Freshmen:
Admission: 9,845 applied, 3,370 admitted, 964 enrolled. ***Average high school GPA:*** 3.6. ***Test scores:*** SAT evidence-based reading and writing scores over 500: 100%; SAT math scores over 500: 100%; ACT scores over 18: 100%; SAT evidence-based reading and writing scores over 600: 88%; SAT math scores over 600: 89%; ACT scores over 24: 98%; SAT evidence-based reading and writing scores over 700: 26%; SAT math scores over 700: 43%; ACT scores over 30: 59%.

Retention: 92% of full-time freshmen returned.

FACULTY
Total: 435, 90% full-time, 91% with terminal degrees.

Student/faculty ratio: 9:1.

ACADEMICS
Calendar: semesters. *Degrees:* bachelor's and master's.

Special study options: advanced placement credit, double majors, honors programs, independent study, internships, off-campus study, part-time degree program, services for LD students, student-designed majors, study abroad, summer session for credit. ***ROTC:*** Army (b).

Unusual degree programs: 3-2 engineering; biology, chemistry.

Computers: 1,154 computers/terminals and 190 ports are available on campus for general student use. Students can access the following: campus intranet, computer help desk, free student e-mail accounts, online (class) grades, online (class) registration, online (class) schedules. Campuswide network is available. 100% of college-owned or -operated housing units are wired for high-speed Internet access. Wireless service is available via entire campus.
Library: Ellen Clarke Bertrand Library. *Books:* 664,918 (physical), 885,255 (digital/electronic); *Serial titles:* 240 (physical), 61,703 (digital/electronic); *Databases:* 239. Weekly public service hours: 125.

STUDENT LIFE
Housing options: on-campus residence required through senior year; coed, women-only, cooperative, special housing for students with disabilities. Campus housing is university owned. Freshman campus housing is guaranteed.

Activities and organizations: drama/theater group, student-run newspaper, radio station, choral group, Black Student Union, Outing Club, Activities and Campus Events, French Club, Catholic Campus Ministries, national fraternities, national sororities.

Athletics Member NCAA. All Division I except football (Division I-AA). ***Intercollegiate sports:*** baseball M, basketball M(s)/W(s), cheerleading M(c)/W(c), crew M(c)/W, cross-country running M/W(s), equestrian sports M(c)/W(c), field hockey W(s), golf M/W(c), ice hockey M(c), lacrosse M(s)/W(s), rock climbing M(c)/W(c), rugby M(c)/W(c), sailing M(c)/W(c), skiing (downhill) W(c), soccer M(s)/W, softball W(s), squash M(c)/W(c), swimming and diving M(s)/W, tennis M/W, track and field M/W(s), ultimate Frisbee M(c)/W(c), volleyball M(c)/W(s), water polo M/W, weight lifting M(c)/W(c), wrestling M(s). ***Intramural sports:*** basketball M/W, cross-country running M/W, golf M/W, racquetball M/W, soccer M/W, softball M/W, squash M/W, table tennis M/W, tennis M/W, ultimate Frisbee M/W, volleyball M/W, weight lifting M, wrestling M.

Campus security: 24-hour emergency response devices and patrols, student patrols, late-night transport/escort service, controlled dormitory access.

Student services: health clinic, personal/psychological counseling, women's center.

COSTS & FINANCIAL AID
Costs (2020–21) ***Comprehensive fee:*** $72,872 includes full-time tuition ($57,882), mandatory fees ($320), and room and board ($14,670). Part-time tuition: $6352 per course. ***College room only:*** $8946. Room and board charges vary according to board plan and housing facility. ***Payment plan:*** tuition prepayment. ***Waivers:*** employees or children of employees.

Financial Aid Of all full-time matriculated undergraduates who enrolled in 2019, 1,715 applied for aid, 1,369 were judged to have need. 600 Federal Work-Study jobs (averaging $1500). 50 state and other part-time jobs (averaging $1500). In 2019, 323 non-need-based awards were made. ***Average percent of need met:*** 92. ***Average financial aid package:*** $37,000. ***Average need-based loan:*** $5500. ***Average need-based gift aid:*** $32,300. ***Average non-need-based aid:*** $12,978. ***Average indebtedness upon graduation:*** $31,000.

APPLYING
Standardized Tests *Required for some:* SAT or ACT (for admission).

Options: electronic application, early decision, deferred entrance.

Application fee: $40.

Required: essay or personal statement, high school transcript, 1 letter of recommendation.

Application deadlines: 1/15 (freshmen), 3/15 (transfers).

Early decision deadline: 11/15.

Notification: 4/1 (freshmen), 5/1 (transfers), 12/15 (early decision).

CONTACT
Dean Kevin Mathes, Dean of Admissions, Bucknell University, 1 Dent Drive, Lewisburg, PA 17837. *Phone:* 570-577-3000. *Fax:* 570-577-3538. *E-mail:* admissions@bucknell.edu.

Cabrini University
Radnor, Pennsylvania
http://www.cabrini.edu/

- **Independent Roman Catholic** comprehensive, founded 1957
- **Suburban** 112-acre campus with easy access to Philadelphia
- **Endowment** $43.7 million
- **Coed**
- **Moderately difficult** entrance level

FACULTY
Student/faculty ratio: 11:1.

ACADEMICS
Calendar: semesters. *Degrees:* bachelor's, master's, and doctoral.
Library: Holy Spirit Library. *Books:* 143,980 (digital/electronic); *Serial titles:* 67 (physical), 68,500 (digital/electronic); *Databases:* 47. Weekly public service hours: 97.

STUDENT LIFE
Housing options: coed, women-only, special housing for students with disabilities. Campus housing is university owned and leased by the school. Freshman applicants given priority for college housing.

Activities and organizations: drama/theater group, student-run newspaper, radio and television station, choral group, Campus Activities and Programming (CAP) Board, Student Government Association (SGA), Black Student Union, Catholic Relief Services (CRS) Ambassadors, Cabrini Friends of Exceptional Children (CFEC), national fraternities, national sororities.

Athletics Member NCAA. All Division III.

Campus security: 24-hour emergency response devices and patrols, student patrols, late-night transport/escort service, controlled dormitory access, Resident Assistants and Directors on nightly duty.

Student services: health clinic, personal/psychological counseling.

COSTS & FINANCIAL AID
Costs (2019–20) ***Comprehensive fee:*** $45,455 includes full-time tuition ($31,875), mandatory fees ($990), and room and board ($12,590). Part-time tuition and fees vary according to course load. ***College room only:*** $7560. Room and board charges vary according to board plan and housing facility.

Financial Aid Of all full-time matriculated undergraduates who enrolled in 2015, 1,197 applied for aid, 1,006 were judged to have need, 258 had their need fully met. 226 Federal Work-Study jobs (averaging $1141). In 2015, 221 non-need-based awards were made. ***Average financial aid package:*** $16,988. ***Average need-based loan:*** $3257. ***Average need-based gift aid:*** $7627. ***Average non-need-based aid:*** $10,210. ***Average indebtedness upon graduation:*** $43,437.

APPLYING
Standardized Tests *Recommended:* SAT or ACT (for admission).

Options: electronic application, deferred entrance.

Application fee: $20.

Required: essay or personal statement, high school transcript, minimum 2.0 GPA. ***Recommended:*** minimum 2.0 GPA, 1 letter of recommendation, interview.

CONTACT
Ms. Shannon Zottola, Assistant Vice President for Enrollment Management, Cabrini University, 610 King of Prussia Road, Radnor, PA 19087-3698. *Phone:* 610-902-1027. *Toll-free phone:* 800-848-1003. *Fax:* 610-902-8508. *E-mail:* admit@cabrini.edu.

Cairn University

Langhorne, Pennsylvania

http://cairn.edu/

CONTACT
Mr. Thomas Sherf, Director of Undergraduate Admissions, Cairn University, 200 Manor Avenue, Langhorne, PA 19047. *Phone:* 215-702-4248. *Toll-free phone:* 800-366-0049. *Fax:* 215-702-4248. *E-mail:* admissions@cairn.edu.

California University of Pennsylvania

California, Pennsylvania

http://www.calu.edu/

- **State-supported** comprehensive, founded 1852, part of Pennsylvania State System of Higher Education
- **Rural** 188-acre campus with easy access to Pittsburgh
- **Endowment** $24.1 million
- **Coed** 5,174 undergraduate students, 81% full-time, 54% women, 46% men
- **Moderately difficult** entrance level, 97% of applicants were admitted

UNDERGRAD STUDENTS
4,212 full-time, 962 part-time. Students come from 49 states and territories; 36 other countries; 7% are from out of state; 14% transferred in; 48% live on campus.

Freshmen:
Admission: 2,909 applied, 2,820 admitted, 1,017 enrolled. ***Average high school GPA:*** 3.2.

Retention: 71% of full-time freshmen returned.

ACADEMICS
Calendar: semesters. *Degrees:* certificates, associate, bachelor's, master's, doctoral, post-master's, and postbachelor's certificates.

Special study options: academic remediation for entering students, accelerated degree program, adult/continuing education programs, advanced placement credit, cooperative education, distance learning, double majors, English as a second language, honors programs, independent study, internships, off-campus study, part-time degree program, services for LD students, study abroad, summer session for credit. ***ROTC:*** Army (b).

Computers: 1,300 computers/terminals and 18,000 ports are available on campus for general student use. Students can access the following: campus intranet, computer help desk, free student e-mail accounts, online (class) grades, online (class) registration, online (class) schedules. 100% of college-owned or -operated housing units are wired for high-speed Internet access. Wireless service is available via entire campus.

Library: Manderino Library. Students can reserve study rooms.

STUDENT LIFE
Housing options: on-campus residence required for freshman year; coed, special housing for students with disabilities. Campus housing is university owned. Freshman campus housing is guaranteed.

Activities and organizations: drama/theater group, student-run newspaper, radio and television station, choral group, marching band, Commuter Council, STAND, Student Activities Board, University Band, Colleges Against Cancer, national fraternities, national sororities.

Athletics ***Intercollegiate sports:*** baseball M(s), basketball M(s)/W(s), cross-country running M(s)/W(s), football M(s), golf M(s)/W(s), soccer M(s)/W(s), softball W(s), swimming and diving W(s), tennis W(s), track and field M(s)/W(s), volleyball W(s). ***Intramural sports:*** archery M(c)/W(c), baseball M(c)/W(c), basketball M/W, cheerleading M(c)/W(c), equestrian sports M(c)/W(c), fencing M(c)/W(c), golf M(c)/W(c), ice hockey M(c)/W(c), lacrosse M(c), rugby M(c)/W(c), soccer M(c)/W(c), ultimate Frisbee M(c), volleyball M(c)/W(c).

Campus security: 24-hour emergency response devices and patrols, student patrols, late-night transport/escort service, controlled dormitory access.

Student services: health clinic, personal/psychological counseling, women's center, legal services, veterans affairs office.

COSTS & FINANCIAL AID
Costs (2019–20) ***Tuition:*** state resident $7716 full-time, $322 per credit hour part-time; nonresident $11,574 full-time, $482 per credit hour part-time. ***Required fees:*** $3186 full-time. ***Room and board:*** $10,186; room only: $6592. Room and board charges vary according to board plan and housing facility. ***Payment plan:*** installment. ***Waivers:*** senior citizens and employees or children of employees.

Financial Aid Of all full-time matriculated undergraduates who enrolled in 2018, 3,849 applied for aid, 3,378 were judged to have need, 474 had their need fully met. In 2018, 217 non-need-based awards were made. ***Average percent of need met:*** 67. ***Average financial aid package:*** $10,525. ***Average need-based loan:*** $4163. ***Average need-based gift aid:*** $6260. ***Average non-need-based aid:*** $1713. ***Average indebtedness upon graduation:*** $42,029.

APPLYING
Standardized Tests *Required:* SAT or ACT (for admission).

Options: electronic application, deferred entrance.

Application fee: $35.

Application deadlines: rolling (freshmen), rolling (transfers).

Notification: continuous (freshmen), continuous (transfers).

CONTACT
Dr. Tracey Sheetz, Dean of Undergraduate Admissions, California University of Pennsylvania, 250 University Avenue, California, PA 15419. *Phone:* 724-938-4404. *Toll-free phone:* 888-412-0479. *Fax:* 724-938-4564. *E-mail:* sheetz@calu.edu.

Carlow University

Pittsburgh, Pennsylvania

http://www.carlow.edu/

- **Independent Roman Catholic** comprehensive, founded 1929
- **Urban** 13-acre campus with easy access to Pittsburgh
- **Coed, primarily women** 1,298 undergraduate students, 80% full-time, 83% women, 17% men
- **Minimally difficult** entrance level, 92% of applicants were admitted

UNDERGRAD STUDENTS
1,037 full-time, 261 part-time. 5% are from out of state; 18% Black or African American, non-Hispanic/Latino; 2% Hispanic/Latino; 3% Asian, non-Hispanic/Latino; 0.1% American Indian or Alaska Native, non-Hispanic/Latino; 4% Two or more races, non-Hispanic/Latino; 3% Race/ethnicity unknown; 0.3% international; 14% transferred in; 28% live on campus.

Freshmen:
Admission: 721 applied, 662 admitted, 163 enrolled. ***Average high school GPA:*** 3.6. ***Test scores:*** SAT evidence-based reading and writing scores

over 500: 76%; SAT math scores over 500: 71%; ACT scores over 18: 92%; SAT evidence-based reading and writing scores over 600: 22%; SAT math scores over 600: 12%; ACT scores over 24: 33%; SAT evidence-based reading and writing scores over 700: 1%; SAT math scores over 700: 1%.

Retention: 78% of full-time freshmen returned.

FACULTY
Total: 245, 44% full-time, 53% with terminal degrees.

Student/faculty ratio: 11:1.

ACADEMICS
Calendar: semesters. *Degrees:* certificates, bachelor's, master's, doctoral, post-master's, and postbachelor's certificates.

Special study options: academic remediation for entering students, accelerated degree program, advanced placement credit, distance learning, double majors, honors programs, independent study, internships, off-campus study, part-time degree program, services for LD students, study abroad, summer session for credit. ***ROTC:*** Army (c), Navy (c), Air Force (c).

Unusual degree programs: 3-2 biology/environmental science and Management with Duquesne University.

Computers: Students can access the following: campus intranet, computer help desk, free student e-mail accounts, online (class) grades, online (class) registration, online (class) schedules. Campuswide network is available. 100% of college-owned or -operated housing units are wired for high-speed Internet access. Wireless service is available via entire campus.
Library: Grace Library.

STUDENT LIFE
Housing options: coed, men-only, women-only. Campus housing is university owned. Freshman applicants given priority for college housing.

Activities and organizations: drama/theater group, student-run newspaper, choral group, Student Government Association, Campus Activities Board, SPiRiT (Student Ambassadors), SNAP (Student Nursing Association), PSEA (School Education Association), national fraternities.

Athletics Member NAIA, USCAA. ***Intercollegiate sports:*** basketball M(s)/W(s), cross-country running M(s)/W(s), soccer W(s), softball W(s), tennis W(s), volleyball W(s).

Campus security: 24-hour emergency response devices and patrols, late-night transport/escort service, controlled dormitory access.

Student services: health clinic, personal/psychological counseling.

COSTS & FINANCIAL AID
Costs (2019–20) ***Comprehensive fee:*** $42,430 includes full-time tuition ($29,652), mandatory fees ($876), and room and board ($11,902). Full-time tuition and fees vary according to course load and program. Part-time tuition: $716 per credit hour. Part-time tuition and fees vary according to course load and program. ***Required fees:*** $15 per credit hour part-time. ***College room only:*** $6142. Room and board charges vary according to board plan. ***Payment plan:*** installment. ***Waivers:*** children of alumni, adult students, and employees or children of employees.

Financial Aid Of all full-time matriculated undergraduates who enrolled in 2018, 1,051 applied for aid, 997 were judged to have need, 229 had their need fully met. In 2018, 94 non-need-based awards were made. ***Average percent of need met:*** 61. ***Average financial aid package:*** $20,076. ***Average need-based loan:*** $3788. ***Average need-based gift aid:*** $4613. ***Average non-need-based aid:*** $9876. ***Average indebtedness upon graduation:*** $40,958.

APPLYING
Standardized Tests *Required:* SAT or ACT (for admission). *Recommended:* SAT (for admission), SAT and SAT Subject Tests or ACT (for admission).

Options: electronic application, deferred entrance.

Required: high school transcript. ***Recommended:*** essay or personal statement, minimum 2.5 GPA, interview.

Application deadlines: rolling (freshmen), rolling (transfers).

Notification: continuous (freshmen), continuous (transfers).

CONTACT
Ms. Wivina Chmura, Director of Undergraduate Admissions, Carlow University, 3333 Fifth Avenue, Pittsburgh, PA 15213. *Phone:* 412-578-8762. *Toll-free phone:* 800-333-CARLOW. *Fax:* 412-578-6668. *E-mail:* admissions@carlow.edu.

Carnegie Mellon University

Pittsburgh, Pennsylvania

http://www.cmu.edu/

- **Independent** university, founded 1900
- **Urban** 153-acre campus with easy access to Pittsburgh
- **Endowment** $2.0 billion
- **Coed** 7,022 undergraduate students, 97% full time, 50% women, 50% men
- **Most difficult** entrance level, 15% of applicants were admitted

UNDERGRAD STUDENTS
6,805 full-time, 217 part-time. Students come from 51 states and territories; 57 other countries; 86% are from out of state; 4% Black or African American, non-Hispanic/Latino; 9% Hispanic/Latino; 31% Asian, non-Hispanic/Latino; 4% Two or more races, non-Hispanic/Latino; 6% Race/ethnicity unknown; 22% international; 0.4% transferred in; 55% live on campus.

Freshmen:
Admission: 27,634 applied, 4,267 admitted, 1,585 enrolled. ***Average high school GPA:*** 3.9. ***Test scores:*** SAT evidence-based reading and writing scores over 500: 100%; SAT math scores over 500: 100%; ACT scores over 18: 100%; SAT evidence-based reading and writing scores over 600: 99%; SAT math scores over 600: 98%; ACT scores over 24: 99%; SAT evidence-based reading and writing scores over 700: 76%; SAT math scores over 700: 89%; ACT scores over 30: 93%.

Retention: 97% of full-time freshmen returned.

FACULTY
Total: 1,183, 91% full-time, 91% with terminal degrees.

Student/faculty ratio: 7:1.

ACADEMICS
Calendar: semesters. *Degrees:* bachelor's, master's, doctoral, post-master's, and postbachelor's certificates.

Special study options: accelerated degree program, advanced placement credit, cooperative education, distance learning, double majors, independent study, internships, off-campus study, part-time degree program, services for LD students, student-designed majors, study abroad, summer session for credit. ***ROTC:*** Army (c), Navy (b), Air Force (c).

Unusual degree programs: 3-2 business administration; engineering; public management and policy.

Computers: Students can access the following: campus intranet, computer help desk, free student e-mail accounts, online (class) grades, online (class) registration, online (class) schedules. Campuswide network is available. 100% of college-owned or -operated housing units are wired for high-speed Internet access. Wireless service is available via entire campus.
Library: Hunt Library plus 2 others. Weekly public service hours: 168; study areas open 24 hours, 5–7 days a week; students can reserve study rooms.

STUDENT LIFE
Housing options: on-campus residence required for freshman year; coed, men-only, women-only, special housing for students with disabilities. Campus housing is university owned. Freshman campus housing is guaranteed.

Activities and organizations: drama/theater group, student-run newspaper, radio station, choral group, marching band, national fraternities, national sororities.

Athletics Member NCAA. All Division III. ***Intercollegiate sports:*** badminton M(c)/W(c), baseball M(c)/W(c), basketball M/W, crew M(c)/W(c), cross-country running M/W, fencing M(c)/W(c), football M, golf M/W, ice hockey M(c)/W(c), lacrosse M(c)/W(c), rowing M(c)/W(c), rugby M(c)/W(c), skiing (downhill) M(c)/W(c), soccer M/W, squash M(c)/W(c), swimming and diving M/W, table tennis M(c)/W(c), tennis M/W, track and field M/W, ultimate Frisbee M(c)/W(c), volleyball M(c)/W, water polo M(c)/W(c), weight lifting M(c)/W(c), wrestling M(c)/W(c). ***Intramural sports:*** badminton M/W, basketball M/W, racquetball M/W, soccer M/W, softball M/W, squash M/W, table tennis

M/W, tennis M/W, ultimate Frisbee M/W, volleyball M/W, water polo M/W.

Campus security: 24-hour emergency response devices and patrols, late-night transport/escort service, controlled dormitory access.

Student services: health clinic, personal/psychological counseling, legal services, veterans affairs office.

COSTS & FINANCIAL AID

Costs (2020–21) ***Comprehensive fee:*** $74,474 includes full-time tuition ($57,560), mandatory fees ($1364), and room and board ($15,550). Part-time tuition: $800 per unit. ***College room only:*** $9210.

Financial Aid Of all full-time matriculated undergraduates who enrolled in 2019, 3,208 applied for aid, 2,670 were judged to have need, 2,041 had their need fully met. In 2019, 328 non-need-based awards were made. ***Average percent of need met:*** 97. ***Average financial aid package:*** $48,843. ***Average need-based loan:*** $4517. ***Average need-based gift aid:*** $43,475. ***Average non-need-based aid:*** $30,380. ***Average indebtedness upon graduation:*** $31,342. ***Financial aid deadline:*** 2/15.

APPLYING

Standardized Tests *Required:* SAT or ACT (for admission). *Recommended:* SAT Subject Tests (for admission).

Options: electronic application, early admission, early decision, deferred entrance.

Application fee: $75.

Required: essay or personal statement, high school transcript. ***Required for some:*** audition/portfolio for fine arts.

Application deadlines: 1/1 (freshmen), 2/15 (transfers).

Early decision deadline: 11/1.

Notification: 4/1 (freshmen), 5/15 (transfers), 12/15 (early decision).

CONTACT

Mr. Greg Edleman, Director of Admission, Carnegie Mellon University, 5000 Forbes Avenue, Pittsburgh, PA 15213. *Phone:* 412-268-2082. *Fax:* 412-268-7838. *E-mail:* admission@andrew.cmu.edu.

Cedar Crest College

Allentown, Pennsylvania

http://www.cedarcrest.edu/

- **Independent** comprehensive, founded 1867, affiliated with United Church of Christ
- **Suburban** 84-acre campus with easy access to Philadelphia
- **Coed, primarily women** 1,216 undergraduate students, 72% full-time, 92% women, 8% men
- **Moderately difficult** entrance level, 61% of applicants were admitted

UNDERGRAD STUDENTS

872 full-time, 344 part-time. 19% are from out of state; 9% Black or African American, non-Hispanic/Latino; 14% Hispanic/Latino; 3% Asian, non-Hispanic/Latino; 0.1% Native Hawaiian or other Pacific Islander, non-Hispanic/Latino; 0.1% American Indian or Alaska Native, non-Hispanic/Latino; 2% Two or more races, non-Hispanic/Latino; 5% Race/ethnicity unknown; 7% international; 2% transferred in; 37% live on campus.

Freshmen:

Admission: 1,375 applied, 837 admitted, 205 enrolled. ***Average high school GPA:*** 3.4. ***Test scores:*** SAT evidence-based reading and writing scores over 500: 75%; SAT math scores over 500: 61%; ACT scores over 18: 76%; SAT evidence-based reading and writing scores over 600: 28%; SAT math scores over 600: 15%; ACT scores over 24: 30%; SAT evidence-based reading and writing scores over 700: 2%; SAT math scores over 700: 1%; ACT scores over 30: 6%.

Retention: 75% of full-time freshmen returned.

FACULTY

Total: 222, 37% full-time, 45% with terminal degrees.

Student/faculty ratio: 9:1.

ACADEMICS

Calendar: semesters. *Degrees:* certificates, bachelor's, master's, doctoral, post-master's, and postbachelor's certificates.

Special study options: academic remediation for entering students, accelerated degree program, advanced placement credit, distance learning, double majors, honors programs, independent study, internships, off-campus study, part-time degree program, services for LD students, student-designed majors, study abroad, summer session for credit.

Computers: Students can access the following: campus intranet, computer help desk, free student e-mail accounts, online (class) grades, online (class) registration, online (class) schedules. Campuswide network is available. 100% of college-owned or -operated housing units are wired for high-speed Internet access. Wireless service is available via entire campus.

Library: Frank M. Cressman Library.

STUDENT LIFE

Housing options: women-only. Campus housing is university owned. Freshman campus housing is guaranteed.

Activities and organizations: drama/theater group, student-run newspaper, radio station, choral group, Student Activities Board, Student Government Association, Commuter Awareness Board, Student Nurse Association, Forensic Student Science organization.

Athletics Member NCAA. All Division III. ***Intercollegiate sports:*** basketball W, cross-country running W, equestrian sports W(c), field hockey W, lacrosse W, soccer W, softball W, swimming and diving W, tennis W, track and field W(c), volleyball W. ***Intramural sports:*** badminton W, basketball W, soccer W, softball W, tennis W, volleyball W.

Campus security: 24-hour emergency response devices and patrols, late-night transport/escort service, controlled dormitory access, crime prevention programs.

Student services: health clinic, personal/psychological counseling.

COSTS & FINANCIAL AID

Costs (2020–21) ***Comprehensive fee:*** $53,889 includes full-time tuition ($40,967), mandatory fees ($600), and room and board ($12,322). Full-time tuition and fees vary according to class time, course load, and program. Part-time tuition: $1366 per credit hour. Part-time tuition and fees vary according to class time, course load, and program. ***College room only:*** $5750. Room and board charges vary according to board plan and housing facility. ***Payment plans:*** installment, deferred payment. ***Waivers:*** employees or children of employees.

Financial Aid Of all full-time matriculated undergraduates who enrolled in 2019, 704 applied for aid, 652 were judged to have need, 106 had their need fully met. In 2019, 61 non-need-based awards were made. ***Average percent of need met:*** 77. ***Average financial aid package:*** $30,972. ***Average need-based loan:*** $4411. ***Average need-based gift aid:*** $27,214. ***Average non-need-based aid:*** $22,147. ***Average indebtedness upon graduation:*** $39,866.

APPLYING

Standardized Tests *Required:* SAT or ACT (for admission).

Options: electronic application, early admission.

Required: essay or personal statement, high school transcript. ***Required for some:*** 2 letters of recommendation. ***Recommended:*** minimum 2.0 GPA, interview.

Application deadlines: rolling (freshmen), rolling (transfers).

Notification: continuous (freshmen), continuous (transfers).

CONTACT

Mary Alice Ozechoski, Vice President of Student Affairs and Traditional Enrollment, Cedar Crest College, 100 College Drive, Allentown, PA 18104. *Phone:* 610-606-4666. *Toll-free phone:* 800-360-1222. *E-mail:* admissions@cedarcrest.edu.

Central Penn College

Summerdale, Pennsylvania

http://www.centralpenn.edu/

CONTACT

Central Penn College, College Hill & Valley Roads, Summerdale, PA 17093-0309. *Toll-free phone:* 800-759-2727.

Chatham University
Pittsburgh, Pennsylvania
http://www.chatham.edu/

- **Independent** university, founded 1869
- **Urban** 427-acre campus with easy access to Pittsburgh, PA
- **Endowment** $81.6 million
- **Coed, primarily women** 1,408 undergraduate students, 81% full-time, 73% women, 27% men
- **Moderately difficult** entrance level, 62% of applicants were admitted

UNDERGRAD STUDENTS
1,142 full-time, 266 part-time. Students come from 39 states and territories; 16 other countries; 23% are from out of state; 5% Black or African American, non-Hispanic/Latino; 5% Hispanic/Latino; 3% Asian, non-Hispanic/Latino; 0.1% Native Hawaiian or other Pacific Islander, non-Hispanic/Latino; 3% Two or more races, non-Hispanic/Latino; 4% Race/ethnicity unknown; 2% international; 7% transferred in; 62% live on campus.

Freshmen:
Admission: 2,531 applied, 1,574 admitted, 315 enrolled. ***Average high school GPA:*** 3.7. ***Test scores:*** SAT evidence-based reading and writing scores over 500: 92%; SAT math scores over 500: 87%; ACT scores over 18: 100%; SAT evidence-based reading and writing scores over 600: 48%; SAT math scores over 600: 36%; ACT scores over 24: 63%; SAT evidence-based reading and writing scores over 700: 8%; SAT math scores over 700: 6%; ACT scores over 30: 16%.

Retention: 80% of full-time freshmen returned.

FACULTY
Total: 344, 37% full-time, 71% with terminal degrees.

Student/faculty ratio: 10:1.

ACADEMICS
Calendar: 4-4-1. *Degrees:* bachelor's, master's, doctoral, and postbachelor's certificates.

Special study options: accelerated degree program, adult/continuing education programs, advanced placement credit, cooperative education, distance learning, double majors, English as a second language, honors programs, independent study, internships, off-campus study, part-time degree program, services for LD students, student-designed majors, study abroad, summer session for credit. ***ROTC:*** Army (c), Navy (c), Air Force (c).

Unusual degree programs: 3-2 business administration; engineering with Carnegie Mellon University, Penn State University, University of Pittsburgh; nursing; social work; arts management with Carnegie Mellon, biology, counseling psychology, film/digital technology, leadership/organizational transformation, occupational therapy, physician assistant studies, business, teaching, writing and creative writing, architecture (landscape and interior), global/public policy.

Computers: 202 computers/terminals and 500 ports are available on campus for general student use. Students can access the following: campus intranet, computer help desk, free student e-mail accounts, online (class) grades, online (class) registration, online (class) schedules. Campuswide network is available. 100% of college-owned or -operated housing units are wired for high-speed Internet access. Wireless service is available via entire campus.

Library: Jennie King Mellon Library. *Books:* 97,602 (physical), 788,185 (digital/electronic); *Serial titles:* 585 (physical), 86,930 (digital/electronic); *Databases:* 70. Weekly public service hours: 99; study areas open 24 hours, 5–7 days a week; students can reserve study rooms.

STUDENT LIFE
Housing options: on-campus residence required through sophomore year; coed, women-only, special housing for students with disabilities. Campus housing is university owned. Freshman campus housing is guaranteed.

Activities and organizations: drama/theater group, student-run newspaper, choral group, Chatham Student Government, Residence Hall Council, Student Athletic Advisory Council (SAAC), Creative Writing Club and MFA Writing Council, Graduate Student Assembly.

Athletics Member NCAA. All Division III. ***Intercollegiate sports:*** baseball M, basketball M/W, cross-country running M/W, ice hockey M/W, lacrosse M/W, soccer M/W, softball W, swimming and diving M/W, track and field M/W, volleyball W. ***Intramural sports:*** basketball W, bowling M/W, cheerleading M/W, soccer M/W, squash M/W, volleyball M/W.

Campus security: 24-hour emergency response devices and patrols, late-night transport/escort service, controlled dormitory access, self-defense education, well-lighted pathways and sidewalks.

Student services: health clinic, personal/psychological counseling, women's center, veterans affairs office.

COSTS & FINANCIAL AID
Costs (2020–21) ***Comprehensive fee:*** $52,755 includes full-time tuition ($38,482), mandatory fees ($1420), and room and board ($12,853). Part-time tuition: $934 per credit hour. ***College room only:*** $6645. Room and board charges vary according to board plan and housing facility.

Financial Aid Of all full-time matriculated undergraduates who enrolled in 2019, 974 applied for aid, 857 were judged to have need, 142 had their need fully met. In 2019, 87 non-need-based awards were made. ***Average percent of need met:*** 65. ***Average financial aid package:*** $31,286. ***Average need-based loan:*** $4089. ***Average need-based gift aid:*** $8926. ***Average non-need-based aid:*** $20,436. ***Average indebtedness upon graduation:*** $35,199.

APPLYING
Options: electronic application, early admission, deferred entrance.

Application fee: $35.

Required: essay or personal statement, high school transcript, minimum 2.0 GPA, 1 letter of recommendation. ***Recommended:*** interview.

Application deadlines: 8/1 (freshmen), rolling (transfers).

Notification: continuous (freshmen), continuous (transfers).

CONTACT
Ms. Amy M. Becher, Vice President for Enrollment Management, Chatham University, Woodland, Berry Hall, Pittsburgh, PA 15232. *Phone:* 800-837-1290. *Toll-free phone:* 800-837-1290. *Fax:* 412-365-1609. *E-mail:* admission@chatham.edu.

Chestnut Hill College
Philadelphia, Pennsylvania
http://www.chc.edu/

- **Independent Roman Catholic** comprehensive, founded 1924
- **Suburban** 75-acre campus with easy access to Philadelphia
- **Endowment** $9.4 million
- **Coed** 1,364 undergraduate students, 82% full-time, 63% women, 37% men
- **Moderately difficult** entrance level, 96% of applicants were admitted

UNDERGRAD STUDENTS
1,118 full-time, 246 part-time. Students come from 27 states and territories; 39 other countries; 22% are from out of state; 5% transferred in; 52% live on campus.

Freshmen:
Admission: 1,286 applied, 1,231 admitted, 207 enrolled. ***Average high school GPA:*** 3.2.

Retention: 79% of full-time freshmen returned.

ACADEMICS
Calendar: semesters. *Degrees:* certificates, associate, bachelor's, master's, doctoral, post-master's, and postbachelor's certificates (profile includes figures from both traditional and accelerated (part-time) programs).

Special study options: academic remediation for entering students, accelerated degree program, adult/continuing education programs, advanced placement credit, cooperative education, double majors, English as a second language, honors programs, independent study, internships, off-campus study, part-time degree program, services for LD students, student-designed majors, study abroad, summer session for credit.

Computers: 70 computers/terminals and 150 ports are available on campus for general student use. Students can access the following: campus intranet, computer help desk, free student e-mail accounts, online (class) grades, online (class) registration, online (class) schedules. Campuswide network is available. 90% of college-owned or -operated housing units are wired for high-speed Internet access. Wireless service is available via classrooms, dorm rooms.

Library: Logue Library. Weekly public service hours: 99; students can reserve study rooms.

STUDENT LIFE
Housing options: coed. Campus housing is university owned.

Activities and organizations: drama/theater group, student-run newspaper, radio and television station, choral group, Student Government, Mask and Foil Drama Club, Association for Musical Performance, Campus Ministry Community Service Group, Business Club.

Athletics ***Intercollegiate sports:*** baseball M(s), basketball M(s)/W(s), bowling W(s), cross-country running M(s)/W(s), football M(s)(c), golf M(s)(c), lacrosse M(s)/W(s), soccer M(s)/W(s), softball W(s), tennis M(s)/W(s), track and field M(s)/W(s), volleyball W(s).

Campus security: 24-hour emergency response devices and patrols, late-night transport/escort service, controlled dormitory access.

Student services: health clinic, personal/psychological counseling.

COSTS & FINANCIAL AID
Costs (2019–20) ***One-time required fee:*** $480. ***Comprehensive fee:*** $48,200 includes full-time tuition ($36,950), mandatory fees ($250), and room and board ($11,000). Part-time tuition: $775 per credit hour. ***Required fees:*** $250 per year part-time. ***Room and board:*** Room and board charges vary according to housing facility. ***Payment plans:*** installment, deferred payment. ***Waivers:*** senior citizens and employees or children of employees.

Financial Aid Of all full-time matriculated undergraduates who enrolled in 2019, 833 applied for aid, 833 were judged to have need, 207 had their need fully met. In 2019, 113 non-need-based awards were made. ***Average percent of need met:*** 63. ***Average financial aid package:*** $28,602. ***Average need-based loan:*** $4485. ***Average need-based gift aid:*** $9788. ***Average non-need-based aid:*** $16,730. ***Average indebtedness upon graduation:*** $47,542.

APPLYING
Standardized Tests *Required:* SAT or ACT (for admission).

Options: electronic application, deferred entrance.

Application fee: $35.

Required: high school transcript. ***Required for some:*** interview. ***Recommended:*** essay or personal statement, .

Application deadlines: rolling (freshmen), rolling (transfers).

Notification: continuous (freshmen), continuous (transfers).

CONTACT
Ms. Stephanie Williams, Chestnut Hill College, 9601 Germantown Avenue, Philadelphia, PA 19118-2693. *Phone:* 215-248-7001. *Toll-free phone:* 800-248-0052. *Fax:* 215-248-7082. *E-mail:* williamss@chc.edu.

Cheyney University of Pennsylvania

Cheyney, Pennsylvania

http://www.cheyney.edu/

CONTACT
Shon Jeffery, Associate Director of Enrollment Management, Cheyney University of Pennsylvania, 1837 University Circle, PO Box 200, Cheyney, PA 19319. *Phone:* 610-399-2255. *Toll-free phone:* 800-CHEYNEY. *E-mail:* spjeffery@cheyney.edu.

Clarion University of Pennsylvania

Clarion, Pennsylvania

http://www.clarion.edu/

- **State-supported** comprehensive, founded 1867, part of Pennsylvania State System of Higher Education
- **Rural** 201-acre campus
- **Endowment** $37.0 million
- **Coed** 3,776 undergraduate students, 79% full-time, 68% women, 32% men
- **Minimally difficult** entrance level, 95% of applicants were admitted

UNDERGRAD STUDENTS
2,995 full-time, 781 part-time. 7% are from out of state; 8% Black or African American, non-Hispanic/Latino; 3% Hispanic/Latino; 0.8% Asian, non-Hispanic/Latino; 0.1% Native Hawaiian or other Pacific Islander, non-Hispanic/Latino; 0.2% American Indian or Alaska Native, non-Hispanic/Latino; 2% Two or more races, non-Hispanic/Latino; 3% Race/ethnicity unknown; 0.4% international; 7% transferred in; 37% live on campus.

Freshmen:
Admission: 2,622 applied, 2,491 admitted, 755 enrolled. ***Average high school GPA:*** 3.5. ***Test scores:*** SAT evidence-based reading and writing scores over 500: 66%; SAT math scores over 500: 62%; ACT scores over 18: 73%; SAT evidence-based reading and writing scores over 600: 18%; SAT math scores over 600: 13%; ACT scores over 24: 25%; SAT evidence-based reading and writing scores over 700: 1%; SAT math scores over 700: 1%.

Retention: 74% of full-time freshmen returned.

FACULTY
Total: 278, 74% full-time, 74% with terminal degrees.

Student/faculty ratio: 18:1.

ACADEMICS
Calendar: semesters. *Degrees:* certificates, bachelor's, master's, doctoral, post-master's, and postbachelor's certificates.

Special study options: academic remediation for entering students, accelerated degree program, adult/continuing education programs, advanced placement credit, cooperative education, distance learning, double majors, English as a second language, honors programs, independent study, internships, off-campus study, part-time degree program, services for LD students, study abroad, summer session for credit. ***ROTC:*** Army (b).

Unusual degree programs: 3-2 engineering with University of Pittsburgh, Case Western Reserve University.

Computers: 950 computers/terminals and 24 ports are available on campus for general student use. Students can access the following: campus intranet, computer help desk, free student e-mail accounts, online (class) grades, online (class) registration, online (class) schedules, Online Learning Management, Student Organization, Career Services, video conferencing systems; web-based personal disk space; other online student services (financial aid, billing, student employment, scholarships etc.). Campuswide network is available. 100% of college-owned or -operated housing units are wired for high-speed Internet access. Wireless service is available via entire campus.

Library: Carlson Library plus 1 other. *Books:* 444,818 (physical), 348,037 (digital/electronic); *Serial titles:* 179 (physical), 57,405 (digital/electronic); *Databases:* 102. Weekly public service hours: 94; students can reserve study rooms.

STUDENT LIFE
Housing options: on-campus residence required through sophomore year; special housing for students with disabilities. Campus housing is university owned. Freshman campus housing is guaranteed.

Activities and organizations: drama/theater group, student-run newspaper, radio and television station, choral group, marching band, The National Student Speech-Language Hearing Association, Phi Eta Sigma freshman honor society, Allies, Black Student Union, Cru, national fraternities, national sororities.

Athletics Member NCAA. All Division II except golf (Division I), wrestling (Division I). ***Intercollegiate sports:*** baseball M(s), basketball M(s)/W(s), cross-country running W(s), football M(s), golf M(s)/W(s), soccer W(s), softball W(s), swimming and diving M(s)/W(s), tennis W(s), track and field W(s), volleyball W(s), wrestling M(s). ***Intramural sports:*** badminton M/W, basketball M/W, equestrian sports M(c)/W(c), golf M/W, racquetball M/W, rock climbing M(c)/W(c), rugby M(c)/W(c), sand volleyball M/W, soccer M/W, softball M/W, table tennis M/W, tennis M/W, track and field M(c)/W(c), ultimate Frisbee M(c)/W(c), volleyball M/W, weight lifting M/W, wrestling M/W.

Campus security: 24-hour emergency response devices and patrols, student patrols, late-night transport/escort service, controlled dormitory access.

Student services: health clinic, personal/psychological counseling, women's center.

COSTS & FINANCIAL AID
Costs (2020–21) ***One-time required fee:*** $50. ***Tuition:*** state resident $7716 full-time, $322 per credit hour part-time; nonresident $11,574 full-time, $482 per credit hour part-time. Full-time tuition and fees vary

according to course load and location. Part-time tuition and fees vary according to course load and location. ***Room and board:*** Room and board charges vary according to board plan and housing facility. ***Payment plans:*** installment, deferred payment. ***Waivers:*** senior citizens and employees or children of employees.

Financial Aid Of all full-time matriculated undergraduates who enrolled in 2018, 2,874 applied for aid, 2,551 were judged to have need, 167 had their need fully met. 314 Federal Work-Study jobs (averaging $1190). 463 state and other part-time jobs (averaging $1851). In 2018, 213 non-need-based awards were made. ***Average percent of need met:*** 50. ***Average financial aid package:*** $10,861. ***Average need-based loan:*** $3893. ***Average need-based gift aid:*** $5834. ***Average non-need-based aid:*** $2291. ***Average indebtedness upon graduation:*** $36,800.

APPLYING

Standardized Tests *Required:* SAT or ACT (for admission). *Required for some:* TOEFL, TSE or IELTS for international students.

Options: electronic application, early admission, deferred entrance.

Application fee: $40.

Required: high school transcript, minimum 2.0 GPA. ***Required for some:*** essay or personal statement, interview, NLN Test for ASN program. ***Recommended:*** essay or personal statement, 2 letters of recommendation, interview.

Application deadlines: rolling (freshmen), rolling (out-of-state freshmen), rolling (transfers).

Notification: continuous (freshmen), continuous (out-of-state freshmen), continuous (transfers).

CONTACT

Ms. Merrilyn Dunlap, Senior Associate Director, Clarion University of Pennsylvania, 314 Becht Hall, 840 Wood Street, Clarion, PA 16214. *Phone:* 814-393-2306. *Toll-free phone:* 800-672-7171. *Fax:* 814-393-2030. *E-mail:* mdunlap@clarion.edu.

Clarks Summit University

South Abington Township, Pennsylvania

http://www.clarkssummitu.edu/

- **Independent Baptist** comprehensive, founded 1932
- **Suburban** 124-acre campus
- **Endowment** $2.1 million
- **Coed**
- **Minimally difficult** entrance level

FACULTY

Student/faculty ratio: 11:1.

ACADEMICS

Calendar: semesters. *Degrees:* certificates, associate, bachelor's, master's, and doctoral.

Library: Murphy Memorial Library.

STUDENT LIFE

Housing options: on-campus residence required through senior year; men-only, women-only. Campus housing is university owned. Freshman campus housing is guaranteed.

Activities and organizations: drama/theater group, choral group.

Athletics Member NCAA, NCCAA. All NCAA Division III.

Campus security: 24-hour patrols, student patrols, controlled dormitory access.

Student services: health clinic, personal/psychological counseling.

FINANCIAL AID

Financial Aid Of all full-time matriculated undergraduates who enrolled in 2015, 72 Federal Work-Study jobs (averaging $1457). ***Average indebtedness upon graduation:*** $29,483.

APPLYING

Standardized Tests *Required:* SAT or ACT (for admission).

Options: electronic application, early admission, deferred entrance.

Application fee: $40.

Required: essay or personal statement, high school transcript, 2 letters of recommendation, Christian testimony. ***Required for some:*** 1 letter of recommendation, interview.

CONTACT

Ms. Patience Schwamb, Director of Student Accounts, Clarks Summit University, 538 Venard Road, Clarks Summit, PA 18411-1297. *Phone:* 570-585-9205. *Toll-free phone:* 800-451-7664. *Fax:* 570-585-9271. *E-mail:* pschwamb@clarkssummitu.edu.

Curtis Institute of Music

Philadelphia, Pennsylvania

http://www.curtis.edu/

CONTACT

Mr. Christopher Hodges, Admissions Officer, Curtis Institute of Music, 1726 Locust Street, Philadelphia, PA 19103-6107. *Phone:* 215-893-5262. *E-mail:* chris.hodges@curtis.edu.

Delaware Valley University

Doylestown, Pennsylvania

http://www.delval.edu/

- **Independent** comprehensive, founded 1896
- **Suburban** 571-acre campus with easy access to Philadelphia
- **Endowment** $33.6 million
- **Coed** 1,924 undergraduate students, 86% full-time, 59% women, 41% men
- **Minimally difficult** entrance level, 93% of applicants were admitted

UNDERGRAD STUDENTS

1,649 full-time, 275 part-time. Students come from 25 states and territories; 8 other countries; 38% are from out of state; 9% Black or African American, non-Hispanic/Latino; 8% Hispanic/Latino; 1% Asian, non-Hispanic/Latino; 0.2% Native Hawaiian or other Pacific Islander, non-Hispanic/Latino; 0.5% American Indian or Alaska Native, non-Hispanic/Latino; 2% Two or more races, non-Hispanic/Latino; 11% Race/ethnicity unknown; 0.2% international; 7% transferred in; 55% live on campus.

Freshmen:

Admission: 1,676 applied, 1,554 admitted, 377 enrolled. ***Average high school GPA:*** 3.3. ***Test scores:*** SAT evidence-based reading and writing scores over 500: 71%; SAT math scores over 500: 69%; ACT scores over 18: 79%; SAT evidence-based reading and writing scores over 600: 25%; SAT math scores over 600: 18%; ACT scores over 24: 42%; SAT evidence-based reading and writing scores over 700: 2%; SAT math scores over 700: 1%; ACT scores over 30: 12%.

Retention: 72% of full-time freshmen returned.

FACULTY

Total: 282, 32% full-time, 22% with terminal degrees.

Student/faculty ratio: 13:1.

ACADEMICS

Calendar: semesters. *Degrees:* certificates, bachelor's, master's, doctoral, and postbachelor's certificates.

Special study options: academic remediation for entering students, adult/continuing education programs, advanced placement credit, distance learning, double majors, honors programs, independent study, internships, part-time degree program, services for LD students, student-designed majors, study abroad, summer session for credit.

Computers: 160 computers/terminals are available on campus for general student use. Students can access the following: campus intranet, computer help desk, free student e-mail accounts, online (class) grades, online (class) registration, online (class) schedules. Campuswide network is available. 100% of college-owned or -operated housing units are wired for high-speed Internet access. Wireless service is available via entire campus.

Library: Joseph Krauskopf Memorial Library. *Books:* 45,500 (physical), 7,830 (digital/electronic); *Serial titles:* 74 (physical), 113,400 (digital/electronic); *Databases:* 44. Weekly public service hours: 92.

STUDENT LIFE

Housing options: on-campus residence required for freshman year; coed. Campus housing is university owned. Freshman campus housing is guaranteed.

Activities and organizations: Animal Lifeline Club, Pre-Vet Club, Dairy Society, Sigma Alpha, A-Day, national sororities.

Athletics Member NCAA. All Division III. ***Intercollegiate sports:*** baseball M, basketball M/W, cheerleading W, cross-country running M/W, equestrian sports M/W, fencing M/W, field hockey W, football M, golf M/W, lacrosse M/W, soccer M/W, softball W, tennis M/W, track and field M/W, volleyball W, wrestling M/W. ***Intramural sports:*** basketball M/W, football W, soccer M/W, softball M/W, volleyball M/W.

Campus security: 24-hour emergency response devices and patrols, late-night transport/escort service, controlled dormitory access.

Student services: health clinic, personal/psychological counseling, veterans affairs office.

COSTS & FINANCIAL AID

Costs (2020–21) ***Comprehensive fee:*** $55,240 includes full-time tuition ($38,070), mandatory fees ($2550), and room and board ($14,620). Full-time tuition and fees vary according to location and program. Part-time tuition: $1049 per credit hour. Part-time tuition and fees vary according to course load, location, and program. ***College room only:*** $6950. Room and board charges vary according to board plan and housing facility. ***Payment plan:*** installment. ***Waivers:*** employees or children of employees.

Financial Aid Of all full-time matriculated undergraduates who enrolled in 2019, 1,465 applied for aid, 1,333 were judged to have need, 210 had their need fully met. In 2019, 287 non-need-based awards were made. ***Average percent of need met:*** 71. ***Average financial aid package:*** $31,252. ***Average need-based loan:*** $4272. ***Average need-based gift aid:*** $27,031. ***Average non-need-based aid:*** $19,443. ***Average indebtedness upon graduation:*** $48,278.

APPLYING

Standardized Tests *Required for some:* SAT or ACT (for admission), TOEFL.

Options: electronic application, deferred entrance.

Application fee: $50.

Required: essay or personal statement, high school transcript, 1 letter of recommendation, Test scores (SAT/ACT), additional short-answer questions for Zoo Science applicants. ***Required for some:*** interview.

Application deadlines: rolling (freshmen), rolling (out-of-state freshmen), rolling (transfers).

Notification: continuous (freshmen), continuous (out-of-state freshmen), continuous (transfers).

CONTACT

Mr. Dwayne Walker, Vice President for Enrollment Management and Director of Admissions, Delaware Valley University, 700 E. Butler Avenue, Doylestown, PA 18901. *Phone:* 215-489-2372. *Toll-free phone:* 800-2DELVAL. *Fax:* 215-230-2968. *E-mail:* dwayne.walker@delval.edu.

DeSales University

Center Valley, Pennsylvania

http://www.desales.edu/

- **Independent Roman Catholic** comprehensive, founded 1964
- **Suburban** 550-acre campus with easy access to Philadelphia, PA
- **Endowment** $87.8 million
- **Coed** 2,492 undergraduate students, 79% full-time, 64% women, 36% men
- **Moderately difficult** entrance level, 79% of applicants were admitted

UNDERGRAD STUDENTS

1,963 full-time, 529 part-time. Students come from 29 states and territories; 5 other countries; 26% are from out of state; 5% Black or African American, non-Hispanic/Latino; 12% Hispanic/Latino; 3% Asian, non-Hispanic/Latino; 0.1% American Indian or Alaska Native, non-Hispanic/Latino; 3% Two or more races, non-Hispanic/Latino; 6% Race/ethnicity unknown; 0.1% international; 6% transferred in; 41% live on campus.

Freshmen:

Admission: 3,272 applied, 2,579 admitted, 500 enrolled. ***Average high school GPA:*** 3.3. ***Test scores:*** SAT evidence-based reading and writing scores over 500: 85%; SAT math scores over 500: 79%; SAT evidence-based reading and writing scores over 600: 42%; SAT math scores over 600: 33%; SAT evidence-based reading and writing scores over 700: 6%; SAT math scores over 700: 8%.

Retention: 80% of full-time freshmen returned.

FACULTY

Total: 405, 32% full-time.

Student/faculty ratio: 13:1.

ACADEMICS

Calendar: semesters. *Degrees:* certificates, bachelor's, master's, doctoral, post-master's, and postbachelor's certificates.

Special study options: academic remediation for entering students, accelerated degree program, adult/continuing education programs, advanced placement credit, cooperative education, distance learning, double majors, external degree program, honors programs, independent study, internships, off-campus study, part-time degree program, services for LD students, student-designed majors, study abroad, summer session for credit. ***ROTC:*** Army (c).

Unusual degree programs: 3-2 medical studies/physician assistant studies.

Computers: 245 computers/terminals are available on campus for general student use. Students can access the following: campus intranet, computer help desk, free student e-mail accounts, online (class) grades, online (class) registration, online (class) schedules. Campuswide network is available. 100% of college-owned or -operated housing units are wired for high-speed Internet access. Wireless service is available via entire campus.

Library: Trexler Library. *Books:* 110,400 (physical), 190,317 (digital/electronic); *Serial titles:* 155 (physical), 17,260 (digital/electronic); *Databases:* 52. Weekly public service hours: 102; students can reserve study rooms.

STUDENT LIFE

Housing options: coed, men-only, women-only, special housing for students with disabilities. Campus housing is university owned. Freshman campus housing is guaranteed.

Activities and organizations: drama/theater group, student-run newspaper, radio and television station, choral group, marching band, College Against Cancer, Outdoor Adventure Club, Student Nursing Association, Criminal Justice Association, Natural Science Club.

Athletics Member NCAA. All Division III. ***Intercollegiate sports:*** baseball M, basketball M/W, cross-country running M/W, field hockey W, golf M, lacrosse M, soccer M/W, softball W, tennis M/W, track and field M/W, volleyball W. ***Intramural sports:*** cheerleading M(c)/W(c), ice hockey M(c), rugby M(c), swimming and diving M(c)/W(c), tennis M(c)/W(c), volleyball M(c).

Campus security: 24-hour emergency response devices and patrols, late-night transport/escort service, controlled dormitory access.

Student services: health clinic, personal/psychological counseling.

COSTS & FINANCIAL AID

Costs (2019–20) ***One-time required fee:*** $200. ***Comprehensive fee:*** $51,700 includes full-time tuition ($37,200), mandatory fees ($1500), and room and board ($13,000). Full-time tuition and fees vary according to class time and course load. Part-time tuition: $1550 per credit hour. Part-time tuition and fees vary according to class time and course load. ***Room and board:*** Room and board charges vary according to board plan and housing facility. ***Payment plans:*** installment, deferred payment. ***Waivers:*** adult students, senior citizens, and employees or children of employees.

Financial Aid Of all full-time matriculated undergraduates who enrolled in 2019, 1,721 applied for aid, 1,521 were judged to have need, 370 had their need fully met. 366 Federal Work-Study jobs (averaging $1966). 335 state and other part-time jobs (averaging $1990). In 2019, 359 non-need-based awards were made. ***Average percent of need met:*** 69. ***Average financial aid package:*** $26,908. ***Average need-based loan:*** $4472. ***Average need-based gift aid:*** $21,264. ***Average non-need-based aid:*** $18,583. ***Average indebtedness upon graduation:*** $40,776.

APPLYING

Standardized Tests *Required:* SAT or ACT (for admission).

Options: electronic application, early admission, deferred entrance.

Required: essay or personal statement, high school transcript, letters of recommendation. ***Recommended:*** interview.

Notification: continuous until 10/6 (freshmen).

CONTACT

Mr. Derrick Wetzel, Director of Admissions, DeSales University, 2755 Station Avenue, Center Valley, PA 18034-9568. *Phone:* 610-282-4443. *Fax:* 610-282-0131. *E-mail:* derrick.wetzell@desales.edu.

DeVry University–Ft. Washington Campus

Fort Washington, Pennsylvania

http://www.devry.edu/

- **Proprietary** comprehensive, founded 2002, part of DeVry University
- **Coed**
- **Minimally difficult** entrance level

FACULTY

Student/faculty ratio: 17:1.

ACADEMICS

Calendar: semesters. *Degrees:* associate, bachelor's, master's, and postbachelor's certificates.
Library: Learning Resource Center.

STUDENT LIFE

Housing options: college housing not available.

FINANCIAL AID

Financial Aid Of all full-time matriculated undergraduates who enrolled in 2007, 254 applied for aid, 244 were judged to have need, 2 had their need fully met. In 2007, 23 non-need-based awards were made. ***Average percent of need met:*** 34. ***Average financial aid package:*** $12,114. ***Average need-based loan:*** $6836. ***Average need-based gift aid:*** $6835. ***Average non-need-based aid:*** $13,057. ***Average indebtedness upon graduation:*** $15,638.

APPLYING

Application fee: $30.

Required: high school transcript, interview.

CONTACT

DeVry University–Ft. Washington Campus, 1140 Virginia Drive, Fort Washington, PA 19034. *Phone:* 215-591-5700. *Toll-free phone:* 866-338-7934.

Dickinson College

Carlisle, Pennsylvania

http://www.dickinson.edu/

- **Independent** 4-year, founded 1773
- **Suburban** 144-acre campus with easy access to Harrisburg
- **Endowment** $451.2 million
- **Coed** 2,133 undergraduate students, 99% full-time, 57% women, 43% men
- **Very difficult** entrance level, 40% of applicants were admitted

UNDERGRAD STUDENTS

2,107 full-time, 26 part-time. Students come from 43 states and territories; 46 other countries; 75% are from out of state; 5% Black or African American, non-Hispanic/Latino; 9% Hispanic/Latino; 4% Asian, non-Hispanic/Latino; 0.2% American Indian or Alaska Native, non-Hispanic/Latino; 4% Two or more races, non-Hispanic/Latino; 0.9% Race/ethnicity unknown; 13% international; 1% transferred in; 100% live on campus.

Freshmen:

Admission: 6,426 applied, 2,574 admitted, 453 enrolled. ***Test scores:*** SAT evidence-based reading and writing scores over 500: 100%; SAT math scores over 500: 100%; ACT scores over 18: 100%; SAT evidence-based reading and writing scores over 600: 87%; SAT math scores over 600: 85%; ACT scores over 24: 97%; SAT evidence-based reading and writing scores over 700: 28%; SAT math scores over 700: 33%; ACT scores over 30: 57%.

Retention: 87% of full-time freshmen returned.

FACULTY

Total: 271, 80% full-time, 88% with terminal degrees.
Student/faculty ratio: 8:1.

ACADEMICS

Calendar: semesters. *Degree:* bachelor's.

Special study options: accelerated degree program, adult/continuing education programs, advanced placement credit, double majors, English as a second language, independent study, internships, off-campus study, part-time degree program, services for LD students, student-designed majors, study abroad, summer session for credit. ***ROTC:*** Army (b).

Unusual degree programs: 3-2 engineering with Case Western Reserve University, Rensselaer Polytechnic Institute; international studies with Johns Hopkins University, Columbia University Mailman School of Public Health, 3-3 law degree with Dickinson School of Law Penn State.

Computers: 1,700 computers/terminals and 5,400 ports are available on campus for general student use. Students can access the following: campus intranet, computer help desk, free student e-mail accounts, online (class) grades, online (class) registration, online (class) schedules. Campuswide network is available. 100% of college-owned or -operated housing units are wired for high-speed Internet access. Wireless service is available via entire campus.

Library: Waidner-Spahr Library. *Books:* 492,695 (physical), 621,247 (digital/electronic); *Serial titles:* 2,985 (physical), 107,495 (digital/electronic); *Databases:* 464. Weekly public service hours: 114; students can reserve study rooms.

STUDENT LIFE

Housing options: on-campus residence required through senior year; coed, special housing for students with disabilities. Campus housing is university owned. Freshman campus housing is guaranteed.

Activities and organizations: drama/theater group, student-run newspaper, radio station, choral group, Multi-Organization Board, Outing Club, Student Senate, Admissions Volunteers, WDCV Radio Station, national fraternities, national sororities.

Athletics Member NCAA. All Division III. ***Intercollegiate sports:*** badminton M(c)/W(c), baseball M/W(c), basketball M/W, cheerleading M(c)/W(c), cross-country running M/W, equestrian sports M(c)/W(c), fencing M(c)/W(c), field hockey W, football M, golf M/W, ice hockey M(c)/W(c), lacrosse M/W, racquetball M(c)/W(c), rock climbing M(c)/W(c), skiing (downhill) M(c)/W(c), soccer M/W, softball W, squash M/W, swimming and diving M/W, tennis M/W, track and field M/W, ultimate Frisbee M(c)/W(c), volleyball M(c)/W. ***Intramural sports:*** baseball M(c), basketball M(c)/W(c), lacrosse M(c), soccer M(c)/W(c), squash M(c)/W(c), tennis M(c)/W(c), volleyball W(c).

Campus security: 24-hour emergency response devices and patrols, student patrols, late-night transport/escort service, controlled dormitory access.

Student services: health clinic, personal/psychological counseling, women's center.

COSTS & FINANCIAL AID

Costs (2020–21) ***One-time required fee:*** $25. ***Comprehensive fee:*** $73,352 includes full-time tuition ($58,130), mandatory fees ($550), and room and board ($14,672). Part-time tuition: $7265 per course. ***Required fees:*** $70 per course part-time. ***College room only:*** $7566. Room and board charges vary according to board plan and housing facility. ***Payment plan:*** installment. ***Waivers:*** senior citizens and employees or children of employees.

Financial Aid Of all full-time matriculated undergraduates who enrolled in 2019, 1,422 applied for aid, 1,336 were judged to have need, 984 had their need fully met. In 2019, 292 non-need-based awards were made. ***Average percent of need met:*** 98. ***Average financial aid package:*** $49,622. ***Average need-based loan:*** $4958. ***Average need-based gift aid:*** $43,188. ***Average non-need-based aid:*** $12,027. ***Average indebtedness upon graduation:*** $27,030. ***Financial aid deadline:*** 1/15.

APPLYING

Standardized Tests *Recommended:* SAT or ACT (for admission).

Options: electronic application, early decision, deferred entrance.

Application fee: $65.

Required: essay or personal statement, high school transcript, 2 letters of recommendation. ***Recommended:*** minimum 3.0 GPA, interview.

Application deadlines: 1/15 (freshmen), 1/15 (out-of-state freshmen), 4/1 (transfers).

Early decision deadline: 11/15 (for plan 1), 1/15 (for plan 2).

Notification: 3/23 (freshmen), 3/23 (out-of-state freshmen), 5/15 (transfers), 12/15 (early decision plan 1), 2/15 (early decision plan 2).

CONTACT

Catherine Davenport, VP Enrollment Management & Dean of Admissions, Dickinson College, PO Box 1773, Admissions Office, Carlisle, PA 17013-2896. *Phone:* 717-245-1231. *Toll-free phone:* 800-644-1773. *Fax:* 717-245-1442. *E-mail:* admissions@dickinson.edu.

Drexel University

Philadelphia, Pennsylvania

http://www.drexel.edu/

- **Independent** university, founded 1891
- **Urban** 96-acre campus with easy access to Philadelphia
- **Endowment** $650.3 million
- **Coed** 15,346 undergraduate students, 90% full-time, 48% women, 52% men
- **Moderately difficult** entrance level, 75% of applicants were admitted

UNDERGRAD STUDENTS

13,878 full-time, 1,468 part-time. 51% are from out of state; 6% Black or African American, non-Hispanic/Latino; 7% Hispanic/Latino; 20% Asian, non-Hispanic/Latino; 0.1% Native Hawaiian or other Pacific Islander, non-Hispanic/Latino; 0.1% American Indian or Alaska Native, non-Hispanic/Latino; 4% Two or more races, non-Hispanic/Latino; 2% Race/ethnicity unknown; 10% international; 3% transferred in; 22% live on campus.

Freshmen:

Admission: 31,824 applied, 23,771 admitted, 3,178 enrolled. ***Average high school GPA:*** 3.7. ***Test scores:*** SAT evidence-based reading and writing scores over 500: 99%; SAT math scores over 500: 99%; ACT scores over 18: 100%; SAT evidence-based reading and writing scores over 600: 72%; SAT math scores over 600: 75%; ACT scores over 24: 85%; SAT evidence-based reading and writing scores over 700: 17%; SAT math scores over 700: 31%; ACT scores over 30: 39%.

Retention: 89% of full-time freshmen returned.

FACULTY

Total: 1,984, 56% full-time, 50% with terminal degrees.

Student/faculty ratio: 11:1.

ACADEMICS

Calendar: quarters. *Degrees:* certificates, bachelor's, master's, doctoral, post-master's, and postbachelor's certificates.

Special study options: academic remediation for entering students, accelerated degree program, adult/continuing education programs, advanced placement credit, cooperative education, distance learning, double majors, English as a second language, freshman honors college, honors programs, independent study, internships, part-time degree program, services for LD students, student-designed majors, study abroad, summer session for credit. ***ROTC:*** Army (b), Navy (c), Air Force (c).

Unusual degree programs: 3-2 business administration; engineering; nursing.

Computers: Students can access the following: campus intranet, computer help desk, free student e-mail accounts, online (class) grades, online (class) registration, online (class) schedules. Campuswide network is available. 100% of college-owned or -operated housing units are wired for high-speed Internet access. Wireless service is available via entire campus.

Library: W. W. Hagerty Library plus 3 others. *Books:* 286,613 (physical), 215,379 (digital/electronic); *Serial titles:* 126 (physical), 51,775 (digital/electronic); *Databases:* 465. Weekly public service hours: 87; study areas open 24 hours, 5–7 days a week; students can reserve study rooms.

STUDENT LIFE

Housing options: on-campus residence required for freshman year; coed. Campus housing is university owned. Freshman campus housing is guaranteed.

Activities and organizations: drama/theater group, student-run newspaper, radio and television station, choral group, Student Government, Black Student Union, Society of Hispanic Professional Engineers, Society of Minority Engineers and Scientists, Campus Activities Board, national fraternities, national sororities.

Athletics Member NCAA. All Division I. ***Intercollegiate sports:*** basketball M(s)/W(s), crew M(s)/W(s), field hockey W(s), golf M(s), lacrosse M(s)/W(s), soccer M(s)/W(s), softball W(s), squash M(s)/W(s), swimming and diving M(s)/W(s), tennis M(s)/W(s), wrestling M(s). ***Intramural sports:*** basketball M/W, fencing M/W, football M, ice hockey M, riflery M/W, sailing M/W, soccer M/W, softball M/W, squash M/W, table tennis M/W, tennis M/W, volleyball M/W, water polo M/W.

Campus security: 24-hour emergency response devices and patrols, late-night transport/escort service, controlled dormitory access.

Student services: health clinic, personal/psychological counseling, women's center, veterans affairs office.

COSTS & FINANCIAL AID

Costs (2019–20) ***Comprehensive fee:*** $68,757 includes full-time tuition ($52,146), mandatory fees ($2370), and room and board ($14,241). Part-time tuition: $1173 per credit hour. Part-time tuition and fees vary according to program. ***Required fees:*** $150 per term part-time. ***College room only:*** $8400. Room and board charges vary according to board plan and housing facility. ***Waivers:*** employees or children of employees.

Financial Aid Of all full-time matriculated undergraduates who enrolled in 2019, 10,053 applied for aid, 8,888 were judged to have need, 2,082 had their need fully met. In 2019, 4499 non-need-based awards were made. ***Average percent of need met:*** 74. ***Average financial aid package:*** $38,995. ***Average need-based loan:*** $10,122. ***Average need-based gift aid:*** $29,367. ***Average non-need-based aid:*** $16,986. ***Average indebtedness upon graduation:*** $72,883. ***Financial aid deadline:*** 2/15.

APPLYING

Standardized Tests *Required:* SAT or ACT (for admission).

Options: electronic application, early decision, early action, deferred entrance.

Application fee: $50.

Required: essay or personal statement, high school transcript, minimum 2.0 GPA. ***Recommended:*** 2 letters of recommendation, interview.

Application deadlines: 1/15 (freshmen), rolling (transfers), 11/1 (early action).

Early decision deadline: 11/1.

Notification: continuous until 4/1 (freshmen), continuous (transfers), 12/15 (early decision), 12/15 (early action).

CONTACT

Evelyn Thimba, Vice President, Dean of Admissions, Drexel University, 3141 Chestnut Street, Philadelphia, PA 19104-2875. *Phone:* 215-895-6712. *Toll-free phone:* 800-2-DREXEL. *E-mail:* evelyn.k.thimba@drexel.edu.

See below for display ad and page 1054 for the College Close-Up.

Duquesne University

Pittsburgh, Pennsylvania

http://www.duq.edu/

- **Independent Roman Catholic** university, founded 1878
- **Urban** 50-acre campus with easy access to Pittsburgh
- **Endowment** $308.2 million
- **Coed**
- **Moderately difficult** entrance level

FACULTY

Student/faculty ratio: 14:1.

ACADEMICS

Calendar: semesters. *Degrees:* bachelor's, master's, doctoral, post-master's, and postbachelor's certificates.

Library: Gumberg Library plus 1 other. *Books:* 562,314 (physical), 342,710 (digital/electronic); *Serial titles:* 123 (physical), 99,402 (digital/electronic); *Databases:* 227. Weekly public service hours: 112; students can reserve study rooms.

STUDENT LIFE

Housing options: on-campus residence required through sophomore year; coed, men-only, women-only, special housing for students with disabilities. Campus housing is university owned. Freshman campus housing is guaranteed.

Activities and organizations: drama/theater group, student-run newspaper, radio and television station, choral group, marching band, International Student's Org (ISO), Red and Blue Crew, Duquesne University Volunteers (DUV), Duquesne Program Council, Residence Hall Association, national fraternities, national sororities.

Athletics Member NCAA. All Division I except football (Division I-AA).

Campus security: 24-hour emergency response devices and patrols, late-night transport/escort service, controlled dormitory access, cameras monitor exterior 24-hours/day, card access for buildings, outside warning siren system.

Student services: health clinic, personal/psychological counseling, veterans affairs office.

COSTS & FINANCIAL AID

Costs (2019–20) ***Comprehensive fee:*** $53,080 includes full-time tuition ($39,992) and room and board ($13,088). Full-time tuition and fees vary according to course load and program. Part-time tuition: $1325 per credit. Part-time tuition and fees vary according to course load and program. ***College room only:*** $7194. Room and board charges vary according to board plan and housing facility. ***Payment plans:*** installment, deferred payment.

Financial Aid Of all full-time matriculated undergraduates who enrolled in 2018, 4,645 applied for aid, 3,982 were judged to have need, 742 had their need fully met. In 2018, 1690 non-need-based awards were made. ***Average percent of need met:*** 71. ***Average financial aid package:*** $26,543. ***Average need-based loan:*** $4251. ***Average need-based gift aid:*** $23,681. ***Average non-need-based aid:*** $15,309. ***Average indebtedness upon graduation:*** $44,243. ***Financial aid deadline:*** 5/1.

APPLYING

Standardized Tests *Required for some:* SAT or ACT (for admission).

Options: electronic application, early admission, early decision, early action, deferred entrance.

Application fee: $50.

Required: high school transcript. ***Required for some:*** essay or personal statement, 1 letter of recommendation, audition for School of Music; 40 hours of volunteer, paid, or shadowing experience for physical therapy. ***Recommended:*** minimum 3.0 GPA, interview.

CONTACT

Ms. Debra Zugates, Director of Admissions, Duquesne University, Administration Building, 600 Forbes Avenue, Pittsburgh, PA 15282-0201. *Phone:* 412-396-5211. *Toll-free phone:* 800-456-0590. *Fax:* 412-396-5644. *E-mail:* admissions@duq.edu.

Eastern University

St. Davids, Pennsylvania

http://www.eastern.edu/

- **Independent Christian** university, founded 1952
- **Suburban** 114-acre campus with easy access to Philadelphia
- **Endowment** $30.5 million
- **Coed** 1,752 undergraduate students, 76% full-time, 69% women, 31% men
- 62% of applicants were admitted

UNDERGRAD STUDENTS

1,328 full-time, 424 part-time. Students come from 36 states and territories; 19 other countries; 40% are from out of state; 21% Black or African American, non-Hispanic/Latino; 18% Hispanic/Latino; 2% Asian, non-Hispanic/Latino; 0.1% Native Hawaiian or other Pacific Islander, non-Hispanic/Latino; 0.1% American Indian or Alaska Native, non-Hispanic/Latino; 2% Two or more races, non-Hispanic/Latino; 7% Race/ethnicity unknown; 2% international; 11% transferred in; 78% live on campus.

Freshmen:

Admission: 2,054 applied, 1,279 admitted, 357 enrolled. ***Average high school GPA:*** 3.6. ***Test scores:*** SAT evidence-based reading and writing scores over 500: 89%; SAT math scores over 500: 78%; ACT scores over 18: 91%; SAT evidence-based reading and writing scores over 600: 37%; SAT math scores over 600: 30%; ACT scores over 24: 46%; SAT evidence-based reading and writing scores over 700: 8%; SAT math scores over 700: 4%; ACT scores over 30: 5%.

Retention: 78% of full-time freshmen returned.

FACULTY
Total: 421, 25% full-time, 38% with terminal degrees.

Student/faculty ratio: 10:1.

ACADEMICS
Calendar: semesters. *Degrees:* certificates, diplomas, associate, bachelor's, master's, doctoral, and post-master's certificates.

Special study options: academic remediation for entering students, accelerated degree program, advanced placement credit, distance learning, double majors, honors programs, independent study, internships, off-campus study, part-time degree program, services for LD students, student-designed majors, study abroad, summer session for credit. ***ROTC:*** Army (c), Air Force (c).

Computers: 68 computers/terminals are available on campus for general student use. Students can access the following: campus intranet, computer help desk, free student e-mail accounts, online (class) grades, online (class) registration, online (class) schedules, BRIGHTSPACE. Campuswide network is available. 100% of college-owned or -operated housing units are wired for high-speed Internet access. Wireless service is available via entire campus.

Library: Warner Memorial Library plus 1 other. *Books:* 150,192 (physical), 604,592 (digital/electronic); *Serial titles:* 60 (physical), 44,003 (digital/electronic); *Databases:* 176. Weekly public service hours: 85; students can reserve study rooms.

STUDENT LIFE
Housing options: on-campus residence required through senior year; men-only, women-only, special housing for students with disabilities. Campus housing is university owned.

Activities and organizations: drama/theater group, student-run newspaper, choral group, Wednesday Night Worship, Ultimate Frisbee, Student Activities Board, Multicultural Awareness Advisory Committee (MAAC), Student Chaplain Program.

Athletics Member NCAA. All Division III. ***Intercollegiate sports:*** baseball M, basketball M/W, cross-country running M/W, field hockey W, golf M/W, lacrosse M/W, soccer M/W, softball W, tennis M/W, track and field M/W, volleyball M/W. ***Intramural sports:*** basketball M/W, soccer M/W, volleyball M/W.

Campus security: 24-hour emergency response devices and patrols, late-night transport/escort service, controlled dormitory access.

Student services: health clinic, personal/psychological counseling.

COSTS & FINANCIAL AID
Costs (2020–21) ***One-time required fee:*** $75. ***Comprehensive fee:*** $46,530 includes full-time tuition ($34,136), mandatory fees ($570), and room and board ($11,824). Full-time tuition and fees vary according to course load, degree level, and program. Part-time tuition: $748 per credit. Part-time tuition and fees vary according to course load, degree level, and program. ***Required fees:*** $285 per term part-time. ***College room only:*** $6290. Room and board charges vary according to housing facility. ***Payment plan:*** installment. ***Waivers:*** children of alumni and employees or children of employees.

Financial Aid Of all full-time matriculated undergraduates who enrolled in 2018, 1,299 applied for aid, 1,192 were judged to have need, 278 had their need fully met. 318 Federal Work-Study jobs (averaging $1059). In 2018, 92 non-need-based awards were made. ***Average percent of need met:*** 81. ***Average financial aid package:*** $24,846. ***Average need-based loan:*** $4172. ***Average need-based gift aid:*** $8460. ***Average non-need-based aid:*** $13,282. ***Average indebtedness upon graduation:*** $40,488.

APPLYING
Standardized Tests *Required for some:* SAT or ACT (for admission).

Options: electronic application, early admission, deferred entrance.

Application fee: $35.

Required: high school transcript, minimum 2.0 GPA, 1 letter of recommendation. ***Required for some:*** essay or personal statement. ***Recommended:*** 2 letters of recommendation, interview.

Application deadlines: rolling (freshmen), rolling (out-of-state freshmen), rolling (transfers).

Notification: continuous (freshmen), continuous (out-of-state freshmen), continuous (transfers).

CONTACT
Katelyn Ambrose, Director of Enrollment, Eastern University, 1300 Eagle Road, St Davids, PA 19087-3696. *Phone:* 800-452-0996. *Toll-free phone:* 800-452-0996. *E-mail:* ugadm@eastern.edu.

East Stroudsburg University of Pennsylvania

East Stroudsburg, Pennsylvania

http://www.esu.edu/

- **State-supported** comprehensive, founded 1893, part of Pennsylvania State System of Higher Education
- **Suburban** 258-acre campus
- **Endowment** $22.2 million
- **Coed**
- **Moderately difficult** entrance level

FACULTY
Student/faculty ratio: 19:1.

ACADEMICS
Calendar: semesters. *Degrees:* certificates, bachelor's, master's, doctoral, post-master's, and postbachelor's certificates.

Library: Kemp Library. *Books:* 227,237 (physical), 411,580 (digital/electronic); *Serial titles:* 3,143 (physical), 76,680 (digital/electronic); *Databases:* 107. Weekly public service hours: 99.

STUDENT LIFE
Housing options: on-campus residence required for freshman year; coed, special housing for students with disabilities. Campus housing is university owned and is provided by a third party. Freshman campus housing is guaranteed.

Activities and organizations: drama/theater group, student-run newspaper, radio station, choral group, marching band, Black Student Union, Council for Exceptional Children, National Student Speech Hearing Language Association, Student Governmnet, Stage II, national fraternities, national sororities.

Athletics Member NCAA. All Division II except golf (Division I).

Campus security: 24-hour emergency response devices and patrols, late-night transport/escort service, controlled dormitory access, self-defense education, shuttle buses, lighted pathways/sidewalks, controlled building access.

Student services: health clinic, personal/psychological counseling, women's center, legal services, veterans affairs office.

COSTS & FINANCIAL AID
Costs (2019–20) ***Tuition:*** state resident $7716 full-time, $322 per credit hour part-time; nonresident $19,290 full-time, $805 per credit hour part-time. Full-time tuition and fees vary according to course load, location, and program. Part-time tuition and fees vary according to location and program. No tuition increase for student's term of enrollment. ***Required fees:*** $2972 full-time, $155 per credit hour part-time, $155 per credit hour part-time. ***Room and board:*** $11,760; room only: $8700. Room and board charges vary according to board plan and housing facility.

Financial Aid Of all full-time matriculated undergraduates who enrolled in 2018, 3,824 applied for aid, 3,269 were judged to have need, 1,468 had their need fully met. ***Average percent of need met:*** 63. ***Average financial aid package:*** $9194. ***Average need-based loan:*** $4220. ***Average need-based gift aid:*** $8634. ***Average indebtedness upon graduation:*** $12,070.

APPLYING
Standardized Tests *Required for some:* SAT or ACT (for admission).

Options: electronic application, deferred entrance.

Application fee: $25.

Required: high school transcript.

CONTACT
Mr. David Bousquet, Vice President of Enrollment Management, East Stroudsburg University of Pennsylvania, 200 Prospect Street, East Stroudsburg, PA 18301. *Phone:* 570-422-3542. *Toll-free phone:* 877-230-5547. *Fax:* 570-422-3933. *E-mail:* admission@esu.edu.

Edinboro University of Pennsylvania
Edinboro, Pennsylvania
http://www.edinboro.edu/

- **State-supported** comprehensive, founded 1857, part of Pennsylvania State System of Higher Education
- **Small-town** 585-acre campus
- **Endowment** $32.2 million
- **Coed** 3,399 undergraduate students, 88% full-time, 58% women, 42% men
- **Minimally difficult** entrance level, 83% of applicants were admitted

UNDERGRAD STUDENTS
2,998 full-time, 401 part-time. Students come from 31 states and territories; 21 other countries; 13% are from out of state; 6% Black or African American, non-Hispanic/Latino; 4% Hispanic/Latino; 1% Asian, non-Hispanic/Latino; 0.3% American Indian or Alaska Native, non-Hispanic/Latino; 4% Two or more races, non-Hispanic/Latino; 2% Race/ethnicity unknown; 1% international; 6% transferred in; 30% live on campus.

Freshmen:
Admission: 2,872 applied, 2,393 admitted, 706 enrolled. ***Average high school GPA:*** 3.5. ***Test scores:*** SAT evidence-based reading and writing scores over 500: 71%; SAT math scores over 500: 70%; ACT scores over 18: 75%; SAT evidence-based reading and writing scores over 600: 25%; SAT math scores over 600: 17%; ACT scores over 24: 24%; SAT evidence-based reading and writing scores over 700: 3%; SAT math scores over 700: 2%; ACT scores over 30: 1%.

Retention: 71% of full-time freshmen returned.

FACULTY
Total: 311, 80% full-time, 74% with terminal degrees.

Student/faculty ratio: 15:1.

ACADEMICS
Calendar: semesters. *Degrees:* certificates, bachelor's, master's, doctoral, post-master's, and postbachelor's certificates.

Special study options: academic remediation for entering students, adult/continuing education programs, advanced placement credit, distance learning, double majors, freshman honors college, honors programs, independent study, internships, off-campus study, services for LD students, student-designed majors, study abroad, summer session for credit. ***ROTC:*** Army (b).

Computers: Students can access the following: campus intranet, computer help desk, free student e-mail accounts, online (class) grades, online (class) registration, online (class) schedules, new students receive technology instruction during orientation, 24-hour computer lab, some software. Campuswide network is available. 100% of college-owned or -operated housing units are wired for high-speed Internet access. Wireless service is available via entire campus.

Library: Baron-Forness Library plus 1 other. *Books:* 310,014 (physical), 456,241 (digital/electronic); *Serial titles:* 73 (physical), 78,643 (digital/electronic); *Databases:* 113. Weekly public service hours: 90; study areas open 24 hours, 5–7 days a week; students can reserve study rooms.

STUDENT LIFE
Housing options: on-campus residence required through sophomore year; coed, special housing for students with disabilities. Campus housing is university owned. Freshman campus housing is guaranteed.

Activities and organizations: drama/theater group, student-run newspaper, radio and television station, choral group, marching band, Student Government Association, University Programming Board, Greek Life, Recreational Sports, Student Leadership (Leadership Edinboro), national fraternities, national sororities.

Athletics Member NCAA. All Division II except wrestling (Division I). ***Intercollegiate sports:*** basketball M(s)/W(s), cross-country running M(s)/W(s), football M(s), lacrosse W(s), soccer W(s), softball W(s), swimming and diving M(s)/W(s), tennis M(s)/W(s), track and field M(s)/W(s), volleyball W(s), wrestling M(s). ***Intramural sports:*** baseball M, basketball M/W, bowling M/W, cheerleading W, equestrian sports M/W, fencing M/W, field hockey M(c)/W(c), football M(c)/W(c), golf M/W, ice hockey M/W, lacrosse M, racquetball M/W, rock climbing M/W, skiing (downhill) M/W, soccer M/W, softball M(c)/W(c), tennis M/W, ultimate Frisbee M/W, volleyball M/W.

Campus security: 24-hour emergency response devices and patrols, late-night transport/escort service, controlled dormitory access, self-defense education.

Student services: health clinic, personal/psychological counseling, women's center, legal services.

COSTS & FINANCIAL AID
Costs (2019–20) ***Tuition:*** state resident $7716 full-time, $322 per credit hour part-time; nonresident $11,574 full-time, $482 per credit hour part-time. Full-time tuition and fees vary according to location and program. Part-time tuition and fees vary according to course load, location, and program. ***Required fees:*** $2827 full-time, $182 per credit hour part-time. ***Room and board:*** $9800; room only: $6660. Room and board charges vary according to board plan and housing facility. ***Payment plans:*** installment, deferred payment. ***Waivers:*** senior citizens and employees or children of employees.

Financial Aid Of all full-time matriculated undergraduates who enrolled in 2018, 3,066 applied for aid, 2,530 were judged to have need, 84 had their need fully met. In 2018, 30 non-need-based awards were made. ***Average percent of need met:*** 48. ***Average financial aid package:*** $9914. ***Average need-based loan:*** $2702. ***Average need-based gift aid:*** $5909. ***Average non-need-based aid:*** $3183. ***Average indebtedness upon graduation:*** $42,694.

APPLYING
Standardized Tests *Required:* SAT or ACT (for admission).

Options: electronic application, deferred entrance.

Application fee: $30.

Required: high school transcript. ***Required for some:*** essay or personal statement, interview, music auditions.

Notification: continuous (freshmen), continuous (transfers).

CONTACT
Ms. Melissa Manning, Associate Director of Undergraduate Admissions, Edinboro University of Pennsylvania, Academy Hall, Edinboro, PA 16444. *Phone:* 814-732-2761. *Toll-free phone:* 888-846-2676. *Fax:* 814-732-2420. *E-mail:* eup_admissions@edinboro.edu.

Elizabethtown College
Elizabethtown, Pennsylvania
http://www.etown.edu/

CONTACT
Ms. Lauren Deibler, Director of Admissions and Coordinator of International Recruitment, Elizabethtown College, One Alpha Drive, Elizabethtown, PA 17022. *Phone:* 717-361-1400. *Fax:* 717-361-1365. *E-mail:* admissions@etown.edu.

See below for display ad and page 1056 for the College Close-Up.

Elizabethtown College School of Continuing and Professional Studies
Elizabethtown, Pennsylvania
http://www.etowndegrees.com/

CONTACT
Ms. Barbara A. Randazzo, Assistant Dean of Enrollment Management, Elizabethtown College School of Continuing and Professional Studies, One Alpha Drive, Elizabethtown College, PA 17022. *Phone:* 717-361-3750. *Toll-free phone:* 800-877-2694. *Fax:* 717-361-1466. *E-mail:* randazzob@etown.edu.

Franklin & Marshall College
Lancaster, Pennsylvania
http://www.fandm.edu/

- **Independent** 4-year, founded 1787
- **Suburban** 209-acre campus with easy access to Philadelphia
- **Coed**
- **Very difficult** entrance level

FACULTY
Student/faculty ratio: 9:1.

ACADEMICS
Calendar: semesters. *Degree:* bachelor's.
Library: Shadek-Fackenthal Library plus 1 other. *Books:* 468,748 (physical), 135,071 (digital/electronic); *Serial titles:* 2,680 (physical), 167,874 (digital/electronic). Weekly public service hours: 110; students can reserve study rooms.

STUDENT LIFE
Housing options: on-campus residence required through senior year; coed, men-only, women-only, cooperative, special housing for students with disabilities. Campus housing is university owned and is provided by a third party. Freshman campus housing is guaranteed.
Activities and organizations: drama/theater group, student-run newspaper, radio station, choral group, Intervarsity, Hillel, Mi Gente Latina, Cia Bella, F&M Players, national fraternities, national sororities.
Athletics Member NCAA. All Division III except wrestling (Division I).
Campus security: 24-hour emergency response devices and patrols, late-night transport/escort service, controlled dormitory access, residence hall security, campus security connected to city police and fire company.
Student services: health clinic, personal/psychological counseling, women's center.

COSTS & FINANCIAL AID
Costs (2019–20) ***One-time required fee:*** $200. ***Comprehensive fee:*** $73,250 includes full-time tuition ($58,615), mandatory fees ($185), and room and board ($14,450). Part-time tuition: $7325 per course. Part-time tuition and fees vary according to course load. ***College room only:*** $8550. Room and board charges vary according to board plan and housing facility.
Financial Aid Of all full-time matriculated undergraduates who enrolled in 2019, 1,429 applied for aid, 1,270 were judged to have need, 746 had their need fully met. In 2019, 22 non-need-based awards were made. ***Average percent of need met:*** 100. ***Average financial aid package:*** $54,166. ***Average need-based loan:*** $3639. ***Average need-based gift aid:*** $49,637. ***Average non-need-based aid:*** $22,222. ***Average indebtedness upon graduation:*** $27,928.

APPLYING
Options: electronic application, early admission, early decision, deferred entrance.
Application fee: $60.
Required: essay or personal statement, high school transcript, 2 letters of recommendation, Common Application Supplement. ***Required for some:*** interview.

CONTACT
Julie Kerich, Director of Admissions, Franklin & Marshall College, PO Box 3003, Lancaster, PA 17604-3003. *Phone:* 717-358-4743. *Toll-free phone:* 877-678-9111. *Fax:* 717-358-4389. *E-mail:* julie.kerich@fandm.edu.

Gannon University
Erle, Pennsylvania
http://www.gannon.edu/

- **Independent Roman Catholic** university, founded 1925
- **Urban** 38-acre campus with easy access to Cleveland, Buffalo, Pittsburgh
- **Coed** 3,432 undergraduate students, 81% full-time, 61% women, 39% men
- **Moderately difficult** entrance level, 76% of applicants were admitted

UNDERGRAD STUDENTS
2,775 full-time, 657 part-time. 28% are from out of state; 5% Black or African American, non-Hispanic/Latino; 4% Hispanic/Latino; 2% Asian, non-Hispanic/Latino; 0.1% Native Hawaiian or other Pacific Islander, non-Hispanic/Latino; 0.1% American Indian or Alaska Native, non-

Hispanic/Latino; 3% Two or more races, non-Hispanic/Latino; 6% Race/ethnicity unknown; 9% international; 3% transferred in; 45% live on campus.

Freshmen:
Admission: 4,727 applied, 3,570 admitted, 734 enrolled. ***Average high school GPA:*** 3.6. ***Test scores:*** SAT evidence-based reading and writing scores over 500: 84%; SAT math scores over 500: 81%; ACT scores over 18: 85%; SAT evidence-based reading and writing scores over 600: 35%; SAT math scores over 600: 35%; ACT scores over 24: 45%; SAT evidence-based reading and writing scores over 700: 4%; SAT math scores over 700: 6%; ACT scores over 30: 9%.
Retention: 82% of full-time freshmen returned.

FACULTY
Total: 373, 63% full-time, 58% with terminal degrees.

Student/faculty ratio: 13:1.

ACADEMICS
Calendar: semesters plus 2 summer sessions. *Degrees:* certificates, associate, bachelor's, master's, doctoral, post-master's, and postbachelor's certificates.

Special study options: academic remediation for entering students, accelerated degree program, adult/continuing education programs, advanced placement credit, cooperative education, distance learning, double majors, English as a second language, honors programs, independent study, internships, off-campus study, part-time degree program, services for LD students, study abroad, summer session for credit. ***ROTC:*** Army (b).

Unusual degree programs: 3-2 business administration; engineering with University of Pittsburgh; occupational therapy, physician assistant, sport and exercise science.

Computers: 386 computers/terminals and 1,425 ports are available on campus for general student use. Students can access the following: campus intranet, computer help desk, free student e-mail accounts, online (class) grades, online (class) registration, online (class) schedules. Campuswide network is available. 100% of college-owned or -operated housing units are wired for high-speed Internet access. Wireless service is available via entire campus.
Library: Nash Library. *Books:* 213,041 (physical), 252,244 (digital/electronic); *Serial titles:* 37 (physical), 52,805 (digital/electronic); *Databases:* 45. Weekly public service hours: 97; students can reserve study rooms.

STUDENT LIFE
Housing options: on-campus residence required through sophomore year; coed. Campus housing is university owned. Freshman campus housing is guaranteed.

Activities and organizations: drama/theater group, student-run newspaper, radio station, choral group, GU Society of Physician Assistant, GU Habitat for Humanity, Activities Programming Board, Student Occupational Therapy Association, Organization of Women Leaders, national fraternities, national sororities.

Athletics Member NCAA. All Division II. ***Intercollegiate sports:*** baseball M(s), basketball M(s)/W(s), cheerleading W(s)(c), cross-country running M(s)/W(s), football M(s), golf M(s)/W(s), gymnastics W(s)(c), lacrosse W(s), rugby M(c), soccer M(s)/W(s), softball W(s), swimming and diving M(s)/W(s), volleyball W(s), water polo M(s)/W(s), wrestling M(s). ***Intramural sports:*** basketball M/W, football M/W, ice hockey M(c), lacrosse M(c), racquetball M/W, rugby M(c)/W(c), sailing M(c)/W(c), soccer M/W(c), ultimate Frisbee M(c)/W(c), volleyball M(c)/W(c).

Campus security: 24-hour emergency response devices and patrols, late-night transport/escort service, controlled dormitory access, security cameras in and outside of campus facilities, including streets and sidewalks.

Student services: health clinic, personal/psychological counseling, veterans affairs office.

FINANCIAL AID
Financial Aid Of all full-time matriculated undergraduates who enrolled in 2019, 2,340 applied for aid, 2,115 were judged to have need, 477 had their need fully met. In 2019, 445 non-need-based awards were made. ***Average percent of need met:*** 74. ***Average financial aid package:*** $27,213. ***Average need-based loan:*** $21,932. ***Average need-based gift aid:*** $23,422. ***Average non-need-based aid:*** $17,388.

APPLYING

Standardized Tests *Required:* SAT or ACT (for admission).

Options: electronic application, deferred entrance.

Application fee: $25.

Required: high school transcript, minimum 2.0 GPA, counselor's recommendation. ***Required for some:*** minimum 3.0 GPA, 2 letters of recommendation, interview. ***Recommended:*** essay or personal statement.

Application deadlines: rolling (freshmen), rolling (transfers).

Notification: continuous (freshmen), continuous (transfers).

CONTACT

Office of Admissions, Gannon University, 109 University Square, Erie, PA 16541. *Phone:* 814-871-7240. *Toll-free phone:* 800-GANNONU. *Fax:* 814-871-5803. *E-mail:* admissions@gannon.edu.

See below for display ad and page 1060 for the College Close-Up.

Geneva College

Beaver Falls, Pennsylvania

http://www.geneva.edu/

- **Independent** comprehensive, founded 1848, affiliated with Reformed Presbyterian Church of North America
- **Small-town** 55-acre campus with easy access to Pittsburgh
- **Endowment** $44.2 million
- **Coed** 1,290 undergraduate students, 87% full-time, 47% women, 53% men
- **Moderately difficult** entrance level, 53% of applicants were admitted

UNDERGRAD STUDENTS

1,116 full-time, 174 part-time. Students come from 33 states and territories; 11 other countries; 27% are from out of state; 8% Black or African American, non-Hispanic/Latino; 2% Hispanic/Latino; 2% Asian, non-Hispanic/Latino; 0.4% American Indian or Alaska Native, non-Hispanic/Latino; 3% Two or more races, non-Hispanic/Latino; 4% Race/ethnicity unknown; 2% international; 3% transferred in; 67% live on campus.

Freshmen:

Admission: 2,801 applied, 1,491 admitted, 314 enrolled. ***Average high school GPA:*** 3.6. ***Test scores:*** SAT evidence-based reading and writing scores over 500: 81%; SAT math scores over 500: 77%; ACT scores over 18: 91%; SAT evidence-based reading and writing scores over 600: 38%; SAT math scores over 600: 28%; ACT scores over 24: 54%; SAT evidence-based reading and writing scores over 700: 6%; SAT math scores over 700: 6%; ACT scores over 30: 14%.

Retention: 73% of full-time freshmen returned.

FACULTY

Total: 213, 31% full-time, 48% with terminal degrees.

Student/faculty ratio: 12:1.

ACADEMICS

Calendar: semesters. *Degrees:* associate, bachelor's, and master's (also offers non-traditional programs in Philadelphia and western Pennsylvania with significant enrollment not reflected in profile).

Special study options: academic remediation for entering students, accelerated degree program, adult/continuing education programs, advanced placement credit, cooperative education, distance learning, double majors, English as a second language, honors programs, independent study, internships, off-campus study, part-time degree program, services for LD students, student-designed majors, study abroad, summer session for credit. ***ROTC:*** Army (c).

Computers: 150 computers/terminals and 400 ports are available on campus for general student use. Students can access the following: campus intranet, computer help desk, free student e-mail accounts, online (class) grades, online (class) registration, online (class) schedules. Campuswide network is available. 100% of college-owned or -operated housing units are wired for high-speed Internet access. Wireless service is available via entire campus.

Library: McCartney Library plus 3 others. *Books:* 140,157 (physical), 12,739 (digital/electronic); *Serial titles:* 30,449 (physical); *Databases:* 54. Weekly public service hours: 84.

STUDENT LIFE

Housing options: men-only, women-only. Campus housing is university owned. Freshman campus housing is guaranteed.

Activities and organizations: drama/theater group, student-run newspaper, choral group, marching band, marching band, Genevans Choir, Intramural sports, ministry groups, discipleship groups.

Athletics Member NCAA, NCCAA. All NCAA Division III. ***Intercollegiate sports:*** baseball M, basketball M/W, cross-country running M/W, football M, golf M/W, soccer M/W, softball W, tennis M/W, track and field M/W, volleyball M(c)/W. ***Intramural sports:*** basketball M/W, cheerleading W(c), football M/W, ice hockey M(c), racquetball M/W, rugby M(c)/W(c), skiing (downhill) M(c)/W(c), soccer M/W, softball M/W, table tennis M/W, ultimate Frisbee M/W, volleyball M/W.

Campus security: 24-hour emergency response devices and patrols, late-night transport/escort service, controlled dormitory access.

Student services: health clinic, personal/psychological counseling.

COSTS & FINANCIAL AID

Costs (2020–21) ***Comprehensive fee:*** $39,890 includes full-time tuition ($28,500), mandatory fees ($540), and room and board ($10,850). Full-time tuition and fees vary according to course load, location, and program. Part-time tuition: $960 per credit hour. Part-time tuition and fees vary according to course load, location, and program. ***Required fees:*** $270 per credit hour part-time. ***College room only:*** $5660. Room and board charges vary according to board plan. ***Payment plan:*** installment.

Financial Aid Of all full-time matriculated undergraduates who enrolled in 2017, 1,023 applied for aid, 927 were judged to have need, 196 had their need fully met. 217 Federal Work-Study jobs (averaging $698). In 2017, 179 non-need-based awards were made. ***Average percent of need met:*** 77. ***Average financial aid package:*** $21,364. ***Average need-based loan:*** $4252. ***Average need-based gift aid:*** $16,975. ***Average non-need-based aid:*** $11,500. ***Average indebtedness upon graduation:*** $36,605.

APPLYING

Standardized Tests *Required:* SAT or ACT (for admission).

Options: electronic application, early admission, deferred entrance.

Application fee: $40.

Required: essay or personal statement, high school transcript, minimum 2.0 GPA. ***Required for some:*** 1 unit of chemistry and physics and 4 units of college-prep mathematics (including trigonometry and pre-calculus) for engineering. ***Recommended:*** minimum 3.0 GPA, 2 letters of recommendation, interview.

Application deadlines: rolling (freshmen), rolling (transfers).

Notification: continuous (freshmen), continuous (transfers).

CONTACT

Mr. David Layton, Associate Vice President for Enrollment, Geneva College, 3200 College Avenue, Beaver Falls, PA 15010-3599. *Phone:* 724-847-6500. *Toll-free phone:* 800-847-8255. *E-mail:* admissions@geneva.edu.

Gettysburg College

Gettysburg, Pennsylvania

http://www.gettysburg.edu/

- **Independent** 4-year, founded 1832, affiliated with Evangelical Lutheran Church in America
- **Suburban** 200-acre campus with easy access to Baltimore and Washington, D.C.
- **Endowment** $313.8 million
- **Coed**
- **Most difficult** entrance level

FACULTY

Student/faculty ratio: 9:1.

ACADEMICS

Calendar: semesters. *Degree:* bachelor's.

Library: Musselman Library. *Books:* 370,500 (physical), 350,000 (digital/electronic); *Databases:* 299. Study areas open 24 hours, 5–7 days a week.

STUDENT LIFE
Housing options: on-campus residence required through senior year; coed, men-only, women-only. Campus housing is university owned. Freshman campus housing is guaranteed.

Activities and organizations: drama/theater group, student-run newspaper, radio and television station, choral group, marching band, community service, music, athletics, student government, national fraternities, national sororities.

Athletics Member NCAA. All Division III.

Campus security: 24-hour emergency response devices and patrols, student patrols, late-night transport/escort service, controlled dormitory access.

Student services: health clinic, personal/psychological counseling, women's center.

COSTS & FINANCIAL AID
Costs (2019–20) ***Comprehensive fee:*** $69,850 includes full-time tuition ($56,390) and room and board ($13,460). ***College room only:*** $7220. Room and board charges vary according to board plan and housing facility.

Financial Aid Of all full-time matriculated undergraduates who enrolled in 2019, 1,849 applied for aid, 1,617 were judged to have need, 1,435 had their need fully met. 381 Federal Work-Study jobs (averaging $690). 1,145 state and other part-time jobs (averaging $825). In 2019, 544 non-need-based awards were made. ***Average percent of need met:*** 90. ***Average financial aid package:*** $44,448. ***Average need-based loan:*** $4809. ***Average need-based gift aid:*** $40,404. ***Average non-need-based aid:*** $16,637. ***Average indebtedness upon graduation:*** $34,630.

APPLYING
Standardized Tests *Required for some:* SAT or ACT (for admission).

Options: electronic application, early admission, early decision, deferred entrance.

Application fee: $60.

Required: essay or personal statement, high school transcript, 2 letters of recommendation. ***Recommended:*** minimum 3.0 GPA, interview, extracurricular activities.

CONTACT
Ms. Gail Sweezey, Director of Admissions, Gettysburg College, 300 North Washington Street, Gettysburg, PA 17325. *Phone:* 717-337-6100. *Toll-free phone:* 800-431-0803. *Fax:* 717-337-6145. *E-mail:* admiss@gettysburg.edu.

Grove City College

Grove City, Pennsylvania

http://www.gcc.edu/

- **Independent Presbyterian** 4-year, founded 1876
- **Small-town** 180-acre campus with easy access to Pittsburgh
- **Endowment** $128.2 million
- **Coed**
- **Moderately difficult** entrance level

FACULTY
Student/faculty ratio: 13:1.

ACADEMICS
Calendar: semesters. *Degree:* bachelor's.
Library: Henry Buhl Library plus 1 other. *Books:* 168,520 (physical), 264,550 (digital/electronic); *Serial titles:* 25 (physical), 45,123 (digital/electronic); *Databases:* 107. Weekly public service hours: 103.

STUDENT LIFE
Housing options: on-campus residence required through senior year; men-only, women-only. Campus housing is university owned. Freshman campus housing is guaranteed.

Activities and organizations: drama/theater group, student-run newspaper, radio and television station, choral group, marching band, Warriors for Christ, Orchesis, Orientation Board, Association for Women Students (AWS), Young Life.

Athletics Member NCAA. All Division III except golf (Division II).

Campus security: 24-hour emergency response devices and patrols, student patrols, late-night transport/escort service, controlled dormitory access.

Student services: health clinic, personal/psychological counseling.

COSTS & FINANCIAL AID
Costs (2019–20) ***Comprehensive fee:*** $28,530 includes full-time tuition ($18,470) and room and board ($10,060). Part-time tuition: $595 per credit hour. ***College room only:*** $6160. Room and board charges vary according to housing facility.

Financial Aid Of all full-time matriculated undergraduates who enrolled in 2019, 1,313 applied for aid, 1,078 were judged to have need, 81 had their need fully met. In 2019, 407 non-need-based awards were made. ***Average percent of need met:*** 49. ***Average financial aid package:*** $7999. ***Average need-based loan:*** $18. ***Average need-based gift aid:*** $7999. ***Average non-need-based aid:*** $3420. ***Average indebtedness upon graduation:*** $40,600. ***Financial aid deadline:*** 4/15.

APPLYING
Standardized Tests *Required:* SAT or ACT (for admission), SAT, ACT, and/or CLT test scores (for admission).

Options: electronic application, early admission, early decision, deferred entrance.

Application fee: $50.

Required: essay or personal statement, high school transcript, 2 letters of recommendation. ***Recommended:*** interview.

CONTACT
Lee S Wishing, VP Student Recruitment, Grove City College, 100 Campus Drive, Grove City, PA 16127-2104. *Phone:* 724-458-3332. *E-mail:* admissions@gcc.edu.

Gwynedd Mercy University

Gwynedd Valley, Pennsylvania

http://www.gmercyu.edu/

- **Independent Roman Catholic** comprehensive, founded 1948
- **Suburban** 170-acre campus with easy access to Philadelphia
- **Endowment** $38.4 million
- **Coed** 2,157 undergraduate students, 79% full-time, 72% women, 28% men
- **Moderately difficult** entrance level, 95% of applicants were admitted

UNDERGRAD STUDENTS
1,702 full-time, 455 part-time. 13% are from out of state; 21% Black or African American, non-Hispanic/Latino; 6% Hispanic/Latino; 7% Asian, non-Hispanic/Latino; 0.3% Native Hawaiian or other Pacific Islander, non-Hispanic/Latino; 0.8% American Indian or Alaska Native, non-Hispanic/Latino; 1% Two or more races, non-Hispanic/Latino; 3% Race/ethnicity unknown; 9% transferred in; 20% live on campus.

Freshmen:
Admission: 1,030 applied, 980 admitted, 239 enrolled. ***Average high school GPA:*** 3.3. ***Test scores:*** SAT evidence-based reading and writing scores over 500: 60%; SAT math scores over 500: 61%; ACT scores over 18: 78%; SAT evidence-based reading and writing scores over 600: 17%; SAT math scores over 600: 11%; ACT scores over 24: 31%; SAT math scores over 700: 2%; ACT scores over 30: 6%.

Retention: 78% of full-time freshmen returned.

FACULTY
Total: 325, 29% full-time, 28% with terminal degrees.

Student/faculty ratio: 10:1.

ACADEMICS
Calendar: semesters. *Degrees:* associate, bachelor's, master's, doctoral, and post-master's certificates.

Special study options: academic remediation for entering students, accelerated degree program, adult/continuing education programs, advanced placement credit, distance learning, double majors, honors programs, independent study, internships, part-time degree program, services for LD students, study abroad, summer session for credit.

Computers: 200 computers/terminals and 1,000 ports are available on campus for general student use. Students can access the following: campus intranet, computer help desk, free student e-mail accounts, online (class) grades, online (class) registration, online (class) schedules. Campuswide network is available. 100% of college-owned or -operated housing units are wired for high-speed Internet access. Wireless service is available via entire campus.

Library: Keiss Library plus 1 other. *Books:* 85,778 (physical), 180,000 (digital/electronic); *Serial titles:* 21 (physical), 111,480 (digital/electronic); *Databases:* 46. Weekly public service hours: 76; students can reserve study rooms.

STUDENT LIFE

Housing options: coed. Campus housing is university owned. Freshman applicants given priority for college housing.

Activities and organizations: student-run newspaper, choral group, Voices of Gwynedd, Athletic Association, Student Government, Program Board, Peer Mentors.

Athletics Member NCAA. All Division III. ***Intercollegiate sports:*** baseball M, basketball M/W, cheerleading W, cross-country running M/W, field hockey W, lacrosse M/W, soccer M/W, softball W, tennis M/W, track and field M/W, volleyball W. ***Intramural sports:*** football M.

Campus security: 24-hour emergency response devices and patrols, late-night transport/escort service, controlled dormitory access.

Student services: health clinic, personal/psychological counseling.

COSTS & FINANCIAL AID

Costs (2020–21) ***Comprehensive fee:*** $48,280 includes full-time tuition ($34,650), mandatory fees ($950), and room and board ($12,680). Full-time tuition and fees vary according to program. Part-time tuition and fees vary according to program. ***College room only:*** $5520. Room and board charges vary according to board plan.

Financial Aid Of all full-time matriculated undergraduates who enrolled in 2019, 1,521 applied for aid, 1,373 were judged to have need, 165 had their need fully met. In 2019, 185 non-need-based awards were made. ***Average percent of need met:*** 60. ***Average financial aid package:*** $22,614. ***Average need-based loan:*** $4282. ***Average need-based gift aid:*** $20,455. ***Average non-need-based aid:*** $15,892. ***Average indebtedness upon graduation:*** $35,827. ***Financial aid deadline:*** 5/1.

APPLYING

Standardized Tests *Required:* SAT or ACT (for admission). *Recommended:* SAT (for admission), ACT (for admission).

Options: electronic application, deferred entrance.

Required for some: essay or personal statement.

Application deadlines: rolling (freshmen), 8/20 (transfers).

Notification: continuous (freshmen), continuous (transfers).

CONTACT

Ms. Michelle Diehl, Director of Admissions, Gwynedd Mercy University, 1325 Sumneytown Pike, Gwynedd Valley, PA 19437-0901. *Phone:* 215-646-7300. *Toll-free phone:* 800-342-5462. *Fax:* 215-641-5556. *E-mail:* admissions@gmercyu.edu.

Harrisburg University of Science and Technology

Harrisburg, Pennsylvania

http://www.HarrisburgU.edu/

CONTACT

Harrisburg University of Science and Technology, 326 Market Street, Harrisburg, PA 17101. *Phone:* 717-901-5150. *Toll-free phone:* 866-HBG-UNIV.

Haverford College

Haverford, Pennsylvania

http://www.haverford.edu/

- **Independent** 4-year, founded 1833
- **Suburban** 216-acre campus with easy access to Philadelphia
- **Endowment** $518.9 million
- **Coed**
- **Most difficult** entrance level

FACULTY

Student/faculty ratio: 9:1.

ACADEMICS

Calendar: semesters. *Degree:* bachelor's.

Library: James P. Magill Library plus 3 others. *Books:* 475,604 (physical), 702,593 (digital/electronic); *Serial titles:* 18,525 (physical), 135,312 (digital/electronic); *Databases:* 91. Study areas open 24 hours, 5–7 days a week; students can reserve study rooms.

STUDENT LIFE

Housing options: on-campus residence required for freshman year; coed, men-only, women-only, special housing for students with disabilities. Campus housing is university owned. Freshman campus housing is guaranteed.

Activities and organizations: drama/theater group, student-run newspaper, radio station, choral group, Volunteer Programs, Student government, Choral groups, Multicultural Groups, Orientation Team/Residential Life Leaders.

Athletics Member NCAA. All Division III.

Campus security: 24-hour emergency response devices and patrols, late-night transport/escort service, controlled dormitory access.

Student services: health clinic, personal/psychological counseling, women's center.

COSTS & FINANCIAL AID

Costs (2019–20) ***One-time required fee:*** $254. ***Comprehensive fee:*** $73,468 includes full-time tuition ($56,200), mandatory fees ($498), and room and board ($16,770). ***College room only:*** $9790.

Financial Aid Of all full-time matriculated undergraduates who enrolled in 2019, 653 applied for aid, 588 were judged to have need, 588 had their need fully met. ***Average percent of need met:*** 100. ***Average financial aid package:*** $54,803. ***Average need-based loan:*** $3607. ***Average need-based gift aid:*** $52,045. ***Average indebtedness upon graduation:*** $11,500.

APPLYING

Standardized Tests *Required:* SAT or ACT (for admission).

Options: electronic application, early admission, early decision, deferred entrance.

Application fee: $65.

Required: essay or personal statement. ***Required for some:*** high school transcript. ***Recommended:*** interview.

CONTACT

Mr. Jess Lord, Dean of Admissions and Financial Aid, Haverford College, 370 Lancaster Avenue, Haverford, PA 19041-1392. *Phone:* 610-896-1350. *Fax:* 610-896-1338. *E-mail:* admission@haverford.edu.

Holy Family University

Philadelphia, Pennsylvania

http://www.holyfamily.edu/

CONTACT

Ms. Lauren Campbell, Director of Admissions, Holy Family University, 9801 Frankford Avenue, Philadelphia, PA 19114-2009. *Phone:* 215-637-3050. *Fax:* 215-281-1022. *E-mail:* admissions@holyfamily.edu.

Hussian College, School of Art

Philadelphia, Pennsylvania

http://www.hussiancollege.edu/

CONTACT

Mr. Mark Cernero, Director of Admissions, Hussian College, School of Art, The Bourse, Suite 300, 111 South Independence Mall East, Philadelphia, PA 19106. *Phone:* 215-574-9600. *Fax:* 215-574-9800. *E-mail:* mcernero@hussianart.edu.

Immaculata University
Immaculata, Pennsylvania
http://www.immaculata.edu/

- **Independent Roman Catholic** university, founded 1920
- **Suburban** 373-acre campus with easy access to Philadelphia
- **Endowment** $19.7 million
- **Coed** 1,503 undergraduate students, 60% full-time, 71% women, 29% men
- **Moderately difficult** entrance level, 81% of applicants were admitted

UNDERGRAD STUDENTS
904 full-time, 599 part-time. 23% are from out of state; 15% Black or African American, non-Hispanic/Latino; 9% Hispanic/Latino; 2% Asian, non-Hispanic/Latino; 0.1% American Indian or Alaska Native, non-Hispanic/Latino; 2% Two or more races, non-Hispanic/Latino; 0.8% Race/ethnicity unknown; 2% international; 3% transferred in; 30% live on campus.

Freshmen:
Admission: 1,969 applied, 1,602 admitted, 259 enrolled. ***Average high school GPA:*** 3.3. ***Test scores:*** SAT evidence-based reading and writing scores over 500: 75%; SAT math scores over 500: 70%; ACT scores over 18: 78%; SAT evidence-based reading and writing scores over 600: 30%; SAT math scores over 600: 21%; ACT scores over 24: 28%; SAT evidence-based reading and writing scores over 700: 3%; SAT math scores over 700: 1%; ACT scores over 30: 11%.

Retention: 86% of full-time freshmen returned.

FACULTY
Total: 311, 27% full-time, 52% with terminal degrees.

Student/faculty ratio: 9:1.

ACADEMICS
Calendar: semesters. *Degrees:* certificates, associate, bachelor's, master's, doctoral, and post-master's certificates.

Special study options: academic remediation for entering students, accelerated degree program, adult/continuing education programs, advanced placement credit, distance learning, double majors, honors programs, independent study, internships, off-campus study, part-time degree program, services for LD students, study abroad, summer session for credit. ***ROTC:*** Army (c).

Unusual degree programs: 3-2 business administration with DeSales University; 3+3 Program with Widener University Law School.

Computers: Students can access the following: campus intranet, computer help desk, free student e-mail accounts, online (class) grades, online (class) registration, online (class) schedules. Campuswide network is available. Wireless service is available via entire campus.
Library: Gabriele Library. Students can reserve study rooms.

STUDENT LIFE
Housing options: coed, men-only, women-only, special housing for students with disabilities. Campus housing is university owned.

Activities and organizations: drama/theater group, student-run newspaper, choral group.

Athletics Member NCAA. All Division III. ***Intercollegiate sports:*** baseball M, basketball M/W, cross-country running M/W, field hockey W, golf M/W, lacrosse M/W, soccer M/W, softball W, swimming and diving M/W, tennis M/W, track and field M/W, volleyball M/W. ***Intramural sports:*** basketball M/W, cheerleading W(c), soccer M/W, softball M/W, volleyball M/W.

Campus security: 24-hour emergency response devices and patrols, late-night transport/escort service, controlled dormitory access.

Student services: health clinic, personal/psychological counseling.

COSTS & FINANCIAL AID
Costs (2020–21) ***Comprehensive fee:*** $40,370 includes full-time tuition ($26,900), mandatory fees ($850), and room and board ($12,620). Full-time tuition and fees vary according to degree level. Part-time tuition: $540 per credit hour. Part-time tuition and fees vary according to degree level. ***College room only:*** $6390. Room and board charges vary according to board plan. ***Payment plan:*** installment. ***Waivers:*** employees or children of employees.

Financial Aid Of all full-time matriculated undergraduates who enrolled in 2018, 728 applied for aid, 639 were judged to have need, 88 had their need fully met. In 2018, 152 non-need-based awards were made. ***Average percent of need met:*** 55. ***Average financial aid package:*** $17,757. ***Average need-based loan:*** $4289. ***Average need-based gift aid:*** $7522. ***Average non-need-based aid:*** $9665. ***Average indebtedness upon graduation:*** $55,126.

APPLYING
Options: electronic application, deferred entrance.

Application fee: $35.

Required: essay or personal statement, high school transcript, minimum 2.0 GPA, 1 letter of recommendation. ***Required for some:*** minimum 3.0 GPA, 2 letters of recommendation, audition for music students. ***Recommended:*** minimum 3.0 GPA, interview.

Application deadlines: rolling (freshmen), rolling (transfers).

Notification: continuous (freshmen), continuous (transfers).

CONTACT
Ms. Christine Rhine, Director of Admissions, Immaculata University, 1145 King Road, Immaculata, PA 19345-0702. *Phone:* 610-647-4400 Ext. 3044. *Toll-free phone:* 877-428-6329. *Fax:* 610-640-0836. *E-mail:* cesbensen@immaculata.edu.

Indiana University of Pennsylvania
Indiana, Pennsylvania
http://www.iup.edu/

- **State-supported** university, founded 1875, part of Pennsylvania State System of Higher Education
- **Small-town** 374-acre campus with easy access to Pittsburgh
- **Endowment** $70.4 million
- **Coed** 14,234 undergraduate students, 95% full-time, 76% women, 24% men
- **Minimally difficult** entrance level, 93% of applicants were admitted

UNDERGRAD STUDENTS
13,489 full-time, 745 part-time. Students come from 29 states and territories; 28 other countries; 5% are from out of state; 12% Black or African American, non-Hispanic/Latino; 5% Hispanic/Latino; 1% Asian, non-Hispanic/Latino; 0.1% American Indian or Alaska Native, non-Hispanic/Latino; 5% Two or more races, non-Hispanic/Latino; 0.9% Race/ethnicity unknown; 2% international; 2% transferred in; 30% live on campus.

Freshmen:
Admission: 10,061 applied, 9,398 admitted, 7,779 enrolled. ***Average high school GPA:*** 3.3. ***Test scores:*** SAT evidence-based reading and writing scores over 500: 59%; SAT math scores over 500: 54%; ACT scores over 18: 66%; SAT evidence-based reading and writing scores over 600: 16%; SAT math scores over 600: 10%; ACT scores over 24: 22%; SAT evidence-based reading and writing scores over 700: 1%; SAT math scores over 700: 1%; ACT scores over 30: 2%.

Retention: 72% of full-time freshmen returned.

FACULTY
Total: 556, 86% full-time.

Student/faculty ratio: 15:1.

ACADEMICS
Calendar: semesters. *Degrees:* certificates, associate, bachelor's, master's, doctoral, post-master's, and postbachelor's certificates.

Special study options: academic remediation for entering students, accelerated degree program, adult/continuing education programs, advanced placement credit, cooperative education, distance learning, double majors, English as a second language, external degree program, freshman honors college, honors programs, independent study, internships, off-campus study, part-time degree program, services for LD students, student-designed majors, study abroad, summer session for credit. ***ROTC:*** Army (b).

Unusual degree programs: 3-2 engineering with Drexel University, University of Pittsburgh; Accelerated Pre-Professional Programs: Pre-chiropractic with Logan College of Chiropractic, New York Chiropractic College, Parker College, Sherman Chiropractic College: Pre-Dentistry with Temple University School of Dentistry; Pre-Optometry with Sal.

Computers: 2,363 computers/terminals and 5,000 ports are available on campus for general student use. Students can access the following:

computer help desk, free student e-mail accounts, online (class) grades, online (class) registration, online (class) schedules. Campuswide network is available. 100% of college-owned or -operated housing units are wired for high-speed Internet access. Wireless service is available via entire campus.
Library: Stapleton Library plus 1 other. *Books:* 514,631 (physical), 100,229 (digital/electronic); *Serial titles:* 4,858 (physical). Weekly public service hours: 101; study areas open 24 hours, 5–7 days a week; students can reserve study rooms.

STUDENT LIFE
Housing options: on-campus residence required for freshman year; coed, women-only, special housing for students with disabilities. Campus housing is university owned. Freshman campus housing is guaranteed.

Activities and organizations: drama/theater group, student-run newspaper, radio and television station, choral group, marching band, Student Government Association, Panhellenic Association, Interfraternity Council, Student Association of Nutrition and Dietetics, Saudi Student Association, national fraternities, national sororities.

Athletics Member NCAA. All Division II. ***Intercollegiate sports:*** baseball M(s), basketball M(s)/W(s), cross-country running M(s)/W(s), field hockey W(s), football M(s), golf M(s), lacrosse W(s), soccer W(s), softball W(s), swimming and diving M(s)/W(s), tennis W(s), track and field M(s)/W(s), volleyball W(s). ***Intramural sports:*** baseball M(c), basketball M/W, cheerleading M(c)/W(c), equestrian sports M(c)/W(c), fencing M(c)/W(c), field hockey W(c), ice hockey M(c)/W(c), lacrosse M(c)/W(c), riflery M(c)/W(c), rugby M(c)/W(c), sailing M(c)/W(c), soccer M/W, swimming and diving M(c)/W(c), tennis M(c)/W(c), ultimate Frisbee M(c)/W(c), volleyball M/W.

Campus security: 24-hour emergency response devices and patrols, late-night transport/escort service, controlled dormitory access.

Student services: health clinic, personal/psychological counseling, legal services, veterans affairs office.

COSTS & FINANCIAL AID
Costs (2019–20) ***Tuition:*** state resident $9570 full-time, $319 per credit hour part-time; nonresident $13,890 full-time, $463 per credit hour part-time. Full-time tuition and fees vary according to course load. Part-time tuition and fees vary according to course load. ***Required fees:*** $3784 full-time, $133 per credit hour part-time, $50 per term part-time. ***Room and board:*** $12,744; room only: $8950. Room and board charges vary according to board plan, housing facility, and location. ***Payment plans:*** installment, deferred payment. ***Waivers:*** senior citizens and employees or children of employees.

Financial Aid Of all full-time matriculated undergraduates who enrolled in 2018, 7,276 applied for aid, 6,177 were judged to have need, 334 had their need fully met. 902 Federal Work-Study jobs (averaging $1797). 830 state and other part-time jobs (averaging $1627). In 2018, 330 non-need-based awards were made. ***Average percent of need met:*** 53. ***Average financial aid package:*** $10,462. ***Average need-based loan:*** $4051. ***Average need-based gift aid:*** $6341. ***Average non-need-based aid:*** $1960. ***Average indebtedness upon graduation:*** $41,222.

APPLYING
Standardized Tests *Required:* SAT or ACT (for admission).

Options: electronic application, early admission, deferred entrance.

Required: high school transcript. ***Recommended:*** essay or personal statement, 2 letters of recommendation.

Application deadlines: rolling (freshmen), rolling (out-of-state freshmen), rolling (transfers).

Notification: continuous (freshmen), continuous (out-of-state freshmen), continuous (transfers).

CONTACT
Indiana University of Pennsylvania, 1011 South Drive, Indiana, PA 15705. *Phone:* 724-357-7544. *Toll-free phone:* 800-442-6830.

Juniata College

Huntingdon, Pennsylvania

http://www.juniata.edu/

- **Independent** comprehensive, founded 1876, affiliated with Church of the Brethren
- **Small-town** 110-acre campus
- **Endowment** $122.3 million
- **Coed**
- **Moderately difficult** entrance level

FACULTY
Student/faculty ratio: 11:1.

ACADEMICS
Calendar: semesters. *Degrees:* certificates, bachelor's, master's, and postbachelor's certificates.
Library: Beeghly Library. *Books:* 139,415 (physical), 467,938 (digital/electronic); *Serial titles:* 379 (physical), 38,606 (digital/electronic); *Databases:* 53. Weekly public service hours: 107.

STUDENT LIFE
Housing options: on-campus residence required through senior year; coed, women-only. Campus housing is university owned. Freshman campus housing is guaranteed.

Activities and organizations: drama/theater group, student-run radio station, choral group, Ministry of Games, Student Government Association, Health Professions Organization, Mud Junkies Ceramics Club, National Society of Leadership and Success.

Athletics Member NCAA. All Division III.

Campus security: 24-hour emergency response devices and patrols, student patrols, late-night transport/escort service, controlled dormitory access.

Student services: health clinic, personal/psychological counseling, women's center.

COSTS & FINANCIAL AID
Costs (2019–20) ***Comprehensive fee:*** $59,875 includes full-time tuition ($46,250), mandatory fees ($825), and room and board ($12,800). Part-time tuition: $1765 per credit hour. ***College room only:*** $6814. Room and board charges vary according to housing facility.

Financial Aid Of all full-time matriculated undergraduates who enrolled in 2018, 1,096 applied for aid, 991 were judged to have need, 191 had their need fully met. In 2018, 313 non-need-based awards were made. ***Average percent of need met:*** 84. ***Average financial aid package:*** $38,359. ***Average need-based loan:*** $5781. ***Average need-based gift aid:*** $32,148. ***Average non-need-based aid:*** $24,404. ***Average indebtedness upon graduation:*** $31,156.

APPLYING
Standardized Tests *Recommended:* SAT (for admission), ACT (for admission), SAT or ACT (for admission).

Options: electronic application, early admission, early decision, early action, deferred entrance.

Required: essay or personal statement, high school transcript, minimum 3.0 GPA, 1 letter of recommendation. ***Recommended:*** interview.

CONTACT
Ms. Terri Bollman-Dalansky, Senior Associate Dean of Admission, Juniata College, 1700 Moore St, Huntingdon, PA 16652. *Phone:* 814-641-3424. *Toll-free phone:* 877-JUNIATA. *Fax:* 814-641-3100. *E-mail:* bollmat@juniata.edu.

Keystone College

La Plume, Pennsylvania

http://www.keystone.edu/

- **Independent** comprehensive, founded 1868
- **Rural** campus
- **Coed** 1,288 undergraduate students, 83% full-time, 58% women, 42% men
- 79% of applicants were admitted

UNDERGRAD STUDENTS
1,067 full-time, 221 part-time. 20% are from out of state; 13% Black or African American, non-Hispanic/Latino; 8% Hispanic/Latino; 0.8%

Asian, non-Hispanic/Latino; 0.1% Native Hawaiian or other Pacific Islander, non-Hispanic/Latino; 0.5% American Indian or Alaska Native, non-Hispanic/Latino; 3% Two or more races, non-Hispanic/Latino; 7% Race/ethnicity unknown; 0.1% international; 3% transferred in; 37% live on campus.

Freshmen:
Admission: 2,051 applied, 1,615 admitted, 343 enrolled. ***Average high school GPA:*** 3.0. ***Test scores:*** SAT evidence-based reading and writing scores over 500: 47%; SAT math scores over 500: 44%; ACT scores over 18: 41%; SAT evidence-based reading and writing scores over 600: 11%; SAT math scores over 600: 6%; SAT evidence-based reading and writing scores over 700: 1%.

Retention: 58% of full-time freshmen returned.

FACULTY
Total: 168, 27% full-time.

Student/faculty ratio: 13:1.

ACADEMICS
Calendar: semesters. *Degrees:* certificates, associate, bachelor's, and master's.

Special study options: academic remediation for entering students, adult/continuing education programs, advanced placement credit, distance learning, double majors, honors programs, independent study, internships, part-time degree program, services for LD students, study abroad, summer session for credit.

Computers: 100 computers/terminals are available on campus for general student use. Students can access the following: campus intranet, computer help desk, free student e-mail accounts, online (class) grades, online (class) registration, online (class) schedules. Campuswide network is available. 100% of college-owned or -operated housing units are wired for high-speed Internet access. Wireless service is available via entire campus.
Library: Miller Library.

STUDENT LIFE
Housing options: on-campus residence required for freshman year; coed, special housing for students with disabilities. Campus housing is university owned. Freshman campus housing is guaranteed.

Activities and organizations: drama/theater group, student-run newspaper, radio station, choral group.

Athletics Member NCAA. All Division III.

Student services: health clinic, personal/psychological counseling.

COSTS
Costs (2020–21) ***Comprehensive fee:*** $28,900 includes full-time tuition ($14,500), mandatory fees ($2500), and room and board ($11,900). Part-time tuition: $575 per credit hour. ***College room only:*** $6000.

APPLYING
Options: electronic application, early admission, deferred entrance.

Required: essay or personal statement, high school transcript. ***Required for some:*** art portfolio for visual arts and art education. ***Recommended:*** interview.

Notification: continuous (freshmen), continuous (transfers).

CONTACT
Keystone College, One College Green, La Plume, PA 18440. *Phone:* 570-945-8111. *Toll-free phone:* 877-4-COLLEGE.

King's College

Wilkes-Barre, Pennsylvania

http://www.kings.edu/

- **Independent Roman Catholic** comprehensive, founded 1946
- **Urban** 48-acre campus
- **Endowment** $84.9 million
- **Coed** 2,231 undergraduate students, 92% full-time, 47% women, 53% men
- **Moderately difficult** entrance level, 81% of applicants were admitted

UNDERGRAD STUDENTS
2,042 full-time, 189 part-time. Students come from 25 states and territories; 8 other countries; 28% are from out of state; 4% Black or African American, non-Hispanic/Latino; 9% Hispanic/Latino; 2% Asian, non-Hispanic/Latino; 0.3% American Indian or Alaska Native, non-Hispanic/Latino; 3% Two or more races, non-Hispanic/Latino; 5% Race/ethnicity unknown; 9% international; 4% transferred in; 47% live on campus.

Freshmen:
Admission: 4,176 applied, 3,380 admitted, 560 enrolled. ***Average high school GPA:*** 3.4. ***Test scores:*** SAT evidence-based reading and writing scores over 500: 75%; SAT math scores over 500: 75%; ACT scores over 18: 90%; SAT evidence-based reading and writing scores over 600: 28%; SAT math scores over 600: 32%; ACT scores over 24: 51%; SAT evidence-based reading and writing scores over 700: 2%; SAT math scores over 700: 3%; ACT scores over 30: 9%.

Retention: 72% of full-time freshmen returned.

FACULTY
Total: 227, 61% full-time, 59% with terminal degrees.

Student/faculty ratio: 13:1.

ACADEMICS
Calendar: semesters. *Degrees:* bachelor's, master's, and postbachelor's certificates.

Special study options: accelerated degree program, adult/continuing education programs, advanced placement credit, distance learning, double majors, English as a second language, honors programs, independent study, internships, off-campus study, part-time degree program, services for LD students, student-designed majors, study abroad, summer session for credit. ***ROTC:*** Army (b), Air Force (c).

Unusual degree programs: 3-2 engineering with University of Notre Dame, Washington University.

Computers: 470 computers/terminals are available on campus for general student use. Students can access the following: computer help desk, free student e-mail accounts, online (class) grades, online (class) registration, online (class) schedules. Campuswide network is available. 100% of college-owned or -operated housing units are wired for high-speed Internet access. Wireless service is available via classrooms, computer labs, dorm rooms, libraries, student centers.
Library: D. Leonard Corgan Library. *Books:* 176,374 (physical); *Databases:* 64. Weekly public service hours: 90; study areas open 24 hours, 5–7 days a week.

STUDENT LIFE
Housing options: on-campus residence required through sophomore year; coed, men-only, women-only, cooperative, special housing for students with disabilities. Campus housing is university owned. Freshman campus housing is guaranteed.

Activities and organizations: drama/theater group, student-run newspaper, radio station, choral group, Association of Campus Events, Student Government Association, Accounting Association, International/Multicultural Club, Biology Club.

Athletics Member NCAA. All Division III. ***Intercollegiate sports:*** baseball M, basketball M/W, cross-country running M/W, field hockey W, football M, golf M/W, ice hockey M/W, lacrosse M/W, soccer M/W, softball W, swimming and diving M/W, tennis M/W, track and field M/W, volleyball M/W, wrestling M. ***Intramural sports:*** basketball M/W, rugby M, soccer M/W.

Campus security: 24-hour emergency response devices and patrols, late-night transport/escort service, controlled dormitory access.

Student services: health clinic, personal/psychological counseling.

COSTS & FINANCIAL AID
Costs (2020–21) ***Comprehensive fee:*** $54,088 includes full-time tuition ($38,062), mandatory fees ($2018), and room and board ($14,008). Part-time tuition: $621 per credit hour. ***Required fees:*** $88 part-time. ***College room only:*** $7364. ***Waivers:*** children of alumni and employees or children of employees.

Financial Aid Of all full-time matriculated undergraduates who enrolled in 2019, 1,733 applied for aid, 1,569 were judged to have need, 288 had their need fully met. 273 Federal Work-Study jobs (averaging $1958). 292 state and other part-time jobs (averaging $991). In 2019, 305 non-need-based awards were made. ***Average percent of need met:*** 75. ***Average financial aid package:*** $28,268. ***Average need-based loan:*** $4353. ***Average need-based gift aid:*** $19,749. ***Average non-need-based aid:*** $17,612. ***Average indebtedness upon graduation:*** $40,818.

APPLYING
Standardized Tests *Recommended:* SAT or ACT (for admission).

Options: electronic application, early decision, early action, deferred entrance.

Application fee: $30.

Required: essay or personal statement, high school transcript. ***Recommended:*** interview.

Application deadlines: rolling (freshmen), rolling (out-of-state freshmen), rolling (transfers), 12/1 (early action).

Early decision deadline: 12/1.

Notification: continuous (freshmen), continuous (out-of-state freshmen), continuous (transfers).

CONTACT
Mr. Robert Reese, Vice President for Enrollment Management, King's College, 133 North River Street, Wilkes-Barre, PA 18711-0801. *Phone:* 570-208-5858. *Toll-free phone:* 888-KINGSPA. *Fax:* 570-208-5971. *E-mail:* admissions@kings.edu.

Kutztown University of Pennsylvania
Kutztown, Pennsylvania
http://www.kutztown.edu/

- **State-supported** comprehensive, founded 1866, part of Pennsylvania State System of Higher Education
- **Rural** 289-acre campus with easy access to Philadelphia
- **Endowment** $32.0 million
- **Coed** 9,108 undergraduate students, 91% full-time, 56% women, 44% men
- **Moderately difficult** entrance level, 89% of applicants were admitted

UNDERGRAD STUDENTS
8,307 full-time, 801 part-time. Students come from 36 states and territories; 34 other countries; 12% are from out of state; 8% Black or African American, non-Hispanic/Latino; 9% Hispanic/Latino; 2% Asian, non-Hispanic/Latino; 0.1% Native Hawaiian or other Pacific Islander, non-Hispanic/Latino; 0.1% American Indian or Alaska Native, non-Hispanic/Latino; 3% Two or more races, non-Hispanic/Latino; 3% Race/ethnicity unknown; 0.8% international; 5% transferred in; 49% live on campus.

Freshmen:
Admission: 6,893 applied, 6,117 admitted, 1,399 enrolled. ***Average high school GPA:*** 3.2. ***Test scores:*** SAT evidence-based reading and writing scores over 500: 72%; SAT math scores over 500: 64%; ACT scores over 18: 77%; SAT evidence-based reading and writing scores over 600: 20%; SAT math scores over 600: 14%; ACT scores over 24: 27%; SAT evidence-based reading and writing scores over 700: 2%; SAT math scores over 700: 1%; ACT scores over 30: 3%.

Retention: 74% of full-time freshmen returned.

FACULTY
Total: 440, 85% full-time, 81% with terminal degrees.

Student/faculty ratio: 17:1.

ACADEMICS
Calendar: semesters. *Degrees:* bachelor's, master's, doctoral, post-master's, and postbachelor's certificates.

Special study options: academic remediation for entering students, accelerated degree program, adult/continuing education programs, advanced placement credit, distance learning, double majors, honors programs, independent study, internships, off-campus study, part-time degree program, services for LD students, student-designed majors, study abroad, summer session for credit. ***ROTC:*** Army (c).

Computers: 1,075 computers/terminals and 100 ports are available on campus for general student use. Students can access the following: computer help desk, free student e-mail accounts, online (class) grades, online (class) registration, online (class) schedules. Campuswide network is available. 100% of college-owned or -operated housing units are wired for high-speed Internet access. Wireless service is available via classrooms, computer centers, computer labs, dorm rooms, learning centers, libraries, student centers.

Library: Rohrbach Library. *Books:* 313,503 (physical), 436,634 (digital/electronic); *Serial titles:* 892 (physical), 32,486 (digital/electronic); *Databases:* 145. Weekly public service hours: 96; students can reserve study rooms.

STUDENT LIFE
Housing options: on-campus residence required through sophomore year; coed, women-only, cooperative. Campus housing is university owned. Freshman campus housing is guaranteed.

Activities and organizations: drama/theater group, student-run newspaper, radio and television station, choral group, marching band, Marching Unit, Honors Club, American Marketing Association Kutztown Chapter, Humans versus Zombies: Kutztown Chapter, Paws for Love, national fraternities, national sororities.

Athletics Member NCAA. All Division II. ***Intercollegiate sports:*** baseball M(s), basketball M(s)/W(s), bowling W(s), cheerleading M(c)/W(c), cross-country running M(s)/W(s), equestrian sports M(c)/W(c), fencing M(c)/W(c), field hockey W(s), football M(s), golf M(c)/W(s), ice hockey M(c), lacrosse M(c)/W(s), rugby M(c)/W(c), soccer M(c)/W(s), softball W(s), swimming and diving W(s), tennis M(s)/W(s), track and field M(s)/W(s), ultimate Frisbee M(c)/W(c), volleyball M(c)/W(s), wrestling M(s). ***Intramural sports:*** basketball M/W, football M/W, rock climbing M/W, soccer M/W, softball M/W, volleyball M/W.

Campus security: 24-hour emergency response devices and patrols, student patrols, late-night transport/escort service, controlled dormitory access, secondary door electronic alarm system in residence halls, 24-hour student desk personnel at main entrance of residence halls.

Student services: health clinic, personal/psychological counseling, women's center.

COSTS & FINANCIAL AID
Costs (2019–20) ***One-time required fee:*** $313. ***Tuition:*** state resident $7716 full-time, $322 per credit part-time; nonresident $11,574 full-time, $805 per credit part-time. Full-time tuition and fees vary according to course load. Part-time tuition and fees vary according to course load. ***Required fees:*** $3234 full-time, $104 per credit part-time. ***Room and board:*** $10,434; room only: $6484. Room and board charges vary according to board plan and housing facility. ***Payment plans:*** installment, deferred payment. ***Waivers:*** senior citizens and employees or children of employees.

Financial Aid Of all full-time matriculated undergraduates who enrolled in 2018, 6,069 applied for aid, 5,139 were judged to have need, 378 had their need fully met. 520 Federal Work-Study jobs (averaging $3030). In 2018, 309 non-need-based awards were made. ***Average percent of need met:*** 43. ***Average financial aid package:*** $9403. ***Average need-based loan:*** $4218. ***Average need-based gift aid:*** $5939. ***Average non-need-based aid:*** $1506. ***Average indebtedness upon graduation:*** $40,592.

APPLYING
Standardized Tests *Required:* SAT or ACT (for admission). *Required for some:* SAT Subject Tests (for admission).

Options: electronic application, early admission, deferred entrance.

Application fee: $35.

Required: high school transcript, minimum 2.0 GPA. ***Required for some:*** audition for music, portfolio and/or art test for arts.

Application deadlines: rolling (freshmen), rolling (transfers).

Notification: continuous (freshmen), continuous (transfers).

CONTACT
Kutztown University of Pennsylvania, 15200 Kutztown Road, Kutztown, PA 19530-0730. *Phone:* 484-646-4144. *Toll-free phone:* 877-628-1915.

Lackawanna College
Scranton, Pennsylvania
http://www.lackawanna.edu/

- **Independent** primarily 2-year, founded 1894
- **Urban** 4-acre campus
- **Endowment** $5.7 million
- **Coed** 1,991 undergraduate students, 67% full-time, 56% women, 44% men
- **Noncompetitive** entrance level, 35% of applicants were admitted

UNDERGRAD STUDENTS
1,335 full-time, 656 part-time. Students come from 16 states and territories; 8% are from out of state; 12% Black or African American, non-Hispanic/Latino; 12% Hispanic/Latino; 1% Asian, non-Hispanic/Latino; 0.2% Native Hawaiian or other Pacific Islander, non-Hispanic/Latino; 0.4% American Indian or Alaska Native, non-Hispanic/Latino; 2% Two or more races, non-Hispanic/Latino; 11% Race/ethnicity unknown; 1% international; 11% transferred in; 17% live on campus.

Freshmen:
Admission: 1,627 applied, 570 admitted, 466 enrolled.
Retention: 100% of full-time freshmen returned.

FACULTY
Total: 193, 17% full-time, 5% with terminal degrees.
Student/faculty ratio: 19:1.

ACADEMICS
Calendar: semesters. *Degrees:* certificates, diplomas, associate, and bachelor's.
Special study options: academic remediation for entering students, adult/continuing education programs, cooperative education, double majors, English as a second language, internships, part-time degree program, services for LD students, summer session for credit.
Computers: 186 computers/terminals are available on campus for general student use. Students can access the following: campus intranet, computer help desk, free student e-mail accounts, online (class) grades, online (class) registration, online (class) schedules. Campuswide network is available. 100% of college-owned or -operated housing units are wired for high-speed Internet access. Wireless service is available via entire campus.
Library: Albright Memorial Library plus 1 other. Students can reserve study rooms.

STUDENT LIFE
Housing options: on-campus residence required through sophomore year; coed, men-only. Campus housing is university owned.
Activities and organizations: Student Government Association, V.O.L.C. (Volunteers of Lackawanna College), Falcon Ambassador Board (FAB), COMMunity Club, Pineapple Club (Hospitality & Culinary Club).
Athletics Member NJCAA. ***Intercollegiate sports:*** baseball M(s), basketball M(s)/W(s), cross-country running M(s)/W(s), football M(s), golf M(s), soccer M(s)/W(s), softball W(s), tennis W(s), volleyball W(s), wrestling M(s). ***Intramural sports:*** cheerleading W.
Campus security: 24-hour emergency response devices and patrols, late-night transport/escort service, controlled dormitory access, patrols by college liaison staff.
Student services: personal/psychological counseling, veterans affairs office.

COSTS & FINANCIAL AID
Costs (2019–20) ***Comprehensive fee:*** $26,430 includes full-time tuition ($15,300), mandatory fees ($830), and room and board ($10,300). Full-time tuition and fees vary according to course load, location, and program. Part-time tuition: $535 per credit. Part-time tuition and fees vary according to course load, location, and program. ***Required fees:*** $415 per term part-time. ***College room only:*** $6700. Room and board charges vary according to board plan. ***Payment plans:*** installment, deferred payment. ***Waivers:*** employees or children of employees.
Financial Aid Of all full-time matriculated undergraduates who enrolled in 2018, 2,718 applied for aid, 2,448 were judged to have need, 33 had their need fully met. In 2018, 27 non-need-based awards were made. ***Average percent of need met:*** 27. ***Average financial aid package:*** $8291. ***Average need-based loan:*** $3331. ***Average need-based gift aid:*** $6733. ***Average non-need-based aid:*** $4987. ***Average indebtedness upon graduation:*** $9496.

APPLYING
Standardized Tests *Recommended:* SAT or ACT (for admission).
Options: electronic application, deferred entrance.
Application fee: $35.
Required: high school transcript, interview.
Application deadlines: rolling (freshmen), rolling (transfers).

CONTACT
Mr. Eddie Perry, Admissions Advisor, Lackawanna College, 501 Vine Street, Scranton, PA 18509. *Phone:* 570-961-7889. *Toll-free phone:* 877-346-3552. *E-mail:* perrye@lackawanna.edu.

Lafayette College
Easton, Pennsylvania
http://www.lafayette.edu/

- **Independent** 4-year, founded 1826, affiliated with Presbyterian Church (U.S.A.)
- **Suburban** 340-acre campus with easy access to New York City, Philadelphia
- **Endowment** $832.1 million
- **Coed** 2,662 undergraduate students, 99% full-time, 51% women, 49% men
- **Very difficult** entrance level, 31% of applicants were admitted

UNDERGRAD STUDENTS
2,633 full-time, 29 part-time. Students come from 47 states and territories; 57 other countries; 81% are from out of state; 5% Black or African American, non-Hispanic/Latino; 7% Hispanic/Latino; 4% Asian, non-Hispanic/Latino; 3% Two or more races, non-Hispanic/Latino; 5% Race/ethnicity unknown; 10% international; 0.7% transferred in; 93% live on campus.

Freshmen:
Admission: 8,521 applied, 2,682 admitted, 698 enrolled. ***Average high school GPA:*** 3.5. ***Test scores:*** SAT evidence-based reading and writing scores over 500: 99%; SAT math scores over 500: 99%; ACT scores over 18: 100%; SAT evidence-based reading and writing scores over 600: 85%; SAT math scores over 600: 86%; ACT scores over 24: 97%; SAT evidence-based reading and writing scores over 700: 27%; SAT math scores over 700: 46%; ACT scores over 30: 60%.
Retention: 94% of full-time freshmen returned.

FACULTY
Total: 296, 82% full-time, 92% with terminal degrees.
Student/faculty ratio: 10:1.

ACADEMICS
Calendar: semesters plus interim January program. *Degree:* bachelor's.
Special study options: academic remediation for entering students, accelerated degree program, advanced placement credit, double majors, honors programs, independent study, internships, off-campus study, part-time degree program, services for LD students, student-designed majors, study abroad, summer session for credit. ***ROTC:*** Army (c).
Computers: 690 computers/terminals and 690 ports are available on campus for general student use. Students can access the following: campus intranet, computer help desk, free student e-mail accounts, online (class) grades, online (class) registration, online (class) schedules. Campuswide network is available. 100% of college-owned or -operated housing units are wired for high-speed Internet access. Wireless service is available via entire campus.
Library: Skillman Library plus 2 others. *Books:* 603,599 (physical), 344,469 (digital/electronic); *Serial titles:* 306 (physical), 68,298 (digital/electronic); *Databases:* 132. Weekly public service hours: 106.

STUDENT LIFE
Housing options: on-campus residence required through senior year; coed, men-only, women-only, special housing for students with disabilities. Campus housing is university owned. Freshman campus housing is guaranteed.
Activities and organizations: drama/theater group, student-run newspaper, radio station, choral group, LAF (Lafayette Activities Forum), Student Government, Crew, International Students Association, Leopards Lair, national fraternities, national sororities.
Athletics Member NCAA. All Division I except football (Division I-AA). ***Intercollegiate sports:*** baseball M, basketball M/W, crew M(c)/W(c), cross-country running M/W, equestrian sports M(c)/W(c), fencing M/W, field hockey W, golf M, ice hockey M(c), lacrosse M/W, rugby M(c)/W(c), skiing (downhill) W(c), soccer M/W, softball W, squash M(c), swimming and diving M/W, tennis M/W, track and field M/W, volleyball W, weight lifting M(c)/W(c), wrestling M(c). ***Intramural sports:*** badminton M/W, baseball M, basketball M/W, bowling M/W, cross-

country running M/W, fencing M/W, field hockey W, football M, golf M/W, lacrosse M/W, racquetball M/W, sailing M(c)/W(c), skiing (cross-country) M(c)/W(c), soccer M/W, softball M/W, squash M/W, swimming and diving M/W, table tennis M/W, tennis M/W, track and field M/W, volleyball M/W, weight lifting M/W, wrestling M.

Campus security: 24-hour emergency response devices and patrols, student patrols, late-night transport/escort service, controlled dormitory access.

Student services: health clinic, personal/psychological counseling, women's center.

COSTS & FINANCIAL AID

Costs (2020–21) ***One-time required fee:*** $750. ***Comprehensive fee:*** $73,926 includes full-time tuition ($56,556), mandatory fees ($496), and room and board ($16,874). Part-time tuition: $613 per credit hour. ***College room only:*** $10,434.

Financial Aid Of all full-time matriculated undergraduates who enrolled in 2019, 1,451 applied for aid, 919 were judged to have need, 919 had their need fully met. 510 Federal Work-Study jobs (averaging $1230). In 2019, 147 non-need-based awards were made. ***Average percent of need met:*** 100. ***Average financial aid package:*** $51,240. ***Average need-based loan:*** $3752. ***Average need-based gift aid:*** $46,031. ***Average non-need-based aid:*** $31,469. ***Average indebtedness upon graduation:*** $30,181.

APPLYING

Standardized Tests *Required:* SAT or ACT (for admission). *Recommended:* SAT Subject Tests (for admission).

Options: electronic application, early admission, early decision, deferred entrance.

Application fee: $65.

Required: essay or personal statement, high school transcript, 1 letter of recommendation. ***Recommended:*** interview.

Application deadlines: 1/15 (freshmen), 5/1 (transfers).

Early decision deadline: 11/15.

Notification: 4/1 (freshmen), continuous (transfers).

CONTACT

Mr. Matthew Hyde, Assistant VP Enrollment Management/Dean of Admissions, Lafayette College, 118 Markle Hall, 730 High Street, Easton, PA 18042-1798. *Phone:* 610-330-5100. *Fax:* 610-330-5355. *E-mail:* hydem@lafayette.edu.

Lancaster Bible College

Lancaster, Pennsylvania

http://www.lbc.edu/

- **Independent nondenominational** comprehensive, founded 1933
- **Suburban** 100-acre campus with easy access to Philadelphia
- **Endowment** $14.3 million
- **Coed** 1,688 undergraduate students, 58% full-time, 52% women, 48% men
- **Minimally difficult** entrance level, 57% of applicants were admitted

UNDERGRAD STUDENTS

986 full-time, 702 part-time. Students come from 17 states and territories; 3 other countries; 30% are from out of state; 25% Black or African American, non-Hispanic/Latino; 5% Hispanic/Latino; 1% Asian, non-Hispanic/Latino; 0.1% Native Hawaiian or other Pacific Islander, non-Hispanic/Latino; 0.1% American Indian or Alaska Native, non-Hispanic/Latino; 9% Two or more races, non-Hispanic/Latino; 14% Race/ethnicity unknown; 0.1% international; 22% transferred in; 54% live on campus.

Freshmen:

Admission: 192 applied, 109 admitted, 190 enrolled. ***Average high school GPA:*** 3.1.

Retention: 81% of full-time freshmen returned.

FACULTY

Total: 86, 51% full-time, 37% with terminal degrees.

Student/faculty ratio: 15:1.

ACADEMICS

Calendar: semesters. *Degrees:* certificates, associate, bachelor's, master's, doctoral, and postbachelor's certificates.

Special study options: academic remediation for entering students, adult/continuing education programs, advanced placement credit, double majors, independent study, internships, part-time degree program, services for LD students, study abroad, summer session for credit.

Computers: 50 computers/terminals are available on campus for general student use. Campuswide network is available.
Library: Lancaster Bible College Library.

STUDENT LIFE

Housing options: on-campus residence required through senior year; men-only, women-only. Campus housing is university owned. Freshman campus housing is guaranteed.

Activities and organizations: drama/theater group, student-run newspaper, choral group, Student Government Association, Student Missionary Fellowship, International Student Fellowship, Resident Affairs Council, Student Intramural Association.

Athletics ***Intercollegiate sports:*** baseball M, basketball M/W, lacrosse W, soccer M/W, volleyball M/W. ***Intramural sports:*** basketball M/W, cheerleading M/W, football M/W, soccer M/W, softball M/W, table tennis M/W, tennis M/W, volleyball M/W.

Campus security: student patrols, late-night transport/escort service, controlled dormitory access.

Student services: health clinic, personal/psychological counseling.

COSTS & FINANCIAL AID

Costs (2019–20) ***One-time required fee:*** $300. ***Comprehensive fee:*** $35,070 includes full-time tuition ($25,390), mandatory fees ($680), and room and board ($9000). Full-time tuition and fees vary according to degree level and student level. Part-time tuition: $840 per credit hour. Part-time tuition and fees vary according to course load and degree level. ***Required fees:*** $35 per credit hour part-time. ***Room and board:*** Room and board charges vary according to board plan. ***Payment plan:*** installment. ***Waivers:*** children of alumni, senior citizens, and employees or children of employees.

Financial Aid Of all full-time matriculated undergraduates who enrolled in 2019, 717 applied for aid, 633 were judged to have need, 211 had their need fully met. 96 Federal Work-Study jobs (averaging $1500). In 2019, 163 non-need-based awards were made. ***Average percent of need met:*** 79. ***Average financial aid package:*** $21,306. ***Average need-based loan:*** $4239. ***Average need-based gift aid:*** $18,463. ***Average non-need-based aid:*** $10,623. ***Average indebtedness upon graduation:*** $32,751.

APPLYING

Standardized Tests *Required:* SAT or ACT (for admission).

Options: early admission, deferred entrance.

Application fee: $25.

Required: essay or personal statement, high school transcript, minimum 2.0 GPA, 3 letters of recommendation. ***Required for some:*** interview.

Application deadlines: rolling (freshmen), rolling (transfers).

Notification: continuous (freshmen), continuous (transfers).

CONTACT

Mr. Jared Yoder, Director of Admissions, Lancaster Bible College, PO Box 83403, Lancaster, PA 17608. *Phone:* 717-569-7071. *Toll-free phone:* 800-544-7335. *Fax:* 717-560-8213. *E-mail:* admissions@lbc.edu.

La Roche University

Pittsburgh, Pennsylvania

http://www.laroche.edu/

- **Independent** comprehensive, founded 1963, affiliated with Roman Catholic Church
- **Suburban** 43-acre campus
- **Endowment** $6.1 million
- **Coed** 1,241 undergraduate students, 86% full-time, 57% women, 43% men
- **Minimally difficult** entrance level, 99% of applicants were admitted

UNDERGRAD STUDENTS

1,070 full-time, 171 part-time. Students come from 20 states and territories; 34 other countries; 11% are from out of state; 10% Black or African American, non-Hispanic/Latino; 5% Hispanic/Latino; 1% Asian, non-Hispanic/Latino; 0.1% Native Hawaiian or other Pacific Islander, non-Hispanic/Latino; 0.1% American Indian or Alaska Native, non-

Hispanic/Latino; 3% Two or more races, non-Hispanic/Latino; 5% Race/ethnicity unknown; 15% international; 14% transferred in; 40% live on campus.

Freshmen:
Admission: 1,220 applied, 1,213 admitted, 205 enrolled. ***Average high school GPA:*** 3.2. ***Test scores:*** SAT evidence-based reading and writing scores over 500: 53%; SAT math scores over 500: 51%; ACT scores over 18: 72%; SAT evidence-based reading and writing scores over 600: 22%; SAT math scores over 600: 14%; ACT scores over 24: 11%; SAT evidence-based reading and writing scores over 700: 2%; SAT math scores over 700: 3%.
Retention: 73% of full-time freshmen returned.

FACULTY
Total: 188, 32% full-time, 38% with terminal degrees.
Student/faculty ratio: 12:1.

ACADEMICS
Calendar: semesters plus summer term. *Degrees:* certificates, associate, bachelor's, master's, doctoral, and postbachelor's certificates.
Special study options: academic remediation for entering students, accelerated degree program, adult/continuing education programs, advanced placement credit, distance learning, double majors, English as a second language, freshman honors college, honors programs, independent study, internships, off-campus study, part-time degree program, services for LD students, student-designed majors, study abroad, summer session for credit. ***ROTC:*** Army (b), Air Force (b).
Computers: 200 computers/terminals are available on campus for general student use. Students can access the following: campus intranet, computer help desk, free student e-mail accounts, online (class) grades, online (class) registration, online (class) schedules. Campuswide network is available. 100% of college-owned or -operated housing units are wired for high-speed Internet access. Wireless service is available via entire campus.
Library: John J. Wright Library plus 1 other. *Books:* 80,000 (physical), 276,600 (digital/electronic); *Serial titles:* 770 (physical), 28 (digital/electronic); *Databases:* 55.

STUDENT LIFE
Housing options: coed. Campus housing is university owned. Freshman campus housing is guaranteed.
Activities and organizations: student-run newspaper, radio station, American Society of Interior Design, student government, Marketing Club.
Athletics Member NCAA. All Division III. ***Intercollegiate sports:*** baseball M, basketball M/W, bowling W, cross-country running M/W, golf M, lacrosse M/W, soccer M/W, softball W, tennis W, volleyball W. ***Intramural sports:*** basketball M/W, weight lifting M/W.
Campus security: 24-hour emergency response devices and patrols, student patrols, late-night transport/escort service, controlled dormitory access.
Student services: health clinic, personal/psychological counseling, veterans affairs office.

COSTS & FINANCIAL AID
Costs (2020–21) ***Comprehensive fee:*** $42,590 includes full-time tuition ($29,470), mandatory fees ($850), and room and board ($12,270). Part-time tuition: $747 per credit hour. ***Required fees:*** $40 per term part-time. ***College room only:*** $7770. Room and board charges vary according to board plan and housing facility. ***Payment plan:*** installment. ***Waivers:*** senior citizens and employees or children of employees.
Financial Aid Of all full-time matriculated undergraduates who enrolled in 2019, 808 applied for aid, 755 were judged to have need, 322 had their need fully met. 127 Federal Work-Study jobs (averaging $1647). In 2019, 54 non-need-based awards were made. ***Average percent of need met:*** 92. ***Average financial aid package:*** $31,428. ***Average need-based loan:*** $3368. ***Average need-based gift aid:*** $6374. ***Average non-need-based aid:*** $20,928. ***Average indebtedness upon graduation:*** $33,433.

APPLYING
Standardized Tests *Recommended:* SAT or ACT (for admission).
Options: electronic application, early admission, deferred entrance.
Application fee: $50.
Required: high school transcript, minimum 2.0 GPA, 2 letters of recommendation. ***Recommended:*** essay or personal statement, minimum 3.0 GPA, interview.
Application deadlines: rolling (freshmen), rolling (transfers).
Notification: 9/15 (freshmen).

CONTACT
La Roche University, 9000 Babcock Boulevard, Pittsburgh, PA 15237. *Phone:* 412-536-1272. *Toll-free phone:* 800-838-4LRC. *Fax:* 412-536-1048. *E-mail:* admissions@laroche.edu.

La Salle University

Philadelphia, Pennsylvania

http://www.lasalle.edu/

- **Independent Roman Catholic** comprehensive, founded 1863
- **Urban** 133-acre campus with easy access to Philadelphia
- **Endowment** $84.3 million
- **Coed**
- **Moderately difficult** entrance level

FACULTY
Student/faculty ratio: 11:1.

ACADEMICS
Calendar: semesters. *Degrees:* associate, bachelor's, master's, doctoral, post-master's, and postbachelor's certificates.
Library: Connelly Library. *Books:* 314,203 (physical), 819,865 (digital/electronic); *Serial titles:* 2,982 (physical), 139,962 (digital/electronic); *Databases:* 88. Weekly public service hours: 96; students can reserve study rooms.

STUDENT LIFE
Housing options: on-campus residence required through sophomore year; coed, men-only, women-only, special housing for students with disabilities. Campus housing is university owned. Freshman campus housing is guaranteed.
Activities and organizations: drama/theater group, student-run newspaper, radio and television station, choral group, Student Government Association, community service organization, La Salle Entertainment Organization, The Explorer (yearbook), The Masque (theater group), national fraternities, national sororities.
Athletics Member NCAA. All Division I.
Campus security: 24-hour emergency response devices and patrols, student patrols, late-night transport/escort service, controlled dormitory access.
Student services: health clinic, personal/psychological counseling, women's center, veterans affairs office.

COSTS & FINANCIAL AID
Costs (2019–20) ***One-time required fee:*** $300. ***Comprehensive fee:*** $46,800 includes full-time tuition ($30,700), mandatory fees ($950), and room and board ($15,150). Full-time tuition and fees vary according to course load and program. Part-time tuition: $1080 per credit hour. Part-time tuition and fees vary according to course load and program. ***Required fees:*** $325 part-time. ***College room only:*** $7990. Room and board charges vary according to board plan and housing facility. ***Payment plans:*** installment, deferred payment.
Financial Aid Of all full-time matriculated undergraduates who enrolled in 2016, 2,765 applied for aid, 2,605 were judged to have need, 366 had their need fully met. 364 Federal Work-Study jobs (averaging $1837). In 2016, 471 non-need-based awards were made. ***Average percent of need met:*** 75. ***Average financial aid package:*** $32,236. ***Average need-based loan:*** $4822. ***Average need-based gift aid:*** $25,432. ***Average non-need-based aid:*** $19,520. ***Average indebtedness upon graduation:*** $37,002.

APPLYING
Standardized Tests *Required for some:* SAT or ACT (for admission).
Options: electronic application, early admission, early action, deferred entrance.
Required: essay or personal statement, high school transcript, 1 letter of recommendation. ***Recommended:*** interview.

CONTACT
Mr. James Plunkett, Executive Director of Undergraduate Admission, La Salle University, 1900 West Olney Avenue, Philadelphia, PA 19141-1199. *Phone:* 215-951-1500. *Toll-free phone:* 800-328-1910. *Fax:* 215-951-1656. *E-mail:* admiss@lasalle.edu.

Lebanon Valley College

Annville, Pennsylvania

http://www.lvc.edu/

- **Independent United Methodist** comprehensive, founded 1866
- **Small-town** 357-acre campus
- **Endowment** $67.5 million
- **Coed**
- **Moderately difficult** entrance level

FACULTY
Student/faculty ratio: 10:1.

ACADEMICS
Calendar: semesters. *Degrees:* bachelor's, master's, doctoral, and postbachelor's certificates.
Library: Vernon and Doris Bishop Library. *Books:* 152,319 (physical), 204,880 (digital/electronic); *Serial titles:* 3,047 (physical), 59,331 (digital/electronic); *Databases:* 256. Weekly public service hours: 101; students can reserve study rooms.

STUDENT LIFE
Housing options: on-campus residence required through senior year; coed, special housing for students with disabilities. Campus housing is university owned. Freshman campus housing is guaranteed.

Activities and organizations: drama/theater group, student-run newspaper, choral group, marching band, Mini-THON, Student Government, Colleges Against Cancer, Wig and Buckle Theater Group, Valleyfest, national fraternities, national sororities.

Athletics Member NCAA. All Division III except golf (Division II).

Campus security: 24-hour emergency response devices and patrols, late-night transport/escort service, controlled dormitory access.

Student services: health clinic, personal/psychological counseling, women's center.

COSTS & FINANCIAL AID
Costs (2019–20) ***Comprehensive fee:*** $57,110 includes full-time tuition ($43,650), mandatory fees ($1260), and room and board ($12,200). ***College room only:*** $5890.

Financial Aid Of all full-time matriculated undergraduates who enrolled in 2019, 1,555 applied for aid, 1,375 were judged to have need, 358 had their need fully met. In 2019, 222 non-need-based awards were made. ***Average percent of need met:*** 82. ***Average financial aid package:*** $35,421. ***Average need-based loan:*** $4032. ***Average need-based gift aid:*** $29,436. ***Average non-need-based aid:*** $22,627. ***Average indebtedness upon graduation:*** $42,880.

APPLYING
Options: electronic application, early decision.

Required: high school transcript. ***Required for some:*** audition for music majors, specific requirements for physical therapy and athletic training programs. ***Recommended:*** 2 letters of recommendation, interview.

CONTACT
Mr. Edwin Wright, Vice President of Enrollment Management, Lebanon Valley College, 101 North College Avenue, Annville, PA 17003. *Phone:* 717-867-6181. *Toll-free phone:* 866-LVC-4ADM. *Fax:* 717-867-6026. *E-mail:* admission@lvc.edu.

Lehigh University

Bethlehem, Pennsylvania

http://www.lehigh.edu/

- **Independent** university, founded 1865
- **Suburban** 2355-acre campus with easy access to Philadelphia
- **Endowment** $1.4 billion
- **Coed** 5,178 undergraduate students, 99% full-time, 46% women, 54% men
- **Most difficult** entrance level, 32% of applicants were admitted

UNDERGRAD STUDENTS
5,107 full-time, 71 part-time. Students come from 49 states and territories; 69 other countries; 73% are from out of state; 4% Black or African American, non-Hispanic/Latino; 9% Hispanic/Latino; 8% Asian, non-Hispanic/Latino; 0.1% Native Hawaiian or other Pacific Islander, non-Hispanic/Latino; 0.1% American Indian or Alaska Native, non-Hispanic/Latino; 4% Two or more races, non-Hispanic/Latino; 4% Race/ethnicity unknown; 9% international; 0.6% transferred in; 61% live on campus.

Freshmen:
Admission: 15,649 applied, 5,023 admitted, 1,406 enrolled. ***Test scores:*** SAT evidence-based reading and writing scores over 500: 100%; SAT math scores over 500: 100%; ACT scores over 18: 100%; SAT evidence-based reading and writing scores over 600: 87%; SAT math scores over 600: 92%; ACT scores over 24: 99%; SAT evidence-based reading and writing scores over 700: 24%; SAT math scores over 700: 56%; ACT scores over 30: 72%.

Retention: 93% of full-time freshmen returned.

FACULTY
Total: 715, 77% full time, 81% with terminal degrees.
Student/faculty ratio: 9:1.

ACADEMICS
Calendar: semesters. *Degrees:* bachelor's, master's, doctoral, post-master's, and postbachelor's certificates.

Special study options: accelerated degree program, advanced placement credit, cooperative education, distance learning, double majors, English as a second language, honors programs, independent study, internships, off-campus study, services for LD students, study abroad, summer session for credit. ***ROTC:*** Army (b).

Unusual degree programs: 3-2 engineering; education.

Computers: 437 computers/terminals are available on campus for general student use. Students can access the following: campus intranet, computer help desk, free student e-mail accounts, online (class) grades, online (class) registration, online (class) schedules. Campuswide network is available. 100% of college-owned or -operated housing units are wired for high-speed Internet access. Wireless service is available via entire campus.

Library: E. W. Fairchild-Martindale Library plus 1 other. *Books:* 739,278 (physical), 471,889 (digital/electronic); *Serial titles:* 7,595 (physical), 60,385 (digital/electronic); *Databases:* 209. Weekly public service hours: 83; students can reserve study rooms.

STUDENT LIFE
Housing options: on-campus residence required through sophomore year; coed, special housing for students with disabilities. Campus housing is university owned. Freshman campus housing is guaranteed.

Activities and organizations: drama/theater group, student-run newspaper, radio station, choral group, marching band, Cheese Club, Outing Club, South Asian Students Association, F1RSt, Marching 97, national fraternities, national sororities.

Athletics Member NCAA. All Division I. ***Intercollegiate sports:*** baseball M(s), basketball M(s)/W(s), crew M(c)/W(s), cross-country running M(s)/W(s), equestrian sports M(c)/W(c), fencing M(c)/W(c), field hockey W(s), football M(s), golf M(s)/W(s), ice hockey M(c), lacrosse M(s)/W(s), rugby M(c)/W(c), skiing (downhill) M(c)/W(c), soccer M(s)/W(s), softball W(s), swimming and diving M(s)/W(s), tennis M(s)/W(s), track and field M(s)/W(s), ultimate Frisbee M(c)/W(c), volleyball M(c)/W(s), water polo M(c)/W(c), wrestling M(s). ***Intramural sports:*** baseball M(c), basketball M(c)/W(c), cheerleading M(c)/W(c), cross-country running M(c)/W(c), field hockey W(c), football M/W, golf M(c)/W(c), gymnastics M(c)/W(c), lacrosse M(c)/W(c), skiing (downhill) M(c)/W(c), soccer M(c)/W(c), softball M/W, volleyball M(c)/W(c), wrestling M(c).

Campus security: 24-hour emergency response devices and patrols, student patrols, late-night transport/escort service, controlled dormitory access, self defense training.

Student services: health clinic, personal/psychological counseling, women's center.

COSTS & FINANCIAL AID
Costs (2020–21) ***Comprehensive fee:*** $72,190 includes full-time tuition ($56,980), mandatory fees ($470), and room and board ($14,740). Part-

time tuition: $2375 per credit hour. ***College room only:*** $8660. Room and board charges vary according to board plan and housing facility. ***Payment plans:*** tuition prepayment, installment. ***Waivers:*** employees or children of employees.

Financial Aid Of all full-time matriculated undergraduates who enrolled in 2019, 2,860 applied for aid, 2,084 were judged to have need, 1,863 had their need fully met. 1,356 Federal Work-Study jobs (averaging $1943). 91 state and other part-time jobs (averaging $1761). In 2019, 233 non-need-based awards were made. ***Average percent of need met:*** 99. ***Average financial aid package:*** $53,951. ***Average need-based loan:*** $4017. ***Average need-based gift aid:*** $47,745. ***Average non-need-based aid:*** $11,202. ***Average indebtedness upon graduation:*** $39,609.

APPLYING

Standardized Tests *Required:* SAT or ACT (for admission). *Recommended:* SAT (for admission), ACT (for admission).

Options: electronic application, early decision, deferred entrance.

Application fee: $70.

Required: essay or personal statement, high school transcript, 2 letters of recommendation.

Application deadlines: 1/1 (freshmen), 3/15 (transfers).

Early decision deadline: 11/1 (for plan 1), 1/1 (for plan 2).

Notification: 3/27 (freshmen), 4/15 (transfers), 12/15 (early decision plan 1), 2/8 (early decision plan 2).

CONTACT

Mr. Bruce Bunnick, Director of Admissions, Lehigh University, 27 Memorial Drive West, Bethlehem, PA 18015. *Phone:* 610-758-3100. *Fax:* 610-758-4361. *E-mail:* admissions@lehigh.edu.

Lincoln University

Lincoln University, Pennsylvania

http://www.lincoln.edu/

- **State-related** comprehensive, founded 1854
- **Rural** 422-acre campus with easy access to Philadelphia
- **Endowment** $44.1 million
- **Coed** 2,040 undergraduate students, 93% full-time, 66% women, 34% men
- **Minimally difficult** entrance level, 83% of applicants were admitted

UNDERGRAD STUDENTS

1,901 full-time, 139 part-time. Students come from 28 states and territories; 10 other countries; 50% are from out of state; 85% Black or African American, non-Hispanic/Latino; 5% Hispanic/Latino; 0.0% Asian, non-Hispanic/Latino; 0.1% American Indian or Alaska Native, non-Hispanic/Latino; 3% Two or more races, non-Hispanic/Latino; 4% Race/ethnicity unknown; 3% international; 4% transferred in; 88% live on campus.

Freshmen:

Admission: 4,429 applied, 3,666 admitted, 445 enrolled. ***Average high school GPA:*** 3.0. ***Test scores:*** SAT evidence-based reading and writing scores over 500: 32%; SAT math scores over 500: 29%; ACT scores over 18: 34%; SAT evidence-based reading and writing scores over 600: 5%; SAT math scores over 600: 2%; ACT scores over 24: 2%; SAT math scores over 700: 1%.

Retention: 71% of full-time freshmen returned.

FACULTY

Total: 208, 48% full-time, 40% with terminal degrees.

Student/faculty ratio: 15:1.

ACADEMICS

Calendar: semesters. *Degrees:* bachelor's and master's.

Special study options: academic remediation for entering students, accelerated degree program, adult/continuing education programs, advanced placement credit, double majors, external degree program, honors programs, independent study, internships, part-time degree program, services for LD students, study abroad, summer session for credit. ***ROTC:*** Army (c).

Computers: 600 computers/terminals are available on campus for general student use. Students can access the following: campus intranet, computer help desk, free student e-mail accounts, online (class) grades, online (class) registration, online (class) schedules. Campuswide network is available. 65% of college-owned or -operated housing units are wired for high-speed Internet access. Wireless service is available via entire campus.

Library: Langston Hughes Memorial Library. *Books:* 177,538 (physical), 133,000 (digital/electronic); *Serial titles:* 37,382 (physical). Weekly public service hours: 96; study areas open 24 hours, 5–7 days a week; students can reserve study rooms.

STUDENT LIFE

Housing options: on-campus residence required for freshman year; coed, men-only, women-only, special housing for students with disabilities. Campus housing is university owned. Freshman applicants given priority for college housing.

Activities and organizations: drama/theater group, student-run newspaper, radio and television station, choral group, marching band, People Standing United (PSU), Student Life and Development, Onyx Dance Troupe, We R "1" Family, Caribbean Student Association, national fraternities, national sororities.

Athletics Member NCAA. All Division II. ***Intercollegiate sports:*** baseball M(s), basketball M(s)/W(s), cheerleading M(s)/W(s), cross-country running M(s)/W(s), football M(s), soccer W(s), softball W(s), track and field M(s)/W(s), volleyball W(s). ***Intramural sports:*** basketball M/W, bowling M/W, football M, lacrosse M(c)/W(c), swimming and diving M/W, volleyball W.

Campus security: 24-hour emergency response devices and patrols, late-night transport/escort service, controlled dormitory access, 24-hour command center, gated entrance/exit, medical transports.

Student services: health clinic, personal/psychological counseling, women's center, veterans affairs office.

COSTS & FINANCIAL AID

Costs (2019–20) ***Tuition:*** state resident $8026 full-time, $335 per credit hour part-time; nonresident $13,396 full-time, $562 per credit hour part-time. Full-time tuition and fees vary according to course load, degree level, location, program, and student level. Part-time tuition and fees vary according to course load, degree level, program, and student level. No tuition increase for student's term of enrollment. ***Required fees:*** $3240 full-time, $145 per credit hour part-time. ***Room and board:*** $9828; room only: $5242. Room and board charges vary according to board plan and housing facility. ***Payment plans:*** installment, deferred payment. ***Waivers:*** children of alumni and employees or children of employees.

Financial Aid Of all full-time matriculated undergraduates who enrolled in 2018, 1,892 applied for aid, 1,770 were judged to have need, 165 had their need fully met. 122 Federal Work-Study jobs (averaging $1716). 25 state and other part-time jobs (averaging $884). In 2018, 45 non-need-based awards were made. ***Average percent of need met:*** 50. ***Average financial aid package:*** $12,732. ***Average need-based loan:*** $3995. ***Average need-based gift aid:*** $7372. ***Average non-need-based aid:*** $10,795. ***Average indebtedness upon graduation:*** $36,567.

APPLYING

Standardized Tests *Required:* SAT or ACT (for admission).

Options: electronic application, deferred entrance.

Required: high school transcript, Standardized Test Scores: SAT or ACT. ***Required for some:*** essay or personal statement, 2 letters of recommendation, interview. ***Recommended:*** essay or personal statement.

Application deadlines: 5/1 (freshmen), 4/1 (transfers).

Notification: continuous (transfers).

CONTACT

Ms. Nikoia Forde, Director, Office of Undergraduate Admissions, Lincoln University, 1570 Baltimore Pike, Lincoln University, PA 19352. *Phone:* 484-365-7275. *Toll-free phone:* 800-790-0191. *Fax:* 484-365-8109. *E-mail:* nforde@lincoln.edu.

Lock Haven University of Pennsylvania

Lock Haven, Pennsylvania

http://www.lockhaven.edu/

- **State-supported** comprehensive, founded 1870, part of Pennsylvania State System of Higher Education
- **Rural** 165-acre campus
- **Endowment** $11.4 million
- **Coed** 2,748 undergraduate students, 90% full-time, 60% women, 40% men
- **Moderately difficult** entrance level, 95% of applicants were admitted

UNDERGRAD STUDENTS

2,480 full-time, 268 part-time. Students come from 17 states and territories; 22 other countries; 5% are from out of state; 7% Black or African American, non-Hispanic/Latino; 3% Hispanic/Latino; 1% Asian, non-Hispanic/Latino; 0.1% Native Hawaiian or other Pacific Islander, non-Hispanic/Latino; 0.3% American Indian or Alaska Native, non-Hispanic/Latino; 2% Two or more races, non-Hispanic/Latino; 2% Race/ethnicity unknown; 0.4% international; 4% transferred in, 31% live on campus.

Freshmen:

Admission: 2,203 applied, 2,089 admitted, 598 enrolled. ***Average high school GPA:*** 3.3. ***Test scores:*** SAT evidence-based reading and writing scores over 500: 61%; SAT math scores over 500: 61%; ACT scores over 18: 67%; SAT evidence-based reading and writing scores over 600: 16%; SAT math scores over 600: 13%; ACT scores over 24: 21%; SAT evidence-based reading and writing scores over 700: 1%; ACT scores over 30: 4%.

Retention: 68% of full-time freshmen returned.

FACULTY

Total: 216, 88% full-time, 80% with terminal degrees.

Student/faculty ratio: 14:1.

ACADEMICS

Calendar: semesters. *Degrees:* associate, bachelor's, and master's.

Special study options: academic remediation for entering students, adult/continuing education programs, advanced placement credit, cooperative education, distance learning, double majors, English as a second language, freshman honors college, honors programs, independent study, internships, off-campus study, part-time degree program, services for LD students, student-designed majors, study abroad, summer session for credit. ***ROTC:*** Army (b).

Unusual degree programs: 3-2 engineering with Penn State University Park.

Computers: 290 computers/terminals are available on campus for general student use. Students can access the following: online (class) registration. Campuswide network is available.

Library: Stevenson Library plus 1 other. *Books:* 239,556 (physical); *Serial titles:* 36,958 (physical); *Databases:* 95. Students can reserve study rooms.

STUDENT LIFE

Housing options: on-campus residence required through sophomore year; coed. Campus housing is university owned. Freshman applicants given priority for college housing.

Activities and organizations: drama/theater group, student-run newspaper, radio and television station, choral group, marching band, Student Government, Residence Hall Association, national fraternities, national sororities.

Athletics Member NCAA. All Division II except field hockey (Division I), wrestling (Division I). ***Intercollegiate sports:*** baseball M(s), basketball M(s)/W(s), cross-country running M(s)/W(s), field hockey W(s), football M(s), lacrosse W(s), soccer M(s)/W(s), softball W(s), swimming and diving W(s), tennis W(s), track and field M(s)/W(s), volleyball W(s), wrestling M(s)/W(s). ***Intramural sports:*** badminton M/W, basketball M/W, cross-country running M/W, fencing M/W, field hockey W, football M, golf M/W, ice hockey M, lacrosse M/W, racquetball M/W, rugby M/W, skiing (cross-country) M/W, skiing (downhill) M/W, soccer M/W, softball M/W, swimming and diving M/W, tennis M/W, track and field M/W, ultimate Frisbee M/W, volleyball M/W, water polo M, weight lifting M/W, wrestling M.

Campus security: 24-hour emergency response devices and patrols, late-night transport/escort service, controlled dormitory access.

Student services: health clinic, personal/psychological counseling, women's center.

COSTS & FINANCIAL AID

Costs (2019–20) ***Tuition:*** state resident $7716 full-time, $322 per credit hour part-time; nonresident $17,290 full-time, $720 per credit hour part-time. Full-time tuition and fees vary according to course load, location, and program. Part-time tuition and fees vary according to course load, location, and program. ***Required fees:*** $3162 full-time, $168 per credit hour part-time. ***Room and board:*** $10,368; room only: $6540. Room and board charges vary according to board plan and housing facility. ***Payment plan:*** installment. ***Waivers:*** minority students, senior citizens, and employees or children of employees.

Financial Aid Of all full-time matriculated undergraduates who enrolled in 2018, 2,480 applied for aid, 2,171 were judged to have need, 127 had their need fully met. In 2018, 52 non-need-based awards were made. ***Average percent of need met:*** 58. ***Average financial aid package:*** $9379. ***Average need-based loan:*** $3853. ***Average need-based gift aid:*** $5793. ***Average non-need-based aid:*** $2848. ***Average indebtedness upon graduation:*** $23,490.

APPLYING

Standardized Tests *Required:* SAT or ACT (for admission).

Options: electronic application, deferred entrance.

Application fee: $25.

Required: high school transcript. ***Required for some:*** essay or personal statement. ***Recommended:*** interview.

Application deadlines: rolling (freshmen), rolling (transfers).

Notification: continuous (freshmen), continuous (transfers).

CONTACT

Lock Haven University of Pennsylvania, 401 North Fairview Street, Lock Haven, PA 17745-2390. *Phone:* 570-484-2109. *Toll-free phone:* 800-332-8900 (in-state); 800-233-8978 (out-of-state).

Lycoming College

Williamsport, Pennsylvania

http://www.lycoming.edu/

- **Independent United Methodist** 4-year, founded 1812
- **Small-town** 35-acre campus
- **Endowment** $207.6 million
- **Coed**
- **Moderately difficult** entrance level

FACULTY

Student/faculty ratio: 12:1.

ACADEMICS

Calendar: semesters. *Degree:* bachelor's.

Library: Snowden Library. *Books:* 135,456 (physical), 134,657 (digital/electronic); *Serial titles:* 1,045 (physical), 18,343 (digital/electronic); *Databases:* 89. Weekly public service hours: 107.

STUDENT LIFE

Housing options: on-campus residence required through senior year; coed, women-only. Campus housing is university owned. Freshman campus housing is guaranteed.

Activities and organizations: drama/theater group, student-run newspaper, radio station, choral group, Campus Activities Board, Lycoming Pom and Dance Club, Society of Physics Students, Black Student Union, Creative Arts Society, national fraternities, national sororities.

Athletics Member NCAA. All Division III except golf (Division II).

Campus security: 24-hour emergency response devices and patrols, student patrols, late-night transport/escort service, controlled dormitory access.

Student services: health clinic, personal/psychological counseling.

COSTS & FINANCIAL AID
Costs (2019–20) ***One-time required fee:*** $225. ***Comprehensive fee:*** $54,634 includes full-time tuition ($40,896), mandatory fees ($730), and room and board ($13,008). Part-time tuition: $1278 per credit hour. ***Room and board:*** Room and board charges vary according to board plan. ***Payment plans:*** installment, deferred payment.

Financial Aid Of all full-time matriculated undergraduates who enrolled in 2019, 1,010 applied for aid, 967 were judged to have need, 247 had their need fully met. In 2019, 149 non-need-based awards were made. ***Average percent of need met:*** 85. ***Average financial aid package:*** $43,039. ***Average need-based loan:*** $4914. ***Average need-based gift aid:*** $35,342. ***Average non-need-based aid:*** $27,854.

APPLYING
Standardized Tests *Recommended:* SAT or ACT (for admission).

Options: electronic application, early decision, early action, deferred entrance.

Required: essay or personal statement, high school transcript, 2 letters of recommendation. ***Recommended:*** minimum 2.3 GPA, interview.

CONTACT
Jessica Hess, Director of Admissions, Lycoming College, 700 College Place, Williamsport, PA 17701. *Phone:* 570-321-4318. *Toll-free phone:* 800-345-3920 Ext. 4026. *Fax:* 570-321-4317. *E-mail:* admissions@lycoming.edu.

Manor College

Jenkintown, Pennsylvania

http://www.manor.edu/

- **Independent Byzantine Catholic** primarily 2-year, founded 1947
- **Suburban** 35-acre campus with easy access to Philadelphia
- **Endowment** $2.8 million
- **Coed**
- **Minimally difficult** entrance level

FACULTY
Student/faculty ratio: 10:1.

ACADEMICS
Calendar: semesters. *Degrees:* certificates, associate, bachelor's, and postbachelor's certificates.
Library: Basileiad Library. *Books:* 27,188 (physical), 5,037 (digital/electronic); *Serial titles:* 3 (physical); *Databases:* 14. Weekly public service hours: 65.

STUDENT LIFE
Housing options: coed. Campus housing is university owned.

Activities and organizations: choral group, Rotoract (student service organization), Vet Tech Club, Campus Activities Board, Macrinian Yearbook, Phi Theta Kappa (honor society).

Athletics Member NJCAA.

Campus security: 24-hour emergency response devices and patrols, late-night transport/escort service.

Student services: personal/psychological counseling, veterans affairs office.

COSTS & FINANCIAL AID
Costs (2019–20) ***Comprehensive fee:*** $25,984 includes full-time tuition ($16,922), mandatory fees ($1100), and room and board ($7962). Full-time tuition and fees vary according to course load and program. Part-time tuition: $689 per credit. Part-time tuition and fees vary according to course load and program. ***Required fees:*** $275 per term part-time.

Financial Aid Of all full-time matriculated undergraduates who enrolled in 2009, 35 Federal Work-Study jobs (averaging $3000). 10 state and other part-time jobs (averaging $3600).

APPLYING
Standardized Tests *Recommended:* SAT or ACT (for admission).

Options: electronic application, deferred entrance.

Required: high school transcript, minimum 2.0 GPA. ***Required for some:*** essay or personal statement, letters of recommendation, interview.

CONTACT
Angelica Crespo, Admissions Office Manager, Manor College, 700 Fox Chase Road, Jenkintown, PA 19046. *Phone:* 215-885-2216 Ext. 212. *Fax:* 215-576-6564. *E-mail:* swalker@manor.edu.

Mansfield University of Pennsylvania

Mansfield, Pennsylvania

http://www.mansfield.edu/

- **State-supported** comprehensive, founded 1857, part of Pennsylvania State System of Higher Education
- **Small-town** 174-acre campus
- **Coed** 1,640 undergraduate students, 90% full-time, 63% women, 37% men
- **Moderately difficult** entrance level, 94% of applicants were admitted

UNDERGRAD STUDENTS
1,484 full-time, 156 part-time. 19% are from out of state; 11% Black or African American, non-Hispanic/Latino; 5% Hispanic/Latino; 0.6% Asian, non-Hispanic/Latino; 0.1% Native Hawaiian or other Pacific Islander, non-Hispanic/Latino; 0.3% American Indian or Alaska Native, non-Hispanic/Latino; 2% Two or more races, non-Hispanic/Latino; 3% Race/ethnicity unknown; 0.8% international; 7% transferred in; 57% live on campus.

Freshmen:
Admission: 1,892 applied, 1,777 admitted, 450 enrolled. ***Average high school GPA:*** 3.4. ***Test scores:*** SAT evidence-based reading and writing scores over 500: 72%; SAT math scores over 500: 68%; SAT evidence-based reading and writing scores over 600: 19%; SAT math scores over 600: 12%; SAT evidence-based reading and writing scores over 700: 2%; SAT math scores over 700: 1%.

Retention: 73% of full-time freshmen returned.

FACULTY
Total: 132, 65% full-time, 67% with terminal degrees.

Student/faculty ratio: 15:1.

ACADEMICS
Calendar: semesters. *Degrees:* associate, bachelor's, master's, and postbachelor's certificates.

Special study options: adult/continuing education programs, part-time degree program. ***ROTC:*** Army (c).

Computers: Students can access the following: campus intranet, computer help desk, free student e-mail accounts, online (class) grades, online (class) registration, online (class) schedules. Campuswide network is available. 100% of college-owned or -operated housing units are wired for high-speed Internet access. Wireless service is available via classrooms, computer centers, computer labs, dorm rooms, learning centers, libraries, student centers.
Library: North Hall Library.

STUDENT LIFE
Housing options: on-campus residence required through sophomore yearCampus housing is university owned. Freshman campus housing is guaranteed.

Activities and organizations: drama/theater group, student-run newspaper, radio and television station, choral group, marching band, national fraternities, national sororities.

Athletics Member NCAA. All Division II. ***Intercollegiate sports:*** baseball M(s), basketball M(s)/W(s), cross-country running M(s)/W(s), field hockey W(s), football M(c), soccer W(s), softball W(s), swimming and diving W, track and field M(s)/W(s). ***Intramural sports:*** badminton M/W, basketball M/W, bowling M/W, cheerleading W, cross-country running M/W, equestrian sports M/W, football M/W, golf M/W, racquetball M/W, skiing (cross-country) M/W, skiing (downhill) M/W, soccer M/W, softball M/W, swimming and diving M/W, tennis M/W, track and field M/W, volleyball M/W, water polo M/W, weight lifting M/W.

Campus security: 24-hour emergency response devices and patrols, student patrols, late-night transport/escort service, controlled dormitory access.

Student services: health clinic, personal/psychological counseling, women's center.

COSTS & FINANCIAL AID
Costs (2020–21) ***Tuition:*** area resident $7716 full-time; state resident $7716 full-time; nonresident $10,032 full-time. ***Required fees:*** $2880 full-time. ***Room and board:*** $10,147; room only: $6600.

Financial Aid Of all full-time matriculated undergraduates who enrolled in 2018, 1,294 applied for aid, 1,169 were judged to have need, 756 had their need fully met. In 2018, 178 non-need-based awards were made. ***Average percent of need met:*** 87. ***Average financial aid package:*** $1858. ***Average need-based loan:*** $2100. ***Average need-based gift aid:*** $1422. ***Average non-need-based aid:*** $1440. ***Average indebtedness upon graduation:*** $42,457.

APPLYING
Standardized Tests *Required for some:* SAT or ACT (for admission).

Options: electronic application.

Required: high school transcript. ***Required for some:*** interview. ***Recommended:*** essay or personal statement, minimum 2.5 GPA.

CONTACT
Ms. Rachel Green, Director of Admissions, Mansfield University of Pennsylvania, Academy Street, Mansfield, PA 16933. *Phone:* 570-662-4813. *Toll-free phone:* 800-577-6826. *E-mail:* admissions@mnsfld.edu.

Marywood University

Scranton, Pennsylvania

http://www.marywood.edu/

- **Independent Roman Catholic** comprehensive, founded 1915
- **Suburban** 123-acre campus
- **Endowment** $40.6 million
- **Coed** 1,809 undergraduate students, 91% full-time, 67% women, 33% men
- **Moderately difficult** entrance level, 78% of applicants were admitted

UNDERGRAD STUDENTS
1,655 full-time, 154 part-time. Students come from 18 states and territories; 7 other countries; 27% are from out of state; 2% Black or African American, non-Hispanic/Latino; 8% Hispanic/Latino; 2% Asian, non-Hispanic/Latino; 0.1% Native Hawaiian or other Pacific Islander, non-Hispanic/Latino; 0.2% American Indian or Alaska Native, non-Hispanic/Latino; 2% Two or more races, non-Hispanic/Latino; 10% Race/ethnicity unknown; 1% international; 5% transferred in; 34% live on campus.

Freshmen:
Admission: 2,005 applied, 1,559 admitted, 361 enrolled. ***Average high school GPA:*** 3.5. ***Test scores:*** SAT evidence-based reading and writing scores over 500: 78%; SAT math scores over 500: 75%; SAT evidence-based reading and writing scores over 600: 27%; SAT math scores over 600: 20%; SAT evidence-based reading and writing scores over 700: 3%; SAT math scores over 700: 3%.

Retention: 86% of full-time freshmen returned.

FACULTY
Total: 372, 41% full-time.

Student/faculty ratio: 11:1.

ACADEMICS
Calendar: semesters. *Degrees:* certificates, bachelor's, master's, doctoral, post-master's, and postbachelor's certificates.

Special study options: adult/continuing education programs, advanced placement credit, double majors, English as a second language, honors programs, independent study, internships, off-campus study, part-time degree program, services for LD students, student-designed majors, study abroad, summer session for credit. ***ROTC:*** Army (c), Air Force (c).

Unusual degree programs: 3-2 physician assistant, communication sciences disorders, criminal justice, biotechnology, health services administration.

Computers: 359 computers/terminals are available on campus for general student use. Students can access the following: computer help desk, free student e-mail accounts, online (class) grades, online (class) registration, online (class) schedules, degree audit, student account management, financial aid self-service, student planning. Campuswide network is available. 100% of college-owned or -operated housing units are wired for high-speed Internet access. Wireless service is available via entire campus.

Library: Learning Commons plus 2 others. *Books:* 185,509 (physical), 225,884 (digital/electronic); *Serial titles:* 62 (physical), 44,458 (digital/electronic); *Databases:* 62. Weekly public service hours: 99; students can reserve study rooms.

STUDENT LIFE

Housing options: on-campus residence required through sophomore year; coed, women-only, special housing for students with disabilities. Campus housing is university owned. Freshman campus housing is guaranteed.

Activities and organizations: drama/theater group, student-run newspaper, radio and television station, choral group, Phi Beta Lambda (Business Club), Marywood Media Group, Volunteers in Action (VIA), Zeta Phi Delta, American Institute of Architects, national fraternities.

Athletics Member NCAA. All Division III. ***Intercollegiate sports:*** baseball M, basketball M/W, cross-country running M/W, field hockey W, golf M/W, lacrosse M/W, rugby M/W, soccer M/W, softball W, swimming and diving M/W, tennis M/W, track and field M/W, volleyball W. ***Intramural sports:*** basketball M/W, skiing (downhill) M(c)/W(c), soccer M/W, volleyball M/W.

Campus security: 24-hour emergency response devices and patrols, late-night transport/escort service, controlled dormitory access, apartments with deadbolts, self-defense education, lighted pathways, seminars on safety.

Student services: health clinic, personal/psychological counseling, veterans affairs office.

COSTS & FINANCIAL AID

Costs (2020–21) ***Comprehensive fee:*** $51,266 includes full-time tuition ($35,178), mandatory fees ($1750), and room and board ($14,338). Part-time tuition: $670 per credit. ***College room only:*** $8138. Room and board charges vary according to board plan and housing facility. ***Payment plan:*** installment. ***Waivers:*** senior citizens and employees or children of employees.

Financial Aid Of all full-time matriculated undergraduates who enrolled in 2019, 1,471 applied for aid, 1,339 were judged to have need, 255 had their need fully met. 950 Federal Work-Study jobs (averaging $1982). In 2019, 274 non-need-based awards were made. ***Average percent of need met:*** 75. ***Average financial aid package:*** $28,358. ***Average need-based loan:*** $4191. ***Average need-based gift aid:*** $24,537. ***Average non-need-based aid:*** $17,539. ***Average indebtedness upon graduation:*** $41,925.

APPLYING

Standardized Tests *Required:* SAT or ACT (for admission).

Options: electronic application, deferred entrance.

Application fee: $35.

Required: essay or personal statement, high school transcript, minimum 2.5 GPA, 1 letter of recommendation. ***Required for some:*** portfolio for art majors, audition for music majors. ***Recommended:*** interview.

Application deadlines: rolling (freshmen), rolling (transfers).

Notification: continuous (freshmen), continuous (transfers).

CONTACT

Ms. Rachel Hartz, Director of Undergraduate Admissions, Marywood University, 2300 Adams Avenue, Scranton, PA 18509. *Phone:* 570-348-6234. *Toll-free phone:* 866-279-9663. *Fax:* 570-961-4763. *E-mail:* yourfuture@marywood.edu.

See below for display ad and page 1080 for the College Close-Up.

Mercyhurst North East

North East, Pennsylvania

http://northeast.mercyhurst.edu/

CONTACT

Travis Lindahl, Director of Admissions, Mercyhurst North East, 16 West Division Street, North East, PA 16428. *Phone:* 814-725-6217. *Toll-free phone:* 866-846-6042. *Fax:* 814-725-6251. *E-mail:* neadmiss@mercyhurst.edu.

Mercyhurst University

Erie, Pennsylvania

http://www.mercyhurst.edu/

CONTACT

Mercyhurst University, 501 East 38th Street, Erie, PA 16546. *Toll-free phone:* 800-825-1926.

Messiah College

Mechanicsburg, Pennsylvania

http://www.messiah.edu/

- **Independent interdenominational** comprehensive, founded 1909
- **Small-town** 485-acre campus
- **Endowment** $138.2 million
- **Coed** 2,709 undergraduate students, 94% full-time, 61% women, 39% men
- **Moderately difficult** entrance level, 76% of applicants were admitted

UNDERGRAD STUDENTS

2,545 full-time, 164 part-time. Students come from 38 states and territories; 28 other countries; 35% are from out of state; 3% Black or African American, non-Hispanic/Latino; 6% Hispanic/Latino; 2% Asian, non-Hispanic/Latino; 0.1% American Indian or Alaska Native, non-Hispanic/Latino; 4% Two or more races, non-Hispanic/Latino; 0.4% Race/ethnicity unknown; 4% international; 3% transferred in; 87% live on campus.

Freshmen:

Admission: 2,640 applied, 2,003 admitted, 606 enrolled. ***Average high school GPA:*** 3.8. ***Test scores:*** SAT evidence-based reading and writing scores over 500: 92%; SAT math scores over 500: 91%; ACT scores over 18: 94%; SAT evidence-based reading and writing scores over 600: 54%; SAT math scores over 600: 47%; ACT scores over 24: 70%; SAT evidence-based reading and writing scores over 700: 12%; SAT math scores over 700: 13%; ACT scores over 30: 28%.

Retention: 89% of full-time freshmen returned.

FACULTY

Total: 364, 55% full-time, 59% with terminal degrees.

Student/faculty ratio: 12:1.

ACADEMICS

Calendar: semesters. *Degrees:* certificates, bachelor's, master's, doctoral, post-master's, and postbachelor's certificates.

Special study options: academic remediation for entering students, accelerated degree program, adult/continuing education programs, advanced placement credit, cooperative education, distance learning, double majors, freshman honors college, honors programs, independent study, internships, off-campus study, part-time degree program, services for LD students, student-designed majors, study abroad, summer session for credit.

Unusual degree programs: 3-2 applied health science or biopsychology/occupational therapy with Thomas Jefferson University, biochemistry/pharmacy with the University of the Sciences in Philadelphia, politics/public policy and management with Carnegie Mellon University.

Computers: 571 computers/terminals are available on campus for general student use. Students can access the following: campus intranet, computer help desk, free student e-mail accounts, online (class) grades, online (class) registration, online (class) schedules, access to software. Campuswide network is available. 100% of college-owned or -operated housing units are wired for high-speed Internet access. Wireless service is available via entire campus.

Library: Murray Library. *Books:* 242,324 (physical), 681,328 (digital/electronic); *Serial titles:* 145 (physical), 454,574 (digital/electronic); *Databases:* 152. Weekly public service hours: 97; students can reserve study rooms.

STUDENT LIFE

Housing options: on-campus residence required through senior year; coed, men-only, women-only, special housing for students with disabilities. Campus housing is university owned. Freshman campus housing is guaranteed.

Activities and organizations: drama/theater group, student-run newspaper, radio station, choral group, Outreach teams, student government, choral groups and ensembles, Small Group Program, Outdoors Club.

Athletics Member NCAA. All Division III. ***Intercollegiate sports:*** baseball M, basketball M/W, cross-country running M/W, field hockey W, lacrosse M/W, soccer M/W, softball W, swimming and diving M/W, tennis M/W, track and field M/W, volleyball M/W, wrestling M. ***Intramural sports:*** basketball M/W, field hockey W(c), football M/W, soccer M/W, softball M/W, ultimate Frisbee M(c)/W(c), volleyball M/W.

Campus security: 24-hour emergency response devices and patrols, student patrols, late-night transport/escort service, controlled dormitory access.

Student services: health clinic, personal/psychological counseling.

COSTS & FINANCIAL AID

Costs (2020–21) ***Comprehensive fee:*** $48,080 includes full-time tuition ($36,340), mandatory fees ($840), and room and board ($10,900). Part-time tuition: $1515 per credit hour. ***College room only:*** $5800. Room and board charges vary according to board plan and housing facility. ***Payment plan:*** installment. ***Waivers:*** adult students, senior citizens, and employees or children of employees.

Financial Aid Of all full-time matriculated undergraduates who enrolled in 2019, 2,148 applied for aid, 1,870 were judged to have need, 360 had their need fully met. 670 Federal Work-Study jobs (averaging $2141). 1,018 state and other part-time jobs (averaging $1871). In 2019, 677 non-need-based awards were made. ***Average percent of need met:*** 73. ***Average financial aid package:*** $26,020. ***Average need-based loan:*** $4828. ***Average need-based gift aid:*** $19,830. ***Average non-need-based aid:*** $14,921. ***Average indebtedness upon graduation:*** $41,859.

APPLYING

Standardized Tests *Required:* SAT or ACT (for admission).

Options: electronic application.

Application fee: $50.

Required: essay or personal statement, high school transcript. ***Required for some:*** interview.

Application deadlines: rolling (freshmen), rolling (transfers).

Notification: continuous (freshmen), continuous (transfers).

CONTACT

Dr. John Chopka, Vice President for Enrollment Management, Messiah College, One College Avenue, Suite 3005, Mechanicsburg, PA 17055. *Phone:* 717-691-6000. *Toll-free phone:* 800-233-4220. *Fax:* 717-691-2307. *E-mail:* admiss@messiah.edu.

Millersville University of Pennsylvania

Millersville, Pennsylvania

http://www.millersville.edu/

- **State-supported** university, founded 1855, part of Pennsylvania State System of Higher Education
- **Small-town** 250-acre campus
- **Endowment** $11.5 million
- **Coed** 6,779 undergraduate students, 81% full-time, 58% women, 42% men
- **Moderately difficult** entrance level, 76% of applicants were admitted

UNDERGRAD STUDENTS

5,499 full-time, 1,280 part-time. Students come from 30 states and territories; 56 other countries; 8% are from out of state; 9% Black or African American, non-Hispanic/Latino; 11% Hispanic/Latino; 3% Asian, non-Hispanic/Latino; 0.5% American Indian or Alaska Native, non-Hispanic/Latino; 1% Two or more races, non-Hispanic/Latino; 1% Race/ethnicity unknown; 0.9% international; 8% transferred in; 32% live on campus.

Freshmen:

Admission: 6,560 applied, 4,979 admitted, 1,334 enrolled. ***Average high school GPA:*** 3.4. ***Test scores:*** SAT evidence-based reading and writing scores over 500: 73%; SAT math scores over 500: 71%; ACT scores over 18: 81%; SAT evidence-based reading and writing scores over 600: 25%; SAT math scores over 600: 18%; ACT scores over 24: 43%; SAT evidence-based reading and writing scores over 700: 2%; SAT math scores over 700: 3%; ACT scores over 30: 8%.

Retention: 77% of full-time freshmen returned.

FACULTY

Total: 474, 58% full-time, 72% with terminal degrees.

Student/faculty ratio: 19:1.

ACADEMICS

Calendar: 4-1-4. *Degrees:* certificates, associate, bachelor's, master's, doctoral, post-master's, and postbachelor's certificates.

Special study options: academic remediation for entering students, accelerated degree program, adult/continuing education programs, advanced placement credit, cooperative education, distance learning, double majors, English as a second language, freshman honors college, honors programs, independent study, internships, off-campus study, part-time degree program, services for LD students, student-designed majors, study abroad, summer session for credit. ***ROTC:*** Army (b).

Unusual degree programs: 3-2 engineering with Penn State University, University of Delaware.

Computers: 430 computers/terminals and 2,500 ports are available on campus for general student use. Students can access the following: campus intranet, computer help desk, free student e-mail accounts, online (class) grades, online (class) registration, online (class) schedules. Campuswide network is available. 100% of college-owned or -operated housing units are wired for high-speed Internet access. Wireless service is available via entire campus.

Library: The Francine G. McNairy Library and Learning Forum at Ganser Hall. *Books:* 265,170 (physical), 58,096 (digital/electronic); *Serial titles:* 4,575 (physical), 230,749 (digital/electronic); *Databases:* 179. Weekly public service hours: 94; students can reserve study rooms.

STUDENT LIFE

Housing options: on-campus residence required through sophomore year; coed, special housing for students with disabilities. Campus housing is university owned. Freshman campus housing is guaranteed.

Activities and organizations: drama/theater group, student-run newspaper, radio and television station, choral group, marching band, University Activities Board, Honors College Student Association, Helping Paws, Team FTK, Marauder Music Productions, national fraternities, national sororities.

Athletics Member NCAA. All Division II. ***Intercollegiate sports:*** baseball M(s), basketball M(s)/W(s), cross-country running W(s), field hockey W(s), football M(s), golf M(s)/W(s), lacrosse W(s), soccer M(s)/W(s), softball W(s), swimming and diving W(s), tennis M(s)/W(s), track and field W(s), volleyball W(s), wrestling M(s). ***Intramural sports:*** badminton M/W, baseball M(c)/W(c), basketball M/W, bowling M(c)/W(c), cheerleading M(c)/W(c), cross-country running M(c)/W(c), equestrian sports M(c)/W(c), fencing M(c)/W(c), football M/W, ice hockey M(c)/W(c), lacrosse M(c), rugby M(c)/W(c), soccer M/W, softball M/W, table tennis M/W, ultimate Frisbee M/W, volleyball M/W.

Campus security: 24-hour emergency response devices and patrols, student patrols, late-night transport/escort service, controlled dormitory access, emergency notification system, crime awareness programs, timely warning alerts, self-defense education, shuttle buses, lighted pathways.

Student services: health clinic, personal/psychological counseling, women's center, veterans affairs office.

COSTS & FINANCIAL AID

Costs (2019–20) ***Tuition:*** state resident $9570 full-time, $319 per credit part-time; nonresident $19,290 full-time, $805 per credit part-time. Full-time tuition and fees vary according to course load. Part-time tuition and fees vary according to course load. ***Required fees:*** $2680 full-time, $112 per credit part-time. ***Room and board:*** $12,980. Room and board charges vary according to board plan and housing facility. ***Payment plan:*** installment. ***Waivers:*** senior citizens and employees or children of employees.

Financial Aid Of all full-time matriculated undergraduates who enrolled in 2018, 4,538 applied for aid, 3,765 were judged to have need, 109 had their need fully met. 233 Federal Work-Study jobs (averaging $1347). 1,297 state and other part-time jobs (averaging $1411). In 2018, 285 non-need-based awards were made. ***Average percent of need met:*** 56. ***Average financial aid package:*** $8997. ***Average need-based loan:*** $4090. ***Average***

need-based gift aid: $6432. ***Average non-need-based aid:*** $3190. ***Average indebtedness upon graduation:*** $32,815.

APPLYING

Standardized Tests *Required:* SAT or ACT (for admission).

Options: electronic application, early admission, deferred entrance.

Application fee: $50.

Required: essay or personal statement, high school transcript, minimum 2.0 GPA, health examination, high school diploma or GED, SAT or ACT scores, audition required for music applicants, portfolio required for art applicants, associate degree in nursing or diploma and RN license required for nursing applicants. ***Required for some:*** 1 letter of recommendation, interview. ***Recommended:*** minimum 3.0 GPA, 2 letters of recommendation.

Application deadlines: rolling (freshmen), rolling (out-of-state freshmen), rolling (transfers).

Notification: continuous (freshmen), continuous (out-of-state freshmen), continuous (transfers).

CONTACT

Ms. Katy A. Charles, Director of Admissions, Millersville University of Pennsylvania, PO Box 1002, Millersville, PA 17551-0302. *Phone:* 717-871-4625. *Toll-free phone:* 800-MU-ADMIT. *Fax:* 717-871-7973. *E-mail:* admissions@millersville.edu.

Misericordia University

Dallas, Pennsylvania

http://www.misericordia.edu/

- **Independent Roman Catholic** comprehensive, founded 1924
- **Small-town** 120-acre campus
- **Endowment** $49.2 million
- **Coed** 1,964 undergraduate students, 81% full-time, 68% women, 32% men
- **Moderately difficult** entrance level, 86% of applicants were admitted

UNDERGRAD STUDENTS

1,584 full-time, 380 part-time. 28% are from out of state; 3% Black or African American, non-Hispanic/Latino; 3% Hispanic/Latino; 1% Asian, non-Hispanic/Latino; 0.2% Native Hawaiian or other Pacific Islander, non-Hispanic/Latino; 0.2% American Indian or Alaska Native, non-Hispanic/Latino; 4% Two or more races, non-Hispanic/Latino; 3% Race/ethnicity unknown; 0.2% international; 4% transferred in; 44% live on campus.

Freshmen:

Admission: 1,547 applied, 1,327 admitted, 414 enrolled. ***Average high school GPA:*** 3.4. ***Test scores:*** SAT evidence-based reading and writing scores over 500: 86%; SAT math scores over 500: 90%; ACT scores over 18: 100%; SAT evidence-based reading and writing scores over 600: 35%; SAT math scores over 600: 33%; ACT scores over 24: 58%; SAT evidence-based reading and writing scores over 700: 2%; SAT math scores over 700: 4%; ACT scores over 30: 2%.

Retention: 51% of full-time freshmen returned.

FACULTY

Total: 298, 48% full-time, 50% with terminal degrees.

Student/faculty ratio: 10:1.

ACADEMICS

Calendar: semesters. *Degrees:* certificates, bachelor's, master's, doctoral, post-master's, and postbachelor's certificates.

Special study options: accelerated degree program, adult/continuing education programs, advanced placement credit, distance learning, double majors, honors programs, independent study, internships, off-campus study, part-time degree program, services for LD students, student-designed majors, study abroad, summer session for credit. ***ROTC:*** Army (c), Air Force (c).

Computers: 150 computers/terminals and 1,000 ports are available on campus for general student use. Students can access the following: campus intranet, computer help desk, free student e-mail accounts, online (class) grades, online (class) registration, online (class) schedules. Campuswide network is available. 100% of college-owned or -operated housing units are wired for high-speed Internet access. Wireless service is available via entire campus.

Library: Mary Kintz Bevevino Library. *Books:* 80,036 (physical), 13,154 (digital/electronic); *Serial titles:* 8,153 (physical), 28,230 (digital/electronic); *Databases:* 111. Students can reserve study rooms.

STUDENT LIFE

Housing options: coed. Campus housing is university owned. Freshman applicants given priority for college housing.

Activities and organizations: drama/theater group, student-run newspaper, radio and television station, choral group, Physical Therapy club, MSOTA, Colleges against Cancer, Dance Ensemble, Medical Imaging club.

Athletics Member NCAA. All Division III except tennis (Division II). ***Intercollegiate sports:*** baseball M, basketball M/W, cross-country running M/W, field hockey W, football M, golf M/W, lacrosse M/W, soccer M/W, softball W, swimming and diving M/W, tennis M/W, track and field M/W, volleyball M/W. ***Intramural sports:*** basketball M/W, football M/W, soccer M/W, softball M/W, tennis M/W, ultimate Frisbee M/W, volleyball M/W.

Campus security: 24-hour emergency response devices and patrols, late-night transport/escort service, controlled dormitory access.

Student services: health clinic, personal/psychological counseling, women's center, veterans affairs office.

COSTS & FINANCIAL AID

Costs (2020–21) ***Comprehensive fee:*** $48,780 includes full-time tuition ($32,800), mandatory fees ($1760), and room and board ($14,220). Part-time tuition: $615 per credit hour. ***College room only:*** $7800.

Financial Aid Of all full-time matriculated undergraduates who enrolled in 2019, 1,465 applied for aid, 1,291 were judged to have need, 339 had their need fully met. In 2019, 172 non-need-based awards were made. ***Average percent of need met:*** 81. ***Average financial aid package:*** $25,422. ***Average need-based loan:*** $8941. ***Average need-based gift aid:*** $19,101. ***Average non-need-based aid:*** $16,206. ***Average indebtedness upon graduation:*** $46,756.

APPLYING

Standardized Tests *Required:* SAT or ACT (for admission).

Options: electronic application, early admission, deferred entrance.

Application fee: $35.

Required: high school transcript. ***Required for some:*** essay or personal statement, minimum 2.5 GPA, 2 letters of recommendation. ***Recommended:*** interview.

Application deadlines: rolling (freshmen), rolling (transfers).

Notification: continuous (freshmen), continuous (transfers).

CONTACT

Mr. Glenn Bozinski, Director of Admissions, Misericordia University, 301 Lake Street, Dallas, PA 18612-1098. *Phone:* 570-675-6264. *Toll-free phone:* 866-262-6363. *Fax:* 570-674-6232. *E-mail:* admiss@misericordia.edu.

See below for display ad and page 1082 for the College Close-Up.

Moore College of Art & Design

Philadelphia, Pennsylvania

http://www.moore.edu/

CONTACT

Ms. Jasmine Zateeny, Assistant Director of Admissions, Recruitment Coordinator, Moore College of Art & Design, 20th and The Parkway, Philadelphia, PA 19103. *Phone:* 215-965-4015. *Toll-free phone:* 800-523-2025. *Fax:* 215-965-8544. *E-mail:* enroll@moore.edu.

Moravian College

Bethlehem, Pennsylvania

http://www.moravian.edu/

- **Independent** comprehensive, founded 1742, affiliated with Moravian Church
- **Suburban** 85-acre campus with easy access to Philadelphia
- **Endowment** $117.9 million
- **Coed** 2,073 undergraduate students, 92% full-time, 61% women, 39% men
- **Moderately difficult** entrance level, 75% of applicants were admitted

UNDERGRAD STUDENTS

1,916 full-time, 157 part-time. Students come from 21 states and territories; 18 other countries; 25% are from out of state; 3% Black or African American, non-Hispanic/Latino; 12% Hispanic/Latino; 2% Asian, non-Hispanic/Latino; 0.1% Native Hawaiian or other Pacific Islander, non-Hispanic/Latino; 0.3% American Indian or Alaska Native, non-Hispanic/Latino; 2% Two or more races, non-Hispanic/Latino; 5% Race/ethnicity unknown; 5% international; 5% transferred in; 52% live on campus.

Freshmen:

Admission: 2,127 applied, 1,599 admitted, 428 enrolled. ***Average high school GPA:*** 3.6. ***Test scores:*** SAT evidence-based reading and writing scores over 500: 89%; SAT math scores over 500: 86%; ACT scores over 18: 95%; SAT evidence-based reading and writing scores over 600: 34%; SAT math scores over 600: 27%; ACT scores over 24: 47%; SAT evidence-based reading and writing scores over 700: 3%; SAT math scores over 700: 2%; ACT scores over 30: 6%.

Retention: 82% of full-time freshmen returned.

FACULTY

Total: 339, 45% full-time, 57% with terminal degrees.

Student/faculty ratio: 11:1.

ACADEMICS

Calendar: semesters. *Degrees:* bachelor's, master's, doctoral, post-master's, and postbachelor's certificates.

Special study options: accelerated degree program, adult/continuing education programs, advanced placement credit, cooperative education, distance learning, double majors, honors programs, independent study, internships, off-campus study, part-time degree program, services for LD students, student-designed majors, study abroad, summer session for credit. ***ROTC:*** Army (c).

Unusual degree programs: 3-2 engineering with Lehigh University, Washington University in St. Louis.

Computers: 230 computers/terminals and 1,700 ports are available on campus for general student use. Students can access the following: campus intranet, computer help desk, free student e-mail accounts, online (class) grades, online (class) registration, online (class) schedules. Campuswide network is available. 100% of college-owned or -operated housing units are wired for high-speed Internet access. Wireless service is available via entire campus.

Library: Reeves Library. *Books:* 225,810 (physical), 288,179 (digital/electronic); *Serial titles:* 164 (physical), 5,827 (digital/electronic); *Databases:* 67. Weekly public service hours: 86.

STUDENT LIFE

Housing options: on-campus residence required through senior year; coed, men-only, women-only, special housing for students with disabilities. Campus housing is university owned. Freshman campus housing is guaranteed.

Activities and organizations: drama/theater group, student-run newspaper, radio station, choral group, marching band, Moravian Activities Council, Black Student Union, Habitat for Humanity, Commuter Student Union, American Association of University Women, national fraternities, national sororities.

Athletics Member NCAA. All Division III. ***Intercollegiate sports:*** baseball M, basketball M/W, cheerleading W(c), cross-country running M/W, equestrian sports W(c), field hockey W, football M, golf M, ice hockey M(c), lacrosse M/W, rugby M(c), soccer M/W, softball W, tennis M/W, track and field M/W, volleyball W. ***Intramural sports:*** basketball M/W, football M/W, soccer M/W, softball M/W, table tennis M/W, tennis M/W, volleyball M/W.

Campus security: 24-hour emergency response devices and patrols, late-night transport/escort service, controlled dormitory access.

Student services: health clinic, personal/psychological counseling, veterans affairs office.

COSTS & FINANCIAL AID

Costs (2020–21) ***One-time required fee:*** $500. ***Comprehensive fee:*** $61,838 includes full-time tuition ($45,321), mandatory fees ($2046), and room and board ($14,471). Full-time tuition and fees vary according to class time and program. Part-time tuition: $1259 per credit. Part-time tuition and fees vary according to class time. ***College room only:*** $8154. Room and board charges vary according to board plan and housing facility. ***Payment plan:*** installment. ***Waivers:*** employees or children of employees.

Financial Aid Of all full-time matriculated undergraduates who enrolled in 2019, 1,665 applied for aid, 1,527 were judged to have need, 249 had their need fully met. In 2019, 315 non-need-based awards were made. ***Average percent of need met:*** 73. ***Average financial aid package:*** $31,338. ***Average need-based loan:*** $4210. ***Average need-based gift aid:*** $27,678. ***Average non-need-based aid:*** $20,998. ***Average indebtedness upon graduation:*** $38,514.

APPLYING

Standardized Tests *Required:* SAT or ACT (for admission).

Options: electronic application, deferred entrance.

Required: essay or personal statement, high school transcript, 1 letter of recommendation. ***Required for some:*** portfolio for art majors; audition for music majors; 3.3 high school GPA, minimum SAT combined score of 1500 (with no section less than 500) or ACT score of 23 for nursing.

Application deadlines: 3/1 (freshmen), 5/1 (transfers).

Notification: continuous until 11/15 (freshmen).

CONTACT

Mr. Scott Dams, Vice President of Enrollment and Marketing, Moravian College, 1200 Main Street, Bethlehem, PA 18018. *Phone:* 610-861-1320. *Toll-free phone:* 800-441-3191. *Fax:* 610-625-7930. *E-mail:* admission@moravian.edu.

Mount Aloysius College

Cresson, Pennsylvania

http://www.mtaloy.edu/

- **Independent Roman Catholic** comprehensive, founded 1939
- **Small-town** 193-acre campus
- **Coed** 1,791 undergraduate students, 54% full-time, 67% women, 33% men
- **Minimally difficult** entrance level, 95% of applicants were admitted

UNDERGRAD STUDENTS

959 full-time, 832 part-time. 5% are from out of state; 3% Black or African American, non-Hispanic/Latino; 1% Hispanic/Latino; 0.8% Asian, non-Hispanic/Latino; 0.3% American Indian or Alaska Native, non-Hispanic/Latino; 9% Race/ethnicity unknown; 5% international; 67% live on campus.

Freshmen:

Admission: 1,407 applied, 1,335 admitted, 246 enrolled. ***Average high school GPA:*** 3.4.

FACULTY

Total: 154, 40% full-time.

Student/faculty ratio: 11:1.

ACADEMICS

Calendar: semesters. *Degrees:* certificates, associate, bachelor's, and master's.

Special study options: academic remediation for entering students, accelerated degree program, advanced placement credit, distance learning, double majors, honors programs, independent study, internships, part-time degree program, student-designed majors, study abroad, summer session for credit.

Computers: Students can access the following: campus intranet, computer help desk, free student e-mail accounts, online (class) grades, online (class) registration, online (class) schedules. Campuswide network is available. 100% of college-owned or -operated housing units are wired for high-speed Internet access. Wireless service is available via entire campus.

Library: Mount Aloysius College Library.

STUDENT LIFE

Housing options: on-campus residence required through sophomore year; coed. Campus housing is university owned. Freshman campus housing is guaranteed.

Activities and organizations: drama/theater group, student-run newspaper, choral group, Student Government, Campus Activity Board, Student Athletic Advisory Committee, Spirit Team, Dance Team.

Athletics Member NCAA. All Division III. ***Intercollegiate sports:*** baseball M, basketball M/W, cross-country running M/W, golf M/W, soccer M/W, softball W, tennis M/W, volleyball W. ***Intramural sports:*** basketball M/W, bowling M/W, cheerleading M(c)/W(c), football M/W, skiing (cross-country) M/W, skiing (downhill) M/W, table tennis M/W, ultimate Frisbee M/W, volleyball M/W, weight lifting M/W.

Campus security: 24-hour emergency response devices and patrols, student patrols, late-night transport/escort service, controlled dormitory access.

Student services: health clinic, personal/psychological counseling.

FINANCIAL AID

Financial Aid Of all full-time matriculated undergraduates who enrolled in 2018, 940 applied for aid, 881 were judged to have need. In 2018, 59 non-need-based awards were made. ***Average percent of need met:*** 37. ***Average financial aid package:*** $22,400. ***Average need-based loan:*** $3300. ***Average need-based gift aid:*** $4970. ***Average non-need-based aid:*** $7000.

APPLYING

Options: electronic application, early admission, deferred entrance.

Application fee: $30.

Required: high school transcript. ***Required for some:*** essay or personal statement, interview. ***Recommended:*** interview.

Application deadlines: rolling (freshmen), rolling (transfers).

Notification: continuous (freshmen), continuous (transfers).

CONTACT

Mr. Frank C. Crouse Jr., Vice President for Enrollment Management/Dean of Admissions, Mount Aloysius College, 7373 Admiral Peary Highway, Cresson, PA 16630-1999. *Phone:* 814-886-6383. *Toll-free phone:* 888-823-2220. *Fax:* 814-886-6441. *E-mail:* admissions@mtaloy.edu.

See below for display ad and page 1086 for the College Close-Up.

Muhlenberg College

Allentown, Pennsylvania

http://www.muhlenberg.edu/

- **Independent** 4-year, founded 1848, affiliated with Lutheran Church
- **Suburban** 75-acre campus with easy access to Philadelphia
- **Endowment** $246.9 million
- **Coed** 2,251 undergraduate students, 97% full-time, 61% women, 39% men
- **Very difficult** entrance level, 66% of applicants were admitted

UNDERGRAD STUDENTS

2,193 full-time, 58 part-time. 73% are from out of state; 4% Black or African American, non-Hispanic/Latino; 9% Hispanic/Latino; 3% Asian, non-Hispanic/Latino; 0.1% American Indian or Alaska Native, non-Hispanic/Latino; 2% Two or more races, non-Hispanic/Latino; 4% Race/ethnicity unknown; 3% international; 1% transferred in.

Freshmen:

Admission: 4,224 applied, 2,798 admitted, 538 enrolled. ***Average high school GPA:*** 3.4. ***Test scores:*** SAT evidence-based reading and writing scores over 500: 97%; SAT math scores over 500: 97%; ACT scores over 18: 100%; SAT evidence-based reading and writing scores over 600: 72%; SAT math scores over 600: 62%; ACT scores over 24: 93%; SAT evidence-based reading and writing scores over 700: 20%; SAT math scores over 700: 15%; ACT scores over 30: 45%.

Retention: 90% of full-time freshmen returned.

FACULTY

Total: 328, 60% full-time, 52% with terminal degrees.

Student/faculty ratio: 9:1.

ACADEMICS

Calendar: semesters. *Degrees:* certificates, associate, and bachelor's.

Special study options: accelerated degree program, adult/continuing education programs, advanced placement credit, double majors, honors programs, independent study, internships, off-campus study, part-time degree program, services for LD students, student-designed majors, study abroad, summer session for credit. ***ROTC:*** Army (c).

Unusual degree programs: 3-2 engineering with Columbia University; forestry with Duke University; dentistry with University of Pennsylvania, medicine with Drexel University, optometry with State University of New York (SUNY) State College of Optometry, occupational and physical therapy with Thomas Jefferson University.

Computers: 450 computers/terminals and 100 ports are available on campus for general student use. Students can access the following: campus intranet, computer help desk, free student e-mail accounts, online (class) grades, online (class) registration, online (class) schedules. Campuswide network is available. 100% of college-owned or -operated housing units are wired for high-speed Internet access. Wireless service is available via entire campus.

Library: Trexler Library. *Books:* 228,069 (physical), 515,579 (digital/electronic); *Serial titles:* 1,183 (physical), 40,276 (digital/electronic); *Databases:* 99. Weekly public service hours: 105; students can reserve study rooms.

STUDENT LIFE

Housing options: on-campus residence required through senior year; coed, women only, special housing for students with disabilities. Campus housing is university owned. Freshman campus housing is guaranteed.

Activities and organizations: drama/theater group, student-run newspaper, radio and television station, choral group, Theater Association, Environmental Action Team, Jefferson School Partnership, Select Choir, Habitat for Humanity, national fraternities, national sororities.

Athletics Member NCAA. All Division III. ***Intercollegiate sports:*** baseball M, basketball M/W, cheerleading M/W, cross-country running M/W, field hockey W, football M, golf M/W, lacrosse M/W, soccer M/W, softball W, tennis M/W, track and field M/W, volleyball W, wrestling M. ***Intramural sports:*** basketball M/W, cross-country running M/W, football M/W, racquetball M/W, rugby M/W, soccer M/W, softball M, swimming and diving M/W, tennis M/W, ultimate Frisbee M/W, volleyball M/W.

Campus security: 24-hour emergency response devices and patrols, late-night transport/escort service, controlled dormitory access.

Student services: health clinic, personal/psychological counseling.

COSTS & FINANCIAL AID

Costs (2019–20) ***One-time required fee:*** $160. ***Comprehensive fee:*** $66,765 includes full-time tuition ($53,865), mandatory fees ($735), and room and board ($12,165). Part-time tuition: $1585 per credit hour. Part-time tuition and fees vary according to program. ***Required fees:*** $368 per term part-time. ***College room only:*** $6615. Room and board charges vary according to board plan, housing facility, and location. ***Payment plan:*** installment. ***Waivers:*** employees or children of employees.

Financial Aid Of all full-time matriculated undergraduates who enrolled in 2018, 1,573 applied for aid, 1,380 were judged to have need, 266 had their need fully met. In 2018, 644 non-need-based awards were made. ***Average percent of need met:*** 81. ***Average financial aid package:*** $37,874. ***Average need-based loan:*** $4384. ***Average need-based gift aid:*** $34,325. ***Average non-need-based aid:*** $14,525. ***Average indebtedness upon graduation:*** $32,963. ***Financial aid deadline:*** 2/1.

APPLYING

Standardized Tests *Required for some:* SAT or ACT (for admission).

Options: electronic application, early admission, early decision, deferred entrance.

Application fee: $50.

Required: essay or personal statement, high school transcript, 2 letters of recommendation. ***Required for some:*** interview, graded paper. ***Recommended:*** interview.

Application deadlines: 2/1 (freshmen), 6/15 (transfers).

Early decision deadline: 11/15 (for plan 1), 2/1 (for plan 2).

Notification: 3/20 (freshmen), continuous until 7/1 (transfers), 12/15 (early decision plan 1), 2/15 (early decision plan 2).

CONTACT

Muhlenberg College, 2400 Chew Street, Allentown, PA 18104-5586.

Neumann University

Aston, Pennsylvania

http://www.neumann.edu/

- **Independent Roman Catholic** comprehensive, founded 1965
- **Suburban** 68-acre campus with easy access to Philadelphia
- **Endowment** $30.8 million
- **Coed**
- **Minimally difficult** entrance level

FACULTY

Student/faculty ratio: 14:1.

ACADEMICS

Calendar: semesters. *Degrees:* associate, bachelor's, master's, doctoral, post-master's, and postbachelor's certificates.
Library: Neumann University Library plus 1 other. *Books:* 51,000 (physical), 161,000 (digital/electronic); *Serial titles:* 20 (physical), 100,000 (digital/electronic); *Databases:* 45. Weekly public service hours: 80; students can reserve study rooms.

STUDENT LIFE

Housing options: coed, special housing for students with disabilities. Campus housing is university owned and leased by the school. Freshman applicants given priority for college housing.

Activities and organizations: drama/theater group, student-run newspaper, radio and television station, choral group, Student Nurses Association, Student Activities Board, Boogie Nights, Knights for Education, Neumann Media.

Athletics Member NCAA. All Division III.

Campus security: 24-hour emergency response devices and patrols, late-night transport/escort service, controlled dormitory access.

Student services: health clinic, personal/psychological counseling, veterans affairs office.

FINANCIAL AID

Financial Aid Of all full-time matriculated undergraduates who enrolled in 2018, 1,338 applied for aid, 1,220 were judged to have need, 115 had their need fully met. In 2018, 204 non-need-based awards were made. ***Average percent of need met:*** 68. ***Average financial aid package:*** $22,378. ***Average need-based loan:*** $4229. ***Average need-based gift aid:*** $8262. ***Average non-need-based aid:*** $12,319. ***Average indebtedness upon graduation:*** $45,011.

APPLYING

Standardized Tests *Required:* SAT or ACT (for admission).

Options: electronic application, deferred entrance.

Application fee: $35.

Required: high school transcript, minimum 2.5 GPA. ***Required for some:*** 1 letter of recommendation. ***Recommended:*** essay or personal statement, interview.

CONTACT

Mr. Edward P. Wright, Director of Undergraduate Admissions, Neumann University, One Neumann Drive, Aston, PA 19014-1298. *Phone:* 610-558-5616. *Toll-free phone:* 800-963-8626. *Fax:* 610-361-2548. *E-mail:* wrighte@neumann.edu.

Peirce College

Philadelphia, Pennsylvania

http://www.peirce.edu/

- **Independent** comprehensive, founded 1865
- **Urban** 1-acre campus
- **Coed, primarily women** 1,089 undergraduate students, 27% full-time, 70% women, 30% men
- **Noncompetitive** entrance level

UNDERGRAD STUDENTS

297 full-time, 792 part-time. 9% are from out of state; 56% Black or African American, non-Hispanic/Latino; 8% Hispanic/Latino; 3% Asian, non-Hispanic/Latino; 0.2% Native Hawaiian or other Pacific Islander, non-Hispanic/Latino; 0.3% American Indian or Alaska Native, non-Hispanic/Latino; 2% Two or more races, non-Hispanic/Latino; 10% Race/ethnicity unknown; 0.6% international.

Freshmen:
Admission: 50 enrolled.
Retention: 50% of full-time freshmen returned.

FACULTY

Total: 81, 33% full-time, 49% with terminal degrees.
Student/faculty ratio: 13:1.

ACADEMICS

Calendar: semesters. *Degrees:* certificates, associate, bachelor's, and master's.

Special study options: accelerated degree program, adult/continuing education programs, advanced placement credit, cooperative education, distance learning, internships, part-time degree program, services for LD students, summer session for credit.

Computers: Students can access the following: campus intranet, computer help desk, free student e-mail accounts, online (class) grades, online (class) registration, online (class) schedules. Campuswide network is available. Wireless service is available via entire campus.
Library: Peirce College Library.

STUDENT LIFE

Housing options: college housing not available.

Campus security: 24-hour emergency response devices and patrols, late-night transport/escort service, 24-hour security cameras.

APPLYING

Options: electronic application.

Required: high school transcript.

CONTACT

Mr. Paul Ballentine, Manager, Admissions, Peirce College, 1420 Pine Street, Philadelphia, PA 19102. *Phone:* 215-670-9214. *Toll-free phone:* 888-467-3472. *Fax:* 215-670-9366. *E-mail:* info@peirce.edu.

Penn State Abington

Abington, Pennsylvania

http://www.abington.psu.edu/

- **State-related** 4-year, founded 1950, part of Pennsylvania State University
- **Small-town** campus
- **Coed** 3,746 undergraduate students, 88% full-time, 49% women, 51% men
- **Very difficult** entrance level, 85% of applicants were admitted

UNDERGRAD STUDENTS

3,283 full-time, 463 part-time. Students come from 31 states and territories; 27 other countries; 9% are from out of state; 12% Black or African American, non-Hispanic/Latino; 11% Hispanic/Latino; 15% Asian, non-Hispanic/Latino; 0.1% Native Hawaiian or other Pacific Islander, non-Hispanic/Latino; 0.1% American Indian or Alaska Native, non-Hispanic/Latino; 3% Two or more races, non-Hispanic/Latino; 2% Race/ethnicity unknown; 14% international; 5% transferred in; 11% live on campus.

Freshmen:
Admission: 4,545 applied, 3,852 admitted, 1,050 enrolled. ***Average high school GPA:*** 3.2. ***Test scores:*** SAT evidence-based reading and writing scores over 500: 76%; SAT math scores over 500: 81%; ACT scores over 18: 94%; SAT evidence-based reading and writing scores over 600: 27%; SAT math scores over 600: 41%; ACT scores over 24: 55%; SAT evidence-based reading and writing scores over 700: 2%; SAT math scores over 700: 20%; ACT scores over 30: 4%.
Retention: 79% of full-time freshmen returned.

FACULTY

Total: 334, 44% full-time, 43% with terminal degrees.
Student/faculty ratio: 16:1.

ACADEMICS

Calendar: semesters. *Degrees:* certificates, associate, bachelor's, and postbachelor's certificates (enrollment figures include students enrolled at The Graduate School at Penn State who are taking courses at this location).

Special study options: adult/continuing education programs, cooperative education, double majors, external degree program, freshman honors college, honors programs, independent study, internships, part-time degree program, study abroad, summer session for credit. ***ROTC:*** Army (c), Air Force (c).

Computers: 83 computers/terminals are available on campus for general student use. Students can access the following: campus intranet, computer help desk, free student e-mail accounts, online (class) grades, online (class) registration, online (class) schedules. Campuswide network is available. 1% of college-owned or -operated housing units are wired for high-speed Internet access. Wireless service is available via entire campus.

Library: Penn State Abington Library. *Books:* 60,000 (physical); *Databases:* 400. Students can reserve study rooms.

STUDENT LIFE

Housing options: coed, special housing for students with disabilities. Campus housing is university owned.

Activities and organizations: drama/theater group, student-run newspaper, radio and television station, choral group.

Athletics Member NCAA. All Division III. ***Intercollegiate sports:*** baseball M, basketball M/W, golf M, soccer M/W, softball W, tennis M/W, volleyball W. ***Intramural sports:*** basketball M/W, cross-country running M/W, football M, soccer M/W, softball M, tennis M/W, volleyball M/W.

Campus security: 24-hour emergency response devices and patrols.

Student services: health clinic, personal/psychological counseling.

COSTS & FINANCIAL AID

Costs (2020–21) ***Tuition:*** area resident $14,532 full-time; state resident $14,532 full-time; nonresident $23,720 full-time. Full-time tuition and fees vary according to course level, degree level, location, program, and student level. Part-time tuition and fees vary according to course level, course load, degree level, location, program, and student level. ***Required fees:*** $992 full-time. ***Room only:*** $8420. ***Payment plans:*** installment, deferred payment. ***Waivers:*** senior citizens and employees or children of employees.

Financial Aid Of all full-time matriculated undergraduates who enrolled in 2018, 2,382 applied for aid, 2,060 were judged to have need, 258 had their need fully met. In 2018, 254 non-need-based awards were made. ***Average percent of need met:*** 57. ***Average financial aid package:*** $10,694. ***Average need-based loan:*** $3988. ***Average need-based gift aid:*** $6118. ***Average non-need-based aid:*** $3423. ***Average indebtedness upon graduation:*** $32,957.

APPLYING

Standardized Tests *Required:* SAT or ACT (for admission).

Options: electronic application, early admission, early action, deferred entrance.

Application fee: $65.

Required: high school transcript, Self-Reported Academic Record. ***Required for some:*** interview. ***Recommended:*** essay or personal statement.

Application deadlines: rolling (freshmen), rolling (transfers).

Notification: continuous (freshmen), continuous (transfers).

CONTACT

Admissions Office, Penn State Abington, 1600 Woodland Road, Abington, PA 19001. *Phone:* 215-881-7600. *Fax:* 215-881-7655. *E-mail:* abingtonadmissions@psu.edu.

Penn State Altoona

Altoona, Pennsylvania

http://www.altoona.psu.edu/

- **State-related** 4-year, founded 1939, part of Pennsylvania State University
- **Suburban** campus
- **Coed** 3,070 undergraduate students, 97% full-time, 45% women, 55% men
- **Very difficult** entrance level, 85% of applicants were admitted

UNDERGRAD STUDENTS

2,990 full-time, 80 part-time. 17% are from out of state; 5% Black or African American, non-Hispanic/Latino; 5% Hispanic/Latino; 3% Asian, non-Hispanic/Latino; 3% Two or more races, non-Hispanic/Latino; 0.9% Race/ethnicity unknown; 7% international; 4% transferred in; 31% live on campus.

Freshmen:
Admission: 6,802 applied, 5,796 admitted, 1,118 enrolled. ***Test scores:*** SAT evidence-based reading and writing scores over 500: 77%; SAT math scores over 500: 79%; ACT scores over 18: 93%; SAT evidence-based reading and writing scores over 600: 24%; SAT math scores over 600: 28%; ACT scores over 24: 48%; SAT evidence-based reading and writing scores over 700: 2%; SAT math scores over 700: 7%; ACT scores over 30: 7%.

Retention: 81% of full-time freshmen returned.

FACULTY

Total: 312, 65% full-time, 46% with terminal degrees.

Student/faculty ratio: 13:1.

ACADEMICS

Calendar: semesters. *Degrees:* certificates, associate, and bachelor's (enrollment figures include students enrolled at The Graduate School at Penn State who are taking courses at this location).

Special study options: accelerated degree program, cooperative education, distance learning, double majors, English as a second language, external degree program, honors programs, independent study, internships, student-designed majors, study abroad. ***ROTC:*** Army (c), Air Force (c).

Computers: Students can access the following: campus intranet, computer help desk, free student e-mail accounts, online (class) grades, online (class) registration, online (class) schedules.

Library: Robert E. Eiche Library.

STUDENT LIFE

Housing options: coed, cooperative, special housing for students with disabilities. Campus housing is university owned.

Activities and organizations: drama/theater group, student-run newspaper, choral group.

Athletics Member NCAA. All Division III. ***Intercollegiate sports:*** baseball M, basketball M/W, cross-country running M/W, golf M/W, soccer M/W, softball W, swimming and diving M/W, tennis M/W. ***Intramural sports:*** badminton M/W, baseball M/W, basketball M/W, football M/W, golf M/W, racquetball M/W, soccer M/W, softball M/W, table tennis M/W, tennis M/W, track and field M/W, volleyball M/W, weight lifting M/W.

Campus security: 24-hour emergency response devices and patrols, late-night transport/escort service.

COSTS & FINANCIAL AID

Costs (2020–21) ***Tuition:*** area resident $14,214 full-time, $592 per credit hour part-time; state resident $14,214 full-time, $592 per credit hour part-time; nonresident $23,924 full-time, $997 per credit hour part-time. ***Required fees:*** $992 full-time. ***Room and board:*** $11,884; room only: $6554.

Financial Aid Of all full-time matriculated undergraduates who enrolled in 2018, 2,468 applied for aid, 2,073 were judged to have need, 562 had their need fully met. In 2018, 249 non-need-based awards were made. ***Average percent of need met:*** 66. ***Average financial aid package:*** $10,597. ***Average need-based loan:*** $3960. ***Average need-based gift aid:*** $6132. ***Average non-need-based aid:*** $3652. ***Average indebtedness upon graduation:*** $43,294.

APPLYING

Standardized Tests *Required:* SAT or ACT (for admission).

Options: electronic application, early admission, early action, deferred entrance.

Application fee: $65.

Required: high school transcript. ***Required for some:*** interview. ***Recommended:*** essay or personal statement.

Application deadlines: rolling (freshmen), rolling (transfers), 11/1 (early action).

Notification: continuous (freshmen), continuous (transfers), 12/24 (early action).

CONTACT
Admissions Office, Penn State Altoona, 3000 Ivyside Park, Altoona, PA 16601. *Phone:* 814-949-5466. *Toll-free phone:* 800-848-9843. *Fax:* 814-949-5564. *E-mail:* aaadmit@psu.edu.

Penn State Beaver

Monaca, Pennsylvania

http://www.br.psu.edu/

- **State-related** 4-year, founded 1964, part of Pennsylvania State University
- **Small-town** campus
- **Coed** 599 undergraduate students, 90% full-time, 43% women, 57% men
- **Moderately difficult** entrance level, 65% of applicants were admitted

UNDERGRAD STUDENTS
537 full-time, 62 part-time. 19% are from out of state; 8% Black or African American, non-Hispanic/Latino; 8% Hispanic/Latino; 4% Asian, non-Hispanic/Latino; 0.2% Native Hawaiian or other Pacific Islander, non-Hispanic/Latino; 4% Two or more races, non-Hispanic/Latino; 0.5% Race/ethnicity unknown; 2% international; 5% transferred in; 27% live on campus.

Freshmen:
Admission: 1,991 applied, 1,303 admitted, 190 enrolled. ***Test scores:*** SAT evidence-based reading and writing scores over 500: 78%; SAT math scores over 500: 77%; ACT scores over 18: 92%; SAT evidence-based reading and writing scores over 600: 28%; SAT math scores over 600: 26%; ACT scores over 24: 36%; SAT evidence-based reading and writing scores over 700: 3%; SAT math scores over 700: 8%.

Retention: 71% of full-time freshmen returned.

FACULTY
Total: 88, 40% full-time, 27% with terminal degrees.

Student/faculty ratio: 11:1.

ACADEMICS
Calendar: semesters. *Degree:* certificates and bachelor's.

Special study options: adult/continuing education programs, distance learning, double majors, external degree program, honors programs, independent study, study abroad.

STUDENT LIFE
Housing options: coed, special housing for students with disabilities. Campus housing is university owned. Freshman campus housing is guaranteed.

Activities and organizations: student-run newspaper, radio station.

Athletics Member NJCAA. ***Intercollegiate sports:*** baseball M, basketball M, softball M/W, volleyball W. ***Intramural sports:*** basketball M/W, cheerleading M(c)/W(c), cross-country running M/W, football M, golf M/W, soccer M/W, softball M/W, table tennis M/W.

COSTS & FINANCIAL AID
Costs (2020–21) ***Tuition:*** area resident $12,718 full-time, $524 per credit hour part-time; state resident $12,718 full-time, $524 per credit hour part-time; nonresident $21,310 full-time, $888 per credit hour part-time. ***Required fees:*** $992 full-time. ***Room and board:*** $11,510; room only: $6180.

Financial Aid Of all full-time matriculated undergraduates who enrolled in 2018, 469 applied for aid, 406 were judged to have need, 98 had their need fully met. In 2018, 78 non-need-based awards were made. ***Average percent of need met:*** 66. ***Average financial aid package:*** $11,100. ***Average need-based loan:*** $4024. ***Average need-based gift aid:*** $6355. ***Average non-need-based aid:*** $2821. ***Average indebtedness upon graduation:*** $38,026.

APPLYING
Standardized Tests *Required:* SAT or ACT (for admission).

Options: electronic application, early admission, early action, deferred entrance.

Application fee: $65.

Required: high school transcript. ***Required for some:*** interview. ***Recommended:*** essay or personal statement.

Application deadlines: rolling (freshmen), rolling (transfers), 11/1 (early action).

Notification: continuous (freshmen), continuous (transfers), 12/24 (early action).

CONTACT
Admissions Office, Penn State Beaver, 100 University Drive, Monaca, PA 15061. *Phone:* 724-773-3800. *Fax:* 724-773-3658. *E-mail:* br-admissions@psu.edu.

Penn State Berks

Reading, Pennsylvania

http://www.bk.psu.edu/

- **State-related** 4-year, founded 1924, part of Pennsylvania State University
- **Suburban** campus
- **Coed** 2,481 undergraduate students, 88% full-time, 39% women, 61% men
- **Very difficult** entrance level

UNDERGRAD STUDENTS
2,187 full-time, 294 part-time. 8% are from out of state; 7% Black or African American, non-Hispanic/Latino; 14% Hispanic/Latino; 5% Asian, non-Hispanic/Latino; 0.2% American Indian or Alaska Native, non-Hispanic/Latino; 3% Two or more races, non-Hispanic/Latino; 1% Race/ethnicity unknown; 4% international; 6% transferred in; 29% live on campus.

Freshmen:
Admission: 640 enrolled. ***Test scores:*** SAT evidence-based reading and writing scores over 500: 79%; SAT math scores over 500: 78%; ACT scores over 18: 85%; SAT evidence-based reading and writing scores over 600: 25%; SAT math scores over 600: 31%; ACT scores over 24: 52%; SAT evidence-based reading and writing scores over 700: 2%; SAT math scores over 700: 6%; ACT scores over 30: 18%.

Retention: 82% of full-time freshmen returned.

FACULTY
Total: 244, 56% full-time, 48% with terminal degrees.

Student/faculty ratio: 13:1.

ACADEMICS
Calendar: semesters. *Degrees:* certificates, associate, and bachelor's (enrollment figures include students enrolled at The Graduate School at Penn State who are taking courses at this location).

Special study options: accelerated degree program, adult/continuing education programs, cooperative education, distance learning, English as a second language, external degree program, honors programs, independent study, internships, part-time degree program, study abroad. ***ROTC:*** Army (c), Air Force (c).

Computers: Students can access the following: campus intranet, computer help desk, free student e-mail accounts, online (class) grades, online (class) registration, online (class) schedules. Campuswide network is available.

Library: Thun Library.

STUDENT LIFE
Housing options: coed, cooperative, special housing for students with disabilities. Campus housing is university owned.

Activities and organizations: drama/theater group, student-run newspaper, choral group.

Athletics Member NJCAA. ***Intercollegiate sports:*** baseball M, basketball M/W, cheerleading M/W, cross-country running M/W, golf M, soccer M/W, softball W, tennis M/W, volleyball W. ***Intramural sports:*** badminton M/W, basketball M/W, football M/W, golf M/W, table tennis M/W, volleyball M/W.

Campus security: 24-hour emergency response devices and patrols, late-night transport/escort service, controlled dormitory access.

COSTS & FINANCIAL AID
Costs (2020–21) ***Tuition:*** area resident $14,214 full-time, $592 per credit hour part-time; state resident $14,214 full-time, $592 per credit hour part-time; nonresident $23,924 full-time, $997 per credit hour part-time. Full-time tuition and fees vary according to course level, degree level, location, program, and student level. Part-time tuition and fees vary according to course level, course load, degree level, location, program, and student level. ***Required fees:*** $992 full-time. ***Room and board:*** $13,080; room

only: $7750. Room and board charges vary according to board plan, housing facility, and location. ***Payment plans:*** installment, deferred payment. ***Waivers:*** senior citizens and employees or children of employees.

Financial Aid Of all full-time matriculated undergraduates who enrolled in 2018, 1,867 applied for aid, 1,522 were judged to have need, 343 had their need fully met. In 2018, 140 non-need-based awards were made. ***Average percent of need met:*** 63. ***Average financial aid package:*** $10,235. ***Average need-based loan:*** $4195. ***Average need-based gift aid:*** $5950. ***Average non-need-based aid:*** $3246. ***Average indebtedness upon graduation:*** $41,278.

APPLYING

Standardized Tests *Required:* SAT or ACT (for admission).

Options: electronic application, early admission, early action, deferred entrance.

Application fee: $65.

Required: high school transcript. ***Required for some:*** interview. ***Recommended:*** essay or personal statement.

Application deadlines: rolling (freshmen), rolling (transfers), 11/1 (early action).

Notification: continuous (freshmen), continuous (transfers), 12/24 (early action).

CONTACT

Admissions Office, Penn State Berks, Tulpehocken Road, PO Box 7009, Reading, PA 19610. *Phone:* 610-396-6060. *Fax:* 610-396-6077. *E-mail:* admissionsbk@psu.edu.

Penn State Brandywine

Media, Pennsylvania

http://www.brandywine.psu.edu/

- **State-related** 4-year, founded 1966, part of Pennsylvania State University
- **Small-town** campus
- **Coed** 1,332 undergraduate students, 91% full-time, 42% women, 58% men
- **Moderately difficult** entrance level, 81% of applicants were admitted

UNDERGRAD STUDENTS

1,211 full-time, 121 part-time. 12% are from out of state; 16% Black or African American, non-Hispanic/Latino; 8% Hispanic/Latino; 12% Asian, non-Hispanic/Latino; 0.1% Native Hawaiian or other Pacific Islander, non-Hispanic/Latino; 0.3% American Indian or Alaska Native, non-Hispanic/Latino; 4% Two or more races, non-Hispanic/Latino; 2% Race/ethnicity unknown; 2% international; 5% transferred in; 20% live on campus.

Freshmen:

Admission: 2,226 applied, 1,798 admitted, 439 enrolled. ***Test scores:*** SAT evidence-based reading and writing scores over 500: 66%; SAT math scores over 500: 73%; ACT scores over 18: 95%; SAT evidence-based reading and writing scores over 600: 23%; SAT math scores over 600: 27%; ACT scores over 24: 38%; SAT evidence-based reading and writing scores over 700: 2%; SAT math scores over 700: 7%; ACT scores over 30: 16%.

Retention: 77% of full-time freshmen returned.

FACULTY

Total: 165, 42% full-time, 38% with terminal degrees.

Student/faculty ratio: 12:1.

ACADEMICS

Calendar: semesters. *Degrees:* certificates, associate, and bachelor's.

Special study options: accelerated degree program, adult/continuing education programs, distance learning, double majors, English as a second language, external degree program, honors programs, independent study, internships, student-designed majors, study abroad. ***ROTC:*** Army (c), Air Force (c).

Computers: Students can access the following: online (class) registration. Campuswide network is available.

STUDENT LIFE

Housing options: coed.

Activities and organizations: student-run newspaper.

Athletics Member NJCAA. ***Intercollegiate sports:*** baseball M, basketball M/W, soccer M/W, tennis M/W, volleyball W. ***Intramural sports:*** basketball M/W, cheerleading M(c)/W(c), golf M/W, ice hockey M(c)/W(c), lacrosse M/W, soccer M/W, softball W(c), tennis M/W, volleyball M(c)/W.

Campus security: late-night transport/escort service, part-time trained security personnel.

COSTS & FINANCIAL AID

Costs (2020–21) ***Tuition:*** area resident $13,484 full-time, $555 per credit hour part-time; state resident $13,484 full-time, $555 per credit hour part-time; nonresident $22,474 full-time, $936 per credit hour part-time. Full-time tuition and fees vary according to course level, degree level, location, program, and student level. Part-time tuition and fees vary according to course level, course load, degree level, location, program, and student level. ***Required fees:*** $992 full-time. ***Room and board:*** $12,586; room only: $7256. Room and board charges vary according to board plan. ***Payment plans:*** installment, deferred payment. ***Waivers:*** senior citizens and employees or children of employees.

Financial Aid Of all full-time matriculated undergraduates who enrolled in 2018, 984 applied for aid, 810 were judged to have need, 172 had their need fully met. In 2018, 106 non-need-based awards were made. ***Average percent of need met:*** 61. ***Average financial aid package:*** $10,439. ***Average need-based loan:*** $3968. ***Average need-based gift aid:*** $6119. ***Average non-need-based aid:*** $4144. ***Average indebtedness upon graduation:*** $33,019.

APPLYING

Standardized Tests *Required:* SAT or ACT (for admission).

Options: electronic application, early admission, early action, deferred entrance.

Application fee: $65.

Required: high school transcript.

Application deadlines: rolling (freshmen), rolling (transfers), 11/1 (early action).

Notification: continuous (freshmen), continuous (transfers), 12/24 (early action).

CONTACT

Admissions Office, Penn State Brandywine, 25 Yearsley Mill Road, Media, PA 19063. *Phone:* 610-892-1200. *Fax:* 610-892-1320. *E-mail:* bwadmissions@psu.edu.

Penn State DuBois

DuBois, Pennsylvania

http://www.ds.psu.edu/

- **State-related** primarily 2-year, founded 1935, part of Pennsylvania State University
- **Small-town** campus
- **Coed** 563 undergraduate students, 78% full-time, 41% women, 59% men
- **Moderately difficult** entrance level, 72% of applicants were admitted

UNDERGRAD STUDENTS

441 full-time, 122 part-time. 5% are from out of state; 3% Black or African American, non-Hispanic/Latino; 2% Hispanic/Latino; 1% Asian, non-Hispanic/Latino; 0.2% Native Hawaiian or other Pacific Islander, non-Hispanic/Latino; 0.2% American Indian or Alaska Native, non-Hispanic/Latino; 1% Two or more races, non-Hispanic/Latino; 0.4% Race/ethnicity unknown; 6% transferred in.

Freshmen:

Admission: 561 applied, 403 admitted, 123 enrolled. ***Test scores:*** SAT evidence-based reading and writing scores over 500: 75%; SAT math scores over 500: 73%; ACT scores over 18: 80%; SAT evidence-based reading and writing scores over 600: 28%; SAT math scores over 600: 30%; SAT evidence-based reading and writing scores over 700: 1%; SAT math scores over 700: 4%.

Retention: 86% of full-time freshmen returned.

FACULTY

Total: 63, 63% full-time, 37% with terminal degrees.

Student/faculty ratio: 10:1.

ACADEMICS
Calendar: semesters. *Degrees:* certificates, associate, and bachelor's.

Special study options: adult/continuing education programs, distance learning, double majors, external degree program, honors programs, independent study, internships, student-designed majors, study abroad.

Computers: Students can access the following: online (class) registration. Campuswide network is available.

STUDENT LIFE
Housing options: college housing not available.

Athletics Member NJCAA. ***Intercollegiate sports:*** basketball M, cross-country running M/W, golf M/W, volleyball W. ***Intramural sports:*** basketball M/W, football M, soccer M/W, table tennis M/W, volleyball M/W.

COSTS & FINANCIAL AID
Costs (2020–21) ***Tuition:*** area resident $12,718 full-time, $524 per credit hour part-time; state resident $12,718 full-time, $524 per credit hour part-time; nonresident $21,310 full-time, $888 per credit hour part-time. Full-time tuition and fees vary according to course level, degree level, location, program, and student level. Part-time tuition and fees vary according to course level, course load, degree level, location, program, and student level. ***Required fees:*** $992 full-time. ***Payment plans:*** installment, deferred payment. ***Waivers:*** senior citizens and employees or children of employees.

Financial Aid Of all full-time matriculated undergraduates who enrolled in 2018, 411 applied for aid, 359 were judged to have need, 67 had their need fully met. In 2018, 32 non-need-based awards were made. ***Average percent of need met:*** 57. ***Average financial aid package:*** $10,140. ***Average need-based loan:*** $3846. ***Average need-based gift aid:*** $5423. ***Average non-need-based aid:*** $2724. ***Average indebtedness upon graduation:*** $33,943.

APPLYING
Standardized Tests *Required:* SAT or ACT (for admission).

Options: electronic application, early admission, early action, deferred entrance.

Application fee: $65.

Required: high school transcript. ***Required for some:*** interview. ***Recommended:*** essay or personal statement.

Application deadlines: rolling (freshmen), rolling (transfers), 11/1 (early action).

Notification: continuous (freshmen), continuous (transfers), 12/24 (early action).

CONTACT
Admissions Office, Penn State DuBois, 1 College Place, DuBois, PA 15801. *Phone:* 814-375-4720. *Toll-free phone:* 800-346-7627. *Fax:* 814-375-4784. *E-mail:* duboisinfo@psi.edu.

Penn State Erie, The Behrend College

Erie, Pennsylvania

http://www.psbehrend.psu.edu/

- **State-related** comprehensive, founded 1948, part of Pennsylvania State University
- **Suburban** 725-acre campus
- **Coed** 7,852 undergraduate students, 96% full-time, 34% women, 66% men
- **Very difficult** entrance level, 84% of applicants were admitted

UNDERGRAD STUDENTS
7,516 full-time, 336 part-time. 10% are from out of state; 3% Black or African American, non-Hispanic/Latino; 4% Hispanic/Latino; 3% Asian, non-Hispanic/Latino; 0.1% Native Hawaiian or other Pacific Islander, non-Hispanic/Latino; 0.1% American Indian or Alaska Native, non-Hispanic/Latino; 3% Two or more races, non-Hispanic/Latino; 1% Race/ethnicity unknown; 8% international; 1% transferred in; 39% live on campus.

Freshmen:
Admission: 4,765 applied, 3,997 admitted, 1,019 enrolled. ***Test scores:*** SAT evidence-based reading and writing scores over 500: 85%; SAT math scores over 500: 88%; ACT scores over 18: 91%; SAT evidence-based reading and writing scores over 600: 36%; SAT math scores over 600: 46%; ACT scores over 24: 50%; SAT evidence-based reading and writing scores over 700: 2%; SAT math scores over 700: 14%; ACT scores over 30: 6%.

Retention: 83% of full-time freshmen returned.

FACULTY
Total: 372, 76% full-time, 47% with terminal degrees.

Student/faculty ratio: 13:1.

ACADEMICS
Calendar: semesters. *Degrees:* certificates, associate, bachelor's, master's, and postbachelor's certificates.

Special study options: accelerated degree program, adult/continuing education programs, cooperative education, distance learning, double majors, external degree program, honors programs, independent study, internships, part-time degree program, study abroad. ***ROTC:*** Army (c).

Computers: Students can access the following: campus intranet, computer help desk, free student e-mail accounts, online (class) grades, online (class) registration, online (class) schedules. Campuswide network is available.

Library: John M. Lilley Library.

STUDENT LIFE
Housing options: coed, men-only, women-only, special housing for students with disabilities. Campus housing is university owned.

Activities and organizations: drama/theater group, student-run newspaper, radio station, choral group.

Athletics Member NCAA. All Division III. ***Intercollegiate sports:*** baseball M, basketball M/W, cheerleading M/W, cross-country running M/W, golf M/W, ice hockey M(c), lacrosse M(c), skiing (downhill) M(c)/W(c), soccer M/W, softball W, swimming and diving M/W, tennis M/W, track and field M/W, volleyball M(c)/W, water polo M/W. ***Intramural sports:*** badminton M/W, basketball M/W, bowling M/W, cross-country running M/W, football M/W, golf M/W, skiing (downhill) M/W, soccer M/W, softball M/W, swimming and diving M/W, table tennis M/W, tennis M/W, volleyball M/W.

Campus security: 24-hour emergency response devices and patrols, student patrols, late-night transport/escort service, controlled dormitory access.

COSTS & FINANCIAL AID
Costs (2020–21) ***Tuition:*** area resident $14,214 full-time, $592 per credit hour part-time; state resident $14,214 full-time, $592 per credit hour part-time; nonresident $23,924 full-time, $997 per credit hour part-time. ***Required fees:*** $992 full-time. ***Room and board:*** $11,884; room only: $6554.

Financial Aid Of all full-time matriculated undergraduates who enrolled in 2018, 3,096 applied for aid, 2,658 were judged to have need, 707 had their need fully met. In 2018, 239 non-need-based awards were made. ***Average percent of need met:*** 66. ***Average financial aid package:*** $10,866. ***Average need-based loan:*** $4346. ***Average need-based gift aid:*** $6274. ***Average non-need-based aid:*** $4174. ***Average indebtedness upon graduation:*** $41,841.

APPLYING
Standardized Tests *Required:* SAT or ACT (for admission).

Options: electronic application, early admission, early action, deferred entrance.

Application fee: $65.

Required: high school transcript. ***Required for some:*** interview. ***Recommended:*** essay or personal statement.

Application deadlines: rolling (freshmen), rolling (transfers), 11/1 (early action).

Notification: continuous (freshmen), continuous (transfers), 12/24 (early action).

CONTACT
Admissions Office, Penn State Erie, The Behrend College, 4701 College Drive, Erie, PA 16563. *Phone:* 814-898-6100. *Toll-free phone:* 866-374-3378. *Fax:* 814-898-6044. *E-mail:* behrend.admissions@psu.edu.

Penn State Fayette, The Eberly Campus

Lemont Furnace, Pennsylvania

http://www.fe.psu.edu/

- **State-related** primarily 2-year, founded 1934, part of Pennsylvania State University
- **Small-town** campus
- **Coed** 589 undergraduate students, 89% full-time, 55% women, 45% men
- **Moderately difficult** entrance level, 63% of applicants were admitted

UNDERGRAD STUDENTS

525 full-time, 64 part-time. 5% are from out of state; 3% Black or African American, non-Hispanic/Latino; 3% Hispanic/Latino; 0.9% Asian, non-Hispanic/Latino; 1% Native Hawaiian or other Pacific Islander, non-Hispanic/Latino; 0.5% American Indian or Alaska Native, non-Hispanic/Latino; 3% Two or more races, non-Hispanic/Latino; 0.9% Race/ethnicity unknown; 0.3% international; 6% transferred in.

Freshmen:

Admission: 638 applied, 401 admitted, 165 enrolled. ***Test scores:*** SAT evidence-based reading and writing scores over 500: 73%; SAT math scores over 500: 70%; ACT scores over 18: 80%; SAT evidence-based reading and writing scores over 600: 19%; SAT math scores over 600: 21%; ACT scores over 24: 20%; SAT evidence-based reading and writing scores over 700: 3%; SAT math scores over 700: 1%; ACT scores over 30: 10%.

Retention: 76% of full-time freshmen returned.

FACULTY

Total: 75, 53% full-time, 29% with terminal degrees.

Student/faculty ratio: 11:1.

ACADEMICS

Calendar: semesters. *Degrees:* certificates, associate, and bachelor's.

Special study options: accelerated degree program, adult/continuing education programs, distance learning, double majors, external degree program, honors programs, independent study, internships, study abroad.

Computers: Students can access the following: online (class) registration. Campuswide network is available.

STUDENT LIFE

Housing options: college housing not available.

Activities and organizations: drama/theater group.

Athletics Member NJCAA. ***Intercollegiate sports:*** baseball M, basketball M, softball W, volleyball W. ***Intramural sports:*** badminton M/W, basketball M/W, cheerleading M(c)/W(c), equestrian sports M(c)/W(c), football M/W, golf M(c)/W(c), softball M/W, tennis M/W, volleyball M/W, weight lifting M/W.

Campus security: student patrols, 8-hour patrols by trained security personnel.

COSTS & FINANCIAL AID

Costs (2020–21) ***Tuition:*** area resident $12,718 full-time, $524 per credit hour part-time; state resident $12,718 full-time, $524 per credit hour part-time; nonresident $21,310 full-time, $888 per credit hour part-time. Full-time tuition and fees vary according to course level, degree level, location, program, and student level. Part-time tuition and fees vary according to course level, course load, degree level, location, program, and student level. ***Required fees:*** $992 full-time. ***Payment plans:*** installment, deferred payment. ***Waivers:*** senior citizens and employees or children of employees.

Financial Aid Of all full-time matriculated undergraduates who enrolled in 2018, 527 applied for aid, 456 were judged to have need, 76 had their need fully met. In 2018, 55 non-need-based awards were made. ***Average percent of need met:*** 61. ***Average financial aid package:*** $11,145. ***Average need-based loan:*** $3975. ***Average need-based gift aid:*** $6060. ***Average non-need-based aid:*** $2567. ***Average indebtedness upon graduation:*** $36,499.

APPLYING

Standardized Tests *Required:* SAT or ACT (for admission).

Options: electronic application, early admission, early action, deferred entrance.

Application fee: $65.

Required: high school transcript. ***Required for some:*** interview. ***Recommended:*** essay or personal statement.

Application deadlines: rolling (freshmen), rolling (transfers), 11/1 (early action).

Notification: continuous (freshmen), continuous (transfers), 12/24 (early action).

CONTACT

Admissions Office, Penn State Fayette, The Eberly Campus, 2201 University Drive, Lemont Furnace, PA 15456. *Phone:* 724-430-4130. *Toll-free phone:* 877-568-4130. *Fax:* 724-430-4175. *E-mail:* feadm@psu.edu.

Penn State Greater Allegheny

McKeesport, Pennsylvania

http://www.ga.psu.edu/

- **State-related** comprehensive, founded 1947, part of Pennsylvania State University
- **Small-town** campus
- **Coed** 439 undergraduate students, 91% full-time, 41% women, 59% men
- **Moderately difficult** entrance level, 77% of applicants were admitted

UNDERGRAD STUDENTS

401 full-time, 38 part-time. 10% are from out of state; 19% Black or African American, non-Hispanic/Latino; 7% Hispanic/Latino; 7% Asian, non-Hispanic/Latino; 0.2% American Indian or Alaska Native, non-Hispanic/Latino; 5% Two or more races, non-Hispanic/Latino; 0.9% Race/ethnicity unknown; 2% international; 7% transferred in; 26% live on campus.

Freshmen:

Admission: 486 applied, 372 admitted, 103 enrolled. ***Test scores:*** SAT evidence-based reading and writing scores over 500: 71%; SAT math scores over 500: 66%; ACT scores over 18: 60%; SAT evidence-based reading and writing scores over 600: 23%; SAT math scores over 600: 18%; ACT scores over 24: 40%; SAT evidence-based reading and writing scores over 700: 8%; SAT math scores over 700: 5%.

Retention: 69% of full-time freshmen returned.

FACULTY

Total: 81, 47% full-time, 35% with terminal degrees.

Student/faculty ratio: 8:1.

ACADEMICS

Calendar: semesters. *Degrees:* certificates, associate, and bachelor's.

Special study options: accelerated degree program, adult/continuing education programs, distance learning, double majors, external degree program, honors programs, independent study, internships, student-designed majors, study abroad. ***ROTC:*** Air Force (c).

Computers: Students can access the following: online (class) registration. Campuswide network is available.

STUDENT LIFE

Housing options: coed, special housing for students with disabilities. Campus housing is university owned. Freshman campus housing is guaranteed.

Activities and organizations: student-run newspaper, radio station.

Athletics Member NJCAA. ***Intercollegiate sports:*** baseball M, basketball M, softball W, volleyball W. ***Intramural sports:*** basketball M/W, cheerleading M(c)/W(c), football M/W, ice hockey M(c), racquetball M/W, skiing (cross-country) M(c)/W(c), skiing (downhill) M(c)/W(c), soccer M(c)/W(c), softball M/W, tennis M/W, volleyball M/W.

Campus security: 24-hour patrols, controlled dormitory access.

COSTS & FINANCIAL AID

Costs (2020–21) ***Tuition:*** area resident $12,718 full-time, $524 per credit hour part-time; state resident $12,718 full-time, $524 per credit hour part-time; nonresident $21,310 full-time, $888 per credit hour part-time. Full-time tuition and fees vary according to course level, degree level, location, program, and student level. Part-time tuition and fees vary according to course level, course load, degree level, location, program, and student level. ***Required fees:*** $992 full-time. ***Room and board:*** $11,510; room only: $6180. Room and board charges vary according to board plan, housing facility, and location. ***Payment plans:*** installment, deferred payment. ***Waivers:*** senior citizens and employees or children of employees.

Financial Aid Of all full-time matriculated undergraduates who enrolled in 2018, 367 applied for aid, 325 were judged to have need, 67 had their need fully met. In 2018, 35 non-need-based awards were made. ***Average percent of need met:*** 67. ***Average financial aid package:*** $12,783. ***Average need-based loan:*** $4008. ***Average need-based gift aid:*** $7104. ***Average non-need-based aid:*** $3099. ***Average indebtedness upon graduation:*** $36,645.

APPLYING
Standardized Tests *Required:* SAT or ACT (for admission).

Options: electronic application, early admission, early action, deferred entrance.

Application fee: $65.

Required: high school transcript.

Application deadlines: rolling (freshmen), rolling (transfers), 11/1 (early action).

Notification: continuous (freshmen), continuous (transfers), 12/24 (early action).

CONTACT
Admissions Office, Penn State Greater Allegheny, 4000 University Drive, McKeesport, PA 15132. *Phone:* 412-675-9010. *Fax:* 412-675-9046. *E-mail:* psuga@psu.edu.

Penn State Harrisburg

Middletown, Pennsylvania

http://www.harrisburg.psu.edu/

- **State-related** comprehensive, founded 1966, part of Pennsylvania State University
- **Small-town** campus
- **Coed** 4,246 undergraduate students, 92% full-time, 39% women, 61% men
- **Very difficult** entrance level, 84% of applicants were admitted

UNDERGRAD STUDENTS
3,914 full-time, 332 part-time. 18% are from out of state; 10% Black or African American, non-Hispanic/Latino; 7% Hispanic/Latino; 12% Asian, non-Hispanic/Latino; 0.1% Native Hawaiian or other Pacific Islander, non-Hispanic/Latino; 0.2% American Indian or Alaska Native, non-Hispanic/Latino; 3% Two or more races, non-Hispanic/Latino; 1% Race/ethnicity unknown; 13% international; 8% transferred in; 16% live on campus.

Freshmen:
Admission: 7,803 applied, 6,529 admitted, 956 enrolled. ***Test scores:*** SAT evidence-based reading and writing scores over 500: 82%; SAT math scores over 500: 82%; ACT scores over 18: 84%; SAT evidence-based reading and writing scores over 600: 35%; SAT math scores over 600: 43%; ACT scores over 24: 66%; SAT evidence-based reading and writing scores over 700: 3%; SAT math scores over 700: 14%; ACT scores over 30: 10%.

Retention: 87% of full-time freshmen returned.

FACULTY
Total: 487, 50% full-time, 48% with terminal degrees.

Student/faculty ratio: 14:1.

ACADEMICS
Calendar: semesters. *Degrees:* certificates, associate, bachelor's, master's, doctoral, and postbachelor's certificates.

Special study options: accelerated degree program, adult/continuing education programs, cooperative education, distance learning, double majors, English as a second language, honors programs, independent study, part-time degree program, student-designed majors, study abroad. ***ROTC:*** Army (c).

Computers: Students can access the following: campus intranet, computer help desk, free student e-mail accounts, online (class) grades, online (class) registration, online (class) schedules. Campuswide network is available.

Library: Penn State Harrisburg Library.

STUDENT LIFE
Housing options: special housing for students with disabilities. Campus housing is university owned.

Activities and organizations: drama/theater group, student-run newspaper, radio station, choral group.

Athletics ***Intercollegiate sports:*** baseball M, basketball M/W, cross-country running M/W, golf M/W, soccer M/W, softball W, tennis M/W, volleyball W. ***Intramural sports:*** badminton M/W, basketball M/W, racquetball M/W, tennis M/W.

Campus security: 24-hour emergency response devices and patrols, student patrols, late-night transport/escort service, controlled dormitory access.

COSTS & FINANCIAL AID
Costs (2020–21) ***Tuition:*** area resident $14,214 full-time, $592 per credit hour part-time; state resident $14,214 full-time, $592 per credit hour part-time; nonresident $23,924 full-time, $997 per credit hour part-time. Full-time tuition and fees vary according to course level, degree level, location, program, and student level. Part-time tuition and fees vary according to course level, course load, degree level, location, program, and student level. ***Required fees:*** $992 full-time. ***Room and board:*** $13,750; room only: $8420. Room and board charges vary according to board plan, housing facility, and location. ***Payment plans:*** installment, deferred payment. ***Waivers:*** senior citizens and employees or children of employees.

Financial Aid Of all full-time matriculated undergraduates who enrolled in 2018, 2,765 applied for aid, 2,391 were judged to have need, 477 had their need fully met. In 2018, 345 non-need-based awards were made. ***Average percent of need met:*** 59. ***Average financial aid package:*** $10,491. ***Average need-based loan:*** $4292. ***Average need-based gift aid:*** $5901. ***Average non-need-based aid:*** $2911. ***Average indebtedness upon graduation:*** $39,036.

APPLYING
Standardized Tests *Required:* SAT or ACT (for admission).

Options: electronic application, early admission, early action, deferred entrance.

Application fee: $65.

Required: high school transcript. ***Required for some:*** interview. ***Recommended:*** essay or personal statement.

Application deadlines: rolling (freshmen), rolling (transfers).

Notification: continuous (freshmen), continuous (transfers).

CONTACT
Admissions Office, Penn State Harrisburg, 777 West Harrisburg Pike, Middletown, PA 17057. *Phone:* 717-948-6250. *Toll-free phone:* 800-222-2056. *Fax:* 717-948-6325. *E-mail:* hbgadmit@psu.edu.

Penn State Hazleton

Hazleton, Pennsylvania

http://www.hn.psu.edu/

- **State-related** 4-year, founded 1934, part of Pennsylvania State University
- **Small-town** campus
- **Coed** 619 undergraduate students, 88% full-time, 51% women, 49% men
- **Moderately difficult** entrance level, 77% of applicants were admitted

UNDERGRAD STUDENTS
544 full-time, 75 part-time. 12% are from out of state; 7% Black or African American, non-Hispanic/Latino; 21% Hispanic/Latino; 3% Asian, non-Hispanic/Latino; 0.2% American Indian or Alaska Native, non-Hispanic/Latino; 3% Two or more races, non-Hispanic/Latino; 0.9% Race/ethnicity unknown; 2% international; 8% transferred in; 30% live on campus.

Freshmen:
Admission: 585 applied, 452 admitted, 160 enrolled. ***Test scores:*** SAT evidence-based reading and writing scores over 500: 68%; SAT math scores over 500: 67%; ACT scores over 18: 78%; SAT evidence-based reading and writing scores over 600: 11%; SAT math scores over 600: 19%; ACT scores over 24: 33%; SAT evidence-based reading and writing scores over 700: 2%; SAT math scores over 700: 2%.

Retention: 76% of full-time freshmen returned.

FACULTY
Total: 75, 61% full-time, 43% with terminal degrees.

Student/faculty ratio: 10:1.

ACADEMICS
Calendar: semesters. *Degrees:* certificates, associate, and bachelor's.

Special study options: accelerated degree program, adult/continuing education programs, distance learning, double majors, English as a second language, external degree program, honors programs, independent study, internships, student-designed majors, study abroad. ***ROTC:*** Air Force (c).

Computers: Students can access the following: online (class) registration. Campuswide network is available.

STUDENT LIFE
Housing options: coed. Campus housing is university owned. Freshman campus housing is guaranteed.

Activities and organizations: drama/theater group, student-run newspaper, choral group.

Athletics Member NJCAA. ***Intercollegiate sports:*** baseball M, basketball M/W, cheerleading M/W, soccer M, softball W(s), tennis M/W, volleyball M/W. ***Intramural sports:*** basketball M/W, skiing (downhill) M(c)/W(c), soccer M/W, volleyball M/W.

Campus security: 24-hour patrols, late-night transport/escort service, controlled dormitory access.

COSTS & FINANCIAL AID
Costs (2020–21) ***Tuition:*** area resident $13,484 full-time, $555 per credit hour part-time; state resident $13,484 full-time, $555 per credit hour part-time; nonresident $22,474 full-time, $936 per credit hour part-time. Full-time tuition and fees vary according to course level, degree level, location, program, and student level. Part-time tuition and fees vary according to course level, course load, degree level, location, program, and student level. ***Required fees:*** $992 full-time. ***Room and board:*** $11,510; room only: $6180. Room and board charges vary according to board plan, housing facility, and location. ***Payment plans:*** installment, deferred payment. ***Waivers:*** senior citizens and employees or children of employees.

Financial Aid Of all full-time matriculated undergraduates who enrolled in 2018, 542 applied for aid, 489 were judged to have need, 120 had their need fully met. In 2018, 60 non-need-based awards were made. ***Average percent of need met:*** 67. ***Average financial aid package:*** $11,656. ***Average need-based loan:*** $3959. ***Average need-based gift aid:*** $6803. ***Average non-need-based aid:*** $3612. ***Average indebtedness upon graduation:*** $38,737.

APPLYING
Standardized Tests *Required:* SAT or ACT (for admission).

Options: electronic application, early admission, early action, deferred entrance.

Application fee: $65.

Required: high school transcript. ***Required for some:*** interview. ***Recommended:*** essay or personal statement.

Application deadlines: rolling (freshmen), rolling (transfers), 11/1 (early action).

Notification: continuous (freshmen), continuous (transfers), 12/24 (early action).

CONTACT
Admissions Office, Penn State Hazleton, 76 University Drive, Hazleton, PA 18202. *Phone:* 570-450-3142. *Toll-free phone:* 800-279-8495. *Fax:* 570-450-3182. *E-mail:* admissions-hn@psu.edu.

Penn State Lehigh Valley
Center Valley, Pennsylvania
http://www.lv.psu.edu/

- **State-related** 4-year, founded 1912, part of Pennsylvania State University
- **Rural** campus
- **Coed** 954 undergraduate students, 84% full-time, 43% women, 57% men
- **Moderately difficult** entrance level, 83% of applicants were admitted

UNDERGRAD STUDENTS
804 full-time, 150 part-time. 5% are from out of state; 6% Black or African American, non-Hispanic/Latino; 18% Hispanic/Latino; 11% Asian, non-Hispanic/Latino; 0.1% American Indian or Alaska Native, non-Hispanic/Latino; 3% Two or more races, non-Hispanic/Latino; 3% Race/ethnicity unknown; 3% international; 9% transferred in.

Freshmen:
Admission: 1,647 applied, 1,367 admitted, 267 enrolled. ***Test scores:*** SAT evidence-based reading and writing scores over 500: 73%; SAT math scores over 500: 75%; ACT scores over 18: 91%; SAT evidence-based reading and writing scores over 600: 31%; SAT math scores over 600: 33%; ACT scores over 24: 64%; SAT evidence-based reading and writing scores over 700: 3%; SAT math scores over 700: 8%; ACT scores over 30: 9%.

Retention: 85% of full-time freshmen returned.

FACULTY
Total: 120, 34% full-time, 26% with terminal degrees.

Student/faculty ratio: 13:1.

ACADEMICS
Calendar: semesters. *Degrees:* certificates, associate, and bachelor's (enrollment figures include students enrolled at The Graduate School at Penn State who are taking courses at this location).

Special study options: adult/continuing education programs, cooperative education, distance learning, double majors, external degree program, honors programs, independent study, internships, part-time degree program, study abroad. ***ROTC:*** Army (c).

Computers: Students can access the following: online (class) registration. Campuswide network is available.

STUDENT LIFE
Housing options: college housing not available.

Activities and organizations: drama/theater group, student-run newspaper, choral group.

Athletics ***Intercollegiate sports:*** baseball M, basketball M/W, bowling M(c)/W(c), cheerleading M/W, cross-country running M/W, football M(c), golf M(c)/W(c), ice hockey M(c)/W(c), skiing (downhill) M(c)/W(c), soccer M(c)/W, tennis M/W, volleyball M(c)/W. ***Intramural sports:*** badminton M/W, basketball M/W, football M/W, golf M/W, soccer M/W, volleyball M/W.

COSTS & FINANCIAL AID
Costs (2020–21) ***Tuition:*** area resident $13,484 full-time, $555 per credit hour part-time; state resident $13,484 full-time, $555 per credit hour part-time; nonresident $22,474 full-time, $936 per credit hour part-time. ***Required fees:*** $992 full-time.

Financial Aid Of all full-time matriculated undergraduates who enrolled in 2018, 618 applied for aid, 533 were judged to have need, 77 had their need fully met. In 2018, 56 non-need-based awards were made. ***Average percent of need met:*** 57. ***Average financial aid package:*** $10,335. ***Average need-based loan:*** $4065. ***Average need-based gift aid:*** $6152. ***Average non-need-based aid:*** $2986. ***Average indebtedness upon graduation:*** $35,834.

APPLYING
Standardized Tests *Required:* SAT or ACT (for admission).

Options: electronic application, early admission, early action, deferred entrance.

Application fee: $65.

Required: high school transcript.

CONTACT
Admissions Office, Penn State Lehigh Valley, 2809 Saucon Valley Road, Center Valley, PA 18034. *Phone:* 610-285-5000. *Fax:* 610-285-5220. *E-mail:* admissions-lv@psu.edu.

Penn State Mont Alto

Mont Alto, Pennsylvania

http://www.ma.psu.edu/

- **State-related** primarily 2-year, founded 1929, part of Pennsylvania State University
- **Small-town** campus
- **Coed** 730 undergraduate students, 80% full-time, 58% women, 42% men
- **Moderately difficult** entrance level, 77% of applicants were admitted

UNDERGRAD STUDENTS
587 full-time, 143 part-time. 15% are from out of state; 5% Black or African American, non-Hispanic/Latino; 7% Hispanic/Latino; 2% Asian, non-Hispanic/Latino; 5% Two or more races, non-Hispanic/Latino; 0.9% Race/ethnicity unknown; 0.4% international; 5% transferred in; 22% live on campus.

Freshmen:
Admission: 712 applied, 550 admitted, 188 enrolled. ***Test scores:*** SAT evidence-based reading and writing scores over 500: 74%; SAT math scores over 500: 76%; ACT scores over 18: 57%; SAT evidence-based reading and writing scores over 600: 20%; SAT math scores over 600: 20%; ACT scores over 24: 29%; SAT math scores over 700: 4%.

Retention: 84% of full-time freshmen returned.

FACULTY
Total: 114, 50% full-time, 25% with terminal degrees.

Student/faculty ratio: 8:1.

ACADEMICS
Calendar: semesters. *Degrees:* certificates, associate, and bachelor's.

Special study options: adult/continuing education programs, distance learning, double majors, external degree program, honors programs, independent study, internships, study abroad. ***ROTC:*** Army (c).

Computers: Students can access the following: online (class) registration. Campuswide network is available.

STUDENT LIFE
Housing options: coed, special housing for students with disabilities. Campus housing is university owned. Freshman campus housing is guaranteed.

Activities and organizations: drama/theater group, student-run newspaper, choral group.

Athletics Member NJCAA. ***Intercollegiate sports:*** basketball M/W, cheerleading M/W, cross-country running M/W, golf M/W, soccer M/W, softball W, tennis M/W, volleyball W. ***Intramural sports:*** badminton M/W, basketball M/W, cheerleading M(c)/W(c), racquetball M/W, soccer M/W, softball W, volleyball M/W.

Campus security: 24-hour patrols, controlled dormitory access.

COSTS & FINANCIAL AID
Costs (2020–21) ***Tuition:*** area resident $12,718 full-time, $524 per credit hour part-time; state resident $12,718 full-time, $524 per credit hour part-time; nonresident $21,310 full-time, $888 per credit hour part-time. Full-time tuition and fees vary according to course level, degree level, location, program, and student level. Part-time tuition and fees vary according to course level, course load, degree level, location, program, and student level. ***Required fees:*** $992 full-time. ***Room and board:*** $11,510; room only: $6180. Room and board charges vary according to board plan, housing facility, and location. ***Payment plans:*** installment, deferred payment. ***Waivers:*** senior citizens and employees or children of employees.

Financial Aid Of all full-time matriculated undergraduates who enrolled in 2018, 529 applied for aid, 456 were judged to have need, 116 had their need fully met. In 2018, 43 non-need-based awards were made. ***Average percent of need met:*** 62. ***Average financial aid package:*** $10,768. ***Average need-based loan:*** $3798. ***Average need-based gift aid:*** $5354. ***Average non-need-based aid:*** $3860. ***Average indebtedness upon graduation:*** $42,611.

APPLYING
Standardized Tests *Required:* SAT or ACT (for admission).

Options: electronic application, early admission, early action, deferred entrance.

Application fee: $65.

Required: high school transcript. ***Required for some:*** interview. ***Recommended:*** essay or personal statement.

Application deadlines: rolling (freshmen), rolling (transfers), 11/1 (early action).

Notification: continuous (freshmen), continuous (transfers), 12/24 (early action).

CONTACT
Admissions Office, Penn State Mont Alto, 1 Campus Drive, Mont Alto, PA 17237. *Phone:* 717-749-6130. *Toll-free phone:* 800-392-6173. *Fax:* 717-749-6132. *E-mail:* psuma@psu.edu.

Penn State New Kensington

New Kensington, Pennsylvania

http://www.nk.psu.edu/

- **State-related** 4-year, founded 1958, part of Pennsylvania State University
- **Small-town** campus
- **Coed** 545 undergraduate students, 86% full-time, 40% women, 60% men
- **Moderately difficult** entrance level, 75% of applicants were admitted

UNDERGRAD STUDENTS
470 full-time, 75 part-time. 4% are from out of state; 4% Black or African American, non-Hispanic/Latino; 1% Hispanic/Latino; 2% Asian, non-Hispanic/Latino; 0.8% American Indian or Alaska Native, non-Hispanic/Latino; 5% Two or more races, non-Hispanic/Latino; 0.9% Race/ethnicity unknown; 0.8% international; 9% transferred in.

Freshmen:
Admission: 542 applied, 407 admitted, 136 enrolled. ***Test scores:*** SAT evidence-based reading and writing scores over 500: 68%; SAT math scores over 500: 73%; ACT scores over 18: 89%; SAT evidence-based reading and writing scores over 600: 16%; SAT math scores over 600: 29%; ACT scores over 24: 44%; SAT evidence-based reading and writing scores over 700: 4%; SAT math scores over 700: 3%; ACT scores over 30: 11%.

Retention: 71% of full-time freshmen returned.

FACULTY
Total: 91, 43% full-time, 34% with terminal degrees.

Student/faculty ratio: 9:1.

ACADEMICS
Calendar: semesters. *Degrees:* certificates, associate, and bachelor's.

Special study options: adult/continuing education programs, distance learning, double majors, external degree program, honors programs, independent study, study abroad. ***ROTC:*** Air Force (c).

Computers: Students can access the following: online (class) registration. Campuswide network is available.

STUDENT LIFE
Housing options: college housing not available.

Activities and organizations: drama/theater group, student-run newspaper.

Athletics Member NJCAA. ***Intercollegiate sports:*** baseball M, basketball M/W, cheerleading M/W, golf M/W, softball W, volleyball W. ***Intramural sports:*** badminton M/W, basketball M/W, bowling M/W, cheerleading M(c)/W(c), football M/W, ice hockey M(c)/W(c), racquetball M/W, skiing (downhill) M(c)/W(c), soccer M/W, softball W, volleyball M/W.

Campus security: part-time trained security personnel.

COSTS & FINANCIAL AID
Costs (2019–20) ***Tuition:*** area resident $12,718 full-time; state resident $12,718 full-time; nonresident $21,310 full-time. Full-time tuition and fees vary according to course level, degree level, location, program, and student level. Part-time tuition and fees vary according to course level, course load, degree level, location, program, and student level. ***Required fees:*** $992 full-time. ***Payment plans:*** installment, deferred payment. ***Waivers:*** senior citizens and employees or children of employees.

Financial Aid Of all full-time matriculated undergraduates who enrolled in 2018, 412 applied for aid, 335 were judged to have need, 66 had their need fully met. In 2018, 50 non-need-based awards were made. ***Average percent of need met:*** 59. ***Average financial aid package:*** $10,095. ***Average need-based loan:*** $3931. ***Average need-based gift aid:*** $5560.

Average non-need-based aid: $2730. *Average indebtedness upon graduation:* $34,304.

APPLYING

Standardized Tests *Required:* SAT or ACT (for admission).

Options: electronic application, early admission, early action, deferred entrance.

Application fee: $65.

Required: high school transcript. *Required for some:* interview. *Recommended:* essay or personal statement.

Application deadlines: rolling (freshmen), rolling (transfers), 11/1 (early action).

Notification: continuous (freshmen), continuous (transfers), 12/24 (early action).

CONTACT

Admissions Office, Penn State New Kensington, 3550 Seventh Street Road, New Kensington, PA 15068. *Phone:* 724-334-5466. *Toll-free phone:* 888-968-7297. *Fax:* 724-334-6111. *E-mail:* nkadmissions@psu.edu.

Penn State Schuylkill

Schuylkill Haven, Pennsylvania

http://www.sl.psu.edu/

- **State-related** 4-year, founded 1934, part of Pennsylvania State University
- **Small-town** campus
- **Coed** 631 undergraduate students, 79% full-time, 59% women, 41% men
- **Moderately difficult** entrance level, 73% of applicants were admitted

UNDERGRAD STUDENTS

500 full-time, 131 part-time. 9% are from out of state; 8% Black or African American, non-Hispanic/Latino; 7% Hispanic/Latino; 1% Asian, non-Hispanic/Latino; 0.2% American Indian or Alaska Native, non-Hispanic/Latino; 2% Two or more races, non-Hispanic/Latino; 0.7% Race/ethnicity unknown; 0.7% international; 8% transferred in; 19% live on campus.

Freshmen:

Admission: 579 applied, 425 admitted, 172 enrolled. *Test scores:* SAT evidence-based reading and writing scores over 500: 63%; SAT math scores over 500: 58%; ACT scores over 18: 79%; SAT evidence-based reading and writing scores over 600: 21%; SAT math scores over 600: 16%; ACT scores over 24: 14%; SAT evidence-based reading and writing scores over 700: 1%; SAT math scores over 700: 6%.

Retention: 73% of full-time freshmen returned.

FACULTY

Total: 76, 51% full-time, 42% with terminal degrees.

Student/faculty ratio: 11:1.

ACADEMICS

Calendar: semesters. *Degrees:* certificates, associate, and bachelor's (bachelor's degree programs completed at the Harrisburg campus).

Special study options: accelerated degree program, adult/continuing education programs, distance learning, double majors, English as a second language, external degree program, honors programs, independent study, internships, study abroad.

Computers: Students can access the following: online (class) registration. Campuswide network is available.

STUDENT LIFE

Housing options: special housing for students with disabilities.

Activities and organizations: drama/theater group, student-run radio station, choral group.

Athletics Member NJCAA. *Intercollegiate sports:* basketball M, cross-country running M/W, golf M, soccer M, softball W, volleyball W. *Intramural sports:* basketball M/W, football M, soccer M/W, softball M/W, table tennis M/W, volleyball M/W.

Campus security: 24-hour patrols, controlled dormitory access.

COSTS & FINANCIAL AID

Costs (2020–21) *Tuition:* area resident $13,484 full-time, $555 per credit hour part-time; state resident $13,484 full-time, $555 per credit hour part-time; nonresident $22,474 full-time, $936 per credit hour part-time. Full-time tuition and fees vary according to course level, degree level, location, program, and student level. Part-time tuition and fees vary according to course level, course load, degree level, location, program, and student level. *Required fees:* $992 full-time. *Room and board:* $6766; room only: $6766. Room and board charges vary according to board plan, housing facility, and location. *Payment plans:* installment, deferred payment. *Waivers:* senior citizens and employees or children of employees.

Financial Aid Of all full-time matriculated undergraduates who enrolled in 2018, 470 applied for aid, 431 were judged to have need, 105 had their need fully met. In 2018, 27 non-need-based awards were made. *Average percent of need met:* 68. *Average financial aid package:* $11,749. *Average need-based loan:* $3920. *Average need-based gift aid:* $6421. *Average non-need-based aid:* $2946. *Average indebtedness upon graduation:* $41,749.

APPLYING

Standardized Tests *Required:* SAT or ACT (for admission).

Options: electronic application, early admission, early action, deferred entrance.

Application fee: $65.

Required: high school transcript.

Application deadlines: rolling (freshmen), rolling (transfers), 11/1 (early action).

Notification: continuous (freshmen), continuous (transfers), 12/24 (early action).

CONTACT

Admissions Office, Penn State Schuylkill, 200 University Drive, Schuylkill Haven, PA 17972. *Phone:* 570-385-6252. *Fax:* 570-385-6272. *E-mail:* sl-admissions@psu.edu.

Penn State Shenango

Sharon, Pennsylvania

http://www.shenango.psu.edu/

- **State-related** 4-year, founded 1965, part of Pennsylvania State University
- **Small-town** campus
- **Coed** 402 undergraduate students, 54% full-time, 73% women, 27% men
- **Moderately difficult** entrance level, 67% of applicants were admitted

UNDERGRAD STUDENTS

216 full-time, 186 part-time. 24% are from out of state; 11% Black or African American, non-Hispanic/Latino; 3% Hispanic/Latino; 1% Asian, non-Hispanic/Latino; 0.3% American Indian or Alaska Native, non-Hispanic/Latino; 6% Two or more races, non-Hispanic/Latino; 1% Race/ethnicity unknown; 0.3% international; 9% transferred in.

Freshmen:

Admission: 165 applied, 110 admitted, 43 enrolled. *Test scores:* SAT evidence-based reading and writing scores over 500: 61%; SAT math scores over 500: 56%; ACT scores over 18: 25%; SAT evidence-based reading and writing scores over 600: 11%; SAT math scores over 600: 11%.

Retention: 69% of full-time freshmen returned.

FACULTY

Total: 61, 51% full-time, 26% with terminal degrees.

Student/faculty ratio: 7:1.

ACADEMICS

Calendar: semesters. *Degrees:* certificates, associate, and bachelor's.

Special study options: accelerated degree program, adult/continuing education programs, distance learning, double majors, external degree program, honors programs, independent study, internships, student-designed majors, study abroad.

Computers: Students can access the following: online (class) registration. Campuswide network is available.

STUDENT LIFE

Housing options: college housing not available.

Activities and organizations: drama/theater group, choral group.

Athletics ***Intramural sports:*** basketball M(c)/W, bowling M/W, football M(c), golf M/W, softball M/W, tennis M/W, volleyball M/W.

COSTS & FINANCIAL AID

Costs (2020–21) ***Tuition:*** area resident $12,474 full-time, $504 per credit hour part-time; state resident $12,474 full-time, $504 per credit hour part-time; nonresident $20,898 full-time, $871 per credit hour part-time. Full-time tuition and fees vary according to course level, degree level, location, program, and student level. Part-time tuition and fees vary according to course level, course load, degree level, location, program, and student level. ***Required fees:*** $876 full-time. ***Payment plans:*** installment, deferred payment. ***Waivers:*** senior citizens and employees or children of employees.

Financial Aid Of all full-time matriculated undergraduates who enrolled in 2018, 203 applied for aid, 188 were judged to have need, 16 had their need fully met. In 2018, 22 non-need-based awards were made. ***Average percent of need met:*** 58. ***Average financial aid package:*** $13,037. ***Average need-based loan:*** $3598. ***Average need-based gift aid:*** $6096. ***Average non-need-based aid:*** $4254. ***Average indebtedness upon graduation:*** $40,515.

APPLYING

Standardized Tests *Required:* SAT or ACT (for admission).

Options: electronic application, early admission, early action, deferred entrance.

Application fee: $65.

Required: high school transcript.

Application deadlines: rolling (freshmen), rolling (transfers), 11/1 (early action).

Notification: continuous (freshmen), continuous (transfers), 12/24 (early action).

CONTACT

Admissions Office, Penn State Shenango, 147 Shenango Avenue, Sharon, PA 16146. *Phone:* 724-983-2803. *Fax:* 724-983-2820. *E-mail:* psushenango@psu.edu.

Penn State University Park

State College, Pennsylvania

http://www.psu.edu/

- **State-related** university, founded 1855, part of The Pennsylvania State University
- **Small-town** 7958-acre campus with easy access to Harrisburg
- **Endowment** $2.8 billion
- **Coed** 40,639 undergraduate students, 97% full-time, 47% women, 53% men
- **Very difficult** entrance level, 49% of applicants were admitted

UNDERGRAD STUDENTS

39,529 full-time, 1,110 part-time. 34% are from out of state; 4% Black or African American, non-Hispanic/Latino; 7% Hispanic/Latino; 6% Asian, non-Hispanic/Latino; 0.1% Native Hawaiian or other Pacific Islander, non-Hispanic/Latino; 0.1% American Indian or Alaska Native, non-Hispanic/Latino; 3% Two or more races, non-Hispanic/Latino; 2% Race/ethnicity unknown; 12% international; 0.8% transferred in; 36% live on campus.

Freshmen:

Admission: 71,903 applied, 35,302 admitted, 8,331 enrolled. ***Test scores:*** SAT evidence-based reading and writing scores over 500: 97%; SAT math scores over 500: 97%; ACT scores over 18: 100%; SAT evidence-based reading and writing scores over 600: 68%; SAT math scores over 600: 69%; ACT scores over 24: 86%; SAT evidence-based reading and writing scores over 700: 13%; SAT math scores over 700: 26%; ACT scores over 30: 33%.

Retention: 94% of full-time freshmen returned.

FACULTY

Total: 3,511, 85% full-time, 68% with terminal degrees.

Student/faculty ratio: 14:1.

ACADEMICS

Calendar: semesters. *Degrees:* certificates, associate, bachelor's, master's, doctoral, and postbachelor's certificates.

Special study options: academic remediation for entering students, accelerated degree program, adult/continuing education programs, advanced placement credit, cooperative education, distance learning, double majors, English as a second language, external degree program, freshman honors college, honors programs, independent study, internships, off-campus study, part-time degree program, services for LD students, student-designed majors, study abroad, summer session for credit. ***ROTC:*** Army (b), Navy (b), Air Force (b).

Unusual degree programs: 3-2 engineering; geoscience.

Computers: 3,154 computers/terminals are available on campus for general student use. Students can access the following: campus intranet, computer help desk, free student e-mail accounts, online (class) grades, online (class) registration, online (class) schedules. Campuswide network is available. 100% of college-owned or -operated housing units are wired for high-speed Internet access. Wireless service is available via classrooms, computer centers, computer labs, dorm rooms, learning centers, libraries, student centers.

Library: Pattee and Paterno Libraries plus 4 others. *Books:* 5.0 million (physical), 2.1 million (digital/electronic); *Serial titles:* 84,993 (physical), 160,000 (digital/electronic); *Databases:* 828. Weekly public service hours: 148; study areas open 24 hours, 5–7 days a week; students can reserve study rooms.

STUDENT LIFE

Housing options: on-campus residence required for freshman year; coed, women-only, special housing for students with disabilities. Campus housing is university owned. Freshman campus housing is guaranteed.

Activities and organizations: drama/theater group, student-run newspaper, radio and television station, choral group, marching band, national fraternities, national sororities.

Athletics Member NCAA, USCAA. All Division I except football (Division I-A). ***Intercollegiate sports:*** baseball M(s), basketball M(s)/W(s), cross-country running M(s)/W(s), fencing M(s)/W(s), field hockey W(s), golf M(s)/W(s), gymnastics M(s)/W(s), ice hockey M(s)(c)/W(s)(c), lacrosse M(s)/W(s), soccer M(s)/W(s), softball W(s), swimming and diving M(s)/W(s), tennis M(s)/W(s), track and field M(s)/W(s), volleyball M(s)/W(s), wrestling M(s). ***Intramural sports:*** archery M(c)/W(c), badminton M(c)/W(c), baseball M/W(c), basketball M/W, bowling M(c)/W(c), cheerleading M(c)/W(c), crew M(c)/W(c), cross-country running M/W, equestrian sports M(c)/W(c), fencing M/W, field hockey M(c)/W(c), football M, golf M/W, gymnastics M/W, ice hockey M/W, lacrosse M(c)/W(c), riflery M(c)/W(c), rowing M(c)/W(c), rugby M(c)/W(c), sailing M(c)/W(c), skiing (downhill) M(c)/W(c), soccer M/W, softball M(c)/W, squash M(c)/W(c), swimming and diving M/W, table tennis M(c)/W(c), tennis M/W, track and field M/W, triathlon M(c)/W(c), ultimate Frisbee M(c)/W(c), volleyball M/W, water polo M(c)/W(c), weight lifting M(c)/W(c), wrestling M/W(c).

Campus security: 24-hour emergency response devices and patrols, student patrols, late-night transport/escort service, controlled dormitory access.

Student services: health clinic, personal/psychological counseling, women's center, legal services, veterans affairs office.

COSTS & FINANCIAL AID

Costs (2020–21) ***Tuition:*** area resident $17,416 full-time, $726 per credit hour part-time; state resident $17,416 full-time, $726 per credit hour part-time; nonresident $34,480 full-time, $1437 per credit hour part-time. ***Required fees:*** $1034 full-time. ***Room and board:*** $11,884; room only: $6554.

Financial Aid Of all full-time matriculated undergraduates who enrolled in 2018, 23,848 applied for aid, 18,000 were judged to have need, 5,466 had their need fully met. In 2018, 3404 non-need-based awards were made. ***Average percent of need met:*** 64. ***Average financial aid package:*** $11,497. ***Average need-based loan:*** $4582. ***Average need-based gift aid:*** $6755. ***Average non-need-based aid:*** $4716. ***Average indebtedness upon graduation:*** $40,128.

APPLYING

Standardized Tests *Required:* SAT or ACT (for admission).

Options: electronic application, early admission, early action, deferred entrance.

Application fee: $65.

Notification: continuous (freshmen), continuous (transfers), 12/24 (early action).

CONTACT
Clark V. Brigger, Executive Director for Undergraduate Admissions, Penn State University Park, 201 Shields Building, University Park, PA 16802. *Phone:* 814-865-5471. *Fax:* 814-863-7590. *E-mail:* admissions@psu.edu.

Penn State Wilkes-Barre

Lehman, Pennsylvania

http://www.wb.psu.edu/

- **State-related** 4-year, founded 1916, part of Pennsylvania State University
- **Rural** campus
- **Coed** 444 undergraduate students, 79% full-time, 36% women, 64% men
- **Moderately difficult** entrance level, 80% of applicants were admitted

UNDERGRAD STUDENTS
350 full-time, 94 part-time. 11% are from out of state; 8% Black or African American, non-Hispanic/Latino; 7% Hispanic/Latino; 2% Asian, non-Hispanic/Latino; 1% Two or more races, non-Hispanic/Latino; 0.3% Race/ethnicity unknown; 8% transferred in.

Freshmen:
Admission: 560 applied, 449 admitted, 113 enrolled. ***Test scores:*** SAT evidence-based reading and writing scores over 500: 72%; SAT math scores over 500: 74%; ACT scores over 18: 60%; SAT evidence-based reading and writing scores over 600: 29%; SAT math scores over 600: 26%; ACT scores over 24: 40%; SAT evidence-based reading and writing scores over 700: 2%; SAT math scores over 700: 5%; ACT scores over 30: 20%.

Retention: 85% of full-time freshmen returned.

FACULTY
Total: 77, 40% full-time, 27% with terminal degrees.

Student/faculty ratio: 8:1.

ACADEMICS
Calendar: semesters. *Degrees:* certificates, associate, and bachelor's (enrollment figures include students enrolled at The Graduate School at Penn State who are taking courses at this location).

Special study options: accelerated degree program, adult/continuing education programs, double majors, external degree program, honors programs, independent study, internships, study abroad. ***ROTC:*** Army (c), Air Force (c).

Computers: Students can access the following: online (class) registration. Campuswide network is available.

STUDENT LIFE
Housing options: college housing not available.

Activities and organizations: student-run newspaper, radio station.

Athletics Member NJCAA. ***Intercollegiate sports:*** baseball M, basketball M, cross-country running M/W, golf M/W, soccer M/W, volleyball W. ***Intramural sports:*** basketball M/W, bowling M(c)/W(c), cheerleading M(c)/W(c), football M, racquetball M/W, softball W, volleyball M(c)/W.

COSTS & FINANCIAL AID
Costs (2020–21) ***Tuition:*** area resident $12,718 full-time, $524 per credit hour part-time; state resident $12,718 full-time, $524 per credit hour part-time; nonresident $21,310 full-time, $888 per credit hour part-time. Full-time tuition and fees vary according to course level, degree level, location, program, and student level. Part-time tuition and fees vary according to course level, course load, degree level, location, program, and student level. ***Required fees:*** $876 full-time. ***Payment plans:*** installment, deferred payment. ***Waivers:*** senior citizens and employees or children of employees.

Financial Aid Of all full-time matriculated undergraduates who enrolled in 2018, 330 applied for aid, 275 were judged to have need, 60 had their need fully met. In 2018, 19 non-need-based awards were made. ***Average percent of need met:*** 64. ***Average financial aid package:*** $11,199. ***Average need-based loan:*** $4076. ***Average need-based gift aid:*** $7088. ***Average non-need-based aid:*** $3212. ***Average indebtedness upon graduation:*** $34,928.

APPLYING
Standardized Tests *Required:* SAT or ACT (for admission).

Options: electronic application, early admission, early action, deferred entrance.

Application fee: $65.

Required: high school transcript.

Application deadlines: rolling (freshmen), rolling (transfers), 11/1 (early action).

Notification: continuous (freshmen), continuous (transfers), 12/24 (early action).

CONTACT
Admissions Office, Penn State Wilkes-Barre, Old Route 115, PO Box PSU, Lehman, PA 18627. *Phone:* 570-675-9238. *Fax:* 570-675-9113. *E-mail:* wbadmissions@psu.edu.

Penn State Worthington Scranton

Dunmore, Pennsylvania

http://www.sn.psu.edu/

CONTACT
Admissions Office, Penn State Worthington Scranton, 120 Ridge View Drive, Dunmore, PA 18512. *Phone:* 570-963-2500. *Fax:* 570-963-2524. *E-mail:* wsadmissions@psu.edu.

Penn State York

York, Pennsylvania

http://www.york.psu.edu/

- **State-related** comprehensive, founded 1926, part of Pennsylvania State University
- **Suburban** campus
- **Coed** 820 undergraduate students, 83% full-time, 39% women, 61% men
- **Moderately difficult** entrance level, 77% of applicants were admitted

UNDERGRAD STUDENTS
680 full-time, 140 part-time. 11% are from out of state; 7% Black or African American, non-Hispanic/Latino; 9% Hispanic/Latino; 6% Asian, non-Hispanic/Latino; 0.4% Native Hawaiian or other Pacific Islander, non-Hispanic/Latino; 4% Two or more races, non-Hispanic/Latino; 2% Race/ethnicity unknown; 15% international; 6% transferred in.

Freshmen:
Admission: 1,837 applied, 1,411 admitted, 202 enrolled. ***Test scores:*** SAT evidence-based reading and writing scores over 500: 77%; SAT math scores over 500: 81%; ACT scores over 18: 100%; SAT evidence-based reading and writing scores over 600: 34%; SAT math scores over 600: 41%; ACT scores over 24: 47%; SAT evidence-based reading and writing scores over 700: 5%; SAT math scores over 700: 13%; ACT scores over 30: 21%.

Retention: 81% of full-time freshmen returned.

FACULTY
Total: 110, 46% full-time, 41% with terminal degrees.

Student/faculty ratio: 10:1.

ACADEMICS
Calendar: semesters. *Degrees:* certificates, associate, bachelor's, and master's (also offers up to 2 years of most bachelor's degree programs offered at University Park campus).

Special study options: accelerated degree program, adult/continuing education programs, distance learning, double majors, English as a second language, external degree program, honors programs, independent study, internships, study abroad.

Computers: Students can access the following: online (class) registration. Campuswide network is available.

STUDENT LIFE
Housing options: college housing not available.

Activities and organizations: drama/theater group, student-run newspaper.

COSTS & FINANCIAL AID
Costs (2020–21) ***Tuition:*** area resident $13,484 full-time, $555 per credit hour part-time; state resident $13,484 full-time, $555 per credit hour part-time; nonresident $22,474 full-time, $936 per credit hour part-time. Full-

time tuition and fees vary according to course level, degree level, location, program, and student level. Part-time tuition and fees vary according to course level, course load, degree level, location, program, and student level. ***Required fees:*** $992 full-time. ***Payment plans:*** installment, deferred payment. ***Waivers:*** senior citizens and employees or children of employees.

Financial Aid Of all full-time matriculated undergraduates who enrolled in 2018, 526 applied for aid, 431 were judged to have need, 85 had their need fully met. In 2018, 84 non-need-based awards were made. ***Average percent of need met:*** 57. ***Average financial aid package:*** $9767. ***Average need-based loan:*** $3885. ***Average need-based gift aid:*** $5708. ***Average non-need-based aid:*** $3416. ***Average indebtedness upon graduation:*** $37,420.

APPLYING

Standardized Tests *Required:* SAT or ACT (for admission).

Options: electronic application, early admission, early action, deferred entrance.

Application fee: $65.

Required: high school transcript.

Application deadlines: rolling (freshmen), rolling (transfers), 11/1 (early action).

Notification: continuous (freshmen), continuous (transfers), 12/24 (early action).

CONTACT

Admissions Office, Penn State York, 1031 Edgecomb Avenue, York, PA 17403. *Phone:* 717-771-4040. *Toll-free phone:* 800-778-6227. *Fax:* 717-771-4005. *E-mail:* ykadmission@psu.edu.

Pennsylvania Academy of the Fine Arts

Philadelphia, Pennsylvania

http://www.pafa.edu/

- **Independent** comprehensive, founded 1805
- **Urban** campus
- **Coed**
- 90% of applicants were admitted

ACADEMICS

Calendar: semesters. *Degrees:* certificates, bachelor's, master's, and postbachelor's certificates.
Library: Arcadia Fine Arts Library.

STUDENT LIFE

Housing options: coed.

Campus security: 24-hour patrols.

COSTS & FINANCIAL AID

Costs (2019–20) ***Tuition:*** $38,926 full-time, $1622 per credit part-time. ***Required fees:*** $1450 full-time. ***Room only:*** $12,010.

Financial Aid Of all full-time matriculated undergraduates who enrolled in 2019, 57 Federal Work-Study jobs (averaging $2000).

APPLYING

Standardized Tests *Required for some:* TOEFL (suggested 600 paper based, 250 computer based, 100 iBT) or IELTS (suggested 6.0 paper based) for international students.

Options: electronic application.

Application fee: $60.

Required: essay or personal statement, minimum 3.0 GPA, 2 letters of recommendation, portfolio of work.

CONTACT

Peter Tran, Director of Admissions Operations, Pennsylvania Academy of the Fine Arts, 128 North Broad Street, Philadelphia, PA 19102. *Phone:* 215-391-4111. *Fax:* 215-569-0153. *E-mail:* ptran@pafa.edu.

Pennsylvania College of Art & Design

Lancaster, Pennsylvania

http://www.pcad.edu/

- **Independent** 4-year, founded 1982
- **Urban** campus with easy access to Philadelphia, Baltimore
- **Coed**
- **Moderately difficult** entrance level

FACULTY

Student/faculty ratio: 13:1.

ACADEMICS

Calendar: semesters. *Degree:* certificates and bachelor's.
Library: Pennsylvania College of Art & Design Library.

STUDENT LIFE

Activities and organizations: Student Council, Anime Club, Student AIGA, Society of Illustrators - Student Group.

Campus security: late-night transport/escort service, trained evening/weekend security personnel.

COSTS

Costs (2019–20) ***Comprehensive fee:*** $37,800 includes full-time tuition ($25,000), mandatory fees ($1600), and room and board ($11,200). Full-time tuition and fees vary according to location. Part-time tuition: $1042 per credit. Part-time tuition and fees vary according to course load and location. ***Required fees:*** $1600 per year part-time. ***College room only:*** $9600. Room and board charges vary according to housing facility.

APPLYING

Options: electronic application, deferred entrance.

Application fee: $40.

Required: essay or personal statement, high school transcript, minimum 2.5 GPA, portfolio. ***Required for some:*** 2 letters of recommendation. ***Recommended:*** interview.

CONTACT

Natalie A Lascek, Director of Admissions Marketing & Recruitment, Pennsylvania College of Art & Design, 204 North Prince Street, PO Box 59, Lancaster, PA 17608-0059. *Phone:* 717-3967833. *Toll-free phone:* 800-689-0379 Ext. 1001. *E-mail:* nlascek@pcad.edu.

Pennsylvania College of Health Sciences

Lancaster, Pennsylvania

http://www.pacollege.edu/

CONTACT

Pennsylvania College of Health Sciences, 850 Greenfield Road, Lancaster, PA 17601. *Toll-free phone:* 800-622-5443.

Pennsylvania College of Technology

Williamsport, Pennsylvania

http://www.pct.edu/

CONTACT

Ashley Murphy, Director of Admissions, Pennsylvania College of Technology, One College Avenue, DIF #119, Williamsport, PA 17701. *Phone:* 570-327-4761 Ext. 7337. *Toll-free phone:* 800-367-9222. *Fax:* 570-321-5551. *E-mail:* admissions@pct.edu.

Pittsburgh Technical College

Oakdale, Pennsylvania

http://www.ptcollege.edu/

CONTACT

Ms. Nancy Goodlin, Admissions Office Assistant, Pittsburgh Technical College, 1111 McKee Road, Oakdale, PA 15071. *Phone:* 412-809-5100. *Toll-free phone:* 800-784-9675. *Fax:* 412-809-5351. *E-mail:* goodlin.nancy@ptcollege.edu.

Point Park University

Pittsburgh, Pennsylvania

http://www.pointpark.edu/

- **Independent** university, founded 1960
- **Urban** campus
- **Endowment** $33.5 million
- **Coed**
- **Moderately difficult** entrance level

FACULTY

Student/faculty ratio: 13:1.

ACADEMICS

Calendar: semesters. *Degrees:* certificates, associate, bachelor's, master's, doctoral, and postbachelor's certificates.

Library: Point Park University Library.

STUDENT LIFE

Housing options: coed, women-only, special housing for students with disabilities. Campus housing is university owned and leased by the school. Freshman campus housing is guaranteed.

Activities and organizations: drama/theater group, student-run newspaper, radio and television station, WPPJ student radio station, The Body Christian Fellowship, Dance Club, Campus Activities Board, Action Sports Club.

Athletics Member NAIA.

Campus security: 24-hour emergency response devices and patrols, late-night transport/escort service, controlled dormitory access, campus patrolled by Accredited Law Enforcement Agency, 24-hour security desk, video security.

Student services: health clinic, personal/psychological counseling, veterans affairs office.

COSTS & FINANCIAL AID

Costs (2019–20) ***Comprehensive fee:*** $45,190 includes full-time tuition ($31,180), mandatory fees ($1570), and room and board ($12,440). Full-time tuition and fees vary according to program. Part-time tuition: $878 per credit. Part-time tuition and fees vary according to program. ***Required fees:*** $878 per credit part-time, $65 per credit part-time. ***College room only:*** $5420. Room and board charges vary according to board plan and housing facility. ***Payment plans:*** installment, deferred payment.

Financial Aid Of all full-time matriculated undergraduates who enrolled in 2017, 2,516 applied for aid, 2,345 were judged to have need, 296 had their need fully met. In 2017, 162 non-need-based awards were made. ***Average percent of need met:*** 71. ***Average financial aid package:*** $25,353. ***Average need-based loan:*** $5380. ***Average need-based gift aid:*** $19,916. ***Average non-need-based aid:*** $13,043. ***Average indebtedness upon graduation:*** $27,924.

APPLYING

Standardized Tests *Required:* SAT or ACT (for admission).

Options: electronic application, deferred entrance.

Application fee: $40.

Required: high school transcript. ***Required for some:*** essay or personal statement, 2 letters of recommendation, interview, audition. ***Recommended:*** minimum 2.5 GPA.

CONTACT

Point Park University, 201 Wood Street, Pittsburgh, PA 15222-1984. *Phone:* 412-392-3430. *Toll-free phone:* 800-321-0129.

The Restaurant School at Walnut Hill College

Philadelphia, Pennsylvania

http://www.walnuthillcollege.edu/

CONTACT

Mr. John English, Director of Admissions, The Restaurant School at Walnut Hill College, 4207 Walnut Street, Philadelphia, PA 19104-3518. *Phone:* 267-295-2353. *Fax:* 215-222-4219. *E-mail:* jenglish@walnuthillcollege.edu.

Robert Morris University

Moon Township, Pennsylvania

http://www.rmu.edu/

- **Independent** university, founded 1921
- **Suburban** 230-acre campus with easy access to Pittsburgh
- **Endowment** $33.6 million
- **Coed**
- **Minimally difficult** entrance level

FACULTY

Student/faculty ratio: 15:1.

ACADEMICS

Calendar: semesters. *Degrees:* bachelor's, master's, doctoral, and postbachelor's certificates.

Library: Robert Morris University Library. *Books:* 97,693 (physical), 172,931 (digital/electronic); *Serial titles:* 244 (physical), 47,791 (digital/electronic); *Databases:* 104. Weekly public service hours: 101; study areas open 24 hours, 5–7 days a week; students can reserve study rooms.

STUDENT LIFE

Housing options: on-campus residence required for freshman year; coed, men-only, women-only, special housing for students with disabilities. Campus housing is university owned. Freshman applicants given priority for college housing.

Activities and organizations: drama/theater group, student-run newspaper, radio and television station, choral group, marching band, Student Government Association, Residence Hall Association, The Saudi Student Club, National Society of Collegiate Scholars, Top Secret Colonials, national fraternities, national sororities.

Athletics Member NCAA. All Division I.

Campus security: 24-hour emergency response devices and patrols, late-night transport/escort service, controlled dormitory access.

Student services: health clinic, personal/psychological counseling, veterans affairs office.

COSTS & FINANCIAL AID

Costs (2019–20) ***Comprehensive fee:*** $22,550 includes full-time tuition ($9800) and room and board ($12,750). Part-time tuition: $6540.

Financial Aid Of all full-time matriculated undergraduates who enrolled in 2017, 2,996 applied for aid, 2,707 were judged to have need, 347 had their need fully met. In 2017, 670 non-need-based awards were made. ***Average percent of need met:*** 71. ***Average financial aid package:*** $22,897. ***Average need-based loan:*** $6650. ***Average need-based gift aid:*** $16,555. ***Average non-need-based aid:*** $12,841. ***Average indebtedness upon graduation:*** $39,856.

APPLYING

Standardized Tests *Required:* SAT or ACT (for admission).

Options: electronic application, deferred entrance.

Application fee: $30.

Required: high school transcript, minimum 2.0 GPA. ***Required for some:*** interview. ***Recommended:*** essay or personal statement, minimum 3.0 GPA, interview.

CONTACT

Enrollment Services Department, Robert Morris University, 6001 University Boulevard, Moon Township, PA 15108-1189. *Phone:* 412-397-5200. *Toll-free phone:* 800-762-0097. *Fax:* 412-397-2425. *E-mail:* admissionsoffice@rmu.edu.

Rosemont College

Rosemont, Pennsylvania

http://www.rosemont.edu/

- **Independent Roman Catholic** comprehensive, founded 1921
- **Suburban** 56-acre campus with easy access to Philadelphia
- **Coed** 572 undergraduate students, 81% full-time, 64% women, 36% men
- **Moderately difficult** entrance level, 92% of applicants were admitted

UNDERGRAD STUDENTS

462 full-time, 110 part-time. Students come from 13 states and territories; 7 other countries; 27% are from out of state; 44% Black or African

American, non-Hispanic/Latino; 7% Hispanic/Latino; 2% Asian, non-Hispanic/Latino; 0.3% Native Hawaiian or other Pacific Islander, non-Hispanic/Latino; 0.2% American Indian or Alaska Native, non-Hispanic/Latino; 3% Two or more races, non-Hispanic/Latino; 6% Race/ethnicity unknown; 2% international; 8% transferred in; 67% live on campus.

Freshmen:

Admission: 784 applied, 722 admitted, 91 enrolled. ***Average high school GPA:*** 3.2. ***Test scores:*** SAT evidence-based reading and writing scores over 500: 60%; SAT math scores over 500: 56%; ACT scores over 18: 50%; SAT evidence-based reading and writing scores over 600: 15%; SAT math scores over 600: 7%; ACT scores over 24: 9%; SAT evidence-based reading and writing scores over 700: 4%; SAT math scores over 700: 2%; ACT scores over 30: 2%.

Retention: 66% of full-time freshmen returned.

FACULTY

Total: 131, 21% full-time, 55% with terminal degrees.

Student/faculty ratio: 10:1.

ACADEMICS

Calendar: semesters. *Degrees:* associate, bachelor's, master's, and postbachelor's certificates.

Special study options: accelerated degree program, adult/continuing education programs, advanced placement credit, distance learning, double majors, external degree program, honors programs, independent study, internships, off-campus study, part-time degree program, services for LD students, student-designed majors, study abroad, summer session for credit.

Computers: Students can access the following: campus intranet, computer help desk, free student e-mail accounts, online (class) grades, online (class) registration, online (class) schedules. Campuswide network is available. 100% of college-owned or -operated housing units are wired for high-speed Internet access. Wireless service is available via entire campus.

Library: Gertrude Kistler Memorial Library plus 1 other. *Books:* 138,609 (physical), 11,583 (digital/electronic); *Serial titles:* 20 (physical), 17,350 (digital/electronic); *Databases:* 45. Students can reserve study rooms.

STUDENT LIFE

Housing options: coed. Campus housing is university owned. Freshman campus housing is guaranteed.

Activities and organizations: drama/theater group, student-run newspaper, choral group.

Athletics Member NCAA. All Division III. ***Intercollegiate sports:*** basketball M/W, cross-country running M/W, golf M, lacrosse M/W, soccer M/W, softball W, tennis M/W, volleyball M/W.

Campus security: 24-hour emergency response devices and patrols, late-night transport/escort service, controlled dormitory access.

Student services: health clinic, personal/psychological counseling.

COSTS & FINANCIAL AID

Costs (2020–21) ***Tuition:*** $735 per credit hour part-time. ***Waivers:*** employees or children of employees.

Financial Aid Of all full-time matriculated undergraduates who enrolled in 2019, 340 applied for aid, 303 were judged to have need, 24 had their need fully met. 168 Federal Work-Study jobs (averaging $1940). 168 state and other part-time jobs (averaging $1940). In 2019, 57 non-need-based awards were made. ***Average percent of need met:*** 73. ***Average financial aid package:*** $22,102. ***Average need-based loan:*** $4310. ***Average need-based gift aid:*** $17,308. ***Average non-need-based aid:*** $6860. ***Average indebtedness upon graduation:*** $39,050.

APPLYING

Standardized Tests *Required for some:* SAT or ACT (for admission).

Options: electronic application, deferred entrance.

Required: high school transcript, minimum 2.0 GPA. ***Required for some:*** essay or personal statement. ***Recommended:*** interview.

Application deadlines: rolling (freshmen), rolling (transfers).

Notification: continuous (transfers).

CONTACT

Mr. Louis Hegyes, Undergraduate College Director, Rosemont College, 1400 Montgomery Avenue, Rosemont, PA 19010. *Phone:* 610-527-0200 Ext. 2601. *Toll-free phone:* 888-2-ROSEMONT. *Fax:* 610-520-4399. *E-mail:* louis.hegyes@rosemont.edu.

Saint Charles Borromeo Seminary, Overbrook

Wynnewood, Pennsylvania

http://www.scs.edu/

CONTACT

Rev. Joseph Shenosky, Vice Rector, Saint Charles Borromeo Seminary, Overbrook, 100 East Wynnewood Road, Wynnewood, PA 19096. *Phone:* 610-785-6520. *E-mail:* jshenosky@scs.edu.

Saint Francis University

Loretto, Pennsylvania

http://www.francis.edu/

- **Independent Roman Catholic** comprehensive, founded 1847
- **Rural** 600-acre campus
- **Endowment** $50.3 million
- **Coed** 2,111 undergraduate students, 70% full-time, 65% women, 35% men
- **Moderately difficult** entrance level, 75% of applicants were admitted

UNDERGRAD STUDENTS

1,485 full-time, 626 part-time. Students come from 37 states and territories; 24 other countries; 24% are from out of state; 7% Black or African American, non-Hispanic/Latino; 1% Hispanic/Latino; 3% Asian, non-Hispanic/Latino; 0.2% Native Hawaiian or other Pacific Islander, non-Hispanic/Latino; 0.4% American Indian or Alaska Native, non-Hispanic/Latino; 2% Two or more races, non-Hispanic/Latino; 3% Race/ethnicity unknown; 2% international; 2% transferred in; 83% live on campus.

Freshmen:

Admission: 1,741 applied, 1,299 admitted, 387 enrolled. ***Average high school GPA:*** 3.7. ***Test scores:*** SAT evidence-based reading and writing scores over 500: 84%; SAT math scores over 500: 82%; ACT scores over 18: 90%; SAT evidence-based reading and writing scores over 600: 42%; SAT math scores over 600: 38%; ACT scores over 24: 52%; SAT evidence-based reading and writing scores over 700: 3%; SAT math scores over 700: 5%; ACT scores over 30: 5%.

Retention: 85% of full-time freshmen returned.

FACULTY

Total: 212, 53% full-time, 48% with terminal degrees.

Student/faculty ratio: 16:1.

ACADEMICS

Calendar: semesters. *Degrees:* certificates, associate, bachelor's, master's, and doctoral.

Special study options: academic remediation for entering students, accelerated degree program, adult/continuing education programs, advanced placement credit, cooperative education, distance learning, double majors, English as a second language, external degree program, freshman honors college, honors programs, independent study, internships, off-campus study, part-time degree program, services for LD students, student-designed majors, study abroad, summer session for credit. ***ROTC:*** Army (b).

Unusual degree programs: 3-2 engineering with Penn State University Park, University of Pittsburgh; forestry with Duke University; Optometry with Salus University, osteopathic medicine with Lake Erie College of Osteopathic Medicine, PharmD Duquesne University & Lake Erie College of Osteopathic Medicine, Dental Lake Erie College of Osteopathic Medicine.

Computers: 1,500 computers/terminals are available on campus for general student use. Students can access the following: campus intranet, computer help desk, free student e-mail accounts, online (class) grades, online (class) registration, online (class) schedules. Campuswide network is available. 95% of college-owned or -operated housing units are wired for high-speed Internet access. Wireless service is available via entire campus.

Library: Saint Francis University Library. *Books:* 60,353 (physical), 1.3 million (digital/electronic); *Databases:* 74.

STUDENT LIFE
Housing options: on-campus residence required through junior year; coed, men-only, women-only. Campus housing is university owned. Freshman campus housing is guaranteed.

Activities and organizations: drama/theater group, student-run newspaper, radio station, choral group, marching band, Student Activities Organization, Club Baseball, Student Government Association, Best Buddies, Cru, national fraternities, national sororities.

Athletics Member NCAA. All Division I. ***Intercollegiate sports:*** basketball M(s)/W(s), bowling W, cross-country running M(s)/W(s), field hockey W(s), football M(s), golf M(s)/W(s)(c), lacrosse W(s), soccer M(s)/W(s), softball W(s), swimming and diving W(s), tennis M(s)/W(s), track and field M(s)/W(s), volleyball M(s)/W(s), water polo M. ***Intramural sports:*** baseball M(c)/W(c), basketball M/W, cheerleading M/W, football M, golf M/W, ice hockey M(c)/W(c), lacrosse W, soccer M/W, softball W, swimming and diving W, tennis M/W, track and field M/W, ultimate Frisbee M/W, volleyball M/W.

Campus security: 24-hour emergency response devices and patrols, late-night transport/escort service, controlled dormitory access.

Student services: health clinic, personal/psychological counseling, veterans affairs office.

COSTS & FINANCIAL AID
Costs (2020–21) ***One-time required fee:*** $110. ***Comprehensive fee:*** $51,850 includes full-time tuition ($38,078), mandatory fees ($1300), and room and board ($12,472). Part-time tuition: $1155 per credit. ***College room only:*** $6148. ***Waivers:*** employees or children of employees.

Financial Aid Of all full-time matriculated undergraduates who enrolled in 2019, 1,318 applied for aid, 1,161 were judged to have need, 258 had their need fully met. In 2019, 267 non-need-based awards were made. ***Average percent of need met:*** 69. ***Average financial aid package:*** $25,319. ***Average need-based loan:*** $3885. ***Average need-based gift aid:*** $22,127. ***Average non-need-based aid:*** $13,880. ***Average indebtedness upon graduation:*** $40,676.

APPLYING
Standardized Tests *Required:* SAT or ACT (for admission).

Options: electronic application, deferred entrance.

Application fee: $30.

Required: essay or personal statement, high school transcript, 1 letter of recommendation. ***Recommended:*** interview.

Application deadlines: rolling (freshmen), rolling (transfers).

Notification: continuous (transfers).

CONTACT
Erin McCloskey, Dean for Enrollment Management, Saint Francis University, 117 Evergreen Drive, PO Box 600, Loretto, PA 15940-0600. *Phone:* 814-472-3100. *Toll-free phone:* 866-DIAL-SFU. *E-mail:* emccloskey@francis.edu.

See below for display ad and page 1106 for the College Close-Up.

Saint Joseph's University

Philadelphia, Pennsylvania

http://www.sju.edu/

- **Independent Roman Catholic (Jesuit)** comprehensive, founded 1851
- **Suburban** 114-acre campus with easy access to Philadelphia
- **Endowment** $280.3 million
- **Coed** 4,783 undergraduate students, 88% full-time, 54% women, 46% men
- **Moderately difficult** entrance level, 75% of applicants were admitted

UNDERGRAD STUDENTS
4,221 full-time, 562 part-time. Students come from 36 states and territories; 36 other countries; 54% are from out of state; 6% Black or African American, non-Hispanic/Latino; 8% Hispanic/Latino; 3% Asian, non-Hispanic/Latino; 0.2% Native Hawaiian or other Pacific Islander, non-Hispanic/Latino; 0.1% American Indian or Alaska Native, non-Hispanic/Latino; 3% Two or more races, non-Hispanic/Latino; 1% Race/ethnicity unknown; 2% international; 2% transferred in; 48% live on campus.

Freshmen:
Admission: 8,692 applied, 6,517 admitted, 1,103 enrolled. ***Average high school GPA:*** 3.7. ***Test scores:*** SAT evidence-based reading and writing scores over 500: 98%; SAT math scores over 500: 96%; ACT scores over 18: 99%; SAT evidence-based reading and writing scores over 600: 59%; SAT math scores over 600: 53%; ACT scores over 24: 75%; SAT evidence-based reading and writing scores over 700: 8%; SAT math scores over 700: 11%; ACT scores over 30: 22%.

Retention: 88% of full-time freshmen returned.

FACULTY
Total: 681, 43% full-time.

Student/faculty ratio: 10:1.

ACADEMICS
Calendar: semesters. *Degrees:* associate, bachelor's, master's, doctoral, post-master's, and postbachelor's certificates.

Special study options: accelerated degree program, adult/continuing education programs, advanced placement credit, cooperative education, distance learning, double majors, English as a second language, honors programs, independent study, internships, off-campus study, part-time degree program, services for LD students, student-designed majors, study abroad, summer session for credit. ***ROTC:*** Army (c), Navy (c), Air Force (b).

Computers: 900 computers/terminals are available on campus for general student use. Students can access the following: campus intranet, computer help desk, free student e-mail accounts, online (class) grades, online (class) registration, online (class) schedules. Campuswide network is available. 100% of college-owned or -operated housing units are wired for high-speed Internet access. Wireless service is available via entire campus.
Library: Post Learning Commons and Drexel Library. *Books:* 271,281 (physical), 467,643 (digital/electronic); *Serial titles:* 3,324 (physical), 76,020 (digital/electronic); *Databases:* 219. Weekly public service hours: 109; students can reserve study rooms.

STUDENT LIFE
Housing options: on-campus residence required through sophomore year; coed, men-only, women-only, special housing for students with disabilities. Campus housing is university owned. Freshman campus housing is guaranteed.

Activities and organizations: drama/theater group, student-run newspaper, radio station, choral group, Student Union Board, Hand-in-Hand, 54th Airborne / Booster Club, Appalachian Experience, Weekly Service, national fraternities, national sororities.

Athletics Member NCAA. All Division I. ***Intercollegiate sports:*** baseball M(s), basketball M(s)/W(s), cheerleading M(c)/W(c), crew M(s)/W(s), cross-country running M(s)/W(s), field hockey W(s), golf M(s), lacrosse M(s)/W(s), soccer M(s)/W(s), softball W(s), tennis M(s)/W(s), track and field M(s)/W(s). ***Intramural sports:*** baseball M(c), basketball M(c)/W(c), fencing W(c), football M/W, golf M(c)/W(c), ice hockey M(c)/W(c), lacrosse M(c)/W(c), rugby M(c)/W(c), soccer M(c)/W(c), softball W, swimming and diving M(c)/W(c), tennis M(c)/W(c), ultimate Frisbee M(c)/W(c), volleyball M(c)/W(c), water polo M(c)/W(c).

Campus security: 24-hour emergency response devices and patrols, late-night transport/escort service, controlled dormitory access.

Student services: health clinic, personal/psychological counseling, veterans affairs office.

COSTS & FINANCIAL AID
Costs (2020–21) ***Comprehensive fee:*** $62,780 includes full-time tuition ($47,740), mandatory fees ($200), and room and board ($14,840). Full-time tuition and fees vary according to course load. Part-time tuition: $584 per credit hour. Part-time tuition and fees vary according to course load. ***College room only:*** $9424. Room and board charges vary according to board plan and housing facility. ***Payment plan:*** installment. ***Waivers:*** employees or children of employees.

Financial Aid Of all full-time matriculated undergraduates who enrolled in 2019, 3,201 applied for aid, 2,598 were judged to have need, 714 had their need fully met. In 2019, 1252 non-need-based awards were made. ***Average percent of need met:*** 79. ***Average financial aid package:*** $32,275. ***Average need-based loan:*** $4380. ***Average need-based gift aid:*** $25,170. ***Average non-need-based aid:*** $15,459.

APPLYING
Options: electronic application, early decision, early action, deferred entrance.

Application fee: $50.

Required: essay or personal statement, high school transcript, 1 letter of recommendation.

Application deadlines: 2/1 (freshmen), 3/1 (transfers), 11/1 (early action).

Early decision deadline: 11/1 (for plan 1), 1/15 (for plan 2).

Notification: 3/15 (freshmen), continuous (transfers), 12/20 (early decision plan 1), 2/15 (early decision plan 2), 12/20 (early action).

CONTACT
Saint Joseph's University, 5600 City Avenue, Philadelphia, PA 19131-1395. *Phone:* 610-660-1300. *Toll-free phone:* 888-BE-A-HAWK (in-state); 800-BE-A-HAWK (out-of-state).

Saint Vincent College

Latrobe, Pennsylvania

http://www.stvincent.edu/

- **Independent Roman Catholic** comprehensive, founded 1846
- **Suburban** 200-acre campus with easy access to Pittsburgh
- **Endowment** $113.4 million
- **Coed** 1,560 undergraduate students, 96% full-time, 47% women, 53% men
- **Moderately difficult** entrance level, 68% of applicants were admitted

UNDERGRAD STUDENTS
1,491 full-time, 69 part-time. Students come from 31 states and territories; 10 other countries; 22% are from out of state; 6% Black or African American, non-Hispanic/Latino; 5% Hispanic/Latino; 1% Asian, non-Hispanic/Latino; 0.1% Native Hawaiian or other Pacific Islander, non-Hispanic/Latino; 0.1% American Indian or Alaska Native, non-Hispanic/Latino; 2% Two or more races, non-Hispanic/Latino; 3% Race/ethnicity unknown; 0.8% international; 2% transferred in; 67% live on campus.

Freshmen:
Admission: 2,025 applied, 1,371 admitted, 359 enrolled. ***Average high school GPA:*** 3.6. ***Test scores:*** SAT evidence-based reading and writing scores over 500: 85%; SAT math scores over 500: 82%; ACT scores over 18: 88%; SAT evidence-based reading and writing scores over 600: 40%; SAT math scores over 600: 34%; ACT scores over 24: 50%; SAT evidence-based reading and writing scores over 700: 5%; SAT math scores over 700: 6%; ACT scores over 30: 12%.

Retention: 81% of full-time freshmen returned.

FACULTY
Total: 224, 46% full-time, 62% with terminal degrees.

Student/faculty ratio: 11:1.

ACADEMICS
Calendar: semesters. *Degrees:* certificates, bachelor's, master's, doctoral, and postbachelor's certificates.

Special study options: advanced placement credit, cooperative education, distance learning, double majors, English as a second language, external degree program, honors programs, independent study, internships, part-time degree program, services for LD students, student-designed majors, study abroad, summer session for credit. ***ROTC:*** Army (c), Air Force (c).

Unusual degree programs: 3-2 engineering with University of Pittsburgh, Penn State University, The Catholic University of America; nursing with Carlow University.

Computers: 296 computers/terminals are available on campus for general student use. Students can access the following: campus intranet, computer help desk, free student e-mail accounts, online (class) grades, online (class) registration, online (class) schedules, program requirement evaluation. Campuswide network is available. 100% of college-owned or -operated housing units are wired for high-speed Internet access. Wireless service is available via entire campus.
Library: Latimer Family Library plus 1 other. *Books:* 226,400 (physical); *Serial titles:* 220 (physical). Weekly public service hours: 84.

STUDENT LIFE
Housing options: coed. Campus housing is university owned. Freshman applicants given priority for college housing.

Activities and organizations: drama/theater group, student-run newspaper, choral group, marching band, Activities Programming Board, Orientation Committee, Campus Ministry, Visionaries of Hope.

Athletics Member NCAA. All Division III. ***Intercollegiate sports:*** baseball M, basketball M/W, bowling W, cheerleading W(c), cross-country running M/W, equestrian sports M(c)/W(c), fencing M(c)/W(c), football M, golf M/W, ice hockey M(c), lacrosse M/W, rugby M(c)/W(c), soccer M/W, softball W, swimming and diving M/W, tennis M/W, track and field M/W, volleyball M/W. ***Intramural sports:*** basketball M/W, football M/W, ultimate Frisbee M/W, volleyball M/W.

Campus security: 24-hour emergency response devices and patrols, late-night transport/escort service, controlled dormitory access.

Student services: health clinic, personal/psychological counseling.

COSTS & FINANCIAL AID
Costs (2019–20) ***Comprehensive fee:*** $49,065 includes full-time tuition ($35,520), mandatory fees ($1384), and room and board ($12,161). Full-time tuition and fees vary according to course load and degree level. Part-time tuition: $1112 per credit hour. Part time tuition and fees vary according to course load and degree level. ***Required fees:*** $100 per term part-time. ***Room and board:*** Room and board charges vary according to board plan and housing facility. ***Payment plan:*** installment. ***Waivers:*** employees or children of employees.

Financial Aid Of all full-time matriculated undergraduates who enrolled in 2019, 1,283 applied for aid, 1,172 were judged to have need, 318 had their need fully met. In 2019, 294 non-need-based awards were made. ***Average percent of need met:*** 82. ***Average financial aid package:*** $32,749. ***Average need-based loan:*** $4417. ***Average need-based gift aid:*** $6620. ***Average non-need-based aid:*** $20,426. ***Average indebtedness upon graduation:*** $36,745.

APPLYING
Standardized Tests *Required:* SAT or ACT (for admission).

Options: early admission, deferred entrance.

Application fee: $25.

Required: essay or personal statement, high school transcript. ***Recommended:*** 3 letters of recommendation, interview.

Application deadlines: 5/1 (freshmen), 7/1 (transfers).

Notification: continuous until 10/1 (freshmen), continuous until 12/1 (transfers).

CONTACT
Ms. Heather Kabala, Dean of Admission, Saint Vincent College, 300 Fraser Purchase Road, Latrobe, PA 15650-2690. *Phone:* 800-782-5549. *Toll-free phone:* 800-782-5549. *Fax:* 724-532-5069. *E-mail:* admission@stvincent.edu.

Seton Hill University

Greensburg, Pennsylvania

http://www.setonhill.edu/

- **Independent Roman Catholic** comprehensive, founded 1883
- **Small-town** 200-acre campus with easy access to Pittsburgh
- **Coed** 1,726 undergraduate students, 92% full-time, 65% women, 35% men
- **Moderately difficult** entrance level, 77% of applicants were admitted

UNDERGRAD STUDENTS
1,584 full-time, 142 part-time. 23% are from out of state; 8% Black or African American, non-Hispanic/Latino; 4% Hispanic/Latino; 2% Asian, non-Hispanic/Latino; 0.2% Native Hawaiian or other Pacific Islander, non-Hispanic/Latino; 0.3% American Indian or Alaska Native, non-Hispanic/Latino; 3% Two or more races, non-Hispanic/Latino; 1% Race/ethnicity unknown; 1% international; 4% transferred in; 51% live on campus.

Freshmen:
Admission: 2,509 applied, 1,927 admitted, 399 enrolled. ***Average high school GPA:*** 3.7. ***Test scores:*** SAT evidence-based reading and writing scores over 500: 77%; SAT math scores over 500: 77%; ACT scores over 18: 88%; SAT evidence-based reading and writing scores over 600: 31%; SAT math scores over 600: 29%; ACT scores over 24: 45%; SAT evidence-based reading and writing scores over 700: 2%; SAT math scores over 700: 4%; ACT scores over 30: 10%.

Retention: 78% of full-time freshmen returned.

FACULTY
Total: 215, 46% full-time, 58% with terminal degrees.

Student/faculty ratio: 14:1.

ACADEMICS
Calendar: semesters. *Degrees:* certificates, bachelor's, master's, post-master's, and postbachelor's certificates.

Special study options: academic remediation for entering students, accelerated degree program, adult/continuing education programs, advanced placement credit, distance learning, double majors, English as a second language, external degree program, honors programs, independent study, internships, off-campus study, part-time degree program, services for LD students, student-designed majors, study abroad, summer session for credit.

Unusual degree programs: 3-2 engineering with University of Pittsburgh, Penn State University Park, Georgia Institute of Technology; physician assistant with Seton Hill University, osteopathic medicine or pharmacy with Lake Erie College of Osteopathic Medicine.

Computers: 66 computers/terminals and 66 ports are available on campus for general student use. Students can access the following: campus intranet, computer help desk, free student e-mail accounts, online (class) grades, online (class) registration, online (class) schedules. Campuswide network is available. 100% of college-owned or -operated housing units are wired for high-speed Internet access. Wireless service is available via entire campus.

Library: Reeves Memorial Library. *Books:* 72,274 (physical), 127,160 (digital/electronic); *Serial titles:* 2,919 (physical); *Databases:* 37. Students can reserve study rooms.

STUDENT LIFE
Housing options: on-campus residence required through junior year; coed. Campus housing is university owned. Freshman campus housing is guaranteed.

Activities and organizations: drama/theater group, student-run newspaper, choral group, marching band, Student Body Activities Council, Future Greek leaders, Dietetics Club, Biology Club, intramurals.

Athletics Member NCAA. All Division II except golf (Division I). ***Intercollegiate sports:*** baseball M(s), basketball M(s)/W(s), cross-country running M(s)/W(s), equestrian sports W(s), field hockey W(s), football M(s), golf W(s), lacrosse M(s)/W(s), soccer M(s)/W(s), softball W(s), tennis W(s), track and field M(s)/W(s), volleyball W(s), wrestling M(s).

Campus security: 24-hour emergency response devices and patrols, late-night transport/escort service, controlled dormitory access.

Student services: health clinic, personal/psychological counseling.

COSTS & FINANCIAL AID
Costs (2020–21) ***Comprehensive fee:*** $50,462 includes full-time tuition ($37,396), mandatory fees ($550), and room and board ($12,516). Part-time tuition: $1003 per credit hour. ***College room only:*** $6902. Room and board charges vary according to board plan and housing facility. ***Payment plan:*** installment.

Financial Aid Of all full-time matriculated undergraduates who enrolled in 2017, 1,412 applied for aid, 1,279 were judged to have need, 252 had their need fully met. In 2017, 256 non-need-based awards were made. ***Average percent of need met:*** 74. ***Average financial aid package:*** $26,634. ***Average need-based loan:*** $6502. ***Average need-based gift aid:*** $21,314. ***Average non-need-based aid:*** $16,077. ***Average indebtedness upon graduation:*** $35,356.

APPLYING
Standardized Tests *Recommended:* SAT or ACT (for admission).

Options: electronic application, deferred entrance.

Required: essay or personal statement, high school transcript, 1 letter of recommendation. ***Required for some:*** portfolio for art, audition for music and theatre. ***Recommended:*** interview.

Application deadlines: 8/15 (freshmen), 8/15 (transfers).

Notification: continuous (freshmen), continuous (transfers).

CONTACT
Mrs. Allison Sasso, Director of Admissions, Seton Hill University, 1 Seton Hill Drive, Greensburg, PA 15601. *Phone:* 724-838-4231. *Toll-free phone:* 800-826-6234. *E-mail:* admit@setonhill.edu.

Shippensburg University of Pennsylvania

Shippensburg, Pennsylvania

http://www.ship.edu/

- **State-supported** comprehensive, founded 1871, part of Pennsylvania State System of Higher Education
- **Rural** 200-acre campus
- **Endowment** $38.9 million
- **Coed**
- 88% of applicants were admitted

FACULTY
Student/faculty ratio: 18:1.

ACADEMICS
Calendar: semesters. *Degrees:* certificates, bachelor's, master's, doctoral, post-master's, and postbachelor's certificates.
Library: Ezra Lehman Memorial Library plus 1 other. *Books:* 359,138 (physical), 189,092 (digital/electronic); *Serial titles:* 50 (physical), 255 (digital/electronic); *Databases:* 106. Weekly public service hours: 97.

STUDENT LIFE
Housing options: on-campus residence required for freshman year; coed. Campus housing is provided by a third party. Freshman campus housing is guaranteed.

Activities and organizations: drama/theater group, student-run newspaper, radio and television station, choral group, marching band, national fraternities, national sororities.

Athletics Member NCAA. All Division II.

Campus security: 24-hour emergency response devices and patrols, late-night transport/escort service, controlled dormitory access, surveillance cameras in certain parking lots and buildings; foot, vehicular and bicycle patrols by security officers.

Student services: health clinic, personal/psychological counseling, women's center, veterans affairs office.

FINANCIAL AID
Financial Aid Of all full-time matriculated undergraduates who enrolled in 2019, 4,259 applied for aid, 3,464 were judged to have need, 397 had their need fully met. 114 Federal Work-Study jobs (averaging $1475). 608 state and other part-time jobs (averaging $2320). In 2019, 533 non-need-based awards were made. ***Average percent of need met:*** 54. ***Average financial aid package:*** $10,154. ***Average need-based loan:*** $3857. ***Average need-based gift aid:*** $7630. ***Average non-need-based aid:*** $5326. ***Average indebtedness upon graduation:*** $37,130.

APPLYING
Standardized Tests *Required:* SAT or ACT (for admission).

Options: electronic application, early admission, early action, deferred entrance.

Application fee: $45.

Required: high school transcript. ***Required for some:*** interview. ***Recommended:*** essay or personal statement, class rank, letters of recommendation.

CONTACT
Mr. William H. Washabaugh, Associate Dean of Admissions, Shippensburg University of Pennsylvania, 1871 Old Main Drive, Shippensburg, PA 17257-2299. *Phone:* 717-477-1231. *Toll-free phone:* 800-822-8028. *Fax:* 717-477-4016. *E-mail:* admiss@ship.edu.

Slippery Rock University of Pennsylvania

Slippery Rock, Pennsylvania

http://www.sru.edu/

- **State-supported** university, founded 1889, part of Pennsylvania State System of Higher Education
- **Small-town** 660-acre campus with easy access to Pittsburgh
- **Endowment** $30.6 million
- **Coed** 7,538 undergraduate students, 93% full-time, 56% women, 44% men
- **Moderately difficult** entrance level, 73% of applicants were admitted

UNDERGRAD STUDENTS
7,032 full-time, 506 part-time. Students come from 47 states and territories; 33 other countries; 9% are from out of state; 7% transferred in; 36% live on campus.

Freshmen:
Admission: 5,369 applied, 3,928 admitted, 1,554 enrolled. ***Average high school GPA:*** 3.4.

Retention: 81% of full-time freshmen returned.

ACADEMICS
Calendar: semesters. *Degrees:* certificates, bachelor's, master's, doctoral, and postbachelor's certificates.

Special study options: academic remediation for entering students, adult/continuing education programs, advanced placement credit, distance learning, double majors, English as a second language, honors programs, independent study, internships, off-campus study, part-time degree program, services for LD students, student-designed majors, study abroad, summer session for credit. ***ROTC:*** Army (b).

Unusual degree programs: 3-2 engineering with Penn State University Park, Youngstown State University, West Virginia University, University of Pittsburg.

Computers: 1,654 computers/terminals and 75 ports are available on campus for general student use. Students can access the following: computer help desk, free student e-mail accounts, online (class) grades, online (class) registration, online (class) schedules. Campuswide network is available. 100% of college-owned or -operated housing units are wired for high-speed Internet access. Wireless service is available via entire campus.
Library: Bailey Library. Weekly public service hours: 98; students can reserve study rooms.

STUDENT LIFE
Housing options: on-campus residence required for freshman year; coed, special housing for students with disabilities. Campus housing is university owned. Freshman campus housing is guaranteed.

Activities and organizations: drama/theater group, student-run newspaper, radio and television station, choral group, marching band, University Program Board, Interfraternity Council/Panhellenic Council, State Government Association, Black Action Society, Gamer's Guild, national fraternities, national sororities.

Athletics ***Intercollegiate sports:*** baseball M(s), basketball M(s)/W(s), cheerleading M(c)/W(c), cross-country running M(s)/W(s), equestrian sports M(c)/W(c), field hockey W(s), football M(s), ice hockey M(c)/W(c), lacrosse M(c)/W(s), rugby M(c)/W(c), soccer M(s)/W(s), softball W(s), tennis M(c)/W(s), track and field M(s)/W(s), volleyball M(c)/W(s). ***Intramural sports:*** badminton M/W, baseball M(c), basketball M/W, football M/W, golf M(c)/W(c), gymnastics M(c)/W(c), soccer M/W, softball M/W, swimming and diving M(c)/W(c), ultimate Frisbee M/W, volleyball M/W, water polo M/W, wrestling M(c).

Campus security: 24-hour emergency response devices and patrols, late-night transport/escort service, controlled dormitory access.

Student services: health clinic, personal/psychological counseling, women's center, legal services, veterans affairs office.

COSTS & FINANCIAL AID
Costs (2019–20) ***Tuition:*** state resident $7716 full-time, $322 per credit hour part-time; nonresident $15,432 full-time, $644 per credit hour part-time. Full-time tuition and fees vary according to course load. Part-time tuition and fees vary according to course load. ***Required fees:*** $2801 full-time, $115 per credit hour part-time. ***Room and board:*** $10,446; room

only: $6876. Room and board charges vary according to board plan and housing facility. ***Payment plan:*** installment. ***Waivers:*** minority students, senior citizens, and employees or children of employees.

Financial Aid Of all full-time matriculated undergraduates who enrolled in 2019, 6,116 applied for aid, 4,703 were judged to have need, 548 had their need fully met. 591 Federal Work-Study jobs (averaging $1506). 908 state and other part-time jobs (averaging $2012). In 2019, 717 non-need-based awards were made. ***Average percent of need met:*** 60. ***Average financial aid package:*** $9560. ***Average need-based loan:*** $4225. ***Average need-based gift aid:*** $5969. ***Average non-need-based aid:*** $3114. ***Average indebtedness upon graduation:*** $37,450.

APPLYING

Standardized Tests *Required:* SAT or ACT (for admission).

Options: electronic application, deferred entrance.

Application fee: $30.

Required: high school transcript. ***Recommended:*** minimum 3.0 GPA.

Application deadlines: rolling (freshmen), rolling (transfers).

Notification: continuous until 6/15 (freshmen), continuous until 6/15 (transfers).

CONTACT

Slippery Rock University of Pennsylvania, 1 Morrow Way, Slippery Rock, PA 16057-1383. *Phone:* 724-738-2015. *Toll-free phone:* 800-SRU-9111.

Strayer University - Allentown

Allentown, Pennsylvania

http://www.strayer.edu/pennsylvania/allentown/

CONTACT

Strayer University - Allentown, 520 Hamilton Street, Suite 100, Allentown, PA 18101-1502. *Toll-free phone:* 888-311-0355.

Strayer University - Center City

Philadelphia, Pennsylvania

http://www.strayer.edu/pennsylvania/center-city/

CONTACT

Strayer University - Center City, 1601 Cherry Street, Suite 100, Philadelphia, PA 19102. *Toll-free phone:* 888-311-0355.

Strayer University–Delaware County Campus

Springfield, Pennsylvania

http://www.strayer.edu/pennsylvania/delaware-county/

CONTACT

Strayer University–Delaware County Campus, 760 West Sproul Road, Suite 200, Springfield, PA 19064. *Toll-free phone:* 888-311-0355.

Strayer University–Lower Bucks County Campus

Trevose, Pennsylvania

http://www.strayer.edu/pennsylvania/lower-bucks-county/

CONTACT

Strayer University–Lower Bucks County Campus, 3800 Horizon Boulevard, Suite 100, Trevose, PA 19053. *Toll-free phone:* 888-311-0355.

Strayer University–Warrendale Campus

Warrendale, Pennsylvania

http://www.strayer.edu/pennsylvania/warrendale/

CONTACT

Strayer University–Warrendale Campus, 802 Warrendale Village Drive, Warrendale, PA 15086. *Toll-free phone:* 888-311-0355.

Susquehanna University

Selinsgrove, Pennsylvania

http://www.susqu.edu/

- **Independent** 4-year, founded 1858, affiliated with Evangelical Lutheran Church in America
- **Small-town** 325-acre campus
- **Endowment** $175.7 million
- **Coed** 2,312 undergraduate students, 95% full-time, 56% women, 44% men
- **Moderately difficult** entrance level, 85% of applicants were admitted

UNDERGRAD STUDENTS

2,200 full-time, 112 part-time. Students come from 30 states and territories; 21 other countries; 35% are from out of state; 6% Black or African American, non-Hispanic/Latino; 6% Hispanic/Latino; 2% Asian, non-Hispanic/Latino; 0.1% Native Hawaiian or other Pacific Islander, non-Hispanic/Latino; 0.1% American Indian or Alaska Native, non-Hispanic/Latino; 3% Two or more races, non-Hispanic/Latino; 6% Race/ethnicity unknown; 2% international; 1% transferred in; 89% live on campus.

Freshmen:

Admission: 4,863 applied, 4,122 admitted, 620 enrolled. ***Average high school GPA:*** 3.7. ***Test scores:*** SAT evidence-based reading and writing scores over 500: 94%; SAT math scores over 500: 94%; ACT scores over 18: 99%; SAT evidence-based reading and writing scores over 600: 54%; SAT math scores over 600: 47%; ACT scores over 24: 64%; SAT evidence-based reading and writing scores over 700: 9%; SAT math scores over 700: 7%; ACT scores over 30: 19%.

Retention: 87% of full-time freshmen returned.

FACULTY

Total: 227, 61% full-time.

Student/faculty ratio: 13:1.

ACADEMICS

Calendar: semesters. *Degrees:* bachelor's and master's (also offers evening associate degree program limited to local adult students).

Special study options: accelerated degree program, adult/continuing education programs, advanced placement credit, distance learning, double majors, English as a second language, honors programs, independent study, internships, off-campus study, part-time degree program, services for LD students, student-designed majors, study abroad, summer session for credit. ***ROTC:*** Army (b).

Unusual degree programs: 3-2 engineering with Columbia University, Washington University-St. Louis, Case Western Reserve University.

Computers: 211 computers/terminals are available on campus for general student use. Students can access the following: campus intranet, computer help desk, free student e-mail accounts, online (class) grades, online (class) registration, online (class) schedules, online voting booth. Campuswide network is available. 100% of college-owned or -operated housing units are wired for high-speed Internet access. Wireless service is available via entire campus.

Library: Blough-Weis Library. *Books:* 154,876 (physical), 435,770 (digital/electronic); *Serial titles:* 523 (physical), 111,780 (digital/electronic); *Databases:* 139. Weekly public service hours: 106; students can reserve study rooms.

STUDENT LIFE

Housing options: on-campus residence required through senior year; coed, cooperative, special housing for students with disabilities. Campus housing is university owned. Freshman campus housing is guaranteed.

Activities and organizations: drama/theater group, student-run newspaper, radio station, choral group, Student Government Association, Alpha Phi Omega, Student Activities Committee, SU Dance Corps, Club Sports, national fraternities, national sororities.

Athletics Member NCAA. All Division III. ***Intercollegiate sports:*** baseball M, basketball M/W, cheerleading M(c)/W(c), crew M(c)/W(c), cross-country running M/W, equestrian sports M(c)/W(c), field hockey W, football M, golf M/W, lacrosse M/W, rugby M(c)/W(c), soccer M/W, softball W, swimming and diving M/W, tennis M/W, track and field M/W, volleyball M(c)/W. ***Intramural sports:*** basketball M/W, racquetball M/W, soccer M/W, softball M/W, tennis M/W, volleyball M/W.

Campus security: 24-hour emergency response devices and patrols, late-night transport/escort service, controlled dormitory access.

Student services: health clinic, personal/psychological counseling.

COSTS & FINANCIAL AID

Costs (2020–21) ***Comprehensive fee:*** $64,820 includes full-time tuition ($50,500), mandatory fees ($640), and room and board ($13,680). Part-time tuition: $1605 per credit hour. ***College room only:*** $7320. Room and board charges vary according to board plan. ***Payment plans:*** tuition prepayment, installment. ***Waivers:*** employees or children of employees.

Financial Aid Of all full-time matriculated undergraduates who enrolled in 2019, 2,007 applied for aid, 1,834 were judged to have need, 396 had their need fully met. In 2019, 421 non-need-based awards were made. ***Average percent of need met:*** 82. ***Average financial aid package:*** $39,750. ***Average need-based loan:*** $4102. ***Average need-based gift aid:*** $35,382. ***Average non-need-based aid:*** $27,871. ***Average indebtedness upon graduation:*** $40,455. ***Financial aid deadline:*** 5/1.

APPLYING

Options: electronic application, early admission, early decision, early action, deferred entrance.

Required: essay or personal statement, high school transcript, minimum 2.5 GPA, 1 letter of recommendation. ***Required for some:*** writing portfolio for creative writing program, audition for music programs, design portfolio for graphic design programs. ***Recommended:*** minimum 3.0 GPA, interview.

Application deadlines: rolling (freshmen), 8/1 (transfers), 11/1 (early action).

Early decision deadline: 11/15.

Notification: continuous (freshmen), continuous (transfers), 12/1 (early decision), 12/1 (early action).

CONTACT

Mr. Philip Betz, Director of Admissions, Susquehanna University, 514 University Avenue, Selinsgrove, PA 17841. *Phone:* 570-372-4260. *Toll-free phone:* 800-326-9672. *Fax:* 570-372-2722. *E-mail:* suadmiss@susqu.edu.

Swarthmore College

Swarthmore, Pennsylvania

http://www.swarthmore.edu/

- **Independent** 4-year, founded 1864
- **Suburban** 425-acre campus with easy access to Philadelphia
- **Endowment** $1.7 million
- **Coed**
- 9% of applicants were admitted

FACULTY

Student/faculty ratio: 8:1.

ACADEMICS

Calendar: semesters. *Degree:* bachelor's.
Library: McCabe Library plus 6 others.

STUDENT LIFE

Housing options: on-campus residence required for freshman year; coed, men-only, women-only, special housing for students with disabilities. Campus housing is university owned. Freshman campus housing is guaranteed.

Activities and organizations: drama/theater group, student-run newspaper, radio station, choral group, Boy Meets Tractor (sketch comedy troupe), Rhythm N' Motion (performing dance styles of the African Diaspora), Multi (community for people who self-identify as multiracial, multiethnic, multicultural, and/or multireligious), Mixed Company (a cappella group), national fraternities, national sororities.

Athletics Member NCAA. All Division III.

Campus security: 24-hour emergency response devices and patrols, late-night transport/escort service.

Student services: health clinic, personal/psychological counseling, women's center.

COSTS & FINANCIAL AID

Costs (2019–20) ***Comprehensive fee:*** $70,744 includes full-time tuition ($54,256), mandatory fees ($400), and room and board ($16,088). ***College room only:*** $8252.

Financial Aid Of all full-time matriculated undergraduates who enrolled in 2019, 995 applied for aid, 906 were judged to have need, 906 had their need fully met. In 2019, 23 non-need-based awards were made. ***Average percent of need met:*** 100. ***Average financial aid package:*** $56,048. ***Average need-based gift aid:*** $54,217. ***Average non-need-based aid:*** $52,223. ***Average indebtedness upon graduation:*** $24,099. ***Financial aid deadline:*** 1/1.

APPLYING

Standardized Tests *Required:* SAT or ACT (for admission).

Options: early admission, early decision, deferred entrance.

Application fee: $60.

Required: essay or personal statement, high school transcript, 3 letters of recommendation.

CONTACT

Swarthmore College, 500 College Avenue, Swarthmore, PA 19081-1397. *Toll-free phone:* 800-667-3110.

Talmudical Yeshiva of Philadelphia

Philadelphia, Pennsylvania

CONTACT

Rabbi Shmuel Kamenetsky, Co-Dean, Talmudical Yeshiva of Philadelphia, 6063 Drexel Road, Philadelphia, PA 19131-1296. *Phone:* 215-473-1212.

Temple University

Philadelphia, Pennsylvania

http://www.temple.edu/

- **State-related** university, founded 1884, part of Commonwealth System of Higher Education
- **Urban** 335-acre campus with easy access to Philadelphia
- **Endowment** $682.2 million
- **Coed** 28,726 undergraduate students, 91% full-time, 54% women, 46% men
- **Moderately difficult** entrance level, 60% of applicants were admitted

UNDERGRAD STUDENTS

26,247 full-time, 2,479 part-time. Students come from 51 states and territories; 112 other countries; 21% are from out of state; 13% Black or African American, non-Hispanic/Latino; 8% Hispanic/Latino; 12% Asian, non-Hispanic/Latino; 0.1% Native Hawaiian or other Pacific Islander, non-Hispanic/Latino; 0.1% American Indian or Alaska Native, non-Hispanic/Latino; 4% Two or more races, non-Hispanic/Latino; 2% Race/ethnicity unknown; 5% international; 8% transferred in; 18% live on campus.

Freshmen:

Admission: 35,599 applied, 21,375 admitted, 4,967 enrolled. ***Average high school GPA:*** 3.5. ***Test scores:*** SAT evidence-based reading and writing scores over 500: 94%; SAT math scores over 500: 94%; ACT scores over 18: 97%; SAT evidence-based reading and writing scores over 600: 62%; SAT math scores over 600: 54%; ACT scores over 24: 75%; SAT evidence-based reading and writing scores over 700: 13%; SAT math scores over 700: 15%; ACT scores over 30: 29%.

Retention: 89% of full-time freshmen returned.

FACULTY

Total: 2,942, 54% full-time, 49% with terminal degrees.

Student/faculty ratio: 13:1.

ACADEMICS

Calendar: semesters. *Degrees:* certificates, diplomas, bachelor's, master's, doctoral, post-master's, and postbachelor's certificates.

Special study options: academic remediation for entering students, accelerated degree program, adult/continuing education programs, advanced placement credit, cooperative education, distance learning, double majors, English as a second language, honors programs,

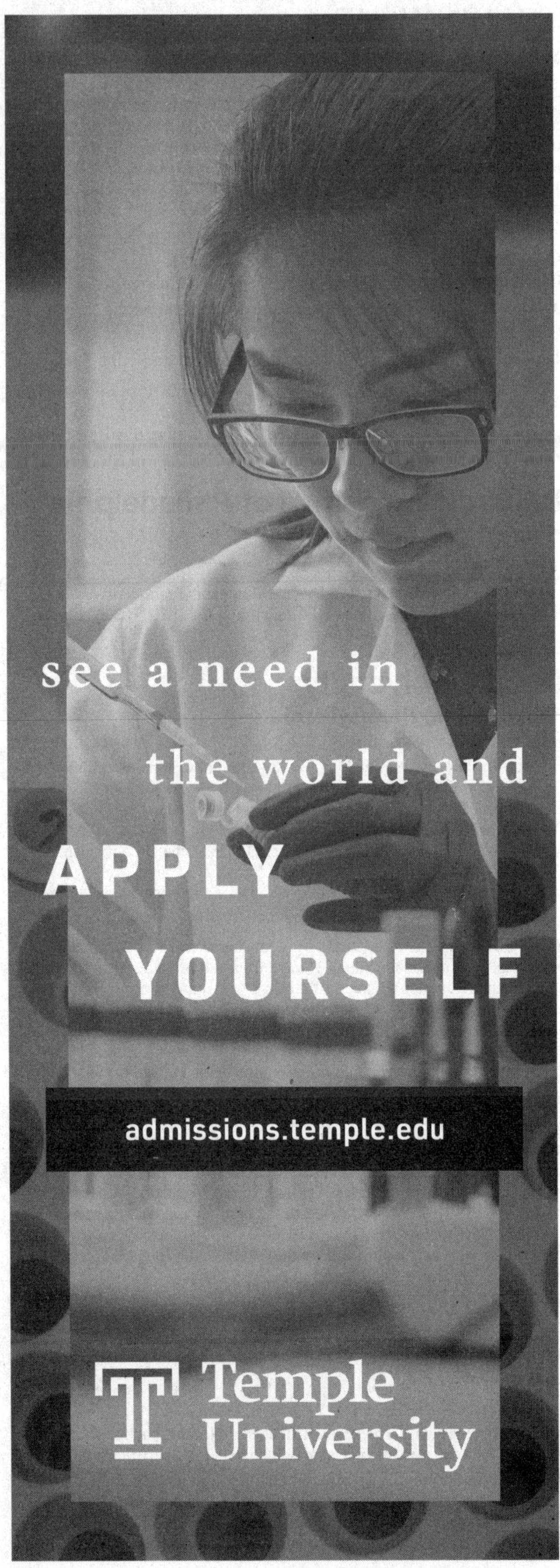

independent study, internships, off-campus study, part-time degree program, services for LD students, study abroad, summer session for credit. ***ROTC:*** Army (b), Navy (c), Air Force (c).

Computers: 11,962 computers/terminals and 67,934 ports are available on campus for general student use. Students can access the following: campus intranet, computer help desk, free student e-mail accounts, online (class) grades, online (class) registration, online (class) schedules, student accounts, Web hosting. Campuswide network is available. 100% of college-owned or -operated housing units are wired for high-speed Internet access. Wireless service is available via entire campus.
Library: Charles Library plus 6 others. *Books:* 2.8 million (physical), 2.3 million (digital/electronic); *Serial titles:* 40,735 (physical), 2.2 million (digital/electronic); *Databases:* 709. Students can reserve study rooms.

STUDENT LIFE
Housing options: coed, special housing for students with disabilities. Campus housing is university owned. Freshman campus housing is guaranteed.

Activities and organizations: drama/theater group, student-run newspaper, radio and television station, choral group, marching band, Temple University Gamers' Guild, Queer Student Union, Habitat for Humanity, Temple University Community Service Association, American Medical Student Association, national fraternities, national sororities.

Athletics Member NCAA. All Division I except football (Division I-A). ***Intercollegiate sports:*** basketball M(s)/W(s), crew M(s), cross-country running M(s)/W(s), fencing W(s), field hockey W(s), golf M(s), gymnastics W(s), lacrosse W(s), rowing W(s), soccer M(s)/W(s), tennis M(s)/W(s), track and field W(s), volleyball W(s). ***Intramural sports:*** badminton M(c)/W(c), baseball M(c)/W(c), basketball M/W, bowling M(c)/W(c), equestrian sports M(c)/W(c), fencing M(c)/W(c), field hockey W(c), football M/W, gymnastics M(c)/W(c), ice hockey M(c), lacrosse M(c)/W(c), rock climbing M(c)/W(c), rugby M(c)/W(c), soccer M(c)/W(c), softball M/W(c), swimming and diving M(c)/W(c), tennis M(c)/W(c), track and field M(c)/W(c), weight lifting M(c)/W(c), wrestling M(c).

Campus security: 24-hour emergency response devices and patrols, student patrols, late-night transport/escort service, controlled dormitory access.

Student services: health clinic, personal/psychological counseling, veterans affairs office.

COSTS & FINANCIAL AID
Costs (2019–20) ***Tuition:*** state resident $18,858 full-time, $670 per credit hour part-time; nonresident $33,236 full-time, $1208 per credit hour part-time. Full-time tuition and fees vary according to course load and program. Part-time tuition and fees vary according to course load and program. ***Required fees:*** $890 full-time, $163 per term part-time. ***Room and board:*** $12,188; room only: $8166. Room and board charges vary according to board plan, housing facility, and location. ***Payment plans:*** installment, deferred payment. ***Waivers:*** employees or children of employees.

Financial Aid Of all full-time matriculated undergraduates who enrolled in 2018, 20,994 applied for aid, 18,138 were judged to have need, 601 had their need fully met. In 2018, 3605 non-need-based awards were made. ***Average percent of need met:*** 61. ***Average financial aid package:*** $12,347. ***Average need-based loan:*** $4260. ***Average need-based gift aid:*** $9596. ***Average non-need-based aid:*** $7953. ***Average indebtedness upon graduation:*** $38,634.

APPLYING
Options: electronic application, early action, deferred entrance.

Application fee: $55.

Required: essay or personal statement, high school transcript. ***Recommended:*** minimum 3.0 GPA, 1 letter of recommendation.

Application deadlines: 2/1 (freshmen), 2/1 (out-of-state freshmen), 6/1 (transfers), 11/1 (early action).

Notification: continuous (freshmen), continuous (out-of-state freshmen), continuous (transfers), 1/10 (early action).

CONTACT
Temple University, 1801 North Broad Street, Philadelphia, PA 19122-6096. *Phone:* 215-204-7200. *Toll-free phone:* 888-340-2222.

See below for display ad and page 1116 for the College Close-Up.

Thiel College

Greenville, Pennsylvania

http://www.thiel.edu/

CONTACT
Mr. Stephen Lazowski, Vice President for Enrollment Management, Thiel College, 75 College Avenue, Greenville, PA 16125. *Phone:* 724-589-2182. *Toll-free phone:* 800-248-4435. *Fax:* 724-589-2013. *E-mail:* admissions@thiel.edu.

Thomas Jefferson University

Philadelphia, Pennsylvania

http://www.jefferson.edu/university.html

CONTACT
Ms. Karen Jacobs, Director of Admissions, Thomas Jefferson University, Edison Building, 130 South Ninth Street, Philadelphia, PA 19107. *Phone:* 215-503-8890. *Toll-free phone:* 877-533-3247. *Fax:* 215-503-7241. *E-mail:* chpadmissions@mail.tju.edu.

University of Pennsylvania

Philadelphia, Pennsylvania

http://www.upenn.edu/

- **Independent** university, founded 1740
- **Urban** 299-acre campus
- **Endowment** $14.6 billion
- **Coed** 10,019 undergraduate students, 98% full-time, 52% women, 48% men
- **Most difficult** entrance level, 8% of applicants were admitted

UNDERGRAD STUDENTS
9,774 full-time, 245 part-time. 80% are from out of state; 8% Black or African American, non-Hispanic/Latino; 10% Hispanic/Latino; 22% Asian, non-Hispanic/Latino; 0.0% Native Hawaiian or other Pacific Islander, non-Hispanic/Latino; 0.1% American Indian or Alaska Native, non-Hispanic/Latino; 5% Two or more races, non-Hispanic/Latino; 2% Race/ethnicity unknown; 13% international; 1% transferred in; 55% live on campus.

Freshmen:
Admission: 44,961 applied, 3,446 admitted, 2,340 enrolled. ***Average high school GPA:*** 3.9. ***Test scores:*** SAT evidence-based reading and writing scores over 500: 100%; SAT math scores over 500: 100%; ACT scores over 18: 100%; SAT evidence-based reading and writing scores over 600: 99%; SAT math scores over 600: 99%; ACT scores over 24: 100%; SAT evidence-based reading and writing scores over 700: 80%; SAT math scores over 700: 91%; ACT scores over 30: 94%.

Retention: 98% of full-time freshmen returned.

FACULTY
Total: 1,960, 81% full-time, 100% with terminal degrees.

Student/faculty ratio: 6:1.

ACADEMICS
Calendar: semesters plus 2 5-week summer sessions. *Degrees:* certificates, associate, bachelor's, master's, doctoral, post-master's, and postbachelor's certificates (also offers evening program with significant enrollment not reflected in profile).

Special study options: academic remediation for entering students, accelerated degree program, adult/continuing education programs, advanced placement credit, cooperative education, distance learning, double majors, English as a second language, honors programs, independent study, internships, off-campus study, part-time degree program, services for LD students, student-designed majors, study abroad, summer session for credit. ***ROTC:*** Army (c), Navy (b), Air Force (c).

Computers: Students can access the following: campus intranet, computer help desk, free student e-mail accounts, online (class) grades, online (class) registration, online (class) schedules, billing information, financial aid application, status, academic records, student services. Campuswide network is available. 100% of college-owned or -operated housing units are wired for high-speed Internet access. Wireless service is available via entire campus.

Library: Van Pelt Library plus 13 others. *Books:* 6.7 million (physical), 2.0 million (digital/electronic); *Serial titles:* 282,857 (physical), 279,206 (digital/electronic). Study areas open 24 hours, 5–7 days a week; students can reserve study rooms.

STUDENT LIFE
Housing options: coed, special housing for students with disabilities. Campus housing is university owned. Freshman campus housing is guaranteed.

Activities and organizations: drama/theater group, student-run newspaper, radio and television station, choral group, marching band, Kite and Key Society, Social Planning and Events Committee, Hillel at Penn, Sports Club Council, Interfraternity Council, national fraternities, national sororities.

Athletics Member NCAA. All Division I except football (Division I-AA). ***Intercollegiate sports:*** baseball M, basketball M/W, crew M/W, cross-country running M/W, fencing M/W, field hockey W, golf M/W, gymnastics W, lacrosse M/W, soccer M/W, softball W, squash M/W, swimming and diving M/W, tennis M/W, track and field M/W, volleyball W, wrestling M. ***Intramural sports:*** badminton M(c)/W(c), baseball M(c)/W(c), basketball M(c)/W(c), cheerleading M/W, equestrian sports M(c)/W(c), fencing W(c), field hockey M(c), golf M(c)/W(c), gymnastics M(c)/W(c), ice hockey M(c)/W(c), lacrosse M/W, rugby M(c)/W(c), sailing M(c)/W(c), skiing (downhill) M(c)/W(c), soccer M/W, softball M/W, squash M/W, swimming and diving M/W, table tennis M/W, tennis M/W, ultimate Frisbee M(c)/W(c), volleyball M/W, water polo M(c)/W(c).

Campus security: 24-hour emergency response devices and patrols, late-night transport/escort service, controlled dormitory access.

Student services: health clinic, personal/psychological counseling, women's center, legal services.

COSTS & FINANCIAL AID
Costs (2020–21) ***Comprehensive fee:*** $76,826 includes full-time tuition ($53,166), mandatory fees ($6876), and room and board ($16,784). Part-time tuition and fees vary according to course load. ***College room only:*** $11,014. Room and board charges vary according to board plan and housing facility. ***Payment plans:*** tuition prepayment, installment. ***Waivers:*** employees or children of employees.

Financial Aid Of all full-time matriculated undergraduates who enrolled in 2017, 4,882 applied for aid, 4,517 were judged to have need, 4,517 had their need fully met. ***Average percent of need met:*** 100. ***Average financial aid package:*** $51,860. ***Average need-based loan:*** $3783. ***Average need-based gift aid:*** $48,787. ***Average indebtedness upon graduation:*** $22,103.

APPLYING
Standardized Tests *Required:* SAT or ACT (for admission). *Recommended:* SAT Subject Tests (for admission).

Options: electronic application, early admission, early decision, deferred entrance.

Application fee: $75.

Required: essay or personal statement, high school transcript, 2 letters of recommendation.

Application deadlines: 1/5 (freshmen), 3/15 (transfers).

Early decision deadline: 11/1.

Notification: continuous until 4/1 (freshmen), 5/15 (transfers), 12/15 (early decision).

CONTACT
University of Pennsylvania, 3451 Walnut Street, Philadelphia, PA 19104. *Phone:* 215-898-7507.

University of Pittsburgh

Pittsburgh, Pennsylvania

http://www.pitt.edu/

- **State-related** university, founded 1787, part of Commonwealth System of Higher Education
- **Urban** 145-acre campus with easy access to Pittsburgh
- **Endowment** $4.2 billion
- **Coed**
- **Very difficult** entrance level

FACULTY
Student/faculty ratio: 14:1.

ACADEMICS
Calendar: semesters plus summer term. *Degrees:* certificates, bachelor's, master's, doctoral, post-master's, and postbachelor's certificates.
Library: Hillman Library plus 16 others. *Books:* 4.3 million (physical), 1.7 million (digital/electronic); *Serial titles:* 108,985 (physical), 261,311 (digital/electronic); *Databases:* 571. Weekly public service hours: 145; study areas open 24 hours, 5–7 days a week; students can reserve study rooms.

STUDENT LIFE
Housing options: coed, cooperative, special housing for students with disabilities. Campus housing is university owned. Freshman campus housing is guaranteed.

Activities and organizations: drama/theater group, student-run newspaper, radio and television station, choral group, marching band, Resident Student Association, Black Action Society, Pitt Program Council, Interfraternity Council, Panhellenic Association, national fraternities, national sororities.

Athletics Member NCAA. All Division I except football (Division I-A).

Campus security: 24-hour emergency response devices and patrols, late-night transport/escort service, controlled dormitory access.

Student services: health clinic, personal/psychological counseling, veterans affairs office.

COSTS & FINANCIAL AID
Costs (2019–20) ***Tuition:*** area resident $18,628 full-time, $776 per credit hour part-time; state resident $18,628 full-time, $776 per credit hour part-time; nonresident $32,656 full-time, $1360 per credit hour part-time. Full-time tuition and fees vary according to location and program. Part-time tuition and fees vary according to location and program. ***Required fees:*** $1090 full-time, $310 per term part-time. ***Room and board:*** $11,250; room only: $6550. Room and board charges vary according to board plan, housing facility, and location.

Financial Aid Of all full-time matriculated undergraduates who enrolled in 2018, 12,593 applied for aid, 9,473 were judged to have need, 870 had their need fully met. In 2018, 713 non-need-based awards were made. ***Average percent of need met:*** 53. ***Average financial aid package:*** $12,362. ***Average need-based loan:*** $4496. ***Average need-based gift aid:*** $10,519. ***Average non-need-based aid:*** $10,206. ***Average indebtedness upon graduation:*** $39,417.

APPLYING
Standardized Tests *Required:* SAT or ACT (for admission).

Options: electronic application.

Application fee: $45.

Required: high school transcript. ***Recommended:*** essay or personal statement, interview.

CONTACT
Marc L. Harding, Chief Enrollment Officer, University of Pittsburgh, 4227 Fifth Avenue, First Floor, Alumni Hall, Pittsburgh, PA 15260. *Phone:* 412-624-7488. *Fax:* 412-648-8815. *E-mail:* oafa@pitt.edu.

University of Pittsburgh at Bradford

Bradford, Pennsylvania

http://www.upb.pitt.edu/

- **State-related** 4-year, founded 1963, part of University of Pittsburgh System
- **Small-town** 317-acre campus with easy access to Buffalo
- **Endowment** $28.5 million
- **Coed** 1,326 undergraduate students, 95% full-time, 57% women, 43% men
- **Minimally difficult** entrance level, 79% of applicants were admitted

UNDERGRAD STUDENTS
1,259 full-time, 67 part-time. Students come from 30 states and territories; 14 other countries; 26% are from out of state; 14% Black or African American, non-Hispanic/Latino; 7% Hispanic/Latino; 3% Asian, non-Hispanic/Latino; 0.4% American Indian or Alaska Native, non-Hispanic/Latino; 4% Two or more races, non-Hispanic/Latino; 3% Race/ethnicity unknown; 2% international; 5% transferred in; 76% live on campus.

Freshmen:
Admission: 2,852 applied, 2,242 admitted, 433 enrolled. ***Average high school GPA:*** 3.3. ***Test scores:*** SAT evidence-based reading and writing scores over 500: 73%; SAT math scores over 500: 69%; ACT scores over 18: 73%; SAT evidence-based reading and writing scores over 600: 23%; SAT math scores over 600: 17%; ACT scores over 24: 27%; SAT math scores over 700: 2%; ACT scores over 30: 3%.

Retention: 68% of full-time freshmen returned.

FACULTY
Total: 149, 51% full-time, 42% with terminal degrees.

Student/faculty ratio: 16:1.

ACADEMICS
Calendar: semesters. *Degrees:* associate and bachelor's.

Special study options: academic remediation for entering students, accelerated degree program, adult/continuing education programs, advanced placement credit, cooperative education, distance learning, double majors, independent study, internships, off-campus study, part-time degree program, services for LD students, student-designed majors, study abroad, summer session for credit. ***ROTC:*** Army (c).

Computers: 133 computers/terminals and 1,200 ports are available on campus for general student use. Students can access the following: computer help desk, free student e-mail accounts, online (class) grades, online (class) registration, online (class) schedules, online bills. Campuswide network is available. 100% of college-owned or -operated housing units are wired for high-speed Internet access. Wireless service is available via entire campus.
Library: T. Edward and Tullah Hanley Library. *Books:* 108,686 (physical), 1.5 million (digital/electronic); *Serial titles:* 72 (physical), 261,311 (digital/electronic); *Databases:* 586. Weekly public service hours: 86; students can reserve study rooms.

STUDENT LIFE
Housing options: on-campus residence required for freshman year; coed, special housing for students with disabilities. Campus housing is university owned. Freshman campus housing is guaranteed.

Activities and organizations: drama/theater group, student-run radio station, choral group, Student Government Association, Student Activities Board, The Source (student newspaper), Alpha Phi Omega, WDRQ (student radio station), national fraternities, national sororities.

Athletics Member NCAA. All Division III. ***Intercollegiate sports:*** baseball M, basketball M/W, bowling W, golf M, ice hockey M, soccer M/W, softball W, swimming and diving M/W, tennis M/W, volleyball W, wrestling M. ***Intramural sports:*** basketball M/W, cheerleading W(c), cross-country running M/W, football M/W, golf M, ice hockey M/W, rock climbing M/W, sand volleyball M/W, soccer M/W, softball M/W, swimming and diving M/W, table tennis M/W, ultimate Frisbee M/W, volleyball M/W, water polo M/W.

Campus security: 24-hour emergency response devices and patrols, late-night transport/escort service, controlled dormitory access.

Student services: health clinic, personal/psychological counseling.

COSTS & FINANCIAL AID
Costs (2019–20) ***One-time required fee:*** $90. ***Tuition:*** area resident $13,198 full-time, $549 per credit hour part-time; state resident $13,198 full-time, $549 per credit hour part-time; nonresident $24,666 full-time, $1027 per credit hour part-time. Full-time tuition and fees vary according to course load and program. Part-time tuition and fees vary according to course load and program. ***Required fees:*** $960 full-time, $165 per term part-time. ***Room and board:*** $10,532; room only: $6468. Room and board charges vary according to board plan and housing facility. ***Payment plan:*** installment. ***Waivers:*** employees or children of employees.

Financial Aid Of all full-time matriculated undergraduates who enrolled in 2018, 1,118 applied for aid, 1,011 were judged to have need, 61 had their need fully met. In 2018, 85 non-need-based awards were made. ***Average percent of need met:*** 60. ***Average financial aid package:*** $14,162. ***Average need-based loan:*** $4067. ***Average need-based gift aid:*** $10,236. ***Average non-need-based aid:*** $6118. ***Average indebtedness upon graduation:*** $38,322.

APPLYING
Standardized Tests *Required:* SAT or ACT (for admission).

Options: electronic application, deferred entrance.

Required: high school transcript, minimum 2.0 GPA. ***Required for some:*** minimum 3.0 GPA, interview. ***Recommended:*** essay or personal statement, 2 letters of recommendation.

Application deadlines: rolling (freshmen), rolling (out-of-state freshmen), rolling (transfers).

Notification: continuous (freshmen), continuous (out-of-state freshmen), continuous (transfers).

CONTACT
Ms. Vicky Pingie, Associate Director of Admissions, University of Pittsburgh at Bradford, 300 Campus Drive, Bradford, PA 16701. *Phone:* 814-362-7552. *Toll-free phone:* 800-872-1787. *Fax:* 814-362-5150. *E-mail:* monti@pitt.edu.

See below for display ad and page 1128 for the College Close-Up.

University of Pittsburgh at Greensburg

Greensburg, Pennsylvania

http://www.greensburg.pitt.edu/

- **State-related** 4-year, founded 1963, part of University of Pittsburgh System
- **Small-town** 219-acre campus with easy access to Pittsburgh
- **Coed** 1,439 undergraduate students, 94% full-time, 56% women, 44% men
- **Moderately difficult** entrance level, 84% of applicants were admitted

UNDERGRAD STUDENTS
1,359 full-time, 80 part-time. 5% are from out of state; 6% Black or African American, non-Hispanic/Latino; 7% Hispanic/Latino; 4% Asian, non-Hispanic/Latino; 4% Two or more races, non-Hispanic/Latino; 3% Race/ethnicity unknown; 0.4% international; 7% transferred in; 46% live on campus.

Freshmen:
Admission: 2,127 applied, 1,783 admitted, 412 enrolled. ***Average high school GPA:*** 3.6. ***Test scores:*** SAT evidence-based reading and writing scores over 500: 82%; SAT math scores over 500: 78%; ACT scores over 18: 90%; SAT evidence-based reading and writing scores over 600: 26%; SAT math scores over 600: 22%; ACT scores over 24: 36%; SAT evidence-based reading and writing scores over 700: 2%; SAT math scores over 700: 1%; ACT scores over 30: 4%.

Retention: 60% of full-time freshmen returned.

ACADEMICS
Calendar: semesters. *Degree:* certificates and bachelor's.

Special study options: academic remediation for entering students, accelerated degree program, adult/continuing education programs, advanced placement credit, distance learning, double majors, independent study, internships, off-campus study, part-time degree program, services for LD students, student-designed majors, study abroad, summer session for credit. ***ROTC:*** Army (b), Air Force (c).

Computers: Students can access the following: campus intranet, computer help desk, free student e-mail accounts, online (class) grades, online (class) registration, online (class) schedules. Campuswide network is available. 100% of college-owned or -operated housing units are wired for high-speed Internet access. Wireless service is available via classrooms, computer centers, computer labs, dorm rooms, learning centers, libraries, student centers.
Library: Millstein Library.

STUDENT LIFE
Housing options: coed. Campus housing is university owned.

Activities and organizations: drama/theater group, student-run newspaper, choral group, Habitat for Humanity, Student Government Association, Student Activities Board, Outdoor Adventure and Community Service, Freshmen Honor Society - Phi Eta Sigma.

Athletics Member NCAA. All Division III. ***Intercollegiate sports:*** baseball M, basketball M/W, cross-country running M/W, golf M, soccer M/W, softball W, tennis M/W, volleyball W. ***Intramural sports:*** baseball M, basketball M/W, bowling M/W, football M/W, golf M/W, racquetball M/W, skiing (cross-country) M/W, skiing (downhill) M/W, soccer M/W, softball M/W, table tennis M/W, tennis M/W, volleyball M/W, weight lifting M/W.

Campus security: 24-hour emergency response devices and patrols, late-night transport/escort service, controlled dormitory access.

Student services: health clinic, personal/psychological counseling.

COSTS & FINANCIAL AID

Costs (2019–20) ***Tuition:*** area resident $13,198 full-time, $549 per credit hour part-time; state resident $13,198 full-time, $549 per credit hour part-time; nonresident $24,666 full-time, $1027 per credit hour part-time. Full-time tuition and fees vary according to program. Part-time tuition and fees vary according to program. ***Required fees:*** $950 full-time, $176 per term part-time. ***Room and board:*** $10,870; room only: $6710. Room and board charges vary according to board plan and housing facility. ***Payment plan:*** installment. ***Waivers:*** senior citizens and employees or children of employees.

Financial Aid Of all full-time matriculated undergraduates who enrolled in 2018, 1,241 applied for aid, 1,084 were judged to have need, 74 had their need fully met. In 2018, 87 non-need-based awards were made. ***Average percent of need met:*** 57. ***Average financial aid package:*** $11,076. ***Average need-based loan:*** $4073. ***Average need-based gift aid:*** $8741. ***Average non-need-based aid:*** $5291. ***Average indebtedness upon graduation:*** $33,844.

APPLYING

Options: electronic application, early admission, deferred entrance.

Required: high school transcript, minimum 2.5 GPA. ***Recommended:*** essay or personal statement, interview.

Application deadlines: rolling (freshmen), rolling (transfers).

Notification: continuous (freshmen), continuous (transfers).

CONTACT

Dana Bearer, Director of Admissions, University of Pittsburgh at Greensburg, 150 Finoli Drive, Greensburg, PA 15601. *Phone:* 724-836-9880. *Fax:* 724-836-7471. *E-mail:* upgadmit@pitt.edu.

University of Pittsburgh at Johnstown

Johnstown, Pennsylvania

http://www.upj.pitt.edu/

- **State-related** 4-year, founded 1927, part of University of Pittsburgh System
- **Suburban** 655-acre campus with easy access to Pittsburgh
- **Coed**
- **Moderately difficult** entrance level

FACULTY

Student/faculty ratio: 17:1.

ACADEMICS

Calendar: semesters. *Degrees:* certificates, associate, and bachelor's.
Library: Owen Library. Study areas open 24 hours, 5–7 days a week.

STUDENT LIFE

Housing options: coed, special housing for students with disabilities. Campus housing is university owned. Freshman campus housing is guaranteed.

Activities and organizations: drama/theater group, student-run newspaper, radio and television station, choral group, Dance Ensemble, Student Senate, Programming Board, academic clubs, national fraternities, national sororities.

Athletics Member NCAA. All Division II.

Campus security: 24-hour emergency response devices and patrols, late-night transport/escort service, controlled dormitory access.

Student services: health clinic, personal/psychological counseling, veterans affairs office.

COSTS & FINANCIAL AID

Costs (2019–20) ***Tuition:*** area resident $13,198 full-time, $549 per credit part-time; state resident $13,198 full-time, $549 per credit part-time; nonresident $24,666 full-time, $1027 per credit part-time. Full-time tuition and fees vary according to program. Part-time tuition and fees vary according to program. ***Required fees:*** $958 full-time. ***Room and board:*** $10,060; room only: $6040. Room and board charges vary according to board plan and housing facility.

Financial Aid Of all full-time matriculated undergraduates who enrolled in 2018, 1,241 applied for aid, 1,084 were judged to have need, 74 had their need fully met. 100 Federal Work-Study jobs (averaging $2400). In 2018, 87 non-need-based awards were made. ***Average percent of need met:*** 57. ***Average financial aid package:*** $11,076. ***Average need-based loan:*** $4073. ***Average need-based gift aid:*** $8741. ***Average non-need-based aid:*** $5291. ***Average indebtedness upon graduation:*** $39,603.

APPLYING

Standardized Tests *Required:* SAT or ACT (for admission).

Options: electronic application, early admission, deferred entrance.

Required: high school transcript, minimum 2.0 GPA. ***Recommended:*** essay or personal statement, 3 letters of recommendation, interview.

CONTACT

Mr. Ryan Clancy, Office of Admissions, University of Pittsburgh at Johnstown, 157 Blackington Hall, Johnstown, PA 15904. *Phone:* 814-269-7050. *Toll-free phone:* 800-765-4875. *E-mail:* upjadmit@pitt.edu.

The University of Scranton

Scranton, Pennsylvania

http://www.scranton.edu/

- **Independent Roman Catholic (Jesuit)** comprehensive, founded 1888
- **Urban** 50-acre campus
- **Endowment** $187.2 million
- **Coed** 3,792 undergraduate students, 96% full-time, 58% women, 42% men
- **Moderately difficult** entrance level, 76% of applicants were admitted

UNDERGRAD STUDENTS

3,626 full-time, 166 part-time. 58% are from out of state; 2% Black or African American, non-Hispanic/Latino; 10% Hispanic/Latino; 3% Asian, non-Hispanic/Latino; 0.3% Native Hawaiian or other Pacific Islander, non-Hispanic/Latino; 0.1% American Indian or Alaska Native, non-Hispanic/Latino; 2% Two or more races, non-Hispanic/Latino; 3% Race/ethnicity unknown; 0.9% international; 1% transferred in; 64% live on campus.

Freshmen:

Admission: 9,545 applied, 7,285 admitted, 996 enrolled. ***Average high school GPA:*** 3.6. ***Test scores:*** SAT evidence-based reading and writing scores over 500: 96%; SAT math scores over 500: 95%; ACT scores over 18: 98%; SAT evidence-based reading and writing scores over 600: 59%; SAT math scores over 600: 54%; ACT scores over 24: 76%; SAT evidence-based reading and writing scores over 700: 10%; SAT math scores over 700: 10%; ACT scores over 30: 16%.

Retention: 88% of full-time freshmen returned.

FACULTY

Total: 465, 60% full-time, 61% with terminal degrees.

Student/faculty ratio: 13:1.

ACADEMICS

Calendar: semesters. *Degrees:* certificates, associate, bachelor's, master's, doctoral, post-master's, and postbachelor's certificates.

Special study options: academic remediation for entering students, accelerated degree program, adult/continuing education programs, advanced placement credit, distance learning, double majors, honors programs, independent study, internships, off-campus study, part-time degree program, services for LD students, student-designed majors, study abroad, summer session for credit. ***ROTC:*** Army (b), Air Force (c).

Computers: 988 computers/terminals are available on campus for general student use. Students can access the following: computer help desk, free student e-mail accounts, online (class) grades, online (class) registration, online (class) schedules. Campuswide network is available. 100% of college-owned or -operated housing units are wired for high-speed Internet access. Wireless service is available via classrooms, computer centers, computer labs, dorm rooms, learning centers, libraries, student centers.

Library: Harry and Jeanette Weinberg Memorial Library. *Books:* 331,804 (physical), 212,028 (digital/electronic); *Serial titles:* 2,677 (physical), 53,194 (digital/electronic); *Databases:* 120. Weekly public service hours: 95; study areas open 24 hours, 5–7 days a week; students can reserve study rooms.

STUDENT LIFE
Housing options: on-campus residence required through sophomore year; coed, men-only, women-only, special housing for students with disabilities. Campus housing is university owned. Freshman campus housing is guaranteed.

Activities and organizations: drama/theater group, student-run newspaper, radio and television station, choral group, Service-oriented student clubs, United Colors, Retreat Programs, Biology/Pre-Medicine clubs, Pre-Law Society.

Athletics Member NCAA. All Division III. ***Intercollegiate sports:*** baseball M, basketball M/W, crew M(c)/W(c), cross-country running M/W, equestrian sports M(c)/W(c), fencing M(c)/W(c), field hockey W, golf M/W, ice hockey M(c), lacrosse M/W, rugby M(c)/W(c), soccer M/W, softball W, swimming and diving M/W, tennis M/W, track and field M/W, ultimate Frisbee M(c)/W(c), volleyball M(c)/W, wrestling M. ***Intramural sports:*** archery M(c)/W(c), badminton M/W, basketball M/W, cheerleading M(c)/W(c), football M/W, skiing (downhill) M(c)/W(c), soccer M/W, softball M/W, ultimate Frisbee M/W, volleyball M/W.

Campus security: 24-hour emergency response devices and patrols, student patrols, late-night transport/escort service, controlled dormitory access, sprinkler systems in all University-owned housing.

Student services: health clinic, personal/psychological counseling, women's center.

COSTS & FINANCIAL AID
Costs (2019–20) ***Comprehensive fee:*** $61,100 includes full-time tuition ($45,390), mandatory fees ($400), and room and board ($15,310). ***College room only:*** $8950. Room and board charges vary according to board plan and housing facility. ***Payment plan:*** installment. ***Waivers:*** senior citizens and employees or children of employees.

Financial Aid Of all full-time matriculated undergraduates who enrolled in 2018, 2,956 applied for aid, 2,552 were judged to have need, 495 had their need fully met. In 2018, 763 non-need-based awards were made. ***Average percent of need met:*** 69. ***Average financial aid package:*** $31,832. ***Average need-based loan:*** $4333. ***Average need-based gift aid:*** $16,402. ***Average non-need-based aid:*** $16,299. ***Average indebtedness upon graduation:*** $41,570.

APPLYING
Standardized Tests *Required:* SAT or ACT (for admission).

Options: electronic application, early admission, early action, deferred entrance.

Required: essay or personal statement, high school transcript, 1 letter of recommendation. ***Required for some:*** interview.

Application deadlines: 3/1 (freshmen), rolling (transfers), 11/15 (early action).

Notification: continuous until 1/5 (freshmen), continuous (transfers), 12/15 (early action).

CONTACT
Mr. Joseph Roback, Associate Vice Provost, Admissions and Enrollment, The University of Scranton, The Estate Room 208, Scranton, PA 18510-4501. *Phone:* 570-941-7540. *Toll-free phone:* 888-SCRANTON. *Fax:* 570-941-5928. *E-mail:* admissions@scranton.edu.

The University of the Arts

Philadelphia, Pennsylvania

http://www.uarts.edu/

- **Independent** comprehensive, founded 1876
- **Urban** 21-acre campus with easy access to Philadelphia
- **Coed**
- **Moderately difficult** entrance level

FACULTY
Student/faculty ratio: 8:1.

ACADEMICS
Calendar: semesters. *Degrees:* diplomas, bachelor's, master's, and postbachelor's certificates.
Library: Albert M. Greenfield Library plus 1 other.

STUDENT LIFE
Housing options: coed. Campus housing is university owned and leased by the school. Freshman applicants given priority for college housing.

Activities and organizations: drama/theater group, choral group.

Campus security: 24-hour emergency response devices and patrols, crime prevention workshops and seminars.

Student services: health clinic, personal/psychological counseling.

FINANCIAL AID
Financial Aid Of all full-time matriculated undergraduates who enrolled in 2017, 1,305 applied for aid, 1,305 were judged to have need, 149 had their need fully met. In 2017, 334 non-need-based awards were made. ***Average percent of need met:*** 62. ***Average financial aid package:*** $29,310. ***Average need-based loan:*** $4103. ***Average need-based gift aid:*** $24,377. ***Average non-need-based aid:*** $16,427. ***Average indebtedness upon graduation:*** $37,575.

APPLYING
Options: electronic application, early admission, deferred entrance.

Application fee: $60.

Required: high school transcript. ***Required for some:*** interview, audition or portfolio required for performing arts programs; portfolio for design, visual arts, film programs. ***Recommended:*** minimum 2.0 GPA.

CONTACT
Ms. Kaitlyn Arillo, Director of Undergraduate Recruitment, The University of the Arts, 320 South Broad Street, Philadelphia, PA 19102-4944. *Phone:* 215-717-6017. *Toll-free phone:* 800-616-ARTS. *Fax:* 215-717-6045. *E-mail:* admissions@uarts.edu.

University of the Sciences

Philadelphia, Pennsylvania

http://www.usciences.edu/

- **Independent** university, founded 1821
- **Urban** 35-acre campus with easy access to Philadelphia
- **Endowment** $174.5 million
- **Coed**
- **Moderately difficult** entrance level

FACULTY
Student/faculty ratio: 9:1.

ACADEMICS
Calendar: semesters. *Degrees:* certificates, bachelor's, master's, doctoral, and postbachelor's certificates.
Library: Joseph W. England Library.

STUDENT LIFE
Housing options: on-campus residence required through sophomore year; coed. Campus housing is university owned and leased by the school. Freshman campus housing is guaranteed.

Activities and organizations: drama/theater group, student-run newspaper, choral group, Student Government Association, Hillel: Jewish Student Association, Pre-Medical Society, Society of Physics Students, American Chemical Society, national fraternities, national sororities.

Athletics Member NCAA, NAIA. All NCAA Division II.

Campus security: 24-hour emergency response devices and patrols, late-night transport/escort service, controlled dormitory access.

Student services: health clinic, personal/psychological counseling.

FINANCIAL AID
Financial Aid ***Average indebtedness upon graduation:*** $46,210.

APPLYING
Standardized Tests *Required:* SAT or ACT (for admission). *Required for some:* TOEFL or IELTS for non-English as first language applicants.

Options: electronic application, deferred entrance.

Application fee: $45.

Required: essay or personal statement, high school transcript, minimum 3.0 GPA, 1 letter of recommendation. ***Required for some:*** interview.

CONTACT
Executive Director of Admission and Enrollment Services, University of the Sciences, 600 South 43rd Street, Philadelphia, PA 19104-4495. *Phone:* 888-996-8747. *Toll-free phone:* 888-996-8747. *Fax:* 215-596-8821. *E-mail:* admit@usciences.edu.

University of Valley Forge

Phoenixville, Pennsylvania

http://www.valleyforge.edu/

CONTACT

Claire M. Eiler, Director of Admissions, University of Valley Forge, 1401 Charlestown Road, Phoenixville, PA 19460. *Phone:* 610-917-1487. *Toll-free phone:* 800-432-8322. *Fax:* 610-917-2069. *E-mail:* admissions@valleyforge.edu.

Ursinus College

Collegeville, Pennsylvania

http://www.ursinus.edu/

- **Independent** 4-year, founded 1869
- **Suburban** 170-acre campus with easy access to Philadelphia
- **Endowment** $144.9 million
- **Coed**
- **Moderately difficult** entrance level

FACULTY

Student/faculty ratio: 11:1.

ACADEMICS

Calendar: semesters. *Degree:* bachelor's.

Library: Myrin Library. *Books:* 175,320 (physical), 396,143 (digital/electronic); *Serial titles:* 797 (physical), 52,952 (digital/electronic); *Databases:* 53. Weekly public service hours: 113.

STUDENT LIFE

Housing options: on-campus residence required through senior year; coed, men-only, women-only, special housing for students with disabilities. Campus housing is university owned. Freshman campus housing is guaranteed.

Activities and organizations: drama/theater group, student-run newspaper, radio and television station, choral group, Campus Activities Board, Ursinus College Student Government, Best Buddies, The Grizzly student newspaper, Gender Sexuality Alliance, national fraternities, national sororities.

Athletics Member NCAA. All Division III except golf (Division II).

Campus security: 24-hour emergency response devices and patrols, student patrols, late-night transport/escort service, controlled dormitory access.

Student services: health clinic, personal/psychological counseling.

COSTS & FINANCIAL AID

Costs (2019–20) ***Comprehensive fee:*** $66,730 includes full-time tuition ($53,610) and room and board ($13,120). Part-time tuition: $1675 per credit hour.

Financial Aid Of all full-time matriculated undergraduates who enrolled in 2018, 1,201 applied for aid, 1,071 were judged to have need, 259 had their need fully met. 605 Federal Work-Study jobs (averaging $1851). In 2018, 318 non-need-based awards were made. ***Average percent of need met:*** 81. ***Average financial aid package:*** $42,001. ***Average need-based loan:*** $4382. ***Average need-based gift aid:*** $35,652. ***Average non-need-based aid:*** $25,984. ***Average indebtedness upon graduation:*** $42,113. ***Financial aid deadline:*** 2/1.

APPLYING

Standardized Tests *Required for some:* SAT or ACT (for admission).

Options: electronic application, early decision, early action, deferred entrance.

Required: essay or personal statement, high school transcript, 1 letter of recommendation. ***Required for some:*** home schooled students must include detailed information about the depth of their curriculum, including reading lists and standardized tests. ***Recommended:*** interview.

CONTACT

Ms. Diane Greenwood, Director of Admission, Ursinus College, 601 E. Main Street, Collegeville, PA 19426. *Phone:* 610-409-3200. *Fax:* 610-409-3197. *E-mail:* admission@ursinus.edu.

Villanova University

Villanova, Pennsylvania

http://www.villanova.edu/

- **Independent Roman Catholic** university, founded 1842
- **Suburban** 254-acre campus with easy access to Philadelphia
- **Coed** 9,565 undergraduate students, 96% full-time, 66% women, 34% men
- **Very difficult** entrance level, 28% of applicants were admitted

UNDERGRAD STUDENTS

9,228 full-time, 337 part-time. Students come from 48 states and territories; 44 other countries; 78% are from out of state; 5% Black or African American, non-Hispanic/Latino; 8% Hispanic/Latino; 6% Asian, non-Hispanic/Latino; 3% Two or more races, non-Hispanic/Latino; 2% Race/ethnicity unknown; 3% international; 0.8% transferred in; 76% live on campus.

Freshmen:

Admission: 22,909 applied, 6,470 admitted, 1,695 enrolled. ***Average high school GPA:*** 4.2. ***Test scores:*** SAT evidence-based reading and writing scores over 500: 100%; SAT math scores over 500: 100%; ACT scores over 18: 100%; SAT evidence-based reading and writing scores over 600: 92%; SAT math scores over 600: 93%; ACT scores over 24: 99%; SAT evidence-based reading and writing scores over 700: 39%; SAT math scores over 700: 64%; ACT scores over 30: 83%.

Retention: 96% of full-time freshmen returned.

FACULTY

Total: 1,066, 60% full-time, 68% with terminal degrees.

Student/faculty ratio: 11:1.

ACADEMICS

Calendar: semesters. *Degrees:* bachelor's, master's, doctoral, post-master's, and postbachelor's certificates.

Special study options: accelerated degree program, adult/continuing education programs, advanced placement credit, cooperative education, distance learning, double majors, English as a second language, external degree program, honors programs, independent study, internships, off-campus study, part-time degree program, services for LD students, study abroad, summer session for credit. ***ROTC:*** Army (b), Navy (b), Air Force (c).

Unusual degree programs: 3-2 engineering; arts/liberal studies, classical studies, communication, criminal justice, political science, psychology, Spanish, religious studies, computer science, biology, chemistry, mathematics, mathematics/applied statistics, human resources development, business information systems/software engineering.

Computers: 700 computers/terminals and 15,000 ports are available on campus for general student use. Students can access the following: campus intranet, computer help desk, free student e-mail accounts, online (class) grades, online (class) registration, online (class) schedules, learning management system with anti-plagiarism software, testing software, online faculty hours, videoconferencing, electronic portfolios, data vaulting/backup service, software. Campuswide network is available. 100% of college-owned or -operated housing units are wired for high-speed Internet access. Wireless service is available via entire campus.

Library: Falvey Memorial Library plus 1 other. Study areas open 24 hours, 5–7 days a week; students can reserve study rooms.

STUDENT LIFE

Housing options: coed, women-only, special housing for students with disabilities. Campus housing is university owned. Freshman campus housing is guaranteed.

Activities and organizations: drama/theater group, student-run newspaper, radio and television station, choral group, marching band, Blue Key Society, New Student Orientation Counselor Program, Special Olympics, Campus Activities Team, Student Government Association, national fraternities, national sororities.

Athletics Member NCAA. All Division I except football (Division I-AA). ***Intercollegiate sports:*** baseball M(s), basketball M(s)/W(s), cheerleading M/W, crew M(c)/W, cross-country running M(s)/W(s), equestrian sports W(c), field hockey W(s), golf M, ice hockey M(c)/W(c), lacrosse M(s)/W(s), sailing M(c)/W(c), skiing (downhill) M(c)/W(c), soccer M(s)/W(s), softball W(s), swimming and diving M/W(s), tennis M/W, track and field M(s)/W(s), volleyball M(c)/W(s), water polo M(c)/W.

Intramural sports: badminton M(c)/W(c), baseball M(c), basketball M(c)/W(c), crew M(c), cross-country running M(c)/W(c), equestrian sports W(c), field hockey W(c), football M, golf M(c)/W(c), ice hockey M(c)/W(c), lacrosse M(c)/W(c), rugby M(c), sailing M(c)/W(c), skiing (downhill) M(c)/W(c), soccer M(c)/W(c), softball M/W, swimming and diving M(c)/W(c), tennis M(c)/W(c), ultimate Frisbee M(c)/W(c), volleyball M(c)/W(c), water polo M(c).

Campus security: 24-hour emergency response devices and patrols, late-night transport/escort service, controlled dormitory access, Nova Alert: email, text messaging for emergency situations.

Student services: health clinic, personal/psychological counseling.

COSTS & FINANCIAL AID

Costs (2020–21) ***Comprehensive fee:*** $69,724 includes full-time tuition ($54,550), mandatory fees ($730), and room and board ($14,444). Part-time tuition: $3031 per credit hour. ***College room only:*** $7744.

Financial Aid Of all full-time matriculated undergraduates who enrolled in 2019, 3,838 applied for aid, 3,084 were judged to have need, 605 had their need fully met. In 2019, 527 non-need-based awards were made. ***Average percent of need met:*** 80. ***Average financial aid package:*** $42,523. ***Average need-based loan:*** $4634. ***Average need-based gift aid:*** $37,187. ***Average non-need-based aid:*** $17,558. ***Average indebtedness upon graduation:*** $36,716. ***Financial aid deadline:*** 1/15.

APPLYING

Standardized Tests *Required:* SAT or ACT (for admission).

Options: electronic application, early admission, early decision, early action, deferred entrance.

Application fee: $80.

Required: essay or personal statement, high school transcript, 1 letter of recommendation.

Application deadlines: 1/15 (freshmen), 6/1 (transfers), 11/1 (early action).

Early decision deadline: 11/1.

Notification: 4/1 (freshmen), continuous (transfers), 12/20 (early decision), 1/15 (early action).

CONTACT

Villanova University, 800 Lancaster Avenue, Villanova, PA 19085-1699.

Washington & Jefferson College

Washington, Pennsylvania

http://www.washjeff.edu/

- **Independent** comprehensive, founded 1781
- **Suburban** 60-acre campus with easy access to Pittsburgh
- **Endowment** $143.6 million
- **Coed** 1,356 undergraduate students, 100% full-time, 49% women, 51% men
- **Very difficult** entrance level, 82% of applicants were admitted

UNDERGRAD STUDENTS

1,350 full-time, 6 part-time. Students come from 36 states and territories; 37 other countries; 23% are from out of state; 1% transferred in; 93% live on campus.

Freshmen:

Admission: 2,806 applied, 2,311 admitted, 351 enrolled. ***Average high school GPA:*** 3.7.

Retention: 81% of full-time freshmen returned.

ACADEMICS

Calendar: 4-1-4. *Degrees:* bachelor's, master's, and postbachelor's certificates.

Special study options: academic remediation for entering students, accelerated degree program, advanced placement credit, double majors, English as a second language, freshman honors college, honors programs, independent study, internships, off-campus study, part-time degree program, services for LD students, student-designed majors, study abroad, summer session for credit. ***ROTC:*** Army (b), Air Force (c).

Unusual degree programs: 3-2 engineering with Columbia University, Case Western Reserve University, Washington University in St. Louis.

Computers: 450 computers/terminals and 2,000 ports are available on campus for general student use. Students can access the following: campus intranet, computer help desk, free student e-mail accounts, online (class) grades, online (class) registration, online (class) schedules. Campuswide network is available. 100% of college-owned or -operated housing units are wired for high-speed Internet access. Wireless service is available via entire campus.

Library: U. Grant Miller Library plus 4 others. Weekly public service hours: 107.

STUDENT LIFE

Housing options: on-campus residence required through senior year, coed, men-only, women-only, special housing for students with disabilities. Campus housing is university owned. Freshman campus housing is guaranteed.

Activities and organizations: drama/theater group, student-run newspaper, radio station, choral group, Student Government Association, Student Activities Board, Black Student Union, Mock Trial, Latino Culture Association, national fraternities, national sororities.

Athletics ***Intercollegiate sports:*** baseball M, basketball M/W, cheerleading M(c)/W(c), cross-country running M/W, equestrian sports M(c)/W(c), field hockey W, football M, golf M/W, ice hockey M(c), lacrosse M/W, rugby M(c)/W(c), soccer M/W, softball W, swimming and diving M/W, tennis M/W, track and field M/W, ultimate Frisbee M(c)/W(c), volleyball M(c)/W, water polo M/W, wrestling M. ***Intramural sports:*** basketball M/W, soccer M/W, tennis M/W, triathlon M/W, volleyball M/W.

Campus security: 24-hour emergency response devices and patrols, late-night transport/escort service, controlled dormitory access.

Student services: health clinic, personal/psychological counseling, women's center.

COSTS & FINANCIAL AID

Costs (2019–20) ***Comprehensive fee:*** $62,382 includes full-time tuition ($48,758), mandatory fees ($580), and room and board ($13,044). Part-time tuition: $1220 per credit hour. ***College room only:*** $7654. Room and board charges vary according to board plan and housing facility. ***Payment plans:*** tuition prepayment, installment. ***Waivers:*** employees or children of employees.

Financial Aid Of all full-time matriculated undergraduates who enrolled in 2018, 1,149 applied for aid, 1,066 were judged to have need, 172 had their need fully met. 663 Federal Work-Study jobs (averaging $1782). 210 state and other part-time jobs (averaging $1708). In 2018, 269 non-need-based awards were made. ***Average percent of need met:*** 81. ***Average financial aid package:*** $39,176. ***Average need-based loan:*** $3739. ***Average need-based gift aid:*** $34,328. ***Average non-need-based aid:*** $23,561. ***Average indebtedness upon graduation:*** $45,306.

APPLYING

Options: electronic application, early admission, early decision, early action, deferred entrance.

Application fee: $25.

Required: essay or personal statement, high school transcript, letters of recommendation. ***Recommended:*** interview.

Early decision deadline: 12/1.

Notification: 4/1 (freshmen), 12/15 (early decision).

CONTACT

Mr. Robert Adkins, Dean of Admission, Washington & Jefferson College, 60 South Lincoln Street, Washington, PA 15301. *Phone:* 724-223-6025. *Toll-free phone:* 888-WANDJAY. *Fax:* 724-223-6534. *E-mail:* admission@washjeff.edu.

Waynesburg University

Waynesburg, Pennsylvania

http://www.waynesburg.edu/

- **Independent** comprehensive, founded 1849, affiliated with Presbyterian Church (U.S.A.)
- **Small-town** 30-acre campus with easy access to Pittsburgh
- **Coed** 1,277 undergraduate students, 97% full-time, 59% women, 41% men
- **Moderately difficult** entrance level, 93% of applicants were admitted

UNDERGRAD STUDENTS
1,239 full-time, 38 part-time. Students come from 31 states and territories; 2 other countries; 22% are from out of state; 0.1% Black or African American, non-Hispanic/Latino; 3% Hispanic/Latino; 0.2% Asian, non-Hispanic/Latino; 85% Native Hawaiian or other Pacific Islander, non-Hispanic/Latino; 3% American Indian or Alaska Native, non-Hispanic/Latino; 3% Two or more races, non-Hispanic/Latino; 3% Race/ethnicity unknown; 0.3% international; 3% transferred in; 80% live on campus.

Freshmen:
Admission: 1,589 applied, 1,470 admitted, 355 enrolled. ***Average high school GPA:*** 3.6.

Retention: 76% of full-time freshmen returned.

FACULTY
Total: 219, 37% full-time, 21% with terminal degrees.

Student/faculty ratio: 12:1.

ACADEMICS
Calendar: semesters. *Degrees:* bachelor's, master's, and doctoral.

Special study options: accelerated degree program, adult/continuing education programs, advanced placement credit, distance learning, double majors, honors programs, independent study, internships, part-time degree program, services for LD students, study abroad, summer session for credit. ***ROTC:*** Army (c), Air Force (c).

Unusual degree programs: 3-2 engineering with Penn State University.

Computers: 160 computers/terminals are available on campus for general student use. Students can access the following: campus intranet, computer help desk, free student e-mail accounts, online (class) grades, online (class) registration, online (class) schedules. Campuswide network is available. 100% of college-owned or -operated housing units are wired for high-speed Internet access. Wireless service is available via entire campus.

Library: Eberly Library. *Books:* 73,884 (physical), 206,831 (digital/electronic); *Serial titles:* 307 (physical), 14,986 (digital/electronic); *Databases:* 36.

STUDENT LIFE
Housing options: on-campus residence required through junior year; men-only, women-only, special housing for students with disabilities. Campus housing is university owned. Freshman campus housing is guaranteed.

Activities and organizations: drama/theater group, student-run newspaper, radio and television station, choral group, Student Activity Board, Waynesburg Outdoor Experience, Criminal Justice Club, Sting Swing, Student Nurses Association.

Athletics Member NCAA. All Division III. ***Intercollegiate sports:*** baseball M, basketball M/W, cross-country running M/W, football M, golf M, lacrosse W, soccer M/W, softball W, tennis M/W, track and field M/W, volleyball W, wrestling M. ***Intramural sports:*** basketball M/W, bowling M/W, racquetball M/W, softball M/W, table tennis M/W, volleyball M/W.

Campus security: 24-hour emergency response devices and patrols, late-night transport/escort service, controlled dormitory access.

Student services: health clinic, personal/psychological counseling.

COSTS & FINANCIAL AID
Costs (2020–21) ***Comprehensive fee:*** $37,530 includes full-time tuition ($25,430), mandatory fees ($1210), and room and board ($10,890). Part-time tuition: $1050 per credit hour. ***College room only:*** $5510. Room and board charges vary according to board plan and housing facility.

Financial Aid Of all full-time matriculated undergraduates who enrolled in 2019, 1,188 applied for aid, 1,049 were judged to have need, 207 had their need fully met. 672 Federal Work-Study jobs (averaging $1193). In 2019, 208 non-need-based awards were made. ***Average percent of need met:*** 82. ***Average financial aid package:*** $21,635. ***Average need-based loan:*** $5581. ***Average need-based gift aid:*** $16,760. ***Average non-need-based aid:*** $11,073. ***Average indebtedness upon graduation:*** $23,316.

APPLYING
Standardized Tests *Required:* SAT or ACT (for admission).

Options: electronic application, early admission.

Application fee: $20.

Required: high school transcript, minimum 2.8 GPA. ***Required for some:*** essay or personal statement, 2 letters of recommendation. ***Recommended:*** minimum 3.0 GPA, interview.

Application deadlines: rolling (freshmen), rolling (transfers).

Notification: continuous (freshmen), continuous (transfers).

CONTACT
Mrs. Jacqueline Palko, Director of Admissions, Waynesburg University, 51 West College Street, Waynesburg, PA 15370. *Phone:* 724-852-3216. *Toll-free phone:* 800-225-7393. *Fax:* 724-627-8124. *E-mail:* admissions@waynesburg.edu.

West Chester University of Pennsylvania

West Chester, Pennsylvania

http://www.wcupa.edu/

- **State-supported** comprehensive, founded 1871, part of Pennsylvania State System of Higher Education
- **Suburban** 409-acre campus with easy access to Philadelphia
- **Endowment** $26.7 million
- **Coed** 14,615 undergraduate students, 89% full-time, 59% women, 41% men
- **Moderately difficult** entrance level, 75% of applicants were admitted

UNDERGRAD STUDENTS
13,044 full-time, 1,571 part-time. Students come from 32 states and territories; 84 other countries; 10% are from out of state; 11% Black or African American, non-Hispanic/Latino; 6% Hispanic/Latino; 2% Asian, non-Hispanic/Latino; 0.1% Native Hawaiian or other Pacific Islander, non-Hispanic/Latino; 0.1% American Indian or Alaska Native, non-Hispanic/Latino; 4% Two or more races, non-Hispanic/Latino; 2% Race/ethnicity unknown; 0.4% international; 8% transferred in; 36% live on campus.

Freshmen:
Admission: 15,085 applied, 11,354 admitted, 2,871 enrolled. ***Average high school GPA:*** 3.4. ***Test scores:*** SAT evidence-based reading and writing scores over 500: 86%; SAT math scores over 500: 83%; ACT scores over 18: 93%; SAT evidence-based reading and writing scores over 600: 32%; SAT math scores over 600: 26%; ACT scores over 24: 42%; SAT evidence-based reading and writing scores over 700: 3%; SAT math scores over 700: 3%; ACT scores over 30: 8%.

Retention: 86% of full-time freshmen returned.

FACULTY
Total: 995, 70% full-time, 68% with terminal degrees.

Student/faculty ratio: 19:1.

ACADEMICS
Calendar: semesters. *Degrees:* bachelor's, master's, doctoral, post-master's, and postbachelor's certificates.

Special study options: academic remediation for entering students, accelerated degree program, adult/continuing education programs, advanced placement credit, distance learning, double majors, English as a second language, freshman honors college, honors programs, independent study, internships, off-campus study, part-time degree program, services for LD students, student-designed majors, study abroad, summer session for credit. ***ROTC:*** Army (b), Air Force (c).

Unusual degree programs: 3-2 engineering with Pennsylvania State University, Thomas Jefferson University (formerly known as Philadelphia University), Columbia University, and Case Western University.

Computers: 2,547 computers/terminals are available on campus for general student use. Students can access the following: campus intranet, computer help desk, free student e-mail accounts, online (class) grades, online (class) registration, online (class) schedules, virtual software. Campuswide network is available. 100% of college-owned or -operated housing units are wired for high-speed Internet access. Wireless service is available via entire campus.

Library: Francis Harvey Green Library plus 1 other. *Books:* 715,684 (physical), 1.2 million (digital/electronic); *Serial titles:* 1,528 (physical), 135,694 (digital/electronic); *Databases:* 271. Weekly public service hours: 134; study areas open 24 hours, 5–7 days a week.

STUDENT LIFE

Housing options: coed, special housing for students with disabilities. Campus housing is university owned. Freshman applicants given priority for college housing.

Activities and organizations: drama/theater group, student-run newspaper, radio and television station, choral group, marching band, Student Government Association, Residence Hall Association, Fraternal Programming Board, Sports Club Council, CRU, national fraternities, national sororities.

Athletics Member NCAA. All Division II. ***Intercollegiate sports:*** baseball M(s), basketball M(s)/W(s), bowling M(c)/W(c), cheerleading W, cross-country running M(s)/W(s), equestrian sports M(c)/W(c), fencing M(c)/W(c), field hockey W(s), football M(s), golf M(s)/W(s), gymnastics W(s), ice hockey M(c)/W(c), lacrosse M(c)/W(s), rugby M(c)/W(s), soccer M(s)/W(s), softball W(s), swimming and diving M(s)/W(s), tennis M(s)/W(s), track and field M(s)/W(s), ultimate Frisbee M(c)/W(c), volleyball M(c)/W(s), water polo M(c)/W(c), wrestling M(c). ***Intramural sports:*** basketball M/W, football M/W, racquetball M/W, soccer M/W, softball M/W, table tennis M/W, tennis M/W, ultimate Frisbee M/W, volleyball M/W.

Campus security: 24-hour emergency response devices and patrols, late-night transport/escort service, controlled dormitory access, Police and Security guards 24/7. Camera systems in campus residence halls, recreational and classroom facilities and outdoor areas.

Student services: health clinic, personal/psychological counseling, women's center, veterans affairs office.

COSTS & FINANCIAL AID

Costs (2019–20) ***Tuition:*** state resident $7716 full-time, $322 per credit part-time; nonresident $19,290 full-time, $805 per credit part-time. Full-time tuition and fees vary according to location. Part-time tuition and fees vary according to location. ***Required fees:*** $2705 full-time, $113 per credit part-time. ***Room and board:*** $9326; room only: $5626. Room and board charges vary according to board plan and housing facility. ***Payment plan:*** installment. ***Waivers:*** senior citizens and employees or children of employees.

Financial Aid Of all full-time matriculated undergraduates who enrolled in 2019, 10,231 applied for aid, 7,495 were judged to have need, 684 had their need fully met. 253 Federal Work-Study jobs (averaging $1691). In 2019, 403 non-need-based awards were made. ***Average percent of need met:*** 47. ***Average financial aid package:*** $8438. ***Average need-based loan:*** $4057. ***Average need-based gift aid:*** $6057. ***Average non-need-based aid:*** $3603. ***Average indebtedness upon graduation:*** $36,469.

APPLYING

Standardized Tests *Required:* SAT or ACT (for admission).

Options: electronic application.

Application fee: $45.

Required: high school transcript, SAT or ACT. ***Required for some:*** essay or personal statement, interview. ***Recommended:*** minimum 3.0 GPA.

Application deadlines: rolling (freshmen), rolling (transfers).

Notification: continuous (freshmen), continuous (transfers).

CONTACT

West Chester University of Pennsylvania, University Avenue and High Street, West Chester, PA 19383. *Phone:* 610-436-3411. *Toll-free phone:* 877-315-2165.

Westminster College

New Wilmington, Pennsylvania

http://www.westminster.edu/

CONTACT

Dr. Thomas H. Stein, Vice President for Enrollment Management, Westminster College, Remick House, 319 S. Market Street, New Wilmington, PA 16172. *Phone:* 724-946-7105. *Toll-free phone:* 800-942-8033. *Fax:* 724-946-7171. *E-mail:* steinth@westminster.edu.

Widener University

Chester, Pennsylvania

http://www.widener.edu/

- **Independent** comprehensive, founded 1821
- **Suburban** 110-acre campus with easy access to Philadelphia
- **Endowment** $91.8 million
- **Coed** 3,345 undergraduate students, 87% full-time, 57% women, 43% men
- **Moderately difficult** entrance level, 70% of applicants were admitted

UNDERGRAD STUDENTS

2,910 full-time, 435 part-time. 40% are from out of state; 13% Black or African American, non-Hispanic/Latino; 5% Hispanic/Latino; 3% Asian, non-Hispanic/Latino; 0.1% American Indian or Alaska Native, non-Hispanic/Latino; 4% Two or more races, non-Hispanic/Latino; 2% Race/ethnicity unknown; 2% international; 3% transferred in; 47% live on campus.

Freshmen:

Admission: 6,422 applied, 4,474 admitted, 770 enrolled. ***Average high school GPA:*** 3.5.

Retention: 80% of full-time freshmen returned.

ACADEMICS

Calendar: semesters. *Degrees:* certificates, associate, bachelor's, master's, doctoral, and post-master's certificates.

Special study options: academic remediation for entering students, accelerated degree program, adult/continuing education programs, advanced placement credit, cooperative education, distance learning, double majors, English as a second language, honors programs, independent study, internships, off-campus study, part-time degree program, services for LD students, student-designed majors, study abroad, summer session for credit. ***ROTC:*** Army (b), Navy (c), Air Force (c).

Unusual degree programs: 3-2 business administration; engineering; social work; physical therapy, education.

Computers: Students can access the following: campus intranet, computer help desk, free student e-mail accounts, online (class) grades, online (class) registration, online (class) schedules. Campuswide network is available. 100% of college-owned or -operated housing units are wired for high-speed Internet access. Wireless service is available via classrooms, computer centers, computer labs, dorm rooms, learning centers, libraries, student centers.

Library: Wolfgram Memorial Library.

STUDENT LIFE

Housing options: on-campus residence required through junior year; coed, men-only, women-only, cooperative. Campus housing is university owned. Freshman campus housing is guaranteed.

Activities and organizations: drama/theater group, student-run television station, choral group, marching band, national fraternities, national sororities.

Athletics ***Intercollegiate sports:*** baseball M, basketball M/W, cheerleading W, cross-country running M/W, field hockey W, football M, golf M/W, lacrosse M/W, soccer M/W, softball W, swimming and diving M/W, track and field M/W, volleyball M/W. ***Intramural sports:*** ice hockey M(c), rugby M(c)/W(c), soccer M(c), volleyball M(c).

Campus security: 24-hour emergency response devices and patrols, late-night transport/escort service, controlled dormitory access.

Student services: health clinic, personal/psychological counseling, veterans affairs office.

COSTS & FINANCIAL AID

Costs (2020–21) ***Comprehensive fee:*** $63,552 includes full-time tuition ($47,770), mandatory fees ($970), and room and board ($14,812). Part-time tuition: $1592 per credit hour. ***College room only:*** $7748. ***Waivers:*** employees or children of employees.

Financial Aid Of all full-time matriculated undergraduates who enrolled in 2019, 2,388 applied for aid, 2,172 were judged to have need, 471 had their need fully met. In 2019, 506 non-need-based awards were made. ***Average percent of need met:*** 74. ***Average financial aid package:*** $35,270. ***Average need-based loan:*** $4505. ***Average need-based gift aid:*** $29,670. ***Average non-need-based aid:*** $25,590.

APPLYING
Standardized Tests *Required:* SAT or ACT (for admission).
Options: electronic application, deferred entrance.
Required: essay or personal statement, high school transcript. ***Required for some:*** minimum 2.9 GPA. ***Recommended:*** interview.
Application deadlines: rolling (freshmen), rolling (transfers).
Notification: continuous (freshmen), continuous (transfers).

CONTACT
Widener University, One University Place, Chester, PA 19013-5792.
Phone: 610-499-4126. *Toll-free phone:* 888-WIDENER.

Wilkes University

Wilkes-Barre, Pennsylvania

http://www.wilkes.edu/

- **Independent** comprehensive, founded 1933
- **Urban** 25-acre campus
- **Endowment** $51.8 million
- **Coed** 2,351 undergraduate students, 90% full-time, 50% women, 50% men
- **Moderately difficult** entrance level, 79% of applicants were admitted

UNDERGRAD STUDENTS
2,110 full-time, 241 part-time. Students come from 31 states and territories; 16 other countries; 28% are from out of state; 4% Black or African American, non-Hispanic/Latino; 7% Hispanic/Latino; 3% Asian, non-Hispanic/Latino; 0.1% Native Hawaiian or other Pacific Islander, non-Hispanic/Latino; 0.2% American Indian or Alaska Native, non-Hispanic/Latino; 3% Two or more races, non-Hispanic/Latino; 3% Race/ethnicity unknown; 6% international; 5% transferred in; 43% live on campus.

Freshmen:
Admission: 3,756 applied, 2,953 admitted, 550 enrolled. ***Average high school GPA:*** 3.6. ***Test scores:*** SAT evidence-based reading and writing scores over 500: 84%; SAT math scores over 500: 83%; ACT scores over 18: 94%; SAT evidence-based reading and writing scores over 600: 30%; SAT math scores over 600: 30%; ACT scores over 24: 45%; SAT evidence-based reading and writing scores over 700: 2%; SAT math scores over 700: 5%; ACT scores over 30: 12%.
Retention: 78% of full-time freshmen returned.

FACULTY
Total: 448, 44% full-time.
Student/faculty ratio: 12:1.

ACADEMICS
Calendar: semesters. *Degrees:* bachelor's, master's, and doctoral.
Special study options: academic remediation for entering students, accelerated degree program, adult/continuing education programs, advanced placement credit, cooperative education, distance learning, double majors, English as a second language, honors programs, independent study, internships, off-campus study, part-time degree program, services for LD students, student-designed majors, study abroad, summer session for credit. ***ROTC:*** Army (c), Air Force (b).
Computers: 1,015 computers/terminals are available on campus for general student use. Students can access the following: campus intranet, computer help desk, free student e-mail accounts, online (class) grades, online (class) registration, online (class) schedules. Campuswide network is available. Wireless service is available via classrooms, dorm rooms, libraries, student centers.
Library: Eugene S. Farley Library. *Books:* 173,872 (physical), 338,879 (digital/electronic); *Serial titles:* 71,253 (digital/electronic); *Databases:* 131. Students can reserve study rooms.

STUDENT LIFE
Housing options: on-campus residence required through sophomore year; coed, men-only, women-only. Campus housing is university owned. Freshman campus housing is guaranteed.
Activities and organizations: drama/theater group, student-run newspaper, radio and television station, choral group, marching band.
Athletics Member NCAA. All Division III except golf (Division II).
Intercollegiate sports: baseball M, basketball M/W, cross-country running M/W, field hockey W, football M, golf M/W, ice hockey M/W, lacrosse M/W, soccer M/W, softball W, swimming and diving M/W, tennis M/W,

volleyball M/W, wrestling M. ***Intramural sports:*** basketball M/W, cheerleading W(c), cross-country running M(c)/W(c), football M, racquetball M(c)/W(c), rock climbing M(c)/W(c), skiing (downhill) M(c)/W(c), softball M/W, ultimate Frisbee M(c)/W(c), volleyball M/W.

Campus security: 24-hour emergency response devices and patrols, late-night transport/escort service, controlled dormitory access.

Student services: health clinic, personal/psychological counseling, veterans affairs office.

COSTS & FINANCIAL AID

Costs (2019–20) ***Comprehensive fee:*** $52,730 includes full-time tuition ($35,814), mandatory fees ($1808), and room and board ($15,108). Part-time tuition: $995 per credit hour. ***Required fees:*** $80 per credit hour part-time. ***Room and board:*** Room and board charges vary according to board plan and housing facility. ***Payment plans:*** installment, deferred payment. ***Waivers:*** employees or children of employees.

Financial Aid Of all full-time matriculated undergraduates who enrolled in 2019, 1,839 applied for aid, 1,703 were judged to have need, 233 had their need fully met. In 2019, 124 non-need-based awards were made. ***Average percent of need met:*** 74. ***Average financial aid package:*** $28,253. ***Average need-based loan:*** $4330. ***Average need-based gift aid:*** $23,365. ***Average non-need-based aid:*** $16,692.

APPLYING

Standardized Tests *Required:* SAT or ACT (for admission).

Options: electronic application, early admission, deferred entrance.

Application fee: $40.

Required: high school transcript. ***Recommended:*** interview.

Application deadlines: rolling (freshmen), rolling (out-of-state freshmen), rolling (transfers).

Notification: continuous (freshmen), continuous (out-of-state freshmen), continuous (transfers).

CONTACT

Kishan Zuber, VP Enrollment Management & Marketing, Wilkes University, 84 West South Street, Wilkes-Barre, PA 18766. *Phone:* 570-408-4400. *Toll-free phone:* 800-945-5378 Ext. 4400. *Fax:* 570-408-4904. *E-mail:* admissions@wilkes.edu.

See below for display ad and page 1140 for the College Close-Up.

Wilson College

Chambersburg, Pennsylvania

http://www.wilson.edu/

CONTACT

Mr. Michael Montana, Director of Admissions, Wilson College, 1015 Philadelphia Avenue, Chambersburg, PA 17201. *Phone:* 717-262-2002 Ext. 3197. *Toll-free phone:* 800-421-8402. *Fax:* 717-262-2546. *E-mail:* admissions@wilson.edu.

Yeshiva Beth Moshe

Scranton, Pennsylvania

CONTACT

Dean, Yeshiva Beth Moshe, 930 Hickory Street, PO Box 1141, Scranton, PA 18505-2124. *Phone:* 717-346-1747.

York College of Pennsylvania

York, Pennsylvania

http://www.ycp.edu/

- **Independent** comprehensive, founded 1787
- **Suburban** 190-acre campus with easy access to Baltimore
- **Endowment** $155.1 million
- **Coed** 4,036 undergraduate students, 91% full-time, 56% women, 44% men
- **Moderately difficult** entrance level, 69% of applicants were admitted

UNDERGRAD STUDENTS

3,685 full-time, 351 part-time. 35% are from out of state; 6% Black or African American, non-Hispanic/Latino; 7% Hispanic/Latino; 2% Asian, non-Hispanic/Latino; 0.1% Native Hawaiian or other Pacific Islander, non-Hispanic/Latino; 0.1% American Indian or Alaska Native, non-Hispanic/Latino; 3% Two or more races, non-Hispanic/Latino; 2% Race/ethnicity unknown; 1% international; 4% transferred in; 55% live on campus.

Freshmen:

Admission: 5,991 applied, 4,126 admitted, 930 enrolled. ***Average high school GPA:*** 3.5. ***Test scores:*** SAT evidence-based reading and writing scores over 500: 79%; SAT math scores over 500: 78%; ACT scores over 18: 86%; SAT evidence-based reading and writing scores over 600: 27%; SAT math scores over 600: 30%; ACT scores over 24: 39%; SAT evidence-based reading and writing scores over 700: 2%; SAT math scores over 700: 3%; ACT scores over 30: 7%.

Retention: 81% of full-time freshmen returned.

FACULTY

Total: 443, 40% full-time, 54% with terminal degrees.

Student/faculty ratio: 15:1.

ACADEMICS

Calendar: semesters. *Degrees:* associate, bachelor's, master's, doctoral, and post-master's certificates.

Special study options: academic remediation for entering students, advanced placement credit, cooperative education, double majors, honors programs, independent study, internships, part-time degree program, services for LD students, student-designed majors, study abroad, summer session for credit.

Unusual degree programs: 3-2 business administration.

Computers: Students can access the following: campus intranet, computer help desk, free student e-mail accounts, online (class) grades, online (class) registration, online (class) schedules. Campuswide network is available. 100% of college-owned or -operated housing units are wired for high-speed Internet access. Wireless service is available via entire campus.

Library: Schmidt Library.

STUDENT LIFE

Housing options: on-campus residence required through senior year; coed, special housing for students with disabilities. Campus housing is university owned. Freshman campus housing is guaranteed.

Activities and organizations: drama/theater group, student-run newspaper, radio and television station, choral group, Pre-Med Society, Ski and Outdoor Club, Habitat for Humanity, Students in Free Enterprise (SIFE), WVYC Radio Station, national fraternities, national sororities.

Athletics Member NCAA. All Division III. ***Intercollegiate sports:*** baseball M, basketball M/W, cheerleading M/W, cross-country running M/W, field hockey W, golf M, lacrosse M/W, soccer M/W, softball W, swimming and diving M/W, tennis M/W, track and field M/W, volleyball W, wrestling M. ***Intramural sports:*** badminton M/W, basketball M/W, equestrian sports M(c)/W(c), football M/W, lacrosse M(c)/W(c), racquetball M/W, rugby M(c)/W(c), soccer M/W, softball M/W, table tennis M/W, tennis M/W, ultimate Frisbee M(c)/W(c), volleyball M/W.

Campus security: 24-hour emergency response devices and patrols, student patrols, late-night transport/escort service, controlled dormitory access.

Student services: health clinic, personal/psychological counseling.

COSTS & FINANCIAL AID

Costs (2020–21) ***Comprehensive fee:*** $33,680 includes full-time tuition ($19,760), mandatory fees ($2030), and room and board ($11,890). Full-time tuition and fees vary according to program. ***College room only:*** $6720. Room and board charges vary according to board plan and housing facility. ***Payment plan:*** installment. ***Waivers:*** employees or children of employees.

Financial Aid Of all full-time matriculated undergraduates who enrolled in 2019, 3,116 applied for aid, 2,488 were judged to have need, 408 had their need fully met. In 2019, 1004 non-need-based awards were made. ***Average percent of need met:*** 58. ***Average financial aid package:*** $14,171. ***Average need-based loan:*** $4150. ***Average need-based gift aid:*** $6172. ***Average non-need-based aid:*** $6270. ***Average indebtedness upon graduation:*** $44,077.

APPLYING

Standardized Tests *Required:* SAT or ACT (for admission).

Options: electronic application, early decision, deferred entrance.

Required: high school transcript, minimum 2.0 GPA. ***Required for some:*** interview. ***Recommended:*** essay or personal statement, 1 letter of recommendation.

Early decision deadline: 12/15.

Notification: continuous (freshmen), continuous (transfers), 10/1 (early decision).

CONTACT

York College of Pennsylvania, 441 Country Club Road, York, PA 17403-3651. *Phone:* 717-815-2240. *Toll-free phone:* 800-455-8018.

RHODE ISLAND

Brown University

Providence, Rhode Island

http://www.brown.edu/

- **Independent** university, founded 1764
- **Urban** 154-acre campus with easy access to Boston
- **Endowment** $3.0 billion
- **Coed** 7,160 undergraduate students, 95% full-time, 53% women, 47% men
- **Most difficult** entrance level, 7% of applicants were admitted

UNDERGRAD STUDENTS

6,826 full-time, 334 part-time. 95% are from out of state; 7% Black or African American, non-Hispanic/Latino; 11% Hispanic/Latino; 17% Asian, non-Hispanic/Latino; 0.2% Native Hawaiian or other Pacific Islander, non-Hispanic/Latino; 0.4% American Indian or Alaska Native, non-Hispanic/Latino; 6% Two or more races, non-Hispanic/Latino; 5% Race/ethnicity unknown; 11% international; 1% transferred in; 72% live on campus.

Freshmen:

Admission: 38,674 applied, 2,733 admitted, 1,660 enrolled. ***Test scores:*** SAT evidence-based reading and writing scores over 500: 100%; SAT math scores over 500: 100%; ACT scores over 18: 100%; SAT evidence-based reading and writing scores over 600: 99%; SAT math scores over 600: 99%; ACT scores over 24: 99%; SAT evidence-based reading and writing scores over 700: 80%; SAT math scores over 700: 87%; ACT scores over 30: 92%.

Retention: 98% of full-time freshmen returned.

FACULTY

Total: 947, 92% full-time, 94% with terminal degrees.

Student/faculty ratio: 6:1.

ACADEMICS

Calendar: semesters. *Degrees:* bachelor's, master's, doctoral, and postbachelor's certificates.

Special study options: adult/continuing education programs, double majors, honors programs, independent study, internships, off-campus study, services for LD students, student-designed majors, study abroad, summer session for credit. ***ROTC:*** Army (c), Navy (c), Air Force (c).

Computers: 320 computers/terminals are available on campus for general student use. Students can access the following: campus intranet, computer help desk, free student e-mail accounts, online (class) grades, online (class) registration, online (class) schedules. Campuswide network is available. 100% of college-owned or -operated housing units are wired for high-speed Internet access. Wireless service is available via entire campus.

Library: John D. Rockefeller Library plus 7 others. *Books:* 2.6 million (physical), 1.8 million (digital/electronic); *Serial titles:* 1,667 (physical), 112,138 (digital/electronic); *Databases:* 415. Study areas open 24 hours, 5–7 days a week; students can reserve study rooms.

STUDENT LIFE

Housing options: on-campus residence required through junior year; coed, cooperative, special housing for students with disabilities. Campus housing is university owned. Freshman campus housing is guaranteed.

Activities and organizations: drama/theater group, student-run newspaper, radio and television station, choral group, marching band, national fraternities, national sororities.

Athletics Member NCAA. All Division I. ***Intercollegiate sports:*** baseball M, basketball M/W, cheerleading M(c)/W(c), crew M/W, cross-country running M/W, equestrian sports W, fencing M/W, field hockey W, football M, golf M/W, gymnastics W, ice hockey M/W, lacrosse M/W, rowing M/W, rugby M(c)/W, sailing M(c)/W(c), skiing (downhill) M(c)/W, soccer M/W, softball W, squash M/W, swimming and diving M/W, tennis M/W, track and field M/W, ultimate Frisbee M(c)/W(c), volleyball M(c)/W, water polo M/W, wrestling M. ***Intramural sports:*** badminton M/W, basketball M/W, bowling M/W, field hockey W(c), football M/W, golf M/W, ice hockey M/W, lacrosse M(c)/W(c), soccer M/W, softball M/W, squash M/W, table tennis M(c)/W(c), tennis M/W, ultimate Frisbee M/W, volleyball M/W.

Campus security: 24-hour emergency response devices and patrols, student patrols, late-night transport/escort service, controlled dormitory access.

Student services: health clinic, personal/psychological counseling, women's center, veterans affairs office.

COSTS & FINANCIAL AID

Costs (2020–21) ***Comprehensive fee:*** $76,504 includes full-time tuition ($59,254), mandatory fees ($1342), and room and board ($15,908). Part-time tuition: $7407 per course. ***College room only:*** $9774.

Financial Aid Of all full-time matriculated undergraduates who enrolled in 2019, 3,105 applied for aid, 2,826 were judged to have need, 2,820 had their need fully met. 1,911 Federal Work-Study jobs (averaging $2587). 420 state and other part-time jobs (averaging $2610). In 2019, 7 non-need-based awards were made. ***Average percent of need met:*** 100. ***Average financial aid package:*** $55,513. ***Average need-based loan:*** $738. ***Average need-based gift aid:*** $52,057. ***Average non-need-based aid:*** $8880. ***Average indebtedness upon graduation:*** $24,304. ***Financial aid deadline:*** 2/1.

APPLYING

Standardized Tests *Required:* SAT or ACT (for admission).

Options: electronic application, early decision, deferred entrance.

Application fee: $75.

Required: essay or personal statement, high school transcript, 2 letters of recommendation, Common Application, Brown Supplemental Questions, Alumni Interview if convenient for the applicant. ***Recommended:*** interview.

Application deadlines: 1/1 (freshmen), 3/1 (transfers).

Early decision deadline: 11/1.

Notification: 3/31 (freshmen), 5/15 (transfers), 12/15 (early decision).

CONTACT

Mr. Logan Powell, Dean of Admission, Brown University, Box 1876, Providence, RI 02912. *Phone:* 401-863-2378. *Fax:* 401-863-9300. *E-mail:* admission_undergraduate@brown.edu.

Bryant University

Smithfield, Rhode Island

http://www.bryant.edu/

- **Independent** comprehensive, founded 1863
- **Suburban** 428-acre campus with easy access to Boston, Providence
- **Endowment** $184.0 million
- **Coed** 3,259 undergraduate students, 98% full-time, 37% women, 63% men
- **Moderately difficult** entrance level, 71% of applicants were admitted

UNDERGRAD STUDENTS

3,205 full-time, 54 part-time. Students come from 38 states and territories; 44 other countries; 87% are from out of state; 3% Black or African American, non-Hispanic/Latino; 6% Hispanic/Latino; 3% Asian, non-Hispanic/Latino; 0.1% Native Hawaiian or other Pacific Islander, non-Hispanic/Latino; 0.2% American Indian or Alaska Native, non-Hispanic/Latino; 2% Two or more races, non-Hispanic/Latino; 1% Race/ethnicity unknown; 8% international; 3% transferred in; 81% live on campus.

Freshmen:

Admission: 7,632 applied, 5,418 admitted, 854 enrolled. ***Average high school GPA:*** 3.4. ***Test scores:*** SAT evidence-based reading and writing scores over 500: 97%; SAT math scores over 500: 99%; ACT scores over

18: 100%; SAT evidence-based reading and writing scores over 600: 54%; SAT math scores over 600: 58%; ACT scores over 24: 86%; SAT evidence-based reading and writing scores over 700: 5%; SAT math scores over 700: 12%; ACT scores over 30: 22%.

Retention: 87% of full-time freshmen returned.

FACULTY

Total: 330, 53% full-time, 59% with terminal degrees.

Student/faculty ratio: 13:1.

ACADEMICS

Calendar: semesters. *Degrees:* bachelor's, master's, and postbachelor's certificates.

Special study options: adult/continuing education programs, advanced placement credit, double majors, English as a second language, honors programs, independent study, internships, off-campus study, part-time degree program, services for LD students, study abroad, summer session for credit. ***ROTC:*** Army (c).

Computers: 526 computers/terminals and 4,652 ports are available on campus for general student use. Students can access the following: campus intranet, computer help desk, free student e-mail accounts, online (class) grades, online (class) registration, online (class) schedules, e-mail, online library, student Web hosts. Campuswide network is available. 100% of college-owned or -operated housing units are wired for high-speed Internet access. Wireless service is available via entire campus.

Library: Douglas and Judith Krupp Library plus 1 other. *Books:* 134,668 (physical), 351,966 (digital/electronic); *Serial titles:* 5,018 (physical), 43,931 (digital/electronic); *Databases:* 68. Weekly public service hours: 110; students can reserve study rooms.

STUDENT LIFE

Housing options: coed, special housing for students with disabilities. Campus housing is university owned. Freshman campus housing is guaranteed.

Activities and organizations: drama/theater group, student-run newspaper, radio and television station, choral group, Collegiate Entrepeneur Organization (CEO), Bryant U Spanish Cultural Org (BUSCO), Her Campus, Bryant Habitat for Humanity, Bryant Outdoor Adventure Club, national fraternities, national sororities.

Athletics Member NCAA. All Division I. ***Intercollegiate sports:*** baseball M(s), basketball M(s)/W(s), bowling M(c)/W(c), cheerleading W(c), crew W(c), cross-country running M(s)/W(s), field hockey W(s), football M(s), golf M(s), ice hockey M(c), lacrosse M(s)/W(s), racquetball M(c)/W(c), rowing W(c), rugby M(c)/W(c), soccer M(s)/W(s), softball W(s), squash M(c)/W(c), swimming and diving M(s)/W(s), tennis M(s)/W(s), track and field M(s)/W(s), ultimate Frisbee M(c)/W(c), volleyball M(c)/W(s). ***Intramural sports:*** badminton M/W, basketball M/W, sand volleyball M/W, soccer M(c)/W, softball M/W, table tennis M/W, tennis M(c)/W(c).

Campus security: 24-hour emergency response devices and patrols, late-night transport/escort service, controlled dormitory access.

Student services: health clinic, personal/psychological counseling, women's center.

COSTS & FINANCIAL AID

Costs (2020–21) ***Comprehensive fee:*** $63,067 includes full-time tuition ($45,966), mandatory fees ($897), and room and board ($16,204). Full-time tuition and fees vary according to program. Part-time tuition: $1139 per credit hour. Part-time tuition and fees vary according to program. ***College room only:*** $9589. Room and board charges vary according to board plan. ***Payment plan:*** installment. ***Waivers:*** employees or children of employees.

Financial Aid Of all full-time matriculated undergraduates who enrolled in 2019, 2,291 applied for aid, 1,939 were judged to have need, 916 had their need fully met. In 2019, 315 non-need-based awards were made. ***Average percent of need met:*** 48. ***Average financial aid package:*** $25,940. ***Average need-based loan:*** $4435. ***Average need-based gift aid:*** $9760. ***Average non-need-based aid:*** $17,182. ***Average indebtedness upon graduation:*** $53,350. ***Financial aid deadline:*** 2/15.

APPLYING

Options: electronic application, early decision, early action, deferred entrance.

Application fee: $50.

Required: essay or personal statement, high school transcript, 1 letter of recommendation, senior year first-quarter grades, three short essay questions in place of test scores. ***Recommended:*** minimum 3.3 GPA, 2 letters of recommendation, interview.

Application deadlines: 2/1 (freshmen), 5/1 (transfers), 11/15 (early action).

Early decision deadline: 11/1 (for plan 1), 1/15 (for plan 2).

Notification: 3/15 (freshmen), continuous (transfers), 12/1 (early decision plan 1), 2/15 (early decision plan 2), 1/15 (early action).

CONTACT

Ms. Michelle Cloutier, Vice President for Enrollment Management, Bryant University, 1150 Douglas Pike, Smithfield, RI 02917. *Phone:* 401-232-6100. *Toll-free phone:* 800-622-7001. *Fax:* 401-232-6741. *E-mail:* admission@bryant.edu.

Johnson & Wales University

Providence, Rhode Island

http://www.jwu.edu/providence/

CONTACT

Amy Podbelski, Dean of Undergraduate Admissions, Johnson & Wales University, 8 Abbott Park Place, Providence, RI 02903-3703. *Phone:* 401-598-2310. *Toll-free phone:* 800-342-5598. *Fax:* 401-598-2948. *E-mail:* pvd@admissions.jwu.edu.

New England Institute of Technology

East Greenwich, Rhode Island

http://www.neit.edu/

- **Independent** comprehensive, founded 1940
- **Suburban** 225-acre campus with easy access to Boston
- **Coed** 2,314 undergraduate students, 87% full-time, 35% women, 65% men
- **Minimally difficult** entrance level

UNDERGRAD STUDENTS

2,020 full-time, 294 part-time. Students come from 13 states and territories; 14 other countries; 33% are from out of state; 1% Black or African American, non-Hispanic/Latino; 10% Hispanic/Latino; 0.2% Asian, non-Hispanic/Latino; 3% Two or more races, non-Hispanic/Latino; 74% Race/ethnicity unknown; 1% international; 19% live on campus.

Freshmen:

Admission: 467 enrolled.

FACULTY

Total: 279, 44% full-time, 16% with terminal degrees.

Student/faculty ratio: 13:1.

ACADEMICS

Calendar: quarters. *Degrees:* associate, bachelor's, master's, and doctoral.

Special study options: academic remediation for entering students, accelerated degree program, adult/continuing education programs, advanced placement credit, cooperative education, distance learning, double majors, internships, part-time degree program, services for LD students, student-designed majors, summer session for credit.

Computers: 1,300 computers/terminals are available on campus for general student use. Students can access the following: campus intranet, computer help desk, free student e-mail accounts, online (class) grades, online (class) registration, online (class) schedules. Campuswide network is available. 100% of college-owned or -operated housing units are wired for high-speed Internet access. Wireless service is available via entire campus.

Library: New England Institute of Technology Library. *Books:* 46,560 (physical), 27,542 (digital/electronic); *Serial titles:* 314 (physical), 92,156 (digital/electronic); *Databases:* 64. Weekly public service hours: 70; students can reserve study rooms.

STUDENT LIFE

Housing options: coed. Campus housing is university owned. Freshman applicants given priority for college housing.

Activities and organizations: student-run radio station, Rotaract Club, Student Physical Therapist Assistant Club, Student Nurses Association, Video Club, Criminal Justice Club.

Athletics ***Intramural sports:*** basketball M(c)/W(c), golf M(c)/W(c), soccer M(c)/W(c).

Campus security: 24-hour emergency response devices and patrols, late-night transport/escort service, controlled dormitory access.

Student services: health clinic, personal/psychological counseling, veterans affairs office.

COSTS & FINANCIAL AID
Costs (2020–21) ***Comprehensive fee:*** $46,050 includes full-time tuition ($30,000), mandatory fees ($1545), and room and board ($14,505). Full-time tuition and fees vary according to program. Part-time tuition: $15,000 per year. Part-time tuition and fees vary according to program. No tuition increase for student's term of enrollment. ***Required fees:*** $1545 per year part-time. ***Payment plans:*** tuition prepayment, installment. ***Waivers:*** employees or children of employees.

Financial Aid Of all full-time matriculated undergraduates who enrolled in 2018, 250 Federal Work-Study jobs (averaging $2290).

APPLYING
Options: electronic application, early admission, deferred entrance.

Application fee: $50.

Required: high school transcript, interview. ***Required for some:*** portfolio for advanced standing.

Application deadlines: rolling (freshmen), rolling (out-of-state freshmen), rolling (transfers).

Notification: continuous (freshmen), continuous (out-of-state freshmen), continuous (transfers).

CONTACT
Scott Freund, Executive Vice President, New England Institute of Technology, One New England Tech Blvd., East Greenwich, RI 02818. *Phone:* 401-739-5000 Ext. 3640. *Toll-free phone:* 800-736-7744. *Fax:* 401-886-0859. *E-mail:* sfreund@neit.edu.

Providence College

Providence, Rhode Island

http://www.providence.edu/

- **Independent Roman Catholic** comprehensive, founded 1917
- **Suburban** 105-acre campus with easy access to Boston
- **Endowment** $238.5 million
- **Coed** 4,379 undergraduate students, 95% full-time, 55% women, 45% men
- **Moderately difficult** entrance level, 49% of applicants were admitted

UNDERGRAD STUDENTS
4,148 full-time, 231 part-time. Students come from 40 states and territories; 24 other countries; 89% are from out of state; 4% Black or African American, non-Hispanic/Latino; 10% Hispanic/Latino; 1% Asian, non-Hispanic/Latino; 0.3% Native Hawaiian or other Pacific Islander, non-Hispanic/Latino; 0.2% American Indian or Alaska Native, non-Hispanic/Latino; 2% Two or more races, non-Hispanic/Latino; 4% Race/ethnicity unknown; 2% international; 1% transferred in; 81% live on campus.

Freshmen:
Admission: 11,421 applied, 5,593 admitted, 1,122 enrolled. ***Average high school GPA:*** 3.5. ***Test scores:*** SAT evidence-based reading and writing scores over 500: 99%; SAT math scores over 500: 99%; ACT scores over 18: 100%; SAT evidence-based reading and writing scores over 600: 82%; SAT math scores over 600: 77%; ACT scores over 24: 94%; SAT evidence-based reading and writing scores over 700: 15%; SAT math scores over 700: 21%; ACT scores over 30: 37%.

Retention: 93% of full-time freshmen returned.

FACULTY
Total: 488, 62% full-time, 73% with terminal degrees.

Student/faculty ratio: 12:1.

ACADEMICS
Calendar: semesters. *Degrees:* certificates, bachelor's, master's, and postbachelor's certificates.

Special study options: adult/continuing education programs, advanced placement credit, distance learning, double majors, honors programs, independent study, internships, off-campus study, part-time degree program, services for LD students, student-designed majors, study abroad, summer session for credit. ***ROTC:*** Army (b).

Unusual degree programs: 3-2 engineering with Columbia University, Washington University in St. Louis; biology/optometry with New England School of Optometry.

Computers: 460 computers/terminals and 5,000 ports are available on campus for general student use. Students can access the following: campus intranet, computer help desk, free student e-mail accounts, online (class) grades, online (class) registration, online (class) schedules. Campuswide network is available. 100% of college-owned or -operated housing units are wired for high-speed Internet access. Wireless service is available via entire campus.

Library: Phillips Memorial Library. *Books:* 286,704 (physical), 1.0 million (digital/electronic); *Serial titles:* 241 (physical), 58,816 (digital/electronic); *Databases:* 397. Weekly public service hours: 116; students can reserve study rooms.

STUDENT LIFE
Housing options: on-campus residence required through junior year; coed, men-only, women-only, special housing for students with disabilities. Campus housing is university owned. Freshman campus housing is guaranteed.

Activities and organizations: drama/theater group, student-run newspaper, radio and television station, choral group, Student Congress, Board of Multicultural Student Affairs, Campus Ministry, Dance Club, Board of Programmers.

Athletics Member NCAA. All Division I. ***Intercollegiate sports:*** basketball M(s)/W(s), cross-country running M(s)/W(s), field hockey W(s), ice hockey M(s)/W(s), lacrosse M(s), soccer M(s)/W(s), softball W(s), swimming and diving M/W, tennis W, track and field M(s)/W(s), volleyball W(s). ***Intramural sports:*** badminton M/W, basketball M(c)/W(c), cheerleading M(c)/W(c), cross-country running M/W, fencing W, football M/W, golf M(c)/W(c), ice hockey M(c)/W, lacrosse M/W(c), racquetball M(c)/W(c), rugby M(c)/W(c), sailing M(c)/W(c), soccer M/W, softball M/W, table tennis M/W, track and field M/W, ultimate Frisbee M(c)/W(c), volleyball M(c)/W(c), water polo M/W, wrestling M(c)/W(c).

Campus security: 24-hour emergency response devices and patrols, late-night transport/escort service, controlled dormitory access.

Student services: health clinic, personal/psychological counseling, legal services.

COSTS & FINANCIAL AID
Costs (2019–20) ***Comprehensive fee:*** $67,578 includes full-time tuition ($51,490), mandatory fees ($948), and room and board ($15,140). Part-time tuition: $2145 per credit hour. ***College room only:*** $8730. ***Payment plan:*** installment. ***Waivers:*** employees or children of employees.

Financial Aid Of all full-time matriculated undergraduates who enrolled in 2019, 2,722 applied for aid, 1,967 were judged to have need, 455 had their need fully met. In 2019, 545 non-need-based awards were made. ***Average percent of need met:*** 84. ***Average financial aid package:*** $36,988. ***Average need-based loan:*** $4564. ***Average need-based gift aid:*** $32,316. ***Average non-need-based aid:*** $21,350. ***Average indebtedness upon graduation:*** $44,529. ***Financial aid deadline:*** 2/1.

APPLYING
Standardized Tests *Required for some:* TOEFL or IELTS if English is not the applicant's first language.

Options: electronic application, early decision, early action, deferred entrance.

Application fee: $65.

Required: essay or personal statement, high school transcript, 2 letters of recommendation.

Application deadlines: 1/15 (freshmen), 4/1 (transfers), 11/1 (early action).

Early decision deadline: 11/15 (for plan 1), 1/15 (for plan 2).

Notification: 4/1 (freshmen), 4/15 (transfers), 1/1 (early decision plan 1), 2/15 (early decision plan 2), 1/1 (early action).

CONTACT
Providence College, 1 Cunningham Square, Providence, RI 02918. *Phone:* 401-865-2535. *Toll-free phone:* 800-721-6444.

Rhode Island College

Providence, Rhode Island

http://www.ric.edu/

- **State-supported** comprehensive, founded 1854
- **Suburban** 180-acre campus with easy access to Boston
- **Endowment** $18.2 million
- **Coed** 6,443 undergraduate students, 77% full-time, 69% women, 31% men
- **Moderately difficult** entrance level, 78% of applicants were admitted

UNDERGRAD STUDENTS
4,953 full-time, 1,490 part-time. 14% are from out of state; 11% Black or African American, non-Hispanic/Latino; 23% Hispanic/Latino; 3% Asian, non-Hispanic/Latino; 0.5% American Indian or Alaska Native, non-Hispanic/Latino; 2% Two or more races, non-Hispanic/Latino; 5% Race/ethnicity unknown; 0.2% international; 10% transferred in; 14% live on campus.

Freshmen:
Admission: 4,749 applied, 3,722 admitted, 964 enrolled. ***Test scores:*** SAT evidence-based reading and writing scores over 500: 51%; SAT math scores over 500: 47%; ACT scores over 18: 52%; SAT evidence-based reading and writing scores over 600: 12%; SAT math scores over 600: 7%; ACT scores over 24: 3%; SAT evidence-based reading and writing scores over 700: 1%; SAT math scores over 700: 1%.

Retention: 75% of full-time freshmen returned.

FACULTY
Total: 742, 45% full-time, 40% with terminal degrees.

Student/faculty ratio: 13:1.

ACADEMICS
Calendar: semesters. *Degrees:* certificates, bachelor's, master's, doctoral, post-master's, and postbachelor's certificates.

Special study options: academic remediation for entering students, adult/continuing education programs, advanced placement credit, double majors, English as a second language, external degree program, honors programs, independent study, internships, off-campus study, part-time degree program, services for LD students, student-designed majors, study abroad, summer session for credit. ***ROTC:*** Army (c).

Unusual degree programs: 3-2 public administration with University of Rhode Island.

Computers: 250 computers/terminals are available on campus for general student use. Students can access the following: computer help desk, free student e-mail accounts, online (class) grades, online (class) registration, online (class) schedules. Campuswide network is available. 100% of college-owned or -operated housing units are wired for high-speed Internet access. Wireless service is available via classrooms, computer centers, computer labs, dorm rooms, learning centers, libraries, student centers.

Library: Adams Library. *Books:* 306,080 (physical), 302,387 (digital/electronic); *Serial titles:* 3,081 (physical), 52,652 (digital/electronic); *Databases:* 123. Weekly public service hours: 80.

STUDENT LIFE
Housing options: coed, special housing for students with disabilities. Campus housing is university owned. Freshman applicants given priority for college housing.

Activities and organizations: drama/theater group, student-run newspaper, radio and television station, choral group, Theta Phi Alpha, Delta Phi Epsilon, Alpha Sigma Tau, Sojourn Collegiate Ministries, Student Community Government, national fraternities, national sororities.

Athletics Member NCAA. All Division III except golf (Division II). ***Intercollegiate sports:*** baseball M, basketball M/W, cross-country running M/W, golf M/W, gymnastics W, lacrosse W, soccer M/W, softball W, swimming and diving W, tennis M/W, track and field M/W, volleyball W, wrestling M. ***Intramural sports:*** badminton M/W, basketball M/W, football M, soccer M/W, softball M/W, swimming and diving M/W, tennis M/W, volleyball M/W, water polo M/W.

Campus security: 24-hour emergency response devices and patrols, late-night transport/escort service, controlled dormitory access.

Student services: health clinic, personal/psychological counseling, women's center, legal services, veterans affairs office.

FINANCIAL AID
Financial Aid Of all full-time matriculated undergraduates who enrolled in 2019, 4,234 applied for aid, 3,547 were judged to have need, 584 had their need fully met. In 2019, 110 non-need-based awards were made. ***Average percent of need met:*** 66. ***Average financial aid package:*** $9843. ***Average need-based loan:*** $3972. ***Average need-based gift aid:*** $7510. ***Average non-need-based aid.*** $2643. ***Average indebtedness upon graduation:*** $25,936.

APPLYING
Standardized Tests *Required:* SAT or ACT (for admission).

Options: electronic application, early admission.

Application fee: $50.

Required: essay or personal statement, high school transcript, 1 letter of recommendation, 1 letter from a guidance counselor. ***Required for some:*** interview. ***Recommended:*** minimum 3.0 GPA.

Notification: continuous until 12/15 (freshmen), continuous (out-of-state freshmen), continuous (transfers).

CONTACT
Jason Anthony, Director of Admissions, Rhode Island College, 600 Mount Pleasant Avenue, Providence, RI 02908-1927. *Phone:* 401-456-8234. *Toll-free phone:* 800-669-5760. *Fax:* 401-456-8817. *E-mail:* admissions@ric.edu.

Rhode Island School of Design

Providence, Rhode Island

http://www.risd.edu/

- **Independent** comprehensive, founded 1877
- **Urban** 19-acre campus with easy access to Boston, MA
- **Endowment** $351.4 million
- **Coed**
- 24% of applicants were admitted

FACULTY
Student/faculty ratio: 10:1.

ACADEMICS
Calendar: 4-1-4. *Degrees:* bachelor's and master's.

Library: Fleet Library. *Books:* 131,412 (physical), 178,450 (digital/electronic); *Serial titles:* 1,662 (physical), 800 (digital/electronic); *Databases:* 48. Weekly public service hours: 89; students can reserve study rooms.

STUDENT LIFE
Housing options: on-campus residence required through sophomore year; coed, special housing for students with disabilities. Campus housing is university owned and leased by the school. Freshman campus housing is guaranteed.

Activities and organizations: drama/theater group, student-run newspaper, radio station, choral group, athletic clubs, Religious clubs, South Asian Student Association, RISD Global Initiative, Community Service Club.

Campus security: 24-hour emergency response devices and patrols, late-night transport/escort service, controlled dormitory access.

Student services: health clinic, personal/psychological counseling, legal services.

COSTS & FINANCIAL AID
Costs (2019–20) ***Comprehensive fee:*** $66,580 includes full-time tuition ($51,800), mandatory fees ($1060), and room and board ($13,720).

Financial Aid Of all full-time matriculated undergraduates who enrolled in 2018, 887 applied for aid, 794 were judged to have need, 28 had their need fully met. ***Average percent of need met:*** 66. ***Average financial aid package:*** $35,064. ***Average need-based loan:*** $6750. ***Average need-based gift aid:*** $30,418. ***Average indebtedness upon graduation:*** $35,398. ***Financial aid deadline:*** 2/15.

APPLYING
Standardized Tests *Required:* SAT or ACT (for admission).

Options: electronic application, early decision, deferred entrance.

Application fee: $60.

Required: essay or personal statement, high school transcript, portfolio, drawing assignments. ***Recommended:*** 3 letters of recommendation.

CONTACT

James O'Hara, Vice President for Enrollment, Rhode Island School of Design, 2 College Street, Providence, RI 02903-2784. *Phone:* 401-454-6300. *Toll-free phone:* 800-364-7473. *Fax:* 401-454-6309. *E-mail:* admissions@risd.edu.

Roger Williams University

Bristol, Rhode Island

http://www.rwu.edu/

- **Independent** comprehensive, founded 1956
- **Small-town** 140-acre campus with easy access to Boston
- **Endowment** $67.6 million
- **Coed** 4,523 undergraduate students, 89% full-time, 51% women, 49% men
- **Moderately difficult** entrance level, 85% of applicants were admitted

UNDERGRAD STUDENTS

4,022 full-time, 501 part-time. Students come from 42 states and territories; 56 other countries; 78% are from out of state; 2% Black or African American, non-Hispanic/Latino; 8% Hispanic/Latino; 2% Asian, non-Hispanic/Latino; 0.2% American Indian or Alaska Native, non-Hispanic/Latino; 2% Two or more races, non-Hispanic/Latino; 7% Race/ethnicity unknown; 1% international; 2% transferred in; 73% live on campus.

Freshmen:

Admission: 8,906 applied, 7,601 admitted, 1,113 enrolled. ***Average high school GPA:*** 3.5. ***Test scores:*** SAT evidence-based reading and writing scores over 500: 89%; SAT math scores over 500: 88%; ACT scores over 18: 95%; SAT evidence-based reading and writing scores over 600: 41%; SAT math scores over 600: 34%; ACT scores over 24: 62%; SAT evidence-based reading and writing scores over 700: 5%; SAT math scores over 700: 4%; ACT scores over 30: 11%.

Retention: 85% of full-time freshmen returned.

FACULTY

Total: 523, 40% full-time, 37% with terminal degrees.

Student/faculty ratio: 14:1.

ACADEMICS

Calendar: semesters. *Degrees:* certificates, associate, bachelor's, master's, doctoral, and postbachelor's certificates.

Special study options: accelerated degree program, adult/continuing education programs, advanced placement credit, cooperative education, distance learning, double majors, English as a second language, freshman honors college, honors programs, independent study, internships, part-time degree program, services for LD students, student-designed majors, study abroad, summer session for credit. ***ROTC:*** Army (b).

Computers: 100 computers/terminals and 300 ports are available on campus for general student use. Students can access the following: campus intranet, computer help desk, free student e-mail accounts, online (class) grades, online (class) registration, online (class) schedules. Campuswide network is available. 20% of college-owned or -operated housing units are wired for high-speed Internet access. Wireless service is available via entire campus.

Library: Roger Williams University Library plus 1 other. *Books:* 219,429 (physical), 448,637 (digital/electronic); *Serial titles:* 493 (physical), 52,585 (digital/electronic); *Databases:* 189. Weekly public service hours: 111; students can reserve study rooms.

STUDENT LIFE

Housing options: on-campus residence required through sophomore year; coed, men-only, special housing for students with disabilities. Campus housing is university owned. Freshman campus housing is guaranteed.

Activities and organizations: drama/theater group, student-run newspaper, radio station, choral group, Campus Entertainment Network, Dance Club, WQRI 88.3 Radio Station, Habitat for Humanity.

Athletics Member NCAA. All Division III. ***Intercollegiate sports:*** baseball M, basketball M/W, crew M(c)/W(c), cross-country running M/W, equestrian sports W, field hockey W, golf M, ice hockey M(c), lacrosse M/W, rugby M(c)/W(c), sailing M/W, soccer M/W, softball W, swimming and diving M/W, tennis M/W, track and field M/W, ultimate Frisbee M(c)/W(c), volleyball M(c)/W, wrestling M. ***Intramural sports:*** basketball M/W, cheerleading W(c), football M/W, gymnastics M(c)/W(c), sand volleyball M/W, soccer M/W, softball M/W, volleyball M/W.

Campus security: 24-hour emergency response devices and patrols, late-night transport/escort service, controlled dormitory access, Rave Guardian Emergency Communication App.

Student services: health clinic, personal/psychological counseling, women's center, veterans affairs office.

COSTS & FINANCIAL AID

Costs (2020–21) ***Comprehensive fee:*** $48,179 includes full-time tuition ($32,789) and room and board ($15,390). ***College room only:*** $8696.

Financial Aid Of all full-time matriculated undergraduates who enrolled in 2019, 3,194 applied for aid, 2,675 were judged to have need, 276 had their need fully met. 1,489 Federal Work-Study jobs (averaging $1825). In 2019, 1248 non-need-based awards were made. ***Average percent of need met:*** 81. ***Average financial aid package:*** $24,895. ***Average need-based loan:*** $4271. ***Average need-based gift aid:*** $16,971. ***Average non-need-based aid:*** $13,553. ***Average indebtedness upon graduation:*** $44,753. ***Financial aid deadline:*** 2/1.

APPLYING

Options: electronic application, early action, deferred entrance.

Application fee: $55.

Required: essay or personal statement, 1 letter of recommendation. ***Required for some:*** high school transcript, portfolio review, audition, specific preparatory courses for visual arts studies, graphic design communications, architecture, creative writing, dance and theater.

Application deadlines: 2/1 (freshmen), rolling (transfers), 11/15 (early action).

Notification: continuous (freshmen), continuous (out-of-state freshmen), continuous (transfers).

CONTACT

Roger Williams University, 1 Old Ferry Road, Bristol, RI 02809. *Toll-free phone:* 800-458-7144.

Salve Regina University

Newport, Rhode Island

http://www.salve.edu/

- **Independent Roman Catholic** comprehensive, founded 1934
- **Suburban** 80-acre campus with easy access to Boston, Providence
- **Endowment** $63.8 million
- **Coed** 2,167 undergraduate students, 96% full-time, 65% women, 35% men
- 74% of applicants were admitted

UNDERGRAD STUDENTS

2,091 full-time, 76 part-time. Students come from 40 states and territories; 16 other countries; 84% are from out of state; 2% Black or African American, non-Hispanic/Latino; 7% Hispanic/Latino; 1% Asian, non-Hispanic/Latino; 0.2% American Indian or Alaska Native, non-Hispanic/Latino; 3% Two or more races, non-Hispanic/Latino; 3% Race/ethnicity unknown; 2% international; 2% transferred in; 59% live on campus.

Freshmen:

Admission: 4,888 applied, 3,606 admitted, 655 enrolled. ***Average high school GPA:*** 3.5. ***Test scores:*** SAT evidence-based reading and writing scores over 500: 97%; SAT math scores over 500: 97%; ACT scores over 18: 99%; SAT evidence-based reading and writing scores over 600: 49%; SAT math scores over 600: 36%; ACT scores over 24: 82%; SAT evidence-based reading and writing scores over 700: 4%; SAT math scores over 700: 4%; ACT scores over 30: 17%.

Retention: 85% of full-time freshmen returned.

FACULTY

Total: 295, 43% full-time, 36% with terminal degrees.

Student/faculty ratio: 13:1.

ACADEMICS
Calendar: semesters. *Degrees:* certificates, associate, bachelor's, master's, doctoral, post-master's, and postbachelor's certificates.

Special study options: accelerated degree program, adult/continuing education programs, advanced placement credit, double majors, English as a second language, honors programs, independent study, internships, off-campus study, part-time degree program, services for LD students, study abroad, summer session for credit. ***ROTC:*** Army (c).

Unusual degree programs: 3-2 business administration; nursing; administration of justice, holistic counseling, international relations, MBA, management, rehabilitation counseling.

Computers: 237 computers/terminals are available on campus for general student use. Students can access the following: campus intranet, computer help desk, free student e-mail accounts, online (class) grades, online (class) registration, online (class) schedules. Campuswide network is available. 100% of college-owned or -operated housing units are wired for high-speed Internet access. Wireless service is available via entire campus.
Library: McKillop Library. *Books:* 148,506 (physical), 437,247 (digital/electronic); *Serial titles:* 134 (physical), 43,668 (digital/electronic); *Databases:* 85. Weekly public service hours: 58; students can reserve study rooms.

STUDENT LIFE
Housing options: on-campus residence required through sophomore year; coed, men-only, women-only. Campus housing is university owned. Freshman campus housing is guaranteed.

Activities and organizations: drama/theater group, student-run newspaper, radio station, choral group, Campus Activities Board, Best Buddies, SRU Dance, Student Nursing Organization, Student Government Association.

Athletics Member NCAA. All Division III. ***Intercollegiate sports:*** baseball M, basketball M/W, cross-country running M/W, equestrian sports W, field hockey W, football M, ice hockey M/W, lacrosse M/W, rugby M(c)/W(c), sailing M/W, soccer M/W, softball W, tennis M/W, track and field W, volleyball W. ***Intramural sports:*** baseball M, basketball M/W, cheerleading W(c), football M/W, golf M/W, ice hockey M, lacrosse M, rugby M(c)/W(c), soccer M/W, softball W, swimming and diving M(c)/W(c), tennis M/W, ultimate Frisbee M/W, volleyball M/W, weight lifting M/W.

Campus security: 24-hour emergency response devices and patrols, late-night transport/escort service, controlled dormitory access.

Student services: health clinic, personal/psychological counseling, veterans affairs office.

COSTS & FINANCIAL AID
Costs (2020–21) ***Comprehensive fee:*** $58,320 includes full-time tuition ($42,220), mandatory fees ($700), and room and board ($15,400). Full-time tuition and fees vary according to course load and location. Part-time tuition: $1407 per credit hour. Part-time tuition and fees vary according to course load and location. ***College room only:*** $9020. Room and board charges vary according to board plan and housing facility. ***Payment plan:*** installment. ***Waivers:*** employees or children of employees.

Financial Aid Of all full-time matriculated undergraduates who enrolled in 2019, 1,824 applied for aid, 1,581 were judged to have need, 211 had their need fully met. In 2019, 468 non-need-based awards were made. ***Average percent of need met:*** 68. ***Average financial aid package:*** $28,725. ***Average need-based loan:*** $4350. ***Average need-based gift aid:*** $24,047. ***Average non-need-based aid:*** $15,964. ***Average indebtedness upon graduation:*** $40,958.

APPLYING
Standardized Tests *Required for some:* SAT or ACT (for admission).

Options: electronic application, early action, deferred entrance.

Application fee: $50.

Required: essay or personal statement, high school transcript, 2 letters of recommendation. ***Recommended:*** minimum 2.7 GPA.

Application deadlines: 2/1 (freshmen), rolling (transfers), 11/1 (early action).

Notification: 12/25 (freshmen), continuous (transfers), 12/25 (early action).

CONTACT
Dean Colleen Emerson, Dean of Undergraduate Admissions, Salve Regina University, 100 Ochre Point Avenue, Newport, RI 02840-4192. *Phone:* 401-341-2908. *Toll-free phone:* 888-GO SALVE. *Fax:* 401-848-2823. *E-mail:* emersonc@salve.edu.

University of Rhode Island

Kingston, Rhode Island

http://www.uri.edu/

CONTACT
Ms. Joanne Lynch, Assistant Dean of Admissions, University of Rhode Island, Undergraduate Admission Office, Newman Hall, 14 Upper College Road, Kingston, RI 02881. *Phone:* 401-874-7110. *Fax:* 401-874-5523. *E-mail:* lynch@uri.edu.

SOUTH CAROLINA

Allen University

Columbia, South Carolina

http://www.allenuniversity.edu/

CONTACT
Terri Parker, Director of Admission, Allen University, 1530 Harden Street, Columbia, SC 29204. *Phone:* 803-376-5733. *Toll-free phone:* 877-625-5368. *E-mail:* tparker@allenuniversity.edu.

Anderson University

Anderson, South Carolina

http://www.andersonuniversity.edu/

- **Independent Baptist** comprehensive, founded 1911
- **Urban** 271-acre campus with easy access to Greenville
- **Endowment** $44.7 million
- **Coed** 2,983 undergraduate students, 85% full-time, 69% women, 31% men
- **Minimally difficult** entrance level, 79% of applicants were admitted

UNDERGRAD STUDENTS
2,550 full-time, 433 part-time. Students come from 35 states and territories; 20 other countries; 19% are from out of state; 5% transferred in; 46% live on campus.

Freshmen:
Admission: 2,322 applied, 1,836 admitted, 681 enrolled. ***Average high school GPA:*** 3.6.

Retention: 75% of full-time freshmen returned.

FACULTY
Total: 341, 43% full-time, 46% with terminal degrees.

Student/faculty ratio: 14:1.

ACADEMICS
Calendar: semesters. *Degrees:* bachelor's, master's, and doctoral.

Special study options: academic remediation for entering students, accelerated degree program, adult/continuing education programs, advanced placement credit, cooperative education, distance learning, double majors, honors programs, independent study, internships, part-time degree program, services for LD students, study abroad, summer session for credit. ***ROTC:*** Army (c), Air Force (c).

Computers: 192 computers/terminals are available on campus for general student use. Students can access the following: campus intranet, computer help desk, free student e-mail accounts, online (class) grades, online (class) registration, online (class) schedules. Campuswide network is available. 100% of college-owned or -operated housing units are wired for high-speed Internet access. Wireless service is available via entire campus.
Library: Thrift Library. *Books:* 90,729 (physical), 99,204 (digital/electronic); *Serial titles:* 14,268 (physical), 174,052 (digital/electronic); *Databases:* 200. Weekly public service hours: 88; students can reserve study rooms.

STUDENT LIFE

Housing options: on-campus residence required through sophomore year; men-only, women-only. Campus housing is university owned. Freshman campus housing is guaranteed.

Activities and organizations: drama/theater group, student-run newspaper, choral group, Baptist Collegiate Ministries, Gamma Beta Phi, Anderson University Education Club, Ducks Unlimited, Council of Exceptional Children.

Athletics Member NCAA. All Division II. ***Intercollegiate sports:*** baseball M(s), basketball M(s)/W(s), cheerleading W(s), cross-country running M(s)/W(s), golf M(s)/W(s), soccer M(s)/W(s), softball W(s), tennis M(s)/W(s), track and field M(s)/W(s), volleyball W(s). ***Intramural sports:*** basketball M/W, football M/W, racquetball M/W, softball M/W, table tennis M/W, ultimate Frisbee M/W, volleyball M/W, weight lifting M.

Campus security: 24-hour emergency response devices and patrols, late-night transport/escort service, controlled dormitory access.

Student services: health clinic, personal/psychological counseling.

COSTS & FINANCIAL AID

Costs (2020–21) ***Comprehensive fee:*** $40,620 includes full time tuition ($26,820), mandatory fees ($3160), and room and board ($10,640). Part-time tuition: $665 per credit hour. ***College room only:*** $5430. ***Payment plan:*** installment.

Financial Aid Of all full-time matriculated undergraduates who enrolled in 2019, 2,366 applied for aid, 1,955 were judged to have need, 603 had their need fully met. 201 Federal Work-Study jobs (averaging $4000). 282 state and other part-time jobs (averaging $850). In 2019, 550 non-need-based awards were made. ***Average percent of need met:*** 73. ***Average financial aid package:*** $21,124. ***Average need-based loan:*** $3896. ***Average need-based gift aid:*** $18,752. ***Average non-need-based aid:*** $12,794. ***Average indebtedness upon graduation:*** $32,609.

APPLYING

Standardized Tests *Required:* SAT or ACT (for admission).

Options: electronic application, deferred entrance.

Application fee: $25.

Required: high school transcript. ***Required for some:*** essay or personal statement, 2 letters of recommendation, interview. ***Recommended:*** minimum 2.9 GPA.

Notification: continuous (freshmen), continuous (transfers).

CONTACT

Mr. William Monts, Director of Admission, Anderson University, 316 Boulevard, Anderson, SC 29621. *Phone:* 864-231-5795. *Toll-free phone:* 800-542-3594. *E-mail:* wmonts@andersonuniversity.edu.

Benedict College

Columbia, South Carolina

http://www.benedict.edu/

CONTACT

Benedict College, 1600 Harden Street, Columbia, SC 29204. *Phone:* 803-705-4491. *Toll-free phone:* 800-868-6598.

Bob Jones University

Greenville, South Carolina

http://www.bju.edu/

CONTACT

Mr. Gary Deedrick, Director of Admission, Bob Jones University, 1700 Wade Hampton Boulevard, Greenville, SC 29614. *Phone:* 864-242-5100. *Toll-free phone:* 800-252-6363. *Fax:* 800-232-9258. *E-mail:* admission@bju.edu.

Charleston Southern University

Charleston, South Carolina

http://www.charlestonsouthern.edu/

CONTACT

Mr. Jim Rhoden, Director of Enrollment Management, Charleston Southern University, Charleston, SC 29423-8087. *Phone:* 843-863-7050. *Toll-free phone:* 800-947-7474. *E-mail:* enroll@csuniv.edu.

The Citadel, The Military College of South Carolina

Charleston, South Carolina

http://www.citadel.edu/

- **State-supported** comprehensive, founded 1842
- **Suburban** 300-acre campus
- **Endowment** $314.4 million
- **Coed, primarily men** 2,923 undergraduate students, 92% full-time, 13% women, 87% men
- 75% of applicants were admitted

UNDERGRAD STUDENTS

2,688 full-time, 235 part-time. Students come from 48 states and territories; 9 other countries; 33% are from out of state; 7% Black or African American, non-Hispanic/Latino; 7% Hispanic/Latino; 2% Asian, non-Hispanic/Latino; 0.2% Native Hawaiian or other Pacific Islander, non-Hispanic/Latino; 0.4% American Indian or Alaska Native, non-Hispanic/Latino; 5% Two or more races, non-Hispanic/Latino; 0.9% Race/ethnicity unknown; 0.9% international; 4% transferred in; 100% live on campus.

Freshmen:

Admission: 2,742 applied, 2,049 admitted, 643 enrolled. ***Average high school GPA:*** 3.8. ***Test scores:*** SAT evidence-based reading and writing scores over 500: 92%; SAT math scores over 500: 88%; ACT scores over 18: 97%; SAT evidence-based reading and writing scores over 600: 39%; SAT math scores over 600: 32%; ACT scores over 24: 43%; SAT evidence-based reading and writing scores over 700: 4%; SAT math scores over 700: 6%; ACT scores over 30: 4%.

Retention: 86% of full-time freshmen returned.

FACULTY

Total: 327, 62% full-time, 74% with terminal degrees.

Student/faculty ratio: 12:1.

ACADEMICS

Calendar: semesters. *Degrees:* bachelor's, master's, post-master's, and postbachelor's certificates.

Special study options: adult/continuing education programs, advanced placement credit, distance learning, double majors, honors programs, independent study, internships, off-campus study, part-time degree program, services for LD students, study abroad, summer session for credit. ***ROTC:*** Army (b), Navy (b), Air Force (b).

Computers: 400 computers/terminals are available on campus for general student use. Students can access the following: campus intranet, computer help desk, free student e-mail accounts, online (class) grades, online (class) registration, online (class) schedules. Campuswide network is available. 100% of college-owned or -operated housing units are wired for high-speed Internet access. Wireless service is available via entire campus.

Library: Daniel Library. *Books:* 173,127 (physical), 424,551 (digital/electronic); *Serial titles:* 64 (physical); *Databases:* 79. Weekly public service hours: 80; students can reserve study rooms.

STUDENT LIFE

Housing options: on-campus residence required through senior year; coed. Campus housing is university owned. Freshman campus housing is guaranteed.

Activities and organizations: student-run newspaper, choral group, marching band, The Republican Society, Semper Fi Society, American Society of Civil Engineers, Campus Outreach, Criminal Justice Society.

Athletics Member NCAA. All Division I except football (Division I-AA). ***Intercollegiate sports:*** baseball M(s), basketball M(s), cross-country running M(s)/W(s), golf W(s), riflery M(s)/W(s), soccer W(s), tennis

M(s), track and field M(s)/W(s), volleyball W(s), wrestling M(s). ***Intramural sports:*** badminton M/W, basketball M/W, fencing M(c)/W(c), football M/W, golf M(c), ice hockey M(c)/W(c), lacrosse M(c), racquetball M/W, riflery M/W, rugby M(c)/W(c), sailing M(c)/W(c), sand volleyball M/W, soccer M/W, softball M/W, swimming and diving M/W, table tennis M/W, tennis M/W, track and field M/W, triathlon M(c)/W(c), ultimate Frisbee M/W, volleyball M(c)/W(c), weight lifting M/W, wrestling M/W.

Campus security: 24-hour patrols.

Student services: health clinic, personal/psychological counseling, veterans affairs office.

COSTS & FINANCIAL AID
Costs (2020–21) ***Tuition:*** area resident $14,483 full-time; state resident $14,483 full-time; nonresident $38,368 full-time. ***Room and board:*** $7957. ***Payment plan:*** installment. ***Waivers:*** senior citizens and employees or children of employees.

Financial Aid Of all full-time matriculated undergraduates who enrolled in 2019, 1,985 applied for aid, 1,491 were judged to have need, 455 had their need fully met. In 2019, 658 non-need-based awards were made. ***Average percent of need met:*** 67. ***Average financial aid package:*** $19,584. ***Average need-based loan:*** $4331. ***Average need-based gift aid:*** $19,036. ***Average non-need-based aid:*** $16,160. ***Average indebtedness upon graduation:*** $28,159.

APPLYING
Standardized Tests *Required:* SAT or ACT (for admission).

Options: electronic application.

Application fee: $40.

Required: high school transcript. ***Recommended:*** interview.

Application deadlines: rolling (freshmen), rolling (transfers).

Notification: continuous (freshmen), continuous (transfers).

CONTACT
Lt. Col. John W. Powell Jr., Director of Admissions, The Citadel, The Military College of South Carolina, 171 Moultrie Street, Charleston, SC 29409. *Phone:* 843-953-5230. *Toll-free phone:* 800-868-1842. *Fax:* 843-953-7036. *E-mail:* john.powell@citadel.edu.

Claflin University

Orangeburg, South Carolina

http://www.claflin.edu/

- **Independent United Methodist** comprehensive, founded 1869
- **Small-town** 46-acre campus with easy access to Columbia
- **Endowment** $21.7 million
- **Coed**
- **Minimally difficult** entrance level

FACULTY
Student/faculty ratio: 14:1.

ACADEMICS
Calendar: semesters. *Degrees:* bachelor's and master's.
Library: H. V. Manning Library plus 1 other.

STUDENT LIFE
Housing options: men-only, women-only. Campus housing is university owned and leased by the school. Freshman applicants given priority for college housing.

Activities and organizations: drama/theater group, student-run newspaper, television station, choral group, Gospel Choir, NAACP, American Chemical Society, Sisters of Service, International Student Association, national fraternities, national sororities.

Athletics Member NCAA. All Division II.

Campus security: 24-hour emergency response devices and patrols, student patrols, controlled dormitory access.

Student services: health clinic, personal/psychological counseling.

FINANCIAL AID
Financial Aid Of all full-time matriculated undergraduates who enrolled in 2017, 2,002 applied for aid, 1,943 were judged to have need, 107 had their need fully met. 233 Federal Work-Study jobs (averaging $1152). In 2017, 68 non-need-based awards were made. ***Average percent of need met:*** 47. ***Average financial aid package:*** $15,962. ***Average need-based loan:*** $4024. ***Average need-based gift aid:*** $12,530. ***Average non-need-based aid:*** $7704. ***Average indebtedness upon graduation:*** $31,747. ***Financial aid deadline:*** 7/15.

APPLYING
Standardized Tests *Required:* SAT or ACT (for admission).

Options: electronic application, deferred entrance.

Application fee: $30.

Required: essay or personal statement, high school transcript, minimum 2.0 GPA.

CONTACT
Claflin University, 400 Magnolia Street, Orangeburg, SC 29115. *Phone:* 803-535-5340. *Toll-free phone:* 800-922-1276.

Clemson University

Clemson, South Carolina

http://www.clemson.edu/

- **State-supported** university, founded 1889
- **Small-town** 1400-acre campus
- **Endowment** $518.6 million
- **Coed** 20,195 undergraduate students, 96% full-time, 50% women, 50% men
- **Very difficult** entrance level, 51% of applicants were admitted

UNDERGRAD STUDENTS
19,486 full-time, 709 part-time. 33% are from out of state; 6% Black or African American, non-Hispanic/Latino; 6% Hispanic/Latino; 3% Asian, non-Hispanic/Latino; 0.0% Native Hawaiian or other Pacific Islander, non-Hispanic/Latino; 0.2% American Indian or Alaska Native, non-Hispanic/Latino; 4% Two or more races, non-Hispanic/Latino; 0.3% Race/ethnicity unknown; 0.7% international; 8% transferred in; 99% live on campus.

Freshmen:
Admission: 29,070 applied, 14,900 admitted, 3,932 enrolled. ***Average high school GPA:*** 4.4. ***Test scores:*** SAT evidence-based reading and writing scores over 500: 99%; SAT math scores over 500: 99%; ACT scores over 18: 99%; SAT evidence-based reading and writing scores over 600: 86%; SAT math scores over 600: 82%; ACT scores over 24: 92%; SAT evidence-based reading and writing scores over 700: 23%; SAT math scores over 700: 34%; ACT scores over 30: 53%.

Retention: 93% of full-time freshmen returned.

FACULTY
Total: 1,763, 77% full-time, 77% with terminal degrees.

Student/faculty ratio: 16:1.

ACADEMICS
Calendar: semesters. *Degrees:* bachelor's, master's, doctoral, and post-master's certificates.

Special study options: academic remediation for entering students, advanced placement credit, cooperative education, distance learning, double majors, English as a second language, freshman honors college, honors programs, independent study, internships, off-campus study, part-time degree program, services for LD students, study abroad, summer session for credit. ***ROTC:*** Army (b), Air Force (b).

Computers: 1,250 computers/terminals are available on campus for general student use. Students can access the following: campus intranet, computer help desk, free student e-mail accounts, online (class) grades, online (class) registration, online (class) schedules. Campuswide network is available. 100% of college-owned or -operated housing units are wired for high-speed Internet access. Wireless service is available via entire campus.

Library: Robert Muldrow Cooper Library plus 1 other. Study areas open 24 hours, 5–7 days a week; students can reserve study rooms.

STUDENT LIFE
Housing options: on-campus residence required for freshman year; coed, men-only, women-only, special housing for students with disabilities. Campus housing is university owned. Freshman campus housing is guaranteed.

Activities and organizations: drama/theater group, student-run newspaper, radio and television station, choral group, marching band,

Student Government, Fellowship of Christian Athletes, Tiger Band, national fraternities, national sororities.

Athletics Member NCAA. All Division I except football (Division I-A). ***Intercollegiate sports:*** baseball M(s), basketball M(s)/W(s), bowling M(c)/W(c), cheerleading M/W, crew M(c)/W(s), cross-country running M(s)/W(s), equestrian sports M(c)/W(c), fencing M(c)/W(c), field hockey M(c)/W(c), golf M(s), ice hockey M(c)/W(c), lacrosse M(c)/W(c), riflery M(c)/W(c), rugby M(c)/W(c), sailing M(c)/W(c), soccer M(s)/W(s), softball W(s)(c), tennis M(s)/W(s), track and field M(s)/W(s), ultimate Frisbee M(c)/W(c), volleyball M(c)/W(s), weight lifting M(c)/W(c), wrestling M(c). ***Intramural sports:*** basketball M/W, golf M/W, racquetball M/W, soccer M/W, softball M/W, swimming and diving M(c)/W(c), table tennis M/W, tennis M(c)/W(c), volleyball M/W, water polo M/W.

Campus security: 24-hour emergency response devices and patrols, late-night transport/escort service, controlled dormitory access.

Student services: health clinic, personal/psychological counseling, legal services.

COSTS & FINANCIAL AID

Costs (2019–20) ***Tuition:*** $641 per credit hour part-time; state resident $13,702 full-time, $641 per credit hour part-time; nonresident $35,056 full-time, $1586 per credit hour part-time. ***Required fees:*** $1268 full-time. ***Room only:*** $6812.

Financial Aid Of all full-time matriculated undergraduates who enrolled in 2019, 13,367 applied for aid, 9,224 were judged to have need, 1,278 had their need fully met. In 2019, 4872 non-need-based awards were made. ***Average percent of need met:*** 50. ***Average financial aid package:*** $11,679. ***Average need-based loan:*** $4351. ***Average need-based gift aid:*** $9711. ***Average non-need-based aid:*** $5421. ***Average indebtedness upon graduation:*** $32,510.

APPLYING

Standardized Tests *Required:* SAT or ACT (for admission).

Options: electronic application, deferred entrance.

Application fee: $70.

Required: high school transcript. ***Recommended:*** essay or personal statement.

Application deadlines: 5/1 (freshmen), 7/1 (transfers).

Notification: continuous (freshmen), continuous (transfers).

CONTACT

Clemson University, Clemson, SC 29634.

Coastal Carolina University

Conway, South Carolina

http://www.coastal.edu/

- **State-supported** comprehensive, founded 1954
- **Suburban** 621-acre campus
- **Endowment** $51.5 million
- **Coed** 9,760 undergraduate students, 90% full-time, 55% women, 45% men
- **Moderately difficult** entrance level, 69% of applicants were admitted

UNDERGRAD STUDENTS

8,810 full-time, 950 part-time. Students come from 52 states and territories; 56 other countries; 50% are from out of state; 18% Black or African American, non-Hispanic/Latino; 5% Hispanic/Latino; 0.8% Asian, non-Hispanic/Latino; 0.1% Native Hawaiian or other Pacific Islander, non-Hispanic/Latino; 0.4% American Indian or Alaska Native, non-Hispanic/Latino; 5% Two or more races, non-Hispanic/Latino; 2% Race/ethnicity unknown; 1% international; 7% transferred in; 45% live on campus.

Freshmen:

Admission: 15,061 applied, 10,373 admitted, 2,304 enrolled. ***Average high school GPA:*** 3.6. ***Test scores:*** SAT evidence-based reading and writing scores over 500: 86%; SAT math scores over 500: 81%; ACT scores over 18: 92%; SAT evidence-based reading and writing scores over 600: 24%; SAT math scores over 600: 17%; ACT scores over 24: 30%; SAT evidence-based reading and writing scores over 700: 2%; SAT math scores over 700: 1%; ACT scores over 30: 4%.

Retention: 68% of full-time freshmen returned.

FACULTY

Total: 775, 63% full-time, 57% with terminal degrees.

Student/faculty ratio: 16:1.

ACADEMICS

Calendar: semesters. *Degrees:* certificates, bachelor's, master's, doctoral, post-master's, and postbachelor's certificates.

Special study options: accelerated degree program, adult/continuing education programs, advanced placement credit, cooperative education, distance learning, double majors, honors programs, independent study, internships, part-time degree program, services for LD students, student-designed majors, study abroad, summer session for credit. ***ROTC:*** Army (b).

Computers: 1,577 computers/terminals are available on campus for general student use. Students can access the following: computer help desk, free student e-mail accounts, online (class) grades, online (class) registration, online (class) schedules. Campuswide network is available. Wireless service is available via entire campus.

Library: Kimbel Library. *Books:* 129,696 (physical), 433,254 (digital/electronic); *Serial titles:* 622 (physical), 79,146 (digital/electronic); *Databases:* 213. Weekly public service hours: 168; study areas open 24 hours, 5–7 days a week; students can reserve study rooms.

STUDENT LIFE

Housing options: on-campus residence required through sophomore year; coed, special housing for students with disabilities. Campus housing is university owned. Freshman campus housing is guaranteed.

Activities and organizations: drama/theater group, student-run newspaper, radio station, choral group, marching band, Outdoor Adventure Club, Surf Club, Alpha Delta Pi, Women of Color, Aqua League (Scuba Club), national fraternities, national sororities.

Athletics Member NCAA. All Division I. ***Intercollegiate sports:*** baseball M(s), basketball M(s)/W(s), cheerleading M(c)/W(c), cross-country running M(s)/W(s), equestrian sports M(c)/W(c), field hockey M(c)/W(c), football M(s), golf M(s)/W(s), lacrosse M(c)/W(s), rugby M(c)/W(c), sailing M(c)/W(c), sand volleyball W(s), soccer M(s)/W(s), softball W(s), swimming and diving M(c)/W(c), tennis M(s)/W(s), track and field M(s)/W(s), volleyball M(c)/W(s), weight lifting M(c)/W(c). ***Intramural sports:*** badminton M/W, basketball M/W, lacrosse M/W, sand volleyball M/W, soccer M/W, softball M/W, table tennis M/W, tennis M/W, volleyball M/W.

Campus security: 24-hour emergency response devices and patrols, late-night transport/escort service, controlled dormitory access.

Student services: health clinic, personal/psychological counseling, women's center, veterans affairs office.

COSTS & FINANCIAL AID

Costs (2019–20) ***Tuition:*** state resident $11,460 full-time, $487 per credit hour part-time; nonresident $27,214 full-time, $1138 per credit hour part-time. Full-time tuition and fees vary according to course load, degree level, and reciprocity agreements. Part-time tuition and fees vary according to course load, degree level, and reciprocity agreements. ***Required fees:*** $180 full-time, $5 per credit hour part-time. ***Room and board:*** $9290; room only: $5440. Room and board charges vary according to board plan and housing facility. ***Payment plan:*** installment. ***Waivers:*** senior citizens and employees or children of employees.

Financial Aid Of all full-time matriculated undergraduates who enrolled in 2018, 7,439 applied for aid, 6,131 were judged to have need, 695 had their need fully met. 315 Federal Work-Study jobs (averaging $1790). 1,568 state and other part-time jobs (averaging $1775). In 2018, 1835 non-need-based awards were made. ***Average percent of need met:*** 48. ***Average financial aid package:*** $11,168. ***Average need-based loan:*** $9620. ***Average need-based gift aid:*** $5337. ***Average non-need-based aid:*** $14,254. ***Average indebtedness upon graduation:*** $37,717.

APPLYING

Standardized Tests *Required:* SAT or ACT (for admission).

Options: electronic application, deferred entrance.

Application fee: $45.

Required: high school transcript, minimum 2.0 GPA. ***Recommended:*** essay or personal statement, 1 letter of recommendation.

Application deadlines: rolling (freshmen), rolling (transfers).

Notification: continuous (freshmen), continuous (transfers).

CONTACT

Coastal Carolina University, PO Box 261954, Conway, SC 29528-6054. *Phone:* 843-349-2170. *Toll-free phone:* 800-277-7000.

Coker College

Hartsville, South Carolina

http://www.coker.edu/

CONTACT

Mr. Adam Connolly, Vice President for Enrollment Management, Coker College, 300 E. College Avenue, Hartsville, SC 29550. *Phone:* 843-383-8050. *Toll-free phone:* 800-950-1908. *Fax:* 843-383-8056. *E-mail:* admissions@coker.edu.

College of Charleston

Charleston, South Carolina

http://www.cofc.edu/

- **State-supported** comprehensive, founded 1770
- **Urban** 66-acre campus
- **Endowment** $92.3 million
- **Coed** 9,600 undergraduate students, 91% full-time, 64% women, 36% men
- **Moderately difficult** entrance level, 78% of applicants were admitted

UNDERGRAD STUDENTS

8,762 full-time, 838 part-time. 35% are from out of state; 7% Black or African American, non-Hispanic/Latino; 6% Hispanic/Latino; 2% Asian, non-Hispanic/Latino; 0.2% Native Hawaiian or other Pacific Islander, non-Hispanic/Latino; 0.4% American Indian or Alaska Native, non-Hispanic/Latino; 4% Two or more races, non-Hispanic/Latino; 1% Race/ethnicity unknown; 1% international; 5% transferred in; 33% live on campus.

Freshmen:

Admission: 11,783 applied, 9,230 admitted, 2,051 enrolled. ***Average high school GPA:*** 4.0. ***Test scores:*** SAT evidence-based reading and writing scores over 500: 96%; SAT math scores over 500: 90%; ACT scores over 18: 97%; SAT evidence-based reading and writing scores over 600: 52%; SAT math scores over 600: 35%; ACT scores over 24: 61%; SAT evidence-based reading and writing scores over 700: 9%; SAT math scores over 700: 5%; ACT scores over 30: 17%.

Retention: 81% of full-time freshmen returned.

FACULTY

Total: 944, 58% full-time, 65% with terminal degrees.

Student/faculty ratio: 14:1.

ACADEMICS

Calendar: semesters. *Degrees:* certificates, bachelor's, master's, post-master's, and postbachelor's certificates (also offers graduate degree programs through University of Charleston, South Carolina).

Special study options: accelerated degree program, adult/continuing education programs, advanced placement credit, cooperative education, distance learning, double majors, English as a second language, external degree program, honors programs, independent study, internships, off-campus study, part-time degree program, services for LD students, study abroad, summer session for credit. ***ROTC:*** Army (c), Air Force (c).

Unusual degree programs: 3-2 computer science, mathematics.

Computers: 325 computers/terminals are available on campus for general student use. Students can access the following: campus intranet, computer help desk, free student e-mail accounts, online (class) grades, online (class) registration, online (class) schedules. Campuswide network is available. 80% of college-owned or -operated housing units are wired for high-speed Internet access. Wireless service is available via entire campus.

Library: Marlene and Nathan Addlestone Library plus 3 others. *Books:* 608,954 (physical), 635,379 (digital/electronic); *Serial titles:* 418 (physical), 89,449 (digital/electronic); *Databases:* 339. Weekly public service hours: 112; students can reserve study rooms.

STUDENT LIFE

Housing options: coed, men-only, women-only, special housing for students with disabilities. Campus housing is university owned. Freshman applicants given priority for college housing.

Activities and organizations: drama/theater group, student-run newspaper, radio and television station, choral group, Student Government Association, Cougar Activities Board, Black Student Union, Charleston Miracle, Intramural Basketball, national fraternities, national sororities.

Athletics Member NCAA. All Division I. ***Intercollegiate sports:*** baseball M(s), basketball M(s)/W(s), cheerleading M/W, cross-country running M(s)/W(s), equestrian sports W, golf M(s)/W(s), sailing M/W, sand volleyball W, soccer M(s)/W(s), softball W(s), tennis M(s)/W(s), volleyball W(s). ***Intramural sports:*** badminton M/W, baseball M(c), basketball M/W, crew M(c)/W(c), fencing M(c)/W(c), golf M(c)/W(c), gymnastics M(c)/W(c), ice hockey M(c)/W(c), lacrosse M(c)/W(c), racquetball M/W, rock climbing M/W, rowing M(c)/W(c), rugby M(c)/W(c), soccer M/W, softball M/W, squash M(c)/W(c), swimming and diving M(c)/W(c), table tennis M/W, tennis M(c)/W(c), ultimate Frisbee M(c)/W(c), volleyball M/W, weight lifting M/W.

Campus security: 24-hour emergency response devices and patrols, student patrols, late-night transport/escort service, controlled dormitory access.

Student services: health clinic, personal/psychological counseling, women's center, veterans affairs office.

COSTS & FINANCIAL AID

Costs (2019–20) ***Tuition:*** state resident $12,518 full-time, $522 per credit hour part-time; nonresident $32,848 full-time, $1369 per credit hour part-time. Full-time tuition and fees vary according to program and student level. Part-time tuition and fees vary according to course load, program, and student level. ***Required fees:*** $460 full-time, $15 per term part-time. ***Room and board:*** $12,123; room only: $7673. Room and board charges vary according to board plan and housing facility. ***Payment plan:*** installment. ***Waivers:*** senior citizens and employees or children of employees.

Financial Aid Of all full-time matriculated undergraduates who enrolled in 2018, 5,974 applied for aid, 4,585 were judged to have need, 680 had their need fully met. In 2018, 1882 non-need-based awards were made. ***Average percent of need met:*** 53. ***Average financial aid package:*** $14,110. ***Average need-based loan:*** $3513. ***Average need-based gift aid:*** $2671. ***Average non-need-based aid:*** $12,252. ***Average indebtedness upon graduation:*** $27,731.

APPLYING

Standardized Tests *Required:* SAT or ACT (for admission). *Required for some:* International applicants not submitting an SAT/ACT score should submit an English language proficiency test score (TOEFL, IELTS, or iTEP).

Options: electronic application, early decision, early action, deferred entrance.

Application fee: $50.

Required: essay or personal statement, high school transcript. ***Required for some:*** letters of recommendation for Honors College.

Application deadlines: 2/15 (freshmen), 6/1 (transfers), 12/1 (early action).

Early decision deadline: 11/1.

Notification: 4/1 (freshmen), continuous (transfers), 12/1 (early decision), 1/15 (early action).

CONTACT

Ms. Suzette Stille, Dean of Admissions, College of Charleston, 66 George Street, Charleston, SC 29424-0001. *Phone:* 843-953-5670. *Fax:* 843-953-6322. *E-mail:* admissions@cofc.edu.

Columbia College

Columbia, South Carolina

http://www.columbiasc.edu/

- **Independent United Methodist** comprehensive, founded 1854
- **Suburban** 59-acre campus
- **Endowment** $20.1 million
- **Coed, primarily women** 1,102 undergraduate students, 69% full-time, 84% women, 16% men
- **Moderately difficult** entrance level, 97% of applicants were admitted

UNDERGRAD STUDENTS

763 full-time, 339 part-time. Students come from 28 states and territories; 4 other countries; 12% are from out of state; 37% Black or African American, non-Hispanic/Latino; 6% Hispanic/Latino; 0.7% Asian, non-Hispanic/Latino; 0.5% American Indian or Alaska Native, non-Hispanic/Latino; 4% Two or more races, non-Hispanic/Latino; 17% Race/ethnicity unknown; 0.9% international; 17% transferred in; 37% live on campus.

Freshmen:

Admission: 819 applied, 791 admitted, 178 enrolled. ***Average high school GPA:*** 3.5. ***Test scores:*** SAT evidence-based reading and writing scores over 500: 44%; SAT math scores over 500: 31%; ACT scores over 18: 44%; SAT evidence-based reading and writing scores over 600: 8%; SAT math scores over 600: 7%; ACT scores over 24: 12%; SAT evidence-based reading and writing scores over 700: 1%; ACT scores over 30: 2%. ***Retention:*** 68% of full-time freshmen returned.

FACULTY

Total: 162, 31% full-time, 40% with terminal degrees.

Student/faculty ratio: 11:1.

ACADEMICS

Calendar: semesters. *Degrees:* bachelor's and master's.

Special study options: academic remediation for entering students, adult/continuing education programs, advanced placement credit, distance learning, double majors, honors programs, independent study, internships, off-campus study, part-time degree program, services for LD students, student-designed majors, study abroad, summer session for credit. ***ROTC:*** Army (c).

Computers: 165 computers/terminals are available on campus for general student use. Students can access the following: campus intranet, computer help desk, free student e-mail accounts, online (class) grades, online (class) registration, online (class) schedules. Campuswide network is available. 100% of college-owned or -operated housing units are wired for high-speed Internet access. Wireless service is available via entire campus.

Library: J. Edens Drake Library. *Books:* 128,000 (physical), 92 (digital/electronic); *Serial titles:* 310 (physical); *Databases:* 84. Weekly public service hours: 70; students can reserve study rooms.

STUDENT LIFE

Housing options: on-campus residence required through sophomore year; women-only. Campus housing is university owned. Freshman campus housing is guaranteed.

Activities and organizations: drama/theater group, student-run newspaper, choral group, national sororities.

Athletics Member NAIA. ***Intercollegiate sports:*** basketball W(s), cross-country running W(s), golf W(s), lacrosse W(s), soccer W(s), softball W(s), swimming and diving W(s), tennis W(s), track and field W(s), volleyball W(s).

Campus security: 24-hour emergency response devices and patrols, late-night transport/escort service, controlled dormitory access.

Student services: health clinic, personal/psychological counseling, women's center, veterans affairs office.

COSTS & FINANCIAL AID

Costs (2020–21) ***One-time required fee:*** $150. ***Comprehensive fee:*** $28,185 includes full-time tuition ($19,890) and room and board ($8295). Full-time tuition and fees vary according to class time and location. Part-time tuition: $650 per semester hour. Part-time tuition and fees vary according to class time and location. No tuition increase for student's term of enrollment. ***Room and board:*** Room and board charges vary according to board plan and housing facility. ***Payment plan:*** installment. ***Waivers:*** employees or children of employees.

Financial Aid Of all full-time matriculated undergraduates who enrolled in 2019, 722 applied for aid, 662 were judged to have need, 49 had their need fully met. In 2019, 57 non-need-based awards were made. ***Average percent of need met:*** 57. ***Average financial aid package:*** $14,022. ***Average need-based loan:*** $3800. ***Average need-based gift aid:*** $10,732. ***Average non-need-based aid:*** $5541. ***Average indebtedness upon graduation:*** $25,241.

APPLYING

Options: electronic application.

Required: high school transcript. ***Required for some:*** interview. ***Recommended:*** essay or personal statement.

Application deadlines: 8/1 (freshmen), 8/1 (transfers).

CONTACT

Mr. Vincent Maloney, Dean of Enrollment Management, Columbia College, 1301 Columbia College Drive, Columbia, SC 29203. *Phone:* 803-786-3608. *Toll-free phone:* 800-277-1301. *E-mail:* vmaloney@columbiasc.edu.

Columbia International University

Columbia, South Carolina

http://www.ciu.edu/

- **Independent nondenominational** university, founded 1923
- **Suburban** 400-acre campus with easy access to Columbia, SC
- **Endowment** $21.1 million
- **Coed** 621 undergraduate students, 86% full-time, 50% women, 50% men
- **Moderately difficult** entrance level, 48% of applicants were admitted

UNDERGRAD STUDENTS

531 full-time, 90 part-time. 52% are from out of state; 19% Black or African American, non-Hispanic/Latino; 6% Hispanic/Latino; 0.9% Asian, non-Hispanic/Latino; 0.2% Native Hawaiian or other Pacific Islander, non-Hispanic/Latino; 0.2% American Indian or Alaska Native, non-Hispanic/Latino; 0.8% Two or more races, non-Hispanic/Latino; 5% Race/ethnicity unknown; 5% international; 72% live on campus.

Freshmen:

Admission: 336 applied, 161 admitted, 146 enrolled. ***Average high school GPA:*** 3.3. ***Test scores:*** SAT evidence-based reading and writing scores over 500: 67%; SAT math scores over 500: 53%; ACT scores over 18: 87%; SAT evidence-based reading and writing scores over 600: 23%; SAT math scores over 600: 11%; ACT scores over 24: 35%; SAT evidence-based reading and writing scores over 700: 4%; SAT math scores over 700: 1%; ACT scores over 30: 6%.

FACULTY

Total: 125, 33% full-time, 64% with terminal degrees.

Student/faculty ratio: 14:1.

ACADEMICS

Calendar: semesters. *Degrees:* certificates, associate, bachelor's, master's, doctoral, post-master's, and postbachelor's certificates.

Special study options: academic remediation for entering students, accelerated degree program, advanced placement credit, cooperative education, distance learning, double majors, honors programs, independent study, internships, off-campus study, part-time degree program, services for LD students, study abroad, summer session for credit.

Unusual degree programs: 3-2 teaching or divinity.

Computers: 106 computers/terminals and 374 ports are available on campus for general student use. Students can access the following: campus intranet, computer help desk, free student e-mail accounts, online (class) grades, online (class) registration, online (class) schedules. Campuswide network is available. 100% of college-owned or -operated housing units are wired for high-speed Internet access. Wireless service is available via classrooms, computer centers, computer labs, dorm rooms, learning centers, libraries, student centers.

Library: G. Allen Fleece Library. *Books:* 32,000 (physical), 100,000 (digital/electronic); *Databases:* 133. Weekly public service hours: 81; students can reserve study rooms.

STUDENT LIFE

Housing options: on-campus residence required through senior year; men-only, women-only, special housing for students with disabilities. Campus housing is university owned. Freshman campus housing is guaranteed.

Activities and organizations: drama/theater group, student-run newspaper, choral group, Student Union, Mu Kappa, Student Missions Connection, GradLife, African American Fellowship Ministries.

Athletics Member NCCAA. ***Intercollegiate sports:*** basketball M(s)/W(s), cross-country running M(s)/W(s), soccer M(s)/W(s). ***Intramural sports:*** basketball M/W, football M/W, soccer M/W, ultimate Frisbee M/W, volleyball M/W.

Campus security: 24-hour emergency response devices and patrols, late-night transport/escort service, controlled dormitory access.

Student services: health clinic, personal/psychological counseling, legal services.

COSTS & FINANCIAL AID

Costs (2020–21) ***Comprehensive fee:*** $8950 includes full-time tuition ($23,550), mandatory fees ($1100), and room and board ($8950). Full-time tuition and fees vary according to course load, program, and reciprocity agreements. Part-time tuition: $980 per credit hour. Part-time tuition and fees vary according to course load, program, and reciprocity agreements. ***Room and board:*** Room and board charges vary according to board plan and housing facility. ***Payment plan:*** installment. ***Waivers:*** employees or children of employees.

Financial Aid Of all full-time matriculated undergraduates who enrolled in 2018, 447 applied for aid, 407 were judged to have need, 54 had their need fully met. In 2018, 77 non-need-based awards were made. ***Average percent of need met:*** 69. ***Average financial aid package:*** $19,354. ***Average need-based loan:*** $3891. ***Average need-based gift aid:*** $16,305. ***Average non-need-based aid:*** $9852. ***Average indebtedness upon graduation:*** $23,695.

APPLYING

Standardized Tests *Required:* SAT or ACT (for admission).

Options: electronic application, deferred entrance.

Application fee: $25.

Required: essay or personal statement, minimum 2.0 GPA, 1 letter of recommendation. ***Required for some:*** interview. ***Recommended:*** high school transcript.

Application deadlines: 8/1 (freshmen), 8/1 (transfers).

Notification: continuous (freshmen), continuous (out-of-state freshmen), continuous (transfers).

CONTACT

Ms. Jen Johnson, Undergraduate Admissions Office, Columbia International University, Columbia, SC 29230-3122. *Phone:* 803-777-2227. *Toll-free phone:* 800-777-2227 Ext. 5024. *Fax:* 803-786-4041. *E-mail:* yesciu@ciu.edu.

Converse College

Spartanburg, South Carolina

http://www.converse.edu/

CONTACT

Admissions, Converse College, 580 East Main Street, Spartanburg, SC 29302. *Phone:* 864-596-9040. *Toll-free phone:* 800-766-1125. *E-mail:* admissions@converse.edu.

Erskine College

Due West, South Carolina

http://www.erskine.edu/

CONTACT

Kasey McNair, Director of Admissions, Erskine College, 2 Washington Street, PO Box 338, Due West, SC 29639. *Phone:* 864-379-8830. *Toll-free phone:* 800-241-8721. *E-mail:* mcnair@erskine.edu.

Francis Marion University

Florence, South Carolina

http://www.fmarion.edu/

- **State-supported** comprehensive, founded 1970
- **Rural** 832-acre campus
- **Coed** 3,800 undergraduate students, 76% full-time, 68% women, 32% men
- **Moderately difficult** entrance level, 69% of applicants were admitted

UNDERGRAD STUDENTS

2,900 full-time, 900 part-time. Students come from 23 states and territories; 30 other countries; 4% are from out of state; 40% Black or African American, non-Hispanic/Latino; 3% Hispanic/Latino; 1% Asian, non-Hispanic/Latino; 0.5% American Indian or Alaska Native, non-Hispanic/Latino; 4% Two or more races, non-Hispanic/Latino; 1% Race/ethnicity unknown; 1% international; 6% transferred in; 41% live on campus.

Freshmen:

Admission: 4,162 applied, 2,860 admitted, 716 enrolled. ***Average high school GPA:*** 3.9. ***Test scores:*** SAT evidence-based reading and writing scores over 500: 58%; SAT math scores over 500: 50%; ACT scores over 18: 56%; SAT evidence-based reading and writing scores over 600: 16%; SAT math scores over 600: 7%; ACT scores over 24: 15%; SAT math scores over 700: 1%; ACT scores over 30: 1%.

Retention: 69% of full-time freshmen returned.

FACULTY

Total: 303, 70% full-time, 74% with terminal degrees.

Student/faculty ratio: 14:1.

ACADEMICS

Calendar: semesters. *Degrees:* bachelor's, master's, doctoral, and post-master's certificates.

Special study options: accelerated degree program, advanced placement credit, cooperative education, distance learning, double majors, honors programs, independent study, internships, off-campus study, part-time degree program, services for LD students, study abroad, summer session for credit. ***ROTC:*** Army (b).

Unusual degree programs: 3-2 engineering with Clemson University.

Computers: 141 computers/terminals are available on campus for general student use. Students can access the following: computer help desk, free student e-mail accounts, online (class) grades, online (class) registration, online (class) schedules, Learning management system. Campuswide network is available. 100% of college-owned or -operated housing units are wired for high-speed Internet access. Wireless service is available via entire campus.

Library: James A. Rogers Library. *Books:* 289,630 (physical), 343,000 (digital/electronic); *Serial titles:* 179 (physical), 34,999 (digital/electronic); *Databases:* 147. Weekly public service hours: 86.

STUDENT LIFE

Housing options: coed, men-only, women-only, special housing for students with disabilities. Campus housing is university owned.

Activities and organizations: drama/theater group, student-run newspaper, choral group, Baptist Collegiate Ministries, University Programming Board, Psychology Club, Student Alumni Association, Young Gifted and Blessed Chorus, national fraternities, national sororities.

Athletics Member NCAA. All Division II except golf (Division I). ***Intercollegiate sports:*** baseball M(s), basketball M(s)/W(s), cross-country running M(s)/W(s), golf M(s), soccer M(s)/W(s), softball W(s), swimming and diving M(c)/W(c), tennis M(s)/W(s), track and field M(s)/W(s), volleyball W(s). ***Intramural sports:*** basketball M/W, football M/W, racquetball M/W, soccer M/W, softball M/W, table tennis M/W, tennis M/W, volleyball M/W.

Campus security: 24-hour emergency response devices and patrols, late-night transport/escort service, controlled dormitory access.

Student services: health clinic, personal/psychological counseling.

FINANCIAL AID

Financial Aid Of all full-time matriculated undergraduates who enrolled in 2017, 2,576 applied for aid, 2,327 were judged to have need, 235 had their need fully met. In 2017, 65 non-need-based awards were made.

Average percent of need met: 64. ***Average financial aid package:*** $12,396. ***Average need-based loan:*** $4142. ***Average need-based gift aid:*** $7682. ***Average non-need-based aid:*** $2252. ***Average indebtedness upon graduation:*** $32,346.

APPLYING

Standardized Tests *Required:* SAT or ACT (for admission).

Options: electronic application, deferred entrance.

Application fee: $41.

Required: high school transcript.

Application deadlines: rolling (freshmen), rolling (out-of-state freshmen), rolling (transfers).

Notification: continuous (freshmen), continuous (out-of-state freshmen), continuous (transfers).

CONTACT

Jamee Freeman, Director of Admissions, Francis Marion University, PO Box 100547, Florence, SC 29502-0547. *Phone:* 843-661-1318. *Toll-free phone:* 800-368-7551. *Fax:* 843-661-4635. *E-mail:* admissions@fmarion.edu.

Furman University

Greenville, South Carolina

http://www.furman.edu/

- **Independent** comprehensive, founded 1826
- **Suburban** 800-acre campus
- **Coed** 2,687 undergraduate students, 97% full-time, 61% women, 39% men
- **Moderately difficult** entrance level, 57% of applicants were admitted

UNDERGRAD STUDENTS

2,614 full-time, 73 part-time. Students come from 48 states and territories; 22 other countries; 70% are from out of state; 6% Black or African American, non-Hispanic/Latino; 5% Hispanic/Latino; 3% Asian, non-Hispanic/Latino; 0.1% Native Hawaiian or other Pacific Islander, non-Hispanic/Latino; 0.2% American Indian or Alaska Native, non-Hispanic/Latino; 3% Two or more races, non-Hispanic/Latino; 1% Race/ethnicity unknown; 3% international; 0.7% transferred in; 96% live on campus.

Freshmen:

Admission: 5,258 applied, 2,987 admitted, 648 enrolled. ***Average high school GPA:*** 3.6. ***Test scores:*** SAT evidence-based reading and writing scores over 500: 100%; SAT math scores over 500: 100%; ACT scores over 18: 100%; SAT evidence-based reading and writing scores over 600: 91%; SAT math scores over 600: 82%; ACT scores over 24: 98%; SAT evidence-based reading and writing scores over 700: 32%; SAT math scores over 700: 29%; ACT scores over 30: 54%.

Retention: 90% of full-time freshmen returned.

FACULTY

Total: 338, 72% full-time, 83% with terminal degrees.

Student/faculty ratio: 10:1.

ACADEMICS

Calendar: semesters. *Degrees:* bachelor's, master's, and postbachelor's certificates.

Special study options: accelerated degree program, adult/continuing education programs, advanced placement credit, double majors, independent study, internships, part-time degree program, services for LD students, student-designed majors, study abroad, summer session for credit. ***ROTC:*** Army (b).

Unusual degree programs: 3-2 engineering with Georgia Institute of Technology, Clemson University, Auburn University, North Carolina State University, Washington University in St. Louis.

Computers: 500 computers/terminals are available on campus for general student use. Students can access the following: campus intranet, computer help desk, free student e-mail accounts, online (class) grades, online (class) registration, online (class) schedules. Campuswide network is available. 100% of college-owned or -operated housing units are wired for high-speed Internet access. Wireless service is available via entire campus.

Library: James Buchanan Duke Library plus 3 others. *Books:* 366,124 (physical), 1.1 million (digital/electronic); *Serial titles:* 501 (physical), 752,337 (digital/electronic); *Databases:* 496. Study areas open 24 hours, 5–7 days a week.

STUDENT LIFE

Housing options: on-campus residence required through senior year; coed, men-only, women-only, special housing for students with disabilities. Campus housing is university owned. Freshman campus housing is guaranteed.

Activities and organizations: drama/theater group, student-run newspaper, radio and television station, choral group, marching band, Heller Service Corps, national fraternities, national sororities.

Athletics Member NCAA. All Division I except football (Division I-AA). ***Intercollegiate sports:*** baseball M(s), basketball M(s)/W(s), cheerleading W(s), cross-country running M(s)/W(s), equestrian sports W(c), golf M(s)/W(s), lacrosse M/W, rugby M(c), soccer M(s)/W(s), softball W(s), swimming and diving M(c)/W(c), tennis M(s)/W(s), track and field M(s)/W(s), ultimate Frisbee M(c)/W(c), volleyball W(s). ***Intramural sports:*** basketball M/W, bowling M/W, racquetball M(c)/W(c), rock climbing M(c)/W(c), soccer M/W, softball M/W, volleyball M/W, weight lifting M(c)/W(c).

Campus security: 24-hour emergency response devices and patrols, student patrols, late-night transport/escort service, controlled dormitory access.

Student services: health clinic, personal/psychological counseling, women's center.

COSTS & FINANCIAL AID

Costs (2020–21) ***Comprehensive fee:*** $65,454 includes full-time tuition ($51,712), mandatory fees ($380), and room and board ($13,362). Part-time tuition: $1616 per credit. Part-time tuition and fees vary according to course load. ***Required fees:*** $380 per year part-time. ***College room only:*** $7312. Room and board charges vary according to board plan, housing facility, and student level. ***Payment plan:*** installment. ***Waivers:*** employees or children of employees.

Financial Aid Of all full-time matriculated undergraduates who enrolled in 2018, 1,528 applied for aid, 1,214 were judged to have need, 528 had their need fully met. In 2018, 1212 non-need-based awards were made. ***Average percent of need met:*** 81. ***Average financial aid package:*** $41,883. ***Average need-based loan:*** $4265. ***Average need-based gift aid:*** $30,365. ***Average non-need-based aid:*** $18,905. ***Average indebtedness upon graduation:*** $34,072. ***Financial aid deadline:*** 3/1.

APPLYING

Options: electronic application, early decision, early action.

Application fee: $50.

Required: essay or personal statement, high school transcript.

Application deadlines: 1/15 (freshmen), 1/15 (transfers), 11/1 (early action).

Early decision deadline: 11/1.

Notification: 3/1 (freshmen), 3/1 (transfers), 11/15 (early decision), 12/20 (early action).

CONTACT

Mr. Brad Pochard, Associate VP for Enrollment Management & Dean of Admission, Furman University, 3300 Poinsett Highway, Greenville, SC 29613. *Phone:* 864-294-2018. *Fax:* 864-294-2018. *E-mail:* admissions@furman.edu.

Lander University

Greenwood, South Carolina

http://www.lander.edu/

CONTACT

Ms. Jennifer M. Mathis, Director of Admissions, Lander University, 320 Stanley Avenue, Greenwood, SC 29649. *Phone:* 864-388-8307. *Toll-free phone:* 888-452-6337. *Fax:* 864-388-8125. *E-mail:* admissions@lander.edu.

Limestone College

Gaffney, South Carolina

http://www.limestone.edu/

- **Independent** comprehensive, founded 1845
- **Suburban** 123-acre campus with easy access to Charlotte
- **Endowment** $20.5 million
- **Coed** 2,129 undergraduate students, 66% full-time, 55% women, 45% men
- **Minimally difficult** entrance level, 74% of applicants were admitted

UNDERGRAD STUDENTS

1,401 full-time, 728 part-time. Students come from 28 states and territories; 30 other countries; 42% are from out of state; 42% Black or African American, non-Hispanic/Latino; 4% Hispanic/Latino; 0.5% Asian, non-Hispanic/Latino; 0.1% Native Hawaiian or other Pacific Islander, non-Hispanic/Latino; 0.5% American Indian or Alaska Native, non-Hispanic/Latino; 3% Two or more races, non-Hispanic/Latino; 2% Race/ethnicity unknown; 4% international; 2% transferred in; 75% live on campus.

Freshmen:

Admission: 337 applied, 249 admitted, 332 enrolled. ***Average high school GPA:*** 3.3. ***Test scores:*** SAT evidence-based reading and writing scores over 500: 69%; SAT math scores over 500: 69%; ACT scores over 18: 77%; SAT evidence-based reading and writing scores over 600: 12%; SAT math scores over 600: 21%; ACT scores over 24: 25%.

Retention: 54% of full-time freshmen returned.

FACULTY

Total: 298, 30% full-time, 37% with terminal degrees.

Student/faculty ratio: 10:1.

ACADEMICS

Calendar: semesters. *Degrees:* associate, bachelor's, and master's.

Special study options: academic remediation for entering students, accelerated degree program, adult/continuing education programs, advanced placement credit, distance learning, double majors, honors programs, independent study, internships, part-time degree program, services for LD students, student-designed majors, summer session for credit.

Computers: 137 computers/terminals are available on campus for general student use. Students can access the following: campus intranet, computer help desk, free student e-mail accounts, online (class) grades, online (class) registration, online (class) schedules. Campuswide network is available. 100% of college-owned or -operated housing units are wired for high-speed Internet access. Wireless service is available via classrooms, dorm rooms, learning centers, libraries, student centers.

Library: A. J. Eastwood Library plus 1 other. *Books:* 67,000 (physical), 239,537 (digital/electronic); *Serial titles:* 111 (physical), 482,082 (digital/electronic); *Databases:* 156. Weekly public service hours: 70.

STUDENT LIFE

Housing options: on-campus residence required through junior year; men-only, women-only. Campus housing is university owned. Freshman applicants given priority for college housing.

Activities and organizations: drama/theater group, choral group, marching band, Fellowship of Christian Athletes, Student Government Association, Student Alumni Leadership Council, Campus Crusade (CRU), Limestone Activities Board (LAB), national fraternities, national sororities.

Athletics Member NCAA. All Division II except golf (Division I). ***Intercollegiate sports:*** baseball M(s), basketball M(s)/W(s), cheerleading M(s)/W(s), cross-country running M(s)/W(s), field hockey W(s), football M(s), golf M(s)/W(s), gymnastics W(s), lacrosse M(s)/W(s), soccer M(s)/W(s), softball W(s), swimming and diving M(s)/W(s), tennis M(s)/W(s), track and field M(s)/W(s), volleyball M(s)/W(s), wrestling M(s)/W(s). ***Intramural sports:*** badminton M/W, basketball M/W, bowling M/W, racquetball M/W, soccer M/W, table tennis M/W, ultimate Frisbee M/W, volleyball M/W, weight lifting M/W.

Campus security: 24-hour emergency response devices and patrols, late-night transport/escort service, controlled dormitory access.

Student services: health clinic, personal/psychological counseling, veterans affairs office.

COSTS & FINANCIAL AID

Costs (2020–21) ***Comprehensive fee:*** $36,200 includes full-time tuition ($25,200), mandatory fees ($1100), and room and board ($9900). Full-time tuition and fees vary according to course load and location. Part-time tuition: $1050 per credit hour. Part-time tuition and fees vary according to course load and location. ***Required fees:*** $60 per credit hour part-time. ***Room and board:*** Room and board charges vary according to board plan and housing facility. ***Payment plans:*** installment, deferred payment. ***Waivers:*** employees or children of employees.

Financial Aid Of all full-time matriculated undergraduates who enrolled in 2018, 1,895 applied for aid, 1,812 were judged to have need, 134 had their need fully met. 91 Federal Work-Study jobs (averaging $2253). In 2018, 66 non-need-based awards were made. ***Average percent of need met:*** 45. ***Average financial aid package:*** $13,019. ***Average need-based loan:*** $3716. ***Average need-based gift aid:*** $10,773. ***Average non-need-based aid:*** $6966. ***Average indebtedness upon graduation:*** $33,427.

APPLYING

Standardized Tests *Required:* SAT or ACT (for admission). *Required for some:* minimum score of 500 on TOEFL or proof of successfully completed ESL program for students whose native language is not English.

Options: electronic application.

Application fee: $25.

Required: high school transcript, minimum 2.0 GPA. ***Recommended:*** 2 letters of recommendation, interview.

Application deadlines: rolling (freshmen), rolling (transfers).

Notification: continuous (freshmen), continuous (transfers).

CONTACT

Ms. Lisa Hobbs, Admissions Office Manager, Limestone College, 1115 College Drive, Gaffney, SC 29340-3799. *Phone:* 864-488-4554. *Toll-free phone:* 800-795-7151. *Fax:* 864-487-8706. *E-mail:* lhobbs@limestone.edu.

Medical University of South Carolina

Charleston, South Carolina

http://www.musc.edu/

CONTACT

Lyla E. Hudson, Director of Admissions, Medical University of South Carolina, 41 Bee Street MSC203, Charleston, SC 29425-2030. *Phone:* 843-792-7408. *E-mail:* hudsonly@musc.edu.

Morris College

Sumter, South Carolina

http://www.morris.edu/

CONTACT

Ms. Gloria Scriven, Assistant Director of Admissions and Records, Morris College, 100 West College Street, Sumter, SC 29150-3502. *Phone:* 803-934-3239. *Toll-free phone:* 866-853-1345. *Fax:* 803-773-8241. *E-mail:* gscriven@morris.edu.

Newberry College

Newberry, South Carolina

http://www.newberry.edu/

CONTACT

Mr. Joel Vander Horst, Dean of Enrollment Management, Newberry College, 2100 College Street, Newberry, SC 29108. *Phone:* 803-947-2110. *Toll-free phone:* 800-845-4955. *Fax:* 803-321-5138. *E-mail:* admissions@newberry.edu.

North Greenville University

Tigerville, South Carolina

http://www.ngu.edu/

- **Independent Southern Baptist** comprehensive, founded 1892
- **Rural** 380-acre campus with easy access to Greenville
- **Endowment** $258.4 million
- **Coed** 2,167 undergraduate students, 80% full-time, 55% women, 45% men
- **Minimally difficult** entrance level, 61% of applicants were admitted

UNDERGRAD STUDENTS

1,736 full-time, 431 part-time. 22% are from out of state; 4% Black or African American, non-Hispanic/Latino; 7% Hispanic/Latino; 3% Asian, non-Hispanic/Latino; 0.7% Native Hawaiian or other Pacific Islander, non-Hispanic/Latino; 0.8% American Indian or Alaska Native, non-Hispanic/Latino; 0.1% Two or more races, non-Hispanic/Latino; 0.2% Race/ethnicity unknown; 77% international; 5% transferred in; 63% live on campus.

Freshmen:

Admission: 1,695 applied, 1,040 admitted, 414 enrolled. ***Average high school GPA:*** 3.6. ***Test scores:*** SAT evidence-based reading and writing scores over 500: 78%; SAT math scores over 500: 70%; ACT scores over 18: 78%; SAT evidence-based reading and writing scores over 600: 35%; SAT math scores over 600: 24%; ACT scores over 24: 32%; SAT evidence-based reading and writing scores over 700: 6%; SAT math scores over 700: 4%; ACT scores over 30: 9%.

FACULTY

Total: 266, 61% full-time, 56% with terminal degrees.

Student/faculty ratio: 13:1.

ACADEMICS

Calendar: semesters. *Degrees:* bachelor's, master's, and doctoral.

Special study options: academic remediation for entering students, accelerated degree program, adult/continuing education programs, advanced placement credit, cooperative education, distance learning, double majors, English as a second language, freshman honors college, honors programs, independent study, internships, part-time degree program, services for LD students, student-designed majors, study abroad, summer session for credit. ***ROTC:*** Army (c).

Unusual degree programs: 3-2 engineering with Clemson University.

Computers: 95 computers/terminals and 6 ports are available on campus for general student use. Students can access the following: campus intranet, computer help desk, free student e-mail accounts, online (class) grades, online (class) schedules. Campuswide network is available. 100% of college-owned or -operated housing units are wired for high-speed Internet access. Wireless service is available via entire campus.

Library: Hester Memorial Library. *Books:* 70,000 (physical), 250,000 (digital/electronic); *Serial titles:* 250 (physical), 150 (digital/electronic); *Databases:* 103. Weekly public service hours: 85.

STUDENT LIFE

Housing options: on-campus residence required through sophomore year; men-only, women-only, special housing for students with disabilities. Campus housing is university owned. Freshman campus housing is guaranteed.

Activities and organizations: drama/theater group, student-run radio station, choral group, marching band, Baptist Student Union, Fellowship of Christians in Service, Fellowship of Christian Athletes, Black Student Fellowship, Education Club.

Athletics Member NCAA, NCCAA. All NCAA Division II. ***Intercollegiate sports:*** baseball M(s), basketball M(s)/W(s), cheerleading M(s)/W(s), cross-country running M(s)/W(s), football M(s), golf M(s)/W(s), lacrosse M(s)/W(s), soccer M(s)/W(s), softball W(s), tennis M(s)/W(s), track and field M(s)/W(s), volleyball M(s)/W(s). ***Intramural sports:*** basketball M/W, bowling M/W, football M, golf M/W, sand volleyball M/W, soccer M/W, softball M/W, table tennis M/W, tennis M/W, ultimate Frisbee M/W, volleyball W, weight lifting M/W.

Campus security: 24-hour emergency response devices and patrols, late-night transport/escort service, controlled dormitory access.

Student services: personal/psychological counseling.

COSTS & FINANCIAL AID

Costs (2020–21) ***Comprehensive fee:*** $32,500 includes full-time tuition ($22,050) and room and board ($10,450). Full-time tuition and fees vary according to course load. Part-time tuition: $545 per credit hour. ***Room and board:*** Room and board charges vary according to housing facility. ***Payment plan:*** installment. ***Waivers:*** employees or children of employees.

Financial Aid Of all full-time matriculated undergraduates who enrolled in 2015, 1,143 applied for aid, 1,143 were judged to have need, 1,143 had their need fully met. In 2015, 1989 non-need-based awards were made. ***Average financial aid package:*** $5783. ***Average need-based gift aid:*** $5783. ***Average non-need-based aid:*** $7081.

APPLYING

Standardized Tests *Required:* SAT or ACT (for admission), CPT (for admission). *Required for some:* CPT. *Recommended:* CPT.

Options: electronic application, deferred entrance.

Application fee: $35.

Required: high school transcript. ***Required for some:*** interview. ***Recommended:*** minimum 2.0 GPA.

Application deadlines: 8/22 (freshmen), 8/26 (transfers).

Notification: continuous (freshmen), continuous (transfers).

CONTACT

North Greenville University, PO Box 1892, Tigerville, SC 29688-1892. *Phone:* 864-977-7052. *Toll-free phone:* 800-468-6642 Ext. 7001.

Presbyterian College

Clinton, South Carolina

http://www.presby.edu/

- **Independent** comprehensive, founded 1880, affiliated with Presbyterian Church (U.S.A.)
- **Small-town** 240-acre campus with easy access to Greenville, Spartanburg
- **Endowment** $90.2 million
- **Coed**
- **Very difficult** entrance level

FACULTY

Student/faculty ratio: 13:1.

ACADEMICS

Calendar: semesters. *Degrees:* bachelor's and doctoral.

Library: James H. Thomason Library. *Books:* 108,925 (physical), 227,396 (digital/electronic); *Serial titles:* 702 (physical), 16,342 (digital/electronic); *Databases:* 71. Study areas open 24 hours, 5–7 days a week; students can reserve study rooms.

STUDENT LIFE

Housing options: on-campus residence required through senior year; coed, men-only, women-only. Campus housing is university owned. Freshman campus housing is guaranteed.

Activities and organizations: drama/theater group, student-run newspaper, choral group, Student Volunteer Services, Intramural sports, Student Union Board, Fellowship of Christian Athletes, Student Government Association, national fraternities, national sororities.

Athletics Member NCAA. All Division I.

Campus security: 24-hour emergency response devices and patrols, late-night transport/escort service, controlled dormitory access.

Student services: health clinic, personal/psychological counseling.

COSTS & FINANCIAL AID

Costs (2019–20) ***Comprehensive fee:*** $50,140 includes full-time tuition ($36,600), mandatory fees ($2860), and room and board ($10,680). Full-time tuition and fees vary according to course load and reciprocity agreements. Part-time tuition: $1525 per credit hour. Part-time tuition and fees vary according to course load. ***Required fees:*** $27 per credit hour part-time, $25 per term part-time. ***College room only:*** $5200. Room and board charges vary according to board plan and housing facility.

Financial Aid Of all full-time matriculated undergraduates who enrolled in 2018, 836 applied for aid, 734 were judged to have need, 247 had their need fully met. In 2018, 102 non-need-based awards were made. ***Average percent of need met:*** 86. ***Average financial aid package:*** $37,073. ***Average need-based loan:*** $3872. ***Average need-based gift aid:*** $31,185.

Average non-need-based aid: $19,998. ***Average indebtedness upon graduation:*** $31,925. ***Financial aid deadline:*** 6/30.

APPLYING
Standardized Tests *Required for some:* SAT or ACT (for admission).

Options: electronic application, early decision, early action, deferred entrance.

Required: essay or personal statement, high school transcript, minimum 2.0 GPA, 1 letter of recommendation. ***Recommended:*** interview.

CONTACT
Mr. Mark O. Fox, Director of Admissions, Presbyterian College, 503 South Broad Street, Clinton, SC 29325. *Phone:* 864-833-8232. *Toll-free phone:* 800-476-7272. *Fax:* 864-833-8195. *E-mail:* mfox@presby.edu.

South Carolina State University

Orangeburg, South Carolina

http://www.scsu.edu/

- **State-supported** comprehensive, founded 1896, part of South Carolina Commission on Higher Education
- **Small-town** 160-acre campus
- **Coed**
- **Minimally difficult** entrance level

FACULTY
Student/faculty ratio: 16:1.

ACADEMICS
Calendar: semesters. *Degrees:* bachelor's, master's, doctoral, and postbachelor's certificates.
Library: Miller F. Whittaker Library. *Books:* 317,233 (physical), 195,578 (digital/electronic); *Serial titles:* 18,334 (digital/electronic); *Databases:* 114. Weekly public service hours: 74; students can reserve study rooms.

STUDENT LIFE
Housing options: special housing for students with disabilities. Campus housing is university owned, leased by the school and is provided by a third party. Freshman applicants given priority for college housing.

Activities and organizations: drama/theater group, student-run newspaper, radio station, choral group, marching band, Student Government Association, Campus Activity Board, NAACP, United Voices of Christ, Student Media, national fraternities, national sororities.

Athletics Member NCAA. All Division I except football (Division I-AA).

Campus security: 24-hour emergency response devices and patrols, late-night transport/escort service, controlled dormitory access.

Student services: health clinic, personal/psychological counseling, veterans affairs office.

COSTS
Costs (2019–20) ***Tuition:*** state resident $9528 full-time, $461 per credit hour part-time; nonresident $20,218 full-time, $906 per credit hour part-time. Full-time tuition and fees vary according to course load and reciprocity agreements. Part-time tuition and fees vary according to course load and reciprocity agreements. ***Required fees:*** $1532 full-time. ***Room and board:*** $9890; room only: $6600. Room and board charges vary according to board plan and housing facility.

APPLYING
Standardized Tests *Required:* SAT or ACT (for admission).

Options: electronic application, deferred entrance.

Application fee: $25.

Required: high school transcript, minimum 2.0 GPA.

CONTACT
Mrs. Gennifer Bookhardt, South Carolina State University, PO Box 7127, 300 College Street NE, Orangeburg, SC 29117. *Phone:* 803-536-7186. *Toll-free phone:* 800-260-5956. *Fax:* 803-536-8990. *E-mail:* admissions@scsu.edu.

Southern Wesleyan University

Central, South Carolina

http://www.swu.edu/

CONTACT
Mrs. Beth Roe, Director of First Year Experience, Southern Wesleyan University, PO Box 1020, 907 Wesleyan Drive, Central, SC 29630-1020. *Phone:* 864-644-5149. *Toll-free phone:* 800-CU-AT-SWU. *Fax:* 864-644-5901. *E-mail:* broe@swu.edu.

South University - Columbia

Columbia, South Carolina

http://www.southuniversity.edu/columbia/

CONTACT
South University - Columbia, 9 Science Court, Columbia, SC 29203. *Phone:* 803-799-9082. *Toll-free phone:* 866-629-3031.

Strayer University–Charleston Campus

North Charleston, South Carolina

http://www.strayer.edu/south-carolina/charleston/

CONTACT
Strayer University–Charleston Campus, 5010 Wetland Crossing, North Charleston, SC 29418. *Toll-free phone:* 888-311-0355.

Strayer University–Columbia Campus

Columbia, South Carolina

http://www.strayer.edu/south-carolina/columbia/

CONTACT
Strayer University–Columbia Campus, 200 Center Point Circle, Suite 300, Columbia, SC 29210. *Toll-free phone:* 888-311-0355.

Strayer University–Greenville Campus

Greenville, South Carolina

http://www.strayer.edu/south-carolina/greenville/

CONTACT
Strayer University–Greenville Campus, 777 Lowndes Hill Road, Building 3, Suite 300, Greenville, SC 29607. *Toll-free phone:* 888-311-0355.

University of South Carolina

Columbia, South Carolina

http://www.sc.edu/

- **State-supported** university, founded 1801, part of University of South Carolina System
- **Urban** 444-acre campus
- **Coed** 27,502 undergraduate students, 96% full-time, 54% women, 46% men
- **Moderately difficult** entrance level, 69% of applicants were admitted

UNDERGRAD STUDENTS
26,400 full-time, 1,102 part-time. 39% are from out of state; 8% Black or African American, non-Hispanic/Latino; 5% Hispanic/Latino; 3% Asian, non-Hispanic/Latino; 0.1% Native Hawaiian or other Pacific Islander, non-Hispanic/Latino; 0.2% American Indian or Alaska Native, non-Hispanic/Latino; 4% Two or more races, non-Hispanic/Latino; 0.7% Race/ethnicity unknown; 3% international; 6% transferred in; 27% live on campus.

Freshmen:
Admission: 31,268 applied, 21,464 admitted, 6,287 enrolled. ***Average high school GPA:*** 4.2. ***Test scores:*** SAT evidence-based reading and writing scores over 500: 99%; SAT math scores over 500: 99%; ACT scores over 18: 100%; SAT evidence-based reading and writing scores over 600: 75%; SAT math scores over 600: 69%; ACT scores over 24:

87%; SAT evidence-based reading and writing scores over 700: 16%; SAT math scores over 700: 22%; ACT scores over 30: 37%.

Retention: 89% of full-time freshmen returned.

FACULTY

Total: 2,235, 70% full-time, 76% with terminal degrees.

Student/faculty ratio: 17:1.

ACADEMICS

Calendar: semesters. *Degrees:* certificates, associate, bachelor's, master's, doctoral, post-master's, and postbachelor's certificates.

Special study options: accelerated degree program, adult/continuing education programs, advanced placement credit, cooperative education, distance learning, double majors, English as a second language, freshman honors college, honors programs, independent study, internships, part-time degree program, services for LD students, student-designed majors, study abroad, summer session for credit. ***ROTC:*** Army (b), Navy (b), Air Force (b).

Computers: Students can access the following: computer help desk, free student e-mail accounts, online (class) grades, online (class) registration, online (class) schedules. Campuswide network is available. 100% of college-owned or -operated housing units are wired for high-speed Internet access. Wireless service is available via entire campus.

Library: Thomas Cooper Library plus 6 others. *Books:* 1.9 million (physical), 971,375 (digital/electronic); *Serial titles:* 73,491 (physical), 19,146 (digital/electronic); *Databases:* 480.

STUDENT LIFE

Housing options: on-campus residence required for freshman year; coed, men-only, women-only, special housing for students with disabilities. Campus housing is university owned. Freshman campus housing is guaranteed.

Activities and organizations: drama/theater group, student-run newspaper, radio and television station, choral group, marching band, national fraternities, national sororities.

Athletics Member NCAA. All Division I. ***Intercollegiate sports:*** baseball M(s), basketball M(s)/W(s), cross-country running W(s), equestrian sports W(s), football M(s), golf M(s)/W(s), soccer M(s)/W(s), softball W(s), swimming and diving M(s)/W(s), tennis M(s)/W(s), track and field M(s)/W(s), volleyball W(s).

Campus security: 24-hour emergency response devices and patrols, student patrols, late-night transport/escort service, controlled dormitory access.

Student services: health clinic, personal/psychological counseling, women's center.

COSTS & FINANCIAL AID

Costs (2019–20) ***Tuition:*** state resident $12,288 full-time, $512 per credit hour part-time; nonresident $33,528 full-time, $1397 per credit hour part-time. Full-time tuition and fees vary according to program and reciprocity agreements. Part-time tuition and fees vary according to course load. ***Required fees:*** $400 full-time, $17 per credit part-time. ***Room and board:*** $10,670; room only: $6700. Room and board charges vary according to board plan, housing facility, and location. ***Payment plan:*** deferred payment. ***Waivers:*** senior citizens and employees or children of employees.

Financial Aid Of all full-time matriculated undergraduates who enrolled in 2019, 16,811 applied for aid, 12,454 were judged to have need, 3,122 had their need fully met. In 2019, 8783 non-need-based awards were made. ***Average percent of need met:*** 72. ***Average financial aid package:*** $9887. ***Average need-based loan:*** $2222. ***Average need-based gift aid:*** $5958. ***Average non-need-based aid:*** $6610. ***Average indebtedness upon graduation:*** $30,449.

APPLYING

Standardized Tests *Required:* SAT or ACT (for admission).

Options: electronic application, early action.

Application fee: $65.

Required: high school transcript, minimum 2.0 GPA.

CONTACT

Dr. Mary Wagner, Director, Undergraduate Admissions, University of South Carolina, Columbia, SC 29208. *Phone:* 803-777-7700. *Toll-free phone:* 800-868-5872. *Fax:* 803-777-0101. *E-mail:* wagnermt@mailbox.sc.edu.

University of South Carolina Aiken

Aiken, South Carolina

http://www.usca.edu/

- **State-supported** comprehensive, founded 1961, part of University of South Carolina System
- **Suburban** 453-acre campus with easy access to Columbia
- **Endowment** $27.4 million
- **Coed** 3,252 undergraduate students, 79% full-time, 65% women, 35% men
- **Moderately difficult** entrance level, 56% of applicants were admitted

UNDERGRAD STUDENTS

2,585 full-time, 667 part-time. Students come from 28 states and territories; 30 other countries; 12% are from out of state; 26% Black or African American, non-Hispanic/Latino; 5% Hispanic/Latino; 1% Asian, non-Hispanic/Latino; 0.1% Native Hawaiian or other Pacific Islander, non-Hispanic/Latino; 0.3% American Indian or Alaska Native, non-Hispanic/Latino; 5% Two or more races, non-Hispanic/Latino; 1% Race/ethnicity unknown; 2% international; 11% transferred in; 27% live on campus.

Freshmen:

Admission: 2,775 applied, 1,547 admitted, 558 enrolled. ***Average high school GPA:*** 4.0. ***Test scores:*** SAT evidence-based reading and writing scores over 500: 72%; SAT math scores over 500: 66%; ACT scores over 18: 73%; SAT evidence-based reading and writing scores over 600: 20%; SAT math scores over 600: 12%; ACT scores over 24: 17%; SAT evidence-based reading and writing scores over 700: 1%; SAT math scores over 700: 1%; ACT scores over 30: 2%.

Retention: 65% of full-time freshmen returned.

FACULTY

Total: 302, 52% full-time, 57% with terminal degrees.

Student/faculty ratio: 14:1.

ACADEMICS

Calendar: semesters. *Degrees:* bachelor's and master's.

Special study options: adult/continuing education programs, advanced placement credit, cooperative education, distance learning, double majors, English as a second language, honors programs, independent study, internships, off-campus study, part-time degree program, services for LD students, student-designed majors, study abroad, summer session for credit.

Computers: 550 computers/terminals and 1,400 ports are available on campus for general student use. Students can access the following: computer help desk, free student e-mail accounts, online (class) grades, online (class) registration, online (class) schedules. Campuswide network is available. 100% of college-owned or -operated housing units are wired for high-speed Internet access. Wireless service is available via entire campus.

Library: Gregg-Graniteville Library. *Books:* 132,606 (physical), 345,793 (digital/electronic); *Serial titles:* 16,359 (physical), 128,203 (digital/electronic); *Databases:* 220. Weekly public service hours: 78; students can reserve study rooms.

STUDENT LIFE

Housing options: on-campus residence required for freshman year; coed, special housing for students with disabilities. Campus housing is university owned. Freshman applicants given priority for college housing.

Activities and organizations: drama/theater group, student-run newspaper, choral group, National Society of Leadership and Success, Pacer Fanatics, Alpha Omicron Pi, Zeta Tau Alpha, Phi Mu, national fraternities, national sororities.

Athletics Member NCAA. All Division II. ***Intercollegiate sports:*** baseball M(s), basketball M(s)/W(s), cross-country running M(s)/W(s), golf M(s), soccer M(s)/W(s), softball W(s), volleyball W(s). ***Intramural sports:*** basketball M/W, cheerleading M(c)/W(c), equestrian sports M(c)/W(c), lacrosse M(c)/W(c), rugby M(c)/W(c), soccer M/W, softball M/W, swimming and diving M(c)/W(c), table tennis M(c)/W(c), tennis M(c)/W(c), ultimate Frisbee M/W, volleyball M/W.

Campus security: 24-hour emergency response devices and patrols, late-night transport/escort service, controlled dormitory access.

Student services: health clinic, personal/psychological counseling, veterans affairs office.

COSTS & FINANCIAL AID
Costs (2019–20) ***Tuition:*** state resident $10,398 full-time, $433 per credit hour part-time; nonresident $20,856 full-time, $869 per credit hour part-time. Full-time tuition and fees vary according to program and reciprocity agreements. Part-time tuition and fees vary according to course load, program, and reciprocity agreements. ***Required fees:*** $362 full-time, $13 per credit hour part-time, $25 per term part-time. ***Room and board:*** $7946; room only: $5192. Room and board charges vary according to board plan and housing facility. ***Payment plan:*** deferred payment. ***Waivers:*** senior citizens and employees or children of employees.

Financial Aid Of all full-time matriculated undergraduates who enrolled in 2017, 2,711 applied for aid, 1,823 were judged to have need, 344 had their need fully met. 61 Federal Work-Study jobs (averaging $2075). 386 state and other part-time jobs (averaging $1844). In 2017, 171 non-need-based awards were made. ***Average percent of need met:*** 62. ***Average financial aid package:*** $11,898. ***Average need-based loan:*** $4113. ***Average need-based gift aid:*** $7264. ***Average non-need-based aid:*** $1775. ***Average indebtedness upon graduation:*** $28,908.

APPLYING
Standardized Tests *Required:* SAT or ACT (for admission).

Options: electronic application, early admission, deferred entrance.

Application fee: $45.

Required: high school transcript.

Application deadlines: 7/1 (freshmen), 7/1 (out-of-state freshmen), 7/1 (transfers).

Notification: continuous (freshmen), continuous (out-of-state freshmen), continuous (transfers).

CONTACT
Mr. Andrew Hendrix, Director of Admissions, University of South Carolina Aiken, 471 University Parkway, Aiken, SC 29801-6309. *Phone:* 803-641-3366. *Toll-free phone:* 888-WOW-USCA. *Fax:* 803-641-3727. *E-mail:* admit@usca.edu.

University of South Carolina Beaufort

Bluffton, South Carolina

http://www.uscb.edu/

- **State-supported** 4-year, founded 1959, part of University of South Carolina system
- **Suburban** 200-acre campus
- **Coed** 2,112 undergraduate students, 84% full-time, 68% women, 32% men
- **Minimally difficult** entrance level, 62% of applicants were admitted

UNDERGRAD STUDENTS
1,775 full-time, 337 part-time. Students come from 37 states and territories; 9 other countries; 16% are from out of state; 21% Black or African American, non-Hispanic/Latino; 9% Hispanic/Latino; 1% Asian, non-Hispanic/Latino; 0.1% Native Hawaiian or other Pacific Islander, non-Hispanic/Latino; 0.5% American Indian or Alaska Native, non-Hispanic/Latino; 5% Two or more races, non-Hispanic/Latino; 2% Race/ethnicity unknown; 1% international; 9% transferred in; 45% live on campus.

Freshmen:
Admission: 2,023 applied, 1,248 admitted, 450 enrolled. ***Average high school GPA:*** 3.8. ***Test scores:*** ACT scores over 18: 68%; ACT scores over 24: 16%; ACT scores over 30: 3%.

Retention: 58% of full-time freshmen returned.

ACADEMICS
Calendar: semesters. *Degrees:* associate, bachelor's, and master's.

Special study options: adult/continuing education programs, advanced placement credit, distance learning, double majors, independent study, internships, part-time degree program, services for LD students, student-designed majors, study abroad, summer session for credit.

Computers: Students can access the following: computer help desk, free student e-mail accounts, online (class) grades, online (class) registration, online (class) schedules. Campuswide network is available. 100% of college-owned or -operated housing units are wired for high-speed Internet access. Wireless service is available via entire campus.

Library: University of South Carolina Beaufort Library plus 1 other. *Books:* 90,519 (physical), 505,463 (digital/electronic); *Serial titles:* 1,861 (physical), 7,031 (digital/electronic); *Databases:* 235. Students can reserve study rooms.

STUDENT LIFE
Housing options: on-campus residence required for freshman year; coed. Campus housing is university owned. Freshman applicants given priority for college housing.

Activities and organizations: drama/theater group, student-run television station, choral group, Student Government Association, Gamma Beta Phi, Black Student Organization, FCA, Environmental Awareness Club, national fraternities, national sororities.

Athletics Member NAIA. ***Intercollegiate sports:*** baseball M(s), cross-country running M(s)/W(s), golf M(s)/W(s), soccer W(s), softball W, track and field M(s)/W(s). ***Intramural sports:*** basketball M/W, soccer M/W, table tennis M/W, tennis M/W, ultimate Frisbee M/W, volleyball M/W.

Campus security: 24-hour emergency response devices, controlled dormitory access, evening security service.

Student services: personal/psychological counseling, veterans affairs office.

FINANCIAL AID
Financial Aid Of all full-time matriculated undergraduates who enrolled in 2015, 21 Federal Work-Study jobs (averaging $2800).

APPLYING
Standardized Tests *Required:* SAT or ACT (for admission).

Options: electronic application, deferred entrance.

Application fee: $40.

Required: high school transcript, prerequisite high school courses. ***Recommended:*** minimum 2.0 GPA.

Application deadlines: rolling (freshmen), rolling (transfers).

Notification: continuous (freshmen), continuous (transfers).

CONTACT
Mr. Matt Cash, University of South Carolina Beaufort, 1 University Boulevard, Bluffton, SC 29909. *Phone:* 843-208-8125. *Fax:* 843-208-8015. *E-mail:* cashmj@sc.edu.

University of South Carolina Lancaster

Lancaster, South Carolina

http://usclancaster.sc.edu/

- **State-supported** primarily 2-year, founded 1959, part of University of South Carolina System
- **Small-town** 17-acre campus with easy access to Charlotte
- **Coed** 1,593 undergraduate students, 50% full-time, 60% women, 40% men
- **Noncompetitive** entrance level, 100% of applicants were admitted

UNDERGRAD STUDENTS
794 full-time, 799 part-time. Students come from 10 states and territories; 2 other countries; 1% are from out of state.

Freshmen:
Admission: 557 applied, 555 admitted.

FACULTY
Total: 105, 60% full-time, 44% with terminal degrees.

Student/faculty ratio: 14:1.

ACADEMICS
Calendar: semesters. *Degrees:* associate and bachelor's.

Special study options: academic remediation for entering students, advanced placement credit, distance learning, honors programs, independent study, internships, part-time degree program, services for LD students.

Computers: 40 computers/terminals and 75 ports are available on campus for general student use. Students can access the following: free student e-mail accounts, online (class) grades, online (class) registration, online

(class) schedules. Campuswide network is available. Wireless service is available via entire campus.
Library: Medford Library. Students can reserve study rooms.

STUDENT LIFE
Housing options: college housing not available.

Activities and organizations: drama/theater group, student-run newspaper.

Athletics Member NJCAA. ***Intercollegiate sports:*** baseball M(s), soccer M(s)/W(s), volleyball W(s).

Student services: personal/psychological counseling.

APPLYING
Standardized Tests *Required:* SAT or ACT (for admission).

Options: electronic application, early admission.

Application fee: $40.

Required: high school transcript, Standardized test scores.

Application deadlines: rolling (freshmen), rolling (out-of-state freshmen), rolling (transfers).

Notification: continuous (freshmen), continuous (out-of-state freshmen), continuous (transfers).

CONTACT
Jennifer Blackmon, Admissions Processor, University of South Carolina Lancaster, PO Box 889, Lancaster, SC 29721. *Phone:* 803-313-7073. *Fax:* 803-313-7116. *E-mail:* jblackmo@mailbox.sc.edu.

University of South Carolina Union

Union, South Carolina

http://uscunion.sc.edu/

- **State-supported** primarily 2-year, founded 1965, part of University of South Carolina System
- **Small-town** 7-acre campus with easy access to Charlotte, North Carolina
- **Endowment** $1.2 million
- **Coed**
- **Minimally difficult** entrance level

FACULTY
Student/faculty ratio: 18:1.

ACADEMICS
Calendar: semesters. *Degrees:* associate and bachelor's.
Library: Union Carnegie Library plus 1 other. Study areas open 24 hours, 5–7 days a week.

STUDENT LIFE
Housing options: college housing not available.

Activities and organizations: drama/theater group, choral group.

Athletics Member NJCAA.

Campus security: 24-hour emergency response devices.

Student services: personal/psychological counseling, veterans affairs office.

FINANCIAL AID
Financial Aid Of all full-time matriculated undergraduates who enrolled in 2018, 16 Federal Work-Study jobs (averaging $3400).

APPLYING
Standardized Tests *Required:* SAT or ACT (for admission).

Options: electronic application.

Application fee: $40.

Required: high school transcript.

CONTACT
Mr. Michael B. Greer, Director of Enrollment Services, University of South Carolina Union, PO Drawer 729, Union, SC 29379-0729. *Phone:* 864-424-8039. *E-mail:* greerm@mailbox.sc.edu.

University of South Carolina Upstate

Spartanburg, South Carolina

http://www.uscupstate.edu/

- **State-supported** comprehensive, founded 1967, part of University of South Carolina System
- **Urban** 330-acre campus with easy access to Charlotte
- **Endowment** $7.7 million
- **Coed**
- **Moderately difficult** entrance level

FACULTY
Student/faculty ratio: 13:1.

ACADEMICS
Calendar: semesters. *Degrees:* bachelor's, master's, and postbachelor's certificates.
Library: University of South Carolina Upstate Library.

STUDENT LIFE
Housing options: coed. Campus housing is university owned. Freshman applicants given priority for college housing.

Activities and organizations: drama/theater group, student-run newspaper, choral group, African-American Association, Campus Activity Board, Student Nurses Association, Student Government Association, Impact, national fraternities, national sororities.

Athletics Member NCAA. All Division I.

Campus security: 24-hour emergency response devices and patrols, late-night transport/escort service, campus security cameras.

Student services: health clinic, personal/psychological counseling, women's center.

FINANCIAL AID
Financial Aid Of all full-time matriculated undergraduates who enrolled in 2017, 3,550 applied for aid, 3,133 were judged to have need, 111 had their need fully met. 39 Federal Work-Study jobs (averaging $4051). In 2017, 110 non-need-based awards were made. ***Average percent of need met:*** 48. ***Average financial aid package:*** $9830. ***Average need-based loan:*** $4076. ***Average need-based gift aid:*** $5336. ***Average non-need-based aid:*** $1813. ***Average indebtedness upon graduation:*** $27,935. ***Financial aid deadline:*** 7/1.

APPLYING
Standardized Tests *Required:* SAT or ACT (for admission).

Options: electronic application, deferred entrance.

Application fee: $40.

Required: high school transcript, minimum 2.0 GPA, college preparatory courses.

CONTACT
Ms. Donette Stewart, Associate Vice Chancellor for Enrollment Services, University of South Carolina Upstate, 800 University Way, Spartanburg, SC 29303. *Phone:* 864-503-5280. *Toll-free phone:* 800-277-8727. *Fax:* 864-503-5727. *E-mail:* dstewart@uscupstate.edu.

Voorhees College

Denmark, South Carolina

http://www.voorhees.edu/

- **Independent Episcopal** 4-year, founded 1897
- **Rural** 350-acre campus
- **Endowment** $5.9 million
- **Coed**
- **Moderately difficult** entrance level

ACADEMICS
Calendar: semesters. *Degree:* bachelor's.
Library: Wright-Potts Library.

STUDENT LIFE
Housing options: coed, men-only, women-only. Campus housing is university owned. Freshman campus housing is guaranteed.

Activities and organizations: drama/theater group, student-run newspaper, radio station, choral group, national fraternities, national sororities.

Athletics Member NAIA.

Campus security: 24-hour emergency response devices and patrols, student patrols, late-night transport/escort service, controlled dormitory access.

Student services: health clinic, personal/psychological counseling, veterans affairs office.

FINANCIAL AID

Financial Aid Of all full-time matriculated undergraduates who enrolled in 2004, 813 applied for aid, 791 were judged to have need, 61 had their need fully met. 223 Federal Work-Study jobs (averaging $2000). In 2004, 65 non-need-based awards were made. ***Average percent of need met:*** 51. ***Average financial aid package:*** $7449. ***Average need-based loan:*** $2840. ***Average need-based gift aid:*** $4805. ***Average non-need-based aid:*** $9582. ***Average indebtedness upon graduation:*** $13,383.

APPLYING

Standardized Tests *Recommended:* SAT or ACT (for admission).

Options: electronic application, deferred entrance.

Application fee: $25.

Required: high school transcript, minimum 2.0 GPA, secondary school GPA. ***Required for some:*** interview.

CONTACT

Adrain West, Dean of Enrollment Management, Voorhees College, PO Box 678, Denmark, SC 29042. *Phone:* 803-780-1269. *Toll-free phone:* 866-237-4570. *E-mail:* west@voorhees.edu.

Winthrop University

Rock Hill, South Carolina

http://www.winthrop.edu/

- **State-supported** comprehensive, founded 1886, part of South Carolina Commission on Higher Education
- **Suburban** 456-acre campus with easy access to Charlotte
- **Coed** 4,887 undergraduate students, 89% full-time, 70% women, 30% men
- **Moderately difficult** entrance level, 69% of applicants were admitted

UNDERGRAD STUDENTS

4,331 full-time, 556 part-time. Students come from 35 states and territories; 66 other countries; 10% are from out of state; 29% Black or African American, non-Hispanic/Latino; 5% Hispanic/Latino; 1% Asian, non-Hispanic/Latino; 0.1% Native Hawaiian or other Pacific Islander, non-Hispanic/Latino; 0.3% American Indian or Alaska Native, non-Hispanic/Latino; 4% Two or more races, non-Hispanic/Latino; 0.1% Race/ethnicity unknown; 1% international; 6% transferred in; 48% live on campus.

Freshmen:

Admission: 6,101 applied, 4,196 admitted, 991 enrolled. ***Average high school GPA:*** 4.0. ***Test scores:*** SAT evidence-based reading and writing scores over 500: 70%; SAT math scores over 500: 61%; ACT scores over 18: 82%; SAT evidence-based reading and writing scores over 600: 28%; SAT math scores over 600: 15%; ACT scores over 24: 31%; SAT evidence-based reading and writing scores over 700: 3%; SAT math scores over 700: 1%; ACT scores over 30: 4%.

Retention: 70% of full-time freshmen returned.

FACULTY

Total: 563, 51% full-time, 59% with terminal degrees.

Student/faculty ratio: 13:1.

ACADEMICS

Calendar: semesters. *Degrees:* certificates, bachelor's, master's, post-master's, and postbachelor's certificates.

Special study options: adult/continuing education programs, advanced placement credit, cooperative education, distance learning, double majors, honors programs, independent study, internships, off-campus study, part-time degree program, services for LD students, student-designed majors, study abroad, summer session for credit. ***ROTC:*** Army (c), Air Force (c).

Computers: 620 computers/terminals are available on campus for general student use. Students can access the following: campus intranet, computer help desk, free student e-mail accounts, online (class) grades, online (class) registration, online (class) schedules, university services. Campuswide network is available. 100% of college-owned or -operated housing units are wired for high-speed Internet access. Wireless service is available via entire campus.

Library: Dacus Library plus 1 other. *Books:* 295,558 (physical), 187,817 (digital/electronic); *Serial titles:* 3,474 (physical), 53,319 (digital/electronic); *Databases:* 87. Weekly public service hours: 144; study areas open 24 hours, 5–7 days a week; students can reserve study rooms.

STUDENT LIFE

Housing options: on-campus residence required through sophomore year; coed, women-only, special housing for students with disabilities. Campus housing is university owned. Freshman campus housing is guaranteed.

Activities and organizations: drama/theater group, student-run newspaper, radio station, choral group, Association of Ebonites, WU Crew, Greek Life, DiGiorgio Student Union, Campus Ministries, national fraternities, national sororities.

Athletics Member NCAA. All Division I. ***Intercollegiate sports:*** baseball M(s), basketball M(s)/W(s), cheerleading M(c)/W(c), cross-country running M(s)/W(s), fencing M(c)/W(c), golf M(s)/W(s)(c), lacrosse M(c)/W, rugby M(c), soccer M(s)/W(s), softball W(s), tennis M(s)/W(s), track and field M(s)/W(s), volleyball W(s). ***Intramural sports:*** badminton M/W, basketball M/W, cross-country running M/W, equestrian sports M(c)/W(c), football M/W, golf M/W, racquetball M/W, soccer M/W, softball M/W, swimming and diving M/W, table tennis M/W, tennis M/W, ultimate Frisbee M/W, volleyball M/W, water polo M/W, weight lifting M/W.

Campus security: 24-hour emergency response devices and patrols, late-night transport/escort service, controlled dormitory access.

Student services: health clinic, personal/psychological counseling, veterans affairs office.

COSTS & FINANCIAL AID

Costs (2019–20) ***Tuition:*** state resident $15,306 full-time, $641 per credit hour part-time; nonresident $29,636 full-time, $1234 per credit hour part-time. Full-time tuition and fees vary according to degree level, reciprocity agreements, and student level. Part-time tuition and fees vary according to degree level and student level. ***Required fees:*** $360 full-time. ***Room and board:*** $9340; room only: $5526. Room and board charges vary according to board plan and housing facility. ***Payment plan:*** installment. ***Waivers:*** senior citizens and employees or children of employees.

Financial Aid Of all full-time matriculated undergraduates who enrolled in 2018, 3,758 applied for aid, 3,275 were judged to have need, 434 had their need fully met. 148 Federal Work-Study jobs (averaging $2002). In 2018, 576 non-need-based awards were made. ***Average percent of need met:*** 56. ***Average financial aid package:*** $13,642. ***Average need-based loan:*** $4185. ***Average need-based gift aid:*** $9191. ***Average non-need-based aid:*** $4329. ***Average indebtedness upon graduation:*** $33,499.

APPLYING

Standardized Tests *Required:* SAT or ACT (for admission).

Options: electronic application, deferred entrance.

Application fee: $40.

Required: high school transcript, minimum 3.0 GPA. ***Required for some:*** essay or personal statement.

Notification: continuous (freshmen), continuous (transfers).

CONTACT

David Rollings, Director of Admissions Ops and Systems, Winthrop University, Joynes Hall 226, Rock Hill, SC 29733. *Phone:* 803-323-2191. *Toll-free phone:* 800-763-0230. *E-mail:* rollingsd@winthrop.edu.

Wofford College

Spartanburg, South Carolina

http://www.wofford.edu/

- **Independent** 4-year, founded 1854, affiliated with United Methodist Church
- **Urban** 170-acre campus
- **Endowment** $194.0 million
- **Coed** 1,667 undergraduate students, 99% full-time, 52% women, 48% men
- **Very difficult** entrance level, 60% of applicants were admitted

UNDERGRAD STUDENTS
1,648 full-time, 19 part-time. 43% are from out of state; 8% Black or African American, non-Hispanic/Latino; 4% Hispanic/Latino; 2% Asian, non-Hispanic/Latino; 0.1% American Indian or Alaska Native, non-Hispanic/Latino; 3% Two or more races, non-Hispanic/Latino; 0.6% Race/ethnicity unknown; 2% international; 1% transferred in; 91% live on campus.

Freshmen:
Admission: 3,786 applied, 2,265 admitted, 474 enrolled. ***Average high school GPA:*** 3.7. ***Test scores:*** SAT evidence-based reading and writing scores over 500: 98%; SAT math scores over 500: 98%; ACT scores over 18: 100%; SAT evidence-based reading and writing scores over 600: 79%; SAT math scores over 600: 69%; ACT scores over 24: 95%; SAT evidence-based reading and writing scores over 700: 16%; SAT math scores over 700: 12%; ACT scores over 30: 34%.

Retention: 92% of full-time freshmen returned.

FACULTY
Total: 166, 87% full-time, 84% with terminal degrees.

Student/faculty ratio: 11:1.

ACADEMICS
Calendar: 4-1-4.

Special study options: accelerated degree program, advanced placement credit, double majors, external degree program, independent study, internships, off-campus study, part-time degree program, student-designed majors, study abroad, summer session for credit. ***ROTC:*** Army (b).

Computers: 233 computers/terminals are available on campus for general student use. Students can access the following: campus intranet, computer help desk, free student e-mail accounts, online (class) grades, online (class) registration, online (class) schedules. Campuswide network is available. Wireless service is available via entire campus.

Library: Sandor Teszler Library. *Books:* 114,660 (physical), 498,046 (digital/electronic); *Serial titles:* 372 (physical), 78,078 (digital/electronic); *Databases:* 201.

STUDENT LIFE
Housing options: on-campus residence required through senior year; coed, special housing for students with disabilities. Campus housing is university owned. Freshman applicants given priority for college housing.

Activities and organizations: drama/theater group, student-run newspaper, choral group, W.A.R. - Wofford Athletics and Recreation, W.A.C. - Wofford Activities Council, Twin Towers - Service Organization, Math Academy, Arcadia Volunteer Corp, national fraternities, national sororities.

Athletics Member NCAA. All Division I except football (Division I-AA). ***Intercollegiate sports:*** baseball M(s), basketball M(s)/W(s), cheerleading W, cross-country running M(s)/W(s), golf M(s)/W(s)(c), lacrosse W(s), riflery M(s)/W(s), soccer M(s)/W(s), tennis M(s)/W(s), track and field M(s)/W(s), volleyball W(s). ***Intramural sports:*** basketball M/W, football M/W, soccer M/W, softball M/W, table tennis M/W, tennis M/W, ultimate Frisbee M/W.

Campus security: 24-hour emergency response devices and patrols, late-night transport/escort service, controlled dormitory access.

Student services: health clinic, personal/psychological counseling.

COSTS & FINANCIAL AID
Costs (2020–21) ***Comprehensive fee:*** $61,440 includes full-time tuition ($46,010), mandatory fees ($1640), and room and board ($13,790). Part-time tuition: $1900 per credit hour. ***College room only:*** $8065. ***Waivers:*** employees or children of employees.

Financial Aid Of all full-time matriculated undergraduates who enrolled in 2019, 1,324 applied for aid, 1,028 were judged to have need, 405 had their need fully met. In 2019, 478 non-need-based awards were made. ***Average percent of need met:*** 83. ***Average financial aid package:*** $39,677. ***Average need-based loan:*** $4286. ***Average need-based gift aid:*** $35,045. ***Average non-need-based aid:*** $19,583. ***Average indebtedness upon graduation:*** $31,107. ***Financial aid deadline:*** 3/1.

APPLYING
Options: electronic application, early decision, early action, deferred entrance.

Application fee: $35.

Required: essay or personal statement, high school transcript. ***Recommended:*** 2 letters of recommendation, interview.

Application deadlines: 1/15 (freshmen), rolling (transfers), 11/15 (early action).

Early decision deadline: 11/1.

Notification: 3/1 (freshmen), continuous (transfers), 12/1 (early decision), 2/1 (early action).

CONTACT
Ms. Britt Shisler, Visit Coordinator, Wofford College, 429 N. Church Street, Spartanburg, SC 29303. *Phone:* 864-597-4132. *Fax:* 864-597-4147. *E-mail:* admission@wofford.edu.

SOUTH DAKOTA

Augustana University
Sioux Falls, South Dakota
http://www.augie.edu/

- **Independent** comprehensive, founded 1860, affiliated with Evangelical Lutheran Church in America
- **Urban** 100-acre campus
- **Endowment** $89.8 million
- **Coed** 1,818 undergraduate students, 95% full-time, 63% women, 37% men
- **Moderately difficult** entrance level, 67% of applicants were admitted

UNDERGRAD STUDENTS
1,727 full-time, 91 part-time. Students come from 33 states and territories; 35 other countries; 49% are from out of state; 2% Black or African American, non-Hispanic/Latino; 3% Hispanic/Latino; 2% Asian, non-Hispanic/Latino; 0.1% Native Hawaiian or other Pacific Islander, non-Hispanic/Latino; 0.8% American Indian or Alaska Native, non-Hispanic/Latino; 2% Two or more races, non-Hispanic/Latino; 0.2% Race/ethnicity unknown; 6% international; 3% transferred in; 65% live on campus.

Freshmen:
Admission: 2,224 applied, 1,488 admitted, 432 enrolled. ***Average high school GPA:*** 3.7. ***Test scores:*** SAT evidence-based reading and writing scores over 500: 94%; SAT math scores over 500: 91%; ACT scores over 18: 98%; SAT evidence-based reading and writing scores over 600: 47%; SAT math scores over 600: 56%; ACT scores over 24: 69%; SAT evidence-based reading and writing scores over 700: 13%; SAT math scores over 700: 28%; ACT scores over 30: 20%.

Retention: 82% of full-time freshmen returned.

FACULTY
Total: 191, 79% full-time, 76% with terminal degrees.

Student/faculty ratio: 11:1.

ACADEMICS
Calendar: 4-1-4. *Degrees:* bachelor's and master's.

Special study options: academic remediation for entering students, accelerated degree program, advanced placement credit, distance learning, double majors, external degree program, honors programs, independent study, internships, off-campus study, part-time degree program, services for LD students, student-designed majors, study abroad, summer session for credit. ***ROTC:*** Army (c), Air Force (c).

Unusual degree programs: 3-2 engineering with Columbia University, Washington University in St. Louis.

Computers: 295 computers/terminals are available on campus for general student use. Students can access the following: campus intranet, computer help desk, free student e-mail accounts, online (class) grades, online (class) registration, online (class) schedules. Campuswide network is available. 100% of college-owned or -operated housing units are wired for high-speed Internet access. Wireless service is available via entire campus.

Library: Mikkelsen Library. Students can reserve study rooms.

STUDENT LIFE

Housing options: on-campus residence required through sophomore year; coed, special housing for students with disabilities. Campus housing is university owned. Freshman campus housing is guaranteed.

Activities and organizations: drama/theater group, student-run newspaper, choral group, Augieholics (student athletics support organization), intramurals, Union Board of Governors (student union), Augie Green, Campus Ministries.

Athletics Member NCAA. All Division II. ***Intercollegiate sports:*** baseball M(s), basketball M(s)/W(s), cheerleading M/W, cross-country running M(s)/W(s), football M(s), golf M(s)/W(s), rugby W(c), soccer M(c)/W(s), softball W(s), swimming and diving W(s), tennis M(s)/W(s), track and field M(s)/W(s), ultimate Frisbee M(c)/W(c), volleyball W(s), wrestling M(s). ***Intramural sports:*** basketball M/W, bowling M/W, cross-country running M/W, football M/W, golf M/W, racquetball M/W, rock climbing M/W, skiing (cross-country) M/W, soccer M/W, softball M/W, swimming and diving M/W, table tennis M/W, tennis M/W, ultimate Frisbee M/W, volleyball M(c)/W(c), weight lifting M/W.

Campus security: 24-hour emergency response devices and patrols, late-night transport/escort service, controlled dormitory access, special "day lighting" night lights throughout the campus grounds.

Student services: health clinic, personal/psychological counseling.

COSTS & FINANCIAL AID

Costs (2020–21) ***Comprehensive fee:*** $44,500 includes full-time tuition ($34,934), mandatory fees ($950), and room and board ($8616). Full-time tuition and fees vary according to course load and degree level. Part-time tuition and fees vary according to course load and degree level. ***College room only:*** $3854. Room and board charges vary according to board plan and housing facility. ***Payment plan:*** installment. ***Waivers:*** employees or children of employees.

Financial Aid Of all full-time matriculated undergraduates who enrolled in 2019, 1,262 applied for aid, 1,056 were judged to have need, 156 had their need fully met. 324 Federal Work-Study jobs (averaging $1788). 152 state and other part-time jobs (averaging $879). In 2019, 653 non-need-based awards were made. ***Average percent of need met:*** 83. ***Average financial aid package:*** $27,245. ***Average need-based loan:*** $4630. ***Average need-based gift aid:*** $24,114. ***Average non-need-based aid:*** $17,674. ***Average indebtedness upon graduation:*** $37,647.

APPLYING

Standardized Tests *Required for some:* SAT or ACT (for admission). *Recommended:* SAT or ACT (for admission).

Options: electronic application, deferred entrance.

Required: high school transcript, minimum 2.7 GPA. ***Required for some:*** minimum ACT score of 20. ***Recommended:*** essay or personal statement, 1 letter of recommendation.

Application deadlines: rolling (freshmen), rolling (transfers).

Notification: continuous until 10/1 (freshmen), continuous (transfers).

CONTACT

Adam Heinitz, Director of Admission, Augustana University, 2001 South Summit Avenue, Sioux Falls, SD 57197. *Phone:* 605-274-5516. *Toll-free phone:* 800-727-2844. *Fax:* 605-274-5518. *E-mail:* admission@augie.edu.

Black Hills State University

Spearfish, South Dakota

http://www.bhsu.edu/

- **State-supported** comprehensive, founded 1883, part of South Dakota Board of Regents
- **Small-town** 123-acre campus
- **Coed** 3,684 undergraduate students, 53% full-time, 63% women, 37% men
- 99% of applicants were admitted

UNDERGRAD STUDENTS

1,944 full-time, 1,738 part-time. 29% are from out of state; 1% Black or African American, non-Hispanic/Latino; 6% Hispanic/Latino; 0.9% Asian, non-Hispanic/Latino; 0.1% Native Hawaiian or other Pacific Islander, non-Hispanic/Latino; 4% American Indian or Alaska Native, non-Hispanic/Latino; 5% Two or more races, non-Hispanic/Latino; 1% Race/ethnicity unknown; 1% international; 5% transferred in.

Freshmen:

Admission: 1,808 applied, 1,787 admitted, 520 enrolled.

Retention: 62% of full-time freshmen returned.

ACADEMICS

Calendar: semesters. *Degrees:* associate, bachelor's, master's, post-master's, and postbachelor's certificates.

Special study options: academic remediation for entering students, accelerated degree program, advanced placement credit, cooperative education, distance learning, double majors, English as a second language, honors programs, independent study, internships, off-campus study, part-time degree program, services for LD students, study abroad, summer session for credit. ***ROTC:*** Army (b).

Computers: Students can access the following: campus intranet, computer help desk, free student e-mail accounts, online (class) grades, online (class) registration, online (class) schedules. Campuswide network is available. 100% of college-owned or -operated housing units are wired for high-speed Internet access. Wireless service is available via classrooms, computer centers, computer labs, dorm rooms, learning centers, libraries, student centers.

Library: E. Y. Berry Library. Students can reserve study rooms.

STUDENT LIFE

Housing options: on-campus residence required through sophomore year; coed, men-only, women-only, special housing for students with disabilities. Campus housing is university owned. Freshman applicants given priority for college housing.

Activities and organizations: drama/theater group, student-run newspaper, radio and television station, choral group, Student Activities Committee, Student Government, national fraternities, national sororities.

Athletics Member NCAA. All Division II. ***Intercollegiate sports:*** basketball M(s)/W(s), cross-country running M(s)/W(s), football M(s), golf W, soccer W(s), track and field M(s)/W(s), volleyball W(s). ***Intramural sports:*** archery M/W, badminton M/W, basketball M/W, bowling M/W, football M, golf M/W, racquetball M/W, skiing (cross-country) M/W, skiing (downhill) M/W, soccer M/W, softball M/W, tennis M/W, volleyball M/W, weight lifting M/W.

Campus security: 24-hour patrols, late-night transport/escort service, controlled dormitory access.

Student services: health clinic, personal/psychological counseling, veterans affairs office.

COSTS

Costs (2019–20) ***Tuition:*** state resident $9009 full-time, $300 per credit hour part-time; nonresident $12,155 full-time, $405 per credit hour part-time. Full-time tuition and fees vary according to course load, location, and reciprocity agreements. Part-time tuition and fees vary according to course load, location, and reciprocity agreements. ***Room and board:*** $7142; room only: $3608. Room and board charges vary according to board plan, housing facility, and location. ***Payment plans:*** installment, deferred payment. ***Waivers:*** senior citizens and employees or children of employees.

APPLYING

Standardized Tests *Required:* SAT or ACT (for admission).

Application fee: $20.

Required: high school transcript, minimum 2.0 high school GPA in core curriculum.

CONTACT

Ms. Barbara O'Malley, Director of Admissions, Black Hills State University, 1200 University Street, Unit 9502, Spearfish, SD 57799-9502. *Phone:* 605-642-6343. *Toll-free phone:* 800-255-2478. *Fax:* 605-642-6254. *E-mail:* admissions@bhsu.edu.

Dakota State University
Madison, South Dakota
http://www.dsu.edu/

- **State-supported** comprehensive, founded 1881, part of South Dakota Board of Regents
- **Rural** 62-acre campus with easy access to Sioux Falls
- **Endowment** $15.8 million
- **Coed** 2,818 undergraduate students, 53% full-time, 38% women, 62% men
- **Moderately difficult** entrance level, 77% of applicants were admitted

UNDERGRAD STUDENTS
1,503 full-time, 1,315 part-time. Students come from 48 states and territories; 31 other countries; 40% are from out of state; 3% Black or African American, non-Hispanic/Latino; 4% Hispanic/Latino; 2% Asian, non-Hispanic/Latino; 0.3% Native Hawaiian or other Pacific Islander, non-Hispanic/Latino; 1% American Indian or Alaska Native, non-Hispanic/Latino; 4% Two or more races, non-Hispanic/Latino; 1% Race/ethnicity unknown; 2% international; 9% transferred in; 38% live on campus.

Freshmen:
Admission: 978 applied, 757 admitted, 425 enrolled. ***Average high school GPA:*** 3.7. ***Test scores:*** SAT evidence-based reading and writing scores over 500: 76%; SAT math scores over 500: 83%; ACT scores over 18: 87%; SAT evidence-based reading and writing scores over 600: 39%; SAT math scores over 600: 37%; ACT scores over 24: 43%; SAT evidence-based reading and writing scores over 700: 10%; SAT math scores over 700: 14%; ACT scores over 30: 9%.

Retention: 66% of full-time freshmen returned.

FACULTY
Total: 148, 71% full-time, 61% with terminal degrees.

Student/faculty ratio: 16:1.

ACADEMICS
Calendar: semesters. *Degrees:* certificates, associate, bachelor's, master's, doctoral, and postbachelor's certificates.

Special study options: academic remediation for entering students, advanced placement credit, cooperative education, distance learning, double majors, honors programs, independent study, internships, off-campus study, part-time degree program, services for LD students, study abroad, summer session for credit. ***ROTC:*** Army (c), Air Force (c).

Computers: 80 computers/terminals are available on campus for general student use. Students can access the following: computer help desk, free student e-mail accounts, online (class) grades, online (class) registration, online (class) schedules. Campuswide network is available. 100% of college-owned or -operated housing units are wired for high-speed Internet access. Wireless service is available via entire campus.
Library: Karl E. Mundt Library & Learning Commons plus 1 other. *Books:* 38,709 (physical), 261,118 (digital/electronic); *Serial titles:* 174 (physical); *Databases:* 124. Weekly public service hours: 85.

STUDENT LIFE
Housing options: on-campus residence required through sophomore year; coed, men-only. Campus housing is university owned. Freshman campus housing is guaranteed.

Activities and organizations: drama/theater group, student-run newspaper, radio station, choral group, Esports Club, Computer Club, Gaming Club, Fellowship of Christian Athletes, Campus Crusade for Christ (Cru).

Athletics Member NAIA. ***Intercollegiate sports:*** baseball M(s), basketball M(s)/W(s), cheerleading M/W, cross-country running M(s)/W(s), football M(s), golf M/W, softball W(s), track and field M(s)/W(s), volleyball W(s). ***Intramural sports:*** basketball M/W, softball W, table tennis M/W, tennis M/W, volleyball W.

Campus security: late-night transport/escort service, controlled dormitory access.

Student services: health clinic, personal/psychological counseling, veterans affairs office.

COSTS & FINANCIAL AID
Costs (2019–20) ***Tuition:*** state resident $7541 full-time, $251 per credit hour part-time; nonresident $10,611 full-time, $354 per credit hour part-time. Full-time tuition and fees vary according to location and reciprocity agreements. Part-time tuition and fees vary according to location and reciprocity agreements. ***Required fees:*** $1995 full-time, $40 per credit hour part-time. ***Room and board:*** $7033; room only: $3805. Room and board charges vary according to board plan and housing facility. ***Payment plan:*** installment. ***Waivers:*** senior citizens and employees or children of employees.

Financial Aid Of all full-time matriculated undergraduates who enrolled in 2018, 1,198 applied for aid, 963 were judged to have need, 97 had their need fully met. 117 Federal Work-Study jobs (averaging $2339). 27 state and other part-time jobs (averaging $6895). In 2018, 137 non-need-based awards were made. ***Average percent of need met:*** 53. ***Average financial aid package:*** $8362. ***Average need-based loan:*** $4024. ***Average need-based gift aid:*** $4754. ***Average non-need-based aid:*** $5209. ***Average indebtedness upon graduation:*** $27,928.

APPLYING
Standardized Tests *Required:* SAT or ACT (for admission).

Options: electronic application, deferred entrance.

Application fee: $20.

Required: high school transcript, minimum 2.6 GPA.

Application deadlines: rolling (freshmen), rolling (out-of-state freshmen), rolling (transfers).

Notification: continuous (freshmen), continuous (out-of-state freshmen), continuous (transfers).

CONTACT
Ms. Tory Bickett, Admissions Senior Secretary, Dakota State University, 820 North Washington, Madison, SD 57042-1799. *Phone:* 605-256-5178. *Toll-free phone:* 888-DSU-9988. *Fax:* 605-256-5020. *E-mail:* admissions@dsu.edu.

Dakota Wesleyan University
Mitchell, South Dakota
http://www.dwu.edu/

- **Independent United Methodist** comprehensive, founded 1885
- **Small-town** 50-acre campus
- **Endowment** $20.9 million
- **Coed**
- **Moderately difficult** entrance level

FACULTY
Student/faculty ratio: 11:1.

ACADEMICS
Calendar: semesters. *Degrees:* associate, bachelor's, and master's.
Library: George and Eleanor McGovern Library plus 1 other.

STUDENT LIFE
Housing options: on-campus residence required through sophomore year; coed, men-only, women-only. Campus housing is university owned and leased by the school. Freshman campus housing is guaranteed.

Activities and organizations: drama/theater group, student-run newspaper, choral group, Future Teachers Organization, Student Nurses Association, Multi-Culture Club, Human Services Club, Student Ministry Council.

Athletics Member NAIA.

Campus security: 24-hour emergency response devices, student patrols, late-night transport/escort service, controlled dormitory access, campus patrol from 2am to 6am by special request only.

Student services: health clinic, personal/psychological counseling.

FINANCIAL AID
Financial Aid Of all full-time matriculated undergraduates who enrolled in 2015, 823 applied for aid, 739 were judged to have need, 49 had their need fully met. 109 Federal Work-Study jobs (averaging $1550). In 2015, 27 non-need-based awards were made. ***Average percent of need met:*** 58. ***Average need-based loan:*** $9320. ***Average need-based gift aid:*** $13,425. ***Average non-need-based aid:*** $10,158. ***Average indebtedness upon graduation:*** $37,564.

APPLYING
Standardized Tests *Required:* SAT or ACT (for admission).

Options: electronic application.

Application fee: $25.

Required: high school transcript. ***Recommended:*** minimum 2.0 GPA.

CONTACT
Mrs. Melissa Herr-Valburg, Director of Admissions, Dakota Wesleyan University, 1200 West University Avenue, Mitchell, SD 57301-4398. *Phone:* 605-995-2600 Ext. 2652. *Toll-free phone:* 800-333-8506. *Fax:* 605-995-2699. *E-mail:* admissions@dwu.edu.

Mount Marty College

Yankton, South Dakota

http://www.mtmc.edu/

- **Independent Roman Catholic** comprehensive, founded 1936
- **Small-town** 80-acre campus
- **Endowment** $28.3 million
- **Coed** 869 undergraduate students, 61% full-time, 57% women, 43% men
- **Minimally difficult** entrance level, 72% of applicants were admitted

UNDERGRAD STUDENTS
526 full-time, 343 part-time. Students come from 28 states and territories; 15 other countries; 52% are from out of state; 5% Black or African American, non-Hispanic/Latino; 7% Hispanic/Latino; 0.6% Asian, non-Hispanic/Latino; 0.2% Native Hawaiian or other Pacific Islander, non-Hispanic/Latino; 3% American Indian or Alaska Native, non-Hispanic/Latino; 0.8% Two or more races, non-Hispanic/Latino; 3% Race/ethnicity unknown; 3% international; 9% transferred in; 65% live on campus.

Freshmen:
Admission: 479 applied, 343 admitted, 119 enrolled. ***Test scores:*** ACT scores over 18: 85%; ACT scores over 24: 31%; ACT scores over 30: 2%.

Retention: 72% of full-time freshmen returned.

FACULTY
Total: 52, 87% full-time, 62% with terminal degrees.

Student/faculty ratio: 11:1.

ACADEMICS
Calendar: semesters. *Degrees:* certificates, associate, bachelor's, master's, doctoral, and post-master's certificates.

Special study options: academic remediation for entering students, accelerated degree program, adult/continuing education programs, advanced placement credit, cooperative education, distance learning, double majors, honors programs, independent study, internships, off-campus study, part-time degree program, services for LD students, student-designed majors, summer session for credit. ***ROTC:*** Army (c).

Computers: 8 computers/terminals are available on campus for general student use. Students can access the following: campus intranet, computer help desk, free student e-mail accounts, online (class) grades, online (class) registration, online (class) schedules. Campuswide network is available. 100% of college-owned or -operated housing units are wired for high-speed Internet access. Wireless service is available via entire campus.

Library: Mother Jerome Schmitt Library. *Books:* 80,420 (physical), 18,075 (digital/electronic); *Serial titles:* 153 (physical); *Databases:* 80. Weekly public service hours: 81; study areas open 24 hours, 5–7 days a week; students can reserve study rooms.

STUDENT LIFE
Housing options: on-campus residence required through senior year; coed, men-only, women-only. Campus housing is university owned. Freshman campus housing is guaranteed.

Activities and organizations: drama/theater group, choral group, Campus Ministry, Student Government Association, Nursing Club, Education Club, Theater Club.

Athletics Member NAIA. ***Intercollegiate sports:*** archery M(s)/W(s), baseball M(s), basketball M(s)/W(s), cheerleading W(s), cross-country running M(s)/W(s), football M(s), golf M(s), riflery M(c)/W(c), soccer M(s)/W(s), softball W(s), tennis M(s)/W(s), track and field M(s)/W(s), volleyball W(s). ***Intramural sports:*** basketball M/W, soccer M/W, softball W, volleyball M/W.

Campus security: 24-hour emergency response devices and patrols, late-night transport/escort service, controlled dormitory access.

Student services: health clinic, personal/psychological counseling.

COSTS & FINANCIAL AID
Costs (2019–20) ***Comprehensive fee:*** $36,272 includes full-time tuition ($25,976), mandatory fees ($2150), and room and board ($8146). Full-time tuition and fees vary according to course load, degree level, and location. Part-time tuition: $540 per credit hour. Part-time tuition and fees vary according to course load, degree level, and location. ***Required fees:*** $45 per credit hour part-time. ***Payment plan:*** installment. ***Waivers:*** employees or children of employees.

Financial Aid Of all full-time matriculated undergraduates who enrolled in 2019, 485 applied for aid, 446 were judged to have need, 201 had their need fully met. In 2019, 35 non-need-based awards were made. ***Average percent of need met:*** 91. ***Average financial aid package:*** $31,753. ***Average need-based loan:*** $4733. ***Average need-based gift aid:*** $19,322. ***Average non-need-based aid:*** $6411.

APPLYING
Standardized Tests *Required:* SAT or ACT (for admission).

Options: electronic application, early admission, deferred entrance.

Application fee: $35.

Required: high school transcript, minimum 2.0 GPA. ***Recommended:*** interview.

Application deadlines: rolling (freshmen), rolling (transfers).

Notification: continuous (freshmen), continuous (transfers).

CONTACT
Katie Harrell, Dean of Enrollment, Mount Marty College, 1105 W. 8th Street, Yankton, SD 57078. *Phone:* 605-668-1545. *Toll-free phone:* 800-658-4552. *E-mail:* katie.harrell@mountmarty.edu.

National American University

Ellsworth AFB, South Dakota

http://www.national.edu/

CONTACT
Admissions Office, National American University, 1000 Ellsworth Street, Rushmore Center, Suite 2400B, Ellsworth AFB, SD 57706.

National American University

Rapid City, South Dakota

http://www.national.edu/

CONTACT
Ms. Angela Beck, Director of Enrollment Management, National American University, 321 Kansas City Street, Rapid City, SD 57701. *Phone:* 605-394-4902. *Toll-free phone:* 800-209-0490. *Fax:* 605-394-4871. *E-mail:* abeck@national.edu.

National American University

Sioux Falls, South Dakota

http://www.national.edu/

CONTACT
Ms. Lisa Houtsma, Director of Admissions, National American University, 5801 South Corporate Place, Sioux Falls, SD 57108. *Phone:* 605-336-4600. *Toll-free phone:* 800-388-5430. *Fax:* 605-336-4605. *E-mail:* lhoutsma@national.edu.

National American University

Watertown, South Dakota

http://www.national.edu/

CONTACT
National American University, 925 29th Street SE, Watertown, SD 57201.

Northern State University

Aberdeen, South Dakota

http://www.northern.edu/

- **State-supported** comprehensive, founded 1901, part of South Dakota Board of Regents
- **Small-town** 72-acre campus
- **Endowment** $30.8 million
- **Coed** 3,008 undergraduate students, 42% full-time, 58% women, 42% men
- **Minimally difficult** entrance level, 84% of applicants were admitted

UNDERGRAD STUDENTS

1,265 full-time, 1,743 part-time. 31% are from out of state; 2% Black or African American, non-Hispanic/Latino; 3% Hispanic/Latino; 2% Asian, non-Hispanic/Latino; 0.2% Native Hawaiian or other Pacific Islander, non-Hispanic/Latino; 2% American Indian or Alaska Native, non-Hispanic/Latino; 4% Two or more races, non-Hispanic/Latino; 0.8% Race/ethnicity unknown; 4% international; 3% transferred in; 41% live on campus.

Freshmen:

Admission: 1,409 applied, 1,190 admitted, 342 enrolled. ***Average high school GPA:*** 3.4. ***Test scores:*** SAT evidence-based reading and writing scores over 500: 69%; SAT math scores over 500: 94%; ACT scores over 18: 83%; SAT evidence-based reading and writing scores over 600: 19%; SAT math scores over 600: 31%; ACT scores over 24: 36%; SAT math scores over 700: 6%; ACT scores over 30: 4%.

Retention: 73% of full-time freshmen returned.

FACULTY

Total: 134, 68% full-time, 61% with terminal degrees.

Student/faculty ratio: 19:1.

ACADEMICS

Calendar: semesters. *Degrees:* certificates, associate, bachelor's, master's, and postbachelor's certificates.

Special study options: academic remediation for entering students, accelerated degree program, adult/continuing education programs, advanced placement credit, distance learning, double majors, English as a second language, freshman honors college, honors programs, independent study, internships, off-campus study, part-time degree program, services for LD students, study abroad, summer session for credit.

Computers: 130 computers/terminals and 20 ports are available on campus for general student use. Students can access the following: campus intranet, computer help desk, free student e-mail accounts, online (class) grades, online (class) registration, online (class) schedules. Campuswide network is available. 100% of college-owned or -operated housing units are wired for high-speed Internet access. Wireless service is available via entire campus.

Library: Beulah Williams Library. *Books:* 156,950 (physical), 15,000 (digital/electronic); *Serial titles:* 7,000 (physical), 250 (digital/electronic); *Databases:* 80. Weekly public service hours: 90; students can reserve study rooms.

STUDENT LIFE

Housing options: on-campus residence required through sophomore year; coed. Campus housing is university owned. Freshman campus housing is guaranteed.

Activities and organizations: drama/theater group, student-run newspaper, choral group, marching band.

Athletics Member NCAA. All Division II. ***Intercollegiate sports:*** baseball M(s), basketball M(s)/W(s), cross-country running M(s)/W(s), football M(s), soccer W(s), softball W(s), swimming and diving W(s), track and field M(s)/W(s), volleyball W(s), wrestling M(s). ***Intramural sports:*** badminton M(c)/W(c), basketball M/W, cheerleading W(c), football M/W, racquetball M/W, rugby M(c)/W(c), soccer M/W, softball M/W, table tennis M/W, ultimate Frisbee M/W, volleyball M/W.

Campus security: 24-hour emergency response devices, controlled dormitory access.

Student services: health clinic, personal/psychological counseling, legal services, veterans affairs office.

COSTS & FINANCIAL AID

Costs (2019–20) ***Tuition:*** state resident $7540 full-time, $292 per credit hour part-time; nonresident $10,611 full-time, $394 per credit hour part-time. Full-time tuition and fees vary according to course load, program, and reciprocity agreements. Part-time tuition and fees vary according to course load, program, and reciprocity agreements. ***Required fees:*** $1210 full-time, $40 per credit hour part-time. ***Room and board:*** $8925; room only: $4701. Room and board charges vary according to board plan and housing facility. ***Payment plan:*** installment. ***Waivers:*** senior citizens and employees or children of employees.

Financial Aid Of all full-time matriculated undergraduates who enrolled in 2018, 1,014 applied for aid, 797 were judged to have need, 201 had their need fully met. In 2018, 120 non-need-based awards were made. ***Average percent of need met:*** 72. ***Average financial aid package:*** $11,007. ***Average need-based loan:*** $4794. ***Average need-based gift aid:*** $5113. ***Average non-need-based aid:*** $1722. ***Average indebtedness upon graduation:*** $29,635.

APPLYING

Standardized Tests *Required:* SAT or ACT (for admission).

Options: electronic application, deferred entrance.

Application fee: $20.

Required: high school transcript, minimum 2.6 GPA.

Application deadlines: rolling (freshmen), rolling (out-of-state freshmen), rolling (transfers).

Notification: continuous (freshmen), continuous (out-of-state freshmen), continuous (transfers).

CONTACT

Dr. Jeremy Reed, Vice President of Enrollment Management and Student Affairs, Northern State University, 1200 South Jay Street, Aberdeen, SD 57401. *Phone:* 605-626-2530. *Toll-free phone:* 800-678-5330. *Fax:* 605-626-2531. *E-mail:* admissions@northern.edu.

Oglala Lakota College

Kyle, South Dakota

http://www.olc.edu/

- **State and locally supported** comprehensive, founded 1970
- **Rural** campus
- **Coed**

FACULTY

Student/faculty ratio: 10:1.

ACADEMICS

Calendar: semesters. *Degrees:* associate, bachelor's, and master's.

Library: Oglala Lakota College Learning Resource Center.

STUDENT LIFE

Housing options: college housing not available.

APPLYING

Options: early admission.

Application fee: $40.

CONTACT

Director of Admissions, Oglala Lakota College, 490 Piya Wiconi Road, Kyle, SD 57752-0490. *Phone:* 605-455-2321 Ext. 236. *E-mail:* lmeseteth@olc.edu.

Presentation College

Aberdeen, South Dakota

http://www.presentation.edu/

CONTACT

Mr. Robert Schuchardt, Vice President for Student Services, Presentation College, 1500 North Main Street, Aberdeen, SD 57401. *Phone:* 605-229-8406. *Toll-free phone:* 800-437-6060. *Fax:* 605-229-8425. *E-mail:* admit@presentation.edu.

Sinte Gleska University

Mission, South Dakota

http://www.sintegleska.edu/

CONTACT

Mr. Jack Herman, Registrar and Director of Admissions, Sinte Gleska University, 101 Antelope Lake Circle, PO Box 105, Mission, SD 57555. *Phone:* 605-856-8100 Ext. 8479.

South Dakota School of Mines and Technology

Rapid City, South Dakota

http://www.sdsmt.edu/

- **State-supported** university, founded 1885, part of South Dakota Board of Regents
- **Suburban** 120-acre campus
- **Endowment** $53.7 million
- **Coed**
- **Moderately difficult** entrance level

FACULTY

Student/faculty ratio: 15:1.

ACADEMICS

Calendar: semesters. *Degrees:* certificates, associate, bachelor's, master's, doctoral, and postbachelor's certificates.

Library: Devereaux Library plus 1 other. *Books:* 130,971 (physical), 142,661 (digital/electronic); *Serial titles:* 1,663 (physical), 23,896 (digital/electronic); *Databases:* 200. Weekly public service hours: 32; students can reserve study rooms.

STUDENT LIFE

Housing options: on-campus residence required through sophomore year; coed, men-only, women-only, special housing for students with disabilities. Campus housing is university owned and leased by the school. Freshman campus housing is guaranteed.

Activities and organizations: drama/theater group, student-run newspaper, radio station, choral group, eSports 144, ASME (American Society of Mechanical Engineers), Skid Snowboard Club 115, AIChe 107, ASCE 105, national fraternities, national sororities.

Athletics Member NCAA. All Division II.

Campus security: 24-hour emergency response devices and patrols, student patrols, late-night transport/escort service, controlled dormitory access.

Student services: health clinic, personal/psychological counseling, veterans affairs office.

FINANCIAL AID

Financial Aid Of all full-time matriculated undergraduates who enrolled in 2015, 1,812 applied for aid, 1,095 were judged to have need, 334 had their need fully met. 148 Federal Work-Study jobs (averaging $1718). In 2015, 405 non-need-based awards were made. ***Average percent of need met:*** 71. ***Average financial aid package:*** $14,262. ***Average need-based loan:*** $4106. ***Average need-based gift aid:*** $4616. ***Average non-need-based aid:*** $3360. ***Average indebtedness upon graduation:*** $32,995.

APPLYING

Standardized Tests *Required:* SAT or ACT (for admission).

Options: electronic application.

Application fee: $20.

Required: high school transcript. ***Recommended:*** minimum 2.8 GPA.

CONTACT

Genene Sigler, Applications Processor, South Dakota School of Mines and Technology, 501 East Saint Joseph Street, Rapid City, SD 57701-3995. *Phone:* 605-394-2414 Ext. 5209. *Toll-free phone:* 800-544-8162. *Fax:* 605-394-1979. *E-mail:* admissions@sdsmt.edu.

South Dakota State University

Brookings, South Dakota

http://www.sdstate.edu/

- **State-supported** university, founded 1881, part of South Dakota Board of Regents
- **Small-town** 387-acre campus
- **Endowment** $145.9 million
- **Coed** 10,073 undergraduate students, 79% full-time, 53% women, 47% men
- 90% of applicants were admitted

UNDERGRAD STUDENTS

7,971 full-time, 2,102 part-time. Students come from 50 states and territories; 80 other countries; 46% are from out of state; 2% Black or African American, non-Hispanic/Latino; 3% Hispanic/Latino; 1% Asian, non-Hispanic/Latino; 1% American Indian or Alaska Native, non-Hispanic/Latino; 2% Two or more races, non-Hispanic/Latino; 0.6% Race/ethnicity unknown; 4% international; 4% transferred in.

Freshmen:

Admission: 5,861 applied, 5,277 admitted, 2,123 enrolled. ***Average high school GPA:*** 3.5. ***Test scores:*** SAT evidence-based reading and writing scores over 500: 83%; SAT math scores over 500: 89%; ACT scores over 18: 91%; SAT evidence-based reading and writing scores over 600: 37%; SAT math scores over 600: 34%; ACT scores over 24: 45%; SAT evidence-based reading and writing scores over 700: 9%; SAT math scores over 700: 12%; ACT scores over 30: 8%.

Retention: 78% of full-time freshmen returned.

FACULTY

Total: 648, 79% full-time, 67% with terminal degrees.

Student/faculty ratio: 17:1.

ACADEMICS

Calendar: semesters. *Degrees:* certificates, associate, bachelor's, master's, doctoral, post-master's, and postbachelor's certificates.

Special study options: academic remediation for entering students, accelerated degree program, adult/continuing education programs, advanced placement credit, cooperative education, distance learning, double majors, English as a second language, freshman honors college, honors programs, independent study, internships, off-campus study, part-time degree program, services for LD students, study abroad, summer session for credit. ***ROTC:*** Army (b), Air Force (b).

Unusual degree programs: 3-2 engineering; economics, athletic training, computer science, data science, human biology, mathematics, sociology, statistics.

Computers: Students can access the following: campus intranet, computer help desk, free student e-mail accounts, online (class) grades, online (class) registration, online (class) schedules. Campuswide network is available. 100% of college-owned or -operated housing units are wired for high-speed Internet access. Wireless service is available via entire campus.

Library: Hilton. M. Briggs Library. *Books:* 523,425 (physical), 176,144 (digital/electronic); *Serial titles:* 31,372 (physical), 82,704 (digital/electronic); *Databases:* 111. Weekly public service hours: 100; students can reserve study rooms.

STUDENT LIFE

Housing options: on-campus residence required through sophomore year; coed, special housing for students with disabilities. Campus housing is university owned. Freshman campus housing is guaranteed.

Activities and organizations: drama/theater group, student-run newspaper, radio station, choral group, marching band, national fraternities, national sororities.

Athletics Member NCAA. All Division I. ***Intercollegiate sports:*** baseball M(s), basketball M(s)/W(s), cross-country running M(s)/W(s), equestrian sports W(s), football M(s), golf M(s)/W(s), soccer W(s), softball W(s), swimming and diving M(s)/W(s), track and field M(s)/W(s), volleyball W(s), wrestling M(s). ***Intramural sports:*** badminton M/W, basketball M/W, bowling M/W, football M/W, golf M/W, ice hockey M(c)/W(c), racquetball M/W, rugby M(c)/W(c), sand volleyball M/W, soccer M/W, softball M/W, swimming and diving M/W, table tennis M/W, tennis M/W, volleyball M/W, weight lifting M/W, wrestling M/W.

Campus security: 24-hour emergency response devices and patrols, student patrols, late-night transport/escort service, controlled dormitory access.

Student services: health clinic, personal/psychological counseling, legal services, veterans affairs office.

COSTS & FINANCIAL AID

Costs (2020–21) ***Tuition:*** state resident $7697 full-time, $257 per credit hour part-time; nonresident $11,172 full-time, $372 per credit hour part-time. Full-time tuition and fees vary according to course level, location, program, and reciprocity agreements. Part-time tuition and fees vary according to course level, location, program, and reciprocity agreements. ***Required fees:*** $1503 full-time, $50 per credit hour part-time. ***Room and board:*** $8307; room only: $4929. Room and board charges vary according to board plan and housing facility. ***Payment plan:*** installment. ***Waivers:*** children of alumni, senior citizens, and employees or children of employees.

Financial Aid ***Average indebtedness upon graduation:*** $31,131.

APPLYING

Standardized Tests *Required:* SAT or ACT (for admission).

Options: electronic application, deferred entrance.

Application fee: $20.

Application deadlines: rolling (freshmen), rolling (transfers).

Notification: continuous (freshmen), continuous (transfers).

CONTACT

Ms. Michelle Kuebler, Assistant Director of Admissions, South Dakota State University, PO Box 2201, Brookings, SD 57007. *Phone:* 605-688-4121. *Toll-free phone:* 800-952-3541. *Fax:* 605-688-6891. *E-mail:* sdsu.admissions@sdstate.edu.

University of Sioux Falls

Sioux Falls, South Dakota

http://www.usiouxfalls.edu/

- **Independent American Baptist Churches in the USA** comprehensive, founded 1883
- **Suburban** 140-acre campus
- **Endowment** $30.4 million
- **Coed**
- **Moderately difficult** entrance level

FACULTY

Student/faculty ratio: 13:1.

ACADEMICS

Calendar: 4-1-4. *Degrees:* certificates, associate, bachelor's, master's, post-master's, and postbachelor's certificates.

Library: Norman B. Mears Library. *Books:* 55,448 (physical), 158,760 (digital/electronic); *Serial titles:* 361 (physical), 30,000 (digital/electronic); *Databases:* 58. Weekly public service hours: 78.

STUDENT LIFE

Housing options: on-campus residence required through sophomore year; coed, women-only. Campus housing is university owned. Freshman campus housing is guaranteed.

Activities and organizations: drama/theater group, student-run newspaper, radio and television station, choral group, Campus Ministries, Student Senate, Fellowship of Christian Athletes, Association for Supervision and Curriculum Development, Service Core.

Athletics Member NCAA. All Division II except golf (Division I).

Campus security: 24-hour emergency response devices and patrols, student patrols, late-night transport/escort service, controlled dormitory access.

Student services: personal/psychological counseling.

COSTS & FINANCIAL AID

Costs (2019–20) ***Comprehensive fee:*** $26,460 includes full-time tuition ($18,610), mandatory fees ($300), and room and board ($7550). Full-time tuition and fees vary according to program. Part-time tuition: $370 per semester hour. Part-time tuition and fees vary according to course load. ***College room only:*** $3970. Room and board charges vary according to board plan and housing facility.

Financial Aid Of all full-time matriculated undergraduates who enrolled in 2018, 956 applied for aid, 782 were judged to have need, 146 had their need fully met. 107 Federal Work-Study jobs (averaging $1500). In 2018, 271 non-need-based awards were made. ***Average percent of need met:*** 76. ***Average financial aid package:*** $12,765. ***Average need-based loan:*** $4405. ***Average need-based gift aid:*** $8292. ***Average non-need-based aid:*** $5474. ***Average indebtedness upon graduation:*** $33,862.

APPLYING

Standardized Tests *Required:* SAT or ACT (for admission).

Options: electronic application, deferred entrance.

Application fee: $25.

Required: high school transcript. ***Required for some:*** essay or personal statement, 2 letters of recommendation, interview. ***Recommended:*** minimum 2.8 GPA.

CONTACT

Mr. Ben Weins, Director of Admissions, University of Sioux Falls, 1101 West 22nd Street, Sioux Falls, SD 57105-1699. *Phone:* 605-331-6700. *Toll-free phone:* 800-888-1047. *Fax:* 605-331-6615. *E-mail:* admissions@usiouxfalls.edu.

University of South Dakota

Vermillion, South Dakota

http://www.usd.edu/

- **State-supported** university, founded 1862, part of South Dakota Board of Regents
- **Small-town** 274-acre campus
- **Endowment** $243.9 million
- **Coed** 12,262 undergraduate students, 79% full-time, 63% women, 37% men
- **Moderately difficult** entrance level, 86% of applicants were admitted

UNDERGRAD STUDENTS

9,686 full-time, 2,576 part-time. 36% are from out of state; 3% Black or African American, non-Hispanic/Latino; 4% Hispanic/Latino; 1% Asian, non-Hispanic/Latino; 0.1% Native Hawaiian or other Pacific Islander, non-Hispanic/Latino; 2% American Indian or Alaska Native, non-Hispanic/Latino; 4% Two or more races, non-Hispanic/Latino; 0.7% Race/ethnicity unknown; 2% international; 4% transferred in; 33% live on campus.

Freshmen:

Admission: 4,434 applied, 3,830 admitted, 1,293 enrolled. ***Average high school GPA:*** 3.4. ***Test scores:*** SAT evidence-based reading and writing scores over 500: 76%; SAT math scores over 500: 70%; ACT scores over 18: 87%; SAT evidence-based reading and writing scores over 600: 26%; SAT math scores over 600: 22%; ACT scores over 24: 38%; SAT evidence-based reading and writing scores over 700: 3%; SAT math scores over 700: 1%; ACT scores over 30: 5%.

Retention: 78% of full-time freshmen returned.

FACULTY

Total: 723, 55% full-time, 53% with terminal degrees.

Student/faculty ratio: 15:1.

ACADEMICS

Calendar: semesters. *Degrees:* certificates, bachelor's, master's, doctoral, and postbachelor's certificates.

Special study options: academic remediation for entering students, accelerated degree program, adult/continuing education programs, advanced placement credit, distance learning, double majors, English as a second language, honors programs, independent study, internships, off-campus study, part-time degree program, services for LD students, student-designed majors, study abroad, summer session for credit. ***ROTC:*** Army (b).

Unusual degree programs: 3-2 business administration; engineering; BA/BS English with MA, BS/MS Physics,BS/MS Computer Science, BA/BS Psychology with MA, BS/MS Biology.

Computers: 975 computers/terminals are available on campus for general student use. Students can access the following: campus intranet, computer help desk, free student e-mail accounts, online (class) grades, online (class) registration, online (class) schedules. Campuswide network is available. 100% of college-owned or -operated housing units are wired for

high-speed Internet access. Wireless service is available via entire campus.

Library: I. D. Weeks Library plus 2 others. *Books:* 528,075 (physical), 152,540 (digital/electronic); *Serial titles:* 4,739 (physical), 154,738 (digital/electronic); *Databases:* 230. Weekly public service hours: 103; students can reserve study rooms.

STUDENT LIFE

Housing options: on-campus residence required through sophomore year; coed, men-only, women-only, special housing for students with disabilities. Campus housing is university owned. Freshman campus housing is guaranteed.

Activities and organizations: drama/theater group, student-run newspaper, radio and television station, choral group, marching band, Dakotathon, International Club, SERVE, Campus Activities Board, national fraternities, national sororities.

Athletics Member NCAA. All Division I. ***Intercollegiate sports:*** basketball M(s)/W(s), cross-country running M(s)/W(s), football M(s), golf M/W(s)(c), soccer W(s), softball W(s), swimming and diving M(s)/W(s), tennis W(s), track and field M(s)/W(s), triathlon W(s), volleyball W(s). ***Intramural sports:*** archery M(c)/W(c), baseball M(c)/W(c), basketball M/W, fencing M(c)/W(c), field hockey W(c), football M, golf M/W, racquetball M/W, rugby W(c), soccer M(c)/W(c), softball M/W, table tennis M/W, tennis M/W, ultimate Frisbee M(c)/W(c), volleyball M/W, weight lifting M/W.

Campus security: 24-hour emergency response devices and patrols, student patrols, late-night transport/escort service, controlled dormitory access.

Student services: health clinic, personal/psychological counseling, legal services, veterans affairs office.

COSTS & FINANCIAL AID

Costs (2020–21) ***Tuition:*** area resident $7697 full-time, $257 per credit hour part-time; state resident $7697 full-time, $257 per credit hour part-time; nonresident $11,172 full-time, $372 per credit hour part-time. ***Required fees:*** $1635 full-time. ***Room and board:*** $8409; room only: $4280.

Financial Aid Of all full-time matriculated undergraduates who enrolled in 2018, 3,931 applied for aid, 2,872 were judged to have need, 415 had their need fully met. In 2018, 956 non-need-based awards were made. ***Average percent of need met:*** 55. ***Average financial aid package:*** $8617. ***Average need-based loan:*** $4051. ***Average need-based gift aid:*** $5067. ***Average non-need-based aid:*** $2348. ***Average indebtedness upon graduation:*** $28,363.

APPLYING

Standardized Tests *Required:* SAT or ACT (for admission).

Options: electronic application, early admission.

Application fee: $20.

CONTACT

Mr. Travis Vlasman, Senior Associate Director of Admissions, University of South Dakota, 414 East Clark Street, Vermillion, SD 57069-2390. *Phone:* 605-658-6228. *Toll-free phone:* 877-269-6837. *Fax:* 605-677-6323. *E-mail:* Travis.Vlasman@usd.edu.

TENNESSEE

American Baptist College

Nashville, Tennessee

http://www.abcnash.edu/

CONTACT

American Baptist College, 1800 Baptist World Center Drive, Nashville, TN 37207.

Aquinas College

Nashville, Tennessee

http://www.aquinascollege.edu/

CONTACT

Ms. Connie Hansom, Director of Admissions, Aquinas College, 4210 Harding Pike, Nashville, TN 37205-2005. *Phone:* 615-297-7545 Ext. 411. *Toll-free phone:* 800-649-9956. *Fax:* 615-279-3893. *E-mail:* hansomc@aquinascollege.edu.

Austin Peay State University

Clarksville, Tennessee

http://www.apsu.edu/

- **State-supported** comprehensive, founded 1927
- **Suburban** 196-acre campus with easy access to Nashville
- **Endowment** $10.2 million
- **Coed** 9,971 undergraduate students, 68% full-time, 58% women, 42% men
- **Moderately difficult** entrance level, 95% of applicants were admitted

UNDERGRAD STUDENTS

6,773 full-time, 3,198 part-time. Students come from 47 states and territories; 25 other countries; 16% are from out of state; 23% Black or African American, non-Hispanic/Latino; 9% Hispanic/Latino; 2% Asian, non-Hispanic/Latino; 0.2% Native Hawaiian or other Pacific Islander, non-Hispanic/Latino; 0.3% American Indian or Alaska Native, non-Hispanic/Latino; 7% Two or more races, non-Hispanic/Latino; 2% Race/ethnicity unknown; 0.6% international; 10% transferred in; 14% live on campus.

Freshmen:

Admission: 7,412 applied, 7,044 admitted, 1,716 enrolled. ***Average high school GPA:*** 3.2. ***Test scores:*** SAT evidence-based reading and writing scores over 500: 70%; SAT math scores over 500: 70%; ACT scores over 18: 83%; SAT evidence-based reading and writing scores over 600: 20%; SAT math scores over 600: 30%; ACT scores over 24: 30%; SAT evidence-based reading and writing scores over 700: 10%; SAT math scores over 700: 15%; ACT scores over 30: 5%.

Retention: 63% of full-time freshmen returned.

FACULTY

Total: 704, 55% full-time.

Student/faculty ratio: 17:1.

ACADEMICS

Calendar: semesters. *Degrees:* certificates, associate, bachelor's, master's, doctoral, post-master's, and postbachelor's certificates.

Special study options: academic remediation for entering students, accelerated degree program, adult/continuing education programs, advanced placement credit, cooperative education, distance learning, double majors, English as a second language, honors programs, independent study, internships, part-time degree program, services for LD students, study abroad, summer session for credit. ***ROTC:*** Army (b), Air Force (c).

Computers: 1,400 computers/terminals are available on campus for general student use. Students can access the following: campus intranet, computer help desk, free student e-mail accounts, online (class) grades, online (class) registration, online (class) schedules. Campuswide network is available. Wireless service is available via entire campus.

Library: Felix G. Woodward Library. *Books:* 197,772 (physical), 419,747 (digital/electronic); *Serial titles:* 53,388 (physical), 60,726 (digital/electronic); *Databases:* 298. Weekly public service hours: 110.

STUDENT LIFE

Housing options: on-campus residence required for freshman year; coed, men-only, women-only, special housing for students with disabilities. Campus housing is university owned.

Activities and organizations: drama/theater group, student-run newspaper, radio and television station, choral group, marching band, national fraternities, national sororities.

Athletics Member NCAA. All Division I except football (Division I-AA). ***Intercollegiate sports:*** baseball M(s), basketball M(s)/W(s), cheerleading M(s)/W(s), cross-country running M(s)/W(s), golf M(s)/W(s)(c), soccer

W(s), softball W(s), tennis M(s)/W(s), track and field W(s), volleyball W(s). ***Intramural sports:*** badminton M/W, basketball M/W, football M/W, golf M/W, racquetball M/W, soccer M/W, softball M/W, table tennis M/W, ultimate Frisbee M/W, volleyball M/W.

Campus security: 24-hour emergency response devices and patrols, student patrols, late-night transport/escort service, controlled dormitory access.

Student services: health clinic, personal/psychological counseling, veterans affairs office.

COSTS & FINANCIAL AID

Costs (2019–20) ***One-time required fee:*** $75. ***Tuition:*** state resident $6720 full-time, $280 per credit hour part-time; nonresident $12,264 full-time, $511 per credit hour part-time. Full-time tuition and fees vary according to location and program. Part-time tuition and fees vary according to location and program. ***Required fees:*** $1583 full-time. ***Room and board:*** $11,114; room only: $7200. Room and board charges vary according to board plan and housing facility. ***Payment plan:*** installment. ***Waivers:*** senior citizens and employees or children of employees.

Financial Aid Of all full-time matriculated undergraduates who enrolled in 2018, 6,460 applied for aid, 5,735 were judged to have need. 127 Federal Work-Study jobs (averaging $3189). 579 state and other part-time jobs (averaging $1747). In 2018, 585 non-need-based awards were made. ***Average financial aid package:*** $5776. ***Average need-based loan:*** $2070. ***Average need-based gift aid:*** $3241. ***Average non-need-based aid:*** $2648. ***Average indebtedness upon graduation:*** $25,938.

APPLYING

Standardized Tests *Required for some:* SAT or ACT (for admission).

Options: electronic application, deferred entrance.

Application fee: $25.

Required: high school transcript. ***Required for some:*** minimum 2.8 GPA.

Notification: continuous (freshmen), continuous (transfers).

CONTACT

Ms. Amy Corlew, Director of Admissions, Austin Peay State University, 601 College Street, Clarksville, TN 37044. *Phone:* 931-221-7661. *Toll-free phone:* 800-844-2778. *Fax:* 931-221-6168. *E-mail:* admissions@apsu.edu.

Baptist College of Health Sciences

Memphis, Tennessee

http://www.bchs.edu/

- **Independent Southern Baptist** comprehensive, founded 1994
- **Urban** 17-acre campus with easy access to Memphis, TN
- **Endowment** $44.6 million
- **Coed, primarily women** 971 undergraduate students, 43% full-time, 89% women, 11% men
- **Moderately difficult** entrance level, 60% of applicants were admitted

UNDERGRAD STUDENTS

420 full-time, 551 part-time. Students come from 17 states and territories; 30% are from out of state; 41% Black or African American, non-Hispanic/Latino; 8% Hispanic/Latino; 2% Asian, non-Hispanic/Latino; 0.1% Native Hawaiian or other Pacific Islander, non-Hispanic/Latino; 2% Two or more races, non-Hispanic/Latino; 0.9% Race/ethnicity unknown; 19% transferred in; 10% live on campus.

Freshmen:

Admission: 413 applied, 246 admitted, 94 enrolled. ***Average high school GPA:*** 3.2. ***Test scores:*** ACT scores over 18: 245%; ACT scores over 24: 78%; ACT scores over 30: 10%.

Retention: 65% of full-time freshmen returned.

FACULTY

Total: 70.

Student/faculty ratio: 9:1.

ACADEMICS

Calendar: trimesters. *Degrees:* associate, bachelor's, and doctoral.

Special study options: accelerated degree program, advanced placement credit, distance learning, double majors, honors programs, part-time degree program, services for LD students, summer session for credit.

Computers: 26 computers/terminals are available on campus for general student use. Students can access the following: campus intranet, computer help desk, free student e-mail accounts, online (class) grades, online (class) registration, online (class) schedules. Campuswide network is available. 100% of college-owned or -operated housing units are wired for high-speed Internet access. Wireless service is available via entire campus.

Library: Health Sciences Library. *Books:* 1,856 (physical), 5,515 (digital/electronic); *Serial titles:* 5 (physical), 136,331 (digital/electronic); *Databases:* 45. Students can reserve study rooms.

STUDENT LIFE

Housing options: coed. Campus housing is university owned.

Activities and organizations: Student Government Association, Student Nursing Association, Allied Health Organization, Active Minds.

Campus security: 24-hour emergency response devices and patrols, late-night transport/escort service, controlled dormitory access, trained security personnel.

Student services: health clinic, personal/psychological counseling.

COSTS

Costs (2020–21) ***Tuition:*** $10,872 full-time, $453 per credit hour part-time. ***Required fees:*** $1340 full-time, $55 per credit hour part-time. ***Room only:*** $3648. ***Payment plan:*** installment. ***Waivers:*** employees or children of employees.

APPLYING

Standardized Tests *Required:* SAT or ACT (for admission).

Options: electronic application.

Application fee: $25.

Required: high school transcript, minimum 2.8 GPA, immunizations, health physical. ***Required for some:*** interview.

CONTACT

Baptist College of Health Sciences, 1003 Monroe Avenue, Memphis, TN 38104. *Phone:* 901-572-2441. *Toll-free phone:* 866-575-2247.

Belhaven University

Memphis, Tennessee

http://memphis.belhaven.edu/

CONTACT

Don Jones, Director of Admission, Belhaven University, 5100 Poplar Avenue, Suite 200, Memphis, TN 38137. *Phone:* 901-888-3343. *Fax:* 901-888-0771. *E-mail:* memphisadmission@belhaven.edu.

Belmont University

Nashville, Tennessee

http://www.belmont.edu/

- **Independent Christian** university, founded 1951
- **Urban** 77-acre campus
- **Endowment** $107.8 million
- **Coed** 6,808 undergraduate students, 96% full-time, 65% women, 35% men
- **Moderately difficult** entrance level, 84% of applicants were admitted

UNDERGRAD STUDENTS

6,563 full-time, 245 part-time. Students come from 51 states and territories; 29 other countries; 70% are from out of state; 5% Black or African American, non-Hispanic/Latino; 6% Hispanic/Latino; 2% Asian, non-Hispanic/Latino; 0.1% Native Hawaiian or other Pacific Islander, non-Hispanic/Latino; 0.3% American Indian or Alaska Native, non-Hispanic/Latino; 4% Two or more races, non-Hispanic/Latino; 1% Race/ethnicity unknown; 1% international; 6% transferred in; 56% live on campus.

Freshmen:

Admission: 7,965 applied, 6,675 admitted, 1,684 enrolled. ***Average high school GPA:*** 3.5. ***Test scores:*** SAT evidence-based reading and writing scores over 500: 98%; SAT math scores over 500: 96%; ACT scores over 18: 99%; SAT evidence-based reading and writing scores over 600: 68%; SAT math scores over 600: 47%; ACT scores over 24: 75%; SAT evidence-based reading and writing scores over 700: 14%; SAT math scores over 700: 10%; ACT scores over 30: 24%.

Retention: 83% of full-time freshmen returned.

FACULTY
Total: 894, 43% full-time, 55% with terminal degrees.

Student/faculty ratio: 14:1.

ACADEMICS
Calendar: semesters. *Degrees:* bachelor's, master's, doctoral, and post-master's certificates.

Special study options: accelerated degree program, adult/continuing education programs, advanced placement credit, cooperative education, distance learning, double majors, English as a second language, honors programs, independent study, internships, off-campus study, part-time degree program, services for LD students, student-designed majors, study abroad, summer session for credit. ***ROTC:*** Army (c), Navy (c), Air Force (c).

Unusual degree programs: 3-2 engineering with Auburn University, Georgia Institute of Technology, University of Tennessee.

Computers: 500 computers/terminals are available on campus for general student use. Students can access the following: campus intranet, free student e-mail accounts, online (class) grades, online (class) registration, online (class) schedules, individual student information via course management system. Campuswide network is available. 100% of college-owned or -operated housing units are wired for high-speed Internet access. Wireless service is available via entire campus.

Library: Lila D. Bunch Library plus 1 other. *Books:* 208,565 (physical), 242,722 (digital/electronic); *Serial titles:* 1,107 (physical), 83,897 (digital/electronic); *Databases:* 344. Weekly public service hours: 127; students can reserve study rooms.

STUDENT LIFE
Housing options: on-campus residence required through sophomore year; coed, men-only, women-only, special housing for students with disabilities. Campus housing is university owned. Freshman campus housing is guaranteed.

Activities and organizations: drama/theater group, student-run newspaper, radio and television station, choral group, marching band, Service Corp, Alpha Sigma Tau, Phi Mu, Phi Kappa Tau, MOB, national fraternities, national sororities.

Athletics Member NCAA. All Division I. ***Intercollegiate sports:*** baseball M(s), basketball M(s)/W(s), cross-country running M(s)/W(s), golf M(s)/W(s)(c), soccer M(s)/W(s), softball W(s), tennis M(s)/W(s), track and field M(s)/W(s), volleyball W(s). ***Intramural sports:*** baseball M, basketball M/W, bowling M/W, cheerleading M/W, football M, golf M, ice hockey M/W, racquetball M/W, soccer M/W, softball M/W, table tennis M/W, tennis M/W, volleyball M/W.

Campus security: 24-hour emergency response devices and patrols, late-night transport/escort service, controlled dormitory access, bicycle patrol.

Student services: health clinic, personal/psychological counseling, women's center.

COSTS & FINANCIAL AID
Costs (2019–20) ***Comprehensive fee:*** $48,170 includes full-time tuition ($34,000), mandatory fees ($1650), and room and board ($12,520). Full-time tuition and fees vary according to course load and location. Part-time tuition: $1280 per credit hour. Part-time tuition and fees vary according to course load and location. ***College room only:*** $6860. Room and board charges vary according to board plan and housing facility. ***Payment plans:*** installment, deferred payment. ***Waivers:*** senior citizens and employees or children of employees.

Financial Aid Of all full-time matriculated undergraduates who enrolled in 2018, 4,388 applied for aid, 3,356 were judged to have need, 315 had their need fully met. In 2018, 1701 non-need-based awards were made. ***Average percent of need met:*** 56. ***Average financial aid package:*** $20,334. ***Average need-based loan:*** $4289. ***Average need-based gift aid:*** $16,511. ***Average non-need-based aid:*** $7988. ***Average indebtedness upon graduation:*** $30,465.

APPLYING
Standardized Tests *Required:* SAT or ACT (for admission).

Options: electronic application, early admission, deferred entrance.

Application fee: $50.

Required: essay or personal statement, high school transcript. ***Required for some:*** interview, resumé of activities.

Application deadlines: 8/1 (freshmen), 8/1 (transfers).

Notification: continuous (freshmen), continuous (transfers).

CONTACT
Mr. David Mee, Associate Provost and Dean of Enrollment, Belmont University, 1900 Belmont Boulevard, Nashville, TN 37212-3757. *Phone:* 615-460-5479. *Fax:* 615-460-5434. *E-mail:* david.mee@belmont.edu.

Bethel University

McKenzie, Tennessee

http://www.bethelu.edu/

- **Independent Cumberland Presbyterian** comprehensive, founded 1842
- **Small-town** 100-acre campus
- **Endowment** $2.9 million
- **Coed** 4,852 undergraduate students, 87% full-time, 57% women, 43% men
- **Minimally difficult** entrance level, 71% of applicants were admitted

UNDERGRAD STUDENTS
4,214 full-time, 638 part-time. Students come from 25 states and territories; 19 other countries; 18% are from out of state; 5% Black or African American, non-Hispanic/Latino; 5% Hispanic/Latino; 4% Asian, non-Hispanic/Latino; 0.1% Native Hawaiian or other Pacific Islander, non-Hispanic/Latino; 0.4% American Indian or Alaska Native, non-Hispanic/Latino; 4% Two or more races, non-Hispanic/Latino; 3% Race/ethnicity unknown; 0.8% international; 2% transferred in; 66% live on campus.

Freshmen:
Admission: 2,184 applied, 1,540 admitted, 562 enrolled. ***Average high school GPA:*** 3.6. ***Test scores:*** ACT scores over 18: 95%; ACT scores over 24: 60%; ACT scores over 30: 14%.

Retention: 85% of full-time freshmen returned.

FACULTY
Total: 469, 44% full-time, 57% with terminal degrees.

Student/faculty ratio: 13:1.

ACADEMICS
Calendar: semesters. *Degrees:* associate, bachelor's, and master's.

Special study options: academic remediation for entering students, accelerated degree program, adult/continuing education programs, advanced placement credit, cooperative education, distance learning, double majors, external degree program, honors programs, independent study, internships, off-campus study, part-time degree program, services for LD students, student-designed majors, summer session for credit. ***ROTC:*** Army (c), Air Force (c).

Computers: 12 computers/terminals and 30 ports are available on campus for general student use. Students can access the following: campus intranet, computer help desk, free student e-mail accounts, online (class) grades, online (class) registration, online (class) schedules. Campuswide network is available. 100% of college-owned or -operated housing units are wired for high-speed Internet access. Wireless service is available via entire campus.

Library: Burroughs Learning Center plus 1 other. *Books:* 24,618 (physical), 175,995 (digital/electronic); *Serial titles:* 26 (physical), 58,233 (digital/electronic); *Databases:* 92. Students can reserve study rooms.

STUDENT LIFE
Housing options: on-campus residence required through junior year; coed, men-only, women-only, cooperative, special housing for students with disabilities. Campus housing is university owned. Freshman applicants given priority for college housing.

Activities and organizations: drama/theater group, choral group, marching band, Campus Crusade for Christ, STEA (Education), Student Government Association, Students in Free Enterprise (SIFE), Arete.

Athletics Member NAIA. ***Intercollegiate sports:*** baseball M(s), basketball M(s)/W(s), bowling M(s)/W(s), cheerleading M(s)/W(s), cross-country running M(s)/W(s), football M(s), golf M(s)/W(s), riflery M(s)/W(s), soccer M(s)/W(s), softball W(s), tennis M(s)/W(s), track and field M(s)/W(s), volleyball W(s). ***Intramural sports:*** basketball M/W, football M, golf M/W, soccer M/W, softball M/W, table tennis M/W, tennis M/W, volleyball M/W.

Campus security: night patrols by trained security personnel.

Student services: personal/psychological counseling.

COSTS

Costs (2019–20) ***Comprehensive fee:*** $26,208 includes full-time tuition ($15,750), mandatory fees ($1260), and room and board ($9198). Full-time tuition and fees vary according to course load and program. Part-time tuition: $476 per credit hour. Part-time tuition and fees vary according to course load and program. ***Required fees:*** $53 per credit hour part-time. ***College room only:*** $5814. Room and board charges vary according to board plan and housing facility. ***Payment plan:*** installment. ***Waivers:*** employees or children of employees.

APPLYING

Standardized Tests *Recommended:* SAT or ACT (for admission).

Options: electronic application, early admission, deferred entrance.

Application fee: $30.

Required: high school transcript, minimum 2.0 GPA. ***Required for some:*** essay or personal statement, interview.

Application deadlines: rolling (freshmen), rolling (transfers).

Notification: continuous (freshmen), continuous (transfers).

CONTACT

Tina Hodges, Admissions Coordinator, Bethel University, 325 Cherry Avenue, McKenzie, TN 38201. *Phone:* 731-352-4030. *Fax:* 731-352-4069. *E-mail:* hodgest@bethelu.edu.

Bryan College

Dayton, Tennessee

http://www.bryan.edu/

- **Independent interdenominational** comprehensive, founded 1930
- **Small-town** 130-acre campus
- **Coed** 1,266 undergraduate students, 54% full-time, 54% women, 46% men
- **Moderately difficult** entrance level, 51% of applicants were admitted

UNDERGRAD STUDENTS

687 full-time, 579 part-time. Students come from 5 other countries; 29% are from out of state; 5% Black or African American, non-Hispanic/Latino; 3% Hispanic/Latino; 0.6% Asian, non-Hispanic/Latino; 0.2% Native Hawaiian or other Pacific Islander, non-Hispanic/Latino; 0.5% American Indian or Alaska Native, non-Hispanic/Latino; 2% Two or more races, non-Hispanic/Latino; 0.8% Race/ethnicity unknown; 4% international; 3% transferred in; 75% live on campus.

Freshmen:

Admission: 990 applied, 505 admitted, 191 enrolled. ***Average high school GPA:*** 3.7. ***Test scores:*** SAT evidence-based reading and writing scores over 500: 83%; SAT math scores over 500: 74%; ACT scores over 18: 96%; SAT evidence-based reading and writing scores over 600: 53%; SAT math scores over 600: 43%; ACT scores over 24: 48%; SAT evidence-based reading and writing scores over 700: 23%; SAT math scores over 700: 8%; ACT scores over 30: 11%.

Retention: 71% of full-time freshmen returned.

FACULTY

Total: 117, 36% full-time, 53% with terminal degrees.

Student/faculty ratio: 13:1.

ACADEMICS

Calendar: semesters. *Degrees:* diplomas, associate, bachelor's, master's, and postbachelor's certificates.

Special study options: academic remediation for entering students, adult/continuing education programs, advanced placement credit, distance learning, double majors, honors programs, independent study, internships, off-campus study, part-time degree program, services for LD students, study abroad, summer session for credit.

Unusual degree programs: 3-2 psychology with Richmont Graduate University.

Computers: 109 computers/terminals and 5 ports are available on campus for general student use. Students can access the following: campus intranet, computer help desk, free student e-mail accounts, online (class) grades, online (class) registration, online (class) schedules, campus-wide wi-fi. Campuswide network is available. 100% of college-owned or -operated housing units are wired for high-speed Internet access. Wireless service is available via entire campus.

Library: Bryan College Library. *Books:* 64,993 (physical), 350,219 (digital/electronic); *Serial titles:* 48 (physical), 85,938 (digital/electronic). Weekly public service hours: 83; students can reserve study rooms.

STUDENT LIFE

Housing options: on-campus residence required through senior year; men-only, women-only, special housing for students with disabilities. Campus housing is university owned. Freshman campus housing is guaranteed.

Activities and organizations: drama/theater group, student-run newspaper, choral group, SSTOP, PALS, Neighbor2Neighbor, Swing Dancing Club, Enactus.

Athletics Member NAIA. ***Intercollegiate sports:*** baseball M(s), basketball M(s)/W(s), cross-country running M(s)/W(s), golf M(s)/W(s), soccer M(s)/W(s), softball W(s), track and field M(s)/W(s), volleyball W(s). ***Intramural sports:*** basketball M/W, cheerleading M(c)/W(c), football M, rugby M(c), soccer M/W, softball M/W, table tennis M/W, ultimate Frisbee M/W, volleyball M/W.

Campus security: controlled dormitory access, police patrols, night watch.

Student services: personal/psychological counseling, veterans affairs office.

COSTS & FINANCIAL AID

Costs (2020–21) ***Comprehensive fee:*** $24,700 includes full-time tuition ($16,900) and room and board ($7800). Full-time tuition and fees vary according to program. Part-time tuition and fees vary according to program. ***Room and board:*** Room and board charges vary according to housing facility. ***Payment plan:*** installment. ***Waivers:*** employees or children of employees.

Financial Aid Of all full-time matriculated undergraduates who enrolled in 2019, 568 applied for aid, 509 were judged to have need, 223 had their need fully met. 150 Federal Work-Study jobs (averaging $2000). ***Average financial aid package:*** $24,217. ***Average need-based loan:*** $3609. ***Average need-based gift aid:*** $14,140. ***Average indebtedness upon graduation:*** $24,630.

APPLYING

Standardized Tests *Required:* SAT or ACT (for admission).

Options: electronic application, early admission, early action, deferred entrance.

Application fee: $35.

Required: high school transcript, minimum 2.0 GPA, minimum ACT score of 18 or RSAT of 960 or CLT 61. ***Required for some:*** essay or personal statement, interview.

Application deadlines: rolling (freshmen), rolling (transfers), rolling (early action).

Notification: continuous (freshmen), continuous (transfers), rolling (early action).

CONTACT

Leigha Miller, Senior Enrollment Counselor, Bryan College, 721 Bryan Drive, Dayton, TN 37321-7000. *Phone:* 423-775-2041 Ext. 579. *Toll-free phone:* 800-277-9522. *Fax:* 423-775-7199. *E-mail:* admissions@bryan.edu.

Carson-Newman University

Jefferson City, Tennessee

http://www.cn.edu/

- **Independent Southern Baptist** comprehensive, founded 1851
- **Small-town** 90-acre campus with easy access to Knoxville
- **Endowment** $54.6 million
- **Coed** 1,774 undergraduate students, 94% full-time, 59% women, 41% men
- **Moderately difficult** entrance level, 66% of applicants were admitted

UNDERGRAD STUDENTS

1,661 full-time, 113 part-time. 19% are from out of state; 9% Black or African American, non-Hispanic/Latino; 3% Hispanic/Latino; 0.7% Asian, non-Hispanic/Latino; 0.1% Native Hawaiian or other Pacific Islander, non-Hispanic/Latino; 0.7% American Indian or Alaska Native, non-Hispanic/Latino; 3% Two or more races, non-Hispanic/Latino; 0.9% Race/ethnicity unknown; 3% international; 6% transferred in; 49% live on campus.

Freshmen:

Admission: 3,736 applied, 2,467 admitted, 483 enrolled. ***Average high school GPA:*** 3.5.

Retention: 63% of full-time freshmen returned.

ACADEMICS

Calendar: semesters. *Degrees:* associate, bachelor's, master's, doctoral, and post-master's certificates.

Special study options: academic remediation for entering students, accelerated degree program, adult/continuing education programs, advanced placement credit, English as a second language, honors programs, internships, off-campus study, part-time degree program, services for LD students, student-designed majors, study abroad, summer session for credit. ***ROTC:*** Army (b).

Unusual degree programs: 3-2 engineering with Georgia Institute of Technology, University of Tennessee, Tennessee Technological University; pharmacy with Campbell University, Mercer University, University of Georgia.

Computers: 200 computers/terminals and 200 ports are available on campus for general student use. Students can access the following: campus intranet, computer help desk, free student e-mail accounts, online (class) grades, online (class) registration, online (class) schedules. Campuswide network is available. 100% of college-owned or -operated housing units are wired for high-speed Internet access. Wireless service is available via entire campus.

Library: Stephens-Burnett Library plus 3 others. Study areas open 24 hours, 5–7 days a week; students can reserve study rooms.

STUDENT LIFE

Housing options: on-campus residence required through junior year; men-only, women-only, special housing for students with disabilities. Campus housing is university owned. Freshman campus housing is guaranteed.

Activities and organizations: drama/theater group, student-run newspaper, choral group, marching band, Baptist Student Union, Fellowship of Christian Athletes, Student Government Association, Student Ambassadors Association, Columbians, national fraternities, national sororities.

Athletics ***Intercollegiate sports:*** baseball M(s), basketball M(s)/W(s), cross-country running M(s)/W(s), football M(s), golf M(s)/W, soccer M(s)/W(s), softball W(s), swimming and diving M(s)/W(s), tennis M(s)/W(s), track and field M(s)/W(s), volleyball W(s). ***Intramural sports:*** badminton M/W, baseball M/W, basketball M/W, football M/W, golf M/W, racquetball M/W, skiing (downhill) M/W, soccer M/W, softball M/W, swimming and diving M/W, table tennis M/W, tennis M/W, volleyball M/W.

Campus security: 24-hour emergency response devices and patrols, late-night transport/escort service, controlled dormitory access.

Student services: health clinic, personal/psychological counseling.

COSTS & FINANCIAL AID

Costs (2019–20) ***Comprehensive fee:*** $37,650 includes full-time tuition ($28,200), mandatory fees ($1300), and room and board ($8150). Part-time tuition: $1175 per credit hour. ***Required fees:*** $385 per term part-time. ***College room only:*** $2990. Room and board charges vary according to board plan and housing facility. ***Payment plans:*** installment, deferred payment. ***Waivers:*** employees or children of employees.

Financial Aid Of all full-time matriculated undergraduates who enrolled in 2018, 1,398 applied for aid, 1,398 were judged to have need, 260 had their need fully met. In 2018, 119 non-need-based awards were made. ***Average percent of need met:*** 76. ***Average financial aid package:*** $24,530. ***Average need-based loan:*** $2715. ***Average need-based gift aid:*** $19,098. ***Average non-need-based aid:*** $10,791. ***Average indebtedness upon graduation:*** $28,014.

APPLYING

Standardized Tests *Required:* SAT or ACT (for admission).

Options: electronic application, deferred entrance.

Required: high school transcript, minimum 2.3 GPA, medical history. ***Required for some:*** essay or personal statement. ***Recommended:*** interview.

Notification: continuous (freshmen), continuous (transfers).

CONTACT

Mr. Aaron Porter, Vice President for Enrollment Management, Carson-Newman University, 1646 Russell Avenue, PO Box 557, Jefferson City, TN 37760. *Phone:* 865-471-3223. *Toll-free phone:* 800-678-9061. *Fax:* 865-471-4817. *E-mail:* cnadmiss@cn.edu.

Christian Brothers University

Memphis, Tennessee

http://www.cbu.edu/

- **Independent Roman Catholic** comprehensive, founded 1871
- **Urban** 75-acre campus with easy access to Memphis
- **Endowment** $38.6 million
- **Coed**
- **Moderately difficult** entrance level

FACULTY

Student/faculty ratio: 13:1.

ACADEMICS

Calendar: semesters. *Degrees:* associate, bachelor's, and master's.

Library: Plough Memorial Library and Media Center. *Books:* 69,362 (physical), 180,750 (digital/electronic); *Serial titles:* 111 (physical), 39 (digital/electronic); *Databases:* 25. Weekly public service hours: 70; students can reserve study rooms.

STUDENT LIFE

Housing options: on-campus residence required through sophomore year; coed, men-only, women-only. Campus housing is university owned. Freshman campus housing is guaranteed.

Activities and organizations: choral group, Black Student Association, Tri-Beta, Hola CBU, Delta Sigma Pi, national fraternities, national sororities.

Athletics Member NCAA. All Division II except golf (Division I).

Campus security: 24-hour emergency response devices and patrols, late-night transport/escort service, controlled dormitory access.

Student services: health clinic, personal/psychological counseling.

FINANCIAL AID

Financial Aid Of all full-time matriculated undergraduates who enrolled in 2018, 1,359 applied for aid, 976 were judged to have need, 168 had their need fully met. 128 Federal Work-Study jobs (averaging $1108). 102 state and other part-time jobs (averaging $1069). In 2018, 368 non-need-based awards were made. ***Average percent of need met:*** 71. ***Average financial aid package:*** $25,525. ***Average need-based loan:*** $2771. ***Average need-based gift aid:*** $20,664. ***Average non-need-based aid:*** $18,501. ***Average indebtedness upon graduation:*** $36,886.

APPLYING

Standardized Tests *Required:* SAT or ACT (for admission).

Options: electronic application, deferred entrance.

Application fee: $25.

Required: essay or personal statement, high school transcript, minimum 2.0 GPA. ***Required for some:*** 2 letters of recommendation. ***Recommended:*** interview.

CONTACT

Ms. Kristi Forman, Director of Admissions, Christian Brothers University, 650 East Parkway South, Memphis, TN 38104. *Phone:* 901-321-3205. *Toll-free phone:* 877-321-4CBU. *Fax:* 901-321-3202. *E-mail:* admissions@cbu.edu.

Cumberland University

Lebanon, Tennessee

http://www.cumberland.edu/

CONTACT

Ms. Beatrice LaChance, Director of Enrollment Services, Cumberland University, One Cumberland Square, Lebanon, TN 37087. *Phone:* 615-

547-1244. *Toll-free phone:* 800-467-0562. *Fax:* 615-444-2569. *E-mail:* admissions@cumberland.edu.

Daymar College

Clarksville, Tennessee

http://www.daymarcollege.edu/

- **Proprietary** primarily 2-year, founded 1987
- **Small-town** campus
- **Coed**
- **Noncompetitive** entrance level

FACULTY
Student/faculty ratio: 7:1.

ACADEMICS
Calendar: quarters. *Degrees:* certificates, diplomas, associate, and bachelor's.

STUDENT LIFE
Housing options: college housing not available.

FINANCIAL AID
Financial Aid Of all full-time matriculated undergraduates who enrolled in 2018, 20 Federal Work-Study jobs (averaging $1000).

APPLYING
Required: high school transcript, interview.

CONTACT
Daymar College, 2691 Trenton Road, Clarksville, TN 37040. *Phone:* 931-552-7600 Ext. 204.

Daymar College

Murfreesboro, Tennessee

http://www.daymarcollege.edu/

- **Proprietary** primarily 2-year
- **Coed**

ACADEMICS
Degrees: certificates, associate, and bachelor's.

CONTACT
Daymar College, 415 Golden Bear Court, Murfreesboro, TN 37128.

DeVry University–Nashville Campus

Nashville, Tennessee

http://www.devry.edu/

CONTACT
Admissions Office, DeVry University–Nashville Campus, 3343 Perimeter Hill Drive, Suite 200, Nashville, TN 37211-4147. *Phone:* 615-445-3456. *Toll-free phone:* 866-338-7934.

East Tennessee State University

Johnson City, Tennessee

http://www.etsu.edu/

- **State-supported** university, founded 1911, part of State University and Community College System of Tennessee
- **Small-town** 366-acre campus
- **Endowment** $113.3 million
- **Coed**
- **Moderately difficult** entrance level

FACULTY
Student/faculty ratio: 15:1.

ACADEMICS
Calendar: semesters. *Degrees:* certificates, bachelor's, master's, doctoral, post-master's, and postbachelor's certificates.
Library: Charles C. Sherrod Library plus 2 others. *Books:* 731,960 (physical), 98,312 (digital/electronic); *Databases:* 210. Study areas open 24 hours, 5–7 days a week; students can reserve study rooms.

STUDENT LIFE
Housing options: coed, men-only, women-only, special housing for students with disabilities. Campus housing is university owned.

Activities and organizations: drama/theater group, student-run newspaper, radio and television station, choral group, marching band, honor societies, Volunteer ETSU, religious groups, residence hall councils, national fraternities, national sororities.

Athletics Member NCAA. All Division I except football (Division I-AA).

Campus security: 24-hour emergency response devices and patrols, student patrols, late-night transport/escort service, controlled dormitory access.

Student services: health clinic, personal/psychological counseling, women's center, veterans affairs office.

FINANCIAL AID
Financial Aid Of all full-time matriculated undergraduates who enrolled in 2015, 8,121 applied for aid, 6,967 were judged to have need, 517 had their need fully met. 359 state and other part-time jobs (averaging $1156). In 2015, 1145 non-need-based awards were made. ***Average percent of need met:*** 54. ***Average financial aid package:*** $10,182. ***Average need-based loan:*** $4198. ***Average need-based gift aid:*** $6449. ***Average non-need-based aid:*** $9680. ***Average indebtedness upon graduation:*** $27,866.

APPLYING
Standardized Tests *Required:* SAT or ACT (for admission).

Options: electronic application, early admission.

Application fee: $25.

Required: high school transcript, minimum 2.3 GPA, minimum 2.3 high school GPA or ACT score of 19.

CONTACT
Mr. Michelle Williams, Director of Admissions, East Tennessee State University, PO Box 70731, Johnson City, TN 37614-0734. *Phone:* 423-439-4213. *Toll-free phone:* 800-462-3878. *Fax:* 423-439-4630. *E-mail:* go2etsu@etsu.edu.

Fisk University

Nashville, Tennessee

http://www.fisk.edu/

CONTACT
Ms. Loretta McDonald, Dean of the Office of Recruitment and Admission, Fisk University, 1000 17th Avenue North, Nashville, TN 37208-3051. *Phone:* 615-329-8503. *Toll-free phone:* 888-702-0022. *Fax:* 615-329-8774. *E-mail:* lmcdonald@fisk.edu.

Freed-Hardeman University

Henderson, Tennessee

http://www.fhu.edu/

- **Independent** comprehensive, founded 1869, affiliated with Church of Christ
- **Small-town** 120-acre campus
- **Coed** 1,648 undergraduate students, 79% full-time, 57% women, 43% men
- **Moderately difficult** entrance level, 88% of applicants were admitted

UNDERGRAD STUDENTS
1,306 full-time, 342 part-time. 39% are from out of state; 4% Black or African American, non-Hispanic/Latino; 0.4% Hispanic/Latino; 0.5% Asian, non-Hispanic/Latino; 0.1% Native Hawaiian or other Pacific Islander, non-Hispanic/Latino; 0.9% American Indian or Alaska Native, non-Hispanic/Latino; 1% Two or more races, non-Hispanic/Latino; 5% Race/ethnicity unknown; 1% international; 6% transferred in; 83% live on campus.

Freshmen:
Admission: 944 applied, 835 admitted, 327 enrolled. ***Average high school GPA:*** 3.7. ***Test scores:*** SAT evidence-based reading and writing scores over 500: 78%; SAT math scores over 500: 78%; ACT scores over 18: 96%; SAT evidence-based reading and writing scores over 600: 45%; SAT math scores over 600: 29%; ACT scores over 24: 57%; SAT evidence-

based reading and writing scores over 700: 9%; SAT math scores over 700: 2%; ACT scores over 30: 18%.

Retention: 83% of full-time freshmen returned.

FACULTY
Total: 178, 56% full-time, 62% with terminal degrees.

Student/faculty ratio: 13:1.

ACADEMICS
Calendar: semesters. *Degrees:* diplomas, associate, bachelor's, master's, doctoral, post-master's, and postbachelor's certificates.

Special study options: academic remediation for entering students, accelerated degree program, advanced placement credit, distance learning, double majors, freshman honors college, honors programs, independent study, internships, off-campus study, part-time degree program, services for LD students, student-designed majors, study abroad, summer session for credit. ***ROTC:*** Army (b).

Unusual degree programs: 3-2 engineering.

Computers: Students can access the following: computer help desk, free student e-mail accounts, online (class) grades, online (class) registration, online (class) schedules. Campuswide network is available. 100% of college-owned or -operated housing units are wired for high-speed Internet access. Wireless service is available via entire campus.
Library: Hope Barber Shull Academic Resource Center plus 1 other. Students can reserve study rooms.

STUDENT LIFE
Housing options: on-campus residence required through senior year; men-only, women-only, special housing for students with disabilities. Campus housing is university owned. Freshman campus housing is guaranteed.

Activities and organizations: drama/theater group, student-run newspaper, radio station, choral group.

Athletics Member NAIA. ***Intercollegiate sports:*** baseball M(s), basketball M(s)/W(s), cheerleading W(s), cross-country running M(s)/W(s), golf M(s)/W(s), soccer M(s)/W(s), softball W(s), track and field M(s)/W(s), volleyball W(s). ***Intramural sports:*** basketball M/W, football M/W, softball M/W, volleyball M/W.

Campus security: 24-hour patrols, controlled dormitory access.

Student services: health clinic, personal/psychological counseling.

COSTS & FINANCIAL AID
Costs (2020–21) ***Comprehensive fee:*** $30,900 includes full-time tuition ($22,950) and room and board ($7950). Part-time tuition: $750 per credit hour. ***College room only:*** $4320.

Financial Aid Of all full-time matriculated undergraduates who enrolled in 2019, 1,224 applied for aid, 958 were judged to have need, 225 had their need fully met. In 2019, 339 non-need-based awards were made. ***Average percent of need met:*** 71. ***Average financial aid package:*** $19,696. ***Average need-based loan:*** $3885. ***Average need-based gift aid:*** $15,341. ***Average non-need-based aid:*** $10,338. ***Average indebtedness upon graduation:*** $29,103.

APPLYING
Standardized Tests *Required:* SAT or ACT (for admission).

Options: electronic application, deferred entrance.

Required: high school transcript, minimum 2.3 GPA. ***Required for some:*** interview.

Application deadlines: rolling (freshmen), rolling (transfers).

Notification: continuous (freshmen), continuous until 9/1 (transfers).

CONTACT
Freed-Hardeman University, 158 East Main Street, Henderson, TN 38340-2399. *Phone:* 731-989-6557. *Toll-free phone:* 800-FHU-FHU-1.

Huntington University of Health Sciences
Knoxville, Tennessee
http://www.huhs.edu/

- **Proprietary** comprehensive, founded 1984
- **Suburban** campus
- **Coed** 117 undergraduate students, 26% full-time, 88% women, 12% men
- **Noncompetitive** entrance level, 100% of applicants were admitted

UNDERGRAD STUDENTS
31 full-time, 86 part-time. Students come from 42 states and territories; 5 other countries; 99% are from out of state; 5% Black or African American, non-Hispanic/Latino; 5% Hispanic/Latino; 2% Asian, non-Hispanic/Latino; 1% American Indian or Alaska Native, non-Hispanic/Latino; 1% Two or more races, non-Hispanic/Latino; 1% Race/ethnicity unknown; 1% international; 9% transferred in.

Freshmen:
Admission: 5 applied, 5 admitted, 5 enrolled.

FACULTY
Total: 18, 17% full-time, 39% with terminal degrees.

Student/faculty ratio: 9:1.

ACADEMICS
Calendar: continuous. *Degrees:* certificates, diplomas, associate, bachelor's, master's, and doctoral (offers only external degree programs conducted through home study).

Special study options: academic remediation for entering students, accelerated degree program, adult/continuing education programs, distance learning, external degree program, independent study, part-time degree program, summer session for credit.

Computers: Students can access the following: online (class) grades.
Library: HUHS Online Library. *Books:* 9,973 (digital/electronic); *Serial titles:* 4,661 (digital/electronic); *Databases:* 11.

STUDENT LIFE
Housing options: college housing not available.

COSTS
Costs (2020–21) ***Tuition:*** $7950 full-time, $265 per credit hour part-time. ***Required fees:*** $325 full-time. ***Payment plan:*** installment. ***Waivers:*** employees or children of employees.

APPLYING
Options: deferred entrance.

Application fee: $75.

Required: minimum 2.0 GPA. ***Required for some:*** high school transcript, interview.

Application deadlines: rolling (freshmen), rolling (out-of-state freshmen), rolling (transfers).

Notification: continuous (freshmen), continuous (out-of-state freshmen), continuous (transfers).

CONTACT
Gregory Scott, Director of Admissions, Huntington University of Health Sciences, 118 Legacy View Way, Knoxville, TN 37918. *Phone:* 865-524-8079 Ext. 1001. *Toll-free phone:* 800-290-4226. *Fax:* 865-524-8339. *E-mail:* admissions@huhs.edu.

Johnson University
Knoxville, Tennessee
http://www.johnsonu.edu/

- **Independent** comprehensive, founded 1893, affiliated with Christian Churches and Churches of Christ
- **Rural** 175-acre campus with easy access to Knoxville
- **Coed** 774 undergraduate students, 78% full-time, 48% women, 52% men
- **Moderately difficult** entrance level, 53% of applicants were admitted

UNDERGRAD STUDENTS
601 full-time, 173 part-time. 57% are from out of state; 4% Black or African American, non-Hispanic/Latino; 3% Hispanic/Latino; 0.1% Asian, non-Hispanic/Latino; 0.1% American Indian or Alaska Native, non-Hispanic/Latino; 2% Two or more races, non-Hispanic/Latino; 4%

Race/ethnicity unknown; 2% international; 10% transferred in; 84% live on campus.

Freshmen:
Admission: 398 applied, 212 admitted, 145 enrolled. ***Average high school GPA:*** 3.5. ***Test scores:*** SAT evidence-based reading and writing scores over 500: 83%; SAT math scores over 500: 81%; ACT scores over 18: 83%; SAT evidence-based reading and writing scores over 600: 38%; SAT math scores over 600: 25%; ACT scores over 24: 38%; SAT evidence-based reading and writing scores over 700: 8%; SAT math scores over 700: 6%; ACT scores over 30: 8%.

FACULTY
Total: 165, 27% full-time, 53% with terminal degrees.

Student/faculty ratio: 10:1.

ACADEMICS
Calendar: semesters. *Degrees:* certificates, associate, bachelor's, master's, doctoral, and post-master's certificates.

Special study options: academic remediation for entering students, accelerated degree program, adult/continuing education programs, advanced placement credit, cooperative education, distance learning, double majors, English as a second language, honors programs, independent study, internships, part-time degree program, services for LD students, study abroad, summer session for credit.

Computers: Students can access the following: campus intranet, computer help desk, free student e-mail accounts, online (class) grades, online (class) registration, online (class) schedules. Campuswide network is available. 100% of college-owned or -operated housing units are wired for high-speed Internet access. Wireless service is available via entire campus.
Library: Glass Memorial Library plus 1 other. Weekly public service hours: 80.

STUDENT LIFE
Housing options: on-campus residence required through senior year; men-only, women-only. Campus housing is university owned.

Activities and organizations: drama/theater group, student-run newspaper, radio station, choral group, Student Government Association, International student Association, Harvesters (Missions), International Justice Mission, Students Promoting Social Unity.

Athletics Member NCCAA. ***Intercollegiate sports:*** baseball M, basketball M/W, cheerleading M/W, cross-country running M/W, soccer M/W, volleyball W. ***Intramural sports:*** basketball M, tennis M/W, ultimate Frisbee M/W, volleyball M/W.

Campus security: 24-hour emergency response devices and patrols, student patrols, controlled dormitory access.

Student services: health clinic, personal/psychological counseling.

COSTS
Costs (2020–21) ***Tuition:*** $16,400 full-time. Full-time tuition and fees vary according to class time, course load, degree level, location, and program. Part-time tuition and fees vary according to class time, course load, degree level, location, and program. ***Required fees:*** $1890 full-time. ***Room only:*** $3500. Room and board charges vary according to board plan, housing facility, and location. ***Payment plan:*** installment. ***Waivers:*** employees or children of employees.

APPLYING
Standardized Tests *Required:* SAT or ACT (for admission).

Options: electronic application, early admission, deferred entrance.

Application fee: $35.

Required: essay or personal statement, high school transcript, minimum 2.5 GPA, 3 letters of recommendation. ***Required for some:*** interview.

Application deadlines: 7/1 (freshmen), 7/1 (transfers).

Notification: continuous (freshmen), continuous (transfers).

CONTACT
Ms. Julee Schultz, Director of Admissions, Johnson University, 7900 Johnson Drive, Knoxville, TN 37998. *Phone:* 865-251-2233. *Toll-free phone:* 800-827-2122. *Fax:* 865-251-2336. *E-mail:* jschultz@johnsonu.edu.

King University

Bristol, Tennessee

http://www.king.edu/

- **Independent** comprehensive, founded 1867, affiliated with Presbyterian Church (U.S.A.)
- **Suburban** 135-acre campus
- **Endowment** $38.5 million
- **Coed** 1,617 undergraduate students, 92% full-time, 65% women, 35% men
- **Moderately difficult** entrance level, 62% of applicants were admitted

UNDERGRAD STUDENTS
1,487 full-time, 130 part-time. Students come from 40 states and territories; 27 other countries; 41% are from out of state; 6% Black or African American, non-Hispanic/Latino; 2% Hispanic/Latino; 1% Asian, non-Hispanic/Latino; 0.3% Native Hawaiian or other Pacific Islander, non-Hispanic/Latino; 0.7% American Indian or Alaska Native, non-Hispanic/Latino; 0.8% Two or more races, non-Hispanic/Latino; 4% Race/ethnicity unknown; 3% international; 4% transferred in; 15% live on campus.

Freshmen:
Admission: 949 applied, 589 admitted, 205 enrolled. ***Average high school GPA:*** 3.5.

Retention: 67% of full-time freshmen returned.

FACULTY
Total: 264, 33% full-time, 51% with terminal degrees.

Student/faculty ratio: 13:1.

ACADEMICS
Calendar: semesters. *Degrees:* associate, bachelor's, master's, doctoral, and post-master's certificates.

Special study options: adult/continuing education programs, advanced placement credit, distance learning, double majors, English as a second language, honors programs, independent study, internships, off-campus study, part-time degree program, services for LD students, student-designed majors, study abroad, summer session for credit. ***ROTC:*** Army (c).

Unusual degree programs: 3-2 engineering with The University of Tennessee.

Computers: 90 computers/terminals and 500 ports are available on campus for general student use. Students can access the following: campus intranet, computer help desk, free student e-mail accounts, online (class) grades, online (class) registration, online (class) schedules, Student Portal. Campuswide network is available. 100% of college-owned or -operated housing units are wired for high-speed Internet access. Wireless service is available via entire campus.
Library: E. W. King Library plus 3 others. *Books:* 79,129 (physical), 212,133 (digital/electronic); *Serial titles:* 179 (physical); *Databases:* 95. Weekly public service hours: 85.

STUDENT LIFE
Housing options: on-campus residence required through junior year; men-only, women-only, special housing for students with disabilities. Campus housing is university owned. Freshman campus housing is guaranteed.

Activities and organizations: drama/theater group, student-run newspaper, choral group, Student Government Association, Women in STEM, King Security and Intelligence Studies Student Group, Enactus, STEA-KE.

Athletics Member NCAA. All Division II. ***Intercollegiate sports:*** baseball M(s), basketball M(s)/W(s), cheerleading M/W(s), cross-country running M(s)/W(s), golf M(s)/W(s), soccer M(s)/W(s), softball W(s), swimming and diving M(s)/W(s), tennis M(s)/W(s), track and field M(s)/W(s), volleyball M(s)/W(s), wrestling M(s)/W(s). ***Intramural sports:*** baseball M/W, basketball M/W, bowling M/W, football M/W, racquetball M(c)/W(c), sand volleyball M(c)/W(c), soccer M/W, softball M/W, table tennis M(c)/W(c), tennis M(c)/W(c), ultimate Frisbee M/W, volleyball M/W.

Campus security: 24-hour emergency response devices and patrols, late-night transport/escort service, controlled dormitory access.

Student services: personal/psychological counseling.

COSTS & FINANCIAL AID
Costs (2020–21) ***One-time required fee:*** $125. ***Comprehensive fee:*** $41,226 includes full-time tuition ($30,106), mandatory fees ($1734), and room and board ($9386). Full-time tuition and fees vary according to degree level, program, and reciprocity agreements. Part-time tuition: $600 per semester hour. Part-time tuition and fees vary according to degree level, program, and reciprocity agreements. ***Required fees:*** $100 per course part-time. ***College room only:*** $4714. Room and board charges vary according to housing facility. ***Payment plan:*** installment. ***Waivers:*** employees or children of employees.

Financial Aid Of all full-time matriculated undergraduates who enrolled in 2019, 1,319 applied for aid, 1,212 were judged to have need, 130 had their need fully met. In 2019, 109 non-need-based awards were made. ***Average percent of need met:*** 63. ***Average financial aid package:*** $16,246. ***Average need-based loan:*** $4403. ***Average need-based gift aid:*** $14,183. ***Average non-need-based aid:*** $10,001. ***Average indebtedness upon graduation:*** $29,417.

APPLYING
Options: electronic application, deferred entrance.

Required: high school transcript. ***Required for some:*** essay or personal statement. ***Recommended:*** minimum 3.0 GPA.

Application deadlines: rolling (freshmen), rolling (transfers).

Notification: continuous (freshmen), continuous (transfers).

CONTACT
Jon Harr, Vice President for Enrollment Management, King University, 1350 King College Road, Bristol, TN 37620. *Phone:* 423-652-4861. *Toll-free phone:* 800-362-0014. *Fax:* 423-652-4727. *E-mail:* admissions@king.edu.

Lane College

Jackson, Tennessee

http://www.lanecollege.edu/

- **Independent** 4-year, founded 1882, affiliated with Christian Methodist Episcopal Church
- **Suburban** 55-acre campus with easy access to Memphis
- **Coed**
- **Minimally difficult** entrance level

FACULTY
Student/faculty ratio: 19:1.

ACADEMICS
Calendar: semesters. *Degree:* bachelor's.
Library: Chambers-McClure Academic Center.

STUDENT LIFE
Housing options: on-campus residence required for freshman year; coed, men-only, women-only. Campus housing is university owned. Freshman applicants given priority for college housing.

Activities and organizations: drama/theater group, choral group, marching band, Student Government Association, Pre-Law Club, Student Christian Association, Drama Club, Sociology Club, national fraternities, national sororities.

Athletics Member NCAA. All Division II.

Campus security: 24-hour emergency response devices and patrols, late-night transport/escort service, surveillance cameras, lighted parking areas.

Student services: health clinic, personal/psychological counseling, legal services, veterans affairs office.

FINANCIAL AID
Financial Aid Of all full-time matriculated undergraduates who enrolled in 2016, 1,365 applied for aid, 1,365 were judged to have need. In 2016, 2 non-need-based awards were made. ***Average financial aid package:*** $12,240. ***Average need-based loan:*** $3568. ***Average need-based gift aid:*** $13,527. ***Average non-need-based aid:*** $4761.

APPLYING
Standardized Tests *Required:* SAT or ACT (for admission).

Options: electronic application, deferred entrance.

Required: high school transcript, 2 letters of recommendation.

CONTACT
Dr. Monica C. Scott, Director of Enrollment Management, Lane College, 545 Lane Avenue, Jackson, TN 38301. *Phone:* 731-426-7533. *Toll-free phone:* 800-960-7533. *Fax:* 731-426-7559. *E-mail:* mclayborne@lanecollege.edu.

Lee University

Cleveland, Tennessee

http://www.leeuniversity.edu/

- **Independent** comprehensive, founded 1918, affiliated with Church of God
- **Small-town** 120-acre campus with easy access to Chattanooga, TN
- **Endowment** $23.9 million
- **Coed** 4,686 undergraduate students, 78% full-time, 61% women, 39% men
- **Moderately difficult** entrance level, 82% of applicants were admitted

UNDERGRAD STUDENTS
3,677 full-time, 1,009 part-time. Students come from 48 states and territories; 51 other countries; 52% are from out of state; 5% Black or African American, non-Hispanic/Latino; 2% Hispanic/Latino; 0.9% Asian, non-Hispanic/Latino; 0.1% Native Hawaiian or other Pacific Islander, non-Hispanic/Latino; 0.4% American Indian or Alaska Native, non-Hispanic/Latino; 4% Two or more races, non-Hispanic/Latino; 3% Race/ethnicity unknown; 3% international; 4% transferred in; 47% live on campus.

Freshmen:
Admission: 2,416 applied, 1,975 admitted, 792 enrolled. ***Average high school GPA:*** 3.7. ***Test scores:*** SAT evidence-based reading and writing scores over 500: 82%; SAT math scores over 500: 71%; ACT scores over 18: 91%; SAT evidence-based reading and writing scores over 600: 44%; SAT math scores over 600: 31%; ACT scores over 24: 60%; SAT evidence-based reading and writing scores over 700: 9%; SAT math scores over 700: 8%; ACT scores over 30: 19%.

Retention: 78% of full-time freshmen returned.

FACULTY
Total: 465, 40% full-time, 54% with terminal degrees.

Student/faculty ratio: 15:1.

ACADEMICS
Calendar: semesters. *Degrees:* bachelor's, master's, doctoral, and post-master's certificates.

Special study options: academic remediation for entering students, adult/continuing education programs, advanced placement credit, cooperative education, distance learning, double majors, English as a second language, external degree program, honors programs, independent study, internships, off-campus study, part-time degree program, services for LD students, student-designed majors, study abroad, summer session for credit.

Computers: 460 computers/terminals and 650 ports are available on campus for general student use. Students can access the following: campus intranet, computer help desk, free student e-mail accounts, online (class) grades, online (class) registration, online (class) schedules. Campuswide network is available. 95% of college-owned or -operated housing units are wired for high-speed Internet access. Wireless service is available via entire campus.

Library: William G. Squires Library plus 2 others. *Books:* 149,928 (physical), 439,290 (digital/electronic); *Serial titles:* 244 (physical), 97,212 (digital/electronic); *Databases:* 136. Weekly public service hours: 93; students can reserve study rooms.

STUDENT LIFE
Housing options: on-campus residence required through sophomore year; men-only, women-only. Campus housing is university owned. Freshman campus housing is guaranteed.

Activities and organizations: drama/theater group, student-run newspaper, choral group, Student Leadership Council, CRU, Big Pal Little Pal, Delta Zeta Tau, Crossover.

Athletics Member NCAA, NCCAA. All NCAA Division II.
Intercollegiate sports: baseball M(s), basketball M(s)/W(s), cross-country running M(s)/W(s), golf M(s)/W(s), lacrosse W(s), soccer M(s)/W(s), softball W(s), tennis M(s)/W(s), track and field M(s)/W(s), volleyball

W(s). ***Intramural sports:*** basketball M/W, bowling M/W, football M/W, golf M/W, racquetball M/W, rugby M(c)/W(c), sand volleyball M/W, soccer M/W, softball M/W, table tennis M/W, tennis M/W, ultimate Frisbee M(c)/W(c), volleyball M/W.

Campus security: 24-hour emergency response devices and patrols, late-night transport/escort service, controlled dormitory access.

Student services: health clinic, personal/psychological counseling, veterans affairs office.

COSTS & FINANCIAL AID

Costs (2020–21) ***Comprehensive fee:*** $27,800 includes full-time tuition ($18,840), mandatory fees ($700), and room and board ($8260). Part-time tuition: $785 per credit hour. ***Required fees:*** $60 per term part-time. ***College room only:*** $4270. Room and board charges vary according to board plan and housing facility. ***Payment plan:*** deferred payment. ***Waivers:*** employees or children of employees.

Financial Aid Of all full-time matriculated undergraduates who enrolled in 2019, 3,278 applied for aid, 2,624 were judged to have need, 437 had their need fully met. 312 Federal Work-Study jobs (averaging $1377). 774 state and other part-time jobs (averaging $1757). In 2019, 617 non-need-based awards were made. ***Average percent of need met:*** 49. ***Average financial aid package:*** $13,991. ***Average need-based loan:*** $4213. ***Average need-based gift aid:*** $11,684. ***Average non-need-based aid:*** $8073. ***Average indebtedness upon graduation:*** $30,846.

APPLYING

Standardized Tests *Required:* SAT or ACT (for admission). *Recommended:* SAT (for admission), ACT (for admission).

Options: electronic application, early admission, deferred entrance.

Application fee: $25.

Required: high school transcript, minimum 2.0 GPA, MMR immunization record. ***Required for some:*** 3 letters of recommendation.

Application deadlines: rolling (freshmen), rolling (out-of-state freshmen), rolling (transfers).

Notification: continuous (freshmen), continuous (out-of-state freshmen), continuous (transfers).

CONTACT

Mr. Phillip Cook, Vice President for Enrollment, Lee University, 1120 N. Ocoee Street, Cleveland, TN 37311. *Phone:* 423-614-8500. *Toll-free phone:* 800-533-9930. *Fax:* 423-614-8533. *E-mail:* admissions@leeuniversity.edu.

LeMoyne-Owen College

Memphis, Tennessee

http://www.loc.edu/

CONTACT

LeMoyne-Owen College, 807 Walker Avenue, Memphis, TN 38126-6595. *Phone:* 901-435-1500. *Toll-free phone:* 800-737-7778.

Lincoln Memorial University

Harrogate, Tennessee

http://www.lmunet.edu/

- **Independent** university, founded 1897
- **Small-town** 1000-acre campus
- **Endowment** $40.8 million
- **Coed** 1,975 undergraduate students, 72% full-time, 71% women, 29% men
- **Moderately difficult** entrance level, 49% of applicants were admitted

UNDERGRAD STUDENTS

1,427 full-time, 548 part-time. 37% are from out of state; 6% Black or African American, non-Hispanic/Latino; 0.3% Hispanic/Latino; 1% Asian, non-Hispanic/Latino; 1% American Indian or Alaska Native, non-Hispanic/Latino; 3% Race/ethnicity unknown; 4% international; 14% transferred in; 38% live on campus.

Freshmen:

Admission: 1,549 applied, 766 admitted, 267 enrolled. ***Average high school GPA:*** 3.5. ***Test scores:*** SAT evidence-based reading and writing scores over 500: 84%; SAT math scores over 500: 76%; ACT scores over 18: 91%; SAT evidence-based reading and writing scores over 600: 31%; SAT math scores over 600: 30%; ACT scores over 24: 38%; SAT math scores over 700: 3%; ACT scores over 30: 8%.

Retention: 77% of full-time freshmen returned.

FACULTY

Total: 323, 74% full-time, 80% with terminal degrees.

Student/faculty ratio: 16:1.

ACADEMICS

Calendar: semesters. *Degrees:* associate, bachelor's, master's, doctoral, and post-master's certificates.

Special study options: academic remediation for entering students, adult/continuing education programs, advanced placement credit, distance learning, double majors, English as a second language, honors programs, independent study, internships, part-time degree program, services for LD students, study abroad, summer session for credit. ***ROTC:*** Army (b).

Computers: 121 computers/terminals are available on campus for general student use. Students can access the following: campus intranet, computer help desk, free student e-mail accounts, online (class) grades, online (class) registration, online (class) schedules. Campuswide network is available. 100% of college-owned or -operated housing units are wired for high-speed Internet access. Wireless service is available via classrooms, computer centers, computer labs, dorm rooms, learning centers, libraries, student centers.

Library: Carnegie-Vincent Library. *Books:* 85,346 (physical), 355,314 (digital/electronic); *Serial titles:* 1,548 (physical), 32,592 (digital/electronic); *Databases:* 225. Weekly public service hours: 92; students can reserve study rooms.

STUDENT LIFE

Housing options: coed, men-only, women-only, special housing for students with disabilities. Campus housing is university owned.

Activities and organizations: drama/theater group, choral group, Enactus, Pre-Vet Club, Pre-Med Club, Fishing Club, Earth Club, national fraternities, national sororities.

Athletics Member NCAA. All Division II. ***Intercollegiate sports:*** baseball M(s), basketball M(s)/W(s), bowling M(s)/W(s), cross-country running M(s)/W(s), golf M(s)/W(s), lacrosse M(s)/W(s), sand volleyball W(s), soccer M(s)/W(s), softball W(s), tennis M(s)/W(s), volleyball W(s). ***Intramural sports:*** basketball M/W, football M/W, soccer M/W, softball M/W, swimming and diving M/W, table tennis M/W, tennis M/W, ultimate Frisbee M/W, volleyball M/W.

Campus security: 24-hour emergency response devices and patrols, late-night transport/escort service.

Student services: health clinic, personal/psychological counseling, veterans affairs office.

COSTS & FINANCIAL AID

Costs (2020–21) ***Comprehensive fee:*** $35,676 includes full-time tuition ($23,040), mandatory fees ($1998), and room and board ($10,638). Part-time tuition: $960 per credit hour.

Financial Aid Of all full-time matriculated undergraduates who enrolled in 2018, 1,358 applied for aid, 1,160 were judged to have need, 47 had their need fully met. In 2018, 78 non-need-based awards were made. ***Average percent of need met:*** 54. ***Average financial aid package:*** $23,472. ***Average need-based loan:*** $8838. ***Average need-based gift aid:*** $14,411. ***Average non-need-based aid:*** $6316. ***Average indebtedness upon graduation:*** $22,290.

APPLYING

Standardized Tests *Required:* SAT or ACT (for admission).

Options: electronic application, deferred entrance.

Required: high school transcript, immunization records, financial aid application. ***Recommended:*** minimum 3.0 GPA.

Application deadlines: rolling (freshmen), rolling (transfers).

Notification: continuous (freshmen), continuous (transfers).

CONTACT

Lincoln Memorial University, 6965 Cumberland Gap Parkway, Harrogate, TN 37752-1901. *Phone:* 423-869-6280. *Toll-free phone:* 800-325-0900.

Lipscomb University

Nashville, Tennessee

http://www.lipscomb.edu/

- **Independent** university, founded 1891, affiliated with Church of Christ
- **Suburban** 89-acre campus
- **Endowment** $79.1 million
- **Coed** 2,859 undergraduate students, 94% full-time, 60% women, 40% men
- **Moderately difficult** entrance level, 63% of applicants were admitted

UNDERGRAD STUDENTS

2,680 full-time, 179 part-time. 36% are from out of state; 7% Black or African American, non-Hispanic/Latino; 7% Hispanic/Latino; 3% Asian, non-Hispanic/Latino; 0.1% Native Hawaiian or other Pacific Islander, non-Hispanic/Latino; 0.2% American Indian or Alaska Native, non-Hispanic/Latino; 3% Two or more races, non-Hispanic/Latino; 2% Race/ethnicity unknown; 4% international; 7% transferred in; 55% live on campus.

Freshmen:

Admission: 3,481 applied, 2,197 admitted, 613 enrolled. ***Average high school GPA:*** 3.7. ***Test scores:*** SAT evidence-based reading and writing scores over 500: 95%; SAT math scores over 500: 92%; ACT scores over 18: 99%; SAT evidence-based reading and writing scores over 600: 55%; SAT math scores over 600: 49%; ACT scores over 24: 69%; SAT evidence-based reading and writing scores over 700: 12%; SAT math scores over 700: 8%; ACT scores over 30: 21%.

FACULTY

Total: 608, 39% full-time, 55% with terminal degrees.

Student/faculty ratio: 13:1.

ACADEMICS

Calendar: semesters. *Degrees:* certificates, bachelor's, master's, doctoral, and postbachelor's certificates.

Special study options: academic remediation for entering students, accelerated degree program, adult/continuing education programs, advanced placement credit, distance learning, double majors, English as a second language, honors programs, independent study, internships, part-time degree program, services for LD students, student-designed majors, study abroad, summer session for credit. ***ROTC:*** Army (c), Air Force (c).

Computers: 150 computers/terminals are available on campus for general student use. Students can access the following: campus intranet, computer help desk, free student e-mail accounts, online (class) grades, online (class) registration, online (class) schedules. Campuswide network is available. 100% of college-owned or -operated housing units are wired for high-speed Internet access. Wireless service is available via entire campus.

Library: Beaman Library plus 1 other. *Books:* 157,824 (physical), 167,520 (digital/electronic); *Serial titles:* 253 (physical), 489 (digital/electronic); *Databases:* 100. Students can reserve study rooms.

STUDENT LIFE

Housing options: on-campus residence required through junior year; men-only, women-only. Campus housing is university owned. Freshman applicants given priority for college housing.

Activities and organizations: drama/theater group, student-run newspaper, radio and television station, choral group, Sigma Pi Beta, business fraternities, Multicultural Association, Alpha Phi Chi men's service club, Pi Kappa Sigma women's service club.

Athletics Member NCAA. All Division I. ***Intercollegiate sports:*** baseball M(s), basketball M(s)/W(s), cross-country running M(s)/W(s), golf M(s)/W(s)(c), ice hockey M(c), soccer M(s)/W(s), softball W(s), tennis M(s)/W(s), track and field M(s)/W(s), volleyball W(s). ***Intramural sports:*** basketball M/W, football M/W, golf M/W, racquetball M/W, sand volleyball M/W, soccer M/W, softball M/W, table tennis M/W, ultimate Frisbee M/W, volleyball M/W.

Campus security: 24-hour emergency response devices and patrols, late-night transport/escort service, controlled dormitory access.

Student services: health clinic, personal/psychological counseling, veterans affairs office.

COSTS & FINANCIAL AID

Costs (2020–21) ***Comprehensive fee:*** $48,548 includes full-time tuition ($32,080), mandatory fees ($2664), and room and board ($13,804).

Financial Aid Of all full-time matriculated undergraduates who enrolled in 2019, 2,605 applied for aid, 1,685 were judged to have need, 606 had their need fully met. In 2019, 803 non-need-based awards were made. ***Average percent of need met:*** 61. ***Average financial aid package:*** $30,420. ***Average need-based loan:*** $5345. ***Average need-based gift aid:*** $26,557. ***Average non-need-based aid:*** $18,668. ***Average indebtedness upon graduation:*** $31,116.

APPLYING

Standardized Tests *Required:* SAT or ACT (for admission).

Options: electronic application, early admission, deferred entrance.

Application fee: $50.

CONTACT

Mr. Johnathan Akin, Assistant Vice President of Undergraduate Admissions, Lipscomb University, One University Park Drive, Nashville, TN 37204-3951. *Phone:* 615-966-6150. *Toll-free phone:* 877-582-4766. *Fax:* 615-966-1804. *E-mail:* admissions@lipscomb.edu.

Martin Methodist College

Pulaski, Tennessee

http://www.martinmethodist.edu/

CONTACT

Lisa Smith, Director of Admissions, Martin Methodist College, 433 West Madison Street, Pulaski, TN 38478-2716. *Phone:* 931-363-9868. *Toll-free phone:* 800-467-1273. *Fax:* 931-363-9818. *E-mail:* admit@martinmethodist.edu.

Maryville College

Maryville, Tennessee

http://www.maryvillecollege.edu/

CONTACT

Ms. Arielle Kilday, Associate Director of Admissions, Maryville College, 502 East Lamar Alexander Parkway, Maryville, TN 37804-5907. *Phone:* 865-981-8042. *Toll-free phone:* 800-597-2687. *Fax:* 865-981-8005. *E-mail:* admissions@maryvillecollege.edu.

Mid-America Baptist Theological Seminary

Cordova, Tennessee

http://www.mabts.edu/

- **Independent Southern Baptist** comprehensive, founded 1972
- **Suburban** campus with easy access to Memphis
- **Endowment** $3.6 million
- **Men only** 51 undergraduate students
- **Noncompetitive** entrance level

UNDERGRAD STUDENTS

Students come from 26 states and territories.

Freshmen:

Admission: 123 applied.

FACULTY

Total: 27, 100% full-time, 100% with terminal degrees.

Student/faculty ratio: 11:1.

ACADEMICS

Calendar: semesters. *Degrees:* associate, bachelor's, master's, and doctoral.

Special study options: accelerated degree program, distance learning, internships, part-time degree program, summer session for credit.

Computers: 10 computers/terminals are available on campus for general student use. Campuswide network is available. 100% of college-owned or -operated housing units are wired for high-speed Internet access. Wireless service is available via entire campus.

Library: Ora Byram Allison Memorial Library. Students can reserve study rooms.

STUDENT LIFE

Housing options: men-only, women-only, special housing for students with disabilities. Campus housing is university owned.

Campus security: 24-hour emergency response devices.

COSTS

Costs (2020–21) ***Tuition:*** $8000 full-time, $325 per credit hour part-time. ***Required fees:*** $350 full-time. ***Room only:*** $3750. ***Payment plan:*** installment. ***Waivers:*** employees or children of employees.

APPLYING

Standardized Tests *Required for some:* SAT or ACT (for admission).

Options: electronic application.

Application fee: $25.

Required: essay or personal statement, 2 letters of recommendation. ***Required for some:*** high school transcript.

Application deadlines: rolling (freshmen), rolling (out-of-state freshmen), rolling (transfers).

CONTACT

Mid-America Baptist Theological Seminary, 2095 Appling Road, Cordova, TN 38016. *Toll-free phone:* 800-968-4508.

Middle Tennessee State University

Murfreesboro, Tennessee

http://www.mtsu.edu/

- **State-supported** university, founded 1911
- **Urban** 500-acre campus with easy access to Nashville
- **Endowment** $92.9 million
- **Coed** 19,461 undergraduate students, 81% full-time, 53% women, 47% men
- **Moderately difficult** entrance level, 94% of applicants were admitted

UNDERGRAD STUDENTS

15,721 full-time, 3,740 part-time. Students come from 43 states and territories; 65 other countries; 7% are from out of state; 19% Black or African American, non-Hispanic/Latino; 7% Hispanic/Latino; 4% Asian, non-Hispanic/Latino; 0.1% Native Hawaiian or other Pacific Islander, non-Hispanic/Latino; 0.2% American Indian or Alaska Native, non-Hispanic/Latino; 4% Two or more races, non-Hispanic/Latino; 0.1% Race/ethnicity unknown; 3% international; 11% transferred in; 17% live on campus.

Freshmen:

Admission: 8,973 applied, 8,409 admitted, 3,312 enrolled. ***Average high school GPA:*** 3.5. ***Test scores:*** SAT evidence-based reading and writing scores over 500: 82%; SAT math scores over 500: 77%; ACT scores over 18: 91%; SAT evidence-based reading and writing scores over 600: 35%; SAT math scores over 600: 34%; ACT scores over 24: 47%; SAT evidence-based reading and writing scores over 700: 10%; SAT math scores over 700: 13%; ACT scores over 30: 10%.

Retention: 76% of full-time freshmen returned.

FACULTY

Total: 1,264, 76% full-time, 69% with terminal degrees.

Student/faculty ratio: 17:1.

ACADEMICS

Calendar: semesters. *Degrees:* certificates, bachelor's, master's, doctoral, post-master's, and postbachelor's certificates.

Special study options: adult/continuing education programs, advanced placement credit, cooperative education, distance learning, double majors, English as a second language, external degree program, freshman honors college, honors programs, independent study, off-campus study, part-time degree program, services for LD students, study abroad, summer session for credit. ***ROTC:*** Army (b), Air Force (c).

Computers: 687 computers/terminals are available on campus for general student use. Students can access the following: computer help desk, free student e-mail accounts, online (class) grades, online (class) registration, online (class) schedules, Office 365, online learning management system. Campuswide network is available. 100% of college-owned or -operated housing units are wired for high-speed Internet access. Wireless service is available via entire campus.

Library: James E. Walker Library plus 4 others. *Books:* 964,669 (physical), 820,847 (digital/electronic); *Serial titles:* 11,397 (physical), 103,008 (digital/electronic); *Databases:* 390. Weekly public service hours: 105; students can reserve study rooms.

STUDENT LIFE

Housing options: coed, men-only, women-only, cooperative, special housing for students with disabilities. Campus housing is university owned.

Activities and organizations: drama/theater group, student-run newspaper, radio and television station, choral group, marching band, Student Government Association, Black Student Union, Alpha Kappa Psi Business Fraternity, Gamma Beta Phi Honors Society, The Point Ministries, national fraternities, national sororities.

Athletics Member NCAA. All Division I except football (Division I-A). ***Intercollegiate sports:*** baseball M(s), basketball M(s)/W(s), cheerleading M(s)/W(s), cross-country running M(s)/W(s), equestrian sports M/W, golf M(s)/W(s), soccer W(s), softball W(s), tennis M(s)/W(s), track and field M(s)/W(s), volleyball W(s). ***Intramural sports:*** badminton M/W, basketball M/W, bowling M(c)/W(c), fencing M(c)/W(c), field hockey M(c)/W(c), football M, ice hockey M(c)/W(c), lacrosse M(c)/W(c), racquetball M(c)/W(c), riflery M(c)/W(c), rock climbing M(c)/W(c), rugby M(c)/W(c), soccer M(c)/W, softball M/W, swimming and diving M/W, tennis M/W, ultimate Frisbee M(c)/W(c), volleyball M(c)/W(c), wrestling M(c).

Campus security: 24-hour emergency response devices and patrols, student patrols, late-night transport/escort service, controlled dormitory access, Tornado Siren, Emergency Alert Text Messages.

Student services: health clinic, personal/psychological counseling, women's center, legal services, veterans affairs office.

COSTS & FINANCIAL AID

Costs (2020–21) ***Tuition:*** state resident $9306 full-time, $300 per credit hour part-time; nonresident $28,606 full-time, $1078 per credit hour part-time. Full-time tuition and fees vary according to course load and program. Part-time tuition and fees vary according to course load and program. ***Required fees:*** $1870 full-time, $78 per credit hour part-time. ***Room and board:*** $8976. Room and board charges vary according to board plan and housing facility. ***Payment plan:*** installment. ***Waivers:*** senior citizens and employees or children of employees.

Financial Aid Of all full-time matriculated undergraduates who enrolled in 2019, 13,642 applied for aid, 10,392 were judged to have need, 1,199 had their need fully met. 286 Federal Work-Study jobs (averaging $2929). In 2019, 2717 non-need-based awards were made. ***Average percent of need met:*** 64. ***Average financial aid package:*** $10,238. ***Average need-based loan:*** $3983. ***Average need-based gift aid:*** $6189. ***Average non-need-based aid:*** $8520. ***Average indebtedness upon graduation:*** $24,936.

APPLYING

Standardized Tests *Required:* SAT or ACT (for admission).

Options: electronic application.

Application fee: $25.

Required: high school transcript, minimum 3.0 GPA. ***Required for some:*** essay or personal statement.

Application deadlines: rolling (freshmen), rolling (out-of-state freshmen), rolling (transfers).

Notification: continuous (freshmen), continuous (out-of-state freshmen), continuous (transfers).

CONTACT

Middle Tennessee State University, 1301 East Main Street, Murfreesboro, TN 37132. *Phone:* 615-898-2233. *Toll-free phone:* 800-331-MTSU.

Mid-South Christian College

Memphis, Tennessee

http://www.midsouthchristian.edu/

CONTACT

Mrs. Wendy Lambert, Student Recruiter, Mid-South Christian College, PO Box 181056, Memphis, TN 38181. *Phone:* 901-375-4400 Ext. 103. *Fax:* 901-375-4085. *E-mail:* wendylambert@midsouthcc.org.

Milligan College

Milligan College, Tennessee

http://www.milligan.edu/

- **Independent Christian** comprehensive, founded 1866
- **Suburban** 235-acre campus
- **Endowment** $45.3 million
- **Coed** 886 undergraduate students, 87% full-time, 53% women, 47% men
- **Moderately difficult** entrance level, 99% of applicants were admitted

UNDERGRAD STUDENTS

767 full-time, 119 part-time. Students come from 27 states and territories; 28 other countries; 34% are from out of state; 4% Black or African American, non-Hispanic/Latino; 4% Hispanic/Latino; 1% Asian, non-Hispanic/Latino; 0.1% Native Hawaiian or other Pacific Islander, non-Hispanic/Latino; 2% Two or more races, non-Hispanic/Latino; 0.3% Race/ethnicity unknown; 7% international; 7% transferred in; 77% live on campus.

Freshmen:

Admission: 548 applied, 542 admitted, 202 enrolled. ***Average high school GPA:*** 3.8. ***Test scores:*** SAT evidence-based reading and writing scores over 500: 92%; SAT math scores over 500: 88%; ACT scores over 18: 98%; SAT evidence-based reading and writing scores over 600: 40%; SAT math scores over 600: 48%; ACT scores over 24: 63%; SAT evidence-based reading and writing scores over 700: 9%; SAT math scores over 700: 10%; ACT scores over 30: 16%.

Retention: 74% of full-time freshmen returned.

FACULTY

Total: 178, 53% full-time, 55% with terminal degrees.

Student/faculty ratio: 9:1.

ACADEMICS

Calendar: semesters. *Degrees:* certificates, bachelor's, master's, doctoral, and postbachelor's certificates.

Special study options: academic remediation for entering students, adult/continuing education programs, advanced placement credit, cooperative education, distance learning, double majors, honors programs, independent study, internships, off-campus study, part-time degree program, student-designed majors, study abroad, summer session for credit. ***ROTC:*** Army (c).

Unusual degree programs: 3-2 pharmacy with East Tennessee State University.

Computers: 102 computers/terminals and 690 ports are available on campus for general student use. Students can access the following: campus intranet, computer help desk, free student e-mail accounts, online (class) grades, online (class) registration, online (class) schedules. Campuswide network is available. 100% of college-owned or -operated housing units are wired for high-speed Internet access. Wireless service is available via classrooms, computer centers, computer labs, dorm rooms, learning centers, libraries, student centers.

Library: P. H. Welshimer Memorial Library plus 1 other. *Books:* 173,100 (physical), 284,410 (digital/electronic); *Serial titles:* 610 (physical), 36,590 (digital/electronic); *Databases:* 96. Weekly public service hours: 89; students can reserve study rooms.

STUDENT LIFE

Housing options: on-campus residence required through senior year; men-only, women-only. Campus housing is university owned. Freshman campus housing is guaranteed.

Activities and organizations: drama/theater group, student-run newspaper, radio and television station, choral group, Student Government Association, Vespers-worship team, LINC-service organization, Campus Activities Board, Club Ultimate-frisbee.

Athletics Member NAIA. ***Intercollegiate sports:*** baseball M(s), basketball M(s)/W(s), cheerleading W(s)(c), cross-country running M(s)/W(s), golf M(s)/W(s), soccer M(s)/W(s), softball W(s), swimming and diving M(s)/W(s), tennis M(s)/W(s), track and field M(s)/W(s), triathlon M(s)(c)/W(s)(c), volleyball M(s)(c)/W(s). ***Intramural sports:*** basketball M/W, football M/W, softball M/W, table tennis M/W, ultimate Frisbee M(c)/W(c), volleyball M/W.

Campus security: 24-hour emergency response devices, student patrols, late-night transport/escort service, controlled dormitory access.

Student services: health clinic, personal/psychological counseling.

COSTS & FINANCIAL AID

Costs (2020–21) ***One-time required fee:*** $75. ***Comprehensive fee:*** $43,000 includes full-time tuition ($34,150), mandatory fees ($1450), and room and board ($7400). Full-time tuition and fees vary according to course load and program. Part-time tuition: $950 per semester hour. Part-time tuition and fees vary according to course load and program. ***Required fees:*** $950 per semester hour part-time, $375 per term part-time. ***College room only:*** $3650. Room and board charges vary according to housing facility. ***Payment plan:*** installment. ***Waivers:*** minority students and employees or children of employees.

Financial Aid Of all full-time matriculated undergraduates who enrolled in 2019, 682 applied for aid, 588 were judged to have need, 188 had their need fully met. 133 Federal Work-Study jobs (averaging $1200). 142 state and other part-time jobs (averaging $1485). In 2019, 147 non-need-based awards were made. ***Average percent of need met:*** 80. ***Average financial aid package:*** $25,811. ***Average need-based loan:*** $4428. ***Average need-based gift aid:*** $22,804. ***Average non-need-based aid:*** $13,614. ***Average indebtedness upon graduation:*** $28,864.

APPLYING

Standardized Tests *Required:* SAT or ACT (for admission).

Options: electronic application, deferred entrance.

Application fee: $30.

Required: essay or personal statement, high school transcript, minimum 2.0 GPA, 2 letters of recommendation. ***Required for some:*** interview. ***Recommended:*** minimum 3.0 GPA.

Application deadlines: 8/28 (freshmen), rolling (transfers).

Notification: continuous (freshmen), continuous (transfers).

CONTACT

Ms. Kristin Wright, Director of Admissions, Milligan College, PO Box 210, Milligan College, TN 37682. *Phone:* 423-461-8730. *Toll-free phone:* 800-262-8337. *Fax:* 423-461-8982. *E-mail:* admissions@milligan.edu.

National College

Bristol, Tennessee

http://www.national-college.edu/

CONTACT

National College, 1328 Highway 11 West, Bristol, TN 37620. *Phone:* 423-878-4440. *Toll-free phone:* 888-9-JOBREADY.

Nossi College of Art

Nashville, Tennessee

http://www.nossi.edu/

- **Proprietary** 4-year, founded 1973
- **Urban** 10-acre campus with easy access to Nashville
- **Coed** 296 undergraduate students, 100% full-time, 59% women, 41% men

UNDERGRAD STUDENTS

296 full-time. Students come from 11 states and territories; 52% are from out of state; 25% Black or African American, non-Hispanic/Latino; 6% Hispanic/Latino; 2% Asian, non-Hispanic/Latino; 0.7% Native Hawaiian or other Pacific Islander, non-Hispanic/Latino; 0.7% American Indian or Alaska Native, non-Hispanic/Latino; 0.7% Two or more races, non-Hispanic/Latino; 0.3% Race/ethnicity unknown; 9% transferred in.

Freshmen:

Admission: 54 enrolled.

Retention: 89% of full-time freshmen returned.

FACULTY
Total: 40, 10% full-time.
Student/faculty ratio: 10:1.

ACADEMICS
Calendar: semesters. *Degrees:* associate and bachelor's.
Special study options: independent study, internships, off-campus study, part-time degree program.
Computers: 22 computers/terminals are available on campus for general student use. Students can access the following: campus intranet, free student e-mail accounts, online (class) grades, online (class) schedules. Wireless service is available via entire campus.
Library: Learning Resource Center.

STUDENT LIFE
Housing options: college housing not available.
Activities and organizations: Kappa Pi, CMA.EDU, Fashion Alliance, Colors Club, national fraternities, national sororities.
Campus security: gated entrance, ID badges for building access, doors are locked at all times.
Student services: personal/psychological counseling.

COSTS
Costs (2020–21) ***Tuition:*** $18,900 full-time. Full-time tuition and fees vary according to degree level. Part-time tuition and fees vary according to degree level. No tuition increase for student's term of enrollment. ***Payment plan:*** installment.

APPLYING
Standardized Tests *Required for some:* ACT (for admission).
Options: electronic application, early admission.
Application fee: $150.
Required: essay or personal statement, high school transcript, interview, portfolio of work.
Notification: continuous (freshmen).

CONTACT
Ms. Mitzi Hatfield, Admissions Director, Nossi College of Art, 590 Cheron Road, Madison, TN 37115. *Phone:* 615-514-2787 (ARTS). *Toll-free phone:* 888-986-ARTS. *Fax:* 615-514-2788. *E-mail:* admissions@nossi.edu.

O'More School of Design at Belmont University

Nashville, Tennessee

http://www.omorecollege.edu/

- **Independent** 4-year, founded 1970
- **Small-town** 7-acre campus with easy access to Nashville
- **Coed**
- **Moderately difficult** entrance level

FACULTY
Student/faculty ratio: 13:1.

ACADEMICS
Calendar: semesters. *Degree:* bachelor's.
Library: McAfee Library. *Books:* 2,242 (physical); *Databases:* 30. Weekly public service hours: 40.

STUDENT LIFE
Housing options: coed, men-only, women-only.
Activities and organizations: Student Activities Council, Magnolia Social, O'More Fashion Association, LeP (Interior Design Association), Graphic Designers Guild.
Campus security: on-campus security/contracted security until 10pm M-F, 24-hour studio key access.

COSTS & FINANCIAL AID
Costs (2019–20) ***Comprehensive fee:*** $48,170 includes full-time tuition ($34,000), mandatory fees ($1650), and room and board ($12,520). Full-time tuition and fees vary according to course load. ***College room only:*** $6860.
Financial Aid Of all full-time matriculated undergraduates who enrolled in 2015, 147 applied for aid, 130 were judged to have need, 18 had their need fully met. 13 Federal Work-Study jobs (averaging $1285). 17 state and other part-time jobs (averaging $2130). In 2015, 34 non-need-based awards were made. ***Average percent of need met:*** 76. ***Average financial aid package:*** $16,617. ***Average need-based loan:*** $4762. ***Average need-based gift aid:*** $13,756. ***Average non-need-based aid:*** $5934. ***Average indebtedness upon graduation:*** $31,773.

APPLYING
Standardized Tests *Required:* SAT or ACT (for admission).
Options: electronic application, early admission, deferred entrance.
Application fee: $50.
Required: high school transcript, interview, minimum 3.0 GPA or ACT score of 20. ***Required for some:*** essay or personal statement.

CONTACT
Tori Bagsby, Admissions Manager, O'More School of Design at Belmont University, 423 South Margin Street, Franklin, TN 37064-2816. *Phone:* 615-794-4254 Ext. 230. *Toll-free phone:* 888-662-1970. *Fax:* 615-790-1662. *E-mail:* tbagsby@omorecollege.edu.

Remington College–Memphis Campus

Memphis, Tennessee

http://www.remingtoncollege.edu/

CONTACT
Randal Hayes, Director of Recruitment, Remington College–Memphis Campus, 2710 Nonconnah Boulevard, Memphis, TN 38132. *Phone:* 901-345-1000. *Toll-free phone:* 800-323-8122. *Fax:* 901-396-8310. *E-mail:* randal.hayes@remingtoncollege.edu.

Rhodes College

Memphis, Tennessee

http://www.rhodes.edu/

- **Independent** comprehensive, founded 1848
- **Urban** 123-acre campus with easy access to Memphis
- **Endowment** $352.2 million
- **Coed** 1,973 undergraduate students, 99% full-time, 58% women, 42% men
- **Very difficult** entrance level, 45% of applicants were admitted

UNDERGRAD STUDENTS
1,945 full-time, 28 part-time. Students come from 46 states and territories; 35 other countries; 71% are from out of state; 10% Black or African American, non-Hispanic/Latino; 7% Hispanic/Latino; 6% Asian, non-Hispanic/Latino; 0.1% Native Hawaiian or other Pacific Islander, non-Hispanic/Latino; 0.2% American Indian or Alaska Native, non-Hispanic/Latino; 5% Two or more races, non-Hispanic/Latino; 0.8% Race/ethnicity unknown; 5% international; 67% live on campus.

Freshmen:
Admission: 5,207 applied, 2,328 admitted, 517 enrolled. ***Average high school GPA:*** 3.7. ***Test scores:*** SAT evidence-based reading and writing scores over 500: 100%; SAT math scores over 500: 99%; ACT scores over 18: 100%; SAT evidence-based reading and writing scores over 600: 88%; SAT math scores over 600: 78%; ACT scores over 24: 96%; SAT evidence-based reading and writing scores over 700: 29%; SAT math scores over 700: 35%; ACT scores over 30: 48%.
Retention: 92% of full-time freshmen returned.

FACULTY
Total: 223, 82% full-time, 94% with terminal degrees.
Student/faculty ratio: 10:1.

ACADEMICS
Calendar: semesters. *Degrees:* bachelor's, master's, and postbachelor's certificates (master's degree in accounting only).
Special study options: advanced placement credit, cooperative education, double majors, honors programs, independent study, internships, off-campus study, part-time degree program, services for LD students, student-designed majors, study abroad, summer session for credit. ***ROTC:*** Army (c), Navy (c), Air Force (c).

Unusual degree programs: 3-2 engineering with Washington University in St. Louis, Christian Brothers University, University of Memphis, The University of Tennessee.

Computers: 1,000 computers/terminals are available on campus for general student use. Students can access the following: campus intranet, computer help desk, free student e-mail accounts, online (class) grades, online (class) registration, online (class) schedules. Campuswide network is available. 100% of college-owned or -operated housing units are wired for high-speed Internet access. Wireless service is available via entire campus.

Library: Paul Barret, Jr. Library. *Books:* 221,803 (physical), 351,899 (digital/electronic); *Serial titles:* 16,497 (physical), 92,422 (digital/electronic); *Databases:* 296. Weekly public service hours: 113.

STUDENT LIFE

Housing options: on-campus residence required through sophomore year; coed, men-only, women-only. Campus housing is university owned. Freshman campus housing is guaranteed.

Activities and organizations: drama/theater group, student-run newspaper, radio and television station, choral group, Rhodes Outdoors Club, South Asian Culture and Advocacy, Rhodes College Crew Team, Gender and Sexuality Alliance, Culture of Consent, national fraternities, national sororities.

Athletics Member NCAA. All Division III except golf (Division II). ***Intercollegiate sports:*** badminton M(c)/W(c), baseball M, basketball M/W, crew M(c)/W(c), cross-country running M/W, equestrian sports M(c)/W(c), fencing M(c)/W(c), field hockey W, football M, golf M/W, ice hockey M(c), lacrosse M/W, rugby M(c), soccer M/W, softball W, swimming and diving M/W, tennis M/W, track and field M/W, ultimate Frisbee M(c)/W(c), volleyball W, wrestling M(c). ***Intramural sports:*** basketball M/W, racquetball M/W, soccer M/W, squash M(c), volleyball M/W.

Campus security: 24-hour emergency response devices and patrols, student patrols, late-night transport/escort service.

Student services: health clinic, personal/psychological counseling, women's center.

COSTS & FINANCIAL AID

Costs (2020–21) ***Tuition:*** Part-time tuition and fees vary according to course load. ***Required fees:*** $310 full-time. ***Room and board:*** $11,631. Room and board charges vary according to board plan. ***Waivers:*** employees or children of employees.

Financial Aid Of all full-time matriculated undergraduates who enrolled in 2018, 1,325 applied for aid, 1,011 were judged to have need, 583 had their need fully met. In 2018, 826 non-need-based awards were made. ***Average percent of need met:*** 91. ***Average financial aid package:*** $42,180. ***Average need-based loan:*** $4622. ***Average need-based gift aid:*** $34,229. ***Average non-need-based aid:*** $27,136. ***Average indebtedness upon graduation:*** $26,155.

APPLYING

Options: electronic application, early admission, early decision, early action, deferred entrance.

Required: essay or personal statement, high school transcript. ***Recommended:*** letters of recommendation, interview.

Application deadlines: 1/15 (freshmen), 5/1 (transfers), 11/15 (early action).

Early decision deadline: 11/1 (for plan 1), 1/15 (for plan 2).

Notification: 4/1 (freshmen), 5/15 (transfers), 12/1 (early decision plan 1), 2/1 (early decision plan 2), 1/15 (early action).

CONTACT

Mr. Carey Thompson, Vice President of Enrollment and Communications, Dean of Admissions, Rhodes College, 2000 N. Parkway, Memphis, TN 38112. *Phone:* 901-843-3700. *Toll-free phone:* 800-844-5969. *Fax:* 901-843-3631. *E-mail:* adminfo@rhodes.edu.

South College

Knoxville, Tennessee

http://www.southcollegetn.edu/

CONTACT

Mr. Walter Hosea, Director of Admissions, South College, 720 North Fifth Avenue, Knoxville, TN 37917. *Phone:* 865-524-3043 Ext. 1825. *E-mail:* whosea@southcollegetn.edu.

Southern Adventist University

Collegedale, Tennessee

http://www.southern.edu/

CONTACT

Jennifer Landivar, Applications Manager, Southern Adventist University, PO Box 370, Collegedale, TN 37315-0370. *Phone:* 423-236-2655. *Toll-free phone:* 800-768-8437. *Fax:* 423-236-1835. *E-mail:* jlandivar@southern.edu.

Strayer University–Knoxville Campus

Knoxville, Tennessee

http://www.strayer.edu/tennessee/knoxville/

CONTACT

Strayer University–Knoxville Campus, 10118 Parkside Drive, Suite 200, Knoxville, TN 37922. *Toll-free phone:* 888-311-0355.

Strayer University–Nashville Campus

Nashville, Tennessee

http://www.strayer.edu/tennessee/nashville/

CONTACT

Strayer University–Nashville Campus, 1809 Dabbs Avenue, Nashville, TN 37210. *Toll-free phone:* 888-311-0355.

Strayer University–Shelby Campus

Memphis, Tennessee

http://www.strayer.edu/tennessee/shelby/

CONTACT

Strayer University–Shelby Campus, 7275 Appling Farms Parkway, Memphis, TN 38133. *Toll-free phone:* 888-311-0355.

Strayer University–Thousand Oaks Campus

Memphis, Tennessee

http://www.strayer.edu/tennessee/thousand-oaks/

CONTACT

Strayer University–Thousand Oaks Campus, 2620 Thousand Oaks Boulevard, Suite 1100, Memphis, TN 38118. *Toll-free phone:* 888-311-0355.

Tennessee State University

Nashville, Tennessee

http://www.tnstate.edu/

CONTACT

Dr. John Cade, Associate Vice President/Interim Vice President, Tennessee State University, 3500 John A. Merritt Boulevard, Nashville, TN 37209. *Phone:* 615-963-5101. *E-mail:* jcade@tnstate.edu.

Tennessee Technological University

Cookeville, Tennessee

http://www.tntech.edu/

- **State-supported** university, founded 1915, part of Tennessee Board of Regents
- **Small-town** campus
- **Endowment** $65.9 million
- **Coed**
- **Moderately difficult** entrance level

FACULTY

Student/faculty ratio: 18:1.

ACADEMICS

Calendar: semesters. *Degrees:* bachelor's, master's, doctoral, post-master's, and postbachelor's certificates.
Library: Angelo and Jennette Volpe Library and Media Center. *Books:* 235,249 (physical), 267,168 (digital/electronic); *Serial titles:* 120,118 (physical); *Databases:* 193.

STUDENT LIFE

Housing options: on-campus residence required for freshman year, coed, men-only, women-only, special housing for students with disabilities. Campus housing is university owned. Freshman campus housing is guaranteed.

Activities and organizations: drama/theater group, student-run newspaper, choral group, marching band, Baptist Collegiate Center, Fellowship of Christian Athletes, University Christian Student Center, Residence Hall Association, national fraternities, national sororities.

Athletics Member NCAA. All Division I except football (Division I-AA).

Campus security: 24-hour emergency response devices and patrols, late-night transport/escort service, controlled dormitory access, student safety organization, lighted pathways.

Student services: health clinic, personal/psychological counseling, women's center, veterans affairs office.

FINANCIAL AID

Financial Aid Of all full-time matriculated undergraduates who enrolled in 2016, 7,301 applied for aid, 5,815 were judged to have need, 538 had their need fully met. 456 Federal Work-Study jobs (averaging $963). In 2016, 1620 non-need-based awards were made. ***Average percent of need met:*** 60. ***Average financial aid package:*** $10,151. ***Average need-based loan:*** $4029. ***Average need-based gift aid:*** $5694. ***Average non-need-based aid:*** $9264. ***Average indebtedness upon graduation:*** $22,018.

APPLYING

Standardized Tests *Required:* SAT or ACT (for admission). *Recommended:* ACT (for admission).

Options: electronic application, early admission, deferred entrance.

Application fee: $25.

Required: high school transcript, minimum 2.5 GPA. ***Recommended:*** interview.

CONTACT

Tennessee Technological University, North Dixie Avenue, Cookeville, TN 38505. *Toll-free phone:* 800-255-8881.

Tennessee Wesleyan University

Athens, Tennessee

http://www.tnwesleyan.edu/

- **Independent United Methodist** comprehensive, founded 1857
- **Small-town** 40-acre campus with easy access to Knoxville, Chattanooga
- **Endowment** $9.4 million
- **Coed** 1,067 undergraduate students, 91% full-time, 62% women, 38% men
- **Minimally difficult** entrance level, 65% of applicants were admitted

UNDERGRAD STUDENTS

969 full-time, 98 part-time. 14% are from out of state; 11% Black or African American, non-Hispanic/Latino; 5% Hispanic/Latino; 0.8% Asian, non-Hispanic/Latino; 0.1% Native Hawaiian or other Pacific Islander, non-Hispanic/Latino; 0.2% American Indian or Alaska Native, non-Hispanic/Latino; 3% Two or more races, non-Hispanic/Latino; 4% Race/ethnicity unknown; 6% international; 22% transferred in; 36% live on campus.

Freshmen:
Admission: 833 applied, 539 admitted, 217 enrolled. ***Average high school GPA:*** 3.4. ***Test scores:*** SAT evidence-based reading and writing scores over 500: 39%; SAT math scores over 500: 61%; ACT scores over 18: 89%; SAT evidence-based reading and writing scores over 600: 12%; SAT math scores over 600: 12%; ACT scores over 24: 34%; SAT math scores over 700: 6%; ACT scores over 30: 7%.

Retention: 70% of full-time freshmen returned.

FACULTY

Total: 138, 48% full-time, 49% with terminal degrees.

Student/faculty ratio: 12:1.

ACADEMICS

Calendar: semesters. *Degrees:* bachelor's and master's (profile includes information for both the main and branch campuses).

Special study options: academic remediation for entering students, accelerated degree program, adult/continuing education programs, advanced placement credit, distance learning, double majors, honors programs, independent study, internships, off-campus study, part-time degree program, services for LD students, student-designed majors, study abroad, summer session for credit. ***ROTC:*** Army (c), Navy (c), Air Force (c).

Computers: 205 computers/terminals and 350 ports are available on campus for general student use. Students can access the following: campus intranet, computer help desk, free student e-mail accounts, online (class) grades, online (class) registration, online (class) schedules. Campuswide network is available. 100% of college-owned or -operated housing units are wired for high-speed Internet access. Wireless service is available via entire campus.
Library: Merner-Pfeiffer Library plus 1 other. *Books:* 52,465 (physical), 356,697 (digital/electronic); *Serial titles:* 82 (physical); *Databases:* 76. Weekly public service hours: 69.

STUDENT LIFE

Housing options: coed, men-only, women-only. Campus housing is university owned. Freshman campus housing is guaranteed.

Activities and organizations: drama/theater group, student-run newspaper, choral group, Student Government Association, national sororities.

Athletics Member NAIA. ***Intercollegiate sports:*** baseball M(s), basketball M(s)/W(s), bowling M(s)/W(s), cheerleading M(s)/W(s), cross-country running M(s)/W(s), golf M(s)/W(s), lacrosse M(s)/W(s), soccer M(s)/W(s), softball W(s), tennis M(s)/W(s), track and field M(s)/W(s), volleyball W(s).

Campus security: 24-hour patrols, late-night transport/escort service, controlled dormitory access, night patrols by trained security personnel.

Student services: health clinic, personal/psychological counseling, veterans affairs office.

COSTS & FINANCIAL AID

Costs (2020–21) ***Comprehensive fee:*** $33,200 includes full-time tuition ($23,900), mandatory fees ($1250), and room and board ($8050). Full-time tuition and fees vary according to program. Part-time tuition: $590 per credit hour. Part-time tuition and fees vary according to program. ***College room only:*** $2230. Room and board charges vary according to board plan and housing facility. ***Payment plans:*** installment, deferred payment. ***Waivers:*** employees or children of employees.

Financial Aid Of all full-time matriculated undergraduates who enrolled in 2019, 847 applied for aid, 778 were judged to have need, 326 had their need fully met. In 2019, 48 non-need-based awards were made. ***Average percent of need met:*** 72. ***Average financial aid package:*** $21,445. ***Average need-based loan:*** $4106. ***Average need-based gift aid:*** $18,790. ***Average non-need-based aid:*** $12,265. ***Average indebtedness upon graduation:*** $24,338.

APPLYING

Standardized Tests *Required:* SAT or ACT (for admission).

Options: electronic application, deferred entrance.

Required: high school transcript, minimum 2.3 GPA, 1 letter of recommendation. ***Required for some:*** essay or personal statement, interview. ***Recommended:*** essay or personal statement.

Application deadlines: rolling (freshmen), rolling (transfers).

Notification: continuous (freshmen), continuous (transfers).

CONTACT
Ms. Joanne Landers, Vice President for Admissions, Tennessee Wesleyan University, 204 East College Street, Athens, TN 37303. *Phone:* 423-746-7504. *Toll-free phone:* 800-PICK-TWU. *Fax:* 423-745-9335. *E-mail:* admissions@twcnet.edu.

Trevecca Nazarene University

Nashville, Tennessee

http://www.trevecca.edu/

- **Independent Nazarene** comprehensive, founded 1901
- **Urban** 80-acre campus with easy access to Nashville, TN
- **Endowment** $32.2 million
- **Coed** 2,390 undergraduate students, 74% full-time, 61% women, 39% men
- **Moderately difficult** entrance level, 62% of applicants were admitted

UNDERGRAD STUDENTS
1,768 full-time, 622 part-time. Students come from 48 states and territories; 28 other countries; 40% are from out of state; 12% Black or African American, non-Hispanic/Latino; 10% Hispanic/Latino; 1% Asian, non-Hispanic/Latino; 0.4% American Indian or Alaska Native, non-Hispanic/Latino; 3% Two or more races, non-Hispanic/Latino; 3% Race/ethnicity unknown; 10% international; 4% transferred in; 61% live on campus.

Freshmen:
Admission: 1,662 applied, 1,036 admitted, 392 enrolled. ***Average high school GPA:*** 3.5. ***Test scores:*** SAT evidence-based reading and writing scores over 500: 89%; SAT math scores over 500: 78%; ACT scores over 18: 96%; SAT evidence-based reading and writing scores over 600: 43%; SAT math scores over 600: 32%; ACT scores over 24: 40%; SAT evidence-based reading and writing scores over 700: 7%; SAT math scores over 700: 12%; ACT scores over 30: 8%.

Retention: 75% of full-time freshmen returned.

FACULTY
Total: 287, 38% full-time, 62% with terminal degrees.

Student/faculty ratio: 24:1.

ACADEMICS
Calendar: semesters. *Degrees:* certificates, associate, bachelor's, master's, doctoral, and post-master's certificates.

Special study options: academic remediation for entering students, adult/continuing education programs, advanced placement credit, distance learning, double majors, internships, services for LD students, study abroad, summer session for credit. ***ROTC:*** Army (c).

Computers: 200 computers/terminals and 1,460 ports are available on campus for general student use. Students can access the following: campus intranet, computer help desk, free student e-mail accounts, online (class) grades, online (class) registration, online (class) schedules, Non-traditional and graduate students are registered through Academic Records. Campuswide network is available. 100% of college-owned or -operated housing units are wired for high-speed Internet access. Wireless service is available via entire campus.

Library: Waggoner Library. *Books:* 86,173 (physical), 54,818 (digital/electronic); *Serial titles:* 381 (physical), 73,116 (digital/electronic); *Databases:* 58. Weekly public service hours: 91; students can reserve study rooms.

STUDENT LIFE
Housing options: on-campus residence required through senior year; men-only, women-only. Campus housing is university owned.

Activities and organizations: drama/theater group, student-run newspaper, choral group, marching band.

Athletics Member NCAA. All Division II except golf (Division I). ***Intercollegiate sports:*** baseball M(s), basketball M(s)/W(s), cross-country running M(s)/W(s), golf M(s)/W(s), soccer M(s)/W(s), softball W(s), track and field M(s)/W(s), volleyball W(s). ***Intramural sports:*** basketball M/W, football M/W, soccer M/W, softball M/W, tennis M/W, ultimate Frisbee M/W, volleyball M/W.

Campus security: 24-hour patrols, late-night transport/escort service, weather alert warning system (phone, email, siren).

Student services: health clinic, personal/psychological counseling.

COSTS & FINANCIAL AID
Costs (2020–21) ***Comprehensive fee:*** $35,998 includes full-time tuition ($25,998), mandatory fees ($900), and room and board ($9100). Full-time tuition and fees vary according to degree level and program. Part-time tuition: $1005 per credit hour. Part-time tuition and fees vary according to course load, degree level, and program. ***College room only:*** $4550. Room and board charges vary according to board plan. ***Payment plan:*** installment.

Financial Aid ***Average indebtedness upon graduation:*** $24,895.

APPLYING
Standardized Tests *Required:* SAT or ACT (for admission).

Options: electronic application, early admission, deferred entrance.

Required: high school transcript, minimum 2.5 GPA, minimum ACT composite score of 18, SAT Evidence-Based Reading and Writing and Math score of 940, medical history and immunization records.

Notification: continuous (freshmen), continuous (transfers).

CONTACT
Ms. Melinda Miller, Director of Undergraduate Admissions, Trevecca Nazarene University, 333 Murfreesboro Road, Nashville, TN 37210. *Phone:* 615-248-1320. *Toll-free phone:* 888-210-4TNU. *Fax:* 615-248-7406. *E-mail:* admissions_und@trevecca.edu.

Tusculum University

Greeneville, Tennessee

http://www.tusculum.edu/

- **Independent Presbyterian** comprehensive, founded 1794
- **Small-town** 140-acre campus
- **Endowment** $21.1 million
- **Coed**
- **Moderately difficult** entrance level

FACULTY
Student/faculty ratio: 17:1.

ACADEMICS
Calendar: semesters. *Degrees:* associate, bachelor's, and master's.

Library: Thomas J. Garland Library plus 2 others. Students can reserve study rooms.

STUDENT LIFE
Housing options: coed, men-only, women-only, special housing for students with disabilities. Campus housing is university owned. Freshman campus housing is guaranteed.

Activities and organizations: drama/theater group, student-run newspaper, radio and television station, choral group, marching band.

Athletics Member NCAA. All Division II.

Campus security: 24-hour emergency response devices and patrols, student patrols, late-night transport/escort service, controlled dormitory access, trained security personnel on duty.

Student services: health clinic, personal/psychological counseling, women's center.

FINANCIAL AID
Financial Aid Of all full-time matriculated undergraduates who enrolled in 2016, 1,286 applied for aid, 1,196 were judged to have need, 103 had their need fully met. 293 Federal Work-Study jobs (averaging $963). In 2016, 72 non-need-based awards were made. ***Average percent of need met:*** 77. ***Average financial aid package:*** $17,079. ***Average need-based loan:*** $4098. ***Average need-based gift aid:*** $9629. ***Average non-need-based aid:*** $8329. ***Average indebtedness upon graduation:*** $33,916.

APPLYING
Standardized Tests *Required:* SAT or ACT (for admission).

Options: electronic application, early admission, early decision, deferred entrance.

CONTACT
Tusculum University, PO Box 50627, Greeneville, TN 37743-9997. *Phone:* 423-636-7300 Ext. 5374. *Toll-free phone:* 800-729-0256. *E-mail:* admissions@tusculum.edu.

Union University

Jackson, Tennessee

http://www.uu.edu/

- **Independent Southern Baptist** comprehensive, founded 1823
- **Suburban** 360-acre campus with easy access to Memphis
- **Endowment** $39.1 million
- **Coed** 2,164 undergraduate students, 83% full-time, 66% women, 34% men
- **Moderately difficult** entrance level, 53% of applicants were admitted

UNDERGRAD STUDENTS
1,796 full-time, 368 part-time. 32% are from out of state; 17% Black or African American, non-Hispanic/Latino; 2% Hispanic/Latino; 2% Asian, non-Hispanic/Latino; 0.1% Native Hawaiian or other Pacific Islander, non-Hispanic/Latino; 1% American Indian or Alaska Native, non-Hispanic/Latino; 2% Race/ethnicity unknown; 2% international; 3% transferred in; 77% live on campus.

Freshmen:
Admission: 2,866 applied, 1,511 admitted, 326 enrolled. ***Average high school GPA:*** 3.8. ***Test scores:*** SAT evidence-based reading and writing scores over 500: 94%; SAT math scores over 500: 87%; ACT scores over 18: 99%; SAT evidence-based reading and writing scores over 600: 51%; SAT math scores over 600: 38%; ACT scores over 24: 64%; SAT evidence-based reading and writing scores over 700: 12%; SAT math scores over 700: 15%; ACT scores over 30: 26%.

Retention: 84% of full-time freshmen returned.

FACULTY
Total: 223, 98% full-time, 82% with terminal degrees.

Student/faculty ratio: 9:1.

ACADEMICS
Calendar: 4-1-4. *Degrees:* associate, bachelor's, master's, and doctoral.

Special study options: academic remediation for entering students, accelerated degree program, adult/continuing education programs, advanced placement credit, distance learning, double majors, English as a second language, external degree program, honors programs, independent study, internships, off-campus study, part-time degree program, services for LD students, study abroad, summer session for credit.

Unusual degree programs: 3-2 pharmacy.

Computers: 202 computers/terminals are available on campus for general student use. Students can access the following: campus intranet, computer help desk, free student e-mail accounts, online (class) grades, online (class) registration, online (class) schedules. Campuswide network is available. 100% of college-owned or -operated housing units are wired for high-speed Internet access. Wireless service is available via entire campus.

Library: The Logos Library plus 1 other. *Books:* 136,991 (physical), 265,352 (digital/electronic); *Serial titles:* 2,362 (physical), 33,609 (digital/electronic); *Databases:* 135. Weekly public service hours: 93; students can reserve study rooms.

STUDENT LIFE
Housing options: on-campus residence required through junior year; men-only, women-only, special housing for students with disabilities. Campus housing is university owned. Freshman applicants given priority for college housing.

Activities and organizations: drama/theater group, student-run newspaper, choral group, Campus Ministries, Student Government Association, Student Activities Council, Students in Free Enterprise (SIFE), national fraternities, national sororities.

Athletics Member NCAA. All Division II. ***Intercollegiate sports:*** baseball M(s), basketball M(s)/W(s), cheerleading M/W(s), cross-country running M(s)/W(s), golf M(s)/W(s), soccer M(s)/W(s), softball W(s), ultimate Frisbee M(c)/W(c), volleyball W(s). ***Intramural sports:*** basketball M/W, cross-country running M/W, football M/W, golf M/W, racquetball M/W, sand volleyball M/W, soccer M/W, softball M/W, swimming and diving M/W, table tennis M/W, ultimate Frisbee M/W, volleyball M/W, weight lifting M/W.

Campus security: 24-hour emergency response devices and patrols, student patrols, late-night transport/escort service.

Student services: health clinic, personal/psychological counseling.

COSTS & FINANCIAL AID
Costs (2020–21) ***Comprehensive fee:*** $45,660 includes full-time tuition ($33,480), mandatory fees ($1300), and room and board ($10,880). Part-time tuition: $1075 per credit hour. ***College room only:*** $8050.

Financial Aid Of all full-time matriculated undergraduates who enrolled in 2019, 1,526 applied for aid, 1,339 were judged to have need, 224 had their need fully met. In 2019, 167 non-need-based awards were made. ***Average percent of need met:*** 86. ***Average financial aid package:*** $24,879. ***Average need-based loan:*** $3922. ***Average need-based gift aid:*** $5830. ***Average non-need-based aid:*** $15,431.

APPLYING
Standardized Tests *Required:* SAT or ACT (for admission).

Options: electronic application, early admission, deferred entrance.

Application fee: $35.

Notification: continuous (freshmen), continuous (transfers).

CONTACT
Mr. Robbie Graves, Director of Enrollment Services, Union University, 1050 Union University Drive, Jackson, TN 38305-3697. *Phone:* 731-661-5590. *Toll-free phone:* 800-33-UNION. *Fax:* 731-661-5589. *E-mail:* rgraves@uu.edu.

University of Memphis

Memphis, Tennessee

http://www.memphis.edu/

- **State-supported** university, founded 1912
- **Urban** 1160-acre campus with easy access to Memphis
- **Endowment** $223.4 million
- **Coed** 17,378 undergraduate students, 69% full-time, 59% women, 41% men
- **Moderately difficult** entrance level, 85% of applicants were admitted

UNDERGRAD STUDENTS
12,066 full-time, 5,312 part-time. Students come from 47 states and territories; 60 other countries; 13% are from out of state; 36% Black or African American, non-Hispanic/Latino; 6% Hispanic/Latino; 4% Asian, non-Hispanic/Latino; 0.1% Native Hawaiian or other Pacific Islander, non-Hispanic/Latino; 0.2% American Indian or Alaska Native, non-Hispanic/Latino; 4% Two or more races, non-Hispanic/Latino; 1% Race/ethnicity unknown; 1% international; 8% transferred in; 17% live on campus.

Freshmen:
Admission: 14,760 applied, 12,513 admitted, 2,683 enrolled. ***Average high school GPA:*** 3.5. ***Test scores:*** SAT evidence-based reading and writing scores over 500: 82%; SAT math scores over 500: 77%; ACT scores over 18: 90%; SAT evidence-based reading and writing scores over 600: 39%; SAT math scores over 600: 30%; ACT scores over 24: 40%; SAT evidence-based reading and writing scores over 700: 7%; SAT math scores over 700: 12%; ACT scores over 30: 8%.

Retention: 78% of full-time freshmen returned.

FACULTY
Total: 1,500, 60% full-time, 51% with terminal degrees.

Student/faculty ratio: 15:1.

ACADEMICS
Calendar: semesters. *Degrees:* bachelor's, master's, doctoral, post-master's, and postbachelor's certificates.

Special study options: accelerated degree program, adult/continuing education programs, advanced placement credit, cooperative education, distance learning, double majors, English as a second language, external degree program, honors programs, independent study, internships, off-campus study, part-time degree program, services for LD students, student-designed majors, study abroad, summer session for credit. ***ROTC:*** Army (b), Navy (b), Air Force (b).

Unusual degree programs: 3-2 business administration; engineering.

Computers: 1,255 computers/terminals and 35 ports are available on campus for general student use. Students can access the following: campus intranet, computer help desk, free student e-mail accounts, online (class) grades, online (class) registration, online (class) schedules. Campuswide network is available. 100% of college-owned or -operated housing units are wired for high-speed Internet access. Wireless service is available via entire campus.
Library: McWherter Library plus 4 others. *Books:* 900,408 (physical), 458,374 (digital/electronic); *Serial titles:* 17,630 (physical), 243,557 (digital/electronic); *Databases:* 398. Weekly public service hours: 91; students can reserve study rooms

STUDENT LIFE
Housing options: coed, men-only, women-only, cooperative, special housing for students with disabilities. Campus housing is university owned.

Activities and organizations: drama/theater group, student-run newspaper, radio station, choral group, marching band, Student Activities Council, Fraternity and Sorority Life, Black Student Association, Student Government Association, Up 'til Dawn- St. Jude Philanthropy, national fraternities, national sororities.

Athletics Member NCAA. All Division I except football (Division I-A). ***Intercollegiate sports:*** baseball M(s), basketball M(s)/W(s), cheerleading M(s)/W(s), cross-country running M(s)/W(s), golf M(s)/W(s), riflery M(s)/W(s), soccer M(s)/W(s), softball W(s), tennis M(s)/W(s), track and field M(s)/W(s), volleyball W(s). ***Intramural sports:*** badminton M/W, basketball M/W, bowling M(c)/W(c), equestrian sports W(c), fencing M(c)/W(c), football M/W, golf M/W, ice hockey M(c), lacrosse M(c), racquetball M/W, rugby M(c), soccer M/W, softball M/W, table tennis M/W, ultimate Frisbee M/W, volleyball M/W, water polo M(c), wrestling M(c).

Campus security: 24-hour emergency response devices and patrols, student patrols, late-night transport/escort service, controlled dormitory access.

Student services: health clinic, personal/psychological counseling, women's center, veterans affairs office.

COSTS & FINANCIAL AID
Costs (2019–20) ***Tuition:*** state resident $8208 full-time, $342 per credit hour part-time; nonresident $15,060 full-time, $502 per credit hour part-time. Full-time tuition and fees vary according to course load, degree level, program, and reciprocity agreements. Part-time tuition and fees vary according to course load, degree level, and program. ***Required fees:*** $1704 full-time, $71 per credit hour part-time. ***Room and board:*** $10,175; room only: $6105. Room and board charges vary according to board plan, housing facility, and location. ***Payment plan:*** installment. ***Waivers:*** senior citizens and employees or children of employees.

Financial Aid Of all full-time matriculated undergraduates who enrolled in 2018, 11,254 applied for aid, 9,366 were judged to have need, 789 had their need fully met. 332 Federal Work-Study jobs (averaging $2625). In 2018, 1526 non-need-based awards were made. ***Average percent of need met:*** 55. ***Average financial aid package:*** $11,767. ***Average need-based loan:*** $4053. ***Average need-based gift aid:*** $6858. ***Average non-need-based aid:*** $6540. ***Average indebtedness upon graduation:*** $30,931.

APPLYING
Standardized Tests *Required:* SAT or ACT (for admission).

Options: electronic application, early admission.

Application fee: $25.

Required: high school transcript. ***Required for some:*** essay or personal statement, minimum 2.0 GPA, 2 letters of recommendation, interview.

Application deadlines: 7/1 (freshmen), 7/1 (out-of-state freshmen), 7/1 (transfers).

Notification: continuous (freshmen), continuous (out-of-state freshmen), continuous (transfers).

CONTACT
Drusilla Welch, Associate Director of Operations for Admissions, University of Memphis, Admissions Operations, 204A Wilder Tower, Memphis, TN 38152. *Phone:* 901-678-3007. *Toll-free phone:* 800-669-2678. *E-mail:* dwelch@memphis.edu.

The University of Tennessee

Knoxville, Tennessee

http://www.utk.edu/

- **State-supported** university, founded 1794, part of University of Tennessee System
- **Urban** 600-acre campus
- **Endowment** $518.9 million
- **Coed** 23,290 undergraduate students, 95% full-time, 51% women, 49% men
- **Moderately difficult** entrance level, 79% of applicants were admitted

UNDERGRAD STUDENTS
22,018 full-time, 1,272 part-time. Students come from 47 states and territories; 55 other countries; 18% are from out of state; 6% Black or African American, non-Hispanic/Latino; 5% Hispanic/Latino; 4% Asian, non-Hispanic/Latino; 0.2% American Indian or Alaska Native, non-Hispanic/Latino; 4% Two or more races, non-Hispanic/Latino; 2% Race/ethnicity unknown; 1% international; 6% transferred in; 34% live on campus.

Freshmen:
Admission: 21,764 applied, 17,160 admitted, 5,254 enrolled. ***Average high school GPA:*** 4.0. ***Test scores:*** SAT evidence-based reading and writing scores over 500: 98%; SAT math scores over 500: 98%; ACT scores over 18: 100%; SAT evidence-based reading and writing scores over 600: 65%; SAT math scores over 600: 58%; ACT scores over 24: 80%; SAT evidence-based reading and writing scores over 700: 12%; SAT math scores over 700: 17%; ACT scores over 30: 30%.

Retention: 87% of full-time freshmen returned.

FACULTY
Total: 1,829, 89% full-time, 83% with terminal degrees.

Student/faculty ratio: 17:1.

ACADEMICS
Calendar: semesters. *Degrees:* bachelor's, master's, doctoral, and postbachelor's certificates.

Special study options: accelerated degree program, advanced placement credit, cooperative education, distance learning, double majors, English as a second language, external degree program, freshman honors college, honors programs, independent study, internships, off-campus study, part-time degree program, services for LD students, student-designed majors, study abroad, summer session for credit. ***ROTC:*** Army (b), Air Force (b).

Computers: 1,045 computers/terminals are available on campus for general student use. Students can access the following: campus intranet, computer help desk, free student e-mail accounts, online (class) grades, online (class) registration, online (class) schedules, Blackboard Course Management System. Campuswide network is available. 100% of college-owned or -operated housing units are wired for high-speed Internet access. Wireless service is available via entire campus.
Library: John C. Hodges Library plus 4 others. *Books:* 1.5 million (physical), 1.1 million (digital/electronic); *Serial titles:* 50,733 (physical), 133,016 (digital/electronic); *Databases:* 736. Weekly public service hours: 160; study areas open 24 hours, 5–7 days a week; students can reserve study rooms.

STUDENT LIFE
Housing options: on-campus residence required for freshman year; coed, men-only, women-only, special housing for students with disabilities. Campus housing is university owned. Freshman campus housing is guaranteed.

Activities and organizations: drama/theater group, student-run newspaper, radio and television station, choral group, marching band, Fraternities/Sororities, Religious organizations, Campus Events Board, Black Cultural Programming Committee, Student Government Association, national fraternities, national sororities.

Athletics Member NCAA. All Division I. ***Intercollegiate sports:*** baseball M(s), basketball M(s)/W(s), crew W(s), cross-country running M/W, football M(s), golf M(s)/W(s), soccer W(s), softball W(s), swimming and diving M(s)/W(s), tennis M(s)/W(s), track and field M(s)/W(s), volleyball W(s). ***Intramural sports:*** badminton M/W, baseball M(c), basketball M/W, bowling M/W, crew M(c)/W(c), cross-country running M(c)/W(c), equestrian sports M(c)/W(c), fencing M(c)/W(c), field hockey M/W, golf M(c)/W(c), gymnastics M(c)/W(c), ice hockey M(c)/W(c), lacrosse

M(c)/W(c), racquetball M/W, rock climbing M(c)/W(c), rowing M(c)/W(c), rugby M(c)/W(c), sailing M(c)/W(c), sand volleyball M/W, skiing (downhill) M(c)/W(c), soccer M/W, softball M/W, swimming and diving M(c)/W(c), table tennis M/W, tennis M/W, triathlon M(c)/W(c), ultimate Frisbee M/W, volleyball M/W, water polo M/W, weight lifting M/W, wrestling M(c)/W(c).

Campus security: 24-hour emergency response devices and patrols, late-night transport/escort service, controlled dormitory access, campus safety educational programs.

Student services: health clinic, personal/psychological counseling, women's center, veterans affairs office.

COSTS & FINANCIAL AID

Costs (2019–20) ***Tuition:*** state resident $11,332 full-time, $378 per credit hour part-time; nonresident $29,522 full-time, $1137 per credit hour part-time. Full-time tuition and fees vary according to course level, location, program, and reciprocity agreements. Part-time tuition and fees vary according to course level, location, program, and reciprocity agreements. ***Required fees:*** $1932 full-time. ***Room and board:*** $11,482. Room and board charges vary according to board plan and housing facility. ***Payment plan:*** installment. ***Waivers:*** senior citizens and employees or children of employees.

Financial Aid Of all full-time matriculated undergraduates who enrolled in 2019, 18,946 applied for aid, 12,028 were judged to have need, 1,682 had their need fully met. 679 Federal Work-Study jobs (averaging $2552). In 2019, 3769 non-need-based awards were made. ***Average percent of need met:*** 57. ***Average financial aid package:*** $13,977. ***Average need-based loan:*** $7016. ***Average need-based gift aid:*** $11,138. ***Average non-need-based aid:*** $6528. ***Average indebtedness upon graduation:*** $27,060.

APPLYING

Standardized Tests *Required:* SAT or ACT (for admission).

Options: electronic application, early action.

Application fee: $50.

Required: essay or personal statement, high school transcript, minimum 2.0 GPA. ***Recommended:*** 1 letter of recommendation.

Application deadlines: 8/20 (freshmen), rolling (out-of-state freshmen), 7/1 (transfers), 11/1 (early action).

Notification: continuous until 9/15 (freshmen), continuous until 9/15 (out-of-state freshmen), continuous (transfers), 12/15 (early action).

CONTACT

Mr. Clayton Alexander, Associate Director, The University of Tennessee, 320 Student Services Building, Knoxville, TN 37996-0230. *Phone:* 865-974-2184. *E-mail:* admissions@utk.edu.

The University of Tennessee at Chattanooga

Chattanooga, Tennessee

http://www.utc.edu/

- **State-supported** comprehensive, founded 1886, part of University of Tennessee System
- **Urban** 425-acre campus
- **Coed** 10,297 undergraduate students, 90% full-time, 56% women, 44% men
- **Moderately difficult** entrance level, 83% of applicants were admitted

UNDERGRAD STUDENTS

9,224 full-time, 1,072 part-time. Students come from 35 states and territories; 34 other countries; 6% are from out of state; 10% Black or African American, non-Hispanic/Latino; 6% Hispanic/Latino; 2% Asian, non-Hispanic/Latino; 0.2% American Indian or Alaska Native, non-Hispanic/Latino; 3% Two or more races, non-Hispanic/Latino; 3% Race/ethnicity unknown; 1% international; 9% transferred in; 35% live on campus.

Freshmen:

Admission: 7,235 applied, 5,990 admitted, 2,310 enrolled. ***Average high school GPA:*** 3.6. ***Test scores:*** SAT evidence-based reading and writing scores over 500: 88%; SAT math scores over 500: 80%; ACT scores over 18: 99%; SAT evidence-based reading and writing scores over 600: 39%; SAT math scores over 600: 29%; ACT scores over 24: 50%; SAT evidence-based reading and writing scores over 700: 6%; SAT math scores over 700: 3%; ACT scores over 30: 9%.

Retention: 71% of full-time freshmen returned.

FACULTY

Total: 717, 67% full-time, 69% with terminal degrees.

Student/faculty ratio: 19:1.

ACADEMICS

Calendar: semesters. *Degrees:* certificates, bachelor's, master's, doctoral, post-master's, and postbachelor's certificates.

Special study options: accelerated degree program, advanced placement credit, cooperative education, distance learning, double majors, English as a second language, freshman honors college, honors programs, independent study, internships, off-campus study, part-time degree program, services for LD students, student-designed majors, study abroad, summer session for credit. ***ROTC:*** Army (b).

Computers: Students can access the following: campus intranet, computer help desk, free student e-mail accounts, online (class) grades, online (class) registration, online (class) schedules. Campuswide network is available. 100% of college-owned or -operated housing units are wired for high-speed Internet access. Wireless service is available via entire campus.

Library: UTC Library plus 1 other. *Books:* 325,387 (physical), 373,007 (digital/electronic); *Databases:* 208. Study areas open 24 hours, 5–7 days a week; students can reserve study rooms.

STUDENT LIFE

Housing options: on-campus residence required for freshman year; coed, special housing for students with disabilities. Campus housing is university owned. Freshman applicants given priority for college housing.

Activities and organizations: drama/theater group, student-run newspaper, choral group, marching band, national fraternities, national sororities.

Athletics Member NCAA. All Division I except football (Division I-AA). ***Intercollegiate sports:*** basketball M(s)/W(s), cross-country running M(s)/W(s), golf M(s)/W(s), soccer W(s), softball W(s), tennis M(s)/W(s), track and field M(s)/W(s), volleyball W(s), wrestling M(s). ***Intramural sports:*** badminton M/W, baseball M(c), basketball M/W, crew M(c)/W(c), cross-country running M/W, fencing M(c)/W(c), golf M/W, racquetball M/W, soccer M/W, swimming and diving M/W, tennis M/W, ultimate Frisbee M(c)/W(c), volleyball W, wrestling M.

Campus security: 24-hour emergency response devices.

Student services: health clinic, personal/psychological counseling, women's center, veterans affairs office.

COSTS & FINANCIAL AID

Costs (2019–20) ***Tuition:*** state resident $7836 full-time, $294 per credit part-time; nonresident $23,954 full-time, $966 per credit part-time. Full-time tuition and fees vary according to degree level and student level. Part-time tuition and fees vary according to degree level. ***Required fees:*** $1820 full-time, $60 per credit part-time, $205 per term part-time. ***Room and board:*** $10,159; room only: $6163. Room and board charges vary according to board plan, housing facility, and location. ***Payment plan:*** installment. ***Waivers:*** senior citizens and employees or children of employees.

Financial Aid Of all full-time matriculated undergraduates who enrolled in 2019, 8,220 applied for aid, 5,616 were judged to have need, 705 had their need fully met. In 2019, 1994 non-need-based awards were made. ***Average percent of need met:*** 63. ***Average financial aid package:*** $10,919. ***Average need-based loan:*** $3571. ***Average need-based gift aid:*** $7907. ***Average non-need-based aid:*** $5904. ***Average indebtedness upon graduation:*** $23,059.

APPLYING

Standardized Tests *Required:* SAT or ACT (for admission).

Options: electronic application, early admission, deferred entrance.

Application fee: $30.

Required: high school transcript, 2.5 GPA with minimum ACT score of 21/SAT of 990 or minimum GPA of 2.85 with minimum ACT score of 18/SAT score of 870.

Application deadlines: 5/1 (freshmen), 7/1 (transfers).

CONTACT
Mr. Jason Lyon, Director of Admissions, The University of Tennessee at Chattanooga, 615 McCallie Avenue, 101 University Center, Department 5105, Chattanooga, TN 37403. *Phone:* 423-425-4662. *Toll-free phone:* 800-882-6627. *Fax:* 423-425-4157. *E-mail:* jason-lyon@utc.edu.

The University of Tennessee at Martin

Martin, Tennessee

http://www.utm.edu/

- **State-supported** comprehensive, founded 1900, part of University of Tennessee System
- **Small-town** 250-acre campus
- **Endowment** $37.1 million
- **Coed** 6,779 undergraduate students, 70% full-time, 61% women, 39% men
- **Moderately difficult** entrance level, 64% of applicants were admitted

UNDERGRAD STUDENTS

4,757 full-time, 2,022 part-time. Students come from 39 states and territories; 21 other countries; 9% are from out of state; 13% Black or African American, non-Hispanic/Latino; 3% Hispanic/Latino; 0.7% Asian, non-Hispanic/Latino; 0.3% American Indian or Alaska Native, non-Hispanic/Latino; 3% Two or more races, non-Hispanic/Latino; 1% international; 7% transferred in; 33% live on campus.

Freshmen:

Admission: 9,158 applied, 5,906 admitted, 1,160 enrolled. ***Average high school GPA:*** 3.6. ***Test scores:*** ACT scores over 18: 99%; ACT scores over 24: 46%; ACT scores over 30: 8%.

Retention: 74% of full-time freshmen returned.

FACULTY

Total: 494, 58% full-time, 50% with terminal degrees.

Student/faculty ratio: 15:1.

ACADEMICS

Calendar: semesters. *Degrees:* bachelor's and master's.

Special study options: accelerated degree program, adult/continuing education programs, advanced placement credit, cooperative education, distance learning, double majors, English as a second language, honors programs, independent study, internships, off-campus study, part-time degree program, services for LD students, student-designed majors, study abroad, summer session for credit. ***ROTC:*** Army (b).

Computers: 1,157 computers/terminals and 2,597 ports are available on campus for general student use. Students can access the following: campus intranet, computer help desk, free student e-mail accounts, online (class) grades, online (class) registration, online (class) schedules, online fee payments, degree progress, financial aid data, housing applications, transcripts. Campuswide network is available. 100% of college-owned or -operated housing units are wired for high-speed Internet access. Wireless service is available via entire campus.

Library: Paul Meek Library. *Books:* 280,270 (physical), 114,346 (digital/electronic); *Serial titles:* 44,595 (physical), 220,785 (digital/electronic); *Databases:* 370. Weekly public service hours: 92; study areas open 24 hours, 5–7 days a week.

STUDENT LIFE

Housing options: on-campus residence required for freshman year; men-only, women-only, special housing for students with disabilities. Campus housing is university owned. Freshman applicants given priority for college housing.

Activities and organizations: drama/theater group, student-run newspaper, radio and television station, choral group, marching band, Student Government Association, Baptist Collegiate Ministry, National Society for Leadership and Success, Phi Eta Sigma, League of Striving Artists, national fraternities, national sororities.

Athletics Member NCAA. All Division I except football (Division I-AA). ***Intercollegiate sports:*** baseball M(s), basketball M(s)/W(s), cheerleading W(s), cross-country running M(s)/W(s), equestrian sports W(s), golf M(s), riflery M(s)/W(s), sand volleyball W(s), soccer W(s), softball W(s), tennis W(s), volleyball W(s). ***Intramural sports:*** basketball M/W, football M/W, golf M/W, racquetball M/W, soccer M/W, softball M/W, table tennis M/W, tennis M/W, ultimate Frisbee M/W, volleyball M/W, water polo M/W.

Campus security: 24-hour emergency response devices and patrols, student patrols, controlled dormitory access.

Student services: health clinic, personal/psychological counseling, women's center, veterans affairs office.

COSTS & FINANCIAL AID

Costs (2019–20) ***Tuition:*** state resident $8214 full-time, $342 per credit hour part-time; nonresident $14,254 full-time, $594 per credit hour part-time. Part-time tuition and fees vary according to course load. ***Required fees:*** $1534 full-time, $64 per credit hour part-time. ***Room and board:*** $6396; room only: $2920. Room and board charges vary according to board plan and housing facility. ***Payment plans:*** installment, deferred payment. ***Waivers:*** senior citizens and employees or children of employees.

Financial Aid Of all full-time matriculated undergraduates who enrolled in 2019, 4,496 applied for aid, 3,547 were judged to have need, 843 had their need fully met. 175 Federal Work-Study jobs (averaging $2376). In 2019, 395 non-need-based awards were made. ***Average percent of need met:*** 45. ***Average financial aid package:*** $11,898. ***Average need-based loan:*** $4144. ***Average need-based gift aid:*** $7010. ***Average non-need-based aid:*** $2022. ***Average indebtedness upon graduation:*** $24,096.

APPLYING

Standardized Tests *Required:* SAT or ACT (for admission).

Options: electronic application, early admission, deferred entrance.

Application fee: $30.

Required: high school transcript, minimum 2.7 GPA.

Application deadlines: rolling (freshmen), rolling (transfers).

Notification: continuous until 8/1 (freshmen), continuous until 8/1 (transfers).

CONTACT

Ms. Destin Tucker, Director of Admission, The University of Tennessee at Martin, 200 Hall-Moody Administration Building, Martin, TN 38238. *Phone:* 731-881-7020. *Toll-free phone:* 800-829-8861. *Fax:* 731-881-7029. *E-mail:* dtucker@utm.edu.

The University of the South

Sewanee, Tennessee

http://www.sewanee.edu/

- **Independent Episcopal** comprehensive, founded 1857
- **Small-town** 13,000-acre campus with easy access to Chattanooga
- **Endowment** $408.8 million
- **Coed** 1,695 undergraduate students, 99% full-time, 51% women, 49% men
- **Very difficult** entrance level, 67% of applicants were admitted

UNDERGRAD STUDENTS

1,671 full-time, 24 part-time. Students come from 44 states and territories; 22 other countries; 79% are from out of state; 4% Black or African American, non-Hispanic/Latino; 5% Hispanic/Latino; 1% Asian, non-Hispanic/Latino; 0.1% American Indian or Alaska Native, non-Hispanic/Latino; 3% Two or more races, non-Hispanic/Latino; 4% international; 0.9% transferred in; 98% live on campus.

Freshmen:

Admission: 3,545 applied, 2,365 admitted, 438 enrolled. ***Test scores:*** SAT evidence-based reading and writing scores over 500: 97%; SAT math scores over 500: 94%; ACT scores over 18: 98%; SAT evidence-based reading and writing scores over 600: 66%; SAT math scores over 600: 63%; ACT scores over 24: 82%; SAT evidence-based reading and writing scores over 700: 16%; SAT math scores over 700: 14%; ACT scores over 30: 34%.

Retention: 88% of full-time freshmen returned.

FACULTY

Total: 232, 75% full-time, 86% with terminal degrees.

Student/faculty ratio: 10:1.

ACADEMICS

Calendar: semesters. *Degrees:* bachelor's, master's, doctoral, post-master's, and postbachelor's certificates.

Special study options: advanced placement credit, double majors, independent study, internships, off-campus study, services for LD students, student-designed majors, study abroad, summer session for credit.

Unusual degree programs: 3-2 engineering with Columbia University, Rensselaer Polytechnic Institute, Vanderbilt University, Washington University in St. Louis.

Computers: 150 computers/terminals and 3,000 ports are available on campus for general student use. Students can access the following: computer help desk, free student e-mail accounts, online (class) grades, online (class) registration, online (class) schedules. Campuswide network is available. 100% of college-owned or -operated housing units are wired for high-speed Internet access. Wireless service is available via entire campus.

Library: Jessie Ball duPont Library. *Books:* 522,116 (physical), 574,014 (digital/electronic); *Serial titles:* 4,136 (physical), 23,827 (digital/electronic); *Databases:* 351. Study areas open 24 hours, 5–7 days a week; students can reserve study rooms.

STUDENT LIFE

Housing options: on-campus residence required through senior year; coed, men-only, women-only. Campus housing is university owned. Freshman campus housing is guaranteed.

Activities and organizations: drama/theater group, student-run newspaper, radio station, choral group, Sewanee Outing Program, Office of Civic Engagement, Organization for Cross Cultural Understanding, Alpha Phi Omega (APO) National Service Fraternity, Black Student Union, national fraternities, national sororities.

Athletics Member NCAA. All Division III. ***Intercollegiate sports:*** baseball M, basketball M/W, cheerleading W, crew M(c)/W(c), cross-country running M/W, equestrian sports M/W, fencing M(c)/W(c), field hockey W, football M, golf M/W, ice hockey M(c)/W(c), lacrosse M/W, rugby M(c)/W(c), soccer M/W, softball W, squash M(c)/W(c), swimming and diving M/W, tennis M/W, track and field M/W, volleyball W. ***Intramural sports:*** basketball M/W, football M/W, soccer M/W, table tennis M/W.

Campus security: 24-hour emergency response devices and patrols, late-night transport/escort service, controlled dormitory access, LiveSafe App.

Student services: health clinic, personal/psychological counseling, women's center.

COSTS & FINANCIAL AID

Costs (2020–21) ***Comprehensive fee:*** $61,680 includes full-time tuition ($47,708), mandatory fees ($272), and room and board ($13,700). Part-time tuition: $1490 per credit hour. ***College room only:*** $7100. ***Payment plan:*** installment. ***Waivers:*** employees or children of employees.

Financial Aid Of all full-time matriculated undergraduates who enrolled in 2019, 997 applied for aid, 739 were judged to have need, 241 had their need fully met. 405 Federal Work-Study jobs (averaging $1629). 160 state and other part-time jobs (averaging $3242). In 2019, 810 non-need-based awards were made. ***Average percent of need met:*** 83. ***Average financial aid package:*** $37,115. ***Average need-based loan:*** $4545. ***Average need-based gift aid:*** $30,501. ***Average non-need-based aid:*** $18,238. ***Average indebtedness upon graduation:*** $31,737.

APPLYING

Standardized Tests *Required for some:* Duolingo English Test, IELTS, PTE Academic, or TOEFL for international students. *Recommended:* SAT or ACT (for admission).

Options: electronic application, early admission, early decision, early action, deferred entrance.

Required: essay or personal statement, high school transcript, 2 letters of recommendation. ***Recommended:*** interview.

Application deadlines: 2/1 (freshmen), 4/1 (transfers), 12/1 (early action).

Early decision deadline: 11/15 (for plan 1), 1/15 (for plan 2).

Notification: continuous (transfers), 12/15 (early decision plan 1), 2/15 (early decision plan 2).

CONTACT

Ms. Lisa Burns, Associate Dean of Admission, The University of the South, 735 University Avenue, Sewanee, TN 37383. *Phone:* 931-598-1238. *Toll-free phone:* 800-522-2234. *Fax:* 931-598-3248. *E-mail:* admiss@sewanee.edu.

Vanderbilt University

Nashville, Tennessee

http://www.vanderbilt.edu/

- **Independent** university, founded 1873
- **Urban** 330-acre campus with easy access to Nashville, TN
- **Endowment** $3.8 billion
- **Coed** 6,886 undergraduate students, 99% full-time, 52% women, 48% men
- **Most difficult** entrance level, 9% of applicants were admitted

UNDERGRAD STUDENTS

6,833 full-time, 53 part-time. 89% are from out of state; 11% Black or African American, non-Hispanic/Latino; 10% Hispanic/Latino; 14% Asian, non-Hispanic/Latino; 0.3% Native Hawaiian or other Pacific Islander, non-Hispanic/Latino; 0.5% American Indian or Alaska Native, non-Hispanic/Latino; 6% Two or more races, non-Hispanic/Latino; 5% Race/ethnicity unknown; 10% international; 3% transferred in; 85% live on campus.

Freshmen:

Admission: 37,310 applied, 3,402 admitted, 1,604 enrolled. ***Average high school GPA:*** 3.8. ***Test scores:*** SAT evidence-based reading and writing scores over 500: 100%; SAT math scores over 500: 100%; ACT scores over 18: 100%; SAT evidence-based reading and writing scores over 600: 98%; SAT math scores over 600: 98%; ACT scores over 24: 98%; SAT evidence-based reading and writing scores over 700: 84%; SAT math scores over 700: 91%; ACT scores over 30: 93%.

Retention: 97% of full-time freshmen returned.

FACULTY

Total: 1,233, 79% full-time, 91% with terminal degrees.

Student/faculty ratio: 7:1.

ACADEMICS

Calendar: semesters. *Degrees:* bachelor's, master's, and doctoral.

Special study options: accelerated degree program, advanced placement credit, cooperative education, double majors, English as a second language, honors programs, independent study, internships, off-campus study, services for LD students, student-designed majors, study abroad, summer session for credit. ***ROTC:*** Army (b), Navy (b), Air Force (c).

Unusual degree programs: 3-2 business administration; engineering; nursing; English, French, German, history, Latin American Studies, mathematics, philosophy, political science, psychology, and medicine, health and society.

Computers: Students can access the following: campus intranet, computer help desk, free student e-mail accounts, online (class) grades, online (class) registration, online (class) schedules, productivity and educational software. Campuswide network is available. Wireless service is available via entire campus.

Library: Jean and Alexander Heard Library plus 7 others. *Books:* 3.1 million (physical), 1.7 million (digital/electronic); *Databases:* 3,700.

STUDENT LIFE

Housing options: on-campus residence required for freshman year; coed, men-only, women-only, special housing for students with disabilities. Campus housing is university owned. Freshman campus housing is guaranteed.

Activities and organizations: drama/theater group, student-run newspaper, radio and television station, choral group, marching band, national fraternities, national sororities.

Athletics Member NCAA. All Division I except football (Division I-A). ***Intercollegiate sports:*** baseball M(s), basketball M(s)/W(s), bowling W(s), cross-country running M(s)/W(s), golf M(s)/W(s), lacrosse W(s), soccer W(s), swimming and diving W(s), tennis M(s)/W(s), track and field W(s). ***Intramural sports:*** badminton M(c)/W(c), baseball M(c), basketball M(c)/W(c), bowling M(c)/W(c), crew M(c)/W(c), cross-country running M(c)/W(c), equestrian sports M(c)/W(c), fencing M(c)/W(c), field hockey M(c)/W(c), golf M(c)/W(c), ice hockey M(c), lacrosse M(c)/W(c), racquetball M(c)/W(c), rowing M(c)/W(c), rugby M(c), sailing M(c)/W(c), sand volleyball M/W, soccer M(c)/W(c), softball M/W, squash M(c)/W(c), swimming and diving M(c)/W(c), table tennis M(c)/W(c), tennis M(c)/W(c), track and field M(c)/W(c), triathlon M(c)/W(c), ultimate Frisbee M/W, volleyball M(c)/W(c), water polo M(c)/W(c).

Campus security: 24-hour emergency response devices and patrols, student patrols, late-night transport/escort service, controlled dormitory access.

Student services: health clinic, personal/psychological counseling, women's center.

COSTS & FINANCIAL AID

Costs (2020–21) ***Comprehensive fee:*** $72,702 includes full-time tuition ($52,781), mandatory fees ($2251), and room and board ($17,670). Part-time tuition: $2199 per credit hour. ***College room only:*** $11,540. Room and board charges vary according to board plan. ***Payment plans:*** tuition prepayment, installment. ***Waivers:*** employees or children of employees.

Financial Aid Of all full-time matriculated undergraduates who enrolled in 2019, 3,807 applied for aid, 3,355 were judged to have need, 3,355 had their need fully met. In 2019, 704 non-need-based awards were made. ***Average percent of need met:*** 100. ***Average financial aid package:*** $54,138. ***Average need-based loan:*** $3436. ***Average need-based gift aid:*** $52,242. ***Average non-need-based aid:*** $25,480. ***Average indebtedness upon graduation:*** $22,727.

APPLYING

Standardized Tests *Required:* SAT or ACT (for admission).

Options: electronic application, early decision, deferred entrance.

Application fee: $50.

Required: essay or personal statement, high school transcript, 3 letters of recommendation, 3 letters of recommendation (2 from teachers in core subject areas and 1 from counselor).

Application deadlines: 1/1 (freshmen), 3/15 (transfers).

Early decision deadline: 11/1 (for plan 1), 1/1 (for plan 2).

Notification: 4/1 (freshmen), 4/15 (transfers), 12/15 (early decision plan 1), 2/15 (early decision plan 2).

CONTACT

Mr. John O. Gaines, Director of Undergraduate Admissions, Vanderbilt University, 2305 West End Avenue, Nashville, TN 37203. *Phone:* 615-936-2811. *Toll-free phone:* 800-288-0432. *Fax:* 615-343-8326. *E-mail:* admissions@vanderbilt.edu.

Visible Music College

Memphis, Tennessee

http://visible.edu/

CONTACT

Visible Music College, 200 Madison Avenue, Memphis, TN 38103.

Watkins College of Art, Design, & Film

Nashville, Tennessee

http://www.watkins.edu/

CONTACT

Ms. Jaime Raybin, Recruiter, Watkins College of Art, Design, & Film, 2298 Rosa L. Parks Boulevard, Nashville, TN 37228. *Phone:* 615-383-4848 Ext. 5397. *Fax:* 615-383-4849. *E-mail:* admissions@watkins.edu.

Welch College

Gallatin, Tennessee

http://www.welch.edu/

CONTACT

Mr. Daniel Webster, Director of Enrollment Services, Welch College, 1045 Bison Trail, Gallatin, TN 37066. *Phone:* 615-675-5295. *Toll-free phone:* 800-763-9222. *Fax:* 615-296-0400. *E-mail:* daniel.webster@welch.edu.

Williamson College

Franklin, Tennessee

http://www.williamsoncc.edu/

CONTACT

Ms. Laura Flowers, Admissions Coordinator, Williamson College, 274 Mallory Station Road, Franklin, TN 37067. *Phone:* 615-771-7821. *Fax:* 615-771-7810. *E-mail:* laura@williamsoncc.edu.

TEXAS

Abilene Christian University

Abilene, Texas

http://www.acu.edu/

- **Independent** university, founded 1906, affiliated with Church of Christ
- **Urban** 262-acre campus
- **Endowment** $444.1 million
- **Coed** 3,525 undergraduate students, 95% full-time, 60% women, 40% men
- **Moderately difficult** entrance level, 62% of applicants were admitted

UNDERGRAD STUDENTS

3,352 full-time, 173 part-time. Students come from 43 states and territories; 38 other countries; 13% are from out of state; 9% Black or African American, non-Hispanic/Latino; 19% Hispanic/Latino; 1% Asian, non-Hispanic/Latino; 0.1% Native Hawaiian or other Pacific Islander, non-Hispanic/Latino; 0.4% American Indian or Alaska Native, non-Hispanic/Latino; 5% Two or more races, non-Hispanic/Latino; 0.5% Race/ethnicity unknown; 3% international; 3% transferred in; 45% live on campus.

Freshmen:

Admission: 11,349 applied, 6,996 admitted, 932 enrolled. ***Average high school GPA:*** 3.6. ***Test scores:*** SAT evidence-based reading and writing scores over 500: 83%; SAT math scores over 500: 79%; ACT scores over 18: 93%; SAT evidence-based reading and writing scores over 600: 36%; SAT math scores over 600: 28%; ACT scores over 24: 52%; SAT evidence-based reading and writing scores over 700: 5%; SAT math scores over 700: 6%; ACT scores over 30: 16%.

Retention: 79% of full-time freshmen returned.

FACULTY

Total: 492, 54% full-time, 69% with terminal degrees.

Student/faculty ratio: 14:1.

ACADEMICS

Calendar: semesters. *Degrees:* certificates, associate, bachelor's, master's, doctoral, post-master's, and postbachelor's certificates.

Special study options: adult/continuing education programs, advanced placement credit, distance learning, double majors, English as a second language, external degree program, honors programs, independent study, internships, off-campus study, part-time degree program, services for LD students, student-designed majors, study abroad, summer session for credit.

Unusual degree programs: 3-2 animal health professions.

Computers: 500 computers/terminals and 3,900 ports are available on campus for general student use. Students can access the following: campus intranet, computer help desk, free student e-mail accounts, online (class) grades, online (class) registration, online (class) schedules. Campuswide network is available. 100% of college-owned or -operated housing units are wired for high-speed Internet access. Wireless service is available via entire campus.

Library: Brown Library. *Books:* 532,096 (physical), 489,972 (digital/electronic); *Serial titles:* 5,941 (physical), 58,956 (digital/electronic); *Databases:* 113. Weekly public service hours: 97; students can reserve study rooms.

STUDENT LIFE

Housing options: on-campus residence required through sophomore year; men-only, women-only, special housing for students with disabilities.

Campus housing is university owned. Freshman campus housing is guaranteed.

Activities and organizations: drama/theater group, student-run newspaper, radio and television station, choral group, marching band, Student Association, Graduate Students Association, Spring Break Campaigns, International Students Association, LYNAY.

Athletics Member NCAA. All Division I. ***Intercollegiate sports:*** baseball M(s), basketball M(s)/W(s), cross-country running M(s)/W(s), football M(s), golf M(s), sand volleyball W, soccer W(s), softball W(s), tennis M(s)/W(s), track and field M(s)/W(s), volleyball W(s). ***Intramural sports:*** basketball M/W, football M/W, golf M(c)/W(c), lacrosse M(c), racquetball M/W, rugby M(c), soccer M(c)/W, softball M/W, table tennis M/W, tennis M/W, volleyball M/W.

Campus security: 24-hour emergency response devices and patrols, student patrols, late-night transport/escort service, controlled dormitory access.

Student services: health clinic, personal/psychological counseling, veterans affairs office.

COSTS & FINANCIAL AID

Costs (2020–21) ***Comprehensive fee:*** $49,150 includes full-time tuition ($37,750), mandatory fees ($50), and room and board ($11,350). Full-time tuition and fees vary according to course load. Part-time tuition and fees vary according to course load. ***College room only:*** $5850. Room and board charges vary according to board plan and housing facility. ***Payment plans:*** tuition prepayment, installment. ***Waivers:*** employees or children of employees.

Financial Aid Of all full-time matriculated undergraduates who enrolled in 2019, 2,583 applied for aid, 2,245 were judged to have need, 692 had their need fully met. In 2019, 1144 non-need-based awards were made. ***Average percent of need met:*** 67. ***Average financial aid package:*** $25,017. ***Average need-based loan:*** $4100. ***Average need-based gift aid:*** $22,497. ***Average non-need-based aid:*** $14,877.

APPLYING

Standardized Tests *Required:* SAT or ACT (for admission).

Options: electronic application, early admission, early action.

Application fee: $50.

Required: high school transcript. ***Required for some:*** essay or personal statement.

Application deadlines: 2/15 (freshmen), rolling (transfers).

Notification: 3/15 (freshmen), continuous until 9/1 (transfers).

CONTACT

Admissions, Abilene Christian University, ACU Box 29000, Abilene, TX 79699-9000. *Phone:* 325-674-2650. *Toll-free phone:* 800-460-6228. *Fax:* 325-674-2130. *E-mail:* info@admissions.acu.edu.

Amberton University

Garland, Texas

http://www.amberton.edu/

CONTACT

Academic Dean, Amberton University, 1700 Eastgate Drive, Garland, TX 75041-5595. *Phone:* 972-279-6511. *E-mail:* advisor@amberton.edu.

American InterContinental University Houston

Houston, Texas

http://www.aiuniv.edu/

CONTACT

American InterContinental University Houston, 9999 Richmond Avenue, Houston, TX 77042. *Phone:* 877-564-6248. *Toll-free phone:* 888-607-9888.

Angelo State University

San Angelo, Texas

http://www.angelo.edu/

- **State-supported** comprehensive, founded 1928, part of Texas Tech University System
- **Urban** 268-acre campus
- **Endowment** $185.4 million
- **Coed** 9,046 undergraduate students, 61% full-time, 59% women, 41% men
- **Moderately difficult** entrance level, 77% of applicants were admitted

UNDERGRAD STUDENTS

5,503 full-time, 3,543 part-time. Students come from 38 states and territories; 26 other countries; 3% are from out of state; 7% Black or African American, non-Hispanic/Latino; 37% Hispanic/Latino; 0.8% Asian, non-Hispanic/Latino; 0.2% Native Hawaiian or other Pacific Islander, non-Hispanic/Latino; 0.5% American Indian or Alaska Native, non-Hispanic/Latino; 3% Two or more races, non-Hispanic/Latino; 0.1% Race/ethnicity unknown; 4% international; 5% transferred in; 22% live on campus.

Freshmen:

Admission: 3,913 applied, 2,997 admitted, 1,260 enrolled. ***Test scores:*** SAT evidence-based reading and writing scores over 500: 65%; SAT math scores over 500: 63%; ACT scores over 18: 75%; SAT evidence-based reading and writing scores over 600: 20%; SAT math scores over 600: 13%; ACT scores over 24: 24%; SAT evidence-based reading and writing scores over 700: 3%; SAT math scores over 700: 1%; ACT scores over 30: 3%.

Retention: 69% of full-time freshmen returned.

FACULTY

Total: 376, 82% full-time, 72% with terminal degrees.

Student/faculty ratio: 20:1.

ACADEMICS

Calendar: semesters. *Degrees:* certificates, bachelor's, master's, doctoral, post-master's, and postbachelor's certificates.

Special study options: academic remediation for entering students, advanced placement credit, distance learning, double majors, English as a second language, honors programs, independent study, internships, part-time degree program, services for LD students, study abroad, summer session for credit. ***ROTC:*** Air Force (b).

Unusual degree programs: 3-2 business administration.

Computers: 953 computers/terminals and 3,900 ports are available on campus for general student use. Students can access the following: campus intranet, computer help desk, free student e-mail accounts, online (class) grades, online (class) registration, online (class) schedules, online courses, tuition payments, book purchase, parking permits, university calendar, discounted hardware and software. Campuswide network is available. 100% of college-owned or -operated housing units are wired for high-speed Internet access. Wireless service is available via entire campus.

Library: Porter Henderson Library. *Books:* 311,098 (physical), 114,849 (digital/electronic); *Serial titles:* 105 (physical), 51,083 (digital/electronic); *Databases:* 234. Weekly public service hours: 137; study areas open 24 hours, 5–7 days a week; students can reserve study rooms.

STUDENT LIFE

Housing options: on-campus residence required through sophomore year; coed, special housing for students with disabilities. Campus housing is university owned.

Activities and organizations: drama/theater group, student-run newspaper, radio and television station, choral group, marching band, Association of Mexican-American Students, Block and Bridle Club, Air Force ROTC, University Center Program Council, Baptist Student Union, national fraternities, national sororities.

Athletics Member NCAA. All Division II. ***Intercollegiate sports:*** baseball M(s), basketball M(s)/W(s), cheerleading M(s)/W(s), cross-country running M(s)/W(s), football M(s), golf W(s), soccer W(s), softball W(s), tennis W(s), track and field M(s)/W(s), volleyball W(s). ***Intramural sports:*** badminton M/W, basketball M/W, football M/W, golf M/W, racquetball M/W, rugby M(c)/W(c), sand volleyball M/W, soccer M/W, softball M/W, table tennis M/W, tennis M(c)/W(c), ultimate Frisbee M(c)/W(c), volleyball M(c)/W(c), weight lifting M(c)/W(c).

Campus security: 24-hour emergency response devices and patrols, late-night transport/escort service, controlled dormitory access.

Student services: health clinic, personal/psychological counseling, veterans affairs office.

COSTS & FINANCIAL AID

Costs (2020–21) ***One-time required fee:*** $100. ***Tuition:*** area resident $5516 full-time, $184 per credit hour part-time; state resident $5516 full-time, $184 per credit hour part-time; nonresident $17,786 full-time, $593 per credit hour part-time. Full-time tuition and fees vary according to course level, course load, degree level, location, and program. Part-time tuition and fees vary according to course level, course load, degree level, location, and program. No tuition increase for student's term of enrollment. ***Required fees:*** $3495 full-time. ***Room and board:*** $9630. Room and board charges vary according to board plan and housing facility. ***Payment plan:*** installment. ***Waivers:*** senior citizens and employees or children of employees.

Financial Aid Of all full-time matriculated undergraduates who enrolled in 2018, 4,696 applied for aid, 4,007 were judged to have need, 560 had their need fully met. 125 Federal Work-Study jobs (averaging $2100). 16 state and other part-time jobs (averaging $1827). In 2018, 1031 non-need-based awards were made. ***Average percent of need met:*** 64. ***Average financial aid package:*** $10,572. ***Average need-based loan:*** $3843. ***Average need-based gift aid:*** $3607. ***Average non-need-based aid:*** $3246. ***Average indebtedness upon graduation:*** $24,496.

APPLYING

Standardized Tests *Required:* SAT or ACT (for admission).

Options: electronic application, deferred entrance.

Application fee: $40.

Required: high school transcript, high school class rank.

Application deadlines: rolling (freshmen), rolling (out-of-state freshmen), rolling (transfers).

Notification: continuous (freshmen), continuous (out-of-state freshmen), continuous (transfers).

CONTACT

Ms. Sharla Adam, Director of Admissions, Angelo State University, 2601 West Avenue N., San Angelo, TX 76909. *Phone:* 325-942-2041. *Toll-free phone:* 800-946-8627. *Fax:* 325-942-2078. *E-mail:* admissions@angelo.edu.

Arlington Baptist University

Arlington, Texas

http://www.abu.edu/

CONTACT

Melissa Hayward, Admissions Specialist, Arlington Baptist University, 3001 West Division, Arlington, TX 76012-3425. *Phone:* 817-461-8741. *Fax:* 817-274-1138. *E-mail:* mhayward@abu.edu.

The Art Institute of Austin, a branch of The Art Institute of Houston

Austin, Texas

http://www.artinstitutes.edu/austin

CONTACT

The Art Institute of Austin, a branch of The Art Institute of Houston, 101 W. Louis Henna Boulevard, Suite 100, Austin, TX 78728. *Phone:* 512-691-1707. *Toll-free phone:* 866-583-7952.

The Art Institute of Dallas, a branch of Miami International University of Art & Design

Dallas, Texas

http://www.artinstitutes.edu/dallas/

CONTACT

The Art Institute of Dallas, a branch of Miami International University of Art & Design, 8080 Park Lane, Suite 100, Dallas, TX 75231-5993. *Phone:* 214-692-8080. *Toll-free phone:* 800-275-4243.

The Art Institute of Houston

Houston, Texas

http://www.artinstitutes.edu/houston/

CONTACT

The Art Institute of Houston, 4140 Southwest Freeway, Houston, TX 77027. *Phone:* 713-623-2040. *Toll-free phone:* 800-275-4244.

The Art Institute of San Antonio, a branch of The Art Institute of Houston

San Antonio, Texas

http://www.artinstitutes.edu/san-antonio/

CONTACT

The Art Institute of San Antonio, a branch of The Art Institute of Houston, 1000 IH-10 West, Suite 200, San Antonio, TX 78230. *Phone:* 210-338-7320. *Toll-free phone:* 888-222-0040.

Austin College

Sherman, Texas

http://www.austincollege.edu/

- **Independent Presbyterian** comprehensive, founded 1849
- **Small-town** 60-acre campus with easy access to Dallas-Fort Worth
- **Coed** 1,294 undergraduate students, 100% full-time, 52% women, 48% men
- **Moderately difficult** entrance level, 51% of applicants were admitted

UNDERGRAD STUDENTS

1,290 full-time, 4 part-time. 10% Black or African American, non-Hispanic/Latino; 24% Hispanic/Latino; 13% Asian, non-Hispanic/Latino; 0.3% Native Hawaiian or other Pacific Islander, non-Hispanic/Latino; 0.3% American Indian or Alaska Native, non-Hispanic/Latino; 3% Two or more races, non-Hispanic/Latino; 0.5% Race/ethnicity unknown; 1% international; 2% transferred in; 74% live on campus.

Freshmen:

Admission: 4,360 applied, 2,236 admitted, 378 enrolled. ***Average high school GPA:*** 3.5. ***Test scores:*** SAT evidence-based reading and writing scores over 500: 97%; SAT math scores over 500: 96%; ACT scores over 18: 98%; SAT evidence-based reading and writing scores over 600: 59%; SAT math scores over 600: 51%; ACT scores over 24: 75%; SAT evidence-based reading and writing scores over 700: 9%; SAT math scores over 700: 12%; ACT scores over 30: 21%.

Retention: 78% of full-time freshmen returned.

FACULTY

Total: 116, 88% full-time, 85% with terminal degrees.

Student/faculty ratio: 12:1.

ACADEMICS

Calendar: 4-1-4. *Degrees:* bachelor's and master's.

Special study options: advanced placement credit, double majors, independent study, internships, off-campus study, part-time degree program, services for LD students, student-designed majors, study abroad, summer session for credit.

Unusual degree programs: 3-2 engineering with University of Texas at Dallas, Texas A&M University, Washington University in St. Louis, Columbia University.

Computers: 160 computers/terminals are available on campus for general student use. Students can access the following: campus intranet, computer help desk, free student e-mail accounts, online (class) grades, online (class) registration, online (class) schedules. Campuswide network is available. 100% of college-owned or -operated housing units are wired for high-speed Internet access. Wireless service is available via entire campus.
Library: Abell Library. *Books:* 227,390 (physical). Study areas open 24 hours, 5–7 days a week; students can reserve study rooms.

STUDENT LIFE
Housing options: on-campus residence required through junior year; coed, men-only, women-only, special housing for students with disabilities. Campus housing is university owned. Freshman campus housing is guaranteed.

Activities and organizations: drama/theater group, student-run newspaper, choral group, Inter-Varsity Christian Fellowship (IVCF), Campus Activity Board (CAB), Indian Cultural Association, Students Today Alumni Tomorrow (STAT), ACtivators.

Athletics Member NCAA. All Division III. ***Intercollegiate sports:*** baseball M, basketball M/W, cheerleading M(c)/W(c), cross-country running M/W, football M, soccer M/W, softball W, swimming and diving M/W, tennis M/W, volleyball W, water polo M/W. ***Intramural sports:*** basketball M/W, football M/W, soccer M/W, softball M/W, ultimate Frisbee M/W, volleyball M/W.

Campus security: 24-hour emergency response devices and patrols, late-night transport/escort service, controlled dormitory access.

Student services: health clinic, personal/psychological counseling.

COSTS & FINANCIAL AID
Costs (2019–20) ***One-time required fee:*** $25. ***Comprehensive fee:*** $53,907 includes full-time tuition ($40,970), mandatory fees ($185), and room and board ($12,752). Part-time tuition: $5850 per course. ***Required fees:*** $90 per term part-time. ***College room only:*** $5900. ***Payment plan:*** installment. ***Waivers:*** employees or children of employees.

Financial Aid Of all full-time matriculated undergraduates who enrolled in 2019, 1,016 applied for aid, 868 were judged to have need, 231 had their need fully met. In 2019, 416 non-need-based awards were made. ***Average percent of need met:*** 89. ***Average financial aid package:*** $39,081. ***Average need-based loan:*** $4197. ***Average need-based gift aid:*** $34,058. ***Average non-need-based aid:*** $24,825.

APPLYING
Standardized Tests *Required for some:* SAT or ACT (for admission).

Options: electronic application, early admission, early decision, early action, deferred entrance.

Required: high school transcript. ***Required for some:*** essay or personal statement. ***Recommended:*** minimum 3.0 GPA, 2 letters of recommendation, interview.

Application deadlines: 3/1 (freshmen), 8/1 (transfers), 12/1 (early action).

Early decision deadline: 11/1.

Notification: 4/1 (freshmen), 12/4 (early decision), 1/15 (early action).

CONTACT
Mrs. Baylee Kowert, Executive Director of Institutional Enrollment, Austin College, 900 North Grand Avenue, Suite 6N, Sherman, TX 75090-4400. *Phone:* 903-813-3000. *Toll-free phone:* 800-596-4276 (in-state); 800-526-4276 (out-of-state). *Fax:* 903-813-3198. *E-mail:* admission@austincollege.edu.

Austin Community College District

Austin, Texas

http://www.austincc.edu/

- **State and locally supported** primarily 2-year, founded 1972
- **Urban** campus with easy access to Austin
- **Endowment** $8.7 million
- **Coed** 41,056 undergraduate students, 22% full-time, 57% women, 43% men
- **Noncompetitive** entrance level

UNDERGRAD STUDENTS
8,939 full-time, 32,117 part-time. Students come from 54 states and territories; 101 other countries; 2% are from out of state; 8% Black or African American, non-Hispanic/Latino; 40% Hispanic/Latino; 5% Asian, non-Hispanic/Latino; 0.2% Native Hawaiian or other Pacific Islander, non-Hispanic/Latino; 0.6% American Indian or Alaska Native, non-Hispanic/Latino; 3% Two or more races, non-Hispanic/Latino; 0.9% Race/ethnicity unknown; 2% international; 10% transferred in.

Freshmen:
Admission: 5,505 enrolled.

FACULTY
Total: 1,893, 32% full-time, 24% with terminal degrees.

Student/faculty ratio: 19:1.

ACADEMICS
Calendar: semesters. *Degrees:* certificates, associate, bachelor's, and postbachelor's certificates.

Special study options: academic remediation for entering students, accelerated degree program, adult/continuing education programs, advanced placement credit, cooperative education, distance learning, English as a second language, honors programs, independent study, internships, part-time degree program, services for LD students, summer session for credit. ***ROTC:*** Army (c), Air Force (c).

Computers: 2,090 computers/terminals are available on campus for general student use. Students can access the following: computer help desk, free student e-mail accounts, online (class) grades, online (class) registration, online (class) schedules. Campuswide network is available. Wireless service is available via entire campus.
Library: Main Library plus 11 others. *Books:* 148,059 (physical), 36,660 (digital/electronic); *Serial titles:* 402 (physical), 94,538 (digital/electronic); *Databases:* 104. Weekly public service hours: 83; students can reserve study rooms.

STUDENT LIFE
Housing options: college housing not available.

Activities and organizations: Intramurals, Students for Environmental Outreach, Phi Theta Kappa (PTK), National Society of Collegiate Scholars, Students for Community Involvement.

Athletics ***Intramural sports:*** basketball M/W, soccer M/W, softball M/W, volleyball W.

Campus security: 24-hour emergency response devices and patrols, late-night transport/escort service.

Student services: personal/psychological counseling, veterans affairs office.

COSTS & FINANCIAL AID
Costs (2019–20) ***Tuition:*** area resident $2010 full-time, $67 per credit hour part-time; state resident $10,290 full-time, $343 per credit hour part-time; nonresident $12,480 full-time, $416 per credit hour part-time. Full-time tuition and fees vary according to course load. Part-time tuition and fees vary according to course load. ***Required fees:*** $540 full-time, $18 per credit hour part-time. ***Payment plan:*** installment. ***Waivers:*** senior citizens and employees or children of employees.

Financial Aid Of all full-time matriculated undergraduates who enrolled in 2019, 4,771 applied for aid, 3,941 were judged to have need. 167 Federal Work-Study jobs (averaging $2987). 15 state and other part-time jobs (averaging $2185). ***Average need-based loan:*** $3286. ***Average need-based gift aid:*** $4779.

APPLYING
Options: electronic application.

Required: high school transcript.

Application deadlines: rolling (freshmen), rolling (transfers).

CONTACT
Mrs. Linda Terry, Executive Director, Admissions and Records, Austin Community College District, 5930 Middle Fiskville Road, Austin, TX 78752. *Phone:* 512-223-7503. *Fax:* 512-223-7963. *E-mail:* admission@austincc.edu.

Austin Graduate School of Theology

Austin, Texas

http://www.austingrad.edu/

CONTACT

Dawn Bond, Director of Admissions, Austin Graduate School of Theology, 7640 Guadalupe Street, Austin, TX 78752. *Phone:* 512-476-2772. *Toll-free phone:* 866-AUS-GRAD. *Fax:* 512-476-3919. *E-mail:* registrar@austingrad.edu.

Baptist Health System School of Health Professions

San Antonio, Texas

http://www.bshp.edu/

CONTACT

Baptist Health System School of Health Professions, 8400 Datapoint Drive, San Antonio, TX 78229.

Baptist Missionary Association Theological Seminary

Jacksonville, Texas

http://www.bmats.edu/

CONTACT

Baptist Missionary Association Theological Seminary, 1530 East Pine Street, Jacksonville, TX 75766-5407. *Phone:* 903-586-2501 Ext. 229. *Toll-free phone:* 800-259-5673.

Baptist University of the Americas

San Antonio, Texas

http://www.bua.edu/

CONTACT

Admissions Counselor, Baptist University of the Americas, 8019 Pan Am Expressway, San Antonio, TX 78224. *Phone:* 210-924-4338 Ext. 229. *Toll-free phone:* 800-721-1396. *Fax:* 210-924-2701. *E-mail:* admissions@bua.edu.

Baylor University

Waco, Texas

http://www.baylor.edu/

- **Independent Baptist** university, founded 1845
- **Urban** 1000-acre campus with easy access to Dallas-Fort Worth
- **Endowment** $1.3 billion
- **Coed** 14,108 undergraduate students, 99% full-time, 60% women, 40% men
- **Moderately difficult** entrance level, 45% of applicants were admitted

UNDERGRAD STUDENTS

13,906 full-time, 202 part-time. Students come from 51 states and territories; 75 other countries; 33% are from out of state; 6% Black or African American, non-Hispanic/Latino; 16% Hispanic/Latino; 7% Asian, non-Hispanic/Latino; 0.1% Native Hawaiian or other Pacific Islander, non-Hispanic/Latino; 0.4% American Indian or Alaska Native, non-Hispanic/Latino; 5% Two or more races, non-Hispanic/Latino; 0.5% Race/ethnicity unknown; 4% international; 3% transferred in; 35% live on campus.

Freshmen:

Admission: 34,582 applied, 15,676 admitted, 3,307 enrolled. ***Test scores:*** SAT evidence-based reading and writing scores over 500: 98%; SAT math scores over 500: 100%; ACT scores over 18: 100%; SAT evidence-based reading and writing scores over 600: 78%; SAT math scores over 600: 77%; ACT scores over 24: 94%; SAT evidence-based reading and writing scores over 700: 19%; SAT math scores over 700: 28%; ACT scores over 30: 45%.

Retention: 88% of full-time freshmen returned.

FACULTY

Total: 1,431, 79% full-time, 68% with terminal degrees.

Student/faculty ratio: 13:1.

ACADEMICS

Calendar: semesters. *Degrees:* bachelor's, master's, doctoral, and post-master's certificates.

Special study options: accelerated degree program, advanced placement credit, double majors, English as a second language, honors programs, internships, part-time degree program, services for LD students, student-designed majors, study abroad, summer session for credit. ***ROTC:*** Army (b), Air Force (b).

Unusual degree programs: 3-2 clinical laboratory science.

Computers: Students can access the following: campus intranet, computer help desk, free student e-mail accounts, online (class) grades, online (class) registration, online (class) schedules. Campuswide network is available. 99% of college-owned or -operated housing units are wired for high-speed Internet access. Wireless service is available via entire campus.

Library: Moody Memorial Library plus 8 others.

STUDENT LIFE

Housing options: on-campus residence required for freshman year; coed, men-only, women-only, cooperative, special housing for students with disabilities. Campus housing is university owned. Freshman campus housing is guaranteed.

Activities and organizations: drama/theater group, student-run newspaper, radio and television station, choral group, marching band, national fraternities, national sororities.

Athletics Member NCAA. All Division I except football (Division I-A). ***Intercollegiate sports:*** baseball M(s), basketball M(s)/W(s), cheerleading M(s)/W(s), cross-country running M(s)/W(s), equestrian sports W(s), golf M(s)/W(s)(c), soccer W(s), softball W(s), tennis M(s)/W(s), track and field M(s)/W(s), volleyball W(s). ***Intramural sports:*** baseball M(c), basketball M/W, bowling M/W, crew M(c)/W(c), cross-country running M/W, fencing M(c), field hockey W(c), football M/W, golf M(c), gymnastics M(c)/W(c), lacrosse M(c)/W(c), racquetball M/W, rock climbing M(c)/W(c), rowing M(c)/W(c), rugby M(c)/W(c), sailing M(c)/W(c), skiing (downhill) M(c)/W(c), soccer M(c)/W(c), softball M/W, swimming and diving M(c)/W(c), table tennis M/W, tennis M(c)/W(c), track and field M/W, triathlon M(c)/W(c), ultimate Frisbee M(c)/W(c), volleyball M(c), water polo M(c)/W(c).

Campus security: 24-hour emergency response devices and patrols, late-night transport/escort service, controlled dormitory access.

Student services: health clinic, personal/psychological counseling, legal services.

COSTS & FINANCIAL AID

Costs (2020–21) ***Comprehensive fee:*** $62,520 includes full-time tuition ($44,544), mandatory fees ($4702), and room and board ($13,274). Part-time tuition: $1856 per semester hour. ***Required fees:*** $196 per semester hour part-time. ***College room only:*** $7200. Room and board charges vary according to board plan, housing facility, and location. ***Payment plan:*** installment. ***Waivers:*** employees or children of employees.

Financial Aid Of all full-time matriculated undergraduates who enrolled in 2019, 8,772 applied for aid, 7,216 were judged to have need, 1,124 had their need fully met. 4,740 Federal Work-Study jobs (averaging $2928). In 2019, 5254 non-need-based awards were made. ***Average percent of need met:*** 66. ***Average financial aid package:*** $32,093. ***Average need-based loan:*** $3300. ***Average need-based gift aid:*** $26,384. ***Average non-need-based aid:*** $16,890. ***Average indebtedness upon graduation:*** $49,610.

APPLYING

Standardized Tests *Required:* SAT or ACT (for admission).

Options: electronic application, early admission, early decision, early action, deferred entrance.

Required: high school transcript. ***Required for some:*** essay or personal statement, minimum 2.5 GPA, 2 letters of recommendation.

Application deadlines: 2/1 (freshmen), rolling (transfers), 11/1 (early action).

Early decision deadline: 11/1.

Notification: 4/10 (freshmen), continuous (transfers), 12/15 (early decision), 1/15 (early action).

CONTACT
Ms. Jessica King Gereghty, Assistant Vice President of Undergraduate Admissions, Baylor University, PO Box 97056, Waco, TX 76798. *Phone:* 254-710-3435. *Toll-free phone:* 800-BAYLORU. *Fax:* 254-710-3436. *E-mail:* admissions@baylor.edu.

Brazosport College

Lake Jackson, Texas

http://www.brazosport.edu/

- **State and locally supported** primarily 2-year, founded 1968
- **Small-town** 160-acre campus with easy access to Houston
- **Coed**
- **Noncompetitive** entrance level

FACULTY
Student/faculty ratio: 17:1.

ACADEMICS
Calendar: semesters. *Degrees:* certificates, associate, and bachelor's.
Library: Brazosport College Library.

STUDENT LIFE
Housing options: college housing not available.

Activities and organizations: drama/theater group, student-run newspaper, choral group.

Campus security: 24-hour patrols.

APPLYING
Options: early admission, deferred entrance.

Required for some: high school transcript.

CONTACT
Brazosport College, 500 College Drive, Lake Jackson, TX 77566-3199. *Phone:* 979-230-3020.

Chamberlain College of Nursing - Houston

Houston, Texas

http://www.chamberlain.edu/

CONTACT
Director of Recruitment, Chamberlain College of Nursing - Houston, 11025 Equity Drive, Houston, TX 77041. *Phone:* 713-277-9800. *Toll-free phone:* 877-751-5783.

Chamberlain College of Nursing - Irving

Irving, Texas

http://www.chamberlain.edu/

CONTACT
Chamberlain College of Nursing - Irving, 4800 Regent Boulevard, Irving, TX 75063. *Toll-free phone:* 866-593-8669.

Chamberlain College of Nursing - Pearland

Pearland, Texas

http://www.chamberlain.edu/

CONTACT
Chamberlain College of Nursing - Pearland, 12000 Shadow Creek Parkway, Pearland, TX 77584. *Toll-free phone:* 877-751-5783.

College of Biblical Studies–Houston

Houston, Texas

http://www.cbshouston.edu/

CONTACT
Admissions Office, College of Biblical Studies–Houston, 7000 Regency Square Boulevard, Houston, TX 77036. *Phone:* 713-772-4253. *Toll-free phone:* 844-227-9673. *E-mail:* admissions@cbshouston.edu.

Collin County Community College District

McKinney, Texas

http://www.collin.edu/

- **State and locally supported** primarily 2-year, founded 1985
- **Suburban** 406-acre campus with easy access to Dallas-Fort Worth
- **Endowment** $11.7 million
- **Coed** 35,144 undergraduate students, 31% full-time, 56% women, 44% men
- 100% of applicants were admitted

UNDERGRAD STUDENTS
10,760 full-time, 24,384 part-time. 72% are from out of state; 13% Black or African American, non-Hispanic/Latino; 23% Hispanic/Latino; 11% Asian, non-Hispanic/Latino; 0.2% Native Hawaiian or other Pacific Islander, non-Hispanic/Latino; 0.3% American Indian or Alaska Native, non-Hispanic/Latino; 4% Two or more races, non-Hispanic/Latino; 2% Race/ethnicity unknown; 3% international; 5% transferred in.

Freshmen:
Admission: 9,625 applied, 9,625 admitted, 5,566 enrolled.

Retention: 66% of full-time freshmen returned.

FACULTY
Total: 1,442, 32% full-time, 28% with terminal degrees.

Student/faculty ratio: 25:1.

ACADEMICS
Calendar: semesters. *Degrees:* certificates, associate, and bachelor's.

Special study options: academic remediation for entering students, adult/continuing education programs, advanced placement credit, cooperative education, distance learning, English as a second language, honors programs, internships, part-time degree program, services for LD students, summer session for credit. ***ROTC:*** Army (c), Air Force (c).

Computers: 3,164 computers/terminals are available on campus for general student use. Students can access the following: computer help desk, free student e-mail accounts, online (class) grades, online (class) registration, online (class) schedules. Campuswide network is available. 100% of college-owned or -operated housing units are wired for high-speed Internet access. Wireless service is available via entire campus.
Library: Collin College Library plus 2 others. *Books:* 248,662 (physical), 53,569 (digital/electronic); *Serial titles:* 741 (physical), 176 (digital/electronic); *Databases:* 185. Weekly public service hours: 75; students can reserve study rooms.

STUDENT LIFE
Activities and organizations: drama/theater group, choral group, Student Government Association, Phi Theta Kappa, Fellowship of Christian University Students, Collin Organized Geek Society, Society of Women Engineers.

Athletics Member NJCAA. ***Intercollegiate sports:*** basketball M(s)/W(s), tennis M(s)/W(s). ***Intramural sports:*** basketball M/W, soccer M/W, volleyball M/W.

Campus security: 24-hour emergency response devices and patrols, late-night transport/escort service.

Student services: personal/psychological counseling, veterans affairs office.

COSTS & FINANCIAL AID
Costs (2020–21) ***Tuition:*** area resident $1560 full-time, $52 per credit hour part-time; state resident $2940 full-time, $98 per credit hour part-time; nonresident $4950 full-time, $165 per credit hour part-time. ***Required fees:*** $64 full-time. ***Room and board:*** $11,655. ***Payment plan:***

installment. ***Waivers:*** senior citizens and employees or children of employees.

Financial Aid Of all full-time matriculated undergraduates who enrolled in 2018, 4,909 applied for aid, 3,782 were judged to have need, 12 had their need fully met. In 2018, 144 non-need-based awards were made. ***Average percent of need met:*** 37. ***Average financial aid package:*** $5797. ***Average need-based loan:*** $2941. ***Average need-based gift aid:*** $4949. ***Average non-need-based aid:*** $1180.

APPLYING

Options: electronic application.

Application deadlines: rolling (freshmen), rolling (transfers).

Notification: continuous (freshmen), continuous (out-of-state freshmen), continuous (transfers).

CONTACT

Mr. Todd E. Fields, Dean Admission/District Registrar, Collin County Community College District, 2800 E. Spring Creek Parkway, Plano, TX 75074. *Phone:* 972-881-5174. *Fax:* 972-881-5175. *E-mail:* tfields@collin.edu.

Concordia University Texas

Austin, Texas

http://www.concordia.edu/

CONTACT

Ms. Kristin Coulter, Director of Admissions, Concordia University Texas, 11400 Concordia University Drive, Austin, TX 78726. *Phone:* 800-865-4282. *Toll-free phone:* 800-865-4282. *Fax:* 512-313-3999. *E-mail:* admissions@concordia.edu.

Criswell College

Dallas, Texas

http://www.criswell.edu/

CONTACT

Sam Hagos, Enrollment Assistant, Criswell College, 4010 Gaston Avenue, Dallas, TX 75246. *Phone:* 214-818-1391. *Toll-free phone:* 800-899-0012. *E-mail:* shagos@criswell.edu.

Dallas Baptist University

Dallas, Texas

http://www.dbu.edu/

- **Independent** comprehensive, founded 1965, affiliated with Baptist General Convention of Texas
- **Suburban** 368-acre campus with easy access to Dallas-Fort Worth
- **Endowment** $51.6 million
- **Coed** 2,883 undergraduate students, 81% full-time, 59% women, 41% men
- **Moderately difficult** entrance level, 90% of applicants were admitted

UNDERGRAD STUDENTS

2,332 full-time, 551 part-time. Students come from 38 states and territories; 43 other countries; 8% are from out of state; 10% Black or African American, non-Hispanic/Latino; 19% Hispanic/Latino; 2% Asian, non-Hispanic/Latino; 0.3% Native Hawaiian or other Pacific Islander, non-Hispanic/Latino; 0.4% American Indian or Alaska Native, non-Hispanic/Latino; 2% Two or more races, non-Hispanic/Latino; 7% international; 6% transferred in; 72% live on campus.

Freshmen:

Admission: 3,241 applied, 2,912 admitted, 572 enrolled. ***Average high school GPA:*** 3.8. ***Test scores:*** SAT evidence-based reading and writing scores over 500: 89%; SAT math scores over 500: 86%; ACT scores over 18: 93%; SAT evidence-based reading and writing scores over 600: 45%; SAT math scores over 600: 30%; ACT scores over 24: 50%; SAT evidence-based reading and writing scores over 700: 6%; SAT math scores over 700: 4%; ACT scores over 30: 11%.

Retention: 72% of full-time freshmen returned.

FACULTY

Total: 610, 22% full-time, 54% with terminal degrees.

Student/faculty ratio: 13:1.

ACADEMICS

Calendar: 4-1-4. *Degrees:* certificates, associate, bachelor's, master's, doctoral, post-master's, and postbachelor's certificates.

Special study options: academic remediation for entering students, accelerated degree program, adult/continuing education programs, advanced placement credit, distance learning, double majors, English as a second language, honors programs, independent study, internships, off-campus study, part-time degree program, services for LD students, study abroad, summer session for credit. ***ROTC:*** Army (c), Air Force (c).

Unusual degree programs: 3-2 business administration; ministry, education, information technology.

Computers: 214 computers/terminals are available on campus for general student use. Students can access the following: computer help desk, free student e-mail accounts, online (class) grades, online (class) registration, online (class) schedules. Campuswide network is available. 100% of college-owned or -operated housing units are wired for high-speed Internet access. Wireless service is available via entire campus.

Library: Vance Memorial Library plus 3 others. *Books:* 250,441 (physical), 151,333 (digital/electronic); *Serial titles:* 582 (physical), 48,819 (digital/electronic); *Databases:* 203. Weekly public service hours: 108.

STUDENT LIFE

Housing options: men-only, women-only, special housing for students with disabilities. Campus housing is university owned. Freshman applicants given priority for college housing.

Activities and organizations: drama/theater group, choral group, Baptist Student Ministry, Student Government Association, Greek Life Organizations, Ministry Fellowship, International Student Organization.

Athletics Member NCAA, NCCAA. All NCAA Division II except baseball (Division I). ***Intercollegiate sports:*** baseball M(s), basketball M(s), bowling M(c), cheerleading W(c), cross-country running M/W(s), golf M/W(s), ice hockey M(c), lacrosse M(c), soccer M/W(s), tennis M/W(s), track and field M/W(s), volleyball W(s). ***Intramural sports:*** basketball M/W, football M/W, golf M/W, soccer M/W, softball M/W, table tennis M/W, tennis M/W, ultimate Frisbee M/W, volleyball M/W.

Campus security: 24-hour emergency response devices and patrols, late-night transport/escort service, controlled dormitory access.

Student services: health clinic, personal/psychological counseling, veterans affairs office.

COSTS & FINANCIAL AID

Costs (2020–21) ***Comprehensive fee:*** $40,508 includes full-time tuition ($30,690), mandatory fees ($1250), and room and board ($8568). Full-time tuition and fees vary according to course load. Part-time tuition: $1023 per credit hour. Part-time tuition and fees vary according to course load. ***Required fees:*** $625 per term part-time. ***College room only:*** $4156. Room and board charges vary according to board plan and housing facility. ***Payment plans:*** installment, deferred payment. ***Waivers:*** employees or children of employees.

Financial Aid Of all full-time matriculated undergraduates who enrolled in 2019, 1,972 applied for aid, 1,471 were judged to have need, 540 had their need fully met. 80 Federal Work-Study jobs (averaging $2897). 21 state and other part-time jobs (averaging $3448). In 2019, 534 non-need-based awards were made. ***Average percent of need met:*** 66. ***Average financial aid package:*** $19,713. ***Average need-based loan:*** $4186. ***Average need-based gift aid:*** $4517. ***Average non-need-based aid:*** $11,289. ***Average indebtedness upon graduation:*** $27,248.

APPLYING

Standardized Tests *Required:* SAT or ACT (for admission).

Options: electronic application, early admission, deferred entrance.

Required: high school transcript, minimum 2.5 GPA, rank in upper 50% of high school class. ***Recommended:*** interview.

Application deadlines: rolling (freshmen), rolling (out-of-state freshmen), rolling (transfers).

Notification: continuous (freshmen), continuous (out-of-state freshmen), continuous (transfers).

CONTACT

Dr. John Borum, Assistant VP for Undergraduate Enrollment, Dallas Baptist University, 3000 Mountain Creek Parkway, Dallas, TX 75211-9299. *Phone:* 214-333-5360. *Toll-free phone:* 800-460-1328. *Fax:* 214-333-5447. *E-mail:* johnb@dbu.edu.

Dallas Christian College

Dallas, Texas

http://www.dallas.edu/

- **Independent** 4-year, founded 1950, affiliated with Christian Churches and Churches of Christ
- **Suburban** 22-acre campus with easy access to Dallas-Fort Worth
- **Endowment** $169,907
- **Coed** 212 undergraduate students, 79% full-time, 40% women, 60% men
- **Moderately difficult** entrance level, 37% of applicants were admitted

UNDERGRAD STUDENTS
167 full-time, 45 part-time. Students come from 11 states and territories; 5 other countries; 16% are from out of state; 24% Black or African American, non-Hispanic/Latino; 15% Hispanic/Latino; 1% Asian, non-Hispanic/Latino; 0.5% Native Hawaiian or other Pacific Islander, non-Hispanic/Latino; 10% Two or more races, non-Hispanic/Latino; 5% Race/ethnicity unknown; 3% international; 13% transferred in; 46% live on campus.

Freshmen:
Admission: 132 applied, 49 admitted, 49 enrolled. ***Average high school GPA:*** 3.1.

Retention: 50% of full-time freshmen returned.

FACULTY
Total: 56, 14% full-time, 29% with terminal degrees.

Student/faculty ratio: 16:1.

ACADEMICS
Calendar: semesters. *Degrees:* associate and bachelor's.

Special study options: academic remediation for entering students, accelerated degree program, adult/continuing education programs, advanced placement credit, distance learning, double majors, independent study, internships, part-time degree program, summer session for credit.

Computers: 16 computers/terminals are available on campus for general student use. Students can access the following: free student e-mail accounts, online (class) grades, online (class) registration, online (class) schedules. Campuswide network is available. 100% of college-owned or -operated housing units are wired for high-speed Internet access. Wireless service is available via entire campus.
Library: The Crawford Library. *Books:* 35,000 (physical), 26,000 (digital/electronic); *Serial titles:* 100 (physical); *Databases:* 60. Weekly public service hours: 52.

STUDENT LIFE
Housing options: on-campus residence required through sophomore year; men-only, women-only. Campus housing is university owned. Freshman campus housing is guaranteed.

Activities and organizations: choral group, Student Government.

Athletics Member NCCAA. ***Intercollegiate sports:*** baseball M, basketball M/W, cross-country running W, soccer M/W, volleyball W. ***Intramural sports:*** basketball M/W, sand volleyball M/W, soccer M/W, table tennis M/W, volleyball M/W.

Campus security: controlled dormitory access.

Student services: personal/psychological counseling.

FINANCIAL AID
Financial Aid Of all full-time matriculated undergraduates who enrolled in 2005, 189 applied for aid, 132 were judged to have need. 36 Federal Work-Study jobs (averaging $1404). In 2005, 26 non-need-based awards were made. ***Average percent of need met:*** 43. ***Average financial aid package:*** $3940. ***Average need-based loan:*** $3589. ***Average need-based gift aid:*** $1282. ***Average non-need-based aid:*** $3664. ***Average indebtedness upon graduation:*** $15,000.

APPLYING
Standardized Tests *Required for some:* SAT or ACT (for admission).

Options: electronic application, deferred entrance.

Application fee: $30.

Required for some: essay or personal statement, high school transcript, interview.

Application deadlines: rolling (freshmen), rolling (transfers).

CONTACT
Ms. Tyese Little, Admissions Counselor, Dallas Christian College, 2700 Christian Parkway, Dallas, TX 75234-7299. *Phone:* 972-241-3371 Ext. 104. *Toll-free phone:* 800-688-1029. *Fax:* 972-241-8021. *E-mail:* tlittle@dallas.edu.

Dallas International University

Dallas, Texas

http://www.diu.edu/

CONTACT
Dallas International University, 7500 West Camp Wisdom Road, Dallas, TX 75236.

Dallas Nursing Institute

Dallas, Texas

http://www.dni.edu/

CONTACT
Dallas Nursing Institute, 12170 N. Abrams Road, Suite 200, Dallas, TX 75243.

DeVry University–Irving Campus

Irving, Texas

http://www.devry.edu/

- **Proprietary** comprehensive, founded 1969, part of DeVry University
- **Suburban** campus
- **Coed**
- **Minimally difficult** entrance level

FACULTY
Student/faculty ratio: 20:1.

ACADEMICS
Calendar: semesters. *Degrees:* associate, bachelor's, master's, and postbachelor's certificates.
Library: Learning Resource Center.

STUDENT LIFE
Housing options: college housing not available.

APPLYING
Options: deferred entrance.

Application fee: $30.

Required: high school transcript, interview.

CONTACT
DeVry University–Irving Campus, 4800 Regent Boulevard, Suite 200, Irving, TX 75063. *Phone:* 972-929-6777. *Toll-free phone:* 866-338-7934.

East Texas Baptist University

Marshall, Texas

http://www.etbu.edu/

- **Independent Baptist** comprehensive, founded 1912
- **Small-town** 250-acre campus
- **Endowment** $69.4 million
- **Coed** 1,471 undergraduate students, 84% full-time, 56% women, 44% men
- **Moderately difficult** entrance level, 59% of applicants were admitted

UNDERGRAD STUDENTS
1,230 full-time, 241 part-time. Students come from 28 states and territories; 6 other countries; 12% are from out of state; 17% Black or African American, non-Hispanic/Latino; 13% Hispanic/Latino; 0.7% Asian, non-Hispanic/Latino; 0.2% Native Hawaiian or other Pacific Islander, non-Hispanic/Latino; 0.5% American Indian or Alaska Native, non-Hispanic/Latino; 4% Two or more races, non-Hispanic/Latino; 0.2% Race/ethnicity unknown; 0.8% international; 7% transferred in; 80% live on campus.

Freshmen:
Admission: 1,777 applied, 1,056 admitted, 345 enrolled. ***Average high school GPA:*** 3.4. ***Test scores:*** SAT evidence-based reading and writing

scores over 500: 54%; SAT math scores over 500: 56%; ACT scores over 18: 75%; SAT evidence-based reading and writing scores over 600: 13%; SAT math scores over 600: 10%; ACT scores over 24: 17%; SAT evidence-based reading and writing scores over 700: 1%; SAT math scores over 700: 1%; ACT scores over 30: 2%.

Retention: 62% of full-time freshmen returned.

FACULTY

Total: 148, 49% full-time, 56% with terminal degrees.

Student/faculty ratio: 14:1.

ACADEMICS

Calendar: semesters. *Degrees:* certificates, bachelor's, and master's.

Special study options: accelerated degree program, adult/continuing education programs, advanced placement credit, distance learning, double majors, English as a second language, honors programs, independent study, internships, off-campus study, part-time degree program, services for LD students, student-designed majors, summer session for credit.

Computers: 301 computers/terminals and 800 ports are available on campus for general student use. Students can access the following: campus intranet, free student e-mail accounts, online (class) grades, online (class) registration, online (class) schedules. Campuswide network is available. 100% of college-owned or -operated housing units are wired for high-speed Internet access. Wireless service is available via entire campus.

Library: Mamye Jarrett Library. *Books:* 96,495 (physical), 478,599 (digital/electronic); *Serial titles:* 403 (physical), 43,364 (digital/electronic); *Databases:* 175. Weekly public service hours: 88; students can reserve study rooms.

STUDENT LIFE

Housing options: on-campus residence required through senior year; men-only, women-only. Campus housing is university owned. Freshman applicants given priority for college housing.

Activities and organizations: drama/theater group, choral group, marching band, Fellowship of Christian Athletes (FCA), Student Foundation, Student Government Association (SGA), Enactus, Chem Club.

Athletics Member NCAA. All Division III. ***Intercollegiate sports:*** baseball M, basketball M/W, cross-country running M/W, football M, golf M/W, soccer M/W, softball W, tennis M/W, track and field M/W, volleyball W. ***Intramural sports:*** basketball M/W, football M/W, sand volleyball M/W, soccer M/W, softball M/W, table tennis M/W, ultimate Frisbee M/W, volleyball M/W.

Campus security: 24-hour emergency response devices and patrols, student patrols, late-night transport/escort service, controlled dormitory access.

Student services: personal/psychological counseling.

COSTS & FINANCIAL AID

Costs (2019–20) ***Comprehensive fee:*** $36,538 includes full-time tuition ($26,100), mandatory fees ($1110), and room and board ($9328). Full-time tuition and fees vary according to program. Part-time tuition: $870 per credit hour. Part-time tuition and fees vary according to program. ***Required fees:*** $46 per credit hour part-time. ***College room only:*** $4576. Room and board charges vary according to board plan and housing facility. ***Payment plan:*** installment. ***Waivers:*** adult students and employees or children of employees.

Financial Aid Of all full-time matriculated undergraduates who enrolled in 2018, 1,208 applied for aid, 1,090 were judged to have need, 156 had their need fully met. 230 Federal Work-Study jobs (averaging $1777). 9 state and other part-time jobs (averaging $1857). In 2018, 204 non-need-based awards were made. ***Average percent of need met:*** 29. ***Average financial aid package:*** $19,534. ***Average need-based loan:*** $3875. ***Average need-based gift aid:*** $5834. ***Average non-need-based aid:*** $12,013. ***Average indebtedness upon graduation:*** $30,351.

APPLYING

Standardized Tests *Required:* SAT or ACT (for admission).

Options: electronic application.

Application fee: $25.

Required: high school transcript.

Application deadlines: 8/25 (freshmen), 8/25 (out-of-state freshmen), 8/25 (transfers).

CONTACT

Mr. Jeremy Johnson, Assistant Vice President for Enrollment, East Texas Baptist University, One Tiger Drive, Marshall, TX 75670. *Phone:* 903-923-2010. *Toll-free phone:* 800-804-ETBU. *Fax:* 903-923-2001. *E-mail:* admissions@etbu.edu.

Galveston College

Galveston, Texas

http://www.gc.edu/

- **State and locally supported** primarily 2-year, founded 1967
- **Small-town** 11-acre campus with easy access to Houston, Texas
- **Coed** 2,306 undergraduate students, 32% full-time, 61% women, 39% men
- **Noncompetitive** entrance level

UNDERGRAD STUDENTS

731 full-time, 1,575 part-time. Students come from 28 states and territories; 17 other countries; 3% are from out of state; 16% Black or African American, non-Hispanic/Latino; 41% Hispanic/Latino; 3% Asian, non-Hispanic/Latino; 0.3% Native Hawaiian or other Pacific Islander, non-Hispanic/Latino; 0.3% American Indian or Alaska Native, non-Hispanic/Latino; 1% Two or more races, non-Hispanic/Latino; 2% Race/ethnicity unknown; 0.9% international; 9% transferred in.

Freshmen:

Admission: 353 enrolled.

Retention: 55% of full-time freshmen returned.

FACULTY

Total: 105, 56% full-time, 21% with terminal degrees.

Student/faculty ratio: 17:1.

ACADEMICS

Calendar: semesters. *Degrees:* certificates, associate, and bachelor's.

Special study options: academic remediation for entering students, adult/continuing education programs, advanced placement credit, cooperative education, distance learning, double majors, honors programs, internships, part-time degree program, services for LD students, study abroad, summer session for credit.

Computers: 690 computers/terminals are available on campus for general student use. Students can access the following: campus intranet, computer help desk, free student e-mail accounts, online (class) grades, online (class) registration, online (class) schedules. Campuswide network is available. 100% of college-owned or -operated housing units are wired for high-speed Internet access. Wireless service is available via entire campus.

Library: David Glenn Hunt Memorial Library. *Books:* 35,214 (physical), 227,610 (digital/electronic); *Serial titles:* 67 (physical), 34,344 (digital/electronic); *Databases:* 117. Students can reserve study rooms.

STUDENT LIFE

Housing options: Campus housing is university owned.

Activities and organizations: drama/theater group, choral group, Fishing Club, Associate Degree in Nursing (ADN) Club, Radiography Club.

Athletics Member NJCAA. ***Intercollegiate sports:*** baseball M(s), softball W(s). ***Intramural sports:*** badminton M/W, basketball M/W, soccer M/W, tennis M/W, volleyball M/W.

Campus security: 24-hour emergency response devices and patrols, late-night transport/escort service.

Student services: personal/psychological counseling, veterans affairs office.

COSTS & FINANCIAL AID

Costs (2020–21) ***Tuition:*** area resident $1350 full-time, $45 per credit hour part-time; state resident $2010 full-time, $67 per credit hour part-time; nonresident $4260 full-time, $142 per credit hour part-time. Full-time tuition and fees vary according to course load. Part-time tuition and fees vary according to course load. ***Required fees:*** $940 full-time, $25 per credit hour part-time, $95 per term part-time. ***Room and board:*** $3194; room only: $1894. ***Payment plan:*** installment. ***Waivers:*** senior citizens.

Financial Aid Of all full-time matriculated undergraduates who enrolled in 2016, 27 Federal Work-Study jobs (averaging $3000). 3 state and other part-time jobs (averaging $3000).

APPLYING
Options: electronic application.
Required for some: high school transcript.
Application deadlines: rolling (freshmen), rolling (transfers).
Notification: continuous (freshmen), continuous (transfers).

CONTACT
Galveston College, 4015 Avenue Q, Galveston, TX 77550. *Phone:* 409-944-1216.

Gemini School of Visual Arts & Communication

Cedar Park, Texas

http://www.geminischool.com/

CONTACT
Gemini School of Visual Arts & Communication, 501 Prize Oaks Drive, Cedar Park, TX 78613.

Grace School of Theology

Conroe, Texas

http://www.gsot.edu/

CONTACT
Grace School of Theology, 3705 College Park Drive Suite 140, Conroe, TX 77384-4894.

Hallmark University

San Antonio, Texas

http://www.hallmarkuniversity.edu/

CONTACT
Ms. Jennifer Sanchez, Director of Admissions, Hallmark University, 10401 IH-10 West, San Antonio, TX 78230. *Phone:* 210-690-9000 Ext. 7540. *Toll-free phone:* 800-880-6600. *Fax:* 210-697-8225. *E-mail:* jsanchez@hallmarkuniversity.edu.

Hardin-Simmons University

Abilene, Texas

http://www.hsutx.edu/

- **Independent Baptist** comprehensive, founded 1891
- **Urban** 220-acre campus
- **Endowment** $212.4 million
- **Coed** 1,742 undergraduate students, 92% full-time, 53% women, 47% men
- **Moderately difficult** entrance level, 84% of applicants were admitted

UNDERGRAD STUDENTS
1,610 full-time, 132 part-time. Students come from 32 states and territories; 26 other countries; 3% are from out of state; 11% Black or African American, non-Hispanic/Latino; 20% Hispanic/Latino; 2% Asian, non-Hispanic/Latino; 0.1% Native Hawaiian or other Pacific Islander, non-Hispanic/Latino; 0.5% American Indian or Alaska Native, non-Hispanic/Latino; 3% Two or more races, non-Hispanic/Latino; 0.6% Race/ethnicity unknown; 3% international; 6% transferred in; 57% live on campus.

Freshmen:
Admission: 2,189 applied, 1,834 admitted, 479 enrolled. ***Average high school GPA:*** 3.6. ***Test scores:*** SAT evidence-based reading and writing scores over 500: 69%; SAT math scores over 500: 66%; ACT scores over 18: 85%; SAT evidence-based reading and writing scores over 600: 21%; SAT math scores over 600: 16%; ACT scores over 24: 25%; SAT evidence-based reading and writing scores over 700: 3%; SAT math scores over 700: 3%; ACT scores over 30: 4%.
Retention: 67% of full-time freshmen returned.

FACULTY
Total: 237, 45% full-time, 63% with terminal degrees.
Student/faculty ratio: 14:1.

ACADEMICS
Calendar: semesters. *Degrees:* bachelor's, master's, doctoral, post-master's, and postbachelor's certificates.
Special study options: academic remediation for entering students, accelerated degree program, adult/continuing education programs, advanced placement credit, distance learning, double majors, honors programs, independent study, internships, off-campus study, part-time degree program, services for LD students, study abroad, summer session for credit.
Unusual degree programs: 3-2 business administration; Doctor of Physical Therapy and Master of Athletic Training.
Computers: 115 computers/terminals are available on campus for general student use. Students can access the following: campus intranet, computer help desk, free student e-mail accounts, online (class) grades, online (class) registration, online (class) schedules. Campuswide network is available. 100% of college-owned or -operated housing units are wired for high-speed Internet access. Wireless service is available via entire campus.
Library: Richardson Library plus 1 other. *Books:* 175,179 (physical), 45,133 (digital/electronic); *Serial titles:* 184 (physical), 111,157 (digital/electronic); *Databases:* 137. Weekly public service hours: 84

STUDENT LIFE
Housing options: on-campus residence required through sophomore year; men-only, women-only. Campus housing is university owned. Freshman campus housing is guaranteed.
Activities and organizations: drama/theater group, student-run newspaper, choral group, marching band, Baptist Student Ministries, Student Government, Alpha Phi Omega, Student Activities Board, Fellowship of Christian Athletes.
Athletics Member NCAA. All Division III. ***Intercollegiate sports:*** baseball M, basketball M/W, cheerleading M(c)/W(c), cross-country running M/W, football M, golf M/W, soccer M/W, softball W, tennis M/W, track and field M/W, volleyball W. ***Intramural sports:*** badminton M/W, basketball M/W, bowling M/W, football M/W, golf M/W, gymnastics M(c)/W(c), lacrosse M(c)/W(c), racquetball M/W, soccer M/W, softball M/W, table tennis M(c)/W(c), tennis M(c)/W(c), ultimate Frisbee M/W, volleyball M/W.
Campus security: 24-hour emergency response devices and patrols, late-night transport/escort service, controlled dormitory access.
Student services: personal/psychological counseling.

COSTS & FINANCIAL AID
Costs (2020–21) ***Comprehensive fee:*** $41,106 includes full-time tuition ($29,526), mandatory fees ($1840), and room and board ($9740). Part-time tuition: $935 per credit hour. Part-time tuition and fees vary according to course load. ***Required fees:*** $500 per term part-time. ***College room only:*** $4840. Room and board charges vary according to board plan and housing facility. ***Payment plan:*** installment. ***Waivers:*** employees or children of employees.
Financial Aid Of all full-time matriculated undergraduates who enrolled in 2018, 1,350 applied for aid, 1,244 were judged to have need, 231 had their need fully met. In 2018, 373 non-need-based awards were made. ***Average percent of need met:*** 74. ***Average financial aid package:*** $24,415. ***Average need-based loan:*** $4107. ***Average need-based gift aid:*** $7088. ***Average non-need-based aid:*** $14,960. ***Average indebtedness upon graduation:*** $36,053.

APPLYING
Standardized Tests *Required:* SAT or ACT (for admission).
Options: electronic application, early admission, deferred entrance.
Required: high school transcript, minimum 2.0 GPA.
Application deadlines: rolling (freshmen), rolling (out-of-state freshmen), rolling (transfers).
Notification: continuous (freshmen), continuous (out-of-state freshmen), continuous (transfers).

CONTACT
Mr. Grant Greenwood, Director of Undergraduate Admissions and Recruiting, Hardin-Simmons University, Box 16050, Abilene, TX 79698-0001. *Phone:* 325-670-1422. *Toll-free phone:* 877-464-7889. *E-mail:* grant.t.greenwood@hsutx.edu.

Houston Baptist University

Houston, Texas

http://www.hbu.edu/

- **Independent Baptist** comprehensive, founded 1960
- **Suburban** 100-acre campus with easy access to Houston
- **Endowment** $105.6 million
- **Coed** 2,632 undergraduate students, 79% full-time, 66% women, 34% men
- **Moderately difficult** entrance level, 70% of applicants were admitted

UNDERGRAD STUDENTS
2,067 full-time, 565 part-time. Students come from 31 states and territories; 40 other countries; 5% are from out of state; 20% Black or African American, non-Hispanic/Latino; 37% Hispanic/Latino; 8% Asian, non-Hispanic/Latino; 0.2% Native Hawaiian or other Pacific Islander, non-Hispanic/Latino; 0.4% American Indian or Alaska Native, non-Hispanic/Latino; 3% Two or more races, non-Hispanic/Latino; 4% Race/ethnicity unknown; 4% international; 10% transferred in; 34% live on campus.

Freshmen:
Admission: 8,441 applied, 5,943 admitted, 727 enrolled. ***Average high school GPA:*** 3.4. ***Test scores:*** SAT evidence-based reading and writing scores over 500: 87%; SAT math scores over 500: 84%; ACT scores over 18: 94%; SAT evidence-based reading and writing scores over 600: 26%; SAT math scores over 600: 21%; ACT scores over 24: 26%; SAT evidence-based reading and writing scores over 700: 2%; SAT math scores over 700: 4%; ACT scores over 30: 3%.

Retention: 71% of full-time freshmen returned.

FACULTY
Total: 303, 46% full-time, 70% with terminal degrees.

Student/faculty ratio: 14:1.

ACADEMICS
Calendar: semesters. *Degrees:* bachelor's, master's, and doctoral.

Special study options: accelerated degree program, advanced placement credit, distance learning, double majors, external degree program, freshman honors college, honors programs, independent study, internships, off-campus study, part-time degree program, services for LD students, summer session for credit. ***ROTC:*** Army (c), Air Force (c).

Unusual degree programs: 3-2 business administration.

Computers: 125 computers/terminals are available on campus for general student use. Students can access the following: campus intranet, computer help desk, free student e-mail accounts, online (class) grades, online (class) registration, online (class) schedules, office software for 5 devices for each student. Campuswide network is available. 100% of college-owned or -operated housing units are wired for high-speed Internet access. Wireless service is available via entire campus.

Library: Moody Library. *Books:* 123,173 (physical); *Serial titles:* 269 (physical), 123,519 (digital/electronic); *Databases:* 95. Weekly public service hours: 82; students can reserve study rooms.

STUDENT LIFE
Housing options: on-campus residence required for freshman year; coed, men-only, women-only, special housing for students with disabilities. Campus housing is university owned. Freshman campus housing is guaranteed.

Activities and organizations: drama/theater group, student-run newspaper, choral group, marching band, Baptist Student Ministry, Filipino Student Association, African Student Association, American Red Cross at HBU, TriBeta, national fraternities, national sororities.

Athletics Member NCAA. All Division I. ***Intercollegiate sports:*** baseball M(s), basketball M(s)/W(s), cross-country running M(s)/W(s), football M(s), golf M(s)/W(s), soccer M(s)/W(s), softball W(s), track and field M(s)/W(s), volleyball W(s). ***Intramural sports:*** basketball M(c)/W(c), football M/W, soccer M(c)/W(c), ultimate Frisbee M/W(c), volleyball M/W(c).

Campus security: 24-hour emergency response devices and patrols, late-night transport/escort service, controlled dormitory access.

Student services: health clinic, personal/psychological counseling, veterans affairs office.

COSTS & FINANCIAL AID
Costs (2020–21) ***Comprehensive fee:*** $43,630 includes full-time tuition ($32,350), mandatory fees ($2150), and room and board ($9130). Part-time tuition: $1350 per semester hour. ***Required fees:*** $1075 per term part-time. ***College room only:*** $4850. Room and board charges vary according to board plan and housing facility. ***Payment plan:*** installment. ***Waivers:*** employees or children of employees.

Financial Aid Of all full-time matriculated undergraduates who enrolled in 2019, 1,683 applied for aid, 1,598 were judged to have need, 234 had their need fully met. 1,022 Federal Work-Study jobs (averaging $990). In 2019, 430 non-need-based awards were made. ***Average percent of need met:*** 70. ***Average financial aid package:*** $29,796. ***Average need-based loan:*** $4001. ***Average need-based gift aid:*** $23,561. ***Average non-need-based aid:*** $15,528. ***Average indebtedness upon graduation:*** $32,538.

APPLYING
Standardized Tests *Required:* SAT or ACT (for admission).

Options: electronic application, deferred entrance.

Required: high school transcript.

Application deadlines: rolling (freshmen), rolling (out-of-state freshmen), rolling (transfers).

Notification: continuous (freshmen), continuous (out-of-state freshmen), continuous (transfers).

CONTACT
Undergraduate Admissions, Houston Baptist University, 7502 Fondren Road, Houston, TX 77074-3298. *Phone:* 281-649-3211. *Toll-free phone:* 800-696-3210. *Fax:* 281-649-3217. *E-mail:* admissions@HBU.edu.

Howard Payne University

Brownwood, Texas

http://www.hputx.edu/

CONTACT
Mrs. P. J. Gramling, Director of Admission, Howard Payne University, 1000 Fisk Street, Brownwood, TX 76801. *Phone:* 325-649-8406. *Toll-free phone:* 800-880-4478. *Fax:* 325-649-8901. *E-mail:* enroll@hputx.edu.

Huston-Tillotson University

Austin, Texas

http://www.htu.edu/

CONTACT
Ms. Shakitha Stinson, Director of Admission, Huston-Tillotson University, 900 Chicon Street, Austin, TX 78702. *Phone:* 512-505-3029. *Fax:* 512-505-3192. *E-mail:* slstinson@htu.edu.

Jarvis Christian College

Hawkins, Texas

http://www.jarvis.edu/

CONTACT
Mr. Brandon Byrd, Director of Admissions and Enrollment, Jarvis Christian College, PO Box 1470, Hawkins, TX 75765-9989. *Phone:* 903-730-4890 Ext. 2201. *Fax:* 903-769-4842.

The King's University

Southlake, Texas

http://www.tku.edu/

CONTACT
Tyler Maxey, Director of Admissions, The King's University, 2121 E. Southlake Boulevard, Southlake, TX 76092. *Phone:* 817-552-7570. *Toll-free phone:* 888-779-8040. *E-mail:* tyler.maxey@tku.edu.

COLLEGES AT-A-GLANCE

Lamar University

Beaumont, Texas

http://www.lamar.edu/

- **State-supported** university, founded 1923, part of Texas State University System
- **Suburban** 292-acre campus with easy access to Houston
- **Endowment** $128.5 million
- **Coed** 8,697 undergraduate students, 60% full-time, 58% women, 42% men
- **Minimally difficult** entrance level, 84% of applicants were admitted

UNDERGRAD STUDENTS
5,243 full-time, 3,454 part-time. Students come from 36 states and territories; 37 other countries; 2% are from out of state; 24% Black or African American, non-Hispanic/Latino; 21% Hispanic/Latino; 5% Asian, non-Hispanic/Latino; 0.1% Native Hawaiian or other Pacific Islander, non-Hispanic/Latino; 0.3% American Indian or Alaska Native, non-Hispanic/Latino; 3% Two or more races, non-Hispanic/Latino; 3% Race/ethnicity unknown; 1% international; 10% transferred in; 25% live on campus.

Freshmen:
Admission: 6,249 applied, 5,237 admitted, 1,297 enrolled. ***Average high school GPA:*** 3.4. ***Test scores:*** SAT evidence-based reading and writing scores over 500: 69%; SAT math scores over 500: 64%; ACT scores over 18: 75%; SAT evidence-based reading and writing scores over 600: 20%; SAT math scores over 600: 13%; ACT scores over 24: 21%; SAT evidence-based reading and writing scores over 700: 3%; SAT math scores over 700: 3%; ACT scores over 30: 4%.

Retention: 66% of full-time freshmen returned.

FACULTY
Total: 597, 78% full-time, 61% with terminal degrees.

Student/faculty ratio: 18:1.

ACADEMICS
Calendar: semesters. *Degrees:* bachelor's, master's, doctoral, post-master's, and postbachelor's certificates.

Special study options: academic remediation for entering students, accelerated degree program, advanced placement credit, cooperative education, distance learning, double majors, English as a second language, freshman honors college, honors programs, independent study, internships, off-campus study, part-time degree program, services for LD students, student-designed majors, study abroad, summer session for credit. ***ROTC:*** Air Force (c).

Computers: 1,104 computers/terminals are available on campus for general student use. Students can access the following: campus intranet, computer help desk, free student e-mail accounts, online (class) grades, online (class) registration, online (class) schedules. Campuswide network is available. 100% of college-owned or -operated housing units are wired for high-speed Internet access. Wireless service is available via entire campus.

Library: Mary and John Gray Library plus 1 other. *Books:* 410,300 (physical), 115,699 (digital/electronic); *Serial titles:* 29,473 (physical), 47,431 (digital/electronic); *Databases:* 140. Weekly public service hours: 90; students can reserve study rooms.

STUDENT LIFE
Housing options: on-campus residence required for freshman year; coed, special housing for students with disabilities. Campus housing is university owned. Freshman campus housing is guaranteed.

Activities and organizations: drama/theater group, student-run newspaper, television station, choral group, marching band, national fraternities, national sororities.

Athletics Member NCAA. All Division I except football (Division I-AA). ***Intercollegiate sports:*** baseball M(s), basketball M(s)/W(s), cheerleading M/W, cross-country running M(s)/W(s), golf M(s)/W(s)(c), soccer W(s), softball W, tennis M(s)/W(s), track and field M(s)/W(s), volleyball W(s). ***Intramural sports:*** badminton M/W, basketball M/W, cross-country running M/W, football M, golf M/W, racquetball M/W, rugby M/W, sailing M/W, soccer M/W, softball M/W, swimming and diving M/W, table tennis M/W, tennis M/W, track and field M/W, volleyball M/W, weight lifting M/W.

Campus security: 24-hour emergency response devices and patrols, student patrols, late-night transport/escort service, controlled dormitory access.

Student services: health clinic, personal/psychological counseling, veterans affairs office.

COSTS & FINANCIAL AID
Costs (2019–20) ***One-time required fee:*** $10. ***Tuition:*** state resident $7541 full-time, $251 per credit hour part-time; nonresident $20,201 full-time, $673 per credit hour part-time. Full-time tuition and fees vary according to course load, location, and program. Part-time tuition and fees vary according to course load, location, and program. No tuition increase for student's term of enrollment. ***Required fees:*** $2801 full-time, $382 per credit hour part-time. ***Room and board:*** $9158; room only: $5868. Room and board charges vary according to board plan. ***Payment plan:*** installment. ***Waivers:*** senior citizens and employees or children of employees.

Financial Aid ***Average indebtedness upon graduation:*** $35,651.

APPLYING
Standardized Tests *Required:* SAT or ACT (for admission).

Options: electronic application, early admission.

Application fee: $25.

Required: high school transcript. ***Required for some:*** essay or personal statement.

CONTACT
Celeste Contreras, Director of Admissions, Lamar University, PO Box 10009, Beaumont, TX 77710. *Phone:* 409-880-8888. *Fax:* 409-880-8463. *E-mail:* admissions@lamar.edu.

LeTourneau University

Longview, Texas

http://www.letu.edu/

- **Independent nondenominational** comprehensive, founded 1946
- **Suburban** 162-acre campus
- **Coed** 2,862 undergraduate students, 47% full-time, 45% women, 55% men
- **Moderately difficult** entrance level, 45% of applicants were admitted

UNDERGRAD STUDENTS
1,347 full-time, 1,515 part-time. Students come from 45 states and territories; 40 other countries; 30% are from out of state; 10% Black or African American, non-Hispanic/Latino; 6% Hispanic/Latino; 1% Asian, non-Hispanic/Latino; 0.2% Native Hawaiian or other Pacific Islander, non-Hispanic/Latino; 1% American Indian or Alaska Native, non-Hispanic/Latino; 6% Two or more races, non-Hispanic/Latino; 6% Race/ethnicity unknown; 5% international; 6% transferred in; 72% live on campus.

Freshmen:
Admission: 2,314 applied, 1,030 admitted, 362 enrolled. ***Average high school GPA:*** 3.6. ***Test scores:*** SAT evidence-based reading and writing scores over 500: 91%; SAT math scores over 500: 93%; ACT scores over 18: 98%; SAT evidence-based reading and writing scores over 600: 56%; SAT math scores over 600: 45%; ACT scores over 24: 62%; SAT evidence-based reading and writing scores over 700: 12%; SAT math scores over 700: 13%; ACT scores over 30: 20%.

Retention: 76% of full-time freshmen returned.

FACULTY
Total: 267, 35% full-time, 52% with terminal degrees.

Student/faculty ratio: 13:1.

ACADEMICS
Calendar: semesters. *Degrees:* certificates, associate, bachelor's, and master's.

Special study options: accelerated degree program, advanced placement credit, cooperative education, distance learning, double majors, English as a second language, freshman honors college, honors programs, independent study, internships, part-time degree program, services for LD students, study abroad, summer session for credit.

Computers: Students can access the following: campus intranet, computer help desk, free student e-mail accounts, online (class) grades, online (class) registration, online (class) schedules. Campuswide network is available. 100% of college-owned or -operated housing units are wired for high-speed Internet access. Wireless service is available via entire campus.

Library: Margaret Estes Library plus 1 other. *Books:* 31,156 (physical), 287,976 (digital/electronic); *Serial titles:* 53,534 (digital/electronic); *Databases:* 106. Weekly public service hours: 93; students can reserve study rooms.

STUDENT LIFE

Housing options: on-campus residence required through junior year; men-only, women-only, special housing for students with disabilities. Campus housing is university owned. Freshman campus housing is guaranteed.

Activities and organizations: drama/theater group, choral group.

Athletics Member NCAA. All Division III. ***Intercollegiate sports:*** baseball M, basketball M/W, cross-country running M/W, golf M/W, rugby M(c)/W(c), soccer M/W, softball W, swimming and diving M(c)/W(c), tennis M/W, track and field M/W, volleyball W. ***Intramural sports:*** badminton M/W, basketball M/W, golf M/W, racquetball M/W, sand volleyball M/W, soccer M/W, softball M/W, swimming and diving M/W, table tennis M/W, tennis M/W, ultimate Frisbee M/W, volleyball M/W.

Campus security: 24-hour patrols, student patrols, late-night transport/escort service, controlled dormitory access.

Student services: personal/psychological counseling.

COSTS & FINANCIAL AID

Costs (2020–21) ***Comprehensive fee:*** $42,560 includes full-time tuition ($31,740), mandatory fees ($750), and room and board ($10,070).

Financial Aid Of all full-time matriculated undergraduates who enrolled in 2019, 999 applied for aid, 892 were judged to have need, 136 had their need fully met. In 2019, 363 non-need-based awards were made. ***Average percent of need met:*** 70. ***Average financial aid package:*** $23,645. ***Average need-based loan:*** $4376. ***Average need-based gift aid:*** $18,618. ***Average non-need-based aid:*** $15,056. ***Average indebtedness upon graduation:*** $36,103. ***Financial aid deadline:*** 8/1.

APPLYING

Standardized Tests *Required for some:* SAT or ACT (for admission).

Options: electronic application, deferred entrance.

Application deadlines: rolling (freshmen), rolling (transfers).

Notification: continuous (freshmen), continuous (transfers).

CONTACT

LeTourneau University, PO Box 7001, Longview, TX 75607-7001. *Toll-free phone:* 800-759-8811.

Lubbock Christian University

Lubbock, Texas

http://www.lcu.edu/

- **Independent** comprehensive, founded 1957, affiliated with Church of Christ
- **Suburban** 120-acre campus
- **Endowment** $19.7 million
- **Coed**
- **Moderately difficult** entrance level

FACULTY

Student/faculty ratio: 13:1.

ACADEMICS

Calendar: semesters. *Degrees:* bachelor's and master's.

Library: University Library. *Books:* 124,676 (physical), 176,165 (digital/electronic); *Serial titles:* 5 (digital/electronic); *Databases:* 92. Weekly public service hours: 93.

STUDENT LIFE

Housing options: on-campus residence required through sophomore year; men-only, women-only. Campus housing is university owned. Freshman campus housing is guaranteed.

Activities and organizations: drama/theater group, student-run newspaper, radio station, choral group, Student Senate, Enactus, Ag Club, Behavioral Science Society, International Student Association.

Athletics Member NCAA. All Division II.

Campus security: 24-hour patrols, late-night transport/escort service, controlled dormitory access.

Student services: health clinic, personal/psychological counseling.

COSTS & FINANCIAL AID

Costs (2019–20) ***Comprehensive fee:*** $31,270 includes full-time tuition ($23,330) and room and board ($7940). Part-time tuition: $755 per credit hour. ***Required fees:*** $60 per term part-time.

Financial Aid Of all full-time matriculated undergraduates who enrolled in 2018, 1,095 applied for aid, 940 were judged to have need, 105 had their need fully met. 632 Federal Work-Study jobs (averaging $1733). 14 state and other part-time jobs (averaging $735). In 2018, 204 non-need-based awards were made. ***Average percent of need met:*** 64. ***Average financial aid package:*** $16,179. ***Average need-based loan:*** $4221. ***Average need-based gift aid:*** $11,974. ***Average non-need-based aid:*** $6569. ***Average indebtedness upon graduation:*** $39,288.

APPLYING

Standardized Tests *Required:* SAT or ACT (for admission).

Options: electronic application, early decision, early action.

Application fee: $25.

Required: high school transcript.

CONTACT

Mr. Chris Hayes, Director of Admissions, Lubbock Christian University, 5601 19th Street, Lubbock, TX 79407. *Phone:* 806-720-7156. *Toll-free phone:* 800-933-7601. *Fax:* 806-720-7162. *E-mail:* admissions@lcu.edu.

McMurry University

Abilene, Texas

http://www.mcm.edu/

- **Independent United Methodist** comprehensive, founded 1923
- **Suburban** 52-acre campus
- **Endowment** $93.8 million
- **Coed** 1,166 undergraduate students, 87% full-time, 51% women, 49% men
- **Moderately difficult** entrance level, 45% of applicants were admitted

UNDERGRAD STUDENTS

1,020 full-time, 146 part-time. Students come from 14 states and territories; 8 other countries; 3% are from out of state; 14% Black or African American, non-Hispanic/Latino; 28% Hispanic/Latino; 0.9% Asian, non-Hispanic/Latino; 0.2% Native Hawaiian or other Pacific Islander, non-Hispanic/Latino; 0.5% American Indian or Alaska Native, non-Hispanic/Latino; 3% Two or more races, non-Hispanic/Latino; 1% Race/ethnicity unknown; 4% international; 10% transferred in; 47% live on campus.

Freshmen:

Admission: 2,116 applied, 962 admitted, 259 enrolled. ***Average high school GPA:*** 3.5.

Retention: 70% of full-time freshmen returned.

FACULTY

Total: 141, 60% full-time, 60% with terminal degrees.

Student/faculty ratio: 10:1.

ACADEMICS

Calendar: semesters plus May term. *Degrees:* bachelor's and master's.

Special study options: academic remediation for entering students, accelerated degree program, adult/continuing education programs, advanced placement credit, distance learning, double majors, English as a second language, honors programs, internships, off-campus study, part-time degree program, services for LD students, student-designed majors, study abroad, summer session for credit.

Computers: 50 computers/terminals and 705 ports are available on campus for general student use. Students can access the following: campus intranet, computer help desk, free student e-mail accounts, online (class) grades, online (class) registration, online (class) schedules, learning management system. Campuswide network is available. 100% of college-owned or -operated housing units are wired for high-speed Internet access. Wireless service is available via entire campus.

Library: Jay-Rollins Library. *Books:* 128,278 (physical), 218,272 (digital/electronic); *Serial titles:* 115 (physical), 384 (digital/electronic); *Databases:* 128. Weekly public service hours; 86.

STUDENT LIFE

Housing options: on-campus residence required through junior year; coed, men-only, women-only. Campus housing is university owned. Freshman campus housing is guaranteed.

Activities and organizations: drama/theater group, student-run newspaper, choral group, marching band, Alpha Phi Omega, Religious Life Council, McMurry Student Government, Campus Activity Board, Servant Leadership.

Athletics Member NCAA, NCCAA. All NCAA Division III. ***Intercollegiate sports:*** baseball M, basketball M/W, cross-country running M/W, football M, golf M/W, soccer M/W, softball W, swimming and diving M/W, tennis M/W, track and field M/W, volleyball W. ***Intramural sports:*** basketball M/W, football M/W, soccer M/W, softball M/W, ultimate Frisbee M/W, volleyball M/W.

Campus security: 24-hour emergency response devices and patrols, late-night transport/escort service, controlled dormitory access, McMurry Alert System.

Student services: health clinic, personal/psychological counseling, veterans affairs office.

COSTS & FINANCIAL AID

Costs (2020–21) ***One-time required fee:*** $210. ***Comprehensive fee:*** $37,498 includes full-time tuition ($28,530), mandatory fees ($90), and room and board ($8878). Full-time tuition and fees vary according to course load. Part-time tuition: $892 per credit hour. Part-time tuition and fees vary according to course load. ***Required fees:*** $3 per credit hour part-time. ***College room only:*** $4224. Room and board charges vary according to board plan and housing facility. ***Payment plan:*** installment. ***Waivers:*** employees or children of employees.

Financial Aid Of all full-time matriculated undergraduates who enrolled in 2017, 823 applied for aid, 777 were judged to have need, 94 had their need fully met. 130 Federal Work-Study jobs (averaging $975). 40 state and other part-time jobs (averaging $1106). In 2017, 103 non-need-based awards were made. ***Average percent of need met:*** 72. ***Average financial aid package:*** $21,941. ***Average need-based loan:*** $4260. ***Average need-based gift aid:*** $16,829. ***Average non-need-based aid:*** $11,582. ***Average indebtedness upon graduation:*** $31,350.

APPLYING

Options: electronic application, deferred entrance.

Application fee: $25.

Required: essay or personal statement, high school transcript, minimum 2.0 GPA. ***Required for some:*** 3 letters of recommendation, interview.

Application deadlines: 8/15 (freshmen), 8/15 (out-of-state freshmen), 8/15 (transfers).

Notification: continuous (freshmen), continuous (transfers).

CONTACT

Ms. Teresa Bridwell, Admission Counselor, McMurry University, 1 McMurry University, #278, Abilene, TX 79697. *Phone:* 325-793-4700. *Toll-free phone:* 800-460-2392. *Fax:* 325-793-4701. *E-mail:* admissions@mcm.edu.

Messenger College

Euless, Texas

http://www.messengercollege.edu/

- **Independent Pentecostal** 4-year, founded 1987
- **Suburban** 3-acre campus with easy access to Dallas-Fort Worth
- **Endowment** $547,736
- **Coed** 46 undergraduate students, 91% full-time, 57% women, 43% men
- **Moderately difficult** entrance level, 20% of applicants were admitted

UNDERGRAD STUDENTS

42 full-time, 4 part-time. Students come from 12 states and territories; 78% are from out of state; 17% Hispanic/Latino; 4% Two or more races, non-Hispanic/Latino; 4% Race/ethnicity unknown; 15% transferred in; 77% live on campus.

Freshmen:

Admission: 15 applied, 3 admitted, 3 enrolled. ***Average high school GPA:*** 3.2.

Retention: 78% of full-time freshmen returned.

FACULTY

Total: 33, 6% full-time, 12% with terminal degrees.

ACADEMICS

Calendar: semesters. *Degrees:* associate and bachelor's.

Special study options: academic remediation for entering students, advanced placement credit, cooperative education, distance learning, double majors, external degree program, honors programs, independent study, internships, part-time degree program.

Computers: 5 computers/terminals are available on campus for general student use. Students can access the following: campus intranet, free student e-mail accounts, online (class) grades, online (class) registration, online (class) schedules. Campuswide network is available. 100% of college-owned or -operated housing units are wired for high-speed Internet access. Wireless service is available via entire campus.

Library: McDole-McDonald Library. *Books:* 12,617 (physical), 10,290 (digital/electronic); *Serial titles:* 12,705 (physical), 14,979 (digital/electronic); *Databases:* 15. Students can reserve study rooms.

STUDENT LIFE

Housing options: men-only, women-only. Campus housing is university owned.

Campus security: 24-hour emergency response devices, student patrols, controlled dormitory access.

COSTS & FINANCIAL AID

Costs (2020–21) ***One-time required fee:*** $100. ***Comprehensive fee:*** $17,540 includes full-time tuition ($9750), mandatory fees ($1320), and room and board ($6470). Part-time tuition: $325 per credit hour. ***Required fees:*** $660 per term part-time. ***College room only:*** $3350. ***Payment plan:*** installment. ***Waivers:*** employees or children of employees.

Financial Aid Of all full-time matriculated undergraduates who enrolled in 2010, 64 applied for aid, 64 were judged to have need. 16 Federal Work-Study jobs (averaging $460). ***Average percent of need met:*** 44. ***Average financial aid package:*** $8338. ***Average need-based loan:*** $3791. ***Average need-based gift aid:*** $5198. ***Average indebtedness upon graduation:*** $20,805.

APPLYING

Standardized Tests *Required for some:* SAT or ACT (for admission).

Options: electronic application, early admission.

Application fee: $35.

Required: essay or personal statement, high school transcript, minimum 2.0 GPA, 3 letters of recommendation, health form. ***Required for some:*** interview.

Application deadlines: 8/14 (freshmen), 8/14 (out-of-state freshmen), 8/14 (transfers).

Notification: continuous (freshmen), continuous (out-of-state freshmen), continuous (transfers).

CONTACT

Olivia Carter, Teaching & Academic Assistant, Messenger College, 400 South Industrial Boulevard, Suite 300, Euless, TX 76040. *Phone:* 817-554-5950 Ext. 165. *Toll-free phone:* 800-385-8940. *Fax:* 817-391-4003. *E-mail:* enrollment@messengercollege.edu.

Midland College

Midland, Texas

http://www.midland.edu/

- **State and locally supported** 4-year, founded 1969
- **Suburban** 163-acre campus
- **Coed** 5,115 undergraduate students, 31% full-time, 60% women, 40% men
- **Noncompetitive** entrance level

UNDERGRAD STUDENTS

1,579 full-time, 3,536 part-time. 7% Black or African American, non-Hispanic/Latino; 43% Hispanic/Latino; 1% Asian, non-Hispanic/Latino; 0.1% Native Hawaiian or other Pacific Islander, non-Hispanic/Latino;

0.5% American Indian or Alaska Native, non-Hispanic/Latino; 0.9% Two or more races, non-Hispanic/Latino; 15% Race/ethnicity unknown; 3% international; 3% transferred in.

Freshmen:
Admission: 790 enrolled.

FACULTY
Student/faculty ratio: 17:1.

ACADEMICS
Calendar: semesters. *Degrees:* certificates, associate, and bachelor's.

Special study options: academic remediation for entering students, advanced placement credit, cooperative education, distance learning, English as a second language, honors programs, off-campus study, services for LD students, summer session for credit.

Computers: 950 computers/terminals are available on campus for general student use. Students can access the following: computer help desk, free student e-mail accounts, online (class) grades, online (class) registration, online (class) schedules. Campuswide network is available. 100% of college-owned or -operated housing units are wired for high-speed Internet access. Wireless service is available via entire campus.
Library: Murray Fasken Learning Resource Center. Weekly public service hours: 84.

STUDENT LIFE
Housing options: coed, men-only, women-only. Campus housing is university owned.

Activities and organizations: drama/theater group, choral group, OIKOS, Midland College Latin American Student Society, Student Government Association, Student Nurses Association, Baptist Student Ministries.

Athletics Member NJCAA. ***Intercollegiate sports:*** baseball M(s), basketball M(s)/W(s), cheerleading M(s)/W(s), golf M(s), softball W(s), volleyball W(s). ***Intramural sports:*** basketball M/W, cheerleading M/W, volleyball M/W.

Campus security: 24-hour patrols, controlled dormitory access.

Student services: personal/psychological counseling, veterans affairs office.

COSTS & FINANCIAL AID
Costs (2019–20) ***Tuition:*** area resident $3840 full-time; state resident $7080 full-time; nonresident $9600 full-time. Full-time tuition and fees vary according to course level, course load, degree level, location, program, reciprocity agreements, and student level. Part-time tuition and fees vary according to course level, course load, degree level, location, program, reciprocity agreements, and student level. ***Required fees:*** $750 full-time. ***Room and board:*** $5000; room only: $2200. ***Payment plan:*** installment. ***Waivers:*** senior citizens and employees or children of employees.

Financial Aid Of all full-time matriculated undergraduates who enrolled in 2017, 5,640 applied for aid, 3,630 were judged to have need, 137 had their need fully met. 30 Federal Work-Study jobs (averaging $49,712). 10 state and other part-time jobs (averaging $24,745). In 2017, 133 non-need-based awards were made. ***Average percent of need met:*** 57. ***Average financial aid package:*** $7934. ***Average need-based loan:*** $2985. ***Average need-based gift aid:*** $4059. ***Average non-need-based aid:*** $1524.

APPLYING
Options: electronic application.

Application deadlines: rolling (freshmen), rolling (transfers).

Notification: continuous (freshmen), continuous (transfers).

CONTACT
Ms. Amy Webb, Enrollment Services and Navigation Director, Midland College, 3600 North Garfield, Midland, TX 79705-6399. *Phone:* 432-685-4816. *E-mail:* amyw@midland.edu.

Midwestern State University

Wichita Falls, Texas

http://www.mwsu.edu/

- **State-supported** comprehensive, founded 1922
- **Urban** 255-acre campus
- **Endowment** $20.9 million
- **Coed**
- **Moderately difficult** entrance level

FACULTY
Student/faculty ratio: 18:1.

ACADEMICS
Calendar: semesters. *Degrees:* associate, bachelor's, master's, and postbachelor's certificates.
Library: Moffett Library plus 1 other. *Books:* 331,562 (physical), 193,374 (digital/electronic); *Databases:* 123.

STUDENT LIFE
Housing options: on-campus residence required through sophomore year; coed, men-only, women-only, special housing for students with disabilities. Campus housing is university owned. Freshman applicants given priority for college housing.

Activities and organizations: drama/theater group, student-run newspaper, television station, choral group, marching band, Caribbean Students Organization, Baptist Student Ministry, Catholic Campus Ministry, African Students Organization, University Programming Board, national fraternities, national sororities.

Athletics Member NCAA. All Division II.

Campus security: 24-hour emergency response devices and patrols, controlled dormitory access.

Student services: health clinic, personal/psychological counseling, legal services, veterans affairs office.

FINANCIAL AID
Financial Aid Of all full-time matriculated undergraduates who enrolled in 2018, 3,150 applied for aid, 2,670 were judged to have need, 488 had their need fully met. In 2018, 859 non-need-based awards were made. ***Average percent of need met:*** 59. ***Average financial aid package:*** $10,596. ***Average need-based loan:*** $6820. ***Average need-based gift aid:*** $8291. ***Average non-need-based aid:*** $3160. ***Average indebtedness upon graduation:*** $49,146.

APPLYING
Standardized Tests *Required:* SAT or ACT (for admission). *Required for some:* SAT and SAT Subject Tests or ACT (for admission).

Options: electronic application.

Application fee: $25.

Required: high school transcript.

CONTACT
Ms. Leah Vineyard, Interim Director of Admissions, Midwestern State University, 3410 Taft Boulevard, Wichita Falls, TX 76308. *Phone:* 940-397-4343. *Toll-free phone:* 800-842-1922. *Fax:* 940-397-4672. *E-mail:* leah.vineyard@mwsu.edu.

National American University

Austin, Texas

http://www.national.edu/

CONTACT
National American University, 13801 Burnet Road, Suite 300, Austin, TX 78727. *Toll-free phone:* 888-628-8392.

National American University

Georgetown, Texas

http://www.national.edu/

CONTACT
National American University, 1015 West University Avenue, Suite 700, Georgetown, TX 78628. *Toll-free phone:* 888-628-8392.

National American University

Houston, Texas

http://www.national.edu/

CONTACT
National American University, 11511 Katy Freeway, Suite 200, Houston, TX 77079. *Toll-free phone:* 855-455-8029.

National American University

Lewisville, Texas

http://www.national.edu/

CONTACT
National American University, 475 State Highway 121 Bypass, Suite 150, Lewisville, TX 75067. *Toll-free phone:* 800-548-0605.

National American University

Mesquite, Texas

http://www.national.edu/

CONTACT
National American University, 18600 LBJ Freeway, Mesquite, TX 75150. *Toll-free phone:* 800-548-0605.

National American University

Richardson, Texas

http://www.national.edu/

CONTACT
National American University, 300 North Coit Road, Suite 225, Richardson, TX 75080. *Toll-free phone:* 800-548-0605.

North American University

Stafford, Texas

http://www.na.edu/

CONTACT
Mr. Shawn Washington, Associate Director of Admissions, North American University, 11929 West Airport Boulevard, Stafford, TX 77477. *Phone:* 832-230-5555. *E-mail:* admissions@na.edu.

Our Lady of the Lake University

San Antonio, Texas

http://www.ollusa.edu/

- **Independent Roman Catholic** comprehensive, founded 1895
- **Urban** 75-acre campus with easy access to San Antonio, TX
- **Endowment** $27.7 million
- **Coed**
- 93% of applicants were admitted

FACULTY
Student/faculty ratio: 11:1.

ACADEMICS
Calendar: semesters plus summer sessions. *Degrees:* bachelor's, master's, and doctoral.
Library: The Sueltenfuss Library. *Books:* 82,924 (physical), 51,160 (digital/electronic); *Serial titles:* 16,651 (physical), 167,665 (digital/electronic); *Databases:* 96. Weekly public service hours: 95; study areas open 24 hours, 5–7 days a week.

STUDENT LIFE
Housing options: coed, women-only, special housing for students with disabilities. Campus housing is university owned.

Activities and organizations: drama/theater group, student-run newspaper, television station, choral group, First Year Connection, Kappa Delta Chi, Epsilon Sigma Alpha, Social Justice Organization, Higher Achievement Through Leadership Opportunities, national sororities.

Athletics Member NAIA.

Campus security: 24-hour emergency response devices and patrols, late-night transport/escort service, controlled dormitory access.

Student services: health clinic, personal/psychological counseling, women's center, veterans affairs office.

FINANCIAL AID
Financial Aid Of all full-time matriculated undergraduates who enrolled in 2016, 1,084 applied for aid, 1,016 were judged to have need, 418 had their need fully met. In 2016, 108 non-need-based awards were made. ***Average percent of need met:*** 84. ***Average financial aid package:*** $22,549. ***Average need-based loan:*** $4785. ***Average need-based gift aid:*** $15,648. ***Average non-need-based aid:*** $8806. ***Average indebtedness upon graduation:*** $34,224.

APPLYING
Standardized Tests *Required:* SAT or ACT (for admission).

Options: early action.

Application fee: $35.

Required: high school transcript, minimum 2.0 GPA.

CONTACT
Shannon Tijerina, Assistant Director of Traditional Admissions, Our Lady of the Lake University, 411 Southwest 24th Street, San Antonio, TX 78207-4689. *Phone:* 210-434-6711 Ext. 4133. *Toll-free phone:* 800-436-6558. *Fax:* 210-431-4036. *E-mail:* sytijeria@lake.ollusa.edu.

Paul Quinn College

Dallas, Texas

http://www.pqc.edu/

CONTACT
Paul Quinn College, 3837 Simpson-Stuart Road, Dallas, TX 75241-4331. *Phone:* 214-379-5494. *Toll-free phone:* 877-346-1063.

Prairie View A&M University

Prairie View, Texas

http://www.pvamu.edu/

- **State-supported** university, founded 1878, part of Texas A&M University System
- **Small-town** 1502-acre campus with easy access to Houston
- **Endowment** $80.9 million
- **Coed** 8,531 undergraduate students, 93% full-time, 64% women, 36% men
- **Moderately difficult** entrance level, 74% of applicants were admitted

UNDERGRAD STUDENTS
7,953 full-time, 578 part-time. Students come from 40 states and territories; 26 other countries; 8% are from out of state; 6% transferred in; 45% live on campus.

Freshmen:
Admission: 7,158 applied, 5,321 admitted, 2,177 enrolled. ***Average high school GPA:*** 3.2.
Retention: 74% of full-time freshmen returned.

ACADEMICS
Calendar: semesters. *Degrees:* bachelor's, master's, doctoral, post-master's, and postbachelor's certificates.

Special study options: academic remediation for entering students, accelerated degree program, advanced placement credit, cooperative education, distance learning, double majors, honors programs, independent study, internships, off-campus study, part-time degree program, services for LD students, study abroad, summer session for credit. ***ROTC:*** Army (b), Navy (b), Air Force (c).

Computers: 3,500 computers/terminals are available on campus for general student use. Students can access the following: campus intranet, computer help desk, free student e-mail accounts, online (class) grades, online (class) registration, online (class) schedules. Campuswide network is available. 100% of college-owned or -operated housing units are wired for high-speed Internet access. Wireless service is available via entire campus.
Library: John B. Coleman Library plus 3 others. Weekly public service hours: 97; students can reserve study rooms.

STUDENT LIFE
Housing options: men-only, women-only, special housing for students with disabilities. Campus housing is university owned. Freshman applicants given priority for college housing.

Activities and organizations: drama/theater group, student-run newspaper, radio and television station, choral group, marching band, Student Government Association, Campus Activities Board, National Association for the Advancement of Colored People, National Society of Black Engineers, Peer Advisors to Leadership Students, national fraternities, national sororities.

Athletics Member NCAA, NAIA. All NCAA Division I except football (Division I-AA). ***Intercollegiate sports:*** baseball M(s), basketball M(s)/W(s), bowling W(s), cheerleading M(s)/W(s), cross-country running M(s)/W(s), golf M(s)/W(s)(c), soccer W(s), softball W(s), tennis M(s)/W(s), track and field M(s)/W(s), volleyball W(s). ***Intramural sports:*** basketball M/W, football M/W, rugby M/W, soccer M, swimming and diving M/W, tennis M/W, volleyball W, weight lifting M/W.

Campus security: 24-hour emergency response devices and patrols, late-night transport/escort service, controlled dormitory access.

Student services: health clinic, personal/psychological counseling, women's center, veterans affairs office.

COSTS & FINANCIAL AID
Costs (2019–20) ***One-time required fee:*** $40. ***Tuition:*** area resident $7043 full-time, $235 per credit hour part-time; state resident $7043 full-time, $235 per credit hour part-time; nonresident $21,912 full-time, $730 per credit hour part-time. Full-time tuition and fees vary according to course load, degree level, program, and reciprocity agreements. Part-time tuition and fees vary according to course load, degree level, program, and reciprocity agreements. No tuition increase for student's term of enrollment. ***Required fees:*** $3743 full-time, $141 per credit hour part-time, $141 per credit hour part-time. ***Room and board:*** $9076; room only: $5890. Room and board charges vary according to board plan, housing facility, and student level. ***Payment plan:*** installment. ***Waivers:*** senior citizens and employees or children of employees.

Financial Aid Of all full-time matriculated undergraduates who enrolled in 2018, 7,424 applied for aid, 6,872 were judged to have need, 650 had their need fully met. 471 Federal Work-Study jobs (averaging $2863). 27 state and other part-time jobs (averaging $2859). In 2018, 171 non-need-based awards were made. ***Average percent of need met:*** 69. ***Average financial aid package:*** $15,404. ***Average need-based loan:*** $7556. ***Average need-based gift aid:*** $8033. ***Average non-need-based aid:*** $7913. ***Average indebtedness upon graduation:*** $32,960.

APPLYING
Standardized Tests *Required:* SAT or ACT (for admission).

Options: electronic application, early admission, deferred entrance.

Application fee: $40.

Notification: 8/15 (freshmen), 8/15 (transfers).

CONTACT
Ms. Nicole Woods, Administrative Assistant, Prairie View A&M University, PO Box 519, MS #1009, Prairie View, TX 77446-0188. *Phone:* 936-261-1000. *E-mail:* admissions@pvamu.edu.

Rice University

Houston, Texas

http://www.rice.edu/

- **Independent** university, founded 1912
- **Urban** 300-acre campus with easy access to Houston
- **Endowment** $6.3 billion
- **Coed** 3,989 undergraduate students, 99% full-time, 48% women, 52% men
- **Most difficult** entrance level, 9% of applicants were admitted

UNDERGRAD STUDENTS
3,942 full-time, 47 part-time. 53% are from out of state; 7% Black or African American, non-Hispanic/Latino; 16% Hispanic/Latino; 26% Asian, non-Hispanic/Latino; 0.2% Native Hawaiian or other Pacific Islander, non-Hispanic/Latino; 0.1% American Indian or Alaska Native, non-Hispanic/Latino; 5% Two or more races, non-Hispanic/Latino; 1% Race/ethnicity unknown; 12% international; 1% transferred in; 70% live on campus.

Freshmen:
Admission: 27,087 applied, 2,361 admitted, 961 enrolled. ***Test scores:*** SAT evidence-based reading and writing scores over 500: 100%; SAT math scores over 500: 100%; ACT scores over 18: 100%; SAT evidence-based reading and writing scores over 600: 98%; SAT math scores over 600: 98%; ACT scores over 24: 98%; SAT evidence-based reading and writing scores over 700: 83%; SAT math scores over 700: 90%; ACT scores over 30: 93%.

Retention: 98% of full-time freshmen returned.

FACULTY
Total: 887, 78% full-time, 90% with terminal degrees.

Student/faculty ratio: 6:1.

ACADEMICS
Calendar: semesters. *Degrees:* bachelor's, master's, and doctoral.

Special study options: accelerated degree program, advanced placement credit, double majors, English as a second language, honors programs, independent study, internships, off-campus study, services for LD students, student-designed majors, study abroad, summer session for credit. ***ROTC:*** Army (c), Navy (b), Air Force (c).

Computers: 245 computers/terminals are available on campus for general student use. Students can access the following: campus intranet, computer help desk, free student e-mail accounts, online (class) grades, online (class) registration, online (class) schedules. Campuswide network is available. 100% of college-owned or -operated housing units are wired for high-speed Internet access. Wireless service is available via entire campus.

Library: Fondren Library. *Books:* 3.0 million (physical), 51,950 (digital/electronic); *Serial titles:* 172,172 (digital/electronic).

STUDENT LIFE
Housing options: coed, special housing for students with disabilities. Campus housing is university owned. Freshman applicants given priority for college housing.

Activities and organizations: drama/theater group, student-run newspaper, radio and television station, choral group, marching band, Drama Club, Community service/volunteer program, intramural sports, College government, Marching Owl Band.

Athletics Member NCAA. All Division I except football (Division I-A). ***Intercollegiate sports:*** badminton M(c)/W(c), baseball M(s), basketball M(s)/W(s), cheerleading W, crew M(c)/W(c), cross-country running M(s)/W(s), equestrian sports W(c), fencing M(c)/W(c), golf M(s), lacrosse M(c), rugby M(c)/W(c), sailing M(c)/W(c), soccer M(c)/W(s), swimming and diving W(s), tennis M(s)/W(s), track and field M(s)/W(s), ultimate Frisbee M(c)/W(c), volleyball M(c)/W(s), water polo M(c)/W(c). ***Intramural sports:*** badminton M/W, basketball M/W, cross-country running M/W, football M, golf M/W, racquetball M/W, soccer M/W, softball M/W, swimming and diving M/W, table tennis M/W, tennis M/W, track and field M/W, ultimate Frisbee M/W, volleyball M/W, water polo M/W.

Campus security: 24-hour emergency response devices and patrols, late-night transport/escort service, controlled dormitory access.

Student services: health clinic, personal/psychological counseling, women's center.

COSTS & FINANCIAL AID
Costs (2019–20) ***Comprehensive fee:*** $63,252 includes full-time tuition ($48,330), mandatory fees ($782), and room and board ($14,140). Part-time tuition: $2014 per credit hour. ***College room only:*** $9700.

Financial Aid Of all full-time matriculated undergraduates who enrolled in 2019, 2,931 applied for aid, 1,729 were judged to have need, 1,708 had their need fully met. In 2019, 379 non-need-based awards were made. ***Average percent of need met:*** 100. ***Average financial aid package:*** $52,493. ***Average need-based loan:*** $3302. ***Average need-based gift aid:*** $48,300. ***Average non-need-based aid:*** $20,318. ***Average indebtedness upon graduation:*** $24,292.

APPLYING
Standardized Tests *Required:* SAT or ACT (for admission). *Recommended:* SAT Subject Tests (for admission).

Options: electronic application, early decision, deferred entrance.

Application fee: $75.

Required: essay or personal statement, high school transcript, 2 letters of recommendation. ***Required for some:*** portfolio for architecture, audition for music. ***Recommended:*** interview.

Application deadlines: 1/1 (freshmen), 3/15 (transfers).

Early decision deadline: 11/1.

Notification: 4/1 (freshmen), continuous until 5/15 (transfers), 12/15 (early decision).

CONTACT

Rice University, 6100 Main Street, PO Box 1892, Houston, TX 77251-1892. *Phone:* 713-348-RICE.

Rio Grande Bible Institute

Edinburg, Texas

http://www.riogrande.edu/

CONTACT

David Loyola, Director of Admissions, Rio Grande Bible Institute, 4300 S US Hwy 281, Edinburg, TX 78539. *Phone:* 956-380-8100. *Fax:* 956-380-8256. *E-mail:* admisiones@riogrande.edu.

St. Edward's University

Austin, Texas

http://www.stedwards.edu/

- **Independent Roman Catholic** comprehensive, founded 1885
- **Urban** 160-acre campus with easy access to Austin
- **Endowment** $94.9 million
- **Coed**
- **Moderately difficult** entrance level

FACULTY

Student/faculty ratio: 13:1.

ACADEMICS

Calendar: semesters. *Degrees:* bachelor's, master's, and postbachelor's certificates.

Library: Munday Library. *Books:* 71,983 (physical), 273,440 (digital/electronic); *Serial titles:* 202 (physical), 121,477 (digital/electronic); *Databases:* 230. Weekly public service hours: 103; students can reserve study rooms.

STUDENT LIFE

Housing options: on-campus residence required for freshman year; coed, special housing for students with disabilities. Campus housing is university owned. Freshman campus housing is guaranteed.

Activities and organizations: drama/theater group, student-run newspaper, radio and television station, choral group, American Medical Student Association, Students for Sustainability, Academy of Science, PRIDE, Asian Student Association.

Athletics Member NCAA. All Division II.

Campus security: 24-hour emergency response devices and patrols, late-night transport/escort service, controlled dormitory access, self-defense education, informal discussions, pamphlets, posters, alcohol awareness meetings, lighted pathways and sidewalks.

Student services: health clinic, personal/psychological counseling, veterans affairs office.

FINANCIAL AID

Financial Aid Of all full-time matriculated undergraduates who enrolled in 2018, 2,662 applied for aid, 2,407 were judged to have need, 357 had their need fully met. In 2018, 164 non-need-based awards were made. ***Average percent of need met:*** 67. ***Average financial aid package:*** $36,366. ***Average need-based loan:*** $4512. ***Average need-based gift aid:*** $22,805. ***Average non-need-based aid:*** $17,934. ***Average indebtedness upon graduation:*** $38,406.

APPLYING

Standardized Tests *Required:* SAT or ACT (for admission).

Options: electronic application, deferred entrance.

Application fee: $50.

Required: essay or personal statement, high school transcript, 1 letter of recommendation. ***Recommended:*** interview.

CONTACT

Ms. Kelsey McClure, Administrative Coordinator, St. Edward's University, 3001 South Congress Avenue, Austin, TX 78704. *Phone:* 512-448-8500. *Toll-free phone:* 800-555-0164. *Fax:* 512-464-8877. *E-mail:* seu.admit@stedwards.edu.

St. Mary's University

San Antonio, Texas

http://www.stmarytx.edu/

- **Independent Roman Catholic** comprehensive, founded 1852
- **Urban** 135-acre campus with easy access to San Antonio
- **Endowment** $196.0 million
- **Coed** 2,270 undergraduate students, 95% full-time, 56% women, 44% men
- **Moderately difficult** entrance level, 79% of applicants were admitted

UNDERGRAD STUDENTS

2,162 full-time, 108 part-time. Students come from 31 states and territories; 30 other countries; 12% are from out of state; 3% Black or African American, non-Hispanic/Latino; 68% Hispanic/Latino; 2% Asian, non-Hispanic/Latino; 0.2% American Indian or Alaska Native, non Hispanic/Latino; 1% Two or more races, non-Hispanic/Latino; 4% Race/ethnicity unknown; 6% international; 4% transferred in; 51% live on campus.

Freshmen:

Admission: 4,861 applied, 3,822 admitted, 545 enrolled. ***Average high school GPA:*** 3.7. ***Test scores:*** SAT evidence-based reading and writing scores over 500: 91%; SAT math scores over 500: 83%; ACT scores over 18: 97%; SAT evidence-based reading and writing scores over 600: 39%; SAT math scores over 600: 30%; ACT scores over 24: 42%; SAT evidence-based reading and writing scores over 700: 3%; SAT math scores over 700: 3%; ACT scores over 30: 7%.

Retention: 74% of full-time freshmen returned.

FACULTY

Total: 384, 58% full-time, 77% with terminal degrees.

Student/faculty ratio: 11:1.

ACADEMICS

Calendar: semesters. *Degrees:* certificates, bachelor's, master's, doctoral, and postbachelor's certificates.

Special study options: academic remediation for entering students, adult/continuing education programs, advanced placement credit, cooperative education, distance learning, double majors, English as a second language, honors programs, independent study, internships, off-campus study, part-time degree program, services for LD students, study abroad, summer session for credit. ***ROTC:*** Army (b), Air Force (c).

Computers: 200 computers/terminals and 125 ports are available on campus for general student use. Students can access the following: campus intranet, computer help desk, free student e-mail accounts, online (class) grades, online (class) registration, online (class) schedules. Campuswide network is available. 100% of college-owned or -operated housing units are wired for high-speed Internet access. Wireless service is available via entire campus.

Library: Louis J. Blume Library plus 1 other. *Books:* 205,522 (physical), 530,643 (digital/electronic); *Serial titles:* 479 (physical), 50,186 (digital/electronic); *Databases:* 139. Weekly public service hours: 100.

STUDENT LIFE

Housing options: on-campus residence required for freshman year; coed, special housing for students with disabilities. Campus housing is university owned. Freshman applicants given priority for college housing.

Activities and organizations: drama/theater group, student-run newspaper, choral group, Alpha Phi Omega (Professional Service Fraternity), Beta Beta Beta Biological Honor Society, Delta Sigma Pi (Professional Business Fraternity), Society of Hispanic Engineers, Pre-Medical Society, national fraternities, national sororities.

Athletics Member NCAA. All Division II. ***Intercollegiate sports:*** baseball M(s), basketball M(s)/W(s), golf M(s), soccer M(s)/W(s), softball W, tennis M(s)/W(s), volleyball W(s). ***Intramural sports:*** badminton M/W, basketball M/W, football M/W, racquetball M/W, rock climbing M/W, sand volleyball M/W, soccer M/W, softball M/W, swimming and diving M/W, table tennis M/W, tennis M/W, ultimate Frisbee M(c)/W(c), volleyball M/W.

Campus security: 24-hour emergency response devices and patrols, late-night transport/escort service, controlled dormitory access.

Student services: health clinic, personal/psychological counseling.

COSTS & FINANCIAL AID
Costs (2020–21) ***Comprehensive fee:*** $45,720 includes full-time tuition ($33,720), mandatory fees ($1020), and room and board ($10,980). Full-time tuition and fees vary according to course load, degree level, program, reciprocity agreements, and student level. Part-time tuition: $1010 per credit hour. Part-time tuition and fees vary according to course load, degree level, program, reciprocity agreements, and student level. ***Required fees:*** $510 per term part-time. ***College room only:*** $7000. Room and board charges vary according to board plan, housing facility, and student level. ***Payment plan:*** installment.

Financial Aid Of all full-time matriculated undergraduates who enrolled in 2018, 1,813 applied for aid, 1,598 were judged to have need, 196 had their need fully met. 447 Federal Work-Study jobs (averaging $2087). 61 state and other part-time jobs (averaging $2430). In 2018, 471 non-need-based awards were made. ***Average percent of need met:*** 77. ***Average financial aid package:*** $28,040. ***Average need-based loan:*** $4235. ***Average need-based gift aid:*** $22,804. ***Average non-need-based aid:*** $18,709. ***Average indebtedness upon graduation:*** $35,111. ***Financial aid deadline:*** 6/1.

APPLYING
Standardized Tests *Required:* SAT or ACT (for admission).

Options: electronic application, deferred entrance.

Required: essay or personal statement, high school transcript, minimum 2.5 GPA, 1 letter of recommendation. ***Required for some:*** interview.

Application deadlines: rolling (freshmen), rolling (transfers).

Notification: continuous (freshmen), continuous (transfers).

CONTACT
Gerardo Salgado, Senior Admission Counselor, St. Mary's University, One Camino Santa Maria, Box #3, San Antonio, TX 78228. *Phone:* 210-436-3126. *Toll-free phone:* 800-367-7868. *Fax:* 210-431-6742. *E-mail:* uadm@stmarytx.edu.

Sam Houston State University

Huntsville, Texas

http://www.shsu.edu/

- **State-supported** university, founded 1879, part of Texas State University System
- **Small-town** campus with easy access to Houston
- **Endowment** $96.5 million
- **Coed** 18,783 undergraduate students, 81% full-time, 62% women, 38% men
- **Moderately difficult** entrance level, 83% of applicants were admitted

UNDERGRAD STUDENTS
15,296 full-time, 3,487 part-time. 2% are from out of state; 18% Black or African American, non-Hispanic/Latino; 25% Hispanic/Latino; 2% Asian, non-Hispanic/Latino; 0.1% Native Hawaiian or other Pacific Islander, non-Hispanic/Latino; 0.6% American Indian or Alaska Native, non-Hispanic/Latino; 3% Two or more races, non-Hispanic/Latino; 2% Race/ethnicity unknown; 1% international; 14% transferred in; 20% live on campus.

Freshmen:
Admission: 11,569 applied, 9,649 admitted, 2,927 enrolled. ***Test scores:*** SAT evidence-based reading and writing scores over 500: 78%; SAT math scores over 500: 68%; ACT scores over 18: 88%; SAT evidence-based reading and writing scores over 600: 19%; SAT math scores over 600: 12%; ACT scores over 24: 21%; SAT evidence-based reading and writing scores over 700: 1%; SAT math scores over 700: 1%; ACT scores over 30: 2%.

Retention: 75% of full-time freshmen returned.

FACULTY
Total: 988, 68% full-time, 73% with terminal degrees.

Student/faculty ratio: 23:1.

ACADEMICS
Calendar: semesters. *Degrees:* bachelor's, master's, doctoral, and postbachelor's certificates.

Special study options: academic remediation for entering students, accelerated degree program, advanced placement credit, distance learning, double majors, English as a second language, external degree program, honors programs, independent study, internships, off-campus study, part-time degree program, services for LD students, study abroad, summer session for credit. ***ROTC:*** Army (b).

Computers: 1,600 computers/terminals and 5,544 ports are available on campus for general student use. Students can access the following: computer help desk, free student e-mail accounts, online (class) grades, online (class) registration, online (class) schedules. Campuswide network is available. 100% of college-owned or -operated housing units are wired for high-speed Internet access. Wireless service is available via entire campus.

Library: Newton Gresham Library. Students can reserve study rooms.

STUDENT LIFE
Housing options: on-campus residence required for freshman year; coed, women-only, special housing for students with disabilities. Campus housing is university owned. Freshman campus housing is guaranteed.

Activities and organizations: drama/theater group, student-run newspaper, radio and television station, choral group, marching band, national fraternities, national sororities.

Athletics Member NCAA. All Division I except football (Division I-AA). ***Intercollegiate sports:*** baseball M(s), basketball M(s)/W(s), bowling W(s), cheerleading M(s)/W(s), cross-country running M(s)/W(s), equestrian sports M/W, golf M(s)/W(s), lacrosse M(c)/W(c), soccer W(s), softball W(s), tennis W(s), track and field M(s)/W(s), ultimate Frisbee M(c)/W(c), volleyball W(s). ***Intramural sports:*** basketball M/W, football M/W, racquetball M/W, riflery M(c), rugby M(c)/W(c), soccer M/W, softball M/W, tennis M(c)/W(c), volleyball M/W.

Campus security: 24-hour emergency response devices and patrols, student patrols, late-night transport/escort service, controlled dormitory access.

Student services: health clinic, personal/psychological counseling, legal services, veterans affairs office.

FINANCIAL AID
Financial Aid Of all full-time matriculated undergraduates who enrolled in 2018, 11,872 applied for aid, 10,307 were judged to have need, 647 had their need fully met. In 2018, 403 non-need-based awards were made. ***Average percent of need met:*** 74. ***Average financial aid package:*** $11,812. ***Average need-based loan:*** $4022. ***Average need-based gift aid:*** $7983. ***Average non-need-based aid:*** $2733. ***Average indebtedness upon graduation:*** $27,207.

APPLYING
Standardized Tests *Required:* SAT or ACT (for admission).

Options: electronic application, early admission.

Application fee: $45.

Required: high school transcript.

Application deadlines: 8/1 (freshmen), 8/1 (transfers).

CONTACT
Ms. Angie Taylor, Director of Admissions, Sam Houston State University, Box 2418, Huntsville, TX 77341. *Phone:* 936-294-1845. *Toll-free phone:* 866-232-7528 Ext. 1828. *Fax:* 936-294-3758. *E-mail:* agb003@shsu.edu.

Schreiner University

Kerrville, Texas

http://www.schreiner.edu/

- **Independent Presbyterian** comprehensive, founded 1923
- **Small-town** 211-acre campus with easy access to San Antonio, Austin
- **Endowment** $72.7 million
- **Coed** 1,257 undergraduate students, 86% full-time, 56% women, 44% men
- **Moderately difficult** entrance level, 93% of applicants were admitted

UNDERGRAD STUDENTS
1,087 full-time, 170 part-time. Students come from 24 states and territories; 4 other countries; 3% are from out of state; 4% Black or

African American, non-Hispanic/Latino; 43% Hispanic/Latino; 1% Asian, non-Hispanic/Latino; 0.1% Native Hawaiian or other Pacific Islander, non-Hispanic/Latino; 0.3% American Indian or Alaska Native, non-Hispanic/Latino; 2% Two or more races, non-Hispanic/Latino; 0.9% international; 4% transferred in; 61% live on campus.

Freshmen:
Admission: 1,194 applied, 1,113 admitted, 310 enrolled. ***Average high school GPA:*** 3.5. ***Test scores:*** SAT evidence-based reading and writing scores over 500: 60%; SAT math scores over 500: 58%; ACT scores over 18: 69%; SAT evidence-based reading and writing scores over 600: 13%; SAT math scores over 600: 13%; ACT scores over 24: 16%; SAT math scores over 700: 1%.

Retention: 64% of full-time freshmen returned.

FACULTY
Total: 123, 50% full-time.

Student/faculty ratio: 14:1.

ACADEMICS
Calendar: semesters. *Degrees:* certificates, associate, bachelor's, and master's.

Special study options: academic remediation for entering students, accelerated degree program, advanced placement credit, cooperative education, distance learning, double majors, honors programs, independent study, internships, part-time degree program, services for LD students, student-designed majors, study abroad, summer session for credit.

Unusual degree programs: 3-2 engineering with University of Texas at Austin, Texas A&M University, University of North Dakota.

Computers: 120 computers/terminals are available on campus for general student use. Students can access the following: campus intranet, computer help desk, free student e-mail accounts, online (class) grades, online (class) registration, online (class) schedules. Campuswide network is available. 100% of college-owned or -operated housing units are wired for high-speed Internet access. Wireless service is available via entire campus.

Library: W. M. Logan Library. *Books:* 75,807 (physical), 201,500 (digital/electronic); *Serial titles:* 45 (physical), 49,182 (digital/electronic); *Databases:* 104. Weekly public service hours: 30; students can reserve study rooms.

STUDENT LIFE
Housing options: on-campus residence required through junior year; coed, special housing for students with disabilities. Campus housing is university owned. Freshman campus housing is guaranteed.

Activities and organizations: drama/theater group, student-run newspaper, choral group, Student Senate, Greek Life, Campus Ministry, honor societies, Hall Councils, national fraternities, national sororities.

Athletics Member NCAA. All Division III. ***Intercollegiate sports:*** baseball M, basketball M/W, cross-country running M/W, golf M/W, soccer M/W, softball W, tennis M/W, track and field M/W, volleyball W. ***Intramural sports:*** cheerleading W, equestrian sports W, riflery M/W, wrestling M/W.

Campus security: 24-hour emergency response devices and patrols, student patrols, late-night transport/escort service, controlled dormitory access.

Student services: health clinic, personal/psychological counseling, veterans affairs office.

COSTS & FINANCIAL AID
Costs (2020–21) ***Comprehensive fee:*** $42,517 includes full-time tuition ($31,938) and room and board ($10,579). Full-time tuition and fees vary according to course load, location, and program. Part-time tuition: $1451 per credit hour. Part-time tuition and fees vary according to course load and program. No tuition increase for student's term of enrollment. ***College room only:*** $4956. Room and board charges vary according to board plan and housing facility. ***Payment plan:*** installment. ***Waivers:*** employees or children of employees.

Financial Aid Of all full-time matriculated undergraduates who enrolled in 2018, 957 applied for aid, 853 were judged to have need, 96 had their need fully met. 124 Federal Work-Study jobs (averaging $2109). In 2018, 90 non-need-based awards were made. ***Average percent of need met:*** 38. ***Average financial aid package:*** $21,816. ***Average need-based loan:*** $3667. ***Average need-based gift aid:*** $8020. ***Average non-need-based aid:*** $12,291. ***Average indebtedness upon graduation:*** $47,330.

APPLYING
Standardized Tests *Required:* SAT or ACT (for admission).

Options: electronic application, deferred entrance.

Application fee: $25.

Required for some: high school transcript.

Application deadlines: 5/1 (freshmen), 5/1 (transfers).

Notification: continuous (freshmen), continuous (transfers).

CONTACT
Danielle Jenschke, Director of Admissions, Schreiner University, 2100 Memorial Boulevard, Kerrville, TX 78028. *Phone:* 830-792-7430. *Toll-free phone:* 800-343-4919. *E-mail:* DRJenschke@schreiner.edu.

Southern Methodist University

Dallas, Texas

http://www.smu.edu/

- **Independent** university, founded 1911, affiliated with United Methodist Church
- **Urban** 234-acre campus with easy access to Dallas-Fort Worth
- **Endowment** $1.5 billion
- **Coed** 6,710 undergraduate students, 97% full-time, 49% women, 51% men
- **Moderately difficult** entrance level, 47% of applicants were admitted

UNDERGRAD STUDENTS
6,519 full-time, 191 part-time. Students come from 53 states and territories; 59 other countries; 55% are from out of state; 4% Black or African American, non-Hispanic/Latino; 12% Hispanic/Latino; 7% Asian, non-Hispanic/Latino; 0.2% American Indian or Alaska Native, non-Hispanic/Latino; 4% Two or more races, non-Hispanic/Latino; 0.4% Race/ethnicity unknown; 7% international; 4% transferred in; 54% live on campus.

Freshmen:
Admission: 13,959 applied, 6,601 admitted, 1,544 enrolled. ***Average high school GPA:*** 3.6. ***Test scores:*** SAT evidence-based reading and writing scores over 500: 99%; SAT math scores over 500: 99%; ACT scores over 18: 100%; SAT evidence-based reading and writing scores over 600: 91%; SAT math scores over 600: 90%; ACT scores over 24: 97%; SAT evidence-based reading and writing scores over 700: 39%; SAT math scores over 700: 57%; ACT scores over 30: 71%.

Retention: 91% of full-time freshmen returned.

FACULTY
Total: 1,151, 66% full-time, 71% with terminal degrees.

Student/faculty ratio: 11:1.

ACADEMICS
Calendar: semesters. *Degrees:* bachelor's, master's, doctoral, post-master's, and postbachelor's certificates.

Special study options: academic remediation for entering students, accelerated degree program, adult/continuing education programs, advanced placement credit, cooperative education, distance learning, double majors, English as a second language, honors programs, independent study, internships, part-time degree program, services for LD students, student-designed majors, study abroad, summer session for credit. ***ROTC:*** Army (b), Air Force (c).

Computers: 758 computers/terminals and 758 ports are available on campus for general student use. Students can access the following: campus intranet, computer help desk, free student e-mail accounts, online (class) grades, online (class) registration, online (class) schedules, online billing/payment processing. Campuswide network is available. 100% of college-owned or -operated housing units are wired for high-speed Internet access. Wireless service is available via classrooms, computer centers, computer labs, dorm rooms, learning centers, libraries, student centers.

Library: Fondren Library plus 7 others. *Books:* 3.0 million (physical), 1.2 million (digital/electronic); *Serial titles:* 16,580 (physical), 139,891 (digital/electronic); *Databases:* 667. Weekly public service hours: 150; study areas open 24 hours, 5–7 days a week; students can reserve study rooms.

STUDENT LIFE

Housing options: on-campus residence required through sophomore year; coed, cooperative, special housing for students with disabilities. Campus housing is university owned. Freshman campus housing is guaranteed.

Activities and organizations: drama/theater group, student-run newspaper, radio and television station, choral group, marching band, Program Council, Student Senate, Student Foundation, Residence Hall Association, SPARC (Students Promoting Awareness, Responsibility, and Citizenship), national fraternities, national sororities.

Athletics Member NCAA. All Division I except football (Division I-A). ***Intercollegiate sports:*** baseball M(c), basketball M(s)/W(s), cheerleading M(s)(c)/W(s)(c), crew W(s), cross-country running W(s), equestrian sports W(s), fencing M(c)/W(c), golf M(s)/W(s), ice hockey M(c), lacrosse M(c), rugby M(c)/W(c), soccer M(s)/W(s), swimming and diving M(s)/W(s), tennis M(s)/W(s), track and field W, volleyball W(s), wrestling M(c). ***Intramural sports:*** basketball M/W, bowling M/W, football M, golf M/W, racquetball M/W, rock climbing M(c)/W(c), soccer M/W, softball M/W, swimming and diving M/W, table tennis M(c)/W(c), tennis M/W, ultimate Frisbee M/W, volleyball M/W, water polo M/W, weight lifting M(c)/W(c).

Campus security: 24-hour emergency response devices and patrols, late-night transport/escort service, controlled dormitory access.

Student services: health clinic, personal/psychological counseling, women's center, veterans affairs office.

COSTS & FINANCIAL AID

Costs (2020–21) ***Comprehensive fee:*** $75,650 includes full-time tuition ($51,958), mandatory fees ($6582), and room and board ($17,110). Part-time tuition: $2171 per credit hour. ***Room and board:*** Room and board charges vary according to board plan. ***Payment plans:*** tuition prepayment, installment. ***Waivers:*** employees or children of employees.

Financial Aid Of all full-time matriculated undergraduates who enrolled in 2019, 2,567 applied for aid, 2,018 were judged to have need, 727 had their need fully met. In 2019, 2659 non-need-based awards were made. ***Average percent of need met:*** 85. ***Average financial aid package:*** $44,634. ***Average need-based loan:*** $4182. ***Average need-based gift aid:*** $22,114. ***Average non-need-based aid:*** $28,717. ***Average indebtedness upon graduation:*** $30,697.

APPLYING

Standardized Tests *Required:* SAT or ACT (for admission). *Required for some:* SAT Subject Tests (for admission).

Options: electronic application, early decision, early action, deferred entrance.

Application fee: $60.

Required: high school transcript, minimum 2.0 GPA, 1 letter of recommendation, statement of good standing from prior institution(s). ***Recommended:*** essay or personal statement, minimum 2.7 GPA.

Application deadlines: 1/15 (freshmen), 4/1 (transfers), 11/1 (early action).

Early decision deadline: 11/1 (for plan 1), 1/15 (for plan 2).

Notification: continuous (freshmen), 12/31 (early decision plan 1), 4/1 (early decision plan 2), 12/31 (early action).

CONTACT

Ms. Elena Hicks, Dean of Undergraduate Admission, Southern Methodist University, PO Box 750181, Dallas, TX 75275-0181. *Phone:* 214-768-3417. *Toll-free phone:* 800-323-0672. *Fax:* 214-768-1083. *E-mail:* ugadmission@smu.edu.

South Texas College

McAllen, Texas

http://www.southtexascollege.edu/

CONTACT

Mr. Matthew Hebbard, Director of Enrollment Services and Registrar, South Texas College, 3201 West Pecan, McAllen, TX 78501. *Phone:* 956-872-2147. *Toll-free phone:* 800-742-7822. *E-mail:* mshebbar@southtexascollege.edu.

South University - Austin

Round Rock, Texas

http://www.southuniversity.edu/austin.aspx

CONTACT

Director of Admissions, South University - Austin, 1220 West Louis Henna Boulevard, Round Rock, TX 78681. *Phone:* 512-516-8800. *Toll-free phone:* 877-659-5706. *Fax:* 512-516-8680.

Southwestern Adventist University

Keene, Texas

http://www.swau.edu/

CONTACT

Ms. Rahneeka Hazelton, Director of Admissions, Southwestern Adventist University, 100 West Hillcrest, Keene, TX 76059. *Phone:* 817-202-6733. *Toll-free phone:* 800-433-2240. *E-mail:* rahneeka@swau.edu.

Southwestern Assemblies of God University

Waxahachie, Texas

http://www.sagu.edu/

CONTACT

Mr. Joshua Martin, Assistant Dean of Admissions, Southwestern Assemblies of God University, 1200 Sycamore Street, Waxahachie, TX 75165. *Phone:* 972-825-4821. *Toll-free phone:* 888-937-7248. *E-mail:* jmartin@sagu.edu.

Southwestern Christian College

Terrell, Texas

http://www.swcc.edu/

CONTACT

Admissions Department, Southwestern Christian College, Box 10, 200 Bowser Street, Terrell, TX 75160. *Phone:* 214-524-3341.

Southwestern University

Georgetown, Texas

http://www.southwestern.edu/

- **Independent Methodist** 4-year, founded 1840
- **Suburban** 700-acre campus with easy access to Austin
- **Endowment** $296.6 million
- **Coed** 1,507 undergraduate students, 99% full-time, 55% women, 45% men
- **Very difficult** entrance level, 49% of applicants were admitted

UNDERGRAD STUDENTS

1,495 full-time, 12 part-time. Students come from 34 states and territories; 16 other countries; 11% are from out of state; 6% Black or African American, non-Hispanic/Latino; 23% Hispanic/Latino; 4% Asian, non-Hispanic/Latino; 0.1% Native Hawaiian or other Pacific Islander, non-Hispanic/Latino; 0.3% American Indian or Alaska Native, non-Hispanic/Latino; 4% Two or more races, non-Hispanic/Latino; 0.8% Race/ethnicity unknown; 1% international; 4% transferred in; 78% live on campus.

Freshmen:

Admission: 4,766 applied, 2,337 admitted, 444 enrolled. ***Average high school GPA:*** 3.5. ***Test scores:*** SAT evidence-based reading and writing scores over 500: 98%; SAT math scores over 500: 97%; ACT scores over 18: 100%; SAT evidence-based reading and writing scores over 600: 66%; SAT math scores over 600: 57%; ACT scores over 24: 70%; SAT evidence-based reading and writing scores over 700: 15%; SAT math scores over 700: 10%; ACT scores over 30: 21%.

Retention: 86% of full-time freshmen returned.

FACULTY

Total: 154, 71% full-time, 88% with terminal degrees.

Student/faculty ratio: 12:1.

ACADEMICS
Calendar: semesters. *Degree:* bachelor's.

Special study options: advanced placement credit, double majors, honors programs, independent study, internships, off-campus study, services for LD students, student-designed majors, study abroad, summer session for credit. ***ROTC:*** Air Force (c).

Unusual degree programs: 3-2 engineering with Engineering school accredited by the Accreditation Board for Engineering and Technology (ABET).

Computers: 395 computers/terminals are available on campus for general student use. Students can access the following: campus intranet, computer help desk, free student e-mail accounts, online (class) grades, online (class) registration, online (class) schedules, transcripts. Campuswide network is available. 100% of college-owned or -operated housing units are wired for high-speed Internet access. Wireless service is available via entire campus.

Library: A. Frank Smith, Jr. Library Center. *Books:* 262,766 (physical), 459,342 (digital/electronic); *Serial titles:* 221 (physical), 86,191 (digital/electronic); *Databases:* 184. Weekly public service hours: 90; study areas open 24 hours, 5–7 days a week.

STUDENT LIFE
Housing options: on-campus residence required through sophomore year; coed, men-only, women-only, special housing for students with disabilities. Campus housing is university owned. Freshman campus housing is guaranteed.

Activities and organizations: drama/theater group, student-run newspaper, radio station, choral group, Students for Environmental Activism and Knowledge (SEAK), Cat Partners, Women's Panhellenic, Men's IFC, Coalition for Diversity and Social Justice, national fraternities, national sororities.

Athletics Member NCAA. All Division III. ***Intercollegiate sports:*** baseball M, basketball M/W, cross-country running M/W, football M, golf M/W, lacrosse M/W, soccer M/W, softball W, swimming and diving M/W, tennis M/W, track and field M/W, volleyball W. ***Intramural sports:*** basketball M/W, cheerleading M(c)/W(c), football M/W, rock climbing M(c)/W(c), sand volleyball M/W, soccer M/W, table tennis M/W, ultimate Frisbee M(c)/W(c), volleyball M/W.

Campus security: 24-hour emergency response devices and patrols, late-night transport/escort service, controlled dormitory access.

Student services: health clinic, personal/psychological counseling, women's center.

COSTS & FINANCIAL AID
Costs (2020–21) ***One-time required fee:*** $200. ***Comprehensive fee:*** $57,570 includes full-time tuition ($45,120) and room and board ($12,450). Part-time tuition: $1880 per credit hour. ***College room only:*** $6800. Room and board charges vary according to board plan, housing facility, and student level. ***Payment plan:*** installment. ***Waivers:*** employees or children of employees.

Financial Aid Of all full-time matriculated undergraduates who enrolled in 2018, 1,059 applied for aid, 903 were judged to have need, 244 had their need fully met. 219 Federal Work-Study jobs (averaging $2199). 433 state and other part-time jobs (averaging $2499). In 2018, 500 non-need-based awards were made. ***Average percent of need met:*** 87. ***Average financial aid package:*** $37,110. ***Average need-based loan:*** $4425. ***Average need-based gift aid:*** $31,848. ***Average non-need-based aid:*** $22,521. ***Average indebtedness upon graduation:*** $34,133.

APPLYING
Standardized Tests *Required for some:* SAT or ACT (for admission).

Options: electronic application, early admission, early decision, early action, deferred entrance.

Required: essay or personal statement, high school transcript, 1 letter of recommendation, counselor recommendation. ***Recommended:*** interview.

Application deadlines: 2/1 (freshmen), 2/1 (out-of-state freshmen), 4/1 (transfers), 12/1 (early action).

Early decision deadline: 11/1.

Notification: 4/1 (freshmen), 4/1 (out-of-state freshmen), 7/1 (transfers), 12/1 (early decision), 3/1 (early action).

CONTACT
Mrs. Christine Bowman, Dean of Enrollment Services, Southwestern University, 1001 East University Avenue, Georgetown, TX 78626. *Phone:* 512-863-1200. *Toll-free phone:* 800-252-3166. *Fax:* 512-863-9601. *E-mail:* admission@southwestern.edu.

Southwest University at El Paso

El Paso, Texas

http://southwestuniversity.edu/

CONTACT
Southwest University at El Paso, 1414 Geronimo Drive, El Paso, TX 79925.

Stephen F. Austin State University

Nacogdoches, Texas

http://www.sfasu.edu/

CONTACT
Mr. Kevin Davis, Associate Director of Admissions, Stephen F. Austin State University, PO Box 13051, SFA Station, Nacogdoches, TX 75962. *Phone:* 936-468-2504. *Toll-free phone:* 800-731-2902. *Fax:* 936-468-3849. *E-mail:* admissions@sfasu.edu.

Strayer University - Cedar Hill

Cedar Hill, Texas

http://www.strayer.edu/texas/cedar-hill/

CONTACT
Strayer University - Cedar Hill, 610 Uptown Boulevard, Suite 3500, Cedar Hill, TX 75104. *Toll-free phone:* 888-311-0355.

Strayer University–North Austin Campus

Austin, Texas

http://www.strayer.edu/texas/north-austin/

CONTACT
Strayer University–North Austin Campus, 8501 North Mopac Expressway, Suite 100, Austin, TX 78759. *Toll-free phone:* 888-311-0355.

Strayer University–North Dallas Campus

Farmers Branch, Texas

http://www.strayer.edu/texas/north-dallas

CONTACT
Strayer University–North Dallas Campus, 2711 LBJ Freeway, Suite 450, Farmers Branch, TX 75234-7315.

Strayer University–Northwest Houston Campus

Houston, Texas

http://www.strayer.edu/texas/northwest-houston/

CONTACT
Strayer University–Northwest Houston Campus, 10343 Sam Houston Park Drive, Suite 110, Houston, TX 77064. *Toll-free phone:* 888-311-0355.

Strayer University–San Antonio Campus

San Antonio, Texas

http://www.strayer.edu/texas/san-antonio

CONTACT
Strayer University–San Antonio Campus, 40 NE Loop 410, Suite 500, San Antonio, TX 78216.

Strayer University–Stafford Campus

Stafford, Texas

http://www.strayer.edu/texas/stafford

CONTACT
Strayer University–Stafford Campus, 12603 Southwest Freeway, Suite 400, Stafford, TX 77477.

Sul Ross State University

Alpine, Texas

http://www.sulross.edu/

CONTACT
Sul Ross State University, PO Box C - 114, Alpine, TX 79832. *Phone:* 432-837-8050. *Toll-free phone:* 888-722-7778.

Tarleton State University

Stephenville, Texas

http://www.tarleton.edu/

- **State-supported** comprehensive, founded 1899, part of Texas A&M University System
- **Small-town** 175-acre campus with easy access to Fort Worth
- **Endowment** $29.8 million
- **Coed** 11,350 undergraduate students, 72% full-time, 62% women, 38% men
- **Moderately difficult** entrance level, 64% of applicants were admitted

UNDERGRAD STUDENTS
8,211 full-time, 3,139 part-time. 2% are from out of state; 8% Black or African American, non-Hispanic/Latino; 21% Hispanic/Latino; 1% Asian, non-Hispanic/Latino; 0.1% Native Hawaiian or other Pacific Islander, non-Hispanic/Latino; 0.4% American Indian or Alaska Native, non-Hispanic/Latino; 4% Two or more races, non-Hispanic/Latino; 0.5% Race/ethnicity unknown; 0.5% international; 13% transferred in; 32% live on campus.

Freshmen:
Admission: 7,175 applied, 4,593 admitted, 1,858 enrolled. ***Test scores:*** SAT math scores over 500: 65%; ACT scores over 18: 80%; SAT math scores over 600: 14%; ACT scores over 24: 21%; ACT scores over 30: 1%.

Retention: 65% of full-time freshmen returned.

FACULTY
Total: 703, 18% full-time.

Student/faculty ratio: 19:1.

ACADEMICS
Calendar: semesters. *Degrees:* certificates, associate, bachelor's, master's, and doctoral.

Special study options: academic remediation for entering students, accelerated degree program, adult/continuing education programs, advanced placement credit, cooperative education, distance learning, double majors, freshman honors college, honors programs, independent study, internships, off-campus study, part-time degree program, services for LD students, study abroad, summer session for credit. ***ROTC:*** Army (b), Air Force (c).

Computers: 1,200 computers/terminals are available on campus for general student use. Students can access the following: campus intranet, computer help desk, free student e-mail accounts, online (class) grades, online (class) registration, online (class) schedules. Campuswide network is available. 100% of college-owned or -operated housing units are wired for high-speed Internet access. Wireless service is available via entire campus.

Library: Dick Smith Library plus 1 other. *Books:* 200,093 (physical), 266,615 (digital/electronic); *Serial titles:* 3,999 (physical), 158,307 (digital/electronic); *Databases:* 311. Students can reserve study rooms.

STUDENT LIFE
Housing options: on-campus residence required through sophomore year; coed, men-only, women-only, cooperative. Campus housing is university owned. Freshman campus housing is guaranteed.

Activities and organizations: drama/theater group, student-run newspaper, radio station, choral group, marching band, Student Government Association, Student Programming Association, Kappa Delta Rho, Delta Zeta, Chi Alpha, national fraternities, national sororities.

Athletics Member NCAA. All Division II. ***Intercollegiate sports:*** baseball M(s), basketball M(s)/W(s), cheerleading M(s)/W(s), cross-country running M(s)/W(s), football M(s), golf W(s), softball W(s), tennis W(s), track and field M(s)/W(s), volleyball W(s). ***Intramural sports:*** archery M/W, basketball M/W, football M/W, golf M/W, racquetball M/W, soccer M/W, softball M/W, table tennis M/W, tennis M/W, volleyball M/W.

Campus security: 24-hour emergency response devices and patrols, student patrols, late-night transport/escort service, controlled dormitory access.

Student services: health clinic, personal/psychological counseling, legal services, veterans affairs office.

COSTS & FINANCIAL AID
Costs (2020–21) ***Tuition:*** state resident $5290 full-time, $174 per credit hour part-time; nonresident $17,869 full-time, $596 per credit hour part-time. Full-time tuition and fees vary according to course load, degree level, program, and student level. Part-time tuition and fees vary according to course load, degree level, program, and student level. No tuition increase for student's term of enrollment. ***Required fees:*** $3848 full-time, $3848 per year part-time. ***Room and board:*** $10,712; room only: $6762. Room and board charges vary according to board plan and housing facility. ***Payment plan:*** installment.

Financial Aid Of all full-time matriculated undergraduates who enrolled in 2019, 6,439 applied for aid, 5,110 were judged to have need, 138 had their need fully met. ***Average percent of need met:*** 53. ***Average financial aid package:*** $9700. ***Average need-based loan:*** $4270. ***Average need-based gift aid:*** $7533. ***Average indebtedness upon graduation:*** $23,820.

APPLYING
Standardized Tests *Required:* SAT or ACT (for admission).

Options: electronic application, early action.

Application fee: $50.

Required: high school transcript.

Application deadlines: 8/20 (freshmen), 8/20 (transfers), 3/1 (early action).

CONTACT
Ms. Cindy Hess, Director of Undergraduate Admissions, Tarleton State University, Box T-0030, Tarleton Station, Stephenville, TX 76402. *Phone:* 254-968-9123. *Toll-free phone:* 800-687-8236. *Fax:* 254-968-9951. *E-mail:* uadm@tarleton.edu.

Texas A&M International University

Laredo, Texas

http://www.tamiu.edu/

- **State-supported** comprehensive, founded 1969, part of Texas A&M University System
- **Urban** 300-acre campus
- **Endowment** $51.9 million
- **Coed** 7,220 undergraduate students, 77% full-time, 61% women, 39% men
- **Moderately difficult** entrance level, 54% of applicants were admitted

UNDERGRAD STUDENTS
5,574 full-time, 1,646 part-time. Students come from 22 states and territories; 29 other countries; 0.7% are from out of state; 0.4% Black or African American, non-Hispanic/Latino; 96% Hispanic/Latino; 0.3% Asian, non-Hispanic/Latino; 0.2% Two or more races, non-

Hispanic/Latino; 0.4% Race/ethnicity unknown; 1% international; 7% transferred in; 9% live on campus.

Freshmen:

Admission: 7,884 applied, 4,287 admitted, 1,297 enrolled. ***Average high school GPA:*** 4.0. ***Test scores:*** SAT evidence-based reading and writing scores over 500: 57%; SAT math scores over 500: 52%; ACT scores over 18: 53%; SAT evidence-based reading and writing scores over 600: 11%; SAT math scores over 600: 9%; ACT scores over 24: 7%; SAT evidence-based reading and writing scores over 700: 1%; SAT math scores over 700: 1%; ACT scores over 30: 1%.

Retention: 79% of full-time freshmen returned.

FACULTY

Total: 400, 58% full-time, 51% with terminal degrees.

Student/faculty ratio: 24:1.

ACADEMICS

Calendar: semesters. *Degrees:* bachelor's, master's, and doctoral.

Special study options: academic remediation for entering students, advanced placement credit, distance learning, double majors, English as a second language, honors programs, independent study, internships, part-time degree program, services for LD students, study abroad, summer session for credit. ***ROTC:*** Army (b).

Computers: 970 computers/terminals are available on campus for general student use. Students can access the following: computer help desk, free student e-mail accounts, online (class) grades, online (class) registration, online (class) schedules. Campuswide network is available. 100% of college-owned or -operated housing units are wired for high-speed Internet access. Wireless service is available via entire campus.

Library: Sue and Radcliff Killam Library. *Books:* 257,033 (physical), 721,976 (digital/electronic); *Serial titles:* 5,376 (physical), 89,109 (digital/electronic); *Databases:* 239. Weekly public service hours: 96; students can reserve study rooms.

STUDENT LIFE

Housing options: coed. Campus housing is university owned.

Activities and organizations: student-run newspaper, choral group, Student Government Association, Campus Activities Board, National Society of Leadership and Success, Greek Association, Student Nurses Association, national fraternities, national sororities.

Athletics ***Intercollegiate sports:*** baseball M(s), basketball M(s)/W(s), cross-country running M(s)/W(s), golf M(s), soccer M(s)/W(s), softball W(s), volleyball W(s). ***Intramural sports:*** badminton M/W, basketball M/W, soccer M/W, softball M/W, table tennis M/W, ultimate Frisbee M/W, volleyball M/W.

Campus security: 24-hour emergency response devices and patrols, late-night transport/escort service, controlled dormitory access, active shooter response training for faculty, staff, and new students; timely on-going threat information dissemination.

Student services: health clinic, personal/psychological counseling, veterans affairs office.

COSTS & FINANCIAL AID

Costs (2020–21) ***Tuition:*** state resident $4773 full-time, $159 per credit hour part-time; nonresident $17,043 full-time, $568 per credit hour part-time. No tuition increase for student's term of enrollment. ***Required fees:*** $4481 full-time, $289 per credit hour part-time, $133 per credit hour part-time. ***Room and board:*** $8809; room only: $5811. ***Payment plans:*** installment, deferred payment. ***Waivers:*** senior citizens.

Financial Aid Of all full-time matriculated undergraduates who enrolled in 2018, 5,174 were judged to have need. ***Average need-based loan:*** $3713. ***Average need-based gift aid:*** $8497. ***Average indebtedness upon graduation:*** $3477. ***Financial aid deadline:*** 6/30.

APPLYING

Standardized Tests *Required:* SAT or ACT (for admission).

Options: electronic application, deferred entrance.

Required: high school transcript.

Notification: continuous (freshmen), continuous (transfers).

CONTACT

Ms. Rosie A. Dickinson, Admissions Director, Office of Admissions, Texas A&M International University, 5201 University Boulevard, Laredo, TX 78041-1900. *Phone:* 956-326-2202. *Toll-free phone:* 888-489-2648. *E-mail:* adms@tamiu.edu.

Texas A&M University

College Station, Texas

http://www.tamu.edu/

- **State-supported** university, founded 1876, part of Texas A&M University System
- **Suburban** campus with easy access to Houston
- **Endowment** $13.5 billion
- **Coed** 53,791 undergraduate students, 89% full-time, 47% women, 53% men
- **Moderately difficult** entrance level, 58% of applicants were admitted

UNDERGRAD STUDENTS

47,667 full-time, 6,124 part-time. Students come from 54 states and territories; 72 other countries; 4% are from out of state; 3% Black or African American, non-Hispanic/Latino; 25% Hispanic/Latino; 9% Asian, non-Hispanic/Latino; 0.1% Native Hawaiian or other Pacific Islander, non-Hispanic/Latino; 0.2% American Indian or Alaska Native, non-Hispanic/Latino; 3% Two or more races, non-Hispanic/Latino; 0.2% Race/ethnicity unknown; 1% international; 5% transferred in; 23% live on campus.

Freshmen:

Admission: 42,899 applied, 24,676 admitted, 10,613 enrolled. ***Test scores:*** SAT evidence-based reading and writing scores over 500: 96%; SAT math scores over 500: 96%; ACT scores over 18: 99%; SAT evidence-based reading and writing scores over 600: 70%; SAT math scores over 600: 70%; ACT scores over 24: 87%; SAT evidence-based reading and writing scores over 700: 19%; SAT math scores over 700: 32%; ACT scores over 30: 45%.

Retention: 93% of full-time freshmen returned.

FACULTY

Total: 3,706, 85% full-time, 77% with terminal degrees.

Student/faculty ratio: 19:1.

ACADEMICS

Calendar: semesters. *Degrees:* bachelor's, master's, doctoral, post-master's, and postbachelor's certificates.

Special study options: academic remediation for entering students, accelerated degree program, advanced placement credit, cooperative education, distance learning, double majors, English as a second language, honors programs, independent study, internships, off-campus study, part-time degree program, services for LD students, study abroad, summer session for credit. ***ROTC:*** Army (b), Navy (b), Air Force (b).

Unusual degree programs: 3-2 business administration; engineering.

Computers: 2,636 computers/terminals are available on campus for general student use. Students can access the following: campus intranet, computer help desk, free student e-mail accounts, online (class) grades, online (class) registration, online (class) schedules, virtual desktops. Campuswide network is available. 100% of college-owned or -operated housing units are wired for high-speed Internet access. Wireless service is available via entire campus.

Library: Sterling C. Evans Library plus 6 others. *Books:* 3.9 million (physical), 1.9 million (digital/electronic); *Serial titles:* 115,870 (physical), 64,422 (digital/electronic); *Databases:* 1,303. Study areas open 24 hours, 5–7 days a week; students can reserve study rooms.

STUDENT LIFE

Housing options: coed, men-only, women-only, cooperative, special housing for students with disabilities. Campus housing is university owned.

Activities and organizations: drama/theater group, student-run newspaper, radio and television station, choral group, marching band, Memorial Student Center, Corps of Cadets, Fish Camp, Student Government, national fraternities, national sororities.

Athletics Member NCAA. All Division I except football (Division I-A). ***Intercollegiate sports:*** baseball M(s), basketball M(s)/W(s), cross-country running M/W, equestrian sports W(s), golf M(s)/W(s), soccer W(s), softball W(s), swimming and diving M(s)/W(s), tennis M(s)/W(s), track and field M(s)/W(s), volleyball W(s). ***Intramural sports:*** archery M(c)/W(c), baseball M(c), basketball M/W, bowling M(c)/W(c), cheerleading W, equestrian sports M(c)/W(c), fencing M(c)/W(c), football M/W, golf M/W, gymnastics M/W, ice hockey M, lacrosse M(c)/W(c), racquetball M(c)/W(c), riflery M(c)/W(c), rowing M(c)/W(c), rugby M(c)/W(c), sailing M(c)/W(c), soccer M/W, softball M/W, table tennis M/W, tennis M/W, triathlon M(c)/W(c), ultimate Frisbee M(c)/W(c), volleyball M(c)/W(c), water polo M(c)/W(c), weight lifting M(c)/W(c), wrestling M(c)/W(c).

Campus security: 24-hour emergency response devices and patrols, late-night transport/escort service, controlled dormitory access, student escorts.

Student services: health clinic, personal/psychological counseling, women's center, legal services.

COSTS & FINANCIAL AID

Costs (2019–20) ***Tuition:*** area resident $7580 full-time, $253 per credit hour part-time; state resident $7580 full-time, $253 per credit hour part-time; nonresident $34,073 full-time, $1136 per credit hour part-time. Full-time tuition and fees vary according to course load and student level. Part-time tuition and fees vary according to course load and student level. No tuition increase for student's term of enrollment. ***Required fees:*** $3652 full-time. ***Room and board:*** $10,400. Room and board charges vary according to housing facility and location. ***Payment plans:*** tuition prepayment, installment. ***Waivers:*** employees or children of employees.

Financial Aid Of all full-time matriculated undergraduates who enrolled in 2018, 30,712 applied for aid, 22,753 were judged to have need, 4,188 had their need fully met. In 2018, 5559 non-need-based awards were made. ***Average percent of need met:*** 69. ***Average financial aid package:*** $17,534. ***Average need-based loan:*** $8788. ***Average need-based gift aid:*** $10,740. ***Average non-need-based aid:*** $4159. ***Average indebtedness upon graduation:*** $24,590.

APPLYING

Standardized Tests *Required:* SAT or ACT (for admission).

Options: electronic application.

Application fee: $75.

Required: essay or personal statement, high school transcript. ***Required for some:*** Apply Texas application, minimum SAT math score of 550 or ACT math score of 24 for the College of Engineering.

Application deadlines: 12/1 (freshmen), 3/15 (transfers).

Notification: continuous until 12/15 (freshmen), continuous (transfers).

CONTACT

Office of Admissions, Texas A&M University, Freshman Admissions, PO Box 30014, College Station, TX 77842-3014. *Phone:* 979-845-1060. *Fax:* 979-845-1808.

Texas A&M University–Central Texas

Killeen, Texas

http://www.tamuct.edu/

- **State-supported** upper-level, founded 2009, part of Texas A&M University System
- **Rural** 672-acre campus with easy access to Austin Metropolitan Area
- **Coed** 1,944 undergraduate students, 37% full-time, 59% women, 41% men
- 62% of applicants were admitted

UNDERGRAD STUDENTS

717 full-time, 1,227 part-time. Students come from 23 states and territories; 1 other country; 4% are from out of state; 28% Black or African American, non-Hispanic/Latino; 25% Hispanic/Latino; 3% Asian, non-Hispanic/Latino; 0.9% Native Hawaiian or other Pacific Islander, non-Hispanic/Latino; 0.5% American Indian or Alaska Native, non-Hispanic/Latino; 2% Two or more races, non-Hispanic/Latino; 1% Race/ethnicity unknown; 0.1% international; 26% transferred in.

Freshmen:

Admission: 39 applied, 24 admitted.

FACULTY

Total: 189, 46% full-time, 74% with terminal degrees.

Student/faculty ratio: 13:1.

ACADEMICS

Calendar: semesters. *Degrees:* bachelor's, master's, post-master's, and postbachelor's certificates.

Special study options: accelerated degree program, advanced placement credit, cooperative education, distance learning, double majors, independent study, internships, off-campus study, part-time degree program, services for LD students, study abroad, summer session for credit. ***ROTC:*** Army (b).

Computers: 48 computers/terminals are available on campus for general student use. Students can access the following: computer help desk, free student e-mail accounts, online (class) grades, online (class) registration, online (class) schedules. Campuswide network is available. Wireless service is available via entire campus.

Library: University Library. *Books:* 87,374 (physical), 427,178 (digital/electronic); *Serial titles:* 159 (physical), 113,218 (digital/electronic); *Databases:* 283. Weekly public service hours: 72; students can reserve study rooms.

STUDENT LIFE

Activities and organizations: TAMUCT Science club, Phi Alpha, Student Association of Social Workers, TAMUCT Psychology Club, National Society for Leadership and Success.

Athletics ***Intramural sports:*** rugby M(c)/W(c).

Campus security: 24-hour emergency response devices and patrols.

Student services: personal/psychological counseling, veterans affairs office.

COSTS & FINANCIAL AID

Costs (2020–21) ***Tuition:*** state resident $6426 full-time, $254 per credit hour part-time; nonresident $16,241 full-time, $677 per credit hour part-time. Full-time tuition and fees vary according to course load. Part-time tuition and fees vary according to course load. No tuition increase for student's term of enrollment. ***Required fees:*** $2270 full-time, $158 per credit hour part-time. ***Room and board:*** $9136; room only: $9136. ***Payment plan:*** installment.

Financial Aid Of all full-time matriculated undergraduates who enrolled in 2018, 680 applied for aid, 489 were judged to have need, 54 had their need fully met. ***Average percent of need met:*** 71. ***Average financial aid package:*** $9505. ***Average need-based loan:*** $4406. ***Average need-based gift aid:*** $6638.

APPLYING

Options: electronic application, deferred entrance.

Application fee: $30.

Notification: continuous (transfers).

CONTACT

Texas A&M University–Central Texas, 1001 Leadership Place, Killeen, TX 76549. *Phone:* 254-519-5438.

Texas A&M University–Commerce

Commerce, Texas

http://www.tamuc.edu/

- **State-supported** university, founded 1889, part of Texas A&M University System
- **Small-town** 2095-acre campus with easy access to Dallas-Fort Worth
- **Endowment** $22.6 million
- **Coed** 8,324 undergraduate students, 67% full-time, 60% women, 40% men
- **Moderately difficult** entrance level, 36% of applicants were admitted

UNDERGRAD STUDENTS

5,609 full-time, 2,715 part-time. Students come from 39 states and territories; 59 other countries; 6% are from out of state; 22% Black or African American, non-Hispanic/Latino; 22% Hispanic/Latino; 2% Asian, non-Hispanic/Latino; 0.2% Native Hawaiian or other Pacific Islander, non-Hispanic/Latino; 0.5% American Indian or Alaska Native, non-Hispanic/Latino; 7% Two or more races, non-Hispanic/Latino; 1% Race/ethnicity unknown; 4% international; 18% transferred in; 31% live on campus.

Freshmen:

Admission: 10,593 applied, 3,816 admitted, 868 enrolled. ***Average high school GPA:*** 3.4. ***Test scores:*** SAT evidence-based reading and writing

scores over 500: 69%; SAT math scores over 500: 66%; ACT scores over 18: 64%; SAT evidence-based reading and writing scores over 600: 22%; SAT math scores over 600: 17%; ACT scores over 24: 28%; SAT evidence-based reading and writing scores over 700: 3%; SAT math scores over 700: 2%; ACT scores over 30: 2%.

Retention: 65% of full-time freshmen returned.

FACULTY

Total: 660, 59% full-time, 62% with terminal degrees.

Student/faculty ratio: 17:1.

ACADEMICS

Calendar: semesters. *Degrees:* bachelor's, master's, doctoral, and postbachelor's certificates.

Special study options: academic remediation for entering students, accelerated degree program, adult/continuing education programs, advanced placement credit, cooperative education, distance learning, double majors, English as a second language, freshman honors college, honors programs, independent study, internships, off-campus study, part-time degree program, services for LD students, student-designed majors, study abroad, summer session for credit. ***ROTC:*** Air Force (c).

Computers: Students can access the following: campus intranet, computer help desk, free student e-mail accounts, online (class) grades, online (class) registration, online (class) schedules. Campuswide network is available. 100% of college-owned or -operated housing units are wired for high-speed Internet access. Wireless service is available via entire campus.

Library: Gee Library. *Books:* 363,482 (physical), 740,828 (digital/electronic); *Serial titles:* 14,396 (physical), 123,135 (digital/electronic); *Databases:* 272. Weekly public service hours: 110; students can reserve study rooms.

STUDENT LIFE

Housing options: on-campus residence required through sophomore year; coed, men-only, women-only, cooperative, special housing for students with disabilities. Campus housing is university owned. Freshman campus housing is guaranteed.

Activities and organizations: drama/theater group, student-run newspaper, television station, choral group, marching band, National Society for Leadership and Success, Alpha Lambda Delta/Phi Eta Sigma Freshman Honor Societies, Catholic Student Organization, Baptist Student Ministry, Chi Omega Sorority, national fraternities, national sororities.

Athletics Member NCAA. All Division II. ***Intercollegiate sports:*** basketball M(s)/W(s), cheerleading M(s)/W(s), cross-country running M(s)/W(s), football M(s), golf M(s)/W(s), soccer W(s), softball W, track and field M(s)/W(s), volleyball W(s). ***Intramural sports:*** archery M/W, badminton M/W, basketball M/W, bowling M/W, cross-country running M/W, equestrian sports M/W, football M/W, golf M/W, racquetball M/W, soccer M, softball M/W, swimming and diving M/W, table tennis M/W, tennis M/W, track and field M/W, volleyball W.

Campus security: 24-hour emergency response devices and patrols, late-night transport/escort service, controlled dormitory access.

Student services: health clinic, personal/psychological counseling, legal services, veterans affairs office.

COSTS & FINANCIAL AID

Costs (2020–21) ***Tuition:*** state resident $4790 full-time, $160 per credit hour part-time; nonresident $17,460 full-time, $582 per credit hour part-time. Full-time tuition and fees vary according to course load, location, program, and reciprocity agreements. Part-time tuition and fees vary according to course load, location, program, and reciprocity agreements. ***Required fees:*** $4168 full-time. ***Room and board:*** $8868. Room and board charges vary according to board plan and housing facility. ***Payment plan:*** installment. ***Waivers:*** senior citizens.

Financial Aid Of all full-time matriculated undergraduates who enrolled in 2019, 4,774 applied for aid, 4,168 were judged to have need, 427 had their need fully met. 135 Federal Work-Study jobs (averaging $1762). 16 state and other part-time jobs (averaging $1342). In 2019, 199 non-need-based awards were made. ***Average percent of need met:*** 51. ***Average financial aid package:*** $10,008. ***Average need-based loan:*** $3734. ***Average need-based gift aid:*** $9305. ***Average non-need-based aid:*** $2207. ***Average indebtedness upon graduation:*** $25,546.

APPLYING

Standardized Tests *Required:* SAT or ACT (for admission).

Options: electronic application, deferred entrance.

Required: high school transcript. ***Required for some:*** interview for honors college.

Application deadlines: 8/15 (freshmen), 8/15 (transfers).

CONTACT

Mr. Jody Todhunter, Director of Admissions, Texas A&M University–Commerce, PO Box 3011, Commerce, TX 75429. *Phone:* 903-886-5072. *Toll-free phone:* 888-868-2682. *Fax:* 903-468-8698. *E-mail:* admissions@tamu-commerce.edu.

Texas A&M University–Corpus Christi

Corpus Christi, Texas

http://www.tamucc.edu/

- **State-supported** university, founded 1947, part of Texas A&M University System
- **Suburban** 317-acre campus
- **Endowment** $13.4 million
- **Coed** 9,323 undergraduate students, 77% full-time, 60% women, 40% men
- **Moderately difficult** entrance level, 83% of applicants were admitted

UNDERGRAD STUDENTS

7,201 full-time, 2,122 part-time. Students come from 45 states and territories; 50 other countries; 3% are from out of state; 5% Black or African American, non-Hispanic/Latino; 51% Hispanic/Latino; 3% Asian, non-Hispanic/Latino; 0.2% American Indian or Alaska Native, non-Hispanic/Latino; 2% Two or more races, non-Hispanic/Latino; 0.9% Race/ethnicity unknown; 2% international; 8% transferred in; 24% live on campus.

Freshmen:

Admission: 9,839 applied, 8,206 admitted, 1,915 enrolled. ***Test scores:*** SAT evidence-based reading and writing scores over 500: 81%; SAT math scores over 500: 77%; ACT scores over 18: 83%; SAT evidence-based reading and writing scores over 600: 31%; SAT math scores over 600: 21%; ACT scores over 24: 29%; SAT evidence-based reading and writing scores over 700: 2%; SAT math scores over 700: 2%; ACT scores over 30: 3%.

Retention: 60% of full-time freshmen returned.

FACULTY

Total: 662, 65% full-time, 55% with terminal degrees.

Student/faculty ratio: 18:1.

ACADEMICS

Calendar: semesters. *Degrees:* bachelor's, master's, doctoral, post-master's, and postbachelor's certificates.

Special study options: academic remediation for entering students, advanced placement credit, cooperative education, distance learning, double majors, English as a second language, honors programs, independent study, internships, off-campus study, part-time degree program, services for LD students, study abroad, summer session for credit. ***ROTC:*** Army (b).

Unusual degree programs: 3-2 business administration; engineering; nursing.

Computers: 750 computers/terminals are available on campus for general student use. Students can access the following: campus intranet, computer help desk, free student e-mail accounts, online (class) grades, online (class) registration, online (class) schedules. Campuswide network is available. 100% of college-owned or -operated housing units are wired for high-speed Internet access. Wireless service is available via entire campus.

Library: Mary and Jeff Bell Library. *Books:* 263,954 (physical), 220,773 (digital/electronic); *Serial titles:* 10,498 (physical), 106,435 (digital/electronic); *Databases:* 228. Weekly public service hours: 106; students can reserve study rooms.

STUDENT LIFE

Housing options: coed. Campus housing is university owned.

Activities and organizations: drama/theater group, student-run newspaper, choral group, Student Accounting Society: Alpha Epsilon

Delta, Student Art Association: Golden Key, Islander Cultural Alliance: Kinesiology Club, Graduate Student Association: Sea Turtle Club, Student Nurses Association, national fraternities, national sororities.

Athletics Member NCAA. All Division I. ***Intercollegiate sports:*** baseball M(s), basketball M(s)/W(s), cheerleading M/W, cross-country running M(s)/W(s), golf W(s), sand volleyball W(s), soccer W(s), softball W(s), tennis M(s)/W(s), track and field M(s)/W(s), volleyball W(s). ***Intramural sports:*** badminton M/W, basketball M/W, rugby M/W, sailing M/W, soccer M/W, table tennis M/W, tennis M/W, volleyball M/W, weight lifting M/W.

Campus security: 24-hour emergency response devices and patrols, late-night transport/escort service, controlled dormitory access.

Student services: health clinic, personal/psychological counseling, veterans affairs office.

COSTS & FINANCIAL AID

Costs (2020–21) ***Tuition:*** state resident $4992 full-time; nonresident $17,107 full-time. ***Room and board:*** $10,220.

Financial Aid Of all full-time matriculated undergraduates who enrolled in 2019, 5,674 applied for aid, 4,763 were judged to have need, 695 had their need fully met. 132 Federal Work-Study jobs (averaging $2891). 216 state and other part-time jobs (averaging $2546). In 2019, 429 non-need-based awards were made. ***Average percent of need met:*** 44. ***Average financial aid package:*** $10,100. ***Average need-based loan:*** $3854. ***Average need-based gift aid:*** $8908. ***Average non-need-based aid:*** $3209. ***Average indebtedness upon graduation:*** $17,748.

APPLYING

Standardized Tests *Required:* SAT or ACT (for admission).

Options: electronic application.

Application fee: $40.

Required: high school transcript, minimum 2.0 GPA.

Application deadlines: 7/1 (freshmen), 7/1 (out-of-state freshmen), 7/1 (transfers).

Notification: continuous (freshmen), continuous (out-of-state freshmen), continuous (transfers).

CONTACT

Ms. Linda Ramon-Barbato, Associate Director of Admissions, Texas A&M University–Corpus Christi, SSC, 6300 Ocean Drive, Unit 5774, Corpus Christi, TX 78412-5774. *Phone:* 361-825-5923. *Toll-free phone:* 800-482-6822. *Fax:* 361-825-5887. *E-mail:* linda.ramon-barbato@tamucc.edu.

Texas A&M University–Kingsville

Kingsville, Texas

http://www.tamuk.edu/

- **State-supported** university, founded 1925, part of Texas A&M University System
- **Small-town** 250-acre campus
- **Coed** 6,174 undergraduate students, 76% full-time, 50% women, 50% men
- **Moderately difficult** entrance level, 77% of applicants were admitted

UNDERGRAD STUDENTS

4,670 full-time, 1,504 part-time. 1% are from out of state; 5% Black or African American, non-Hispanic/Latino; 73% Hispanic/Latino; 0.8% Asian, non-Hispanic/Latino; 0.2% Native Hawaiian or other Pacific Islander, non-Hispanic/Latino; 0.1% American Indian or Alaska Native, non-Hispanic/Latino; 0.7% Two or more races, non-Hispanic/Latino; 0.3% Race/ethnicity unknown; 4% international; 6% transferred in; 26% live on campus.

Freshmen:

Admission: 6,330 applied, 4,892 admitted, 987 enrolled. ***Average high school GPA:*** 3.4. ***Test scores:*** SAT evidence-based reading and writing scores over 500: 62%; SAT math scores over 500: 61%; ACT scores over 18: 66%; SAT evidence-based reading and writing scores over 600: 13%; SAT math scores over 600: 12%; ACT scores over 24: 16%; SAT evidence-based reading and writing scores over 700: 1%; SAT math scores over 700: 1%; ACT scores over 30: 2%.

Retention: 65% of full-time freshmen returned.

FACULTY

Total: 440, 73% full-time, 71% with terminal degrees.

Student/faculty ratio: 17:1.

ACADEMICS

Calendar: semesters. *Degrees:* bachelor's, master's, doctoral, post-master's, and postbachelor's certificates.

Special study options: academic remediation for entering students, adult/continuing education programs, advanced placement credit, distance learning, double majors, English as a second language, honors programs, independent study, internships, off-campus study, part-time degree program, services for LD students, study abroad, summer session for credit. ***ROTC:*** Army (b).

Computers: Students can access the following: campus intranet, computer help desk, free student e-mail accounts, online (class) grades, online (class) registration, online (class) schedules. Campuswide network is available.

Library: James C. Jernigan Library. Students can reserve study rooms.

STUDENT LIFE

Housing options: on-campus residence required for freshman year; coed, men-only, women-only. Campus housing is university owned. Freshman campus housing is guaranteed.

Activities and organizations: drama/theater group, student-run newspaper, radio and television station, choral group, marching band, national fraternities, national sororities.

Athletics Member NCAA. All Division II. ***Intercollegiate sports:*** baseball M, basketball M/W, cross-country running M/W, football M, golf W, softball W, tennis W, track and field M/W, volleyball W. ***Intramural sports:*** badminton M/W, basketball M/W, racquetball M/W, soccer M/W, softball M/W, tennis M/W, ultimate Frisbee M/W, volleyball W.

Campus security: controlled dormitory access.

Student services: health clinic, personal/psychological counseling, veterans affairs office.

COSTS & FINANCIAL AID

Costs (2020–21) ***Tuition:*** area resident $4801 full-time, $188 per credit hour part-time; state resident $4801 full-time, $188 per credit hour part-time; nonresident $18,191 full-time, $640 per credit hour part-time. Full-time tuition and fees vary according to course load and degree level. Part-time tuition and fees vary according to course load and degree level. No tuition increase for student's term of enrollment. ***Required fees:*** $4335 full-time. ***Room and board:*** $8848. Room and board charges vary according to board plan and housing facility. ***Payment plan:*** installment. ***Waivers:*** senior citizens and employees or children of employees.

Financial Aid Of all full-time matriculated undergraduates who enrolled in 2018, 4,359 applied for aid, 3,944 were judged to have need, 540 had their need fully met. In 2018, 304 non-need-based awards were made. ***Average percent of need met:*** 66. ***Average financial aid package:*** $10,618. ***Average need-based loan:*** $8889. ***Average need-based gift aid:*** $7536. ***Average non-need-based aid:*** $5592. ***Average indebtedness upon graduation:*** $30,726.

APPLYING

Standardized Tests *Required:* SAT or ACT (for admission).

Options: electronic application, deferred entrance.

Application fee: $25.

Required for some: essay or personal statement, high school transcript, minimum 2.0 GPA, 2 letters of recommendation, written statement and two letters of recommendation for alternate admissions process.

Application deadlines: rolling (freshmen), rolling (transfers).

CONTACT

Laura Knippers, Associate Director of Admissions, Texas A&M University–Kingsville, MSC 128, 700 University Boulevard, Kingsville, TX 78363. *Phone:* 361-593-2311. *Toll-free phone:* 800-687-6000. *E-mail:* laura.knippers@tamuk.edu.

Texas A&M University–San Antonio

San Antonio, Texas

http://www.tamusa.edu/

CONTACT
Ms. Jennifer Zamarripa, Director of Admissions and Registrar, Texas A&M University–San Antonio, One University Way, San Antonio, TX 78224. *Phone:* 210-932-6201. *E-mail:* jennifer.zamarripa@tamusa.tamus.edu.

Texas A&M University–Texarkana

Texarkana, Texas

http://www.tamut.edu/

CONTACT
Ms. Chrissy Gonzalez, Assistant Director of Admissions, Texas A&M University–Texarkana, Texarkana, TX 75505-5518. *Phone:* 903-223-3180. *E-mail:* admissions@tamut.edu.

Texas Christian University

Fort Worth, Texas

http://www.tcu.edu/

- **Independent** university, founded 1873, affiliated with Christian Church (Disciples of Christ)
- **Suburban** 302-acre campus with easy access to Dallas-Fort Worth
- **Endowment** $1.6 billion
- **Coed** 9,474 undergraduate students, 97% full-time, 58% women, 42% men
- **Very difficult** entrance level, 47% of applicants were admitted

UNDERGRAD STUDENTS
9,219 full-time, 255 part-time. Students come from 52 states and territories; 75 other countries; 46% are from out of state; 5% Black or African American, non-Hispanic/Latino; 15% Hispanic/Latino; 3% Asian, non-Hispanic/Latino; 0.2% Native Hawaiian or other Pacific Islander, non-Hispanic/Latino; 0.6% American Indian or Alaska Native, non-Hispanic/Latino; 2% Two or more races, non-Hispanic/Latino; 1% Race/ethnicity unknown; 5% international; 4% transferred in; 52% live on campus.

Freshmen:
Admission: 19,028 applied, 8,966 admitted, 2,159 enrolled. ***Test scores:*** SAT evidence-based reading and writing scores over 500: 96%; SAT math scores over 500: 96%; ACT scores over 18: 99%; SAT evidence-based reading and writing scores over 600: 65%; SAT math scores over 600: 64%; ACT scores over 24: 85%; SAT evidence-based reading and writing scores over 700: 13%; SAT math scores over 700: 19%; ACT scores over 30: 36%.
Retention: 91% of full-time freshmen returned.

FACULTY
Total: 1,087, 66% full-time, 70% with terminal degrees.
Student/faculty ratio: 13:1.

ACADEMICS
Calendar: semesters. *Degrees:* certificates, diplomas, bachelor's, master's, doctoral, post-master's, and postbachelor's certificates.
Special study options: accelerated degree program, advanced placement credit, distance learning, double majors, English as a second language, honors programs, independent study, internships, part-time degree program, services for LD students, student-designed majors, study abroad, summer session for credit. ***ROTC:*** Army (b), Air Force (b).
Computers: 1,400 computers/terminals and 11,000 ports are available on campus for general student use. Students can access the following: campus intranet, computer help desk, free student e-mail accounts, online (class) grades, online (class) registration, online (class) schedules. Campuswide network is available. 100% of college-owned or -operated housing units are wired for high-speed Internet access. Wireless service is available via entire campus.
Library: Mary Couts Burnett Library. *Books:* 1.4 million (physical), 1.4 million (digital/electronic); *Serial titles:* 11,084 (physical), 154,528 (digital/electronic); *Databases:* 598. Weekly public service hours: 139; study areas open 24 hours, 5–7 days a week; students can reserve study rooms.

STUDENT LIFE
Housing options: on-campus residence required through sophomore year; coed, men-only, women-only, special housing for students with disabilities. Campus housing is university owned. Freshman campus housing is guaranteed.
Activities and organizations: drama/theater group, student-run newspaper, radio and television station, choral group, marching band, College Republicans, National Society of Collegiate Scholars, Entrepreneurship Club, Dream Outside the Box, American Marketing Association, national fraternities, national sororities.
Athletics Member NCAA. All Division I. ***Intercollegiate sports:*** baseball M(s), basketball M(s)/W(s), cross-country running M(s)/W(s), equestrian sports W(s), football M(s), golf M(s)/W(s)(c), gymnastics M(c)/W(c), ice hockey M(c), lacrosse M(c)/W(c), riflery W(s), rock climbing M(c)/W(c), rowing M(c)/W(c), rugby M(c)/W(c), sand volleyball W(s), soccer M(c)/W(s), swimming and diving M(s)/W(s), tennis M(s)/W(s), track and field M(s)/W(s), triathlon M(c)/W(c), ultimate Frisbee M(c)/W(c), volleyball M(c)/W(s), water polo M(c)/W(c). ***Intramural sports:*** baseball M(c), basketball M/W, bowling M/W, football M/W, golf M(c)/W(c), racquetball M/W, sand volleyball M/W, soccer M/W(c), table tennis M/W, tennis M(c)/W(c), ultimate Frisbee M/W, volleyball M/W(c).
Campus security: 24-hour emergency response devices and patrols, late-night transport/escort service, controlled dormitory access.
Student services: health clinic, personal/psychological counseling, women's center, veterans affairs office.

COSTS & FINANCIAL AID
Costs (2020–21) ***Comprehensive fee:*** $65,700 includes full-time tuition ($51,570), mandatory fees ($90), and room and board ($14,040). Part-time tuition: $2180 per credit hour. Part-time tuition and fees vary according to course load. ***Required fees:*** $45 per term part-time. ***College room only:*** $8340. Room and board charges vary according to board plan and housing facility. ***Payment plan:*** installment. ***Waivers:*** employees or children of employees.
Financial Aid Of all full-time matriculated undergraduates who enrolled in 2019, 4,696 applied for aid, 3,576 were judged to have need, 877 had their need fully met. 1,323 Federal Work-Study jobs (averaging $2370). In 2019, 2914 non-need-based awards were made. ***Average percent of need met:*** 64. ***Average financial aid package:*** $33,516. ***Average need-based loan:*** $4352. ***Average need-based gift aid:*** $31,070. ***Average non-need-based aid:*** $19,133. ***Average indebtedness upon graduation:*** $47,931. ***Financial aid deadline:*** 5/1.

APPLYING
Standardized Tests *Required:* SAT or ACT (for admission).
Options: electronic application, early decision, early action, deferred entrance.
Application fee: $50.
Required: essay or personal statement, high school transcript, 2 letters of recommendation.
Application deadlines: 2/1 (freshmen), 8/1 (transfers), 11/1 (early action).
Early decision deadline: 11/1.
Notification: 4/1 (freshmen), continuous (transfers), 12/1 (early decision), 12/15 (early action).

CONTACT
Mandy Castro, Director of Freshman Admission, Texas Christian University, Office of Admission, Box 297013, Fort Worth, TX 76129. *Phone:* 817-257-7490. *Toll-free phone:* 800-828-3764. *Fax:* 817-257-7268. *E-mail:* frogmail@tcu.edu.

Texas College

Tyler, Texas

http://www.texascollege.edu/

CONTACT
Mr. Ronald MsDowell, Director of Financial Aid, Texas College, 2404 North Grand Avenue, Tyler, TX 75702. *Phone:* 903-593-8311 Ext. 2297.

Toll-free phone: 800-306-6299. *Fax:* 903-593-6551. *E-mail:* rmcdowell@texascollege.edu.

Texas Lutheran University

Seguin, Texas

http://www.tlu.edu/

- **Independent** comprehensive, founded 1891, affiliated with Evangelical Lutheran Church
- **Suburban** 196-acre campus with easy access to San Antonio, Austin
- **Coed** 1,445 undergraduate students, 96% full time, 51% women, 49% men
- **Moderately difficult** entrance level, 56% of applicants were admitted

UNDERGRAD STUDENTS

1,380 full-time, 65 part-time. 2% are from out of state; 9% Black or African American, non-Hispanic/Latino; 40% Hispanic/Latino; 0.8% Asian, non-Hispanic/Latino; 0.1% Native Hawaiian or other Pacific Islander, non-Hispanic/Latino; 0.2% American Indian or Alaska Native, non-Hispanic/Latino; 2% Two or more races, non-Hispanic/Latino; 1% Race/ethnicity unknown; 0.6% international; 4% transferred in; 47% live on campus.

Freshmen:

Admission: 3,000 applied, 1,672 admitted, 409 enrolled. ***Test scores:*** SAT evidence-based reading and writing scores over 500: 77%; SAT math scores over 500: 70%; ACT scores over 18: 88%; SAT evidence-based reading and writing scores over 600: 22%; SAT math scores over 600: 16%; ACT scores over 24: 32%; SAT evidence-based reading and writing scores over 700: 2%; SAT math scores over 700: 2%; ACT scores over 30: 7%.

Retention: 73% of full-time freshmen returned.

FACULTY

Total: 135, 63% full-time, 67% with terminal degrees.

Student/faculty ratio: 14:1.

ACADEMICS

Calendar: semesters. *Degrees:* bachelor's and master's.

Special study options: advanced placement credit, double majors, external degree program, honors programs, independent study, internships, part-time degree program, services for LD students, study abroad, summer session for credit. ***ROTC:*** Army (c), Navy (c).

Computers: Students can access the following: campus intranet, computer help desk, free student e-mail accounts, online (class) grades, online (class) registration, online (class) schedules, free printing. Campuswide network is available. 100% of college-owned or -operated housing units are wired for high-speed Internet access. Wireless service is available via entire campus.

Library: Blumberg Memorial Library plus 1 other. Weekly public service hours: 86; students can reserve study rooms.

STUDENT LIFE

Housing options: coed, special housing for students with disabilities. Campus housing is university owned. Freshman campus housing is guaranteed.

Activities and organizations: drama/theater group, student-run newspaper, choral group, Alpha Lambda Delta, Pre Health Professions Club, Xi Tau, Sigma Phi Theta, Mexican American Student Association.

Athletics Member NCAA. All Division III except golf (Division II). ***Intercollegiate sports:*** baseball M, basketball M/W, cross-country running M/W, football M, golf M/W, soccer M/W, softball W, tennis M/W, track and field M/W, volleyball W. ***Intramural sports:*** basketball M/W, bowling M/W, football M, racquetball M/W, softball M/W, tennis M/W, volleyball M/W.

Campus security: 24-hour emergency response devices and patrols, late-night transport/escort service, controlled dormitory access.

Student services: health clinic, personal/psychological counseling, women's center.

COSTS & FINANCIAL AID

Costs (2019–20) ***One-time required fee:*** $400. ***Comprehensive fee:*** $41,300 includes full-time tuition ($30,550), mandatory fees ($310), and room and board ($10,440). Full-time tuition and fees vary according to course load. Part-time tuition: $1010 per credit hour. ***Required fees:*** $155 per term part-time. ***College room only:*** $5870. Room and board charges vary according to board plan and housing facility. ***Payment plan:*** installment. ***Waivers:*** children of alumni and employees or children of employees.

Financial Aid Of all full-time matriculated undergraduates who enrolled in 2019, 1,233 applied for aid, 1,089 were judged to have need, 251 had their need fully met. In 2019, 261 non-need-based awards were made. ***Average percent of need met:*** 81. ***Average financial aid package:*** $26,094. ***Average need-based loan:*** $3711. ***Average need-based gift aid:*** $22,738. ***Average non-need-based aid:*** $17,152. ***Average indebtedness upon graduation:*** $29,735.

APPLYING

Standardized Tests *Required:* SAT or ACT (for admission).

Options: electronic application.

Required: high school transcript. ***Required for some:*** letters of recommendation.

CONTACT

Mrs. Alecia McCain, Director for Admissions Recruiting, Texas Lutheran University, 1000 West Court Street, Seguin, TX 78155-5999. *Phone:* 830-372-6078. *Toll-free phone:* 800-771-8521. *Fax:* 830-372-8096. *E-mail:* almccain@tlu.edu.

Texas Southern University

Houston, Texas

http://www.tsu.edu/

- **State-supported** university, founded 1947
- **Urban** 147-acre campus with easy access to Houston, TX
- **Endowment** $58.0 million
- **Coed** 7,092 undergraduate students, 85% full-time, 59% women, 41% men
- **Noncompetitive** entrance level, 91% of applicants were admitted

UNDERGRAD STUDENTS

6,032 full-time, 1,060 part-time. Students come from 43 states and territories; 40 other countries; 10% are from out of state; 82% Black or African American, non-Hispanic/Latino; 8% Hispanic/Latino; 1% Asian, non-Hispanic/Latino; 0.1% Native Hawaiian or other Pacific Islander, non-Hispanic/Latino; 0.1% American Indian or Alaska Native, non-Hispanic/Latino; 3% Two or more races, non-Hispanic/Latino; 5% international; 10% transferred in; 25% live on campus.

Freshmen:

Admission: 8,554 applied, 7,772 admitted, 1,475 enrolled. ***Average high school GPA:*** 3.1.

Retention: 53% of full-time freshmen returned.

FACULTY

Total: 709, 55% full-time.

Student/faculty ratio: 16:1.

ACADEMICS

Calendar: semesters. *Degrees:* certificates, bachelor's, master's, doctoral, and postbachelor's certificates.

Special study options: academic remediation for entering students, accelerated degree program, adult/continuing education programs, advanced placement credit, cooperative education, distance learning, double majors, English as a second language, external degree program, honors programs, independent study, internships, off-campus study, part-time degree program, services for LD students, study abroad, summer session for credit. ***ROTC:*** Army (b), Navy (c), Air Force (c).

Computers: Students can access the following: computer help desk, free student e-mail accounts, online (class) grades, online (class) registration, online (class) schedules, learning management system. Campuswide network is available. 100% of college-owned or -operated housing units are wired for high-speed Internet access. Wireless service is available via entire campus.

Library: Library Learning Center plus 1 other. Study areas open 24 hours, 5–7 days a week; students can reserve study rooms.

STUDENT LIFE

Housing options: on-campus residence required for freshman year; coed, men-only, women-only. Campus housing is university owned. Freshman campus housing is guaranteed.

Activities and organizations: drama/theater group, student-run newspaper, radio station, choral group, marching band, Debate Team, University Program Council, Student Government Association, Band, Greek Letter Organizations, national fraternities, national sororities.

Athletics Member NCAA. All Division I except football (Division I-AA). ***Intercollegiate sports:*** baseball M(s), basketball M(s)/W(s), bowling W(s), cross-country running M(s)/W(s), golf M(s)/W(s), soccer W(s), softball W(s), tennis M(s)/W(s), track and field M(s)/W(s), volleyball W(s). ***Intramural sports:*** basketball M/W, bowling W, cheerleading M/W, softball W, swimming and diving M/W, tennis M/W, track and field M/W, volleyball W.

Campus security: 24-hour emergency response devices and patrols, student patrols, late-night transport/escort service, controlled dormitory access.

Student services: health clinic, personal/psychological counseling, women's center, legal services, veterans affairs office.

FINANCIAL AID

Financial Aid Of all full-time matriculated undergraduates who enrolled in 2018, 5,793 applied for aid, 5,793 were judged to have need, 5,303 had their need fully met. 317 Federal Work-Study jobs (averaging $4000). 23 state and other part-time jobs (averaging $4000). ***Average percent of need met:*** 100. ***Average financial aid package:*** $18,324. ***Average need-based loan:*** $3900. ***Average need-based gift aid:*** $7500. ***Average indebtedness upon graduation:*** $23,390.

APPLYING

Standardized Tests *Required:* SAT or ACT (for admission).

Options: electronic application, early admission.

Application fee: $42.

Required: high school transcript, minimum 2.5 GPA. ***Required for some:*** TSI (Texas Success Initiative) Assessment, minimum ACT score of 17/SAT 820.

Application deadlines: 8/14 (freshmen), 8/14 (out-of-state freshmen), 8/14 (transfers).

Notification: continuous (transfers).

CONTACT

Office of Admissions, Texas Southern University, 3100 Cleburne Street, Houston, TX 77004-4598. *Phone:* 713-313-7071. *Fax:* 713-313-7851. *E-mail:* admissions@tsu.edu.

Texas State University

San Marcos, Texas

http://www.txstate.edu/

- **State-supported** university, founded 1899, part of Texas State University System
- **Suburban** 491-acre campus with easy access to San Antonio, Austin
- **Endowment** $204.9 million
- **Coed** 33,917 undergraduate students, 82% full-time, 58% women, 42% men
- **Moderately difficult** entrance level, 81% of applicants were admitted

UNDERGRAD STUDENTS

27,923 full-time, 5,994 part-time. Students come from 49 states and territories; 50 other countries; 2% are from out of state; 9% Black or African American, non-Hispanic/Latino; 40% Hispanic/Latino; 3% Asian, non-Hispanic/Latino; 0.1% Native Hawaiian or other Pacific Islander, non-Hispanic/Latino; 0.3% American Indian or Alaska Native, non-Hispanic/Latino; 4% Two or more races, non-Hispanic/Latino; 0.2% Race/ethnicity unknown; 0.5% international; 10% transferred in; 20% live on campus.

Freshmen:

Admission: 23,583 applied, 19,134 admitted, 6,362 enrolled. ***Test scores:*** SAT evidence-based reading and writing scores over 500: 83%; SAT math scores over 500: 79%; ACT scores over 18: 78%; SAT evidence-based reading and writing scores over 600: 29%; SAT math scores over 600: 19%; ACT scores over 24: 33%; SAT evidence-based reading and writing scores over 700: 3%; SAT math scores over 700: 2%; ACT scores over 30: 2%.

Retention: 76% of full-time freshmen returned.

FACULTY

Total: 2,077, 67% full-time, 60% with terminal degrees.

Student/faculty ratio: 20:1.

ACADEMICS

Calendar: semesters. *Degrees:* bachelor's, master's, doctoral, and postbachelor's certificates.

Special study options: academic remediation for entering students, accelerated degree program, adult/continuing education programs, advanced placement credit, cooperative education, distance learning, double majors, English as a second language, external degree program, freshman honors college, honors programs, independent study, internships, off-campus study, part-time degree program, services for LD students, study abroad, summer session for credit. ***ROTC:*** Army (b), Air Force (b).

Unusual degree programs: 3-2 business administration; engineering with University of Texas at Austin, Texas A&M University, Texas Tech University, University of Texas at San Antonio.

Computers: 3,233 computers/terminals are available on campus for general student use. Students can access the following: computer help desk, free student e-mail accounts, online (class) grades, online (class) registration, online (class) schedules. Campuswide network is available. 100% of college-owned or -operated housing units are wired for high-speed Internet access. Wireless service is available via entire campus.

Library: Alkek Library plus 1 other. *Books:* 1.9 million (physical), 664,569 (digital/electronic); *Serial titles:* 200,587 (physical), 129,479 (digital/electronic); *Databases:* 503. Weekly public service hours: 103; students can reserve study rooms.

STUDENT LIFE

Housing options: on-campus residence required for freshman year; coed, men-only, women-only, special housing for students with disabilities. Campus housing is university owned. Freshman campus housing is guaranteed.

Activities and organizations: drama/theater group, student-run newspaper, radio station, choral group, marching band, Veterans Alliance of Texas State, Texas State Strutters (Dance performance group), Student Foundation, Sport Clubs Alliance, Student Association for Campus Activities, national fraternities, national sororities.

Athletics Member NCAA. All Division I. ***Intercollegiate sports:*** baseball M(s), basketball M(s)/W(s), cheerleading M(c)/W(c), cross-country running M(s)/W(s), equestrian sports M(c)/W(c), fencing M(c)/W(c), football M(s), golf M(s)/W(s), gymnastics M(c)/W(c), ice hockey M(c), lacrosse M(c)/W(c), rugby M(c)/W(c), soccer M(c)/W(s), softball M(c)/W(s), tennis M(c)/W(s), track and field M(s)/W(s), ultimate Frisbee M(c)/W(c), volleyball W(s), water polo M(c)/W(c), weight lifting M(c)/W(c), wrestling M(c)/W(c). ***Intramural sports:*** basketball M/W, bowling M/W, cross-country running M/W, football M/W, golf M/W, racquetball M/W, rock climbing M/W, soccer M/W, softball M/W, tennis M/W, ultimate Frisbee M/W, volleyball M/W.

Campus security: 24-hour emergency response devices and patrols, late-night transport/escort service, controlled dormitory access, Emergency Notification System (electronic signs) within classrooms and offices.

Student services: health clinic, personal/psychological counseling, legal services, veterans affairs office.

COSTS & FINANCIAL AID

Costs (2020–21) ***Tuition:*** state resident $8920 full-time, $297 per credit hour part-time; nonresident $21,190 full-time, $706 per credit hour part-time. Full-time tuition and fees vary according to course load. Part-time tuition and fees vary according to course load. No tuition increase for student's term of enrollment. ***Required fees:*** $2630 full-time, $51 per credit hour part-time, $464 per term part-time. ***Room only:*** $7646. Room and board charges vary according to board plan and housing facility. ***Payment plan:*** installment. ***Waivers:*** employees or children of employees.

Financial Aid Of all full-time matriculated undergraduates who enrolled in 2019, 27,198 applied for aid, 16,459 were judged to have need, 3,189 had their need fully met. 1,556 Federal Work-Study jobs (averaging $2297). 43 state and other part-time jobs (averaging $3358). In 2019, 1267 non-need-based awards were made. ***Average percent of need met:*** 63. ***Average financial aid package:*** $11,730. ***Average need-based loan:*** $4067. ***Average need-based gift aid:*** $8081. ***Average non-need-based aid:*** $3395. ***Average indebtedness upon graduation:*** $24,950.

APPLYING

Standardized Tests *Required:* SAT or ACT (for admission). *Required for some:* TOEFL for international students. *Recommended:* SAT (for admission), ACT (for admission).

Options: electronic application, early admission, deferred entrance.

Application fee: $75.

Required: essay or personal statement, high school transcript, SAT or ACT Test Scores.

Application deadlines: 3/1 (freshmen), 7/1 (transfers).

Notification: continuous (freshmen), continuous (transfers).

CONTACT

Texas State University, 429 N. Guadalupe Street, San Marcos, TX 78666. *Phone:* 512-245-2364. *Fax:* 512-245-8100. *E-mail:* admissions@txstate.edu.

Texas Tech University

Lubbock, Texas

http://www.ttu.edu/

- **State-supported** university, founded 1923, part of Texas Tech University System
- **Urban** 1839-acre campus
- **Endowment** $749.1 million
- **Coed** 32,125 undergraduate students, 87% full-time, 48% women, 52% men
- **Moderately difficult** entrance level, 69% of applicants were admitted

UNDERGRAD STUDENTS

28,062 full-time, 4,063 part-time. Students come from 51 states and territories; 103 other countries; 6% are from out of state; 6% Black or African American, non-Hispanic/Latino; 29% Hispanic/Latino; 3% Asian, non-Hispanic/Latino; 0.1% Native Hawaiian or other Pacific Islander, non-Hispanic/Latino; 0.4% American Indian or Alaska Native, non-Hispanic/Latino; 3% Two or more races, non-Hispanic/Latino; 0.5% Race/ethnicity unknown; 3% international; 8% transferred in; 26% live on campus.

Freshmen:

Admission: 25,384 applied, 17,493 admitted, 6,145 enrolled. ***Average high school GPA:*** 3.6. ***Test scores:*** SAT evidence-based reading and writing scores over 500: 94%; SAT math scores over 500: 94%; ACT scores over 18: 99%; SAT evidence-based reading and writing scores over 600: 43%; SAT math scores over 600: 39%; ACT scores over 24: 57%; SAT evidence-based reading and writing scores over 700: 4%; SAT math scores over 700: 7%; ACT scores over 30: 10%.

Retention: 87% of full-time freshmen returned.

FACULTY

Total: 1,802, 89% full-time.

Student/faculty ratio: 20:1.

ACADEMICS

Calendar: semesters. *Degrees:* bachelor's, master's, doctoral, and postbachelor's certificates.

Special study options: academic remediation for entering students, accelerated degree program, advanced placement credit, cooperative education, distance learning, double majors, English as a second language, external degree program, freshman honors college, honors programs, independent study, internships, off-campus study, part-time degree program, services for LD students, student-designed majors, study abroad, summer session for credit. ***ROTC:*** Army (b), Air Force (b).

Unusual degree programs: 3-2 business administration; engineering; agribusiness, agricultural & applied economics, architecture, environmental design, hospitality & retail management, interdisciplinary studies, languages & cultures, mathematics, music education, personal financial planning, political science, psycho.

Computers: 1,934 computers/terminals and 3,250 ports are available on campus for general student use. Students can access the following: campus intranet, computer help desk, free student e-mail accounts, online (class) grades, online (class) registration, online (class) schedules, online degree plans, accounts, transcripts, financial aid, course and instructor evaluations, scholarship applications and submissions. Campuswide network is available. 100% of college-owned or -operated housing units are wired for high-speed Internet access. Wireless service is available via entire campus.

Library: Texas Tech Library plus 3 others. *Books:* 2.9 million (physical), 160,584 (digital/electronic); *Serial titles:* 1,464 (physical), 200,332 (digital/electronic); *Databases:* 405. Weekly public service hours: 146; study areas open 24 hours, 5–7 days a week; students can reserve study rooms.

STUDENT LIFE

Housing options: on-campus residence required for freshman year; coed, men-only, women-only, special housing for students with disabilities. Campus housing is university owned. Freshman campus housing is guaranteed.

Activities and organizations: drama/theater group, student-run newspaper, radio station, choral group, marching band, Society of Petroleum Engineers, Hispanic Student Society, Pre-Nursing Association, Alpha Lambda Delta and Phi Eta Sigma, Catholic Student Association, national fraternities, national sororities.

Athletics Member NCAA. All Division I except football (Division I-A). ***Intercollegiate sports:*** baseball M(s), basketball M(s)/W(s), cross-country running M(s)/W(s), golf M(s)/W(s), soccer W(s), softball W(s), tennis M(s)/W(s), track and field M(s)/W(s), volleyball W(s). ***Intramural sports:*** archery M/W, badminton M(c)/W(c), baseball M(c), basketball M/W, bowling M/W, equestrian sports M(c)/W(c), fencing M(c)/W(c), golf M/W, gymnastics M(c)/W(c), ice hockey M(c), lacrosse M(c)/W(c), racquetball M/W, rock climbing M(c)/W(c), rugby M(c)/W(c), sand volleyball M/W, soccer M/W, softball M/W, swimming and diving M(c)/W(c), table tennis M/W, tennis M/W, triathlon M(c)/W(c), ultimate Frisbee M(c)/W(c), volleyball M/W, water polo M(c)/W(c), weight lifting M/W, wrestling M(c)/W(c).

Campus security: 24-hour emergency response devices and patrols, late-night transport/escort service, controlled dormitory access, TechAlert system, bike registration, crime prevention programs.

Student services: health clinic, personal/psychological counseling, legal services, veterans affairs office.

COSTS & FINANCIAL AID

Costs (2019–20) ***Tuition:*** state resident $8430 full-time, $281 per credit hour part-time; nonresident $20,880 full-time, $696 per credit hour part-time. Full-time tuition and fees vary according to course load, location, program, and reciprocity agreements. Part-time tuition and fees vary according to course load, location, program, and reciprocity agreements. ***Required fees:*** $2890 full-time, $56 per credit hour part-time, $612 per term part-time. ***Room and board:*** $9772; room only: $6236. Room and board charges vary according to board plan and housing facility. ***Payment plan:*** installment. ***Waivers:*** senior citizens and employees or children of employees.

Financial Aid Of all full-time matriculated undergraduates who enrolled in 2016, 16,239 applied for aid, 13,251 were judged to have need, 1,075 had their need fully met. 360 Federal Work-Study jobs (averaging $2520). 6 state and other part-time jobs (averaging $1296). In 2016, 3132 non-need-based awards were made. ***Average percent of need met:*** 67. ***Average financial aid package:*** $15,085. ***Average need-based loan:*** $5307. ***Average need-based gift aid:*** $7786. ***Average non-need-based aid:*** $3564. ***Average indebtedness upon graduation:*** $30,759.

APPLYING

Standardized Tests *Required:* SAT or ACT (for admission).

Options: electronic application.

Application fee: $75.

Required: high school transcript. ***Recommended:*** essay or personal statement, 3 letters of recommendation.

Application deadlines: 8/1 (freshmen), rolling (transfers).

Notification: 9/1 (freshmen), continuous (transfers).

CONTACT

Texas Tech University, 2500 Broadway, Lubbock, TX 79409. *Phone:* 806-742-1480.

Texas Wesleyan University
Fort Worth, Texas
http://www.txwes.edu/

CONTACT
Mrs. Djuana Young, Associate Vice President for Enrollment, Admissions, Texas Wesleyan University, 1201 Wesleyan Street, Fort Worth, TX 76105-1536. *Phone:* 817-531-4422. *Toll-free phone:* 800-580-8980. *Fax:* 817-531-7515. *E-mail:* admissions@txwes.edu.

Texas Woman's University
Denton, Texas
http://www.twu.edu/

- **State-supported** university, founded 1901
- **Suburban** 270-acre campus with easy access to Dallas-Fort Worth
- **Endowment** $79.6 million
- **Coed, primarily women** 10,591 undergraduate students, 66% full-time, 87% women, 13% men
- **Moderately difficult** entrance level, 93% of applicants were admitted

UNDERGRAD STUDENTS
7,032 full-time, 3,559 part-time. Students come from 39 states and territories; 30 other countries; 2% are from out of state; 18% Black or African American, non-Hispanic/Latino; 33% Hispanic/Latino; 9% Asian, non-Hispanic/Latino; 0.1% Native Hawaiian or other Pacific Islander, non-Hispanic/Latino; 0.4% American Indian or Alaska Native, non-Hispanic/Latino; 3% Two or more races, non-Hispanic/Latino; 0.6% Race/ethnicity unknown; 2% international; 12% transferred in; 25% live on campus.

Freshmen:
Admission: 5,651 applied, 5,278 admitted, 1,301 enrolled. ***Average high school GPA:*** 3.2. ***Test scores:*** SAT evidence-based reading and writing scores over 500: 64%; SAT math scores over 500: 58%; ACT scores over 18: 66%; SAT evidence-based reading and writing scores over 600: 22%; SAT math scores over 600: 15%; ACT scores over 24: 20%; SAT evidence-based reading and writing scores over 700: 2%; SAT math scores over 700: 2%; ACT scores over 30: 3%.

Retention: 73% of full-time freshmen returned.

FACULTY
Total: 912, 56% full-time, 55% with terminal degrees.

Student/faculty ratio: 17:1.

ACADEMICS
Calendar: semesters. *Degrees:* bachelor's, master's, doctoral, post-master's, and postbachelor's certificates.

Special study options: academic remediation for entering students, accelerated degree program, adult/continuing education programs, advanced placement credit, cooperative education, distance learning, double majors, external degree program, honors programs, independent study, internships, off-campus study, part-time degree program, services for LD students, study abroad, summer session for credit. ***ROTC:*** Army (c), Navy (c), Air Force (c).

Computers: 296 computers/terminals are available on campus for general student use. Students can access the following: campus intranet, computer help desk, free student e-mail accounts, online (class) grades, online (class) registration, online (class) schedules. Campuswide network is available. 100% of college-owned or -operated housing units are wired for high-speed Internet access. Wireless service is available via entire campus.

Library: Blagg-Huey Library. *Books:* 389,891 (physical), 551,571 (digital/electronic); *Serial titles:* 163,695 (physical), 265,681 (digital/electronic); *Databases:* 306. Weekly public service hours: 116; students can reserve study rooms.

STUDENT LIFE
Housing options: on-campus residence required through sophomore year; coed, women-only, special housing for students with disabilities. Campus housing is university owned. Freshman campus housing is guaranteed.

Activities and organizations: drama/theater group, student-run newspaper, choral group, Residence Hall Association, Helping Hands Service Ambassadors, Athenian Honor Society, Women's Health Student Advocate Association, University Network Intercultural Team and Education, national fraternities, national sororities.

Athletics Member NCAA. All Division II. ***Intercollegiate sports:*** basketball W(s), gymnastics W(s), soccer W(s), softball W(s), volleyball W(s). ***Intramural sports:*** basketball M/W, football M/W, sand volleyball M/W, soccer M/W, tennis M/W, volleyball M/W.

Campus security: 24-hour emergency response devices and patrols, late-night transport/escort service, controlled dormitory access.

Student services: health clinic, personal/psychological counseling, women's center, legal services, veterans affairs office.

COSTS & FINANCIAL AID
Costs (2020–21) ***Tuition:*** area resident $6789 full-time, $226 per credit hour part-time; state resident $6789 full-time, $226 per credit hour part-time; nonresident $19,449 full-time, $648 per credit hour part-time. Full-time tuition and fees vary according to course load and program. Part-time tuition and fees vary according to course load and program. No tuition increase for student's term of enrollment. ***Required fees:*** $2959 full-time, $99 per credit hour part-time. ***Room and board:*** $9050. Room and board charges vary according to board plan and housing facility. ***Payment plan:*** installment. ***Waivers:*** senior citizens.

Financial Aid Of all full-time matriculated undergraduates who enrolled in 2018, 5,333 applied for aid, 4,591 were judged to have need, 1,529 had their need fully met. 262 Federal Work-Study jobs (averaging $3410). 65 state and other part-time jobs (averaging $1152). In 2018, 486 non-need-based awards were made. ***Average percent of need met:*** 86. ***Average financial aid package:*** $14,151. ***Average need-based loan:*** $6766. ***Average need-based gift aid:*** $7877. ***Average non-need-based aid:*** $4465. ***Average indebtedness upon graduation:*** $22,206. ***Financial aid deadline:*** 3/15.

APPLYING
Standardized Tests *Required for some:* SAT or ACT (for admission).

Options: electronic application, early admission, deferred entrance.

Application fee: $50.

Required: minimum 2.0 GPA, Transcripts from prior colleges attended. ***Required for some:*** high school transcript.

Application deadlines: 8/25 (freshmen), 8/25 (transfers).

Notification: continuous (freshmen), continuous (transfers).

CONTACT
Ms. Nikki Young, Director of Admissions, Texas Woman's University, P.O. Box 425589, Denton, TX 76204. *Phone:* 940-898-3188. *Toll-free phone:* 866-809-6130. *Fax:* 940-898-3081. *E-mail:* admissions@twu.edu.

Trinity University
San Antonio, Texas
http://www.trinity.edu/

- **Independent** comprehensive, founded 1869, affiliated with Presbyterian Church
- **Urban** 117-acre campus with easy access to San Antonio
- **Endowment** $1.3 billion
- **Coed** 2,528 undergraduate students, 98% full-time, 53% women, 47% men
- **Very difficult** entrance level, 29% of applicants were admitted

UNDERGRAD STUDENTS
2,476 full-time, 52 part-time. Students come from 47 states and territories; 68 other countries; 24% are from out of state; 4% Black or African American, non-Hispanic/Latino; 21% Hispanic/Latino; 8% Asian, non-Hispanic/Latino; 0.1% Native Hawaiian or other Pacific Islander, non-Hispanic/Latino; 0.4% American Indian or Alaska Native, non-Hispanic/Latino; 5% Two or more races, non-Hispanic/Latino; 1% Race/ethnicity unknown; 4% international; 1% transferred in; 81% live on campus.

Freshmen:
Admission: 9,864 applied, 2,837 admitted, 637 enrolled. ***Average high school GPA:*** 3.7. ***Test scores:*** SAT evidence-based reading and writing scores over 500: 100%; SAT math scores over 500: 100%; ACT scores over 18: 100%; SAT evidence-based reading and writing scores over 600: 95%; SAT math scores over 600: 92%; ACT scores over 24: 100%; SAT

evidence-based reading and writing scores over 700: 39%; SAT math scores over 700: 38%; ACT scores over 30: 65%.

Retention: 92% of full-time freshmen returned.

FACULTY

Total: 354, 73% full-time, 83% with terminal degrees.

Student/faculty ratio: 9:1.

ACADEMICS

Calendar: semesters. *Degrees:* bachelor's and master's.

Special study options: accelerated degree program, advanced placement credit, double majors, honors programs, independent study, internships, off-campus study, part-time degree program, services for LD students, student-designed majors, study abroad, summer session for credit. ***ROTC:*** Army (c), Air Force (c).

Computers: 500 computers/terminals and 2,000 ports are available on campus for general student use. Students can access the following: campus intranet, computer help desk, free student e-mail accounts, online (class) grades, online (class) registration, online (class) schedules. Campuswide network is available. 100% of college-owned or -operated housing units are wired for high-speed Internet access. Wireless service is available via entire campus.

Library: Elizabeth Huth Coates Library plus 1 other. *Books:* 688,626 (physical); *Serial titles:* 1,590 (physical), 120,000 (digital/electronic); *Databases:* 297. Weekly public service hours: 96; students can reserve study rooms.

STUDENT LIFE

Housing options: on-campus residence required through junior year; coed. Campus housing is university owned. Freshman campus housing is guaranteed.

Activities and organizations: drama/theater group, student-run newspaper, radio and television station, choral group, Tiger Stand Band, Alpha Phi Omega, Association of Student Representatives, Acabellas/Trinitones, Multicultural Network.

Athletics Member NCAA. All Division III except golf (Division II). ***Intercollegiate sports:*** baseball M, basketball M/W, cross-country running M/W, fencing M(c)/W(c), football M, golf M/W, lacrosse M(c)/W(c), soccer M/W, softball W, swimming and diving M/W, tennis M/W, track and field M/W, volleyball W. ***Intramural sports:*** basketball M/W, cross-country running M/W, equestrian sports M(c)/W(c), football M, racquetball M/W, soccer M/W, softball M/W, swimming and diving M/W, table tennis M/W, tennis M/W, ultimate Frisbee M/W, volleyball M/W.

Campus security: 24-hour emergency response devices and patrols, late-night transport/escort service, controlled dormitory access.

Student services: health clinic, personal/psychological counseling.

COSTS & FINANCIAL AID

Costs (2020–21) ***Comprehensive fee:*** $60,196 includes full-time tuition ($45,840), mandatory fees ($616), and room and board ($13,740). Full-time tuition and fees vary according to course load. Part-time tuition: $1910 per credit hour. Part-time tuition and fees vary according to course load. ***Required fees:*** $13 per credit hour part-time. ***College room only:*** $8690. Room and board charges vary according to board plan. ***Payment plan:*** installment. ***Waivers:*** employees or children of employees.

Financial Aid Of all full-time matriculated undergraduates who enrolled in 2019, 1,487 applied for aid, 1,097 were judged to have need, 435 had their need fully met. In 2019, 1318 non-need-based awards were made. ***Average percent of need met:*** 92. ***Average financial aid package:*** $41,170. ***Average need-based loan:*** $4721. ***Average need-based gift aid:*** $33,705. ***Average non-need-based aid:*** $22,746. ***Average indebtedness upon graduation:*** $43,005.

APPLYING

Standardized Tests *Required:* SAT or ACT (for admission).

Options: electronic application, early decision, early action, deferred entrance.

Required: essay or personal statement, high school transcript, 2 letters of recommendation. ***Recommended:*** interview.

Application deadlines: 1/15 (freshmen), 4/1 (transfers), 11/1 (early action).

Early decision deadline: 11/1 (for plan 1), 1/15 (for plan 2).

Notification: 3/15 (freshmen), 5/1 (transfers), 12/1 (early decision plan 1), 2/1 (early decision plan 2), 12/15 (early action).

CONTACT

Office of Admissions, Trinity University, One Trinity Place, Northrup Hall 140, San Antonio, TX 78212-7200. *Phone:* 210-999-7207. *Toll-free phone:* 800-TRINITY. *Fax:* 210-999-8164. *E-mail:* admissions@trinity.edu.

Tyler Junior College

Tyler, Texas

http://www.tjc.edu/

- **State and locally supported** primarily 2-year, founded 1926
- **Suburban** 137-acre campus
- **Endowment** $42.2 million
- **Coed**
- **Noncompetitive** entrance level

FACULTY

Student/faculty ratio: 20:1.

ACADEMICS

Calendar: semesters. *Degrees:* certificates, diplomas, associate, and bachelor's.

Library: Vaughn Library and Learning Resource Center. *Books:* 85,418 (physical), 135,816 (digital/electronic); *Databases:* 100. Weekly public service hours: 74.

STUDENT LIFE

Housing options: coed, men-only, women-only. Campus housing is university owned and is provided by a third party.

Activities and organizations: drama/theater group, student-run newspaper, choral group, marching band, Student Government, Religious Affiliation Clubs, Phi Theta Kappa, national sororities.

Athletics Member NJCAA.

Campus security: 24-hour emergency response devices and patrols, controlled dormitory access.

Student services: health clinic, personal/psychological counseling, veterans affairs office.

COSTS & FINANCIAL AID

Costs (2019–20) ***Tuition:*** $32 per credit hour part-time; state resident $32 per credit hour part-time; nonresident $56 per credit hour part-time. ***Required fees:*** $59 per credit hour part-time, $120 per term part-time. ***Room and board:*** Room and board charges vary according to housing facility.

Financial Aid Of all full-time matriculated undergraduates who enrolled in 2018, 4,359 applied for aid, 3,789 were judged to have need, 50 had their need fully met. In 2018, 647 non-need-based awards were made. ***Average percent of need met:*** 57. ***Average financial aid package:*** $3822. ***Average need-based loan:*** $1017. ***Average need-based gift aid:*** $2700. ***Average non-need-based aid:*** $1227. ***Average indebtedness upon graduation:*** $14,743. ***Financial aid deadline:*** 6/1.

APPLYING

Options: electronic application, early admission.

Required: high school transcript.

CONTACT

Tyler Junior College, PO Box 9020, Tyler, TX 75711-9020. *Toll-free phone:* 800-687-5680.

University of Dallas

Irving, Texas

http://www.udallas.edu/

- **Independent Roman Catholic** university, founded 1955
- **Suburban** 215-acre campus with easy access to Dallas-Fort Worth
- **Endowment** $74.1 million
- **Coed** 1,475 undergraduate students, 98% full-time, 53% women, 47% men
- **Moderately difficult** entrance level, 45% of applicants were admitted

UNDERGRAD STUDENTS

1,443 full-time, 32 part-time. Students come from 49 states and territories; 20 other countries; 48% are from out of state; 2% Black or African American, non-Hispanic/Latino; 25% Hispanic/Latino; 7% Asian, non-Hispanic/Latino; 0.1% Native Hawaiian or other Pacific Islander, non-

Hispanic/Latino; 0.3% American Indian or Alaska Native, non-Hispanic/Latino; 3% Two or more races, non-Hispanic/Latino; 1% Race/ethnicity unknown; 3% international; 3% transferred in; 55% live on campus.

Freshmen:

Admission: 4,676 applied, 2,120 admitted, 382 enrolled. ***Average high school GPA:*** 3.9. ***Test scores:*** SAT evidence-based reading and writing scores over 500: 98%; SAT math scores over 500: 96%; ACT scores over 18: 99%; SAT evidence-based reading and writing scores over 600: 73%; SAT math scores over 600: 55%; ACT scores over 24: 78%; SAT evidence-based reading and writing scores over 700: 26%; SAT math scores over 700: 14%; ACT scores over 30: 37%.

Retention: 85% of full-time freshmen returned.

FACULTY

Total: 231, 62% full-time, 72% with terminal degrees.

Student/faculty ratio: 11:1.

ACADEMICS

Calendar: semesters. *Degrees:* bachelor's, master's, doctoral, post-master's, and postbachelor's certificates.

Special study options: advanced placement credit, double majors, independent study, internships, off-campus study, part-time degree program, services for LD students, student-designed majors, study abroad, summer session for credit. ***ROTC:*** Army (c), Air Force (c).

Unusual degree programs: 3-2 engineering with University of Texas at Arlington; nursing with Texas Woman's University.

Computers: 125 computers/terminals are available on campus for general student use. Students can access the following: campus intranet, computer help desk, free student e-mail accounts, online (class) grades, online (class) registration, online (class) schedules. Campuswide network is available. 100% of college-owned or -operated housing units are wired for high-speed Internet access. Wireless service is available via entire campus.

Library: Cowan-Blakley Memorial Library. *Books:* 240,269 (physical), 248,867 (digital/electronic); *Serial titles:* 283 (physical), 189 (digital/electronic); *Databases:* 219. Weekly public service hours: 99; students can reserve study rooms.

STUDENT LIFE

Housing options: on-campus residence required through junior year; men-only, women-only. Campus housing is university owned. Freshman campus housing is guaranteed.

Activities and organizations: drama/theater group, student-run newspaper, choral group, CAB (Campus Activities Board), Crusaders for Life, Student Government, Best Buddies, Alexander Hamilton Society.

Athletics Member NCAA. All Division III. ***Intercollegiate sports:*** baseball M, basketball M/W, cross-country running M/W, golf M/W, lacrosse M/W, soccer M/W, softball W, track and field M/W, volleyball W. ***Intramural sports:*** basketball M/W, rugby M(c), sailing M(c)/W(c), soccer M/W, softball M/W, swimming and diving M(c)/W(c), tennis M(c)/W(c), ultimate Frisbee M(c)/W(c), volleyball M/W.

Campus security: 24-hour emergency response devices and patrols, controlled dormitory access.

Student services: health clinic, personal/psychological counseling, veterans affairs office.

COSTS & FINANCIAL AID

Costs (2020–21) ***Comprehensive fee:*** $57,890 includes full-time tuition ($41,660), mandatory fees ($3150), and room and board ($13,080). Full-time tuition and fees vary according to course load. Part-time tuition: $1750 per credit hour. Part-time tuition and fees vary according to course load. ***Required fees:*** $1575 per term part-time. ***College room only:*** $7046. Room and board charges vary according to board plan, housing facility, and location. ***Payment plan:*** installment. ***Waivers:*** employees or children of employees.

Financial Aid Of all full-time matriculated undergraduates who enrolled in 2018, 1,035 applied for aid, 922 were judged to have need, 186 had their need fully met. In 2018, 391 non-need-based awards were made. ***Average percent of need met:*** 79. ***Average financial aid package:*** $34,469. ***Average need-based loan:*** $4322. ***Average need-based gift aid:*** $29,804. ***Average non-need-based aid:*** $21,207. ***Average indebtedness upon graduation:*** $34,205.

APPLYING

Standardized Tests *Required for some:* SAT or ACT (for admission).

Options: electronic application, early action, deferred entrance.

Application fee: $50.

Required: essay or personal statement, 1 letter of recommendation. ***Required for some:*** high school transcript, interview.

Application deadlines: 8/1 (freshmen), 8/1 (out-of-state freshmen), 8/1 (transfers), 12/1 (early action).

Notification: continuous (freshmen), continuous (out-of-state freshmen), continuous (transfers), 1/15 (early action).

CONTACT

Michael Probus, Director of Undergraduate Admission, University of Dallas, 1845 East Northgate Drive, Irving, TX 75062-4736. *Phone:* 800-628-6999. *Toll-free phone:* 800-628-6999. *Fax:* 972-721-5017. *E-mail:* crusader@udallas.edu.

University of Houston

Houston, Texas

http://www.uh.edu/

- **State-supported** university, founded 1927, part of University of Houston System
- **Urban** 858-acre campus with easy access to Houston
- **Endowment** $868.2 million
- **Coed** 38,597 undergraduate students, 73% full-time, 50% women, 50% men
- **Moderately difficult** entrance level, 65% of applicants were admitted

UNDERGRAD STUDENTS

28,368 full-time, 10,229 part-time. Students come from 47 states and territories; 106 other countries; 2% are from out of state; 10% Black or African American, non-Hispanic/Latino; 36% Hispanic/Latino; 23% Asian, non-Hispanic/Latino; 0.1% Native Hawaiian or other Pacific Islander, non-Hispanic/Latino; 0.1% American Indian or Alaska Native, non-Hispanic/Latino; 3% Two or more races, non-Hispanic/Latino; 2% Race/ethnicity unknown; 4% international; 12% transferred in; 17% live on campus.

Freshmen:

Admission: 25,393 applied, 16,500 admitted, 5,680 enrolled. ***Average high school GPA:*** 3.7. ***Test scores:*** SAT evidence-based reading and writing scores over 500: 96%; SAT math scores over 500: 97%; ACT scores over 18: 98%; SAT evidence-based reading and writing scores over 600: 59%; SAT math scores over 600: 58%; ACT scores over 24: 60%; SAT evidence-based reading and writing scores over 700: 9%; SAT math scores over 700: 13%; ACT scores over 30: 13%.

Retention: 85% of full-time freshmen returned.

FACULTY

Total: 2,406, 64% full-time, 77% with terminal degrees.

Student/faculty ratio: 23:1.

ACADEMICS

Calendar: semesters. *Degrees:* bachelor's, master's, and doctoral.

Special study options: academic remediation for entering students, adult/continuing education programs, advanced placement credit, cooperative education, distance learning, double majors, freshman honors college, honors programs, independent study, internships, off-campus study, part-time degree program, services for LD students, study abroad, summer session for credit. ***ROTC:*** Army (b), Navy (c), Air Force (b).

Unusual degree programs: 3-2 business administration.

Computers: 1,010 computers/terminals and 94,316 ports are available on campus for general student use. Students can access the following: campus intranet, computer help desk, free student e-mail accounts, online (class) grades, online (class) registration, online (class) schedules, Bus loop schedule; Academic calendar; Student media; Alerts; Social Media Directory. Campuswide network is available. 100% of college-owned or -operated housing units are wired for high-speed Internet access. Wireless service is available via entire campus.

Library: M. D. Anderson Library plus 4 others. *Books:* 1.9 million (physical), 794,332 (digital/electronic); *Serial titles:* 54,042 (physical), 142,038 (digital/electronic); *Databases:* 419. Weekly public service hours: 122; study areas open 24 hours, 5–7 days a week; students can reserve study rooms.

STUDENT LIFE

Housing options: coed, special housing for students with disabilities. Campus housing is university owned.

Activities and organizations: drama/theater group, student-run newspaper, radio and television station, choral group, marching band, Metropolitan Volunteer Program, Student Program Board, Alpha Epsilon Delta Texas Delta Chapter, Filipino Student Association, Pharmacy Council, national fraternities, national sororities.

Athletics Member NCAA. All Division I except football (Division I-A). ***Intercollegiate sports:*** baseball M(s), basketball M(s)/W(s), cross-country running M(s)/W(s), golf M(s)/W(s), soccer W(s), softball W(s), swimming and diving W(s), tennis W(s), track and field M(s)/W(s), volleyball W(s). ***Intramural sports:*** badminton M/W, basketball M/W, bowling M(c)/W, fencing M(c), field hockey W(c), golf M/W, racquetball M/W, rock climbing M/W, soccer M/W, softball M/W, swimming and diving M/W, table tennis M/W, tennis M/W, track and field M/W, ultimate Frisbee M(c)/W(c), volleyball M/W(c), water polo M(c)/W(c), weight lifting M/W.

Campus security: 24-hour emergency response devices and patrols, student patrols, late-night transport/escort service, controlled dormitory access.

Student services: health clinic, personal/psychological counseling, women's center, legal services, veterans affairs office.

COSTS & FINANCIAL AID

Costs (2019–20) ***Tuition:*** state resident $10,274 full-time, $342 per credit hour part-time; nonresident $25,934 full-time, $864 per credit hour part-time. Full-time tuition and fees vary according to course level, course load, degree level, program, and student level. Part-time tuition and fees vary according to course level, course load, degree level, program, and student level. No tuition increase for student's term of enrollment. ***Required fees:*** $1002 full-time. ***Room and board:*** $9368. Room and board charges vary according to board plan and housing facility. ***Payment plans:*** installment, deferred payment. ***Waivers:*** senior citizens.

Financial Aid Of all full-time matriculated undergraduates who enrolled in 2019, 20,296 applied for aid, 17,733 were judged to have need, 2,100 had their need fully met. 513 Federal Work-Study jobs (averaging $4127). 98 state and other part-time jobs (averaging $4434). In 2019, 928 non-need-based awards were made. ***Average percent of need met:*** 59. ***Average financial aid package:*** $12,716. ***Average need-based loan:*** $7113. ***Average need-based gift aid:*** $9099. ***Average non-need-based aid:*** $4747. ***Average indebtedness upon graduation:*** $22,858.

APPLYING

Standardized Tests *Required:* SAT or ACT (for admission).

Options: electronic application.

Application fee: $75.

Required: high school transcript.

Application deadlines: 6/1 (freshmen), 6/1 (out-of-state freshmen), 6/26 (transfers).

Notification: continuous (freshmen), continuous (out-of-state freshmen), continuous (transfers).

CONTACT

Mardell Maxwell, Exec Director, Admissions, University of Houston, Welcome Center, 4400 University Boulevard, Houston, TX 77204-2023. *Phone:* 713-743-1010. *Fax:* 713-743-9633. *E-mail:* mrmaxwe2@central.uh.edu.

University of Houston–Clear Lake

Houston, Texas

http://www.uhcl.edu/

- **State-supported** comprehensive, founded 1971, part of University of Houston System
- **Suburban** 524-acre campus with easy access to Houston
- **Coed** 6,425 undergraduate students, 52% full-time, 62% women, 38% men
- **Minimally difficult** entrance level, 78% of applicants were admitted

UNDERGRAD STUDENTS

3,356 full-time, 3,069 part-time. Students come from 19 other countries; 0.1% are from out of state; 7% Black or African American, non-Hispanic/Latino; 43% Hispanic/Latino; 7% Asian, non-Hispanic/Latino; 0.1% Native Hawaiian or other Pacific Islander, non-Hispanic/Latino; 0.2% American Indian or Alaska Native, non-Hispanic/Latino; 3% Two or more races, non-Hispanic/Latino; 1% Race/ethnicity unknown; 1% international; 23% transferred in; 3% live on campus.

Freshmen:

Admission: 1,311 applied, 1,024 admitted, 336 enrolled. ***Average high school GPA:*** 3.4. ***Test scores:*** SAT evidence-based reading and writing scores over 500: 85%; SAT math scores over 500: 88%; ACT scores over 18: 84%; SAT evidence-based reading and writing scores over 600: 28%; SAT math scores over 600: 21%; ACT scores over 24: 27%; SAT evidence-based reading and writing scores over 700: 3%; SAT math scores over 700: 5%; ACT scores over 30: 3%.

Retention: 81% of full-time freshmen returned.

FACULTY

Total: 494, 56% full-time.

Student/faculty ratio: 17:1.

ACADEMICS

Calendar: semesters. *Degrees:* bachelor's, master's, doctoral, post-master's, and postbachelor's certificates.

Special study options: academic remediation for entering students, advanced placement credit, distance learning, double majors, English as a second language, independent study, internships, off-campus study, part-time degree program, services for LD students, study abroad, summer session for credit.

Computers: 723 computers/terminals are available on campus for general student use. Students can access the following: campus intranet, computer help desk, free student e-mail accounts, online (class) grades, online (class) registration, online (class) schedules. Campuswide network is available. 100% of college-owned or -operated housing units are wired for high-speed Internet access. Wireless service is available via entire campus.

Library: Alfred R. Neuman Library. *Books:* 443,716 (physical), 584,631 (digital/electronic); *Serial titles:* 5,400 (physical), 90,919 (digital/electronic); *Databases:* 215. Weekly public service hours: 89; students can reserve study rooms.

STUDENT LIFE

Housing options: special housing for students with disabilities. Campus housing is university owned. Freshman applicants given priority for college housing.

Activities and organizations: drama/theater group, student-run newspaper, national sororities.

Athletics ***Intramural sports:*** badminton M/W, basketball M/W, bowling M/W, football M/W, table tennis M/W, tennis M/W, volleyball M/W.

Campus security: 24-hour emergency response devices and patrols, student patrols, late-night transport/escort service, controlled dormitory access.

Student services: health clinic, personal/psychological counseling, women's center, veterans affairs office.

COSTS & FINANCIAL AID

Costs (2020–21) ***Tuition:*** area resident $7176 full-time; state resident $7176 full-time; nonresident $23,970 full-time. ***Required fees:*** $785 full-time. ***Room and board:*** $5109. ***Payment plan:*** installment. ***Waivers:*** employees or children of employees.

Financial Aid Of all full-time matriculated undergraduates who enrolled in 2016, 1,916 applied for aid, 1,810 were judged to have need, 66 had their need fully met. In 2016, 252 non-need-based awards were made. ***Average percent of need met:*** 45. ***Average financial aid package:*** $8767. ***Average need-based loan:*** $4452. ***Average need-based gift aid:*** $6891. ***Average non-need-based aid:*** $2149.

APPLYING

Standardized Tests *Required:* SAT or ACT (for admission).

Options: electronic application, deferred entrance.

Application fee: $45.

Required: high school transcript, State of Texas Uniform Admission Policy criteria. ***Required for some:*** essay or personal statement, 2 letters of recommendation.

Application deadlines: 8/1 (freshmen), 8/1 (out-of-state freshmen).

CONTACT
University of Houston–Clear Lake, 2700 Bay Area Boulevard, Houston, TX 77058-1002.

University of Houston–Downtown

Houston, Texas

http://www.uhd.edu/

- **State-supported** comprehensive, founded 1974, part of University of Houston System
- **Urban** 24-acre campus
- **Coed** 13,136 undergraduate students, 50% full-time, 60% women, 40% men
- **Noncompetitive** entrance level, 89% of applicants were admitted

UNDERGRAD STUDENTS
6,629 full-time, 6,507 part-time. 2% are from out of state; 18% Black or African American, non-Hispanic/Latino; 54% Hispanic/Latino; 9% Asian, non-Hispanic/Latino; 0.2% Native Hawaiian or other Pacific Islander, non-Hispanic/Latino; 0.2% American Indian or Alaska Native, non-Hispanic/Latino; 1% Two or more races, non-Hispanic/Latino; 0.9% Race/ethnicity unknown; 2% international; 17% transferred in.

Freshmen:
Admission: 5,617 applied, 4,981 admitted, 1,467 enrolled. ***Test scores:*** SAT evidence-based reading and writing scores over 500: 52%; SAT math scores over 500: 55%; ACT scores over 18: 57%; SAT evidence-based reading and writing scores over 600: 7%; SAT math scores over 600: 5%; ACT scores over 24: 4%; ACT scores over 30: 1%.

Retention: 73% of full-time freshmen returned.

FACULTY
Total: 730, 50% full-time, 65% with terminal degrees.

Student/faculty ratio: 19:1.

ACADEMICS
Calendar: semesters. *Degrees:* bachelor's, master's, and postbachelor's certificates.

Special study options: academic remediation for entering students, advanced placement credit, distance learning, double majors, honors programs, independent study, internships, off-campus study, part-time degree program, services for LD students, study abroad, summer session for credit. ***ROTC:*** Army (c), Air Force (c).

Computers: Students can access the following: computer help desk, free student e-mail accounts, online (class) grades, online (class) registration, online (class) schedules. Campuswide network is available. Wireless service is available via entire campus.
Library: W. I. Dykes Library. Study areas open 24 hours, 5–7 days a week; students can reserve study rooms.

STUDENT LIFE
Housing options: college housing not available.

Activities and organizations: drama/theater group, student-run newspaper, radio station, marching band, Student Government Association, Campus Activities Board, Professional Accounting Society, American Marketing Association, Bilingual Education Student Organization, national fraternities, national sororities.

Athletics ***Intramural sports:*** badminton M/W, baseball M(c), basketball M(c)/W(c), bowling M/W, cheerleading M(c)/W(c), soccer M(c)/W(c), tennis M/W, volleyball M(c)/W(c), weight lifting M(c)/W(c).

Campus security: 24-hour emergency response devices and patrols, late-night transport/escort service.

Student services: health clinic, personal/psychological counseling, legal services, veterans affairs office.

COSTS & FINANCIAL AID
Costs (2020–21) ***Tuition:*** area resident $7208 full-time, $240 per credit hour part-time; state resident $7208 full-time, $240 per credit hour part-time; nonresident $19,568 full-time, $649 per credit hour part-time. ***Required fees:*** $1456 full-time.

Financial Aid Of all full-time matriculated undergraduates who enrolled in 2019, 5,294 applied for aid, 5,066 were judged to have need, 549 had their need fully met. In 2019, 78 non-need-based awards were made. ***Average percent of need met:*** 59. ***Average financial aid package:*** $8452. ***Average need-based loan:*** $4231. ***Average need-based gift aid:*** $5993. ***Average non-need-based aid:*** $2742. ***Average indebtedness upon graduation:*** $4902.

APPLYING
Standardized Tests *Required:* SAT or ACT (for admission).

Options: electronic application, deferred entrance.

Application fee: $50.

Required: high school transcript.

CONTACT
Mr. Jordan Green, Assistant Director, Customer Services Undergraduate Admissions, University of Houston–Downtown, One Main Street, Suite GSB308, Houston, TX 77002. *Phone:* 713-221-8021. *Fax:* 713-221-8157. *E-mail:* uhdadmit@uhd.edu.

University of Houston–Victoria

Victoria, Texas

http://www.uhv.edu/

- **State-supported** upper-level, founded 1973, part of University of Houston System
- **Small-town** 20-acre campus
- **Endowment** $7.5 million
- **Coed**
- **Minimally difficult** entrance level

FACULTY
Student/faculty ratio: 18:1.

ACADEMICS
Calendar: semesters. *Degrees:* bachelor's, master's, post-master's, and postbachelor's certificates.
Library: VC/UHV Library.

STUDENT LIFE
Housing options: coed. Campus housing is university owned. Freshman applicants given priority for college housing.

Athletics Member NAIA.

Campus security: 24-hour emergency response devices and patrols, controlled dormitory access.

Student services: personal/psychological counseling.

COSTS & FINANCIAL AID
Costs (2019–20) ***Tuition:*** $307 per credit hour part-time; state resident $729 per credit hour part-time; nonresident $729 per credit hour part-time.

Financial Aid Of all full-time matriculated undergraduates who enrolled in 2017, 1,433 applied for aid, 1,318 were judged to have need, 206 had their need fully met. In 2017, 57 non-need-based awards were made. ***Average percent of need met:*** 69. ***Average financial aid package:*** $10,272. ***Average need-based loan:*** $3978. ***Average need-based gift aid:*** $6351. ***Average non-need-based aid:*** $1376. ***Average indebtedness upon graduation:*** $6382.

APPLYING
Standardized Tests *Required for some:* SAT or ACT (for admission).

Options: electronic application, deferred entrance.

CONTACT
Mrs. Trudy Wortham, Registrar, University of Houston–Victoria, 3007 North Ben Wilson, Victoria, TX 77901. *Phone:* 361-485-4521 Ext. 4184. *Toll-free phone:* 877-970-4848 Ext. 110. *E-mail:* worthamt@uhv.edu.

University of Mary Hardin-Baylor

Belton, Texas

http://www.umhb.edu/

- **Independent Southern Baptist** comprehensive, founded 1845
- **Small-town** 340-acre campus with easy access to Austin
- **Endowment** $92.2 million
- **Coed** 3,361 undergraduate students, 93% full-time, 65% women, 35% men
- **Moderately difficult** entrance level, 87% of applicants were admitted

UNDERGRAD STUDENTS

3,113 full-time, 248 part-time. Students come from 34 states and territories; 25 other countries; 5% are from out of state; 14% Black or African American, non-Hispanic/Latino; 23% Hispanic/Latino; 2% Asian, non-Hispanic/Latino; 0.1% Native Hawaiian or other Pacific Islander, non-Hispanic/Latino; 0.6% American Indian or Alaska Native, non-Hispanic/Latino; 3% Two or more races, non-Hispanic/Latino; 3% Race/ethnicity unknown; 0.9% international; 6% transferred in; 59% live on campus.

Freshmen:

Admission: 15,355 applied, 13,417 admitted, 868 enrolled. ***Average high school GPA:*** 3.4. ***Test scores:*** SAT evidence-based reading and writing scores over 500: 78%; SAT math scores over 500: 76%; ACT scores over 18: 90%; SAT evidence-based reading and writing scores over 600: 29%; SAT math scores over 600: 20%; ACT scores over 24: 35%; SAT evidence-based reading and writing scores over 700: 3%; SAT math scores over 700: 1%; ACT scores over 30: 8%.

Retention: 66% of full-time freshmen returned.

FACULTY

Total: 281, 59% full-time, 65% with terminal degrees.

Student/faculty ratio: 17:1.

ACADEMICS

Calendar: semesters. *Degrees:* bachelor's, master's, doctoral, and post-master's certificates.

Special study options: academic remediation for entering students, adult/continuing education programs, advanced placement credit, distance learning, double majors, English as a second language, honors programs, independent study, internships, off-campus study, part-time degree program, services for LD students, study abroad, summer session for credit. ***ROTC:*** Army (b), Air Force (c).

Unusual degree programs: 3-2 business administration.

Computers: 275 computers/terminals and 1,000 ports are available on campus for general student use. Students can access the following: campus intranet, computer help desk, free student e-mail accounts, online (class) grades, online (class) registration, online (class) schedules. Campuswide network is available. 100% of college-owned or -operated housing units are wired for high-speed Internet access. Wireless service is available via entire campus.

Library: Townsend Memorial Library. *Books:* 195,754 (physical), 29,300 (digital/electronic); *Serial titles:* 236 (physical), 399,560 (digital/electronic); *Databases:* 145. Weekly public service hours: 99; students can reserve study rooms.

STUDENT LIFE

Housing options: men-only, women-only, special housing for students with disabilities. Campus housing is university owned. Freshman applicants given priority for college housing.

Activities and organizations: student-run newspaper, choral group, Baptist Student Ministry, Student Government Association, Nursing Student Association, Campus Activities Board, Search Cru.

Athletics Member NCAA. All Division III. ***Intercollegiate sports:*** baseball M, basketball M/W, cross-country running M/W, football M, golf M/W, soccer M/W, softball W, tennis M/W, volleyball W. ***Intramural sports:*** basketball M/W, football M/W, golf M/W, soccer M/W, softball M/W, table tennis M/W, tennis M/W, ultimate Frisbee M/W, volleyball M/W.

Campus security: 24-hour emergency response devices and patrols, late-night transport/escort service, controlled dormitory access.

Student services: health clinic, personal/psychological counseling, veterans affairs office.

COSTS & FINANCIAL AID

Costs (2020–21) ***Comprehensive fee:*** $38,582 includes full-time tuition ($27,450), mandatory fees ($2350), and room and board ($8782). Full-time tuition and fees vary according to course load and degree level. Part-time tuition: $915 per credit hour. ***Required fees:*** $75 per credit hour part-time. ***Room and board:*** Room and board charges vary according to board plan and housing facility. ***Payment plan:*** installment. ***Waivers:*** employees or children of employees.

Financial Aid Of all full-time matriculated undergraduates who enrolled in 2019, 2,793 applied for aid, 2,520 were judged to have need, 178 had their need fully met. In 2019, 352 non-need-based awards were made. ***Average percent of need met:*** 57. ***Average financial aid package:*** $18,818. ***Average need-based loan:*** $4047. ***Average need-based gift aid:*** $15,216. ***Average non-need-based aid:*** $8416. ***Average indebtedness upon graduation:*** $34,104.

APPLYING

Standardized Tests *Required:* SAT or ACT (for admission).

Options: electronic application, early admission, deferred entrance.

Application fee: $35.

Required: high school transcript. ***Required for some:*** essay or personal statement, interview.

Application deadlines: rolling (freshmen), rolling (transfers).

Notification: continuous (freshmen), continuous (transfers).

CONTACT

Mr. Nick Jones, Associate Director, Admissions and Recruiting, University of Mary Hardin-Baylor, 900 College Street UMHB Box 8004, Belton, TX 76513. *Phone:* 254-295-4249. *Toll-free phone:* 800-727-8642. *E-mail:* njones@umhb.edu.

University of North Texas

Denton, Texas

http://www.unt.edu/

- **State-supported** university, founded 1890, part of University of North Texas System
- **Suburban** 875-acre campus with easy access to Dallas-Fort Worth
- **Endowment** $150.0 million
- **Coed** 32,126 undergraduate students, 81% full-time, 53% women, 47% men
- **Moderately difficult** entrance level, 71% of applicants were admitted

UNDERGRAD STUDENTS

26,090 full-time, 6,036 part-time. Students come from 50 states and territories; 142 other countries; 4% are from out of state; 14% Black or African American, non-Hispanic/Latino; 27% Hispanic/Latino; 7% Asian, non-Hispanic/Latino; 0.1% Native Hawaiian or other Pacific Islander, non-Hispanic/Latino; 0.3% American Indian or Alaska Native, non-Hispanic/Latino; 4% Two or more races, non-Hispanic/Latino; 0.6% Race/ethnicity unknown; 4% international; 13% transferred in; 19% live on campus.

Freshmen:

Admission: 19,761 applied, 14,083 admitted, 5,510 enrolled. ***Test scores:*** SAT evidence-based reading and writing scores over 500: 92%; SAT math scores over 500: 90%; ACT scores over 18: 93%; SAT evidence-based reading and writing scores over 600: 45%; SAT math scores over 600: 34%; ACT scores over 24: 41%; SAT evidence-based reading and writing scores over 700: 8%; SAT math scores over 700: 8%; ACT scores over 30: 7%.

Retention: 79% of full-time freshmen returned.

FACULTY

Total: 1,715, 66% full-time, 66% with terminal degrees.

Student/faculty ratio: 24:1.

ACADEMICS

Calendar: semesters. *Degrees:* bachelor's, master's, doctoral, and postbachelor's certificates.

Special study options: academic remediation for entering students, accelerated degree program, advanced placement credit, cooperative education, distance learning, double majors, English as a second language, freshman honors college, honors programs, independent study, internships, off-campus study, part-time degree program, services for LD students, study abroad, summer session for credit. ***ROTC:*** Army (b), Air Force (b).

Computers: 925 computers/terminals are available on campus for general student use. Students can access the following: campus intranet, computer help desk, free student e-mail accounts, online (class) grades, online (class) schedules. Campuswide network is available. 100% of college-owned or -operated housing units are wired for high-speed Internet access. Wireless service is available via entire campus.

Library: Willis Library plus 5 others. *Books:* 2.0 million (physical), 1.4 million (digital/electronic); *Serial titles:* 38,339 (physical), 185,694 (digital/electronic); *Databases:* 430. Weekly public service hours: 168; study areas open 24 hours, 5–7 days a week; students can reserve study rooms.

STUDENT LIFE

Housing options: on-campus residence required for freshman year; coed, men-only, women-only, special housing for students with disabilities. Campus housing is university owned. Freshman applicants given priority for college housing.

Activities and organizations: drama/theater group, student-run newspaper, radio and television station, choral group, marching band, Student Government Association, Residence Hall Association, Panhellenic Association, Interfraternity Council, Black Student Union, national fraternities, national sororities.

Athletics Member NCAA. All Division I except football (Division I-A). ***Intercollegiate sports:*** archery M(c)/W(c), badminton M(c)/W(c), baseball M(c), basketball M(s)/W(s), bowling M(c)/W(c), cross-country running M(s)/W(s), equestrian sports M(c)/W(c), fencing M(c)/W(c), golf M(s)/W(s), ice hockey M(c)/W(c), lacrosse M(c)/W(c), racquetball M(c)/W(c), rugby M(c), sailing M(c)/W(c), soccer M(c)/W(s), softball M/W(s), swimming and diving W(s), table tennis M(c)/W(c), tennis M(c)/W, track and field M(s)/W(s), ultimate Frisbee M(c)/W(c), volleyball M(c)/W(s), wrestling M(c)/W(c). ***Intramural sports:*** basketball M/W, football M, racquetball M/W, soccer M/W, softball M/W, table tennis M/W, tennis M/W, ultimate Frisbee M/W, volleyball M/W.

Campus security: 24-hour emergency response devices and patrols, late-night transport/escort service, controlled dormitory access.

Student services: health clinic, personal/psychological counseling, legal services, veterans affairs office.

COSTS & FINANCIAL AID

Costs (2019–20) ***Tuition:*** $303 per credit hour part-time; state resident $303 per credit hour part-time; nonresident $718 per credit hour part-time.

Financial Aid Of all full-time matriculated undergraduates who enrolled in 2019, 19,363 applied for aid, 15,789 were judged to have need, 1,479 had their need fully met. In 2019, 3141 non-need-based awards were made. ***Average percent of need met:*** 53. ***Average financial aid package:*** $11,601. ***Average need-based loan:*** $3969. ***Average need-based gift aid:*** $8553. ***Average non-need-based aid:*** $6269. ***Average indebtedness upon graduation:*** $22,307.

APPLYING

Standardized Tests *Required:* SAT or ACT (for admission).

Options: electronic application, early admission, deferred entrance.

Application fee: $75.

Required: high school transcript. ***Required for some:*** essay or personal statement.

Application deadlines: 8/1 (freshmen), rolling (transfers).

Notification: continuous (freshmen), continuous (transfers).

CONTACT

Mr. Randall Nunn, Associate Director of Admissions, University of North Texas, Denton, TX 76203. *Phone:* 940-565-3920. *Toll-free phone:* 800-868-8211. *E-mail:* randall.nunn@unt.edu.

University of North Texas at Dallas

Dallas, Texas

http://untdallas.edu/

- **State-supported** comprehensive, founded 2001, part of University of North Texas System
- **Urban** 264-acre campus with easy access to Dallas-Fort Worth
- **Endowment** $823,724
- **Coed**
- 83% of applicants were admitted

FACULTY

Student/faculty ratio: 17:1.

ACADEMICS

Degrees: bachelor's, master's, and doctoral.

Library: UNTD Library. *Books:* 3,980 (physical), 44,401 (digital/electronic); *Serial titles:* 330 (physical), 10,899 (digital/electronic); *Databases:* 281.

STUDENT LIFE

Activities and organizations: national fraternities, national sororities.

Campus security: 24-hour emergency response devices, late-night transport/escort service.

Student services: personal/psychological counseling, veterans affairs office.

COSTS & FINANCIAL AID

Costs (2019–20) ***Tuition:*** area resident $7840 full-time; state resident $7840 full-time, $261 per credit hour part-time; nonresident $20,511 full-time, $683 per credit hour part-time. Full-time tuition and fees vary according to degree level. Part-time tuition and fees vary according to degree level. No tuition increase for student's term of enrollment. ***Required fees:*** $300 full-time, $10 per credit hour part-time. ***Room and board:*** $8948. Room and board charges vary according to board plan and housing facility.

Financial Aid Of all full-time matriculated undergraduates who enrolled in 2017, 1,469 applied for aid, 1,400 were judged to have need, 77 had their need fully met. In 2017, 152 non-need-based awards were made. ***Average percent of need met:*** 46. ***Average financial aid package:*** $9796. ***Average need-based loan:*** $4230. ***Average need-based gift aid:*** $6835. ***Average non-need-based aid:*** $6012. ***Average indebtedness upon graduation:*** $6566.

APPLYING

Standardized Tests *Required:* SAT or ACT (for admission).

Options: electronic application.

Application fee: $40.

Required: high school transcript.

CONTACT

Mr. Jason Faulk, Director of Undergraduate Admission, University of North Texas at Dallas, 7300 University Hill Drive, Admin (B1)105, Dallas 76039. *Phone:* 972-780-3642. *E-mail:* admissions@untdallas.edu.

University of Phoenix–Dallas Campus

Dallas, Texas

http://www.phoenix.edu/

CONTACT

Marc Booker, Senior Director, Office of Admissions and Evaluation, University of Phoenix–Dallas Campus, 4035 South Riverpoint Parkway, Mail Stop CF-L101, Phoenix, AZ 85040. *Phone:* 602-557-4609. *Toll-free phone:* 866-766-0766. *Fax:* 480-643-1156.

University of Phoenix–Houston Campus

Houston, Texas

http://www.phoenix.edu/

CONTACT

Marc Booker, Senior Director, Office of Admissions and Evaluation, University of Phoenix–Houston Campus, 4305 South Riverpoint Parkway,

Mail Stop CF-L101, Phoenix, AZ 85040. *Phone:* 602-557-4609. *Toll-free phone:* 866-766-0766. *Fax:* 480-643-1156.

University of Phoenix–San Antonio Campus

San Antonio, Texas

http://www.phoenix.edu/

CONTACT

University of Phoenix–San Antonio Campus, 8200 IH-10 West, San Antonio, TX 78230. *Toll-free phone:* 866-766-0766.

University of St. Thomas

Houston, Texas

http://www.stthom.edu/

- **Independent Roman Catholic** comprehensive, founded 1947
- **Urban** 23-acre campus with easy access to Houston, TX
- **Endowment** $102.4 million
- **Coed** 2,174 undergraduate students, 78% full-time, 62% women, 38% men
- **Moderately difficult** entrance level, 87% of applicants were admitted

UNDERGRAD STUDENTS

1,693 full-time, 481 part-time. Students come from 34 states and territories; 50 other countries; 3% are from out of state; 7% Black or African American, non-Hispanic/Latino; 47% Hispanic/Latino; 12% Asian, non-Hispanic/Latino; 0.2% Native Hawaiian or other Pacific Islander, non-Hispanic/Latino; 0.2% American Indian or Alaska Native, non-Hispanic/Latino; 2% Two or more races, non-Hispanic/Latino; 4% Race/ethnicity unknown; 7% international; 11% transferred in; 21% live on campus.

Freshmen:

Admission: 1,101 applied, 961 admitted, 343 enrolled. ***Average high school GPA:*** 3.7. ***Test scores:*** SAT evidence-based reading and writing scores over 500: 91%; SAT math scores over 500: 91%; ACT scores over 18: 99%; SAT evidence-based reading and writing scores over 600: 38%; SAT math scores over 600: 38%; ACT scores over 24: 40%; SAT evidence-based reading and writing scores over 700: 5%; SAT math scores over 700: 7%; ACT scores over 30: 11%.

Retention: 84% of full-time freshmen returned.

FACULTY

Total: 356, 42% full-time, 63% with terminal degrees.

Student/faculty ratio: 12:1.

ACADEMICS

Calendar: semesters. *Degrees:* associate, bachelor's, master's, doctoral, and postbachelor's certificates.

Special study options: accelerated degree program, adult/continuing education programs, advanced placement credit, cooperative education, distance learning, double majors, honors programs, independent study, internships, off-campus study, part-time degree program, services for LD students, study abroad, summer session for credit. ***ROTC:*** Army (c), Air Force (c).

Unusual degree programs: 3-2 business administration; engineering with University of Notre Dame, University of Houston, Texas A&M University, The Catholic University of America; nursing.

Computers: 74 computers/terminals and 800 ports are available on campus for general student use. Students can access the following: campus intranet, computer help desk, free student e-mail accounts, online (class) grades, online (class) registration, online (class) schedules. Campuswide network is available. 100% of college-owned or -operated housing units are wired for high-speed Internet access. Wireless service is available via entire campus.

Library: Doherty Library. *Books:* 262,245 (physical), 2,496 (digital/electronic); *Serial titles:* 74,347 (physical), 74,347 (digital/electronic); *Databases:* 274. Weekly public service hours: 100; students can reserve study rooms.

STUDENT LIFE

Housing options: coed, men-only, women-only, special housing for students with disabilities. Campus housing is university owned. Freshman applicants given priority for college housing.

Activities and organizations: drama/theater group, student-run newspaper, choral group, Health Occupations Students of America (HOSA), Filipino Student Association (FSA), Tri-Beta, Psi Chi, Pre-Health Professional Society.

Athletics Member NAIA. ***Intercollegiate sports:*** baseball M, basketball M(s)/W(s), cross-country running M(s)/W(s), golf M(s)/W(s), soccer M(s)/W(s), tennis M/W, volleyball W(s). ***Intramural sports:*** badminton M(c)/W(c), baseball M(c)/W(c), basketball M(c)/W(c), cheerleading M(c)/W(c), fencing M(c)/W(c), sand volleyball M(c)/W(c), soccer M(c)/W(c), table tennis M(c)/W(c), tennis M(c)/W(c).

Campus security: 24-hour patrols, late-night transport/escort service, controlled dormitory access.

Student services: personal/psychological counseling.

COSTS & FINANCIAL AID

Costs (2020–21) ***Comprehensive fee:*** $41,030 includes full-time tuition ($30,800), mandatory fees ($760), and room and board ($9470). Part-time tuition: $1100 per credit hour. Part-time tuition and fees vary according to course load. ***College room only:*** $5880. Room and board charges vary according to board plan and housing facility. ***Payment plans:*** installment, deferred payment. ***Waivers:*** employees or children of employees.

Financial Aid Of all full-time matriculated undergraduates who enrolled in 2019, 1,260 applied for aid, 1,181 were judged to have need, 109 had their need fully met. 72 Federal Work-Study jobs (averaging $3854). 1 state and other part-time job (averaging $4000). In 2019, 395 non-need-based awards were made. ***Average percent of need met:*** 70. ***Average financial aid package:*** $25,335. ***Average need-based loan:*** $4470. ***Average need-based gift aid:*** $22,983. ***Average non-need-based aid:*** $12,558. ***Average indebtedness upon graduation:*** $25,969.

APPLYING

Standardized Tests *Required for some:* SAT or ACT (for admission).

Options: electronic application, deferred entrance.

Required: minimum 2.8 GPA. ***Recommended:*** 3 letters of recommendation.

Application deadlines: 8/15 (freshmen), 8/15 (out-of-state freshmen), 8/15 (transfers).

Notification: continuous until 10/1 (freshmen), continuous until 10/1 (out-of-state freshmen), continuous until 10/1 (transfers), 10/1 (early decision plan 1), 10/1 (early decision plan 2), 10/1 (early action).

CONTACT

Mr. Ryan Konkright, Director of Undergrdauate Admissions, University of St. Thomas, 3800 Montrose Boulevard, Houston, TX 77006-4696. *Phone:* 713-525-3500. *Toll-free phone:* 800-856-8565. *Fax:* 713-525-3558. *E-mail:* admissions@stthom.edu.

The University of Texas at Arlington

Arlington, Texas

http://www.uta.edu/

CONTACT

Dr. Hans Gatterdam, Executive Director of Admissions, Records and Registration, The University of Texas at Arlington, UTA Box 19088, 701 South Nedderman Drive, Arlington, TX 76019-0088. *Phone:* 817-272-3275. *Fax:* 817-272-5114.

The University of Texas at Austin

Austin, Texas

http://www.utexas.edu/

- **State-supported** university, founded 1883, part of University of Texas System
- **Urban** 431-acre campus with easy access to Austin
- **Endowment** $4.0 billion
- **Coed**
- **Moderately difficult** entrance level

FACULTY
Student/faculty ratio: 18:1.

ACADEMICS
Calendar: semesters. *Degrees:* certificates, bachelor's, master's, doctoral, and postbachelor's certificates.

Library: PCL (Perry Castaneda Library) plus 19 others. *Books:* 11.5 million (physical), 1.5 million (digital/electronic); *Serial titles:* 252,967 (physical), 471,535 (digital/electronic); *Databases:* 941. Weekly public service hours: 94; study areas open 24 hours, 5–7 days a week; students can reserve study rooms.

STUDENT LIFE
Housing options: coed, men-only, women-only, special housing for students with disabilities. Campus housing is university owned. Freshman applicants given priority for college housing.

Activities and organizations: drama/theater group, student-run newspaper, radio and television station, choral group, marching band, Alpha Phi Omega, University Panhellenic Council, Asian Business Students Association, Longhorn Band Student Organization, Campus Events + Entertainment, national fraternities, national sororities.

Athletics Member NCAA. All Division I except football (Division I-A).

Campus security: 24-hour emergency response devices and patrols, late-night transport/escort service, controlled dormitory access.

Student services: health clinic, personal/psychological counseling, women's center, legal services, veterans affairs office.

COSTS & FINANCIAL AID
Costs (2019–20) ***Tuition:*** state resident $10,824 full-time; nonresident $38,326 full-time. Full-time tuition and fees vary according to course load and program. Part-time tuition and fees vary according to course load and program. No tuition increase for student's term of enrollment. ***Room and board:*** $11,812. Room and board charges vary according to housing facility.

Financial Aid Of all full-time matriculated undergraduates who enrolled in 2018, 23,064 applied for aid, 15,377 were judged to have need, 2,697 had their need fully met. In 2018, 546 non-need-based awards were made. ***Average percent of need met:*** 68. ***Average financial aid package:*** $12,306. ***Average need-based loan:*** $4081. ***Average need-based gift aid:*** $9659. ***Average non-need-based aid:*** $2982. ***Average indebtedness upon graduation:*** $24,263.

APPLYING
Standardized Tests *Required:* SAT or ACT (for admission).

Options: electronic application.

Application fee: $75.

Required: essay or personal statement, high school transcript.

CONTACT
Miguel Wasielewski, Executive Director of Admissions, The University of Texas at Austin, Office of Admissions, PO Box 8058, PO Box 8058, Austin, TX 78713-8058. *Phone:* 512-475-7399. *E-mail:* admissions@austin.utexas.edu.

The University of Texas at Dallas

Richardson, Texas

http://www.utdallas.edu/

- **State-supported** university, founded 1969, part of University of Texas System
- **Suburban** 500-acre campus with easy access to Dallas-Fort Worth
- **Endowment** $558.5 million
- **Coed** 20,994 undergraduate students, 85% full-time, 43% women, 57% men
- **Very difficult** entrance level, 80% of applicants were admitted

UNDERGRAD STUDENTS
17,941 full-time, 3,053 part-time. Students come from 49 states and territories; 68 other countries; 5% are from out of state; 6% Black or African American, non-Hispanic/Latino; 19% Hispanic/Latino; 33% Asian, non-Hispanic/Latino; 0.2% Native Hawaiian or other Pacific Islander, non-Hispanic/Latino; 0.1% American Indian or Alaska Native, non-Hispanic/Latino; 4% Two or more races, non-Hispanic/Latino; 2% Race/ethnicity unknown; 5% international; 9% transferred in; 24% live on campus.

Freshmen:
Admission: 14,147 applied, 11,260 admitted, 4,073 enrolled. ***Test scores:*** SAT evidence-based reading and writing scores over 500: 99%; SAT math scores over 500: 99%; ACT scores over 18: 100%; SAT evidence-based reading and writing scores over 600: 82%; SAT math scores over 600: 86%; ACT scores over 24: 88%; SAT evidence-based reading and writing scores over 700: 30%; SAT math scores over 700: 48%; ACT scores over 30: 48%.

Retention: 88% of full-time freshmen returned.

FACULTY
Total: 1,361, 68% full-time, 73% with terminal degrees.

Student/faculty ratio: 24:1.

ACADEMICS
Calendar: semesters. *Degrees:* bachelor's, master's, doctoral, and postbachelor's certificates.

Special study options: academic remediation for entering students, accelerated degree program, adult/continuing education programs, advanced placement credit, cooperative education, distance learning, double majors, freshman honors college, honors programs, independent study, internships, part-time degree program, services for LD students, student-designed majors, study abroad, summer session for credit. ***ROTC:*** Army (c), Air Force (c).

Unusual degree programs: 3-2 engineering with Abilene Christian University, Austin College, Paul Quinn College, Texas Woman's University.

Computers: 170 computers/terminals are available on campus for general student use. Students can access the following: computer help desk, free student e-mail accounts, online (class) grades, online (class) registration, online (class) schedules. Campuswide network is available. 100% of college-owned or -operated housing units are wired for high-speed Internet access. Wireless service is available via classrooms, computer centers, dorm rooms, libraries, student centers.

Library: Eugene McDermott Library plus 1 other. *Books:* 567,164 (physical), 1.5 million (digital/electronic); *Serial titles:* 77,304 (physical), 165,725 (digital/electronic); *Databases:* 596. Weekly public service hours: 152; study areas open 24 hours, 5–7 days a week; students can reserve study rooms.

STUDENT LIFE
Housing options: coed. Campus housing is university owned. Freshman applicants given priority for college housing.

Activities and organizations: drama/theater group, student-run newspaper, radio and television station, choral group, Student Government Association, Golden Key National Honor Society, Muslim Students Association, Indian Student Association, Friendship Association of Chinese Students and Scholars, national fraternities, national sororities.

Athletics Member NCAA. All Division III. ***Intercollegiate sports:*** baseball M, basketball M/W, cross-country running M/W, golf M/W, soccer M/W, softball W, tennis M/W, volleyball W. ***Intramural sports:*** archery M(c)/W(c), badminton M(c)/W(c), basketball M/W, cheerleading M/W, cross-country running M(c)/W(c), fencing M(c)/W(c), gymnastics M(c)/W(c), lacrosse M(c), rock climbing M(c)/W(c), rugby M(c)/W(c), soccer M(c)/W(c), swimming and diving M(c)/W(c), table tennis M(c)/W(c), tennis M(c)/W(c), ultimate Frisbee M(c)/W(c), volleyball M(c)/W(c), weight lifting M(c)/W(c), wrestling M(c)/W(c).

Campus security: 24-hour emergency response devices and patrols, student patrols, late-night transport/escort service, controlled dormitory access.

Student services: health clinic, personal/psychological counseling, women's center, legal services, veterans affairs office.

COSTS & FINANCIAL AID
Costs (2019–20) ***Tuition:*** state resident $13,442 full-time; nonresident $38,168 full-time. Full-time tuition and fees vary according to course load and degree level. Part-time tuition and fees vary according to course load and degree level. No tuition increase for student's term of enrollment. ***Room and board:*** $11,532. Room and board charges vary according to board plan and housing facility. ***Payment plan:*** installment. ***Waivers:*** senior citizens and employees or children of employees.

Financial Aid Of all full-time matriculated undergraduates who enrolled in 2018, 10,450 applied for aid, 8,620 were judged to have need, 1,247 had their need fully met. In 2018, 3484 non-need-based awards were made. ***Average percent of need met:*** 65. ***Average financial aid package:*** $13,776. ***Average need-based loan:*** $4445. ***Average need-based gift aid:*** $9706. ***Average non-need-based aid:*** $11,842. ***Average indebtedness upon graduation:*** $23,176.

APPLYING
Standardized Tests *Required:* SAT or ACT (for admission). *Required for some:* THEA.

Options: electronic application, deferred entrance.

Application fee: $50.

Required: essay or personal statement, high school transcript. ***Required for some:*** interview. ***Recommended:*** 3 letters of recommendation.

Notification: continuous (freshmen), continuous (transfers).

CONTACT
Enrollment Services, The University of Texas at Dallas, 800 West Campbell Road, Mail Station ROC12, Richardson, TX 75083-0688. *Phone:* 972-883-2270. *Toll-free phone:* 800-889-2443. *Fax:* 972-883-2599. *E-mail:* admission@utdallas.edu.

The University of Texas at El Paso

El Paso, Texas

http://www.utep.edu/

- **State-supported** university, founded 1913, part of University of Texas System
- **Urban** 360-acre campus with easy access to El Paso, TX
- **Coed** 21,427 undergraduate students, 65% full-time, 54% women, 46% men
- **Minimally difficult** entrance level, 100% of applicants were admitted

UNDERGRAD STUDENTS
13,858 full-time, 7,569 part-time. Students come from 53 states and territories; 80 other countries; 4% are from out of state; 2% Black or African American, non-Hispanic/Latino; 85% Hispanic/Latino; 0.8% Asian, non-Hispanic/Latino; 0.1% Native Hawaiian or other Pacific Islander, non-Hispanic/Latino; 0.2% American Indian or Alaska Native, non-Hispanic/Latino; 0.9% Two or more races, non-Hispanic/Latino; 0.5% Race/ethnicity unknown; 5% international; 8% transferred in.

Freshmen:
Admission: 10,972 applied, 10,971 admitted, 3,063 enrolled. ***Average high school GPA:*** 3.3. ***Test scores:*** SAT evidence-based reading and writing scores over 500: 55%; SAT math scores over 500: 54%; ACT scores over 18: 69%; SAT evidence-based reading and writing scores over 600: 14%; SAT math scores over 600: 10%; ACT scores over 24: 15%; SAT evidence-based reading and writing scores over 700: 1%; SAT math scores over 700: 1%; ACT scores over 30: 1%.

Retention: 75% of full-time freshmen returned.

FACULTY
Total: 1,354, 59% full-time.

Student/faculty ratio: 25:1.

ACADEMICS
Calendar: semesters. *Degrees:* certificates, diplomas, bachelor's, master's, and doctoral.

Special study options: academic remediation for entering students, advanced placement credit, distance learning, double majors, external degree program, honors programs, independent study, off-campus study, part-time degree program, services for LD students, study abroad, summer session for credit. ***ROTC:*** Army (b).

Computers: Students can access the following: computer help desk, free student e-mail accounts, online (class) grades, online (class) registration, online (class) schedules. Campuswide network is available. 100% of college-owned or -operated housing units are wired for high-speed Internet access. Wireless service is available via entire campus.
Library: University Library. *Books:* 914,412 (physical), 407,455 (digital/electronic); *Serial titles:* 15,278 (physical), 101,613 (digital/electronic); *Databases:* 395. Students can reserve study rooms.

STUDENT LIFE
Housing options: coed. Campus housing is university owned.

Activities and organizations: drama/theater group, student-run newspaper, radio station, choral group, marching band, The National Society of Leadership and Success, The National Society of Collegiate Scholars, Institute of Electrical and Electronics Engineers (IEEE), Medical Professions Organization, Latinos in Science and Engineering/Society of Hispanic Professional Engineers, national fraternities, national sororities.

Athletics Member NCAA. All Division I except football (Division I-A). ***Intercollegiate sports:*** basketball M(s)/W(s), cross-country running M(s)/W(s), golf M(s)/W(s), riflery M(s)/W, soccer W(s), softball W(s), tennis W(s), track and field M(s)/W(s), volleyball W(s). ***Intramural sports:*** archery M/W, badminton M/W, basketball M/W, bowling M/W, fencing M, field hockey M/W, golf M/W, gymnastics M/W, ice hockey M(c), racquetball M/W, rock climbing M/W, sand volleyball M/W, skiing (downhill) M, soccer M/W, squash M/W, swimming and diving M/W, tennis M/W, track and field M/W, volleyball M/W, water polo M/W, weight lifting M, wrestling M/W.

Campus security: 24-hour emergency response devices and patrols, late-night transport/escort service.

Student services: health clinic, personal/psychological counseling, women's center, legal services.

COSTS & FINANCIAL AID
Costs (2019–20) ***Tuition:*** area resident $7193 full-time, $294 per credit hour part-time; state resident $7193 full-time, $294 per credit hour part-time; nonresident $22,556 full-time, $806 per credit hour part-time. Full-time tuition and fees vary according to course load, degree level, and program. Part-time tuition and fees vary according to course load, degree level, and program. No tuition increase for student's term of enrollment. ***Required fees:*** $1768 full-time. ***Room and board:*** $9496; room only: $5200. ***Payment plan:*** installment.

Financial Aid Of all full-time matriculated undergraduates who enrolled in 2017, 12,305 applied for aid, 10,363 were judged to have need, 1,622 had their need fully met. In 2017, 655 non-need-based awards were made. ***Average percent of need met:*** 55. ***Average financial aid package:*** $11,820. ***Average need-based loan:*** $6172. ***Average need-based gift aid:*** $7873. ***Average non-need-based aid:*** $4229. ***Average indebtedness upon graduation:*** $23,632.

APPLYING
Standardized Tests *Required:* SAT or ACT (for admission). *Recommended:* ACT (for admission).

Options: electronic application, deferred entrance.

Required: high school transcript.

CONTACT
Mr. Michael J. Talamantes, Director of Admissions and Recruitment, The University of Texas at El Paso, Academic Services Building, Room 102, El Paso, TX 779968. *Phone:* 915-747-5890. *Toll-free phone:* 877-74MINER. *Fax:* 915-747-5890. *E-mail:* futureminer@utep.edu.

The University of Texas at San Antonio

San Antonio, Texas

http://www.utsa.edu/

- **State-supported** university, founded 1969, part of University of Texas System
- **Suburban** 725-acre campus with easy access to San Antonio
- **Endowment** $134.5 million
- **Coed** 28,275 undergraduate students, 79% full-time, 50% women, 50% men
- **Moderately difficult** entrance level, 77% of applicants were admitted

UNDERGRAD STUDENTS
22,414 full-time, 5,861 part-time. 2% are from out of state; 9% Black or African American, non-Hispanic/Latino; 58% Hispanic/Latino; 6% Asian, non-Hispanic/Latino; 0.2% Native Hawaiian or other Pacific Islander, non-Hispanic/Latino; 0.2% American Indian or Alaska Native, non-Hispanic/Latino; 4% Two or more races, non-Hispanic/Latino; 0.5% Race/ethnicity unknown; 2% international; 11% transferred in; 8% live on campus.

Freshmen:
Admission: 17,122 applied, 13,113 admitted, 4,599 enrolled. ***Test scores:*** SAT evidence-based reading and writing scores over 500: 86%; SAT math

scores over 500: 84%; ACT scores over 18: 89%; SAT evidence-based reading and writing scores over 600: 36%; SAT math scores over 600: 27%; ACT scores over 24: 34%; SAT evidence-based reading and writing scores over 700: 4%; SAT math scores over 700: 4%; ACT scores over 30: 5%.

Retention: 74% of full-time freshmen returned.

FACULTY

Total: 1,301, 75% full-time, 74% with terminal degrees.

Student/faculty ratio: 25:1.

ACADEMICS

Calendar: semesters. *Degrees:* certificates, bachelor's, master's, doctoral, and postbachelor's certificates.

Special study options: academic remediation for entering students, accelerated degree program, adult/continuing education programs, advanced placement credit, cooperative education, distance learning, double majors, English as a second language, honors programs, independent study, internships, off-campus study, part-time degree program, services for LD students, student-designed majors, study abroad, summer session for credit. ***ROTC:*** Army (b), Air Force (b).

Computers: 510 computers/terminals and 104 ports are available on campus for general student use. Students can access the following: campus intranet, computer help desk, free student e-mail accounts, online (class) grades, online (class) registration, online (class) schedules. Campuswide network is available. 100% of college-owned or -operated housing units are wired for high-speed Internet access. Wireless service is available via entire campus.

Library: John Peace Library plus 3 others. Students can reserve study rooms.

STUDENT LIFE

Housing options: coed. Campus housing is university owned.

Activities and organizations: student-run newspaper, choral group, marching band, Student Government, VOICES, Chi Alpha Christian Fellowship, Hispanic Student Association, Panhellenic Council, national fraternities, national sororities.

Athletics Member NCAA. All Division I. ***Intercollegiate sports:*** badminton M(c)/W(c), baseball M(s), basketball M(s)/W(s), cross-country running M(s)/W(s), fencing M(c)/W(c), football M(s), golf M(s)/W(s), ice hockey M(c), lacrosse M(c)/W(c), racquetball M(c)/W(c), rock climbing M(c)/W(c), rugby M(c)/W(c), soccer M(c)/W(s), softball W(s), swimming and diving M(c)/W(c), table tennis M(c)/W(c), tennis M(s)/W(s), track and field M(s)/W(s), ultimate Frisbee M(c)/W(c), volleyball M(c)/W(s), weight lifting M(c)/W(c), wrestling M(c). ***Intramural sports:*** badminton M/W, baseball M(c), basketball M/W, cross-country running M/W, football M, golf M/W, racquetball M/W, soccer M/W, softball M/W, table tennis M/W, tennis M/W, track and field M/W, ultimate Frisbee M/W, volleyball M/W.

Campus security: 24-hour emergency response devices and patrols, late-night transport/escort service, controlled dormitory access, close to 1000 security cameras, Reverse 911 emergency telephone notification system, warning speaker arrays.

Student services: health clinic, personal/psychological counseling, women's center, veterans affairs office.

COSTS & FINANCIAL AID

Costs (2019–20) ***Tuition:*** area resident $6887 full-time, $230 per credit hour part-time; state resident $6887 full-time, $230 per credit hour part-time; nonresident $21,889 full-time, $730 per credit hour part-time. Full-time tuition and fees vary according to course level and program. Part-time tuition and fees vary according to course level and program. No tuition increase for student's term of enrollment. ***Required fees:*** $2836 full-time, $1111 per term part-time. ***Room and board:*** $7590; room only: $4770. Room and board charges vary according to housing facility. ***Payment plans:*** installment, deferred payment. ***Waivers:*** employees or children of employees.

Financial Aid Of all full-time matriculated undergraduates who enrolled in 2018, 17,732 applied for aid, 15,265 were judged to have need, 672 had their need fully met. In 2018, 2694 non-need-based awards were made. ***Average percent of need met:*** 51. ***Average financial aid package:*** $10,241. ***Average need-based loan:*** $4119. ***Average need-based gift aid:*** $7611. ***Average non-need-based aid:*** $1711. ***Average indebtedness upon graduation:*** $24,214.

APPLYING

Standardized Tests *Required:* SAT or ACT (for admission).

Options: electronic application.

Application fee: $70.

Required: high school transcript. ***Required for some:*** transfer applicants with less than 30 hours must meet freshman requirements and have a 2.25 GPA on a 4.0 scale and submit all college transcripts; transfer applicants with 30 or more completed hours must have a 2.25 GPA on a 4.0 scale and submit all college transcripts. ***Recommended:*** essay or personal statement, 1 letter of recommendation.

Application deadlines: 6/1 (freshmen), 6/1 (transfers).

Notification: continuous (freshmen), continuous (out-of-state freshmen), continuous (transfers).

CONTACT

Mrs. Beverly Woodson Day, Director of Admissions, The University of Texas at San Antonio, One UTSA Circle, San Antonio, TX 78249. *Phone:* 210-458-4536. *Toll-free phone:* 800-669-0919. *Fax:* 210-458-2001. *E-mail:* prospects@utsa.edu.

The University of Texas at Tyler

Tyler, Texas

http://www.uttyler.edu/

- **State-supported** comprehensive, founded 1971, part of University of Texas System
- **Urban** 200-acre campus
- **Coed**
- **Moderately difficult** entrance level

FACULTY

Student/faculty ratio: 19:1.

ACADEMICS

Calendar: semesters. *Degrees:* bachelor's, master's, doctoral, post-master's, and postbachelor's certificates.

Library: Robert Muntz Library.

STUDENT LIFE

Housing options: on-campus residence required for freshman year; coed. Campus housing is university owned and is provided by a third party. Freshman applicants given priority for college housing.

Activities and organizations: student-run newspaper, choral group, national fraternities, national sororities.

Athletics Member NCAA. All Division III.

Campus security: 24-hour emergency response devices and patrols, late-night transport/escort service, controlled dormitory access.

COSTS & FINANCIAL AID

Costs (2019–20) ***Tuition:*** area resident $6540 full-time; state resident $6540 full-time; nonresident $20,550 full-time. ***Required fees:*** $2202 full-time. ***Room and board:*** $9502; room only: $5754.

Financial Aid Of all full-time matriculated undergraduates who enrolled in 2018, 3,861 applied for aid, 3,728 were judged to have need, 110 had their need fully met. In 2018, 17 non-need-based awards were made. ***Average percent of need met:*** 38. ***Average financial aid package:*** $8519. ***Average need-based loan:*** $3419. ***Average need-based gift aid:*** $7397. ***Average non-need-based aid:*** $3198. ***Average indebtedness upon graduation:*** $19,691.

APPLYING

Standardized Tests *Required:* SAT or ACT (for admission).

Options: electronic application, deferred entrance.

Application fee: $60.

Required: high school transcript.

CONTACT

Ms. Sarah Bowdin, Interim Assistant Vice President for Enrollment Management, The University of Texas at Tyler, 3900 University Boulevard, Tyler, TX 75799-0001. *Phone:* 903-566-7057. *Toll-free phone:* 800-UTTYLER. *Fax:* 903-566-7068. *E-mail:* admissions@uttyler.edu.

The University of Texas Health Science Center at Houston

Houston, Texas

http://www.uthouston.edu/

CONTACT
The University of Texas Health Science Center at Houston, PO Box 20036, Houston, TX 77225-0036. *Phone:* 713-500-3388.

The University of Texas Health Science Center at San Antonio

San Antonio, Texas

http://www.uthscsa.edu/

CONTACT
The University of Texas Health Science Center at San Antonio, 7703 Floyd Curl Drive, San Antonio, TX 78229-3900. *Phone:* 210-567-2659.

The University of Texas MD Anderson Cancer Center

Houston, Texas

http://www.mdanderson.org/education-and-research/

CONTACT
The University of Texas MD Anderson Cancer Center, 1515 Holcombe Boulevard, Houston, TX 77030.

The University of Texas Medical Branch

Galveston, Texas

http://www.utmb.edu/

CONTACT
The University of Texas Medical Branch, 301 University Boulevard, Galveston, TX 77555. *Phone:* 409-772-1215.

The University of Texas of the Permian Basin

Odessa, Texas

http://www.utpb.edu/

- **State-supported** comprehensive, founded 1969, part of The University of Texas System
- **Urban** 600-acre campus
- **Endowment** $42.2 million
- **Coed** 4,347 undergraduate students, 43% full-time, 58% women, 42% men
- **Moderately difficult** entrance level, 79% of applicants were admitted

UNDERGRAD STUDENTS
1,862 full-time, 2,485 part-time. Students come from 42 states and territories; 36 other countries; 6% Black or African American, non-Hispanic/Latino; 54% Hispanic/Latino; 3% Asian, non-Hispanic/Latino; 0.3% Native Hawaiian or other Pacific Islander, non-Hispanic/Latino; 0.3% American Indian or Alaska Native, non-Hispanic/Latino; 3% Two or more races, non-Hispanic/Latino; 2% Race/ethnicity unknown; 5% international; 20% live on campus.

Freshmen:
Admission: 1,162 applied, 915 admitted, 311 enrolled. ***Test scores:*** SAT evidence-based reading and writing scores over 500: 62%; SAT math scores over 500: 62%; ACT scores over 18: 70%; SAT evidence-based reading and writing scores over 600: 17%; SAT math scores over 600: 18%; ACT scores over 24: 18%; SAT evidence-based reading and writing scores over 700: 1%; SAT math scores over 700: 3%; ACT scores over 30: 2%.

Retention: 60% of full-time freshmen returned.

FACULTY
Total: 280, 61% full-time, 52% with terminal degrees.

Student/faculty ratio: 19:1.

ACADEMICS
Calendar: semesters. *Degrees:* bachelor's, master's, and postbachelor's certificates.

Special study options: academic remediation for entering students, accelerated degree program, advanced placement credit, cooperative education, distance learning, double majors, English as a second language, honors programs, independent study, internships, part-time degree program, services for LD students, study abroad, summer session for credit.

Unusual degree programs: 3-2 business administration; engineering; nursing; social work.

Computers: 511 computers/terminals are available on campus for general student use. Students can access the following: campus intranet, computer help desk, free student e-mail accounts, online (class) grades, online (class) registration, online (class) schedules. Campuswide network is available. 100% of college-owned or -operated housing units are wired for high-speed Internet access. Wireless service is available via entire campus.

Library: J. Conrad Dunagan Library. *Books:* 207,582 (physical), 3.4 million (digital/electronic); *Serial titles:* 57,446 (physical), 136,464 (digital/electronic); *Databases:* 271. Weekly public service hours: 86; students can reserve study rooms.

STUDENT LIFE
Housing options: coed. Campus housing is university owned.

Activities and organizations: drama/theater group, student-run newspaper, choral group, marching band, The American Society for Mechanical Engineers, The Student Veteran Association, Marketing Experiences, The National Society for Leadership and Success, Students in Free Enterprise, national fraternities.

Athletics Member NCAA. All Division II except golf (Division I). ***Intercollegiate sports:*** baseball M(s), basketball M(s)/W(s), cheerleading M(s)/W(s), cross-country running M(s)/W(s), football M(s), golf M(s)/W(s), soccer M(s)/W(s), softball W(s), swimming and diving M(s)/W(s), tennis M(s)/W(s), volleyball W(s). ***Intramural sports:*** basketball M/W, bowling M/W, cross-country running M/W, golf M/W, soccer M/W, softball W, swimming and diving M/W, tennis M/W, volleyball M/W.

Campus security: 24-hour emergency response devices and patrols, late-night transport/escort service, controlled dormitory access.

Student services: health clinic, personal/psychological counseling, veterans affairs office.

COSTS & FINANCIAL AID
Costs (2020–21) ***Tuition:*** area resident $7641 full-time, $203 per credit hour part-time; state resident $7641 full-time, $203 per credit hour part-time; nonresident $8915 full-time, $288 per credit hour part-time. Full-time tuition and fees vary according to course load, degree level, and location. No tuition increase for student's term of enrollment. ***Required fees:*** $2299 full-time, $1270 per year part-time. ***Room and board:*** $9846; room only: $6076. Room and board charges vary according to board plan and housing facility. ***Payment plan:*** installment. ***Waivers:*** senior citizens.

Financial Aid Of all full-time matriculated undergraduates who enrolled in 2018, 2,371 applied for aid, 2,066 were judged to have need, 306 had their need fully met. In 2018, 985 non-need-based awards were made. ***Average percent of need met:*** 100. ***Average financial aid package:*** $17,965. ***Average need-based loan:*** $4207. ***Average need-based gift aid:*** $17,554. ***Average non-need-based aid:*** $2398. ***Average indebtedness upon graduation:*** $13,445.

APPLYING
Standardized Tests *Required:* SAT or ACT (for admission).

Options: electronic application.

Application fee: $40.

Required: high school transcript.

Application deadlines: 7/15 (freshmen), 7/15 (transfers).

Notification: continuous (freshmen), continuous (transfers).

CONTACT
The University of Texas of the Permian Basin, 4901 East University Boulevard, Odessa, TX 79762-0001. *Phone:* 432-552-2605. *Toll-free phone:* 866-552-UTPB.

The University of Texas Rio Grande Valley

Edinburg, Texas

http://www.utrgv.edu/

- **State-supported** university, founded 1927, part of University of Texas System
- **Small-town** 685-acre campus with easy access to McAllen, Edinburg, Mission
- **Endowment** $98.0 million
- **Coed** 24,965 undergraduate students, 80% full-time, 57% women, 43% men
- **Noncompetitive** entrance level, 80% of applicants were admitted

UNDERGRAD STUDENTS
19,922 full-time, 5,043 part-time. Students come from 38 states and territories; 48 other countries; 1% are from out of state; 0.4% Black or African American, non-Hispanic/Latino; 92% Hispanic/Latino; 1% Asian, non-Hispanic/Latino; 0.3% Two or more races, non-Hispanic/Latino; 2% Race/ethnicity unknown; 2% international; 7% transferred in; 3% live on campus.

Freshmen:
Admission: 10,680 applied, 8,523 admitted, 4,793 enrolled. ***Test scores:*** SAT evidence-based reading and writing scores over 500: 68%; SAT math scores over 500: 64%; ACT scores over 18: 74%; SAT evidence-based reading and writing scores over 600: 19%; SAT math scores over 600: 11%; ACT scores over 24: 13%; SAT evidence-based reading and writing scores over 700: 1%; SAT math scores over 700: 1%; ACT scores over 30: 1%.

Retention: 77% of full-time freshmen returned.

FACULTY
Total: 1,433, 76% full-time.

ACADEMICS
Calendar: semesters. *Degrees:* bachelor's, master's, doctoral, and postbachelor's certificates.

Special study options: academic remediation for entering students, accelerated degree program, adult/continuing education programs, advanced placement credit, cooperative education, distance learning, double majors, English as a second language, honors programs, independent study, internships, off-campus study, part-time degree program, services for LD students, study abroad, summer session for credit. ***ROTC:*** Army (b).

Unusual degree programs: 3-2 business administration.

Computers: Students can access the following: campus intranet, computer help desk, free student e-mail accounts, online (class) grades, online (class) registration, online (class) schedules. Campuswide network is available. 66% of college-owned or -operated housing units are wired for high-speed Internet access. Wireless service is available via entire campus.

Library: University Library plus 4 others. *Books:* 546,403 (digital/electronic); *Serial titles:* 47,627 (digital/electronic); *Databases:* 230. Students can reserve study rooms.

STUDENT LIFE
Housing options: men-only, women-only, special housing for students with disabilities. Campus housing is university owned.

Activities and organizations: drama/theater group, student-run newspaper, radio and television station, choral group, Alpha Lambda Delta National Honor Society for First-Year Students, The National Society of Collegiate Scholars, Golden Key International Honor Society, Pre-Medical Bio-Medical Society, Environmental Awareness Club, national fraternities, national sororities.

Athletics Member NCAA. All Division I. ***Intercollegiate sports:*** baseball M(s), basketball M(s)/W(s), cross-country running M(s)/W(s), golf M(s)/W(s), soccer M(s)/W(s), tennis M(s)/W(s), track and field M(s)/W(s), volleyball W(s). ***Intramural sports:*** basketball M/W, football M, soccer M/W, volleyball M/W.

Campus security: 24-hour emergency response devices and patrols, late-night transport/escort service.

Student services: health clinic, personal/psychological counseling, veterans affairs office.

COSTS & FINANCIAL AID
Costs (2020–21) ***Tuition:*** area resident $7232 full-time, $430 per credit hour part-time; state resident $7232 full-time, $430 per credit hour part-time; nonresident $19,502 full-time, $839 per credit hour part-time. Full-time tuition and fees vary according to degree level and program. Part-time tuition and fees vary according to degree level and program. No tuition increase for student's term of enrollment. ***Required fees:*** $1684 full-time, $194 per credit hour part-time. ***Room and board:*** $8342. Room and board charges vary according to board plan and housing facility. ***Payment plans:*** installment, deferred payment. ***Waivers:*** employees or children of employees.

Financial Aid Of all full-time matriculated undergraduates who enrolled in 2017, 14,435 applied for aid, 13,829 were judged to have need, 345 had their need fully met. 764 Federal Work-Study jobs (averaging $2694). 428 state and other part-time jobs (averaging $2056). In 2017, 389 non-need-based awards were made. ***Average percent of need met:*** 78. ***Average financial aid package:*** $10,132. ***Average need-based loan:*** $4417. ***Average need-based gift aid:*** $10,676. ***Average non-need-based aid:*** $3329. ***Average indebtedness upon graduation:*** $16,129.

APPLYING
Standardized Tests *Required:* SAT or ACT (for admission).

Options: electronic application.

Required: high school transcript, minimum 2.0 GPA. ***Required for some:*** interview.

Application deadlines: 7/1 (freshmen), 7/1 (transfers).

Notification: continuous (freshmen).

CONTACT
Ms. Hilary Balli, Admissions Officer, The University of Texas Rio Grande Valley, 1201 W. University Drive, ESSBL 1.162, Edinburg, TX 78539. *Phone:* 956-665-2926. *Toll-free phone:* 888-882-4026. *Fax:* 956-665-2687. *E-mail:* hilary.balli01@utrgv.edu.

University of the Incarnate Word

San Antonio, Texas

http://www.uiw.edu/

- **Independent Roman Catholic** comprehensive, founded 1881
- **Urban** 200-acre campus with easy access to San Antonio
- **Endowment** $142.1 million
- **Coed** 5,368 undergraduate students, 76% full-time, 61% women, 39% men
- **Minimally difficult** entrance level, 94% of applicants were admitted

UNDERGRAD STUDENTS
4,093 full-time, 1,275 part-time. Students come from 46 states and territories; 44 other countries; 5% are from out of state; 7% Black or African American, non-Hispanic/Latino; 54% Hispanic/Latino; 2% Asian, non-Hispanic/Latino; 0.3% Native Hawaiian or other Pacific Islander, non-Hispanic/Latino; 0.4% American Indian or Alaska Native, non-Hispanic/Latino; 2% Two or more races, non-Hispanic/Latino; 6% Race/ethnicity unknown; 4% international; 9% transferred in; 23% live on campus.

Freshmen:
Admission: 6,291 applied, 5,911 admitted, 1,012 enrolled. ***Average high school GPA:*** 3.6. ***Test scores:*** SAT evidence-based reading and writing scores over 500: 69%; SAT math scores over 500: 66%; ACT scores over 18: 78%; SAT evidence-based reading and writing scores over 600: 22%; SAT math scores over 600: 14%; ACT scores over 24: 21%; SAT evidence-based reading and writing scores over 700: 2%; SAT math scores over 700: 1%; ACT scores over 30: 2%.

Retention: 73% of full-time freshmen returned.

FACULTY
Total: 770, 44% full-time, 47% with terminal degrees.

Student/faculty ratio: 14:1.

ACADEMICS
Calendar: semesters. *Degrees:* diplomas, associate, bachelor's, master's, and doctoral.

Special study options: academic remediation for entering students, accelerated degree program, adult/continuing education programs, advanced placement credit, cooperative education, distance learning, double majors, English as a second language, freshman honors college, honors programs, independent study, internships, off-campus study, part-time degree program, services for LD students, study abroad, summer session for credit. ***ROTC:*** Army (c).

Unusual degree programs: 3-2 business administration; accounting.

Computers: 406 computers/terminals are available on campus for general student use. Students can access the following: computer help desk, free student e-mail accounts, online (class) grades, online (class) registration, online (class) schedules. Campuswide network is available. 100% of college-owned or -operated housing units are wired for high-speed Internet access. Wireless service is available via entire campus.
Library: J. E. and M. E. Mabee Library plus 1 other. *Books:* 159,953 (physical), 60,292 (digital/electronic); *Serial titles:* 1,063 (physical), 86,652 (digital/electronic); *Databases:* 206. Weekly public service hours: 105.

STUDENT LIFE
Housing options: coed, men-only, women-only, special housing for students with disabilities. Campus housing is university owned.

Activities and organizations: drama/theater group, student-run newspaper, radio and television station, choral group, marching band, Business Club, Biology Club, Student Government Association, International Students Association, Multicultural Greek Council, national fraternities, national sororities.

Athletics Member NCAA. All Division I except football (Division I-AA), softball (Division II). ***Intercollegiate sports:*** baseball M(s), basketball M(s)/W(s), cross-country running M(s)/W(s), golf M(s)/W(s)(c), soccer M(s)/W(s), softball W(s), swimming and diving M(s)/W(s), tennis M(s)/W(s), track and field M(s)/W(s), volleyball W(s). ***Intramural sports:*** basketball M/W, cheerleading M/W, football M/W, racquetball M/W, soccer M/W, softball M/W, tennis M/W, ultimate Frisbee M/W, volleyball M/W, water polo M/W.

Campus security: 24-hour emergency response devices and patrols, late-night transport/escort service, controlled dormitory access.

Student services: health clinic, personal/psychological counseling, veterans affairs office.

COSTS & FINANCIAL AID
Costs (2020–21) ***Comprehensive fee:*** $45,300 includes full-time tuition ($31,020), mandatory fees ($1266), and room and board ($13,014). Full-time tuition and fees vary according to program. Part-time tuition: $950 per credit hour. Part-time tuition and fees vary according to program. ***Room and board:*** Room and board charges vary according to board plan and housing facility. ***Payment plans:*** installment, deferred payment. ***Waivers:*** employees or children of employees.

Financial Aid Of all full-time matriculated undergraduates who enrolled in 2017, 3,571 applied for aid, 3,374 were judged to have need, 248 had their need fully met. In 2017, 2 non-need-based awards were made. ***Average percent of need met:*** 58. ***Average financial aid package:*** $20,157. ***Average need-based loan:*** $3744. ***Average need-based gift aid:*** $15,472. ***Average non-need-based aid:*** $2356. ***Average indebtedness upon graduation:*** $38,722.

APPLYING
Standardized Tests *Required:* SAT or ACT (for admission).

Options: electronic application, deferred entrance.

Application fee: $20.

Required: high school transcript. ***Required for some:*** essay or personal statement. ***Recommended:*** minimum 2.0 GPA, interview.

Application deadlines: rolling (freshmen), rolling (transfers).

Notification: continuous (freshmen), continuous (transfers).

CONTACT
Ms. Jessica Delarosa, Director of Undergraduate Admissions, University of the Incarnate Word, 4301 Broadway Avenue, San Antonio, TX 78209. *Phone:* 210-829-6005. *Toll-free phone:* 800-749-WORD. *Fax:* 210-829-3921. *E-mail:* jsdelaro@uiwtx.edu.

Wade College

Dallas, Texas

http://www.wadecollege.edu/

CONTACT
Wade College, Infomart, 1950 North Stemmons Freeway, Suite 4080, LB 562, Dallas, TX 75207. *Phone:* 214-637-3530. *Toll-free phone:* 800-624-4850.

Wayland Baptist University

Plainview, Texas

http://www.wbu.edu/

- **Independent Baptist** comprehensive, founded 1908
- **Small-town** 80-acre campus
- **Endowment** $82.8 million
- **Coed** 3,543 undergraduate students, 25% full-time, 43% women, 42% men
- **Minimally difficult** entrance level, 97% of applicants were admitted

UNDERGRAD STUDENTS
869 full-time, 2,143 part-time. Students come from 45 states and territories; 20 other countries; 30% are from out of state; 18% Black or African American, non-Hispanic/Latino; 32% Hispanic/Latino; 2% Asian, non-Hispanic/Latino; 0.9% Native Hawaiian or other Pacific Islander, non-Hispanic/Latino; 0.8% American Indian or Alaska Native, non-Hispanic/Latino; 4% Two or more races, non-Hispanic/Latino; 4% Race/ethnicity unknown; 1% international; 9% transferred in; 73% live on campus.

Freshmen:
Admission: 635 applied, 619 admitted, 249 enrolled. ***Average high school GPA:*** 3.3. ***Test scores:*** SAT evidence-based reading and writing scores over 500: 45%; SAT math scores over 500: 45%; ACT scores over 18: 57%; SAT evidence-based reading and writing scores over 600: 8%; SAT math scores over 600: 7%; ACT scores over 24: 20%; SAT evidence-based reading and writing scores over 700: 1%; SAT math scores over 700: 1%; ACT scores over 30: 2%.

Retention: 41% of full-time freshmen returned.

FACULTY
Total: 537, 30% full-time.

Student/faculty ratio: 6:1.

ACADEMICS
Calendar: semesters. *Degrees:* associate, bachelor's, master's, and doctoral (branch locations in Anchorage, AK; Amarillo, TX; Luke Air Force Base, AZ; Glorieta, NM; Aiea, HI; Lubbock, TX; San Antonio, TX; Wichita Falls, TX).

Special study options: academic remediation for entering students, accelerated degree program, adult/continuing education programs, advanced placement credit, distance learning, double majors, external degree program, honors programs, part-time degree program, services for LD students, study abroad, summer session for credit. ***ROTC:*** Army (c), Air Force (c).

Unusual degree programs: 3-2 engineering with Texas Tech University.

Computers: 840 computers/terminals are available on campus for general student use. Students can access the following: computer help desk, free student e-mail accounts, online (class) grades, online (class) registration, online (class) schedules. Campuswide network is available. 100% of college-owned or -operated housing units are wired for high-speed Internet access. Wireless service is available via classrooms, computer labs, dorm rooms, libraries, student centers.
Library: J.E. and L.E. Mabee Learning Resource Center. *Books:* 130,903 (physical), 49,479 (digital/electronic); *Serial titles:* 555,663 (digital/electronic); *Databases:* 104.

STUDENT LIFE
Housing options: on-campus residence required through junior year; men-only, women-only. Campus housing is university owned. Freshman campus housing is guaranteed.

Activities and organizations: drama/theater group, student-run newspaper, radio and television station, choral group, marching band, Student Government, Wayland Singers, Baptist Student Ministries,

International Choir, President's Ambassadors, national fraternities, national sororities.

Athletics Member NAIA. ***Intercollegiate sports:*** baseball M(s), basketball M(s)/W(s), cheerleading M(s)/W(s), cross-country running M(s)/W(s), football M(s), golf M(s)/W(s), soccer M(s)/W(s), track and field M(s)/W(s), volleyball W(s), wrestling M(s)/W(s). ***Intramural sports:*** basketball M/W, football M, soccer M/W, volleyball M/W.

Campus security: 24-hour emergency response devices and patrols, security lighting, campus police department.

Student services: health clinic, personal/psychological counseling.

COSTS & FINANCIAL AID

Costs (2020–21) ***Comprehensive fee:*** $31,020 includes full-time tuition ($21,990), mandatory fees ($1308), and room and board ($7722). Full-time tuition and fees vary according to course load and location. Part-time tuition and fees vary according to course load and location. ***College room only:*** $2674. Room and board charges vary according to board plan and housing facility. ***Payment plan:*** installment.

Financial Aid Of all full-time matriculated undergraduates who enrolled in 2019, 708 applied for aid, 647 were judged to have need, 64 had their need fully met. In 2019, 93 non-need-based awards were made. ***Average percent of need met:*** 59. ***Average financial aid package:*** $14,139. ***Average need-based loan:*** $3958. ***Average need-based gift aid:*** $11,049. ***Average non-need-based aid:*** $6149. ***Average indebtedness upon graduation:*** $29,555.

APPLYING

Standardized Tests *Required:* SAT or ACT (for admission).

Options: electronic application.

Application fee: $35.

Required: high school transcript. ***Required for some:*** interview.

Application deadlines: 8/1 (freshmen), rolling (transfers).

Notification: continuous (freshmen), continuous (transfers).

CONTACT

Ms. Debbie Stennett, Director of Student Admissions, Wayland Baptist University, 1900 West 7th Street, CMB 1294, Plainview, TX 79072. *Phone:* 806-291-3500. *Toll-free phone:* 800-588-1928. *Fax:* 806-291-1973. *E-mail:* admityou@wbu.edu.

Weatherford College

Weatherford, Texas

http://www.wc.edu/

- **State and locally supported** primarily 2-year, founded 1869
- **Small-town** 94-acre campus with easy access to Dallas-Fort Worth
- **Coed** 5,637 undergraduate students
- **Noncompetitive** entrance level

UNDERGRAD STUDENTS

Students come from 28 other countries; 7% live on campus.

FACULTY

Total: 220, 43% full-time.

Student/faculty ratio: 22:1.

ACADEMICS

Calendar: semesters. *Degrees:* certificates, diplomas, associate, and bachelor's.

Special study options: academic remediation for entering students, adult/continuing education programs, cooperative education, distance learning, freshman honors college, honors programs, internships, part-time degree program, services for LD students, student-designed majors, summer session for credit. ***ROTC:*** Army (c), Air Force (c).

Computers: 85 computers/terminals are available on campus for general student use. Students can access the following: computer help desk, free student e-mail accounts, online (class) grades, online (class) registration, online (class) schedules, online catalog. Campuswide network is available. 100% of college-owned or -operated housing units are wired for high-speed Internet access. Wireless service is available via entire campus.

Library: Speaker Jim Wright Library. *Books:* 50,220 (physical). Students can reserve study rooms.

STUDENT LIFE

Housing options: coed. Campus housing is university owned.

Activities and organizations: drama/theater group, choral group, Black Awareness Student Organization, Criminal Justice Club, Phi Theta Kappa.

Athletics Member NJCAA. ***Intercollegiate sports:*** baseball M(s), basketball M(s)/W(s), cheerleading M(s)/W(s), equestrian sports M(s)/W(s), softball W(s).

Campus security: 24-hour emergency response devices and patrols, late-night transport/escort service.

Student services: personal/psychological counseling, veterans affairs office.

COSTS

Costs (2019–20) ***Tuition:*** area resident $2136 full-time, $89 per semester hour part-time; state resident $3432 full-time, $143 per semester hour part-time; nonresident $4848 full-time, $202 per semester hour part-time. Full-time tuition and fees vary according to course load and program. Part-time tuition and fees vary according to course load and program. ***Required fees:*** $240 full-time, $10 per semester hour part-time. ***Room and board:*** $7673. Room and board charges vary according to board plan. ***Payment plan:*** installment. ***Waivers:*** senior citizens and employees or children of employees.

APPLYING

Options: electronic application, early admission.

Recommended: high school transcript.

Notification: continuous (freshmen), continuous (transfers).

CONTACT

Mr. Ralph Willingham, Director of Admissions, Weatherford College, 225 College Park Drive, Weatherford, TX 76086-5699. *Phone:* 817-598-6248. *Toll-free phone:* 800-287-5471. *Fax:* 817-598-6205. *E-mail:* rwillingham@wc.edu.

West Coast University

Dallas, Texas

http://www.westcoastuniversity.edu/

CONTACT

West Coast University, 8435 N. Stemmons Freeway, Dallas, TX 75247. *Toll-free phone:* 866-508-2684.

West Texas A&M University

Canyon, Texas

http://www.wtamu.edu/

- **State-supported** comprehensive, founded 1909, part of Texas A&M University System
- **Small-town** 128-acre campus
- **Endowment** $80.4 million
- **Coed**
- **Moderately difficult** entrance level

FACULTY

Student/faculty ratio: 18:1.

ACADEMICS

Calendar: semesters. *Degrees:* bachelor's, master's, and doctoral.

Library: Cornette Library plus 3 others. *Books:* 305,487 (physical), 516,531 (digital/electronic); *Serial titles:* 12,207 (physical), 12,592 (digital/electronic); *Databases:* 181. Weekly public service hours: 91; students can reserve study rooms.

STUDENT LIFE

Housing options: on-campus residence required through sophomore year; coed, men-only, women-only, special housing for students with disabilities. Campus housing is university owned. Freshman campus housing is guaranteed.

Activities and organizations: drama/theater group, student-run newspaper, radio station, choral group, marching band, Residence Hall Association, Wesley, Student Government, SAGE, Baptist Student Ministries, national fraternities, national sororities.

Athletics Member NCAA. All Division II.

Campus security: 24-hour emergency response devices and patrols, late-night transport/escort service, controlled dormitory access.

Student services: health clinic, personal/psychological counseling, veterans affairs office.

COSTS & FINANCIAL AID

Costs (2019–20) ***Tuition:*** area resident $5854 full-time, $289 per credit hour part-time; state resident $5854 full-time, $289 per credit hour part-time; nonresident $7440 full-time, $342 per credit hour part-time. Full-time tuition and fees vary according to course load, degree level, program, and student level. Part-time tuition and fees vary according to course load, degree level, program, and student level. No tuition increase for student's term of enrollment. ***Required fees:*** $2834 full-time. ***Room and board:*** $7196. Room and board charges vary according to board plan and housing facility.

Financial Aid Of all full-time matriculated undergraduates who enrolled in 2019, 4,812 applied for aid, 3,530 were judged to have need, 238 had their need fully met. In 2019, 651 non-need-based awards were made. ***Average percent of need met:*** 58. ***Average financial aid package:*** $9628. ***Average need-based loan:*** $4015. ***Average need-based gift aid:*** $7398. ***Average non-need-based aid:*** $2304. ***Average indebtedness upon graduation:*** $28,132.

APPLYING

Standardized Tests *Required:* SAT or ACT (for admission).

Options: electronic application, deferred entrance.

Application fee: $55.

Required: high school transcript, class rank and Texas high school curriculum or equivalent.

CONTACT

Mrs. Tana Miller, Assistant Vice President for SEES/Registrar, West Texas A&M University, WTAMU Box 60907, Canyon, TX 79016-0001. *Phone:* 806-651-4911. *Toll-free phone:* 800-99-WTAMU. *Fax:* 806-651-5285. *E-mail:* tmiller@wtamu.edu.

Wiley College

Marshall, Texas

http://www.wileyc.edu/

CONTACT

Ms. Alvena Jones, Interim Director of Admissions/Recruitment, Wiley College, 711 Wiley Avenue, Marshall, TX 75670-5199. *Phone:* 903-927-3222. *Toll-free phone:* 800-658-6889. *Fax:* 903-923-8878. *E-mail:* ajones@wileyc.edu.

UTAH

Ameritech College of Healthcare

Draper, Utah

http://www.ameritech.edu/

CONTACT

Ameritech College of Healthcare, 12257 South Business Park Drive, Suite 108, Draper, UT 84020-6545.

Brigham Young University

Provo, Utah

http://www.byu.edu/

- **Independent** university, founded 1875, affiliated with The Church of Jesus Christ of Latter-day Saints, part of Church Education System (CES) of The Church of Jesus Christ of Latter-day Saints
- **Suburban** 557-acre campus with easy access to Salt Lake City
- **Coed** 31,292 undergraduate students, 90% full-time, 50% women, 50% men
- **Moderately difficult** entrance level, 67% of applicants were admitted

UNDERGRAD STUDENTS

28,288 full-time, 3,004 part-time. 68% are from out of state; 0.4% Black or African American, non-Hispanic/Latino; 7% Hispanic/Latino; 2% Asian, non-Hispanic/Latino; 0.7% Native Hawaiian or other Pacific Islander, non-Hispanic/Latino; 0.2% American Indian or Alaska Native, non-Hispanic/Latino; 4% Two or more races, non-Hispanic/Latino; 1% Race/ethnicity unknown; 4% international; 3% transferred in; 15% live on campus.

Freshmen:

Admission: 10,500 applied, 7,086 admitted, 5,731 enrolled. ***Average high school GPA:*** 3.9. ***Test scores:*** SAT evidence-based reading and writing scores over 500: 98%; SAT math scores over 500: 98%; ACT scores over 18: 100%; SAT evidence-based reading and writing scores over 600: 82%; SAT math scores over 600: 77%; ACT scores over 24: 89%; SAT evidence-based reading and writing scores over 700: 31%; SAT math scores over 700: 32%; ACT scores over 30: 43%.

Retention: 90% of full-time freshmen returned.

FACULTY

Total: 1,851, 69% full-time, 73% with terminal degrees.

Student/faculty ratio: 20:1.

ACADEMICS

Calendar: semesters. *Degrees:* bachelor's, master's, doctoral, post-master's, and postbachelor's certificates.

Special study options: adult/continuing education programs, external degree program, off-campus study, part-time degree program. ***ROTC:*** Army (b), Air Force (b).

Computers: Students can access the following: campus intranet, computer help desk, online (class) grades, online (class) registration, online (class) schedules. Campuswide network is available.

Library: Harold B. Lee Library plus 2 others.

STUDENT LIFE

Housing options: men-only, women-only, special housing for students with disabilities. Campus housing is university owned.

Athletics Member NCAA. All Division I except football (Division I-A). ***Intercollegiate sports:*** baseball M(s), basketball M(s)/W(s), cheerleading M(s)/W(s), cross-country running M(s)/W(s), golf M(s)/W(s), gymnastics W(s), lacrosse M(c), racquetball M/W, rugby M(c), soccer M(c)/W(s), softball W(s), swimming and diving M(s)/W(s), tennis M(s)/W(s), track and field M(s)/W(s), volleyball M(s)/W(s). ***Intramural sports:*** badminton W, basketball M/W, field hockey M, football M/W, golf M/W, racquetball M/W, soccer M/W, softball M/W, table tennis M/W, tennis M/W, ultimate Frisbee M/W, volleyball M/W, water polo M/W, wrestling M.

Campus security: 24-hour emergency response devices and patrols, late-night transport/escort service, controlled dormitory access.

COSTS & FINANCIAL AID

Costs (2020–21) ***Comprehensive fee:*** $13,778 includes full-time tuition ($5970) and room and board ($7808). Part-time tuition: $304 per credit hour.

Financial Aid Of all full-time matriculated undergraduates who enrolled in 2018, 17,104 applied for aid, 13,909 were judged to have need, 467 had their need fully met. In 2018, 7623 non-need-based awards were made. ***Average percent of need met:*** 35. ***Average financial aid package:*** $8257. ***Average need-based loan:*** $4034. ***Average need-based gift aid:*** $5712. ***Average non-need-based aid:*** $4579. ***Average indebtedness upon graduation:*** $14,672.

APPLYING

Standardized Tests *Required:* SAT or ACT (for admission).

Options: electronic application, early admission, deferred entrance.

Application fee: $35.

Required: essay or personal statement, high school transcript, 1 letter of recommendation, interview.

CONTACT

Dean of Admissions, Brigham Young University, A-153 Abraham Smoot Building, Provo, UT 84602. *Phone:* 801-422-2507. *Fax:* 801-422-0005. *E-mail:* admissions@byu.edu.

Broadview University–West Jordan

West Jordan, Utah

http://www.broadviewuniversity.edu/

CONTACT
Broadview University–West Jordan, 1902 West 7800 South, West Jordan, UT 84088. *Toll-free phone:* 866-304-4224.

Careers Unlimited

Orem, Utah

http://www.ucdh.edu/

CONTACT
Careers Unlimited, 1176 South 1480 West, Orem, UT 84058.

Dixie State University

St. George, Utah

http://www.dixie.edu/

- **State-supported** 4-year, founded 1911, part of Utah System of Higher Education
- **Small-town** 117-acre campus
- **Endowment** $14.4 million
- **Coed**
- **Noncompetitive** entrance level

FACULTY
Student/faculty ratio: 22:1.

ACADEMICS
Calendar: semesters. *Degrees:* certificates, diplomas, associate, and bachelor's.
Library: Val A. Browning Library. *Books:* 92,371 (physical), 133,819 (digital/electronic); *Serial titles:* 265 (physical), 41,536 (digital/electronic); *Databases:* 126. Weekly public service hours: 96.

STUDENT LIFE
Housing options: coed, men-only. Campus housing is university owned.
Activities and organizations: drama/theater group, student-run newspaper, radio and television station, choral group, marching band, Dixie Spirit, Outdoor Club, Association of Women Students, intramurals, Futbol Club.
Athletics Member NCAA. All Division II.
Campus security: 24-hour emergency response devices and patrols.
Student services: health clinic, personal/psychological counseling, women's center.

FINANCIAL AID
Financial Aid Of all full-time matriculated undergraduates who enrolled in 2017, 4,368 applied for aid, 3,939 were judged to have need, 1,737 had their need fully met. 112 Federal Work-Study jobs (averaging $3776). 49 state and other part-time jobs (averaging $3698). In 2017, 54 non-need-based awards were made. ***Average percent of need met:*** 53. ***Average financial aid package:*** $10,573. ***Average need-based loan:*** $4240. ***Average need-based gift aid:*** $6956. ***Average non-need-based aid:*** $1493. ***Average indebtedness upon graduation:*** $24,044. ***Financial aid deadline:*** 6/30.

APPLYING
Options: electronic application, early admission, deferred entrance.
Application fee: $65.
Required: high school transcript.

CONTACT
Dixie State University, 225 South 700 East, St. George, UT 84770-3876. *Phone:* 435-652-7698.

Eagle Gate College

Layton, Utah

http://eaglegatecollege.edu/

CONTACT
Eagle Gate College, 915 North 400 West, Layton, UT 84041. *Phone:* 801-546-7500. *Toll-free phone:* 866-29-EAGLE.

Eagle Gate College

Murray, Utah

http://eaglegatecollege.edu/

CONTACT
Eagle Gate College, 5588 South Green Street, Murray, UT 84123. *Phone:* 801-333-8100. *Toll-free phone:* 866-29-EAGLE.

Independence University

Salt Lake City, Utah

http://www.independence.edu/

CONTACT
Ms. Deborah Hopkins, Enrollment Manager, Independence University, 4021 South 700 East, Suite 400, Salt Lake City, UT 84107. *Toll-free phone:* 800-917-6391.

Midwives College of Utah

Salt Lake City, Utah

http://www.midwifery.edu/

CONTACT
Mel Smith-Tourville, Admissions Director, Midwives College of Utah, 1174 East Graystone Way, Suite 2, Suite 2, Salt Lake City, UT 84106. *Phone:* 801-649-5230. *Toll-free phone:* 866-680-2756. *Fax:* 866-207-2024. *E-mail:* admission@midwifery.edu.

Neumont College of Computer Science

Salt Lake City, Utah

http://www.neumont.edu/

CONTACT
Neumont College of Computer Science, 143 South Main Street, Salt Lake City, UT 84111. *Toll-free phone:* 888-NEUMONT.

New Charter University

Salt Lake City, Utah

http://www.new.edu/

- **Proprietary** comprehensive, founded 1994
- **Suburban** campus with easy access to Salt Lake City, UT
- **Coed** 32 undergraduate students, 100% full-time, 38% women, 63% men
- **Noncompetitive** entrance level

UNDERGRAD STUDENTS
32 full-time. Students come from 11 states and territories; 5 other countries; 10% are from out of state; 17% Black or African American, non-Hispanic/Latino; 3% Hispanic/Latino; 17% Asian, non-Hispanic/Latino; 20% Race/ethnicity unknown.

FACULTY
Total: 15, 67% with terminal degrees.
Student/faculty ratio: 5:1.

ACADEMICS
Degrees: certificates, associate, bachelor's, and master's (offers primarily external degree programs).
Special study options: accelerated degree program, adult/continuing education programs, advanced placement credit, distance learning, external degree program, independent study, off-campus study, part-time degree program, summer session for credit.
Computers: Campuswide network is available.

STUDENT LIFE
Housing options: college housing not available.

COSTS
Costs (2020–21) ***Tuition:*** $897 per term part-time. Full-time tuition and fees vary according to reciprocity agreements. Part-time tuition and fees vary according to reciprocity agreements. No tuition increase for student's term of enrollment. ***Required fees:*** $50 per term part-time. ***Payment plan:*** installment. ***Waivers:*** employees or children of employees.

APPLYING
Options: electronic application.

Required: high school transcript, valid government photo identification.

CONTACT
Mr. Stephen Mann, Admissions Representative, New Charter University, 50 Broadway suite 300, Salt Lake City, UT 84101. *Phone:* 801-515-3085. *Toll-free phone:* 888-639-1388. *Fax:* 801-855-5922. *E-mail:* enroll@new.edu.

Nightingale College
Ogden, Utah
http://www.nightingale.edu/

- **Proprietary** primarily 2-year
- **Suburban** campus with easy access to Salt Lake City
- **Coed**
- 75% of applicants were admitted

FACULTY
Student/faculty ratio: 7:1.

ACADEMICS
Calendar: semesters. *Degrees:* diplomas, associate, and bachelor's.

APPLYING
Standardized Tests *Required:* Nightingale Entrance Exam (for admission).

Options: electronic application, early admission.

Application fee: $100.

Required: essay or personal statement, high school transcript, interview.

CONTACT
Nightingale College, 4155 Harrison Boulevard #100, Ogden, UT 84403.

Southern Utah University
Cedar City, Utah
http://www.suu.edu/

- **State-supported** comprehensive, founded 1897, part of Utah System of Higher Education
- **Small-town** 130-acre campus
- **Endowment** $273.2 million
- **Coed**
- **Moderately difficult** entrance level

FACULTY
Student/faculty ratio: 19:1.

ACADEMICS
Calendar: semesters. *Degrees:* certificates, diplomas, associate, bachelor's, and master's.
Library: Gerald R Sherratt Library. *Books:* 241,434 (physical), 441,219 (digital/electronic); *Serial titles:* 676 (physical), 22,603 (digital/electronic); *Databases:* 218. Students can reserve study rooms.

STUDENT LIFE
Housing options: coed, special housing for students with disabilities. Campus housing is university owned.

Activities and organizations: drama/theater group, student-run newspaper, radio and television station, choral group, national fraternities, national sororities.

Athletics Member NCAA. All Division I.

Campus security: 24-hour emergency response devices, student patrols, late-night transport/escort service, controlled dormitory access.

Student services: health clinic, personal/psychological counseling, women's center.

COSTS & FINANCIAL AID
Costs (2019–20) ***Tuition:*** area resident $6006 full-time, $200 per credit hour part-time; state resident $6006 full-time, $200 per credit hour part-time; nonresident $19,822 full-time, $661 per credit hour part-time. Full-time tuition and fees vary according to program. Part-time tuition and fees vary according to course load and program. ***Required fees:*** $764 full-time, $37 per credit hour part-time. ***Room and board:*** $7349; room only: $3325. Room and board charges vary according to board plan and housing facility.

Financial Aid Of all full-time matriculated undergraduates who enrolled in 2018, 4,756 applied for aid, 4,013 were judged to have need, 512 had their need fully met. In 2018, 1927 non-need-based awards were made. ***Average percent of need met:*** 62. ***Average financial aid package:*** $10,078. ***Average need-based loan:*** $3572. ***Average need-based gift aid:*** $4987. ***Average non-need-based aid:*** $6767. ***Average indebtedness upon graduation:*** $16,958.

APPLYING
Standardized Tests *Required:* SAT or ACT (for admission).

Options: electronic application, deferred entrance.

Application fee: $50.

Required: high school transcript.

CONTACT
Southern Utah University, 351 West University Boulevard, Cedar City, UT 84720-2498. *Phone:* 435-586-7740.

Stevens-Henager College
Logan, Utah
http://www.stevenshenager.edu/

CONTACT
Stevens-Henager College, 755 South Main Street, Logan, UT 84321. *Toll-free phone:* 800-622-2640.

Stevens-Henager College
Orem, Utah
http://www.stevenshenager.edu/

CONTACT
Stevens-Henager College, 1476 South Sandhill Road, Orem, UT 84058. *Toll-free phone:* 800-622-2640.

Stevens-Henager College
St. George, Utah
http://www.stevenshenager.edu/

CONTACT
Stevens-Henager College, 720 South River Road, Suite C-130, St. George, UT 84790. *Toll-free phone:* 800-622-2640.

Stevens-Henager College
Salt Lake City, Utah
http://www.stevenshenager.edu/

CONTACT
Stevens-Henager College, 383 West Vine Street, Salt Lake City, UT 84123. *Toll-free phone:* 800-622-2640.

Stevens-Henager College
West Haven, Utah
http://www.stevenshenager.edu/

CONTACT
Admissions Office, Stevens-Henager College, 1890 South 1350 West, West Haven, UT 84401. *Phone:* 801-394-7791. *Toll-free phone:* 800-622-2640.

University of Utah

Salt Lake City, Utah

http://www.utah.edu/

- **State-supported** university, founded 1850, part of Utah System of Higher Education
- **Urban** 1535-acre campus with easy access to Salt Lake City
- **Endowment** $1.1 billion
- **Coed** 24,485 undergraduate students, 76% full-time, 47% women, 53% men
- **Moderately difficult** entrance level, 62% of applicants were admitted

UNDERGRAD STUDENTS

18,628 full-time, 5,857 part-time. Students come from 52 states and territories; 75 other countries; 22% are from out of state; 1% Black or African American, non-Hispanic/Latino; 13% Hispanic/Latino; 6% Asian, non-Hispanic/Latino; 0.4% Native Hawaiian or other Pacific Islander, non-Hispanic/Latino; 0.4% American Indian or Alaska Native, non-Hispanic/Latino; 6% Two or more races, non-Hispanic/Latino; 0.9% Race/ethnicity unknown; 5% international; 5% transferred in; 13% live on campus.

Freshmen:

Admission: 24,403 applied, 15,159 admitted, 4,249 enrolled. ***Average high school GPA:*** 3.7. ***Test scores:*** SAT evidence-based reading and writing scores over 500: 96%; SAT math scores over 500: 96%; ACT scores over 18: 97%; SAT evidence-based reading and writing scores over 600: 67%; SAT math scores over 600: 64%; ACT scores over 24: 66%; SAT evidence-based reading and writing scores over 700: 19%; SAT math scores over 700: 26%; ACT scores over 30: 24%.

Retention: 89% of full-time freshmen returned.

FACULTY

Total: 2,167, 66% full-time, 67% with terminal degrees.

Student/faculty ratio: 17:1.

ACADEMICS

Calendar: semesters. *Degrees:* bachelor's, master's, doctoral, post-master's, and postbachelor's certificates.

Special study options: academic remediation for entering students, accelerated degree program, advanced placement credit, cooperative education, distance learning, double majors, English as a second language, freshman honors college, honors programs, independent study, internships, off-campus study, part-time degree program, services for LD students, student-designed majors, study abroad, summer session for credit. ***ROTC:*** Army (b), Navy (b), Air Force (b).

Unusual degree programs: 3-2 engineering; nursing; computer science, chemistry, math, public policy.

Computers: 1,099 computers/terminals are available on campus for general student use. Students can access the following: campus intranet, computer help desk, free student e-mail accounts, online (class) grades, online (class) registration, online (class) schedules, online classes. Campuswide network is available. 100% of college-owned or -operated housing units are wired for high-speed Internet access. Wireless service is available via entire campus.

Library: J. Willard Marriott Library plus 3 others. *Books:* 2.5 million (physical), 1.5 million (digital/electronic); *Serial titles:* 480 (physical), 10,075 (digital/electronic); *Databases:* 321. Students can reserve study rooms.

STUDENT LIFE

Housing options: coed, men-only, women-only, special housing for students with disabilities. Campus housing is university owned.

Activities and organizations: drama/theater group, student-run newspaper, radio and television station, choral group, marching band, Yellow for Life, Women in Business, Tek Club, Red Cross at the U, Campus Contraceptive Initiative, national fraternities, national sororities.

Athletics Member NCAA. All Division I. ***Intercollegiate sports:*** baseball M(s), basketball M(s)/W(s), cheerleading M(s)/W(s), cross-country running W(s), football M(s), golf M(s), gymnastics W(s), ice hockey M(c), lacrosse M(s)/W(c), rugby M(c), sand volleyball W(s), skiing (cross-country) M(s)/W(s), skiing (downhill) M(s)/W(s), soccer M(c)/W(s), softball W(s), swimming and diving M(s)/W(s), tennis M(s)/W(s), track and field W(s), volleyball M(c)/W(s), water polo M(c)/W(c). ***Intramural sports:*** basketball M/W, lacrosse M(c), sand volleyball M/W, skiing (downhill) M(c)/W(c), soccer M/W, swimming and diving M(c)/W(c), tennis M(c)/W(c), track and field M(c)/W(c), triathlon M(c)/W(c), ultimate Frisbee M(c)/W(c), volleyball M/W, water polo M/W.

Campus security: 24-hour emergency response devices and patrols, student patrols, late-night transport/escort service, controlled dormitory access.

Student services: health clinic, personal/psychological counseling, women's center, legal services, veterans affairs office.

COSTS & FINANCIAL AID

Costs (2020–21) ***Tuition:*** area resident $8252 full-time; state resident $8252 full-time, $232 per credit hour part-time; nonresident $28,886 full-time, $797 per credit hour part-time. Full-time tuition and fees vary according to course level, course load, degree level, location, program, and student level. Part-time tuition and fees vary according to course level, course load, degree level, location, program, and student level. ***Required fees:*** $1246 full-time. ***Room and board:*** $10,201; room only: $5757. Room and board charges vary according to board plan, housing facility, and location. ***Payment plans:*** installment, deferred payment. ***Waivers:*** senior citizens and employees or children of employees.

Financial Aid Of all full-time matriculated undergraduates who enrolled in 2019, 10,988 applied for aid, 8,413 were judged to have need, 1,055 had their need fully met. 1,223 Federal Work-Study jobs (averaging $4702). In 2019, 6338 non-need-based awards were made. ***Average percent of need met:*** 65. ***Average financial aid package:*** $23,875. ***Average need-based loan:*** $4271. ***Average need-based gift aid:*** $8361. ***Average non-need-based aid:*** $7234. ***Average indebtedness upon graduation:*** $19,656.

APPLYING

Standardized Tests *Required:* SAT or ACT (for admission).

Options: electronic application, early admission, early action, deferred entrance.

Application fee: $55.

Required: high school transcript.

Application deadlines: 4/1 (freshmen), 4/1 (transfers), 12/1 (early action).

Notification: continuous (freshmen), continuous (out-of-state freshmen), continuous (transfers).

CONTACT

Moana Hansen-Kofe, Associate Director, Office of Admissions, University of Utah, 201 S. 1460 E., Room 250 S., Salt Lake City, UT 84112. *Phone:* 801-5851320. *Toll-free phone:* 800-685-8856. *E-mail:* mhansen@sa.utah.edu.

Utah State University

Logan, Utah

http://www.usu.edu/

- **State-supported** university, founded 1888, part of Utah System of Higher Education
- **Urban** 456-acre campus with easy access to Salt Lake City
- **Endowment** $406.1 million
- **Coed** 24,669 undergraduate students, 69% full-time, 55% women, 45% men
- **Moderately difficult** entrance level, 91% of applicants were admitted

UNDERGRAD STUDENTS

17,063 full-time, 7,606 part-time. Students come from 53 states and territories; 52 other countries; 27% are from out of state; 0.8% Black or African American, non-Hispanic/Latino; 6% Hispanic/Latino; 1% Asian, non-Hispanic/Latino; 0.4% Native Hawaiian or other Pacific Islander, non-Hispanic/Latino; 2% American Indian or Alaska Native, non-Hispanic/Latino; 2% Two or more races, non-Hispanic/Latino; 4% Race/ethnicity unknown; 1% international; 5% transferred in.

Freshmen:

Admission: 15,276 applied, 13,894 admitted, 4,411 enrolled. ***Average high school GPA:*** 3.6. ***Test scores:*** SAT evidence-based reading and writing scores over 500: 87%; SAT math scores over 500: 86%; ACT scores over 18: 91%; SAT evidence-based reading and writing scores over 600: 48%; SAT math scores over 600: 42%; ACT scores over 24: 53%;

SAT evidence-based reading and writing scores over 700: 10%; SAT math scores over 700: 13%; ACT scores over 30: 17%.

Retention: 74% of full-time freshmen returned.

FACULTY

Total: 1,282, 79% full-time, 68% with terminal degrees.

Student/faculty ratio: 20:1.

ACADEMICS

Calendar: semesters. *Degrees:* certificates, associate, bachelor's, master's, doctoral, and postbachelor's certificates.

Special study options: academic remediation for entering students, accelerated degree program, adult/continuing education programs, advanced placement credit, cooperative education, distance learning, double majors, English as a second language, freshman honors college, honors programs, independent study, internships, off-campus study, part-time degree program, services for LD students, student-designed majors, study abroad, summer session for credit. ***ROTC:*** Army (b), Air Force (b).

Computers: 1,000 computers/terminals are available on campus for general student use. Students can access the following: computer help desk, free student e-mail accounts, online (class) grades, online (class) registration, online (class) schedules. Campuswide network is available. 100% of college-owned or -operated housing units are wired for high-speed Internet access. Wireless service is available via classrooms, computer centers, computer labs, dorm rooms, learning centers, libraries, student centers.

Library: Merrill-Cazier Library plus 4 others. *Books:* 1.2 million (physical), 844,425 (digital/electronic); *Serial titles:* 48,814 (physical), 95,990 (digital/electronic); *Databases:* 430. Weekly public service hours: 101; students can reserve study rooms.

STUDENT LIFE

Housing options: coed, men-only, women-only, special housing for students with disabilities. Campus housing is university owned.

Activities and organizations: drama/theater group, student-run newspaper, radio station, choral group, marching band, Latter-Day Saints Student Association, multicultural clubs, volunteer groups, college councils, national fraternities, national sororities.

Athletics Member NCAA. All Division I except football (Division I-A). ***Intercollegiate sports:*** baseball M(c), basketball M(s)/W(s), cross-country running M(s)/W(s), equestrian sports M(c)/W(c), golf M(s), gymnastics W(s), ice hockey M(c), racquetball M(c)/W(c), rugby M(c)/W(c), soccer M(c)/W(s), softball W(s), tennis M(s)/W(s), track and field M(s)/W(s), ultimate Frisbee M(c)/W(c), volleyball M(c)/W(s). ***Intramural sports:*** basketball M/W, football M/W, lacrosse M(c)/W(c), sand volleyball M/W, soccer M/W, softball M/W, swimming and diving M(c)/W(c), volleyball M/W, water polo M(c)/W(c), weight lifting M(c)/W(c).

Campus security: 24-hour emergency response devices and patrols, student patrols, late-night transport/escort service.

Student services: health clinic, personal/psychological counseling, women's center, legal services, veterans affairs office.

COSTS & FINANCIAL AID

Costs (2020–21) ***Tuition:*** state resident $6732 full-time; nonresident $21,677 full-time. Full-time tuition and fees vary according to course level, course load, program, and reciprocity agreements. Part-time tuition and fees vary according to course level, course load, program, and reciprocity agreements. ***Required fees:*** $1128 full-time. ***Room and board:*** $5960; room only: $2410. Room and board charges vary according to board plan and housing facility. ***Payment plan:*** deferred payment. ***Waivers:*** minority students, children of alumni, adult students, senior citizens, and employees or children of employees.

Financial Aid Of all full-time matriculated undergraduates who enrolled in 2019, 11,396 applied for aid, 9,131 were judged to have need, 884 had their need fully met. In 2019, 2647 non-need-based awards were made. ***Average percent of need met:*** 56. ***Average financial aid package:*** $11,738. ***Average need-based loan:*** $4338. ***Average need-based gift aid:*** $5035. ***Average non-need-based aid:*** $3235. ***Average indebtedness upon graduation:*** $21,171.

APPLYING

Standardized Tests *Required:* SAT or ACT (for admission).

Options: electronic application, deferred entrance.

Application fee: $50.

Required: high school transcript. ***Recommended:*** minimum 2.8 GPA.

Application deadlines: rolling (freshmen), rolling (transfers).

Notification: continuous (freshmen), continuous (transfers).

CONTACT

Mr. Jeff Sorenson, Assistant Director, Admissions Office, Utah State University, 0160 Old Main Hill, Logan, UT 84322-0160. *Phone:* 435-797-1079. *Toll-free phone:* 800-488-8108. *Fax:* 435-797-3708. *E-mail:* admit@usu.edu.

Utah Valley University

Orem, Utah

http://www.uvu.edu/

- **State-supported** comprehensive, founded 1941, affiliated with Advent Christian Church, part of Utah System of Higher Education
- **Suburban** 524-acre campus with easy access to Salt Lake City
- **Coed** 41,186 undergraduate students, 48% full-time, 48% women, 52% men
- 100% of applicants were admitted

UNDERGRAD STUDENTS

19,799 full-time, 21,387 part-time. Students come from 50 states and territories; 71 other countries; 12% are from out of state; 1% Black or African American, non-Hispanic/Latino; 12% Hispanic/Latino; 1% Asian, non-Hispanic/Latino; 0.8% Native Hawaiian or other Pacific Islander, non-Hispanic/Latino; 0.5% American Indian or Alaska Native, non-Hispanic/Latino; 4% Two or more races, non-Hispanic/Latino; 0.9% Race/ethnicity unknown; 2% international; 7% transferred in.

Freshmen:

Admission: 11,190 applied, 11,190 admitted, 4,764 enrolled. ***Average high school GPA:*** 3.4.

Retention: 65% of full-time freshmen returned.

FACULTY

Total: 1,914, 39% full-time, 32% with terminal degrees.

Student/faculty ratio: 24:1.

ACADEMICS

Calendar: semesters. *Degrees:* certificates, diplomas, associate, bachelor's, master's, and postbachelor's certificates.

Special study options: academic remediation for entering students, advanced placement credit, cooperative education, distance learning, double majors, English as a second language, honors programs, independent study, internships, off-campus study, part-time degree program, services for LD students, student-designed majors, study abroad, summer session for credit. ***ROTC:*** Army (b), Air Force (c).

Computers: Students can access the following: campus intranet, computer help desk, free student e-mail accounts, online (class) grades, online (class) registration, online (class) schedules. Campuswide network is available. Wireless service is available via entire campus.

Library: Utah Valley University Library plus 1 other. *Books:* 194,315 (physical), 341,537 (digital/electronic); *Serial titles:* 16,301 (physical), 602,769 (digital/electronic); *Databases:* 220. Students can reserve study rooms.

STUDENT LIFE

Housing options: college housing not available.

Activities and organizations: drama/theater group, student-run newspaper, television station, choral group, national fraternities, national sororities.

Athletics Member NCAA. All Division I. ***Intercollegiate sports:*** baseball M(s), basketball M(s)/W(s), cross-country running M(s)/W(s), golf M(s)/W(s)(c), soccer W(s), softball W(s), track and field M(s)/W(s), volleyball W(s), wrestling M(s).

Campus security: 24-hour emergency response devices and patrols, late-night transport/escort service.

Student services: health clinic, personal/psychological counseling, women's center, legal services, veterans affairs office.

FINANCIAL AID

Financial Aid Of all full-time matriculated undergraduates who enrolled in 2019, 12,748 applied for aid, 10,786 were judged to have need, 870 had their need fully met. In 2019, 566 non-need-based awards were made.

Average percent of need met: 63. ***Average financial aid package:*** $8019. ***Average need-based loan:*** $2704. ***Average need-based gift aid:*** $5344. ***Average non-need-based aid:*** $6149. ***Average indebtedness upon graduation:*** $22,424.

APPLYING

Options: electronic application, deferred entrance.

Application fee: $35.

Notification: continuous (freshmen), continuous (out-of-state freshmen), continuous (transfers).

CONTACT

Mr. Kristopher Coles, Director of Admissions, Utah Valley University, 800 West University Parkway, Orem, UT 84058-5999. *Phone:* 801-863-6368. *Fax:* 801-863-7229. *E-mail:* coleskr@uvu.edu.

Weber State University

Ogden, Utah

http://www.weber.edu/

- **State-supported** comprehensive, founded 1889, part of Utah System of Higher Education
- **Urban** 504-acre campus with easy access to Salt Lake City
- **Endowment** $149.0 million
- **Coed** 28,833 undergraduate students, 41% full-time, 56% women, 44% men
- **Noncompetitive** entrance level, 89% of applicants were admitted

UNDERGRAD STUDENTS

11,844 full-time, 16,989 part-time. 10% are from out of state; 2% Black or African American, non-Hispanic/Latino; 12% Hispanic/Latino; 2% Asian, non-Hispanic/Latino; 0.6% Native Hawaiian or other Pacific Islander, non-Hispanic/Latino; 0.5% American Indian or Alaska Native, non-Hispanic/Latino; 4% Two or more races, non-Hispanic/Latino; 3% Race/ethnicity unknown; 1% international; 2% transferred in; 4% live on campus.

Freshmen:

Admission: 6,852 applied, 6,102 admitted, 3,303 enrolled. ***Average high school GPA:*** 3.4. ***Test scores:*** ACT scores over 18: 78%; ACT scores over 24: 31%; ACT scores over 30: 5%.

Retention: 65% of full-time freshmen returned.

FACULTY

Total: 1,539, 35% full-time, 22% with terminal degrees.

Student/faculty ratio: 21:1.

ACADEMICS

Calendar: semesters. *Degrees:* certificates, associate, bachelor's, master's, doctoral, post-master's, and postbachelor's certificates.

Special study options: academic remediation for entering students, accelerated degree program, adult/continuing education programs, advanced placement credit, cooperative education, distance learning, double majors, English as a second language, external degree program, freshman honors college, honors programs, independent study, internships, off-campus study, part-time degree program, services for LD students, student-designed majors, study abroad, summer session for credit. ***ROTC:*** Army (b), Navy (c), Air Force (c).

Computers: 650 computers/terminals are available on campus for general student use. Students can access the following: campus intranet, computer help desk, free student e-mail accounts, online (class) grades, online (class) registration, online (class) schedules. Campuswide network is available. 100% of college-owned or -operated housing units are wired for high-speed Internet access. Wireless service is available via entire campus.

Library: Stewart Library. *Books:* 498,531 (physical); *Serial titles:* 425 (physical); *Databases:* 223,410.

STUDENT LIFE

Housing options: coed, men-only, women-only, special housing for students with disabilities. Campus housing is university owned.

Activities and organizations: drama/theater group, student-run newspaper, radio and television station, choral group, marching band, LDSSA (Latter-day Saint Student Association), SAA (Student Alumni Association), GSA (Gay-Straight Alliance), Chinese Club, Golden Key Honor Society, national fraternities, national sororities.

Athletics Member NCAA. All Division I. ***Intercollegiate sports:*** archery M(c)/W(c), baseball M(c), basketball M(s)/W(s), bowling M(c)/W(c), cheerleading M(s)/W(s), cross-country running M(s)/W(s), football M(s), golf M(s)/W(s)(c), ice hockey M(c), lacrosse M(c), racquetball M/W, rugby M(c), skiing (downhill) W(c), soccer M(c)/W(s), softball W(s), swimming and diving M(c)/W(c), tennis M(s)(c)/W(s)(c), track and field M(s)/W(s), volleyball M(c)/W(s), weight lifting M(c)/W(c), wrestling M(c). ***Intramural sports:*** racquetball M(c)/W(c), rock climbing M/W, tennis M(c)/W(c), ultimate Frisbee M(c)/W(c), volleyball M(c)/W(c).

Campus security: 24-hour emergency response devices and patrols, student patrols, late-night transport/escort service, controlled dormitory access.

Student services: health clinic, personal/psychological counseling, women's center, legal services, veterans affairs office.

COSTS & FINANCIAL AID

Costs (2019–20) ***Tuition:*** state resident $4990 full-time, $2944 per year part-time; nonresident $14,973 full-time, $8834 per year part-time. Full-time tuition and fees vary according to course level, course load, degree level, program, and reciprocity agreements. Part-time tuition and fees vary according to course level, course load, degree level, program, and reciprocity agreements. ***Required fees:*** $977 full-time, $612 per year part-time. ***Room and board:*** $8400. Room and board charges vary according to board plan and housing facility. ***Payment plan:*** installment. ***Waivers:*** senior citizens and employees or children of employees.

Financial Aid Of all full-time matriculated undergraduates who enrolled in 2018, 7,229 applied for aid, 6,181 were judged to have need, 2,023 had their need fully met. In 2018, 2226 non-need-based awards were made. ***Average financial aid package:*** $6895. ***Average need-based loan:*** $3553. ***Average need-based gift aid:*** $5351. ***Average non-need-based aid:*** $3841. ***Average indebtedness upon graduation:*** $21,690.

APPLYING

Standardized Tests *Required for some:* ACCUPLACER. *Recommended:* SAT or ACT (for admission).

Options: electronic application, early admission, deferred entrance.

Application fee: $30.

Required: high school transcript.

Notification: continuous (freshmen), continuous (out-of-state freshmen), continuous (transfers).

CONTACT

Andrew Young, Associate Director of Admissions, Weber State University, 1137 University Circle, Ogden, UT 84408-1137. *Phone:* 801-626-6050. *Toll-free phone:* 800-848-7700 (in-state); 800-848-7770 (out-of-state). *Fax:* 801-626-6747. *E-mail:* andrewyoung@weber.edu.

Western Governors University

Salt Lake City, Utah

http://www.wgu.edu/

CONTACT

Western Governors University, 4001 South 700 East, Suite 700, Salt Lake City, UT 84107. *Phone:* 801-274-3280 Ext. 336. *Toll-free phone:* 866-225-5948.

Westminster College

Salt Lake City, Utah

http://www.westminstercollege.edu/

- **Independent** comprehensive, founded 1875
- **Suburban** 27-acre campus
- **Endowment** $81.2 million
- **Coed** 1,740 undergraduate students, 95% full-time, 61% women, 39% men
- **Moderately difficult** entrance level, 92% of applicants were admitted

UNDERGRAD STUDENTS

1,649 full-time, 91 part-time. Students come from 43 states and territories; 41 other countries; 39% are from out of state; 2% Black or African American, non-Hispanic/Latino; 12% Hispanic/Latino; 3% Asian, non-Hispanic/Latino; 0.5% Native Hawaiian or other Pacific Islander, non-Hispanic/Latino; 0.3% American Indian or Alaska Native, non-Hispanic/Latino; 5% Two or more races, non-Hispanic/Latino; 3%

Race/ethnicity unknown; 4% international; 6% transferred in; 35% live on campus.

Freshmen:
Admission: 1,666 applied, 1,530 admitted, 283 enrolled. ***Average high school GPA:*** 3.6. ***Test scores:*** SAT evidence-based reading and writing scores over 500: 88%; SAT math scores over 500: 84%; ACT scores over 18: 92%; SAT evidence-based reading and writing scores over 600: 52%; SAT math scores over 600: 38%; ACT scores over 24: 54%; SAT evidence-based reading and writing scores over 700: 6%; SAT math scores over 700: 2%; ACT scores over 30: 11%.

Retention: 80% of full-time freshmen returned.

FACULTY
Total: 384, 39% full-time, 50% with terminal degrees.

Student/faculty ratio: 9:1.

ACADEMICS
Calendar: semesters. *Degrees:* bachelor's, master's, doctoral, and postbachelor's certificates.

Special study options: academic remediation for entering students, accelerated degree program, adult/continuing education programs, advanced placement credit, cooperative education, distance learning, double majors, English as a second language, freshman honors college, honors programs, independent study, internships, off-campus study, part-time degree program, services for LD students, student-designed majors, study abroad, summer session for credit. ***ROTC:*** Army (c), Navy (c), Air Force (c).

Unusual degree programs: 3-2 engineering with University of Southern California, Washington University in St. Louis.

Computers: 82 computers/terminals are available on campus for general student use. Students can access the following: campus intranet, computer help desk, free student e-mail accounts, online (class) grades, online (class) registration, online (class) schedules. Campuswide network is available. 100% of college-owned or -operated housing units are wired for high-speed Internet access. Wireless service is available via entire campus.

Library: Giovale Library plus 1 other. *Books:* 84,255 (physical), 257,900 (digital/electronic); *Serial titles:* 93 (physical), 201,876 (digital/electronic); *Databases:* 100. Students can reserve study rooms.

STUDENT LIFE
Housing options: on-campus residence required through sophomore year; coed, special housing for students with disabilities. Campus housing is university owned. Freshman campus housing is guaranteed.

Activities and organizations: drama/theater group, student-run newspaper, Westminster Ski and Snowboard Club (WSSC), Residence Hall Association (Residential Government), Feminist Club, Latin X, Theatre Society.

Athletics Member NCAA. All Division II. ***Intercollegiate sports:*** basketball M(s)/W(s), cross-country running M(s)/W(s), golf M(s)/W(s), lacrosse M(s)/W(s), skiing (downhill) M(s)/W(s), soccer M(s)/W(s), track and field M(s)/W(s), volleyball W(s). ***Intramural sports:*** badminton M/W, basketball M/W, football M/W, rock climbing M/W, skiing (cross-country) M/W, soccer M/W, volleyball M/W.

Campus security: 24-hour emergency response devices and patrols, student patrols, late-night transport/escort service, controlled dormitory access.

Student services: health clinic, personal/psychological counseling, veterans affairs office.

COSTS & FINANCIAL AID
Costs (2020–21) ***One-time required fee:*** $300. ***Comprehensive fee:*** $49,057 includes full-time tuition ($37,440), mandatory fees ($520), and room and board ($11,097). Full-time tuition and fees vary according to course load. Part-time tuition: $1558 per credit hour. Part-time tuition and fees vary according to course load. ***Required fees:*** $154 per term part-time. ***College room only:*** $7506. Room and board charges vary according to board plan and housing facility. ***Waivers:*** employees or children of employees.

Financial Aid Of all full-time matriculated undergraduates who enrolled in 2019, 1,218 applied for aid, 1,038 were judged to have need, 219 had their need fully met. In 2019, 459 non-need-based awards were made. ***Average percent of need met:*** 80. ***Average financial aid package:*** $29,823. ***Average need-based loan:*** $4567. ***Average need-based gift aid:*** $24,569. ***Average non-need-based aid:*** $16,679. ***Average indebtedness upon graduation:*** $25,219.

APPLYING
Standardized Tests *Required:* SAT or ACT (for admission).

Options: electronic application, deferred entrance.

Required: essay or personal statement, high school transcript, minimum 2.5 GPA, 1 letter of recommendation. ***Recommended:*** interview.

Application deadlines: rolling (freshmen), rolling (transfers).

Notification: continuous (freshmen), continuous (transfers).

CONTACT
Quincey Otuafi, Director of Undergraduate Admissions, Westminster College, 1840 South 1300 East, Salt Lake City, UT 84105-3697. *Phone:* 801-832-2200. *Toll-free phone:* 800-748-4753. *Fax:* 801-832-3101. *E-mail:* admission@westminstercollege.edu.

VERMONT

Bennington College

Bennington, Vermont

http://www.bennington.edu/

- **Independent** comprehensive, founded 1932
- **Small-town** 440-acre campus with easy access to Albany, NY
- **Endowment** $40.6 million
- **Coed** 733 undergraduate students, 94% full-time, 65% women, 35% men
- **Very difficult** entrance level, 61% of applicants were admitted

UNDERGRAD STUDENTS
687 full-time, 46 part-time. Students come from 38 states and territories; 60 other countries; 96% are from out of state; 4% Black or African American, non-Hispanic/Latino; 10% Hispanic/Latino; 1% Asian, non-Hispanic/Latino; 0.1% Native Hawaiian or other Pacific Islander, non-Hispanic/Latino; 0.3% American Indian or Alaska Native, non-Hispanic/Latino; 4% Two or more races, non-Hispanic/Latino; 4% Race/ethnicity unknown; 19% international; 0.5% transferred in; 98% live on campus.

Freshmen:
Admission: 1,344 applied, 817 admitted, 179 enrolled. ***Average high school GPA:*** 3.5. ***Test scores:*** SAT evidence-based reading and writing scores over 500: 100%; SAT math scores over 500: 97%; ACT scores over 18: 100%; SAT evidence-based reading and writing scores over 600: 95%; SAT math scores over 600: 69%; ACT scores over 24: 87%; SAT evidence-based reading and writing scores over 700: 50%; SAT math scores over 700: 28%; ACT scores over 30: 70%.

Retention: 83% of full-time freshmen returned.

FACULTY
Total: 121, 48% full-time, 69% with terminal degrees.

Student/faculty ratio: 10:1.

ACADEMICS
Calendar: semesters plus winter work term in January and February. *Degrees:* bachelor's and master's.

Special study options: advanced placement credit, double majors, English as a second language, independent study, internships, off-campus study, services for LD students, student-designed majors, study abroad.

Computers: 130 computers/terminals are available on campus for general student use. Students can access the following: campus intranet, computer help desk, free student e-mail accounts, online (class) grades, online (class) registration, online (class) schedules. Campuswide network is available. 100% of college-owned or -operated housing units are wired for high-speed Internet access. Wireless service is available via entire campus.

Library: Crossett Library plus 1 other. *Books:* 94,505 (physical), 194,000 (digital/electronic); *Serial titles:* 299 (physical), 28,186 (digital/electronic); *Databases:* 50. Weekly public service hours: 126; students can reserve study rooms.

STUDENT LIFE
Housing options: on-campus residence required through senior year; coed. Campus housing is university owned. Freshman campus housing is guaranteed.

Activities and organizations: drama/theater group, student-run radio station, choral group, Student Educational Policies Committee, Soccer Club, DREAM, FLoW Student Collective, Programming & Activity Council.

Athletics ***Intramural sports:*** archery M(c)/W(c), basketball M(c)/W(c), equestrian sports M(c)/W(c), skiing (cross-country) M(c)/W(c), skiing (downhill) M(c)/W(c), soccer M(c)/W(c), swimming and diving M(c)/W(c), ultimate Frisbee M(c)/W(c), volleyball M(c)/W(c).

Campus security: 24-hour emergency response devices and patrols, late-night transport/escort service, controlled dormitory access, prevention/awareness program.

Student services: health clinic, personal/psychological counseling.

COSTS & FINANCIAL AID
Costs (2020–21) ***One-time required fee:*** $660. ***Comprehensive fee:*** $74,964 includes full-time tuition ($57,350), mandatory fees ($774), and room and board ($16,840). Full-time tuition and fees vary according to degree level. Part-time tuition: $2390 per credit hour. ***College room only:*** $9140. Room and board charges vary according to board plan. ***Payment plan:*** installment. ***Waivers:*** employees or children of employees.

Financial Aid Of all full-time matriculated undergraduates who enrolled in 2018, 672 applied for aid, 476 were judged to have need, 69 had their need fully met. 349 Federal Work-Study jobs (averaging $2136). 122 state and other part-time jobs (averaging $2097). In 2018, 224 non-need-based awards were made. ***Average percent of need met:*** 83. ***Average financial aid package:*** $45,551. ***Average need-based loan:*** $3440. ***Average need-based gift aid:*** $41,440. ***Average non-need-based aid:*** $27,277. ***Average indebtedness upon graduation:*** $29,443. ***Financial aid deadline:*** 1/3.

APPLYING
Options: electronic application, early admission, early decision, early action, deferred entrance.

Required: essay or personal statement, high school transcript, 2 letters of recommendation, graded analytic paper. ***Recommended:*** interview.

Application deadlines: 1/15 (freshmen), 3/15 (transfers), 12/1 (early action).

Early decision deadline: 11/15 (for plan 1), 1/15 (for plan 2).

Notification: 3/23 (freshmen), 5/1 (transfers), 12/13 (early decision plan 1), 2/7 (early decision plan 2), 1/31 (early action).

CONTACT
Ms. Tonya Strong, Director of Admissions, Bennington College, One College Drive, Bennington, VT 05201-6003. *Phone:* 802-440-4316. *Toll-free phone:* 800-833-6845. *Fax:* 802-440-4320. *E-mail:* admissions@bennington.edu.

Castleton University

Castleton, Vermont

http://www.castleton.edu/

- **State-supported** comprehensive, founded 1787, part of Vermont State Colleges System
- **Rural** 165-acre campus
- **Endowment** $7.5 million
- **Coed**
- **Moderately difficult** entrance level

FACULTY
Student/faculty ratio: 13:1.

ACADEMICS
Calendar: semesters. *Degrees:* associate, bachelor's, master's, post-master's, and postbachelor's certificates.
Library: Calvin Coolidge Library.

STUDENT LIFE
Housing options: on-campus residence required for freshman year; coed. Campus housing is university owned. Freshman campus housing is guaranteed.

Activities and organizations: drama/theater group, student-run newspaper, radio station, choral group, marching band, community service, clubs in the academic majors, Women's issues organization, Spanish and International, Skiing/Snowboarding.

Athletics Member NCAA. All Division III.

Campus security: 24-hour emergency response devices and patrols, student patrols, late-night transport/escort service, controlled dormitory access.

Student services: health clinic, personal/psychological counseling.

FINANCIAL AID
Financial Aid Of all full-time matriculated undergraduates who enrolled in 2013, 325 Federal Work-Study jobs (averaging $1249).

APPLYING
Standardized Tests *Required:* SAT or ACT (for admission).

Options: electronic application, deferred entrance.

Application fee: $40.

Required: essay or personal statement, high school transcript, minimum 3.0 GPA, 2 letters of recommendation.

CONTACT
Mr. Maurice Ouimet Jr., Dean of Enrollment, Castleton University, 62 Alumni Drive, Woodruff Hall, Castleton, VT 05735. *Phone:* 802-468-1213. *Toll-free phone:* 800-639-8521. *Fax:* 802-468-1476. *E-mail:* info@castleton.edu.

Champlain College

Burlington, Vermont

http://www.champlain.edu/

- **Independent** comprehensive, founded 1878
- **Suburban** 27-acre campus with easy access to Montreal
- **Endowment** $25.0 million
- **Coed** 2,078 undergraduate students, 97% full-time, 36% women, 64% men
- **Moderately difficult** entrance level, 85% of applicants were admitted

UNDERGRAD STUDENTS
2,024 full-time, 54 part-time. Students come from 40 states and territories; 18 other countries; 78% are from out of state; 3% Black or African American, non-Hispanic/Latino; 7% Hispanic/Latino; 3% Asian, non-Hispanic/Latino; 0.1% American Indian or Alaska Native, non-Hispanic/Latino; 4% Two or more races, non-Hispanic/Latino; 7% Race/ethnicity unknown; 0.6% international; 3% transferred in; 72% live on campus.

Freshmen:
Admission: 3,629 applied, 3,090 admitted, 524 enrolled. ***Average high school GPA:*** 3.4. ***Test scores:*** SAT evidence-based reading and writing scores over 500: 95%; SAT math scores over 500: 90%; ACT scores over 18: 98%; SAT evidence-based reading and writing scores over 600: 59%; SAT math scores over 600: 46%; ACT scores over 24: 76%; SAT evidence-based reading and writing scores over 700: 13%; SAT math scores over 700: 9%; ACT scores over 30: 20%.

Retention: 83% of full-time freshmen returned.

FACULTY
Total: 273, 42% full-time, 42% with terminal degrees.

Student/faculty ratio: 12:1.

ACADEMICS
Calendar: semesters. *Degrees:* certificates, associate, bachelor's, master's, and postbachelor's certificates.

Special study options: adult/continuing education programs, advanced placement credit, cooperative education, distance learning, double majors, independent study, internships, off-campus study, part-time degree program, services for LD students, study abroad, summer session for credit. ***ROTC:*** Army (c).

Computers: 640 computers/terminals are available on campus for general student use. Students can access the following: campus intranet, computer help desk, free student e-mail accounts, online (class) grades, online (class) registration, online (class) schedules. Campuswide network is available. 100% of college-owned or -operated housing units are wired for high-speed Internet access. Wireless service is available via entire campus.

Library: Miller Information Commons. *Books:* 51,197 (physical), 262,675 (digital/electronic); *Serial titles:* 148 (physical), 83,772 (digital/electronic); *Databases:* 151. Weekly public service hours: 105; students can reserve study rooms.

STUDENT LIFE

Housing options: coed, women-only, special housing for students with disabilities. Campus housing is university owned. Freshman campus housing is guaranteed.

Activities and organizations: drama/theater group, student-run newspaper, radio station, choral group, Diversity Champlain, International Club, community service organization, Champlain Players (theater group), Outing Club/Skiing Snowboarding Club.

Athletics ***Intramural sports:*** basketball M/W, cross-country running M(c)/W(c), equestrian sports M(c)/W(c), fencing W, football M/W, ice hockey M, lacrosse M, rock climbing M/W, rugby M(c)/W(c), skiing (cross-country) M/W, skiing (downhill) M(c)/W(c), soccer M/W, table tennis M/W, tennis M/W, ultimate Frisbee M/W, volleyball M/W.

Campus security: 24-hour emergency response devices and patrols, late-night transport/escort service, controlled dormitory access.

Student services: health clinic, personal/psychological counseling, women's center.

COSTS & FINANCIAL AID

Costs (2019–20) ***Comprehensive fee:*** $57,594 includes full-time tuition ($41,728), mandatory fees ($100), and room and board ($15,766). Part-time tuition: $1762 per credit hour. ***Payment plan:*** tuition prepayment.

Financial Aid Of all full-time matriculated undergraduates who enrolled in 2019, 1,530 applied for aid, 1,321 were judged to have need, 241 had their need fully met. In 2019, 206 non-need-based awards were made. ***Average percent of need met:*** 75. ***Average financial aid package:*** $31,913. ***Average need-based loan:*** $3850. ***Average need-based gift aid:*** $25,089. ***Average non-need-based aid:*** $16,137. ***Average indebtedness upon graduation:*** $36,976.

APPLYING

Options: electronic application, early admission, early decision, deferred entrance.

Required: essay or personal statement, high school transcript, letters of recommendation. ***Required for some:*** portfolio for creative media, filmmaking, game art and animation, game design, and graphic design and digital media majors.

Application deadlines: 2/15 (freshmen), rolling (transfers).

Early decision deadline: 11/15.

Notification: 3/15 (freshmen), continuous (transfers), 12/15 (early decision).

CONTACT

Diane Soboski, Director of Undergraduate Admissions, Champlain College, PO Box 670, Burlington, VT 05401. *Phone:* 802-865-5740. *Toll-free phone:* 800-570-5858. *Fax:* 802-860-2767. *E-mail:* admission@champlain.edu.

College of St. Joseph

Rutland, Vermont

http://www.csj.edu/

CONTACT

Mr. Alan Young, Dean of Admissions, College of St. Joseph, 71 Clement Road, Rutland, VT 05701-3899. *Phone:* 802-773-5227. *Toll-free phone:* 877-270-9998. *Fax:* 802-776-5310. *E-mail:* admissions@csj.edu.

Goddard College

Plainfield, Vermont

http://www.goddard.edu/

CONTACT

Admissions Office, Goddard College, 123 Pitkin Road, Plainfield, VT 05667-9432. *Phone:* 800-906-8312. *Toll-free phone:* 800-906-8312. *Fax:* 802-454-1029. *E-mail:* admissions@goddard.edu.

Landmark College

Putney, Vermont

http://www.landmark.edu/

CONTACT

Admissions Main Desk, Landmark College, Admissions Office, River Road South, Putney, VT 05346. *Phone:* 802-387-6718. *Fax:* 802-387-6868. *E-mail:* admissions@landmark.edu.

Marlboro College

Marlboro, Vermont

http://www.marlboro.edu/

CONTACT

Marlboro College, PO Box A, South Road, Marlboro, VT 05344. *Toll-free phone:* 800-343-0049.

Middlebury College

Middlebury, Vermont

http://www.middlebury.edu/

- **Independent** comprehensive, founded 1800
- **Small-town** 350-acre campus
- **Endowment** $1.1 billion
- **Coed** 2,580 undergraduate students, 99% full-time, 53% women, 47% men
- **Most difficult** entrance level, 17% of applicants were admitted

UNDERGRAD STUDENTS

2,556 full-time, 24 part-time. Students come from 52 states and territories; 68 other countries; 94% are from out of state; 4% Black or African American, non-Hispanic/Latino; 10% Hispanic/Latino; 7% Asian, non-Hispanic/Latino; 0.1% American Indian or Alaska Native, non-Hispanic/Latino; 5% Two or more races, non-Hispanic/Latino; 1% Race/ethnicity unknown; 10% international; 0.3% transferred in; 95% live on campus.

Freshmen:

Admission: 9,227 applied, 1,542 admitted, 605 enrolled. ***Test scores:*** SAT evidence-based reading and writing scores over 500: 100%; SAT math scores over 500: 100%; ACT scores over 18: 100%; SAT evidence-based reading and writing scores over 600: 97%; SAT math scores over 600: 95%; ACT scores over 24: 99%; SAT evidence-based reading and writing scores over 700: 53%; SAT math scores over 700: 64%; ACT scores over 30: 87%.

Retention: 96% of full-time freshmen returned.

FACULTY

Total: 357, 84% full-time, 94% with terminal degrees.

Student/faculty ratio: 8:1.

ACADEMICS

Calendar: 4-1-4. *Degrees:* bachelor's, master's, and doctoral.

Special study options: accelerated degree program, advanced placement credit, double majors, honors programs, independent study, internships, off-campus study, services for LD students, student-designed majors, study abroad, summer session for credit. ***ROTC:*** Army (c).

Unusual degree programs: 3-2 engineering with Columbia University, Dartmouth College.

Computers: Students can access the following: campus intranet, computer help desk, free student e-mail accounts, online (class) grades, online (class) registration, online (class) schedules, personal Web pages, file servers. Campuswide network is available. Wireless service is available via entire campus.

Library: Davis Family Library plus 2 others. Weekly public service hours: 112; students can reserve study rooms.

STUDENT LIFE

Housing options: on-campus residence required through junior year; coed, special housing for students with disabilities. Campus housing is university owned. Freshman campus housing is guaranteed.

Activities and organizations: drama/theater group, student-run newspaper, radio station, choral group, Middlebury College Activities

Board, Middlebury Mountain Club, Student Government Association, International Students Organization, WRMC.

Athletics ***Intercollegiate sports:*** baseball M, basketball M/W, cross-country running M/W, field hockey W, football M, golf M/W, ice hockey M/W, lacrosse M/W, skiing (cross-country) M/W, skiing (downhill) M(c)/W, soccer M/W, softball W, squash M/W, swimming and diving M/W, tennis M/W, track and field M/W, volleyball W. ***Intramural sports:*** badminton M(c)/W(c), basketball M/W, crew M(c)/W(c), equestrian sports M(c)/W(c), fencing M(c), field hockey W(c), football M/W, golf M/W, ice hockey M/W, rugby M(c)/W(c), sailing M(c)/W(c), soccer M/W, softball M/W, squash M/W, tennis M/W, ultimate Frisbee M(c)/W(c), volleyball M(c), water polo M(c)/W(c).

Campus security: 24-hour emergency response devices and patrols, student patrols, late-night transport/escort service, controlled dormitory access.

Student services: health clinic, personal/psychological counseling, women's center.

COSTS & FINANCIAL AID

Costs (2019–20) ***Comprehensive fee:*** $72,248 includes full-time tuition ($55,790), mandatory fees ($426), and room and board ($16,032). ***Payment plan:*** tuition prepayment.

Financial Aid Of all full-time matriculated undergraduates who enrolled in 2019, 1,303 applied for aid, 1,165 were judged to have need, 1,165 had their need fully met. In 2019, 4 non-need-based awards were made. ***Average percent of need met:*** 100. ***Average financial aid package:*** $53,261. ***Average need-based loan:*** $4252. ***Average need-based gift aid:*** $49,992. ***Average non-need-based aid:*** $20,000. ***Average indebtedness upon graduation:*** $19,838.

APPLYING

Standardized Tests *Required:* SAT and SAT Subject Tests or ACT (for admission).

Options: electronic application, early admission, early decision, deferred entrance.

Application fee: $65.

Required: essay or personal statement, high school transcript, 2 letters of recommendation. ***Recommended:*** interview.

Application deadlines: 1/1 (freshmen), 3/1 (transfers).

Early decision deadline: 11/1.

Notification: 3/31 (freshmen), 4/10 (transfers), 12/15 (early decision).

CONTACT

Mr. Greg Buckles, Dean of Admissions, Middlebury College, Emma Willard House, Middlebury, VT 05753-6002. *Phone:* 802-443-3000. *Fax:* 802-443-2056. *E-mail:* admissions@middlebury.edu.

New England Culinary Institute

Montpelier, Vermont

http://www.neci.edu/

- **Proprietary** primarily 2-year, founded 1980
- **Small-town** campus
- **Coed**
- **Moderately difficult** entrance level

FACULTY

Student/faculty ratio: 6:1.

ACADEMICS

Calendar: quarters. *Degrees:* certificates, associate, and bachelor's.
Library: New England Culinary Institute Library.

STUDENT LIFE

Housing options: on-campus residence required for freshman year; coed, men-only, women-only. Campus housing is leased by the school. Freshman applicants given priority for college housing.

Activities and organizations: American Culinary Federation, Slow Food, Student Council, Special Guest Lecture Series, Student Ambassadors (leadership program).

Campus security: 24-hour emergency response devices, student patrols.

FINANCIAL AID

Financial Aid Of all full-time matriculated undergraduates who enrolled in 2018, 320 Federal Work-Study jobs (averaging $1000).

APPLYING

Standardized Tests *Recommended:* SAT or ACT (for admission).

Options: electronic application, early admission, deferred entrance.

Application fee: $35.

Required: essay or personal statement, high school transcript, 1 letter of recommendation, interview. ***Recommended:*** culinary experience.

CONTACT

Adonica Williams, New England Culinary Institute, 7 School Street, Montpelier, VT 05602-3115. *Phone:* 802-225-3210. *Toll-free phone:* 877-223-6324. *Fax:* 802-225-3280. *E-mail:* admissions@neci.edu.

Northern Vermont University–Johnson

Johnson, Vermont

http://www.northernvermont.edu/

CONTACT

Bethany Harrington, Admissions Specialist, Northern Vermont University–Johnson, 337 College Hill, Johnson, VT 05656. *Phone:* 802-635-1219. *Toll-free phone:* 800-635-2356. *Fax:* 802-635-1230. *E-mail:* admissions@jsc.edu.

Northern Vermont University–Lyndon

Lyndonville, Vermont

http://www.northernvermont.edu/

CONTACT

Ms. Cheri Goldrick, Admissions Assistant, Northern Vermont University–Lyndon, 1001 College Road, PO Box 919, Lyndonville, VT 05851. *Phone:* 802-626-6451. *Toll-free phone:* 800-225-1998. *Fax:* 802-626-6335. *E-mail:* admissions@lyndonstate.edu.

Norwich University

Northfield, Vermont

http://www.norwich.edu/

CONTACT

Norwich University, 158 Harmon Drive, Northfield, VT 05663. *Phone:* 802-485-2658. *Toll-free phone:* 800-468-6679.

Saint Michael's College

Colchester, Vermont

http://www.smcvt.edu/

CONTACT

Mr. Michael Stefanowicz, Director of Admission, Saint Michael's College, One Winooski Park, Colchester, VT 05439. *Phone:* 802-654-2108. *Toll-free phone:* 800-762-8000. *Fax:* 802-654-2906. *E-mail:* admission@smcvt.edu.

Southern Vermont College

Bennington, Vermont

http://www.svc.edu/

CONTACT

Southern Vermont College, 897 Monument Avenue, Bennington, VT 05201. *Phone:* 802-447-6300. *Fax:* 802-681-2868. *E-mail:* admissions@svc.edu.

Sterling College

Craftsbury Common, Vermont

http://www.sterlingcollege.edu/

CONTACT

Tim Patterson, Director of Admission and Financial Aid, Sterling College, PO Box 72, Craftsbury Common, VT 05827. *Phone:* 802-586-7711 Ext. 135. *Toll-free phone:* 800-648-3591 Ext. 100. *Fax:* 802-586-2596. *E-mail:* tpatterson@sterlingcollege.edu.

University of Vermont

Burlington, Vermont

http://www.uvm.edu/

- **State-supported** university, founded 1791
- **Suburban** 459-acre campus
- **Endowment** $566.7 million
- **Coed** 11,443 undergraduate students, 92% full-time, 59% women, 41% men
- **Moderately difficult** entrance level, 67% of applicants were admitted

UNDERGRAD STUDENTS

10,501 full-time, 942 part-time. Students come from 50 states and territories; 43 other countries; 72% are from out of state; 1% Black or African American, non-Hispanic/Latino; 4% Hispanic/Latino; 3% Asian, non-Hispanic/Latino; 3% Two or more races, non-Hispanic/Latino; 3% Race/ethnicity unknown; 4% international; 3% transferred in; 51% live on campus.

Freshmen:

Admission: 19,233 applied, 12,943 admitted, 2,636 enrolled. ***Average high school GPA:*** 3.7. ***Test scores:*** SAT evidence-based reading and writing scores over 500: 99%; SAT math scores over 500: 98%; ACT scores over 18: 100%; SAT evidence-based reading and writing scores over 600: 78%; SAT math scores over 600: 69%; ACT scores over 24: 93%; SAT evidence-based reading and writing scores over 700: 20%; SAT math scores over 700: 18%; ACT scores over 30: 49%.

Retention: 87% of full-time freshmen returned.

FACULTY

Total: 804, 77% full-time, 73% with terminal degrees.

Student/faculty ratio: 18:1.

ACADEMICS

Calendar: semesters. *Degrees:* bachelor's, master's, doctoral, post-master's, and postbachelor's certificates.

Special study options: adult/continuing education programs, advanced placement credit, cooperative education, distance learning, double majors, freshman honors college, honors programs, independent study, internships, off-campus study, part-time degree program, services for LD students, student-designed majors, study abroad, summer session for credit. ***ROTC:*** Army (b).

Unusual degree programs: 3-2 law with Vermont Law School.

Computers: 530 computers/terminals and 300 ports are available on campus for general student use. Students can access the following: campus intranet, computer help desk, free student e-mail accounts, online (class) grades, online (class) registration, online (class) schedules, Web pages, online course support, learning management system. Campuswide network is available. 100% of college-owned or -operated housing units are wired for high-speed Internet access. Wireless service is available via entire campus.

Library: David W. Howe Memorial Library plus 3 others. *Books:* 1.2 million (physical), 334,751 (digital/electronic); *Serial titles:* 42,611 (physical), 90,435 (digital/electronic); *Databases:* 395. Weekly public service hours: 102; study areas open 24 hours, 5–7 days a week; students can reserve study rooms.

STUDENT LIFE

Housing options: on-campus residence required through sophomore year; coed. Campus housing is university owned. Freshman campus housing is guaranteed.

Activities and organizations: drama/theater group, student-run newspaper, radio and television station, choral group, Ski and Snowboard Club, Outing Club, Volunteer in Action, Climbing Team, Cycling Team, national fraternities, national sororities.

Athletics Member NCAA. All Division I. ***Intercollegiate sports:*** badminton M(c)/W(c), baseball M(c)/W(c), basketball M(s)/W(s), cheerleading M(c)/W(c), crew M(c)/W(c), cross-country running M(s)/W(s), equestrian sports M(c)/W(c), fencing M(c)/W(c), field hockey M(c)/W(s), football M(c)/W(c), golf M(c), gymnastics M(c)/W(c), ice hockey M(s)/W(s), lacrosse M(s)/W(s), riflery M(c)/W(c), rock climbing M(c)/W(c), rowing M(c)/W, rugby M(c)/W(c), sailing M(c)/W(c), skiing (cross-country) M(s)/W(s), skiing (downhill) M(s)/W(s), soccer M(s)/W(s), softball W(c), squash M(c)/W(c), swimming and diving M(c)/W(s), table tennis M(c)/W(c), tennis M(c)/W(c), track and field M(s)/W(s), triathlon M(c)/W(c), ultimate Frisbee M(c)/W(c), volleyball M(c)/W(c), water polo M(c)/W(c), weight lifting M(c)/W(c), wrestling M(c)/W(c). ***Intramural sports:*** badminton M/W, basketball M/W, football M/W, ice hockey M/W, soccer M/W, tennis M/W, ultimate Frisbee M/W, volleyball M/W.

Campus security: 24-hour emergency response devices and patrols, student patrols, controlled dormitory access.

Student services: health clinic, personal/psychological counseling, women's center, legal services, veterans affairs office.

COSTS & FINANCIAL AID

Costs (2020–21) ***Tuition:*** state resident $16,392 full-time, $683 per credit hour part-time; nonresident $41,280 full-time, $1720 per credit hour part-time. Full-time tuition and fees vary according to reciprocity agreements. Part-time tuition and fees vary according to course load and reciprocity agreements. ***Required fees:*** $2670 full-time, $10 per credit hour part-time. ***Room and board:*** $13,354; room only: $8681. Room and board charges vary according to board plan and housing facility. ***Payment plan:*** installment. ***Waivers:*** employees or children of employees.

Financial Aid Of all full-time matriculated undergraduates who enrolled in 2017, 7,053 applied for aid, 5,654 were judged to have need, 892 had their need fully met. 1,500 Federal Work-Study jobs (averaging $1600). In 2017, 3119 non-need-based awards were made. ***Average percent of need met:*** 68. ***Average financial aid package:*** $26,256. ***Average need-based loan:*** $4604. ***Average need-based gift aid:*** $17,169. ***Average non-need-based aid:*** $13,726. ***Average indebtedness upon graduation:*** $32,950.

APPLYING

Standardized Tests *Required:* SAT or ACT (for admission).

Options: electronic application, early admission, early action, deferred entrance.

Application fee: $55.

Required: essay or personal statement, high school transcript, 1 letter of recommendation. ***Required for some:*** audition for music or music education.

Application deadlines: 1/15 (freshmen), 1/15 (out-of-state freshmen), 4/15 (transfers), 11/1 (early action).

Notification: 3/31 (freshmen), 3/31 (out-of-state freshmen), continuous (transfers), 12/15 (early action).

CONTACT

Mr. Ryan Hargraves, Director of Admissions, University of Vermont, Office of Admissions, 194 South Prospect Street, Burlington, VT 05401. *Phone:* 802-656-3370. *Fax:* 802-656-8611. *E-mail:* admissions@uvm.edu.

Vermont Technical College

Randolph Center, Vermont

http://www.vtc.edu/

- **State-supported** comprehensive, founded 1866, part of Vermont State Colleges System
- **Rural** 544-acre campus
- **Endowment** $5.5 million
- **Coed** 1,671 undergraduate students, 65% full-time, 46% women, 54% men
- **Moderately difficult** entrance level, 68% of applicants were admitted

UNDERGRAD STUDENTS

1,089 full-time, 582 part-time. Students come from 26 states and territories; 20 other countries; 14% are from out of state; 1% Black or African American, non-Hispanic/Latino; 2% Hispanic/Latino; 1% Asian, non-Hispanic/Latino; 0.2% American Indian or Alaska Native, non-Hispanic/Latino; 30% Two or more races, non-Hispanic/Latino; 1% Race/ethnicity unknown; 1% international; 20% transferred in; 44% live on campus.

Freshmen:

Admission: 1,087 applied, 740 admitted, 202 enrolled. ***Average high school GPA:*** 3.1. ***Test scores:*** SAT evidence-based reading and writing scores over 500: 71%; SAT math scores over 500: 75%; ACT scores over 18: 67%; SAT evidence-based reading and writing scores over 600: 23%; SAT math scores over 600: 21%; ACT scores over 24: 23%; SAT

evidence-based reading and writing scores over 700: 1%; SAT math scores over 700: 4%; ACT scores over 30: 3%.

Retention: 89% of full-time freshmen returned.

FACULTY

Total: 214, 38% full-time, 20% with terminal degrees.

Student/faculty ratio: 8:1.

ACADEMICS

Calendar: semesters. *Degrees:* certificates, diplomas, associate, bachelor's, and master's.

Special study options: academic remediation for entering students, accelerated degree program, advanced placement credit, cooperative education, distance learning, double majors, English as a second language, honors programs, independent study, internships, part-time degree program, services for LD students, summer session for credit. ***ROTC:*** Army (c).

Computers: 480 computers/terminals and 600 ports are available on campus for general student use. Students can access the following: campus intranet, computer help desk, free student e-mail accounts, online (class) grades, online (class) registration, online (class) schedules, online (network) file storage. Campuswide network is available. 98% of college-owned or -operated housing units are wired for high-speed Internet access. Wireless service is available via entire campus.

Library: Hartness Library. *Books:* 42,000 (physical), 200,000 (digital/electronic); *Serial titles:* 58,000 (digital/electronic). Weekly public service hours: 82; students can reserve study rooms.

STUDENT LIFE

Housing options: on-campus residence required through sophomore year; coed, men-only, women-only, special housing for students with disabilities. Campus housing is university owned.

Activities and organizations: student-run radio station, choral group, Student Council (student government), Adventurer's Guild (board and video gaming), WVTC (student radio station), Outing Club, Veterinary Technology Club.

Athletics Member USCAA. ***Intercollegiate sports:*** basketball M/W, cross-country running M/W, soccer M/W, track and field M/W. ***Intramural sports:*** basketball M/W, bowling M/W, racquetball M/W, rock climbing M(c)/W(c), skiing (downhill) M(c)/W(c), soccer M/W, ultimate Frisbee M/W, volleyball M/W.

Campus security: 24-hour emergency response devices and patrols, late-night transport/escort service, controlled dormitory access.

Student services: health clinic, personal/psychological counseling, veterans affairs office.

COSTS & FINANCIAL AID

Costs (2020–21) ***Tuition:*** state resident $14,712 full-time, $613 per credit part-time; nonresident $28,128 full-time, $1172 per credit part-time. Full-time tuition and fees vary according to course load, program, and reciprocity agreements. Part-time tuition and fees vary according to program. ***Required fees:*** $1759 full-time, $78 per term part-time. ***Room and board:*** $11,694; room only: $7100. Room and board charges vary according to board plan and location. ***Payment plans:*** installment, deferred payment. ***Waivers:*** senior citizens and employees or children of employees.

Financial Aid Of all full-time matriculated undergraduates who enrolled in 2019, 982 applied for aid, 884 were judged to have need, 23 had their need fully met. 253 Federal Work-Study jobs (averaging $1006). In 2019, 85 non-need-based awards were made. ***Average percent of need met:*** 44. ***Average financial aid package:*** $14,270. ***Average need-based loan:*** $3868. ***Average need-based gift aid:*** $7060. ***Average non-need-based aid:*** $4624. ***Average indebtedness upon graduation:*** $24,410.

APPLYING

Standardized Tests *Required for some:* SAT (for admission).

Options: electronic application.

Application fee: $47.

Required: high school transcript. ***Required for some:*** essay or personal statement, 2 letters of recommendation. ***Recommended:*** minimum 3.0 GPA, 2 letters of recommendation, interview.

Application deadlines: rolling (freshmen), rolling (out-of-state freshmen), rolling (transfers).

Notification: continuous (freshmen), continuous (out-of-state freshmen), continuous (transfers).

CONTACT

Jessica Van Deren, Assistant Dean of Admissions, Vermont Technical College, PO Box 500, Randolph Center, VT 05061. *Phone:* 802-728-1244. *Toll-free phone:* 800-442-VTC1. *Fax:* 802-728-1390. *E-mail:* admissions@vtc.edu.

VIRGINIA

American National University - Danville

Danville, Virginia

http://www.an.edu/

- **Proprietary** primarily 2-year, founded 1975, part of National College of Business and Technology
- **Small-town** campus
- **Coed**
- **Noncompetitive** entrance level

ACADEMICS

Calendar: quarters. *Degrees:* diplomas, associate, and bachelor's.

FINANCIAL AID

Financial Aid Of all full-time matriculated undergraduates who enrolled in 2018, 3 Federal Work-Study jobs.

APPLYING

Options: electronic application.

Required for some: high school transcript. ***Recommended:*** interview.

CONTACT

Admissions Office, American National University - Danville, 336 Old Riverside Drive, Danville, VA 24541. *Phone:* 434-793-6822. *Toll-free phone:* 888-9-JOBREADY.

American National University - Roanoke Valley

Salem, Virginia

http://www.an.edu/

- **Proprietary** comprehensive, founded 1886, part of National College of Business and Technology
- **Urban** 3-acre campus
- **Coed**
- **Noncompetitive** entrance level

ACADEMICS

Calendar: quarters. *Degrees:* certificates, diplomas, associate, bachelor's, and master's.

STUDENT LIFE

Housing options: college housing not available.

FINANCIAL AID

Financial Aid Of all full-time matriculated undergraduates who enrolled in 2018, 6 Federal Work-Study jobs.

APPLYING

Required: high school transcript. ***Recommended:*** interview.

CONTACT

Director of Admissions, American National University - Roanoke Valley, 1813 East Main Street, Salem, VA 24153. *Phone:* 540-986-1800. *Toll-free phone:* 888-9-JOBREADY. *Fax:* 540-444-4198.

Argosy University, Northern Virginia
Arlington, Virginia
http://www.argosy.edu/locations/northern-virginia/

CONTACT
Argosy University, Northern Virginia, 1550 Wilson Boulevard, Suite 600, Arlington, VA 22209. *Phone:* 703-526-5800. *Toll-free phone:* 866-703-2777.

The Art Institute of Virginia Beach, a branch of The Art Institute of Atlanta
Virginia Beach, Virginia
http://www.artinstitutes.edu/virginia-beach/

CONTACT
The Art Institute of Virginia Beach, a branch of The Art Institute of Atlanta, Two Columbus Center, 4500 Main Street, Suite 100, Virginia Beach, VA 23462. *Phone:* 757-493-6700. *Toll-free phone:* 877-437-4428.

Averett University
Danville, Virginia
http://www.averett.edu/

- **Independent** comprehensive, founded 1859, affiliated with Baptist General Association of Virginia
- **Small-town** 185-acre campus with easy access to Greensboro, NC
- **Endowment** $29.4 million
- **Coed** 903 undergraduate students, 97% full-time, 44% women, 56% men
- **Moderately difficult** entrance level, 65% of applicants were admitted

UNDERGRAD STUDENTS
876 full-time, 27 part-time. 40% are from out of state; 28% Black or African American, non-Hispanic/Latino; 4% Hispanic/Latino; 0.8% Asian, non-Hispanic/Latino; 0.6% Native Hawaiian or other Pacific Islander, non-Hispanic/Latino; 0.7% American Indian or Alaska Native, non-Hispanic/Latino; 4% Two or more races, non-Hispanic/Latino; 0.6% Race/ethnicity unknown; 7% international; 6% transferred in; 56% live on campus.

Freshmen:
Admission: 2,725 applied, 1,772 admitted, 232 enrolled. ***Average high school GPA:*** 3.2. ***Test scores:*** SAT evidence-based reading and writing scores over 500: 42%; SAT math scores over 500: 40%; ACT scores over 18: 49%; SAT evidence-based reading and writing scores over 600: 6%; SAT math scores over 600: 7%; ACT scores over 24: 11%.

Retention: 69% of full-time freshmen returned.

FACULTY
Total: 124, 44% full-time, 39% with terminal degrees.

Student/faculty ratio: 10:1.

ACADEMICS
Calendar: semesters. *Degrees:* associate and bachelor's.

Special study options: academic remediation for entering students, adult/continuing education programs, advanced placement credit, distance learning, double majors, honors programs, independent study, internships, off-campus study, part-time degree program, services for LD students, student-designed majors, study abroad, summer session for credit.

Computers: 150 computers/terminals and 25 ports are available on campus for general student use. Students can access the following: computer help desk, free student e-mail accounts, online (class) grades, online (class) registration, online (class) schedules. Campuswide network is available. 100% of college-owned or -operated housing units are wired for high-speed Internet access. Wireless service is available via entire campus.

Library: Mary B. Blount Library. *Books:* 86,432 (physical), 313,632 (digital/electronic); *Serial titles:* 98 (physical), 35,069 (digital/electronic); *Databases:* 160. Weekly public service hours: 81; students can reserve study rooms.

STUDENT LIFE
Housing options: on-campus residence required through junior year; coed, men-only, women-only, special housing for students with disabilities. Campus housing is university owned. Freshman campus housing is guaranteed.

Activities and organizations: drama/theater group, choral group, Cougar Activities Board (CAB), Student Athletic Advisory Committee (SAAC), Student Government Association (SGA), FOCUS/Christian Student Fellowship, Rainbow Club, national fraternities.

Athletics Member NCAA. All Division III. ***Intercollegiate sports:*** baseball M, basketball M/W, cheerleading M(c)/W(c), cross country running M/W, equestrian sports M(c)/W(c), football M, golf M, lacrosse M/W, soccer M/W, softball W, tennis M/W, volleyball W, wrestling M. ***Intramural sports:*** soccer M/W, volleyball M/W.

Campus security: 24-hour emergency response devices and patrols, late-night transport/escort service, controlled dormitory access.

Student services: health clinic, personal/psychological counseling, veterans affairs office.

COSTS & FINANCIAL AID
Costs (2019–20) ***Comprehensive fee:*** $42,170 includes full-time tuition ($35,450), mandatory fees ($150), and room and board ($6570). Full-time tuition and fees vary according to class time, course load, degree level, location, and program. Part-time tuition: $1105 per credit hour. Part-time tuition and fees vary according to class time, course load, degree level, location, and program. ***Required fees:*** $40 per term part-time. ***College room only:*** $3990. Room and board charges vary according to board plan and housing facility. ***Payment plan:*** installment. ***Waivers:*** senior citizens and employees or children of employees.

Financial Aid Of all full-time matriculated undergraduates who enrolled in 2019, 798 applied for aid, 746 were judged to have need, 86 had their need fully met. In 2019, 130 non-need-based awards were made. ***Average percent of need met:*** 73. ***Average financial aid package:*** $27,096. ***Average need-based loan:*** $3754. ***Average need-based gift aid:*** $23,713. ***Average non-need-based aid:*** $16,235. ***Average indebtedness upon graduation:*** $33,711.

APPLYING
Standardized Tests *Required:* SAT or ACT (for admission), TOEFL for international students (for admission).

Options: electronic application, deferred entrance.

Required: high school transcript, minimum 2.5 GPA. ***Recommended:*** essay or personal statement, 1 letter of recommendation, interview.

Notification: continuous (freshmen), continuous (transfers).

CONTACT
Mr. Joel Nester, Director of Admissions and International Counselor, Averett University, 420 West Main Street, English Hall, Danville, VA 24541. *Phone:* 434-791-5663. *Toll-free phone:* 800-AVERETT. *E-mail:* joel.nester@averett.edu.

Bethel College
Hampton, Virginia
http://www.bcva.edu/

CONTACT
Ms. Nanette Bartholomew, Student Affairs, Bethel College, 1705 Todds Lane, Hampton, VA 23666. *Phone:* 757-826-1883 Ext. 215.

Bluefield College
Bluefield, Virginia
http://www.bluefield.edu/

CONTACT
Mr. Matthew Hamilton, Director of Traditional Admissions, Bluefield College, 3000 College Avenue, Bluefield, VA 24605-1799. *Phone:* 276-326-4602. *Toll-free phone:* 800-872-0175. *Fax:* 276-326-4395. *E-mail:* mrh263676@bluefield.edu.

Bon Secours Memorial College of Nursing

Richmond, Virginia

http://www.bsmcon.edu/

CONTACT

Bon Secours Memorial College of Nursing, 8550 Magellan Parkway, Suite 1100, Richmond, VA 23227-1149. *Toll-free phone:* 866-238-7414.

Bridgewater College

Bridgewater, Virginia

http://www.bridgewater.edu/

- **Independent** comprehensive, founded 1880, affiliated with Church of the Brethren
- **Small-town** 300-acre campus
- **Endowment** $96.9 million
- **Coed** 1,713 undergraduate students, 100% full-time, 55% women, 45% men
- **Moderately difficult** entrance level, 67% of applicants were admitted

UNDERGRAD STUDENTS

1,707 full-time, 6 part-time. Students come from 29 states and territories; 16 other countries; 23% are from out of state; 15% Black or African American, non-Hispanic/Latino; 7% Hispanic/Latino; 1% Asian, non-Hispanic/Latino; 0.2% Native Hawaiian or other Pacific Islander, non-Hispanic/Latino; 0.4% American Indian or Alaska Native, non-Hispanic/Latino; 6% Two or more races, non-Hispanic/Latino; 3% Race/ethnicity unknown; 2% international; 3% transferred in; 81% live on campus.

Freshmen:

Admission: 6,279 applied, 4,225 admitted, 487 enrolled. ***Average high school GPA:*** 3.6. ***Test scores:*** SAT evidence-based reading and writing scores over 500: 73%; SAT math scores over 500: 67%; ACT scores over 18: 79%; SAT evidence-based reading and writing scores over 600: 27%; SAT math scores over 600: 19%; ACT scores over 24: 30%; SAT evidence-based reading and writing scores over 700: 3%; SAT math scores over 700: 3%; ACT scores over 30: 3%.

Retention: 72% of full-time freshmen returned.

FACULTY

Total: 165, 70% full-time, 70% with terminal degrees.

Student/faculty ratio: 13:1.

ACADEMICS

Calendar: semesters. *Degrees:* bachelor's and master's.

Special study options: adult/continuing education programs, advanced placement credit, distance learning, double majors, honors programs, independent study, internships, off-campus study, part-time degree program, services for LD students, study abroad, summer session for credit.

Unusual degree programs: 3-2 engineering with Virginia Polytechnic Institute and State University; 3-2 athletic training (internal); 4-1 digital media strategy (internal); 3-4 Veterinary Science with Virginia Tech.

Computers: 149 computers/terminals and 700 ports are available on campus for general student use. Students can access the following: campus intranet, computer help desk, free student e-mail accounts, online (class) grades, online (class) registration, online (class) schedules, Canvas, campus bulletin board system. Campuswide network is available. 100% of college-owned or -operated housing units are wired for high-speed Internet access. Wireless service is available via entire campus.

Library: John Kenny Forrer Learning Commons. *Books:* 105,776 (physical), 23,752 (digital/electronic); *Serial titles:* 264 (physical), 130 (digital/electronic); *Databases:* 110.

STUDENT LIFE

Housing options: on-campus residence required through senior year; coed, women-only, special housing for students with disabilities. Campus housing is university owned.

Activities and organizations: drama/theater group, student-run newspaper, radio station, choral group, Eagle Productions (program board), Physics Club, Active Minds, BC Allies.

Athletics Member NCAA. All Division III. ***Intercollegiate sports:*** baseball M, basketball M/W, cheerleading M(c)/W(c), cross-country running M/W, equestrian sports M(c)/W(c), field hockey W, football M, golf M/W, lacrosse M/W, soccer M/W, softball W, swimming and diving M/W, tennis M/W, track and field M/W, volleyball W. ***Intramural sports:*** badminton M/W, basketball M/W, bowling M/W, football M/W, golf M/W, racquetball M/W, sand volleyball M/W, soccer M/W, softball M/W, table tennis M/W, tennis M/W, ultimate Frisbee M/W, volleyball M/W.

Campus security: 24-hour emergency response devices and patrols, controlled dormitory access, emergency alert system.

Student services: health clinic, personal/psychological counseling.

COSTS & FINANCIAL AID

Costs (2020–21) ***Comprehensive fee:*** $51,080 includes full-time tuition ($36,800), mandatory fees ($920), and room and board ($13,360). ***Room and board:*** Room and board charges vary according to housing facility. ***Waivers:*** employees or children of employees.

Financial Aid Of all full-time matriculated undergraduates who enrolled in 2019, 1,533 applied for aid, 1,430 were judged to have need, 386 had their need fully met. 396 Federal Work-Study jobs (averaging $1482). 91 state and other part-time jobs (averaging $1162). In 2019, 268 non-need-based awards were made. ***Average percent of need met:*** 83. ***Average financial aid package:*** $36,959. ***Average need-based loan:*** $4174. ***Average need-based gift aid:*** $33,808. ***Average non-need-based aid:*** $24,033. ***Average indebtedness upon graduation:*** $31,871.

APPLYING

Standardized Tests *Required:* SAT or ACT (for admission).

Options: electronic application, deferred entrance.

Required: high school transcript. ***Recommended:*** minimum 3.0 GPA.

Application deadlines: 5/1 (freshmen), rolling (transfers).

Notification: continuous (freshmen), continuous (transfers).

CONTACT

Mr. Jarret L. Smith, Director of Admissions, Bridgewater College, 402 East College Street, Bridgewater, VA 22812. *Phone:* 540-828-5469. *Toll-free phone:* 800-759-8328. *Fax:* 540-828-5481. *E-mail:* admissions@bridgewater.edu.

Bryant & Stratton College–Hampton Campus

Hampton, Virginia

http://www.bryantstratton.edu/

CONTACT

Bryant & Stratton College–Hampton Campus, 4410 East Claiborne Square, Suite 233, Hampton, VA 23666.

Bryant & Stratton College–Richmond Campus

Richmond, Virginia

http://www.bryantstratton.edu/

CONTACT

Mr. David K. Mayle, Director of Admissions, Bryant & Stratton College–Richmond Campus, 8141 Hull Street Road, Richmond, VA 23235-6411. *Phone:* 804-745-2444. *Fax:* 804-745-6884. *E-mail:* tlawson@bryanstratton.edu.

Bryant & Stratton College–Virginia Beach Campus

Virginia Beach, Virginia

http://www.bryantstratton.edu/

CONTACT

Bryant & Stratton College–Virginia Beach Campus, 301 Centre Pointe Drive, Virginia Beach, VA 23462. *Phone:* 757-499-7900 Ext. 173.

Centura College

Virginia Beach, Virginia

http://www.centuracollege.edu/

CONTACT
Admissions Office, Centura College, 2697 Dean Drive, Suite 100, Virginia Beach, VA 23452. *Phone:* 757-340-2121. *Toll-free phone:* 877-575-5627. *Fax:* 757-340-9704.

Chamberlain College of Nursing - Tysons Corner

Vienna, Virginia

http://www.chamberlain.edu/

CONTACT
Admissions, Chamberlain College of Nursing - Tysons Corner, 1951 Kidwell Drive, Vienna, VA 22182. *Phone:* 703-416-7300. *Toll-free phone:* 877-751-5783.

Christendom College

Front Royal, Virginia

http://www.christendom.edu/

CONTACT
Mr. Sam Phillips, Director of Admissions, Christendom College, 134 Christendom Drive, Front Royal, VA 22630. *Phone:* 800-877-5456 Ext. 1290. *Toll-free phone:* 800-877-5456. *E-mail:* sam.phillips@christendom.edu.

Christopher Newport University

Newport News, Virginia

http://www.cnu.edu/

- **State-supported** comprehensive, founded 1960
- **Suburban** 260-acre campus with easy access to Virginia Beach
- **Endowment** $35.4 million
- **Coed**
- **Moderately difficult** entrance level

FACULTY
Student/faculty ratio: 15:1.

ACADEMICS
Calendar: semesters. *Degrees:* bachelor's and master's.
Library: Paul and Rosemary Trible Library. *Books:* 229,577 (physical), 578,114 (digital/electronic); *Serial titles:* 745 (physical), 65,202 (digital/electronic); *Databases:* 282. Weekly public service hours: 101; study areas open 24 hours, 5–7 days a week; students can reserve study rooms.

STUDENT LIFE
Housing options: on-campus residence required through junior year; coed. Campus housing is university owned. Freshman campus housing is guaranteed.

Activities and organizations: drama/theater group, student-run newspaper, radio and television station, choral group, marching band, Intervarsity Christian Fellowship, Alpha Delta Pi, Delta Gamma, Gamma Phi Beta, Alpha Phi, national fraternities, national sororities.

Athletics Member NCAA. All Division III except golf (Division II).

Campus security: 24-hour emergency response devices and patrols, late-night transport/escort service, controlled dormitory access.

Student services: health clinic, personal/psychological counseling, veterans affairs office.

COSTS & FINANCIAL AID
Costs (2019–20) ***Tuition:*** state resident $9100 full-time, $378 per credit hour part-time; nonresident $21,566 full-time, $897 per credit hour part-time. Full-time tuition and fees vary according to course load. Part-time tuition and fees vary according to course load. ***Required fees:*** $5824 full-time, $244 per credit hour part-time. ***Room and board:*** $11,760; room only: $7238. Room and board charges vary according to board plan and housing facility.

Financial Aid Of all full-time matriculated undergraduates who enrolled in 2019, 3,128 applied for aid, 2,043 were judged to have need, 447 had their need fully met. 131 Federal Work-Study jobs (averaging $1517). 1,401 state and other part-time jobs (averaging $2184). In 2019, 778 non-need-based awards were made. ***Average percent of need met:*** 69. ***Average financial aid package:*** $10,790. ***Average need-based loan:*** $5410. ***Average need-based gift aid:*** $7839. ***Average non-need-based aid:*** $3674. ***Average indebtedness upon graduation:*** $32,878.

APPLYING
Standardized Tests *Required for some:* SAT or ACT (for admission).

Options: electronic application, early admission, early decision, early action, deferred entrance.

Application fee: $65.

Required: essay or personal statement, high school transcript. ***Required for some:*** interview. ***Recommended:*** minimum 3.5 GPA, 2 letters of recommendation.

CONTACT
Mr. Rob J. Lange III, Dean of Admission, Christopher Newport University, Office of Admission, 1 Avenue of the Arts, Newport News, VA 23606-3072. *Phone:* 757-594-7015. *Toll-free phone:* 800-333-4268. *Fax:* 757-594-7333. *E-mail:* admit@cnu.edu.

Culinary Institute of Virginia

Norfolk, Virginia

http://www.chefva.com/

CONTACT
Director of Admissions, Culinary Institute of Virginia, 2428 Almeda Avenue, Suite 316, Norfolk, VA 23513. *Phone:* 757-858-2433. *Toll-free phone:* 866-619-CHEF. *E-mail:* hsadmissions@chefva.com.

DeVry University–Arlington Campus

Arlington, Virginia

http://www.devry.edu/

- **Proprietary** comprehensive, founded 2001, part of DeVry University
- **Coed**
- **Minimally difficult** entrance level

FACULTY
Student/faculty ratio: 17:1.

ACADEMICS
Calendar: semesters. *Degrees:* associate, bachelor's, master's, and postbachelor's certificates.
Library: Learning Resource Center.

STUDENT LIFE
Housing options: college housing not available.

FINANCIAL AID
Financial Aid Of all full-time matriculated undergraduates who enrolled in 2007, 175 applied for aid, 164 were judged to have need, 9 had their need fully met. In 2007, 21 non-need-based awards were made. ***Average percent of need met:*** 38. ***Average financial aid package:*** $11,581. ***Average need-based loan:*** $7979. ***Average need-based gift aid:*** $5610. ***Average non-need-based aid:*** $18,172. ***Average indebtedness upon graduation:*** $12,479.

APPLYING
Options: deferred entrance.

Application fee: $30.

Required: high school transcript, interview.

CONTACT
DeVry University–Arlington Campus, 2450 Crystal Drive, Arlington, VA 22202. *Phone:* 703-414-4000. *Toll-free phone:* 866-338-7934.

DeVry University–Chesapeake Campus

Chesapeake, Virginia

http://www.devry.edu/

CONTACT

Admissions Office, DeVry University–Chesapeake Campus, 1317 Executive Boulevard, Suite 100, Chesapeake, VA 23320-3671. *Phone:* 757-382-5680. *Toll-free phone:* 866-338-7934.

Eastern Mennonite University

Harrisonburg, Virginia

http://www.emu.edu/

- **Independent Mennonite** comprehensive, founded 1917
- **Small-town** 93-acre campus
- **Endowment** $33.1 million
- **Coed** 980 undergraduate students, 85% full-time, 61% women, 39% men
- **Moderately difficult** entrance level, 65% of applicants were admitted

UNDERGRAD STUDENTS

830 full-time, 150 part-time. Students come from 28 states and territories; 30 other countries; 37% are from out of state; 9% Black or African American, non-Hispanic/Latino; 8% Hispanic/Latino; 2% Asian, non-Hispanic/Latino; 0.3% Native Hawaiian or other Pacific Islander, non-Hispanic/Latino; 0.1% American Indian or Alaska Native, non-Hispanic/Latino; 5% Two or more races, non-Hispanic/Latino; 4% Race/ethnicity unknown; 3% international; 4% transferred in; 44% live on campus.

Freshmen:

Admission: 1,435 applied, 927 admitted, 204 enrolled. ***Average high school GPA:*** 3.6. ***Test scores:*** SAT evidence-based reading and writing scores over 500: 73%; SAT math scores over 500: 73%; ACT scores over 18: 86%; SAT evidence-based reading and writing scores over 600: 34%; SAT math scores over 600: 24%; ACT scores over 24: 44%; SAT evidence-based reading and writing scores over 700: 3%; SAT math scores over 700: 3%; ACT scores over 30: 11%.

Retention: 85% of full-time freshmen returned.

FACULTY

Total: 204, 44% full-time, 54% with terminal degrees.

Student/faculty ratio: 10:1.

ACADEMICS

Calendar: semesters. *Degrees:* certificates, associate, bachelor's, master's, doctoral, and postbachelor's certificates.

Special study options: adult/continuing education programs, advanced placement credit, distance learning, double majors, English as a second language, honors programs, independent study, internships, off-campus study, part-time degree program, services for LD students, study abroad, summer session for credit.

Unusual degree programs: 3-2 engineering with The Catholic University of America.

Computers: 100 computers/terminals are available on campus for general student use. Students can access the following: campus intranet, computer help desk, free student e-mail accounts, online (class) grades, online (class) registration, online (class) schedules. Campuswide network is available. 100% of college-owned or -operated housing units are wired for high-speed Internet access. Wireless service is available via entire campus.

Library: Sadie Hartzler Library. *Books:* 138,611 (physical), 256,672 (digital/electronic); *Serial titles:* 2,076 (physical), 70,423 (digital/electronic); *Databases:* 161. Weekly public service hours: 92.

STUDENT LIFE

Housing options: on-campus residence required through junior year; coed, cooperative, special housing for students with disabilities. Campus housing is university owned. Freshman campus housing is guaranteed.

Activities and organizations: drama/theater group, student-run newspaper, choral group, Young People's Christian Association, Student Government Association, Student Education Association, Creation Care Council, Black Student Union.

Athletics Member NCAA. All Division III. ***Intercollegiate sports:*** baseball M, basketball M/W, cross-country running M/W, field hockey W, golf M/W, lacrosse W, soccer M/W, softball W, track and field M/W, triathlon W, volleyball M/W. ***Intramural sports:*** basketball M/W, football M/W, golf M/W, lacrosse M(c), rock climbing M/W, soccer M/W, softball M/W, table tennis M/W, tennis M/W, volleyball M/W.

Campus security: 24-hour emergency response devices, controlled dormitory access.

Student services: health clinic, personal/psychological counseling.

COSTS & FINANCIAL AID

Costs (2020–21) ***Comprehensive fee:*** $50,950 includes full-time tuition ($38,850), mandatory fees ($370), and room and board ($11,730). Part-time tuition: $1430 per credit hour. Part-time tuition and fees vary according to course load. ***Required fees:*** $18 per credit hour part-time. ***College room only:*** $6760. Room and board charges vary according to board plan and housing facility. ***Payment plan:*** installment. ***Waivers:*** employees or children of employees.

Financial Aid Of all full-time matriculated undergraduates who enrolled in 2019, 775 applied for aid, 717 were judged to have need, 126 had their need fully met. 243 Federal Work-Study jobs (averaging $1043). 45 state and other part time jobs (averaging $1196). In 2019, 179 non need based awards were made. ***Average percent of need met:*** 69. ***Average financial aid package:*** $33,326. ***Average need-based loan:*** $8217. ***Average need-based gift aid:*** $21,552. ***Average non-need-based aid:*** $17,264. ***Average indebtedness upon graduation:*** $43,893.

APPLYING

Standardized Tests *Required:* SAT or ACT (for admission).

Options: electronic application, deferred entrance.

Application fee: $25.

Required: high school transcript, minimum 2.2 GPA, Community Lifestyle Commitment. ***Required for some:*** 2 letters of recommendation. ***Recommended:*** interview.

Application deadlines: rolling (freshmen), rolling (transfers).

Notification: continuous (freshmen), continuous (transfers).

CONTACT

Matthew Ruth, Director of Admissions, Eastern Mennonite University, 1200 Park Road, Harrisonburg, VA 22802. *Phone:* 540-432-4118. *Toll-free phone:* 800-368-2665. *Fax:* 540-432-4444. *E-mail:* admiss@emu.edu.

ECPI University

Virginia Beach, Virginia

http://www.ecpi.edu/

- **Proprietary** comprehensive, founded 1966
- **Suburban** campus
- **Coed** 13,350 undergraduate students, 97% full-time, 59% women, 40% men
- **Moderately difficult** entrance level, 74% of applicants were admitted

UNDERGRAD STUDENTS

13,005 full-time, 137 part-time. Students come from 52 states and territories; 4 other countries; 7% are from out of state; 37% Black or African American, non-Hispanic/Latino; 11% Hispanic/Latino; 3% Asian, non-Hispanic/Latino; 0.5% Native Hawaiian or other Pacific Islander, non-Hispanic/Latino; 0.6% American Indian or Alaska Native, non-Hispanic/Latino; 3% Two or more races, non-Hispanic/Latino; 7% Race/ethnicity unknown; 17% transferred in.

Freshmen:

Admission: 5,701 applied, 4,208 admitted, 1,385 enrolled.

Retention: 47% of full-time freshmen returned.

FACULTY

Total: 1,164, 37% full-time, 10% with terminal degrees.

Student/faculty ratio: 11:1.

ACADEMICS

Calendar: continuous. *Degrees:* certificates, diplomas, associate, bachelor's, and master's.

Special study options: academic remediation for entering students, accelerated degree program, adult/continuing education programs, advanced placement credit, cooperative education, distance learning, double majors, independent study, internships, off-campus study, part-time degree program, services for LD students, study abroad, summer session for credit.

Computers: 6,500 computers/terminals are available on campus for general student use. Students can access the following: campus intranet, computer help desk, free student e-mail accounts, online (class) grades, online (class) registration, online (class) schedules. Campuswide network is available. Wireless service is available via entire campus.
Library: ECPI-Virginia Beach Campus Library plus 13 others. *Books:* 17,128 (physical), 197,849 (digital/electronic); *Serial titles:* 79 (physical); *Databases:* 81. Weekly public service hours: 62; students can reserve study rooms.

STUDENT LIFE
Housing options: college housing not available.

Activities and organizations: Student Electronic Technicians Association (SETA), Institute of Electrical and Electronic Engineers (IEEE), Phi Theta Kappa Honor Society, Information Technology Exchange (ITE), Medical Student Association, national fraternities, national sororities.

Campus security: building and parking lot security.

Student services: personal/psychological counseling, veterans affairs office.

COSTS
Costs (2020–21) ***Tuition:*** $16,584 full-time. Full-time tuition and fees vary according to course load, degree level, location, program, and reciprocity agreements. No tuition increase for student's term of enrollment. ***Payment plans:*** tuition prepayment, installment. ***Waivers:*** employees or children of employees.

APPLYING
Standardized Tests *Required:* (for admission).

Options: electronic application, deferred entrance.

Application fee: $45.

Required: high school transcript, interview, Entrance Exam. ***Required for some:*** minimum 2.5 GPA.

Notification: continuous (freshmen), continuous (transfers).

CONTACT
Mr. Chad Samuelson, University Director of Student Recruitment, ECPI University, 5555 Greenwich Road, Virginia Beach, VA 23462. *Phone:* 757-671-7171 Ext. 55839. *Toll-free phone:* 844-611-0766. *E-mail:* csamuelson@ecpi.edu.

Emory & Henry College

Emory, Virginia

http://www.ehc.edu/

- **Independent United Methodist** comprehensive, founded 1836
- **Rural** 335-acre campus
- **Endowment** $81.8 million
- **Coed** 1,019 undergraduate students, 97% full-time, 51% women, 49% men
- **Moderately difficult** entrance level, 73% of applicants were admitted

UNDERGRAD STUDENTS
988 full-time, 31 part-time. Students come from 31 states and territories; 5 other countries; 58% are from out of state; 9% Black or African American, non-Hispanic/Latino; 3% Hispanic/Latino; 0.5% Asian, non-Hispanic/Latino; 0.1% Native Hawaiian or other Pacific Islander, non-Hispanic/Latino; 4% Two or more races, non-Hispanic/Latino; 3% Race/ethnicity unknown; 0.2% international; 5% transferred in; 78% live on campus.

Freshmen:
Admission: 1,646 applied, 1,203 admitted, 271 enrolled. ***Average high school GPA:*** 3.6. ***Test scores:*** SAT evidence-based reading and writing scores over 500: 69%; SAT math scores over 500: 64%; ACT scores over 18: 71%; SAT evidence-based reading and writing scores over 600: 27%; SAT math scores over 600: 13%; ACT scores over 24: 33%; SAT evidence-based reading and writing scores over 700: 1%; SAT math scores over 700: 2%; ACT scores over 30: 2%.

Retention: 77% of full-time freshmen returned.

FACULTY
Total: 181, 54% full-time, 60% with terminal degrees.

Student/faculty ratio: 11:1.

ACADEMICS
Calendar: semesters. *Degrees:* bachelor's, master's, and doctoral.

Special study options: academic remediation for entering students, advanced placement credit, cooperative education, double majors, honors programs, independent study, internships, part-time degree program, services for LD students, student-designed majors, study abroad, summer session for credit. ***ROTC:*** Army (c).

Computers: 200 computers/terminals and 200 ports are available on campus for general student use. Students can access the following: campus intranet, computer help desk, free student e-mail accounts, online (class) grades, online (class) registration, online (class) schedules. Campuswide network is available. 100% of college-owned or -operated housing units are wired for high-speed Internet access. Wireless service is available via entire campus.
Library: Kelly Library plus 1 other. *Books:* 162,516 (physical), 113,380 (digital/electronic); *Serial titles:* 432 (physical), 79,160 (digital/electronic); *Databases:* 106. Weekly public service hours: 93.

STUDENT LIFE
Housing options: on-campus residence required through senior year; coed, men-only, women-only, special housing for students with disabilities. Campus housing is university owned. Freshman campus housing is guaranteed.

Activities and organizations: drama/theater group, student-run newspaper, radio and television station, choral group, marching band, E&H Outdoor Program, Alpha Psi Omega Honors Fraternity, Alpha Phi Omega Honors Fraternity, Blue Key/ Cardinal Key Honors Society, The Emory Activities Board.

Athletics Member NCAA. All Division III. ***Intercollegiate sports:*** baseball M, basketball M/W, cheerleading W(c), cross-country running M/W, equestrian sports M(s)/W(s), football M, golf M/W, soccer M/W, softball W, swimming and diving M/W, tennis M/W, track and field M/W, volleyball W. ***Intramural sports:*** basketball M/W, football M/W, racquetball M/W, rugby M(c)/W(c), sand volleyball M/W, soccer M/W, table tennis M/W, tennis M/W, ultimate Frisbee M/W, volleyball M/W.

Campus security: 24-hour emergency response devices and patrols, late-night transport/escort service, controlled dormitory access.

Student services: health clinic, personal/psychological counseling.

COSTS & FINANCIAL AID
Costs (2020–21) ***Comprehensive fee:*** $48,425 includes full-time tuition ($34,500), mandatory fees ($800), and room and board ($13,125). Part-time tuition: $1350 per credit hour. ***Required fees:*** $50 per term part-time. ***College room only:*** $6900. ***Payment plan:*** installment. ***Waivers:*** employees or children of employees.

Financial Aid Of all full-time matriculated undergraduates who enrolled in 2019, 941 applied for aid, 876 were judged to have need, 198 had their need fully met. 400 Federal Work-Study jobs (averaging $1925). In 2019, 105 non-need-based awards were made. ***Average percent of need met:*** 84. ***Average financial aid package:*** $37,101. ***Average need-based loan:*** $3955. ***Average need-based gift aid:*** $29,846. ***Average non-need-based aid:*** $20,368. ***Average indebtedness upon graduation:*** $30,360.

APPLYING
Standardized Tests *Required:* SAT or ACT (for admission).

Options: electronic application, early decision.

Required: high school transcript. ***Recommended:*** interview.

Application deadlines: rolling (freshmen), rolling (transfers).

Early decision deadline: 11/15 (for plan 1), 1/15 (for plan 2).

Notification: continuous (freshmen), continuous (transfers), 12/15 (early decision).

CONTACT
Ms. Jennifer Pearce, Vice President for Enrollment and External Affairs, Emory & Henry College, PO Box 947, Emory, VA 24327-0947. *Phone:* 276-944-6968. *Toll-free phone:* 800-848-5493. *E-mail:* jpearce@ehc.edu.

Ferrum College

Ferrum, Virginia

http://www.ferrum.edu/

- **Independent United Methodist** 4-year, founded 1913
- **Rural** 720-acre campus
- **Coed**
- **Minimally difficult** entrance level

FACULTY

Student/faculty ratio: 14:1.

ACADEMICS

Calendar: semesters. *Degree:* bachelor's.
Library: Stanley Library.

STUDENT LIFE

Housing options: on-campus residence required through senior year; coed, men-only, women-only, special housing for students with disabilities. Campus housing is university owned. Freshman campus housing is guaranteed.

Activities and organizations: drama/theater group, student-run newspaper, radio station, choral group, Student Government Association, Agriculture Club, BACCHUS, Panther Productions, African American Student Association, Students in Free Enterprise (SIFE), national sororities.

Athletics Member NCAA. All Division III.

Campus security: 24-hour emergency response devices and patrols, student patrols, late-night transport/escort service, controlled dormitory access.

Student services: health clinic, personal/psychological counseling.

COSTS & FINANCIAL AID

Costs (2019–20) ***Comprehensive fee:*** $47,810 includes full-time tuition ($35,250), mandatory fees ($115), and room and board ($12,445). Part-time tuition: $710 per credit hour.

Financial Aid Of all full-time matriculated undergraduates who enrolled in 2015, 1,214 applied for aid, 1,214 were judged to have need, 105 had their need fully met. In 2015, 55 non-need-based awards were made. ***Average percent of need met:*** 72. ***Average financial aid package:*** $30,418. ***Average need-based loan:*** $4576. ***Average need-based gift aid:*** $12,783. ***Average non-need-based aid:*** $12,087. ***Average indebtedness upon graduation:*** $30,353.

APPLYING

Standardized Tests *Required:* SAT or ACT (for admission).

Options: electronic application, early admission, deferred entrance.

Application fee: $25.

Required: high school transcript. ***Required for some:*** interview. ***Recommended:*** essay or personal statement, minimum 2.0 GPA, interview.

CONTACT

Ms. Gilda Q. Woods, Associate Vice President for Enrollment Management and Dean of Admissions, Ferrum College, Spilman-Daniel House, PO Box 1000, Ferrum, VA 24088-9001. *Phone:* 540-365-4290. *Toll-free phone:* 800-868-9797. *Fax:* 540-365-4266. *E-mail:* admissions@ferrum.edu.

George Mason University

Fairfax, Virginia

http://www.gmu.edu/

- **State-supported** university, founded 1972
- **Suburban** 817-acre campus with easy access to Washington, DC
- **Endowment** $99.8 million
- **Coed** 26,662 undergraduate students, 81% full-time, 49% women, 51% men
- **Moderately difficult** entrance level, 87% of applicants were admitted

UNDERGRAD STUDENTS

21,672 full-time, 4,990 part-time. Students come from 50 states and territories; 108 other countries; 10% are from out of state; 11% Black or African American, non-Hispanic/Latino; 16% Hispanic/Latino; 21% Asian, non-Hispanic/Latino; 0.2% Native Hawaiian or other Pacific Islander, non-Hispanic/Latino; 0.1% American Indian or Alaska Native, non-Hispanic/Latino; 5% Two or more races, non-Hispanic/Latino; 3% Race/ethnicity unknown; 6% international; 11% transferred in; 23% live on campus.

Freshmen:
Admission: 19,554 applied, 16,962 admitted, 3,763 enrolled. ***Average high school GPA:*** 3.7. ***Test scores:*** SAT evidence-based reading and writing scores over 500: 96%; SAT math scores over 500: 95%; ACT scores over 18: 99%; SAT evidence-based reading and writing scores over 600: 58%; SAT math scores over 600: 51%; ACT scores over 24: 78%; SAT evidence-based reading and writing scores over 700: 11%; SAT math scores over 700: 14%; ACT scores over 30: 26%.

Retention: 86% of full-time freshmen returned.

FACULTY

Total: 2,860, 48% full-time.

Student/faculty ratio: 17:1.

ACADEMICS

Calendar: semesters. *Degrees:* bachelor's, master's, doctoral, post-master's, and postbachelor's certificates.

Special study options: accelerated degree program, adult/continuing education programs, advanced placement credit, cooperative education, distance learning, double majors, English as a second language, freshman honors college, honors programs, independent study, internships, off-campus study, part-time degree program, services for LD students, student-designed majors, study abroad, summer session for credit. ***ROTC:*** Army (b), Air Force (c).

Computers: 622 computers/terminals and 45,871 ports are available on campus for general student use. Students can access the following: campus intranet, computer help desk, free student e-mail accounts, online (class) grades, online (class) registration, online (class) schedules. Campuswide network is available. 100% of college-owned or -operated housing units are wired for high-speed Internet access. Wireless service is available via entire campus.

Library: Fenwick Library plus 3 others. *Books:* 115,412 (physical), 162,436 (digital/electronic); *Serial titles:* 908 (physical), 119,174 (digital/electronic); *Databases:* 806. Weekly public service hours: 95; study areas open 24 hours, 5–7 days a week; students can reserve study rooms.

STUDENT LIFE

Housing options: coed, special housing for students with disabilities. Campus housing is university owned. Freshman campus housing is guaranteed.

Activities and organizations: drama/theater group, student-run newspaper, radio and television station, choral group, Catholic Campus Ministry, Indian Student Association, Black Student Alliance, Muslim Student Association, CRU (Campus Crusade for Christ), national fraternities, national sororities.

Athletics Member NCAA. All Division I. ***Intercollegiate sports:*** baseball M(s), basketball M(s)/W(s), crew W(s), cross-country running M(s)/W(s), golf M(s), lacrosse W(s), soccer M(s)/W(s), softball W(s), swimming and diving M(s)/W(s), tennis M(s)/W(s), track and field M(s)/W(s), volleyball M(s)/W(s), wrestling M(s). ***Intramural sports:*** badminton M(c)/W(c), baseball M(c), basketball M/W, bowling M(c)/W(c), crew M(c)/W(c), cross-country running M(c)/W(c), equestrian sports M(c)/W(c), fencing M(c)/W(c), field hockey M(c)/W(c), football M(c), golf M/W, ice hockey M(c), lacrosse M(c)/W(c), rugby M(c)/W(c), soccer M(c)/W(c), softball M/W(c), swimming and diving M/W, tennis M(c)/W(c), track and field M(c)/W(c), ultimate Frisbee M(c)/W(c), volleyball M(c)/W(c), water polo M/W, wrestling M(c).

Campus security: 24-hour emergency response devices and patrols, student patrols, late-night transport/escort service, controlled dormitory access.

Student services: health clinic, personal/psychological counseling, women's center, veterans affairs office.

COSTS & FINANCIAL AID

Costs (2019–20) ***Tuition:*** state resident $9060 full-time, $378 per credit hour part-time; nonresident $32,520 full-time, $1355 per credit hour part-time. Full-time tuition and fees vary according to course load. Part-time tuition and fees vary according to course load. ***Required fees:*** $3504 full-time, $146 per credit hour part-time. ***Room and board:*** $11,705. Room and board charges vary according to board plan and housing facility. ***Payment plans:*** installment, deferred payment. ***Waivers:*** senior citizens and employees or children of employees.

Financial Aid Of all full-time matriculated undergraduates who enrolled in 2017, 13,964 applied for aid, 11,574 were judged to have need, 218 had their need fully met. 626 Federal Work-Study jobs (averaging $2050). In 2017, 1441 non-need-based awards were made. ***Average percent of need met:*** 55. ***Average financial aid package:*** $14,053. ***Average need-based loan:*** $4411. ***Average need-based gift aid:*** $6752. ***Average non-need-based aid:*** $4998. ***Average indebtedness upon graduation:*** $30,790.

APPLYING

Standardized Tests *Required for some:* SAT or ACT (for admission).

Options: electronic application, early admission, early action, deferred entrance.

Application fee: $70.

Required: high school transcript. ***Required for some:*** essay or personal statement, audition for dance and music, portfolio for art and visual technology and computer game design, interview and audition or portfolio for theater. ***Recommended:*** 3 letters of recommendation.

Application deadlines: 1/15 (freshmen), 3/1 (transfers), 11/15 (early action).

Notification: 4/1 (transfers), 12/15 (early action).

CONTACT

Melissa Bevacqua, Director, Undergraduate Admissions, George Mason University, 4400 University Drive, MSN 3A4, Fairfax, VA 22030-4444. *Phone:* 703-993-2291. *Toll-free phone:* 888-627-6612. *Fax:* 703-993-2392. *E-mail:* mbevacqu@gmu.edu.

Hampden-Sydney College

Hampden-Sydney, Virginia

http://www.hsc.edu/

- **Independent** 4-year, founded 1776, affiliated with Presbyterian Church (U.S.A.)
- **Rural** 1343-acre campus with easy access to Richmond, Lynchburg, Charlottesville
- **Endowment** $176.3 million
- **Men only** 993 undergraduate students, 100% full-time
- **Moderately difficult** entrance level, 57% of applicants were admitted

UNDERGRAD STUDENTS

993 full-time. Students come from 30 states and territories; 4 other countries; 30% are from out of state; 5% Black or African American, non-Hispanic/Latino; 5% Hispanic/Latino; 0.7% Asian, non-Hispanic/Latino; 0.3% American Indian or Alaska Native, non-Hispanic/Latino; 3% Two or more races, non-Hispanic/Latino; 1% Race/ethnicity unknown; 0.3% international; 0.8% transferred in; 98% live on campus.

Freshmen:

Admission: 3,056 applied, 1,755 admitted, 228 enrolled. ***Average high school GPA:*** 3.4. ***Test scores:*** SAT evidence-based reading and writing scores over 500: 84%; SAT math scores over 500: 84%; ACT scores over 18: 92%; SAT evidence-based reading and writing scores over 600: 43%; SAT math scores over 600: 38%; ACT scores over 24: 51%; SAT evidence-based reading and writing scores over 700: 7%; SAT math scores over 700: 8%; ACT scores over 30: 13%.

Retention: 79% of full-time freshmen returned.

FACULTY

Total: 114, 83% full-time, 86% with terminal degrees.

Student/faculty ratio: 10:1.

ACADEMICS

Calendar: semesters. *Degree:* bachelor's.

Special study options: academic remediation for entering students, advanced placement credit, cooperative education, double majors, honors programs, independent study, internships, off-campus study, study abroad, summer session for credit. ***ROTC:*** Army (c).

Unusual degree programs: 3-2 engineering with University of Virginia, Old Dominion University.

Computers: 200 computers/terminals are available on campus for general student use. Students can access the following: campus intranet, computer help desk, free student e-mail accounts, online (class) grades, online (class) registration, online (class) schedules. Campuswide network is available. 100% of college-owned or -operated housing units are wired for high-speed Internet access. Wireless service is available via entire campus.

Library: Walter M. Bortz III Library. *Books:* 213,700 (physical), 179,858 (digital/electronic); *Serial titles:* 81 (physical), 87,069 (digital/electronic); *Databases:* 101. Weekly public service hours: 99; students can reserve study rooms.

STUDENT LIFE

Housing options: on-campus residence required through senior year; men-only, special housing for students with disabilities. Campus housing is university owned. Freshman campus housing is guaranteed.

Activities and organizations: drama/theater group, student-run newspaper, radio station, choral group, Republican Society, Pre-Health Society, Outdoors Club, Tiger Athletic Club, Pre-Law Society, national fraternities.

Athletics Member NCAA. All Division III. ***Intercollegiate sports:*** baseball M, basketball M, crew M(c), cross-country running M, fencing M(c), football M, golf M, lacrosse M, riflery M(c), rugby M(c), soccer M, swimming and diving M, tennis M, ultimate Frisbee M(c). ***Intramural sports:*** archery M(c), basketball M, fencing M(c), football M, lacrosse M(c), racquetball M(c), riflery M(c), soccer M, softball M, swimming and diving M(c), volleyball M, water polo M(c), wrestling M(c).

Campus security: 24-hour emergency response devices and patrols.

Student services: health clinic, personal/psychological counseling.

COSTS & FINANCIAL AID

Costs (2020–21) ***Comprehensive fee:*** $61,986 includes full-time tuition ($45,690), mandatory fees ($2420), and room and board ($13,876). Part-time tuition: $1430 per credit hour. ***Room and board:*** Room and board charges vary according to board plan.

Financial Aid Of all full-time matriculated undergraduates who enrolled in 2019, 770 applied for aid, 661 were judged to have need, 173 had their need fully met. 140 Federal Work-Study jobs (averaging $1404). In 2019, 312 non-need-based awards were made. ***Average percent of need met:*** 80. ***Average financial aid package:*** $34,703. ***Average need-based loan:*** $4014. ***Average need-based gift aid:*** $31,288. ***Average non-need-based aid:*** $18,814. ***Average indebtedness upon graduation:*** $41,316.

APPLYING

Standardized Tests *Required:* SAT or ACT (for admission). *Recommended:* SAT and SAT Subject Tests or ACT (for admission).

Options: electronic application, early admission, early decision, early action.

Application fee: $30.

Required: essay or personal statement, high school transcript, 2 letters of recommendation. ***Recommended:*** interview.

Early decision deadline: 11/1.

Notification: 4/15 (freshmen), 7/31 (transfers), 12/1 (early decision), 12/1 (early action).

CONTACT

Dean Jason Ferguson, Dean of Admissions, Hampden-Sydney College, PO Box 667, Hampden-Sydney, VA 23943-0667. *Phone:* 434-223-6327. *Toll-free phone:* 800-755-0733. *Fax:* 434-223-6346. *E-mail:* hsapp@hsc.edu.

Hampton University

Hampton, Virginia

http://www.hamptonu.edu/

- **Independent** comprehensive, founded 1868
- **Urban** 314-acre campus with easy access to Norfolk
- **Endowment** $282.5 million
- **Coed** 3,799 undergraduate students, 96% full-time, 67% women, 33% men
- **Moderately difficult** entrance level, 36% of applicants were admitted

UNDERGRAD STUDENTS

3,651 full-time, 148 part-time. Students come from 44 states and territories; 22 other countries; 73% are from out of state; 96% Black or African American, non-Hispanic/Latino; 1% Hispanic/Latino; 0.3%

Asian, non-Hispanic/Latino; 0.1% Native Hawaiian or other Pacific Islander, non-Hispanic/Latino; 0.4% American Indian or Alaska Native, non-Hispanic/Latino; 0.4% Race/ethnicity unknown; 0.7% international; 2% transferred in; 57% live on campus.

Freshmen:

Admission: 12,130 applied, 4,391 admitted, 704 enrolled. ***Average high school GPA:*** 3.7. ***Test scores:*** SAT evidence-based reading and writing scores over 500: 93%; SAT math scores over 500: 74%; ACT scores over 18: 100%; SAT evidence-based reading and writing scores over 600: 22%; SAT math scores over 600: 11%; ACT scores over 24: 33%; SAT evidence-based reading and writing scores over 700: 3%; SAT math scores over 700: 2%; ACT scores over 30: 6%.

Retention: 77% of full-time freshmen returned.

FACULTY

Total: 311, 81% full-time, 74% with terminal degrees.

Student/faculty ratio: 14:1.

ACADEMICS

Calendar: semesters. *Degrees:* certificates, associate, bachelor's, master's, doctoral, and post-master's certificates.

Special study options: academic remediation for entering students, accelerated degree program, adult/continuing education programs, advanced placement credit, cooperative education, distance learning, double majors, English as a second language, honors programs, independent study, internships, off-campus study, part-time degree program, services for LD students, study abroad, summer session for credit. ***ROTC:*** Army (b), Navy (b).

Computers: 1,500 computers/terminals are available on campus for general student use. Students can access the following: campus intranet, computer help desk, free student e-mail accounts, online (class) grades, online (class) registration, online (class) schedules, learning management system. Campuswide network is available. 100% of college-owned or -operated housing units are wired for high-speed Internet access. Wireless service is available via entire campus.

Library: William R. and Norma B. Harvey Library plus 4 others. *Books:* 327,841 (physical), 113,623 (digital/electronic); *Serial titles:* 4,783 (physical), 55,592 (digital/electronic); *Databases:* 145. Study areas open 24 hours, 5–7 days a week; students can reserve study rooms.

STUDENT LIFE

Housing options: on-campus residence required for freshman year; coed, men-only, women-only, special housing for students with disabilities. Campus housing is university owned. Freshman applicants given priority for college housing.

Activities and organizations: drama/theater group, student-run newspaper, radio station, choral group, marching band, Student Government, Student leaders, Student Union Board, Student recruitment team, Resident assistants, national fraternities, national sororities.

Athletics Member NCAA. All Division I. ***Intercollegiate sports:*** basketball M(s)/W(s), bowling W(s), cheerleading W, cross-country running M(s)/W(s), football M(s), golf M(s)/W(s)(c), lacrosse M(s), sailing M(s)/W(s), soccer W, softball W(s), tennis M(s)/W(s), track and field M(s)/W(s), triathlon W, volleyball W(s). ***Intramural sports:*** badminton M/W, basketball M/W, bowling W, football M, lacrosse M/W, soccer M, softball W, swimming and diving M/W, table tennis M/W, triathlon W, volleyball W.

Campus security: 24-hour emergency response devices and patrols.

Student services: health clinic, personal/psychological counseling, women's center, veterans affairs office.

COSTS & FINANCIAL AID

Costs (2020–21) ***Comprehensive fee:*** $42,398 includes full-time tuition ($26,198), mandatory fees ($3214), and room and board ($12,986). Full-time tuition and fees vary according to course load, degree level, location, program, and reciprocity agreements. Part-time tuition and fees vary according to class time, course load, location, and reciprocity agreements. ***Required fees:*** $665 per credit hour part-time. ***College room only:*** $6754. Room and board charges vary according to board plan, housing facility, and location. ***Payment plans:*** installment, deferred payment. ***Waivers:*** employees or children of employees.

Financial Aid Of all full-time matriculated undergraduates who enrolled in 2018, 2,356 applied for aid, 1,855 were judged to have need, 762 had their need fully met. 215 Federal Work-Study jobs (averaging $1376). In 2018, 54 non-need-based awards were made. ***Average percent of need met:*** 43. ***Average financial aid package:*** $5952. ***Average need-based loan:*** $5885. ***Average need-based gift aid:*** $7115. ***Average non-need-based aid:*** $6932. ***Average indebtedness upon graduation:*** $33,680. ***Financial aid deadline:*** 4/15.

APPLYING

Standardized Tests *Required for some:* SAT or ACT (for admission).

Options: electronic application, early admission, early action, deferred entrance.

Application fee: $35.

Required: essay or personal statement, high school transcript, minimum 2.5 GPA, 1 letter of recommendation. ***Required for some:*** interview, audition for music.

Application deadlines: 3/1 (freshmen), 11/1 (early action).

Notification: 12/15 (early action).

CONTACT

Ms. Patra Johnson, Director, Freshman Studies, Hampton University, 204 Student Center, Hampton, VA 23668. *Phone:* 757-727-5901. *Toll-free phone:* 800-624-3328. *Fax:* 757-727-5095. *E-mail:* patra.johnson@hamptonu.edu.

Hollins University

Roanoke, Virginia

http://www.hollins.edu/

- **Independent** comprehensive, founded 1842
- **Suburban** 475-acre campus
- **Endowment** $182.7 million
- **Undergraduate: women only; graduate: coed** 668 undergraduate students, 99% full-time, 100% women, 0% men
- **Moderately difficult** entrance level, 71% of applicants were admitted

UNDERGRAD STUDENTS

659 full-time, 9 part-time. Students come from 39 states and territories; 22 other countries; 48% are from out of state; 9% Black or African American, non-Hispanic/Latino; 8% Hispanic/Latino; 2% Asian, non-Hispanic/Latino; 0.5% Native Hawaiian or other Pacific Islander, non-Hispanic/Latino; 0.2% American Indian or Alaska Native, non-Hispanic/Latino; 7% Two or more races, non-Hispanic/Latino; 1% Race/ethnicity unknown; 10% international; 3% transferred in; 83% live on campus.

Freshmen:

Admission: 3,244 applied, 2,311 admitted, 185 enrolled. ***Average high school GPA:*** 3.7. ***Test scores:*** SAT evidence-based reading and writing scores over 500: 93%; SAT math scores over 500: 85%; ACT scores over 18: 99%; SAT evidence-based reading and writing scores over 600: 53%; SAT math scores over 600: 38%; ACT scores over 24: 69%; SAT evidence-based reading and writing scores over 700: 13%; SAT math scores over 700: 7%; ACT scores over 30: 26%.

Retention: 75% of full-time freshmen returned.

FACULTY

Total: 102, 66% full-time, 85% with terminal degrees.

Student/faculty ratio: 9:1.

ACADEMICS

Calendar: 4-1-4. *Degrees:* bachelor's, master's, and post-master's certificates.

Special study options: accelerated degree program, advanced placement credit, cooperative education, double majors, independent study, internships, off-campus study, part-time degree program, services for LD students, student-designed majors, study abroad.

Computers: 102 computers/terminals and 1,000 ports are available on campus for general student use. Students can access the following: campus intranet, computer help desk, free student e-mail accounts, online (class) grades, online (class) registration, online (class) schedules. Campuswide network is available.

Library: Wyndham Robertson Library plus 1 other. *Books:* 211,223 (physical), 288,069 (digital/electronic); *Serial titles:* 1,250 (physical), 64,491 (digital/electronic); *Databases:* 142. Weekly public service hours: 94.

STUDENT LIFE
Housing options: on-campus residence required through senior year; women-only, special housing for students with disabilities. Campus housing is university owned. Freshman campus housing is guaranteed.

Activities and organizations: drama/theater group, choral group, Hollins Activity Board, Model UN/Model Arab League, Assoc. or Countries, Cultures, Events, & National Traditions (ACCENT), Arts Association, Entrpreneurship Club.

Athletics Member NCAA. All Division III. ***Intercollegiate sports:*** basketball W, cross-country running W, equestrian sports W, lacrosse W, soccer W, swimming and diving W, tennis W, volleyball W.

Campus security: 24-hour emergency response devices and patrols, late-night transport/escort service, controlled dormitory access.

Student services: health clinic, personal/psychological counseling, women's center.

COSTS & FINANCIAL AID
Costs (2019–20) ***Comprehensive fee:*** $53,940 includes full-time tuition ($39,360), mandatory fees ($650), and room and board ($13,930). Part-time tuition: $1233 per credit hour. ***Required fees:*** $325 per year part-time. ***Room and board:*** Room and board charges vary according to board plan. ***Payment plans:*** tuition prepayment, installment. ***Waivers:*** employees or children of employees.

Financial Aid Of all full-time matriculated undergraduates who enrolled in 2019, 536 applied for aid, 494 were judged to have need, 119 had their need fully met. 135 Federal Work-Study jobs (averaging $1500). 165 state and other part-time jobs (averaging $1500). In 2019, 165 non-need-based awards were made. ***Average percent of need met:*** 85. ***Average financial aid package:*** $38,450. ***Average need-based loan:*** $4473. ***Average need-based gift aid:*** $32,163. ***Average non-need-based aid:*** $34,877. ***Average indebtedness upon graduation:*** $33,691.

APPLYING
Standardized Tests *Required:* SAT or ACT (for admission).

Options: electronic application, early admission, early decision, early action, deferred entrance.

Required: essay or personal statement, high school transcript, 1 letter of recommendation. ***Recommended:*** interview.

Application deadlines: rolling (freshmen), 11/15 (early action).

Early decision deadline: 11/1.

Notification: continuous (freshmen), 11/15 (early decision), 12/1 (early action).

CONTACT
Ms. Madeline Aliff, Director of Recruitment, Hollins University, 7916 Williamson Road, Box 9707, Roanoke, VA 24020. *Phone:* 540-362-6401. *Toll-free phone:* 800-456-9595. *Fax:* 540-362-6218. *E-mail:* huadm@hollins.edu.

IGlobal University

Vienna, Virginia

http://www.igu.edu/

CONTACT
IGlobal University, 8133 Leesburg Pike, #230, Vienna, VA 22182.

James Madison University

Harrisonburg, Virginia

http://www.jmu.edu/

- **State-supported** comprehensive, founded 1908
- **Small-town** 721-acre campus
- **Coed** 19,895 undergraduate students, 94% full-time, 58% women, 42% men
- **Very difficult** entrance level, 77% of applicants were admitted

UNDERGRAD STUDENTS
18,798 full-time, 1,097 part-time. 22% are from out of state; 5% Black or African American, non-Hispanic/Latino; 7% Hispanic/Latino; 5% Asian, non-Hispanic/Latino; 0.1% Native Hawaiian or other Pacific Islander, non-Hispanic/Latino; 0.1% American Indian or Alaska Native, non-Hispanic/Latino; 5% Two or more races, non-Hispanic/Latino; 2% Race/ethnicity unknown; 2% international; 4% transferred in; 32% live on campus.

Freshmen:
Admission: 23,578 applied, 18,097 admitted, 4,455 enrolled. ***Test scores:*** SAT evidence-based reading and writing scores over 500: 98%; SAT math scores over 500: 96%; ACT scores over 18: 98%; SAT evidence-based reading and writing scores over 600: 60%; SAT math scores over 600: 49%; ACT scores over 24: 69%; SAT evidence-based reading and writing scores over 700: 8%; SAT math scores over 700: 6%; ACT scores over 30: 14%.

Retention: 89% of full-time freshmen returned.

FACULTY
Total: 1,592, 67% full-time, 60% with terminal degrees.

Student/faculty ratio: 16:1.

ACADEMICS
Calendar: semesters. *Degrees:* bachelor's, master's, and doctoral (also offers specialist in education degree).

Special study options: accelerated degree program, adult/continuing education programs, advanced placement credit, distance learning, double majors, freshman honors college, honors programs, independent study, internships, off-campus study, part-time degree program, services for LD students, study abroad, summer session for credit. ***ROTC:*** Army (b), Air Force (c).

Unusual degree programs: 3-2 forestry with Virginia Polytechnic Institute and State University.

Computers: Students can access the following: campus intranet, computer help desk, free student e-mail accounts, online (class) grades, online (class) registration, online (class) schedules. Campuswide network is available. Wireless service is available via entire campus.
Library: Carrier Library plus 2 others. Students can reserve study rooms.

STUDENT LIFE
Housing options: on-campus residence required for freshman year; coed, special housing for students with disabilities. Campus housing is university owned. Freshman campus housing is guaranteed.

Activities and organizations: drama/theater group, student-run newspaper, radio and television station, choral group, marching band, national fraternities, national sororities.

Athletics Member NCAA. All Division I except football (Division I-AA). ***Intercollegiate sports:*** baseball M(s), basketball M(s)/W(s), cheerleading M/W, cross-country running W(s), field hockey W(s), golf M(s)/W(s), lacrosse W(s), soccer M(s)/W(s), softball W(s), swimming and diving W(s), tennis M(s)/W(s), track and field W(s), volleyball W(s). ***Intramural sports:*** archery M(c)/W(c), baseball M(c), basketball M/W, bowling M/W, cheerleading W(c), crew M(c)/W(c), cross-country running M(c)/W(c), equestrian sports M(c)/W(c), fencing M(c)/W(c), field hockey W(c), football M/W, golf M/W, gymnastics M(c)/W(c), ice hockey M(c)/W(c), lacrosse M(c)/W(c), racquetball M/W, rugby M(c)/W(c), skiing (downhill) M(c)/W(c), soccer M/W, softball M/W, squash M(c)/W(c), swimming and diving M(c)/W(c), table tennis M/W, tennis M/W, track and field M(c)/W(c), ultimate Frisbee M(c)/W(c), volleyball M/W, water polo M(c)/W(c), wrestling M(c).

Campus security: 24-hour emergency response devices and patrols, student patrols, late-night transport/escort service, controlled dormitory access, lighted pathways.

Student services: health clinic, personal/psychological counseling, women's center.

COSTS & FINANCIAL AID
Costs (2019–20) ***Tuition:*** state resident $6620 full-time, $220 per credit hour part-time; nonresident $23,834 full-time, $777 per credit hour part-time. ***Required fees:*** $4956 full-time. ***Room and board:*** $10,582; room only: $5510. Room and board charges vary according to board plan. ***Waivers:*** employees or children of employees.

Financial Aid Of all full-time matriculated undergraduates who enrolled in 2019, 11,213 applied for aid, 7,508 were judged to have need, 4,995 had their need fully met. In 2019, 231 non-need-based awards were made. ***Average percent of need met:*** 37. ***Average financial aid package:*** $9333. ***Average need-based loan:*** $4219. ***Average need-based gift aid:*** $7604. ***Average non-need-based aid:*** $5954. ***Average indebtedness upon graduation:*** $28,554.

APPLYING
Options: electronic application, early action, deferred entrance.
Application fee: $70.
Required: high school transcript. ***Recommended:*** minimum 3.0 GPA.
Application deadlines: 1/15 (freshmen), 11/1 (early action).
Notification: 4/1 (freshmen), 1/15 (early action).

CONTACT
James Madison University, 800 South Main Street, Harrisonburg, VA 22807. *Phone:* 540-568-5681.

Jefferson College of Health Sciences

Roanoke, Virginia

http://www.jchs.edu/

CONTACT
Jefferson College of Health Sciences, 101 Elm Avenue SE, Roanoke, VA 24013. *Phone:* 540-985-8309. *Toll-free phone:* 888-985-8483.

Liberty University

Lynchburg, Virginia

http://www.liberty.edu/

- **Independent nondenominational** comprehensive, founded 1971
- **Suburban** 6500-acre campus
- **Coed** 13,117 undergraduate students, 95% full-time, 55% women, 45% men
- **Minimally difficult** entrance level, 35% of applicants were admitted

UNDERGRAD STUDENTS
12,513 full-time, 604 part-time. Students come from 52 states and territories; 75 other countries; 60% are from out of state; 4% Black or African American, non-Hispanic/Latino; 7% Hispanic/Latino; 2% Asian, non-Hispanic/Latino; 0.1% Native Hawaiian or other Pacific Islander, non-Hispanic/Latino; 0.3% American Indian or Alaska Native, non-Hispanic/Latino; 3% Two or more races, non-Hispanic/Latino; 9% Race/ethnicity unknown; 4% international; 6% transferred in; 58% live on campus.

Freshmen:
Admission: 20,183 applied, 6,979 admitted, 3,256 enrolled. ***Average high school GPA:*** 3.5. ***Test scores:*** SAT evidence-based reading and writing scores over 500: 89%; SAT math scores over 500: 82%; ACT scores over 18: 94%; SAT evidence-based reading and writing scores over 600: 47%; SAT math scores over 600: 34%; ACT scores over 24: 57%; SAT evidence-based reading and writing scores over 700: 10%; SAT math scores over 700: 8%; ACT scores over 30: 19%.
Retention: 85% of full-time freshmen returned.

ACADEMICS
Calendar: semesters. *Degrees:* certificates, associate, bachelor's, master's, doctoral, post-master's, and postbachelor's certificates (also offers external degree program with significant enrollment not reflected in profile).
Special study options: academic remediation for entering students, accelerated degree program, advanced placement credit, cooperative education, distance learning, double majors, English as a second language, external degree program, honors programs, independent study, internships, off-campus study, part-time degree program, services for LD students, student-designed majors, study abroad, summer session for credit. ***ROTC:*** Army (b), Air Force (c).
Computers: 1,640 computers/terminals are available on campus for general student use. Students can access the following: computer help desk, free student e-mail accounts, online (class) grades, online (class) registration, online (class) schedules. Campuswide network is available. 100% of college-owned or -operated housing units are wired for high-speed Internet access. Wireless service is available via entire campus.
Library: Jerry Falwell Library plus 2 others. *Books:* 336,202 (physical), 978,080 (digital/electronic); *Serial titles:* 2,987 (physical), 156,971 (digital/electronic); *Databases:* 451. Weekly public service hours: 100; students can reserve study rooms.

STUDENT LIFE
Housing options: on-campus residence required through senior year; men-only, women-only, special housing for students with disabilities. Campus housing is university owned. Freshman campus housing is guaranteed.
Activities and organizations: drama/theater group, student-run newspaper, radio station, choral group, marching band, Campus Serve.
Athletics Member NCAA. All Division I except football (Division I-AA). ***Intercollegiate sports:*** baseball M(s), basketball M(s)/W(s), cheerleading M(s)/W(s), crew M(c)/W(c), cross-country running M(s)/W(s), equestrian sports M(c)/W(c), field hockey W(s), golf M(s), ice hockey M(c)/W(c), lacrosse W(s), riflery M(c)/W(c), rock climbing M(c)/W(c), sand volleyball M(c)/W(c), soccer M(s)/W(s), softball W(s), swimming and diving W(s), tennis M(s)/W(s), track and field M(s)/W(s), triathlon M(c)/W(c), volleyball M(c)/W(s). ***Intramural sports:*** archery M(c)/W(c), basketball M/W, football M/W, gymnastics M(c)/W(c), lacrosse M(c), racquetball M(c)/W(c), skiing (downhill) M(c)/W(c), soccer M/W, softball M/W, table tennis M/W, tennis M/W, ultimate Frisbee M(c)/W(c), volleyball M/W, wrestling M(c)/W(c).
Campus security: 24-hour patrols, late-night transport/escort service, 24-hour emergency dispatch.
Student services: health clinic, personal/psychological counseling, veterans affairs office.

COSTS & FINANCIAL AID
Costs (2020–21) ***Comprehensive fee:*** $35,372 includes full-time tuition ($23,800), mandatory fees ($1110), and room and board ($10,462). Part-time tuition: $815 per credit hour. ***College room only:*** $6760.
Financial Aid Of all full-time matriculated undergraduates who enrolled in 2018, 11,310 applied for aid, 8,851 were judged to have need, 988 had their need fully met. In 2018, 2322 non-need-based awards were made. ***Average percent of need met:*** 56. ***Average financial aid package:*** $15,336. ***Average need-based loan:*** $4244. ***Average need-based gift aid:*** $11,262. ***Average non-need-based aid:*** $7440. ***Average indebtedness upon graduation:*** $20,876. ***Financial aid deadline:*** 3/1.

APPLYING
Standardized Tests *Required:* SAT or ACT (for admission).
Options: electronic application.
Application fee: $50.
Required: essay or personal statement, high school transcript, minimum 2.0 GPA. ***Recommended:*** minimum 2.0 GPA.
Application deadlines: rolling (freshmen), rolling (transfers).
Notification: continuous (freshmen), continuous (transfers).

CONTACT
"Jason" Chris Jones, Director of Admissions, Liberty University, 1971 University Boulevard, Lynchburg, VA 24515. *Phone:* 434-592-3966. *Toll-free phone:* 800-543-5317. *Fax:* 800-542-2311. *E-mail:* admissions@liberty.edu.

Longwood University

Farmville, Virginia

http://www.longwood.edu/

- **State-supported** comprehensive, founded 1839
- **Small-town** 60-acre campus with easy access to Richmond
- **Endowment** $59.1 million
- **Coed** 3,859 undergraduate students, 89% full-time, 68% women, 32% men
- **Moderately difficult** entrance level, 74% of applicants were admitted

UNDERGRAD STUDENTS
3,439 full-time, 420 part-time. 1% are from out of state; 10% Black or African American, non-Hispanic/Latino; 6% Hispanic/Latino; 0.9% Asian, non-Hispanic/Latino; 0.1% Native Hawaiian or other Pacific Islander, non-Hispanic/Latino; 0.2% American Indian or Alaska Native, non-Hispanic/Latino; 5% Two or more races, non-Hispanic/Latino; 2% Race/ethnicity unknown; 1% international; 4% transferred in; 59% live on campus.

Freshmen:
Admission: 5,374 applied, 3,984 admitted, 799 enrolled. ***Average high school GPA:*** 3.5. ***Test scores:*** SAT evidence-based reading and writing

scores over 500: 73%; SAT math scores over 500: 62%; ACT scores over 18: 73%; SAT evidence-based reading and writing scores over 600: 23%; SAT math scores over 600: 11%; ACT scores over 24: 25%; SAT evidence-based reading and writing scores over 700: 2%; ACT scores over 30: 3%.

Retention: 76% of full-time freshmen returned.

FACULTY

Total: 355, 74% full-time, 79% with terminal degrees.

Student/faculty ratio: 13:1.

ACADEMICS

Calendar: semesters. *Degrees:* bachelor's, master's, post-master's, and postbachelor's certificates.

Special study options: accelerated degree program, distance learning, double majors, English as a second language, honors programs, independent study, internships, off-campus study, services for LD students, study abroad, summer session for credit. ***ROTC:*** Army (b).

Unusual degree programs: 3-2 engineering with University of Virginia, Old Dominion University, Virginia Polytechnic Institute and State University.

Computers: 291 computers/terminals and 701 ports are available on campus for general student use. Students can access the following: campus intranet, computer help desk, free student e-mail accounts, online (class) grades, online (class) schedules. Campuswide network is available. 100% of college-owned or -operated housing units are wired for high-speed Internet access. Wireless service is available via entire campus.

Library: The Janet D. Greenwood Library. *Books:* 216,525 (physical), 333,909 (digital/electronic); *Serial titles:* 2,667 (physical), 403 (digital/electronic); *Databases:* 295. Weekly public service hours: 93.

STUDENT LIFE

Housing options: on-campus residence required through sophomore year; coed, women-only, special housing for students with disabilities. Campus housing is university owned. Freshman campus housing is guaranteed.

Activities and organizations: drama/theater group, student-run newspaper, radio station, choral group, Alpha Lambda Delta, Student Nursing Association, Longwood University, Bare Naked Ladies, Chi Alpha, Sigma Alpha Pi, national fraternities, national sororities.

Athletics Member NCAA. All Division I. ***Intercollegiate sports:*** baseball M(s), basketball M(s)/W(s), cross-country running M(s)/W(s), field hockey W(s), football M(c), golf M(s)/W(s), lacrosse W(s), soccer M(s)/W(s), softball W(s), tennis M(s)/W(s). ***Intramural sports:*** baseball M(c), basketball M(c)/W(c), cheerleading M/W, equestrian sports M(c)/W(c), field hockey M(c)/W(c), football M/W, golf M/W, lacrosse M(c)/W(c), racquetball M/W, rock climbing M/W, rugby W(c), sand volleyball M/W, soccer M(c)/W(c), softball M/W(c), swimming and diving M(c)/W(c), table tennis M/W, tennis M/W, ultimate Frisbee M/W, volleyball M/W, weight lifting M/W, wrestling M(c).

Campus security: 24-hour emergency response devices and patrols, late-night transport/escort service, controlled dormitory access.

Student services: health clinic, personal/psychological counseling.

COSTS & FINANCIAL AID

Costs (2019–20) ***Tuition:*** state resident $7940 full-time, $273 per credit hour part-time; nonresident $23,900 full-time, $805 per credit hour part-time. Full-time tuition and fees vary according to course load and program. Part-time tuition and fees vary according to course load and program. ***Required fees:*** $5580 full-time, $186 per credit hour part-time, $186 per credit hour part-time. ***Room and board:*** $11,668; room only: $7762. Room and board charges vary according to board plan, housing facility, and location. ***Payment plan:*** installment. ***Waivers:*** senior citizens and employees or children of employees.

Financial Aid Of all full-time matriculated undergraduates who enrolled in 2018, 2,945 applied for aid, 2,343 were judged to have need, 235 had their need fully met. In 2018, 450 non-need-based awards were made. ***Average percent of need met:*** 74. ***Average financial aid package:*** $11,422. ***Average need-based loan:*** $4203. ***Average need-based gift aid:*** $6476. ***Average non-need-based aid:*** $4242. ***Average indebtedness upon graduation:*** $30,133.

APPLYING

Standardized Tests *Required:* SAT or ACT (for admission).

Options: electronic application, early decision, early action, deferred entrance.

Application fee: $50.

Required: essay or personal statement, high school transcript. ***Recommended:*** 3 letters of recommendation.

Application deadlines: 3/1 (freshmen), 3/1 (transfers), 12/3 (early action).

Early decision deadline: 11/1.

Notification: 6/1 (freshmen), continuous until 6/1 (transfers).

CONTACT

Mr. Jason Faulk, Dean of Admissions, Longwood University, 201 High Street, Farmville, VA 23909. *Phone:* 434-395-2809. *Toll-free phone:* 800-281-4677. *Fax:* 434-395-2332. *E-mail:* faulkjc@longwood.edu.

Mary Baldwin University

Staunton, Virginia

http://www.marybaldwin.edu/

- **Independent** comprehensive, founded 1842
- **Small-town** 59-acre campus
- **Endowment** $35.1 million
- **Coed, primarily women**
- **Moderately difficult** entrance level

FACULTY

Student/faculty ratio: 9:1.

ACADEMICS

Calendar: 4-1-4. *Degrees:* certificates, bachelor's, master's, doctoral, and postbachelor's certificates.

Library: Grafton Library. *Books:* 104,405 (physical), 367,524 (digital/electronic); *Serial titles:* 348 (physical), 31,879 (digital/electronic); *Databases:* 76. Weekly public service hours: 92; students can reserve study rooms.

STUDENT LIFE

Housing options: on-campus residence required through senior year; coed, women-only. Campus housing is university owned. Freshman campus housing is guaranteed.

Activities and organizations: drama/theater group, choral group, marching band, Minority Clubs United, Greater Things Dance Ministry, MBU Cheer, Ladies of Elegance, Math Club.

Athletics Member NCAA. All Division III.

Campus security: 24-hour emergency response devices and patrols, late-night transport/escort service, controlled dormitory access.

Student services: health clinic, personal/psychological counseling.

FINANCIAL AID

Financial Aid Of all full-time matriculated undergraduates who enrolled in 2018, 924 applied for aid, 855 were judged to have need, 73 had their need fully met. 226 Federal Work-Study jobs (averaging $1300). 84 state and other part-time jobs (averaging $1389). In 2018, 69 non-need-based awards were made. ***Average percent of need met:*** 91. ***Average financial aid package:*** $27,093. ***Average need-based loan:*** $4069. ***Average need-based gift aid:*** $23,495. ***Average non-need-based aid:*** $17,317. ***Average indebtedness upon graduation:*** $37,097.

APPLYING

Standardized Tests *Required:* SAT or ACT (for admission).

Options: electronic application, early admission, deferred entrance.

Required: high school transcript. ***Required for some:*** essay or personal statement, 1 letter of recommendation, interview. ***Recommended:*** 1 letter of recommendation.

CONTACT

Mr. Matthew Munsey, Director of Admissions, Mary Baldwin University, Frederick and New Streets, Staunton, VA 24401. *Phone:* 540-887-7211. *Toll-free phone:* 800-468-2262. *Fax:* 540-887-7292. *E-mail:* mmunsey@marybaldwin.edu.

Marymount University

Arlington, Virginia

http://www.marymount.edu/

- **Independent** comprehensive, founded 1950, affiliated with Roman Catholic Church
- **Suburban** 21-acre campus with easy access to Washington, DC
- **Endowment** $46.9 million
- **Coed** 2,158 undergraduate students, 90% full-time, 65% women, 35% men
- **Moderately difficult** entrance level, 81% of applicants were admitted

UNDERGRAD STUDENTS

1,951 full-time, 207 part-time. Students come from 40 states and territories; 72 other countries; 38% are from out of state; 16% Black or African American, non-Hispanic/Latino; 22% Hispanic/Latino; 8% Asian, non-Hispanic/Latino; 0.2% Native Hawaiian or other Pacific Islander, non-Hispanic/Latino; 0.2% American Indian or Alaska Native, non-Hispanic/Latino; 3% Two or more races, non-Hispanic/Latino; 4% Race/ethnicity unknown; 16% international; 10% transferred in; 31% live on campus.

Freshmen:

Admission: 3,315 applied, 2,684 admitted, 392 enrolled. ***Average high school GPA:*** 3.3. ***Test scores:*** SAT evidence-based reading and writing scores over 500: 68%; SAT math scores over 500: 64%; ACT scores over 18: 62%; SAT evidence-based reading and writing scores over 600: 26%; SAT math scores over 600: 23%; ACT scores over 24: 28%; SAT evidence-based reading and writing scores over 700: 5%; SAT math scores over 700: 1%; ACT scores over 30: 6%.

Retention: 72% of full-time freshmen returned.

FACULTY

Total: 347, 48% full-time, 62% with terminal degrees.

Student/faculty ratio: 12:1.

ACADEMICS

Calendar: semesters plus 2 summer terms. *Degrees:* certificates, bachelor's, master's, doctoral, post-master's, and postbachelor's certificates.

Special study options: academic remediation for entering students, accelerated degree program, advanced placement credit, distance learning, double majors, honors programs, independent study, internships, off-campus study, part-time degree program, services for LD students, student-designed majors, study abroad, summer session for credit. ***ROTC:*** Army (c), Air Force (c).

Unusual degree programs: 3-2 business administration; information technology, health sciences.

Computers: 270 computers/terminals are available on campus for general student use. Students can access the following: campus intranet, computer help desk, free student e-mail accounts, online (class) grades, online (class) registration, online (class) schedules, Online drive space. Campuswide network is available. 100% of college-owned or -operated housing units are wired for high-speed Internet access. Wireless service is available via entire campus.

Library: Emerson C. Reinsch Library plus 1 other. Weekly public service hours: 104; students can reserve study rooms.

STUDENT LIFE

Housing options: on-campus residence required through sophomore year; coed, women-only, special housing for students with disabilities. Campus housing is university owned. Freshman applicants given priority for college housing.

Activities and organizations: drama/theater group, student-run newspaper, choral group, Fashion Club, Student Nurses Association, International Club, Blue Crew (spirit), Marymount Actors Guild.

Athletics Member NCAA. All Division III. ***Intercollegiate sports:*** baseball M, basketball M/W, cheerleading W(c), cross-country running M/W, golf M/W, lacrosse M/W, soccer M/W, swimming and diving M/W, tennis M/W, triathlon M(c)/W(c), volleyball M/W. ***Intramural sports:*** basketball M/W, soccer M/W, ultimate Frisbee M/W, volleyball M/W, water polo M/W.

Campus security: 24-hour emergency response devices and patrols, student patrols, late-night transport/escort service, controlled dormitory access.

Student services: health clinic, personal/psychological counseling, veterans affairs office.

COSTS & FINANCIAL AID

Costs (2020–21) ***One-time required fee:*** $490. ***Comprehensive fee:*** $48,350 includes full-time tuition ($33,200), mandatory fees ($750), and room and board ($14,400). Part-time tuition: $1090 per credit hour. ***Required fees:*** $22 per credit hour part-time. ***Room and board:*** Room and board charges vary according to board plan and housing facility. ***Payment plan:*** installment. ***Waivers:*** senior citizens and employees or children of employees.

Financial Aid Of all full-time matriculated undergraduates who enrolled in 2019, 1,342 applied for aid, 1,219 were judged to have need, 196 had their need fully met. 872 Federal Work-Study jobs (averaging $1934). In 2019, 465 non-need-based awards were made. ***Average percent of need met:*** 64. ***Average financial aid package:*** $25,938. ***Average need-based loan:*** $4374. ***Average need-based gift aid:*** $7382. ***Average non-need-based aid:*** $14,687. ***Average indebtedness upon graduation:*** $33,682.

APPLYING

Standardized Tests *Required for some:* SAT or ACT (for admission).

Options: electronic application, early action, deferred entrance.

Application fee: $40.

Required: high school transcript, minimum 2.6 GPA, 1 letter of recommendation. ***Required for some:*** essay or personal statement, interview. ***Recommended:*** essay or personal statement.

Application deadlines: rolling (freshmen), rolling (transfers), 11/15 (early action).

Notification: continuous (freshmen), continuous (transfers), 12/14 (early action).

CONTACT

Undergraduate Admissions, Marymount University, 2807 North Glebe Road, Arlington, VA 22207. *Phone:* 703-284-1500. *Toll-free phone:* 800-548-7638. *Fax:* 703-522-0349. *E-mail:* admissions@marymount.edu.

Norfolk State University

Norfolk, Virginia

http://www.nsu.edu/

- **State-supported** comprehensive, founded 1935, part of State Council of Higher Education for Virginia
- **Urban** 134-acre campus
- **Coed**
- **Moderately difficult** entrance level

ACADEMICS

Calendar: semesters. *Degrees:* associate, bachelor's, master's, and doctoral.

Library: Lymon Beecher Brooks Library.

STUDENT LIFE

Housing options: men-only, women-only. Campus housing is university owned.

Athletics Member NCAA. All Division I.

Campus security: 24-hour emergency response devices and patrols, late-night transport/escort service.

FINANCIAL AID

Financial Aid ***Financial aid deadline:*** 5/31.

APPLYING

Standardized Tests *Required:* SAT or ACT (for admission).

Options: electronic application, deferred entrance.

Required: high school transcript, minimum 2.3 GPA.

CONTACT

Mr. Kevin M. Holmes, Director of Recruitment and Admissions, Norfolk State University, 700 Park Avenue, Norfolk, VA 23504. *Phone:* 757-823-9222. *Toll-free phone:* 800-274-1821. *Fax:* 757-823-2078. *E-mail:* admissions@nsu.edu.

Old Dominion University

Norfolk, Virginia

http://www.odu.edu/

- **State-supported** university, founded 1930
- **Urban** 251-acre campus with easy access to Virginia Beach
- **Endowment** $267.1 million
- **Coed** 19,176 undergraduate students, 77% full-time, 55% women, 45% men
- **Moderately difficult** entrance level, 89% of applicants were admitted

UNDERGRAD STUDENTS

14,702 full-time, 4,474 part-time. Students come from 50 states and territories; 62 other countries; 8% are from out of state; 32% Black or African American, non-Hispanic/Latino; 9% Hispanic/Latino; 5% Asian, non-Hispanic/Latino; 0.2% Native Hawaiian or other Pacific Islander, non-Hispanic/Latino; 0.2% American Indian or Alaska Native, non-Hispanic/Latino; 7% Two or more races, non-Hispanic/Latino; 2% Race/ethnicity unknown; 1% international; 10% transferred in; 25% live on campus.

Freshmen:

Admission: 13,761 applied, 12,293 admitted, 3,145 enrolled. ***Average high school GPA:*** 3.3. ***Test scores:*** SAT evidence-based reading and writing scores over 500: 75%; SAT math scores over 500: 68%; ACT scores over 18: 78%; SAT evidence-based reading and writing scores over 600: 27%; SAT math scores over 600: 19%; ACT scores over 24: 25%; SAT evidence-based reading and writing scores over 700: 2%; SAT math scores over 700: 2%; ACT scores over 30: 3%.

Retention: 80% of full-time freshmen returned.

FACULTY

Total: 1,551, 56% full-time, 65% with terminal degrees.

Student/faculty ratio: 17:1.

ACADEMICS

Calendar: semesters. *Degrees:* certificates, bachelor's, master's, doctoral, post-master's, and postbachelor's certificates.

Special study options: accelerated degree program, adult/continuing education programs, advanced placement credit, cooperative education, distance learning, double majors, English as a second language, freshman honors college, honors programs, independent study, internships, off-campus study, part-time degree program, services for LD students, student-designed majors, study abroad, summer session for credit. ***ROTC:*** Army (b), Navy (b).

Unusual degree programs: 3-2 business administration; engineering; nursing; International Studies, Dental Hygiene, Communication/Humanities, Interdisciplinary Studies/Humanities, Women's Studies/Humanities, Computer Science, Philosophy/Humanities, Accounting, Math, Art History, Studio Arts, Fine Arts, Geography, Economics, P.

Computers: 1,662 computers/terminals and 14,236 ports are available on campus for general student use. Students can access the following: campus intranet, computer help desk, free student e-mail accounts, online (class) grades, online (class) registration, online (class) schedules, online courses. Campuswide network is available. 100% of college-owned or -operated housing units are wired for high-speed Internet access. Wireless service is available via entire campus.

Library: Patricia W. and Douglas Perry Library plus 3 others. *Books:* 1.2 million (physical), 1.4 million (digital/electronic); *Serial titles:* 16,705 (physical), 145,084 (digital/electronic); *Databases:* 488. Weekly public service hours: 146; study areas open 24 hours, 5–7 days a week; students can reserve study rooms.

STUDENT LIFE

Housing options: coed, women-only, special housing for students with disabilities. Campus housing is university owned. Freshman campus housing is guaranteed.

Activities and organizations: drama/theater group, student-run newspaper, radio station, choral group, marching band, Asian Pacific American Student Union, Student Government Association, Student Veterans Association, Colleges Against Cancer, Student Activities Council, national fraternities, national sororities.

Athletics Member NCAA. All Division I. ***Intercollegiate sports:*** baseball M(s), basketball M(s)/W(s), cheerleading M(s)/W(s), crew M(c)/W(s), equestrian sports M(c)/W(c), field hockey W(s), football M(s), golf M(s)/W(s), ice hockey M(c)/W(c), lacrosse M(c)/W(s), rugby M(c)/W(c), sailing M/W, soccer M(s)/W(s), softball W(c), swimming and diving M(s)/W(s), tennis M(s)/W(s), volleyball M(c)/W(s), wrestling M(s). ***Intramural sports:*** badminton M/W, basketball M/W, golf M/W, racquetball M/W, soccer M/W, softball M/W, table tennis M/W, ultimate Frisbee M/W, volleyball M/W.

Campus security: 24-hour emergency response devices and patrols, student patrols, late-night transport/escort service, controlled dormitory access.

Student services: health clinic, personal/psychological counseling, women's center, veterans affairs office.

COSTS & FINANCIAL AID

Costs (2019–20) ***Tuition:*** state resident $10,680 full-time, $356 per credit hour part-time; nonresident $30,840 full-time, $1028 per credit hour part-time. Full-time tuition and fees vary according to location. Part-time tuition and fees vary according to location. ***Required fees:*** $340 full-time, $70 per term part-time. ***Room and board:*** $12,836; room only: $7538. Room and board charges vary according to board plan, housing facility, location, and student level. ***Payment plans:*** installment, deferred payment. ***Waivers:*** senior citizens and employees or children of employees.

Financial Aid Of all full-time matriculated undergraduates who enrolled in 2019, 11,796 applied for aid, 9,932 were judged to have need, 1,283 had their need fully met. In 2019, 1061 non-need-based awards were made. ***Average percent of need met:*** 44. ***Average financial aid package:*** $11,108. ***Average need-based loan:*** $4206. ***Average need-based gift aid:*** $7747. ***Average non-need-based aid:*** $5392. ***Average indebtedness upon graduation:*** $31,142. ***Financial aid deadline:*** 3/15.

APPLYING

Standardized Tests *Required for some:* SAT or ACT (for admission).

Options: electronic application, early admission, early action, deferred entrance.

Application fee: $50.

Required: high school transcript, minimum 2.7 GPA. ***Required for some:*** test scores. ***Recommended:*** essay or personal statement, 1 letter of recommendation.

Application deadlines: 2/1 (freshmen), 5/1 (transfers), 12/1 (early action).

Notification: continuous (freshmen), continuous (transfers), 1/15 (early action).

CONTACT

Ms. Shereen Williams, Customer Service Manager, Admissions Office, Old Dominion University, 108 Rollins Hall, 5215 Hampton Boulevard, Norfolk, VA 23529. *Phone:* 757-683-3648. *Toll-free phone:* 800-348-7926. *Fax:* 757-683-3255. *E-mail:* admissions@odu.edu.

Patrick Henry College

Purcellville, Virginia

http://www.phc.edu/

- **Independent nondenominational** 4-year, founded 2000
- **Small-town** 119-acre campus with easy access to Washington, DC
- **Endowment** $1.7 million
- **Coed** 311 undergraduate students, 84% full-time, 49% women, 51% men
- **Moderately difficult** entrance level, 86% of applicants were admitted

UNDERGRAD STUDENTS

260 full-time, 51 part-time. Students come from 39 states and territories; 83% are from out of state; 0.6% Black or African American, non-Hispanic/Latino; 5% Hispanic/Latino; 4% Asian, non-Hispanic/Latino; 0.6% Native Hawaiian or other Pacific Islander, non-Hispanic/Latino; 23% Race/ethnicity unknown; 0.3% transferred in; 79% live on campus.

Freshmen:

Admission: 125 applied, 107 admitted, 73 enrolled. ***Average high school GPA:*** 3.9. ***Test scores:*** SAT evidence-based reading and writing scores over 500: 98%; SAT math scores over 500: 94%; ACT scores over 18: 100%; SAT evidence-based reading and writing scores over 600: 93%; SAT math scores over 600: 54%; ACT scores over 24: 100%; SAT

evidence-based reading and writing scores over 700: 49%; SAT math scores over 700: 19%; ACT scores over 30: 50%.

Retention: 90% of full-time freshmen returned.

FACULTY

Total: 42, 43% full-time, 62% with terminal degrees.

Student/faculty ratio: 11:1.

ACADEMICS

Calendar: semesters. *Degree:* bachelor's.

Special study options: accelerated degree program, advanced placement credit, cooperative education, distance learning, double majors, independent study, internships, off-campus study, study abroad, summer session for credit.

Computers: 10 computers/terminals and 100 ports are available on campus for general student use. Students can access the following: campus intranet, computer help desk, free student e-mail accounts, online (class) grades, online (class) registration, online (class) schedules. Campuswide network is available. 100% of college-owned or -operated housing units are wired for high-speed Internet access. Wireless service is available via entire campus.

Library: Patrick Henry College Library. *Books:* 34,177 (physical), 254,740 (digital/electronic); *Serial titles:* 471 (physical), 17,617 (digital/electronic); *Databases:* 15. Weekly public service hours: 75; students can reserve study rooms.

STUDENT LIFE

Housing options: on-campus residence required through sophomore year; men-only, women-only. Campus housing is university owned. Freshman applicants given priority for college housing.

Activities and organizations: drama/theater group, student-run newspaper, choral group, Drama Club, Eden Troupe, Student Government, Chorale, College Republicans, Debate/Moot Court.

Athletics ***Intercollegiate sports:*** baseball M, basketball M/W, soccer M/W. ***Intramural sports:*** baseball M, basketball M/W, fencing M(c)/W(c), football M(c)/W(c), racquetball M(c)/W(c), riflery M(c), sand volleyball M(c)/W(c), soccer M/W, table tennis M(c)/W(c), tennis M/W, ultimate Frisbee M/W, volleyball M/W.

Campus security: 24-hour emergency response devices, student patrols, late-night transport/escort service, controlled dormitory access, After hours patrols by trained security personnel.

Student services: personal/psychological counseling.

COSTS & FINANCIAL AID

Costs (2020–21) ***Comprehensive fee:*** $39,420 includes full-time tuition ($28,400) and room and board ($11,020). Full-time tuition and fees vary according to course load and location. Part-time tuition: $1184 per credit hour. Part-time tuition and fees vary according to course load and location. ***College room only:*** $5000. Room and board charges vary according to board plan, housing facility, and location. ***Payment plans:*** installment, deferred payment. ***Waivers:*** employees or children of employees.

Financial Aid Of all full-time matriculated undergraduates who enrolled in 2019, 67 applied for aid, 60 were judged to have need, 15 had their need fully met. In 2019, 184 non-need-based awards were made. ***Average percent of need met:*** 58. ***Average financial aid package:*** $15,461. ***Average need-based gift aid:*** $5766. ***Average non-need-based aid:*** $14,010. ***Average indebtedness upon graduation:*** $50,668. ***Financial aid deadline:*** 3/1.

APPLYING

Standardized Tests *Required:* SAT or ACT (for admission).

Options: electronic application, deferred entrance.

Application fee: $40.

Required: essay or personal statement, high school transcript, interview, official transcripts from all colleges attended. ***Required for some:*** 2 letters of recommendation.

Application deadlines: 7/15 (freshmen), 7/15 (out-of-state freshmen), 7/15 (transfers).

Notification: continuous until 7/15 (freshmen), continuous until 7/15 (out-of-state freshmen), continuous until 7/15 (transfers).

CONTACT

Mr. Stephen Pierce, Director of Student Recruitment, Patrick Henry College, 10 Patrick Henry Circle, Purcellville, VA 20132. *Phone:* 540-441-8110. *Toll-free phone:* 888-338-1776. *Fax:* 540-441-8119. *E-mail:* admission@phc.edu.

Radford University

Radford, Virginia

http://www.radford.edu/

- **State-supported** university, founded 1910
- **Small-town** 204-acre campus
- **Endowment** $56.7 million
- **Coed** 7,967 undergraduate students, 94% full-time, 61% women, 39% men
- **Minimally difficult** entrance level, 75% of applicants were admitted

UNDERGRAD STUDENTS

7,494 full-time, 473 part-time. Students come from 40 states and territories; 54 other countries; 7% are from out of state; 17% Black or African American, non-Hispanic/Latino; 7% Hispanic/Latino; 2% Asian, non-Hispanic/Latino; 0.1% Native Hawaiian or other Pacific Islander, non-Hispanic/Latino; 0.3% American Indian or Alaska Native, non-Hispanic/Latino; 6% Two or more races, non-Hispanic/Latino; 3% Race/ethnicity unknown; 0.8% international; 8% transferred in; 46% live on campus.

Freshmen:

Admission: 16,013 applied, 12,061 admitted, 1,651 enrolled. ***Average high school GPA:*** 3.3. ***Test scores:*** SAT evidence-based reading and writing scores over 500: 67%; SAT math scores over 500: 56%; ACT scores over 18: 72%; SAT evidence-based reading and writing scores over 600: 17%; SAT math scores over 600: 8%; ACT scores over 24: 22%; SAT evidence-based reading and writing scores over 700: 1%; ACT scores over 30: 3%.

Retention: 71% of full-time freshmen returned.

FACULTY

Total: 873, 61% full-time, 59% with terminal degrees.

Student/faculty ratio: 15:1.

ACADEMICS

Calendar: semesters. *Degrees:* certificates, bachelor's, master's, doctoral, post-master's, and postbachelor's certificates.

Special study options: accelerated degree program, advanced placement credit, distance learning, double majors, English as a second language, freshman honors college, honors programs, independent study, internships, off-campus study, part-time degree program, services for LD students, student-designed majors, study abroad, summer session for credit. ***ROTC:*** Army (b).

Computers: 900 computers/terminals are available on campus for general student use. Students can access the following: campus intranet, computer help desk, free student e-mail accounts, online (class) grades, online (class) registration, online (class) schedules, online financial aid status and student accounts payable. Campuswide network is available. 100% of college-owned or -operated housing units are wired for high-speed Internet access. Wireless service is available via entire campus.

Library: McConnell Library. *Books:* 254,680 (physical), 603,676 (digital/electronic); *Serial titles:* 414 (physical), 25,185 (digital/electronic); *Databases:* 481. Students can reserve study rooms.

STUDENT LIFE

Housing options: on-campus residence required through sophomore year; coed, special housing for students with disabilities. Campus housing is university owned. Freshman campus housing is guaranteed.

Activities and organizations: drama/theater group, student-run newspaper, radio station, choral group, Radford Crafty, American Sign Language Club, Radford Student Programming and Campus Events (R-SPaCE), National Society for Collegiate Scholars, Scholar-Citizen Initiative Student Organization, national fraternities, national sororities.

Athletics Member NCAA. All Division I. ***Intercollegiate sports:*** baseball M(s), basketball M(s)/W(s), cross-country running M(s)/W(s), golf M(s)/W(s)(c), lacrosse W(s), soccer M(s)/W(s), softball W(s), tennis M(s)/W(s), track and field W(s), volleyball W(s). ***Intramural sports:*** archery M(c)/W(c), basketball M/W, bowling M(c)/W(c), cheerleading

M(c)/W(c), cross-country running M/W, equestrian sports M(c)/W(c), field hockey W(c), football M/W, ice hockey M(c)/W(c), lacrosse M(c)/W(c), riflery M(c)/W(c), rugby M(c)/W(c), skiing (downhill) M(c)/W(c), soccer M(c)/W(c), softball M/W, swimming and diving M(c)/W(c), table tennis M/W, tennis M/W, ultimate Frisbee M/W, volleyball M/W, wrestling M(c)/W(c).

Campus security: 24-hour emergency response devices and patrols, late-night transport/escort service, controlled dormitory access.

Student services: health clinic, personal/psychological counseling, veterans affairs office.

COSTS & FINANCIAL AID

Costs (2019–20) ***Tuition:*** state resident $7922 full-time, $329 per credit hour part-time; nonresident $19,557 full-time, $814 per credit hour part-time. Full-time tuition and fees vary according to course load, location, and program. Part-time tuition and fees vary according to course load, location, and program. ***Required fees:*** $3428 full-time, $143 per credit hour part-time. ***Room and board:*** $9637; room only: $5281. Room and board charges vary according to board plan, housing facility, and location. ***Payment plan:*** installment. ***Waivers:*** senior citizens and employees or children of employees.

Financial Aid Of all full-time matriculated undergraduates who enrolled in 2019, 6,295 applied for aid, 5,154 were judged to have need, 663 had their need fully met. 502 Federal Work-Study jobs (averaging $2071). 284 state and other part-time jobs (averaging $2027). In 2019, 517 non-need-based awards were made. ***Average percent of need met:*** 76. ***Average financial aid package:*** $11,147. ***Average need-based loan:*** $4201. ***Average need-based gift aid:*** $8551. ***Average non-need-based aid:*** $3538. ***Average indebtedness upon graduation:*** $32,261.

APPLYING

Standardized Tests *Recommended:* SAT or ACT (for admission).

Options: electronic application, early admission, early action, deferred entrance.

Required: high school transcript.

Application deadlines: 2/1 (freshmen), 6/1 (transfers), 12/1 (early action).

Notification: 4/1 (freshmen), continuous (transfers), 1/15 (early action).

CONTACT

Ms. Rebekah LePlante, Senior Associate Director, Radford University, PO Box 6903, Radford, VA 24142. *Phone:* 540-831-5371. *Fax:* 540-831-5038. *E-mail:* admissions@radford.edu.

Randolph College

Lynchburg, Virginia

http://www.randolphcollege.edu/

- **Independent Methodist** comprehensive, founded 1891
- **Suburban** 100-acre campus
- **Coed** 565 undergraduate students, 96% full-time, 62% women, 39% men
- **Moderately difficult** entrance level, 98% of applicants were admitted

UNDERGRAD STUDENTS

545 full-time, 20 part-time. 21% are from out of state; 16% Black or African American, non-Hispanic/Latino; 8% Hispanic/Latino; 3% Asian, non-Hispanic/Latino; 0.5% Native Hawaiian or other Pacific Islander, non-Hispanic/Latino; 0.7% American Indian or Alaska Native, non-Hispanic/Latino; 7% Two or more races, non-Hispanic/Latino; 1% Race/ethnicity unknown; 3% international; 4% transferred in; 77% live on campus.

Freshmen:

Admission: 1,077 applied, 1,054 admitted, 143 enrolled. ***Average high school GPA:*** 3.6. ***Test scores:*** SAT evidence-based reading and writing scores over 500: 75%; SAT math scores over 500: 69%; ACT scores over 18: 82%; SAT evidence-based reading and writing scores over 600: 28%; SAT math scores over 600: 19%; ACT scores over 24: 32%; SAT evidence-based reading and writing scores over 700: 4%; SAT math scores over 700: 2%.

Retention: 68% of full-time freshmen returned.

FACULTY

Total: 69, 100% full-time, 96% with terminal degrees.

Student/faculty ratio: 8:1.

ACADEMICS

Calendar: semesters. *Degrees:* bachelor's and master's.

Special study options: adult/continuing education programs, part-time degree program.

Computers: Students can access the following: campus intranet, computer help desk, free student e-mail accounts, online (class) grades, online (class) registration, online (class) schedules. Campuswide network is available. Wireless service is available via entire campus.

Library: Lipscomb Library.

STUDENT LIFE

Housing options: on-campus residence required through senior year; coed. Campus housing is university owned. Freshman campus housing is guaranteed.

Athletics Member NCAA. All Division III. ***Intercollegiate sports:*** basketball M/W, cross-country running M/W, equestrian sports M/W, lacrosse M/W, soccer M/W, softball W, tennis M/W, volleyball W.

Campus security: 24-hour emergency response devices and patrols, late-night transport/escort service.

COSTS & FINANCIAL AID

Costs (2020–21) ***Comprehensive fee:*** $36,610 includes full-time tuition ($25,000), mandatory fees ($610), and room and board ($11,000). Part-time tuition: $1688 per credit hour.

Financial Aid Of all full-time matriculated undergraduates who enrolled in 2019, 480 applied for aid, 445 were judged to have need, 96 had their need fully met. In 2019, 94 non-need-based awards were made. ***Average percent of need met:*** 78. ***Average financial aid package:*** $35,737. ***Average need-based loan:*** $5244. ***Average need-based gift aid:*** $31,680. ***Average non-need-based aid:*** $26,035. ***Average indebtedness upon graduation:*** $42,569.

APPLYING

Standardized Tests *Required:* SAT or ACT (for admission).

Options: electronic application, early action, deferred entrance.

Required: essay or personal statement, high school transcript, 2 letters of recommendation. ***Recommended:*** interview.

Notification: rolling (early action).

CONTACT

Michael Quinn, Randolph College, 2500 Rivermont Avenue, Lynchburg, VA 24503-1555. *Phone:* 434-947-8100. *Toll-free phone:* 800-745-7692. *Fax:* 434-947-8996. *E-mail:* admissions@randolphcollege.edu.

Randolph-Macon College

Ashland, Virginia

http://www.rmc.edu/

- **Independent United Methodist** 4-year, founded 1830
- **Suburban** 124-acre campus with easy access to Richmond
- **Endowment** $168.8 million
- **Coed** 1,543 undergraduate students, 99% full-time, 53% women, 47% men
- **Moderately difficult** entrance level, 71% of applicants were admitted

UNDERGRAD STUDENTS

1,520 full-time, 23 part-time. Students come from 27 states and territories; 26 other countries; 22% are from out of state; 10% Black or African American, non-Hispanic/Latino; 4% Hispanic/Latino; 1% Asian, non-Hispanic/Latino; 0.2% Native Hawaiian or other Pacific Islander, non-Hispanic/Latino; 0.3% American Indian or Alaska Native, non-Hispanic/Latino; 5% Two or more races, non-Hispanic/Latino; 1% Race/ethnicity unknown; 2% international; 3% transferred in; 80% live on campus.

Freshmen:

Admission: 2,460 applied, 1,744 admitted, 432 enrolled. ***Average high school GPA:*** 3.7. ***Test scores:*** SAT evidence-based reading and writing scores over 500: 91%; SAT math scores over 500: 85%; ACT scores over 18: 93%; SAT evidence-based reading and writing scores over 600: 44%; SAT math scores over 600: 29%; ACT scores over 24: 52%; SAT evidence-based reading and writing scores over 700: 5%; SAT math scores over 700: 4%; ACT scores over 30: 8%.

Retention: 84% of full-time freshmen returned.

FACULTY
Total: 180, 63% full-time, 76% with terminal degrees.
Student/faculty ratio: 11:1.

ACADEMICS
Calendar: 4-1-4. *Degree:* bachelor's.
Special study options: academic remediation for entering students, accelerated degree program, advanced placement credit, double majors, honors programs, independent study, internships, off-campus study, part-time degree program, services for LD students, study abroad, summer session for credit. ***ROTC:*** Army (c).
Unusual degree programs: 3-2 business administration; engineering with University of Virginia; forestry with Duke University; accounting with Virginia Commonwealth University, BS/MD with Eastern VA Medical School.
Computers: Students can access the following: campus intranet, computer help desk, free student e-mail accounts, online (class) registration, online (class) schedules. Campuswide network is available. 100% of college-owned or -operated housing units are wired for high-speed Internet access. Wireless service is available via entire campus.
Library: McGraw-Page Library. *Books:* 132,434 (physical), 459,977 (digital/electronic); *Serial titles:* 409 (physical), 171,572 (digital/electronic); *Databases:* 177. Study areas open 24 hours, 5–7 days a week; students can reserve study rooms.

STUDENT LIFE
Housing options: on-campus residence required through junior year; coed, men-only, women-only, special housing for students with disabilities. Campus housing is university owned. Freshman campus housing is guaranteed.
Activities and organizations: drama/theater group, student-run newspaper, radio and television station, choral group, marching band, Habitat for Humanity, Macon Outdoors, Relay for Life, College Panhellenic Council, national fraternities, national sororities.
Athletics Member NCAA. All Division III. ***Intercollegiate sports:*** baseball M, basketball M/W, cheerleading M(c)/W(c), equestrian sports M(c)/W(c), field hockey W, football M, golf M/W, lacrosse M/W, soccer M/W, softball W, swimming and diving M/W, tennis M/W, volleyball M/W. ***Intramural sports:*** badminton M/W, basketball M/W, cross-country running M(c)/W(c), football M/W, lacrosse M/W, racquetball M/W, rugby M/W, soccer M/W, softball M/W, table tennis M/W, tennis M/W, ultimate Frisbee M/W, volleyball M/W.
Campus security: 24-hour emergency response devices and patrols, late-night transport/escort service, controlled dormitory access.
Student services: health clinic, personal/psychological counseling, women's center.

COSTS & FINANCIAL AID
Costs (2020–21) ***One-time required fee:*** $100. ***Comprehensive fee:*** $56,620 includes full-time tuition ($42,490), mandatory fees ($1450), and room and board ($12,680). Full-time tuition and fees vary according to course load. Part-time tuition: $4720 per course. Part-time tuition and fees vary according to course load. ***Required fees:*** $150 per term part-time. ***College room only:*** $7000. Room and board charges vary according to board plan and housing facility. ***Payment plan:*** installment. ***Waivers:*** employees or children of employees.
Financial Aid Of all full-time matriculated undergraduates who enrolled in 2019, 1,310 applied for aid, 1,065 were judged to have need, 345 had their need fully met. In 2019, 437 non-need-based awards were made. ***Average percent of need met:*** 82. ***Average financial aid package:*** $31,700. ***Average need-based loan:*** $3904. ***Average need-based gift aid:*** $28,452. ***Average non-need-based aid:*** $22,777. ***Average indebtedness upon graduation:*** $22,206.

APPLYING
Standardized Tests *Required:* SAT or ACT (for admission).
Options: electronic application, early admission, early action, deferred entrance.
Required: essay or personal statement, high school transcript, minimum 2.0 GPA, 1 letter of recommendation. ***Recommended:*** interview.
Application deadlines: 3/1 (freshmen), 4/1 (transfers), 11/15 (early action).
Notification: 4/1 (freshmen), continuous until 5/1 (transfers).

CONTACT
Erin Slater, Director of Admissions, Randolph-Macon College, PO Box 5005, Ashland, VA 23005-5505. *Phone:* 804-752-7305. *Toll-free phone:* 800-888-1762. *Fax:* 804-752-4707. *E-mail:* admissions@rmc.edu.

Regent University

Virginia Beach, Virginia

http://www.regent.edu/

- **Independent Christian** comprehensive, founded 1977
- **Suburban** 70-acre campus
- **Coed** 4,413 undergraduate students, 54% full-time, 61% women, 39% men
- **Minimally difficult** entrance level, 86% of applicants were admitted

UNDERGRAD STUDENTS
2,380 full-time, 2,033 part-time. Students come from 50 states and territories; 19 other countries; 59% are from out of state; 27% Black or African American, non-Hispanic/Latino; 9% Hispanic/Latino; 2% Asian, non-Hispanic/Latino; 0.3% Native Hawaiian or other Pacific Islander, non-Hispanic/Latino; 0.4% American Indian or Alaska Native, non-Hispanic/Latino; 5% Two or more races, non-Hispanic/Latino; 2% Race/ethnicity unknown; 0.5% international; 19% transferred in; 16% live on campus.

Freshmen:
Admission: 2,344 applied, 2,005 admitted, 386 enrolled. ***Average high school GPA:*** 3.4. ***Test scores:*** SAT evidence-based reading and writing scores over 500: 83%; SAT math scores over 500: 67%; ACT scores over 18: 84%; SAT evidence-based reading and writing scores over 600: 38%; SAT math scores over 600: 24%; ACT scores over 24: 38%; SAT evidence-based reading and writing scores over 700: 8%; SAT math scores over 700: 3%; ACT scores over 30: 7%.
Retention: 78% of full-time freshmen returned.

FACULTY
Total: 785, 18% full-time, 68% with terminal degrees.
Student/faculty ratio: 19:1.

ACADEMICS
Calendar: trimesters. *Degrees:* certificates, associate, bachelor's, master's, doctoral, post-master's, and postbachelor's certificates.
Special study options: academic remediation for entering students, adult/continuing education programs, advanced placement credit, distance learning, double majors, external degree program, freshman honors college, honors programs, internships, off-campus study, part-time degree program, services for LD students, study abroad, summer session for credit. ***ROTC:*** Army (c), Navy (c).
Unusual degree programs: 3-2 business administration with Regent University; nursing with Regent University.
Computers: 70 computers/terminals and 75 ports are available on campus for general student use. Students can access the following: campus intranet, computer help desk, free student e-mail accounts, online (class) grades, online (class) registration, online (class) schedules. Campuswide network is available. 100% of college-owned or -operated housing units are wired for high-speed Internet access. Wireless service is available via entire campus.
Library: Regent University Library plus 1 other. *Books:* 306,180 (physical), 729,410 (digital/electronic); *Serial titles:* 51,444 (physical), 93,389 (digital/electronic); *Databases:* 419. Students can reserve study rooms.

STUDENT LIFE
Housing options: on-campus residence required for freshman year; men-only, women-only, special housing for students with disabilities. Campus housing is university owned. Freshman applicants given priority for college housing.
Activities and organizations: drama/theater group, student-run newspaper, choral group, College Student Leadership Board, Student Activities Board, Psychology Club, Student Alumni Ambassadors (SAA), Undergraduate Debate Association, national fraternities, national sororities.
Athletics Member NCCAA. ***Intercollegiate sports:*** basketball M/W, cheerleading W, cross-country running M/W, soccer M/W, track and field

M/W, volleyball W. ***Intramural sports:*** basketball M/W, soccer M/W, softball M/W, ultimate Frisbee M/W, volleyball M/W.

Campus security: 24-hour emergency response devices and patrols, student patrols, late-night transport/escort service, controlled dormitory access.

Student services: personal/psychological counseling, veterans affairs office.

COSTS & FINANCIAL AID

Costs (2020–21) ***Comprehensive fee:*** $27,340 includes full-time tuition ($18,720), mandatory fees ($1400), and room and board ($7220). Part-time tuition: $624 per credit hour. ***Required fees:*** $700 per term part-time. ***College room only:*** $4700. Room and board charges vary according to housing facility. ***Payment plan:*** installment. ***Waivers:*** employees or children of employees.

Financial Aid Of all full-time matriculated undergraduates who enrolled in 2019, 2,031 applied for aid, 1,808 were judged to have need, 185 had their need fully met. In 2019, 244 non-need-based awards were made. ***Average percent of need met:*** 60. ***Average financial aid package:*** $8704. ***Average need-based loan:*** $3913. ***Average need-based gift aid:*** $8141. ***Average non-need-based aid:*** $5929. ***Average indebtedness upon graduation:*** $32,982.

APPLYING

Standardized Tests *Required for some:* SAT or ACT (for admission).

Options: electronic application, deferred entrance.

Application fee: $50.

Required: high school transcript. ***Required for some:*** essay or personal statement, minimum 3.0 GPA.

Application deadlines: rolling (freshmen), rolling (out-of-state freshmen), 8/1 (transfers).

Notification: continuous (freshmen), continuous (out-of-state freshmen), continuous (transfers).

CONTACT

Mrs. Heidi Cece, Associate Vice President, Enrollment Management, Regent University, 1000 Regent University Drive, Virginia Beach, VA 23464. *Phone:* 800-373-5504. *Toll-free phone:* 800-373-5504. *Fax:* 757-352-4839. *E-mail:* admissions@regent.edu.

Roanoke College

Salem, Virginia

http://www.roanoke.edu/

- **Independent** 4-year, founded 1842, affiliated with Evangelical Lutheran Church in America
- **Suburban** 80-acre campus
- **Endowment** $129.2 million
- **Coed** 2,005 undergraduate students, 97% full-time, 58% women, 42% men
- **Moderately difficult** entrance level, 75% of applicants were admitted

UNDERGRAD STUDENTS

1,942 full-time, 63 part-time. Students come from 37 states and territories; 31 other countries; 45% are from out of state; 5% Black or African American, non-Hispanic/Latino; 5% Hispanic/Latino; 1% Asian, non-Hispanic/Latino; 0.1% Native Hawaiian or other Pacific Islander, non-Hispanic/Latino; 0.2% American Indian or Alaska Native, non-Hispanic/Latino; 4% Two or more races, non-Hispanic/Latino; 2% international; 3% transferred in; 79% live on campus.

Freshmen:

Admission: 5,453 applied, 4,079 admitted, 553 enrolled. ***Average high school GPA:*** 3.6. ***Test scores:*** SAT evidence-based reading and writing scores over 500: 92%; SAT math scores over 500: 84%; ACT scores over 18: 94%; SAT evidence-based reading and writing scores over 600: 47%; SAT math scores over 600: 35%; ACT scores over 24: 57%; SAT evidence-based reading and writing scores over 700: 7%; SAT math scores over 700: 6%; ACT scores over 30: 9%.

Retention: 78% of full-time freshmen returned.

FACULTY

Total: 210, 79% full-time, 77% with terminal degrees.

Student/faculty ratio: 11:1.

ACADEMICS

Calendar: semesters. *Degree:* bachelor's.

Special study options: accelerated degree program, adult/continuing education programs, advanced placement credit, distance learning, double majors, English as a second language, honors programs, independent study, internships, off-campus study, part-time degree program, services for LD students, study abroad, summer session for credit.

Unusual degree programs: 3-2 engineering with Virginia Polytechnic Institute and State University.

Computers: 228 computers/terminals and 1,600 ports are available on campus for general student use. Students can access the following: campus intranet, computer help desk, free student e-mail accounts, online (class) grades, online (class) registration, online (class) schedules, discounts on computer hardware and software purchases, free office software, free security software. Campuswide network is available. 100% of college-owned or -operated housing units are wired for high-speed Internet access. Wireless service is available via entire campus.

Library: Fintel Library. *Books:* 188,768 (physical), 246,675 (digital/electronic); *Serial titles:* 184 (physical), 115,657 (digital/electronic); *Databases:* 298. Weekly public service hours: 93; students can reserve study rooms.

STUDENT LIFE

Housing options: on-campus residence required through senior year; coed, men-only, women-only, special housing for students with disabilities. Campus housing is university owned. Freshman campus housing is guaranteed.

Activities and organizations: drama/theater group, student-run newspaper, radio station, choral group, Habitat for Humanity, Black Student Alliance, Board Game Alliance, Toys Like Me, Biology Club, national fraternities, national sororities.

Athletics Member NCAA. All Division III. ***Intercollegiate sports:*** baseball M, basketball M/W, cross-country running M/W, field hockey W, golf M, lacrosse M/W, soccer M/W, softball W, swimming and diving M/W, tennis M/W, track and field M/W, volleyball W. ***Intramural sports:*** badminton M/W, baseball M(c), basketball M/W, cheerleading M(c)/W(c), equestrian sports W(c), football M/W, golf M(c)/W(c), ice hockey M(c), rock climbing M(c)/W(c), rugby M(c)/W(c), soccer M(c)/W(c), softball M/W, tennis M(c)/W(c), ultimate Frisbee M(c)/W(c), volleyball M(c)/W(c).

Campus security: 24-hour emergency response devices and patrols, late-night transport/escort service, controlled dormitory access.

Student services: health clinic, personal/psychological counseling.

COSTS & FINANCIAL AID

Costs (2020–21) ***One-time required fee:*** $150. ***Comprehensive fee:*** $61,450 includes full-time tuition ($45,200), mandatory fees ($1670), and room and board ($14,580). Full-time tuition and fees vary according to course load. Part-time tuition: $2160 per course. Part-time tuition and fees vary according to course load. ***Required fees:*** $62 per term part-time. ***College room only:*** $6770. Room and board charges vary according to board plan and housing facility. ***Payment plan:*** installment. ***Waivers:*** senior citizens and employees or children of employees.

Financial Aid Of all full-time matriculated undergraduates who enrolled in 2019, 1,629 applied for aid, 1,466 were judged to have need, 326 had their need fully met. In 2019, 455 non-need-based awards were made. ***Average percent of need met:*** 84. ***Average financial aid package:*** $38,476. ***Average need-based loan:*** $4261. ***Average need-based gift aid:*** $32,220. ***Average non-need-based aid:*** $24,930. ***Average indebtedness upon graduation:*** $37,335.

APPLYING

Standardized Tests *Required for some:* SAT or ACT (for admission).

Options: electronic application, early admission, early decision, deferred entrance.

Application fee: $30.

Required: high school transcript. ***Required for some:*** applicants may choose to apply test-optional, ACT or SAT scores will be considered if submitted, some applicants may be asked to provide test scores. ***Recommended:*** essay or personal statement, 1 letter of recommendation, interview.

Application deadlines: 3/15 (freshmen), 3/15 (out-of-state freshmen), 8/1 (transfers).

Early decision deadline: 11/15.

Notification: continuous until 4/1 (freshmen), continuous until 4/1 (out-of-state freshmen), continuous until 8/15 (transfers), 12/15 (early decision).

CONTACT
Roanoke College, Admissions Office, 221 College Lane, Salem, VA 24153-3794. *Phone:* 800-388-2276. *Toll-free phone:* 800-388-2276. *E-mail:* admissions@roanoke.edu.

Sentara College of Health Sciences
Chesapeake, Virginia
http://www.sentara.edu/

- **Independent** 4-year, founded 1892
- **Urban** campus with easy access to Virginia Beach
- **Coed** 440 undergraduate students, 53% full-time, 92% women, 8% men

UNDERGRAD STUDENTS
231 full-time, 209 part-time. Students come from 4 states and territories; 10% Black or African American, non-Hispanic/Latino; 4% Hispanic/Latino; 8% Asian, non-Hispanic/Latino; 0.9% Native Hawaiian or other Pacific Islander, non-Hispanic/Latino; 0.2% American Indian or Alaska Native, non-Hispanic/Latino; 5% Two or more races, non-Hispanic/Latino; 2% Race/ethnicity unknown.

ACADEMICS
Calendar: semesters. *Degrees:* associate and bachelor's.

Special study options: academic remediation for entering students, adult/continuing education programs, advanced placement credit, distance learning, part-time degree program, services for LD students, summer session for credit.

Computers: 13 computers/terminals are available on campus for general student use. Students can access the following: free student e-mail accounts, online (class) grades. Campuswide network is available. Wireless service is available via entire campus.
Library: Sentara Healthcare Library.

STUDENT LIFE
Housing options: college housing not available.

Activities and organizations: Sentara Nursing Student Association (SNSA), Alpha Eta National Honor Society for Allied Health Professionals, Sigma Theta Tau International Nursing Honor Society, Chi Kappa Chapter (STTI), Student Community Outreach Program of Excellence (SCOPE).

Campus security: 24-hour emergency response devices.

Student services: personal/psychological counseling.

COSTS
Costs (2019–20) ***One-time required fee:*** $85. ***Tuition:*** $10,556 full-time, $364 per credit hour part-time. Full-time tuition and fees vary according to course level, course load, degree level, and program. Part-time tuition and fees vary according to course level, course load, degree level, and program. ***Required fees:*** $2471 full-time, $2471 per year part-time.

APPLYING
Standardized Tests *Required:* ATI Teas (BSN, CVT, ST) (for admission).

Options: electronic application.

Application fee: $85.

Required for some: high school transcript, minimum 3.5 GPA, For our BSN, early Admission option: earn courses, cumulative GPA of 3.3 on all college transcripts.

Notification: 6/1 (transfers).

CONTACT
Sentara College of Health Sciences, 1441 Crossways Boulevard, Crossways I, Suite 105, Chesapeake, VA 23320. *Phone:* 757-388-2604.

Shenandoah University
Winchester, Virginia
http://www.su.edu/

- **Independent United Methodist** university, founded 1875
- **Suburban** 359-acre campus with easy access to Washington, D.C.
- **Endowment** $68.1 million
- **Coed** 2,040 undergraduate students, 98% full-time, 60% women, 40% men
- **Moderately difficult** entrance level, 74% of applicants were admitted

UNDERGRAD STUDENTS
1,989 full-time, 51 part-time. Students come from 42 states and territories; 18 other countries; 39% are from out of state; 12% Black or African American, non-Hispanic/Latino; 7% Hispanic/Latino; 3% Asian, non-Hispanic/Latino; 0.4% Native Hawaiian or other Pacific Islander, non-Hispanic/Latino; 1% American Indian or Alaska Native, non-Hispanic/Latino; 0.7% Two or more races, non-Hispanic/Latino; 14% Race/ethnicity unknown; 2% international; 6% transferred in; 52% live on campus.

Freshmen:
Admission: 2,322 applied, 1,727 admitted, 503 enrolled. ***Average high school GPA:*** 3.5. ***Test scores:*** SAT evidence-based reading and writing scores over 500: 79%; SAT math scores over 500: 70%; ACT scores over 18: 79%; SAT evidence-based reading and writing scores over 600: 33%; SAT math scores over 600: 20%; ACT scores over 24: 42%; SAT evidence-based reading and writing scores over 700: 2%; SAT math scores over 700: 3%; ACT scores over 30: 5%.

Retention: 84% of full-time freshmen returned.

FACULTY
Total: 507, 53% full-time, 60% with terminal degrees.

Student/faculty ratio: 9:1.

ACADEMICS
Calendar: semesters. *Degrees:* certificates, bachelor's, master's, doctoral, post-master's, and postbachelor's certificates.

Special study options: accelerated degree program, adult/continuing education programs, advanced placement credit, distance learning, double majors, English as a second language, independent study, internships, off-campus study, part-time degree program, services for LD students, student-designed majors, study abroad, summer session for credit.

Unusual degree programs: 3-2 occupational therapy (3-2.5), athletic training, public health.

Computers: 32 computers/terminals and 218 ports are available on campus for general student use. Students can access the following: campus intranet, computer help desk, free student e-mail accounts, online (class) grades, online (class) registration, online (class) schedules, online student account information. Campuswide network is available. 100% of college-owned or -operated housing units are wired for high-speed Internet access. Wireless service is available via entire campus.
Library: Alson H. Smith, Jr. Library plus 1 other. *Books:* 121,000 (physical), 372,566 (digital/electronic); *Serial titles:* 1,050 (physical), 66,729 (digital/electronic); *Databases:* 135. Weekly public service hours: 96; students can reserve study rooms.

STUDENT LIFE
Housing options: on-campus residence required through sophomore year; coed, special housing for students with disabilities. Campus housing is university owned. Freshman campus housing is guaranteed.

Activities and organizations: drama/theater group, student-run newspaper, radio station, choral group, Student Government Association, Graduate Student Assembly, Campus Activities Network, Athletic Training Club, Variety of Groups for Professional Fraternities.

Athletics Member NCAA. All Division III except golf (Division II). ***Intercollegiate sports:*** baseball M, basketball M/W, cross-country running M/W, field hockey W, football M, golf M/W, lacrosse M/W, soccer M/W, softball W, tennis M/W, track and field M/W, volleyball W. ***Intramural sports:*** basketball M/W, cheerleading M(c)/W(c), football M/W, sand volleyball M/W, soccer M/W, softball M/W, table tennis M/W, ultimate Frisbee M/W, volleyball M/W.

Campus security: 24-hour emergency response devices and patrols, late-night transport/escort service, controlled dormitory access, LiveSafe mobile app, anonymous reporting, side-door alarms, campus shuttle, Safe in Sixty Seconds Program, Safe Walk/Safe Ride Program.

Student services: health clinic, personal/psychological counseling, women's center, veterans affairs office.

COSTS & FINANCIAL AID
Costs (2020–21) ***Comprehensive fee:*** $44,640 includes full-time tuition ($32,510), mandatory fees ($1320), and room and board ($10,810). Full-time tuition and fees vary according to course load and program. Part-time tuition: $950 per credit hour. Part-time tuition and fees vary according to course load and program. ***Required fees:*** $100 part-time. ***Room and board:*** Room and board charges vary according to board plan and housing facility. ***Payment plan:*** installment. ***Waivers:*** employees or children of employees.

Financial Aid Of all full-time matriculated undergraduates who enrolled in 2019, 1,793 applied for aid, 1,516 were judged to have need, 273 had their need fully met. In 2019, 449 non-need-based awards were made. ***Average percent of need met:*** 66. ***Average financial aid package:*** $21,001. ***Average need-based loan:*** $4321. ***Average need-based gift aid:*** $6678. ***Average non-need-based aid:*** $13,253. ***Average indebtedness upon graduation:*** $36,370.

APPLYING
Standardized Tests *Required:* SAT or ACT (for admission).

Options: electronic application, deferred entrance.

Application fee: $30.

Required: high school transcript. ***Required for some:*** essay or personal statement, interview, audition for conservatory applicants, interview for some Conservatory programs and for Guaranteed Admission for Health Professions programs.

Application deadlines: rolling (freshmen), rolling (out-of-state freshmen), rolling (transfers).

Notification: continuous (freshmen), continuous (out-of-state freshmen), continuous (transfers).

CONTACT
Mr. Thomas McKenna, Associate Director of Admissions, Shenandoah University, 1460 University Drive, Wilkins Building, Admissions Office, Winchester, VA 22601-5195. *Phone:* 540-545-7327. *Toll-free phone:* 800-432-2266. *Fax:* 540-665-4627. *E-mail:* admit@su.edu.

Southern Virginia University

Buena Vista, Virginia

http://www.svu.edu/

- **Independent Latter-day Saints** 4-year, founded 1867
- **Small-town** 155-acre campus
- **Endowment** $1.0 million
- **Coed**
- **Moderately difficult** entrance level

FACULTY
Student/faculty ratio: 16:1.

ACADEMICS
Calendar: semesters. *Degree:* bachelor's.
Library: Von Canon Library.

STUDENT LIFE
Housing options: on-campus residence required through sophomore year; men-only, women-only. Campus housing is university owned. Freshman applicants given priority for college housing.

Activities and organizations: drama/theater group, choral group, Student Association, LDS Institute of Religion.

Athletics Member NAIA.

Campus security: 24-hour emergency response devices and patrols.

Student services: health clinic, personal/psychological counseling.

FINANCIAL AID
Financial Aid Of all full-time matriculated undergraduates who enrolled in 2007, 545 applied for aid, 477 were judged to have need, 62 had their need fully met. 164 Federal Work-Study jobs (averaging $1000). 19 state and other part-time jobs (averaging $2168). In 2007, 102 non-need-based awards were made. ***Average percent of need met:*** 60. ***Average financial aid package:*** $11,719. ***Average need-based loan:*** $3993. ***Average need-based gift aid:*** $8756. ***Average non-need-based aid:*** $6489. ***Average indebtedness upon graduation:*** $15,444. ***Financial aid deadline:*** 5/1.

APPLYING
Standardized Tests *Required:* SAT or ACT (for admission).

Application fee: $35.

Required: high school transcript, ecclesiastical endorsement. ***Required for some:*** essay or personal statement, interview. ***Recommended:*** minimum 2.0 GPA.

CONTACT
Mr. Tony Caputo, Dean of Admissions, Southern Virginia University, One University Hill Drive, Buena Vista, VA 24416. *Phone:* 540-261-2756. *Toll-free phone:* 800-229-8420. *Fax:* 540-261-8559. *E-mail:* admissions@southernvirginia.edu.

South University - Richmond

Glen Allen, Virginia

http://www.southuniversity.edu/richmond

CONTACT
South University - Richmond, 2151 Old Brick Road, Glen Allen, VA 23060. *Phone:* 804-727-6800. *Toll-free phone:* 888-422-5076.

South University - Virginia Beach

Virginia Beach, Virginia

http://www.southuniversity.edu/virginia-beach

CONTACT
South University - Virginia Beach, 301 Bendix Road, Suite 100, Virginia Beach, VA 23452. *Phone:* 757-493-6900. *Toll-free phone:* 877-206-1845.

Stratford University

Alexandria, Virginia

http://www.stratford.edu/

CONTACT
Admissions, Stratford University, 2900 Eisenhower Avenue, Alexandria, VA 22314. *Phone:* 571-699-3200. *Toll-free phone:* 800-444-0804. *E-mail:* alexandriaadmissions@stratford.edu.

Stratford University

Falls Church, Virginia

http://www.stratford.edu/

CONTACT
Admissions, Stratford University, 7777 Leesburg Pike, Falls Church, VA 22043. *Phone:* 703-821-8570. *Toll-free phone:* 800-444-0804. *E-mail:* fcadmissions@stratford.edu.

Stratford University

Glen Allen, Virginia

http://www.stratford.edu/

CONTACT
Admissions, Stratford University, 11104 West Broad Street, Glen Allen, VA 23060. *Phone:* 804-290-4231. *Toll-free phone:* 877-373-5173. *E-mail:* gaadmissions@stratford.edu.

Stratford University

Newport News, Virginia

http://www.stratford.edu/

CONTACT
Admissions, Stratford University, 836 J. Clyde Morris Boulevard, Newport News, VA 23601. *Phone:* 757-873-4235. *Toll-free phone:* 855-873-4235. *E-mail:* newportnewsadmissions@stratford.edu.

Stratford University
Virginia Beach, Virginia
http://www.stratford.edu/

CONTACT
Admissions, Stratford University, 555 South Independence Boulevard, Virginia Beach, VA 23452. *Phone:* 757-497-4466. *Toll-free phone:* 866-528-8363. *E-mail:* virginiabeachadmissions@stratford.edu.

Stratford University
Woodbridge, Virginia
http://www.stratford.edu/

CONTACT
Admissions, Stratford University, 14349 Gideon Drive, Woodbridge, VA 22192. *Phone:* 703-897-1982. *Toll-free phone:* 888-546-1250. *E-mail:* woodbridgeadmissions@stratford.edu.

Strayer University - Alexandria
Alexandria, Virginia
http://www.strayer.edu/virginia/alexandria/

CONTACT
Strayer University - Alexandria, 2730 Eisenhower Avenue, Alexandria, VA 22314. *Toll-free phone:* 888-311-0355.

Strayer University - Arlington
Arlington, Virginia
http://www.strayer.edu/virginia/arlington/

CONTACT
Strayer University - Arlington, 2121 15th Street North, Arlington, VA 22201. *Toll-free phone:* 888-311-0355.

Strayer University–Chesapeake Campus
Chesapeake, Virginia
http://www.strayer.edu/virginia/chesapeake/

CONTACT
Strayer University–Chesapeake Campus, 676 Independence Parkway, Suite 300, Chesapeake, VA 23320. *Toll-free phone:* 888-311-0355.

Strayer University–Chesterfield Campus
Midlothian, Virginia
http://www.strayer.edu/virginia/chesterfield/

CONTACT
Strayer University–Chesterfield Campus, 15521 Midlothian Turnpike, Suite 401, Midlothian, VA 23113. *Toll-free phone:* 888-311-0355.

Strayer University–Fredericksburg Campus
Fredericksburg, Virginia
http://www.strayer.edu/virginia/fredericksburg/

CONTACT
Strayer University–Fredericksburg Campus, 150 Riverside Parkway, Suite 100, Fredericksburg, VA 22406. *Toll-free phone:* 888-311-0355.

Strayer University–Henrico Campus
Glen Allen, Virginia
http://www.strayer.edu/virginia/henrico/

CONTACT
Strayer University–Henrico Campus, 11501 Nuckols Road, Glen Allen, VA 23059. *Toll-free phone:* 888-311-0355.

Strayer University–Loudoun Campus
Ashburn, Virginia
http://www.strayer.edu/virginia/loudoun/

CONTACT
Strayer University–Loudoun Campus, 45150 Russell Branch Parkway, Suite 200, Ashburn, VA 20147. *Toll-free phone:* 888-311-0355.

Strayer University–Manassas Campus
Manassas, Virginia
http://www.strayer.edu/virginia/manassas/

CONTACT
Strayer University–Manassas Campus, 9990 Battleview Parkway, Manassas, VA 20109. *Toll-free phone:* 888-311-0355.

Strayer University–Newport News Campus
Newport News, Virginia
http://www.strayer.edu/virginia/newport-news/

CONTACT
Strayer University–Newport News Campus, 99 Old Oyster Point Road, Newport News, VA 23602. *Toll-free phone:* 888-311-0355.

Strayer University–Virginia Beach Campus
Virginia Beach, Virginia
http://www.strayer.edu/virginia/virginia-beach/

CONTACT
Strayer University–Virginia Beach Campus, 249 Central Park Avenue, Suite 350, Virginia Beach, VA 23462. *Toll-free phone:* 888-311-0355.

Strayer University–Woodbridge Campus
Woodbridge, Virginia
http://www.strayer.edu/virginia/woodbridge/

CONTACT
Strayer University–Woodbridge Campus, 13385 Minnieville Road, Woodbridge, VA 22192. *Toll-free phone:* 888-311-0355.

Sweet Briar College
Sweet Briar, Virginia
http://www.sbc.edu/

- **Independent** comprehensive, founded 1901
- **Rural** 3250-acre campus
- **Endowment** $74.8 million
- **Women only**
- **Minimally difficult** entrance level

FACULTY
Student/faculty ratio: 5:1.

ACADEMICS
Calendar: semesters. *Degrees:* bachelor's and master's.

Library: Mary Helen Cochran Library plus 1 other. *Books:* 245,124 (physical); *Serial titles:* 1,215 (physical), 31,479 (digital/electronic); *Databases:* 214. Study areas open 24 hours, 5–7 days a week.

STUDENT LIFE

Housing options: on-campus residence required through senior year; women-only. Campus housing is university owned. Freshman campus housing is guaranteed.

Activities and organizations: drama/theater group, student-run newspaper, radio station, choral group.

Athletics Member NCAA. All Division III.

Campus security: 24-hour emergency response devices and patrols, student patrols, late-night transport/escort service, controlled dormitory access, front gate security.

Student services: health clinic, personal/psychological counseling, women's center, veterans affairs office.

COSTS & FINANCIAL AID

Costs (2019–20) ***Comprehensive fee:*** $35,220 includes full-time tuition ($21,420), mandatory fees ($600), and room and board ($13,200).

Financial Aid Of all full-time matriculated undergraduates who enrolled in 2016, 281 applied for aid, 257 were judged to have need, 61 had their need fully met. In 2016, 20 non-need-based awards were made. ***Average percent of need met:*** 81. ***Average financial aid package:*** $34,064. ***Average need-based loan:*** $7457. ***Average need-based gift aid:*** $28,297. ***Average non-need-based aid:*** $29,940. ***Average indebtedness upon graduation:*** $31,269.

APPLYING

Standardized Tests *Required for some:* SAT or ACT (for admission).

Options: electronic application, deferred entrance.

Required: essay or personal statement, high school transcript. ***Recommended:*** 2 letters of recommendation.

CONTACT

Elizabeth Clarke, Dir. Admissions Strategy, Sweet Briar College, PO Box 1052, Sweet Briar, VA 24595. *Phone:* 434-381-6720. *Toll-free phone:* 800-381-6142. *E-mail:* admissions@sbc.edu.

University of Lynchburg

Lynchburg, Virginia

http://www.lynchburg.edu/

- **Independent** comprehensive, founded 1903, affiliated with Christian Church (Disciples of Christ)
- **Suburban** 264-acre campus
- **Endowment** $109.7 million
- **Coed**
- **Moderately difficult** entrance level

FACULTY

Student/faculty ratio: 11:1.

ACADEMICS

Calendar: semesters. *Degrees:* bachelor's, master's, doctoral, post-master's, and postbachelor's certificates.

Library: Knight-Capron Library. *Books:* 109,236 (physical), 323,591 (digital/electronic); *Serial titles:* 109 (physical), 58,732 (digital/electronic); *Databases:* 98. Study areas open 24 hours, 5–7 days a week; students can reserve study rooms.

STUDENT LIFE

Housing options: on-campus residence required through junior year; coed, special housing for students with disabilities. Campus housing is university owned. Freshman campus housing is guaranteed.

Activities and organizations: drama/theater group, student-run newspaper, choral group, Student Government Association, Student Activities Board, Enrollment Student Ambassadors, Emergency Services, Greek Life, national fraternities, national sororities.

Athletics Member NCAA. All Division III.

Campus security: 24-hour emergency response devices and patrols, late-night transport/escort service, controlled dormitory access.

Student services: health clinic, personal/psychological counseling, veterans affairs office.

FINANCIAL AID

Financial Aid Of all full-time matriculated undergraduates who enrolled in 2018, 1,687 applied for aid, 1,547 were judged to have need, 323 had

their need fully met. In 2018, 463 non-need-based awards were made. ***Average percent of need met:*** 76. ***Average financial aid package:*** $29,919. ***Average need-based loan:*** $3399. ***Average need-based gift aid:*** $26,512. ***Average non-need-based aid:*** $19,944. ***Average indebtedness upon graduation:*** $36,076.

APPLYING

Standardized Tests *Required:* SAT or ACT (for admission).

Options: electronic application, early admission, early decision, deferred entrance.

Application fee: $30.

Required: high school transcript. ***Recommended:*** essay or personal statement, 2 letters of recommendation, interview.

CONTACT

Ms. Sharon Walters-Bower, Director of Admissions, University of Lynchburg, 1501 Lakeside Drive, Lynchburg, VA 24501-3199. *Phone:* 434-544-8300. *Toll-free phone:* 800-426-8101. *Fax:* 434-544-8653. *E-mail:* admissions@lynchburg.edu.

See below for display ad and page 1124 for the College Close-Up.

University of Management and Technology

Arlington, Virginia

http://www.umtweb.edu/

- **Proprietary** comprehensive, founded 1998
- **Urban** campus with easy access to Washington, DC
- **Coed** 1,029 undergraduate students, 18% full-time, 8% women, 14% men

UNDERGRAD STUDENTS

181 full-time, 45 part-time.

FACULTY

Student/faculty ratio: 4:1.

ACADEMICS

Calendar: continuous. *Degrees:* certificates, associate, bachelor's, master's, doctoral, post-master's, and postbachelor's certificates.

Special study options: adult/continuing education programs, part-time degree program.

Computers: Students can access the following: campus intranet, online (class) grades, online (class) registration, online (class) schedules. Campuswide network is available. Wireless service is available via entire campus.

Library: *Books:* 9,104 (physical), 569 (digital/electronic); *Serial titles:* 1,008 (physical), 25,739 (digital/electronic); *Databases:* 73.

STUDENT LIFE

Student services: veterans affairs office.

COSTS & FINANCIAL AID

Costs (2020–21) ***Tuition:*** $9360 full-time. ***Required fees:*** $90 full-time. ***Waivers:*** employees or children of employees.

Financial Aid Of all full-time matriculated undergraduates who enrolled in 2014, 71 applied for aid, 67 were judged to have need, 67 had their need fully met. ***Average percent of need met:*** 100. ***Average financial aid package:*** $16,980. ***Average need-based loan:*** $3414. ***Average need-based gift aid:*** $3989. ***Average indebtedness upon graduation:*** $15,415.

APPLYING

Application fee: $30.

CONTACT

Mr. Kenny Hickey, University of Management and Technology, 1901 Fort Myer Drive, Arlington, VA 22209-1609. *Phone:* 703-516-0035. *Toll-free phone:* 800-924-4883. *E-mail:* kenny.hickey@umtweb.edu.

University of Mary Washington

Fredericksburg, Virginia

http://www.umw.edu/

- **State-supported** comprehensive, founded 1908
- **Small-town** 234-acre campus with easy access to Richmond; Washington, D.C.
- **Endowment** $50.0 million
- **Coed** 4,182 undergraduate students, 88% full-time, 64% women, 36% men
- **Very difficult** entrance level, 75% of applicants were admitted

UNDERGRAD STUDENTS

3,694 full-time, 488 part-time. 9% are from out of state; 7% Black or African American, non-Hispanic/Latino; 11% Hispanic/Latino; 4% Asian, non-Hispanic/Latino; 0.1% Native Hawaiian or other Pacific Islander, non-Hispanic/Latino; 0.1% American Indian or Alaska Native, non-Hispanic/Latino; 6% Two or more races, non-Hispanic/Latino; 3% Race/ethnicity unknown; 0.8% international; 7% transferred in; 57% live on campus.

Freshmen:

Admission: 5,939 applied, 4,438 admitted, 891 enrolled. ***Average high school GPA:*** 3.6. ***Test scores:*** SAT evidence-based reading and writing scores over 500: 94%; SAT math scores over 500: 88%; ACT scores over 18: 100%; SAT evidence-based reading and writing scores over 600: 55%; SAT math scores over 600: 35%; ACT scores over 24: 59%; SAT evidence-based reading and writing scores over 700: 13%; SAT math scores over 700: 6%; ACT scores over 30: 11%.

Retention: 80% of full-time freshmen returned.

FACULTY

Total: 395, 65% full-time, 71% with terminal degrees.

Student/faculty ratio: 13:1.

ACADEMICS

Calendar: semesters. *Degrees:* certificates, bachelor's, master's, and postbachelor's certificates.

Special study options: accelerated degree program, adult/continuing education programs, advanced placement credit, distance learning, double majors, honors programs, independent study, internships, part-time degree program, services for LD students, student-designed majors, study abroad, summer session for credit. ***ROTC:*** Army (c).

Computers: 579 computers/terminals are available on campus for general student use. Students can access the following: campus intranet, computer help desk, free student e-mail accounts, online (class) grades, online (class) registration, online (class) schedules, student Web hosting. Campuswide network is available. 100% of college-owned or -operated housing units are wired for high-speed Internet access. Wireless service is available via entire campus.

Library: Simpson Library plus 2 others. *Books:* 373,290 (physical), 243,338 (digital/electronic); *Serial titles:* 3,164 (physical), 76,994 (digital/electronic); *Databases:* 210. Weekly public service hours: 90; students can reserve study rooms.

STUDENT LIFE

Housing options: on-campus residence required through sophomore year; coed, women-only, special housing for students with disabilities. Campus housing is university owned. Freshman campus housing is guaranteed.

Activities and organizations: drama/theater group, student-run newspaper, radio station, choral group, Class Council, Campus Programming Board, Community Outreach and Participation, Association of Residence Halls, Student Government Association.

Athletics Member NCAA. All Division III. ***Intercollegiate sports:*** baseball M, basketball M/W, crew M(c)/W(c), cross-country running M/W, equestrian sports M/W, field hockey W, golf M/W, lacrosse M/W, rugby M(c)/W(c), soccer M/W, softball W, swimming and diving M/W, tennis M/W, track and field M/W, volleyball W. ***Intramural sports:*** badminton M/W, baseball M(c), basketball M/W, cheerleading M(c)/W(c), fencing M(c)/W(c), field hockey W(c), football M/W, lacrosse M(c)/W(c), sand volleyball M/W, soccer M(c)/W(c), softball W, swimming and diving M(c)/W(c), tennis M(c)/W(c), ultimate Frisbee M(c)/W(c), volleyball M(c)/W(c).

Campus security: 24-hour emergency response devices and patrols, student patrols, late-night transport/escort service, controlled dormitory access, self-defense and safety classes. Guardian App.

Student services: health clinic, personal/psychological counseling, veterans affairs office.

COSTS & FINANCIAL AID
Costs (2019–20) ***Tuition:*** area resident $8678 full-time, $335 per credit hour part-time; state resident $8678 full-time, $335 per credit hour part-time; nonresident $25,102 full-time, $1016 per credit hour part-time. Full-time tuition and fees vary according to course load, degree level, and location. Part-time tuition and fees vary according to course load, degree level, and location. ***Required fees:*** $4592 full-time, $132 part-time, $132 part-time. ***Room and board:*** $11,500; room only: $7382. Room and board charges vary according to board plan and housing facility. ***Payment plan:*** installment. ***Waivers:*** senior citizens.

Financial Aid Of all full-time matriculated undergraduates who enrolled in 2018, 2,668 applied for aid, 1,861 were judged to have need, 196 had their need fully met. In 2018, 1054 non-need-based awards were made. ***Average percent of need met:*** 44. ***Average financial aid package:*** $10,336. ***Average need-based loan:*** $4075. ***Average need-based gift aid:*** $3503. ***Average non-need-based aid:*** $3558. ***Average indebtedness upon graduation:*** $31,157. ***Financial aid deadline:*** 6/1.

APPLYING
Standardized Tests *Required for some:* SAT or ACT (for admission).

Options: electronic application, early admission, early decision, early action, deferred entrance.

Application fee: $50.

Required: essay or personal statement, high school transcript.

Application deadlines: 2/1 (freshmen), 4/1 (transfers), 11/15 (early action).

Early decision deadline: 11/1.

Notification: 4/1 (freshmen), 5/15 (transfers), 12/10 (early decision), 1/31 (early action).

CONTACT
Ms. Melissa Yakabouski, Director of Undergraduate Admissions, University of Mary Washington, 1301 College Avenue, Fredericksburg, VA 22401-5358. *Phone:* 540-654-1669. *Toll-free phone:* 800-468-5614. *Fax:* 540-654-1857. *E-mail:* myak@umw.edu.

University of Richmond
Richmond, Virginia
http://www.richmond.edu/

- **Independent** comprehensive, founded 1830
- **Suburban** 350-acre campus
- **Endowment** $2.5 billion
- **Coed** 3,161 undergraduate students, 94% full-time, 52% women, 48% men
- **Very difficult** entrance level, 28% of applicants were admitted

UNDERGRAD STUDENTS
2,979 full-time, 182 part-time. Students come from 50 states and territories; 69 other countries; 76% are from out of state; 7% Black or African American, non-Hispanic/Latino; 9% Hispanic/Latino; 7% Asian, non-Hispanic/Latino; 0.1% American Indian or Alaska Native, non-Hispanic/Latino; 5% Two or more races, non-Hispanic/Latino; 4% Race/ethnicity unknown; 9% international; 1% transferred in; 91% live on campus.

Freshmen:
Admission: 12,356 applied, 3,500 admitted, 832 enrolled. ***Test scores:*** SAT evidence-based reading and writing scores over 500: 100%; SAT math scores over 500: 100%; ACT scores over 18: 100%; SAT evidence-based reading and writing scores over 600: 90%; SAT math scores over 600: 88%; ACT scores over 24: 99%; SAT evidence-based reading and writing scores over 700: 34%; SAT math scores over 700: 54%; ACT scores over 30: 77%.

Retention: 94% of full-time freshmen returned.

FACULTY
Total: 599, 68% full-time, 85% with terminal degrees.

Student/faculty ratio: 8:1.

ACADEMICS
Calendar: semesters. *Degrees:* certificates, bachelor's, master's, and doctoral.

Special study options: advanced placement credit, double majors, English as a second language, honors programs, independent study, internships, off-campus study, part-time degree program, services for LD students, student-designed majors, study abroad, summer session for credit. ***ROTC:*** Army (b).

Unusual degree programs: 3-2 engineering with Columbia University, University of Virginia; Duke University Environmental Studies, Virginia Commonwealth University Environmental Studies.

Computers: 971 computers/terminals and 4,608 ports are available on campus for general student use. Students can access the following: campus intranet, computer help desk, free student e-mail accounts, online (class) grades, online (class) registration, online (class) schedules. Campuswide network is available. 100% of college-owned or -operated housing units are wired for high-speed Internet access. Wireless service is available via entire campus.

Library: Boatwright Memorial Library plus 2 others. *Books:* 541,881 (physical), 598,842 (digital/electronic); *Serial titles:* 405 (physical), 154,436 (digital/electronic); *Databases:* 405. Weekly public service hours: 100; study areas open 24 hours, 5–7 days a week; students can reserve study rooms.

STUDENT LIFE
Housing options: coed, men-only, women-only, special housing for students with disabilities. Campus housing is university owned. Freshman campus housing is guaranteed.

Activities and organizations: drama/theater group, student-run newspaper, radio station, choral group, Greek Life, Sport Clubs, SpiderBoard Concert, SpiderFest, Block Parties, national fraternities, national sororities.

Athletics Member NCAA. All Division I except football (Division I-AA). ***Intercollegiate sports:*** baseball M(s), basketball M(s)/W(s), cross-country running M/W(s), field hockey W(s), golf M(s)/W(s)(c), lacrosse M(s)/W(s), soccer W(s), swimming and diving W(s), tennis M(s)/W(s), track and field W(s). ***Intramural sports:*** archery M(c)/W(c), badminton M(c)/W(c), baseball M(c), basketball M/W, crew M(c)/W(c), equestrian sports M(c)/W(c), field hockey M(c)/W(c), golf M/W, ice hockey M(c)/W(c), lacrosse M(c)/W(c), racquetball M/W, rugby M(c)/W(c), soccer M/W, softball M/W, squash M/W, swimming and diving M(c)/W(c), table tennis M/W, tennis M/W, track and field M(c)/W(c), ultimate Frisbee M(c)/W(c), volleyball M/W, water polo M(c)/W(c), wrestling M(c)/W(c).

Campus security: 24-hour emergency response devices and patrols, late-night transport/escort service, controlled dormitory access.

Student services: health clinic, personal/psychological counseling, women's center.

COSTS & FINANCIAL AID
Costs (2020–21) ***Comprehensive fee:*** $70,290 includes full-time tuition ($56,860) and room and board ($13,430). Part-time tuition: $2320 per credit hour. Part-time tuition and fees vary according to course load. ***College room only:*** $6300. ***Payment plans:*** tuition prepayment, deferred payment. ***Waivers:*** employees or children of employees.

Financial Aid Of all full-time matriculated undergraduates who enrolled in 2019, 1,578 applied for aid, 1,242 were judged to have need, 1,031 had their need fully met. 661 Federal Work-Study jobs (averaging $1400). In 2019, 615 non-need-based awards were made. ***Average percent of need met:*** 100. ***Average financial aid package:*** $52,064. ***Average need-based loan:*** $3650. ***Average need-based gift aid:*** $45,919. ***Average non-need-based aid:*** $23,820. ***Average indebtedness upon graduation:*** $28,341.

APPLYING
Standardized Tests *Required:* SAT or ACT (for admission).

Options: electronic application, early decision, early action, deferred entrance.

Application fee: $50.

Required: essay or personal statement, high school transcript, 1 letter of recommendation.

Application deadlines: 1/15 (freshmen), 2/15 (transfers), 11/1 (early action).

Early decision deadline: 11/1.

Notification: 4/1 (freshmen), 4/15 (transfers), 12/15 (early decision), 1/20 (early action).

CONTACT

Mr. Gil Villanueva, Dean of Admission, University of Richmond, Queally Center for Admission and Career Services, 30 UR Drive, University of Richmond, VA 23173. *Phone:* 804-289-8640. *Toll-free phone:* 800-700-1662. *Fax:* 804-287-6003. *E-mail:* admissions@richmond.edu.

University of Valley Forge Virginia Campus

Woodbridge, Virginia

http://www.valleyforge.edu/

CONTACT

Admissions Coordinator, University of Valley Forge Virginia Campus, 13909 Smoketown Road, Woodbridge, VA 22192. *Phone:* 703-580-4810 Ext. 210. *Toll-free phone:* 800-432-8322.

University of Virginia

Charlottesville, Virginia

http://www.virginia.edu/

- **State-supported** university, founded 1819
- **Suburban** 1167-acre campus with easy access to Richmond
- **Coed** 17,011 undergraduate students, 96% full-time, 55% women, 45% men
- **Most difficult** entrance level, 24% of applicants were admitted

UNDERGRAD STUDENTS

16,280 full-time, 731 part-time. Students come from 52 states and territories; 85 other countries; 28% are from out of state; 7% Black or African American, non-Hispanic/Latino; 7% Hispanic/Latino; 15% Asian, non-Hispanic/Latino; 0.1% Native Hawaiian or other Pacific Islander, non-Hispanic/Latino; 0.1% American Indian or Alaska Native, non-Hispanic/Latino; 5% Two or more races, non-Hispanic/Latino; 5% Race/ethnicity unknown; 4% international; 4% transferred in; 39% live on campus.

Freshmen:

Admission: 40,839 applied, 9,778 admitted, 3,920 enrolled. ***Average high school GPA:*** 4.3. ***Test scores:*** SAT evidence-based reading and writing scores over 500: 100%; SAT math scores over 500: 100%; ACT scores over 18: 100%; SAT evidence-based reading and writing scores over 600: 95%; SAT math scores over 600: 93%; ACT scores over 24: 97%; SAT evidence-based reading and writing scores over 700: 58%; SAT math scores over 700: 66%; ACT scores over 30: 79%.

Retention: 97% of full-time freshmen returned.

FACULTY

Total: 1,601, 95% full-time, 93% with terminal degrees.

Student/faculty ratio: 14:1.

ACADEMICS

Calendar: semesters. *Degrees:* certificates, bachelor's, master's, doctoral, post-master's, and postbachelor's certificates.

Special study options: accelerated degree program, adult/continuing education programs, advanced placement credit, cooperative education, distance learning, double majors, English as a second language, honors programs, independent study, internships, part-time degree program, services for LD students, student-designed majors, study abroad, summer session for credit. ***ROTC:*** Army (b), Navy (b), Air Force (b).

Unusual degree programs: 3-2 public policy.

Computers: Students can access the following: campus intranet, computer help desk, free student e-mail accounts, online (class) grades, online (class) registration, online (class) schedules, online course management tool. Campuswide network is available. 100% of college-owned or -operated housing units are wired for high-speed Internet access. Wireless service is available via classrooms, computer centers, computer labs, dorm rooms, learning centers, libraries, student centers.

Library: Alderman Library plus 14 others. *Books:* 5.3 million (physical), 1.5 million (digital/electronic); *Serial titles:* 121,969 (physical), 290,269 (digital/electronic); *Databases:* 1,456. Weekly public service hours: 149; study areas open 24 hours, 5–7 days a week; students can reserve study rooms.

STUDENT LIFE

Housing options: on-campus residence required for freshman year; coed. Campus housing is university owned. Freshman campus housing is guaranteed.

Activities and organizations: drama/theater group, student-run newspaper, radio and television station, choral group, marching band, Madison House, Student Council, University Guides, The Cavalier Daily, national fraternities, national sororities.

Athletics Member NCAA. All Division I. ***Intercollegiate sports:*** baseball M(s), basketball M(s)/W(s), cross-country running M(s)/W(s), field hockey W(s), football M(s), golf M(s)/W(s), lacrosse M(s)/W(s), rowing W(s), soccer M(s)/W(s), softball W(s), squash M(s)/W(s), swimming and diving M(s)/W(s), tennis M(s)/W(s), track and field M(s)/W(s), volleyball W(s), wrestling M(s). ***Intramural sports:*** archery M(c)/W(c), badminton M(c)/W(c), baseball M(c), basketball M(c)/W(c), cheerleading M(c)/W(c), cross-country running M(c)/W(c), equestrian sports M(c)/W(c), fencing M(c)/W(c), field hockey W(c), football M, golf M(c)/W(c), gymnastics M(c)/W(c), ice hockey M(c), lacrosse W(c), racquetball M(c)/W(c), riflery M(c)/W(c), rock climbing M(c)/W(c), rowing M(c), rugby M(c)/W(c), sailing M(c)/W(c), skiing (downhill) M(c)/W(c), soccer M(c)/W(c), softball W(c), squash M(c)/W(c), swimming and diving M(c)/W(c), tennis M(c)/W(c), track and field M(c)/W(c), ultimate Frisbee M(c)/W(c), volleyball M(c)/W(c), water polo M(c)/W(c), wrestling M(c)/W(c).

Campus security: 24-hour emergency response devices and patrols, student patrols, late-night transport/escort service, controlled dormitory access.

Student services: health clinic, personal/psychological counseling, women's center, legal services.

COSTS & FINANCIAL AID

Costs (2020–21) ***Tuition:*** area resident $15,755 full-time, $510 per credit hour part-time; state resident $15,755 full-time, $510 per credit hour part-time; nonresident $50,516 full-time, $1614 per credit hour part-time. Full-time tuition and fees vary according to program and student level. Part-time tuition and fees vary according to program and student level. No tuition increase for student's term of enrollment. ***Required fees:*** $3123 full-time, $3123 per year part-time. ***Room and board:*** $12,350; room only: $6960. Room and board charges vary according to board plan and housing facility. ***Payment plan:*** installment. ***Waivers:*** senior citizens and employees or children of employees.

Financial Aid Of all full-time matriculated undergraduates who enrolled in 2019, 10,186 applied for aid, 5,740 were judged to have need, 5,740 had their need fully met. 1,192 Federal Work-Study jobs (averaging $3241). In 2019, 769 non-need-based awards were made. ***Average percent of need met:*** 100. ***Average financial aid package:*** $30,591. ***Average need-based loan:*** $5999. ***Average need-based gift aid:*** $24,726. ***Average non-need-based aid:*** $5140. ***Average indebtedness upon graduation:*** $26,023.

APPLYING

Standardized Tests *Required:* SAT or ACT (for admission).

Options: electronic application, early decision, early action, deferred entrance.

Application fee: $70.

Required: essay or personal statement, high school transcript, 2 letters of recommendation.

Application deadlines: 1/6 (freshmen), 1/6 (out-of-state freshmen), 3/1 (transfers), 11/1 (early action).

Early decision deadline: 10/15.

Notification: 4/1 (freshmen), 4/1 (out-of-state freshmen).

CONTACT

Mr. Gregory W. Roberts, Dean of Admission, University of Virginia, PO Box 400160, Charlottesville, VA 22904-4727. *Phone:* 434-982-3200. *Fax:* 434-924-7674. *E-mail:* undergradadmission@virginia.edu.

The University of Virginia's College at Wise

Wise, Virginia

http://www.uvawise.edu/

CONTACT

Mr. Russell D. Necessary, Vice Chancellor for Enrollment Management and Student Life, The University of Virginia's College at Wise, 1 College Avenue, Wise, VA 24293. *Phone:* 276-328-0322. *Toll-free phone:* 888-282-9324. *Fax:* 276-328-0251. *E-mail:* admissions@uvawise.edu.

Virginia Baptist College

Fredericksburg, Virginia

http://www.vbc.edu/

CONTACT

Virginia Baptist College, 4111 Plank Road, Fredericksburg, VA 22407.

Virginia Commonwealth University

Richmond, Virginia

http://www.vcu.edu/

- **State-supported** university, founded 1838
- **Urban** 169-acre campus
- **Endowment** $144.1 million
- **Coed** 23,172 undergraduate students, 87% full-time, 61% women, 39% men
- 78% of applicants were admitted

UNDERGRAD STUDENTS

20,099 full-time, 3,073 part-time. Students come from 48 states and territories; 79 other countries; 7% are from out of state; 19% Black or African American, non-Hispanic/Latino; 11% Hispanic/Latino; 14% Asian, non-Hispanic/Latino; 0.1% Native Hawaiian or other Pacific Islander, non-Hispanic/Latino; 0.2% American Indian or Alaska Native, non-Hispanic/Latino; 7% Two or more races, non-Hispanic/Latino; 3% Race/ethnicity unknown; 2% international; 7% transferred in; 27% live on campus.

Freshmen:

Admission: 19,199 applied, 14,973 admitted, 4,461 enrolled. ***Average high school GPA:*** 3.7. ***Test scores:*** SAT evidence-based reading and writing scores over 500: 93%; SAT math scores over 500: 87%; ACT scores over 18: 95%; SAT evidence-based reading and writing scores over 600: 50%; SAT math scores over 600: 33%; ACT scores over 24: 56%; SAT evidence-based reading and writing scores over 700: 9%; SAT math scores over 700: 8%; ACT scores over 30: 17%.

Retention: 83% of full-time freshmen returned.

FACULTY

Total: 2,133, 60% full-time, 55% with terminal degrees.

Student/faculty ratio: 17:1.

ACADEMICS

Calendar: semesters. *Degrees:* certificates, bachelor's, master's, doctoral, post-master's, and postbachelor's certificates.

Special study options: academic remediation for entering students, accelerated degree program, adult/continuing education programs, advanced placement credit, cooperative education, distance learning, double majors, English as a second language, freshman honors college, honors programs, independent study, internships, off-campus study, part-time degree program, services for LD students, student-designed majors, study abroad, summer session for credit. ***ROTC:*** Army (c).

Computers: 2,281 computers/terminals and 90,000 ports are available on campus for general student use. Students can access the following: campus intranet, computer help desk, free student e-mail accounts, online (class) grades, online (class) registration, online (class) schedules. Campuswide network is available. 100% of college-owned or -operated housing units are wired for high-speed Internet access. Wireless service is available via entire campus.

Library: Cabell Library and Thompkins McCaw Library plus 3 others. *Books:* 1.4 million (physical), 1.3 million (digital/electronic); *Serial titles:* 30,840 (physical), 173,813 (digital/electronic); *Databases:* 505. Weekly public service hours: 146; study areas open 24 hours, 5–7 days a week; students can reserve study rooms.

STUDENT LIFE

Housing options: coed. Campus housing is university owned. Freshman applicants given priority for college housing.

Activities and organizations: drama/theater group, student-run newspaper, radio and television station, choral group, national fraternities, national sororities.

Athletics Member NCAA. All Division I. ***Intercollegiate sports:*** baseball M(s), basketball M(s)/W(s), cross-country running M/W, field hockey W(s), golf M(s), lacrosse W(s), soccer M(s)/W(s), tennis M(s)/W(s), track and field M(s)/W(s), volleyball W(s). ***Intramural sports:*** badminton M(c), baseball M(c), basketball M(c)/W(c), crew M(c), equestrian sports M(c), field hockey M(c), ice hockey M(c), lacrosse M(c)/W(c), rowing M(c), rugby M(c)/W(c), skiing (downhill) M(c), soccer M(c)/W(c), softball W(c), swimming and diving M(c)/W(c), table tennis M(c)/W(c), tennis M(c)/W(c), triathlon M(c)/W(c), ultimate Frisbee M(c)/W(c), volleyball M(c)/W(c), water polo M(c), wrestling M(c).

Campus security: 24-hour emergency response devices and patrols, student patrols, late-night transport/escort service, controlled dormitory access, security personnel in res. halls, RAD classes/special event coverage, more than 90 sworn officers and 200 security personnel.

Student services: health clinic, personal/psychological counseling, women's center, veterans affairs office.

FINANCIAL AID

Financial Aid Of all full-time matriculated undergraduates who enrolled in 2017, 14,326 applied for aid, 12,299 were judged to have need, 414 had their need fully met. 816 Federal Work-Study jobs (averaging $2230). 1 state and other part-time job (averaging $500). In 2017, 1471 non-need-based awards were made. ***Average percent of need met:*** 51. ***Average financial aid package:*** $12,040. ***Average need-based loan:*** $4338. ***Average need-based gift aid:*** $9775. ***Average non-need-based aid:*** $7368. ***Average indebtedness upon graduation:*** $32,617.

APPLYING

Standardized Tests *Required for some:* SAT or ACT (for admission).

Options: electronic application, early admission, deferred entrance.

Application fee: $65.

Required: essay or personal statement, high school transcript.

Application deadlines: 1/15 (freshmen), 1/15 (out-of-state freshmen), 3/15 (transfers).

Notification: continuous until 4/1 (freshmen), continuous until 4/15 (out-of-state freshmen), continuous until 5/1 (transfers).

CONTACT

Virginia Commonwealth University, 901 West Franklin Street, Richmond, VA 23284-9005. *Phone:* 804-828-6125. *Toll-free phone:* 800-841-3638.

Virginia International University

Fairfax, Virginia

http://www.viu.edu/

CONTACT

Admissions Department, Virginia International University, 4401 Village Drive, Fairfax, VA 22030. *Phone:* 703-591-7042 Ext. 313. *Toll-free phone:* 800-514-6848. *Fax:* 703-591-7048. *E-mail:* admissions@viu.edu.

Virginia Military Institute

Lexington, Virginia

http://www.vmi.edu/

- **State-supported** 4-year, founded 1839
- **Small-town** 134-acre campus
- **Endowment** $381.9 million
- **Coed**
- **Moderately difficult** entrance level

FACULTY

Student/faculty ratio: 10:1.

ACADEMICS

Calendar: semesters. *Degree:* bachelor's.

Library: Preston Library. *Books:* 280,000 (physical), 240,000 (digital/electronic); *Databases:* 150. Weekly public service hours: 113.

STUDENT LIFE
Housing options: on-campus residence required through senior year; coed. Campus housing is university owned. Freshman campus housing is guaranteed.

Activities and organizations: drama/theater group, student-run newspaper, choral group, marching band, Newman Club, Officers Christian Fellowship, strength and fitness organizations, Promaji, Pre-Law Society.

Athletics Member NCAA. All Division I.

Campus security: 24-hour emergency response devices and patrols, student patrols.

Student services: health clinic, personal/psychological counseling.

COSTS & FINANCIAL AID
Costs (2019–20) ***Tuition:*** area resident $9284 full-time; state resident $9284 full-time; nonresident $36,128 full-time. ***Required fees:*** $9578 full-time. ***Room and board:*** $9482; room only: $2840.

Financial Aid Of all full-time matriculated undergraduates who enrolled in 2018, 1,155 applied for aid, 921 were judged to have need, 404 had their need fully met. In 2018, 167 non-need-based awards were made. ***Average percent of need met:*** 80. ***Average financial aid package:*** $26,987. ***Average need-based loan:*** $441. ***Average need-based gift aid:*** $12,636. ***Average non-need-based aid:*** $6747. ***Average indebtedness upon graduation:*** $31,893.

APPLYING
Standardized Tests *Required:* SAT or ACT (for admission).

Options: electronic application, early decision.

Application fee: $40.

Required: high school transcript. ***Recommended:*** essay or personal statement, 2 letters of recommendation, interview, statement of good standing from prior institution.

CONTACT
Office of Admissions, Virginia Military Institute, Lexington, VA 24450. *Phone:* 800-767-4207. *Toll-free phone:* 800-767-4207. *Fax:* 540-464-7746. *E-mail:* admissions@vmi.edu.

See below for display ad and page 1134 for the College Close-Up.

Virginia Polytechnic Institute and State University

Blacksburg, Virginia

http://www.vt.edu/

- **State-supported** university, founded 1872
- **Small-town** 2600-acre campus
- **Endowment** $1.1 billion
- **Coed**
- **Moderately difficult** entrance level

FACULTY
Student/faculty ratio: 14:1.

ACADEMICS
Calendar: semesters. *Degrees:* bachelor's, master's, doctoral, post-master's, and postbachelor's certificates.
Library: Newman Library plus 2 others. Study areas open 24 hours, 5–7 days a week.

STUDENT LIFE
Housing options: on-campus residence required for freshman year; coed, men-only, women-only, special housing for students with disabilities. Campus housing is university owned. Freshman campus housing is guaranteed.

Activities and organizations: drama/theater group, student-run newspaper, radio and television station, choral group, marching band, Virginia Tech Union, Student Government Association, International student organizations, national fraternities, national sororities.

Athletics Member NCAA. All Division I except football (Division I-A).

Campus security: 24-hour emergency response devices and patrols, student patrols, late-night transport/escort service, controlled dormitory access.

Student services: health clinic, personal/psychological counseling, women's center, legal services, veterans affairs office.

COSTS & FINANCIAL AID

Costs (2019–20) ***Tuition:*** state resident $11,750 full-time; nonresident $32,385 full-time. Full-time tuition and fees vary according to course load and program. Part-time tuition and fees vary according to course load and program. ***Required fees:*** $2200 full-time. ***Room and board:*** $9460; room only: $5478. Room and board charges vary according to board plan and housing facility.

Financial Aid Of all full-time matriculated undergraduates who enrolled in 2017, 16,636 applied for aid, 11,042 were judged to have need, 1,693 had their need fully met. In 2017, 2269 non-need-based awards were made. ***Average percent of need met:*** 56. ***Average financial aid package:*** $10,980. ***Average need-based loan:*** $4692. ***Average need-based gift aid:*** $7432. ***Average non-need-based aid:*** $3696. ***Average indebtedness upon graduation:*** $31,494. ***Financial aid deadline:*** 1/15.

APPLYING

Standardized Tests *Required:* SAT or ACT (for admission).

Options: electronic application, early admission, early decision, deferred entrance.

Application fee: $60.

Required: high school transcript. ***Recommended:*** essay or personal statement.

CONTACT

Mr. Juan P. Espinoza, Associated Vice Provost for Enrollment Management and Director of Undergraduate Admissions, Virginia Polytechnic Institute and State University, Blacksburg, VA 24061. *Phone:* 540-231-6267. *Fax:* 540-231-3242. *E-mail:* admissions@vt.edu.

Virginia State University

Petersburg, Virginia

http://www.vsu.edu/

- **State-supported** comprehensive, founded 1882, part of State Council of Higher Education for Virginia
- **Suburban** 236-acre campus with easy access to Richmond
- **Endowment** $32.5 million
- **Coed**
- **Minimally difficult** entrance level

FACULTY

Student/faculty ratio: 14:1.

ACADEMICS

Calendar: semesters. *Degrees:* bachelor's, master's, doctoral, and postbachelor's certificates.

Library: Johnston Memorial Library. *Books:* 434,496 (physical); *Serial titles:* 5,805 (physical); *Databases:* 245. Weekly public service hours: 82.

STUDENT LIFE

Housing options: on-campus residence required for freshman year; coed, men-only, women-only. Campus housing is university owned. Freshman applicants given priority for college housing.

Activities and organizations: drama/theater group, student-run newspaper, choral group, marching band, AbstraKt Entertainment, Golden Key Honor Society, The Betterment of Brothers and Sisters, Diversified Virtue Entertainment, Sankofa, national fraternities, national sororities.

Athletics Member NCAA. All Division II.

Campus security: 24-hour emergency response devices and patrols, late-night transport/escort service, controlled dormitory access.

Student services: health clinic, personal/psychological counseling.

COSTS & FINANCIAL AID

Costs (2019–20) ***Tuition:*** state resident $5540 full-time, $395 per credit hour part-time; nonresident $16,542 full-time, $902 per credit hour part-time. Full-time tuition and fees vary according to course load. Part-time tuition and fees vary according to course load. ***Required fees:*** $3614 full-time, $10 per credit hour part-time. ***Room and board:*** $11,544; room only: $6744. Room and board charges vary according to board plan and housing facility.

Financial Aid Of all full-time matriculated undergraduates who enrolled in 2017, 3,952 applied for aid, 3,952 were judged to have need, 591 had their need fully met. 300 Federal Work-Study jobs (averaging $2000). 150 state and other part-time jobs (averaging $3000). In 2017, 433 non-need-based awards were made. ***Average percent of need met:*** 60. ***Average financial aid package:*** $12,250. ***Average need-based loan:*** $6500. ***Average need-based gift aid:*** $7036. ***Average non-need-based aid:*** $1000. ***Average indebtedness upon graduation:*** $28,250.

APPLYING

Standardized Tests *Required:* SAT or ACT (for admission).

Options: electronic application.

Application fee: $25.

Required: high school transcript, minimum 2.2 GPA, 2 letters of recommendation. ***Recommended:*** essay or personal statement.

CONTACT

Mr. Rodney Hall, Director of Enrollment Services, Virginia State University, Office of Admissions, Petersburg, VA 23806. *Phone:* 804-524-2954. *Toll-free phone:* 800-871-7611. *Fax:* 804-524-5055. *E-mail:* rhall@vsu.edu.

Virginia Union University

Richmond, Virginia

http://www.vuu.edu/

CONTACT

Ms. Danitra Morrison, Assistant Director of Admissions, Virginia Union University, 1500 North Lombardy Street, Richmond, VA 23220-1170. *Phone:* 804-257-5853. *Toll-free phone:* 800-368-3227. *Fax:* 804-342-3511. *E-mail:* dvmorrison@vuu.edu.

Virginia University of Lynchburg

Lynchburg, Virginia

http://www.vul.edu/

CONTACT

Ms. Cheryl Glass, Director of Admissions, Virginia University of Lynchburg, 2058 Garfield Avenue, Lynchburg, VA 24501. *Phone:* 434-528-5276 Ext. 106. *Fax:* 434-528-4275. *E-mail:* cglass@vul.edu.

Virginia Wesleyan University

Virginia Beach, Virginia

http://www.vwu.edu/

- **Independent United Methodist** comprehensive, founded 1961
- **Urban** 284-acre campus with easy access to Hampton Roads
- **Endowment** $56.6 million
- **Coed** 1,387 undergraduate students, 90% full-time, 59% women, 41% men
- **Moderately difficult** entrance level, 77% of applicants were admitted

UNDERGRAD STUDENTS

1,245 full-time, 142 part-time. 23% are from out of state; 23% Black or African American, non-Hispanic/Latino; 8% Hispanic/Latino; 2% Asian, non-Hispanic/Latino; 0.4% Native Hawaiian or other Pacific Islander, non-Hispanic/Latino; 0.6% American Indian or Alaska Native, non-Hispanic/Latino; 7% Two or more races, non-Hispanic/Latino; 4% Race/ethnicity unknown; 0.6% international; 6% transferred in; 68% live on campus.

Freshmen:

Admission: 2,323 applied, 1,785 admitted, 344 enrolled. ***Average high school GPA:*** 3.4. ***Test scores:*** SAT evidence-based reading and writing scores over 500: 70%; SAT math scores over 500: 62%; ACT scores over 18: 86%; SAT evidence-based reading and writing scores over 600: 26%; SAT math scores over 600: 20%; ACT scores over 24: 57%; SAT evidence-based reading and writing scores over 700: 5%; SAT math scores over 700: 5%; ACT scores over 30: 19%.

Retention: 59% of full-time freshmen returned.

FACULTY
Total: 131, 69% full-time, 79% with terminal degrees.

Student/faculty ratio: 12:1.

ACADEMICS
Calendar: 4-1-4. *Degrees:* certificates, bachelor's, and master's.

Special study options: academic remediation for entering students, adult/continuing education programs, advanced placement credit, double majors, external degree program, freshman honors college, honors programs, independent study, internships, off-campus study, part-time degree program, services for LD students, student-designed majors, study abroad, summer session for credit. ***ROTC:*** Army (c).

Unusual degree programs: 3-2 engineering with Old Dominion University; forestry with Duke University; medicine with Eastern Virginia Medical School, law with Regent University, pharmacy with Shenandoah University, occupational therapy with Washington University in St. Louis.

Computers: 137 computers/terminals are available on campus for general student use. Students can access the following: campus intranet, computer help desk, free student e-mail accounts, online (class) grades, online (class) registration, online (class) schedules. Campuswide network is available. 100% of college-owned or -operated housing units are wired for high-speed Internet access. Wireless service is available via entire campus.

Library: H. C. Hofheimer II Library plus 1 other. *Books:* 118,216 (physical), 256,770 (digital/electronic); *Serial titles:* 111 (physical), 71,260 (digital/electronic); *Databases:* 73. Weekly public service hours: 93; study areas open 24 hours, 5–7 days a week; students can reserve study rooms.

STUDENT LIFE
Housing options: on-campus residence required through senior year; coed, women-only, special housing for students with disabilities. Campus housing is university owned. Freshman campus housing is guaranteed.

Activities and organizations: drama/theater group, student-run newspaper, choral group, Wesleyan Activities Council, community service, Student Government Association, student newspaper, Black Student Union, national fraternities, national sororities.

Athletics Member NCAA. All Division III. ***Intercollegiate sports:*** baseball M, basketball M/W, cheerleading W, cross-country running M/W, field hockey W, golf M/W, lacrosse M/W, soccer M/W, softball W, swimming and diving M/W, tennis M/W, track and field M/W, volleyball W. ***Intramural sports:*** basketball M/W, crew M(c)/W(c), fencing M(c)/W(c), field hockey W, football M/W, racquetball M/W, soccer M/W, softball M/W, table tennis M/W, ultimate Frisbee M/W, volleyball M/W.

Campus security: 24-hour emergency response devices and patrols, late-night transport/escort service, controlled dormitory access, well-lit pathways.

Student services: health clinic, personal/psychological counseling, women's center, veterans affairs office.

COSTS & FINANCIAL AID
Costs (2020–21) ***Comprehensive fee:*** $10,338 includes full-time tuition ($36,010), mandatory fees ($900), and room and board ($10,338). Part-time tuition: $1500 per credit hour.

Financial Aid Of all full-time matriculated undergraduates who enrolled in 2018, 1,120 applied for aid, 1,054 were judged to have need, 107 had their need fully met. 193 Federal Work-Study jobs (averaging $1013). In 2018, 193 non-need-based awards were made. ***Average percent of need met:*** 62. ***Average financial aid package:*** $25,553. ***Average need-based loan:*** $8181. ***Average need-based gift aid:*** $23,099. ***Average non-need-based aid:*** $18,738. ***Average indebtedness upon graduation:*** $32,515.

APPLYING
Standardized Tests *Required:* SAT or ACT (for admission).

Options: electronic application, deferred entrance.

Required: high school transcript. ***Required for some:*** interview. ***Recommended:*** letters of recommendation.

Application deadlines: rolling (freshmen), rolling (transfers).

Notification: continuous (freshmen), continuous (transfers).

CONTACT
Ms. Elizabeth Clarke, Assistant Vice President for Enrollment, Virginia Wesleyan University, 5817 Wesleyan Drive, Virginia Beach, VA 23455. *Phone:* 757-455-3208. *Toll-free phone:* 800-737-8684. *Fax:* 757-461-5238. *E-mail:* admissions@vwu.edu.

Washington and Lee University

Lexington, Virginia

http://www.wlu.edu/

- **Independent** comprehensive, founded 1749
- **Small-town** 415-acre campus
- **Endowment** $1.7 billion
- **Coed** 1,860 undergraduate students, 99% full-time, 50% women, 50% men
- **Most difficult** entrance level, 19% of applicants were admitted

UNDERGRAD STUDENTS
1,845 full-time, 15 part-time. Students come from 49 states and territories; 28 other countries; 82% are from out of state; 3% Black or African American, non-Hispanic/Latino; 6% Hispanic/Latino; 4% Asian, non-Hispanic/Latino; 4% Two or more races, non-Hispanic/Latino; 0.5% Race/ethnicity unknown; 4% international; 0.3% transferred in; 74% live on campus.

Freshmen:
Admission: 6,178 applied, 1,147 admitted, 462 enrolled. ***Test scores:*** SAT evidence-based reading and writing scores over 500: 100%; ACT scores over 18: 100%; SAT evidence-based reading and writing scores over 600: 99%; SAT math scores over 600: 110%; ACT scores over 24: 100%; SAT evidence-based reading and writing scores over 700: 52%; SAT math scores over 700: 66%; ACT scores over 30: 98%.

Retention: 98% of full-time freshmen returned.

FACULTY
Total: 321, 78% full-time, 91% with terminal degrees.

Student/faculty ratio: 8:1.

ACADEMICS
Calendar: 4-4-2. *Degree:* bachelor's and doctoral.

Special study options: advanced placement credit, double majors, honors programs, independent study, internships, off-campus study, services for LD students, student-designed majors, study abroad. ***ROTC:*** Army (c).

Computers: 180 computers/terminals and 540 ports are available on campus for general student use. Students can access the following: campus intranet, computer help desk, free student e-mail accounts, online (class) grades, online (class) registration, online (class) schedules. Campuswide network is available. 100% of college-owned or -operated housing units are wired for high-speed Internet access. Wireless service is available via entire campus.

Library: James G. Leyburn Library plus 2 others. *Books:* 1.1 million (physical), 1.2 million (digital/electronic); *Serial titles:* 11,972 (digital/electronic). Study areas open 24 hours, 5–7 days a week; students can reserve study rooms.

STUDENT LIFE
Housing options: on-campus residence required through junior year; coed, men-only, women-only, special housing for students with disabilities. Campus housing is university owned. Freshman campus housing is guaranteed.

Activities and organizations: drama/theater group, student-run newspaper, radio and television station, choral group, Mock Convention, General Activities Board, Nabors Service League, Outing Club, Sports Clubs, national fraternities, national sororities.

Athletics Member NCAA. All Division III except golf (Division II). ***Intercollegiate sports:*** baseball M, basketball M/W, cross-country running M/W, equestrian sports M/W, field hockey W, football M, golf M/W, lacrosse M/W, rugby M(c), soccer M/W, swimming and diving M/W, tennis M/W, track and field M/W, volleyball W, wrestling M. ***Intramural sports:*** badminton M/W, baseball M(c), cheerleading M/W, equestrian sports W(c), golf M/W, ice hockey M(c), rock climbing M(c)/W(c), table tennis M/W, tennis M/W, track and field M/W, ultimate Frisbee M/W, volleyball W.

Campus security: 24-hour emergency response devices and patrols, late-night transport/escort service, controlled dormitory access, Emergency Alert System.

Student services: health clinic, personal/psychological counseling.

COSTS & FINANCIAL AID
Costs (2020–21) ***Required fees:*** $56,170 full-time. ***Room and board:*** $15,810; room only: $8365. Room and board charges vary according to board plan. ***Waivers:*** employees or children of employees.

Financial Aid Of all full-time matriculated undergraduates who enrolled in 2019, 903 applied for aid, 833 were judged to have need, 833 had their need fully met. 226 Federal Work-Study jobs (averaging $2000). 380 state and other part-time jobs (averaging $2000). In 2019, 156 non-need-based awards were made. ***Average percent of need met:*** 100. ***Average financial aid package:*** $57,291. ***Average need-based loan:*** $587. ***Average need-based gift aid:*** $49,745. ***Average non-need-based aid:*** $41,636. ***Average indebtedness upon graduation:*** $22,415.

APPLYING
Standardized Tests *Required:* SAT or ACT (for admission).

Options: electronic application, early decision, deferred entrance.

Application fee: $60.

Required: high school transcript, 3 letters of recommendation. ***Recommended:*** essay or personal statement, interview.

Application deadlines: 1/1 (freshmen), 4/1 (transfers).

Early decision deadline: 11/1.

Notification: 4/1 (freshmen), continuous (transfers), 12/22 (early decision).

CONTACT
Sally S. Richmond, Vice President for Admissions and Financial Aid, Washington and Lee University, 204 West Washington Street, Lexington, VA 24450-2116. *Phone:* 540-458-8710. *Fax:* 540-458-8062. *E-mail:* admissions@wlu.edu.

William & Mary

Williamsburg, Virginia

http://www.wm.edu/

- **State-supported** university, founded 1693
- **Small-town** 1200-acre campus with easy access to Richmond
- **Endowment** $995.9 million
- **Coed** 6,256 undergraduate students, 99% full-time, 58% women, 42% men
- **Most difficult** entrance level, 38% of applicants were admitted

UNDERGRAD STUDENTS
6,190 full-time, 66 part-time. Students come from 54 states and territories; 49 other countries; 31% are from out of state; 7% Black or African American, non-Hispanic/Latino; 10% Hispanic/Latino; 8% Asian, non-Hispanic/Latino; 0.1% Native Hawaiian or other Pacific Islander, non-Hispanic/Latino; 0.2% American Indian or Alaska Native, non-Hispanic/Latino; 6% Two or more races, non-Hispanic/Latino; 5% Race/ethnicity unknown; 6% international; 3% transferred in; 70% live on campus.

Freshmen:
Admission: 14,680 applied, 5,532 admitted, 1,530 enrolled. ***Average high school GPA:*** 4.3. ***Test scores:*** SAT evidence-based reading and writing scores over 500: 100%; SAT math scores over 500: 100%; ACT scores over 18: 100%; SAT evidence-based reading and writing scores over 600: 95%; SAT math scores over 600: 91%; ACT scores over 24: 97%; SAT evidence-based reading and writing scores over 700: 56%; SAT math scores over 700: 57%; ACT scores over 30: 77%.

Retention: 95% of full-time freshmen returned.

ACADEMICS
Calendar: semesters. *Degrees:* bachelor's, master's, doctoral, post-master's, and postbachelor's certificates.

Special study options: accelerated degree program, advanced placement credit, distance learning, double majors, external degree program, honors programs, independent study, internships, off-campus study, part-time degree program, services for LD students, student-designed majors, study abroad, summer session for credit. ***ROTC:*** Army (b).

Unusual degree programs: 3-2 elementary education, secondary education, special education, chemistry, public policy.

Computers: 400 computers/terminals and 8,000 ports are available on campus for general student use. Students can access the following: campus intranet, computer help desk, free student e-mail accounts, online (class) grades, online (class) registration, online (class) schedules. Campuswide network is available. 100% of college-owned or -operated housing units are wired for high-speed Internet access. Wireless service is available via entire campus.

Library: Earl Gregg Swem Library plus 5 others. *Books:* 1.4 million (physical), 2.6 million (digital/electronic); *Serial titles:* 40,730 (physical), 201,557 (digital/electronic); *Databases:* 645. Weekly public service hours: 110; study areas open 24 hours, 5–7 days a week; students can reserve study rooms.

STUDENT LIFE
Housing options: on-campus residence required through sophomore year; coed, special housing for students with disabilities. Campus housing is university owned. Freshman campus housing is guaranteed.

Activities and organizations: drama/theater group, student-run newspaper, radio and television station, choral group, Alma Mater Productions, Student Assembly, Residence Hall Association, Alpha Phi Omega, International Relations Club, national fraternities, national sororities.

Athletics Member NCAA. All Division I. ***Intercollegiate sports:*** baseball M(s), basketball M(s)/W(s), cross-country running M(s)/W(s), field hockey W(s), football M(s), golf M(s)/W(s), gymnastics M(s)/W(s), lacrosse W(s), soccer M(s)/W(s), swimming and diving M/W(s), tennis M(s)/W(s), track and field M(s)/W(s), volleyball W(s). ***Intramural sports:*** badminton M(c)/W(c), baseball M(c), basketball M/W, cheerleading M(c)/W(c), crew M(c)/W(c), cross-country running M(c)/W(c), equestrian sports M(c)/W(c), fencing M(c)/W(c), field hockey M(c)/W(c), football M/W, golf M(c)/W(c), gymnastics M(c)/W(c), ice hockey M(c), lacrosse M(c)/W(c), racquetball M(c)/W(c), rock climbing M(c)/W(c), rowing M(c)/W(c), rugby M(c)/W(c), sailing M(c)/W(c), soccer M/W, softball M/W, squash M(c)/W(c), swimming and diving M(c)/W(c), table tennis M(c)/W(c), tennis M(c)/W(c), triathlon M(c)/W(c), ultimate Frisbee M(c)/W(c), volleyball M/W, water polo M(c)/W(c), weight lifting M/W, wrestling M(c).

Campus security: 24-hour emergency response devices and patrols, late-night transport/escort service, controlled dormitory access.

Student services: health clinic, personal/psychological counseling, legal services.

COSTS & FINANCIAL AID
Costs (2019–20) ***Tuition:*** state resident $17,434 full-time, $425 per credit hour part-time; nonresident $40,089 full-time, $1278 per credit hour part-time. Full-time tuition and fees vary according to course load, program, and student level. Part-time tuition and fees vary according to course load and program. No tuition increase for student's term of enrollment. ***Required fees:*** $6194 full-time. ***Room and board:*** $12,926; room only: $7958. Room and board charges vary according to board plan and housing facility. ***Payment plan:*** installment. ***Waivers:*** senior citizens and employees or children of employees.

Financial Aid Of all full-time matriculated undergraduates who enrolled in 2018, 3,497 applied for aid, 2,395 were judged to have need, 549 had their need fully met. 653 Federal Work-Study jobs (averaging $1092). In 2018, 346 non-need-based awards were made. ***Average percent of need met:*** 81. ***Average financial aid package:*** $24,609. ***Average need-based loan:*** $3566. ***Average need-based gift aid:*** $18,222. ***Average non-need-based aid:*** $7661. ***Average indebtedness upon graduation:*** $28,895.

APPLYING
Standardized Tests *Required:* SAT or ACT (for admission).

Options: electronic application, early admission, early decision, deferred entrance.

Application fee: $75.

Required: essay or personal statement, high school transcript, 1 letter of recommendation. ***Recommended:*** 2 letters of recommendation.

Application deadlines: 1/1 (freshmen), 3/1 (transfers).

Early decision deadline: 11/1.

Notification: 4/1 (freshmen), 5/1 (transfers), 12/1 (early decision).

CONTACT
Mr. David Trott, Associate Dean of Admission, William & Mary, PO Box 8795, Williamsburg, VA 23187-8795. *Phone:* 757-221-3059. *Fax:* 757-221-1242. *E-mail:* admission@wm.edu.

WASHINGTON

Antioch University Seattle

Seattle, Washington

http://www.antioch.edu/seattle/

CONTACT
Admissions Office, Antioch University Seattle, 2400 3rd Avenue, Suite 200, Seattle, WA 98121. *Phone:* 206-268-4202. *Toll-free phone:* 888-268-4477. *E-mail:* admissions@antiochseattle.edu.

Argosy University, Seattle

Seattle, Washington

http://www.argosy.edu/locations/seattle/

CONTACT
Argosy University, Seattle, 2601-A Elliott Avenue, Seattle, WA 98121. *Phone:* 206-283-4500. *Toll-free phone:* 866-283-2777.

The Art Institute of Seattle

Seattle, Washington

http://www.artinstitutes.edu/seattle/

CONTACT
The Art Institute of Seattle, 2323 Elliott Avenue, Seattle, WA 98121-1642. *Phone:* 206-448-6600. *Toll-free phone:* 800-275-2471.

Bastyr University

Kenmore, Washington

http://www.bastyr.edu/

CONTACT
Ms. Lauren Marani, Assistant Director of Admissions, Bastyr University, 14500 Juanita Drive NE, Kenmore, WA 98028-4966. *Phone:* 425-602-1300. *Fax:* 425-602-3090. *E-mail:* admissions@bastyr.edu.

Bellevue College

Bellevue, Washington

http://www.bellevuecollege.edu/

- **State-supported** primarily 2-year, founded 1966, part of Washington State Board for Community and Technical Colleges
- **Suburban** 96-acre campus with easy access to Seattle
- **Coed**
- **Noncompetitive** entrance level

ACADEMICS
Calendar: quarters. *Degrees:* certificates, associate, and bachelor's.
Library: Bellevue Community College Library.

STUDENT LIFE
Housing options: college housing not available.

Activities and organizations: drama/theater group, student-run newspaper, radio station.

Student services: health clinic, personal/psychological counseling, women's center.

FINANCIAL AID
Financial Aid Of all full-time matriculated undergraduates who enrolled in 2018, 65 Federal Work-Study jobs (averaging $3400). 43 state and other part-time jobs (averaging $3000).

APPLYING
Options: electronic application.

Application fee: $28.

CONTACT
Morenika Jacobs, Associate Dean of Enrollment Services, Bellevue College, 3000 Landerholm Circle, SE, Bellevue, WA 98007-6484. *Phone:* 425-564-2205. *Fax:* 425-564-4065.

Cascadia College

Bothell, Washington

http://www.cascadia.edu/

- **State-supported** primarily 2-year, founded 1999, part of Washington State Board for Community and Technical Colleges
- **Suburban** 128-acre campus with easy access to Seattle, WA
- **Coed** 3,757 undergraduate students, 41% full-time, 36% women, 37% men
- **Noncompetitive** entrance level

UNDERGRAD STUDENTS
1,529 full-time, 1,230 part-time. Students come from 12 states and territories; 3% Black or African American, non-Hispanic/Latino; 18% Hispanic/Latino; 15% Asian, non-Hispanic/Latino; 0.4% Native Hawaiian or other Pacific Islander, non-Hispanic/Latino; 0.8% American Indian or Alaska Native, non-Hispanic/Latino; 16% Two or more races, non-Hispanic/Latino; 17% Race/ethnicity unknown; 12% international.

Freshmen:
Admission: 2,939 applied.

FACULTY
Total: 129, 24% full-time.

ACADEMICS
Calendar: quarters. *Degrees:* certificates, diplomas, associate, and bachelor's.

Special study options: academic remediation for entering students, accelerated degree program, adult/continuing education programs, advanced placement credit, cooperative education, distance learning, double majors, English as a second language, independent study, internships, off-campus study, part-time degree program, services for LD students, study abroad, summer session for credit.

Computers: Students can access the following: campus intranet, computer help desk, free student e-mail accounts, online (class) grades, online (class) registration, online (class) schedules. Campuswide network is available. Wireless service is available via entire campus.
Library: Campus Library. *Books:* 90,000 (physical), 600,000 (digital/electronic); *Serial titles:* 600 (physical), 100,000 (digital/electronic); *Databases:* 600. Weekly public service hours: 86; students can reserve study rooms.

STUDENT LIFE
Housing options: college housing not available.

Activities and organizations: drama/theater group, student-run newspaper.

Athletics ***Intramural sports:*** basketball M/W, football M/W, soccer M/W.

Campus security: 24-hour emergency response devices, late-night transport/escort service.

Student services: personal/psychological counseling, veterans affairs office.

APPLYING
Options: electronic application.

Application fee: $30.

Application deadlines: rolling (freshmen), rolling (transfers).

Notification: continuous (freshmen), continuous (transfers).

CONTACT
Ms. Erin Blakeney, Dean for Student Success, Cascadia College, 18345 Campus Way, NE, Bothell, WA 98011. *Phone:* 425-352-8000. *Fax:* 425-352-8137. *E-mail:* admissions@cascadia.edu.

Central Washington University

Ellensburg, Washington

http://www.cwu.edu/

- **State-supported** comprehensive, founded 1891
- **Small-town** 380-acre campus with easy access to Seattle
- **Endowment** $5.7 million
- **Coed** 10,884 undergraduate students, 91% full-time, 52% women, 48% men
- **Moderately difficult** entrance level, 88% of applicants were admitted

UNDERGRAD STUDENTS

9,913 full-time, 971 part-time. 6% are from out of state; 4% Black or African American, non-Hispanic/Latino; 17% Hispanic/Latino; 4% Asian, non-Hispanic/Latino; 1% Native Hawaiian or other Pacific Islander, non-Hispanic/Latino; 0.5% American Indian or Alaska Native, non-Hispanic/Latino; 8% Two or more races, non-Hispanic/Latino; 11% Race/ethnicity unknown; 3% international; 12% transferred in; 26% live on campus.

Freshmen:

Admission: 9,914 applied, 8,675 admitted, 2,294 enrolled. ***Average high school GPA:*** 3.1. ***Test scores:*** SAT evidence-based reading and writing scores over 500: 62%; SAT math scores over 500: 61%; ACT scores over 18: 57%; SAT evidence-based reading and writing scores over 600: 13%; SAT math scores over 600: 18%; ACT scores over 24: 21%; SAT evidence-based reading and writing scores over 700: 1%; SAT math scores over 700: 1%; ACT scores over 30: 1%.

Retention: 71% of full-time freshmen returned.

FACULTY

Total: 641, 63% full-time, 58% with terminal degrees.

Student/faculty ratio: 22:1.

ACADEMICS

Calendar: quarters. *Degrees:* certificates, bachelor's, master's, post-master's, and postbachelor's certificates.

Special study options: academic remediation for entering students, advanced placement credit, cooperative education, distance learning, double majors, English as a second language, freshman honors college, honors programs, independent study, internships, off-campus study, part-time degree program, services for LD students, student-designed majors, study abroad, summer session for credit. ***ROTC:*** Army (b), Air Force (b).

Computers: 791 computers/terminals and 3,100 ports are available on campus for general student use. Students can access the following: campus intranet, computer help desk, free student e-mail accounts, online (class) grades, online (class) registration, online (class) schedules, online data storage, office software. Campuswide network is available. 100% of college-owned or -operated housing units are wired for high-speed Internet access. Wireless service is available via entire campus.

Library: James E. Brooks Library plus 2 others. *Books:* 548,805 (physical), 341,967 (digital/electronic); *Serial titles:* 8,719 (physical), 98,119 (digital/electronic); *Databases:* 240. Weekly public service hours: 101; students can reserve study rooms.

STUDENT LIFE

Housing options: on-campus residence required for freshman year; coed, special housing for students with disabilities. Campus housing is university owned. Freshman campus housing is guaranteed.

Activities and organizations: drama/theater group, student-run newspaper, radio and television station, choral group, marching band, SISTERS, Brother 2 Brother, Cosplay, Alpha Kappa Si, Society of Human Resource Management.

Athletics Member NCAA. All Division II. ***Intercollegiate sports:*** archery M(c)/W(c), baseball M(s), basketball M(s)/W(s), bowling M(c)/W(c), cheerleading M/W, cross-country running M(s)/W(s), equestrian sports M(c)/W(c), fencing M(c)/W(c), football M(s), golf M(c), ice hockey M(c)/W(c), lacrosse M(c)/W(c), rock climbing M(c)/W(c), rugby M(s)/W(s), soccer M(c)/W(s), softball W(s), swimming and diving M(c)/W(c), tennis M(c)/W(c), track and field M(s)/W(s), ultimate Frisbee M(c)/W(c), volleyball W(s), water polo M(c)/W(c), wrestling M(c)/W(c). ***Intramural sports:*** badminton M/W, basketball M/W, rock climbing M/W, skiing (cross-country) M/W, soccer M/W, softball M/W, table tennis M/W, tennis M/W, volleyball M/W.

Campus security: 24-hour emergency response devices and patrols, late-night transport/escort service, controlled dormitory access, alert update system: emergency notification across digital platforms, Rape Aggression Defense System: realistic self-defense for women.

Student services: health clinic, personal/psychological counseling, veterans affairs office.

COSTS & FINANCIAL AID

Costs (2020–21) ***Tuition:*** area resident $6318 full-time, $1895 per term part-time; state resident $6318 full-time, $1895 per term part-time; nonresident $21,999 full-time, $6600 per term part-time. Full-time tuition and fees vary according to course load, degree level, location, and program. Part-time tuition and fees vary according to course load, degree level, location, and program. ***Required fees:*** $1244 full-time, $61 per credit part-time, $612 per quarter part-time. ***Room and board:*** $12,637; room only: $6188. Room and board charges vary according to board plan, housing facility, and location. ***Payment plan:*** installment. ***Waivers:*** children of alumni, senior citizens, and employees or children of employees.

Financial Aid Of all full-time matriculated undergraduates who enrolled in 2018, 7,606 applied for aid, 6,115 were judged to have need, 402 had their need fully met. 151 Federal Work-Study jobs (averaging $2138), 162 state and other part-time jobs (averaging $2240). In 2018, 25 non-need-based awards were made. ***Average percent of need met:*** 59. ***Average financial aid package:*** $10,892. ***Average need-based loan:*** $4092. ***Average need-based gift aid:*** $8878. ***Average non-need-based aid:*** $1587. ***Average indebtedness upon graduation:*** $24,498.

APPLYING

Standardized Tests *Required:* SAT or ACT (for admission).

Options: electronic application.

Application fee: $50.

Required: high school transcript, minimum 2.0 GPA. ***Required for some:*** essay or personal statement, interview.

Application deadlines: rolling (out-of-state freshmen), 3/1 (transfers).

Notification: continuous (freshmen), continuous (out-of-state freshmen), continuous (transfers).

CONTACT

Mr. Josh Hibbard, Vice President of Enrollment Management, Central Washington University, 400 East University Way, Ellensburg, WA 98926-7463. *Phone:* 509-963-1211. *Fax:* 509-963-3065. *E-mail:* admissions@cwu.edu.

Charter College

Vancouver, Washington

http://www.chartercollege.edu/

- **Proprietary** comprehensive
- **Coed**

CONTACT

Charter College, 17720 SE Mill Plain Boulevard, Suite 170, Vancouver, WA 98683.

City University of Seattle

Seattle, Washington

http://www.cityu.edu/

CONTACT

Student Services Center, City University of Seattle, 11900 NE First Street, Bellevue, WA 98005. *Phone:* 888-422-4898. *Toll-free phone:* 800-426-5596. *E-mail:* info@cityu.edu.

Clark College

Vancouver, Washington

http://www.clark.edu/

CONTACT

Ms. Vanessa Watkins, Associate Director of Entry Services, Clark College, Vancouver, WA 98663. *Phone:* 360-992-2308. *Fax:* 360-992-2867. *E-mail:* admissions@clark.edu.

Cornish College of the Arts

Seattle, Washington

http://www.cornish.edu/

CONTACT

Ms. Sharron Starling, Director of Admissions, Cornish College of the Arts, 1000 Lenora Street, Seattle, WA 98121. *Phone:* 206-726-5017. *Toll-free phone:* 800-726-ARTS. *Fax:* 206-720-1011. *E-mail:* admissions@cornish.edu.

DigiPen Institute of Technology

Redmond, Washington

http://www.digipen.edu/

- **Proprietary** comprehensive, founded 1988
- **Suburban** 3-acre campus with easy access to Seattle
- **Coed**
- **Minimally difficult** entrance level

FACULTY

Student/faculty ratio: 11:1.

ACADEMICS

Calendar: semesters. *Degrees:* bachelor's and master's.
Library: DigiPen Library. *Books:* 5,946 (physical), 196,396 (digital/electronic); *Serial titles:* 36 (physical), 6,756 (digital/electronic); *Databases:* 11. Weekly public service hours: 84.

STUDENT LIFE

Housing options: coed, men-only, women-only, special housing for students with disabilities. Campus housing is leased by the school and is provided by a third party. Freshman applicants given priority for college housing.

Activities and organizations: choral group, PRISM Club, Cage of the Week Club, Halo Club, Outbreak Club, Wellness Club.

Campus security: 24-hour patrols, late-night transport/escort service, controlled dormitory access, on-site security during campus hours.

Student services: personal/psychological counseling.

COSTS & FINANCIAL AID

Costs (2019–20) ***One-time required fee:*** $150. ***Tuition:*** $32,400 full-time, $1045 per credit part-time. Full-time tuition and fees vary according to course load, degree level, and program. Part-time tuition and fees vary according to course load, degree level, and program. ***Required fees:*** $200 full-time. ***Room only:*** $7500. Room and board charges vary according to board plan and housing facility.

Financial Aid Of all full-time matriculated undergraduates who enrolled in 2018, 592 applied for aid, 512 were judged to have need. 22 Federal Work-Study jobs (averaging $2000). In 2018, 10 non-need-based awards were made. ***Average percent of need met:*** 24. ***Average financial aid package:*** $7966. ***Average need-based loan:*** $3695. ***Average need-based gift aid:*** $7860. ***Average non-need-based aid:*** $6028. ***Average indebtedness upon graduation:*** $28,539.

APPLYING

Standardized Tests *Required for some:* SAT or ACT (for admission).

Options: electronic application, deferred entrance.

Application fee: $60.

Required: essay or personal statement, high school transcript, minimum 2.5 GPA. ***Required for some:*** pre-calculus for Bachelor of Science, art portfolio for BFA in Digital Art and Animation, performance portfolio for BA in Music and Sound Design, design portfolio for Bachelor of Art in Game Design. ***Recommended:*** 2 letters of recommendation.

CONTACT

Ms. Emily Kirby, Director of Admissions, DigiPen Institute of Technology, 9931 Willows Road NE, Redmond, WA 98052. *Phone:* 425-629-4862. *Toll-free phone:* 866-478-5236. *Fax:* 425-558-0378. *E-mail:* admissions@digipen.edu.

Eastern Washington University

Cheney, Washington

http://www.ewu.edu/

- **State-supported** comprehensive, founded 1882
- **Suburban** 335-acre campus with easy access to Spokane
- **Coed** 10,671 undergraduate students, 89% full-time, 55% women, 45% men
- 96% of applicants were admitted

UNDERGRAD STUDENTS

9,458 full-time, 1,213 part-time. 6% are from out of state; 4% Black or African American, non-Hispanic/Latino; 17% Hispanic/Latino; 3% Asian, non-Hispanic/Latino; 0.5% Native Hawaiian or other Pacific Islander, non-Hispanic/Latino; 1% American Indian or Alaska Native, non-Hispanic/Latino; 8% Two or more races, non-Hispanic/Latino; 4% Race/ethnicity unknown; 3% international; 10% transferred in; 46% live on campus.

Freshmen:

Admission: 5,299 applied, 5,069 admitted, 1,810 enrolled. ***Average high school GPA:*** 3.2. ***Test scores:*** SAT evidence-based reading and writing scores over 500: 59%; SAT math scores over 500: 58%; ACT scores over 18: 68%; SAT evidence-based reading and writing scores over 600: 17%; SAT math scores over 600: 12%; ACT scores over 24: 25%; SAT evidence-based reading and writing scores over 700: 1%; SAT math scores over 700: 2%; ACT scores over 30: 2%.

Retention: 70% of full-time freshmen returned.

FACULTY

Total: 694, 66% full-time, 52% with terminal degrees.

Student/faculty ratio: 18:1.

ACADEMICS

Calendar: quarters. *Degrees:* certificates, bachelor's, master's, doctoral, and postbachelor's certificates.

Special study options: academic remediation for entering students, accelerated degree program, adult/continuing education programs, advanced placement credit, distance learning, double majors, English as a second language, honors programs, independent study, internships, off-campus study, part-time degree program, services for LD students, student-designed majors, study abroad, summer session for credit. ***ROTC:*** Army (b).

Unusual degree programs: 3-2 exercise science/occupational therapy, therapeutic recreation, interdisciplinary studies.

Computers: Students can access the following: campus intranet, computer help desk, free student e-mail accounts, online (class) grades, online (class) registration, online (class) schedules, network disk storage; discounted software; laptops, still and video cameras, projectors for checkout; print credit; black white laser, color laser, and color photo options, large format print service. Campuswide network is available. 100% of college-owned or -operated housing units are wired for high-speed Internet access. Wireless service is available via entire campus.
Library: John F. Kennedy Library. Students can reserve study rooms.

STUDENT LIFE

Housing options: on-campus residence required for freshman year; coed, special housing for students with disabilities. Campus housing is university owned. Freshman campus housing is guaranteed.

Activities and organizations: drama/theater group, student-run newspaper, radio station, choral group, marching band, national fraternities, national sororities.

Athletics Member NCAA. All Division I except football (Division I-AA). ***Intercollegiate sports:*** archery M(c)/W(c), baseball M(c), basketball M(s)/W(s), cheerleading W(c), cross-country running M(s)/W(s), equestrian sports M(c)/W(c), fencing M(c)/W(c), golf W(s)(c), ice hockey M(c)/W(c), rugby M(c)/W(c), soccer M(c)/W(s), softball W(c), tennis M(s)/W(s), track and field M(s)/W(s), volleyball W(s). ***Intramural sports:*** baseball M/W, basketball M/W, bowling M/W, cross-country running M/W, football M/W, golf W, racquetball M/W, soccer M/W, softball M/W, tennis M/W, track and field M/W, ultimate Frisbee M(c)/W(c), volleyball M/W, wrestling M(c)/W(c).

Campus security: 24-hour emergency response devices and patrols, student patrols, late-night transport/escort service, controlled dormitory access.

Student services: health clinic, personal/psychological counseling, women's center.

COSTS & FINANCIAL AID

Costs (2019–20) ***Tuition:*** area resident $6522 full-time; state resident $6522 full-time, $218 per credit hour part-time; nonresident $24,018 full-time, $801 per credit hour part-time. ***Required fees:*** $939 full-time. ***Room and board:*** $12,708; room only: $7260.

Financial Aid Of all full-time matriculated undergraduates who enrolled in 2018, 7,445 applied for aid, 5,141 were judged to have need, 384 had their need fully met. 199 Federal Work-Study jobs (averaging $2857). 151 state and other part-time jobs (averaging $2977). In 2018, 676 non-need-based awards were made. ***Average percent of need met:*** 61. ***Average financial aid package:*** $13,326. ***Average need-based loan:*** $3952.

Average need-based gift aid: $8616. *Average non-need-based aid:* $3641. *Average indebtedness upon graduation:* $23,301.

APPLYING
Standardized Tests *Required:* SAT or ACT (for admission).

Options: deferred entrance.

Application fee: $60.

Required: high school transcript, minimum 2.0 GPA. ***Required for some:*** essay or personal statement. ***Recommended:*** minimum 3.0 GPA.

CONTACT
Jana Jaraysi, Director of Recruitment, Eastern Washington University, 304 Sutton Hall, Cheney, WA 99004-2447. *Phone:* 509-359-2450. *Fax:* 509-359-6692. *E-mail:* admissions@ewu.edu.

The Evergreen State College

Olympia, Washington

http://www.evergreen.edu/

- **State-supported** comprehensive, founded 1967, part of Washington State Public Baccalaureate Institution
- **Rural** 1000-acre campus with easy access to Seattle
- **Endowment** $13.4 million
- **Coed**
- **Moderately difficult** entrance level

FACULTY
Student/faculty ratio: 21:1.

ACADEMICS
Calendar: quarters. *Degrees:* bachelor's and master's.
Library: Daniel J. Evans Library. *Books:* 377,812 (physical), 216,358 (digital/electronic); *Serial titles:* 69 (physical), 73,705 (digital/electronic); *Databases:* 103. Weekly public service hours: 77; students can reserve study rooms.

STUDENT LIFE
Housing options: coed, special housing for students with disabilities. Campus housing is university owned. Freshman campus housing is guaranteed.

Activities and organizations: drama/theater group, student-run newspaper, radio and television station, choral group, Flaming Eggplant, Geoduck Student Union, Cooper Point Journal, Gaming Guild, Myco-Collective.

Athletics Member NCAA, NAIA. All NCAA Division II.

Campus security: 24-hour emergency response devices and patrols, student patrols, late-night transport/escort service, controlled dormitory access, car lockouts, jump-starts.

Student services: health clinic, personal/psychological counseling, women's center, veterans affairs office.

FINANCIAL AID
Financial Aid Of all full-time matriculated undergraduates who enrolled in 2018, 2,174 applied for aid, 1,937 were judged to have need, 88 had their need fully met. In 2018, 33 non-need-based awards were made. *Average percent of need met:* 63. *Average financial aid package:* $13,549. *Average need-based loan:* $4210. *Average need-based gift aid:* $10,923. *Average non-need-based aid:* $3225. *Average indebtedness upon graduation:* $20,488.

APPLYING
Standardized Tests *Required:* SAT or ACT (for admission).

Options: electronic application, deferred entrance.

Application fee: $50.

Required: high school transcript, minimum 2.0 GPA. ***Required for some:*** essay or personal statement.

CONTACT
Eric Pedersen, Director of Admissions, The Evergreen State College, 2700 Evergreen Parkway, NW, Olympia, WA 98505. *Phone:* 360-867-6170. *Fax:* 360-867-5114. *E-mail:* admissions@evergreen.edu.

Faith International University

Tacoma, Washington

http://www.faithseminary.edu/

CONTACT
Faith International University, 3504 North Pearl Street, Tacoma, WA 98407. *Toll-free phone:* 888-777-7675.

Gonzaga University

Spokane, Washington

http://www.gonzaga.edu/

- **Independent Roman Catholic** university, founded 1887
- **Urban** 152-acre campus
- **Endowment** $294.7 million
- **Coed** 5,238 undergraduate students, 98% full-time, 53% women, 47% men
- **Moderately difficult** entrance level, 62% of applicants were admitted

UNDERGRAD STUDENTS
5,138 full-time, 100 part-time. Students come from 47 states and territories; 35 other countries; 52% are from out of state; 1% Black or African American, non-Hispanic/Latino; 11% Hispanic/Latino; 6% Asian, non-Hispanic/Latino; 0.4% Native Hawaiian or other Pacific Islander, non-Hispanic/Latino; 0.5% American Indian or Alaska Native, non-Hispanic/Latino; 7% Two or more races, non-Hispanic/Latino; 2% Race/ethnicity unknown; 1% international; 2% transferred in; 51% live on campus.

Freshmen:
Admission: 9,279 applied, 5,744 admitted, 1,248 enrolled. ***Average high school GPA:*** 3.8. ***Test scores:*** SAT evidence-based reading and writing scores over 500: 99%; SAT math scores over 500: 100%; ACT scores over 18: 99%; SAT evidence-based reading and writing scores over 600: 78%; SAT math scores over 600: 76%; ACT scores over 24: 86%; SAT evidence-based reading and writing scores over 700: 14%; SAT math scores over 700: 24%; ACT scores over 30: 28%.

Retention: 94% of full-time freshmen returned.

FACULTY
Total: 844, 54% full-time, 48% with terminal degrees.

Student/faculty ratio: 11:1.

ACADEMICS
Calendar: semesters. *Degrees:* bachelor's, master's, and doctoral.

Special study options: accelerated degree program, adult/continuing education programs, advanced placement credit, distance learning, double majors, English as a second language, honors programs, independent study, internships, off-campus study, part-time degree program, services for LD students, study abroad, summer session for credit. ***ROTC:*** Army (b).

Unusual degree programs: 3-2 business administration.

Computers: Students can access the following: campus intranet, computer help desk, free student e-mail accounts, online (class) grades, online (class) registration, online (class) schedules. Campuswide network is available. 100% of college-owned or -operated housing units are wired for high-speed Internet access. Wireless service is available via entire campus.
Library: Ralph E. and Helen Higgins Foley Center plus 1 other. *Books:* 285,132 (physical), 152,695 (digital/electronic); *Serial titles:* 50,046 (physical), 55,687 (digital/electronic); *Databases:* 356. Weekly public service hours: 112; study areas open 24 hours, 5–7 days a week; students can reserve study rooms.

STUDENT LIFE
Housing options: on-campus residence required through sophomore year; coed, men-only, women-only, special housing for students with disabilities. Campus housing is university owned. Freshman campus housing is guaranteed.

Activities and organizations: drama/theater group, student-run newspaper, radio and television station, choral group, Kennel Club, Ski and Snowboard Club, Alpha Kappa Psi, Queer Student Union, Society of Women Engineers.

Athletics Member NCAA. All Division I. ***Intercollegiate sports:*** baseball M(s), basketball M(s)/W(s), cross-country running M(s)/W(s), golf M(s)/W(s), rowing M/W(s), soccer M(s)/W(s), tennis M(s)/W(s), track and field M(s)/W(s), volleyball W(s). ***Intramural sports:*** badminton M/W, basketball M/W, cheerleading M(c)/W(c), football M/W, golf M(c)/W(c), ice hockey M(c)/W(c), lacrosse M(c)/W(c), racquetball M/W, rugby M(c)/W(c), skiing (downhill) M(c)/W(c), soccer M(c)/W(c), softball M/W, swimming and diving M(c)/W(c), tennis M/W, track and field M(c)/W(c), triathlon M(c)/W(c), ultimate Frisbee M(c)/W(c), volleyball M/W, water polo M(c)/W(c), weight lifting M(c)/W(c), wrestling M.

Campus security: 24-hour emergency response devices and patrols, late-night transport/escort service, controlled dormitory access.

Student services: health clinic, personal/psychological counseling, veterans affairs office.

COSTS & FINANCIAL AID

Costs (2020–21) ***Comprehensive fee:*** $59,871 includes full-time tuition ($46,060), mandatory fees ($860), and room and board ($12,951). Full-time tuition and fees vary according to course load, location, program, and reciprocity agreements. Part-time tuition: $1255 per credit. Part-time tuition and fees vary according to course load, location, program, and reciprocity agreements. ***Required fees:*** $165 per term part-time. ***College room only:*** $6670. Room and board charges vary according to board plan, housing facility, and location. ***Payment plans:*** installment, deferred payment. ***Waivers:*** employees or children of employees.

Financial Aid Of all full-time matriculated undergraduates who enrolled in 2018, 3,465 applied for aid, 2,726 were judged to have need, 635 had their need fully met. 452 Federal Work-Study jobs (averaging $2012). 140 state and other part-time jobs (averaging $2328). In 2018, 2830 non-need-based awards were made. ***Average percent of need met:*** 78. ***Average financial aid package:*** $30,766. ***Average need-based loan:*** $4744. ***Average need-based gift aid:*** $7435. ***Average non-need-based aid:*** $16,064. ***Average indebtedness upon graduation:*** $29,685.

APPLYING

Standardized Tests *Required:* Traditionally, SAT or ACT tests are required but Gonzaga has suspended the requirement for Fall 2021 due to COVID-19. (for admission).

Options: electronic application, deferred entrance.

Application fee: $50.

Required: essay or personal statement, high school transcript, 1 letter of recommendation. ***Recommended:*** interview.

Application deadlines: 2/1 (freshmen), 6/1 (transfers).

Notification: 3/15 (freshmen), continuous (transfers).

CONTACT

Ms. Erin Hays, Director of Undergraduate Admissions, Gonzaga University, 502 East Boone Avenue, Spokane, WA 99258-0102. *Phone:* 800-322-2584 Ext. 6507. *Toll-free phone:* 800-322-2584 Ext. 6572. *E-mail:* admissions@gonzaga.edu.

Heritage University

Toppenish, Washington

http://www.heritage.edu/

CONTACT

Olivia Gutierrez, Director of Admissions, Heritage University, 3240 Fort Road, Toppenish, WA 98948-9599. *Phone:* 509-865-8697. *Toll-free phone:* 888-272-6190. *Fax:* 509-865-4469. *E-mail:* admissions@heritage.edu.

Northwest College of Art & Design

Tacoma, Washington

http://www.ncad.edu/

- **Proprietary** 4-year, founded 1982
- **Urban** campus with easy access to Seattle
- **Coed**

FACULTY

Student/faculty ratio: 5:1.

ACADEMICS

Calendar: semesters. *Degree:* bachelor's.

Library: Northwest College of Art & Design Library plus 1 other. *Books:* 1,686 (physical); *Serial titles:* 366 (physical). Weekly public service hours: 40.

COSTS & FINANCIAL AID

Costs (2019–20) ***Tuition:*** $18,000 full-time, $765 per credit hour part-time. Part-time tuition and fees vary according to course load. No tuition increase for student's term of enrollment. ***Required fees:*** $100 full-time, $100 per year part-time.

Financial Aid Of all full-time matriculated undergraduates who enrolled in 2016, 91 applied for aid, 91 were judged to have need, 72 had their need fully met. ***Average percent of need met:*** 63. ***Average financial aid package:*** $12,093. ***Average need-based loan:*** $7995. ***Average need-based gift aid:*** $10,549. ***Average non-need-based aid:*** $1413.

APPLYING

Required: essay or personal statement, high school transcript, interview, 5 piece portfolio.

CONTACT

Mrs. Ashley Miller, Admissions Representative, Northwest College of Art & Design, 1126 Pacific Avenue, Suite 101, Tacoma, WA 98402. *Phone:* 253-2721126. *Toll-free phone:* 800-769-ARTS. *Fax:* 253-5729058. *E-mail:* amiller@ncad.edu.

Northwest Indian College

Bellingham, Washington

http://www.nwic.edu/

CONTACT

Office of Admissions, Northwest Indian College, 2522 Kwina Road, Bellingham, WA 98226. *Phone:* 360-676-2772. *Toll-free phone:* 866-676-2772. *Fax:* 360-392-4333. *E-mail:* admissions@nwic.edu.

Northwest University

Kirkland, Washington

http://www.northwestu.edu/

- **Independent** comprehensive, founded 1934, affiliated with Assemblies of God
- **Suburban** 56-acre campus with easy access to Seattle
- **Endowment** $8.1 million
- **Coed** 1,871 undergraduate students, 74% full-time, 60% women, 40% men
- **Moderately difficult** entrance level, 92% of applicants were admitted

UNDERGRAD STUDENTS

1,377 full-time, 494 part-time. Students come from 34 states and territories; 24 other countries; 26% are from out of state; 6% Black or African American, non-Hispanic/Latino; 10% Hispanic/Latino; 6% Asian, non-Hispanic/Latino; 2% Native Hawaiian or other Pacific Islander, non-Hispanic/Latino; 2% American Indian or Alaska Native, non-Hispanic/Latino; 5% Two or more races, non-Hispanic/Latino; 8% Race/ethnicity unknown; 0.8% international; 13% transferred in; 55% live on campus.

Freshmen:

Admission: 562 applied, 519 admitted, 215 enrolled. ***Average high school GPA:*** 3.4. ***Test scores:*** SAT evidence-based reading and writing scores over 500: 339%; SAT math scores over 500: 320%; ACT scores over 18: 142%; SAT evidence-based reading and writing scores over 600: 180%; SAT math scores over 600: 120%; ACT scores over 24: 73%; SAT evidence-based reading and writing scores over 700: 28%; SAT math scores over 700: 21%; ACT scores over 30: 9%.

Retention: 80% of full-time freshmen returned.

FACULTY

Total: 252, 33% full-time, 15% with terminal degrees.

Student/faculty ratio: 14:1.

ACADEMICS

Calendar: semesters. *Degrees:* certificates, diplomas, associate, bachelor's, master's, and doctoral.

Special study options: academic remediation for entering students, accelerated degree program, adult/continuing education programs, advanced placement credit, cooperative education, double majors, English as a second language, independent study, internships, part-time degree program, study abroad, summer session for credit. ***ROTC:*** Army (c), Air Force (c).

Computers: 160 computers/terminals are available on campus for general student use. Students can access the following: campus intranet, computer help desk, free student e-mail accounts, online (class) grades, online (class) registration, online (class) schedules, online classes. Campuswide network is available. 100% of college-owned or -operated housing units are wired for high-speed Internet access. Wireless service is available via entire campus.

Library: Hurst Library. *Books:* 170,000 (physical); *Serial titles:* 7,000 (physical); *Databases:* 81. Weekly public service hours: 91; study areas open 24 hours, 5–7 days a week; students can reserve study rooms.

STUDENT LIFE

Housing options: on-campus residence required through sophomore year; men-only, women-only. Campus housing is university owned. Freshman campus housing is guaranteed.

Activities and organizations: drama/theater group, student-run newspaper, choral group, Student Ministries, Pursuit (worship service), Northwest University Business Club, Environmental Stewardship Club.

Athletics Member NAIA. ***Intercollegiate sports:*** basketball M(s)/W(s), cross-country running M(s)/W(s), soccer M(s)/W(s), softball W(s), track and field M(s)/W(s), volleyball W(s).

Campus security: 24-hour emergency response devices and patrols, late-night transport/escort service, controlled dormitory access.

Student services: health clinic, personal/psychological counseling.

COSTS & FINANCIAL AID

Costs (2020–21) ***Comprehensive fee:*** $43,400 includes full-time tuition ($33,500), mandatory fees ($480), and room and board ($9420). ***College room only:*** $4710. Room and board charges vary according to housing facility. ***Payment plan:*** installment.

Financial Aid Of all full-time matriculated undergraduates who enrolled in 2018, 1,154 applied for aid, 989 were judged to have need, 158 had their need fully met. 75 Federal Work-Study jobs (averaging $1887). 3 state and other part-time jobs (averaging $1904). In 2018, 197 non-need-based awards were made. ***Average percent of need met:*** 72. ***Average financial aid package:*** $19,906. ***Average need-based loan:*** $3995. ***Average need-based gift aid:*** $16,435. ***Average non-need-based aid:*** $11,371. ***Average indebtedness upon graduation:*** $24,825.

APPLYING

Standardized Tests *Required:* SAT or ACT (for admission).

Options: electronic application, early action, deferred entrance.

Application fee: $30.

Required: essay or personal statement, high school transcript, minimum 2.3 GPA, 2 letters of recommendation. ***Required for some:*** interview.

Application deadlines: 8/1 (freshmen), 8/1 (transfers), 1/15 (early action).

Notification: continuous (freshmen), continuous (transfers), 2/15 (early action).

CONTACT

Andy Hall, Northwest University, 5520 108th Avenue NE, PO Box 579, Kirkland, WA 98083-0579. *Phone:* 425-889-5212. *Toll-free phone:* 800-669-3781. *Fax:* 425-889-5224. *E-mail:* admissions@northwestu.edu.

Olympic College

Bremerton, Washington

http://www.olympic.edu/

- **State-supported** primarily 2-year, founded 1946, part of Washington State Board for Community and Technical Colleges
- **Suburban** 33-acre campus with easy access to Seattle, Tacoma
- **Coed**
- **Noncompetitive** entrance level

ACADEMICS

Calendar: quarters. *Degrees:* certificates, diplomas, associate, and bachelor's.

Library: Haselwood Library plus 1 other. Students can reserve study rooms.

STUDENT LIFE

Housing options: coed. Campus housing is university owned.

Activities and organizations: drama/theater group, student-run newspaper, choral group, International Club, Armed Forces Club, Gay/Straight Alliance, Engineering Club, Clay Club.

Campus security: 24-hour emergency response devices and patrols, student patrols, late-night transport/escort service.

Student services: personal/psychological counseling.

FINANCIAL AID

Financial Aid Of all full-time matriculated undergraduates who enrolled in 2018, 105 Federal Work-Study jobs (averaging $2380). 31 state and other part-time jobs (averaging $2880).

APPLYING

Options: electronic application.

Required for some: essay or personal statement, high school transcript, 2 letters of recommendation.

CONTACT

Ms. Nora Downard, Program Manager, Olympic College, 1600 Chester Avenue, Bremerton, WA 98337-1699. *Phone:* 360-475-7445. *Toll-free phone:* 800-259-6718. *Fax:* 360-475-7202. *E-mail:* ndownard@olympic.edu.

Pacific Lutheran University

Tacoma, Washington

http://www.plu.edu/

- **Independent** comprehensive, founded 1890, affiliated with Evangelical Lutheran Church in America
- **Suburban** 156-acre campus with easy access to Seattle
- **Endowment** $99.8 million
- **Coed**
- **Moderately difficult** entrance level

FACULTY

Student/faculty ratio: 15:1.

ACADEMICS

Calendar: 4-1-4. *Degrees:* certificates, bachelor's, master's, doctoral, and post-master's certificates.

Library: Robert A. L. Mortvedt Library. *Books:* 222,754 (physical), 40,703 (digital/electronic); *Serial titles:* 34,315 (physical); *Databases:* 118. Weekly public service hours: 80; students can reserve study rooms.

STUDENT LIFE

Housing options: on-campus residence required through sophomore year; coed, women-only, special housing for students with disabilities. Campus housing is university owned. Freshman campus housing is guaranteed.

Activities and organizations: drama/theater group, student-run newspaper, radio and television station, choral group, Chemistry Club, Delta Iota Chi, Black Student Union, APISA, Na Hoaloha O Hawaii.

Athletics Member NCAA. All Division III.

Campus security: 24-hour emergency response devices and patrols, student patrols, late-night transport/escort service, controlled dormitory access.

Student services: health clinic, personal/psychological counseling, women's center.

COSTS & FINANCIAL AID

Costs (2019–20) ***Comprehensive fee:*** $54,550 includes full-time tuition ($43,264), mandatory fees ($410), and room and board ($10,876). Part-time tuition: $1352 per credit hour. ***College room only:*** $4940.

Financial Aid Of all full-time matriculated undergraduates who enrolled in 2018, 2,254 applied for aid, 2,033 were judged to have need, 466 had their need fully met. 683 Federal Work-Study jobs (averaging $3219). 577 state and other part-time jobs (averaging $3092). In 2018, 100 non-need-based awards were made. ***Average percent of need met:*** 87. ***Average financial aid package:*** $33,622. ***Average need-based loan:*** $4752. ***Average need-based gift aid:*** $9797. ***Average non-need-based aid:*** $12,604. ***Average indebtedness upon graduation:*** $25,449.

APPLYING

Standardized Tests *Required:* SAT or ACT (for admission).

Options: electronic application, deferred entrance.

Application fee: $40.

Required: essay or personal statement, high school transcript, 1 letter of recommendation. ***Required for some:*** interview. ***Recommended:*** minimum 2.5 GPA.

CONTACT

Melody A. Ferguson, Director of Admission, Pacific Lutheran University, 12180 Park Avenue S., Tacoma, WA 98447. *Phone:* 253-535-7151. *Toll-free phone:* 800-274-6758. *Fax:* 253-536-5136. *E-mail:* admission@plu.edu.

Peninsula College

Port Angeles, Washington

http://www.pencol.edu/

CONTACT

Ms. Pauline Marvin, Peninsula College, 1502 East Lauridsen Boulevard, Port Angeles, WA 98362. *Phone:* 360-417-6596. *Toll-free phone:* 877-452-9277. *Fax:* 360-457-8100. *E-mail:* admissions@pencol.edu.

Pima Medical Institute - Seattle

Seattle, Washington

http://www.pmi.edu/

CONTACT

Admissions Office, Pima Medical Institute - Seattle, 9709 Third Avenue NE, Suite 400, Seattle, WA 98115. *Phone:* 206-322-6100. *Toll-free phone:* 800-477-PIMA.

Renton Technical College

Renton, Washington

http://www.rtc.edu/

- **State-supported** primarily 2-year, founded 1942, part of Washington State Board for Community and Technical Colleges
- **Suburban** 30-acre campus with easy access to Seattle
- **Endowment** $837,103
- **Coed**
- **Noncompetitive** entrance level

FACULTY

Student/faculty ratio: 16:1.

ACADEMICS

Calendar: quarters. *Degrees:* certificates, diplomas, associate, and bachelor's.

Library: Renton Technical College Library. *Books:* 24,464 (physical), 64,437 (digital/electronic); *Serial titles:* 354 (physical), 19,981 (digital/electronic); *Databases:* 22. Weekly public service hours: 62.

STUDENT LIFE

Housing options: college housing not available.

Campus security: patrols by security, security system.

Student services: personal/psychological counseling, veterans affairs office.

APPLYING

Standardized Tests *Required for some:* ACT ASSET, CLEP, ACCUPLACER, DSP.

Options: electronic application, early admission.

Application fee: $30.

Required for some: essay or personal statement, high school transcript, interview.

CONTACT

Patrick Brown, Director of Enrollment Services/Registrar, Renton Technical College, 3000 NE Fourth Street, Renton, WA 98056. *Phone:* 425-2352352 Ext. 5537. *E-mail:* pbrown@rtc.edu.

Saint Martin's University

Lacey, Washington

http://www.stmartin.edu/

- **Independent Roman Catholic** comprehensive, founded 1895
- **Suburban** 300-acre campus with easy access to Seattle
- **Endowment** $21.8 million
- **Coed**
- **Moderately difficult** entrance level

FACULTY

Student/faculty ratio: 11:1.

ACADEMICS

Calendar: semesters. *Degrees:* certificates, bachelor's, master's, post-master's, and postbachelor's certificates.

Library: O'Grady Library. *Books:* 88,291 (physical), 233,172 (digital/electronic); *Serial titles:* 98 (physical), 54,407 (digital/electronic); *Databases:* 114. Weekly public service hours: 88; students can reserve study rooms.

STUDENT LIFE

Housing options: on-campus residence required through sophomore year; coed. Campus housing is university owned. Freshman campus housing is guaranteed.

Activities and organizations: drama/theater group, student-run newspaper, choral group.

Athletics Member NCAA. All Division II except golf (Division I).

Campus security: 24-hour emergency response devices and patrols, student patrols, late-night transport/escort service, controlled dormitory access, close-circuit TV cameras throughout campus, emergency text messaging/notification.

Student services: health clinic, personal/psychological counseling.

COSTS & FINANCIAL AID

Costs (2019–20) ***Comprehensive fee:*** $50,560 includes full-time tuition ($38,150), mandatory fees ($410), and room and board ($12,000). Part-time tuition: $1275 per credit. ***College room only:*** $5750. Room and board charges vary according to board plan and housing facility.

Financial Aid Of all full-time matriculated undergraduates who enrolled in 2017, 882 applied for aid, 820 were judged to have need, 204 had their need fully met. In 2017, 129 non-need-based awards were made. ***Average percent of need met:*** 79. ***Average financial aid package:*** $29,720. ***Average need-based loan:*** $4028. ***Average need-based gift aid:*** $26,817. ***Average non-need-based aid:*** $15,107. ***Average indebtedness upon graduation:*** $26,761.

APPLYING

Standardized Tests *Required:* SAT or ACT (for admission).

Options: electronic application, deferred entrance.

Required: essay or personal statement, high school transcript, 1 letter of recommendation.

CONTACT

Dr. Pamela Holsinger-Fuchs, Dean of Enrollment, Saint Martin's University, 5000 Abbey Way SE, Lacey, WA 98503. *Phone:* 360-438-4592. *Toll-free phone:* 800-368-8803. *Fax:* 360-412-6189. *E-mail:* admissions@stmartin.edu.

Seattle Pacific University

Seattle, Washington

http://www.spu.edu/

CONTACT

Ineliz Soto-Fuller, Director of Undergraduate Admissions, Seattle Pacific University, 3307 3rd Avenue, West, Seattle, WA 98119-1997. *Phone:* 206-281-2021. *Toll-free phone:* 800-366-3344. *Fax:* 206-281-2544. *E-mail:* admissions@spu.edu.

Seattle University

Seattle, Washington

http://www.seattleu.edu/

- **Independent Roman Catholic** comprehensive, founded 1891
- **Urban** 50-acre campus with easy access to Seattle
- **Coed** 4,700 undergraduate students, 95% full-time, 61% women, 39% men
- **Moderately difficult** entrance level, 78% of applicants were admitted

UNDERGRAD STUDENTS

4,455 full-time, 245 part-time. Students come from 50 states and territories; 101 other countries; 59% are from out of state; 3% Black or African American, non-Hispanic/Latino; 12% Hispanic/Latino; 18% Asian, non-Hispanic/Latino; 0.8% Native Hawaiian or other Pacific Islander, non-Hispanic/Latino; 0.3% American Indian or Alaska Native, non-Hispanic/Latino; 9% Two or more races, non-Hispanic/Latino; 5% Race/ethnicity unknown; 11% international; 9% transferred in; 50% live on campus.

Freshmen:

Admission: 7,968 applied, 6,253 admitted, 930 enrolled. ***Average high school GPA:*** 3.7. ***Test scores:*** SAT evidence-based reading and writing scores over 500: 97%; SAT math scores over 500: 88%; ACT scores over 18: 99%; SAT evidence-based reading and writing scores over 600: 60%; SAT math scores over 600: 54%; ACT scores over 24: 78%; SAT evidence-based reading and writing scores over 700: 15%; SAT math scores over 700: 12%; ACT scores over 30: 31%.

Retention: 88% of full-time freshmen returned.

FACULTY

Total: 760, 69% full-time, 76% with terminal degrees.

Student/faculty ratio: 11:1.

ACADEMICS

Calendar: quarters. *Degrees:* bachelor's, master's, doctoral, post-master's, and postbachelor's certificates.

Special study options: accelerated degree program, adult/continuing education programs, advanced placement credit, double majors, English as a second language, freshman honors college, honors programs, independent study, internships, off-campus study, part-time degree program, services for LD students, student-designed majors, study abroad, summer session for credit. ***ROTC:*** Army (b), Navy (c), Air Force (c).

Computers: 467 computers/terminals are available on campus for general student use. Students can access the following: campus intranet, computer help desk, free student e-mail accounts, online (class) grades, online (class) registration, online (class) schedules. Campuswide network is available. 99% of college-owned or -operated housing units are wired for high-speed Internet access. Wireless service is available via entire campus.

Library: Lemieux Library & McGoldrick Learning Commons plus 1 other. *Books:* 472,572 (physical), 257,641 (digital/electronic); *Serial titles:* 118,353 (physical), 8,597 (digital/electronic); *Databases:* 235. Students can reserve study rooms.

STUDENT LIFE

Housing options: on-campus residence required through sophomore year; coed, special housing for students with disabilities. Campus housing is university owned. Freshman campus housing is guaranteed.

Activities and organizations: drama/theater group, student-run newspaper, radio station, choral group, Student Government of Seattle University (SGSU), Student Events and Activities Council (SEAC), Redzone, Dance Marathon, Hui 'O Nani Hawaii Club.

Athletics Member NCAA. All Division I. ***Intercollegiate sports:*** baseball M, basketball M(s)/W(s), cheerleading M(c)/W(c), crew W(c), cross-country running M(s)/W(s), golf M(s), soccer M(s)/W(s), softball W(s), swimming and diving M(s)/W(s), tennis M/W, track and field M(s)/W(s), volleyball W(s). ***Intramural sports:*** archery M(c)/W(c), basketball M/W, crew M(c)/W(c), fencing W, field hockey M, football M/W, riflery M(c)/W(c), rock climbing M/W, skiing (downhill) M(c)/W(c), soccer M/W, softball M/W, tennis M/W, ultimate Frisbee M/W, volleyball M/W, water polo M/W.

Campus security: 24-hour emergency response devices and patrols, late-night transport/escort service, controlled dormitory access.

Student services: health clinic, personal/psychological counseling, women's center.

COSTS & FINANCIAL AID

Costs (2020–21) ***Comprehensive fee:*** $61,170 includes full-time tuition ($47,565), mandatory fees ($825), and room and board ($12,780). Part-time tuition: $1057 per credit hour. ***College room only:*** $8730. Room and board charges vary according to board plan and housing facility. ***Waivers:*** employees or children of employees.

Financial Aid Of all full-time matriculated undergraduates who enrolled in 2019, 3,043 applied for aid, 2,473 were judged to have need, 724 had their need fully met. 581 Federal Work-Study jobs (averaging $2.2 million). 513 state and other part-time jobs (averaging $2.4 million). In 2019, 246 non-need-based awards were made. ***Average percent of need met:*** 81. ***Average financial aid package:*** $39,057. ***Average need-based loan:*** $5954. ***Average need-based gift aid:*** $28,308. ***Average non-need-based aid:*** $15,110. ***Average indebtedness upon graduation:*** $28,053.

APPLYING

Options: electronic application, early action, deferred entrance.

Application fee: $55.

Required: essay or personal statement, high school transcript, minimum 2.5 GPA, 2 letters of recommendation.

Application deadlines: rolling (freshmen), 3/1 (transfers), 11/15 (early action).

Notification: continuous until 3/1 (freshmen), continuous (transfers).

CONTACT

Seattle University, 902 12th Avenue, PO Box 222000, Seattle, WA 98122-1090. *Toll-free phone:* 800-542-0833 (in-state); 800-426-7123 (out-of-state).

University of Puget Sound

Tacoma, Washington

http://www.pugetsound.edu/

- **Independent** comprehensive, founded 1888
- **Urban** 97-acre campus with easy access to Seattle
- **Endowment** $369.0 million
- **Coed** 2,299 undergraduate students, 99% full-time, 59% women, 41% men
- **Moderately difficult** entrance level, 84% of applicants were admitted

UNDERGRAD STUDENTS

2,271 full-time, 28 part-time. 75% are from out of state; 2% Black or African American, non-Hispanic/Latino; 10% Hispanic/Latino; 7% Asian, non-Hispanic/Latino; 0.5% Native Hawaiian or other Pacific Islander, non-Hispanic/Latino; 0.2% American Indian or Alaska Native, non-Hispanic/Latino; 10% Two or more races, non-Hispanic/Latino; 3% Race/ethnicity unknown; 0.4% international; 2% transferred in; 67% live on campus.

Freshmen:

Admission: 5,181 applied, 4,343 admitted, 615 enrolled. ***Average high school GPA:*** 3.6. ***Test scores:*** SAT evidence-based reading and writing scores over 500: 97%; SAT math scores over 500: 95%; ACT scores over 18: 97%; SAT evidence-based reading and writing scores over 600: 85%; SAT math scores over 600: 59%; ACT scores over 24: 85%; SAT evidence-based reading and writing scores over 700: 33%; SAT math scores over 700: 17%; ACT scores over 30: 33%.

Retention: 81% of full-time freshmen returned.

FACULTY

Total: 291, 79% full-time.

Student/faculty ratio: 11:1.

ACADEMICS

Calendar: semesters. *Degrees:* bachelor's, master's, and doctoral.

Special study options: advanced placement credit, cooperative education, double majors, honors programs, independent study, internships, part-time degree program, services for LD students, student-designed majors, study abroad, summer session for credit. ***ROTC:*** Army (c).

Unusual degree programs: 3-2 engineering with Washington University in St. Louis, Columbia University, University of Southern California.

Computers: 329 computers/terminals are available on campus for general student use. Students can access the following: campus intranet, computer help desk, free student e-mail accounts, online (class) grades, online (class) registration, online (class) schedules, financial aid, admission, student employment. Campuswide network is available. 100% of college-owned or -operated housing units are wired for high-speed Internet access. Wireless service is available via entire campus.
Library: Collins Memorial Library.

STUDENT LIFE
Housing options: on-campus residence required through sophomore year; coed, special housing for students with disabilities. Campus housing is university owned. Freshman campus housing is guaranteed.

Activities and organizations: drama/theater group, student-run newspaper, radio station, choral group, Puget Sound Outdoors, Repertory Dance Group, Ka Ohana me ke Aloha, Student Theatre Productions, Relay for Life, national fraternities, national sororities.

Athletics Member NCAA. All Division III except golf (Division II). ***Intercollegiate sports:*** baseball M, basketball M/W, cheerleading M/W, crew M/W, cross-country running M/W, fencing M(c)/W(c), football M, golf M/W, ice hockey M(c)/W(c), lacrosse M(c)/W, rugby M(c)/W(c), sailing M(c)/W(c), skiing (downhill) W(c), soccer M/W, softball W, swimming and diving M/W, tennis M/W, track and field M/W, ultimate Frisbee M(c)/W(c), volleyball W. ***Intramural sports:*** basketball M/W, football M(c)/W, soccer M/W, softball M/W, volleyball M/W.

Campus security: 24-hour emergency response devices and patrols, student patrols, late-night transport/escort service, controlled dormitory access.

Student services: health clinic, personal/psychological counseling.

COSTS & FINANCIAL AID
Costs (2020–21) ***Comprehensive fee:*** $67,280 includes full-time tuition ($53,520), mandatory fees ($280), and room and board ($13,480). Full-time tuition and fees vary according to course load. Part-time tuition: $1690 per unit. Part-time tuition and fees vary according to course load. ***College room only:*** $7230. Room and board charges vary according to board plan and housing facility. ***Payment plans:*** installment, deferred payment. ***Waivers:*** employees or children of employees.

Financial Aid Of all full-time matriculated undergraduates who enrolled in 2019, 1,563 applied for aid, 1,270 were judged to have need, 196 had their need fully met. 495 Federal Work-Study jobs (averaging $3265). 935 state and other part-time jobs (averaging $2722). In 2019, 993 non-need-based awards were made. ***Average percent of need met:*** 80. ***Average financial aid package:*** $38,542. ***Average need-based loan:*** $4367. ***Average need-based gift aid:*** $33,262. ***Average non-need-based aid:*** $19,681. ***Average indebtedness upon graduation:*** $36,290.

APPLYING
Options: electronic application, early decision, early action, deferred entrance.

Application fee: $60.

Required: essay or personal statement, high school transcript, 2 letters of recommendation. ***Recommended:*** minimum 3.0 GPA, interview.

Early decision deadline: 11/15.

Notification: 12/15 (early decision), 1/15 (early action).

CONTACT
Laura Martin-Fedich, Vice President for Enrollment, University of Puget Sound, 1500 North Warner Street, CMB 1062, Tacoma, WA 98416. *Phone:* 253-879-3211. *Toll-free phone:* 800-396-7191. *Fax:* 253-879-3993. *E-mail:* admission@pugetsound.edu.

University of Washington
Seattle, Washington
http://www.washington.edu/

- **State-supported** university, founded 1861, part of University of Washington
- **Urban** 634-acre campus with easy access to Seattle, WA
- **Endowment** $3.5 billion
- **Coed** 32,046 undergraduate students, 92% full-time, 54% women, 46% men
- **Very difficult** entrance level, 52% of applicants were admitted

UNDERGRAD STUDENTS
29,332 full-time, 2,714 part-time. Students come from 51 states and territories; 83 other countries; 19% are from out of state; 3% Black or African American, non-Hispanic/Latino; 9% Hispanic/Latino; 26% Asian, non-Hispanic/Latino; 0.4% Native Hawaiian or other Pacific Islander, non-Hispanic/Latino; 0.4% American Indian or Alaska Native, non-Hispanic/Latino; 8% Two or more races, non-Hispanic/Latino; 1% Race/ethnicity unknown; 16% international; 5% transferred in; 29% live on campus.

Freshmen:
Admission: 45,579 applied, 23,592 admitted, 6,992 enrolled. ***Average high school GPA:*** 3.8. ***Test scores:*** SAT evidence-based reading and writing scores over 500: 96%; SAT math scores over 500: 97%; ACT scores over 18: 98%; SAT evidence-based reading and writing scores over 600: 76%; SAT math scores over 600: 82%; ACT scores over 24: 87%; SAT evidence-based reading and writing scores over 700: 26%; SAT math scores over 700: 50%; ACT scores over 30: 54%.

Retention: 95% of full-time freshmen returned.

FACULTY
Total: 2,445, 75% full-time, 64% with terminal degrees.

Student/faculty ratio: 21:1.

ACADEMICS
Calendar: quarters. *Degrees:* bachelor's, master's, doctoral, and post-master's certificates.

Special study options: adult/continuing education programs, advanced placement credit, cooperative education, distance learning, double majors, English as a second language, external degree program, honors programs, independent study, internships, off-campus study, part-time degree program, services for LD students, student-designed majors, study abroad, summer session for credit. ***ROTC:*** Army (b), Navy (b), Air Force (b).

Computers: 859 computers/terminals are available on campus for general student use. Students can access the following: computer help desk, free student e-mail accounts, online (class) grades, online (class) registration, online (class) schedules. Campuswide network is available. 100% of college-owned or -operated housing units are wired for high-speed Internet access. Wireless service is available via entire campus.
Library: Odegaard Undergraduate Library plus 12 others. *Books:* 7.9 million (physical), 1.3 million (digital/electronic); *Serial titles:* 175,094 (physical), 193,793 (digital/electronic); *Databases:* 621. Weekly public service hours: 124; study areas open 24 hours, 5–7 days a week; students can reserve study rooms.

STUDENT LIFE
Housing options: coed, special housing for students with disabilities. Campus housing is university owned.

Activities and organizations: drama/theater group, student-run newspaper, radio and television station, choral group, marching band, Interfraternity Council/Pan-Hellenic Council, Taiwanese Student Association, Chinese Student Association, Yacht Club, Asian American Intervarsity Christian Fellowship/Muslim Students Association, national fraternities, national sororities.

Athletics Member NCAA, NAIA. All NCAA Division I except football (Division I-A). ***Intercollegiate sports:*** baseball M(s), basketball M(s)/W(s), cheerleading M/W, crew M(s)/W(s), cross-country running M(s)/W(s), golf M(s)/W(s)(c), gymnastics W(s), ice hockey M(c), rowing M(s)/W(s), rugby M(c)/W(c), soccer M(s)/W(s), softball W(s), tennis M(s)/W(s), track and field M(s)/W(s), volleyball W(s). ***Intramural sports:*** archery M(c)/W(c), badminton M/W, baseball M(c)/W(c), basketball M/W, bowling M/W(c), crew M(c)/W(c), equestrian sports M(c)/W(c), football M/W, lacrosse M(c)/W(c), racquetball M/W, rock climbing M/W, rowing M/W, sailing M(c)/W(c), skiing (cross-country) M(c)/W(c), skiing (downhill) M(c)/W(c), soccer M/W, softball M/W, squash M(c)/W(c), swimming and diving M/W, table tennis M(c)/W(c), tennis M/W, triathlon M(c)/W(c), ultimate Frisbee M/W, volleyball M/W, water polo M(c)/W(c), wrestling M(c)/W(c).

Campus security: 24-hour emergency response devices and patrols, late-night transport/escort service, controlled dormitory access.

Student services: health clinic, personal/psychological counseling, women's center, legal services, veterans affairs office.

COSTS & FINANCIAL AID
Costs (2019–20) ***Tuition:*** state resident $10,370 full-time, $345 per credit part-time; nonresident $37,071 full-time, $1235 per credit part-time. Full-time tuition and fees vary according to course load and location. Part-time tuition and fees vary according to course load and location. ***Required fees:*** $1095 full-time, $28 per credit part-time. ***Room and board:*** $13,296. Room and board charges vary according to board plan, housing facility, and location. ***Waivers:*** senior citizens and employees or children of employees.

Financial Aid Of all full-time matriculated undergraduates who enrolled in 2019, 16,628 applied for aid, 12,085 were judged to have need, 2,271 had their need fully met. In 2019, 2461 non-need-based awards were made. ***Average percent of need met:*** 77. ***Average financial aid package:*** $17,487. ***Average need-based loan:*** $5077. ***Average need-based gift aid:*** $16,746. ***Average non-need-based aid:*** $4673. ***Average indebtedness upon graduation:*** $19,198.

APPLYING
Standardized Tests *Required:* SAT or ACT (for admission).

Options: electronic application, early admission.

Application fee: $80.

Required: essay or personal statement. ***Required for some:*** high school transcript.

Application deadlines: 11/15 (freshmen), 2/15 (transfers).

Notification: 3/15 (freshmen), 6/30 (transfers).

CONTACT
University of Washington, Seattle, WA 98195. *Phone:* 206-543-0852.

University of Washington, Bothell

Bothell, Washington

http://www.uwb.edu/

- **State-supported** comprehensive, founded 1990, part of University of Washington
- **Suburban** 127-acre campus with easy access to Seattle
- **Endowment** $5.0 million
- **Coed** 5,350 undergraduate students, 87% full-time, 48% women, 52% men
- **Minimally difficult** entrance level, 74% of applicants were admitted

UNDERGRAD STUDENTS
4,631 full-time, 719 part-time. Students come from 24 states and territories; 28 other countries; 2% are from out of state; 7% Black or African American, non-Hispanic/Latino; 10% Hispanic/Latino; 31% Asian, non-Hispanic/Latino; 0.5% Native Hawaiian or other Pacific Islander, non-Hispanic/Latino; 0.4% American Indian or Alaska Native, non-Hispanic/Latino; 6% Two or more races, non-Hispanic/Latino; 1% Race/ethnicity unknown; 8% international; 12% transferred in; 6% live on campus.

Freshmen:
Admission: 4,242 applied, 3,145 admitted, 829 enrolled. ***Average high school GPA:*** 3.4. ***Test scores:*** SAT evidence-based reading and writing scores over 500: 77%; SAT math scores over 500: 85%; ACT scores over 18: 84%; SAT evidence-based reading and writing scores over 600: 34%; SAT math scores over 600: 39%; ACT scores over 24: 45%; SAT evidence-based reading and writing scores over 700: 5%; SAT math scores over 700: 12%; ACT scores over 30: 15%.

Retention: 83% of full-time freshmen returned.

FACULTY
Total: 336, 58% full-time, 51% with terminal degrees.

Student/faculty ratio: 20:1.

ACADEMICS
Calendar: quarters. *Degrees:* bachelor's, master's, and postbachelor's certificates.

Special study options: adult/continuing education programs, advanced placement credit, cooperative education, distance learning, double majors, English as a second language, honors programs, independent study, internships, off-campus study, part-time degree program, services for LD students, student-designed majors, study abroad, summer session for credit. ***ROTC:*** Army (c), Navy (c), Air Force (c).

Computers: 195 computers/terminals are available on campus for general student use. Students can access the following: campus intranet, computer help desk, free student e-mail accounts, online (class) grades, online (class) registration, online (class) schedules. Campuswide network is available. 100% of college-owned or -operated housing units are wired for high-speed Internet access. Wireless service is available via classrooms, computer centers, computer labs, dorm rooms, learning centers, libraries, student centers.

Library: Campus Library. *Books:* 114,697 (physical), 1.3 million (digital/electronic); *Serial titles:* 1,297 (physical), 193,793 (digital/electronic); *Databases:* 621. Weekly public service hours: 86; students can reserve study rooms.

STUDENT LIFE
Housing options: coed, special housing for students with disabilities. Campus housing is university owned. Freshman applicants given priority for college housing.

Activities and organizations: student-run newspaper, radio station, Campus Events Board, Social Justice Organizers, Associated Students of University of Washington Bothell (ASUWB), Recreation and Intramurals Program, Club Council.

Athletics ***Intramural sports:*** basketball M/W, football M/W, soccer M/W, softball M/W, tennis M/W, ultimate Frisbee M(c)/W(c), volleyball M/W.

Campus security: 24-hour emergency response devices and patrols, late-night transport/escort service.

Student services: personal/psychological counseling, veterans affairs office.

COSTS & FINANCIAL AID
Costs (2019–20) ***Tuition:*** state resident $10,370 full-time, $345 per credit part-time; nonresident $37,071 full-time, $1235 per credit part-time. Full-time tuition and fees vary according to course load. Part-time tuition and fees vary according to course load. ***Required fees:*** $1020 full-time, $28 per credit part-time. ***Room and board:*** $12,636. Room and board charges vary according to board plan, housing facility, and location. ***Waivers:*** senior citizens and employees or children of employees.

Financial Aid Of all full-time matriculated undergraduates who enrolled in 2019, 3,114 applied for aid, 2,596 were judged to have need, 250 had their need fully met. In 2019, 43 non-need-based awards were made. ***Average percent of need met:*** 70. ***Average financial aid package:*** $15,117. ***Average need-based loan:*** $5817. ***Average need-based gift aid:*** $14,410. ***Average non-need-based aid:*** $6719. ***Average indebtedness upon graduation:*** $18,449.

APPLYING
Standardized Tests *Required:* SAT or ACT (for admission).

Options: electronic application.

Application fee: $60.

Required: essay or personal statement, high school transcript, minimum 2.0 GPA.

Application deadlines: rolling (freshmen), 5/1 (transfers).

Notification: continuous (freshmen), continuous (transfers).

CONTACT
University of Washington, Bothell, 18115 Campus Way NE, Bothell, WA 98011. *Phone:* 425-352-5000.

University of Washington, Tacoma

Tacoma, Washington

http://www.tacoma.uw.edu/

- **State-supported** comprehensive, founded 1990, part of University of Washington
- **Urban** 31-acre campus with easy access to Seattle
- **Endowment** $48.2 million
- **Coed** 4,588 undergraduate students, 89% full-time, 52% women, 48% men
- **Moderately difficult** entrance level, 87% of applicants were admitted

UNDERGRAD STUDENTS
4,066 full-time, 522 part-time. Students come from 27 states and territories; 19 other countries; 2% are from out of state; 9% Black or African American, non-Hispanic/Latino; 15% Hispanic/Latino; 21% Asian, non-Hispanic/Latino; 1% Native Hawaiian or other Pacific

Islander, non-Hispanic/Latino; 0.7% American Indian or Alaska Native, non-Hispanic/Latino; 8% Two or more races, non-Hispanic/Latino; 2% Race/ethnicity unknown; 3% international; 18% transferred in; 6% live on campus.

Freshmen:

Admission: 2,026 applied, 1,769 admitted, 655 enrolled. ***Average high school GPA:*** 3.4. ***Test scores:*** SAT evidence-based reading and writing scores over 500: 74%; SAT math scores over 500: 71%; ACT scores over 18: 65%; SAT evidence-based reading and writing scores over 600: 24%; SAT math scores over 600: 26%; ACT scores over 24: 26%; SAT evidence-based reading and writing scores over 700: 3%; SAT math scores over 700: 4%; ACT scores over 30: 4%.

Retention: 80% of full-time freshmen returned.

FACULTY

Total: 348, 72% full-time, 54% with terminal degrees.

Student/faculty ratio: 15:1.

ACADEMICS

Calendar: quarters. *Degrees:* bachelor's, master's, doctoral, and postbachelor's certificates.

Special study options: academic remediation for entering students, advanced placement credit, distance learning, double majors, honors programs, independent study, internships, off-campus study, part-time degree program, services for LD students, student-designed majors, study abroad, summer session for credit. ***ROTC:*** Army (c), Navy (c), Air Force (c).

Computers: 97 computers/terminals are available on campus for general student use. Students can access the following: campus intranet, computer help desk, free student e-mail accounts, online (class) grades, online (class) registration, online (class) schedules, learning management system, course management system. Campuswide network is available. 100% of college-owned or -operated housing units are wired for high-speed Internet access. Wireless service is available via entire campus.

Library: University of Washington Tacoma Library. *Books:* 134,653 (physical), 1.3 million (digital/electronic); *Serial titles:* 1,389 (physical), 193,793 (digital/electronic); *Databases:* 621. Weekly public service hours: 84; students can reserve study rooms.

STUDENT LIFE

Housing options: Campus housing is university owned. Freshman applicants given priority for college housing.

Activities and organizations: drama/theater group, student-run newspaper, choral group, Accounting Student Association, International Student Association, Partners in Action to Transform Healthcare (PATH), Asian Pacific Islander Student Union (APISU).

Athletics ***Intramural sports:*** badminton M/W, basketball M/W, soccer M(c)/W(c), volleyball M(c)/W(c), wrestling M(c)/W(c).

Campus security: 24-hour emergency response devices and patrols, late-night transport/escort service, key card access to buildings after hours.

Student services: health clinic, personal/psychological counseling, veterans affairs office.

COSTS & FINANCIAL AID

Costs (2019–20) ***Tuition:*** state resident $10,370 full-time, $345 per credit part-time; nonresident $37,071 full-time, $1235 per credit part-time. Full-time tuition and fees vary according to course load. Part-time tuition and fees vary according to course load. ***Required fees:*** $1269 full-time, $28 per credit part-time. ***Room and board:*** $12,636. Room and board charges vary according to housing facility and location. ***Waivers:*** senior citizens and employees or children of employees.

Financial Aid Of all full-time matriculated undergraduates who enrolled in 2019, 3,287 applied for aid, 2,865 were judged to have need, 301 had their need fully met. In 2019, 264 non-need-based awards were made. ***Average percent of need met:*** 71. ***Average financial aid package:*** $15,316. ***Average need-based loan:*** $6025. ***Average need-based gift aid:*** $14,268. ***Average non-need-based aid:*** $2951. ***Average indebtedness upon graduation:*** $16,716.

APPLYING

Standardized Tests *Required:* SAT or ACT (for admission).

Options: electronic application, deferred entrance.

Application fee: $60.

Required: essay or personal statement, high school transcript.

Application deadlines: 6/30 (freshmen), 7/31 (transfers).

Notification: continuous (freshmen), continuous (transfers).

CONTACT

Ms. Megan Cooley, Associate Director of University Recruitment, University of Washington, Tacoma, 1900 Commerce Street, Tacoma, WA 98402-3100. *Phone:* 253-692-4738. *Toll-free phone:* 800-736-7750. *Fax:* 253-692-4414. *E-mail:* uwtinfo@uw.edu.

Walla Walla University

College Place, Washington

http://www.wallawalla.edu/

- **Independent Seventh-day Adventist** comprehensive, founded 1892
- **Small-town** 77-acre campus
- **Coed** 1,683 undergraduate students, 93% full-time, 50% women, 50% men
- **Moderately difficult** entrance level, 75% of applicants were admitted

UNDERGRAD STUDENTS

1,566 full-time, 117 part-time. 64% are from out of state; 2% Black or African American, non-Hispanic/Latino; 18% Hispanic/Latino; 5% Asian, non-Hispanic/Latino; 0.3% Native Hawaiian or other Pacific Islander, non-Hispanic/Latino; 0.2% American Indian or Alaska Native, non-Hispanic/Latino; 8% Two or more races, non-Hispanic/Latino; 1% Race/ethnicity unknown; 3% international; 4% transferred in; 62% live on campus.

Freshmen:

Admission: 1,700 applied, 1,274 admitted, 423 enrolled. ***Average high school GPA:*** 3.6.

Retention: 78% of full-time freshmen returned.

FACULTY

Total: 189, 48% full-time, 41% with terminal degrees.

Student/faculty ratio: 15:1.

ACADEMICS

Calendar: quarters. *Degrees:* certificates, associate, bachelor's, and master's.

Special study options: academic remediation for entering students, advanced placement credit, cooperative education, distance learning, double majors, freshman honors college, honors programs, independent study, internships, off-campus study, part-time degree program, services for LD students, study abroad, summer session for credit.

Computers: Students can access the following: campus intranet, computer help desk, free student e-mail accounts, online (class) grades, online (class) registration, online (class) schedules, online forum, online classifieds, online student directory. Campuswide network is available. 100% of college-owned or -operated housing units are wired for high-speed Internet access. Wireless service is available via entire campus.

Library: Peterson Memorial Library plus 3 others.

STUDENT LIFE

Housing options: on-campus residence required through junior year; men-only, women-only, special housing for students with disabilities. Campus housing is university owned. Freshman campus housing is guaranteed.

Activities and organizations: drama/theater group, student-run newspaper, television station, choral group, Associated Students of Walla Walla University, Campus Ministries, Village Club, OPS Club (Men's residence hall club), AGA Club (women's residence hall club).

Athletics Member NAIA. ***Intercollegiate sports:*** basketball M/W, soccer M, softball W, volleyball W. ***Intramural sports:*** basketball M/W, football M/W, ice hockey M, softball W, table tennis M/W, volleyball M/W.

Campus security: 24-hour emergency response devices and patrols, student patrols, late-night transport/escort service, controlled dormitory access.

Student services: health clinic, personal/psychological counseling.

COSTS & FINANCIAL AID

Costs (2020–21) ***Comprehensive fee:*** $38,307 includes full-time tuition ($28,908), mandatory fees ($1023), and room and board ($8376). Part-time tuition: $803 per credit hour. ***College room only:*** $4554.

Financial Aid Of all full-time matriculated undergraduates who enrolled in 2018, 1,129 applied for aid, 936 were judged to have need, 324 had their need fully met. In 2018, 466 non-need-based awards were made. ***Average percent of need met:*** 93. ***Average financial aid package:*** $24,027. ***Average need-based loan:*** $4771. ***Average need-based gift aid:*** $6973. ***Average non-need-based aid:*** $9971. ***Average indebtedness upon graduation:*** $35,777.

APPLYING

Standardized Tests *Required:* SAT or ACT (for admission).

Options: electronic application, deferred entrance.

Application fee: $40.

Required: high school transcript, minimum 2.5 GPA.

Application deadlines: rolling (freshmen), rolling (transfers).

Notification: continuous (freshmen), continuous (transfers).

CONTACT

Mr. Dallas Weis, Director of Admissions, Walla Walla University, Marketing and Enrollment Services, 204 S. College Avenue, College Place, WA 99324. *Phone:* 509-527-2327. *Toll-free phone:* 800-541-8900. *Fax:* 509-527-2397.

Washington State University

Pullman, Washington

http://www.wsu.edu/

- **State-supported** university, founded 1890
- **Small-town** 620-acre campus with easy access to Spokane
- **Endowment** $1.1 billion
- **Coed** 18,629 undergraduate students, 95% full-time, 50% women, 50% men
- **Moderately difficult** entrance level, 79% of applicants were admitted

UNDERGRAD STUDENTS

17,728 full-time, 901 part-time. Students come from 50 states and territories; 77 other countries; 18% are from out of state; 3% Black or African American, non-Hispanic/Latino; 15% Hispanic/Latino; 6% Asian, non-Hispanic/Latino; 0.4% Native Hawaiian or other Pacific Islander, non-Hispanic/Latino; 0.5% American Indian or Alaska Native, non-Hispanic/Latino; 7% Two or more races, non-Hispanic/Latino; 2% Race/ethnicity unknown; 4% international; 6% transferred in; 25% live on campus.

Freshmen:

Admission: 20,762 applied, 16,305 admitted, 4,193 enrolled. ***Average high school GPA:*** 3.5. ***Test scores:*** SAT evidence-based reading and writing scores over 500: 83%; SAT math scores over 500: 83%; ACT scores over 18: 90%; SAT evidence-based reading and writing scores over 600: 36%; SAT math scores over 600: 33%; ACT scores over 24: 45%; SAT evidence-based reading and writing scores over 700: 5%; SAT math scores over 700: 6%; ACT scores over 30: 10%.

Retention: 80% of full-time freshmen returned.

FACULTY

Total: 1,830, 72% full-time, 77% with terminal degrees.

Student/faculty ratio: 16:1.

ACADEMICS

Calendar: semesters. *Degrees:* certificates, bachelor's, master's, doctoral, post-master's, and postbachelor's certificates.

Special study options: academic remediation for entering students, accelerated degree program, adult/continuing education programs, advanced placement credit, cooperative education, distance learning, double majors, English as a second language, external degree program, freshman honors college, honors programs, independent study, internships, off-campus study, part-time degree program, services for LD students, student-designed majors, study abroad, summer session for credit. ***ROTC:*** Army (b), Navy (c), Air Force (b).

Computers: 2,500 computers/terminals and 2,500 ports are available on campus for general student use. Students can access the following: campus intranet, computer help desk, free student e-mail accounts, online (class) grades, online (class) registration, online (class) schedules. Campuswide network is available. 100% of college-owned or -operated housing units are wired for high-speed Internet access. Wireless service is available via classrooms, computer centers, computer labs, dorm rooms, learning centers, libraries, student centers.

Library: Holland and Terrell Libraries plus 3 others. *Books:* 2.4 million (physical), 790,000 (digital/electronic); *Serial titles:* 136,000 (digital/electronic); *Databases:* 216. Weekly public service hours: 140; students can reserve study rooms.

STUDENT LIFE

Housing options: on-campus residence required for freshman year; coed, men-only, women-only, cooperative, special housing for students with disabilities. Campus housing is university owned. Freshman campus housing is guaranteed.

Activities and organizations: drama/theater group, student-run newspaper, radio and television station, choral group, marching band, Panhellenic Association - Sororities, Interfraternity Council - Fraternities, Student Entertainment Board, International Students Council, ChiLaStAl (Chicana/o Latina/o Student Alliance), national fraternities, national sororities.

Athletics Member NCAA. All Division I except football (Division I-A). ***Intercollegiate sports:*** baseball M(s), basketball M(s)/W(s), bowling M(c)/W(c), cheerleading M/W, crew M(c)/W(s), cross-country running M(s)/W(s), equestrian sports W(c), fencing M(c)/W(c), golf M(s)/W(s)(c), ice hockey M(c)/W(c), lacrosse M(c)/W(c), rowing M(c)/W, rugby M(c)/W(c), skiing (cross-country) M(c)/W(c), skiing (downhill) W(c), soccer M(c)/W(s), softball W(c), swimming and diving W(s), tennis M(c)/W(s), track and field M(s)/W(s), triathlon M(c)/W(c), ultimate Frisbee M(c)/W(c), volleyball M(c)/W(s), water polo W(c), weight lifting M(c)/W(c), wrestling M(c). ***Intramural sports:*** badminton M/W, basketball M/W, football M/W, golf M/W, racquetball M/W, rock climbing M/W, sand volleyball M/W, soccer M/W, softball M/W, table tennis M/W, tennis M/W, triathlon M/W, ultimate Frisbee M/W, volleyball M/W.

Campus security: 24-hour emergency response devices and patrols, student patrols, late-night transport/escort service, controlled dormitory access.

Student services: health clinic, personal/psychological counseling, women's center, legal services.

COSTS & FINANCIAL AID

Costs (2019–20) ***Tuition:*** state resident $9953 full-time, $526 per credit part-time; nonresident $24,531 full-time, $1254 per credit part-time. Full-time tuition and fees vary according to course load, location, and reciprocity agreements. Part-time tuition and fees vary according to course load, location, and reciprocity agreements. ***Required fees:*** $1888 full-time. ***Room and board:*** $11,648; room only: $7150. Room and board charges vary according to board plan, housing facility, and location. ***Waivers:*** senior citizens and employees or children of employees.

Financial Aid Of all full-time matriculated undergraduates who enrolled in 2018, 17,007 applied for aid, 13,219 were judged to have need, 1,502 had their need fully met. In 2018, 4546 non-need-based awards were made. ***Average percent of need met:*** 64. ***Average financial aid package:*** $13,167. ***Average need-based loan:*** $4069. ***Average need-based gift aid:*** $11,416. ***Average non-need-based aid:*** $4702. ***Average indebtedness upon graduation:*** $25,899. ***Financial aid deadline:*** 1/31.

APPLYING

Standardized Tests *Required:* SAT or ACT (for admission).

Options: electronic application.

Application fee: $50.

Required: high school transcript, minimum 2.0 GPA. ***Recommended:*** essay or personal statement.

Application deadlines: 1/31 (freshmen), rolling (out-of-state freshmen), 1/31 (transfers).

Notification: continuous until 11/1 (freshmen), continuous (out-of-state freshmen), continuous until 11/1 (transfers).

CONTACT

Ms. Wendy Peterson, Director of Admissions, Washington State University, PO Box 641067, Pullman, WA 99164-1067. *Phone:* 888-468-6978. *Toll-free phone:* 888-468-6978. *Fax:* 509-335-4902. *E-mail:* admissions@wsu.edu.

Washington State University–Global Campus

Pullman, Washington

http://www.globalcampus.wsu.edu/

CONTACT

Ms. Wendy Peterson, Director of Admissions, Washington State University–Global Campus, 370 Lighty Student Services Building, PO Box 641067, Pullman, WA 99164-1067. *Phone:* 509-335-5586. *Toll-free phone:* 800-222-4978. *Fax:* 509-335-4902. *E-mail:* admissions@wsu.edu.

Washington State University–Spokane

Spokane, Washington

http://www.spokane.wsu.edu/

- **State-supported** upper-level, founded 1989
- **Urban** 48-acre campus
- **Coed** 534 undergraduate students, 97% full-time, 85% women, 15% men
- **Moderately difficult** entrance level

UNDERGRAD STUDENTS

519 full-time, 15 part-time. Students come from 11 states and territories; 8 other countries; 8% are from out of state; 3% Black or African American, non-Hispanic/Latino; 11% Hispanic/Latino; 5% Asian, non-Hispanic/Latino; 0.7% American Indian or Alaska Native, non-Hispanic/Latino; 5% Two or more races, non-Hispanic/Latino; 3% Race/ethnicity unknown; 2% international; 12% transferred in.

Freshmen:

Admission: 5 applied.

ACADEMICS

Calendar: semesters. *Degrees:* bachelor's, master's, and doctoral.

Special study options: accelerated degree program, adult/continuing education programs, advanced placement credit, cooperative education, distance learning, double majors, English as a second language, external degree program, freshman honors college, honors programs, independent study, internships, off-campus study, part-time degree program, services for LD students, student-designed majors, study abroad, summer session for credit.

Computers: Campuswide network is available. Wireless service is available via entire campus.

STUDENT LIFE

Housing options: college housing not available.

Activities and organizations: ASWSU Spokane, Simulation Club, Multicultural Club, IHI Open School (Interprofessional Club), Diversity Club.

Campus security: 24-hour emergency response devices and patrols.

Student services: personal/psychological counseling, veterans affairs office.

COSTS

Costs (2019–20) ***Tuition:*** state resident $9953 full-time, $527 per credit part-time; nonresident $24,531 full-time, $1256 per credit part-time. Full-time tuition and fees vary according to course load, location, and reciprocity agreements. Part-time tuition and fees vary according to course load, location, and reciprocity agreements. ***Required fees:*** $766 full-time. ***Waivers:*** senior citizens and employees or children of employees.

APPLYING

Standardized Tests *Required:* SAT or ACT (for admission).

Options: electronic application.

Application fee: $50.

Notification: continuous until 11/1 (transfers).

CONTACT

Washington State University–Spokane, 412 East Spokane Falls Boulevard, PO Box 1495, Spokane, WA 99210-1495. *Phone:* 509-335-5586.

Washington State University–Tri-Cities

Richland, Washington

http://www.tricities.wsu.edu/

- **State-supported** comprehensive, founded 1989
- **Urban** 84-acre campus
- **Coed** 1,603 undergraduate students, 80% full-time, 56% women, 44% men
- **Moderately difficult** entrance level, 68% of applicants were admitted

UNDERGRAD STUDENTS

1,282 full-time, 321 part-time. Students come from 17 states and territories; 6 other countries; 4% are from out of state; 1% Black or African American, non-Hispanic/Latino; 38% Hispanic/Latino; 4% Asian, non-Hispanic/Latino; 0.2% Native Hawaiian or other Pacific Islander, non-Hispanic/Latino; 0.4% American Indian or Alaska Native, non-Hispanic/Latino; 3% Two or more races, non-Hispanic/Latino; 3% Race/ethnicity unknown; 0.4% international; 13% transferred in.

Freshmen:

Admission: 510 applied, 346 admitted, 201 enrolled. ***Average high school GPA:*** 3.4. ***Test scores:*** SAT evidence-based reading and writing scores over 500: 72%; SAT math scores over 500: 75%; ACT scores over 18: 65%; SAT evidence-based reading and writing scores over 600: 29%; SAT math scores over 600: 26%; ACT scores over 24: 22%; SAT evidence-based reading and writing scores over 700: 3%; SAT math scores over 700: 3%; ACT scores over 30: 4%.

Retention: 73% of full-time freshmen returned.

ACADEMICS

Calendar: semesters. *Degrees:* certificates, bachelor's, master's, doctoral, and postbachelor's certificates.

Special study options: accelerated degree program, adult/continuing education programs, advanced placement credit, cooperative education, distance learning, double majors, English as a second language, external degree program, independent study, internships, part-time degree program, services for LD students, study abroad, summer session for credit.

Computers: Students can access the following: campus intranet, computer help desk, free student e-mail accounts, online (class) grades, online (class) registration. Campuswide network is available. Wireless service is available via entire campus.

Library: Max E. Benitz Memorial Library plus 2 others.

STUDENT LIFE

Housing options: coed. Campus housing is university owned.

Activities and organizations: American Society of Civil Engineers, Environmental Club, Gaming Club, Pre-Health Club, Robotics Club.

Athletics ***Intercollegiate sports:*** rugby M(c), soccer M(c)/W(c), volleyball W(c). ***Intramural sports:*** basketball M/W, football M/W, tennis M/W, ultimate Frisbee M/W.

Campus security: 24-hour emergency response devices.

Student services: personal/psychological counseling, veterans affairs office.

COSTS

Costs (2019–20) ***Tuition:*** state resident $9953 full-time, $523 per credit part-time; nonresident $24,531 full-time, $1252 per credit part-time. Full-time tuition and fees vary according to course load, location, and reciprocity agreements. Part-time tuition and fees vary according to course load, location, and reciprocity agreements. ***Required fees:*** $812 full-time. ***Room and board:*** $11,648; room only: $7150. Room and board charges vary according to housing facility and location. ***Waivers:*** senior citizens and employees or children of employees.

APPLYING

Standardized Tests *Required:* SAT or ACT (for admission).

Options: electronic application.

Application fee: $50.

Required: high school transcript, minimum 2.0 GPA. ***Recommended:*** essay or personal statement.

Application deadlines: 1/31 (freshmen), 1/31 (transfers).

Notification: continuous until 11/1 (freshmen), continuous (out-of-state freshmen), continuous until 11/1 (transfers).

CONTACT

Washington State University–Tri-Cities, 2710 Crimson Way, Richland, WA 99354. *Phone:* 509-372-7250.

Washington State University–Vancouver

Vancouver, Washington

http://www.vancouver.wsu.edu/

- **State-supported** comprehensive, founded 1989
- **Suburban** 351-acre campus with easy access to Portland, OR
- **Coed** 3,170 undergraduate students, 81% full-time, 53% women, 47% men
- **Moderately difficult** entrance level, 62% of applicants were admitted

UNDERGRAD STUDENTS

2,578 full-time, 592 part-time. Students come from 23 states and territories; 14 other countries; 4% are from out of state; 2% Black or African American, non-Hispanic/Latino; 14% Hispanic/Latino; 8% Asian, non-Hispanic/Latino; 0.6% Native Hawaiian or other Pacific Islander, non-Hispanic/Latino; 0.3% American Indian or Alaska Native, non-Hispanic/Latino; 6% Two or more races, non-Hispanic/Latino; 3% Race/ethnicity unknown; 1% international; 20% transferred in.

Freshmen:

Admission: 1,204 applied, 749 admitted, 383 enrolled. ***Average high school GPA:*** 3.4.

Retention: 72% of full-time freshmen returned.

ACADEMICS

Calendar: semesters. *Degrees:* certificates, bachelor's, master's, and doctoral.

Special study options: accelerated degree program, adult/continuing education programs, advanced placement credit, cooperative education, distance learning, double majors, English as a second language, external degree program, honors programs, independent study, internships, off-campus study, part-time degree program, services for LD students, student-designed majors, study abroad, summer session for credit. ***ROTC:*** Army (c), Air Force (c).

Computers: Students can access the following: free student e-mail accounts, online (class) grades, online (class) registration, online (class) schedules. Campuswide network is available. Wireless service is available via classrooms, computer centers, computer labs, learning centers, libraries, student centers.

Library: WSU Vancouver Library plus 1 other. Students can reserve study rooms.

STUDENT LIFE

Housing options: college housing not available.

Activities and organizations: student-run newspaper, radio station.

Athletics ***Intramural sports:*** basketball M/W, soccer M/W, ultimate Frisbee M/W, volleyball M/W.

Campus security: 24-hour emergency response devices and patrols, student patrols.

Student services: personal/psychological counseling, veterans affairs office.

COSTS

Costs (2019–20) ***Tuition:*** state resident $9953 full-time, $526 per credit part-time; nonresident $24,531 full-time, $1255 per credit part-time. Full-time tuition and fees vary according to course load, location, and reciprocity agreements. Part-time tuition and fees vary according to course load, location, and reciprocity agreements. ***Required fees:*** $599 full-time. ***Waivers:*** senior citizens and employees or children of employees.

APPLYING

Standardized Tests *Required:* SAT or ACT (for admission).

Options: electronic application.

Application fee: $50.

Required: high school transcript, minimum 2.0 GPA. ***Recommended:*** essay or personal statement.

Application deadlines: 1/31 (freshmen), 1/31 (transfers).

Notification: continuous until 11/1 (freshmen), continuous (out-of-state freshmen), continuous until 11/1 (transfers).

CONTACT

Ms. Kim Hiatt, Associate Director of Admissions, Washington State University–Vancouver, 14204 NE Salmon Creek Avenue, Vancouver, WA 98686. *Phone:* 360-546-9779. *Fax:* 360-546-9032. *E-mail:* van.admissions@wsu.edu.

Western Washington University

Bellingham, Washington

http://www.wwu.edu/

- **State-supported** comprehensive, founded 1893
- **Urban** 223-acre campus with easy access to Seattle, WA and Vancouver, BC Canada
- **Endowment** $92.8 million
- **Coed** 15,240 undergraduate students, 91% full-time, 57% women, 43% men
- **Moderately difficult** entrance level, 90% of applicants were admitted

UNDERGRAD STUDENTS

13,887 full-time, 1,353 part-time. Students come from 48 states and territories; 47 other countries; 12% are from out of state; 2% Black or African American, non-Hispanic/Latino; 10% Hispanic/Latino; 6% Asian, non-Hispanic/Latino; 0.2% Native Hawaiian or other Pacific Islander, non-Hispanic/Latino; 0.4% American Indian or Alaska Native, non-Hispanic/Latino; 9% Two or more races, non-Hispanic/Latino; 2% Race/ethnicity unknown; 0.9% international; 8% transferred in; 26% live on campus.

Freshmen:

Admission: 10,513 applied, 9,502 admitted, 3,116 enrolled. ***Average high school GPA:*** 3.4. ***Test scores:*** SAT evidence-based reading and writing scores over 500: 90%; SAT math scores over 500: 86%; ACT scores over 18: 95%; SAT evidence-based reading and writing scores over 600: 51%; SAT math scores over 600: 37%; ACT scores over 24: 63%; SAT evidence-based reading and writing scores over 700: 10%; SAT math scores over 700: 8%; ACT scores over 30: 19%.

Retention: 82% of full-time freshmen returned.

FACULTY

Total: 984, 68% full-time, 76% with terminal degrees.

Student/faculty ratio: 19:1.

ACADEMICS

Calendar: quarters. *Degrees:* certificates, bachelor's, master's, doctoral, and post-master's certificates.

Special study options: academic remediation for entering students, advanced placement credit, cooperative education, distance learning, double majors, English as a second language, external degree program, honors programs, independent study, internships, off-campus study, part-time degree program, services for LD students, student-designed majors, study abroad, summer session for credit.

Computers: 2,268 computers/terminals are available on campus for general student use. Students can access the following: computer help desk, free student e-mail accounts, online (class) grades, online (class) registration, online (class) schedules. Campuswide network is available. 100% of college-owned or -operated housing units are wired for high-speed Internet access. Wireless service is available via entire campus.

Library: Western Libraries plus 1 other. *Books:* 643,793 (physical), 562,625 (digital/electronic); *Serial titles:* 22,841 (physical), 146,893 (digital/electronic); *Databases:* 121. Weekly public service hours: 97; students can reserve study rooms.

STUDENT LIFE

Housing options: coed, special housing for students with disabilities. Campus housing is university owned. Freshman campus housing is guaranteed.

Activities and organizations: drama/theater group, student-run newspaper, radio and television station, choral group, Intramurals,

Residence Hall Association, Associated Students, Outdoor Center, Ethnic Student Center.

Athletics Member NCAA. All Division II. ***Intercollegiate sports:*** basketball M(s)/W(s), crew W(s), cross-country running M(s)/W(s), golf M(s)/W(s), soccer M(s)/W(s), softball M/W(s), track and field M(s)/W(s), volleyball W(s). ***Intramural sports:*** badminton M/W, baseball M(c), basketball M/W, crew M(c)/W(c), equestrian sports M(c)/W(c), field hockey W(c), football M/W, golf M/W, ice hockey M(c), lacrosse M(c)/W(c), rock climbing M(c)/W(c), rugby M(c)/W(c), sailing M(c)/W(c), skiing (downhill) M(c)/W(c), soccer M/W, softball M/W, swimming and diving M(c)/W(c), table tennis M/W, tennis M(c)/W(c), ultimate Frisbee M(c)/W(c), volleyball M/W, water polo M(c)/W(c), wrestling M(c)/W(c).

Campus security: 24-hour emergency response devices and patrols, student patrols, late-night transport/escort service, controlled dormitory access.

Student services: health clinic, personal/psychological counseling, women's center, veterans affairs office.

COSTS & FINANCIAL AID

Costs (2019–20) ***One-time required fee:*** $280. ***Tuition:*** state resident $7213 full-time, $240 per credit hour part-time; nonresident $23,562 full-time, $785 per credit hour part-time. Full-time tuition and fees vary according to course load, location, and reciprocity agreements. Part-time tuition and fees vary according to course load, location, and reciprocity agreements. ***Required fees:*** $1128 full-time. ***Room and board:*** $12,037; room only: $7852. Room and board charges vary according to board plan, housing facility, and location. ***Waivers:*** senior citizens and employees or children of employees.

Financial Aid Of all full-time matriculated undergraduates who enrolled in 2019, 9,422 applied for aid, 6,522 were judged to have need, 1,068 had their need fully met. 181 Federal Work-Study jobs (averaging $4439). 486 state and other part-time jobs (averaging $4392). In 2019, 345 non-need-based awards were made. ***Average percent of need met:*** 79. ***Average financial aid package:*** $18,108. ***Average need-based loan:*** $4352. ***Average need-based gift aid:*** $9302. ***Average non-need-based aid:*** $2002. ***Average indebtedness upon graduation:*** $22,466.

APPLYING

Standardized Tests *Required:* SAT or ACT (for admission).

Options: electronic application, early action, deferred entrance.

Application fee: $60.

Required: high school transcript. ***Required for some:*** essay or personal statement.

Application deadlines: 1/31 (freshmen), 3/1 (transfers), 11/1 (early action).

Notification: continuous until 3/31 (freshmen), continuous until 5/1 (transfers), 12/31 (early action).

CONTACT

Cezar Mesquita, Director of Admissions, Western Washington University, 516 High Street, Bellingham, WA 98225-5996. *Phone:* 360-650-3440. *E-mail:* admissions@wwu.edu.

Whitman College

Walla Walla, Washington

http://www.whitman.edu/

- **Independent** 4-year, founded 1859
- **Small-town** 117-acre campus
- **Endowment** $518.3 million
- **Coed**
- **Very difficult** entrance level

FACULTY

Student/faculty ratio: 9:1.

ACADEMICS

Calendar: semesters. *Degree:* bachelor's.

Library: Penrose Library plus 1 other. *Books:* 406,675 (physical), 305,206 (digital/electronic); *Serial titles:* 5,082 (physical), 98,012 (digital/electronic); *Databases:* 206. Weekly public service hours: 84; study areas open 24 hours, 5–7 days a week; students can reserve study rooms.

STUDENT LIFE

Housing options: on-campus residence required through sophomore year; coed, women-only. Campus housing is university owned. Freshman campus housing is guaranteed.

Activities and organizations: drama/theater group, student-run newspaper, radio station, choral group, national fraternities, national sororities.

Athletics Member NCAA. All Division III.

Campus security: 24-hour emergency response devices and patrols, student patrols, late-night transport/escort service, controlled dormitory access.

Student services: health clinic, personal/psychological counseling, women's center.

COSTS & FINANCIAL AID

Costs (2019–20) ***Comprehensive fee:*** $67,332 includes full-time tuition ($53,420), mandatory fees ($400), and room and board ($13,512). Part-time tuition: $2226 per credit. Part-time tuition and fees vary according to course load. ***College room only:*** $6020. Room and board charges vary according to board plan and housing facility.

Financial Aid Of all full-time matriculated undergraduates who enrolled in 2018, 738 applied for aid, 638 were judged to have need, 193 had their need fully met. 470 Federal Work-Study jobs (averaging $2462). 55 state and other part-time jobs (averaging $1706). In 2018, 484 non-need-based awards were made. ***Average percent of need met:*** 94. ***Average financial aid package:*** $43,371. ***Average need-based loan:*** $4279. ***Average need-based gift aid:*** $38,369. ***Average non-need-based aid:*** $12,212. ***Average indebtedness upon graduation:*** $25,356. ***Financial aid deadline:*** 1/15.

APPLYING

Standardized Tests *Required for some:* SAT or ACT (for admission).

Options: electronic application, early decision, deferred entrance.

Application fee: $50.

Required: high school transcript. ***Required for some:*** statement of good standing from prior institutions. ***Recommended:*** essay or personal statement, interview.

CONTACT

Whitman College, Penrose House, 345 Boyer Avenue, Walla Walla, WA 99362. *Phone:* 509-527-5176. *Toll-free phone:* 877-462-9448. *E-mail:* admission@whitman.edu.

Whitworth University

Spokane, Washington

http://www.whitworth.edu/

- **Independent Presbyterian** comprehensive, founded 1890
- **Suburban** 200-acre campus
- **Endowment** $151.2 million
- **Coed** 2,355 undergraduate students, 98% full-time, 60% women, 40% men
- **Moderately difficult** entrance level, 91% of applicants were admitted

UNDERGRAD STUDENTS

2,304 full-time, 51 part-time. Students come from 35 states and territories; 38 other countries; 26% are from out of state; 2% Black or African American, non-Hispanic/Latino; 10% Hispanic/Latino; 5% Asian, non-Hispanic/Latino; 0.8% Native Hawaiian or other Pacific Islander, non-Hispanic/Latino; 0.7% American Indian or Alaska Native, non-Hispanic/Latino; 9% Two or more races, non-Hispanic/Latino; 0.9% Race/ethnicity unknown; 4% international; 4% transferred in; 51% live on campus.

Freshmen:

Admission: 3,731 applied, 3,387 admitted, 696 enrolled. ***Average high school GPA:*** 3.6.

Retention: 82% of full-time freshmen returned.

ACADEMICS

Calendar: 4-1-4. *Degrees:* bachelor's, master's, post-master's, and postbachelor's certificates.

Special study options: adult/continuing education programs, advanced placement credit, double majors, honors programs, independent study, internships, off-campus study, part-time degree program, services for LD students, student-designed majors, study abroad, summer session for credit. ***ROTC:*** Army (c).

Unusual degree programs: 3-2 engineering with Seattle Pacific University, University of Southern California, Washington University in St. Louis, Columbia University, Washington State University; nursing with Washington State University; athletic training at Whitworth University.

Computers: 280 computers/terminals and 950 ports are available on campus for general student use. Students can access the following: campus intranet, computer help desk, free student e-mail accounts, online (class) grades, online (class) registration, online (class) schedules, learning management system. Campuswide network is available. 100% of college-owned or -operated housing units are wired for high-speed Internet access. Wireless service is available via entire campus.
Library: Harriet Cheney Cowles Library. Weekly public service hours: 97; students can reserve study rooms.

STUDENT LIFE
Housing options: on-campus residence required through sophomore year; coed, men-only, women-only. Campus housing is university owned. Freshman campus housing is guaranteed.

Activities and organizations: drama/theater group, student-run newspaper, radio station, choral group, International Club, Whitworth Student Investment Group, En Christo, Hawaiian Club, Swing and Ballroom Dance Club.

Athletics ***Intercollegiate sports:*** baseball M, basketball M/W, cross-country running M/W, football M, golf M/W, lacrosse W, soccer M/W, softball W, swimming and diving M/W, tennis M/W, track and field M/W, volleyball W. ***Intramural sports:*** badminton M/W, basketball M(c)/W, cheerleading M(c)/W(c), football M/W, soccer M/W, softball M/W, table tennis M/W, tennis M/W, ultimate Frisbee M(c)/W(c), volleyball M/W.

Campus security: 24-hour emergency response devices and patrols, late-night transport/escort service, controlled dormitory access.

Student services: health clinic, personal/psychological counseling.

COSTS & FINANCIAL AID
Costs (2020–21) ***Comprehensive fee:*** $58,400 includes full-time tuition ($45,050), mandatory fees ($1200), and room and board ($12,150). Part-time tuition: $1877 per credit hour. ***Required fees:*** $537 per term part-time. ***Room and board:*** Room and board charges vary according to board plan and housing facility. ***Payment plan:*** installment. ***Waivers:*** senior citizens and employees or children of employees.

Financial Aid Of all full-time matriculated undergraduates who enrolled in 2018, 1,821 applied for aid, 1,631 were judged to have need, 310 had their need fully met. 848 Federal Work-Study jobs (averaging $2774). 71 state and other part-time jobs (averaging $3646). In 2018, 583 non-need-based awards were made. ***Average percent of need met:*** 81. ***Average financial aid package:*** $38,637. ***Average need-based loan:*** $4492. ***Average need-based gift aid:*** $30,617. ***Average non-need-based aid:*** $20,509. ***Average indebtedness upon graduation:*** $29,442.

APPLYING
Standardized Tests *Required for some:* SAT or ACT (for admission).

Options: electronic application, early admission, early action, deferred entrance.

Required: essay or personal statement, high school transcript, 1 letter of recommendation. ***Required for some:*** minimum 3.0 GPA, 2 letters of recommendation, interview.

Application deadlines: rolling (freshmen), rolling (out-of-state freshmen), rolling (transfers), 1/15 (early action).

Notification: continuous (freshmen), continuous (out-of-state freshmen), continuous (transfers), rolling (early action).

CONTACT
Ms. Lara Ramsay, Director of Admission, Whitworth University, 300 West, Hawthorne Road, Spokane, WA 99251. *Phone:* 509-777-4347. *Toll-free phone:* 800-533-4668. *Fax:* 509-777-3758. *E-mail:* admission@whitworth.edu.

WEST VIRGINIA

Alderson Broaddus University

Philippi, West Virginia

http://www.ab.edu/

CONTACT
Mr. Erika L. Thon, Director of Admissions, Alderson Broaddus University, 101 College Hill Drive, Campus Box 2003, Philippi, WV 26416. *Phone:* 304-457-6256. *Toll-free phone:* 800 263 1549. *Fax:* 304 457-6239. *E-mail:* thonel@ab.edu.

American Public University System

Charles Town, West Virginia

http://www.apus.edu/

- **Proprietary** comprehensive, founded 1991
- **Rural** campus with easy access to Washington, DC
- **Coed** 37,335 undergraduate students, 6% full-time, 36% women, 64% men
- **Noncompetitive** entrance level

UNDERGRAD STUDENTS
2,425 full-time, 34,910 part-time. 16% Black or African American, non-Hispanic/Latino; 14% Hispanic/Latino; 2% Asian, non-Hispanic/Latino; 1% Native Hawaiian or other Pacific Islander, non-Hispanic/Latino; 0.6% American Indian or Alaska Native, non-Hispanic/Latino; 4% Two or more races, non-Hispanic/Latino; 7% Race/ethnicity unknown; 0.7% international; 14% transferred in.

Freshmen:
Admission: 1,398 enrolled.

ACADEMICS
Calendar: courses start on the first Monday of each month. *Degrees:* certificates, associate, bachelor's, master's, doctoral, and postbachelor's certificates (profile includes American Public University, American Military University and American Community College).

Special study options: advanced placement credit, distance learning, independent study, internships, part-time degree program, services for LD students, summer session for credit.

Computers: Students can access the following: free student e-mail accounts, online (class) grades, online (class) registration, online (class) schedules.
Library: APUS Online Library.

STUDENT LIFE
Housing options: college housing not available.

APPLYING
Options: electronic application.

Required: high school transcript.

CONTACT
Mr. Greg Hill, Assistant Vice President, Prospect Management and Undergraduate Admissions, American Public University System, 111 West Congress Street, Charles Town, WV 25414. *Phone:* 877-468-6268. *Toll-free phone:* 877-755-2787. *Fax:* 304-724-3788. *E-mail:* info@apus.edu.

Appalachian Bible College

Mount Hope, West Virginia

http://www.abc.edu/

CONTACT
Miss Megan Mullens, Admissions Assistant, Appalachian Bible College, 161 College Drive, Mount Hope, WV 25880. *Phone:* 304-877-6428 Ext. 313. *Toll-free phone:* 800-678-9ABC. *Fax:* 304-877-5082. *E-mail:* admissions@abc.edu.

Bethany College

Bethany, West Virginia

http://www.bethanywv.edu/

CONTACT

Ms. Mollie Cecere, Director of Enrollment, Bethany College, Center for Enrollment and Financial Aid, 31 E. Campus Drive #4, Bethany, WV 26032. *Phone:* 304-829-7611. *Toll-free phone:* 800-922-7611. *Fax:* 304-829-7142. *E-mail:* enrollment@bethanywv.edu.

Bluefield State College

Bluefield, West Virginia

http://www.bluefieldstate.edu/

- **State-supported** 4-year, founded 1895, part of West Virginia Higher Education Policy Commission
- **Small-town** 45-acre campus
- **Coed**
- **Noncompetitive** entrance level

FACULTY

Student/faculty ratio: 13:1.

ACADEMICS

Calendar: semesters. *Degrees:* associate and bachelor's.
Library: Hardway Library.

STUDENT LIFE

Housing options: college housing not available.

Activities and organizations: drama/theater group, student-run newspaper, radio station, choral group, national fraternities, national sororities.

Athletics Member NCAA. All Division II.

Campus security: 24-hour emergency response devices and patrols, student patrols.

Student services: health clinic, personal/psychological counseling.

FINANCIAL AID

Financial Aid Of all full-time matriculated undergraduates who enrolled in 2017, 1,380 applied for aid, 1,150 were judged to have need, 140 had their need fully met. 55 Federal Work-Study jobs (averaging $3000). In 2017, 10 non-need-based awards were made. ***Average percent of need met:*** 67. ***Average financial aid package:*** $3500. ***Average need-based loan:*** $4250. ***Average need-based gift aid:*** $3700. ***Average non-need-based aid:*** $850. ***Average indebtedness upon graduation:*** $29,000.

APPLYING

Standardized Tests *Required:* SAT or ACT (for admission).

Options: early admission, deferred entrance.

Required: high school transcript, minimum 2.0 GPA.

CONTACT

Bluefield State College, 219 Rock Street, Bluefield, WV 24701-2198. *Phone:* 304-327-4067. *Toll-free phone:* 800-344-8892 Ext. 4065 (in-state); 800-654-7798 Ext. 4065 (out-of-state).

Concord University

Athens, West Virginia

http://www.concord.edu/

- **State-supported** comprehensive, founded 1872, part of State College System of West Virginia
- **Rural** 100-acre campus
- **Endowment** $24.5 million
- **Coed**
- **Minimally difficult** entrance level

FACULTY

Student/faculty ratio: 15:1.

ACADEMICS

Calendar: semesters. *Degrees:* bachelor's, master's, and post-master's certificates.
Library: J. Frank Marsh Library. *Books:* 162,020 (physical), 34,329 (digital/electronic); *Serial titles:* 68 (physical), 110 (digital/electronic); *Databases:* 14. Weekly public service hours: 77; study areas open 24 hours, 5–7 days a week; students can reserve study rooms.

STUDENT LIFE

Housing options: coed, men-only, women-only. Campus housing is university owned. Freshman campus housing is guaranteed.

Activities and organizations: drama/theater group, student-run newspaper, radio and television station, choral group, marching band, Service Groups, student government, student-run publications, intramurals, Student Activities Committee, national fraternities, national sororities.

Athletics Member NCAA. All Division II.

Campus security: 24-hour emergency response devices and patrols, student patrols, late-night transport/escort service, controlled dormitory access.

Student services: health clinic, personal/psychological counseling, veterans affairs office.

COSTS & FINANCIAL AID

Costs (2019–20) ***Tuition:*** state resident $8050 full-time, $336 per credit hour part-time; nonresident $17,702 full-time, $738 per credit hour part-time. Full-time tuition and fees vary according to course load and program. Part-time tuition and fees vary according to course load and program. ***Required fees:*** $335 full-time. ***Room and board:*** $9762; room only: $5118. Room and board charges vary according to board plan.

Financial Aid Of all full-time matriculated undergraduates who enrolled in 2018, 1,420 applied for aid, 1,222 were judged to have need, 458 had their need fully met. 180 Federal Work-Study jobs (averaging $2041). In 2018, 221 non-need-based awards were made. ***Average percent of need met:*** 83. ***Average financial aid package:*** $8491. ***Average need-based loan:*** $3335. ***Average need-based gift aid:*** $5995. ***Average non-need-based aid:*** $4096. ***Average indebtedness upon graduation:*** $21,176. ***Financial aid deadline:*** 4/15.

APPLYING

Standardized Tests *Required:* SAT or ACT (for admission).

Options: electronic application, early admission.

Required: high school transcript, minimum 2.0 GPA. ***Required for some:*** essay or personal statement, interview. ***Recommended:*** interview.

CONTACT

Mr. Jamie Ealy, Vice President of Enrollment Management, Concord University, 1000 Vermillion Street, Athens, WV 24712. *Phone:* 304-384-6305. *Toll-free phone:* 888-384-5249. *Fax:* 304-384-9044. *E-mail:* admissions@concord.edu.

Davis & Elkins College

Elkins, West Virginia

http://www.dewv.edu/

- **Independent Presbyterian** 4-year, founded 1904
- **Small-town** 170-acre campus
- **Endowment** $22.7 million
- **Coed**
- **Moderately difficult** entrance level

FACULTY

Student/faculty ratio: 10:1.

ACADEMICS

Calendar: 4-1-4. *Degrees:* associate and bachelor's.
Library: Booth Library.

STUDENT LIFE

Housing options: on-campus residence required through senior year; coed, men-only, women-only, special housing for students with disabilities. Campus housing is university owned. Freshman campus housing is guaranteed.

Activities and organizations: drama/theater group, student-run newspaper, radio station, choral group, Beta Alpha Beta, campus radio station, Student Nurses Association, Student Education Association, International Student Organization, national fraternities, national sororities.

Athletics Member NCAA, NAIA, NCCAA. All NCAA Division II.

Campus security: 24-hour emergency response devices, late-night transport/escort service, controlled dormitory access, late night security personnel.

Student services: health clinic, personal/psychological counseling.

FINANCIAL AID

Financial Aid Of all full-time matriculated undergraduates who enrolled in 2006, 473 applied for aid, 422 were judged to have need, 92 had their need fully met. 184 Federal Work-Study jobs (averaging $770). 49 state and other part-time jobs (averaging $1200). In 2006, 120 non-need-based awards were made. ***Average percent of need met:*** 70. ***Average financial aid package:*** $12,635. ***Average need-based loan:*** $4132. ***Average need-based gift aid:*** $4516. ***Average non-need-based aid:*** $5840. ***Average indebtedness upon graduation:*** $23,973.

APPLYING

Standardized Tests *Required:* SAT or ACT (for admission).

Options: electronic application, early admission, deferred entrance.

Application fee: $35.

Required: high school transcript, minimum 2.0 GPA. ***Required for some:*** essay or personal statement, 2 letters of recommendation, interview. ***Recommended:*** essay or personal statement, interview.

CONTACT

Ms. Reneé Heckel, Director of Enrollment Management, Davis & Elkins College, 100 Campus Drive, Elkins, WV 26241. *Phone:* 304-637-1974. *Toll-free phone:* 800-624-3157. *Fax:* 304-637-1800. *E-mail:* admiss@davisandelkins.edu.

Fairmont State University

Fairmont, West Virginia

http://www.fairmontstate.edu/

- **State-supported** comprehensive, founded 1865, part of State College System of West Virginia
- **Small-town** 120-acre campus
- **Endowment** $22.6 million
- **Coed**
- **Minimally difficult** entrance level

FACULTY

Student/faculty ratio: 15:1.

ACADEMICS

Calendar: semesters. *Degrees:* associate, bachelor's, and master's.

Library: Musick Library. Study areas open 24 hours, 5–7 days a week.

STUDENT LIFE

Housing options: on-campus residence required through sophomore year; coed, men-only, women-only. Campus housing is university owned. Freshman campus housing is guaranteed.

Activities and organizations: drama/theater group, student-run newspaper, choral group, marching band, Alpha Phi Omega, Circle K, Society for Non-traditional Students, Criminal Justice Club, Honors Association, national fraternities, national sororities.

Athletics Member NCAA. All Division II.

Campus security: 24-hour emergency response devices and patrols, student patrols, controlled dormitory access.

Student services: health clinic, personal/psychological counseling, legal services.

FINANCIAL AID

Financial Aid Of all full-time matriculated undergraduates who enrolled in 2016, 2,912 applied for aid, 2,279 were judged to have need, 198 had their need fully met. In 2016, 294 non-need-based awards were made. ***Average percent of need met:*** 70. ***Average financial aid package:*** $9060. ***Average need-based loan:*** $3594. ***Average need-based gift aid:*** $6629. ***Average non-need-based aid:*** $7995. ***Average indebtedness upon graduation:*** $25,291.

APPLYING

Standardized Tests *Required:* SAT or ACT (for admission).

Options: electronic application.

Required: high school transcript. ***Recommended:*** minimum 2.0 GPA.

CONTACT

Mrs. Amie Fazalare, Director of Recruiting, Fairmont State University, 1201 Locust Avenue, Fairmont, WV 26554. *Phone:* 304-367-4892. *Toll-free phone:* 800-641-5678. *Fax:* 304-367-4789. *E-mail:* admit@fairmontstate.edu.

Glenville State College

Glenville, West Virginia

http://www.glenville.edu/

- **State-supported** 4-year, founded 1872, part of West Virginia Higher Education Policy Commission
- **Rural** 331-acre campus
- **Endowment** $8.7 million
- **Coed** 1,577 undergraduate students, 63% full-time, 40% women, 60% men
- **Noncompetitive** entrance level, 100% of applicants were admitted

UNDERGRAD STUDENTS

999 full-time, 578 part-time. 16% are from out of state; 14% Black or African American, non-Hispanic/Latino; 3% Hispanic/Latino; 0.4% Asian, non-Hispanic/Latino; 0.4% American Indian or Alaska Native, non-Hispanic/Latino; 3% Two or more races, non-Hispanic/Latino; 3% Race/ethnicity unknown; 1% international; 5% transferred in; 51% live on campus.

Freshmen:

Admission: 2,550 applied, 2,548 admitted, 352 enrolled. ***Average high school GPA:*** 3.1. ***Test scores:*** SAT evidence-based reading and writing scores over 500: 39%; SAT math scores over 500: 39%; ACT scores over 18: 61%; SAT evidence-based reading and writing scores over 600: 8%; SAT math scores over 600: 3%; ACT scores over 24: 14%; ACT scores over 30: 1%.

Retention: 60% of full-time freshmen returned.

FACULTY

Total: 120, 48% full-time, 37% with terminal degrees.

Student/faculty ratio: 15:1.

ACADEMICS

Calendar: semesters. *Degrees:* associate and bachelor's.

Special study options: academic remediation for entering students, accelerated degree program, adult/continuing education programs, advanced placement credit, cooperative education, distance learning, double majors, honors programs, internships, off-campus study, part-time degree program, services for LD students, student-designed majors, study abroad, summer session for credit.

Computers: 183 computers/terminals and 599 ports are available on campus for general student use. Students can access the following: campus intranet, computer help desk, free student e-mail accounts, online (class) grades, online (class) registration, online (class) schedules, WebVista, Wimba Classroom. Campuswide network is available. 100% of college-owned or -operated housing units are wired for high-speed Internet access. Wireless service is available via entire campus.

Library: Robert F. Kidd Library plus 1 other. *Books:* 117,347 (physical), 64,412 (digital/electronic); *Serial titles:* 3,857 (physical), 10,004 (digital/electronic); *Databases:* 62. Weekly public service hours: 71.

STUDENT LIFE

Housing options: on-campus residence required through sophomore year; coed, men-only, women-only. Campus housing is university owned. Freshman campus housing is guaranteed.

Activities and organizations: drama/theater group, student-run newspaper, choral group, marching band, Music Educators National Conference, Student Government Association, Student Support Services, Student Advisory Committee, Glenville Student Action, national fraternities.

Athletics Member NCAA. All Division II. ***Intercollegiate sports:*** basketball M(s)/W(s), cross-country running M(s)/W(s), football M(s), golf M(s)/W(s), softball W(s), track and field M(s)/W(s), volleyball W(s). ***Intramural sports:*** basketball M/W, fencing M/W, rock climbing M/W, softball M/W, swimming and diving M/W, table tennis M/W, tennis M/W, volleyball M/W.

Campus security: 24-hour emergency response devices and patrols, student patrols, late-night transport/escort service, controlled dormitory access.

Student services: health clinic, personal/psychological counseling.

FINANCIAL AID

Financial Aid Of all full-time matriculated undergraduates who enrolled in 2018, 979 applied for aid, 939 were judged to have need, 38 had their need fully met. In 2018, 3 non-need-based awards were made. ***Average percent of need met:*** 63. ***Average financial aid package:*** $14,529. ***Average need-based loan:*** $3999. ***Average need-based gift aid:*** $5464. ***Average non-need-based aid:*** $958. ***Average indebtedness upon graduation:*** $7917. ***Financial aid deadline:*** 4/15.

APPLYING

Standardized Tests *Required:* SAT or ACT (for admission).

Options: electronic application, early action, deferred entrance.

Application fee: $25.

Required: high school transcript, minimum 3.0 GPA, college preparatory program. ***Required for some:*** interview.

Notification: continuous (freshmen).

CONTACT

Ms. Ashley Weir, Admission Counselor, Glenville State College, 200 High Street, Glenville, WV 26351-1200. *Phone:* 304-462-4128 Ext. 6133. *Toll-free phone:* 800-924-2010. *Fax:* 304-462-8619. *E-mail:* ashley.weir@glenville.edu.

Marshall University

Huntington, West Virginia

http://www.marshall.edu/

- **State-supported** university, founded 1837
- **Urban** 114-acre campus
- **Coed** 9,415 undergraduate students, 76% full-time, 58% women, 42% men
- **Moderately difficult** entrance level, 87% of applicants were admitted

UNDERGRAD STUDENTS

7,123 full-time, 2,292 part-time. Students come from 45 states and territories; 48 other countries; 18% are from out of state; 6% Black or African American, non-Hispanic/Latino; 2% Hispanic/Latino; 1% Asian, non-Hispanic/Latino; 0.1% Native Hawaiian or other Pacific Islander, non-Hispanic/Latino; 0.3% American Indian or Alaska Native, non-Hispanic/Latino; 3% Two or more races, non-Hispanic/Latino; 1% Race/ethnicity unknown; 2% international; 5% transferred in.

Freshmen:

Admission: 6,451 applied, 5,605 admitted, 1,769 enrolled. ***Average high school GPA:*** 3.6. ***Test scores:*** SAT evidence-based reading and writing scores over 500: 68%; SAT math scores over 500: 59%; ACT scores over 18: 86%; SAT evidence-based reading and writing scores over 600: 25%; SAT math scores over 600: 12%; ACT scores over 24: 34%; SAT evidence-based reading and writing scores over 700: 2%; SAT math scores over 700: 1%; ACT scores over 30: 6%.

Retention: 72% of full-time freshmen returned.

FACULTY

Total: 739, 63% full-time, 59% with terminal degrees.

Student/faculty ratio: 18:1.

ACADEMICS

Calendar: semesters. *Degrees:* certificates, bachelor's, master's, doctoral, post-master's, and postbachelor's certificates.

Special study options: academic remediation for entering students, accelerated degree program, adult/continuing education programs, advanced placement credit, cooperative education, distance learning, double majors, English as a second language, honors programs, independent study, internships, off-campus study, part-time degree program, services for LD students, study abroad, summer session for credit. ***ROTC:*** Army (b).

Computers: 1,200 computers/terminals and 500 ports are available on campus for general student use. Students can access the following: campus intranet, computer help desk, free student e-mail accounts, online (class) grades, online (class) registration, online (class) schedules, virtual computer lab: remote and Web conferencing. Campuswide network is available. 100% of college-owned or -operated housing units are wired for high-speed Internet access. Wireless service is available via classrooms, computer centers, computer labs, dorm rooms, learning centers, libraries, student centers.

Library: John Deaver Drinko Library plus 1 other. *Books:* 399,500 (physical), 253,337 (digital/electronic); *Serial titles:* 2,039 (physical), 51,798 (digital/electronic); *Databases:* 148. Weekly public service hours: 133; study areas open 24 hours, 5–7 days a week; students can reserve study rooms.

STUDENT LIFE

Housing options: on-campus residence required through sophomore year; coed, women-only, special housing for students with disabilities. Campus housing is university owned. Freshman campus housing is guaranteed.

Activities and organizations: drama/theater group, student-run newspaper, radio and television station, choral group, marching band, Campus Crusade for Christ, Gamma Beta Phi, The International Students' Organization, Newman Association, Phi Alpha Theta, national fraternities, national sororities.

Athletics Member NCAA. All Division I except football (Division I-A). ***Intercollegiate sports:*** baseball M(s), basketball M(s)/W(s), cross-country running M(s)/W(s), golf M(s)/W(s)(c), lacrosse M(c), rugby M(c)/W(c), soccer M(s)/W(s), softball W(s), swimming and diving W(s), tennis W(s), track and field M(s)/W(s), volleyball W(s). ***Intramural sports:*** basketball M/W, bowling M/W, football M/W, golf M/W, racquetball M/W, soccer M/W, softball M/W, swimming and diving M/W, table tennis M/W, tennis M/W, track and field M/W, volleyball M/W.

Campus security: 24-hour emergency response devices and patrols, student patrols, late-night transport/escort service, controlled dormitory access.

Student services: health clinic, personal/psychological counseling, women's center, legal services, veterans affairs office.

COSTS & FINANCIAL AID

Costs (2020–21) ***Tuition:*** area resident $7190 full-time, $300 per credit hour part-time; state resident $7190 full-time, $300 per credit hour part-time; nonresident $18,044 full-time, $752 per credit hour part-time. Full-time tuition and fees vary according to degree level, location, program, and reciprocity agreements. Part-time tuition and fees vary according to course load, degree level, location, program, and reciprocity agreements. ***Required fees:*** $1342 full-time. ***Room and board:*** $10,644; room only: $6648. Room and board charges vary according to board plan and housing facility. ***Payment plan:*** installment. ***Waivers:*** children of alumni, senior citizens, and employees or children of employees.

Financial Aid Of all full-time matriculated undergraduates who enrolled in 2019, 6,291 applied for aid, 5,047 were judged to have need, 1,560 had their need fully met. In 2019, 928 non-need-based awards were made. ***Average percent of need met:*** 46. ***Average financial aid package:*** $11,618. ***Average need-based loan:*** $6554. ***Average need-based gift aid:*** $6774. ***Average non-need-based aid:*** $3193. ***Average indebtedness upon graduation:*** $27,472.

APPLYING

Standardized Tests *Required:* SAT or ACT (for admission).

Options: electronic application, deferred entrance.

Application fee: $40.

Required for some: high school transcript.

Application deadlines: rolling (freshmen), rolling (transfers).

Notification: continuous (freshmen), continuous (transfers).

CONTACT

Dr. Tammy Johnson, Director of Admissions, Marshall University, 1 John Marshall Drive, Huntington, WV 25755. *Phone:* 800-642-3499. *Toll-free phone:* 800-642-3499. *Fax:* 304-696-3135. *E-mail:* admissions@marshall.edu.

Ohio Valley University

Vienna, West Virginia

http://www.ovu.edu/

- **Independent** comprehensive, founded 1960, affiliated with Church of Christ
- **Small-town** 299-acre campus
- **Coed** 304 undergraduate students, 89% full-time, 43% women, 57% men
- **Minimally difficult** entrance level, 43% of applicants were admitted

UNDERGRAD STUDENTS

272 full-time, 32 part-time. 67% are from out of state, 5% Black or African American, non-Hispanic/Latino; 4% Hispanic/Latino; 0.4% Asian, non-Hispanic/Latino; 0.7% American Indian or Alaska Native, non-Hispanic/Latino; 2% Two or more races, non-Hispanic/Latino; 9% Race/ethnicity unknown; 19% international; 13% transferred in; 44% live on campus.

Freshmen:

Admission: 740 applied, 318 admitted, 58 enrolled. ***Average high school GPA:*** 3.2. ***Test scores:*** SAT evidence-based reading and writing scores over 500: 60%; SAT math scores over 500: 50%; ACT scores over 18: 74%; SAT evidence-based reading and writing scores over 600: 27%; SAT math scores over 600: 20%; ACT scores over 24: 19%; SAT math scores over 700: 7%; ACT scores over 30: 2%.

FACULTY

Total: 66, 20% full-time, 32% with terminal degrees.

Student/faculty ratio: 10:1.

ACADEMICS

Calendar: semesters. *Degrees:* certificates, associate, bachelor's, and master's.

Special study options: academic remediation for entering students, adult/continuing education programs, advanced placement credit, distance learning, double majors, English as a second language, honors programs, independent study, internships, off-campus study, part-time degree program, services for LD students, student-designed majors, study abroad, summer session for credit.

Computers: Students can access the following: campus intranet, computer help desk, free student e-mail accounts, online (class) grades, online (class) registration, online (class) schedules. Campuswide network is available. Wireless service is available via entire campus.

Library: Icy Belle Library.

STUDENT LIFE

Housing options: on-campus residence required through sophomore year; men-only, women-only. Campus housing is university owned. Freshman campus housing is guaranteed.

Activities and organizations: drama/theater group, student-run newspaper, choral group, Social Clubs, intramural sports, Theatre Production, A cappella Choir, Ambassadors.

Athletics Member NCAA. All Division II. ***Intercollegiate sports:*** baseball M(s), basketball M(s)/W(s), cross-country running M(s)/W(s), golf M(s)/W(s), lacrosse M(s), soccer M(s)/W(s), softball W(s), volleyball W(s), wrestling M(s). ***Intramural sports:*** basketball M/W, bowling M/W, football M/W, golf M/W, soccer M/W, softball M/W, volleyball M/W.

Campus security: 24-hour emergency response devices and patrols, controlled dormitory access.

FINANCIAL AID

Financial Aid Of all full-time matriculated undergraduates who enrolled in 2018, 346 applied for aid, 303 were judged to have need, 49 had their need fully met. 50 Federal Work-Study jobs (averaging $1000). 10 state and other part-time jobs (averaging $1000). In 2018, 80 non-need-based awards were made. ***Average percent of need met:*** 59. ***Average financial aid package:*** $16,224. ***Average need-based loan:*** $3691. ***Average need-based gift aid:*** $13,295. ***Average non-need-based aid:*** $5492. ***Average indebtedness upon graduation:*** $25,815.

APPLYING

Standardized Tests *Required:* SAT or ACT (for admission).

Options: electronic application.

Required: high school transcript. ***Required for some:*** essay or personal statement, interview.

CONTACT

Mrs. Valerie Wright, Admissions Office Manager, Ohio Valley University, 1 Campus View Drive, Vienna, WV 26105. *Phone:* 304-865-6200. *Toll-free phone:* 877-446-8668. *Fax:* 304-865-6001. *E-mail:* admissions@ovu.edu.

Potomac State College of West Virginia University

Keyser, West Virginia

http://www.potomacstatecollege.edu/

- **State-supported** primarily 2-year, founded 1901, part of West Virginia Higher Education Policy Commission
- **Small-town** 18-acre campus
- **Coed**
- **Noncompetitive** entrance level

FACULTY

Student/faculty ratio: 22:1.

ACADEMICS

Calendar: semesters. *Degrees:* associate and bachelor's.

Library: Mary F. Shipper Library. *Books:* 7,011 (physical), 617,383 (digital/electronic); *Serial titles:* 19 (physical), 93,783 (digital/electronic); *Databases:* 687.

STUDENT LIFE

Housing options: on-campus residence required through sophomore year; coed. Campus housing is university owned. Freshman applicants given priority for college housing.

Activities and organizations: drama/theater group, student-run newspaper, choral group, Agriculture and Forestry Club, Black Student Alliance, Gamers and Geeks Club, Campus and Community Ministries.

Athletics Member NJCAA.

Campus security: 24-hour patrols, late-night transport/escort service, controlled dormitory access.

Student services: health clinic, personal/psychological counseling, veterans affairs office.

COSTS & FINANCIAL AID

Costs (2019–20) ***Tuition:*** state resident $4536 full-time, $189 per credit hour part-time; nonresident $11,544 full-time, $481 per credit hour part-time. Full-time tuition and fees vary according to degree level and program. Part-time tuition and fees vary according to degree level. ***Room and board:*** $8780. Room and board charges vary according to board plan and housing facility.

Financial Aid Of all full-time matriculated undergraduates who enrolled in 2017, 1,059 applied for aid, 843 were judged to have need, 73 had their need fully met. In 2017, 57 non-need-based awards were made. ***Average percent of need met:*** 65. ***Average financial aid package:*** $4355. ***Average need-based loan:*** $3039. ***Average need-based gift aid:*** $3418. ***Average non-need-based aid:*** $1907. ***Average indebtedness upon graduation:*** $18,208.

APPLYING

Options: electronic application.

Required: high school transcript.

CONTACT

Ms. Beth Little, Director of Enrollment Services, Potomac State College of West Virginia University, 75 Arnold Street, Keyser, WV 26726. *Phone:* 304-788-6820. *Toll-free phone:* 800-262-7332 Ext. 6820. *Fax:* 304-788-6939. *E-mail:* go2psc@mail.wvu.edu.

Salem International University

Salem, West Virginia

http://www.salemu.edu/

CONTACT

Mrs. Brenda Davis, Admissions Representative, Salem International University, PO Box 500, Salem, WV 26426-0500. *Phone:* 304-326-1359. *Toll-free phone:* 888-235-5024. *Fax:* 304-326-1592. *E-mail:* admissions@salemiu.edu.

Shepherd University

Shepherdstown, West Virginia

http://www.shepherd.edu/

- **State-supported** comprehensive, founded 1871, part of West Virginia Higher Education Policy Commission
- **Small-town** 325-acre campus with easy access to Washington, D.C.
- **Endowment** $24.2 million
- **Coed** 3,200 undergraduate students, 74% full-time, 58% women, 42% men
- **Moderately difficult** entrance level, 96% of applicants were admitted

UNDERGRAD STUDENTS

2,354 full-time, 846 part-time. Students come from 51 states and territories; 18 other countries; 32% are from out of state; 8% Black or African American, non-Hispanic/Latino; 7% Hispanic/Latino; 1% Asian, non-Hispanic/Latino; 0.1% Native Hawaiian or other Pacific Islander, non-Hispanic/Latino; 0.4% American Indian or Alaska Native, non-Hispanic/Latino; 4% Two or more races, non-Hispanic/Latino; 2% Race/ethnicity unknown; 1% international; 8% transferred in; 36% live on campus.

Freshmen:

Admission: 1,370 applied, 1,319 admitted, 483 enrolled. ***Average high school GPA:*** 3.5. ***Test scores:*** ACT scores over 18: 89%; ACT scores over 24: 38%; ACT scores over 30: 6%.

Retention: 71% of full-time freshmen returned.

FACULTY

Total: 321, 44% full-time, 55% with terminal degrees.

Student/faculty ratio: 14:1.

ACADEMICS

Calendar: semesters. *Degrees:* bachelor's, master's, and doctoral.

Special study options: academic remediation for entering students, adult/continuing education programs, advanced placement credit, cooperative education, distance learning, double majors, English as a second language, honors programs, independent study, internships, part-time degree program, services for LD students, study abroad, summer session for credit. ***ROTC:*** Air Force (c).

Unusual degree programs: 3-2 business administration; biochemistry (biopharmaceutical science) with West Virginia University and Marshall University.

Computers: 567 computers/terminals and 25 ports are available on campus for general student use. Students can access the following: computer help desk, free student e-mail accounts, online (class) grades, online (class) registration, online (class) schedules, virtual labs. Campuswide network is available. 100% of college-owned or -operated housing units are wired for high-speed Internet access. Wireless service is available via entire campus.

Library: Scarborough Library. *Books:* 175,775 (physical), 240,078 (digital/electronic); *Serial titles:* 361 (physical), 108,401 (digital/electronic); *Databases:* 97. Weekly public service hours: 87; study areas open 24 hours, 5–7 days a week; students can reserve study rooms.

STUDENT LIFE

Housing options: on-campus residence required through senior year; coed, special housing for students with disabilities. Campus housing is university owned. Freshman campus housing is guaranteed.

Activities and organizations: drama/theater group, student-run newspaper, radio station, choral group, marching band, Relay for Life, Student Government Association, Ram Marching Band, Sigma Sigma Sigma, Program Board, national fraternities, national sororities.

Athletics Member NCAA. All Division II. ***Intercollegiate sports:*** baseball M(s), basketball M(s)/W(s), football M(s), golf M(s), lacrosse W(s), soccer M(s)/W(s), softball W(s), tennis M(s)/W(s), volleyball W(s). ***Intramural sports:*** basketball M/W, football M/W, racquetball M/W, sand volleyball M/W, soccer M/W, volleyball M/W.

Campus security: 24-hour emergency response devices and patrols, late-night transport/escort service, controlled dormitory access, student security in academic buildings, RAVE emergency alert system.

Student services: health clinic, personal/psychological counseling, veterans affairs office.

COSTS & FINANCIAL AID

Costs (2020–21) ***Tuition:*** state resident $7784 full-time, $325 per credit hour part-time; nonresident $18,224 full-time, $760 per credit hour part-time. Full-time tuition and fees vary according to program and reciprocity agreements. Part-time tuition and fees vary according to program. ***Room and board:*** $10,654. Room and board charges vary according to board plan and housing facility. ***Payment plan:*** installment. ***Waivers:*** minority students, senior citizens, and employees or children of employees.

Financial Aid Of all full-time matriculated undergraduates who enrolled in 2019, 2,266 applied for aid, 1,510 were judged to have need, 411 had their need fully met. 91 Federal Work-Study jobs (averaging $1025). 350 state and other part-time jobs (averaging $1400). In 2019, 609 non-need-based awards were made. ***Average percent of need met:*** 78. ***Average financial aid package:*** $2795. ***Average need-based loan:*** $3967. ***Average need-based gift aid:*** $5666. ***Average non-need-based aid:*** $10,139. ***Average indebtedness upon graduation:*** $28,371.

APPLYING

Standardized Tests *Required:* SAT or ACT (for admission).

Options: electronic application, early admission, early action, deferred entrance.

Application fee: $45.

Required: high school transcript, minimum 2.0 GPA. ***Recommended:*** essay or personal statement, minimum 3.0 GPA, 2 letters of recommendation.

Application deadlines: rolling (freshmen), rolling (transfers), 11/15 (early action).

Notification: continuous until 8/15 (freshmen), continuous until 8/15 (transfers), 12/15 (early action).

CONTACT

Ms. Kristen Lorenz, Director of Admissions, Shepherd University, PO Box 5000, Shepherdstown, WV 25443-5000. *Phone:* 304-876-5212. *Toll-free phone:* 800-344-5231. *Fax:* 304-876-5165. *E-mail:* admission@shepherd.edu.

Strayer University–Teays Valley Campus

Scott Depot, West Virginia

http://www.strayer.edu/west-virginia/teays-valley/

CONTACT

Strayer University–Teays Valley Campus, 135 Corporate Center Drive, Scott Depot, WV 25560. *Toll-free phone:* 888-311-0355.

University of Charleston

Charleston, West Virginia

http://www.ucwv.edu/

- **Independent** comprehensive, founded 1888
- **Small-town** 40-acre campus
- **Coed** 1,907 undergraduate students, 61% full-time, 44% women, 56% men
- **Moderately difficult** entrance level, 50% of applicants were admitted

UNDERGRAD STUDENTS

1,172 full-time, 735 part-time. 51% are from out of state; 9% Black or African American, non-Hispanic/Latino; 3% Hispanic/Latino; 1% Asian, non-Hispanic/Latino; 0.3% Native Hawaiian or other Pacific Islander, non-Hispanic/Latino; 1% American Indian or Alaska Native, non-Hispanic/Latino; 27% Race/ethnicity unknown; 7% international; 16% transferred in; 32% live on campus.

Freshmen:

Admission: 2,454 applied, 1,228 admitted, 282 enrolled.

Retention: 65% of full-time freshmen returned.

ACADEMICS

Calendar: semesters. *Degrees:* associate, bachelor's, master's, and doctoral.

Special study options: academic remediation for entering students, adult/continuing education programs, advanced placement credit, distance learning, double majors, external degree program, freshman honors college, honors programs, independent study, internships, off-campus study, part-time degree program, services for LD students, summer session for credit. ***ROTC:*** Army (c).

Computers: 200 computers/terminals are available on campus for general student use. Students can access the following: campus intranet, computer help desk, free student e-mail accounts, online (class) grades, online (class) registration, online (class) schedules. Campuswide network is available. Wireless service is available via entire campus.

Library: Schoenbaum Library plus 1 other. *Books:* 189,000 (physical), 210,000 (digital/electronic); *Databases:* 56. Students can reserve study rooms.

STUDENT LIFE

Housing options: on-campus residence required through sophomore year; coed, special housing for students with disabilities. Campus housing is university owned. Freshman campus housing is guaranteed.

Activities and organizations: choral group, marching band, Student Activities Board, American Society of Interior Designers, Student Government Association, Capito Association of Nursing Students, International Student Organization, national fraternities, national sororities.

Athletics Member NCAA. All Division II. ***Intercollegiate sports:*** baseball M(s), basketball M(s)/W(s), cheerleading M(s)/W(s), cross-country running M(s)/W(s), football M(s), golf M(s)/W(s), lacrosse W(s), soccer M(s)/W(s), softball W(s), tennis M(s)/W(s), track and field M(s)/W(s), volleyball M(s)/W(s). ***Intramural sports:*** basketball M/W, bowling M/W, football M/W, tennis M/W, volleyball M/W, water polo M/W.

Campus security: 24-hour emergency response devices and patrols, student patrols, late-night transport/escort service, controlled dormitory access, radio connection to city police and ambulance.

Student services: health clinic, personal/psychological counseling, veterans affairs office.

FINANCIAL AID

Financial Aid ***Financial aid deadline:*** 8/15.

APPLYING

Options: electronic application, deferred entrance.

Application fee: $25.

Required: high school transcript, minimum 2.3 GPA. ***Required for some:*** interview. ***Recommended:*** essay or personal statement.

Application deadlines: rolling (freshmen), rolling (transfers).

Notification: continuous (freshmen), continuous (transfers).

CONTACT

Sandy Dolin, Application Coordinator, University of Charleston, 2300 MacCorkle Avenue, SE, Charleston, WV 25304. *Phone:* 304-357-4752. *Toll-free phone:* 800-995-GOUC. *E-mail:* admissions@ucwv.edu.

West Liberty University

West Liberty, West Virginia

http://www.westliberty.edu/

- **State-supported** comprehensive, founded 1837, part of West Virginia Higher Education Policy Commission
- **Rural** campus
- **Coed** 2,183 undergraduate students, 84% full-time, 64% women, 36% men
- **Minimally difficult** entrance level, 71% of applicants were admitted

UNDERGRAD STUDENTS

1,837 full-time, 346 part-time. 31% are from out of state; 3% Black or African American, non-Hispanic/Latino; 0.7% Hispanic/Latino; 0.6% Asian, non-Hispanic/Latino; 2% Two or more races, non-Hispanic/Latino; 16% Race/ethnicity unknown; 2% international; 10% transferred in; 39% live on campus.

Freshmen:

Admission: 1,829 applied, 1,292 admitted, 465 enrolled. ***Average high school GPA:*** 3.5. ***Test scores:*** ACT scores over 18: 72%; ACT scores over 24: 26%; ACT scores over 30: 5%.

Retention: 70% of full-time freshmen returned.

ACADEMICS

Calendar: semesters. *Degrees:* associate, bachelor's, and master's.

Special study options: academic remediation for entering students, accelerated degree program, adult/continuing education programs, advanced placement credit, cooperative education, distance learning, double majors, external degree program, honors programs, independent study, internships, off-campus study, part-time degree program, services for LD students, student-designed majors, study abroad, summer session for credit.

Computers: Students can access the following: campus intranet, computer help desk, free student e-mail accounts, online (class) grades, online (class) registration, online (class) schedules. Campuswide network is available. 100% of college-owned or -operated housing units are wired for high-speed Internet access. Wireless service is available via classrooms, computer labs, dorm rooms, learning centers, libraries, student centers.

Library: Paul N. Elbin Library.

STUDENT LIFE

Housing options: coed, men-only, women-only, special housing for students with disabilities. Campus housing is university owned.

Athletics Member NCAA. All Division II. ***Intercollegiate sports:*** baseball M(s), basketball M(s)/W(s), cross-country running M(s)/W(s), football M(s), golf M(s)/W(s), softball W(s), tennis M(s)/W(s), track and field M(s)/W(s), volleyball W(s), wrestling M(s). ***Intramural sports:*** basketball M/W, golf M/W, racquetball M/W, softball M/W, table tennis M/W, tennis M/W, volleyball M/W.

Campus security: 24-hour emergency response devices and patrols, controlled dormitory access.

COSTS & FINANCIAL AID

Costs (2019–20) ***Tuition:*** area resident $7990 full-time; state resident $7990 full-time; nonresident $15,930 full-time. Full-time tuition and fees vary according to course load, degree level, and program. Part-time tuition and fees vary according to course load, degree level, and program. ***Room and board:*** $9614; room only: $5150. Room and board charges vary according to board plan, housing facility, and location. ***Payment plans:*** installment, deferred payment. ***Waivers:*** senior citizens and employees or children of employees.

Financial Aid Of all full-time matriculated undergraduates who enrolled in 2010, 2,138 applied for aid, 1,799 were judged to have need, 391 had their need fully met. In 2010, 43 non-need-based awards were made. ***Average percent of need met:*** 70. ***Average financial aid package:*** $7990. ***Average need-based loan:*** $3974. ***Average need-based gift aid:*** $5196. ***Average non-need-based aid:*** $1507. ***Average indebtedness upon graduation:*** $25,000.

APPLYING

Standardized Tests *Required:* SAT or ACT (for admission).

Options: electronic application.

Required: high school transcript, minimum 2.0 GPA. ***Recommended:*** interview.

CONTACT

Ms. Stephanie North, Admissions Counselor, West Liberty University, 208 University Drive, West Liberty, WV 26074. *Phone:* 304-336-8078. *Toll-free phone:* 800-732-6204 (in-state); 866-WESTLIB (out-of-state). *Fax:* 304-336-8403. *E-mail:* wladmsn1@westliberty.edu.

West Virginia State University

Institute, West Virginia

http://www.wvstateu.edu/

- **State-supported** comprehensive, founded 1891, part of West Virginia four-year public higher education system
- **Small-town** 98-acre campus
- **Endowment** $7.1 million
- **Coed**
- **Minimally difficult** entrance level

FACULTY

Student/faculty ratio: 13:1.

ACADEMICS

Calendar: semesters. *Degrees:* bachelor's, master's, post-master's, and postbachelor's certificates.
Library: Drain-Jordan Library. *Books:* 135,848 (physical), 25,361 (digital/electronic); *Serial titles:* 1,454 (physical), 33,375 (digital/electronic); *Databases:* 28. Weekly public service hours: 82.

STUDENT LIFE

Housing options: on-campus residence required through sophomore year; coed, special housing for students with disabilities. Campus housing is university owned.

Activities and organizations: student-run newspaper, radio station, choral group, marching band, Student Social Work Organization 20, WVSU College Chapter - NAACP 17, CHOICES Peer Educators 13, WVSU International Student Services 13, C.E. Jones Historical Society 12, national fraternities, national sororities.

Athletics Member NCAA. All Division II.

Campus security: 24-hour emergency response devices and patrols, late-night transport/escort service, controlled dormitory access.

Student services: health clinic, personal/psychological counseling, veterans affairs office.

COSTS & FINANCIAL AID

Costs (2019–20) ***Tuition:*** state resident $8050 full-time, $332 per credit hour part-time; nonresident $17,166 full-time, $746 per credit hour part-time. ***Required fees:*** $700 full-time. ***Room and board:*** $12,486; room only: $7852.

Financial Aid ***Financial aid deadline:*** 6/15.

APPLYING

Standardized Tests *Required:* SAT or ACT (for admission).

Options: electronic application.

Application fee: $20.

Required: high school transcript, minimum 2.0 GPA, minimum ACT composite score of 18 (870 SAT).

CONTACT

Jameelah Means, Interim Director of Admissions, West Virginia State University, PO Box 1000, Ferrell Hall, Room 106, Institute, WV 25112-1000. *Phone:* 304-204-4340. *Toll-free phone:* 800-987-2112. *Fax:* 304-766-5182. *E-mail:* jmeans9@wvstateu.edu.

West Virginia University

Morgantown, West Virginia

http://www.wvu.edu/

- **State-supported** university, founded 1867, part of West Virginia Higher Education Policy Commission
- **Small-town** 1892-acre campus with easy access to Pittsburgh
- **Endowment** $574.9 million
- **Coed** 21,086 undergraduate students, 92% full-time, 50% women, 50% men
- **Moderately difficult** entrance level

UNDERGRAD STUDENTS

19,369 full-time, 1,717 part-time. 41% are from out of state; 4% Black or African American, non-Hispanic/Latino; 4% Hispanic/Latino; 2% Asian, non-Hispanic/Latino; 0.1% Native Hawaiian or other Pacific Islander, non-Hispanic/Latino; 0.1% American Indian or Alaska Native, non-Hispanic/Latino; 4% Two or more races, non-Hispanic/Latino; 0.7% Race/ethnicity unknown; 5% international.

Freshmen:
Admission: 4,949 enrolled. ***Average high school GPA:*** 3.5. ***Test scores:*** SAT evidence-based reading and writing scores over 500: 83%; SAT math scores over 500: 79%; ACT scores over 18: 90%; SAT evidence-based reading and writing scores over 600: 34%; SAT math scores over 600: 28%; ACT scores over 24: 45%; SAT evidence-based reading and writing scores over 700: 4%; SAT math scores over 700: 4%; ACT scores over 30: 9%.

ACADEMICS

Calendar: semesters. *Degrees:* bachelor's, master's, and doctoral.

Special study options: academic remediation for entering students, accelerated degree program, adult/continuing education programs, advanced placement credit, distance learning, double majors, English as a second language, external degree program, honors programs, independent study, internships, off-campus study, part-time degree program, services for LD students, student-designed majors, study abroad, summer session for credit. ***ROTC:*** Army (b), Air Force (b).

Unusual degree programs: 3-2 education, business/foreign language, occupational therapy, physical therapy, social work.

Computers: 1,800 computers/terminals and 900 ports are available on campus for general student use. Students can access the following: campus intranet, computer help desk, free student e-mail accounts, online (class) grades, online (class) registration, online (class) schedules. Campuswide network is available. 100% of college-owned or -operated housing units are wired for high-speed Internet access. Wireless service is available via entire campus.
Library: Downtown Library Complex plus 5 others. *Books:* 1.1 million (physical), 621,166 (digital/electronic); *Serial titles:* 56,340 (physical), 96,553 (digital/electronic); *Databases:* 975. Study areas open 24 hours, 5–7 days a week; students can reserve study rooms.

STUDENT LIFE

Housing options: on-campus residence required for freshman year; coed, men-only, women-only, cooperative, special housing for students with disabilities. Campus housing is university owned. Freshman campus housing is guaranteed.

Activities and organizations: drama/theater group, student-run newspaper, radio station, choral group, marching band, Residential Hall Association, Alpha Phi Omega, WVU Greek System, Mountaineer Maniacs, Campus Crusade for Christ, national fraternities, national sororities.

Athletics Member NCAA. All Division I except football (Division I-A). ***Intercollegiate sports:*** baseball M(s), basketball M(s)/W(s), crew W(s), cross-country running W(s), golf M(s), gymnastics W(s), riflery M(s)/W(s), soccer M(s)/W(s), swimming and diving M(s)/W(s), tennis W(s), track and field W(s), volleyball W(s), wrestling M(s). ***Intramural sports:*** archery M(c)/W(c), baseball M(c), basketball M(c)/W(c), bowling M(c)/W(c), cheerleading M(c)/W(c), crew M(c)/W(c), cross-country running M(c)/W(c), equestrian sports M(c)/W(c), fencing M(c)/W(c), field hockey M(c)/W(c), football M, golf M(c), ice hockey M(c), lacrosse M(c)/W(c), racquetball M(c)/W(c), riflery M(c)/W(c), rock climbing M(c)/W(c), rugby M(c)/W(c), skiing (cross-country) M(c)/W(c), skiing (downhill) M(c)/W(c), soccer M(c)/W(c), softball M(c)/W(c), swimming and diving M(c)/W(c), table tennis M(c)/W(c), tennis M(c)/W(c), track and field M(c)/W(c), ultimate Frisbee M(c)/W(c), volleyball M(c)/W(c), weight lifting M(c), wrestling M(c).

Campus security: 24-hour emergency response devices and patrols, student patrols, late-night transport/escort service, controlled dormitory access, patrol officers just for housing.

Student services: health clinic, personal/psychological counseling, women's center, legal services, veterans affairs office.

COSTS & FINANCIAL AID

Costs (2019–20) ***Tuition:*** state resident $8972 full-time, $374 per credit hour part-time; nonresident $25,320 full-time, $1055 per credit hour part-time. Full-time tuition and fees vary according to location, program, and reciprocity agreements. Part-time tuition and fees vary according to course load, location, program, and reciprocity agreements. ***Room and board:*** $11,062. Room and board charges vary according to board plan, housing facility, and location. ***Payment plan:*** installment. ***Waivers:*** senior citizens and employees or children of employees.

Financial Aid Of all full-time matriculated undergraduates who enrolled in 2017, 16,394 applied for aid, 10,783 were judged to have need, 1,160 had their need fully met. In 2017, 3344 non-need-based awards were made. ***Average financial aid package:*** $7488. ***Average need-based loan:*** $4225. ***Average need-based gift aid:*** $5812. ***Average non-need-based aid:*** $4737. ***Average indebtedness upon graduation:*** $32,541. ***Financial aid deadline:*** 3/1.

APPLYING

Standardized Tests *Required:* SAT or ACT (for admission).

Options: electronic application, early admission, deferred entrance.

Application fee: $65.

Required: high school transcript, minimum 2.0 GPA. ***Required for some:*** essay or personal statement, minimum 2.3 GPA.

Application deadlines: 8/1 (freshmen), 8/1 (transfers).

Notification: continuous (transfers).

CONTACT

Ms. Marilyn Potts, Director of Admissions, West Virginia University, PO Box 6009, Morgantown, WV 26506-6009. *Phone:* 304-293-2121. *Toll-free phone:* 800-344-9881. *Fax:* 304-293-3080. *E-mail:* marilyn.potts@mail.wvu.edu.

West Virginia University at Parkersburg

Parkersburg, West Virginia

http://www.wvup.edu/

CONTACT

Christine Post, Associate Dean of Enrollment Management, West Virginia University at Parkersburg, 300 Campus Drive, Parkersburg, WV 26104. *Phone:* 304-424-8223 Ext. 223. *Toll-free phone:* 800-WVA-WVUP. *Fax:* 304-424-8332. *E-mail:* christine.post@mail.wvu.edu.

West Virginia University Institute of Technology

Beckley, West Virginia

http://www.wvutech.edu/

- **State-supported** 4-year, founded 1895
- **Small-town** 114-acre campus
- **Endowment** $532.6 million
- **Coed**
- **Minimally difficult** entrance level

FACULTY

Student/faculty ratio: 13:1.

ACADEMICS

Calendar: semesters. *Degrees:* bachelor's and postbachelor's certificates.
Library: Vining Library plus 1 other. *Books:* 14,844 (physical), 586,819 (digital/electronic); *Serial titles:* 154 (physical), 95,919 (digital/electronic). Students can reserve study rooms.

STUDENT LIFE

Housing options: on-campus residence required through sophomore year; coed. Campus housing is university owned. Freshman campus housing is guaranteed.

Activities and organizations: drama/theater group, student-run newspaper, Christian Student Union, Student Activities Board, Alpha Phi Omega, Student Government Association, American Society of Mechanical Engineers, national fraternities, national sororities.

Athletics Member NAIA, USCAA.

Campus security: 24-hour emergency response devices and patrols.

Student services: health clinic, personal/psychological counseling, veterans affairs office.

COSTS & FINANCIAL AID

Costs (2019–20) ***Tuition:*** state resident $7560 full-time, $315 per credit hour part-time; nonresident $18,912 full-time, $788 per credit hour part-time. Full-time tuition and fees vary according to program. Part-time tuition and fees vary according to course load and program. ***Room and board:*** $11,628. Room and board charges vary according to board plan and housing facility.

Financial Aid Of all full-time matriculated undergraduates who enrolled in 2017, 940 applied for aid, 736 were judged to have need, 46 had their need fully met. In 2017, 25 non-need-based awards were made. ***Average financial aid package:*** $7441. ***Average need-based loan:*** $3781. ***Average need-based gift aid:*** $3086. ***Average non-need-based aid:*** $2843. ***Average indebtedness upon graduation:*** $28,859.

APPLYING

Standardized Tests *Required:* SAT or ACT (for admission). *Required for some:* TOEFL or IELTS.

Options: electronic application, early admission.

Required: high school transcript, minimum 2.0 GPA, minimum ACT composite score of 18 or 870 SAT math and verbal or minimum 3.0 high school GPA.

CONTACT

William Allen Jr., Dean of Enrollment Services, West Virginia University Institute of Technology, Old Main Box 80, 405 Fayette Pike, Montgomery, WV 25136. *Phone:* 304-442-3146. *Toll-free phone:* 888-554-8324. *Fax:* 304-442-3067. *E-mail:* tech-admissions@mail.wvu.edu.

West Virginia Wesleyan College

Buckhannon, West Virginia

http://www.wvwc.edu/

CONTACT

John Waltz, Vice President for Enrollment Management, West Virginia Wesleyan College, 59 College Avenue, Buckhannon, WV 26201. *Phone:* 304-473-8510. *Toll-free phone:* 800-722-9933. *Fax:* 304-473-8108. *E-mail:* admission@wvwc.edu.

Wheeling Jesuit University

Wheeling, West Virginia

http://www.wju.edu/

- **Independent Roman Catholic (Jesuit)** comprehensive, founded 1954
- **Suburban** 65-acre campus with easy access to Pittsburgh
- **Endowment** $12.5 million
- **Coed**
- **Moderately difficult** entrance level

FACULTY

Student/faculty ratio: 11:1.

ACADEMICS

Calendar: semesters. *Degrees:* bachelor's, master's, doctoral, post-master's, and postbachelor's certificates.
Library: Bishop Hodges Library. *Books:* 134,540 (physical), 165,927 (digital/electronic); *Serial titles:* 107 (physical), 42 (digital/electronic); *Databases:* 69. Weekly public service hours: 85; students can reserve study rooms.

STUDENT LIFE

Housing options: on-campus residence required through sophomore year; coed, men-only, women-only, special housing for students with disabilities. Campus housing is university owned and is provided by a third party. Freshman campus housing is guaranteed.

Activities and organizations: drama/theater group, student-run newspaper, choral group, Campus Activity Board (CAB), Theater Guild, Student Senate, International Student Club, Campus Ministry.

Athletics Member NCAA. All Division II except rugby (Division I).

Campus security: 24-hour patrols, late-night transport/escort service, controlled dormitory access, cameras at residence hall entrances.

Student services: health clinic, personal/psychological counseling.

FINANCIAL AID

Financial Aid Of all full-time matriculated undergraduates who enrolled in 2018, 687 applied for aid, 591 were judged to have need, 171 had their need fully met. 118 Federal Work-Study jobs (averaging $2800). 38 state and other part-time jobs (averaging $2800). In 2018, 143 non-need-based awards were made. ***Average percent of need met:*** 93. ***Average financial aid package:*** $26,835. ***Average need-based loan:*** $3941. ***Average need-based gift aid:*** $9173. ***Average non-need-based aid:*** $18,916. ***Average indebtedness upon graduation:*** $34,151. ***Financial aid deadline:*** 8/1.

APPLYING

Standardized Tests *Required:* SAT or ACT (for admission).

Options: electronic application, deferred entrance.

Application fee: $25.

Required: high school transcript. ***Required for some:*** interview. ***Recommended:*** essay or personal statement, minimum 3.0 GPA, 2 letters of recommendation, interview.

CONTACT

Mr. Christopher Rouhier, Senior Admissions Representative, Wheeling Jesuit University, 316 Washington Avenue, Wheeling, WV 26003. *Phone:*

304-243-2106. *Toll-free phone:* 800-624-6992 Ext. 2359. *Fax:* 304-243-2397. *E-mail:* crouhier@wju.edu.

WISCONSIN

Alverno College

Milwaukee, Wisconsin

http://www.alverno.edu/

- **Independent Roman Catholic** comprehensive, founded 1887
- **Urban** 46-acre campus
- **Endowment** $31.7 million
- **Undergraduate: women only; graduate: coed** 1,104 undergraduate students, 82% full-time, 99% women, 1% men
- **Moderately difficult** entrance level, 67% of applicants were admitted

UNDERGRAD STUDENTS
906 full-time, 198 part-time. Students come from 20 states and territories; 3 other countries; 9% are from out of state; 14% Black or African American, non-Hispanic/Latino; 33% Hispanic/Latino; 5% Asian, non-Hispanic/Latino; 0.7% American Indian or Alaska Native, non-Hispanic/Latino; 5% Two or more races, non-Hispanic/Latino; 0.1% Race/ethnicity unknown; 0.4% international; 11% transferred in; 16% live on campus.

Freshmen:
Admission: 800 applied, 539 admitted, 170 enrolled. ***Average high school GPA:*** 3.2. ***Test scores:*** ACT scores over 18: 78%; ACT scores over 24: 15%; ACT scores over 30: 1%.

Retention: 71% of full-time freshmen returned.

FACULTY
Total: 238, 37% full-time, 42% with terminal degrees.

Student/faculty ratio: 9:1.

ACADEMICS
Calendar: semesters. *Degrees:* associate, bachelor's, master's, doctoral, post-master's, and postbachelor's certificates (also offers weekend program with significant enrollment not reflected in profile).

Special study options: academic remediation for entering students, accelerated degree program, adult/continuing education programs, advanced placement credit, distance learning, double majors, honors programs, independent study, internships, part-time degree program, services for LD students, student-designed majors, study abroad, summer session for credit. ***ROTC:*** Army (c), Air Force (c).

Unusual degree programs: 3-2 math/computer science with UW-Milwaukee; fresh water sciences with UW-Milwaukee.

Computers: 646 computers/terminals are available on campus for general student use. Students can access the following: campus intranet, computer help desk, free student e-mail accounts, online (class) registration, online (class) schedules. Campuswide network is available. 100% of college-owned or -operated housing units are wired for high-speed Internet access. Wireless service is available via classrooms, computer centers, computer labs, dorm rooms, libraries.

Library: Alverno College Library. *Books:* 58,739 (physical), 182,187 (digital/electronic); *Serial titles:* 823 (physical), 27,896 (digital/electronic); *Databases:* 66. Weekly public service hours: 85.

STUDENT LIFE
Housing options: on-campus residence required through sophomore year; women-only. Campus housing is university owned. Freshman campus housing is guaranteed.

Activities and organizations: drama/theater group, student-run newspaper, radio station, choral group, Alverno Cru, CHICA, Ebongrey Gaming Organization, Psych Forum, Gay-Straight Alliance.

Athletics Member NCAA. All Division III. ***Intercollegiate sports:*** basketball W, cross-country running W, golf W, soccer W, softball W, tennis W, volleyball W.

Campus security: 24-hour emergency response devices and patrols, late-night transport/escort service, controlled dormitory access, well-lit parking lots and pathways, emergency first-aid and CPR, crisis intervention team and plan in place.

Student services: health clinic, personal/psychological counseling.

COSTS & FINANCIAL AID
Costs (2019–20) ***Comprehensive fee:*** $38,256 includes full-time tuition ($28,656), mandatory fees ($800), and room and board ($8800). Full-time tuition and fees vary according to program. Part-time tuition: $1194 per credit hour. Part-time tuition and fees vary according to program. ***Room and board:*** Room and board charges vary according to board plan and housing facility. ***Payment plans:*** installment, deferred payment. ***Waivers:*** employees or children of employees.

Financial Aid Of all full-time matriculated undergraduates who enrolled in 2019, 849 applied for aid, 811 were judged to have need. 267 Federal Work-Study jobs (averaging $1148). In 2019, 82 non-need-based awards were made. ***Average financial aid package:*** $21,594. ***Average need-based loan:*** $3986. ***Average need-based gift aid:*** $17,715. ***Average non-need-based aid:*** $12,533. ***Average indebtedness upon graduation:*** $38,959.

APPLYING
Standardized Tests *Required:* SAT or ACT (for admission).

Options: electronic application, deferred entrance.

Required: essay or personal statement, high school transcript, minimum 2.0 college GPA. ***Recommended:*** minimum 2.0 GPA, interview.

Application deadlines: rolling (freshmen), rolling (transfers).

Notification: continuous (freshmen), continuous (transfers).

CONTACT
Ms. Janet Stikel, Director of Admissions, Alverno College, 3400 South 43 Street, PO Box 343922, Milwaukee, WI 53234-3922. *Phone:* 414-382-6110. *Toll-free phone:* 800-933-3401. *Fax:* 414-382-6055. *E-mail:* admissions@alverno.edu.

Bellin College

Green Bay, Wisconsin

http://www.bellincollege.edu/

CONTACT
Kathryn Wall, Director of Enrollment Management, Bellin College, 3201 Eaton Road, Green Bay, WI 54311. *Phone:* 920-433-6651. *Toll-free phone:* 800-236-8707. *E-mail:* admissions@bellincollege.edu.

Beloit College

Beloit, Wisconsin

http://www.beloit.edu/

- **Independent** 4-year, founded 1846
- **Small-town** 84-acre campus with easy access to Chicago, Milwaukee
- **Endowment** $160.9 million
- **Coed** 1,143 undergraduate students, 95% full-time, 55% women, 45% men
- 62% of applicants were admitted

UNDERGRAD STUDENTS
1,082 full-time, 61 part-time. 82% are from out of state; 7% Black or African American, non-Hispanic/Latino; 13% Hispanic/Latino; 4% Asian, non-Hispanic/Latino; 0.4% Native Hawaiian or other Pacific Islander, non-Hispanic/Latino; 0.2% American Indian or Alaska Native, non-Hispanic/Latino; 4% Two or more races, non-Hispanic/Latino; 3% Race/ethnicity unknown; 18% international; 1% transferred in; 87% live on campus.

Freshmen:
Admission: 3,657 applied, 2,269 admitted, 259 enrolled. ***Average high school GPA:*** 3.4. ***Test scores:*** SAT evidence-based reading and writing scores over 500: 85%; SAT math scores over 500: 90%; ACT scores over 18: 97%; SAT evidence-based reading and writing scores over 600: 55%; SAT math scores over 600: 58%; ACT scores over 24: 78%; SAT evidence-based reading and writing scores over 700: 13%; SAT math scores over 700: 26%; ACT scores over 30: 35%.

Retention: 79% of full-time freshmen returned.

FACULTY
Total: 106, 87% full-time, 90% with terminal degrees.

Student/faculty ratio: 11:1.

ACADEMICS
Calendar: semesters. *Degree:* bachelor's.

Special study options: adult/continuing education programs, advanced placement credit, external degree program, independent study, internships, off-campus study, services for LD students, student-designed majors, study abroad, summer session for credit.

Unusual degree programs: 3-2 engineering with Columbia University, Rensselaer Polytechnic Institute, Washington University in St. Louis; forestry with Duke University.

Computers: 300 computers/terminals are available on campus for general student use. Students can access the following: campus intranet, computer help desk, free student e-mail accounts, online (class) grades, online (class) registration, online (class) schedules. Campuswide network is available. 100% of college-owned or -operated housing units are wired for high-speed Internet access. Wireless service is available via entire campus.

Library: Morse Library and Black Information Center. *Books:* 207,000 (physical), 210,000 (digital/electronic); *Serial titles:* 11,700 (physical), 76,000 (digital/electronic); *Databases:* 151. Weekly public service hours: 109; students can reserve study rooms.

STUDENT LIFE
Housing options: on-campus residence required through junior year; coed, women-only. Campus housing is university owned. Freshman campus housing is guaranteed.

Activities and organizations: drama/theater group, student-run newspaper, radio and television station, choral group, BSFFA - Beloit Science Fiction and Fantasy Association, Ceramics Club, Anthropology Club, Yoga Club, Outdoor Environmental Club, national fraternities, national sororities.

Athletics Member NCAA. All Division III. ***Intercollegiate sports:*** baseball M, basketball M/W, cross-country running M/W, football M, ice hockey M(c)/W(c), lacrosse M/W, soccer M/W, softball W, swimming and diving M/W, tennis W, track and field M/W, volleyball W. ***Intramural sports:*** archery M(c)/W(c), badminton M/W, basketball M/W, fencing M(c), field hockey W(c), football M, golf M(c)/W(c), racquetball M/W, sailing M(c)/W(c), skiing (downhill) M(c)/W(c), soccer M/W, ultimate Frisbee M/W, volleyball M/W.

Campus security: 24-hour emergency response devices and patrols, late-night transport/escort service, controlled dormitory access.

Student services: health clinic, personal/psychological counseling, women's center.

COSTS & FINANCIAL AID
Costs (2020–21) ***Comprehensive fee:*** $63,036 includes full-time tuition ($52,858), mandatory fees ($490), and room and board ($9688). Part-time tuition: $1652 per credit hour. ***College room only:*** $5518.

Financial Aid Of all full-time matriculated undergraduates who enrolled in 2019, 725 applied for aid, 665 were judged to have need, 206 had their need fully met. In 2019, 386 non-need-based awards were made. ***Average percent of need met:*** 95. ***Average financial aid package:*** $48,229. ***Average need-based loan:*** $7320. ***Average need-based gift aid:*** $37,603. ***Average non-need-based aid:*** $31,593. ***Average indebtedness upon graduation:*** $23,534. ***Financial aid deadline:*** 3/1.

APPLYING
Standardized Tests *Required for some:* SAT or ACT (for admission).

Options: electronic application, early admission, early decision, early action, deferred entrance.

Required: essay or personal statement, high school transcript, 1 letter of recommendation. ***Recommended:*** interview.

Application deadlines: 1/15 (freshmen), rolling (transfers), 12/1 (early action).

Early decision deadline: 11/1 (for plan 1), 1/15 (for plan 2).

Notification: continuous (freshmen), continuous (transfers), 12/1 (early decision), 1/1 (early action).

CONTACT
Ms. Kate Virgo, Interim Director of Enrollment Operations, Beloit College, 700 College Street, Beloit, WI 53511-5596. *Phone:* 608-363-2380. *Toll-free phone:* 800-9-BELOIT. *Fax:* 608-363-2179. *E-mail:* virgok@beloit.edu.

Bryant & Stratton College–Bayshore Campus

Glendale, Wisconsin

http://www.bryantstratton.edu/

CONTACT
Bryant & Stratton College–Bayshore Campus, 500 West Silver Spring Drive, Bayshore Town Center, Suite K340, Glendale, WI 53217.

Bryant & Stratton College–Milwaukee Campus

Milwaukee, Wisconsin

http://www.bryantstratton.edu/

CONTACT
Mr. Dan Basile, Director of Admissions, Bryant & Stratton College–Milwaukee Campus, 310 West Wisconsin Avenue, Suite 500 East, Milwaukee, WI 53203-2214. *Phone:* 414-276-5200.

Bryant & Stratton College–Wauwatosa Campus

Wauwatosa, Wisconsin

http://www.bryantstratton.edu/

CONTACT
Bryant & Stratton College–Wauwatosa Campus, 10950 West Potter Road, Wauwatosa, WI 53226. *Phone:* 414-302-7000 Ext. 502.

Cardinal Stritch University

Milwaukee, Wisconsin

http://www.stritch.edu/

- **Independent Roman Catholic** university, founded 1937
- **Suburban** 40-acre campus with easy access to Milwaukee
- **Endowment** $19.4 million
- **Coed**
- **Moderately difficult** entrance level

FACULTY
Student/faculty ratio: ####:1.

ACADEMICS
Calendar: semesters. *Degrees:* certificates, associate, bachelor's, master's, doctoral, post-master's, and postbachelor's certificates.
Library: Cardinal Stritch University Library. *Books:* 122,184 (physical), 146,127 (digital/electronic); *Serial titles:* 66 (physical), 68 (digital/electronic); *Databases:* 71. Weekly public service hours: 90.

STUDENT LIFE
Housing options: on-campus residence required for freshman year; coed. Campus housing is university owned and leased by the school. Freshman campus housing is guaranteed.

Activities and organizations: drama/theater group, choral group, Student Government, Student Programming Board, Hispanic Club, University Ministry, Circle K International, national fraternities.

Athletics Member NAIA.

Campus security: 24-hour emergency response devices and patrols, controlled dormitory access.

Student services: health clinic, personal/psychological counseling.

COSTS & FINANCIAL AID
Costs (2019–20) ***Comprehensive fee:*** $40,744 includes full-time tuition ($31,798) and room and board ($8946). Full-time tuition and fees vary according to degree level, program, and reciprocity agreements. Part-time tuition: $992 per credit hour. Part-time tuition and fees vary according to course load, degree level, program, and reciprocity agreements. ***Room and board:*** Room and board charges vary according to board plan and housing facility.

Financial Aid Of all full-time matriculated undergraduates who enrolled in 2019, 514 applied for aid, 484 were judged to have need, 59 had their need fully met. In 2019, 209 non-need-based awards were made. ***Average***

percent of need met: 72. ***Average financial aid package:*** $24,461. ***Average need-based loan:*** $3701. ***Average need-based gift aid:*** $20,657. ***Average non-need-based aid:*** $19,124. ***Average indebtedness upon graduation:*** $33,553.

APPLYING
Standardized Tests *Required for some:* SAT or ACT (for admission), TOEFL for international students.

Options: electronic application, deferred entrance.

Required for some: high school transcript, minimum 2.0 GPA.

CONTACT
Mary-Grace Linse, Associate Director of Undergraduate Admissions, Cardinal Stritch University, 6801 N. Yates Road, Milwaukee, WI 53217. *Phone:* 414-410-4052. *Toll-free phone:* 800-347-8822 Ext. 4040. *Fax:* 414-410-4058. *E-mail:* admissions@stritch.edu.

Carroll University

Waukesha, Wisconsin

http://www.carrollu.edu/

CONTACT
Mr. James Wiseman, Vice President of Enrollment, Carroll University, 100 North East Avenue, Waukesha, WI 53186-5593. *Phone:* 262-524-7221. *Toll-free phone:* 800-CARROLL. *Fax:* 262-524-7139. *E-mail:* info@carrollu.edu.

Carthage College

Kenosha, Wisconsin

http://www.carthage.edu/

- **Independent** comprehensive, founded 1847, affiliated with Evangelical Lutheran Church in America
- **Suburban** 72-acre campus with easy access to Chicago, Milwaukee
- **Coed** 2,654 undergraduate students, 96% full-time, 58% women, 42% men
- **Moderately difficult** entrance level, 68% of applicants were admitted

UNDERGRAD STUDENTS
2,548 full-time, 106 part-time. Students come from 39 states and territories; 19 other countries; 62% are from out of state; 5% Black or African American, non-Hispanic/Latino; 14% Hispanic/Latino; 231% Asian, non-Hispanic/Latino; 0.2% Native Hawaiian or other Pacific Islander, non-Hispanic/Latino; 0.5% American Indian or Alaska Native, non-Hispanic/Latino; 3% Two or more races, non-Hispanic/Latino; 5% Race/ethnicity unknown; 1% international; 3% transferred in; 65% live on campus.

Freshmen:
Admission: 7,018 applied, 4,772 admitted, 687 enrolled. ***Average high school GPA:*** 3.3. ***Test scores:*** SAT evidence-based reading and writing scores over 500: 79%; SAT math scores over 500: 79%; ACT scores over 18: 92%; SAT evidence-based reading and writing scores over 600: 31%; SAT math scores over 600: 32%; ACT scores over 24: 51%; SAT evidence-based reading and writing scores over 700: 4%; SAT math scores over 700: 5%; ACT scores over 30: 12%.

Retention: 76% of full-time freshmen returned.

FACULTY
Total: 313, 55% full-time, 51% with terminal degrees.

Student/faculty ratio: 12:1.

ACADEMICS
Calendar: 4-1-4. *Degrees:* bachelor's and master's.

Special study options: accelerated degree program, adult/continuing education programs, advanced placement credit, distance learning, double majors, honors programs, internships, off-campus study, part-time degree program, services for LD students, student-designed majors, study abroad, summer session for credit. ***ROTC:*** Army (c), Air Force (c).

Unusual degree programs: 3-2 engineering with Case Western Reserve University; occupational therapy with Washington University in St. Louis.

Computers: 130 computers/terminals are available on campus for general student use. Students can access the following: campus intranet, computer help desk, free student e-mail accounts, online (class) grades, online (class) registration, online (class) schedules. Campuswide network is available. 96% of college-owned or -operated housing units are wired for high-speed Internet access. Wireless service is available via entire campus.
Library: Hedberg Library. *Books:* 100,005 (physical), 329,322 (digital/electronic); *Serial titles:* 3,844 (physical), 579,112 (digital/electronic); *Databases:* 378. Students can reserve study rooms.

STUDENT LIFE
Housing options: on-campus residence required through junior year; coed, men-only, women-only. Campus housing is university owned. Freshman campus housing is guaranteed.

Activities and organizations: drama/theater group, student-run newspaper, radio station, choral group, Tau Sigma Chi, Alpha Phi Omega, Intervarsity Christian Fellowship, Alpha Lambda Delta, Beta Beta Beta, national fraternities, national sororities.

Athletics Member NCAA. All Division III. ***Intercollegiate sports:*** baseball M, basketball M/W, bowling M(c)/W(c), cross-country running M/W, football M, golf M/W, ice hockey M(c)/W(c), lacrosse M/W, soccer M/W, softball W, swimming and diving M/W, tennis M/W, track and field M/W, volleyball M/W, water polo M/W. ***Intramural sports:*** basketball M/W, football M/W, racquetball M/W, rock climbing M/W, soccer M/W, softball M/W, volleyball M/W.

Campus security: 24-hour emergency response devices and patrols, student patrols, late-night transport/escort service, controlled dormitory access.

Student services: health clinic, personal/psychological counseling.

COSTS & FINANCIAL AID
Costs (2020–21) ***Comprehensive fee:*** $75,400 includes full-time tuition ($31,500), mandatory fees ($31,500), and room and board ($12,400). ***Room and board:*** Room and board charges vary according to housing facility. ***Payment plan:*** installment. ***Waivers:*** children of alumni, adult students, and employees or children of employees.

Financial Aid ***Average indebtedness upon graduation:*** $54,496.

APPLYING
Standardized Tests *Recommended:* SAT and SAT Subject Tests or ACT (for admission).

Options: electronic application, early action, deferred entrance.

Application fee: $35.

Required: high school transcript. ***Required for some:*** minimum 2.3 GPA, 2 letters of recommendation, statement of good standing from prior institution(s). ***Recommended:*** essay or personal statement, interview.

Application deadlines: rolling (freshmen), rolling (transfers).

Notification: continuous (freshmen), continuous (transfers).

CONTACT
Mr. Nick Mulvey, Vice President for Enrollment, Carthage College, 2001 Alford Park Drive, Kenosha, WI 53140. *Phone:* 262-551-5762. *Toll-free phone:* 800-351-4058. *E-mail:* admissions@carthage.edu.

Columbia College of Nursing

Glendale, Wisconsin

http://www.ccon.edu/

- **Independent** upper-level, founded 1901
- **Urban** 1-acre campus with easy access to Milwaukee
- **Endowment** $700,000
- **Coed, primarily women**
- **Moderately difficult** entrance level

FACULTY
Student/faculty ratio: 9:1.

ACADEMICS
Calendar: semesters. *Degrees:* bachelor's and master's (nursing degree is awarded in conjunction with Mount Mary College).
Library: Columbia St. Mary's Library.

STUDENT LIFE
Housing options: college housing not available.

Activities and organizations: Student Senate, Student Nurses Association.

Campus security: 24-hour emergency response devices and patrols, student patrols, late-night transport/escort service, security card entrances to academic areas.

Student services: health clinic, personal/psychological counseling.

FINANCIAL AID

Financial Aid Of all full-time matriculated undergraduates who enrolled in 2015, 110 applied for aid, 101 were judged to have need, 8 had their need fully met. In 2015, 17 non-need-based awards were made. ***Average percent of need met:*** 40. ***Average financial aid package:*** $11,039. ***Average need-based loan:*** $5646. ***Average need-based gift aid:*** $5917. ***Average non-need-based aid:*** $2882.

APPLYING

Standardized Tests *Required:* SAT or ACT (for admission).

Options: electronic application.

Application fee: $25.

CONTACT

Columbia College of Nursing, 4425 North Port Washington Road, Glendale, WI 53212. *Phone:* 414-326-2336.

Concordia University Wisconsin

Mequon, Wisconsin

http://www.cuw.edu/

- **Independent** comprehensive, founded 1881, affiliated with Lutheran Church–Missouri Synod, part of Concordia University System
- **Suburban** 192-acre campus with easy access to Milwaukee
- **Coed** 3,308 undergraduate students, 70% full-time, 63% women, 37% men
- **Moderately difficult** entrance level, 64% of applicants were admitted

UNDERGRAD STUDENTS

2,317 full-time, 991 part-time. 38% are from out of state; 10% Black or African American, non-Hispanic/Latino; 0.4% Hispanic/Latino; 2% Asian, non-Hispanic/Latino; 0.1% Native Hawaiian or other Pacific Islander, non-Hispanic/Latino; 0.8% American Indian or Alaska Native, non-Hispanic/Latino; 3% Two or more races, non-Hispanic/Latino; 5% Race/ethnicity unknown; 6% international; 2% transferred in; 43% live on campus.

Freshmen:

Admission: 3,772 applied, 2,419 admitted, 578 enrolled. ***Average high school GPA:*** 3.5. ***Test scores:*** ACT scores over 18: 95%; ACT scores over 24: 47%; ACT scores over 30: 9%.

Retention: 81% of full-time freshmen returned.

FACULTY

Total: 414, 50% full-time, 49% with terminal degrees.

Student/faculty ratio: 12:1.

ACADEMICS

Calendar: 4-1-4. *Degrees:* certificates, associate, bachelor's, master's, doctoral, and post-master's certificates.

Special study options: academic remediation for entering students, accelerated degree program, adult/continuing education programs, advanced placement credit, distance learning, double majors, English as a second language, independent study, internships, off-campus study, part-time degree program, services for LD students, student-designed majors, study abroad, summer session for credit.

Computers: Students can access the following: computer help desk, free student e-mail accounts. Campuswide network is available.
Library: Rinker Memorial Library.

STUDENT LIFE

Housing options: men-only, women-only. Campus housing is university owned. Freshman applicants given priority for college housing.

Activities and organizations: drama/theater group, student-run newspaper, radio station, choral group.

Athletics Member NCAA. All Division III. ***Intercollegiate sports:*** baseball M, basketball M/W, cross-country running M/W, football M, golf M/W, ice hockey M/W, soccer M/W, softball W, tennis M/W, track and field M/W, volleyball W, wrestling M. ***Intramural sports:*** basketball M/W, softball M/W, volleyball M/W.

Campus security: 24-hour patrols, student patrols, late-night transport/escort service, controlled dormitory access.

Student services: health clinic, personal/psychological counseling.

COSTS & FINANCIAL AID

Costs (2020–21) ***Comprehensive fee:*** $42,652 includes full-time tuition ($30,890), mandatory fees ($292), and room and board ($11,470). Full-time tuition and fees vary according to program. Part-time tuition: $1287 per credit hour. Part-time tuition and fees vary according to program. ***College room only:*** $8600. Room and board charges vary according to board plan.

Financial Aid Of all full-time matriculated undergraduates who enrolled in 2019, 2,125 applied for aid, 1,791 were judged to have need, 533 had their need fully met. In 2019, 426 non-need-based awards were made. ***Average percent of need met:*** 75. ***Average financial aid package:*** $25,017. ***Average need-based loan:*** $7893. ***Average need-based gift aid:*** $16,758. ***Average non-need-based aid:*** $15,333. ***Average indebtedness upon graduation:*** $36,651.

APPLYING

Standardized Tests *Required:* SAT or ACT (for admission).

Required: high school transcript, minimum 2.0 GPA. ***Required for some:*** essay or personal statement, minimum 3.0 GPA, 3 letters of recommendation. ***Recommended:*** interview.

Notification: continuous (freshmen).

CONTACT

Ms. Julie Schroeder, Concordia University Wisconsin, Admissions Office, 12800 North Lake Drive, Mequon, WI 53097. *Phone:* 262-243-4305 Ext. 4305. *Toll-free phone:* 888-628-9472. *E-mail:* admission@cuw.edu.

Edgewood College

Madison, Wisconsin

http://www.edgewood.edu/

- **Independent Roman Catholic** comprehensive, founded 1927
- **Urban** 55-acre campus
- **Endowment** $41.9 million
- **Coed** 1,407 undergraduate students, 85% full-time, 73% women, 27% men
- **Moderately difficult** entrance level, 72% of applicants were admitted

UNDERGRAD STUDENTS

1,191 full-time, 216 part-time. Students come from 20 states and territories; 16 other countries; 9% are from out of state; 4% Black or African American, non-Hispanic/Latino; 9% Hispanic/Latino; 2% Asian, non-Hispanic/Latino; 0.2% Native Hawaiian or other Pacific Islander, non-Hispanic/Latino; 0.4% American Indian or Alaska Native, non-Hispanic/Latino; 4% Two or more races, non-Hispanic/Latino; 2% Race/ethnicity unknown; 3% international; 7% transferred in; 37% live on campus.

Freshmen:

Admission: 1,397 applied, 1,011 admitted, 239 enrolled. ***Average high school GPA:*** 3.5. ***Test scores:*** SAT evidence-based reading and writing scores over 500: 70%; SAT math scores over 500: 70%; ACT scores over 18: 92%; SAT evidence-based reading and writing scores over 600: 40%; SAT math scores over 600: 30%; ACT scores over 24: 45%; ACT scores over 30: 4%.

Retention: 79% of full-time freshmen returned.

FACULTY

Total: 256, 56% full-time, 55% with terminal degrees.

Student/faculty ratio: 10:1.

ACADEMICS

Calendar: semesters. *Degrees:* certificates, bachelor's, master's, doctoral, and postbachelor's certificates.

Special study options: academic remediation for entering students, accelerated degree program, adult/continuing education programs, advanced placement credit, cooperative education, distance learning, double majors, honors programs, independent study, internships, off-campus study, part-time degree program, services for LD students, student-designed majors, study abroad, summer session for credit. ***ROTC:*** Army (c), Navy (c), Air Force (c).

Computers: 180 computers/terminals and 200 ports are available on campus for general student use. Students can access the following: campus intranet, computer help desk, free student e-mail accounts, online (class) grades, online (class) registration, online (class) schedules. Campuswide network is available. 100% of college-owned or -operated housing units are wired for high-speed Internet access. Wireless service is available via entire campus.
Library: Oscar Rennebohm Library. *Books:* 73,015 (physical), 200,204 (digital/electronic); *Serial titles:* 65 (physical), 38,100 (digital/electronic); *Databases:* 87. Weekly public service hours: 98; students can reserve study rooms.

STUDENT LIFE
Housing options: on-campus residence required through sophomore year; coed, cooperative, special housing for students with disabilities. Campus housing is university owned. Freshman campus housing is guaranteed.

Activities and organizations: drama/theater group, student-run newspaper, Child Life Association, Black Student Union, Edgewood Empowered, Esports, Asian Student Association.

Athletics Member NCAA. All Division III. ***Intercollegiate sports:*** baseball M, basketball M/W, cross-country running M/W, golf M/W, soccer M/W, softball W, tennis M/W, track and field M/W, volleyball W. ***Intramural sports:*** basketball M/W, soccer M/W, swimming and diving M/W, volleyball M/W.

Campus security: 24-hour emergency response devices and patrols, student patrols, late-night transport/escort service, controlled dormitory access, lighted pathways/sidewalks, Eagle Alert System, Public Address System, Safe Ride Shuttle, extensive video surveillance system.

Student services: health clinic, personal/psychological counseling, veterans affairs office.

COSTS & FINANCIAL AID
Costs (2020–21) *Comprehensive fee:* $43,400 includes full-time tuition ($31,700) and room and board ($11,700). Full-time tuition and fees vary according to degree level. Part-time tuition: $994 per credit. Part-time tuition and fees vary according to course load and degree level. ***Room and board:*** Room and board charges vary according to housing facility. ***Payment plan:*** installment. ***Waivers:*** employees or children of employees.

Financial Aid Of all full-time matriculated undergraduates who enrolled in 2018, 1,056 applied for aid, 927 were judged to have need, 128 had their need fully met. 504 Federal Work-Study jobs (averaging $1971). 416 state and other part-time jobs (averaging $1976). In 2018, 235 non-need-based awards were made. ***Average percent of need met:*** 75. ***Average financial aid package:*** $22,736. ***Average need-based loan:*** $5424. ***Average need-based gift aid:*** $16,946. ***Average non-need-based aid:*** $7856. ***Average indebtedness upon graduation:*** $37,332.

APPLYING
Standardized Tests *Required:* SAT or ACT (for admission).

Options: electronic application, deferred entrance.

Application fee: $30.

Required: high school transcript, minimum 2.5 GPA, applicants must meet 2 out of 3 requirements: high school GPA of 2.5 on a 4.0 scale, rank in top 50% of high school graduating class, composite score of 18 on the ACT or an equivalent SAT score. ***Required for some:*** essay or personal statement, 2 letters of recommendation, interview.

Application deadlines: 8/1 (freshmen), 8/1 (out-of-state freshmen), 8/1 (transfers).

Notification: continuous until 8/1 (freshmen), continuous until 8/1 (out-of-state freshmen), continuous until 8/1 (transfers).

CONTACT
Dr. Amber Schultz, Vice President for Enrollment Management, Edgewood College, 1000 Edgewood College Drive, Madison, WI 53711-1997. *Phone:* 608-663-2294. *Toll-free phone:* 800-444-4861 Ext. 2294. *Fax:* 608-663-2214. *E-mail:* admissions@edgewood.edu.

Herzing University
Brookfield, Wisconsin
http://www.herzing.edu/brookfield

CONTACT
Herzing University, 555 South Executive Drive, Brookfield, WI 53005. *Toll-free phone:* 800-596-0724.

Herzing University
Kenosha, Wisconsin
http://www.herzing.edu/kenosha

CONTACT
Herzing University, 4006 Washington Road, Kenosha, WI 53144. *Toll-free phone:* 800-596-0724.

Herzing University
Madison, Wisconsin
http://www.herzing.edu/madison/

CONTACT
Herzing University, 5218 East Terrace Drive, Madison, WI 53718. *Toll-free phone:* 800-596-0724.

Herzing University Online
Menomonee Falls, Wisconsin
http://www.herzingonline.edu/

CONTACT
Herzing University Online, W140N8917 Lilly Road, Menomonee Falls, WI 53051. *Toll-free phone:* 866-508-0748.

Lakeland University
Plymouth, Wisconsin
http://www.lakeland.edu/

- **Independent** comprehensive, founded 1862, affiliated with United Church of Christ
- **Rural** 240-acre campus with easy access to Milwaukee
- **Endowment** $12.1 million
- **Coed**
- **Minimally difficult** entrance level

FACULTY
Student/faculty ratio: 13:1.

ACADEMICS
Calendar: 4-4-1. *Degrees:* bachelor's and master's.
Library: Esch Memorial Library.

STUDENT LIFE
Housing options: on-campus residence required through senior year; coed, men-only, women-only. Campus housing is university owned. Freshman campus housing is guaranteed.

Activities and organizations: drama/theater group, student-run newspaper, choral group, Lakeland College Campus Activities Board, Student Association, Black Student Union, Mortar Board, Global Students Association.

Athletics Member NCAA. All Division III.

Campus security: 24-hour emergency response devices, student patrols, late-night transport/escort service, controlled dormitory access.

Student services: health clinic, personal/psychological counseling.

FINANCIAL AID
Financial Aid Of all full-time matriculated undergraduates who enrolled in 2012, 1,411 applied for aid, 1,264 were judged to have need, 116 had their need fully met. 425 Federal Work-Study jobs (averaging $2500). 100 state and other part-time jobs (averaging $2500). In 2012, 139 non-need-based awards were made. ***Average percent of need met:*** 63. ***Average financial aid package:*** $13,003. ***Average need-based loan:*** $4150. ***Average need-based gift aid:*** $9895. ***Average non-need-based aid:*** $7433. ***Average indebtedness upon graduation:*** $30,105. ***Financial aid deadline:*** 7/1.

APPLYING

Standardized Tests *Required:* SAT or ACT (for admission).

Options: electronic application, deferred entrance.

Application fee: $100.

Required: essay or personal statement, high school transcript, minimum 2.0 GPA. ***Required for some:*** interview.

CONTACT

Mr. Nick Spaeth, Director of Admissions, Lakeland University, PO Box 359, Nash Visitors Center, Sheboygan, WI 53082-0359. *Phone:* 920-565-1007. *Toll-free phone:* 800-569-2166. *Fax:* 920-565-1215. *E-mail:* admissions@lakeland.edu.

Lawrence University

Appleton, Wisconsin

http://www.lawrence.edu/

- **Independent** 4-year, founded 1847
- **Small-town** 88-acre campus
- **Endowment** $339.8 million
- **Coed** 2,850 undergraduate students, 98% full-time, 54% women, 46% men
- **Very difficult** entrance level, 62% of applicants were admitted

UNDERGRAD STUDENTS

2,794 full-time, 56 part-time. 75% are from out of state; 6% Black or African American, non-Hispanic/Latino; 10% Hispanic/Latino; 6% Asian, non-Hispanic/Latino; 0.1% Native Hawaiian or other Pacific Islander, non-Hispanic/Latino; 0.4% American Indian or Alaska Native, non-Hispanic/Latino; 4% Two or more races, non-Hispanic/Latino; 0.4% Race/ethnicity unknown; 12% international; 0.7% transferred in; 95% live on campus.

Freshmen:

Admission: 3,463 applied, 2,150 admitted, 386 enrolled. ***Average high school GPA:*** 3.5. ***Test scores:*** SAT evidence-based reading and writing scores over 500: 98%; SAT math scores over 500: 98%; ACT scores over 18: 100%; SAT evidence-based reading and writing scores over 600: 77%; SAT math scores over 600: 78%; ACT scores over 24: 85%; SAT evidence-based reading and writing scores over 700: 30%; SAT math scores over 700: 37%; ACT scores over 30: 40%.

Retention: 87% of full-time freshmen returned.

FACULTY

Total: 197, 89% full-time, 89% with terminal degrees.

Student/faculty ratio: 8:1.

ACADEMICS

Calendar: trimesters. *Degree:* bachelor's.

Special study options: advanced placement credit, double majors, independent study, internships, off-campus study, part-time degree program, services for LD students, student-designed majors, study abroad.

Unusual degree programs: 3-2 engineering with Columbia University, Rensselaer Polytechnic Institute, Washington University in St. Louis; forestry with Duke University; occupational therapy with Washington University in St. Louis, law with Marquette University.

Computers: 250 computers/terminals and 400 ports are available on campus for general student use. Students can access the following: campus intranet, computer help desk, free student e-mail accounts, online (class) grades, online (class) registration, online (class) schedules, online transcripts, financial aid, financial account information. Campuswide network is available. 100% of college-owned or -operated housing units are wired for high-speed Internet access. Wireless service is available via entire campus.

Library: Seeley G. Mudd Library. *Books:* 553,969 (physical), 220,704 (digital/electronic); *Serial titles:* 544 (physical), 68,015 (digital/electronic); *Databases:* 160. Weekly public service hours: 110; students can reserve study rooms.

STUDENT LIFE

Housing options: on-campus residence required through senior year; coed, women-only, cooperative, special housing for students with disabilities. Campus housing is university owned. Freshman campus housing is guaranteed.

Activities and organizations: drama/theater group, student-run newspaper, radio station, choral group, Gaming, Dance, Lawrence International, Outdoor Recreation Club, Sustainable Lawrence University Gardens (SLUG), national fraternities, national sororities.

Athletics Member NCAA. All Division III. ***Intercollegiate sports:*** baseball M, basketball M/W, crew M(c)/W(c), cross-country running M/W, fencing M/W, football M, ice hockey M/W(c), soccer M/W, softball W, swimming and diving M/W, tennis M/W, track and field M/W, ultimate Frisbee M(c)/W(c), volleyball W. ***Intramural sports:*** badminton M/W, basketball M/W, golf M(c)/W(c), rock climbing M(c)/W(c), sailing M(c)/W(c), skiing (downhill) M/W, soccer M/W, table tennis M/W, triathlon M(c)/W(c), volleyball M/W, water polo M/W.

Campus security: 24-hour emergency response devices and patrols, student patrols, late-night transport/escort service, controlled dormitory access, evening patrols by trained security personnel.

Student services: health clinic, personal/psychological counseling.

COSTS & FINANCIAL AID

Costs (2019–20) ***Comprehensive fee:*** $59,841 includes full-time tuition ($48,822), mandatory fees ($300), and room and board ($10,719). ***College room only:*** $5448. ***Waivers:*** employees or children of employees.

Financial Aid Of all full-time matriculated undergraduates who enrolled in 2019, 1,032 applied for aid, 867 were judged to have need, 434 had their need fully met. In 2019, 501 non-need-based awards were made. ***Average percent of need met:*** 94. ***Average financial aid package:*** $43,652. ***Average need-based loan:*** $4135. ***Average need-based gift aid:*** $37,000. ***Average non-need-based aid:*** $25,449. ***Average indebtedness upon graduation:*** $28,828.

APPLYING

Standardized Tests *Required for some:* English Language Proficiency Exam (SAT/TOEFL/IELTS/ACT).

Options: electronic application, early admission, early decision, early action, deferred entrance.

Required: essay or personal statement, high school transcript, 1 letter of recommendation. ***Required for some:*** audition for music majors. ***Recommended:*** minimum 3.0 GPA, interview.

Application deadlines: 1/15 (freshmen), 7/1 (transfers), 12/1 (early action).

Early decision deadline: 11/1.

Notification: continuous until 4/1 (freshmen), continuous until 7/15 (transfers), 12/1 (early decision), 1/25 (early action).

CONTACT

Ms. Mary Beth Petrie, Admissions Director, Lawrence University, 711 East Boldt Way, Admissions Office, Appleton, WI 54911. *Phone:* 920-832-6502. *Toll-free phone:* 800-227-0982. *Fax:* 920-832-6782. *E-mail:* marybeth.petrie@lawrence.edu.

Maranatha Baptist University

Watertown, Wisconsin

http://www.mbu.edu/

CONTACT

Jonathan Sheeley, Director of Admissions, Maranatha Baptist University, 745 West Main Street, Watertown, WI 53094. *Phone:* 920-206-2327. *Toll-free phone:* 800-622-2947. *Fax:* 920-261-9109. *E-mail:* admissions@mbu.edu.

Marian University

Fond du Lac, Wisconsin

http://www.marianuniversity.edu/

CONTACT

Shannon LaLuzerne, Dean of Admission, Marian University, 45 S. National Avenue, Fond du Lac, WI 54935-4699. *Phone:* 920-923-7650. *Toll-free phone:* 800-2-MARIAN. *E-mail:* admission@marianuniversity.edu.

Marquette University
Milwaukee, Wisconsin
http://www.marquette.edu/

- **Independent Roman Catholic (Jesuit)** university, founded 1881
- **Urban** 107-acre campus with easy access to Milwaukee
- **Coed** 8,515 undergraduate students, 96% full-time, 54% women, 46% men
- **Moderately difficult** entrance level, 83% of applicants were admitted

UNDERGRAD STUDENTS
8,175 full-time, 340 part-time. 70% are from out of state; 4% Black or African American, non-Hispanic/Latino; 14% Hispanic/Latino; 7% Asian, non-Hispanic/Latino; 0.1% Native Hawaiian or other Pacific Islander, non-Hispanic/Latino; 0.2% American Indian or Alaska Native, non-Hispanic/Latino; 3% Two or more races, non-Hispanic/Latino; 0.9% Race/ethnicity unknown; 2% international; 2% transferred in; 46% live on campus.

Freshmen:
Admission: 15,078 applied, 12,509 admitted, 1,977 enrolled. ***Test scores:*** SAT evidence-based reading and writing scores over 500: 96%; SAT math scores over 500: 97%; ACT scores over 18: 100%; SAT evidence-based reading and writing scores over 600: 61%; SAT math scores over 600: 57%; ACT scores over 24: 79%; SAT evidence-based reading and writing scores over 700: 9%; SAT math scores over 700: 16%; ACT scores over 30: 24%.

Retention: 90% of full-time freshmen returned.

FACULTY
Total: 1,244, 56% full-time, 73% with terminal degrees.

Student/faculty ratio: 14:1.

ACADEMICS
Calendar: semesters. *Degrees:* bachelor's, master's, doctoral, post-master's, and postbachelor's certificates.

Special study options: accelerated degree program, adult/continuing education programs, advanced placement credit, cooperative education, distance learning, double majors, English as a second language, honors programs, independent study, internships, off-campus study, part-time degree program, services for LD students, student-designed majors, study abroad, summer session for credit. ***ROTC:*** Army (b), Navy (b), Air Force (b).

Unusual degree programs: 3-2 business administration; engineering; nursing; exercise science/clinical and translational rehabilitation health sciences, speech and language pathology, international affairs, physical therapy.

Computers: Students can access the following: campus intranet, computer help desk, free student e-mail accounts, online (class) grades, online (class) registration, online (class) schedules, AV Software, MATLAB, Printwise. Campuswide network is available. 100% of college-owned or -operated housing units are wired for high-speed Internet access. Wireless service is available via classrooms, computer centers, computer labs, dorm rooms, learning centers, libraries, student centers.

Library: Raynor Memorial Libraries plus 1 other. Study areas open 24 hours, 5–7 days a week; students can reserve study rooms.

STUDENT LIFE
Housing options: on-campus residence required through sophomore year; coed, men-only, women-only, cooperative, special housing for students with disabilities. Campus housing is university owned. Freshman campus housing is guaranteed.

Activities and organizations: drama/theater group, student-run newspaper, radio and television station, choral group, Student Government, club sports, community service organizations, band/jazz/orchestra, Residence Hall Association, national fraternities, national sororities.

Athletics Member NCAA. All Division I. ***Intercollegiate sports:*** basketball M(s)/W(s), cheerleading M/W, cross-country running M(s)/W(s), golf M(s), lacrosse M(s)/W(s), soccer M(s)/W(s), tennis M(s)/W(s), track and field M(s)/W(s), volleyball W(s). ***Intramural sports:*** badminton M/W, baseball M(c), basketball M(c)/W(c), crew M(c)/W(c), cross-country running M(c)/W(c), equestrian sports M(c)/W(c), fencing M(c), field hockey W(c), football M/W, golf M(c)/W(c), ice hockey M(c), lacrosse M(c)/W(c), rowing M(c)/W(c), rugby M(c)/W(c), sailing M(c)/W(c), sand volleyball M/W, skiing (downhill) M(c)/W(c), soccer M(c)/W(c), softball M/W(c), swimming and diving M(c)/W(c), table tennis M(c)/W(c), tennis M(c)/W(c), ultimate Frisbee M(c)/W(c), volleyball M(c)/W(c), water polo M(c)/W(c), weight lifting M/W.

Campus security: 24-hour emergency response devices and patrols, student patrols, late-night transport/escort service.

Student services: health clinic, personal/psychological counseling.

COSTS & FINANCIAL AID
Costs (2020–21) ***Comprehensive fee:*** $59,322 includes full-time tuition ($44,970), mandatory fees ($696), and room and board ($13,656). Full-time tuition and fees vary according to course load and program. Part-time tuition: $1115 per credit hour. Part-time tuition and fees vary according to program. ***College room only:*** $8956. Room and board charges vary according to housing facility. ***Payment plan:*** installment. ***Waivers:*** senior citizens and employees or children of employees.

Financial Aid Of all full-time matriculated undergraduates who enrolled in 2019, 5,884 applied for aid, 4,822 were judged to have need, 1,192 had their need fully met. In 2019, 3100 non-need-based awards were made. ***Average percent of need met:*** 78. ***Average financial aid package:*** $32,164. ***Average need-based loan:*** $5924. ***Average need-based gift aid:*** $25,967. ***Average non-need-based aid:*** $14,936. ***Average indebtedness upon graduation:*** $38,173.

APPLYING
Options: electronic application, deferred entrance.

Required: essay or personal statement, high school transcript, minimum 2.5 GPA. ***Recommended:*** minimum 3.4 GPA.

Notification: 12/23 (freshmen), continuous (transfers).

CONTACT
Mr. Brian Troyer, Dean of Undergraduate Admissions, Marquette University, PO Box 1881, Milwaukee, WI 53201-1881. *Phone:* 414-288-7004. *Toll-free phone:* 800-222-6544. *Fax:* 414-288-3764. *E-mail:* admissions@marquette.edu.

Milwaukee Institute of Art and Design
Milwaukee, Wisconsin
http://www.miad.edu/

CONTACT
David Sigman, Director of Admissions, Milwaukee Institute of Art and Design, 273 East Erie Street, Milwaukee, WI 53202. *Phone:* 414-847-3200. *Toll-free phone:* 888-749-MIAD. *Fax:* 414-291-8077. *E-mail:* admissions@miad.edu.

Milwaukee School of Engineering
Milwaukee, Wisconsin
http://www.msoe.edu/

- **Independent** comprehensive, founded 1903
- **Urban** 22-acre campus
- **Endowment** $65.0 million
- **Coed, primarily men** 2,566 undergraduate students, 97% full-time, 26% women, 74% men
- **Moderately difficult** entrance level, 62% of applicants were admitted

UNDERGRAD STUDENTS
2,478 full-time, 88 part-time. 35% are from out of state; 2% Black or African American, non-Hispanic/Latino; 8% Hispanic/Latino; 5% Asian, non-Hispanic/Latino; 0.2% American Indian or Alaska Native, non-Hispanic/Latino; 3% Two or more races, non-Hispanic/Latino; 7% Race/ethnicity unknown; 6% international; 4% transferred in; 43% live on campus.

Freshmen:
Admission: 3,552 applied, 2,192 admitted, 582 enrolled. ***Average high school GPA:*** 3.7. ***Test scores:*** SAT math scores over 500: 99%; ACT scores over 18: 100%; SAT math scores over 600: 77%; ACT scores over 24: 86%; SAT math scores over 700: 29%; ACT scores over 30: 30%.

Retention: 85% of full-time freshmen returned.

FACULTY
Total: 270, 58% full-time, 65% with terminal degrees.

Student/faculty ratio: 13:1.

ACADEMICS

Calendar: quarters. *Degrees:* certificates, bachelor's, master's, and postbachelor's certificates.

Special study options: academic remediation for entering students, accelerated degree program, adult/continuing education programs, advanced placement credit, double majors, honors programs, independent study, internships, part-time degree program, services for LD students, study abroad, summer session for credit. ***ROTC:*** Army (c), Navy (c), Air Force (c).

Computers: 50 computers/terminals are available on campus for general student use. Students can access the following: campus intranet, computer help desk, free student e-mail accounts, online (class) grades, online (class) registration, online (class) schedules. Campuswide network is available. 100% of college-owned or -operated housing units are wired for high-speed Internet access. Wireless service is available via entire campus.

Library: Walter Schroeder. *Books:* 51,408 (physical), 370,802 (digital/electronic); *Serial titles:* 345 (physical), 114,238 (digital/electronic); *Databases:* 124. Weekly public service hours: 96; students can reserve study rooms.

STUDENT LIFE

Housing options: on-campus residence required through sophomore year; coed, special housing for students with disabilities. Campus housing is university owned. Freshman campus housing is guaranteed.

Activities and organizations: drama/theater group, student-run radio station, choral group, Student Union Board, Greek Council, Student Government Association, Residence Hall Association, Intervarsity Christian Fellowship, national fraternities, national sororities.

Athletics Member NCAA. All Division III. ***Intercollegiate sports:*** baseball M, basketball M/W, cheerleading M/W, crew M/W, cross-country running M/W, golf M, ice hockey M, lacrosse M, soccer M/W, softball W, tennis M/W, track and field M/W, volleyball M/W, wrestling M. ***Intramural sports:*** badminton M(c)/W(c), basketball M/W, bowling M(c)/W(c), fencing M(c)/W(c), football M/W, rugby M(c), soccer M/W, softball M/W, ultimate Frisbee M(c)/W(c), volleyball M/W, weight lifting M(c)/W(c).

Campus security: 24-hour emergency response devices and patrols, late-night transport/escort service, controlled dormitory access.

Student services: health clinic, personal/psychological counseling, women's center.

COSTS & FINANCIAL AID

Costs (2020–21) ***Tuition:*** $41,820 full-time, $727 per credit hour part-time. Full-time tuition and fees vary according to course load. Part-time tuition and fees vary according to course load. ***Required fees:*** $1755 full-time. ***Room only:*** $6339. Room and board charges vary according to board plan and housing facility. ***Payment plan:*** installment. ***Waivers:*** employees or children of employees.

Financial Aid Of all full-time matriculated undergraduates who enrolled in 2018, 2,188 applied for aid, 1,974 were judged to have need, 362 had their need fully met. In 2018, 427 non-need-based awards were made. ***Average percent of need met:*** 76. ***Average financial aid package:*** $30,355. ***Average need-based loan:*** $4130. ***Average need-based gift aid:*** $27,042. ***Average non-need-based aid:*** $15,202. ***Average indebtedness upon graduation:*** $36,150.

APPLYING

Standardized Tests *Required:* SAT or ACT (for admission).

Options: electronic application, deferred entrance.

Required: high school transcript, minimum 3.0 GPA. ***Required for some:*** essay or personal statement, interview.

Application deadlines: 1/1 (freshmen), rolling (out-of-state freshmen), 1/1 (transfers).

Notification: continuous until 10/1 (freshmen), continuous (out-of-state freshmen), continuous until 10/1 (transfers).

CONTACT

Seandra Mitchell, Director, Undergraduate Admission, Milwaukee School of Engineering, 1025 N. Broadway, Milwaukee, WI 53202. *Phone:* 414-277-6762. *Toll-free phone:* 800-332-6763. *E-mail:* mitchell@msoe.edu.

Mount Mary University

Milwaukee, Wisconsin

http://www.mtmary.edu/

- **Independent Roman Catholic** comprehensive, founded 1913
- **Urban** 80-acre campus with easy access to Milwaukee
- **Endowment** $17.0 million
- **Undergraduate: women only; graduate: coed**
- **Moderately difficult** entrance level

FACULTY

Student/faculty ratio: 12:1.

ACADEMICS

Calendar: semesters. *Degrees:* bachelor's, master's, doctoral, post-master's, and postbachelor's certificates.

Library: The Patrick and Beatrice Haggerty Library. *Books:* 77,098 (physical), 142,434 (digital/electronic); *Serial titles:* 5,268 (physical), 155,028 (digital/electronic); *Databases:* 92. Students can reserve study rooms.

STUDENT LIFE

Housing options: on-campus residence required for freshman year; women-only. Campus housing is university owned. Freshman applicants given priority for college housing.

Activities and organizations: student-run newspaper, choral group, Programming and Activities Council, Student Government Association, International Club, Caroline Hall Council, Department Affiliated Clubs.

Athletics Member NCAA. All Division III.

Campus security: 24-hour emergency response devices and patrols, late-night transport/escort service, controlled dormitory access.

Student services: personal/psychological counseling.

FINANCIAL AID

Financial Aid Of all full-time matriculated undergraduates who enrolled in 2018, 619 applied for aid, 594 were judged to have need, 53 had their need fully met. 100 Federal Work-Study jobs (averaging $1620). 76 state and other part-time jobs (averaging $1580). In 2018, 42 non-need-based awards were made. ***Average percent of need met:*** 70. ***Average financial aid package:*** $25,352. ***Average need-based loan:*** $4433. ***Average need-based gift aid:*** $20,616. ***Average non-need-based aid:*** $13,289. ***Average indebtedness upon graduation:*** $27,854.

APPLYING

Standardized Tests *Required:* SAT or ACT (for admission).

Options: electronic application, deferred entrance.

Required: high school transcript. ***Required for some:*** essay or personal statement, 1 letter of recommendation. ***Recommended:*** minimum 2.5 GPA.

CONTACT

Liz Saffold, Admission Counselor Assistant/Receptionist, Mount Mary University, 2900 North Menomonee River Parkway, Milwaukee, WI 53222. *Phone:* 414-930-3000 Ext. 219. *Toll-free phone:* 800-321-6265. *Fax:* 414-256-0180. *E-mail:* mmu-admiss@mtmary.edu.

Northland College

Ashland, Wisconsin

http://www.northland.edu/

CONTACT

Teege Mettille, Executive Director of Admissions, Northland College, 1411 Ellis Avenue, Ashland, WI 54806. *Phone:* 715-682-1224. *Toll-free phone:* 800-753-1840 (in-state); 800-753-1040 (out-of-state). *Fax:* 715-682-1258. *E-mail:* admit@northland.edu.

Purdue University Global

Milwaukee, Wisconsin

http://www.purdueglobal.edu/

CONTACT

Purdue University Global, 201 West Wisconsin Avenue, Milwaukee, WI 53203.

Rasmussen College Green Bay

Green Bay, Wisconsin

http://www.rasmussen.edu/

- **Proprietary** 4-year, part of Rasmussen College System
- **Suburban** campus
- **Coed** 397 undergraduate students, 55% full-time, 91% women, 9% men
- 100% of applicants were admitted

UNDERGRAD STUDENTS
217 full-time, 180 part-time. Students come from 51 states and territories; 27% are from out of state; 7% Black or African American, non-Hispanic/Latino; 5% Hispanic/Latino; 2% Asian, non-Hispanic/Latino; 2% American Indian or Alaska Native, non-Hispanic/Latino; 4% Two or more races, non-Hispanic/Latino; 12% Race/ethnicity unknown.

Freshmen:
Admission: 114 applied, 114 admitted, 55 enrolled.

ACADEMICS
Calendar: quarters. *Degrees:* certificates, diplomas, associate, and bachelor's.

Special study options: academic remediation for entering students, accelerated degree program, adult/continuing education programs, distance learning, double majors, internships, part-time degree program, summer session for credit.

Computers: 137 computers/terminals are available on campus for general student use. Students can access the following: computer help desk, free student e-mail accounts, online (class) grades, online (class) schedules. Campuswide network is available. Wireless service is available via entire campus.
Library: Rasmussen College Library - Green Bay.

STUDENT LIFE
Housing options: college housing not available.

APPLYING
Options: early admission, deferred entrance.

Required: high school transcript, minimum 2.0 GPA. ***Required for some:*** interview.

Application deadlines: rolling (freshmen), rolling (transfers).

CONTACT
Ms. Susan Hammerstrom, Director of Admissions, Rasmussen College Green Bay, 904 South Taylor Street, Suite 100, Green Bay, WI 54303. *Phone:* 920-593-8400. *Toll-free phone:* 888-549-6755. *E-mail:* susan.hammerstrom@rasmussen.edu.

Rasmussen College Wausau

Wausau, Wisconsin

http://www.rasmussen.edu/

- **Proprietary** 4-year, part of Rasmussen College System
- **Suburban** campus
- **Coed** 271 undergraduate students, 58% full-time, 89% women, 11% men
- 100% of applicants were admitted

UNDERGRAD STUDENTS
156 full-time, 115 part-time. Students come from 51 states and territories; 27% are from out of state; 1% Black or African American, non-Hispanic/Latino; 2% Hispanic/Latino; 5% Asian, non-Hispanic/Latino; 1% American Indian or Alaska Native, non-Hispanic/Latino; 1% Two or more races, non-Hispanic/Latino; 18% Race/ethnicity unknown.

Freshmen:
Admission: 49 applied, 49 admitted, 39 enrolled.

ACADEMICS
Calendar: quarters. *Degrees:* certificates, diplomas, associate, and bachelor's.

Computers: 74 computers/terminals are available on campus for general student use. Students can access the following: computer help desk, free student e-mail accounts, online (class) grades, online (class) schedules. Campuswide network is available. Wireless service is available via entire campus.
Library: Rasmussen College Library - Wausau.

STUDENT LIFE
Housing options: college housing not available.

COSTS
Costs (2019–20) ***Tuition:*** $12,785 full-time, $11,486 per year part-time. Full-time tuition and fees vary according to course level, course load, degree level, location, and program. Part-time tuition and fees vary according to course level, course load, degree level, location, and program. No tuition increase for student's term of enrollment. ***Required fees:*** $2900 full-time, $2385 per year part-time. ***Payment plans:*** installment, deferred payment. ***Waivers:*** employees or children of employees.

APPLYING
Options: early admission, deferred entrance.

Required: high school transcript, minimum 2.0 GPA. ***Required for some:*** interview.

Application deadlines: rolling (freshmen), rolling (transfers).

CONTACT
Ms. Susan Hammerstrom, Director of Admissions, Rasmussen College Wausau, 1101 Westwood Drive, Wausau, WI 54401. *Phone:* 715 841 8000. *Toll-free phone:* 888-549-6755. *E-mail:* susan.hammerstrom@rasmussen.edu.

Ripon College

Ripon, Wisconsin

http://www.ripon.edu/

CONTACT
Office of Admission, Ripon College, 300 Seward Street, PO Box 248, Ripon, WI 54971. *Phone:* 920-748-8337. *Toll-free phone:* 800-947-4766. *Fax:* 920-748-8335. *E-mail:* adminfo@ripon.edu.

St. Norbert College

De Pere, Wisconsin

http://www.snc.edu/

- **Independent Roman Catholic** comprehensive, founded 1898
- **Suburban** 113-acre campus
- **Endowment** $145.8 million
- **Coed** 2,000 undergraduate students, 98% full-time, 58% women, 42% men
- **Moderately difficult** entrance level, 80% of applicants were admitted

UNDERGRAD STUDENTS
1,962 full-time, 38 part-time. 22% are from out of state; 2% Black or African American, non-Hispanic/Latino; 5% Hispanic/Latino; 1% Asian, non-Hispanic/Latino; 0.1% Native Hawaiian or other Pacific Islander, non-Hispanic/Latino; 1% American Indian or Alaska Native, non-Hispanic/Latino; 1% Two or more races, non-Hispanic/Latino; 0.8% Race/ethnicity unknown; 1% international; 1% transferred in; 86% live on campus.

Freshmen:
Admission: 3,355 applied, 2,677 admitted, 538 enrolled. ***Average high school GPA:*** 3.5. ***Test scores:*** SAT evidence-based reading and writing scores over 500: 80%; SAT math scores over 500: 76%; ACT scores over 18: 96%; SAT evidence-based reading and writing scores over 600: 48%; SAT math scores over 600: 44%; ACT scores over 24: 58%; SAT evidence-based reading and writing scores over 700: 13%; SAT math scores over 700: 11%; ACT scores over 30: 13%.
Retention: 82% of full-time freshmen returned.

FACULTY
Total: 200, 69% full-time, 77% with terminal degrees.
Student/faculty ratio: 13:1.

ACADEMICS
Calendar: semesters. *Degrees:* certificates, bachelor's, master's, and postbachelor's certificates.

Special study options: academic remediation for entering students, advanced placement credit, distance learning, double majors, English as a second language, honors programs, independent study, internships, off-campus study, part-time degree program, services for LD students, student-designed majors, study abroad, summer session for credit. ***ROTC:*** Army (b).

Computers: 167 computers/terminals are available on campus for general student use. Students can access the following: campus intranet, computer help desk, free student e-mail accounts, online (class) grades, online (class) registration, online (class) schedules. Campuswide network is available. 100% of college-owned or -operated housing units are wired for high-speed Internet access. Wireless service is available via classrooms, computer centers, computer labs, dorm rooms, learning centers, libraries, student centers.

Library: Miriam B. and James J. Mulva Library plus 1 other. *Books:* 252,444 (physical), 207,312 (digital/electronic); *Serial titles:* 103,421 (physical), 103,236 (digital/electronic). Weekly public service hours: 116; students can reserve study rooms.

STUDENT LIFE

Housing options: on-campus residence required through senior year; coed, women-only, special housing for students with disabilities. Campus housing is university owned. Freshman campus housing is guaranteed.

Activities and organizations: drama/theater group, student-run newspaper, radio and television station, choral group, Pre-Health Science Club, Adventure Club, CC Hams, BUD, American Medical Student Association, national fraternities, national sororities.

Athletics Member NCAA. All Division III except golf (Division II). ***Intercollegiate sports:*** baseball M, basketball M/W, cross-country running M/W, football M, golf M/W, ice hockey M/W, soccer M/W, softball W, swimming and diving M/W, tennis M/W, track and field M/W, volleyball M/W. ***Intramural sports:*** basketball M/W, cheerleading W, football M/W, rowing M(c)/W(c), skiing (downhill) M(c)/W(c), soccer M/W, triathlon M(c)/W(c), ultimate Frisbee M(c)/W(c), volleyball M/W.

Campus security: 24-hour emergency response devices and patrols, student patrols, late-night transport/escort service, controlled dormitory access.

Student services: health clinic, personal/psychological counseling, women's center.

COSTS & FINANCIAL AID

Costs (2020–21) ***Comprehensive fee:*** $51,770 includes full-time tuition ($40,070), mandatory fees ($815), and room and board ($10,885). Full-time tuition and fees vary according to course load. Part-time tuition: $1252 per credit hour. Part-time tuition and fees vary according to course load. ***College room only:*** $6046. Room and board charges vary according to board plan and housing facility. ***Payment plan:*** installment. ***Waivers:*** employees or children of employees.

Financial Aid Of all full-time matriculated undergraduates who enrolled in 2018, 1,725 applied for aid, 1,511 were judged to have need, 458 had their need fully met. In 2018, 527 non-need-based awards were made. ***Average percent of need met:*** 79. ***Average financial aid package:*** $27,009. ***Average need-based loan:*** $4379. ***Average need-based gift aid:*** $21,549. ***Average non-need-based aid:*** $14,932. ***Average indebtedness upon graduation:*** $40,265.

APPLYING

Standardized Tests *Required:* SAT or ACT (for admission).

Options: electronic application, deferred entrance.

Required: high school transcript. ***Recommended:*** essay or personal statement, interview.

Application deadlines: rolling (freshmen), rolling (out-of-state freshmen), rolling (transfers).

Notification: continuous (freshmen), continuous (out-of-state freshmen), continuous (transfers).

CONTACT

Mr. Mark Selin, Executive Director of Enrollment and Marketing, St. Norbert College, 100 Grant Street, De Pere, WI 54115-2099. *Phone:* 920-403-3005. *Toll-free phone:* 800-236-4878. *Fax:* 920-403-4072. *E-mail:* admit@snc.edu.

Silver Lake College of the Holy Family

Manitowoc, Wisconsin

http://www.sl.edu/

CONTACT

Daniel Connolly, Director of Enrollment Management, Silver Lake College of the Holy Family, 2406 South Alverno Road, Manitowoc, WI 54220-9319. *Phone:* 920-686-6175. *Toll-free phone:* 800-236-4752 Ext. 175. *Fax:* 920-686-6322. *E-mail:* dan.connolly@sl.edu.

University of Wisconsin–Baraboo/Sauk County

Baraboo, Wisconsin

http://www.baraboo.uwc.edu/

CONTACT

University of Wisconsin–Baraboo/Sauk County, 1006 Connie Road, Baraboo, WI 53913.

University of Wisconsin–Barron County

Rice Lake, Wisconsin

http://www.barron.uwc.edu/

CONTACT

University of Wisconsin–Barron County, 1800 College Drive, Rice Lake, WI 54868.

University of Wisconsin–Eau Claire

Eau Claire, Wisconsin

http://www.uwec.edu/

- **State-supported** comprehensive, founded 1916, part of University of Wisconsin System
- **Small-town** 337-acre campus with easy access to Minneapolis-St. Paul
- **Endowment** $72.9 million
- **Coed** 10,068 undergraduate students, 94% full-time, 62% women, 38% men
- **Moderately difficult** entrance level, 89% of applicants were admitted

UNDERGRAD STUDENTS

9,461 full-time, 607 part-time. Students come from 43 states and territories; 26 other countries; 31% are from out of state; 1% Black or African American, non-Hispanic/Latino; 4% Hispanic/Latino; 3% Asian, non-Hispanic/Latino; 0.2% American Indian or Alaska Native, non-Hispanic/Latino; 3% Two or more races, non-Hispanic/Latino; 0.1% Race/ethnicity unknown; 2% international; 5% transferred in; 20% live on campus.

Freshmen:

Admission: 5,568 applied, 4,972 admitted, 2,321 enrolled. ***Average high school GPA:*** 3.4. ***Test scores:*** SAT evidence-based reading and writing scores over 500: 83%; SAT math scores over 500: 85%; ACT scores over 18: 98%; SAT evidence-based reading and writing scores over 600: 46%; SAT math scores over 600: 51%; ACT scores over 24: 48%; SAT evidence-based reading and writing scores over 700: 5%; SAT math scores over 700: 9%; ACT scores over 30: 6%.

Retention: 82% of full-time freshmen returned.

FACULTY

Total: 611, 67% full-time, 67% with terminal degrees.

Student/faculty ratio: 22:1.

ACADEMICS

Calendar: semesters. *Degrees:* certificates, associate, bachelor's, master's, doctoral, post-master's, and postbachelor's certificates.

Special study options: academic remediation for entering students, accelerated degree program, advanced placement credit, cooperative education, distance learning, double majors, English as a second language, external degree program, honors programs, independent study, internships, off-campus study, part-time degree program, services for LD students, student-designed majors, study abroad, summer session for credit. ***ROTC:*** Army (b).

Computers: 900 computers/terminals and 10,000 ports are available on campus for general student use. Students can access the following: campus intranet, computer help desk, free student e-mail accounts, online (class) grades, online (class) registration, online (class) schedules, course management system, online library databases and card catalog, other online library services (e.g. Interlibrary loan), library reference staff online chat, check open seats in computer labs, laptop check out, poster printing. Campuswide network is available. 100% of college-owned or -operated housing units are wired for high-speed Internet access. Wireless service is available via entire campus.

Library: William D. McIntyre Library. *Books:* 429,451 (physical), 175,741 (digital/electronic); *Serial titles:* 110 (physical), 216,577 (digital/electronic); *Databases:* 200. Weekly public service hours: 89; study areas open 24 hours, 5–7 days a week; students can reserve study rooms.

STUDENT LIFE

Housing options: on-campus residence required through sophomore year; coed. Campus housing is university owned. Freshman campus housing is guaranteed.

Activities and organizations: drama/theater group, student-run newspaper, radio and television station, choral group, marching band, Student Wisconsin Education Association, Pre- Professional Health Club, Kinesiology Club, RHA (Residence Hall Association), Intervarsity Christian Fellowship, national fraternities, national sororities.

Athletics Member NCAA. All Division III. ***Intercollegiate sports:*** basketball M/W, cross-country running M/W, football M, golf M/W, gymnastics W, ice hockey M/W, soccer W, softball W, swimming and diving M/W, tennis M/W, track and field M/W, volleyball W, wrestling M. ***Intramural sports:*** badminton M/W, baseball M(c)/W(c), basketball M/W, bowling M(c)/W(c), cheerleading M(c)/W(c), equestrian sports M(c)/W(c), football M/W, ice hockey M/W, lacrosse M(c)/W(c), rugby M(c)/W(c), sand volleyball M/W, skiing (cross-country) M(c)/W(c), soccer M/W, softball M/W, table tennis M(c)/W(c), tennis M/W, triathlon M(c)/W(c), ultimate Frisbee M/W, volleyball M/W.

Campus security: 24-hour emergency response devices and patrols, student patrols, late-night transport/escort service, controlled dormitory access.

Student services: health clinic, personal/psychological counseling, women's center, legal services, veterans affairs office.

COSTS & FINANCIAL AID

Costs (2019–20) ***Tuition:*** state resident $7361 full-time, $307 per credit part-time; nonresident $15,637 full-time, $652 per credit part-time. Full-time tuition and fees vary according to program and reciprocity agreements. Part-time tuition and fees vary according to program and reciprocity agreements. ***Required fees:*** $1479 full-time, $62 per credit part-time. ***Room and board:*** $8216; room only: $5226. Room and board charges vary according to board plan and housing facility. ***Payment plan:*** installment. ***Waivers:*** senior citizens.

Financial Aid Of all full-time matriculated undergraduates who enrolled in 2018, 7,066 applied for aid, 4,710 were judged to have need, 972 had their need fully met. 4,004 Federal Work-Study jobs (averaging $1673). In 2018, 672 non-need-based awards were made. ***Average percent of need met:*** 82. ***Average financial aid package:*** $9434. ***Average need-based loan:*** $3869. ***Average need-based gift aid:*** $6494. ***Average non-need-based aid:*** $2156. ***Average indebtedness upon graduation:*** $27,129.

APPLYING

Standardized Tests *Required:* SAT or ACT (for admission).

Options: electronic application.

Application fee: $50.

Required: essay or personal statement, high school transcript.

Application deadlines: 8/20 (freshmen), 8/20 (transfers).

Notification: continuous (freshmen), continuous (transfers).

CONTACT

Albert Colom, Vice Chancellor, University of Wisconsin–Eau Claire, PO Box 4004, Eau Claire, WI 54702-4004. *Phone:* 715-836-5415. *Fax:* 715-831-4799. *E-mail:* admissions@uwec.edu.

University of Wisconsin–Green Bay

Green Bay, Wisconsin

http://www.uwgb.edu/

- **State-supported** comprehensive, founded 1968, part of University of Wisconsin System
- **Suburban** 700-acre campus with easy access to Milwaukee
- **Endowment** $28.0 million
- **Coed** 8,661 undergraduate students, 55% full-time, 63% women, 37% men
- **Moderately difficult** entrance level, 79% of applicants were admitted

UNDERGRAD STUDENTS

4,800 full-time, 3,861 part-time. 2% Black or African American, non-Hispanic/Latino; 7% Hispanic/Latino; 4% Asian, non-Hispanic/Latino; 1% American Indian or Alaska Native, non-Hispanic/Latino; 4% Two or more races, non-Hispanic/Latino; 0.4% Race/ethnicity unknown; 1% international; 8% transferred in.

Freshmen:

Admission: 3,222 applied, 2,532 admitted, 1,417 enrolled. ***Average high school GPA:*** 3.5. ***Test scores:*** ACT scores over 18: 79%; ACT scores over 24: 26%; ACT scores over 30: 3%.

FACULTY

Total: 358, 62% full-time.

Student/faculty ratio: 22:1.

ACADEMICS

Calendar: semesters. *Degrees:* associate, bachelor's, master's, and doctoral.

Special study options: academic remediation for entering students, accelerated degree program, adult/continuing education programs, advanced placement credit, cooperative education, distance learning, double majors, English as a second language, external degree program, independent study, internships, off-campus study, part-time degree program, services for LD students, student-designed majors, study abroad, summer session for credit. ***ROTC:*** Army (c).

Unusual degree programs: 3-2 business administration; engineering with University of Wisconsin–Milwaukee; nursing; social work.

Computers: 550 computers/terminals are available on campus for general student use. Students can access the following: computer help desk, free student e-mail accounts, online (class) grades, online (class) registration, online (class) schedules, online degree progress, online financial records and bill paying. Campuswide network is available. 100% of college-owned or -operated housing units are wired for high-speed Internet access. Wireless service is available via entire campus.

Library: Cofrin Library. *Books:* 353,331 (physical); *Serial titles:* 7,592 (physical); *Databases:* 179. Weekly public service hours: 100; students can reserve study rooms.

STUDENT LIFE

Activities and organizations: drama/theater group, choral group, Good Times, Psychology and Human Development Club, Student Ambassadors, Residence Hall Apartment Association, Student Government Association.

Athletics Member NCAA. All Division I. ***Intercollegiate sports:*** basketball M(s)/W(s), cross-country running M(s)/W(s), golf M(s)/W(s), skiing (cross-country) M(s)/W(s), soccer M(s)/W(s), softball W(s), swimming and diving M(s)/W(s), tennis M(s)/W(s), volleyball W(s). ***Intramural sports:*** basketball M/W, bowling M/W, cheerleading M/W, football M/W, golf M/W, racquetball M/W, sailing M/W, skiing (cross-country) M/W, soccer M/W, softball M/W, swimming and diving M/W, tennis M/W, ultimate Frisbee M/W, volleyball M/W, weight lifting M/W.

Campus security: 24-hour emergency response devices and patrols, late-night transport/escort service, controlled dormitory access.

Student services: health clinic, personal/psychological counseling, veterans affairs office.

COSTS & FINANCIAL AID

Costs (2020–21) ***Tuition:*** area resident $6298 full-time, $328 per credit hour part-time; state resident $6298 full-time, $328 per credit hour part-time; nonresident $14,148 full-time, $670 per credit hour part-time. ***Required fees:*** $1580 full-time. ***Room and board:*** $6790; room only: $4020.

Financial Aid Of all full-time matriculated undergraduates who enrolled in 2018, 3,765 applied for aid, 2,815 were judged to have need, 640 had their need fully met. In 2018, 143 non-need-based awards were made. ***Average percent of need met:*** 81. ***Average financial aid package:*** $10,813. ***Average need-based loan:*** $5518. ***Average need-based gift aid:*** $6762. ***Average non-need-based aid:*** $1726. ***Average indebtedness upon graduation:*** $24,668.

APPLYING

Standardized Tests *Required for some:* SAT or ACT (for admission).

Options: electronic application, deferred entrance.

Application fee: $50.

Required: essay or personal statement, high school transcript. ***Required for some:*** interview.

Application deadlines: rolling (freshmen), rolling (transfers).

Notification: continuous (freshmen), continuous (transfers).

CONTACT

Ms. Jen Jones, Director of Admissions, University of Wisconsin–Green Bay, 2420 Nicolet Drive, Green Bay, WI 54311-7001. *Phone:* 920-465-2111. *Fax:* 920-465-5754. *E-mail:* uwgb@uwgb.edu.

University of Wisconsin–La Crosse

La Crosse, Wisconsin

http://www.uwlax.edu/

- **State-supported** comprehensive, founded 1909, part of University of Wisconsin System
- **Small-town** 128-acre campus
- **Endowment** $26.6 million
- **Coed** 9,595 undergraduate students, 94% full-time, 56% women, 44% men
- **Moderately difficult** entrance level, 80% of applicants were admitted

UNDERGRAD STUDENTS

9,051 full-time, 544 part-time. Students come from 43 states and territories; 30 other countries; 18% are from out of state; 0.7% Black or African American, non-Hispanic/Latino; 4% Hispanic/Latino; 2% Asian, non-Hispanic/Latino; 0.2% American Indian or Alaska Native, non-Hispanic/Latino; 3% Two or more races, non-Hispanic/Latino; 0.1% Race/ethnicity unknown; 0.5% international; 4% transferred in; 35% live on campus.

Freshmen:

Admission: 5,843 applied, 4,670 admitted, 2,194 enrolled. ***Test scores:*** SAT evidence-based reading and writing scores over 500: 97%; SAT math scores over 500: 95%; ACT scores over 18: 100%; SAT evidence-based reading and writing scores over 600: 54%; SAT math scores over 600: 59%; ACT scores over 24: 61%; SAT evidence-based reading and writing scores over 700: 5%; SAT math scores over 700: 13%; ACT scores over 30: 7%.

Retention: 84% of full-time freshmen returned.

FACULTY

Total: 647, 72% full-time, 71% with terminal degrees.

Student/faculty ratio: 19:1.

ACADEMICS

Calendar: semesters. *Degrees:* certificates, bachelor's, master's, doctoral, post-master's, and postbachelor's certificates.

Special study options: academic remediation for entering students, advanced placement credit, distance learning, double majors, independent study, internships, off-campus study, part-time degree program, services for LD students, study abroad, summer session for credit. ***ROTC:*** Army (b).

Unusual degree programs: 3-2 engineering with University of Wisconsin-Madison; University of Wisconsin-Milwaukee; University of Wisconsin-Platteville; University of Minnesota-Duluth; Winona State University; physical therapy and physics; physical therapy and biology.

Computers: Students can access the following: campus intranet, computer help desk, free student e-mail accounts, online (class) grades, online (class) registration, online (class) schedules. Campuswide network is available. 100% of college-owned or -operated housing units are wired for high-speed Internet access. Wireless service is available via entire campus.

Library: Murphy Library plus 1 other. *Books:* 482,242 (physical), 906,635 (digital/electronic); *Serial titles:* 8,751 (physical), 133,564 (digital/electronic); *Databases:* 251. Weekly public service hours: 107; students can reserve study rooms.

STUDENT LIFE

Housing options: on-campus residence required for freshman year; coed, special housing for students with disabilities. Campus housing is university owned. Freshman applicants given priority for college housing.

Activities and organizations: drama/theater group, student-run newspaper, radio and television station, choral group, marching band, Sports and Activities Club, Residential Hall Council, Religious/Spiritual Organizations, Human Diversity Organizations, Departmental/Professional, national fraternities, national sororities.

Athletics Member NCAA, NAIA. All NCAA Division III. ***Intercollegiate sports:*** baseball M, basketball M/W, cross-country running M/W, football M, golf W, gymnastics W, lacrosse W, soccer W, softball W, swimming and diving M/W, tennis M/W, track and field M/W, volleyball W, wrestling M. ***Intramural sports:*** archery M(c)/W(c), badminton M/W, basketball M/W, bowling M(c)/W(c), equestrian sports M(c)/W(c), ice hockey M(c)/W(c), lacrosse M(c)/W(c), rugby M(c)/W(c), skiing (cross-country) M(c)/W(c), skiing (downhill) M(c)/W(c), soccer M/W, softball M/W, table tennis M(c)/W(c), tennis M/W, triathlon M(c)/W(c), ultimate Frisbee M/W, volleyball M/W, weight lifting M(c)/W(c).

Campus security: 24-hour emergency response devices and patrols, late-night transport/escort service, controlled dormitory access.

Student services: health clinic, personal/psychological counseling, legal services, veterans affairs office.

COSTS & FINANCIAL AID

Costs (2019–20) ***Tuition:*** state resident $7585 full-time, $316 per credit hour part-time; nonresident $16,254 full-time, $684 per credit hour part-time. Full-time tuition and fees vary according to reciprocity agreements. Part-time tuition and fees vary according to course load and reciprocity agreements. ***Required fees:*** $1368 full-time, $110 per credit hour part-time. ***Room and board:*** $6465; room only: $3921. Room and board charges vary according to board plan and housing facility. ***Payment plan:*** installment. ***Waivers:*** senior citizens.

Financial Aid Of all full-time matriculated undergraduates who enrolled in 2018, 6,773 applied for aid, 4,134 were judged to have need, 957 had their need fully met. In 2018, 708 non-need-based awards were made. ***Average percent of need met:*** 69. ***Average financial aid package:*** $7947. ***Average need-based loan:*** $3863. ***Average need-based gift aid:*** $6382. ***Average non-need-based aid:*** $1648. ***Average indebtedness upon graduation:*** $25,926.

APPLYING

Standardized Tests *Required:* SAT or ACT (for admission).

Options: electronic application.

Application fee: $50.

Required: essay or personal statement, high school transcript.

Application deadlines: rolling (freshmen), rolling (transfers).

Notification: continuous (freshmen), continuous (transfers).

CONTACT

Mr. Corey Sjoquist, Director of Admissions, University of Wisconsin–La Crosse, 1725 State Street, La Crosse, WI 54601. *Phone:* 608-785-8939. *Fax:* 608-785-8940. *E-mail:* admissions@uwlax.edu.

University of Wisconsin–Madison

Madison, Wisconsin

http://www.wisc.edu/

- **State-supported** university, founded 1848, part of University of Wisconsin System
- **Urban** 936-acre campus with easy access to Milwaukee
- **Endowment** $3.0 billion
- **Coed** 32,648 undergraduate students, 90% full-time, 51% women, 49% men
- **Very difficult** entrance level, 53% of applicants were admitted

UNDERGRAD STUDENTS
29,412 full-time, 3,236 part-time. Students come from 52 states and territories; 79 other countries; 35% are from out of state; 2% Black or African American, non-Hispanic/Latino; 5% Hispanic/Latino; 6% Asian, non-Hispanic/Latino; 0.1% Native Hawaiian or other Pacific Islander, non-Hispanic/Latino; 0.2% American Indian or Alaska Native, non-Hispanic/Latino; 3% Two or more races, non-Hispanic/Latino; 2% Race/ethnicity unknown; 10% international; 3% transferred in; 26% live on campus.

Freshmen:
Admission: 43,921 applied, 23,287 admitted, 6,862 enrolled. ***Average high school GPA:*** 3.9. ***Test scores:*** SAT evidence-based reading and writing scores over 500: 100%; SAT math scores over 500: 100%; ACT scores over 18: 100%; SAT evidence-based reading and writing scores over 600: 90%; SAT math scores over 600: 93%; ACT scores over 24: 96%; SAT evidence-based reading and writing scores over 700: 31%; SAT math scores over 700: 67%; ACT scores over 30: 51%.

Retention: 95% of full-time freshmen returned.

FACULTY
Total: 3,012, 83% full-time, 86% with terminal degrees.

Student/faculty ratio: 17:1.

ACADEMICS
Calendar: semesters. *Degrees:* bachelor's, master's, doctoral, and postbachelor's certificates.

Special study options: accelerated degree program, adult/continuing education programs, advanced placement credit, cooperative education, distance learning, double majors, English as a second language, honors programs, independent study, internships, part-time degree program, services for LD students, student-designed majors, study abroad, summer session for credit. ***ROTC:*** Army (b), Navy (b), Air Force (b).

Unusual degree programs: 3-2 business administration.

Computers: 1,000 computers/terminals are available on campus for general student use. Students can access the following: computer help desk, free student e-mail accounts, online (class) grades, online (class) registration, online (class) schedules. Campuswide network is available. 100% of college-owned or -operated housing units are wired for high-speed Internet access. Wireless service is available via entire campus.
Library: Memorial Library plus 40 others. Study areas open 24 hours, 5–7 days a week; students can reserve study rooms.

STUDENT LIFE
Housing options: coed, men-only, women-only, cooperative. Campus housing is university owned. Freshman applicants given priority for college housing.

Activities and organizations: drama/theater group, student-run newspaper, radio station, choral group, marching band, national fraternities, national sororities.

Athletics Member NCAA. All Division I. ***Intercollegiate sports:*** basketball M(s)/W(s), cheerleading M/W, crew M/W, cross-country running M(s)/W(s), fencing M(c)/W(c), football M(s), golf M(s)/W(s), ice hockey M(s)/W(s), lacrosse M(c)/W(c), racquetball M(c)/W(c), rugby M(c)/W(c), sailing M(c)/W(c), soccer M(s)/W(s), softball W(s), swimming and diving M(s)/W(s), tennis M(s)/W(s), track and field M(s)/W(s), ultimate Frisbee M(c)/W(c), volleyball M(c)/W(s), water polo M(c)/W(c), wrestling M(s). ***Intramural sports:*** archery M(c)/W(c), badminton M(c)/W(c), baseball M(c), basketball M/W, cheerleading M(c)/W(c), fencing M(c)/W(c), field hockey M(c)/W(c), golf M(c)/W(c), gymnastics M(c)/W(c), ice hockey M(c)/W(c), lacrosse M(c)/W(c), racquetball M(c)/W(c), rugby M(c)/W(c), soccer M(c)/W(c), softball W, swimming and diving M(c)/W(c), table tennis M(c)/W(c), tennis M(c)/W(c), track and field M(c)/W(c), ultimate Frisbee M(c)/W(c), volleyball M(c)/W(c), water polo M(c)/W(c), wrestling M(c)/W(c).

Campus security: 24-hour emergency response devices and patrols, late-night transport/escort service, controlled dormitory access.

Student services: health clinic, personal/psychological counseling, women's center, veterans affairs office.

COSTS & FINANCIAL AID
Costs (2019–20) ***Tuition:*** state resident $9273 full-time, $386 per credit part-time; nonresident $36,333 full-time, $1514 per credit part-time. Full-time tuition and fees vary according to program and reciprocity agreements. Part-time tuition and fees vary according to course load, program, and reciprocity agreements. ***Required fees:*** $1452 full-time, $109 per credit part-time. ***Room and board:*** $11,558. Room and board charges vary according to board plan and housing facility. ***Payment plan:*** installment.

Financial Aid Of all full-time matriculated undergraduates who enrolled in 2019, 16,460 applied for aid, 10,367 were judged to have need, 4,221 had their need fully met. In 2019, 1049 non-need-based awards were made. ***Average percent of need met:*** 80. ***Average financial aid package:*** $17,473. ***Average need-based loan:*** $4799. ***Average need-based gift aid:*** $15,143. ***Average non-need-based aid:*** $5502. ***Average indebtedness upon graduation:*** $27,973.

APPLYING
Standardized Tests *Required:* SAT or ACT (for admission).

Options: electronic application, early action, deferred entrance.

Application fee: $60.

Required: essay or personal statement, high school transcript. ***Recommended:*** 2 letters of recommendation.

Application deadlines: 2/1 (freshmen), 3/1 (transfers), 11/1 (early action).

Notification: 3/31 (freshmen), 4/30 (transfers), 1/31 (early action).

CONTACT
Office of Admissions and Recruitment, University of Wisconsin–Madison, 702 West Johnson Street, Suite 101, Madison, WI 53706-1481. *Phone:* 608-262-3961. *Fax:* 608-262-7706. *E-mail:* onwisconsin@admissions.wisc.edu.

University of Wisconsin–Marshfield/Wood County

Marshfield, Wisconsin

http://marshfield.uwc.edu/

CONTACT
University of Wisconsin–Marshfield/Wood County, 2000 West 5th Street, Marshfield, WI 54449.

University of Wisconsin–Milwaukee

Milwaukee, Wisconsin

http://www.uwm.edu/

- **State-supported** university, founded 1956, part of University of Wisconsin System
- **Urban** 104-acre campus with easy access to Milwaukee
- **Endowment** $167.2 million
- **Coed** 21,509 undergraduate students, 81% full-time, 53% women, 47% men
- **Moderately difficult** entrance level, 95% of applicants were admitted

UNDERGRAD STUDENTS
17,442 full-time, 4,067 part-time. 12% are from out of state; 7% Black or African American, non-Hispanic/Latino; 12% Hispanic/Latino; 7% Asian, non-Hispanic/Latino; 0.1% Native Hawaiian or other Pacific Islander, non-Hispanic/Latino; 0.3% American Indian or Alaska Native, non-Hispanic/Latino; 4% Two or more races, non-Hispanic/Latino; 0.2% Race/ethnicity unknown; 3% international; 7% transferred in; 17% live on campus.

Freshmen:
Admission: 8,946 applied, 8,481 admitted, 3,753 enrolled. ***Average high school GPA:*** 3.2. ***Test scores:*** SAT evidence-based reading and writing scores over 500: 87%; SAT math scores over 500: 83%; ACT scores over 18: 87%; SAT evidence-based reading and writing scores over 600: 37%; SAT math scores over 600: 37%; ACT scores over 24: 32%; SAT evidence-based reading and writing scores over 700: 6%; SAT math scores over 700: 5%; ACT scores over 30: 4%.

Retention: 76% of full-time freshmen returned.

FACULTY
Total: 1,646, 57% full-time, 44% with terminal degrees.

Student/faculty ratio: 19:1.

ACADEMICS
Calendar: semesters. *Degrees:* certificates, associate, bachelor's, master's, doctoral, post-master's, and postbachelor's certificates.

Special study options: academic remediation for entering students, accelerated degree program, adult/continuing education programs, advanced placement credit, cooperative education, distance learning, double majors, English as a second language, external degree program, freshman honors college, honors programs, independent study, internships, off-campus study, part-time degree program, services for LD students, student-designed majors, study abroad, summer session for credit. ***ROTC:*** Army (c), Navy (c), Air Force (c).

Computers: 500 computers/terminals are available on campus for general student use. Students can access the following: campus intranet, computer help desk, free student e-mail accounts, online (class) grades, online (class) registration, online (class) schedules. Campuswide network is available. 100% of college-owned or -operated housing units are wired for high-speed Internet access. Wireless service is available via classrooms, computer centers, computer labs, dorm rooms, learning centers, libraries, student centers.

Library: Golda Meir Library. *Books:* 2.5 million (physical), 178,268 (digital/electronic); *Serial titles:* 112,752 (physical). Students can reserve study rooms.

STUDENT LIFE
Housing options: on-campus residence required for freshman year; coed, special housing for students with disabilities. Campus housing is university owned. Freshman applicants given priority for college housing.

Activities and organizations: drama/theater group, student-run newspaper, radio station, choral group, national fraternities, national sororities.

Athletics Member NCAA. All Division I. ***Intercollegiate sports:*** baseball M(s), basketball M(s)/W(s), bowling M(c)/W(c), cross-country running M(s)/W(s), equestrian sports M(c)/W(c), football M(c)/W(c), ice hockey M(c)/W(c), lacrosse M(c)/W(c), rugby M(c)/W(c), sailing M(c)/W(c), soccer M(s)/W(s), swimming and diving M(s)/W(s), tennis W(s), track and field M(s)/W(s), ultimate Frisbee M(c)/W(c), volleyball M(c)/W(s). ***Intramural sports:*** badminton M/W, baseball M(c)/W(c), basketball M/W, cross-country running M/W, football M/W, racquetball M/W, skiing (downhill) M(c)/W(c), soccer M/W, swimming and diving M/W, tennis M(c)/W(c), track and field M(c)/W(c), volleyball M/W.

Campus security: 24-hour emergency response devices and patrols, student patrols, late-night transport/escort service, controlled dormitory access.

Student services: health clinic, personal/psychological counseling, women's center, legal services.

COSTS & FINANCIAL AID
Costs (2019–20) ***Tuition:*** area resident $9588 full-time; state resident $9588 full-time, $399 per credit hour part-time; nonresident $20,868 full-time, $882 per credit hour part-time. Full-time tuition and fees vary according to degree level, location, and reciprocity agreements. Part-time tuition and fees vary according to degree level, location, and reciprocity agreements. ***Room and board:*** $10,792.

Financial Aid Of all full-time matriculated undergraduates who enrolled in 2018, 12,895 applied for aid, 10,454 were judged to have need, 683 had their need fully met. In 2018, 543 non-need-based awards were made. ***Average percent of need met:*** 49. ***Average financial aid package:*** $8904. ***Average need-based loan:*** $3991. ***Average need-based gift aid:*** $6662. ***Average non-need-based aid:*** $1705. ***Average indebtedness upon graduation:*** $37,261.

APPLYING
Standardized Tests *Required for some:* SAT or ACT (for admission), TOEFL for students whose native language is not English and who were not educated in an entirely English-speaking country.

Options: electronic application, deferred entrance.

Application fee: $50.

Required: high school transcript. ***Recommended:*** essay or personal statement.

Application deadlines: rolling (freshmen), 8/10 (transfers).

Notification: continuous (freshmen), continuous (transfers).

CONTACT
Mr. Patrick Fay, Interim Director, Undergraduate Admissions, University of Wisconsin–Milwaukee, PO Box 413, Milwaukee, WI 53201-0413. *Phone:* 414-229-4445. *E-mail:* uwmlook@uwm.edu.

University of Wisconsin–Oshkosh

Oshkosh, Wisconsin

http://www.uwosh.edu/

- **State-supported** comprehensive, founded 1871, part of University of Wisconsin System
- **Suburban** 192-acre campus with easy access to Milwaukee
- **Coed**
- **Moderately difficult** entrance level

FACULTY
Student/faculty ratio: 22:1.

ACADEMICS
Calendar: semesters. *Degrees:* certificates, associate, bachelor's, master's, doctoral, and postbachelor's certificates.
Library: Forrest R. Polk Library.

STUDENT LIFE
Housing options: on-campus residence required through sophomore year; coed. Campus housing is university owned. Freshman campus housing is guaranteed.

Activities and organizations: drama/theater group, student-run newspaper, radio and television station, choral group, national fraternities, national sororities.

Athletics Member NCAA. All Division III.

Campus security: 24-hour emergency response devices and patrols, student patrols, late-night transport/escort service, controlled dormitory access.

Student services: health clinic, personal/psychological counseling, women's center, legal services.

FINANCIAL AID
Financial Aid Of all full-time matriculated undergraduates who enrolled in 2016, 6,769 applied for aid, 5,421 were judged to have need, 1,944 had their need fully met. In 2016, 184 non-need-based awards were made. ***Average percent of need met:*** 71. ***Average financial aid package:*** $8558. ***Average need-based loan:*** $4827. ***Average need-based gift aid:*** $6495. ***Average non-need-based aid:*** $2410. ***Average indebtedness upon graduation:*** $32,502.

APPLYING
Standardized Tests *Required:* ACT (for admission).

Options: electronic application, deferred entrance.

Application fee: $50.

Required: high school transcript. ***Recommended:*** essay or personal statement.

CONTACT
Associate Director of Admissions, University of Wisconsin–Oshkosh, 800 Algoma Boulevard, Oshkosh, WI 54901. *Phone:* 920-424-0202. *E-mail:* oshadmuw@uwosh.edu.

University of Wisconsin–Parkside

Kenosha, Wisconsin

http://www.uwp.edu/

- **State-supported** comprehensive, founded 1968, part of University of Wisconsin System
- **Suburban** 700-acre campus with easy access to Chicago, Milwaukee
- **Coed** 3,938 undergraduate students, 80% full-time, 55% women, 45% men
- **Moderately difficult** entrance level, 89% of applicants were admitted

UNDERGRAD STUDENTS
3,143 full-time, 795 part-time. 16% are from out of state; 8% Black or African American, non-Hispanic/Latino; 19% Hispanic/Latino; 4% Asian, non-Hispanic/Latino; 0.2% Native Hawaiian or other Pacific Islander, non-Hispanic/Latino; 0.2% American Indian or Alaska Native, non-

Hispanic/Latino; 4% Two or more races, non-Hispanic/Latino; 1% international; 10% transferred in; 21% live on campus.

Freshmen:

Admission: 1,676 applied, 1,485 admitted, 634 enrolled. ***Average high school GPA:*** 3.1. ***Test scores:*** SAT evidence-based reading and writing scores over 500: 64%; SAT math scores over 500: 61%; ACT scores over 18: 71%; SAT evidence-based reading and writing scores over 600: 16%; SAT math scores over 600: 18%; ACT scores over 24: 20%; SAT evidence-based reading and writing scores over 700: 3%; SAT math scores over 700: 3%; ACT scores over 30: 2%.

Retention: 72% of full-time freshmen returned.

FACULTY

Total: 282, 57% full-time, 56% with terminal degrees.

Student/faculty ratio: 17:1.

ACADEMICS

Calendar: semesters. *Degrees:* certificates, associate, bachelor's, and master's.

Special study options: academic remediation for entering students, adult/continuing education programs, advanced placement credit, distance learning, double majors, English as a second language, honors programs, independent study, internships, off-campus study, part-time degree program, services for LD students, student-designed majors, study abroad, summer session for credit. ***ROTC:*** Army (b), Air Force (c).

Unusual degree programs: 3-2 molecular biology; pharmacy with Rosalind-Franklin University.

Computers: 376 computers/terminals are available on campus for general student use. Students can access the following: campus intranet, computer help desk, free student e-mail accounts, online (class) grades, online (class) registration, online (class) schedules, Online tutoring; Online advising. Campuswide network is available. 100% of college-owned or -operated housing units are wired for high-speed Internet access. Wireless service is available via entire campus.

Library: UWP Library. *Books:* 406,756 (physical); *Serial titles:* 1,277 (physical). Weekly public service hours: 75; students can reserve study rooms.

STUDENT LIFE

Housing options: on-campus residence required through sophomore year; coed, special housing for students with disabilities. Campus housing is university owned.

Activities and organizations: drama/theater group, student-run newspaper, radio station, choral group, Habitat for Humanity, Criminal Justice Association, Next Level Gaming, Parkside Asian Organization, Active Minds, national fraternities, national sororities.

Athletics Member NCAA. All Division II. ***Intercollegiate sports:*** baseball M(s), basketball M(s)/W(s), cross-country running M(s)/W(s), golf M(s), soccer M(s)/W(s), softball W(s), track and field M(s)/W(s), volleyball W(s), wrestling M(s). ***Intramural sports:*** badminton M/W, basketball M/W, football M/W, racquetball M/W, rugby M(c), soccer M/W, softball M/W, table tennis M/W, tennis M/W, volleyball M/W.

Campus security: 24-hour emergency response devices and patrols, late-night transport/escort service, controlled dormitory access, Self-defense training.

Student services: health clinic, personal/psychological counseling, women's center, veterans affairs office.

COSTS & FINANCIAL AID

Costs (2019–20) ***One-time required fee:*** $260. ***Tuition:*** state resident $6298 full-time, $262 per credit hour part-time; nonresident $14,568 full-time, $607 per credit hour part-time. Full-time tuition and fees vary according to course load, program, and reciprocity agreements. Part-time tuition and fees vary according to course load, program, and reciprocity agreements. ***Required fees:*** $1123 full-time, $47 per credit hour part-time. ***Room and board:*** $8200; room only: $4562. Room and board charges vary according to board plan and housing facility. ***Payment plan:*** installment. ***Waivers:*** senior citizens.

Financial Aid Of all full-time matriculated undergraduates who enrolled in 2018, 2,479 applied for aid, 2,080 were judged to have need, 226 had their need fully met. In 2018, 302 non-need-based awards were made. ***Average percent of need met:*** 61. ***Average financial aid package:*** $9133. ***Average need-based loan:*** $4402. ***Average need-based gift aid:*** $6346. ***Average non-need-based aid:*** $3204. ***Average indebtedness upon graduation:*** $29,551.

APPLYING

Standardized Tests *Required for some:* SAT or ACT (for admission). *Recommended:* SAT and SAT Subject Tests or ACT (for admission), SAT Subject Tests (for admission).

Options: electronic application.

Application fee: $50.

Required: high school transcript, minimum of 17 high school units distribution.

Application deadlines: rolling (freshmen), rolling (transfers).

Notification: continuous (freshmen), continuous (transfers).

CONTACT

Troy Moldenhauer, Director, Admissions and Recruitment, University of Wisconsin–Parkside, PO Box 2000, 900 Wood Road, Kenosha, WI 53141-2000. *Phone:* 262-595-2355. *Fax:* 262-595-2006. *E-mail:* moldenht@uwp.edu.

University of Wisconsin–Platteville

Platteville, Wisconsin

http://www.uwplatt.edu/

- **State-supported** comprehensive, founded 1866, part of University of Wisconsin System
- **Small-town** 821-acre campus
- **Endowment** $28.6 million
- **Coed** 7,449 undergraduate students, 87% full-time, 37% women, 63% men
- 86% of applicants were admitted

UNDERGRAD STUDENTS

6,458 full-time, 991 part-time. 22% are from out of state; 1% Black or African American, non-Hispanic/Latino; 5% Hispanic/Latino; 1% Asian, non-Hispanic/Latino; 0.1% Native Hawaiian or other Pacific Islander, non-Hispanic/Latino; 0.2% American Indian or Alaska Native, non-Hispanic/Latino; 2% Two or more races, non-Hispanic/Latino; 0.3% Race/ethnicity unknown; 1% international; 6% transferred in; 43% live on campus.

Freshmen:

Admission: 3,416 applied, 2,931 admitted, 1,492 enrolled. ***Test scores:*** SAT evidence-based reading and writing scores over 500: 84%; SAT math scores over 500: 88%; ACT scores over 18: 93%; SAT evidence-based reading and writing scores over 600: 36%; SAT math scores over 600: 41%; ACT scores over 24: 43%; SAT evidence-based reading and writing scores over 700: 3%; SAT math scores over 700: 7%; ACT scores over 30: 6%.

Retention: 74% of full-time freshmen returned.

FACULTY

Total: 494, 58% full-time, 46% with terminal degrees.

Student/faculty ratio: 20:1.

ACADEMICS

Calendar: semesters. *Degrees:* certificates, associate, bachelor's, master's, and postbachelor's certificates.

Special study options: academic remediation for entering students, adult/continuing education programs, advanced placement credit, cooperative education, distance learning, double majors, English as a second language, external degree program, independent study, internships, off-campus study, part-time degree program, services for LD students, student-designed majors, study abroad, summer session for credit. ***ROTC:*** Army (c).

Computers: 200 computers/terminals and 50 ports are available on campus for general student use. Students can access the following: campus intranet, computer help desk, free student e-mail accounts, online (class) grades, online (class) registration, online (class) schedules. Campuswide network is available. 100% of college-owned or -operated housing units are wired for high-speed Internet access. Wireless service is available via entire campus.

Library: Karrmann Library plus 1 other. *Books:* 167,304 (physical), 59,292 (digital/electronic); *Serial titles:* 1,151 (physical), 44,687 (digital/electronic); *Databases:* 123. Weekly public service hours: 87.

STUDENT LIFE
Housing options: on-campus residence required through sophomore year; coed, men-only, women-only, special housing for students with disabilities. Campus housing is university owned. Freshman campus housing is guaranteed.

Activities and organizations: drama/theater group, student-run newspaper, radio and television station, choral group, marching band, Criminal Justice Association, Platteville Gaming Association, Dodgeball, American Society of Mechanical Engineers, Outdoor Adventure Club, national fraternities, national sororities.

Athletics Member NCAA. All Division III. ***Intercollegiate sports:*** baseball M, basketball M/W, bowling M(c)/W(c), cross-country running M/W, football M, golf W, ice hockey M(c)/W(c), lacrosse M(c)/W(c), rugby M(c)/W(c), soccer M/W, softball W, track and field M/W, ultimate Frisbee M(c)/W(c), volleyball M(c)/W, wrestling M. ***Intramural sports:*** badminton M/W, basketball M/W, bowling M(c)/W(c), cheerleading M(c)/W(c), football M/W, racquetball M/W, soccer M/W, softball M/W, tennis M/W, ultimate Frisbee M/W, volleyball M/W, water polo M/W.

Campus security: 24-hour emergency response devices and patrols, student patrols, late-night transport/escort service, controlled dormitory access.

Student services: health clinic, personal/psychological counseling, women's center, veterans affairs office.

COSTS & FINANCIAL AID
Costs (2020–21) ***Tuition:*** area resident $6298 full-time, $262 per credit hour part-time; state resident $6298 full-time, $262 per credit hour part-time; nonresident $14,148 full-time, $590 per credit hour part-time. ***Required fees:*** $1548 full-time. ***Room and board:*** $7770; room only: $4690.

Financial Aid Of all full-time matriculated undergraduates who enrolled in 2018, 5,381 applied for aid, 3,732 were judged to have need, 484 had their need fully met. In 2018, 897 non-need-based awards were made. ***Average percent of need met:*** 59. ***Average financial aid package:*** $5738. ***Average need-based loan:*** $3618. ***Average need-based gift aid:*** $5541. ***Average non-need-based aid:*** $2992. ***Average indebtedness upon graduation:*** $29,707.

APPLYING
Standardized Tests *Required:* SAT or ACT (for admission).

Options: deferred entrance.

Required: high school transcript. ***Recommended:*** essay or personal statement.

CONTACT
Ms. Heidi Tuescher-Gille, Director of Admission and Enrollment Services, University of Wisconsin–Platteville, 1 University Plaza, 1300 Ullsvik Hall, Platteville, WI 53818-3099. *Phone:* 608-342-1125. *Toll-free phone:* 877-897-5288. *Fax:* 608-342-1122. *E-mail:* tuescheh@uwplatt.edu.

University of Wisconsin–Richland
Richland Center, Wisconsin
http://richland.uwc.edu/

CONTACT
University of Wisconsin–Richland, 1200 Highway 14 West, Richland Center, WI 53581.

University of Wisconsin–River Falls
River Falls, Wisconsin
http://www.uwrf.edu/

- **State-supported** comprehensive, founded 1874, part of University of Wisconsin System
- **Suburban** 303-acre campus with easy access to Minneapolis-St. Paul
- **Endowment** $25.8 million
- **Coed**
- **Moderately difficult** entrance level

FACULTY
Student/faculty ratio: 18:1.

ACADEMICS
Calendar: semesters. *Degrees:* certificates, associate, bachelor's, master's, post-master's, and postbachelor's certificates.
Library: Chalmer Davee Library. *Books:* 268,085 (physical), 433,534 (digital/electronic); *Serial titles:* 35 (physical). Weekly public service hours: 46; study areas open 24 hours, 5–7 days a week; students can reserve study rooms.

STUDENT LIFE
Housing options: on-campus residence required through sophomore year; coed, women-only, special housing for students with disabilities. Campus housing is university owned. Freshman campus housing is guaranteed.

Activities and organizations: drama/theater group, student-run newspaper, radio and television station, choral group, Intervarsity Christian Fellowship, UW Pre-Vet Club, National Association for Music Education, Aspiring Educators, Agricultural Business and Marketing Society, national fraternities, national sororities.

Athletics Member NCAA. All Division III.

Campus security: 24-hour emergency response devices and patrols, student patrols, late-night transport/escort service, controlled dormitory access.

Student services: health clinic, personal/psychological counseling, veterans affairs office.

FINANCIAL AID
Financial Aid Of all full-time matriculated undergraduates who enrolled in 2018, 3,896 applied for aid, 2,719 were judged to have need, 56 had their need fully met. 383 Federal Work-Study jobs (averaging $1242). In 2018, 573 non-need-based awards were made. ***Average percent of need met:*** 54. ***Average financial aid package:*** $6896. ***Average need-based loan:*** $3767. ***Average need-based gift aid:*** $5127. ***Average non-need-based aid:*** $1947. ***Average indebtedness upon graduation:*** $26,814.

APPLYING
Standardized Tests *Required:* SAT or ACT (for admission). *Recommended:* ACT (for admission).

Options: electronic application, deferred entrance.

Application fee: $50.

Required: essay or personal statement, high school transcript. ***Recommended:*** rank in upper 40% of high school class.

CONTACT
Sarah Nelson, Director of Admissions, University of Wisconsin–River Falls, 410 South Third Street, Admissions Office - 112 South Hall, River Falls, WI 54022. *Phone:* 715-425-3500. *E-mail:* admissions@uwrf.edu.

University of Wisconsin–Rock County
Janesville, Wisconsin
http://rock.uwc.edu/

CONTACT
University of Wisconsin–Rock County, 2909 Kellogg Avenue, Janesville, WI 53546. *Toll-free phone:* 888-INFO-UWC.

University of Wisconsin–Stevens Point
Stevens Point, Wisconsin
http://www.uwsp.edu/

- **State-supported** comprehensive, founded 1894, part of University of Wisconsin System
- **Small-town** 400-acre campus
- **Endowment** $28.6 million
- **Coed**
- **Moderately difficult** entrance level

FACULTY
Student/faculty ratio: 18:1.

ACADEMICS
Calendar: semesters. *Degrees:* associate, bachelor's, master's, and doctoral.
Library: Learning Resources Center plus 1 other. *Books:* 420,414 (physical), 247,207 (digital/electronic); *Serial titles:* 7,192 (physical),

133,235 (digital/electronic); *Databases:* 204. Study areas open 24 hours, 5–7 days a week; students can reserve study rooms.

STUDENT LIFE
Housing options: on-campus residence required through sophomore year; coed, men-only, women-only. Campus housing is university owned. Freshman applicants given priority for college housing.

Activities and organizations: drama/theater group, student-run newspaper, radio and television station, choral group, The Wildlife Society, Student Impact, WWSP 90-FM radio station, Gender and Sexuality Alliance, Student Wisconsin Education Association, national fraternities, national sororities.

Athletics Member NCAA. All Division III.

Campus security: 24-hour emergency response devices and patrols, student patrols, late-night transport/escort service, controlled dormitory access.

Student services: health clinic, personal/psychological counseling, women's center, veterans affairs office.

COSTS & FINANCIAL AID
Costs (2019–20) ***Tuition:*** area resident $6698 full-time, $279 per credit part-time; state resident $6698 full-time, $279 per credit part-time; nonresident $15,401 full-time, $642 per credit part-time. Full-time tuition and fees vary according to course load, location, program, reciprocity agreements, and student level. Part-time tuition and fees vary according to course load, location, program, reciprocity agreements, and student level. ***Required fees:*** $1592 full-time. ***Room and board:*** $7428; room only: $4422. Room and board charges vary according to board plan and housing facility. ***Payment plans:*** installment, deferred payment.

Financial Aid Of all full-time matriculated undergraduates who enrolled in 2018, 5,351 applied for aid, 3,987 were judged to have need, 2,342 had their need fully met. In 2018, 759 non-need-based awards were made. ***Average percent of need met:*** 75. ***Average financial aid package:*** $9520. ***Average need-based loan:*** $4619. ***Average need-based gift aid:*** $6382. ***Average non-need-based aid:*** $1497. ***Average indebtedness upon graduation:*** $31,669.

APPLYING
Standardized Tests *Required:* SAT or ACT (for admission).

Options: electronic application, deferred entrance.

Application fee: $50.

Required: high school transcript. ***Recommended:*** essay or personal statement, 3 letters of recommendation.

CONTACT
Mr. William Jordan, Director of Admissions, University of Wisconsin–Stevens Point, 102 Student Services Center, Stevens Point, WI 54481. *Phone:* 715-346-4021. *Fax:* 715-346-3296. *E-mail:* bjordan@uwsp.edu.

University of Wisconsin–Stout

Menomonie, Wisconsin

http://www.uwstout.edu/

- **State-supported** comprehensive, founded 1891, part of University of Wisconsin System
- **Small-town** 120-acre campus with easy access to Minneapolis-St. Paul
- **Coed** 7,289 undergraduate students, 82% full-time, 43% women, 57% men
- **Moderately difficult** entrance level, 88% of applicants were admitted

UNDERGRAD STUDENTS
5,995 full-time, 1,294 part-time. 34% are from out of state; 2% Black or African American, non-Hispanic/Latino; 3% Hispanic/Latino; 4% Asian, non-Hispanic/Latino; 0.1% Native Hawaiian or other Pacific Islander, non-Hispanic/Latino; 0.4% American Indian or Alaska Native, non-Hispanic/Latino; 3% Two or more races, non-Hispanic/Latino; 0.2% Race/ethnicity unknown; 2% international; 39% live on campus.

Freshmen:
Admission: 3,227 applied, 2,842 admitted, 1,491 enrolled. ***Average high school GPA:*** 3.3. ***Test scores:*** ACT scores over 18: 88%; ACT scores over 24: 36%; ACT scores over 30: 5%.

Retention: 72% of full-time freshmen returned.

FACULTY
Total: 463, 82% full-time, 70% with terminal degrees.

Student/faculty ratio: 18:1.

ACADEMICS
Calendar: 4-1-4. *Degrees:* certificates, bachelor's, master's, doctoral, post-master's, and postbachelor's certificates.

Special study options: accelerated degree program, adult/continuing education programs, cooperative education, distance learning, double majors, English as a second language, external degree program, honors programs, independent study, internships, off-campus study, part-time degree program, services for LD students, study abroad, summer session for credit. ***ROTC:*** Army (b), Air Force (c).

Computers: Students can access the following: computer help desk, free student e-mail accounts, online (class) grades, online (class) registration, online (class) schedules. Campuswide network is available. 100% of college-owned or -operated housing units are wired for high-speed Internet access. Wireless service is available via entire campus.

Library: Library Learning Center.

STUDENT LIFE
Housing options: on-campus residence required through sophomore year; coed, special housing for students with disabilities. Campus housing is university owned. Freshman campus housing is guaranteed.

Activities and organizations: drama/theater group, student-run newspaper, radio station, choral group, marching band, national fraternities, national sororities.

Athletics Member NCAA. All Division III. ***Intercollegiate sports:*** baseball M, basketball M/W, cross-country running M/W, football M, gymnastics W, ice hockey M/W(c), soccer M(c)/W, softball W, tennis W, track and field M/W, volleyball M(c)/W. ***Intramural sports:*** baseball M, basketball M/W, bowling M(c)/W(c), football M/W, golf M/W, ice hockey M/W, racquetball M/W, rugby M(c)/W(c), skiing (cross-country) M(c)/W(c), skiing (downhill) M(c)/W(c), softball M/W, ultimate Frisbee M/W, volleyball M/W.

Campus security: 24-hour emergency response devices and patrols, student patrols, controlled dormitory access.

Student services: health clinic, personal/psychological counseling, legal services.

COSTS & FINANCIAL AID
Costs (2020–21) ***Tuition:*** area resident $7014 full-time, $315 per credit hour part-time; state resident $7014 full-time, $315 per credit hour part-time; nonresident $14,981 full-time, $581 per credit hour part-time. ***Required fees:*** $2449 full-time. ***Room and board:*** $6944; room only: $4400.

Financial Aid Of all full-time matriculated undergraduates who enrolled in 2019, 4,615 applied for aid, 3,120 were judged to have need, 507 had their need fully met. In 2019, 265 non-need-based awards were made. ***Average percent of need met:*** 81. ***Average financial aid package:*** $11,079. ***Average need-based loan:*** $4015. ***Average need-based gift aid:*** $6655. ***Average non-need-based aid:*** $1853. ***Average indebtedness upon graduation:*** $31,372.

APPLYING
Standardized Tests *Required:* SAT or ACT (for admission).

Options: electronic application, deferred entrance.

Application fee: $50.

Required: high school transcript. ***Required for some:*** minimum 2.8 GPA. ***Recommended:*** minimum 2.5 GPA.

Application deadlines: rolling (freshmen), rolling (out-of-state freshmen), rolling (transfers).

Notification: continuous until 9/1 (freshmen), continuous (out-of-state freshmen), continuous (transfers).

CONTACT
Dr. Pamela Holsinger-Fuchs, Executive Director of Enrollment Services, University of Wisconsin–Stout, Admissions, Bowman Hall, Menomonie, WI 54751. *Phone:* 715-232-2639. *Toll-free phone:* 800-HI-STOUT. *Fax:* 715-232-1667. *E-mail:* admissions@uwstout.edu.

University of Wisconsin–Superior

Superior, Wisconsin

http://www.uwsuper.edu/

- **State-supported** comprehensive, founded 1893, part of University of Wisconsin System
- **Suburban** 230-acre campus
- **Coed** 2,257 undergraduate students, 76% full-time, 63% women, 37% men
- **Minimally difficult** entrance level, 78% of applicants were admitted

UNDERGRAD STUDENTS

1,715 full-time, 542 part-time. 46% are from out of state; 2% Black or African American, non-Hispanic/Latino; 3% Hispanic/Latino; 1% Asian, non-Hispanic/Latino; 2% American Indian or Alaska Native, non-Hispanic/Latino; 4% Two or more races, non-Hispanic/Latino; 0.2% Race/ethnicity unknown; 9% international; 13% transferred in; 31% live on campus.

Freshmen:

Admission: 897 applied, 696 admitted, 327 enrolled. ***Average high school GPA:*** 3.2. ***Test scores:*** SAT evidence-based reading and writing scores over 500: 82%; SAT math scores over 500: 82%; ACT scores over 18: 78%; SAT evidence-based reading and writing scores over 600: 18%; SAT math scores over 600: 27%; ACT scores over 24: 23%; SAT math scores over 700: 18%; ACT scores over 30: 4%.

Retention: 64% of full-time freshmen returned.

FACULTY

Total: 224, 53% full-time, 43% with terminal degrees.

Student/faculty ratio: 14:1.

ACADEMICS

Calendar: semesters. *Degrees:* certificates, associate, bachelor's, master's, post-master's, and postbachelor's certificates.

Special study options: academic remediation for entering students, accelerated degree program, adult/continuing education programs, advanced placement credit, cooperative education, distance learning, double majors, English as a second language, external degree program, independent study, internships, off-campus study, part-time degree program, services for LD students, student-designed majors, study abroad, summer session for credit. ***ROTC:*** Air Force (c).

Unusual degree programs: 3-2 engineering with Michigan Technological University, University of Wisconsin–Madison; forestry with Michigan Technological University.

Computers: 375 computers/terminals are available on campus for general student use. Students can access the following: campus intranet, computer help desk, free student e-mail accounts, online (class) grades, online (class) registration, online (class) schedules. Campuswide network is available. 100% of college-owned or -operated housing units are wired for high-speed Internet access. Wireless service is available via entire campus.

Library: Jim Dan Hill Library.

STUDENT LIFE

Housing options: on-campus residence required through sophomore year; coed, special housing for students with disabilities. Campus housing is university owned. Freshman campus housing is guaranteed.

Activities and organizations: drama/theater group, student-run newspaper, radio station, choral group.

Athletics Member NCAA. All Division III. ***Intercollegiate sports:*** baseball M, basketball M/W, cross-country running M/W, ice hockey M/W, soccer M/W, softball W, tennis M/W, track and field M/W, volleyball W. ***Intramural sports:*** badminton M/W, baseball M(c), basketball M/W, bowling M/W, football M/W, ice hockey M(c)/W(c), racquetball M/W, riflery M/W, rock climbing M/W, soccer M/W, softball M/W, swimming and diving M/W, table tennis M/W, tennis M(c)/W(c), ultimate Frisbee M(c)/W(c), volleyball M(c)/W(c).

Campus security: 24-hour emergency response devices and patrols, student patrols, late-night transport/escort service, controlled dormitory access.

Student services: health clinic, personal/psychological counseling, women's center, veterans affairs office.

COSTS & FINANCIAL AID

Costs (2019–20) ***Tuition:*** state resident $6535 full-time; nonresident $14,108 full-time. Full-time tuition and fees vary according to course load and reciprocity agreements. Part-time tuition and fees vary according to course load and reciprocity agreements. ***Required fees:*** $1597 full-time. ***Room and board:*** $7280; room only: $4586. Room and board charges vary according to board plan and housing facility. ***Payment plan:*** installment.

Financial Aid Of all full-time matriculated undergraduates who enrolled in 2019, 1,316 applied for aid, 1,043 were judged to have need, 211 had their need fully met. In 2019, 84 non-need-based awards were made. ***Average percent of need met:*** 84. ***Average financial aid package:*** $11,230. ***Average need-based loan:*** $3405. ***Average need-based gift aid:*** $5175. ***Average non-need-based aid:*** $3401. ***Average indebtedness upon graduation:*** $31,490.

APPLYING

Standardized Tests *Required:* SAT or ACT (for admission).

Options: electronic application, early admission, deferred entrance.

Application fee: $44.

Required: high school transcript. ***Required for some:*** interview. ***Recommended:*** essay or personal statement.

Notification: continuous until 9/16 (freshmen), continuous (transfers).

CONTACT

University of Wisconsin–Superior, Belknap and Catlin, PO Box 2000, Superior, WI 54880-4500.

University of Wisconsin–Waukesha

Waukesha, Wisconsin

http://www.waukesha.uwc.edu/

CONTACT

University of Wisconsin–Waukesha, 1500 North University Drive, Waukesha, WI 53188.

University of Wisconsin–Whitewater

Whitewater, Wisconsin

http://www.uww.edu/

- **State-supported** comprehensive, founded 1868, part of University of Wisconsin System
- **Small-town** 400-acre campus with easy access to Milwaukee
- **Coed**
- **Moderately difficult** entrance level

FACULTY

Student/faculty ratio: 20:1.

ACADEMICS

Calendar: semesters. *Degrees:* associate, bachelor's, master's, and doctoral.

Library: Andersen Library. Students can reserve study rooms.

STUDENT LIFE

Housing options: on-campus residence required through sophomore year; coed, special housing for students with disabilities. Campus housing is university owned. Freshman campus housing is guaranteed.

Activities and organizations: drama/theater group, student-run newspaper, radio and television station, choral group, marching band, Adult Student Connection, Pan Hellenic Council, Sigma Alpha Lambda (Academic Honors), Cru (Faith-Related Organization), National Society of Leadership and Success, national fraternities, national sororities.

Athletics Member NCAA. All Division III.

Campus security: 24-hour emergency response devices and patrols, student patrols, late-night transport/escort service, controlled dormitory access.

Student services: health clinic, personal/psychological counseling, women's center, legal services, veterans affairs office.

COSTS & FINANCIAL AID

Costs (2019–20) ***Tuition:*** state resident $6519 full-time, $272 per credit hour part-time; nonresident $15,240 full-time, $635 per credit hour part-time. Full-time tuition and fees vary according to course load, degree level, location, and reciprocity agreements. ***Required fees:*** $1176 full-time. ***Room and board:*** $6878; room only: $4298. Room and board charges vary according to board plan and housing facility. ***Payment plans:*** installment, deferred payment.

Financial Aid Of all full-time matriculated undergraduates who enrolled in 2018, 7,327 applied for aid, 5,226 were judged to have need, 2,130 had their need fully met. 496 Federal Work-Study jobs (averaging $1083). 2,308 state and other part-time jobs (averaging $1982). In 2018, 600 non-need-based awards were made. ***Average percent of need met:*** 63. ***Average financial aid package:*** $8430. ***Average need-based loan:*** $3943. ***Average need-based gift aid:*** $6243. ***Average non-need-based aid:*** $2027. ***Average indebtedness upon graduation:*** $28,008.

APPLYING

Standardized Tests *Required:* SAT or ACT (for admission).

Options: electronic application, deferred entrance.

Application fee: $50.

Required: high school transcript. ***Recommended:*** essay or personal statement.

CONTACT

Mr. Jeremy Reed, Director of Admissions, University of Wisconsin–Whitewater, 800 West Main Street, Whitewater, WI 53190-1790. *Phone:* 262-472-1440. *E-mail:* uwwadmit@uww.edu.

Viterbo University

La Crosse, Wisconsin

http://www.viterbo.edu/

- **Independent Roman Catholic** comprehensive, founded 1890
- **Suburban** 72-acre campus
- **Coed**
- **Moderately difficult** entrance level

FACULTY

Student/faculty ratio: 12:1.

ACADEMICS

Calendar: semesters. *Degrees:* certificates, associate, bachelor's, master's, doctoral, post-master's, and postbachelor's certificates.

Library: Todd Wehr Memorial Library. *Books:* 69,288 (physical), 236 (digital/electronic); *Serial titles:* 105 (physical), 75 (digital/electronic); *Databases:* 36. Weekly public service hours: 97; study areas open 24 hours, 5–7 days a week; students can reserve study rooms.

STUDENT LIFE

Housing options: on-campus residence required for freshman year; coed. Campus housing is university owned. Freshman campus housing is guaranteed.

Activities and organizations: drama/theater group, student-run newspaper, choral group, Student Activities Board (SAB), Viterbo Student Nurses Association (VSNA), Education Club, Colleges Against Cancer (CAL), Residence Hall Association.

Athletics Member NAIA.

Campus security: 24-hour emergency response devices and patrols, late-night transport/escort service, controlled dormitory access, lighted pathways, emergency evacuation plan, self-defense education programs, security cameras.

Student services: health clinic, personal/psychological counseling, veterans affairs office.

COSTS

Costs (2019–20) ***Comprehensive fee:*** $37,945 includes full-time tuition ($27,960), mandatory fees ($690), and room and board ($9295). Part-time tuition: $825 per credit. ***College room only:*** $4125.

APPLYING

Standardized Tests *Required:* SAT or ACT (for admission).

Options: electronic application, deferred entrance.

Required: high school transcript, minimum 2.0 GPA. ***Required for some:*** essay or personal statement, interview, audition for theater and music, portfolio for art.

CONTACT

Mr. Eric Schmidt, Freshman Admission Counselor/Associate Director for Admission, Viterbo University, 900 Viterbo Drive, La Crosse, WI 54601. *Phone:* 608-796-3017. *Toll-free phone:* 800-VITERBO. *E-mail:* admission@viterbo.edu.

Wisconsin Lutheran College

Milwaukee, Wisconsin

http://www.wlc.edu/

CONTACT

Wisconsin Lutheran College, 8800 West Bluemound Road, Milwaukee, WI 53226-9942.

WYOMING

University of Wyoming

Laramie, Wyoming

http://www.uwyo.edu/

- **State-supported** university, founded 1886
- **Small-town** 835-acre campus
- **Endowment** $517.5 million
- **Coed** 9,807 undergraduate students, 85% full-time, 51% women, 49% men
- **Moderately difficult** entrance level, 96% of applicants were admitted

UNDERGRAD STUDENTS

8,332 full-time, 1,475 part-time. Students come from 50 states and territories; 60 other countries; 35% are from out of state; 1% Black or African American, non-Hispanic/Latino; 7% Hispanic/Latino; 1% Asian, non-Hispanic/Latino; 0.1% Native Hawaiian or other Pacific Islander, non-Hispanic/Latino; 0.6% American Indian or Alaska Native, non-Hispanic/Latino; 4% Two or more races, non-Hispanic/Latino; 10% Race/ethnicity unknown; 3% international; 10% transferred in; 25% live on campus.

Freshmen:

Admission: 5,326 applied, 5,112 admitted, 1,760 enrolled. ***Average high school GPA:*** 3.5. ***Test scores:*** SAT evidence-based reading and writing scores over 500: 87%; SAT math scores over 500: 86%; ACT scores over 18: 96%; SAT evidence-based reading and writing scores over 600: 47%; SAT math scores over 600: 44%; ACT scores over 24: 59%; SAT evidence-based reading and writing scores over 700: 8%; SAT math scores over 700: 9%; ACT scores over 30: 15%.

Retention: 76% of full-time freshmen returned.

FACULTY

Total: 731, 99% full-time, 85% with terminal degrees.

Student/faculty ratio: 15:1.

ACADEMICS

Calendar: semesters. *Degrees:* certificates, bachelor's, master's, doctoral, and postbachelor's certificates.

Special study options: accelerated degree program, advanced placement credit, cooperative education, distance learning, double majors, English as a second language, external degree program, honors programs, independent study, internships, off-campus study, part-time degree program, services for LD students, student-designed majors, study abroad, summer session for credit. ***ROTC:*** Army (b), Air Force (b).

Computers: 1,683 computers/terminals and 10 ports are available on campus for general student use. Students can access the following: campus intranet, computer help desk, free student e-mail accounts, online (class) grades, online (class) registration, online (class) schedules. Campuswide network is available. 100% of college-owned or -operated housing units are wired for high-speed Internet access. Wireless service is available via classrooms, computer centers, computer labs, dorm rooms, learning centers, libraries, student centers.

Library: William Robertson Coe Library plus 4 others. *Books:* 1.5 million (physical), 2.2 million (digital/electronic); *Serial titles:* 56,672 (physical), 156,775 (digital/electronic); *Databases:* 1,273. Study areas open 24 hours, 5–7 days a week; students can reserve study rooms.

STUDENT LIFE
Housing options: on-campus residence required for freshman year; coed, men-only, women-only, special housing for students with disabilities. Campus housing is university owned. Freshman campus housing is guaranteed.

Activities and organizations: drama/theater group, student-run newspaper, radio and television station, choral group, marching band, national fraternities, national sororities.

Athletics Member NCAA. All Division I except football (Division I-A). ***Intercollegiate sports:*** baseball M(c), basketball M(s)/W(s), cross-country running M(s)/W(s), equestrian sports M(c)/W(c), fencing M(c)/W(c), golf M(s)/W(s)(c), ice hockey M(c)/W(c), lacrosse M(c)/W(c), racquetball M(c)/W(c), riflery M(c)/W(c), rugby M(c)/W(c), skiing (cross-country) M(c)/W(c), skiing (downhill) W(c), soccer M(c)/W(s), softball W(c), swimming and diving M(s)/W(s), tennis M(c)/W(s), track and field M(s)/W(s), triathlon M(c)/W(c), volleyball W(s), water polo M(c), wrestling M(s). ***Intramural sports:*** badminton M/W, basketball M/W, bowling M/W, football M/W, golf M/W, racquetball M(c)/W(c), soccer M/W, softball M/W, swimming and diving M/W, table tennis M/W, tennis M/W, track and field M/W, triathlon M/W, ultimate Frisbee M/W, volleyball M/W, water polo M/W, weight lifting M/W, wrestling M/W.

Campus security: 24-hour emergency response devices and patrols, student patrols, late-night transport/escort service, controlled dormitory access.

Student services: health clinic, personal/psychological counseling, women's center, legal services, veterans affairs office.

COSTS & FINANCIAL AID
Costs (2020–21) ***One-time required fee:*** $40. ***Tuition:*** area resident $4350 full-time, $139 per credit hour part-time; state resident $4350 full-time, $139 per credit hour part-time; nonresident $18,090 full-time, $558 per credit hour part-time. Full-time tuition and fees vary according to course load, location, program, and reciprocity agreements. Part-time tuition and fees vary according to course load, location, program, and reciprocity agreements. ***Required fees:*** $1441 full-time. ***Room and board:*** $10,615; room only: $4583. Room and board charges vary according to board plan and housing facility. ***Payment plan:*** installment. ***Waivers:*** children of alumni, senior citizens, and employees or children of employees.

Financial Aid Of all full-time matriculated undergraduates who enrolled in 2018, 5,791 applied for aid, 4,067 were judged to have need, 654 had their need fully met. 250 Federal Work-Study jobs (averaging $2135). In 2018, 1714 non-need-based awards were made. ***Average percent of need met:*** 59. ***Average financial aid package:*** $10,431. ***Average need-based loan:*** $3729. ***Average need-based gift aid:*** $5185. ***Average non-need-based aid:*** $4084. ***Average indebtedness upon graduation:*** $23,444.

APPLYING
Standardized Tests *Required:* SAT or ACT (for admission).

Options: electronic application, deferred entrance.

Application fee: $40.

Required: high school transcript, minimum 3.0 GPA, pre-college curriculum, minimum ACT composite score of 21 or SAT of 980.

Application deadlines: 8/10 (freshmen), 8/10 (out-of-state freshmen), 8/10 (transfers).

Notification: continuous (freshmen), continuous (out-of-state freshmen), continuous (transfers).

CONTACT
Katie Carroll, Assistant Director of Admissions, University of Wyoming, 1000 E. University Avenue, Dept 3435, Laramie, WY 82071. *Phone:* 307-766-4261. *Toll-free phone:* 800-342-5996. *Fax:* 307-766-4042. *E-mail:* admissions@uwyo.edu.

AMERICAN SAMOA

American Samoa Community College

Pago Pago, American Samoa

http://www.amsamoa.edu/

CONTACT
Elizabeth Leuma, Admissions Officer, American Samoa Community College, PO Box 2609, Pago Pago 96799, American Samoa. *Phone:* 684-699-9155 Ext. 411. *Fax:* 684-699-1083.

GUAM

Pacific Islands University

Mangilao, Guam

http://www.piu.edu/

CONTACT
Ethel Laco, Admissions Office, Pacific Islands University, 172 Kinney's Road, Mangilao, GU 96913. *Phone:* 671-734-1812. *Fax:* 671-734-1813. *E-mail:* guamcampus@pibc.edu.

University of Guam

Mangilao, Guam

http://www.uog.edu/

- **Territory-supported** comprehensive, founded 1952
- **Suburban** 100-acre campus
- **Coed** 3,215 undergraduate students, 80% full-time, 56% women, 44% men
- **Noncompetitive** entrance level, 90% of applicants were admitted

UNDERGRAD STUDENTS
2,578 full-time, 637 part-time. Students come from 39 states and territories; 10 other countries; 0.6% are from out of state; 0.5% Black or African American, non-Hispanic/Latino; 0.7% Hispanic/Latino; 46% Asian, non-Hispanic/Latino; 46% Native Hawaiian or other Pacific Islander, non-Hispanic/Latino; 0.1% American Indian or Alaska Native, non-Hispanic/Latino; 3% Race/ethnicity unknown; 0.8% international; 4% transferred in.

Freshmen:
Admission: 503 applied, 455 admitted, 416 enrolled. ***Average high school GPA:*** 3.5.

Retention: 77% of full-time freshmen returned.

FACULTY
Total: 287, 50% full-time.

Student/faculty ratio: 16:1.

ACADEMICS
Calendar: semesters. *Degrees:* certificates, bachelor's, master's, and postbachelor's certificates.

Special study options: academic remediation for entering students, accelerated degree program, advanced placement credit, cooperative education, distance learning, double majors, English as a second language, honors programs, independent study, internships, off-campus study, part-time degree program, services for LD students, study abroad, summer session for credit. ***ROTC:*** Army (b).

Computers: 262 computers/terminals and 262 ports are available on campus for general student use. Students can access the following: campus intranet, free student e-mail accounts, online (class) grades, online (class) registration, online (class) schedules, Free Microsoft Office Suite. Campuswide network is available. 100% of college-owned or -operated housing units are wired for high-speed Internet access. Wireless service is available via classrooms, computer centers, computer labs, dorm rooms, learning centers, libraries, student centers.
Library: University of Guam Robert F. Kennedy Memorial Library. *Books:* 120,789 (physical), 232,406 (digital/electronic); *Serial titles:* 111

(physical); *Databases:* 128. Weekly public service hours: 60; study areas open 24 hours, 5–7 days a week; students can reserve study rooms.

STUDENT LIFE

Housing options: coed. Campus housing is university owned.

Activities and organizations: drama/theater group, student-run newspaper, radio station, choral group, American Marketing Association, Student Nurses Association of Guam, Social Work Student Alliance, Association of Early Childhood Education International, Public Administration and Legal Studies.

Athletics ***Intramural sports:*** basketball M/W, crew M(c)/W(c), soccer M/W, softball M(c)/W(c), volleyball M/W.

Campus security: 24-hour emergency response devices and patrols, late-night transport/escort service, Sexual Harassment Training Requirement for all Students, Faculty, Staff, and Administrators.

Student services: health clinic, personal/psychological counseling, women's center.

COSTS

Costs (2020–21) ***Tuition:*** area resident $5040 full-time, $210 per credit hour part-time; territory resident $5040 full-time, $210 per credit hour part-time; nonresident $12,096 full-time, $504 per credit hour part-time. Full-time tuition and fees vary according to course load and degree level. Part-time tuition and fees vary according to course load and degree level. ***Required fees:*** $764 full-time, $382 part-time. ***Room and board:*** $3850; room only: $2250. ***Payment plan:*** installment. ***Waivers:*** senior citizens and employees or children of employees.

APPLYING

Options: electronic application, deferred entrance.

Application fee: $52.

Required: high school transcript.

Application deadlines: 6/1 (freshmen), 6/1 (out-of-state freshmen), 6/1 (transfers).

Notification: continuous (freshmen), continuous (out-of-state freshmen), continuous (transfers).

CONTACT

Ms. Betty Jean Bailey, Records Supervisor, University of Guam, Admissions and Records Office, UOG Station, Mangilao, GU 96923. *Phone:* 671-735-2213. *Fax:* 671-735-2203. *E-mail:* admitme@triton.uog.edu.

NORTHERN MARIANA ISLANDS

Northern Marianas College

Saipan, Northern Mariana Islands

http://www.marianas.edu/

CONTACT

Ms. Leilani M. Basa-Alam, Admission Specialist, Northern Marianas College, PO Box 501250, Saipan, MP 96950-1250. *Phone:* 670-234-3690 Ext. 1539. *Fax:* 670-235-4967. *E-mail:* leilanib@nmcnet.edu.

PUERTO RICO

Albizu University - San Juan

San Juan, Puerto Rico

http://www.albizu.edu/

CONTACT

Albizu University - San Juan, 151 Tanca Street, San Juan, PR 00901.

American University of Puerto Rico - Bayamon

Bayamon, Puerto Rico

http://www.aupr.edu/

CONTACT

Ms. Keren Llanos Figueroa, Director of Admissions, American University of Puerto Rico - Bayamon, PO Box 2037, Bayamon, PR 00960-2037. *Phone:* 787-620-2040 Ext. 2020. *Fax:* 787-785-7377. *E-mail:* kllanos@aupr.edu.

American University of Puerto Rico - Manati

Manati, Puerto Rico

http://www.aupr.edu/

CONTACT

American University of Puerto Rico - Manati, Carretera Estatal #2 Km. 48.7, PO Box 1082, Manati, PR 00674-1082.

Atenas College

Manati, Puerto Rico

http://www.atenascollege.edu/

CONTACT

Atenas College, Paseo de La Atenas #101 Altos, Manati, PR 00674.

Atlantic University College

Guaynabo, Puerto Rico

http://www.atlanticu.edu/

CONTACT

Ms. Zaida Perez, Admission's Officer, Atlantic University College, PO Box 3918, Guaynabo, PR 00970. *Phone:* 787-720-1022 Ext. 13. *E-mail:* admisiones@atlanticcollege.edu.

Bayamón Central University

Bayamón, Puerto Rico

http://www.ucb.edu.pr/

- **Independent Roman Catholic** comprehensive, founded 1970
- **Urban** 55-acre campus with easy access to San Juan
- **Endowment** $1.0 million
- **Coed** 1,077 undergraduate students, 77% full-time, 66% women, 34% men
- 78% of applicants were admitted

UNDERGRAD STUDENTS

834 full-time, 243 part-time. Students come from 1 other state; 2 other countries; 99% Hispanic/Latino; 0.8% international; 5% transferred in.

Freshmen:

Admission: 231 applied, 180 admitted, 166 enrolled. ***Average high school GPA:*** 3.0.

Retention: 78% of full-time freshmen returned.

FACULTY

Total: 112, 21% full-time.

Student/faculty ratio: 17:1.

ACADEMICS

Calendar: semesters for undergraduate programs, trimesters for graduate programs. *Degrees:* certificates, associate, bachelor's, master's, post-master's, and postbachelor's certificates.

Special study options: academic remediation for entering students, accelerated degree program, cooperative education, distance learning, honors programs, part-time degree program, services for LD students, summer session for credit. ***ROTC:*** Army (c), Air Force (c).

Computers: 150 computers/terminals are available on campus for general student use. Students can access the following: computer help desk, free

student e-mail accounts, online (class) grades. Campuswide network is available. Wireless service is available via entire campus.
Library: Blibliotека Dra. Margot Arce de Vazquez plus 1 other. *Books:* 62,165 (physical), 140,545 (digital/electronic); *Serial titles:* 305 (physical), 310,109 (digital/electronic); *Databases:* 62. Weekly public service hours: 50; students can reserve study rooms.

STUDENT LIFE
Housing options: men-only, women-only. Campus housing is university owned.

Athletics ***Intercollegiate sports:*** basketball M(s)/W(s), cross-country running M(s)/W(s), swimming and diving M(s)/W(s), table tennis M(s)/W(s), track and field M(s)/W(s), volleyball M(s)/W(s). ***Intramural sports:*** basketball M/W, track and field M/W, volleyball M/W.

Campus security: 24-hour patrols.

Student services: health clinic, personal/psychological counseling, veterans affairs office.

COSTS
Costs (2020–21) ***Comprehensive fee:*** $11,984 includes full-time tuition ($5290), mandatory fees ($970), and room and board ($5724). ***College room only:*** $4500.

APPLYING
Standardized Tests *Required:* CEEB (for admission).

Options: electronic application.

Application fee: $25.

Required: high school transcript. ***Recommended:*** minimum 2.0 GPA.

Application deadlines: rolling (freshmen), rolling (transfers).

Notification: continuous (freshmen), continuous (transfers).

CONTACT
Bayamón Central University, PO Box 1725, Bayamón, PR 00960-1725. *Phone:* 787-786-3030 Ext. 2102.

Caribbean University

Bayamón, Puerto Rico

http://www.caribbean.edu/

CONTACT
Caribbean University, Box 493, Bayamón, PR 00960-0493. *Phone:* 787-780-0070 Ext. 1129.

Caribbean University–Carolina

Carolina, Puerto Rico

http://www.caribbean.edu/

CONTACT
Caribbean University–Carolina, Calle Ignacio Arzuaga #208, Carolina, PR 00985.

Caribbean University–Ponce

Ponce, Puerto Rico

http://www.caribbean.edu/

CONTACT
Caribbean University–Ponce, Ave. Ednita Nazario #1015, Ponce, PR 00716-7733.

Caribbean University–Vega Baja

Vega Baja, Puerto Rico

http://www.caribbean.edu/

CONTACT
Caribbean University–Vega Baja, Carr 671 K.M. 5, Sector El Criollo, Bo. Algarrobo, Vega Baja, PR 00964.

Centro de Estudios Multidisciplinarios

Bayamon, Puerto Rico

http://www.cemcollege.edu/

CONTACT
Centro de Estudios Multidisciplinarios, Calle Degetau #25, Bayamon, PR 00961.

Centro de Estudios Multidisciplinarios

Humacao, Puerto Rico

http://www.cemcollege.edu/

CONTACT
Centro de Estudios Multidisciplinarios, Calle Dr. Vidal #8 y #53, Humacao, PR 00791. *Phone:* 787-850-8333.

Centro de Estudios Multidisciplinarios

Mayaguez, Puerto Rico

http://www.cemcollege.edu/

CONTACT
Centro de Estudios Multidisciplinarios, Calle Cristy #56, Mayaguez, PR 00680.

Centro de Estudios Multidisciplinarios

Rio Piedras, Puerto Rico

http://www.cemcollege.edu/

CONTACT
Admissions Department, Centro de Estudios Multidisciplinarios, Calle 13 #1206, Ext. San Agustin, Rio Piedras, PR 00926. *Phone:* 787-765-4210 Ext. 115. *Toll-free phone:* 877-779-CDEM.

Colegio Universitario de San Juan

San Juan, Puerto Rico

http://www.cunisanjuan.edu/

- **City-supported** 4-year, founded 1971
- **Urban** 5-acre campus
- **Coed** 1,059 undergraduate students, 79% full-time, 60% women, 40% men
- **Noncompetitive** entrance level, 85% of applicants were admitted

UNDERGRAD STUDENTS
837 full-time, 222 part-time. 100% Hispanic/Latino; 12% transferred in.

Freshmen:
Admission: 101 applied, 86 admitted, 86 enrolled. ***Average high school GPA:*** 2.8.
Retention: 51% of full-time freshmen returned.

ACADEMICS
Calendar: semesters. *Degrees:* certificates, diplomas, associate, and bachelor's.

Special study options: academic remediation for entering students, cooperative education, English as a second language, independent study, internships, off-campus study, part-time degree program, services for LD students, summer session for credit.

Computers: 319 computers/terminals are available on campus for general student use. Students can access the following: campus intranet, free student e-mail accounts, online (class) grades, online (class) registration, Portal students. Campuswide network is available. Wireless service is available via entire campus.

Library: Access to Information Center. *Books:* 18,013 (physical), 87,751 (digital/electronic); *Serial titles:* 82,010 (digital/electronic); *Databases:* 77. Weekly public service hours: 81; students can reserve study rooms.

STUDENT LIFE
Activities and organizations: Students Coluncil.

Athletics ***Intramural sports:*** basketball M/W, volleyball M/W.

Student services: health clinic, personal/psychological counseling, veterans affairs office.

COSTS
Costs (2020–21) ***Tuition:*** area resident $2040 full-time; commonwealth resident $2040 full-time; nonresident $2040 full-time. Full-time tuition and fees vary according to course load and program. Part-time tuition and fees vary according to course load and program. ***Required fees:*** $330 full-time. ***Room and board:*** $7350. ***Payment plan:*** installment. ***Waivers:*** employees or children of employees.

APPLYING
Options: electronic application.

Application fee: $15.

Required: high school transcript, minimum 2.0 GPA, medical history. ***Required for some:*** interview.

Notification: continuous (freshmen), continuous (transfers).

CONTACT
Colegio Universitario de San Juan, Jose R. Oliver Street, Hato Rey, PR 00918. *Phone:* 787-787-480-2402.

Columbia Central University

Caguas, Puerto Rico

http://www.columbiacentral.edu/

- **Proprietary** comprehensive, founded 1966
- **Urban** 6-acre campus with easy access to San Juan
- **Coed**
- **Noncompetitive** entrance level

FACULTY
Student/faculty ratio: 17:1.

ACADEMICS
Calendar: semesters. *Degrees:* certificates, associate, bachelor's, and master's.
Library: Efrain Sola Bezares Library plus 1 other. *Books:* 9,494 (physical), 759 (digital/electronic); *Serial titles:* 19 (physical), 13,966 (digital/electronic); *Databases:* 26. Weekly public service hours: 81; students can reserve study rooms.

STUDENT LIFE
Campus security: 24-hour patrols.

Student services: personal/psychological counseling.

COSTS & FINANCIAL AID
Costs (2019–20) ***Comprehensive fee:*** $16,707 includes full-time tuition ($9630), mandatory fees ($180), and room and board ($6897). Full-time tuition and fees vary according to program. Part-time tuition: $1605 per term. Part-time tuition and fees vary according to program. ***Required fees:*** $60 per term part-time.

Financial Aid Of all full-time matriculated undergraduates who enrolled in 2008, 974 applied for aid, 818 were judged to have need. 61 Federal Work-Study jobs (averaging $982). ***Average percent of need met:*** 11. ***Average financial aid package:*** $4035.

APPLYING
Options: electronic application.

Application fee: $10.

Required: high school transcript, minimum 2.0 GPA. ***Required for some:*** essay or personal statement, 3 letters of recommendation, interview, Immunization Certificate for candidates who are under 21.

CONTACT
Mrs. Brendaliz Zayas, Vice President of Student Affairs and Enrollment, Columbia Central University, PO Box 8517, Caguas, PR 00726, Puerto Rico. *Phone:* 787-743-4041 Ext. 224. *Fax:* 787-744-7031. *E-mail:* bzayas@columbiacentral.edu.

Columbia Central University

Yauco, Puerto Rico

http://www.columbiacentral.edu/

- **Proprietary** 4-year, founded 1966
- **Urban** campus with easy access to Ponce, Mayaguez
- **Coed**
- **Minimally difficult** entrance level

FACULTY
Student/faculty ratio: 10:1.

ACADEMICS
Calendar: trimesters. *Degrees:* certificates, associate, and bachelor's.
Library: Centro de Informacion y Recursos Integrados (CIRI). *Books:* 2,362 (physical), 759 (digital/electronic); *Serial titles:* 547 (physical), 231,831 (digital/electronic); *Databases:* 26. Weekly public service hours: 64; students can reserve study rooms.

STUDENT LIFE
Housing options: college housing not available.
Activities and organizations: Student Association Pharmacy Technicians, Student Association Graphic Design, Student Council.

Campus security: trained security personnel during hours of operation.

Student services: personal/psychological counseling.

APPLYING
Options: electronic application, deferred entrance.

Application fee: $10.

Required: high school transcript, minimum 2.0 GPA.

CONTACT
Mrs. Carmen Ivette Pabon, Admissions Coordinator, Columbia Central University, PO Box 3062, Yauco, PR 00698. *Phone:* 787-856-0945 Ext. 117. *Fax:* 787-267-0994. *E-mail:* cipabon@columbiacentral.edu.

Conservatorio de Musica de Puerto Rico

San Juan, Puerto Rico

http://www.cmpr.edu/

CONTACT
Mrs. Ana Marta Arraiza, Admission Coordinator, Conservatorio de Musica de Puerto Rico, 951 Ponce de Leon Avenue, San Juan, PR 00907-3373. *Phone:* 787-751-0160 Ext. 275. *Fax:* 787-758-9511. *E-mail:* aarraiza2@cmpr.gobierno.pr.

Dewey University–Carolina

Carolina, Puerto Rico

http://www.dewey.edu/

CONTACT
Dewey University–Carolina, Carr. #3, Km. 11, Parque Industrial de Carolina, Lote 7, Carolina, PR 00986.

Dewey University–Hato Rey

Hato Rey, Puerto Rico

http://www.dewey.edu/

CONTACT
Dewey University–Hato Rey, 427 Avenida Barbosa, Hato Rey, PR 00923.

Dewey University–Manati

Manati, Puerto Rico

http://www.dewey.edu/

CONTACT
Dewey University–Manati, Carr. 604, Km. 49.1 Barrio Tierras Nuevas, Salientes, Manati, PR 00674. *Toll-free phone:* 866-773-3939.

EDIC College

Caguas, Puerto Rico

http://www.ediccollege.edu/

CONTACT
EDIC College, Ave. Rafael Cordero Calle Génova Urb. Caguas Norte, Caguas, PR 00726.

EDP University of Puerto Rico

Hato Rey, Puerto Rico

http://www.edpuniversity.edu/

CONTACT
Mr. Oscar Morales, Dean of Student Affairs, EDP University of Puerto Rico, Avenue Ponce de Leon, #560, Hato Rey, PR 00918, Puerto Rico. *Phone:* 787-765-3560 Ext. 2272. *Fax:* 787-777-0024. *E-mail:* oscarmorales@edpuniversity.edu.

EDP University of Puerto Rico–San Sebastian

San Sebastian, Puerto Rico

http://www.edpuniversity.edu/

- **Independent** comprehensive, founded 1976
- **Rural** campus
- **Coed** 1,066 undergraduate students, 67% full-time, 67% women, 33% men
- **Minimally difficult** entrance level

UNDERGRAD STUDENTS
715 full-time, 351 part-time. 100% Hispanic/Latino; 0.1% international.

Freshmen:
Admission: 145 enrolled. ***Average high school GPA:*** 3.0.
Retention: 80% of full-time freshmen returned.

FACULTY
Total: 113, 30% full-time, 13% with terminal degrees.
Student/faculty ratio: 31:1.

ACADEMICS
Calendar: semesters. *Degrees:* associate, bachelor's, and master's.
Special study options: academic remediation for entering students, accelerated degree program, adult/continuing education programs, cooperative education, distance learning, external degree program, independent study, internships, services for LD students, summer session for credit.
Computers: 194 computers/terminals are available on campus for general student use. Students can access the following: computer help desk, free student e-mail accounts, online (class) grades, online (class) registration, online (class) schedules. Campuswide network is available. Wireless service is available via entire campus.
Library: Juan S. Robles Library. *Books:* 11,880 (physical), 222,080 (digital/electronic); *Serial titles:* 8 (physical), 25,590 (digital/electronic); *Databases:* 14. Weekly public service hours: 85; students can reserve study rooms.

STUDENT LIFE
Housing options: college housing not available.
Activities and organizations: student-run radio station, Nursing, Physical Therapy, Information Systems (SITA), Pharmacy, Digital Fashion Design.
Campus security: private security.
Student services: personal/psychological counseling.

COSTS & FINANCIAL AID
Costs (2019–20) ***Tuition:*** $5280 full-time, $176 per credit hour part-time. Full-time tuition and fees vary according to course load and program. Part-time tuition and fees vary according to course load and program. ***Required fees:*** $920 full-time, $4600 per term part-time. ***Payment plan:*** installment. ***Waivers:*** employees or children of employees.
Financial Aid Of all full-time matriculated undergraduates who enrolled in 2012, 1,098 applied for aid, 1,097 were judged to have need. 32 Federal Work-Study jobs (averaging $1714). ***Average percent of need met:*** 92. ***Average financial aid package:*** $5000. ***Average need-based loan:*** $2601. ***Average need-based gift aid:*** $4545.

APPLYING
Standardized Tests *Required:* College Board exam or institutional entrance test (for admission).
Application fee: $15.
Required: high school transcript, minimum 1.6 GPA. ***Required for some:*** essay or personal statement, minimum 2.5 GPA, interview.
Application deadlines: rolling (freshmen), rolling (out-of-state freshmen), rolling (transfers).

CONTACT
EDP University of Puerto Rico–San Sebastian, Avenue Betances #49, San Sebastian, PR 00685. *Phone:* 787-896-2252 Ext. 3300.

Escuela de Artes Plasticas y Diseño de Puerto Rico

San Juan, Puerto Rico

http://www.eap.edu/

- **Commonwealth-supported** 4-year, founded 1966
- **Urban** campus
- **Endowment** $2.5 million
- **Coed**
- **Moderately difficult** entrance level

FACULTY
Student/faculty ratio: 12:1.

ACADEMICS
Calendar: semesters 3 semesters each calendar year; participant in Year Round Pell. *Degree:* bachelor's.
Library: Francisco Oller Library. *Books:* 23,366 (physical); *Serial titles:* 449 (digital/electronic); *Databases:* 3. Weekly public service hours: 59.

STUDENT LIFE
Activities and organizations: Student government, CINEAP, Arte-Sanacion.
Campus security: 24-hour emergency response devices and patrols, security cameras.
Student services: personal/psychological counseling.

COSTS & FINANCIAL AID
Costs (2019–20) ***Tuition:*** area resident $2860 full-time, $90 per credit hour part-time; commonwealth resident $2860 full-time, $90 per credit hour part-time; nonresident $5020 full-time, $180 per credit hour part-time. Full-time tuition and fees vary according to course load. ***Required fees:*** $602 full-time, $489 per year part-time. ***Room and board:*** $8144.
Financial Aid Of all full-time matriculated undergraduates who enrolled in 2007, 276 applied for aid, 276 were judged to have need. 10 Federal Work-Study jobs (averaging $1850). ***Average percent of need met:*** 82. ***Financial aid deadline:*** 5/25.

APPLYING
Standardized Tests *Recommended:* SAT (for admission).
Application fee: $25.
Required: high school transcript, minimum 2.0 GPA, portfolio or seminar.

CONTACT
Alicea Denizard, Officer of Admissions, Escuela de Artes Plasticas y Diseño de Puerto Rico, PO Box 902112, San Juan, PR 00902-1112. *Phone:* 787-725-8120 Ext. 373. *E-mail:* admisiones@eap.edu.

Humacao Community College

Humacao, Puerto Rico

http://www.hccpr.edu/

CONTACT
Mrs. Arlene Osorio, Recruitment and Promotion Official, Humacao Community College, PO Box 9139, Humacao, PR 00792, Puerto Rico. *Phone:* 787-852-1430 Ext. 225. *Fax:* 787-850-1577. *E-mail:* arlene.osorio@hccpr.edu.

Inter American University of Puerto Rico, Aguadilla Campus

Aguadilla, Puerto Rico

http://www.aguadilla.inter.edu/

- **Independent** comprehensive, founded 1957, part of Inter American University of Puerto Rico
- **Small-town** 50-acre campus
- **Endowment** $239.0 million
- **Coed** 3,667 undergraduate students, 86% full-time, 58% women, 42% men
- **Moderately difficult** entrance level

UNDERGRAD STUDENTS
3,141 full-time, 526 part-time. Students come from 23 states and territories; 1 other country; 2% are from out of state; 0.1% Black or African American, non-Hispanic/Latino; 100% Hispanic/Latino; 0.1% American Indian or Alaska Native, non-Hispanic/Latino; 5% transferred in.

Freshmen:
Admission: 1,748 applied, 797 enrolled. ***Average high school GPA:*** 3.1.

FACULTY
Total: 228, 35% full-time, 100% with terminal degrees.

Student/faculty ratio: 30:1.

ACADEMICS
Calendar: semesters. *Degrees:* certificates, diplomas, bachelor's, and master's.

Special study options: academic remediation for entering students, accelerated degree program, adult/continuing education programs, advanced placement credit, cooperative education, distance learning, double majors, English as a second language, external degree program, honors programs, independent study, internships, part-time degree program, services for LD students, study abroad, summer session for credit. ***ROTC:*** Army (b), Air Force (b).

Computers: 861 computers/terminals are available on campus for general student use. Students can access the following: campus intranet, free student e-mail accounts, online (class) grades, online (class) registration, online (class) schedules. Campuswide network is available. Wireless service is available via entire campus.
Library: Manuel Mendez Ballester Information Access Center. *Books:* 62,162 (physical), 249,610 (digital/electronic); *Serial titles:* 100 (physical); *Databases:* 75. Weekly public service hours: 80; students can reserve study rooms.

STUDENT LIFE
Housing options: college housing not available.

Activities and organizations: drama/theater group, student-run newspaper, choral group, Criminal Justice Association, Microbiot Science Association, Social Workers Association, Nursing Association, Psychology Association.

Athletics *Intercollegiate sports:* baseball M(s), basketball M(s)/W(s), cross-country running M(s)/W(s), soccer M(s)/W(s), softball M(s)/W(s), swimming and diving M(s)/W(s), table tennis M(s)/W(s), tennis M(s)/W(s), track and field M(s)/W(s), volleyball M(s)/W(s), weight lifting M(s)/W(s), wrestling M(s)/W(s). ***Intramural sports:*** basketball M/W, cross-country running M/W, soccer M/W, softball M/W, table tennis M/W, tennis M/W, track and field M/W, volleyball M/W, weight lifting M/W.

Campus security: 24-hour emergency response devices and patrols.

Student services: personal/psychological counseling, veterans affairs office.

COSTS & FINANCIAL AID
Costs (2019–20) *Tuition:* $4560 full-time, $190 per credit part-time. Full-time tuition and fees vary according to course load. Part-time tuition and fees vary according to course load. ***Required fees:*** $694 full-time, $283 per semester part-time. ***Payment plan:*** deferred payment. ***Waivers:*** employees or children of employees.

Financial Aid Of all full-time matriculated undergraduates who enrolled in 2018, 3,180 applied for aid, 3,160 were judged to have need, 1 had their need fully met. ***Average percent of need met:*** 13. ***Average need-based gift aid:*** $2933.

APPLYING
Standardized Tests *Required:* SAT or ACT (for admission), PAA (for admission).

Options: electronic application.

CONTACT
Mrs. Daisy Irizarry, Administrative Assistant, Inter American University of Puerto Rico, Aguadilla Campus, PO Box 20,000, Road 459 Intersection 463, Aguadilla, PR 00605. *Phone:* 787-891-0925 Ext. 2181. *Fax:* 787-882-3020.

Inter American University of Puerto Rico, Arecibo Campus

Arecibo, Puerto Rico

http://www.arecibo.inter.edu/

CONTACT
Ms. Provi Montalvo, Admission Director, Inter American University of Puerto Rico, Arecibo Campus, PO Box 4050, Arecibo, PR 00614-4050. *Phone:* 787-878-5475. *Fax:* 787-880-1624. *E-mail:* pmontalvo@arecibo.inter.edu.

Inter American University of Puerto Rico, Barranquitas Campus

Barranquitas, Puerto Rico

http://www.br.inter.edu/

- **Independent** comprehensive, founded 1957, part of Inter American University of Puerto Rico
- **Suburban** 32-acre campus with easy access to 35 miles from San Juan
- **Endowment** $252.2 million
- **Coed** 1,514 undergraduate students, 86% full-time, 66% women, 34% men
- 90% of applicants were admitted

UNDERGRAD STUDENTS
1,295 full-time, 219 part-time. 100% Hispanic/Latino; 0.1% American Indian or Alaska Native, non-Hispanic/Latino; 2% transferred in.

Freshmen:
Admission: 1,166 applied, 1,052 admitted, 433 enrolled.
Retention: 71% of full-time freshmen returned.

FACULTY
Total: 134, 22% full-time, 20% with terminal degrees.

Student/faculty ratio: 20:1.

ACADEMICS
Calendar: semesters. *Degrees:* certificates, associate, bachelor's, master's, and doctoral.

Special study options: adult/continuing education programs, cooperative education, distance learning, English as a second language, external degree program, honors programs, off-campus study, part-time degree program, services for LD students, summer session for credit. ***ROTC:*** Army (c).

Computers: 378 computers/terminals and 378 ports are available on campus for general student use. Students can access the following: campus intranet, computer help desk, free student e-mail accounts, online (class) grades, online (class) registration, online (class) schedules. Campuswide network is available. Wireless service is available via entire campus.
Library: Centro de Acceso a la Informacion (CAI), Recinto de Barranquitas. *Books:* 40,386 (physical), 275,704 (digital/electronic); *Serial titles:* 60 (physical), 58,313 (digital/electronic); *Databases:* 83. Weekly public service hours: 72; students can reserve study rooms.

STUDENT LIFE
Activities and organizations: Nursing Student Organization, Sport Organization, Culinary Arts Student Organization, Criminal Justice Student Organization.

Athletics ***Intercollegiate sports:*** baseball M(s), basketball M(s), cross-country running M/W, softball M/W, tennis M/W, volleyball M(s)/W(s). ***Intramural sports:*** basketball M, cross-country running M/W, softball M/W, table tennis M/W, tennis M/W, track and field M/W, volleyball M/W, weight lifting M/W.

Campus security: 24-hour emergency response devices and patrols.

Student services: health clinic, veterans affairs office.

COSTS

Costs (2020–21) ***Tuition:*** $5700 full-time, $3040 per year part-time. Full-time tuition and fees vary according to course load, degree level, and program. Part-time tuition and fees vary according to course load, degree level, and program. ***Required fees:*** $732 full-time, $694 per year part-time, $347 per term part-time. ***Payment plan:*** deferred payment. ***Waivers:*** minority students and employees or children of employees.

APPLYING

Standardized Tests *Required:* CEEB (for admission). *Required for some:* SAT or ACT (for admission). *Recommended:* SAT (for admission), SAT Subject Tests (for admission).

Options: electronic application.

Required: high school transcript, interview, statement of good standing from prior institution(s).

Application deadlines: rolling (freshmen), rolling (transfers).

CONTACT

Mrs. Lydia Arce, Registration Manager, Inter American University of Puerto Rico, Barranquitas Campus, PO Box 517, Barranquitas, PR 00794. *Phone:* 787-857-3600 Ext. 2054. *E-mail:* larce@br.inter.edu.

Inter American University of Puerto Rico, Bayamón Campus

Bayamón, Puerto Rico

http://bayamon.inter.edu/

- **Independent** comprehensive, founded 1912, part of Inter American University of Puerto Rico
- **Suburban** 51-acre campus with easy access to San Juan
- **Endowment** $252.2 million
- **Coed** 4,396 undergraduate students, 88% full-time, 43% women, 57% men
- 27% of applicants were admitted

UNDERGRAD STUDENTS

3,856 full-time, 540 part-time. Students come from 12 states and territories; 5 other countries; 0.6% are from out of state; 0.2% Black or African American, non-Hispanic/Latino; 99% Hispanic/Latino; 0.4% American Indian or Alaska Native, non-Hispanic/Latino; 4% transferred in; 1% live on campus.

Freshmen:

Admission: 3,639 applied, 976 admitted, 876 enrolled. ***Average high school GPA:*** 3.3.

Retention: 76% of full-time freshmen returned.

FACULTY

Total: 248, 36% full-time, 36% with terminal degrees.

Student/faculty ratio: 29:1.

ACADEMICS

Calendar: semesters. *Degrees:* certificates, associate, bachelor's, and master's.

Special study options: accelerated degree program, adult/continuing education programs, advanced placement credit, cooperative education, distance learning, external degree program, honors programs, independent study, internships, part-time degree program, services for LD students, study abroad, summer session for credit. ***ROTC:*** Army (c).

Computers: 730 computers/terminals and 4,500 ports are available on campus for general student use. Students can access the following: computer help desk, free student e-mail accounts, online (class) grades, online (class) registration. Campuswide network is available. Wireless service is available via entire campus.

Library: Centro de Acceso a la Informacion plus 1 other. *Books:* 27,751 (physical), 250,984 (digital/electronic); *Serial titles:* 104 (physical), 2 (digital/electronic); *Databases:* 67. Weekly public service hours: 79; students can reserve study rooms.

STUDENT LIFE

Housing options: men-only, women-only. Campus housing is university owned.

Activities and organizations: drama/theater group, student-run radio station, choral group, Asociación de Estudiantes de Enfermería (AEE), Aeronautical Student Association (ASA), Student Chapter of the American Society of Mechanical Engineers (ASME), Sociedad Unidos por la Ciencia (SCUC), Student Chapter of the Society of the Women Engineers (SWE).

Athletics ***Intercollegiate sports:*** baseball M(s), basketball M(s)/W(s), softball M(s)/W(s), swimming and diving M(s)/W(s), table tennis M(s)/W(s), track and field M(s)/W(s), volleyball M(s)/W(s), weight lifting M(s). ***Intramural sports:*** basketball M/W, softball M/W, swimming and diving M/W, table tennis M/W, tennis M/W, track and field M/W, volleyball M/W, weight lifting M.

Campus security: 24-hour patrols, controlled dormitory access.

Student services: health clinic, personal/psychological counseling, veterans affairs office.

COSTS & FINANCIAL AID

Costs (2020–21) ***Comprehensive fee:*** $14,543 includes full-time tuition ($4560), mandatory fees ($1452), and room and board ($8531). Full-time tuition and fees vary according to course level, course load, degree level, and program. Part-time tuition: $190 per credit. Part-time tuition and fees vary according to course level, course load, degree level, and program. ***Required fees:*** $190 per credit part-time, $1054 per year part-time. ***College room only:*** $5342. ***Payment plan:*** deferred payment. ***Waivers:*** employees or children of employees.

Financial Aid Of all full-time matriculated undergraduates who enrolled in 2018, 2,578 applied for aid, 2,539 were judged to have need. ***Average percent of need met:*** 26. ***Average financial aid package:*** $3917. ***Average need-based loan:*** $2152. ***Average need-based gift aid:*** $3544.

APPLYING

Standardized Tests *Required:* PAA (for admission). *Required for some:* SAT (for admission), SAT Subject Tests (for admission).

Options: electronic application, early admission, deferred entrance.

Required: high school transcript, minimum 2.0 GPA. ***Required for some:*** minimum 2.5 GPA for engineering program.

Notification: continuous (freshmen), continuous (transfers).

CONTACT

Mrs. Aurelis Baez, Director of Students Services, Inter American University of Puerto Rico, Bayamón Campus, 500 Dr. John Will Harris Road, Bayamon, PR 00957-6257. *Phone:* 787-279-1912 Ext. 2017. *Fax:* 787-279-205. *E-mail:* abaez@bayamon.inter.edu.

Inter American University of Puerto Rico, Fajardo Campus

Fajardo, Puerto Rico

http://www.fajardo.inter.edu/

- **Independent** comprehensive, founded 1965, part of Inter American University of Puerto Rico
- **Small-town** 11-acre campus with easy access to San Juan
- **Endowment** $4.3 million
- **Coed**
- **Moderately difficult** entrance level

FACULTY

Student/faculty ratio: 11:1.

ACADEMICS

Calendar: semesters. *Degrees:* certificates, associate, bachelor's, and master's.

Library: Antonio S. Belaval Library plus 1 other. *Books:* 47,697 (physical), 262,990 (digital/electronic); *Databases:* 36. Students can reserve study rooms.

STUDENT LIFE

Housing options: college housing not available.

Activities and organizations: choral group, Future Teachers Association, Criminal Justice Student Association, Honor Program Association, Computer Science Association, Social Work Association.

Campus security: 24-hour patrols.

Student services: personal/psychological counseling.

COSTS

Costs (2019–20) ***Tuition:*** $187 per credit hour part-time.

APPLYING

Standardized Tests *Required:* College Board exam (for admission).

Options: electronic application, early admission, deferred entrance.

Required: high school transcript. ***Required for some:*** interview.

CONTACT

Ms. Ghisita M. Garcia, Administrative Assistant II, Inter American University of Puerto Rico, Fajardo Campus, Call Box 70003, Fajardo, PR 00738-7003. *Phone:* 787-863-2390 Ext. 2210. *Fax:* 787-860-3470. *E-mail:* ghisita.garcia@fajardo.inter.edu.

Inter American University of Puerto Rico, Guayama Campus

Guayama, Puerto Rico

http://www.guayama.inter.edu/

- **Independent** comprehensive, founded 1958, part of Inter American University of Puerto Rico
- **Small-town** 50-acre campus with easy access to San Juan
- **Coed**
- **Moderately difficult** entrance level

FACULTY

Student/faculty ratio: 20:1.

ACADEMICS

Calendar: semesters. *Degrees:* certificates, associate, bachelor's, and master's.

Library: Information Access Center. Weekly public service hours: 60.

STUDENT LIFE

Housing options: college housing not available.

Activities and organizations: student-run radio station, Natural Science and Technology, Nursing Student Association, Office Professionals, Medical Billers Organization, Pharmacy Technicians.

Campus security: 24-hour patrols.

Student services: health clinic, personal/psychological counseling, veterans affairs office.

FINANCIAL AID

Financial Aid Of all full-time matriculated undergraduates who enrolled in 2015, 1,039 applied for aid, 1,036 were judged to have need, 1 had their need fully met. ***Average percent of need met:*** 29. ***Average financial aid package:*** $4163. ***Average need-based loan:*** $2279. ***Average need-based gift aid:*** $3301.

APPLYING

Standardized Tests *Required:* PAA (for admission). *Recommended:* SAT (for admission).

Options: electronic application.

Required: high school transcript, minimum 2.0 GPA. ***Required for some:*** interview.

CONTACT

Mrs. Laura E. Ferrer, Director of Admissions, Inter American University of Puerto Rico, Guayama Campus, Call Box 10004, Guayama, PR 00785. *Phone:* 787-864-2222 Ext. 2220. *Fax:* 787-864-8232. *E-mail:* laura.ferrer@guayama.inter.edu.

Inter American University of Puerto Rico, Metropolitan Campus

San Juan, Puerto Rico

http://metro.inter.edu/

- **Independent** comprehensive, founded 1960, part of Inter American University of Puerto Rico
- **Urban** campus with easy access to San Juan
- **Endowment** $252.2 million
- **Coed** 5,508 undergraduate students, 79% full-time, 57% women, 43% men
- **Moderately difficult** entrance level, 26% of applicants were admitted

UNDERGRAD STUDENTS

4,367 full-time, 1,141 part-time. 0.6% Black or African American, non-Hispanic/Latino; 98% Hispanic/Latino; 0.1% Asian, non-Hispanic/Latino; 0.3% American Indian or Alaska Native, non-Hispanic/Latino; 8% transferred in.

Freshmen:

Admission: 3,136 applied, 817 admitted, 668 enrolled.

Retention: 74% of full-time freshmen returned.

FACULTY

Total: 466, 39% full-time, 57% with terminal degrees.

ACADEMICS

Calendar: trimesters. *Degrees:* certificates, associate, bachelor's, master's, doctoral, post-master's, and postbachelor's certificates.

Special study options: accelerated degree program, adult/continuing education programs, cooperative education, distance learning, English as a second language, external degree program, honors programs, independent study, internships, part-time degree program, services for LD students, study abroad, summer session for credit. ***ROTC:*** Army (c), Navy (c), Air Force (c).

Computers: 637 computers/terminals are available on campus for general student use. Students can access the following: campus intranet, computer help desk, free student e-mail accounts, online (class) grades, online (class) registration, online (class) schedules. Campuswide network is available. Wireless service is available via classrooms, computer centers, computer labs, learning centers, libraries, student centers.

Library: Centro de Acceso a la Informacion plus 1 other. *Books:* 120,253 (physical), 160,731 (digital/electronic); *Serial titles:* 822 (physical); *Databases:* 53. Students can reserve study rooms.

STUDENT LIFE

Housing options: college housing not available.

Activities and organizations: drama/theater group, student-run newspaper, choral group, International Entrepreneurship, Club Rotaract, Roots and Shoots Inter Metro, Chemical Students Association, Biomedical Students Association.

Athletics ***Intercollegiate sports:*** baseball M, basketball M/W, soccer M, softball W, table tennis M/W, tennis M/W, track and field M/W, volleyball M/W, weight lifting M/W. ***Intramural sports:*** basketball M/W, softball M, table tennis M/W, track and field M/W, volleyball M/W, weight lifting M/W.

Campus security: 24-hour emergency response devices and patrols, Video Security System.

Student services: personal/psychological counseling, women's center, veterans affairs office.

COSTS & FINANCIAL AID

Costs (2019–20) ***Tuition:*** $6840 full-time, $190 per credit part-time. ***Required fees:*** $1956 full-time, $248 per term part-time. ***Payment plan:*** deferred payment. ***Waivers:*** employees or children of employees.

Financial Aid Of all full-time matriculated undergraduates who enrolled in 1999, 4,328 applied for aid, 3,935 were judged to have need, 29 had their need fully met. ***Average percent of need met:*** 11. ***Average financial aid package:*** $2144. ***Average need-based loan:*** $1149. ***Average need-based gift aid:*** $1617. ***Financial aid deadline:*** 4/30.

APPLYING

Standardized Tests *Required:* CEEB (for admission). *Required for some:* SAT or ACT (for admission).

Options: electronic application.

Required: high school transcript, minimum 2.0 GPA.

Application deadlines: 5/15 (freshmen), 5/15 (transfers).

CONTACT
Inter American University of Puerto Rico, Metropolitan Campus, PO Box 191293, San Juan, PR 00919-1293. *Phone:* 787-250-1912 Ext. 2204.

Inter American University of Puerto Rico, Ponce Campus

Mercedita, Puerto Rico

http://www.ponce.inter.edu/

CONTACT
Mr. Franco Diaz, Admissions Officer, Inter American University of Puerto Rico, Ponce Campus, 104 Turpo Industrial Park, Road #1, Mercedita, PR 00715-1602. *Phone:* 787-284-1912 Ext. 2025. *Fax:* 787-841-0103. *E-mail:* fidiaz@ponce.inter.edu.

Inter American University of Puerto Rico, San Germán Campus

San Germán, Puerto Rico

http://www.sg.inter.edu/

- **Independent** university, founded 1912, part of Inter American University of Puerto Rico
- **Small-town** 289-acre campus with easy access to Ponce, Aguadilla, Mayaguez
- **Endowment** $252.2 million
- **Coed** 3,766 undergraduate students, 89% full-time, 53% women, 47% men
- **Moderately difficult** entrance level, 44% of applicants were admitted

UNDERGRAD STUDENTS
3,337 full-time, 429 part-time. Students come from 5 other countries; 0.4% are from out of state; 0.2% Black or African American, non-Hispanic/Latino; 99% Hispanic/Latino; 0.1% American Indian or Alaska Native, non-Hispanic/Latino; 3% transferred in; 7% live on campus.

Freshmen:
Admission: 1,929 applied, 844 admitted, 825 enrolled. ***Average high school GPA:*** 3.3.

Retention: 80% of full-time freshmen returned.

FACULTY
Total: 296, 32% full-time, 45% with terminal degrees.

Student/faculty ratio: 24:1.

ACADEMICS
Calendar: semesters. *Degrees:* certificates, associate, bachelor's, master's, doctoral, and postbachelor's certificates.

Special study options: academic remediation for entering students, accelerated degree program, adult/continuing education programs, advanced placement credit, cooperative education, distance learning, double majors, English as a second language, external degree program, honors programs, independent study, internships, off-campus study, part-time degree program, services for LD students, summer session for credit. ***ROTC:*** Army (c), Navy (c), Air Force (c).

Computers: 950 computers/terminals are available on campus for general student use. Students can access the following: campus intranet, computer help desk, free student e-mail accounts, online (class) grades, online (class) registration, online (class) schedules. Campuswide network is available. Wireless service is available via entire campus.

Library: Juan Cancio Ortiz Library. *Books:* 125,151 (physical), 3,850 (digital/electronic); *Serial titles:* 154 (physical), 571,242 (digital/electronic); *Databases:* 86. Weekly public service hours: 69.

STUDENT LIFE
Housing options: men-only, women-only. Campus housing is university owned.

Activities and organizations: choral group, Tomorrows Leaders Association, Business Professionals of America, Sociedad de Honor en Biologia Beta Beta Beta (TriBeta), Asociacion Estudiantes de Enfermería, Asociacion de Estudiantes del Programa de Honor, national fraternities.

Athletics ***Intercollegiate sports:*** baseball M(s), basketball M(s)/W(s), cross-country running M(s)/W(s), sand volleyball M/W, soccer M/W, softball W, swimming and diving M/W, table tennis M(s)/W(s), tennis M(s)/W(s), track and field M(s)/W(s), volleyball M(s)/W(s), weight lifting M(s)/W(s), wrestling M. ***Intramural sports:*** baseball M, basketball M/W, cheerleading M/W, cross-country running M/W, softball M/W, table tennis M/W, tennis M/W, track and field M/W, volleyball M/W, weight lifting M/W.

Campus security: 24-hour patrols.

Student services: health clinic, personal/psychological counseling.

COSTS & FINANCIAL AID
Costs (2019–20) ***Comprehensive fee:*** $10,896 includes full-time tuition ($5700), mandatory fees ($732), and room and board ($4464). Full-time tuition and fees vary according to degree level. Part-time tuition: $190 per credit. Part-time tuition and fees vary according to degree level. ***Required fees:*** $190 per credit part-time, $732 per year part-time. ***College room only:*** $2400. Room and board charges vary according to board plan and housing facility. ***Payment plan:*** installment. ***Waivers:*** employees or children of employees.

Financial Aid Of all full-time matriculated undergraduates who enrolled in 2009, 2,797 applied for aid, 2,755 were judged to have need, 4 had their need fully met. ***Average percent of need met:*** 12. ***Average financial aid package:*** $2009. ***Average need-based loan:*** $3080. ***Average need-based gift aid:*** $642.

APPLYING
Standardized Tests *Required:* CEEB (for admission). *Required for some:* SAT or ACT (for admission).

Options: electronic application, early admission.

Required: high school transcript, medical history, vaccination. ***Required for some:*** 1 letter of recommendation, interview. ***Recommended:*** essay or personal statement, minimum 2.0 GPA.

Notification: continuous (freshmen), continuous (transfers).

CONTACT
Prof. Mildred Camacho, Director of Admissions, Inter American University of Puerto Rico, San Germán Campus, PO Box 5100, San German, PR 00683-5008. *Phone:* 787-264-1912 Ext. 7283. *Toll-free phone:* 800-981-8075. *Fax:* 787-892-7020. *E-mail:* milcama@intersg.edu.

National University College

Arecibo, Puerto Rico

http://www.nuc.edu/

CONTACT
National University College, Calle Manuel Pérez Avilés, Avenida Víctor Rojas, Arecibo, PR 00612.

National University College

Bayamón, Puerto Rico

http://www.nuc.edu/

CONTACT
Admissions, National University College, PO Box 2036, National College Plaza Building, Bayamón, PR 00960. *Toll-free phone:* 800-780-5134.

National University College

Caguas, Puerto Rico

http://www.nuc.edu/

CONTACT
National University College, 190 Avenida Gautier Benitez Esquina Avenida Federico Degatau, Caguas, PR 00725. *Toll-free phone:* 800-780-5134.

National University College

Ponce, Puerto Rico

http://www.nuc.edu/

CONTACT
National University College, PO Box 801243, Ponce, PR 00716.

National University College

Rio Grande, Puerto Rico

http://www.nuc.edu/

CONTACT
National University College, Carretera #3 Km. 22.1, Bo. Ciénaga Baja, Rio Grande, PR 00745. *Toll-free phone:* 800-981-0812.

Polytechnic University of Puerto Rico

Hato Rey, Puerto Rico

http://www.pupr.edu/

- **Independent** comprehensive, founded 1966
- **Urban** 10-acre campus with easy access to San Juan
- **Endowment** $16.1 million
- **Coed** 3,689 undergraduate students, 48% full-time, 24% women, 76% men
- **Minimally difficult** entrance level, 86% of applicants were admitted

UNDERGRAD STUDENTS
1,788 full-time, 1,901 part-time. Students come from 7 states and territories; 3 other countries; 100% Hispanic/Latino; 0.1% Race/ethnicity unknown; 7% transferred in.

Freshmen:
Admission: 862 applied, 739 admitted, 569 enrolled. ***Average high school GPA:*** 3.4.
Retention: 86% of full-time freshmen returned.

FACULTY
Total: 221, 59% full-time, 33% with terminal degrees.
Student/faculty ratio: 20:1.

ACADEMICS
Calendar: trimesters. *Degrees:* associate, bachelor's, master's, and doctoral.
Special study options: academic remediation for entering students, advanced placement credit, distance learning, English as a second language, honors programs, independent study, internships, student-designed majors, summer session for credit. ***ROTC:*** Army (c).
Computers: 800 computers/terminals and 800 ports are available on campus for general student use. Students can access the following: campus intranet, computer help desk, free student e-mail accounts, online (class) grades, online (class) registration, online (class) schedules. Campuswide network is available. 100% of college-owned or -operated housing units are wired for high-speed Internet access. Wireless service is available via entire campus.
Library: Biblioteca de la Universidad Politecnica de Puerto Rico. *Books:* 67,161 (physical), 114,078 (digital/electronic); *Serial titles:* 1,766 (physical), 24,595 (digital/electronic); *Databases:* 44. Weekly public service hours: 82; study areas open 24 hours, 5–7 days a week; students can reserve study rooms.

STUDENT LIFE
Housing options: coed. Campus housing is university owned.
Activities and organizations: choral group, ASCE (American Society of Civil Engineering), PRWEA (Puerto Rico Water and Environment Association), ACI (American Concrete Institute), SAE PUPR AERO DESIGN TEAM, SHPE (Society of Hispanic Professional Engineers).
Athletics ***Intercollegiate sports:*** track and field M(s)/W(s), volleyball M(s)/W(s), weight lifting M(s)/W(s).
Campus security: 24-hour emergency response devices and patrols, late-night transport/escort service, controlled dormitory access, over 350 security cameras on campus.
Student services: health clinic, personal/psychological counseling, veterans affairs office.

COSTS
Costs (2020–21) ***Comprehensive fee:*** $20,568 includes full-time tuition ($7740), mandatory fees ($900), and room and board ($11,928). Full-time tuition and fees vary according to course level, degree level, location, and program. Part-time tuition: $215 per credit hour. Part-time tuition and fees vary according to course level, degree level, location, and program. ***Required fees:*** $300 per term part-time. ***College room only:*** $4950. ***Payment plan:*** deferred payment. ***Waivers:*** employees or children of employees.

APPLYING
Standardized Tests *Recommended:* CEEB or PEAU.
Options: electronic application.
Application fee: $30.
Required: high school transcript, minimum 2.0 GPA.

CONTACT
Ms. Teresa Cardona, Director of Admissions, Polytechnic University of Puerto Rico, PO Box 192017, San Juan, PR 00919-2017. *Phone:* 787-622-8000 Ext. 240. *Fax:* 787-764-8712. *E-mail:* tcardona@pupr.edu.

Pontifical Catholic University of Puerto Rico

Ponce, Puerto Rico

http://www.pucpr.edu/

CONTACT
Sra. Ana O. Bonilla, Director of Admissions, Pontifical Catholic University of Puerto Rico, 2250 Avenida Las Americas Avenue, Suite 584, Ponce, PR 00717-9777. *Phone:* 787-841-2000 Ext. 1004. *Toll-free phone:* 800-961-7696. *Fax:* 787-840-4295. *E-mail:* admissions@email.pucpr.edu.

Pontifical Catholic University of Puerto Rico–Arecibo Campus

Arecibo, Puerto Rico

http://www.pucpr.edu/arecibo/

- **Independent** comprehensive, affiliated with Roman Catholic Church
- **Coed**
- 99% of applicants were admitted

ACADEMICS
Degrees: associate, bachelor's, and master's.

CONTACT
Pontifical Catholic University of Puerto Rico–Arecibo Campus, Bo. Santana Carr. 662 Km. 2.3, Arecibo, PR 00614-4045.

Pontifical Catholic University of Puerto Rico–Mayaguez Campus

Mayaguez, Puerto Rico

http://www.pucpr.edu/mayaguez/

- **Independent** comprehensive, affiliated with Roman Catholic Church
- **Coed**
- 96% of applicants were admitted

FACULTY
Student/faculty ratio: 20:1.

ACADEMICS
Degrees: associate, bachelor's, and master's.

CONTACT
Pontifical Catholic University of Puerto Rico–Mayaguez Campus, 482 Sur Calle Ramon Emerito Betances, Mayaguez, PR 00680.

Theological University of the Caribbean

Saint Just, Puerto Rico

http://www.utcpr.edu/

- **Independent Pentecostal** comprehensive, founded 1956
- **Suburban** 4-acre campus with easy access to San Juan
- **Endowment** $1.0 million
- **Coed**
- 100% of applicants were admitted

FACULTY
Student/faculty ratio: 23:1.

ACADEMICS
Calendar: semesters. *Degrees:* certificates, diplomas, associate, bachelor's, and master's.
Library: Juan L. Lugo Library plus 1 other. *Books:* 17,258 (physical); *Serial titles:* 45 (physical). Weekly public service hours: 61.

STUDENT LIFE
Housing options: coed. Campus housing is university owned.

Activities and organizations: Student Council, Missionary Evangelistic Association, Ministerial Association, FESI, Free Night.

Campus security: patrols by security personnel at night since 6:00 pm to midnight; Security Cameras.

Student services: personal/psychological counseling.

COSTS & FINANCIAL AID
Costs (2019–20) ***Tuition:*** $4524 full-time, $21 per credit hour part-time. ***Required fees:*** $1000 full-time, $154 per credit hour part-time, $3696 per term part-time.

Financial Aid Of all full-time matriculated undergraduates who enrolled in 2017, 251 applied for aid, 251 were judged to have need. ***Average financial aid package:*** $4054. ***Average need-based loan:*** $1899. ***Average need-based gift aid:*** $4054. ***Average indebtedness upon graduation:*** $8906. ***Financial aid deadline:*** 6/30.

APPLYING
Options: early admission.

Application fee: $45.

Required: high school transcript, medical certificate, certificate of immunization, 1 2x2 photo, Bible content exam.

CONTACT
Mrs. Avianny Paulino, Recruitment Officer, Theological University of the Caribbean, PO Box 901, Saint Just, PR 00978-901. *Phone:* 787-761-0640 Ext. 1246. *Fax:* 787-748-9220. *E-mail:* promocion@utcpr.edu.

Universidad Adventista de las Antillas

Mayagüez, Puerto Rico

https://www.uaa.edu/esp/

- **Independent Seventh-day Adventist** comprehensive, founded 1957
- **Rural** 284-acre campus
- **Coed** 1,058 undergraduate students, 90% full-time, 62% women, 38% men
- **Minimally difficult** entrance level, 34% of applicants were admitted

UNDERGRAD STUDENTS
956 full-time, 102 part-time. Students come from 23 other countries; 19% are from out of state; 1% Black or African American, non-Hispanic/Latino; 96% Hispanic/Latino; 0.1% Asian, non-Hispanic/Latino; 2% international; 28% live on campus.

Freshmen:
Admission: 318 applied, 107 admitted, 106 enrolled.
Retention: 73% of full-time freshmen returned.

FACULTY
Total: 107, 40% full-time, 44% with terminal degrees.

ACADEMICS
Calendar: semesters. *Degrees:* associate, bachelor's, and master's.

Special study options: academic remediation for entering students, advanced placement credit, cooperative education, double majors, English as a second language, internships, part-time degree program, services for LD students, summer session for credit.

Computers: 50 computers/terminals are available on campus for general student use. Students can access the following: campus intranet, computer help desk, free student e-mail accounts, online (class) grades, online (class) registration, online (class) schedules. Campuswide network is available. 95% of college-owned or -operated housing units are wired for high-speed Internet access. Wireless service is available via classrooms, computer centers, computer labs, dorm rooms, learning centers, libraries, student centers.
Library: Dennis Soto Library. *Books:* 67,322 (physical); *Databases:* 42. Weekly public service hours: 67; students can reserve study rooms.

STUDENT LIFE
Housing options: on-campus residence required for freshman year; men-only, women-only. Campus housing is university owned. Freshman applicants given priority for college housing.

Activities and organizations: student-run newspaper, choral group, Score Group, Gymnastic Club, Student Council, Green Movement, 3AM.

Athletics ***Intramural sports:*** basketball M/W, soccer M/W, volleyball M/W.

Campus security: 24-hour emergency response devices and patrols, student patrols, controlled dormitory access.

Student services: health clinic, personal/psychological counseling.

FINANCIAL AID
Financial Aid ***Average indebtedness upon graduation:*** $4801.

APPLYING
Standardized Tests *Recommended:* SAT or ACT (for admission), CEEB.

Options: electronic application, early admission.

Application fee: $20.

Required: high school transcript, minimum 2.0 GPA, 1 letter of recommendation. ***Required for some:*** essay or personal statement, interview.

Application deadlines: 7/15 (freshmen), 7/15 (transfers).

CONTACT
Mrs. Yolanda Ferrer, Director of Admissions, Universidad Adventista de las Antillas, Oficina de Admisiones, PO Box 118, Mayaguez, PR 00681-0118. *Phone:* 787-834-9595 Ext. 2208. *Fax:* 787-834-9597. *E-mail:* admissions@uaa.edu.

Universidad Central del Caribe

Bayamón, Puerto Rico

http://www.uccaribe.edu/

CONTACT
Admissions Department, Universidad Central del Caribe, PO Box 60-327, Bayamón, PR 00960-6032. *Phone:* 787-740-1611.

Universidad del Este

Carolina, Puerto Rico

http://www.suagm.edu/une/

CONTACT
Universidad del Este, PO Box 2010, Carolina, PR 00984. *Phone:* 787-257-7373 Ext. 3401.

Universidad del Turabo

Gurabo, Puerto Rico

http://www.suagm.edu/ut/

CONTACT
Universidad del Turabo, PO Box 3030, Gurabo, PR 00778-3030. *Phone:* 787-743-7979 Ext. 4351.

Universidad Metropolitana

San Juan, Puerto Rico

http://www.suagm.edu/umet/

CONTACT

Mrs. Yadira Rivera Lugo, Director of Admissions, Universidad Metropolitana, Box 21150, San Juan, PR 00928-1150. *Phone:* 787-766-1717 Ext. 6683. *Toll-free phone:* 800-747-8362. *E-mail:* yrivera@suagm.edu.

Universidad Pentecostal Mizpa

San Juan, Puerto Rico

http://www.mizpa.edu/

CONTACT

Omar Alicea, Recruitment, Universidad Pentecostal Mizpa, Bo Caimito Road 199, Apartado 20966, San Juan, PR 00928-0966. *Phone:* 787-720-4476. *Fax:* 787-720-2012.

University of Puerto Rico–Aguadilla

Aguadilla, Puerto Rico

http://www.uprag.edu/

- **Commonwealth-supported** 4-year, founded 1972, part of University of Puerto Rico System
- **Suburban** 32-acre campus
- **Coed**
- **Moderately difficult** entrance level

FACULTY

Student/faculty ratio: 24:1.

ACADEMICS

Calendar: semesters. *Degrees:* associate and bachelor's.

STUDENT LIFE

Housing options: college housing not available.

Activities and organizations: choral group.

Campus security: 24-hour patrols.

APPLYING

Standardized Tests *Required:* SAT (for admission), SAT Subject Tests (for admission), PAA (for admission).

Options: early admission, deferred entrance.

Application fee: $30.

Required: high school transcript.

CONTACT

Ms. Melba Serrano Lugo, Admissions Officer, University of Puerto Rico–Aguadilla, PO Box 6150, Aguadilla, PR 00604. *Phone:* 787-890-2681 Ext. 280.

University of Puerto Rico–Arecibo

Arecibo, Puerto Rico

http://www.upra.edu/

- **Commonwealth-supported** 4-year, founded 1967, part of University of Puerto Rico System
- **Urban** 44-acre campus with easy access to San Juan
- **Coed**
- **Very difficult** entrance level

FACULTY

Student/faculty ratio: 23:1.

ACADEMICS

Calendar: semesters. *Degrees:* associate and bachelor's.
Library: General Library.

STUDENT LIFE

Activities and organizations: drama/theater group, choral group, marching band.

Campus security: 24-hour emergency response devices and patrols.

Student services: health clinic, personal/psychological counseling.

FINANCIAL AID

Financial Aid Of all full-time matriculated undergraduates who enrolled in 1999, 274 Federal Work-Study jobs (averaging $1100). ***Financial aid deadline:*** 6/2.

APPLYING

Standardized Tests *Required:* SAT Subject Tests (for admission), PAA or SAT, CEEB (for admission).

Application fee: $20.

Required: high school transcript.

CONTACT

University of Puerto Rico–Arecibo, Carretera 653 Km. 0.8, Sector Las Dunas, PO Box 4010, Arecibo, PR 00614. *Phone:* 787-878-2830 Ext. 4101.

University of Puerto Rico–Bayamón

Bayamón, Puerto Rico

http://www.uprb.edu/

- **Commonwealth-supported** 4-year, founded 1971, part of University of Puerto Rico System
- **Urban** 78-acre campus with easy access to San Juan
- **Coed**
- **Very difficult** entrance level

FACULTY

Student/faculty ratio: 20:1.

ACADEMICS

Calendar: semesters. *Degrees:* associate and bachelor's.
Library: Centro Recursos para el Aprendizaje. *Books:* 54,105 (physical), 4,871 (digital/electronic); *Serial titles:* 386 (physical), 2,947 (digital/electronic); *Databases:* 103. Weekly public service hours: 78; students can reserve study rooms.

STUDENT LIFE

Housing options: college housing not available.

Activities and organizations: drama/theater group, choral group, The National Society of Collegiate Scholars at UPRB (NSCS), American Medical Student Association (AMSA), Med Life Capitulo Vaquero, Asociacion de Estudiantes de Computadoras (AECC), Asociacion de Estudiantes de Contabilidad (ASEC).

Athletics Member NCAA. All Division II.

Campus security: 24-hour patrols.

Student services: health clinic, personal/psychological counseling.

COSTS & FINANCIAL AID

Costs (2019–20) ***Tuition:*** commonwealth resident $3910 full-time, $115 per credit part-time; nonresident $5865 full-time, $173 per credit part-time. Full-time tuition and fees vary according to class time, course load, and program. Part-time tuition and fees vary according to class time, course load, and program. No tuition increase for student's term of enrollment. ***Required fees:*** $174 full-time.

Financial Aid Of all full-time matriculated undergraduates who enrolled in 2016, 315 Federal Work-Study jobs (averaging $1111).

APPLYING

Standardized Tests *Required:* College Board exam (for admission).

Options: electronic application.

Application fee: $30.

Required: high school transcript.

CONTACT

Ms. Carmen I. Montes Burgos, Director, Office of Admissions, University of Puerto Rico–Bayamón, OPEI Office, Street 174 #170 Minillas Industrial Park, Bayamon, PR 00959-1919. *Phone:* 787-993-8952 Ext. 4016. *Fax:* 787-993-8929. *E-mail:* carmen.montes1@upr.edu.

University of Puerto Rico–Carolina

Carolina, Puerto Rico

http://www.uprc.edu/

- **Commonwealth-supported** 4-year, founded 1974, part of University of Puerto Rico System
- **Urban** 60-acre campus with easy access to San Juan
- **Coed**
- **Moderately difficult** entrance level

FACULTY
Student/faculty ratio: 21:1.

ACADEMICS
Calendar: quarters. *Degrees:* associate and bachelor's.
Library: Learning Resource Center, Prof. Jose Paulino Fernandez-Miranda.

STUDENT LIFE
Activities and organizations: drama/theater group, choral group, marching band.

Student services: health clinic, personal/psychological counseling.

APPLYING
Standardized Tests *Required:* SAT (for admission), ACT (for admission), SAT Subject Tests (for admission), CEEB (for admission).

Application fee: $20.

Required: high school transcript.

CONTACT
Ms. Celia Mendez, Admissions Officer, University of Puerto Rico–Carolina, PO Box 4800, Carolina, PR 00984-4800. *Phone:* 787-757-1485.

University of Puerto Rico–Cayey

Cayey, Puerto Rico

http://www.cayey.upr.edu/

- **Commonwealth-supported** 4-year, founded 1967, part of University of Puerto Rico System
- **Urban** 177-acre campus with easy access to San Juan
- **Coed**
- **Moderately difficult** entrance level

FACULTY
Student/faculty ratio: 25:1.

ACADEMICS
Calendar: semesters. *Degrees:* associate and bachelor's.
Library: Victor M. Pons Library.

STUDENT LIFE
Activities and organizations: drama/theater group, choral group, marching band, Asociacion de Estudiantes de Psicologia Psy-Chi, Sociedad Honoraria de Biologia - Tri Beta, Asociacion Cristiana Universitaria-CONFRA, Asociacion de Estudiantes del Programa de Estudios de Honor, GAIA, national fraternities, national sororities.

Campus security: 24-hour emergency response devices and patrols, late-night transport/escort service.

Student services: health clinic, personal/psychological counseling, women's center.

FINANCIAL AID
Financial Aid Of all full-time matriculated undergraduates who enrolled in 2000, 2,866 applied for aid, 2,819 were judged to have need. 281 Federal Work-Study jobs (averaging $1260). ***Average financial aid package:*** $4200. ***Average need-based loan:*** $3000. ***Average need-based gift aid:*** $3300.

APPLYING
Standardized Tests *Required:* CEEB (for admission). *Required for some:* SAT (for admission).

Options: early admission, early decision.

Application fee: $20.

Required: high school transcript.

CONTACT
University of Puerto Rico–Cayey, 205 Avenue Antonio R. Barcelo, Cayey, PR 00736. *Phone:* 787-738-2161 Ext. 2233.

University of Puerto Rico–Humacao

Humacao, Puerto Rico

http://www.uprh.edu/

- **Commonwealth-supported** 4-year, founded 1962, part of University of Puerto Rico System
- **Suburban** 62-acre campus with easy access to San Juan
- **Coed**
- **Moderately difficult** entrance level

FACULTY
Student/faculty ratio: 16:1.

ACADEMICS
Calendar: semesters. *Degrees:* associate and bachelor's.
Library: Aguedo Mojica Marrero. *Books:* 101,475 (physical), 200 (digital/electronic); *Serial titles:* 15 (physical), 43,942 (digital/electronic); *Databases:* 7. Weekly public service hours: 92; study areas open 24 hours, 5–7 days a week; students can reserve study rooms.

STUDENT LIFE
Housing options: college housing not available.

Activities and organizations: drama/theater group, student-run newspaper, radio and television station, choral group, marching band, Accounting Students Association, Management Students Association, Microbiology Students Association, Human Resources Students Association, Biology Students Association.

Campus security: 24-hour emergency response devices and patrols, late-night transport/escort service, 24-hour gate security.

Student services: personal/psychological counseling, women's center.

FINANCIAL AID
Financial Aid Of all full-time matriculated undergraduates who enrolled in 2001, 3,515 applied for aid, 2,883 were judged to have need, 7 had their need fully met. 278 Federal Work-Study jobs (averaging $1318). ***Average percent of need met:*** 50. ***Average financial aid package:*** $3929. ***Average need-based loan:*** $3295. ***Average need-based gift aid:*** $3664. ***Average indebtedness upon graduation:*** $2749. ***Financial aid deadline:*** 6/30.

APPLYING
Standardized Tests *Required:* Pruebas de Evaluacion y Admision Universitaria (PEAU) (for admission).

Options: electronic application, deferred entrance.

Required: high school transcript. ***Required for some:*** interview.

CONTACT
Mrs. Debbie García, Admissions Officer, University of Puerto Rico–Humacao, Call Box 860, Humacao, PR 00792. *Phone:* 787-850-9301. *Fax:* 787-850-9428. *E-mail:* debbie.garcia@upr.edu.

University of Puerto Rico–Mayagüez

Mayagüez, Puerto Rico

http://www.uprm.edu/

- **Commonwealth-supported** university, founded 1911, part of University of Puerto Rico System
- **Urban** 315-acre campus
- **Coed**
- **Moderately difficult** entrance level

FACULTY
Student/faculty ratio: 22:1.

ACADEMICS
Calendar: semesters. *Degrees:* bachelor's, master's, and doctoral.
Library: General Library plus 1 other.

STUDENT LIFE
Activities and organizations: drama/theater group, student-run newspaper, choral group, marching band, national fraternities, national sororities.

Campus security: 24-hour emergency response devices and patrols.

Student services: health clinic, personal/psychological counseling.

COSTS & FINANCIAL AID

Costs (2019–20) ***One-time required fee:*** $179. ***Tuition:*** Full-time tuition and fees vary according to course load and student level. Part-time tuition and fees vary according to course load and student level. ***Room and board:*** Room and board charges vary according to student level.

Financial Aid Of all full-time matriculated undergraduates who enrolled in 2018, 9,734 applied for aid, 9,464 were judged to have need, 15 had their need fully met. 1,096 Federal Work-Study jobs (averaging $1099). In 2018, 63 non-need-based awards were made. ***Average financial aid package:*** $6856. ***Average need-based loan:*** $3257. ***Average need-based gift aid:*** $5409. ***Average non-need-based aid:*** $1512. ***Average indebtedness upon graduation:*** $4378.

APPLYING

Standardized Tests *Required:* SAT Subject Tests (for admission), PEAU, CEEB (for admission).

Options: early action.

Application fee: $30.

Required: high school transcript.

CONTACT

Ms. Sheila Marty-Rodriquez, Director, Admissions Office, University of Puerto Rico–Mayagüez, PO Box 9000, Mayagüez, PR 00681-9000. *Phone:* 787-265-5465. *Fax:* 787-265-5465. *E-mail:* smarty@uprm.edu.

University of Puerto Rico-Medical Sciences Campus

San Juan, Puerto Rico

http://www.rcm.upr.edu/

- **Commonwealth-supported** university, founded 1950, part of University of Puerto Rico System
- **Urban** 11-acre campus
- **Coed, primarily women**
- **Moderately difficult** entrance level

FACULTY

Student/faculty ratio: 2:1.

ACADEMICS

Calendar: semesters. *Degrees:* certificates, associate, bachelor's, master's, doctoral, and postbachelor's certificates (bachelor's degree is upper-level).

Library: Medical Sciences Library.

STUDENT LIFE

Housing options: college housing not available.

Campus security: 24-hour emergency response devices.

FINANCIAL AID

Financial Aid Of all full-time matriculated undergraduates who enrolled in 2007, 299 applied for aid, 285 were judged to have need, 6 had their need fully met. 45 Federal Work-Study jobs (averaging $953). ***Average percent of need met:*** 47. ***Average financial aid package:*** $5436. ***Average need-based loan:*** $4195. ***Average need-based gift aid:*** $4082. ***Average indebtedness upon graduation:*** $4240. ***Financial aid deadline:*** 5/25.

APPLYING

Application fee: $30.

CONTACT

University of Puerto Rico-Medical Sciences Campus, PO Box 365067, San Juan, PR 00936-5067. *Phone:* 787-758-2525 Ext. 5214.

University of Puerto Rico–Ponce

Ponce, Puerto Rico

http://www.uprp.edu/

- **Commonwealth-supported** 4-year, founded 1970, part of University of Puerto Rico System
- **Urban** 86-acre campus with easy access to San Juan
- **Coed** 2,540 undergraduate students, 94% full-time, 58% women, 42% men
- **Moderately difficult** entrance level, 73% of applicants were admitted

UNDERGRAD STUDENTS

2,381 full-time, 159 part-time. Students come from 1 other state; 100% Hispanic/Latino; 11% transferred in.

Freshmen:

Admission: 1,561 applied, 1,146 admitted, 513 enrolled. ***Average high school GPA:*** 3.6.

Retention: 80% of full-time freshmen returned.

FACULTY

Total: 164, 44% full-time, 40% with terminal degrees.

Student/faculty ratio: 15:1.

ACADEMICS

Calendar: semesters. *Degrees:* associate and bachelor's.

Special study options: academic remediation for entering students, accelerated degree program, advanced placement credit, English as a second language, freshman honors college, honors programs, internships, part-time degree program, summer session for credit. ***ROTC:*** Army (b).

Computers: 81 computers/terminals and 132 ports are available on campus for general student use. Students can access the following: campus intranet, free student e-mail accounts, online (class) registration, online (class) schedules. Campuswide network is available. Wireless service is available via entire campus.

Library: Adelina Coppin. *Books:* 66,237 (physical), 780 (digital/electronic); *Serial titles:* 356 (physical); *Databases:* 83. Weekly public service hours: 6; students can reserve study rooms.

STUDENT LIFE

Housing options: college housing not available.

Activities and organizations: drama/theater group, choral group, marching band.

Athletics ***Intercollegiate sports:*** baseball M, basketball M(s)/W(s), cross-country running M(s)/W(s), table tennis M/W, tennis M(s), track and field M(s)/W(s), volleyball M(s)/W(s), weight lifting M(s)/W(s). ***Intramural sports:*** basketball M/W, cross-country running M/W, racquetball M/W, softball M/W, table tennis M/W, tennis M/W, track and field M/W, volleyball M/W, weight lifting M/W.

Campus security: 24-hour patrols.

Student services: health clinic, personal/psychological counseling, veterans affairs office.

FINANCIAL AID

Financial Aid Of all full-time matriculated undergraduates who enrolled in 1998, 3,461 applied for aid, 3,133 were judged to have need. ***Average percent of need met:*** 40. ***Financial aid deadline:*** 6/30.

APPLYING

Standardized Tests *Required:* CEEB University Evaluation and Admissions Tests (PEAU) (for admission).

Options: early admission.

Application fee: $20.

Required: high school transcript.

Application deadlines: 11/15 (freshmen), 2/23 (transfers).

Notification: 3/4 (freshmen), continuous until 5/15 (transfers).

CONTACT

University of Puerto Rico–Ponce, PO Box 7186, Ponce, PR 00732-7186. *Phone:* 787-844-8181 Ext. 2533.

University of Puerto Rico-Rio Piedras

San Juan, Puerto Rico

http://www.uprrp.edu/

- **Commonwealth-supported** university, founded 1903, part of University of Puerto Rico System
- **Urban** 281-acre campus
- **Coed**
- **Very difficult** entrance level

FACULTY

Student/faculty ratio: 15:1.

ACADEMICS
Calendar: semesters. *Degrees:* bachelor's, master's, doctoral, post-master's, and postbachelor's certificates.
Library: Jose M. Lazaro Library plus 10 others.

STUDENT LIFE
Housing options: coed. Campus housing is university owned.

Activities and organizations: drama/theater group, student-run radio station, choral group, national fraternities, national sororities.

Athletics Member NCAA, NAIA. All NCAA Division II.

Campus security: 24-hour emergency response devices, late-night transport/escort service.

Student services: health clinic, personal/psychological counseling, legal services.

FINANCIAL AID
Financial Aid ***Financial aid deadline:*** 4/25.

APPLYING
Standardized Tests *Required:* SAT (for admission), College Entrance Examination Board (CEEB) Aptitude Test in mathematics and verbal reasoning and the Academic Achievement Test in English, mathematics and Spanish (for admission).

Options: electronic application.

Application fee: $30.

Required: high school transcript. ***Required for some:*** interview.

CONTACT
Mrs. Cruz B. Valentín, Director of Admissions, University of Puerto Rico-Rio Piedras, PO Box 23300, San Juan, PR 00931-3300. *Phone:* 787-764-0000 Ext. 85700.

University of Puerto Rico–Utuado

Utuado, Puerto Rico

http://www.uprutuado.edu/

- **Commonwealth-supported** 4-year, founded 1979, part of University of Puerto Rico System
- **Small-town** 180-acre campus with easy access to San Juan
- **Coed**
- **Moderately difficult** entrance level

FACULTY
Student/faculty ratio: 15:1.

ACADEMICS
Calendar: semesters. *Degrees:* associate and bachelor's.
Library: Centro de Recursos para el Aprendizaje.

STUDENT LIFE
Housing options: college housing not available.

Activities and organizations: drama/theater group, choral group, national fraternities, national sororities.

Campus security: 24-hour emergency response devices and patrols.

Student services: health clinic, personal/psychological counseling.

FINANCIAL AID
Financial Aid Of all full-time matriculated undergraduates who enrolled in 2006, 143 Federal Work-Study jobs. ***Financial aid deadline:*** 6/15.

APPLYING
Standardized Tests *Required:* SAT Subject Tests (for admission), CEEB (for admission).

Options: electronic application, early admission, deferred entrance.

Application fee: $20.

CONTACT
Mrs. Maria Robles Serrano, Admissions Officer, University of Puerto Rico–Utuado, PO Box 2500, Utuado, PR 00641-2500. *Phone:* 787-894-2828 Ext. 2240.

University of the Sacred Heart

San Juan, Puerto Rico

http://www.sagrado.edu/

CONTACT
Mr. Luis Heviquez, Director of Admissions, University of the Sacred Heart, PO Box 12383, San Juan, PR 00914-0383. *Phone:* 787-728-1515 Ext. 3237.

VIRGIN ISLANDS

University of the Virgin Islands

St. Thomas, Virgin Islands

http://www.uvi.edu/

- **Territory-supported** comprehensive, founded 1962
- **Small-town** 518-acre campus
- **Coed** 1,850 undergraduate students, 68% full-time, 69% women, 31% men
- **Noncompetitive** entrance level, 98% of applicants were admitted

UNDERGRAD STUDENTS
1,251 full-time, 599 part-time. Students come from 36 states and territories; 15 other countries; 5% are from out of state; 71% Black or African American, non-Hispanic/Latino; 11% Hispanic/Latino; 0.8% Asian, non-Hispanic/Latino; 0.2% American Indian or Alaska Native, non-Hispanic/Latino; 1% Two or more races, non-Hispanic/Latino; 5% Race/ethnicity unknown; 6% international; 4% transferred in.

Freshmen:
Admission: 914 applied, 899 admitted, 382 enrolled. ***Average high school GPA:*** 2.9.

Retention: 66% of full-time freshmen returned.

FACULTY
Total: 195, 45% full-time, 41% with terminal degrees.

Student/faculty ratio: 13:1.

ACADEMICS
Calendar: semesters. *Degrees:* associate, bachelor's, master's, doctoral, and post-master's certificates.

Special study options: academic remediation for entering students, adult/continuing education programs, advanced placement credit, cooperative education, distance learning, double majors, English as a second language, external degree program, honors programs, independent study, internships, off-campus study, part-time degree program, services for LD students, study abroad, summer session for credit. ***ROTC:*** Army (b).

Unusual degree programs: 3-2 engineering with Columbia University, University of Florida, University of South Carolina.

Computers: 500 computers/terminals are available on campus for general student use. Students can access the following: campus intranet, computer help desk, free student e-mail accounts, online (class) grades, online (class) registration, online (class) schedules. Campuswide network is available. 100% of college-owned or -operated housing units are wired for high-speed Internet access. Wireless service is available via entire campus.
Library: Ralph M. Paiewonsky Library. Study areas open 24 hours, 5–7 days a week; students can reserve study rooms.

STUDENT LIFE
Housing options: coed, men-only, women-only. Campus housing is university owned.

Activities and organizations: drama/theater group, student-run newspaper, radio station, choral group, Student Government Association, Golden Key Honor Society, Student Nurses Association, National Student Exchange Club, St. Kitts and Nevis, national sororities.

Athletics Member NAIA. ***Intercollegiate sports:*** basketball M(s)/W(s)(c), cross-country running M(c)/W(c), soccer M(s)(c), track and field M(c)/W(c), volleyball M(c)/W(c).

Campus security: 24-hour emergency response devices and patrols.

Student services: health clinic, personal/psychological counseling.

COSTS & FINANCIAL AID

Costs (2020–21) ***Tuition:*** territory resident $4631 full-time, $154 per credit part-time; nonresident $13,892 full-time, $463 per credit part-time. Full-time tuition and fees vary according to reciprocity agreements. Part-time tuition and fees vary according to course load and reciprocity agreements. ***Required fees:*** $604 full-time, $254 per term part-time. ***Room and board:*** $9900; room only: $4120. Room and board charges vary according to board plan and housing facility. ***Payment plan:*** installment. ***Waivers:*** senior citizens and employees or children of employees.

Financial Aid Of all full-time matriculated undergraduates who enrolled in 2007, 1,202 applied for aid, 1,118 were judged to have need, 10 had their need fully met. 39 Federal Work-Study jobs (averaging $2130). 28 state and other part-time jobs (averaging $1900). In 2007, 5 non-need-based awards were made. ***Average financial aid package:*** $4450. ***Average need-based loan:*** $3240. ***Average need-based gift aid:*** $3440. ***Average non-need-based aid:*** $8500. ***Average indebtedness upon graduation:*** $9480.

APPLYING

Options: electronic application, early admission, deferred entrance.

Application fee: $25.

Recommended: high school transcript, minimum 2.0 GPA.

Application deadlines: 4/30 (freshmen), 4/30 (transfers).

Notification: continuous until 10/1 (freshmen).

CONTACT

University of the Virgin Islands, 2 John Brewers Bay, St. Thomas, VI 00802. *Toll-free phone:* 877-468-6884.

CANADA

CANADA

Acadia University

Wolfville, Nova Scotia, Canada

http://www.acadiau.ca/

- **Province-supported** comprehensive, founded 1838
- **Small-town** 250-acre campus with easy access to Halifax, Nova Scotia
- **Coed**
- **Moderately difficult** entrance level

FACULTY

Student/faculty ratio: 15:1.

ACADEMICS

Calendar: Canadian standard year. *Degrees:* certificates, bachelor's, master's, doctoral, and postbachelor's certificates.
Library: Vaughan Memorial Library.

STUDENT LIFE

Housing options: coed, women-only. Campus housing is university owned. Freshman campus housing is guaranteed.

Activities and organizations: drama/theater group, student-run newspaper, radio station, choral group, Dance Acadia, Power Cheerleading, Water Watch Canada, LINC, Biology.

Athletics Member CIS.

Campus security: 24-hour emergency response devices and patrols, student patrols, late-night transport/escort service, controlled dormitory access, video surveillance, emergency response, emergency notification, emergency management planning.

Student services: health clinic, personal/psychological counseling, women's center, legal services.

APPLYING

Options: electronic application, deferred entrance.

Application fee: $40 Canadian dollars.

Required: high school transcript, minimum 2.5 GPA. ***Required for some:*** essay or personal statement, 1 letter of recommendation, interview, auditions for music programs.

CONTACT

Ms. Leigh-Ann Murphy, Manager of Admissions, Acadia University, 15 University Avenue, Wolfville, NS B4P 2R6, Canada. *Phone:* 902-585-1016. *Toll-free phone:* 877-585-1121. *Fax:* 902-585-1092. *E-mail:* admissions@acadiau.ca.

Alberta Bible College

Calgary, Alberta, Canada

http://www.abccampus.ca/

CONTACT

Craig Reid, Recruitment Officer, Alberta Bible College, 635 Northmount Drive, NW, Calgary, AB T2K 3J6, Canada. *Phone:* 403-282-2994 Ext. 225. *Toll-free phone:* 877-542-9492. *E-mail:* admissions@abccampus.ca.

Alberta College of Art & Design

Calgary, Alberta, Canada

http://www.acad.ca/

CONTACT

Alberta College of Art & Design, 1407 14 Avenue NW, Calgary, AB T2N 4R3, Canada. *Toll-free phone:* 800-251-8290.

Ambrose University

Calgary, Alberta, Canada

http://www.ambrose.edu/

CONTACT

Kalie Eeles, Enrolment Coordinator, Ambrose University, 150 Ambrose Circle SW, Calgary, AB T3H 0L5, Canada. *Phone:* 403-410-2000 Ext. 2954. *Toll-free phone:* 800-461-1222. *Fax:* 403-571-6556. *E-mail:* enrolment@ambrose.edu.

Athabasca University

Athabasca, Alberta, Canada

http://www.athabascau.ca/

CONTACT

Information Centre, Athabasca University, 1 University Drive, Athabasca, AB T9S 3A3, Canada. *Phone:* 800-788-9041. *Toll-free phone:* 800-788-9041. *Fax:* 780-675-6437.

Bishop's University

Sherbrooke, Quebec, Canada

http://www.ubishops.ca/

CONTACT

Mr. Doug McCooeye, Manager Student Recruitment, Admissions and Student Exchange, Bishop's University, 2600 College Street, Sherbrooke, QC J1M 1Z7, Canada. *Phone:* 819-822-9600 Ext. 2206. *Toll-free phone:* 877-822-8200. *E-mail:* admissions@ubishops.ca.

Booth University College

Winnipeg, Manitoba, Canada

http://www.boothuc.ca/

CONTACT

Chantel Burt, Director of Admission, Booth University College, 447 Webb Place, Winnipeg, MB R3B 2P2, Canada. *Phone:* 204-924-4867. *Toll-free phone:* 877-942-6684. *E-mail:* cburt@boothcollege.ca.

Brandon University

Brandon, Manitoba, Canada

http://www.brandonu.ca/

- **Province-supported** comprehensive, founded 1899
- **Small-town** 30-acre campus
- **Endowment** $34.8 million
- **Coed** 3,180 undergraduate students, 72% full-time, 70% women, 30% men
- **Noncompetitive** entrance level, 93% of applicants were admitted

UNDERGRAD STUDENTS

2,284 full-time, 896 part-time. Students come from 13 provinces and territories; 88 other countries; 6% are from out of state; 9% live on campus.

Freshmen:

Admission: 2,820 applied, 2,616 admitted.

Retention: 71% of full-time freshmen returned.

FACULTY

Total: 242, 93% full-time, 76% with terminal degrees.

Student/faculty ratio: 11:1.

ACADEMICS

Calendar: Canadian standard year. *Degrees:* certificates, bachelor's, and master's.

Special study options: academic remediation for entering students, accelerated degree program, cooperative education, distance learning, double majors, English as a second language, honors programs, off-campus study, part-time degree program, services for LD students, student-designed majors, study abroad, summer session for credit.

Unusual degree programs: 3-2 education.

Computers: 160 computers/terminals are available on campus for general student use. Students can access the following: computer help desk, free student e-mail accounts, online (class) grades, online (class) registration, online (class) schedules. Campuswide network is available. Wireless service is available via entire campus.

Library: John E. Robbins Library.

STUDENT LIFE

Housing options: coed, men-only, women-only. Campus housing is university owned. Freshman campus housing is guaranteed.

Activities and organizations: drama/theater group, student-run newspaper, radio station, choral group, Psychology Club, zoology club, Inter-Varsity Christian Fellowship, International Students Club, Business Administration Club.

Athletics Member CIS. ***Intercollegiate sports:*** basketball M(s)/W(s), soccer M(s)/W(s), volleyball M(s)/W(s). ***Intramural sports:*** badminton M/W, baseball M/W, bowling M/W, cheerleading M/W, soccer M/W, volleyball M/W, weight lifting M/W.

Campus security: 24-hour emergency response devices, controlled dormitory access, night residence hall security personnel.

Student services: personal/psychological counseling.

COSTS

Costs (2020–21) ***Tuition:*** area resident $4287 full-time, $143 per credit hour part-time; nonresident $529 per credit hour part-time; International tuition $15,862 full-time. Full-time tuition and fees vary according to class time, course level, course load, degree level, location, program, reciprocity agreements, and student level. Part-time tuition and fees vary according to class time, course level, course load, degree level, location, program, reciprocity agreements, and student level. ***Required fees:*** $996 full-time, $19 per credit hour part-time, $133 per term part-time. ***Room and board:*** $10,511; room only: $6303. Room and board charges vary according to board plan, gender, and location. ***Payment plan:*** installment. ***Waivers:*** senior citizens and employees or children of employees.

APPLYING

Options: electronic application, deferred entrance.

Application fee: $70 Canadian dollars.

Required: high school transcript. ***Required for some:*** criminal and child abuse registry checks.

Application deadlines: 8/15 (freshmen), 8/15 (out-of-state freshmen), 8/15 (transfers).

Notification: continuous until 9/30 (freshmen), continuous until 9/30 (transfers).

CONTACT

Leanne Barcellona, Director of Admissions, Brandon University, 270 18th Street, Brandon, MB R7A 6A9, Canada. *Phone:* 204-727-7352. *Toll-free phone:* 800-644-7644. *Fax:* 204-728-3221. *E-mail:* BarcellonaL@BrandonU.ca.

Briercrest College

Caronport, Saskatchewan, Canada

http://www.briercrest.ca/

CONTACT

Mr. Ralph Troshke, Director of Enrolment, Briercrest College, 510 College Drive, Caronport, SK S0H 0S0, Canada. *Phone:* 306-756-3200. *Toll-free phone:* 800-667-5199. *Fax:* 800-667-5199. *E-mail:* admissions@briercrest.ca.

British Columbia Institute of Technology

Burnaby, British Columbia, Canada

http://www.bcit.ca/

CONTACT

Ms. Anna Dosen, Supervisor of Admissions, British Columbia Institute of Technology, 3700 Willingdon Avenue, Burnaby, BC V5G 3H2, Canada. *Phone:* 604-432-8496. *Toll-free phone:* 866-434-1610. *Fax:* 604-431-6917.

Brock University

St. Catharines, Ontario, Canada

http://www.brocku.ca/

- **Province-supported** university, founded 1964
- **Urban** 540-acre campus with easy access to Toronto, ON and Buffalo, NY
- **Coed**

FACULTY

Student/faculty ratio: 30:1.

ACADEMICS

Calendar: Canadian standard year. *Degrees:* certificates, bachelor's, master's, and doctoral.

Library: James A. Gibson Library plus 1 other. *Books:* 492,672 (physical). Students can reserve study rooms.

STUDENT LIFE

Housing options: coed, special housing for students with disabilities. Campus housing is university owned and leased by the school. Freshman campus housing is guaranteed.

Activities and organizations: drama/theater group, student-run newspaper, radio and television station, choral group, International Students Association, Brock University Student Association, Business Administration Association, Brock Christian Fellowship, Ace Brock.

Athletics Member CIS.

Campus security: 24-hour emergency response devices and patrols, student patrols, late-night transport/escort service, controlled dormitory access.

Student services: health clinic, personal/psychological counseling, women's center.

COLLEGES AT-A-GLANCE

COSTS
Costs (2019–20) ***Tuition:*** province resident $7210 Canadian dollars full-time; nonresident $7210 Canadian dollars full-time; International tuition $27,160 Canadian dollars full-time. Full-time tuition and fees vary according to course load, degree level, program, and student level. Part-time tuition and fees vary according to course load, program, and student level. ***Room and board:*** $7780 Canadian dollars. Room and board charges vary according to board plan and housing facility.

APPLYING
Standardized Tests *Required:* SAT or ACT (for admission).

Options: electronic application.

Required: high school transcript. ***Required for some:*** essay or personal statement, interview, audition for Dramatic Arts and Music programs, profile questionnaire for Concurrent Education programs. ***Recommended:*** minimum 3.0 GPA.

CONTACT
Mrs. Lynn Thompson-Dovi, Admissions Officer, International Undergraduate, Brock University, 1812 Sir Isaac Brock Way, L2S 3A1, Canada. *Phone:* 905-688-5550 Ext. 3431. *E-mail:* central@brocku.ca.

Cape Breton University
Sydney, Nova Scotia, Canada
http://www.cbu.ca/

CONTACT
Cape Breton University, Box 5300, 1250 Grand Lake Road, Sydney, NS B1P 6L2, Canada. *Phone:* 902-563-1117. *Toll-free phone:* 888-959-9995.

Capilano University
North Vancouver, British Columbia, Canada
http://www.capilanou.ca/

- **Public** 4-year, founded 1967, part of British Columbia's Advanced Education system
- **Suburban** 44-hectare campus with easy access to Vancouver
- **Endowment** $7.6 million
- **Coed**
- **Noncompetitive** entrance level

FACULTY
Student/faculty ratio: 17:1.

ACADEMICS
Calendar: semesters. *Degrees:* certificates, diplomas, associate, bachelor's, and postbachelor's certificates.
Library: Capilano University Library. *Books:* 73,290 (physical), 178,273 (digital/electronic); *Serial titles:* 122 (physical), 34,260 (digital/electronic); *Databases:* 136. Weekly public service hours: 73; students can reserve study rooms.

STUDENT LIFE
Housing options: coed, men-only, women-only, special housing for students with disabilities. Campus housing is leased by the school. Freshman applicants given priority for college housing.

Activities and organizations: student-run newspaper, radio station, choral group.

Campus security: 24-hour emergency response devices and patrols, late-night transport/escort service.

Student services: health clinic, personal/psychological counseling, women's center, legal services.

COSTS
Costs (2019–20) ***Tuition:*** province resident $3986 Canadian dollars full-time, $133 Canadian dollars per credit part-time; nonresident $3986 Canadian dollars full-time, $133 Canadian dollars per credit part-time; International tuition $17,853 Canadian dollars full-time. Full-time tuition and fees vary according to course level, degree level, and program. Part-time tuition and fees vary according to course level, degree level, and program. ***Required fees:*** $264 Canadian dollars full-time, $13 Canadian dollars per credit part-time, $29 Canadian dollars per term part-time.

APPLYING
Options: electronic application, early admission.

Required for some: essay or personal statement, minimum 2.0 GPA.

CONTACT
Capilano University, 2055 Purcell Way, North Vancouver, BC V7J 3H5, Canada.

Carleton University
Ottawa, Ontario, Canada
http://www.carleton.ca/

CONTACT
Ms. Jean Mullan, Director, Undergraduate Recruitment Office, Carleton University, 1125 Colonel By Drive, Ottawa, ON K1S 5B6, Canada. *Phone:* 613-520-3663. *Toll-free phone:* 888-354-4414. *E-mail:* liaison@admissions.carleton.ca.

Centennial College
Scarborough, Ontario, Canada
http://www.centennialcollege.ca/

CONTACT
Centennial College, PO Box 631, Station 'A', Scarborough, ON M1K 5E9, Canada. *Toll-free phone:* 800-268-4419.

Columbia Bible College
Abbotsford, British Columbia, Canada
http://www.columbiabc.edu/

CONTACT
Nathan Martin, Admissions Coordinator, Columbia Bible College, 2940 Clearbrook Road, Abbotsford, BC V2T 2Z8, Canada. *Phone:* 604-853-3358 Ext. 309. *Toll-free phone:* 800-283-0881. *Fax:* 604-853-3063. *E-mail:* nathan.martin@columbiabc.edu.

Concordia University
Montréal, Quebec, Canada
http://www.concordia.ca/

- **Province-supported** university, founded 1974, part of Quebec University Network
- **Urban** 52-acre campus with easy access to Montreal
- **Coed**
- **Moderately difficult** entrance level

FACULTY
Student/faculty ratio: 25:1.

ACADEMICS
Calendar: semesters. *Degrees:* certificates, diplomas, bachelor's, master's, doctoral, and postbachelor's certificates.
Library: Webster Library plus 1 other. *Books:* 994,394 (physical), 556,907 (digital/electronic); *Serial titles:* 18,752 (physical), 140,024 (digital/electronic); *Databases:* 1,000. Weekly public service hours: 70; study areas open 24 hours, 5–7 days a week; students can reserve study rooms.

STUDENT LIFE
Housing options: coed, special housing for students with disabilities. Campus housing is university owned. Freshman applicants given priority for college housing.

Activities and organizations: drama/theater group, student-run newspaper, radio and television station, choral group, Undergraduate Student Union, departmental clubs, religious clubs, ethnic clubs, social action groups, national fraternities, national sororities.

Athletics Member CIS.

Campus security: 24-hour emergency response devices and patrols, student patrols, late-night transport/escort service, controlled dormitory access.

Student services: health clinic, personal/psychological counseling, women's center.

FINANCIAL AID

Financial Aid Of all full-time matriculated undergraduates who enrolled in 2018, 349 state and other part-time jobs (averaging $1286). ***Financial aid deadline:*** 3/31.

APPLYING

Options: electronic application, deferred entrance.

Application fee: $100 Canadian dollars.

Required: high school transcript, minimum 2.5 GPA. ***Required for some:*** essay or personal statement, minimum 3.7 GPA, 2 letters of recommendation, interview, portfolio and/or auditions are for performing and visual arts, interview/essay/portfolio for communications, letter of intent and interview for some education programs.

CONTACT

Dr. Matthew Stiegemeyer, Director, Student Recruitment (Enrolment and Student Services), Concordia University, 1455 de Maisonneuve Boulevard West, Building LB-718, Montreal, QC H3G 1M8, Canada. *Phone:* 514-848-2424 Ext. 4781. *Fax:* 514-848-2837. *E-mail:* matthew.stiegemeyer@concordia.ca.

Concordia University of Edmonton

Edmonton, Alberta, Canada

http://www.concordia.ab.ca/

CONTACT

Student and Enrollment Services, Concordia University of Edmonton, 7128 Ada Boulevard, Edmonton, AB T5B 4E4, Canada. *Phone:* 780-479-9220. *Toll-free phone:* 866-479-5200. *Fax:* 780-378-8460. *E-mail:* admits@concordia.ab.ca.

Crandall University

Moncton, New Brunswick, Canada

http://www.crandallu.ca/

CONTACT

Mrs. Lorrie Weir, Admissions Administrative Assistant, Crandall University, Box 6004, Moncton, NB E1C 9L7, Canada. *Phone:* 506-858-8970 Ext. 434. *Toll-free phone:* 888-968-6228. *Fax:* 506-863-6460. *E-mail:* admissions@crandallu.ca.

Dalhousie University

Halifax, Nova Scotia, Canada

http://www.dal.ca/

CONTACT

Ashley Jordan, Assistant Registrar, Associate Director Admissions, Dalhousie University, Office of the Registrar, Halifax, NS B3H 4H6, Canada. *Phone:* 902-494-1833. *Fax:* 902-494-1630. *E-mail:* admissions@dal.ca.

Emily Carr University of Art + Design

Vancouver, British Columbia, Canada

http://www.ecuad.ca/

CONTACT

Sara Liao, Admissions, Emily Carr University of Art + Design, 1399 Johnston Street, Vancouver, BC V6H 3R9, Canada. *Phone:* 604-844-3800. *Toll-free phone:* 800-832-7788. *Fax:* 604-844-3801. *E-mail:* admissions@ecuad.ca.

Emmanuel Bible College

Kitchener, Ontario, Canada

http://www.emmanuelbiblecollege.ca/

CONTACT

Emmanuel Bible College, 100 Fergus Avenue, Kitchener, ON N2A 2H2, Canada. *Phone:* 519-894-8900 Ext. 224.

Eston College

Eston, Saskatchewan, Canada

http://www.estoncollege.ca/

CONTACT

Admissions, Eston College, 730 1st Street E., Box 579, Eston, SK S0L 1A0, Canada. *Phone:* 306-962-3621. *Toll-free phone:* 888-440-3424. *Fax:* 306-962-3810. *E-mail:* admissions@estoncollege.ca.

HEC Montreal

Montréal, Quebec, Canada

http://www.hec.ca/

- **Province-supported** comprehensive, founded 1910, part of Universite de Montreal
- **Urban** 9-acre campus with easy access to Montreal, QC
- **Coed** 10,830 undergraduate students, 49% full-time, 52% women, 48% men
- **Moderately difficult** entrance level, 76% of applicants were admitted

UNDERGRAD STUDENTS

5,317 full-time, 5,513 part-time. Students come from 6 provinces and territories; 62 other countries; 0.6% are from out of state.

Freshmen:

Admission: 3,089 applied, 2,352 admitted, 1,049 enrolled.

Retention: 97% of full-time freshmen returned.

FACULTY

Total: 809, 37% full-time, 35% with terminal degrees.

Student/faculty ratio: 22:1.

ACADEMICS

Calendar: trimesters. *Degrees:* certificates, bachelor's, master's, doctoral, and postbachelor's certificates.

Special study options: academic remediation for entering students, adult/continuing education programs, distance learning, English as a second language, honors programs, independent study, off-campus study, part-time degree program, student-designed majors, study abroad, summer session for credit.

Computers: 159 computers/terminals are available on campus for general student use. Students can access the following: campus intranet, computer help desk, free student e-mail accounts, online (class) grades, online (class) registration, online (class) schedules, learning management system, corporate calendar and Web sites for resources available for classes. Campuswide network is available. 100% of college-owned or -operated housing units are wired for high-speed Internet access. Wireless service is available via entire campus.

Library: HEC Montreal Library plus 1 other. *Books:* 123,221 (physical), 219,302 (digital/electronic); *Serial titles:* 952 (physical), 112,671 (digital/electronic); *Databases:* 156. Weekly public service hours: 100; students can reserve study rooms.

STUDENT LIFE

Housing options: coed. Campus housing is university owned. Freshman applicants given priority for college housing.

Activities and organizations: student-run newspaper, AEMBA (MBA Students' Association), AEHEC (BBA Students'; Association), AEPC (Certificate Students'; Association), AECS (Graduate Students'; Association).

Campus security: 24-hour emergency response devices and patrols.

Student services: health clinic, personal/psychological counseling.

COSTS & FINANCIAL AID

Costs (2019–20) ***Tuition:*** province resident $2544 full-time, $85 per credit part-time; nonresident $7940 full-time, $265 per credit part-time; International tuition $26,000 full-time. Full-time tuition and fees vary according to program. Part-time tuition and fees vary according to program. ***Required fees:*** $1571 full-time, $49 per credit part-time, $85 per term part-time. ***Room and board:*** $3960. Room and board charges vary according to board plan. ***Waivers:*** employees or children of employees.

Financial Aid Of all full-time matriculated undergraduates who enrolled in 2018, 2,400 applied for aid, 2,400 were judged to have need. 10 state and other part-time jobs (averaging $3900). ***Average financial aid***

package: $7900. ***Average need-based loan:*** $3300. ***Average need-based gift aid:*** $6600. ***Average indebtedness upon graduation:*** $3300.

APPLYING
Options: electronic application, deferred entrance.

Application fee: $92 Canadian dollars.

Required: high school transcript. ***Required for some:*** R score, collegial/college performance rating.

Application deadlines: 3/1 (freshmen), 2/15 (out-of-state freshmen).

CONTACT
Mrs. Geneviève Gélinas, Assistant Registrar, HEC Montreal, 3000 Chemin de la Cote-Sainte-Catherine, Montreal, QC H3T 2A7, Canada. *Phone:* 514-340-6050. *Fax:* 514-340-5640.

Heritage College and Seminary
Cambridge, Ontario, Canada
http://www.heritagecambridge.com/

CONTACT
Mr. Mark Walther, Assistant Dean of Students, Heritage College and Seminary, New York, NY 10023-6588. *Phone:* 519-651-2869 Ext. 251. *Toll-free phone:* 800-465-1961. *Fax:* 519-651-2870. *E-mail:* mwalther@heritagecollege.net.

Horizon College & Seminary
Saskatoon, Saskatchewan, Canada
http://www.horizon.edu/

CONTACT
Mrs. Jenn Lundy, Assistant Registrar, Horizon College & Seminary, 1303 Jackson Avenue, Saskatoon, SK S7H 2M9, Canada. *Phone:* 306-374-6655 Ext. 225. *Toll-free phone:* 877-374-6655. *Fax:* 306-373-6968. *E-mail:* admissions@horizon.edu.

The King's University
Edmonton, Alberta, Canada
http://www.kingsu.ca/

- **Independent interdenominational** 4-year, founded 1979
- **Suburban** 20-acre campus
- **Endowment** $2.5 million
- **Coed** 730 undergraduate students, 95% full-time, 54% women, 46% men
- **Minimally difficult** entrance level, 72% of applicants were admitted

UNDERGRAD STUDENTS
690 full-time, 40 part-time. Students come from 76 provinces and territories; 14 other countries; 9% are from out of state; 11% transferred in; 22% live on campus.

Freshmen:
Admission: 399 applied, 289 admitted, 144 enrolled. ***Average high school GPA:*** 3.0.

Retention: 64% of full-time freshmen returned.

FACULTY
Total: 92, 49% full-time, 59% with terminal degrees.

Student/faculty ratio: 14:1.

ACADEMICS
Calendar: Canadian standard year. *Degrees:* certificates, diplomas, bachelor's, and postbachelor's certificates.

Special study options: advanced placement credit, double majors, English as a second language, independent study, internships, off-campus study, services for LD students, study abroad, summer session for credit.

Computers: 76 computers/terminals are available on campus for general student use. Students can access the following: computer help desk, free student e-mail accounts, online (class) grades, online (class) registration, online (class) schedules. Campuswide network is available. 100% of college-owned or -operated housing units are wired for high-speed Internet access. Wireless service is available via entire campus.
Library: Simona Maaskant. *Books:* 75,000 (physical), 326,525 (digital/electronic); *Serial titles:* 120 (physical), 125,000 (digital/electronic); *Databases:* 60. Weekly public service hours: 68.

STUDENT LIFE
Housing options: coed, men-only, women-only. Campus housing is university owned. Freshman applicants given priority for college housing.

Activities and organizations: drama/theater group, student-run newspaper, choral group, Zumba Club, Pokemon Go Club, King's Science Society, King's Own Historical Society, King's Helping Hands.

Athletics ***Intercollegiate sports:*** badminton M(s)/W(s), basketball M(s)/W(s), soccer M(s)/W(s), volleyball M(s)/W(s). ***Intramural sports:*** basketball M/W, ice hockey M, soccer M/W, volleyball M/W.

Campus security: 24-hour emergency response devices, student patrols, controlled dormitory access, email and text alert system.

Student services: personal/psychological counseling.

COSTS & FINANCIAL AID
Costs (2020–21) ***Comprehensive fee:*** $21,635 includes full-time tuition ($13,082), mandatory fees ($1267), and room and board ($7286). Full-time tuition and fees vary according to course load. Part-time tuition: $422 per credit. Part-time tuition and fees vary according to course load. ***Required fees:*** $256 per term part-time. ***College room only:*** $3800. Room and board charges vary according to board plan and housing facility. ***Payment plan:*** installment. ***Waivers:*** employees or children of employees.

Financial Aid ***Financial aid deadline:*** 3/31.

APPLYING
Options: electronic application.

Application fee: $70 Canadian dollars.

Required: high school transcript, minimum 2.0 GPA, 1 letter of recommendation. ***Required for some:*** essay or personal statement, interview.

Application deadlines: rolling (freshmen), rolling (transfers).

Notification: 8/15 (freshmen), 8/15 (transfers).

CONTACT
Ms. Hilda Buisman, Director of Admissions, The King's University, 9125-50 Street, Edmonton, AB T6B 2H3, Canada. *Phone:* 780-465-3500 Ext. 8031. *Toll-free phone:* 800-661-8582. *Fax:* 780-465-3534. *E-mail:* admissions@kingsu.ca.

Kingswood University
Sussex, New Brunswick, Canada
http://www.kingswood.edu/

CONTACT
Mrs. Shelley Vail, Associate Director for Admissions and Financial Aid, Kingswood University, PO Box 5125, Sussex, NB E4E 5L2, Canada. *Phone:* 506-432-4422. *Toll-free phone:* 888-432-4422. *Fax:* 506-432-4442. *E-mail:* vails@kingswood.edu.

Lakehead University
Thunder Bay, Ontario, Canada
http://www.lakeheadu.ca/

- **Province-supported** comprehensive, founded 1965
- **Suburban** 345-acre campus
- **Endowment** $37.0 million
- **Coed**
- **Moderately difficult** entrance level

ACADEMICS
Calendar: Canadian standard year. *Degrees:* certificates, diplomas, bachelor's, master's, doctoral, and postbachelor's certificates.
Library: Chancellor Norman M. Paterson Library plus 1 other.

STUDENT LIFE
Housing options: coed, special housing for students with disabilities. Campus housing is university owned. Freshman campus housing is guaranteed.

Activities and organizations: student-run newspaper, radio station, choral group, Outdoor Recreation Students Association, Engineering Students Society, Business Association, Educational Students Association, Native Students Association.

Athletics Member CIS.

Campus security: 24-hour emergency response devices and patrols, student patrols, late-night transport/escort service, controlled dormitory access.

Student services: health clinic, personal/psychological counseling, women's center.

COSTS

Costs (2019–20) ***Tuition:*** $1197 Canadian dollars per course part-time. Full-time tuition and fees vary according to course level, degree level, location, program, and student level. Part-time tuition and fees vary according to course level, course load, degree level, location, program, and student level. ***Required fees:*** $109 Canadian dollars part-time. ***Room and board:*** Room and board charges vary according to board plan, housing facility, and location.

APPLYING

Standardized Tests *Required:* SAT or ACT (for admission).

Options: electronic application, early admission, deferred entrance.

Application fee: $125 Canadian dollars.

Required: portfolio for visual arts program, audition for music program, portfolio for media studies. ***Required for some:*** essay or personal statement, high school transcript. ***Recommended:*** minimum 3.0 GPA.

CONTACT

Mr. Nicholas Chamut, Manager of Undergraduate Admissions, Lakehead University, 955 Oliver Road, Thunder Bay, ON P7B 5E1, Canada. *Phone:* 807-343-8676. *Toll-free phone:* 800-465-3959. *Fax:* 807-766-7209. *E-mail:* admissions@lakeheadu.ca.

Laurentian University

Sudbury, Ontario, Canada

http://www.laurentian.ca/

CONTACT

Laurentian University, 935 Ramsey Lake Road, P3E 2C6, Canada. *Phone:* 800-263-4188. *Toll-free phone:* 800-263-4188. *E-mail:* explore@laurentian.ca.

Master's College and Seminary

Peterborough, Ontario, Canada

http://www.mcs.edu/

- **Independent Pentecostal** 4-year, founded 1939
- **Suburban** campus with easy access to Toronto
- **Endowment** $970,384
- **Coed** 227 undergraduate students
- **Noncompetitive** entrance level, 87% of applicants were admitted

UNDERGRAD STUDENTS

Students come from 7 provinces and territories; 1 other country; 21% are from out of state; 65% live on campus.

Freshmen:

Admission: 83 applied, 72 admitted.

Retention: 88% of full-time freshmen returned.

FACULTY

Total: 24, 21% full-time, 25% with terminal degrees.

Student/faculty ratio: 15:1.

ACADEMICS

Calendar: semesters. *Degree:* certificates, diplomas, and bachelor's.

Special study options: academic remediation for entering students, distance learning, independent study, internships, off-campus study, part-time degree program, services for LD students, summer session for credit.

Computers: 6 computers/terminals are available on campus for general student use. Students can access the following: computer help desk, free student e-mail accounts, online (class) grades, online (class) registration, online (class) schedules. Campuswide network is available. 100% of college-owned or -operated housing units are wired for high-speed Internet access. Wireless service is available via entire campus.

Library: Robert and Shirley Taitinger Learning Commons. *Books:* 35,418 (physical), 5,422 (digital/electronic); *Serial titles:* 542 (physical). Weekly public service hours: 71.

STUDENT LIFE

Housing options: on-campus residence required for freshman year; men-only, women-only. Campus housing is university owned. Freshman campus housing is guaranteed.

Campus security: 24-hour emergency response devices, controlled dormitory access.

Student services: personal/psychological counseling.

COSTS

Costs (2020–21) ***One-time required fee:*** $542. ***Comprehensive fee:*** $17,560 includes full-time tuition ($7488), mandatory fees ($1532), and room and board ($8540). Full-time tuition and fees vary according to course load, location, and program. Part-time tuition: $234 per credit hour. Part-time tuition and fees vary according to course load, location, and program. ***Required fees:*** $32 per credit hour part-time. ***Room and board:*** Room and board charges vary according to board plan. ***Payment plan:*** deferred payment. ***Waivers:*** senior citizens and employees or children of employees.

APPLYING

Options: electronic application, deferred entrance.

Application fee: $75 Canadian dollars.

Required: essay or personal statement, high school transcript, 3 letters of recommendation, Christian commitment. ***Required for some:*** interview. ***Recommended:*** minimum 2.0 GPA.

Application deadlines: 8/1 (freshmen), 8/1 (transfers).

Notification: continuous (freshmen), continuous (transfers).

CONTACT

Ms. Shelley Tinlin, Admissions Counsellor, Master's College and Seminary, 780 Argyle Street, Peterborough, ON K9H 5T2, Canada. *Phone:* 800-295-6368 Ext. 251. *Toll-free phone:* 800-295-6368. *Fax:* 705-749-0417. *E-mail:* shelley.tinlin@mcs.edu.

McGill University

Montréal, Quebec, Canada

http://www.mcgill.ca/

CONTACT

Enrollment Services, McGill University, 845 Sherbrooke Street West, James Administration Building, Room 205, Montreal, QC H3A 2T5, Canada. *Phone:* 514-398-3910. *Fax:* 514-398-4193. *E-mail:* admissions@mcgill.ca.

McMaster University

Hamilton, Ontario, Canada

http://www.mcmaster.ca/

- **Province-supported** university, founded 1887
- **Suburban** 300-acre campus with easy access to Toronto
- **Endowment** $631.7 million
- **Coed**
- **Very difficult** entrance level

FACULTY

Student/faculty ratio: 25:1.

ACADEMICS

Calendar: Canadian standard year. *Degrees:* certificates, diplomas, bachelor's, master's, and doctoral.

Library: Mills Memorial Library plus 4 others.

STUDENT LIFE

Housing options: coed, women-only, special housing for students with disabilities. Campus housing is university owned. Freshman applicants given priority for college housing.

Activities and organizations: drama/theater group, student-run newspaper, radio station, choral group, Inter-Varsity Christian Fellowship, African-Caribbean Student Association, Chinese Students' Association, AIESEC (international leadership organization), Southeast Asian-American Society.

Athletics Member CIS.

Campus security: 24-hour emergency response devices and patrols, student patrols, late-night transport/escort service, controlled dormitory access.

Student services: health clinic, personal/psychological counseling, women's center, legal services.

COSTS

Costs (2019–20) ***Tuition:*** $201 Canadian dollars per unit part-time; province resident $6093 Canadian dollars full-time, $201 Canadian dollars per unit part-time; nonresident $6093 Canadian dollars full-time, $201 Canadian dollars per unit part-time; International tuition $30,824 Canadian dollars full-time. Full-time tuition and fees vary according to course load, degree level, program, and student level. Part-time tuition and fees vary according to course load, degree level, program, and student level. ***Required fees:*** $1167 Canadian dollars full-time, $10 Canadian dollars per year part-time. ***Room and board:*** $11,640 Canadian dollars; room only: $6885 Canadian dollars. Room and board charges vary according to board plan and housing facility.

APPLYING

Standardized Tests *Required:* SAT or ACT (for admission)

Options: electronic application, deferred entrance.

Application fee: $150 Canadian dollars.

Required: high school transcript. ***Required for some:*** essay or personal statement, interview.

CONTACT

Olivia Demerling, Admissions Officer, McMaster University, 1280 Main Street West, Hamilton, ON L8S 4M2, Canada. *Phone:* 905-525-4600. *Fax:* 905-527-1105. *E-mail:* admitmac@mcmaster.ca.

Memorial University of Newfoundland

St. John's, Newfoundland and Labrador, Canada

http://www.mun.ca/

CONTACT

Ms. Marian Abbott, Admissions Office, Memorial University of Newfoundland, Elizabeth Avenue, St. John's, NL A1C 5S7, Canada. *Phone:* 709-737-3705. *E-mail:* sturecru@morgan.ucs.mun.ca.

Mount Allison University

Sackville, New Brunswick, Canada

http://www.mta.ca/

- **Province-supported** comprehensive, founded 1839
- **Small-town** 50-acre campus
- **Endowment** $65.0 million
- **Coed**
- **Moderately difficult** entrance level

FACULTY

Student/faculty ratio: 16:1.

ACADEMICS

Calendar: Canadian standard year. *Degrees:* certificates, bachelor's, and master's.

Library: Ralph Pickard Bell Library plus 3 others. Students can reserve study rooms.

STUDENT LIFE

Housing options: coed, women-only, cooperative. Campus housing is university owned. Freshman campus housing is guaranteed.

Activities and organizations: drama/theater group, student-run newspaper, radio station, choral group, Commerce Society, Windsor Theatre, President's Leadership Development Certificate, Leadership Mount Allison, Garnet and Gold Society.

Athletics Member CIS.

Campus security: 24-hour emergency response devices, late-night transport/escort service.

Student services: health clinic, personal/psychological counseling.

COSTS

Costs (2019–20) ***Tuition:*** province resident $8085 Canadian dollars full-time, $809 Canadian dollars per course part-time; nonresident $8770 Canadian dollars full-time, $877 Canadian dollars per course part-time; International tuition $18,130 Canadian dollars full-time. Full-time tuition and fees vary according to course load and degree level. Part-time tuition and fees vary according to course load and degree level. ***Required fees:*** $1022 Canadian dollars full-time, $115 Canadian dollars per year part-time. ***Room and board:*** $10,625 Canadian dollars; room only: $4896 Canadian dollars. Room and board charges vary according to board plan and housing facility.

APPLYING

Options: electronic application, deferred entrance.

Application fee: $50 Canadian dollars.

Required: high school transcript, minimum 2.5 GPA. ***Required for some:*** essay or personal statement, interview. ***Recommended:*** 2 letters of recommendation.

CONTACT

Mr. Curtis Michaelis, Manager of Admissions, Mount Allison University, 65 York Street, Sackville, NB E4L 1E4, Canada. *Phone:* 506-364-3294. *Fax:* 506-364-2272. *E-mail:* admissions@mta.ca.

Mount Royal University

Calgary, Alberta, Canada

http://www.mtroyal.ca/

CONTACT

Admissions Office, Mount Royal University, 4825 Mount Royal Gate SW, Calgary, AB T3E 6K6, Canada. *Phone:* 403-440-5000. *Toll-free phone:* 877-440-5001.

Mount Saint Vincent University

Halifax, Nova Scotia, Canada

http://www.msvu.ca/

CONTACT

Ms. Heidi Tattrie, Assistant Registrar/Admissions, Mount Saint Vincent University, 166 Bedford Highway, Halifax, NS B3M2J6, Canada. *Phone:* 902-457-6117. *Toll-free phone:* 877-733-6788. *Fax:* 902-457-6498. *E-mail:* admissions@msvu.ca.

Ner Israel Yeshiva College of Toronto

Thornhill, Ontario, Canada

http://www.neryisroel.info/

- **Independent Jewish** comprehensive, founded 1959
- 14-acre campus
- **Men only**
- **Very difficult** entrance level

UNDERGRAD STUDENTS

Students come from 3 provinces and territories; 2 other countries.

ACADEMICS

Calendar: Canadian standard year. *Degrees:* bachelor's and master's.

Special study options: summer session for credit.

STUDENT LIFE

Housing options: on-campus residence required through senior year.

Student services: personal/psychological counseling.

APPLYING

Required: high school transcript, 2 letters of recommendation, interview.

Application deadlines: 8/15 (freshmen), 8/15 (transfers).

CONTACT

Ner Israel Yeshiva College of Toronto, 8950 Bathurst Street, Thornhill, ON L4J 8A7, Canada. *Phone:* 905-731-1224.

Nipissing University

North Bay, Ontario, Canada

http://www.nipissingu.ca/

CONTACT

Ms. Lori-Ann Beckford, Assistant Registrar, Liaison, Nipissing University, 100 College Drive, Box 5002, North Bay, ON P1B 8L7,

Canada. *Phone:* 705-474-3461 Ext. 4518. *Fax:* 705-474-1947. *E-mail:* liaison@nipissingu.ca.

NSCAD University

Halifax, Nova Scotia, Canada

http://www.nscad.ca/

CONTACT
Mr. Terry Bailey, Director of Admissions and Enrollment Services, NSCAD University, 5163 Duke Street, Halifax, NS B3J 3J6, Canada. *Phone:* 902-494-8129. *Toll-free phone:* 888-444-5989. *Fax:* 902-425-2987. *E-mail:* admissions@nscad.ca.

Okanagan College

Kelowna, British Columbia, Canada

http://www.okanagan.bc.ca/

CONTACT
Mr. Allan Hickey, Associate Registrar Systems, Okanagan College, 1000 K.L.O. Road, Kelowna, BC V1Y 4X8, Canada. *Phone:* 250-762-5445 Ext. 4332. *Toll-free phone:* 877-755-2266. *E-mail:* ahickey@okanagan.bc.ca.

Polytechnique Montréal

Montréal, Quebec, Canada

http://www.polymtl.ca/

CONTACT
Polytechnique Montréal, CP 6079, Succursale Centre-Ville, Montréal, QC H3C 3A7, Canada.

Prairie Bible Institute

Three Hills, Alberta, Canada

http://www.prairie.edu/

CONTACT
Mr. Kevin Kirk, Vice President, Marketing and Enrollment Management, Prairie Bible Institute, 350 5th Avenue, NE, Box 4000, Three Hills, AB T0M 2N0, Canada. *Phone:* 403-443-5511 Ext. 3007. *Toll-free phone:* 800-661-2425. *E-mail:* admissions@prairie.edu.

Providence University College & Theological Seminary

Otterburne, Manitoba, Canada

http://www.prov.ca/

CONTACT
Mr. Adrian Enns, Director of College Enrollment, Providence University College & Theological Seminary, 10 College Crescent, Otterburne, MB R0A 1G0, Canada. *Phone:* 204-433-7488. *Toll-free phone:* 800-668-7768. *Fax:* 204-433-7158. *E-mail:* info@prov.ca.

Queen's University at Kingston

Kingston, Ontario, Canada

http://www.queensu.ca/

- **Province-supported** university, founded 1841
- **Urban** 160-acre campus
- **Endowment** $710.3 million
- **Coed**
- **Most difficult** entrance level

FACULTY
Student/faculty ratio: 15:1.

ACADEMICS
Calendar: Canadian standard year. *Degrees:* certificates, bachelor's, master's, and doctoral.
Library: Joseph S. Stauffer Library plus 4 others.

STUDENT LIFE
Housing options: coed, men-only, women-only, cooperative, special housing for students with disabilities. Campus housing is university owned. Freshman campus housing is guaranteed.

Activities and organizations: drama/theater group, student-run newspaper, radio station, choral group, marching band, Arts and Sciences Undergraduate Society, Alma Mater Society, Engineering Society, Commerce Society, dance club.

Athletics Member CIS.

Campus security: 24-hour emergency response devices and patrols, student patrols, late-night transport/escort service, controlled dormitory access.

Student services: health clinic, personal/psychological counseling, women's center, legal services.

FINANCIAL AID
Financial Aid Of all full-time matriculated undergraduates who enrolled in 2012, 431 state and other part-time jobs (averaging $1200). ***Average financial aid package:*** $8796.

APPLYING
Standardized Tests *Required:* SAT or ACT (for admission).

Options: deferred entrance.

Application fee: $230 Canadian dollars.

Required: essay or personal statement, high school transcript, minimum 2.7 GPA. ***Required for some:*** 1 letter of recommendation.

CONTACT
Ms. Iveta Reinikovaite, Admission Coordinator, Queen's University at Kingston, Undergraduate Admissions, Gordon Hall, 74 Union Street, Kingston, ON K7L 3N6, Canada. *Phone:* 613-533-2218. *Fax:* 613-533-6810. *E-mail:* admission@queensu.ca.

Redeemer University College

Ancaster, Ontario, Canada

http://www.redeemer.ca/

- **Independent interdenominational** 4-year, founded 1980
- **Small-town** 86-acre campus with easy access to Toronto
- **Coed**
- 94% of applicants were admitted

FACULTY
Student/faculty ratio: 11:1.

ACADEMICS
Calendar: semesters. *Degree:* certificates and bachelor's.
Library: Peter Turkstra Library. *Books:* 92,733 (physical); *Serial titles:* 93 (physical), 9,387 (digital/electronic); *Databases:* 21. Students can reserve study rooms.

STUDENT LIFE
Housing options: on-campus residence required through sophomore year; men-only, women-only. Campus housing is university owned. Freshman campus housing is guaranteed.

Activities and organizations: drama/theater group, student-run newspaper, choral group, Church in the Box, Service Learning Trips, Deedz, Athletics and Recreation, Concert Choir.

Campus security: 24-hour emergency response devices, student patrols, late-night transport/escort service, controlled dormitory access.

Student services: personal/psychological counseling.

COSTS & FINANCIAL AID
Costs (2019–20) ***Comprehensive fee:*** $18,969 Canadian dollars includes full-time tuition ($9800 Canadian dollars), mandatory fees ($621 Canadian dollars), and room and board ($8548 Canadian dollars). Part-time tuition: $980 Canadian dollars per course. ***Required fees:*** $43 Canadian dollars part-time. ***College room only:*** $6200 Canadian dollars.

Financial Aid Of all full-time matriculated undergraduates who enrolled in 2010, 640 applied for aid, 607 were judged to have need, 200 had their need fully met. 385 state and other part-time jobs (averaging $1238). In 2010, 99 non-need-based awards were made. ***Average percent of need met:*** 82. ***Average financial aid package:*** $12,582. ***Average need-based loan:*** $7464. ***Average need-based gift aid:*** $4587. ***Average non-need-***

based aid: $3061. ***Average indebtedness upon graduation:*** $23,598. ***Financial aid deadline:*** 3/31.

APPLYING

Standardized Tests *Required for some:* SAT or ACT (for admission).

Options: electronic application, deferred entrance.

Application fee: $40 Canadian dollars.

Required: essay or personal statement, high school transcript, minimum 2.0 GPA, 1 letter of recommendation. ***Required for some:*** interview.

CONTACT

Mr. Willem deRuijter, Director, Admissions, Redeemer University College, 777 Garner Road East, Ancaster, ON L9K 1J4, Canada. *Phone:* 905-648-2131 Ext. 4471. *Toll-free phone:* 800-263-6467. *Fax:* 905-648-2134. *E-mail:* recruitment@redeemer.ca.

Rocky Mountain College

Calgary, Alberta, Canada

http://www.rockymountaincollege.ca/

CONTACT

Rocky Mountain College, 4039 Brentwood Road, NW, Calgary, AB T2L 1L1, Canada. *Phone:* 403-284-5100 Ext. 222. *Toll-free phone:* 877-YOUnRMC.

Royal Military College of Canada

Kingston, Ontario, Canada

http://www.rmc.ca/

CONTACT

Royal Military College of Canada, PO Box 17000, Station Forces, Kingston, ON K7K 7B4, Canada. *Phone:* 613-541-6000 Ext. 6579.

Royal Roads University

Victoria, British Columbia, Canada

http://www.royalroads.ca/

CONTACT

Royal Roads University, 2005 Sooke Road, Victoria, BC V9B 5Y2, Canada. *Phone:* 250-391-2511. *Toll-free phone:* 800-788-8028.

Ryerson University

Toronto, Ontario, Canada

http://www.ryerson.ca/

CONTACT

Michelle Beaton, Manager of International Student Recruitment, Ryerson University, 350 Victoria Street, Toronto, ON M5B 2K3, Canada. *Phone:* 416-979-5080. *Fax:* 416-979-5067. *E-mail:* inquire@ryerson.ca.

St. Francis Xavier University

Antigonish, Nova Scotia, Canada

http://www.stfx.ca/

CONTACT

Ms. Sarah Murray, Admissions Officer, St. Francis Xavier University, PO Box 5000, Antigonish, NS B2G 2W5, Canada. *Phone:* 902-867-2219. *Toll-free phone:* 877-867-7839 (in-state); 877-867-STFX (out-of-state). *Fax:* 902-867-2329. *E-mail:* mbarry@stfx.ca.

Saint Mary's University

Halifax, Nova Scotia, Canada

http://www.smu.ca/

CONTACT

Mr. Greg Ferguson, Director of Admissions, Saint Mary's University, Halifax, NS B3H 3C3, Canada. *Phone:* 902-420-5415. *Fax:* 902-496-8100. *E-mail:* greg.ferguson@smu.ca.

Saint Paul University

Ottawa, Ontario, Canada

http://www.ustpaul.ca/

CONTACT

Admission and Recruitment Office, Saint Paul University, 223 Main Street, Ottawa, ON K1S 1C4, Canada. *Phone:* 613-236-1393 Ext. 8990. *Toll-free phone:* 800-637-6859. *Fax:* 613-782-3014. *E-mail:* admission@ustpaul.ca.

St. Thomas University - New Brunswick

Fredericton, New Brunswick, Canada

http://www.stu.ca/

- **Independent Roman Catholic** 4-year, founded 1910
- **Urban** 16-acre campus
- **Endowment** $16.1 million
- **Coed** 1,850 undergraduate students, 96% full-time, 74% women, 26% men
- **Moderately difficult** entrance level, 79% of applicants were admitted

UNDERGRAD STUDENTS

1,772 full-time, 78 part-time. Students come from 10 provinces and territories; 46 other countries; 15% are from out of state; 3% American Indian or Alaska Native, non-Hispanic/Latino; 87% Race/ethnicity unknown; 10% international; 5% transferred in; 20% live on campus.

Freshmen:

Admission: 1,194 applied, 939 admitted, 520 enrolled. ***Average high school GPA:*** 3.3.

Retention: 78% of full-time freshmen returned.

FACULTY

Total: 187, 56% full-time, 72% with terminal degrees.

Student/faculty ratio: 16:1.

ACADEMICS

Calendar: semesters. *Degrees:* certificates, bachelor's, and postbachelor's certificates.

Special study options: academic remediation for entering students, accelerated degree program, advanced placement credit, double majors, English as a second language, honors programs, independent study, internships, off-campus study, part-time degree program, services for LD students, student-designed majors, study abroad, summer session for credit.

Computers: 88 computers/terminals are available on campus for general student use. Students can access the following: computer help desk, free student e-mail accounts, online (class) grades, online (class) registration, online (class) schedules, learning management system. Campuswide network is available. 100% of college-owned or -operated housing units are wired for high-speed Internet access. Wireless service is available via entire campus.

Library: Harriet Irving Library plus 2 others. *Books:* 976,313 (physical), 532,787 (digital/electronic); *Serial titles:* 2,449 (physical), 44,800 (digital/electronic). Weekly public service hours: 113; students can reserve study rooms.

STUDENT LIFE

Housing options: coed, women-only, special housing for students with disabilities. Campus housing is university owned. Freshman campus housing is guaranteed.

Activities and organizations: drama/theater group, student-run newspaper, radio station, choral group, Theatre St. Thomas, St. Thomas Student Union, Criminology Society, Model UN, International Students' Association.

Athletics Member CIS. ***Intercollegiate sports:*** basketball M/W, cross-country running M/W, golf M/W, ice hockey W, soccer M/W, track and field M/W, volleyball M/W. ***Intramural sports:*** badminton M/W, basketball M/W, cross-country running M/W, fencing M/W, football M, ice hockey M/W, rock climbing M/W, soccer M/W, softball M/W, squash M/W, swimming and diving M/W, table tennis M/W, track and field M/W, ultimate Frisbee M/W, volleyball M/W, water polo M/W.

Campus security: 24-hour emergency response devices and patrols, student patrols, late-night transport/escort service, controlled dormitory access.

Student services: health clinic, personal/psychological counseling, women's center.

COSTS & FINANCIAL AID

Costs (2019–20) ***Comprehensive fee:*** $17,191 includes full-time tuition ($7149), mandatory fees ($908), and room and board ($9134). Full-time tuition and fees vary according to course load, degree level, and program. Part-time tuition: $717 per course. Part-time tuition and fees vary according to course load. ***Required fees:*** $57 per course part-time. ***Room and board:*** Room and board charges vary according to board plan, housing facility, and location. ***Payment plans:*** installment, deferred payment. ***Waivers:*** senior citizens and employees or children of employees.

Financial Aid ***Financial aid deadline:*** 3/1.

APPLYING

Options: electronic application, early action.

Application fee: $55 Canadian dollars.

Required: essay or personal statement, high school transcript, minimum 3.0 GPA. ***Required for some:*** interview.

Application deadlines: 8/31 (freshmen), 8/31 (transfers), 12/7 (early action).

Notification: continuous (freshmen), continuous (transfers).

CONTACT

Ms. Michelle Wright, Director of Admissions, St. Thomas University - New Brunswick, Duffie Hall, Fredericton, NB E3B 5G3, Canada. *Phone:* 506-452-0532. *Fax:* 506-452-0617. *E-mail:* admissions@stu.ca.

Simon Fraser University

Burnaby, British Columbia, Canada

http://www.sfu.ca/

- **Province-supported** university, founded 1965
- **Suburban** 174-hectare campus with easy access to Vancouver
- **Coed** 25,425 undergraduate students, 51% full-time, 54% women, 46% men
- **Moderately difficult** entrance level, 58% of applicants were admitted

UNDERGRAD STUDENTS

12,919 full-time, 12,506 part-time. 7% are from out of state; 3% transferred in.

Freshmen:

Admission: 15,852 applied, 9,171 admitted, 2,956 enrolled.

Retention: 86% of full-time freshmen returned.

FACULTY

Total: 984, 99% full-time, 90% with terminal degrees.

Student/faculty ratio: 22:1.

ACADEMICS

Calendar: trimesters. *Degrees:* certificates, diplomas, bachelor's, master's, doctoral, post-master's, and postbachelor's certificates.

Special study options: academic remediation for entering students, adult/continuing education programs, advanced placement credit, cooperative education, distance learning, double majors, English as a second language, honors programs, independent study, internships, off-campus study, part-time degree program, services for LD students, study abroad, summer session for credit.

Computers: 200 computers/terminals and 30 ports are available on campus for general student use. Students can access the following: computer help desk, free student e-mail accounts, online (class) grades, online (class) registration, online (class) schedules. Campuswide network is available. 100% of college-owned or -operated housing units are wired for high-speed Internet access. Wireless service is available via entire campus.

Library: Bennett Library plus 2 others. *Books:* 1.5 million (physical), 1.1 million (digital/electronic); *Serial titles:* 2,500 (physical), 98,000 (digital/electronic). Weekly public service hours: 103; students can reserve study rooms.

STUDENT LIFE

Housing options: coed, special housing for students with disabilities. Campus housing is university owned. Freshman applicants given priority for college housing.

Activities and organizations: student-run newspaper, radio station, The Peak Newspaper, orientation/peer leaders, Crisis line, Women's Centre, Simon Fraser Public Interest Research Group.

Athletics Member NCAA. All Division II. ***Intercollegiate sports:*** basketball M(s)/W(s), cross-country running M(s)/W(s), football M(s), golf M(s)/W, gymnastics M, soccer M(s)/W(s), softball W(s), swimming and diving M(s)/W(s), track and field M(s)/W(s), volleyball W(s), wrestling M(s)/W(s). ***Intramural sports:*** archery M(c)/W(c), badminton M(c)/W(c), basketball M/W, cheerleading M(c)/W(c), crew M(c)/W(c), fencing M(c)/W(c), field hockey W(c), football M/W, golf W(c), gymnastics W(c), ice hockey M(c)/W(c), lacrosse M(c), rugby M(c)/W(c), soccer M/W, softball M/W, squash M(c)/W(c), table tennis M(c)/W(c), tennis M/W, ultimate Frisbee M(c)/W(c), volleyball M(c)/W(c), water polo M(c)/W(c).

Campus security: 24-hour emergency response devices and patrols, student patrols, late-night transport/escort service, controlled dormitory access, safe-walk stations, 24-hour safe study area.

Student services: health clinic, personal/psychological counseling, women's center.

APPLYING

Standardized Tests *Required for some:* SAT or ACT (for admission).

Options: electronic application, deferred entrance.

Required: high school transcript, minimum 3.0 GPA. ***Required for some:*** essay or personal statement, interview.

Application deadlines: 2/28 (freshmen), 2/28 (transfers).

Notification: continuous until 6/30 (freshmen), continuous until 5/30 (transfers).

CONTACT

Louise Legris, Director of Admissions, Simon Fraser University, 8888 University Drive, MBC 3200, Burnaby, BC V5A 1S6, Canada. *Phone:* 778-782-3498. *Fax:* 778-782-4969.

Southern Alberta Institute of Technology

Calgary, Alberta, Canada

http://www.sait.ca/

CONTACT

Southern Alberta Institute of Technology, 1301 16th Avenue NW, Calgary, AB T2M 0L4, Canada. *Phone:* 403-284-8857. *Toll-free phone:* 877-284-SAIT.

Steinbach Bible College

Steinbach, Manitoba, Canada

http://www.sbcollege.ca/

- **Independent Mennonite** 4-year, founded 1936
- **Urban** 16-acre campus with easy access to Winnipeg
- **Coed** 118 undergraduate students, 67% full-time, 55% women, 45% men
- **Minimally difficult** entrance level, 78% of applicants were admitted

UNDERGRAD STUDENTS

79 full-time, 39 part-time.

Freshmen:

Admission: 59 applied, 46 admitted.

Retention: 56% of full-time freshmen returned.

FACULTY

Total: 20, 30% with terminal degrees.

ACADEMICS

Calendar: semesters. *Degrees:* certificates, associate, and bachelor's.

STUDENT LIFE

Housing options: Campus housing is university owned.

APPLYING
Options: electronic application.

Application fee: $50 Canadian dollars.

CONTACT
Mrs. Kaylene Buhler, Admissions Counselor, Steinbach Bible College, 50 PTH 12 North, Steinbach, MB R5G 1T4, Canada. *Phone:* 204-326-6451 Ext. 232. *Toll-free phone:* 800-230-8478. *Fax:* 204-326-6908. *E-mail:* info@sbcollege.ca.

Summit Pacific College

Abbotsford, British Columbia, Canada

http://www.summitpacific.ca/

CONTACT
Ms. Melody Deeley, Admissions and Registration, Summit Pacific College, Box 1700, Abbotsford, BC V2S 7E7, Canada. *Phone:* 604-851-7225. *Toll-free phone:* 800-976-8388. *E-mail:* registrar@summitpacific.ca.

Télé-université

Québec, Quebec, Canada

http://www.teluq.uquebec.ca/

CONTACT
Ms. Louise Bertrand, Registraire, Télé-université, 455, rue de l'Église, C.P. 4800, succ. Terminus, Québec, QC G1K 9H5, Canada. *Phone:* 418-657-2262 Ext. 5307. *Toll-free phone:* 888-843-4333.

Thompson Rivers University

Kamloops, British Columbia, Canada

http://www.tru.ca/

- **Province-supported** comprehensive, founded 1970, part of Ministry of Advanced Education, Province of British Columbia
- **Small-town** 100-acre campus
- **Endowment** $16.1 million
- **Coed**
- 82% of applicants were admitted

ACADEMICS
Calendar: semesters. *Degrees:* certificates, diplomas, associate, bachelor's, master's, and postbachelor's certificates.
Library: Thompson Rivers University Library plus 2 others.

STUDENT LIFE
Housing options: coed. Campus housing is university owned and is provided by a third party.

Activities and organizations: drama/theater group, student-run newspaper, radio station, choral group, national fraternities, national sororities.

Athletics Member CIS.

Campus security: 24-hour emergency response devices and patrols, student patrols, late-night transport/escort service, controlled dormitory access.

Student services: health clinic, personal/psychological counseling.

FINANCIAL AID
Financial Aid Of all full-time matriculated undergraduates who enrolled in 2009, 85 state and other part-time jobs (averaging $2400). ***Financial aid deadline:*** 3/1.

APPLYING
Options: electronic application, early admission, early decision, deferred entrance.

Application fee: $26 Canadian dollars.

Required: high school transcript. ***Required for some:*** essay or personal statement, interview.

CONTACT
Mr. Josh Keller, Director, Student Recruitment and Liaison, Thompson Rivers University, 900 McGill Road, Kamloops, BC V2C 0C8, Canada. *Phone:* 250-828-5008. *Fax:* 250-828-5159. *E-mail:* jkeller@tru.ca.

Trent University

Peterborough, Ontario, Canada

http://www.trentu.ca/

CONTACT
Mr. Kevin Whitmore, Director, Recruitment and Admissions, Trent University, 1600 West Bank Drive, Peterborough, ON K9J 7B8, Canada. *Phone:* 705-748-1011 Ext. 7748. *Fax:* 705-748-1629. *E-mail:* admissions@trentu.ca.

Trinity Western University

Langley, British Columbia, Canada

http://www.twu.ca/

CONTACT
Trinity Western University, 7600 Glover Road, Langley, BC V2Y 1Y1, Canada. *Toll-free phone:* 888-468-6898.

Tyndale University College & Seminary

Toronto, Ontario, Canada

http://www.tyndale.ca/

- **Independent interdenominational** comprehensive, founded 1894
- **Urban** 56-acre campus
- **Endowment** $2.0 million
- **Coed**
- **Moderately difficult** entrance level

FACULTY
Student/faculty ratio: 23:1.

ACADEMICS
Calendar: semesters. *Degrees:* certificates, bachelor's, master's, and doctoral.
Library: J. William Horsey Library.

STUDENT LIFE
Housing options: men-only, women-only. Campus housing is university owned. Freshman applicants given priority for college housing.

Activities and organizations: drama/theater group, student-run newspaper, choral group, choir, student government, Urban Ministry Team, Steadfast drama team.

Campus security: 24-hour patrols, student patrols, late-night transport/escort service, controlled dormitory access.

Student services: personal/psychological counseling.

COSTS
Costs (2019–20) ***Comprehensive fee:*** $22,850 Canadian dollars includes full-time tuition ($14,640 Canadian dollars), mandatory fees ($1290 Canadian dollars), and room and board ($6920 Canadian dollars). Full-time tuition and fees vary according to course load. Part-time tuition: $1464 Canadian dollars per course. Part-time tuition and fees vary according to course load. ***Required fees:*** $129 Canadian dollars per course part-time. ***College room only:*** $3720 Canadian dollars. Room and board charges vary according to board plan.

APPLYING
Options: electronic application, deferred entrance.

Application fee: $50 Canadian dollars.

Required: high school transcript, minimum 2.0 GPA, all post-secondary transcripts. ***Required for some:*** 1 letter of recommendation, interview. ***Recommended:*** essay or personal statement.

CONTACT
Justin Hackett, Director, Admissions, Tyndale University College & Seminary, 3377 Bayview Avenue, Toronto, ON M2M 3S4, Canada. *Phone:* 416-218-6757. *Toll-free phone:* 877-896-3253. *E-mail:* admissions@tydale.ca.

Université de Moncton

Moncton, New Brunswick, Canada

http://www.umoncton.ca/

- **Province-supported** comprehensive, founded 1963
- **Urban** 400-acre campus
- **Endowment** $19.8 million
- **Coed**
- **Moderately difficult** entrance level

FACULTY
Student/faculty ratio: 12:1.

ACADEMICS
Calendar: semesters. *Degrees:* bachelor's, master's, and doctoral (doctoral degree in French studies only).
Library: Bibliothéque Champlain plus 2 others.

STUDENT LIFE
Housing options: coed, women-only, special housing for students with disabilities.

Activities and organizations: drama/theater group, student-run newspaper, radio station, choral group, Amnesty International, student radio station, business clubs, Improvisational League, WSC.

Athletics Member CIS.

Campus security: 24-hour emergency response devices and patrols, controlled dormitory access, student security attendants in residences 8 pm to 2 am.

Student services: health clinic, personal/psychological counseling.

COSTS & FINANCIAL AID
Costs (2019–20) ***Tuition:*** $6771 Canadian dollars full-time. ***Room only:*** $3210 Canadian dollars.

Financial Aid Of all full-time matriculated undergraduates who enrolled in 2016, 1,385 were judged to have need. In 2016, 454 non-need-based awards were made. ***Average financial aid package:*** $9489. ***Average need-based gift aid:*** $4289. ***Average non-need-based aid:*** $2391. ***Financial aid deadline:*** 3/10.

APPLYING
Options: deferred entrance.

Application fee: $30.

Required: high school transcript, French examination. ***Required for some:*** essay or personal statement, minimum 2.0 GPA, 1 letter of recommendation, interview.

CONTACT
Miss Nicole Savois, Chief Admission Officer, Université de Moncton, Moncton, NB E1A 3E9, Canada. *Phone:* 506-858-4115. *Toll-free phone:* 800-363-8336. *E-mail:* gallanrm@umoncton.ca.

Université de Montréal

Montréal, Quebec, Canada

http://www.umontreal.ca/

CONTACT
Mme. Marie-Claude Binette, Registrar, Université de Montréal, Bureau du registraire, CP 6128, Succursale Centre-Ville, Montreal, QC H3C 3J7, Canada. *Phone:* 514-343-2214. *Toll-free phone:* 866-977-7076 (in-state); 800-977-0761 (out-of-state). *Fax:* 514-343-2097. *E-mail:* marie-claude.binette@umontreal.ca.

Université de Saint-Boniface

Saint-Boniface, Manitoba, Canada

http://www.ustboniface.ca/

CONTACT
Université de Saint-Boniface, 200 avenue de la Cathèdrale, Saint-Boniface, MB R2H 0H7, Canada.

Université de Sherbrooke

Sherbrooke, Quebec, Canada

http://www.usherbrooke.ca/

- **Independent** university, founded 1954
- **Urban** 800-acre campus with easy access to Montreal
- **Coed**
- **Moderately difficult** entrance level

ACADEMICS
Calendar: Canadian standard year. *Degrees:* certificates, diplomas, bachelor's, master's, and doctoral.
Library: Bibliotheque Roger-Maltais plus 5 others. Weekly public service hours: 73; students can reserve study rooms.

STUDENT LIFE
Housing options: coed, cooperative. Campus housing is university owned and is provided by a third party.

Activities and organizations: drama/theater group, student-run newspaper, radio station, choral group.

Athletics Member CIS.

Campus security: 24-hour emergency response devices and patrols, late-night transport/escort service.

Student services: health clinic, personal/psychological counseling.

COSTS & FINANCIAL AID
Costs (2019–20) ***Tuition:*** Full-time tuition and fees vary according to course load, location, program, and reciprocity agreements. Part-time tuition and fees vary according to course load, location, program, and reciprocity agreements. ***Required fees:*** $14 Canadian dollars per credit part-time, $67 Canadian dollars per term part-time. ***Room and board:*** $9200 Canadian dollars; room only: $4992 Canadian dollars. Room and board charges vary according to location.

Financial Aid ***Financial aid deadline:*** 3/31.

APPLYING
Options: electronic application.

Application fee: $75 Canadian dollars.

Required: high school transcript. ***Required for some:*** interview, Test of French level, Casper test.

CONTACT
Mme. Lisa BEDARD, Admissions Officer, Université de Sherbrooke, 2500 boulevard de l'Universite, Sherbrooke, QC J1K 2R1. *Phone:* 819-821-7687. *Toll-free phone:* 800-267-UDES.

Université du Québec à Chicoutimi

Chicoutimi, Quebec, Canada

http://www.uqac.ca/

CONTACT
Jean Wauthier, Admissions Officer, Université du Québec à Chicoutimi, 555, boulevard de L'Université, Chicoutimi, QC G7H 2B1, Canada. *Phone:* 418-545-5005. *E-mail:* czoccast@uqac.uquebec.ca.

Université du Québec à Montréal

Montréal, Quebec, Canada

http://www.uqam.ca/

CONTACT
Ms. Lucille Boisselle-Roy, Admissions Officer, Université du Québec à Montréal, CP 8888, Succursale Centreville, Montréal, QC H2L 4S8, Canada. *Phone:* 514-987-3132. *E-mail:* admission@uqam.ca.

Université du Québec à Rimouski

Rimouski, Quebec, Canada

http://www.uqar.ca/

CONTACT
Ms. Marie Saint-Laurent, Admissions Officer, Université du Québec à Rimouski, 300 Allee des Ursulines, CP3300, Rimouski QC G5L 3A1, Canada. *Phone:* 418-724-1433. *E-mail:* philippe_horth@uqar.uquebec.ca.

Université du Québec à Trois-Rivières

Trois-Rivières, Quebec, Canada

http://www.uqtr.ca/

CONTACT

Ms. Jean Bois, Admissions Officer, Université du Québec à Trois-Rivières, 3351 blvd des Forges, Case post 500, Trois-Rivières, QC G9A 5H7, Canada. *Phone:* 819-376-5011. *Toll-free phone:* 800-365-0922. *Fax:* 819-376-5232. *E-mail:* registraire@uqtr.ca.

Université du Québec, École de technologie supérieure

Montréal, Quebec, Canada

http://www.etsmtl.ca/

CONTACT

Mme. Francine Gamache, Registraire, Université du Québec, École de technologie supérieure, 1100, rue Notre Dame Ouest, Montréal, QC H3C 1K3, Canada. *Phone:* 514-396-8885. *E-mail:* admission@ets.mtl.ca.

Université du Québec en Abitibi-Témiscamingue

Rouyn-Noranda, Quebec, Canada

http://www.uqat.ca/

CONTACT

Mrs. Monique Fay, Admissions Officer, Université du Québec en Abitibi-Témiscamingue, 445 boulevard de l'Université, Rouyn-Noranda, QC J9X 5E4, Canada. *Phone:* 819-762-0971. *E-mail:* micheline.chevalier@uqat.uquebec.ca.

Université du Québec en Outaouais

Gatineau, Quebec, Canada

http://www.uqo.ca/

CONTACT

Registrar's Office, Université du Québec en Outaouais, CP 1250, Succursale Hull, 101 Saint-Jean-Bosco, 101 rue Saint-Jean-Bosco, Gatineau, QC J8X 3X7, Canada. *Phone:* 819-595-3900 Ext. 1850. *Toll-free phone:* 800-567-1283. *Fax:* 819-773-1835. *E-mail:* registraire@uqo.ca.

Université Laval

Québec, Quebec, Canada

http://www.ulaval.ca/

CONTACT

Promotion and Recruitment Division, Université Laval, Quebec, QC G1K 7P4, Canada. *Phone:* 418-656-2764. *Toll-free phone:* 877-785-2825. *Fax:* 418-656-5216. *E-mail:* info@dap.ulaval.ca.

Université Sainte-Anne

Church Point, Nova Scotia, Canada

http://www.usainteanne.ca/

- **Province-supported** comprehensive, founded 1890
- **Rural** 115-acre campus
- **Endowment** $2.7 million
- **Coed**
- **Moderately difficult** entrance level

ACADEMICS

Calendar: semesters. *Degrees:* certificates, diplomas, bachelor's, and master's.
Library: Bibliothèque Louis-R.-Comeau plus 1 other. *Books:* 76,000 (physical); *Serial titles:* 52 (physical); *Databases:* 27. Weekly public service hours: 78.

STUDENT LIFE

Housing options: coed, special housing for students with disabilities. Campus housing is university owned and is provided by a third party.

Activities and organizations: drama/theater group, Student Organization, Enactus, Club de Plein Air, Education Committee, Association des étudiants internationaux de l'Université Sainte-Anne.

Athletics Member CIS.

Campus security: 24-hour emergency response devices and patrols, student patrols, late-night transport/escort service, 14-hour patrols by trained security personnel.

Student services: health clinic, personal/psychological counseling.

FINANCIAL AID

Financial Aid Of all full-time matriculated undergraduates who enrolled in 2013, 3 were judged to have need. ***Financial aid deadline:*** 11/15.

APPLYING

Options: electronic application, early admission, deferred entrance.

Application fee: $50.

Required: high school transcript. ***Required for some:*** essay or personal statement, 3 letters of recommendation, criminal record check.

CONTACT

Ms. Nora Saulnier, Admissions Officer, Université Sainte-Anne, 1695, Highway 1, Church Point, NS B0W 1M0. *Phone:* 902-769-2114 Ext. 7116. *E-mail:* admission@usainteanne.ca.

University of Alberta

Edmonton, Alberta, Canada

http://www.ualberta.ca/

CONTACT

Melissa Padfield, Deputy Registrar, University of Alberta, Administration Building, Edmonton, AB T6G 2M7, Canada. *Phone:* 780-492-3113. *Toll-free phone:* 855-492-3113. *Fax:* 780-492-7172.

The University of British Columbia

Vancouver, British Columbia, Canada

http://www.ubc.ca/

- **Province-supported** university, founded 1915
- **Urban** 1000-acre campus with easy access to Vancouver
- **Endowment** $1.2 billion
- **Coed**
- **Very difficult** entrance level

FACULTY

Student/faculty ratio: 15:1.

ACADEMICS

Calendar: Canadian standard year. *Degrees:* certificates, diplomas, bachelor's, master's, doctoral, and postbachelor's certificates.
Library: UBC Library plus 9 others.

STUDENT LIFE

Housing options: coed, men-only, women-only, special housing for students with disabilities. Campus housing is university owned. Freshman applicants given priority for college housing.

Activities and organizations: drama/theater group, student-run newspaper, radio station, choral group, Ski and Board Club, Dance Club, AIESEC (international leadership organization), UBC Film Society, Varsity Outdoors Club, national fraternities, national sororities.

Athletics Member NAIA, CIS.

Campus security: 24-hour emergency response devices and patrols, student patrols, late-night transport/escort service, 24-hour desk attendants in residence halls.

Student services: health clinic, personal/psychological counseling, women's center, legal services.

FINANCIAL AID

Financial Aid Of all full-time matriculated undergraduates who enrolled in 2016, 13,714 were judged to have need. 1,902 state and other part-time jobs (averaging $1849). In 2016, 4969 non-need-based awards were made. ***Average financial aid package:*** $11,550. ***Average need-based loan:*** $7924. ***Average need-based gift aid:*** $5034. ***Average non-need-based aid:*** $3509. ***Financial aid deadline:*** 9/15.

APPLYING
Standardized Tests *Required for some:* SAT or ACT (for admission), SAT or ACT plus Writing required of applicants following US curriculum.

Options: electronic application, deferred entrance.

Application fee: $108 Canadian dollars.

Required: essay or personal statement, high school transcript, minimum 2.6 GPA.

CONTACT
The University of British Columbia, 2075 Wesbrook Mall, Vancouver, BC V6T 1Z1, Canada. *Phone:* 604-822-3014.

The University of British Columbia–Okanagan Campus

Kelowna, British Columbia, Canada

http://www.ok.ubc.ca/

- **Province-supported** university, founded 2005, part of University of British Columbia
- **Urban** 500-acre campus with easy access to Kelowna
- **Endowment** $1.2 billion
- **Coed**
- **Moderately difficult** entrance level

FACULTY
Student/faculty ratio: 18:1.

ACADEMICS
Calendar: semesters. *Degrees:* certificates, diplomas, bachelor's, master's, doctoral, and postbachelor's certificates.
Library: UBC Library.

STUDENT LIFE
Housing options: coed, men-only, women-only. Campus housing is university owned. Freshman campus housing is guaranteed.

Activities and organizations: drama/theater group, student-run newspaper, radio station, choral group, Film Club, International Student Club, UBCSUO Mountain Riders Ski and Snowboard Club, Engineers without Borders, Model United Nations Club, national fraternities.

Athletics Member CIS.

Campus security: 24-hour emergency response devices and patrols, controlled dormitory access, 24-hour desk attendants in residence halls.

Student services: health clinic, personal/psychological counseling, women's center, legal services.

FINANCIAL AID
Financial Aid ***Financial aid deadline:*** 12/10.

APPLYING
Standardized Tests *Required for some:* SAT or ACT (for admission).

Options: electronic application, deferred entrance.

Application fee: $108 Canadian dollars.

Required: essay or personal statement, high school transcript, minimum 2.6 GPA.

CONTACT
International Student Recruitment, The University of British Columbia–Okanagan Campus, UC222 University Centre, 3333 University Way, Kelowna, BC V1V 1V7, Canada. *Phone:* 250-807-9447. *Fax:* 250-807-8552.

University of Calgary

Calgary, Alberta, Canada

http://www.ucalgary.ca/

CONTACT
Mr. Kaili Xu, Associate Registrar, Undergraduate Admissions, University of Calgary, 2500 University Drive NW, Calgary, AB T2N 1N4, Canada. *Phone:* 403-210-7625. *E-mail:* future.students@ucalgary.ca.

University of Guelph

Guelph, Ontario, Canada

http://www.uoguelph.ca/

- **Province-supported** university, founded 1964
- **Suburban** 1017-acre campus with easy access to Toronto
- **Endowment** $419.1 million
- **Coed**
- **Moderately difficult** entrance level

FACULTY
Student/faculty ratio: 23:1.

ACADEMICS
Calendar: trimesters. *Degrees:* certificates, diplomas, associate, bachelor's, master's, and doctoral.
Library: University of Guelph Library plus 1 other. *Books:* 1.3 million (physical), 35,000 (digital/electronic); *Serial titles:* 1,617 (physical), 21,287 (digital/electronic); *Databases:* 280. Students can reserve study rooms.

STUDENT LIFE
Housing options: coed, women-only, cooperative, special housing for students with disabilities. Campus housing is university owned and is provided by a third party. Freshman campus housing is guaranteed.

Activities and organizations: drama/theater group, student-run newspaper, radio station, choral group, Guelph Gryphon Athletics, Habitat for Humanity, Curtain Call Productions, West Indian Students Association, OXFAM-Guelph Chapter.

Athletics Member CIS.

Campus security: 24-hour emergency response devices and patrols, student patrols, late-night transport/escort service, controlled dormitory access, video camera surveillance in parking lots, alarms in women's locker room.

Student services: health clinic, personal/psychological counseling, women's center, legal services.

COSTS
Costs (2019–20) ***Tuition:*** province resident $6091 Canadian dollars full-time, $1217 Canadian dollars per credit part-time; nonresident $6091 Canadian dollars full-time, $4860 Canadian dollars per credit part-time. Full-time tuition and fees vary according to course load, degree level, and program. Part-time tuition and fees vary according to program. ***Required fees:*** $24,300 Canadian dollars full-time, $567 Canadian dollars per credit part-time. ***Room and board:*** $11,700 Canadian dollars; room only: $6345 Canadian dollars. Room and board charges vary according to board plan and housing facility.

APPLYING
Standardized Tests *Required:* SAT or ACT (for admission).

Options: electronic application, early admission, deferred entrance.

Application fee: $150 Canadian dollars.

Required: high school transcript, minimum 3.0 GPA. ***Required for some:*** essay or personal statement.

CONTACT
Ms. Janette Hogan, Assistant Registrar, Admissions, University of Guelph, L-3 University Centre, Guelph, ON N1G 2W1, Canada. *Phone:* 519-824-4120 Ext. 58529. *Fax:* 519-766-9481. *E-mail:* jhogan@uoguelph.ca.

University of King's College

Halifax, Nova Scotia, Canada

http://www.ukings.ca/

CONTACT
Ms. Tara Wigglesworth-Hines, Assistant Registrar/Admissions, University of King's College, Registrar's Office, Halifax, NS B3H 3A1, Canada. *Phone:* 902-422-1271. *Fax:* 902-425-8183. *E-mail:* admissions@ukings.ns.ca.

University of Lethbridge

Lethbridge, Alberta, Canada

http://www.uleth.ca/

CONTACT

Registrar's Office, University of Lethbridge, 4401 University Drive, Lethbridge, AB T1K 3M4, Canada. *Phone:* 403-320-5700. *Fax:* 403-329-5159. *E-mail:* regoffice@uleth.ca.

University of Manitoba

Winnipeg, Manitoba, Canada

http://www.umanitoba.ca/

CONTACT

Mr. Peter Dueck, Director of Enrollment Services, University of Manitoba, Winnipeg, MB R3T 2N2, Canada. *Phone:* 204-474-6382.

University of New Brunswick Fredericton

Fredericton, New Brunswick, Canada

http://www.unb.ca/

CONTACT

University of New Brunswick Fredericton, PO Box 4400, Fredericton, NB E3B 5A3, Canada. *Phone:* 506-453-4865.

University of New Brunswick Saint John

Saint John, New Brunswick, Canada

http://www.unb.ca/

CONTACT

University of New Brunswick Saint John, PO Box 5050, Saint John, NB E2L 4L5, Canada.

University of Northern British Columbia

Prince George, British Columbia, Canada

http://www.unbc.ca/

CONTACT

Pamela Flagel, Associate Registrar Enrollment, University of Northern British Columbia, Office of the Registrar, 3333 University Way, Prince George, BC V2N 4Z9, Canada. *Phone:* 250-960-6300. *Fax:* 250-960-6330. *E-mail:* registrar-info@unbc.ca.

University of Ottawa

Ottawa, Ontario, Canada

http://www.uottawa.ca/

CONTACT

University of Ottawa, 550 Cumberland Street, Ottawa, ON K1N 6N5, Canada. *Phone:* 613-562-5800 Ext. 1594.

University of Prince Edward Island

Charlottetown, Prince Edward Island, Canada

http://home.upei.ca/

CONTACT

University of Prince Edward Island, 550 University Avenue, Charlottetown, PE C1A 4P3, Canada. *Phone:* 902-566-0634.

University of Regina

Regina, Saskatchewan, Canada

http://www.uregina.ca/

- **Province-supported** university, founded 1974
- **Urban** 76-hectare campus
- **Endowment** $48.7 million
- **Coed**
- **Minimally difficult** entrance level

FACULTY

Student/faculty ratio: 23:1.

ACADEMICS

Calendar: semesters. *Degrees:* certificates, diplomas, bachelor's, master's, doctoral, and postbachelor's certificates.

Library: Dr. John Archer Library plus 5 others. *Books:* 806,988 (physical), 802,795 (digital/electronic); *Serial titles:* 163,120 (physical), 131,946 (digital/electronic); *Databases:* 519. Weekly public service hours: 105; students can reserve study rooms.

STUDENT LIFE

Housing options: special housing for students with disabilities. Campus housing is university owned. Freshman campus housing is guaranteed.

Activities and organizations: drama/theater group, student-run newspaper, University of Regina Students' Union, Biology Undergraduate and Graduate Society, Institute of Electrical and Electronics Engineers (IEEE) U of R Students Branch, UR Toastmasters, Inter-Varsity Christian Fellowship.

Athletics Member CIS.

Campus security: 24-hour emergency response devices and patrols, controlled dormitory access, CCTV, card access and some alarm monitoring.

Student services: health clinic, personal/psychological counseling, women's center.

COSTS

Costs (2019–20) ***Tuition:*** province resident $6713 Canadian dollars full-time, $224 Canadian dollars per credit hour part-time; International tuition $20,138 Canadian dollars full-time. ***Required fees:*** $817 Canadian dollars full-time. ***Room and board:*** $7102 Canadian dollars; room only: $6404 Canadian dollars.

APPLYING

Standardized Tests *Required for some:* SAT or ACT (for admission).

Options: electronic application, early admission, early action, deferred entrance.

Application fee: $100 Canadian dollars.

Required: high school transcript, minimum 2.3 GPA. ***Required for some:*** essay or personal statement, 2 letters of recommendation, interview, portfolio, audition, 2.3 minimum GPA.

CONTACT

Ms. Christine McBain, Associate Director, Enrolment Services, University of Regina, 3737 Wascana Parkway, Regina, SK S4S 0A2, Canada. *Phone:* 306-585-5345. *Toll-free phone:* 800-644-4756. *Fax:* 306-337-2525. *E-mail:* enrolment.services@uregina.ca.

University of Saskatchewan

Saskatoon, Saskatchewan, Canada

http://www.usask.ca/

CONTACT

University of Saskatchewan, 105 Administration Place, Saskatoon, SK S7N 5A2, Canada. *Phone:* 306-966-5788.

University of the Fraser Valley

Abbotsford, British Columbia, Canada

http://www.ufv.ca/

- **Province-supported** comprehensive, founded 1974
- **Urban** 64-hectare campus with easy access to Vancouver
- **Endowment** $10.5 million
- **Coed** 9,814 undergraduate students, 77% full-time, 58% women, 42% men

UNDERGRAD STUDENTS
7,516 full-time, 2,298 part-time. Students come from 9 provinces and territories; 77 other countries.

Freshmen:
Admission: 815 enrolled.
Retention: 78% of full-time freshmen returned.

FACULTY
Total: 732, 45% full-time, 32% with terminal degrees.

ACADEMICS
Calendar: semesters. *Degrees:* certificates, diplomas, associate, bachelor's, master's, and postbachelor's certificates.

Special study options: academic remediation for entering students, adult/continuing education programs, advanced placement credit, cooperative education, distance learning, double majors, English as a second language, honors programs, independent study, internships, off-campus study, part-time degree program, services for LD students, student-designed majors, study abroad, summer session for credit.

Computers: Students can access the following: computer help desk, free student e-mail accounts, online (class) grades, online (class) registration, online (class) schedules. Wireless service is available via entire campus.
Library: Peter Jones Library plus 3 others. *Books:* 159,000 (physical), 311,000 (digital/electronic). Students can reserve study rooms.

STUDENT LIFE
Housing options: coed. Campus housing is university owned. Freshman applicants given priority for college housing.

Activities and organizations: drama/theater group, student-run newspaper, radio station.

Athletics Member CIS. ***Intercollegiate sports:*** basketball M(s)/W(s), soccer M(s)/W(s), wrestling M(c)/W(c). ***Intramural sports:*** badminton M/W, baseball M(c), basketball M/W, cross-country running M(c)/W(c), golf M/W, rowing M/W, rugby W(c), soccer M/W, volleyball M/W, wrestling M(c)/W(c).

Campus security: 24-hour emergency response devices and patrols, late-night transport/escort service, controlled dormitory access.

Student services: personal/psychological counseling.

COSTS
Costs (2020–21) ***Tuition:*** province resident $5070 full-time, $169 per credit part-time; nonresident $5070 full-time, $169 per credit part-time; International tuition $18,900 full-time. Full-time tuition and fees vary according to course load. Part-time tuition and fees vary according to course load. ***Required fees:*** $508 full-time, $156 per term part-time. ***Room and board:*** $8107; room only: $6107. Room and board charges vary according to board plan. ***Waivers:*** senior citizens and employees or children of employees.

APPLYING
Options: electronic application, early admission, deferred entrance.

Application fee: $49 Canadian dollars.

Required: high school transcript. ***Required for some:*** essay or personal statement, 2 letters of recommendation, interview, minimum GPA of 2.0 to 2.67.

Notification: continuous (freshmen), continuous (transfers).

CONTACT
Mr. Daniel Goertz, Recruitment Coordinator, University of the Fraser Valley, 33844 King Road, Abbotsford, BC V2S 7M8, Canada. *Phone:* 604-504-7441 Ext. 4693. *Toll-free phone:* 888-504-7441. *E-mail:* daniel.goertz@ufv.ca.

University of Toronto

Toronto, Ontario, Canada

http://www.utoronto.ca/

- **Province-supported** university, founded 1827
- **Urban** 714-hectare campus with easy access to Greater Toronto Area
- **Endowment** $2.4 billion
- **Coed** 70,728 undergraduate students, 100% full-time, 52% women, 48% men
- **Very difficult** entrance level

UNDERGRAD STUDENTS
70,728 full-time. Students come from 12 provinces and territories; 168 other countries; 6% are from out of state; 14% live on campus.

FACULTY
Total: 14,420.

Student/faculty ratio: 24:1.

ACADEMICS
Calendar: fall/winter terms and a summer session. *Degrees:* certificates, diplomas, bachelor's, master's, doctoral, and postbachelor's certificates.

Special study options: adult/continuing education programs, cooperative education, double majors, English as a second language, independent study, internships, off-campus study, part-time degree program, services for LD students, study abroad, summer session for credit.

Computers: 2,000 computers/terminals are available on campus for general student use. Students can access the following: campus intranet, computer help desk, free student e-mail accounts, online (class) grades, online (class) registration, online (class) schedules. Campuswide network is available. Wireless service is available via entire campus.
Library: See library.utoronto.ca plus 43 others. *Books:* 19.4 million (physical), 6.0 million (digital/electronic). Students can reserve study rooms.

STUDENT LIFE
Housing options: coed, women-only. Campus housing is university owned. Freshman campus housing is guaranteed.

Activities and organizations: drama/theater group, student-run newspaper, radio station, choral group, national fraternities, national sororities.

Athletics Member CIS. ***Intercollegiate sports:*** archery M/W, badminton M/W, basketball M/W, crew M, cross-country running M/W, fencing M/W, field hockey W, football M, golf M, gymnastics M/W, ice hockey M/W, rugby M, skiing (cross-country) M/W, skiing (downhill) M/W, soccer M/W, squash M/W, swimming and diving M/W, tennis M/W, track and field M/W, volleyball M/W, wrestling M. ***Intramural sports:*** archery M/W, badminton M/W, basketball M/W, crew M, fencing M/W, field hockey W, football M/W, gymnastics M/W, ice hockey M/W, lacrosse M/W, racquetball M, rugby M, skiing (downhill) M/W, soccer M/W, squash M/W, swimming and diving M/W, tennis M/W, track and field M/W, volleyball M/W, water polo M/W.

Campus security: 24-hour emergency response devices and patrols, student patrols, late-night transport/escort service.

Student services: health clinic, personal/psychological counseling, women's center, legal services.

APPLYING
Standardized Tests *Required:* SAT and SAT Subject Tests or ACT (for admission).

Options: electronic application, deferred entrance.

Application fee: $255 Canadian dollars.

Required: high school transcript. ***Required for some:*** essay or personal statement, interview, audition for music and theatre programs.

Application deadlines: 1/19 (freshmen), 7/1 (transfers).

Notification: continuous (freshmen), continuous (transfers).

CONTACT
University of Toronto, 27 King's College Circle, Toronto, ON M5S 1A1, Canada. *Phone:* 416-978-2190. *Fax:* 416-978-7022.

University of Victoria

Victoria, British Columbia, Canada

http://www.uvic.ca/

CONTACT
Mr. Bruno Rocca, Student Recruitment Director, University of Victoria, PO Box 1700, STN CSC, Victoria, BC V8W 2Y2, Canada. *Phone:* 250-721-8121 Ext. 8109. *Fax:* 250-721-6225. *E-mail:* admit@uvic.ca.

University of Waterloo

Waterloo, Ontario, Canada

http://www.uwaterloo.ca/

- **Province-supported** university, founded 1957
- **Suburban** 1112-acre campus with easy access to Toronto
- **Endowment** $412.9 million
- **Coed** 33,322 undergraduate students
- **Moderately difficult** entrance level

FACULTY

Student/faculty ratio: 26:1.

ACADEMICS

Calendar: trimesters. *Degrees:* bachelor's, master's, and doctoral.

Special study options: cooperative education, distance learning, double majors, English as a second language, honors programs, internships, off-campus study, part-time degree program, services for LD students, study abroad.

Computers: 6,000 computers/terminals are available on campus for general student use. Students can access the following: campus intranet, computer help desk, free student e-mail accounts, online (class) grades, online (class) registration, online (class) schedules. Campuswide network is available. Wireless service is available via entire campus.

Library: Dana Porter Library plus 11 others. Students can reserve study rooms.

STUDENT LIFE

Housing options: coed. Campus housing is university owned. Freshman campus housing is guaranteed.

Activities and organizations: drama/theater group, student-run newspaper, choral group, marching band, national fraternities, national sororities.

Athletics ***Intercollegiate sports:*** badminton M/W, baseball M, basketball M/W, cheerleading M/W, cross-country running M/W, field hockey W, football M, golf M, ice hockey M/W, rugby M/W, skiing (cross-country) M/W, soccer M/W, squash M/W, swimming and diving M/W, tennis M/W, track and field M/W, volleyball M/W. ***Intramural sports:*** archery M(c)/W(c), badminton M(c)/W(c), baseball M/W, basketball M/W, bowling M/W, crew M(c)/W(c), cross-country running M(c)/W(c), equestrian sports M(c)/W(c), fencing M(c), field hockey W(c), football M/W, golf M(c)/W(c), ice hockey M/W, racquetball M(c)/W(c), rock climbing M(c)/W(c), sailing M(c)/W(c), skiing (cross-country) M(c)/W(c), skiing (downhill) M(c)/W(c), soccer M(c)/W(c), softball M/W, squash M(c)/W(c), swimming and diving M(c)/W(c), table tennis M(c)/W(c), tennis M/W, ultimate Frisbee M(c)/W(c), volleyball M/W, water polo M(c)/W(c), weight lifting M(c)/W(c).

Campus security: 24-hour emergency response devices and patrols, student patrols, late-night transport/escort service, controlled dormitory access.

Student services: health clinic, personal/psychological counseling, women's center, legal services.

COSTS

Costs (2020–21) ***Tuition:*** province resident $683 per course part-time; nonresident $3652 per course part-time. Full-time tuition and fees vary according to course load, degree level, program, and student level. Part-time tuition and fees vary according to course load, degree level, program, and student level. ***Required fees:*** $1200 full-time. ***Room and board:*** $7260; room only: $4797. Room and board charges vary according to board plan, housing facility, and location. ***Payment plan:*** deferred payment. ***Waivers:*** senior citizens and employees or children of employees.

APPLYING

Options: electronic application, early admission, deferred entrance.

Application fee: $125 Canadian dollars.

Required: high school transcript. ***Required for some:*** essay or personal statement, interview. ***Recommended:*** essay or personal statement.

Notification: continuous until 5/26 (freshmen).

CONTACT

University of Waterloo, 200 University Avenue West, Waterloo, ON N2L 3G1, Canada. *Phone:* 519-888-4567. *E-mail:* myapplication@uwaterloo.ca.

The University of Western Ontario

London, Ontario, Canada

http://www.uwo.ca/

- **Province-supported** university, founded 1878
- **Suburban** 1200-acre campus
- **Coed** 23,041 undergraduate students, 95% full-time, 57% women, 43% men
- **Very difficult** entrance level, 58% of applicants were admitted

UNDERGRAD STUDENTS

21,921 full-time, 1,120 part-time. Students come from 116 other countries; 78% live on campus.

Freshmen:

Admission: 33,924 applied, 19,537 admitted. ***Average high school GPA:*** ####.

Retention: 94% of full-time freshmen returned.

FACULTY

Total: 1,406

ACADEMICS

Calendar: Canadian standard year. *Degrees:* certificates, diplomas, bachelor's, master's, doctoral, and postbachelor's certificates.

Special study options: academic remediation for entering students, accelerated degree program, adult/continuing education programs, advanced placement credit, cooperative education, distance learning, double majors, English as a second language, honors programs, independent study, internships, off-campus study, part-time degree program, services for LD students, student-designed majors, study abroad, summer session for credit.

Computers: 414 computers/terminals are available on campus for general student use. Students can access the following: campus intranet, computer help desk, free student e-mail accounts, online (class) grades, online (class) registration, online (class) schedules. Campuswide network is available. 100% of college-owned or -operated housing units are wired for high-speed Internet access. Wireless service is available via classrooms, computer centers, computer labs, learning centers, libraries, student centers.

Library: Western Libraries plus 7 others. *Books:* 3.4 million (physical), 2.0 million (digital/electronic); *Serial titles:* 4,149 (physical), 156,899 (digital/electronic); *Databases:* 1,004. Weekly public service hours: 103; students can reserve study rooms.

STUDENT LIFE

Housing options: coed, men-only, women-only, special housing for students with disabilities. Campus housing is university owned. Freshman campus housing is guaranteed.

Activities and organizations: drama/theater group, student-run newspaper, radio and television station, choral group, marching band, Pre-Medical Society, Western Investment Club, Purple Spur Society, Pre-Business Students' Network, Pre-Law Society, national fraternities, national sororities.

Athletics Member CIS. ***Intercollegiate sports:*** badminton M/W, baseball M, basketball M(s)/W(s), cheerleading M/W, crew M/W, cross-country running M/W, equestrian sports W, fencing M/W, field hockey W, football M(s), golf M/W, ice hockey M(s)/W(s), lacrosse M/W, rugby M(s)/W, soccer M(s)/W, softball W, squash M(s)/W, swimming and diving M(s)/W(s), table tennis M/W, tennis M(s)/W(s), track and field M(s)/W(s), ultimate Frisbee M/W, volleyball M(s)/W(s), water polo M, wrestling M(s)/W(s). ***Intramural sports:*** badminton M/W, basketball M/W, equestrian sports M(c)/W(c), fencing M(c)/W(c), ice hockey M/W, rock climbing M(c)/W(c), soccer M/W, squash M(c)/W(c), table tennis M(c)/W(c), tennis M(c)/W(c), track and field M(c)/W(c), ultimate Frisbee M/W, volleyball M/W, water polo M/W.

Campus security: 24-hour emergency response devices and patrols, student patrols, late-night transport/escort service, controlled dormitory access, Campus Community Police, SERT: Student Emergency Response Team, Western Foot Patrol.

Student services: health clinic, personal/psychological counseling, legal services.

COSTS & FINANCIAL AID
Costs (2020–21) ***Tuition:*** province resident $6050 full-time; International tuition $31,042 full-time. Full-time tuition and fees vary according to program. Part-time tuition and fees vary according to course load and program. ***Required fees:*** $1605 full-time. ***Room and board:*** $15,116; room only: $9542. Room and board charges vary according to board plan, housing facility, and location. ***Payment plan:*** installment. ***Waivers:*** employees or children of employees.

Financial Aid Of all full-time matriculated undergraduates who enrolled in 2017, 1,412 state and other part-time jobs (averaging $2444).

APPLYING
Standardized Tests *Required for some:* SAT or ACT (for admission).

Options: electronic application, early decision, deferred entrance.

Application fee: $150 Canadian dollars.

Required: high school transcript, minimum 3.5 GPA. ***Required for some:*** supplemental profile, interview or audition.

Application deadlines: 6/1 (freshmen), 6/1 (out-of-state freshmen), 6/1 (transfers).

Early decision deadline: 3/1.

Notification: continuous (freshmen), continuous (out-of-state freshmen), rolling (early decision).

CONTACT
Undergraduate Recruitment and Admissions, The University of Western Ontario, Western University, London, ON N6A 3K7, Canada. *Phone:* 519-661-2100. *Fax:* 519-661-3710. *E-mail:* welcome@uwo.ca.

University of Windsor
Windsor, Ontario, Canada
http://www.uwindsor.ca/

CONTACT
Ms. Charlene Yates, Associate Registrar, University of Windsor, Office of the Registrar, 401 Sunset Avenue, Windsor, ON N9B 3P4, Canada. *Phone:* 519-253-3000 Ext. 3332. *Toll-free phone:* 800-864-2860. *Fax:* 519-971-3653. *E-mail:* registrar@uwindsor.ca.

The University of Winnipeg
Winnipeg, Manitoba, Canada
http://www.uwinnipeg.ca/

- **Province-supported** comprehensive, founded 1967
- **Urban** 8-acre campus
- **Endowment** $16.8 million
- **Coed**
- **Moderately difficult** entrance level

FACULTY
Student/faculty ratio: 35:1.

ACADEMICS
Calendar: Canadian standard year. *Degrees:* bachelor's and master's.

STUDENT LIFE
Housing options: coed. Campus housing is university owned and leased by the school. Freshman applicants given priority for college housing.

Activities and organizations: drama/theater group, student-run newspaper, radio station, choral group, Woman's Centre, LGBT (Lesbian Gay Bisexual Transgender), radio station, International Resource Centre, Aboriginal Student Centre, national fraternities.

Athletics Member CIS.

Campus security: 24-hour emergency response devices and patrols, student patrols, video controlled external access.

Student services: health clinic, personal/psychological counseling, women's center.

FINANCIAL AID
Financial Aid ***Financial aid deadline:*** 3/1.

APPLYING
Options: early admission, deferred entrance.

Application fee: $60.

Required: minimum 2.0 GPA. ***Required for some:*** high school transcript, interview.

CONTACT
Mr. Colin Russell, Registrar, The University of Winnipeg, 515 Portage Avenue, Winnipeg, MB R3B 2E9, Canada. *Phone:* 204-786-9776. *Fax:* 204-786-8656. *E-mail:* admissions@uwinnipeg.ca.

Vancouver Island University
Nanaimo, British Columbia, Canada
http://www.viu.ca/

CONTACT
Mr. Andrew Amour, Associate Registrar, Admissions and Registration, Vancouver Island University, 900 Fifth Street, Nanaimo, BC V9R 5S5, Canada. *Phone:* 250-740-6355. *Fax:* 250-740-6479.

Vanguard College
Edmonton, Alberta, Canada
http://www.vanguardcollege.com/

CONTACT
Vanguard College, 12140 103rd Street, Edmonton, AB T5G 2J9, Canada. *Phone:* 780-452-0808 Ext. 231. *Toll-free phone:* 866-222-0808. *E-mail:* admissions@vanguardcollege.com.

Wilfrid Laurier University
Waterloo, Ontario, Canada
http://www.wlu.ca/

- **Province-supported** comprehensive, founded 1911
- **Urban** 40-acre campus with easy access to Toronto
- **Coed**
- **Minimally difficult** entrance level

FACULTY
Student/faculty ratio: 25:1.

ACADEMICS
Calendar: Canadian standard year. *Degrees:* certificates, diplomas, bachelor's, master's, and doctoral.
Library: Wilfrid Laurier University Library plus 1 other.

STUDENT LIFE
Housing options: coed, men-only, women-only, special housing for students with disabilities. Campus housing is university owned. Freshman campus housing is guaranteed.

Activities and organizations: drama/theater group, student-run newspaper, radio station, Habitat for Humanity of WLU, Laurier Musical Theatre, East Meets West, Laurier SOS, Laurier Ski and Snowboarding Club, national fraternities, national sororities.

Athletics Member CIS.

Campus security: 24-hour emergency response devices and patrols, student patrols, late-night transport/escort service, controlled dormitory access.

Student services: health clinic, personal/psychological counseling, women's center, legal services.

FINANCIAL AID
Financial Aid ***Financial aid deadline:*** 1/17.

APPLYING
Standardized Tests *Required for some:* SAT or ACT (for admission).

Options: electronic application, early admission, early decision, deferred entrance.

Application fee: $150 Canadian dollars.

Required: high school transcript. ***Required for some:*** essay or personal statement, interview, audition for music programs.

CONTACT
Wilfrid Laurier University, 75 University Avenue West, Waterloo, ON N2L 3C5, Canada. *Phone:* 519-884-0710 Ext. 6099.

York University
Toronto, Ontario, Canada
http://www.yorku.ca/

CONTACT
International Recruitment, York University, N301 Bennett Centre for Student Services, 4700 Keele Street, Toronto, ON M3J 1P3, Canada. *Phone:* 416-736-5825. *Fax:* 416-736-5741. *E-mail:* intlenq@yorku.ca.

INTERNATIONAL

BULGARIA

American University in Bulgaria
Blagoevgrad, Bulgaria
http://www.aubg.edu/

- **Independent** comprehensive, founded 1991
- **Small-town** 12-acre campus with easy access to Sofia, Bulgaria
- **Endowment** $27.4 million
- **Coed**
- **Very difficult** entrance level

FACULTY
Student/faculty ratio: 16:1.

ACADEMICS
Calendar: semesters. *Degrees:* bachelor's and master's.
Library: Panitza Library. *Books:* 122,369 (physical), 326,128 (digital/electronic); *Serial titles:* 170 (physical), 62,637 (digital/electronic); *Databases:* 34. Weekly public service hours: 56; study areas open 24 hours, 5–7 days a week; students can reserve study rooms.

STUDENT LIFE
Housing options: on-campus residence required through senior year; coed, special housing for students with disabilities. Campus housing is university owned. Freshman campus housing is guaranteed.

Activities and organizations: drama/theater group, student-run newspaper, radio station, choral group, Computer Science Student Union, AUBG Political Science Club, Better Community Club, AUBG Broadway Performance Club, Business Club.

Campus security: 24-hour emergency response devices and patrols, controlled dormitory access.

Student services: health clinic, personal/psychological counseling.

COSTS
Costs (2019–20) ***Comprehensive fee:*** $14,650 includes full-time tuition ($12,300), mandatory fees ($610), and room and board ($1740). Part-time tuition: $1025 per credit hour. ***College room only:*** $1440.

APPLYING
Standardized Tests *Required for some:* TOEFL, IELTS, or ESOL for students whose primary language is not English. *Recommended:* SAT or ACT (for admission).

Options: electronic application, early admission, deferred entrance.

Required: essay or personal statement, high school transcript, minimum 3.0 GPA, 2 letters of recommendation.

CONTACT
Ms. Boriana Shalyavska, Director of Admissions, American University in Bulgaria, 1 Izmirliev Square, 1st Floor, Blagoevgrad 2700. *Phone:* 359-73 888 218. *Fax:* 359-73 883 227. *E-mail:* admissions@aubg.edu.

EGYPT

The American University in Cairo
Cairo, Egypt
http://www.aucegypt.edu/

- **Independent** comprehensive, founded 1919
- **Suburban** 260-acre campus with easy access to Cairo
- **Endowment** $519
- **Coed**
- **Very difficult** entrance level

FACULTY
Student/faculty ratio: 10:1.

ACADEMICS
Calendar: semesters. *Degrees:* diplomas, bachelor's, master's, and doctoral (majority of students are Egyptians; enrollment open to all nationalities).
Library: American University in Cairo Library plus 1 other. *Books:* 546,020 (physical), 311,887 (digital/electronic); *Databases:* 123. Weekly public service hours: 80; students can reserve study rooms.

STUDENT LIFE
Housing options: men-only, women-only, special housing for students with disabilities. Campus housing is university owned and leased by the school. Freshman applicants given priority for college housing.

Activities and organizations: drama/theater group, student-run newspaper, choral group, AIESEC, Theater and Film Club, VIA, ACT, Mashrou3 Kheir.

Campus security: 24-hour emergency response devices and patrols, controlled dormitory access.

Student services: health clinic, personal/psychological counseling.

FINANCIAL AID
Financial Aid ***Average financial aid package:*** $3711. ***Average need-based gift aid:*** $2991. ***Financial aid deadline:*** 3/14.

APPLYING
Standardized Tests *Required for some:* SAT or ACT (for admission), SAT Subject Tests (for admission).

Options: electronic application, early admission, early action, deferred entrance.

Application fee: $85.

Required: essay or personal statement, high school transcript, minimum 2.0 GPA.

CONTACT
Ms. Randa Kamel, Chief Enrollment Officer, The American University in Cairo, AUC Avenue, PO Box 74 New Cairo 11835, Cairo, Egypt. *Phone:* 202-26154601. *E-mail:* randakamel@aucegypt.edu.

FRANCE

The American University of Paris

Paris, France

http://www.aup.edu/

- **Independent** comprehensive, founded 1962
- **Urban** campus with easy access to Paris, France
- **Endowment** $852,072
- **Coed** 1,000 undergraduate students, 92% full-time, 70% women, 30% men
- **Moderately difficult** entrance level, 76% of applicants were admitted

UNDERGRAD STUDENTS
922 full-time, 78 part-time. Students come from 47 states and territories; 105 other countries; 5% transferred in.

Freshmen:
Admission: 1,293 applied, 981 admitted, 169 enrolled. ***Average high school GPA:*** 3.3.

Retention: 69% of full-time freshmen returned.

FACULTY
Total: 136, 61% full-time, 72% with terminal degrees.

Student/faculty ratio: 8:1.

ACADEMICS
Calendar: semesters. *Degrees:* bachelor's and master's.

Special study options: advanced placement credit, double majors, English as a second language, honors programs, independent study, internships, off-campus study, part-time degree program, student-designed majors, study abroad, summer session for credit.

Computers: 155 computers/terminals are available on campus for general student use. Students can access the following: campus intranet, computer help desk, free student e-mail accounts, online (class) grades, online (class) registration, online (class) schedules, free office software. Campuswide network is available. Wireless service is available via entire campus.
Library: AUP Library. *Books:* 41,927 (physical), 545,019 (digital/electronic); *Serial titles:* 28 (physical), 44,960 (digital/electronic); *Databases:* 48. Students can reserve study rooms.

STUDENT LIFE
Housing options: on-campus residence required for freshman yearCampus housing is university owned.

Activities and organizations: drama/theater group, student-run newspaper, television station, choral group, AUP Student Media (ASM) - Print, Video, Audio, Student Government Association (SGA), Sports Association, BVSyria (Refugee Assistance), Environmental and Community Services Committee.

Athletics *Intercollegiate sports:* basketball M, equestrian sports M/W, volleyball W. ***Intramural sports:*** badminton M(c)/W(c), basketball M, cheerleading M(c)/W(c), equestrian sports M/W, volleyball W.

Campus security: 24-hour emergency response devices, valid student ID required for all building entries.

Student services: personal/psychological counseling.

COSTS & FINANCIAL AID
Costs (2020–21) *One-time required fee:* $460. ***Comprehensive fee:*** $44,016 includes full-time tuition ($31,456), mandatory fees ($1580), and room and board ($10,980). Full-time tuition and fees vary according to degree level. Part-time tuition: $960 per credit hour. Part-time tuition and fees vary according to course load and degree level. ***College room only:*** $8640. Room and board charges vary according to housing facility. ***Payment plan:*** installment. ***Waivers:*** children of alumni and employees or children of employees.

Financial Aid Of all full-time matriculated undergraduates who enrolled in 2018, 289 applied for aid, 260 were judged to have need, 13 had their need fully met. In 2018, 21 non-need-based awards were made. ***Average percent of need met:*** 18. ***Average financial aid package:*** $12,353. ***Average need-based loan:*** $4502. ***Average need-based gift aid:*** $10,385. ***Average non-need-based aid:*** $4088. ***Average indebtedness upon graduation:*** $79,256.

APPLYING
Standardized Tests *Required for some:* TOEFL, TOEIC or IELTS for students whose primary language is not English. *Recommended:* SAT or ACT (for admission).

Options: electronic application, deferred entrance.

Application fee: $70.

Required: essay or personal statement, high school transcript, 2 letters of recommendation. ***Recommended:*** minimum 3.0 GPA, interview.

Application deadlines: 3/15 (freshmen), 3/15 (transfers).

Notification: continuous (freshmen), continuous (transfers).

CONTACT
International Admissions Office Counselors, The American University of Paris, 5 boulevard de la Tour Maubourg, Paris 75007, France. *Phone:* -+33 1 40 62 07 20. *Fax:* +33 1 47 05 34 32. *E-mail:* admissions@aup.edu.

The New School–Parsons Paris

Paris, France

http://www.newschool.edu/parsons-paris/

CONTACT
Mr. Mike Fakih, Director of Admissions, The New School–Parsons Paris, 79 Fifth Avenue, 5th floor, New York, NY 10011. *Phone:* 212-229-5150. *Toll-free phone:* 800-292-3040. *E-mail:* fakihm@newschool.edu.

Paris College of Art

Paris, France

http://www.paris.edu/

- **Independent** comprehensive
- **Urban** campus with easy access to Paris, France
- **Coed**

FACULTY
Student/faculty ratio: 3:1.

ACADEMICS
Calendar: semesters. *Degrees:* certificates, bachelor's, and master's.

Special study options: academic remediation for entering students, accelerated degree program, adult/continuing education programs, cooperative education, English as a second language, independent study, internships, off-campus study, part-time degree program, services for LD students, study abroad, summer session for credit.

Computers: Students can access the following: campus intranet, computer help desk, free student e-mail accounts, online (class) grades, online (class) schedules. Campuswide network is available. Wireless service is available via entire campus.

STUDENT LIFE
Housing options: college housing not available.

Activities and organizations: student-run radio station.

Student services: personal/psychological counseling.

FINANCIAL AID
Financial Aid *Financial aid deadline:* 8/1.

APPLYING
Options: electronic application, early action.

Required: essay or personal statement, high school transcript, interview, artistic portfolio. ***Required for some:*** letters of recommendation.

Application deadlines: rolling (freshmen), rolling (out-of-state freshmen), rolling (transfers), rolling (early action).

Early decision deadline: rolling (for plan 1), rolling (for plan 2).

Notification: continuous (freshmen), continuous (out-of-state freshmen), continuous (transfers), rolling (early decision plan 1), rolling (early decision plan 2), rolling (early action).

CONTACT
Paris College of Art, 15 rue Fénelon, 75010 Paris, France.

Schiller International University - Paris

Paris, France

http://www.schiller.edu/

CONTACT
Schiller International University - Paris, 9 rue d'Yvart, F-75015 Paris, France. *Toll-free phone:* 800-261-9571 (in-state); 800-261-9751 (out-of-state).

GERMANY

Schiller International University

Heidelberg, Germany

http://www.schiller.edu/

CONTACT
Ms. Kamala Dontamsetti, Associate Director of Admissions, Schiller International University, 300 East Bay Drive, Largo, FL 33770. *Phone:* 727-736-5082 Ext. 234. *Toll-free phone:* 800-261-9571 (in-state); 800-261-9751 (out-of-state). *Fax:* 727-734-0359. *E-mail:* kamala_dontamsetti@schiller.edu.

GREECE

American College of Thessaloniki

Pylea, Greece

http://www.act.edu/

- **Independent** comprehensive, founded 1886
- **Suburban** 62-acre campus with easy access to Thessaloniki
- **Endowment** $6.6 million
- **Coed** 547 undergraduate students, 87% full-time, 56% women, 44% men
- **Minimally difficult** entrance level, 91% of applicants were admitted

UNDERGRAD STUDENTS
476 full-time, 71 part-time. Students come from 27 other countries; 0.4% transferred in.

Freshmen:
Admission: 134 applied, 122 admitted, 92 enrolled. ***Average high school GPA:*** 3.5.

Retention: 95% of full-time freshmen returned.

FACULTY
Total: 55, 40% full-time, 64% with terminal degrees.

Student/faculty ratio: 18:1.

ACADEMICS
Calendar: semesters. *Degrees:* certificates, bachelor's, and master's.

Special study options: academic remediation for entering students, accelerated degree program, advanced placement credit, double majors, English as a second language, honors programs, independent study, internships, part-time degree program, services for LD students, study abroad, summer session for credit.

Computers: 165 computers/terminals and 30 ports are available on campus for general student use. Students can access the following: campus intranet, computer help desk, free student e-mail accounts, online (class) grades, online (class) schedules. Campuswide network is available. 100% of college-owned or -operated housing units are wired for high-speed Internet access. Wireless service is available via entire campus.

Library: Bissell Library plus 1 other. *Books:* 28,605 (physical), 201,768 (digital/electronic); *Serial titles:* 22 (physical), 72,165 (digital/electronic); *Databases:* 33. Weekly public service hours: 54; students can reserve study rooms.

STUDENT LIFE
Housing options: coed. Campus housing is university owned. Freshman applicants given priority for college housing.

Activities and organizations: drama/theater group, student-run newspaper, radio station, Model MUN, Tennis Club, Kick Boxing Club, Painting Club, Cinema Club.

Athletics *Intercollegiate sports:* basketball M/W, lacrosse M, soccer M/W, table tennis M/W, tennis M/W, volleyball M/W. ***Intramural sports:*** basketball M, lacrosse M/W, sailing M/W, sand volleyball M/W, soccer M/W, table tennis M/W, tennis M/W, volleyball M/W.

Campus security: 24-hour emergency response devices and patrols, controlled dormitory access.

Student services: health clinic, personal/psychological counseling.

COSTS
Costs (2020–21) ***One-time required fee:*** $70. ***Tuition:*** $8550 full-time, $285 per credit part-time. ***Required fees:*** $50 full-time, $285 per credit part-time. ***Payment plans:*** installment, deferred payment. ***Waivers:*** employees or children of employees.

APPLYING
Options: electronic application, deferred entrance.

Application fee: 75 euros.

Required: high school transcript, CV. ***Required for some:*** essay or personal statement, interview. ***Recommended:*** minimum 2.0 GPA.

Application deadlines: rolling (freshmen), rolling (transfers).

Notification: continuous (freshmen), continuous (transfers).

CONTACT
Mr. Manolis Maou, Director of Admissions, American College of Thessaloniki, 17 Sevenidi st, PO Box 21021, 55535 Pylaia, Greece. *Phone:* 30-2310398380. *Fax:* 30-2310398389. *E-mail:* emaou@act.edu.

DEREE - The American College of Greece

Athens, Greece

http://www.acg.edu/

- **Independent** comprehensive, founded 1875
- **Suburban** 64-acre campus with easy access to Athens
- **Coed**
- **Moderately difficult** entrance level

FACULTY
Student/faculty ratio: 11:1.

ACADEMICS
Calendar: semesters 2 summer sessions. *Degrees:* bachelor's, master's, and postbachelor's certificates.

Library: John S. Bailey Library plus 1 other. *Books:* 129,000 (physical), 316,000 (digital/electronic); *Serial titles:* 60 (physical), 13,000 (digital/electronic); *Databases:* 45. Weekly public service hours: 72; students can reserve study rooms.

STUDENT LIFE
Housing options: coed, special housing for students with disabilities. Campus housing is university owned. Freshman applicants given priority for college housing.

Activities and organizations: drama/theater group, student-run newspaper, choral group, DEREE Ambassadors, DEREE Orientation Leaders, Debate Club, DEREE SAB (Student Activities Board), Innovation and Entrepreneurship Clib.

Campus security: 24-hour emergency response devices and patrols, controlled dormitory access.

Student services: health clinic, personal/psychological counseling.

COSTS & FINANCIAL AID
Costs (2019–20) ***Tuition:*** $13,120 full-time. No tuition increase for student's term of enrollment. ***Required fees:*** $1240 full-time.

Financial Aid ***Financial aid deadline:*** 9/1.

APPLYING
Options: electronic application, deferred entrance.

Required: essay or personal statement, high school transcript, minimum 2.1 GPA, 1 letter of recommendation, interview.

CONTACT
Ms. Loukia Kanatsouli, Dean of Enrollment and International Students, DEREE - The American College of Greece, 6 Gravias Street, Aghia Paraskevi, Athens 15342, Greece. *Phone:* 30-210-600-9800 Ext. 1474. *Fax:* 30-210-608-2344. *E-mail:* lkanatsouli@acg.edu.

IRELAND

American College Dublin

Dublin, Ireland

http://www.amcd.ie/

CONTACT
American College Dublin, 2 Merrion Square, Dublin 2, Ireland.

Institute of Public Administration

Dublin, Ireland

http://www.ipa.ie/

CONTACT
Dr. Denis O'Brien, Registrar, Institute of Public Administration, 57-61 Lansdowne Road, Dublin 4, Ireland. *Phone:* 353-1-240-3600. *Fax:* 353-1-668-9135. *E-mail:* undergrad@ipa.ie.

ITALY

The American University of Rome

Rome, Italy

http://www.aur.edu/

CONTACT
Ms. Jessica York, Admissions Counselor, The American University of Rome, Via Pietro Roselli 4, Rome 00153, Italy. *Phone:* -+39 0658330919. *Toll-free phone:* 877-592-1287. *Fax:* +39 0658330992. *E-mail:* admissions@aur.edu.

John Cabot University

Rome, Italy

http://www.johncabot.edu/

- **Independent** comprehensive, founded 1972
- **Urban** campus with easy access to Rome
- **Coed** 1,497 undergraduate students
- 58% of applicants were admitted

UNDERGRAD STUDENTS
Students come from 40 states and territories; 70 other countries; 46% live on campus.

Freshmen:
Admission: 791 applied, 461 admitted. ***Average high school GPA:*** 3.1.
Retention: 98% of full-time freshmen returned.

FACULTY
Total: 150, 23% full-time, 63% with terminal degrees.
Student/faculty ratio: 9:1.

ACADEMICS
Calendar: semesters. *Degrees:* associate, bachelor's, and master's.
Special study options: adult/continuing education programs, advanced placement credit, double majors, English as a second language, freshman honors college, honors programs, independent study, internships, part-

time degree program, services for LD students, study abroad, summer session for credit.

Computers: 153 computers/terminals are available on campus for general student use. Students can access the following: campus intranet, computer help desk, free student e-mail accounts, online (class) grades, online (class) registration, online (class) schedules. Campuswide network is available. 100% of college-owned or -operated housing units are wired for high-speed Internet access. Wireless service is available via entire campus.
Library: Frohring Library. *Books:* 34,218 (physical); *Databases:* 39. Weekly public service hours: 86; students can reserve study rooms.

STUDENT LIFE
Housing options: coed, men-only, women-only, special housing for students with disabilities. Campus housing is university owned. Freshman campus housing is guaranteed.

Activities and organizations: drama/theater group, student-run newspaper, Student Government, Model United Nations, Student Newspaper, Queer Alliance Club, Grassroots.

Athletics ***Intercollegiate sports:*** basketball M/W, soccer M/W, volleyball M/W. ***Intramural sports:*** basketball M/W, cheerleading M/W, cross-country running M/W, skiing (downhill) M/W, soccer M/W, volleyball M/W, weight lifting M(c)/W(c).

Campus security: 24-hour emergency response devices and patrols, controlled dormitory access.

Student services: health clinic, personal/psychological counseling.

COSTS
Costs (2020–21) ***Comprehensive fee:*** $38,310 includes full-time tuition ($25,900), mandatory fees ($230), and room and board ($12,180). Full-time tuition and fees vary according to course load. Part-time tuition: $1250 per semester hour. Part-time tuition and fees vary according to course load. No tuition increase for student's term of enrollment. ***Required fees:*** $230 per year part-time. ***College room only:*** $9800. Room and board charges vary according to board plan and housing facility. ***Payment plan:*** installment. ***Waivers:*** children of alumni and employees or children of employees.

APPLYING
Standardized Tests *Required for some:* SAT or ACT (for admission), SAT and SAT Subject Tests or ACT (for admission).

Options: early admission, early decision, early action, deferred entrance.

Application fee: $50.

Required: essay or personal statement, high school transcript, 2 letters of recommendation, interview. ***Required for some:*** English Proficiency for non-US applicants. ***Recommended:*** minimum 2.5 GPA.

Application deadlines: 3/31 (freshmen), 3/1 (out-of-state freshmen), 6/1 (transfers), 11/15 (early action).

Early decision deadline: 11/15.

Notification: 8/5 (freshmen), 4/1 (out-of-state freshmen), 6/15 (transfers), 12/15 (early action).

CONTACT
Ms. Stefania Corrado, Associate Coordinator of DS Admissions, John Cabot University, Roma 00165. *Phone:* 855-528-7662. *Toll-free phone:* 855-528-7662. *E-mail:* admissions@johncabot.edu.

See below for display ad and page 1068 for the College Close-Up.

KENYA

United States International University–Africa

Nairobi, Kenya

http://www.usiu.ac.ke/

CONTACT
United States International University–Africa, PO Box 14634, Thika Road Kasarani, Nairobi 00800, Kenya. *Phone:* 254-02-3606563.

LEBANON

American University of Beirut

Beirut, Lebanon

http://www.aub.edu.lb/

- **Independent** university, founded 1866
- **Urban** 61-acre campus with easy access to Beirut
- **Endowment** $769.0 million
- **Coed** 7,357 undergraduate students, 95% full-time, 50% women, 50% men
- 72% of applicants were admitted

UNDERGRAD STUDENTS
7,023 full-time, 334 part-time. Students come from 87 other countries; 0.3% transferred in; 14% live on campus.

Freshmen:
Admission: 5,150 applied, 3,685 admitted, 1,766 enrolled. ***Test scores:*** SAT evidence-based reading and writing scores over 500: 87%; SAT math scores over 500: 98%; SAT evidence-based reading and writing scores over 600: 36%; SAT math scores over 600: 73%; SAT evidence-based reading and writing scores over 700: 3%; SAT math scores over 700: 31%.
Retention: 92% of full-time freshmen returned.

FACULTY
Total: 1,214, 77% full-time.

Student/faculty ratio: 11:1.

ACADEMICS
Calendar: semesters. *Degrees:* certificates, diplomas, bachelor's, master's, doctoral, and postbachelor's certificates.

Special study options: academic remediation for entering students, advanced placement credit, double majors, English as a second language, honors programs, independent study, internships, services for LD students, study abroad, summer session for credit.

Computers: 2,450 computers/terminals and 1,320 ports are available on campus for general student use. Students can access the following: campus intranet, computer help desk, free student e-mail accounts, online (class) grades, online (class) registration, online (class) schedules. Campuswide network is available. 100% of college-owned or -operated housing units are wired for high-speed Internet access. Wireless service is available via entire campus.
Library: Jafet Library plus 3 others. *Books:* 400,000 (physical), 1.1 million (digital/electronic); *Serial titles:* 5,000 (physical), 140,000 (digital/electronic); *Databases:* 350. Weekly public service hours: 107.

STUDENT LIFE
Housing options: on-campus residence required for freshman year; men-only, women-only. Campus housing is university owned. Freshman campus housing is guaranteed.

Activities and organizations: drama/theater group, student-run newspaper, choral group, Red Cross Club, Biology Society, Business Society, Music Club, Institute of Electrical and Electronics Engineer IEEE.

Athletics ***Intercollegiate sports:*** archery M/W, badminton M/W, basketball M/W, cheerleading M/W, football M, rugby M/W, soccer M/W, swimming and diving M/W, table tennis M/W, tennis M/W, track and field M/W, ultimate Frisbee M/W, volleyball M/W, water polo M. ***Intramural sports:*** archery M/W, badminton M/W, basketball M/W, cheerleading M/W, football M, rugby M/W, soccer M/W, swimming and diving M/W, table tennis M/W, tennis M/W, track and field M/W, ultimate Frisbee M/W, volleyball M/W, weight lifting M/W.

Campus security: 24-hour emergency response devices and patrols, late-night transport/escort service, controlled dormitory access.

Student services: health clinic, personal/psychological counseling, legal services.

COSTS & FINANCIAL AID
Costs (2019–20) ***Tuition:*** $11,625 full-time, $775 per credit part-time. Full-time tuition and fees vary according to course load, degree level, and program. Part-time tuition and fees vary according to course load, degree level, and program. ***Required fees:*** $917 full-time, $917 per term part-time. ***Room only:*** $1538. Room and board charges vary according to

housing facility and location. ***Payment plan:*** deferred payment. ***Waivers:*** employees or children of employees.

Financial Aid Of all full-time matriculated undergraduates who enrolled in 2018, 4,111 applied for aid, 3,204 were judged to have need. 34 state and other part-time jobs (averaging $2440). In 2018, 40 non-need-based awards were made. ***Average need-based loan:*** $6229. ***Average non-need-based aid:*** $25,966. ***Average indebtedness upon graduation:*** $19,144.

APPLYING

Standardized Tests *Required:* SAT (for admission). *Required for some:* SAT Subject Tests (for admission), TOEFL, IELTS.

Options: electronic application, early admission, early action, deferred entrance.

Application fee: $80.

Required: high school transcript. ***Required for some:*** essay or personal statement, 2 letters of recommendation, interview.

Application deadlines: 12/20 (freshmen), 12/20 (out-of-state freshmen), 4/30 (transfers).

Early decision deadline: 10/31.

Notification: 3/30 (freshmen), 3/30 (out-of-state freshmen), continuous until 6/30 (transfers), 1/31 (early decision).

CONTACT

Dr. Antoine Sabbagh, Director of Admissions Office, American University of Beirut, PO Box 11-0236, Riad El-Solh, 1107 2020. *Phone:* 1-374374 Ext. 2592. *Fax:* 1-750775. *E-mail:* admissions@aub.edu.lb.

Lebanese American University

Beirut, Lebanon

http://www.lau.edu.lb/

- **Private** comprehensive, founded 1835
- **Urban** 50-acre campus with easy access to Beirut, Byblos, Tripoli
- **Endowment** $543.4 million
- **Coed** 7,149 undergraduate students, 95% full-time, 50% women, 50% men
- **Moderately difficult** entrance level, 91% of applicants were admitted

UNDERGRAD STUDENTS

6,758 full-time, 391 part-time. Students come from 78 other countries; 19% are from out of state; 1% transferred in; 5% live on campus.

Freshmen:

Admission: 4,708 applied, 4,274 admitted, 1,630 enrolled. ***Average high school GPA:*** 3.0. ***Test scores:*** SAT evidence-based reading and writing scores over 500: 61%; SAT math scores over 500: 91%; SAT evidence-based reading and writing scores over 600: 19%; SAT math scores over 600: 54%; SAT evidence-based reading and writing scores over 700: 2%; SAT math scores over 700: 16%.

Retention: 87% of full-time freshmen returned.

FACULTY

Total: 799, 40% full-time, 50% with terminal degrees.

Student/faculty ratio: 15:1.

ACADEMICS

Calendar: semesters. *Degrees:* bachelor's, master's, doctoral, and postbachelor's certificates.

Special study options: academic remediation for entering students, advanced placement credit, double majors, honors programs, internships, part-time degree program, services for LD students, study abroad, summer session for credit.

Computers: 1,713 computers/terminals and 2,200 ports are available on campus for general student use. Students can access the following: campus intranet, computer help desk, free student e-mail accounts, online (class) grades, online (class) registration, online (class) schedules, online forms requests, online and mobile course management system. Campuswide network is available. 100% of college-owned or -operated housing units are wired for high-speed Internet access. Wireless service is available via entire campus.

Library: LAU Libraries plus 3 others. *Books:* 392,642 (physical), 578,822 (digital/electronic); *Serial titles:* 452 (physical), 134,766 (digital/electronic); *Databases:* 162. Weekly public service hours: 88; students can reserve study rooms.

STUDENT LIFE

Housing options: men-only, women-only, special housing for students with disabilities. Campus housing is university owned.

Activities and organizations: drama/theater group, choral group, Event Organization Club, Astronomy Club, Human Rights Club, International Affairs Club, Red Cross Club.

Athletics ***Intercollegiate sports:*** badminton M/W, basketball M/W, cross-country running M/W, rugby M, soccer M, swimming and diving M/W, table tennis M/W, tennis M/W, track and field M/W, volleyball M/W. ***Intramural sports:*** badminton M/W, basketball M/W, swimming and diving M/W, table tennis M/W, tennis M/W, volleyball M/W.

Campus security: 24-hour emergency response devices and patrols.

Student services: health clinic, personal/psychological counseling, women's center.

COSTS & FINANCIAL AID

Costs (2019–20) ***Tuition:*** $18,273 full-time, $800 per credit part-time. Full-time tuition and fees vary according to course load, degree level, and program. Part-time tuition and fees vary according to course load, degree level, and program. ***Required fees:*** $415 full-time, $235 per year part-time. ***Room only:*** Room and board charges vary according to housing facility and location. ***Payment plans:*** installment, deferred payment. ***Waivers:*** employees or children of employees.

Financial Aid Of all full-time matriculated undergraduates who enrolled in 2018, 3,799 applied for aid, 3,446 were judged to have need. 2,801 state and other part-time jobs (averaging $1797). In 2018, 748 non-need-based awards were made. ***Average financial aid package:*** $7854. ***Average need-based loan:*** $1436. ***Average need-based gift aid:*** $4854. ***Average non-need-based aid:*** $8199. ***Average indebtedness upon graduation:*** $5024. ***Financial aid deadline:*** 4/15.

APPLYING

Standardized Tests *Required:* SAT or ACT (for admission). *Required for some:* SAT and SAT Subject Tests or ACT (for admission), SAT Subject Tests (for admission), Institutional English Test (English Entrance Exam EEE) or International TOFEL.

Options: electronic application, deferred entrance.

Application fee: $85.

Required: high school transcript, minimum 2.0 GPA.

Application deadlines: 7/15 (freshmen), 7/15 (out-of-state freshmen), 7/15 (transfers).

Notification: continuous (freshmen), continuous (out-of-state freshmen), continuous (transfers).

CONTACT

Mrs. Nada Hajj, University Director of Admissions, Lebanese American University, PO Box 13-5053 Chouran Beirut 1102 2801, Lebanon, Beirut. *Phone:* 961-1786456 Ext. 1111. *Fax:* 961-1867098. *E-mail:* nhajj@lau.edu.lb.

MEXICO

Instituto Tecnológico y de Estudios Superiores de Monterrey, Campus Central de Veracruz

Córdoba, Mexico

http://www.itesm.mx/

CONTACT

Ing. Luis Pablo Villareal, Registrar, Instituto Tecnológico y de Estudios Superiores de Monterrey, Campus Central de Veracruz, Avenida Eugenio Garza Sada 1, Apartado Postal 314, 94500 Córdoba, Veracruz, Mexico. *Phone:* -27-13-23-40 Ext. 123.

Instituto Tecnológico y de Estudios Superiores de Monterrey, Campus Chiapas

Tuxtla Gutiérrez, Mexico

http://www.itesm.mx/

CONTACT

Lic. Luis Enrique Cancino, Registrar, Instituto Tecnológico y de Estudios Superiores de Monterrey, Campus Chiapas, Carretera a Tapanatepec Km 149&746, Apartado Postal 312, 29000 Tuxtla Gutiérrez, Chiapas, Mexico. *Phone:* -96-15-1723.

Instituto Tecnológico y de Estudios Superiores de Monterrey, Campus Chihuahua

Chihuahua, Mexico

http://www.itesm.mx/

CONTACT

Ing. Juan Manuel Fernandez, Registrar, Instituto Tecnológico y de Estudios Superiores de Monterrey, Campus Chihuahua, Colegio Militar 4700, Colonia Nombre de Dios, Apartado Postal 728, 31300 Chihuahua, Chihuahua, Mexico. *Phone:* -14-17-48-58 Ext. 117.

Instituto Tecnológico y de Estudios Superiores de Monterrey, Campus Ciudad de México

Ciudad de Mexico, Mexico

http://www.itesm.mx/

CONTACT

Admissions Office, Instituto Tecnológico y de Estudios Superiores de Monterrey, Campus Ciudad de México, Calle del Puente #222 esquina con Periférico, 14380 Colonia Huipulco, Tlalpan, MDF, Mexico. *Phone:* -5-673-6488.

Instituto Tecnológico y de Estudios Superiores de Monterrey, Campus Ciudad Juárez

Ciudad Juárez, Mexico

http://www.itesm.mx/

CONTACT

Lic. Alberto Trejo, Registrar, Instituto Tecnológico y de Estudios Superiores de Monterrey, Campus Ciudad Juárez, Boulevard Tomas Fernandez y Avenida A J Bermudez, Apartado Postal 3105-J, 32320 Ciudad Juárez, Chihuahua, Mexico. *Phone:* -16-17-88-07 Ext. 113.

Instituto Tecnológico y de Estudios Superiores de Monterrey, Campus Ciudad Obregón

Ciudad Obregón, Mexico

http://www.itesm.mx/

CONTACT

Lic. Judith Almeida, Registrar, Instituto Tecnológico y de Estudios Superiores de Monterrey, Campus Ciudad Obregón, Dr Norman E Borlaug Km 14, Apartado Postal 662, 85000 Ciudad Obregón, Sonora, Mexico. *Phone:* -64-15-03-12.

Instituto Tecnológico y de Estudios Superiores de Monterrey, Campus Colima

Colima, Mexico

http://www.itesm.mx/

CONTACT

Lic. Manuel Perez Rivera, Registrar, Instituto Tecnológico y de Estudios Superiores de Monterrey, Campus Colima, Prolongacion Ignacio Sandoval s/n, Fraccionamiento Jardines de Vista Hermosa, Apartado Postal 190, 28010 Colima, Colima, Mexico. *Phone:* -33-12-53-39.

Instituto Tecnológico y de Estudios Superiores de Monterrey, Campus Cuernavaca

Temixco, Mexico

http://www.itesm.mx/

CONTACT

Lic. Miguel Angel Machua, Registrar, Instituto Tecnológico y de Estudios Superiores de Monterrey, Campus Cuernavaca, Paseo de la Reforma 182-A, Colonia Lomas de Cuernavaca, 62000 Temixco, Morelos, Mexico. *Phone:* -73 18 49 57.

Instituto Tecnológico y de Estudios Superiores de Monterrey, Campus Estado de México

Estado de Mexico, Mexico

http://www.itesm.mx/

CONTACT

Prof. Jose de Jesus Molina, Registrar, Instituto Tecnológico y de Estudios Superiores de Monterrey, Campus Estado de México, Carretera Lago de Guadalupe Km. 3.5, Atizapan de Zaragoza, Estado de Mexico 52926, Mexico. *Phone:* -5-873-3600.

Instituto Tecnológico y de Estudios Superiores de Monterrey, Campus Guadalajara

Zapopan, Mexico

http://www.itesm.mx/

CONTACT

Ms. Janet Martell Sotomayor, Registration Director, Instituto Tecnológico y de Estudios Superiores de Monterrey, Campus Guadalajara, Avenida General Ramón Corona 2514, Colonia Nuevo Mexico, 45140 Zapopan, Jalisco, Mexico. *Phone:* -3-669-3006.

Instituto Tecnológico y de Estudios Superiores de Monterrey, Campus Hidalgo

Pachuca, Mexico

http://www.itesm.mx/

CONTACT

Lic. Lizbet Melo, Registrar, Instituto Tecnológico y de Estudios Superiores de Monterrey, Campus Hidalgo, Boulevard Felipe Angeles s/n al lado de la Unidad Deportiva, Apartado Postal 337, 42090 Pachuca, Hidalgo, Mexico. *Phone:* -714-25-00 Ext. 128.

Instituto Tecnológico y de Estudios Superiores de Monterrey, Campus Laguna

Torreón, Mexico

http://www.itesm.mx/

CONTACT
Ing. Aroldo Camargo Soto, Registrar, Instituto Tecnológico y de Estudios Superiores de Monterrey, Campus Laguna, Paseo del Tecnologico s/n Ampliacion La Rosita, Apartado Postal 506, 27250 Torreón, Coahuila, Mexico. *Phone:* -17-20-66-61 Ext. 23.

Instituto Tecnológico y de Estudios Superiores de Monterrey, Campus León

León, Mexico

http://www.itesm.mx/

CONTACT
Lic. Eddie Villegas, Registrar, Instituto Tecnológico y de Estudios Superiores de Monterrey, Campus León, Avenida Eugenio Garza Sada s/n Colonia Cerro Gordo, Apartado Postal 872, 37120 León, Guanajuato, Mexico. *Phone:* -47-17-10-00 Ext. 131.

Instituto Tecnológico y de Estudios Superiores de Monterrey, Campus Monterrey

Monterrey, Mexico

http://www.itesm.mx/

CONTACT
Lic. Carlos Ordoñez, International Student Advisor, Instituto Tecnológico y de Estudios Superiores de Monterrey, Campus Monterrey, Avenida Eugenio Garza Sada 2501 Sur Colonia Tecnnologico, Sucursal de Correos J, 64849 Monterrey, Nuevo León, Mexico. *Phone:* -52 81 8328 4065 Ext. 3942.

Instituto Tecnológico y de Estudios Superiores de Monterrey, Campus Querétaro

Santiago de Querétaro, Mexico

http://www.itesm.mx/

CONTACT
Lic. Marco Vinicio Lopez, Registrar, Instituto Tecnológico y de Estudios Superiores de Monterrey, Campus Querétaro, Avenida Epigmenio González #500, Apartado Postal 37, 76130 Querétaro, Querétaro, Mexico. *Phone:* -42-17-38-25 Ext. 156.

Instituto Tecnológico y de Estudios Superiores de Monterrey, Campus Saltillo

Saltillo, Mexico

http://www.itesm.mx/

CONTACT
Lic. Esteban Ramos, Registrar, Instituto Tecnológico y de Estudios Superiores de Monterrey, Campus Saltillo, Prolongacion Juan de la Barrera 1241 Ote, Apartado Postal 539, 25270 Saltillo, Coahuila, Mexico. *Phone:* -84-15-06-90 Ext. 12.

Instituto Tecnológico y de Estudios Superiores de Monterrey, Campus San Luis Potosí

San Luis Potosí, Mexico

http://www.itesm.mx/

CONTACT
Ing. Consuelo Gonzalez, Registrar, Instituto Tecnológico y de Estudios Superiores de Monterrey, Campus San Luis Potosí, Avenida Robles 600, Colonia Jacarandas, Apartado Postal 1473 Suc E, 78140 San Luis Potosí, SLP, Mexico. *Phone:* -48 13-3441 Ext. 14.

Instituto Tecnológico y de Estudios Superiores de Monterrey, Campus Sinaloa

Culiacán, Mexico

http://www.itesm.mx/

CONTACT
Lic. Hugo Guerrero, Registrar, Instituto Tecnológico y de Estudios Superiores de Monterrey, Campus Sinaloa, Boulevard Culiacán 3773, Apartado Postal 69-F, 80800 Culiacán, Sinaloa, Mexico. *Phone:* -67-14-03-69.

Instituto Tecnológico y de Estudios Superiores de Monterrey, Campus Sonora Norte

Hermosillo, Mexico

http://www.itesm.mx/

CONTACT
Ing. Victor Eduardo Perez Orozco, Library and Admissions/Registration Director, Instituto Tecnológico y de Estudios Superiores de Monterrey, Campus Sonora Norte, Carretera Hermosillo-Nogales Km 9, Apartado Postal 216, 83000 Hermosillo, Sonora, Mexico. *Phone:* -62-15-52-05 Ext. 131.

Instituto Tecnológico y de Estudios Superiores de Monterrey, Campus Tampico

Altimira, Mexico

http://www.itesm.mx/

CONTACT
Ing. Javier Ponce, Registrar, Instituto Tecnológico y de Estudios Superiores de Monterrey, Campus Tampico, Boulevard Petrocel Km 1.3, Corredor Industrial, Carretera Tampico-Mante, 89120 Altimira, Tamaulipas, Mexico. *Phone:* -126-4-19-79.

Instituto Tecnológico y de Estudios Superiores de Monterrey, Campus Toluca

Toluca, Mexico

http://www.itesm.mx/

CONTACT
Ing. Victor M. Martinez Orta, Registrar, Instituto Tecnológico y de Estudios Superiores de Monterrey, Campus Toluca, Ex-hacienda La Pila, 100 metros al norte de San Antonio Buenavista, 50252 Toluca, Estado de Mexico, Mexico. *Phone:* -72-74-11-92.

Instituto Tecnológico y de Estudios Superiores de Monterrey, Campus Zacatecas

Zacatecas, Mexico

http://www.itesm.mx/

CONTACT
Lic. de Lourdes Zorrilla, Business Affairs Director and Registrar, Instituto Tecnológico y de Estudios Superiores de Monterrey, Campus Zacatecas, Calzada Pedro Coronel #16, Frente al Club Bernades, Municipio de Guadalupe, 98000 Zacatecas, Zacatecas, Mexico. *Phone:* -49 23-00-40.

Instituto Tecnológico y de Estudios Superiores de Monterrey, Campus Irapuato

Irapuato, Mexico

http://www.itesm.mx/

CONTACT
Ing. Marcela Beltrán, Registrar, Instituto Tecnológico y de Estudios Superiores de Monterrey, Campus Irapuato, Paseo Mirador del Valle No. 445, Col. Villas de Irapuato, Apartado Postal 568, 36660 Irapuato, Guanajuato, Mexico. *Phone:* -46-230342.

Universidad de las Americas, A.C.

Mexico City, Mexico

http://www.udladf.mx/

CONTACT
Universidad de las Americas, A.C., Calle de Puebla 223, Col. Roma, 06700 Mexico City, Mexico.

Universidad de las Américas Puebla

Puebla, Mexico

http://www.udlap.mx/

CONTACT
Miss Madet Ruisenor-Quintero, Director of Student Enrollment Office, Universidad de las Américas Puebla, Ex-Hacienda Santa Catarina Martir, Cholula, Puebla 72820, Mexico. *Phone:* -52 229-2024.

Universidad de Monterrey

San Pedro Garza Garcia, Mexico

http://www.udem.edu.mx/

CONTACT
Universidad de Monterrey, Av. Ignacio Morones Prieto 4500 Pte, 66238 San Pedro Garza Garcia, NL, Mexico. *Toll-free phone:* 800-801-UDEM.

MONACO

The International University of Monaco

Monte Carlo, Monaco

http://www.monaco.edu/

CONTACT
Dr. Gisele Dudognon, Director of Admissions, The International University of Monaco, 2, Avenue Albert II, MC-98000 Principality of Monaco, Monaco. *Phone:* -377 97986 994. *Fax:* 377 92052 830. *E-mail:* gdudognon@monaco.edu.

SOUTH AFRICA

University of South Africa

Pretoria, South Africa

http://www.unisa.ac.za/

CONTACT
Contact Centre, University of South Africa, PO Box 392, Pretoria 0003, South Africa. *Phone:* 27-11 670-9000. *Fax:* 012 429 4150. *E-mail:* study-info@unisa.ac.za.

SPAIN

Saint Louis University–Madrid Campus

Madrid, Spain

http://www.slu.edu/madrid

CONTACT
Ms. Heidi Buffington, Director of Admissions, Saint Louis University–Madrid Campus, Avenida del Valle, 34, Madrid 28003, Spain. *Phone:* -34 91-554-5858 Ext. 206. *Fax:* 34 91-554-6202. *E-mail:* heidi.buffington@slu.edu.

Schiller International University - Madrid

Madrid, Spain

http://www.schiller.edu/

CONTACT
Ms. Kamala Dontamsetti, Associate Director of Admissions, Schiller International University - Madrid, 300 East Bay Drive, Largo, FL 33700. *Phone:* 727-736-5082 Ext. 234. *Toll-free phone:* 800-261-9571 (in-state); 800-261-9751 (out-of-state). *Fax:* 727-734-0359. *E-mail:* admissions@schiller.edu.

SWITZERLAND

Ecole Hôtelière de Lausanne

Lausanne, Switzerland

http://www.ehl.edu/

CONTACT
Ecole Hôtelière de Lausanne, Route de Cojonnex 18, Le Chalet-a-Gobet, CH-1000 Lausanne 25, Switzerland. *Phone:* -41 21 785 1111.

Franklin University Switzerland

Sorengo, Switzerland

http://www.fus.edu/

CONTACT
Franklin University Switzerland, Via Ponte Tresa 29, CH-6924 Sorengo, Switzerland.

Glion Institute of Higher Education

Glion-sur-Montreux, Switzerland

http://www.glion.edu/

CONTACT
Admissions, Glion Institute of Higher Education, Route de Glion 111, CH-1823 Glion-sur-Montreux, Switzerland. *Phone:* 41-0 21 989 26 77. *Fax:* 41-0 21 989 26 78. *E-mail:* info@glion.edu.

International University in Geneva

Geneva, Switzerland

http://www.iun.ch/

- **Private** comprehensive
- **Urban** campus
- **Coed** 112 undergraduate students, 100% full-time, 47% women, 53% men
- **Moderately difficult** entrance level

UNDERGRAD STUDENTS
112 full-time. Students come from 62 other countries; 6% transferred in.

Freshmen:
Admission: 29 enrolled. ***Average high school GPA:*** 2.5.
Retention: 94% of full-time freshmen returned.

FACULTY
Total: 44, 18% full-time, 36% with terminal degrees.

Student/faculty ratio: 7:1.

ACADEMICS
Calendar: trimesters. *Degrees:* bachelor's, master's, and doctoral.

Special study options: academic remediation for entering students, accelerated degree program, advanced placement credit, double majors, English as a second language, independent study, off-campus study, part-time degree program, study abroad, summer session for credit.

Computers: 30 computers/terminals are available on campus for general student use. Students can access the following: campus intranet, computer help desk, free student e-mail accounts, online (class) schedules. Campuswide network is available. Wireless service is available via classrooms, student centers.
Library: IUG Library.

STUDENT LIFE
Housing options: college housing not available.

Activities and organizations: student-run newspaper, UNICEF, United Nations Women Bazaar, WUFUNA, Harvard MUN.

Athletics *Intercollegiate sports:* basketball M, bowling M/W, football M, sand volleyball W, tennis M/W, volleyball W.

Student services: personal/psychological counseling.

APPLYING
Options: electronic application, early decision, early action, deferred entrance.

Application fee: $150.

Required: essay or personal statement, high school transcript, minimum 2.0 GPA, 1 letter of recommendation. ***Required for some:*** interview.

Application deadlines: rolling (freshmen), rolling (transfers).

Notification: continuous (freshmen), continuous (transfers).

CONTACT
Ms. Olga Bulankina, Director of Bachelor Admissions, International University in Geneva, Geneva 1215, Switzerland. *Phone:* -41 22710-7110. *Fax:* 41 22710-7111. *E-mail:* bachelor@iun.ch.

Les Roches International School of Hotel Management

Bluche, Switzerland

http://www.lesroches.edu/

CONTACT
Enrollment Management Department, Les Roches International School of Hotel Management, CH-3975 Bluche, Switzerland. *Phone:* 41-021 989 26 44. *Fax:* 41-021 989 26 45. *E-mail:* info@lesroches.edu.

TAIWAN

Christ's College

Taipei, Taiwan

http://www.cct.edu.tw/

CONTACT
Ms. Lucy Li, Recruiter, Christ's College, No. 51, Ziqiang Road, Tamsui District, New Taipei City 251, Taiwan. *Phone:* -+886-2-2809-7661. *Fax:* +886-2-8809-1084. *E-mail:* lucyli@christs-college.org.

UNITED ARAB EMIRATES

The American University in Dubai

Dubai, United Arab Emirates

http://www.aud.edu/

CONTACT
Mrs. Carol Maalouf, Director of Admissions, The American University in Dubai, PO Box 28282, Dubai, United Arab Emirates. *Phone:* -971 4 399 9000 Ext. 170. *Fax:* 971 4 399 8899. *E-mail:* admissions@aud.edu.

American University of Sharjah

Sharjah, United Arab Emirates

http://www.aus.edu/

- **Independent** comprehensive, founded 1997
- **Suburban** campus with easy access to Sharjah and Dubai
- **Coed**
- **Moderately difficult** entrance level

FACULTY
Student/faculty ratio: 15:1.

ACADEMICS
Calendar: semesters. *Degrees:* bachelor's and master's.
Library: University Library.

STUDENT LIFE
Housing options: men-only, women-only. Campus housing is university owned.

Activities and organizations: drama/theater group, student-run newspaper, radio station, choral group.

Campus security: 24-hour emergency response devices and patrols, late-night transport/escort service, controlled dormitory access.

Student services: health clinic, personal/psychological counseling, women's center.

APPLYING
Options: electronic application, early admission, early decision, deferred entrance.

Required: high school transcript.

CONTACT
American University of Sharjah, PO Box 26666, Sharjah, United Arab Emirates. *Phone:* -+971 6 515 1000. *Fax:* + 971 6 515 2200. *E-mail:* inforequest@aus.edu.

United Arab Emirates University

Al-Ain, United Arab Emirates

http://www.uaeu.ac.ae/

CONTACT
United Arab Emirates University, PO Box 15551, Al Ain, Abu Dhabi, United Arab Emirates.

UNITED KINGDOM

Hult International Business School

London, United Kingdom

http://www.hult.edu/

- **Independent** comprehensive, founded 1959
- **Urban** campus with easy access to San Francisco, London, Boston
- **Coed**
- **Moderately difficult** entrance level

FACULTY
Student/faculty ratio: 15:1.

ACADEMICS
Calendar: 5-term academic calendar: required fall, winter, spring terms; optional Summer 1, Summer 2 terms. *Degrees:* bachelor's, master's, and doctoral.
Library: Main Library plus 3 others. *Books:* 198,590 (digital/electronic); *Databases:* 23.

STUDENT LIFE
Housing options: on-campus residence required through sophomore year; coed. Campus housing is leased by the school. Freshman applicants given priority for college housing.

Activities and organizations: drama/theater group, student-run newspaper, choral group, Language Cafe, Model United Nations, International Law Society, Hult RISE (charity club), Consultancy Club.

Campus security: 24-hour emergency response devices and patrols, controlled dormitory access.

Student services: personal/psychological counseling.

COSTS
Costs (2019–20) ***One-time required fee:*** $850. ***Comprehensive fee:*** $59,650 includes full-time tuition ($41,650) and room and board ($18,000). ***College room only:*** $14,000.

APPLYING
Standardized Tests *Required for some:* SAT or ACT (for admission), TOEFL, IELTS, or PTE for non-native English speakers.

Options: electronic application.

Application fee: 75 British pounds.

Required: essay or personal statement, high school transcript, 2 letters of recommendation. ***Required for some:*** interview.

CONTACT
Mr. Niccolo Del Monte, Vice President, Undergraduate Enrollment, Hult International Business School, 35 Commercial Road, London E1 1LD, United Kingdom. *Phone:* -44 207 341 8555. *E-mail:* niccolo.delmonte@hult.edu.

London Metropolitan University

London, United Kingdom

http://www.londonmet.ac.uk/

CONTACT
London Metropolitan University, 166-220 Holloway Road, London N7 8DB, United Kingdom.

Open University

Milton Keynes, United Kingdom

http://www.open.ac.uk/

CONTACT
Open University, Walton Hall, Milton Keynes MK7 6AA, United Kingdom.

Regent's University London

London, United Kingdom

http://www.regents.ac.uk/

CONTACT
Admissions Director, Regent's University London, Inner Circle, Regent's Park, London NW1 4NS, United Kingdom. *Phone:* 44-0 207 487 7505. *Fax:* 44-0 207 487 7425. *E-mail:* bacl@regents.ac.uk.

Richmond, The American International University in London

Richmond, United Kingdom

http://www.richmond.ac.uk/

- **Independent** comprehensive, founded 1972
- **Urban** 5-acre campus with easy access to London
- **Coed** 1,035 undergraduate students, 99% full-time, 64% women, 36% men
- **Moderately difficult** entrance level, 65% of applicants were admitted

UNDERGRAD STUDENTS
1,024 full-time, 11 part-time. Students come from 46 states and territories; 97 other countries; 54% live on campus.

Freshmen:
Admission: 1,550 applied, 1,012 admitted, 210 enrolled. ***Average high school GPA:*** 3.5.

FACULTY
Total: 106, 39% full-time, 44% with terminal degrees.
Student/faculty ratio: 17:1.

ACADEMICS
Calendar: semesters. *Degrees:* bachelor's, master's, and postbachelor's certificates.

Special study options: academic remediation for entering students, advanced placement credit, double majors, independent study, internships, services for LD students, study abroad, summer session for credit.

Computers: 425 computers/terminals are available on campus for general student use. Students can access the following: campus intranet, computer help desk, free student e-mail accounts, online (class) grades, online (class) registration, online (class) schedules. Campuswide network is available. 100% of college-owned or -operated housing units are wired for high-speed Internet access. Wireless service is available via entire campus.
Library: Taylor Library plus 2 others.

STUDENT LIFE
Housing options: coed, men-only, women-only. Campus housing is university owned. Freshman campus housing is guaranteed.

Activities and organizations: drama/theater group, student-run newspaper, radio station, choral group, Student Union, Green Project, community service, Richmond International Society, Model United Nations.

Athletics ***Intercollegiate sports:*** rugby M, soccer M/W. ***Intramural sports:*** basketball M/W, rugby M, soccer M/W, swimming and diving M/W, table tennis M/W, tennis M/W, volleyball M/W, weight lifting M/W.

Campus security: 24-hour patrols.

Student services: health clinic, personal/psychological counseling.

COSTS
Costs (2020–21) ***Room and board:*** Room and board charges vary according to housing facility. ***Payment plan:*** installment.

APPLYING
Options: electronic application, deferred entrance.

Required: essay or personal statement, high school transcript, minimum 2.5 GPA, 1 letter of recommendation. ***Required for some:*** interview.

Application deadlines: rolling (freshmen), rolling (transfers).

Notification: continuous (freshmen), continuous (transfers).

CONTACT
Mr. Bryan Witham, Sr. Director of US Operations, Richmond, The American International University in London, 343 Congress Street, Suite

3100, Boston, MA 02210-1214. *Phone:* 617-958-9534. *E-mail:* us_admissions@richmond.ac.uk.

College Close-Ups

NOTICE: Certain portions of or information contained in this book have been submitted and paid for by the educational institution identified, and such institutions take full responsibility for the accuracy, timeliness, completeness and functionality of such content. Such portions or information include (i) each display ad in the "Profiles" section from pages 53 through 1037 that comprises a half or full page of information covering a single educational institution, and (ii) each two-page description in the "College Close-Up" section from pages 1039 through 1141.

ALLEGHENY COLLEGE

MEADVILLE, PENNSYLVANIA

The College

One of Loren Pope's 40 "Colleges That Change Lives," Allegheny is known as one of the most innovative liberal arts colleges in the nation. On its historic campus—where the liberal arts and sciences have been taught for more than 200 years—students dive deep into majors and minors in areas that may, at first glance, seem unrelated: biology and economics, political science and music, history and psychology. Allegheny students share an abiding passion for learning and life, a spirit of camaraderie, and a respect for shared inquiry that spans all areas of study. Neuroscience majors play in the Civic Symphony and build houses during Alternative Spring Break. Students prepare for law school while playing basketball and interning in Washington, D.C. Computer science majors present work in philosophy at national conferences.

Building on the intersection of academic disciplines and passions, every student completes the comprehensive Senior Project under the guidance of a faculty adviser in his or her major field. The project demonstrates the skills most prized by employers and graduate schools: the ability to complete a major assignment, work independently, analyze and synthesize information, and to write and speak persuasively.

Allegheny students are encouraged to explore all of their interests and to look at academic disciplines from multiple perspectives, which leads them to extraordinary outcomes. Biochemistry majors use the skills they learned in communication arts to start marketing careers with the Environmental Protection Agency. English majors collaborate with the College's pre-health advisers and enjoy acceptance rates to medical school between 80 and 100 percent—twice the national average. And over 95 percent of Allegheny's job-seeking graduates find employment within six months.

Leaders in business, government, medicine, education, and community service frequently declare that the future belongs to individuals who are innovators, inventors, and big-picture thinkers, those who think outside the lines, both analytically and creatively. It is this preparation for the global marketplace, and for life, that Allegheny, with its emphasis on pursuing all your interests, is nationally known for providing.

Location

Central campus looks like a traditional college with a rich liberal arts heritage and tradition, with its 79 acres of rolling lawns and brick walkways, historic buildings, and century-old oaks and elms. A 203-acre recreational complex and a 283-acre nature reserve complement state-of-the-art classrooms, labs, theaters, studios and other facilities.

The campus overlooks the town of Meadville, a county seat that features a courthouse, hospital, a variety of industries, and more. Allegheny students connect with the community in many ways, from running after-school programs to taking in the latest movies, from creating art installations to checking out live music.

Allegheny students live in a section of the country that most people get to see only on vacation. Northwest Pennsylvania is a nature-lover's paradise of verdant, undisturbed forests and streams and lakes that are gems of biodiversity. It's no wonder that the College has one of the oldest Outing Clubs in the country.

Allegheny is ideally situated within two hours of the social and transportation hubs of Pittsburgh, Cleveland, and Buffalo. Being just close enough to major cities allows for frequent excursions to major sporting events, concerts, and other attractions.

Majors and Degrees

Allegheny students can earn the Bachelor of Arts (B.A.) or the Bachelor of Science (B.S.) degree in the following programs of study; art (studio); art, science, and innovation; biochemistry; biology; business; chemistry; communication arts; community and justice studies; computer science; creative writing; economics; English; environmental geology; environmental science & sustainability; French; geology; global health studies; history; integrative informatics; international studies; mathematics; music; neuroscience; philosophy; physics; political science; psychology; religious studies; Spanish; theatre; women's, gender, and sexuality studies; and self-designed majors.

In addition to the above majors, minors are available in: astronomy, black studies, Chinese, Chinese studies, classical studies, dance and movement studies, education studies, energy & society, environmental writing, French studies, German, Jewish studies, journalism in the public interest, Latin American and Caribbean studies, Middle East and North African studies, music history, music performance, music theory, and writing.

Dedicated advisers are available for students interested in: pre-dental, pre-law, pre-medicine, pre-nursing, pre-pharmacy, and pre-veterinary.

Students may also take advantage of accelerated master's and doctoral degree programs, teacher certification programs, and engineering cooperative programs with other top institutions.

Academic Programs

Allegheny College believes so strongly in allowing students to study varied subjects that it is built right into its curriculum; it is one of the few liberal arts colleges nationally that requires students to choose a minor as well as a major. This may make the school sound more difficult, but most students at Allegheny are individuals for whom the most difficult thing would be to give up some vital part of themselves. Some Allegheny students have majors and minors that complement each other in predictable ways—an international studies major with a minor in French, for example. But there are other students whose majors and minors represent very different aspects of themselves—an environmental science & sustainability major with a minor in creative writing or a chemistry major with a minor in history. Coupled with experiential learning and the distinctive Senior Project, seeing academic disciplines from multiple perspectives leads to extraordinary outcomes.

During the first two years, every Allegheny student participates in seminars that focus on written and oral communication as well as academic and career advising, and the faculty instructor serves as adviser for both years. This progressive course sequence, in addition to the Junior Seminar and Senior Project, helps students create a four-year experience to match all of their needs and goals.

Under the guidance of a faculty adviser in his or her major field, every student completes the Senior Project, a significant piece of original scholarly work with a creative, analytical, or experimental focus. The project mirrors a master's thesis and requires project management skills, independent work, writing and presentation skills, and the ability to analyze and synthesize information. Allegheny has required a senior capstone experience since the college's first commencement ceremony in 1821. The Council on Undergraduate Research recognized Allegheny as the top baccalaureate college in the nation for providing high-quality research experiences to undergraduates.

In the National Survey of Student Engagement, responses by college freshmen placed Allegheny within the top 10 percent in the United States for both a supportive campus environment and level of academic challenge.

Off-Campus Programs

Allegheny College recognizes the enormous academic, professional, and personal value of studying off-campus, nationally or internationally. Allegheny students can experience multiple off-campus adventures, learning with an eclectic group of students with diverse academic majors and interests. The Gateway facilitates a variety of opportunities through study abroad, career services, community service, and more.

The College sponsors semester and year-long study-away programs, some of which require skills in languages other than English, and others with no language requirements. More than 190 Allegheny students and faculty participate in 40 Allegheny-sponsored study abroad programs in 20 countries.

In addition, faculty members lead students each year on intensive three-week experiential learning seminars. These for-credit, faculty-designed programs occur at the end of each spring semester. Recent excursions took students to Austria, the Czech Republic, England, Germany, India, Japan, Turkey, and South Africa.

The Office of Career Education maintains a database of 2,500 internship and shadowing opportunities, including especially popular ones in Boston, New York City, Los Angeles, and Washington, D.C. Students at Allegheny can choose among several kinds of internships, including academic internships taken for credit that often take place during a spring or fall semester and noncredit internships throughout the summer.

Academic Facilities

Allegheny boasts the nationally acclaimed Steffee Hall of Life Sciences, which incorporates state-of-the-art labs located right next to classrooms and faculty offices. An environmental science & sustainability center features the best in sustainable practices with a living wall, aquaponics equipment, and solar panels. Students also benefit from the GIS learning lab, planetarium, and seismographic network station.

The multimillion-dollar Vukovich Center for Communication Arts, which meets LEED certification standards and has a rooftop garden, features a learning theater, scene and costume shops, and video production facilities. Language students enjoy a multimedia learning lab, and dancers work in bright, functional studio and performance spaces. The Bowman, Penelec, and Megahan art galleries display student and faculty work as well as visiting exhibits.

Allegheny's Learning Commons provides academic support to all students through professional guidance, peer mentors, training, and effective learning tools. The center is housed in Pelletier Library, which offers more than 900,000 volumes, as well as extensive digital resources, research tools, and unique meeting spaces.

Costs

For 2019–20, tuition and fees were $ 50,480. The standard first-year room and board was $15,204.

Financial Aid

Through the generous support of its alumni, Allegheny is able to provide over $52 million in achievement-based scholarships; need-based grant assistance; and aid awarded to students from federal, state, and private sources. Allegheny's financial assistance allows many students the opportunity to make a college choice based on value and fit, rather than financial constraints.

Allegheny's Trustee Scholarships are awarded without regard to financial need to students who have balanced academic excellence with other distinctive activities while in high school. Awards range up to $148,000, distributed equally over four years of study at Allegheny (up to $37,000 per year), and renew automatically.

Faculty

Whether it's conducting research, teaching a First-Year Seminar, leading a three-week study tour, co-authoring an article or making an authentic French dinner, faculty work and learn alongside students every day. There's no graduate school buffer between undergraduates and faculty. Students don't have to wait behind graduate students for research positions on faculty-led projects or compete against hundreds of other students for the lead roles in plays or an editorship at the literary magazine.

Of the 173 full-time faculty members, 91 percent have earned the highest degree in their fields. The student to faculty ratio is 11:1, and introductory classes have an average of 19 students. Advanced classes have an average of 12 students, and some seminars have fewer than 10. Of all classes, 88 percent have fewer than 30 students.

Every student has a faculty adviser for the first two years and a faculty adviser in his/her major field for the final two years. Culminating with their work guiding students through the Senior Project, faculty members are not only supportive and engaging teachers but true leaders and mentors.

Student Government

The Allegheny Student Government is the official voice and administrative unit of the student body. This extremely active and influential organization concerns itself with the quality of the educational, cultural, and social aspects of the Allegheny community. Its members organize and coordinate programs of a cocurricular and extracurricular nature and sponsor more than 120 student-run clubs and organizations.

Students serve on every major college committee, including faculty searches, sustainability efforts, and strategic planning. Their presence exemplifies the importance placed on student participation and represents the influence students have on the institution.

Admission Requirements

From the time a prospective student first contacts Allegheny, the College's holistic approach is directed to addressing his or her unique character, needs, and aspirations. During the application process, primary attention is focused on those criteria that indicate academic promise, including difficulty of high school classes, GPA, and class rank. Careful consideration is also given to those personal qualities that are important in the total success of the college experience: school and community activities, recommendation letters, and the personal essay. Students are encouraged to share additional information through the College's application supplement and an interview and visit. Allegheny embraces the concept that standardized test scores do not exclusively reflect a student's full range of abilities or potential to succeed in college. As a result, Allegheny is test optional. ACT and SAT I scores are optional for U.S. citizens and permanent residents.

The result is a highly personalized approach to the selection of students that remains consistent with the aims of the College, respects the individuality of each applicant, and ensures equal consideration of every candidate. The College encourages diversity and actively seeks students from all ethnic, religious, racial, political, geographic, and socioeconomic backgrounds.

Application and Information

Office of Admissions
Allegheny College
520 North Main Street
Meadville, Pennsylvania 16335
Phone: 814-332-4351
800-521-5293 (toll-free)
Fax: 814-337-0431
E-mail: admissions@allegheny.edu
Web site: http://www.allegheny.edu/admissions
http://www.allegheny.edu/distinctions
http://www.allegheny.edu/visit
http://www.allegheny.edu/apply

Recognized among Loren Pope's 40 "Colleges That Change Lives," Allegheny College is one of the nation's most historic and innovative institutions of higher education. Allegheny is one of the only colleges in the country that requires students to choose both a major and minor, ensuring they develop the skills needed to be analytical and creative.

BARNARD COLLEGE

NEW YORK, NEW YORK

The College

The founders of Barnard College were among the pioneers in the late nineteenth-century crusade who sought to make access to higher education available to women. Founded in 1889 and formally partnered with Columbia University since 1900, the College serves more than 2,650 students today from almost every state and more than fifty countries. It offers the intimacy of a small college with the added advantages of a large research university. Barnard remains affiliated with Columbia, with students at both schools regularly cross-registering for courses taught at either institution. Barnard students have access to the University's resources and graduates receive their degree from Columbia. At the same time, Barnard College remains a small, independent liberal arts college, devoted solely to the undergraduate education of women. The College maintains its own Board of Trustees, faculty, administrative staff, endowment, admissions process, and sole ownership of its property and physical plant.

The self-contained Barnard campus occupies 4+ acres of urban property along Broadway between 116th and 120th streets and serves as an oasis from the hustle and bustle of New York City. Its location on the upper west side of Manhattan grants students access to thousands of internship opportunities in addition to unparalleled cultural, intellectual, and social resources. Forty-five percent of students identify as students of color, and 13 percent come from non-college backgrounds.

Location

Barnard is located north of Central Park on the upper west side of Manhattan, in the safe and student-friendly Morningside Heights neighborhood. The campus is directly across from Columbia University, and has numerous educational and cultural institutions as neighbors, including the Jewish Theological Seminary, Bank Street School of Education, St. John the Divine church, and Grant's tomb. Abounding with cultural, educational, internship, and professional opportunities and more than 500,000 college students, New York is Barnard's laboratory.

Majors and Degrees

Students can earn a Bachelor of Arts (B.A.) in the following subjects: Africana studies, American studies, ancient studies, anthropology, architecture, art history, Asian and Middle Eastern cultures, astronomy, biochemistry, biological sciences, chemistry, classics (Greek and Latin), comparative literature, computer science, dance, economics, education, English, environmental biology science or studies, European studies, film studies, French, German, history, human rights, Italian, Jewish studies, mathematics and applied mathematics, medieval and Renaissance studies, music, neuroscience, philosophy, physics, political science, psychology, religion, Russian and Slavic studies, sociology, Spanish and Latin American cultures, statistics, theater, urban studies, and women's, gender, and sexuality studies. The College provides an excellent education program, leading to teaching certification with a specific urban studies track, and prepares students for graduate programs in health and medicine, law, and business..

Barnard College also offers double- and joint-degree programs in cooperation with other schools within the Columbia community as well as several 4+1 programs for a graduate degree. The 4+1 programs are in partnership with a number of Columbia's programs: the School of International and Public Affairs (SIPA), the School of Engineering and Applied Sciences (SEAS), the Mailman School of Public Health, the Harriman Institute for Russian, European and Eastern European Studies, the Graduate School of Arts and Sciences Oral History program (OHMA), and the Graduate School of Arts and Sciences Quantitative Methods in the Social Sciences program (QMSS). Barnard also offers a double-degree program with List College of the Jewish Theological Seminary and lessons exchange programs with Manhattan School of Music and The Juilliard School.

Academic Programs

Two required courses, First-Year Seminar and First-Year Writing, set the foundation for a Barnard education with small seminar classes, limited to 16 students. In addition to these First-Year Experience courses, Barnard's flexible general education requirements are organized around Foundation Requirements in four subject areas and Modes of Thinking that connect to six themes. A generous list of courses allows for students to choose which options interest them most. Barnard students shape their educational experience by choosing courses that enhance the way they view the world.

Advanced placement and I.B. credit are available. Barnard operates on a two-semester calendar, with classes beginning in early September. The fall semester ends in mid-December; classes resume for the spring semester in mid-January and end in mid-May.

Off-Campus Programs

As an independent partner of Columbia University, Barnard offers students open access to courses, libraries, and other facilities of the University. With special permission, students may also register for selected classes in Columbia's graduate and professional schools. Barnard has a rich history and tradition of study abroad dating back to the 1930s. Today, qualified students are eligible to study in nearly 100 programs in more than fifty countries worldwide and nearly forty percent of Barnard students spend a semester or year abroad. Students are currently studying in Argentina, Australia, Austria, Bolivia, Brazil, Chile, China, Costa Rica, Czech Republic, Denmark, Ecuador, England, France, Germany, Greece, Hungary, Ireland, Israel, Italy, Japan, Jordan, Kenya, Madagascar, Netherlands, New Zealand, Panama, Peru, Russia, Scotland, Senegal, South Africa, Spain, Switzerland, and other locations. Students may also participate in a domestic exchange with Spelman College in Atlanta or Howard University in Washington, D.C.

Barnard's location offers its students a variety of work experiences and 75 percent of students will complete one or more internships.

Academic Facilities

Barnard's campus blends classic and modern architecture. The Cheryl and Philip Milstein Teaching and Learning Center, which opened in fall 2018, serves as the academic hub in the heart of the Barnard College campus. The 128,000 square-foot building includes a 40,000 square-foot library and centers for pedagogy, media, data analysis, movement, and design. The Center includes the Vagelos Computational Science Center, homes for the Barnard Center for Research on Women and the Athena Center for Leadership Studies, and social and study spaces for students. Historic Milbank Hall anchors the north end of campus, topped by the 2,500-square-foot Arthur Ross Greenhouse, housing administrative and faculty offices in addition to the Minor Latham Playhouse.

The south end of the campus, referred to as the Quad, contains the Brooks, Reid, Hewitt, and Sulzberger residence halls; first-year students are housed in the Quad. Additional housing (twelve residence halls in total) provides those entering as first-years guaranteed housing for four years of continuous enrollment at Barnard. The Diana Center, a 70,000 square-foot student center, added a new element of design in 2010. Its seven-story glass structure stretches across campus, linking the historic gates of the entrance at the south end of campus, to one of the original campus buildings, Milbank Hall, on the north.

Costs

Tuition and fees for 2019-20 are $55,781. Room and board costs are an additional $17,856.

Financial Aid

Financial aid at Barnard is awarded based upon demonstrated need. Federal funds and institutional grants are administered as determined by federal and institutional methodology. Barnard provides no merit or athletic scholarships. Once need has been established, Barnard covers 100 percent of demonstrated need with a combination of grants, loans, and work-study or student employment. Approximately 40 percent of the students at Barnard receive some form of financial aid.

Barnard College has a need-blind admission policy in which first-year applicants who are U.S. citizens or permanent residents are judged solely on merit without reference to financial circumstances. International and transfer students are considered for need-based aid from a limited pool of funding.

Faculty

Barnard College employs more than 300 teaching faculty members with a student-faculty ratio of 9:1. Barnard's faculty includes editors of leading scholarly journals, prize-winning novelists and translators, and frequent winners of awards from respected foundations, corporations, and government agencies. They are actively engaged in research and publication in their respective fields, but they regard teaching as their primary commitment. From the start of their time at the College, all students have faculty advisers who assist them in selecting courses and designing individual academic programs, in addition to a vast network of decanal, staff, and peer advising.

Student Life

Barnard women have access to more than eighty clubs and organizations on the College campus alone. Add to this list the hundreds of additional dually recognized clubs with members from both Barnard and Columbia, provided for through Barnard's long-standing partnership with the University, and strong friendships develop among students from both sides of Broadway. Student groups include performance groups, academic and pre-professional, ethnic and cultural, language, community service, and publications. Social interaction and cooperation between Barnard and Columbia groups is virtually seamless, with Barnard women regularly joining and leading a variety of Columbia organizations. Students, faculty members, and administrators also serve on tripartite committees and share responsibility for policy on curriculum, housing, financial aid, orientation, and the library.

On Barnard's campus, every student service is designed to meet the needs of a women-focused community. Primary Health Services, Furman Counseling Center, the academic advising program, and a unique Career Development and graduate school/fellowships advising Center called Beyond Barnard create programs to provide the kind of support young women may need as they navigate their academic experiences and life beyond college. The Athena Center for Leadership studies also provides Barnard students with the unique opportunity to become an Athena scholar and dedicate a portion of their studies to leadership development, history, and skills, culminating in a senior capstone project.

Admission Requirements

The Committee on Admissions selects motivated women of proven academic strength who exhibit intellectual and personal maturity. Careful consideration is given to candidates' high school records, recommendations, writing skills, standardized test scores (optional for students entering in 2021), special abilities and interests, and personal and educational context.

Admission to Barnard is highly selective and candidates for admission to the first-year class are expected to have taken a highly rigorous college-preparatory program. Students educated in a non-English-speaking setting or who have studied in English for less than four years must also take the TOEFL or IELTS exam. Interview opportunities are available for first-year students, but are not required. Barnard also enrolls a robust transfer class for fall and spring semesters and offers visiting student opportunities.

Application and Information

Applicants for first-year admission should apply in the fall of their senior year of high school. Applications must be received by January 1 and must include the non-refundable application fee. Students are notified in late March. Well-qualified high school seniors who have selected Barnard as their first-choice college are encouraged to apply under the binding early decision plan. Early decision applications must be submitted by November 1. Barnard accepts sophomore and junior transfer students. Transfer and visiting student applications must be submitted by March 15 for consideration for September entrance and by November 1 for consideration for January entrance.

For more information about Barnard College, students should contact:

Dean of Admissions
Barnard College, Office of Admissions
3009 Broadway
New York, New York 10027
Phone: 212-854-2014
Fax: 212-280-8797
E-mail: admissions@barnard.edu
Website: http://www.admissions.barnard.edu

A view of Milbank Hall from the Diana Center, Barnard's multipurpose student center.

BOSTON COLLEGE

CHESTNUT HILL, MASSACHUSETTS

The University

Boston College (BC) was founded in 1863 by the Jesuits to serve the sons of Boston's Irish immigrants. Today a coeducational university on more than 239 acres in Chestnut Hill, BC may seem a world apart from the small school in the crowded heart of Boston that was its first home. Through more than fifteen decades of growth and change, however, BC has held fast to the Jesuit ideals that inspired its founders. A Jesuit education today, as a century ago, is grounded in the liberal arts and in a commitment to the service of others.

Undergraduates may enroll in the Morrissey College of Arts and Sciences, the Wallace E. Carroll School of Management, the Connell School of Nursing, or the Lynch School of Education.

BC's approximately 9,000 undergraduates come from many backgrounds. The university draws from nearly all fifty states and more than sixty countries. Students' religious and cultural backgrounds are similarly diverse. Today, the university's AHANA (African American, Hispanic, Asian, and Native American) and international students make up over 30 percent of the undergraduate student body.

In today's complex and increasingly diverse world, the university believes that the best education is one that broadens a student's capacity to reason, think, and make critical judgments in a wide range of areas. Thus, each BC student fulfills a core of liberal arts courses from which he or she can pursue degrees in more than fifty areas of study and choose from more than 1,400 course offerings throughout the university.

According to several recent national publications, BC is in the top tier of the nation's colleges and universities. The foundation for that achievement is the university's scholars and researchers—860 full-time professionals who make up the faculty. The kinship between teachers and students is one of the hallmarks of a BC education; that relationship is nurtured by a student-teacher ratio of 10.6:1. The median class size at the university is 20 students.

At BC, learning continues beyond the classroom in more than 300 student-run organizations. These include student government, honor societies, language and cultural organizations, performance ensembles, political groups, pre-professional clubs, publications, and service organizations. BC also sponsors thirteen varsity teams for men and sixteen for women, all of which compete at the NCAA Division I level. The College also supports over sixty club and intramural sports.

Boston College's public affairs office maintains university profiles on major social networking sites including: Twitter (http://twitter.com/BostonCollege), Facebook (http://www.facebook.com/BostonCollege), YouTube (http://www.youtube.com/bostoncollege), Instagram (http://instagram.com/BostonCollege), and LinkedIn (https://www.linkedin.com/school/boston-college/).

Location

Located in the Chestnut Hill section of Newton, BC sits on the doorstep of one of America's great cities, a center of culture and education for more than three centuries. It is an energetic, cosmopolitan city that draws life and enthusiasm from the more than 200,000 college students in residence during the academic year. Located just 6 miles from downtown Boston and with easy access to the city via the trolley system that stops at the foot of the campus, BC offers the best of both worlds: a scenic suburban setting neighboring an exciting metropolitan center.

Majors and Degrees

The College of Arts and Sciences (A&S) is the oldest and largest of the four undergraduate schools at BC. A&S students must complete thirty-eight 1-semester courses, thirty-two of which are in A&S departments. The normal course load is five courses per semester for the first three years and four courses per semester during the senior year. The undergraduate curriculum includes the university core curriculum and ten to twelve courses in the major field, with the remainder of courses chosen as electives. A&S offers degrees in the following areas: African and African Diaspora Studies, art history, biochemistry, biology, chemistry, classical studies, communication, computer science, economics, English, environmental geosciences, environmental studies, film studies, French, geology, geological studies, geophysics, German studies, Hispanic studies, history, independent major, international studies, Islamic civilizations and societies, Italian, linguistics, mathematics, music, neuroscience, philosophy, physics, political science, psychology, Russian, Slavic studies, sociology, studio art, theater, and theology. Pre-professional advisement is also available in medical, dental, veterinary, and legal programs. Students can also select from twenty-one departmental minors, or seventeen interdisciplinary minors.

The Carroll School of Management educates students to be leaders in business and industry and in public agencies, educational institutions, and service organizations. The Carroll School offers concentrations in accounting, business analytics, computer science, corporate reporting and analysis, economics, entrepreneurship, finance, general management, information systems, management and leadership, managing for social impact, marketing, and operations management.

The Lynch School of Education and Human Development prepares students for education and human services professions. Programs provide a general education, professional preparation, and specialized education in the major field. Fieldwork in area schools is closely linked to course work in each specialization. The Lynch School awards degrees upon completion of thirty-eight courses, including the university core curriculum, a major field of study in education, and a second major in a subject field or an interdisciplinary area in A&S that complements the student's program. Areas of specialization include applied psychology and human development, elementary education, and secondary education. The Lynch School also offers interdisciplinary majors in American heritages, general science, mathematics/computer science, and perspectives on Spanish America.

The Connell School of Nursing offers a four-year program of study leading to a Bachelor of Science degree. The three major components to the curriculum are nursing major courses, electives, and the required university core curriculum. In all courses, principles of wellness, illness, rehabilitation, and health maintenance serve as a theoretical basis in preparing students for professional nursing practice. Nursing courses include traditional classes, simulated and audiovisual laboratory activities on campus, and clinical learning activities in health-care settings.

Academic Programs

Every BC education is centered on a core curriculum of 15 required courses designed to guide students on journeys of interdisciplinary inquiry to discover how to think about the world. Students explore new ways of knowing and being, helping them discern who they want to be, how they want to live—and why. While the core, which is continually reviewed by a committee of faculty members, varies somewhat by school, its common elements include literature, natural science, writing, philosophy, theology, social science, history, mathematics, fine arts, and cultural diversity.

There are a wide variety of extraordinary academic programs available to BC students to enhance their educational experience. They include, among others, Undergraduate Faculty Research Fellows, PULSE, and Perspectives on Western Culture.

Off-Campus Programs

BC encourages all students to take part in internship programs. Approximately 87 percent of BC undergraduates participate in at least one internship or pre-practicum placement during their college years. Internships can be paid or unpaid and may take place during the academic year or the summer; some carry academic credit.

BC students may take on the challenge of international study in more than sixty programs administered by BC at universities in more than forty countries. BC students who study abroad typically do so in their junior year, but there is also a range of full-year and summer-abroad opportunities. The Office of International Programs helps students with program selection and applications and maintains a library of reference books and professional evaluations of international study programs.

Academic Facilities

BC's eight libraries contain more than 3.2 million printed volumes, over 4.3 million items in microform, over 1 million e-books, over 313,000 government documents, 42,082 serial subscriptions, and a wide collection of films and archival items. The resources of the library system range from some of Europe's earliest printed books to hundreds of computerized databases. Students with personal computers have dorm-room access to these databases as well as to Quest and other library information sources through Agora, the campus information network. BC also offers a 24/7 "Ask a Librarian" e-mail service and the capability to text questions to a librarian. In addition, all of BC's libraries and classrooms offer a wireless network that provides access to these resources and the Internet.

Research laboratories in the state-of-the-art science facilities have been specially designed to accommodate the advanced instrumentation required for modern science and to provide flexibility for accommodating new equipment. The $85-million expansion to the Higgins Biology and Physics Center was carefully designed to place classrooms, laboratories, computer facilities, and office space in proximity and to facilitate interaction among faculty members, researchers, and students. In addition to the Center's seventeen teaching laboratories, special working labs are designed and outfitted for research and teaching in the fields of biology and physics.

Boston College opened Stokes Hall in January 2013. This $78-million facility is strategically designed to foster interdisciplinary collaboration among BC's humanities departments and enhanced student-faculty interaction, with thirty-six state-of-the-art classrooms and 200 faculty offices for the Classical Studies, English, History, Philosophy, and Theology departments. Stokes Hall also houses the Academic Advising Center, College of Arts and Sciences Honors Department, and Office of First Year Experience, as well as common areas, conference rooms, a coffee shop, and an outdoor garden and plaza that provide multiple meeting spaces to connect students and faculty.

In 2016, BC opened a new residence hall with 490 beds, as well as a new museum of art which hosts modern architecture with larger space for exhibits, functions, and meetings.

In 2018, BC opened the newly constructed Fish Field House which provides 115,700 square feet of indoor practice space for football, as well as re-designed outdoor athletics fields for baseball and soccer. In 2019, the 244,000 square foot Margot Connell Recreation Center was opened featuring a fitness center, rock climbing wall, jogging track, aquatics center, wood-floor basketball courts, tennis courts, and multi-purpose rooms for spin, yoga, and fitness classes.

Costs

Tuition for the 2019–20 academic year was $57,910 which included a student activity fee and campus health fee of $1,130. The total for room and board was $14,826, which included the board plan. Freshman mandatory fees include a one-time required charge of $575 for first-year orientation and student identification.

Financial Aid

BC maintains a financial aid program to assist deserving and qualified students who might otherwise not be able to attend the university. Boston College is committed to providing funds to meet the full demonstrated need of every admitted student who applies for financial aid. Overall, 68 percent of students receive some form of financial aid with the University awarding over $160 million annually in need-based scholarships and grants. Assistance for freshmen alone included over $40 million in need-based scholarships and grants. The university offers financial aid to students based on need as demonstrated by completion of the College Scholarship Service's Financial Aid PROFILE and the Free Application for Federal Student Aid (FAFSA). All requirements and deadlines and complete instructions are available in BC admission literature. An application for financial aid in no way affects a decision on admission.

Each year, BC chooses 15 incoming freshmen as Presidential Scholars to receive merit-based, full-tuition scholarships. Students are selected from Early Decision and Regular Decision applicants who submit their BC applications by the November 1 priority scholarship deadline.

Faculty

BC has 860 full-time faculty members. Of these faculty members, 98 percent hold doctoral degrees. Approximately 50 Jesuits live on BC-owned property and make up one of the largest Apostolic Jesuit communities in the world. About a quarter of those members are active in the College's administration and teaching.

Student Government

The Undergraduate Government of Boston College (UGBC), formed in 1968, is led by the president and vice president, who are elected in the spring of each year by the entire student body. UGBC's goal is to serve the students by providing services and opportunities and by representing them in the best manner possible to the university community. To accomplish this goal, UGBC provides many educational, social, and cultural programs, such as concerts, lectures, roundtables, and more.

Admission Requirements

The undergraduate admission staff pays particular attention to students who have done well in a demanding college-preparatory curriculum, including Advanced Placement (AP) and honors courses when available. For the class of 2023, there were 35,552 applications for 2,297 places. The majority of incoming freshmen ranked comfortably in the top 10 percent of their high school class. The SAT scores of the middle half of admitted freshmen were 1370-1490. On the ACT, scores of the middle half were between 31 and 34.

Application and Information

Students applying to Boston College for a place in the freshman class must complete both the Common Application and the Boston College Supplemental Application. All applicants should submit the BC Supplemental Application as soon as they have decided to apply to Boston College. Students are encouraged to review the electronic application instructions on BC's website at https://www.bc.edu/content/bc-web/admission.html and then apply at http://www.commonapp.org.

Students applying through the regular decision program must submit the Common Application and all other required forms, along with the $80 application fee, by January 1. Candidates are notified of action taken on their application in early April.

Students with superior academic credentials who view Boston College as their top choice may apply through the Early Decision 1 or Early Decision 2 programs. Applicants who apply for Early Decision 1 and submit their application forms by November 1st, along with the $80 application fee, will be notified of their admissions decision by December 15th. Applicants who apply for Early Decision 2 and submit their application forms by January 1st, along with the $80 application fee, will be notified of their admissions decision by February 15th.

BC accepts approximately 120 transfer students each year. Transfer candidates should request applications for transfer admission from the Office of Undergraduate Admission or via the website at http://www.bc.edu/transfer. In addition to high school records and standardized test results, transfer applicants must furnish transcripts from all postsecondary institutions they have attended.

For more information, students should contact:

Office of Undergraduate Admission
Devlin Hall 208
Boston College
Chestnut Hill, Massachusetts 02467
Phone: 617-552-3100
800-360-2522 (toll-free)
Fax: 617-552-0798
Website: http://www.bc.edu

BOSTON UNIVERSITY

BOSTON, MASSACHUSETTS

The University

Located in the heart of historic Boston, Boston University (BU) is a private teaching and research university ranked #40 in the nation by U.S. News & World Report. With ten undergraduate schools and colleges; over 300 programs of study; more than 650+ in-depth, global courses; and more than 100 study-abroad programs, the challenges at BU are vast and varied. BU students come from all fifty states and more than 100 countries; they are bright, driven, and inquisitive. Students study with world-renowned faculty, 90 percent of whom have a Ph.D. or equivalent. Faculty members include Fulbright scholars, Guggenheim scholars, Sloan Research fellows, Pulitzer Prize winners, and more. With an average class size of 27 and a 10:1 student-to-faculty ratio, these professors become more than just a face students see in class. There are hundreds of research projects that allow undergraduates to work directly with faculty as early as their first year through the Undergraduate Research Opportunities Program (UROP).

Location

Students experience the city as an extension of campus. Boston provides an environment rich in intellectual and cultural stimuli thanks to its remarkable concentration of higher education institutions, world-renowned medical centers, and historic and cultural attractions. The city provides many opportunities for impressive internship and research positions and is home to world-class attractions including the Museum of Fine Arts, Fenway Park, Boston Symphony Orchestra, and a thriving theater district. With four years of guaranteed campus housing, and 75 percent of undergraduates living on campus all four years, the campus feels like a true residential community in the heart of Boston.

Majors and Degrees

Of the University's seventeen schools and colleges, ten offer opportunities for undergraduate study.

As BU's largest academic division, the College of Arts & Sciences (CAS) offers a diverse learning community with world-class research faculty. Students may major in American studies; ancient Greek; ancient Greek and Latin; anthropology; anthropology and religion; archaeology; architectural studies; astronomy; astronomy and physics; biochemistry and molecular biology; biology; biology with a specialization in behavioral biology; biology with a specialization in cell biology, molecular biology, and genetics; biology with a specialization in ecology and conservation biology; biology with a specialization in neurobiology; chemistry; chemistry with specialization in biochemistry; chemistry with specialization in teaching; Chinese language and literature; classical civilization; classics and philosophy; classics and religion; comparative literature; computer science; earth and environmental sciences; economics; economics and mathematics; English; environmental analysis and policy; French and linguistics; French studies; geophysics and planetary sciences; German language and literature; history; history of art and architecture; Italian studies; Japanese and linguistics; Japanese language and literature; Latin; linguistics; linguistics and philosophy; linguistics and speech, language, and hearing sciences (also offered in Sargent); marine science; mathematics (includes statistics); mathematics and computer science; mathematics and mathematics education; mathematics and philosophy; neuroscience; philosophy; philosophy and neuroscience; philosophy and physics; philosophy and political science; philosophy and psychology; philosophy and religion; physics; political science; pre-dentistry; pre-law; pre-medicine; pre-veterinary medicine; psychology; religion; Russian language and literature; sociology; Spanish; and Spanish and linguistics. Special curricula include a seven-year accelerated program in liberal arts and medicine; the Modular Medical/Dental Integrated Curriculum (MMEDIC); the BU dual-degree program; the Wheelock/CAS double-degree program; and various combined B.A./M.A. degree programs.

The College of Fine Arts (CFA) offers programs in the School of Music (composition and theory, music education, performance, and nonperformance), the School of Theatre (acting, design, stage management, production, and theater arts/performing), and the School of Visual Arts (art education, graphic design, painting, printmaking, and sculpture).

The College of General Studies (CGS) offers spring admission to the Boston-London Experience. This demanding, two-year program in the liberal arts and sciences stresses an interdisciplinary and global approach to learning. Students begin course work in Boston in January with classes in the humanities, social sciences, and rhetoric, before gaining global perspectives in London during a six-week summer term of intensive study. Students complete the CGS curriculum in their sophomore year, then continue into one of BU's degree-granting schools or colleges to complete their studies. For students who are unable to go abroad, a similar program is offered during the summer in Boston.

Located in one of the largest media markets in the nation, the College of Communication (COM) offers majors in advertising; film and television (production, writing, management); journalism (with specialization available in broadcast, magazine, news-editorial, online, and photojournalism); media science; and public relations.

Majors in the College of Engineering (ENG) include biomedical engineering (a program consistently ranked among the top in the country by U.S. News & World Report), computer engineering, electrical engineering, mechanical engineering, and mechanical engineering with specialization in aerospace.

The College of Health & Rehabilitation Sciences: Sargent College is one of the oldest and top-ranked health sciences schools in the country. It offers programs in behavior and health; health science; human physiology; a combined major in linguistics and speech, language, and hearing sciences; nutrition; and speech, language, and hearing sciences. Also offered is a six-year B.S./D.P.T. program.

The Frederick S. Pardee School of Global Studies is housed within the CAS and is dedicated to advancing human progress and educating the next generation of global leaders. The school's education, research, and initiatives aim to produce globally competent citizens and leaders. Consisting of two divisions—international studies and regional studies—the school offers programs in Asian studies, European studies, international relations, Latin American studies, and Middle East and North Africa studies.

Located in one of the hospitality and tourism capitals of the world, the School of Hospitality Administration (SHA) offers a rigorous program in the management of hotels, restaurants, food and beverage service, travel and tourism, and entertainment. SHA offers majors in hospitality and communication and hospitality administration, with concentrations in event management, hospitality marketing, and hospitality real estate development.

With a unique global curriculum, the Questrom School of Business offers concentrations in accounting, entrepreneurship, finance, general management, health and life sciences management, global business, law, management information systems, marketing, operations and technology management, organizational behavior, real estate, retailing, and strategy.

Areas of concentration in the Wheelock College of Education & Human Development include bilingual education (includes TESOL), deaf studies, early childhood education, elementary education, English education, mathematics education, modern foreign languages education, science education, social studies education, and special education. The Wheelock/CAS double-degree program is also offered.

Academic Programs

A Boston University education combines the elements of a traditional liberal arts education with training for the professions.

Highly qualified freshmen may also be invited to participate in the prestigious Arvind & Chandan Nandlal Kilachand Honors College.

Students complete general education requirements through the BU Hub, an innovative general education program that is integrated with majors and minors and enables students to develop six core capacities. Students take courses of interest while exploring areas ranging from global citizenship to scientific and social inquiry to ethical reasoning or digital communication. The Hub is robust in its options for experiential learning and co-curriculars, and its signature feature, the BU Cross-College Challenge, offers an opportunity to work with a team of students and faculty drawn from across BU's schools and colleges.

Boston University has more than 100 study-abroad opportunities that take students around the world for courses, internships, and fieldwork. Opportunities are offered on six continents, in over twenty-five countries, and in cities such as Auckland, Dresden, London, Los Angeles, Madrid, Paris, Shanghai, Sydney, and Washington, D.C. Programs offered include studies in art/architecture, business/economics, engineering, health and human services, journalism/communications, visual/performing arts, and many more.

Boston University operates on a calendar of two semesters and two summer terms. Students generally take four courses each semester.

Academic Facilities

The Yawkey Center for Student Services is home to BU's Center for Career Development, Educational Resource Center, Pre-Professional Advising Office with pre-med and pre-law advising services, and the two-story Marciano Commons dining hall. The Engineering Product Innovation Center (EPIC) is a 15,000-square-foot facility where undergraduates can experiment with developing new products, from design to manufacturing. The BUild Lab: IDG Capital Student Innovation Center fosters innovation and entrepreneurship across the campus and any area of study. Students can connect with advisers, find funding sources, collaborate with other students on projects, and get help with matters from design and prototyping to legal advice and marketing. West campus features the modern Student Village, including Agganis Arena; the Fitness & Recreation Center, complete with a 35-foot rock-climbing wall; and high-rise, apartment-style dorms. The Questrom School of Business building also offers technologically advanced educational facilities, with a dedicated career center and management library. The Joan & Edgar Booth Theatre and College of Fine Arts Production Center, studio space for visual arts students, practice rooms for music, and a 575-seat music performance center are indicative of BU's support for the arts. More than 2.8 million library volumes and over 4.7 million microform units are contained in Mugar Memorial Library, where the Twentieth-Century Archives are held, including the papers of Dr. Martin Luther King, Jr., Theodore Roosevelt, Robert Frost, and Bette Davis.

Costs

Tuition for 2020–19 is $56,854, estimated room and board costs are $16,640, and University and college fees are $1,218. These costs are exclusive of books, supplies, transportation, and personal expenses.

Financial Assistance

For US students enrolling in college for the first time, BU will meet 100% of your demonstrated need. A student's financial aid package will make up the difference between the cost of attendance and what they can afford. Additionally, a student's BU need-based scholarship will not be reduced during their four years at BU. Eligibility for BU need-based scholarship aid is established and confirmed in the first year when students file the CSS Profile™ and the FAFSA. After the first year, the Profile™ is not required. Learn more at go.bu.edu/affordableBU. In addition, the Trustee Scholarship (full tuition) and the Presidential Scholarship ($25,000) are offered based on merit to the highest achieving students who apply for admission.

Admission Requirements

The Board of Admissions considers each candidate individually. Primary emphasis is placed on the strength of the secondary school record, but required test scores, character, breadth of interest, school recommendations, and other personal qualifications are also carefully evaluated. Students are required to submit the SAT or the ACT, with the exception of students applying for fall 2021/spring 2022 and those applying to the College of Fine Arts. A full listing of the standardized testing requirements and BU's fall 2021/spring 2022 optional testing policy can be found on the BU Admissions website at www.bu.edu/admissions/apply/. Secondary school graduation or an equivalency diploma is required of all candidates; for the College of Fine Arts a prescreening, audition, or a portfolio may be required, depending on the program of interest. For the accelerated medical program, interviews and SAT Subject Test scores are required; however, students applying for fall 2021/spring 2022 are not required to submit SAT Subject Test scores. Boston University offers programs of early decision (binding agreement), early decision 2 (binding agreement), and deferred admission.

Transfer applicants are considered for September or January admission. Transfer students are not eligible for admission to the accelerated liberal arts/medical program or the six-year Bachelor of Science in Health Studies/Doctor of Physical Therapy program. January admission to the College of Fine Arts School of Theatre, the College of General Studies, and the Questrom School of Business is also not available to transfer students.

Boston University admits qualified students to all its programs and activities regardless of their race, color, national origin, religion, sex, age, or disability.

Application and Information

Boston University accepts either the Common Application or the Coalition Application. Information on applying is available online at www.bu.edu/admissions/apply/. The deadline for regular decision applications is January 1. Applicants for early decision must apply by November 1. Accelerated medical program applications are due November 15. The deadline for the Trustee Scholarship (full tuition) and the Presidential Scholarship ($25,000) is December 1. Transfer students applying for September admission should submit their applications, CSS Profile, and FAFSA forms by March 1 or by November 1 for January admission.

Boston University Admissions
233 Bay State Road
Boston, Massachusetts 02215
Phone: 617-353-2300
E-mail: admissions@bu.edu
Website: http://www.bu.edu/admissions
http://www.facebook.com/BUadmissions
https://twitter.com/ApplyToBU
https://www.instagram.com/applytobu

Students at Boston University find that nothing separates them from Boston's world-class museums, vibrant culture, legendary sports teams, rich history, or world-renowned scientific and medical communities.

BRYN MAWR COLLEGE

BRYN MAWR, PENNSYLVANIA

The College

At Bryn Mawr College, students turn a passion for learning into a life of purpose. Every year, almost 1,400 undergraduate students and 300 graduate students from around the world gather on Bryn Mawr College's historic campus to study with leading scholars, conduct advanced research, and expand the boundaries of what's possible. As a women's college, Bryn Mawr supports academic excellence, opportunity for women, respect for the individual, and purposeful action in the world.

The College is known for its academic excellence and consistently ranks among the top feeder schools to premier graduate and professional schools. Students can pursue independent and interdepartmental majors, as well as minors and concentrations. Bryn Mawr's academic offerings are enriched by partnerships with Haverford, Swarthmore, and the University of Pennsylvania. Bryn Mawr's relationship with Haverford College is particularly close: the two colleges, just 10 minutes apart, share majors, courses, departments, dining, and many activities. Many Bryn Mawr courses also create connections – intellectual, professional, and social – with extensive offerings in nearby Philadelphia.

Bryn Mawr's well-resourced Career and Civic Engagement Center supports students in connecting deep learning to action through programs in civic engagement, professional development, and hands-on study, including extensive opportunities for internships, research, and service in nearby Philadelphia and beyond. Bryn Mawr's prestigious graduates are agents of change in every arena, including the first woman to be president of Harvard University, one of the first women to receive the Nobel Peace Prize, and the first and only woman to receive four Academy Awards. 97% of graduates have positive career outcomes one year out of college. Bryn Mawr offers innovative learning experiences like 360° Course Clusters, in which a cohort of students takes several courses together to engage multiple perspectives of a topic or theme. 360° participants hone their arguments and insights through writing and research, develop strategies for teamwork that push the limits of their talents and creativity, and work with professors and scholars to promote big-picture thinking. Each 360° includes an experiential learning component like travel abroad or local community work.

Similarly, Bryn Mawr offers a Tri-Co Philly program in conjunction with Haverford and Swarthmore Colleges. This semester-long, non-residential program uses curricular and co-curricular activities to help students engage with the diversity, complexity, innovation, and systems of the city.

Bryn Mawr students share a commitment to a community that is based on inclusion and support, reinforced by the College's Honor Code, a set of principles stressing personal integrity and mutual respect. In the words of one graduating senior, "This is a place where being yourself makes you feel part of something larger than yourself. A strong sense of self is what we all have in common."

Diversity is central to Bryn Mawr's commitment to racial justice and equity across all dimensions. Students of color and international students make up 53 percent of the undergraduate enrollment. Bryn Mawr's students come from 50 U.S. states, districts, and territories and 44 other countries. Above all else, Bryn Mawr students share a tremendous respect for individual differences. The diversity of perspectives that Bryn Mawr students experience, in and out of the classroom, is central to the College's commitment to academic excellence and its support for thoughtful, active work in the world.

Bryn Mawr is a charter member of the Centennial Conference and is home to twelve NCAA varsity athletic teams. Students may compete in badminton, basketball, crew, cross-country, field hockey, lacrosse, soccer, swimming, tennis, indoor track and field, outdoor track and field, and volleyball. The Bern Schwartz Fitness and Athletic Center offers enhanced spaces for training, fitness, and aquatics.

Bryn Mawr students participate in and lead more than 100 active student organizations. The tri-college community of Haverford, Swarthmore, and Bryn Mawr also sponsors many student groups and activities. The College sponsors a wide-ranging assortment of events, including a top-rated performing arts and reading series. Home to a thriving arts scene, the College boasts a theater for 500+, a teaching theater, scene shop, music rooms, and performance spaces, and several dance studios. Other performance spaces include the Pembroke Dance Studio and the Denbigh Dance Studio.

Location

Students at Bryn Mawr have the best of it all in terms of location. The campus itself is a picture-perfect example of Collegiate Gothic architecture that it has been used as the backdrop for several motion pictures. A quick 5-minute walk into the suburban town of Bryn Mawr finds an eclectic mix of funky independent and favorite franchise coffee shops, eateries, and retailers; an historic movie theater; and a commuter train that can take students to the heart of Philadelphia in about 20 minutes. Philadelphia has a bustling arts scene and nightlife and is home to more than 250,000 college students. Bryn Mawr students enjoy a rich academic and social life on their own campus, on tri-college campuses, and in Philadelphia.

Almost all students live on campus in one of thirteen main residence halls. Two of the buildings are listed on the National Register of Historic Places, and one is also a National Historic Landmark

Majors and Degrees

Bryn Mawr College grants the Bachelor of Arts (A.B.) degree with majors, minors, and concentrations in more than forty areas: Africana studies; anthropology; Arabic, astronomy; biology; biochemistry and molecular biology; chemistry; child and family studies; Chinese; classical and Near Eastern archaeology; classical culture and society; classical languages; comparative literature; computational methods; computer science; creative writing; dance; East Asian languages and cultures; economics; education; English; environmental studies; film studies; fine arts; French and Francophone studies; gender and sexuality studies; geoarchaeology; geology; German and German studies; Greek; growth and structure of cities; Hebrew and Judaic studies; health studies; history; history of art; international studies; Italian studies; Japanese; Latin; Latin American, Iberian, and Latina/o studies; linguistics; mathematics; Middle Eastern studies; museum studies; music; neurosciences; peace, conflict, and social justice studies; philosophy; physics; political science; psychology; religion; Romance languages; Russian; sociology; Spanish; theater studies; and visual studies. In consultation with faculty and academic advisers, students may apply to partnership programs for combined undergraduate/graduate degrees from the University of Pennsylvania in engineering, education, city planning, and bioethics. Other partnership programs are available from Aberystwyth University, Boston University in public health, Zhejiang University in Chinese studies, University of Rochester in optics, and Indiana University in law. Combined undergraduate programs in engineering are also available through Cal Tech and Columbia University.

There are approximately 3,000 course exchanges between Bryn Mawr and Haverford each year, selected from a jointly published course list. Bryn Mawr students may major in any of Haverford's coordinate departments or in astronomy, classics, fine arts, music, religion, or visual studies while earning a Bachelor of Arts degree from Bryn Mawr. Students may also apply to obtain their master's through the combined A.B./M.A. program in chemistry, classical and Near Eastern archaeology, French, Greek, Latin, and classical studies, history of art, mathematics, and physics or the combined A.B./M.S.S. with Bryn Mawr's Graduate School of Social Work and Social Research.

Academic Programs

The Bryn Mawr curriculum is designed to encourage breadth of learning and depth of scholarship. At some point during their first three years at Bryn Mawr, students are required to complete Approaches to Inquiry, a curriculum designed to introduce possibilities and problems in scientific investigation, critical interpretation, cross-cultural analysis, and inquiry into the past. Many options are available to fulfill these requirements and students are encouraged to explore many areas of interest. Innovative curricular options include interdisciplinary programs like the Growth and Structure of Cities and the Environmental Studies programs; 360° Course Clusters; Tri-Co Philly program, and Focus Courses, which are demanding, half-semester courses that may ignite a new intellectual passion. The curriculum encourages independence within a rigorous but flexible framework. Students choose and plan their major in consultation with a dean and faculty adviser. Some students take advantage of this freedom to design an independent major, while others fashion their own intellectual perspectives by enrolling in courses that span academic fields or participating in independent research experiences. Students may also freely enroll in courses and even major at Haverford College. With certain restrictions, full-time Bryn Mawr students may also take courses at Swarthmore College, the University of Pennsylvania, and Villanova University during the academic year without paying additional fees.

Off-Campus Programs

Bryn Mawr is only 20 minutes by car or seven short stops by train from Philadelphia, the nation's sixth-largest city. Philadelphia is an incredible resource for Bryn Mawr—a truly accessible city, rich with cultural and professional opportunities, including the Philadelphia Museum of Art, the Philadelphia Orchestra, the Pennsylvania Ballet, numerous theaters, professional sports teams, and some of the nation's most important historic sites. Students may also take advantage of internship opportunities in Center City law firms, art galleries, government agencies, hospitals, TV studios, banks, and schools. Student also have easy access to New York City and Washington D.C. via train and bus. Bryn Mawr students can take advantage of one of Bryn Mawr's many study-abroad opportunities.

Academic Facilities

Bryn Mawr ranks highly among U.S. colleges and universities in the percentage of graduates going on to earn a Ph.D. Bryn Mawr students have unlimited access to libraries and laboratories equal to those of many graduate programs, allowing students to pursue independent research at a level unavailable at most undergraduate institutions. These resources include an extensive array of laboratory equipment for the study of science, such as a robotics lab, laser with rangefinder, DNA analyzers, and a geological subsurface profiling system. The first phase of the Park Science Building renovation to update and expand the many laboratory spaces and equipment was recently completed. More than 1 million volumes in a network of open-stack libraries are available to Bryn Mawr students, as well as access to the libraries of both Haverford and Swarthmore Colleges via the Tripod Library System.

In addition, the College has recently enhanced several of its buildings to increase sustainability practices and support student inquiry in all of the liberal arts, including a $19-million renovation of the Marjorie Goodhart Theater which consists of a new state-of-the-art theater, practice rooms, a teaching theater, and scene shop; the upgrade of Dalton Hall, home to Bryn Mawr's social science labs and classrooms; and Bettws-y-Coed, a center for the study of psychology complete with new labs, faculty offices, and meeting rooms. Four former faculty residences have also been renovated to house the student activities village, Cambrian Row.

Costs

In 2020–21, Bryn Mawr tuition, room and board, and fees totaled $74,330.

Financial Aid

To apply for financial aid, students must submit the Free Application for Federal Student Aid (FAFSA), the College Scholarship Service (CSS) Profile form, and if applicable, the CSS Noncustodial Parent Profile. The College also requires a signed copy of the custodial and noncustodial parents' prior-prior year federal income tax returns, including W-2 forms, and all schedules and attachments. The student's federal income tax return is only required if the student is selected for verification. Tax returns must be submitted to The College Board's Institutional Documentation Service (IDOC). Applicants who are not citizens of the U.S. may file the (CSS) Profile. Prospective first-year students are notified of admission and financial aid decisions simultaneously. Students must apply for financial aid in their first year to be considered for aid in subsequent years.

Faculty

The Bryn Mawr faculty has 159 full-time members, of whom 65 percent are women and 26 percent are professors of color. The College's student-faculty ratio is 9:1. Few colleges or universities can genuinely claim the intellectual curiosity, intensity, and passion found at Bryn Mawr. Classes are small (many have fewer than 15 students), and faculty members come to know their students as individuals. That means more than just being on a first-name basis. In fact, Bryn Mawr faculty members, world-renowned leaders in their fields, regard their students as junior colleagues, fully capable of working at a high level, developing their own ideas, and making important contributions. It is in this way that, perhaps more than at any other school, Bryn Mawr feels like a graduate school on an undergraduate level.

Student Government

Bryn Mawr's culture of innovative leadership dates back to 1892 and the founding of the Student Self-Government Association (SGA), the oldest undergraduate governing body in the country. SGA gives Bryn Mawr students the responsibility of running many campus organizations and activities and participating in discussions and resolutions of important issues, such as curriculum and faculty appointments.

Admission Requirements

Every year, Bryn Mawr receives many more outstanding applications for admission than can be admitted into the first-year class of about 375 students. As members of the Common Application and Coalition Application, Bryn Mawr practices holistic review, with admission decisions based on a number of factors. Strength of the applicant's high school curriculum within the context of the high school and academic performance are of significant importance. Other factors considered are a student's writing, recommendations from the high school counselor and academic teachers, test scores (optional for U.S. citizens and permanent residents), involvement in school and community, and diverse or unique perspectives and talents a student might bring to the Bryn Mawr community. A school program giving good preparation for study at Bryn Mawr includes four years of English grammar, composition, and literature; at least three years of mathematics (preferably up to statistics, pre-calculus, or calculus); three years of one modern or ancient language, or a good foundation in two languages; work in history; and at least three courses in science, including two lab sciences (preferably biology, chemistry, or physics). Non-U.S. citizens and non-U.S. permanent residents are required to submit standardized test scores (SAT I or ACT) as well as either the TOEFL or IELTS if their primary language is not English and/or their language of instruction over the past four years has not been English. Complete details may be found on the Bryn Mawr website. An interview, either with an admissions representative or with a local alumnae/i representative, is strongly recommended, but not required. Bryn Mawr accepts the Common Application and Coalition Application and waives the application fees when students apply online. Application forms should be submitted by November 15 for fall early decision applicants, by January 1 for winter early decision applicants, and by January 15 for regular decision applicants. Transfer students must complete a minimum of two years of work at Bryn Mawr to qualify for the A.B. degree.

Application and Information

The Office of Admissions is open from 9 a.m. to 5 p.m. on weekdays and some Saturdays throughout the year. Please visit the College website http://www.brynmawr.edu/admissions to plan a visit. Bryn Mawr accepts both the Common Application (http://www.commonapplication.org) and the Coalition Application (http://www.coalitionforcollegeaccess.org/). For additional information, prospective students should contact:

Bryn Mawr College Office of Admissions
101 North Merion Avenue
Bryn Mawr, Pennsylvania 19010-2899
Phone: 610-526-5152
Fax: 610-526-7471
E-mail: admissions@brynmawr.edu
Websites: http://www.brynmawr.edu
http://www.brynmawr.edu/admissions/
http://www.themawryouknow.blogs.brynmawr.edu
http://www.facebook.com/BMCadmissions
http://www.instagram.com/bmc_admissions
http://twitter.com/BrynMawrCollege

Bryn Mawr means "big hill" in Welsh.

COLUMBIA UNIVERSITY
Columbia College/The Fu Foundation School of Engineering and Applied Science
NEW YORK, NEW YORK

The University

Columbia College and The Fu Foundation School of Engineering and Applied Science (Columbia Engineering) offer their students the unique advantages proved by both a major research university and a small, selective college. Students benefit from over 250 years of rich history and distinction, easy access to the immense resources of New York City and a dynamic residential community where "Columbia Blue" is worn with pride at events ranging from Lions' basketball games to the World Leaders Forum, from the *Varsity Show* to the annual tree-lighting ceremony.

The Columbia College student body is composed of approximately 4,500 students; the Columbia Engineering student body has roughly 1,500. Students come from all fifty states and over ninety countries. They represent a dazzling array of ethnic, social, economic, cultural, religious, and geographic backgrounds. The diversity of Columbia's student body reflects the diversity of New York City, the world's most international city. Columbia guarantees four years of on-campus housing to all entering first-year students. More than 95 percent of undergraduates remain in University residence halls for all four years.

Columbia students take part in extracurricular groups of all kinds: artistic (theater, music, dance, film, and visual arts), athletic (thirty-one Division I varsity sports and dozens of club and intramural sports), communications (the *Columbia Daily Spectator*, the *Columbia Journal of Literary Criticism*, WKCR-FM, and many others), community service (Big Brother/Big Sister programs, after-hours tutoring programs, a volunteer ambulance squad, and partnerships with dozens of hospitals, soup kitchens, and homeless shelters), and pre-professional (the Charles Drew Pre-Medical Society, the Society of Hispanic Professional Engineers, and more). Other groups represent students' ethnic, religious, political, and gender identities. There are twenty-eight fraternities and sororities. Alfred Lerner Hall houses office and meeting space for student organizations, a black box theatre, a cinema, the Berick Center for Student Advising, and many dining options.

Location

Columbia shares its Manhattan neighborhood, Morningside Heights, with a number of other notable institutions: Barnard College, the Cathedral of St. John the Divine, Union Theological Seminary, Jewish Theological Seminary, and the Manhattan School of Music, to name a few. Many faculty members from Columbia and the other surrounding schools make their homes in the neighborhood. Morningside Heights is an area known for bookstores, wonderfully varied restaurants, and merchants that cater to student tastes, student budgets, and student hours. Columbia students enjoy a college town community in addition to the opportunities New York City has to offer.

Students are encouraged to take advantage of New York's breathtaking variety of cultural, recreational, and professional resources. Through the Columbia Arts Initiative, students can receive discounted tickets to Broadway shows, film screenings, art galleries, and cultural events in New York City. Passport to NYC offers students free access to over thirty museums throughout the city. Columbia students can be found any day of the week exploring the Metropolitan Museum of Art, the Museum of Modern Art, the Guggenheim Museum, the Museum of African Art, or the Museo del Barrio. They might be discovering the theatrical offerings on, off, or "off-off" Broadway; attending the opera, ballet, or symphony at Lincoln Center; enjoying jazz in Greenwich Village or amateur night at the Apollo; sampling *pai gwat* in Chinatown; or jogging in Central Park. Columbia's Center for Career Education offers students opportunities to explore career pathways in depth; nowhere else in the world does the concentration of industries allow such a range of possibilities for internships and post-graduate employment. New York's public transportation system puts the entire city within easy reach of Columbia students; the campus is directly served by a subway line and five bus routes.

Majors and Degrees

Columbia College grants the B.A. degree in more than eighty programs of study in the humanities, social sciences, and pure sciences, including many interdisciplinary majors. Columbia Engineering grants the B.S. degree in sixteen engineering fields. A five-year program that begins in either school allows students to receive both a B.A. from Columbia College and a B.S. from Columbia Engineering.

Joint degree programs offer selected students the opportunity to combine their undergraduate work with study in Columbia University's schools of law and international affairs and with the Juilliard School.

Academic Programs

Columbia College is known for its Core Curriculum, a set of common courses required of all undergraduates and considered the necessary general education for students, regardless of their choice in major. The communal learning—with all students encountering the same texts and issues at the same time—and the critical dialogue experienced in small seminars are the distinctive features of the Core. Begun in 1919, the Core Curriculum is one of the founding experiments in liberal higher education in the United States, and it remains vibrant a century later. One of the signature courses in the Core is Contemporary Civilization, a year-long historical survey of Western civilization's religious, political, and moral philosophies; another is Literature Humanities, a year-long introduction to Western culture's most seminal and meaningful literary works. A second year of humanities offers a semester each of music and art appreciation, encouraging students to experience the cultural treasures of New York City. The Global Core requirement enlarges the scope of inquiry beyond the Western focus in order to promote learning and thought about the variety of cultures and the diversity of traditions that interact in the United States and the world today. Frontiers of Science outlines the approaches that scientists take to answer compelling problems in the natural world and introduces students to scientific research methods. University Writing equips students with the ability and thoughtfulness to read and write essays in order to participate in the academic conversations that form Columbia's intellectual community. The Core is the critical examination of challenging ideas. It's a shared connection with classmates, professors, and other Columbians since 1919. Core classrooms are places where the pursuit of better questions is just as important as the pursuit of better answers.

The strength of Columbia Engineering's education is in its unique vision—Engineering for Humanity—preparing students not only to be world-class engineers but also to be global leaders across industries who are equipped and motivated to address the most pressing global challenges in the areas of sustainability, health, security, connectivity, and creativity. In addition to taking rigorous math and science courses typically offered at top undergraduate programs, Columbia Engineering students benefit from programming that fosters innovation and entrepreneurship, and are also required to take courses in the liberal arts alongside their College counterparts, providing them with interdisciplinary tools for real-world problem solving. This type of broad academic exposure is what alumni often cite as the foundation of their later academic and professional success.

Another hallmark of the Columbia Engineering education is the Art of Engineering, where first-year students are introduced to the field through interactive lectures, hands-on group projects, and guest speakers. Past examples of projects include mathematically modeling the U.S. elections, designing vital signs monitors, and modifying a laser pointer to transmit digital data over long distances. In addition to the technical issues discussed in the course, other key issues of importance in professional engineering such as ethics, project management, and societal impact are addressed.

Off-Campus Programs

Columbia maintains a network of global centers, developing opportunities for research, scholarship, teaching, and service across borders. With nine international locations ranging from Turkey to Chile and from Kenya to China, undergraduate options include summer Arabic language programs in Amman, Jordan, or a semester-long French literature program in Paris. Columbia also has direct enrollment agreements with many partner institutions abroad, as well as a growing number of exchange programs with universities abroad.

Altogether, Columbia students, with the help of advisers from the Center for Global Engagement, may choose from over 150 study-abroad programs on nearly every continent.

Academic Facilities

Columbia has the fifth-largest research library system in the world, consisting of 12 million volumes and 26 million manuscripts within 3,000 collections. The LEED Gold–certified Northwest Corner Building houses cutting-edge labs that bring together researchers in biology, chemistry, physics, and engineering, as well as a science library, lecture hall, and café. Students may also make use of an electronic music lab, a cyclotron, an oral history collection, the facilities and programs of the Lamont-Doherty Earth Observatory, and oceanographic research ships.

Costs

Tuition for the 2019-20 academic year was $58,920. Room and board for all first-year students was $14,490. With typical fees, books, and supplies, the total cost of a year at Columbia was approximately $79,814.

Financial Aid

Columbia awards more than $174 million annually in scholarships and grants, and the average amount awarded is $55,690. Additionally, 50 percent of Columbia students receive grants from the university. All first-year candidates who are U.S. citizens, have U.S. permanent resident or political refugee status, or are undocumented students who reside in the U.S. are considered for admission without regard to their financial need. International students who do not fit into the above categories should be aware that their admissions process is not need-blind; their financial need is taken into account at the time of admission. Regardless of citizenship, Columbia meets the full demonstrated need of every student admitted as a first-year or transfer student. All financial aid at Columbia is based on need, in the form of grants and student work only, not loans. Prospective students should go to http://cc-seas.financialaid.columbia.edu/ for information on specific requirements and deadlines.

Faculty

The student-to-faculty ratio is 6:1. Core Curriculum classes are capped at 22 students, and 80 percent of classes have 20 students or fewer. The Columbia faculty is committed to both teaching and research, and all faculty members, including the president of the University, teach undergraduates.

Admission Requirements

The Columbia first-year class of 1,400 students is selected from a much larger pool of applicants through a holistic, committee-based review process. There are no specific course requirements for admission, but applicants must present evidence that they are prepared for college work in a variety of disciplines as required for the Columbia degree. Accordingly, the following preparation is strongly recommended: 4 years of English, including meaningful work in literature and writing; 3 (preferably 4) years of mathematics, including pre-calculus and calculus where offered; 3 (preferably 4) years of history and social studies; 3 or more years of the same foreign language; and 3 (preferably 4) years of laboratory science (including chemistry and physics where available). Modifying the preparatory program just outlined—by taking more work in some subjects and less in others—is not only acceptable but may be desirable in individual cases.

Standardized tests are required for admission, according to the following guidelines. Students must take *either* the SAT *or* the ACT, and they may self-report their scores. Students who take the SAT more than once are evaluated on the highest score they receive in any individual section. Applicants taking the ACT more than once are evaluated on the highest score received in any individual section. The writing component of both exams is not required. Only admitted students who choose to enroll at Columbia must have their official scores sent by the testing agency.

While Columbia does not require SAT or ACT writing tests or SAT Subject Tests, students who have taken these exams may submit their results if they wish them to be considered. Transfer students may enter Columbia in the fall term only. Columbia College and Columbia Engineering each have a Visiting Students Program, which allow students to attend for one or both semesters of their sophomore, junior, or senior year.

Application and Information

Students may apply via the Common Application or the Coalition Application. Students for whom Columbia is their definite first choice are encouraged to apply early decision. The early decision deadline is November 1, and candidates are notified by mid-December. Students admitted to Columbia under early decision are required to matriculate at Columbia and withdraw their applications to other colleges. The regular decision deadline is January 1, and candidates are notified by April 1. Admitted students must respond to Columbia's offer of admission by May 1.

For further information, interested students should contact:

Undergraduate Admissions
Columbia University
1130 Amsterdam Avenue, MC 2807
New York, New York 10027
Phone: 212-854-2522
Fax: 212-854-1209
E-mail: ugrad-ask@columbia.edu
Website: http://undergrad.admissions.columbia.edu/
http://www.youtube.com/columbiaadmissions
http://www.instagram.com/columbiaadmissions

Columbia University in the City of New York, a place unlike any other.

DEAN COLLEGE

FRANKLIN, MASSACHUSETTS

The College

Founded in 1865, Dean is a unique New England college awarding both four-year baccalaureate and two-year associate degrees. Students may choose from over two-dozen academic programs supported by state-of-the-art facilities, a dedicated teaching faculty, and professional advising known for exceptional personalized academic support.

Located 45 minutes outside Boston in the town of Franklin, Massachusetts, Dean's attractive 100-acre campus is home to WGAO-FM, the Joan Phelps Palladino School of Dance, and several buildings listed on the National Register of Historic Places. There are two fitness centers, a gymnasium, and athletic fields, as well as a library learning commons, an advising center, a 214-seat theater, and numerous dance studios.

Nearly all of Dean's 1,200 full-time students live on campus, and housing is available for all four years. The student body is impressively diverse with more than 30 states and 25 countries represented (and an additional 500 part-time students). The College sponsors 16 NCAA Division III athletic teams, an Honors Program, internship and study abroad opportunities, an executive lecture series, and dozens of clubs, performance groups, and student organizations.

Dean College graduates are very successful. Of those receiving a bachelor's degree last year, 96 percent were employed or attending graduate school within a year. Among associate degree graduates, 98 percent were accepted as transfers to highly selective universities across the United States or had plans to continue their bachelor's degree at Dean.

Location

Dean's home town, Franklin, is a charming, historic Massachusetts community. The suburban setting is safe and convenient to downtown Boston with many local stores and restaurants to support an active college campus. The Commuter Rail—just three blocks from Dean—provides frequent train service to Boston, and students can reach popular destinations such as baseball's Fenway Park, the TD Garden, Museum of Fine Arts, and Harvard Square in less than an hour. Providence, Rhode Island, is even closer (40 minutes) where students can shop at Providence Place or see events at the Dunkin' Donuts Center and Rhode Island Center for the Performing Arts.

The area's biggest attractions are only minutes from Dean: Patriot Place and Gillette Stadium (home of the New England Patriots), the fashionable Wrentham Outlets, and Xfinity Center outdoor amphitheater. For day trips, students can easily get to the beaches on Cape Cod, see Newport's mansions, or reach the mountains in nearby New Hampshire and Vermont.

Areas of Study

Dean College offers a wide range of Bachelor's and Associate Degree Programs across four academic schools: the School of the Arts, School of Business, Palladino School of Dance, and School of Liberal Arts.

Areas of study include: arts and entertainment management, athletic coaching and recreation management, pre-athletic training, biology, business management, communications, criminal justice and homeland security, dance (B.A. and B.F.A. degrees), early childhood education, English, entertainment industry management, exercise science, family and childhood studies, global studies, health and the human experience, health sciences, history, human services, individually designed programs, liberal arts and studies, marketing, pre-law, pre-nursing, psychology, sociology, sport management, sports broadcasting, and theatre (acting, musical theatre, and technical theatre).

Academic Programs

Dean is accredited by the New England Association of Schools and Colleges. Bachelor's degree candidates must complete a required internship or other experiential learning opportunity related to their major.

The Honors Program at Dean offers academically talented students an opportunity to engage in stimulating and challenging courses, seminars, and colloquia. Students who meet the honors entrance criteria enroll in special course sections reserved for honors students or may enhance non-honors courses with additional intensive readings and analysis approved by the instructors. The Honors Program also offers exciting academic and cultural activities outside the traditional classroom environment.

Study-abroad and study-away opportunities are increasingly popular at Dean. Students may choose programs across the globe through cooperative arrangements facilitated by the College, such as programs in London and Buenos Aires, or take advantage of Dean's relationship with the Washington Center Program for study and internships in Washington, D.C.

The Dean Leadership Institute sponsors an Executive Lecture Series that brings leaders in business, media, and the arts to campus. Featured speakers share their insights into post-graduate opportunities and help build each student's career network. Recent guests include Bert Jacobs (Life is Good), Anne Finucane (Bank of America), and Michael Spillane (Nike).

The Arch Learning Community provides comprehensive support for students with diagnosed learning differences. Arch students receive dedicated academic advising and coaching as well as a cohort educational model specially designed to help students maximize their academic and personal potential. The program works with students to find success within the rigors of a traditional college curriculum.

Academic Facilities

Students have access to a wide range of facilities, including the Green Family Library-Learning Commons and E. Ross Anderson Library, Berenson Writing Center, and Morton Family Learning Center—all housed under one roof. Together, these form the hub of Dean's academic support efforts. There are print and online resources for class projects, academic coaches to provide professional one-on-one mentoring, peer and professional tutoring services, the Technology Service Center, and space for weekly faculty drop-in sessions where students can participate in group or individual advising.

Other academic facilities include the A.W. Pierce Technology and Science Center, which houses science and computer labs as well as the Alden Center high-tech master classroom; the Dean College Children's Center, an on-campus pre-school, which doubles as a learning laboratory for student teachers; and Campus Center, where students can find the Advising Center, Main Stage Theater, Guidrey Center, student activities office, and newly renovated classrooms featuring cutting-edge technology.

Costs

The basic costs related to attending Dean College for 2019–20 are $40,414 for tuition and fees and $17,258 for room and board.

Financial Aid

Dean College awards more than $25 million in scholarships and grants annually to assist their students in funding their educations. Ninety-five percent of Dean students receive some form of merit-based aid with an average award amount of $23,000 per year. These awards are based solely on the information students provide in their application for admission—not financial need—and help to reduce the average cost of attendance by over 30 percent. In addition, most students apply for—and receive—federal and state financial aid, which is separate from (and can be added to) Dean's scholarship awards.

Student financial aid packages are generally a combination of grants, loans, and work-study, contingent upon demonstrated need and the availability of funds. The College participates in all Federal Title IV and Federal Family Education Loan Programs. Students must submit the Free Application for Federal Student Aid (FAFSA) in order to be considered for need-based aid. Upon receipt of a valid FAFSA, full-time students are considered for all of the financial aid programs that Dean administers. Residents of Massachusetts and other reciprocal states may also be eligible for state scholarships, grants, or loans.

Faculty

Dean's dedicated faculty members, advisers, and educational specialists—some of the best in their respective fields—offer direct, personal involvement to help students obtain the full value of their college experience. The average class size is 18 students.

Student Government

The Student Government Association serves as a liaison between the student body and Dean College administration. It disseminates information about College policies, seeks out student opinion, allocates funds collected from the activities fee to clubs and organizations through a budget request process, and coordinates the activities of various clubs, groups, and organizations campus wide.

Admission Requirements

Every application to Dean is carefully reviewed by the Admission Committee. In addition to the application form, students must submit an official high school transcript. A letter of recommendation from a guidance counselor or teacher, a personal statement or essay, and SAT or ACT scores are all optional. Interviews are not required but are offered as students visit campus. Students applying for the dance and theatre programs must audition.

Application and Information

Students who identify Dean as a top choice may choose to apply under the early action plan, with an application deadline of November 1 or December 1. The College accepts applications on a rolling basis thereafter, though it is recommended that applications be submitted by March 15 to ensure access to the highest level of financial aid and priority in housing and class registration. Once an application is complete, an admissions decision is typically made within four weeks.

For more information, contact:

Office of Admissions
Dean College
99 Main Street
Franklin, Massachusetts 02038
Phone: 508-541-1508
877-TRY-DEAN (toll-free)
E-mail: admissions@dean.edu
Website: http://www.dean.edu

Dean Hall, built in 1865 when Dean College was established.

DREXEL UNIVERSITY

PHILADELPHIA, PENNSYLVANIA

The University

Drexel University is a comprehensive global research university that has maintained a reputation for academic excellence since its founding in 1891. The University's use-inspired approach to learning prepares undergraduates for a variety of careers and graduate school. Cooperative education is a vital part of a Drexel education. Students gain professional experience in jobs related to their career interests by alternating classroom study with periods of meaningful employment. The 2019 undergraduate enrollment numbered 14,696 full-time students representing 46 states and 127 other countries. International students compose about 15 percent of the undergraduate population. Drexel University grants bachelor's, master's, and doctoral degrees—as well as certificates—in a variety of programs.

Drexel offers 18 Division I varsity athletic programs and competes in the Colonial Athletic Association Conference. The University also sponsors intramural and club sports.

There is always something to do on campus, including events such as dances, lectures, excursions, community service projects, free movie screenings from the Campus Activities Board (CAB), and other activities related to Drexel's more than 30 active fraternities and sororities. Students can also take part in performing arts groups in dance, theater, and music. In all, there are over 350 student organizations.

Location

Drexel is located in the heart of Philadelphia, the nation's sixth-largest city, and shares its University City neighborhood with five other universities. With thousands of college student residents, University City is a great place for students to spend their college years—in an urban campus setting, surrounded by the amenities of the city and the diversity of their peers. Philadelphia is home to some of the nation's best historical and cultural attractions and offers a vibrant social and cultural scene, dynamic arts, and highly competitive professional athletic teams. Drexel's location offers easy access to public transportation and the Drexel shuttle provides convenient, free transportation between campuses for Drexel students. Adjacent to Drexel's University City Campus, Amtrak's 30th Street Station is a hub for trains and buses to the Philadelphia suburbs, New York City, Washington, DC, and the Philadelphia International Airport.

Academic Disciplines

Whatever their interests, students at Drexel are at the forefront of their fields. Drexel offers more than 80 undergraduate majors and as many minors. Academic majors include fields such as business, computing and informatics, culinary arts and science, education, engineering, entrepreneurship, exploratory studies, health professions, hospitality, humanities and social sciences, media arts and design, nursing, public health, sciences, and undeclared.

Academic Enhancement Programs

Qualified students can apply to the Honors Program, one of many exciting opportunities offered by the Pennoni Honors College. The Honors Program offers enhanced academic and extracurricular options to talented students through course work, speakers, social activities, and travel. Honors students receive benefits such as small Honors classes, Honors housing, free tickets to cultural events in Philadelphia, Honors-specific advising and mentoring, and priority registration for classes. Students in the Honors Program who satisfy the requirements are eligible for Graduation with Honors or, for the most accomplished students, Graduation with Distinction.

Drexel is an R1-level comprehensive research institution committed to use-inspired research with real-world applications. Research at Drexel is driven by faculty from all disciplines and students are encouraged to seek opportunities to partner with world-renowned faculty or develop independent research projects. The STAR (Students Tackling Advanced Research) Scholars program invites qualified students to participate in faculty-mentored research projects in their chosen fields as early as their first year. Students who take part in research may be eligible for stipends or academic credit.

Opportunities for Enrichment

Drexel's experiential learning model recognizes the importance of both academic and professional preparation. Drexel's cooperative education program (Drexel Co-op) provides professional employment experiences for students, giving them the opportunity to test-drive a career before they enter the workforce. The benefits are obvious—during their time at Drexel, students experience up to three different co-ops (up to 18 months). Drexel Co-op connects them with industry leaders and brings their cooperative education experiences back into the classroom. Plus, the majority of co-ops are paid and, of those that are, the median six-month salary is more than $18,000. Drexel Co-op experiences enable students to graduate having already built a professional network, and they typically receive higher starting salaries than their counterparts from other schools.

Drexel brings an international dimension to University life through its academic programs, study and cooperative education abroad, major research projects, global classrooms, conferences, and cultural events. Last year, Drexel students participated in over 140 unique study abroad experiences, and the year before that, the University offered over 175 international co-op opportunities. These students represented every major, and with programs in Africa, Asia, Europe, Latin America, and the Pacific, the possibilities presented are as varied as the interests of Drexel students.

Students can also become civically engaged and fulfill public service and leadership roles at Drexel's Lindy Center for Civic Engagement. Last year alone, Drexel students performed over 50,000 hours of volunteer service in support of our surrounding neighborhoods and communities.

Academic Facilities

Drexel has three campus locations: University City Campus, Center City Campus, and Queen Lane Campus. The University's library system comprises the W. W. Hagerty Library, the Library Learning Terrace, the Legal Research Center, and three health sciences libraries. The W. W. Hagerty Library, the University's central library located on the University City campus, maintains subscriptions to nearly 12,000 electronic journals, which are accessed via the library website, along with academic journals and 200 databases. Students may borrow laptops for use in the library. The Library Learning Terrace, a 3,000-square-foot flexible learning space located in a residence hall and staffed by librarians, enables students to learn and research collaboratively through a variety of technologies. The Legal Research Center on the third floor of the Kline School of Law shares University databases while continuing to acquire new material. The additional libraries on the health sciences campuses provide study space, 75,000 books, and network access to the same set of online journals and databases.

The University comprises many state-of-the-art spaces for students. One popular student location is the 12-story, 177,500-square-foot Gerri C. LeBow Hall, which houses the LeBow

College of Business, along with the Chestnut Square complex, which features mixed-use housing and retail, including a Shake Shack. The URBN Center houses the Westphal College of Media Arts & Design, providing space for exhibitions, labs, studios, and a black box theater. The five-story, 130,000-square-foot Papadakis Integrated Sciences Building features classrooms and North America's largest biowall. In addition, The Summit at University City provides more student housing and mixed-use commercial space.

Costs

For the 2020–21 academic year, Drexel's estimated cost of attendance for a full-time undergraduate student starting as a first-year student includes $53,868 in tuition, $2,405 in fees, and $16,008 in room and board. Students also incur additional costs for books (which vary by program), a computer for personal use, transportation, and miscellaneous personal costs.

Financial Aid

First-year students eligible for merit and/or need-based funds were awarded financial aid in the 2019–20 academic year. The average scholarship and grant aid offered to first-year students in the 2019–20 academic year was $30,753. All incoming students are encouraged to submit both the CSS Profile and the Free Application for Federal Student Aid (FAFSA) by specific deadlines. Financial aid notifications to students begin mid-December for students accepted during Early Action and Early Decision. The Drexel Liberty Scholars Program also provides 50 full-tuition and fees scholarships to low-income students who live in Philadelphia. The Drexel Global Scholar program grants full-tuition scholarships to exceptional international students who are also committed to global leadership.

Faculty

The University requires faculty members engaged in research and graduate-level teaching to also teach at the undergraduate level, allowing all students to benefit from the research activities of the faculty. Specially selected faculty members serve as advisors for first-year students. The student–faculty ratio is 11:1.

Admission Requirements

All colleges within the University require completion of a college-preparatory program in high school that includes at least 3 years of mathematics and 1 year of laboratory science. Students applying to a major in the sciences or business and engineering are required to take 4 years of mathematics (through trigonometry) and 2 years of laboratory science. Engineering requires 4 years of mathematics (through trigonometry and precalculus), chemistry, and physics. Biomedical engineering requires 1 year of calculus and 1 year of physics. Computer science and software engineering require 4 years of math (including trigonometry and calculus) and 2 years of lab science. The quality of academic performance is more important than merely meeting minimum requirements. The strength of preparation is judged primarily by rigor of course work or relative grade point average (GPA), by the degree of improvement in the quality of the academic record, and by the comments and recommendations from principals, school counselors, or teachers. First-year applicants are required to submit standardized test scores—including the SAT, ACT, SAT Subject, AP, or IB—and can also utilize Drexel's flexible testing policy. Students who were admitted and enrolled in the fall of 2019 had an average SAT math score (25th–75th percentiles) of 600–710 and an average SAT critical reading score (25th–75th percentiles) of 590–680. The essay from the Common Application or personal statement is required of all full-time applicants (except nursing ACE). Applicants to the Westphal College of Media Arts & Design or those seeking a custom-designed major may also be required to submit a writing supplement or portfolio. Transfer applicants should complete a minimum of 24 college credits from a regionally accredited institution. Transfer applicants who have fewer than 24 college credits prior to their application will also need to submit their high school transcript and SAT or ACT scores.

Application and Information

There are a few different ways for full-time undergraduate students to apply for admission. First-year students may submit either the Common Application or the Coalition Application. There is a $50 application fee and all Common Application and Coalition Application waivers are honored. First-year students may apply under Early Action, Early Decision, or Regular Decision options. Early Decision is binding and, if admitted, students must withdraw all other applications and commit to enrolling at Drexel. Early Action and Early Decision deadlines are November 1, with admission decisions rendered in mid-December. Applications for Regular Decision have a deadline of January 15, with admission decisions rendered no later than April 1. Applications for the BS+MD Early Assurance degree program are due on November 1. Drexel subscribes to the College Board candidate's reply date of May 1. More information can be found at https://drexel.edu/undergrad/apply. Full-time undergraduate transfer students may apply using the Common Application or the Drexel University Application. For transfer application deadlines, please visit https://drexel.edu/undergrad/apply/deadlines.

Undergraduate Admissions
Drexel University
3141 Chestnut Street
Philadelphia, Pennsylvania 19104-2876
Phone: 215-895-2400; 800-2-DREXEL (toll-free)
Fax: 215-895-1285
E-mail: enroll@drexel.edu
Website: drexel.edu/admissions (admissions)
drexel.edu/undergrad/apply (application)
@DrexelAdmission (Instagram)
facebook.com/DrexelAdmission (Facebook)
twitter.com/DrexelAdmission (Twitter)
drexeladmission (Snapchat)

Drexel students on Chestnut St. in University City, Philadelphia, Pennsylvania.

COLLEGE CLOSE-UPS

ELIZABETHTOWN COLLEGE
ELIZABETHTOWN, PENNSYLVANIA

The College

Founded in 1899, and located in Lancaster County, Pennsylvania, Elizabethtown College offers students 58 majors, over 100 minors and concentrations in health and sciences, engineering, communications, fine arts, and other professional studies. A selective, private institution, the College is grounded by its motto, "Educate for Service," and links classroom instruction with experiential learning through Signature Learning Experiences (SLEs), which supplement classroom learning and include choices in supervised research, cross-cultural experiences, community-based learning, internships, and capstone courses. SLEs prepare students for lives of purpose and are the hallmarks of the Elizabethtown experience.

Home to more than 1,800 students in our programs, hailing from 28 states and 23 countries, approximately 84 percent live on the 204-acre campus in residence halls, townhouses and apartments, and college-owned houses called student-directed learning communities, where students commit to community-focused service work.

In addition to an active intramural and club sports program, Blue Jay Athletics fields 24 NCAA Division III teams for Men (Baseball, Basketball, Cross Country, Golf, Lacrosse, Soccer, Swimming, Tennis, indoor and outdoor Track & Field, Volleyball, Wrestling) and Women (Basketball, Cross Country, Field Hockey, Golf, Lacrosse, Soccer, Softball, Swimming, Tennis, indoor and outdoor Track & Field, Volleyball). The College also added an Esports team in 2019.

The Center for Student Success offers academic advising, individual academic coaching, tutoring, and writing support for all students. Student Wellness provides individual and group counseling in a diversity affirming environment, delivers health services in partnership with Penn State Health, and offers robust health promotion programs through The Well. Career Services assists with career exploration, job shadow, and internship options, and prepares students for the job search process. The Center for Student Involvement promotes strengths-based initiatives for cultivating lives of purpose and meaning including the Called to Lead program, civic and community engagement and interfaith programs.

The Office of Diversity is committed to valuing and fostering the diversity reflected in our life together and in the world beyond the campus. The Mosaic House serves as a gathering place for students of diverse backgrounds and interests.

The campus offers five dining venues: The Marketplace (traditional dining); The Jay's Nest (deli/quick-serve/convenience store); The Blue Bean (which proudly serves Starbucks); The Jay Truck (food truck); and a smoothie bar and cafe in the Bowers Center for Sports, Fitness & Well-Being. Recreational spaces and offerings include Thompson Gymnasium, an outdoor mondo-surface track, a swimming pool and lots of walking/running paths and green space. The newly opened Bowers Center for Sports, Fitness and Well-being, with more than 78,000 square feet, will house wellness programming, intramural and club sports, intercollegiate athletics, fitness studios, cardio, strength and conditioning areas, a 180-meter indoor track, wellness classrooms and areas for meditation and yoga, meeting and gathering spaces for students, a smoothie bar, spin studio, training and athletic treatment areas, and office space for health educators and campus recreation. The KAV is a multipurpose entertainment and educational space. Leffler Chapel and Performance Center features an 840-seat auditorium. The campus events calendar boasts more than 125 arts and cultural happenings each academic year, not including student-run programming from OSA and the 80+ campus clubs.

Elizabethtown holds accreditations from the Middle States Commission for Higher Education (MSCHE), American Chemical Society for Clinical Lab Services (ACS), National Association of Schools of Music (NASM), National Council on Social Work Education (CSWE), Accreditation Council for Occupational Therapy Education (ACOTE), Association of Collegiate Business Schools and Programs (ACBSP), and the Accreditation Board for Engineering and Technology Inc. for Computer Engineering and Engineering (ABET).

Location

Elizabethtown borough is a community of close to 12,000 people located in historic Lancaster County in south-central Pennsylvania, 20 minutes from Harrisburg (state capital), Hershey, and Lancaster; 90 minutes from Philadelphia and Baltimore; and a few hours from New York City and Washington, D.C. The Amtrak station in Elizabethtown offers train service to and from New York, Philadelphia, and Pittsburgh. The Harrisburg International Airport is 15 minutes away.

Majors and Degrees

Bachelor of Arts degrees awarded: Communications, Criminal Justice, Economics, English, English Education (7-12), Fine Arts, Fine Arts Education (K-12), French, German, Graphic Design, History, Individualized, Interfaith Leadership Studies, Japanese, Legal Studies, Music, Philosophy, Political Science, Psychology, Religious Studies, Sociology-Anthropology, Spanish, and Spanish Education (K-12).

Bachelor of Science degrees awarded: Accounting, Actuarial Science, Biochemistry (Pre-Medicine), Biology (Allied Health, Biological Science, Pre-medicine), Biology Education (7-12), Biotechnology, Business Administration (Accounting, Economics, Entrepreneurship and Family Business, Finance, Management, Marketing), Business Data Science, Chemistry (ACS Professional, Chemical Physics, Chemistry Management, Forensic Science, Premedical) , Chemistry Education (7-12), Chemistry Laboratory Sciences, Computer Engineering, Computer Science, Data Science, Early Childhood Education (Pre-K through 4, Dual Special Education Certification, English as a Second Language), Elementary & Middle-level Education (English as a Second Language) (4-8), Engineering (Biomedical, Civil, Electrical, Environmental, Industrial and Systems, Mechanical), Environmental Science,, Finance, Financial Economics, Health Science, Information Systems, Individualized, International Business (Accounting, Economics, Entrepreneurship & Family Business, Finance, Management, Marketing, Self-Designed), Marketing, Mathematical Business, Mathematics (Applied Mathematics, Pure Mathematics), Mathematics Education (7-12), Neuroscience, Physics, Physics Education (7-12). Also awarded: Bachelor of Music degree in Music Education (K-12) and Music Therapy and the Bachelor of Social Work.

Masters degrees awarded are a Master of Occupational Therapy; a Master of Public Policy (4+1); a Master of Special Education (4+1); a Master of Education in Curriculum and Instruction in Peace Education; a Master of Music Education; and a Master of Physician Assistant Studies. The School of Continuing and Professional Studies offers a Master of Business Administration and a Master of Science in Strategic Leadership, Master of Education in Special Education, and graduate certificates in Health Care Administration and Strategic Leadership with more than 100 minors, concentrations, endorsements, and certifications are offered.

A Doctorate degree is awarded in Occupational Therapy.

The College offers a variety of cooperative programs that allow qualified students to combine undergraduate studies with direct admission into graduate school. These include a special partnership with Northumbria University in the UK; the Law Early Admissions Program with Drexel University Thomas R. Kline School of Law, Duquesne University School of Law, and Widener University Schools of Law; the 4+1 Masters in Molecular Medicine with Drexel University College of Medicine; a Masters of Public Health with Penn State College of Medicine; the Physician Assistant Program with Penn State College of Medicine; the Primary Care Program with Penn State College of Medicine; the Cardiovascular Invasive Specialty Program with Pennsylvania College of Health Sciences; the 3+4 or 4+4 Doctor of Dental Medicine with Lake Erie College of Osteopathic Medicine; 4+4 Doctor of Dental Surgery with West Virginia University School of Dentistry; and the 3+4 or 4+4 Doctor of Pharmaceutical with Lake Erie College of Osteopathic Medicine.

Academic Programs

An interdisciplinary first-year seminar and a strong core curriculum create a solid foundation for a student's chosen area of study. The core develops critical analysis and communication skills that ensure adaptability in the ever-changing global marketplace. Independent and directed studies, undergraduate research, and internships are available.

The Elizabethtown College Honors Program offers top students a highly selective program of study with the opportunity for a stipend to fund professional development, research, or travel-related study.

Called to Lead is a leadership-building program that helps students aspire to lead purposeful lives. Scholarship and Creative Arts Days, held each spring, give students of all majors and class years the opportunity to showcase their research or creative works. The Center for Global Understanding and Peacemaking, Bowers Writers House, and The Young Center for Anabaptist and Pietist Studies all offer a variety of academic programming that further reinforce classroom experiences. The Social Enterprise Institute offers students the opportunity to collaborate with faculty and industry fellows to create sustainable social and economic value both domestically and internationally. The Momentum program, a pre-orientation program, helps first-generation college students prepare for the academic expectations of Elizabethtown.

Off-Campus Programs

During their time at Elizabethtown, each student is guaranteed to experience at least two of the following Signature Learning Experiences: undergraduate research, study abroad, community-based learning, internships/fieldwork, and capstone course work.

Students may study abroad for a semester in 45 different locations on six continents through the College's affiliate programs. Short-term academic study tours or service-learning trips are offered. The Center for Community and Civic Engagement offers numerous community-based learning experiences locally, regionally, and nationally.

Academic Facilities

The High Library contains more than 241,000 volumes and an extensive collection of journals and other research materials; computers and printers; conference rooms; and private, individual, and group study areas. Librarians help students with research projects and using library resources effectively.

The campus features numerous academic buildings, including the James B. Hoover Center for Business and The Masters Center for Science, Mathematics, and Engineering. The Baugher Student center is home to the Tempest Theatre and a dance studio, and Zug Memorial Hall houses a recital hall and private and group practice rooms. Steinman Center for Communications and Arts features a television studio, radio station, and office space for the College newspaper. The College houses three art galleries and the Masters Mineral Gallery.

Elizabethtown is home to The Young Center for Anabaptist and Pietist Studies, a world-renowned research center focusing on the Amish and other similar religions. The High Center, a local research and resource center for family-owned businesses, partners with academic departments for events and programs. The Social Enterprise Institute brings together faculty members, industry fellows of the Institute and students, to collaborate on social enterprise development initiatives.

Costs

For 2019–20, tuition was $32,960 and room and meals are $12,060, for a total comprehensive fee of $45,020. Students should also plan for an additional $2,150 for books, transportation, and personal expenses, for a total cost of $45,860. Financial aid is based on this figure.

Financial Aid

Elizabethtown has a teaching faculty of 123 full-time professors. The student-faculty ratio is 11:1. Of the full-time faculty members, 91.9 percent hold a Ph.D. or the highest earned degree in their field. In addition to being assigned a faculty adviser for the First-Year Seminar program, when students declare a major, they are also assigned a new faculty adviser within the academic department of their declared major.

Faculty

Elizabethtown has a teaching faculty of 124 full-time professors. The student-faculty ratio is 11:1. Of the full-time faculty members, 94 percent hold a Ph.D. or the highest earned degree in their field. In addition to being assigned a faculty adviser for the First-Year Seminar program, when students declare a major, they are also assigned a new faculty adviser within the academic department of their declared major.

Student Government

Students play an active role in campus governance through Student Senate. Representative members of Student Senate are elected from each class. They advocate for students, coordinate special events, and allocate funds for student activities and the more than eighty student-directed clubs and organizations.

Admission Requirements

Elizabethtown believes the right fit is more than just SAT scores and GPA; other admission factors considered at the College are academic, cocurricular, and social fit. Admissions decisions are made without regard to sex, sexual orientation, race, religion, physical handicap, or place of residence. On average, 71 percent of all applicants are accepted. The middle 50 percent of enrolled students scored between 1070 and 1290 on the evidence-based reading and writing section and mathematics section of the SAT, and 63 percent were in the top 25 percent of their high school class.

The College is a diverse and exciting community, one that is composed of students who display leadership abilities and special talents. Campus interviews are highly recommended but not required for most students, although the College reserves the right to require interviews in special cases. Applicants to the Honors Program and occupational therapy program are required to interview. Auditions are required for music students.

Early admission is available for highly qualified high school juniors.

Application and Information

The College operates on a rolling admission basis—applications are processed as they are received—and the application deadline is April 1. Students can apply using the Common Application or online at the College's website. Applicants must submit a high school transcript, SAT or ACT scores, and a personal statement, essay, or graded paper. Early application is strongly recommended. Accepted students should notify the College of their decision to attend by May 1. Students who are interested in the Elizabethtown College Honors Program must submit a completed application by January 15.

For more information, students should contact:

Lauren Deibler, Director of Admissions
Elizabethtown College
One Alpha Drive
Elizabethtown, Pennsylvania 17022-2298
Phone: 717-361-1400; Fax: 717-361-1365
E-mail: admissions@etown.edu; Website: http://www.etown.edu

Elizabethtown College, home to about 1,800 students, offers more than 58 majors, 45 minors, and 48 concentrations.

EMERSON COLLEGE

BOSTON, MASSACHUSETTS

Emerson
COLLEGE

The College

Foundedin1880andlocatedintheheartofBoston,Massachusetts, Emerson College is the nation's premier institution for the study of communication and the arts. Students may choose from nearly 30 undergraduate programs supported by state-of-the-art facilities and a nationally renowned faculty. Emerson's campus is home to WERS-FM, the oldest noncommercial radio station in Boston; the historic 1,200-seat Cutler Majestic Theatre; and Ploughshares, the award-winning literary journal for new writing. Emerson College offers educational programs that prepare undergraduate and graduate students to assume positions of responsibility and leadership in communication and the arts and to pursue scholarship and work that brings innovation to these disciplines.

Originally a small, regional school of oratory, Emerson has evolved into a diverse, coeducational, and multi-faceted degree-granting institution with a liberal arts rather than conservatory orientation. But its mission and focus remains largely the same: to explore and push the boundaries of communication, art, and culture and, thereby, to contribute to the advancement of society. Many of the College's 39,000+ alumni remain active participants in the life of Emerson. Although concentrated in Massachusetts, California, and New York, Emersonians can be found working in virtually every major media, entertainment, or arts enterprise across the country.

The College's 3,817 undergraduate and 718 graduate students come from across the United States and seven-ty countries. Many undergraduate students live on campus, some in special learning communities, such as the Writers' Block, Film Immersion, and Performing Cultures. There is a fitness center, athletic field, and five residence halls, one of which includes our campus center and a recently renovated residence hall that houses all first year students, meeting spaces and will house numerous dining options as well. Emerson opened a new 18-story residence hall and a new 18,000 square-foot Dining Center in fall 2017, as well as a new student center in May 2019. Emerson is fully accredited by the New England Association of Schools and Colleges as authorized by the Commission on Institutions of Higher Education. Emerson is also accredited by the Council on Academic Accreditation of the American Speech-Language-Hearing Association and the Massachusetts Department of Education.

Location

Emerson College is located in Boston, Massachusetts, the most popular college city in the U.S. Emerson's campus is in the heart of downtown Boston and the city's Theatre District, just steps from the Massachusetts State House, Boston Common, the historic Freedom Trail, Boston Public Garden, Chinatown, and countless restaurants and museums. Emerson College's Boston campus is located at the gateway to the city's bustling Theatre District, in close proximity to cultural resources, media outlets, and public transportation. It comprises a cluster of over a dozen buildings near the intersection of Boylston and Tremont Streets (adjacent to the historic Boston Common) plus the magnificent Paramount Center, a performing arts and residence center on nearby Washington Street. The College also has facilities in Los Angeles and the Netherlands. The Boston campus has been assembled during the past 30 years as the College moved to the Theatre District from the Back Bay. Since 1993, Emerson has invested more than $500 million in preserving and restoring historic spaces and also creating new facilities. Emerson's decision to create the "Campus on the Common" is widely credited with reviving and revitalizing this section of Boston, attracting the development of private residences, hotels, restaurants, and other retail spaces. Emerson is continuing its legacy of preservation and restoration through its recently completed renovation of the Colonial Theatre and the Little Building residence hall, which re-opened in Fall 2019. Since these projects have been completed, the College is able to house nearly 70 percent of its students and has preserved several additional historic spaces for future generations.

Majors and Degrees

Boston's Emerson College offers Bachelor of Arts, Bachelor of Fine Arts, and Bachelor of Science degrees. Undergraduates can major in acting; business of creative enterprises; comedic arts; communication disorders; communication studies; creative writing; film art; journalism; marketing communication; media arts production; media studies; musical theatre; political communication; production; public relations; sports communication; stage and production management; stage and screen design/technology; theatre; theatre design/technology; theatre education; theatre education and performance; theatre and performance; or writing, literature, and publishing. The individually-designed interdisciplinary program also allows students to create their own major from the multitude of programs offered in communication, arts, and the liberal arts with faculty approval.

Academic Programs

The Institute for Liberal Arts and Interdisciplinary Studies is also home to Emerson's highly competitive Honors Program. Emerson offers a wide range of student support services including the Academic Advising Center, Career Development Services, Student Accessibility Services, and the Lacerte Family Writing and Academic Resource Center. Emerson College is committed to creating a campus environment that supports and promotes superior research, premier creative activities, and innovative scholarly pursuits. The mission of the Office of Research and Creative Scholarship (ORCS) is to serve the Emerson community by providing information, personal assistance, services, and programs to those who seek financial support for scholarly endeavors. The Office also provides college-wide leadership in the development of research and sponsored program activities, and works closely with faculty, staff and senior administrators in shaping the effort to build a more robust program of grants and sponsored research.

Off-Campus Programs

Hundreds of internship placements exist throughout Boston Hundreds of internship placements exist throughout Boston and in major cities across the country, including Emerson College's Los Angeles center—a state-of-the-art facility, home to a residential study and internship program in the hub of the global entertainment industry. Emerson also offers a semester-long program in Washington, DC. Students also have the option to register for courses with six other arts colleges in Boston through the ProArts Consortium. The Office of Internationalization and Global Engagement (IGE) seeks to enhance global engagement by utilizing Emerson's collective talent, energy, human and financial resources to support compelling transformation and change in international education across disciplines and around the world. Students can study abroad at the College's castle in the Netherlands; 20+ additional study abroad opportunities in China, the Czech Republic, Greece, Spain, and more. Emerson's Global Portal programs provide students the freedom to complete joint degrees in Boston and abroad. The Global BFA in Film Art gives students the opportunity to study at Paris College of Art in the heart of the City of Lights. The partnership with Franklin University Switzerland allows students to choose between two majors: International & Political Communication and Business of Creative Enterprises.

Academic Facilities

More than half of Emerson's facilities are new or renovated since 2019. Students have access to the highest quality equipment, clinical facilities devoted to communication disorders research and treatment, and an integrated digital newsroom for aspiring journalists. The College also owns more performance space than any other institution in Boston. The eleven-story Tufte Performance and Production Center has rehearsal space, a theatre design/technology center, makeup lab, and costume shop. Emerson's Paramount Center performance facility houses a sound stage, black box theater, scene shop, film screening room, and residence hall. Other performance facilities include the Cutler Majestic Theatre, a 1,200-seat Broadway-style theatre, renovated in 2002, and the Bill Bordy Auditorium and Theater.

Emerson has one of the largest installations of film, video, and audio post-production facilities of any college in the country. Digital production labs contain workstations with multimedia production and digital video/audio applications. Emerson has been designated a New Media Center since 1995. Emerson also has numerous radio, television, and film outlets and facilities. Clinical facilities include the Robbins Speech, Language and Hearing Center in the Department of Communication Sciences and Disorders. Graduate students work with patients and participate in a variety of Emerson-run clinics that are widely recognized in the field. In addition, the Iwasaki Library houses more than 180,000 volumes and serial subscriptions, 10,000 micro-forms, 11,000 audiovisual materials, and 8,000 e-books. Students can access the resources of a dozen cooperating libraries through Emerson College's membership in the Fenway Library Consortium.

Costs

In the 2020–21 academic year, full-time undergraduate student tuition is $50,528, room and board (for a double room) is $19,138, and the student services fee is $908.

Financial Aid

Emerson offers a variety of financial assistance programs. Approximately 77 percent of Emerson's student body receives financial assistance to help pay for their education. Sources of support may include institutional gift aid, academic scholarships, need-based grants, loan programs, work-study, and payment plans. There are also merit scholarships available through the Office of Undergraduate Admission. All applicants are automatically reviewed for eligibility for these merit scholarships once they have submitted their application.

Faculty

With a student-faculty ratio of 13:1, students at Emerson College develop close relationships with remarkably talented and active instructors who are experts in their fields. Emerson's 479 full- and part-time faculty members are nationally recognized and award-winning authors, directors, researchers, producers, journalists, playwrights, actors, and more. The majority of the faculty has earned doctorates or the highest degree obtainable in their field.

Student Life

Emerson students are doers and learners, creating and collaborating even after class is over for the day. The College offers more than 100 student organizations and performance groups, student publications, and honor societies. Emerson also supports 14 NCAA Division III men's and women's athletic teams. The College has five residence halls, four of which are newly renovated or brand new within the last 10 years. Students use the nearby Boston Common for relaxation and recreational activities such as tennis, softball, running, Quidditch, and ice-skating. The Field at Rotch Playground, located a mile from campus, serves as a practice and playing field while the Bobbi Brown and Steven Plofker Gym is the site for men's and women's basketball and volleyball games and other events.

Admission Requirements

Admission is competitive; each year, more than 13,000 applications are received for a class of approximately 900 new first-year students. Selection is based on academic promise as indicated by secondary school performance, recommendations, and writing competency. Emerson has a Test Optional admission policy. Students are welcome to submit SAT or ACT scores or may submit a test optional essay or major-related creative sample in their place. TOEFL, IELTS or other exams are required if English is not the first language. Emerson also considers personal qualities as seen in extracurricular activities, community involvement, and demonstrated leadership.

Application and Information

Emerson College accepts the Common Application and the Emerson Application. Students are required to complete all parts of their chosen application, including the Emerson-specific questions and writing supplement. There are additional requirements for students applying to Performing Arts programs, Comedic Arts, Film Art or Media Arts Production.

The deadline for fall admission for first-year students is January 15 (Early Action and Early Decision are November 1), and for transfer students, the priority deadline is March 15. The spring admission priority deadline is November 1 for first-year students and transfer students.

Emerson College Admissions
120 Boylston Street
Boston, Massachusetts 02116
United States
Phone: 617-824-8600
E-mail: admission@emerson.edu
Website: www.emerson.edu

GANNON UNIVERSITY
ERIE, PENNSYLVANIA

Believe in the possibilities.

The University

Gannon University is a place where lives are transformed, lifelong friendships made, and futures forged, a place where possibilities are discovered and become reality.

A Catholic, diocesan university founded in 1925, Gannon is more than a brick-and-mortar institution. It is a close-knit family of dedicated faculty, staff, and students inspired to solve problems, meet challenges, and make a difference in the process. It is a family that values faith, leadership, inclusiveness, and social responsibility—and puts those values into action locally and across the world.

Gannon's expert faculty and staff prepare students to be global citizens and leaders through innovative programs that are grounded in the liberal arts, sciences, and professional specializations and complemented by unique research, internship, and travel-abroad opportunities. Students don't have to imagine themselves interning at a Fortune 500 company, building an instrument for a NASA-funded project, or being immersed in the culture and history of Italy or Thailand or Spain. It happens at Gannon every day.

School pride doesn't end with academics. The entire Gannon community rallies around the Golden Knights and Lady Knights who excel in NCAA Division II athletics. Student-athletes can take their pick of 21 scholarship-granting varsity sports and year-round intramural and club sports. The campus includes the Recreation and Wellness Center, which recently underwent an expansion project that included a complete interior renovation, new cardio equipment, new locker rooms, and the addition of a 51,300 square-foot, indoor fieldhouse that features an 80-yard practice facility open to all students.

Students looking for a different kind of team can participate in service-learning projects or join any of more than 130 student clubs and organizations that offer a chance to bond with new friends over shared interests—two of the many ways Gannon students make memories that last a lifetime.

Location

Located in downtown Erie, Pennsylvania, Gannon is within walking distance of shops, restaurants, theaters, and professional sports venues and just minutes from Erie's bayfront and the beaches of Presque Isle State Park. Cleveland, Buffalo, and Pittsburgh all are within a two-hour drive.

Gannon's residence halls, apartments, academic buildings, administrative offices, and chapel are centered around the Waldron Campus Center—the heart of Gannon's campus—where members of the University's community meet, dine, study, and socialize. All campus housing is within three blocks of the cafeteria, Recreation and Wellness Center, library, and classrooms, creating a special, close-knit atmosphere in an urban setting. Students live and work near many of the businesses, organizations, and government agencies that are active partners in providing hands-on learning opportunities, including internships and service-learning experiences.

Majors and Degrees

The challenge at Gannon is not a lack of career paths—it's which one to choose. Students have their pick of more than 100 undergraduate, graduate, and online academic programs, all taught by faculty members who are experts in their field.

The College of Humanities, Education and Social Sciences offers programs in advertising communication, criminal justice, digital media communication, English, foreign language and international studies, foreign language and literature, history, interdisciplinary studies, journalism communications, legal studies, mortuary science, performance for media and stage, philosophy, political science, prelaw, a 3+3 prelaw program that includes early admission to Duquesne University, psychology, public relations, public service and global affairs, social work, theatre and communication arts, theatre technologies and design, or theology.

Future educators can choose from several programs in the School of Education including early childhood education PreK–4, early childhood education PreK–4/special education PreK–8, middle level education 4–8 and middle level education 4–8/special education PreK–8, and secondary education (in biology, English, mathematics and social studies).

The Morosky College of Health Professions and Sciences offers the following degrees: athletic training (master's), medical laboratory science, nursing, nutrition and human performance, occupational therapy (five-year direct-entry master's and a doctorate offered at the Ruskin, Florida campus), physical therapy (direct-entry doctorate), physician assistant (five-year direct-entry master's), public health, radiologic sciences, respiratory care, sport and exercise science, and undecided health science.

Degrees are also offered in biochemistry, biology, chemical engineering (cooperative program), chemistry, freshwater and marine biology, mathematics and science. Students who wish to enter chiropractic, dental, medical, optometry, pharmacy, podiatry, or veterinary school can choose from among 11 preprofessional programs.

The College of Engineering and Business offers degrees in biomedical engineering, computer science, electrical engineering (including a five-year co-op program), environmental engineering, industrial engineering, information systems, mechanical engineering (including a five-year co-op program), software engineering, and a dual-degree program in partnership with Esslingen University of Applied Sciences in which students earn bachelor's degrees in software engineering or computer science as well as software technology.

The most recent additions include programs in cyber engineering and cybersecurity with an Institute for Cyber Health and Knowledge that will serve as the global headquarters for academic, industry, and business owners to design, integrate and protect cybernetic intelligence and data systems worldwide.

Programs in the Dahlkemper School of Business include accounting, economics, entrepreneurship, finance, healthcare management, international management, management, management information systems, marketing, risk management and insurance, sport management and marketing, and supply chain management.

Academic Programs

Gannon's academic calendar consists of two full semesters running from August to December and from January to May, with optional summer classes. Basic graduation requirements for bachelor's degree candidates are 128 credit hours, including completion of requirements for the major and the liberal studies program. Associate degree students must complete 60 to 68 credit hours, depending on the program.

Academic Facilities

Nash Library, the hub of academic life at Gannon, reopened in 2017, following a complete exterior and interior renovation of the 82,000 square-foot building. The transformed library features new student study spaces, group collaboration spaces, the University's Writing and Research and S.T.E.M. centers, a full-service information technology help desk, new spaces for the university's archives and special collections, a reading room and a coffeehouse. The renovation follows the recent reopening of Beyer Hall after a 40,000 square-foot expansion project that created a collaborative space where students from around the world come together to learn, participate in campus life and organizations, and discover ways to engage the world.

Also new this year is the Donald M. and Judith C. Alstadt Environmental Center, waterfront property on 3.57 acres at the edge of the Allegheny National Forest that will be used by Gannon students and faculty to live, learn, and conduct research in a setting that offers unparalleled direct access to diverse ecosystems.

Gannon's academic facilities do more than house programs. They are the spaces where students learn by doing.

The Center for Business Ingenuity brings together the Dahlkemper School of business, Gannon's Small Business Development Center, and the Erie Technology Incubator under one roof, creating unprecedented collaboration between business students, entrepreneurs, business faculty, and consultants in a facility that looks and feels like a major corporate headquarters.

Gannon's mechanical, biomedical, and industrial and robotics engineering programs are located in another exceptional learning environment, the Center for Advanced Engineering, also home to the industrial engineering laboratory and the only biomedical engineering lab of its kind in the region.

Budding biologists, doctors, physicists, chemists, and engineers will spend much of their time in the Zurn Science Center, which houses laboratory space, an open-engineering computer lab, and 3-D printers for student use. Criminal justice students can investigate simulated crime scenes, conduct research in a state-of-the-art forensics lab, and train in interrogation rooms and a virtual reality firearms simulator in the forensic investigation center.

The Morosky College of Health Professions and Sciences is located in the Robert H. Morosky Academic Center, a 99,000 square-foot facility that includes classrooms, labs, and a state-of-the-art patient simulation center, the largest and most comprehensive one in the region. Nursing, respiratory care, radiologic science, physician assistant, and occupational therapy students come together at the center to take part in collaborative, hands-on learning.

Gannon's advertising, digital media communication, journalism, and theater programs, along with Gannon's award-winning radio station and student newspaper, are housed in the new Center for Communication Arts. Other academic buildings include the A. J. Palumbo Center, home to the College of Humanities, Education and Social Sciences, and Scottino Hall, home to the acclaimed Schuster Theatre.

Costs

Full-time tuition for 2020-21 is $16,780 per semester ($17,795 for engineering and health sciences), or $33,560 per academic year ($35,590for engineering and health sciences). Tuition for part-time students is $810-$875 per credit hour. Room and board range from $6,425 to $8,210 per semester. The total cost for the academic year at Gannon is $34,526 for commuting students and between $47,376 and $52,976 for resident students, depending on the program of study.

Financial Aid

Gannon is dedicated to ensuring a high-quality education is within everyone's reach: More than $27 million in student scholarship and financial aid is provided to 94 percent of undergraduate students. Students seeking financial aid can file the admissions and financial aid applications as early as October 1 and should file by the preferred deadline of March 15. Numerous employment and scholarship opportunities are available to qualified students. Each year the University offers its top incoming freshmen the ability to compete for full-tuition scholarships. The application deadline for this competition is December 15 with an on-campus competition in late January or early February.

Faculty

Gannon's faculty numbers more than 400 and 69 percent of the full-time faculty members have either doctoral or terminal degrees. The student-to-faculty ratio is 13:1, and average class size is approximately 25 students.

Admission Requirements

Gannon University actively recruits students of all races, faith traditions, and ages from all geographic regions of North America and abroad. Applicants must submit scores (including senior-year scores) on either the SAT or ACT; an up-to-date official transcript of the high school record (plus official college transcripts for transfer applicants); and a completed application form. Applications can be completed online at www.gannon.edu/apply or via the Common Application.

Admission decisions are based upon numerous factors, most importantly the high school record as demonstrated through grades and SAT and/or ACT scores and other test scores that may be available. Recommendations and personal statements also affect admission decisions. Transfer and international students should check with the admissions office for special application procedures.

Application and Information

Gannon operates on a rolling admissions basis; there is no deadline for filing applications with the exception of the physician assistant program, which has a deadline of November 15 for the fall semester. Due to the competitiveness of some programs, students interested in the nursing or occupational therapy programs are strongly encouraged to file applications in September. Early applications are recommended, as are enrollment deposits.

To find out more, contact:
Office of Admissions
Gannon University
109 University Square
Erie, Pennsylvania 16541
Phone: 814-871-7240
800-GANNON-U (426-6668, toll-free)
Fax: 814-871-5803
E-mail: admissions@gannon.edu
Website: http://www.gannon.edu

COLLEGE CLOSE-UPS

GRAND VIEW UNIVERSITY

DES MOINES, IOWA

The University

Grand View University is a liberal arts institution that offers a high-quality education to a diverse student body in a career-oriented curriculum at its modern campus in Des Moines, Iowa. Founded in 1896, Grand View welcomes traditional students, adult learners, and graduate students representing a wide range of ethnic, religious, and cultural backgrounds.

At Grand View, students find a winning combination of high-quality programs, experienced professors, and student experiences that will prepare them for successful careers. With 2,000 students and an average class size of 17, learning is an interactive process at Grand View—students engage in lively discussions, work on real-world projects, and participate in career-related work experiences.

Grand View stands out from other universities because of its partnerships with leading businesses and organizations in Des Moines, which has led to challenging internships and stellar job placement—for more than two decades nearly 100 percent of GV graduates have found jobs right after graduation or continued their education.

Students are encouraged to develop leadership and team skills through involvement in campus organizations, which include intercollegiate and intramural athletics, speech and theater groups, academic clubs, student government, musical ensembles, and honor societies. Grand View's student leadership program provides opportunities for students with or without leadership experience to seek and develop critical thinking, interpersonal, and networking skills.

Student athletes compete in baseball, basketball, bowling, competitive cheer (coed), cross-country, Esports, football, golf, shooting sports (coed), soccer, tennis, track and field, volleyball, and men's and women's wrestling, and women's basketball, bowling, competitive dance, cross-country, golf, soccer, softball, tennis, track and field, and volleyball. Grand View is a member of the Heart of America Conference of the National Association of Intercollegiate Athletics. Athletic scholarships are available.

Location

Grand View is located in Des Moines, a metropolitan area of more than half a million people in central Iowa. In essence, Grand View's campus is the entire city of Des Moines because students aren't limited by the confines of a small campus or small town. Nationally recognized companies that have their corporate offices in Des Moines include DuPont/Pioneer, the Principal Financial Group, Meredith Corporation, Wells Fargo Home Mortgage, and the *Des Moines Register*.

The recreation and cultural options are endless. In a given day, students can catch an Iowa Cubs professional baseball doubleheader, head down to the Court Avenue district for great food and nightlife, or take in a concert at Wells Fargo Arena. A thriving arts program in Des Moines features the Des Moines Metro Opera, Ballet Iowa, the Des Moines Symphony, the Des Moines Art Center, the Des Moines Playhouse, and many others. The summer Des Moines Arts Festival is ranked third in the nation.

Majors and Degrees

Grand View University offers 40 majors in areas such as accounting, applied mathematics, art education, biology, biochemistry, biotechnology, business administration (with concentrations in areas such as finance, human resource management, management, and marketing), business analytics, communication and media practice, computer science, criminal justice, , elementary education, English, graphic design, game design, kinesiology, history, human services, liberal arts, management information systems, music, music education, nursing, organizational studies, paralegal studies, physical education, political studies (pre-law or public administration), psychology, secondary education, Spanish for careers and professionals, studio arts, theater arts, and theology.

The university also offers five master's degree programs: the Master of Science in Organizational Leadership, the Master of Science in Clinical Mental Health Counseling, the Master of Education, Master of Science in Sport Management and Master of Science in Athletic Training. Grand View also has a Athletic Training 3+2 program that pairs a kinesiology undergraduate degree with an MSAT.

Academic Programs

Grand View operates on a 4-4-1 academic calendar. The first semester runs from late August to December. The second semester begins in early January and ends in late April. Three one-month summer sessions are offered in May, June, and July, as is a summer trimester evening program.

Grand View's general education core takes an innovative, integrated approach to developing essential abilities employers seek in graduates, such as writing, speaking, analysis, problem-solving, and critical thinking. Through their coursework, students can gain the personal and intellectual depth that will help them thrive in today's knowledge-based economy and in their communities.

The GV Honors Program is a selective, application-based opportunity to receive Honors recognition upon graduation. Students who capitalize on this program will undergo an exploration of humanity, society and life's purpose. GV Honors students will develop strong communication skills through discussions and collaborative learning opportunities - on and off campus. Begin learning in a completely new way, strengthen leadership skills and engage with peers and professors who share similar levels of intellectual curiosity.An active study-abroad program gives students opportunities to learn in an international setting, particularly through a partnership with the Danish Institute for Study Abroad, IBA, and China's Tianfu University.

Costs

For 2020-21, the comprehensive cost for first-year students living on campus is approximately $39,406, which includes tuition, an activity fee, a technology fee, a parking fee, and room and board. Students have several residential and meal plan options that affect cost. Health services and Internet access are also included in the comprehensive fee.

Financial Aid and Affordability

All incoming Grand View first-year students are automatically enrolled in GV COMPLETE, an innovative program that allows students to plan and finance their entire degree right from the beginning, with a four-year financing plan,a four-year academic plan and capped tuition and room and board increases. GV COMPLETE is designed to help make a Grand View education more affordable and transparent and to encourage four-year graduation.

In 2018-19, 99 percent of Grand View students received financial assistance. The average first-year full-time award package exceeds $27,300 with more than $19,600 in grants and scholarships, and the remainder in work-study and student loans. The amount of aid is determined through a combination of merit and analysis of need as determined through the Free Application for Federal Student Aid. The priority deadline for financial aid is January 15. Students receive notification of financial aid packages following acceptance of admission to the university and receipt of their financial aid analysis of need

Faculty

There are approximately 94 full-time faculty members and 120 part-time faculty members. More than 62 percent of full-time faculty members hold terminal degrees. All classes are taught by professors; no graduate or teaching assistants instruct Grand View classes.

Student Government

Students participate in Grand View governance. The Student Activities Council and Viking Council plan student activities that promote educational, social, cultural, and recreational aspects of student life. Students serve as representatives on faculty and staff search committees, programming committees, and student life committees.

Admission Requirements

Applicants' files are reviewed to determine their preparation for a Grand View education. Official high school transcripts and submission of ACT or SAT scores are required for applicants with less than 24 semester hours of college credit. Applicants transferring from another college are required to submit official transcripts from all colleges previously attended.

Application and Information

For more information about Grand View, students should contact:
Admissions Office
Grand View University
1200 Grandview Avenue
Des Moines, Iowa 50316
Phone: 515-263-2810
800-444-6083 (toll-free)
Fax: 515-263-2974
E-mail: admissions@grandview.edu
Website: http://www.grandview.edu
https://www.facebook.com/GrandViewUniversity (Facebook)

Grand View students in downtown Des Moines.

COLLEGE CLOSE-UPS

HILLSDALE COLLEGE
HILLSDALE, MICHIGAN

COLLEGE CLOSE-UPS

The College

Hillsdale College is a private, independent, nonsectarian, Christian institution of higher learning founded in 1844 by men and women who described themselves as "grateful to God for the inestimable blessings" resulting from civil and religious liberty and as "believing that the diffusion of sound learning is essential to the perpetuity of those blessings." The College has maintained institutional independence since its founding by refusing to accept aid from or control by federal authorities. Private support from a national constituency has enabled Hillsdale to continue its trusteeship of the intellectual and spiritual inheritance tracing to Athens and Jerusalem, a heritage finding its clearest expression in the American experiment of self-government under law.

The undergraduate enrollment for fall 2019 was 1,468—52 percent men and 48 percent women—from 49 states and 11 foreign countries. Approximately 31 percent of students are from Michigan. The entering freshman class in 2019 had the following mid-range scores: high school grade-point average of 3.89–4.0, ACT of 29–33, and SAT of 1310–1450. All Hillsdale students sign an Honor Code challenging self-government and committing them to honesty, duty, and respect.

Location

Hillsdale College is located in Hillsdale, Michigan (population 8,000) near the Indiana and Ohio borders. Stores, churches, restaurants, and coffee shops are within walking distance of the campus.

Majors and Degrees

Hillsdale awards Bachelor of Arts and Bachelor of Science degrees in accounting, applied mathematics, art, biochemistry, biology, chemistry, classics, economics, English, exercise science, financial management, French, German, Greek, history, Latin, marketing/management, mathematics, music, philosophy, physical education, physics, politics, psychology, religion, rhetoric and public address, Spanish, sport management, sport psychology, and theater. Interdisciplinary majors are available in American studies, Christian studies, comparative literature, European studies, international studies in business and foreign language, political economy, and sociology and social thought. Preprofessional programs are offered in allied health sciences (including optometry, pharmacy, and physical therapy), dentistry, education, engineering, journalism, law, medicine and osteopathy, theology, and veterinary medicine. Hillsdale also offers two graduate programs—one in politics and one in government.

The Academic Program

Hillsdale operates on a two-semester schedule. Two 3-week summer sessions are also offered.

The College offers a classical liberal arts curriculum. Every Hillsdale College student is required to complete a structured core of courses in the humanities, natural sciences, and social sciences. Required courses include Western and American Heritage, U.S. Constitution, Great Books in the Western and British/American Traditions, Classical Logic and Rhetoric, Western Philosophical Tradition, and Western Theological Tradition. To graduate, students must complete a minimum 124 hours of course work and fulfill the requirements of at least one major field. The B.A. program includes a foreign language proficiency requirement. The B.S. program requires additional studies in mathematics and the natural sciences.

The Center for Constructive Alternatives conducts four week-long symposia during the academic year, bringing distinguished scholars and public figures to the campus. All students are required to enroll in at least one seminar for credit during their time at Hillsdale.

The Collegiate Scholars Program enriches the academic experience of high-performing students through seminars, campus lectures and discussions, retreats, subsidized foreign travel, and the completion of an interdisciplinary senior thesis.

Off-Campus Programs

For forty years, the Washington-Hillsdale Internship Program (WHIP) has provided students the opportunity to participate in full-time, academically intensive internships in Washington, D.C. Past interns and fellows have been placed in locations such as the U.S. Senate, the White House, and the Smithsonian Institution, as well as news and media outlets. Students complement their internships with classes at Hillsdale's Allan P. Kirby, Jr. Center for Constitutional Studies and Citizenship.

Hillsdale students are able to study abroad for a summer or a semester at one of the more than thirty colleges of Oxford University. Hillsdale also offers a summer business program in cooperation with Regent's College in London, England, and the opportunity to study at the University of St. Andrews in St. Andrews, Scotland. Science students benefit from Hillsdale's 685-acre field research laboratory in northern Michigan, a marine biology course in the Florida Keys, and internship opportunities with the Omaha Zoo. Foreign language students frequently study abroad in Argentina, France, Germany, and Spain.

Academic Facilities

The Hillsdale College Mossey Library features a collection of more than 270,000 books and media volumes, including rare and special holdings such as the Ludwig von Mises and Russell Kirk collections.

Lane and Kendall Halls contain classroom space and faculty offices for the humanities and social sciences, as well as a special laboratory for experimental psychology. Strosacker Science Center and the Herbert Henry Dow Science Building provide classrooms and laboratories for the natural sciences. The Joseph H. Moss Family Laboratory Wing includes state-of-the-art laboratories and a greenhouse. Slayton Arboretum is a 48-acre campus garden and bird sanctuary used by students to conduct research. At the Mary Randall Preschool, children are taught by students specializing in early childhood education and psychology. Hillsdale Academy, a K–12 private school, provides additional classroom observation opportunities.

The Roche Sports Complex houses the Dawn Tibbetts Potter Arena, with a student fitness center and basketball/volleyball courts, the John "Jack" McAvoy Natatorium for swimming and diving, an exercise physiology and sports medicine facility, four racquetball courts, and a weight/fitness room. Adjacent is the Frank "Muddy" Waters Stadium, featuring an artificial surface football field; all-weather, Olympic-quality eight-lane running track; and fields for soccer, baseball, and women's softball. The Margot V. Biermann Athletic Center houses four acrylic tennis courts and a six-lane, 200-meter NCAA regulation Mondo surface track. In addition to serving as a course for Hillsdale's cross-country teams and offering a driving range for the golf team, Hayden Park, located northeast of campus, provides a place for club and intramural sports, mountain biking, cross-country skiing, and general outdoor recreation. The 113-acre John Anthony Halter Shooting Sports Education Center, located five miles from the main campus, features seven American trap fields, a five-stand sporting clays field, a small arms range, a skeet field for both American and International skeet, an Olympic bunker, an outdoor Olympic archery range, a 20-station sporting clays course, and a lodge and education center.

The Fine Arts Building is home to the departments of art and theater. It features Daughtrey Gallery, a prop- and scene-construction shop, a sound studio, graphics lab, black box theatre, and the Markel Auditorium, a 353-seat performance hall (with orchestra pit). Howard Music Hall houses the McNamara Rehearsal Hall, Conrad Recital Hall, studio space for percussion and jazz studies, offices, and practice rooms.

The Grewcock Student Union houses the cafeteria, bookstore, student mail center, offices for student activities and publications, a lounge and game area, and AJ's Café. The 27,000-square-foot Christ Chapel serves as a performance venue, a center for campus spiritual life, and a symbol of Hillsdale's Christian roots and identity.

Faculty

The faculty consists of 146 full-time members with a 9:1 student-teacher ratio and average class sizes of 15. The size and closeness of the College community enable personal attention and faculty mentorship. Each student has a faculty advisor for core and major coursework.

Athletics

Hillsdale's Charger athletes compete in 14 intercollegiate NCAA Division II varsity sports as part of the Great Midwest Athletic Conference. Hillsdale College sponsors varsity basketball, cross-country, swimming, softball, tennis, indoor and outdoor track and field, and volleyball for women, and varsity baseball, basketball, cross-country, golf, football, tennis, and indoor and outdoor track and field for men.

Student Life

Four national fraternities, three national sororities, a newspaper and radio station, and more than 100 other social, academic, spiritual, and service organizations provide Hillsdale students with diverse cocurricular opportunities. A resident drama troupe and dance company, a concert choir and chamber chorale, a jazz program, instrumental chamber ensembles, and a symphony orchestra and band constitute the College's performing arts organizations. The Student Activities Board hosts campus-wide social functions throughout the year, including events like Garden Party, Homecoming, President's Ball, and Centralhallapalooza.

Hillsdale students are housed in single-sex dormitories, fraternity and sorority houses, and off-campus houses. Each College-owned residence hall is supervised by a resident director and resident advisers. All freshmen (except commuters) are required to live on campus; upper-class students seeking to live off campus must apply to the deans.

Student services provided by the College include career planning and placement counseling; academic advising and tutoring; and a health service staffed by a resident nurse, counselors, and visiting medical professionals.

Costs

Annual tuition for the 2019–20 academic year was $27,090, room was $5,640, board was $5,750, and mandatory fees were $1,278. Books, supplies, and personal expenses (including travel, recreation, and clothing) are estimated at $3,200 per year.

Financial Aid

Academic scholarships are awarded on a competitive basis, regardless of financial need. The application for admission also serves as the application for merit-based aid. Athletic scholarships are awarded on a competitive basis in men's baseball, football, and golf; men's and women's basketball, tennis, track, and cross-country; and women's swimming, softball, and volleyball. The art and music departments also award a select number of scholarships based on strength of portfolio/audition. To apply for aid on the basis of financial need, students are required to file Hillsdale's Confidential Family Financial Statement (CFFS). Because Hillsdale does not accept government funds, either directly for its operations or indirectly in the form of student aid, the FAFSA is not applicable; government funds are replaced with private dollars. Grants and loans are available from the College.

Admission Requirements

A formal application to Hillsdale College includes: (1) a completed application form; (2) the scores from either the Scholastic Aptitude Test (SAT), the American College Test (ACT), or the Classic Learning Test (CLT); (3) an official transcript of high school grades (and post-secondary grades, if available); (4) thoughtful essay and short answer responses; (5) two academic letters of recommendation; and (6) a résumé of extracurricular activities, volunteerism, leadership, and work experience. An interview is recommended, but not required. Transfer students must include a Dean of Students Transfer Form and official college transcript(s). Students who come from a non-English speaking country must submit all required documents in English and must complete the SAT, ACT, or CLT to demonstrate proficiency in English as well as academic preparedness.

Application and Information

Students may apply to Hillsdale College any time after the completion of the junior year of high school. A formal application includes a completed application form accompanied by a nonrefundable fee of $35 (free if submitted online) and all required credentials. Application plans include early decision (November 1), spring admission (December 15), priority scholarship (January 1), and regular decision (April 1). Hillsdale College has been distinguished since its founding in 1844 by voluntarily adhering to a nondiscriminatory admissions policy regarding race, religion, sex, and national or ethnic origin. All records and forms should be mailed to:

Admissions Office
Hillsdale College
33 East College Street
Hillsdale, Michigan 49242-1298
Phone: 517-607-2327
Fax: 517-607-2223
E-mail: admissions@hillsdale.edu
Website: http://www.hillsdale.edu

Central Hall, on the campus of Hillsdale College, stands as an enduring symbol of the school's independence.

COLLEGE CLOSE-UPS

HOFSTRA UNIVERSITY

HEMPSTEAD, NEW YORK

The University

Since its founding in 1935, Hofstra has evolved into an internationally renowned university that continues to achieve recognition as an institution of academic excellence. Hofstra has 28 academic accreditations and 32 total accreditations, and consistently earns recognition on the best college lists of U.S. News & World Report, The Princeton Review, Fiske Guide to Colleges, PayScale College ROI and Salary Reports, and Forbes magazine. Additionally, Hofstra has consistently been named to the President's Higher Education Community Service Honor Roll and is the only university to host three consecutive U.S. presidential debates (2008, 2012, and 2016).

Hofstra offers more than 160 undergraduate and more than 165 graduate program options. More than 100 dual degree program options are also offered, giving students the opportunity to earn both a graduate and undergraduate degree in less time than if each degree was pursued separately. Students can choose from internationally recognized programs within Hofstra's various schools and colleges:

- Academic Health Sciences Center, including the Donald and Barbara Zucker School of Medicine at Hofstra/Northwell; the Hofstra Northwell School of Graduate Nursing and Physician Assistant Studies at Hofstra University; and the School of Health Professions and Human Services.
- Frank G. Zarb School of Business
- Fred DeMatteis School of Engineering and Applied Science
- Hofstra College of Liberal Arts and Sciences, including the Peter S. Kalikow School of Government, Public Policy, and International Affairs; the School of Education; the School of Humanities, Fine and Performing Arts; and the School of Natural Sciences and Mathematics
- Honors College
- Lawrence Herbert School of Communication
- Maurice A. Deane School of Law
- Hofstra University Continuing Education
- Students live and learn in one of the university's 35 residence halls, each with a community and life of its own. Hofstra hosts hundreds of social, academic, and cultural events each year, drawing together scholars, business leaders, authors, celebrities, health care professionals, politicians, and journalists from across the nation and around the world.
- The David S. Mack Sports and Exhibition Complex, a 5,025-seat arena, is home to various Hofstra Pride athletic teams. It is also the site for events such as commencements, exhibitions, trade shows, televised political events—including U.S. presidential debates—and concerts. Other recreational and athletic facilities include an indoor, Olympic-size swimming pool; a state-of-the-art fitness center; and various athletic fields. In addition, Hofstra offers 21 varsity sports that compete at the NCAA Division I level; 29 local/national fraternities and sororities; and more than 220 academic, media, multicultural, performance, preprofessional, religious, social/political, and sports clubs and organizations.

Location

Hofstra's 244-acre suburban campus is a short train ride from all the cultural, recreational, internship, and career opportunities New York City has to offer—and only minutes from beautiful beaches, shopping malls, restaurants, and two major airports.

Majors and Degrees

The Bachelor of Arts (B.A.) is awarded in African studies; American studies; anthropology; art history; Asian studies; biology; chemistry; Chinese; Chinese studies; classics; comparative literature and languages; computer science; criminology; dance; drama; early childhood education and childhood education (with dual major in another discipline); economics; elementary education; engineering science; English; English education; film studies and production; fine arts; foreign language education (French, German, Italian, Russian, Spanish); French; geography; geology; German; global studies; Hebrew; history; individually designed B.A. major in humanities, natural sciences, or social sciences; Italian; Japanese and Japanese studies; Jewish studies; journalism; labor studies; Latin, Latin American and Caribbean studies, liberal arts; linguistics; mass media studies; math education (with a dual major in another discipline); mathematical economics; mathematics; music; philosophy; physics; political science; pre-health with a concentration in humanities and social sciences; psychology; public relations; public policy and public service; radio production and studies; religion; rhetorical studies; Russian; science education (biology, chemistry, earth science, physics); science technology, engineering and mathematics (STEM); social studies education (with a dual major in another discipline); sociology; Spanish; speech-language-hearing sciences; sustainability studies; television production and studies; urban ecology; and women's studies.

The Bachelor of Business Administration (B.B.A.) is awarded in accounting, business analytics, entrepreneurship, finance, information systems, international business, legal studies in business, management, marketing, and supply chain management.

The Bachelor of Science (B.S.) is offered in applied physics, athletic training, biochemistry, biology, business economics, chemistry, civil engineering, community health, computer engineering, computer science, computer science and mathematics (dual major), early childhood education/childhood education, electrical engineering, environmental resources, exercise science, fine arts, forensic science, geographic information systems, geology, health education, health science, industrial engineering, mathematical business economics, mathematical finance, mathematics, mechanical engineering, music, neuroscience, philosophy, physics, pre-medical, psychology, sustainability studies, urban ecology, video/television, video/television and business, video/television and film, and video/television.

The Bachelor of Science in Education (B.S.Ed.) is offered with specializations in dance, fine arts, music, and physical education.

The Bachelor of Engineering (B.E.) is offered in engineering science with specializations in biomedical engineering and civil engineering.

The Bachelor of Fine Arts (B.F.A.) is awarded in theater arts and dance.

Combined (dual) degrees offered include Bachelor of Arts/Juris Doctor (B.A./J.D.), in collaboration with the Maurice A. Deane School of Law; Juris Doctor/Master of Business Administration (J.D./MBA) in collaboration with the Maurice A. Deane School of Law and the Frank G. Zarb School of Business; Juris Doctor/Master of Public Health (J.D./M.P.H.) in collaboration with the Maurice A. Dean School of Law and the School of Health Professions and Human Services; Medical Doctorate/Master of Public Health in collaboration with the Donald and Barbara Zucker School of Medicine at Hofstra/Northwell and the School of Health Professions and Human Services; B.S./M.S. in physician assistant studies; B.S./M.D. and B.A./M.D., through the Donald and Barbara Zucker School of Medicine at Hofstra/Northwell; and various majors and concentrations leading to the B.A./MBA, B.S./MBA, B.A./M.S.Ed., B.A./M.A., B.A./M.S., B.S./M.S., B.B.A./M.S.Ed., B.B.A./M.S., B.B.A./MBA, B.S./M.S.Ed., B.S./M.A., B.A./M.F.A., M.A./MBA, and M.D./Ph.D.

Academic Programs

Requirements for graduation vary among schools and majors. A liberal arts core curriculum is an integral part of all areas of concentration. The University calendar is organized on a traditional fall and spring semester system, and offers an optional January session and three optional Summer sessions (between May and August).

Hofstra offers innovative programs designed to meet the needs of its diverse student body. These include Honors College, Legal Education Accelerated Program (LEAP), Hofstra 4+4 Program, First-Year Connections, and living/learning communities.

Honors College students can elect to study in any of the University's undergraduate programs and are involved in all fields of advanced study.

The Legal Education Accelerated Program allows students to earn both a B.A. and a J.D. in just six years.

The Hofstra 4+4 Program allows students to earn both a bachelor's degree (B.A. or B.S.) and M.D. in eight years in collaboration with the Donald and Barbara Zucker School of Medicine at Hofstra/Northwell.

First-Year Connections, an optional integrated academic and social program, helps first-year students connect with one another as well as with all the resources and opportunities offered at the University. The program offers seminars and course clusters, that satisfy general education requirements for all majors, and features small classes taught by distinguished faculty.

Through Hofstra's living/learning communities, students are exposed to environments that are intellectually stimulating, supportive, and conducive to building lasting friendships and a memorable first-year experience. These communities are associated with several first-year clusters and seminars, giving students the opportunity to live with students who are in their classes and who share their interests.

Off-Campus Programs

Hofstra extends learning beyond the classroom through varied internship programs and study-abroad opportunities. The internship programs take advantage of Hofstra's proximity to New York City, allowing students to gain real-life experience in areas such as finance, business, media, advertising, and entertainment. Through study-abroad programs in Europe, Asia, South America, and other locations, students can explore the world while earning college credits. More information is available at hofstra.edu/studyabroad.

Academic Facilities

Hofstra students connect with the real world through experiential learning and build leadership skills by participating in service projects that give back to the community. Students have the opportunity to work in cutting-edge facilities, including the Martin B. Greenberg Trading Room; a big data lab; a robotics and advanced manufacturing lab; a cell and tissue engineering lab; and WRHU-88.7FM Radio Hofstra University, recipient of two prestigious Marconi Awards from the National Association of Broadcasters and among the top college radio stations in the country.

Costs

The 2018–19 annual tuition and fees for a full-time undergraduate student were $44,640. The cost of a housing and dining plan was approximately $16,768. The current full tuition and fees schedule is available at hofstra.edu/tuition.

Financial Aid

Hofstra University works hard to make a private college education affordable for students and families, and offers several financial aid options for new undergraduates, including interest-free payment plans and a four-year locked-in rate for tuition and fees (hofstra.edu/lockedintuitionrate) that can help students manage costs from admission through graduation. Detailed information can be found at hofstra.edu/FinancialAid.

Faculty

All classes at Hofstra are taught by distinguished faculty members who are committed to excellence in teaching, scholarly research, and service. With an average undergraduate class size of 21 and a student-faculty ratio of 13:1, students are encouraged to debate, question, conduct research, discuss, and think critically in an open, collaborative learning environment.

Student Government

The Student Government Association (SGA) is Hofstra University's student-run governing body and is comprised of full-time undergraduate students; the SGA acts as a liaison between Hofstra students and the University's faculty, administration, and Board of Trustees. In addition, SGA plans and executes multiple programs and initiatives throughout the academic year, and oversees and finances of more than 200 clubs and organizations.

Admission Requirements

Hofstra is a competitive institution that seeks to enroll students who demonstrate academic ability, intellectual curiosity, and the motivation to succeed and contribute to the campus community. Careful consideration is given to a student's high school record, types of courses taken, SAT or ACT scores (if applicable), letters of recommendation, extracurricular involvement, and the personal essay. Submitting standardized test scores to Hofstra is optional. Prospective students should visit hofstra.edu/testing policy for more information. The most competitive applicants will have followed a rigorous college preparatory curriculum and will have taken advantage of honors and advanced placement–level courses where appropriate. The Office of Admission prefers a high school curriculum that includes 4 years of English, 3 to 4 years of social studies, 2 to 3 years of foreign language, 3 years of mathematics (4 years for engineering applicants), and 3 years of science (4 years for engineering applicants). Campus visits are strongly recommended. Hofstra accepts applications from first-year, transfer, and international students.

Application and Information

For students whose first choice is Hofstra, there are two early action periods: (1) When an application is submitted by November 15, notification is made to the student by December 15; and (2) When an application is submitted by December 15, notification is made to the student by January 15. Students applying for regular decision are considered on a rolling basis.

First-year applicants must submit an application, $70 application fee, high school transcript, SAT or ACT scores (if applicable), essay, and letter of recommendation. Hofstra accepts applications via mail or online and participates in the Common Application.

For more information, contact:
Hofstra University
Office of Undergraduate Admission
100 Hofstra University
Hempstead, New York 11549-1000
Phone: 516-463-6700
Fax: 516-463-5100
E-mail: admission@hofstra.edu
Website: http://www.hofstra.edu/admission

Hofstra students live and learn in the best of both worlds. Professors teach in traditional classroom settings, but lectures expand into the world beyond. With NYC only a 45-minute train ride away, students can immerse themselves in diverse cultural and entertainment activities, while applying what they learn in the classroom at internships and co-op programs.

JOHN CABOT UNIVERSITY

ROME, ITALY

The University

John Cabot University (JCU) was founded in 1972 and is the first overseas American university in Italy with regional accreditation by the Middle States Commission on Higher Education. JCU is a liberal arts university following the American system of education but with a distinctive European and international character. Located in the historic center of Rome, the University has unparalleled access to history, culture, and the active international communities associated with the United Nations organizations and embassies present in the city. With a commitment to a serious liberal arts education and a unique relationship with leading multinational corporations, media, and other cultural and international organizations, JCU provides students with the academic training and opportunities to participate in exclusive internships that will allow them to enter directly into challenging careers after graduation, or to continue their studies at prestigious graduate programs.

The University has a diverse and unique student body, comprised of American, Italian, and international students from more than 80 countries. This group is complemented by visiting students from universities across the United States. The visiting students bring their own regional diversity, which enhances the international environment at JCU, resulting in a dynamic and engaging student body. JCU's commitment to creating a student community of both degree-seeking and visiting students results in the friendly, close community of a small campus, with the wide-ranging networks that come from studying with a large pool of students from across the United States.

The average class size is 15 students, and there are approximately 100 full- and part-time faculty members with advanced degrees from prestigious universities all over the world. Students work closely with professors and receive the individual attention needed to develop their academic abilities. JCU graduates are accepted into acclaimed graduate programs in the United States, the United Kingdom, and Europe, such as Columbia University, Johns Hopkins University, London School of Economics, and the University of Oxford.

The University is licensed by the Delaware Department of Education to award its degrees and is authorized by the Italian Ministry of Research and Instruction to operate as an institution of American higher education in Rome. John Cabot University was accredited in 2003 by the Middle States Commission on Higher Education (http://www.msche.org).

Location

John Cabot University is located in Rome, Italy, in the picturesque Trastevere neighborhood, just down the river from the Vatican; across the river from Piazza Navona, the Pantheon, and the Spanish Steps; and a short walk from the Colosseum and Roman Forum. The University has three campuses within a 15-minute walk from each other and student residences with 24/7 security next to campus. The Guarini Campus consists of a main building with three floors and an adjacent wing connected by terraces and courtyards. The property offers students a quiet atmosphere in which to study and interact, while historic, bustling Rome is just a few steps away. Surrounded by the gardens of the Accademia dei Lincei (the National Academy of Sciences, of which Galileo was an early member) and the Villa Farnesina of Raphael's famous frescoes, the Guarini Campus is buttressed by the Aurelian Wall of the Roman Empire. The Guarini Campus is approached through the Porta Settimiana, which was built in the third century and later rebuilt by Pope Alexander VI Borgia in 1498. JCU also has spacious classrooms, a cafeteria, and the Student Services office in the Tiber Campus, which is located along the banks of the Tiber River. JCU's Critelli Campus, also along the Tiber River, was opened in 2018 and houses administrative offices as well as classrooms. All three campuses are equipped with WiFi, and classrooms are furnished with multimedia equipment. JCU's fine arts and art history classes often meet at famous monuments such as the Colosseum and the Forum. In essence, all of Rome is John Cabot University's campus, and students take advantage of JCU's urban setting, meeting with friends and faculty at local cafés as well as in many of the piazzas that are tucked away within the streets of Rome's historic center.

Majors and Degrees

John Cabot University offers the Bachelor of Arts degree in 14 majors: Art History, Business Administration, Classical Studies, Communications, Economics and Finance, English Literature, History, Humanistic Studies, International Affairs, International Business, Italian Studies, Marketing, Political Science, and Psychological Science. JCU also offers a joint degree in communications with the University of Milan, as well as a dual degree in marketing with Pace University in New York City. Students may select minors in all of the major areas except international business, as well as in Creative Writing, Entrepreneurship, Legal Studies, and Philosophy. John Cabot offers the Associate of Arts degree in all major fields of study. JCU also introduced a master's degree in Art History in 2017, the first graduate degree program in art history based entirely in Rome offered by a US-accredited university.

Each of these programs is designed to offer a unique learning and living experience in a setting rich in history, culture, and geopolitical interaction. All majors are complemented by internship opportunities at the United Nations, museums, and international firms in Rome. JCU's Career Services Center offers support for students' preparation and transition into post-graduate activities, with 600+ internship and job opportunities each year. JCU's 10,000-member alumni network spans 110 countries and includes business leaders, politicians, diplomats, artists, scholars, and entrepreneurs, providing additional opportunities for graduates to continue their career development through international connections.

Academic Programs

The American higher education system encourages experimentation and breadth, particularly during the first two years of the university experience. The curricula of the University's programs are divided into two basic categories: the general distribution requirements of the first two years of study, which give the student a broad exposure to the basic disciplines of the liberal arts educational experience, and the specific requirements of each degree awarded by the University.

The general distribution requirements and other introductory courses equip the student to select an area of specialization as a degree candidate. The degree requirements include 10-12 core courses deemed by faculty members to be essential to the discipline of the degree. Other requisites include electives that support the core program and allow the student to take courses in other discipline areas of particular interest.

The academic year is divided into two semesters of 15 weeks each, beginning in late August and mid-January. In one semester, a student normally takes five courses, earning 15 credits in the semester and 30 credits in the year. Two 5-week summer sessions allow students to take one or two additional courses per summer session. To earn the Bachelor of Arts degree, a student must complete 120 credits (40 courses); to earn the Associate of Arts degree, a student must complete 60 credits (20 courses).

JCU accepts up to 60 transfer credits, including the IB diploma, AP exams, UK A-Levels, and other college-level courses.

Special programs include English language preparation for university study (ENLUS) for non-native English speakers, after which students who successfully complete the program may transfer directly into one of JCU's degree programs.

Off-Campus Programs

The Going Global program at JCU offers degree-seeking students the opportunity to study at partner universities in the United States, Mexico, Europe, Africa, Asia, and the Middle East. This opportunity contributes to educational growth and cultural awareness and helps prepare students for careers in international fields.

Academic Facilities

The Frohring Library provides the latest in online access to academic journals and indexes and is the University center for research in support of the academic programs as well as a quiet place for study and pleasure reading. The University's computer laboratories contain desktop computers (Macs and PCs) equipped with the latest software as well as printers and a full-color scanner. The University is equipped with high-speed WiFi across campus, a studio art facility, a fitness center, a cafeteria, and a digital media lab.

Costs

Tuition for 2020–21 is $25,900 and housing costs begin at $4,900 per semester.

Financial Aid

US citizens and eligible non-citizens attending JCU may apply for Title IV Federal Student Aid, including Federal Direct Subsidized, Unsubsidized, and Parent Loans for Undergraduate Students (PLUS). Academic scholarships are awarded by the University each year, based on merit and need; they include the Presidential Scholarship, the Italian Merit Scholarship, the Expansion Scholarship for Latin American students, the Dean's List Scholarship, and the assistance grant. JCU certifies enrollment for US veterans and their dependents studying on the Post-9/11 GI Bill.

Faculty

The University has a distinguished faculty of professors from around the world who are actively engaged in research. In addition to teaching, faculty members take part in academic advising and co-curricular activities, such as field trips, lectures, and seminars.

Student Government

Student Government at JCU contributes significantly to the quality of student life. A Student Senate is elected each year to represent students' interests, acting as a link between students, faculty, and staff. The Student Government works with a faculty adviser in planning social, cultural, intellectual, and sports activities to respond to students' interests and needs.

Admission Requirements

Successful applicants must have a scholastic record demonstrating a commitment to their studies and the ability to succeed at college-level work.

The previous school's documentation of the applicant's academic ability, motivation, character, and contribution to school life is very important. The University does not prescribe a fixed secondary school course of study but considers both the quality and breadth of the student's record. Results of the SAT or the ACT are required for high school students graduating from an American secondary school.

The University is open to all applicants without regard to race, national origin, religion, or gender.

For applicants coming from the US secondary school system, a standard college-preparatory program is expected. For applicants from other national systems, an essential requirement is successful completion of a secondary school program permitting university admission in the respective system. Students holding the Italian Diploma di Maturità, the International Baccalaureate, or other equivalent academic credentials may be granted advanced standing.

Applicants who did not attend an English-language secondary school or university for at least two years must demonstrate sufficient preparation in the English language. Standardized test scores, such as the Test of English as a Foreign Language (TOEFL) or the International English Language Testing System (IELTS) are required.

Application and Information

Admissions decisions are based on the review of official transcripts, results of standardized tests, the student's GPA, final examination results, a personal statement, an interview, and letters of recommendation from teachers or school counselors. A completed application must be accompanied by a non-refundable application fee of $50. Students may complete the application online or apply through the Common Application. The University has four application deadlines for fall: November 15 (Early Action), March 1 (Regular Decision), June 1 (Late Decision), and July 31 (Late Decision II, only available to students who do not require a study visa). The spring application deadlines are October 15 (Regular Decision), November 15 (Late Decision), and December 15 (Late Decision II, only available to students who do not require a study visa). Candidates are urged to submit their application and supporting documents as early as possible, as greater scholarship funds may be available.

Students may apply online at: https://students.johncabot.edu/

For additional information, prospective students should contact:

Admissions Office
John Cabot University
Caroline Critelli Guarini Campus
Piazza Giuseppe Gioachino Belli, 11
00153 Rome
Italy
Phone: 1-855-JCU-ROMA (toll free)
E-mail: admissions@johncabot.edu
Website: http://www.johncabot.edu
https://www.facebook.com/JohnCabotUniversity
http://twitter.com/JohnCabotRome
http://instagram.com/johncabotuniversity

John Cabot University is located in the picturesque Trastevere neighborhood, just down the river from the Vatican, and a short walk from the Colosseum and Roman Forum.

COLLEGE CLOSE-UPS

JOHNS HOPKINS UNIVERSITY

Krieger School of Arts and Sciences and Whiting School of Engineering

BALTIMORE, MARYLAND

The University

As America's first research institution, Johns Hopkins University is the place for the most curious students to collaborate. Since 1876, the university has made extraordinary discoveries, advanced innovative solutions, and created a place where all students can see their big ideas brought to life. Hopkins emphasizes the importance of exploration and discovery in the undergraduate experience—learning occurs through hands-on experiences across all academic disciplines and within every subject imaginable. The academic experience is built around freedom, which allows students to create their own unique interdisciplinary paths. They choose classes they are genuinely interested in, not just required to take, so there's a real sense of curiosity around learning that extends beyond the classroom setting.

Collaborative learning is fundamental to the academic culture and cross-disciplinary partnerships occur between students of all academic areas. Hopkins professors, another invaluable resource, are enthusiastic about teaching and often include undergraduates in their own groundbreaking research. Students get to know their professors and classmates the way they would at a small liberal arts college but have all of the opportunities of a major research institution with a global reach. As a part of this community, undergraduates not only work alongside experts who share their interests but they also run with projects of their own design. In fact, the university remains a national leader of research funding and students in all programs within the Krieger School of Arts & Sciences and Whiting School of Engineering gain practical experiences through research conducted both on and off campus. Every day, faculty and students together create meaningful contributions to academic discourse and make important discoveries. About 75 percent of students across all disciplines participate in research, which takes place in labs, museums, and unconventional places throughout campus and the city of Baltimore. The Homewood campus brings together students with varied interests. Diversity of thought, culture, and experiences cultivates a dynamic, open-minded environment. With over 400 student-run organizations, students find leadership opportunities and the chance to get involved on campus and in their local and global communities.

Location

Located in Baltimore, Maryland, the undergraduate Homewood campus is a traditional college campus with all the advantages of a major city just beyond its front gates. The 140-acre campus, featuring grassy quads and brick buildings, is surrounded by residential areas and neighborhoods that boast one-of-a-kind boutiques, restaurants, historic theaters, and a thriving arts and entertainment district. Baltimore's cultural and networking resources make it an extension of the classroom and an integral part of a Hopkins education. The experiences Hopkins students find in Baltimore create lasting memories and offer preparation for future success in a wide variety of industries. An entrepreneurial hub, Baltimore is the ideal environment to build professional networks, access coveted internships and careers, and get startups off the ground. Undergrads intern at major corporations, government agencies, and nonprofits and make lasting connections with help from the broader Hopkins network. Hopkins students also embrace the University's long-standing commitment to Baltimore and use their skills to make an impact on the city that becomes their second home.

Majors and Degrees

Academics at Hopkins are interdisciplinary and collaboration is encouraged—between students and faculty and across disciplines. The majority of programs combine different areas of study to enable students to make connections across academic boundaries and discover new interests. This establishes a dynamic, engaging learning environment where students from various backgrounds bring an array of perspectives to class discussions. More than 60 percent of Hopkins students pursue a double major or minor, often creating unique combinations like electrical engineering and romance languages or biomedical engineering and business. The full list of majors and minors can be found at apply.jhu.edu/majors.

Academic Programs

Undergraduates in all programs in the Krieger School of Arts & Sciences and Whiting School of Engineering gain practical experience through innovative research. Several funded programs, such as the Provost's Undergraduate Research Award and the Woodrow Wilson Undergraduate Research Fellowship, are available to give participants the chance to complete projects of their own design. Students also encounter real-world experiences—like implementing marketing plans for local companies and heading startup businesses on campus through the Center for Leadership Education—as well as classes in business, marketing, and communications, accounting and financial management, leadership studies, and entrepreneurship and management. Students can pursue their creative interests through the Center for Visual Arts, which offers nearly 40 studio courses and state-of-the-art equipment for student use. Students interested in pursuing law or medicine can choose any major/minor combination alongside a pre-law or pre-med advising track offered through the Office of Pre-Professional Advising. The biomedical engineering (BME) program at Johns Hopkins, widely regarded as one of the best in the world, is the only undergraduate limited-enrollment major.

Several combined programs are available for undergraduates who want to broaden their educational experience. The Peabody Double Degree Program allows qualified students to simultaneously earn a bachelor of music from the Johns Hopkins Peabody Institute and a B.A or B.S. from Johns Hopkins University. The Direct Matriculation Programs: Master's in International Studies and Master's in Global Health Studies, allow qualified students displaying a strong interest in either area to pursue a combined bachelor's/master's degree with the Johns Hopkins School of Advanced International Studies (SAIS) or the Johns Hopkins Bloomberg School of Public Health. The University also offers the Army ROTC program on campus and the Air Force ROTC program in cooperation with the University of Maryland, College Park.

Off-Campus Programs

Off campus, the city of Baltimore provides unique academic, cultural, and pre-professional experiences. Some classes partner with local organizations to give students practical experiences that complement classroom lectures—like documenting the history of African American life, literature, and art in Baltimore through the Billie Holiday Project, documenting the history of African American life, literature, and art in Baltimore through the Billie Holiday Project, engineering a "fish ladder" at Maryland's Bloede Dam or replicating ancient Greek pottery work at Baltimore Clayworks. Due to the vast network of Hopkins schools and facilities that extends throughout Baltimore (and abroad), undergraduates have the chance to take courses and participate in research at the other renowned divisions of Johns Hopkins University, including the Peabody Conservatory, the School of Nursing, the Bloomberg

School of Public Health, the Nitze School of Advanced International Studies, the School of Education, the Carey Business School, and the School of Medicine. In addition to local programs and opportunities, each year about one-third of our students study abroad in nearly 50 countries all over the globe. The University also participates in a cooperative program with other colleges in the Baltimore area, such as the Maryland Institute College of Art (MICA), which Hopkins partnered with to open the Johns Hopkins–MICA Film Centre.

Academic Facilities

Collaborative learning is embedded within the academic environment and many of the newest buildings were designed to foster collaboration across disciplines. Brody Learning Commons (BLC) is one of the most popular places for students to gather, study, and work together. Designed with student input, the building is directly connected to the library and contains the latest learning technology—like interactive projectors that allow students to write on walls and video teleconferencing capabilities—in an eco-friendly, energy-efficient space. The Undergraduate Teaching Labs (UTL), a 105,000-square-foot facility equipped with the latest lab technology, enables synergistic, cross-disciplinary partnerships and research opportunities. Malone Hall was built in 2014 and is a hub for the computer science department, where faculty and students work on innovative projects. The Milton S. Eisenhower Library on the Homewood campus is part of the University's Sheridan Libraries, which include the rare books collection, the Albert D. Hutzler Undergraduate Reading Room, and the George Peabody Library. Together, these libraries provide one of the most comprehensive learning resources in the world. Two on-campus creative centers provide resources for students in the arts: The Mattin Student Arts Center contains theaters, a dance studio, music practice rooms, film and digital labs, darkrooms, and art studios; the Digital Media Center offers digital tools like high-end computers and cameras that enable digital and audio composition and editing, animation, virtual painting, 3-D modeling, and workshops for programs like Adobe After Effects. Less than a 10 minute-walk from campus, our FastForward U innovation hub allows student entrepreneurs to collaborate, strategize, prototype, and get their ideas off the ground with funding opportunities. Additionally, a new Student Center is being built and expected to open in 2024 as a nonacademic, campus social space.

Costs

Costs for 2019-20 were $55,350 for tuition and $16,310 for room and meals, plus personal expenses like books and travel. (Expenses such as travel and room and meals vary based on choices.)

Financial Aid

Johns Hopkins University's philosophy is anchored around a simple approach: Enrolling the brightest minds. Period. The University is need-blind for domestic students (including those with DACA and undocumented status) and meets 100% of demonstrated need for every admitted student without loans. Students who are primed to thrive on a campus where diversity of thought drives our academic culture shouldn't be limited by their family's ability to pay. With the potential to graduate debt-free, equipped with an education that opens doors, Hopkins students have the freedom to boldly explore ways to apply their knowledge and talents. More details, including financial aid application requirements and deadlines and net price calculator tools, are available at finaid.jhu.edu.

Faculty

As a global research university, Johns Hopkins attracts esteemed faculty. Professors are enthusiastic about teaching, often including undergraduates in their own groundbreaking research, and are always accessible to advise and assist students. It's not unusual for faculty to brainstorm research ideas with students over coffee, debate philosophical theories during office hours, and mentor students throughout their four years on campus and beyond.

Admission Requirements

Johns Hopkins seeks students who are eager to take advantage of the resources and opportunities at the University and who will contribute to the campus community. The student's academic character, intellectual curiosity, impact and initiative, and extracurricular involvement play a significant role in application review. A student's intellectual interests and accomplishments are of primary importance, and the admissions committee considers each applicant's scholastic record, standardized test results, essays, and recommendations from secondary school officials. In addition to the application and the Hopkins supplement, first-year applicants are required to submit a school-specific essay, other required documents include: two teacher recommendations, the secondary school report, and scores on the SAT or the ACT (unofficial test scores accepted; learn more at apply.jhu.edu/testing). The University enrolls a first-year class of approximately 1,300 scholars from across the globe. In addition, transfer students from other colleges and universities are admitted to the sophomore and junior classes. Prospective students should refer to apply.jhu.edu/apply for more information about the application process.

Application and Information

Johns Hopkins accepts the Coalition for College application and the Common Application both with a Johns Hopkins supplement. Students who are certain Johns Hopkins is the place for them should consider applying under the Early Decision plan. This requires that the application be submitted by November 1. The deadline for the Regular Decision application is usually January 1. (Note: Deadlines can vary slightly from year to year; see apply.jhu.edu/apply for specific dates.) Notification is given by December 15 for those applying under the Early Decision plan and by April 1 for Regular Decision students. Students wishing to enroll in the biomedical engineering (BME) program must indicate BME as their first choice major on their application. Students applying to the Direct Matriculation Program: Master's in International Studies or Direct Matriculation Program: Master's in Global Health Studies (DMP) must submit an additional application and essay to be considered. First-year students who apply to the BME major or Direct Matriculation Program receive notification at the time of their admission to Johns Hopkins University. Students interested in pursuing a research project of their own design can also apply to the Woodrow Wilson Undergraduate Research Fellowship, which awards up to $10,000 to arts and sciences undergraduates. The Wilson Fellowship application deadline is in January and the date varies slightly from year to year.

Office of Undergraduate Admissions
Johns Hopkins University
Mason Hall
3400 N. Charles Street
Baltimore, Maryland 21218-2683
Phone: 410-516-8171
Fax: 410-516-6025
E-mail: gotojhu@jhu.edu
Website: https://apply.jhu.edu

Johns Hopkins undergrads walking to class on the Homewood campus.

LINFIELD COLLEGE

McMINNVILLE, OREGON

The College

Linfield University (1858) is an independent, coeducational, residential, university featuring robust programs throughout the liberal arts and sciences, as well as pre-professional programs dedicated to providing an educational environment conducive to learning and participation. There are 1,500 full-time students on the McMinnville campus. These students come primarily from the thirteen Western states (nineteen states overall) but also from nineteen other countries. Students of color make up 34 percent of the student body, and 3 percent of students are international. Most students are between 18 and 22. Linfield is primarily residential, with fifteen residence halls, each accommodating between 10 and 100 residents. Each hall establishes its own calendar of social, educational, and recreational events throughout the year. Students who reside on campus eat their meals in the College dining hall. Apartments are available for upper-division students. Social clubs, professional organizations, four sororities and three fraternities, service clubs, and almost forty other organizations, including a new marching band, play an important role in the daily life of a Linfield student. Linfield's winning athletics tradition fosters participation at all levels of competition. Women compete in intercollegiate basketball, cross-country, golf, lacrosse, soccer, softball, swimming, tennis, indoor and outdoor track and field, and volleyball. Men compete in intercollegiate baseball, basketball, cross-country, football, golf, soccer, swimming, tennis, and indoor and outdoor track and field. Linfield also has an extensive and active year-round intramural program.

Linfield hosts the Oregon Nobel Laureate Symposium, one of five such symposiums worldwide. At each symposium, several Nobel laureates come to share their backgrounds and expertise within the context of a basic theme. The Linfield–Good Samaritan School of Nursing, an academic unit of the College at its Portland campus, prepares students for careers in nursing. In 2006, the Portland campus programs became open only to transfer admission and in 2021 moved to a new facility on twenty acres. The new campus will provide additional opportunities, including larger experiential learning labs.

Location

Located in McMinnville, 40 miles southwest of Portland, Linfield College is a leader in the cultural, educational, and recreational events of the fast-growing community of 35,000. Linfield is situated on 189 acres with most classrooms no more than a 10-minute walk from any of the twenty-two on-campus apartment buildings and residence halls. With most students living on campus, Linfield offers a welcoming and lively community.

Coffeehouses, cinemas, boutiques, a community theater, the Evergreen Air and Space Museum (including an IMAX theater and water park), bowling alleys, and a wide variety of restaurants are within walking distance for Linfield students. The central Oregon coast is an hour to the west, and the outdoor activity areas of the Oregon Cascade Range, including year-round skiing at Mount Hood, are two hours to the east. Salem, the state capital of Oregon, is 25 miles to the southeast, and Eugene is 80 miles south. Rainfall in western Oregon averages 42 inches annually and the winter temperature averages 41°F.

Majors and Degrees

Linfield offers nearly 50 major and minor academic programs across the three units of the university. Within the College of Arts and Sciences, students may pursue anthropology, applied physics, applied physics: engineering focus, biochemistry and molecular biology, biology, chemistry, communication arts, computer science, creative writing, digital art, economics, elementary education, environmental studies, French, global and cultural studies: Latin American/Latinex studies, global and cultural studies: French and Francophone Studies, global and cultural studies: Japanese studies, history, exercise science, intercultural communication, international relations, Japanese, journalism and media studies, law rights and justice, literature, mathematics, mathematics: data science focus, music, philosophy, physics, physics: material science focus, political science, psychology, public health: health promotiuon, religious studies, secondary education, sociology, Spanish, studio art, theatre arts and wine studies. Within the School of Business, students may pursue accounting, finance, international business, management, marketing, sport management. The School of Nursing offers a Bachelor of Science in Nursing. Most academic majors can also be studied as a minor. Additional minors include entrepreneurship, Chinese studies, leadership and ethics across the disciplines and neuroscience. The University has programs to prepare students for advanced study in any health profession, including medicine, as well as law.

Academic Programs

The academic year is divided into two 15-week semesters (fall and spring) and a four-week winter term in January. The January Term offers regular departmental courses and off-campus and international study. Academic courses are assigned 1–5 semester credit hours each; 125 credits are required for a B.A. or a B.S. degree. Students divide their time equally among required general education courses, a major area of study, and elective subjects. The Linfield Curriculum courses, selected to provide a solid foundation in the liberal arts, require students to take 3 semester hours in each of the six Modes of Inquiry as well as one upper-division course in one of these areas. These Modes of Inquiry are as follows: Vital Past; Ultimate Questions; Individuals, Systems, and Societies; Natural World; Creative Studies; and Quantitative Reasoning. In addition, students are required to take a writing-intensive course, a course addressing global pluralisms, and a course dealing with United States pluralism. Individually designed majors are available with faculty approval. Students majoring in a foreign language spend an academic year in a country in which the language being studied is the native tongue.

Through the college's English Language and Culture Program, Linfield offers courses designed to help international students whose native language is not English to achieve competence in academic and social English skills, so that they may work effectively in their undergraduate classes at Linfield.

Off-Campus Programs

Off-campus educational experiences include the Semester Abroad program, involving four months of study in Australia, Austria, Chile, China, Ecuador, England, France, Germany, Hong Kong, Ireland, Japan, Korea, New Zealand, Norway, and Spain. Transportation for the first round-trip is included in the cost of tuition, and most of these study programs cost the same as a semester on campus. January Term study-abroad programs for four weeks are also offered. Recent offerings included Health Care in Kenya; China's Solutions to Energy Issues in the Twenty-first Century; Art and Visual Culture of Catalonia, Spain; and Australia: From Colony to Asian Power.

Academic Facilities

In recent years, the College has opened two residence halls, six apartment buildings, the James F. Miller Fine Arts Center, the

Marshall Theatre and communication arts facility, the Vivian A. Bull Center for Music, and the Nicholson Library. The library covers 56,000 square feet and combines traditional collections of books and journals with the new and changing digital and electronic technology to provide access to the web and web-based designs. The studio theater has an audience seating capacity of up to 140 and includes space for set construction and design.

In 2011, Linfield reopened the former library to provide new classroom and office space for the departments of business, economics, English, and philosophy. This state-of-the-art facility, T. J. Day Hall, includes the Program for Liberal Arts and Civic Engagement (PLACE). PLACE connects the Linfield student experience with civic discourse and real-world application. T. J. Day Hall is Linfield's first LEED-certified Gold building, underscoring the University's commitment to sustainability and conservation.

Murdock and Graf Halls house the biology, chemistry, and physics departments and up-to-date laboratories and equipment. Other facilities include art galleries and studios, an experimental psychology lab, dance and music studios, a preschool, and a 425-seat auditorium that houses a three-manual, 48-rank Casavant pipe organ. Linfield students benefit from a communications and technology network that includes phone service, voice mail, e-mail, and wireless Internet connections in each residence hall room. In addition, there is wireless access in the library and all other areas of the campus.

The Health and Physical Education/Recreation Complex houses three gymnasiums; weight rooms; fitness laboratories with a hydrostatic weighing tank, a metabolic and pulmonary measuring system, and an electrocardiovascular exercise ECG system; an eight-lane, 25-yard indoor pool; handball and racquetball courts; classrooms; offices; and a 28,000-square-foot field house.

Costs

For 2020–21, tuition and fees are $44,670 per two-semester year, room and board is $12,930.

Financial Aid

Eligibility for most of Linfield's assistance programs is based on need as determined by a federally approved needs analysis processor. The only form required for need-based programs is the Free Application for Federal Student Aid (FAFSA). Linfield participates in the federal grant, loan, and work programs, and other forms of financial assistance on the basis of demonstrated need.

The University awards scholarships to full-time students based on scholastic achievement, independent of financial need. These academic scholarships vary from 30 to 60 percent of tuition. A number of criteria are used when determining scholarships, including grade point average, strength of curriculum, and standardized test scores, if submitted. Linfield sponsors special scholarships for National Merit finalists. The University also sponsors an annual Scholarship and Visit Weekend program in February. Participation is limited to high school seniors who meet particular academic requirements and apply by December 1. Each academic department offers prizes ranging from $12,000 to $20,000, divided over the student's four years at Linfield. Scholarships are also available to students from the departments of music, theater, and communication who demonstrate outstanding leadership and community service. Financial assistance for non–U.S. citizens is limited to partial-tuition scholarships and the opportunity to work part-time on campus.

Faculty

There are 137 faculty members, each of whom is committed to undergraduate teaching and scholarship. Eighty-eight percent have doctoral or other terminal degrees within their field. The student-faculty ratio on the McMinnville campus is 11:1, and faculty members serve as academic advisers. There are no teaching assistants.

Student Government

Students have a significant voice in establishing and changing University policies and regulations. The Student Senate, chosen through campus elections, is the focus of student opinion and debate. Students are represented on most University governing councils and committees with faculty members and trustees, and they are encouraged to express and implement their ideas on academic or extracurricular matters.

Admission Requirements

Admission to Linfield University is selective. Admission is granted to students who are likely to grow and succeed in a personal and challenging liberal arts environment. Each applicant is judged on individual merit, based on high school performance, a writing sample, recommendations from teachers and counselors, precollege standardized test results (ACT or SAT), if submitted, and the depth and quality of an applicant's involvement in community and school activities. Linfield is a member of the Common Application. Students may opt to pursue Linfield's test optional admission process, as well.

International students whose education has been in a language other than English must submit certified English translations of their academic work. Proficiency in English is required, as demonstrated by an official English proficiency exam score report.

Application and Information

The early action deadline is November 1 (with notification by January 15) and the regular decision priority deadline is February 1 (with notification by April 1).

Interviews are not required, but students are encouraged to visit. Appointments should be made in advance and can be requested online at http://www.linfield.edu/. The Linfield website provides students with information on academic programs, student life, and athletics.

Interested students are encouraged to contact:

Office of Admission
Linfield University
900 SE Baker Street
McMinnville, Oregon 97128
Phone: 503-883-2213
800-640-2287 (toll-free)
Fax: 503-883-2472
E-mail: admission@linfield.edu
Website: http://www.linfield.edu/admission
https://www.facebook.com/LinfieldCollege/
https://twitter.com/linfieldcollege
https://www.instagram.com/linfieldcollege/

Linfield University's McMinnville campus is located 1 hour southwest of Portland, Oregon's largest city, on nearly 200 acres. Nearly sixty buildings, many built in Georgian colonial style, house forty academic departments among a grove of oak trees.

COLLEGE CLOSE-UPS

LOYOLA UNIVERSITY MARYLAND

BALTIMORE, MARYLAND

COLLEGE CLOSE-UPS

The University

Loyola University Maryland's time-tested, distinctly taught Jesuit approach to education allows students to master the tools and develop the traits needed to learn, lead, and serve in our diverse and ever-changing world. Loyola is everything Jesuit education should be: rigorous, values oriented, communal, and spiritually uplifting. Your experiences here will be some of the most transformative of your life—and some of the most rewarding. They will help you become even more than you knew you could be: more knowledgeable, capable, confident, and committed to changing lives—others' and your own. You'll be prepared and eager to face whatever the future holds in your life and career that follow.

With just under 4,000 undergraduates from 40 states, 40+ countries, and six continents, Loyola is big enough to inspire and challenge you, yet small enough to be welcoming, personal, and accessible. Surrounded by people from different backgrounds and with diverse interests, you will be immersed in an experience that is sure to be rich and guaranteed to surprise you. You will feel comfortable taking risks, asking bold questions, and trying new things. And you will forge deep, meaningful relationships with your peers, professors, coaches, classmates, and neighbors.

As a Loyola student, you will embrace new perspectives and expand your possibilities, shatter your preconceptions, find your joy, and divine your truths. So that when you graduate, you'll be ready: Ready to meet the complex demands of today—and to anticipate and adapt to the needs of tomorrow. Ready to forge a career that's true to who you are. Readyto build a life you love and create the world you imagine. More than ready. Loyola ready.

Location

Loyola's beautiful Evergreen campus is in a residential area of North Baltimore, five miles from the city's Inner Harbor area. This location offers students the best of both worlds: the advantage of quiet residential living on 80 wooded acres that offer grassy quadrangles, Gothic-style buildings, nationally-ranked residence halls, and state-of-the-art classrooms and facilities—all within a few minutes of the attractions and amenities of city life. Make no mistake; with 160,000 students at 14 universities, Baltimore is very much a college town. The fourth-largest metropolitan area in the United States, Baltimore/Washington D.C. offers a wide variety of theaters, museums, professional and intercollegiate sports events, and historical points of interest. Loyola attracts the types of students who are also attracted to Baltimore, people eager to shape their lives—and their city—according to their ideals. Whether you dream of forming your own tech startup, opening a craft brewery, or becoming a social activist in a region that's ripe for change, Baltimore is the ideal place to begin.

Majors and Degrees

Loyola offers more than 30 majors and more than 45 minors. The Bachelor of Arts degree is awarded in art history, classical civilization, classics, communication, comparative cultures and literary studies, computer science, economics, elementary education, English, fine arts, French, global studies, history, philosophy, political science, psychology, sociology, Spanish, speech-language-hearing sciences, theology, and writing. The Bachelor of Business Administration degree is awarded in accounting, business economics, finance, information systems, international business, management, and marketing. The Bachelor of Science degree is awarded in biology, chemistry, computer science, data science, engineering (with concentrations in mechanical, computer, electrical, and materials), forensic studies, mathematics, statistics, and physics.

Academic Programs

At Loyola, you won't have to choose between focused, effective career preparation and the profound, life-long benefits of a liberal arts education. In fact, it's a false choice. Because the skills that will give you the security in the new world of work are the very capabilities that define us as human beings. There's a simple reason a comprehensive liberal arts experience has been the Jesuit education standard for hundreds of years: It works. No other academic foundation better prepares you to meet the various and complex challenges you will face in your life—today, tomorrow, and 20 years from now.

The curriculum at Loyola is divided into three parts: the core, the major, and electives. The core contains courses essential to the liberal arts foundation of a Jesuit education: a classical or foreign language, literature, writing, natural and applied science, social science, fine arts, history, philosophy, ethics, diversity, and theology, and these courses are completed by all students throughout their years. Majors enable students to pursue their specialized area of study in depth. Electives give students the opportunity to broaden their intellectual and cultural background in areas of special interest. Through service-learning, research, practicums, field experience, internships, and independent study, students extend classroom learning throughout their coursework and obtain valuable skills and experience.

Messina, Loyola's first-year experience, is designed to help students adjust quickly to college-level work and forge a clear path to success at Loyola and in the life and career that will follow. Messina offers a similarly distinctive and powerful beginning, an opportunity to explore a wide range of academic disciplines, appreciate their interconnectedness, and take to heart the importance of learning in a student's personal and intellectual growth.

University Programs

Pre-Professional Programs: To prepare for graduate study, students may enroll in one of three pre-professional programs: pre-health, pre-medical, or pre-law. Loyola's Pre-Law Advisory Program guides, supports, and prepares students of every major who attend law school. Loyola graduates average a 90% law school acceptance rate, with several students accepted in Top 25 programs each year and a significant percentage accepted in Top 50 programs.

Loyola's Pre-Health Programs prepare students for careers in a variety of medical specialties and nursing—while providing the support, mentorship, and access to internships and real-world experience students need for professional school. That's why our graduates are accepted at rates that are much higher than the national average. Loyola graduates averaged a 77% medical school acceptance rate between 2015-2019 (national annual average is 39%) and a 76% dental school acceptance rate (national annual average is 41%).

Study Abroad: Nearly two-thirds of students participate in Loyola's nationally ranked study abroad program, which includes programs and exchanges taught in English, total immersion programs taught in the host country's native language, and combinations of the two. Accommodating all majors, Loyola offers study abroad programs in Accra, Ghana; Amsterdam, Netherlands; Athens, Greece; Auckland, New Zealand; Bangkok, Thailand; Beijing, China; Berlin, Germany;

Budapest, Hungary; Cape Town, South Africa; Copenhagen, Denmark; Cork, Ireland; Dubai, United Arab Emirates; Glasgow, Scotland; Leuven, Belgium; Lyon, France; Madrid, Spain; Melbourne, Australia; Montpellier, France; Newcastle, England; Osaka, Ja-pan; Paris, France; Rome, Italy; Santiago, Dominican Republic; Santiago, Chile; Seoul, South Korea; Singapore; and Stockholm, Sweden. Loyola also offers summer and winter study tours and assists students in applying to a variety of non-Loyola affiliated international study programs each year.

Mentorship & Guidance: Nothing sets Loyola apart more than the role mentorship and guidance play in your experience. With a faculty-student ratio of approximately 12:1 and an average class size of 20, students are individually taught—and taught as individuals. Our 350+ full-time faculty are committed teachers and advisors, scholars, and experts and in their fields. Loyola professors push students to the limits of their intellect and imagination. In fact, few things will transform your life as much as your relationships with your professors. They are your guides, coaches, mentors, personal advisors, and champions. Your confidants when you need a listening ear. Your compass when you lose your way. They know what you're capable of—sometimes even better than you do—and are personally invested in your success. Their insights, guidance, encouragement, and faith in your potential will stay with you for the rest of your life.

Costs

For 2020-21, tuition for all undergraduate students is $49,700 per year. Housing costs are $10,580 or $11,920, de-pending upon the specific residence hall in which the student lives. The base meal plan for first-year residential students is $5,240 per year and student fees are estimated at $1,400.

Financial Aid

Loyola believes that the cost of a high-quality education should not be a deterrent to prospective applicants. In recognition of the concern students and families have with finding adequate resources to meet these costs, our financial aid program is designed to make Loyola affordable and accessible for all qualified students and their families. Approximately 92 percent of all undergraduates receive some form of aid from federal, state, institutional, and private sources, and our average financial aid package for first time students is $35,650.

To apply for need-based financial aid, students are required to submit the Free Application for Federal Student Aid (FAFSA) and CSS Profile Application. All applicants (first-year, transfer, and international) are eligible to receive merit-based scholarships, and every student who completes an application for admission is automatically considered for merit scholarships. Students are notified of their merit scholarship award at the time of admission. Loyola is also pleased to offer both need-based financial aid and merit-based scholarships to undocumented and Deferred Action for Child-hood Arrivals (DACA) students.

Faculty

With a faculty-student ratio of approximately 12:1 and an average class size of 20, students are individually taught—and taught as individuals. Our 359 full-time faculty are committed teachers and advisors, scholars, and experts and in their fields; 70 percent are tenured or on the tenure track. Loyola professors push students to the limits of their intellect and imagination. Beyond academic rigor, the cornerstone of intellectual life at Loyola is relationships between faculty and students: relationships that help students discover strengths, that instill confidence—and that celebrate and champion achievement. Ask any Loyola graduate what made the difference in their academic journey, and they'll not only say it was their professors, but they'll likely name a name and share a story, a specific example, of a meaningful relationship with a faculty member who became a mentor.

Admission Requirements

The admission evaluation at Loyola combines an analysis of academic information submitted along with a review of recommendations, the record of extracurricular involvement and evidence of special talent, leadership, and service. The admission committee does not use a formula or have strict cutoffs. Instead, the admission office's goal is to conduct a balanced and individual review, taking a number of factors into account. Submission of SAT and ACT scores is optional for all first-year applicants, excluding home-school students. Students may apply early action (nonbinding) or regular decision (nonbinding).

First-year students apply online using the Common Application and are required to submit the following materials: official high school transcript(s), high school counselor recommendation letter, high school teacher, recommendation letter, SAT/ACT scores (optional), personal essay, and $60 application fee. Transfer students apply online using the Common Application for transfer students and are required to submit the following material: the college report/ Registrar's Report from each institution attended, official high school transcript(s), official college transcript(s) including current semester courses, and $60 application fee.

Application and Information

Interested students seeking to enroll at Loyola may apply online using the Common Application. Each applicant must submit a school counselor letter of recommendation, a teacher letter of recommendation, and a personal statement. Applicants for financial aid must file the Free Application for Federal Student Aid (FAFSA) to be considered for federal student aid in addition to the CSS Profile application to be considered for all forms of institutionally funded need-based aid. A $60 application fee must accompany the application for admission. Learn more at https://www.loyola.edu/undergraduate

For additional information, students are encouraged to contact:

Office of Undergraduate Admission
Loyola University Maryland
4501 North Charles Street
Baltimore, Maryland 21210-2699
Phone: 410-617-5012
800-221-9107 (toll-free)
Website: http://www.loyola.edu/undergraduate
http://www.facebook.com/LoyolaMarylandAdmission
https://twitter.com/LOYOLAdmission
https://instagram.com/LOYOLAdmission

Loyola University Maryland has a vibrant and active student community. Whether you're looking for adventure, leadership, professional experiences, friendship, or the latest foodie trends, we're confident that Loyola has a place for you.

LUTHER COLLEGE

DECORAH, IOWA

LUTHER COLLEGE

The College

Luther College is home to more than 1,900 undergraduates who explore big questions and take action to benefit people, communities, and society. Luther's 60+ academic programs, experiential approach to learning, and welcoming community inspire students to learn actively, live purposefully, and lead courageously for a lifetime of impact.

Ranked among the nation's top 100 liberal arts colleges, Luther is a Phi Beta Kappa campus in the Lutheran tradition (ELCA). It is nationally recognized for its engaging Paideia program and commitment to sustainability, as well as its number of Rhodes and Fulbright scholars and percentage of students who study abroad.

Location

Decorah, a warm and vibrant town of 8,000 people, is situated in the bluff country of the Midwest's Driftless Region. Featured in Smithsonian Magazine's annual list of the 20 best small towns to visit in America and named on Forbes' "America's Prettiest Towns" list, Decorah boasts three waterfalls and hundreds of miles of hiking and biking trails. The Upper Iowa River, which borders Luther's campus, offers great kayaking, canoeing, tubing, and fishing. Named a top-ten college town by Business Insider, Decorah has a charming downtown with fun coffee shops, restaurants, shops, and more.

The Decorah region is the perfect place to learn outside the classroom. Its stunning natural areas—from the bluffs, to the river, to the woods and prairies—offer lots of places to conduct field research. Nursing and pre-med students gain clinical experience at medical centers in town and at Mayo Clinic in Rochester, Minn., just a short drive away. Management, accounting, and visual communication students intern at local businesses. Future educators student-teach at area schools, and future social workers get involved with various social services in town.

All of this is possible because the close-knit and supportive Decorah community—home to many Luther alumni—is eager to welcome, mentor, and employ Luther students.

Academic Programs

Luther offers 60+ majors and pre-professional programs that prepare students with deep expertise in their area of interest as well as broad knowledge that helps them think in new and unexpected ways. By learning across disciplines, in small classes, and through spirited discussion-based courses, students learn to build the collaborative skills, social conscience, and critical thinking abilities that set them apart in work and life. From day one, classes at Luther encourage students to innovate, reflect, communicate, problem-solve, and lead—ultimately allowing them to live with meaning and purpose.

A Luther education isn't limited to the classroom. From the woods and river and fields on campus, to life-changing study-away trips, to meaningful internships and work-study positions, students constantly grow their knowledge base and realize new interests.

Luther is big enough to offer the type of research opportunities found in graduate schools but small enough to ensure that undergraduate students can take part. In the sciences and mathematics, students join professors in the labs and field, help design and run experiments, and publish and present findings. In the humanities and social sciences, students also publish and present work, take part in sociology and psychology studies and archaeological digs, and initiate creative projects, like producing a short film.

Luther faculty believe the best education connects students with global issues and helps them engage with the larger world. The college offers study-away programs in more than 25 countries—from Malta to New Zealand to Tanzania—and in several domestic locations. Luther consistently ranks among the top 20 baccalaureate colleges in the nation for the percentage of students studying abroad.

More than two-thirds of Luther students complete at least one internship, externship, or paid work experience before graduating. These opportunities enable them to see academic interests in the context of the working world, investigate career fields, and build professional networks and resumes.

Luther offers one of the largest and most respected undergraduate music programs in the country, with more than 40 percent of the student body participating each year in five choirs, three bands, three orchestras, and two jazz bands—in addition to opera, composition, handbell choir, faculty-directed chamber groups, applied lessons, and master classes.

Luther student musicians have plenty of opportunities for meaningful performances, from Austria to Brazil. Luther touring groups have been sharing the gift of music with audiences across the country and around the globe for more than 130 years. The college's renowned Christmas at Luther performance involves multiple choirs and instrumental ensembles and regularly airs on television, radio, and online. Each spring, Luther's Music Department presents a fully staged and costumed opera, in addition to performing musical theatre, operetta, and opera scenes in the fall and January terms.

Luther is committed to the idea that music is important in the lives of all students. Any student, regardless of major, is eligible to audition for renewable music scholarships and ensembles.

Costs

For 2020-21, the comprehensive fee is $55,720, which includes tuition, room, board, a technology fee, and a health and wellbeing fee. Private music lessons are $550 per credit. It is estimated that an additional $1,040 is adequate for books.

Financial Aid

Luther strives to make a college education affordable for all students through scholarships, work-study opportunities, loans, and grants. In 2019–20, the college offered more than $50 million in financial aid. All students who are legally eligible to work in the United States are offered a work study job if they apply for one, and nearly three-quarters of students work on campus.

Student Life

Students come to Luther from cities, small towns, and 74 countries around the world. They tend to be friendly, funny, open, adventurous, and committed to social justice and the environment. And although they are motivated to achieve, they create a campus community that is warm, welcoming, and supportive.

Ninety percent of students live on campus, which is part of what creates such an engaged student body and deep sense of community. Luther offers 80+ student organizations, from mock trial to PRIDE to improv and dance troupes, as well as a student newspaper and radio station.

A constant stream of performers—including, recently, Lizzo and Pentatonix—lectures, films, music recitals, athletic games, and other events ensures that there's always something to do on campus.

Luther is a member of NCAA Division III, a non-scholarship division of college athletics. Student-athletes who choose to attend

Luther are seeking balance between an outstanding academic experience and the opportunity to participate in a nationally recognized sports program. The college offers 19 NCAA Division III teams and has won 246 conference titles. Luther student athletes have won 29 individual national championships, 42 NCAA Postgraduate Scholarships, 69 CoSIDA Academic All-American honors, 342 All-American honors, and 2,276 All-Academic team honors.

From Florida to Arizona to Europe, Luther student athletes travel far and wide to compete against the very best. While they're at Luther, they train in top-notch facilities, including a top-of-the-line synthetic turf and pad system in Carlson Stadium, a stunning on-campus cross country course, newly renovated tennis courts and softball/baseball stadiums, a golf performance center with a TrackMan launch monitor, an aquatic center with an eight-lane competition pool with diving wells, and many other assets.

More than 45 percent of Luther students play intramural sports. From pickleball to sand volleyball to Wii bowling and badminton, students relieve stress, have fun, and make new friends through Luther's 30+ intramural teams and leagues. Students can also join club teams for men's and women's rugby and Ultimate Frisbee.

Luther graduates have stellar employment and graduate school placement rates. More than 98 percent of 2018 Luther graduates report being employed, continuing their education, doing service work, or not intentionally seeking employment by the end of 2018.

Luther alumni live in more than 100 countries and in all 50 states. They lead and work at employers from Mayo Clinic to Google to Habitat for Humanity to the United Nations. Each year, Luther's campus doubles as enthusiastic alumni return to celebrate Homecoming.

Students share in the governance of the College and participate in social and cultural programming. They have full membership on most College committees, majority representation in the Community Assembly, and nonvoting representation on the Board of Regents.

Faculty

There are 175 full-time faculty members; 95 percent hold a Ph.D., first professional, or other terminal degree. The student-faculty ratio is 11:1.

Admission Requirements

Admission is selective. An applicant must be a graduate of an accredited high school and have completed at least four years of English, three years of mathematics, three years of social science, and two units of natural science. It is strongly recommended that the applicant have at least two years of a foreign language. Transfer students may enroll at the beginning of the fall or spring semester or the January term.

Application and Information

An application, SAT or ACT scores, an educator's reference, a personal statement/essay, and a transcript of previous academic work are required for admission. On-campus interviews are recommended but not required. For more information about Luther, students should contact:

Admissions Office
Luther College
700 College Drive
Decorah, Iowa 52101-1042
Phone: 563-387-1287
800-458-8437 (toll-free)
Fax: 563-387-2159
E-mail: admissions@luther.edu (admissions)
finaid@luther.edu (financial aid)
global@luther.edu (international)
Website: http://admissions.luther.edu
http://www.facebook.com/luthercollege1861
http://twitter.com/luthercollege

Luther College students learn in a community that emphasizes challenging academics, a world-class music program, competitive athletics, and opportunities to put their classroom learning to the test through internships, independent research, and study abroad. Typically, 97 percent of Luther graduates are employed, attending graduate school, or engaged in an internship or volunteer work within eight months of graduation.

MANHATTAN COLLEGE

RIVERDALE, NEW YORK

The College

Manhattan College has more than sixty programs that build upon a strong liberal arts foundation and offer professional preparation in business, education and health, liberal arts, science, and engineering. Learning extends beyond the classroom through internships in New York City and beyond.

The College is one of only a few U.S. colleges to have chapters of all five of these distinguished national honor societies: Phi Beta Kappa, Beta Gamma Sigma, Kappa Delta Pi, Sigma Xi, and Beta Pi.

In MONEY magazine's annual ranking of the most transformative colleges in America, Manhattan College is #1, "thanks to its proven ability to change the lives of its students."Following in the Lasallian Catholic tradition, many Manhattan College students actively define their commitment to social justice by balancing their traditional lifestyles with immersion and service experiences around the city, country, and world.

Following in the Lasallian Catholic tradition, many Manhattan College students actively define their commitment to social justice by balancing their traditional lifestyles with immersion and service experiences around the city, country, and world.

Each year, Campus Ministry and Social Action (CMSA) organizes several L.O.V.E. programs (Lasallian Outreach Volunteer Experience), which give students the opportunity to travel to some of the world's poorest areas in New Orleans, West Virginia, Kenya, Ecuador, and the Dominican Republic to volunteer with people of very different socioeconomic backgrounds.

Closer to home, the Lasallian Collegians volunteer on campus and in New York City by arranging school blood drives, toy drives, soup kitchen trips, and food runs. In addition, the Arches offers freshman students the opportunity to live in a community in Lee Hall and take one class together each semester of their freshman year that incorporates cultural excursions and service projects in New York City. Many former Arches students say the friendships they made through the program last well beyond graduation.

The tight-knit College community is comprised of 3,894 students. With a 13:1 student-to-faculty ratio, professors know students personally and care about their success. The majority of students live on the traditional collegiate campus, just a subway ride from midtown Manhattan.

Location

Manhattan College's 23-acre campus is located 10 miles north of midtown Manhattan in the suburban Riverdale section of the Bronx, about a mile from Westchester County. The College is located in the world's greatest cultural hub, where renowned museums and landmarks serve as off-campus classrooms. Students have access to internship and job opportunities at some of the country's most prestigious companies. From Fortune 500 companies to independent start-ups, students can find an organization in New York City to support their career goals.

Majors and Degrees

Business: The O'Malley School of Business, accredited by AACSB International, has programs leading to a Bachelor of Science in Business Administration degree with majors in accounting, business analytics, computer information systems, economics, finance, global business studies, management, and marketing.

In addition, Manhattan College also offers the following graduate programs: the Bachelor of Science in Professional Accounting/Master of Business Administration and the Bachelor of Science in Business/Master of Business Administration, which offer students the opportunity to complete a five-year multiple award program.

Education and Health: The School of Education and Health offers a curriculum leading to a Bachelor of Arts degree in childhood education, childhood/special education (dual program), and adolescent education. The kinesiology curriculum leads to a Bachelor of Science degree in physical education and exercise science. The health curriculum leads to a Bachelor of Science degree in public health. Curricula in radiological and health sciences lead to a Bachelor of Science in radiation therapy or nuclear medicine technology. In addition, the School of Education and Health offers the five-year childhood/special education program, which allows the student to receive a bachelor's and master's degree with eligibility to pursue certification for grades 1–6 in regular and special education. The School of Education and Health also offers master's degrees and professional diplomas in school counseling, mental health counseling, special education, and school building leadership. All programs are approved by the New York State Education Department and accredited by the Teacher Education Accreditation Council (TEAC).

Engineering: The School of Engineering has a well-deserved reputation as one of the best college engineering schools in the nation and offers programs leading to a Bachelor of Science degree in chemical, civil, computer, electrical, and mechanical engineering. The program is fully accredited by the Educational Accreditation Commission of ABET. Graduate programs are also available in chemical, civil, computer, electrical, environmental, and mechanical engineering.

Liberal Arts: The curriculum of the School of Liberal Arts provides programs that lead to a Bachelor of Arts or Bachelor of Science degree with majors in the humanities and the social sciences, including art history, communication, economics, English, French, political science, history, labor studies, philosophy, psychology, religious studies, sociology, and Spanish. Interdisciplinary majors include international studies, peace studies, sound studies, environmental science, and urban studies.

Science: In the School of Science, programs lead to a Bachelor of Science or Bachelor of Arts degree with majors in biochemistry, biology, chemistry, computer science, environmental science, mathematics, and physics. Pre-medical, pre-dental, and pre–veterinary studies programs are also available. In addition, Manhattan College also offers the following graduate programs: Applied Mathematics–Data Analytics and Computer Science.

Academic Programs

The core curriculum shared by the Schools of Liberal Arts and Science studies some of the vital works of humankind, explores new ideas, examines the meaning of scientific experimentation, and encourages a student to develop his or her thinking and leadership abilities. The major programs offer advanced work in specific humanistic and scientific disciplines and opportunities to work on research projects in collaboration with faculty scholars.

In the School of Engineering, all engineering students follow a common core curriculum during the first two years and choose a major at the beginning of the junior year. Each curriculum includes a generous selection of courses in basic sciences, the engineering sciences, humanistic studies, and mathematics.

The O'Malley School of Business prepares students for positions of executive responsibility in business, government, and nonprofit organizations. The business curriculum is based on a strong commitment to liberal education and is well balanced between professional business courses, humanities, sciences, and social sciences. This is a reflection of the school's belief that executives should be broadly educated and should involve themselves, as well as their organizations, in efforts to solve social problems.

The School of Education and Health prepares students for teaching, counseling, and health professions. Students complete the College's core curriculum in liberal arts and sciences and then complete a major in various programs in the school's three departments: education, kinesiology, and radiological and health professions. All programs include internships/practicums in schools, hospitals, or other institutions. Graduates of the school's teacher-preparation programs receive New York State provisional teaching certification.

The school also offers a five-year B.A./M.S. program in childhood/special education and special education.

Off-Campus Programs

Manhattan College also offers study-abroad programs in many countries; arrangements can be made to study in a country of choice. Students in the O'Malley School of Business may participate in the International Field Studies Seminar. As participants, they spend time in another country studying the effect of that environment on international firms. Career services and co-op education integrate classroom theory with the practical experience of a job in industry, business, the social services, the arts, or government. Portions of the education courses are conducted in New York City schools, so that student teachers may gain experience in urban education at an early stage.

Academic Facilities

There are more than forty scientific and engineering laboratories at Manhattan, including the Research and Learning Center, as well as a modern language laboratory and a computer information systems laboratory. Manhattan's O'Malley Library is a state-of-the-art facility featuring modern accommodations for study and research.

The Raymond W. Kelly ('63) Student Commons, which opened in the fall of 2014, is a 70,000-square-foot building, which has quickly become a focal point on campus. It enhances the College's ability to integrate academics and student life, and provides space for fitness and wellness programming, cultural and community events, dining, student activities, and student collaboration.

The Higgins Engineering and Science Center is slated to open in the Fall of 2020. It will provide the necessary resources for a 21st-century education in engineering and the sciences. Fourteen ultramodern laboratories will support and expand teaching and research in each of the College's engineering and science disciplines. There also will be space for collaborative learning and interdisciplinary partnerships among students and faculty.

Costs

For 2019–20, the tuition for Manhattan College new students will be $40,400 per year plus program fee. Room and board for the year will be $16,870.

Financial Aid

Manhattan grants or administers financial assistance in the form of tuition awards to students on the basis of need and/or ability. Need is evaluated by submitting the FAFSA. In addition to a merit scholarship fund, Manhattan offers endowed scholarships, special category scholarships and student athletic grants, Federal Pell Grants, Federal Supplemental Educational Opportunity Grants, student loans, Federal Work-Study Program awards, and New York State financial assistance are also available to students who qualify. Forty-eight percent of all students receive merit aid with 94 percent of the students receiving aid.

Faculty

Manhattan's faculty has 219 full-time faculty members. Ninety-three percent of the faculty members hold doctorates. They are available to students for informal guidance and counseling and serve as official moderators of many campus organizations.

Admission Requirements and Application Information

An application for admission to Manhattan College may be submitted using the Common Application or a Manhattan College Application. An application fee of $75 is required.

In reviewing applications for admission, the most emphasis is placed upon student course selection and the rigor of the course curriculum as well as on cumulative grade point average. All applicants must have completed a minimum of 16 units in academic subjects to be qualified for admission.

Applicants for freshman admission need to submit SAT or ACT scores. Only a student's highest scores are considered for admission and scholarship eligibility.

Grades and examination scores alone do not adequately evaluate a student's ability to be successful in college. Therefore, appropriate character references are considered important when reviewing candidates for admission. One letter of recommendation from a teacher or guidance counselor is required. Applicants must also submit a brief personal statement or college essay.

Interviews are recommended but not required as part of the admissions process.

Applications are reviewed on a rolling admission basis. Manhattan will consider for admission any qualified student upon completion of the junior year. Students must continue to demonstrate progress at the same academic level in their senior year and that all secondary school graduation requirements must be met, and a diploma issued, in order to enroll. Junior college or other transfer students are welcome. Manhattan College requires applicants whose native language is not English to take the Test of English as a Foreign Language (TOEFL), IELTS, the SAT, or ACT exam. The average SAT score is 1100–1240.

The high school report, recommendation letters, and transcript must be submitted by the high school guidance counselor. There is a rolling admissions policy and a March 1 priority deadline for financial aid applications.

For more information, contact:

Tara Fay-Reilly
Director of Undergraduate Admissions
Manhattan College
Riverdale, New York 10471
United States
Phone: 718-862-7200
800-MC2-XCEL (toll-free)
E-mail: admit@manhattan.edu
Website: http://www.manhattan.edu

Manhattan College centers a great deal of its campus activity around the main quadrangle.

MARYWOOD UNIVERSITY

SCRANTON, PENNSYLVANIA

The University

Marywood University enrolls more than 2,600 students in its undergraduate, graduate, and doctoral programs. Founded in 1915 by the Sisters, Servants of the Immaculate Heart of Mary, the University provides a framework for educational excellence that enables students to develop fully as persons and to master professional and leadership skills necessary for meeting human needs.

Students at Marywood have the opportunity to build on their academic interests and proactively shape their educational experience. Marywood believes in the power of the individual and in the premise that education is the most empowering tool.

Marywood is fully accredited by the Commission on Higher Education of the Middle States Association of Colleges and Schools. Program-specific accreditations are available to review online at www.marywood.edu/academics.

Marywood's athletic programs provide students with opportunities to play on competitive intercollegiate, club, and intramural teams. Students compete on an intercollegiate basis in baseball, basketball, cross-country, field hockey, golf, lacrosse, rugby, soccer, softball, swimming/diving, tennis, track and field, and volleyball. Marywood is a member of NCAA Division III, the Atlantic East Conference, and the Eastern College Athletic Conference.

Prospective students can connect with Marywood through social networks including Facebook (facebook.com/marywoodu), Twitter (twitter.com/marywoodu), and YouTube (youtube.com/marywoodu).

Location

Marywood's campus is part of an attractive residential area of Scranton, in northeastern Pennsylvania. With a population of 78,000, Scranton is the fifth-largest city in Pennsylvania. Marywood is close to many major cities of the Northeast; traveling by car, it is 2½ hours to New York and Philadelphia, 4 hours to Washington, D.C., and 5½ hours to Boston. Several airlines serve the Wilkes-Barre/Scranton International Airport, which is 20 minutes from the campus. The Pocono Mountains, offering spectacular scenery and an abundance of outdoor recreational opportunities, including downhill skiing, are a short distance from campus.

Academic Programs

All students are required to complete a core curriculum in the liberal arts in addition to the courses in their major. Opportunities for undergraduates abound through double majors, honors and independent-study programs, practicums, internships, and study abroad. Army and Air Force ROTC programs are available.

Majors and Degrees

At the undergraduate level, Marywood awards the Bachelor of Arts (B.A.), Bachelor of Architecture (B.Arch.), Bachelor of Business Administration (B.B.A.), Bachelor of Environmental Design in Architecture (B.E.D.A.), Bachelor of Fine Arts (B.F.A.), Bachelor of Interior Architecture (B.I.A.), Bachelor of Music (B.M.), Bachelor of Science (B.S.), Bachelor of Science in Nursing (B.S.N.), and Bachelor of Social Work (B.S.W.).

Marywood University offers majors in the following areas of study: accounting, ad hoc (self-designed), architecture and interior architecture/design, art (studio: ceramics, painting, sculpture, illustration; design: graphic design, photography), art therapy, arts administration (art, music, theater), athletic training, aviation management, biology, biology secondary education, biotechnology, communication sciences and disorders (speech-language pathology), computer science, criminal justice, cyber security (information security), early childhood and elementary education, early childhood and elementary education/special education, English (literature and writing), English secondary education, environmental science, exercise science, film, TV, and digital production, financial planning, health services administration, history, history/pre-law, history secondary education, hospitality management, international business, journalism, management, marketing, mathematics, mathematics secondary education, medical laboratory science, music education, music performance, music therapy, nursing, nutrition and dietetics, philosophy, pre-physician assistant studies, psychology, psychology/clinical practice, public relations and image management, religious studies, respiratory therapy, retail business management, sociology, social work, Spanish, Spanish secondary education, sports media, and theater.

Off-Campus Programs

Study-abroad opportunities are available in countries such as Australia, Canada, England, France, Mexico, and Spain. Through Studio Art Centers International (SACI), art students may study in Florence, Italy.

Academic Facilities

In recent years, the University has made major improvements to campus, including new athletic, residence, and dining facilities, and one of the finest studio arts facilities in the northeast. The Learning Commons is a 21st century–style library featuring four levels of open, accessible, and technologically advanced facilities. The Insalaco Center for Studio Arts features 60,000 square feet of fully equipped studios, labs, and classroom spaces for a broad variety of artistic disciplines. The Center for Architectural Studies offers students two levels of studio space in a spacious, adaptive re-use of Marywood's former gymnasium and pool space. A Center for Communication Arts offers a wide range of media tools, including a soundstage for television production and audio recording, a radio station, video and editing rooms, an animation studio, and print journalism facilities.

Costs

Tuition for full-time students (12–18 credits per semester) for the 2020-21 academic year is a flat fee of $35,181. There is also a general fee of $1,500 for full-time students. Costs for room and board for a full academic year are approximately $14,400, depending on which meal plan is selected and the desired room occupancy.

Financial Aid

Marywood offers a comprehensive program of financial aid to assist students in meeting educational costs. Eligibility for federal and state programs is based on demonstrated financial need, as determined by a federal eligibility formula that analyzes family income and assets. In addition, approximately $31 million in institutional aid is awarded annually to Marywood students. Applicants to Marywood are considered for all financial assistance programs for which they qualify. Candidates are required to submit the Free Application for Federal Student Aid (FAFSA) and the Marywood application form.

Faculty

Among faculty members at Marywood, 152 are full-time. The student-faculty ratio is 12:1. Faculty members are evaluated on their teaching and on their scholarly and artistic activities.

Student Government

All matriculated students in the undergraduate school are members of the Student Government Association (SGA). The SGA operates with a number of committees, including the Student Council, the Resident Committee, and the Commuter Committee. The association plays a key role in establishing a positive campus environment.

Admission Requirements

Candidates for admission should demonstrate reasonable progress toward graduation in an accredited secondary school, have graduated from a secondary school, or offer evidence of an equivalent secondary education. Each candidate should show satisfactory academic preparation in 16 units of subject matter, including 4 units of English, 3 units of social studies, 2 units of mathematics, 1 unit of science with laboratory, and 6 additional units. Prospective students should check with the Office of University Admissions regarding current standardized test requirements.

In addition to fulfilling general admission requirements, candidates for admission to a degree program in architecture, art, music, nursing, pre–physician assistant studies, and speech language pathology must meet special standards established by the department. Prior to enrollment, music, theater, and art candidates are required to audition or to present an art portfolio.

For certain programs, candidates without the recommended distribution of units may be eligible for admission if their course work as a whole and the results of their tests offer evidence of a strong foundation for college work. Candidates who are deficient in required course work may complete the appropriate work during the summer or first year in college.

A student who demonstrates satisfactory academic performance at another college may apply for admission as a transfer student. Academic courses presented for transfer should be equivalents of courses required by the programs of study at Marywood. Students should have earned a grade of C or higher in their course work; C– will not transfer. A student should expect to earn a minimum of 42 credits at Marywood; ordinarily, at least one half of the credits required for a major must also be earned at Marywood.

International candidates are required to meet the academic standards for admission, demonstrate proficiency in the use of the English language, and submit documentation of having sufficient funds to cover educational and living expenses for the duration of study. To certify proficiency in the use of English, international applicants whose primary language is not English must submit scores from the Test of English as a Foreign Language (TOEFL) or the IELTS.

Application and Information

Applications for admission are considered on a rolling basis; however, candidates are strongly encouraged to submit applications by March 1. Applications received after March 1 are considered on the basis of available space in particular programs. To be considered for admission, freshman applicants must submit to the Office of University Admissions a completed application, a nonrefundable $35 application fee (waived if applying online), an official high school transcript, an official report of scores from the SAT or ACT, and at least one letter of recommendation. Students can apply online at www.marywood.edu/admissions/applying.

Transfer students must submit a completed application, a nonrefundable $35 application fee (waived if applying online), an official high school transcript, official academic transcript(s) reflecting all college course work for which the candidate has enrolled, and at least one letter of recommendation.

All submitted credentials become the property of Marywood and are not returnable to the applicant. Admission standards and policies are free of discrimination on grounds of race, color, national origin, sex, age, or disability.

For further information, interested students should contact:

Rachel Hartz, Director of Undergraduate Admissions
Office of University Admissions
Marywood University
2300 Adams Avenue
Scranton, Pennsylvania 18509
Phone: 570-348-6234
Fax: 570-961-4763
E-mail: yourfuture@marywood.edu
Website: http://www.marywood.edu/admissions
www.facebook.com/marywoodu
www.twitter.com/marywoodu
www.youtube.com/marywoodu

The majestic Rotunda located in the Liberal Arts Center on Marywood's campus.

MISERICORDIA UNIVERSITY

DALLAS, PENNSYLVANIA

The University

Misericordia University is a high-quality liberal arts and professional studies institution rooted in service to others and committed to challenging academics and the personal attention students deserve. Founded by the Religious Sisters of Mercy in 1924, Misericordia offers undergraduate and graduate programs to resident and commuter students, as well as adult students. Current enrollment is more than 2,500 men and women.

The University cultivates a spirit of community service and a lifelong love of learning in its students through extracurricular activities, experiential learning, and challenging academic programs. In the National Survey of Student Engagement, Misericordia students say they are more involved in learning and have better relationships with faculty members and peers than students at other similar institutions. Misericordia is also ranked in the top tier of U.S. News & World Report's America's Best Regional Universities–North Category 2019.

Misericordia operates twelve residential facilities, including five residence halls, a town house complex, and off-campus housing, with a total capacity of more than 1,100 students. This includes three nearby homes are reserved for upper-level students. Residents have a number of options, including single rooms and wellness housing. Each residence hall offers study rooms, laundry facilities, and recreational lounges. The Metz Dining Hall is located in the Banks Student Life Center, which also houses a "We Proudly Brew Starbucks" coffee shop, a Chick-fil-A Express, and the Chopping Block restaurant, and the renovated Student Union that features flat-screen televisions as well as pool and foosball tables.

There are numerous campus activities. Besides Student Government, there are over 40 chartered student clubs and organizations. Cultural events, Campus Ministry, intramural and intercollegiate athletic programs including esports, performing arts shows, art exhibits, and many other social activities complement the academic experience. The Metz Field House provides enhanced facilities for student athletes. In keeping with the University's tradition of Mercy, Service, Justice, and Hospitality, students have opportunities to develop leadership potential through service projects. Misericordia earned a spot on the President's National Community Service Honor Roll for the past several years.

On spring break, students have served the needy in rural Appalachia, the Gulf Coast, Texas, California, Philadelphia, and the South Bronx. Students have volunteered abroad in Jamaica, Guyana, and Romania.

Personalized attention is the key to the support available in the Student Success Center. A psychologist, counselors, therapists, and peer counselors conduct workshops each semester on a variety of topics, including test anxiety, stress management, time management, and goal setting. Many services are free of charge to students and contacts are confidential.

First-year students may join the Guaranteed Placement Program (GPP) through the Insalaco Center for Career Development. The GPP program includes academic standards, cocurricular activities (such as leadership and service projects), internships, resume development, etiquette development, and interviewing skills. If a student fulfills the program's requirements and is not employed in his or her field or enrolled in graduate or professional school within six months of graduation, a paid internship is assured. The center also co-presents the Choice Program, which offers special guidance for students who have not declared a major. Opportunities for career exploration, cooperative education, and internships help students develop the skills they need to be successful when they enter the working world.

Student Health Services staff members provide first aid, assessment and treatment of common illnesses, and referrals for more serious health conditions. Health center activities are directed by a nurse practitioner. A self-care room offers reference materials and up-to-date information on personal health concerns. All services are confidential.

A rapidly evolving world has increased the number of adults who seek higher education. Misericordia offers bachelor's, master's, and doctoral programs for adult learners in several formats. The Ruth Matthews Bourger Women with Children program provides housing and support services for single women with children who are working toward their undergraduate degree. Convenient evening, online, and weekend formats also are available for people with families and full-time jobs.

Master's degrees are available in education, nurse practitioner studies, occupational therapy, physician assistant, speech/language pathology, business administration, and organizational management. A doctoral program in physical therapy is available to students entering in a full-time format, and doctoral programs in occupational therapy and nursing practice are available for graduate students via part-time study, including online and in-class components.

The University is fully accredited by the Middle States Association of Colleges and Schools. The medical imaging, nursing, occupational therapy, physical therapy, social work, and speech-language pathology programs are accredited by the National League for Nursing Accrediting Commission, the Council on Social Work Education, the Joint Review Committee on Education in Radiologic Technology, the American Occupational Therapy Association, the American Physical Therapy Association, and the American Speech-Language and Hearing Association. The ARC-PA has granted Accreditation - Provisional status to the Misericordia University Physician Assistant Program.

Location

Located in northeastern Pennsylvania, Misericordia University is the oldest four-year institution of higher education in Luzerne County. Expansive lawns and thick stands of trees dominate the 127-acre upper and expanding lower campuses. It is 9 miles from the city of Wilkes-Barre. The area offers shopping centers, malls, cinemas, skiing, professional sporting events, and a variety of cultural activities. Pennsylvania's largest natural lake and two state parks are nearby, as are Pocono ski resorts. Metropolitan New York and Philadelphia are each within a 3-hour drive. Public and university-sponsored transportation serves the campus.

Majors and Degrees

Misericordia University awards the Bachelor of Arts (B.A.) degree in English, history, government, law and national security, medical and health humanities, and philosophy. The Bachelor of Science (B.S.) degree is awarded in accounting, biochemistry, biology, business administration, chemistry, clinical laboratory science, computer science, diagnostic medical sonography, early childhood and special education, health care management, health science, information technology, mass communications and design, mathematics, medical imaging, middle level education, professional studies, psychology, secondary education, sport management, and statistics. The Bachelor of Science in Nursing (B.S.N.) is awarded to nursing majors, and a Bachelor of Social Work (B.S.W.) is awarded to social work majors. Specializations in exercise science, IT security, marketing, medical science, patient navigation, pre-law, respiratory therapy, sport communications, surgical technology, and preprofessional occupations are also available. Certificate programs include addictions counseling, diagnostic medical sonography, patient navigation, post-professional pediatrics certificate for occupational therapists and physical therapists, and secondary education. These may be taken in support of several degrees offered by Misericordia or as stand-alone programs.

The University also offers five-year entry-level graduate majors in occupational therapy and speech-language pathology. Students graduate with a master's degree in speech-language pathology or occupational therapy and a bachelor's degree in health sciences. The physical therapy program is a 6½-year doctoral program. Students graduate with a bachelor's degree in one of several areas and a Doctor of Physical Therapy (D.P.T.) degree.

Academic Programs

Candidates for any bachelor's degree must fulfill a 49-credit liberal arts core curriculum and must complete the requirements of at least one major (credits vary, but no less than 30 credits in a major). The typical requirement for a baccalaureate degree is a total of 121 credits. Other options include minors, specializations, and free electives. Interested students should consult the academic catalog for the most current information.

Courses are offered on a semester basis, beginning in August and January and ending in December and May. Summer, weekend, online, and accelerated courses are also available.

Academic Facilities

The chemistry, physics, and biology departments all have fully equipped research laboratories available to students in these fields. State-of-the-art equipment includes high-performance liquid chromatography (HPLC), a rotary evaporator, and a new gas chromatograph mass spectrometer. The science building contains a gross anatomy laboratory, a rare asset for a university of this size. The University also houses an energized radiation laboratory for the medical imaging program. The Passan Hall–College of Health Sciences provides classrooms and high-tech laboratories for the occupational therapy, physical therapy, speech-language pathology, and nursing programs in a facility devoted to these majors.

In addition to the four main computer labs, most other campus buildings and common areas offer wireless Internet access. The University operates MyMU, a secure online portal where students can access e-mail, course schedules, class registration tools, and student account and registration information from a single sign-on.

Mercy Hall, the original administrative building, offers multi-purpose academic classrooms and facilities. Many key student service departments, including the registrar, student accounts, and financial aid are centralized in one area in Mercy Hall. Sandy and Marlene Insalaco Hall houses the Pauly Friedman Art Gallery, Intermetzo Café, computer labs, an ensemble room, fine arts classroom, music teaching and practice areas, and the Assistive Technology Research Institute.

The new Michael and Tina MacDowell Residence Hall hosts three ultramodern classrooms on the first floor.

The three-story Mark Kintz Bevevino Library covers 37,500 square feet and houses stacks for 90,000 volumes. Materials include information and communication technology and a reference section that offers books, serials, and a variety of periodicals as well as reference search tools.

Costs

Full-time undergraduate tuition for 2019-2020 was $32,800 per year. The general fee was $1,760. Housing options include traditional rooms, suites, town houses, and lower-campus housing. The median room cost was $8,320. The median board cost is $4,303.

Financial Aid

All students applying for financial aid must complete the Free Application for Federal Student Aid (FAFSA) by May 1, but it can be completed as early as October 1 of senior year. This is used for Federal Pell Grants, Federal Supplemental Educational Opportunity Grants (FSEOG), subsidized and unsubsidized Federal Direct Student Loans, Federal Perkins Loans, nursing loans, and the Federal Work-Study Program. This application is also the basis upon which state and institutional aid is awarded. The University also offers a no-interest monthly payment plan. Many scholarships are available including $20 million in presidential scholarships based on academic ability and $4.6 million in McAuley Awards for students who have experience in leadership roles and volunteer service.

The average 2018-19 financial aid package for first-time, full-time undergraduate students with financial need was $25,409.

Faculty

There are 143 full-time faculty members. A student-faculty ratio of 10.4:1 results in students receiving a great deal of individual attention from a highly qualified faculty; 80 percent of the faculty members hold doctorates. Besides student academic advising, the faculty members also serve as advisers to clubs.

Student Government

An active student government organization serves as a liaison between the students and the faculty and staff members. The administration enables students to become involved by serving as student representatives on various University committees.

Admission Requirements

Misericordia University admits applicants based on their secondary school record, high school recommendation, extracurricular activities, and personal promise. The University requires SAT or ACT scores.

Transfer students with a cumulative average of at least 2.0 (4.0 scale) may be considered for admission and may receive advanced standing. Some majors require a 2.5 or higher cumulative average. Transfer students must submit official high school transcripts and transcripts of work completed at other colleges and universities.

Application and Information

Applicants must submit the free online application, available at misericordia.edu/apply, transcripts, and SAT or ACT scores.

The University considers applications on a rolling basis. Usually, candidates are notified of the admission decision within three weeks of receipt of all required materials.

For more information, students should contact:

Office of Admissions
Misericordia University
301 Lake Street
Dallas, Pennsylvania 18612-1090
Phone: 570-674-6461
866-262-6363 (toll free)
Fax: 570-675-2441
E-mail: admiss@misericordia.edu
Website: http://admissions.misericordia.edu
www.twitter.com/misericordiaUAD
www.facebook.com/misericordiauniversity
www.facebook.com/misericoridau
www.snapchat.com/misericordiau
www.instagram.com/misericordiau

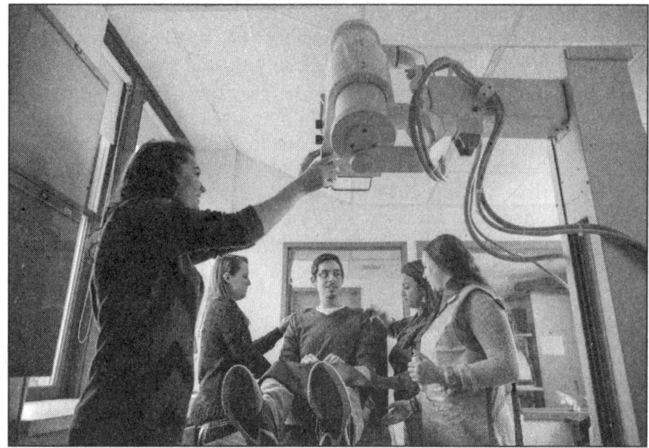

Misericordia University offers multiple medical and health science degree options on the undergraduate and graduate levels.

MOLLOY COLLEGE

ROCKVILLE CENTRE, NEW YORK

The College

What college offers a great education with small classes, wonderful internships, community service projects, and international trips, plus an amazing campus life program to round out the college experience? Welcome to Molloy College, where you can truly "live your story. Molloy, an independent, private Catholic college based in Rockville Centre, New York was founded in 1955 by the Sisters of Saint Dominic of Amityville, New York. The College serves a student population of more than 4,900 undergraduate and graduate students. Molloy students can earn degrees in a variety of outstanding academic programs, including nursing, business, education, social work, music therapy, and many more.

Prospective students are always looking for an academic environment that offers the best fit for the student and the best value for their tuition dollar. Molloy was recently named by *The Wall Street Journal* as the #18 ranked "value-added" college in the nation, a testament to our tremendous academic programs. Molloy also earned important recognition from another source, when *Newsday* produced an enrollment overview of the many private colleges in the Long Island region. While most of Molloy's competitors struggled in the 2012-2017 period, Molloy "saw the largest increase, rising more than 11 percent."

Molloy continues to earn recognition in many areas. College Factual recently named Molloy the #1 college for health professions, as well as naming Molloy's undergraduate nursing program the best in the nation. The College's music therapy program is ranked 16th in the nation by TheBestSchools.org. In addition, the College's residence halls were voted Best in New York by Niche.com, and these rankings also referenced Molloy's freshmen retention rate, which is among the highest in the country (89 percent). Also of note, Molloy graduates' starting salaries have ranked among the highest in the U.S. in surveys conducted by Georgetown University and PayScale.com.

Location and Environment

Molloy is located on the South Shore of Long Island in the Village of Rockville Centre. Its proximity to New York City—just a short train ride away from the 30-acre campus—allows students to benefit from the cultural, social, and professional opportunities that Manhattan has to offer. Molloy's location in the New York metro region provides its students with numerous opportunities for internships and clinical placements, critical for helping students land their first job upon graduation.

Molloy College also offers off-campus locations for study at the Suffolk Center in East Farmingdale and at area hospitals and schools, all designed to provide convenience for graduate and continuing education students. Most recently, Molloy opened a new facility at 50 Broadway in lower Manhattan. The new building houses the Molloy/CAP21 B.F.A. musical conservatory program, in addition to hosting a variety of lectures and other academic programs.

Majors and Degrees

Molloy offers the A.A. degree in liberal arts; the A.A.S. degree in cardiovascular technology; and the B.A. or B.S. degree in accounting, art, biology, business management, communications, computer science, computer information systems, criminal justice, economics; education, English, earth and environmental studies, finance, history, interdisciplinary studies, marketing, mathematics, modern languages, music, music therapy, new media, nuclear medicine technology, nursing, philosophy, political science, psychology, respiratory care, sociology, speech language pathology/audiology, and theology; the B.S.W. degree in Social Work; and the B.F.A. in art, music, and theatre arts. Teacher certification programs are available in childhood (1–6), adolescence (7–12), special education, and birth–grade 2 childhood special education.

On the graduate level, Molloy offers a Master of Science degree as well as post-master's certification in nursing and education. M.B.A. programs are available in business, accounting, healthcare, marketing, and personal financial planning; a master's program in clinical mental health counseling was recently launched as well. A master's in social work is offered through Molloy's partnership with Fordham University. Molloy also offers graduate degrees in criminal justice, music therapy, and speech-language pathology. The College offers three doctoral programs: a Ph.D. in nursing and a Doctor of Nursing Practice (D.N.P.), as well as an Ed.D. in Education.

Students interested in pre-dental, pre-law, pre-medical, or pre-veterinary programs are offered special advisement. Articulation agreements with community colleges and established transfer credit policies ensure ease of transferability. Experienced admissions counselors will evaluate transfer applicants' credits and help plan toward a path toward degree completion.

Academic Programs

At Molloy, small class size, engaging and experienced faculty, and renowned academic programs help ensure student success, both in the classroom and beyond.

Molloy strives to make the college experience convenient for all students. The College offers evening and weekend classes, many in online and hybrid formats, with accelerated schedules designed to accommodate students' busy schedules. Additionally, there are numerous online programs available during daytime hours as well. The College also recently launched a five-year program with St. John's University that provides an accelerated pathway to a master's degree. Students in Molloy's School of Arts and Sciences can earn their bachelor's at Molloy and a master's at St. John's in only five years, providing them with a key edge in the marketplace while saving them time (and $) over more traditional paths to a master's.

A minimum of 128 credit hours is required for a baccalaureate degree; these courses include a strong liberal arts general education curriculum for every major field of study. Students may choose a double major, and many minors are available. Molloy has a 4-1-4 academic calendar. Students may earn CLEP and CPE credit, and advanced placement credit is granted for a score of 3 or better on the AP exam. Qualified full-time students may participate in the Army ROTC program at Hofstra University or St. John's University on a cross-enrolled basis. Molloy students may also elect Air Force ROTC on a cross-enrolled basis with New York Institute of Technology.

Off-Campus Programs

The vast majority of students at Molloy enjoy an internship at some point in their academic careers. These real-world experiences are a crucial part of the learning process and ensure that students enter their chosen field ready to make strong contributions. Molloy's location in the New York metro region provides its students with numerous opportunities for all-important internships and clinical placements that can lead to a full-time job. Molloy students are also instilled with the belief that they can make a difference beyond the classroom. As part of Molloy's tradition of service, students become involved in projects that help underserved populations in New York City,

New Orleans, Puerto Rico and Haiti, to name but a few locations. Through the College's international education program, students seek enrichment and greater understanding of the world by participating in trips to Europe, Japan, South America, and other locales around the globe.

Facilities

In recent years, Molloy has added a number of new facilities, including three residence halls, a student center, and a performing arts theatre, all of which enhance the student experience. Additionally, Molloy recently opened the Barbara H. Hagan School of Nursing & Health Sciences to support its nationally ranked nursing program. The College opened its newest residence hall in fall 2019. Molloy is a wireless campus and its computer labs house more than 325 PCs. Many departments have their own computer labs with state-of-the-art equipment.

The James E. Tobin (JET) Library is the center of academic research on the Molloy College campus. Beyond the library's physical collection of books, media, and periodicals, it also provides 24/7 access to over 250,000 ebooks as well as full text to over 170 million articles contained within its 80+ subscription databases. The facility itself contains reference computers, three classrooms, a media center, and designated areas for both group and private study. The Information Commons, located in the Public Square, offers an additional 40 computers as well as four study rooms that can be reserved in advance. Reference services are available to both on-campus and remote researchers in a variety of ways, including a chat service that is available all of the hours the library is open. Additionally, the Public Square provides numerous music studios, for both individual and group study.The Wilbur Arts Center features art studios, a cable television studio, and the Lucille B. Hays Theatre. The school also has six science labs, a language lab, the education resource center, new state-of-the-art nursing labs, and a behavioral sciences research facility.

Costs

For 2019-20, tuition was $31,330 and required fees were $1,190. Students can expect to spend about $1,400 on books.

Financial Aid

Financial aid, which is based on academic achievement and financial need, is awarded to more than 85 percent of the student body. Aid is awarded in the form of scholarships, grants, loans, and Federal Work-Study Program employment. Merit-based scholarships and grants are also available. Students are required to complete the FAFSA application every year. Full- and partial-tuition scholarships are available through the following: Molloy Scholars, Presidential Dominican Scholarships, Presidential Business Scholarships, Dean Scholarships, Academic Achievement, Fine Arts Scholarships, Community Service Awards, and other funded scholarships. The Transfer Scholarship Program awards partial-tuition scholarships to students transferring into Molloy College with at least a 3.0 cumulative GPA. Nursing transfers are required to have a 3.3 GPA to be eligible for a transfer scholarship. Athletic grants (Division II only) are awarded to full-time students who show superior athletic ability in baseball, basketball, bowling, cross-country, equestrian, field hockey, indoor and outdoor track, lacrosse, soccer, softball, tennis, or volleyball. Most recently, Molloy announced that it would be offering scholarships for students participating in e-sports.

Faculty

Molloy's 10:1 undergraduate student-faculty ratio reflects the College's commitment to its students. In addition, the College has increased the number of faculty members by more than 10 percent in recent years. Of those faculty members, more than 77 percent have doctoral degrees.

Student Organizations and Activities

Molloy offers plenty of opportunities for its 4,900+ undergraduate and graduate students. There are more than 50 academic programs, approximately 60 clubs and honor societies, various service opportunities, and NCAA Division II athletics, providing abundant opportunities for each student to not only strive for academic excellence, but also explore new interests, pursue athletics, and enrich the community.

Admission Requirements

While Molloy is a selective college, admissions counselors respect each individual applicant and consider the whole student—not just test scores—when making admissions decision. Prospective freshmen must submit their high school credentials, SAT or ACT scores, the Molloy application, and a $40 nonrefundable application fee. While not required, a personal interview is strongly suggested. Entrance requirements include graduation from high school or equivalent with 20.5 units, including the following: 4 units of English, 3 units of a foreign language, 3 units of mathematics, 4 units of social studies, and 3 units of science. Those who plan to major in mathematics must have 4 units of high school mathematics and 2 units of science, including either chemistry or physics. Biology majors must have biology, chemistry, physics, and 4 units of mathematics. Nursing majors must have biology and chemistry. Cardio-respiratory science majors must have biology, chemistry, and mathematics. Nuclear medicine majors must have high school algebra and biology. Applicants lacking above requirements are reviewed on an individual basis.

Application Information

Molloy College offers rolling admissions at the undergraduate level. Early action on admission will be made promptly on applications received by December 1 of the senior year from well-qualified students who have filed all their credentials with the admissions office. Prospective students are invited to visit the campus. Questions or requests for more information can be directed to:

Undergraduate Admissions
Molloy College
1000 Hempstead Avenue
Rockville Centre, New York 11571
Phone: 516-323-4000
888-4-MOLLOY (toll-free)
E-mail: admissions@molloy.edu
Website: http://www.molloy.edu
http://www.facebook.com/GoMolloy
http://www.twitter.com/MolloyCollege

MOUNT ALOYSIUS COLLEGE

CRESSON, PENNSYLVANIA

The College

Mount Aloysius College is a private, comprehensive, Catholic liberal arts college sponsored by the Sisters of Mercy. The College welcomes people of all faith traditions. Established in 1853, Mount Aloysius College offers both undergraduate and graduate education. Since the founding of the College, nearly 17,000 students have become proud Mount Aloysius alumni. The College is committed to providing small class sizes, and students benefit from accessible faculty and staff. Mount Aloysius students come mostly from throughout Pennsylvania and the mid-Atlantic Region. There are approximately 1,000 full-time, undergraduate students.

Mount Aloysius College is one of 17 Mercy Colleges nationwide. Students are encouraged to synthesize faith with learning, to develop competence with compassion, to apply their talents and gifts to the service of others, and to assume leadership in their community.

Student activities play a distinctive role in personal growth. At Mount Aloysius College, there are approximately 100 organized clubs, groups, honor societies, and an intramural sports program. Activities include a student newspaper, residence hall associations, student government, cheerleading, dance team, scholarship-funded theater and choir programs, and a student activity planning board. Mount Aloysius fun includes social events, intramural sports, athletic events, comedians, live music, theater, educational events, campus forums, and awesome guest lectures.

Mount Aloysius College is a member of NCAA Division III. Athletic programs involve both women and men and include basketball, cross-country, golf, soccer, and tennis. Men's baseball and women's bowling, softball, lacrosse, and volleyball are also offered. Athletes benefit from the Ray S. and Louise S. Walker Athletic Field Complex, which includes a softball, turfed baseball field and soccer field. The Calandra-Smith baseball complex houses the Mountie Stables which offer players and fans lockers, showers, a press box, and concession facilities. The College's soccer field was recently updated to include a turf field, bleachers, a press box and stadium lighting.

The Athletic Convocation and Wellness Center is a spectacular 87,400 square-foot multipurpose facility on the western edge of the beautiful 193-acre campus. This facility takes Mount Aloysius athletics to a new level and adds a welcomed special events venue to the southern Allegheny Mountains. This Center houses a main gymnasium and events venue with seating for over 2,500, home and visitor locker rooms, training facilities, high-tech classrooms, a conference center, and office space. On the ground floor, a new state-of-the-art wellness center offers both cardio and resistance training in a spacious, modern environment.

The Bertschi Center and Technology Commons—with open architecture, vivid colors, and glass walls offering great views of the campus and surrounding mountains—is an additional social, technology, and special events venue that serves both commuter and resident students.

The main campus building is a picturesque structure dating to 1897. It houses the admissions, financial aid, security, health, and academic offices, along with the Office of the President, classrooms, and the Wolf-Kuhn Art Gallery. Cosgrave Center is the hub of campus life. The building contains the Dining Hall, Snack Bar, Bookstore, Child Care Center (part of the elementary education/early childhood program at the College), lounges, recreational rooms, student affairs offices, and meeting rooms. Residence halls include Ihmsen Hall; the Misciagna Residence—a state-of-the-art residence hall, providing 25 suites and private bathrooms; McAuley Hall featuring double and single rooms, a large multipurpose room, and study lounge; and Saint Gert's and Saint Joseph's residence halls. Alumni Hall is a historic, multipurpose facility used for College drama, musicals, lectures, and performing arts events. The College operates 12 months per year and opens its facilities to the Southern Allegheny community.

The College is 100 percent wireless, and smart classrooms are located throughout the campus.

Mount Aloysius is fully accredited by the Middle States Association of Colleges and Schools and approved by the Pennsylvania Department of Education.

In addition to its undergraduate programs—both associate and bachelor's degrees—Mount Aloysius offers master's degree programs in business administration and counseling.

Location

Mount Aloysius College is located in the scenic Southern Allegheny Mountains of west-central Pennsylvania, in the town of Cresson. Convenient and accessible from U.S. Route 22, the College's setting is rural but mere minutes from State College, Altoona, Johnstown, and Pittsburgh, Pennsylvania. Outdoor lovers are at home here. The area has warm, beautiful summers; brisk, breathtaking autumns; invigorating winters; and cool, blooming springs. Facilities are available for biking, golfing, swimming, horseback riding, waterskiing, boating, hiking, spelunking, cross-country and downhill skiing, picnicking, and amusement parks. A well-kept system of State Parks is convenient to the College as are shopping malls, golf courses, and numerous historical sites. Outdoor opportunities on campus include a 9-hole disc golf course, fishing pond, clay sports team, obstacle course, a hiking trail, and more.

Majors and Degrees

Mount Aloysius College awards bachelor's and associate degrees in the arts, sciences, and health studies fields in both career-oriented and traditional liberal arts programs. Baccalaureate degrees are available in accounting (includes a fifth-year MBA option), American Sign Language/English interpreter education, behavioral and social science, biology and general science, business administration (includes a fifth-year MBA option), computer science, criminology, dentistry (4-4), elementary/early childhood education and secondary education (with certifications), English, natural science, history/political science, humanities, information technology, math/science, medical imaging, natural resource management, nursing (RN-BSN program), nursing (2+2), nursing (traditional BSN), occupational therapy (3-2), osteopathic medicine (3-4), pharmacy (3-3), physical therapy (4-3), physician assistant studies (3-2), prelaw, psychology, ultrasonography, and undeclared. The College now also offers degrees in communication studies and cybersecurity and digital forensics. Associate degrees are offered in applied technology, business administration, criminology, early childhood studies, general studies, legal studies, liberal arts, nursing, physical therapist assistant studies, radiography/medical imaging, and surgical technology. The College also confers the MBA and a master's degree in community counseling.

Academic Programs

Whether preparing students for careers upon graduation or for graduate school, Mount Aloysius recognizes the importance of a liberal arts education. In addition to receiving solid preparation for a chosen career, every student at the College receives a foundation in the arts, sciences, and humanities through an outstanding core curriculum. Strong emphasis is placed on the specialized courses within each program of study, and many academic programs combine classroom experience with internships and related training at area clinical sites, agencies, and institutions. In addition to its regular academic programs, Mount Aloysius offers independent and directed study with a commitment to service, a central component of a Mercy education. The College has an excellent honors program and academic services area. The academic calendar has two traditional semesters and optional summer sessions.

Off-Campus Programs

An important feature of many academic programs is off-campus training. The majority of the College's programs of study require credit-yielding practicums at partnering hospitals, public and private schools, or health or human service agencies. Students in all health programs benefit from required clinical training during their time at the College.

Academic Facilities

The Mount Aloysius College Library is a state-of-the-art learning and study facility offering unprecedented access to a world of information. With a cybersecurity lab and more than 80,000 print and nonprint titles, the Library is an impressive, 31,000 square-foot facility with ample seating, four group-study rooms, reading lounge, and an unparalleled 18,000-volume Ecumenical Collection donated by Pastor Gerald Myers. This facility is completely automated, with an online catalog and access to remote libraries and the Internet through more than 30 workstations. The Library also houses the Information Technology Center, home to 15 multimedia workstations and the latest educational software.

The Learning Center for Health Science & Technology is a 45,000 square-foot facility which houses all laboratory science courses and certain allied health programs providing state-of-the-art instructional resources. The building includes simulation labs that resemble real hospital wings, study lounges and classrooms. The Learning Center for Health Science and Technology offers students science- and health-oriented learning environments that nearly mirror their clinical sites. The full scope of the Mount Aloysius Learning Center for Science and Technology includes: a new nursing simulation lab, a new and expanded medical imaging suite, a renovated and expanded surgical technology suite, anatomy and physiology labs, a renovated and expanded ultrasound suite and upgraded laboratories for chemistry and biology.

Academic Hall is home to the College Honors Program. It houses classrooms, labs, seminar rooms, faculty offices, and a state-of-the-art American Sign Language lab. The College is proud of its bridge to the past and its progress in providing 21st-century learning facilities.

Costs

Annual tuition and fees for the 2018–19 academic year for full-time students were $21,870; room and board were $10,176. Up-to-date cost information is available online at https://www.mtaloy.edu/admissions/tuition-fees/.

Financial Aid

Mount Aloysius prides itself on affordability. 98 percent of MAC students receive some sort of financial aid. The average annual aid package is $12,000. Many MAC students hail from proud families of modest means and many are first-generation students. The College understands the expense involved in acquiring a quality education and encourages students to apply for all available aid. Through the Office of Financial Aid, the College assists students in applying for state and federal grants, loans, work-study awards, merit scholarships, need-based aid and more. The College awards academic monies based on GPA and SAT or ACT scores. These awards are renewable over a four-year period and range from $1,500 to $14,000 per year. Mount Aloysius College participates in all federal and state programs. U.S. News & World Report has ranked Mount Aloysius College as one of the best-priced private liberal arts colleges in the United States.

Faculty

The Mount Aloysius faculty consists of approximately 175 members, whose primary responsibility is teaching and advising students. Many faculty members hold advanced or terminal degrees and are expected to maintain close instructional ties with students. Many professors hold national, professional certificates in such disciplines as criminology, education, law, and nursing. The Mount Aloysius student-faculty ratio of 11:1 allows close contact between students and faculty members, providing personal attention in a highly structured environment—a key ingredient in the College's academic philosophy.

Student Government

The Student Government Association (SGA) represents students on all issues that concern the College. The SGA appoints student representatives to all student-oriented College committees. The College encourages student participation in the general governance structure and other matters concerning the development and implementation of policies on residential student life.

Recognitions

Mount Aloysius was recently named one of 100 Best Value Colleges in the U.S. It is a College of Distinction, a Catholic College of Distinction and a Pennsylvania College of Distinction; three separate academic areas—business, education, and nursing—have also earned College of Distinction status. It has also received the Homeschooling Parent's Seal of Approval. Mount Aloysius was one of four colleges deemed "an engine of opportunity" in a White House Report. In the past year, the College's Theatre productions have earned several awards from the prestigious Kennedy Center. The Nursing Division boasts NCLEX pass rates that beat both state and national averages. The American Sign Language/English Interpreter program is an accredited bachelor's program. Mount Aloysius College has also been designated as a Military Friendly College.

Admission Requirements

The College enrolls a freshman class of approximately 350 students. The total class of 550 includes transfer students. Admission is selective, based on academic promise, as indicated by a student's secondary school performance and activities, standardized test scores, and special experience and talents. Applicants are required to have or expected to earn a diploma from an approved secondary school or a GED diploma. Submission of official transcripts and SAT or ACT scores is no longer required but will be reviewed. In addition to the general admission requirements, specific admission requirements exist for the health programs.

For further information, students should visit the College's website at http://www.mtaloy.edu. Prospective students are encouraged to visit the scenic 193-acre campus. The College is open Monday to Friday from 8:30 a.m. to 5 p.m. and on select weekends.

Application and Information

To apply for admission to Mount Aloysius College, candidates are encouraged to submit their application and $30 application fee to the Office of Undergraduate and Graduate Admissions.

In addition, students may apply online.

For further information, students should contact:

Office of Undergraduate and Graduate Admissions
Mount Aloysius College
7373 Admiral Peary Highway
Cresson, Pennsylvania 16630
Phone: 814-886-6383
888-823-2220 (toll-free)
Fax: 814-886-6441
E-mail: admissions@mtaloy.edu
Website: http://www.mtaloy.edu

Mount Aloysius College, located on a beautiful 193-acre campus in Cresson, Pennsylvania provides a safe, vibrant learning community. Nestled in the southern Allegheny Mountains, Mount Aloysius is one of 17 U.S. Mercy colleges and universities. Mount Aloysius offers year-round recreational and cultural opportunities. Students enjoy both the security of the campus and the proximity to State College to the east and Pittsburgh to the west. Mount Aloysius College is minutes away from all the amenities of Altoona and Johnstown, Pennsylvania. Interstate highways, the Pennsylvania Turnpike, AMTRAK train service, bus service, and several regional airports—including Pittsburgh International Airport—make Mount Aloysius College convenient from anywhere.

NEW COLLEGE OF FLORIDA

SARASOTA, FLORIDA

The College

New College of Florida offers students an environment designed to promote depth in thinking, free exchange of ideas, and highly individualized interaction with faculty members. In 2001, New College was designated as the official public Honors College in the liberal arts and sciences for the State University System of Florida. Regularly featured as a leading educational value, New College is also known as one of the nation's top producers of Fulbright scholarship recipients, with one of the highest numbers of annual Fulbright awards per capita among all colleges and universities. Through the Fulbright program, more than 80 New College graduates have traveled to 33 countries on six continents since our founding in 1960.

About 80 percent of New College graduates go on to pursue advanced degrees, in recent years including at Harvard, Yale, MIT, Georgetown, Berkeley, and Oxford. New College's student population is 837, of whom approximately 62 percent are women. Approximately 20 percent of students are out-of-state or overseas residents. The College has begun a growth initiative, with plans to increase enrollment to 1,200 by 2024.

The College's 110-acre bayfront location near the Gulf of Mexico includes basketball, racquetball, and tennis courts; a multipurpose soccer, softball, and athletic field; a running trail; a 25-meter swimming pool; and a comprehensive fitness center. The New College sailing team is part of the Inter-Collegiate Sailing Association of North America (ICSA). Students may compete in recreational and intramural sports including soccer, tennis, fencing, flag football, softball, and swimming. Sailboats, kayaks, and canoes are also available free of charge. The College's membership in the local Cross College Alliance provides recreational opportunities and access to course work with Ringling College of Art and Design, USF at Sarasota-Manatee, and State College of Florida, as well as internships through FSU's Ringling Museum. Off-campus study opportunities are available by individual arrangement and through partnerships with EcoLeague, the National Student Exchange, and the Consortium for Innovative Environments in Learning.

Location

On the coastline in southwest Florida, New College serves On the coastline in southwest Florida, 50 miles south of Tampa. Sarasota is noted for its beautiful white-sand beaches; professional theater, orchestra, opera, and ballet companies; an abundance of art and music venues; and outdoor festivals. New College next-door neighbor is the John and Mable Ringling Museum of Art, which offers students free entry to view its Baroque, Renaissance, and Asian art collections.

Major airlines serve the Sarasota-Bradenton International Airport. Bus service links the campus to downtown, shopping malls, parks, and beaches. Bicycling is popular, and students are welcome to have a car on campus.

Majors and Degrees

New College awards the Bachelor of Arts degree in liberal arts and sciences, and a Master of Science in Data Science. Each of the College's undergraduate majors includes work that students design in consultation with faculty members. Concentrations include Anthropology; Applied Mathematics; Art; Art History; Biology; Biopsychology; Chemistry (including Biochemistry); Chinese Language and Culture; Classics; Computer Science; Economics; English; Environmental Studies; French Language and Literature; Gender Studies; German Studies/German Language and Literature; History; Humanities; International and Area Studies (including Caribbean and Latin American Studies, East Asian Studies, and European Studies); Literature; Marine Biology; Mathematics; Music; Natural Sciences; Philosophy; Physics; Political Science; Psychology; Religion; Russian Language and Literature; Social Sciences; Sociology; Spanish Language and Literature; Statistics; Theater, Dance and Performance Studies; and Urban Studies. Creative Writing, Finance, Greek, Latin, Medieval and Renaissance Studies, Neuroscience, or Rhetoric and Writing may be pursued as part of a combined concentration; another option is to pursue a special program area of concentration with faculty approval. Programs are available to earn certificates in Bloomberg Market Concepts and Geographic Information Systems, as well as to become a Certified Financial Analyst. The Center for Career Engagement and Opportunity (CEO) works with faculty to build credit-bearing internships into your program, in addition to providing personalized career coaching from day one, career fairs and reverse career fairs, assistance with resume-writing and interviewing, and connecting you to job opportunities. The CEO also provides advising for graduate school and other advanced degree programs, including medical school, law school, business school, and veterinary school.

Academic Programs

New College students work closely with their faculty. Average class size is 14, and students regularly customize their programs with seminars, individual and small tutorials, independent research, internships, and off-campus experiences. At the end of each semester, students receive detailed narrative evaluations that are far more comprehensive than grades, as well as satisfactory/unsatisfactory assessments of their work from their professors. The program provides assistance and substantial feedback to support and challenge students in doing their best work. About 80 percent of New College graduates go on to pursue advanced degrees, in recent years including at Harvard, Yale, MIT, Georgetown, Berkeley, and Oxford.

Graduation requirements include satisfactory completion of seven academic contracts (a set of academic courses and other goals for the semester, planned by the student and faculty adviser), three independent study projects, a senior thesis or project, and an oral baccalaureate examination. In addition to the requirements for individual majors, students must complete eight courses within the liberal arts curriculum, with at least one course each in the humanities, social sciences, natural sciences, and diverse perspectives. Students must also meet basic proficiency in mathematics and English language and advanced proficiency in written and oral English language.

The College operates on a 4-1-4 calendar year, including a January interterm when students undertake independent study projects, such as library, laboratory, or field research; internships; and performing arts projects.

Off-Campus Programs

New College believes that internships, fieldwork, and independent research can make a significant contribution to an undergraduate education, and facilitates such study through its flexible, individualized curriculum and special support services. New College is a member of the National Student Exchange, which provides access to nearly 200 universities with programs in the U.S. and abroad (many with comparable tuition costs) and the Consortium for Innovative Environments in Learning. New College is also a member of the Cross-College Alliance with four other higher education institutions in the Sarasota area that allow students to cross-register for courses at each other's campuses.

Academic Facilities

New College's Jane Bancroft Cook Library holds over 225,000 volumes, and provides access to over 2,500 serials, 200 databases, and 26,000 e-books. As a member of the public State University System of Florida Libraries, the Cook Library provides access to over 11 million items, with access to electronic serial titles (including scholarly journals), newspapers, digital images and videos, and datasets. A comprehensive online interlibrary loan system gives students convenient access to holdings of libraries worldwide. Library staff offer research instruction, digital services, data management and grant compliance services, workshops, lectures, seminars, and other offerings. The Library's Academic Resource Center provides comprehensive writing support services, quantitative resources, and language study support. Silent study space, individual study carrels, collaborative work space, and workshop and group study rooms accommodate a variety of learning styles.

The Harry Sudakoff Conference Center hosts visiting lecturers, meetings of campus and community organizations, and special events. The Caples Fine Arts Complex includes the 264-seat Mildred Sainer Music and Arts Pavilion, which features student, local, and national performances; the Lota Mundy Music Building, which houses eight music practice rooms and the Benjamin and Barbara Slavin Electronic Music Studio; the Christianne Felsmann Fine Arts Building; the Betty Isermann Fine Arts Gallery and Studio; and a sculpture studio.

The R.V. Heiser Natural Sciences Complex houses laboratories, classrooms, offices, a state-of-the-art optical spectroscopy and nanomaterials laboratory, a research greenhouse, herbarium, a computer lab, two electron microscopes, an auditorium, and facilities for the College's master's program in Data Science. The Rhoda and Jack Pritzker Marine Biology Research Center, one of the leading marine research centers in southwest Florida, features culture rooms, laboratories, and aquariums with water drawn from Sarasota Bay.

The College's 35,000 square-foot Academic Center, which opened in 2011, was awarded LEED Gold certification by the U.S. Green Building Council. It includes a state-of-the-art computer lab, classrooms, faculty offices, and a student lounge.

Costs

For the 2020--2021 academic year, estimated tuition and fees at New College of Florida are $6,916 for Florida residents, $29,944 for out-of-state residents. Room and board costs are estimated at $9,529.

Financial Aid

Approximately 96 percent of New College students receive some form of financial assistance, including academic scholarships and need-based financial aid. To apply for federal and need-based financial aid, students should file the Free Application for Federal Student Aid (FAFSA). November 1 is the priority date for need-based financial aid. No additional forms are required for most of the College's scholarship programs. The overwhelming majority of admitted freshmen and transfers (including students on the F-1 visa), are provided scholarship funding to attend New College.

Faculty

Of New College's full-time faculty members, 97 percent hold the highest degree awarded in their field of study, usually the doctorate. They are drawn to an environment that emphasizes excellence in teaching and fosters a close-knit community of scholars. Faculty members sponsor individual students in the formulation of their academic programs, gradually moving toward a form of mentorship through which joint research is sometimes pursued. The student-faculty ratio is 8:1.

Student Government

Student input is a decisive factor in campus governance. Elected student representatives serve on the Board of Trustees and most major policymaking committees, and are voting participants in divisional and campus-wide faculty meetings. The New College Student Alliance, the College's student government, has authority over funding for recreational events, social events, student clubs and organizations on campus, and allocation of the Green Fee for environmentally friendly projects.

Admission Requirements

New College of Florida seeks highly capable students eager to take responsibility for their own education. Course selection and academic records are primary components of the application review. Middle 50 percent numbers for fall 2019 freshmen are 3.55-4.28 for the GPA, and 1170-1330 on the SAT or 26-29 on the ACT; 73% of freshman applicants were offered admission.

All prospective students may apply for entrance to the fall term. Scores for the SAT or ACT may be required for most students. The application fee is waived. In addition to the admission application, the College requires all transcripts and may require a recommendation. (Freshman applicants may substitute the Self-Reported Student Record for the high school transcript requirement.)

Application and Information

You can apply either through the New College application on the College's website, or through the Common Application. Applications are reviewed on a rolling basis.

Inquiries and application requests should be directed to:

Sonia Wu
Associate Dean of Admissions and Financial Aid
New College of Florida
5800 Bay Shore Road
Sarasota, Florida 34243-2109
United States
Phone: 941-487-5000
Fax: 941-487-5001
E-mail: admissions@ncf.edu
Website: http://www.ncf.edu
http://www.facebook.com/newcollegeofflorida
http://twitter.com/NewCollegeofFL
http://www.youtube.com/user/NewCollegeofFL

New College of Florida's historic waterfront campus features spectacular sunsets, wetlands, an intertidal lagoon, and boat access.

NORTHEASTERN UNIVERSITY

BOSTON, MASSACHUSETTS

The University

Founded in 1898, Northeastern is a global research university and the recognized leader in experience-driven lifelong learning. Northeastern's world-renowned experiential approach empowers their students, faculty, alumni, and partners to create impact far beyond the confines of discipline, degree, and campus. The academic curriculum is enhanced by experiential learning through research, professional, global, and service experiences. Anchored by the world's largest, most innovative cooperative education program, Northeastern prepares students for a lifetime of achievement and allows them to make an impact on the world before they graduate.

The current undergraduate enrollment of 18,191is comprised of students of all backgrounds and interests, giving Northeastern its diverse culture and community. Students can participate in more than 400 student clubs and organizations, engage in cutting-edge research with faculty from various disciplines, and perform with an award-winning a cappella group. They can join Northeastern's student-run venture accelerator, IDEA, play varsity or club basketball, tutor local children, and more. Students have countless opportunities to make lifelong friendships, to try something brand new—a class, a sport, or a career path—to hone their leadership skills and find a place where they belong. Quiet corners of the campus feel far from city streets and give students a secluded haven to read, write, or relax. The 73-acre campus is dynamic and welcoming, a beautiful stretch of leafy green in the heart of Boston.

Location

Northeastern's Boston campus is located in the heart of the city, where the distinctive neighborhoods of Back Bay, South End, Fenway, and Roxbury meet. Over half of the student body lives on campus and many of the residence halls have amazing views of the Boston skyline.

The Back Bay area, known for its many cultural and educational institutions, is just steps away from Symphony Hall, the New England Conservatory of Music, the Museum of Fine Arts, and the Isabella Stewart Gardner Museum. The South End is home to elegant Victorian row houses, a vibrant arts scene, hidden gardens, and some of the finest dining in Boston. The Fenway area, with its beautiful rose garden, bicycle and jogging paths, and Fenway Park (home of the Boston Red Sox), is just a few blocks away.

In addition to the Boston campus, Northeastern has a growing network of global locations including Charlotte, Portland, San Francisco and Silicon Valley, Seattle, Toronto, and London. Students also have the option to engage in a variety of high-quality study abroad opportunities such as Northeastern's award-winning Dialogue of Civilizations program.

Majors and Degrees

Northeastern offers over 220 majors and more than 130 combined majors across eight colleges and programs. Combined majors are unique, hybrid degree programs that help students explore their passions through several academic fields while staying on track towards graduation. Half of Northeastern students have more than just a major—either a double major, a combined major, a major and a minor, or another combination.

The College of Arts, Media and Design awards undergraduate degrees in architecture, architecture studies, art: art, visual studies, communication studies, design, game art and animation, games, journalism, landscape architecture, media and screen studies, media arts, music, music industry, music technology, studio art, and theatre.

The D'Amore-McKim School of Business offers two degree options: business administration and international business. The college offers concentrations in accounting, entrepreneurship and innovation, finance, healthcare management and consulting, management, management information systems, marketing, marketing analytics, and supply chain management.

The Khoury College of Computer Sciences awards degrees in computer science, cybersecurity, and data science. Khoury also offers combined majors that pair computer science with over 30 different academic fields.

The College of Engineering offers degrees in bioengineering, chemical, civil, computer, electrical, environmental, industrial, and mechanical engineering.

The Bouvé College of Health Sciences awards degrees in health science, nursing, pharmaceutical sciences, pharmacy, and speech language pathology and audiology.

The College of Science offers degrees in applied physics, behavioral neuroscience, biochemistry, biology, biomedical physics, cell and molecular biology, chemistry, ecology and evolutionary biology, environmental science, environmental studies, linguistics, marine biology, mathematics, physics, and psychology.

The College of Social Sciences and Humanities awards undergraduate degrees in Africana studies, American Sign Language, Asian studies, criminal justice, cultural anthropology, economics, English, history, human services, international affairs, philosophy, political science, PPE (politics, philosophy, and economics), religious studies, sociology, and Spanish.

The Explore Program for undeclared students offers a wide array of academic opportunities designed to help students who feel strongly about exploring their options before making a commitment to a major. The program provides the support and guidance students need to explore and eventually choose one of Northeastern's undergraduate programs.

Academic Programs

At the heart of a Northeastern education are award-winning faculty mentors, a rigorous and innovative curriculum, undergraduate research, and global experiences that challenge and transform. Northeastern's innovative programs encompass over 220 majors and 130 combined majors, along with a variety of concentrations and minors as well as honors, pre-professional, and study-abroad programs.

Northeastern's approach to education integrates a challenging academic curriculum with immersive experiences including research, service, global opportunities, and the university's signature cooperative education program (co-op), enabling students to make deep connections between their field of study and the world around them. Personalized, guided, and supported flexibility enables students to choose their unique path and gain real-world experience, creating a strong professional network and giving students confidence—as well as a significant edge in the job market. Students learn which careers are a good fit for them—and which are not—all before graduating. Over half of students are offered full-time jobs from previous co-op employers. Northeastern partners with over 3,100 co-op employers around the globe, including some of the world's largest and most reputable companies: Apple, Dana-Farber Cancer Institute, General Electric, Hill Holiday, Facebook, Google, Pixar, PricewaterhouseCoopers, SpaceX, and Vogue, just to name a few.

The University Honors Program allows students to participate in enriched educational experiences and offers opportunities that include honors sections of required academic courses, honors seminars, funding for independent research and travel, faculty mentorship, Living Learning Communities (honors housing), and specialized study abroad.

Academic Facilities

Northeastern is home to more than 60 research centers and undergraduates have ample opportunities to work alongside their professors to aid and conduct research on a variety of topics. The 220,000 square-foot Interdisciplinary Science and Engineering Complex has further evolved Northeastern's research enterprise by providing state-of-the-art infrastructure and fostering collaboration across disciplines.

The university library system is comprised of Snell Library, a 240,000-square-foot central library on the Boston campus, the School of Law Library, and a supplemental collection at the Nahant Marine Science Center. Snell also houses the Digital Media Commons, a dedicated media lab and digital creativity space that offers flexible work areas, professional-grade technology, high-power computer workstations, printers, scanners, a 3D printing studio, and a recording studio.

Costs

For the 2019–20 academic year, the estimated tuition is $52,420 and room and board fees are estimated at $16,930. Regardless of time to degree, tuition is charged only while students are earning academic credit. All tuition and fees are subject to approval and revision by the Board of Trustees. For the most up to date information, please visit studentfinance.northeastern.edu.

Financial Aid

The university operates a substantial aid program designed to make attendance feasible for all qualified students. Northeastern is dedicated to meeting full demonstrated need for incoming domestic financial aid applicants. By coordinating the resources of the university and various public and private scholarship programs, the Office of Student Financial Services was able to provide $296 million in grant and scholarship assistance. More than 75 percent of students receive some form of financial aid. Northeastern participates in all federal aid programs. Financial aid is based on need and academic merit and may consist of scholarships, grants, loans, work-study employment, or any combination of these funds. To apply, students must file the Free Application for Federal Student Aid (FAFSA) and a CSS Profile form, available through the College Board, by the priority filing deadline that corresponds with their application type.

Faculty

The university has more than 1,371 full-time faculty members with a variety of research and teaching interests. Academic counselors in each college work closely with students to assist them in developing programs suited to their interests and abilities. Co-op advisors assist students in resume-building and honing interview skills, while helping students develop contacts with businesses to support networking and professional opportunities.

Admission Requirements

Students may enter the university with advanced credit on the basis of test scores on Advanced Placement (AP) examinations, the International Baccalaureate (IB) examinations, or with successful completion of accredited college-level courses. In addition to the application for admission, prospective freshmen must submit official high school transcript(s) (or official GED score reports); official transcripts for any college-level coursework taken while a secondary-school student; written recommendations from their secondary school counselor and a teacher; and scores from the SAT (Northeastern's College Board code is 3667) or ACT, including the writing section. Please visit the university's website for additional admission requirements for specific student populations including transfer, international, and military (northeastern.edu/admissions).

Application and Information

Admission to Northeastern is selective and competitive. For the freshman class entering in Fall 2019, the university received more than 62,000 applications for 2,800 seats in the freshman class. Students are reviewed in the context of their environment, with attention paid to their academic course selections and rigor, academic achievement, extracurricular involvement and impact, and their potential fit with Northeastern, including the demonstration of personal traits like leadership, adaptability, a global perspective, or an entrepreneurial spirit.

Northeastern offers four decision plans for first year students: Early Decision I, Early Action, Early Decision II, and Regular Decision. The deadline for Early Decision I is November 1, and the deadline for Early Decision II is January 1; both of these programs are binding admission programs. Students who have carefully explored their college options and have decided that Northeastern is where they want to enroll may choose to apply under the Early Decision program. November 1 is the deadline for Early Action, and January 1 is the deadline for Regular Decision; both of these programs are non-binding. For transfer students, the admissions deadlines are April 1 for fall and October 1 for spring admission. Fall and spring transfer admission decisions are made on a space-available, rolling basis.

Please visit the university's website for application requirements and additional admission details for specific student populations (northeastern.edu/admissions).

Northeastern offers a variety of visit options including information sessions and campus tours. For more information, or to register, visit northeastern.edu/admissions/connect/visit. For more information, students should contact:

The Office of Undergraduate Admissions
240 West Village F
Northeastern University
360 Huntington Avenue
Boston, Massachusetts 02115
Phone: 617-373-2200
E-mail: admissions@northeastern.edu
Website: northeastern.edu/admissions

Northeastern's Centennial Common—a typical quad where students relax, study, and hang out with friends.

NORTHERN ARIZONA UNIVERSITY

FLAGSTAFF, ARIZONA

COLLEGE CLOSE-UPS

The University

Founded in 1899, Northern Arizona University (NAU) is a fully accredited, four-year public university centered on student success. For those interested in a collaborative community with a breadth of stellar programs and a dedicated research agenda, NAU offers an environment ideal for academic achievement, personal growth, professional outcomes, and adventure.

The university's Flagstaff campus offers the amenities of a big campus with a small-campus feel—all in a beautiful mountain location that ranks among the best college towns in the nation. NAU also offers more than 20 statewide locations, as well as online and competency-based learning programs. Innovative 2NAU partnerships with numerous Arizona community colleges give students affordable and convenient options for transferring into an NAU bachelor's degree program.

NAU offers a comprehensive range of nearly 100 majors to choose from and many nationally ranked programs taught by professors who work alongside you as mentors and teammates. Students have an abundance of opportunities to participate in important research and creative and scholarly projects alongside passionate faculty, with nearly 3,000 students participating in research and professional internships each year. Through the "Accelerated Program," high-achieving students can even work simultaneously on select master's degrees and graduate in as few as five years with both a bachelor's and a master's degree. And students can find everything they need to accomplish their goals, including programs and support services that are second to none—from enrollment through graduation and beyond.

Students who live in one of 14 Western states can save nearly 40 percent on the out-of-state tuition rate through the Western Undergraduate Exchange (WUE). Every major at NAU is eligible for the WUE rate.

Location

With a population of about 70,000, Flagstaff is a vibrant high-elevation mountain town that breaks Arizona's desert stereotype. Temperatures rarely exceed 90 degrees in the summer, fall brings a brilliant change of color, winter snowfall averages more than 100 inches, and spring bursts with blossoms. The region's unparalleled natural scenery is enhanced by hundreds of great restaurants and a robust arts and entertainment scene. The four-season climate provides recreational opportunities that range from scenic hiking and biking to skiing and snowboarding. The campus sits just 75 miles south of the Grand Canyon—close enough that studies might bring students there to collect water samples from the Colorado River, discuss issues related to Native populations, or explore the art and culture of the region.

Flagstaff's charm, location, and recreational opportunities consistently earn top honors and distinctions from national publications. Time.com named it one of the nation's happiest cities, and the American Institute for Economic Research named Flagstaff the No. 1 Best College Town in Arizona and No. 3 in the nation. Outside Magazine has named Flagstaff among the best places to live in the United States. Prospective students can explore some of the most popular local sights through NAU's fully immersive online tours: nau.edu/explore.

In addition to Northern Arizona University's Flagstaff campus, NAU has locations throughout the state that provide a convenient way for students to complete an NAU degree at an Arizona community college. Online options allow students to take classes that work with their schedule and location.

Academics

NAU offers nearly 100 bachelor's degrees, about 65 master's degrees, about 20 doctoral degrees, and a wide range of minors, certificates, and emphases, so students are sure to find a program that's right for them. Majors and programs are organized by academic discipline under nine colleges: the College of Arts and Letters; the College of Education; the College of Engineering, Informatics and Applied Sciences; The College of the Environment, Forestry and Natural Sciences; the College of Health and Human Services; the College of Social and Behavioral Sciences; The W. A. Franke College of Business; the Honors College; and the Graduate College. Some of the most popular majors include biomedical science, criminology and criminal justice, nursing, mechanical engineering, elementary education, and hotel and restaurant management.

Through the Honors College, students can pursue a rewarding and enriching academic path that emphasizes small, interactive classes where students gain critical-thinking skills that appeal to employers and graduate schools. The new 200,000-square foot Honors College facility provides meaningful engagement living and working with other motivated students who share a passion for learning.

To complete a bachelor's degree at NAU, students must complete 120 units of credit, including all liberal studies and capstone requirements, and all requirements for a student's specific academic plan. Other requirements, such as a minimum GPA, also apply. Detailed information can be found at nau.edu/academics.

Beyond the Classroom

A degree from NAU represents a quality educational experience—one that incorporates a practical learning approach beyond any textbook. Nearly 600 NAU students each year travel to partner institutions in one of more than 60 foreign countries as part of our international-award-winning study-abroad experiences. Those wishing to stay closer to home can study at one of 200 U.S. institutions through the National Student Exchange program. An internationalization strategy at NAU incorporates global cultures into every discipline. And the Interdisciplinary Global Programs in a STEM field, business, or hospitality infuse language, culture, and a year abroad into students' studies—participants graduate with two degrees: one in their field of study and one in their chosen foreign language.

A signature of the NAU undergraduate experience is a focus on engaged and active learning. Nearly 3,000 students each year engage in practical research opportunities alongside skilled faculty and mentors. More than 1,000 students convene each spring for the Undergraduate Symposium, a large-scale event where students share their research and discoveries and present scholarly and creative work to their peers, professors, and the Flagstaff community.

NAU also takes advantage of its prime location with world-class outdoor education opportunities. An interdisciplinary Grand Canyon semester offers students immersion in the science, culture, and politics of one of the truly unique regions of the U.S. Flagstaff is the world's first International Dark Sky City and offers unparalleled night skies and stargazing facilities for astronomical research, including the Discovery Channel Telescope, the world's fifth-largest. And the 50,000-acre Centennial Forest offers forestry majors and students in other environmental studies programs the chance to conduct research and practice maintenance of a variety of ecosystems.

Facilities

With nearly 90 percent of freshmen choosing to live on campus, students begin to build their community the moment they arrive at NAU. Freshman housing options are based upon each student's academic interests, so they select a room in the Residential College that aligns with their major and career interests and live alongside others who are on a similar journey. Multiple Academic Success Centers on campus provide distinct types of tutoring, most at no cost. And the 225,000-square-foot Cline Library offers an array of services, research materials, and study spaces, and students can reserve rooms, check out laptops, and get help with technology or writing.

NAU is ranked as one of the top 100 research universities without a medical school by the National Science Foundation. The visually striking, five-story Science and Health Building serves as a symbol of the university's rise to scientific and research prominence. This is where students interested in medicine, dentistry, research, or science education will take some of their first steps toward a professional career. The university's one-of-a-kind Native American Cultural Center was built with input from 22 tribes and reflects NAU's commitment to Indigenous students and to helping others learn more about these cultures.

NAU's Aquatic and Tennis Complex attracts international athletes and Olympic teams for high-altitude training, and a world-class recreation facility at the Health and Learning Center offers a 38-foot climbing wall, an indoor jogging track, a fully equipped weight room, cardio studio, and much more.

A visit to campus is the best way to learn more about the university's impressive facilities; for those who can't make it to Flagstaff in person, NAU's online virtual tour is the next best thing: nau.edu/virtualtour.

Costs

NAU tuition and fees for 2020–21 are $11,896 per academic year for Arizona residents and $26,516 for non-residents. Under the Western Undergraduate Exchange (WUE) program, students from 14 qualifying states pay a tuition rate nearly 40 percent lower than the out-of-state rate. The 2020–21 WUE tuition and fee rate is $17,221 per academic year. Tuition rates are set each spring by the Arizona Board of Regents. Room, board, books, transportation, and personal expenses vary by student and are not included in the tuition costs. Students and parents can estimate their total cost of attendance (before scholarships and financial aid) by visiting nau.edu/calculator.

Financial Aid

Students are automatically considered for merit scholarships when they apply. Arizona residents might be eligible for the Lumberjack Scholars Award, which covers up to 100 percent of the cost of in-state tuition. Non-residents might be eligible for a number of awards including the President's Excellence Scholarship, valued at $36,000 over four years. NAU's friendly financial aid staff is available to help students explore other opportunities such as private scholarships, grants, and loans in order to make their education as affordable as possible. More details regarding financial aid can be found at nau.edu/finaid.

Faculty

Northern Arizona University is designed for discovery. The faculty and staff care about student success and encourage students to push past their limits and develop new strengths. From biology to social sciences, professors weave interactive learning into NAU's curriculum, providing students with the hands-on experience they need to succeed and opportunities to make original contributions to a field of study.

NAU professors from a variety of disciplines are among the leading experts in their fields, such as astronomy professor David Trilling, who is one of the world's foremost asteroid researchers and works on several NASA-funded projects investigating hundreds of asteroids, including those that could strike Earth. Biology professor Kiisa Nishikawa's muscle function theory is improving prosthetic devices and neuromuscular disease treatment. And entomology professor Rich Hofstetter studies how loud rock music might slow the infestation of bark beetles, which destroy pine trees and increase wildfire danger in Southwestern forests.

Student Clubs and Organizations

Getting involved in campus life is one of the best ways students can gain leadership skills and define their own NAU experience. Northern Arizona University offers more than 400 clubs and organizations ranging from sport clubs and intramurals to sororities and fraternities. There is also a wide range of leadership, academic, and service organizations related to almost every hobby, passion, or academic interest students might have.

Studies have shown that students who are involved in campus activities are more likely to be successful; it's also a great way to meet new friends. NAU students can join organizations such as First Jacks, which empowers first-generation college students toward personal and academic success; or find a sense of 'ohana, or family, with the HAPA Hawaiian Club. The university's thriving intramural sports program ranges from favorites such as basketball and soccer to unique sports such as Canoe Battleship and even Quidditch. If a student can't find the exact club they're looking for, they can always start one of their own! Whatever a student's interest, pursuits, or background, there is a club or organization offering a sense of community and a chance to get involved.

Admission Requirements and Application Information

NAU applicants will be offered admission if they demonstrate a 3.0 high school core GPA and have no deficiencies in the 16 required college preparatory courses. Students will be considered for admission if they have a 2.5 high school core GPA and no more than one deficiency in any two areas of the college preparatory courses. Additionally, applicants with mathematics and science combination deficiencies are not admissible.

Students can apply online at nau.edu/apply. They are required to access their high school transcripts and self-report them on the online application. ACT and SAT scores are not required to apply or for scholarship eligibility, but could increase the amount of scholarships a student might receive. Test scores will never count against NAU applicants in admission or scholarship decisions. A $25 application fee is required. Deadlines and additional details are available online at nau.edu/admissions.

Northern Arizona University
University Admissions
P.O. Box 4084
Student and Academic Services Building (#60)
Flagstaff, Arizona 86011-4084
Phone: 888-628-2968 (toll-free)
Fax: 928-523-6023
Email: admissions@nau.edu
Website: nau.edu

Consistently named among the nation's top college towns, Flagstaff is a vibrant, high-elevation mountain town that breaks Arizona's desert stereotype.

COLLEGE CLOSE-UPS

OHIO NORTHERN UNIVERSITY

ADA, OHIO

The University

Ohio Northern University (ONU) has a 96 percent job and graduate school placement rate. Its long-standing success is partly because of excellent professors, partly because of ambitious students, and partly because the University has always been rooted in relationships and the future. At ONU, students forge strong connections with their professors and classmates. They receive individualized attention to discover their passions and achieve at a high level. ONU students move toward a career long before they graduate—and ONU's alumni successes prove it. With top-ranked programs and opportunities outside the classroom, any path a student chooses at ONU is grounded in concrete applications for the future. Established in 1871 and comprised of five colleges (Arts & Sciences, Business Administration, Engineering, Pharmacy, and Law), ONU's beautiful residential campus is made up of more than sixty modern residences and academic buildings and provides a vibrant campus experience.

Students can choose from a variety of campus activities including more than 200 student organizations; four national sororities and seven national fraternities; fine arts, music, and theatrical events; and intramural and club sports. Residence hall living is an integral part of the educational program, contributing to a student's personal development. There are nine residence halls on campus as well as eight campus apartment complexes and an Affinity Housing complex.

The ONU Polar Bears compete successfully at the NCAA Division III level in twenty-three varsity sports as part of the highly respected Ohio Athletic Conference. ONU has twelve men's teams (baseball, basketball, cross-country, football, golf, lacrosse, soccer, swimming and diving, tennis, indoor and outdoor track, and wrestling) and eleven women's teams (basketball, cross-country, fast-pitch softball, golf, lacrosse, soccer, swimming and diving, tennis, indoor and outdoor track, and volleyball). In fall 2019, ONU began competing in esports.

Location

Ohio Northern University's campus is situated on 342 beautiful acres in the village of Ada (population 5,500). Located in northwestern Ohio, ONU is easily accessible by major highways and conveniently located near major cities such as Columbus, Dayton, Toledo, and Fort Wayne, Indiana.

Majors and Degrees

Ohio Northern University offers the undergraduate degrees: Bachelor of Arts, Bachelor of Fine Arts, Bachelor of Music, Bachelor of Science, Bachelor of Science in Business Administration, Bachelor of Science in Civil Engineering, Bachelor of Science in Medical Laboratory Science, Bachelor of Science in Computer Engineering, Bachelor of Science in Electrical Engineering, Bachelor of Science in Mechanical Engineering, and Bachelor of Science in Nursing. In addition to the undergraduate programs, ONU offers a Master of Science in Accounting; Juris Doctor; and Doctor of Pharmacy (Pharm.D.), which is a 0-6, direct entry program. The 3+3 Law Admissions Program leads to an approved bachelor's degree plus a juris doctorate degree. Majors considered for the 3+3 Admissions Program include business administration; chemistry; creative writing; literature; history; philosophy; philosophy, politics, and economics (PPE); political science; religion; and sociology.

Majors are offered in accounting; art education; biochemistry; biology; chemistry; civil engineering; communication studies; computer engineering; computer science; construction management; creative writing; criminal justice; data analytics; early childhood education; electrical engineering; engineering education; engineering exploratory; environmental and field biology; exercise physiology; finance; forensic biology; graphic design; history; international theatre production; language arts education; literature; management; manufacturing technology; marketing; mathematics; mechanical engineering; medical laboratory science; middle childhood education; molecular biology; music; music education; musical theatre; nursing; pharmaceutical and healthcare business; pharmacy; philosophy; philosophy, politics, and economics; physics; political science; psychology; public health; public relations; religion; social studies; sociology; Spanish; sport management; statistics; studio arts; technology education; theatre; writing and multimedia studies; youth ministry; undecided business; undecided general studies; and undecided sciences.

Special preprofessional programs are available in dentistry, law, medicine, occupational therapy, physical therapy, physician assistant, seminary, and veterinary medicine. Teacher licensure programs are offered at the early childhood, middle childhood, adolescent/young adult, and multiage levels within 16 programs and two endorsement areas.

ONU designed its academic programs to offer optimal flexibility. Many ONU students double major or add minors or concentrations to expand their career options for the future. Changes in programs of study are updated at www.onu.edu.

Academic Programs

The Getty College of Arts & Sciences creatively combines a traditional liberal arts education with cutting-edge preprofessional studies. The college offers more than 50 majors in six schools: Center for Teacher Education; Visual and Performing Arts; Health and Behavioral Sciences; Humanities and Global Cultures; Science, Mathematics and Technology; and Social Sciences and Human Interaction. Students can earn a Bachelor of Arts, Bachelor of Fine Arts, Bachelor of Music, Bachelor of Science, Bachelor of Science in Medical Laboratory Science, or Bachelor of Science in Nursing.

Thirteen students in the sciences have been honored by the Barry M. Goldwater Scholarship and Excellence in Education Foundation in the past eleven years. The college has also been recognized as one of the top 200 programs in the nation for creative students in Creative Colleges: A Guide for Student Actors, Artists, Dancers, Musicians and Writers.

Working closely with dedicated faculty members, students complete the general education requirements, delve deeply into advanced courses, and engage in high-impact learning through research, internships, practicum experiences, study abroad, and more.

The Dicke College of Business Administration focuses on creating ethical, entrepreneurial, and professional business and civic leaders. The college offers a rigorous academic curriculum with a signature program in pharmaceutical and healthcare business. Internships are required by the college and are available year-round. There are international programs, including study abroad, work abroad, and study tours. An office of experiential learning supports students looking for these opportunities. The course of study for the Bachelor of Science in Business Administration includes a four-year business core experience themed around strategic business planning. Personal attention and mentoring from faculty members, small intimate classes, and active student organizations combine with an emphasis on experiential learning, global awareness, and the entrepreneurial spirit. The college is accredited by the AACSB International—The Association to Advance Collegiate Schools of Business. The Dicke College of Business Administration is ranked by Bloomberg Businessweek among the top 50 undergraduate business programs in the United States and No. 1 in Ohio for teaching quality.

The T. J. Smull College of Engineering is noted for its hands-on learning; small, intimate classes; dedicated, accessible professors; and world-class, top-ranked instruction. Ranked thirtieth in the nation for undergraduate engineering programs by U.S. News & World Report, ONU's engineering and computer science programs prepare graduates who think critically, lead confidently, and have solid technical foundations upon which to build successful long-term careers. From strong lab components to a host of experiential learning opportunities, ONU's faculty is committed to helping its students achieve their educational goals and realize their dreams. The college features six accredited, disciplinary majors in civil, computer, electrical, and mechanical engineering; computer science; and engineering education, a degree option supporting the demand for high school math teachers with engineering degrees. A new, state-of-the-art engineering building opened in fall 2019.

The courses for the first academic year are essentially the same for each degree program, offering students an easy track to move from one program to another if initially uncertain which disciplines they prefer to study.

An optional five-year co-op program is available for students in each program, provided they maintain a minimum 2.5 GPA. The college focuses on high-impact learning as an essential part of an engineering education; thus, in addition to a co-op program, students apply their classroom learning in freshman design projects, senior capstone projects, national design competitions, and numerous engineering projects in community service (EPICS). Further, many opportunities are available for valuable work experience through the co-op and internship programs, with a historically high job-placement rate for graduates.

For more than 130 years, the Raabe College of Pharmacy has offered distinctive, challenging, and comprehensive training for some of the nation's most talented pharmacists. This University signature program features a six-year Doctor of Pharmacy (Pharm.D.) degree accredited by the American Council on Pharmaceutical Education. This program is direct-entry, admitting students immediately from high school into the college's professional program. This approach enables students to take pharmacy courses from the very first day. A rigorous curriculum utilizes an innovative modular format to organize learning around the human body systems and patient care implementation.

Cutting-edge clinical facilities include the Pharmacy Skills Center, where students access state-of-the-art compounding/counseling pods with portable OTC simulation stations. Students gain considerable experience through a strong undergraduate research program and through the college's on-campus pharmacy facility. Faculty members are teaching-focused but remain current in their research disciplines. Upon graduation, students are well schooled in every aspect of pharmacy and have a high placement rate.

Off-Campus Programs

Many majors may take part in study-abroad programs developed in consultation with faculty members. Field experiences and internships are available to most majors. Externships are required of all pharmacy majors and place students in retail and clinical experiences. Teacher licensure requires one semester of primary or secondary classroom teaching experience under the supervision of practicing teachers. Additional opportunities include computer science and mathematics co-op programs (professional practice), engineering co-op programs (professional practice, domestic and international), and an honors program. All off-campus learning experiences carry credit.

Academic Facilities

Among the nineteen modern academic buildings on campus, the newest is the James Lehr Kennedy Engineering Building. This 105,000-square-foot facility is a sleek, innovative space for learning and collaborating. Every lab and workspace is available to engineering students starting their first year.

The Mathile Center for the Natural Sciences is a 95,145-square-foot student-centered academic research and learning facility that blends hands-on teaching excellence with advanced technology in a functional modern environment.

The College of Business Administration's Dicke Hall offers students a modern setting for high-tech classrooms, meeting rooms and a 150-seat lecture forum.

ONU's Heterick Memorial Library and the Taggart Law Library provide information resources and services to support course offerings and foster independent study.

The Freed Center for the Performing Arts houses Communications and Theatre Arts classrooms and features a 550-seat theater/concert hall, a 120-seat studio theater, and television and radio production facilities. WONB Radio is the voice of ONU.

Costs

Tuition and fees charges for the 2020-21 year are $33,470 for the Colleges of Arts & Sciences and Business Administration; $38,320 for the College of Engineering; and $39,570 for the College of Pharmacy. These totals do not include room and board.

Financial Aid

Even with one of the highest returns on investment in the nation, ONU invests more than $52 million toward merit-based scholarships and need-based resources. The average ONU student receives approximately $23,500 in scholarships and grants. To be considered, the student should submit the FAFSA to the University along with the admission application.

Faculty

More than 200 full-time faculty members bring extensive academic, work, travel, and life experience to their classrooms. Ohio Northern values excellence, innovation, technology, diversity, and its people. With an 11:1 student-faculty ratio, students get lots of personal attention from professors who are passionate about teaching and mentoring.

Student Government

The Student Senate provides self-government in many areas of student life and seeks to further ideals of character and service to the University. The Student Senate serves as the official representative group of the student body to the University administration and agencies in matters pertaining to the student body.

Admission Requirements

High school students applying for admission to the University should present an official transcript indicating at least 16 total units of study, including work in specific academic areas as indicated by each college. Applicants are also required to submit scores on the ACT and/or SAT. For scholarship purposes, the traditional sections of the ACT and the SAT are considered. An on-campus interview is also recommended.

Application and Information

In the colleges of Arts & Sciences, Business Administration, and Engineering, a student's file is considered complete when it contains the application, official high school transcript, and ACT and/or SAT scores. The College of Pharmacy requires an essay and a recommendation in addition to the previous items.

The College of Pharmacy's priority application deadline is December 1 for entering freshmen. A campus visit is strongly encouraged for consideration for admittance into this college.

Requests for catalogs or additional information should be directed to:

Office of Admissions
Ohio Northern University
525 South Main Street
Ada, Ohio 45810
Phone: 888-408-4668 (toll-free)
Fax: 419-772-2821
E-mail: admissions-ug@onu.edu
Website: www.onu.edu
www.facebook.com/ohionorthern
www.twitter.com/ohionorthern

BUILDING ENGINEERS - The James Lehr Kennedy Engineering Building, our new home of the T.J. Smull College of Engineering, opened in Fall 2019. The innovative 105,000-square-foot facility features space for collaboration, class projects and community-building, and a state-of-the-art cybersecurity laboratory and high-speed computing cluster, keeping ONU on the cutting edge of educating engineers who make a difference. ONU engineers are improving our world by finding new ways to design, build and use technology. We're ranked among the top 50 undergraduate engineering schools in the nation, and our engineering education major is one of the first of its kind.

PACE UNIVERSITY

NEW YORK CITY AND WESTCHESTER, NEW YORK

The University

Founded in 1906, Pace University is a leading private metropolitan university that offers an exceptional liberal arts education combined with superior professional preparation, two strategic undergraduate New York locations, and robust scholarships and financial aid. The diverse student population of 8,914 undergraduates (6,284 in New York City and 2,630 in Westchester) is enrolled in more than 3,000 courses across 100-plus majors and combined, accelerated bachelor's and graduate degree programs. These are offered through five undergraduate schools and colleges: the Lubin School of Business, the Dyson College of Arts and Sciences, the Seidenberg School of Computer Science and Information Systems, the School of Education, and the College of Health Professions. Pace facilitates more than 5,000 internships, co-op experiences, practicums, field experiences, and clinical assignments every year.

Many student-led clubs and organizations are active on the campus, including the Pace Advertising Club, African Students Association, the Pace Association for Collegiate Entrepreneurs, the Student Government Association, and the Collegiate Psychology Club. Pace also offers many campus activities, including student government associations, fraternities, sororities, two campus newspapers, two literary magazines, two yearbooks, and two campus broadcasting systems. Athletic facilities are available for students, and intercollegiate sports include baseball, basketball, cross-country, cheerleading, dance, women's field hockey, football, lacrosse, women's soccer, women's softball, swimming and diving, and women's volleyball.

The student body is diverse, representing forty-nine states, five U.S. territories, and more than 100 countries.

Location

Pace University is a multicampus institution with campuses in both New York City and Westchester, New York. Both locations are within reach of cultural, business, and social resources and opportunities. The New York City campus is located in the heart of the Financial District in lower Manhattan, and within a short walking distance of Wall Street and the South Street Seaport. Lincoln Center, Broadway theaters, museums, and many world-famous attractions are minutes away by public transportation. Located 35 miles north of New York City, the newly renovated Westchester campus offers a traditional college experience: state-of-the-art science and video production labs, competitive athletics, fraternities and sororities, and access to internship opportunities at many Fortune 500 companies.

Students can take courses at either campus, and housing is available in both New York City and Westchester residence halls.

Majors and Degrees

The following programs are offered at both the New York City and Westchester campuses. The Bachelor of Business Administration (B.B.A.) is offered with majors in accounting (with concentrations in forensic accounting and internal auditing), accounting—public, finance, general business, information systems, international management, management (with concentrations in business, entrepreneurship, health care, hospitality and tourism, and human resources), and marketing (with concentrations in advertising and integrated marketing communications, global marketing management, and sports marketing). In addition, a five-year combined B.B.A./M.B.A in public accounting is available for qualified students. The Bachelor of Arts (B.A.) degree is granted in adolescent education (with concentrations in biology, chemistry, earth science, English, history/social studies, mathematics, and Spanish), applied psychology and human relations, biology, childhood education, computer science, early childhood education, economics, environmental studies, film and screen studies, health science, history, information systems, liberal studies, mathematics, philosophy and religious studies, political science, and psychology. The Bachelor of Science (B.S.) degree is offered in biochemistry, biology, business economics, chemistry, computer science, criminal justice, economics, environmental science, health science, information systems, information systems, information technology, mathematics, professional computer studies, and professional studies.

Certain programs are available only on one campus. The B.S. programs in biology–pre-professional (occupational therapy, optometry, and podiatry) and forensic science; the B.B.A. programs in arts and entertainment management, and business analytics; the B.F.A. programs in acting, art, commercial dance, musical theater, and production and design for stage and screen; and the B.A. programs in acting; acting for film, television, voice-overs, and commercials; American studies; art; art history; communication science and disorders; communication studies; directing; English language and literature; language, culture, and world trade; global Asia studies; global professional studies; Latin American studies; modern languages and culture; peace and justice studies; sociology-anthropology; Spanish; stage management; teaching students with speech and language disabilities; theater arts (acting and design/technical); and women's and gender studies are offered only at the New York City campus. The B.A. programs in biological psychology, communication arts and journalism, communications, digital journalism, digital cinema and filmmaking, English, English and communications, education, global professional studies, and personality and social psychology, and the B.S. programs in nursing are available at the Westchester campus only.

Pace University offers a five-year engineering programs in cooperation with Manhattan College and Rensselaer Polytechnic Institute. Students attend Pace for three years and either Manhattan College or Rensselaer for two years. Upon successful completion, students receive a B.S. degree in chemistry from Pace and either a Bachelor of Chemical Engineering (B.C.E.) in chemical engineering from Manhattan or a B.S. degree in engineering from Rensselaer.

Academic Programs

The Pace Path is an innovative program unique to Pace University that helps each student become successful in college, career, and life. Each student develops strengths in managing oneself, interpersonal relations, and organizational awareness through co-curricular activities with an academic program. This is accomplished through collaboration with Pace faulty, advisers, staff, coaches, and mentors. The Pace Path is framed by Pace's historic mission of *Opportunitas* and prepares innovative thinkers through a powerful combination of knowledge in the professions, real-world experience, and rigorous liberal arts curriculum.

The Pforzheimer Honors College is a highly esteemed opportunity at Pace—a community of talented undergraduate scholars studying under the distinguished faculty of the University's five undergraduate schools and colleges. It is a place to excel and realize potential.

Pace University's internship program is nationally recognized and offers qualified students the opportunity to gain experience in their field of study while earning a four-year degree. Students can choose full-time, part-time, or summer positions working in an area directly related to their major course of study. Over 4,000 Pace students participate each year in internships, faculty-sponsored research, consulting projects, fieldwork, and practicums—Pace's Career Services team is one of the largest in the New York Metropolitan area.

Academic Facilities

Pace University opened its second new high-rise (34 stories) residence hall on its New York City campus in fall 2015. It is the tallest university residence hall in the world. In addition, there are brand new science labs, art studios, an honors student lounge, and School of Performing Arts studios. The Westchester campus had the most visible and dramatic changes with new modern residence halls, enlarged student centers, digital video/filmmaking facilities, new environmental center with indoor and outdoor classrooms, expanded athletic fields, and new field house.

Costs

For the 2018–19 academic year, undergraduate tuition was $43,624 per year for full-time study. The cost for an on-campus double-occupancy room and board was $16,600–$19,200, with different housing options available.

Financial Aid

Pace University strives to provide opportunities to students of diverse backgrounds and varied circumstances and is committed to offering financial aid to students to the fullest extent of its resources. University-sponsored scholarships are awarded to students on the basis of academic merit, service to the community, and financial need. The goal is to offer every student as much financial assistance as possible, based upon availability and need. Last year, ninety-two percent of first-year students received financial aid. Pace's comprehensive student financial aid assistance program includes scholarships, grants, on-campus employment, student loans (federal and alternative plans), and tuition payment plans. Pace participates in all federal financial aid programs and the New York State Tuition Assistance Program (TAP) and honors awards from other states' incentive grant programs.

Students should submit the Free Application for Federal Student Aid (FAFSA) by November 15 for priority consideration for the fall semester. Pace University's new Net Price Calculator (www.pace.edu/calculator) is an online tool designed to help students and their families estimate their financial aid package. Many find that Pace is actually more affordable than similar public and private colleges due to the scholarship and financial aid awards offered to families.

Faculty

First and foremost, Pace University professors are dedicated teachers. All Pace classes are taught by professors. Students will never take a course taught by a teaching assistant. Faculty members also bring real-world experience and scholarship into the classroom through their work with outside companies and organizations and by leading cutting-edge research projects. Faculty members come from the best graduate and doctoral programs in the country. Professors—90 percent of whom hold Ph.D.'s—have earned degrees from the University of Pennsylvania, Harvard, Brown, Columbia, and Yale. Pace professors work closely with students to not only broaden their academic horizons, but to show how their work in the classroom is applicable to their future careers.

Admission Requirements

A minimum of 16 academic units from an accredited secondary school, or equivalent, are required. Academic subjects in high school should be distributed as follows: 4 years of English, 3–4 years of college-preparatory mathematics, 2 years of foreign language, 3–4 years of history/social science, 2 years of laboratory science, and 2–3 units of academic electives. All domestic applicants are required to take either the SAT or ACT examination and have results forwarded to the University. International students are required to take the TOEFL, IELTS, or PTE.

Application and Information

Students can apply online at www.pace.edu/apply.

For more information contact:

Pace University
861 Bedford Road
Pleasantville, New York 10570-2799
Phone: 800-874-7223 (toll-free)
E-mail: infoctr@pace.edu
Website: http://www.pace.edu

PEPPERDINE UNIVERSITY
Seaver College
MALIBU, CALIFORNIA

PEPPERDINE

The University and The College

Pepperdine University is a private, faith-based university committed to the highest standards of academic excellence and Christian values, where students are strengthened for lives of purpose, service, and leadership.

Seaver College, Pepperdine's undergraduate liberal arts college, is comprised of approximately 3,400 students, 53 percent of which come from California. Thirty-four percent hail from the other forty-nine states, and 13 percent are international. The 2019–20 freshmen class had an average high school GPA of 3.76. It's this diversity of backgrounds and worldviews that helps contribute to Pepperdine's unique educational experience.

Nestled between the Santa Monica Mountains and the Pacific Ocean, Pepperdine's Malibu campus provides fantastic on-campus housing options for all students. Students are required to live on campus during their first and second years, and also have premium residence halls available as upperclassmen.

Students have a wide range of extracurricular activities and organizations to choose from, including social, honor, service, spiritual, professional, divisional, and special interest clubs. Pepperdine provides students with interests in communications and media the chance to be involved with the campus radio station, weekly student newspaper and television broadcast.

Pepperdine has 17 Division One men's and women's athletic programs that have won an impressive 13 national team championships and 12 individual national championships. As a member of the West Coast Conference, the University houses a 3,500-seat gymnasium, an Olympic-size swimming pool, a tennis pavilion and sixteen additional tennis courts, an intramural field, and a 2,000-seat baseball stadium.

Pepperdine's graduate schools include the School of Law, School of Public Policy, School of Education and Psychology, and the George L. Graziado School of Business and Management. These distinguished programs offer master's degrees in law, dispute resolution, public policy, business, and more.

Location

Overlooking the Pacific Ocean in scenic Malibu, California, and less than an hour from downtown Los Angeles, Seaver's Malibu campus offers both the benefits of a small coastal community and the advantages of proximity to a major metropolitan area.

Malibu is a pristine beach community with excellent restaurants, a movie theater, and shopping centers complete with banking facilities and industry-leading brands. The winding seashore and rugged beauty of Malibu connects students to a litany of nightlife options in Santa Monica, Hollywood, and Los Angeles. Malibu's clean air provides an environment conducive to study, while the moderate climate permits year-round outdoor recreation. In addition to making use of the physical education facilities on campus, students can enjoy swimming, surfing, horseback riding, fishing, hiking, boating, kayaking, and other activities in the vicinity. As an international epicenter of culture, industry, and trade, Los Angeles provides students with a one-of-a-kind living experience.

Majors and Degrees

Students can choose from forty-five majors and thirty-seven minors. Seaver College awards the Bachelor of Arts in advertising, art, art history, biology, chemistry, communication, creative writing, economics, English, film studies, French, German, Hispanic studies (Spanish), history, integrated marketing communication, international studies, Italian, journalism, liberal arts, math education, media production, music, natural science, philosophy, political science, psychology, public relations, religion, sociology, sport administration, sports medicine, theater and music, theater and media production, and theater arts.

The Bachelor of Science is awarded in accounting, biology, business administration, chemistry, computer science and mathematics, international business, mathematics, nutritional science, physics, and sports medicine. A teacher education program offers credentials in single or multiple subjects.

Academic Programs

The academic programs at Seaver College provide students with a liberal arts education in a Christian atmosphere that sharpens critical thinking, improves information literacy, and builds a learning community. Students must complete 128 units for the B.A. or B.S. degree, including 64 units in general education requirements and 40 or more in upper-division studies.

Major requirements may be fulfilled through three basic arrangements. Students who specialize in a discipline must complete at least 24 units of upper-division work in their chosen discipline. Students may choose an interdisciplinary major, entailing at least 40 units of upper-division work, with courses ranging broadly across disciplinary lines within a division and on occasion crossing divisional lines, in one of the following fields of study: communication, English, humanities, international studies, liberal arts, or religion. Alternatively, students may initiate a contract major by presenting an application for specific upper-division courses to the Dean of Seaver College.

Seaver College functions on a semester plan; the regular academic year consists of two semesters from late August to April. In addition to the regular academic year, summer sessions run from early May to August.

At Seaver, instruction and study are adapted both to students' abilities and to the nature of the course content, instead of utilizing only the traditional lecture method. Programs involve several types of learning experiences: seminars, integrated lectures, individual study, fieldwork, and laboratories. Students are never taught by a teacher's assistant at Pepperdine; the average class size is 19 students and a student-to-faculty ratio of 13:1 fosters an environment where professors are invested in the growth and success of their students.

The Dean's List of undergraduate students is published each semester, comprised of the top 10 percent of the class with a grade point index no lower than 3.5. Other honors include cum laude for students graduating with a scholastic level of at least 3.5, magna cum laude for 3.7, and summa cum laude for 3.9.

Off-Campus Programs

At Seaver, students have the opportunity to study abroad in Buenos Aires, Argentina; Florence, Italy; Heidelberg, Germany; Lausanne, Switzerland; London, England; and Shanghai, China. The academic programs emphasize European, Latin American, or Asian history and culture. Seaver also offers an internship-based program in Washington, D.C. and summer special interest programs in Spain, Thailand, East Africa, and the Middle East. Classes are taught by Seaver faculty members. Serious study and the daily experiences of living in another country give students a special depth of understanding of other cultures and a broader world perspective.

The Buenos Aires program accommodates approximately 60 students who live in the homes of carefully selected host families. The Florence program houses approximately 55 students who live in a Florentine villa and residential complex with classrooms, a library, a computer facility, and recreational facilities. The Heidelberg program has space for approximately 50 students at the Moore Haus, located near the city's famous castle. Classes are held in modern facilities in downtown Heidelberg. The Lausanne program accommodates about 70 students. The Pepperdine facility is located in La Croisée near the center of Lausanne, which has a picturesque view of Lake Geneva and the French Alps. The London program has space for approximately 40 students in the Knightsbridge area. In addition to living quarters, the facility includes classrooms, a library, a computer room, offices, and a student center. The Shanghai program accommodates approximately 40 students who live in the Pepperdine-owned jia, meaning "house," which is located in the French Concession area near the American Consulate. The majority of the international program facilities are University-owned.

Academic Facilities

The Malibu campus is home to academic complexes containing seminar and lecture rooms, art studios, communication facilities, science and computer laboratories, mini-theaters, a recital hall, and administrative offices. The newly renovated Payson Library is the global gateway to knowledge and provides students access to thousands of online journals, articles, and periodicals through various databases. Payson Library serves as a sanctuary for study, learning, and research by encouraging discovery, contemplation, social discourse, and creative expression.

The 300-seat George Elkins Auditorium is used for public presentations and lectures. The Center for the Arts facility includes the renowned Frederick R. Weisman Museum of Art and the Smothers Theatre, which seats 450 people and is used for dance, music, and theater performances. The Center for Communication and Business building houses a state-of-the-art radio and television production center where students have the opportunity to work on Pepperdine's cable television and radio stations.

Costs

Costs for the 2019–20 academic year were $55,640 for tuition, $15,670 for room and board, and $252 for additional campus life fees.

Financial Aid

Approximately 88 percent of Seaver's students receive some form of financial assistance through scholarships, loans, grants, work-study programs, or jobs within the University. To be eligible for financial assistance from institutional resources, an undergraduate student must be enrolled in at least 12 units. To ensure full consideration, the Free Application for Federal Student Aid (FAFSA) should be submitted by the priority deadlines of November 1 for early action and February 15 for regular decision for the fall semester and October 15 for the spring semester. Students who qualify should also apply for the Cal Grant (California residents only). Prospective students will receive their estimated financial assistance award after admission to the University but prior to the enrollment deadline.

Faculty

Seaver College's faculty includes men and women of high academic distinction whose primary focus is instruction with a secondary focus on research. Fifty-four percent of faculty members are full-time, and 85 percent of full-time faculty members hold a doctorate or terminal degree in their field. Upon enrollment, each student is assigned an academic adviser from among the faculty members. A qualified counseling staff is also available to assist with personal, professional, and academic needs.

Student Government

The Student Government Association (SGA) is composed of student leaders dedicated to providing Pepperdine's students with quality representation through innovative advocacy programs. SGA serves as the voice of the students to the Seaver administration and works in coordination with the Student Activities Office in establishing activities and maintaining school policies. Seaver has more than 1,000 programmed on-campus events each year including movies, sightseeing trips, guest performances, dances, speakers, and more. Pepperdine has eight nationally recognized sororities and five fraternities and there are over 110 different student clubs and organizations on campus that focus on a range of interests, including academic, language, art, music, dance, drama, sports, and politics.

Admission Requirements

Applicants are admitted on the basis of their academic record, SAT or ACT scores, and personal information and references. Transfer applicants are high school graduates who have taken any transferable college units after graduating high school. Students who took colleges courses prior to graduating high school are not considered transfer students and should apply as a first-year student. To ensure full consideration for the fall semester, students should apply by the early action deadline of November 1 or regular application deadline of January 15. October 1 is the regular deadline for the spring semester. Decision letter dates are announced in the current application form.

Seaver College seeks to enroll a diverse student body. As such, Pepperdine University does not unlawfully discriminate on the basis of any status or condition protected by applicable federal or state law in the administration of its educational policies, admission, financial assistance, employment, educational programs, or activities.

Application and Information

To request information, students should contact:

Office of Admission
Seaver College
Pepperdine University
Malibu, California 90263-4392
Phone: 310-506-4392
E-mail: admission-seaver@pepperdine.edu
Website: http://seaver.pepperdine.edu/admission
https://seaver.pepperdine.edu/admission/risingtide (Docuseries)
http://instagram.com/seaveradmission# (Instagram)
http://on.fb.me/Seaver_Admission (Facebook)
http://twitter.com/#!/SeaverAdmission (Twitter)
http://bit.ly/YouTube_Pepperdine (YouTube)
http://pinterest.com/seaveradmission/ (Pinterest)

The 830-acre Malibu campus of Pepperdine University, Seaver College, overlooks the Pacific Ocean, 30 miles west of Los Angeles, California.

REED COLLEGE

PORTLAND, OREGON

The College

Referred to as one of the most intellectual colleges in the country, Reed is known for its high standards of scholarly practice, creative thinking, and engaged citizenship. A genuine enthusiasm for academic work and intellectual exchange is valued, and the Honor Principle, Reed's ethos that guides both academic and campus life, ensures personal responsibility and mutual respect within its small community of 1,483 students and 143 faculty members. More than four-fifths of Reed's students come from outside the Northwest, with one-fifth from the Northeast and one-tenth from outside of the United States. Over 40 percent of Reed's students identify with historically underrepresented racial and ethnic backgrounds. Reed's twenty-seven residence halls enable approximately 80 percent of students to live on campus.

At its founding, Reed rejected fraternal societies and varsity sports. The goal was to foster a climate of inclusivity and collaboration focused on academics. This atmosphere persists, with student groups—social, religious, and cultural—open to all and wellness and the development of athletic skills taking precedence over competition.

Location

Reed's 116-acre wooded campus is located in a residential section of southeast Portland. The city, a welcoming metropolis, offers a thriving local music scene, diverse restaurants and food carts, tranquil Japanese and Chinese gardens, noisy downtown clubs, a plethora of bridges and bike paths, and the largest independent bookstore in the world. Just 90 minutes west of Portland are the wild beaches of the Pacific Ocean; 90 minutes east are the ski slopes of Mount Hood, where Reed owns a ski cabin for use by the college community.

Majors and Degrees

Reed College awards the Bachelor of Arts degree in a variety of traditional fields as well as in interdisciplinary combinations. Students may select from the following majors: American studies, anthropology, art, biochemistry and molecular biology, biology, chemistry, chemistry-physics, Chinese literature, classics, classics-religion, comparative literature, comparative race and ethnicity studies, computer science, dance, dance-theater, economics, English literature, environmental studies, French literature, German literature, history, history-literature, international and comparative policy studies, linguistics, literature-theater, mathematics, mathematics-computer science, mathematics-physics, music, neuroscience, philosophy, physics, political science, psychology, religion, religion-political science, Russian literature, sociology, Spanish literature, and theatre.

Students may also design their own interdisciplinary majors. The approval of such special programs, which link two or more disciplines, is reviewed by the student's adviser and the departments concerned.

Reed offers several combined 3-2 programs, which allow students to graduate with degrees from Reed and an affiliated institution. Science programs and institutions include engineering (California Institute of Technology, Columbia University, and Rensselaer Polytechnic Institute) and forestry-environmental sciences (Duke University). The college also has a combined program in visual arts (Pacific Northwest College of Art).

Academic Programs

Hallmarks of academic life at Reed include the small-group conference method of teaching and its reliance on active student participation; a de-emphasizing of grades coupled with comprehensive narrative feedback; a yearlong interdisciplinary humanities program; and distribution requirements that balance breadth of learning with the depth of designing an in-depth senior thesis. In addition to fulfilling the requirements for the major, taking the humanities course, and writing the senior thesis, students must satisfy a distributional requirement, consisting of core classes from each of the following academic groups: arts, literature, and languages; history and social sciences; laboratory sciences and mathematics.

Off-Campus Programs

Reed participates in domestic exchange programs with Howard University in Washington, D.C.; Sarah Lawrence College in New York; and Sea Education Association in Massachusetts. In addition, Reed provides study-abroad opportunities for students in Argentina, Australia, Botswana, China, Costa Rica, Cuba, the Czech Republic, Ecuador, Egypt, England, France, Germany, Greece, Hungary, Ireland, Israel, Italy, Lebanon, Morocco, Palestine, Russia, Scotland, South Africa, Spain, Taiwan, Tanzania, Turkey, and Turks and Caicos. Students may also arrange independent study plans in consultation with appropriate faculty members, the director for off-campus studies, and the registrar.

Academic Facilities

Students have access to Reed's substantial library collection by searching the online catalog in the library or from any computer on the campus network. Through its participation in Summit, a union catalog of Oregon and Washington academic libraries, Reed provides online access to other library catalogs and databases. Students may borrow materials directly from academic libraries in the Portland area, as well as from collections worldwide through interlibrary loan. In addition, the Reed library houses a first-rate art gallery, a language lab, and a multimedia resource facility. The Reed library is open 18 hours most days and 24 hours a day during examinations.

The science laboratories at Reed are among the best equipped of any undergraduate college in the United States. These include the A.A. Knowlton Laboratory of Physics, the Arthur F. Scott Laboratory of Chemistry, and the L.E. Griffin Memorial Biology Building. Reed's nuclear research reactor (the only such reactor in the country that is staffed primarily by undergraduates) and radiochemistry lab are actively used for student research, instruction, and training. For those interested in the arts, the campus houses studio art facilities, performing arts facilities, twenty instrumental practice rooms, a computer music laboratory, a recording system, and an 800-seat auditorium. In fall 2013, Reed opened a new $28-million Performing Arts Building, representing the important role the arts play at Reed. Other popular facilities include a radio station and Reed's newly expanded sports center, which offers a climbing wall and a nationally recognized outdoor program.

Costs

Tuition for 2019–20 is $58,130, and room and board is $14,620. The student body fee is $310, bringing the yearly total cost to approximately $73,060. The cost of books and incidental expenses averages approximately $2,000.

Financial Aid

Over half of the Reed student body receives financial assistance from the college. The need-based financial aid program makes Reed accessible to students from a wide range of economic backgrounds. The college guarantees to meet the full demonstrated need of all continuing students in good academic standing who complete their financial aid applications on time. Reed's own funds are the primary source of grants to students; the average financial aid package for the incoming class of 2023 was $45,490.. Reed also administers federal and state grants as well as federally subsidized loan programs. Campus employment and work-study programs are available. The size of a financial aid award is based solely upon analysis of the student's need. The average amount awarded to all students receiving financial aid in 2019-20 was $47,547, which included grants, loans, and work opportunities. Reed students' average graduating loan debt for all four years is $21,081, well below the national average.

Faculty

All classes at Reed are taught by professors rather than by teaching assistants. Classes are small, averaging about 15 students. The opportunity to work closely with faculty members is noted by students as one of the great benefits of a Reed education. Reed faculty members point to the opportunity to work with students who are serious scholars as one of the great benefits of teaching at Reed. Faculty members commit themselves primarily to teaching, with scholarly and scientific research furthering this primary goal; they view students as partners in learning, often serving as coauthors and co-investigators on professional papers and research projects. This close association is due, in large part, to a 10:1 student-faculty ratio and the one-on-one relationship between thesis adviser (a professor) and student during the senior year.

Student Government

The Student Senate is the central body in student governance. The Senate consists of the student body president, vice president, and 8 student representatives, all elected by the students. Its two primary functions are to allocate student body funds and to represent student interests and concerns to the faculty, administration, and Reed College Board of Trustees. The Senate distributes approximately $40,000 each semester to the many student organizations on campus. As agreed under the community constitution, students participate fully in discussions and decisions on a wide variety of issues. The Student Committee on Academic Policy and Planning participates in debate about the curriculum at Reed; many other committees, from the Library Board to the Reactor Committee, have substantial student input. The Senate and student body president make all student appointments to such committees.

Admission Requirements

Reed welcomes applications from first-year and transfer candidates who are genuinely committed to the pursuit of a liberal arts education and a rigorous academic program. Those applicants are admitted who, in the view of the Admission Committee, are most likely to become successful members of and contribute significantly and honorably to the Reed community. The college is committed to maintaining a student body distinguished by its intellectual passion and its diverse range of backgrounds, interests, and talents.

Admission decisions are based on many factors, but academic accomplishments and talents are given the greatest weight in the selection process. A strong secondary school preparation, including honors and advanced courses where available, improves a student's chances for admission. Such a program usually includes 4 years of English and 3 to 4 years of mathematics (through pre-calculus), science, foreign language, and history or social studies. Given the wide variation in high school programs and quality, however, there are no fixed requirements for secondary school courses. Applicants are expected to have obtained a secondary school diploma prior to enrollment, although exceptions are occasionally made. There are no cutoff points for high school or college grades or for test scores.

Reed recognizes qualities of character—in particular, motivation, intellectual curiosity, individual responsibility, and community and social consciousness—as important considerations in the selection process, beyond a demonstrated commitment to academic excellence. Thus, the Admission Committee looks for students whose accomplishments and interests in various fields of endeavor will contribute to the overall liveliness of the Reed community. Personal interviews, either on or off campus, are not a requirement in the admission process but are recommended whenever possible. Applications for early decision should be submitted by November 15 (Option I) or December 20 (Option II), early action applications should be submitted by November 15, regular freshman admission by January 15, and transfer candidates by March 1.

Application and Information

The Office of Admission is open Monday through Friday from 8:30 a.m. until 5 p.m. (Pacific time) all year, except for major holidays. The Admission Office is also open on select Saturdays in the spring and fall. In the case that the campus is closed, the Office of Admission offers virtual information sessions, interviews, and other sessions online at reed.edu/apply/visit/virtual-visits.html. Reed College uses both the Coalition Application and the Common Application; students can find a complete list of application requirements online at reed.edu/apply/guide-to-applying.

For further information or to arrange a campus tour, overnight stay, information session, or interview, students should contact:

Office of Admission
Reed College
3203 Southeast Woodstock Boulevard
Portland, Oregon 97202-8199
Phone: 503-777-7511
800-547-4750 (toll-free)
Fax: 503-777-7553
E-mail: admission@reed.edu
Website: reed.edu

Students at Reed College have a great appreciation for intellectual inquiry and passionate discussion, wherever it can be found.

RIDER UNIVERSITY
LAWRENCEVILLE, NEW JERSEY

The University

When students join Rider University's vibrant living-and-learning community, life—and learning—is never the same. Here, students discover powerful new ways to connect to the world around them. Rider's gifted faculty and supportive staff gives students the ability to find their interests, develop their skills, and take the first step toward a future with infinite possibilities. The Rider campus is a train ride from Philadelphia and New York City, and just minutes from historic Princeton. Located in central New Jersey, Rider offers students great opportunities for exploration, culture, leadership development, internships, and jobs.

Students are at the heart of everything that happens at Rider. The University's student-centered commitment begins with professors who are focused on teaching and mentoring students. That commitment is shared by the entire University community, where every staff member is available to support students and their goals. It's a unique environment dedicated to giving students the self-confidence, skills and strong foundation essential for professional and personal success. Students come to Rider from 39 states, two U.S. territories, and more than 60 countries. Each year, Rider enrolls 3,900 undergraduate and 930 graduate students.

The greatest legacy of a Rider education is measured by the success of its alumni. Rider alumni have gone on to great success at many of the country's top-ranked graduate and professional schools. They have competed for and won prestigious internships, research grants, scholarships, and fellowships—including numerous Fulbright Scholars.

The outcomes of a Rider education are clear: 9 out of 10 Rider graduates are employed full- or part-time, pursuing graduate study, or involved in a volunteer or fellowship position within six months of graduating. And, over 250+ Rider alumni are presidents, CEOs, and leaders of national or international corporations or organizations.

Location

Rider's central location between two vibrant metropolitan centers—New York and Philadelphia—offers many opportunities for adventure, exploration, culture and shopping. Rider is just minutes away from downtown Princeton, incredible nature trails, shopping malls, and more. Students can head an hour in any direction to laze at the beach, downhill ski, or enjoy the sights and sounds of the big city. Whether it's for sightseeing or shows, auditions or internships, Rider is only an hour by train to the heart of Manhattan or to downtown Philadelphia.

Majors and Degrees

At Rider, students can choose from 100 undergraduate majors and minors, as well as 50+ graduate degree and certificate programs through five colleges/schools: The Norm Brodsky College of Business; College of Liberal Arts and Sciences; College of Education and Human Services; Westminster College of the Arts; and College of Continuing Studies. Interdisciplinary majors are plentiful, and dual majors are encouraged.

Academic Programs

Lessons learned in the classroom at Rider are complemented and reinforced with rich hands-on experiences. Students have the opportunity to participate in impressive professional internships, student-faculty research, honors and study-abroad programs, and volunteer experiences.

Rider students do lab work, perform on stage, hold leadership roles on campus, and work at the TV station as early as freshman year. Education majors are guaranteed 700 hours of classroom experience through field placements that begin in the sophomore year. Each year, Rider students complete more than 1,000 internships, co-ops, and field placements as part of their degree studies. Rider's award-winning Model UN program, innovative Global Village class, and a wealth of study-abroad and international partnership programs provide opportunities for students to experience the world in a new way.

Learning is enhanced by course work that reflects the latest best practices and technology, and guest lectures by leading experts. With plenty of real-world opportunities in nearby New York and Philadelphia, these great cities are true learning laboratories for students. By building on these experiences, achievements, credentials, and contacts, Rider students discover what they love to do most—and stand out from the competition when they graduate.

Each of Rider's colleges has a career advisor who specializes in providing the support and preparation needed to move students from their majors to relevant careers. Students begin planning for the future in their first semester, using the expert resources of the Career Development and Success Center to create a compelling professional portfolio and a targeted resume. More information is available online at www.rider.edu/careers.

Students also have opportunities to develop polished interview skills through interactive workshops and alumni videos, launch their job search through the Rider career "handshake" site, and shadow and network with 60,000+ Rider alumni. Rider also hosts career fairs each semester attended by hundreds of employers who come to campus to recruit candidates.

Costs

Rider is proud to be private and affordable. As a student, you will benefit from the many advantages of Rider's private university experience, and generous scholarship and financial aid programs personalized to you and your family's needs. Rider focuses on making its bottom-line costs extremely competitive with most public colleges and universities.

For the 2019–20 academic year, tuition was $21,860 per semester for full-time students. There is a student activities fee of $145 per semester and a technology fee of $225 per semester. There may be additional fees associated with certain academic programs. Housing options ranged from $5,010 to $6,640 per semester, depending on the type of residence selected. Meal plans ranged from $2,685 to $2,765 per semester. Additional details can be found online at http://www.rider.edu/offices-services/financial-aid-scholarships/tuition-fees/housing-and-dining-rates.

Financial Aid

Financial aid is personal and tailored to each student's needs and circumstances, starting with the assigning of a personal financial aid advisor to each student. Ninety-nine percent of students receive Rider-funded scholarships and gift aid with a total of $95.3M awarded by Rider annually. The average annual student assistance package at Rider is more than $35,000. More information on financial aid and scholarship availability can be found at http://www.rider.edu/offices-services/financial-aid-scholarships.

Faculty

Rider's professors are passionate about their disciplines, but teaching is their top priority. They are distinguished authors, educators, scholars, scientists, performing artists, and researchers; 97% percent hold a doctorate or the highest degree in their field. With an average class size of 21 and a 10:1 student/faculty ratio, classes at Rider are small and students receive the attention that they deserve.

Student Life

Rider's focus on engaged learning helps students grow, professionally and personally, through abundant global and cultural experiences, honors and leadership development programs, service-learning opportunities, and exposure to the arts. Rider's vibrant and active campus community includes student government, 150+ student organizations with 2,000+ students holding leadership positions, fraternities and sororities, plus 20 NCAA Division I men's and women's teams. Students can also get involved in our 28 club and intramural sports. Getting involved offers students the chance to inspire and lead others, manage budgets, plan successful events, and engage in big-picture thinking.

Admission Requirements

Rider University welcomes students with a variety of academic backgrounds. When reviewing an application for admission, the Undergraduate Admission Office takes a holistic approach by assessing academic performance, letters of recommendation, and admission essay. Once the committee has reviewed the entirety of the student's academic experience, an admission decision will be made.

Potential students must submit official transcripts from their high school or for any college work they may have completed while in high school, a letter of recommendation and a $50 nonrefundable application fee. Students may request a fee waiver. Rider is Test Optional so students may apply to the University without submitting the results of their standardized testing. For those students submitting scores from the SAT or ACT test, the writing section is not required.

Application and Information

The application deadlines for the fall semester are the following: Early Action (nonbinding), November 15; musical theatre, December 1; and scholarship consideration deadline, January 15. For spring admission, the scholarship deadline is December 15. For transfer students, the spring scholarship deadline and the application deadline are April 1.

Campus tours are offered Monday through Friday at 10 a.m. and 1 p.m. and select Saturdays at 11 a.m. Rider hosts Open Houses and "Bronc for a Day" events as well. To explore all of the opportunities Rider has to offer for prospective students, go to rider.edu/visit.

For details on application dates and more, visit http://www.rider.edu/applynow.
Office of Admission
Rider University
2083 Lawrenceville Road
Lawrenceville, New Jersey 08648
Phone: 609-896-5000 (Main)
800-257-9026 (Admission)
E-mail: admissions@rider.edu
Website: http://www.rider.edu

Rider University's vibrant and engaged learning community brings together people from diverse backgrounds, talents, and perspectives to explore subjects, tackle problems, share ideas, embark on adventures, and create solutions.

RIVIER UNIVERSITY

NASHUA, NEW HAMPSHIRE

The University

Rivier University, a private Catholic university founded in 1933 by the Sisters of the Presentation of Mary, has earned a reputation for excellence with distinguished academic programs. Rivier offers many of the region's leading programs at the undergraduate, graduate, postgraduate, and doctoral levels.

Rivier's School of Undergraduate Studies enrolls approximately 1,400 students, including more than 940 full-time day students. With a 12:1 student-faculty ratio, day students have plenty of opportunities to connect with faculty and become active members of the academic community.

The majority of undergraduate students enroll from the six New England states. Rivier also attracts students from all over the United States as well as international students representing countries in Africa, Asia, Europe, and the Middle East. Students who live on campus reside in four modern residence halls, some with suite-style options. Rivier also provides substance-free housing and honors housing. The Dion Center features the University's student center and the newly renovated Dining Center which offers a healthy, upscale dining experience. The commuter lounge, a campus store, student development offices, and meeting rooms are also available in the Dion Center.

The Office of Student Affairs, the Student Government Association, and more than 13 student clubs and organizations provide a calendar of social, cultural, and recreational activities, including concerts, live entertainment, films, and sporting events. The University and student organizations frequently organize outings, including trips to locations such as Boston and New York. Students also enjoy performances by the University Dance Team and Rivier Theater Company.

Rivier's orientation for new students introduces them to the University's wide array of services, such as academic advisers, the Academic Support Center, and peer tutors. The Health Services Center and the Wellness and Counseling Center ensure students' physical and emotional well-being. Campus Ministry staff coordinate spiritual activities and service opportunities.

Be Remarkable

University programs feature a strong liberal arts foundation and proactive professional preparation. Students are encouraged to "Be Remarkable" through Rivier's unique combination of classroom learning, real-world experiences, and career preparation. Vocational exploration begins in the first year, and a personal, four-year academic and professional action plan is offered to each student, charting a path to achieving their goals. Close collaboration between academics, Student Advising, faculty, and the Career Development Center facilitates students' achievement and tracks progress on their plans.

Employment Promise Program

Rivier University has instituted an innovative Employment Promise Program to enhance career preparation and employability of students in all academic disciplines. The program demonstrates the University's confidence in its educational experience marked by distinctive academic programs, committed faculty, and active learning. Through this initiative, the University promises invested students that they will secure a job within nine months of graduation. If they do not, they will receive additional support in the form of payment of monthly federal subsidized student loans for up to one year or enrollment in up to six Rivier master's degree courses tuition-free. Rivier is the only institution in New Hampshire to offer this program.

Athletics

Rivier is a Division III member of the NCAA and sponsors 13 intercollegiate sports. Rivier Raiders compete in men's and women's soccer, volleyball, cross-country, basketball, and lacrosse; men's baseball; and women's field hockey and softball. The men's volleyball team has been nationally ranked every year since 2001 and recently captured heir 9th NCAA championship. The Muldoon Health and Fitness Center is home to Rivier's varsity athletics, fitness activities, and recreation programs including volleyball, floor hockey, basketball, weight training, indoor soccer, and more. The campus also has a turf rectangular field and a natural grass softball field, as well as a beach volleyball court and cross-country trail. Student athletes can take advantage of an on-campus athletic training clinic for injury assessment and rehabilitation. Rivier is constructing a new Athletics Pavilion, elevating the game-day experience for athletes and fans. Features will include spectator seating, team rooms and conference space, a training room, locker rooms, and a press box.

Location

Nashua (population approximately 87,000) is located in southern New Hampshire. The city of Boston lies within easy access 40 miles to the south. Local access to public transportation provides for easy travel to and from the campus. Recreational activities abound year-round at nearby lakes and ski areas, in the White Mountains to the north, and at the seacoast, just an hour's drive to the east. The Manchester airport is a 15-minute drive from campus, convenient for students who must access air travel.

Majors and Degrees

Rivier University awards Bachelor of Arts and Bachelor of Science degrees in the following areas: biology, biology education, biotechnology, business, criminal justice, cybersecurity management, early childhood education, education and community leadership, elementary education, English, English education, finance, global studies, history, homeland and international security, human development, human services, liberal studies, marketing, mathematics, mathematics education, nursing, political science, psychology (with optional track in substance use disorders), public health, secondary education, social studies education, sociology, special education, and sport management. The University offers preprofessional programs in law, dentistry, medicine, and veterinary medicine.

Academic Programs

Professional studies and liberal arts programs prepare students for a rapidly changing, highly technological, and global society. The broad-based curriculum focuses on preparing students for rewarding careers and furthering their personal growth. The University launched a new core curriculum, offering opportunities for service learning, servant leadership, civic engagement, and community service to support the intellectual growth of students and enhance student leadership. Students choose from courses in three areas: humanities and social sciences, mathematics and natural sciences, and languages in the core complement. The new core is aligned with the Association of American Colleges and Universities' (AAC&U) essential learning outcomes, which provide Rivier graduates with the strong intellectual and practical skills that are in demand in the workplace. A bachelor's degree requires a minimum of 120 credits with a grade point average of at least 2.0. For an associate degree, the student must complete a minimum of 60 credits with a grade point average of at least 2.0.

All departments encourage qualified students to pursue internships in their field of study. Students in Rivier's public health major will work alongside public health professionals at local agencies, and a study-abroad component offers first-hand global perspective and experience. Education majors student teach in local schools. Nursing majors complete clinical rotations in healthcare facilities throughout southern New Hampshire and northern Massachusetts. History, law, and political science majors may work in a law office, business, legal-assistance agency, or government agency. Sociology and psychology majors work with local social service agencies. English and marketing majors work in public relations, broadcasting, or corporate communications positions. Business majors work in advertising, management, and technology.

Honors and awards for students include placement on the dean's list, membership in Kappa Gamma Pi or Psi Chi, listing in *Who's Who Among Students in American Universities and Colleges*, listing in *The National Dean's List*, and degrees with honors. Academically talented students may also apply to the four-year Global Scholars Honors Program.

The academic year is divided into two 14-week semesters. Students usually take five courses each semester. Additional courses are offered during the summer. Academic credit may be granted to incoming freshmen on the basis of Advanced Placement test and CLEP examination scores. Students may also "challenge" courses and receive credit by special examination.

Off-Campus Programs

Through Rivier University's membership in the New Hampshire College and University Council, a sixteen-member consortium of senior and two-year colleges, Rivier students may register for courses at any of the member colleges and receive transfer credits.

Academic Facilities

Academic facilities include Memorial Hall, which houses 14 classrooms, the Office of Global Engagement, faculty offices, a lecture hall, a behavioral science lab, and Rivier's art gallery. The Academic Computer Center features up to 68 workstations with a full range of cutting-edge software and Internet/email access. Regina Library provides access to more than 90,000 print volumes, 45,000 e-books and over 90 research databases, as well as more than 3 million volumes in 12 area libraries on virtually every academic subject. The Writing and Resource Center offers assistance from professional writing consultants as well as peer tutors. Other academic facilities include nursing and science laboratories; a physical assessment lab and nursing skills simulation lab, which provide nursing students with practical experience using blood pressure cuffs, ophthalmoscopes, IV pumps, high-fidelity patient simulators, and more; the McLean Center for Finance and Economics; the BAE Student Research Lab; a clinical psychology lab; electronic classrooms offering multimedia learning tools; and the Benoit Education Center, which houses the eight-classroom Landry Early Childhood Center, observation rooms, and an educational resource center. A new 35,000 square foot Science Center is scheduled for Fall 2020.

Costs

Tuition and fees for the academic year 2019–20 are $32,440; room and board, $13,790; and books and supplies, approximately $1,400.

Financial Aid

Financial aid is awarded on the basis of the financial need of the student and family. Approximately 98 percent of Rivier's full-time undergraduate students receive financial aid from the University or from government or private sources. Federal aid includes Federal Pell Grants, Federal Supplemental Educational Opportunity Grants, Federal Perkins Loans, Federal Direct Stafford Student Loans, the Federal Direct PLUS loan program, and the Federal Work-Study Program. To be considered for financial aid, a student must file the Free Application for Federal Student Aid (FAFSA) with the federal government as soon as possible after October 1 for the coming year. FAFSA results should be on file with the University Financial Aid Office prior to March 1 for the following academic year. Each applicant is assessed individually to determine the best combination of grant, work, scholarship, and loan amounts to meet the need of the student. The University awards more than $13 million in institutional need-based and merit-based scholarships and grants annually. For more information, students should contact the Office of Financial Aid.

Faculty

The University employs 64 full-time faculty members. Part-time instructors in specialized areas are working professionals who bring current knowledge and expertise in their field to their classes. All classes are taught by faculty members, and department chairs serve as academic advisers to students in their major programs.

Student Government

Every full-time day student automatically becomes a member of the Student Government Association (SGA) upon registration and payment of the student activity fee. The SGA's main goals are to stimulate active participation in all University functions; to establish and maintain effective channels of communication among members of the University community and the community at large; to foster a mutual trust; to encourage a spirit of cooperation; and to initiate new endeavors. The SGA also supervises student clubs and organizations and oversees their finances. The SGA Executive Board serves as the channel of communication through which the views of the students on institutional policies reach the University administration.

Admission Requirements

Applicants for admission should ordinarily have completed, in an accredited high school, a minimum of 16 academic units, including 4 of English, 2 of a modern foreign language (optional), 3 of mathematics, 2 of social science, 1 of laboratory science, and 3 of electives. The most successful candidates are in the upper half of their class, with at least a B average. The University does not require SAT or ACT scores as part of a student's overall admissions file, except for nursing students. While nursing students are required to provide SAT or ACT scores, all other students have the option to submit their scores. A personal interview is strongly recommended but not required.

Rivier welcomes applications from qualified transfer candidates from accredited institutions, as well as applications from international students. Transfer students must forward transcripts of all previous college work and a high school transcript. International students must fulfill the requirements for general admission; they may also be required to submit Test of English as a Foreign Language (TOEFL) scores. Deferred admission may be granted to students who wish to postpone entrance for up to one year, provided they have not been enrolled full-time at another postsecondary institution.

Application and Information

Applications must be accompanied by an essay, one letter of recommendation, and a high school transcript. The School of Undergraduate Studies employs a system of rolling admission that allows qualified students to be admitted approximately one month after their application is completed. Transfers should apply by June 1 for fall admission and by December 1 for spring admission. Those applying for financial aid should observe the March 1 deadline. Interviews are arranged through the Admissions Office. Students may apply online using the Common Application or the application on the University's website.

For an application or additional information, please contact:

Office of Undergraduate Admissions
Rivier University
420 South Main Street
Nashua, New Hampshire 03060
Phone: 603-897-8507
Fax: 603-891-1799
E-mail: admissions@rivier.edu
Website: http://www.rivier.edu

Students enjoy Rivier's great location in the heart of New England—approximately an hour's drive from Boston, the mountains, and the seacoast.

SAINT FRANCIS UNIVERSITY

LORETTO, PENNSYLVANIA

The University

As the first Franciscan university in the nation, Saint Francis University has been educating competent, caring professionals for 170 years. The private, Catholic, coeducational institution founded by the Franciscan Friars of the Third Order Regular, welcomes students of all faiths and currently enrolls more than 2,600 students from more than 20 countries.

The University offers highly targeted, career-focused programs grounded in the liberal arts tradition of inquiry and self-discovery. The values of respect, drive, generosity, and joy run deep in the University culture and help to prepare ethical, knowledgeable professionals with a passion to shape the world. This holistic approach to career preparation is supported by respected faculty who work closely with students in small settings to meet individual goals.

Saint Francis students are encouraged to make a difference through research and service projects, and many start as early as their freshman year. Undergraduate students work alongside Ph.D. faculty members conducting research and service projects as part of classes and through specialized learning centers such as the Center for Watershed Research and Service, The Keirn Family World War II Museum, the Center for the Study of Occupational Regulation, and the Center for Rural Cancer Survivorship.

Every student is encouraged to look beyond the classroom for career and personal growth through service leadership, undergraduate research, internships, and global opportunities. Saint Francis students graduate with a custom transcript in addition to their academic transcript known as their L.I.S.T. (Leadership, Involvement, Service Transcript) that quantifies these co-curricular accomplishments for employers.

The University is home to a vibrant campus life experience which capitalizes on its natural, rural setting as well as activities organized through student leaders. There are more than 50 official clubs and organizations including Campus Ministry, club sports, Greek Life, the Literary Guild, and marching band. Athletics also plays a major role in the student life with over twenty NCAA Division I sports for men and women ranging from football to water polo.

Location

Saint Francis University's picturesque campus is situated on 600 acres in the heart of the Allegheny Mountains. The campus is located in the borough of Loretto, which has a population of approximately 1,400. The campus is 6 miles from the county seat of Ebensburg, which has a population of 4,000. The cities of Johnstown and Altoona are within 25 miles of Loretto and have populations of 35,000 and 55,000, respectively. The University is a 90-minute drive east of Pittsburgh.

Majors and Degrees

Saint Francis University offers more than 60 academic majors and a wide variety of minors and concentrations through three distinct academic schools. Each school couples classroom curriculum with embedded research and outreach centers for in-depth experiences.

School of Science, Technology, Engineering, Arts & Mathematics: aquarium and zoo sciences, arts and letters, aviation concentration, biology, biochemistry, chemistry, computer science, cybersecurity administration, engineering, English, environmental engineering, history, mathematics, petroleum and natural gas engineering, philosophy, political sciences, pre-law, pre-professional (dentistry, optometry, pharmacy, veterinary), religious studies, Spanish, and women's studies.

School of Business: accounting, business analytics, communications, criminal justice, digital media, economics, entrepreneurship concentration, finance, healthcare management, management, management information systems (M.I.S.), marketing, MBA (5-year, undergraduate entry), and sociology.

School of Health Sciences and Education: early childhood education, exercise physiology, healthcare studies (pre–allied health, pre-occupational therapy, pre-physician assistant), middle childhood education, nursing, occupational therapy (5-year master's degree), physical therapy (6-year doctorate program), and physician assistant sciences (5-year master's degree), psychology, public health and social work.

The University is accredited by the Middle States Association of Colleges and Schools. Many departmental programs also hold program-level accreditations. A complete list of accreditations may be found in the University catalog or online at www.francis.edu.

Academic Programs

The program of study leading to a bachelor's degree is usually completed in eight semesters. To qualify for graduation, a student must follow a program of study approved by the University that totals at least 128 credits distributed among liberal arts courses, major requirements, collateral requirements, and general electives. All students, regardless of major, are required to complete the University's general education program of 58 credits. A majority of academic programs integrate hands-on learning opportunities using undergraduate research, clinical fieldwork experiences, study abroad, or independent study.

Off-Campus Programs

Students at Saint Francis University may, with permission of the University's administration, spend their junior year of study abroad or may earn credit for participation in summer programs conducted in Canada, France, Germany, Spain, and other countries by accredited American colleges and universities.

Students are encouraged to take advantage of the University's study abroad facility in Ambialet, France, anytime throughout their academic career. The Semester in France program offers study for students within any major for the same tuition costs as studying on campus.

A number of departments offer students the opportunity for off-campus study. For some majors, such as nursing, occupational therapy, physical therapy, physician assistant science, education, medical technology, and social work, internships and/or clinical rotations are required. Saint Francis University strongly encourages students in all other academic majors to complement their field of study with an internship, study abroad, a community service experience, or academic research with a faculty member.

Academic Facilities

The Campus Mall is flanked by academic buildings dedicated to each of the three academic schools. The newest construction projects include a re-imagined space for The Shields School of Business and a state-of-the art 70,000 square-foot science center. Currently underway is a 10,000 square-foot addition to the Sullivan Hall, which will provide health science majors a new space to practice real-world healthcare scenarios. These projects complement the DiSepio Institute for Rural Health and Wellness Center which provides a clinical training area for health sciences. Students in the School of STEAM conduct archival research in the newly opened Keirn Family World War II Museum.

Costs

For 2020-21, tuition is $38,078. In addition, there are fees for expenses associated with lodging, food, insurance, facilities, technology, orientation, and travel. The estimated total per student ranged from $50,500 to $51,500. Detailed cost breakdowns are available on the University website, www.francis.edu.

Financial Aid

Approximately 98 percent of the Saint Francis University student body receives financial aid. In addition to participating in federal and state need-based student aid programs, Saint Francis University offers its own substantial grant program and a generous scholarship program that is based on SAT or ACT scores, high school average, and class rank. Academic awards range from $1,000 to $18,000 annually.

Faculty

Faculty members are chosen for their knowledge of subject matter, as well as for their ability to communicate. Of the teaching faculty at Saint Francis University, 82 percent hold a doctorate or the highest degree attainable in their specific field of expertise. No teaching assistants or graduate students teach classes at Saint Francis University.

Student Clubs and Organizations

Saint Francis University offers an extensive list of co-curricular organizations for students. Over 60 clubs and organizations allow students to choose to become involved in areas of interest. A Greek life community, Student Government Association, and Student Activities Organization provide students additional leadership and involvement opportunities. Several club sport teams are available for students.

Admission Requirements

The admission committee considers applicants and renders decisions on the basis of the secondary school record, the recommendation of the secondary school principal or counselor, and the results of the SAT or ACT. Applicants to the School of Health Science should be aware of specified application requirements and deadlines. Applicants should have a minimum of 16 academic units and are strongly encouraged to visit the University campus for an admission interview and tour. Interviews and campus tours are available Monday through Friday throughout the year and select Saturday mornings while classes are in session.

Transfer students must submit a formal transfer application and a college clearance form in addition to official transcripts from each high school and college previously attended. Transfer students receive an advanced standing evaluation after an offer of admission has been made.

Saint Francis University, an equal opportunity/affirmative action employer, complies with applicable federal and state laws regarding nondiscrimination and affirmative action, including Title IX of the Educational Amendments of 1972, Titles VI and VII of the Civil Rights Act of 1964, and Section 504 of the Rehabilitation Act of 1973. Saint Francis University is committed to a policy of non-discrimination and equal opportunity in employment, education programs and activities, and admissions that includes all persons regardless of race, gender, color, religion, national origin or ancestry, age, marital status, disability, or Vietnam-era veteran status. Inquiries or complaints may be addressed to the University's Director of Human Resources/Affirmative Action/Title IX Coordinator, Saint Francis University, Loretto, Pennsylvania 15940; telephone: 814-472-3264. For other University information, students should call 814-472-3000 or visit the website at www.francis.edu.

Application and Information

The University operates under a rolling admission policy. The occupational therapy and physical therapy programs have a January 15 priority application deadline. The Physician Assistant Sciences program has a November 15 priority application deadline. For more information about Saint Francis University, students should contact:

Vice President for Enrollment Management
Saint Francis University
P.O. Box 600
Loretto, Pennsylvania 15940
Phone: 814-472-3100
866-342-5738 (toll-free)
E-mail: admissions@francis.edu
Website: http://www.francis.edu
http://www.facebook.com/SaintFrancisUniversity
http://twitter.com/SaintFrancisPA
https://www.instagram.com/saintfrancispa

Following a year-long $7 million renovation and expansion project, Schwab Hall recently welcomed students once more. Schwab Hall has been re-imagined as home to The Shields School of Business. The project was funded entirely by donations from alumni and friends of the University and carefully designed with the needs of our students at the forefront.

SAINT MARY'S COLLEGE

NOTRE DAME, INDIANA

The College

Saint Mary's College is a Catholic undergraduate women's college located in Notre Dame, Indiana, offering graduate programs for women and men. The Sisters of the Holy Cross founded the College in 1844.

Saint Mary's College has an undergraduate community of 1,450 academically motivated women from 44 states and nine countries determined to make the world a better place. As a women's college, our students are more likely to speak up, ask for instruction, and become leaders when integrated into co-ed classes and work settings. At Saint Mary's, accomplished, passionate, confident, women express themselves, share their dreams, support and encourage each other, are inspired, and strive to inspire. Ninety-one percent of the school's graduates complete their degrees in four years, and whether they choose new careers, graduate school, or postgraduate service, Saint Mary's alumnae are prepared for life.

Saint Mary's unique relationship with the University of Notre Dame provides access to the exciting atmosphere of a large university—just across the street. Students at both schools can take courses at either institution. Saint Mary's students can audition for Notre Dame's legendary marching band or work for The Observer, the student newspaper for Saint Mary's and Notre Dame. In addition, students participate in dances, concerts, lectures, and social organizations on both campuses. Holy Cross College is also just next door to Saint Mary's College and completes the tri-campus community; each founded by Holy Cross congregations.

Saint Mary's residential campus becomes the students' second home. Saint Mary's five residence halls include Opus Hall, which offers apartment-style living for seniors on campus. Residence halls host events and compete with each other in intramural athletics. Each hall also sponsors a local nonprofit organization that provides students with service opportunities. All residence halls have chapels, and the Church of Our Lady of Loretto, the main worship space, offers daily Mass on campus.

As an NCAA Division III school and a member of the Michigan Intercollegiate Athletic Association (MIAA), Saint Mary's sponsors eight varsity teams in basketball, cross country, golf, lacrosse, soccer, softball, tennis, and volleyball. Club sports, co-sponsored with Notre Dame, include gymnastics, figure skating, and many more. In addition, Saint Mary's offers many intramural sports. The new Angela Athletic & Wellness Complex opened in spring of 2018, complete with a training and fitness center with weight and cardio machines, an indoor track, fitness classes for every level, a café, and study spaces.

Location

Saint Mary's beautiful 140-acre campus, set alongside the Saint Joseph River, is across the street from the University of Notre Dame, next door to Holy Cross College, minutes north of the city of South Bend (population 101,000), 90 miles from Chicago and 140 miles from Indianapolis. The South Bend community provides opportunities for internships, field practicums, and volunteer service. Eighty-three percent of Saint Mary's students engage in service by the time they graduate (the national average is 55 percent).

Majors and Degrees

Saint Mary's College offers more than 50 academic programs including accounting, biology, business, English, global studies, Math, pre-law, and more. There are also more than 40 options for minors, including American history, anthropology, computer science, justice studies, Latin American studies, and women's studies.

Saint Mary's also offers four coeducational graduate degrees: a Master of Science in Data Science, a Master of Science in Speech Language Pathology, a Doctor of Nursing Practice, and a Master in Autism Studies.

In addition, the Five-Year Dual Degree in Engineering Program with the University of Notre Dame leads to a bachelor's degree from Saint Mary's College and a Bachelor of Science in Engineering degree from Notre Dame in aerospace, chemical, civil, computer, electrical, environmental, or mechanical engineering.

Saint Mary's education department, accredited by the National Council for Accreditation of Teacher Education, offers an elementary education major (grades K–6) and a secondary education minor (grades 5–12). With an elementary education major, students can also receive mild intervention licensure (K–6) and an Indiana reading licensure (P–12). Saint Mary's also offers minors in English as a second language and early childhood education.

The rigorous nursing program and clinical instruction at Saint Mary's emphasizes relationship-centered nursing care with individuals, families, groups, and communities informed by professional nursing standards. A Bachelor of Science in Nursing (BSN) degree is high in demand and the nursing department teaches the knowledge and skills to take the NCLEX-RN licensure exam.

Academic Programs

In addition to completing the required credit hours in her chosen field, every undergraduate student completes a senior comprehensive in her major (a thesis, a research or creative project, or a written or oral examination). All undergraduate students must also complete a writing-intensive "W" course, usually in the first year, and an advanced portfolio of writing in the major discipline, usually in the senior year. The "W" prepares students to think deeply and express themselves clearly in a written format.

Off-Campus Programs

Intercultural competence is a cornerstone of the liberal arts education. Saint Mary's combines that with travel and adventure through study-abroad experiences in more than 15 locations. Saint Mary's students may also study through a cooperative program with the University of Notre Dame. Domestic programs include a semester at American University in Washington, D.C. for political science majors, opportunities for student teachers in Africa and Ireland, and pilgrimages through Campus Ministry.

Academic Facilities

Librarians at the Cushwa-Leighton Library help students navigate research assignments, using a collection of over 228,000 books, dozens of online databases, and thousands of online journals. The recently renovated library also houses a 24/7 study space and research help is available in person or by phone, email, or live online chat.

Laboratory facilities are available for biology, chemistry, and physics in the newly renovated Science Hall, and for psychology and language students. Art studios, music practice rooms, O'Laughlin Auditorium, and Little Theatre provide space for fine arts creation, practice, and performance.

The Early Childhood Development Center provides education and psychology majors with a unique opportunity to work with young children on campus.

Costs

Expenses for the 2020–21 academic year include tuition and fees, $45,720 room and board, $13,470 (average).

Financial Aid

The College strives to make a Saint Mary's education available for every admitted student by offering financial aid packages that might include institutional need-based assistance, merit scholarships, and work-study opportunities in addition to state and federal grants and loans. In fact, 100 percent of admitted students receive financial aid.

Faculty

Saint Mary's professors are experts in their fields of study and mentors to their students inside and outside the classroom. Our small class sizes allow students to connect with their professors. Students are encouraged to ask questions, work together, and get involved in various projects. Our faculty typically know each student by name so there is no getting lost in the shuffle. Most importantly, they become mentors and advisors, leading our students towards academic and professional success.

Student Government

The Student Government Association (SGA) is a dynamic student-led organization that sponsors extracurricular and co-curricular activities including service projects, social events, and learning experiences. It provides student participants with leadership opportunities that often include leadership training. SGA has voting representatives on the president's two highest advisory boards, the Student Affairs Council and the Academic Affairs Council. A student is also a voting member of the College's Board of Trustees.

Admission Requirements

Applicants for undergraduate admission to Saint Mary's College should be impending graduates of an accredited high school. Home-schooled students are also encouraged to apply. All applicants must complete a four-year, college-preparatory curriculum that consists of a minimum of 16 academic (Carnegie) units where one unit represents one full year of study. The minimum requirements are: four units of English, two units of the same foreign language, three units of college-preparatory mathematics (beginning with algebra I), two units of laboratory science, and two units of history or social science. The remaining required units should consist of three additional units in the above listed subjects.

Applications must include an academic transcript showing current rank and senior-year courses (if available), a secondary school report, and SAT or ACT scores. Saint Mary's offers students the ability to apply without their test scores. In order for students to qualify for this, they must have a minimum 3.2 GPA out of 4.0. In lieu of test scores, they are asked to submit an academic writing sample and an academic teacher recommendation from grades 10-12 and an essay. There is no application fee, and Saint Mary's is a member of the Common Application.

Saint Mary's encourages students to visit the campus for a tour and informational meeting with an admission counselor. Arrangements to attend classes, meet with coaches, stay overnight, or have an admission meeting via phone or Skype can be made by contacting the Office of Admission.

Application and Information

Saint Mary's has two application and notification programs: early decision and modified rolling regular admission. Students who have selected Saint Mary's as their first choice for admission may apply under the early decision program. The application deadline is November 15, and the notification date is January 15. Students who apply for modified rolling admission, and those whose application files are complete on or before the end of November are notified of the admission decision prior to the Christmas holiday. After that, applications are reviewed in the order in which they become complete. The priority application deadline for regular admission is February 15. Applications are accepted, however, as long as space is available.

Interested students are encouraged to contact:

Office of Admission
Saint Mary's College
Notre Dame, Indiana 46556-5001
Call (574) 284-4587
Text (574) 213-0281
Email admission@saintmarys.edu
Visit saintmarys.edu
@saintmaryscollege on Facebook and Instagram

We promise you discovery. Discovery of yourselves, discovery of the universe, and your place in it.
—Sister Madeleva Wolfe, CSC,
President of Saint Mary's College from 1934–1961

SETON HALL UNIVERSITY

SOUTH ORANGE, NEW JERSEY

The University

As one of the nation's leading Catholic universities, Seton Hall provides great minds with rigorous and challenging academic opportunities in over ninety academic programs that are highly ranked by the Princeton Review, *U.S. News & World Report,* and *Bloomberg Businessweek.* Seton Hall offers all the advantages of a large research university—national reputation; challenging academic programs; notable alumni; state-of-the-art facilities; renowned faculty; and extensive opportunities for internships, research, and scholarship— with all the benefits of a small, supportive, and nurturing environment. The 14:1 student-to-faculty ratio and average class size of 21 students means faculty members know more about each student than just their name.

The University's accomplished faculty members include Fulbright Scholars, prominent researchers, authors, artists, filmmakers, former school superintendents and principals, leaders in nursing, former ambassadors, analysts, and lawmakers—all of whom are dedicated to their fields and their students. They have graduated from some of the nation's leading institutions, including Seton Hall, Harvard, Columbia, Yale, Princeton, and Dartmouth. While faculty members shine in the lecture halls and on the national stage every day, they also meet regularly with students outside the classroom and help them learn to think critically.

Seton Hall offers more than 17,000 internship opportunities, and over 81 percent of students have an internship—or two—on their resume before graduation. This is just one of the reasons Seton Hall graduates have an employment rate of over 93 percent and mid-career earnings 50 percent higher than the national average. Seton Hall was recently ranked in the top 5 in the nation for providing internship opportunities. This national reputation coupled with the University's stellar academic programs draws over 550 employers to campus each year to recruit graduates.

Seton Hall is a Catholic university with a 160-year tradition of educational excellence. A welcoming community, Seton Hall embraces students of all faiths and inspires them to become servant-leaders who make a difference in the world. The University community performs over 40,000 hours of community service annually.

Location

Nestled in the suburban village of South Orange, New Jersey, Seton Hall provides small-town charm combined with big-city opportunities. The University's 58-acre, suburban, park-like campus sits proudly in this picturesque town with tree-lined streets; historic, gracious homes; and quaint shops just 14 miles from New York City—close to all the action, but not engulfed by it.

The bustling town center—with diners, pizzerias, banks, pharmacies, Starbucks, Cold Stone Creamery, a gourmet marketplace, South Orange Performing Arts Center, a movie theater, and more—is just a 5-minute walk from campus. The train station, right in the center of town, provides a direct link to NYC's Penn Station, just 30 minutes away.

The University takes full advantage of all the Big Apple has to offer; after all, it's where the worlds of entertainment, art, publishing, global finance, international diplomacy, and fashion collide. NYC is also one of the world's largest job markets, brimming with internship and job placement opportunities in a variety of companies. Seton Hall students have interned at leading companies like Goldman Sachs, American Express, CNN, the U.S. Secret Service, the United Nations, The *New York Times*, Prudential, The Museum of Natural History, Lockheed Martin, NBC, Sony Music, JPMorgan Chase, Lincoln Center and more.

One of the wealthiest states in the nation, New Jersey is brimming with opportunity. Seton Hall's backyard boasts a powerhouse corporate corridor of more than fifty Fortune 500 companies, pharmaceutical giants, and major corporations. For students, this means networking, internships, and career opportunities.

Academic Programs

Seton Hall is a place where great minds are exposed to even greater opportunities. This is evident in the dozens of student and alumni national scholars and fellows, including 20 prestigious Fulbright Scholars since 2009, as well as Rhodes, Udall, Pickering, Marshall, Critical Language, and Truman Scholars and more than 100,000 alumni who are now successful as CEOs, judges, doctors, principals, CFOs, journalists, nurses, diplomats, and more. About 1,000 Seton Hall graduates have served in executive positions at firms like Oppenheimer, Visiting Nurse Service of New York, American Express, and Merrill Lynch. They have served as elected officials in Washington, D.C., and in hundreds of state capitals and town halls throughout the country. In New Jersey alone, almost 20 percent of the state legislators holds a Seton Hall degree.

Seton Hall's commitment to academic excellence is evident in the more than ninety academic programs offered through six undergraduate schools and colleges. In addition, the University has recently opened a medical school in partnership with Hackensack Meridian Health and is also offering a joint bachelor's/MD program to incoming freshman.

Majors and Degrees

Accounting•
Accounting (5-year B.S./M.S. dual-degree∞)
Africana Studies•
American Humanics√
Ancient Greek†
Anthropology•
Applied Scientific Mathematics†
Arabic†
Archaeology†
Art (Art History•, Fine Arts•, Graphic Interactive and Advertising Design•)
Art (B.A./M.A. in Museum Professions)∞
Asian Studies•
Athletic Training (5-year B.S./M.S. or B.A./M.S. dual-degree)∞
Biochemistry
Biology (B.A. or B.S.)
Broadcasting, Visual and Interactive Media•
Business Administration•‡
Catholic Studies•‡
Catholic Theology•
Chemistry•
Classical Culture†
Classical Languages†
Classical Studies•
Communication•
Communication (B.A./M.A. in Communication or Public Relations)∞
Computer Graphics√
Computer Science•
Creative Writing
Criminal Justice•
Data Visualization and Analysis√
Digital Media and Video√
Digital Media Production for the Web√
Diplomacy and International Relations•
Diplomacy and International Relations (B.S./M.A. dual degree)∞
Early Childhood (integrated with elementary and special education)
Elementary Education (integrated with early childhood and special education)
Education with Speech Language Pathology (6-year B.S.E./M.S. dual- degree)∞
Economics (B.A. or B.S.)
Engineering (Biomedical, Chemical, Civil, Computer, Electrical, Industrial, Mechanical)§
English•
Entrepreneurial Studies√
Entrepreneurship
Environmental Sciences†
Environmental Studies•
Ethics and Applied Ethics†
Finance
French•
Gerontology√
Graphic, Interactive, and Advertising Design
History•
Information Technologies√
Information Technology Management‡
International Business
International Relations
Italian•
Italian Studies†
Journalism•
Latin†
Latin America and Latino/Latina Studies•
Law (3+3, B.S. in International Relations, B.S. in Business or B.A. in Political Science/J.D.)∞
Legal Studies in Business†
Liberal Studies

Management
Marketing
Mathematical Finance
Mathematics•
M.B.A. (5-year B.S./M.B.A. or B.A./ M.B.A. dual-degree)∞
Medicine (Joint bachelors/MD)
Modern Languages
Music (Comprehensive Music/ Music Education, Music Performance•)
Music History†
Music Technology†
Musical Theatre†
Nonprofit Studies†
Nursing
Occupational Therapy (6-year B.A./M.S. dual-degree)∞
Online Course Development and Management√
Philosophical Theology√
Philosophy•
Physical Therapy (6-year B.S./D.P.T. dual-degree)∞
Physician Assistant (6-year B.S./M.S. dual-degree)∞
Physics (B.A. or B.S.)•
Political Science•
Pre-Dental*
Pre-Law*
Pre-Medical*
Pre-Optometry*
Pre-Veterinary*
Psychology (B.A. or B.S.)•
Public Relations
Religion•
Russian†
Russian and East European Studies†√
Secondary Education (optional integration with special education)
Social and Behavioral Sciences
Social Work•
Sociology•
Spanish•
Special Education (integrated with early childhood, elementary, and secondary education)
Speech Language Pathology (6-year with Bachelors in Education or Psychology)∞
Sport Management•
Supply Chain Management√
Theatre and Performance•
Web Design√
Women and Gender Studies†
Writing†
Undecided

• Minor also available
† Minor only
√ Certificate program only
‡ Certificate program also available
§ Dual-degree program with New Jersey Institute of Technology
∞ Seton Hall dual-degree program
* Pre-professional programs (students must also select a major)

Campus Facilities

Seton Hall places a strong emphasis on the use of state-of-the-art technology, facilities, and support services to aid in its students' development. Many investments have been made to the campus infrastructure, including the recent construction of a new academic classroom building, new residence hall space, newly renovated cafeteria, new esports facility, new Interprofessional Health Sciences Campus, new organic chemistry labs, newly renovated soccer field, and a new recreation and fitness center. In addition, the campus boasts a state-of-the-art research library complete with a computerized catalog and 200 computer terminals. The Science and Technology Center is home to state-of-the-future biology and chemistry labs, an atrium, and auditorium, as well as an observatory and greenhouse.

The campus also offers many unique learning labs, such as a Mock Trading Room, Patient Simulation Laboratory, Market Research Center, a student-run radio station (ranked the number-one noncommercial radio station by the National Association of Broadcasters), and Sport Polling Center. All incoming students are provided a new, fully loaded laptop computer.

Costs

Seton Hall offers a flat-tuition rate for students taking between 12 and 18 credit hours. The 2019–20 tuition and fees were $44,080. Room and board costs vary depending on meal plans; however, the average rate is $15,222.

Financial Aid

Paying for college is a major investment. Seton Hall University has been rated as one of the best schools in the nation for return on investment and is committed to providing students with the resources needed to make their dreams a reality. The University gives over $100 million in aid each year; 98 percent of students receive some form of financial aid, and 97 percent receive scholarships or grants directly from the University. Most scholarships are automatically awarded upon admission and do not require separate applications. However, there are also several special scholarships for which students can apply; more information on those is available online at www.shu.edu/scholarships. Seton Hall also provides need-based aid to eligible students who complete the Free Application for Federal Student Aid (FAFSA) form by November 1.

Student Organizations and Activities

On campus, Seton Hall leaders learn to put their ideas into action; discover something new; become part of a community; and build trust, spirit, and lasting friendships. Extracurricular activities abound, with over 130 clubs and organizations, twenty-two Greek societies, fourteen Division 1 Big East athletic teams, and extensive club and intramural sports. Students can audition for one of the many theater productions each year; broadcast at the number-one ranked college radio station in the nation, WSOU-FM, which attracts more than 120,000 listeners a week from the NYC area; be part of the Brownson Speech and Debate team, which has been ranked among the top 20 college and university forensic teams for years; or write for one of three student newspapers. More than two thirds of Seton Hall students participate in clubs and organizations and over 50 percent participate in club or intramural sports.

Admissions Process

Seton Hall takes a holistic approach to reviewing applications for admission, considering academic performance in high school, grades and the rigor of the curriculum, and SAT and/or ACT scores. These are essential indicators of a potential student's ability to succeed at Seton Hall. A personal essay, recommendations, extracurricular activities, and demonstrated interest in the University are also considerations. Students can apply using the Common Application or the Seton Hall application, located on the admission.shu.edu website.

The typical student who entered Seton Hall last year had an average GPA of 3.6 (B+), an average SAT score of 1235 and/or an average ACT score of 27.

Application and Information

Potential students are encouraged to visit Seton Hall in person. Tours are offered Mondays through Fridays at 10 a.m. and 2 p.m. and on Saturdays at 10 a.m., noon, and 2 p.m. Open houses are offered in mid-October, mid-November, mid-February, and late April. Visits can be scheduled online at www.shu.edu/visiting

For more information, prospective students should contact:

Office of Undergraduate Admissions
Seton Hall University
400 South Orange Avenue
South Orange, New Jersey 07079
Phone: 800-THE-HALL (843-4255; toll-free)
E-mail: thehall@shu.edu
Website: http://www.admissions.shu.edu

Students enjoy a spring day on the University Green, the scenic pathway located at the heart of Seton Hall's campus.

STATE UNIVERSITY OF NEW YORK AT OSWEGO

OSWEGO, NEW YORK

OSWEGO
STATE UNIVERSITY OF NEW YORK

The University

Founded in 1861, SUNY Oswego is one of 13 comprehensive colleges in the 64-campus State University of New York (SUNY) system with an excellent academic reputation and a commitment to teaching, learning, research, and service. Inspired by a shared commitment to excellence and the desire to transcend traditional higher education boundaries, SUNY Oswego provides a transformative experience to a diverse student body. Total enrollment, including part-time and graduate students, is approximately 8,000 students including 6,800 undergraduates. More than 130 liberal arts and career-oriented programs are offered through the College of Liberal Arts and Sciences; School of Business; School of Communication, Media, and the Arts; and School of Education.

Located on 700 acres on the southern shore of Lake Ontario, the spacious tree-lined campus consists of over 50 academic and residential buildings. Twelve residence halls and The Village townhouse complex offer a variety of on campus housing opportunities. More than 200 registered extracurricular organizations cover a wide range of social, academic, cultural, and intellectual interests. Theater, art, film, music, dance, and discussion events fill the campus cultural calendar throughout the school year as well. There are 24 NCAA Division III intercollegiate sports for men and women, along with a full complement of competitive club sports and intramural athletics.

SUNY Oswego receives more than 14,000 applications for some 1,400 freshman and transfer openings each fall. It has been recognized by a number of authoritative guides for its outstanding academic opportunities and high academic standards. In recent years, SUNY Oswego has been cited for excellence and selectivity in U.S. News & World Report's Top Regional Universities in the North and Best Colleges Guide, Colleges of Distinction, and in both the Princeton Review's Best Northeastern Colleges and their Best Value Colleges.

Over the past 20 years, SUNY Oswego has invested more than $900 million in academic, residential, and infrastructure enhancements to better support the mission of the college and improve the experience of its students. Recently completed projects include the comprehensive $49 million renewal of Park and Wilber Halls for the School of Education; a $53 million renovation of Tyler Hall—a 100,000-square foot visual and performing arts building—that now provides art, theatre, and music students access to digital-age instructional tools and program delivery; the $118-million Richard S. Shineman Center for Science, Engineering, and Innovation; a new Biological Field Station lab facility and contemporary, sustainable renovations to Scales Hall and Waterbury Hall—two of four lakeside residential halls on the Oswego campus.

Location

With a population of nearly 18,000, the city of Oswego is a modest-sized, friendly upstate New York community. It is the country's oldest freshwater port and one of the leading ports on the Great Lakes and St. Lawrence Seaway. The city and its surrounding area are known for summer and winter recreation, including camping, boating, sailing, fishing, tennis, golf, ice skating, alpine and cross-country skiing, snowboarding, and sledding. The campus is conveniently located 35 miles northwest of Syracuse and 65 miles east of Rochester. Students traveling by rail or air may utilize bus service to Oswego through the Regional Transportation Center located adjacent to one of the largest malls in the northeast, Destiny USA in Syracuse.

Majors and Degrees

SUNY Oswego awards the Bachelor of Arts (B.A.), Bachelor of Science (B.S.), and Bachelor of Fine Arts (B.F.A.) degrees.

Through the College of Liberal Arts and Sciences, students can earn a baccalaureate degree in American studies; anthropology; applied mathematics; applied mathematical economics; biochemistry; biology; chemistry; cinema and screen studies; cognitive science; computer science; creative writing; criminal justice; economics; electrical and computer engineering; English; French; gender and women's studies; geochemistry; geology; German; global and international studies; history; human development; information science; language and international trade; linguistics; mathematics; meteorology; philosophy; philosophy, politics, and economics; philosophy-psychology; physics; political science; psychology; public justice; sociology; software engineering; Spanish; and zoology.

The School of Business offers B.S. degree programs in accounting; business administration; finance; human resource management; marketing; operations management and information systems; and risk management and insurance. The globally respected Association for the Advancement of Collegiate Schools of Business International (AACSB) extended, in fall 2018, the accreditation of SUNY Oswego's School of Business for five years, following a rigorous Continuous Improvement Review. The AACSB commended Oswego's School of Business —first AACSB-accredited in 2002—for a variety of strengths, innovations, and unique features, and specifically noted high levels of student satisfaction with faculty and staff, advisement, internship supervision, business-based student organizations, and other applied-learning opportunities.

The School of Communication, Media, and the Arts offers baccalaureate degree programs in art; broadcasting and mass communication; communication; graphic design; journalism; music, audio recording; public relations; and theater.

The School of Education offers B.S. degree programs in adolescence education; career and technical educator preparation; childhood education; teaching English to speakers of other languages (TESOL); technology education; technology management; and wellness management.

In addition, four innovative five-year combined bachelor's and master's programs are available: a bachelor's degree in accounting with an M.B.A., a bachelor's in psychology with an M.B.A., a bachelor's in psychology with a master's in human computer interaction, and a bachelor's in broadcasting and mass communication with an M.B.A.

Cooperative programs include a 3+3 program leading to a B.S./D.P.T. in physical therapy from SUNY Upstate Medical University; and a 3+4 pre-optometry program leading to a bachelor's in chemistry from Oswego and an O.D. in optometry from SUNY College of Optometry.

Academic Programs

Oswego offers students a broad range of courses in the liberal arts and in pre-professional and professional studies. In addition to core courses within a major, all students must satisfy general education requirements designed to strengthen basic writing and analytical proficiency, give students awareness of their cultural heritage, and provide a level of literacy in the social and behavioral sciences, natural sciences, and humanities.

Before arriving on campus, students are assigned an advisor who specializes in their academic major. Advisors assist students with academic, personal, and career concerns, and collaborate in scheduling courses needed for graduation. The college has a strong reputation for working with undeclared students and helping them to discover and apply their education passions.

Students may be selected for the college's honors program, which provides a challenging academic experience for high achievers regardless of major.

Off-Campus Programs

Opportunities exist for students to broaden their knowledge of other countries by participating in one of 80 different summer or semester overseas academic programs offered. This includes options in short study-abroad quarter courses offering an intensive curriculum followed by a one-to-two-week experience in a foreign country.

SUNY Oswego provides many opportunities for students to engage in experiential education through internships, undergraduate research, and service learning. Internships and other field experiences are available for students from all disciplines through EXCEL: Experiential Courses and Engaged Learning. In addition, a formalized cooperative education program (co-op) is available to students from over 25 major areas. Each year, more than 1,300 Oswego students participate in internships, co-ops, and service-learning activities on campus, in the local area, and throughout the world.

Academic Facilities

Penfield Library is a high-tech information center supporting the curriculum, teaching, and research of SUNY Oswego. Through Interlibrary Loan, Penfield can provide additional materials from libraries all over the world.

Campus-wide computer technology service professionals support students in their classroom, residence, and Internet activities. Wireless access is available throughout the campus. The campus maintains hundreds of Mac and Windows-based computers.

Adjacent to the campus, the college maintains the 330-acre Rice Creek Field Station, with its $5.5-million modern, 7,200-square-foot lab facility which opened its doors in the fall of 2013. The facility has two lab/classrooms, a lecture room, and exhibit areas with an indoor viewing gallery, providing a unique vista of the creek and pond. College classes and community education programs are regularly held at the field station, which ranks among the five most extensively used facilities of its kind in the country.

Tyler Hall, Oswego's newly renovated fine arts center, has an art gallery that features annual traveling exhibitions, locally produced theme exhibitions, and the best work of students and faculty members. Tyler Hall's Waterman Theatre hosts student plays, musical performances, and productions by internationally renowned traveling artists. Other new facilities support musical performances and audio production opportunities.

The WRVO Stations, the college's 50,000-watt public radio outlet, provides outstanding on-campus internship opportunities. Communication Department facilities also include two new all-digital television studios, a modern radio lab, and two new journalism labs in Lanigan Hall. Student-run TV and radio stations and the college newspaper are located in the Marano Campus Center facilities.

Costs

Tuition for 2019–20 was $3,535 per semester for New York State residents and $8,490 per semester for nonresidents. Room and board charges were approximately $7,145 per semester for entering students, depending on the meal plan, and additional fees totaled approximately $1,647 per year. SUNY Oswego guarantees that a student's initial first-year costs for room and board will be frozen for up to four consecutive years.

Financial Aid

Need-based financial assistance consists of grants, loans, and part-time employment. Oswego offers more than $84 million in aid to its students annually. Students interested in financial aid must file a Free Application for Federal Student Aid (FAFSA). New York State residents also need to file an application for the state's Tuition Assistance Program (TAP).

Oswego offers a very generous merit scholarship program. Students receive more than $6.5 million annually in merit scholarships and approximately 45 percent of first-year students receive one. The average four-year renewable scholarship is more than $3,600 per year. Through New York State's Excelsior Scholarship program, a large number of New York students are also eligible for free tuition at SUNY Oswego. For scholarship qualifications and details, visit http://www.oswego.edu/admissions/scholarships.

Faculty

With approximately 88 percent of SUNY Oswego faculty holding doctoral or other terminal degrees, students can be assured of the opportunity for an outstanding undergraduate education. The student-faculty ratio is approximately 17:1. While dedicated to teaching first and foremost, Oswego's faculty members are also actively engaged in research—often in partnership with undergraduate students.

Admission Requirements

Admission to SUNY Oswego is competitive, with high school average, academic program, and standardized test scores being the most important criteria for applicants. Special talents such as artistic, musical, athletic, and creative writing skills are also considered. The Committee on Admissions accepts results of either the ACT or the SAT. A campus admissions visit is encouraged.

Transfer students in good standing are encouraged to apply for admission. The average GPA for entering transfer students is 3.0.

Application and Information

Oswego accepts both The Common Application and the SUNY Application for admission. Both applications are available online at http://www.oswego.edu/apply. Oswego evaluates applications as they are completed and as space remains available. Applications completed by November 15 will be considered for Early Action. Early Action applicants will be notified of our decision by December 15. Applications completed by January 15 for the fall term or October 15 for the spring term are ensured equal consideration. Applications received after those dates are welcomed, although considered as space remains available. Regular admission applicants for the fall term will receive their decision beginning January 15, and spring applicants will receive their decision beginning November 15.

Prospective students and their parents are encouraged to visit the campus to participate in a student-guided tour and speak with an admissions counselor. Visits can be scheduled online at www.oswego.edu/admissions. Interested candidates can also call the Office of Admissions in advance to schedule a visit.

For further information, students should contact:

Office of Admissions
229 Sheldon Hall
SUNY Oswego
Oswego, New York 13126
Phone: 315-312-2250
Fax: 315-312-3260
E-mail: admiss@oswego.edu
Website: http://www.oswego.edu/admissions

SUNY Oswego is located on 700+ acres on the southern shore of Lake Ontario.

COLLEGE CLOSE-UPS

STOCKTON UNIVERSITY

GALLOWAY, NEW JERSEY

The University

Thinking translates into doing at Stockton. Students gain hands-on experience in Nursing, Exercise Science, Occupational Therapy or Physical Therapy in state-of-the-art facilities on campus; use cutting-edge technology to preserve historic underwater wreck sites or analyze the seafloor's ecosystems at Stockton's Marine Field Station and on the five-vessel research fleet; study artistic techniques firsthand through a partnership with the Noyes Museum of Art or at the Philadelphia Museum of Art; bask in the beautiful, 1,600-acre campus in the Pinelands National Reserve, a perfect setting for Stockton's nationally renowned Environmental and Marine Science programs, or live and learn at a new coastal residential campus just steps from the beach and Boardwalk in Atlantic City.

Stockton students engage with Fulbright Scholars, Guggenheim Fellows, and Pulitzer-awarded authors. Small classes are guided by professors who care as much about teaching as research, allowing for discussion, debate, and discovery in the classroom and beyond.

Founded in 1969, Stockton offers extensive service-learning opportunities and has become an international leader in alternative energy research and conservation efforts.

The University offers bachelor's, master's, and doctoral degree programs designed to challenge the brightest students, providing many of the academic, technological, and cultural advantages of a large university, but with the communal spirit typical of smaller colleges.

Stockton enrolls nearly 10,000 students from New Jersey, the Mid-Atlantic states, and abroad, providing unique educational programs with a curriculum focused on developing the students' analytic and creative capabilities through the encouragement of individually planned courses of study.

The Stockton experience is enhanced with 200+ ways to get involved with clubs, organizations, and activities. In addition to extensive intramural and club sports, a Rocket League E-Sports team, NCAA Division III sports teams offered include men's baseball, basketball, lacrosse, and soccer, women's basketball, field hockey, golf, lacrosse, soccer, softball, tennis, rowing and volleyball, and men's and women's cross-country and track and field.

Stockton provides on-campus housing for almost 4,000 students in traditional residence halls, apartments, campus-owned facilities, and at the Residential Complex at Stockton University Atlantic City. All complexes are furnished and air conditioned, with cable TV and Internet. Others choose to live off campus in nearby apartment complexes or winter rentals in local shore towns.

Beyond its undergraduate programs, Stockton offers the following graduate degrees: Doctor of Nursing Practice, Doctor of Physical Therapy, and Doctor of Education in Organizational Leadership; Master of Arts in American Studies, Counseling, Criminal Justice, Education, Holocaust & Genocide Studies, and Instructional Technology; Master of Business Administration; Master of Business Administration in Healthcare Administration and Leadership; Master of Science in Coastal Zone Management, Communication Disorders, Data Science & Strategic Analytics, Nursing, and Occupational Therapy; Master of Social Work; and a Professional Science Master's in Environmental Science. Certificate and endorsement programs are offered in Administration and Leadership, Adult Gerontology Primary Care Nurse Practitioner, American Studies, Bilingual/Bicultural Education, Data Science, Energy, ESL (English as a second language), Family Nurse Practitioner, Forensic Science, Forensic Psychology, Genocide Prevention, Geographic Information Systems, Gerontology, Homeland Security, Learning Disabilities Teacher Consultant, Middle School Endorsement, New Jersey Standard Supervisor Endorsement, Preschool–Grade 3 Endorsement, Reading Specialist, Special Education, and Student Assistance Coordinator.

Stockton University is accredited by the Commission on Higher Education of the Middle States Association of Colleges and Schools. In addition, the School of Business is accredited by the Association to Advance Collegiate Schools of Business, the Social Work program is accredited by the Council on Social Work Education; teacher education is approved by the New Jersey Department of Education, the National Association of State Directors of Teacher Education and Certification, and the Teacher Education Accreditation Council; nursing is accredited by the New Jersey Board of Nursing and the Commission on Collegiate Nursing Education; chemistry is accredited by the American Chemical Society; physical therapy is accredited by the Commission on Accreditation in Physical Therapy Education of the American Physical Therapy Association; environmental health is accredited by the National Environmental Health Sciences and Protection Accreditation Council; occupational therapy is accredited by the Accreditation Council for Occupational Therapy Education of the American Occupational Therapy Association; communication disorders is accredited by the Council on Academic Accreditation in Audiology and Speech-Language Pathology; the Biochemistry and Molecular Biology Program is accredited by the American Society for biochemistry and molecular biology, and criminal justice is accredited by the Academy of Criminal Justice Sciences.

Location

Stockton's main campus in Galloway, New Jersey, is nestled in the environmentally protected Pinelands National Reserve, just minutes west of Atlantic City, an hour from Philadelphia, and two hours from New York City. Steps from the beach and Boardwalk, Stockton University Atlantic City includes the John F. Scarpa Academic Center and Residential Complex, allowing the University to support its surrounding communities and expand the hospitality, tourism & event management, organizational leadership, business studies, social work, and community leadership and civic engagement programs. Courses are also offered online and at the Hammonton, Manahawkin, and Woodbine locations. Collaboration with the Sam Azeez Museum of Woodbine Heritage and the Noyes Museum of Art provides enriching exhibitions and educational programs.

Majors and Degrees

The Bachelor of Arts, Bachelor of Fine Arts and Bachelor of Science degrees are offered in studies in the arts (visual and performing), Africana studies, biochemistry/molecular biology, biology, business studies (accounting, business analytics, finance, financial planning, management, marketing), chemistry, communication studies, computer information systems, computer science, computing, criminal justice (forensic psychology/investigation, homeland security), economics, education, environmental science/studies, exercise science, geology, health science, historical studies, hospitality, tourism & event management, languages & culture studies, liberal studies, literature, marine science, mathematics, nursing, philosophy & religion, physics, political science, psychology, public health, social work, sociology & anthropology, studio art, and sustainability.

Stockton also offers pre-professional preparation in dentistry, law, medicine, pharmacy, veterinary medicine, communication disorders (speech therapy/audiology), occupational therapy, physical therapy, and physician assistant studies, with the master's degree in Occupational Therapy, Communication Disorders, and Doctorate in Physical Therapy completed at Stockton. The university also has an accelerated seven-year dual-degree articulation agreements with Rowan School of Osteopathic Medicine; a five-year BS-MSPA that combines a B.S. in Health Science from Stockton with a master's in

Physician Assistant Studies from Jefferson University; and five-year, dual-degree programs with New Jersey Institute of Technology, Rowan University and Rutgers University for engineering. In addition, students can graduate from Stockton with a Bachelor of Science degree in Biochemistry/Molecular Biology and finish their Doctor of Pharmacy degree through the Ernest Mario School of Pharmacy at Rutgers University.

Academic Programs

To earn a baccalaureate degree from Stockton, students must satisfactorily complete a minimum of 128 semester credits. Degree programs include a combination of general studies and major studies. Bachelor of Arts students must earn 64 credits in general studies; Bachelor of Science students must earn 48. General studies courses are cross-disciplinary courses designed to introduce students to all major areas of the curriculum and to the intellectual skills necessary for success in college. Students select courses from each major curricular area. The only required courses within general studies are basic studies (up to three); students may be exempt from these courses based on testing. Bachelor of Arts students must earn 64 credits in major studies; Bachelor of Science students must earn 80. Requirements are carefully structured and emphasize sequences of specific courses.

Stockton students can influence what and how they learn. The preceptorial system enables students to work closely with a faculty-staff preceptor in planning and evaluating courses and in exploring career paths.

Off-Campus Programs

Off-campus experiences for credit are a requirement for most programs, namely in the form of internships, research projects, and field studies. Stockton sends more students to the Washington Internship Program than any other college or university outside the Washington, D.C., area.

Study abroad, Semester at Sea, study-tours and an honors program provide additional opportunities.

The office of Career Education and Development, as well as academic offices, coordinate off-campus internships; education abroad is coordinated by the Office of Global Engagement.

Academic Facilities

Stockton's campuses in Galloway and Atlantic City serve as living-learning centers, with academic, recreational, and living spaces mixed to promote interaction among students, faculty, and staff. Facilities include interactive and electronic classrooms, an extensive library containing the Sara & Sam Schoffer Holocaust Resource Center, an art gallery, and performing arts center. New academic facilities include Unified Science Center 2, a 58,000 square-foot addition to USC 1, the 38,000 square-foot John F. Scarpa Health Sciences Center as well as the John F. Scarpa Academic Center.

Costs

Costs for the 2019–20 academic year were $14,317 for in-state students and $21,605 for out-of-state students (flat-rate tuition up to 40 credits per year, fees); on-campus housing and board were $12,542 (double-occupancy residence room, Ultimate meal plan). Books, supplies, transportation, and personal items are extra. Costs are subject to change.

Financial Aid

Financial aid is available as scholarships, grants, loans, and work-study. Need-based financial aid is awarded according to student and family need. Students seeking financial aid should file the Free Application for Federal Student Aid (FAFSA) as soon as possible after October 1. Stockton offers aggressive and generous merit-based aid awards to academically talented freshman and transfer students based on grade point average, standardized test scores, and college-level performance.

Faculty

Stockton's faculty represent highly diverse academic, training, and social backgrounds, with 91 percent holding terminal degrees in their field. Faculty members work closely with students through individualized research opportunities, and share social, recreational, and cultural programs with students and staff. This arrangement supports the exceptional rapport and learning relationships among students and faculty members.

Student Government

The Stockton University Student Senate consists of 27 student members. The advisory council is made up of one faculty member and two staff members. Student senators hold office for one year. The Student Senate reviews and makes recommendations on budgets of funded student organizations and acts as the official representative of the student body.

Admission Requirements

Stockton operates on rolling admission. Fall admission deadline is rolling for most freshmen, with special program deadlines posted on the university's website. Transfer deadline for fall admission is August 31. Spring (January) admission deadline for all students is January 10. Students may apply for admission to the fall or spring term and are notified of the decision as soon as their application file is completed and has been reviewed. Some freshman applicants must submit ACT and/or SAT scores. All students must submit official transcripts from all educational institutions attended. Admission is selective.

Armed Services veterans and those who have been away from formal education for some time are encouraged to apply. Stockton makes no distinction between part- and full-time students in offering admission.

Stockton offers special admission to a limited number of New Jersey students from educationally and financially disadvantaged backgrounds. Students wishing to explore this opportunity should contact the Office of Admissions.

Application and Information

For more information, contact:
Chief Enrollment Management Officer
Stockton University
101 Vera King Farris Drive
Galloway, New Jersey 08205-9441
Phone: 609-652-4261
Fax: 609-626-5541
E-mail: admissions@stockton.edu
Website: admissions.stockton.edu
Social Media: Facebook.com/StocktonUniversity
Twitter.com/@Stockton_edu
Instagram.com/stocktonuniversity

Stockton University students can choose from 160+ academic programs, including a customized major, with every class providing hands-on, real-world experience. Students live and learn on the main campus in a beautiful park-like setting and at the new coastal/urban campus steps from the beach and Boardwalk in Atlantic City.

TEMPLE UNIVERSITY

PHILADELPHIA, PENNSYLVANIA

The University

Temple University attracts some of the most diverse, driven and motivated minds from across the nation and around the world. These students and faculty bring the university to life and move Temple forward and upward in academics, athletics, research and the arts. Powering Temple's ascent are innovative approaches to admissions and affordability; a campus transformation; plentiful creative and research opportunities; rigorous academic programs; an indelible bond with the city of Philadelphia; and groundbreaking work in science, research and technology.

Temple is home to about 40,000 students, is the thirty-first largest public, four-year institution in the United States and offers more than 570 academic programs in 17 schools and colleges, on eight campuses, including locations in Japan and Italy.

More than 3,800 distinguished faculty members; five professional schools; and dozens of renowned programs make Temple an academic powerhouse. Students enjoy the advantages and atmosphere of a large urban, public research university with the individualized attention that comes from a 14:1 student-to-faculty ratio.

The majority of first-year students live on campus, where they are steps away from classes; a state-of-the-art TECH Center; the library; fitness and recreation facilities; dining options such as cafés, dining halls and food trucks; and the many arts, cultural, sports and scholarly events that happen daily at Temple and throughout the city.

By living and learning in an urban environment, Temple students are well prepared for the world. Employers laud Owls for their tenacity, teamwork and talent. Students also have access to an immense alumni network 332,000 strong for guidance, job opportunities and mentoring.

Location

Each of Temple's distinct campuses has its own personality and environment, from urban to suburban to international. Temple's Main Campus is located just 1.5 miles from the center of Philadelphia, one of the largest cities on the East Coast. Philadelphia is among the most walkable cities in the U.S.—meaning students can easily access all the city has to offer, including more than 100 museums, a thriving restaurant scene, numerous athletic events, and the largest urban landscaped park in the country. The professional world is also right outside Temple's door: There are thousands of opportunities for hands-on learning and internships in the Philadelphia area, and the University's more than 100,000 alumni in the region love to hire Temple graduates.

Temple's other seven campuses include a location in Tokyo—the largest and oldest American university in Japan—and another in Rome, Italy. Temple University Harrisburg is located in the heart of Pennsylvania's capital city. The University's campus in Ambler, Pennsylvania, is the hub of the University's environmental programs and home to a 187-acre arboretum that serves as a living laboratory. In addition to Main Campus, Temple's Philadelphia campuses are the Health Sciences Center just north of Main Campus, and the Center City and Podiatric Medicine campuses, both a short subway ride away in downtown Philadelphia.

Majors and Degrees

Temple offers more than 160 undergraduate degree programs, making it easy for students to follow, or discover, their passions. Students who need time to decide on a major can explore their interests through the University Studies program. Those who would like to accelerate their education can apply to one of Temple's many dual-degree programs.

The Tyler School of Art offers a B.F.A. with concentrations in ceramics, glass, fibers and materials studies, graphic and interactive design, metals/jewelry/CAD-CAM, painting, photography, printmaking, and sculpture (all concentrations available with entrepreneurial studies); a B.A. in art history, art therapy, and visual studies; and a B.S. in art education. Tyler's architecture program confers a B.S. in historic preservation, architecture (pre-professional), and facilities management. B.S. programs are offered in community development and in horticulture and landscape architecture.

The Fox School of Business offers a B.B.A. in accounting; actuarial science; business management; economics; entrepreneurship and innovation management; finance; financial planning; human resource management; international business; legal studies; management information systems; marketing, real estate, risk management and insurance, and supply chain management. The school also offers a B.S. in statistical science and data analytics.

The College of Education offers a B.A. in adult and organizational development and a B.S. in career and technical education, early childhood–elementary education, human development and community engagement, middle-grades education (4–8), and secondary education combined with a second major or subject area.

The College of Engineering offers a B.S. in bioengineering; civil engineering; construction engineering technology; electrical engineering; engineering (general program); engineering technology; environmental engineering; industrial and systems engineering; and mechanical engineering.

The College of Liberal Arts offers a B.A. in Africology and African American studies; American studies; anthropology; Asian studies; Chinese; classics; criminal justice; economics; English; environmental studies; French; gender, sexuality, and women's studies; geography and urban studies; German language and cultural studies; global studies; history; interdisciplinary German studies; interdisciplinary liberal arts; Italian; Jewish studies; Latin American studies; liberal studies; mathematical economics; neuroscience: systems, behaviors, and plasticity; philosophy; political science; psychology; religion; sociology; and Spanish. Temple University Japan offers a B.A. in general studies; international affairs; Japanese; and psychological studies.

The Klein College of Media and Communication offers a B.A. in advertising, communication and social influence, communication studies, journalism, media studies and production, and public relations.

The Boyer College of Music and Dance offers a B.S. in music and music technology; and a B.M. in jazz studies composition, jazz studies performance (instrumental or vocal); composition; music education, music education with jazz studies component; music history (instrumental or vocal); theory; music therapy, music therapy with jazz studies component, performance (instrumental or vocal); and piano pedagogy. A B.F.A. is offered in dance.

The College of Public Health offers a B.S. in exercise and sport science; health information management; health professions; kinesiology; nursing; public health; recreational therapy; speech, language, and hearing science.

The College of Science and Technology offers a B.A. in biology; chemistry; computer science; geology; information science and technology; mathematical economics; mathematics; natural sciences; and physics. The college also offers a B.S. in applied mathematics; biochemistry; biology; biology with teaching; biophysics; chemistry; chemistry with teaching; computer science; computer science and physics; data science; Earth and space science with teaching; environmental science; general science with teaching; geology; information science and technology; mathematics; mathematics and computer science with teaching; mathematics with teaching; mathematics and computer science; mathematics and physics; natural sciences; neuroscience: cellular and molecular; pharmaceutical sciences; physics; and physics with teaching.

The School of Social Work offers the B.S.W. degree.

The School of Theater, Film, and Media Arts offers a B.A. in film and media arts; and theater as well as a B.F.A. in film and media arts; and musical theater.

The School of Sport Tourism and Hospitality Management offers a B.S. in sport and recreation management and in tourism and hospitality management.

Academic Programs

Students are attracted to Temple because of its diversity and quality of academic programs: More than 570 are offered, including more than 160 undergraduate degree programs. The University provides all of the resources and opportunities of a large, world-class research institution and the individual attention of a small college—with a 14:1 student-to-faculty ratio.

All students complete the General Education curriculum, a cross-section of courses that focuses on making connections locally and globally and looks at cutting-edge issues from multiple angles. Flexibility in coursework offers each student a unique and transformative experience.

Some students pursue common interests in Living and Learning Communities. Academically qualified students take on extra intellectual challenges through the Honors Program. Temple's study abroad programs offer opportunities to take learning around the world.

The Diamond Research Scholars program provides students with the opportunity to engage in a focused, mentored research or creative arts project. TUteach allows students to graduate with a bachelor of science in a math or science field and the qualifications to earn a middle or high school teaching certificate. Through various special academic programs, students can work directly with renowned faculty and present at professional conferences, publish in peer-reviewed journals, and premiere music and dance at venues around the globe.

And to keep students on track academically, Fly in 4 was established. It's a program unique to Temple and helps students create academic plans to ensure they graduate in four years to limit debt. If students meet all of the programs obligations and are still unable to graduate in four years, Temple pays for the remaining coursework.

Academic Facilities

Whether in a high-tech classroom or the University's Science Education and Research Center (SERC), Temple students learn in world-class facilities. At SERC, which is home to 68 research and teaching labs and leading-edge technologies, students work with faculty on real-world projects, making the connection between understanding science and putting advanced research techniques into practice.

At the TECH Center—among the largest student computer labs in the country—students can collaborate in breakout rooms, edit video in a specialized lab, get assistance from the 24-hour help desk, or work on one of 700 computers. There are more than 100 other computer labs on campus and 90 percent of classrooms are smart classrooms.

Costs

Typical tuition and fees for the 2018–19 academic year were $19,618 for Pennsylvania residents and $33,058 for out-of-state residents (tuition rates vary by major). Room and board on Main Campus for the academic year were about $11,916.

Financial Aid

Temple offers a multitude of options to help make college more affordable. A variety of scholarships, grants, loans, and work-study programs are available: 70 percent of first-year students receive need-based financial aid, and Temple awards more than $100 million in scholarships each year. Four-year academic merit scholarships for talented freshmen range from $2,000 to full tuition, and several include summer stipends for research, internships, and study abroad.

Most incoming freshmen—more than 90 percent—commit to Temple's Fly in 4 program, an innovative plan which helps students limit their debt and enter the workforce sooner by graduating in four years. The program also offers 500 need-based grants per entering class to help reduce the need for students to work for pay while studying. Based on the Free Application for Federal Student Aid (FAFSA), eligible students receive $4,000 per year.

Faculty

Students at Temple learn from and collaborate with faculty at the forefront of their fields—winners of prestigious teaching and research awards, scientists doing groundbreaking research, and working artists who exhibit all over the world.

Temple faculty members are also known for their practical experience—a marketing class may be led by a successful entrepreneur; music lessons by a member of the Philadelphia Orchestra. Marine biologists, newspaper editors, published authors, practicing architects, and healthcare professionals all bring their expertise to the classroom.

And the roster of outstanding faculty members is growing. Renowned faculty join Temple from leading universities and research centers including Princeton University, MIT, and the Cleveland Clinic.

Admission Requirements

Temple's admissions process is holistic; every aspect of the student's academic history is considered. Typically, students have a B+ average or better in a strong college-prep curriculum in grades 9–12. For students submitting test scores, the average SAT score in 2018 was 1237, and the average ACT composite was 27. Temple Option is an admissions path for determined and tenacious students who have the ability to succeed in college but may not perform well on standardized tests. When students apply with Temple Option, they show their potential by answering open-ended questions rather than submitting SAT or ACT scores.

For freshman admissions, high school grades (quality of courses and grade trends), standardized test scores or Temple Option responses, and other factors are considered. Temple uses a sliding scale rather than absolute cutoffs. Students self-report their high school transcripts online through TUportal once they apply. Official standardized test scores must be sent directly to the admissions office. SAT subject tests and personal interviews are not required.

The application fee is $55; most students apply online through Temple or the Common Application.

Temple offers rolling admissions and early action decision plans for the fall semester. Those interested in early action must submit a completed application by November 1 and will receive notification by mid-January. The rolling admissions deadline is February 1; freshman decisions begin in early fall.

Applicants are considered transfer students if they have taken 15 or more college-level credits after high school. If this is not the case, they should apply as freshman students. In admissions decisions, careful consideration is given to the quality of a student's program, number of credits earned, and GPA. The mean GPA for new transfer students is 3.15 (on a 4.0 scale). The architecture, nursing, and pharmacy programs have higher minimum GPA requirements. For most programs, transfer students must complete the application process by June 1 for the fall semester or by November 1 for the spring semester. The fall priority deadline for the health information management and nursing programs is February 1. SAT or ACT scores are not required if an applicant has earned at least 15 college-level credits.

Application and Information

A completed file contains an application form accompanied by a nonrefundable application fee, a secondary-school transcript (sent by the student's school), and SAT or ACT scores (sent directly by the testing agencies) or responses to the Temple Option questions.

For additional information, students may contact:

Office of Undergraduate Admissions
Temple University
Philadelphia, Pennsylvania 19122-6096
United States
Phone: 215-204-7200
888-340-2222 (toll-free)
E-mail: askanowl@temple.edu
Website: nextstop.temple.edu
Facebook: facebook.com/TempleU
Twitter: @admissionsTU
Instagram: @admissionsTU
Snapchat: @admissionsTU

At Temple University, students get a full campus experience—complete with state-of-the-art facilities and labs, and bountiful, green social spaces—while being in the heart of a destination city.

UNIVERSITY OF CALIFORNIA SAN DIEGO

UC San Diego

SAN DIEGO, CALIFORNIA

COLLEGE CLOSE-UPS

The University

The University of California San Diego—one of the world's top public research universities—is defined by a culture of risk-taking, collaboration, and innovation. Established in 1960, UC San Diego has been shaped by exceptional scholars who aren't afraid to look deeper, challenge expectations and transform conventional wisdom in order to make our world better.

The 1,200-acre campus is located on a sunny cliff overlooking the Pacific Ocean in the La Jolla neighborhood of San Diego, Calif.—the heart of one of the most densely concentrated innovation hubs in the nation. The campus is consistently ranked among the top 10 best public universities in the nation and top 20 in the world for research, teaching, public service and post-graduation career prospects. The university is organized into seven undergraduate residential colleges, five academic divisions—Arts and Humanities, Biological Sciences, Jacobs School of Engineering, Physical Sciences, and Social Sciences—and five professional and graduate schools, including the Rady School of Management, School of Global Policy and Strategy, School of Medicine, Scripps Institution of Oceanography/School of Marine Sciences, and Skaggs School of Pharmacy and Pharmaceutical Sciences.

Over the last 50 years, 16 Nobel laureates have taught on campus. Over 160 current faculty are members of one or more of the prestigious national academies, while numerous others have garnered such awards as the MacArthur Fellowship, National Medal of Science, Pulitzer Prize, Fields Medal and Academy Award. The university's 200,000 alumni are making an impact, including activist Alicia Garza, who co-founded the Black Lives Matter movement; astronaut Jessica Meir, who recently conducted physiological experiments for NASA on the International Space Station; entrepreneur Suman Kanuganti, who co-created smart glasses that allow the vision-impaired to navigate the world; and the trio who created Wong Fu Productions, a digital production company that has amassed over 3M subscribers around the world, led by Wesley Chan, Ted Fu and Philip Wang.

UC San Diego is an ever-evolving campus, with big transformational plans over the next five years to accommodate the growing needs of the university. The Torrey Pines Living and Learning Neighborhood will open in fall 2020, a mixed-use community with student housing and state-of-the-art academic facilities; while the Design and Innovation Center will offer a hub for creativity, collaboration, and entrepreneurship in 2021. Also, the Blue Line Trolley extension will connect campus to the entire regional community, from the U.S.-Mexico border (approximately 30 miles away from the campus) through downtown and directly into the heart of our university in La Jolla, in late 2021.

UC San Diego is committed to achieving inclusive excellence. Through innovative programs and scholarships, the campus offers access to higher education for students from all backgrounds, including first generation students and those from underserved communities. The university was recently ranked fourth in the nation for providing access to low-income students by The New York Times. In addition, UC San Diego graduates the largest percentage of women with STEM degrees, and has been named one of the top 10 most LGBTQ-friendly public universities. Students are invited to engage in open dialogue, develop leadership skills and learn about social issues at six campus community centers. In addition, students can take part in numerous cultural events and celebrations of diversity, from Raza Awareness Week to the annual UC San Diego Powwow and Martin Luther King Jr. Parade and Day of Service.

Majors and Degrees

The campus offers more than 100 undergraduate degree programs spanning five academic divisions, as well as master's and doctoral degree programs in 60 academic departments. A complete list of undergraduate degree programs can be found at http://ucsd.edu/academics detail.html.

Academic Programs

UC San Diego's academic programs, taught by highly regarded scholars, prepare students to stand out and lead change. Every UC San Diego undergraduate belongs to one of seven colleges when they are admitted to UC San Diego. Students may select from the full range of available majors regardless of college assignment.

A student-centered university, UC San Diego offers supplemental learning, tutoring and career development programs to equip students to thrive academically. At the Teaching + Learning Commons, students develop transferable skills, participate in peer-facilitated study groups, and are matched with experiential learning projects. Additionally, new students are connected to a Success Coach from their undergraduate college who helps them create a success plan including research, leadership experience, faculty interaction and more.

Across campus, nearly a dozen makerspaces and incubators offer resources, training, and mentorship opportunities to help students launch their big ideas. At The Basement, students gain business guidance and funding ideas from alumni and industry mentors. For hands-on projects, the EnVision Arts and Engineering Maker Studio contains tools to design, fabricate and prototype, including 3-D printers, welding stations, and laser cutters.

Students apply their learning outside the classroom through faculty-mentored research, service learning projects, study abroad and professional internships. Undergraduates can explore opportunities through the Research Experience and Applied Learning Portal, get matched with real-world training opportunities through the Academic Internship Program, and become immersed in the culture of another country through the Study Abroad Office.

Costs

For the 2019-20 academic year, tuition and fees for California residents were $14,451; nonresidents paid a supplemental tuition of $29,754. The estimated cost of on-campus housing and meals was $14,295. Books and supplies were estimated at $1,128.

Financial Aid

For prospective students and their families, budgeting, costs and how to pay for college can seem complicated. UC San Diego offers information and advising to help students understand the big picture and the bottom line. Students may utilize a wide array of grants, loans, scholarships, veteran's benefits, work-study and other means to finance their education.

Through financial aid and scholarships, our campus offers a pathway to education at an affordable price. In total, 70% of UC San Diego undergraduates receive financial aid. And in 2013, UC San Diego launched the Chancellor's Associates Scholars Program to support the educational dreams of low-income students from schools across California that enroll historically underserved populations. The scholarship, when combined with other financial aid, covers all tuition and fees.

Student Life

Students find community among six residential colleges—with a seventh arriving in fall 2020. The campus is on track to become the nation's largest residential campus by 2028, offering students a four-year housing guarantee at 20% below market rate. Each of the colleges has distinct neighborhoods, residence facilities, staff, traditions and general education requirements. Students bond over shared classes and annual events, from the summertime watermelon drop to the 1960s-inspired Muirstock concert and the annual chocolate festival.

Transfer students find community at The Village at Torrey Pines and the Rita Atkinson Residences. They organize a variety of events, programs and gatherings to enhance educational and social experiences while providing exposure to diverse ideas and viewpoints of fellow students. Graduate students have the option to reside in one of six housing communities on or nearby campus, with amenities for couples and students with children.

Located just a short walk to the beach, surf culture is prevalent on campus. In 2018, UC San Diego was ranked first nationally among "Top 10 Surf Colleges" by Surfer magazine. The campus features a competitive surf team, classes on the physics of surfing as well as opportunities to learn how to ride the salty swells. When students aren't immersed in the sea, they unwind at one of dozens of campuswide events, including Triton Fest, a month-long fall kickoff experience that has featured a haunted trail, go-kart racing and outdoor movie night; Winter Game Fest, the largest student-run gaming festival on the West Coast; and the Sun God Festival, a day-long carnival and concert.

The university features nearly 500 student organizations on campus and more than 40 Greek organizations. In addition, UC San Diego students are very active in their community through a number of co-curricular community service programs; more than 70 student organizations have a primary focus on service.

UC San Diego's Triton Athletics includes 23 intercollegiate sports teams, which have garnered 30 national championship titles. Beginning July 1, 2020, the university will begin competing in the National Collegiate Athletic Association (NCAA) Division 1 Big West Conference, and audiences from around the country can tune in to watch home games on ESPN3. Students can also take part in dozens of sports clubs and intramural leagues, choose from hundreds of recreation classes, and venture into the wild with the campus's Outback Adventures.

Admission Requirements

UC San Diego looks for students at the first-year level who are well-prepared to succeed in a rigorous and challenging academic setting. Admission is highly competitive and applicants must exceed the minimum requirements. Every application, including the personal insight questions, is reviewed by a minimum of two individuals.

In addition to the 14 factors that are detailed on the University of California admissions website, first-year applicants must earn a high school diploma (or equivalent); complete a rigorous array of college preparatory classes with a C grade or better (detailed on the university's website); earn a GPA of 3.0 or better (California residents) or 3.4 or better (nonresidents); submit scores from either ACT Plus Writing, SAT Reasoning Test with critical reading, math, and writing; answers to the UC personal insight questions; and an optional portfolio for students who want to major in history, literature, music, philosophy, theatre and dance, and visual arts. Meeting these requirements does not guarantee admission. Students admitted to UC San Diego exceed UC admission requirements.

Application and Information

The University of California application (available online) must be submitted by November 30. In December, applicants will receive an email that confirms receipt of their application, along with instructions on how to log into UC San Diego's application status portal. The FAFSA or California Dream Act application must be filed by March 2. First-year admission decisions will be posted by the end of March.

Successful applicants must exceed minimum UC admission requirements. Enrollment goals are established annually. The campus does not select students on the basis of academic major or choice of UC San Diego undergraduate college.

For more information, prospective students may contact:

Office of Admissions
University of California San Diego
9500 Gilman Drive
La Jolla, California 92093
Phone: 858-534-4831
Fax: 858-534-5629
E-mail: admissionsreply@ucsd.edu
Website: admissions.ucsd.edu; admissions.ucsd.edu/español

UC San Diego Geisel Library

COLLEGE CLOSE-UPS

UNIVERSITY OF COLORADO BOULDER

BOULDER, COLORADO

The University

The University of Colorado Boulder (CU Boulder) is a dynamic community of scholars and learners situated on one of the most spectacular college campuses in the country. CU Boulder is one of thirty-six U.S. public institutions belonging to the prestigious Association of American Universities (AAU) and has an established reputation for world-class teaching, research, and service to the global society.

At the cornerstone of the university experience are CU Boulder's innovative academic programs, hands-on opportunities, and rigorous coursework that will prepare students for a complex global society. Within the supportive learning community, students will interact with world-renowned faculty—which include Nobel laureates, MacArthur "genius grant" fellows, U.S. Professor of the Year awardees and National Medal of Science winners—who listen, question and help students refine their ideas to develop a broad understanding of the world, strong leadership skills and an enhanced ability to think critically.

CU Boulder offers more than 110 undergraduate and graduate programs; 84 bachelor's majors; 40 concurrent bachelor's/master's degree programs; more than 30 minors and 29 certificate programs; 12 research institutes and more than 75 research centers.

With hands-on experience, world-class education and the ability to think critically, globally and creatively, CU Boulder graduates benefit from a strong salary potential, high employment rates and the opportunity to find and excel in a career they are passionate about.

Location

Students at CU Boulder get to live in spectacular surroundings and learn in a campus environment of extraordinary opportunities.

The city of Boulder is a fitting home for this institution. It's known as the number-one place for entrepreneurs (Livability, 2017), the number one mid-sized metro area in the nation (Amer. Institute for Economic Research, 2017) and the top metro area for female entrepreneurship (version 2.0 Communications, 2017). Ranked the number-one college town in America (American Institute of Economic Research, 2017) and smartest city in America (Bloomberg, 2017), Boulder is known as one of the best places to live because of its beautiful setting, its 45,000 acres of open space, and its lively atmosphere.

Home to more than 100,000 residents, Boulder has a mild, dry climate with more than 300 days of sunshine per year. Over 300 miles of bike lanes, bike paths, bike routes, designated shoulders and paths in and around Boulder, as well as a convenient bus system, provide excellent options for getting around town.

Majors and Degrees

CU Boulder has eight colleges, schools and programs. Amongst them, CU Boulder offers more than 4,000 academic courses across 150 fields of study, enabling students to create an academic experience that is unique.

College of Arts and Sciences: The oldest and largest college at CU Boulder and intellectual core of the university, conducting research, scholarship, creative work and education in more than 60 fields. CU Boulder's research generates new knowledge, solving some of the world's most critical problems. The College offers 50 majors, 25 minors and 10 certificate programs; there are 10 different residential academic programs available to students during their first year of studies.

College of Engineering and Applied Science: The top-ranked engineering programs in Colorado and the entire Rocky Mountain region are found in this college, with a full range of degree programs that emphasize hands-on, active learning and a tradition of research excellence. Engineers Without Borders began at CU in 2000 and has since grown to 206 chapters in 34 countries.

College of Media, Communication and Information (CMCI): Students learn and prepare to be leaders in the ever-changing information society. CMCI students and faculty think across boundaries, innovate around emerging problems and create culture that transcends convention. CU offers six student media outlets and six affiliated centers and labs.

College of Music: CU Boulder is the home of one of the country's top public music programs. A talented and active faculty of musicians, composers and scholars teach an impressive series of programs, ranging from performance to music theory. The college offers 7 degree plans and more than 30 fields of study. The College of Music's library contains more than 150,000 volumes, scores, recordings and periodicals.

Leeds School of Business: Students can earn undergraduate, master's and doctoral degrees from the top-ranked Colorado business school, also one of the best business schools in the Rocky Mountain and Midwest regions. Leeds has several points of pride: 88 percent of internships are paid; 92 percent of 2016 graduates were in a job within three months of graduation; and about 200 students annually take part in the Leeds First-Year Global Experience program (offered in 11 countries); and 8 global initiative programs give students the opportunity to travel and learn about international business.

School of Education: CU Boulder is a proud national leader in the field of education, working professionally with colleagues and communities to deliver outstanding undergraduate and graduate programs for classroom teachers and future scholars alike. More than half of the college's alumni teach in Colorado public schools. Students log many hours of field experience and in turn, 100 percent of recent graduates were employed within six months.

Program in Environmental Design (ENVD): This program fosters an innovative interdisciplinary education to prepare students for practice and advanced study in numerous design-based fields, as well as to apply design thinking to a variety of other possible careers. ENVD houses a state-of-the-art design fabrication lab that includes woodworking tools, metal welding and shaping equipment.

Program in Exploratory Studies: This program provides resources and guidance to help students discover and shape their academic and career journey. The Program in Exploratory Studies exposes students to all CU Boulder has to offer and helps students find a major that merges their interests and skills.

Preprofessional Study Programs in Health and Law: These programs prepare undergraduate students for future advanced education in their field of interest through specialized advising, resources and networking opportunities—all of which help to determine if it is the right fit.

Academic Programs

CU Boulder offers students a wealth of opportunities to engage in hands-on learning and scholarly research in fields as diverse as literature and biology. Programs include the Undergraduate Research Opportunities Program, which funds research projects and scholarly and creative work; the Engineering Active Learning Program, which gives students the chance to gain hands-on engineering experience while forging professional connections through internships; the Biological Sciences Initiative Scholars in STEM Undergraduate Research, which helps students gain research experience as paid research assistants; and the Herbst Program of Humanities for engineering students, a unique program that encourages engineering students to develop thinking skills that incorporate humanities disciplines.

A group of programs, referred to as Top Scholars, is designed to enhance the educational opportunities for high-achieving students who are seeking the challenge of becoming more critical and analytical thinkers.

The CU LEAD Alliance and Scholarship Program is a set of academic learning. LEAD stands for Leadership, Excellence, Achievement and Diversity, and the students, faculty and staff in these communities work together to help students from diverse and underrepresented backgrounds succeed at CU Boulder.

Off-Campus Programs

Studying abroad is a unique opportunity for students to learn from other cultures, enhance their resumes, travel the world and grow as individuals. Education Abroad gives students the chance to earn academic credit while taking classes in another country. The Education Abroad Office administers 450 CU Boulder sponsored programs in 66 countries.

Costs

Estimated tuition, fees, on-campus housing (double room), and meals (19 per week) for the 2019–20 academic year for Colorado residents ranges from $28,478 to $33,782, based on course of study. The totals for nonresidents range from $54,296 to $57,692, based on course of study.

In April 2016, the University of Colorado Board of Regents approved a four-year guarantee of tuition and mandatory fee costs for undergraduate resident and nonresident students. The purpose of this guarantee is to provide financial predictability for students and families to understand the required costs each year. The CU Boulder Guarantee will allow students and families to understand not just first-year tuition and mandatory fee costs, but the cost of fees throughout four years of study.

Financial Aid

Approximately 18,300 undergraduate students received over $320 million in federal, state and university aid in 2018–19. Of that total, almost $170 million was in the form of grants, scholarships and work-study. Prospective students are encouraged to complete the Free Application for Federal Student Aid (FAFSA) by February 15 to ensure full consideration for limited funds. The FAFSA is available starting October 1 and must be completed each year. Incoming students are automatically considered for some scholarships, but more are available via the CU Boulder Scholarship Application between November 1 and March 13.

Faculty

CU Boulder and its nationally and internationally ranked faculty have built a global reputation for outstanding teaching, research and creative work across more than 150 academic fields. CU Boulder faculty members are leaders in their fields but are also dedicated to working closely with undergraduate students. Among faculty members, there are: the 2004 and 2013 National Professor of the Year; 5 Nobel Laureates; 9 recipients of MacArthur Fellowships (also known as the "genius grant"); 89 faculty who are part of the National Academies of Science, Arts and Sciences, Engineering, or Education; and more than 100 Fulbright fellows. The student to faculty ratio is 18:1.

Student Life

Estimated CU Boulder's inclusive community offers many ways to get involved and make lifelong friends. CU Boulder has one of the most active college campuses in the nation, where recreation, sports and student groups play a key role in the campus experience. More than 3,500 students are enrolled in Residential Academic Programs and Living and Learning communities. CU Boulder has 33 competitive club sports, including crew, hockey, snowboarding and swimming, while 12+ intramural sports provide opportunity for campus competition in sports like broomball, inner-tube water polo and flag football.

Students also have the opportunity to serve the greater good through volunteerism and civic engagement, whether it's around the world or across the street. More than 8,000 students serve each year through the CU Boulder Volunteer Resource Center.

Admission Requirements

CU Boulder's mission is to enroll an incoming class of highly qualified, intellectually curious and actively involved students who have demonstrated high levels of maturity and personal integrity as well as a commitment to serving their communities. While admission is competitive, applicants will be considered on an individual basis relative to a prediction of academic success in the college to which they apply.

The primary factor in admission decisions is academic achievement: classroom performance in core academic and prerequisite courses, the rigor of those courses and the best combination of scores on the SAT or ACT.

While academics and test scores play a large role in admission decisions, secondary factors, such as school and community involvement, also help assess the overall qualities of an applicant.

Application and Information

Materials needed for application include the online application, a $50 application fee, a personal essay and writing supplement, a letter of recommendation, high school transcript or equivalency and SAT or ACT scores. The Early Action deadline is November 15 and the Regular Decision deadline is January 15.

Office of Admissions
University of Colorado at Boulder
552 UCB
Boulder, Colorado 80309
Phone: 303-492-6301
Fax: 303-492-7115
E-mail: admissions@colorado.edu
Website: http://www.colorado.edu/admissions

UNIVERSITY OF DENVER
DENVER, COLORADO

The University

Since its founding in 1864, the University of Denver (DU) has grown into one of the West's premier private universities. As the oldest private university in the Rocky Mountain region, the University is home to not only a top-ranked undergraduate program, but also a number of world-renowned research centers and professional programs, including the Josef Korbel School of International Studies, the Sturm College of Law, the Daniel Felix Ritchie School of Engineering & Computer Science, and the Daniels College of Business. A student-centered research university with a liberal arts philosophy, DU develops knowledge in students through classroom academics, hands-on educational experiences and global learning adventures, putting students on the path toward lives and careers that will shape the world.

The DU community brings together 5,774 traditional undergraduate students and 7,157 graduate students from 50 states and over 80 countries. In an environment that prizes innovation, cross-disciplinary study, and adventurous learning partnerships, students embark on a personalized educational journey inspired and framed by a spirit of exploration and openness. Whatever their backgrounds and majors, DU students are engaged and active, taking advantage of the region's many recreational and cultural opportunities—everything from world-class skiing and white-water rafting to award-winning professional theater at the Denver Center for the Performing Arts and alternative music shows at Red Rocks Amphitheatre. On campus, students attend performances at the three-venue Newman Center for the Performing Arts and cheer for the 17 varsity teams that compete in NCAA Division I Athletics at the Ritchie Center for Sports & Wellness. DU has claimed many athletic successes over the years including eight national hockey titles, one lacrosse title, several All-American gymnasts and 24 national championship skiing titles.

The University of Denver is accredited by the Higher Learning Commission. The Carnegie Foundation classifies the University of Denver as a Doctoral/Research University–Extensive.

Location

The University of Denver is built to inspire. Nestled in the Denver metro area, the 130-acre campus is located just eight miles from bustling downtown Denver and 30 minutes from the Rocky Mountains. With 300 days of sunshine and beautiful views year-round, this is a place students are excited to call home. DU's tree-shaded campus is surrounded by pleasant urban neighborhoods offering coffee shops, retail stores, and diverse restaurants. The institution is located along a light-rail line and major bus lines, providing access to the city's arts districts, shopping centers, sports arenas, and an extensive network of parks. DU students can ride all public transportation for free, using their University-supplied CollegePass smart cards.

Majors and Degrees

Whether a student already has a career in mind or they're just exploring what moves them, DU has a program that will inspire them to make their mark. There are over 100 areas of study available to undergrads, and students can further match degrees with their passions with a minor or a concentration. Areas of study include the arts, business, computer science, engineering, humanities, international studies, mathematics, natural sciences, and social sciences. Students who are interested in pre-professional programs can choose from law, medical, dental, and veterinary programs that prepare them for professional study beyond their undergraduate degree.

In addition, the University offers 4+1 and 3+2 dual-degree programs that allow students to complete both a bachelor's and master's degree in five years or less. These dual-degree programs are offered in education, social work, computer science, engineering, accounting, art history, international studies, public policy, and geographic information science. There is also a six-year B.A. or B.S./J.D. program in conjunction with DU's Sturm College of Law.

Academic Programs

Undergraduate programs at the University operate on the quarter system and emphasize experiential, dynamic, and cross-disciplinary learning, providing students with the culture and tools to create a positive impact and make meaningful, lasting contributions to their communities and professions. The University will work with students to help them discover the programs they want to build their future around. Start with liberal arts coursework as well as major-related classes, then blend formal degree programs with professional education to launch an inspiring career. These foundational courses in mathematics and computer science, the arts and humanities, natural sciences, and social sciences (DU's Common Curriculum) ensures students have a wide base of knowledge upon graduation.

First-year students also enroll in a First-Year Seminar. Limited to a small cohort of around 20 students, these seminars focus on a topic that reflects the professor's research interests. This professor, who serves as a mentor throughout the student's first year, introduces the class to university-level work and inquiry, while also advising students on everything from time management to University procedures. The seminar is complemented by a two-quarter writing sequence that trains students to conduct research, construct arguments, and write persuasively for the academic setting. The University's emphasis on writing continues throughout the next three years, with upper-division writing-intensive classes across the disciplines. By the time they graduate, DU students have developed the communication skills that are essential for career success.

A DU education takes students out of the classroom and into communities where they can learn by making an impact. The academic programs incorporate real-world learning, connecting students with the professional environments they'll strive toward after graduation. Because the University believes in the value of hands-on learning, students are encouraged to collaborate with faculty members and peers on research projects and creative endeavors. Through the Partners in Scholarship (PinS) program, DU sponsors student work through grants that fund field studies, research trips, and special materials. At year's end, students share their research and findings at a special symposium for their peers.

Thanks to opportunities like these, the University's academic programs earn high marks from students. In the 2018 National Survey of Student Engagement (NSSE), first-year students and seniors at over 500 participating U.S. colleges and universities reported their satisfaction with their own campus. National results revealed that DU students reported significantly higher levels of satisfaction than the average of students at all other participating mid-size private schools for involvement in collaborative learning, quantitative reasoning, reflective and integrative learning, interaction with faculty members, and the quality of interactions on campus.

Global Opportunities

Studying abroad is an important part of the DU experience—a chance to immerse students in a new perspective and use that knowledge and understanding to strengthen their studies, their community and their career. The Office of International Education guides students through the entire process, from finding a program that meets their needs and goals, to applying, to working to ensure any health or safety concerns are addressed.

With more than 150 DU Partner Programs offered in over 50 countries, DU students find experiences that advance their current academic work and passions. The Cherrington Global Scholars program helps offset some of the significant costs of studying abroad on these programs, like roundtrip airfare and visa fees.

On average, just over 77 percent of all DU students participate, ranking the University 3rd in the nation for the percentage of students studying abroad.

In addition to academics, students explore and surround themselves with new cultures and ideas while making connections with locals and other program participants. Prior to departure, students develop cross-cultural communication skills that help them maximize these experiences abroad in a required Exploring Global Citizenship course.

Academic Facilities

The University has invested hundreds of millions of dollars in new buildings and learning centers to ensure that students can prepare for the challenges awaiting them after graduation. These include the Robert and Judi Newman Center for the Performing Arts, home to the University's celebrated Lamont School of Music and host to a performing arts series known for its adventurous offerings; the Knoebel School of Hospitality Management, home to a full-production kitchen, a beverage-management center, a 120-person dining hall, a student-run coffee shop, and a student-faculty-staff commons; and the Anderson Academic Commons, which serves as the library and hub of the University with a central campus location, multimedia software support services, and a full complement of individual and group study areas and rooms. DU recently opened the Daniel Felix Ritchie School of Engineering and Computer Science, which allows dramatic expansion of both current programming and new STEM initiatives, including the Knoebel Center for the Study of Aging as well as the Sie Complex, part of the Korbel School of International Studies. Both facilities make use of state-of-the-art tools to enhance the ability of students to gain the knowledge and skills needed to excel in their careers.

With a state-of-the-art fitness center, a natatorium, a field house, two ice arenas, a gymnastics venue, a lacrosse stadium, a soccer stadium, and a tennis pavilion, the Ritchie Center for Sports and Wellness brings students and members of the Denver community together to exercise, try new sports, and cheer on the Pioneer athletic teams to victory.

Three new physical spaces are currently under construction as well —a Community Commons that brings the entire DU community together; a first-year residence hall that builds a sense of community from day one; and a Pioneer Career Achievement Center that connects students to DU's 140,000+ global alumni.

Cost of Attendance

For the 2020–21 academic year, tuition will be $52,596, fees are estimated at $1,179, and on-campus room and board costs are $14,178, for a total of $67,953. Because the University of Denver is a private institution, costs are the same for in-state and out-of-state students.

Financial Aid

The University of Denver offers two types of financial assistance to students: need-based aid, which includes scholarships, grants, loans, and work-study based on financial need; and merit-based awards, which include scholarships based on merit or special talent. Each year, the Financial Aid office awards over $159 million in need- and merit-based assistance to undergraduate students. About 85% of full-time DU undergraduates receive some form of financial assistance.

To recognize achievement in the classroom, the sports arena, leadership, and in music, theatre, and art, the University sponsors a number of merit- and talent-based scholarships. Although the requirements vary from scholarship to scholarship, most are renewable each year if the student maintains a specified minimum GPA. More information regarding scholarships can be found at http://www.du.edu/financialaid.

Need-based financial aid is computed using a number of factors, including family income, assets, size, and the number of family members attending college at the same time. DU utilizes both the CSS Profile and the Free Application for Federal Student Aid (FAFSA) to determine need-based aid. Need-based awards generally combine scholarships, grants, loans, and work-study opportunities from a variety of federal, state, and institutional sources. The financial aid offer may also include any competitive scholarships the student has been awarded at the point of admission. To help determine how much need- and merit-based aid might be available to a prospective student and his or her family, DU offers access to a comprehensive net price calculator, found at www.du.edu/estimator.

The priority deadline for applying for financial aid is November 15 for Early Action and Early Decision I applicants, and February 1 for Regular Decision and Early Decision II applicants. Because some financial aid funds are limited, students who complete their financial aid applications in a timely manner are more likely to maximize financial aid resources. Students who simultaneously complete both their application checklist as well as their financial aid applications will receive notification of both their admission decision and need-based award package (a student's financial aid package cannot be determined until they are officially admitted to DU). More information on applying for financial aid at DU is available at http://www.du.edu/financialaid.

Faculty

DU professors teach more than 99% of undergraduate courses, ensuring students work closely with faculty members and the intensity of the learning environment is maximized. The average class size is 23 students; 80% of undergraduate classes have fewer than 30 students and 94% of classes have fewer than 50 students.

Committed teachers, innovative researchers, and prolific publishers, University of Denver professors often include undergraduate students in their research projects and fieldwork. It is not uncommon for an undergraduate student to share publication credit with a professor or to participate in groundbreaking research with tangible, transformational benefits for humankind.

Student Government

At the University of Denver, the student population is represented by the Undergraduate Student Government (USG), whose elected representatives participate in the University's legislative process and communicate student interests to the administration. In addition, USG oversees the allocation of the student activities fee and the licensing of DU's 100-plus student organizations. In the past few years this group has worked extensively on matters ranging from sustainability to diversity and academic affairs to spirit on campus.

USG includes senators from each major, each geographic area (on-campus, off-campus), and each class (senior, junior, etc.). The USG Executive Board includes an advisor, graduate advisor, president, vice president, and a cabinet of members.

Admission Requirements

Admission to the University of Denver is selective. Students are evaluated individually on the basis of their academic record, test scores (when submitted, as DU is a test-optional institution), essay, and recommendations. In making its admission decisions, the University seeks to foster an academic community of geographically, ethnically, and economically diverse learners. The admission committee seeks students who are committed to integrity, innovation, inclusiveness, leadership, academic excellence, and community engagement.

Applicants are required to submit either the Common Application or the DU Pioneer Application—both are posted on the DU website. In addition, applicants are required to submit their high school transcripts, an essay, and a high school counselor recommendation. If students wish to submit an ACT or SAT test score, that score will also be evaluated. Students may submit a teacher recommendation and/or a ZeeMee profile, although neither are required.

Application and Information

The University of Denver offers four application programs for first-year domestic students seeking fall quarter admission. Early Action (deadline of November 1) is a nonbinding program leading to an admission decision in mid-December. Early Decision I (also a November 1 deadline) is a binding program leading to an admission decision in early December. Regular Decision and Early Decision II (deadline of January 15 for both), which are nonbinding and binding respectively, are the final admission programs for fall quarter consideration. Regular Decision applicants and Early Decision II applicants receive their admission decision in early March.

To learn more about the University of Denver, students should contact:

Undergraduate Admission
University of Denver
2197 South University Boulevard
Denver, Colorado, 80208-9401
United States
Phone: 303-871-2036
E-mail: admission@du.edu
Website: http://www.du.edu/admission
http://www.youtube.com/uofdenver
https://www.instagram.com/duadmission/
http://www.facebook.com/uofdenveradmission
http://twitter.com/uofdenver
https://www.du.edu/zeemee

UNIVERSITY OF LYNCHBURG FORMERLY LYNCHBURG COLLEGE

LYNCHBURG, VIRGINIA

The College

The University of Lynchburg is a vibrant learning community where students are empowered to discover their abilities and passions, connect with professors and the community, and achieve more than they dreamed possible. Formerly known as Lynchburg College, the University remains committed to a student-centered approach to instruction and has expanded active, engaged, and relevant learning opportunities across disciplines and throughout the University's curricula.

A fully accredited, coeducational, residential university affiliated with the Christian Church (Disciples of Christ), the University of Lynchburg offers 52 undergraduate majors, 60 minors, and 14 pre-professional programs, all supported by a strong liberal arts foundation. The University's graduate studies program includes three doctoral degrees and 14 master's programs. The University of Lynchburg is nationally recognized by such publications as The Princeton Review's "The Best 384 Colleges" (2019), U.S. News & World Report (Best Regional Universities category and Best Colleges for Veterans in the South), and the John Templeton Foundation's Honor Roll of Character-Building Colleges. Lynchburg is one of the 45 colleges and universities featured in Loren Pope's "Colleges That Change Lives."

The University of Lynchburg is home to 2,800 undergraduate and graduate students, representing 45 states and 25 foreign countries. The University community is largely residential with 75% of the full-time undergraduate student body living on campus.

Set against the backdrop of the Blue Ridge Mountains, in the heart of Lynchburg, Virginia, the 250-acre campus features more than 40 buildings, many of Georgian Revival-style architecture. The main campus forms an elliptical pattern with Hopwood Hall at the east end and Snidow Chapel at the west end, symbolically linking the principles of faith and reason, the vision of Dr. Josephus Hopwood, the University's founder. The Drysdale Student Center is the hub for student activities with multiple dining options, a fitness room, club and student organization meeting spaces, the campus store, and the veterans center.

The University community is a busy place, with a wide variety of activities, including service and honors organizations, such as the national Bonner Leader Program; more than 60 clubs and organizations; 12 fraternities and sororities; and opportunities to participate in dramatic productions, student publications, religious activities, and musical performances. The Outdoor Leadership Program provides adventure-based leadership and team-building opportunities for individuals and groups. Community service (lynchburg.edu/volunteering-and-service) is a distinguishing feature at Lynchburg. Last year, students, faculty, and staff contributed more than 70,000 volunteer hours to the community. The University has been on the President's Higher Education Community Service Honor Roll for the past seven years.

The University of Lynchburg encourages students to develop and maintain a sustainable lifestyle and supports sustainability initiatives on campus. One of the greenest universities in Virginia, Lynchburg gets 100% of its electricity from landfill gas. Other initiatives include recycling, a student-run garden, the climate commitment, a community bike project, and free bus rides for students.

The intercollegiate athletics program (lynchburgsports.com/landing/index) sponsors 22 NCAA Division III teams for men and women, along with equestrian and cheer programs. Lynchburg's NCAA programs compete in the Old Dominion Athletic Conference (ODAC), and the equestrian program fields teams in the National Collegiate Equestrian Association (NCEA) and Intercollegiate Horse Shows Association (IHSA). In 2014, Lynchburg's women's soccer team won the NCAA Division III championship, bringing home the first team national championship in the history of the institution. Lynchburg students can also play a variety of intramural and club sports. Turner Gymnasium includes exercise and fitness areas, a dance studio, and one of the top exercise physiology labs in Virginia.

Shellenberger Field, named for Lynchburg's legendary soccer coach, is state-of-the-art with artificial turf, an eight-lane track, night lighting, and a 3,000-spectator capacity stadium with chair and bleacher seating. The field hosts men's and women's soccer, lacrosse, track and field, field hockey, and intramural and club sports. Moon Field is home to Lynchburg's softball team and the track-and-field events of javelin, hammer, shot put, and discus. Fox Field is one of the best baseball fields in the ODAC, with batting cages, a press box, and seating for up to 1,000 spectators.

Location

The University of Lynchburg (lynchburg.edu) is located in Central Virginia, 100 miles from Richmond, Virginia, 180 miles southwest of Washington, D.C., and 50 miles east of Roanoke, Virginia. Air, bus, and railroad transportation place Lynchburg within easy reach of urban centers. Greater Lynchburg is a growing business and industrial center with a population of more than 260,000. The city is noted for its pleasant climate, its growing arts and music scene, historic landmarks, and its close proximity to the Blue Ridge Mountains.

Majors and Degrees

The University of Lynchburg offers the Bachelor of Arts degree in: accounting, Africana studies, art (art therapy, graphic design, or studio art), business administration, chemistry, communication studies (communication and social influence, convergent journalism, electronic media, or public relations), criminology, criminology-philosophy, economics (financial or general), English, environmental studies, French, history, intelligence studies, international relations and security studies, liberal arts studies, management (general or human resource), marketing, music (instrumental performance, liberal arts, or vocal performance), music education (instrumental education or vocal education), philosophy, philosophy-political science, political science, religious studies, sociology, Spanish, sport management, and theatre (design/technical, general, or performance). The Bachelor of Science degree is offered in: biology, biomedical science, chemistry, computer science, elementary education, environmental science, exercise physiology, health and physical education, health promotion, information technology, mathematics, nursing, physics, psychological science, special education - general curriculum (K-12), and statistics and data science. More information is available at lynchburg.edu/majors-and-minors.

Pre-professional and professional courses are available in art therapy, dentistry, engineering, forestry and wildlife management, law, library science, medicine, ministry and ministry-related occupations, museum studies, occupational therapy, optometry, pharmacy, physical therapy, and veterinary medicine.

Academic Programs

To be eligible for a degree, a student must complete at least 124 semester hours of college-level academic work with a grade point average of at least 2.0 or higher on all work undertaken in the major field.

The curriculum at the University of Lynchburg is divided into two general areas: general education requirements and the major, providing students with breadth and depth of study. General education requirements are selected from the broad disciplines of world literature, fine arts, philosophy, religious studies, mathematics, history, social science, laboratory science, foreign languages, and health and movement science. Additional hours are available for students to explore coursework in free elective hours of their choice, or students may devote their free elective hours to a minor.

The Westover Honors College (lynchburg.edu/academics/westover-honors-college) is designed to attract, stimulate, challenge, and fulfill academically gifted students through a challenging curriculum that promotes intellectual curiosity and independent thinking, and places strong emphasis on creative problem-solving.

Off-Campus Programs

Lynchburg students are encouraged to engage in foreign-study programs, particularly Lynchburg's study abroad program (lynchburg.edu/study-abroad).

More than 1,000 internships (lynchburg.edu/career-services) are available locally, nationally, and internationally, and are integral to a Lynchburg education. As members of the Tri-College Consortium of Virginia, Lynchburg maintains cooperative relationships for sharing facilities and offerings with Randolph College and Sweet Briar College.

Academic Facilities

The University of Lynchburg has 23 computer labs with both PCs and Macs. New students may bring a computer of their own or use one of the many available on campus. All residence hall rooms are wired for network access and the intranet, which serves the University community. Wireless internet access is available in most areas of the campus.

The University has several active-learning classrooms where students can write on the walls, collaborate in the cloud with the help of Chromecast-enabled monitors, and easily rearrange the room thanks to wheeled tables and chairs.

Hobbs-Sigler Hall provides an outstanding learning environment for students studying biology, chemistry, physics, biomedical sciences, environmental science, psychology, mathematics, nursing, and computer science. A cadaver lab, cutting-edge research labs, online weather station, GIS and remote-sensing software, and digitizer are just some of the learning tools available. The science center is also used during the summer by the Virginia Governor's School for Math and Science to provide programming for selected high school students.

Schewel Hall, a $12-million classroom and laboratory facility, houses the College of Business, the communication studies program, and visual arts classes. This 67,000 square-foot facility includes technology-based classrooms, computer laboratories, and specialized teaching-learning settings, including a stock exchange trading room, a digital darkroom, and a multimedia development center with television and recording studios. Sydnor Performance Hall provides an excellent venue for concerts, lectures, and other programs, with seating for 250 people.

Daura Gallery (lynchburg.edu/daura-gallery) is the major repository of more than 1,000 works by Pierre Daura, the Catalan-American artist for whom the gallery is named. Daura Gallery features traveling exhibitions throughout the academic year and is the site of the Senior Art Show, where selected student works are exhibited.

Claytor Nature Center, located on nearly 500 acres in nearby Bedford County, provides an outdoor classroom and laboratory for hands-on, field-based environmental study and research. Donated to the institution by the late A. Boyd Claytor III, a member of the University of Lynchburg Board of Trustees, the property features lakes, woodlands, wetlands, grasslands, rare plants, formal gardens, a primitive campground, and three miles of hiking trails. The land is managed for environmental conservation and restoration through agreements with the Virginia Outdoors Foundation and the USDA's Natural Resources Conservation Service. The A. Boyd Claytor III Education and Research Facility, a 7,700 square-foot multipurpose building, offers Lynchburg students and regional K–12 students and teachers an ideal location for learning with seminar, laboratory, classroom, conference, and retreat spaces.

The Belk Observatory sits at one of the highest points at Claytor (approximately 960 feet above sea level) and is one of the most publicly accessible dark-sky observatories in Virginia. The observatory features an RC Optical Systems 20-inch (0.51 meter) Truss Ritchey-Chrétien telescope with a 177-square-foot dome housing, and an observation deck equipped with 12 piers for mounting smaller telescopes. The control room is equipped with instrumentation that allows Lynchburg to conduct extensive stellar and planetary research and pursue astronomical research with other regional colleges and universities.

The Chandler Eco-Lodge, a 16-bed facility at Claytor, provides overnight accommodations for students and researchers who wish to study outside the classroom. The 2,100 square-foot lodge is built with energy-efficient and low-impact design and includes a constructed wetland to handle wastewater.

Costs

Total charges for residential students for the 2020-21 session are $52,140: $38,720 tuition, $11,450 room and board, and $970 student fees (lynchburg.edu/undergraduate-admission/tuition-fees).

Financial Aid

The University of Lynchburg administers a financial aid program of more than $40 million annually. These resources are awarded to students for meritorious achievement and/or for demonstrated need. The University offers academic scholarships (lynchburg.edu/financial-aid/scholarships) that range from $20,000 to $24,000 and are based on performance and accomplishments at the high school or community college level. In addition, the University offers scholarship competitions, with awards ranging from $1,000 to $5,000, which are awarded in conjunction with other academic scholarships. The competitions are based on academic performance, leadership, community service and talent. These awards are renewable each year until the student graduates, as long as the recipient maintains a qualifying minimum academic average each year. Students are identified to receive these scholarships through the admission application; no separate application is necessary. Free early aid estimates are available for students. One hundred percent of last year's entering class received academic and/or need-based financial aid. The average amount of aid received was $30,000.

To determine eligibility for need-based financial aid, the student should complete the Free Application for Federal Student Aid (FAFSA). FAFSA results determine the student's eligibility for federally funded grants and loans, and other support, such as work-study opportunities. In addition, students from Virginia are eligible to apply for the Virginia Tuition Assistance Grant.

Faculty

The University of Lynchburg's faculty members are outstanding scholars who are leaders in their disciplines. Of the 190 full-time members, 83% hold the doctorate or terminal degree in their fields. The student-to-faculty ratio is 11:1, which allows for personal attention and student-faculty collaborative research, both of which are essential to the Lynchburg experience. While Lynchburg faculty are involved in various research and writing projects, University policy requires teaching to be their top priority.

Admission Requirements

A candidate for admission to the University of Lynchburg (lynchburg.edu/undergraduate-admission) should be a graduate of an approved secondary school with a minimum of 16 academic units or the equivalent, as shown by examination. It is required that the academic work include major emphases in the areas of English, foreign language, social science, natural sciences, and mathematics. An applicant must demonstrate above-average academic ability in all areas of study, as admission is competitive. In support of the record, a student must present satisfactory scores on the ACT or SAT (critical reading and math scores are used to determine admission decisions and merit scholarship awards). It is recommended that all students have a personal interview and visit the campus beginning the spring semester of their junior year or during their senior year. Enrollment office hours during the academic year are 9 a.m. to 5 p.m. Monday through Friday and 10 a.m. to noon on Saturday.

Application and Information

The University operates on an early semester calendar. The first semester begins in late August and ends before Christmas, and the second semester runs from mid-January to early May. An optional winter term abroad, on campus, or online is also offered.

Early decision admission applications must be received by November 15 (lynchburg.edu/undergraduate-admission/freshman-application-steps); notification of acceptance is made by December 15. All other applications are processed on a rolling admission basis. Applicants are usually notified of the status of their application within two to four weeks of the date their application file is completed.

For information, students should contact:

Sharon Walters-Bower, Director of Admissions
University of Lynchburg
1501 Lakeside Drive
Lynchburg, Virginia 24501
Phone: 434-544-8300
800-426-8101 (toll-free)
Fax: 434-544-8653
Email: admissions@lynchburg.edu
Website: lynchburg.edu

The iconic LOVE works sculpture at the University of Lynchburg serves as a visible reminder of the University's commitment to embracing all people and to our past as Lynchburg College (LC).

COLLEGE CLOSE-UPS

UNIVERSITY OF MAINE

ORONO, MAINE

The University

The University of Maine (UMaine) offers the extensive academic opportunities expected from a major research university, with the close-knit feel of a small college. The University of Maine is Maine's Flagship University, offering the most comprehensive academic experience in the state. There are over 100 majors and academic programs, 75 master's degree programs, and 35 doctoral programs. All majors benefit from a strong foundation in the liberal arts. Top students are invited to join the Honors College, one of the country's oldest and most prestigious honors colleges in the nation. UMaine is also the state's only public research university, housing facilities with an international reputation for excellence. UMaine students have extraordinary opportunities to gain real-world experience through research and experiential learning. Undergraduates have the opportunity to collaborate with faculty, conduct fieldwork, and participate in internships around the world. Wildlife ecology majors learn about animal behavior by working in the field with wildlife biologists and black bear cubs. Many engineering students secure co-ops that typically lead to employment immediately after graduation. Education majors have the opportunity to take advantage of urban, rural, and international student-teaching opportunities. There are over 200 student organizations, such as the student investment club that manages a $3.5-million real-money portfolio, Greek Life, Division I athletics, and many more.

Location

There's no place like Maine. UMaine students are surrounded by the great outdoors and have ample opportunity to explore everything the state has to offer. Orono is nestled between the Stillwater and Penobscot rivers. The campus has a traditional New England feel with ivy-covered brick buildings, towering pines, and beautiful fall foliage. Some of the best skiing in the Northeast is within easy driving distance. Beautiful tourist attractions such as Bar Harbor, Acadia National Park, Baxter State Park, and the northern terminus of the Appalachian Trail are just a short drive from campus. The University of Maine is 10 minutes from the city of Bangor, Maine's third-largest city, with its own international airport.

Majors and Degrees

UMaine offers over 100 majors and programs across six colleges at the undergraduate level: the College of Education and Human Development; College of Engineering; College of Liberal Arts and Sciences; College of Natural Sciences, Forestry, and Agriculture; the Maine Business School; and the Honors College. In addition, UMaine offers the Explorations program, designed to help undecided students identify a major across the vast academic opportunities available and find the best fit for a degree program. The Division of Lifelong Learning offers online classes, Summer University, Winter Session, and distance-learning opportunities for students who need a flexible class schedule.

Academic Programs

UMaine provides a comprehensive academic and student experience, yielding graduates who are well-educated, well-adjusted, and well-prepared to succeed after graduation and assume leadership roles within their respective careers. The University seeks to foster excellence and innovation through inspired, dedicated teaching by ensuring there is a constant discovery of new knowledge for students. In addition to their major or concentration within their degree programs, University of Maine students benefit from a solid liberal arts foundation. Students develop and refine the qualities needed to fully engage with the world around them, regardless of their academic discipline.

Undergraduate research is a major component of the learning atmosphere. The University of Maine offers students true hands-on research experience, as early as their first year on campus. UMaine is the state's largest research university, providing rich and diverse opportunities for undergraduates to publish findings, travel the globe, and work alongside UMaine's world-class scholars and researchers. The Center for Undergraduate Research connects students with faculty projects applicable to their academic interests and future careers. The abundance of research opportunities also provides students with great mentoring connections between faculty and students that carry benefits beyond the classroom. The skills students develop through research creates applicants who are much more competitive in the workplace and graduate school.

Campus Programs

Students will get a full and enriching college experience at UMaine. The University of Maine hosts many on-campus programs and opportunities for students to explore and meet new people. There are over 200 clubs and organizations for students to get involved in, such as Greek Life, Woodsmen's Team, Robotics Club, Spanish Club, and more. The Campus Activities Board also puts on free events during the school year, including movies, karaoke, game nights, and astronomy shows. Students can join an athletic team or cheer the UMaine Black Bears Division I teams to victory for free during the year.

There are many ways to explore Maine off campus as well through outdoor recreation, music and food festivals, museums, and much more. Bangor, a 10-minute drive from campus, hosts Waterfront Concerts, First Friday Artwalks and the Bangor State Fair.

Through UMaine study-abroad programs, students explore globally while enhancing their education by taking courses, researching or volunteering. UMaine students have traveled to China to study emerging financial markets, to Italy to learn about Renaissance art history, to Turkey to study film, and to Brazil to look at our world's diverse ecosystem.

Academic Facilities

The University of Maine is home to state-of-the-art research facilities, classrooms, and teaching laboratories. Fogler Library is the state's largest library and located in the heart of campus. It houses more than 1.4 million volumes, 1.6 million microforms, and 2.3 million U.S. and Canadian government publications. It's also the archive of papers written by famous UMaine Alumnus Stephen King. Students have access to UMaine's Capital Markets Training Laboratory with state-of-the-art technology and 12 Bloomberg Terminals that provide hands-on learning in finance. The Advanced Structures & Composites Center's integrated labs include the world's largest 3D printer and he Alfond W2 Ocean Engineering Lab, a 1:50-scale offshore model testing facility that can create scaled wind and wave conditions that represent some of the worst storms possible anywhere on Earth. The Virtual Environment and Multimodal Interaction Laboratory (VEMI) is a research facility that combines fully immersive virtual reality with augmented reality technologies in an integrated research and development environment. Students from all interests and majors collaborate in VEMI Lab research in areas such as aging, vision impairment, and virtual realities. The Innovative Media Research and Commercialization Center (IMRC) and the Wyeth Family Studio Art Center contain facilities for training, research, development, and commercialization. Students have access to many different labs, such as a fabrication studio, electronics lab, audio and video production labs, 3-D printing and design, and prototype production. The University of Maine is also a cultural hub. It is home to the region's premier performing arts center, the Collins Center for the Arts, as well as several museums and galleries.

Costs

For the 2019–20 academic year, tuition for in-state undergraduate students is estimated at $9,000, and $29,310 for out-of-state residents. Canadian residents and students who qualify for the New England Regional Program (NEBHE) will pay an estimated $14,400 for tuition. The average credit load for full-time students is 15 credit hours per semester or 30 credit hours for the academic year. Required university fees are estimated at $2,438 per year for a full-time student. These fees include a variety of healthcare services and admission to cultural, recreational, and athletic events. Books and supplies cost, on average, about $1,000, and room and board estimated cost is $13,254 for one academic year.

Financial Aid

UMaine requires all financial aid applicants to file the Free Application for Federal Student Aid (FAFSA). The priority deadline to apply for aid is March 1. Awards usually consist of a combination of several types of aid, ranging from grants and scholarships to work-study jobs and student loans. Students are encouraged to apply by the Early Action deadline of December 1 to ensure admission in selective academic programs and receive merit scholarships based on high school achievement, as demonstrated by high school rank, grade point average, and standardized test results (SAT and ACT). Additional information on application deadlines and merit scholarships is available online at go.umaine.edu.

Faculty

UMaine is known for its beautiful and vast campus, large student body, and family atmosphere. Students will get to know each other quickly, but even more importantly, so will their professors. UMaine's professors have an open-door policy and encourage students to meet with them outside of class. Undergraduate classes are taught by professors, and many faculty go on to be academic and professional mentors for their students. Students have the opportunity to work alongside UMaine's renowned scholars and scientists in research and other academic ventures.

Student Government

Student Government, Inc. is the independent representative body for UMaine's undergraduate students. An elected president, vice president, and vice president of financial affairs direct and coordinate student clubs and programs at the University of Maine. Student Government works closely with the Office of the Vice President for Student Life and appoints 200 student representatives to various university committees. These students assist with the planning and implementation of residence hall programs, student discipline, athletics, and cultural activities on campus.

Admission Requirements

Admission to the University of Maine is a highly competitive and selective process. Successful applicants hold high scholastic achievement, intellectual curiosity, and extracurricular involvement that promise success at the University of Maine. The holistic selection process looks at the strength of the high school curriculum, grades received, class rank, counselor recommendation, and SAT or ACT scores for admission consideration. Additional information such as essays and community involvement may help the admissions committee evaluate student applications. UMaine recognizes advanced work completed in secondary schools in Advanced Placement tests, honors, or higher education courses. Students who pass examinations may be exempt from certain courses at UMaine.

Application and Information

Applicants may submit electronic or paper versions of the Common Application, the University of Maine Mobile Application, or the ApplyMaine Application. Required documents for all applicants include official high school or college transcripts, counselor recommendations, and SAT or ACT scores. Students above the age of 20 do not need to submit SAT or ACT test scores. Students are encouraged to apply by December 1 to ensure admission in selective academic programs and receive merit scholarship–based application review. More information on application deadlines and merit scholarships can be found on the University's website at go.umaine.edu. Applications and all supporting documents (i.e., SAT or ACT scores, transcripts, essays, etc.) should be sent to UMS Processing, P.O. Box 412, Bangor, ME 04402-0412. For additional information on the application process, prospective students can contact:

Office of Admissions
5713 Chadbourne Hall
University of Maine
Orono, Maine 04469-5713
Phone: 207-581-1561
Fax: 207-581-1213
E-mail: umaineadmissions@maine.edu
Website: go.umaine.edu
facebook.com/UMaineAdmissions
twitter.com@GoUMaine
instagram.com@university.of.maine
linkedin.com/edu/school?id=18586
pinterest.com/GoUMaine/

The University of Maine features over 100 research labs and students typically engage in hands-on research during their first year of college. The Alfond W2 Ocean Engineering Lab (pictured) is capable of realistically simulating scaled wind and wave conditions from the nicest day to the worst storms possible anywhere on Earth.

UNIVERSITY OF PITTSBURGH AT BRADFORD

BRADFORD, PENNSYLVANIA

The University

The University of Pittsburgh at Bradford (Pitt-Bradford) can take students beyond. Students will go beyond smart by having real-world experiences that will take them beyond the intellectual aspects of college and give them the skills they need to succeed; beyond fun by participating in an active student life, a friendly residence-life environment, excellent athletic and cultural facilities, and a wide range of recreational opportunities; beyond borders by being exposed to the world through many study-abroad opportunities; beyond expectations by having a college experience that can transform them; and beyond success by achieving a life that has impact and one in which they are happy, healthy, productive members of society.

At Pitt-Bradford, students live and learn on a safe, welcoming, and inclusive campus, where they receive personalized attention from committed professors who work at their side. In addition, students earn a degree from the University of Pittsburgh, which commands respect around the world.

Students can work out in a state-of-the-art fitness center or swim in the six-lane swimming pool in the Richard E. and Ruth McDowell Sport and Fitness Center. The building also houses facilities for intercollegiate and intramural athletic events.

The Frame-Westerberg Commons offers a place to eat, gather, and participate in campus life. The building houses the dining hall, where students can help themselves to a wide assortment of meals; a bookstore, which features an after-hours convenience store; offices for many student clubs and organizations; and areas to read or relax.

There are more than sixty clubs and organizations, from the campus radio station and literary magazine to academic clubs, honor societies, and fraternities and sororities. Pitt-Bradford competes in Division III of the NCAA and fields seven men's teams in baseball, basketball, golf, soccer, swimming, tennis, and wrestling, and seven women's teams in basketball, bowling, soccer, softball, swimming, tennis, and volleyball. Pitt-Bradford also has an ice hockey club sport, an esports club team and cheerleading.

Location

Pitt-Bradford encompasses 319 acres in the foothills of the Allegheny Mountains, only steps from the Allegheny National Forest. Pitt-Bradford also is a short drive from larger cities such as Buffalo, New York (80 miles north); Pittsburgh (160 miles southeast); and Erie, Pennsylvania (90 miles west). Pitt-Bradford can also be reached easily by car and plane.

At Pitt-Bradford, students have many opportunities to participate in co-curricular opportunities in the region, including cross-country and downhill skiing, snowboarding, snowshoeing, ice skating, biking, fishing, hiking, and hunting.

Majors and Degrees

Students may pursue four-year degrees in accounting, applied mathematics; biology; biology education 7–12; broadcast communications; business, computer and information technology K–12; business management; chemistry; chemistry education 7–12; communications, computer information systems and technology; criminal justice; early level education PreK–4; economics; energy science and technology; English; English education 7–12; environmental studies; exercise science; forensic science; general studies; health and physical education K–12; history/political science; hospitality management; interdisciplinary arts; international affairs; mathematics education 7–12; nursing; physical sciences; psychology; radiological science; social studies education 7–12; sociology; sport and recreation management; and writing.

Pitt-Bradford also offers associate degrees in engineering science, information systems, liberal studies, nursing (RN), and petroleum technology.

Students may also study engineering for up to two years at Pitt-Bradford and then complete a program at the Oakland campus in bioengineering, chemical and petroleum engineering, civil and environmental engineering, electrical and computer engineering, industrial engineering, materials science and engineering, or mechanical engineering.

Pitt-Bradford also offers programs for students to continue their studies in many of the University of Pittsburgh's graduate and professional programs such as medicine, dentistry, and law.

Pitt-Bradford also offers the first two years of study leading to the doctorate in pharmacy. Students must complete the program at the Oakland campus, where admission is competitive. The Pittsburgh School of Pharmacy pre-admits some qualified high school seniors, pending completion of the first two years of the pre-professional program at Pitt-Bradford.

The University also has an agreement with Lake Erie College of Osteopathic Medicine (LECOM), which allows qualifying students to continue their education in medicine at LECOM after their third year at Pitt-Bradford. Students who have successfully completed their first year of medical school classes at LECOM will receive their bachelor's degree from Pitt-Bradford. They will then continue at LECOM to finish their medical studies.

Academic Programs

The academic programs stress critical-thinking and communication skills and encourage hands-on learning through field experience, internships, and faculty-student collaboration on research. A Pitt-Bradford bachelor's degree requires 120–128 credit hours (requirements differ slightly among programs). Students need to complete between 60 and 70 credit hours to earn an associate degree.

The accounting major prepares students for the workplace, which has a growing need for accountants. The major also prepares students to earn a master's degree in either professional accountancy or business administration. They'll also develop skills in the virtual reality lab.

The biology program prepares students for careers in health-related professions, education, and research; technical positions in governmental agencies; and careers with food, pharmaceutical, chemical, and biotechnology companies. Most students interested in medicine, dentistry, optometry, pharmacy, osteopathy, physical therapy, occupational therapy, podiatry, chiropractic medicine, veterinary medicine, preclinical dietetics and nutrition, and a variety of careers in health and rehabilitation sciences are biology majors.

Students who choose to major in broadcast communications, English, or writing are able to broadcast over the college radio station, WDRQ; and publish original works in the award-winning student literary magazine, *Baily's Beads*. Students also have access to an all-digital television studio and two digital radio facilities.

Students who choose a major in computer information systems and technology will get a broad IT background and gain hands-on lab experiences. Students will learn programming applications, network development, systems design and analysis, web technologies, multimedia applications, database development, and systems administration. They'll also develop skills in the virtual reality lab.

In the criminal justice program, students are able to intern with local and regional police departments, county court and probation offices, and a federal prison. State-of-the-art crime-scene investigatory tools enable students to work a crime scene using many of the same tools as professional law enforcement agents. In the Crime Scene Investigation (CSI) House students can process simulated crime scenes and collect evidence just like the pros.

An education major prepares a student for a career as a teacher in a world of rapid political, economic, scientific, and cultural change. The Education Department seeks to graduate students who have general knowledge and specific content knowledge, as well as sound theory and practice.

The nursing program at Pitt-Bradford offers an Associate of Science degree that can be completed in two years and a Bachelor of Science in Nursing degree that requires two additional years. Students may commence this program upon completion of the associate degree.

In psychology, students gain knowledge in the scientific and theoretical aspects of psychology as well as the application of this knowledge. The major prepares students for graduate work in psychology and related disciplines and for employment in social service agencies, mental health centers, industries, and not-for-profit and governmental agencies.

Students may relocate to another University of Pittsburgh campus to complete academic programs not offered at Pitt-Bradford, but they may earn no more than 70 credits before transferring. All students in the arts and sciences may relocate, provided they are in good standing. Engineering students may relocate if they maintain a grade point average of at least 3.0.

Academic Facilities

In addition to the T. Edward and Tullah Hanley Library on campus, Pitt-Bradford students have online access to the entire University of Pittsburgh library system.

Blaisdell Hall, the fine arts and communication arts building, houses the art, communication arts, interdisciplinary arts, theater, and music programs and features state-of-the-art equipment. Students can find a computer graphics lab, two art studios, a music/theater rehearsal hall, and a radio and television studio. The building also houses a multipurpose theater and serves as the cultural center for the region by housing plays, concerts, lectures, and other arts-related events.

Fisher Hall houses the science programs, such as biology, chemistry, engineering, engineering science and technology, petroleum technology, and physics. The science labs are filled with up-to-date scientific equipment, enabling students to perform a variety of experiments. The building also has two computer-aided learning centers and, on the roof, a campus greenhouse.

In Swarts Hall, students take courses in business, education, sociology, anthropology, psychology, history/political science, languages, English, writing, and criminal justice. The building also houses a nursing suite and multimedia classrooms that can turn a typical class into an audio and visual experience.

There is more to the Richard E. and Ruth McDowell Sport and Fitness Center than sports. The building also houses the exercise science, and sport and recreation management programs.

In the Ceramic Studio, students get their hands dirty—literally. Students have sixteen motorized pottery wheels, a manual kick wheel, a worktable, and a kiln to help turn slabs of clay into art.

Costs

For 2019–20, tuition for full-time students was $6,599 per fifteen-week term for Pennsylvania residents and $12,333 for nonresidents. Nursing tuition was $8,454 per term for Pennsylvania residents and $15,727 for nonresidents. Room and board expenses were $4,806 per term. Other costs include an activity fee of $100 per term, a wellness fee of $75 per term, a parking and transportation fee of $40 per term, and a computer fee of $175 per term. Books and supplies cost approximately $500 per term.

Financial Aid

Pitt-Bradford believes that the cost of a college education should not be a deterrent to any student regardless of family financial circumstances. Nearly all students–94% – who apply for assistance receive some form of financial aid, including grants, scholarships, loans and work-study opportunities administered through the Financial Aid Office. During 2019–20, the average financial aid award was roughly $19,171 for Pennsylvania students and $24,102 for out-of-state students. All aid applicants must submit the Free Application for Federal Student Aid (FAFSA) by March 1 to receive priority consideration. Pennsylvania residents who complete the FAFSA by March 1 are also eligible for Pennsylvania Higher Education Assistance Agency (PHEAA) grants. Students who live outside of Pennsylvania should contact their state agency to learn more about the prerequisites for grants.

The University awards merit-based scholarships to those who demonstrate exceptional academic achievement. Additionally, students who receive a Federal Pell Grant will have it matched dollar for dollar by the university. The University ROTC program is another possible source of aid. The University encourages veterans to contact the VA about educational benefits.

To learn more about financial assistance, students should contact the Financial Aid Office or visit the financial aid website at http://www.upb.pitt.edu/financialaid.

Faculty

Pitt-Bradford's 75 full-time faculty members hold doctorates and master's degrees from some of the most prestigious universities in the nation, including Cornell, Harvard, Stanford, and the University of Pittsburgh. Teaching is the primary activity of the faculty, and personal attention is emphasized in the classroom. Faculty members welcome the chance to meet with their students and know them by name. The student-faculty ratio is 15:1.

Student Government

Because Pitt-Bradford is a personalized campus, opportunities for leadership abound. Many students become campus leaders as early as their sophomore year. Regardless of students' background or interests, most find many places to become involved at Pitt-Bradford.

The Student Activities Council schedules comedy performances, lectures, art exhibits, movies, and trips to such cities as Toronto, Niagara Falls, Cooperstown, and New York City.

Admission Requirements

The Admissions Committee considers three primary factors in evaluating an applicant's ability to succeed in college work: the high school record, the results of standardized tests (SAT or ACT), and the high school's recommendations. In addition, personal qualifications, extracurricular activities, and potential to contribute to the college community may be taken into consideration.

Application and Information

Pitt-Bradford has a rolling admissions program, and students may apply at any time. All candidates are notified as soon as action is taken on their application.

Candidates for admission should complete and return the paper application with a nonrefundable $45 fee. However, students can apply online at no charge. Students must also submit an official copy of their high school record and scores from either the SAT or ACT. In addition to fulfilling the above requirements, transfer applicants must submit all official college transcripts and must have a minimum cumulative grade point average of 2.0.

The Office of Admissions welcomes campus visits by students and their families; such visits help students arrive at a final decision about Pitt-Bradford. Interviews and tours are scheduled Monday through Friday, 9 a.m. to 3 p.m., and on selected Saturdays. Arrangements can be made by contacting the Office of Admissions or by going online to http://www.upb.pitt.edu/visit.

For application forms, catalogs, and further information, students should contact:

Office of Admissions
University of Pittsburgh at Bradford
300 Campus Drive
Bradford, Pennsylvania 16701-2898
Phone: 814-362-7555
800-872-1787 (toll-free)
Website: http://www.upb.pitt.edu
http://www.facebook.com/PittBradford
https://twitter.com/PittBradford
http://www.instagram.com/upittbradford

UNIVERSITY OF SAN FRANCISCO
SAN FRANCISCO, CALIFORNIA

COLLEGE CLOSE-UPS

The University

The University of San Francisco—a private, Jesuit university—reflects the diverse and dynamic city that surrounds it. USF provides students from all backgrounds an education that is intensely personalized, intellectually inspiring, and designed expressly to help them change the world for the better.

USF enrolls 6,577 undergraduate and 4,059 graduate students, offers more than 100 undergraduate and graduate degree programs, and boasts a network of over 110,000 alumni who live in all 50 states, six U.S. territories, and 135 countries. The school's campus, in the geographic heart of San Francisco, puts students right in the middle of everything San Francisco has to offer.

USF is one of the most diverse university campuses in the United States. Living and learning in a community that comprises students from 50 states and 98 countries is a unique opportunity. USF guarantees two semesters of housing to all first-time, first-year students who enroll for the fall semester. Approximately 90 percent of incoming first-years live on campus. Any new student who is not a first-time, first-year student may apply for housing and will be assigned housing based on availability.

The University offers six on-campus residence halls and one off-campus residence hall. Housing for first-time first-year students is in Gillson, Hayes-Healy, Lone Mountain, and Fromm. A new residence hall opening in the fall of 2021 will add 600 additional beds, a new dining commons, and more event spaces. Housing for upper-division students under the age of 21 is in Toler. Pedro Arrupe, 12 blocks from campus, offers housing for upper-division students of all ages. Housing for upper-division students ages 21+ is in Loyola Village (apartment-style living). Fulton House, a single-family home and cottage, is reserved for specific graduate student populations. St. Anne, in the Inner Sunset district, houses law students. Each residence hall has laundry facilities, study rooms/spaces, community kitchens, television lounges, and 24-hour front desk staff (except St. Anne and Fulton House, which do not have desk operations).

University Center, in the heart of campus, is home to the USF bookstore, Center for Academic and Student Achievement, Career Services Center, and the Cultural Centers, which bring students together to increase their understanding and embrace their roles as members of a diverse local and global community.

The Koret Health and Recreation Center provides facilities for court games, weight training, massage, personal training, and various aquatic activities in an Olympic-size pool. Spin, yoga, and Pilates mat are just some of the free classes offered at Koret. Outdoor adventures include horseback riding, skiing/snowboarding, and sea kayaking. Intramural and club sports include basketball, soccer, flag football, sailing, table tennis, karate, lacrosse, rugby, water polo, Ultimate (Frisbee), and volleyball. NCAA Division I sports include baseball, basketball, cross-country, golf, soccer, tennis, track and field, and women's volleyball and sand volleyball.

Dining venues are located all over campus. The Market Café in University Center offers a food court with a variety of choices, including global and vegetarian options. Other dining options include Wolf & Kettle Café, Crossroads Café, and Kendrick Café in the School of Law.

Location

USF's 55-acre campus is located in the center of one of the world's most dynamic cities, just minutes from the Financial District, Golden Gate Park, Fisherman's Wharf, and the Pacific Ocean. Students take advantage of the opportunities available in San Francisco including concerts, museums, theater, dining, the ballet, opera, and major sporting events. The city also offers a wide range of research, community involvement, internship, and employment opportunities.

Majors and Degrees

The College of Arts and Sciences offers both B.A. and B.S. degrees. The School of Management offers B.S. and B.S.B.A. degrees. The School of Nursing and Health Professions offers a direct-entry, four-year B.S. in Nursing for qualified high school and transfer applicants. Major programs include accounting, advertising, architecture and community design, art history/arts management, Asian studies, biology, chemistry, communication studies, comparative literature and culture, computer science, critical diversity studies, data science, design, economics, English, engineering with concentrations in environmental, sustainable built environments, electrical and computer engineering, entrepreneurship and innovation, environmental science, environmental studies, finance, fine arts, French studies, history, hospitality management, international business, international studies, Japanese studies, kinesiology, Latin American studies, marketing, management, mathematics, media studies, nursing, performing arts and social justice, philosophy, physics, politics, psychology, sociology, Spanish, theology and religious studies, and urban studies.

USF offers 71 minors and special programs, including astronomy; African studies; Asia Pacific studies; Black Achievement Success and Engagement (BASE) program; Catholic studies and social thought; ethnic studies; film studies; Honors College; Jewish studies and social justice; Latin@/Chican@ studies; Middle Eastern studies; neuroscience; 4+3 dual degrees in law, premedical, and other pre-professional health studies; public relations; an undergraduate and a five-year dual-degree teacher preparation program that results in teacher certification at the elementary or secondary level; and the School of Management honors cohort program.

Academic Programs

The University of San Francisco offers a well-rounded education that prepares students not only for successful careers but also for fulfilling lives. A baccalaureate degree is issued upon the successful completion of a 128-credit curriculum consisting of 44 credits in core requirements chosen from six specified categories, with the remainder of credits being taken as part of major requirements and electives. The academic year is based on two semesters, with summer sessions and a winter intersession also available. USF101, a 1-unit course available to first-semester undergraduates, helps students learn about USF's Jesuit mission, join the campus community, navigate the university's academic requirements and resources, and map their individual paths to graduation.

USF accepts Advanced Placement (AP) credits, as certified by the College Board's Advanced Placement Program exams; the International Baccalaureate program courses; and the College-Level Examination Program (CLEP). Students in the College of Arts and Sciences may earn a bachelor's degree in three years with a combination of Advanced Placement credits and an academically rigorous schedule.

The USF Pre-Professional Health Committee serves to guide and recommend students to medical and dental professional schools as well as to schools for pharmacy, optometry, veterinary medicine, and podiatry. A student may complete the premedical or other pre–health science requirements as part of, or in addition to, the requirements of an academic major. The Pre-Professional Health Committee assists students with the application process, collects and mails recommendations to professional schools, conducts interviews in preparation for application, and endorses approved candidates via a committee letter of recommendation sent to all professional schools selected by the student.

The St. Ignatius Institute offers a core curriculum based on the great books of Western civilization. Any undergraduate student, regardless of major, may take Institute courses to meet core curriculum requirements. The University also offers Army ROTC, which offers scholarships for qualified applicants and continuing students.

Off-Campus Programs

The USF Center for Global Education offers over 100 semester-long programs including exchange programs with Jesuit and

Catholic-affiliated universities in Argentina, Australia, Brazil, Chile, China, Colombia, Ecuador, England, France, Greece, Ireland, Japan, Korea, Mexico, Netherlands, Peru, Philippines, Spain, Taiwan, Turkey, and Uruguay. The Center also offers internship-specific programs in a broad range of fields including arts, business, hospitality, international relations, plus field study programs focused on global issues such as sustainable development, public health, human rights, and climate change.

Because all USF students are encouraged to be civically and politically engaged, the Leo T. McCarthy Center for Public Service and the Common Good creates partnerships between local communities and USF. Students participate in community engaged learning to understand community organizing, advocacy, policy, power, and privilege and to change the world in ways both small and large.

Academic Facilities

USF students have access to Gleeson Library's 2.2 million holdings and to Lo Schiavo Center for Science and Innovation, which houses a digital lecture hall; spaces for collaborative learning; and labs for chemistry, toxicology, advanced biotechnology, and mathematics. Cowell Hall, the base for nursing classes and the Nursing Skills Laboratory, includes the Instructional Media Center. Malloy Hall, headquarters for the School of Management, houses a computer lab and special seminar rooms. Kalmanovitz Hall houses all programs in the humanities and social sciences and features state-of-the-art classrooms, a rooftop sculpture garden, and 17 laboratories for language, writing, media, and psychology. The 281 Masonic building is home to the Performing Arts and Social Justice department, the first program in the nation that trains young artists to create a humane and just society through their craft. The Presentation Theater and Lone Mountain Studio Theater offer space for theatrical productions and guest speakers. In fall 2021, USF will open the Innovation Hive, a space for students to utilize 3D printers, woodworking tools, and more to create their visions.

Costs

Tuition and fees for the 2020–21 school year are $51,930. Room and board are $15,990 for the academic year.

Financial Aid

A variety of financial aid programs are available at the University, including scholarships, grants, loans, and campus employment. Domestic students who wish to be considered for financial aid must file the Free Application for Federal Student Aid (FAFSA). More than two thirds of all USF students receive some type of financial aid. In addition to need-based financial aid, the University has a generous academic scholarship program based on the applicant's high school record and test scores. Eligible students are identified during the admission process and can apply as early action, early decision, or regular action applicants. Scholarship recipients are expected to maintain a competitive GPA while enrolled at USF.

Faculty

The University has 1,184 full- and part-time faculty members; 96% of full-time faculty hold doctoral or terminal degrees in the fields they teach. USF fosters a close relationship between students and faculty members. This is reflected in the small classes (fewer than 25 students), the low student-to-faculty ratio (13:1), and the faculty members' availability for advising. The central focus of faculty is on classroom teaching and working with students on research. Classes are not taught by student teachers or teachers' assistants.

Student Clubs and Organizations

Undergraduates participate in over 100 student associations, including fraternities and sororities, honor societies, student media, performing arts groups, and culturally focused clubs. Annual events sponsored by student organizations range from Campus Movie Fest to theater productions and cultural events such as Black Cultural Dinner, Barrio Fiesta, Lu'au, Culturescape, and Dia de la Mujer. Students also participate in Campus Activities Board–sponsored events including Fright Night, Holiday Roller Rink, Donaroo Spring Concert, Spring Carnival, and Late Nights at Crossroads.

All undergraduates are members of the Associated Students of the University of San Francisco (ASUSF). ASUSF Senate is the official representative body of undergraduate students at USF, composed of an executive board and student senators. The ASUSF government has three functions: to represent the official student viewpoint, to recommend policies, and to fund activities and services.

Admission Requirements

The University seeks students who are sincerely interested in pursuing a well-rounded education and who hope to make a positive difference in the world. The admission process is selective, and each application is reviewed individually. To enhance the quality and diversity of its student body, USF welcomes men and women of all races, nationalities, and religious beliefs—or no religious belief—to apply. Eligibility is based on high school coursework and GPA, the application essay, an academic recommendation, extracurricular involvement, and test scores. Domestic applicants are not required to submit SAT or ACT test scores. International applicants are required to submit TOEFL or IELTS test scores; however, if an international applicant submits sufficient SAT or ACT test scores, the TOEFL or IELTS may be waived.

Application and Information

A completed application includes the application form, the application fee, a personal essay, all academic transcripts, optional standardized test scores, and one letter of recommendation. For the fall semester, the application deadlines are: November 1 for early action and early decision (freshmen), January 15 for regular decision (freshmen), and March 1 (transfers). USF is a Common Application school.

Office of Admission
University of San Francisco
2130 Fulton Street
San Francisco, California 94117-1080
Phone: 415-422-6563
Toll free outside CA (1-)800-CALL-USF
E-mail: admission@usfca.edu
Website: www.usfca.edu
Instagram: @usfca_admission
Facebook: www.facebook.com/University.of.San.Francisco
Twitter: @usfca

THE UNIVERSITY OF TULSA

TULSA, OKLAHOMA

The University

The University of Tulsa (TU) is a private, comprehensive degree-granting university that provides high-quality education in the arts, humanities, sciences, engineering, business, education, applied health sciences and law. Fully accredited by the North Central Association of Colleges and Universities, TU comprises the Kendall College of Arts and Sciences, the Collins College of Business, the College of Engineering and Natural Sciences, the Oxley College of Health Sciences, the College of Law and a Graduate School.

The university is an NCAA Division IA participant currently in the American Athletic Conference. TU, which maintains a covenant relationship with the Presbyterian Church (U.S.A.), is a force for good locally, through its True Blue Neighbors initiatives (with more than 100,000 volunteer hours per year), as well as through various student programs that include projects such as producing assistive devices for people with disabilities and working on international projects that provide self-sustaining sources of energy and hot water.

TU's 11:1 student-faculty ratio, average class size of 20 and emphasis on individual attention anchor an educational culture where students receive both rigorous challenges and comprehensive support. In 2018, TU graduates had a 96 percent placement rate in full-time jobs or graduate/professional schools.

Extracurricular opportunities include intramural sports, special interest clubs, preprofessional organizations, national fraternities and sororities, community service organizations, student government, departmental honorary groups and campus ministries.

Total fall 2019 enrollment was 4,380, with 3,269 undergraduates and 1,111 graduate and law students. The ratio of men to women is 54:46, 33 percent of the students are multicultural, and 14 percent international. TU's diverse student population comes from Oklahoma, 42 states and the District of Columbia, and 66 countries.

Location

TU is a 220-acre residential campus in midtown Tulsa, Oklahoma. Tulsa's prominent industries include energy, telecommunications, technology, data processing, manufacturing, health care, aerospace, transportation and education, all of which provide TU students with opportunities for internships and employment after graduation. The Tulsa metropolitan area has about 950,000 residents. Cultural assets include the Performing Arts Center, BOK Center (venue for popular entertainers), acclaimed ballet and opera companies, a symphony, Philbrook Museum, Gilcrease Museum, Tulsa Arts District and cultural festivals. Professional sports in Tulsa include baseball, soccer and hockey. The River Parks system provides facilities for outdoor activities with jogging and biking trails; Guthrie Green is a popular arts, music, and food truck destination; and the Gathering Place Park is a vibrant, inclusive space designed to bring Tulsans of all ages and backgrounds together.

Majors and Degrees

The Kendall College of Arts and Sciences grants the Bachelor of Arts, Bachelor of Fine Arts, Bachelor of Music, Bachelor of Music Education, and Bachelor of Science degrees with majors in anthropology, art, art history, arts management, creative writing, earth and environmental sciences, economics, education, English, environmental policy, film studies, French, German, history, media studies, music, organizational studies, political science, psychology, sociology, Spanish, women's and gender studies and self-designed majors.

The Collins College of Business awards the Bachelor of Science in Business Administration degree in accounting (accelerated master's), business administration (accelerated master's), computer information systems, economics, energy management, international business and languages, finance, management and marketing. Management majors may choose specializations in business law, entrepreneurship and family business management, or human resource management. The college is home to several specialized centers, including the Energy Management program, Family Owned Business Institute, and the Risk Management Center.

The Oxley College of Health Sciences offers the Bachelor of Science degree in nursing, athletic training (accelerated master's), exercise and sport science and speech-language pathology.

The College of Engineering and Natural Sciences offers the Bachelor of Arts degree in biology, earth & environmental sciences, and physics; and the Bachelor of Science degree in applied mathematics, biochemistry, biological science (options in pre-medicine, pre-dentistry, and pre–veterinary science), chemical engineering, chemistry, computer science, computer simulation and gaming, cyber security, electrical and computer engineering, electrical engineering, engineering physics, geosciences, mathematics, mechanical engineering, petroleum engineering, and physics. The college features state-of-the-art research facilities for all majors. Since 1995, more than 60 TU engineering students have received the prestigious Barry M. Goldwater Scholarship, the nation's premier award for undergraduate students in engineering, math, or science, and 67 National Science Foundation fellowships.

Minors are available in major fields of study, as well as advertising; African American studies; bioinformatics; biomedical engineering; business administration; business analytics; Chinese; coaching; computational sciences; creative writing; cyber security; early intervention; energy business; geology; high performance computing; innovation and entrepreneurship; international business; law, policy and social justice; medieval and early modern studies; Portuguese; and sport management.

Academic Programs

The Tulsa Curriculum links a broad, humanities-based core and writing-across-the-curriculum approach for all students with a highly flexible group of majors and minors. TU students can receive an education that is well-rounded, in-depth and uniquely personalized. Candidates for graduation must complete at least 124 semester hours of course work, with more hours required of engineering and business administration majors.

The Honors Program engages students in a critical examination of the major epochs and ideas of Western thought and culture through careful study of primary texts. The acclaimed Tulsa Undergraduate Research Challenge (TURC) program combines advanced research in most disciplines, scholarship, and community service.

The TU Institute for Information Security is developing defenses against cyber-attacks and comprised infrastructure. The center supports the university's National Security Agency (NSA)–accredited certificate program in information assurance, a curriculum that integrates information security with computer law and policy issues. TU has been designated a Center of Excellence in information assurance by the NSA and is one of six pioneer institutions selected by the National Science Foundation for the Federal Cyber Service Initiative (Cyber Corps).

Air Force ROTC is available through a satellite program.

Qualified students may receive credit through Advanced Placement testing. Students who complete the International Baccalaureate diploma can receive up to 30 college credit hours.

The University of Tulsa operates on a semester calendar. The fall term begins in late August and the spring term in mid-January.

Off-Campus Programs

The university is supportive of study-abroad and internship experiences. The Center for Global Education helps students locate the perfect program, whether for TU credit or as an intern or volunteer. Students choose from hundreds of opportunities offered around the world through a direct exchange with an international university, an affiliate-sponsored program, or as part of a faculty-led course. Internship opportunities are also available in Tulsa and throughout the nation.

Academic Facilities

TU's libraries, historic McFarlin Library and Mabee Legal Information Center, house more than 4 million items. McFarlin holdings include over 990,000 volumes, 680,000 titles, 450,000 e-books, 54,000 electronic periodicals, 9,900 videos, and 11,900 recordings. McFarlin's special collections rare book holdings number over 125,000 volumes and are internationally recognized, particularly for holdings of Native American history and law, along with nineteenth- and twentieth-century Irish, English, and American literature. McFarlin is home to the papers of 2001 Nobel Laureate V. S. Naipaul. The 12,000 square-foot Academic Technology Center annex was dedicated in 2009, adding computer labs, a coffee shop, and restored reading rooms.

The College of Engineering and Natural Sciences added J. Newton Rayzor Hall, a $14-million home for the Tandy School of Computer Science and Department of Electrical Engineering with 24 integrated classrooms and state-of-the-art teaching/research laboratories; and Stephenson Hall, the 38,600 square-foot home for the Department of Mechanical Engineering and McDougall School of Petroleum Engineering. The university's flagship Keplinger Hall was recently renovated. Additional research facilities are housed at Tulsa's North Campus where government- and industry-funded research consortia explore innovations and solve problems faced by the petroleum industry while fostering student learning.

Helmerich Hall, which houses the Collins College of Business, includes innovative learning spaces such as the Williams Student Services Center and Studio Blue. The Risk Management Center combines the latest in trading-floor technology and advanced study in risk management theories and techniques.

The Roxana Rózsa and Robert Eugene Lorton Performance Center houses the School of Music and the Department of Film Studies. The 77,000 square-foot facility includes a 600-seat concert hall, specialized rehearsal and practice rooms, and a film production suite with postproduction editing and scoring capabilities.

The Oxley College of Health Sciences moved is located in downtown Tulsa, occupying 50,000 square feet of the building at 1215 South Boulder. To accommodate travel between the main campus and the college, the university operates continuous shuttle routes for students, faculty, and staff. Oxley expands TU's downtown presence, which also includes the Henry Zarrow Center for Art and Education in the Tulsa Arts District.

The Donald W. Reynolds Center is the campus arena and convocation center, home for TU basketball and volleyball, and includes cutting-edge facilities for video editing and training.

The Allen Chapman Student Union offers dining options and meeting spaces. Meals and snacks are also available in the Pat Case Dining Center, the Collins Fitness Center, and the McFarlin Library Café.

The 29,000 square-foot Case Athletic Complex is home to the Golden Hurricane football program and adjoins the H. A. Chapman Stadium where players enjoy one of the nation's elite college football training and playing environments.

The university's 34-acre sports and recreation complex features a 64,000 square-foot fitness center, the Michael D. Case Tennis Center, track, NCAA soccer and softball fields and intramural fields.

TU manages the city's Gilcrease Museum, home to the world's largest collection of art and artifacts of the American West. The two entities have expanded into the Tulsa Arts District to open the Henry Zarrow Center for Art and Education, providing classes and studio space. In 2014, the university opened the Helmerich Center for American Research at Gilcrease Museum to house the museum's library and archive. Faculty, students, and scholars from around the world visit the 25,000 square-foot facility to conduct research and present symposia on their research topics.

Costs

For 2020-21, the typical cost for students living on campus is $42,950 for tuition, $12,062 for room and board, and fees of $1,035. Additional miscellaneous expenses (including books) average about $4,500 per year.

Financial Aid

In 2019, 98 percent of entering students received some form of financial aid (including grants, scholarships, work-study, and loans). TU offers a limited number of highly competitive Presidential Scholarships that cover full tuition, room, and board. All applicants may be considered for a range of university scholarships based on academic merit. Performance scholarships are available in music and theater by audition. The University of Tulsa participates in National Merit and National Achievement Scholarship Corporation's Finalist program and the National Hispanic Scholar Program. Applicants for aid should submit the Free Application for Federal Student Aid (FAFSA) by January 15 for priority consideration.

Faculty

The University has 355 full-time faculty members, with 94 percent having earned the highest degree in their field of study. The faculty is primarily a teaching faculty, although most of its members are also involved in funded research or publishing activities.

Admission Requirements

The University of Tulsa seeks students whose academic background indicates potential for success in the university's rigorous academic environment. Performance in high school college-preparatory subjects and scores on the SAT or ACT are key factors in the admission evaluation, but each applicant is reviewed holistically. Each applicant's counselor recommendation; extracurricular activities; and indicators of leadership, creativity, and focus are all taken into consideration. Campus visits and interviews are highly recommended but not required.

Application and Information

TU has a nonbinding, early action freshman admission plan with an application deadline of November 1. Decisions are mailed within five weeks. Applications received after November 1 are reviewed under a rolling admission process with notifications made on an ongoing basis in early January.

An application, high school transcript, ACT or SAT score results, and a guidance counselor recommendation are required. TU accepts the Common Application or its own online or paper application form. TU adheres to the national Candidate's Reply Date of May 1.

For more information, students should contact:

Office of Undergraduate Admission
The University of Tulsa
800 South Tucker Drive
Tulsa, Oklahoma 74104-3189
Phone: 918-631-2307 (in Tulsa)
800-331-3050 (toll-free)
Fax: 918-631-5008
E-mail: admission@utulsa.edu
Website: https://admission.utulsa.edu

The Kendall Bell plays a big part in TU's most well-known tradition. After completing their last final exam of their last year at TU, students ring the bell to recognize their hard work of the past and their optimism for the future..

VIRGINIA MILITARY INSTITUTE

LEXINGTON, VIRGINIA

The Institute

the Virginia Military Institute (VMI) is the nation`s oldest state-supported military college, founded in 1839 in Lexington, Virginia, and located at the southern end of the Shenandoah Valley. VMI offers qualified young men and women a demanding combination of academic study and rigorous military training that exists nowhere else, and grants B.A. and B.S. degrees in fourteen disciplines within the general fields of engineering, science, and liberal arts. The Institute`s emphasis on qualities of honor, integrity, and responsibility contributes to its unique educational philosophy. Professional leadership training is provided to all cadets through the Reserve Officers` Training Corps (ROTC) programs, maintained at VMI by the Department of Defense. Cadets may pursue commissions in the U.S. Army, Air Force, Navy, or Marine Corps.

In every field of endeavor, whether it is leadership in business, industry, public service, education, the professions, or careers in the military, success comes early to a high number of VMI graduates. In an independent survey of college graduates seeking employment, armed forces commission, or admission to graduate or professional school following graduation, over 95 percent of VMI graduates met their goal by the following October.

VMI`s breadth is diverse. The curricula for the selected major begin in the first year. More than 25 percent of cadets major in civil, electrical, or mechanical engineering, and more than 50 percent of cadets major in liberal arts fields. The two most popular fields are economics/ business and international studies.

The academic excellence of VMI and its stature among institutions of higher education are highlighted by the fact that U.S. News and World Report ranks VMI among the nation`s top public liberal arts colleges annually. Its engineering programs remain in the top tier of best undergraduate accredited programs at schools offering only bachelor`s or master`s degrees.

VMI`s alumni support is unparalleled in many ways, especially in their financial support. The National Association of College and University Business Officers has reported that VMI has one of the largest endowments per student of any public institution.

VMI alumni include Nobel Peace Prize winner George C. Marshall, 11 Rhodes scholars, and 39 college presidents. VMI alumni have distinguished themselves in every American conflict since the Mexican War, and they include 7 Medal of Honor recipients and 265 general and flag officers. Well over 1,000 alumni have served in war zones and in support of operations in the war on terror since 2001.

After nearly 160 years of preparing young men for distinguished leadership roles, VMI made the transition to being coeducational in 1997, successfully assimilation women in the Corps of Cadets. The Institute graduated its first women cadets in May 1999.

Today, approximately 1,700 young men and women in the VMI Corps of Cadets represent forty-four states and nine other countries. More than 100 cadets study abroad each year, one third compete in intercollegiate athletics, and all have significant leadership opportunities.

All cadets reside in Barracks, at the centerpiece of the VMI Post. The original structure was built in 1850 and is a National Historic Landmark. An additional wing was added in 1949. A third section of the Barracks was completed in 2008. All cadet rooms are equipped for computer technology.

VMI cadets uphold an honor system as old as the Institute. An oath of honor is taken by each cadet, "not to lie, cheat, or steal, nor tolerate those who do," and the oath is practiced in daily life. As it is basic to cadet life, it is ingrained and builds strong character. Honor is at the cornerstone of every cade`s lifelong commitment to integrity, duty, self-discipline, and self-reliance.

One of the oldest VMI traditions is the orientation and instruction provided to new cadets by older cadets. Regardless of background or prior training, every cadet in the first year at VMI is a Rat, and each is a Brother Rat to the other. They live under the Rat system until Break Out in late winter, and their bonds formed by the experience last a lifetime.

VMI places great emphasis on physical fitness and training programs, whether cadets participate in athletics, ROTC training, or physical education programs. VMI offers eighteen intercollegiate athletics programs at the NCAA Division I level and supports numerous club sports and intramural activities. The VMI "Keydet" Club is one of the oldest and most productive athletic foundations in the country, raising more than $3.3 million annually for athletic scholarships and grants-in-aid to 450 cadets in all eighteen sports. Athletic grounds and facilities are within easy access to the Post

VMI is a member of the Southern conference.

Location

Lexington is in Rockbridge County, Virginia, an area rich in history and natural beauty. VMI adjoins the campus of Washington and Lee University, the nation`s ninth-oldest institution of higher learning. Both colleges are within walking distance to historic downtown Lexington, a popular tourist destination. Interstate Highways 81 and 64 intersect only minutes from VMI, north of Lexington`s downtown area. U.S. Highways 11 (north-south) and 60 (east-west), the area`s crossroads for two centuries, intersect in downtown Lexington. Air service to VMI is available from Roanoke Regional Airport, less than an hour`s drive from Lexington.

Majors and Degrees

VMI offers the baccalaureate degree in fourteen curricula. The B.S. is awarded in applied math, civil engineering, computer science, electrical engineering, mechanical engineering, psychology, and physics. The B.A. is conferred in economics and business, English, history, international studies, and modern languages. A B.S. or B.A. can be earned in biology and chemistry. A course of study leading to a B.S. or B.A. is chosen upon entering VMI, but a transfer from one major field of study to another is permitted.

Academic Programs

VMI`s demanding academic program reflects, established needs and emerging trends of an ever-changing, global society. A newly funded undergraduate research initiative extends though summer, affording cadets and faculty members financial incentives and continuous support for a wide range of investigative projects. The Institute's international programs include faculty and student exchanges with more than a dozen international academies and universities, seven international internships and numerous study-abroad programs each semester and during the summer. VMI is accredited by the Southern Association of Colleges and Schools and is a member of American Council on Education, the Association of American Colleges, the College Entrance Examination Board, and the Association of Virginia Colleges. VMI`s engineering and computer science programs and ABET-accredited, the chemistry program is accredited by ACS.

Academic Facilities

The VMI Post covers 134 acres, of which 12 acres are designated a National Historic District. VMI`s academic facilities, Superintendent`s quarters, library, alumni hall, and other administrative buildings, along with Barracks, encircle a 12-acre parade ground used for marching drills, weekly parades, training exercises and social gatherings. The physics department has laser optics and nuclear physics laboratories and operates an observatory with a 20-inch reflecting telescope. The George C. Marshall Research Museum and the VMI Museum are located on Post.

Faculty

All VMI faculty members teach in the classroom, and almost 100 percent of full-time faculty members hold doctoral or terminal degrees. The cadet-faculty ratio is 12:1, permitting a close, mentor relationship between a cadet and instructor. Faculty research is conducted in partnership with cadets. ROTC instructors are experienced military officers and make an outstanding contribution to cadet leadership training.

Student Government

VMI has two systems of student government. The regimental system oversees cadet accountability for conduct, appearance, military training, and all ceremonial functions. The regiment of the Corps is divided into two battalions of with nine line companies plus a band company.

Although Institute regulations govern the discipline of cadets, a large measure of supervision resides in each of the four closely-knit classes within the Corps. The class system administers the Corps` standards and the privileges accorded each class and governs with the regimental system to oversee cadet appearance and conduct.

Representatives to the Honor Court are elected from the Corps, by the Corps, to enforce the rules of the honor system and prosecute Honor Court cases.

Admission Requirements

Applicants must be unmarried, 16 to 22 years of age (a one-year age waiver may be granted for an applicant who has served in active duty in the armed forces or in certain other circumstances), physically fit for enrollment in ROTC, and graduated from an accredited secondary school with 16 or more academic units. Recommended course credits include 4 English, 3 social studies, 3 laboratory sciences, 3 foreign language, 3 mathematics (including 2 years of algebra and 1 of geometry) and 2 electives. The average GPA of incoming freshman is approximately 3.6. Other qualifications include rank in the upper 50 percent of the senior class (significance of rank depends on class size and other factors), above-average scores on SAT or ACT, and satisfactory character recommendations. Extracurricular activities are viewed as favorable indicators of leadership and character traits. Transfer students are accepted, but six semesters of residency at VMI are required. Admissions standards are applied without regard to gender, race, nationality, or religion, and all factors are weighed in the final determination of the applicant`s qualifications.

Application and Information

An application may be submitted anytime between August 1 and February 1 (priority deadline) of the senior year in high school and should be accompanied by a nonrefundable $40 application fee, a transcript of the school record for grade 9 through the last completed semester, and SAT or ACT scores. Visits to the Institute are highly recommended. Open House visits are held throughout the academic year.

Interested Students should contact:
Director of Admissions
Virginia Military Institute
Lexington, Virginia 24450
Phone: 540-464-7211
800-767-4207
Fax: 540-464-7746
E-mail: admissions@vmi.edu
Web site: http://www.vmi.edu

WESTMONT COLLEGE

SANTA BARBARA, CALIFORNIA

The College

Westmont College helps students unite both spirit and mind through a liberal arts education that offers rigorous training in every area of human knowledge and fosters a deep love of God. The college's nationally ranked program focuses entirely on undergraduates and helps them develop deep relationships by living in a residential Christian community. Westmont professors lead semesters on four continents to help students develop a global perspective.

Learning at Westmont extends beyond the classroom as students participate in a variety of student clubs, activities and service projects. Athletes can compete with a Warrior team or play for a club sport or intramural league. Musicians have the opportunity to perform with accomplished choirs and instrumental groups, the theater program stages classic plays and an exciting Fringe Festival, and art students study in beautifully designed studios and exhibit artwork in the Westmont Ridley-Tree Museum of Art. Other possibilities include the student newspaper, literary magazine, or yearbook; intercultural clubs and political organizations; or volunteer opportunities in the community. Chapel, an integral part of a Westmont education, features inspiring speakers who encourage students to grow in their faith. Attendance is required three days a week.

Westmont's Office of Career Planning and Calling helps students discover their strengths and weaknesses then prepare for a career by encouraging them to participate in internships. Westmont's professors and classes also provide preparation for graduate school; Westmont alumni have attended some of the finest universities in the world, such as UCLA, Stanford, Harvard, Yale, Princeton, Cambridge, the University of Chicago, and others.

The college's 1,200 students come from more than 30 states and 16 countries, with the highest percentage from California. About 61 percent are women, 36 percent are students of color, and 2 percent are international students. Ninety-five percent of students live in the six residence halls on campus or the apartment complex off campus. Westmont belongs to the National Association of Intercollegiate Athletics and the Golden State Athletic Conference and competes in intercollegiate sports for men and women in basketball, cross-country, golf, soccer, tennis, and track and field and in baseball (men) and swimming and volleyball (women). Club teams for men include polo, rugby, soccer, volleyball, Ultimate (Frisbee), and golf; women's club teams are polo, cheer, and golf. Both men and women can participate in intramural sports.

Location

Located in scenic Santa Barbara, Westmont's 111-acre wooded campus lies between the Santa Ynez Mountains and the Pacific Ocean. Students enjoy the beach and mountain trails year-round. The local community offers a wealth of culture, including museums, theaters, libraries, concerts, lectures and historic sites.

Majors and Degrees

Westmont awards Bachelor of Arts (B.A.) and Bachelor of Science (B.S.) degrees in more than 100 academic majors, minors, and programs: alternative major, art, art history, biology, chemistry, communication studies, computer science, economics and business, data analytics, education, engineering, engineering physics, English, English and modern languages, European studies, French, history, kinesiology, liberal studies, mathematics, music, philosophy, physics, political science, psychology, religious studies, social science, sociology and anthropology, Spanish, and theater arts. also offers a The California Commission for Teacher Preparation and Licensing accredits the teacher-preparation program, and students may qualify for either the single-subject or the multiple-subject credential. Pre-professional programs include athletic training, dentistry, engineering, law, medicine, ministry and missionary studies, pharmacy, physical therapy, and veterinary studies. Minors include anthropology, biblical languages, coaching, environmental studies, ethnic studies, film studies, gender studies, global studies, movement science and writing.

Academic Programs

All majors and programs of study feature thought-provoking and inspiring ways to integrate belief, thought and action to reach a deeper, more accurate understanding of the world and achieve a wider impact. Professors demand critical thinking and encourage exploration of the world of ideas through a wide range of opportunities and organizations. For example, students consider issues of science and religion through the Pascal Society and attend lectures in the humanities sponsored by the Erasmus Society. At Westmont, an exclusively undergraduate college, students can engage in significant research projects in the sciences and all disciplines by assisting professors in their scholarly work and completing independent study. Professors, staff members, and alumni seek to help students grow through their questions toward an ever-deeper faith.

Global Education

Westmont professors lead the college's global education programs, including Europe Semester, which offers the broadest geographical scope. England Semester combines travel and residential study of literature in the British Isles. At Westmont in Cairo students live in a developing world megalopolis at the heart of the Islamic world. Westmont in Jerusalem lets students explore the ancient world of Jesus and modern Israel-Palestine. Through Westmont in Mexico, students gain skills for effective cross-cultural living and improve their Spanish-speaking skills. Westmont in East Asia takes participants to Seoul, Shanghai, and Singapore to learn about globalization, culture, society, and Christianity. Westmont in Northern Europe features extended stays in London, Berlin, and Northern Ireland and focuses on conflict and peace-making. Global Health: Uganda gives medical and public-health-related majors an international field placement at a local organization in Uganda. Students can take part in a meaningful internship during Westmont in San Francisco and grapple with big questions while staying in a historic mansion in a vibrant area of the city. The Summer Session in Singapore combines academic study, an internship, and some travel in the region. At Westmont Downtown, participants live in downtown Santa Barbara, study social entrepreneurship, and spend 20 hours a week in a significant internship. Westmont's membership in the Christian College Consortium (CCC) lets students explore additional opportunities and programs led by other colleges, such as language and cultural study in places such as France, Spain, and Latin America; a Washington Semester in the nation's capital; and the Consortium Visitor Program, in which students spend a semester at another of the CCC's 13 campuses.

Academic Facilities

Westmont's newest buildings include the Global Leadership Center, Adams Center for the Visual Arts, which features the Westmont Ridley-Tree Museum of Art, Winter Hall for Science and Mathematics, and the Westmont Observatory with the powerful Keck Telescope. The tri-level Roger John Voskuyl Library, named for Westmont's third president, provides resources and services that support the teaching and research needs of faculty, staff, students and the surrounding community. The library collections include 237,000 books, media items, music scores, and microforms; 300 print periodical titles; 105 online databases with access to 12,000 online periodicals; and access to additional resources through the Gold Coast Library Network, Camino, and Interlibrary Loan Services. Westmont's network consists of both wired and wireless components. Wireless coverage extends to all campus buildings and most outdoor areas, with a total Internet bandwidth of 135 Mb/s. Students obtain Google Apps accounts through Westmont that provide email, a calendar, document sharing, and 4 GB of storage per student. The college provides a computer lab with 27 dual-platform iMacs located on the main floor of the library. Westmont's Learning Commons, a 21st-century space in the library, brings together library, technology and other campus services in an environment that fosters collaborative and creative work and social interaction. Voskuyl Library also houses departments that provide student support services: Academic Advising and Disability Services, Internship Programs, Writer's Corner, and Information Technology. Porter Theatre contains state-of-the-art equipment for dramatic productions and concerts, including the Black Box Theatre. Mericos H. Whittier Science Building and Winter Hall for Science and Mathematics house the college's science program and equipment, including an ultracentrifuge, a liquid scintillation counter for measuring radioactivity, physiographic units, and other equipment for advanced physiological studies.

Costs

Tuition and fees for 2020–2021 are $46,980 and room and board for the academic year are $15,040. The cost of books and personal expenses are estimated at $3,000.

Financial Aid

Westmont provides generous financial aid and encourages all students to apply regardless of their financial resources. Ninety-five percent of students receive some form of financial assistance. Westmont offers awards worth 85 percent of tuition through the Augustinian Scholars Program to 60 students each year, available only to first-year applicants who apply via nonbinding early action. A select group of these applicants participate in a formal competition on campus; interested students should contact the Office of Admissions for more information. Other merit awards in the financial aid program—President's, Ruth Kerr, Wallace L. Emerson, and Founders Scholarships and the Warrior Academic Award—range from $15,000 to $25,000. Transfer students may be eligible for scholarships ranging from $11,500 to $17,500, offered to students with impressive academic achievement. Westmont also gives awards to those who demonstrate strength in art, music, theater arts, dance, cultural diversity, and athletics. After submitting the Free Application for Federal Student Aid (FAFSA), students may be eligible for state grants, aid from federal programs, institutional grants, loans, and work-study programs.

Faculty

One of Westmont's highest priorities is attracting and retaining Christian teachers and scholars with outstanding credentials and a love for students. Students get to know professors personally and will likely spend time with them outside of class. The college's 96 full-time and 58 part-time professors are dedicated to integrating faith and learning and being actively involved in the lives of students. The student-faculty ratio is 11:1; the average class size is 17. Ninety-eight percent of tenure-track faculty members hold a terminal degree. Professors are committed to teaching at the undergraduate level and advise either incoming first-year students or majors in their department. Although teaching is their primary scholarly activity, many professors engage in research, write books, and publish articles in leading journals and periodicals.

Student Government

The Westmont College Student Association (WCSA) is a self-governing body. Students elect WCSA representatives, who are responsible for organizing social, cultural, and educational activities. They actively participate as voting members on most faculty committees, and allocate the student budget to various clubs and organizations. Westmont Student Ministries, another student-managed organization, organizes a range of outreach programs and ministries on and off campus.

Admission Requirements

Westmont selects candidates for admission from prospective students who demonstrate their preparation for the academic stimulation and spiritual vitality central to Westmont's character. All applicants must submit one academic letter of recommendation, official high school or college transcripts, and official SAT or ACT scores. A pastoral/character reference is optional. An interview is strongly encouraged. For transfer students from an accredited two- or four-year college or university or a Bible college or university that is accredited by the American Association of Bible Colleges, the evaluation is based on achievement in solid, transferable course work; an assessment of the personal areas covered by the application (as stated above); and the quality of the written responses. High school records must also be submitted by transfer students having completed fewer than 24 semester units or 36 quarter units.

Application and Information

Students may enroll at Westmont at the beginning of either the fall or spring semester. The college offers an early-action plan. High school seniors interested in applying Early Action 1 must submit an application by October 15, and those interested in applying Early Action 2 must submit an application by November 1. Notifications are mailed by December 1 and January 1, respectively. The priority deadline for regular decision is January 15 for first-year applicants and March 15 for transfers. Notifications are mailed on a rolling basis. Applications should be submitted online via the Common Application or the Westmont Application. No application fee is required. The Office of Admission encourages prospective students to complete the application process as early as possible.

Visitors are welcome any time. Guests may stay overnight in the residence halls, attend classes and chapel, speak with professors or coaches, audition for a music program, share a portfolio with the art department, interview with an admissions counselor, and eat meals with Westmont students. Several Preview Day events are held each semester. Westmont seeks to enroll a well-rounded and varied first-year class while creating a dynamic and culturally and traditionally diverse community of learners possessing a variety of attributes, accomplishments, backgrounds, and interests.

For more information regarding admissions students should contact:

Office of Admission
Westmont College
955 La Paz Road
Santa Barbara, California 93108
Phone: 800-777-9011 (toll-free)
Fax: 805-565-6234
E-mail: admissions@westmont.edu
Website: http://www.westmont.edu/
http://www.facebook.com/westmont
http://twitter.com/westmontnews

Discover a premiere liberal arts college on one of the most beautiful college campuses in the country.

WHEATON COLLEGE

WHEATON, ILLINOIS

The College

Ranked by *U.S. News & World Report* as one of the nation's top liberal arts colleges, Wheaton College attracts exceptional students from all fifty states and as many as ninety countries. An interdenominational Christian liberal arts college, Wheaton takes the pursuit of faith and learning seriously. In addition to upholding an academically rigorous curriculum, Wheaton is committed to being a community that fearlessly pursues God's truth; invests in developing whole, well-rounded students; and prepares its graduates to lead lives that make a difference in the world.

The student body at Wheaton College consists of approximately 2,400 undergraduates (including 150+ students in the Conservatory of Music), approximately 80 percent of which come from outside Illinois.

Wheaton College's nearly 160-year history demonstrates the benefits of stable leadership in private Christian higher education—it has had only 8 presidents since it was founded in 1860. Wheaton has been faithful to its original precepts, and its legacy is shown in the lives of its graduates. Many distinguished graduate schools currently enroll Wheaton graduates, including Notre Dame, Princeton, SMU, Yale, and the Universities of Chicago and Missouri–Kansas City; several of the Big Ten music schools; and the A.R.T./MXAT Institute for Advanced Theater Training at Harvard. Wheaton alumni also excel in a wealth of endeavors around the world, with many holding positions in business and finance, government and foreign service, teaching, ministry, law, medicine, and the arts. Wheaton graduates actively contribute to their communities and churches, and no matter what position they hold, they strive to make a difference in the world around them.

Wheaton offers a rich, life-changing education, with graduates trained for life, not just jobs. Students are taught to think, reason, and express themselves effectively. They are equipped to attain knowledge and measure it against the truth of God's word, understand the importance of service, and value faith that embraces both theological accuracy and actively living it out. Developing strong, life-long relationships—with classmates, professors, and Jesus Christ—is a priority. Graduates are well-positioned for whatever they want to pursue and prepared to face the challenges of life. The Wheaton experience is distinctive, and living and learning at Wheaton is extraordinary. As a visiting lecturer recently observed, "I was so impressed by the enthusiasm of the Wheaton students to shape the world, and to make it a better place. And they are approaching this goal in practical ways. Some colleges are full of dour cynics. Wheaton is the opposite—brimming with optimists!"

Location

Wheaton's 80-acre campus is located in a residential suburb (population 55,000) 25 miles west of Chicago. The educational and cultural features of the Chicago metropolitan area are easily accessible by train and regularly visited by students.

Majors and Degrees

Wheaton grants the Bachelor of Arts and Bachelor of Science degrees and, through the Wheaton Conservatory of Music, the Bachelor of Music and Bachelor of Music Education degrees.

The following majors are available in the arts and sciences: anthropology, applied health science, archaeology, art, biblical and theological studies, biology, business/economics, chemistry, Christian education and ministry, classical languages (Greek, Hebrew, Latin), communication, computer science, economics, education, English, environmental studies, geology, history, interdisciplinary studies, international relations, mathematics, modern languages (Chinese, French, German, and Spanish), music, philosophy, physics, political science, psychology, sociology, and urban studies.

The Wheaton Conservatory of Music offers a full range of professional music majors, including composition, education, history/literature, performance, music with elective studies in an outside field, and music with an emphasis in a music-related field (such as media/film music, pedagogy, conducting, and collaborative piano). Students seeking these professional music degrees are accepted directly into the program by audition.

An on-campus program in military science leads to a commission in the U.S. Army at graduation. In addition to the majors offered, Wheaton has programs leading to teacher certification and to athletic training certification as well as programs preparing students for careers in business, health professions, law, and ministry.

Academic Programs

Because of the College's strong commitment to developing effective servant/leaders for society worldwide and the church, there is a particularly strong integration of faith and learning in all degree programs. A new general education curriculum, Christ at the Core, implemented in fall '16, brings a well-rounded, Christ-centered academic experience while allowing increased freedom and flexibility among cohorts.

Students must demonstrate core competencies (either by examination or by taking prescribed courses) as essential skills for the pursuit of knowledge: First Year Writing, Modern and Classical Languages, Oral Communication and Wellness.

SHARED CORE classes foster developmental learning with special attention to integrating faith with learning.

THEMATIC CORE courses allow students to shape their own learning experience to their intellectual needs and vocational calling through the many creative course offerings within ten multidisciplinary themes. A student may be granted advanced placement or college credit on the basis of examination (including SAT Subject Tests, AP, or IB).

Wheaton offers ten natural science majors—applied health science, biology, chemistry, computer science, environmental studies, geology, liberal arts engineering, liberal arts nursing, mathematics, and physics—in six academic departments. Also, 3-2 programs are offered in engineering and nursing, alongside a five-year cooperative engineering program with Illinois Institute of Technology and other engineering schools. The Wheaton faculty members engage the study of science authoritatively, enthusiastically, and creatively in the classrooms and laboratories and beyond the campus. They are creative and offer more than two dozen general education courses in the natural sciences as well as the majors listed above. The programming includes the use of state-of-the-art technologies and techniques on the main Wheaton campus, cutting edge geological and biological studies in a large science station in the scientifically rich area of the Black Hills of South Dakota, and marine biology studies in Belize.

Off-Campus Programs

Wheaton offers a variety of off-campus opportunities to enhance students' programs of study. The Wheaton Passage program is a popular pre-orientation experience available to new students at the College's Northwoods Campus in the wilderness of northern Wisconsin, or the Urban track available to students wishing to experience time in Chicago prior to transitioning to Wheaton. Another program, Human Needs and Global Resources (HNGR), combines classroom study with a six-month, field-based, service-learning internship in the Global South. A similar program in urban studies, Wheaton in Chicago, focuses on urban issues in U.S. cities and includes a semester living in College-owned housing in urban Chicago.

The Aequitas Program in Urban Leadership provides $20,000 in merit scholarships, additional funded study opportunities, and a challenging and supportive cohort experience to 10-12 outstanding students from many different majors.

Other special summer programs for credit include field study at the Wheaton College Science Station in the Black Hills of South Dakota; working with youth at HoneyRock Camp; interdisciplinary study in East Asia; the study of English literature in England; language study in France, Germany, and Spain; the Wheaton in the Holy Lands program, involving biblical and archaeological studies; the Arts in London program, which includes course work in music, theater, and art; and an international study program based in England and the Netherlands, offering courses in economics, political science, and psychology. Wheaton is a member of the Council of Christian Colleges and Universities, based in Washington, D.C. The council's activities increase students' learning opportunities by bringing special programs to campus and by providing off-campus study.

Off-campus programs include American Studies in Washington, D.C.; the Washington Journalism Center in Washington, D.C.; the Los Angeles Film Studies Center; the Contemporary Music Center in Martha's Vineyard; Latin American Studies in Costa Rica; Middle East Studies in Cairo; the Australia Studies Center; China Studies Program; the Scholar's Semester in Oxford; Russia Studies Program; and Uganda Studies Program. Wheaton is also affiliated with the International Sustainable Development Studies Institute in Chiang Mai, Thailand. In addition, Wheaton's membership in the Christian College Consortium allows students a semester of study at one of the other twelve consortium colleges in the CCCU.

Academic Facilities

A new Welcome Center housing undergraduate admissions and the new Armerding Center for Music and the Arts opened in Fall 2017, with the new Concert Hall to follow during the 2019-2020 school year.

An $80-million science and mathematics facility opened in Fall 2010. The 128,000-square-feet of space includes eight teaching labs and research space designed to promote collaborative teacher-student research.

In 2009, an $11 million renovation of Adams Hall added art gallery and studio space. Edman Chapel, often the venue for concerts by world-class musicians, has undergone a $9 million renovation that added rehearsal space, including a large rehearsal room named for alum John Nelson, former conductor of Ensemble Orchestral de Paris.

In 2008, Wheaton's Memorial Student Center reopened after an extensive renovation to house the Wheaton Center for Faith, Politics and Economics. The facility provides classroom, research, and public discussion space geared toward the study of economics, politics, and values in business, government, and ministry. Other recent additions to campus facilities include the Todd Beamer Student Center (2004); the Wade Center (2001), which houses the books and papers of seven British authors, including C. S. Lewis and J. R. R. Tolkien; and the Chrouser Sports Complex (2000).

Costs

Tuition for the 2019-20 is $37,700; room and board are $10,510. The Wheaton Fund (supported by alumni, parents, and friends of Wheaton) subsidizes what would be the actual cost of tuition by nearly a third.

Financial Aid

Realizing that a private college education is a sizable investment, Wheaton is committed to providing the necessary need-based financial aid so students can attend. Last year Wheaton awarded over $34 million in grants and scholarships.

For first-time, full-time freshman who have financial need and were awarded any financial aid, the average amount of need-based scholarship or grant awarded for 2018-19 was $27,000.

The Center for Vocation and Career helps students to secure part-time jobs, as well as future employment, including Canvas to engage sophomores, employer recruiting, job fairs, professional development, and Wheaton in Network (WiN) alumni networking resources for upperclass students.

Faculty

Ninety-four percent of Wheaton's 222 full-time faculty members hold terminal degrees. The professors' primary commitment as educators and advisers is enriched by their considerable research, publishing, and artistic activities. In addition, the professors are active Christians who strive to show how a profound commitment to God's word structures a vision of all of life, including intellectual life. They are dedicated to honoring a Christian perspective and to modeling Christ's love to their students.

All undergraduate courses are taught by faculty members.

To ensure a rich range of perspectives and expertise, every department at Wheaton has at least 3 full-time professors, and most have 5 to 10. The student-faculty ratio is 10:1.

Student Government

Student Government ensures a student voice in institutional affairs and provides a wide range of opportunities to develop leadership abilities. Student Government's vision is "To further the educational, spiritual, and relational development of the Wheaton College community as elected servant leaders representing student initiative, concern, creativity, and enthusiasm."

Besides Student Government, there are over forty academic, cultural, social justice, and entertainment student groups on campus. In addition, the Office of Christian Outreach provides opportunities for student ministry through student-run mission trips and ministries in urban and suburban Chicago.

Admission Requirements

Wheaton is a selective college that seeks to enroll students who evidence a vital Christian experience, high moral character, personal integrity, social concern, strong academic ability and motivation, and the desire to pursue Christian higher education as defined in the aims and objectives of the College. These qualities are evaluated by consideration of each applicant's academic record, autobiographical essays, test scores, recommendations, optional interview, and participation in extracurricular activities. For students applying to the Conservatory of Music, strong consideration is given to the evaluation of the required audition.

Applicants must have a high school diploma or the equivalent, and at the time of graduation should have completed a college-preparatory curriculum with a minimum of 18 acceptable units.

Satisfactory scores on the SAT or on the ACT examination are required of all applicants to the freshman class. The middle 50 percent range of scores for those admitted is 27–32 (ACT) and 1220–1440 composite score on the SAT.

Application and Information

An application packet, complete with detailed instructions and requirements, can be obtained from the Admissions Office or online. For early action (nonbinding), students seeking admission in the fall term should apply to either the College of Arts and Sciences or the Conservatory of Music by November 1. The regular action deadline is January 10; the transfer application deadline is March 1. An admissions counselor can provide more information about Wheaton in general or the application process in particular.

Further information is available from:

Admissions Office
Wheaton College
501 College Avenue
Wheaton, Illinois 60187
Phone: 630-752-5005
800-222-2419
E-mail: admissions@wheaton.edu
Website: wheaton.edu
wheaton.edu/connect

Historic Blanchard Hall overlooks Wheaton's front of campus.

WILKES UNIVERSITY

WILKES-BARRE, PENNSYLVANIA

The University

Wilkes University offers the opportunities of a large university and the personal attention of a small institution. Its unique program mix and variety of extracurricular activities let students build their educational experience to suit their goals and interests.

Students may notice something unexpected: professors genuinely interested in their thoughts and aspirations. All Wilkes students have opportunities to gain real-world experience, whether starting a business, conducting research, or using high-tech instruments that even graduate students at other institutions rarely touch.

Located at the foothills of the Pocono Mountains, along the shore of the Susquehanna River and within walking distance of downtown Wilkes-Barre, Pennsylvania, Wilkes University is a private, comprehensive institution with about 2,400 undergraduate students.

The University includes the College of Arts, Humanities, and Social Sciences; the College of Science and Engineering; the Nesbitt School of Pharmacy; the Passan School of Nursing; the Sidhu School of Business and Leadership; the School of Education; and University College (for students still deciding on a major). Wilkes offers bachelor's and master's degrees in the humanities, social and natural sciences, engineering, business administration, nursing, and education as well as the Master of Fine Arts, Doctor of Pharmacy, Doctor of Education, Doctor of Nursing Practice, and Doctor of Philosophy in nursing degrees.

The Wilkes campus features a parklike quadrangle surrounded by modern classroom buildings and historic nineteenth-century mansions that have been restored as student residences and academic buildings. Facilities include the Cohen Science Center, a sports and conference center, a financial trading room, a new media and communication center, and new engineering facilities with state-of-the-art laboratories.

Programs provide students with a liberal arts foundation that cultivates independent thinking and prepares them for professional life or for graduate or professional school. Academic advising integrated with career planning is stressed, and hands-on experiences are provided in laboratory, internship, and cooperative education settings. Free tutorial services are available to all students.

The University is accredited by the Middle States Association of Colleges and Schools and has specialized accreditation in the sciences, engineering, nursing, education, and business. Ninety-six percent of students are employed or attending graduate/professional school within one year of receiving their degrees.

First-year students enrolling prior to May 1 are guaranteed housing, and all students may have cars on campus. Campus housing is available for all four years. Residence halls include modern, multifloored buildings and historic mansions.

Student activities complement academic life. Intercollegiate athletics encompass 23 Division III sports, including swimming and women's and men's ice hockey. About 80 clubs and organizations recognize student achievement and provide opportunities for leadership development, professional growth, and community service. The award-winning e-mentor program links current students with incoming freshmen to ease the transition to college life.

Location

Wilkes-Barre is a medium-sized city of about 43,000. Nearby recreational facilities include Pocono Mountain ski resorts; PNC Field, home of a Triple A baseball team; the Mohegan Sun Arena, home to a professional hockey team; golf courses; state parks; tennis courts; and harness racing.

The University is located in the historic district, which features a performing arts center, the Wilkes University/King's College Barnes and Noble bookstore, a fourteen-screen movie complex, and numerous shops and restaurants. Other offerings include art galleries, ethnic and community festivals, and libraries and museums. The city is approximately 2 hours from New York City and Philadelphia.

Wilkes-Barre lies near the intersection of Interstates 80, 81, and 476 and within 6 hours of Washington, D.C., and Boston. The Wilkes-Barre/Scranton International Airport is about 20 minutes from campus.

Majors and Degrees

Wilkes University offers Bachelor of Arts, Bachelor of Fine Arts, Bachelor of Business Administration, and Bachelor of Science degrees, as well as a guaranteed-seat Doctor of Pharmacy program. Majors offered are: accounting; applied and engineering sciences; biochemistry; biology; chemistry; communication studies; computer information systems; computer science; corporate finance; criminology; digital design and media art; earth and environmental sciences; electrical engineering; education (elementary and early childhood, middle-level, secondary with a subject-area major, and special education certification); engineering management; English; environmental engineering; financial investments; geology; history; hospitality leadership; international studies; management; marketing; mathematics; mechanical engineering; medical laboratory sciences; musical theatre; neuroscience; nursing; philosophy; physics; political science; psychology; public administration; sociology; Spanish; sports management; supply chain management; theatre arts; and theatre design and technology. Wilkes also offers the six-year guaranteed-seat pharmacy program, a pharmacy/M.B.A. dual degree program, a 4+1 M.B.A. program, and a 4+1 B.S./M.S. in bioengineering.

Premedical and prelaw preparation programs are strong. Other preprofessional programs include dentistry, occupational therapy, optometry, physical therapy, physician assistant, podiatry, and veterinary science. A full-time director of health sciences and student success advises students who wish to continue study in a professional health-care field. The University offers an affiliated program in medicine with the Penn State College of Medicine at Hershey; in optometry with the Pennsylvania College of Optometry and the State University of New York (SUNY) College of Optometry; in podiatry with Temple University School of Podiatric Medicine; in occupational therapy with Temple University; in physical therapy with Drexel University, Temple University, and Widener University; and in medical technology/medical laboratory sciences with Robert Packer Hospital.

Academic Programs

Through a rigorous curriculum that emphasizes hands-on experience, Wilkes helps prepare students in all majors to adapt to a technologically and socially evolving world. To graduate, students must complete a core curriculum from 120 to 136 credits, depending on their major.

At Wilkes, we help translate your ambition into reality. Our Center for Career Development and Internships can help you clarify goals, assess skills, and find the internship experiences that will build your resume and launch your career. Services include internship and career fairs, career coaching, resume assistance, practice interviews, career development workshops and networking opportunities.

The University operates on a dual-semester calendar, with optional summer sessions and a January intersession. Advanced Placement test credits, College Level Examination Program (CLEP) credits, and International Baccalaureate (I.B.) credits are accepted.

Off-Campus Programs

A cooperative education (internship) program is available to all students, with credit applicable in most majors. Many government offices and private businesses in northeastern Pennsylvania, as well as in New York City, Philadelphia, Harrisburg, and Washington, D.C., employ Wilkes students. A study-abroad adviser works with interested students, placing them in the situation best suited to their academic pursuits. Students have recently attended programs in Costa Rica, England, Spain, Tanzania, and Uganda.

Academic Facilities

Wilkes University recently invested $100 million in campus upgrades. The new Mark Engineering Center has cutting-edge flex labs, additive manufacturing, 3-D visualization and high-performance computing; the Cohen Science Center boasts four floors of state-of-the-art laboratories designed for interdisciplinary research and study; the Karambelas Media and Communication Center is equipped with a professional television studio and radio station; the Sidhu School of Business offers a trading room with an electronic stock ticker, and even has a Starbucks in the lobby. In addition, the newly renovated Farley Library is one of the largest resource libraries in the region, the NeuroTraining and Research Center is utilized by the campus community to enhance academic, athletic and artistic performance, and the Darte Performing Arts Center contains a 500-seat theatre, a 45-seat black box theatre and a dance studio.

Costs

For the 2020–21 academic year, tuition is $36,888 per year, and room and board are $15,400. Fees are $1,864 annually.

Financial Aid

Financial aid is available to students who demonstrate quality academic ability and/or financial need, as verified by the Free Application for Federal Student Aid (FAFSA). Merit-based and need-based aid is available for qualified students. Scholarships ranging from $14,000 to $21,000 per year are available to students based on academic ability, regardless of financial need. Approximately 90 percent of students receive some type of financial assistance.

Faculty

Wilkes University has a nationally recruited full-time faculty of 196 members, approximately 92 percent of whom have earned Ph.D.'s or terminal degrees in their chosen field. Faculty evaluation criteria emphasize teaching excellence and effective advising, while recognizing continued scholarly activities. The student-faculty ratio is 12:1.

Admission Requirements

SAT or ACT scores are required. In cases where a student has taken the examination more than once, scores from the highest testing in each category are used. Freshman applicants should either have completed or be in the process of completing a college-preparatory course of study, including 3 to 4 years of mathematics, social studies, science, and English. Additional courses should be elected in academic subjects according to individual interests. Acceptable electives include foreign language and computing, among others. Students who have not followed this pattern may still qualify for admission if there is other strong evidence of preparation for college work. Letters of recommendation are not required but may be submitted. Students intending to pursue a major in pharmacy should have completed algebra I and II, geometry, and trigonometry prior to enrollment. Students intending to major in nursing should have completed courses in biology and chemistry. An audition is required for all prospective musical theatre and theatre arts students. Transfer students must submit a transcript from every college previously attended.

Wilkes University is an Equal Opportunity/Affirmative Action institution. No applicant shall be denied admission to the University because of race, color, gender, religion, national or ethnic origin, sexual orientation, or handicap.

Application and Information

Applications for admission should be completed early in the senior year of secondary school. Applications are reviewed after all of the student's credentials have been received. Notification of the University's decision reaches the student two to four weeks after the application file is complete. Priority deadline for all applications is March 1; applications for the Guaranteed Seat Pharmacy Program must be received by February 1. Other health science programs may have additional deadlines.

Contact the Admissions Office for more information.

Admissions Office
Wilkes University
84 West South Street
Wilkes-Barre, Pennsylvania 18766
Phone: 570-408-4400
800-945-5378 Ext. 4400 (toll-free)
Website: http://www.wilkes.edu

Indexes

Majors

ACCOUNTING

Abilene Christian U (TX)
Adams State U (CO)
Albion Coll (MI)
Alfred U (NY)
American Public U System (WV)
American U (DC)
Anderson U (IN)
Anderson U (SC)
Andrews U (MI)
Angelo State U (TX)
Appalachian State U (NC)
Aquinas Coll (MI)
Arcadia U (PA)
Arizona State U at the Tempe campus (AZ)
Arizona State U at the West campus (AZ)
Arkansas Tech U (AR)
Assumption Coll (MA)
Athens State U (AL)
Auburn U (AL)
Auburn U at Montgomery (AL)
Augsburg U (MN)
Augustana Coll (IL)
Augustana U (SD)
Aurora U (IL)
Austin Peay State U (TN)
Averett U (VA)
Avila U (MO)
Azusa Pacific U (CA)
Babson Coll (MA)
Baker U (KS)
Ball State U (IN)
Barry U (FL)
Baruch Coll of the City U of New York (NY)
Bayamón Central U (PR)
Bay Atlantic U (DC)
Baylor U (TX)
Belhaven U (MS)
Belmont Abbey Coll (NC)
Belmont U (TN)
Bemidji State U (MN)
Benedictine Coll (KS)
Benedictine U (IL)
Bentley U (MA)
Berry Coll (GA)
Bethel U (IN)
Binghamton U, State U of New York (NY)
Biola U (CA)
Black Hills State U (SD)
Bluffton U (OH)
Boise State U (ID)
Boston Coll (MA)
Bowling Green State U (OH)
Bradley U (IL)
Brenau U (GA)
Bridgewater State U (MA)
Bryant U (RI)
Butler U (IN)
Caldwell U (NJ)
California Baptist U (CA)
California Lutheran U (CA)
California State U, Dominguez Hills (CA)
California State U, Fresno (CA)
California State U, Fullerton (CA)
California State U, Long Beach (CA)
California State U, Northridge (CA)
California State U, San Bernardino (CA)
California State U, San Marcos (CA)
California State U, Stanislaus (CA)
California U of Pennsylvania (PA)
Calumet Coll of Saint Joseph (IN)
Calvin Coll (MI)
Cameron U (OK)
Campbellsville U (KY)
Capital U (OH)
Carlow U (PA)
Carson-Newman U (TN)
Carthage Coll (WI)
Catawba Coll (NC)
The Catholic U of America (DC)
Cedar Crest Coll (PA)
Cedarville U (OH)
Central Christian Coll of Kansas (KS)
Central Coll (IA)
Central Connecticut State U (CT)
Central Methodist U (MO)
Central Michigan U (MI)
Central State U (OH)
Central Washington U (WA)
Champlain Coll (VT)
Chatham U (PA)
Chestnut Hill Coll (PA)
The Citadel, The Military Coll of South Carolina (SC)
Claremont McKenna Coll (CA)
Clarion U of Pennsylvania (PA)
Clark Atlanta U (GA)
Clayton State U (GA)
Clemson U (SC)
Coastal Carolina U (SC)
Coe Coll (IA)
Colegio Universitario de San Juan, San Juan (PR)
Coll of Charleston (SC)
The Coll of Idaho (ID)
Coll of Saint Benedict (MN)
The Coll of Saint Rose (NY)
The Coll of St. Scholastica (MN)
Coll of Staten Island of the City U of New York (NY)
Coll of the Holy Cross (MA)
Coll of the Ozarks (MO)
The Coll of Westchester (NY)
Columbia Coll (MO)
Columbia Coll (SC)
Concordia Coll (MN)
Concordia U Chicago (IL)
Concordia U, St. Paul (MN)
Concordia U Wisconsin (WI)
Creighton U (NE)
Culver-Stockton Coll (MO)
Dakota State U (SD)
Dallas Baptist U (TX)
Davenport U, Grand Rapids (MI)
Delta State U (MS)
DePaul U (IL)
DeSales U (PA)
Dickinson State U (ND)
Dillard U (LA)
Doane U (NE)
Dominican Coll (NY)
Dominican U (IL)
Drake U (IA)
Drexel U (PA)
Drury U (MO)
D'Youville Coll (NY)
East Carolina U (NC)
East Central U (OK)
Eastern Illinois U (IL)
Eastern Kentucky U (KY)
Eastern Mennonite U (VA)
Eastern Michigan U (MI)
Eastern New Mexico U (NM)
Eastern Washington U (WA)
ECPI U, Virginia Beach (VA)
Edgewood Coll (WI)
Edinboro U of Pennsylvania (PA)
Elms Coll (MA)
Elon U (NC)
Emmanuel Coll (MA)
Emory & Henry Coll (VA)
Emory U (GA)
Emporia State U (KS)
Endicott Coll (MA)
Fairfield U (CT)
Fairleigh Dickinson U (NJ)
Fayetteville State U (NC)
Felician U (NJ)
Fisher Coll (MA)
Fitchburg State U (MA)
Flagler Coll (FL)
Florida A&M U (FL)
Florida Atlantic U (FL)
Florida Gulf Coast U (FL)
Florida Inst of Technology (FL)
Florida National U (FL)
Florida Southern Coll (FL)
Florida State U (FL)
Fordham U (NY)
Fort Lewis Coll (CO)
Framingham State U (MA)
Francis Marion U (SC)
Franklin Coll (IN)
Freed-Hardeman U (TN)
Friends U (KS)
Furman U (SC)
Gallaudet U (DC)
Gannon U (PA)
Geneva Coll (PA)
George Fox U (OR)
Georgetown Coll (KY)
Georgetown U (DC)
The George Washington U (DC)
Georgia Coll & State U (GA)
Georgian Court U (NJ)
Georgia Southern U (GA)
Georgia State U (GA)
Gonzaga U (WA)
Gordon Coll (MA)
Goshen Coll (IN)
Governors State U (IL)
Graceland U (IA)
Grambling State U (LA)
Grand Valley State U (MI)
Guilford Coll (NC)
Gustavus Adolphus Coll (MN)
Gwynedd Mercy U (PA)
Hamline U (MN)
Hampton U (VA)
Harding U (AR)
Hardin-Simmons U (TX)
Harris-Stowe State U (MO)
HEC Montreal (QC, Canada)
High Point U (NC)
Hillsdale Coll (MI)
Hofstra U (NY)
Hope Coll (MI)
Houston Baptist U (TX)
Howard U (DC)
Husson U (ME)
Illinois Coll (IL)
Illinois State U (IL)
Illinois Wesleyan U (IL)
Immaculata U (PA)
Indiana State U (IN)
Indiana U of Pennsylvania (PA)
Inter American U of Puerto Rico, Aguadilla Campus (PR)
Inter American U of Puerto Rico, Barranquitas Campus (PR)
Inter American U of Puerto Rico, Bayamón Campus (PR)
Inter American U of Puerto Rico, San Germán Campus (PR)
Iona Coll (NY)
Iowa State U of Science and Technology (IA)
Ithaca Coll (NY)
Jacksonville State U (AL)
Jacksonville U (FL)
James Madison U (VA)
John Brown U (AR)
John Carroll U (OH)
Kansas State U (KS)
Kansas Wesleyan U (KS)
Kean U (NJ)
Keiser U, Fort Lauderdale (FL)
Kennesaw State U (GA)
Keuka Coll (NY)
King's Coll (PA)
LaGrange Coll (GA)
Lamar U (TX)
La Roche U (PA)
Lasell Coll (MA)
La Sierra U (CA)
Lawrence Technological U (MI)
Lee U (TN)
Lehigh U (PA)
Lehman Coll of the City U of New York (NY)
Le Moyne Coll (NY)
Lenoir-Rhyne U (NC)
LeTourneau U (TX)
Lewis U (IL)
Liberty U (VA)
Limestone Coll (SC)
Lincoln Memorial U (TN)
Lincoln U (MO)
Lincoln U (PA)
Lindenwood U (MO)
Linfield Coll (OR)
Lipscomb U (TN)
Lock Haven U of Pennsylvania (PA)
Loras Coll (IA)
Louisiana State U and A&M Coll (LA)
Louisiana State U in Shreveport (LA)
Louisiana Tech U (LA)
Loyola Marymount U (CA)
Loyola U Chicago (IL)
Loyola U Maryland (MD)
Loyola U New Orleans (LA)
Madonna U (MI)
Malone U (OH)
Manhattan Coll (NY)
Manhattanville Coll (NY)
Mansfield U of Pennsylvania (PA)
Marian U (IN)
Marietta Coll (OH)
Marquette U (WI)
Marshall U (WV)
Marymount California U (CA)
Marymount Manhattan Coll (NY)
Maryville U of Saint Louis (MO)
Marywood U (PA)
McKendree U (IL)
McMurry U (TX)
McNeese State U (LA)
Mercer U, Macon (GA)
Mercy Coll (NY)
Meredith Coll (NC)
Merrimack Coll (MA)
Messiah Coll (PA)
Miami U (OH)
Miami U Hamilton (OH)
Miami U Middletown (OH)
Michigan State U (MI)
Michigan Technological U (MI)
Mid-America Christian U (OK)
MidAmerica Nazarene U (KS)
Middle Tennessee State U (TN)
Midway U (KY)
Milligan Coll (TN)
Millikin U (IL)
Minnesota State U Mankato (MN)
Minot State U (ND)
Misericordia U (PA)
Mississippi State U (MS)
Missouri Southern State U (MO)
Missouri State U (MO)
Missouri Valley Coll (MO)
Molloy Coll (NY)
Montclair State U (NJ)
Moravian Coll (PA)
Morehead State U (KY)
Mount Aloysius Coll (PA)
Mount Marty Coll (SD)
Mount Mercy U (IA)
Mount Saint Mary Coll (NY)
Mount Saint Mary's U (CA)
Mount St. Mary's U (MD)
Mount Vernon Nazarene U (OH)
Muhlenberg Coll (PA)
Murray State U (KY)
Muskingum U (OH)
National U (CA)
Nazareth Coll of Rochester (NY)
Nebraska Wesleyan U (NE)
New England Coll (NH)
Newman U (KS)
New Mexico Highlands U (NM)
New York Inst of Technology (NY)
New York U (NY)
Niagara U (NY)
Nichols Coll (MA)
North Carolina Central U (NC)
North Central U (MN)
Northeastern Illinois U (IL)
Northeastern State U (OK)
Northern Arizona U (AZ)
Northern Illinois U (IL)
Northern State U (SD)
North Greenville U (SC)
Northwest Christian U (OR)
Northwestern Coll (IA)
Northwestern State U of Louisiana (LA)
Northwest Missouri State U (MO)
Northwest Nazarene U (ID)
Northwest U (WA)
Notre Dame Coll (OH)
Nova Southeastern U (FL)
Nyack Coll (NY)
Oakland U (MI)
Oglethorpe U (GA)
Ohio Dominican U (OH)
The Ohio State U (OH)
Ohio Valley U (WV)
Ohio Wesleyan U (OH)
Oklahoma Baptist U (OK)
Oklahoma State U (OK)
Old Dominion U (VA)
Olivet Nazarene U (IL)
Oral Roberts U (OK)
Ottawa U (KS)
Pace U, Pleasantville Campus (NY)
Pacific U (OR)
Palm Beach Atlantic U (FL)
Peirce Coll (PA)
Penn State Abington (PA)
Penn State Altoona (PA)
Penn State Beaver (PA)
Penn State Berks (PA)
Penn State Brandywine (PA)
Penn State DuBois (PA)
Penn State Erie, The Behrend Coll (PA)
Penn State Fayette, The Eberly Campus (PA)
Penn State Greater Allegheny (PA)
Penn State Hazleton (PA)
Penn State Lehigh Valley (PA)
Penn State Mont Alto (PA)
Penn State New Kensington (PA)
Penn State Schuylkill (PA)
Penn State Shenango (PA)
Penn State U Park (PA)
Penn State Wilkes-Barre (PA)
Penn State York (PA)
Pepperdine U, Malibu (CA)
Pittsburg State U (KS)
Point Loma Nazarene U (CA)
Prairie View A&M U (TX)
Providence Coll (RI)
Purdue U Fort Wayne (IN)
Purdue U Northwest (IN)
Queens Coll of the City U of New York (NY)
Queens U of Charlotte (NC)
Radford U (VA)
Ramapo Coll of New Jersey (NJ)
Randolph-Macon Coll (VA)
Rasmussen Coll Bloomington (MN)
Rasmussen Coll Brooklyn Park (MN)
Rasmussen Coll Eagan (MN)
Rasmussen Coll Fargo (ND)
Rasmussen Coll Fort Myers (FL)
Rasmussen Coll Kansas City/Overland Park (KS)
Rasmussen Coll Lake Elmo/Woodbury (MN)
Rasmussen Coll Land O' Lakes (FL)
Rasmussen Coll Mankato (MN)
Rasmussen Coll Moorhead (MN)
Rasmussen Coll New Port Richey (FL)
Rasmussen Coll Ocala (FL)
Rasmussen Coll Rockford (IL)
Rasmussen Coll St. Cloud (MN)
Rasmussen Coll Tampa/Brandon (FL)
Rasmussen Coll Topeka (KS)
Regent U (VA)
Rhode Island Coll (RI)
Roberts Wesleyan Coll (NY)
Rochester U (MI)
Rocky Mountain Coll (MT)
Roger Williams U (RI)
Rosemont Coll (PA)
Sacred Heart U (CT)
The Sage Colls (NY)
Saginaw Valley State U (MI)
St. Ambrose U (IA)
St. Bonaventure U (NY)
St. Catherine U (MN)
St. Cloud State U (MN)
Saint Francis U (PA)

St. John Fisher Coll (NY)
Saint John's U (MN)
Saint Joseph's U (PA)
Saint Leo U (FL)
Saint Louis U (MO)
Saint Mary-of-the-Woods Coll (IN)
Saint Mary's Coll (IN)
Saint Mary's Coll of California (CA)
St. Mary's U (TX)
Saint Mary's U of Minnesota (MN)
St. Norbert Coll (WI)
St. Thomas Aquinas Coll (NY)
St. Thomas U - Florida (FL)
Saint Vincent Coll (PA)
Salem State U (MA)
Salisbury U (MD)
Salve Regina U (RI)
Samford U (AL)
Sam Houston State U (TX)
San Diego State U (CA)
San Francisco State U (CA)
San Jose State U (CA)
Santa Clara U (CA)
Schreiner U (TX)
Scripps Coll (CA)
Seattle U (WA)
Seton Hill U (PA)
Shepherd U (WV)
Siena Coll (NY)
Siena Heights U (MI)
Slippery Rock U of Pennsylvania (PA)
Southeastern Louisiana U (LA)
Southeastern U (FL)
Southeast Missouri State U (MO)
Southern Arkansas U–Magnolia (AR)
Southern California Inst of Technology (CA)
Southern Illinois U Carbondale (IL)
Southern Illinois U Edwardsville (IL)
Southern Methodist U (TX)
Southwest Baptist U (MO)
Southwestern Coll (KS)
Spring Arbor U (MI)
Spring Hill Coll (AL)
State U of New York at Fredonia (NY)
State U of New York at New Paltz (NY)
State U of New York at Oswego (NY)
State U of New York Coll at Geneseo (NY)
State U of New York Coll at Old Westbury (NY)
State U of New York Coll at Oneonta (NY)
Stetson U (FL)
Stevenson U (MD)
Suffolk U (MA)
Sullivan U (KY)
SUNY Brockport (NY)
Susquehanna U (PA)
Tarleton State U (TX)
Taylor U (IN)
Temple U (PA)
Tennessee Wesleyan U (TN)
Texas A&M Intl U (TX)
Texas A&M U (TX)
Texas A&M U–Central Texas (TX)
Texas A&M U–Commerce (TX)
Texas A&M U–Corpus Christi (TX)
Texas A&M U–Kingsville (TX)
Texas Christian U (TX)
Texas Lutheran U (TX)
Texas Southern U (TX)
Texas State U (TX)
Texas Tech U (TX)
Texas Woman's U (TX)
Tiffin U (OH)
Towson U (MD)
Transylvania U (KY)
Trevecca Nazarene U (TN)
Trine U (IN)
Trinity U (TX)
Troy U (AL)
Truman State U (MO)
Tulane U (LA)
Union U (TN)
Universidad Adventista de las Antillas (PR)
U at Albany, State U of New York (NY)
U at Buffalo, the State U of New York (NY)
The U of Akron (OH)
The U of Alabama (AL)
The U of Alabama at Birmingham (AL)
The U of Alabama in Huntsville (AL)
U of Alaska Fairbanks (AK)
The U of Arizona (AZ)
U of Arkansas (AR)
U of Arkansas at Little Rock (AR)
U of Central Arkansas (AR)
U of Central Florida (FL)
U of Charleston (WV)
U of Cincinnati (OH)
U of Colorado Boulder (CO)
U of Dayton (OH)
U of Denver (CO)
U of Detroit Mercy (MI)
U of Dubuque (IA)
The U of Findlay (OH)
U of Guam (GU)
U of Hartford (CT)
U of Hawaii at Manoa (HI)
U of Houston (TX)
U of Houston–Clear Lake (TX)
U of Houston–Downtown (TX)
U of Idaho (ID)
U of Illinois at Chicago (IL)
U of Illinois at Springfield (IL)
The U of Iowa (IA)
U of Jamestown (ND)
The U of Kansas (KS)
U of Kentucky (KY)
U of La Verne (CA)
U of Louisiana at Lafayette (LA)
U of Louisiana at Monroe (LA)
U of Louisville (KY)
U of Maine (ME)
U of Maine at Presque Isle (ME)
U of Mary Hardin-Baylor (TX)
U of Maryland Global Campus (MD)
U of Massachusetts Amherst (MA)
U of Massachusetts Dartmouth (MA)
U of Memphis (TN)
U of Miami (FL)
U of Michigan–Dearborn (MI)
U of Michigan–Flint (MI)
U of Minnesota, Duluth (MN)
U of Minnesota, Twin Cities Campus (MN)
U of Missouri–St. Louis (MO)
U of Montana (MT)
U of Montevallo (AL)
U of Nebraska–Lincoln (NE)
U of Nevada, Las Vegas (NV)
U of Nevada, Reno (NV)
U of New Haven (CT)
The U of North Carolina at Charlotte (NC)
The U of North Carolina at Greensboro (NC)
The U of North Carolina at Pembroke (NC)
U of North Dakota (ND)
U of Northern Iowa (IA)
U of North Florida (FL)
U of North Texas (TX)
U of Northwestern–St. Paul (MN)
U of Notre Dame (IN)
U of Oregon (OR)
U of Pennsylvania (PA)
U of Pittsburgh at Bradford (PA)
U of Pittsburgh at Greensburg (PA)
U of Portland (OR)
U of Providence (MT)
U of Puerto Rico–Ponce (PR)
U of Richmond (VA)
U of St. Francis (IL)
U of Saint Francis (IN)
U of Saint Joseph (CT)
U of Saint Mary (KS)
U of St. Thomas (TX)
U of San Diego (CA)
U of San Francisco (CA)
The U of Scranton (PA)
U of South Alabama (AL)
U of South Carolina (SC)
U of South Dakota (SD)
U of Southern Indiana (IN)
U of Southern Maine (ME)
U of Southern Mississippi (MS)
U of South Florida (FL)
U of South Florida, St. Petersburg (FL)
The U of Tampa (FL)
The U of Tennessee (TN)
The U of Tennessee at Chattanooga (TN)
The U of Tennessee at Martin (TN)
The U of Texas at Dallas (TX)
The U of Texas at El Paso (TX)
The U of Texas at San Antonio (TX)
The U of Texas of the Permian Basin (TX)
The U of Texas Rio Grande Valley (TX)
U of the Incarnate Word (TX)
U of the Virgin Islands (VI)
The U of Toledo (OH)
U of Toronto (ON, Canada)
The U of Tulsa (OK)
U of Utah (UT)
U of Washington (WA)
U of Washington, Bothell (WA)
U of Washington, Tacoma (WA)
U of Waterloo (ON, Canada)
The U of West Alabama (AL)
The U of Western Ontario (ON, Canada)
U of West Florida (FL)
U of West Georgia (GA)
U of Wisconsin–Eau Claire (WI)
U of Wisconsin–Green Bay (WI)
U of Wisconsin–La Crosse (WI)
U of Wisconsin–Madison (WI)
U of Wisconsin–Milwaukee (WI)
U of Wisconsin–Parkside (WI)
U of Wisconsin–Platteville (WI)
U of Wisconsin–Superior (WI)
U of Wyoming (WY)
Upper Iowa U (IA)
Utah State U (UT)
Utah Valley U (UT)
Utica Coll (NY)
Valdosta State U (GA)
Valparaiso U (IN)
Vanguard U of Southern California (CA)
Villanova U (PA)
Virginia Commonwealth U (VA)
Wake Forest U (NC)
Walla Walla U (WA)
Wartburg Coll (IA)
Washington & Jefferson Coll (PA)
Washington State U (WA)
Washington State U–Tri-Cities (WA)
Washington State U–Vancouver (WA)
Washington U in St. Louis (MO)
Waynesburg U (PA)
Wayne State U (MI)
Webber Intl U (FL)
Weber State U (UT)
Wesleyan Coll (GA)
West Chester U of Pennsylvania (PA)
Western Carolina U (NC)
Western Colorado U (CO)
Western Connecticut State U (CT)
Western Kentucky U (KY)
Western Michigan U (MI)
Western New England U (MA)
Western New Mexico U (NM)
Western Washington U (WA)
West Liberty U (WV)
Westminster Coll (UT)
West Virginia U (WV)
Whitworth U (WA)
Wichita State U (KS)
Widener U (PA)
Wilkes U (PA)
William & Mary (VA)
William Jewell Coll (MO)
William Paterson U of New Jersey (NJ)
William Penn U (IA)
Wilmington Coll (OH)
Wingate U (NC)
Wittenberg U (OH)
Wofford Coll (SC)
Woodbury U (CA)
Wright State U (OH)
Wright State U–Lake Campus (OH)
Xavier U (OH)
Xavier U of Louisiana (LA)
Yeshiva U (NY)
York Coll of Pennsylvania (PA)
Youngstown State U (OH)

ACCOUNTING AND BUSINESS/MANAGEMENT

Babson Coll (MA)
Bethel U (TN)
Chaminade U of Honolulu (HI)
Chestnut Hill Coll (PA)
East Carolina U (NC)
EDP U of Puerto Rico–San Sebastian (PR)
Hope Coll (MI)
Husson U (ME)
Mercy Coll (NY)
Northwest Christian U (OR)
Rasmussen Coll Fort Myers (FL)
Rasmussen Coll Green Bay (WI)
Rasmussen Coll Land O' Lakes (FL)
Rasmussen Coll New Port Richey (FL)
Rasmussen Coll Ocala (FL)
Rasmussen Coll Tampa/Brandon (FL)
Rasmussen Coll Wausau (WI)
Rocky Mountain Coll (MT)
Santa Clara U (CA)
Sierra Nevada Coll (NV)
U of Providence (MT)
The U of Western Ontario (ON, Canada)
Walla Walla U (WA)
Washington and Lee U (VA)
Worcester State U (MA)

ACCOUNTING AND COMPUTER SCIENCE

Saint Mary-of-the-Woods Coll (IN)

ACCOUNTING AND FINANCE

Babson Coll (MA)
Bentley U (MA)
Bethel U (MN)
Bridgewater State U (MA)
Bryant U (RI)
Bucknell U (PA)
Central Christian Coll of Kansas (KS)
Clarkson U (NY)
Drake U (IA)
East Central U (OK)
Eastern U (PA)
Ferris State U (MI)
Fordham U (NY)
Granite State Coll (NH)
Northwest U (WA)
Ohio Christian U (OH)
Saint Francis U (PA)
Salem State U (MA)
U of Miami (FL)
U of North Dakota (ND)
U of Southern Maine (ME)
U of Waterloo (ON, Canada)
The U of Western Ontario (ON, Canada)
Western New England U (MA)

ACCOUNTING RELATED

Bentley U (MA)
Brigham Young U (UT)
Eastern Michigan U (MI)
Guilford Coll (NC)
Gwynedd Mercy U (PA)
Maryville U of Saint Louis (MO)
McDaniel Coll (MD)
Rocky Mountain Coll (MT)
Southwest Baptist U (MO)
State U of New York at New Paltz (NY)
State U of New York at Oswego (NY)
U of New Haven (CT)
U of Northern Iowa (IA)

ACCOUNTING TECHNOLOGY AND BOOKKEEPING

Ferris State U (MI)
Lewis-Clark State Coll (ID)
Missouri Valley Coll (MO)
Rowan U (NJ)
Trine U (IN)
The U of Akron (OH)
U of Miami (FL)

ACOUSTICS

Columbia Coll Chicago (IL)
New York U (NY)

ACTING

Academy of Art U (CA)
Anderson U (SC)
Arcadia U (PA)
Augsburg U (MN)
Averett U (VA)
Barry U (FL)
Baylor U (TX)
Belmont U (TN)
Bennington Coll (VT)
Bradley U (IL)
Brenau U (GA)
Brigham Young U (UT)
California Baptist U (CA)
California State U, Long Beach (CA)
Central Christian Coll of Kansas (KS)
Central Washington U (WA)
Coll of the Ozarks (MO)
Columbia Coll Chicago (IL)
DePaul U (IL)
Drake U (IA)
Elon U (NC)
Emory & Henry Coll (VA)
Florida Southern Coll (FL)
Florida State U (FL)
Freed-Hardeman U (TN)
Gannon U (PA)
Hofstra U (NY)
Illinois Wesleyan U (IL)
Ithaca Coll (NY)
Kean U (NJ)
Liberty U (VA)
Lindenwood U (MO)
Lipscomb U (TN)
Marymount Manhattan Coll (NY)
Michigan State U (MI)
Nebraska Wesleyan U (NE)
Notre Dame Coll (OH)
Oakland U (MI)
Oral Roberts U (OK)
Penn State Abington (PA)
Penn State Altoona (PA)
Penn State Beaver (PA)
Penn State Berks (PA)
Penn State Brandywine (PA)
Penn State DuBois (PA)
Penn State Erie, The Behrend Coll (PA)
Penn State Fayette, The Eberly Campus (PA)
Penn State Greater Allegheny (PA)
Penn State Hazleton (PA)
Penn State Lehigh Valley (PA)
Penn State Mont Alto (PA)
Penn State New Kensington (PA)
Penn State Schuylkill (PA)
Penn State Shenango (PA)
Penn State U Park (PA)
Penn State Wilkes-Barre (PA)
Penn State York (PA)
Pepperdine U, Malibu (CA)
Regent U (VA)
Rhode Island Coll (RI)
Salem State U (MA)
Seton Hill U (PA)
Shenandoah U (VA)
Stevenson U (MD)
Texas Christian U (TX)
Towson U (MD)
Trinity U (TX)
U of Cincinnati (OH)
U of Hartford (CT)
U of Maryland, Baltimore County (MD)
U of Miami (FL)
U of Nevada, Las Vegas (NV)
U of Northern Iowa (IA)
U of Washington (WA)
Western Michigan U (MI)
Whitworth U (WA)
Worcester State U (MA)
Wright State U (OH)

ACTUARIAL SCIENCE

Alfred U (NY)
Anderson U (SC)
Appalachian State U (NC)
Arcadia U (PA)
Arizona State U at the Tempe campus (AZ)
Assumption Coll (MA)
Aurora U (IL)
Ball State U (IN)
Baruch Coll of the City U of New York (NY)
Bentley U (MA)
Bowling Green State U (OH)
Bradley U (IL)

Brigham Young U (UT)
Butler U (IN)
California Baptist U (CA)
Calvin Coll (MI)
Carnegie Mellon U (PA)
Central Coll (IA)
Central Michigan U (MI)
Central Washington U (WA)
Concordia U Wisconsin (WI)
DePaul U (IL)
Drake U (IA)
Eastern Michigan U (MI)
Edinboro U of Pennsylvania (PA)
Ferris State U (MI)
Florida State U (FL)
Franklin Coll (IN)
Georgia State U (GA)
High Point U (NC)
Indiana U Northwest (IN)
Indiana U South Bend (IN)
Iowa State U of Science and Technology (IA)
Maryville U of Saint Louis (MO)
Messiah Coll (PA)
Michigan State U (MI)
Middle Tennessee State U (TN)
Milwaukee School of Eng (WI)
Mount Mercy U (IA)
New York U (NY)
Niagara U (NY)
Northwestern Coll (IA)
Oakland U (MI)
The Ohio State U (OH)
Olivet Nazarene U (IL)
Penn State Abington (PA)
Penn State Altoona (PA)
Penn State Beaver (PA)
Penn State Berks (PA)
Penn State Brandywine (PA)
Penn State DuBois (PA)
Penn State Erie, The Behrend Coll (PA)
Penn State Fayette, The Eberly Campus (PA)
Penn State Greater Allegheny (PA)
Penn State Hazleton (PA)
Penn State Lehigh Valley (PA)
Penn State Mont Alto (PA)
Penn State New Kensington (PA)
Penn State Schuylkill (PA)
Penn State Shenango (PA)
Penn State Wilkes-Barre (PA)
Penn State York (PA)
Purdue U Fort Wayne (IN)
Queens Coll of the City U of New York (NY)
Roanoke Coll (VA)
Saint Joseph's U (PA)
Saint Mary's U of Minnesota (MN)
Siena Coll (NY)
Simon Fraser U (BC, Canada)
Spring Arbor U (MI)
Temple U (PA)
Texas Christian U (TX)
U at Albany, State U of New York (NY)
U of California, Santa Barbara (CA)
U of Central Florida (FL)
The U of Iowa (IA)
U of Michigan–Dearborn (MI)
U of Michigan–Flint (MI)
U of Missouri–St. Louis (MO)
U of Nebraska–Lincoln (NE)
U of Pennsylvania (PA)
The U of Texas at Dallas (TX)
The U of Texas at San Antonio (TX)
U of Toronto (ON, Canada)
U of Waterloo (ON, Canada)
The U of Western Ontario (ON, Canada)
U of Wisconsin–Eau Claire (WI)
U of Wisconsin–Madison (WI)
U of Wisconsin–Milwaukee (WI)
Valparaiso U (IN)
Vanguard U of Southern California (CA)
Wartburg Coll (IA)
Western New England U (MA)
Xavier U (OH)

ADMINISTRATIVE ASSISTANT AND SECRETARIAL SCIENCE
Bayamón Central U (PR)
EDP U of Puerto Rico–San Sebastian (PR)
Lewis-Clark State Coll (ID)
Universidad Adventista de las Antillas (PR)
Valdosta State U (GA)
Weber State U (UT)

ADULT AND CONTINUING EDUCATION
Auburn U (AL)
Boise Bible Coll (ID)
Eastern Washington U (WA)
Louisiana State U and A&M Coll (LA)
U of the Fraser Valley (BC, Canada)

ADULT AND CONTINUING EDUCATION ADMINISTRATION
Penn State Abington (PA)
Penn State Altoona (PA)
Penn State Beaver (PA)
Penn State Berks (PA)
Penn State Brandywine (PA)
Penn State DuBois (PA)
Penn State Erie, The Behrend Coll (PA)
Penn State Fayette, The Eberly Campus (PA)
Penn State Greater Allegheny (PA)
Penn State Hazleton (PA)
Penn State Lehigh Valley (PA)
Penn State Mont Alto (PA)
Penn State New Kensington (PA)
Penn State Schuylkill (PA)
Penn State Shenango (PA)
Penn State Wilkes-Barre (PA)
Penn State York (PA)

ADULT DEVELOPMENT AND AGING
Georgia Gwinnett Coll (GA)
Madonna U (MI)
Rhode Island Coll (RI)
St. Thomas U - New Brunswick (NB, Canada)

ADULT HEALTH NURSING
King U (TN)
Worcester State U (MA)

ADVERTISING
Adams State U (CO)
Appalachian State U (NC)
Ball State U (IN)
Barry U (FL)
Bowling Green State U (OH)
Bradley U (IL)
Brigham Young U (UT)
California State U, Fullerton (CA)
Central Michigan U (MI)
The Coll of St. Scholastica (MN)
Columbia Coll Chicago (IL)
Drake U (IA)
Fashion Inst of Technology (NY)
Ferris State U (MI)
Florida State U (FL)
Gannon U (PA)
Grand Valley State U (MI)
Harding U (AR)
Iona Coll (NY)
Iowa State U of Science and Technology (IA)
Lamar U (TX)
Lee U (TN)
Loyola U Chicago (IL)
Marquette U (WI)
Michigan State U (MI)
Murray State U (KY)
New York Inst of Technology (NY)
Northwest Missouri State U (MO)
Pace U, Pleasantville Campus (NY)
Penn State Abington (PA)
Penn State Altoona (PA)
Penn State Beaver (PA)
Penn State Berks (PA)
Penn State Brandywine (PA)
Penn State DuBois (PA)
Penn State Erie, The Behrend Coll (PA)
Penn State Fayette, The Eberly Campus (PA)
Penn State Greater Allegheny (PA)
Penn State Hazleton (PA)
Penn State Lehigh Valley (PA)
Penn State Mont Alto (PA)
Penn State New Kensington (PA)
Penn State Schuylkill (PA)
Penn State Shenango (PA)
Penn State U Park (PA)
Penn State Wilkes-Barre (PA)
Penn State York (PA)
Pepperdine U, Malibu (CA)
Portland State U (OR)
Rowan U (NJ)
Salem State U (MA)
Sam Houston State U (TX)
San Diego State U (CA)
San Jose State U (CA)
South Dakota State U (SD)
Southern Methodist U (TX)
Spring Arbor U (MI)
Suffolk U (MA)
Susquehanna U (PA)
Temple U (PA)
Texas State U (TX)
Texas Tech U (TX)
Union U (TN)
The U of Alabama (AL)
U of Central Florida (FL)
U of Idaho (ID)
U of Memphis (TN)
U of Miami (FL)
U of Oregon (OR)
U of San Francisco (CA)
U of South Carolina (SC)
U of Southern Indiana (IN)
U of Southern Mississippi (MS)
The U of Tennessee (TN)
The U of Texas at El Paso (TX)
Washington State U (WA)
Washington U in St. Louis (MO)
Waynesburg U (PA)
Wesleyan Coll (GA)
Western Kentucky U (KY)
Western Michigan U (MI)
Western New England U (MA)
Widener U (PA)
Xavier U (OH)
Youngstown State U (OH)

AERONAUTICAL/AEROSPACE ENGINEERING TECHNOLOGY
American Public U System (WV)
Bowling Green State U (OH)
LeTourneau U (TX)

AERONAUTICS/AVIATION/AEROSPACE SCIENCE AND TECHNOLOGY
Andrews U (MI)
Arizona State U at the Polytechnic campus (AZ)
Averett U (VA)
Bowling Green State U (OH)
Bridgewater State U (MA)
Delta State U (MS)
Eastern Kentucky U (KY)
Florida Inst of Technology (FL)
Indiana State U (IN)
Kansas State U (KS)
LeTourneau U (TX)
Lewis U (IL)
Liberty U (VA)
Louisiana Tech U (LA)
Middle Tennessee State U (TN)
The Ohio State U (OH)
Oklahoma State U (OK)
Polk State Coll (FL)
Saint Louis U (MO)
San Jose State U (CA)
South Dakota State U (SD)
Texas Lutheran U (TX)
Texas Southern U (TX)
U of Memphis (TN)
U of North Dakota (ND)
U of North Texas (TX)
Walla Walla U (WA)

AEROSPACE, AERONAUTICAL AND ASTRONAUTICAL/SPACE ENGINEERING
Arizona State U at the Tempe campus (AZ)
Auburn U (AL)
California Polytechnic State U, San Luis Obispo (CA)
California State Polytechnic U, Pomona (CA)
California State U, Long Beach (CA)
Clarkson U (NY)
Florida Inst of Technology (FL)
Georgia Inst of Technology (GA)
Illinois Inst of Technology (IL)
Iowa State U of Science and Technology (IA)
Mississippi State U (MS)
Missouri U of Science and Technology (MO)
Morehead State U (KY)
New York U (NY)
The Ohio State U (OH)
Oklahoma State U (OK)
Penn State Abington (PA)
Penn State Altoona (PA)
Penn State Beaver (PA)
Penn State Berks (PA)
Penn State Brandywine (PA)
Penn State DuBois (PA)
Penn State Erie, The Behrend Coll (PA)
Penn State Fayette, The Eberly Campus (PA)
Penn State Greater Allegheny (PA)
Penn State Hazleton (PA)
Penn State Lehigh Valley (PA)
Penn State Mont Alto (PA)
Penn State New Kensington (PA)
Penn State Schuylkill (PA)
Penn State Shenango (PA)
Penn State U Park (PA)
Penn State Wilkes-Barre (PA)
Penn State York (PA)
Saint Louis U (MO)
San Diego State U (CA)
San Jose State U (CA)
Stanford U (CA)
Texas A&M U (TX)
U at Buffalo, the State U of New York (NY)
The U of Alabama (AL)
The U of Alabama in Huntsville (AL)
The U of Arizona (AZ)
U of California, Irvine (CA)
U of California, Los Angeles (CA)
U of California, San Diego (CA)
U of Central Florida (FL)
U of Cincinnati (OH)
U of Colorado Boulder (CO)
The U of Kansas (KS)
U of Miami (FL)
U of Michigan (MI)
U of Minnesota, Twin Cities Campus (MN)
U of Notre Dame (IN)
The U of Tennessee (TN)
U of Toronto (ON, Canada)
U of Virginia (VA)
U of Washington (WA)
Western Michigan U (MI)
West Virginia U (WV)
Wichita State U (KS)
Worcester Polytechnic Inst (MA)

AEROSPACE GROUND EQUIPMENT TECHNOLOGY
Liberty U (VA)

AFRICAN AMERICAN/BLACK STUDIES
American U (DC)
Amherst Coll (MA)
Arizona State U at the Tempe campus (AZ)
Bates Coll (ME)
Bennington Coll (VT)
Berea Coll (KY)
Binghamton U, State U of New York (NY)
Boston Coll (MA)
Bowling Green State U (OH)
Brandeis U (MA)
Brown U (RI)
California State U, Dominguez Hills (CA)
California State U, Fresno (CA)
California State U, Fullerton (CA)
California State U, Long Beach (CA)
California State U, Los Angeles (CA)
California State U, Northridge (CA)
City Coll of the City U of New York (NY)
Claremont McKenna Coll (CA)
Clemson U (SC)
Coe Coll (IA)
Colby Coll (ME)
Coll of Charleston (SC)
Coll of Staten Island of the City U of New York (NY)
The Coll of Wooster (OH)
Cornell U (NY)
Dartmouth Coll (NH)
DePaul U (IL)
DePauw U (IN)
Dominican U (IL)
Drew U (NJ)
Earlham Coll (IN)
East Carolina U (NC)
Eastern Michigan U (MI)
Emory U (GA)
Florida A&M U (FL)
Florida State U (FL)
Fordham U (NY)
Georgia State U (GA)
Guilford Coll (NC)
Hampshire Coll (MA)
Harvard U (MA)
Hobart and William Smith Colls (NY)
Howard U (DC)
Indiana State U (IN)
Indiana U Bloomington (IN)
Indiana U Northwest (IN)
Indiana U-Purdue U Indianapolis (IN)
Johns Hopkins U (MD)
Knox Coll (IL)
Lake Forest Coll (IL)
Lehman Coll of the City U of New York (NY)
Loyola Marymount U (CA)
Loyola U Chicago (IL)
Marquette U (WI)
Mercer U, Macon (GA)
Miami U (OH)
Miami U Hamilton (OH)
Miami U Middletown (OH)
Middlebury Coll (VT)
Middle Tennessee State U (TN)
Mount Holyoke Coll (MA)
New York U (NY)
Northwestern U (IL)
Oberlin Coll (OH)
Occidental Coll (CA)
The Ohio State U (OH)
Ohio Wesleyan U (OH)
Old Dominion U (VA)
Penn State Abington (PA)
Penn State Altoona (PA)
Penn State Beaver (PA)
Penn State Berks (PA)
Penn State Brandywine (PA)
Penn State DuBois (PA)
Penn State Erie, The Behrend Coll (PA)
Penn State Fayette, The Eberly Campus (PA)
Penn State Greater Allegheny (PA)
Penn State Hazleton (PA)
Penn State Lehigh Valley (PA)
Penn State Mont Alto (PA)
Penn State New Kensington (PA)
Penn State Schuylkill (PA)
Penn State Shenango (PA)
Penn State U Park (PA)
Penn State Wilkes-Barre (PA)
Penn State York (PA)
Pitzer Coll (CA)
Pomona Coll (CA)
Portland State U (OR)
Princeton U (NJ)
Queens Coll of the City U of New York (NY)
Ramapo Coll of New Jersey (NJ)
Rhode Island Coll (RI)
Saint Louis U (MO)
San Diego State U (CA)
San Francisco State U (CA)
San Jose State U (CA)
Scripps Coll (CA)
Smith Coll (MA)
Southern Illinois U Carbondale (IL)
Southern Methodist U (TX)
Stanford U (CA)
State U of New York at New Paltz (NY)
State U of New York Coll at Cortland (NY)
State U of New York Coll at Geneseo (NY)
Stockton U (NJ)
Stony Brook U, State U of New York (NY)
SUNY Brockport (NY)
Temple U (PA)
U at Albany, State U of New York (NY)
U at Buffalo, the State U of New York (NY)

MAJORS LISTING

The U of Alabama (AL)
The U of Alabama at Birmingham (AL)
The U of Arizona (AZ)
U of California, Berkeley (CA)
U of California, Irvine (CA)
U of California, Los Angeles (CA)
U of California, Riverside (CA)
U of California, Santa Barbara (CA)
U of Central Arkansas (AR)
U of Cincinnati (OH)
U of Houston (TX)
U of Illinois at Chicago (IL)
The U of Iowa (IA)
The U of Kansas (KS)
U of Louisville (KY)
U of Maryland, Baltimore County (MD)
U of Massachusetts Amherst (MA)
U of Massachusetts Boston (MA)
U of Memphis (TN)
U of Miami (FL)
U of Michigan (MI)
U of Michigan–Dearborn (MI)
U of Michigan–Flint (MI)
U of Minnesota, Twin Cities Campus (MN)
U of Montana (MT)
U of Nevada, Las Vegas (NV)
U of New Mexico (NM)
The U of North Carolina at Chapel Hill (NC)
The U of North Carolina at Charlotte (NC)
The U of North Carolina at Greensboro (NC)
U of Northern Colorado (CO)
U of Notre Dame (IN)
U of Pennsylvania (PA)
U of Puget Sound (WA)
U of South Carolina (SC)
U of South Florida (FL)
The U of Toledo (OH)
U of Virginia (VA)
U of Wisconsin–Madison (WI)
U of Wisconsin–Milwaukee (WI)
U of Wyoming (WY)
Vanderbilt U (TN)
Virginia Commonwealth U (VA)
Washington U in St. Louis (MO)
Wayne State U (MI)
Wesleyan U (CT)
Western Michigan U (MI)
Wheaton Coll (MA)
William & Mary (VA)
William Paterson U of New Jersey (NJ)
Yale U (CT)

AFRICAN LANGUAGES
U of California, Los Angeles (CA)
U of Wisconsin–Madison (WI)

AFRICAN STUDIES
Agnes Scott Coll (GA)
Augustana Coll (IL)
Barnard Coll (NY)
Bowdoin Coll (ME)
Bowling Green State U (OH)
Carleton Coll (MN)
Coll of the Holy Cross (MA)
Davidson Coll (NC)
Dickinson Coll (PA)
Emory U (GA)
Hampshire Coll (MA)
Hobart and William Smith Colls (NY)
Hofstra U (NY)
Illinois Wesleyan U (IL)
Kennesaw State U (GA)
Lehigh U (PA)
Lincoln U (PA)
Loyola U Chicago (IL)
Middlebury Coll (VT)
Northwestern U (IL)
Portland State U (OR)
Rowan U (NJ)
Sarah Lawrence Coll (NY)
Simmons U (MA)
Tulane U (LA)
Union Coll (NY)
United States Military Acad (NY)
The U of Iowa (IA)
The U of Kansas (KS)
U of Pennsylvania (PA)
U of Richmond (VA)
U of Toronto (ON, Canada)
Washington U in St. Louis (MO)
Willamette U (OR)
Yale U (CT)

AGRIBUSINESS
Abilene Christian U (TX)
Adams State U (CO)
American U of Beirut (Lebanon)
Angelo State U (TX)
Arkansas Tech U (AR)
Brigham Young U (UT)
Colorado State U (CO)
Delaware Valley U (PA)
Eastern New Mexico U (NM)
Florida A&M U (FL)
Iowa State U of Science and Technology (IA)
Kent State U at Tuscarawas (OH)
Middle Tennessee State U (TN)
Mississippi State U (MS)
Missouri State U (MO)
Northwest Missouri State U (MO)
Penn State Abington (PA)
Penn State Altoona (PA)
Penn State Beaver (PA)
Penn State Berks (PA)
Penn State Brandywine (PA)
Penn State DuBois (PA)
Penn State Erie, The Behrend Coll (PA)
Penn State Fayette, The Eberly Campus (PA)
Penn State Greater Allegheny (PA)
Penn State Hazleton (PA)
Penn State Lehigh Valley (PA)
Penn State Mont Alto (PA)
Penn State New Kensington (PA)
Penn State Schuylkill (PA)
Penn State Shenango (PA)
Penn State U Park (PA)
Penn State Wilkes-Barre (PA)
Penn State York (PA)
Sam Houston State U (TX)
South Dakota State U (SD)
Southeast Missouri State U (MO)
Tarleton State U (TX)
Texas A&M U (TX)
Texas A&M U–Commerce (TX)
Texas A&M U–Kingsville (TX)
Texas State U (TX)
U of Arkansas (AR)
U of Idaho (ID)
The U of Tennessee at Martin (TN)
U of Wisconsin–Platteville (WI)
U of Wyoming (WY)
Vermont Tech Coll (VT)
Washington State U (WA)

AGRICULTURAL AND DOMESTIC ANIMAL SERVICES RELATED
Saint Mary-of-the-Woods Coll (IN)

AGRICULTURAL AND EXTENSION EDUCATION
The Ohio State U (OH)
Penn State Abington (PA)
Penn State Altoona (PA)
Penn State Beaver (PA)
Penn State Berks (PA)
Penn State Brandywine (PA)
Penn State DuBois (PA)
Penn State Erie, The Behrend Coll (PA)
Penn State Fayette, The Eberly Campus (PA)
Penn State Greater Allegheny (PA)
Penn State Hazleton (PA)
Penn State Lehigh Valley (PA)
Penn State Mont Alto (PA)
Penn State New Kensington (PA)
Penn State Schuylkill (PA)
Penn State Shenango (PA)
Penn State Wilkes-Barre (PA)
Penn State York (PA)
U of Arkansas (AR)
The U of Tennessee (TN)

AGRICULTURAL AND FOOD PRODUCTS PROCESSING
Angelo State U (TX)
Kansas State U (KS)
The Ohio State U (OH)
Texas A&M U (TX)
U of Nebraska–Lincoln (NE)
Washington State U (WA)

AGRICULTURAL AND HORTICULTURAL PLANT BREEDING
Washington State U (WA)

AGRICULTURAL BUSINESS AND MANAGEMENT
Brigham Young U (UT)
California Polytechnic State U, San Luis Obispo (CA)
California State Polytechnic U, Pomona (CA)
California State U, Fresno (CA)
Clemson U (SC)
Coll of the Ozarks (MO)
Florida Southern Coll (FL)
Graceland U (IA)
Kansas State U (KS)
Louisiana State U and A&M Coll (LA)
Louisiana Tech U (LA)
Michigan State U (MI)
Missouri Valley Coll (MO)
Montana State U (MT)
Oklahoma State U (OK)
Southern Arkansas U–Magnolia (AR)
State U of New York Coll of Agriculture and Technology at Cobleskill (NY)
State U of New York Coll of Technology at Alfred (NY)
Texas A&M U (TX)
Texas Tech U (TX)
The U of Arizona (AZ)
U of Louisiana at Monroe (LA)
U of Nebraska at Kearney (NE)
U of Nebraska–Lincoln (NE)
The U of Tennessee (TN)
U of the Fraser Valley (BC, Canada)
U of Wisconsin–Madison (WI)
Upper Iowa U (IA)
Utah State U (UT)
Wilmington Coll (OH)

AGRICULTURAL BUSINESS AND MANAGEMENT RELATED
Penn State New Kensington (PA)
U of Minnesota, Twin Cities Campus (MN)

AGRICULTURAL BUSINESS TECHNOLOGY
Auburn U (AL)
Iowa State U of Science and Technology (IA)
The U of Arizona (AZ)
U of Wisconsin–Platteville (WI)

AGRICULTURAL COMMUNICATION/ JOURNALISM
Auburn U (AL)
California Polytechnic State U, San Luis Obispo (CA)
Kansas State U (KS)
Oklahoma State U (OK)
Sam Houston State U (TX)
South Dakota State U (SD)
Texas A&M U (TX)
Texas Tech U (TX)
U of Idaho (ID)
U of Nebraska–Lincoln (NE)
U of Wisconsin–Madison (WI)
U of Wyoming (WY)
Utah State U (UT)

AGRICULTURAL ECONOMICS
Auburn U (AL)
Brigham Young U (UT)
Clemson U (SC)
Colorado State U (CO)
Cornell U (NY)
Kansas State U (KS)
Mississippi State U (MS)
The Ohio State U (OH)
Oklahoma State U (OK)
South Dakota State U (SD)
Southern Illinois U Carbondale (IL)
Texas A&M U (TX)
Texas Tech U (TX)
U of Idaho (ID)
U of Kentucky (KY)
U of Nebraska–Lincoln (NE)
U of Wisconsin–Madison (WI)
West Virginia U (WV)

AGRICULTURAL ENGINEERING
Auburn U (AL)
California Polytechnic State U, San Luis Obispo (CA)
Clemson U (SC)
Cornell U (NY)
Florida A&M U (FL)
Iowa State U of Science and Technology (IA)
Kansas State U (KS)
Michigan State U (MI)
Missouri U of Science and Technology (MO)
The Ohio State U (OH)
Oklahoma State U (OK)
Penn State Abington (PA)
Penn State Beaver (PA)
Penn State Brandywine (PA)
Penn State DuBois (PA)
Penn State Erie, The Behrend Coll (PA)
Penn State Fayette, The Eberly Campus (PA)
Penn State Greater Allegheny (PA)
Penn State Hazleton (PA)
Penn State Lehigh Valley (PA)
Penn State Mont Alto (PA)
Penn State New Kensington (PA)
Penn State Schuylkill (PA)
Penn State Shenango (PA)
Penn State U Park (PA)
Penn State Wilkes-Barre (PA)
Penn State York (PA)
South Dakota State U (SD)
Texas A&M U (TX)
U of California, Los Angeles (CA)
U of Hawaii at Manoa (HI)
U of Kentucky (KY)
U of Minnesota, Twin Cities Campus (MN)
The U of Tennessee (TN)
U of Wisconsin–Madison (WI)
Walla Walla U (WA)

AGRICULTURAL/FARM SUPPLIES RETAILING AND WHOLESALING
Texas A&M U (TX)

AGRICULTURAL MECHANIZATION
California Polytechnic State U, San Luis Obispo (CA)
Kansas State U (KS)
Montana State U (MT)
Penn State Abington (PA)
Penn State Altoona (PA)
Penn State Beaver (PA)
Penn State Berks (PA)
Penn State Brandywine (PA)
Penn State DuBois (PA)
Penn State Erie, The Behrend Coll (PA)
Penn State Fayette, The Eberly Campus (PA)
Penn State Greater Allegheny (PA)
Penn State Hazleton (PA)
Penn State Lehigh Valley (PA)
Penn State Mont Alto (PA)
Penn State New Kensington (PA)
Penn State Schuylkill (PA)
Penn State Shenango (PA)
Penn State Wilkes-Barre (PA)
Penn State York (PA)
Sam Houston State U (TX)
South Dakota State U (SD)
U of Idaho (ID)
U of Nebraska–Lincoln (NE)

AGRICULTURAL PRODUCTION
Eastern Kentucky U (KY)
South Dakota State U (SD)
The U of Arizona (AZ)
Utah State U (UT)
Washington State U (WA)

AGRICULTURAL PUBLIC SERVICES RELATED
Iowa State U of Science and Technology (IA)
Oklahoma State U (OK)
U of Kentucky (KY)

AGRICULTURAL TEACHER EDUCATION
Arkansas Tech U (AR)
Auburn U (AL)
California Polytechnic State U, San Luis Obispo (CA)
California State Polytechnic U, Pomona (CA)
California State U, Fresno (CA)
Central State U (OH)
Clemson U (SC)
Coll of the Ozarks (MO)
Colorado State U (CO)
Eastern New Mexico U (NM)
Emmanuel Coll (GA)
Iowa State U of Science and Technology (IA)
Kansas State U (KS)
Louisiana Tech U (LA)
Michigan State U (MI)
Mississippi State U (MS)
Missouri State U (MO)
Montana State U (MT)
Northwest Missouri State U (MO)
The Ohio State U (OH)
Oklahoma State U (OK)
Sam Houston State U (TX)
South Dakota State U (SD)
Southeast Missouri State U (MO)
Southern Arkansas U–Magnolia (AR)
State U of New York at Oswego (NY)
U of Idaho (ID)
U of Minnesota, Twin Cities Campus (MN)
U of Nebraska–Lincoln (NE)
U of Nevada, Reno (NV)
U of Wisconsin–Platteville (WI)
U of Wyoming (WY)
Utah State U (UT)
Washington State U (WA)
West Virginia U (WV)
Wilmington Coll (OH)

AGRICULTURE
American U of Beirut (Lebanon)
Angelo State U (TX)
Auburn U (AL)
Austin Peay State U (TN)
Berea Coll (KY)
California State U, Stanislaus (CA)
Cameron U (OK)
Cornell U (NY)
Dickinson State U (ND)
Eastern New Mexico U (NM)
Florida A&M U (FL)
Hampshire Coll (MA)
Illinois State U (IL)
Iowa State U of Science and Technology (IA)
Lincoln U (MO)
McNeese State U (LA)
Missouri State U (MO)
Montana State U (MT)
Morehead State U (KY)
Northwest Missouri State U (MO)
Penn State Abington (PA)
Penn State Altoona (PA)
Penn State Beaver (PA)
Penn State Berks (PA)
Penn State Brandywine (PA)
Penn State DuBois (PA)
Penn State Erie, The Behrend Coll (PA)
Penn State Fayette, The Eberly Campus (PA)
Penn State Greater Allegheny (PA)
Penn State Hazleton (PA)
Penn State Lehigh Valley (PA)
Penn State Mont Alto (PA)
Penn State New Kensington (PA)
Penn State Schuylkill (PA)
Penn State Shenango (PA)
Penn State U Park (PA)
Penn State Wilkes-Barre (PA)
Penn State York (PA)
Prairie View A&M U (TX)
Sam Houston State U (TX)
South Dakota State U (SD)
Southern Arkansas U–Magnolia (AR)
Southern Illinois U Carbondale (IL)
Tarleton State U (TX)
Texas A&M U (TX)
Texas A&M U–Commerce (TX)
Texas A&M U–Kingsville (TX)
Texas State U (TX)
Texas Tech U (TX)
Truman State U (MO)
U of Guam (GU)

U of Maine at Presque Isle (ME)
U of Nebraska–Lincoln (NE)
U of Nevada, Reno (NV)
The U of Tennessee at Martin (TN)
U of Vermont (VT)
Washington State U (WA)
Western Kentucky U (KY)
Wilmington Coll (OH)

AGRICULTURE AND AGRICULTURE OPERATIONS RELATED
California State U, Stanislaus (CA)
Emmanuel Coll (GA)
Murray State U (KY)
The Ohio State U (OH)
Penn State U Park (PA)
The U of Arizona (AZ)
U of Kentucky (KY)
U of Nebraska–Lincoln (NE)

AGROECOLOGY AND SUSTAINABLE AGRICULTURE
Central State U (OH)
Delaware Valley U (PA)
Goshen Coll (IN)
Guilford Coll (NC)
Mississippi State U (MS)
U of Idaho (ID)
U of Maine (ME)
U of Massachusetts Amherst (MA)
U of New Hampshire (NH)
U of Wyoming (WY)
Washington State U (WA)
Xavier U (OH)

AGRONOMY AND CROP SCIENCE
Auburn U (AL)
California Polytechnic State U, San Luis Obispo (CA)
California State U, Fresno (CA)
Coll of the Ozarks (MO)
Delaware Valley U (PA)
Iowa State U of Science and Technology (IA)
Kansas State U (KS)
Mississippi State U (MS)
Missouri State U (MO)
Northwest Missouri State U (MO)
Penn State Abington (PA)
Penn State Altoona (PA)
Penn State Beaver (PA)
Penn State Berks (PA)
Penn State Brandywine (PA)
Penn State DuBois (PA)
Penn State Erie, The Behrend Coll (PA)
Penn State Fayette, The Eberly Campus (PA)
Penn State Greater Allegheny (PA)
Penn State Hazleton (PA)
Penn State Mont Alto (PA)
Penn State New Kensington (PA)
Penn State Shenango (PA)
Penn State Wilkes-Barre (PA)
Penn State York (PA)
South Dakota State U (SD)
State U of New York Coll of Agriculture and Technology at Cobleskill (NY)
Tarleton State U (TX)
Texas A&M U (TX)
Texas A&M U–Kingsville (TX)
The U of Arizona (AZ)
U of Arkansas (AR)
U of Idaho (ID)
U of Kentucky (KY)
U of Nebraska–Lincoln (NE)
U of Vermont (VT)
U of Wisconsin–Madison (WI)
U of Wisconsin–Platteville (WI)
Washington State U (WA)

AIR AND SPACE OPERATIONS TECHNOLOGY
U of Utah (UT)

AIR FORCE ROTC/AIR SCIENCE
The U of Iowa (IA)

AIRFRAME MECHANICS AND AIRCRAFT MAINTENANCE TECHNOLOGY
Kansas State U (KS)

AIRLINE PILOT AND FLIGHT CREW
Auburn U (AL)
Austin Peay State U (TN)
Baylor U (TX)
Bridgewater State U (MA)
California Baptist U (CA)
Central Washington U (WA)
Delta State U (MS)
Eastern Kentucky U (KY)
Eastern Michigan U (MI)
Farmingdale State Coll (NY)
Hesston Coll (KS)
Indiana State U (IN)
Jacksonville U (FL)
Kansas State U (KS)
LeTourneau U (TX)
Lynn U (FL)
Rocky Mountain Coll (MT)
Texas A&M U–Central Texas (TX)
U of Dubuque (IA)
U of Louisiana at Monroe (LA)
U of North Dakota (ND)
Utah State U (UT)
Utah Valley U (UT)
Western Michigan U (MI)
Westminster Coll (UT)

AIR TRAFFIC CONTROL
Arizona State U at the Polytechnic campus (AZ)
Hampton U (VA)
Lewis U (IL)
Lynn U (FL)
U of North Dakota (ND)

AIR TRANSPORTATION RELATED
California Baptist U (CA)
Florida Inst of Technology (FL)
Inter American U of Puerto Rico, Bayamón Campus (PR)
U of North Dakota (ND)

ALLIED HEALTH AND MEDICAL ASSISTING SERVICES RELATED
Azusa Pacific U (CA)
Cedarville U (OH)
The Ohio State U (OH)
The Ohio State U at Lima (OH)
Ramapo Coll of New Jersey (NJ)
U of Vermont (VT)
Widener U (PA)

ALLIED HEALTH DIAGNOSTIC, INTERVENTION, AND TREATMENT PROFESSIONS RELATED
Coll of Saint Elizabeth (NJ)
Fairleigh Dickinson U (NJ)
Georgian Court U (NJ)
Hofstra U (NY)
Immaculata U (PA)
Indiana State U (IN)
Millersville U of Pennsylvania (PA)
Point Loma Nazarene U (CA)
Ramapo Coll of New Jersey (NJ)
Sacred Heart U (CT)
Tennessee Wesleyan U (TN)
U of Nebraska at Kearney (NE)
The U of North Carolina at Charlotte (NC)
Weber State U (UT)

AMERICAN GOVERNMENT AND POLITICS
Arizona Christian U (AZ)
Belmont Abbey Coll (NC)
Bridgewater State U (MA)
Emmanuel Coll (MA)
Emory & Henry Coll (VA)
Fitchburg State U (MA)
Gallaudet U (DC)
Lenoir-Rhyne U (NC)
Misericordia U (PA)
United States Military Acad (NY)
The U of Akron (OH)
U of Montana (MT)
Wayland Baptist U (TX)
Western Michigan U (MI)

AMERICAN HISTORY
Salem State U (MA)
Sarah Lawrence Coll (NY)
United States Military Acad (NY)
U of Washington, Tacoma (WA)
The U of Western Ontario (ON, Canada)
William Peace U (NC)

AMERICAN INDIAN/NATIVE AMERICAN STUDIES
Arizona State U at the Tempe campus (AZ)
Augsburg U (MN)
Bemidji State U (MN)
Black Hills State U (SD)
Brandon U (MB, Canada)
California State U, San Marcos (CA)
Colgate U (NY)
Dartmouth Coll (NH)
East Central U (OK)
Fort Lewis Coll (CO)
Hampshire Coll (MA)
Northeastern State U (OK)
Northern Arizona U (AZ)
Northwest U (WA)
Portland State U (OR)
St. Thomas U - New Brunswick (NB, Canada)
San Diego State U (CA)
San Francisco State U (CA)
South Dakota State U (SD)
Stanford U (CA)
U of Alaska Fairbanks (AK)
The U of Arizona (AZ)
U of California, Berkeley (CA)
U of California, Los Angeles (CA)
U of California, Riverside (CA)
U of Hawaii at Manoa (HI)
U of Minnesota, Duluth (MN)
U of Minnesota, Morris (MN)
U of Minnesota, Twin Cities Campus (MN)
U of Montana (MT)
U of New Mexico (NM)
The U of North Carolina at Pembroke (NC)
U of North Dakota (ND)
U of Science and Arts of Oklahoma (OK)
U of South Dakota (SD)
U of Toronto (ON, Canada)
U of Washington (WA)
The U of Western Ontario (ON, Canada)
U of Wisconsin–Eau Claire (WI)
U of Wisconsin–Green Bay (WI)
U of Wyoming (WY)
Western New England U (MA)

AMERICAN LITERATURE
U of California, Los Angeles (CA)
Washington U in St. Louis (MO)

AMERICAN NATIVE/NATIVE AMERICAN EDUCATION
The Coll of St. Scholastica (MN)
Northeastern State U (OK)

AMERICAN NATIVE/NATIVE AMERICAN LANGUAGES
Bemidji State U (MN)
U of Alaska Fairbanks (AK)
U of Minnesota, Twin Cities Campus (MN)

AMERICAN SIGN LANGUAGE (ASL)
Augustana U (SD)
California State U, Sacramento (CA)
Keuka Coll (NY)
Lamar U (TX)
Liberty U (VA)
Madonna U (MI)
North Central U (MN)
St. Catherine U (MN)
U of Houston (TX)
The U of Kansas (KS)
U of Utah (UT)
U of Wisconsin–Milwaukee (WI)
Utah Valley U (UT)

AMERICAN SIGN LANGUAGE RELATED
Eastern Kentucky U (KY)

AMERICAN STUDIES
American U (DC)
Amherst Coll (MA)
Augustana U (SD)
Austin Coll (TX)
Barnard Coll (NY)
Bates Coll (ME)
Baylor U (TX)
Bethany Lutheran Coll (MN)
Bowling Green State U (OH)
Brandeis U (MA)
Brown U (RI)
California State Polytechnic U, Pomona (CA)
California State U, Fullerton (CA)
California State U, Long Beach (CA)
California State U, San Bernardino (CA)
Carleton Coll (MN)
Claremont McKenna Coll (CA)
Coe Coll (IA)
Colby Coll (ME)
Coll of Saint Elizabeth (NJ)
Coll of Staten Island of the City U of New York (NY)
Cornell U (NY)
Creighton U (NE)
DePaul U (IL)
Dickinson Coll (PA)
Dominican U (IL)
Emmanuel Coll (MA)
Emory U (GA)
Fairfield U (CT)
Fordham U (NY)
George Fox U (OR)
Georgetown Coll (KY)
Georgetown U (DC)
The George Washington U (DC)
Goucher Coll (MD)
Hampshire Coll (MA)
Hillsdale Coll (MI)
Hobart and William Smith Colls (NY)
Hofstra U (NY)
Illinois Wesleyan U (IL)
Indiana U Bloomington (IN)
Kansas State U (KS)
Kenyon Coll (OH)
Knox Coll (IL)
Lake Forest Coll (IL)
Lehman Coll of the City U of New York (NY)
Lenoir-Rhyne U (NC)
Lesley U (MA)
Lipscomb U (TN)
Manhattanville Coll (NY)
Miami U (OH)
Miami U Hamilton (OH)
Miami U Middletown (OH)
Middlebury Coll (VT)
Mount Saint Mary's U (CA)
Muhlenberg Coll (PA)
Nazareth Coll of Rochester (NY)
New York U (NY)
Northwestern U (IL)
Occidental Coll (CA)
Oglethorpe U (GA)
Oklahoma State U (OK)
Pace U, Pleasantville Campus (NY)
Penn State Abington (PA)
Penn State Berks (PA)
Penn State Brandywine (PA)
Penn State Erie, The Behrend Coll (PA)
Penn State Harrisburg (PA)
Penn State Lehigh Valley (PA)
Penn State Schuylkill (PA)
Penn State York (PA)
Pitzer Coll (CA)
Pomona Coll (CA)
Providence Coll (RI)
Queens Coll of the City U of New York (NY)
Ramapo Coll of New Jersey (NJ)
Roger Williams U (RI)
Rollins Coll (FL)
Rowan U (NJ)
St. John Fisher Coll (NY)
Saint Louis U (MO)
St. Olaf Coll (MN)
Salve Regina U (RI)
San Francisco State U (CA)
Scripps Coll (CA)
Siena Coll (NY)
Skidmore Coll (NY)
Smith Coll (MA)
Springfield Coll (MA)
Stanford U (CA)
State U of New York at Oswego (NY)
State U of New York Coll at Geneseo (NY)
State U of New York Coll at Old Westbury (NY)
Stetson U (FL)
Stony Brook U, State U of New York (NY)
Temple U (PA)
Tennessee Wesleyan U (TN)
Towson U (MD)
Tulane U (LA)
Union Coll (NY)
U at Buffalo, the State U of New York (NY)
The U of Alabama (AL)
U of California, Berkeley (CA)
U of Hawaii at Manoa (HI)
The U of Iowa (IA)
The U of Kansas (KS)
U of Kentucky (KY)
U of Maryland, Baltimore County (MD)
U of Massachusetts Boston (MA)
U of Massachusetts Lowell (MA)
U of Miami (FL)
U of Michigan (MI)
U of Minnesota, Twin Cities Campus (MN)
U of New Mexico (NM)
The U of North Carolina at Chapel Hill (NC)
U of Notre Dame (IN)
U of Pennsylvania (PA)
U of Pittsburgh at Greensburg (PA)
U of Richmond (VA)
U of Southern Mississippi (MS)
U of South Florida (FL)
The U of Texas at Dallas (TX)
The U of Texas at San Antonio (TX)
The U of the South (TN)
The U of Toledo (OH)
U of Toronto (ON, Canada)
U of Washington, Bothell (WA)
U of Washington, Tacoma (WA)
The U of Western Ontario (ON, Canada)
U of Wyoming (WY)
Utah State U (UT)
Valparaiso U (IN)
Vanderbilt U (TN)
Virginia Wesleyan U (VA)
Washington Coll (MD)
Washington U in St. Louis (MO)
Wesleyan U (CT)
Western Connecticut State U (CT)
Western Washington U (WA)
Wheaton Coll (MA)
Whitworth U (WA)
William & Mary (VA)
Williams Coll (MA)
Yale U (CT)

ANALYTICAL CHEMISTRY
The U of Western Ontario (ON, Canada)
West Chester U of Pennsylvania (PA)

ANATOMY
Howard U (DC)
Minnesota State U Mankato (MN)
Oakland U (MI)
Tulane U (LA)
U of Utah (UT)
The U of Western Ontario (ON, Canada)

ANCIENT/CLASSICAL GREEK
Amherst Coll (MA)
Augustana Coll (IL)
Barnard Coll (NY)
Baylor U (TX)
Brigham Young U (UT)
California State U, Long Beach (CA)
Carleton Coll (MN)
Colgate U (NY)
DePauw U (IN)
Emory U (GA)
Hampden-Sydney Coll (VA)
Hillsdale Coll (MI)
Hobart and William Smith Colls (NY)
Indiana U Bloomington (IN)
Kenyon Coll (OH)
Loyola U Chicago (IL)
Loyola U New Orleans (LA)
Mount Holyoke Coll (MA)
Multnomah U (OR)
New York U (NY)
Queens Coll of the City U of New York (NY)

Randolph-Macon Coll (VA)
Rice U (TX)
St. Olaf Coll (MN)
Samford U (AL)
Sarah Lawrence Coll (NY)
Smith Coll (MA)
Southwestern U (TX)
Stanford U (CA)
Trinity U (TX)
U of California, Berkeley (CA)
U of California, Los Angeles (CA)
The U of Iowa (IA)
U of Michigan (MI)
The U of North Carolina at Greensboro (NC)
U of Notre Dame (IN)
U of Richmond (VA)
The U of the South (TN)
U of Vermont (VT)
U of Washington (WA)
The U of Western Ontario (ON, Canada)
Wabash Coll (IN)
Wake Forest U (NC)
Washington U in St. Louis (MO)
Yale U (CT)

ANCIENT NEAR EASTERN AND BIBLICAL LANGUAGES
Baylor U (TX)
Belmont U (TN)
Carson-Newman U (TN)
Columbia Intl U (SC)
Concordia U Wisconsin (WI)
Houston Baptist U (TX)
Northwest Nazarene U (ID)
Northwest U (WA)
Oklahoma Baptist U (OK)
Toccoa Falls Coll (GA)
Union U (TN)
U of Toronto (ON, Canada)
U of Washington (WA)
Walla Walla U (WA)

ANCIENT STUDIES
Barnard Coll (NY)
Bates Coll (ME)
Bowdoin Coll (ME)
Colby Coll (ME)
Creighton U (NE)
Dartmouth Coll (NH)
Emory U (GA)
Fordham U (NY)
Loyola Marymount U (CA)
Mount Holyoke Coll (MA)
Ohio Wesleyan U (OH)
Rollins Coll (FL)
Saint Joseph's U (PA)
St. Olaf Coll (MN)
The U of Iowa (IA)
The U of Kansas (KS)
U of Maryland, Baltimore County (MD)
U of Miami (FL)
U of Michigan (MI)
U of Nebraska–Lincoln (NE)
U of Richmond (VA)
Vanderbilt U (TN)
Washington U in St. Louis (MO)
Wesleyan U (CT)
Wheaton Coll (MA)

ANIMAL-ASSISTED THERAPY
Aurora U (IL)
Averett U (VA)
State U of New York Coll of Agriculture and Technology at Cobleskill (NY)

ANIMAL BEHAVIOR AND ETHOLOGY
Bucknell U (PA)
Hampshire Coll (MA)
Indiana U Bloomington (IN)
U of New England (ME)
U of Toronto (ON, Canada)
The U of Western Ontario (ON, Canada)

ANIMAL GENETICS
Clemson U (SC)
Jacksonville State U (AL)
Ohio Wesleyan U (OH)
U of Toronto (ON, Canada)

ANIMAL/LIVESTOCK HUSBANDRY AND PRODUCTION
Delaware Valley U (PA)
Texas A&M U (TX)

ANIMAL PHYSIOLOGY
California State U, Fresno (CA)
Minnesota State U Mankato (MN)
San Jose State U (CA)
The U of Akron (OH)
U of Toronto (ON, Canada)

ANIMAL SCIENCES
Abilene Christian U (TX)
Angelo State U (TX)
Auburn U (AL)
California Polytechnic State U, San Luis Obispo (CA)
California State Polytechnic U, Pomona (CA)
California State U, Fresno (CA)
Clemson U (SC)
Coll of the Ozarks (MO)
Colorado State U (CO)
Cornell U (NY)
Delaware Valley U (PA)
Iowa State U of Science and Technology (IA)
Kansas State U (KS)
Louisiana State U and A&M Coll (LA)
Louisiana Tech U (LA)
Michigan State U (MI)
Middle Tennessee State U (TN)
Mississippi State U (MS)
Missouri State U (MO)
Montana State U (MT)
Northwest Missouri State U (MO)
The Ohio State U (OH)
Oklahoma State U (OK)
Penn State Abington (PA)
Penn State Altoona (PA)
Penn State Beaver (PA)
Penn State Berks (PA)
Penn State Brandywine (PA)
Penn State DuBois (PA)
Penn State Erie, The Behrend Coll (PA)
Penn State Fayette, The Eberly Campus (PA)
Penn State Greater Allegheny (PA)
Penn State Hazleton (PA)
Penn State Lehigh Valley (PA)
Penn State Mont Alto (PA)
Penn State New Kensington (PA)
Penn State Schuylkill (PA)
Penn State Shenango (PA)
Penn State U Park (PA)
Penn State Wilkes-Barre (PA)
Penn State York (PA)
Sam Houston State U (TX)
South Dakota State U (SD)
Southern Illinois U Carbondale (IL)
Tarleton State U (TX)
Texas A&M U (TX)
Texas A&M U–Commerce (TX)
Texas A&M U–Kingsville (TX)
Texas State U (TX)
Texas Tech U (TX)
The U of Arizona (AZ)
U of Arkansas (AR)
The U of Findlay (OH)
U of Hawaii at Manoa (HI)
U of Idaho (ID)
U of Kentucky (KY)
U of Maine (ME)
U of Massachusetts Amherst (MA)
U of Minnesota, Twin Cities Campus (MN)
U of Nebraska–Lincoln (NE)
U of New Hampshire (NH)
The U of Tennessee (TN)
U of Vermont (VT)
U of Wisconsin–Madison (WI)
U of Wisconsin–Platteville (WI)
U of Wyoming (WY)
Utah State U (UT)
Washington State U (WA)
West Virginia U (WV)

ANIMAL SCIENCES RELATED
Delaware Valley U (PA)
Penn State Abington (PA)
Penn State Beaver (PA)
Penn State Brandywine (PA)
Penn State DuBois (PA)
Penn State Erie, The Behrend Coll (PA)
Penn State Fayette, The Eberly Campus (PA)
Penn State Greater Allegheny (PA)
Penn State Hazleton (PA)
Penn State Lehigh Valley (PA)
Penn State Mont Alto (PA)
Penn State New Kensington (PA)
Penn State Schuylkill (PA)
Penn State Shenango (PA)
Penn State Wilkes-Barre (PA)
Penn State York (PA)

ANIMAL TRAINING
Saint Francis U (PA)

ANIMATION, INTERACTIVE TECHNOLOGY, VIDEO GRAPHICS AND SPECIAL EFFECTS
Academy of Art U (CA)
American Acad of Art (IL)
Arizona State U at the Tempe campus (AZ)
Bennington Coll (VT)
Bradley U (IL)
Brigham Young U (UT)
Chatham U (PA)
Cleveland Inst of Art (OH)
Columbia Coll Chicago (IL)
Davenport U, Grand Rapids (MI)
DePaul U (IL)
Drury U (MO)
Eastern Michigan U (MI)
Fashion Inst of Technology (NY)
Ferris State U (MI)
Florida State U (FL)
George Mason U (VA)
Gulf Coast State Coll (FL)
Lawrence Technological U (MI)
Loyola Marymount U (CA)
Lynn U (FL)
Massachusetts Coll of Art and Design (MA)
Middle Tennessee State U (TN)
Minneapolis Coll of Art and Design (MN)
New England Inst of Technology (RI)
New Jersey Inst of Technology (NJ)
New York U (NY)
Platt Coll San Diego (CA)
Regent U (VA)
Sam Houston State U (TX)
State U of New York Coll of Technology at Alfred (NY)
U of California, Santa Cruz (CA)
U of Hawaii–West Oahu (HI)
U of Idaho (ID)
U of Northwestern–St. Paul (MN)
The U of Tampa (FL)
U of the Incarnate Word (TX)

ANTHROPOLOGY
Agnes Scott Coll (GA)
Albion Coll (MI)
American U (DC)
Amherst Coll (MA)
Appalachian State U (NC)
Arizona State U at the Tempe campus (AZ)
Auburn U (AL)
Augustana Coll (IL)
Augustana U (SD)
Austin Coll (TX)
Ball State U (IN)
Bates Coll (ME)
Baylor U (TX)
Beloit Coll (WI)
Bennington Coll (VT)
Binghamton U, State U of New York (NY)
Biola U (CA)
Boise State U (ID)
Bowdoin Coll (ME)
Brandeis U (MA)
Bridgewater State U (MA)
Brown U (RI)
Bucknell U (PA)
Butler U (IN)
California State Polytechnic U, Pomona (CA)
California State U, Bakersfield (CA)
California State U, Dominguez Hills (CA)
California State U, Fresno (CA)
California State U, Fullerton (CA)
California State U, Long Beach (CA)
California State U, Los Angeles (CA)
California State U, Northridge (CA)
California State U, Sacramento (CA)
California State U, San Bernardino (CA)
California State U, San Marcos (CA)
California State U, Stanislaus (CA)
California U of Pennsylvania (PA)
Carleton Coll (MN)
The Catholic U of America (DC)
Central Coll (IA)
Central Connecticut State U (CT)
Central Michigan U (MI)
Central Washington U (WA)
City Coll of the City U of New York (NY)
Clarion U of Pennsylvania (PA)
Clemson U (SC)
Coastal Carolina U (SC)
Colby Coll (ME)
Colgate U (NY)
Coll of Charleston (SC)
The Coll of Idaho (ID)
Coll of the Holy Cross (MA)
The Coll of Wooster (OH)
The Colorado Coll (CO)
Colorado State U (CO)
Cornell Coll (IA)
Cornell U (NY)
Dartmouth Coll (NH)
Davidson Coll (NC)
DePaul U (IL)
DePauw U (IN)
Dickinson Coll (PA)
Drake U (IA)
Drew U (NJ)
Drexel U (PA)
East Carolina U (NC)
Eastern Kentucky U (KY)
Eastern Michigan U (MI)
Eastern New Mexico U (NM)
Eastern Washington U (WA)
Edinboro U of Pennsylvania (PA)
Elon U (NC)
Emory U (GA)
Florida Atlantic U (FL)
Florida Gulf Coast U (FL)
Florida State U (FL)
Fordham U (NY)
Fort Lewis Coll (CO)
Furman U (SC)
George Mason U (VA)
Georgetown U (DC)
The George Washington U (DC)
Georgia Southern U (GA)
Georgia State U (GA)
Grand Valley State U (MI)
Grinnell Coll (IA)
Gustavus Adolphus Coll (MN)
Hamline U (MN)
Hampshire Coll (MA)
Hanover Coll (IN)
Harvard U (MA)
Hobart and William Smith Colls (NY)
Hofstra U (NY)
Howard U (DC)
Illinois State U (IL)
Illinois Wesleyan U (IL)
Indiana U Bloomington (IN)
Indiana U Northwest (IN)
Indiana U of Pennsylvania (PA)
Indiana U-Purdue U Indianapolis (IN)
Indiana U South Bend (IN)
Inter American U of Puerto Rico, San Germán Campus (PR)
Iowa State U of Science and Technology (IA)
Ithaca Coll (NY)
Jacksonville State U (AL)
James Madison U (VA)
John Jay Coll of Criminal Justice of the City U of New York (NY)
Johns Hopkins U (MD)
Kansas State U (KS)
Kennesaw State U (GA)
Kenyon Coll (OH)
Kutztown U of Pennsylvania (PA)
Lafayette Coll (PA)
Lake Forest Coll (IL)
Lawrence U (WI)
Lee U (TN)
Lehigh U (PA)
Lehman Coll of the City U of New York (NY)
Lincoln U (PA)
Lindenwood U (MO)
Linfield Coll (OR)
Longwood U (VA)
Louisiana State U and A&M Coll (LA)
Loyola U Chicago (IL)
Marquette U (WI)
Miami U (OH)
Miami U Hamilton (OH)
Miami U Middletown (OH)
Michigan State U (MI)
Michigan Technological U (MI)
Middlebury Coll (VT)
Middle Tennessee State U (TN)
Millersville U of Pennsylvania (PA)
Minnesota State U Mankato (MN)
Mississippi State U (MS)
Missouri State U (MO)
Montana State U (MT)
Montclair State U (NJ)
Mount Holyoke Coll (MA)
Muhlenberg Coll (PA)
Muskingum U (OH)
Nazareth Coll of Rochester (NY)
New Coll of Florida (FL)
New York U (NY)
Northeastern Illinois U (IL)
Northern Arizona U (AZ)
Northern Illinois U (IL)
Northern Kentucky U (KY)
Northwestern U (IL)
Oakland U (MI)
Oberlin Coll (OH)
The Ohio State U (OH)
Oklahoma Baptist U (OK)
Penn State Abington (PA)
Penn State Altoona (PA)
Penn State Beaver (PA)
Penn State Berks (PA)
Penn State Brandywine (PA)
Penn State DuBois (PA)
Penn State Erie, The Behrend Coll (PA)
Penn State Fayette, The Eberly Campus (PA)
Penn State Greater Allegheny (PA)
Penn State Hazleton (PA)
Penn State Lehigh Valley (PA)
Penn State Mont Alto (PA)
Penn State New Kensington (PA)
Penn State Schuylkill (PA)
Penn State Shenango (PA)
Penn State U Park (PA)
Penn State Wilkes-Barre (PA)
Penn State York (PA)
Pitzer Coll (CA)
Pomona Coll (CA)
Portland State U (OR)
Princeton U (NJ)
Purchase Coll, State U of New York (NY)
Purdue U Fort Wayne (IN)
Queens Coll of the City U of New York (NY)
Radford U (VA)
Rhode Island Coll (RI)
Rhodes Coll (TN)
Rice U (TX)
Rollins Coll (FL)
St. Cloud State U (MN)
St. John Fisher Coll (NY)
Saint Louis U (MO)
Saint Mary's Coll of California (CA)
St. Mary's Coll of Maryland (MD)
St. Thomas U - New Brunswick (NB, Canada)
Saint Vincent Coll (PA)
San Diego State U (CA)
San Francisco State U (CA)
San Jose State U (CA)
Santa Clara U (CA)
Sarah Lawrence Coll (NY)
Scripps Coll (CA)
Seattle U (WA)
Skidmore Coll (NY)
Smith Coll (MA)
Southern Illinois U Carbondale (IL)
Southern Illinois U Edwardsville (IL)
Southern Methodist U (TX)
Southwestern U (TX)
Stanford U (CA)
State U of New York at New Paltz (NY)
State U of New York at Oswego (NY)

State U of New York Coll at Cortland (NY)
State U of New York Coll at Geneseo (NY)
State U of New York Coll at Oneonta (NY)
State U of New York Coll at Potsdam (NY)
Stony Brook U, State U of New York (NY)
SUNY Brockport (NY)
Susquehanna U (PA)
Temple U (PA)
Texas A&M U (TX)
Texas Christian U (TX)
Texas State U (TX)
Texas Tech U (TX)
Transylvania U (KY)
Trinity U (TX)
Troy U (AL)
Tulane U (LA)
Union Coll (NY)
U at Albany, State U of New York (NY)
U at Buffalo, the State U of New York (NY)
The U of Akron (OH)
The U of Alabama (AL)
The U of Alabama at Birmingham (AL)
U of Alaska Fairbanks (AK)
The U of Arizona (AZ)
U of Arkansas (AR)
U of Arkansas at Little Rock (AR)
U of California, Berkeley (CA)
U of California, Irvine (CA)
U of California, Los Angeles (CA)
U of California, Merced (CA)
U of California, Riverside (CA)
U of California, San Diego (CA)
U of California, Santa Barbara (CA)
U of California, Santa Cruz (CA)
U of Central Florida (FL)
U of Cincinnati (OH)
U of Colorado Boulder (CO)
U of Colorado Colorado Springs (CO)
U of Colorado Denver (CO)
U of Denver (CO)
U of Guam (GU)
U of Hawaii at Manoa (HI)
U of Houston (TX)
U of Houston–Clear Lake (TX)
U of Idaho (ID)
U of Illinois at Chicago (IL)
The U of Iowa (IA)
The U of Kansas (KS)
U of Kentucky (KY)
U of La Verne (CA)
U of Louisiana at Lafayette (LA)
U of Louisville (KY)
U of Maine (ME)
U of Maryland, Baltimore County (MD)
U of Mary Washington (VA)
U of Massachusetts Amherst (MA)
U of Massachusetts Boston (MA)
U of Memphis (TN)
U of Miami (FL)
U of Michigan (MI)
U of Michigan–Dearborn (MI)
U of Michigan–Flint (MI)
U of Minnesota, Duluth (MN)
U of Minnesota, Morris (MN)
U of Minnesota, Twin Cities Campus (MN)
U of Missouri–St. Louis (MO)
U of Montana (MT)
U of Nebraska–Lincoln (NE)
U of Nevada, Las Vegas (NV)
U of Nevada, Reno (NV)
U of New Hampshire (NH)
U of New Mexico (NM)
The U of North Carolina at Chapel Hill (NC)
The U of North Carolina at Charlotte (NC)
The U of North Carolina at Greensboro (NC)
The U of North Carolina Wilmington (NC)
U of North Dakota (ND)
U of Northern Colorado (CO)
U of Northern Iowa (IA)
U of North Florida (FL)
U of North Texas (TX)
U of Notre Dame (IN)
U of Oregon (OR)
U of Pennsylvania (PA)
U of Pittsburgh at Greensburg (PA)
U of Richmond (VA)
U of San Diego (CA)
U of South Alabama (AL)
U of South Carolina (SC)
U of South Dakota (SD)
U of Southern Indiana (IN)
U of Southern Mississippi (MS)
U of South Florida (FL)
U of South Florida, St. Petersburg (FL)
The U of Tennessee (TN)
The U of Texas at El Paso (TX)
The U of Texas at San Antonio (TX)
The U of Texas Rio Grande Valley (TX)
U of the Fraser Valley (BC, Canada)
The U of the South (TN)
The U of Toledo (OH)
U of Toronto (ON, Canada)
The U of Tulsa (OK)
U of Utah (UT)
U of Vermont (VT)
U of Virginia (VA)
U of Washington (WA)
U of Waterloo (ON, Canada)
The U of Western Ontario (ON, Canada)
U of West Florida (FL)
U of West Georgia (GA)
U of Wisconsin–Madison (WI)
U of Wisconsin–Milwaukee (WI)
U of Wyoming (WY)
Utah State U (UT)
Vanderbilt U (TN)
Virginia Commonwealth U (VA)
Wake Forest U (NC)
Washington Coll (MD)
Washington State U (WA)
Washington State U–Vancouver (WA)
Washington U in St. Louis (MO)
Wayne State U (MI)
Weber State U (UT)
Wesleyan U (CT)
West Chester U of Pennsylvania (PA)
Western Carolina U (NC)
Western Colorado U (CO)
Western Connecticut State U (CT)
Western Kentucky U (KY)
Western Michigan U (MI)
Western Oregon U (OR)
Western Washington U (WA)
Wheaton Coll (IL)
Wheaton Coll (MA)
Wichita State U (KS)
Widener U (PA)
Willamette U (OR)
William & Mary (VA)
William Paterson U of New Jersey (NJ)
William Peace U (NC)
Williams Coll (MA)
Wright State U (OH)
Wright State U–Lake Campus (OH)
Yale U (CT)
Youngstown State U (OH)

ANTHROPOLOGY RELATED
Bridgewater State U (MA)
Butler U (IN)
California Baptist U (CA)
U of California, San Diego (CA)
U of Michigan (MI)
The U of Western Ontario (ON, Canada)
Western Washington U (WA)

APPAREL AND ACCESSORIES MARKETING
Woodbury U (CA)

APPAREL AND TEXTILE MANUFACTURING
Academy of Art U (CA)
Ball State U (IN)
Fashion Inst of Technology (NY)
FIDM/Fashion Inst of Design & Merchandising, Los Angeles Campus (CA)
Michigan State U (MI)
Utah State U (UT)

APPAREL AND TEXTILE MARKETING MANAGEMENT
Academy of Art U (CA)
Auburn U (AL)
Central Washington U (WA)
Colorado State U (CO)
East Central U (OK)
South Dakota State U (SD)
U of Nebraska–Lincoln (NE)
U of the Incarnate Word (TX)
Wayne State U (MI)

APPAREL AND TEXTILES
Academy of Art U (CA)
Appalachian State U (NC)
Auburn U (AL)
Bowling Green State U (OH)
California State Polytechnic U, Pomona (CA)
California State U, Long Beach (CA)
East Carolina U (NC)
Framingham State U (MA)
Georgia Southern U (GA)
Illinois State U (IL)
Indiana State U (IN)
Indiana U Bloomington (IN)
Iowa State U of Science and Technology (IA)
Jacksonville State U (AL)
Kansas State U (KS)
Lamar U (TX)
Liberty U (VA)
Lipscomb U (TN)
Louisiana State U and A&M Coll (LA)
Michigan State U (MI)
Middle Tennessee State U (TN)
Mississippi State U (MS)
Missouri State U (MO)
Northern Illinois U (IL)
The Ohio State U (OH)
Southern Illinois U Carbondale (IL)
Texas A&M U–Kingsville (TX)
The U of Akron (OH)
The U of Alabama (AL)
U of Arkansas (AR)
U of Hawaii at Manoa (HI)
U of Idaho (ID)
U of Kentucky (KY)
U of Minnesota, Twin Cities Campus (MN)
U of Nebraska–Lincoln (NE)
The U of North Carolina at Greensboro (NC)
U of Northern Iowa (IA)
U of Southern Mississippi (MS)
U of Utah (UT)
U of Wisconsin–Madison (WI)
U of Wisconsin–Stout (WI)
Washington State U (WA)
Western Kentucky U (KY)

APPLIED AND PROFESSIONAL ETHICS
Carnegie Mellon U (PA)
Carson-Newman U (TN)
Drexel U (PA)
Mount Saint Mary's U (CA)
Nazarene Bible Coll (CO)
U of Michigan–Flint (MI)
Western Michigan U (MI)

APPLIED BEHAVIOR ANALYSIS
Ball State U (IN)
Florida Inst of Technology (FL)
Saint Joseph's U (PA)
U of North Texas (TX)
Western Michigan U (MI)

APPLIED ECONOMICS
Augsburg U (MN)
Binghamton U, State U of New York (NY)
Bowling Green State U (OH)
Brigham Young U (UT)
Bryant U (RI)
Carnegie Mellon U (PA)
Farmingdale State Coll (NY)
HEC Montreal (QC, Canada)
Illinois Inst of Technology (IL)
Ithaca Coll (NY)
Penn State Abington (PA)
Penn State Beaver (PA)
Penn State Brandywine (PA)
Penn State DuBois (PA)
Penn State Erie, The Behrend Coll (PA)
Penn State Fayette, The Eberly Campus (PA)
Penn State Greater Allegheny (PA)
Penn State Hazleton (PA)
Penn State Lehigh Valley (PA)
Penn State Mont Alto (PA)
Penn State New Kensington (PA)
Penn State Schuylkill (PA)
Penn State Shenango (PA)
Penn State Wilkes-Barre (PA)
Penn State York (PA)
The U of Akron (OH)
The U of Arizona (AZ)
U of Dayton (OH)
U of Massachusetts Amherst (MA)
U of Minnesota, Twin Cities Campus (MN)
U of Northern Iowa (IA)
U of San Francisco (CA)
U of Waterloo (ON, Canada)
Utah State U (UT)
Wabash Coll (IN)

APPLIED HORTICULTURE/ HORTICULTURE OPERATIONS
Colorado State U (CO)
Farmingdale State Coll (NY)
South Dakota State U (SD)
Texas A&M U (TX)
U of Maine (ME)
U of Massachusetts Amherst (MA)

APPLIED LINGUISTICS
Caldwell U (NJ)
Johnson U Florida (FL)
Portland State U (OR)
U of Alaska Southeast (AK)
U of California, Santa Cruz (CA)
U of Idaho (ID)

APPLIED MATHEMATICS
American U (DC)
American U of Beirut (Lebanon)
Arizona State U at the Polytechnic campus (AZ)
Arizona State U at the West campus (AZ)
Auburn U (AL)
Augustana Coll (IL)
Azusa Pacific U (CA)
Baylor U (TX)
Bennington Coll (VT)
Bethel U (IN)
Biola U (CA)
Boise State U (ID)
Brandeis U (MA)
Brown U (RI)
Bryant U (RI)
California State U, Fullerton (CA)
California State U, Long Beach (CA)
Central Michigan U (MI)
Clarkson U (NY)
Coastal Carolina U (SC)
Colgate U (NY)
The Coll of Idaho (ID)
East Central U (OK)
Elon U (NC)
Emmaus Bible Coll (IA)
Emory U (GA)
Endicott Coll (MA)
Farmingdale State Coll (NY)
Ferris State U (MI)
Fitchburg State U (MA)
Florida Inst of Technology (FL)
Florida Polytechnic U (FL)
Florida State U (FL)
Geneva Coll (PA)
The George Washington U (DC)
Georgia Inst of Technology (GA)
Gonzaga U (WA)
Hampden-Sydney Coll (VA)
Harvard U (MA)
Hillsdale Coll (MI)
Illinois Inst of Technology (IL)
Indiana U South Bend (IN)
Inter American U of Puerto Rico, San Germán Campus (PR)
Iona Coll (NY)
John Jay Coll of Criminal Justice of the City U of New York (NY)
Johns Hopkins U (MD)
Kennesaw State U (GA)
Kettering U (MI)
King U (TN)
Lee U (TN)
Lipscomb U (TN)
Loyola Marymount U (CA)
Loyola U Chicago (IL)
Loyola U Maryland (MD)
Maryville U of Saint Louis (MO)
Missouri U of Science and Technology (MO)
New Coll of Florida (FL)
New Jersey Inst of Technology (NJ)
New York City Coll of Technology of the City U of New York (NY)
New York U (NY)
Northwestern U (IL)
Penn State Harrisburg (PA)
Portland State U (OR)
Rice U (TX)
Roger Williams U (RI)
Saginaw Valley State U (MI)
Saint Mary's Coll (IN)
San Diego State U (CA)
San Francisco State U (CA)
San Jose State U (CA)
Siena Heights U (MI)
Simon Fraser U (BC, Canada)
Southeastern U (FL)
State U of New York at Oswego (NY)
State U of New York Coll at Geneseo (NY)
Stony Brook U, State U of New York (NY)
Temple U (PA)
Texas A&M U (TX)
Texas State U (TX)
Trevecca Nazarene U (TN)
U at Buffalo, the State U of New York (NY)
The U of Akron (OH)
U of California, Berkeley (CA)
U of California, Los Angeles (CA)
U of California, Merced (CA)
U of California, San Diego (CA)
U of Colorado Boulder (CO)
The U of Findlay (OH)
U of Houston–Downtown (TX)
U of Idaho (ID)
The U of Iowa (IA)
U of Jamestown (ND)
U of Massachusetts Lowell (MA)
U of Miami (FL)
U of New England (ME)
U of New Hampshire (NH)
U of New Haven (CT)
The U of North Carolina at Chapel Hill (NC)
U of North Florida (FL)
U of Northwestern–St. Paul (MN)
U of Pittsburgh at Bradford (PA)
U of Pittsburgh at Greensburg (PA)
U of Saint Mary (KS)
The U of Scranton (PA)
U of South Carolina Aiken (SC)
The U of Tennessee at Chattanooga (TN)
U of the Virgin Islands (VI)
U of Toronto (ON, Canada)
The U of Tulsa (OK)
U of Utah (UT)
U of Waterloo (ON, Canada)
The U of Western Ontario (ON, Canada)
U of Wisconsin–Madison (WI)
U of Wisconsin–Milwaukee (WI)
U of Wisconsin–Stout (WI)
Valdosta State U (GA)
Washington State U (WA)
Washington State U–Vancouver (WA)
Washington U in St. Louis (MO)
Weber State U (UT)
Wentworth Inst of Technology (MA)
Wesleyan Coll (GA)
Western Michigan U (MI)
Western Washington U (WA)
Wheaton Coll (IL)
William Penn U (IA)
Yale U (CT)

APPLIED MATHEMATICS RELATED
Arizona State U at the Tempe campus (AZ)
Averett U (VA)
Belmont U (TN)
Berea Coll (KY)
Bucknell U (PA)
Georgia Inst of Technology (GA)

Inter American U of Puerto Rico, Metropolitan Campus (PR)
Merrimack Coll (MA)
The Ohio State U (OH)
U of California, Santa Barbara (CA)
U of Washington (WA)
U of Waterloo (ON, Canada)
U of Wisconsin–Milwaukee (WI)
Whitworth U (WA)
Willamette U (OR)

APPLIED PSYCHOLOGY
Arizona State U at the Polytechnic campus (AZ)
Belhaven U (MS)
Carson-Newman U (TN)
Farmingdale State Coll (NY)
Gwynedd Mercy U (PA)
Loyola U Chicago (IL)
Miami U (OH)
Miami U Hamilton (OH)
Miami U Middletown (OH)
Mount Saint Mary's U (CA)
Multnomah U (OR)
New York U (NY)
Ottawa U (KS)
Pace U, Pleasantville Campus (NY)
State U of New York Coll of Technology at Canton (NY)
United States Military Acad (NY)
U of Saint Mary (KS)

AQUACULTURE
Auburn U (AL)
Clemson U (SC)
U of New England (ME)

AQUATIC BIOLOGY/ LIMNOLOGY
Bemidji State U (MN)
Florida Inst of Technology (FL)
Gannon U (PA)
Stetson U (FL)
Texas State U (TX)
U of South Carolina (SC)
Western Michigan U (MI)

ARABIC
American U (DC)
Baylor U (TX)
Binghamton U, State U of New York (NY)
California U of Pennsylvania (PA)
DePaul U (IL)
Emory U (GA)
Georgetown U (DC)
Lebanese American U (Lebanon)
Michigan State U (MI)
Middlebury Coll (VT)
Montclair State U (NJ)
The Ohio State U (OH)
Portland State U (OR)
United States Military Acad (NY)
The U of Arizona (AZ)
U of Arkansas (AR)
U of California, Los Angeles (CA)
U of Cincinnati (OH)
U of Notre Dame (IN)
U of Toronto (ON, Canada)
U of Utah (UT)
Washington U in St. Louis (MO)
Western Kentucky U (KY)

ARCHEOLOGY
American U of Beirut (Lebanon)
Biola U (CA)
Bowdoin Coll (ME)
Bridgewater State U (MA)
Brown U (RI)
Coll of Charleston (SC)
The Coll of Wooster (OH)
Cornell Coll (IA)
Cornell U (NY)
Dickinson Coll (PA)
The George Washington U (DC)
Johns Hopkins U (MD)
New York U (NY)
Oberlin Coll (OH)
Penn State Abington (PA)
Penn State Altoona (PA)
Penn State Beaver (PA)
Penn State Berks (PA)
Penn State Brandywine (PA)
Penn State DuBois (PA)
Penn State Erie, The Behrend Coll (PA)
Penn State Fayette, The Eberly Campus (PA)
Penn State Greater Allegheny (PA)
Penn State Hazleton (PA)
Penn State Lehigh Valley (PA)
Penn State Mont Alto (PA)
Penn State New Kensington (PA)
Penn State Schuylkill (PA)
Penn State Shenango (PA)
Penn State U Park (PA)
Penn State Wilkes-Barre (PA)
Penn State York (PA)
Saint Mary's Coll of California (CA)
Simon Fraser U (BC, Canada)
Stanford U (CA)
State U of New York Coll at Potsdam (NY)
U of California, San Diego (CA)
U of Cincinnati (OH)
The U of North Carolina at Chapel Hill (NC)
U of Toronto (ON, Canada)
U of Wisconsin–La Crosse (WI)
Washington U in St. Louis (MO)
Wesleyan U (CT)
Western Washington U (WA)
Wheaton Coll (IL)
Yale U (CT)

ARCHITECTURAL AND BUILDING SCIENCES
Carnegie Mellon U (PA)
Georgia Inst of Technology (GA)
Iowa State U of Science and Technology (IA)
Lawrence Technological U (MI)
Miami U Hamilton (OH)
Miami U Middletown (OH)
New Jersey Inst of Technology (NJ)
New York Inst of Technology (NY)
Oklahoma State U (OK)
State U of New York Coll of Technology at Delhi (NY)
The U of Arizona (AZ)
U of Massachusetts Amherst (MA)
U of Utah (UT)
Washington U in St. Louis (MO)
Woodbury U (CA)

ARCHITECTURAL DRAFTING AND CAD/CADD
Academy of Art U (CA)

ARCHITECTURAL ENGINEERING
Auburn U (AL)
California Polytechnic State U, San Luis Obispo (CA)
Drexel U (PA)
Illinois Inst of Technology (IL)
Inter American U of Puerto Rico, Bayamón Campus (PR)
Kansas State U (KS)
Lawrence Technological U (MI)
Milwaukee School of Eng (WI)
Missouri U of Science and Technology (MO)
Oklahoma State U (OK)
Penn State Abington (PA)
Penn State Altoona (PA)
Penn State Beaver (PA)
Penn State Berks (PA)
Penn State Brandywine (PA)
Penn State DuBois (PA)
Penn State Erie, The Behrend Coll (PA)
Penn State Fayette, The Eberly Campus (PA)
Penn State Greater Allegheny (PA)
Penn State Hazleton (PA)
Penn State Lehigh Valley (PA)
Penn State Mont Alto (PA)
Penn State New Kensington (PA)
Penn State Schuylkill (PA)
Penn State Shenango (PA)
Penn State U Park (PA)
Penn State Wilkes-Barre (PA)
Penn State York (PA)
Texas A&M U–Kingsville (TX)
The U of Alabama (AL)
The U of Arizona (AZ)
U of Cincinnati (OH)
U of Colorado Boulder (CO)
U of Detroit Mercy (MI)
The U of Kansas (KS)
U of Miami (FL)
U of Waterloo (ON, Canada)
U of Wyoming (WY)
Worcester Polytechnic Inst (MA)

ARCHITECTURAL ENGINEERING TECHNOLOGY
Farmingdale State Coll (NY)
Ferris State U (MI)
Fitchburg State U (MA)
Indiana U-Purdue U Indianapolis (IN)
New England Inst of Technology (RI)
State U of New York Coll of Technology at Alfred (NY)
U of Hartford (CT)
U of Southern Mississippi (MS)
Vermont Tech Coll (VT)
Washington U in St. Louis (MO)

ARCHITECTURAL HISTORY AND CRITICISM
Amherst Coll (MA)
Brown U (RI)
Coll of the Holy Cross (MA)
Cornell U (NY)
DePaul U (IL)
The U of Kansas (KS)
U of Miami (FL)
U of San Diego (CA)
U of Virginia (VA)

ARCHITECTURAL TECHNOLOGY
Indiana State U (IN)
New York City Coll of Technology of the City U of New York (NY)
New York Inst of Technology (NY)
Washington U in St. Louis (MO)
Western Kentucky U (KY)

ARCHITECTURE
Academy of Art U (CA)
American U of Beirut (Lebanon)
Andrews U (MI)
Arizona State U at the Tempe campus (AZ)
Auburn U (AL)
Ball State U (IN)
Barnard Coll (NY)
Benedictine Coll (KS)
Bennington Coll (VT)
Boston Architectural Coll (MA)
California Baptist U (CA)
California Polytechnic State U, San Luis Obispo (CA)
California State Polytechnic U, Pomona (CA)
Carnegie Mellon U (PA)
The Catholic U of America (DC)
City Coll of the City U of New York (NY)
Clemson U (SC)
Cornell Coll (IA)
Cornell U (NY)
Drexel U (PA)
Drury U (MO)
Dunwoody Coll of Technology (MN)
Florida A&M U (FL)
Florida Atlantic U (FL)
Georgia Inst of Technology (GA)
Hampshire Coll (MA)
Hampton U (VA)
Hobart and William Smith Colls (NY)
Howard U (DC)
Illinois Inst of Technology (IL)
Inter American U of Puerto Rico, San Germán Campus (PR)
Ithaca Coll (NY)
Kean U (NJ)
Kennesaw State U (GA)
Lebanese American U (Lebanon)
Lehigh U (PA)
Louisiana State U and A&M Coll (LA)
Louisiana Tech U (LA)
Marywood U (PA)
Massachusetts Coll of Art and Design (MA)
Miami U (OH)
Middlebury Coll (VT)
Mississippi State U (MS)
New Jersey Inst of Technology (NJ)
New York Inst of Technology (NY)
The Ohio State U (OH)
Penn State U Park (PA)
Polytechnic U of Puerto Rico (PR)
Portland State U (OR)
Prairie View A&M U (TX)
Pratt Inst (NY)
Princeton U (NJ)
Rice U (TX)
Roger Williams U (RI)
Sarah Lawrence Coll (NY)
Smith Coll (MA)
South Dakota State U (SD)
Southern Illinois U Carbondale (IL)
State U of New York Coll of Technology at Alfred (NY)
Texas A&M U (TX)
Texas Tech U (TX)
Tulane U (LA)
U at Buffalo, the State U of New York (NY)
The U of Arizona (AZ)
U of Arkansas (AR)
U of California, Berkeley (CA)
U of California, Los Angeles (CA)
U of Central Florida (FL)
U of Cincinnati (OH)
U of Colorado Denver (CO)
U of Detroit Mercy (MI)
U of Hawaii at Manoa (HI)
U of Houston (TX)
U of Idaho (ID)
U of Illinois at Chicago (IL)
The U of Kansas (KS)
U of Kentucky (KY)
U of Louisiana at Lafayette (LA)
U of Memphis (TN)
U of Miami (FL)
U of Michigan (MI)
U of Minnesota, Twin Cities Campus (MN)
U of Nebraska–Lincoln (NE)
U of Nevada, Las Vegas (NV)
U of New Mexico (NM)
The U of North Carolina at Charlotte (NC)
U of Notre Dame (IN)
U of Oregon (OR)
U of Pennsylvania (PA)
U of San Francisco (CA)
The U of Tennessee (TN)
The U of Texas at San Antonio (TX)
U of Toronto (ON, Canada)
U of Utah (UT)
U of Virginia (VA)
U of Washington (WA)
U of Waterloo (ON, Canada)
U of Wisconsin–Milwaukee (WI)
Washington State U (WA)
Washington U in St. Louis (MO)
Wentworth Inst of Technology (MA)
Yale U (CT)

ARCHITECTURE RELATED
Ball State U (IN)
Drury U (MO)
Eugene Lang Coll of Liberal Arts (NY)
Lipscomb U (TN)
Mount Holyoke Coll (MA)
New Jersey Inst of Technology (NJ)
Parsons School of Design (NY)
The U of Arizona (AZ)
U of Illinois at Chicago (IL)
U of Louisiana at Lafayette (LA)
U of Utah (UT)
Washington U in St. Louis (MO)

AREA STUDIES RELATED
Augsburg U (MN)
Bridgewater State U (MA)
Carleton Coll (MN)
Colgate U (NY)
Eastern Michigan U (MI)
Hofstra U (NY)
Illinois Wesleyan U (IL)
Lake Forest Coll (IL)
Millersville U of Pennsylvania (PA)
New York U (NY)
Northeastern State U (OK)
Northwestern U (IL)
Ramapo Coll of New Jersey (NJ)
St. Ambrose U (IA)
Stanford U (CA)
U of Alaska Fairbanks (AK)
U of California, Santa Barbara (CA)
U of Michigan–Dearborn (MI)
The U of North Carolina at Chapel Hill (NC)
U of Richmond (VA)
U of San Francisco (CA)
U of Virginia (VA)
U of Washington (WA)
Utah State U (UT)
Virginia Commonwealth U (VA)
Washington U in St. Louis (MO)
Williams Coll (MA)

ARMY ROTC/MILITARY SCIENCE
Iowa State U of Science and Technology (IA)
Jacksonville State U (AL)
Minnesota State U Mankato (MN)
Northwest U (WA)
The U of Iowa (IA)

ARMY ROTC, MILITARY SCIENCE AND OPERATIONS RELATED
Western Kentucky U (KY)

ART
Albion Coll (MI)
Alfred U (NY)
Alverno Coll (WI)
American Acad of Art (IL)
Amherst Coll (MA)
Andrews U (MI)
Appalachian State U (NC)
Aquinas Coll (MI)
Arcadia U (PA)
Arizona State U at the Tempe campus (AZ)
Arkansas Tech U (AR)
Athens State U (AL)
Auburn U at Montgomery (AL)
Augustana Coll (IL)
Augustana U (SD)
Austin Coll (TX)
Austin Peay State U (TN)
Averett U (VA)
Avila U (MO)
Azusa Pacific U (CA)
Ball State U (IN)
Barton Coll (NC)
Bates Coll (ME)
Baylor U (TX)
Belhaven U (MS)
Belmont U (TN)
Bemidji State U (MN)
Benedictine Coll (KS)
Berea Coll (KY)
Berry Coll (GA)
Bethel U (MN)
Binghamton U, State U of New York (NY)
Biola U (CA)
Birmingham-Southern Coll (AL)
Black Hills State U (SD)
Bluffton U (OH)
Bowling Green State U (OH)
Bradley U (IL)
Brown U (RI)
Bucknell U (PA)
Caldwell U (NJ)
California Lutheran U (CA)
California State Polytechnic U, Pomona (CA)
California State U, Bakersfield (CA)
California State U, Dominguez Hills (CA)
California State U, Fresno (CA)
California State U, Fullerton (CA)
California State U, Long Beach (CA)
California State U, Los Angeles (CA)
California State U, Monterey Bay (CA)
California State U, Northridge (CA)
California State U, Sacramento (CA)
California State U, San Bernardino (CA)
California State U, Stanislaus (CA)
California U of Pennsylvania (PA)
Calvin Coll (MI)
Cameron U (OK)
Campbellsville U (KY)
Capital U (OH)
Carnegie Mellon U (PA)
Carson-Newman U (TN)
The Catholic U of America (DC)
Cedar Crest Coll (PA)
Central Christian Coll of Kansas (KS)
Central Coll (IA)
Central Connecticut State U (CT)
Central Michigan U (MI)

Central State U (OH)
Central Washington U (WA)
City Coll of the City U of New York (NY)
Clarion U of Pennsylvania (PA)
Clark Atlanta U (GA)
Clemson U (SC)
Coe Coll (IA)
Colby Coll (ME)
Colby-Sawyer Coll (NH)
Colgate U (NY)
The Coll of Idaho (ID)
Coll of Saint Benedict (MN)
Coll of Saint Elizabeth (NJ)
Coll of Saint Mary (NE)
The Coll of St. Scholastica (MN)
Columbia Coll (MO)
Concordia Coll (MN)
Concordia U Chicago (IL)
Concordia U, St. Paul (MN)
Concordia U Wisconsin (WI)
Cornell Coll (IA)
Creighton U (NE)
Culver-Stockton Coll (MO)
Dallas Baptist U (TX)
Davidson Coll (NC)
DePaul U (IL)
Dickinson Coll (PA)
Dickinson State U (ND)
Dillard U (LA)
Doane U (NE)
Dominican U of California (CA)
Drake U (IA)
Earlham Coll (IN)
East Central U (OK)
Eastern Illinois U (IL)
Eastern Kentucky U (KY)
Eastern Mennonite U (VA)
Eastern Michigan U (MI)
Eastern New Mexico U (NM)
Eastern Oregon U (OR)
Edgewood Coll (WI)
Edinboro U of Pennsylvania (PA)
Elms Coll (MA)
Elon U (NC)
Emporia State U (KS)
Evangel U (MO)
Fairleigh Dickinson U (NJ)
Fayetteville State U (NC)
Felician U (NJ)
Florida Atlantic U (FL)
Florida Gulf Coast U (FL)
Fort Lewis Coll (CO)
Framingham State U (MA)
Francis Marion U (SC)
Freed-Hardeman U (TN)
Friends U (KS)
George Fox U (OR)
The George Washington U (DC)
Georgia Coll & State U (GA)
Georgian Court U (NJ)
Georgia Southern U (GA)
Gonzaga U (WA)
Gordon Coll (MA)
Goshen Coll (IN)
Governors State U (IL)
Graceland U (IA)
Grinnell Coll (IA)
Guilford Coll (NC)
Gustavus Adolphus Coll (MN)
Hampton U (VA)
Hanover Coll (IN)
Hardin-Simmons U (TX)
Hillsdale Coll (MI)
Hobart and William Smith Colls (NY)
Hollins U (VA)
Howard U (DC)
Illinois Coll (IL)
Illinois State U (IL)
Illinois Wesleyan U (IL)
Indiana State U (IN)
Indiana U Bloomington (IN)
Indiana U East (IN)
Indiana U Kokomo (IN)
Indiana U of Pennsylvania (PA)
Indiana U South Bend (IN)
Indiana U Southeast (IN)
Inter American U of Puerto Rico, San Germán Campus (PR)
Ithaca Coll (NY)
Jacksonville State U (AL)
Jacksonville U (FL)
James Madison U (VA)
Kalamazoo Coll (MI)
Kansas State U (KS)
Kean U (NJ)
Kennesaw State U (GA)
Lafayette Coll (PA)
Lake Forest Coll (IL)
La Sierra U (CA)
Lehigh U (PA)
Lehman Coll of the City U of New York (NY)
Lesley U (MA)
Lewis U (IL)
Lincoln Memorial U (TN)
Linfield Coll (OR)
Lock Haven U of Pennsylvania (PA)
Louisiana Tech U (LA)
Loyola U Maryland (MD)
Marian U (IN)
Marietta Coll (OH)
Marshall U (WV)
McDaniel Coll (MD)
McNeese State U (LA)
Mercer U, Macon (GA)
Miami U (OH)
Miami U Hamilton (OH)
Miami U Middletown (OH)
Michigan State U (MI)
Middle Tennessee State U (TN)
Millersville U of Pennsylvania (PA)
Minnesota State U Mankato (MN)
Minot State U (ND)
Missouri Southern State U (MO)
Missouri State U (MO)
Missouri Valley Coll (MO)
Montana State U (MT)
Montclair State U (NJ)
Moravian Coll (PA)
Mount Mercy U (IA)
Mount Saint Mary's U (CA)
Mount Vernon Nazarene U (OH)
Muhlenberg Coll (PA)
Muskingum U (OH)
Nazareth Coll of Rochester (NY)
Nebraska Wesleyan U (NE)
New England Coll (NH)
New Jersey Inst of Technology (NJ)
Newman U (KS)
New Mexico Highlands U (NM)
North Carolina Central U (NC)
Northeastern Illinois U (IL)
Northeastern State U (OK)
Northern Illinois U (IL)
Northern State U (SD)
Northwestern Coll (IA)
Northwestern U (IL)
Northwest Nazarene U (ID)
Oakland City U (IN)
Oberlin Coll (OH)
Occidental Coll (CA)
Oglethorpe U (GA)
Ohio Dominican U (OH)
The Ohio State U (OH)
Oklahoma Baptist U (OK)
Oklahoma State U (OK)
Old Dominion U (VA)
Olivet Nazarene U (IL)
Oral Roberts U (OK)
Otis Coll of Art and Design (CA)
Ottawa U (KS)
Pacific U (OR)
Penn State Abington (PA)
Penn State Altoona (PA)
Penn State Beaver (PA)
Penn State Berks (PA)
Penn State Brandywine (PA)
Penn State DuBois (PA)
Penn State Erie, The Behrend Coll (PA)
Penn State Fayette, The Eberly Campus (PA)
Penn State Greater Allegheny (PA)
Penn State Hazleton (PA)
Penn State Lehigh Valley (PA)
Penn State Mont Alto (PA)
Penn State New Kensington (PA)
Penn State Schuylkill (PA)
Penn State Shenango (PA)
Penn State U Park (PA)
Penn State Wilkes-Barre (PA)
Penn State York (PA)
Pepperdine U, Malibu (CA)
Pittsburg State U (KS)
Pomona Coll (CA)
Portland State U (OR)
Pratt Inst (NY)
Providence Coll (RI)
Purchase Coll, State U of New York (NY)
Purdue U Fort Wayne (IN)
Radford U (VA)
Rhodes Coll (TN)
Rice U (TX)
Roanoke Coll (VA)
Roberts Wesleyan Coll (NY)
Rocky Mountain Coll (MT)
Roger Williams U (RI)
Rollins Coll (FL)
Sacred Heart U (CT)
Saginaw Valley State U (MI)
St. Catherine U (MN)
St. Cloud State U (MN)
Saint John's U (MN)
Saint Joseph's U (PA)
Saint Mary's Coll (IN)
Saint Mary's Coll of California (CA)
St. Mary's Coll of Maryland (MD)
St. Norbert Coll (WI)
St. Olaf Coll (MN)
Salem State U (MA)
Salisbury U (MD)
Sam Houston State U (TX)
San Diego State U (CA)
San Francisco State U (CA)
San Jose State U (CA)
Scripps Coll (CA)
Shepherd U (WV)
Siena Heights U (MI)
Sierra Nevada Coll (NV)
Simmons U (MA)
Simon Fraser U (BC, Canada)
Skidmore Coll (NY)
Slippery Rock U of Pennsylvania (PA)
Smith Coll (MA)
Southeastern Louisiana U (LA)
Southeast Missouri State U (MO)
Southern Arkansas U–Magnolia (AR)
Southern Illinois U Carbondale (IL)
Southern Illinois U Edwardsville (IL)
Southwest Baptist U (MO)
Spring Arbor U (MI)
Springfield Coll (MA)
Stanford U (CA)
State U of New York at Fredonia (NY)
State U of New York at Oswego (NY)
State U of New York Coll at Old Westbury (NY)
State U of New York Coll at Oneonta (NY)
State U of New York Coll at Potsdam (NY)
State U of New York Empire State Coll (NY)
Sterling Coll (KS)
Stetson U (FL)
Stony Brook U, State U of New York (NY)
Susquehanna U (PA)
Tarleton State U (TX)
Taylor U (IN)
Texas A&M U–Corpus Christi (TX)
Texas Lutheran U (TX)
Texas State U (TX)
Texas Tech U (TX)
Texas Woman's U (TX)
Tiffin U (OH)
Towson U (MD)
Transylvania U (KY)
Trinity U (TX)
Troy U (AL)
Truman State U (MO)
Tulane U (LA)
Union U (TN)
U at Albany, State U of New York (NY)
U at Buffalo, the State U of New York (NY)
The U of Alabama at Birmingham (AL)
The U of Alabama in Huntsville (AL)
U of Alaska Fairbanks (AK)
U of Arkansas (AR)
U of Arkansas at Little Rock (AR)
U of California, Berkeley (CA)
U of California, Los Angeles (CA)
U of California, Riverside (CA)
U of California, San Diego (CA)
U of California, Santa Cruz (CA)
U of Central Arkansas (AR)
U of Central Florida (FL)
U of Charleston (WV)
U of Dallas (TX)
U of Denver (CO)
The U of Findlay (OH)
U of Hawaii at Manoa (HI)
U of Houston (TX)
U of Idaho (ID)
The U of Iowa (IA)
U of Jamestown (ND)
U of La Verne (CA)
U of Louisiana at Lafayette (LA)
U of Maine at Presque Isle (ME)
U of Massachusetts Boston (MA)
U of Memphis (TN)
U of Miami (FL)
U of Michigan (MI)
U of Minnesota, Duluth (MN)
U of Minnesota, Twin Cities Campus (MN)
U of Montana (MT)
U of Montevallo (AL)
U of Nebraska at Kearney (NE)
U of Nevada, Las Vegas (NV)
U of Nevada, Reno (NV)
U of New Hampshire (NH)
U of New Mexico (NM)
The U of North Carolina at Greensboro (NC)
U of North Dakota (ND)
U of Northern Iowa (IA)
U of North Florida (FL)
U of North Texas (TX)
U of Oregon (OR)
U of Pikeville (KY)
U of Providence (MT)
U of Puget Sound (WA)
U of Saint Mary (KS)
U of San Diego (CA)
U of Science and Arts of Oklahoma (OK)
U of South Alabama (AL)
U of South Dakota (SD)
U of Southern Indiana (IN)
U of South Florida (FL)
U of South Florida, St. Petersburg (FL)
The U of Tampa (FL)
The U of Tennessee at Chattanooga (TN)
The U of Texas at El Paso (TX)
The U of Texas at San Antonio (TX)
The U of Texas of the Permian Basin (TX)
The U of Texas Rio Grande Valley (TX)
U of the Incarnate Word (TX)
U of the Pacific (CA)
The U of Toledo (OH)
U of Utah (UT)
U of Virginia (VA)
U of Washington (WA)
The U of Western Ontario (ON, Canada)
U of West Florida (FL)
U of West Georgia (GA)
U of Wisconsin–Eau Claire (WI)
U of Wisconsin–Green Bay (WI)
U of Wisconsin–La Crosse (WI)
U of Wisconsin–Madison (WI)
U of Wisconsin–Milwaukee (WI)
U of Wisconsin–Parkside (WI)
U of Wisconsin–Platteville (WI)
U of Wyoming (WY)
Upper Iowa U (IA)
Utah State U (UT)
Valdosta State U (GA)
Valley City State U (ND)
Valparaiso U (IN)
Virginia Wesleyan U (VA)
Wabash Coll (IN)
Walla Walla U (WA)
Warren Wilson Coll (NC)
Wartburg Coll (IA)
Washington & Jefferson Coll (PA)
Washington Coll (MD)
Washington U in St. Louis (MO)
Wayland Baptist U (TX)
Waynesburg U (PA)
Wayne State Coll (NE)
Wayne State U (MI)
Weber State U (UT)
Western Carolina U (NC)
Western Connecticut State U (CT)
Western Michigan U (MI)
Western New Mexico U (NM)
Western Oregon U (OR)
Western Washington U (WA)
Westfield State U (MA)
Westminster Coll (UT)
Westmont Coll (CA)
West Virginia U (WV)
Wheaton Coll (IL)
Whitworth U (WA)
Wichita State U (KS)
Willamette U (OR)
William & Mary (VA)
William Paterson U of New Jersey (NJ)
William Penn U (IA)
Williams Coll (MA)
Winthrop U (SC)
Wittenberg U (OH)
Worcester State U (MA)
Wright State U (OH)
Wright State U–Lake Campus (OH)
Xavier U (OH)
Xavier U of Louisiana (LA)
Yale U (CT)
Youngstown State U (OH)

ART HISTORY, CRITICISM AND CONSERVATION

Academy of Art U (CA)
Adams State U (CO)
Agnes Scott Coll (GA)
Albion Coll (MI)
Alfred U (NY)
American U (DC)
The American U of Paris (France)
Aquinas Coll (MI)
Arcadia U (PA)
Augsburg U (MN)
Augustana Coll (IL)
Baker U (KS)
Barnard Coll (NY)
Baylor U (TX)
Belmont U (TN)
Beloit Coll (WI)
Bennington Coll (VT)
Binghamton U, State U of New York (NY)
Birmingham-Southern Coll (AL)
Boston Coll (MA)
Bowdoin Coll (ME)
Bowling Green State U (OH)
Bradley U (IL)
Brandeis U (MA)
Bridgewater State U (MA)
Bucknell U (PA)
California State Polytechnic U, Pomona (CA)
California State U, Dominguez Hills (CA)
California State U, Fullerton (CA)
California State U, Long Beach (CA)
California State U, Stanislaus (CA)
Carleton Coll (MN)
Carthage Coll (WI)
The Catholic U of America (DC)
Central Michigan U (MI)
Centre Coll (KY)
Chatham U (PA)
City Coll of the City U of New York (NY)
Clark U (MA)
Coastal Carolina U (SC)
Coe Coll (IA)
Colby Coll (ME)
Coll of Charleston (SC)
Coll of the Holy Cross (MA)
The Coll of Wooster (OH)
The Colorado Coll (CO)
Columbia Coll Chicago (IL)
Cornell Coll (IA)
Cornell U (NY)
Creighton U (NE)
Dartmouth Coll (NH)
DePaul U (IL)
DePauw U (IN)
Dominican U of California (CA)
Drake U (IA)
Drew U (NJ)
Drury U (MO)
Eastern Michigan U (MI)
Eastern Washington U (WA)
Elon U (NC)
Emory U (GA)
Fairfield U (CT)
Ferris State U (MI)
Flagler Coll (FL)
Florida Southern Coll (FL)
Florida State U (FL)

Fordham U (NY)
Franklin Coll (IN)
Furman U (SC)
Gallaudet U (DC)
George Mason U (VA)
Georgetown U (DC)
The George Washington U (DC)
Goucher Coll (MD)
Grand Valley State U (MI)
Grinnell Coll (IA)
Gustavus Adolphus Coll (MN)
Hamline U (MN)
Hampshire Coll (MA)
Hanover Coll (IN)
Harvard U (MA)
Hobart and William Smith Colls (NY)
Hofstra U (NY)
Hollins U (VA)
Holy Apostles Coll and Sem (CT)
Hope Coll (MI)
Indiana U Bloomington (IN)
Indiana U-Purdue U Indianapolis (IN)
Ithaca Coll (NY)
Jacksonville U (FL)
James Madison U (VA)
John Cabot U (Italy)
John Carroll U (OH)
Johns Hopkins U (MD)
Kalamazoo Coll (MI)
Kennesaw State U (GA)
Kenyon Coll (OH)
Knox Coll (IL)
Kutztown U of Pennsylvania (PA)
Lake Forest Coll (IL)
Lawrence U (WI)
Lehigh U (PA)
Lehman Coll of the City U of New York (NY)
Lewis & Clark Coll (OR)
Lindenwood U (MO)
Loyola Marymount U (CA)
Loyola U Chicago (IL)
Loyola U Maryland (MD)
Manhattanville Coll (NY)
Mansfield U of Pennsylvania (PA)
Massachusetts Coll of Art and Design (MA)
McDaniel Coll (MD)
Merrimack Coll (MA)
Messiah Coll (PA)
Miami U (OH)
Miami U Hamilton (OH)
Miami U Middletown (OH)
Michigan State U (MI)
Middlebury Coll (VT)
Minnesota State U Mankato (MN)
Missouri State U (MO)
Mount Holyoke Coll (MA)
Muhlenberg Coll (PA)
Nazareth Coll of Rochester (NY)
New Coll of Florida (FL)
New York U (NY)
Niagara U (NY)
Northern Illinois U (IL)
Northwestern U (IL)
Oakland U (MI)
Oberlin Coll (OH)
Oglethorpe U (GA)
The Ohio State U (OH)
Ohio Wesleyan U (OH)
Old Dominion U (VA)
Penn State Abington (PA)
Penn State Altoona (PA)
Penn State Beaver (PA)
Penn State Berks (PA)
Penn State Brandywine (PA)
Penn State DuBois (PA)
Penn State Erie, The Behrend Coll (PA)
Penn State Fayette, The Eberly Campus (PA)
Penn State Greater Allegheny (PA)
Penn State Hazleton (PA)
Penn State Lehigh Valley (PA)
Penn State Mont Alto (PA)
Penn State New Kensington (PA)
Penn State Schuylkill (PA)
Penn State Shenango (PA)
Penn State U Park (PA)
Penn State Wilkes-Barre (PA)
Penn State York (PA)
Pepperdine U, Malibu (CA)
Pomona Coll (CA)
Portland State U (OR)
Pratt Inst (NY)
Princeton U (NJ)
Providence Coll (RI)
Purchase Coll, State U of New York (NY)
Queens Coll of the City U of New York (NY)
Queens U of Charlotte (NC)
Randolph Coll (VA)
Randolph-Macon Coll (VA)
Rhode Island Coll (RI)
Rice U (TX)
Roanoke Coll (VA)
Roger Williams U (RI)
Rollins Coll (FL)
Rosemont Coll (PA)
St. Ambrose U (IA)
St. Catherine U (MN)
St. Cloud State U (MN)
Saint Louis U (MO)
St. Mary's Coll of Maryland (MD)
St. Olaf Coll (MN)
Saint Vincent Coll (PA)
Salem State U (MA)
Salve Regina U (RI)
San Diego State U (CA)
San Francisco Art Inst (CA)
San Jose State U (CA)
Santa Clara U (CA)
Sarah Lawrence Coll (NY)
Scripps Coll (CA)
Seattle U (WA)
Seton Hill U (PA)
Siena Heights U (MI)
Skidmore Coll (NY)
Smith Coll (MA)
Southern Methodist U (TX)
Southwestern U (TX)
Stanford U (CA)
State U of New York at Fredonia (NY)
State U of New York at New Paltz (NY)
State U of New York Coll at Cortland (NY)
State U of New York Coll at Geneseo (NY)
State U of New York Coll at Oneonta (NY)
State U of New York Coll at Potsdam (NY)
Stetson U (FL)
Stony Brook U, State U of New York (NY)
Suffolk U (MA)
Susquehanna U (PA)
Temple U (PA)
Texas Christian U (TX)
Texas State U (TX)
Towson U (MD)
Transylvania U (KY)
Trinity U (TX)
Tulane U (LA)
U at Albany, State U of New York (NY)
U at Buffalo, the State U of New York (NY)
The U of Akron (OH)
The U of Alabama (AL)
The U of Arizona (AZ)
U of Arkansas (AR)
U of California, Berkeley (CA)
U of California, Irvine (CA)
U of California, Los Angeles (CA)
U of California, Riverside (CA)
U of California, San Diego (CA)
U of California, Santa Barbara (CA)
U of California, Santa Cruz (CA)
U of Cincinnati (OH)
U of Colorado Boulder (CO)
U of Dallas (TX)
U of Dayton (OH)
U of Denver (CO)
U of Hartford (CT)
U of Houston (TX)
U of Illinois at Chicago (IL)
The U of Iowa (IA)
The U of Kansas (KS)
U of Kentucky (KY)
U of La Verne (CA)
U of Louisville (KY)
U of Maine (ME)
U of Mary Washington (VA)
U of Massachusetts Amherst (MA)
U of Massachusetts Dartmouth (MA)
U of Memphis (TN)
U of Miami (FL)
U of Michigan (MI)
U of Michigan–Dearborn (MI)
U of Michigan–Flint (MI)
U of Minnesota, Duluth (MN)
U of Minnesota, Morris (MN)
U of Minnesota, Twin Cities Campus (MN)
U of Missouri–St. Louis (MO)
U of Nebraska–Lincoln (NE)
U of Nevada, Las Vegas (NV)
U of Nevada, Reno (NV)
U of New Mexico (NM)
The U of North Carolina at Chapel Hill (NC)
The U of North Carolina at Charlotte (NC)
The U of North Carolina Wilmington (NC)
U of Northern Iowa (IA)
U of North Florida (FL)
U of North Texas (TX)
U of Notre Dame (IN)
U of Oregon (OR)
U of Pennsylvania (PA)
U of Richmond (VA)
U of Saint Francis (IN)
U of Saint Joseph (CT)
U of San Diego (CA)
U of San Francisco (CA)
U of South Carolina (SC)
U of South Florida (FL)
The U of Tennessee (TN)
The U of Texas at El Paso (TX)
The U of Texas at San Antonio (TX)
U of the Pacific (CA)
The U of the South (TN)
The U of Toledo (OH)
The U of Tulsa (OK)
U of Utah (UT)
U of Vermont (VT)
U of Washington (WA)
U of Waterloo (ON, Canada)
The U of Western Ontario (ON, Canada)
U of West Florida (FL)
U of Wisconsin–Madison (WI)
U of Wisconsin–Milwaukee (WI)
U of Wisconsin–Superior (WI)
U of Wyoming (WY)
Utah State U (UT)
Vanderbilt U (TN)
Villanova U (PA)
Virginia Commonwealth U (VA)
Wake Forest U (NC)
Washington and Lee U (VA)
Washington U in St. Louis (MO)
Wayne State U (MI)
Wesleyan U (CT)
Western Kentucky U (KY)
Western Michigan U (MI)
Western Washington U (WA)
West Virginia U (WV)
Wheaton Coll (MA)
Whitworth U (WA)
Willamette U (OR)
William & Mary (VA)
William Paterson U of New Jersey (NJ)
Williams Coll (MA)
Winthrop U (SC)
Wittenberg U (OH)
Wofford Coll (SC)
Wright State U (OH)
Wright State U–Lake Campus (OH)
Yale U (CT)
Youngstown State U (OH)

ARTIFICIAL INTELLIGENCE

Carnegie Mellon U (PA)
Indiana U Bloomington (IN)

ARTS, ENTERTAINMENT, AND MEDIA MANAGEMENT

Anderson U (IN)
Belmont U (TN)
Butler U (IN)
California State U, San Marcos (CA)
Champlain Coll (VT)
Columbia Coll Chicago (IL)
Dean Coll (MA)
Drexel U (PA)
Drury U (MO)
Elon U (NC)
Kansas Wesleyan U (KS)
Loyola U New Orleans (LA)
Millikin U (IL)
National U (CA)
Schreiner U (TX)
Shenandoah U (VA)
State U of New York at Fredonia (NY)
U of Central Florida (FL)
The U of Findlay (OH)
U of Kentucky (KY)
U of Wisconsin–Green Bay (WI)

ARTS, ENTERTAINMENT, AND MEDIA MANAGEMENT RELATED

Belmont U (TN)
Delta State U (MS)
Loyola U New Orleans (LA)
U of New Haven (CT)
Wesleyan Coll (GA)

ART TEACHER EDUCATION

Academy of Art U (CA)
Adams State U (CO)
Alfred U (NY)
Alverno Coll (WI)
Anderson U (SC)
Andrews U (MI)
Appalachian State U (NC)
Arkansas Tech U (AR)
Augustana Coll (IL)
Augustana U (SD)
Averett U (VA)
Baker U (KS)
Baylor U (TX)
Belmont U (TN)
Beloit Coll (WI)
Benedictine Coll (KS)
Berry Coll (GA)
Bethany Lutheran Coll (MN)
Bethel U (IN)
Bethel U (MN)
Birmingham-Southern Coll (AL)
Boise State U (ID)
Bowling Green State U (OH)
Bradley U (IL)
Bridgewater State U (MA)
California Lutheran U (CA)
California State U, Long Beach (CA)
Calvin Coll (MI)
Campbellsville U (KY)
Capital U (OH)
Carlow U (PA)
Carson-Newman U (TN)
Central Christian Coll of Kansas (KS)
Central Connecticut State U (CT)
Central Michigan U (MI)
Central State U (OH)
City Coll of the City U of New York (NY)
Coe Coll (IA)
Coll of Saint Mary (NE)
Coll of the Ozarks (MO)
Concordia Coll (MN)
Concordia U Chicago (IL)
Concordia U, St. Paul (MN)
Concordia U Wisconsin (WI)
Culver-Stockton Coll (MO)
DePaul U (IL)
Dickinson State U (ND)
East Carolina U (NC)
East Central U (OK)
Eastern Michigan U (MI)
Eastern Washington U (WA)
Edgewood Coll (WI)
Edinboro U of Pennsylvania (PA)
Emory & Henry Coll (VA)
Evangel U (MO)
Fayetteville State U (NC)
Ferris State U (MI)
Flagler Coll (FL)
Florida Southern Coll (FL)
Francis Marion U (SC)
Friends U (KS)
Gallaudet U (DC)
Georgia Southern U (GA)
Georgia State U (GA)
Goshen Coll (IN)
Graceland U (IA)
Grand Valley State U (MI)
Gustavus Adolphus Coll (MN)
Hampton U (VA)
Harding U (AR)
Hardin-Simmons U (TX)
Hofstra U (NY)
Hope Coll (MI)
Houston Baptist U (TX)
Indiana State U (IN)
Indiana U Bloomington (IN)
Indiana U-Purdue U Indianapolis (IN)
Indiana U South Bend (IN)
Inter American U of Puerto Rico, San Germán Campus (PR)
Ithaca Coll (NY)
Jacksonville U (FL)
Kansas State U (KS)
Kansas Wesleyan U (KS)
Kennesaw State U (GA)
Kutztown U of Pennsylvania (PA)
Lee U (TN)
Lehman Coll of the City U of New York (NY)
Lincoln Memorial U (TN)
Lincoln U (MO)
Lipscomb U (TN)
Louisiana Tech U (LA)
Manhattanville Coll (NY)
Marywood U (PA)
Massachusetts Coll of Art and Design (MA)
McKendree U (IL)
McMurry U (TX)
Meredith Coll (NC)
Messiah Coll (PA)
Miami U (OH)
Miami U Hamilton (OH)
Miami U Middletown (OH)
Michigan State U (MI)
Middle Tennessee State U (TN)
Millikin U (IL)
Minnesota State U Mankato (MN)
Minot State U (ND)
Missouri State U (MO)
Molloy Coll (NY)
Mount Mercy U (IA)
Mount Vernon Nazarene U (OH)
Muskingum U (OH)
Nazareth Coll of Rochester (NY)
New York U (NY)
Northeastern State U (OK)
Northern Arizona U (AZ)
Northern Illinois U (IL)
Northern State U (SD)
Northwestern Coll (IA)
Northwest Missouri State U (MO)
Northwest Nazarene U (ID)
Nova Southeastern U (FL)
Ohio Dominican U (OH)
The Ohio State U (OH)
Ohio Wesleyan U (OH)
Olivet Nazarene U (IL)
Oral Roberts U (OK)
Ottawa U (KS)
Pacific U (OR)
Palm Beach Atlantic U (FL)
Penn State Abington (PA)
Penn State Altoona (PA)
Penn State Beaver (PA)
Penn State Berks (PA)
Penn State Brandywine (PA)
Penn State DuBois (PA)
Penn State Erie, The Behrend Coll (PA)
Penn State Fayette, The Eberly Campus (PA)
Penn State Greater Allegheny (PA)
Penn State Hazleton (PA)
Penn State Lehigh Valley (PA)
Penn State Mont Alto (PA)
Penn State New Kensington (PA)
Penn State Schuylkill (PA)
Penn State Shenango (PA)
Penn State U Park (PA)
Penn State Wilkes-Barre (PA)
Penn State York (PA)
Point Loma Nazarene U (CA)
Portland State U (OR)
Pratt Inst (NY)
Purdue U Fort Wayne (IN)
Queens Coll of the City U of New York (NY)
Rhode Island Coll (RI)
Roanoke Coll (VA)
Rocky Mountain Coll (MT)
Saginaw Valley State U (MI)
St. Ambrose U (IA)
St. Catherine U (MN)
St. Cloud State U (MN)
Saint Joseph's U (PA)
Saint Mary-of-the-Woods Coll (IN)
St. Mary's U (TX)
Saint Vincent Coll (PA)
Salem State U (MA)
Seton Hill U (PA)

Siena Heights U (MI)
Southeast Missouri State U (MO)
Southern Arkansas U–Magnolia (AR)
Southwest Baptist U (MO)
Southwestern Oklahoma State U (OK)
Spring Arbor U (MI)
State U of New York at New Paltz (NY)
State U of New York Coll at Potsdam (NY)
Sterling Coll (KS)
Taylor U (IN)
Texas Christian U (TX)
Texas Lutheran U (TX)
Towson U (MD)
Transylvania U (KY)
Union U (TN)
The U of Akron (OH)
The U of Arizona (AZ)
U of Arkansas (AR)
U of Cincinnati (OH)
U of Dayton (OH)
U of Denver (CO)
The U of Findlay (OH)
U of Illinois at Chicago (IL)
The U of Iowa (IA)
The U of Kansas (KS)
U of Kentucky (KY)
U of Maine (ME)
U of Mary Hardin-Baylor (TX)
U of Massachusetts Dartmouth (MA)
U of Michigan–Flint (MI)
U of Minnesota, Duluth (MN)
U of New Mexico (NM)
The U of North Carolina at Greensboro (NC)
The U of North Carolina at Pembroke (NC)
U of Northern Iowa (IA)
U of North Florida (FL)
U of Northwestern–St. Paul (MN)
U of Providence (MT)
U of St. Francis (IL)
U of Saint Francis (IN)
U of South Carolina (SC)
U of South Dakota (SD)
U of Southern Maine (ME)
The U of Tennessee at Chattanooga (TN)
U of Vermont (VT)
U of Wisconsin–Madison (WI)
U of Wisconsin–Milwaukee (WI)
U of Wisconsin–Stout (WI)
U of Wisconsin–Superior (WI)
U of Wyoming (WY)
Upper Iowa U (IA)
Ursuline Coll (OH)
Utah Valley U (UT)
Valdosta State U (GA)
Valley City State U (ND)
Valparaiso U (IN)
Virginia Commonwealth U (VA)
Virginia Wesleyan U (VA)
Walla Walla U (WA)
Washington & Jefferson Coll (PA)
Washington U in St. Louis (MO)
Wayne State Coll (NE)
Weber State U (UT)
Western Carolina U (NC)
Western Michigan U (MI)
Western New Mexico U (NM)
Western Washington U (WA)
West Liberty U (WV)
Whitworth U (WA)
Wilmington Coll (OH)
Xavier U of Louisiana (LA)
Youngstown State U (OH)

ART THERAPY
Alverno Coll (WI)
Arcadia U (PA)
Bluffton U (OH)
Bowling Green State U (OH)
Capital U (OH)
Carlow U (PA)
Cedar Crest Coll (PA)
Concordia U Chicago (IL)
Edgewood Coll (WI)
Emmanuel Coll (MA)
Harding U (AR)
Houston Baptist U (TX)
Howard U (DC)
Kansas Wesleyan U (KS)
Lesley U (MA)
Lipscomb U (TN)
Marywood U (PA)
Miami U Hamilton (OH)
Miami U Middletown (OH)
Millikin U (IL)
Northwestern Coll (IA)
St. Thomas Aquinas Coll (NY)
Seton Hill U (PA)
Sierra Nevada Coll (NV)
Springfield Coll (MA)
U of Saint Francis (IN)
The U of Tampa (FL)
U of Wisconsin–Superior (WI)
Ursuline Coll (OH)

ASIAN AMERICAN STUDIES
Arizona State U at the Tempe campus (AZ)
Binghamton U, State U of New York (NY)
California State U, Fullerton (CA)
California State U, Long Beach (CA)
California State U, Los Angeles (CA)
California State U, Northridge (CA)
New York U (NY)
Pitzer Coll (CA)
Pomona Coll (CA)
San Francisco State U (CA)
Scripps Coll (CA)
Stanford U (CA)
U of California, Berkeley (CA)
U of California, Irvine (CA)
U of California, Los Angeles (CA)
U of California, Riverside (CA)
U of California, Santa Barbara (CA)
U of Denver (CO)

ASIAN HISTORY
Sarah Lawrence Coll (NY)
U of Washington, Tacoma (WA)

ASIAN STUDIES
American U (DC)
Amherst Coll (MA)
Arizona State U at the Tempe campus (AZ)
Augustana Coll (IL)
Austin Coll (TX)
Barnard Coll (NY)
Baylor U (TX)
Belmont U (TN)
Bennington Coll (VT)
Berea Coll (KY)
Binghamton U, State U of New York (NY)
Birmingham-Southern Coll (AL)
Bowdoin Coll (ME)
Bowling Green State U (OH)
California State U, Long Beach (CA)
California State U, Sacramento (CA)
Calvin Coll (MI)
Carleton Coll (MN)
Carthage Coll (WI)
City Coll of the City U of New York (NY)
Claremont McKenna Coll (CA)
Clark U (MA)
Coe Coll (IA)
Colgate U (NY)
Coll of Saint Benedict (MN)
Coll of the Holy Cross (MA)
The Colorado Coll (CO)
Cornell U (NY)
Dartmouth Coll (NH)
Florida State U (FL)
Furman U (SC)
The George Washington U (DC)
Gonzaga U (WA)
Hobart and William Smith Colls (NY)
Illinois Wesleyan U (IL)
Indiana U of Pennsylvania (PA)
John Carroll U (OH)
Kean U (NJ)
Kennesaw State U (GA)
Kenyon Coll (OH)
Knox Coll (IL)
Lake Forest Coll (IL)
Lehigh U (PA)
Lewis & Clark Coll (OR)
Loyola Marymount U (CA)
McDaniel Coll (MD)
Northwestern U (IL)
Old Dominion U (VA)
Penn State U Park (PA)
Pepperdine U, Malibu (CA)
Pomona Coll (CA)
Randolph-Macon Coll (VA)
Rice U (TX)
Rollins Coll (FL)
Saint John's U (MN)
Saint Joseph's U (PA)
Saint Mary's Coll of California (CA)
St. Mary's Coll of Maryland (MD)
St. Olaf Coll (MN)
San Diego State U (CA)
Sarah Lawrence Coll (NY)
Scripps Coll (CA)
Seattle U (WA)
Skidmore Coll (NY)
State U of New York at New Paltz (NY)
Stony Brook U, State U of New York (NY)
Suffolk U (MA)
Temple U (PA)
Trinity U (TX)
Tulane U (LA)
Union Coll (NY)
U at Albany, State U of New York (NY)
U at Buffalo, the State U of New York (NY)
U of California, Berkeley (CA)
U of California, Riverside (CA)
U of California, Santa Barbara (CA)
U of Cincinnati (OH)
U of Colorado Boulder (CO)
U of Hawaii at Manoa (HI)
The U of Iowa (IA)
U of Louisville (KY)
U of Maryland, Baltimore County (MD)
U of Maryland Global Campus (MD)
U of Massachusetts Boston (MA)
U of Michigan (MI)
U of Montana (MT)
U of Nevada, Las Vegas (NV)
U of New Mexico (NM)
The U of North Carolina at Chapel Hill (NC)
U of Northern Colorado (CO)
U of Oregon (OR)
U of Richmond (VA)
U of San Francisco (CA)
The U of the South (TN)
The U of Toledo (OH)
U of Toronto (ON, Canada)
U of Utah (UT)
U of Vermont (VT)
U of Washington (WA)
The U of Western Ontario (ON, Canada)
U of Wisconsin–Madison (WI)
Utah State U (UT)
Vanderbilt U (TN)
Washington State U (WA)
Washington U in St. Louis (MO)
Western Kentucky U (KY)
Willamette U (OR)
William Paterson U of New Jersey (NJ)
Williams Coll (MA)

ASIAN STUDIES (EAST)
Austin Coll (TX)
Bates Coll (ME)
Binghamton U, State U of New York (NY)
Brandeis U (MA)
Brown U (RI)
Bucknell U (PA)
Colby Coll (ME)
Davidson Coll (NC)
DePaul U (IL)
DePauw U (IN)
Dickinson Coll (PA)
Emory & Henry Coll (VA)
Emory U (GA)
The George Washington U (DC)
Grand Valley State U (MI)
Hampshire Coll (MA)
Harvard U (MA)
Hofstra U (NY)
Indiana U Bloomington (IN)
Johns Hopkins U (MD)
Kalamazoo Coll (MI)
Lawrence U (WI)
Miami U (OH)
Miami U Hamilton (OH)
Miami U Middletown (OH)
Middlebury Coll (VT)
Mount Holyoke Coll (MA)
New York U (NY)
Oberlin Coll (OH)
Occidental Coll (CA)
Ohio Wesleyan U (OH)
Penn State Abington (PA)
Penn State Altoona (PA)
Penn State Beaver (PA)
Penn State Berks (PA)
Penn State Brandywine (PA)
Penn State DuBois (PA)
Penn State Erie, The Behrend Coll (PA)
Penn State Fayette, The Eberly Campus (PA)
Penn State Greater Allegheny (PA)
Penn State Hazleton (PA)
Penn State Lehigh Valley (PA)
Penn State Mont Alto (PA)
Penn State New Kensington (PA)
Penn State Schuylkill (PA)
Penn State Shenango (PA)
Penn State York (PA)
Portland State U (OR)
Princeton U (NJ)
Queens Coll of the City U of New York (NY)
Simmons U (MA)
Smith Coll (MA)
Stanford U (CA)
Trinity U (TX)
United States Military Acad (NY)
U at Albany, State U of New York (NY)
The U of Arizona (AZ)
U of California, Irvine (CA)
U of Montana (MT)
U of Pennsylvania (PA)
U of Toronto (ON, Canada)
The U of Western Ontario (ON, Canada)
Valparaiso U (IN)
Washington U in St. Louis (MO)
Wayne State U (MI)
Wesleyan U (CT)
Western Washington U (WA)
Willamette U (OR)
Wittenberg U (OH)
Yale U (CT)

ASIAN STUDIES (SOUTH)
Binghamton U, State U of New York (NY)
Brown U (RI)
Hampshire Coll (MA)
Indiana U Bloomington (IN)
Middlebury Coll (VT)
Mount Holyoke Coll (MA)
U of Pennsylvania (PA)
U of Toronto (ON, Canada)
U of Washington (WA)

ASIAN STUDIES (SOUTHEAST)
U of California, Berkeley (CA)
U of Washington (WA)

ASIAN STUDIES (URAL-ALTAIC AND CENTRAL)
Indiana U Bloomington (IN)

ASTRONOMY
Amherst Coll (MA)
Ball State U (IN)
Barnard Coll (NY)
Baylor U (TX)
Benedictine Coll (KS)
Bennington Coll (VT)
Berry Coll (GA)
Brigham Young U (UT)
Central Michigan U (MI)
Cornell U (NY)
Dartmouth Coll (NH)
Drake U (IA)
George Mason U (VA)
Hampshire Coll (MA)
Howard U (DC)
Indiana U Bloomington (IN)
Lehigh U (PA)
Minnesota State U Mankato (MN)
Mount Holyoke Coll (MA)
Northern Arizona U (AZ)
Northwestern U (IL)
The Ohio State U (OH)
Ohio Wesleyan U (OH)
Penn State Abington (PA)
Penn State Altoona (PA)
Penn State Beaver (PA)
Penn State Berks (PA)
Penn State Brandywine (PA)
Penn State DuBois (PA)
Penn State Erie, The Behrend Coll (PA)
Penn State Fayette, The Eberly Campus (PA)
Penn State Greater Allegheny (PA)
Penn State Hazleton (PA)
Penn State Lehigh Valley (PA)
Penn State Mont Alto (PA)
Penn State New Kensington (PA)
Penn State Schuylkill (PA)
Penn State Shenango (PA)
Penn State U Park (PA)
Penn State Wilkes-Barre (PA)
Penn State York (PA)
Pomona Coll (CA)
Rice U (TX)
San Diego State U (CA)
San Francisco State U (CA)
Smith Coll (MA)
State U of New York at New Paltz (NY)
Stony Brook U, State U of New York (NY)
Union Coll (NY)
The U of Arizona (AZ)
U of Colorado Boulder (CO)
U of Hawaii at Manoa (HI)
The U of Iowa (IA)
The U of Kansas (KS)
U of Massachusetts Amherst (MA)
U of Michigan (MI)
U of Montana (MT)
The U of Toledo (OH)
U of Virginia (VA)
U of Washington (WA)
The U of Western Ontario (ON, Canada)
Valdosta State U (GA)
Valparaiso U (IN)
Villanova U (PA)
Wayne State U (MI)
Wesleyan U (CT)
Williams Coll (MA)
Yale U (CT)
Youngstown State U (OH)

ASTRONOMY AND ASTROPHYSICS RELATED
Butler U (IN)
Coll of Charleston (SC)
Emory U (GA)
Florida Inst of Technology (FL)
Harvard U (MA)
Texas Christian U (TX)
U of Wyoming (WY)
Wheaton Coll (MA)

ASTROPHYSICS
Agnes Scott Coll (GA)
Barnard Coll (NY)
Baylor U (TX)
Carnegie Mellon U (PA)
Colgate U (NY)
DePaul U (IL)
Florida State U (FL)
Illinois Inst of Technology (IL)
Lehigh U (PA)
Michigan State U (MI)
Ohio Wesleyan U (OH)
Princeton U (NJ)
Rice U (TX)
San Francisco State U (CA)
U of California, Berkeley (CA)
U of California, Los Angeles (CA)
U of California, Santa Cruz (CA)
U of Cincinnati (OH)
U of Hawaii at Manoa (HI)
U of Minnesota, Twin Cities Campus (MN)
U of New Mexico (NM)
The U of Western Ontario (ON, Canada)
U of Wisconsin–Madison (WI)
Villanova U (PA)
Williams Coll (MA)
Yale U (CT)

ATHLETIC TRAINING
Alfred U (NY)
Anderson U (IN)
Anderson U (SC)
Aquinas Coll (MI)
Augustana U (SD)
Averett U (VA)

Azusa Pacific U (CA)
Ball State U (IN)
Bethel U (MN)
Bowling Green State U (OH)
Bridgewater State U (MA)
Brigham Young U (UT)
California State U, Fullerton (CA)
California State U, Long Beach (CA)
California State U, Northridge (CA)
California U of Pennsylvania (PA)
Capital U (OH)
Carthage Coll (WI)
Catawba Coll (NC)
Cedarville U (OH)
Central Christian Coll of Kansas (KS)
Central Coll (IA)
Central Connecticut State U (CT)
Central Methodist U (MO)
Central Michigan U (MI)
Colby-Sawyer Coll (NH)
Concordia U Wisconsin (WI)
Culver-Stockton Coll (MO)
DePauw U (IN)
Dominican Coll (NY)
East Carolina U (NC)
East Central U (OK)
Eastern Illinois U (IL)
Eastern Kentucky U (KY)
Eastern Michigan U (MI)
Eastern Washington U (WA)
East Texas Baptist U (TX)
Emory & Henry Coll (VA)
Emporia State U (KS)
Endicott Coll (MA)
Florida Gulf Coast U (FL)
Florida State U (FL)
George Fox U (OR)
Georgetown Coll (KY)
Georgia Coll & State U (GA)
Georgia Southern U (GA)
Grand Valley State U (MI)
Gustavus Adolphus Coll (MN)
Harding U (AR)
Hardin-Simmons U (TX)
Hofstra U (NY)
Hope Coll (MI)
Illinois State U (IL)
Indiana U Bloomington (IN)
Iowa State U of Science and Technology (IA)
Ithaca Coll (NY)
James Madison U (VA)
Kansas State U (KS)
Kean U (NJ)
King's Coll (PA)
Lasell Coll (MA)
Lee U (TN)
Lewis U (IL)
Liberty U (VA)
Limestone Coll (SC)
Lincoln Memorial U (TN)
Longwood U (VA)
Loras Coll (IA)
Marietta Coll (OH)
Marquette U (WI)
Marshall U (WV)
Marywood U (PA)
McKendree U (IL)
Messiah Coll (PA)
Miami U (OH)
Miami U Hamilton (OH)
Miami U Middletown (OH)
Michigan State U (MI)
Middle Tennessee State U (TN)
Minot State U (ND)
Missouri State U (MO)
Missouri Valley Coll (MO)
Montclair State U (NJ)
Muskingum U (OH)
Nebraska Wesleyan U (NE)
North Carolina Central U (NC)
Northern Illinois U (IL)
Northwest Nazarene U (ID)
The Ohio State U (OH)
Oklahoma Baptist U (OK)
Olivet Nazarene U (IL)
Pacific U (OR)
Palm Beach Atlantic U (FL)
Penn State U Park (PA)
Radford U (VA)
Rowan U (NJ)
Sacred Heart U (CT)
Saginaw Valley State U (MI)
St. Cloud State U (MN)
Salem State U (MA)
Salisbury U (MD)
Sam Houston State U (TX)
San Diego State U (CA)
Slippery Rock U of Pennsylvania (PA)
Southeastern Louisiana U (LA)
Southeast Missouri State U (MO)
Southern Arkansas U–Magnolia (AR)
Southwest Baptist U (MO)
Southwestern Coll (KS)
Springfield Coll (MA)
State U of New York Coll at Cortland (NY)
Sterling Coll (KS)
Stony Brook U, State U of New York (NY)
SUNY Brockport (NY)
Texas A&M U–Corpus Christi (TX)
Texas Christian U (TX)
Texas Lutheran U (TX)
Texas State U (TX)
Tiffin U (OH)
Towson U (MD)
Troy U (AL)
Union U (TN)
The U of Akron (OH)
The U of Alabama (AL)
U of Central Florida (FL)
U of Cincinnati (OH)
The U of Iowa (IA)
The U of Kansas (KS)
U of Louisiana at Lafayette (LA)
U of Maine (ME)
U of Miami (FL)
U of Michigan (MI)
U of Minnesota, Duluth (MN)
U of Montana (MT)
U of Nebraska–Lincoln (NE)
U of Nevada, Las Vegas (NV)
U of New England (ME)
U of New Hampshire (NH)
The U of North Carolina at Pembroke (NC)
U of North Dakota (ND)
U of Northern Colorado (CO)
U of Northern Iowa (IA)
U of North Florida (FL)
U of Pittsburgh at Bradford (PA)
U of Puerto Rico–Ponce (PR)
U of Southern Maine (ME)
U of Southern Mississippi (MS)
The U of Tampa (FL)
The U of Texas of the Permian Basin (TX)
U of the Incarnate Word (TX)
The U of Tulsa (OK)
U of Utah (UT)
U of Vermont (VT)
The U of West Alabama (AL)
U of Wisconsin–La Crosse (WI)
U of Wisconsin–Madison (WI)
U of Wisconsin–Milwaukee (WI)
Upper Iowa U (IA)
Valdosta State U (GA)
Valley City State U (ND)
Washington State U (WA)
Wayne State Coll (NE)
Weber State U (UT)
West Chester U of Pennsylvania (PA)
Western Carolina U (NC)
Western Michigan U (MI)
Westfield State U (MA)
Wichita State U (KS)
William Paterson U of New Jersey (NJ)
Wilmington Coll (OH)
Wingate U (NC)
Winthrop U (SC)
Wright State U (OH)
Wright State U–Lake Campus (OH)
Xavier U (OH)
Youngstown State U (OH)

ATMOSPHERIC SCIENCES AND METEOROLOGY

Ball State U (IN)
Cornell U (NY)
George Mason U (VA)
Indiana U Bloomington (IN)
Millersville U of Pennsylvania (PA)
Northern Illinois U (IL)
The Ohio State U (OH)
Penn State Abington (PA)
Penn State Altoona (PA)
Penn State Beaver (PA)
Penn State Berks (PA)
Penn State Brandywine (PA)
Penn State DuBois (PA)
Penn State Erie, The Behrend Coll (PA)
Penn State Fayette, The Eberly Campus (PA)
Penn State Greater Allegheny (PA)
Penn State Hazleton (PA)
Penn State Lehigh Valley (PA)
Penn State Mont Alto (PA)
Penn State New Kensington (PA)
Penn State Schuylkill (PA)
Penn State Shenango (PA)
Penn State U Park (PA)
Penn State Wilkes-Barre (PA)
Penn State York (PA)
Saint Louis U (MO)
San Jose State U (CA)
State U of New York at Oswego (NY)
State U of New York Coll at Oneonta (NY)
State U of New York Maritime Coll (NY)
Stony Brook U, State U of New York (NY)
SUNY Brockport (NY)
Texas A&M U (TX)
Texas A&M U–Corpus Christi (TX)
U at Albany, State U of New York (NY)
U of California, Berkeley (CA)
U of Colorado Boulder (CO)
The U of Kansas (KS)
U of Louisiana at Monroe (LA)
U of Louisville (KY)
U of Miami (FL)
U of Michigan (MI)
U of Nebraska–Lincoln (NE)
U of Nevada, Reno (NV)
U of North Dakota (ND)
U of Utah (UT)
U of Washington (WA)
U of Waterloo (ON, Canada)
U of Wisconsin–Madison (WI)
Utah State U (UT)
Valparaiso U (IN)
Western Connecticut State U (CT)

ATMOSPHERIC SCIENCES AND METEOROLOGY RELATED

East Carolina U (NC)
Indiana U Bloomington (IN)
U of California, Los Angeles (CA)
U of California, San Diego (CA)
U of Michigan (MI)

ATOMIC/MOLECULAR PHYSICS

San Diego State U (CA)
U of Waterloo (ON, Canada)

AUDIOLOGY

Biola U (CA)
California State U, Long Beach (CA)
Northwestern U (IL)
The Ohio State U (OH)
Portland State U (OR)
Queens Coll of the City U of New York (NY)
U of Montevallo (AL)
Western Michigan U (MI)

AUDIOLOGY AND SPEECH-LANGUAGE PATHOLOGY

Andrews U (MI)
Auburn U (AL)
Auburn U at Montgomery (AL)
Augustana U (SD)
Ball State U (IN)
Biola U (CA)
Bluffton U (OH)
Bowling Green State U (OH)
California State U, Fresno (CA)
California State U, Long Beach (CA)
California State U, Sacramento (CA)
Calvin Coll (MI)
The Coll of Idaho (ID)
The Coll of Saint Rose (NY)
Delta State U (MS)
East Carolina U (NC)
Eastern Kentucky U (KY)
Eastern New Mexico U (NM)
The George Washington U (DC)
Hofstra U (NY)
Illinois State U (IL)
Indiana State U (IN)
Indiana U Bloomington (IN)
Indiana U of Pennsylvania (PA)
Iona Coll (NY)
Lehman Coll of the City U of New York (NY)
Longwood U (VA)
Louisiana State U and A&M Coll (LA)
Louisiana Tech U (LA)
Marymount Manhattan Coll (NY)
Marywood U (PA)
Miami U (OH)
Miami U Hamilton (OH)
Miami U Middletown (OH)
Middle Tennessee State U (TN)
Minnesota State U Mankato (MN)
Missouri State U (MO)
Murray State U (KY)
Nazareth Coll of Rochester (NY)
New York U (NY)
Northeastern State U (OK)
Northwestern U (IL)
Old Dominion U (VA)
Purdue U Fort Wayne (IN)
Southeastern Louisiana U (LA)
Southern Illinois U Edwardsville (IL)
State U of New York at Fredonia (NY)
State U of New York Coll at Cortland (NY)
Towson U (MD)
U at Buffalo, the State U of New York (NY)
The U of Alabama (AL)
U of Arkansas (AR)
U of Arkansas at Little Rock (AR)
U of Central Arkansas (AR)
U of Central Florida (FL)
The U of Iowa (IA)
U of Kentucky (KY)
U of Louisiana at Lafayette (LA)
U of Louisiana at Monroe (LA)
U of Minnesota, Twin Cities Campus (MN)
U of Montana (MT)
U of New Mexico (NM)
The U of North Carolina at Greensboro (NC)
U of Northern Colorado (CO)
U of North Texas (TX)
U of Southern Mississippi (MS)
U of South Florida (FL)
The U of Tennessee (TN)
The U of Texas at Dallas (TX)
U of the Pacific (CA)
The U of Tulsa (OK)
U of Utah (UT)
U of Virginia (VA)
U of Wisconsin–Madison (WI)
U of Wisconsin–Milwaukee (WI)
U of Wyoming (WY)
Washington State U (WA)
Washington State U–Spokane (WA)
West Chester U of Pennsylvania (PA)
Western Michigan U (MI)
West Virginia U (WV)
Yeshiva U (NY)

AUDIOVISUAL COMMUNICATIONS TECHNOLOGIES RELATED

Husson U (ME)
St. Thomas Aquinas Coll (NY)

AUDITING

Babson Coll (MA)
Bradley U (IL)
Carlow U (PA)
Davenport U, Grand Rapids (MI)
State U of New York Coll of Technology at Delhi (NY)
Tiffin U (OH)

AUTOBODY/COLLISION AND REPAIR TECHNOLOGY

Lewis-Clark State Coll (ID)

AUTOMATION ENGINEER TECHNOLOGY

ECPI U, Virginia Beach (VA)
Millersville U of Pennsylvania (PA)
State U of New York Coll of Technology at Delhi (NY)

AUTOMOBILE/AUTOMOTIVE MECHANICS TECHNOLOGY

Benjamin Franklin Inst of Technology (MA)
Lewis-Clark State Coll (ID)
Walla Walla U (WA)

AUTOMOTIVE ENGINEERING TECHNOLOGY

Benjamin Franklin Inst of Technology (MA)
Ferris State U (MI)
Indiana State U (IN)
Minnesota State U Mankato (MN)
Pittsburg State U (KS)
Southern Illinois U Carbondale (IL)
Weber State U (UT)

AVIATION/AIRWAY MANAGEMENT

Auburn U (AL)
Averett U (VA)
Baylor U (TX)
Bridgewater State U (MA)
California Baptist U (CA)
California State U, Los Angeles (CA)
Central Washington U (WA)
Eastern Michigan U (MI)
Eastern New Mexico U (NM)
Farmingdale State Coll (NY)
Florida Inst of Technology (FL)
Hampton U (VA)
Indiana State U (IN)
Inter American U of Puerto Rico, Bayamón Campus (PR)
Jacksonville U (FL)
LeTourneau U (TX)
Lewis U (IL)
Liberty U (VA)
Louisiana Tech U (LA)
Lynn U (FL)
Marywood U (PA)
Minnesota State U Mankato (MN)
The Ohio State U (OH)
Rocky Mountain Coll (MT)
Salem State U (MA)
South Dakota State U (SD)
Southern Illinois U Carbondale (IL)
Texas A&M U–Central Texas (TX)
U of Dubuque (IA)
U of North Dakota (ND)
U of the Fraser Valley (BC, Canada)
U of Waterloo (ON, Canada)
The U of Western Ontario (ON, Canada)
Vermont Tech Coll (VT)
Western Michigan U (MI)
Westminster Coll (UT)

AVIONICS MAINTENANCE TECHNOLOGY

Southern Illinois U Carbondale (IL)
Utah State U (UT)
Western Michigan U (MI)

BAKING AND PASTRY ARTS

The Culinary Inst of America (NY)

BALLET

Brigham Young U (UT)
Friends U (KS)
Indiana U Bloomington (IN)
Marymount Manhattan Coll (NY)
Texas Christian U (TX)
U of Utah (UT)

BANKING AND FINANCIAL SUPPORT SERVICES

Hampton U (VA)
Hardin-Simmons U (TX)
Husson U (ME)
Northern State U (SD)
Sam Houston State U (TX)
State U of New York Coll of Agriculture and Technology at Cobleskill (NY)
Texas Southern U (TX)
U of Nebraska–Lincoln (NE)
U of North Florida (FL)
U of the Incarnate Word (TX)
West Liberty U (WV)
Youngstown State U (OH)

BEHAVIORAL ASPECTS OF HEALTH

Baptist Coll of Health Sciences (TN)
Taylor U (IN)

U of Houston–Downtown (TX)
U of Massachusetts Dartmouth (MA)
U of Vermont (VT)

BEHAVIORAL SCIENCES
Andrews U (MI)
Athens State U (AL)
Bemidji State U (MN)
Brown U (RI)
California Baptist U (CA)
California State U, Dominguez Hills (CA)
Carnegie Mellon U (PA)
Central Washington U (WA)
Chaminade U of Honolulu (HI)
Columbia Coll (SC)
East Texas Baptist U (TX)
Evangel U (MO)
Felician U (NJ)
George Fox U (OR)
Glenville State Coll (WV)
Gwynedd Mercy U (PA)
Inter American U of Puerto Rico, San Germán Campus (PR)
Johns Hopkins U (MD)
Loyola U Chicago (IL)
Minnesota State U Mankato (MN)
Nova Southeastern U (FL)
Purdue U Northwest (IN)
Rochester U (MI)
Rowan U (NJ)
San Jose State U (CA)
Sterling Coll (KS)
Tabor Coll (KS)
Tennessee Wesleyan U (TN)
Trevecca Nazarene U (TN)
U of Houston–Clear Lake (TX)
The U of Kansas (KS)
U of West Georgia (GA)
U of Wisconsin–Green Bay (WI)
Widener U (PA)
York Coll of Pennsylvania (PA)

BIBLICAL STUDIES
Abilene Christian U (TX)
Anderson U (SC)
Andrews U (MI)
Arizona Christian U (AZ)
Azusa Pacific U (CA)
The Baptist Coll of Florida (FL)
Belhaven U (MS)
Belmont U (TN)
Bethel U (MN)
Bethesda U (CA)
Biola U (CA)
Bluffton U (OH)
Boise Bible Coll (ID)
Bryan Coll (TN)
California Baptist U (CA)
Calvin Coll (MI)
Campbellsville U (KY)
Carolina Christian Coll (NC)
Carson-Newman U (TN)
Cedarville U (OH)
Central Christian Coll of Kansas (KS)
Coll of the Ozarks (MO)
Covenant Coll (GA)
Dallas Baptist U (TX)
Dallas Christian Coll (TX)
Eastern U (PA)
Ecclesia Coll (AR)
Emmaus Bible Coll (IA)
Evangel U (MO)
Freed-Hardeman U (TN)
Geneva Coll (PA)
George Fox U (OR)
Goshen Coll (IN)
Harding U (AR)
Hardin-Simmons U (TX)
Hope Intl U (CA)
Houston Baptist U (TX)
Johnson U (TN)
Johnson U Florida (FL)
Kentucky Mountain Bible Coll (KY)
Lancaster Bible Coll (PA)
Lee U (TN)
LeTourneau U (TX)
Lipscomb U (TN)
Malone U (OH)
Master's Coll and Sem (ON, Canada)
Messiah Coll (PA)
MidAmerica Nazarene U (KS)
Milligan Coll (TN)
Mount Vernon Nazarene U (OH)
Multnomah U (OR)
Nazarene Bible Coll (CO)
North Central U (MN)
North Greenville U (SC)
Northwest Christian U (OR)
Northwest Nazarene U (ID)
Northwest U (WA)
Nyack Coll (NY)
Ohio Valley U (WV)
Oklahoma Baptist U (OK)
Olivet Nazarene U (IL)
Oral Roberts U (OK)
Palm Beach Atlantic U (FL)
Roberts Wesleyan Coll (NY)
Samford U (AL)
Southeastern U (FL)
Southwest Baptist U (MO)
Spring Arbor U (MI)
Taylor U (IN)
Toccoa Falls Coll (GA)
Truett McConnell U (GA)
Union U (TN)
The U of Findlay (OH)
U of Minnesota, Twin Cities Campus (MN)
U of Northwestern–St. Paul (MN)
The U of Western Ontario (ON, Canada)
Vanguard U of Southern California (CA)
Waynesburg U (PA)
Wheaton Coll (IL)
Whitworth U (WA)

BILINGUAL AND MULTILINGUAL EDUCATION
California State U, Stanislaus (CA)
Calvin Coll (MI)
Houston Baptist U (TX)
Loyola U Chicago (IL)
Northeastern Illinois U (IL)
State U of New York Coll at Old Westbury (NY)
Texas A&M Intl U (TX)
Texas Christian U (TX)
The U of Findlay (OH)
The U of Texas at San Antonio (TX)
U of Wisconsin–Milwaukee (WI)

BIOCHEMICAL ENGINEERING
U of Colorado Boulder (CO)

BIOCHEMISTRY
Abilene Christian U (TX)
Adams State U (CO)
Agnes Scott Coll (GA)
Albion Coll (MI)
Allegheny Coll (PA)
American U (DC)
Anderson U (IN)
Andrews U (MI)
Arizona State U at the Tempe campus (AZ)
Auburn U (AL)
Augustana Coll (IL)
Augustana U (SD)
Austin Coll (TX)
Azusa Pacific U (CA)
Baker U (KS)
Barnard Coll (NY)
Bates Coll (ME)
Baylor U (TX)
Beloit Coll (WI)
Benedictine Coll (KS)
Bennington Coll (VT)
Berry Coll (GA)
Bethany Lutheran Coll (MN)
Binghamton U, State U of New York (NY)
Biola U (CA)
Boston Coll (MA)
Bowdoin Coll (ME)
Bowling Green State U (OH)
Bradley U (IL)
Brandeis U (MA)
Bridgewater Coll (VA)
Bridgewater State U (MA)
Brown U (RI)
Bucknell U (PA)
Butler U (IN)
California Lutheran U (CA)
California Polytechnic State U, San Luis Obispo (CA)
California State U, Dominguez Hills (CA)
California State U, Fullerton (CA)
California State U, Long Beach (CA)
California State U, Los Angeles (CA)
California State U, Northridge (CA)
California State U, San Marcos (CA)
Calvin Coll (MI)
Capital U (OH)
Carson-Newman U (TN)
The Catholic U of America (DC)
Cedar Crest Coll (PA)
Central Coll (IA)
Central Connecticut State U (CT)
Central Michigan U (MI)
Central Washington U (WA)
Chaminade U of Honolulu (HI)
Chatham U (PA)
Chestnut Hill Coll (PA)
City Coll of the City U of New York (NY)
Claremont McKenna Coll (CA)
Clemson U (SC)
Coastal Carolina U (SC)
Coe Coll (IA)
Colby Coll (ME)
Colgate U (NY)
Coll of Saint Benedict (MN)
Coll of Saint Elizabeth (NJ)
The Coll of Saint Rose (NY)
The Coll of St. Scholastica (MN)
Coll of Staten Island of the City U of New York (NY)
The Coll of Wooster (OH)
The Colorado Coll (CO)
Colorado State U (CO)
Columbia Coll (MO)
Columbia Coll (SC)
Concordia U, St. Paul (MN)
Cornell Coll (IA)
Dartmouth Coll (NH)
DePaul U (IL)
DePauw U (IN)
DeSales U (PA)
Doane U (NE)
Dominican U (IL)
Drake U (IA)
Drew U (NJ)
Drury U (MO)
Earlham Coll (IN)
East Carolina U (NC)
Eastern Mennonite U (VA)
Eastern Michigan U (MI)
Eastern New Mexico U (NM)
Eastern U (PA)
Edinboro U of Pennsylvania (PA)
Elon U (NC)
Emmanuel Coll (MA)
Fairfield U (CT)
Fairleigh Dickinson U (NJ)
Ferris State U (MI)
Florida Gulf Coast U (FL)
Florida Inst of Technology (FL)
Florida State U (FL)
Fort Lewis Coll (CO)
Framingham State U (MA)
Freed-Hardeman U (TN)
Friends U (KS)
Gannon U (PA)
Geneva Coll (PA)
George Fox U (OR)
Georgetown Coll (KY)
Georgetown U (DC)
Georgia Inst of Technology (GA)
Georgian Court U (NJ)
Gonzaga U (WA)
Gordon Coll (MA)
Grand Valley State U (MI)
Grinnell Coll (IA)
Gustavus Adolphus Coll (MN)
Hamline U (MN)
Hanover Coll (IN)
Harding U (AR)
Harvard U (MA)
High Point U (NC)
Hillsdale Coll (MI)
Hobart and William Smith Colls (NY)
Hofstra U (NY)
Husson U (ME)
Illinois Inst of Technology (IL)
Illinois State U (IL)
Indiana U Bloomington (IN)
Indiana U East (IN)
Indiana U Kokomo (IN)
Indiana U Northwest (IN)
Indiana U of Pennsylvania (PA)
Indiana U South Bend (IN)
Iona Coll (NY)
Iowa State U of Science and Technology (IA)
Ithaca Coll (NY)
John Brown U (AR)
Kansas State U (KS)
Kennesaw State U (GA)
Kenyon Coll (OH)
Kettering U (MI)
Keuka Coll (NY)
King U (TN)
Knox Coll (IL)
Kutztown U of Pennsylvania (PA)
Lafayette Coll (PA)
LaGrange Coll (GA)
Lamar U (TX)
La Roche U (PA)
La Sierra U (CA)
Lawrence Technological U (MI)
Lawrence U (WI)
Lee U (TN)
Lehigh U (PA)
Lehman Coll of the City U of New York (NY)
Le Moyne Coll (NY)
Lewis & Clark Coll (OR)
Lewis U (IL)
Liberty U (VA)
Lipscomb U (TN)
Loras Coll (IA)
Louisiana State U and A&M Coll (LA)
Loyola Marymount U (CA)
Loyola U Chicago (IL)
Loyola U New Orleans (LA)
Madonna U (MI)
Malone U (OH)
Manhattan Coll (NY)
Manhattanville Coll (NY)
Mansfield U of Pennsylvania (PA)
Marietta Coll (OH)
Marymount U (VA)
Maryville U of Saint Louis (MO)
McMurry U (TX)
Mercer U, Macon (GA)
Merrimack Coll (MA)
Messiah Coll (PA)
Miami U (OH)
Miami U Hamilton (OH)
Miami U Middletown (OH)
Michigan State U (MI)
Middlebury Coll (VT)
Middle Tennessee State U (TN)
Minnesota State U Mankato (MN)
Misericordia U (PA)
Mississippi State U (MS)
Missouri Southern State U (MO)
Montclair State U (NJ)
Moravian Coll (PA)
Mount Holyoke Coll (MA)
Mount Mercy U (IA)
Mount Saint Mary's U (CA)
Mount St. Mary's U (MD)
Muhlenberg Coll (PA)
Nazareth Coll of Rochester (NY)
Nebraska Wesleyan U (NE)
New Jersey Inst of Technology (NJ)
Newman U (KS)
New York U (NY)
Niagara U (NY)
Northwestern Coll (IA)
Northwestern U (IL)
Northwest Nazarene U (ID)
Oakland U (MI)
Oberlin Coll (OH)
Occidental Coll (CA)
The Ohio State U (OH)
Oklahoma Baptist U (OK)
Oklahoma State U (OK)
Old Dominion U (VA)
Oral Roberts U (OK)
Pace U, Pleasantville Campus (NY)
Penn State Abington (PA)
Penn State Altoona (PA)
Penn State Beaver (PA)
Penn State Berks (PA)
Penn State Brandywine (PA)
Penn State DuBois (PA)
Penn State Erie, The Behrend Coll (PA)
Penn State Fayette, The Eberly Campus (PA)
Penn State Greater Allegheny (PA)
Penn State Hazleton (PA)
Penn State Lehigh Valley (PA)
Penn State Mont Alto (PA)
Penn State New Kensington (PA)
Penn State Schuylkill (PA)
Penn State Shenango (PA)
Penn State U Park (PA)
Penn State Wilkes-Barre (PA)
Penn State York (PA)
Pitzer Coll (CA)
Point Loma Nazarene U (CA)
Portland State U (OR)
Providence Coll (RI)
Purchase Coll, State U of New York (NY)
Purdue U Fort Wayne (IN)
Queens U of Charlotte (NC)
Ramapo Coll of New Jersey (NJ)
Rhode Island Coll (RI)
Rice U (TX)
Roanoke Coll (VA)
Roberts Wesleyan Coll (NY)
Roger Williams U (RI)
Rollins Coll (FL)
Rose-Hulman Inst of Technology (IN)
Rosemont Coll (PA)
Rowan U (NJ)
Sacred Heart U (CT)
Saginaw Valley State U (MI)
St. Bonaventure U (NY)
St. Catherine U (MN)
St. Cloud State U (MN)
Saint Francis U (PA)
Saint John's U (MN)
Saint Joseph's U (PA)
Saint Louis U (MO)
Saint Mary's Coll of California (CA)
St. Mary's Coll of Maryland (MD)
St. Mary's U (TX)
Saint Mary's U of Minnesota (MN)
St. Thomas Aquinas Coll (NY)
Saint Vincent Coll (PA)
Salem State U (MA)
Samford U (AL)
San Francisco State U (CA)
San Jose State U (CA)
Santa Clara U (CA)
Schreiner U (TX)
Scripps Coll (CA)
Seattle U (WA)
Seton Hill U (PA)
Siena Coll (NY)
Simon Fraser U (BC, Canada)
Smith Coll (MA)
South Dakota State U (SD)
Southern Methodist U (TX)
Southwestern Coll (KS)
Southwestern U (TX)
Spring Arbor U (MI)
Spring Hill Coll (AL)
State U of New York at Fredonia (NY)
State U of New York at New Paltz (NY)
State U of New York at Oswego (NY)
State U of New York Coll at Geneseo (NY)
State U of New York Coll at Old Westbury (NY)
State U of New York Coll at Oneonta (NY)
State U of New York Coll at Potsdam (NY)
Stetson U (FL)
Stevens Inst of Technology (NJ)
Stevenson U (MD)
Stockton U (NJ)
Stony Brook U, State U of New York (NY)
Suffolk U (MA)
SUNY Brockport (NY)
Susquehanna U (PA)
Tabor Coll (KS)
Taylor U (IN)
Temple U (PA)
Texas A&M U (TX)
Texas Christian U (TX)
Texas State U (TX)
Texas Tech U (TX)
Texas Woman's U (TX)
Trine U (IN)
Trinity U (TX)
Tulane U (LA)
Union Coll (NY)
U at Albany, State U of New York (NY)

U at Buffalo, the State U of New York (NY)
The U of Akron (OH)
The U of Arizona (AZ)
U of California, Los Angeles (CA)
U of California, Riverside (CA)
U of California, San Diego (CA)
U of Charleston (WV)
U of Cincinnati (OH)
U of Colorado Boulder (CO)
U of Colorado Colorado Springs (CO)
U of Dallas (TX)
U of Dayton (OH)
U of Denver (CO)
U of Detroit Mercy (MI)
U of Hawaii at Manoa (HI)
U of Houston (TX)
U of Idaho (ID)
U of Illinois at Chicago (IL)
U of Illinois at Springfield (IL)
The U of Iowa (IA)
U of Jamestown (ND)
The U of Kansas (KS)
U of Maine (ME)
U of Mary Hardin-Baylor (TX)
U of Massachusetts Boston (MA)
U of Miami (FL)
U of Michigan (MI)
U of Michigan–Dearborn (MI)
U of Michigan–Flint (MI)
U of Minnesota, Duluth (MN)
U of Minnesota, Twin Cities Campus (MN)
U of Missouri–St. Louis (MO)
U of Montana (MT)
U of Nebraska–Lincoln (NE)
U of Nevada, Las Vegas (NV)
U of Nevada, Reno (NV)
U of New England (ME)
U of New Mexico (NM)
The U of North Carolina at Greensboro (NC)
U of Northern Iowa (IA)
U of North Texas (TX)
U of Northwestern–St. Paul (MN)
U of Notre Dame (IN)
U of Oregon (OR)
U of Pennsylvania (PA)
U of Puget Sound (WA)
U of St. Francis (IL)
U of Saint Joseph (CT)
U of St. Thomas (TX)
U of San Diego (CA)
The U of Scranton (PA)
U of Southern Indiana (IN)
The U of Tampa (FL)
The U of Texas at Dallas (TX)
The U of Texas at El Paso (TX)
The U of Texas at San Antonio (TX)
U of the Incarnate Word (TX)
U of the Pacific (CA)
The U of the South (TN)
The U of Toledo (OH)
U of Toronto (ON, Canada)
The U of Tulsa (OK)
U of Vermont (VT)
U of Washington (WA)
U of Washington, Bothell (WA)
U of Waterloo (ON, Canada)
The U of Western Ontario (ON, Canada)
U of Wisconsin–La Crosse (WI)
U of Wisconsin–Madison (WI)
U of Wisconsin–Milwaukee (WI)
Ursuline Coll (OH)
Utah State U (UT)
Valparaiso U (IN)
Vanguard U of Southern California (CA)
Villanova U (PA)
Wabash Coll (IN)
Walla Walla U (WA)
Wartburg Coll (IA)
Washington & Jefferson Coll (PA)
Washington and Lee U (VA)
Washington State U (WA)
Washington U in St. Louis (MO)
Weber State U (UT)
West Chester U of Pennsylvania (PA)
Western Kentucky U (KY)
Western Michigan U (MI)
Western Washington U (WA)
West Virginia U (WV)
Wheaton Coll (MA)
Whitworth U (WA)
Widener U (PA)
Wilkes U (PA)
William Jewell Coll (MO)
Worcester Polytechnic Inst (MA)
Worcester State U (MA)
Wright State U (OH)
Wright State U–Lake Campus (OH)
Xavier U of Louisiana (LA)
Yeshiva U (NY)
Youngstown State U (OH)

BIOCHEMISTRY AND MOLECULAR BIOLOGY
Anderson U (SC)
Aquinas Coll (MI)
Belmont U (TN)
Benedictine U (IL)
Bethel U (IN)
Bethel U (MN)
California State U, Long Beach (CA)
Centre Coll (KY)
Coll of the Ozarks (MO)
Dickinson Coll (PA)
Florida Southern Coll (FL)
Goucher Coll (MD)
Hampden-Sydney Coll (VA)
Harding U (AR)
Hardin-Simmons U (TX)
Hope Coll (MI)
Houston Baptist U (TX)
Lake Forest Coll (IL)
La Sierra U (CA)
Lincoln U (PA)
Linfield Coll (OR)
Marquette U (WI)
Michigan State U (MI)
Michigan Technological U (MI)
Middlebury Coll (VT)
Nebraska Wesleyan U (NE)
New York U (NY)
Rhodes Coll (TN)
St. Cloud State U (MN)
Salve Regina U (RI)
Simmons U (MA)
U of California, Irvine (CA)
U of Maryland, Baltimore County (MD)
U of Massachusetts Amherst (MA)
U of Minnesota, Duluth (MN)
U of New Hampshire (NH)
U of Waterloo (ON, Canada)
The U of Western Ontario (ON, Canada)
Wittenberg U (OH)

BIOCHEMISTRY, BIOPHYSICS AND MOLECULAR BIOLOGY RELATED
Amherst Coll (MA)
California Baptist U (CA)
Indiana U Kokomo (IN)
St. Mary's U (TX)
Towson U (MD)
U of Miami (FL)
U of Waterloo (ON, Canada)
The U of Western Ontario (ON, Canada)
Wichita State U (KS)
Xavier U (OH)

BIOENGINEERING AND BIOMEDICAL ENGINEERING
Alfred U (NY)
Arizona State U at the Tempe campus (AZ)
Binghamton U, State U of New York (NY)
Brown U (RI)
Bucknell U (PA)
California Baptist U (CA)
California Polytechnic State U, San Luis Obispo (CA)
California State U, Long Beach (CA)
The Catholic U of America (DC)
City Coll of the City U of New York (NY)
Clemson U (SC)
Colorado School of Mines (CO)
Colorado State U (CO)
Dartmouth Coll (NH)
Drexel U (PA)
Elon U (NC)
Endicott Coll (MA)
Fairfield U (CT)
Florida A&M U (FL)
Florida Gulf Coast U (FL)
Florida Inst of Technology (FL)
Gannon U (PA)
George Mason U (VA)
Georgia Inst of Technology (GA)
Harding U (AR)
Harvard U (MA)
Hofstra U (NY)
Illinois Inst of Technology (IL)
Indiana U-Purdue U Indianapolis (IN)
Johns Hopkins U (MD)
Lawrence Technological U (MI)
Lehigh U (PA)
LeTourneau U (TX)
Louisiana State U and A&M Coll (LA)
Louisiana Tech U (LA)
Loyola U Chicago (IL)
Marquette U (WI)
Marshall U (WV)
Messiah Coll (PA)
Miami U (OH)
Miami U Hamilton (OH)
Miami U Middletown (OH)
Michigan Technological U (MI)
Milwaukee School of Eng (WI)
Mississippi State U (MS)
New Jersey Inst of Technology (NJ)
New York U (NY)
Northern Illinois U (IL)
Northwestern U (IL)
The Ohio State U (OH)
Oral Roberts U (OK)
Penn State Abington (PA)
Penn State Altoona (PA)
Penn State Beaver (PA)
Penn State Berks (PA)
Penn State Brandywine (PA)
Penn State DuBois (PA)
Penn State Erie, The Behrend Coll (PA)
Penn State Fayette, The Eberly Campus (PA)
Penn State Greater Allegheny (PA)
Penn State Hazleton (PA)
Penn State Lehigh Valley (PA)
Penn State Mont Alto (PA)
Penn State New Kensington (PA)
Penn State Schuylkill (PA)
Penn State Shenango (PA)
Penn State U Park (PA)
Penn State Wilkes-Barre (PA)
Penn State York (PA)
Regis Coll (MA)
Rice U (TX)
Rose-Hulman Inst of Technology (IN)
Rowan U (NJ)
Saint Louis U (MO)
San Jose State U (CA)
Santa Clara U (CA)
Southern California Inst of Technology (CA)
Stanford U (CA)
Stevens Inst of Technology (NJ)
Stevenson U (MD)
Stony Brook U, State U of New York (NY)
Temple U (PA)
Texas A&M U (TX)
Trine U (IN)
Tulane U (LA)
Union Coll (NY)
U at Buffalo, the State U of New York (NY)
The U of Akron (OH)
The U of Alabama at Birmingham (AL)
The U of Arizona (AZ)
U of Arkansas (AR)
U of California, Berkeley (CA)
U of California, Irvine (CA)
U of California, Merced (CA)
U of California, Riverside (CA)
U of California, San Diego (CA)
U of Cincinnati (OH)
U of Colorado Denver (CO)
U of Hartford (CT)
U of Houston (TX)
U of Illinois at Chicago (IL)
The U of Iowa (IA)
U of Louisville (KY)
U of Maine (ME)
U of Massachusetts Amherst (MA)
U of Massachusetts Dartmouth (MA)
U of Massachusetts Lowell (MA)
U of Memphis (TN)
U of Miami (FL)
U of Michigan (MI)
U of Michigan–Dearborn (MI)
U of Minnesota, Twin Cities Campus (MN)
U of Nevada, Reno (NV)
U of New Hampshire (NH)
The U of North Carolina at Chapel Hill (NC)
U of North Texas (TX)
U of Pennsylvania (PA)
U of South Carolina (SC)
U of South Dakota (SD)
The U of Tennessee (TN)
The U of Texas at Dallas (TX)
The U of Texas at San Antonio (TX)
U of the Pacific (CA)
The U of Toledo (OH)
U of Toronto (ON, Canada)
U of Utah (UT)
U of Vermont (VT)
U of Virginia (VA)
U of Washington (WA)
U of Waterloo (ON, Canada)
U of Wisconsin–Madison (WI)
Valparaiso U (IN)
Vanderbilt U (TN)
Virginia Commonwealth U (VA)
Walla Walla U (WA)
Washington State U (WA)
Washington U in St. Louis (MO)
Wayne State U (MI)
Wentworth Inst of Technology (MA)
West Chester U of Pennsylvania (PA)
Western New England U (MA)
West Virginia U (WV)
Wichita State U (KS)
Widener U (PA)
Worcester Polytechnic Inst (MA)
Wright State U (OH)
Wright State U–Lake Campus (OH)
Yale U (CT)

BIOETHICS/MEDICAL ETHICS
Houston Baptist U (TX)
U of Miami (FL)
U of Richmond (VA)

BIOINFORMATICS
Arizona State U at the Tempe campus (AZ)
Baylor U (TX)
California State U, San Bernardino (CA)
Davenport U, Grand Rapids (MI)
Iowa State U of Science and Technology (IA)
Lebanese American U (Lebanon)
Loyola U Chicago (IL)
Marquette U (WI)
Michigan Technological U (MI)
New Jersey Inst of Technology (NJ)
New York City Coll of Technology of the City U of New York (NY)
Portland State U (OR)
Ramapo Coll of New Jersey (NJ)
Rowan U (NJ)
St. Bonaventure U (NY)
Saint Vincent Coll (PA)
U at Buffalo, the State U of New York (NY)
The U of Alabama at Birmingham (AL)
The U of Arizona (AZ)
U of California, San Diego (CA)
U of California, Santa Cruz (CA)
U of Denver (CO)
U of Maryland, Baltimore County (MD)
U of Memphis (TN)
U of Pennsylvania (PA)
U of St. Thomas (TX)
U of Waterloo (ON, Canada)
The U of Western Ontario (ON, Canada)
Virginia Commonwealth U (VA)
Wheaton Coll (MA)
Whitworth U (WA)
Worcester State U (MA)

BIOLOGICAL AND BIOMEDICAL SCIENCES RELATED
Baptist Coll of Health Sciences (TN)
Bethel U (MN)
Biola U (CA)
Central Michigan U (MI)
Central Washington U (WA)
Cornell U (NY)
Dakota State U (SD)
Grand Valley State U (MI)
Guilford Coll (NC)
Indiana U Bloomington (IN)
Indiana U East (IN)
Inter American U of Puerto Rico, Bayamón Campus (PR)
Mount Aloysius Coll (PA)
New York Inst of Technology (NY)
New York U (NY)
Penn State Abington (PA)
Penn State Altoona (PA)
Penn State Beaver (PA)
Penn State Berks (PA)
Penn State Brandywine (PA)
Penn State DuBois (PA)
Penn State Erie, The Behrend Coll (PA)
Penn State Fayette, The Eberly Campus (PA)
Penn State Greater Allegheny (PA)
Penn State Hazleton (PA)
Penn State Lehigh Valley (PA)
Penn State Mont Alto (PA)
Penn State New Kensington (PA)
Penn State Schuylkill (PA)
Penn State Shenango (PA)
Penn State U Park (PA)
Penn State Wilkes-Barre (PA)
Penn State York (PA)
The Sage Colls (NY)
Saint Mary's Coll of California (CA)
Scripps Coll (CA)
Siena Coll (NY)
State U of New York Coll of Agriculture and Technology at Cobleskill (NY)
Trevecca Nazarene U (TN)
Union Coll (NY)
U of Cincinnati (OH)
U of Maryland Global Campus (MD)
U of Michigan (MI)
U of New Hampshire (NH)
U of North Dakota (ND)
U of Puerto Rico–Ponce (PR)
U of Utah (UT)
U of Wisconsin–Parkside (WI)
Ursuline Coll (OH)
Washington U in St. Louis (MO)

BIOLOGICAL AND PHYSICAL SCIENCES
Alfred U (NY)
Arcadia U (PA)
Averett U (VA)
Baker U (KS)
Bemidji State U (MN)
Bennington Coll (VT)
California State U, Fresno (CA)
Calumet Coll of Saint Joseph (IN)
Calvin Coll (MI)
Clarion U of Pennsylvania (PA)
Concordia U Chicago (IL)
Covenant Coll (GA)
Delta State U (MS)
Dominican U (IL)
Drexel U (PA)
Eastern Michigan U (MI)
Edinboro U of Pennsylvania (PA)
Emory U (GA)
Eugene Lang Coll of Liberal Arts (NY)
Fairleigh Dickinson U (NJ)
Fordham U (NY)
Indiana U Kokomo (IN)
Indiana U of Pennsylvania (PA)
Indiana U-Purdue U Indianapolis (IN)
Johns Hopkins U (MD)
King's Coll (PA)
Lawrence U (WI)
Mansfield U of Pennsylvania (PA)
Maryville U of Saint Louis (MO)
Michigan State U (MI)
Middle Tennessee State U (TN)
Minnesota State U Mankato (MN)
Mississippi State U (MS)

Moravian Coll (PA)
New York U (NY)
Northwestern U (IL)
Northwest Missouri State U (MO)
Penn State Abington (PA)
Penn State Altoona (PA)
Penn State Beaver (PA)
Penn State Berks (PA)
Penn State Brandywine (PA)
Penn State DuBois (PA)
Penn State Erie, The Behrend Coll (PA)
Penn State Fayette, The Eberly Campus (PA)
Penn State Greater Allegheny (PA)
Penn State Hazleton (PA)
Penn State Lehigh Valley (PA)
Penn State Mont Alto (PA)
Penn State New Kensington (PA)
Penn State Schuylkill (PA)
Penn State Shenango (PA)
Penn State U Park (PA)
Penn State Wilkes-Barre (PA)
Penn State York (PA)
Portland State U (OR)
Roberts Wesleyan Coll (NY)
St. Norbert Coll (WI)
Sam Houston State U (TX)
San Francisco State U (CA)
Sierra Nevada Coll (NV)
Simon Fraser U (BC, Canada)
Southern Arkansas U–Magnolia (AR)
State U of New York at Fredonia (NY)
Stony Brook U, State U of New York (NY)
Texas State U (TX)
Texas Tech U (TX)
Troy U (AL)
Union Coll (NY)
Union U (TN)
The U of Alabama at Birmingham (AL)
U of Alaska Fairbanks (AK)
U of Denver (CO)
U of Houston–Downtown (TX)
U of Massachusetts Amherst (MA)
U of Northern Iowa (IA)
U of Notre Dame (IN)
U of Oregon (OR)
U of Puget Sound (WA)
U of Southern Indiana (IN)
U of Southern Mississippi (MS)
U of South Florida (FL)
The U of Texas at San Antonio (TX)
U of Waterloo (ON, Canada)
The U of West Alabama (AL)
U of West Florida (FL)
U of Wisconsin–Platteville (WI)
U of Wisconsin–Superior (WI)
Upper Iowa U (IA)
Virginia Commonwealth U (VA)
Washington State U (WA)
Washington State U–Tri-Cities (WA)
Washington U in St. Louis (MO)
Wesleyan U (CT)
Western New Mexico U (NM)
Western Washington U (WA)
Wilmington Coll (OH)
Xavier U (OH)

BIOLOGICAL/BIOSYSTEMS ENGINEERING

Auburn U (AL)
Iowa State U of Science and Technology (IA)
Oakland U (MI)
The U of Arizona (AZ)
U of Arkansas (AR)
U of California, San Diego (CA)
U of Idaho (ID)
U of Nebraska–Lincoln (NE)
Utah State U (UT)

BIOLOGY/BIOLOGICAL SCIENCES

Abilene Christian U (TX)
Adams State U (CO)
Agnes Scott Coll (GA)
Albion Coll (MI)
Alfred U (NY)
Allegheny Coll (PA)
Alverno Coll (WI)
American U (DC)
Amherst Coll (MA)
Anderson U (IN)
Anderson U (SC)
Andrews U (MI)
Angelo State U (TX)
Appalachian State U (NC)
Aquinas Coll (MI)
Arcadia U (PA)
Arizona Christian U (AZ)
Arizona State U at the Polytechnic campus (AZ)
Arizona State U at the Tempe campus (AZ)
Arizona State U at the West campus (AZ)
Arkansas Tech U (AR)
Assumption Coll (MA)
Athens State U (AL)
Auburn U (AL)
Auburn U at Montgomery (AL)
Augsburg U (MN)
Augustana Coll (IL)
Augustana U (SD)
Aurora U (IL)
Austin Coll (TX)
Austin Peay State U (TN)
Averett U (VA)
Avila U (MO)
Azusa Pacific U (CA)
Baker U (KS)
Ball State U (IN)
Barnard Coll (NY)
Barry U (FL)
Barton Coll (NC)
Bates Coll (ME)
Bayamón Central U (PR)
Baylor U (TX)
Becker Coll (MA)
Belhaven U (MS)
Belmont Abbey Coll (NC)
Belmont U (TN)
Beloit Coll (WI)
Bemidji State U (MN)
Benedictine Coll (KS)
Benedictine U (IL)
Bennington Coll (VT)
Berea Coll (KY)
Berry Coll (GA)
Bethany Lutheran Coll (MN)
Bethel U (IN)
Bethel U (MN)
Bethel U (TN)
Binghamton U, State U of New York (NY)
Biola U (CA)
Birmingham-Southern Coll (AL)
Black Hills State U (SD)
Bluffton U (OH)
Boise State U (ID)
Boston Coll (MA)
Bowdoin Coll (ME)
Bowling Green State U (OH)
Bradley U (IL)
Brandeis U (MA)
Brandon U (MB, Canada)
Brenau U (GA)
Bridgewater Coll (VA)
Bridgewater State U (MA)
Brown U (RI)
Bryan Coll (TN)
Bryant U (RI)
Bryn Athyn Coll of the New Church (PA)
Bucknell U (PA)
Butler U (IN)
Caldwell U (NJ)
California Baptist U (CA)
California Lutheran U (CA)
California Polytechnic State U, San Luis Obispo (CA)
California State Polytechnic U, Pomona (CA)
California State U, Bakersfield (CA)
California State U, Dominguez Hills (CA)
California State U, Fresno (CA)
California State U, Fullerton (CA)
California State U, Long Beach (CA)
California State U, Los Angeles (CA)
California State U, Monterey Bay (CA)
California State U, Northridge (CA)
California State U, Sacramento (CA)
California State U, San Bernardino (CA)
California State U, San Marcos (CA)
California State U, Stanislaus (CA)
California U of Pennsylvania (PA)
Calvin Coll (MI)
Cameron U (OK)
Campbellsville U (KY)
Capital U (OH)
Carleton Coll (MN)
Carlow U (PA)
Carnegie Mellon U (PA)
Carson-Newman U (TN)
Carthage Coll (WI)
Catawba Coll (NC)
The Catholic U of America (DC)
Cazenovia Coll (NY)
Cedar Crest Coll (PA)
Cedarville U (OH)
Central Coll (IA)
Central Connecticut State U (CT)
Central Methodist U (MO)
Central State U (OH)
Central Washington U (WA)
Centre Coll (KY)
Chaminade U of Honolulu (HI)
Chatham U (PA)
Chestnut Hill Coll (PA)
The Citadel, The Military Coll of South Carolina (SC)
City Coll of the City U of New York (NY)
Claremont McKenna Coll (CA)
Clarion U of Pennsylvania (PA)
Clark Atlanta U (GA)
Clarkson U (NY)
Clark U (MA)
Clayton State U (GA)
Clemson U (SC)
Coastal Carolina U (SC)
Coe Coll (IA)
Colby Coll (ME)
Colby-Sawyer Coll (NH)
Colgate U (NY)
Coll of Charleston (SC)
The Coll of Idaho (ID)
Coll of Saint Benedict (MN)
Coll of Saint Elizabeth (NJ)
Coll of Saint Mary (NE)
The Coll of Saint Rose (NY)
The Coll of St. Scholastica (MN)
Coll of Staten Island of the City U of New York (NY)
Coll of the Holy Cross (MA)
The Coll of Wooster (OH)
Colorado State U (CO)
Columbia Coll (MO)
Columbia Coll (SC)
Concordia Coll (MN)
Concordia U Chicago (IL)
Concordia U, St. Paul (MN)
Concordia U Wisconsin (WI)
Cornell Coll (IA)
Cornell U (NY)
Covenant Coll (GA)
Creighton U (NE)
Culver-Stockton Coll (MO)
Dallas Baptist U (TX)
Dartmouth Coll (NH)
Davidson Coll (NC)
Dean Coll (MA)
Delaware Valley U (PA)
Delta State U (MS)
DePaul U (IL)
DePauw U (IN)
DeSales U (PA)
Dickinson Coll (PA)
Dickinson State U (ND)
Dillard U (LA)
Doane U (NE)
Dominican Coll (NY)
Dominican U (IL)
Dominican U of California (CA)
Drake U (IA)
Drew U (NJ)
Drexel U (PA)
Drury U (MO)
D'Youville Coll (NY)
Earlham Coll (IN)
East Carolina U (NC)
East Central U (OK)
Eastern Illinois U (IL)
Eastern Kentucky U (KY)
Eastern Mennonite U (VA)
Eastern Michigan U (MI)
Eastern New Mexico U (NM)
Eastern Oregon U (OR)
Eastern U (PA)
Eastern Washington U (WA)
East Texas Baptist U (TX)
Edgewood Coll (WI)
Edinboro U of Pennsylvania (PA)
Elms Coll (MA)
Elon U (NC)
Emmanuel Coll (GA)
Emmanuel Coll (MA)
Emory & Henry Coll (VA)
Emory U (GA)
Emporia State U (KS)
Evangel U (MO)
Excelsior Coll (NY)
Fairfield U (CT)
Fairleigh Dickinson U (NJ)
Farmingdale State Coll (NY)
Fayetteville State U (NC)
Felician U (NJ)
Ferris State U (MI)
Fisher Coll (MA)
Fitchburg State U (MA)
Florida A&M U (FL)
Florida Atlantic U (FL)
Florida Gulf Coast U (FL)
Florida Inst of Technology (FL)
Florida Southern Coll (FL)
Florida State U (FL)
Fordham U (NY)
Framingham State U (MA)
Francis Marion U (SC)
Franklin Coll (IN)
Freed-Hardeman U (TN)
Friends U (KS)
Furman U (SC)
Gallaudet U (DC)
Gannon U (PA)
Geneva Coll (PA)
George Fox U (OR)
George Mason U (VA)
Georgetown Coll (KY)
Georgetown U (DC)
The George Washington U (DC)
Georgia Coll & State U (GA)
Georgia Gwinnett Coll (GA)
Georgia Inst of Technology (GA)
Georgian Court U (NJ)
Georgia Southern U (GA)
Georgia State U (GA)
Glenville State Coll (WV)
Gonzaga U (WA)
Gordon Coll (MA)
Goshen Coll (IN)
Goucher Coll (MD)
Governors State U (IL)
Graceland U (IA)
Grambling State U (LA)
Grand Valley State U (MI)
Grinnell Coll (IA)
Guilford Coll (NC)
Gustavus Adolphus Coll (MN)
Gwynedd Mercy U (PA)
Hamline U (MN)
Hampden-Sydney Coll (VA)
Hampshire Coll (MA)
Hampton U (VA)
Hanover Coll (IN)
Harding U (AR)
Hardin-Simmons U (TX)
Harris-Stowe State U (MO)
Harvard U (MA)
High Point U (NC)
Hillsdale Coll (MI)
Hobart and William Smith Colls (NY)
Hofstra U (NY)
Hollins U (VA)
Hope Coll (MI)
Houston Baptist U (TX)
Howard U (DC)
Husson U (ME)
Illinois Coll (IL)
Illinois Inst of Technology (IL)
Illinois State U (IL)
Illinois Wesleyan U (IL)
Immaculata U (PA)
Indiana State U (IN)
Indiana U Bloomington (IN)
Indiana U East (IN)
Indiana U Kokomo (IN)
Indiana U Northwest (IN)
Indiana U of Pennsylvania (PA)
Indiana U-Purdue U Indianapolis (IN)
Indiana U South Bend (IN)
Indiana U Southeast (IN)
Inter American U of Puerto Rico, Aguadilla Campus (PR)
Inter American U of Puerto Rico, Barranquitas Campus (PR)
Inter American U of Puerto Rico, Bayamón Campus (PR)
Inter American U of Puerto Rico, Metropolitan Campus (PR)
Inter American U of Puerto Rico, San Germán Campus (PR)
Iona Coll (NY)
Iowa State U of Science and Technology (IA)
Ithaca Coll (NY)
Jacksonville State U (AL)
Jacksonville U (FL)
James Madison U (VA)
John Brown U (AR)
John Carroll U (OH)
Johns Hopkins U (MD)
Kalamazoo Coll (MI)
Kansas State U (KS)
Kansas Wesleyan U (KS)
Kean U (NJ)
Kennesaw State U (GA)
Kenyon Coll (OH)
Kettering U (MI)
Keuka Coll (NY)
King's Coll (PA)
The King's U (AB, Canada)
King U (TN)
Knox Coll (IL)
Kutztown U of Pennsylvania (PA)
Lafayette Coll (PA)
LaGrange Coll (GA)
Lake Forest Coll (IL)
Lamar U (TX)
La Roche U (PA)
Lasell Coll (MA)
La Sierra U (CA)
Lawrence U (WI)
Lebanese American U (Lebanon)
Lee U (TN)
Lehigh U (PA)
Lehman Coll of the City U of New York (NY)
Le Moyne Coll (NY)
Lenoir-Rhyne U (NC)
LeTourneau U (TX)
Lewis & Clark Coll (OR)
Lewis-Clark State Coll (ID)
Lewis U (IL)
Liberty U (VA)
Life U (GA)
Limestone Coll (SC)
Lincoln Memorial U (TN)
Lincoln U (MO)
Lincoln U (PA)
Lindenwood U (MO)
Linfield Coll (OR)
Lipscomb U (TN)
Lock Haven U of Pennsylvania (PA)
Longwood U (VA)
Loras Coll (IA)
Louisiana State U and A&M Coll (LA)
Louisiana State U in Shreveport (LA)
Louisiana Tech U (LA)
Loyola Marymount U (CA)
Loyola U Chicago (IL)
Loyola U Maryland (MD)
Loyola U New Orleans (LA)
Lynn U (FL)
Madonna U (MI)
Malone U (OH)
Manhattan Coll (NY)
Manhattanville Coll (NY)
Mansfield U of Pennsylvania (PA)
Marian U (IN)
Marietta Coll (OH)
Marquette U (WI)
Marshall U (WV)
Marymount California U (CA)
Marymount Manhattan Coll (NY)
Marymount U (VA)
Maryville U of Saint Louis (MO)
Marywood U (PA)
Mayville State U (ND)
McDaniel Coll (MD)
McKendree U (IL)
McMurry U (TX)
McNeese State U (LA)
Mercer U, Macon (GA)
Mercy Coll (NY)
Mercy Coll of Ohio (OH)
Meredith Coll (NC)
Merrimack Coll (MA)

Messiah Coll (PA)
Miami Dade Coll (FL)
Miami U (OH)
Miami U Hamilton (OH)
Miami U Middletown (OH)
Michigan State U (MI)
Michigan Technological U (MI)
Mid-America Christian U (OK)
MidAmerica Nazarene U (KS)
Middlebury Coll (VT)
Middle Tennessee State U (TN)
Midway U (KY)
Millersville U of Pennsylvania (PA)
Milligan Coll (TN)
Millikin U (IL)
Minnesota State U Mankato (MN)
Minot State U (ND)
Misericordia U (PA)
Mississippi State U (MS)
Missouri Southern State U (MO)
Missouri State U (MO)
Missouri U of Science and Technology (MO)
Missouri Valley Coll (MO)
Molloy Coll (NY)
Montana State U (MT)
Montana Technological U (MT)
Montclair State U (NJ)
Moravian Coll (PA)
Morehead State U (KY)
Mount Aloysius Coll (PA)
Mount Holyoke Coll (MA)
Mount Marty Coll (SD)
Mount Mercy U (IA)
Mount Saint Mary Coll (NY)
Mount Saint Mary's U (CA)
Mount St. Mary's U (MD)
Mount Vernon Nazarene U (OH)
Muhlenberg Coll (PA)
Murray State U (KY)
National U (CA)
Nazareth Coll of Rochester (NY)
Nebraska Wesleyan U (NE)
New Coll of Florida (FL)
New England Coll (NH)
New Jersey Inst of Technology (NJ)
Newman U (KS)
New Mexico Highlands U (NM)
New Mexico Inst of Mining and Technology (NM)
New York Inst of Technology (NY)
New York U (NY)
Niagara U (NY)
North Carolina Central U (NC)
North Central U (MN)
Northeastern Illinois U (IL)
Northeastern State U (OK)
Northern Arizona U (AZ)
Northern Illinois U (IL)
Northern Kentucky U (KY)
Northern State U (SD)
North Greenville U (SC)
Northwest Christian U (OR)
Northwestern Coll (IA)
Northwestern State U of Louisiana (LA)
Northwestern U (IL)
Northwest Missouri State U (MO)
Northwest Nazarene U (ID)
Northwest U (WA)
Notre Dame Coll (OH)
Nova Southeastern U (FL)
Nyack Coll (NY)
Oakland City U (IN)
Oakland U (MI)
Oberlin Coll (OH)
Occidental Coll (CA)
Oglethorpe U (GA)
Ohio Dominican U (OH)
The Ohio State U (OH)
The Ohio State U at Lima (OH)
The Ohio State U at Marion (OH)
Ohio Wesleyan U (OH)
Oklahoma Baptist U (OK)
Oklahoma State U (OK)
Old Dominion U (VA)
Olivet Nazarene U (IL)
Oral Roberts U (OK)
Ottawa U (KS)
Pace U, Pleasantville Campus (NY)
Pacific U (OR)
Palm Beach Atlantic U (FL)
Penn State Abington (PA)
Penn State Altoona (PA)
Penn State Beaver (PA)
Penn State Berks (PA)
Penn State Brandywine (PA)
Penn State DuBois (PA)
Penn State Erie, The Behrend Coll (PA)
Penn State Fayette, The Eberly Campus (PA)
Penn State Greater Allegheny (PA)
Penn State Hazleton (PA)
Penn State Lehigh Valley (PA)
Penn State Mont Alto (PA)
Penn State New Kensington (PA)
Penn State Schuylkill (PA)
Penn State Shenango (PA)
Penn State U Park (PA)
Penn State Wilkes-Barre (PA)
Penn State York (PA)
Pepperdine U, Malibu (CA)
Pittsburg State U (KS)
Pitzer Coll (CA)
Point Loma Nazarene U (CA)
Pomona Coll (CA)
Portland State U (OR)
Prairie View A&M U (TX)
Providence Coll (RI)
Purchase Coll, State U of New York (NY)
Purdue U Fort Wayne (IN)
Purdue U Northwest (IN)
Queens Coll of the City U of New York (NY)
Queens U of Charlotte (NC)
Radford U (VA)
Ramapo Coll of New Jersey (NJ)
Randolph Coll (VA)
Randolph-Macon Coll (VA)
Regis Coll (MA)
Rhode Island Coll (RI)
Rhodes Coll (TN)
Rice U (TX)
Roanoke Coll (VA)
Roberts Wesleyan Coll (NY)
Rochester U (MI)
Rocky Mountain Coll (MT)
Rogers State U (OK)
Roger Williams U (RI)
Rollins Coll (FL)
Rose-Hulman Inst of Technology (IN)
Rosemont Coll (PA)
Rowan U (NJ)
Sacred Heart U (CT)
The Sage Colls (NY)
Saginaw Valley State U (MI)
St. Ambrose U (IA)
St. Bonaventure U (NY)
St. Catherine U (MN)
St. Cloud State U (MN)
Saint Francis U (PA)
St. John Fisher Coll (NY)
Saint John's U (MN)
Saint Joseph's U (PA)
Saint Leo U (FL)
Saint Louis U (MO)
Saint Mary-of-the-Woods Coll (IN)
Saint Mary's Coll (IN)
Saint Mary's Coll of California (CA)
St. Mary's Coll of Maryland (MD)
St. Mary's U (TX)
Saint Mary's U of Minnesota (MN)
St. Norbert Coll (WI)
St. Olaf Coll (MN)
St. Petersburg Coll (FL)
St. Thomas Aquinas Coll (NY)
St. Thomas U - Florida (FL)
Saint Vincent Coll (PA)
Salem State U (MA)
Salisbury U (MD)
Salve Regina U (RI)
Samford U (AL)
Sam Houston State U (TX)
San Diego State U (CA)
San Francisco State U (CA)
San Jose State U (CA)
Santa Clara U (CA)
Sarah Lawrence Coll (NY)
Schreiner U (TX)
Scripps Coll (CA)
Seattle U (WA)
Seton Hill U (PA)
Shenandoah U (VA)
Shepherd U (WV)
Siena Coll (NY)
Siena Heights U (MI)
Simmons U (MA)
Simon Fraser U (BC, Canada)
Skidmore Coll (NY)
Slippery Rock U of Pennsylvania (PA)
Smith Coll (MA)
South Dakota State U (SD)
Southeastern Louisiana U (LA)
Southeastern U (FL)
Southeast Missouri State U (MO)
Southern Arkansas U–Magnolia (AR)
Southern Illinois U Carbondale (IL)
Southern Illinois U Edwardsville (IL)
Southern Methodist U (TX)
Southwest Baptist U (MO)
Southwestern Coll (KS)
Southwestern Oklahoma State U (OK)
Southwestern U (TX)
Spring Arbor U (MI)
Springfield Coll (MA)
Spring Hill Coll (AL)
Stanford U (CA)
State U of New York at Fredonia (NY)
State U of New York at New Paltz (NY)
State U of New York at Oswego (NY)
State U of New York Coll at Cortland (NY)
State U of New York Coll at Geneseo (NY)
State U of New York Coll at Old Westbury (NY)
State U of New York Coll at Oneonta (NY)
State U of New York Coll at Potsdam (NY)
Sterling Coll (KS)
Stetson U (FL)
Stevens Inst of Technology (NJ)
Stevenson U (MD)
Stockton U (NJ)
Stony Brook U, State U of New York (NY)
Suffolk U (MA)
SUNY Brockport (NY)
Susquehanna U (PA)
Tabor Coll (KS)
Tarleton State U (TX)
Taylor U (IN)
Tennessee Wesleyan U (TN)
Texas A&M Intl U (TX)
Texas A&M U (TX)
Texas A&M U–Central Texas (TX)
Texas A&M U–Commerce (TX)
Texas A&M U–Corpus Christi (TX)
Texas A&M U–Kingsville (TX)
Texas Christian U (TX)
Texas Lutheran U (TX)
Texas State U (TX)
Texas Tech U (TX)
Texas Woman's U (TX)
Toccoa Falls Coll (GA)
Towson U (MD)
Transylvania U (KY)
Trevecca Nazarene U (TN)
Trine U (IN)
Trinity U (TX)
Troy U (AL)
Truett McConnell U (GA)
Truman State U (MO)
Tulane U (LA)
Union Coll (NY)
Union U (TN)
United States Military Acad (NY)
Universidad Adventista de las Antillas (PR)
U at Albany, State U of New York (NY)
U at Buffalo, the State U of New York (NY)
The U of Akron (OH)
The U of Alabama (AL)
The U of Alabama at Birmingham (AL)
The U of Alabama in Huntsville (AL)
U of Alaska Fairbanks (AK)
U of Alaska Southeast (AK)
The U of Arizona (AZ)
U of Arkansas (AR)
U of Arkansas at Little Rock (AR)
U of California, Berkeley (CA)
U of California, Irvine (CA)
U of California, Los Angeles (CA)
U of California, Merced (CA)
U of California, Riverside (CA)
U of California, San Diego (CA)
U of California, Santa Barbara (CA)
U of California, Santa Cruz (CA)
U of Central Arkansas (AR)
U of Central Florida (FL)
U of Charleston (WV)
U of Cincinnati (OH)
U of Colorado Colorado Springs (CO)
U of Colorado Denver (CO)
U of Dallas (TX)
U of Dayton (OH)
U of Denver (CO)
U of Detroit Mercy (MI)
U of Dubuque (IA)
The U of Findlay (OH)
U of Guam (GU)
U of Hartford (CT)
U of Hawaii at Manoa (HI)
U of Houston (TX)
U of Houston–Clear Lake (TX)
U of Houston–Downtown (TX)
U of Idaho (ID)
U of Illinois at Chicago (IL)
U of Illinois at Springfield (IL)
The U of Iowa (IA)
U of Jamestown (ND)
The U of Kansas (KS)
U of Kentucky (KY)
U of La Verne (CA)
U of Louisiana at Lafayette (LA)
U of Louisiana at Monroe (LA)
U of Louisville (KY)
U of Maine (ME)
U of Maine at Presque Isle (ME)
U of Mary Hardin-Baylor (TX)
U of Maryland, Baltimore County (MD)
U of Mary Washington (VA)
U of Massachusetts Amherst (MA)
U of Massachusetts Boston (MA)
U of Massachusetts Dartmouth (MA)
U of Massachusetts Lowell (MA)
U of Memphis (TN)
U of Miami (FL)
U of Michigan (MI)
U of Michigan–Dearborn (MI)
U of Michigan–Flint (MI)
U of Minnesota, Duluth (MN)
U of Minnesota, Morris (MN)
U of Minnesota, Twin Cities Campus (MN)
U of Missouri–St. Louis (MO)
U of Montana (MT)
U of Montevallo (AL)
U of Nebraska at Kearney (NE)
U of Nebraska–Lincoln (NE)
U of Nevada, Las Vegas (NV)
U of Nevada, Reno (NV)
U of New England (ME)
U of New Hampshire (NH)
U of New Haven (CT)
U of New Mexico (NM)
The U of North Carolina at Chapel Hill (NC)
The U of North Carolina at Charlotte (NC)
The U of North Carolina at Greensboro (NC)
The U of North Carolina at Pembroke (NC)
The U of North Carolina Wilmington (NC)
U of North Dakota (ND)
U of Northern Colorado (CO)
U of Northern Iowa (IA)
U of North Florida (FL)
U of North Texas (TX)
U of Northwestern–St. Paul (MN)
U of Notre Dame (IN)
U of Oregon (OR)
U of Pennsylvania (PA)
U of Pikeville (KY)
U of Pittsburgh at Bradford (PA)
U of Pittsburgh at Greensburg (PA)
U of Portland (OR)
U of Providence (MT)
U of Puget Sound (WA)
U of Richmond (VA)
U of St. Francis (IL)
U of Saint Francis (IN)
U of Saint Joseph (CT)
U of Saint Mary (KS)
U of St. Thomas (TX)
U of San Diego (CA)
U of San Francisco (CA)
U of Science and Arts of Oklahoma (OK)
The U of Scranton (PA)
U of South Alabama (AL)
U of South Carolina (SC)
U of South Carolina Aiken (SC)
U of South Carolina Beaufort (SC)
U of South Dakota (SD)
U of Southern Indiana (IN)
U of Southern Maine (ME)
U of Southern Mississippi (MS)
U of South Florida (FL)
U of South Florida, St. Petersburg (FL)
The U of Tampa (FL)
The U of Tennessee (TN)
The U of Tennessee at Chattanooga (TN)
The U of Tennessee at Martin (TN)
The U of Texas at Dallas (TX)
The U of Texas at El Paso (TX)
The U of Texas at San Antonio (TX)
The U of Texas of the Permian Basin (TX)
The U of Texas Rio Grande Valley (TX)
U of the Fraser Valley (BC, Canada)
U of the Incarnate Word (TX)
U of the Pacific (CA)
The U of the South (TN)
U of the Virgin Islands (VI)
The U of Toledo (OH)
U of Toronto (ON, Canada)
The U of Tulsa (OK)
U of Utah (UT)
U of Vermont (VT)
U of Virginia (VA)
U of Washington (WA)
U of Washington, Bothell (WA)
U of Waterloo (ON, Canada)
The U of West Alabama (AL)
The U of Western Ontario (ON, Canada)
U of West Florida (FL)
U of West Georgia (GA)
U of Wisconsin–Eau Claire (WI)
U of Wisconsin–Green Bay (WI)
U of Wisconsin–La Crosse (WI)
U of Wisconsin–Madison (WI)
U of Wisconsin–Milwaukee (WI)
U of Wisconsin–Platteville (WI)
U of Wisconsin–Superior (WI)
U of Wyoming (WY)
Upper Iowa U (IA)
Ursuline Coll (OH)
Utah State U (UT)
Utah Valley U (UT)
Utica Coll (NY)
Valdosta State U (GA)
Valley City State U (ND)
Valparaiso U (IN)
Vanderbilt U (TN)
Vanguard U of Southern California (CA)
Villanova U (PA)
Virginia Commonwealth U (VA)
Virginia Wesleyan U (VA)
Wabash Coll (IN)
Wake Forest U (NC)
Walla Walla U (WA)
Warren Wilson Coll (NC)
Wartburg Coll (IA)
Washington & Jefferson Coll (PA)
Washington and Lee U (VA)
Washington Coll (MD)
Washington State U (WA)
Washington State U–Tri-Cities (WA)
Washington State U–Vancouver (WA)
Washington U in St. Louis (MO)
Wayland Baptist U (TX)
Waynesburg U (PA)
Wayne State Coll (NE)
Wayne State U (MI)
Wesleyan Coll (GA)
Wesleyan U (CT)
West Chester U of Pennsylvania (PA)
Western Carolina U (NC)
Western Colorado U (CO)
Western Connecticut State U (CT)
Western Kentucky U (KY)
Western Michigan U (MI)

Western New England U (MA)
Western New Mexico U (NM)
Western Oregon U (OR)
Western Washington U (WA)
Westfield State U (MA)
West Liberty U (WV)
Westminster Coll (UT)
Westmont Coll (CA)
West Virginia U (WV)
Wheaton Coll (IL)
Wheaton Coll (MA)
Whitworth U (WA)
Wichita State U (KS)
Widener U (PA)
Wilkes U (PA)
Willamette U (OR)
William & Mary (VA)
William Jewell Coll (MO)
William Paterson U of New Jersey (NJ)
William Peace U (NC)
William Penn U (IA)
Williams Coll (MA)
Wilmington Coll (OH)
Wingate U (NC)
Winthrop U (SC)
Wittenberg U (OH)
Wofford Coll (SC)
Worcester Polytechnic Inst (MA)
Worcester State U (MA)
Wright State U (OH)
Xavier U (OH)
Xavier U of Louisiana (LA)
Yale U (CT)
Yeshiva U (NY)
York Coll of Pennsylvania (PA)
Youngstown State U (OH)

BIOLOGY/BIOTECHNOLOGY LABORATORY TECHNICIAN
Davenport U, Grand Rapids (MI)
Edinboro U of Pennsylvania (PA)
MiraCosta Coll (CA)
Penn State Abington (PA)
Penn State Altoona (PA)
Penn State Beaver (PA)
Penn State Berks (PA)
Penn State Brandywine (PA)
Penn State DuBois (PA)
Penn State Erie, The Behrend Coll (PA)
Penn State Fayette, The Eberly Campus (PA)
Penn State Greater Allegheny (PA)
Penn State Hazleton (PA)
Penn State Lehigh Valley (PA)
Penn State Mont Alto (PA)
Penn State New Kensington (PA)
Penn State Schuylkill (PA)
Penn State Shenango (PA)
Penn State U Park (PA)
Penn State Wilkes-Barre (PA)
Penn State York (PA)
State U of New York at Fredonia (NY)
State U of New York Coll at Oneonta (NY)
Ursuline Coll (OH)

BIOLOGY TEACHER EDUCATION
Abilene Christian U (TX)
Adams State U (CO)
Albion Coll (MI)
Aquinas Coll (MI)
Arizona Christian U (AZ)
Arkansas Tech U (AR)
Augustana Coll (IL)
Ball State U (IN)
Baylor U (TX)
Bethel U (IN)
Biola U (CA)
Bowling Green State U (OH)
Bradley U (IL)
Bridgewater State U (MA)
Bryan Coll (TN)
California State U, Long Beach (CA)
Calvin Coll (MI)
Campbellsville U (KY)
Cedarville U (OH)
Central Methodist U (MO)
Central Michigan U (MI)
Central State U (OH)
Central Washington U (WA)
City Coll of the City U of New York (NY)
Coll of Saint Mary (NE)
The Coll of Saint Rose (NY)
Coll of Staten Island of the City U of New York (NY)
Coll of the Ozarks (MO)
Concordia U Chicago (IL)
Concordia U, St. Paul (MN)
Culver-Stockton Coll (MO)
Daytona State Coll (FL)
Dickinson State U (ND)
Dominican Coll (NY)
East Central U (OK)
Eastern Kentucky U (KY)
Eastern Michigan U (MI)
Eastern Washington U (WA)
East Texas Baptist U (TX)
Edgewood Coll (WI)
Emory & Henry Coll (VA)
Evangel U (MO)
Ferris State U (MI)
Fitchburg State U (MA)
Florida Inst of Technology (FL)
Florida Southern Coll (FL)
Florida SouthWestern State Coll (FL)
Florida State U (FL)
Fort Lewis Coll (CO)
Francis Marion U (SC)
Franklin Coll (IN)
Friends U (KS)
Glenville State Coll (WV)
Goshen Coll (IN)
Grand Valley State U (MI)
Gustavus Adolphus Coll (MN)
Gwynedd Mercy U (PA)
Harding U (AR)
Hofstra U (NY)
Hope Coll (MI)
Houston Baptist U (TX)
Illinois State U (IL)
Immaculata U (PA)
Indiana U Bloomington (IN)
Indiana U Northwest (IN)
Indiana U South Bend (IN)
Indiana U Southeast (IN)
Inter American U of Puerto Rico, Aguadilla Campus (PR)
Inter American U of Puerto Rico, Barranquitas Campus (PR)
Inter American U of Puerto Rico, San Germán Campus (PR)
Iona Coll (NY)
Ithaca Coll (NY)
Kansas Wesleyan U (KS)
Kennesaw State U (GA)
Keuka Coll (NY)
Lee U (TN)
Le Moyne Coll (NY)
Lincoln Memorial U (TN)
Lincoln U (MO)
Lipscomb U (TN)
Louisiana Tech U (LA)
Madonna U (MI)
Manhattanville Coll (NY)
Marywood U (PA)
Mayville State U (ND)
McMurry U (TX)
Merrimack Coll (MA)
Messiah Coll (PA)
Miami Dade Coll (FL)
Miami U Hamilton (OH)
Miami U Middletown (OH)
Michigan State U (MI)
MidAmerica Nazarene U (KS)
Midway U (KY)
Millikin U (IL)
Minot State U (ND)
Misericordia U (PA)
Missouri State U (MO)
Mount Vernon Nazarene U (OH)
Nazareth Coll of Rochester (NY)
New York U (NY)
Niagara U (NY)
Northern Arizona U (AZ)
Northern State U (SD)
Northwestern Coll (IA)
Northwest Missouri State U (MO)
Northwest Nazarene U (ID)
Northwest U (WA)
Notre Dame Coll (OH)
Oakland City U (IN)
Ohio Dominican U (OH)
Ohio Wesleyan U (OH)
Ottawa U (KS)
Pace U, Pleasantville Campus (NY)
Pittsburg State U (KS)
Providence Coll (RI)
Purdue U Fort Wayne (IN)
Queens Coll of the City U of New York (NY)
Roanoke Coll (VA)
Roberts Wesleyan Coll (NY)
Rocky Mountain Coll (MT)
Saginaw Valley State U (MI)
St. Ambrose U (IA)
St. Catherine U (MN)
St. Cloud State U (MN)
Saint Francis U (PA)
St. John Fisher Coll (NY)
Saint Joseph's U (PA)
Saint Mary's U of Minnesota (MN)
St. Petersburg Coll (FL)
Salve Regina U (RI)
Schreiner U (TX)
Seattle U (WA)
Seton Hill U (PA)
Southeastern U (FL)
Southwest Baptist U (MO)
Spring Arbor U (MI)
Spring Hill Coll (AL)
State U of New York at New Paltz (NY)
State U of New York Coll at Cortland (NY)
State U of New York Coll at Old Westbury (NY)
State U of New York Coll at Oneonta (NY)
State U of New York Coll at Potsdam (NY)
Sterling Coll (KS)
Taylor U (IN)
Trevecca Nazarene U (TN)
Trine U (IN)
Universidad Adventista de las Antillas (PR)
U of California, Irvine (CA)
U of Dubuque (IA)
The U of Findlay (OH)
U of Illinois at Chicago (IL)
The U of Iowa (IA)
U of Jamestown (ND)
U of Louisiana at Monroe (LA)
U of Maine (ME)
U of Mary Hardin-Baylor (TX)
U of Maryland, Baltimore County (MD)
U of Nebraska–Lincoln (NE)
U of Nevada, Reno (NV)
U of Pikeville (KY)
U of Providence (MT)
U of South Dakota (SD)
U of Waterloo (ON, Canada)
U of Wisconsin–Superior (WI)
Utah State U (UT)
Utah Valley U (UT)
Utica Coll (NY)
Valley City State U (ND)
Valparaiso U (IN)
Washington U in St. Louis (MO)
Waynesburg U (PA)
Wayne State Coll (NE)
Weber State U (UT)
Western Michigan U (MI)
Western Washington U (WA)
Widener U (PA)
Wingate U (NC)
Xavier U (OH)
Xavier U of Louisiana (LA)
York Coll of Pennsylvania (PA)
Youngstown State U (OH)

BIOMATHEMATICS, BIOINFORMATICS, AND COMPUTATIONAL BIOLOGY RELATED
Florida Inst of Technology (FL)
Florida State U (FL)
La Sierra U (CA)
Scripps Coll (CA)
U of California, Los Angeles (CA)
Washington U in St. Louis (MO)
Worcester Polytechnic Inst (MA)
Worcester State U (MA)

BIOMEDICAL SCIENCES
AdventHealth U (FL)
Alverno Coll (WI)
Auburn U (AL)
Bradley U (IL)
Bridgewater State U (MA)
Brigham Young U (UT)
Central Michigan U (MI)
Central Washington U (WA)
Charles R. Drew U of Medicine and Science (CA)
City Coll of the City U of New York (NY)
Coll of the Ozarks (MO)
Colorado State U (CO)
Concordia U Wisconsin (WI)
East Central U (OK)
Eastern Kentucky U (KY)
Edgewood Coll (WI)
Fitchburg State U (MA)
Florida Inst of Technology (FL)
Georgetown Coll (KY)
Inter American U of Puerto Rico, Metropolitan Campus (PR)
Keiser U, Fort Lauderdale (FL)
Keuka Coll (NY)
La Sierra U (CA)
Lewis U (IL)
Liberty U (VA)
Madonna U (MI)
Marquette U (WI)
Marymount Manhattan Coll (NY)
Maryville U of Saint Louis (MO)
McMurry U (TX)
Michigan State U (MI)
Morehead State U (KY)
Multnomah U (OR)
New Mexico Inst of Mining and Technology (NM)
North Carolina Central U (NC)
Northern Arizona U (AZ)
Oakland U (MI)
The Ohio State U (OH)
Portland State U (OR)
Radford U (VA)
Rowan U (NJ)
St. Ambrose U (IA)
St. Cloud State U (MN)
Sam Houston State U (TX)
State U of New York at Fredonia (NY)
Susquehanna U (PA)
Tarleton State U (TX)
Texas A&M U (TX)
Texas A&M U–Corpus Christi (TX)
Texas A&M U–Kingsville (TX)
Troy U (AL)
U at Buffalo, the State U of New York (NY)
The U of Alabama at Birmingham (AL)
U of California, Santa Cruz (CA)
U of Central Florida (FL)
U of Colorado Denver (CO)
U of Michigan–Flint (MI)
U of Minnesota, Duluth (MN)
U of New England (ME)
U of New Hampshire (NH)
U of Northern Iowa (IA)
U of Pennsylvania (PA)
U of Saint Mary (KS)
U of South Alabama (AL)
U of South Carolina Aiken (SC)
U of South Dakota (SD)
U of South Florida (FL)
The U of Texas Rio Grande Valley (TX)
U of Washington, Tacoma (WA)
U of Waterloo (ON, Canada)
Washington State U (WA)
Western Michigan U (MI)

BIOMEDICAL TECHNOLOGY
Indiana U-Purdue U Indianapolis (IN)

BIOMETRY/BIOMETRICS
Carnegie Mellon U (PA)
Cornell U (NY)
Stanford U (CA)

BIOPHYSICS
Andrews U (MI)
Arizona State U at the Tempe campus (AZ)
Augsburg U (MN)
Brandeis U (MA)
Brigham Young U (UT)
Brown U (RI)
Carnegie Mellon U (PA)
Claremont McKenna Coll (CA)
Elon U (NC)
Emory U (GA)
Illinois Inst of Technology (IL)
Iowa State U of Science and Technology (IA)
Johns Hopkins U (MD)
La Sierra U (CA)
Lipscomb U (TN)
Loyola U Chicago (IL)
Loyola U New Orleans (LA)
Marquette U (WI)
Miami U (OH)
Miami U Hamilton (OH)
Miami U Middletown (OH)
New Jersey Inst of Technology (NJ)
Oakland U (MI)
Pitzer Coll (CA)
Regent U (VA)
Rowan U (NJ)
Scripps Coll (CA)
Southern Methodist U (TX)
State U of New York Coll at Geneseo (NY)
Temple U (PA)
Texas Christian U (TX)
U at Buffalo, the State U of New York (NY)
U of California, Los Angeles (CA)
U of California, San Diego (CA)
U of Michigan (MI)
U of Pennsylvania (PA)
U of San Diego (CA)
The U of Scranton (PA)
U of Southern Indiana (IN)
U of Toronto (ON, Canada)
The U of Western Ontario (ON, Canada)
Walla Walla U (WA)
Washington & Jefferson Coll (PA)
Washington U in St. Louis (MO)
Whitworth U (WA)

BIOPSYCHOLOGY
Augsburg U (MN)
Bucknell U (PA)
Carnegie Mellon U (PA)
Geneva Coll (PA)
Grand Valley State U (MI)
Immaculata U (PA)
Inter American U of Puerto Rico, Metropolitan Campus (PR)
Liberty U (VA)
Life U (GA)
Messiah Coll (PA)
New Coll of Florida (FL)
Oglethorpe U (GA)
Ohio Dominican U (OH)
Saint Mary's Coll of California (CA)
Spring Hill Coll (AL)
U of California, Santa Barbara (CA)
Washington U in St. Louis (MO)

BIOSTATISTICS
Emmanuel Coll (MA)
Indiana U-Purdue U Indianapolis (IN)
Saint Louis U (MO)
Simmons U (MA)
Tulane U (LA)
The U of North Carolina at Chapel Hill (NC)
The U of Scranton (PA)
U of Waterloo (ON, Canada)
The U of Western Ontario (ON, Canada)

BIOTECHNOLOGY
Andrews U (MI)
Arizona State U at the West campus (AZ)
Auburn U (AL)
California State Polytechnic U, Pomona (CA)
California State U, San Marcos (CA)
City Coll of the City U of New York (NY)
Colorado State U (CO)
Endicott Coll (MA)
Ferris State U (MI)
Fitchburg State U (MA)
Florida Gulf Coast U (FL)
Florida Southern Coll (FL)
Indiana U Bloomington (IN)
Indiana U East (IN)
Indiana U-Purdue U Indianapolis (IN)
Inter American U of Puerto Rico, Aguadilla Campus (PR)
Inter American U of Puerto Rico, Barranquitas Campus (PR)
Inter American U of Puerto Rico, Bayamón Campus (PR)
James Madison U (VA)
Keiser U, Fort Lauderdale (FL)

Liberty U (VA)
Manhattan Coll (NY)
Marywood U (PA)
Montana State U (MT)
New York Inst of Technology (NY)
St. Cloud State U (MN)
South Dakota State U (SD)
State U of New York Coll of Agriculture and Technology at Cobleskill (NY)
Stevenson U (MD)
U at Buffalo, the State U of New York (NY)
U of California, San Diego (CA)
U of Central Florida (FL)
U of Hawaii at Manoa (HI)
U of Houston (TX)
U of Houston–Downtown (TX)
U of Idaho (ID)
The U of Kansas (KS)
U of Kentucky (KY)
U of Maryland, Baltimore County (MD)
U of Nevada, Reno (NV)
The U of North Carolina at Pembroke (NC)
U of Puerto Rico–Ponce (PR)
U of Waterloo (ON, Canada)
Ursuline Coll (OH)
Utah Valley U (UT)
William Paterson U of New Jersey (NJ)
Worcester State U (MA)

BLOOD BANK TECHNOLOGY
Rasmussen Coll St. Cloud (MN)

BOTANY/PLANT BIOLOGY
Auburn U (AL)
Brandon U (MB, Canada)
California State U, Long Beach (CA)
Miami U (OH)
Miami U Hamilton (OH)
Miami U Middletown (OH)
Michigan State U (MI)
Ohio Wesleyan U (OH)
Oklahoma State U (OK)
Portland State U (OR)
San Francisco State U (CA)
Southern Illinois U Carbondale (IL)
The U of Akron (OH)
U of California, Berkeley (CA)
U of California, Riverside (CA)
U of Hawaii at Manoa (HI)
U of Maine (ME)
U of Nebraska–Lincoln (NE)
U of Providence (MT)
U of Toronto (ON, Canada)
U of Utah (UT)
U of Vermont (VT)
U of Washington (WA)
U of Wisconsin–Madison (WI)
U of Wyoming (WY)
Utah Valley U (UT)
Weber State U (UT)
Western New Mexico U (NM)

BOTANY/PLANT BIOLOGY RELATED
U of Hawaii at Manoa (HI)
U of Minnesota, Twin Cities Campus (MN)
Utah State U (UT)

BRASS INSTRUMENTS
Liberty U (VA)
The U of Arizona (AZ)
The U of Kansas (KS)
Vanderbilt U (TN)
Youngstown State U (OH)

BROADCAST JOURNALISM
Auburn U (AL)
Barry U (FL)
Belmont U (TN)
Biola U (CA)
Bluffton U (OH)
Bowling Green State U (OH)
Brigham Young U (UT)
California State U, Long Beach (CA)
Cameron U (OK)
Central State U (OH)
Central Washington U (WA)
Concordia U Chicago (IL)
Drake U (IA)
Evangel U (MO)
Gonzaga U (WA)
Goshen Coll (IN)
Hampton U (VA)
Harding U (AR)
Howard U (DC)
Johnson U Florida (FL)
Marywood U (PA)
Mount Vernon Nazarene U (OH)
Northern Kentucky U (KY)
North Greenville U (SC)
Ohio Wesleyan U (OH)
Pacific U (OR)
Southwestern Coll (KS)
State U of New York at Oswego (NY)
Suffolk U (MA)
SUNY Brockport (NY)
Trevecca Nazarene U (TN)
Union U (TN)
U of Miami (FL)
U of Nebraska–Lincoln (NE)
U of North Texas (TX)
The U of Scranton (PA)
U of South Carolina (SC)
Wartburg Coll (IA)
Washington State U (WA)
Western Kentucky U (KY)
Youngstown State U (OH)

BUILDING/CONSTRUCTION FINISHING, MANAGEMENT, AND INSPECTION RELATED
Andrews U (MI)
California State U, Long Beach (CA)
Minnesota State U Mankato (MN)
Pratt Inst (NY)

BUILDING/CONSTRUCTION SITE MANAGEMENT
Rowan U (NJ)
State U of New York Coll of Technology at Delhi (NY)
The U of Texas at San Antonio (TX)

BUSINESS ADMINISTRATION AND MANAGEMENT
Abilene Christian U (TX)
Adams State U (CO)
Agnes Scott Coll (GA)
Albion Coll (MI)
Alfred U (NY)
Alverno Coll (WI)
American Public U System (WV)
American U (DC)
The American U of Paris (France)
Anderson U (IN)
Anderson U (SC)
Andrews U (MI)
Angelo State U (TX)
Appalachian State U (NC)
Aquinas Coll (MI)
Arcadia U (PA)
Arizona Christian U (AZ)
Arizona State U at the Polytechnic campus (AZ)
Arizona State U at the Tempe campus (AZ)
Arizona State U at the West campus (AZ)
Arkansas Tech U (AR)
Assumption Coll (MA)
Athens State U (AL)
Auburn U (AL)
Auburn U at Montgomery (AL)
Augsburg U (MN)
Augustana Coll (IL)
Augustana U (SD)
Aurora U (IL)
Austin Coll (TX)
Austin Peay State U (TN)
Avila U (MO)
Azusa Pacific U (CA)
Babson Coll (MA)
Ball State U (IN)
The Baptist Coll of Florida (FL)
Barry U (FL)
Barton Coll (NC)
Baruch Coll of the City U of New York (NY)
Bayamón Central U (PR)
Bay Atlantic U (DC)
Baylor U (TX)
Beacon Coll (FL)
Becker Coll (MA)
Belhaven U (MS)
Belmont Abbey Coll (NC)
Belmont U (TN)
Bemidji State U (MN)
Benedictine Coll (KS)
Bentley U (MA)
Berea Coll (KY)
Berry Coll (GA)
Bethany Lutheran Coll (MN)
Bethel U (IN)
Bethel U (MN)
Bethel U (TN)
Binghamton U, State U of New York (NY)
Biola U (CA)
Birmingham-Southern Coll (AL)
Black Hills State U (SD)
Bluffton U (OH)
Boise State U (ID)
Boston Coll (MA)
Bowling Green State U (OH)
Bradley U (IL)
Brandon U (MB, Canada)
Brenau U (GA)
Bridgewater Coll (VA)
Bridgewater State U (MA)
Bryan Coll (TN)
Bryant U (RI)
Bucknell U (PA)
Caldwell U (NJ)
California Lutheran U (CA)
California Polytechnic State U, San Luis Obispo (CA)
California State Polytechnic U, Pomona (CA)
California State U, Bakersfield (CA)
California State U, Dominguez Hills (CA)
California State U, Fresno (CA)
California State U, Fullerton (CA)
California State U, Long Beach (CA)
California State U, Los Angeles (CA)
California State U, Monterey Bay (CA)
California State U, Northridge (CA)
California State U, Sacramento (CA)
California State U, San Bernardino (CA)
California State U, San Marcos (CA)
California State U, Stanislaus (CA)
California U of Pennsylvania (PA)
Calumet Coll of Saint Joseph (IN)
Calvin Coll (MI)
Cameron U (OK)
Campbellsville U (KY)
Capital U (OH)
Carlow U (PA)
Carnegie Mellon U (PA)
Carson-Newman U (TN)
Carthage Coll (WI)
Catawba Coll (NC)
The Catholic U of America (DC)
Cazenovia Coll (NY)
Cedar Crest Coll (PA)
Cedarville U (OH)
Central Coll (IA)
Central Connecticut State U (CT)
Central Methodist U (MO)
Central Michigan U (MI)
Central Washington U (WA)
Chaminade U of Honolulu (HI)
Champlain Coll (VT)
Charter Oak State Coll (CT)
Chestnut Hill Coll (PA)
The Citadel, The Military Coll of South Carolina (SC)
City Coll of the City U of New York (NY)
Clarion U of Pennsylvania (PA)
Clark Atlanta U (GA)
Clarkson U (NY)
Clark U (MA)
Clayton State U (GA)
Clemson U (SC)
Coastal Carolina U (SC)
Coe Coll (IA)
Cogswell Polytechnical Coll (CA)
Colby-Sawyer Coll (NH)
Coll of Charleston (SC)
The Coll of Idaho (ID)
Coll of Saint Benedict (MN)
Coll of Saint Elizabeth (NJ)
Coll of Saint Mary (NE)
The Coll of Saint Rose (NY)
The Coll of St. Scholastica (MN)
Coll of the Ozarks (MO)
The Coll of Westchester (NY)
Colorado State U (CO)
Columbia Coll (MO)
Columbia Coll (SC)
Concordia Coll (MN)
Concordia U Chicago (IL)
Concordia U, St. Paul (MN)
Concordia U Wisconsin (WI)
Creighton U (NE)
Culver-Stockton Coll (MO)
Dakota State U (SD)
Dallas Baptist U (TX)
Dallas Christian Coll (TX)
Davenport U, Grand Rapids (MI)
Dean Coll (MA)
Delaware Valley U (PA)
Delta State U (MS)
DePaul U (IL)
DeSales U (PA)
Dickinson State U (ND)
Dillard U (LA)
Doane U (NE)
Dominican Coll (NY)
Dominican U (IL)
Dominican U of California (CA)
Drake U (IA)
Drew U (NJ)
Drury U (MO)
Dunwoody Coll of Technology (MN)
D'Youville Coll (NY)
Earlham Coll (IN)
East Carolina U (NC)
East Central U (OK)
Eastern Illinois U (IL)
Eastern Kentucky U (KY)
Eastern Mennonite U (VA)
Eastern Michigan U (MI)
Eastern New Mexico U (NM)
Eastern U (PA)
Eastern Washington U (WA)
East Texas Baptist U (TX)
Ecclesia Coll (AR)
ECPI U, Virginia Beach (VA)
Edgewood Coll (WI)
Edinboro U of Pennsylvania (PA)
Emmanuel Coll (MA)
Emmaus Bible Coll (IA)
Emory & Henry Coll (VA)
Emory U (GA)
Emporia State U (KS)
Endicott Coll (MA)
Evangel U (MO)
Excelsior Coll (NY)
Fairfield U (CT)
Fairleigh Dickinson U (NJ)
Farmingdale State Coll (NY)
Fayetteville State U (NC)
Felician U (NJ)
Ferris State U (MI)
Fisher Coll (MA)
Fitchburg State U (MA)
Flagler Coll (FL)
Florida A&M U (FL)
Florida Atlantic U (FL)
Florida Gulf Coast U (FL)
Florida Inst of Technology (FL)
Florida National U (FL)
Florida Southern Coll (FL)
Florida State U (FL)
Fordham U (NY)
Fort Lewis Coll (CO)
Francis Marion U (SC)
Freed-Hardeman U (TN)
Friends U (KS)
Furman U (SC)
Gallaudet U (DC)
Gannon U (PA)
Geneva Coll (PA)
George Fox U (OR)
George Mason U (VA)
Georgetown Coll (KY)
Georgetown U (DC)
The George Washington U (DC)
Georgia Coll & State U (GA)
Georgia Inst of Technology (GA)
Georgian Court U (NJ)
Georgia Southern U (GA)
Georgia State U (GA)
Glenville State Coll (WV)
Gonzaga U (WA)
Gordon Coll (MA)
Goucher Coll (MD)
Governors State U (IL)
Graceland U (IA)
Grambling State U (LA)
Granite State Coll (NH)
Guilford Coll (NC)
Gustavus Adolphus Coll (MN)
Hamline U (MN)
Hampton U (VA)
Harding U (AR)
Hardin-Simmons U (TX)
Harris-Stowe State U (MO)
HEC Montreal (QC, Canada)
High Point U (NC)
Hofstra U (NY)
Hope Coll (MI)
Hope Intl U (CA)
Houston Baptist U (TX)
Howard U (DC)
Husson U (ME)
Illinois Coll (IL)
Illinois Inst of Technology (IL)
Illinois State U (IL)
Illinois Wesleyan U (IL)
Immaculata U (PA)
Indiana State U (IN)
Indiana U East (IN)
Indiana U Kokomo (IN)
Indiana U Northwest (IN)
Indiana U of Pennsylvania (PA)
Indiana U South Bend (IN)
Indiana U Southeast (IN)
Inter American U of Puerto Rico, Aguadilla Campus (PR)
Inter American U of Puerto Rico, Metropolitan Campus (PR)
Inter American U of Puerto Rico, San Germán Campus (PR)
Intl U in Geneva (Switzerland)
Iona Coll (NY)
Ithaca Coll (NY)
Jacksonville State U (AL)
Jacksonville U (FL)
James Madison U (VA)
John Brown U (AR)
John Cabot U (Italy)
Johnson U (TN)
Johnson U Florida (FL)
Kansas State U (KS)
Kansas Wesleyan U (KS)
Kean U (NJ)
Keiser U, Fort Lauderdale (FL)
Kennesaw State U (GA)
Kent State U at Tuscarawas (OH)
Kettering U (MI)
Keuka Coll (NY)
The King's Coll (NY)
King's Coll (PA)
The King's U (AB, Canada)
King U (TN)
Knox Coll (IL)
Kutztown U of Pennsylvania (PA)
Lackawanna Coll (PA)
LaGrange Coll (GA)
Lancaster Bible Coll (PA)
Lasell Coll (MA)
La Sierra U (CA)
Lawrence Technological U (MI)
Lebanese American U (Lebanon)
Lee U (TN)
Lehman Coll of the City U of New York (NY)
Lenoir-Rhyne U (NC)
Lesley U (MA)
LeTourneau U (TX)
Lewis-Clark State Coll (ID)
Lewis U (IL)
Liberty U (VA)
Limestone Coll (SC)
Lincoln Memorial U (TN)
Lincoln U (MO)
Lincoln U (PA)
Lindenwood U (MO)
Linfield Coll (OR)
Lipscomb U (TN)
Lock Haven U of Pennsylvania (PA)
Longwood U (VA)
Loras Coll (IA)
Louisiana State U and A&M Coll (LA)
Louisiana State U in Shreveport (LA)
Louisiana Tech U (LA)
Loyola Marymount U (CA)
Loyola U Chicago (IL)
Loyola U New Orleans (LA)
Lynn U (FL)
Madonna U (MI)
Malone U (OH)
Manhattanville Coll (NY)
Mansfield U of Pennsylvania (PA)

Marian U (IN)
Marietta Coll (OH)
Marquette U (WI)
Marshall U (WV)
Marymount California U (CA)
Marymount Manhattan Coll (NY)
Marymount U (VA)
Maryville U of Saint Louis (MO)
Marywood U (PA)
Mayville State U (ND)
McDaniel Coll (MD)
McKendree U (IL)
McMurry U (TX)
McNeese State U (LA)
Mercy Coll (NY)
Meredith Coll (NC)
Merrimack Coll (MA)
Messiah Coll (PA)
Miami U (OH)
Miami U Hamilton (OH)
Miami U Middletown (OH)
Michigan State U (MI)
Michigan Technological U (MI)
Mid-America Christian U (OK)
MidAmerica Nazarene U (KS)
Middle Tennessee State U (TN)
Midland Coll (TX)
Millersville U of Pennsylvania (PA)
Milligan Coll (TN)
Millikin U (IL)
Milwaukee School of Eng (WI)
Minnesota State U Mankato (MN)
Minot State U (ND)
Misericordia U (PA)
Mississippi State U (MS)
Missouri State U (MO)
Missouri U of Science and Technology (MO)
Missouri Valley Coll (MO)
Molloy Coll (NY)
Montclair State U (NJ)
Moravian Coll (PA)
Morehead State U (KY)
Mount Aloysius Coll (PA)
Mount Marty Coll (SD)
Mount Mercy U (IA)
Mount Saint Mary Coll (NY)
Mount Saint Mary's U (CA)
Mount Vernon Nazarene U (OH)
Muhlenberg Coll (PA)
Murray State U (KY)
Muskingum U (OH)
National U (CA)
Nazareth Coll of Rochester (NY)
Nebraska Wesleyan U (NE)
New England Coll (NH)
New England Inst of Technology (RI)
New Jersey Inst of Technology (NJ)
Newman U (KS)
New Mexico Highlands U (NM)
New Mexico Inst of Mining and Technology (NM)
New York Inst of Technology (NY)
Niagara U (NY)
Nichols Coll (MA)
North Carolina Central U (NC)
North Central U (MN)
Northeastern Illinois U (IL)
Northeastern State U (OK)
Northern Arizona U (AZ)
Northern Illinois U (IL)
Northern Kentucky U (KY)
Northern State U (SD)
North Greenville U (SC)
Northwest Christian U (OR)
Northwestern Coll (IA)
Northwestern State U of Louisiana (LA)
Northwest Missouri State U (MO)
Northwest Nazarene U (ID)
Northwest U (WA)
Notre Dame Coll (OH)
Nova Southeastern U (FL)
Nyack Coll (NY)
Oakland City U (IN)
Oglethorpe U (GA)
Ohio Christian U (OH)
Ohio Dominican U (OH)
The Ohio State U (OH)
The Ohio State U at Lima (OH)
The Ohio State U at Mansfield (OH)
The Ohio State U at Marion (OH)
The Ohio State U at Newark (OH)
Ohio Valley U (WV)
Ohio Wesleyan U (OH)
Oklahoma State U (OK)
Old Dominion U (VA)
Olivet Nazarene U (IL)
Oral Roberts U (OK)
Ottawa U (KS)
Pacific U (OR)
Palm Beach Atlantic U (FL)
Peirce Coll (PA)
Penn State Beaver (PA)
Penn State Brandywine (PA)
Penn State DuBois (PA)
Penn State Erie, The Behrend Coll (PA)
Penn State Fayette, The Eberly Campus (PA)
Penn State Greater Allegheny (PA)
Penn State Harrisburg (PA)
Penn State Hazleton (PA)
Penn State Mont Alto (PA)
Penn State New Kensington (PA)
Penn State Shenango (PA)
Penn State Wilkes-Barre (PA)
Penn State York (PA)
Pepperdine U, Malibu (CA)
Point Loma Nazarene U (CA)
Polk State Coll (FL)
Polytechnic U of Puerto Rico (PR)
Prairie View A&M U (TX)
Providence Coll (RI)
Purdue U Fort Wayne (IN)
Purdue U Northwest (IN)
Queens U of Charlotte (NC)
Radford U (VA)
Ramapo Coll of New Jersey (NJ)
Rasmussen Coll Bloomington (MN)
Rasmussen Coll Brooklyn Park (MN)
Rasmussen Coll Eagan (MN)
Rasmussen Coll Fargo (ND)
Rasmussen Coll Fort Myers (FL)
Rasmussen Coll Kansas City/ Overland Park (KS)
Rasmussen Coll Lake Elmo/ Woodbury (MN)
Rasmussen Coll Land O' Lakes (FL)
Rasmussen Coll Mankato (MN)
Rasmussen Coll Moorhead (MN)
Rasmussen Coll New Port Richey (FL)
Rasmussen Coll Ocala (FL)
Rasmussen Coll Rockford (IL)
Rasmussen Coll St. Cloud (MN)
Rasmussen Coll Tampa/Brandon (FL)
Rasmussen Coll Topeka (KS)
Regent U (VA)
Rhode Island Coll (RI)
Rhodes Coll (TN)
Rice U (TX)
Richmond, The American Intl U in London (United Kingdom)
Roanoke Coll (VA)
Roberts Wesleyan Coll (NY)
Rochester U (MI)
Rocky Mountain Coll (MT)
Rogers State U (OK)
Roger Williams U (RI)
Rollins Coll (FL)
Rosemont Coll (PA)
Rowan U (NJ)
Sacred Heart U (CT)
The Sage Colls (NY)
Saginaw Valley State U (MI)
St. Ambrose U (IA)
St. Bonaventure U (NY)
St. Catherine U (MN)
St. Cloud State U (MN)
Saint Francis U (PA)
St. John Fisher Coll (NY)
Saint John's U (MN)
Saint Joseph's U (PA)
Saint Leo U (FL)
Saint Louis U (MO)
Saint Mary's Coll (IN)
St. Mary's U (TX)
St. Norbert Coll (WI)
St. Petersburg Coll (FL)
St. Thomas Aquinas Coll (NY)
St. Thomas U - Florida (FL)
Saint Vincent Coll (PA)
Salem State U (MA)
Salisbury U (MD)
Salve Regina U (RI)
Samford U (AL)
Sam Houston State U (TX)
San Diego State U (CA)
San Francisco State U (CA)
San Jose State U (CA)
Schreiner U (TX)
Seattle U (WA)
Seton Hill U (PA)
Shenandoah U (VA)
Shepherd U (WV)
Siena Heights U (MI)
Sierra Nevada Coll (NV)
Simmons U (MA)
Simon Fraser U (BC, Canada)
Slippery Rock U of Pennsylvania (PA)
Southeastern Louisiana U (LA)
Southeastern U (FL)
Southeast Missouri State U (MO)
Southern Arkansas U–Magnolia (AR)
Southern Illinois U Carbondale (IL)
Southern Illinois U Edwardsville (IL)
Southern Methodist U (TX)
Southwest Baptist U (MO)
Southwestern Coll (KS)
Southwestern Oklahoma State U (OK)
Spring Arbor U (MI)
Springfield Coll (MA)
Spring Hill Coll (AL)
State U of New York at Fredonia (NY)
State U of New York at New Paltz (NY)
State U of New York at Oswego (NY)
State U of New York Coll at Geneseo (NY)
State U of New York Coll at Old Westbury (NY)
State U of New York Coll at Potsdam (NY)
State U of New York Coll of Technology at Alfred (NY)
State U of New York Coll of Technology at Delhi (NY)
Sterling Coll (KS)
Stetson U (FL)
Stevens Inst of Technology (NJ)
Stevenson U (MD)
Stockton U (NJ)
Stony Brook U, State U of New York (NY)
Suffolk U (MA)
Sullivan U (KY)
SUNY Brockport (NY)
Susquehanna U (PA)
Taylor U (IN)
Tennessee Wesleyan U (TN)
Texas A&M Intl U (TX)
Texas A&M U (TX)
Texas A&M U–Central Texas (TX)
Texas A&M U–Commerce (TX)
Texas A&M U–Corpus Christi (TX)
Texas A&M U–Kingsville (TX)
Texas Christian U (TX)
Texas Lutheran U (TX)
Texas Southern U (TX)
Texas State U (TX)
Texas Tech U (TX)
Texas Woman's U (TX)
Tiffin U (OH)
Toccoa Falls Coll (GA)
Towson U (MD)
Trevecca Nazarene U (TN)
Trine U (IN)
Trinity U (TX)
Troy U (AL)
Truett McConnell U (GA)
Truman State U (MO)
Tulane U (LA)
Union U (TN)
United States Military Acad (NY)
Universidad Adventista de las Antillas (PR)
U at Albany, State U of New York (NY)
U at Buffalo, the State U of New York (NY)
The U of Akron (OH)
The U of Alabama (AL)
The U of Alabama at Birmingham (AL)
The U of Alabama in Huntsville (AL)
U of Alaska Fairbanks (AK)
U of Alaska Southeast (AK)
The U of Arizona (AZ)
U of Arkansas (AR)
U of Arkansas at Little Rock (AR)
U of California, Berkeley (CA)
U of California, Irvine (CA)
U of California, Merced (CA)
U of California, Riverside (CA)
U of Central Arkansas (AR)
U of Central Florida (FL)
U of Cincinnati (OH)
U of Colorado Boulder (CO)
U of Colorado Colorado Springs (CO)
U of Colorado Denver (CO)
U of Dallas (TX)
U of Denver (CO)
U of Detroit Mercy (MI)
U of Dubuque (IA)
The U of Findlay (OH)
U of Guam (GU)
U of Hartford (CT)
U of Hawaii at Manoa (HI)
U of Hawaii–West Oahu (HI)
U of Houston (TX)
U of Houston–Clear Lake (TX)
U of Houston–Downtown (TX)
U of Idaho (ID)
U of Illinois at Chicago (IL)
U of Illinois at Springfield (IL)
The U of Iowa (IA)
U of Jamestown (ND)
The U of Kansas (KS)
U of La Verne (CA)
U of Louisiana at Lafayette (LA)
U of Louisiana at Monroe (LA)
U of Maine (ME)
U of Management and Technology (VA)
U of Mary Hardin-Baylor (TX)
U of Maryland Global Campus (MD)
U of Mary Washington (VA)
U of Massachusetts Amherst (MA)
U of Massachusetts Boston (MA)
U of Massachusetts Dartmouth (MA)
U of Massachusetts Lowell (MA)
U of Memphis (TN)
U of Miami (FL)
U of Michigan (MI)
U of Michigan–Dearborn (MI)
U of Michigan–Flint (MI)
U of Minnesota, Duluth (MN)
U of Minnesota, Morris (MN)
U of Montevallo (AL)
U of Nebraska at Kearney (NE)
U of Nebraska–Lincoln (NE)
U of Nevada, Las Vegas (NV)
U of Nevada, Reno (NV)
U of New England (ME)
U of New Hampshire (NH)
U of New Haven (CT)
U of New Mexico (NM)
The U of North Carolina at Chapel Hill (NC)
The U of North Carolina at Charlotte (NC)
The U of North Carolina at Greensboro (NC)
The U of North Carolina at Pembroke (NC)
The U of North Carolina Wilmington (NC)
U of North Dakota (ND)
U of Northern Colorado (CO)
U of Northern Iowa (IA)
U of North Florida (FL)
U of Northwestern–St. Paul (MN)
U of Pennsylvania (PA)
U of Pikeville (KY)
U of Pittsburgh at Bradford (PA)
U of Pittsburgh at Greensburg (PA)
U of Portland (OR)
U of Providence (MT)
U of Puget Sound (WA)
U of Richmond (VA)
U of Saint Francis (IN)
U of Saint Joseph (CT)
U of Saint Mary (KS)
U of St. Thomas (TX)
U of San Diego (CA)
U of San Francisco (CA)
The U of Scranton (PA)
U of South Alabama (AL)
U of South Carolina (SC)
U of South Carolina Aiken (SC)
U of South Carolina Beaufort (SC)
U of South Dakota (SD)
U of Southern Indiana (IN)
U of Southern Maine (ME)
U of Southern Mississippi (MS)
U of South Florida (FL)
U of South Florida, St. Petersburg (FL)
The U of Tampa (FL)
The U of Tennessee (TN)
The U of Tennessee at Chattanooga (TN)
The U of Tennessee at Martin (TN)
The U of Texas at El Paso (TX)
The U of Texas at San Antonio (TX)
The U of Texas of the Permian Basin (TX)
The U of Texas Rio Grande Valley (TX)
U of the Fraser Valley (BC, Canada)
U of the Incarnate Word (TX)
U of the Pacific (CA)
U of the Virgin Islands (VI)
The U of Toledo (OH)
U of Toronto (ON, Canada)
The U of Tulsa (OK)
U of Utah (UT)
U of Vermont (VT)
U of Washington (WA)
U of Washington, Bothell (WA)
U of Washington, Tacoma (WA)
U of Waterloo (ON, Canada)
The U of West Alabama (AL)
The U of Western Ontario (ON, Canada)
U of West Florida (FL)
U of West Georgia (GA)
U of Wisconsin–Eau Claire (WI)
U of Wisconsin–Green Bay (WI)
U of Wisconsin–La Crosse (WI)
U of Wisconsin–Madison (WI)
U of Wisconsin–Parkside (WI)
U of Wisconsin–Stout (WI)
U of Wisconsin–Superior (WI)
U of Wyoming (WY)
Upper Iowa U (IA)
Ursuline Coll (OH)
Utah State U (UT)
Utah Valley U (UT)
Utica Coll (NY)
Valdosta State U (GA)
Valley City State U (ND)
Valparaiso U (IN)
Vanguard U of Southern California (CA)
Vermont Tech Coll (VT)
Villanova U (PA)
Virginia Wesleyan U (VA)
Walla Walla U (WA)
Wartburg Coll (IA)
Washington and Lee U (VA)
Washington Coll (MD)
Washington State U (WA)
Washington State U–Tri-Cities (WA)
Washington State U–Vancouver (WA)
Washington U in St. Louis (MO)
Wayland Baptist U (TX)
Waynesburg U (PA)
Wayne State Coll (NE)
Webber Intl U (FL)
Weber State U (UT)
Wesleyan Coll (GA)
West Chester U of Pennsylvania (PA)
Western Carolina U (NC)
Western Colorado U (CO)
Western Connecticut State U (CT)
Western Kentucky U (KY)
Western Michigan U (MI)
Western New England U (MA)
Western New Mexico U (NM)
Western Washington U (WA)
Westfield State U (MA)
West Liberty U (WV)
West Virginia U (WV)
Wheaton Coll (MA)
Whitworth U (WA)
Wichita State U (KS)
Widener U (PA)
Wilkes U (PA)
William & Mary (VA)
William Jewell Coll (MO)
William Paterson U of New Jersey (NJ)
William Peace U (NC)

William Penn U (IA)
Wilmington Coll (OH)
Wingate U (NC)
Winthrop U (SC)
Wittenberg U (OH)
Woodbury U (CA)
Worcester State U (MA)
Wright State U (OH)
Xavier U (OH)
Xavier U of Louisiana (LA)
Yeshiva U (NY)
York Coll of Pennsylvania (PA)
Youngstown State U (OH)

BUSINESS ADMINISTRATION, MANAGEMENT AND OPERATIONS RELATED
Adams State U (CO)
Alverno Coll (WI)
Augsburg U (MN)
Austin Coll (TX)
Babson Coll (MA)
Benedictine U (IL)
Bentley U (MA)
Bethel U (TN)
Bowling Green State U (OH)
California State U, San Bernardino (CA)
Calumet Coll of Saint Joseph (IN)
Capital U (OH)
Carnegie Mellon U (PA)
Cazenovia Coll (NY)
Central Michigan U (MI)
Central Washington U (WA)
Clayton State U (GA)
Columbia Coll (SC)
Davenport U, Grand Rapids (MI)
Daytona State Coll (FL)
Dominican U of California (CA)
Eastern Oregon U (OR)
Florida Inst of Technology (FL)
Florida SouthWestern State Coll (FL)
Gulf Coast State Coll (FL)
Hofstra U (NY)
Inter American U of Puerto Rico, Metropolitan Campus (PR)
Jacksonville U (FL)
Lackawanna Coll (PA)
La Roche U (PA)
Le Moyne Coll (NY)
Limestone Coll (SC)
Lincoln Memorial U (TN)
Loyola U Chicago (IL)
Malone U (OH)
Mayville State U (ND)
Mercer U, Macon (GA)
Miami Dade Coll (FL)
Millikin U (IL)
Missouri State U (MO)
Northwest Christian U (OR)
Northwest U (WA)
Oakland U (MI)
Pensacola State Coll (FL)
Polk State Coll (FL)
Saint Mary's Coll of California (CA)
St. Petersburg Coll (FL)
St. Thomas U - Florida (FL)
San Jose State U (CA)
Shenandoah U (VA)
Siena Coll (NY)
Spring Hill Coll (AL)
State U of New York at New Paltz (NY)
Texas Tech U (TX)
Trine U (IN)
The U of Alabama at Birmingham (AL)
U of Charleston (WV)
U of Houston–Clear Lake (TX)
U of Illinois at Springfield (IL)
U of Louisville (KY)
U of Maryland, Baltimore County (MD)
U of Maryland Global Campus (MD)
U of Miami (FL)
U of Michigan–Dearborn (MI)
U of Pennsylvania (PA)
U of Puerto Rico–Ponce (PR)
U of Southern Maine (ME)
U of Waterloo (ON, Canada)
The U of Western Ontario (ON, Canada)
U of Wyoming (WY)
Washington U in St. Louis (MO)
Waynesburg U (PA)

Western New England U (MA)
Wichita State U (KS)
Widener U (PA)
Worcester State U (MA)

BUSINESS AND PERSONAL/ FINANCIAL SERVICES MARKETING
Walla Walla U (WA)

BUSINESS AUTOMATION/ TECHNOLOGY/DATA ENTRY
HEC Montreal (QC, Canada)
Mount Vernon Nazarene U (OH)
The U of Tampa (FL)

BUSINESS/COMMERCE
Adams State U (CO)
Alverno Coll (WI)
American Coll of Thessaloniki (Greece)
Anderson U (SC)
Auburn U at Montgomery (AL)
Austin Coll (TX)
Avila U (MO)
Azusa Pacific U (CA)
Baker U (KS)
Ball State U (IN)
Bayamón Central U (PR)
Baylor U (TX)
Belmont U (TN)
Bentley U (MA)
Bethel U (IN)
Bowling Green State U (OH)
Brandeis U (MA)
Brenau U (GA)
Bryn Athyn Coll of the New Church (PA)
Bucknell U (PA)
California Baptist U (CA)
California State U, Dominguez Hills (CA)
California U of Pennsylvania (PA)
The Catholic U of America (DC)
Central Christian Coll of Kansas (KS)
Central State U (OH)
Champlain Coll (VT)
Clayton State U (GA)
Columbia Coll (MO)
Covenant Coll (GA)
Davenport U, Grand Rapids (MI)
Delta State U (MS)
Dickinson State U (ND)
Drake U (IA)
Drexel U (PA)
Earlham Coll (IN)
East Central U (OK)
Eastern Kentucky U (KY)
Eastern Michigan U (MI)
East Texas Baptist U (TX)
Edgewood Coll (WI)
Excelsior Coll (NY)
Fort Lewis Coll (CO)
Framingham State U (MA)
Franklin Coll (IN)
Georgia Gwinnett Coll (GA)
Glenville State Coll (WV)
Goshen Coll (IN)
Grand Valley State U (MI)
HEC Montreal (QC, Canada)
Hofstra U (NY)
Hollins U (VA)
Husson U (ME)
Indiana State U (IN)
Indiana U Bloomington (IN)
Indiana U Kokomo (IN)
Indiana U Northwest (IN)
Indiana U of Pennsylvania (PA)
Indiana U-Purdue U Indianapolis (IN)
Indiana U South Bend (IN)
Indiana U Southeast (IN)
Jacksonville U (FL)
John Brown U (AR)
Kalamazoo Coll (MI)
Kansas State U (KS)
Lackawanna Coll (PA)
Lamar U (TX)
La Sierra U (CA)
Limestone Coll (SC)
Loyola U Chicago (IL)
Loyola U Maryland (MD)
Loyola U New Orleans (LA)
Marymount Manhattan Coll (NY)
Maryville U of Saint Louis (MO)
McMurry U (TX)
Mercer U, Macon (GA)

MidAmerica Nazarene U (KS)
Middle Tennessee State U (TN)
Midway U (KY)
Missouri Southern State U (MO)
Missouri State U (MO)
Montana State U (MT)
Montana Technological U (MT)
Morehead State U (KY)
Mount Mercy U (IA)
Mount St. Mary's U (MD)
Mount Vernon Nazarene U (OH)
Multnomah U (OR)
Murray State U (KY)
Nebraska Wesleyan U (NE)
New Charter U (UT)
New York U (NY)
Niagara U (NY)
Nichols Coll (MA)
Northeastern Illinois U (IL)
Northwest Christian U (OR)
Northwest U (WA)
Oakland U (MI)
The Ohio State U (OH)
The Ohio State U at Lima (OH)
The Ohio State U at Mansfield (OH)
The Ohio State U at Marion (OH)
The Ohio State U at Newark (OH)
Ohio Valley U (WV)
Ohio Wesleyan U (OH)
Pace U, Pleasantville Campus (NY)
Penn State Abington (PA)
Penn State Altoona (PA)
Penn State Berks (PA)
Penn State Lehigh Valley (PA)
Penn State Schuylkill (PA)
Pittsburg State U (KS)
Purdue U Fort Wayne (IN)
Purdue U Northwest (IN)
Ramapo Coll of New Jersey (NJ)
Randolph Coll (VA)
Randolph-Macon Coll (VA)
Regis Coll (MA)
Saginaw Valley State U (MI)
St. Cloud State U (MN)
Saint Mary's Coll of California (CA)
St. Thomas U - Florida (FL)
Saint Vincent Coll (PA)
Sam Houston State U (TX)
Santa Clara U (CA)
Schreiner U (TX)
Seattle U (WA)
Siena Coll (NY)
Skidmore Coll (NY)
Southeastern U (FL)
Southern Arkansas U–Magnolia (AR)
Southwest Baptist U (MO)
Southwestern U (TX)
State U of New York at New Paltz (NY)
State U of New York Empire State Coll (NY)
Suffolk U (MA)
Sullivan U (KY)
Tabor Coll (KS)
Temple U (PA)
Texas A&M U–Commerce (TX)
Texas A&M U–Corpus Christi (TX)
Texas A&M U–Kingsville (TX)
Texas Christian U (TX)
Texas Tech U (TX)
Texas Woman's U (TX)
Transylvania U (KY)
Trine U (IN)
The U of Akron (OH)
The U of Arizona (AZ)
U of Arkansas (AR)
U of Arkansas at Little Rock (AR)
U of Central Florida (FL)
U of Cincinnati (OH)
U of Denver (CO)
U of Hawaii at Manoa (HI)
U of Houston–Clear Lake (TX)
U of Houston–Downtown (TX)
The U of Kansas (KS)
U of Kentucky (KY)
U of Massachusetts Dartmouth (MA)
U of Missouri–St. Louis (MO)
U of Montana (MT)
U of Nevada, Reno (NV)
U of North Texas (TX)
U of Notre Dame (IN)
U of Oregon (OR)
U of Puget Sound (WA)
U of Saint Francis (IN)

U of Science and Arts of Oklahoma (OK)
U of South Alabama (AL)
U of South Dakota (SD)
U of South Florida (FL)
The U of Texas at Dallas (TX)
The U of Texas at El Paso (TX)
The U of Texas at San Antonio (TX)
U of Utah (UT)
U of Virginia (VA)
The U of Western Ontario (ON, Canada)
U of West Florida (FL)
U of Wisconsin–Milwaukee (WI)
U of Wisconsin–Platteville (WI)
Virginia Commonwealth U (VA)
Wake Forest U (NC)
Washington & Jefferson Coll (PA)
Washington U in St. Louis (MO)
Webber Intl U (FL)
Western New England U (MA)
Western New Mexico U (NM)
Western Oregon U (OR)
West Virginia U (WV)
Worcester Polytechnic Inst (MA)
Wright State U (OH)
Wright State U–Lake Campus (OH)
Youngstown State U (OH)

BUSINESS/CORPORATE COMMUNICATIONS
Aquinas Coll (MI)
Augustana U (SD)
Babson Coll (MA)
Baruch Coll of the City U of New York (NY)
Bentley U (MA)
Chestnut Hill Coll (PA)
Concordia U Chicago (IL)
Inter American U of Puerto Rico, Metropolitan Campus (PR)
Marietta Coll (OH)
Marquette U (WI)
Mercy Coll (NY)
National U (CA)
Nichols Coll (MA)
Penn State Abington (PA)
Point Loma Nazarene U (CA)
Saint Leo U (FL)
Stevens Inst of Technology (NJ)
Stevenson U (MD)
Susquehanna U (PA)
U of New England (ME)
The U of Western Ontario (ON, Canada)

BUSINESS FAMILY AND CONSUMER SCIENCES/ HUMAN SCIENCES
Brigham Young U (UT)
U of Houston (TX)

BUSINESS, MANAGEMENT, AND MARKETING RELATED
Alfred U (NY)
American U (DC)
Arizona State U at the Polytechnic campus (AZ)
Arizona State U at the Tempe campus (AZ)
Arizona State U at the West campus (AZ)
Athens State U (AL)
Benedictine U (IL)
Bentley U (MA)
Bowling Green State U (OH)
Bradley U (IL)
Bridgewater State U (MA)
California State U, Dominguez Hills (CA)
Eastern U (PA)
Elms Coll (MA)
FIDM/Fashion Inst of Design & Merchandising, Los Angeles Campus (CA)
Hofstra U (NY)
Keuka Coll (NY)
Los Angeles Film School (CA)
Loyola U Chicago (IL)
Messiah Coll (PA)
Missouri U of Science and Technology (MO)
Multnomah U (OR)
Nebraska Wesleyan U (NE)
New Jersey Inst of Technology (NJ)
New York U (NY)

North Central U (MN)
Northwest Christian U (OR)
Notre Dame Coll (OH)
Penn State U Park (PA)
Polytechnic U of Puerto Rico (PR)
Roberts Wesleyan Coll (NY)
St. Ambrose U (IA)
Saint Mary's U of Minnesota (MN)
Seton Hill U (PA)
Sierra Nevada Coll (NV)
Skidmore Coll (NY)
Southern California Inst of Technology (CA)
Southwest Baptist U (MO)
Southwestern Coll (KS)
State U of New York Coll of Agriculture and Technology at Cobleskill (NY)
State U of New York Coll of Technology at Alfred (NY)
State U of New York Coll of Technology at Canton (NY)
State U of New York Coll of Technology at Delhi (NY)
State U of New York Maritime Coll (NY)
Susquehanna U (PA)
Tiffin U (OH)
Trevecca Nazarene U (TN)
Troy U (AL)
U of Louisiana at Lafayette (LA)
U of Southern Mississippi (MS)
The U of Western Ontario (ON, Canada)
U of Wisconsin–Stout (WI)
Ursuline Coll (OH)
Utica Coll (NY)
Walla Walla U (WA)
William Peace U (NC)
Worcester Polytechnic Inst (MA)
Xavier U (OH)

BUSINESS/MANAGERIAL ECONOMICS
Allegheny Coll (PA)
Andrews U (MI)
Angelo State U (TX)
Aquinas Coll (MI)
Arkansas Tech U (AR)
Auburn U (AL)
Ball State U (IN)
Baruch Coll of the City U of New York (NY)
Baylor U (TX)
Belmont U (TN)
Beloit Coll (WI)
Benedictine U (IL)
Bentley U (MA)
Berry Coll (GA)
Boise State U (ID)
Boston Coll (MA)
Bowling Green State U (OH)
Bradley U (IL)
California State U, Fullerton (CA)
California State U, Long Beach (CA)
Campbellsville U (KY)
Capital U (OH)
Carson-Newman U (TN)
Cedarville U (OH)
Central Washington U (WA)
Chatham U (PA)
Clarion U of Pennsylvania (PA)
Clark Atlanta U (GA)
Coastal Carolina U (SC)
The Coll of Saint Rose (NY)
The Coll of Wooster (OH)
DePaul U (IL)
Eastern Michigan U (MI)
Eastern Washington U (WA)
Fairleigh Dickinson U (NJ)
Fort Lewis Coll (CO)
Francis Marion U (SC)
Gannon U (PA)
Georgetown Coll (KY)
The George Washington U (DC)
Georgia Coll & State U (GA)
Georgia Inst of Technology (GA)
Georgia Southern U (GA)
Georgia State U (GA)
Grambling State U (LA)
Grand Valley State U (MI)
Gustavus Adolphus Coll (MN)
Hampden-Sydney Coll (VA)
HEC Montreal (QC, Canada)
Hofstra U (NY)
Hope Coll (MI)

Husson U (ME)
Illinois Coll (IL)
Inter American U of Puerto Rico, Bayamón Campus (PR)
Inter American U of Puerto Rico, Metropolitan Campus (PR)
Inter American U of Puerto Rico, San Germán Campus (PR)
Iowa State U of Science and Technology (IA)
James Madison U (VA)
Kennesaw State U (GA)
Lake Forest Coll (IL)
Lamar U (TX)
Lehigh U (PA)
Lewis U (IL)
Limestone Coll (SC)
Lincoln Memorial U (TN)
Lipscomb U (TN)
Louisiana State U and A&M Coll (LA)
Louisiana Tech U (LA)
Loyola U Chicago (IL)
Loyola U New Orleans (LA)
Marquette U (WI)
Marshall U (WV)
Marymount Manhattan Coll (NY)
Miami U (OH)
Miami U Hamilton (OH)
Miami U Middletown (OH)
Middle Tennessee State U (TN)
Mississippi State U (MS)
Missouri Southern State U (MO)
Missouri Valley Coll (MO)
Molloy Coll (NY)
New York U (NY)
Niagara U (NY)
Nichols Coll (MA)
Northern Arizona U (AZ)
Northern Kentucky U (KY)
Northwest Missouri State U (MO)
Oakland U (MI)
Oglethorpe U (GA)
The Ohio State U (OH)
Ohio Wesleyan U (OH)
Oklahoma State U (OK)
Old Dominion U (VA)
Ottawa U (KS)
Pace U, Pleasantville Campus (NY)
Patrick Henry Coll (VA)
Penn State Abington (PA)
Penn State Altoona (PA)
Penn State Beaver (PA)
Penn State Berks (PA)
Penn State Brandywine (PA)
Penn State DuBois (PA)
Penn State Erie, The Behrend Coll (PA)
Penn State Fayette, The Eberly Campus (PA)
Penn State Greater Allegheny (PA)
Penn State Hazleton (PA)
Penn State Lehigh Valley (PA)
Penn State Mont Alto (PA)
Penn State New Kensington (PA)
Penn State Schuylkill (PA)
Penn State Shenango (PA)
Penn State Wilkes-Barre (PA)
Penn State York (PA)
Purdue U Fort Wayne (IN)
Saginaw Valley State U (MI)
St. Cloud State U (MN)
Saint Louis U (MO)
Salisbury U (MD)
Samford U (AL)
Sam Houston State U (TX)
Santa Clara U (CA)
Seattle U (WA)
Shenandoah U (VA)
South Dakota State U (SD)
Southern Illinois U Carbondale (IL)
Spring Hill Coll (AL)
State U of New York Coll at Oneonta (NY)
State U of New York Coll at Potsdam (NY)
Stetson U (FL)
Suffolk U (MA)
Susquehanna U (PA)
Tarleton State U (TX)
Texas A&M U–Corpus Christi (TX)
Texas State U (TX)
Troy U (AL)
Union Coll (NY)
Union U (TN)
The U of Alabama (AL)
The U of Alabama at Birmingham (AL)
The U of Alabama in Huntsville (AL)
The U of Arizona (AZ)
U of Arkansas (AR)
U of California, Irvine (CA)
U of California, Los Angeles (CA)
U of California, Riverside (CA)
U of California, Santa Cruz (CA)
U of Central Florida (FL)
U of Dayton (OH)
U of Denver (CO)
U of Idaho (ID)
The U of Iowa (IA)
U of Kentucky (KY)
U of Louisiana at Lafayette (LA)
U of Louisville (KY)
U of Mary Hardin-Baylor (TX)
U of Massachusetts Amherst (MA)
U of Memphis (TN)
U of Miami (FL)
U of Nebraska–Lincoln (NE)
The U of North Carolina at Charlotte (NC)
The U of North Carolina at Greensboro (NC)
U of North Dakota (ND)
U of North Florida (FL)
U of North Texas (TX)
U of San Diego (CA)
U of South Carolina (SC)
U of Southern Mississippi (MS)
U of South Florida, St. Petersburg (FL)
The U of Tennessee (TN)
The U of Tennessee at Chattanooga (TN)
The U of Tennessee at Martin (TN)
The U of Texas at El Paso (TX)
The U of Texas at San Antonio (TX)
The U of Texas of the Permian Basin (TX)
U of the Incarnate Word (TX)
The U of Western Ontario (ON, Canada)
U of West Florida (FL)
U of West Georgia (GA)
U of Wyoming (WY)
Utica Coll (NY)
Valdosta State U (GA)
Villanova U (PA)
Virginia Commonwealth U (VA)
Washington U in St. Louis (MO)
Weber State U (UT)
West Chester U of Pennsylvania (PA)
Western Kentucky U (KY)
Western Michigan U (MI)
West Liberty U (WV)
Westminster Coll (UT)
Westmont Coll (CA)
West Virginia U (WV)
Wheaton Coll (IL)
Wichita State U (KS)
Widener U (PA)
Wilmington Coll (OH)
Wofford Coll (SC)
Wright State U (OH)
Wright State U–Lake Campus (OH)
Xavier U (OH)
Youngstown State U (OH)

BUSINESS OPERATIONS SUPPORT AND SECRETARIAL SERVICES RELATED
State U of New York at New Paltz (NY)

BUSINESS STATISTICS
Ball State U (IN)
Baruch Coll of the City U of New York (NY)
Baylor U (TX)
Ferris State U (MI)
HEC Montreal (QC, Canada)
Hofstra U (NY)
Iowa State U of Science and Technology (IA)
Loyola U New Orleans (LA)
Marian U (IN)
Maryville U of Saint Louis (MO)
Mid-America Christian U (OK)
New York U (NY)
The U of Alabama (AL)
U of Denver (CO)
U of Miami (FL)
U of New Haven (CT)
The U of Tennessee (TN)

BUSINESS TEACHER EDUCATION
Adams State U (CO)
Arizona Christian U (AZ)
Arkansas Tech U (AR)
Auburn U (AL)
Avila U (MO)
Ball State U (IN)
Baylor U (TX)
Black Hills State U (SD)
Bowling Green State U (OH)
California State U, Dominguez Hills (CA)
Campbellsville U (KY)
Carson-Newman U (TN)
Coll of Saint Mary (NE)
Concordia Coll (MN)
Concordia U Wisconsin (WI)
Dakota State U (SD)
Dickinson State U (ND)
Doane U (NE)
East Central U (OK)
Eastern Kentucky U (KY)
Eastern Michigan U (MI)
Eastern Washington U (WA)
Emmanuel Coll (GA)
Emory & Henry Coll (VA)
Evangel U (MO)
Fayetteville State U (NC)
Ferris State U (MI)
Friends U (KS)
Glenville State Coll (WV)
Goshen Coll (IN)
Gwynedd Mercy U (PA)
Hampton U (VA)
Hofstra U (NY)
Illinois State U (IL)
Immaculata U (PA)
Indiana State U (IN)
Lee U (TN)
Lehman Coll of the City U of New York (NY)
Lincoln U (MO)
Louisiana Tech U (LA)
Middle Tennessee State U (TN)
Minot State U (ND)
Mississippi State U (MS)
Missouri State U (MO)
Morehead State U (KY)
Mount Vernon Nazarene U (OH)
New York U (NY)
Niagara U (NY)
Northwestern Coll (IA)
Northwest Missouri State U (MO)
Oakland City U (IN)
Ohio Wesleyan U (OH)
Oral Roberts U (OK)
Ottawa U (KS)
Portland State U (OR)
St. Ambrose U (IA)
St. Petersburg Coll (FL)
Saint Vincent Coll (PA)
Sam Houston State U (TX)
Southern Arkansas U–Magnolia (AR)
Trevecca Nazarene U (TN)
Union U (TN)
U of Minnesota, Twin Cities Campus (MN)
U of Nebraska at Kearney (NE)
U of Nebraska–Lincoln (NE)
U of Northern Iowa (IA)
U of Southern Mississippi (MS)
Upper Iowa U (IA)
Utah State U (UT)
Utah Valley U (UT)
Utica Coll (NY)
Valley City State U (ND)
Walla Walla U (WA)
Wayland Baptist U (TX)
Wayne State Coll (NE)
Weber State U (UT)
Western Michigan U (MI)
Western New Mexico U (NM)
William Penn U (IA)
Wilmington Coll (OH)

CAD/CADD DRAFTING/ DESIGN TECHNOLOGY
Academy of Art U (CA)
Eastern Michigan U (MI)
Murray State U (KY)
Trine U (IN)

CANADIAN STUDIES
Brandon U (MB, Canada)
U of Toronto (ON, Canada)
U of Washington (WA)
U of Waterloo (ON, Canada)
The U of Western Ontario (ON, Canada)
Western Washington U (WA)

CARDIOVASCULAR TECHNOLOGY
Louisiana State U Health Sciences Center (LA)
Saint Mary's U of Minnesota (MN)
Weber State U (UT)

CARIBBEAN STUDIES
Hofstra U (NY)
Northwestern U (IL)

CELL AND MOLECULAR BIOLOGY
Adams State U (CO)
Binghamton U, State U of New York (NY)
Bradley U (IL)
Bridgewater State U (MA)
Bucknell U (PA)
Carnegie Mellon U (PA)
Cedarville U (OH)
Central Washington U (WA)
The Colorado Coll (CO)
Fort Lewis Coll (CO)
Grand Valley State U (MI)
Harvard U (MA)
John Carroll U (OH)
John Jay Coll of Criminal Justice of the City U of New York (NY)
Johns Hopkins U (MD)
Limestone Coll (SC)
Loyola U New Orleans (LA)
Marymount U (VA)
Missouri State U (MO)
Northeastern State U (OK)
Northwest Nazarene U (ID)
Sacred Heart U (CT)
Salem State U (MA)
Seattle U (WA)
Texas A&M U (TX)
Texas Tech U (TX)
The U of Arizona (AZ)
U of California, Berkeley (CA)
U of California, Irvine (CA)
U of California, Los Angeles (CA)
U of California, Riverside (CA)
U of California, San Diego (CA)
U of California, Santa Cruz (CA)
U of Colorado Boulder (CO)
U of Hawaii at Manoa (HI)
The U of Kansas (KS)
U of Puget Sound (WA)
U of St. Thomas (TX)
U of Utah (UT)
U of Washington (WA)
Western New Mexico U (NM)
Western Washington U (WA)

CELL BIOLOGY AND ANATOMICAL SCIENCES RELATED
Tulane U (LA)
U of Mary Hardin-Baylor (TX)
Yale U (CT)

CELL BIOLOGY AND ANATOMY
Dallas Baptist U (TX)
The U of Western Ontario (ON, Canada)

CELL BIOLOGY AND HISTOLOGY
Beloit Coll (WI)
California State U, Dominguez Hills (CA)
California State U, Fresno (CA)
California State U, Long Beach (CA)
California State U, San Marcos (CA)
The Coll of Saint Rose (NY)
Johns Hopkins U (MD)
Mansfield U of Pennsylvania (PA)
Montana State U (MT)
Northwestern U (IL)
San Francisco State U (CA)
Tulane U (LA)
U of California, San Diego (CA)
U of Minnesota, Duluth (MN)
U of Minnesota, Twin Cities Campus (MN)
U of Utah (UT)

CELTIC LANGUAGES
U of California, Berkeley (CA)
U of Notre Dame (IN)

CERAMIC ARTS AND CERAMICS
Adams State U (CO)
Alfred U (NY)
Anderson U (SC)
Aquinas Coll (MI)
Arcadia U (PA)
Bennington Coll (VT)
Bowling Green State U (OH)
Bradley U (IL)
Brigham Young U (UT)
California State U, Long Beach (CA)
Central Washington U (WA)
Cleveland Inst of Art (OH)
Coll of the Ozarks (MO)
Columbia Coll (MO)
Edinboro U of Pennsylvania (PA)
Hofstra U (NY)
Howard U (DC)
Inter American U of Puerto Rico, San Germán Campus (PR)
Marywood U (PA)
Massachusetts Coll of Art and Design (MA)
Minnesota State U Mankato (MN)
Northwest Nazarene U (ID)
Portland State U (OR)
Pratt Inst (NY)
Rhode Island Coll (RI)
Seton Hill U (PA)
State U of New York at New Paltz (NY)
The U of Akron (OH)
U of Dallas (TX)
U of Hartford (CT)
The U of Iowa (IA)
The U of Kansas (KS)
U of Miami (FL)
U of Michigan (MI)
U of Oregon (OR)
U of Washington (WA)
Washington U in St. Louis (MO)

CERAMIC SCIENCES AND ENGINEERING
Alfred U (NY)
Missouri U of Science and Technology (MO)

CHEMICAL AND BIOMOLECULAR ENGINEERING
Florida State U (FL)
Johns Hopkins U (MD)
Milwaukee School of Eng (WI)
New York U (NY)
Stony Brook U, State U of New York (NY)
U of Washington (WA)

CHEMICAL ENGINEERING
American U of Beirut (Lebanon)
Arizona State U at the Tempe campus (AZ)
Auburn U (AL)
Benedictine Coll (KS)
Brown U (RI)
Bucknell U (PA)
California Baptist U (CA)
California State Polytechnic U, Pomona (CA)
California State U, Long Beach (CA)
Calvin Coll (MI)
Carnegie Mellon U (PA)
City Coll of the City U of New York (NY)
Clarkson U (NY)
Clemson U (SC)
Colorado School of Mines (CO)
Colorado State U (CO)
Cornell U (NY)
Drexel U (PA)
Elon U (NC)
Florida A&M U (FL)
Florida Inst of Technology (FL)
Florida State U (FL)
Georgia Inst of Technology (GA)
Hampton U (VA)
Howard U (DC)

Illinois Inst of Technology (IL)
Iowa State U of Science and Technology (IA)
Johns Hopkins U (MD)
Kansas State U (KS)
Kettering U (MI)
Lafayette Coll (PA)
Lamar U (TX)
Lehigh U (PA)
Louisiana State U and A&M Coll (LA)
Louisiana Tech U (LA)
Manhattan Coll (NY)
Miami U (OH)
Miami U Hamilton (OH)
Miami U Middletown (OH)
Michigan State U (MI)
Michigan Technological U (MI)
Mississippi State U (MS)
Missouri U of Science and Technology (MO)
Montana State U (MT)
New Jersey Inst of Technology (NJ)
New Mexico Inst of Mining and Technology (NM)
New York U (NY)
Northwestern U (IL)
The Ohio State U (OH)
Oklahoma State U (OK)
Penn State Abington (PA)
Penn State Altoona (PA)
Penn State Beaver (PA)
Penn State Berks (PA)
Penn State Brandywine (PA)
Penn State DuBois (PA)
Penn State Erie, The Behrend Coll (PA)
Penn State Fayette, The Eberly Campus (PA)
Penn State Greater Allegheny (PA)
Penn State Hazleton (PA)
Penn State Lehigh Valley (PA)
Penn State Mont Alto (PA)
Penn State New Kensington (PA)
Penn State Schuylkill (PA)
Penn State Shenango (PA)
Penn State U Park (PA)
Penn State Wilkes-Barre (PA)
Penn State York (PA)
Polytechnic U of Puerto Rico (PR)
Prairie View A&M U (TX)
Princeton U (NJ)
Rice U (TX)
Rose-Hulman Inst of Technology (IN)
Rowan U (NJ)
San Jose State U (CA)
Stanford U (CA)
Stevens Inst of Technology (NJ)
Texas A&M U (TX)
Texas A&M U–Kingsville (TX)
Texas Tech U (TX)
Trine U (IN)
Tulane U (LA)
United States Military Acad (NY)
U at Buffalo, the State U of New York (NY)
The U of Akron (OH)
The U of Alabama (AL)
The U of Alabama in Huntsville (AL)
The U of Arizona (AZ)
U of Arkansas (AR)
U of California, Berkeley (CA)
U of California, Irvine (CA)
U of California, Los Angeles (CA)
U of California, Riverside (CA)
U of California, San Diego (CA)
U of California, Santa Barbara (CA)
U of Cincinnati (OH)
U of Colorado Boulder (CO)
U of Dayton (OH)
U of Houston (TX)
U of Idaho (ID)
U of Illinois at Chicago (IL)
The U of Iowa (IA)
The U of Kansas (KS)
U of Kentucky (KY)
U of Louisiana at Lafayette (LA)
U of Louisville (KY)
U of Maine (ME)
U of Maryland, Baltimore County (MD)
U of Massachusetts Amherst (MA)
U of Massachusetts Lowell (MA)
U of Michigan (MI)
U of Minnesota, Duluth (MN)
U of Minnesota, Twin Cities Campus (MN)
U of Nebraska–Lincoln (NE)
U of Nevada, Reno (NV)
U of New Hampshire (NH)
U of New Haven (CT)
U of New Mexico (NM)
U of North Dakota (ND)
U of Notre Dame (IN)
U of Pennsylvania (PA)
U of South Alabama (AL)
U of South Carolina (SC)
U of South Florida (FL)
The U of Tennessee (TN)
The U of Tennessee at Chattanooga (TN)
The U of Texas at San Antonio (TX)
The U of Texas of the Permian Basin (TX)
The U of Toledo (OH)
U of Toronto (ON, Canada)
The U of Tulsa (OK)
U of Utah (UT)
U of Virginia (VA)
U of Washington (WA)
U of Waterloo (ON, Canada)
The U of Western Ontario (ON, Canada)
U of Wisconsin–Madison (WI)
U of Wyoming (WY)
Vanderbilt U (TN)
Villanova U (PA)
Virginia Commonwealth U (VA)
Washington State U (WA)
Washington U in St. Louis (MO)
Wayne State U (MI)
Western Michigan U (MI)
West Virginia U (WV)
Widener U (PA)
Worcester Polytechnic Inst (MA)
Xavier U (OH)
Yale U (CT)
Youngstown State U (OH)

CHEMICAL ENGINEERING TECHNOLOGY
United States Military Acad (NY)

CHEMICAL PHYSICS
Adams State U (CO)
Aquinas Coll (MI)
Augustana U (SD)
Bowdoin Coll (ME)
Carnegie Mellon U (PA)
Centre Coll (KY)
Harvard U (MA)
Michigan State U (MI)
Saginaw Valley State U (MI)
Simon Fraser U (BC, Canada)
Susquehanna U (PA)
U of Waterloo (ON, Canada)

CHEMICAL TECHNOLOGY
U of Cincinnati (OH)

CHEMISTRY
Abilene Christian U (TX)
Adams State U (CO)
Agnes Scott Coll (GA)
Albion Coll (MI)
Alfred U (NY)
Allegheny Coll (PA)
Alverno Coll (WI)
American U (DC)
American U of Beirut (Lebanon)
Amherst Coll (MA)
Anderson U (IN)
Andrews U (MI)
Angelo State U (TX)
Appalachian State U (NC)
Aquinas Coll (MI)
Arcadia U (PA)
Arizona State U at the Tempe campus (AZ)
Arkansas Tech U (AR)
Assumption Coll (MA)
Athens State U (AL)
Auburn U (AL)
Auburn U at Montgomery (AL)
Augsburg U (MN)
Augustana Coll (IL)
Augustana U (SD)
Aurora U (IL)
Austin Coll (TX)
Austin Peay State U (TN)
Averett U (VA)
Azusa Pacific U (CA)
Baker U (KS)
Ball State U (IN)
Barnard Coll (NY)
Barry U (FL)
Barton Coll (NC)
Bates Coll (ME)
Bayamón Central U (PR)
Baylor U (TX)
Belhaven U (MS)
Belmont U (TN)
Beloit Coll (WI)
Bemidji State U (MN)
Benedictine Coll (KS)
Benedictine U (IL)
Bennington Coll (VT)
Berea Coll (KY)
Berry Coll (GA)
Bethany Lutheran Coll (MN)
Bethel U (IN)
Bethel U (MN)
Bethel U (TN)
Binghamton U, State U of New York (NY)
Biola U (CA)
Birmingham-Southern Coll (AL)
Black Hills State U (SD)
Bluffton U (OH)
Boise State U (ID)
Boston Coll (MA)
Bowdoin Coll (ME)
Bowling Green State U (OH)
Bradley U (IL)
Brandeis U (MA)
Brandon U (MB, Canada)
Bridgewater Coll (VA)
Bridgewater State U (MA)
Brown U (RI)
Bucknell U (PA)
Butler U (IN)
Caldwell U (NJ)
California Baptist U (CA)
California Lutheran U (CA)
California Polytechnic State U, San Luis Obispo (CA)
California State Polytechnic U, Pomona (CA)
California State U, Bakersfield (CA)
California State U, Dominguez Hills (CA)
California State U, Fresno (CA)
California State U, Fullerton (CA)
California State U, Long Beach (CA)
California State U, Los Angeles (CA)
California State U, Northridge (CA)
California State U, Sacramento (CA)
California State U, San Bernardino (CA)
California State U, San Marcos (CA)
California State U, Stanislaus (CA)
California U of Pennsylvania (PA)
Calvin Coll (MI)
Cameron U (OK)
Campbellsville U (KY)
Capital U (OH)
Carleton Coll (MN)
Carlow U (PA)
Carnegie Mellon U (PA)
Carson-Newman U (TN)
Carthage Coll (WI)
Catawba Coll (NC)
The Catholic U of America (DC)
Cedar Crest Coll (PA)
Cedarville U (OH)
Central Coll (IA)
Central Connecticut State U (CT)
Central Methodist U (MO)
Central Michigan U (MI)
Central State U (OH)
Central Washington U (WA)
Centre Coll (KY)
Chaminade U of Honolulu (HI)
Chatham U (PA)
Chestnut Hill Coll (PA)
The Citadel, The Military Coll of South Carolina (SC)
City Coll of the City U of New York (NY)
Claremont McKenna Coll (CA)
Clarion U of Pennsylvania (PA)
Clark Atlanta U (GA)
Clarkson U (NY)
Clark U (MA)
Clayton State U (GA)
Clemson U (SC)
Coastal Carolina U (SC)
Coe Coll (IA)
Colby Coll (ME)
Colgate U (NY)
Coll of Charleston (SC)
The Coll of Idaho (ID)
Coll of Saint Benedict (MN)
Coll of Saint Elizabeth (NJ)
Coll of Saint Mary (NE)
The Coll of Saint Rose (NY)
The Coll of St. Scholastica (MN)
Coll of Staten Island of the City U of New York (NY)
Coll of the Holy Cross (MA)
Coll of the Ozarks (MO)
The Coll of Wooster (OH)
The Colorado Coll (CO)
Colorado School of Mines (CO)
Colorado State U (CO)
Columbia Coll (MO)
Columbia Coll (SC)
Concordia Coll (MN)
Concordia U Chicago (IL)
Concordia U, St. Paul (MN)
Cornell Coll (IA)
Cornell U (NY)
Covenant Coll (GA)
Creighton U (NE)
Culver-Stockton Coll (MO)
Dartmouth Coll (NH)
Davidson Coll (NC)
Delaware Valley U (PA)
Delta State U (MS)
DePaul U (IL)
DePauw U (IN)
DeSales U (PA)
Dickinson Coll (PA)
Dickinson State U (ND)
Dillard U (LA)
Doane U (NE)
Dominican U (IL)
Dominican U of California (CA)
Drake U (IA)
Drew U (NJ)
Drexel U (PA)
Drury U (MO)
D'Youville Coll (NY)
Earlham Coll (IN)
East Carolina U (NC)
East Central U (OK)
Eastern Illinois U (IL)
Eastern Kentucky U (KY)
Eastern Mennonite U (VA)
Eastern Michigan U (MI)
Eastern New Mexico U (NM)
Eastern U (PA)
Eastern Washington U (WA)
East Texas Baptist U (TX)
Edgewood Coll (WI)
Edinboro U of Pennsylvania (PA)
Elms Coll (MA)
Elon U (NC)
Emmanuel Coll (MA)
Emory & Henry Coll (VA)
Emory U (GA)
Emporia State U (KS)
Evangel U (MO)
Fairfield U (CT)
Fairleigh Dickinson U (NJ)
Fayetteville State U (NC)
Ferris State U (MI)
Fitchburg State U (MA)
Florida A&M U (FL)
Florida Atlantic U (FL)
Florida Gulf Coast U (FL)
Florida Inst of Technology (FL)
Florida Southern Coll (FL)
Florida State U (FL)
Fordham U (NY)
Fort Lewis Coll (CO)
Framingham State U (MA)
Francis Marion U (SC)
Franklin Coll (IN)
Freed-Hardeman U (TN)
Friends U (KS)
Furman U (SC)
Gallaudet U (DC)
Gannon U (PA)
Geneva Coll (PA)
George Fox U (OR)
George Mason U (VA)
Georgetown Coll (KY)
Georgetown U (DC)
The George Washington U (DC)
Georgia Coll & State U (GA)
Georgia Gwinnett Coll (GA)
Georgia Inst of Technology (GA)
Georgian Court U (NJ)
Georgia Southern U (GA)
Georgia State U (GA)
Glenville State Coll (WV)
Gonzaga U (WA)
Goshen Coll (IN)
Goucher Coll (MD)
Governors State U (IL)
Graceland U (IA)
Grambling State U (LA)
Grand Valley State U (MI)
Grinnell Coll (IA)
Guilford Coll (NC)
Gustavus Adolphus Coll (MN)
Hamline U (MN)
Hampden-Sydney Coll (VA)
Hampshire Coll (MA)
Hampton U (VA)
Hanover Coll (IN)
Harding U (AR)
Hardin-Simmons U (TX)
Harvard U (MA)
High Point U (NC)
Hillsdale Coll (MI)
Hobart and William Smith Colls (NY)
Hofstra U (NY)
Hollins U (VA)
Hope Coll (MI)
Houston Baptist U (TX)
Howard U (DC)
Illinois Coll (IL)
Illinois Inst of Technology (IL)
Illinois State U (IL)
Illinois Wesleyan U (IL)
Immaculata U (PA)
Indiana State U (IN)
Indiana U Bloomington (IN)
Indiana U Kokomo (IN)
Indiana U Northwest (IN)
Indiana U of Pennsylvania (PA)
Indiana U-Purdue U Indianapolis (IN)
Indiana U South Bend (IN)
Indiana U Southeast (IN)
Inter American U of Puerto Rico, Metropolitan Campus (PR)
Inter American U of Puerto Rico, San Germán Campus (PR)
Iona Coll (NY)
Iowa State U of Science and Technology (IA)
Ithaca Coll (NY)
Jacksonville State U (AL)
Jacksonville U (FL)
James Madison U (VA)
John Brown U (AR)
John Carroll U (OH)
Johns Hopkins U (MD)
Kalamazoo Coll (MI)
Kansas State U (KS)
Kansas Wesleyan U (KS)
Kean U (NJ)
Kennesaw State U (GA)
Kenyon Coll (OH)
Kettering U (MI)
King's Coll (PA)
The King's U (AB, Canada)
King U (TN)
Knox Coll (IL)
Kutztown U of Pennsylvania (PA)
Lafayette Coll (PA)
LaGrange Coll (GA)
Lake Forest Coll (IL)
Lamar U (TX)
La Roche U (PA)
La Sierra U (CA)
Lawrence Technological U (MI)
Lawrence U (WI)
Lebanese American U (Lebanon)
Lee U (TN)
Lehigh U (PA)
Lehman Coll of the City U of New York (NY)
Le Moyne Coll (NY)
LeTourneau U (TX)
Lewis & Clark Coll (OR)
Lewis-Clark State Coll (ID)
Lewis U (IL)
Liberty U (VA)
Limestone Coll (SC)
Lincoln Memorial U (TN)
Lincoln U (MO)
Lincoln U (PA)
Lindenwood U (MO)

Linfield Coll (OR)
Lipscomb U (TN)
Lock Haven U of Pennsylvania (PA)
Longwood U (VA)
Loras Coll (IA)
Louisiana State U and A&M Coll (LA)
Louisiana State U in Shreveport (LA)
Louisiana Tech U (LA)
Loyola Marymount U (CA)
Loyola U Chicago (IL)
Loyola U Maryland (MD)
Loyola U New Orleans (LA)
Madonna U (MI)
Malone U (OH)
Manhattan Coll (NY)
Manhattanville Coll (NY)
Mansfield U of Pennsylvania (PA)
Marian U (IN)
Marietta Coll (OH)
Marquette U (WI)
Marshall U (WV)
Maryville U of Saint Louis (MO)
Mayville State U (ND)
McDaniel Coll (MD)
McKendree U (IL)
McMurry U (TX)
McNeese State U (LA)
Mercer U, Macon (GA)
Meredith Coll (NC)
Merrimack Coll (MA)
Messiah Coll (PA)
Miami U (OH)
Miami U Hamilton (OH)
Miami U Middletown (OH)
Michigan State U (MI)
Michigan Technological U (MI)
MidAmerica Nazarene U (KS)
Middlebury Coll (VT)
Middle Tennessee State U (TN)
Millersville U of Pennsylvania (PA)
Milligan Coll (TN)
Millikin U (IL)
Minnesota State U Mankato (MN)
Minot State U (ND)
Misericordia U (PA)
Mississippi State U (MS)
Missouri Southern State U (MO)
Missouri State U (MO)
Missouri U of Science and Technology (MO)
Montana State U (MT)
Montana Technological U (MT)
Montclair State U (NJ)
Moravian Coll (PA)
Morehead State U (KY)
Mount Holyoke Coll (MA)
Mount Marty Coll (SD)
Mount Mercy U (IA)
Mount Saint Mary Coll (NY)
Mount Saint Mary's U (CA)
Mount St. Mary's U (MD)
Mount Vernon Nazarene U (OH)
Muhlenberg Coll (PA)
Murray State U (KY)
Muskingum U (OH)
Nazareth Coll of Rochester (NY)
Nebraska Wesleyan U (NE)
New Coll of Florida (FL)
New Jersey Inst of Technology (NJ)
Newman U (KS)
New Mexico Highlands U (NM)
New Mexico Inst of Mining and Technology (NM)
New York City Coll of Technology of the City U of New York (NY)
New York Inst of Technology (NY)
New York U (NY)
Niagara U (NY)
North Carolina Central U (NC)
Northeastern Illinois U (IL)
Northeastern State U (OK)
Northern Arizona U (AZ)
Northern Illinois U (IL)
Northern Kentucky U (KY)
Northern State U (SD)
Northwestern Coll (IA)
Northwestern U (IL)
Northwest Missouri State U (MO)
Northwest Nazarene U (ID)
Notre Dame Coll (OH)
Nova Southeastern U (FL)
Oakland U (MI)
Oberlin Coll (OH)
Occidental Coll (CA)
Oglethorpe U (GA)
Ohio Dominican U (OH)
The Ohio State U (OH)
Ohio Wesleyan U (OH)
Oklahoma Baptist U (OK)
Oklahoma State U (OK)
Old Dominion U (VA)
Olivet Nazarene U (IL)
Oral Roberts U (OK)
Pace U, Pleasantville Campus (NY)
Pacific U (OR)
Penn State Abington (PA)
Penn State Altoona (PA)
Penn State Beaver (PA)
Penn State Berks (PA)
Penn State Brandywine (PA)
Penn State DuBois (PA)
Penn State Erie, The Behrend Coll (PA)
Penn State Fayette, The Eberly Campus (PA)
Penn State Greater Allegheny (PA)
Penn State Hazleton (PA)
Penn State Lehigh Valley (PA)
Penn State Mont Alto (PA)
Penn State New Kensington (PA)
Penn State Schuylkill (PA)
Penn State Shenango (PA)
Penn State U Park (PA)
Penn State Wilkes-Barre (PA)
Penn State York (PA)
Pepperdine U, Malibu (CA)
Pittsburg State U (KS)
Pitzer Coll (CA)
Point Loma Nazarene U (CA)
Pomona Coll (CA)
Portland State U (OR)
Prairie View A&M U (TX)
Princeton U (NJ)
Providence Coll (RI)
Purchase Coll, State U of New York (NY)
Purdue U Fort Wayne (IN)
Purdue U Northwest (IN)
Queens Coll of the City U of New York (NY)
Queens U of Charlotte (NC)
Radford U (VA)
Ramapo Coll of New Jersey (NJ)
Randolph Coll (VA)
Randolph-Macon Coll (VA)
Rhode Island Coll (RI)
Rhodes Coll (TN)
Rice U (TX)
Roanoke Coll (VA)
Roberts Wesleyan Coll (NY)
Rocky Mountain Coll (MT)
Roger Williams U (RI)
Rollins Coll (FL)
Rose-Hulman Inst of Technology (IN)
Rosemont Coll (PA)
Rowan U (NJ)
Sacred Heart U (CT)
Saginaw Valley State U (MI)
St. Ambrose U (IA)
St. Bonaventure U (NY)
St. Catherine U (MN)
St. Cloud State U (MN)
Saint Francis U (PA)
St. John Fisher Coll (NY)
Saint John's U (MN)
Saint Joseph's U (PA)
Saint Louis U (MO)
Saint Mary's Coll (IN)
Saint Mary's Coll of California (CA)
St. Mary's Coll of Maryland (MD)
St. Mary's U (TX)
Saint Mary's U of Minnesota (MN)
St. Norbert Coll (WI)
St. Olaf Coll (MN)
St. Thomas U - Florida (FL)
Saint Vincent Coll (PA)
Salem State U (MA)
Salisbury U (MD)
Salve Regina U (RI)
Samford U (AL)
Sam Houston State U (TX)
San Diego State U (CA)
San Francisco State U (CA)
San Jose State U (CA)
Santa Clara U (CA)
Sarah Lawrence Coll (NY)
Schreiner U (TX)
Scripps Coll (CA)
Seattle U (WA)
Seton Hill U (PA)
Shenandoah U (VA)
Shepherd U (WV)
Siena Coll (NY)
Siena Heights U (MI)
Simmons U (MA)
Simon Fraser U (BC, Canada)
Skidmore Coll (NY)
Slippery Rock U of Pennsylvania (PA)
Smith Coll (MA)
South Dakota State U (SD)
Southeastern Louisiana U (LA)
Southeast Missouri State U (MO)
Southern Arkansas U–Magnolia (AR)
Southern Illinois U Carbondale (IL)
Southern Illinois U Edwardsville (IL)
Southern Methodist U (TX)
Southwest Baptist U (MO)
Southwestern Coll (KS)
Southwestern Oklahoma State U (OK)
Southwestern U (TX)
Spring Arbor U (MI)
Spring Hill Coll (AL)
Stanford U (CA)
State U of New York at Fredonia (NY)
State U of New York at New Paltz (NY)
State U of New York at Oswego (NY)
State U of New York Coll at Cortland (NY)
State U of New York Coll at Geneseo (NY)
State U of New York Coll at Old Westbury (NY)
State U of New York Coll at Oneonta (NY)
State U of New York Coll at Potsdam (NY)
Sterling Coll (KS)
Stetson U (FL)
Stevens Inst of Technology (NJ)
Stevenson U (MD)
Stockton U (NJ)
Stony Brook U, State U of New York (NY)
Suffolk U (MA)
SUNY Brockport (NY)
Susquehanna U (PA)
Tabor Coll (KS)
Tarleton State U (TX)
Taylor U (IN)
Tennessee Wesleyan U (TN)
Texas A&M Intl U (TX)
Texas A&M U (TX)
Texas A&M U–Commerce (TX)
Texas A&M U–Corpus Christi (TX)
Texas A&M U–Kingsville (TX)
Texas Christian U (TX)
Texas Lutheran U (TX)
Texas Southern U (TX)
Texas State U (TX)
Texas Tech U (TX)
Texas Woman's U (TX)
Towson U (MD)
Transylvania U (KY)
Trevecca Nazarene U (TN)
Trine U (IN)
Trinity U (TX)
Troy U (AL)
Truman State U (MO)
Tulane U (LA)
Union Coll (NY)
Union U (TN)
United States Military Acad (NY)
U at Albany, State U of New York (NY)
U at Buffalo, the State U of New York (NY)
The U of Akron (OH)
The U of Alabama (AL)
The U of Alabama at Birmingham (AL)
The U of Alabama in Huntsville (AL)
U of Alaska Fairbanks (AK)
The U of Arizona (AZ)
U of Arkansas (AR)
U of Arkansas at Little Rock (AR)
U of California, Berkeley (CA)
U of California, Irvine (CA)
U of California, Los Angeles (CA)
U of California, Merced (CA)
U of California, Riverside (CA)
U of California, San Diego (CA)
U of California, Santa Barbara (CA)
U of California, Santa Cruz (CA)
U of Central Arkansas (AR)
U of Central Florida (FL)
U of Charleston (WV)
U of Cincinnati (OH)
U of Colorado Boulder (CO)
U of Colorado Colorado Springs (CO)
U of Colorado Denver (CO)
U of Dallas (TX)
U of Dayton (OH)
U of Denver (CO)
U of Detroit Mercy (MI)
U of Dubuque (IA)
The U of Findlay (OH)
U of Guam (GU)
U of Hartford (CT)
U of Hawaii at Manoa (HI)
U of Houston (TX)
U of Houston–Clear Lake (TX)
U of Houston–Downtown (TX)
U of Idaho (ID)
U of Illinois at Chicago (IL)
U of Illinois at Springfield (IL)
The U of Iowa (IA)
U of Jamestown (ND)
The U of Kansas (KS)
U of Kentucky (KY)
U of La Verne (CA)
U of Louisiana at Lafayette (LA)
U of Louisville (KY)
U of Maine (ME)
U of Mary Hardin-Baylor (TX)
U of Maryland, Baltimore County (MD)
U of Mary Washington (VA)
U of Massachusetts Amherst (MA)
U of Massachusetts Boston (MA)
U of Massachusetts Dartmouth (MA)
U of Massachusetts Lowell (MA)
U of Memphis (TN)
U of Miami (FL)
U of Michigan (MI)
U of Michigan–Dearborn (MI)
U of Michigan–Flint (MI)
U of Minnesota, Duluth (MN)
U of Minnesota, Morris (MN)
U of Minnesota, Twin Cities Campus (MN)
U of Missouri–St. Louis (MO)
U of Montana (MT)
U of Montevallo (AL)
U of Nebraska at Kearney (NE)
U of Nebraska–Lincoln (NE)
U of Nevada, Las Vegas (NV)
U of New England (ME)
U of New Hampshire (NH)
U of New Haven (CT)
U of New Mexico (NM)
The U of North Carolina at Chapel Hill (NC)
The U of North Carolina at Charlotte (NC)
The U of North Carolina at Greensboro (NC)
The U of North Carolina at Pembroke (NC)
The U of North Carolina Wilmington (NC)
U of North Dakota (ND)
U of Northern Colorado (CO)
U of Northern Iowa (IA)
U of North Florida (FL)
U of North Texas (TX)
U of Notre Dame (IN)
U of Oregon (OR)
U of Pennsylvania (PA)
U of Pikeville (KY)
U of Pittsburgh at Bradford (PA)
U of Pittsburgh at Greensburg (PA)
U of Portland (OR)
U of Providence (MT)
U of Puget Sound (WA)
U of Richmond (VA)
U of Saint Francis (IN)
U of Saint Joseph (CT)
U of Saint Mary (KS)
U of St. Thomas (TX)
U of San Diego (CA)
U of San Francisco (CA)
U of Science and Arts of Oklahoma (OK)
The U of Scranton (PA)
U of South Alabama (AL)
U of South Carolina (SC)
U of South Carolina Aiken (SC)
U of South Dakota (SD)
U of Southern Indiana (IN)
U of Southern Maine (ME)
U of Southern Mississippi (MS)
U of South Florida (FL)
The U of Tampa (FL)
The U of Tennessee (TN)
The U of Tennessee at Chattanooga (TN)
The U of Tennessee at Martin (TN)
The U of Texas at Dallas (TX)
The U of Texas at El Paso (TX)
The U of Texas at San Antonio (TX)
The U of Texas of the Permian Basin (TX)
The U of Texas Rio Grande Valley (TX)
U of the Fraser Valley (BC, Canada)
U of the Incarnate Word (TX)
U of the Pacific (CA)
The U of the South (TN)
U of the Virgin Islands (VI)
The U of Toledo (OH)
The U of Tulsa (OK)
U of Utah (UT)
U of Vermont (VT)
U of Virginia (VA)
U of Washington (WA)
U of Washington, Bothell (WA)
U of Waterloo (ON, Canada)
The U of West Alabama (AL)
The U of Western Ontario (ON, Canada)
U of West Florida (FL)
U of West Georgia (GA)
U of Wisconsin–Eau Claire (WI)
U of Wisconsin–Green Bay (WI)
U of Wisconsin–La Crosse (WI)
U of Wisconsin–Madison (WI)
U of Wisconsin–Milwaukee (WI)
U of Wisconsin–Parkside (WI)
U of Wisconsin–Platteville (WI)
U of Wisconsin–Superior (WI)
U of Wyoming (WY)
Upper Iowa U (IA)
Ursuline Coll (OH)
Utah State U (UT)
Utah Valley U (UT)
Utica Coll (NY)
Valdosta State U (GA)
Valley City State U (ND)
Valparaiso U (IN)
Vanderbilt U (TN)
Vanguard U of Southern California (CA)
Villanova U (PA)
Virginia Commonwealth U (VA)
Virginia Wesleyan U (VA)
Wabash Coll (IN)
Wake Forest U (NC)
Walla Walla U (WA)
Warren Wilson Coll (NC)
Wartburg Coll (IA)
Washington & Jefferson Coll (PA)
Washington and Lee U (VA)
Washington Coll (MD)
Washington State U (WA)
Washington U in St. Louis (MO)
Wayland Baptist U (TX)
Waynesburg U (PA)
Wayne State Coll (NE)
Wayne State U (MI)
Weber State U (UT)
Wesleyan U (CT)
West Chester U of Pennsylvania (PA)
Western Carolina U (NC)
Western Colorado U (CO)
Western Connecticut State U (CT)
Western Kentucky U (KY)
Western Michigan U (MI)
Western New England U (MA)
Western New Mexico U (NM)
Western Oregon U (OR)
Western Washington U (WA)
Westfield State U (MA)
West Liberty U (WV)
Westminster Coll (UT)
Westmont Coll (CA)
West Virginia U (WV)
Wheaton Coll (IL)

Wheaton Coll (MA)
Whitworth U (WA)
Wichita State U (KS)
Widener U (PA)
Wilkes U (PA)
Willamette U (OR)
William & Mary (VA)
William Jewell Coll (MO)
William Paterson U of New Jersey (NJ)
Williams Coll (MA)
Wilmington Coll (OH)
Wingate U (NC)
Winthrop U (SC)
Wittenberg U (OH)
Wofford Coll (SC)
Worcester Polytechnic Inst (MA)
Worcester State U (MA)
Wright State U (OH)
Xavier U (OH)
Xavier U of Louisiana (LA)
Yale U (CT)
Yeshiva U (NY)
York Coll of Pennsylvania (PA)
Youngstown State U (OH)

CHEMISTRY RELATED
Bridgewater Coll (VA)
Bridgewater State U (MA)
Carnegie Mellon U (PA)
Chatham U (PA)
Coll of Charleston (SC)
Dartmouth Coll (NH)
Eastern Oregon U (OR)
Eastern U (PA)
Ferris State U (MI)
Florida Inst of Technology (FL)
Harvard U (MA)
Inter American U of Puerto Rico, Bayamón Campus (PR)
Kansas Wesleyan U (KS)
LeTourneau U (TX)
Mercer U, Macon (GA)
Michigan Technological U (MI)
Palm Beach Atlantic U (FL)
Saginaw Valley State U (MI)
Saint Vincent Coll (PA)
Sam Houston State U (TX)
Stony Brook U, State U of New York (NY)
Taylor U (IN)
U at Buffalo, the State U of New York (NY)
U of California, Berkeley (CA)
U of California, Santa Barbara (CA)
U of Denver (CO)
U of Notre Dame (IN)
The U of Scranton (PA)
U of Southern Mississippi (MS)
U of the Pacific (CA)
U of Wisconsin–Eau Claire (WI)
U of Wisconsin–Milwaukee (WI)
Washington U in St. Louis (MO)
Wayne State U (MI)
Western Michigan U (MI)

CHEMISTRY TEACHER EDUCATION
Adams State U (CO)
Albion Coll (MI)
Aquinas Coll (MI)
Arkansas Tech U (AR)
Augustana Coll (IL)
Ball State U (IN)
Baylor U (TX)
Bethel U (IN)
Bowling Green State U (OH)
Bradley U (IL)
Calvin Coll (MI)
Campbellsville U (KY)
Cedarville U (OH)
Central Methodist U (MO)
Central Michigan U (MI)
Central State U (OH)
Central Washington U (WA)
City Coll of the City U of New York (NY)
Coll of Saint Mary (NE)
Coll of Staten Island of the City U of New York (NY)
Coll of the Ozarks (MO)
Concordia U Chicago (IL)
Concordia U, St. Paul (MN)
Daytona State Coll (FL)
Dickinson State U (ND)
East Central U (OK)
Eastern Michigan U (MI)
Eastern Washington U (WA)
Emory & Henry Coll (VA)
Evangel U (MO)
Ferris State U (MI)
Florida Inst of Technology (FL)
Geneva Coll (PA)
Glenville State Coll (WV)
Goshen Coll (IN)
Grand Valley State U (MI)
Gustavus Adolphus Coll (MN)
Hofstra U (NY)
Hope Coll (MI)
Immaculata U (PA)
Indiana U Bloomington (IN)
Indiana U Northwest (IN)
Indiana U South Bend (IN)
Inter American U of Puerto Rico, San Germán Campus (PR)
Ithaca Coll (NY)
Kansas Wesleyan U (KS)
Keuka Coll (NY)
Lee U (TN)
Le Moyne Coll (NY)
Lincoln Memorial U (TN)
Lincoln U (MO)
Lipscomb U (TN)
Louisiana Tech U (LA)
Madonna U (MI)
Manhattanville Coll (NY)
Martin Luther Coll (MN)
Mayville State U (ND)
McMurry U (TX)
Merrimack Coll (MA)
Messiah Coll (PA)
Miami Dade Coll (FL)
Miami U Hamilton (OH)
Miami U Middletown (OH)
Michigan State U (MI)
Millikin U (IL)
Minot State U (ND)
Misericordia U (PA)
Mount Marty Coll (SD)
Mount Vernon Nazarene U (OH)
Nazareth Coll of Rochester (NY)
New York U (NY)
Niagara U (NY)
Northern Arizona U (AZ)
Northern State U (SD)
Northwest Missouri State U (MO)
Northwest Nazarene U (ID)
Notre Dame Coll (OH)
Ohio Dominican U (OH)
Ohio Wesleyan U (OH)
Pace U, Pleasantville Campus (NY)
Pepperdine U, Malibu (CA)
Pittsburg State U (KS)
Providence Coll (RI)
Purdue U Fort Wayne (IN)
Queens Coll of the City U of New York (NY)
Rhode Island Coll (RI)
Roanoke Coll (VA)
Roberts Wesleyan Coll (NY)
Saginaw Valley State U (MI)
St. Ambrose U (IA)
St. Catherine U (MN)
St. Cloud State U (MN)
Saint Francis U (PA)
St. John Fisher Coll (NY)
Saint Joseph's U (PA)
Saint Mary's U of Minnesota (MN)
Schreiner U (TX)
Seattle U (WA)
Seton Hill U (PA)
South Dakota State U (SD)
Southwest Baptist U (MO)
Spring Arbor U (MI)
State U of New York at New Paltz (NY)
State U of New York Coll at Cortland (NY)
State U of New York Coll at Old Westbury (NY)
State U of New York Coll at Oneonta (NY)
State U of New York Coll at Potsdam (NY)
Sterling Coll (KS)
Taylor U (IN)
Transylvania U (KY)
Trevecca Nazarene U (TN)
Trine U (IN)
U of California, San Diego (CA)
U of Dubuque (IA)
U of Illinois at Chicago (IL)
The U of Iowa (IA)
U of Jamestown (ND)
U of Louisiana at Monroe (LA)
U of Maine (ME)
U of Mary Hardin-Baylor (TX)
U of Maryland, Baltimore County (MD)
U of Michigan–Dearborn (MI)
U of Nebraska–Lincoln (NE)
U of Nevada, Reno (NV)
U of Pikeville (KY)
U of Providence (MT)
U of Waterloo (ON, Canada)
U of Wisconsin–Superior (WI)
Utah State U (UT)
Utah Valley U (UT)
Utica Coll (NY)
Valley City State U (ND)
Valparaiso U (IN)
Washington U in St. Louis (MO)
Waynesburg U (PA)
Wayne State Coll (NE)
Weber State U (UT)
Western Michigan U (MI)
Western Washington U (WA)
Widener U (PA)
Xavier U (OH)
Xavier U of Louisiana (LA)

CHILD CARE AND SUPPORT SERVICES MANAGEMENT
Brigham Young U (UT)
Chestnut Hill Coll (PA)
Ferris State U (MI)
Framingham State U (MA)
Iowa State U of Science and Technology (IA)
Oklahoma State U (OK)
Seton Hill U (PA)
Siena Heights U (MI)
State U of New York Coll of Agriculture and Technology at Cobleskill (NY)
State U of New York Coll of Technology at Canton (NY)
Texas Tech U (TX)
The U of Texas Rio Grande Valley (TX)
U of the Fraser Valley (BC, Canada)
Worcester State U (MA)

CHILD-CARE PROVISION
Brigham Young U (UT)
Wayne State Coll (NE)

CHILD DEVELOPMENT
Appalachian State U (NC)
Aquinas Coll (MI)
Auburn U (AL)
Bluffton U (OH)
Bowling Green State U (OH)
Brigham Young U (UT)
California State U, Fresno (CA)
California State U, Long Beach (CA)
California State U, Northridge (CA)
California State U, Sacramento (CA)
Cameron U (OK)
Carson-Newman U (TN)
Central Michigan U (MI)
Charter Oak State Coll (CT)
Coll of the Ozarks (MO)
Concordia U, St. Paul (MN)
Eastern Washington U (WA)
Hampton U (VA)
Harding U (AR)
Kansas State U (KS)
Lesley U (MA)
Lewis-Clark State Coll (ID)
Louisiana Tech U (LA)
Madonna U (MI)
Meredith Coll (NC)
Michigan State U (MI)
Minnesota State U Mankato (MN)
Mount Saint Mary's U (CA)
North Central U (MN)
Olivet Nazarene U (IL)
Point Loma Nazarene U (CA)
Portland State U (OR)
St. Bonaventure U (NY)
Santa Clara U (CA)
Seton Hill U (PA)
Southwest Baptist U (MO)
Springfield Coll (MA)
State U of New York Coll at Oneonta (NY)
Texas Tech U (TX)
Texas Woman's U (TX)
The U of Akron (OH)
U of Alaska Fairbanks (AK)
U of Houston–Clear Lake (TX)
U of La Verne (CA)
U of Saint Joseph (CT)
U of Saint Mary (KS)
U of Virginia (VA)
The U of Western Ontario (ON, Canada)
Vanderbilt U (TN)
Weber State U (UT)
Western Michigan U (MI)
West Virginia U (WV)
Youngstown State U (OH)

CHINESE
Ball State U (IN)
Bates Coll (ME)
Beloit Coll (WI)
Bennington Coll (VT)
Bryant U (RI)
Butler U (IN)
California State U, Long Beach (CA)
California State U, Los Angeles (CA)
Calvin Coll (MI)
Carnegie Mellon U (PA)
Carthage Coll (WI)
Colgate U (NY)
Coll of the Holy Cross (MA)
Concordia Coll (MN)
Dartmouth Coll (NH)
Davidson Coll (NC)
DePaul U (IL)
Dickinson Coll (PA)
Emory U (GA)
Florida State U (FL)
Georgetown U (DC)
The George Washington U (DC)
Grinnell Coll (IA)
Hobart and William Smith Colls (NY)
Hofstra U (NY)
Lawrence U (WI)
Lehigh U (PA)
Messiah Coll (PA)
Michigan State U (MI)
Middlebury Coll (VT)
Nazareth Coll of Rochester (NY)
New Coll of Florida (FL)
Occidental Coll (CA)
The Ohio State U (OH)
Pacific U (OR)
Penn State U Park (PA)
Pomona Coll (CA)
Portland State U (OR)
Queens Coll of the City U of New York (NY)
St. Olaf Coll (MN)
San Francisco State U (CA)
San Jose State U (CA)
Sarah Lawrence Coll (NY)
Scripps Coll (CA)
Southern Methodist U (TX)
Stanford U (CA)
Temple U (PA)
Trinity U (TX)
Union Coll (NY)
United States Military Acad (NY)
U of California, Berkeley (CA)
U of California, Los Angeles (CA)
U of California, Riverside (CA)
U of California, San Diego (CA)
U of California, Santa Barbara (CA)
U of Colorado Boulder (CO)
U of Hawaii at Manoa (HI)
U of Houston (TX)
The U of Iowa (IA)
U of Kentucky (KY)
U of Massachusetts Amherst (MA)
U of Notre Dame (IN)
U of Oregon (OR)
U of Puget Sound (WA)
The U of Tulsa (OK)
U of Utah (UT)
U of Vermont (VT)
U of Washington (WA)
The U of Western Ontario (ON, Canada)
U of Wisconsin–Madison (WI)
Utah State U (UT)
Wake Forest U (NC)
Washington State U (WA)
Washington U in St. Louis (MO)
Western Kentucky U (KY)
Western Washington U (WA)
Wheaton Coll (IL)
Williams Coll (MA)
Wofford Coll (SC)
Yale U (CT)

CHINESE STUDIES
Ball State U (IN)
DePaul U (IL)
Drew U (NJ)
Furman U (SC)
New York U (NY)
Oakland U (MI)
U at Albany, State U of New York (NY)
U of California, Irvine (CA)
U of Minnesota, Duluth (MN)
U of North Dakota (ND)
U of Richmond (VA)
The U of Tulsa (OK)
U of Washington (WA)
The U of Western Ontario (ON, Canada)
Willamette U (OR)
William & Mary (VA)

CHRISTIAN STUDIES
Anderson U (SC)
Bethel U (TN)
Bryan Coll (TN)
California Baptist U (CA)
The Coll of St. Scholastica (MN)
Coll of the Holy Cross (MA)
Concordia U Wisconsin (WI)
Ecclesia Coll (AR)
Gordon Coll (MA)
Hardin-Simmons U (TX)
Hillsdale Coll (MI)
Houston Baptist U (TX)
Lee U (TN)
Liberty U (VA)
Loyola U New Orleans (LA)
Marian U (IN)
McMurry U (TX)
Messenger Coll (TX)
Oklahoma Baptist U (OK)
Point Loma Nazarene U (CA)
Roanoke Coll (VA)
Saint Mary's U of Minnesota (MN)
St. Thomas U - New Brunswick (NB, Canada)
Steinbach Bible Coll (MB, Canada)
Tabor Coll (KS)
Tennessee Wesleyan U (TN)
Toccoa Falls Coll (GA)
Truett McConnell U (GA)
U of Dubuque (IA)
U of Mary Hardin-Baylor (TX)
Whitworth U (WA)

CINEMATOGRAPHY AND FILM/VIDEO PRODUCTION
Academy of Art U (CA)
American U (DC)
Anderson U (IN)
Belmont U (TN)
Bennington Coll (VT)
Binghamton U, State U of New York (NY)
Biola U (CA)
Brigham Young U (UT)
California Inst of the Arts (CA)
California Lutheran U (CA)
California State U, Long Beach (CA)
California State U, Northridge (CA)
Central Washington U (WA)
City Coll of the City U of New York (NY)
Clayton State U (GA)
Columbia Coll Chicago (IL)
DePaul U (IL)
Drexel U (PA)
Eastern New Mexico U (NM)
Eastern Washington U (WA)
Fairleigh Dickinson U (NJ)
Fashion Inst of Technology (NY)
FIDM/Fashion Inst of Design & Merchandising, Los Angeles Campus (CA)
Fitchburg State U (MA)
George Fox U (OR)
George Mason U (VA)
Goshen Coll (IN)
High Point U (NC)
Ithaca Coll (NY)
John Brown U (AR)
Keiser U, Fort Lauderdale (FL)
La Sierra U (CA)
Lee U (TN)

Liberty U (VA)
Lindenwood U (MO)
Loyola Marymount U (CA)
Loyola U New Orleans (LA)
Lynn U (FL)
Marymount Manhattan Coll (NY)
Massachusetts Coll of Art and Design (MA)
Messiah Coll (PA)
Miami Dade Coll (FL)
Middle Tennessee State U (TN)
Minneapolis Coll of Art and Design (MN)
Montana State U (MT)
Montclair State U (NJ)
Mount Saint Mary's U (CA)
New England Inst of Technology (RI)
New Mexico Highlands U (NM)
New York U (NY)
Oakland U (MI)
Occidental Coll (CA)
Pace U, Pleasantville Campus (NY)
Palm Beach Atlantic U (FL)
Pratt Inst (NY)
Purchase Coll, State U of New York (NY)
Regent U (VA)
St. Ambrose U (IA)
San Francisco Art Inst (CA)
Sarah Lawrence Coll (NY)
School of Visual Arts (NY)
Southeastern U (FL)
Southern Illinois U Carbondale (IL)
Southern Methodist U (TX)
Stanford U (CA)
Stevenson U (MD)
Taylor U (IN)
The U of Arizona (AZ)
U of California, Riverside (CA)
U of Central Florida (FL)
U of Illinois at Chicago (IL)
The U of Iowa (IA)
U of Miami (FL)
U of Montana (MT)
The U of North Carolina Wilmington (NC)
U of Saint Francis (IN)
U of West Georgia (GA)
Virginia Commonwealth U (VA)
Walla Walla U (WA)
Wayne State U (MI)
Woodbury U (CA)
York Coll of Pennsylvania (PA)

CITY/URBAN, COMMUNITY AND REGIONAL PLANNING
Appalachian State U (NC)
Arizona State U at the Tempe campus (AZ)
Ball State U (IN)
Bridgewater State U (MA)
California Polytechnic State U, San Luis Obispo (CA)
California State Polytechnic U, Pomona (CA)
Cornell U (NY)
East Carolina U (NC)
Eastern Kentucky U (KY)
Eastern Michigan U (MI)
Eastern Washington U (WA)
Florida Atlantic U (FL)
Indiana U of Pennsylvania (PA)
Miami U (OH)
Miami U Hamilton (OH)
Miami U Middletown (OH)
Michigan State U (MI)
Minnesota State U Mankato (MN)
Missouri State U (MO)
The Ohio State U (OH)
Parsons School of Design (NY)
Portland State U (OR)
Rowan U (NJ)
Salisbury U (MD)
South Dakota State U (SD)
Texas A&M U (TX)
Texas State U (TX)
The U of Akron (OH)
The U of Arizona (AZ)
U of Cincinnati (OH)
U of New Hampshire (NH)
U of North Texas (TX)
U of Virginia (VA)
U of Washington (WA)
U of Waterloo (ON, Canada)
West Chester U of Pennsylvania (PA)
Western Michigan U (MI)
Westfield State U (MA)

CIVIL ENGINEERING
American U of Beirut (Lebanon)
Angelo State U (TX)
Arizona State U at the Tempe campus (AZ)
Auburn U (AL)
Benedictine Coll (KS)
Boise State U (ID)
Bradley U (IL)
Bucknell U (PA)
California Baptist U (CA)
California Polytechnic State U, San Luis Obispo (CA)
California State Polytechnic U, Pomona (CA)
California State U, Fresno (CA)
California State U, Long Beach (CA)
California State U, Los Angeles (CA)
California State U, Northridge (CA)
California State U, Sacramento (CA)
Calvin Coll (MI)
Carnegie Mellon U (PA)
The Catholic U of America (DC)
Central Connecticut State U (CT)
The Citadel, The Military Coll of South Carolina (SC)
City Coll of the City U of New York (NY)
Clarkson U (NY)
Clemson U (SC)
Colorado School of Mines (CO)
Colorado State U (CO)
Cornell U (NY)
Drexel U (PA)
Fairleigh Dickinson U (NJ)
Florida A&M U (FL)
Florida Atlantic U (FL)
Florida Gulf Coast U (FL)
Florida Inst of Technology (FL)
Florida State U (FL)
George Fox U (OR)
George Mason U (VA)
The George Washington U (DC)
Georgia Inst of Technology (GA)
Georgia Southern U (GA)
Gonzaga U (WA)
Hofstra U (NY)
Howard U (DC)
Illinois Inst of Technology (IL)
Iowa State U of Science and Technology (IA)
Johns Hopkins U (MD)
Kansas State U (KS)
Kennesaw State U (GA)
King's Coll (PA)
Lafayette Coll (PA)
Lamar U (TX)
Lawrence Technological U (MI)
Lebanese American U (Lebanon)
Lehigh U (PA)
LeTourneau U (TX)
Liberty U (VA)
Lipscomb U (TN)
Louisiana State U and A&M Coll (LA)
Louisiana Tech U (LA)
Loyola Marymount U (CA)
Manhattan Coll (NY)
Marquette U (WI)
Merrimack Coll (MA)
Messiah Coll (PA)
Michigan State U (MI)
Michigan Technological U (MI)
Milwaukee School of Eng (WI)
Minnesota State U Mankato (MN)
Mississippi State U (MS)
Missouri U of Science and Technology (MO)
Montana State U (MT)
Montana Technological U (MT)
New Jersey Inst of Technology (NJ)
New Mexico Inst of Mining and Technology (NM)
New York U (NY)
Northern Arizona U (AZ)
Northwestern U (IL)
The Ohio State U (OH)
Oklahoma State U (OK)
Old Dominion U (VA)
Penn State Abington (PA)
Penn State Altoona (PA)
Penn State Beaver (PA)
Penn State Berks (PA)
Penn State Brandywine (PA)
Penn State DuBois (PA)
Penn State Erie, The Behrend Coll (PA)
Penn State Fayette, The Eberly Campus (PA)
Penn State Greater Allegheny (PA)
Penn State Harrisburg (PA)
Penn State Hazleton (PA)
Penn State Lehigh Valley (PA)
Penn State Mont Alto (PA)
Penn State New Kensington (PA)
Penn State Schuylkill (PA)
Penn State Shenango (PA)
Penn State U Park (PA)
Penn State Wilkes-Barre (PA)
Penn State York (PA)
Polytechnic U of Puerto Rico (PR)
Portland State U (OR)
Prairie View A&M U (TX)
Princeton U (NJ)
Purdue U Fort Wayne (IN)
Purdue U Northwest (IN)
Rice U (TX)
Roger Williams U (RI)
Rose-Hulman Inst of Technology (IN)
Rowan U (NJ)
Saint Louis U (MO)
San Diego State U (CA)
San Francisco State U (CA)
San Jose State U (CA)
Santa Clara U (CA)
Seattle U (WA)
South Dakota State U (SD)
Southern Illinois U Carbondale (IL)
Southern Illinois U Edwardsville (IL)
Southern Methodist U (TX)
Stanford U (CA)
Stevens Inst of Technology (NJ)
Stony Brook U, State U of New York (NY)
Tarleton State U (TX)
Temple U (PA)
Texas A&M U (TX)
Texas A&M U–Corpus Christi (TX)
Texas A&M U–Kingsville (TX)
Texas Southern U (TX)
Texas State U (TX)
Texas Tech U (TX)
Trine U (IN)
United States Military Acad (NY)
U at Buffalo, the State U of New York (NY)
The U of Akron (OH)
The U of Alabama (AL)
The U of Alabama at Birmingham (AL)
The U of Alabama in Huntsville (AL)
U of Alaska Fairbanks (AK)
The U of Arizona (AZ)
U of Arkansas (AR)
U of California, Berkeley (CA)
U of California, Irvine (CA)
U of California, Los Angeles (CA)
U of Central Florida (FL)
U of Cincinnati (OH)
U of Colorado Boulder (CO)
U of Colorado Denver (CO)
U of Dayton (OH)
U of Detroit Mercy (MI)
U of Guam (GU)
U of Hartford (CT)
U of Hawaii at Manoa (HI)
U of Houston (TX)
U of Idaho (ID)
U of Illinois at Chicago (IL)
The U of Iowa (IA)
The U of Kansas (KS)
U of Kentucky (KY)
U of Louisiana at Lafayette (LA)
U of Louisville (KY)
U of Maine (ME)
U of Massachusetts Amherst (MA)
U of Massachusetts Dartmouth (MA)
U of Massachusetts Lowell (MA)
U of Memphis (TN)
U of Miami (FL)
U of Michigan (MI)
U of Minnesota, Duluth (MN)
U of Minnesota, Twin Cities Campus (MN)
U of Missouri–St. Louis (MO)
U of Nebraska–Lincoln (NE)
U of Nevada, Las Vegas (NV)
U of Nevada, Reno (NV)
U of New Hampshire (NH)
U of New Haven (CT)
U of New Mexico (NM)
The U of North Carolina at Charlotte (NC)
U of North Dakota (ND)
U of North Florida (FL)
U of Notre Dame (IN)
U of Portland (OR)
U of South Alabama (AL)
U of South Carolina (SC)
U of South Florida (FL)
The U of Tennessee (TN)
The U of Tennessee at Chattanooga (TN)
The U of Texas at El Paso (TX)
The U of Texas at San Antonio (TX)
The U of Texas Rio Grande Valley (TX)
U of the Pacific (CA)
The U of Toledo (OH)
U of Toronto (ON, Canada)
U of Utah (UT)
U of Vermont (VT)
U of Virginia (VA)
U of Washington (WA)
U of Waterloo (ON, Canada)
The U of Western Ontario (ON, Canada)
U of Wisconsin–Madison (WI)
U of Wisconsin–Milwaukee (WI)
U of Wisconsin–Platteville (WI)
U of Wyoming (WY)
Utah State U (UT)
Valparaiso U (IN)
Vanderbilt U (TN)
Villanova U (PA)
Walla Walla U (WA)
Washington State U (WA)
Washington State U–Tri-Cities (WA)
Wayne State U (MI)
Wentworth Inst of Technology (MA)
Western Kentucky U (KY)
Western Michigan U (MI)
Western New England U (MA)
West Virginia U (WV)
Widener U (PA)
William Jewell Coll (MO)
Worcester Polytechnic Inst (MA)
Youngstown State U (OH)

CIVIL ENGINEERING RELATED
California Polytechnic State U, San Luis Obispo (CA)
William Penn U (IA)

CIVIL ENGINEERING TECHNOLOGY
Cedarville U (OH)
Indiana State U (IN)
Lincoln U (MO)
Murray State U (KY)
New England Inst of Technology (RI)
State U of New York Coll of Technology at Canton (NY)
Texas Southern U (TX)
U of Houston–Downtown (TX)
U of Maine (ME)
U of Massachusetts Lowell (MA)
The U of North Carolina at Charlotte (NC)
Youngstown State U (OH)

CLASSICAL, ANCIENT MEDITERRANEAN AND NEAR EASTERN STUDIES AND ARCHAEOLOGY
Baylor U (TX)
Bowdoin Coll (ME)
Butler U (IN)
Calvin Coll (MI)
Colgate U (NY)
Emory U (GA)
Florida State U (FL)
Hampshire Coll (MA)
Hanover Coll (IN)
Kalamazoo Coll (MI)
Knox Coll (IL)
Randolph-Macon Coll (VA)
U of California, Berkeley (CA)
U of California, Los Angeles (CA)
U of Illinois at Chicago (IL)
U of Michigan (MI)
U of Toronto (ON, Canada)

CLASSICS AND CLASSICAL LANGUAGES
Agnes Scott Coll (GA)
Amherst Coll (MA)
Augustana Coll (IL)
Augustana U (SD)
Austin Coll (TX)
Ball State U (IN)
Barnard Coll (NY)
Baylor U (TX)
Beloit Coll (WI)
Binghamton U, State U of New York (NY)
Boston Coll (MA)
Bowdoin Coll (ME)
Bowling Green State U (OH)
Brandeis U (MA)
Brown U (RI)
Bucknell U (PA)
Carleton Coll (MN)
Carthage Coll (WI)
The Catholic U of America (DC)
Centre Coll (KY)
Claremont McKenna Coll (CA)
Clark U (MA)
Colby Coll (ME)
Colgate U (NY)
Coll of Charleston (SC)
Coll of Saint Benedict (MN)
Coll of the Holy Cross (MA)
The Coll of Wooster (OH)
The Colorado Coll (CO)
Cornell Coll (IA)
Cornell U (NY)
Creighton U (NE)
Dartmouth Coll (NH)
DePauw U (IN)
Dickinson Coll (PA)
Drew U (NJ)
Earlham Coll (IN)
Emory U (GA)
Fordham U (NY)
Furman U (SC)
Georgetown U (DC)
The George Washington U (DC)
Grand Valley State U (MI)
Grinnell Coll (IA)
Gustavus Adolphus Coll (MN)
Hampden-Sydney Coll (VA)
Hanover Coll (IN)
Harvard U (MA)
Hillsdale Coll (MI)
Hobart and William Smith Colls (NY)
Hofstra U (NY)
Hollins U (VA)
Hope Coll (MI)
Houston Baptist U (TX)
Howard U (DC)
Illinois Wesleyan U (IL)
Indiana U Bloomington (IN)
John Cabot U (Italy)
Johns Hopkins U (MD)
Kenyon Coll (OH)
Knox Coll (IL)
Lawrence U (WI)
Lehman Coll of the City U of New York (NY)
Lewis & Clark Coll (OR)
Loyola U Chicago (IL)
Loyola U Maryland (MD)
Manhattan Coll (NY)
Marquette U (WI)
Mercer U, Macon (GA)
Miami U (OH)
Miami U Hamilton (OH)
Miami U Middletown (OH)
Middlebury Coll (VT)
Montclair State U (NJ)
Mount Holyoke Coll (MA)
New York U (NY)
Northwestern U (IL)
Oberlin Coll (OH)
The Ohio State U (OH)
Ohio Wesleyan U (OH)
Penn State Abington (PA)
Penn State Altoona (PA)
Penn State Beaver (PA)
Penn State Berks (PA)
Penn State Brandywine (PA)
Penn State DuBois (PA)

Penn State Erie, The Behrend Coll (PA)
Penn State Fayette, The Eberly Campus (PA)
Penn State Greater Allegheny (PA)
Penn State Hazleton (PA)
Penn State Lehigh Valley (PA)
Penn State Mont Alto (PA)
Penn State New Kensington (PA)
Penn State Schuylkill (PA)
Penn State Shenango (PA)
Penn State U Park (PA)
Penn State Wilkes-Barre (PA)
Penn State York (PA)
Pitzer Coll (CA)
Pomona Coll (CA)
Princeton U (NJ)
Queens Coll of the City U of New York (NY)
Randolph Coll (VA)
Randolph-Macon Coll (VA)
Rice U (TX)
Saint John's U (MN)
Saint Joseph's U (PA)
Saint Louis U (MO)
Saint Mary's Coll of California (CA)
St. Olaf Coll (MN)
Samford U (AL)
San Diego State U (CA)
San Francisco State U (CA)
Santa Clara U (CA)
Scripps Coll (CA)
Siena Coll (NY)
Skidmore Coll (NY)
Smith Coll (MA)
Southwestern U (TX)
Stanford U (CA)
Temple U (PA)
Texas A&M U (TX)
Transylvania U (KY)
Trinity U (TX)
Truman State U (MO)
Tulane U (LA)
Union Coll (NY)
U at Buffalo, the State U of New York (NY)
The U of Akron (OH)
The U of Arizona (AZ)
U of Arkansas (AR)
U of California, Berkeley (CA)
U of California, Irvine (CA)
U of California, Riverside (CA)
U of California, San Diego (CA)
U of California, Santa Barbara (CA)
U of California, Santa Cruz (CA)
U of Cincinnati (OH)
U of Colorado Boulder (CO)
U of Dallas (TX)
U of Hawaii at Manoa (HI)
U of Illinois at Chicago (IL)
The U of Iowa (IA)
The U of Kansas (KS)
U of Kentucky (KY)
U of Mary Washington (VA)
U of Massachusetts Amherst (MA)
U of Massachusetts Boston (MA)
U of Miami (FL)
U of Michigan (MI)
U of Minnesota, Twin Cities Campus (MN)
U of Montana (MT)
U of Nebraska–Lincoln (NE)
U of New Hampshire (NH)
U of New Mexico (NM)
The U of North Carolina at Chapel Hill (NC)
The U of North Carolina at Greensboro (NC)
U of North Dakota (ND)
U of Notre Dame (IN)
U of Oregon (OR)
U of Pennsylvania (PA)
U of Puget Sound (WA)
The U of Scranton (PA)
U of South Carolina (SC)
U of South Florida (FL)
The U of Tennessee (TN)
U of the Pacific (CA)
The U of the South (TN)
U of Toronto (ON, Canada)
U of Utah (UT)
U of Vermont (VT)
U of Virginia (VA)
U of Washington (WA)
U of Waterloo (ON, Canada)
The U of Western Ontario (ON, Canada)
U of Wisconsin–Madison (WI)
U of Wisconsin–Milwaukee (WI)
Valparaiso U (IN)
Vanderbilt U (TN)
Villanova U (PA)
Virginia Wesleyan U (VA)
Wabash Coll (IN)
Wake Forest U (NC)
Washington and Lee U (VA)
Washington U in St. Louis (MO)
Wayne State U (MI)
Wesleyan U (CT)
Willamette U (OR)
William & Mary (VA)
Williams Coll (MA)
Wright State U (OH)
Xavier U (OH)
Yale U (CT)
Yeshiva U (NY)

CLASSICS AND CLASSICAL LANGUAGES RELATED
Austin Coll (TX)
California State U, Long Beach (CA)
Florida State U (FL)
Gonzaga U (WA)
Lee U (TN)
Loyola U New Orleans (LA)
Marquette U (WI)
New Coll of Florida (FL)
Providence Coll (RI)
Tulane U (LA)
U of California, Los Angeles (CA)
Wheaton Coll (IL)
Wheaton Coll (MA)
Xavier U (OH)

CLINICAL, COUNSELING AND APPLIED PSYCHOLOGY RELATED
Northwest Christian U (OR)
Saint Mary's Coll of California (CA)

CLINICAL LABORATORY SCIENCE/MEDICAL TECHNOLOGY
Anderson U (IN)
Andrews U (MI)
Arkansas Tech U (AR)
Auburn U (AL)
Augustana U (SD)
Austin Peay State U (TN)
Ball State U (IN)
Barry U (FL)
Baylor U (TX)
Bemidji State U (MN)
Benedictine U (IL)
Bowling Green State U (OH)
Bradley U (IL)
Brigham Young U (UT)
Caldwell U (NJ)
California State U, Dominguez Hills (CA)
Campbellsville U (KY)
The Catholic U of America (DC)
Clarion U of Pennsylvania (PA)
Coll of Saint Elizabeth (NJ)
Coll of Saint Mary (NE)
The Coll of Saint Rose (NY)
Coll of Staten Island of the City U of New York (NY)
Coll of the Ozarks (MO)
DePaul U (IL)
East Carolina U (NC)
East Central U (OK)
Eastern Illinois U (IL)
Eastern Kentucky U (KY)
Eastern Mennonite U (VA)
Eastern Michigan U (MI)
Eastern New Mexico U (NM)
Edinboro U of Pennsylvania (PA)
Evangel U (MO)
Fairleigh Dickinson U (NJ)
Farmingdale State Coll (NY)
Ferris State U (MI)
Florida Gulf Coast U (FL)
Florida Southern Coll (FL)
Gannon U (PA)
George Mason U (VA)
The George Washington U (DC)
Georgian Court U (NJ)
Howard U (DC)
Illinois Coll (IL)
Illinois State U (IL)
Indiana State U (IN)
Indiana U of Pennsylvania (PA)
Indiana U-Purdue U Indianapolis (IN)
Indiana U South Bend (IN)
Indiana U Southeast (IN)
Inter American U of Puerto Rico, Metropolitan Campus (PR)
Inter American U of Puerto Rico, San Germán Campus (PR)
Kansas State U (KS)
Kean U (NJ)
Keuka Coll (NY)
King's Coll (PA)
Lincoln Memorial U (TN)
Lincoln U (MO)
Louisiana State U Health Sciences Center (LA)
Louisiana Tech U (LA)
Loyola U Chicago (IL)
Malone U (OH)
Mansfield U of Pennsylvania (PA)
Marian U (IN)
Marquette U (WI)
Marshall U (WV)
Maryville U of Saint Louis (MO)
Marywood U (PA)
Mayville State U (ND)
McNeese State U (LA)
Mercy Coll (NY)
Miami U (OH)
Miami U Hamilton (OH)
Miami U Middletown (OH)
Michigan State U (MI)
Michigan Technological U (MI)
Minnesota State U Mankato (MN)
Minot State U (ND)
Mississippi State U (MS)
Missouri Southern State U (MO)
Missouri State U (MO)
Mount Marty Coll (SD)
Mount Mercy U (IA)
Muskingum U (OH)
National U (CA)
Nazareth Coll of Rochester (NY)
Northeastern State U (OK)
Northern Illinois U (IL)
Northern State U (SD)
Northwestern Coll (IA)
Northwest Missouri State U (MO)
Oakland U (MI)
The Ohio State U (OH)
Old Dominion U (VA)
Oral Roberts U (OK)
Pittsburg State U (KS)
Purdue U Fort Wayne (IN)
Purdue U Northwest (IN)
Radford U (VA)
Ramapo Coll of New Jersey (NJ)
Roberts Wesleyan Coll (NY)
Saginaw Valley State U (MI)
St. Catherine U (MN)
St. Cloud State U (MN)
Saint Francis U (PA)
Saint Louis U (MO)
Saint Mary's U of Minnesota (MN)
St. Thomas Aquinas Coll (NY)
Salem State U (MA)
Salisbury U (MD)
Salve Regina U (RI)
Sam Houston State U (TX)
Seton Hill U (PA)
South Dakota State U (SD)
Southeast Missouri State U (MO)
Southern Arkansas U–Magnolia (AR)
Southwest Baptist U (MO)
Southwestern Oklahoma State U (OK)
State U of New York at Fredonia (NY)
Stevenson U (MD)
Stony Brook U, State U of New York (NY)
SUNY Brockport (NY)
Tarleton State U (TX)
Texas A&M U–Corpus Christi (TX)
Texas Southern U (TX)
Texas State U (TX)
Texas Woman's U (TX)
Union U (TN)
U at Buffalo, the State U of New York (NY)
The U of Akron (OH)
U of Central Florida (FL)
U of Cincinnati (OH)
The U of Findlay (OH)
U of Hawaii at Manoa (HI)
U of Illinois at Springfield (IL)
The U of Iowa (IA)
U of Jamestown (ND)
The U of Kansas (KS)
U of Kentucky (KY)
U of Louisiana at Monroe (LA)
U of Maine (ME)
U of Massachusetts Dartmouth (MA)
U of Massachusetts Lowell (MA)
U of Montana (MT)
U of New England (ME)
U of New Haven (CT)
The U of North Carolina at Chapel Hill (NC)
U of North Dakota (ND)
U of North Texas (TX)
U of St. Francis (IL)
U of Saint Francis (IN)
U of South Dakota (SD)
U of Southern Mississippi (MS)
U of South Florida (FL)
The U of Tennessee (TN)
The U of Texas at El Paso (TX)
The U of Texas Rio Grande Valley (TX)
The U of Toledo (OH)
U of Utah (UT)
U of Vermont (VT)
U of Washington (WA)
U of West Florida (FL)
U of Wisconsin–La Crosse (WI)
U of Wisconsin–Milwaukee (WI)
U of Wyoming (WY)
Valley City State U (ND)
Virginia Commonwealth U (VA)
Wake Forest U (NC)
Walla Walla U (WA)
Wartburg Coll (IA)
Wayne State U (MI)
Western Connecticut State U (CT)
Western Kentucky U (KY)
Western New Mexico U (NM)
West Liberty U (WV)
West Virginia U (WV)
Wichita State U (KS)
Wilkes U (PA)
Wright State U (OH)
Wright State U–Lake Campus (OH)
Xavier U (OH)
York Coll of Pennsylvania (PA)
Youngstown State U (OH)

CLINICAL/MEDICAL LABORATORY ASSISTANT
Baptist Coll of Health Sciences (TN)

CLINICAL/MEDICAL LABORATORY SCIENCE AND ALLIED PROFESSIONS RELATED
Allen Coll (IA)
Auburn U (AL)
Colby-Sawyer Coll (NH)
The Coll of Idaho (ID)
East Texas Baptist U (TX)
Gwynedd Mercy U (PA)
Misericordia U (PA)
New Jersey Inst of Technology (NJ)
Saint Louis U (MO)
U of Idaho (ID)
U of Massachusetts Lowell (MA)
U of Minnesota, Twin Cities Campus (MN)
U of Saint Mary (KS)

CLINICAL/MEDICAL LABORATORY TECHNOLOGY
Auburn U (AL)
Auburn U at Montgomery (AL)
Barry U (FL)
Maryville U of Saint Louis (MO)
Penn State DuBois (PA)
Purdue U Fort Wayne (IN)
Rhode Island Coll (RI)
U of Montana (MT)
U of New Mexico (NM)
U of Science and Arts of Oklahoma (OK)
Weber State U (UT)

CLINICAL/MEDICAL SOCIAL WORK
Eastern New Mexico U (NM)
New Mexico Highlands U (NM)

CLINICAL NURSE SPECIALIST
LeTourneau U (TX)

CLINICAL NUTRITION
Life U (GA)
Loyola U Chicago (IL)
Southern Illinois U Edwardsville (IL)
Texas Christian U (TX)
U of North Dakota (ND)

CLINICAL PSYCHOLOGY
Augsburg U (MN)
Biola U (CA)
Illinois Inst of Technology (IL)
Sam Houston State U (TX)
Simon Fraser U (BC, Canada)
U of Mary Hardin-Baylor (TX)

COGNITIVE PSYCHOLOGY AND PSYCHOLINGUISTICS
Brown U (RI)
Dartmouth Coll (NH)
Fitchburg State U (MA)
Northwestern U (IL)
Scripps Coll (CA)
State U of New York at Oswego (NY)
Tulane U (LA)
U of California, San Diego (CA)
Washington U in St. Louis (MO)
Yale U (CT)

COGNITIVE SCIENCE
California State U, Fresno (CA)
California State U, Stanislaus (CA)
Carleton Coll (MN)
Carnegie Mellon U (PA)
George Fox U (OR)
Hampshire Coll (MA)
Indiana U Bloomington (IN)
Johns Hopkins U (MD)
Lehigh U (PA)
Loyola U New Orleans (LA)
New York U (NY)
Occidental Coll (CA)
Pomona Coll (CA)
Sarah Lawrence Coll (NY)
Scripps Coll (CA)
Simmons U (MA)
Simon Fraser U (BC, Canada)
State U of New York at Oswego (NY)
Susquehanna U (PA)
United States Military Acad (NY)
U of California, Berkeley (CA)
U of California, Irvine (CA)
U of California, Los Angeles (CA)
U of California, Merced (CA)
U of California, San Diego (CA)
U of California, Santa Cruz (CA)
U of Michigan (MI)
U of Minnesota, Duluth (MN)
U of Pennsylvania (PA)
U of Richmond (VA)
The U of Texas at Dallas (TX)
Vanderbilt U (TN)
Washington U in St. Louis (MO)

COLLEGE STUDENT COUNSELING AND PERSONNEL SERVICES
Bowling Green State U (OH)
Indiana U Bloomington (IN)

COMMERCIAL AND ADVERTISING ART
Academy of Art U (CA)
American Acad of Art (IL)
Ball State U (IN)
Bemidji State U (MN)
Biola U (CA)
Black Hills State U (SD)
Bowling Green State U (OH)
California State U, Fresno (CA)
California State U, Long Beach (CA)
California U of Pennsylvania (PA)
Carson-Newman U (TN)
Clark U (MA)
The Coll of Saint Rose (NY)
The Coll of Westchester (NY)
Columbia Coll Chicago (IL)
Concordia U Wisconsin (WI)
Dallas Baptist U (TX)
Dominican U (IL)
Drake U (IA)
Fashion Inst of Technology (NY)
Kutztown U of Pennsylvania (PA)
Lewis U (IL)
Lipscomb U (TN)
Louisiana Tech U (LA)

Marietta Coll (OH)
Massachusetts Coll of Art and Design (MA)
Mercy Coll (NY)
Miami U (OH)
Miami U Hamilton (OH)
Miami U Middletown (OH)
Millikin U (IL)
Minnesota State U Mankato (MN)
New York City Coll of Technology of the City U of New York (NY)
New York Inst of Technology (NY)
New York U (NY)
Northwest Nazarene U (ID)
Oral Roberts U (OK)
Otis Coll of Art and Design (CA)
Paier Coll of Art, Inc. (CT)
Portland State U (OR)
Pratt Inst (NY)
Purchase Coll, State U of New York (NY)
Purdue U Fort Wayne (IN)
St. Norbert Coll (WI)
Salem State U (MA)
Sam Houston State U (TX)
School of Visual Arts (NY)
Seattle U (WA)
Seton Hill U (PA)
Southwest Baptist U (MO)
State U of New York at Fredonia (NY)
State U of New York at Oswego (NY)
State U of New York Coll at Potsdam (NY)
U of Cincinnati (OH)
U of Minnesota, Duluth (MN)
The U of Tennessee (TN)
U of the Pacific (CA)
Upper Iowa U (IA)
Walla Walla U (WA)
Wartburg Coll (IA)
Waynesburg U (PA)
West Liberty U (WV)
Woodbury U (CA)
York Coll of Pennsylvania (PA)

COMMERCIAL PHOTOGRAPHY
Appalachian State U (NC)
Cazenovia Coll (NY)
Dallas Baptist U (TX)
Fashion Inst of Technology (NY)
Framingham State U (MA)
Nossi Coll of Art (TN)
School of Visual Arts (NY)

COMMUNICATION
Albion Coll (MI)
Angelo State U (TX)
Arizona Christian U (AZ)
Averett U (VA)
Bethany Lutheran Coll (MN)
Bethel U (IN)
Bethel U (MN)
Biola U (CA)
Boston Coll (MA)
Bradley U (IL)
Brenau U (GA)
California State U, Northridge (CA)
California State U, San Marcos (CA)
Carlow U (PA)
Carthage Coll (WI)
Cazenovia Coll (NY)
Central Washington U (WA)
Coll of the Ozarks (MO)
Columbia Coll Chicago (IL)
Concordia Coll (MN)
Cornell U (NY)
Dallas Baptist U (TX)
DePaul U (IL)
DeSales U (PA)
Dominican Coll (NY)
Drury U (MO)
Eastern Illinois U (IL)
Eastern New Mexico U (NM)
Edgewood Coll (WI)
Florida Inst of Technology (FL)
Fordham U (NY)
Geneva Coll (PA)
Goshen Coll (IN)
High Point U (NC)
Jacksonville State U (AL)
John Brown U (AR)
John Cabot U (Italy)
Kansas Wesleyan U (KS)
Kutztown U of Pennsylvania (PA)
Lake Forest Coll (IL)
Lamar U (TX)
Lasell Coll (MA)
Lebanese American U (Lebanon)
Le Moyne Coll (NY)
Lenoir-Rhyne U (NC)
Liberty U (VA)
Limestone Coll (SC)
Marquette U (WI)
Marymount Manhattan Coll (NY)
Marymount U (VA)
Mercy Coll (NY)
Miami U (OH)
Miami U Hamilton (OH)
Miami U Middletown (OH)
Michigan State U (MI)
Milligan Coll (TN)
Misericordia U (PA)
Mount Mercy U (IA)
New York Inst of Technology (NY)
Northwest Christian U (OR)
Northwest Missouri State U (MO)
Northwest U (WA)
Nyack Coll (NY)
Oakland City U (IN)
Oakland U (MI)
Oglethorpe U (GA)
Pepperdine U, Malibu (CA)
Portland State U (OR)
Purchase Coll, State U of New York (NY)
Queens U of Charlotte (NC)
Randolph-Macon Coll (VA)
Regent U (VA)
Regis Coll (MA)
Roanoke Coll (VA)
Rowan U (NJ)
Sacred Heart U (CT)
St. Cloud State U (MN)
St. John Fisher Coll (NY)
Saint Joseph's U (PA)
Saint Louis U (MO)
Saint Mary's Coll (IN)
Siena Coll (NY)
Slippery Rock U of Pennsylvania (PA)
Southeastern U (FL)
Southwestern Coll (KS)
Southwestern Oklahoma State U (OK)
Spring Hill Coll (AL)
State U of New York Coll at Potsdam (NY)
State U of New York Coll of Technology at Delhi (NY)
Stetson U (FL)
Tarleton State U (TX)
Tennessee Wesleyan U (TN)
Texas A&M Intl U (TX)
Texas A&M U (TX)
Texas A&M U–Commerce (TX)
Texas A&M U–Corpus Christi (TX)
Texas A&M U–Kingsville (TX)
Toccoa Falls Coll (GA)
Towson U (MD)
Trinity U (TX)
U of California, San Diego (CA)
U of California, Santa Barbara (CA)
U of Colorado Colorado Springs (CO)
U of Dubuque (IA)
U of Houston (TX)
U of Houston–Clear Lake (TX)
U of Illinois at Chicago (IL)
U of Illinois at Springfield (IL)
U of Maine (ME)
U of Massachusetts Amherst (MA)
U of Massachusetts Boston (MA)
U of Michigan–Flint (MI)
U of Missouri–St. Louis (MO)
U of North Dakota (ND)
U of San Diego (CA)
The U of Scranton (PA)
The U of Tampa (FL)
The U of Tennessee at Chattanooga (TN)
The U of Tennessee at Martin (TN)
The U of Texas at El Paso (TX)
The U of Texas at San Antonio (TX)
The U of Texas of the Permian Basin (TX)
U of Wisconsin–Eau Claire (WI)
U of Wisconsin–Green Bay (WI)
Utah State U (UT)
Valparaiso U (IN)
Whitworth U (WA)
Wichita State U (KS)
William Peace U (NC)
Wingate U (NC)
Woodbury U (CA)
Xavier U (OH)
Youngstown State U (OH)

COMMUNICATION AND JOURNALISM RELATED
Auburn U (AL)
Augustana Coll (IL)
Benedictine U (IL)
Berry Coll (GA)
Bowling Green State U (OH)
Brigham Young U (UT)
California Lutheran U (CA)
Carlow U (PA)
Chestnut Hill Coll (PA)
Dominican Coll (NY)
Dominican U of California (CA)
Drexel U (PA)
Endicott Coll (MA)
Farmingdale State Coll (NY)
Florida Inst of Technology (FL)
Friends U (KS)
Immaculata U (PA)
Lehman Coll of the City U of New York (NY)
Madonna U (MI)
Malone U (OH)
Manhattanville Coll (NY)
Marquette U (WI)
Merrimack Coll (MA)
Minot State U (ND)
New York U (NY)
Northern Arizona U (AZ)
The Ohio State U (OH)
Penn State Abington (PA)
Penn State Altoona (PA)
Penn State Beaver (PA)
Penn State Berks (PA)
Penn State Brandywine (PA)
Penn State DuBois (PA)
Penn State Erie, The Behrend Coll (PA)
Penn State Fayette, The Eberly Campus (PA)
Penn State Greater Allegheny (PA)
Penn State Hazleton (PA)
Penn State Lehigh Valley (PA)
Penn State Mont Alto (PA)
Penn State New Kensington (PA)
Penn State Schuylkill (PA)
Penn State Shenango (PA)
Penn State U Park (PA)
Penn State Wilkes-Barre (PA)
Penn State York (PA)
Pepperdine U, Malibu (CA)
Rosemont Coll (PA)
Sacred Heart U (CT)
Siena Heights U (MI)
Springfield Coll (MA)
Sterling Coll (KS)
Trevecca Nazarene U (TN)
U of Guam (GU)
U of Miami (FL)
U of Minnesota, Duluth (MN)
U of Minnesota, Twin Cities Campus (MN)
U of Wisconsin–Green Bay (WI)
Washington U in St. Louis (MO)
West Virginia U (WV)

COMMUNICATION AND MEDIA RELATED
Academy of Art U (CA)
Auburn U (AL)
Austin Coll (TX)
Belmont U (TN)
Bennington Coll (VT)
Biola U (CA)
Butler U (IN)
Cameron U (OK)
Carthage Coll (WI)
The Coll of Saint Rose (NY)
Columbia Intl U (SC)
DePaul U (IL)
DeSales U (PA)
Emory U (GA)
Fairleigh Dickinson U (NJ)
Florida State U (FL)
Georgetown Coll (KY)
Granite State Coll (NH)
Kennesaw State U (GA)
King's Coll (PA)
King U (TN)
La Roche U (PA)
Lasell Coll (MA)
Loyola U Chicago (IL)
Lynn U (FL)
Marquette U (WI)
Molloy Coll (NY)
Montclair State U (NJ)
Morehead State U (KY)
New Jersey Inst of Technology (NJ)
New York U (NY)
Northeastern Illinois U (IL)
Northwestern U (IL)
Pace U, Pleasantville Campus (NY)
Penn State Erie, The Behrend Coll (PA)
Pitzer Coll (CA)
Ramapo Coll of New Jersey (NJ)
Roger Williams U (RI)
Rollins Coll (FL)
Saint Francis U (PA)
St. Thomas U - Florida (FL)
Salve Regina U (RI)
Slippery Rock U of Pennsylvania (PA)
Southern Methodist U (TX)
Southwestern Coll (KS)
Spring Arbor U (MI)
Stanford U (CA)
U of Colorado Boulder (CO)
U of Oregon (OR)
The U of West Alabama (AL)
The U of Western Ontario (ON, Canada)
Virginia Wesleyan U (VA)
Washington & Jefferson Coll (PA)
William Peace U (NC)
Worcester State U (MA)

COMMUNICATION DISORDERS SCIENCES AND SERVICES RELATED
Elms Coll (MA)
Marquette U (WI)
Saint Mary's Coll (IN)
U of New Hampshire (NH)

COMMUNICATION SCIENCES AND DISORDERS
Appalachian State U (NC)
Arizona State U at the Tempe campus (AZ)
Auburn U (AL)
Augustana Coll (IL)
Baylor U (TX)
Biola U (CA)
Bowling Green State U (OH)
Bridgewater State U (MA)
Butler U (IN)
California State U, Fresno (CA)
California State U, Fullerton (CA)
California State U, Long Beach (CA)
California State U, Los Angeles (CA)
California State U, Northridge (CA)
California U of Pennsylvania (PA)
Central Michigan U (MI)
Eastern Illinois U (IL)
Florida State U (FL)
Governors State U (IL)
Hampton U (VA)
Harding U (AR)
Hardin-Simmons U (TX)
Ithaca Coll (NY)
Jacksonville U (FL)
Kansas State U (KS)
Lamar U (TX)
Maryville U of Saint Louis (MO)
Mercy Coll (NY)
Minnesota State U Mankato (MN)
Minot State U (ND)
Mount Vernon Nazarene U (OH)
Northern Arizona U (AZ)
Northern Illinois U (IL)
Northwestern U (IL)
Penn State Abington (PA)
Penn State Altoona (PA)
Penn State Beaver (PA)
Penn State Berks (PA)
Penn State Brandywine (PA)
Penn State DuBois (PA)
Penn State Erie, The Behrend Coll (PA)
Penn State Fayette, The Eberly Campus (PA)
Penn State Greater Allegheny (PA)
Penn State Hazleton (PA)
Penn State Lehigh Valley (PA)
Penn State Mont Alto (PA)
Penn State New Kensington (PA)
Penn State Schuylkill (PA)
Penn State Shenango (PA)
Penn State U Park (PA)
Penn State Wilkes-Barre (PA)
Penn State York (PA)
Portland State U (OR)
Purdue U Fort Wayne (IN)
Queens Coll of the City U of New York (NY)
Radford U (VA)
Rhode Island Coll (RI)
St. Cloud State U (MN)
Saint Louis U (MO)
Saint Mary's Coll (IN)
Samford U (AL)
San Diego State U (CA)
San Francisco State U (CA)
San Jose State U (CA)
Southeastern U (FL)
Southeast Missouri State U (MO)
Southern Illinois U Carbondale (IL)
Springfield Coll (MA)
State U of New York at Fredonia (NY)
State U of New York at New Paltz (NY)
Texas A&M Intl U (TX)
Texas A&M U–Kingsville (TX)
Texas State U (TX)
Texas Woman's U (TX)
Truman State U (MO)
The U of Akron (OH)
The U of Arizona (AZ)
U of Cincinnati (OH)
U of Colorado Boulder (CO)
U of Houston (TX)
The U of Kansas (KS)
U of Maine (ME)
U of Massachusetts Amherst (MA)
U of Minnesota, Duluth (MN)
U of Nebraska at Kearney (NE)
U of North Dakota (ND)
U of Northern Iowa (IA)
U of Oregon (OR)
U of South Alabama (AL)
U of South Dakota (SD)
The U of Texas Rio Grande Valley (TX)
U of Vermont (VT)
U of Wisconsin–Eau Claire (WI)
Utah State U (UT)
Wayne State U (MI)
Western Carolina U (NC)
Western Kentucky U (KY)
Western Washington U (WA)
Wichita State U (KS)
William Paterson U of New Jersey (NJ)
Winthrop U (SC)
Worcester State U (MA)
Xavier U of Louisiana (LA)

COMMUNICATIONS TECHNOLOGIES AND SUPPORT SERVICES RELATED
Alverno Coll (WI)
Chestnut Hill Coll (PA)
DePaul U (IL)
Framingham State U (MA)
Lesley U (MA)
Minot State U (ND)
U of Wisconsin–Platteville (WI)

COMMUNICATIONS TECHNOLOGY
Eastern Michigan U (MI)
Inter American U of Puerto Rico, Bayamón Campus (PR)
Messiah Coll (PA)

COMMUNITY HEALTH AND PREVENTIVE MEDICINE
Ball State U (IN)
Bowling Green State U (OH)
Charles R. Drew U of Medicine and Science (CA)
Florida Gulf Coast U (FL)
Florida State U (FL)
George Mason U (VA)
Georgia Coll & State U (GA)
Governors State U (IL)
Hofstra U (NY)
Indiana U Bloomington (IN)
Louisiana State U in Shreveport (LA)
Mansfield U of Pennsylvania (PA)
Moravian Coll (PA)

Murray State U (KY)
National U (CA)
Radford U (VA)
St. Cloud State U (MN)
South Dakota State U (SD)
State U of New York Coll at Potsdam (NY)
U of La Verne (CA)
U of the Incarnate Word (TX)
U of Wisconsin–Eau Claire (WI)
U of Wisconsin–La Crosse (WI)
Western Kentucky U (KY)

COMMUNITY HEALTH SERVICES COUNSELING
Becker Coll (MA)
Bethel U (MN)
Eastern Washington U (WA)
Indiana State U (IN)
Indiana U-Purdue U Indianapolis (IN)
James Madison U (VA)
Northeastern Illinois U (IL)
Purdue U Fort Wayne (IN)
Rhode Island Coll (RI)
Texas A&M U (TX)
The U of Arizona (AZ)
U of Central Arkansas (AR)
The U of Kansas (KS)
U of Massachusetts Lowell (MA)
U of Pennsylvania (PA)
The U of Western Ontario (ON, Canada)
U of West Florida (FL)
Western Connecticut State U (CT)
Western Washington U (WA)
Whitworth U (WA)
Worcester State U (MA)
Wright State U (OH)
Wright State U–Lake Campus (OH)
Youngstown State U (OH)

COMMUNITY ORGANIZATION AND ADVOCACY
Allegheny Coll (PA)
Alverno Coll (WI)
Arizona State U at the Downtown Phoenix campus (AZ)
Arizona State U at the West campus (AZ)
Bemidji State U (MN)
Central Michigan U (MI)
Columbia Coll (SC)
Emory & Henry Coll (VA)
Guilford Coll (NC)
Madonna U (MI)
Miami U Hamilton (OH)
Miami U Middletown (OH)
Nazareth Coll of Rochester (NY)
New York U (NY)
Northwestern U (IL)
Portland State U (OR)
Providence Coll (RI)
Saint Louis U (MO)
Siena Heights U (MI)
Southern Arkansas U–Magnolia (AR)
State U of New York Empire State Coll (NY)
U of Alaska Fairbanks (AK)
U of California, Santa Cruz (CA)
U of Colorado Boulder (CO)
U of Massachusetts Boston (MA)

COMMUNITY PSYCHOLOGY
Clayton State U (GA)
Northwestern U (IL)
Rogers State U (OK)
St. Cloud State U (MN)
U of Miami (FL)
U of Washington, Bothell (WA)

COMPARATIVE LITERATURE
The American U of Paris (France)
Barnard Coll (NY)
Barry U (FL)
Beloit Coll (WI)
Binghamton U, State U of New York (NY)
Brandeis U (MA)
Brown U (RI)
California State U, Fullerton (CA)
California State U, Long Beach (CA)
City Coll of the City U of New York (NY)
Clark U (MA)
Coll of the Holy Cross (MA)
The Coll of Wooster (OH)
The Colorado Coll (CO)
Cornell U (NY)
Dartmouth Coll (NH)
Emory U (GA)
Fairleigh Dickinson U (NJ)
Fordham U (NY)
Georgetown U (DC)
Harvard U (MA)
Hillsdale Coll (MI)
Hobart and William Smith Colls (NY)
Hofstra U (NY)
Indiana U Bloomington (IN)
Inter American U of Puerto Rico, San Germán Campus (PR)
Middlebury Coll (VT)
Minnesota State U Mankato (MN)
New York U (NY)
Northwestern U (IL)
Northwest U (WA)
Oberlin Coll (OH)
Occidental Coll (CA)
The Ohio State U (OH)
Ohio Wesleyan U (OH)
Pacific U (OR)
Penn State Abington (PA)
Penn State Altoona (PA)
Penn State Beaver (PA)
Penn State Berks (PA)
Penn State Brandywine (PA)
Penn State DuBois (PA)
Penn State Erie, The Behrend Coll (PA)
Penn State Fayette, The Eberly Campus (PA)
Penn State Greater Allegheny (PA)
Penn State Hazleton (PA)
Penn State Lehigh Valley (PA)
Penn State Mont Alto (PA)
Penn State New Kensington (PA)
Penn State Schuylkill (PA)
Penn State Shenango (PA)
Penn State U Park (PA)
Penn State Wilkes-Barre (PA)
Penn State York (PA)
Princeton U (NJ)
Queens Coll of the City U of New York (NY)
St. Catherine U (MN)
San Diego State U (CA)
San Francisco State U (CA)
Sarah Lawrence Coll (NY)
Smith Coll (MA)
Stanford U (CA)
State U of New York Coll at Geneseo (NY)
State U of New York Coll at Old Westbury (NY)
Stony Brook U, State U of New York (NY)
The U of Arizona (AZ)
U of California, Berkeley (CA)
U of California, Irvine (CA)
U of California, Los Angeles (CA)
U of California, Merced (CA)
U of California, Riverside (CA)
U of California, San Diego (CA)
U of California, Santa Barbara (CA)
U of California, Santa Cruz (CA)
The U of Iowa (IA)
U of Massachusetts Amherst (MA)
U of Michigan (MI)
U of Minnesota, Twin Cities Campus (MN)
U of New Mexico (NM)
U of Oregon (OR)
U of Pennsylvania (PA)
U of Pittsburgh at Greensburg (PA)
U of San Francisco (CA)
U of South Carolina (SC)
The U of Texas at Dallas (TX)
U of Toronto (ON, Canada)
U of Utah (UT)
U of Virginia (VA)
U of Washington (WA)
The U of Western Ontario (ON, Canada)
U of Wisconsin–Madison (WI)
U of Wisconsin–Milwaukee (WI)
Washington U in St. Louis (MO)
Willamette U (OR)
Williams Coll (MA)
Yale U (CT)

COMPUTATIONAL AND APPLIED MATHEMATICS
American Public U System (WV)
Arizona State U at the West campus (AZ)
Bryant U (RI)
Emmanuel Coll (MA)
Florida State U (FL)
Linfield Coll (OR)
Maryville U of Saint Louis (MO)
Saint Mary's Coll (IN)
Saint Mary's Coll of California (CA)
Shenandoah U (VA)
Shepherd U (WV)
U of Notre Dame (IN)
U of South Florida, St. Petersburg (FL)
William Jewell Coll (MO)
Wittenberg U (OH)

COMPUTATIONAL BIOLOGY
Colby Coll (ME)
Florida State U (FL)
Lipscomb U (TN)

COMPUTATIONAL MATHEMATICS
Arizona State U at the Tempe campus (AZ)
Carnegie Mellon U (PA)
Coll of Saint Benedict (MN)
Loyola U New Orleans (LA)
Marquette U (WI)
McKendree U (IL)
Michigan State U (MI)
The Ohio State U (OH)
Purdue U Fort Wayne (IN)
Saint John's U (MN)
Siena Coll (NY)
Simmons U (MA)
Southwestern U (TX)
U of California, Los Angeles (CA)
U of California, San Diego (CA)
U of Washington (WA)
U of Waterloo (ON, Canada)

COMPUTATIONAL SCIENCE
American U (DC)
Colorado State U (CO)
Florida State U (FL)
Hamline U (MN)
Indiana U Bloomington (IN)
Indiana U East (IN)
Indiana U Kokomo (IN)
Indiana U-Purdue U Indianapolis (IN)
Indiana U South Bend (IN)
Indiana U Southeast (IN)
Mercer U, Macon (GA)
Northern Arizona U (AZ)
Point Loma Nazarene U (CA)
Siena Coll (NY)
U of Michigan–Dearborn (MI)
U of New England (ME)
U of South Carolina Beaufort (SC)
Vanguard U of Southern California (CA)
Washington State U (WA)
Washington State U–Vancouver (WA)

COMPUTER AND INFORMATION SCIENCES
Alverno Coll (WI)
American U (DC)
Anderson U (SC)
Andrews U (MI)
Angelo State U (TX)
Aquinas Coll (MI)
Arcadia U (PA)
Arizona State U at the Tempe campus (AZ)
Arkansas Tech U (AR)
Assumption Coll (MA)
Athens State U (AL)
Auburn U (AL)
Avila U (MO)
Azusa Pacific U (CA)
Ball State U (IN)
Barnard Coll (NY)
Beacon Coll (FL)
Becker Coll (MA)
Belmont U (TN)
Bennington Coll (VT)
Bentley U (MA)
Berea Coll (KY)
Bethel U (IN)
Bethel U (MN)
Binghamton U, State U of New York (NY)
Boston Coll (MA)
Bowling Green State U (OH)
Bradley U (IL)
Bucknell U (PA)
Butler U (IN)
Caldwell U (NJ)
California Lutheran U (CA)
California State U, Fresno (CA)
California U of Pennsylvania (PA)
Carthage Coll (WI)
Catawba Coll (NC)
The Catholic U of America (DC)
Central Connecticut State U (CT)
Champlain Coll (VT)
Chestnut Hill Coll (PA)
The Citadel, The Military Coll of South Carolina (SC)
Clarion U of Pennsylvania (PA)
Clark Atlanta U (GA)
Clemson U (SC)
Coastal Carolina U (SC)
Coll of Charleston (SC)
The Coll of St. Scholastica (MN)
Colorado State U (CO)
Columbia Coll (SC)
Concordia U Chicago (IL)
Cornell U (NY)
Covenant Coll (GA)
Dakota State U (SD)
Dallas Baptist U (TX)
Davidson Coll (NC)
DeSales U (PA)
Dickinson State U (ND)
Doane U (NE)
Dominican Coll (NY)
East Central U (OK)
Eastern Kentucky U (KY)
Eastern Michigan U (MI)
Eastern New Mexico U (NM)
Eastern Oregon U (OR)
Eastern Washington U (WA)
Edgewood Coll (WI)
Edinboro U of Pennsylvania (PA)
Elms Coll (MA)
Elon U (NC)
Emmanuel Coll (GA)
Emmaus Bible Coll (IA)
Emporia State U (KS)
Fairfield U (CT)
Fairleigh Dickinson U (NJ)
Felician U (NJ)
Fisher Coll (MA)
Fitchburg State U (MA)
Florida A&M U (FL)
Florida Atlantic U (FL)
Florida Gulf Coast U (FL)
Florida State U (FL)
Fordham U (NY)
Framingham State U (MA)
Francis Marion U (SC)
Freed-Hardeman U (TN)
Gallaudet U (DC)
Gannon U (PA)
Geneva Coll (PA)
George Fox U (OR)
George Mason U (VA)
The George Washington U (DC)
Georgia Inst of Technology (GA)
Georgia Southern U (GA)
Georgia State U (GA)
Goucher Coll (MD)
Graceland U (IA)
Grand Valley State U (MI)
Guilford Coll (NC)
Gwynedd Mercy U (PA)
Hope Coll (MI)
Husson U (ME)
Illinois Inst of Technology (IL)
Indiana State U (IN)
Indiana U of Pennsylvania (PA)
Jacksonville State U (AL)
Jacksonville U (FL)
James Madison U (VA)
John Jay Coll of Criminal Justice of the City U of New York (NY)
Johns Hopkins U (MD)
Kalamazoo Coll (MI)
Kansas State U (KS)
Kean U (NJ)
Keiser U, Fort Lauderdale (FL)
Kennesaw State U (GA)
King's Coll (PA)
Kutztown U of Pennsylvania (PA)
Lamar U (TX)
La Roche U (PA)
Lehman Coll of the City U of New York (NY)
Le Moyne Coll (NY)
Lenoir-Rhyne U (NC)
Lewis-Clark State Coll (ID)
Liberty U (VA)
Lincoln Memorial U (TN)
Lincoln U (PA)
Lindenwood U (MO)
Lock Haven U of Pennsylvania (PA)
Loyola Marymount U (CA)
Loyola U Chicago (IL)
Loyola U New Orleans (LA)
Mansfield U of Pennsylvania (PA)
Marquette U (WI)
Marshall U (WV)
Mayville State U (ND)
McDaniel Coll (MD)
McMurry U (TX)
Mercy Coll (NY)
Miami Dade Coll (FL)
Miami U (OH)
Miami U Hamilton (OH)
Miami U Middletown (OH)
Michigan State U (MI)
MidAmerica Nazarene U (KS)
Millersville U of Pennsylvania (PA)
Milligan Coll (TN)
Minot State U (ND)
Misericordia U (PA)
Mississippi State U (MS)
Missouri Southern State U (MO)
Missouri U of Science and Technology (MO)
Molloy Coll (NY)
Montclair State U (NJ)
Morehead State U (KY)
Mount St. Mary's U (MD)
New England Coll (NH)
New England Inst of Technology (RI)
New Jersey Inst of Technology (NJ)
New Mexico Highlands U (NM)
New York Inst of Technology (NY)
New York U (NY)
Niagara U (NY)
North Central U (MN)
Northern Kentucky U (KY)
Northwest Christian U (OR)
Northwestern U (IL)
Northwest Missouri State U (MO)
Nova Southeastern U (FL)
Oakland U (MI)
Occidental Coll (CA)
The Ohio State U (OH)
Oklahoma Baptist U (OK)
Oklahoma State U (OK)
Old Dominion U (VA)
Oral Roberts U (OK)
Pace U, Pleasantville Campus (NY)
Palm Beach Atlantic U (FL)
Penn State Abington (PA)
Penn State Altoona (PA)
Penn State Beaver (PA)
Penn State Berks (PA)
Penn State Brandywine (PA)
Penn State DuBois (PA)
Penn State Erie, The Behrend Coll (PA)
Penn State Fayette, The Eberly Campus (PA)
Penn State Greater Allegheny (PA)
Penn State Harrisburg (PA)
Penn State Hazleton (PA)
Penn State Lehigh Valley (PA)
Penn State Mont Alto (PA)
Penn State New Kensington (PA)
Penn State Schuylkill (PA)
Penn State Shenango (PA)
Penn State U Park (PA)
Penn State Wilkes-Barre (PA)
Penn State York (PA)
Pittsburg State U (KS)
Polytechnic U of Puerto Rico (PR)
Portland State U (OR)
Prairie View A&M U (TX)
Purdue U Fort Wayne (IN)
Ramapo Coll of New Jersey (NJ)
Rhode Island Coll (RI)
Rice U (TX)
Roger Williams U (RI)
Rollins Coll (FL)
Rowan U (NJ)
Sacred Heart U (CT)
Saginaw Valley State U (MI)

St. Bonaventure U (NY)
St. Catherine U (MN)
St. John Fisher Coll (NY)
Saint Leo U (FL)
Saint Louis U (MO)
St. Mary's Coll of Maryland (MD)
St. Mary's U (TX)
St. Norbert Coll (WI)
St. Thomas Aquinas Coll (NY)
Saint Vincent Coll (PA)
Salem State U (MA)
Salisbury U (MD)
Samford U (AL)
Sam Houston State U (TX)
Shepherd U (WV)
Siena Coll (NY)
Siena Heights U (MI)
Sierra Nevada Coll (NV)
Simmons U (MA)
Skidmore Coll (NY)
Slippery Rock U of Pennsylvania (PA)
South Dakota State U (SD)
Southeast Missouri State U (MO)
Southern Arkansas U–Magnolia (AR)
Southern Illinois U Edwardsville (IL)
Southwest Baptist U (MO)
Southwestern Oklahoma State U (OK)
Southwestern U (TX)
Springfield Coll (MA)
Spring Hill Coll (AL)
State U of New York at New Paltz (NY)
State U of New York Coll at Old Westbury (NY)
State U of New York Coll at Potsdam (NY)
Sterling Coll (KS)
Stetson U (FL)
Stevenson U (MD)
Stockton U (NJ)
Stony Brook U, State U of New York (NY)
Suffolk U (MA)
Susquehanna U (PA)
Tarleton State U (TX)
Temple U (PA)
Tennessee Wesleyan U (TN)
Texas A&M U–Central Texas (TX)
Texas A&M U–Commerce (TX)
Texas A&M U–Corpus Christi (TX)
Texas A&M U–Kingsville (TX)
Texas Christian U (TX)
Texas Southern U (TX)
Texas State U (TX)
Texas Tech U (TX)
Texas Woman's U (TX)
Tiffin U (OH)
Transylvania U (KY)
Trinity U (TX)
Troy U (AL)
Truman State U (MO)
Tulane U (LA)
Union Coll (NY)
United States Military Acad (NY)
U at Albany, State U of New York (NY)
The U of Alabama (AL)
The U of Alabama at Birmingham (AL)
The U of Alabama in Huntsville (AL)
U of Alaska Fairbanks (AK)
The U of Arizona (AZ)
U of Arkansas (AR)
U of California, Irvine (CA)
U of California, Los Angeles (CA)
U of Central Arkansas (AR)
U of Central Florida (FL)
U of Cincinnati (OH)
U of Colorado Denver (CO)
U of Dayton (OH)
U of Denver (CO)
U of Dubuque (IA)
The U of Findlay (OH)
U of Hartford (CT)
U of Hawaii at Manoa (HI)
U of Houston (TX)
U of Houston–Clear Lake (TX)
U of Houston–Downtown (TX)
The U of Kansas (KS)
U of Kentucky (KY)
U of La Verne (CA)
U of Louisiana at Lafayette (LA)
U of Mary Hardin-Baylor (TX)
U of Maryland Global Campus (MD)
U of Mary Washington (VA)
U of Massachusetts Boston (MA)
U of Massachusetts Dartmouth (MA)
U of Michigan (MI)
U of Michigan–Dearborn (MI)
U of Montana (MT)
U of Nebraska at Kearney (NE)
U of Nebraska–Lincoln (NE)
U of Nevada, Reno (NV)
U of New Hampshire (NH)
U of New Haven (CT)
U of New Mexico (NM)
U of North Dakota (ND)
U of North Florida (FL)
U of North Texas (TX)
U of Notre Dame (IN)
U of Oregon (OR)
U of Pikeville (KY)
U of Pittsburgh at Greensburg (PA)
U of Providence (MT)
U of Puerto Rico–Ponce (PR)
U of Puget Sound (WA)
U of Richmond (VA)
U of Saint Mary (KS)
U of San Francisco (CA)
U of South Carolina (SC)
U of South Carolina Aiken (SC)
U of South Dakota (SD)
U of Southern Indiana (IN)
U of Southern Mississippi (MS)
U of South Florida (FL)
The U of Tampa (FL)
The U of Texas at Dallas (TX)
The U of Texas at El Paso (TX)
The U of Texas at San Antonio (TX)
The U of Texas of the Permian Basin (TX)
U of the Fraser Valley (BC, Canada)
U of the Incarnate Word (TX)
U of Virginia (VA)
U of Washington, Bothell (WA)
U of Washington, Tacoma (WA)
The U of Western Ontario (ON, Canada)
U of West Florida (FL)
U of West Georgia (GA)
U of Wisconsin–Eau Claire (WI)
U of Wisconsin–La Crosse (WI)
U of Wisconsin–Madison (WI)
U of Wisconsin–Milwaukee (WI)
U of Wisconsin–Platteville (WI)
Utah State U (UT)
Utica Coll (NY)
Valdosta State U (GA)
Valley City State U (ND)
Virginia Commonwealth U (VA)
Wake Forest U (NC)
Wartburg Coll (IA)
Washington State U (WA)
Washington State U–Tri-Cities (WA)
Washington U in St. Louis (MO)
Waynesburg U (PA)
Wayne State Coll (NE)
Wayne State U (MI)
Webber Intl U (FL)
Weber State U (UT)
West Chester U of Pennsylvania (PA)
Western Kentucky U (KY)
Western Michigan U (MI)
Western Washington U (WA)
Westminster Coll (UT)
Westmont Coll (CA)
Widener U (PA)
Wilkes U (PA)
Willamette U (OR)
William & Mary (VA)
William Paterson U of New Jersey (NJ)
Winthrop U (SC)
Worcester State U (MA)
Wright State U (OH)
Wright State U–Lake Campus (OH)
Xavier U of Louisiana (LA)
Yale U (CT)
Yeshiva U (NY)
Youngstown State U (OH)

COMPUTER AND INFORMATION SCIENCES AND SUPPORT SERVICES RELATED

Alfred U (NY)
Arizona State U at the West campus (AZ)
Coll of Staten Island of the City U of New York (NY)
Ferris State U (MI)
Georgian Court U (NJ)
Hofstra U (NY)
Lehigh U (PA)
Limestone Coll (SC)
Marshall U (WV)
Mayville State U (ND)
Missouri U of Science and Technology (MO)
New York U (NY)
St. Bonaventure U (NY)
State U of New York Coll of Agriculture and Technology at Cobleskill (NY)
U at Albany, State U of New York (NY)
U of Northern Iowa (IA)
U of Notre Dame (IN)
U of Providence (MT)
U of Washington, Bothell (WA)
Washington U in St. Louis (MO)

COMPUTER AND INFORMATION SCIENCES RELATED

California State U, Dominguez Hills (CA)
California State U, Monterey Bay (CA)
Carnegie Mellon U (PA)
Coll of Charleston (SC)
The Colorado Coll (CO)
Eastern Illinois U (IL)
Gwynedd Mercy U (PA)
Hofstra U (NY)
Lewis U (IL)
Limestone Coll (SC)
Missouri State U (MO)
New York U (NY)
Northern Kentucky U (KY)
Taylor U (IN)
U of New Haven (CT)
U of Northern Iowa (IA)
U of Providence (MT)
U of Wisconsin–Stout (WI)
West Virginia U (WV)
Wichita State U (KS)

COMPUTER AND INFORMATION SYSTEMS SECURITY

American Public U System (WV)
Arkansas Tech U (AR)
Assumption Coll (MA)
Aurora U (IL)
Bentley U (MA)
California Baptist U (CA)
Central Connecticut State U (CT)
Central Washington U (WA)
Charter Oak State Coll (CT)
Collin County Comm Coll District (TX)
Columbia Coll (MO)
Dakota State U (SD)
Dallas Baptist U (TX)
Davenport U, Grand Rapids (MI)
DePaul U (IL)
Donnelly Coll (KS)
Drexel U (PA)
ECPI U, Virginia Beach (VA)
Excelsior Coll (NY)
Felician U (NJ)
Ferris State U (MI)
Gannon U (PA)
Guilford Coll (NC)
Hofstra U (NY)
Illinois State U (IL)
Immaculata U (PA)
Inter American U of Puerto Rico, Bayamón Campus (PR)
Iona Coll (NY)
Kennesaw State U (GA)
LeTourneau U (TX)
Lewis U (IL)
Liberty U (VA)
Limestone Coll (SC)
Lindenwood U (MO)
Lipscomb U (TN)
Loyola U Chicago (IL)
Marshall U (WV)
Marywood U (PA)
Mercy Coll (NY)
Messiah Coll (PA)
Michigan Technological U (MI)
Mississippi State U (MS)
Mount St. Mary's U (MD)
Northern Kentucky U (KY)
Northwest Missouri State U (MO)
Oklahoma State U Inst of Technology (OK)
Old Dominion U (VA)
Pensacola State Coll (FL)
Point Loma Nazarene U (CA)
Radford U (VA)
Randolph-Macon Coll (VA)
Rasmussen Coll Blaine (MN)
Rasmussen Coll Bloomington (MN)
Rasmussen Coll Brooklyn Park (MN)
Rasmussen Coll Eagan (MN)
Rasmussen Coll Fargo (ND)
Rasmussen Coll Fort Myers (FL)
Rasmussen Coll Green Bay (WI)
Rasmussen Coll Kansas City/Overland Park (KS)
Rasmussen Coll Lake Elmo/Woodbury (MN)
Rasmussen Coll Land O' Lakes (FL)
Rasmussen Coll Mankato (MN)
Rasmussen Coll Moorhead (MN)
Rasmussen Coll New Port Richey (FL)
Rasmussen Coll Ocala (FL)
Rasmussen Coll St. Cloud (MN)
Rasmussen Coll Tampa/Brandon (FL)
Rasmussen Coll Topeka (KS)
Rasmussen Coll Wausau (WI)
Sacred Heart U (CT)
St. Ambrose U (IA)
St. Bonaventure U (NY)
St. Cloud State U (MN)
Saint Francis U (PA)
Saint Leo U (FL)
Sam Houston State U (TX)
Southeast Missouri State U (MO)
State U of New York Coll of Technology at Alfred (NY)
State U of New York Coll of Technology at Canton (NY)
Stetson U (FL)
Stevens Inst of Technology (NJ)
Sullivan U (KY)
Taylor U (IN)
Trine U (IN)
U of Cincinnati (OH)
U of Colorado Colorado Springs (CO)
U of Illinois at Springfield (IL)
U of Maine at Presque Isle (ME)
U of Maryland Global Campus (MD)
U of Miami (FL)
U of Michigan–Dearborn (MI)
U of North Dakota (ND)
U of Providence (MT)
The U of Tampa (FL)
The U of Texas at San Antonio (TX)
Walla Walla U (WA)
Wentworth Inst of Technology (MA)
Western Washington U (WA)

COMPUTER ENGINEERING

Anderson U (IN)
Arizona State U at the Tempe campus (AZ)
Arkansas Tech U (AR)
Auburn U (AL)
Bethel U (MN)
Binghamton U, State U of New York (NY)
Bowling Green State U (OH)
Bradley U (IL)
Brown U (RI)
Bucknell U (PA)
California Baptist U (CA)
California Polytechnic State U, San Luis Obispo (CA)
California State Polytechnic U, Pomona (CA)
California State U, Fresno (CA)
California State U, Fullerton (CA)
California State U, Long Beach (CA)
California State U, Northridge (CA)
California State U, Sacramento (CA)
California State U, San Bernardino (CA)
Capital U (OH)
Cedarville U (OH)
Central Michigan U (MI)
Clarkson U (NY)
Clemson U (SC)
Coll of Saint Elizabeth (NJ)
Colorado State U (CO)
Drexel U (PA)
Elon U (NC)
Fairfield U (CT)
Florida A&M U (FL)
Florida Atlantic U (FL)
Florida Inst of Technology (FL)
Florida Polytechnic U (FL)
Florida State U (FL)
Fort Lewis Coll (CO)
George Fox U (OR)
George Mason U (VA)
The George Washington U (DC)
Georgia Inst of Technology (GA)
Grand Valley State U (MI)
Hampton U (VA)
Harding U (AR)
High Point U (NC)
Hofstra U (NY)
Howard U (DC)
Illinois Inst of Technology (IL)
Indiana U-Purdue U Indianapolis (IN)
Iowa State U of Science and Technology (IA)
Johns Hopkins U (MD)
Kansas State U (KS)
Kettering U (MI)
Lawrence Technological U (MI)
Lebanese American U (Lebanon)
Lehigh U (PA)
LeTourneau U (TX)
Lewis U (IL)
Liberty U (VA)
Lipscomb U (TN)
Louisiana State U and A&M Coll (LA)
Loyola U Chicago (IL)
Manhattan Coll (NY)
Marquette U (WI)
Merrimack Coll (MA)
Miami U (OH)
Miami U Hamilton (OH)
Miami U Middletown (OH)
Michigan State U (MI)
Michigan Technological U (MI)
Milwaukee School of Eng (WI)
Minnesota State U Mankato (MN)
Mississippi State U (MS)
Missouri U of Science and Technology (MO)
Montana State U (MT)
New Jersey Inst of Technology (NJ)
New York U (NY)
Northern Arizona U (AZ)
Northwestern U (IL)
Oakland U (MI)
The Ohio State U (OH)
Oklahoma State U (OK)
Old Dominion U (VA)
Oral Roberts U (OK)
Penn State Abington (PA)
Penn State Altoona (PA)
Penn State Beaver (PA)
Penn State Berks (PA)
Penn State Brandywine (PA)
Penn State DuBois (PA)
Penn State Erie, The Behrend Coll (PA)
Penn State Fayette, The Eberly Campus (PA)
Penn State Greater Allegheny (PA)
Penn State Hazleton (PA)
Penn State Lehigh Valley (PA)
Penn State Mont Alto (PA)
Penn State New Kensington (PA)
Penn State Schuylkill (PA)
Penn State Shenango (PA)
Penn State U Park (PA)
Penn State Wilkes-Barre (PA)
Penn State York (PA)
Point Loma Nazarene U (CA)
Polytechnic U of Puerto Rico (PR)
Portland State U (OR)
Prairie View A&M U (TX)
Purdue U Fort Wayne (IN)

Purdue U Northwest (IN)
Regent U (VA)
Rice U (TX)
Roger Williams U (RI)
Rose-Hulman Inst of Technology (IN)
Sacred Heart U (CT)
St. Cloud State U (MN)
Saint Louis U (MO)
St. Mary's U (TX)
San Diego State U (CA)
San Francisco State U (CA)
San Jose State U (CA)
Santa Clara U (CA)
Shepherd U (WV)
Southern Illinois U Carbondale (IL)
Southern Illinois U Edwardsville (IL)
Southern Methodist U (TX)
State U of New York at New Paltz (NY)
Stevens Inst of Technology (NJ)
Stony Brook U, State U of New York (NY)
Taylor U (IN)
Texas A&M U (TX)
Texas Tech U (TX)
Trine U (IN)
U at Albany, State U of New York (NY)
U at Buffalo, the State U of New York (NY)
The U of Akron (OH)
The U of Alabama (AL)
The U of Alabama in Huntsville (AL)
U of Alaska Fairbanks (AK)
U of Arkansas (AR)
U of California, Irvine (CA)
U of California, Los Angeles (CA)
U of California, Merced (CA)
U of California, Riverside (CA)
U of California, San Diego (CA)
U of California, Santa Barbara (CA)
U of California, Santa Cruz (CA)
U of Central Florida (FL)
U of Cincinnati (OH)
U of Colorado Boulder (CO)
U of Colorado Colorado Springs (CO)
U of Dayton (OH)
U of Denver (CO)
U of Hartford (CT)
U of Houston (TX)
U of Houston–Clear Lake (TX)
U of Idaho (ID)
U of Illinois at Chicago (IL)
The U of Kansas (KS)
U of Kentucky (KY)
U of Louisiana at Lafayette (LA)
U of Louisville (KY)
U of Maine (ME)
U of Maryland, Baltimore County (MD)
U of Massachusetts Amherst (MA)
U of Massachusetts Boston (MA)
U of Massachusetts Dartmouth (MA)
U of Massachusetts Lowell (MA)
U of Memphis (TN)
U of Miami (FL)
U of Michigan (MI)
U of Michigan–Dearborn (MI)
U of Minnesota, Twin Cities Campus (MN)
U of Nebraska–Lincoln (NE)
U of Nevada, Las Vegas (NV)
U of Nevada, Reno (NV)
U of New Hampshire (NH)
U of New Haven (CT)
U of New Mexico (NM)
The U of North Carolina at Charlotte (NC)
U of North Texas (TX)
U of Notre Dame (IN)
U of Pennsylvania (PA)
U of Portland (OR)
The U of Scranton (PA)
U of South Alabama (AL)
U of South Carolina (SC)
U of South Florida (FL)
The U of Tennessee (TN)
The U of Tennessee at Chattanooga (TN)
The U of Texas at Dallas (TX)
The U of Texas at San Antonio (TX)
The U of Texas Rio Grande Valley (TX)
U of the Pacific (CA)
The U of Toledo (OH)
U of Toronto (ON, Canada)
U of Utah (UT)
U of Virginia (VA)
U of Washington (WA)
U of Washington, Bothell (WA)
U of Waterloo (ON, Canada)
The U of Western Ontario (ON, Canada)
U of West Florida (FL)
U of Wisconsin–La Crosse (WI)
U of Wisconsin–Madison (WI)
U of Wisconsin–Milwaukee (WI)
U of Wisconsin–Stout (WI)
U of Wyoming (WY)
Utah State U (UT)
Valparaiso U (IN)
Vanderbilt U (TN)
Villanova U (PA)
Virginia Commonwealth U (VA)
Walla Walla U (WA)
Washington State U (WA)
Washington U in St. Louis (MO)
Weber State U (UT)
Wentworth Inst of Technology (MA)
Western Michigan U (MI)
Western New England U (MA)
West Virginia U (WV)
Wichita State U (KS)
Wright State U (OH)
Wright State U–Lake Campus (OH)
Xavier U of Louisiana (LA)
York Coll of Pennsylvania (PA)

COMPUTER ENGINEERING RELATED

Auburn U (AL)
U of California, Santa Cruz (CA)
U of Massachusetts Dartmouth (MA)

COMPUTER ENGINEERING TECHNOLOGIES RELATED

Eastern Kentucky U (KY)
Inter American U of Puerto Rico, Bayamón Campus (PR)

COMPUTER ENGINEERING TECHNOLOGY

Ball State U (IN)
California State U, Long Beach (CA)
California U of Pennsylvania (PA)
Central Connecticut State U (CT)
Central Washington U (WA)
Eastern Michigan U (MI)
Farmingdale State Coll (NY)
Indiana State U (IN)
Indiana U-Purdue U Indianapolis (IN)
Kennesaw State U (GA)
LeTourneau U (TX)
Minnesota State U Mankato (MN)
New York City Coll of Technology of the City U of New York (NY)
Prairie View A&M U (TX)
Purdue U Fort Wayne (IN)
Sam Houston State U (TX)
State U of New York Coll of Technology at Alfred (NY)
Texas Southern U (TX)
U of Arkansas at Little Rock (AR)
U of Cincinnati (OH)
U of Dayton (OH)
U of Hartford (CT)
U of Houston (TX)
U of Houston–Downtown (TX)
U of Memphis (TN)
U of Southern Mississippi (MS)
Vermont Tech Coll (VT)

COMPUTER GRAPHICS

Academy of Art U (CA)
Bennington Coll (VT)
Champlain Coll (VT)
Clarkson U (NY)
Dakota State U (SD)
DePaul U (IL)
Elms Coll (MA)
Los Angeles Film School (CA)
Pratt Inst (NY)
Purdue U Northwest (IN)
Rogers State U (OK)
Springfield Coll (MA)
State U of New York at Fredonia (NY)
State U of New York Coll at Oneonta (NY)
Sullivan U (KY)
Texas A&M U (TX)
U of Dubuque (IA)
U of Houston (TX)
U of Mary Hardin-Baylor (TX)
U of Miami (FL)
The U of North Carolina Wilmington (NC)
U of Pennsylvania (PA)
Whitworth U (WA)

COMPUTER HARDWARE ENGINEERING

Auburn U (AL)
Santa Clara U (CA)
Utah Valley U (UT)

COMPUTER/INFORMATION TECHNOLOGY SERVICES ADMINISTRATION RELATED

Chestnut Hill Coll (PA)
Concordia U, St. Paul (MN)
Eastern Illinois U (IL)
Granite State Coll (NH)
Gulf Coast State Coll (FL)
Limestone Coll (SC)
Marywood U (PA)
Missouri State U (MO)
New York U (NY)
Purdue U Fort Wayne (IN)
St. Petersburg Coll (FL)
Southwestern Coll (KS)
U at Buffalo, the State U of New York (NY)
U of California, Santa Cruz (CA)
The U of Findlay (OH)
U of Guam (GU)
U of Maryland, Baltimore County (MD)
U of Northern Iowa (IA)
U of Providence (MT)

COMPUTER PROGRAMMING

Champlain Coll (VT)
Cogswell Polytechnical Coll (CA)
Columbia Coll Chicago (IL)
Davenport U, Grand Rapids (MI)
DePaul U (IL)
Farmingdale State Coll (NY)
Gannon U (PA)
Husson U (ME)
Inter American U of Puerto Rico, San Germán Campus (PR)
Le Moyne Coll (NY)
Limestone Coll (SC)
Missouri Valley Coll (MO)
New England Inst of Technology (RI)
Northwest Christian U (OR)
Rowan U (NJ)
Siena Coll (NY)
Southeast Missouri State U (MO)
Southwestern Coll (KS)
The U of Akron (OH)
U of Michigan–Dearborn (MI)
U of Providence (MT)
The U of Western Ontario (ON, Canada)
Walla Walla U (WA)
Western Colorado U (CO)
Worcester State U (MA)
Youngstown State U (OH)

COMPUTER PROGRAMMING RELATED

The U of Akron (OH)

COMPUTER PROGRAMMING (SPECIFIC APPLICATIONS)

Academy of Art U (CA)
DePaul U (IL)
ECPI U, Virginia Beach (VA)
Jacksonville U (FL)
Kennesaw State U (GA)
State U of New York Coll of Technology at Alfred (NY)
U of Washington, Bothell (WA)
Yale U (CT)

COMPUTER SCIENCE

Abilene Christian U (TX)
Adams State U (CO)
Allegheny Coll (PA)
American Coll of Thessaloniki (Greece)
American U of Beirut (Lebanon)
The American U of Paris (France)
Amherst Coll (MA)
Anderson U (IN)
Andrews U (MI)
Appalachian State U (NC)
Arcadia U (PA)
Arizona State U at the Tempe campus (AZ)
Athens State U (AL)
Auburn U at Montgomery (AL)
Augsburg U (MN)
Augustana Coll (IL)
Augustana U (SD)
Aurora U (IL)
Austin Coll (TX)
Austin Peay State U (TN)
Azusa Pacific U (CA)
Baker U (KS)
Barry U (FL)
Baylor U (TX)
Becker Coll (MA)
Belhaven U (MS)
Beloit Coll (WI)
Bemidji State U (MN)
Benedictine Coll (KS)
Benedictine U (IL)
Bennington Coll (VT)
Bethany Lutheran Coll (MN)
Binghamton U, State U of New York (NY)
Biola U (CA)
Boise State U (ID)
Boston Coll (MA)
Bowdoin Coll (ME)
Bradley U (IL)
Brandeis U (MA)
Brandon U (MB, Canada)
Bridgewater Coll (VA)
Bridgewater State U (MA)
Brown U (RI)
California Baptist U (CA)
California Lutheran U (CA)
California Polytechnic State U, San Luis Obispo (CA)
California State Polytechnic U, Pomona (CA)
California State U, Bakersfield (CA)
California State U, Dominguez Hills (CA)
California State U, Fresno (CA)
California State U, Fullerton (CA)
California State U, Long Beach (CA)
California State U, Los Angeles (CA)
California State U, Northridge (CA)
California State U, Sacramento (CA)
California State U, San Bernardino (CA)
California State U, San Marcos (CA)
California State U, Stanislaus (CA)
Calvin Coll (MI)
Cameron U (OK)
Capital U (OH)
Carleton Coll (MN)
Carnegie Mellon U (PA)
Carson-Newman U (TN)
Carthage Coll (WI)
The Catholic U of America (DC)
Cedarville U (OH)
Central Coll (IA)
Central Methodist U (MO)
Central Michigan U (MI)
Central State U (OH)
Central Washington U (WA)
Centre Coll (KY)
Champlain Coll (VT)
City Coll of the City U of New York (NY)
Clark Atlanta U (GA)
Clarkson U (NY)
Clark U (MA)
Clayton State U (GA)
Coe Coll (IA)
Colby Coll (ME)
Colgate U (NY)
Coll of Saint Benedict (MN)
The Coll of Saint Rose (NY)
Coll of Staten Island of the City U of New York (NY)
Coll of the Holy Cross (MA)
Coll of the Ozarks (MO)
The Coll of Wooster (OH)
Colorado School of Mines (CO)
Columbia Coll (MO)
Concordia Coll (MN)
Concordia U, St. Paul (MN)
Concordia U Wisconsin (WI)
Cornell Coll (IA)
Cornell U (NY)
Creighton U (NE)
Dallas Baptist U (TX)
Dartmouth Coll (NH)
DePaul U (IL)
DePauw U (IN)
DeSales U (PA)
Dickinson Coll (PA)
Dillard U (LA)
Doane U (NE)
Dominican U (IL)
Drake U (IA)
Drew U (NJ)
Drexel U (PA)
Earlham Coll (IN)
East Carolina U (NC)
Eastern Illinois U (IL)
Eastern Kentucky U (KY)
Eastern Mennonite U (VA)
Eastern Michigan U (MI)
Eastern U (PA)
Elon U (NC)
Emory U (GA)
Endicott Coll (MA)
Evangel U (MO)
Fairleigh Dickinson U (NJ)
Fayetteville State U (NC)
Fitchburg State U (MA)
Florida Inst of Technology (FL)
Florida Southern Coll (FL)
Franklin Coll (IN)
Furman U (SC)
Gannon U (PA)
George Mason U (VA)
Georgetown U (DC)
The George Washington U (DC)
Georgia Coll & State U (GA)
Georgia State U (GA)
Glenville State Coll (WV)
Gonzaga U (WA)
Gordon Coll (MA)
Goshen Coll (IN)
Goucher Coll (MD)
Governors State U (IL)
Grambling State U (LA)
Grinnell Coll (IA)
Gustavus Adolphus Coll (MN)
Hampden-Sydney Coll (VA)
Hampshire Coll (MA)
Hampton U (VA)
Hanover Coll (IN)
Harding U (AR)
Hardin-Simmons U (TX)
Harvard U (MA)
High Point U (NC)
Hobart and William Smith Colls (NY)
Hofstra U (NY)
Houston Baptist U (TX)
Howard U (DC)
Illinois Coll (IL)
Illinois Inst of Technology (IL)
Illinois State U (IL)
Illinois Wesleyan U (IL)
Indiana U Bloomington (IN)
Indiana U Kokomo (IN)
Indiana U Northwest (IN)
Indiana U-Purdue U Indianapolis (IN)
Indiana U South Bend (IN)
Indiana U Southeast (IN)
Inter American U of Puerto Rico, Aguadilla Campus (PR)
Inter American U of Puerto Rico, Barranquitas Campus (PR)
Inter American U of Puerto Rico, Bayamón Campus (PR)
Inter American U of Puerto Rico, Metropolitan Campus (PR)
Inter American U of Puerto Rico, San Germán Campus (PR)
Iona Coll (NY)
Iowa State U of Science and Technology (IA)
Ithaca Coll (NY)
John Carroll U (OH)
Kennesaw State U (GA)
Kettering U (MI)
King's Coll (PA)
The King's U (AB, Canada)
Knox Coll (IL)
Lafayette Coll (PA)

Lake Forest Coll (IL)
La Roche U (PA)
La Sierra U (CA)
Lawrence Technological U (MI)
Lebanese American U (Lebanon)
Lehigh U (PA)
Lehman Coll of the City U of New York (NY)
LeTourneau U (TX)
Lewis & Clark Coll (OR)
Lewis-Clark State Coll (ID)
Lewis U (IL)
Limestone Coll (SC)
Lindenwood U (MO)
Linfield Coll (OR)
Lipscomb U (TN)
Longwood U (VA)
Loras Coll (IA)
Louisiana State U and A&M Coll (LA)
Louisiana State U in Shreveport (LA)
Louisiana Tech U (LA)
Loyola U Maryland (MD)
Madonna U (MI)
Malone U (OH)
Manhattan Coll (NY)
Manhattanville Coll (NY)
Mansfield U of Pennsylvania (PA)
Marian U (IN)
Marietta Coll (OH)
Marywood U (PA)
McKendree U (IL)
McNeese State U (LA)
Mercer U, Macon (GA)
Mercy Coll (NY)
Meredith Coll (NC)
Merrimack Coll (MA)
Messiah Coll (PA)
Michigan Technological U (MI)
MidAmerica Nazarene U (KS)
Middlebury Coll (VT)
Middle Tennessee State U (TN)
Milligan Coll (TN)
Millikin U (IL)
Milwaukee School of Eng (WI)
Minot State U (ND)
Missouri State U (MO)
Missouri U of Science and Technology (MO)
Missouri Valley Coll (MO)
Montana State U (MT)
Montana Technological U (MT)
Moravian Coll (PA)
Mount Holyoke Coll (MA)
Mount Vernon Nazarene U (OH)
Murray State U (KY)
Muskingum U (OH)
National U (CA)
New Coll of Florida (FL)
New England Inst of Technology (RI)
New Jersey Inst of Technology (NJ)
New Mexico Inst of Mining and Technology (NM)
New York U (NY)
Northeastern Illinois U (IL)
Northeastern State U (OK)
Northern Arizona U (AZ)
Northern Illinois U (IL)
Northwestern Coll (IA)
Northwestern U (IL)
Northwest Nazarene U (ID)
Nova Southeastern U (FL)
Nyack Coll (NY)
Oberlin Coll (OH)
Ohio Dominican U (OH)
Ohio Wesleyan U (OH)
Oklahoma Baptist U (OK)
Olivet Nazarene U (IL)
Oral Roberts U (OK)
Pace U, Pleasantville Campus (NY)
Pacific U (OR)
Palm Beach Atlantic U (FL)
Penn State Erie, The Behrend Coll (PA)
Polytechnic U of Puerto Rico (PR)
Pomona Coll (CA)
Portland State U (OR)
Prairie View A&M U (TX)
Princeton U (NJ)
Providence Coll (RI)
Purdue U Fort Wayne (IN)
Purdue U Northwest (IN)
Queens Coll of the City U of New York (NY)
Radford U (VA)
Randolph-Macon Coll (VA)
Rasmussen Coll Blaine (MN)
Rasmussen Coll Bloomington (MN)
Rasmussen Coll Brooklyn Park (MN)
Rasmussen Coll Eagan (MN)
Rasmussen Coll Fargo (ND)
Rasmussen Coll Fort Myers (FL)
Rasmussen Coll Green Bay (WI)
Rasmussen Coll Lake Elmo/ Woodbury (MN)
Rasmussen Coll Land O' Lakes (FL)
Rasmussen Coll Mankato (MN)
Rasmussen Coll Moorhead (MN)
Rasmussen Coll New Port Richey (FL)
Rasmussen Coll Ocala (FL)
Rasmussen Coll St. Cloud (MN)
Rasmussen Coll Tampa/Brandon (FL)
Rasmussen Coll Topeka (KS)
Rasmussen Coll Wausau (WI)
Regent U (VA)
Rhode Island Coll (RI)
Rhodes Coll (TN)
Roanoke Coll (VA)
Rocky Mountain Coll (MT)
Roger Williams U (RI)
Rose-Hulman Inst of Technology (IN)
Rowan U (NJ)
Saginaw Valley State U (MI)
St. Ambrose U (IA)
St. Bonaventure U (NY)
St. Cloud State U (MN)
Saint Francis U (PA)
Saint John's U (MN)
Saint Louis U (MO)
St. Mary's U (TX)
Saint Mary's U of Minnesota (MN)
St. Norbert Coll (WI)
St. Olaf Coll (MN)
St. Thomas U - Florida (FL)
San Diego State U (CA)
San Francisco State U (CA)
San Jose State U (CA)
Sarah Lawrence Coll (NY)
Scripps Coll (CA)
Seattle U (WA)
Seton Hill U (PA)
Simon Fraser U (BC, Canada)
Smith Coll (MA)
Southeastern Louisiana U (LA)
Southern California Inst of Technology (CA)
Southern Illinois U Carbondale (IL)
Southern Illinois U Edwardsville (IL)
Southern Methodist U (TX)
Southwest Baptist U (MO)
Southwestern Coll (KS)
Spring Arbor U (MI)
Springfield Coll (MA)
Stanford U (CA)
State U of New York at Fredonia (NY)
State U of New York at Oswego (NY)
State U of New York Coll at Old Westbury (NY)
State U of New York Coll at Oneonta (NY)
State U of New York Coll at Potsdam (NY)
Stetson U (FL)
Stevens Inst of Technology (NJ)
Stockton U (NJ)
Suffolk U (MA)
Susquehanna U (PA)
Tarleton State U (TX)
Taylor U (IN)
Texas A&M U (TX)
Texas Lutheran U (TX)
Texas State U (TX)
Tiffin U (OH)
Towson U (MD)
Trine U (IN)
Tulane U (LA)
Union U (TN)
Universidad Adventista de las Antillas (PR)
U at Albany, State U of New York (NY)
U at Buffalo, the State U of New York (NY)
The U of Akron (OH)
U of Alaska Fairbanks (AK)
The U of Arizona (AZ)
U of Arkansas (AR)
U of Arkansas at Little Rock (AR)
U of California, Berkeley (CA)
U of California, Irvine (CA)
U of California, Riverside (CA)
U of California, San Diego (CA)
U of California, Santa Barbara (CA)
U of California, Santa Cruz (CA)
U of Colorado Boulder (CO)
U of Colorado Colorado Springs (CO)
U of Dallas (TX)
U of Dayton (OH)
U of Denver (CO)
U of Detroit Mercy (MI)
The U of Findlay (OH)
U of Guam (GU)
U of Hawaii at Manoa (HI)
U of Houston–Clear Lake (TX)
U of Idaho (ID)
U of Illinois at Chicago (IL)
U of Illinois at Springfield (IL)
The U of Iowa (IA)
U of Jamestown (ND)
U of La Verne (CA)
U of Louisiana at Lafayette (LA)
U of Louisiana at Monroe (LA)
U of Maine (ME)
U of Management and Technology (VA)
U of Mary Hardin-Baylor (TX)
U of Maryland, Baltimore County (MD)
U of Massachusetts Amherst (MA)
U of Massachusetts Lowell (MA)
U of Memphis (TN)
U of Miami (FL)
U of Michigan–Flint (MI)
U of Minnesota, Duluth (MN)
U of Minnesota, Morris (MN)
U of Minnesota, Twin Cities Campus (MN)
U of Missouri–St. Louis (MO)
U of Montana (MT)
U of Nevada, Las Vegas (NV)
U of New Haven (CT)
The U of North Carolina at Chapel Hill (NC)
The U of North Carolina at Charlotte (NC)
The U of North Carolina at Greensboro (NC)
The U of North Carolina at Pembroke (NC)
The U of North Carolina Wilmington (NC)
U of Northern Iowa (IA)
U of Northwestern–St. Paul (MN)
U of Pittsburgh at Bradford (PA)
U of Portland (OR)
U of Providence (MT)
U of Puget Sound (WA)
U of St. Francis (IL)
U of St. Thomas (TX)
U of San Diego (CA)
U of San Francisco (CA)
The U of Scranton (PA)
U of South Alabama (AL)
U of Southern Indiana (IN)
U of Southern Maine (ME)
The U of Tennessee (TN)
The U of Tennessee at Chattanooga (TN)
The U of Tennessee at Martin (TN)
The U of Texas Rio Grande Valley (TX)
U of the Pacific (CA)
The U of the South (TN)
U of the Virgin Islands (VI)
U of Toronto (ON, Canada)
The U of Tulsa (OK)
U of Utah (UT)
U of Vermont (VT)
U of Washington (WA)
U of Washington, Bothell (WA)
U of Waterloo (ON, Canada)
The U of Western Ontario (ON, Canada)
U of Wisconsin–Green Bay (WI)
U of Wisconsin–Milwaukee (WI)
U of Wisconsin–Parkside (WI)
U of Wisconsin–Superior (WI)
U of Wyoming (WY)
Utah Valley U (UT)
Valparaiso U (IN)
Vanderbilt U (TN)
Villanova U (PA)
Virginia Wesleyan U (VA)
Wabash Coll (IN)
Walla Walla U (WA)
Wartburg Coll (IA)
Washington and Lee U (VA)
Washington Coll (MD)
Washington State U (WA)
Washington State U–Tri-Cities (WA)
Washington State U–Vancouver (WA)
Washington U in St. Louis (MO)
Wayland Baptist U (TX)
Weber State U (UT)
Wentworth Inst of Technology (MA)
Wesleyan U (CT)
Western Carolina U (NC)
Western Connecticut State U (CT)
Western Michigan U (MI)
Western New England U (MA)
Western Oregon U (OR)
Westfield State U (MA)
Westminster Coll (UT)
West Virginia U (WV)
Wheaton Coll (IL)
Wheaton Coll (MA)
Whitworth U (WA)
Widener U (PA)
Willamette U (OR)
William Penn U (IA)
Williams Coll (MA)
Wilmington Coll (OH)
Wittenberg U (OH)
Wofford Coll (SC)
Worcester Polytechnic Inst (MA)
Xavier U (OH)
Xavier U of Louisiana (LA)
Yeshiva U (NY)
York Coll of Pennsylvania (PA)
Youngstown State U (OH)

COMPUTER SOFTWARE AND MEDIA APPLICATIONS RELATED

Academy of Art U (CA)
Champlain Coll (VT)
Coll of Charleston (SC)
Dakota State U (SD)
DePaul U (IL)
Elms Coll (MA)
Florida Polytechnic U (FL)
Franklin Coll (IN)
Inter American U of Puerto Rico, Bayamón Campus (PR)
LeTourneau U (TX)
Limestone Coll (SC)
Loyola U Chicago (IL)
New York U (NY)
Northwest Christian U (OR)
Pace U, Pleasantville Campus (NY)
State U of New York Coll of Agriculture and Technology at Cobleskill (NY)
U of Denver (CO)
U of Providence (MT)
U of Utah (UT)
The U of Western Ontario (ON, Canada)
U of Wisconsin–Stout (WI)
Worcester Polytechnic Inst (MA)

COMPUTER SOFTWARE ENGINEERING

Arizona State U at the Polytechnic campus (AZ)
Auburn U (AL)
Aurora U (IL)
Bethel U (MN)
Bowling Green State U (OH)
California Baptist U (CA)
Clarkson U (NY)
Drexel U (PA)
Dunwoody Coll of Technology (MN)
Florida Gulf Coast U (FL)
Florida Inst of Technology (FL)
Iowa State U of Science and Technology (IA)
Keiser U, Fort Lauderdale (FL)
Kennesaw State U (GA)
Lawrence Technological U (MI)
Loyola U Chicago (IL)
Miami U (OH)
Miami U Hamilton (OH)
Miami U Middletown (OH)
Michigan Technological U (MI)
Milwaukee School of Eng (WI)
Montana Technological U (MT)
Notre Dame Coll (OH)
Nova Southeastern U (FL)
Ohio Dominican U (OH)
Penn State Erie, The Behrend Coll (PA)
Point Loma Nazarene U (CA)
Rose-Hulman Inst of Technology (IN)
St. Cloud State U (MN)
Saint Leo U (FL)
St. Mary's U (TX)
State U of New York at Oswego (NY)
Stevens Inst of Technology (NJ)
Trine U (IN)
U of California, Irvine (CA)
U of Detroit Mercy (MI)
U of Houston (TX)
U of Massachusetts Dartmouth (MA)
U of Miami (FL)
U of Nebraska–Lincoln (NE)
U of Northern Colorado (CO)
The U of Scranton (PA)
The U of Texas at Dallas (TX)
U of Toronto (ON, Canada)
U of Waterloo (ON, Canada)
The U of Western Ontario (ON, Canada)
U of Wisconsin–Platteville (WI)
Upper Iowa U (IA)
Utah Valley U (UT)
Valley City State U (ND)
Vermont Tech Coll (VT)
Washington State U (WA)
Wichita State U (KS)
William Penn U (IA)

COMPUTER SOFTWARE TECHNOLOGY

Cogswell Polytechnical Coll (CA)
Farmingdale State Coll (NY)
Sam Houston State U (TX)

COMPUTER SYSTEMS ANALYSIS

Aquinas Coll (MI)
Arkansas Tech U (AR)
Austin Peay State U (TN)
California Polytechnic State U, San Luis Obispo (CA)
Calvin Coll (MI)
Davenport U, Grand Rapids (MI)
Dunwoody Coll of Technology (MN)
HEC Montreal (QC, Canada)
Lindenwood U (MO)
Miami U Hamilton (OH)
Miami U Middletown (OH)
Missouri State U (MO)
Northern Arizona U (AZ)
Pittsburg State U (KS)
Purdue U Northwest (IN)
Saginaw Valley State U (MI)
St. Ambrose U (IA)
Texas Christian U (TX)
Tiffin U (OH)
U of Denver (CO)
U of Houston (TX)
U of Illinois at Springfield (IL)
U of Louisiana at Lafayette (LA)
U of Minnesota, Twin Cities Campus (MN)
U of North Dakota (ND)
U of Providence (MT)
U of Vermont (VT)
U of Washington, Bothell (WA)

COMPUTER SYSTEMS NETWORKING AND TELECOMMUNICATIONS

Bayamón Central U (PR)
Champlain Coll (VT)
Davenport U, Grand Rapids (MI)
DePaul U (IL)
EDP U of Puerto Rico–San Sebastian (PR)
Ferris State U (MI)
Illinois State U (IL)
Inter American U of Puerto Rico, Aguadilla Campus (PR)
Inter American U of Puerto Rico, Bayamón Campus (PR)
Iona Coll (NY)
Kansas State U (KS)
Kean U (NJ)
Keiser U, Fort Lauderdale (FL)

Lindenwood U (MO)
Montana Technological U (MT)
Mount Vernon Nazarene U (OH)
Stevenson U (MD)
Tiffin U (OH)
The U of Akron (OH)
U of Minnesota, Duluth (MN)
U of Minnesota, Twin Cities Campus (MN)
The U of North Carolina at Greensboro (NC)
U of Pennsylvania (PA)
U of Providence (MT)
U of Toronto (ON, Canada)
U of Wisconsin–Stout (WI)
Utah Valley U (UT)
Weber State U (UT)
Wentworth Inst of Technology (MA)

COMPUTER TEACHER EDUCATION
Abilene Christian U (TX)
Aquinas Coll (MI)
Arkansas Tech U (AR)
Baylor U (TX)
Bowling Green State U (OH)
Concordia U Chicago (IL)
Dakota State U (SD)
Eastern Michigan U (MI)
Edgewood Coll (WI)
Grand Valley State U (MI)
McMurry U (TX)
Michigan State U (MI)
Roanoke Coll (VA)
Utica Coll (NY)

COMPUTER TECHNOLOGY/ COMPUTER SYSTEMS TECHNOLOGY
ECPI U, Virginia Beach (VA)
Florida Atlantic U (FL)
New England Inst of Technology (RI)
Point Loma Nazarene U (CA)
Wayne State U (MI)

CONDENSED MATTER AND MATERIALS PHYSICS
Michigan Technological U (MI)
Rowan U (NJ)

CONDUCTING
McMurry U (TX)
The New School Coll of Performing Arts (NY)

CONSERVATION BIOLOGY
Cedar Crest Coll (PA)
Central Michigan U (MI)
Florida Inst of Technology (FL)
Seattle U (WA)
U of Idaho (ID)
The U of Western Ontario (ON, Canada)
U of Wisconsin–Madison (WI)
Utah State U (UT)

CONSTRUCTION ENGINEERING
American U of Beirut (Lebanon)
Arizona State U at the Tempe campus (AZ)
Bowling Green State U (OH)
Bradley U (IL)
California State U, Long Beach (CA)
The Citadel, The Military Coll of South Carolina (SC)
Iowa State U of Science and Technology (IA)
Kennesaw State U (GA)
Lamar U (TX)
Marquette U (WI)
National U (CA)
New York U (NY)
Texas A&M U–Commerce (TX)
Texas Tech U (TX)
The U of Alabama (AL)
U of Arkansas at Little Rock (AR)
U of Houston (TX)
U of Nebraska–Lincoln (NE)
U of New Mexico (NM)
The U of Texas at El Paso (TX)
U of Utah (UT)
Washington State U (WA)

CONSTRUCTION ENGINEERING TECHNOLOGY
Bemidji State U (MN)
Bowling Green State U (OH)
Bradley U (IL)
California Baptist U (CA)
California State Polytechnic U, Pomona (CA)
California State U, Fresno (CA)
California State U, Long Beach (CA)
California State U, Sacramento (CA)
Colorado State U (CO)
Fairleigh Dickinson U (NJ)
Farmingdale State Coll (NY)
Fitchburg State U (MA)
Florida A&M U (FL)
Florida Gulf Coast U (FL)
Florida Inst of Technology (FL)
Georgia Southern U (GA)
Kansas State U (KS)
Louisiana Tech U (LA)
Michigan State U (MI)
Montana State U (MT)
Oklahoma State U (OK)
Pittsburg State U (KS)
Prairie View A&M U (TX)
Purdue U Fort Wayne (IN)
Purdue U Northwest (IN)
Sam Houston State U (TX)
San Diego State U (CA)
Southern Illinois U Edwardsville (IL)
Tarleton State U (TX)
Temple U (PA)
Texas A&M U (TX)
Texas State U (TX)
The U of Akron (OH)
U of Arkansas at Little Rock (AR)
U of Houston (TX)
U of Nebraska–Lincoln (NE)
U of North Florida (FL)
U of North Texas (TX)
The U of Toledo (OH)
Wayne State U (MI)
Western Carolina U (NC)
Western Kentucky U (KY)

CONSTRUCTION MANAGEMENT
Appalachian State U (NC)
Arizona State U at the Tempe campus (AZ)
Ball State U (IN)
Boise State U (ID)
California State U, Fresno (CA)
California State U, Northridge (CA)
Central Connecticut State U (CT)
Central Washington U (WA)
Clemson U (SC)
Drexel U (PA)
Dunwoody Coll of Technology (MN)
Eastern Illinois U (IL)
Eastern Kentucky U (KY)
Eastern Michigan U (MI)
Ferris State U (MI)
Illinois State U (IL)
Indiana State U (IN)
John Brown U (AR)
Kennesaw State U (GA)
Lawrence Technological U (MI)
Louisiana State U and A&M Coll (LA)
Michigan State U (MI)
Michigan Technological U (MI)
Middle Tennessee State U (TN)
Milwaukee School of Eng (WI)
Mississippi State U (MS)
Missouri State U (MO)
National U (CA)
New England Inst of Technology (RI)
Northern Arizona U (AZ)
Northern Kentucky U (KY)
Pittsburg State U (KS)
Roger Williams U (RI)
South Dakota State U (SD)
State U of New York Coll of Technology at Alfred (NY)
State U of New York Coll of Technology at Delhi (NY)
U of Louisiana at Monroe (LA)
U of Minnesota, Twin Cities Campus (MN)
U of Nevada, Las Vegas (NV)
U of Northern Iowa (IA)
U of Wisconsin–Stout (WI)
U of Wyoming (WY)
Utah Valley U (UT)
Vermont Tech Coll (VT)
Washington State U (WA)
Weber State U (UT)
Wentworth Inst of Technology (MA)
Western Carolina U (NC)
Western Nevada Coll (NV)

CONSTRUCTION TRADES
Utica Coll (NY)

CONSUMER ECONOMICS
Louisiana Tech U (LA)
South Dakota State U (SD)
The U of Tennessee (TN)
U of Utah (UT)

CONSUMER MERCHANDISING/ RETAILING MANAGEMENT
Academy of Art U (CA)
Bradley U (IL)
HEC Montreal (QC, Canada)
San Francisco State U (CA)
Simmons U (MA)
U of Memphis (TN)

CONSUMER SERVICES AND ADVOCACY
Carson-Newman U (TN)
State U of New York Coll at Oneonta (NY)
Texas State U (TX)

CORRECTIONS
Adams State U (CO)
Bowling Green State U (OH)
California State U, Stanislaus (CA)
Eastern Kentucky U (KY)
Jacksonville State U (AL)
John Jay Coll of Criminal Justice of the City U of New York (NY)
Lee U (TN)
Lewis-Clark State Coll (ID)
Minnesota State U Mankato (MN)
Missouri Valley Coll (MO)
Portland State U (OR)
Southeast Missouri State U (MO)
Spring Arbor U (MI)
Texas State U (TX)
Tiffin U (OH)
U of New Mexico (NM)
U of Providence (MT)
Western Oregon U (OR)
Youngstown State U (OH)

CORRECTIONS ADMINISTRATION
U of Providence (MT)

CORRECTIONS AND CRIMINAL JUSTICE RELATED
Anderson U (SC)
Averett U (VA)
Cameron U (OK)
Cedarville U (OH)
Emporia State U (KS)
Gwynedd Mercy U (PA)
Inter American U of Puerto Rico, Aguadilla Campus (PR)
John Jay Coll of Criminal Justice of the City U of New York (NY)
La Roche U (PA)
Limestone Coll (SC)
McMurry U (TX)
Muskingum U (OH)
Northwestern Coll (IA)
Oakland U (MI)
Rasmussen Coll Bloomington (MN)
Rasmussen Coll Brooklyn Park (MN)
Rasmussen Coll Eagan (MN)
Rasmussen Coll Fargo (ND)
Rasmussen Coll Fort Myers (FL)
Rasmussen Coll Kansas City/ Overland Park (KS)
Rasmussen Coll Lake Elmo/ Woodbury (MN)
Rasmussen Coll Land O' Lakes (FL)
Rasmussen Coll Mankato (MN)
Rasmussen Coll Moorhead (MN)
Rasmussen Coll New Port Richey (FL)
Rasmussen Coll Ocala (FL)
Rasmussen Coll St. Cloud (MN)
Rasmussen Coll Tampa/Brandon (FL)
Rasmussen Coll Topeka (KS)
Roger Williams U (RI)
Saint Mary's U of Minnesota (MN)
Sam Houston State U (TX)
State U of New York Coll of Technology at Canton (NY)
The U of Alabama at Birmingham (AL)
U of Alaska Fairbanks (AK)
U of Michigan–Flint (MI)
U of Providence (MT)
U of Saint Joseph (CT)

COSTUME DESIGN
Academy of Art U (CA)
Bennington Coll (VT)
Brenau U (GA)
FIDM/Fashion Inst of Design & Merchandising, Los Angeles Campus (CA)
Marymount Manhattan Coll (NY)

COUNSELING PSYCHOLOGY
Arizona Christian U (AZ)
Averett U (VA)
Avila U (MO)
Boise Bible Coll (ID)
Delaware Valley U (PA)
Eastern Washington U (WA)
Ecclesia Coll (AR)
Emmanuel Coll (MA)
Emmaus Bible Coll (IA)
Fort Lewis Coll (CO)
Geneva Coll (PA)
Hope Intl U (CA)
Lesley U (MA)
Mount Saint Mary's U (CA)
Newman U (KS)
Northwestern U (IL)
St. Cloud State U (MN)
Toccoa Falls Coll (GA)
Trinity Coll of Florida (FL)
U of Jamestown (ND)
Wayne State Coll (NE)

COUNSELOR EDUCATION/ SCHOOL COUNSELING AND GUIDANCE
Bowling Green State U (OH)
Brandon U (MB, Canada)
East Central U (OK)
Howard U (DC)
Lancaster Bible Coll (PA)
Sam Houston State U (TX)
U of South Dakota (SD)

CRAFTS, FOLK ART AND ARTISANRY
Bowling Green State U (OH)
Bridgewater State U (MA)
Brigham Young U (UT)
Kutztown U of Pennsylvania (PA)
Purdue U Fort Wayne (IN)
Virginia Commonwealth U (VA)

CREATIVE WRITING
Adams State U (CO)
Agnes Scott Coll (GA)
Albion Coll (MI)
The American U of Paris (France)
Anderson U (SC)
Arcadia U (PA)
Arkansas Tech U (AR)
Augsburg U (MN)
Augustana Coll (IL)
Austin Coll (TX)
Belhaven U (MS)
Beloit Coll (WI)
Bemidji State U (MN)
Bennington Coll (VT)
Berry Coll (GA)
Binghamton U, State U of New York (NY)
Biola U (CA)
Bowling Green State U (OH)
Bradley U (IL)
Brandeis U (MA)
Bridgewater State U (MA)
Brown U (RI)
Bucknell U (PA)
Butler U (IN)
California Baptist U (CA)
California State U, Long Beach (CA)
Capital U (OH)
Carlow U (PA)
Carnegie Mellon U (PA)
Carson-Newman U (TN)
Catawba Coll (NC)
Central Washington U (WA)
Chatham U (PA)
City Coll of the City U of New York (NY)
Coe Coll (IA)
Colby Coll (ME)
Colby-Sawyer Coll (NH)
The Coll of Idaho (ID)
The Colorado Coll (CO)
Columbia Coll Chicago (IL)
Cornell Coll (IA)
Dartmouth Coll (NH)
Dominican U of California (CA)
Drew U (NJ)
Eastern Michigan U (MI)
Emory & Henry Coll (VA)
Emory U (GA)
Fairleigh Dickinson U (NJ)
Florida Southern Coll (FL)
Florida State U (FL)
Franklin Coll (IN)
George Mason U (VA)
Guilford Coll (NC)
Hamline U (MN)
Hampshire Coll (MA)
Hofstra U (NY)
Hollins U (VA)
Ithaca Coll (NY)
Johns Hopkins U (MD)
Knox Coll (IL)
La Sierra U (CA)
Lee U (TN)
Lehman Coll of the City U of New York (NY)
Lewis-Clark State Coll (ID)
Linfield Coll (OR)
Loras Coll (IA)
Loyola U Maryland (MD)
Loyola U New Orleans (LA)
Malone U (OH)
Marymount Manhattan Coll (NY)
McMurry U (TX)
Mercer U, Macon (GA)
Miami U (OH)
Miami U Hamilton (OH)
Miami U Middletown (OH)
Minnesota State U Mankato (MN)
Morehead State U (KY)
Murray State U (KY)
New England Coll (NH)
New York U (NY)
Northeastern State U (OK)
Oakland U (MI)
Oberlin Coll (OH)
Ohio Wesleyan U (OH)
Pacific U (OR)
Pepperdine U, Malibu (CA)
Portland State U (OR)
Pratt Inst (NY)
Providence Coll (RI)
Purchase Coll, State U of New York (NY)
Queens U of Charlotte (NC)
Randolph Coll (VA)
Rhode Island Coll (RI)
Roanoke Coll (VA)
Rocky Mountain Coll (MT)
Roger Williams U (RI)
Saginaw Valley State U (MI)
St. Catherine U (MN)
Saint Mary-of-the-Woods Coll (IN)
Saint Mary's Coll (IN)
St. Thomas Aquinas Coll (NY)
San Francisco State U (CA)
Sarah Lawrence Coll (NY)
Seattle U (WA)
Seton Hill U (PA)
Siena Heights U (MI)
Sierra Nevada Coll (NV)
Southeastern U (FL)
Southern Methodist U (TX)
Southwestern Coll (KS)
State U of New York at Oswego (NY)
State U of New York Coll at Potsdam (NY)
Sterling Coll (KS)
Stony Brook U, State U of New York (NY)
Suffolk U (MA)
Susquehanna U (PA)
Truman State U (MO)
The U of Arizona (AZ)
U of California, Riverside (CA)
U of California, San Diego (CA)
U of Cincinnati (OH)
U of Denver (CO)
The U of Findlay (OH)
U of Houston (TX)
U of Idaho (ID)
U of La Verne (CA)

U of Miami (FL)
U of Michigan (MI)
U of Montana (MT)
The U of North Carolina Wilmington (NC)
U of Pittsburgh at Bradford (PA)
U of Pittsburgh at Greensburg (PA)
U of Providence (MT)
U of Puget Sound (WA)
The U of Texas at El Paso (TX)
The U of Western Ontario (ON, Canada)
Valparaiso U (IN)
Warren Wilson Coll (NC)
Washington U in St. Louis (MO)
Waynesburg U (PA)
Weber State U (UT)
Western Michigan U (MI)
Western New England U (MA)
Western Washington U (WA)
Wheaton Coll (MA)
Wichita State U (KS)
Yeshiva U (NY)

CRIMINALISTICS AND CRIMINAL SCIENCE
Saint Leo U (FL)
Seattle U (WA)
Tiffin U (OH)
Weber State U (UT)

CRIMINAL JUSTICE/LAW ENFORCEMENT ADMINISTRATION
Abilene Christian U (TX)
Adams State U (CO)
Alfred U (NY)
Anderson U (IN)
Anderson U (SC)
Arizona State U at the Downtown Phoenix campus (AZ)
Arizona State U at the West campus (AZ)
Athens State U (AL)
Austin Peay State U (TN)
Averett U (VA)
Azusa Pacific U (CA)
Becker Coll (MA)
Belhaven U (MS)
Bemidji State U (MN)
Bethel U (TN)
Boise State U (ID)
Bowling Green State U (OH)
Bradley U (IL)
California Baptist U (CA)
California Lutheran U (CA)
California State U, Bakersfield (CA)
California State U, Long Beach (CA)
California State U, Sacramento (CA)
Campbellsville U (KY)
Carthage Coll (WI)
Catawba Coll (NC)
Charter Oak State Coll (CT)
Chestnut Hill Coll (PA)
The Citadel, The Military Coll of South Carolina (SC)
Clarion U of Pennsylvania (PA)
Colegio Universitario de San Juan, San Juan (PR)
The Coll of Saint Rose (NY)
Columbia Coll (MO)
Concordia U Wisconsin (WI)
Culver-Stockton Coll (MO)
Delaware Valley U (PA)
Drexel U (PA)
East Central U (OK)
Eastern Kentucky U (KY)
East Texas Baptist U (TX)
Elms Coll (MA)
Emmanuel Coll (GA)
Evangel U (MO)
Excelsior Coll (NY)
Fairleigh Dickinson U (NJ)
Fayetteville State U (NC)
Ferris State U (MI)
Florida National U (FL)
Florida SouthWestern State Coll (FL)
The George Washington U (DC)
Georgia Coll & State U (GA)
Grand Valley State U (MI)
Gustavus Adolphus Coll (MN)
Hampton U (VA)
Harris-Stowe State U (MO)
Husson U (ME)
Indiana U East (IN)
Iona Coll (NY)
Jacksonville State U (AL)
John Jay Coll of Criminal Justice of the City U of New York (NY)
Kansas Wesleyan U (KS)
Kean U (NJ)
Keiser U, Fort Lauderdale (FL)
Keuka Coll (NY)
Lackawanna Coll (PA)
Limestone Coll (SC)
Lincoln Memorial U (TN)
Lincoln U (MO)
Lock Haven U of Pennsylvania (PA)
Lynn U (FL)
Mansfield U of Pennsylvania (PA)
Marymount California U (CA)
Marymount U (VA)
Marywood U (PA)
Mercy Coll (NY)
Merrimack Coll (MA)
Miami U (OH)
Miami U Hamilton (OH)
Miami U Middletown (OH)
Michigan State U (MI)
Mid-America Christian U (OK)
MidAmerica Nazarene U (KS)
Middle Tennessee State U (TN)
Millikin U (IL)
Missouri Southern State U (MO)
Missouri Valley Coll (MO)
Mount Aloysius Coll (PA)
Mount Mercy U (IA)
Mount Vernon Nazarene U (OH)
Muskingum U (OH)
National U (CA)
New England Coll (NH)
New England Inst of Technology (RI)
Newman U (KS)
New York Inst of Technology (NY)
Nichols Coll (MA)
Northeastern State U (OK)
Northern Arizona U (AZ)
North Greenville U (SC)
Northwest Nazarene U (ID)
Northwest U (WA)
Notre Dame Coll (OH)
Olivet Nazarene U (IL)
Ottawa U (KS)
Pace U, Pleasantville Campus (NY)
Penn State Abington (PA)
Penn State Altoona (PA)
Penn State Beaver (PA)
Penn State Berks (PA)
Penn State Brandywine (PA)
Penn State DuBois (PA)
Penn State Erie, The Behrend Coll (PA)
Penn State Fayette, The Eberly Campus (PA)
Penn State Greater Allegheny (PA)
Penn State Hazleton (PA)
Penn State Lehigh Valley (PA)
Penn State Mont Alto (PA)
Penn State New Kensington (PA)
Penn State Schuylkill (PA)
Penn State Shenango (PA)
Penn State U Park (PA)
Penn State Wilkes-Barre (PA)
Penn State York (PA)
Portland State U (OR)
Regent U (VA)
Roberts Wesleyan Coll (NY)
Rogers State U (OK)
Roger Williams U (RI)
St. Mary's U (TX)
St. Thomas Aquinas Coll (NY)
St. Thomas U - Florida (FL)
Salem State U (MA)
Salve Regina U (RI)
Sam Houston State U (TX)
San Francisco State U (CA)
Shenandoah U (VA)
Southwest Baptist U (MO)
Springfield Coll (MA)
State U of New York at Fredonia (NY)
State U of New York at Oswego (NY)
State U of New York Coll of Technology at Alfred (NY)
State U of New York Coll of Technology at Canton (NY)
Sterling Coll (KS)
Stevenson U (MD)
Tarleton State U (TX)
Texas A&M U–Central Texas (TX)
Tiffin U (OH)
Toccoa Falls Coll (GA)
Trevecca Nazarene U (TN)
Trine U (IN)
U at Albany, State U of New York (NY)
U of Colorado Colorado Springs (CO)
U of Colorado Denver (CO)
U of Dayton (OH)
The U of Findlay (OH)
U of Guam (GU)
U of Louisville (KY)
U of Maine at Presque Isle (ME)
U of Management and Technology (VA)
U of Mary Hardin-Baylor (TX)
U of Massachusetts Lowell (MA)
U of Memphis (TN)
U of New Haven (CT)
U of Northern Iowa (IA)
U of Pittsburgh at Bradford (PA)
U of Pittsburgh at Greensburg (PA)
U of Providence (MT)
U of St. Francis (IL)
U of South Alabama (AL)
U of South Carolina (SC)
U of South Dakota (SD)
The U of Tennessee at Chattanooga (TN)
The U of Tennessee at Martin (TN)
The U of Texas Rio Grande Valley (TX)
U of the Incarnate Word (TX)
U of Wisconsin–Parkside (WI)
Utah Valley U (UT)
Utica Coll (NY)
Villanova U (PA)
Virginia Commonwealth U (VA)
Waynesburg U (PA)
Webber Intl U (FL)
Western New Mexico U (NM)
Western Oregon U (OR)
West Liberty U (WV)
Widener U (PA)
Wilmington Coll (OH)
Wingate U (NC)
York Coll of Pennsylvania (PA)
Youngstown State U (OH)

CRIMINAL JUSTICE/POLICE SCIENCE
Bemidji State U (MN)
Bowling Green State U (OH)
East Central U (OK)
Eastern Illinois U (IL)
Eastern Kentucky U (KY)
Ferris State U (MI)
George Mason U (VA)
Gwynedd Mercy U (PA)
Howard U (DC)
Inter American U of Puerto Rico, Metropolitan Campus (PR)
Inter American U of Puerto Rico, San Germán Campus (PR)
Jacksonville State U (AL)
John Jay Coll of Criminal Justice of the City U of New York (NY)
Lackawanna Coll (PA)
Malone U (OH)
Middle Tennessee State U (TN)
Midway U (KY)
Minnesota State U Mankato (MN)
Oklahoma Baptist U (OK)
Rowan U (NJ)
Sam Houston State U (TX)
Texas A&M Intl U (TX)
Texas State U (TX)
U of Hartford (CT)
U of Pittsburgh at Greensburg (PA)
U of Providence (MT)
U of the Virgin Islands (VI)
U of Toronto (ON, Canada)
U of Washington, Tacoma (WA)
Washington State U (WA)
Washington State U–Vancouver (WA)
Weber State U (UT)
Western Connecticut State U (CT)
Western Oregon U (OR)

CRIMINAL JUSTICE/SAFETY
American Public U System (WV)
American U (DC)
Angelo State U (TX)
Appalachian State U (NC)
Arkansas Tech U (AR)
Athens State U (AL)
Auburn U at Montgomery (AL)
Aurora U (IL)
Ball State U (IN)
Barton Coll (NC)
Belmont Abbey Coll (NC)
Benedictine U (IL)
Bethel U (IN)
Bluffton U (OH)
Bowling Green State U (OH)
Bridgewater State U (MA)
Bryan Coll (TN)
Caldwell U (NJ)
California State U, Dominguez Hills (CA)
California State U, Fresno (CA)
California State U, Fullerton (CA)
California State U, Los Angeles (CA)
California State U, San Bernardino (CA)
California State U, Stanislaus (CA)
California U of Pennsylvania (PA)
Calumet Coll of Saint Joseph (IN)
Cazenovia Coll (NY)
Central Methodist U (MO)
Central State U (OH)
Central Washington U (WA)
Chaminade U of Honolulu (HI)
Champlain Coll (VT)
Charter Oak State Coll (CT)
Clark Atlanta U (GA)
Clayton State U (GA)
Coe Coll (IA)
Coll of the Ozarks (MO)
Columbia Coll (SC)
Concordia U, St. Paul (MN)
Dallas Baptist U (TX)
Davenport U, Grand Rapids (MI)
Dean Coll (MA)
Delta State U (MS)
DeSales U (PA)
Dominican Coll (NY)
East Carolina U (NC)
Eastern New Mexico U (NM)
ECPI U, Virginia Beach (VA)
Edgewood Coll (WI)
Edinboro U of Pennsylvania (PA)
Endicott Coll (MA)
Felician U (NJ)
Fisher Coll (MA)
Fitchburg State U (MA)
Florida A&M U (FL)
Florida Atlantic U (FL)
Florida Gulf Coast U (FL)
Freed-Hardeman U (TN)
Friends U (KS)
Gannon U (PA)
Georgia Gwinnett Coll (GA)
Georgian Court U (NJ)
Georgia State U (GA)
Governors State U (IL)
Graceland U (IA)
Grambling State U (LA)
Granite State Coll (NH)
Guilford Coll (NC)
Harding U (AR)
Hardin-Simmons U (TX)
Harris-Stowe State U (MO)
High Point U (NC)
Hope Intl U (CA)
Houston Baptist U (TX)
Husson U (ME)
Illinois State U (IL)
Immaculata U (PA)
Indiana U Bloomington (IN)
Indiana U Kokomo (IN)
Indiana U Northwest (IN)
Indiana U-Purdue U Indianapolis (IN)
Indiana U South Bend (IN)
Indiana U Southeast (IN)
Inter American U of Puerto Rico, Bayamón Campus (PR)
Iowa State U of Science and Technology (IA)
Keiser U, Fort Lauderdale (FL)
Kennesaw State U (GA)
Kent State U at Tuscarawas (OH)
King's Coll (PA)
King U (TN)
Kutztown U of Pennsylvania (PA)
Lackawanna Coll (PA)
Lamar U (TX)
La Roche U (PA)
La Sierra U (CA)
Lenoir-Rhyne U (NC)
Lewis U (IL)
Liberty U (VA)
Limestone Coll (SC)
Lincoln U (PA)
Lindenwood U (MO)
Lipscomb U (TN)
Longwood U (VA)
Loras Coll (IA)
Louisiana State U in Shreveport (LA)
Loyola U Chicago (IL)
Madonna U (MI)
Marshall U (WV)
McNeese State U (LA)
Michigan State U (MI)
Minot State U (ND)
Molloy Coll (NY)
Mount Marty Coll (SD)
Mount Vernon Nazarene U (OH)
Murray State U (KY)
Nebraska Wesleyan U (NE)
New Charter U (UT)
New Mexico Highlands U (NM)
Nichols Coll (MA)
North Carolina Central U (NC)
Northeastern Illinois U (IL)
Northern Kentucky U (KY)
Northern State U (SD)
Northwestern State U of Louisiana (LA)
Northwest U (WA)
Nova Southeastern U (FL)
Nyack Coll (NY)
Oakland City U (IN)
Ohio Christian U (OH)
Olivet Nazarene U (IL)
Penn State Abington (PA)
Penn State Altoona (PA)
Penn State Erie, The Behrend Coll (PA)
Penn State Fayette, The Eberly Campus (PA)
Penn State Harrisburg (PA)
Penn State Schuylkill (PA)
Penn State Wilkes-Barre (PA)
Pittsburg State U (KS)
Polk State Coll (FL)
Portland State U (OR)
Prairie View A&M U (TX)
Radford U (VA)
Rhode Island Coll (RI)
Roanoke Coll (VA)
Rosemont Coll (PA)
Rowan U (NJ)
Sacred Heart U (CT)
Saginaw Valley State U (MI)
St. Ambrose U (IA)
St. Cloud State U (MN)
Saint Leo U (FL)
Saint Louis U (MO)
St. Thomas U - Florida (FL)
Sam Houston State U (TX)
San Diego State U (CA)
San Jose State U (CA)
Seattle U (WA)
Seton Hill U (PA)
Siena Heights U (MI)
Southeastern Louisiana U (LA)
Southeastern U (FL)
Southern Arkansas U–Magnolia (AR)
Southern Illinois U Edwardsville (IL)
Southwestern Coll (KS)
Southwestern Oklahoma State U (OK)
State U of New York Coll at Oneonta (NY)
State U of New York Coll at Potsdam (NY)
State U of New York Coll of Technology at Delhi (NY)
Sullivan U (KY)
SUNY Brockport (NY)
Tarleton State U (TX)
Temple U (PA)
Tennessee Wesleyan U (TN)
Texas A&M U–Commerce (TX)
Texas A&M U–Corpus Christi (TX)
Texas A&M U–Kingsville (TX)
Texas Christian U (TX)
Texas State U (TX)
Texas Woman's U (TX)
Troy U (AL)
Truett McConnell U (GA)
Truman State U (MO)
The U of Akron (OH)

The U of Alabama (AL)
U of Arkansas (AR)
U of Arkansas at Little Rock (AR)
U of Central Florida (FL)
U of Cincinnati (OH)
U of Detroit Mercy (MI)
U of Dubuque (IA)
U of Houston–Downtown (TX)
U of Illinois at Chicago (IL)
U of Illinois at Springfield (IL)
U of Jamestown (ND)
U of Louisiana at Lafayette (LA)
U of Louisiana at Monroe (LA)
U of Maryland Global Campus (MD)
U of Massachusetts Boston (MA)
U of Michigan–Dearborn (MI)
U of Nebraska at Kearney (NE)
U of Nevada, Las Vegas (NV)
The U of North Carolina at Charlotte (NC)
The U of North Carolina at Pembroke (NC)
U of North Dakota (ND)
U of Northern Colorado (CO)
U of North Florida (FL)
U of North Texas (TX)
U of Northwestern–St. Paul (MN)
U of Pikeville (KY)
U of Providence (MT)
U of Richmond (VA)
U of Saint Francis (IN)
The U of Scranton (PA)
U of South Dakota (SD)
U of Southern Indiana (IN)
U of Southern Mississippi (MS)
The U of Texas at El Paso (TX)
The U of Texas at San Antonio (TX)
The U of Texas of the Permian Basin (TX)
The U of Texas Rio Grande Valley (TX)
U of the Fraser Valley (BC, Canada)
U of the Incarnate Word (TX)
The U of Toledo (OH)
U of West Florida (FL)
U of Wisconsin–Eau Claire (WI)
U of Wisconsin–Milwaukee (WI)
U of Wisconsin–Platteville (WI)
U of Wisconsin–Superior (WI)
U of Wyoming (WY)
Valdosta State U (GA)
Virginia Wesleyan U (VA)
Wayne State Coll (NE)
Wayne State U (MI)
Weber State U (UT)
West Chester U of Pennsylvania (PA)
Western Carolina U (NC)
Western Michigan U (MI)
Western New England U (MA)
Western New Mexico U (NM)
Westfield State U (MA)
Westminster Coll (UT)
Wichita State U (KS)
William Paterson U of New Jersey (NJ)
Woodbury U (CA)
Worcester State U (MA)
Xavier U (OH)
Youngstown State U (OH)

CRIMINOLOGY
Adams State U (CO)
Arcadia U (PA)
Assumption Coll (MA)
Auburn U (AL)
Avila U (MO)
Barry U (FL)
Benedictine Coll (KS)
Biola U (CA)
Butler U (IN)
California State Polytechnic U, Pomona (CA)
California State U, Fresno (CA)
California State U, San Marcos (CA)
California State U, Stanislaus (CA)
Capital U (OH)
Carlow U (PA)
Cedar Crest Coll (PA)
Central Connecticut State U (CT)
Chatham U (PA)
Concordia U Chicago (IL)
DePaul U (IL)
Dominican U (IL)
Drexel U (PA)
Drury U (MO)
Eastern Michigan U (MI)
Eastern U (PA)
Eastern Washington U (WA)
Emmanuel Coll (MA)
Fairleigh Dickinson U (NJ)
Flagler Coll (FL)
Florida Southern Coll (FL)
Florida State U (FL)
Fort Lewis Coll (CO)
Framingham State U (MA)
Geneva Coll (PA)
Gonzaga U (WA)
Hamline U (MN)
Hofstra U (NY)
Husson U (ME)
Indiana State U (IN)
Indiana U of Pennsylvania (PA)
John Jay Coll of Criminal Justice of the City U of New York (NY)
Lasell Coll (MA)
Lee U (TN)
Le Moyne Coll (NY)
LeTourneau U (TX)
Loyola U New Orleans (LA)
Marquette U (WI)
Maryville U of Saint Louis (MO)
McMurry U (TX)
Mercer U, Macon (GA)
Meredith Coll (NC)
Mississippi State U (MS)
Missouri State U (MO)
Mount Saint Mary Coll (NY)
Mount Saint Mary's U (CA)
Mount St. Mary's U (MD)
Niagara U (NY)
Northern Arizona U (AZ)
Ohio Dominican U (OH)
The Ohio State U (OH)
The Ohio State U at Mansfield (OH)
The Ohio State U at Marion (OH)
Old Dominion U (VA)
Randolph-Macon Coll (VA)
St. Bonaventure U (NY)
St. John Fisher Coll (NY)
Saint Joseph's U (PA)
Saint Mary-of-the-Woods Coll (IN)
St. Mary's U (TX)
St. Thomas U - New Brunswick (NB, Canada)
Saint Vincent Coll (PA)
Simon Fraser U (BC, Canada)
Slippery Rock U of Pennsylvania (PA)
Spring Hill Coll (AL)
State U of New York Coll at Cortland (NY)
State U of New York Coll at Old Westbury (NY)
State U of New York Coll of Technology at Canton (NY)
Stockton U (NJ)
Tabor Coll (KS)
Texas A&M U–Kingsville (TX)
Tiffin U (OH)
U at Buffalo, the State U of New York (NY)
The U of Akron (OH)
The U of Alabama (AL)
U of California, Irvine (CA)
U of Denver (CO)
U of Houston–Clear Lake (TX)
U of La Verne (CA)
U of Massachusetts Dartmouth (MA)
U of Memphis (TN)
U of Miami (FL)
U of Minnesota, Duluth (MN)
U of Minnesota, Twin Cities Campus (MN)
U of Missouri–St. Louis (MO)
U of Nevada, Reno (NV)
U of New Hampshire (NH)
The U of North Carolina Wilmington (NC)
U of Northern Iowa (IA)
U of Saint Mary (KS)
U of St. Thomas (TX)
U of Southern Maine (ME)
U of South Florida (FL)
U of South Florida, St. Petersburg (FL)
The U of Tampa (FL)
The U of Texas at Dallas (TX)
The U of Texas of the Permian Basin (TX)
U of Toronto (ON, Canada)
U of Utah (UT)
The U of Western Ontario (ON, Canada)
U of West Georgia (GA)
Upper Iowa U (IA)
Ursuline Coll (OH)
Valparaiso U (IN)
Virginia Wesleyan U (VA)
Wartburg Coll (IA)
Western Kentucky U (KY)
West Virginia U (WV)
Whitworth U (WA)
Wilkes U (PA)
William Peace U (NC)
William Penn U (IA)
Wittenberg U (OH)
Wright State U (OH)
Wright State U–Lake Campus (OH)

CRISIS/EMERGENCY/DISASTER MANAGEMENT
American Public U System (WV)
Arapahoe Comm Coll (CO)
Arkansas Tech U (AR)
Columbia Coll (SC)
Immaculata U (PA)
Kansas Wesleyan U (KS)
Lee U (TN)
Northwest Missouri State U (MO)
Notre Dame Coll (OH)
Ohio Christian U (OH)
Rowan U (NJ)
Saint Louis U (MO)
Southeast Missouri State U (MO)
State U of New York Coll of Technology at Canton (NY)
Texas Southern U (TX)
Truckee Meadows Comm Coll (NV)
U at Albany, State U of New York (NY)
U of Alaska Fairbanks (AK)
U of Central Florida (FL)
U of New Haven (CT)
U of Northern Iowa (IA)
U of North Texas (TX)
Upper Iowa U (IA)

CRITICAL INFRASTRUCTURE PROTECTION
Anderson U (SC)
Bethel U (IN)
Drury U (MO)
George Mason U (VA)
Indiana State U (IN)

CROP PRODUCTION
U of Idaho (ID)

CULINARY ARTS
Coll of the Ozarks (MO)
The Culinary Inst of America (NY)
Drexel U (PA)
Inter American U of Puerto Rico, Barranquitas Campus (PR)
State U of New York Coll of Technology at Delhi (NY)

CULINARY ARTS RELATED
U of Nevada, Las Vegas (NV)

CULINARY SCIENCE
The Culinary Inst of America (NY)
Mississippi State U (MS)
Texas Woman's U (TX)

CULTURAL ANTHROPOLOGY
Arcadia U (PA)
Bennington Coll (VT)
Creighton U (NE)
Eugene Lang Coll of Liberal Arts (NY)

CULTURAL RESOURCE MANAGEMENT AND POLICY ANALYSIS
California State U, Dominguez Hills (CA)
U of Waterloo (ON, Canada)

CULTURAL STUDIES/ CRITICAL THEORY AND ANALYSIS
American Public U System (WV)
Arizona State U at the West campus (AZ)
Bryant U (RI)
Northern Arizona U (AZ)
Occidental Coll (CA)
Rollins Coll (FL)
Samford U (AL)
The U of Tampa (FL)
Western Kentucky U (KY)
Willamette U (OR)

CURRICULUM AND INSTRUCTION
Eastern Washington U (WA)
Lasell Coll (MA)
Sam Houston State U (TX)
U of South Dakota (SD)
The U of Western Ontario (ON, Canada)

CUSTOMER SERVICE MANAGEMENT
Drexel U (PA)
U of North Texas (TX)

CYBER/COMPUTER FORENSICS AND COUNTERTERRORISM
Champlain Coll (VT)
Chestnut Hill Coll (PA)
The Coll of Saint Rose (NY)
Davenport U, Grand Rapids (MI)
Eastern Kentucky U (KY)
Farmingdale State Coll (NY)
Friends U (KS)
Keiser U, Fort Lauderdale (FL)
National U (CA)
Northeastern State U (OK)
Oakland U (MI)
Regent U (VA)
Regis Coll (MA)
Roger Williams U (RI)
Sullivan U (KY)
Tiffin U (OH)
The U of Alabama at Birmingham (AL)
U of the Incarnate Word (TX)

CYBER/ELECTRONIC OPERATIONS AND WARFARE
Excelsior Coll (NY)
Gannon U (PA)
Hampton U (VA)
Indiana U Bloomington (IN)
Iowa State U of Science and Technology (IA)
LeTourneau U (TX)
Maryville U of Saint Louis (MO)
The U of Arizona (AZ)

CYTOTECHNOLOGY
Barry U (FL)
Edgewood Coll (WI)
Illinois Coll (IL)
Indiana U-Purdue U Indianapolis (IN)
Marshall U (WV)
Saint Mary's U of Minnesota (MN)
The U of Alabama at Birmingham (AL)

DAIRY SCIENCE
California Polytechnic State U, San Luis Obispo (CA)
Delaware Valley U (PA)
Eastern New Mexico U (NM)
Iowa State U of Science and Technology (IA)
South Dakota State U (SD)
U of New Hampshire (NH)
U of Wisconsin–Madison (WI)

DANCE
Agnes Scott Coll (GA)
American U (DC)
Anderson U (IN)
Anderson U (SC)
Appalachian State U (NC)
Arizona State U at the Tempe campus (AZ)
Ball State U (IN)
Barnard Coll (NY)
Bates Coll (ME)
Belhaven U (MS)
Beloit Coll (WI)
Bennington Coll (VT)
Bowling Green State U (OH)
Brenau U (GA)
Butler U (IN)
California Inst of the Arts (CA)
California State U, Fresno (CA)
California State U, Fullerton (CA)
California State U, Long Beach (CA)
California State U, Sacramento (CA)
Cedar Crest Coll (PA)
Coll of Charleston (SC)
The Colorado Coll (CO)
Colorado State U (CO)
Columbia Coll (SC)
Columbia Coll Chicago (IL)
Dean Coll (MA)
DeSales U (PA)
Dickinson Coll (PA)
Dominican U of California (CA)
East Carolina U (NC)
Eastern Michigan U (MI)
Eastern U (PA)
Elon U (NC)
Emory U (GA)
Florida Southern Coll (FL)
Florida State U (FL)
Fordham U (NY)
George Mason U (VA)
The George Washington U (DC)
Georgian Court U (NJ)
Gonzaga U (WA)
Goucher Coll (MD)
Grand Valley State U (MI)
Gustavus Adolphus Coll (MN)
Hampshire Coll (MA)
High Point U (NC)
Hobart and William Smith Colls (NY)
Hofstra U (NY)
Hollins U (VA)
Hope Coll (MI)
Indiana U Bloomington (IN)
Jacksonville U (FL)
Kennesaw State U (GA)
Kenyon Coll (OH)
La Roche U (PA)
Lehman Coll of the City U of New York (NY)
Lindenwood U (MO)
Loyola Marymount U (CA)
Loyola U Chicago (IL)
Madonna U (MI)
Manhattanville Coll (NY)
Marymount Manhattan Coll (NY)
Meredith Coll (NC)
Messiah Coll (PA)
Middlebury Coll (VT)
Middle Tennessee State U (TN)
Missouri Valley Coll (MO)
Montclair State U (NJ)
Mount Holyoke Coll (MA)
Muhlenberg Coll (PA)
Nazareth Coll of Rochester (NY)
New York U (NY)
Northwestern U (IL)
Nova Southeastern U (FL)
Oakland U (MI)
Oberlin Coll (OH)
The Ohio State U (OH)
Oral Roberts U (OK)
Palm Beach Atlantic U (FL)
Pomona Coll (CA)
Portland State U (OR)
Purchase Coll, State U of New York (NY)
Radford U (VA)
Randolph Coll (VA)
Rhode Island Coll (RI)
Roger Williams U (RI)
Rowan U (NJ)
Saint Mary's Coll of California (CA)
St. Olaf Coll (MN)
Sam Houston State U (TX)
San Diego State U (CA)
San Francisco State U (CA)
San Jose State U (CA)
Sarah Lawrence Coll (NY)
Scripps Coll (CA)
Seton Hill U (PA)
Shenandoah U (VA)
Simon Fraser U (BC, Canada)
Skidmore Coll (NY)
Slippery Rock U of Pennsylvania (PA)
Smith Coll (MA)
Southern Methodist U (TX)
Springfield Coll (MA)
State U of New York at Fredonia (NY)
State U of New York Coll at Potsdam (NY)
SUNY Brockport (NY)
Temple U (PA)
Texas Christian U (TX)

Texas State U (TX)
Texas Tech U (TX)
Texas Woman's U (TX)
Towson U (MD)
Troy U (AL)
Tulane U (LA)
U at Buffalo, the State U of New York (NY)
The U of Akron (OH)
The U of Alabama (AL)
The U of Arizona (AZ)
U of Arkansas at Little Rock (AR)
U of California, Berkeley (CA)
U of California, Irvine (CA)
U of California, Los Angeles (CA)
U of California, Riverside (CA)
U of California, San Diego (CA)
U of California, Santa Barbara (CA)
U of Cincinnati (OH)
U of Colorado Boulder (CO)
U of Hartford (CT)
U of Hawaii at Manoa (HI)
U of Houston (TX)
U of Idaho (ID)
The U of Iowa (IA)
The U of Kansas (KS)
U of Kentucky (KY)
U of Maryland, Baltimore County (MD)
U of Massachusetts Amherst (MA)
U of Michigan (MI)
U of Michigan–Flint (MI)
U of Minnesota, Twin Cities Campus (MN)
U of Montana (MT)
U of Nebraska–Lincoln (NE)
U of Nevada, Las Vegas (NV)
U of Nevada, Reno (NV)
U of New Mexico (NM)
The U of North Carolina at Charlotte (NC)
The U of North Carolina at Greensboro (NC)
U of North Texas (TX)
U of Oregon (OR)
U of Richmond (VA)
U of Saint Francis (IN)
U of St. Thomas (TX)
U of South Carolina (SC)
U of Southern Mississippi (MS)
U of South Florida (FL)
The U of Tampa (FL)
The U of Texas at El Paso (TX)
The U of Texas Rio Grande Valley (TX)
U of Utah (UT)
U of Vermont (VT)
U of Washington (WA)
U of Wisconsin–Madison (WI)
U of Wisconsin–Milwaukee (WI)
Utah Valley U (UT)
Valdosta State U (GA)
Virginia Commonwealth U (VA)
Wayne State U (MI)
Weber State U (UT)
Wesleyan U (CT)
Western Kentucky U (KY)
Western Michigan U (MI)
Western Oregon U (OR)
Western Washington U (WA)
Westminster Coll (UT)
Winthrop U (SC)
Wittenberg U (OH)
Wright State U (OH)
Wright State U–Lake Campus (OH)

DANCE RELATED
Anderson U (IN)
Brigham Young U (UT)
California State U, Long Beach (CA)
Drexel U (PA)
Marymount Manhattan Coll (NY)
Western Michigan U (MI)
Youngstown State U (OH)

DANISH
U of Washington (WA)

DATA MODELING/ WAREHOUSING AND DATABASE ADMINISTRATION
Aquinas Coll (MI)
Central Washington U (WA)
Champlain Coll (VT)
Eastern U (PA)
Florida Polytechnic U (FL)
Lewis U (IL)
Limestone Coll (SC)
Northwest Missouri State U (MO)
Saint Vincent Coll (PA)
U of Michigan (MI)
U of North Dakota (ND)

DATA PROCESSING AND DATA PROCESSING TECHNOLOGY
California State U, San Marcos (CA)
Campbellsville U (KY)
Dickinson State U (ND)
U of Dubuque (IA)
U of Northwestern–St. Paul (MN)
U of San Francisco (CA)
U of Southern Mississippi (MS)
Wesleyan Coll (GA)

DEAF STUDIES
California State U, Northridge (CA)
Coll of the Holy Cross (MA)
Columbia Coll Chicago (IL)
Towson U (MD)

DENTAL HYGIENE
Ball State U (IN)
Clayton State U (GA)
Creighton U (NE)
Eastern Washington U (WA)
Farmingdale State Coll (NY)
Ferris State U (MI)
Howard U (DC)
Indiana U Northwest (IN)
Indiana U-Purdue U Indianapolis (IN)
Indiana U South Bend (IN)
Lewis U (IL)
Louisiana State U Health Sciences Center (LA)
Loyola U Chicago (IL)
Minnesota State U Mankato (MN)
New York U (NY)
Northern Arizona U (AZ)
The Ohio State U (OH)
Old Dominion U (VA)
Regis Coll (MA)
Rhode Island Coll (RI)
St. Petersburg Coll (FL)
Southern Illinois U Carbondale (IL)
Texas A&M U (TX)
Texas Woman's U (TX)
U of Detroit Mercy (MI)
U of Hawaii at Manoa (HI)
U of Louisiana at Monroe (LA)
U of Louisville (KY)
U of Michigan (MI)
U of Minnesota, Twin Cities Campus (MN)
U of New England (ME)
U of New Haven (CT)
U of New Mexico (NM)
The U of North Carolina at Chapel Hill (NC)
U of South Dakota (SD)
U of Southern Indiana (IN)
U of Washington (WA)
U of Wyoming (WY)
Utah Valley U (UT)
Vermont Tech Coll (VT)
Virginia Commonwealth U (VA)
Weber State U (UT)
Western Kentucky U (KY)
West Liberty U (WV)
West Virginia U (WV)
Wichita State U (KS)
Youngstown State U (OH)

DENTAL LABORATORY TECHNOLOGY
Indiana U-Purdue U Indianapolis (IN)

DENTAL SERVICES AND ALLIED PROFESSIONS RELATED
Indiana U-Purdue U Indianapolis (IN)

DESIGN AND APPLIED ARTS RELATED
Allegheny Coll (PA)
Alverno Coll (WI)
Arizona State U at the Tempe campus (AZ)
Auburn U (AL)
Augsburg U (MN)
Azusa Pacific U (CA)
Bemidji State U (MN)
Butler U (IN)
Carnegie Mellon U (PA)
Drexel U (PA)
Eugene Lang Coll of Liberal Arts (NY)
Farmingdale State Coll (NY)
Fashion Inst of Technology (NY)
Ferris State U (MI)
Guilford Coll (NC)
Hampshire Coll (MA)
Harding U (AR)
Hofstra U (NY)
Howard U (DC)
Inter American U of Puerto Rico, San Germán Campus (PR)
Iowa State U of Science and Technology (IA)
Mansfield U of Pennsylvania (PA)
Marymount Manhattan Coll (NY)
McMurry U (TX)
Merrimack Coll (MA)
Minnesota State U Mankato (MN)
Montclair State U (NJ)
New York Inst of Technology (NY)
Otis Coll of Art and Design (CA)
Parsons School of Design (NY)
Penn State Altoona (PA)
Penn State Berks (PA)
Penn State U Park (PA)
Portland State U (OR)
Pratt Inst (NY)
Roberts Wesleyan Coll (NY)
Salem State U (MA)
School of Visual Arts (NY)
Schreiner U (TX)
Southern Methodist U (TX)
State U of New York at Fredonia (NY)
U of California, Los Angeles (CA)
The U of Findlay (OH)
U of Illinois at Chicago (IL)
U of Oregon (OR)
U of Wisconsin–Stout (WI)
Ursuline Coll (OH)
Virginia Commonwealth U (VA)
Washington U in St. Louis (MO)

DESIGN AND VISUAL COMMUNICATIONS
American U (DC)
Anderson U (IN)
Andrews U (MI)
Auburn U (AL)
Barton Coll (NC)
Belmont U (TN)
Bennington Coll (VT)
Bethesda U (CA)
Biola U (CA)
Boise State U (ID)
Bowling Green State U (OH)
California Inst of the Arts (CA)
California State U, Monterey Bay (CA)
Carnegie Mellon U (PA)
Cazenovia Coll (NY)
Cedarville U (OH)
Central Connecticut State U (CT)
The Coll of Saint Rose (NY)
Coll of the Ozarks (MO)
Concordia U, St. Paul (MN)
Endicott Coll (MA)
Eugene Lang Coll of Liberal Arts (NY)
Farmingdale State Coll (NY)
Ferris State U (MI)
FIDM/Fashion Inst of Design & Merchandising, Los Angeles Campus (CA)
Gordon Coll (MA)
Graceland U (IA)
Houston Baptist U (TX)
Indiana U Bloomington (IN)
Inter American U of Puerto Rico, Metropolitan Campus (PR)
Iowa State U of Science and Technology (IA)
Kean U (NJ)
La Roche U (PA)
Lawrence Technological U (MI)
Lehigh U (PA)
Lewis U (IL)
Liberty U (VA)
Loyola U Chicago (IL)
Loyola U New Orleans (LA)
Madonna U (MI)
Marymount Manhattan Coll (NY)
Marymount U (VA)
Maryville U of Saint Louis (MO)
Massachusetts Coll of Art and Design (MA)
Millersville U of Pennsylvania (PA)
Missouri State U (MO)
Muskingum U (OH)
Nazareth Coll of Rochester (NY)
New Mexico Highlands U (NM)
New York City Coll of Technology of the City U of New York (NY)
Northern Arizona U (AZ)
Northern Kentucky U (KY)
The Ohio State U (OH)
Oral Roberts U (OK)
Otis Coll of Art and Design (CA)
Paris Coll of Art (France)
Radford U (VA)
Saginaw Valley State U (MI)
Saint Mary-of-the-Woods Coll (IN)
St. Thomas Aquinas Coll (NY)
San Francisco State U (CA)
Southern Illinois U Carbondale (IL)
Spring Arbor U (MI)
Stevenson U (MD)
Texas Christian U (TX)
Texas State U (TX)
U of Arkansas (AR)
U of Cincinnati (OH)
U of Dayton (OH)
U of Hartford (CT)
The U of Kansas (KS)
U of Maryland, Baltimore County (MD)
U of Michigan–Flint (MI)
U of North Texas (TX)
U of Notre Dame (IN)
U of Saint Francis (IN)
U of San Francisco (CA)
U of Utah (UT)
U of Washington (WA)
U of Wisconsin–Green Bay (WI)
Utah Valley U (UT)
Washington U in St. Louis (MO)
Western Washington U (WA)
West Virginia U (WV)

DESKTOP PUBLISHING AND DIGITAL IMAGING DESIGN
California Baptist U (CA)
New England Inst of Technology (RI)

DEVELOPMENTAL AND CHILD PSYCHOLOGY
Boston Coll (MA)
Bridgewater State U (MA)
California State U, Bakersfield (CA)
California State U, Stanislaus (CA)
Carson-Newman U (TN)
Eastern Washington U (WA)
East Texas Baptist U (TX)
Emmanuel Coll (MA)
Fitchburg State U (MA)
Hampton U (VA)
Minnesota State U Mankato (MN)
Mount Saint Mary's U (CA)
Saint Mary's Coll of California (CA)
Texas Christian U (TX)
U of California, San Diego (CA)
U of Detroit Mercy (MI)
U of Minnesota, Twin Cities Campus (MN)
U of Saint Francis (IN)
The U of Texas at Dallas (TX)
U of Wisconsin–Green Bay (WI)
Utica Coll (NY)
Vanderbilt U (TN)
Western Washington U (WA)

DEVELOPMENTAL BIOLOGY AND EMBRYOLOGY
U of California, Santa Barbara (CA)

DEVELOPMENT ECONOMICS AND INTERNATIONAL DEVELOPMENT
Calvin Coll (MI)
Clark U (MA)
Eastern Mennonite U (VA)
Illinois Inst of Technology (IL)
Messiah Coll (PA)
Penn State Altoona (PA)
Penn State Berks (PA)
Point Loma Nazarene U (CA)
Stetson U (FL)
U of California, Los Angeles (CA)
U of Dayton (OH)
U of Richmond (VA)
U of St. Thomas (TX)
U of San Francisco (CA)
U of the Fraser Valley (BC, Canada)
U of Vermont (VT)
Williams Coll (MA)

DIAGNOSTIC MEDICAL SONOGRAPHY AND ULTRASOUND TECHNOLOGY
AdventHealth U (FL)
Allen Coll (IA)
Baptist Coll of Health Sciences (TN)
Benedictine U (IL)
The George Washington U (DC)
Grand Valley State U (MI)
Lewis U (IL)
Misericordia U (PA)
Nebraska Methodist Coll (NE)
Newman U (KS)
Nova Southeastern U (FL)
Regis Coll (MA)
Rhode Island Coll (RI)
Seattle U (WA)
The U of Findlay (OH)
Weber State U (UT)

DIESEL MECHANICS TECHNOLOGY
Lewis-Clark State Coll (ID)

DIETETICS
Abilene Christian U (TX)
Appalachian State U (NC)
Ball State U (IN)
Bowling Green State U (OH)
Bradley U (IL)
California Polytechnic State U, San Luis Obispo (CA)
California State Polytechnic U, Pomona (CA)
California State U, Fresno (CA)
California State U, Long Beach (CA)
California State U, San Bernardino (CA)
Carson-Newman U (TN)
Central Michigan U (MI)
Central Washington U (WA)
Coll of Saint Elizabeth (NJ)
Coll of the Ozarks (MO)
Dominican U (IL)
D'Youville Coll (NY)
East Carolina U (NC)
Eastern Illinois U (IL)
Eastern Michigan U (MI)
Florida State U (FL)
Georgia State U (GA)
Harding U (AR)
Illinois State U (IL)
Immaculata U (PA)
Indiana State U (IN)
Iowa State U of Science and Technology (IA)
Jacksonville State U (AL)
Kansas State U (KS)
Keiser U, Fort Lauderdale (FL)
Lebanese American U (Lebanon)
Lehman Coll of the City U of New York (NY)
Life U (GA)
Lipscomb U (TN)
Louisiana Tech U (LA)
Mansfield U of Pennsylvania (PA)
Marshall U (WV)
Marywood U (PA)
Meredith Coll (NC)
Messiah Coll (PA)
Miami U (OH)
Miami U Hamilton (OH)
Miami U Middletown (OH)
Michigan State U (MI)
Minnesota State U Mankato (MN)
Missouri State U (MO)
Northeastern State U (OK)
Northern Illinois U (IL)
Northwest Missouri State U (MO)
The Ohio State U (OH)
Olivet Nazarene U (IL)
Point Loma Nazarene U (CA)
Queens Coll of the City U of New York (NY)
Rowan U (NJ)
St. Catherine U (MN)
Saint Louis U (MO)
San Francisco State U (CA)
Seton Hill U (PA)
Simmons U (MA)

South Dakota State U (SD)
State U of New York Coll at Oneonta (NY)
Texas A&M U–Kingsville (TX)
Texas Christian U (TX)
Texas Southern U (TX)
Texas Tech U (TX)
The U of Akron (OH)
U of Arkansas (AR)
U of Cincinnati (OH)
U of Dayton (OH)
U of Illinois at Chicago (IL)
U of Louisiana at Lafayette (LA)
U of New Haven (CT)
U of North Dakota (ND)
U of Northern Colorado (CO)
U of North Florida (FL)
U of Southern Mississippi (MS)
The U of Texas at San Antonio (TX)
U of Vermont (VT)
The U of Western Ontario (ON, Canada)
U of Wisconsin–Stout (WI)
Utah State U (UT)
Wayne State U (MI)
West Chester U of Pennsylvania (PA)
Western Carolina U (NC)
Western Michigan U (MI)
Youngstown State U (OH)

DIETETICS AND CLINICAL NUTRITION SERVICES RELATED
Andrews U (MI)
Bowling Green State U (OH)
Madonna U (MI)
Texas Christian U (TX)
Western Michigan U (MI)

DIGITAL ARTS
Academy of Art U (CA)
Austin Coll (TX)
Bennington Coll (VT)
Bowling Green State U (OH)
Bridgewater Coll (VA)
Central Michigan U (MI)
Champlain Coll (VT)
Concordia U Chicago (IL)
Delta State U (MS)
Florida Southern Coll (FL)
Fordham U (NY)
Georgian Court U (NJ)
Hamline U (MN)
Kennesaw State U (GA)
King U (TN)
Kutztown U of Pennsylvania (PA)
Linfield Coll (OR)
Lipscomb U (TN)
Louisiana State U in Shreveport (LA)
Marymount California U (CA)
Maryville U of Saint Louis (MO)
Otis Coll of Art and Design (CA)
Point Loma Nazarene U (CA)
Rhode Island Coll (RI)
Roberts Wesleyan Coll (NY)
San Francisco Art Inst (CA)
Southwestern Coll (KS)
State U of New York Coll at Potsdam (NY)
Stetson U (FL)
Tiffin U (OH)
U of Central Florida (FL)
U of Kentucky (KY)
U of Massachusetts Dartmouth (MA)
U of New Mexico (NM)
U of Puget Sound (WA)
U of Saint Francis (IN)
The U of Tampa (FL)
The U of Texas at Dallas (TX)
The U of Toledo (OH)
U of Wisconsin–Stout (WI)
Wartburg Coll (IA)

DIGITAL COMMUNICATION AND MEDIA/MULTIMEDIA
Abilene Christian U (TX)
Academy of Art U (CA)
Anderson U (SC)
Arizona State U at the Polytechnic campus (AZ)
Ball State U (IN)
Baylor U (TX)
Bennington Coll (VT)
Bethany Lutheran Coll (MN)
Bethel U (MN)
Bluffton U (OH)
Bowling Green State U (OH)
Bradley U (IL)
Butler U (IN)
California Lutheran U (CA)
California State U, Dominguez Hills (CA)
Calvin Coll (MI)
Carson-Newman U (TN)
Cedar Crest Coll (PA)
Cedarville U (OH)
Central Washington U (WA)
Columbia Coll Chicago (IL)
Columbia Intl U (SC)
Concordia U Wisconsin (WI)
Eastern Illinois U (IL)
Eastern Mennonite U (VA)
Endicott Coll (MA)
Eugene Lang Coll of Liberal Arts (NY)
Fitchburg State U (MA)
Florida Atlantic U (FL)
Florida Gulf Coast U (FL)
Florida State U (FL)
Fordham U (NY)
Fort Lewis Coll (CO)
Georgia Inst of Technology (GA)
Georgian Court U (NJ)
Georgia Southern U (GA)
Grand Valley State U (MI)
Granite State Coll (NH)
Harding U (AR)
High Point U (NC)
Indiana U Bloomington (IN)
Indiana U Kokomo (IN)
Indiana U-Purdue U Indianapolis (IN)
Indiana U South Bend (IN)
Ithaca Coll (NY)
Kutztown U of Pennsylvania (PA)
Lawrence Technological U (MI)
Lee U (TN)
Lewis U (IL)
Liberty U (VA)
Limestone Coll (SC)
Lincoln U (PA)
Loyola U Chicago (IL)
Loyola U New Orleans (LA)
Lynn U (FL)
Manhattanville Coll (NY)
Marquette U (WI)
Marymount California U (CA)
Maryville U of Saint Louis (MO)
Marywood U (PA)
Messiah Coll (PA)
Miami U (OH)
Miami U Hamilton (OH)
Miami U Middletown (OH)
Middle Tennessee State U (TN)
Minneapolis Coll of Art and Design (MN)
Mount Mercy U (IA)
Mount Saint Mary Coll (NY)
Muskingum U (OH)
National U (CA)
New York Inst of Technology (NY)
New York U (NY)
North Greenville U (SC)
Saginaw Valley State U (MI)
St. Bonaventure U (NY)
Saint Francis U (PA)
St. John Fisher Coll (NY)
San Diego State U (CA)
Seattle U (WA)
Southeastern U (FL)
State U of New York at New Paltz (NY)
State U of New York Coll of Technology at Canton (NY)
Stevenson U (MD)
Texas A&M U (TX)
Texas A&M U–Commerce (TX)
Texas State U (TX)
Texas Tech U (TX)
Tiffin U (OH)
Trevecca Nazarene U (TN)
U of Cincinnati (OH)
U of Colorado Colorado Springs (CO)
U of Denver (CO)
U of Detroit Mercy (MI)
U of Hartford (CT)
U of Idaho (ID)
U of Maine (ME)
U of Miami (FL)
U of Northern Iowa (IA)
U of South Carolina Aiken (SC)
U of South Florida, St. Petersburg (FL)
The U of Tampa (FL)
The U of Texas at El Paso (TX)
U of the Incarnate Word (TX)
U of Toronto (ON, Canada)
U of Waterloo (ON, Canada)
The U of Western Ontario (ON, Canada)
Valdosta State U (GA)
Valparaiso U (IN)
Washington State U (WA)
Washington State U–Tri-Cities (WA)
Washington State U–Vancouver (WA)
Western Michigan U (MI)
Wilkes U (PA)
William Jewell Coll (MO)
William Peace U (NC)
William Penn U (IA)

DIRECTING AND THEATRICAL PRODUCTION
Anderson U (SC)
Augsburg U (MN)
Averett U (VA)
Belmont U (TN)
Bennington Coll (VT)
Binghamton U, State U of New York (NY)
Bradley U (IL)
Brigham Young U (UT)
California Inst of the Arts (CA)
California State U, Long Beach (CA)
Columbia Coll Chicago (IL)
Drake U (IA)
Emory & Henry Coll (VA)
Hofstra U (NY)
Lipscomb U (TN)
Marymount Manhattan Coll (NY)
Nebraska Wesleyan U (NE)
Pepperdine U, Malibu (CA)
Rochester U (MI)
Texas Christian U (TX)
U of Washington (WA)
Whitworth U (WA)

DISABILITY STUDIES
Arizona State U at the West campus (AZ)
Aurora U (IL)
Florida State U (FL)
The U of Western Ontario (ON, Canada)

DISPUTE RESOLUTION
Arizona State U at the West campus (AZ)
Life U (GA)
Missouri State U (MO)

DIVINITY/MINISTRY
Anderson U (SC)
Azusa Pacific U (CA)
The Baptist Coll of Florida (FL)
Belmont U (TN)
Bethel U (IN)
Bethesda U (CA)
Biola U (CA)
Carson-Newman U (TN)
Central Christian Coll of Kansas (KS)
Ecclesia Coll (AR)
Hardin-Simmons U (TX)
Houston Baptist U (TX)
Johnson U (TN)
Johnson U Florida (FL)
Master's Coll and Sem (ON, Canada)
Messenger Coll (TX)
Mid-America Christian U (OK)
Milligan Coll (TN)
Nazarene Bible Coll (CO)
North Central U (MN)
Northwest Nazarene U (ID)
Northwest U (WA)
Ohio Christian U (OH)
Oklahoma Baptist U (OK)
Regent U (VA)
Roberts Wesleyan Coll (NY)
Southeastern U (FL)
Steinbach Bible Coll (MB, Canada)
Toccoa Falls Coll (GA)
Trevecca Nazarene U (TN)

DOCUMENTARY PRODUCTION
Andrews U (MI)
Columbia Coll Chicago (IL)
Ithaca Coll (NY)
Mount Saint Mary's U (CA)
U at Albany, State U of New York (NY)

DRAFTING AND DESIGN TECHNOLOGY
Academy of Art U (CA)
East Carolina U (NC)
East Central U (OK)
Lewis-Clark State Coll (ID)
Sam Houston State U (TX)
Texas Southern U (TX)
Trine U (IN)
Western Michigan U (MI)

DRAFTING/DESIGN ENGINEERING TECHNOLOGIES RELATED
Central Michigan U (MI)
Weber State U (UT)

DRAMA AND DANCE TEACHER EDUCATION
Adams State U (CO)
Austin Coll (TX)
Ball State U (IN)
Belmont U (TN)
Boise State U (ID)
Bridgewater State U (MA)
Butler U (IN)
Catawba Coll (NC)
Central Connecticut State U (CT)
Central Washington U (WA)
Coll of the Ozarks (MO)
Columbia Coll (SC)
East Carolina U (NC)
East Texas Baptist U (TX)
Edgewood Coll (WI)
Hofstra U (NY)
Hope Coll (MI)
Lee U (TN)
Lipscomb U (TN)
Meredith Coll (NC)
Montclair State U (NJ)
Ohio Wesleyan U (OH)
St. Catherine U (MN)
State U of New York Coll at Potsdam (NY)
Sterling Coll (KS)
Trevecca Nazarene U (TN)
The U of Akron (OH)
The U of Iowa (IA)
U of South Dakota (SD)
Utah Valley U (UT)
Valparaiso U (IN)
Washington U in St. Louis (MO)
Wayne State Coll (NE)
Weber State U (UT)
Xavier U (OH)

DRAMA THERAPY
Howard U (DC)

DRAMATIC/THEATER ARTS
Abilene Christian U (TX)
Agnes Scott Coll (GA)
Albion Coll (MI)
Alfred U (NY)
Allegheny Coll (PA)
American U (DC)
Amherst Coll (MA)
Anderson U (SC)
Angelo State U (TX)
Appalachian State U (NC)
Aquinas Coll (MI)
Arcadia U (PA)
Arizona State U at the Tempe campus (AZ)
Auburn U (AL)
Augsburg U (MN)
Augustana Coll (IL)
Augustana U (SD)
Austin Peay State U (TN)
Averett U (VA)
Avila U (MO)
Baker U (KS)
Ball State U (IN)
Barnard Coll (NY)
Barry U (FL)
Barton Coll (NC)
Bates Coll (ME)
Baylor U (TX)
Belhaven U (MS)
Belmont U (TN)
Beloit Coll (WI)
Bemidji State U (MN)
Benedictine Coll (KS)
Bennington Coll (VT)
Berea Coll (KY)
Bethany Lutheran Coll (MN)
Bethel U (IN)
Bethel U (MN)
Bethel U (TN)
Binghamton U, State U of New York (NY)
Biola U (CA)
Birmingham-Southern Coll (AL)
Boise State U (ID)
Boston Coll (MA)
Bowling Green State U (OH)
Bradley U (IL)
Brandeis U (MA)
Brenau U (GA)
Bridgewater Coll (VA)
Bridgewater State U (MA)
Brown U (RI)
Bryan Coll (TN)
Bucknell U (PA)
Butler U (IN)
California Baptist U (CA)
California Lutheran U (CA)
California Polytechnic State U, San Luis Obispo (CA)
California State Polytechnic U, Pomona (CA)
California State U, Bakersfield (CA)
California State U, Dominguez Hills (CA)
California State U, Fresno (CA)
California State U, Fullerton (CA)
California State U, Long Beach (CA)
California State U, Los Angeles (CA)
California State U, Northridge (CA)
California State U, Sacramento (CA)
California State U, San Bernardino (CA)
California State U, San Marcos (CA)
California State U, Stanislaus (CA)
California U of Pennsylvania (PA)
Capital U (OH)
Carleton Coll (MN)
Carnegie Mellon U (PA)
Carson-Newman U (TN)
Carthage Coll (WI)
Catawba Coll (NC)
The Catholic U of America (DC)
Cedar Crest Coll (PA)
Cedarville U (OH)
Central Coll (IA)
Central Connecticut State U (CT)
Central Methodist U (MO)
Central Michigan U (MI)
Centre Coll (KY)
City Coll of the City U of New York (NY)
Claremont McKenna Coll (CA)
Clark U (MA)
Clayton State U (GA)
Coastal Carolina U (SC)
Coe Coll (IA)
Colby Coll (ME)
Colgate U (NY)
Coll of Charleston (SC)
The Coll of Idaho (ID)
Coll of Saint Benedict (MN)
Coll of Staten Island of the City U of New York (NY)
Coll of the Holy Cross (MA)
Coll of the Ozarks (MO)
The Coll of Wooster (OH)
The Colorado Coll (CO)
Colorado State U (CO)
Columbia Coll Chicago (IL)
Concordia Coll (MN)
Concordia U Chicago (IL)
Concordia U, St. Paul (MN)
Cornell Coll (IA)
Cornell U (NY)
Covenant Coll (GA)
Creighton U (NE)
Culver-Stockton Coll (MO)
Dartmouth Coll (NH)
Davidson Coll (NC)
Dean Coll (MA)
DePaul U (IL)
DePauw U (IN)
DeSales U (PA)

Dickinson Coll (PA)
Dickinson State U (ND)
Dillard U (LA)
Doane U (NE)
Dominican U (IL)
Drake U (IA)
Drew U (NJ)
Drury U (MO)
Earlham Coll (IN)
East Carolina U (NC)
East Central U (OK)
Eastern Illinois U (IL)
Eastern Michigan U (MI)
Eastern New Mexico U (NM)
Eastern Oregon U (OR)
Eastern Washington U (WA)
East Texas Baptist U (TX)
Edgewood Coll (WI)
Emory & Henry Coll (VA)
Emory U (GA)
Emporia State U (KS)
Eugene Lang Coll of Liberal Arts (NY)
Fairfield U (CT)
Fairleigh Dickinson U (NJ)
Fitchburg State U (MA)
Flagler Coll (FL)
Florida A&M U (FL)
Florida Atlantic U (FL)
Florida Gulf Coast U (FL)
Florida Southern Coll (FL)
Florida State U (FL)
Fordham U (NY)
Fort Lewis Coll (CO)
Francis Marion U (SC)
Franklin Coll (IN)
Friends U (KS)
Furman U (SC)
George Fox U (OR)
George Mason U (VA)
Georgetown Coll (KY)
The George Washington U (DC)
Georgia Coll & State U (GA)
Georgia Southern U (GA)
Gonzaga U (WA)
Gordon Coll (MA)
Goshen Coll (IN)
Goucher Coll (MD)
Governors State U (IL)
Grinnell Coll (IA)
Guilford Coll (NC)
Gustavus Adolphus Coll (MN)
Hamline U (MN)
Hampshire Coll (MA)
Hampton U (VA)
Hanover Coll (IN)
Harding U (AR)
Hardin-Simmons U (TX)
High Point U (NC)
Hillsdale Coll (MI)
Hofstra U (NY)
Hollins U (VA)
Hope Coll (MI)
Howard U (DC)
Illinois Coll (IL)
Illinois State U (IL)
Illinois Wesleyan U (IL)
Indiana State U (IN)
Indiana U Bloomington (IN)
Indiana U Northwest (IN)
Indiana U of Pennsylvania (PA)
Indiana U South Bend (IN)
Ithaca Coll (NY)
Jacksonville State U (AL)
Jacksonville U (FL)
James Madison U (VA)
Kalamazoo Coll (MI)
Kansas State U (KS)
Kansas Wesleyan U (KS)
Kean U (NJ)
Kennesaw State U (GA)
Kenyon Coll (OH)
King's Coll (PA)
King U (TN)
Knox Coll (IL)
Lafayette Coll (PA)
LaGrange Coll (GA)
Lake Forest Coll (IL)
Lamar U (TX)
Lawrence U (WI)
Lehigh U (PA)
Lehman Coll of the City U of New York (NY)
Le Moyne Coll (NY)
Lenoir-Rhyne U (NC)
Lewis & Clark Coll (OR)
Lewis U (IL)
Liberty U (VA)
Limestone Coll (SC)
Lindenwood U (MO)
Linfield Coll (OR)
Lipscomb U (TN)
Louisiana State U and A&M Coll (LA)
Loyola Marymount U (CA)
Loyola U Chicago (IL)
Loyola U New Orleans (LA)
Lynn U (FL)
Marian U (IN)
Marietta Coll (OH)
Marquette U (WI)
Marywood U (PA)
McDaniel Coll (MD)
McMurry U (TX)
Mercer U, Macon (GA)
Meredith Coll (NC)
Merrimack Coll (MA)
Messiah Coll (PA)
Miami U (OH)
Miami U Hamilton (OH)
Miami U Middletown (OH)
Michigan State U (MI)
Middlebury Coll (VT)
Middle Tennessee State U (TN)
Millikin U (IL)
Minnesota State U Mankato (MN)
Missouri Southern State U (MO)
Missouri State U (MO)
Missouri Valley Coll (MO)
Molloy Coll (NY)
Montclair State U (NJ)
Morehead State U (KY)
Mount Holyoke Coll (MA)
Mount Vernon Nazarene U (OH)
Muhlenberg Coll (PA)
Murray State U (KY)
Muskingum U (OH)
Nazareth Coll of Rochester (NY)
Nebraska Wesleyan U (NE)
New Coll of Florida (FL)
New England Coll (NH)
The New School Coll of Performing Arts (NY)
New York U (NY)
Niagara U (NY)
North Carolina Central U (NC)
North Central U (MN)
Northeastern State U (OK)
Northern Arizona U (AZ)
Northern Illinois U (IL)
Northern Kentucky U (KY)
Northern State U (SD)
North Greenville U (SC)
Northwestern Coll (IA)
Northwestern State U of Louisiana (LA)
Northwestern U (IL)
Northwest Missouri State U (MO)
Northwest U (WA)
Nova Southeastern U (FL)
Oakland U (MI)
Oberlin Coll (OH)
Occidental Coll (CA)
Oglethorpe U (GA)
The Ohio State U (OH)
The Ohio State U at Lima (OH)
Ohio Wesleyan U (OH)
Oklahoma Baptist U (OK)
Oklahoma State U (OK)
Old Dominion U (VA)
Oral Roberts U (OK)
Pacific U (OR)
Palm Beach Atlantic U (FL)
Pepperdine U, Malibu (CA)
Pomona Coll (CA)
Portland State U (OR)
Prairie View A&M U (TX)
Providence Coll (RI)
Purchase Coll, State U of New York (NY)
Purdue U Fort Wayne (IN)
Queens Coll of the City U of New York (NY)
Radford U (VA)
Ramapo Coll of New Jersey (NJ)
Randolph Coll (VA)
Randolph-Macon Coll (VA)
Rhode Island Coll (RI)
Rhodes Coll (TN)
Roanoke Coll (VA)
Rochester U (MI)
Rocky Mountain Coll (MT)
Roger Williams U (RI)
Sacred Heart U (CT)
The Sage Colls (NY)
Saginaw Valley State U (MI)
St. Ambrose U (IA)
St. Bonaventure U (NY)
St. Catherine U (MN)
St. Cloud State U (MN)
Saint John's U (MN)
Saint Louis U (MO)
Saint Mary's Coll (IN)
Saint Mary's Coll of California (CA)
St. Mary's Coll of Maryland (MD)
Saint Mary's U of Minnesota (MN)
St. Norbert Coll (WI)
St. Olaf Coll (MN)
Salem State U (MA)
Salisbury U (MD)
Salve Regina U (RI)
Samford U (AL)
Sam Houston State U (TX)
San Diego State U (CA)
San Francisco State U (CA)
San Jose State U (CA)
Santa Clara U (CA)
Sarah Lawrence Coll (NY)
Schreiner U (TX)
Scripps Coll (CA)
Seattle U (WA)
Seton Hill U (PA)
Shepherd U (WV)
Siena Heights U (MI)
Simon Fraser U (BC, Canada)
Skidmore Coll (NY)
Slippery Rock U of Pennsylvania (PA)
Smith Coll (MA)
South Dakota State U (SD)
Southeast Missouri State U (MO)
Southern Arkansas U–Magnolia (AR)
Southern Illinois U Carbondale (IL)
Southern Illinois U Edwardsville (IL)
Southern Methodist U (TX)
Southwest Baptist U (MO)
Southwestern Coll (KS)
Southwestern U (TX)
Spring Hill Coll (AL)
Stanford U (CA)
State U of New York at Fredonia (NY)
State U of New York at New Paltz (NY)
State U of New York at Oswego (NY)
State U of New York Coll at Geneseo (NY)
State U of New York Coll at Oneonta (NY)
State U of New York Coll at Potsdam (NY)
Sterling Coll (KS)
Stetson U (FL)
Stevenson U (MD)
Stony Brook U, State U of New York (NY)
Suffolk U (MA)
SUNY Brockport (NY)
Susquehanna U (PA)
Tabor Coll (KS)
Tarleton State U (TX)
Taylor U (IN)
Tennessee Wesleyan U (TN)
Texas A&M U (TX)
Texas A&M U–Commerce (TX)
Texas A&M U–Corpus Christi (TX)
Texas A&M U–Kingsville (TX)
Texas Christian U (TX)
Texas Lutheran U (TX)
Texas Southern U (TX)
Texas State U (TX)
Texas Tech U (TX)
Texas Woman's U (TX)
Towson U (MD)
Transylvania U (KY)
Trevecca Nazarene U (TN)
Trinity U (TX)
Truman State U (MO)
Tulane U (LA)
Union U (TN)
U at Albany, State U of New York (NY)
U at Buffalo, the State U of New York (NY)
The U of Akron (OH)
The U of Alabama (AL)
The U of Alabama at Birmingham (AL)
The U of Arizona (AZ)
U of Arkansas (AR)
U of Arkansas at Little Rock (AR)
U of California, Berkeley (CA)
U of California, Irvine (CA)
U of California, Los Angeles (CA)
U of California, San Diego (CA)
U of California, Santa Barbara (CA)
U of California, Santa Cruz (CA)
U of Central Arkansas (AR)
U of Central Florida (FL)
U of Cincinnati (OH)
U of Colorado Boulder (CO)
U of Colorado Denver (CO)
U of Dallas (TX)
U of Dayton (OH)
U of Denver (CO)
U of Detroit Mercy (MI)
The U of Findlay (OH)
U of Hawaii at Manoa (HI)
U of Idaho (ID)
U of Illinois at Chicago (IL)
U of Illinois at Springfield (IL)
The U of Iowa (IA)
U of Jamestown (ND)
The U of Kansas (KS)
U of Kentucky (KY)
U of La Verne (CA)
U of Louisville (KY)
U of Maine (ME)
U of Maryland, Baltimore County (MD)
U of Massachusetts Amherst (MA)
U of Memphis (TN)
U of Miami (FL)
U of Michigan (MI)
U of Michigan–Flint (MI)
U of Minnesota, Duluth (MN)
U of Minnesota, Morris (MN)
U of Minnesota, Twin Cities Campus (MN)
U of Missouri–St. Louis (MO)
U of Montana (MT)
U of Montevallo (AL)
U of Nebraska at Kearney (NE)
U of Nebraska–Lincoln (NE)
U of Nevada, Las Vegas (NV)
U of Nevada, Reno (NV)
U of New Hampshire (NH)
U of New Mexico (NM)
The U of North Carolina at Chapel Hill (NC)
The U of North Carolina at Charlotte (NC)
The U of North Carolina at Greensboro (NC)
The U of North Carolina at Pembroke (NC)
The U of North Carolina Wilmington (NC)
U of North Dakota (ND)
U of Northern Colorado (CO)
U of Northern Iowa (IA)
U of North Texas (TX)
U of Northwestern–St. Paul (MN)
U of Notre Dame (IN)
U of Oregon (OR)
U of Pennsylvania (PA)
U of Portland (OR)
U of Puget Sound (WA)
U of Richmond (VA)
U of Saint Mary (KS)
U of St. Thomas (TX)
U of San Diego (CA)
U of Science and Arts of Oklahoma (OK)
The U of Scranton (PA)
U of South Alabama (AL)
U of South Carolina (SC)
U of South Dakota (SD)
U of Southern Indiana (IN)
U of Southern Maine (ME)
U of Southern Mississippi (MS)
U of South Florida (FL)
The U of Tampa (FL)
The U of Tennessee (TN)
The U of Tennessee at Chattanooga (TN)
The U of Texas at El Paso (TX)
The U of Texas Rio Grande Valley (TX)
U of the Fraser Valley (BC, Canada)
U of the Incarnate Word (TX)
U of the Pacific (CA)
The U of the South (TN)
The U of Toledo (OH)
The U of Tulsa (OK)
U of Utah (UT)
U of Vermont (VT)
U of Virginia (VA)
U of Washington (WA)
U of Waterloo (ON, Canada)
U of West Florida (FL)
U of West Georgia (GA)
U of Wisconsin–Eau Claire (WI)
U of Wisconsin–Green Bay (WI)
U of Wisconsin–La Crosse (WI)
U of Wisconsin–Madison (WI)
U of Wisconsin–Milwaukee (WI)
U of Wisconsin–Parkside (WI)
U of Wyoming (WY)
Utah State U (UT)
Utah Valley U (UT)
Valdosta State U (GA)
Valparaiso U (IN)
Vanderbilt U (TN)
Vanguard U of Southern California (CA)
Virginia Commonwealth U (VA)
Virginia Wesleyan U (VA)
Wabash Coll (IN)
Wake Forest U (NC)
Washington and Lee U (VA)
Washington Coll (MD)
Washington U in St. Louis (MO)
Wayland Baptist U (TX)
Wayne State Coll (NE)
Wayne State U (MI)
Weber State U (UT)
Wesleyan U (CT)
West Chester U of Pennsylvania (PA)
Western Carolina U (NC)
Western Connecticut State U (CT)
Western Kentucky U (KY)
Western Oregon U (OR)
Western Washington U (WA)
Westfield State U (MA)
Westminster Coll (UT)
Westmont Coll (CA)
West Virginia U (WV)
Whitworth U (WA)
Wichita State U (KS)
Wilkes U (PA)
Willamette U (OR)
William & Mary (VA)
William Jewell Coll (MO)
William Peace U (NC)
William Penn U (IA)
Williams Coll (MA)
Wilmington Coll (OH)
Winthrop U (SC)
Wittenberg U (OH)
Wofford Coll (SC)
Wright State U (OH)
Wright State U–Lake Campus (OH)
Xavier U (OH)
Yale U (CT)
York Coll of Pennsylvania (PA)
Youngstown State U (OH)

DRAMATIC/THEATER ARTS AND STAGECRAFT RELATED
Adams State U (CO)
Aquinas Coll (MI)
Benedictine Coll (KS)
Brigham Young U (UT)
Catawba Coll (NC)
Columbia Coll Chicago (IL)
Drake U (IA)
Fayetteville State U (NC)
Indiana U South Bend (IN)
Lee U (TN)
Marymount Manhattan Coll (NY)
Pepperdine U, Malibu (CA)
Saint Leo U (FL)
Seton Hill U (PA)
Southern Illinois U Carbondale (IL)
Southwestern Coll (KS)
U of Miami (FL)
U of Michigan–Flint (MI)
U of Northern Colorado (CO)
Western Kentucky U (KY)
Western Michigan U (MI)
Wheaton Coll (MA)
William Peace U (NC)

DRAWING
Adams State U (CO)
American Acad of Art (IL)
Aquinas Coll (MI)
Bennington Coll (VT)
Biola U (CA)
Birmingham-Southern Coll (AL)

Bowling Green State U (OH)
Bradley U (IL)
Brigham Young U (UT)
California State U, Long Beach (CA)
Carson-Newman U (TN)
Central Washington U (WA)
Cleveland Inst of Art (OH)
Drake U (IA)
Edinboro U of Pennsylvania (PA)
Ferris State U (MI)
Georgia State U (GA)
Inter American U of Puerto Rico, San Germán Campus (PR)
Lewis U (IL)
Minneapolis Coll of Art and Design (MN)
Minnesota State U Mankato (MN)
New England Coll (NH)
Oakland U (MI)
Otis Coll of Art and Design (CA)
Portland State U (OR)
Pratt Inst (NY)
Purdue U Fort Wayne (IN)
School of Visual Arts (NY)
Seton Hill U (PA)
State U of New York at Fredonia (NY)
U of Hartford (CT)
The U of Iowa (IA)
U of Michigan (MI)
Washington U in St. Louis (MO)

DRIVER AND SAFETY TEACHER EDUCATION
New York U (NY)
U of Northern Iowa (IA)

DUTCH/FLEMISH
U of California, Berkeley (CA)

EARLY CHILDHOOD EDUCATION
Adams State U (CO)
Alverno Coll (WI)
Aquinas Coll (MI)
Arcadia U (PA)
Arizona State U at the Tempe campus (AZ)
Auburn U (AL)
Ball State U (IN)
Barton Coll (NC)
Bayamón Central U (PR)
Baylor U (TX)
Becker Coll (MA)
Belmont U (TN)
Berry Coll (GA)
Bethel U (IN)
Bethesda U (CA)
Bluffton U (OH)
Boise State U (ID)
Bradley U (IL)
Bridgewater State U (MA)
Brigham Young U (UT)
Bucknell U (PA)
Butler U (IN)
California Baptist U (CA)
California State U, Dominguez Hills (CA)
California State U, Los Angeles (CA)
California State U, San Bernardino (CA)
California State U, San Marcos (CA)
California State U, Stanislaus (CA)
California U of Pennsylvania (PA)
Calvin Coll (MI)
Cameron U (OK)
Capital U (OH)
Carlow U (PA)
Carson-Newman U (TN)
The Catholic U of America (DC)
Cazenovia Coll (NY)
Cedar Crest Coll (PA)
Cedarville U (OH)
Central Connecticut State U (CT)
Central Methodist U (MO)
Central Michigan U (MI)
Central State U (OH)
Central Washington U (WA)
Chaminade U of Honolulu (HI)
Champlain Coll (VT)
Charter Oak State Coll (CT)
Chatham U (PA)
Chestnut Hill Coll (PA)
City Coll of the City U of New York (NY)
Clarion U of Pennsylvania (PA)
Clark Atlanta U (GA)
Clemson U (SC)
Coastal Carolina U (SC)
Colby-Sawyer Coll (NH)
Coll of Charleston (SC)
The Coll of Saint Rose (NY)
Coll of the Ozarks (MO)
Colorado State U (CO)
Columbia Coll (SC)
Concordia U Chicago (IL)
Concordia U, St. Paul (MN)
Dean Coll (MA)
DePaul U (IL)
DeSales U (PA)
Dominican U (IL)
East Central U (OK)
Eastern Michigan U (MI)
Eastern New Mexico U (NM)
Eastern Oregon U (OR)
Eastern U (PA)
Eastern Washington U (WA)
Edinboro U of Pennsylvania (PA)
Elms Coll (MA)
Elon U (NC)
Endicott Coll (MA)
Evangel U (MO)
Fayetteville State U (NC)
Fitchburg State U (MA)
Florida A&M U (FL)
Florida Atlantic U (FL)
Florida Gulf Coast U (FL)
Fort Lewis Coll (CO)
Framingham State U (MA)
Francis Marion U (SC)
Freed-Hardeman U (TN)
Gannon U (PA)
Georgia Coll & State U (GA)
Georgia Gwinnett Coll (GA)
Gordon Coll (MA)
Governors State U (IL)
Granite State Coll (NH)
Harding U (AR)
Hardin-Simmons U (TX)
Harris-Stowe State U (MO)
Hofstra U (NY)
Illinois Coll (IL)
Illinois State U (IL)
Indiana U Bloomington (IN)
Indiana U Kokomo (IN)
Indiana U of Pennsylvania (PA)
Indiana U-Purdue U Indianapolis (IN)
Inter American U of Puerto Rico, San Germán Campus (PR)
Iona Coll (NY)
Iowa State U of Science and Technology (IA)
Kennesaw State U (GA)
Kent State U at Tuscarawas (OH)
King's Coll (PA)
Kutztown U of Pennsylvania (PA)
Lancaster Bible Coll (PA)
Lasell Coll (MA)
Lee U (TN)
Liberty U (VA)
Limestone Coll (SC)
Lindenwood U (MO)
Lock Haven U of Pennsylvania (PA)
Louisiana State U and A&M Coll (LA)
Louisiana State U in Shreveport (LA)
Louisiana Tech U (LA)
Loyola U Chicago (IL)
Lynn U (FL)
Madonna U (MI)
Malone U (OH)
Martin Luther Coll (MN)
Marywood U (PA)
Mayville State U (ND)
McMurry U (TX)
McNeese State U (LA)
Mercy Coll (NY)
Merrimack Coll (MA)
Messiah Coll (PA)
Miami Dade Coll (FL)
Miami U (OH)
Miami U Hamilton (OH)
Miami U Middletown (OH)
Michigan State U (MI)
Middle Tennessee State U (TN)
Millersville U of Pennsylvania (PA)
Milligan Coll (TN)
Millikin U (IL)
Misericordia U (PA)
Missouri State U (MO)
Missouri Valley Coll (MO)
Morehead State U (KY)
Mount Aloysius Coll (PA)
Mount Saint Mary Coll (NY)
Mount Vernon Nazarene U (OH)
Murray State U (KY)
Muskingum U (OH)
National U (CA)
Newman U (KS)
New York U (NY)
Northeastern Illinois U (IL)
Northeastern State U (OK)
Northern Illinois U (IL)
North Greenville U (SC)
Northwest Christian U (OR)
Northwestern State U of Louisiana (LA)
Oakland City U (IN)
Ohio Christian U (OH)
Ohio Dominican U (OH)
Ohio Wesleyan U (OH)
Oklahoma Baptist U (OK)
Old Dominion U (VA)
Olivet Nazarene U (IL)
Oral Roberts U (OK)
Ottawa U (KS)
Polk State Coll (FL)
Purdue U Northwest (IN)
Regent U (VA)
Regis Coll (MA)
Rhode Island Coll (RI)
Roberts Wesleyan Coll (NY)
Rochester U (MI)
Rowan U (NJ)
St. Ambrose U (IA)
St. Cloud State U (MN)
Saint Vincent Coll (PA)
Salem State U (MA)
Salisbury U (MD)
Salve Regina U (RI)
San Diego State U (CA)
San Francisco State U (CA)
Schreiner U (TX)
Slippery Rock U of Pennsylvania (PA)
South Dakota State U (SD)
Southeastern Louisiana U (LA)
Southeastern U (FL)
Southern Arkansas U–Magnolia (AR)
Southern Illinois U Carbondale (IL)
Southern Illinois U Edwardsville (IL)
Southwest Baptist U (MO)
Southwestern Coll (KS)
Southwestern Oklahoma State U (OK)
Springfield Coll (MA)
Spring Hill Coll (AL)
State U of New York Coll at Geneseo (NY)
State U of New York Coll at Old Westbury (NY)
State U of New York Coll at Potsdam (NY)
Stevenson U (MD)
Susquehanna U (PA)
Tennessee Wesleyan U (TN)
Texas Christian U (TX)
Towson U (MD)
Trevecca Nazarene U (TN)
The U of Akron (OH)
The U of Alabama at Birmingham (AL)
U of Arkansas at Little Rock (AR)
U of Central Florida (FL)
U of Cincinnati (OH)
U of Colorado Colorado Springs (CO)
U of Dayton (OH)
U of Hartford (CT)
U of Hawaii at Manoa (HI)
The U of Kansas (KS)
U of Kentucky (KY)
U of Louisiana at Lafayette (LA)
U of Massachusetts Boston (MA)
U of Michigan–Dearborn (MI)
U of Michigan–Flint (MI)
U of Missouri–St. Louis (MO)
U of Nevada, Las Vegas (NV)
U of New Mexico (NM)
The U of North Carolina at Chapel Hill (NC)
The U of North Carolina at Greensboro (NC)
U of North Dakota (ND)
U of Northern Colorado (CO)
U of Northern Iowa (IA)
U of North Florida (FL)
U of Northwestern–St. Paul (MN)
U of Science and Arts of Oklahoma (OK)
The U of Scranton (PA)
U of South Alabama (AL)
U of South Carolina Aiken (SC)
U of South Carolina Beaufort (SC)
U of Southern Indiana (IN)
U of South Florida (FL)
The U of Tennessee at Chattanooga (TN)
U of the Virgin Islands (VI)
U of Utah (UT)
U of Vermont (VT)
U of West Florida (FL)
U of Wisconsin–Milwaukee (WI)
U of Wisconsin–Parkside (WI)
U of Wisconsin–Stout (WI)
Utah State U (UT)
Valdosta State U (GA)
Vanderbilt U (TN)
Virginia Commonwealth U (VA)
Wayland Baptist U (TX)
Wayne State Coll (NE)
Weber State U (UT)
West Chester U of Pennsylvania (PA)
Western Kentucky U (KY)
Western Michigan U (MI)
Western New Mexico U (NM)
Western Washington U (WA)
Wheaton Coll (MA)
Widener U (PA)
William Paterson U of New Jersey (NJ)
Worcester State U (MA)
Wright State U (OH)
Wright State U–Lake Campus (OH)
Xavier U (OH)
Xavier U of Louisiana (LA)
Yeshiva U (NY)
York Coll of Pennsylvania (PA)
Youngstown State U (OH)

EARTH SCIENCE EDUCATION
Albion Coll (MI)
Ball State U (IN)
Boise State U (ID)
Calvin Coll (MI)
Coll of Staten Island of the City U of New York (NY)
Eastern Kentucky U (KY)
Florida Inst of Technology (FL)
Pace U, Pleasantville Campus (NY)
Queens Coll of the City U of New York (NY)
St. Cloud State U (MN)
State U of New York Coll at Potsdam (NY)
Western Michigan U (MI)
Western Washington U (WA)
Worcester State U (MA)

EAST ASIAN LANGUAGES
Arizona State U at the Tempe campus (AZ)
Austin Coll (TX)
Indiana U Bloomington (IN)
Smith Coll (MA)
The U of Kansas (KS)
U of Pennsylvania (PA)
U of Puget Sound (WA)
The U of Western Ontario (ON, Canada)
Washington and Lee U (VA)

EAST ASIAN LANGUAGES RELATED
Dartmouth Coll (NH)
Northwestern U (IL)
Occidental Coll (CA)
U of Minnesota, Twin Cities Campus (MN)
Washington U in St. Louis (MO)

ECOLOGY
Barry U (FL)
Beloit Coll (WI)
Bemidji State U (MN)
Bennington Coll (VT)
California State U, Dominguez Hills (CA)
California State U, Fresno (CA)
California State U, Long Beach (CA)
California State U, San Marcos (CA)
Central Washington U (WA)
Clark U (MA)
Coll of the Ozarks (MO)
Colorado State U (CO)
East Central U (OK)
Georgetown Coll (KY)
Iowa State U of Science and Technology (IA)
Jacksonville State U (AL)
Le Moyne Coll (NY)
Minnesota State U Mankato (MN)
Molloy Coll (NY)
New York U (NY)
Northern State U (SD)
Northwestern U (IL)
Oberlin Coll (OH)
Oklahoma State U (OK)
Olivet Nazarene U (IL)
Rice U (TX)
St. Cloud State U (MN)
Salisbury U (MD)
San Diego State U (CA)
San Francisco State U (CA)
Siena Coll (NY)
Sierra Nevada Coll (NV)
Stony Brook U, State U of New York (NY)
Susquehanna U (PA)
Tulane U (LA)
The U of Akron (OH)
U of California, Los Angeles (CA)
U of California, San Diego (CA)
U of California, Santa Barbara (CA)
U of California, Santa Cruz (CA)
U of Denver (CO)
U of Minnesota, Twin Cities Campus (MN)
U of Northern Iowa (IA)
U of North Texas (TX)
U of Waterloo (ON, Canada)
The U of Western Ontario (ON, Canada)
Washington U in St. Louis (MO)
Yale U (CT)

ECOLOGY AND EVOLUTIONARY BIOLOGY
Bradley U (IL)
Colby Coll (ME)
The Colorado Coll (CO)
Loyola U New Orleans (LA)
Princeton U (NJ)
The U of Arizona (AZ)
U of California, Irvine (CA)
U of California, San Diego (CA)
U of Colorado Boulder (CO)
The U of Kansas (KS)
U of Michigan (MI)
The U of Texas at El Paso (TX)
Vanderbilt U (TN)

ECOLOGY, EVOLUTION, SYSTEMATICS AND POPULATION BIOLOGY RELATED
Hofstra U (NY)
U of Colorado Boulder (CO)
U of Washington (WA)

E-COMMERCE
Bemidji State U (MN)
Lewis U (IL)
Limestone Coll (SC)
Seattle U (WA)
Trevecca Nazarene U (TN)
The U of Akron (OH)
U of La Verne (CA)
U of Pennsylvania (PA)
The U of Scranton (PA)
U of the Incarnate Word (TX)
The U of Toledo (OH)
U of Toronto (ON, Canada)
Western Michigan U (MI)
Winthrop U (SC)

ECONOMETRICS AND QUANTITATIVE ECONOMICS
American U (DC)
Amherst Coll (MA)
Bowdoin Coll (ME)
Bucknell U (PA)
Carnegie Mellon U (PA)
Clarkson U (NY)
Colgate U (NY)
The Colorado Coll (CO)
Davidson Coll (NC)
Dickinson Coll (PA)

Drexel U (PA)
Emory U (GA)
Grinnell Coll (IA)
Hampden-Sydney Coll (VA)
High Point U (NC)
Hofstra U (NY)
Ithaca Coll (NY)
Knox Coll (IL)
Lake Forest Coll (IL)
Marquette U (WI)
Miami U Hamilton (OH)
Miami U Middletown (OH)
Mount Holyoke Coll (MA)
New York U (NY)
Portland State U (OR)
Providence Coll (RI)
St. Cloud State U (MN)
St. Olaf Coll (MN)
Scripps Coll (CA)
State U of New York at Oswego (NY)
U of California, Irvine (CA)
U of California, Santa Barbara (CA)
U of Dayton (OH)
U of Minnesota, Twin Cities Campus (MN)
U of Northern Iowa (IA)
U of Richmond (VA)
U of San Francisco (CA)
U of Utah (UT)
The U of West Alabama (AL)
U of Wyoming (WY)
Wake Forest U (NC)
Washington U in St. Louis (MO)
Weber State U (UT)
Wesleyan U (CT)
Western Kentucky U (KY)
Western Michigan U (MI)
Wheaton Coll (IL)
Williams Coll (MA)
Youngstown State U (OH)

ECONOMICS

Adams State U (CO)
Agnes Scott Coll (GA)
Albion Coll (MI)
Allegheny Coll (PA)
American U (DC)
American U of Beirut (Lebanon)
Amherst Coll (MA)
Appalachian State U (NC)
Aquinas Coll (MI)
Arizona State U at the Tempe campus (AZ)
Assumption Coll (MA)
Auburn U (AL)
Auburn U at Montgomery (AL)
Augsburg U (MN)
Augustana Coll (IL)
Augustana U (SD)
Austin Coll (TX)
Babson Coll (MA)
Baker U (KS)
Ball State U (IN)
Barnard Coll (NY)
Barry U (FL)
Baruch Coll of the City U of New York (NY)
Bates Coll (ME)
Baylor U (TX)
Belmont Abbey Coll (NC)
Beloit Coll (WI)
Bemidji State U (MN)
Benedictine Coll (KS)
Benedictine U (IL)
Bennington Coll (VT)
Berea Coll (KY)
Bethel U (IN)
Bethel U (MN)
Binghamton U, State U of New York (NY)
Birmingham-Southern Coll (AL)
Bluffton U (OH)
Boise State U (ID)
Boston Coll (MA)
Bowdoin Coll (ME)
Bowling Green State U (OH)
Bradley U (IL)
Brandeis U (MA)
Brandon U (MB, Canada)
Bridgewater Coll (VA)
Bridgewater State U (MA)
Brown U (RI)
Bucknell U (PA)
Butler U (IN)
Caldwell U (NJ)
California Lutheran U (CA)
California Polytechnic State U, San Luis Obispo (CA)
California State Polytechnic U, Pomona (CA)
California State U, Bakersfield (CA)
California State U, Fresno (CA)
California State U, Fullerton (CA)
California State U, Long Beach (CA)
California State U, Los Angeles (CA)
California State U, Northridge (CA)
California State U, Sacramento (CA)
California State U, San Bernardino (CA)
California State U, San Marcos (CA)
California State U, Stanislaus (CA)
Calvin Coll (MI)
Campbellsville U (KY)
Capital U (OH)
Carleton Coll (MN)
Carnegie Mellon U (PA)
Carthage Coll (WI)
Catawba Coll (NC)
The Catholic U of America (DC)
Central Coll (IA)
Central Connecticut State U (CT)
Central Michigan U (MI)
Central Washington U (WA)
Centre Coll (KY)
City Coll of the City U of New York (NY)
Claremont McKenna Coll (CA)
Clarion U of Pennsylvania (PA)
Clark U (MA)
Clemson U (SC)
Coastal Carolina U (SC)
Coe Coll (IA)
Colby Coll (ME)
Colgate U (NY)
Coll of Charleston (SC)
Coll of Saint Benedict (MN)
Coll of Staten Island of the City U of New York (NY)
Coll of the Holy Cross (MA)
The Coll of Wooster (OH)
The Colorado Coll (CO)
Colorado School of Mines (CO)
Colorado State U (CO)
Concordia U Wisconsin (WI)
Cornell Coll (IA)
Cornell U (NY)
Creighton U (NE)
Dartmouth Coll (NH)
DePaul U (IL)
DePauw U (IN)
DeSales U (PA)
Dickinson Coll (PA)
Dillard U (LA)
Doane U (NE)
Dominican U (IL)
Drew U (NJ)
Drexel U (PA)
Drury U (MO)
Earlham Coll (IN)
East Carolina U (NC)
Eastern Illinois U (IL)
Eastern Kentucky U (KY)
Eastern Mennonite U (VA)
Eastern Michigan U (MI)
Eastern Oregon U (OR)
Eastern Washington U (WA)
Edgewood Coll (WI)
Edinboro U of Pennsylvania (PA)
Emmanuel Coll (MA)
Emory & Henry Coll (VA)
Emporia State U (KS)
Eugene Lang Coll of Liberal Arts (NY)
Fairfield U (CT)
Fairleigh Dickinson U (NJ)
Fitchburg State U (MA)
Flagler Coll (FL)
Florida A&M U (FL)
Florida Atlantic U (FL)
Florida Gulf Coast U (FL)
Florida Southern Coll (FL)
Florida State U (FL)
Fordham U (NY)
Framingham State U (MA)
Francis Marion U (SC)
Franklin Coll (IN)
Furman U (SC)
George Fox U (OR)
George Mason U (VA)
Georgetown U (DC)
The George Washington U (DC)
Georgia Southern U (GA)
Georgia State U (GA)
Gonzaga U (WA)
Gordon Coll (MA)
Goucher Coll (MD)
Governors State U (IL)
Graceland U (IA)
Grand Valley State U (MI)
Grinnell Coll (IA)
Guilford Coll (NC)
Gustavus Adolphus Coll (MN)
Hamline U (MN)
Hampden-Sydney Coll (VA)
Hampshire Coll (MA)
Hampton U (VA)
Hanover Coll (IN)
Harding U (AR)
Hardin-Simmons U (TX)
Harvard U (MA)
Hillsdale Coll (MI)
Hobart and William Smith Colls (NY)
Hofstra U (NY)
Hollins U (VA)
Hope Coll (MI)
Howard U (DC)
Illinois Coll (IL)
Illinois State U (IL)
Illinois Wesleyan U (IL)
Indiana State U (IN)
Indiana U Bloomington (IN)
Indiana U Northwest (IN)
Indiana U of Pennsylvania (PA)
Indiana U-Purdue U Indianapolis (IN)
Indiana U South Bend (IN)
Indiana U Southeast (IN)
Inter American U of Puerto Rico, San Germán Campus (PR)
Iona Coll (NY)
Iowa State U of Science and Technology (IA)
Ithaca Coll (NY)
Jacksonville State U (AL)
Jacksonville U (FL)
James Madison U (VA)
John Cabot U (Italy)
John Carroll U (OH)
John Jay Coll of Criminal Justice of the City U of New York (NY)
Johns Hopkins U (MD)
Kalamazoo Coll (MI)
Kansas State U (KS)
Kean U (NJ)
Kenyon Coll (OH)
King's Coll (PA)
Lafayette Coll (PA)
La Sierra U (CA)
Lawrence U (WI)
Lebanese American U (Lebanon)
Lehman Coll of the City U of New York (NY)
Le Moyne Coll (NY)
Lenoir-Rhyne U (NC)
Lewis & Clark Coll (OR)
Limestone Coll (SC)
Lincoln Memorial U (TN)
Lindenwood U (MO)
Linfield Coll (OR)
Longwood U (VA)
Loras Coll (IA)
Louisiana State U and A&M Coll (LA)
Loyola Marymount U (CA)
Loyola U Maryland (MD)
Loyola U New Orleans (LA)
Manhattan Coll (NY)
Manhattanville Coll (NY)
Marietta Coll (OH)
Marquette U (WI)
Marshall U (WV)
Marymount U (VA)
McDaniel Coll (MD)
McKendree U (IL)
Mercer U, Macon (GA)
Meredith Coll (NC)
Merrimack Coll (MA)
Messiah Coll (PA)
Miami U (OH)
Miami U Hamilton (OH)
Miami U Middletown (OH)
Michigan State U (MI)
Michigan Technological U (MI)
Middlebury Coll (VT)
Middle Tennessee State U (TN)
Millersville U of Pennsylvania (PA)
Milligan Coll (TN)
Minnesota State U Mankato (MN)
Mississippi State U (MS)
Missouri State U (MO)
Missouri U of Science and Technology (MO)
Missouri Valley Coll (MO)
Montana State U (MT)
Montclair State U (NJ)
Moravian Coll (PA)
Mount Holyoke Coll (MA)
Mount St. Mary's U (MD)
Muhlenberg Coll (PA)
Murray State U (KY)
Muskingum U (OH)
Nebraska Wesleyan U (NE)
New Coll of Florida (FL)
New York U (NY)
Niagara U (NY)
Nichols Coll (MA)
Northeastern Illinois U (IL)
Northern Illinois U (IL)
Northern State U (SD)
Northwestern Coll (IA)
Northwestern U (IL)
Northwest Missouri State U (MO)
Oakland U (MI)
Oberlin Coll (OH)
Occidental Coll (CA)
Oglethorpe U (GA)
Ohio Dominican U (OH)
The Ohio State U (OH)
Ohio Wesleyan U (OH)
Oklahoma State U (OK)
Old Dominion U (VA)
Olivet Nazarene U (IL)
Pace U, Pleasantville Campus (NY)
Pacific U (OR)
Penn State Abington (PA)
Penn State Altoona (PA)
Penn State Beaver (PA)
Penn State Berks (PA)
Penn State Brandywine (PA)
Penn State DuBois (PA)
Penn State Erie, The Behrend Coll (PA)
Penn State Fayette, The Eberly Campus (PA)
Penn State Greater Allegheny (PA)
Penn State Hazleton (PA)
Penn State Lehigh Valley (PA)
Penn State Mont Alto (PA)
Penn State New Kensington (PA)
Penn State Schuylkill (PA)
Penn State Shenango (PA)
Penn State U Park (PA)
Penn State Wilkes-Barre (PA)
Penn State York (PA)
Pepperdine U, Malibu (CA)
Pittsburg State U (KS)
Pitzer Coll (CA)
Pomona Coll (CA)
Portland State U (OR)
Princeton U (NJ)
Providence Coll (RI)
Purchase Coll, State U of New York (NY)
Purdue U Fort Wayne (IN)
Queens Coll of the City U of New York (NY)
Radford U (VA)
Ramapo Coll of New Jersey (NJ)
Randolph Coll (VA)
Randolph-Macon Coll (VA)
Rhode Island Coll (RI)
Rhodes Coll (TN)
Rice U (TX)
Richmond, The American Intl U in London (United Kingdom)
Roanoke Coll (VA)
Roger Williams U (RI)
Rollins Coll (FL)
Rose-Hulman Inst of Technology (IN)
Rowan U (NJ)
Sacred Heart U (CT)
Saginaw Valley State U (MI)
St. Ambrose U (IA)
St. Catherine U (MN)
St. Cloud State U (MN)
Saint Francis U (PA)
St. John Fisher Coll (NY)
Saint John's U (MN)
Saint Joseph's U (PA)
Saint Leo U (FL)
Saint Mary's Coll (IN)
Saint Mary's Coll of California (CA)
St. Mary's Coll of Maryland (MD)
St. Mary's U (TX)
St. Norbert Coll (WI)
St. Olaf Coll (MN)
St. Thomas U - Florida (FL)
St. Thomas U - New Brunswick (NB, Canada)
Saint Vincent Coll (PA)
Salem State U (MA)
Salisbury U (MD)
Salve Regina U (RI)
Samford U (AL)
San Diego State U (CA)
San Francisco State U (CA)
San Jose State U (CA)
Santa Clara U (CA)
Sarah Lawrence Coll (NY)
Scripps Coll (CA)
Seattle U (WA)
Seton Hill U (PA)
Shepherd U (WV)
Siena Coll (NY)
Simmons U (MA)
Simon Fraser U (BC, Canada)
Skidmore Coll (NY)
Smith Coll (MA)
South Dakota State U (SD)
Southeast Missouri State U (MO)
Southern Illinois U Carbondale (IL)
Southern Illinois U Edwardsville (IL)
Southern Methodist U (TX)
Southwestern U (TX)
Stanford U (CA)
State U of New York at Fredonia (NY)
State U of New York at New Paltz (NY)
State U of New York at Oswego (NY)
State U of New York Coll at Cortland (NY)
State U of New York Coll at Geneseo (NY)
State U of New York Coll at Oneonta (NY)
State U of New York Coll at Potsdam (NY)
Stetson U (FL)
Stockton U (NJ)
Stony Brook U, State U of New York (NY)
Suffolk U (MA)
Susquehanna U (PA)
Tarleton State U (TX)
Temple U (PA)
Texas A&M U (TX)
Texas Christian U (TX)
Texas Lutheran U (TX)
Texas Southern U (TX)
Texas State U (TX)
Texas Tech U (TX)
Towson U (MD)
Transylvania U (KY)
Trinity U (TX)
Troy U (AL)
Truman State U (MO)
Tulane U (LA)
Union Coll (NY)
Union U (TN)
United States Military Acad (NY)
U at Albany, State U of New York (NY)
U at Buffalo, the State U of New York (NY)
The U of Akron (OH)
U of Alaska Fairbanks (AK)
The U of Arizona (AZ)
U of Arkansas (AR)
U of California, Berkeley (CA)
U of California, Irvine (CA)
U of California, Los Angeles (CA)
U of California, Merced (CA)
U of California, Riverside (CA)
U of California, San Diego (CA)
U of California, Santa Barbara (CA)
U of California, Santa Cruz (CA)
U of Central Arkansas (AR)
U of Central Florida (FL)
U of Cincinnati (OH)
U of Colorado Boulder (CO)
U of Colorado Colorado Springs (CO)
U of Colorado Denver (CO)
U of Dallas (TX)
U of Dayton (OH)

U of Denver (CO)
U of Detroit Mercy (MI)
The U of Findlay (OH)
U of Hartford (CT)
U of Hawaii at Manoa (HI)
U of Houston (TX)
U of Idaho (ID)
U of Illinois at Chicago (IL)
U of Illinois at Springfield (IL)
The U of Iowa (IA)
The U of Kansas (KS)
U of Kentucky (KY)
U of La Verne (CA)
U of Louisville (KY)
U of Maine (ME)
U of Maryland, Baltimore County (MD)
U of Mary Washington (VA)
U of Massachusetts Amherst (MA)
U of Massachusetts Boston (MA)
U of Massachusetts Dartmouth (MA)
U of Massachusetts Lowell (MA)
U of Memphis (TN)
U of Miami (FL)
U of Michigan (MI)
U of Michigan–Dearborn (MI)
U of Michigan–Flint (MI)
U of Minnesota, Duluth (MN)
U of Minnesota, Morris (MN)
U of Minnesota, Twin Cities Campus (MN)
U of Missouri–St. Louis (MO)
U of Montana (MT)
U of Nebraska at Kearney (NE)
U of Nebraska–Lincoln (NE)
U of Nevada, Las Vegas (NV)
U of Nevada, Reno (NV)
U of New Hampshire (NH)
U of New Haven (CT)
U of New Mexico (NM)
The U of North Carolina at Chapel Hill (NC)
The U of North Carolina at Greensboro (NC)
The U of North Carolina Wilmington (NC)
U of North Dakota (ND)
U of Northern Colorado (CO)
U of Northern Iowa (IA)
U of North Florida (FL)
U of North Texas (TX)
U of Notre Dame (IN)
U of Oregon (OR)
U of Pennsylvania (PA)
U of Pittsburgh at Bradford (PA)
U of Portland (OR)
U of Puget Sound (WA)
U of Richmond (VA)
U of St. Francis (IL)
U of St. Thomas (TX)
U of San Diego (CA)
U of San Francisco (CA)
U of Science and Arts of Oklahoma (OK)
The U of Scranton (PA)
U of South Carolina (SC)
U of South Dakota (SD)
U of Southern Indiana (IN)
U of Southern Maine (ME)
U of South Florida (FL)
U of South Florida, St. Petersburg (FL)
The U of Tampa (FL)
The U of Tennessee (TN)
The U of Tennessee at Chattanooga (TN)
The U of Texas at Dallas (TX)
The U of Texas Rio Grande Valley (TX)
U of the Fraser Valley (BC, Canada)
U of the Pacific (CA)
The U of the South (TN)
The U of Toledo (OH)
U of Toronto (ON, Canada)
U of Utah (UT)
U of Vermont (VT)
U of Virginia (VA)
U of Washington (WA)
U of Waterloo (ON, Canada)
The U of Western Ontario (ON, Canada)
U of West Florida (FL)
U of West Georgia (GA)
U of Wisconsin–Eau Claire (WI)
U of Wisconsin–Green Bay (WI)
U of Wisconsin–La Crosse (WI)
U of Wisconsin–Madison (WI)
U of Wisconsin–Milwaukee (WI)
U of Wisconsin–Parkside (WI)
U of Wisconsin–Platteville (WI)
U of Wisconsin–Superior (WI)
Utah State U (UT)
Utah Valley U (UT)
Utica Coll (NY)
Valparaiso U (IN)
Vanderbilt U (TN)
Villanova U (PA)
Wabash Coll (IN)
Wake Forest U (NC)
Walla Walla U (WA)
Wartburg Coll (IA)
Washington & Jefferson Coll (PA)
Washington and Lee U (VA)
Washington Coll (MD)
Washington State U (WA)
Washington U in St. Louis (MO)
Wayne State U (MI)
Weber State U (UT)
Western Colorado U (CO)
Western Connecticut State U (CT)
Western Kentucky U (KY)
Western Michigan U (MI)
Western New England U (MA)
Western Oregon U (OR)
Western Washington U (WA)
Westfield State U (MA)
Westminster Coll (UT)
West Virginia U (WV)
Wheaton Coll (IL)
Wheaton Coll (MA)
Whitworth U (WA)
Wichita State U (KS)
Widener U (PA)
Willamette U (OR)
William & Mary (VA)
William Jewell Coll (MO)
William Paterson U of New Jersey (NJ)
Wilmington Coll (OH)
Winthrop U (SC)
Wittenberg U (OH)
Wofford Coll (SC)
Worcester Polytechnic Inst (MA)
Worcester State U (MA)
Wright State U (OH)
Wright State U–Lake Campus (OH)
Xavier U (OH)
Yale U (CT)
Yeshiva U (NY)
York Coll of Pennsylvania (PA)
Youngstown State U (OH)

ECONOMICS RELATED
Augsburg U (MN)
Barnard Coll (NY)
Bay Atlantic U (DC)
Bryan Coll (TN)
Central Washington U (WA)
Centre Coll (KY)
The Colorado Coll (CO)
Emory & Henry Coll (VA)
Lindenwood U (MO)
Muhlenberg Coll (PA)
Susquehanna U (PA)
U of California, Riverside (CA)
U of California, San Diego (CA)
U of Detroit Mercy (MI)
U of Maine (ME)
U of Minnesota, Duluth (MN)
U of Richmond (VA)
U of San Francisco (CA)
Valparaiso U (IN)
Washington & Jefferson Coll (PA)
Wayne State U (MI)
Western Washington U (WA)
Wittenberg U (OH)
Xavier U (OH)

EDUCATION
Alverno Coll (WI)
Arcadia U (PA)
Auburn U (AL)
Augsburg U (MN)
Avila U (MO)
The Baptist Coll of Florida (FL)
Barnard Coll (NY)
Barry U (FL)
Baylor U (TX)
Belmont Abbey Coll (NC)
Beloit Coll (WI)
Bemidji State U (MN)
Bennington Coll (VT)
Berea Coll (KY)
Bethany Lutheran Coll (MN)
Bethel U (IN)
Bethel U (MN)
Biola U (CA)
Birmingham-Southern Coll (AL)
Boise Bible Coll (ID)
Bowdoin Coll (ME)
Bowling Green State U (OH)
Bradley U (IL)
Brandeis U (MA)
Brandon U (MB, Canada)
Brenau U (GA)
Brown U (RI)
Bucknell U (PA)
Carson-Newman U (TN)
The Catholic U of America (DC)
Cedar Crest Coll (PA)
Central Methodist U (MO)
Central Washington U (WA)
City Coll of the City U of New York (NY)
Clark Atlanta U (GA)
Clark U (MA)
Coe Coll (IA)
Colby Coll (ME)
Colgate U (NY)
Coll of Saint Mary (NE)
The Colorado Coll (CO)
Columbia Coll (SC)
Concordia Coll (MN)
Concordia U Chicago (IL)
Concordia U, St. Paul (MN)
Concordia U Wisconsin (WI)
Dallas Christian Coll (TX)
Dominican Coll (NY)
Dominican U (IL)
Eastern Washington U (WA)
East Texas Baptist U (TX)
Elms Coll (MA)
Elon U (NC)
Emory U (GA)
Fitchburg State U (MA)
Fort Lewis Coll (CO)
Furman U (SC)
Gallaudet U (DC)
Glenville State Coll (WV)
Goshen Coll (IN)
Guilford Coll (NC)
Gustavus Adolphus Coll (MN)
Gwynedd Mercy U (PA)
Hampshire Coll (MA)
Hampton U (VA)
Harris-Stowe State U (MO)
Hope Intl U (CA)
Howard U (DC)
Illinois Coll (IL)
Illinois Wesleyan U (IL)
Inter American U of Puerto Rico, Barranquitas Campus (PR)
Inter American U of Puerto Rico, San Germán Campus (PR)
Jacksonville State U (AL)
Jacksonville U (FL)
John Carroll U (OH)
Keuka Coll (NY)
LaGrange Coll (GA)
Lake Forest Coll (IL)
Lancaster Bible Coll (PA)
Lebanese American U (Lebanon)
Lesley U (MA)
Liberty U (VA)
Limestone Coll (SC)
Lincoln Memorial U (TN)
Lindenwood U (MO)
Lipscomb U (TN)
Loyola U Maryland (MD)
Manhattan Coll (NY)
Manhattanville Coll (NY)
Mansfield U of Pennsylvania (PA)
Marian U (IN)
Marietta Coll (OH)
Mayville State U (ND)
Merrimack Coll (MA)
Miami Dade Coll (FL)
Miami U (OH)
Miami U Hamilton (OH)
Miami U Middletown (OH)
Michigan State U (MI)
Minnesota State U Mankato (MN)
Missouri Southern State U (MO)
Missouri Valley Coll (MO)
Mount Marty Coll (SD)
Mount Saint Mary's U (CA)
Mount Vernon Nazarene U (OH)
Muskingum U (OH)
Nazareth Coll of Rochester (NY)
New England Coll (NH)
Newman U (KS)
New York U (NY)
Niagara U (NY)
Northwestern U (IL)
Northwest U (WA)
Nova Southeastern U (FL)
Ohio Christian U (OH)
Ohio Dominican U (OH)
The Ohio State U (OH)
Ohio Wesleyan U (OH)
Oklahoma Baptist U (OK)
Pacific U (OR)
Purdue U Fort Wayne (IN)
Regent U (VA)
Regis Coll (MA)
Rhodes Coll (TN)
Roger Williams U (RI)
Rosemont Coll (PA)
Rowan U (NJ)
Saginaw Valley State U (MI)
St. Catherine U (MN)
Saint Francis U (PA)
Saint Louis U (MO)
St. Thomas Aquinas Coll (NY)
St. Thomas U - New Brunswick (NB, Canada)
Salem State U (MA)
Schreiner U (TX)
Simmons U (MA)
Simon Fraser U (BC, Canada)
Skidmore Coll (NY)
Smith Coll (MA)
Southeastern U (FL)
Southern Methodist U (TX)
Southwest Baptist U (MO)
Southwestern U (TX)
Springfield Coll (MA)
State U of New York at Fredonia (NY)
State U of New York at Oswego (NY)
State U of New York Coll at Geneseo (NY)
State U of New York Coll at Oneonta (NY)
State U of New York Empire State Coll (NY)
Stetson U (FL)
Susquehanna U (PA)
Tabor Coll (KS)
Taylor U (IN)
Tennessee Wesleyan U (TN)
Texas Christian U (TX)
Texas Lutheran U (TX)
Tiffin U (OH)
Trine U (IN)
Union U (TN)
U of Alaska Southeast (AK)
U of Arkansas (AR)
U of Arkansas at Little Rock (AR)
U of California, Irvine (CA)
U of Charleston (WV)
U of Colorado Denver (CO)
U of Dallas (TX)
U of Detroit Mercy (MI)
U of Hawaii at Manoa (HI)
U of Hawaii–West Oahu (HI)
U of Massachusetts Amherst (MA)
U of Massachusetts Boston (MA)
U of Miami (FL)
U of Michigan–Dearborn (MI)
U of Michigan–Flint (MI)
U of Minnesota, Duluth (MN)
U of Missouri–St. Louis (MO)
U of Montana (MT)
U of Nevada, Las Vegas (NV)
U of North Texas (TX)
U of Oregon (OR)
U of Pikeville (KY)
U of Pittsburgh at Greensburg (PA)
U of Portland (OR)
U of Saint Francis (IN)
U of Saint Mary (KS)
U of South Dakota (SD)
The U of Texas at San Antonio (TX)
U of the Fraser Valley (BC, Canada)
U of the Pacific (CA)
U of Toronto (ON, Canada)
The U of Tulsa (OK)
U of Utah (UT)
U of Vermont (VT)
U of Washington, Bothell (WA)
U of Washington, Tacoma (WA)
The U of Western Ontario (ON, Canada)
U of Wisconsin–Green Bay (WI)
U of Wisconsin–Milwaukee (WI)
U of Wisconsin–Platteville (WI)
Upper Iowa U (IA)
Vanderbilt U (TN)
Vanguard U of Southern California (CA)
Washington & Jefferson Coll (PA)
Washington U in St. Louis (MO)
Western New Mexico U (NM)
West Liberty U (WV)
Whitworth U (WA)
Wilkes U (PA)
William Penn U (IA)
Wilmington Coll (OH)
Wittenberg U (OH)
Xavier U (OH)
Xavier U of Louisiana (LA)
Youngstown State U (OH)

EDUCATIONAL ADMINISTRATION AND SUPERVISION RELATED
The U of Western Ontario (ON, Canada)

EDUCATIONAL ASSESSMENT, EVALUATION, AND RESEARCH RELATED
Penn State Altoona (PA)
Penn State Berks (PA)
Penn State U Park (PA)

EDUCATIONAL, INSTRUCTIONAL, AND CURRICULUM SUPERVISION
Millikin U (IL)
Saint Joseph's U (PA)
Sam Houston State U (TX)

EDUCATIONAL/ INSTRUCTIONAL TECHNOLOGY
Academy of Art U (CA)
Bayamón Central U (PR)
Bowling Green State U (OH)
Bridgewater State U (MA)
Eastern Washington U (WA)
Jacksonville State U (AL)
Mississippi State U (MS)
Rhode Island Coll (RI)
Sam Houston State U (TX)
State U of New York Coll at Potsdam (NY)
Tiffin U (OH)
U of Michigan–Dearborn (MI)
The U of Western Ontario (ON, Canada)
Wayne State U (MI)
Western Oregon U (OR)
Widener U (PA)

EDUCATIONAL LEADERSHIP AND ADMINISTRATION
Avila U (MO)
Bradley U (IL)
Eastern Washington U (WA)
Howard U (DC)
Jacksonville State U (AL)
Notre Dame Coll (OH)
Sam Houston State U (TX)
U of the Fraser Valley (BC, Canada)

EDUCATIONAL PSYCHOLOGY
Jacksonville State U (AL)
Mississippi State U (MS)
Saint Vincent Coll (PA)

EDUCATIONAL STATISTICS AND RESEARCH METHODS
Bucknell U (PA)

EDUCATION (MULTIPLE LEVELS)
Adams State U (CO)
Anderson U (SC)
Arcadia U (PA)
Assumption Coll (MA)
Augustana U (SD)
Austin Peay State U (TN)
Averett U (VA)
Biola U (CA)
Birmingham-Southern Coll (AL)
Bowling Green State U (OH)
Coll of Charleston (SC)
Coll of Saint Elizabeth (NJ)
Coll of Saint Mary (NE)
The Coll of Saint Rose (NY)

The Coll of St. Scholastica (MN)
Columbia Intl U (SC)
Concordia U Chicago (IL)
Concordia U Wisconsin (WI)
DePaul U (IL)
Dominican U (IL)
Eastern Washington U (WA)
Emory & Henry Coll (VA)
Fairleigh Dickinson U (NJ)
Florida Southern Coll (FL)
Gannon U (PA)
Geneva Coll (PA)
Georgetown Coll (KY)
Gwynedd Mercy U (PA)
Hamline U (MN)
Harding U (AR)
Hofstra U (NY)
Illinois Coll (IL)
King U (TN)
Lindenwood U (MO)
Manhattan Coll (NY)
Merrimack Coll (MA)
Middle Tennessee State U (TN)
Molloy Coll (NY)
Mount Saint Mary Coll (NY)
New England Coll (NH)
Niagara U (NY)
Northwest Christian U (OR)
Northwestern Coll (IA)
Notre Dame Coll (OH)
Ohio Wesleyan U (OH)
Saint Mary-of-the-Woods Coll (IN)
Samford U (AL)
Slippery Rock U of Pennsylvania (PA)
Stockton U (NJ)
Tennessee Wesleyan U (TN)
Texas Lutheran U (TX)
Troy U (AL)
U of Central Florida (FL)
U of Louisiana at Lafayette (LA)
U of Louisville (KY)
U of Memphis (TN)
U of Michigan–Flint (MI)
U of Minnesota, Duluth (MN)
U of Nebraska–Lincoln (NE)
U of Providence (MT)
U of South Florida, St. Petersburg (FL)
The U of Tennessee at Martin (TN)
The U of Toledo (OH)
The U of West Alabama (AL)
Virginia Wesleyan U (VA)
Wake Forest U (NC)
Walla Walla U (WA)
Washington U in St. Louis (MO)
Wayland Baptist U (TX)
Western Kentucky U (KY)
Western New Mexico U (NM)
William Jewell Coll (MO)

EDUCATION RELATED
Arcadia U (PA)
Arizona State U at the Tempe campus (AZ)
Arizona State U at the West campus (AZ)
Becker Coll (MA)
Bowling Green State U (OH)
Brigham Young U (UT)
Butler U (IN)
California State Polytechnic U, Pomona (CA)
Concordia U, St. Paul (MN)
Eastern Oregon U (OR)
Edgewood Coll (WI)
Fort Lewis Coll (CO)
Gonzaga U (WA)
Indiana U Bloomington (IN)
Lancaster Bible Coll (PA)
Lee U (TN)
Mount Holyoke Coll (MA)
Northwest Missouri State U (MO)
Northwest Nazarene U (ID)
Ottawa U (KS)
Rowan U (NJ)
Saginaw Valley State U (MI)
Saint Mary-of-the-Woods Coll (IN)
Saint Mary's U of Minnesota (MN)
St. Petersburg Coll (FL)
State U of New York at New Paltz (NY)
Towson U (MD)
The U of Arizona (AZ)
U of Maine at Presque Isle (ME)
U of Miami (FL)
U of Minnesota, Duluth (MN)
U of Minnesota, Twin Cities Campus (MN)
U of Northern Iowa (IA)
U of South Alabama (AL)
U of Utah (UT)
U of Washington (WA)
U of Waterloo (ON, Canada)
The U of West Alabama (AL)
U of Wisconsin–Madison (WI)
Vanderbilt U (TN)
Western Michigan U (MI)

EDUCATION (SPECIFIC LEVELS AND METHODS) RELATED
Appalachian State U (NC)
Bayamón Central U (PR)
Brigham Young U (UT)
Emory & Henry Coll (VA)
Felician U (NJ)
Inter American U of Puerto Rico, Metropolitan Campus (PR)
Inter American U of Puerto Rico, San Germán Campus (PR)
King U (TN)
Lenoir-Rhyne U (NC)
Mercer U, Macon (GA)
Ottawa U (KS)
Roanoke Coll (VA)
Rowan U (NJ)
State U of New York Coll at Potsdam (NY)
U of Northwestern–St. Paul (MN)
Utah State U (UT)
Washington U in St. Louis (MO)
Xavier U (OH)

EDUCATION (SPECIFIC SUBJECT AREAS) RELATED
Anderson U (SC)
Andrews U (MI)
Appalachian State U (NC)
Augsburg U (MN)
Averett U (VA)
Avila U (MO)
Ball State U (IN)
Bayamón Central U (PR)
Baylor U (TX)
Bowling Green State U (OH)
Brigham Young U (UT)
Eastern Kentucky U (KY)
Eastern Michigan U (MI)
Florida Inst of Technology (FL)
Florida State U (FL)
Graceland U (IA)
Indiana U Bloomington (IN)
Knox Coll (IL)
Louisiana Tech U (LA)
Madonna U (MI)
Marywood U (PA)
Minot State U (ND)
Missouri State U (MO)
Murray State U (KY)
New York U (NY)
North Central U (MN)
Northwest Missouri State U (MO)
Old Dominion U (VA)
Pittsburg State U (KS)
Roanoke Coll (VA)
U of Kentucky (KY)
U of Minnesota, Duluth (MN)
U of Nebraska–Lincoln (NE)
U of Wisconsin–Eau Claire (WI)
U of Wisconsin–Stout (WI)
Wartburg Coll (IA)
Wayne State Coll (NE)
Weber State U (UT)
Western Michigan U (MI)

ELECTRICAL AND ELECTRONIC ENGINEERING TECHNOLOGIES RELATED
Excelsior Coll (NY)
LeTourneau U (TX)
Penn State Berks (PA)
Southern Illinois U Carbondale (IL)

ELECTRICAL AND ELECTRONICS ENGINEERING
American Public U System (WV)
Anderson U (IN)
Arizona State U at the Tempe campus (AZ)
Arkansas Tech U (AR)
Auburn U (AL)
Baylor U (TX)
Bethel U (MN)
Binghamton U, State U of New York (NY)
Boise State U (ID)
Bradley U (IL)
Brown U (RI)
Bucknell U (PA)
California Polytechnic State U, San Luis Obispo (CA)
California State Polytechnic U, Pomona (CA)
California State U, Fresno (CA)
California State U, Fullerton (CA)
California State U, Long Beach (CA)
California State U, Los Angeles (CA)
California State U, Northridge (CA)
California State U, Sacramento (CA)
Calvin Coll (MI)
Carnegie Mellon U (PA)
The Catholic U of America (DC)
Cedarville U (OH)
Central Michigan U (MI)
The Citadel, The Military Coll of South Carolina (SC)
City Coll of the City U of New York (NY)
Clarkson U (NY)
Clemson U (SC)
Coll of Staten Island of the City U of New York (NY)
Colorado School of Mines (CO)
Colorado State U (CO)
Cornell U (NY)
Dominican U (IL)
Drexel U (PA)
Dunwoody Coll of Technology (MN)
Eastern Illinois U (IL)
Eastern Washington U (WA)
Fairfield U (CT)
Fairleigh Dickinson U (NJ)
Florida A&M U (FL)
Florida Atlantic U (FL)
Florida Inst of Technology (FL)
Florida Polytechnic U (FL)
Florida State U (FL)
Franklin W. Olin Coll of Eng (MA)
Gannon U (PA)
George Fox U (OR)
George Mason U (VA)
The George Washington U (DC)
Georgia Inst of Technology (GA)
Georgia Southern U (GA)
Gonzaga U (WA)
Grand Valley State U (MI)
Hampton U (VA)
Harding U (AR)
High Point U (NC)
Hofstra U (NY)
Houston Baptist U (TX)
Howard U (DC)
Illinois Inst of Technology (IL)
Indiana U-Purdue U Indianapolis (IN)
Inter American U of Puerto Rico, Bayamón Campus (PR)
Iowa State U of Science and Technology (IA)
Jacksonville U (FL)
Johns Hopkins U (MD)
Kansas State U (KS)
Kennesaw State U (GA)
Kettering U (MI)
Lafayette Coll (PA)
Lamar U (TX)
Lawrence Technological U (MI)
Lebanese American U (Lebanon)
Lehigh U (PA)
LeTourneau U (TX)
Lewis U (IL)
Liberty U (VA)
Louisiana State U and A&M Coll (LA)
Louisiana Tech U (LA)
Loyola Marymount U (CA)
Manhattan Coll (NY)
Marquette U (WI)
Marshall U (WV)
Merrimack Coll (MA)
Messiah Coll (PA)
Miami U (OH)
Miami U Hamilton (OH)
Miami U Middletown (OH)
Michigan State U (MI)
Michigan Technological U (MI)
Milligan Coll (TN)
Milwaukee School of Eng (WI)
Minnesota State U Mankato (MN)
Mississippi State U (MS)
Missouri U of Science and Technology (MO)
Montana State U (MT)
Montana Technological U (MT)
Mount Vernon Nazarene U (OH)
National U (CA)
New England Inst of Technology (RI)
New Jersey Inst of Technology (NJ)
New Mexico Highlands U (NM)
New Mexico Inst of Mining and Technology (NM)
New York Inst of Technology (NY)
New York U (NY)
Northern Arizona U (AZ)
Northern Illinois U (IL)
Northwestern U (IL)
Oakland U (MI)
The Ohio State U (OH)
Oklahoma State U (OK)
Old Dominion U (VA)
Oral Roberts U (OK)
Penn State Abington (PA)
Penn State Altoona (PA)
Penn State Beaver (PA)
Penn State Berks (PA)
Penn State Brandywine (PA)
Penn State DuBois (PA)
Penn State Erie, The Behrend Coll (PA)
Penn State Fayette, The Eberly Campus (PA)
Penn State Greater Allegheny (PA)
Penn State Harrisburg (PA)
Penn State Hazleton (PA)
Penn State Lehigh Valley (PA)
Penn State Mont Alto (PA)
Penn State New Kensington (PA)
Penn State Schuylkill (PA)
Penn State Shenango (PA)
Penn State U Park (PA)
Penn State Wilkes-Barre (PA)
Penn State York (PA)
Polytechnic U of Puerto Rico (PR)
Portland State U (OR)
Prairie View A&M U (TX)
Princeton U (NJ)
Purdue U Fort Wayne (IN)
Purdue U Northwest (IN)
Rice U (TX)
Roger Williams U (RI)
Rose-Hulman Inst of Technology (IN)
Rowan U (NJ)
Saginaw Valley State U (MI)
St. Cloud State U (MN)
Saint Louis U (MO)
St. Mary's U (TX)
San Diego State U (CA)
San Francisco State U (CA)
San Jose State U (CA)
Santa Clara U (CA)
Seattle U (WA)
South Dakota State U (SD)
Southern California Inst of Technology (CA)
Southern Illinois U Carbondale (IL)
Southern Illinois U Edwardsville (IL)
Southern Methodist U (TX)
Stanford U (CA)
State U of New York at New Paltz (NY)
State U of New York at Oswego (NY)
State U of New York Maritime Coll (NY)
Stevens Inst of Technology (NJ)
Stony Brook U, State U of New York (NY)
Tarleton State U (TX)
Temple U (PA)
Texas A&M U (TX)
Texas A&M U–Commerce (TX)
Texas A&M U–Corpus Christi (TX)
Texas A&M U–Kingsville (TX)
Texas Southern U (TX)
Texas State U (TX)
Texas Tech U (TX)
Trine U (IN)
Tulane U (LA)
Union Coll (NY)
United States Military Acad (NY)
U at Buffalo, the State U of New York (NY)
The U of Akron (OH)
The U of Alabama (AL)
The U of Alabama at Birmingham (AL)
The U of Alabama in Huntsville (AL)
U of Alaska Fairbanks (AK)
U of Arkansas (AR)
U of California, Berkeley (CA)
U of California, Irvine (CA)
U of California, Los Angeles (CA)
U of California, Riverside (CA)
U of California, San Diego (CA)
U of California, Santa Barbara (CA)
U of California, Santa Cruz (CA)
U of Central Florida (FL)
U of Cincinnati (OH)
U of Colorado Boulder (CO)
U of Colorado Colorado Springs (CO)
U of Colorado Denver (CO)
U of Dayton (OH)
U of Denver (CO)
U of Detroit Mercy (MI)
U of Hartford (CT)
U of Hawaii at Manoa (HI)
U of Houston (TX)
U of Idaho (ID)
U of Illinois at Chicago (IL)
The U of Iowa (IA)
The U of Kansas (KS)
U of Kentucky (KY)
U of Louisiana at Lafayette (LA)
U of Louisville (KY)
U of Maine (ME)
U of Massachusetts Amherst (MA)
U of Massachusetts Boston (MA)
U of Massachusetts Dartmouth (MA)
U of Massachusetts Lowell (MA)
U of Memphis (TN)
U of Miami (FL)
U of Michigan (MI)
U of Michigan–Dearborn (MI)
U of Minnesota, Duluth (MN)
U of Minnesota, Twin Cities Campus (MN)
U of Missouri–St. Louis (MO)
U of Nebraska–Lincoln (NE)
U of Nevada, Las Vegas (NV)
U of Nevada, Reno (NV)
U of New Hampshire (NH)
U of New Haven (CT)
U of New Mexico (NM)
The U of North Carolina at Charlotte (NC)
U of North Dakota (ND)
U of North Florida (FL)
U of North Texas (TX)
U of Notre Dame (IN)
U of Pennsylvania (PA)
U of Portland (OR)
U of San Diego (CA)
The U of Scranton (PA)
U of South Alabama (AL)
U of South Carolina (SC)
U of Southern Maine (ME)
U of South Florida (FL)
The U of Tennessee (TN)
The U of Tennessee at Chattanooga (TN)
The U of Texas at Dallas (TX)
The U of Texas at El Paso (TX)
The U of Texas at San Antonio (TX)
The U of Texas of the Permian Basin (TX)
The U of Texas Rio Grande Valley (TX)
U of the Pacific (CA)
The U of Toledo (OH)
U of Toronto (ON, Canada)
The U of Tulsa (OK)
U of Utah (UT)
U of Vermont (VT)
U of Virginia (VA)
U of Washington (WA)
U of Washington, Bothell (WA)
U of Washington, Tacoma (WA)
U of Waterloo (ON, Canada)
The U of Western Ontario (ON, Canada)
U of West Florida (FL)
U of Wisconsin–Madison (WI)
U of Wisconsin–Milwaukee (WI)
U of Wisconsin–Platteville (WI)
U of Wyoming (WY)

Utah State U (UT)
Valparaiso U (IN)
Vanderbilt U (TN)
Villanova U (PA)
Virginia Commonwealth U (VA)
Walla Walla U (WA)
Washington State U (WA)
Washington State U–Tri-Cities (WA)
Washington State U–Vancouver (WA)
Washington U in St. Louis (MO)
Wayne State U (MI)
Weber State U (UT)
Wentworth Inst of Technology (MA)
Western Carolina U (NC)
Western Kentucky U (KY)
Western Michigan U (MI)
Western New England U (MA)
Western Washington U (WA)
West Virginia U (WV)
Wichita State U (KS)
Widener U (PA)
Wilkes U (PA)
Worcester Polytechnic Inst (MA)
Wright State U (OH)
Wright State U–Lake Campus (OH)
Yale U (CT)
York Coll of Pennsylvania (PA)
Youngstown State U (OH)

ELECTRICAL, ELECTRONIC AND COMMUNICATIONS ENGINEERING TECHNOLOGY
Benedictine Coll (KS)
Bowling Green State U (OH)
California State Polytechnic U, Pomona (CA)
California State U, Long Beach (CA)
California U of Pennsylvania (PA)
Central Connecticut State U (CT)
Central Washington U (WA)
Eastern Michigan U (MI)
Fairleigh Dickinson U (NJ)
Farmingdale State Coll (NY)
Ferris State U (MI)
Fitchburg State U (MA)
Florida A&M U (FL)
Hampton U (VA)
Indiana State U (IN)
Indiana U-Purdue U Indianapolis (IN)
Inter American U of Puerto Rico, Aguadilla Campus (PR)
Inter American U of Puerto Rico, San Germán Campus (PR)
Jacksonville State U (AL)
Kennesaw State U (GA)
LeTourneau U (TX)
Louisiana Tech U (LA)
Miami Dade Coll (FL)
Michigan Technological U (MI)
Middle Tennessee State U (TN)
Minnesota State U Mankato (MN)
New York City Coll of Technology of the City U of New York (NY)
Northern Kentucky U (KY)
Northwestern State U of Louisiana (LA)
Oklahoma State U (OK)
Penn State Erie, The Behrend Coll (PA)
Pittsburg State U (KS)
Prairie View A&M U (TX)
Purdue U Fort Wayne (IN)
Purdue U Northwest (IN)
Sam Houston State U (TX)
South Dakota State U (SD)
State U of New York Coll of Technology at Alfred (NY)
State U of New York Coll of Technology at Canton (NY)
Texas A&M U (TX)
Texas Southern U (TX)
Troy U (AL)
The U of Akron (OH)
U of Arkansas at Little Rock (AR)
U of Cincinnati (OH)
U of Dayton (OH)
U of Hartford (CT)
U of Houston (TX)
U of Maine (ME)
U of Massachusetts Lowell (MA)
U of Memphis (TN)
The U of North Carolina at Charlotte (NC)
U of North Texas (TX)
U of Southern Mississippi (MS)
U of Wisconsin–Green Bay (WI)
Valencia Coll (FL)
Vermont Tech Coll (VT)
Wayne State U (MI)
Weber State U (UT)
Western Carolina U (NC)
Youngstown State U (OH)

ELECTRICAL, ELECTRONICS AND COMMUNICATIONS ENGINEERING RELATED
Marquette U (WI)
The U of Alabama (AL)
The U of Arizona (AZ)
U of Miami (FL)

ELECTRICAL/ELECTRONICS EQUIPMENT INSTALLATION AND REPAIR
Lewis-Clark State Coll (ID)

ELECTROMECHANICAL ENGINEERING
Wentworth Inst of Technology (MA)

ELECTROMECHANICAL TECHNOLOGY
Murray State U (KY)
Purdue U Northwest (IN)
State U of New York Coll of Technology at Alfred (NY)
U of Hartford (CT)
U of Northern Iowa (IA)
The U of Tennessee at Chattanooga (TN)
The U of Toledo (OH)
Vermont Tech Coll (VT)
Wayne State U (MI)

ELECTRONEURODIAGNOSTIC / ELECTROENCEPHALOGRAPHIC TECHNOLOGY
Baptist Coll of Health Sciences (TN)

ELEMENTARY AND MIDDLE SCHOOL ADMINISTRATION/ PRINCIPALSHIP
The Ohio State U (OH)

ELEMENTARY EDUCATION
Abilene Christian U (TX)
Alfred U (NY)
Alverno Coll (WI)
American U (DC)
Anderson U (IN)
Anderson U (SC)
Andrews U (MI)
Appalachian State U (NC)
Aquinas Coll (MI)
Arcadia U (PA)
Arizona Christian U (AZ)
Arizona State U at the Polytechnic campus (AZ)
Arizona State U at the Tempe campus (AZ)
Arizona State U at the West campus (AZ)
Arkansas Tech U (AR)
Athens State U (AL)
Auburn U (AL)
Auburn U at Montgomery (AL)
Augsburg U (MN)
Augustana Coll (IL)
Augustana U (SD)
Aurora U (IL)
Austin Coll (TX)
Avila U (MO)
Baker U (KS)
Ball State U (IN)
The Baptist Coll of Florida (FL)
Barry U (FL)
Barton Coll (NC)
Bayamón Central U (PR)
Baylor U (TX)
Belhaven U (MS)
Belmont Abbey Coll (NC)
Belmont U (TN)
Beloit Coll (WI)
Bemidji State U (MN)
Benedictine Coll (KS)
Benedictine U (IL)
Bethany Lutheran Coll (MN)
Bethel U (IN)
Bethel U (MN)
Bethel U (TN)
Biola U (CA)
Birmingham-Southern Coll (AL)
Black Hills State U (SD)
Boise State U (ID)
Boston Coll (MA)
Bowling Green State U (OH)
Bradley U (IL)
Brandon U (MB, Canada)
Brenau U (GA)
Bridgewater State U (MA)
Bryan Coll (TN)
Bryn Athyn Coll of the New Church (PA)
Bucknell U (PA)
Butler U (IN)
Caldwell U (NJ)
Calumet Coll of Saint Joseph (IN)
Calvin Coll (MI)
Cameron U (OK)
Campbellsville U (KY)
Carson-Newman U (TN)
Carthage Coll (WI)
Catawba Coll (NC)
The Catholic U of America (DC)
Cedar Crest Coll (PA)
Central Christian Coll of Kansas (KS)
Central Coll (IA)
Central Connecticut State U (CT)
Central Methodist U (MO)
Central Washington U (WA)
Chaminade U of Honolulu (HI)
Champlain Coll (VT)
Chatham U (PA)
Chestnut Hill Coll (PA)
City Coll of the City U of New York (NY)
Clark U (MA)
Clayton State U (GA)
Clemson U (SC)
Coastal Carolina U (SC)
Coe Coll (IA)
Coll of Charleston (SC)
Coll of Saint Benedict (MN)
Coll of Saint Mary (NE)
The Coll of Saint Rose (NY)
The Coll of St. Scholastica (MN)
Coll of Staten Island of the City U of New York (NY)
Coll of the Ozarks (MO)
Columbia Coll (SC)
Concordia Coll (MN)
Concordia U Chicago (IL)
Concordia U, St. Paul (MN)
Concordia U Wisconsin (WI)
Cornell Coll (IA)
Covenant Coll (GA)
Creighton U (NE)
Culver-Stockton Coll (MO)
Dakota State U (SD)
Dallas Baptist U (TX)
Daytona State Coll (FL)
Delta State U (MS)
DePaul U (IL)
DeSales U (PA)
Dickinson State U (ND)
Doane U (NE)
Dominican Coll (NY)
Dominican U (IL)
Donnelly Coll (KS)
Drake U (IA)
Drexel U (PA)
Drury U (MO)
East Carolina U (NC)
East Central U (OK)
Eastern Illinois U (IL)
Eastern Kentucky U (KY)
Eastern Michigan U (MI)
Eastern New Mexico U (NM)
East Texas Baptist U (TX)
Edgewood Coll (WI)
Elms Coll (MA)
Elon U (NC)
Emmanuel Coll (GA)
Emmanuel Coll (MA)
Emmaus Bible Coll (IA)
Emporia State U (KS)
Endicott Coll (MA)
Evangel U (MO)
Fayetteville State U (NC)
Felician U (NJ)
Ferris State U (MI)
Fitchburg State U (MA)
Flagler Coll (FL)
Florida A&M U (FL)
Florida Atlantic U (FL)
Florida Gulf Coast U (FL)
Florida Southern Coll (FL)
Florida SouthWestern State Coll (FL)
Florida State U (FL)
Fort Lewis Coll (CO)
Framingham State U (MA)
Francis Marion U (SC)
Franklin Coll (IN)
Freed-Hardeman U (TN)
Friends U (KS)
Furman U (SC)
Geneva Coll (PA)
George Fox U (OR)
Georgetown Coll (KY)
Georgia Gwinnett Coll (GA)
Georgian Court U (NJ)
Georgia Southern U (GA)
Glenville State Coll (WV)
Gordon Coll (MA)
Goshen Coll (IN)
Governors State U (IL)
Graceland U (IA)
Grambling State U (LA)
Grand Valley State U (MI)
Guilford Coll (NC)
Gustavus Adolphus Coll (MN)
Hampton U (VA)
Hanover Coll (IN)
Harding U (AR)
Harris-Stowe State U (MO)
High Point U (NC)
Hofstra U (NY)
Hope Coll (MI)
Hope Intl U (CA)
Houston Baptist U (TX)
Husson U (ME)
Illinois Coll (IL)
Illinois State U (IL)
Illinois Wesleyan U (IL)
Indiana State U (IN)
Indiana U Bloomington (IN)
Indiana U East (IN)
Indiana U Kokomo (IN)
Indiana U Northwest (IN)
Indiana U-Purdue U Indianapolis (IN)
Indiana U South Bend (IN)
Indiana U Southeast (IN)
Inter American U of Puerto Rico, Aguadilla Campus (PR)
Inter American U of Puerto Rico, Metropolitan Campus (PR)
Inter American U of Puerto Rico, San Germán Campus (PR)
Iona Coll (NY)
Iowa State U of Science and Technology (IA)
Jacksonville State U (AL)
Jacksonville U (FL)
John Brown U (AR)
Johnson U (TN)
Johnson U Florida (FL)
Kansas State U (KS)
Kansas Wesleyan U (KS)
Kean U (NJ)
Keiser U, Fort Lauderdale (FL)
Kennesaw State U (GA)
Kentucky Mountain Bible Coll (KY)
Keuka Coll (NY)
King's Coll (PA)
The King's U (AB, Canada)
Knox Coll (IL)
Kutztown U of Pennsylvania (PA)
LaGrange Coll (GA)
Lancaster Bible Coll (PA)
La Roche U (PA)
Lasell Coll (MA)
La Sierra U (CA)
Lee U (TN)
Le Moyne Coll (NY)
Lenoir-Rhyne U (NC)
Lesley U (MA)
LeTourneau U (TX)
Lewis-Clark State Coll (ID)
Lewis U (IL)
Liberty U (VA)
Limestone Coll (SC)
Lincoln Memorial U (TN)
Lincoln U (MO)
Lindenwood U (MO)
Linfield Coll (OR)
Lipscomb U (TN)
Loras Coll (IA)
Louisiana State U and A&M Coll (LA)
Louisiana State U in Shreveport (LA)
Louisiana Tech U (LA)
Loyola U Chicago (IL)
Loyola U Maryland (MD)
Lynn U (FL)
Madonna U (MI)
Manhattan Coll (NY)
Manhattanville Coll (NY)
Mansfield U of Pennsylvania (PA)
Marian U (IN)
Marietta Coll (OH)
Marquette U (WI)
Martin Luther Coll (MN)
Marymount U (VA)
Maryville U of Saint Louis (MO)
Marywood U (PA)
Mayville State U (ND)
McDaniel Coll (MD)
McKendree U (IL)
McMurry U (TX)
McNeese State U (LA)
Mercer U, Macon (GA)
Merrimack Coll (MA)
Michigan State U (MI)
Mid-America Christian U (OK)
MidAmerica Nazarene U (KS)
Middlebury Coll (VT)
Midway U (KY)
Millikin U (IL)
Minnesota State U Mankato (MN)
Minot State U (ND)
Mississippi State U (MS)
Missouri Southern State U (MO)
Missouri State U (MO)
Missouri Valley Coll (MO)
Molloy Coll (NY)
Montana State U (MT)
Morehead State U (KY)
Mount Marty Coll (SD)
Mount Mercy U (IA)
Mount Saint Mary's U (CA)
Mount St. Mary's U (MD)
Multnomah U (OR)
Murray State U (KY)
National U (CA)
Nebraska Wesleyan U (NE)
New England Coll (NH)
Newman U (KS)
New Mexico Highlands U (NM)
New York U (NY)
Niagara U (NY)
North Carolina Central U (NC)
North Central U (MN)
Northeastern Illinois U (IL)
Northeastern State U (OK)
Northern Arizona U (AZ)
Northern Illinois U (IL)
Northern Kentucky U (KY)
Northern State U (SD)
North Greenville U (SC)
Northwest Christian U (OR)
Northwestern Coll (IA)
Northwestern State U of Louisiana (LA)
Northwest Nazarene U (ID)
Northwest U (WA)
Nova Southeastern U (FL)
Nyack Coll (NY)
Oakland City U (IN)
Oakland U (MI)
The Ohio State U (OH)
The Ohio State U at Lima (OH)
The Ohio State U at Mansfield (OH)
The Ohio State U at Marion (OH)
The Ohio State U at Newark (OH)
Ohio Valley U (WV)
Ohio Wesleyan U (OH)
Oklahoma Baptist U (OK)
Oklahoma State U (OK)
Old Dominion U (VA)
Olivet Nazarene U (IL)
Oral Roberts U (OK)
Ottawa U (KS)
Pace U, Pleasantville Campus (NY)
Pacific U (OR)
Palm Beach Atlantic U (FL)
Penn State Abington (PA)
Penn State Altoona (PA)
Penn State Beaver (PA)
Penn State Berks (PA)
Penn State Brandywine (PA)
Penn State DuBois (PA)
Penn State Erie, The Behrend Coll (PA)
Penn State Fayette, The Eberly Campus (PA)
Penn State Greater Allegheny (PA)
Penn State Harrisburg (PA)
Penn State Hazleton (PA)

Penn State Lehigh Valley (PA)
Penn State Mont Alto (PA)
Penn State New Kensington (PA)
Penn State Schuylkill (PA)
Penn State Shenango (PA)
Penn State U Park (PA)
Penn State Wilkes-Barre (PA)
Penn State York (PA)
Pittsburg State U (KS)
Point Loma Nazarene U (CA)
Polk State Coll (FL)
Purdue U Fort Wayne (IN)
Purdue U Northwest (IN)
Queens Coll of the City U of New York (NY)
Queens U of Charlotte (NC)
Regis Coll (MA)
Rhode Island Coll (RI)
Roanoke Coll (VA)
Rochester U (MI)
Rocky Mountain Coll (MT)
Roger Williams U (RI)
Rollins Coll (FL)
Rosemont Coll (PA)
Rowan U (NJ)
The Sage Colls (NY)
Saginaw Valley State U (MI)
St. Ambrose U (IA)
St. Bonaventure U (NY)
St. Catherine U (MN)
St. Cloud State U (MN)
Saint Francis U (PA)
St. John Fisher Coll (NY)
Saint John's U (MN)
Saint Joseph's U (PA)
Saint Leo U (FL)
Saint Mary-of-the-Woods Coll (IN)
Saint Mary's Coll (IN)
Saint Mary's U of Minnesota (MN)
St. Norbert Coll (WI)
St. Petersburg Coll (FL)
St. Thomas Aquinas Coll (NY)
St. Thomas U - Florida (FL)
Salem State U (MA)
Salisbury U (MD)
Salve Regina U (RI)
Schreiner U (TX)
Seton Hill U (PA)
Shenandoah U (VA)
Shepherd U (WV)
Siena Heights U (MI)
Simmons U (MA)
Skidmore Coll (NY)
Southeastern Louisiana U (LA)
Southeastern U (FL)
Southeast Missouri State U (MO)
Southern Illinois U Carbondale (IL)
Southern Illinois U Edwardsville (IL)
Southwest Baptist U (MO)
Southwestern Coll (KS)
Southwestern Oklahoma State U (OK)
Spring Arbor U (MI)
Springfield Coll (MA)
Spring Hill Coll (AL)
State U of New York at Fredonia (NY)
State U of New York at New Paltz (NY)
State U of New York at Oswego (NY)
State U of New York Coll at Cortland (NY)
State U of New York Coll at Geneseo (NY)
State U of New York Coll at Old Westbury (NY)
State U of New York Coll at Oneonta (NY)
State U of New York Coll at Potsdam (NY)
Sterling Coll (KS)
Stetson U (FL)
Stevenson U (MD)
Tabor Coll (KS)
Taylor U (IN)
Tennessee Wesleyan U (TN)
Texas Christian U (TX)
Texas Lutheran U (TX)
Toccoa Falls Coll (GA)
Towson U (MD)
Transylvania U (KY)
Trevecca Nazarene U (TN)
Trine U (IN)
Trinity Coll of Florida (FL)
Troy U (AL)
Truett McConnell U (GA)
Union U (TN)
Universidad Adventista de las Antillas (PR)
The U of Alabama (AL)
The U of Alabama at Birmingham (AL)
The U of Alabama in Huntsville (AL)
U of Alaska Fairbanks (AK)
U of Alaska Southeast (AK)
The U of Arizona (AZ)
U of Arkansas (AR)
U of Arkansas at Little Rock (AR)
U of Central Florida (FL)
U of Charleston (WV)
U of Cincinnati (OH)
U of Colorado Boulder (CO)
U of Colorado Colorado Springs (CO)
U of Detroit Mercy (MI)
U of Dubuque (IA)
The U of Findlay (OH)
U of Guam (GU)
U of Hartford (CT)
U of Hawaii at Manoa (HI)
U of Idaho (ID)
U of Illinois at Chicago (IL)
U of Illinois at Springfield (IL)
The U of Iowa (IA)
U of Jamestown (ND)
The U of Kansas (KS)
U of Kentucky (KY)
U of Louisiana at Lafayette (LA)
U of Louisiana at Monroe (LA)
U of Louisville (KY)
U of Maine (ME)
U of Maine at Presque Isle (ME)
U of Mary Hardin-Baylor (TX)
U of Miami (FL)
U of Michigan (MI)
U of Michigan–Flint (MI)
U of Minnesota, Morris (MN)
U of Minnesota, Twin Cities Campus (MN)
U of Missouri–St. Louis (MO)
U of Montana (MT)
U of Montevallo (AL)
U of Nebraska at Kearney (NE)
U of Nebraska–Lincoln (NE)
U of Nevada, Las Vegas (NV)
U of Nevada, Reno (NV)
U of New England (ME)
U of New Mexico (NM)
The U of North Carolina at Chapel Hill (NC)
The U of North Carolina at Charlotte (NC)
The U of North Carolina at Greensboro (NC)
The U of North Carolina at Pembroke (NC)
The U of North Carolina Wilmington (NC)
U of North Dakota (ND)
U of Northern Colorado (CO)
U of Northern Iowa (IA)
U of North Florida (FL)
U of Northwestern–St. Paul (MN)
U of Pennsylvania (PA)
U of Pikeville (KY)
U of Pittsburgh at Bradford (PA)
U of Portland (OR)
U of Providence (MT)
U of Puerto Rico–Ponce (PR)
U of St. Francis (IL)
U of Saint Francis (IN)
U of Saint Mary (KS)
U of Science and Arts of Oklahoma (OK)
The U of Scranton (PA)
U of South Alabama (AL)
U of South Carolina (SC)
U of South Carolina Aiken (SC)
U of South Carolina Beaufort (SC)
U of South Dakota (SD)
U of Southern Indiana (IN)
U of Southern Mississippi (MS)
U of South Florida (FL)
U of South Florida, St. Petersburg (FL)
The U of Tampa (FL)
The U of Texas at San Antonio (TX)
U of the Incarnate Word (TX)
U of the Virgin Islands (VI)
The U of Tulsa (OK)
U of Utah (UT)
U of Vermont (VT)
The U of Western Ontario (ON, Canada)
U of West Florida (FL)
U of West Georgia (GA)
U of Wisconsin–Eau Claire (WI)
U of Wisconsin–La Crosse (WI)
U of Wisconsin–Madison (WI)
U of Wisconsin–Milwaukee (WI)
U of Wisconsin–Parkside (WI)
U of Wisconsin–Platteville (WI)
U of Wisconsin–Superior (WI)
U of Wyoming (WY)
Upper Iowa U (IA)
Utah State U (UT)
Utah Valley U (UT)
Utica Coll (NY)
Valley City State U (ND)
Valparaiso U (IN)
Vanderbilt U (TN)
Vanguard U of Southern California (CA)
Virginia Commonwealth U (VA)
Virginia Wesleyan U (VA)
Walla Walla U (WA)
Wartburg Coll (IA)
Washington State U (WA)
Washington State U–Tri-Cities (WA)
Washington State U–Vancouver (WA)
Washington U in St. Louis (MO)
Wayland Baptist U (TX)
Waynesburg U (PA)
Wayne State Coll (NE)
Wayne State U (MI)
Webber Intl U (FL)
Weber State U (UT)
Wesleyan Coll (GA)
Western Carolina U (NC)
Western Colorado U (CO)
Western Connecticut State U (CT)
Western Kentucky U (KY)
Western Michigan U (MI)
Western New England U (MA)
Western New Mexico U (NM)
Western Washington U (WA)
Westfield State U (MA)
West Liberty U (WV)
Westminster Coll (UT)
West Virginia U (WV)
Wheaton Coll (IL)
Wheaton Coll (MA)
Whitworth U (WA)
Wichita State U (KS)
Widener U (PA)
Wilkes U (PA)
William & Mary (VA)
William Jewell Coll (MO)
William Paterson U of New Jersey (NJ)
William Peace U (NC)
William Penn U (IA)
Wilmington Coll (OH)
Wingate U (NC)
Winthrop U (SC)
Worcester State U (MA)
Wright State U–Lake Campus (OH)
Xavier U (OH)
Xavier U of Louisiana (LA)
Yeshiva U (NY)
Youngstown State U (OH)

EMERGENCY MEDICAL TECHNOLOGY (EMT PARAMEDIC)
Central Washington U (WA)
Concordia U Chicago (IL)
Creighton U (NE)
Eastern Kentucky U (KY)
The George Washington U (DC)
Loyola U Chicago (IL)
Radford U (VA)
Springfield Coll (MA)
The U of Arizona (AZ)
U of Maryland, Baltimore County (MD)
U of New Haven (CT)
U of New Mexico (NM)
U of South Alabama (AL)
U of Washington (WA)
Western Carolina U (NC)

ENERGY MANAGEMENT AND SYSTEMS TECHNOLOGY
Creighton U (NE)
Excelsior Coll (NY)
Ferris State U (MI)
Fitchburg State U (MA)
Illinois State U (IL)
Vermont Tech Coll (VT)

ENGINEERING
Abilene Christian U (TX)
Albion Coll (MI)
Andrews U (MI)
Arcadia U (PA)
Arizona State U at the Polytechnic campus (AZ)
Auburn U (AL)
Augsburg U (MN)
Aurora U (IL)
Azusa Pacific U (CA)
Ball State U (IN)
Barry U (FL)
Bates Coll (ME)
Baylor U (TX)
Beloit Coll (WI)
Bennington Coll (VT)
Bethel U (IN)
Binghamton U, State U of New York (NY)
Biola U (CA)
Bradley U (IL)
Brown U (RI)
Bryan Coll (TN)
California Baptist U (CA)
California State Polytechnic U, Pomona (CA)
California State U, Long Beach (CA)
California State U, Los Angeles (CA)
California State U, San Marcos (CA)
Calvin Coll (MI)
Carthage Coll (WI)
The Catholic U of America (DC)
Central Coll (IA)
Clarkson U (NY)
Clark U (MA)
Coll of the Ozarks (MO)
Colorado School of Mines (CO)
Cornell Coll (IA)
Cornell U (NY)
Dartmouth Coll (NH)
Dominican U (IL)
Drexel U (PA)
East Carolina U (NC)
East Central U (OK)
Eastern Mennonite U (VA)
Endicott Coll (MA)
Florida Inst of Technology (FL)
Fort Lewis Coll (CO)
Framingham State U (MA)
Franklin W. Olin Coll of Eng (MA)
Geneva Coll (PA)
George Fox U (OR)
The George Washington U (DC)
Gonzaga U (WA)
Hanover Coll (IN)
Harvard U (MA)
Hope Coll (MI)
Houston Baptist U (TX)
Illinois Inst of Technology (IL)
Indiana State U (IN)
Indiana U-Purdue U Indianapolis (IN)
Inter American U of Puerto Rico, Bayamón Campus (PR)
Inter American U of Puerto Rico, San Germán Campus (PR)
James Madison U (VA)
John Brown U (AR)
Johns Hopkins U (MD)
Lafayette Coll (PA)
LaGrange Coll (GA)
LeTourneau U (TX)
Loyola U Maryland (MD)
Manhattan Coll (NY)
Marian U (IN)
Marshall U (WV)
McNeese State U (LA)
Mercer U, Macon (GA)
Messiah Coll (PA)
Miami U (OH)
Miami U Hamilton (OH)
Miami U Middletown (OH)
Michigan State U (MI)
Michigan Technological U (MI)
Milwaukee School of Eng (WI)
Missouri U of Science and Technology (MO)
Montana State U (MT)
New Jersey Inst of Technology (NJ)
New Mexico Highlands U (NM)
New York U (NY)
Northwestern U (IL)
Oglethorpe U (GA)
Old Dominion U (VA)
Olivet Nazarene U (IL)
Oral Roberts U (OK)
Ottawa U (KS)
Princeton U (NJ)
Purdue U Northwest (IN)
Roger Williams U (RI)
Rowan U (NJ)
Saginaw Valley State U (MI)
Saint Francis U (PA)
Saint Louis U (MO)
Saint Mary's Coll of California (CA)
Saint Vincent Coll (PA)
San Diego State U (CA)
San Jose State U (CA)
Santa Clara U (CA)
Schreiner U (TX)
Seattle U (WA)
Southern Arkansas U–Magnolia (AR)
Stanford U (CA)
Stony Brook U, State U of New York (NY)
Tarleton State U (TX)
Taylor U (IN)
Temple U (PA)
Texas Christian U (TX)
Trine U (IN)
The U of Akron (OH)
The U of Alabama at Birmingham (AL)
U of California, Irvine (CA)
U of California, San Diego (CA)
U of Cincinnati (OH)
U of Colorado Boulder (CO)
U of Denver (CO)
U of Detroit Mercy (MI)
U of Hartford (CT)
U of Hawaii at Manoa (HI)
The U of Iowa (IA)
U of Mary Hardin-Baylor (TX)
U of Michigan (MI)
U of Michigan–Dearborn (MI)
U of Nebraska–Lincoln (NE)
U of Nevada, Las Vegas (NV)
U of New Haven (CT)
U of Northwestern–St. Paul (MN)
U of Portland (OR)
U of San Diego (CA)
U of Southern Indiana (IN)
The U of Tennessee at Chattanooga (TN)
The U of Tennessee at Martin (TN)
The U of Texas at El Paso (TX)
U of the Incarnate Word (TX)
U of Toronto (ON, Canada)
U of Utah (UT)
U of Vermont (VT)
U of Virginia (VA)
The U of Western Ontario (ON, Canada)
U of Wisconsin–Platteville (WI)
Wake Forest U (NC)
Walla Walla U (WA)
Washington and Lee U (VA)
Washington U in St. Louis (MO)
Wentworth Inst of Technology (MA)
Western Carolina U (NC)
Westmont Coll (CA)
Whitworth U (WA)
Widener U (PA)
Wilkes U (PA)
Wright State U (OH)
Youngstown State U (OH)

ENGINEERING CHEMISTRY
Oakland U (MI)

ENGINEERING DESIGN
Carnegie Mellon U (PA)
Earlham Coll (IN)

ENGINEERING/INDUSTRIAL MANAGEMENT
Arizona State U at the Tempe campus (AZ)
Bowling Green State U (OH)
California State U, Long Beach (CA)
Clarkson U (NY)
Eastern Kentucky U (KY)
Eastern Michigan U (MI)

Illinois Inst of Technology (IL)
Kansas State U (KS)
Kennesaw State U (GA)
Mercer U, Macon (GA)
Miami U (OH)
Miami U Hamilton (OH)
Miami U Middletown (OH)
Michigan Technological U (MI)
Middle Tennessee State U (TN)
Missouri Southern State U (MO)
Missouri State U (MO)
Missouri U of Science and Technology (MO)
Morehead State U (KY)
New York Inst of Technology (NY)
New York U (NY)
Pittsburg State U (KS)
Pitzer Coll (CA)
Purdue U Northwest (IN)
Saginaw Valley State U (MI)
St. Mary's U (TX)
Stanford U (CA)
State U of New York Coll of Technology at Canton (NY)
Stevens Inst of Technology (NJ)
Texas State U (TX)
Trine U (IN)
United States Military Acad (NY)
The U of Arizona (AZ)
U of Illinois at Chicago (IL)
U of Management and Technology (VA)
U of Northwestern–St. Paul (MN)
The U of Scranton (PA)
The U of Tennessee at Chattanooga (TN)
U of the Incarnate Word (TX)
U of the Pacific (CA)
Utah State U (UT)
Valparaiso U (IN)
Western Michigan U (MI)
Widener U (PA)
Wilkes U (PA)
William Penn U (IA)

ENGINEERING MECHANICS
Johns Hopkins U (MD)
Lehigh U (PA)
New York U (NY)
U of Cincinnati (OH)
U of Wisconsin–Madison (WI)

ENGINEERING PHYSICS/ APPLIED PHYSICS
Adams State U (CO)
Anderson U (IN)
Arizona State U at the Polytechnic campus (AZ)
Arkansas Tech U (AR)
Augustana Coll (IL)
Augustana U (SD)
Austin Peay State U (TN)
Belmont U (TN)
Bemidji State U (MN)
Benedictine Coll (KS)
Biola U (CA)
Brown U (RI)
Central Washington U (WA)
Colorado School of Mines (CO)
Cornell U (NY)
Dartmouth Coll (NH)
Doane U (NE)
Drew U (NJ)
Eastern Michigan U (MI)
Elon U (NC)
Florida Polytechnic U (FL)
Fordham U (NY)
Goshen Coll (IN)
Hamline U (MN)
Hampden-Sydney Coll (VA)
Illinois Inst of Technology (IL)
Jacksonville U (FL)
John Carroll U (OH)
Kansas Wesleyan U (KS)
Kettering U (MI)
Lehigh U (PA)
LeTourneau U (TX)
Linfield Coll (OR)
Loras Coll (IA)
Loyola Marymount U (CA)
Miami U (OH)
Miami U Hamilton (OH)
Miami U Middletown (OH)
Murray State U (KY)
New York U (NY)
Northeastern State U (OK)
Northern Kentucky U (KY)
Northwest Nazarene U (ID)
Oakland U (MI)
The Ohio State U (OH)
Oral Roberts U (OK)
Point Loma Nazarene U (CA)
Providence Coll (RI)
Randolph Coll (VA)
Randolph-Macon Coll (VA)
Rose-Hulman Inst of Technology (IN)
Saint Louis U (MO)
Samford U (AL)
Santa Clara U (CA)
Siena Coll (NY)
Southeast Missouri State U (MO)
Southwestern Oklahoma State U (OK)
Stevens Inst of Technology (NJ)
Tarleton State U (TX)
Taylor U (IN)
Trevecca Nazarene U (TN)
U at Buffalo, the State U of New York (NY)
The U of Arizona (AZ)
U of California, Berkeley (CA)
U of California, San Diego (CA)
U of Colorado Boulder (CO)
U of Illinois at Chicago (IL)
The U of Kansas (KS)
U of Maine (ME)
U of Massachusetts Boston (MA)
U of Michigan (MI)
U of Minnesota, Duluth (MN)
U of Nevada, Reno (NV)
U of New Hampshire (NH)
U of St. Thomas (TX)
U of the Pacific (CA)
The U of Tulsa (OK)
The U of Western Ontario (ON, Canada)
U of Wisconsin–Madison (WI)
U of Wisconsin–Platteville (WI)
Vanguard U of Southern California (CA)
Westmont Coll (CA)
Whitworth U (WA)
Worcester Polytechnic Inst (MA)
Wright State U (OH)
Xavier U (OH)
Yale U (CT)

ENGINEERING RELATED
Agnes Scott Coll (GA)
Alfred U (NY)
Auburn U (AL)
California State U, Long Beach (CA)
Claremont McKenna Coll (CA)
The Coll of Idaho (ID)
Eastern Illinois U (IL)
Indiana U-Purdue U Indianapolis (IN)
Lehigh U (PA)
Loyola U Chicago (IL)
Madonna U (MI)
Maryville U of Saint Louis (MO)
Massachusetts Maritime Acad (MA)
Michigan State U (MI)
Mississippi State U (MS)
New York U (NY)
Northwestern U (IL)
The Ohio State U (OH)
Ohio Wesleyan U (OH)
Penn State Altoona (PA)
Penn State Berks (PA)
Penn State U Park (PA)
Polytechnic U of Puerto Rico (PR)
Rose-Hulman Inst of Technology (IN)
State U of New York at Oswego (NY)
Stevens Inst of Technology (NJ)
U at Albany, State U of New York (NY)
The U of Alabama in Huntsville (AL)
U of California, San Diego (CA)
U of Colorado Colorado Springs (CO)
U of Hartford (CT)
U of Miami (FL)
U of New Hampshire (NH)
The U of North Carolina Wilmington (NC)
U of Pennsylvania (PA)
U of Washington (WA)
U of Waterloo (ON, Canada)
The U of Western Ontario (ON, Canada)
U of Wisconsin–Madison (WI)
Washington U in St. Louis (MO)
Waynesburg U (PA)
Western Michigan U (MI)
Wheaton Coll (IL)
York Coll of Pennsylvania (PA)

ENGINEERING-RELATED TECHNOLOGIES
New Jersey Inst of Technology (NJ)

ENGINEERING SCIENCE
Arizona State U at the Polytechnic campus (AZ)
Benedictine U (IL)
Bethany Lutheran Coll (MN)
Bethel U (MN)
California Polytechnic State U, San Luis Obispo (CA)
Coastal Carolina U (SC)
Colorado State U (CO)
Cornell Coll (IA)
Hanover Coll (IN)
Hofstra U (NY)
Lincoln U (PA)
Muskingum U (OH)
New Jersey Inst of Technology (NJ)
New York U (NY)
Northwestern U (IL)
Ohio Wesleyan U (OH)
Penn State Abington (PA)
Penn State Altoona (PA)
Penn State Beaver (PA)
Penn State Berks (PA)
Penn State Brandywine (PA)
Penn State DuBois (PA)
Penn State Erie, The Behrend Coll (PA)
Penn State Fayette, The Eberly Campus (PA)
Penn State Greater Allegheny (PA)
Penn State Hazleton (PA)
Penn State Lehigh Valley (PA)
Penn State Mont Alto (PA)
Penn State New Kensington (PA)
Penn State Schuylkill (PA)
Penn State Shenango (PA)
Penn State U Park (PA)
Penn State Wilkes-Barre (PA)
Penn State York (PA)
Portland State U (OR)
St. Mary's U (TX)
Shepherd U (WV)
Simon Fraser U (BC, Canada)
Smith Coll (MA)
State U of New York Coll at Oneonta (NY)
Trinity U (TX)
Tulane U (LA)
U of California, Berkeley (CA)
U of California, San Diego (CA)
U of Michigan (MI)
U of Michigan–Flint (MI)
U of New Mexico (NM)
U of Pittsburgh at Bradford (PA)
U of Portland (OR)
U of South Carolina (SC)
U of Toronto (ON, Canada)
The U of Western Ontario (ON, Canada)
Vanderbilt U (TN)
Wartburg Coll (IA)
Washington and Lee U (VA)
Wright State U (OH)
Wright State U–Lake Campus (OH)
Yale U (CT)

ENGINEERING TECHNOLOGIES AND ENGINEERING RELATED
Ball State U (IN)
Bowling Green State U (OH)
Daytona State Coll (FL)
East Carolina U (NC)
East Central U (OK)
Eastern Washington U (WA)
Francis Marion U (SC)
Morehead State U (KY)
New York Inst of Technology (NY)
New York U (NY)
Northeastern State U (OK)
Northern Kentucky U (KY)
Old Dominion U (VA)
Pittsburg State U (KS)
Rogers State U (OK)
State U of New York Coll of Technology at Alfred (NY)
U of Hartford (CT)
The U of North Carolina at Charlotte (NC)
The U of West Alabama (AL)

ENGINEERING TECHNOLOGY
Austin Peay State U (TN)
Berry Coll (GA)
California State Polytechnic U, Pomona (CA)
California State U, Long Beach (CA)
Drexel U (PA)
Eastern Illinois U (IL)
Eastern New Mexico U (NM)
Grambling State U (LA)
Illinois State U (IL)
Indiana State U (IN)
Kansas State U (KS)
Kennesaw State U (GA)
Kent State U at Tuscarawas (OH)
Lawrence Technological U (MI)
Lenoir-Rhyne U (NC)
Miami U (OH)
Miami U Hamilton (OH)
Miami U Middletown (OH)
Middle Tennessee State U (TN)
Morehead State U (KY)
New Jersey Inst of Technology (NJ)
New York Inst of Technology (NY)
New York U (NY)
Northern Illinois U (IL)
Southeastern Louisiana U (LA)
Southeast Missouri State U (MO)
Southern Illinois U Carbondale (IL)
Southwestern Oklahoma State U (OK)
Temple U (PA)
Texas A&M U (TX)
Texas State U (TX)
U of Memphis (TN)
The U of Texas Rio Grande Valley (TX)
The U of West Alabama (AL)
U of West Florida (FL)
U of Wisconsin–Stout (WI)
Walla Walla U (WA)
Wentworth Inst of Technology (MA)
Western Carolina U (NC)
Wichita State U (KS)
William Penn U (IA)
Youngstown State U (OH)

ENGLISH
Abilene Christian U (TX)
Adams State U (CO)
Agnes Scott Coll (GA)
Albion Coll (MI)
Alfred U (NY)
Allegheny Coll (PA)
Alverno Coll (WI)
American Coll of Thessaloniki (Greece)
American Public U System (WV)
Amherst Coll (MA)
Anderson U (IN)
Anderson U (SC)
Andrews U (MI)
Angelo State U (TX)
Appalachian State U (NC)
Aquinas Coll (MI)
Arcadia U (PA)
Arizona State U at the Polytechnic campus (AZ)
Arizona State U at the Tempe campus (AZ)
Arizona State U at the West campus (AZ)
Arkansas Tech U (AR)
Assumption Coll (MA)
Athens State U (AL)
Auburn U (AL)
Auburn U at Montgomery (AL)
Augsburg U (MN)
Augustana Coll (IL)
Augustana U (SD)
Aurora U (IL)
Austin Coll (TX)
Austin Peay State U (TN)
Averett U (VA)
Avila U (MO)
Azusa Pacific U (CA)
Baker U (KS)
Ball State U (IN)
Barnard Coll (NY)
Barry U (FL)
Barton Coll (NC)
Baruch Coll of the City U of New York (NY)
Bates Coll (ME)
Bayamón Central U (PR)
Baylor U (TX)
Belhaven U (MS)
Belmont Abbey Coll (NC)
Belmont U (TN)
Beloit Coll (WI)
Bemidji State U (MN)
Benedictine Coll (KS)
Benedictine U (IL)
Bennington Coll (VT)
Bentley U (MA)
Berea Coll (KY)
Berry Coll (GA)
Bethany Lutheran Coll (MN)
Bethel U (IN)
Bethel U (MN)
Bethel U (TN)
Binghamton U, State U of New York (NY)
Biola U (CA)
Birmingham-Southern Coll (AL)
Black Hills State U (SD)
Bluffton U (OH)
Boise State U (ID)
Boston Coll (MA)
Bowdoin Coll (ME)
Bowling Green State U (OH)
Bradley U (IL)
Brandeis U (MA)
Brandon U (MB, Canada)
Brenau U (GA)
Bridgewater Coll (VA)
Bridgewater State U (MA)
Brown U (RI)
Bryan Coll (TN)
Bryn Athyn Coll of the New Church (PA)
Bucknell U (PA)
Butler U (IN)
Caldwell U (NJ)
California Baptist U (CA)
California Lutheran U (CA)
California Polytechnic State U, San Luis Obispo (CA)
California State Polytechnic U, Pomona (CA)
California State U, Bakersfield (CA)
California State U, Dominguez Hills (CA)
California State U, Fresno (CA)
California State U, Fullerton (CA)
California State U, Long Beach (CA)
California State U, Los Angeles (CA)
California State U, Northridge (CA)
California State U, Sacramento (CA)
California State U, San Bernardino (CA)
California State U, San Marcos (CA)
California State U, Stanislaus (CA)
California U of Pennsylvania (PA)
Calumet Coll of Saint Joseph (IN)
Calvin Coll (MI)
Cameron U (OK)
Campbellsville U (KY)
Capital U (OH)
Carleton Coll (MN)
Carlow U (PA)
Carnegie Mellon U (PA)
Carson-Newman U (TN)
Carthage Coll (WI)
Catawba Coll (NC)
The Catholic U of America (DC)
Cazenovia Coll (NY)
Cedar Crest Coll (PA)
Cedarville U (OH)
Central Christian Coll of Kansas (KS)
Central Coll (IA)
Central Connecticut State U (CT)
Central Methodist U (MO)
Central Michigan U (MI)
Central State U (OH)
Central Washington U (WA)
Centre Coll (KY)
Chaminade U of Honolulu (HI)
Chatham U (PA)

Chestnut Hill Coll (PA)
The Citadel, The Military Coll of South Carolina (SC)
City Coll of the City U of New York (NY)
Claremont McKenna Coll (CA)
Clarion U of Pennsylvania (PA)
Clark Atlanta U (GA)
Clark U (MA)
Clayton State U (GA)
Clemson U (SC)
Coastal Carolina U (SC)
Coe Coll (IA)
Colby Coll (ME)
Colgate U (NY)
Coll of Charleston (SC)
The Coll of Idaho (ID)
Coll of Saint Benedict (MN)
Coll of Saint Elizabeth (NJ)
Coll of Saint Mary (NE)
The Coll of Saint Rose (NY)
The Coll of St. Scholastica (MN)
Coll of Staten Island of the City U of New York (NY)
Coll of the Holy Cross (MA)
Coll of the Ozarks (MO)
The Coll of Wooster (OH)
The Colorado Coll (CO)
Colorado State U (CO)
Columbia Coll (MO)
Columbia Coll (SC)
Columbia Coll Chicago (IL)
Columbia Intl U (SC)
Concordia Coll (MN)
Concordia U Chicago (IL)
Concordia U, St. Paul (MN)
Concordia U Wisconsin (WI)
Cornell Coll (IA)
Cornell U (NY)
Covenant Coll (GA)
Creighton U (NE)
Culver-Stockton Coll (MO)
Dallas Baptist U (TX)
Dartmouth Coll (NH)
Davidson Coll (NC)
Dean Coll (MA)
Delaware Valley U (PA)
Delta State U (MS)
DePaul U (IL)
DePauw U (IN)
DeSales U (PA)
Dickinson Coll (PA)
Dickinson State U (ND)
Dillard U (LA)
Doane U (NE)
Dominican Coll (NY)
Dominican U (IL)
Dominican U of California (CA)
Drake U (IA)
Drew U (NJ)
Drury U (MO)
D'Youville Coll (NY)
East Carolina U (NC)
East Central U (OK)
Eastern Illinois U (IL)
Eastern Kentucky U (KY)
Eastern Mennonite U (VA)
Eastern Michigan U (MI)
Eastern New Mexico U (NM)
Eastern Oregon U (OR)
Eastern Washington U (WA)
East Texas Baptist U (TX)
Edgewood Coll (WI)
Edinboro U of Pennsylvania (PA)
Elms Coll (MA)
Elon U (NC)
Emmanuel Coll (GA)
Emmanuel Coll (MA)
Emory & Henry Coll (VA)
Emory U (GA)
Emporia State U (KS)
Endicott Coll (MA)
Evangel U (MO)
Fairfield U (CT)
Fairleigh Dickinson U (NJ)
Fayetteville State U (NC)
Felician U (NJ)
Fitchburg State U (MA)
Flagler Coll (FL)
Florida A&M U (FL)
Florida Atlantic U (FL)
Florida Gulf Coast U (FL)
Florida State U (FL)
Fordham U (NY)
Fort Lewis Coll (CO)
Framingham State U (MA)
Francis Marion U (SC)
Franklin Coll (IN)
Freed-Hardeman U (TN)
Friends U (KS)
Furman U (SC)
Gallaudet U (DC)
Geneva Coll (PA)
George Fox U (OR)
George Mason U (VA)
Georgetown Coll (KY)
Georgetown U (DC)
The George Washington U (DC)
Georgia Coll & State U (GA)
Georgia Gwinnett Coll (GA)
Georgian Court U (NJ)
Georgia Southern U (GA)
Georgia State U (GA)
Glenville State Coll (WV)
Gonzaga U (WA)
Gordon Coll (MA)
Goshen Coll (IN)
Goucher Coll (MD)
Governors State U (IL)
Graceland U (IA)
Grambling State U (LA)
Grand Valley State U (MI)
Granite State Coll (NH)
Grinnell Coll (IA)
Guilford Coll (NC)
Gustavus Adolphus Coll (MN)
Gwynedd Mercy U (PA)
Hamline U (MN)
Hampden-Sydney Coll (VA)
Hampshire Coll (MA)
Hampton U (VA)
Hanover Coll (IN)
Harding U (AR)
Hardin-Simmons U (TX)
Harvard U (MA)
High Point U (NC)
Hillsdale Coll (MI)
Hobart and William Smith Colls (NY)
Hofstra U (NY)
Hollins U (VA)
Hope Coll (MI)
Hope Intl U (CA)
Houston Baptist U (TX)
Howard U (DC)
Husson U (ME)
Illinois Coll (IL)
Illinois State U (IL)
Immaculata U (PA)
Indiana State U (IN)
Indiana U Bloomington (IN)
Indiana U East (IN)
Indiana U Kokomo (IN)
Indiana U Northwest (IN)
Indiana U of Pennsylvania (PA)
Indiana U-Purdue U Indianapolis (IN)
Indiana U South Bend (IN)
Indiana U Southeast (IN)
Inter American U of Puerto Rico, Metropolitan Campus (PR)
Inter American U of Puerto Rico, San Germán Campus (PR)
Iona Coll (NY)
Iowa State U of Science and Technology (IA)
Ithaca Coll (NY)
Jacksonville State U (AL)
Jacksonville U (FL)
James Madison U (VA)
John Brown U (AR)
John Carroll U (OH)
John Jay Coll of Criminal Justice of the City U of New York (NY)
Johns Hopkins U (MD)
Kalamazoo Coll (MI)
Kansas State U (KS)
Kansas Wesleyan U (KS)
Kean U (NJ)
Kennesaw State U (GA)
Kent State U at Tuscarawas (OH)
Kenyon Coll (OH)
Keuka Coll (NY)
The King's Coll (NY)
King's Coll (PA)
The King's U (AB, Canada)
King U (TN)
Knox Coll (IL)
Kutztown U of Pennsylvania (PA)
Lafayette Coll (PA)
LaGrange Coll (GA)
Lake Forest Coll (IL)
Lamar U (TX)
La Roche U (PA)
Lasell Coll (MA)
La Sierra U (CA)
Lawrence Technological U (MI)
Lawrence U (WI)
Lebanese American U (Lebanon)
Lee U (TN)
Lehigh U (PA)
Lehman Coll of the City U of New York (NY)
Le Moyne Coll (NY)
Lenoir-Rhyne U (NC)
Lesley U (MA)
LeTourneau U (TX)
Lewis & Clark Coll (OR)
Lewis-Clark State Coll (ID)
Lewis U (IL)
Liberty U (VA)
Limestone Coll (SC)
Lincoln Memorial U (TN)
Lincoln U (MO)
Lincoln U (PA)
Lindenwood U (MO)
Lipscomb U (TN)
Lock Haven U of Pennsylvania (PA)
Longwood U (VA)
Loras Coll (IA)
Louisiana State U and A&M Coll (LA)
Louisiana State U in Shreveport (LA)
Louisiana Tech U (LA)
Loyola Marymount U (CA)
Loyola U Chicago (IL)
Loyola U Maryland (MD)
Madonna U (MI)
Malone U (OH)
Manhattan Coll (NY)
Manhattanville Coll (NY)
Mansfield U of Pennsylvania (PA)
Marian U (IN)
Marietta Coll (OH)
Marquette U (WI)
Marshall U (WV)
Marymount U (VA)
Maryville U of Saint Louis (MO)
Marywood U (PA)
Mayville State U (ND)
McDaniel Coll (MD)
McKendree U (IL)
McMurry U (TX)
McNeese State U (LA)
Mercer U, Macon (GA)
Mercy Coll (NY)
Meredith Coll (NC)
Merrimack Coll (MA)
Messiah Coll (PA)
Miami U (OH)
Miami U Hamilton (OH)
Miami U Middletown (OH)
Michigan State U (MI)
Michigan Technological U (MI)
Mid-America Christian U (OK)
MidAmerica Nazarene U (KS)
Middle Tennessee State U (TN)
Midway U (KY)
Millersville U of Pennsylvania (PA)
Milligan Coll (TN)
Millikin U (IL)
Minnesota State U Mankato (MN)
Minot State U (ND)
Misericordia U (PA)
Mississippi State U (MS)
Missouri Southern State U (MO)
Missouri State U (MO)
Missouri U of Science and Technology (MO)
Missouri Valley Coll (MO)
Molloy Coll (NY)
Montana State U (MT)
Montclair State U (NJ)
Moravian Coll (PA)
Morehead State U (KY)
Mount Aloysius Coll (PA)
Mount Holyoke Coll (MA)
Mount Marty Coll (SD)
Mount Mercy U (IA)
Mount Saint Mary Coll (NY)
Mount Saint Mary's U (CA)
Mount St. Mary's U (MD)
Mount Vernon Nazarene U (OH)
Muhlenberg Coll (PA)
Multnomah U (OR)
Murray State U (KY)
Muskingum U (OH)
National U (CA)
Nazareth Coll of Rochester (NY)
Nebraska Wesleyan U (NE)
New Coll of Florida (FL)
Newman U (KS)
New Mexico Highlands U (NM)
New York Inst of Technology (NY)
New York U (NY)
Niagara U (NY)
Nichols Coll (MA)
North Carolina Central U (NC)
North Central U (MN)
Northeastern Illinois U (IL)
Northeastern State U (OK)
Northern Arizona U (AZ)
Northern Illinois U (IL)
Northern Kentucky U (KY)
Northern State U (SD)
North Greenville U (SC)
Northwest Christian U (OR)
Northwestern State U of Louisiana (LA)
Northwestern U (IL)
Northwest Missouri State U (MO)
Northwest Nazarene U (ID)
Northwest U (WA)
Notre Dame Coll (OH)
Nova Southeastern U (FL)
Nyack Coll (NY)
Oakland City U (IN)
Oakland U (MI)
Oberlin Coll (OH)
Oglethorpe U (GA)
Ohio Christian U (OH)
Ohio Dominican U (OH)
The Ohio State U (OH)
The Ohio State U at Lima (OH)
The Ohio State U at Mansfield (OH)
The Ohio State U at Marion (OH)
The Ohio State U at Newark (OH)
Ohio Wesleyan U (OH)
Oklahoma State U (OK)
Old Dominion U (VA)
Olivet Nazarene U (IL)
Oral Roberts U (OK)
Ottawa U (KS)
Pace U, Pleasantville Campus (NY)
Pacific U (OR)
Palm Beach Atlantic U (FL)
Penn State Abington (PA)
Penn State Altoona (PA)
Penn State Beaver (PA)
Penn State Berks (PA)
Penn State Brandywine (PA)
Penn State DuBois (PA)
Penn State Erie, The Behrend Coll (PA)
Penn State Fayette, The Eberly Campus (PA)
Penn State Greater Allegheny (PA)
Penn State Harrisburg (PA)
Penn State Hazleton (PA)
Penn State Lehigh Valley (PA)
Penn State Mont Alto (PA)
Penn State New Kensington (PA)
Penn State Schuylkill (PA)
Penn State Shenango (PA)
Penn State U Park (PA)
Penn State Wilkes-Barre (PA)
Penn State York (PA)
Pepperdine U, Malibu (CA)
Pittsburg State U (KS)
Point Loma Nazarene U (CA)
Pomona Coll (CA)
Portland State U (OR)
Prairie View A&M U (TX)
Princeton U (NJ)
Providence Coll (RI)
Purdue U Fort Wayne (IN)
Purdue U Northwest (IN)
Queens Coll of the City U of New York (NY)
Radford U (VA)
Randolph Coll (VA)
Randolph-Macon Coll (VA)
Regent U (VA)
Regis Coll (MA)
Rhode Island Coll (RI)
Rhodes Coll (TN)
Rice U (TX)
Roanoke Coll (VA)
Roberts Wesleyan Coll (NY)
Rochester U (MI)
Roger Williams U (RI)
Rollins Coll (FL)
Rosemont Coll (PA)
Rowan U (NJ)
Sacred Heart U (CT)
The Sage Colls (NY)
Saginaw Valley State U (MI)
St. Ambrose U (IA)
St. Bonaventure U (NY)
St. Catherine U (MN)
St. Cloud State U (MN)
Saint Francis U (PA)
St. John Fisher Coll (NY)
Saint John's U (MN)
Saint Joseph's U (PA)
Saint Leo U (FL)
Saint Louis U (MO)
Saint Mary-of-the-Woods Coll (IN)
Saint Mary's Coll (IN)
Saint Mary's Coll of California (CA)
St. Mary's Coll of Maryland (MD)
St. Mary's U (TX)
St. Norbert Coll (WI)
St. Olaf Coll (MN)
St. Thomas Aquinas Coll (NY)
St. Thomas U - Florida (FL)
St. Thomas U - New Brunswick (NB, Canada)
Saint Vincent Coll (PA)
Salem State U (MA)
Salisbury U (MD)
Salve Regina U (RI)
Samford U (AL)
Sam Houston State U (TX)
San Diego State U (CA)
San Francisco State U (CA)
San Jose State U (CA)
Santa Clara U (CA)
Schreiner U (TX)
Scripps Coll (CA)
Seattle U (WA)
Seton Hill U (PA)
Shenandoah U (VA)
Shepherd U (WV)
Siena Coll (NY)
Siena Heights U (MI)
Sierra Nevada Coll (NV)
Simmons U (MA)
Simon Fraser U (BC, Canada)
Skidmore Coll (NY)
Slippery Rock U of Pennsylvania (PA)
Smith Coll (MA)
South Dakota State U (SD)
Southeastern Louisiana U (LA)
Southeastern U (FL)
Southeast Missouri State U (MO)
Southern Arkansas U–Magnolia (AR)
Southern Illinois U Carbondale (IL)
Southern Illinois U Edwardsville (IL)
Southern Methodist U (TX)
Southwest Baptist U (MO)
Southwestern Oklahoma State U (OK)
Southwestern U (TX)
Spring Arbor U (MI)
Springfield Coll (MA)
Spring Hill Coll (AL)
Stanford U (CA)
State U of New York at Fredonia (NY)
State U of New York at New Paltz (NY)
State U of New York at Oswego (NY)
State U of New York Coll at Cortland (NY)
State U of New York Coll at Geneseo (NY)
State U of New York Coll at Oneonta (NY)
State U of New York Coll at Potsdam (NY)
Sterling Coll (KS)
Stetson U (FL)
Stevenson U (MD)
Stockton U (NJ)
Stony Brook U, State U of New York (NY)
Suffolk U (MA)
SUNY Brockport (NY)
Susquehanna U (PA)
Tabor Coll (KS)
Tarleton State U (TX)
Taylor U (IN)
Temple U (PA)
Tennessee Wesleyan U (TN)
Texas A&M Intl U (TX)
Texas A&M U (TX)
Texas A&M U–Central Texas (TX)
Texas A&M U–Commerce (TX)

Texas A&M U–Corpus Christi (TX)
Texas A&M U–Kingsville (TX)
Texas Christian U (TX)
Texas Lutheran U (TX)
Texas Southern U (TX)
Texas State U (TX)
Texas Tech U (TX)
Texas Woman's U (TX)
Tiffin U (OH)
Toccoa Falls Coll (GA)
Towson U (MD)
Transylvania U (KY)
Trevecca Nazarene U (TN)
Trine U (IN)
Trinity U (TX)
Troy U (AL)
Truett McConnell U (GA)
Truman State U (MO)
Tulane U (LA)
Union Coll (NY)
Union U (TN)
United States Military Acad (NY)
U at Albany, State U of New York (NY)
U at Buffalo, the State U of New York (NY)
The U of Akron (OH)
The U of Alabama (AL)
The U of Alabama at Birmingham (AL)
The U of Alabama in Huntsville (AL)
U of Alaska Fairbanks (AK)
U of Alaska Southeast (AK)
The U of Arizona (AZ)
U of Arkansas (AR)
U of Arkansas at Little Rock (AR)
U of California, Berkeley (CA)
U of California, Irvine (CA)
U of California, Los Angeles (CA)
U of California, Merced (CA)
U of California, Riverside (CA)
U of California, San Diego (CA)
U of California, Santa Barbara (CA)
U of Central Arkansas (AR)
U of Central Florida (FL)
U of Charleston (WV)
U of Cincinnati (OH)
U of Colorado Boulder (CO)
U of Colorado Colorado Springs (CO)
U of Colorado Denver (CO)
U of Dallas (TX)
U of Dayton (OH)
U of Denver (CO)
U of Detroit Mercy (MI)
U of Dubuque (IA)
U of Guam (GU)
U of Hartford (CT)
U of Hawaii at Manoa (HI)
U of Houston (TX)
U of Houston–Clear Lake (TX)
U of Houston–Downtown (TX)
U of Idaho (ID)
U of Illinois at Chicago (IL)
U of Illinois at Springfield (IL)
The U of Iowa (IA)
U of Jamestown (ND)
The U of Kansas (KS)
U of Kentucky (KY)
U of La Verne (CA)
U of Louisiana at Lafayette (LA)
U of Louisiana at Monroe (LA)
U of Louisville (KY)
U of Maine (ME)
U of Maine at Presque Isle (ME)
U of Mary Hardin-Baylor (TX)
U of Maryland, Baltimore County (MD)
U of Maryland Global Campus (MD)
U of Mary Washington (VA)
U of Massachusetts Amherst (MA)
U of Massachusetts Boston (MA)
U of Massachusetts Dartmouth (MA)
U of Massachusetts Lowell (MA)
U of Memphis (TN)
U of Miami (FL)
U of Michigan (MI)
U of Michigan–Dearborn (MI)
U of Michigan–Flint (MI)
U of Minnesota, Duluth (MN)
U of Minnesota, Morris (MN)
U of Minnesota, Twin Cities Campus (MN)
U of Missouri–St. Louis (MO)
U of Montana (MT)
U of Montevallo (AL)
U of Nebraska at Kearney (NE)
U of Nebraska–Lincoln (NE)
U of Nevada, Las Vegas (NV)
U of Nevada, Reno (NV)
U of New England (ME)
U of New Hampshire (NH)
U of New Haven (CT)
U of New Mexico (NM)
The U of North Carolina at Chapel Hill (NC)
The U of North Carolina at Charlotte (NC)
The U of North Carolina at Greensboro (NC)
The U of North Carolina at Pembroke (NC)
The U of North Carolina Wilmington (NC)
U of North Dakota (ND)
U of Northern Colorado (CO)
U of Northern Iowa (IA)
U of North Florida (FL)
U of North Texas (TX)
U of Northwestern–St. Paul (MN)
U of Notre Dame (IN)
U of Oregon (OR)
U of Pennsylvania (PA)
U of Pikeville (KY)
U of Pittsburgh at Bradford (PA)
U of Pittsburgh at Greensburg (PA)
U of Portland (OR)
U of Providence (MT)
U of Puget Sound (WA)
U of Richmond (VA)
U of St. Francis (IL)
U of Saint Francis (IN)
U of Saint Joseph (CT)
U of Saint Mary (KS)
U of St. Thomas (TX)
U of San Diego (CA)
U of San Francisco (CA)
U of Science and Arts of Oklahoma (OK)
The U of Scranton (PA)
U of South Alabama (AL)
U of South Carolina (SC)
U of South Carolina Aiken (SC)
U of South Carolina Beaufort (SC)
U of South Dakota (SD)
U of Southern Indiana (IN)
U of Southern Maine (ME)
U of Southern Mississippi (MS)
U of South Florida (FL)
U of South Florida, St. Petersburg (FL)
The U of Tampa (FL)
The U of Tennessee (TN)
The U of Tennessee at Chattanooga (TN)
The U of Tennessee at Martin (TN)
The U of Texas at El Paso (TX)
The U of Texas at San Antonio (TX)
The U of Texas of the Permian Basin (TX)
The U of Texas Rio Grande Valley (TX)
U of the Fraser Valley (BC, Canada)
U of the Incarnate Word (TX)
U of the Pacific (CA)
The U of the South (TN)
U of the Virgin Islands (VI)
The U of Toledo (OH)
U of Toronto (ON, Canada)
The U of Tulsa (OK)
U of Utah (UT)
U of Vermont (VT)
U of Virginia (VA)
U of Washington (WA)
U of Waterloo (ON, Canada)
The U of West Alabama (AL)
The U of Western Ontario (ON, Canada)
U of West Florida (FL)
U of West Georgia (GA)
U of Wisconsin–Eau Claire (WI)
U of Wisconsin–Green Bay (WI)
U of Wisconsin–La Crosse (WI)
U of Wisconsin–Madison (WI)
U of Wisconsin–Milwaukee (WI)
U of Wisconsin–Parkside (WI)
U of Wisconsin–Platteville (WI)
U of Wisconsin–Superior (WI)
U of Wyoming (WY)
Upper Iowa U (IA)
Ursuline Coll (OH)
Utah State U (UT)
Utah Valley U (UT)
Utica Coll (NY)
Valdosta State U (GA)
Valley City State U (ND)
Valparaiso U (IN)
Vanderbilt U (TN)
Vanguard U of Southern California (CA)
Villanova U (PA)
Virginia Commonwealth U (VA)
Virginia Wesleyan U (VA)
Wabash Coll (IN)
Wake Forest U (NC)
Walla Walla U (WA)
Warren Wilson Coll (NC)
Wartburg Coll (IA)
Washington & Jefferson Coll (PA)
Washington and Lee U (VA)
Washington Coll (MD)
Washington State U (WA)
Washington State U–Tri-Cities (WA)
Washington State U–Vancouver (WA)
Washington U in St. Louis (MO)
Wayland Baptist U (TX)
Waynesburg U (PA)
Wayne State Coll (NE)
Wayne State U (MI)
Weber State U (UT)
Wesleyan Coll (GA)
Wesleyan U (CT)
West Chester U of Pennsylvania (PA)
Western Carolina U (NC)
Western Colorado U (CO)
Western Connecticut State U (CT)
Western Kentucky U (KY)
Western Michigan U (MI)
Western New England U (MA)
Western New Mexico U (NM)
Western Oregon U (OR)
Western Washington U (WA)
Westfield State U (MA)
West Liberty U (WV)
Westminster Coll (UT)
Westmont Coll (CA)
West Virginia U (WV)
Wheaton Coll (IL)
Wheaton Coll (MA)
Whitworth U (WA)
Wichita State U (KS)
Widener U (PA)
Wilkes U (PA)
Willamette U (OR)
William & Mary (VA)
William Jewell Coll (MO)
William Paterson U of New Jersey (NJ)
William Peace U (NC)
William Penn U (IA)
Williams Coll (MA)
Wilmington Coll (OH)
Wingate U (NC)
Winthrop U (SC)
Wittenberg U (OH)
Wofford Coll (SC)
Worcester State U (MA)
Wright State U (OH)
Wright State U–Lake Campus (OH)
Xavier U (OH)
Xavier U of Louisiana (LA)
Yale U (CT)
Yeshiva U (NY)
York Coll of Pennsylvania (PA)
Youngstown State U (OH)

ENGLISH AS A SECOND/ FOREIGN LANGUAGE (TEACHING)

American U (DC)
Augsburg U (MN)
Bayamón Central U (PR)
Bethel U (IN)
Bethel U (MN)
Bluffton U (OH)
Brigham Young U (UT)
California State U, Stanislaus (CA)
Calvin Coll (MI)
The Catholic U of America (DC)
Concordia Coll (MN)
Concordia U, St. Paul (MN)
Concordia U Wisconsin (WI)
Doane U (NE)
Eastern Washington U (WA)
Fort Lewis Coll (CO)
Goshen Coll (IN)
Inter American U of Puerto Rico, Aguadilla Campus (PR)
Inter American U of Puerto Rico, Barranquitas Campus (PR)
Inter American U of Puerto Rico, Metropolitan Campus (PR)
Inter American U of Puerto Rico, San Germán Campus (PR)
Lee U (TN)
Le Moyne Coll (NY)
Molloy Coll (NY)
Multnomah U (OR)
New York U (NY)
Niagara U (NY)
Northwest U (WA)
The Ohio State U (OH)
Queens Coll of the City U of New York (NY)
Roanoke Coll (VA)
Roberts Wesleyan Coll (NY)
Salisbury U (MD)
Simmons U (MA)
Union U (TN)
The U of Findlay (OH)
U of Guam (GU)
U of Hawaii at Manoa (HI)
U of Northern Iowa (IA)
U of Northwestern–St. Paul (MN)
The U of Texas at San Antonio (TX)
U of Wisconsin–Milwaukee (WI)

ENGLISH/FRENCH AS A SECOND/FOREIGN LANGUAGE (TEACHING) RELATED

Bethel U (IN)

ENGLISH LANGUAGE AND LITERATURE RELATED

The Baptist Coll of Florida (FL)
Binghamton U, State U of New York (NY)
Dakota State U (SD)
Doane U (NE)
Drexel U (PA)
Earlham Coll (IN)
Eastern U (PA)
Emmanuel Coll (MA)
Florida State U (FL)
Harvard U (MA)
Hofstra U (NY)
John Cabot U (Italy)
Loyola U New Orleans (LA)
Middlebury Coll (VT)
Patrick Henry Coll (VA)
Pitzer Coll (CA)
Saint Mary's U of Minnesota (MN)
Southeastern U (FL)
State U of New York Coll at Potsdam (NY)
State U of New York Empire State Coll (NY)
U of Michigan (MI)
U of Pennsylvania (PA)
U of Providence (MT)
Washington U in St. Louis (MO)
Wesleyan U (CT)
Western Kentucky U (KY)

ENGLISH/LANGUAGE ARTS TEACHER EDUCATION

Abilene Christian U (TX)
Adams State U (CO)
Albion Coll (MI)
Alverno Coll (WI)
Anderson U (IN)
Anderson U (SC)
Appalachian State U (NC)
Aquinas Coll (MI)
Arizona Christian U (AZ)
Arkansas Tech U (AR)
Auburn U (AL)
Augustana Coll (IL)
Averett U (VA)
Ball State U (IN)
The Baptist Coll of Florida (FL)
Barry U (FL)
Bayamón Central U (PR)
Baylor U (TX)
Bethany Lutheran Coll (MN)
Bethel U (IN)
Bethel U (MN)
Boise State U (ID)
Bowling Green State U (OH)
Bradley U (IL)
Bridgewater State U (MA)
Bryan Coll (TN)
California State U, Long Beach (CA)
Cameron U (OK)
Campbellsville U (KY)
Capital U (OH)
The Catholic U of America (DC)
Cedarville U (OH)
Central Michigan U (MI)
Central State U (OH)
Central Washington U (WA)
Coll of Saint Mary (NE)
The Coll of Saint Rose (NY)
Coll of Staten Island of the City U of New York (NY)
Coll of the Ozarks (MO)
Concordia U Chicago (IL)
Covenant Coll (GA)
Culver-Stockton Coll (MO)
Dakota State U (SD)
Delta State U (MS)
Dickinson State U (ND)
Dominican Coll (NY)
East Carolina U (NC)
East Central U (OK)
Eastern Kentucky U (KY)
Eastern Michigan U (MI)
Eastern Washington U (WA)
East Texas Baptist U (TX)
Emmanuel Coll (GA)
Emory & Henry Coll (VA)
Ferris State U (MI)
Fitchburg State U (MA)
Flagler Coll (FL)
Florida A&M U (FL)
Florida Atlantic U (FL)
Florida Southern Coll (FL)
Florida SouthWestern State Coll (FL)
Florida State U (FL)
Franklin Coll (IN)
Friends U (KS)
Glenville State Coll (WV)
Goshen Coll (IN)
Grambling State U (LA)
Grand Valley State U (MI)
Granite State Coll (NH)
Harding U (AR)
Hardin-Simmons U (TX)
Hofstra U (NY)
Hope Coll (MI)
Houston Baptist U (TX)
Husson U (ME)
Immaculata U (PA)
Indiana U Bloomington (IN)
Indiana U Northwest (IN)
Indiana U-Purdue U Indianapolis (IN)
Indiana U South Bend (IN)
Inter American U of Puerto Rico, San Germán Campus (PR)
Iona Coll (NY)
Ithaca Coll (NY)
John Brown U (AR)
Kansas Wesleyan U (KS)
Kennesaw State U (GA)
Keuka Coll (NY)
Lee U (TN)
Le Moyne Coll (NY)
LeTourneau U (TX)
Lewis-Clark State Coll (ID)
Limestone Coll (SC)
Lincoln U (MO)
Lipscomb U (TN)
Louisiana Tech U (LA)
Madonna U (MI)
Malone U (OH)
Manhattanville Coll (NY)
Martin Luther Coll (MN)
Marywood U (PA)
Mayville State U (ND)
McMurry U (TX)
Merrimack Coll (MA)
Messiah Coll (PA)
Miami U (OH)
Miami U Hamilton (OH)
Miami U Middletown (OH)
MidAmerica Nazarene U (KS)
Midway U (KY)
Millikin U (IL)
Minot State U (ND)
Misericordia U (PA)
Missouri State U (MO)
Mount Marty Coll (SD)
Mount Vernon Nazarene U (OH)

National U (CA)
Nazareth Coll of Rochester (NY)
Nebraska Wesleyan U (NE)
New York U (NY)
Niagara U (NY)
Northeastern State U (OK)
Northern Arizona U (AZ)
Northern State U (SD)
North Greenville U (SC)
Northwestern Coll (IA)
Northwest Missouri State U (MO)
Northwest Nazarene U (ID)
Northwest U (WA)
Notre Dame Coll (OH)
Nova Southeastern U (FL)
Oakland City U (IN)
Ohio Dominican U (OH)
The Ohio State U (OH)
Oklahoma Baptist U (OK)
Olivet Nazarene U (IL)
Oral Roberts U (OK)
Ottawa U (KS)
Pace U, Pleasantville Campus (NY)
Palm Beach Atlantic U (FL)
Pepperdine U, Malibu (CA)
Pittsburg State U (KS)
Providence Coll (RI)
Purdue U Fort Wayne (IN)
Queens Coll of the City U of New York (NY)
Rhode Island Coll (RI)
Roanoke Coll (VA)
Roberts Wesleyan Coll (NY)
Rocky Mountain Coll (MT)
Roger Williams U (RI)
Saginaw Valley State U (MI)
St. Catherine U (MN)
St. Cloud State U (MN)
Saint Francis U (PA)
St. John Fisher Coll (NY)
Saint Joseph's U (PA)
Saint Mary's U of Minnesota (MN)
Salve Regina U (RI)
Schreiner U (TX)
Seton Hill U (PA)
Slippery Rock U of Pennsylvania (PA)
Southeastern Louisiana U (LA)
Southeastern U (FL)
Southeast Missouri State U (MO)
Southwest Baptist U (MO)
Southwestern Coll (KS)
Southwestern Oklahoma State U (OK)
Spring Arbor U (MI)
Spring Hill Coll (AL)
State U of New York at New Paltz (NY)
State U of New York Coll at Oneonta (NY)
State U of New York Coll at Potsdam (NY)
Sterling Coll (KS)
Taylor U (IN)
Texas Christian U (TX)
Tiffin U (OH)
Toccoa Falls Coll (GA)
Trevecca Nazarene U (TN)
Trine U (IN)
The U of Akron (OH)
U of Dubuque (IA)
The U of Findlay (OH)
U of Idaho (ID)
U of Illinois at Chicago (IL)
U of Jamestown (ND)
U of Louisiana at Monroe (LA)
U of Maine (ME)
U of Mary Hardin-Baylor (TX)
U of Michigan–Flint (MI)
U of Nebraska–Lincoln (NE)
U of Nevada, Reno (NV)
The U of North Carolina at Greensboro (NC)
The U of North Carolina at Pembroke (NC)
U of Northern Colorado (CO)
U of Northwestern–St. Paul (MN)
U of Pikeville (KY)
U of Providence (MT)
U of St. Francis (IL)
U of South Dakota (SD)
U of South Florida (FL)
U of Vermont (VT)
U of Wisconsin–Milwaukee (WI)
U of Wisconsin–Superior (WI)
Utah State U (UT)
Utah Valley U (UT)
Utica Coll (NY)
Valley City State U (ND)
Valparaiso U (IN)
Washington U in St. Louis (MO)
Wayland Baptist U (TX)
Waynesburg U (PA)
Wayne State Coll (NE)
Weber State U (UT)
Western Carolina U (NC)
Western Michigan U (MI)
Widener U (PA)
William Penn U (IA)
Wingate U (NC)
York Coll of Pennsylvania (PA)
Youngstown State U (OH)

ENGLISH LITERATURE (BRITISH AND COMMONWEALTH)
Gannon U (PA)
New York U (NY)
Purchase Coll, State U of New York (NY)
Purdue U Fort Wayne (IN)
Saint Mary's Coll (IN)
Washington U in St. Louis (MO)

ENTOMOLOGY
Cornell U (NY)
Michigan State U (MI)
The Ohio State U (OH)
Oklahoma State U (OK)
Texas A&M U (TX)
U of California, Riverside (CA)
U of Idaho (ID)
U of Nebraska–Lincoln (NE)
U of Wisconsin–Madison (WI)

ENTREPRENEURIAL AND SMALL BUSINESS RELATED
Babson Coll (MA)
Fairleigh Dickinson U (NJ)
Fashion Inst of Technology (NY)
Flagler Coll (FL)
Fort Lewis Coll (CO)
Lipscomb U (TN)
New York Inst of Technology (NY)
Penn State U Park (PA)
Worcester State U (MA)

ENTREPRENEURSHIP
American Public U System (WV)
The American U of Paris (France)
Arizona State U at the Tempe campus (AZ)
Auburn U at Montgomery (AL)
Avila U (MO)
Azusa Pacific U (CA)
Babson Coll (MA)
Ball State U (IN)
Baruch Coll of the City U of New York (NY)
Baylor U (TX)
Belmont U (TN)
Binghamton U, State U of New York (NY)
Boston Coll (MA)
Bradley U (IL)
Brigham Young U (UT)
Bryant U (RI)
Butler U (IN)
California Baptist U (CA)
California State U, Dominguez Hills (CA)
California State U, Fullerton (CA)
Carnegie Mellon U (PA)
Central Michigan U (MI)
Clarkson U (NY)
Columbia Coll (MO)
Dallas Baptist U (TX)
Davenport U, Grand Rapids (MI)
Dominican U (IL)
Drexel U (PA)
East Central U (OK)
Eastern Michigan U (MI)
Eastern U (PA)
Elon U (NC)
Endicott Coll (MA)
Florida State U (FL)
Fort Lewis Coll (CO)
Gannon U (PA)
George Fox U (OR)
Georgia State U (GA)
Governors State U (IL)
Grand Valley State U (MI)
Hampshire Coll (MA)
HEC Montreal (QC, Canada)
High Point U (NC)
Hofstra U (NY)
Husson U (ME)
Illinois Wesleyan U (IL)
Inter American U of Puerto Rico, Aguadilla Campus (PR)
Inter American U of Puerto Rico, Barranquitas Campus (PR)
Inter American U of Puerto Rico, Bayamón Campus (PR)
Inter American U of Puerto Rico, Metropolitan Campus (PR)
Inter American U of Puerto Rico, San Germán Campus (PR)
Iowa State U of Science and Technology (IA)
Jacksonville U (FL)
Kansas State U (KS)
Kennesaw State U (GA)
Lamar U (TX)
Lasell Coll (MA)
Lenoir-Rhyne U (NC)
Lindenwood U (MO)
Lipscomb U (TN)
Louisiana State U and A&M Coll (LA)
Loyola Marymount U (CA)
Loyola U Chicago (IL)
Lynn U (FL)
Marquette U (WI)
Marymount Manhattan Coll (NY)
Mercer U, Macon (GA)
Mercy Coll (NY)
Miami U Hamilton (OH)
Miami U Middletown (OH)
Middle Tennessee State U (TN)
Millikin U (IL)
Minneapolis Coll of Art and Design (MN)
Missouri State U (MO)
Mount St. Mary's U (MD)
North Central U (MN)
Oklahoma State U (OK)
Pace U, Pleasantville Campus (NY)
Point Loma Nazarene U (CA)
Purdue U Northwest (IN)
Rochester U (MI)
Rollins Coll (FL)
Rowan U (NJ)
St. Cloud State U (MN)
Saint Louis U (MO)
St. Mary's U (TX)
Saint Mary's U of Minnesota (MN)
Salem State U (MA)
Samford U (AL)
Sam Houston State U (TX)
Seton Hill U (PA)
Shenandoah U (VA)
Sierra Nevada Coll (NV)
South Dakota State U (SD)
Stetson U (FL)
Suffolk U (MA)
Temple U (PA)
Texas Christian U (TX)
Trine U (IN)
The U of Arizona (AZ)
U of Central Arkansas (AR)
U of Dayton (OH)
U of Hartford (CT)
U of Hawaii at Manoa (HI)
U of Houston (TX)
U of Illinois at Chicago (IL)
U of Miami (FL)
U of Michigan–Flint (MI)
U of Minnesota, Duluth (MN)
U of Nevada, Las Vegas (NV)
U of New England (ME)
The U of North Carolina at Greensboro (NC)
The U of North Carolina at Pembroke (NC)
U of North Dakota (ND)
U of North Texas (TX)
U of St. Francis (IL)
U of San Francisco (CA)
U of South Dakota (SD)
U of South Florida, St. Petersburg (FL)
The U of Tampa (FL)
The U of Tennessee at Chattanooga (TN)
The U of Texas at San Antonio (TX)
The U of Texas Rio Grande Valley (TX)
The U of Toledo (OH)
U of Utah (UT)
U of Vermont (VT)
U of Washington (WA)
The U of Western Ontario (ON, Canada)
Vermont Tech Coll (VT)
Washington State U (WA)
Washington U in St. Louis (MO)
Waynesburg U (PA)
Western Carolina U (NC)
Western Kentucky U (KY)
Western Michigan U (MI)
Western New England U (MA)
West Virginia U (WV)
Wichita State U (KS)
Wilkes U (PA)
Wittenberg U (OH)
Xavier U (OH)
York Coll of Pennsylvania (PA)

ENVIRONMENTAL BIOLOGY
Barnard Coll (NY)
Beloit Coll (WI)
Bennington Coll (VT)
Bridgewater State U (MA)
California State Polytechnic U, Pomona (CA)
Cazenovia Coll (NY)
Cedar Crest Coll (PA)
Central Washington U (WA)
Colby Coll (ME)
Edinboro U of Pennsylvania (PA)
Ferris State U (MI)
Fitchburg State U (MA)
Iona Coll (NY)
Jacksonville State U (AL)
Liberty U (VA)
Lindenwood U (MO)
Michigan State U (MI)
Minnesota State U Mankato (MN)
Northern Arizona U (AZ)
Northwestern Coll (IA)
Roberts Wesleyan Coll (NY)
Saint Mary's U of Minnesota (MN)
Salem State U (MA)
State U of New York Coll at Cortland (NY)
Texas A&M U (TX)
Tulane U (LA)
U of Dayton (OH)
Washington U in St. Louis (MO)
Wingate U (NC)

ENVIRONMENTAL CHEMISTRY
Beloit Coll (WI)
Bennington Coll (VT)
Central Washington U (WA)
Colby Coll (ME)
Florida State U (FL)
Lawrence Technological U (MI)
Queens U of Charlotte (NC)
Rhode Island Coll (RI)
Roberts Wesleyan Coll (NY)
U of California, San Diego (CA)
Vanguard U of Southern California (CA)
Worcester State U (MA)

ENVIRONMENTAL DESIGN/ ARCHITECTURE
Arizona State U at the Tempe campus (AZ)
Auburn U (AL)
Ball State U (IN)
Bennington Coll (VT)
Boston Architectural Coll (MA)
Bowling Green State U (OH)
Cornell U (NY)
Delaware Valley U (PA)
Florida Atlantic U (FL)
Marywood U (PA)
Montana State U (MT)
Otis Coll of Art and Design (CA)
Stony Brook U, State U of New York (NY)
U at Buffalo, the State U of New York (NY)
U of Colorado Boulder (CO)
U of Hawaii at Manoa (HI)
U of Houston (TX)
U of Massachusetts Amherst (MA)
U of Memphis (TN)
U of Minnesota, Twin Cities Campus (MN)
U of New Mexico (NM)
U of Pennsylvania (PA)
Utah State U (UT)

ENVIRONMENTAL EDUCATION
U of Dubuque (IA)
U of Nevada, Reno (NV)

ENVIRONMENTAL ENGINEERING TECHNOLOGY
Appalachian State U (NC)
Bowling Green State U (OH)
Brown U (RI)
California State U, Long Beach (CA)
City Coll of the City U of New York (NY)
Florida State U (FL)
Michigan State U (MI)
United States Military Acad (NY)
The U of Findlay (OH)
U of Wisconsin–Green Bay (WI)

ENVIRONMENTAL/ ENVIRONMENTAL HEALTH ENGINEERING
Arizona State U at the Polytechnic campus (AZ)
Arizona State U at the Tempe campus (AZ)
Bucknell U (PA)
California Polytechnic State U, San Luis Obispo (CA)
Central State U (OH)
Clarkson U (NY)
Clemson U (SC)
Colorado School of Mines (CO)
Colorado State U (CO)
Drexel U (PA)
East Central U (OK)
Elon U (NC)
Florida Gulf Coast U (FL)
Florida Polytechnic U (FL)
Gannon U (PA)
The George Washington U (DC)
Georgia Inst of Technology (GA)
Indiana U of Pennsylvania (PA)
Johns Hopkins U (MD)
Kennesaw State U (GA)
Lafayette Coll (PA)
Lehigh U (PA)
Louisiana State U and A&M Coll (LA)
Loyola U Chicago (IL)
Manhattan Coll (NY)
Marquette U (WI)
Michigan Technological U (MI)
Missouri U of Science and Technology (MO)
Montana Technological U (MT)
New Jersey Inst of Technology (NJ)
New Mexico Inst of Mining and Technology (NM)
New York U (NY)
Northern Arizona U (AZ)
Northwestern U (IL)
The Ohio State U (OH)
Oral Roberts U (OK)
Penn State Abington (PA)
Penn State Altoona (PA)
Penn State Beaver (PA)
Penn State Berks (PA)
Penn State Brandywine (PA)
Penn State DuBois (PA)
Penn State Erie, The Behrend Coll (PA)
Penn State Fayette, The Eberly Campus (PA)
Penn State Greater Allegheny (PA)
Penn State Harrisburg (PA)
Penn State Hazleton (PA)
Penn State Lehigh Valley (PA)
Penn State Mont Alto (PA)
Penn State New Kensington (PA)
Penn State Schuylkill (PA)
Penn State Shenango (PA)
Penn State U Park (PA)
Penn State Wilkes-Barre (PA)
Penn State York (PA)
Polytechnic U of Puerto Rico (PR)
Portland State U (OR)
Rice U (TX)
Roger Williams U (RI)
Saint Francis U (PA)
San Diego State U (CA)
Seattle U (WA)
Southern Methodist U (TX)
Stanford U (CA)
Stevens Inst of Technology (NJ)
Tarleton State U (TX)

Taylor U (IN)
Temple U (PA)
Texas A&M U–Kingsville (TX)
Texas Tech U (TX)
Tulane U (LA)
United States Military Acad (NY)
U at Buffalo, the State U of New York (NY)
The U of Alabama (AL)
The U of Arizona (AZ)
U of California, Berkeley (CA)
U of California, Irvine (CA)
U of California, Merced (CA)
U of California, Riverside (CA)
U of Central Florida (FL)
U of Cincinnati (OH)
U of Colorado Boulder (CO)
U of Massachusetts Lowell (MA)
U of Miami (FL)
U of Michigan (MI)
U of Minnesota, Twin Cities Campus (MN)
U of Nevada, Reno (NV)
U of New Hampshire (NH)
U of North Dakota (ND)
U of Notre Dame (IN)
U of Pennsylvania (PA)
The U of Toledo (OH)
U of Vermont (VT)
U of Washington (WA)
U of Waterloo (ON, Canada)
The U of Western Ontario (ON, Canada)
U of Wisconsin–Platteville (WI)
Utah State U (UT)
Valparaiso U (IN)
Wilkes U (PA)
Worcester Polytechnic Inst (MA)
Yale U (CT)

ENVIRONMENTAL HEALTH
American U of Beirut (Lebanon)
Baylor U (TX)
Boise State U (ID)
Bowling Green State U (OH)
California State U, Northridge (CA)
Central Michigan U (MI)
Colorado State U (CO)
Dickinson State U (ND)
East Carolina U (NC)
East Central U (OK)
Eastern Kentucky U (KY)
Illinois State U (IL)
Indiana U Bloomington (IN)
Missouri Southern State U (MO)
Oakland U (MI)
Old Dominion U (VA)
Rhode Island Coll (RI)
Texas Southern U (TX)
U of Arkansas at Little Rock (AR)
U of Massachusetts Lowell (MA)
The U of North Carolina at Chapel Hill (NC)
U of Saint Francis (IN)
U of Washington (WA)
West Chester U of Pennsylvania (PA)
Western Carolina U (NC)
Western Kentucky U (KY)
Willamette U (OR)

ENVIRONMENTAL SCIENCE
Abilene Christian U (TX)
Albion Coll (MI)
Alverno Coll (WI)
American Public U System (WV)
American U (DC)
The American U of Paris (France)
Appalachian State U (NC)
Arizona State U at the West campus (AZ)
Arkansas Tech U (AR)
Assumption Coll (MA)
Auburn U (AL)
Auburn U at Montgomery (AL)
Averett U (VA)
Ball State U (IN)
Barnard Coll (NY)
Bayamón Central U (PR)
Baylor U (TX)
Belmont U (TN)
Benedictine U (IL)
Bennington Coll (VT)
Berry Coll (GA)
Bethel U (MN)
Biola U (CA)
Bradley U (IL)
Bridgewater Coll (VA)
Brigham Young U (UT)
Brown U (RI)
Bryant U (RI)
Bucknell U (PA)
California Baptist U (CA)
California Lutheran U (CA)
California State U, Fresno (CA)
California State U, Long Beach (CA)
California State U, Monterey Bay (CA)
California U of Pennsylvania (PA)
Calvin Coll (MI)
Capital U (OH)
Carthage Coll (WI)
Catawba Coll (NC)
Cedarville U (OH)
Central Methodist U (MO)
Central Michigan U (MI)
Central Washington U (WA)
Chatham U (PA)
Chestnut Hill Coll (PA)
Clarion U of Pennsylvania (PA)
Clarkson U (NY)
Coe Coll (IA)
Colby Coll (ME)
Colgate U (NY)
The Coll of Wooster (OH)
The Colorado Coll (CO)
Colorado State U (CO)
Columbia Coll (MO)
Creighton U (NE)
Dallas Baptist U (TX)
Delaware Valley U (PA)
DePaul U (IL)
Dickinson Coll (PA)
Dickinson State U (ND)
Dominican U (IL)
Drake U (IA)
Drexel U (PA)
Earlham Coll (IN)
Eastern New Mexico U (NM)
Eastern U (PA)
Eastern Washington U (WA)
Edgewood Coll (WI)
Edinboro U of Pennsylvania (PA)
Elon U (NC)
Emory & Henry Coll (VA)
Endicott Coll (MA)
Fairleigh Dickinson U (NJ)
Flagler Coll (FL)
Florida A&M U (FL)
Florida Inst of Technology (FL)
Florida State U (FL)
Fordham U (NY)
Fort Lewis Coll (CO)
Framingham State U (MA)
Freed-Hardeman U (TN)
Gannon U (PA)
Geneva Coll (PA)
George Mason U (VA)
Georgia Coll & State U (GA)
Georgia Gwinnett Coll (GA)
Goshen Coll (IN)
Hollins U (VA)
Husson U (ME)
Indiana U Bloomington (IN)
Indiana U-Purdue U Indianapolis (IN)
Inter American U of Puerto Rico, Aguadilla Campus (PR)
Inter American U of Puerto Rico, Barranquitas Campus (PR)
Inter American U of Puerto Rico, Bayamón Campus (PR)
Inter American U of Puerto Rico, San Germán Campus (PR)
Iowa State U of Science and Technology (IA)
Ithaca Coll (NY)
John Carroll U (OH)
Johns Hopkins U (MD)
Kennesaw State U (GA)
Keuka Coll (NY)
King's Coll (PA)
Knox Coll (IL)
Kutztown U of Pennsylvania (PA)
Lamar U (TX)
La Sierra U (CA)
Lewis U (IL)
Lincoln U (PA)
Linfield Coll (OR)
Lipscomb U (TN)
Longwood U (VA)
Louisiana State U and A&M Coll (LA)
Loyola Marymount U (CA)
Loyola U Chicago (IL)
Loyola U New Orleans (LA)
Madonna U (MI)
Marietta Coll (OH)
Marshall U (WV)
Maryville U of Saint Louis (MO)
Marywood U (PA)
Massachusetts Maritime Acad (MA)
McMurry U (TX)
Merrimack Coll (MA)
Messiah Coll (PA)
Miami U (OH)
Miami U Hamilton (OH)
Miami U Middletown (OH)
Michigan State U (MI)
Michigan Technological U (MI)
Montana State U (MT)
Moravian Coll (PA)
Muhlenberg Coll (PA)
Muskingum U (OH)
Nazareth Coll of Rochester (NY)
New England Coll (NH)
New Jersey Inst of Technology (NJ)
New York U (NY)
Niagara U (NY)
Northern Arizona U (AZ)
Northern Kentucky U (KY)
Northwestern U (IL)
Northwest U (WA)
Nova Southeastern U (FL)
Oakland U (MI)
Ohio Dominican U (OH)
The Ohio State U (OH)
Oklahoma State U (OK)
Pace U, Pleasantville Campus (NY)
Patrick Henry Coll (VA)
Point Loma Nazarene U (CA)
Portland State U (OR)
Queens Coll of the City U of New York (NY)
Queens U of Charlotte (NC)
Ramapo Coll of New Jersey (NJ)
Randolph Coll (VA)
Rhodes Coll (TN)
Rocky Mountain Coll (MT)
Roger Williams U (RI)
St. Cloud State U (MN)
Saint Francis U (PA)
Saint Joseph's U (PA)
Saint Louis U (MO)
Saint Mary's Coll of California (CA)
St. Mary's U (TX)
St. Norbert Coll (WI)
Saint Vincent Coll (PA)
Salisbury U (MD)
Samford U (AL)
Sam Houston State U (TX)
San Diego State U (CA)
San Francisco State U (CA)
Santa Clara U (CA)
Scripps Coll (CA)
Seattle U (WA)
Siena Coll (NY)
Siena Heights U (MI)
Sierra Nevada Coll (NV)
Simmons U (MA)
Simon Fraser U (BC, Canada)
Skidmore Coll (NY)
South Dakota State U (SD)
Southeast Missouri State U (MO)
Southern Illinois U Edwardsville (IL)
Southern Methodist U (TX)
State U of New York Coll at Cortland (NY)
Stetson U (FL)
Stevenson U (MD)
Stockton U (NJ)
Suffolk U (MA)
SUNY Brockport (NY)
Tarleton State U (TX)
Taylor U (IN)
Temple U (PA)
Texas A&M U (TX)
Texas A&M U–Commerce (TX)
Texas A&M U–Corpus Christi (TX)
Texas Christian U (TX)
Texas State U (TX)
Troy U (AL)
United States Military Acad (NY)
U at Albany, State U of New York (NY)
The U of Alabama (AL)
The U of Arizona (AZ)
U of Arkansas (AR)
U of California, Irvine (CA)
U of California, Los Angeles (CA)
U of California, Riverside (CA)
U of California, San Diego (CA)
U of Denver (CO)
U of Dubuque (IA)
U of Hawaii at Manoa (HI)
U of Houston (TX)
U of Houston–Clear Lake (TX)
U of Idaho (ID)
U of Illinois at Chicago (IL)
The U of Iowa (IA)
U of Louisiana at Lafayette (LA)
U of Maine (ME)
U of Maine at Presque Isle (ME)
U of Maryland, Baltimore County (MD)
U of Massachusetts Amherst (MA)
U of Massachusetts Boston (MA)
U of Massachusetts Lowell (MA)
U of Michigan–Dearborn (MI)
U of Minnesota, Duluth (MN)
U of Minnesota, Morris (MN)
U of Minnesota, Twin Cities Campus (MN)
U of Nevada, Reno (NV)
U of New England (ME)
U of New Hampshire (NH)
U of New Haven (CT)
U of New Mexico (NM)
The U of North Carolina at Chapel Hill (NC)
The U of North Carolina at Pembroke (NC)
The U of North Carolina Wilmington (NC)
U of Northern Iowa (IA)
U of Notre Dame (IN)
U of Oregon (OR)
U of St. Francis (IL)
U of Saint Francis (IN)
U of San Diego (CA)
U of San Francisco (CA)
The U of Scranton (PA)
U of South Carolina (SC)
U of Southern Indiana (IN)
U of Southern Maine (ME)
U of South Florida (FL)
U of South Florida, St. Petersburg (FL)
The U of Tennessee at Chattanooga (TN)
The U of Texas at El Paso (TX)
The U of Texas at San Antonio (TX)
The U of Texas Rio Grande Valley (TX)
U of the Incarnate Word (TX)
The U of Toledo (OH)
U of Utah (UT)
U of Vermont (VT)
U of Virginia (VA)
U of Washington (WA)
U of Washington, Bothell (WA)
U of Washington, Tacoma (WA)
U of Waterloo (ON, Canada)
The U of Western Ontario (ON, Canada)
U of West Florida (FL)
U of Wisconsin–Green Bay (WI)
U of Wisconsin–Madison (WI)
U of Wisconsin–Milwaukee (WI)
U of Wisconsin–Stout (WI)
U of Wisconsin–Superior (WI)
U of Wyoming (WY)
Upper Iowa U (IA)
Utah Valley U (UT)
Valley City State U (ND)
Valparaiso U (IN)
Villanova U (PA)
Walla Walla U (WA)
Wartburg Coll (IA)
Washington & Jefferson Coll (PA)
Washington Coll (MD)
Washington State U (WA)
Washington State U–Tri-Cities (WA)
Washington State U–Vancouver (WA)
Washington U in St. Louis (MO)
Wayland Baptist U (TX)
Wayne State U (MI)
Western Carolina U (NC)
Western Washington U (WA)
Westfield State U (MA)
Wheaton Coll (IL)
Wheaton Coll (MA)
Willamette U (OR)
Williams Coll (MA)
Winthrop U (SC)
Wittenberg U (OH)
Worcester State U (MA)
Wright State U (OH)
Wright State U–Lake Campus (OH)
Youngstown State U (OH)

ENVIRONMENTAL STUDIES
Albion Coll (MI)
Alfred U (NY)
American U (DC)
The American U of Paris (France)
Amherst Coll (MA)
Appalachian State U (NC)
Aquinas Coll (MI)
Arizona State U at the Polytechnic campus (AZ)
Arizona State U at the Tempe campus (AZ)
Augsburg U (MN)
Augustana Coll (IL)
Austin Coll (TX)
Bates Coll (ME)
Baylor U (TX)
Beloit Coll (WI)
Bemidji State U (MN)
Bennington Coll (VT)
Bethel U (MN)
Binghamton U, State U of New York (NY)
Birmingham-Southern Coll (AL)
Black Hills State U (SD)
Boise State U (ID)
Boston Coll (MA)
Bowdoin Coll (ME)
Bowling Green State U (OH)
Brandeis U (MA)
Brown U (RI)
Bucknell U (PA)
Butler U (IN)
California State U, Monterey Bay (CA)
California State U, Sacramento (CA)
California State U, San Marcos (CA)
California U of Pennsylvania (PA)
Calvin Coll (MI)
Carleton Coll (MN)
Catawba Coll (NC)
Central Coll (IA)
Central Michigan U (MI)
Central Washington U (WA)
Centre Coll (KY)
Chaminade U of Honolulu (HI)
Champlain Coll (VT)
Chatham U (PA)
Claremont McKenna Coll (CA)
Coe Coll (IA)
Colby Coll (ME)
Colby-Sawyer Coll (NH)
Colgate U (NY)
The Coll of Idaho (ID)
Coll of Saint Benedict (MN)
The Coll of St. Scholastica (MN)
Coll of the Holy Cross (MA)
The Coll of Wooster (OH)
The Colorado Coll (CO)
Columbia Coll (SC)
Concordia Coll (MN)
Concordia U Wisconsin (WI)
Cornell Coll (IA)
Dartmouth Coll (NH)
Davidson Coll (NC)
DePauw U (IN)
Dickinson Coll (PA)
Doane U (NE)
Drake U (IA)
Drew U (NJ)
Drexel U (PA)
Earlham Coll (IN)
Eastern Kentucky U (KY)
Eastern Mennonite U (VA)
Edgewood Coll (WI)
Elon U (NC)
Emory & Henry Coll (VA)
Emory U (GA)
Eugene Lang Coll of Liberal Arts (NY)
Fairfield U (CT)
Florida A&M U (FL)
Florida Gulf Coast U (FL)
Florida Southern Coll (FL)
Florida State U (FL)

Fordham U (NY)
Fort Lewis Coll (CO)
Framingham State U (MA)
Furman U (SC)
Georgetown U (DC)
The George Washington U (DC)
Gonzaga U (WA)
Goucher Coll (MD)
Guilford Coll (NC)
Gustavus Adolphus Coll (MN)
Hamline U (MN)
Hampshire Coll (MA)
Hampton U (VA)
Harvard U (MA)
Hobart and William Smith Colls (NY)
Hofstra U (NY)
Hollins U (VA)
Illinois Coll (IL)
Illinois Wesleyan U (IL)
Indiana U Bloomington (IN)
Indiana U South Bend (IN)
Indiana U Southeast (IN)
Inter American U of Puerto Rico, San Germán Campus (PR)
Iona Coll (NY)
Iowa State U of Science and Technology (IA)
Ithaca Coll (NY)
John Carroll U (OH)
Johns Hopkins U (MD)
Kansas Wesleyan U (KS)
Kenyon Coll (OH)
King's Coll (PA)
The King's U (AB, Canada)
Knox Coll (IL)
Lake Forest Coll (IL)
Lasell Coll (MA)
Lawrence U (WI)
Lehigh U (PA)
Le Moyne Coll (NY)
Lenoir-Rhyne U (NC)
Lesley U (MA)
Lewis & Clark Coll (OR)
Lincoln Memorial U (TN)
Linfield Coll (OR)
Louisiana Tech U (LA)
Loyola Marymount U (CA)
Loyola U Chicago (IL)
Loyola U New Orleans (LA)
Lynn U (FL)
Malone U (OH)
Manhattanville Coll (NY)
Mansfield U of Pennsylvania (PA)
Marietta Coll (OH)
Marquette U (WI)
Marymount Manhattan Coll (NY)
McDaniel Coll (MD)
McKendree U (IL)
Meredith Coll (NC)
Merrimack Coll (MA)
Michigan State U (MI)
Middlebury Coll (VT)
Millikin U (IL)
Minnesota State U Mankato (MN)
Moravian Coll (PA)
Mount Holyoke Coll (MA)
Mount St. Mary's U (MD)
Muskingum U (OH)
New Coll of Florida (FL)
New Mexico Highlands U (NM)
New Mexico Inst of Mining and Technology (NM)
New York U (NY)
Northeastern Illinois U (IL)
Northern Arizona U (AZ)
Northern Illinois U (IL)
Northwestern U (IL)
Oberlin Coll (OH)
Occidental Coll (CA)
Ohio Wesleyan U (OH)
Pace U, Pleasantville Campus (NY)
Pacific U (OR)
Penn State Altoona (PA)
Penn State U Park (PA)
Pitzer Coll (CA)
Pomona Coll (CA)
Portland State U (OR)
Purchase Coll, State U of New York (NY)
Queens Coll of the City U of New York (NY)
Queens U of Charlotte (NC)
Ramapo Coll of New Jersey (NJ)
Randolph Coll (VA)
Randolph-Macon Coll (VA)
Rhode Island Coll (RI)
Roanoke Coll (VA)
Rocky Mountain Coll (MT)
Rollins Coll (FL)
Rowan U (NJ)
St. Bonaventure U (NY)
St. Cloud State U (MN)
Saint Francis U (PA)
Saint John's U (MN)
Saint Louis U (MO)
Saint Mary's Coll of California (CA)
St. Mary's Coll of Maryland (MD)
St. Olaf Coll (MN)
St. Thomas U - New Brunswick (NB, Canada)
Saint Vincent Coll (PA)
Salve Regina U (RI)
San Diego State U (CA)
San Francisco State U (CA)
San Jose State U (CA)
Santa Clara U (CA)
Scripps Coll (CA)
Seattle U (WA)
Shenandoah U (VA)
Shepherd U (WV)
Siena Coll (NY)
Skidmore Coll (NY)
Smith Coll (MA)
Southwestern U (TX)
Stanford U (CA)
State U of New York Coll at Cortland (NY)
State U of New York Coll at Oneonta (NY)
State U of New York Coll at Potsdam (NY)
State U of New York Coll of Agriculture and Technology at Cobleskill (NY)
Stetson U (FL)
Stockton U (NJ)
Stony Brook U, State U of New York (NY)
Suffolk U (MA)
Susquehanna U (PA)
Temple U (PA)
Tennessee Wesleyan U (TN)
Texas A&M U (TX)
Trine U (IN)
Trinity U (TX)
Tulane U (LA)
U of Alaska Southeast (AK)
The U of Arizona (AZ)
U of California, Irvine (CA)
U of California, San Diego (CA)
U of California, Santa Barbara (CA)
U of California, Santa Cruz (CA)
U of Central Florida (FL)
U of Cincinnati (OH)
U of Colorado Boulder (CO)
U of Denver (CO)
U of Dubuque (IA)
U of Illinois at Springfield (IL)
The U of Iowa (IA)
The U of Kansas (KS)
U of Kentucky (KY)
U of Maine at Presque Isle (ME)
U of Maryland, Baltimore County (MD)
U of Miami (FL)
U of Michigan (MI)
U of Minnesota, Duluth (MN)
U of Minnesota, Morris (MN)
U of Montana (MT)
U of Nebraska–Lincoln (NE)
U of Nevada, Las Vegas (NV)
U of New England (ME)
The U of North Carolina at Chapel Hill (NC)
The U of North Carolina at Pembroke (NC)
The U of North Carolina Wilmington (NC)
U of North Dakota (ND)
U of Oregon (OR)
U of Pennsylvania (PA)
U of Pittsburgh at Bradford (PA)
U of Portland (OR)
U of Puget Sound (WA)
U of Richmond (VA)
U of San Diego (CA)
U of San Francisco (CA)
U of Southern Indiana (IN)
U of Southern Maine (ME)
The U of Tampa (FL)
U of the Fraser Valley (BC, Canada)
U of the Pacific (CA)
The U of the South (TN)
The U of Toledo (OH)
U of Toronto (ON, Canada)
The U of Tulsa (OK)
U of Utah (UT)
U of Vermont (VT)
U of Washington (WA)
U of Washington, Bothell (WA)
U of Washington, Tacoma (WA)
U of Waterloo (ON, Canada)
The U of Western Ontario (ON, Canada)
U of Wisconsin–Green Bay (WI)
U of Wisconsin–Madison (WI)
U of Wyoming (WY)
Utah State U (UT)
Villanova U (PA)
Virginia Commonwealth U (VA)
Virginia Wesleyan U (VA)
Walla Walla U (WA)
Warren Wilson Coll (NC)
Washington & Jefferson Coll (PA)
Washington and Lee U (VA)
Washington Coll (MD)
Washington U in St. Louis (MO)
Waynesburg U (PA)
Wesleyan Coll (GA)
Wesleyan U (CT)
Western Colorado U (CO)
Western Michigan U (MI)
Western Washington U (WA)
Westminster Coll (UT)
Widener U (PA)
William Paterson U of New Jersey (NJ)
William Peace U (NC)
Williams Coll (MA)
Winthrop U (SC)
Wofford Coll (SC)
Yale U (CT)

ENVIRONMENTAL TOXICOLOGY
Clarkson U (NY)

EPIDEMIOLOGY
Indiana U Bloomington (IN)
The U of Western Ontario (ON, Canada)

EQUESTRIAN STUDIES
Averett U (VA)
Becker Coll (MA)
Colorado State U (CO)
Delaware Valley U (PA)
Emory & Henry Coll (VA)
Midway U (KY)
Rocky Mountain Coll (MT)
Saint Mary-of-the-Woods Coll (IN)
Texas A&M U–Commerce (TX)
The U of Findlay (OH)

ETHICS
Bridgewater State U (MA)
Drake U (IA)
Millikin U (IL)
Southeastern Baptist Theological Sem (NC)
U of Washington, Bothell (WA)
The U of Western Ontario (ON, Canada)

ETHNIC, CULTURAL MINORITY, GENDER, AND GROUP STUDIES RELATED
Albion Coll (MI)
Allegheny Coll (PA)
American U (DC)
The American U of Paris (France)
Beloit Coll (WI)
Bethel U (MN)
Boise State U (ID)
Bowdoin Coll (ME)
Bowling Green State U (OH)
California Polytechnic State U, San Luis Obispo (CA)
California State Polytechnic U, Pomona (CA)
California State U, Los Angeles (CA)
California State U, Stanislaus (CA)
Carleton Coll (MN)
Central Michigan U (MI)
Chatham U (PA)
The Colorado Coll (CO)
Colorado State U (CO)
Columbia Coll Chicago (IL)
Cornell Coll (IA)
Davidson Coll (NC)
Edgewood Coll (WI)
Grinnell Coll (IA)
Guilford Coll (NC)
Hampshire Coll (MA)
Indiana U Bloomington (IN)
Indiana U South Bend (IN)
John Jay Coll of Criminal Justice of the City U of New York (NY)
Kalamazoo Coll (MI)
Lawrence U (WI)
Mount Holyoke Coll (MA)
New Coll of Florida (FL)
New York U (NY)
Northeastern Illinois U (IL)
The Ohio State U (OH)
Pitzer Coll (CA)
Portland State U (OR)
San Diego State U (CA)
Sarah Lawrence Coll (NY)
Skidmore Coll (NY)
Stanford U (CA)
U at Buffalo, the State U of New York (NY)
U of California, Berkeley (CA)
U of California, Irvine (CA)
U of California, Riverside (CA)
U of Colorado Colorado Springs (CO)
U of Dayton (OH)
U of Denver (CO)
U of Hawaii at Manoa (HI)
U of Houston (TX)
U of Illinois at Chicago (IL)
U of Kentucky (KY)
U of Minnesota, Duluth (MN)
U of Nebraska–Lincoln (NE)
U of Nevada, Reno (NV)
U of Utah (UT)
U of Washington, Tacoma (WA)
The U of Western Ontario (ON, Canada)
Washington State U (WA)
Washington U in St. Louis (MO)
Wayne State U (MI)
Wesleyan U (CT)
Western Kentucky U (KY)
Western Washington U (WA)
Westfield State U (MA)
Williams Coll (MA)
Xavier U (OH)
Yale U (CT)

ETHNIC STUDIES
Arizona State U at the West campus (AZ)
California State U, San Marcos (CA)
Kansas State U (KS)
Messiah Coll (PA)
Saint Mary's Coll of California (CA)
St. Olaf Coll (MN)
Santa Clara U (CA)
Sarah Lawrence Coll (NY)
Texas Christian U (TX)
U of California, Merced (CA)
U of California, San Diego (CA)
U of California, Santa Cruz (CA)
U of Colorado Boulder (CO)
U of Colorado Denver (CO)
U of Oregon (OR)
U of San Diego (CA)
Willamette U (OR)
Worcester State U (MA)

EUROPEAN HISTORY
Salem State U (MA)
Sarah Lawrence Coll (NY)
U of Idaho (ID)
U of Washington, Tacoma (WA)

EUROPEAN STUDIES
Amherst Coll (MA)
Barnard Coll (NY)
Bowling Green State U (OH)
Brandeis U (MA)
Coll of Saint Benedict (MN)
Emory & Henry Coll (VA)
Georgetown Coll (KY)
The George Washington U (DC)
Gonzaga U (WA)
Hampshire Coll (MA)
Hillsdale Coll (MI)
Hobart and William Smith Colls (NY)
Middlebury Coll (VT)
New York U (NY)
Pepperdine U, Malibu (CA)
Portland State U (OR)
Saint John's U (MN)
Saint Mary's Coll of California (CA)
San Diego State U (CA)
Scripps Coll (CA)
Stony Brook U, State U of New York (NY)
Trinity U (TX)
United States Military Acad (NY)
U of California, Irvine (CA)
U of California, Los Angeles (CA)
The U of Kansas (KS)
The U of North Carolina at Chapel Hill (NC)
U of Northern Colorado (CO)
U of Richmond (VA)
U of South Carolina (SC)
U of Toronto (ON, Canada)
U of Vermont (VT)
U of Washington (WA)
Vanderbilt U (TN)
Washington U in St. Louis (MO)
Westmont Coll (CA)

EUROPEAN STUDIES (WESTERN)
Bates Coll (ME)
Illinois Wesleyan U (IL)
Seattle U (WA)
Willamette U (OR)

EVOLUTIONARY BIOLOGY
Bennington Coll (VT)
Harvard U (MA)
Rice U (TX)
Tulane U (LA)
Yale U (CT)

EXECUTIVE ASSISTANT/ EXECUTIVE SECRETARY
Bowling Green State U (OH)
U of Puerto Rico–Ponce (PR)

EXERCISE PHYSIOLOGY
Anderson U (SC)
Auburn U (AL)
Baylor U (TX)
Bethany Lutheran Coll (MN)
Biola U (CA)
California Baptist U (CA)
Central Coll (IA)
Central Washington U (WA)
Chestnut Hill Coll (PA)
Coll of Charleston (SC)
The Coll of St. Scholastica (MN)
Concordia U Wisconsin (WI)
Creighton U (NE)
Dallas Baptist U (TX)
East Carolina U (NC)
Fitchburg State U (MA)
Florida Southern Coll (FL)
Gonzaga U (WA)
Ithaca Coll (NY)
Marquette U (WI)
Merrimack Coll (MA)
Northern Kentucky U (KY)
Northwest Christian U (OR)
Saint Francis U (PA)
Shenandoah U (VA)
Skidmore Coll (NY)
State U of New York Coll at Potsdam (NY)
Taylor U (IN)
Texas A&M U–Central Texas (TX)
U at Buffalo, the State U of New York (NY)
U of California, Irvine (CA)
U of Colorado Colorado Springs (CO)
U of Dayton (OH)
U of Massachusetts Amherst (MA)
U of Miami (FL)
U of Minnesota, Twin Cities Campus (MN)
U of Southern Maine (ME)
The U of Toledo (OH)
U of Wisconsin–Superior (WI)
Washington State U (WA)
Washington State U–Spokane (WA)
West Virginia U (WV)

EXPERIMENTAL PSYCHOLOGY
Brandeis U (MA)
Claremont McKenna Coll (CA)
Mount Holyoke Coll (MA)
Purdue U Fort Wayne (IN)
Saint Mary's Coll of California (CA)
Tiffin U (OH)

The U of Arizona (AZ)
U of California, Santa Barbara (CA)
U of Mary Hardin-Baylor (TX)
U of Michigan (MI)
U of South Carolina (SC)
Washington U in St. Louis (MO)

FACILITIES PLANNING AND MANAGEMENT
Eastern Michigan U (MI)
Missouri State U (MO)
New England Inst of Technology (RI)
New York City Coll of Technology of the City U of New York (NY)

FAMILY AND COMMUNITY SERVICES
Auburn U (AL)
Bowling Green State U (OH)
East Carolina U (NC)
Harding U (AR)
Iowa State U of Science and Technology (IA)
John Brown U (AR)
La Roche U (PA)
Merrimack Coll (MA)
Messiah Coll (PA)
Michigan State U (MI)
Mount St. Mary's U (MD)
Oklahoma Baptist U (OK)
Stevenson U (MD)
Texas Tech U (TX)
Toccoa Falls Coll (GA)
Union U (TN)
The U of Alabama (AL)
U of Miami (FL)
U of Northern Iowa (IA)
U of Wisconsin–Madison (WI)
Western Michigan U (MI)
Worcester State U (MA)
Youngstown State U (OH)

FAMILY AND CONSUMER ECONOMICS RELATED
Bowling Green State U (OH)
Brigham Young U (UT)
California State U, Fresno (CA)
California State U, Sacramento (CA)
Carson-Newman U (TN)
Howard U (DC)
Minnesota State U Mankato (MN)
U of Hawaii at Manoa (HI)
U of Minnesota, Twin Cities Campus (MN)
U of Nebraska at Kearney (NE)
U of Nebraska–Lincoln (NE)

FAMILY AND CONSUMER SCIENCES/HOME ECONOMICS TEACHER EDUCATION
Ball State U (IN)
Baylor U (TX)
Bowling Green State U (OH)
Bradley U (IL)
Carson-Newman U (TN)
Central Washington U (WA)
East Carolina U (NC)
East Central U (OK)
Eastern Kentucky U (KY)
Harding U (AR)
Jacksonville State U (AL)
Louisiana Tech U (LA)
Messiah Coll (PA)
Minnesota State U Mankato (MN)
Missouri State U (MO)
New York U (NY)
Pittsburg State U (KS)
Queens Coll of the City U of New York (NY)
St. Catherine U (MN)
Seton Hill U (PA)
South Dakota State U (SD)
Southeast Missouri State U (MO)
State U of New York Coll at Oneonta (NY)
The U of Akron (OH)
U of Wisconsin–Stout (WI)
Utah State U (UT)
Wayne State Coll (NE)
Western Kentucky U (KY)
Western Michigan U (MI)
Winthrop U (SC)

FAMILY AND CONSUMER SCIENCES/HUMAN SCIENCES
Auburn U (AL)
Ball State U (IN)
Baylor U (TX)
Berea Coll (KY)
Bowling Green State U (OH)
Bradley U (IL)
Bridgewater Coll (VA)
Brigham Young U (UT)
California State U, Long Beach (CA)
California State U, Northridge (CA)
Carson-Newman U (TN)
Central Washington U (WA)
Colorado State U (CO)
Delta State U (MS)
East Central U (OK)
Eastern Illinois U (IL)
Florida State U (FL)
Harding U (AR)
Illinois State U (IL)
Indiana U of Pennsylvania (PA)
Iowa State U of Science and Technology (IA)
Jacksonville State U (AL)
Kansas State U (KS)
Liberty U (VA)
Lipscomb U (TN)
Madonna U (MI)
Meredith Coll (NC)
Miami U (OH)
Miami U Hamilton (OH)
Miami U Middletown (OH)
Minnesota State U Mankato (MN)
Mississippi State U (MS)
Montana State U (MT)
Montclair State U (NJ)
New Mexico Highlands U (NM)
New York U (NY)
North Carolina Central U (NC)
Northwestern State U of Louisiana (LA)
Olivet Nazarene U (IL)
Pittsburg State U (KS)
Prairie View A&M U (TX)
Queens Coll of the City U of New York (NY)
St. Catherine U (MN)
Sam Houston State U (TX)
San Francisco State U (CA)
Seton Hill U (PA)
Shepherd U (WV)
Southeastern Louisiana U (LA)
Southeast Missouri State U (MO)
State U of New York Coll at Oneonta (NY)
Tarleton State U (TX)
Texas A&M U–Kingsville (TX)
Texas Southern U (TX)
Texas Tech U (TX)
Texas Woman's U (TX)
The U of Alabama (AL)
U of California, San Diego (CA)
U of Central Arkansas (AR)
U of Kentucky (KY)
U of Montevallo (AL)
U of New Mexico (NM)
U of Saint Joseph (CT)
The U of Tennessee at Martin (TN)
The U of Western Ontario (ON, Canada)
U of Wyoming (WY)
Washington State U (WA)
Wayne State Coll (NE)
Youngstown State U (OH)

FAMILY AND CONSUMER SCIENCES/HUMAN SCIENCES BUSINESS SERVICES RELATED
Brigham Young U (UT)

FAMILY AND CONSUMER SCIENCES/HUMAN SCIENCES RELATED
Auburn U (AL)
California State U, Long Beach (CA)
U of Utah (UT)

FAMILY PRACTICE NURSING
Grand Valley State U (MI)
Michigan State U (MI)
Pace U, Pleasantville Campus (NY)
Texas A&M U–Commerce (TX)
The U of Western Ontario (ON, Canada)

FAMILY PSYCHOLOGY
Arizona Christian U (AZ)

FAMILY RESOURCE MANAGEMENT
Arizona State U at the Tempe campus (AZ)
Brigham Young U (UT)
Middle Tennessee State U (TN)
The Ohio State U (OH)
Texas Tech U (TX)
The U of Alabama (AL)
The U of Arizona (AZ)
U of Utah (UT)

FAMILY SYSTEMS
Anderson U (IN)
Ball State U (IN)
Bowling Green State U (OH)
Central Michigan U (MI)
Central Washington U (WA)
Lipscomb U (TN)
Spring Arbor U (MI)
Towson U (MD)
The U of Akron (OH)
U of Southern Mississippi (MS)
Weber State U (UT)
Western Michigan U (MI)

FARM AND RANCH MANAGEMENT
Texas A&M U (TX)
Texas Christian U (TX)

FASHION AND FABRIC CONSULTING
Academy of Art U (CA)
U of Houston–Downtown (TX)

FASHION/APPAREL DESIGN
Academy of Art U (CA)
Arizona State U at the Tempe campus (AZ)
Baylor U (TX)
Belmont U (TN)
Bennington Coll (VT)
Bowling Green State U (OH)
Brenau U (GA)
Carson-Newman U (TN)
Cazenovia Coll (NY)
Clark Atlanta U (GA)
Columbia Coll Chicago (IL)
Dominican U (IL)
Drexel U (PA)
Eugene Lang Coll of Liberal Arts (NY)
Fashion Inst of Technology (NY)
Ferris State U (MI)
FIDM/Fashion Inst of Design & Merchandising, Los Angeles Campus (CA)
Howard U (DC)
Indiana U Bloomington (IN)
Lasell Coll (MA)
Lebanese American U (Lebanon)
Marymount U (VA)
Massachusetts Coll of Art and Design (MA)
Meredith Coll (NC)
Miami U Hamilton (OH)
Miami U Middletown (OH)
Michigan State U (MI)
Montclair State U (NJ)
Otis Coll of Art and Design (CA)
Paris Coll of Art (France)
Parsons School of Design (NY)
Pratt Inst (NY)
St. Catherine U (MN)
Stevenson U (MD)
Texas Tech U (TX)
Texas Woman's U (TX)
U of Cincinnati (OH)
U of Massachusetts Dartmouth (MA)
U of North Texas (TX)
U of the Incarnate Word (TX)
Ursuline Coll (OH)
Virginia Commonwealth U (VA)
Washington U in St. Louis (MO)
Western Michigan U (MI)
Woodbury U (CA)

FASHION MERCHANDISING
Academy of Art U (CA)
Baylor U (TX)
Belmont U (TN)
Bowling Green State U (OH)
Brenau U (GA)
California State U, Long Beach (CA)
Carson-Newman U (TN)
Cazenovia Coll (NY)
Central Michigan U (MI)
Columbia Coll (SC)
Dominican U (IL)
East Central U (OK)
Eastern Illinois U (IL)
Eastern Kentucky U (KY)
Eastern Michigan U (MI)
Fashion Inst of Technology (NY)
Fisher Coll (MA)
Harding U (AR)
High Point U (NC)
Immaculata U (PA)
Indiana U of Pennsylvania (PA)
Lasell Coll (MA)
Lipscomb U (TN)
Lynn U (FL)
Marymount Manhattan Coll (NY)
Marymount U (VA)
Meredith Coll (NC)
Olivet Nazarene U (IL)
Sacred Heart U (CT)
St. Catherine U (MN)
Sam Houston State U (TX)
State U of New York Coll at Oneonta (NY)
Stevenson U (MD)
Texas Christian U (TX)
Texas State U (TX)
Texas Tech U (TX)
Texas Woman's U (TX)
U of North Texas (TX)
Ursuline Coll (OH)
Western Michigan U (MI)
Youngstown State U (OH)

FIBER, TEXTILE AND WEAVING ARTS
Adams State U (CO)
Bowling Green State U (OH)
California State U, Long Beach (CA)
Cornell U (NY)
Massachusetts Coll of Art and Design (MA)
Portland State U (OR)
The U of Kansas (KS)
U of Michigan (MI)
U of Oregon (OR)

FILIPINO/TAGALOG
U of Hawaii at Manoa (HI)

FILM/CINEMA/VIDEO STUDIES
The American U of Paris (France)
Amherst Coll (MA)
Augsburg U (MN)
Barnard Coll (NY)
Belhaven U (MS)
Bennington Coll (VT)
Biola U (CA)
Boston Coll (MA)
Bowling Green State U (OH)
Brandeis U (MA)
Brigham Young U (UT)
Brown U (RI)
California Baptist U (CA)
California State U, Long Beach (CA)
California State U, Northridge (CA)
California State U, Sacramento (CA)
Carleton Coll (MN)
Carson-Newman U (TN)
Central Washington U (WA)
Champlain Coll (VT)
Claremont McKenna Coll (CA)
Clark U (MA)
Coe Coll (IA)
Colgate U (NY)
Coll of Staten Island of the City U of New York (NY)
Coll of the Holy Cross (MA)
The Colorado Coll (CO)
Cornell U (NY)
Dartmouth Coll (NH)
DeSales U (PA)
Dominican U (IL)
Eastern Michigan U (MI)
Eastern Washington U (WA)
Edinboro U of Pennsylvania (PA)
Emory U (GA)
Eugene Lang Coll of Liberal Arts (NY)
Fashion Inst of Technology (NY)
Florida Southern Coll (FL)
Fordham U (NY)
Georgia State U (GA)
Grand Valley State U (MI)
Houston Baptist U (TX)
Howard U (DC)
Jacksonville U (FL)
Johns Hopkins U (MD)
Kenyon Coll (OH)
Lafayette Coll (PA)
La Sierra U (CA)
Lawrence U (WI)
Lipscomb U (TN)
Los Angeles Film School (CA)
Loyola Marymount U (CA)
McDaniel Coll (MD)
Miami U (OH)
Miami U Hamilton (OH)
Miami U Middletown (OH)
Michigan State U (MI)
Middlebury Coll (VT)
Mount Holyoke Coll (MA)
Muhlenberg Coll (PA)
National U (CA)
New York U (NY)
Northwestern U (IL)
Northwest U (WA)
Oakland U (MI)
The Ohio State U (OH)
Pace U, Pleasantville Campus (NY)
Penn State Abington (PA)
Penn State Altoona (PA)
Penn State Beaver (PA)
Penn State Berks (PA)
Penn State Brandywine (PA)
Penn State DuBois (PA)
Penn State Erie, The Behrend Coll (PA)
Penn State Fayette, The Eberly Campus (PA)
Penn State Greater Allegheny (PA)
Penn State Hazleton (PA)
Penn State Lehigh Valley (PA)
Penn State Mont Alto (PA)
Penn State New Kensington (PA)
Penn State Schuylkill (PA)
Penn State Shenango (PA)
Penn State U Park (PA)
Penn State Wilkes-Barre (PA)
Penn State York (PA)
Pepperdine U, Malibu (CA)
Portland State U (OR)
Queens Coll of the City U of New York (NY)
Rhode Island Coll (RI)
St. Cloud State U (MN)
San Francisco State U (CA)
Sarah Lawrence Coll (NY)
School of Visual Arts (NY)
Seattle U (WA)
Simon Fraser U (BC, Canada)
Smith Coll (MA)
Stanford U (CA)
State U of New York at Fredonia (NY)
Stevenson U (MD)
U at Buffalo, the State U of New York (NY)
U of Alaska Fairbanks (AK)
The U of Arizona (AZ)
U of Arkansas at Little Rock (AR)
U of California, Berkeley (CA)
U of California, Irvine (CA)
U of California, Los Angeles (CA)
U of California, Riverside (CA)
U of California, San Diego (CA)
U of California, Santa Barbara (CA)
U of Cincinnati (OH)
U of Colorado Boulder (CO)
U of Denver (CO)
U of Hartford (CT)
U of Idaho (ID)
The U of Iowa (IA)
The U of Kansas (KS)
U of Louisiana at Lafayette (LA)
U of Mary Hardin-Baylor (TX)
U of Michigan (MI)
U of Nebraska–Lincoln (NE)
U of Nevada, Las Vegas (NV)
U of New Mexico (NM)
U of Oregon (OR)
U of Pennsylvania (PA)
U of Pikeville (KY)
U of Richmond (VA)
The U of Tampa (FL)
The U of Toledo (OH)
The U of Tulsa (OK)
U of Utah (UT)
U of Vermont (VT)
U of Washington (WA)
U of Waterloo (ON, Canada)

The U of Western Ontario (ON, Canada)
U of Wisconsin–Milwaukee (WI)
Vanderbilt U (TN)
Washington U in St. Louis (MO)
Wayne State U (MI)
Wesleyan U (CT)
Wheaton Coll (MA)
Wright State U (OH)
Wright State U–Lake Campus (OH)
Yale U (CT)

FILM/VIDEO AND PHOTOGRAPHIC ARTS RELATED
Arizona State U at the Tempe campus (AZ)
Birmingham-Southern Coll (AL)
Brigham Young U (UT)
Chatham U (PA)
Coe Coll (IA)
Fairfield U (CT)
Florida State U (FL)
Georgia Gwinnett Coll (GA)
Hampshire Coll (MA)
Hollins U (VA)
Ithaca Coll (NY)
La Roche U (PA)
Louisiana State U and A&M Coll (LA)
Mount Saint Mary's U (CA)
Nossi Coll of Art (TN)
The Ohio State U (OH)
Portland State U (OR)
Pratt Inst (NY)
Saint Joseph's U (PA)
School of Visual Arts (NY)
Spring Arbor U (MI)
U of California, Santa Cruz (CA)
U of Illinois at Chicago (IL)
U of Minnesota, Twin Cities Campus (MN)
Western Michigan U (MI)
Woodbury U (CA)

FINANCE
Abilene Christian U (TX)
Adams State U (CO)
Albion Coll (MI)
Alfred U (NY)
American U (DC)
Anderson U (IN)
Andrews U (MI)
Angelo State U (TX)
Appalachian State U (NC)
Arcadia U (PA)
Arizona State U at the Tempe campus (AZ)
Arkansas Tech U (AR)
Auburn U (AL)
Auburn U at Montgomery (AL)
Augsburg U (MN)
Aurora U (IL)
Austin Coll (TX)
Austin Peay State U (TN)
Avila U (MO)
Babson Coll (MA)
Ball State U (IN)
Barry U (FL)
Baruch Coll of the City U of New York (NY)
Bayamón Central U (PR)
Baylor U (TX)
Belmont Abbey Coll (NC)
Belmont U (TN)
Benedictine Coll (KS)
Benedictine U (IL)
Bentley U (MA)
Berry Coll (GA)
Binghamton U, State U of New York (NY)
Boise State U (ID)
Boston Coll (MA)
Bowling Green State U (OH)
Bradley U (IL)
Bridgewater State U (MA)
Bryant U (RI)
Butler U (IN)
California State U, Bakersfield (CA)
California State U, Dominguez Hills (CA)
California State U, Fresno (CA)
California State U, Long Beach (CA)
California State U, Northridge (CA)
California State U, San Marcos (CA)
California State U, Stanislaus (CA)
California U of Pennsylvania (PA)
Calvin Coll (MI)
Carnegie Mellon U (PA)
Carthage Coll (WI)
The Catholic U of America (DC)
Cedarville U (OH)
Central Connecticut State U (CT)
Central Michigan U (MI)
Central Washington U (WA)
Champlain Coll (VT)
The Citadel, The Military Coll of South Carolina (SC)
Clarion U of Pennsylvania (PA)
Clemson U (SC)
Coastal Carolina U (SC)
Coll of Charleston (SC)
The Coll of Saint Rose (NY)
The Coll of St. Scholastica (MN)
Columbia Coll (MO)
Concordia Coll (MN)
Concordia U, St. Paul (MN)
Creighton U (NE)
Culver-Stockton Coll (MO)
Dakota State U (SD)
Dallas Baptist U (TX)
Davenport U, Grand Rapids (MI)
Delta State U (MS)
DePaul U (IL)
DeSales U (PA)
Dickinson State U (ND)
Dominican U (IL)
Drake U (IA)
Drexel U (PA)
Drury U (MO)
East Carolina U (NC)
East Central U (OK)
Eastern Illinois U (IL)
Eastern Kentucky U (KY)
Eastern Michigan U (MI)
Eastern Washington U (WA)
Edinboro U of Pennsylvania (PA)
Elon U (NC)
Emmanuel Coll (MA)
Endicott Coll (MA)
Fairfield U (CT)
Fairleigh Dickinson U (NJ)
Fayetteville State U (NC)
Ferris State U (MI)
Fisher Coll (MA)
Fitchburg State U (MA)
Flagler Coll (FL)
Florida Atlantic U (FL)
Florida Gulf Coast U (FL)
Florida State U (FL)
Fordham U (NY)
Fort Lewis Coll (CO)
Framingham State U (MA)
Francis Marion U (SC)
Freed-Hardeman U (TN)
Friends U (KS)
Gannon U (PA)
George Fox U (OR)
Georgetown Coll (KY)
Georgetown U (DC)
The George Washington U (DC)
Georgian Court U (NJ)
Georgia Southern U (GA)
Georgia State U (GA)
Gordon Coll (MA)
Grand Valley State U (MI)
Hamline U (MN)
Hampton U (VA)
Harding U (AR)
Hardin-Simmons U (TX)
HEC Montreal (QC, Canada)
High Point U (NC)
Hillsdale Coll (MI)
Hofstra U (NY)
Houston Baptist U (TX)
Howard U (DC)
Husson U (ME)
Illinois Coll (IL)
Illinois State U (IL)
Immaculata U (PA)
Indiana State U (IN)
Indiana U of Pennsylvania (PA)
Inter American U of Puerto Rico, Bayamón Campus (PR)
Inter American U of Puerto Rico, San Germán Campus (PR)
Iona Coll (NY)
Jacksonville State U (AL)
Jacksonville U (FL)
James Madison U (VA)
John Carroll U (OH)
Kansas State U (KS)
Kean U (NJ)
Keiser U, Fort Lauderdale (FL)
Kennesaw State U (GA)
The King's Coll (NY)
King's Coll (PA)
Lake Forest Coll (IL)
Lamar U (TX)
La Roche U (PA)
Lasell Coll (MA)
La Sierra U (CA)
Lawrence Technological U (MI)
Lehigh U (PA)
Le Moyne Coll (NY)
Lenoir-Rhyne U (NC)
LeTourneau U (TX)
Lewis U (IL)
Lincoln Memorial U (TN)
Lincoln U (PA)
Lindenwood U (MO)
Linfield Coll (OR)
Loras Coll (IA)
Louisiana State U and A&M Coll (LA)
Louisiana State U in Shreveport (LA)
Louisiana Tech U (LA)
Loyola Marymount U (CA)
Loyola U Chicago (IL)
Loyola U Maryland (MD)
Loyola U New Orleans (LA)
Malone U (OH)
Manhattan Coll (NY)
Manhattanville Coll (NY)
Marian U (IN)
Marietta Coll (OH)
Marquette U (WI)
Marshall U (WV)
Marymount Manhattan Coll (NY)
McMurry U (TX)
McNeese State U (LA)
Mercer U, Macon (GA)
Merrimack Coll (MA)
Messiah Coll (PA)
Miami U (OH)
Miami U Hamilton (OH)
Miami U Middletown (OH)
Michigan State U (MI)
Michigan Technological U (MI)
Middle Tennessee State U (TN)
Millikin U (IL)
Minnesota State U Mankato (MN)
Minot State U (ND)
Mississippi State U (MS)
Missouri State U (MO)
Missouri Valley Coll (MO)
Molloy Coll (NY)
Morehead State U (KY)
Mount Mercy U (IA)
Mount Vernon Nazarene U (OH)
Murray State U (KY)
National U (CA)
Nazareth Coll of Rochester (NY)
New England Coll (NH)
New Mexico Highlands U (NM)
New York Inst of Technology (NY)
New York U (NY)
Nichols Coll (MA)
Northeastern Illinois U (IL)
Northeastern State U (OK)
Northern Arizona U (AZ)
Northern Illinois U (IL)
Northern State U (SD)
Northwest Missouri State U (MO)
Northwest Nazarene U (ID)
Notre Dame Coll (OH)
Nova Southeastern U (FL)
Oakland U (MI)
Ohio Dominican U (OH)
The Ohio State U (OH)
Oklahoma Baptist U (OK)
Oklahoma State U (OK)
Old Dominion U (VA)
Oral Roberts U (OK)
Ottawa U (KS)
Pace U, Pleasantville Campus (NY)
Pacific U (OR)
Palm Beach Atlantic U (FL)
Penn State Abington (PA)
Penn State Altoona (PA)
Penn State Beaver (PA)
Penn State Berks (PA)
Penn State Brandywine (PA)
Penn State DuBois (PA)
Penn State Erie, The Behrend Coll (PA)
Penn State Fayette, The Eberly Campus (PA)
Penn State Greater Allegheny (PA)
Penn State Harrisburg (PA)
Penn State Hazleton (PA)
Penn State Lehigh Valley (PA)
Penn State Mont Alto (PA)
Penn State New Kensington (PA)
Penn State Schuylkill (PA)
Penn State Shenango (PA)
Penn State U Park (PA)
Penn State Wilkes-Barre (PA)
Penn State York (PA)
Pepperdine U, Malibu (CA)
Pittsburg State U (KS)
Point Loma Nazarene U (CA)
Polytechnic U of Puerto Rico (PR)
Prairie View A&M U (TX)
Providence Coll (RI)
Purdue U Fort Wayne (IN)
Purdue U Northwest (IN)
Queens Coll of the City U of New York (NY)
Queens U of Charlotte (NC)
Radford U (VA)
Ramapo Coll of New Jersey (NJ)
Rhode Island Coll (RI)
Richmond, The American Intl U in London (United Kingdom)
Roger Williams U (RI)
Rosemont Coll (PA)
Rowan U (NJ)
Sacred Heart U (CT)
Saginaw Valley State U (MI)
St. Ambrose U (IA)
St. Bonaventure U (NY)
Saint Francis U (PA)
St. John Fisher Coll (NY)
Saint Joseph's U (PA)
Saint Louis U (MO)
Saint Mary's Coll of California (CA)
St. Mary's U (TX)
Saint Mary's U of Minnesota (MN)
St. Thomas Aquinas Coll (NY)
St. Thomas U - Florida (FL)
Saint Vincent Coll (PA)
Salem State U (MA)
Salisbury U (MD)
Salve Regina U (RI)
Samford U (AL)
Sam Houston State U (TX)
San Diego State U (CA)
San Francisco State U (CA)
San Jose State U (CA)
Santa Clara U (CA)
Schreiner U (TX)
Seattle U (WA)
Siena Coll (NY)
Sierra Nevada Coll (NV)
Simmons U (MA)
Slippery Rock U of Pennsylvania (PA)
Southeastern Louisiana U (LA)
Southeastern U (FL)
Southeast Missouri State U (MO)
Southern Illinois U Carbondale (IL)
Southern Methodist U (TX)
Southwestern Coll (KS)
Spring Arbor U (MI)
State U of New York at Fredonia (NY)
State U of New York at New Paltz (NY)
State U of New York at Oswego (NY)
State U of New York Coll at Old Westbury (NY)
State U of New York Coll of Technology at Canton (NY)
Stetson U (FL)
Suffolk U (MA)
SUNY Brockport (NY)
Susquehanna U (PA)
Tarleton State U (TX)
Taylor U (IN)
Temple U (PA)
Tennessee Wesleyan U (TN)
Texas A&M Intl U (TX)
Texas A&M U (TX)
Texas A&M U–Central Texas (TX)
Texas A&M U–Commerce (TX)
Texas A&M U–Corpus Christi (TX)
Texas A&M U–Kingsville (TX)
Texas Christian U (TX)
Texas Lutheran U (TX)
Texas State U (TX)
Texas Tech U (TX)
Texas Woman's U (TX)
Tiffin U (OH)
Trine U (IN)
Trinity U (TX)
Tulane U (LA)
Union U (TN)
The U of Alabama (AL)
The U of Alabama at Birmingham (AL)
The U of Alabama in Huntsville (AL)
The U of Arizona (AZ)
U of Arkansas (AR)
U of Arkansas at Little Rock (AR)
U of Central Arkansas (AR)
U of Central Florida (FL)
U of Charleston (WV)
U of Cincinnati (OH)
U of Colorado Boulder (CO)
U of Dayton (OH)
U of Denver (CO)
The U of Findlay (OH)
U of Hartford (CT)
U of Hawaii at Manoa (HI)
U of Houston (TX)
U of Houston–Clear Lake (TX)
U of Houston–Downtown (TX)
U of Idaho (ID)
U of Illinois at Chicago (IL)
The U of Iowa (IA)
The U of Kansas (KS)
U of Kentucky (KY)
U of Louisiana at Lafayette (LA)
U of Louisiana at Monroe (LA)
U of Louisville (KY)
U of Maine (ME)
U of Mary Hardin-Baylor (TX)
U of Maryland Global Campus (MD)
U of Massachusetts Amherst (MA)
U of Massachusetts Dartmouth (MA)
U of Memphis (TN)
U of Miami (FL)
U of Michigan–Dearborn (MI)
U of Michigan–Flint (MI)
U of Minnesota, Duluth (MN)
U of Minnesota, Twin Cities Campus (MN)
U of Montana (MT)
U of Montevallo (AL)
U of Nebraska–Lincoln (NE)
U of Nevada, Las Vegas (NV)
U of Nevada, Reno (NV)
U of New Haven (CT)
The U of North Carolina at Charlotte (NC)
The U of North Carolina at Greensboro (NC)
U of North Dakota (ND)
U of Northern Iowa (IA)
U of North Florida (FL)
U of North Texas (TX)
U of Northwestern–St. Paul (MN)
U of Notre Dame (IN)
U of Pennsylvania (PA)
U of Portland (OR)
U of Puerto Rico–Ponce (PR)
U of St. Francis (IL)
U of Saint Francis (IN)
U of St. Thomas (TX)
U of San Diego (CA)
U of San Francisco (CA)
The U of Scranton (PA)
U of South Alabama (AL)
U of South Carolina (SC)
U of South Dakota (SD)
U of Southern Indiana (IN)
U of Southern Maine (ME)
U of Southern Mississippi (MS)
U of South Florida (FL)
U of South Florida, St. Petersburg (FL)
The U of Tampa (FL)
The U of Tennessee (TN)
The U of Tennessee at Chattanooga (TN)
The U of Tennessee at Martin (TN)
The U of Texas at Dallas (TX)
The U of Texas at El Paso (TX)
The U of Texas at San Antonio (TX)
The U of Texas of the Permian Basin (TX)
The U of Texas Rio Grande Valley (TX)
U of the Incarnate Word (TX)
The U of the South (TN)
The U of Toledo (OH)
U of Toronto (ON, Canada)

The U of Tulsa (OK)
U of Utah (UT)
U of Washington (WA)
U of Washington, Tacoma (WA)
The U of West Alabama (AL)
The U of Western Ontario (ON, Canada)
U of West Florida (FL)
U of West Georgia (GA)
U of Wisconsin–Eau Claire (WI)
U of Wisconsin–La Crosse (WI)
U of Wisconsin–Madison (WI)
U of Wisconsin–Milwaukee (WI)
U of Wyoming (WY)
Utah State U (UT)
Utah Valley U (UT)
Valdosta State U (GA)
Valparaiso U (IN)
Villanova U (PA)
Wake Forest U (NC)
Walla Walla U (WA)
Wartburg Coll (IA)
Washington State U (WA)
Washington State U–Vancouver (WA)
Washington U in St. Louis (MO)
Waynesburg U (PA)
Wayne State U (MI)
Webber Intl U (FL)
Weber State U (UT)
West Chester U of Pennsylvania (PA)
Western Carolina U (NC)
Western Connecticut State U (CT)
Western Kentucky U (KY)
Western Michigan U (MI)
Western New England U (MA)
Western Washington U (WA)
Westminster Coll (UT)
West Virginia U (WV)
Whitworth U (WA)
Wichita State U (KS)
Wilkes U (PA)
William & Mary (VA)
William Paterson U of New Jersey (NJ)
Wingate U (NC)
Wittenberg U (OH)
Wofford Coll (SC)
Worcester State U (MA)
Wright State U (OH)
Wright State U–Lake Campus (OH)
Xavier U (OH)
Yeshiva U (NY)
York Coll of Pennsylvania (PA)
Youngstown State U (OH)

FINANCE AND FINANCIAL MANAGEMENT SERVICES RELATED
Babson Coll (MA)
Brenau U (GA)
Dominican Coll (NY)
Hofstra U (NY)
James Madison U (VA)
Minot State U (ND)
San Jose State U (CA)
Simmons U (MA)
State U of New York at New Paltz (NY)
U of Northern Iowa (IA)
The U of Tampa (FL)
Virginia Commonwealth U (VA)
Westminster Coll (UT)

FINANCIAL FORENSICS AND FRAUD INVESTIGATION
Champlain Coll (VT)
John Jay Coll of Criminal Justice of the City U of New York (NY)
Keiser U, Fort Lauderdale (FL)
Mount St. Mary's U (MD)

FINANCIAL MATHEMATICS
American U (DC)
Anderson U (IN)
Carnegie Mellon U (PA)
Concordia Coll (MN)
Hofstra U (NY)
Knox Coll (IL)
Lee U (TN)
Lehigh U (PA)
LeTourneau U (TX)
Southwest Baptist U (MO)
Stevens Inst of Technology (NJ)
Trinity U (TX)
U of California, Los Angeles (CA)
U of Cincinnati (OH)
U of Kentucky (KY)

FINANCIAL PLANNING AND SERVICES
Baylor U (TX)
Bethel U (IN)
Brigham Young U (UT)
Bryant U (RI)
Central Michigan U (MI)
The Coll of Saint Rose (NY)
Edinboro U of Pennsylvania (PA)
HEC Montreal (QC, Canada)
Iowa State U of Science and Technology (IA)
John Carroll U (OH)
Kansas State U (KS)
Maryville U of Saint Louis (MO)
Marywood U (PA)
Merrimack Coll (MA)
Roger Williams U (RI)
Saint Joseph's U (PA)
St. Mary's U (TX)
San Diego State U (CA)
Southern Methodist U (TX)
State U of New York Coll of Technology at Alfred (NY)
Suffolk U (MA)
Temple U (PA)
The U of Akron (OH)
U of Jamestown (ND)
U of Minnesota, Duluth (MN)
U of Wisconsin–Madison (WI)
Utah Valley U (UT)
Western Michigan U (MI)
Widener U (PA)
William Paterson U of New Jersey (NJ)
Youngstown State U (OH)

FINE AND STUDIO ARTS MANAGEMENT
Aquinas Coll (MI)
Belhaven U (MS)
Butler U (IN)
Chatham U (PA)
Coll of Charleston (SC)
The Coll of Idaho (ID)
Columbia Coll Chicago (IL)
Concordia U Chicago (IL)
Culver-Stockton Coll (MO)
DePaul U (IL)
Dickinson State U (ND)
Eastern Michigan U (MI)
Fashion Inst of Technology (NY)
Indiana U Bloomington (IN)
Lasell Coll (MA)
Lenoir-Rhyne U (NC)
Lipscomb U (TN)
Marywood U (PA)
Messiah Coll (PA)
Miami U (OH)
Miami U Hamilton (OH)
Miami U Middletown (OH)
Minot State U (ND)
Parsons School of Design (NY)
Purchase Coll, State U of New York (NY)
Queens U of Charlotte (NC)
Randolph-Macon Coll (VA)
Saint Vincent Coll (PA)
Seton Hill U (PA)
Simmons U (MA)
Spring Hill Coll (AL)
State U of New York at Fredonia (NY)
State U of New York Coll at Potsdam (NY)
The U of Iowa (IA)
The U of North Carolina at Greensboro (NC)
U of Oregon (OR)
The U of Tulsa (OK)
U of Waterloo (ON, Canada)
Upper Iowa U (IA)
Waynesburg U (PA)
Westminster Coll (UT)
Whitworth U (WA)

FINE ARTS RELATED
Academy of Art U (CA)
Alfred U (NY)
Ball State U (IN)
Benedictine U (IL)
Binghamton U, State U of New York (NY)
Birmingham-Southern Coll (AL)
Bowdoin Coll (ME)
Bowling Green State U (OH)
Bryn Athyn Coll of the New Church (PA)
California State U, Long Beach (CA)
Cleveland Inst of Art (OH)
The Coll of Saint Rose (NY)
Covenant Coll (GA)
Edinboro U of Pennsylvania (PA)
Ferris State U (MI)
Fordham U (NY)
Hampshire Coll (MA)
Kenyon Coll (OH)
Loyola U Maryland (MD)
Madonna U (MI)
Manhattanville Coll (NY)
Marywood U (PA)
New York U (NY)
Oakland U (MI)
The Ohio State U (OH)
Portland State U (OR)
Pratt Inst (NY)
Purchase Coll, State U of New York (NY)
St. Thomas Aquinas Coll (NY)
Seattle U (WA)
Seton Hill U (PA)
Skidmore Coll (NY)
Stevens Inst of Technology (NJ)
The U of Akron (OH)
U of California, Los Angeles (CA)
U of Denver (CO)
U of Guam (GU)
U of Hartford (CT)
U of Maryland, Baltimore County (MD)
U of Mary Washington (VA)
U of Massachusetts Lowell (MA)
U of Michigan (MI)
U of New Haven (CT)
U of Washington (WA)
U of Wisconsin–Milwaukee (WI)
U of Wisconsin–Superior (WI)
Widener U (PA)

FINE/STUDIO ARTS
Abilene Christian U (TX)
Academy of Art U (CA)
Agnes Scott Coll (GA)
Albion Coll (MI)
Alfred U (NY)
Allegheny Coll (PA)
American U (DC)
The American U of Paris (France)
Amherst Coll (MA)
Andrews U (MI)
Angelo State U (TX)
Appalachian State U (NC)
Aquinas Coll (MI)
Arcadia U (PA)
Arkansas Tech U (AR)
Auburn U (AL)
Augsburg U (MN)
Baker U (KS)
Barton Coll (NC)
Baylor U (TX)
Beacon Coll (FL)
Belmont U (TN)
Beloit Coll (WI)
Bemidji State U (MN)
Benedictine U (IL)
Bennington Coll (VT)
Bethany Lutheran Coll (MN)
Bethel U (IN)
Bethel U (MN)
Binghamton U, State U of New York (NY)
Biola U (CA)
Birmingham-Southern Coll (AL)
Boston Coll (MA)
Bowdoin Coll (ME)
Bowling Green State U (OH)
Bradley U (IL)
Brandeis U (MA)
Brenau U (GA)
Bridgewater Coll (VA)
Bridgewater State U (MA)
Brigham Young U (UT)
Brown U (RI)
Bucknell U (PA)
Caldwell U (NJ)
California Inst of the Arts (CA)
California Polytechnic State U, San Luis Obispo (CA)
California State U, Fullerton (CA)
California State U, Long Beach (CA)
California State U, Stanislaus (CA)
California U of Pennsylvania (PA)
Calvin Coll (MI)
Carleton Coll (MN)
Carlow U (PA)
Carthage Coll (WI)
Cazenovia Coll (NY)
Cedarville U (OH)
Central Washington U (WA)
Centre Coll (KY)
Chatham U (PA)
Chestnut Hill Coll (PA)
Clark U (MA)
Coastal Carolina U (SC)
Coe Coll (IA)
Colby-Sawyer Coll (NH)
Coll of Charleston (SC)
The Coll of Idaho (ID)
Coll of Staten Island of the City U of New York (NY)
Coll of the Holy Cross (MA)
The Coll of Wooster (OH)
The Colorado Coll (CO)
Colorado State U (CO)
Columbia Coll (SC)
Columbia Coll Chicago (IL)
Concordia U, St. Paul (MN)
Cornell U (NY)
Creighton U (NE)
Culver-Stockton Coll (MO)
Dallas Baptist U (TX)
Dartmouth Coll (NH)
DePauw U (IN)
Dominican U (IL)
Drake U (IA)
Drew U (NJ)
Drury U (MO)
East Carolina U (NC)
Eastern Kentucky U (KY)
Eastern Washington U (WA)
Edinboro U of Pennsylvania (PA)
Emmanuel Coll (MA)
Emory & Henry Coll (VA)
Endicott Coll (MA)
Eugene Lang Coll of Liberal Arts (NY)
Fairfield U (CT)
Fashion Inst of Technology (NY)
Flagler Coll (FL)
Florida A&M U (FL)
Florida Southern Coll (FL)
Florida State U (FL)
Fort Lewis Coll (CO)
Furman U (SC)
Gallaudet U (DC)
Georgetown Coll (KY)
Georgetown U (DC)
The George Washington U (DC)
Georgia Southern U (GA)
Goucher Coll (MD)
Grinnell Coll (IA)
Guilford Coll (NC)
Hamline U (MN)
Hampden-Sydney Coll (VA)
Harding U (AR)
Hardin-Simmons U (TX)
High Point U (NC)
Hobart and William Smith Colls (NY)
Hofstra U (NY)
Hope Coll (MI)
Houston Baptist U (TX)
Illinois State U (IL)
Indiana State U (IN)
Indiana U Bloomington (IN)
Indiana U Kokomo (IN)
Indiana U Northwest (IN)
Indiana U of Pennsylvania (PA)
Indiana U-Purdue U Indianapolis (IN)
Indiana U South Bend (IN)
Indiana U Southeast (IN)
Ithaca Coll (NY)
Jacksonville U (FL)
Kansas State U (KS)
Kean U (NJ)
Kenyon Coll (OH)
Knox Coll (IL)
Kutztown U of Pennsylvania (PA)
Lafayette Coll (PA)
Lamar U (TX)
La Sierra U (CA)
Lebanese American U (Lebanon)
Lee U (TN)
Lewis & Clark Coll (OR)
Liberty U (VA)
Limestone Coll (SC)
Lincoln U (MO)
Lincoln U (PA)
Linfield Coll (OR)
Lipscomb U (TN)
Lock Haven U of Pennsylvania (PA)
Louisiana State U and A&M Coll (LA)
Loyola Marymount U (CA)
Loyola U Chicago (IL)
Loyola U New Orleans (LA)
Manhattanville Coll (NY)
Marietta Coll (OH)
Marymount Manhattan Coll (NY)
Marymount U (VA)
Maryville U of Saint Louis (MO)
Massachusetts Coll of Art and Design (MA)
McKendree U (IL)
McMurry U (TX)
Meredith Coll (NC)
Messiah Coll (PA)
Michigan State U (MI)
Middlebury Coll (VT)
Millikin U (IL)
Minneapolis Coll of Art and Design (MN)
Minnesota State U Mankato (MN)
Missouri Southern State U (MO)
Molloy Coll (NY)
Montana State U (MT)
Morehead State U (KY)
Mount Holyoke Coll (MA)
Muhlenberg Coll (PA)
Murray State U (KY)
Nazareth Coll of Rochester (NY)
New Coll of Florida (FL)
New England Coll (NH)
New York U (NY)
Northern Arizona U (AZ)
Northern Illinois U (IL)
Northern Kentucky U (KY)
Northern State U (SD)
North Greenville U (SC)
Northwestern State U of Louisiana (LA)
Northwest Missouri State U (MO)
Nova Southeastern U (FL)
Oberlin Coll (OH)
Oglethorpe U (GA)
Ohio Wesleyan U (OH)
Oklahoma Baptist U (OK)
Oral Roberts U (OK)
Otis Coll of Art and Design (CA)
Paier Coll of Art, Inc. (CT)
Palm Beach Atlantic U (FL)
Paris Coll of Art (France)
Parsons School of Design (NY)
Pitzer Coll (CA)
Portland State U (OR)
Pratt Inst (NY)
Purdue U Fort Wayne (IN)
Queens Coll of the City U of New York (NY)
Queens U of Charlotte (NC)
Randolph Coll (VA)
Randolph-Macon Coll (VA)
Rice U (TX)
Roger Williams U (RI)
Rosemont Coll (PA)
The Sage Colls (NY)
Saginaw Valley State U (MI)
St. Catherine U (MN)
St. Cloud State U (MN)
Saint Louis U (MO)
St. Mary's Coll of Maryland (MD)
Saint Mary's U of Minnesota (MN)
Saint Vincent Coll (PA)
Salisbury U (MD)
Salve Regina U (RI)
Samford U (AL)
Sam Houston State U (TX)
San Diego State U (CA)
San Jose State U (CA)
Santa Clara U (CA)
Sarah Lawrence Coll (NY)
School of Visual Arts (NY)
Seattle U (WA)
Seton Hill U (PA)
Sierra Nevada Coll (NV)
Smith Coll (MA)
South Dakota State U (SD)
Southern Arkansas U–Magnolia (AR)
Southern Illinois U Carbondale (IL)
Southern Methodist U (TX)
Southwestern U (TX)
Spring Hill Coll (AL)

Stanford U (CA)
State U of New York at Fredonia (NY)
State U of New York Coll at Cortland (NY)
State U of New York Coll at Oneonta (NY)
State U of New York Coll at Potsdam (NY)
Stockton U (NJ)
Suffolk U (MA)
Susquehanna U (PA)
Tabor Coll (KS)
Tarleton State U (TX)
Taylor U (IN)
Texas A&M Intl U (TX)
Texas A&M U–Commerce (TX)
Texas A&M U–Kingsville (TX)
Texas Christian U (TX)
Texas State U (TX)
Towson U (MD)
Truman State U (MO)
Tulane U (LA)
Union Coll (NY)
U at Buffalo, the State U of New York (NY)
The U of Akron (OH)
The U of Alabama (AL)
The U of Arizona (AZ)
U of Arkansas at Little Rock (AR)
U of California, Irvine (CA)
U of California, San Diego (CA)
U of California, Santa Barbara (CA)
U of Central Florida (FL)
U of Cincinnati (OH)
U of Colorado Boulder (CO)
U of Colorado Denver (CO)
U of Dallas (TX)
U of Dayton (OH)
U of Houston–Clear Lake (TX)
U of Idaho (ID)
U of Illinois at Chicago (IL)
U of Illinois at Springfield (IL)
U of Jamestown (ND)
The U of Kansas (KS)
U of Kentucky (KY)
U of La Verne (CA)
U of Louisiana at Monroe (LA)
U of Louisville (KY)
U of Maine (ME)
U of Maine at Presque Isle (ME)
U of Mary Hardin-Baylor (TX)
U of Massachusetts Amherst (MA)
U of Miami (FL)
U of Michigan–Flint (MI)
U of Minnesota, Duluth (MN)
U of Minnesota, Morris (MN)
U of Missouri–St. Louis (MO)
U of Nebraska–Lincoln (NE)
U of New England (ME)
U of New Hampshire (NH)
The U of North Carolina at Chapel Hill (NC)
The U of North Carolina at Charlotte (NC)
The U of North Carolina at Greensboro (NC)
The U of North Carolina at Pembroke (NC)
The U of North Carolina Wilmington (NC)
U of Northern Colorado (CO)
U of Northern Iowa (IA)
U of North Florida (FL)
U of North Texas (TX)
U of Northwestern–St. Paul (MN)
U of Notre Dame (IN)
U of Oregon (OR)
U of Pennsylvania (PA)
U of Providence (MT)
U of Richmond (VA)
U of Saint Francis (IN)
U of St. Thomas (TX)
U of San Francisco (CA)
U of Science and Arts of Oklahoma (OK)
U of South Carolina (SC)
U of South Carolina Aiken (SC)
U of South Carolina Beaufort (SC)
U of Southern Maine (ME)
U of Southern Mississippi (MS)
U of South Florida (FL)
The U of Tennessee (TN)
The U of Texas at El Paso (TX)
The U of Texas at San Antonio (TX)
U of the Fraser Valley (BC, Canada)
U of the Incarnate Word (TX)
U of the Pacific (CA)
The U of the South (TN)
The U of Tulsa (OK)
U of Vermont (VT)
U of Waterloo (ON, Canada)
The U of Western Ontario (ON, Canada)
U of West Florida (FL)
Vanderbilt U (TN)
Wake Forest U (NC)
Walla Walla U (WA)
Washington and Lee U (VA)
Washington State U (WA)
Washington State U–Tri-Cities (WA)
Washington U in St. Louis (MO)
Wayland Baptist U (TX)
Wesleyan Coll (GA)
Wesleyan U (CT)
West Chester U of Pennsylvania (PA)
Western Carolina U (NC)
Western Colorado U (CO)
Western Kentucky U (KY)
Western Michigan U (MI)
Western New Mexico U (NM)
Westminster Coll (UT)
Wheaton Coll (MA)
Whitworth U (WA)
Wichita State U (KS)
Willamette U (OR)
William Paterson U of New Jersey (NJ)
Wittenberg U (OH)
Wright State U–Lake Campus (OH)
Xavier U (OH)
York Coll of Pennsylvania (PA)
Youngstown State U (OH)

FIRE/ARSON INVESTIGATION AND PREVENTION
Eastern Kentucky U (KY)

FIRE PREVENTION AND SAFETY TECHNOLOGY
Athens State U (AL)
Eastern Kentucky U (KY)
Oklahoma State U (OK)
U of New Haven (CT)

FIRE PROTECTION RELATED
The U of Akron (OH)
U of New Haven (CT)

FIRE SCIENCE/FIREFIGHTING
American Public U System (WV)
Columbia Coll (SC)
Hampton U (VA)
John Jay Coll of Criminal Justice of the City U of New York (NY)
Lewis-Clark State Coll (ID)
Madonna U (MI)
Providence Coll (RI)
Utah Valley U (UT)

FIRE SERVICES ADMINISTRATION
Bowling Green State U (OH)
California State U, Los Angeles (CA)
Colorado State U (CO)
Eastern Kentucky U (KY)
Eastern Oregon U (OR)
Fayetteville State U (NC)
John Jay Coll of Criminal Justice of the City U of New York (NY)
Liberty U (VA)
St. Thomas U - Florida (FL)
Salem State U (MA)
Southern Illinois U Carbondale (IL)
U of Cincinnati (OH)
Western Oregon U (OR)

FISHING AND FISHERIES SCIENCES AND MANAGEMENT
Mansfield U of Pennsylvania (PA)
Michigan State U (MI)
Texas A&M U (TX)
U of Alaska Fairbanks (AK)
U of Idaho (ID)
U of Minnesota, Twin Cities Campus (MN)
Utah State U (UT)

FLIGHT INSTRUCTION
South Dakota State U (SD)

U of North Dakota (ND)

FOLKLORE
Indiana U Bloomington (IN)
U of Oregon (OR)

FOODS AND NUTRITION RELATED
Bennington Coll (VT)
California State U, Long Beach (CA)
The U of Arizona (AZ)
U of Minnesota, Twin Cities Campus (MN)

FOOD SCIENCE
Auburn U (AL)
California Polytechnic State U, San Luis Obispo (CA)
California State Polytechnic U, Pomona (CA)
Clemson U (SC)
Cornell U (NY)
Delaware Valley U (PA)
Dominican U (IL)
East Central U (OK)
Florida A&M U (FL)
Framingham State U (MA)
Iowa State U of Science and Technology (IA)
Kansas State U (KS)
Michigan State U (MI)
Mississippi State U (MS)
The Ohio State U (OH)
Oklahoma State U (OK)
Penn State Abington (PA)
Penn State Altoona (PA)
Penn State Beaver (PA)
Penn State Berks (PA)
Penn State Brandywine (PA)
Penn State DuBois (PA)
Penn State Erie, The Behrend Coll (PA)
Penn State Fayette, The Eberly Campus (PA)
Penn State Greater Allegheny (PA)
Penn State Hazleton (PA)
Penn State Lehigh Valley (PA)
Penn State Mont Alto (PA)
Penn State New Kensington (PA)
Penn State Schuylkill (PA)
Penn State Shenango (PA)
Penn State U Park (PA)
Penn State Wilkes-Barre (PA)
Penn State York (PA)
San Jose State U (CA)
Simmons U (MA)
South Dakota State U (SD)
Texas Tech U (TX)
U of Arkansas (AR)
U of Idaho (ID)
U of Kentucky (KY)
U of Maine (ME)
U of Massachusetts Amherst (MA)
U of Minnesota, Twin Cities Campus (MN)
U of Nebraska–Lincoln (NE)
The U of Tennessee (TN)
U of Wisconsin–Madison (WI)
Utah State U (UT)
Washington State U (WA)
Western Michigan U (MI)

FOOD SCIENCE AND TECHNOLOGY RELATED
Appalachian State U (NC)
Middle Tennessee State U (TN)
Saint Francis U (PA)
The U of Arizona (AZ)

FOOD SERVICE AND DINING ROOM MANAGEMENT
Michigan State U (MI)

FOOD SERVICE SYSTEMS ADMINISTRATION
Dominican U (IL)
Lamar U (TX)
Lipscomb U (TN)
The Ohio State U (OH)
Point Loma Nazarene U (CA)
Sam Houston State U (TX)
Simmons U (MA)
State U of New York Coll at Oneonta (NY)
U of Wisconsin–Stout (WI)
Western Michigan U (MI)

FOODS, NUTRITION, AND WELLNESS
Andrews U (MI)
Arizona State U at the Downtown Phoenix campus (AZ)
Auburn U (AL)
Benedictine U (IL)
Bluffton U (OH)
Bowling Green State U (OH)
Bradley U (IL)
California State U, Fresno (CA)
Carson-Newman U (TN)
Cedar Crest Coll (PA)
Charles R. Drew U of Medicine and Science (CA)
Dominican U (IL)
Eastern Kentucky U (KY)
Framingham State U (MA)
Georgia Southern U (GA)
Howard U (DC)
Indiana State U (IN)
Indiana U of Pennsylvania (PA)
Jacksonville State U (AL)
James Madison U (VA)
Lehman Coll of the City U of New York (NY)
Life U (GA)
Lincoln U (MO)
Madonna U (MI)
Middle Tennessee State U (TN)
Minnesota State U Mankato (MN)
Montclair State U (NJ)
Murray State U (KY)
New York U (NY)
Oklahoma State U (OK)
Point Loma Nazarene U (CA)
Prairie View A&M U (TX)
Radford U (VA)
St. Catherine U (MN)
Samford U (AL)
Sam Houston State U (TX)
South Dakota State U (SD)
Texas A&M U (TX)
Texas State U (TX)
Texas Woman's U (TX)
The U of Akron (OH)
U of Arkansas (AR)
U of Idaho (ID)
U of Kentucky (KY)
U of Nebraska–Lincoln (NE)
U of New Mexico (NM)
The U of North Carolina at Chapel Hill (NC)
U of Saint Joseph (CT)
The U of Tennessee (TN)
U of Toronto (ON, Canada)
U of Utah (UT)
The U of Western Ontario (ON, Canada)
Utah State U (UT)
Washington State U (WA)
Wayne State U (MI)
Youngstown State U (OH)

FOOD TECHNOLOGY AND PROCESSING
Brigham Young U (UT)
California State U, Los Angeles (CA)
State U of New York Coll of Agriculture and Technology at Cobleskill (NY)

FOREIGN LANGUAGES AND LITERATURES
Alfred U (NY)
Arkansas Tech U (AR)
Auburn U (AL)
Auburn U at Montgomery (AL)
Augustana U (SD)
Austin Peay State U (TN)
Benedictine Coll (KS)
Bennington Coll (VT)
Butler U (IN)
California Polytechnic State U, San Luis Obispo (CA)
Cameron U (OK)
The Citadel, The Military Coll of South Carolina (SC)
Clemson U (SC)
Coastal Carolina U (SC)
Colorado State U (CO)
Covenant Coll (GA)
East Carolina U (NC)
Eastern Illinois U (IL)
Elon U (NC)
Emory & Henry Coll (VA)
Emporia State U (KS)
Framingham State U (MA)
Francis Marion U (SC)
Gannon U (PA)
George Mason U (VA)
Georgia Coll & State U (GA)
Georgia Inst of Technology (GA)
Iowa State U of Science and Technology (IA)
James Madison U (VA)
Kansas State U (KS)
Kenyon Coll (OH)
Knox Coll (IL)
Lamar U (TX)
Lewis & Clark Coll (OR)
Lock Haven U of Pennsylvania (PA)
Longwood U (VA)
Marshall U (WV)
Middle Tennessee State U (TN)
Millersville U of Pennsylvania (PA)
Mississippi State U (MS)
Montana State U (MT)
Nebraska Wesleyan U (NE)
New York U (NY)
Northern Arizona U (AZ)
Oakland U (MI)
Old Dominion U (VA)
Penn State Berks (PA)
Penn State Lehigh Valley (PA)
Portland State U (OR)
Purdue U Northwest (IN)
Radford U (VA)
Roger Williams U (RI)
Saint Mary's Coll of California (CA)
St. Mary's Coll of Maryland (MD)
Scripps Coll (CA)
Slippery Rock U of Pennsylvania (PA)
Southern Illinois U Carbondale (IL)
Southern Illinois U Edwardsville (IL)
Stanford U (CA)
State U of New York Coll at Old Westbury (NY)
Stockton U (NJ)
Texas A&M U (TX)
Texas Tech U (TX)
Towson U (MD)
Truman State U (MO)
Tulane U (LA)
Union Coll (NY)
Union U (TN)
The U of Alabama (AL)
The U of Alabama at Birmingham (AL)
The U of Alabama in Huntsville (AL)
U of Alaska Fairbanks (AK)
U of Arkansas at Little Rock (AR)
U of California, Riverside (CA)
U of California, San Diego (CA)
U of Central Arkansas (AR)
U of Dayton (OH)
U of Hartford (CT)
U of Houston (TX)
U of Idaho (ID)
U of Louisiana at Lafayette (LA)
U of Louisiana at Monroe (LA)
U of Maryland, Baltimore County (MD)
U of Mary Washington (VA)
U of Massachusetts Lowell (MA)
U of Memphis (TN)
U of Minnesota, Twin Cities Campus (MN)
U of Missouri–St. Louis (MO)
U of Montevallo (AL)
U of New Mexico (NM)
The U of North Carolina at Chapel Hill (NC)
The U of North Carolina at Greensboro (NC)
U of North Dakota (ND)
U of Northern Colorado (CO)
The U of Scranton (PA)
U of South Alabama (AL)
U of Southern Mississippi (MS)
U of South Florida (FL)
U of South Florida, St. Petersburg (FL)
The U of Tennessee (TN)
The U of Tennessee at Chattanooga (TN)
The U of Texas at San Antonio (TX)
U of Wisconsin–Platteville (WI)
Utica Coll (NY)

Virginia Commonwealth U (VA)
Washington Coll (MD)
Wayne State Coll (NE)
Wayne State U (MI)
West Chester U of Pennsylvania (PA)
Western Washington U (WA)
West Virginia U (WV)
Wichita State U (KS)
Widener U (PA)
Winthrop U (SC)
Wright State U (OH)
Youngstown State U (OH)

FOREIGN LANGUAGES RELATED
Arizona State U at the Tempe campus (AZ)
Augustana U (SD)
Averett U (VA)
Bennington Coll (VT)
Binghamton U, State U of New York (NY)
Clemson U (SC)
Framingham State U (MA)
Georgia Southern U (GA)
Indiana State U (IN)
Kennesaw State U (GA)
Miami U (OH)
Miami U Hamilton (OH)
Miami U Middletown (OH)
Murray State U (KY)
New York U (NY)
Purchase Coll, State U of New York (NY)
Saint Mary's Coll of California (CA)
United States Military Acad (NY)
U of Alaska Fairbanks (AK)
U of California, Berkeley (CA)
U of California, Los Angeles (CA)
U of Hawaii at Manoa (HI)
U of Washington (WA)
U of West Georgia (GA)
Wayne State U (MI)
Yale U (CT)

FOREIGN LANGUAGE TEACHER EDUCATION
Arkansas Tech U (AR)
Auburn U (AL)
Ball State U (IN)
Baylor U (TX)
Bowling Green State U (OH)
Calvin Coll (MI)
Coll of Staten Island of the City U of New York (NY)
Concordia Coll (MN)
Eastern Michigan U (MI)
Florida Southern Coll (FL)
Grand Valley State U (MI)
Hofstra U (NY)
Iona Coll (NY)
Loyola U Chicago (IL)
Messiah Coll (PA)
Miami U (OH)
Miami U Hamilton (OH)
Miami U Middletown (OH)
Nazareth Coll of Rochester (NY)
New York U (NY)
The Ohio State U (OH)
Ohio Wesleyan U (OH)
Oral Roberts U (OK)
Pace U, Pleasantville Campus (NY)
Penn State Abington (PA)
Penn State Altoona (PA)
Penn State Beaver (PA)
Penn State Berks (PA)
Penn State Brandywine (PA)
Penn State DuBois (PA)
Penn State Erie, The Behrend Coll (PA)
Penn State Fayette, The Eberly Campus (PA)
Penn State Greater Allegheny (PA)
Penn State Mont Alto (PA)
Penn State Shenango (PA)
Penn State U Park (PA)
Penn State York (PA)
Providence Coll (RI)
Queens Coll of the City U of New York (NY)
Rhode Island Coll (RI)
Roger Williams U (RI)
Saint Francis U (PA)
Seton Hill U (PA)
Southeast Missouri State U (MO)
State U of New York Coll at Old Westbury (NY)
U of Dayton (OH)
The U of Findlay (OH)
U of Maine (ME)
U of Mary Hardin-Baylor (TX)
U of Minnesota, Duluth (MN)
U of Nebraska–Lincoln (NE)
U of Northern Iowa (IA)
U of South Dakota (SD)
U of South Florida (FL)
U of Vermont (VT)
U of Wisconsin–Milwaukee (WI)
Valparaiso U (IN)
Vanderbilt U (TN)
Virginia Wesleyan U (VA)
Wayne State Coll (NE)
Youngstown State U (OH)

FORENSIC CHEMISTRY
Arizona State U at the West campus (AZ)
Bowling Green State U (OH)
Chestnut Hill Coll (PA)
Eastern Kentucky U (KY)
Edinboro U of Pennsylvania (PA)
Emmanuel Coll (MA)
Lamar U (TX)
LeTourneau U (TX)
Loyola U New Orleans (LA)
Maryville U of Saint Louis (MO)
Mount Mercy U (IA)
Palm Beach Atlantic U (FL)
U of Saint Francis (IN)
Western Carolina U (NC)
Western New England U (MA)

FORENSIC PSYCHOLOGY
The Coll of Saint Rose (NY)
Florida Inst of Technology (FL)
John Jay Coll of Criminal Justice of the City U of New York (NY)
Maryville U of Saint Louis (MO)
Northwest Christian U (OR)
Oklahoma Baptist U (OK)
St. Ambrose U (IA)
Tiffin U (OH)
U of New Haven (CT)
Walla Walla U (WA)

FORENSIC SCIENCE AND TECHNOLOGY
American Public U System (WV)
Becker Coll (MA)
Bryan Coll (TN)
Cedar Crest Coll (PA)
Cedarville U (OH)
Chaminade U of Honolulu (HI)
Chestnut Hill Coll (PA)
The Coll of Saint Rose (NY)
Columbia Coll (MO)
Eastern Kentucky U (KY)
Eastern New Mexico U (NM)
Farmingdale State Coll (NY)
Fayetteville State U (NC)
Florida Gulf Coast U (FL)
Friends U (KS)
Gannon U (PA)
George Mason U (VA)
Hofstra U (NY)
Husson U (ME)
Indiana U-Purdue U Indianapolis (IN)
Inter American U of Puerto Rico, Aguadilla Campus (PR)
Inter American U of Puerto Rico, Barranquitas Campus (PR)
Inter American U of Puerto Rico, Bayamón Campus (PR)
Inter American U of Puerto Rico, Metropolitan Campus (PR)
Jacksonville State U (AL)
John Jay Coll of Criminal Justice of the City U of New York (NY)
King U (TN)
Lasell Coll (MA)
Lewis U (IL)
Liberty U (VA)
Loyola U Chicago (IL)
Lynn U (FL)
Madonna U (MI)
Miami U (OH)
Miami U Hamilton (OH)
Miami U Middletown (OH)
Middle Tennessee State U (TN)
Mount Marty Coll (SD)
New Jersey Inst of Technology (NJ)
Newman U (KS)
New Mexico Highlands U (NM)
Northwest Nazarene U (ID)
Penn State Altoona (PA)
Penn State Berks (PA)
Penn State U Park (PA)
Roberts Wesleyan Coll (NY)
Roger Williams U (RI)
Saint Francis U (PA)
Saint Louis U (MO)
St. Mary's U (TX)
St. Thomas Aquinas Coll (NY)
Sam Houston State U (TX)
Seton Hill U (PA)
State U of New York Coll of Technology at Alfred (NY)
Texas A&M U (TX)
Tiffin U (OH)
Towson U (MD)
Trine U (IN)
U of Central Florida (FL)
U of Dubuque (IA)
The U of Findlay (OH)
U of Maryland Global Campus (MD)
U of Nebraska–Lincoln (NE)
U of New Haven (CT)
U of North Dakota (ND)
U of Pittsburgh at Bradford (PA)
U of Providence (MT)
The U of Scranton (PA)
U of Southern Mississippi (MS)
The U of Tampa (FL)
The U of Texas at El Paso (TX)
U of Toronto (ON, Canada)
U of Wisconsin–Platteville (WI)
Utah Valley U (UT)
Virginia Commonwealth U (VA)
Waynesburg U (PA)
Weber State U (UT)
Western New England U (MA)
West Virginia U (WV)
Wichita State U (KS)
York Coll of Pennsylvania (PA)
Youngstown State U (OH)

FOREST/FOREST RESOURCES MANAGEMENT
Clemson U (SC)
U of California, Berkeley (CA)
U of Idaho (ID)
U of Montana (MT)
U of Nevada, Reno (NV)
U of Toronto (ON, Canada)
West Virginia U (WV)

FORESTRY
Beloit Coll (WI)
California Polytechnic State U, San Luis Obispo (CA)
Colorado State U (CO)
Lenoir-Rhyne U (NC)
Louisiana Tech U (LA)
Michigan State U (MI)
Michigan Technological U (MI)
New Mexico Highlands U (NM)
Southern Illinois U Carbondale (IL)
Texas A&M U (TX)
U of California, Berkeley (CA)
U of Idaho (ID)
U of Maine (ME)
U of Montana (MT)
U of New Hampshire (NH)
The U of Tennessee (TN)
U of Toronto (ON, Canada)
U of Vermont (VT)
Washington State U (WA)

FORESTRY RELATED
Auburn U (AL)
Northwest Missouri State U (MO)
U of Minnesota, Twin Cities Campus (MN)
U of Montana (MT)
U of Wisconsin–Parkside (WI)

FOREST SCIENCES AND BIOLOGY
Auburn U (AL)
Colorado State U (CO)
Iowa State U of Science and Technology (IA)
Mississippi State U (MS)
Northern Arizona U (AZ)
Penn State Abington (PA)
Penn State Altoona (PA)
Penn State Beaver (PA)
Penn State Berks (PA)
Penn State Brandywine (PA)
Penn State DuBois (PA)
Penn State Erie, The Behrend Coll (PA)
Penn State Fayette, The Eberly Campus (PA)
Penn State Greater Allegheny (PA)
Penn State Hazleton (PA)
Penn State Lehigh Valley (PA)
Penn State Mont Alto (PA)
Penn State New Kensington (PA)
Penn State Schuylkill (PA)
Penn State Shenango (PA)
Penn State U Park (PA)
Penn State Wilkes-Barre (PA)
Penn State York (PA)
U of Idaho (ID)
U of Kentucky (KY)
The U of the South (TN)
U of Wisconsin–Madison (WI)
Utah State U (UT)

FOREST TECHNOLOGY
Penn State Abington (PA)
Penn State Altoona (PA)
Penn State Beaver (PA)
Penn State Berks (PA)
Penn State Brandywine (PA)
Penn State DuBois (PA)
Penn State Erie, The Behrend Coll (PA)
Penn State Fayette, The Eberly Campus (PA)
Penn State Greater Allegheny (PA)
Penn State Hazleton (PA)
Penn State Lehigh Valley (PA)
Penn State Mont Alto (PA)
Penn State New Kensington (PA)
Penn State Schuylkill (PA)
Penn State Shenango (PA)
Penn State Wilkes-Barre (PA)
Penn State York (PA)

FRANCHISING
St. Catherine U (MN)

FRENCH
Agnes Scott Coll (GA)
Albion Coll (MI)
Allegheny Coll (PA)
American U (DC)
Amherst Coll (MA)
Andrews U (MI)
Aquinas Coll (MI)
Arizona State U at the Tempe campus (AZ)
Auburn U (AL)
Augsburg U (MN)
Augustana Coll (IL)
Augustana U (SD)
Austin Coll (TX)
Baker U (KS)
Ball State U (IN)
Barnard Coll (NY)
Barry U (FL)
Bates Coll (ME)
Baylor U (TX)
Belmont U (TN)
Beloit Coll (WI)
Benedictine Coll (KS)
Bennington Coll (VT)
Berea Coll (KY)
Berry Coll (GA)
Binghamton U, State U of New York (NY)
Boise State U (ID)
Boston Coll (MA)
Bowling Green State U (OH)
Bradley U (IL)
Brandon U (MB, Canada)
Bridgewater Coll (VA)
Bucknell U (PA)
Butler U (IN)
California Lutheran U (CA)
California State U, Fresno (CA)
California State U, Fullerton (CA)
California State U, Long Beach (CA)
California State U, Los Angeles (CA)
California State U, Northridge (CA)
California State U, Sacramento (CA)
California State U, San Bernardino (CA)
Calvin Coll (MI)
Capital U (OH)
Carleton Coll (MN)
Carnegie Mellon U (PA)
Carthage Coll (WI)
The Catholic U of America (DC)
Central Coll (IA)
Central Connecticut State U (CT)
Central Michigan U (MI)
Central Washington U (WA)
Centre Coll (KY)
Chestnut Hill Coll (PA)
City Coll of the City U of New York (NY)
Claremont McKenna Coll (CA)
Clark Atlanta U (GA)
Clark U (MA)
Clayton State U (GA)
Coe Coll (IA)
Colby Coll (ME)
Colgate U (NY)
Coll of Charleston (SC)
Coll of Saint Benedict (MN)
Coll of Staten Island of the City U of New York (NY)
Coll of the Holy Cross (MA)
The Coll of Wooster (OH)
The Colorado Coll (CO)
Concordia Coll (MN)
Cornell Coll (IA)
Cornell U (NY)
Creighton U (NE)
Dartmouth Coll (NH)
Davidson Coll (NC)
DePaul U (IL)
DePauw U (IN)
Dickinson Coll (PA)
Doane U (NE)
Dominican U (IL)
Drew U (NJ)
Drury U (MO)
Earlham Coll (IN)
Eastern Kentucky U (KY)
Eastern Michigan U (MI)
Eastern Washington U (WA)
Elon U (NC)
Emory & Henry Coll (VA)
Fairfield U (CT)
Fairleigh Dickinson U (NJ)
Florida Atlantic U (FL)
Florida State U (FL)
Fordham U (NY)
Franklin Coll (IN)
Furman U (SC)
Georgetown U (DC)
The George Washington U (DC)
Georgia State U (GA)
Gonzaga U (WA)
Goucher Coll (MD)
Grand Valley State U (MI)
Grinnell Coll (IA)
Guilford Coll (NC)
Gustavus Adolphus Coll (MN)
Hampden-Sydney Coll (VA)
Hanover Coll (IN)
Harding U (AR)
High Point U (NC)
Hillsdale Coll (MI)
Hobart and William Smith Colls (NY)
Hofstra U (NY)
Hollins U (VA)
Hope Coll (MI)
Howard U (DC)
Illinois Coll (IL)
Illinois State U (IL)
Illinois Wesleyan U (IL)
Indiana U Bloomington (IN)
Indiana U Northwest (IN)
Indiana U-Purdue U Indianapolis (IN)
Indiana U South Bend (IN)
Indiana U Southeast (IN)
Iona Coll (NY)
Ithaca Coll (NY)
Jacksonville State U (AL)
Jacksonville U (FL)
John Carroll U (OH)
Johns Hopkins U (MD)
Kalamazoo Coll (MI)
Kenyon Coll (OH)
King's Coll (PA)
Knox Coll (IL)
Lafayette Coll (PA)
Lake Forest Coll (IL)
Lawrence U (WI)
Lee U (TN)
Lehigh U (PA)
Lehman Coll of the City U of New York (NY)
Le Moyne Coll (NY)
Lewis & Clark Coll (OR)

Lincoln U (PA)
Lindenwood U (MO)
Linfield Coll (OR)
Lipscomb U (TN)
Louisiana State U and A&M Coll (LA)
Louisiana Tech U (LA)
Loyola Marymount U (CA)
Loyola U Chicago (IL)
Loyola U Maryland (MD)
Loyola U New Orleans (LA)
Manhattan Coll (NY)
Marquette U (WI)
McDaniel Coll (MD)
Mercer U, Macon (GA)
Merrimack Coll (MA)
Messiah Coll (PA)
Miami U (OH)
Miami U Hamilton (OH)
Miami U Middletown (OH)
Michigan State U (MI)
Middlebury Coll (VT)
Minnesota State U Mankato (MN)
Missouri Southern State U (MO)
Missouri State U (MO)
Montclair State U (NJ)
Moravian Coll (PA)
Mount Holyoke Coll (MA)
Mount Saint Mary's U (CA)
Mount St. Mary's U (MD)
Muhlenberg Coll (PA)
Muskingum U (OH)
Nazareth Coll of Rochester (NY)
Nebraska Wesleyan U (NE)
New Coll of Florida (FL)
New York U (NY)
Niagara U (NY)
Northeastern Illinois U (IL)
Northern Kentucky U (KY)
Northwestern U (IL)
Oakland U (MI)
Oberlin Coll (OH)
Occidental Coll (CA)
Oglethorpe U (GA)
The Ohio State U (OH)
Ohio Wesleyan U (OH)
Oklahoma State U (OK)
Oral Roberts U (OK)
Pacific U (OR)
Penn State Abington (PA)
Penn State Altoona (PA)
Penn State Beaver (PA)
Penn State Berks (PA)
Penn State Brandywine (PA)
Penn State DuBois (PA)
Penn State Erie, The Behrend Coll (PA)
Penn State Fayette, The Eberly Campus (PA)
Penn State Greater Allegheny (PA)
Penn State Hazleton (PA)
Penn State Lehigh Valley (PA)
Penn State Mont Alto (PA)
Penn State New Kensington (PA)
Penn State Schuylkill (PA)
Penn State Shenango (PA)
Penn State U Park (PA)
Penn State Wilkes-Barre (PA)
Penn State York (PA)
Pepperdine U, Malibu (CA)
Pittsburg State U (KS)
Point Loma Nazarene U (CA)
Pomona Coll (CA)
Portland State U (OR)
Princeton U (NJ)
Providence Coll (RI)
Purdue U Fort Wayne (IN)
Queens Coll of the City U of New York (NY)
Queens U of Charlotte (NC)
Randolph Coll (VA)
Randolph-Macon Coll (VA)
Rhode Island Coll (RI)
Rhodes Coll (TN)
Rice U (TX)
Roanoke Coll (VA)
Saginaw Valley State U (MI)
St. Catherine U (MN)
St. Cloud State U (MN)
St. John Fisher Coll (NY)
Saint John's U (MN)
Saint Joseph's U (PA)
Saint Louis U (MO)
Saint Mary's Coll of California (CA)
St. Norbert Coll (WI)
St. Olaf Coll (MN)
St. Thomas U - New Brunswick (NB, Canada)
Salisbury U (MD)
Salve Regina U (RI)
Samford U (AL)
Sam Houston State U (TX)
San Diego State U (CA)
San Francisco State U (CA)
San Jose State U (CA)
Santa Clara U (CA)
Sarah Lawrence Coll (NY)
Scripps Coll (CA)
Seattle U (WA)
Siena Coll (NY)
Simmons U (MA)
Simon Fraser U (BC, Canada)
Skidmore Coll (NY)
Slippery Rock U of Pennsylvania (PA)
Smith Coll (MA)
South Dakota State U (SD)
Southern Methodist U (TX)
Southwestern U (TX)
Stanford U (CA)
State U of New York at Fredonia (NY)
State U of New York at New Paltz (NY)
State U of New York at Oswego (NY)
State U of New York Coll at Cortland (NY)
State U of New York Coll at Geneseo (NY)
State U of New York Coll at Oneonta (NY)
State U of New York Coll at Potsdam (NY)
Stetson U (FL)
Stony Brook U, State U of New York (NY)
SUNY Brockport (NY)
Susquehanna U (PA)
Temple U (PA)
Tennessee Wesleyan U (TN)
Texas A&M U (TX)
Texas Christian U (TX)
Texas State U (TX)
Transylvania U (KY)
Trinity U (TX)
Tulane U (LA)
Union Coll (NY)
Union U (TN)
United States Military Acad (NY)
U at Buffalo, the State U of New York (NY)
The U of Akron (OH)
The U of Arizona (AZ)
U of Arkansas (AR)
U of Arkansas at Little Rock (AR)
U of California, Berkeley (CA)
U of California, Irvine (CA)
U of California, Los Angeles (CA)
U of California, Riverside (CA)
U of California, San Diego (CA)
U of California, Santa Barbara (CA)
U of Central Arkansas (AR)
U of Central Florida (FL)
U of Cincinnati (OH)
U of Colorado Boulder (CO)
U of Colorado Denver (CO)
U of Dallas (TX)
U of Dayton (OH)
U of Denver (CO)
U of Hawaii at Manoa (HI)
U of Houston (TX)
U of Idaho (ID)
U of Illinois at Chicago (IL)
The U of Iowa (IA)
U of Jamestown (ND)
The U of Kansas (KS)
U of Kentucky (KY)
U of La Verne (CA)
U of Louisville (KY)
U of Maine (ME)
U of Massachusetts Amherst (MA)
U of Massachusetts Boston (MA)
U of Massachusetts Dartmouth (MA)
U of Miami (FL)
U of Michigan (MI)
U of Michigan–Dearborn (MI)
U of Minnesota, Duluth (MN)
U of Minnesota, Morris (MN)
U of Minnesota, Twin Cities Campus (MN)
U of Montana (MT)
U of Nebraska at Kearney (NE)
U of Nebraska–Lincoln (NE)
U of Nevada, Las Vegas (NV)
U of Nevada, Reno (NV)
U of New Hampshire (NH)
U of New Mexico (NM)
The U of North Carolina at Charlotte (NC)
The U of North Carolina Wilmington (NC)
U of North Dakota (ND)
U of North Texas (TX)
U of Notre Dame (IN)
U of Oregon (OR)
U of Pennsylvania (PA)
U of Puget Sound (WA)
U of Richmond (VA)
U of St. Thomas (TX)
U of San Diego (CA)
U of San Francisco (CA)
The U of Scranton (PA)
U of South Carolina (SC)
U of South Dakota (SD)
U of Southern Indiana (IN)
U of Southern Maine (ME)
U of South Florida (FL)
The U of Tennessee (TN)
The U of Texas at El Paso (TX)
U of the Pacific (CA)
The U of the South (TN)
The U of Toledo (OH)
U of Toronto (ON, Canada)
The U of Tulsa (OK)
U of Utah (UT)
U of Vermont (VT)
U of Virginia (VA)
U of Washington (WA)
U of Waterloo (ON, Canada)
The U of Western Ontario (ON, Canada)
U of West Florida (FL)
U of Wisconsin–Eau Claire (WI)
U of Wisconsin–Green Bay (WI)
U of Wisconsin–La Crosse (WI)
U of Wisconsin–Madison (WI)
U of Wisconsin–Milwaukee (WI)
U of Wyoming (WY)
Utah State U (UT)
Valdosta State U (GA)
Valparaiso U (IN)
Vanderbilt U (TN)
Villanova U (PA)
Virginia Wesleyan U (VA)
Wabash Coll (IN)
Wake Forest U (NC)
Walla Walla U (WA)
Washington & Jefferson Coll (PA)
Washington and Lee U (VA)
Washington Coll (MD)
Washington State U (WA)
Washington U in St. Louis (MO)
Weber State U (UT)
Western Carolina U (NC)
Western Michigan U (MI)
Western Washington U (WA)
Westmont Coll (CA)
Wheaton Coll (IL)
Whitworth U (WA)
Widener U (PA)
Willamette U (OR)
William & Mary (VA)
Williams Coll (MA)
Wittenberg U (OH)
Wofford Coll (SC)
Wright State U (OH)
Wright State U–Lake Campus (OH)
Xavier U (OH)
Xavier U of Louisiana (LA)
Yale U (CT)

FRENCH AS A SECOND/ FOREIGN LANGUAGE (TEACHING)
Saginaw Valley State U (MI)
U of Toronto (ON, Canada)
U of Wisconsin–Milwaukee (WI)

FRENCH LANGUAGE TEACHER EDUCATION
Albion Coll (MI)
Andrews U (MI)
Auburn U (AL)
Augustana Coll (IL)
Austin Coll (TX)
Boise State U (ID)
California Lutheran U (CA)
Calvin Coll (MI)
The Catholic U of America (DC)
Central Washington U (WA)
Eastern Kentucky U (KY)
Eastern Michigan U (MI)
Eastern Washington U (WA)
Grand Valley State U (MI)
Harding U (AR)
Hofstra U (NY)
Hope Coll (MI)
Indiana U South Bend (IN)
Iona Coll (NY)
Ithaca Coll (NY)
Lee U (TN)
Le Moyne Coll (NY)
Lipscomb U (TN)
Louisiana Tech U (LA)
Manhattanville Coll (NY)
Merrimack Coll (MA)
Messiah Coll (PA)
Miami U (OH)
Miami U Hamilton (OH)
Miami U Middletown (OH)
Michigan State U (MI)
Missouri State U (MO)
New York U (NY)
Niagara U (NY)
Ohio Wesleyan U (OH)
Pittsburg State U (KS)
Providence Coll (RI)
Purdue U Fort Wayne (IN)
Queens Coll of the City U of New York (NY)
Rhode Island Coll (RI)
Roanoke Coll (VA)
St. Catherine U (MN)
St. Cloud State U (MN)
St. John Fisher Coll (NY)
Saint Joseph's U (PA)
Salve Regina U (RI)
State U of New York Coll at Cortland (NY)
State U of New York Coll at Oneonta (NY)
State U of New York Coll at Potsdam (NY)
The U of Akron (OH)
U of Illinois at Chicago (IL)
The U of Iowa (IA)
U of Maine (ME)
U of Nebraska–Lincoln (NE)
U of South Dakota (SD)
U of Toronto (ON, Canada)
U of Waterloo (ON, Canada)
Utah State U (UT)
Valparaiso U (IN)
Washington U in St. Louis (MO)
Weber State U (UT)
Western Michigan U (MI)
Western Washington U (WA)
Whitworth U (WA)
Widener U (PA)
Xavier U of Louisiana (LA)

FRENCH STUDIES
American U (DC)
Arcadia U (PA)
Barnard Coll (NY)
Bowdoin Coll (ME)
Brandeis U (MA)
Brown U (RI)
Carleton Coll (MN)
Coe Coll (IA)
The Colorado Coll (CO)
Emory & Henry Coll (VA)
Emory U (GA)
Fordham U (NY)
Lewis & Clark Coll (OR)
Linfield Coll (OR)
Manhattanville Coll (NY)
Moravian Coll (PA)
Rhode Island Coll (RI)
Saint Joseph's U (PA)
Scripps Coll (CA)
Skidmore Coll (NY)
Smith Coll (MA)
Southern Methodist U (TX)
U of New Hampshire (NH)
U of North Florida (FL)
U of Waterloo (ON, Canada)
The U of Western Ontario (ON, Canada)
Wesleyan U (CT)
Wheaton Coll (MA)

FUNERAL DIRECTION/ SERVICE
Wayne State U (MI)

FUNERAL SERVICE AND MORTUARY SCIENCE
Cincinnati Coll of Mortuary Science (OH)
Gannon U (PA)
Southern Illinois U Carbondale (IL)
U of Minnesota, Twin Cities Campus (MN)
Upper Iowa U (IA)

FURNITURE DESIGN AND MANUFACTURING
Edinboro U of Pennsylvania (PA)
Minneapolis Coll of Art and Design (MN)

GAME AND INTERACTIVE MEDIA DESIGN
Abilene Christian U (TX)
Academy of Art U (CA)
Arkansas Tech U (AR)
Becker Coll (MA)
Boise State U (ID)
Bradley U (IL)
Champlain Coll (VT)
Cleveland Inst of Art (OH)
Cogswell Polytechnical Coll (CA)
Columbia Coll Chicago (IL)
DePaul U (IL)
Drexel U (PA)
Drury U (MO)
Fitchburg State U (MA)
Florida Southern Coll (FL)
Freed-Hardeman U (TN)
High Point U (NC)
Indiana U Bloomington (IN)
Inter American U of Puerto Rico, Barranquitas Campus (PR)
Inter American U of Puerto Rico, Bayamón Campus (PR)
Keiser U, Fort Lauderdale (FL)
Kennesaw State U (GA)
Loyola U New Orleans (LA)
Miami U Hamilton (OH)
Miami U Middletown (OH)
New England Inst of Technology (RI)
Sacred Heart U (CT)
Sarah Lawrence Coll (NY)
Southern Arkansas U–Magnolia (AR)
Southwestern Coll (KS)
State U of New York Coll of Technology at Alfred (NY)
U of California, Irvine (CA)
U of Denver (CO)
U of Miami (FL)
U of Saint Francis (IN)
Wichita State U (KS)
William Peace U (NC)
Woodbury U (CA)
Worcester Polytechnic Inst (MA)

GAY/LESBIAN STUDIES
Bennington Coll (VT)
Cornell U (NY)
Hampshire Coll (MA)
Sarah Lawrence Coll (NY)
The U of Western Ontario (ON, Canada)

GENERAL STUDIES
Alfred U (NY)
Alverno Coll (WI)
American Public U System (WV)
Andrews U (MI)
Aquinas Coll (MI)
Austin Coll (TX)
Austin Peay State U (TN)
Azusa Pacific U (CA)
Belmont U (TN)
Bethel U (MN)
Boise State U (ID)
Brandon U (MB, Canada)
Brenau U (GA)
California State U, San Bernardino (CA)
California State U, San Marcos (CA)
Calumet Coll of Saint Joseph (IN)
Cameron U (OK)
The Catholic U of America (DC)
Champlain Coll (VT)
Clarion U of Pennsylvania (PA)
Coll of the Ozarks (MO)
Columbia Coll (MO)
Columbia Intl U (SC)
Concordia U Chicago (IL)
Concordia U, St. Paul (MN)

Concordia U Wisconsin (WI)
Cornell U (NY)
Dakota State U (SD)
Dean Coll (MA)
Delta State U (MS)
DePaul U (IL)
DeSales U (PA)
Drexel U (PA)
Earlham Coll (IN)
East Carolina U (NC)
East Central U (OK)
Eastern Kentucky U (KY)
Eastern New Mexico U (NM)
Emory & Henry Coll (VA)
Emporia State U (KS)
Fairfield U (CT)
Fairleigh Dickinson U (NJ)
Felician U (NJ)
Ferris State U (MI)
Florida Inst of Technology (FL)
Florida Polytechnic U (FL)
Friends U (KS)
George Mason U (VA)
Georgia Southern U (GA)
Granite State Coll (NH)
Hampton U (VA)
Harding U (AR)
Illinois State U (IL)
Indiana U-Purdue U Indianapolis (IN)
Jacksonville U (FL)
Kansas Wesleyan U (KS)
Kent State U at Tuscarawas (OH)
Kutztown U of Pennsylvania (PA)
LaGrange Coll (GA)
Lamar U (TX)
La Roche U (PA)
Lasell Coll (MA)
La Sierra U (CA)
Le Moyne Coll (NY)
Lewis U (IL)
Liberty U (VA)
Lipscomb U (TN)
Louisiana State U in Shreveport (LA)
Louisiana Tech U (LA)
Loyola U Chicago (IL)
Madonna U (MI)
Marshall U (WV)
Marywood U (PA)
Mayville State U (ND)
McNeese State U (LA)
Mercy Coll (NY)
Middle Tennessee State U (TN)
Milligan Coll (TN)
Minot State U (ND)
Misericordia U (PA)
Mississippi State U (MS)
Missouri Valley Coll (MO)
Molloy Coll (NY)
Montana Technological U (MT)
Morehead State U (KY)
Mount Marty Coll (SD)
Murray State U (KY)
National U (CA)
Nebraska Wesleyan U (NE)
New Jersey Inst of Technology (NJ)
New Mexico Inst of Mining and Technology (NM)
New York City Coll of Technology of the City U of New York (NY)
New York U (NY)
Northeastern State U (OK)
North Greenville U (SC)
Northwestern State U of Louisiana (LA)
Northwestern U (IL)
Northwest U (WA)
Nova Southeastern U (FL)
Oakland City U (IN)
Ohio Wesleyan U (OH)
Oklahoma State U (OK)
Palm Beach Atlantic U (FL)
Portland State U (OR)
Providence Coll (RI)
Purdue U Fort Wayne (IN)
Regis Coll (MA)
Roberts Wesleyan Coll (NY)
Rowan U (NJ)
Sacred Heart U (CT)
Saginaw Valley State U (MI)
St. Cloud State U (MN)
Saint Louis U (MO)
Saint Mary's Coll of California (CA)
Salem State U (MA)
Sam Houston State U (TX)
San Diego State U (CA)
Schoolcraft Coll (MI)
Seton Hill U (PA)
Shenandoah U (VA)
Shepherd U (WV)
Siena Coll (NY)
Siena Heights U (MI)
Simmons U (MA)
Simon Fraser U (BC, Canada)
Slippery Rock U of Pennsylvania (PA)
South Dakota State U (SD)
Southeastern Louisiana U (LA)
Southeastern U (FL)
Southeast Missouri State U (MO)
Southern Arkansas U–Magnolia (AR)
Southwestern Coll (KS)
Springfield Coll (MA)
Spring Hill Coll (AL)
State U of New York at New Paltz (NY)
State U of New York Coll of Technology at Alfred (NY)
State U of New York Maritime Coll (NY)
Tarleton State U (TX)
Texas A&M U–Commerce (TX)
Texas Christian U (TX)
Texas Southern U (TX)
Texas State U (TX)
Texas Tech U (TX)
Texas Woman's U (TX)
Tiffin U (OH)
Toccoa Falls Coll (GA)
Trevecca Nazarene U (TN)
Trinity Coll of Florida (FL)
The U of Alabama at Birmingham (AL)
U of Alaska Southeast (AK)
U of Central Florida (FL)
U of Charleston (WV)
U of Cincinnati (OH)
U of Dayton (OH)
U of Hartford (CT)
U of Idaho (ID)
U of Kentucky (KY)
U of La Verne (CA)
U of Louisiana at Lafayette (LA)
U of Louisiana at Monroe (LA)
U of Management and Technology (VA)
U of Mary Hardin-Baylor (TX)
U of Maryland, Baltimore County (MD)
U of Massachusetts Amherst (MA)
U of Memphis (TN)
U of Miami (FL)
U of Michigan (MI)
U of Nebraska at Kearney (NE)
U of Nevada, Reno (NV)
U of New Mexico (NM)
U of North Dakota (ND)
U of Northern Iowa (IA)
U of North Texas (TX)
U of St. Thomas (TX)
U of South Dakota (SD)
U of South Florida (FL)
U of South Florida, St. Petersburg (FL)
The U of Tampa (FL)
The U of Texas at San Antonio (TX)
U of the Fraser Valley (BC, Canada)
The U of Toledo (OH)
U of Washington (WA)
U of Washington, Bothell (WA)
U of Washington, Tacoma (WA)
U of Wyoming (WY)
Utah State U (UT)
Valley City State U (ND)
Warren Wilson Coll (NC)
Western Kentucky U (KY)
Western New Mexico U (NM)
West Virginia U (WV)
Whitworth U (WA)
Wichita State U (KS)
Widener U (PA)
William Penn U (IA)
Worcester State U (MA)
York Coll of Pennsylvania (PA)
Youngstown State U (OH)

GENETICS
Cedar Crest Coll (PA)
Iowa State U of Science and Technology (IA)
Ohio Wesleyan U (OH)
The U of Alabama at Birmingham (AL)
U of California, Irvine (CA)
U of New Hampshire (NH)
The U of Western Ontario (ON, Canada)
U of Wisconsin–Madison (WI)
Washington State U (WA)

GENETICS RELATED
The George Washington U (DC)

GENOME SCIENCES/ GENOMICS
Florida Inst of Technology (FL)
Northwestern Coll (IA)
U of New Haven (CT)

GEOCHEMISTRY
Bowling Green State U (OH)
Bridgewater State U (MA)
Brown U (RI)
Grand Valley State U (MI)
State U of New York at New Paltz (NY)
State U of New York at Oswego (NY)
State U of New York Coll at Cortland (NY)
State U of New York Coll at Geneseo (NY)
U of California, San Diego (CA)
U of Waterloo (ON, Canada)
Washington U in St. Louis (MO)
Western Michigan U (MI)

GEOGRAPHIC INFORMATION SCIENCE AND CARTOGRAPHY
Arizona State U at the Tempe campus (AZ)
Auburn U at Montgomery (AL)
Binghamton U, State U of New York (NY)
Brigham Young U (UT)
Central Michigan U (MI)
Central Washington U (WA)
DePaul U (IL)
East Central U (OK)
Eastern Kentucky U (KY)
Edinboro U of Pennsylvania (PA)
Farmingdale State Coll (NY)
Front Range Comm Coll (CO)
Hofstra U (NY)
Kennesaw State U (GA)
Michigan State U (MI)
Northwest Missouri State U (MO)
The Ohio State U (OH)
Oklahoma State U (OK)
Radford U (VA)
Rowan U (NJ)
Salem State U (MA)
South Dakota State U (SD)
State U of New York Coll at Oneonta (NY)
State U of New York Coll at Potsdam (NY)
Texas A&M U (TX)
Texas State U (TX)
United States Military Acad (NY)
U at Buffalo, the State U of New York (NY)
The U of Akron (OH)
The U of Arizona (AZ)
U of Cincinnati (OH)
U of Oregon (OR)
The U of Texas at Dallas (TX)
U of Utah (UT)
The U of Western Ontario (ON, Canada)
U of Wisconsin–Eau Claire (WI)
U of Wisconsin–Madison (WI)
Western Michigan U (MI)
Worcester State U (MA)

GEOGRAPHY
Adams State U (CO)
Appalachian State U (NC)
Aquinas Coll (MI)
Arizona State U at the Tempe campus (AZ)
Auburn U (AL)
Augustana Coll (IL)
Ball State U (IN)
Bemidji State U (MN)
Bennington Coll (VT)
Bowling Green State U (OH)
Brandon U (MB, Canada)
Bridgewater State U (MA)
Bucknell U (PA)
California State Polytechnic U, Pomona (CA)
California State U, Dominguez Hills (CA)
California State U, Fresno (CA)
California State U, Fullerton (CA)
California State U, Long Beach (CA)
California State U, Los Angeles (CA)
California State U, Northridge (CA)
California State U, Sacramento (CA)
California State U, San Bernardino (CA)
California State U, Stanislaus (CA)
California U of Pennsylvania (PA)
Calvin Coll (MI)
Carthage Coll (WI)
Central Connecticut State U (CT)
Central Michigan U (MI)
Central Washington U (WA)
City Coll of the City U of New York (NY)
Clark U (MA)
Colgate U (NY)
Coll of Staten Island of the City U of New York (NY)
Colorado State U (CO)
Concordia U Chicago (IL)
Dartmouth Coll (NH)
DePaul U (IL)
East Carolina U (NC)
Eastern Illinois U (IL)
Eastern Kentucky U (KY)
Eastern Michigan U (MI)
Eastern Washington U (WA)
Edinboro U of Pennsylvania (PA)
Emory & Henry Coll (VA)
Fayetteville State U (NC)
Fitchburg State U (MA)
Florida Atlantic U (FL)
Florida State U (FL)
Framingham State U (MA)
George Mason U (VA)
The George Washington U (DC)
Georgia Coll & State U (GA)
Georgia Southern U (GA)
Georgia State U (GA)
Grand Valley State U (MI)
Gustavus Adolphus Coll (MN)
Hofstra U (NY)
Illinois State U (IL)
Indiana State U (IN)
Indiana U Bloomington (IN)
Indiana U of Pennsylvania (PA)
Indiana U-Purdue U Indianapolis (IN)
Indiana U Southeast (IN)
Jacksonville State U (AL)
Jacksonville U (FL)
James Madison U (VA)
Kansas State U (KS)
Kennesaw State U (GA)
Kutztown U of Pennsylvania (PA)
Lehman Coll of the City U of New York (NY)
Louisiana State U and A&M Coll (LA)
Louisiana Tech U (LA)
Marshall U (WV)
Miami U (OH)
Miami U Hamilton (OH)
Miami U Middletown (OH)
Michigan State U (MI)
Middlebury Coll (VT)
Millersville U of Pennsylvania (PA)
Minnesota State U Mankato (MN)
Missouri Southern State U (MO)
Missouri State U (MO)
Montclair State U (NJ)
Mount Holyoke Coll (MA)
Northeastern Illinois U (IL)
Northeastern State U (OK)
Northern Arizona U (AZ)
Northern Illinois U (IL)
Northern Kentucky U (KY)
Northwestern U (IL)
Northwest Missouri State U (MO)
The Ohio State U (OH)
Ohio Wesleyan U (OH)
Oklahoma State U (OK)
Old Dominion U (VA)
Olivet Nazarene U (IL)
Penn State Abington (PA)
Penn State Altoona (PA)
Penn State Beaver (PA)
Penn State Berks (PA)
Penn State Brandywine (PA)
Penn State DuBois (PA)
Penn State Erie, The Behrend Coll (PA)
Penn State Fayette, The Eberly Campus (PA)
Penn State Greater Allegheny (PA)
Penn State Hazleton (PA)
Penn State Lehigh Valley (PA)
Penn State Mont Alto (PA)
Penn State New Kensington (PA)
Penn State Schuylkill (PA)
Penn State Shenango (PA)
Penn State U Park (PA)
Penn State Wilkes-Barre (PA)
Penn State York (PA)
Pittsburg State U (KS)
Portland State U (OR)
Rhode Island Coll (RI)
Rocky Mountain Coll (MT)
Rowan U (NJ)
Saginaw Valley State U (MI)
St. Cloud State U (MN)
Salem State U (MA)
Salisbury U (MD)
Samford U (AL)
Sam Houston State U (TX)
San Diego State U (CA)
San Francisco State U (CA)
San Jose State U (CA)
Sarah Lawrence Coll (NY)
Simon Fraser U (BC, Canada)
Slippery Rock U of Pennsylvania (PA)
South Dakota State U (SD)
Southern Illinois U Carbondale (IL)
Southern Illinois U Edwardsville (IL)
State U of New York at New Paltz (NY)
State U of New York Coll at Cortland (NY)
State U of New York Coll at Geneseo (NY)
State U of New York Coll at Oneonta (NY)
Taylor U (IN)
Texas A&M U (TX)
Texas Christian U (TX)
Texas State U (TX)
Texas Tech U (TX)
Towson U (MD)
United States Military Acad (NY)
U at Albany, State U of New York (NY)
U at Buffalo, the State U of New York (NY)
The U of Akron (OH)
The U of Alabama (AL)
U of Alaska Fairbanks (AK)
The U of Arizona (AZ)
U of Arkansas (AR)
U of California, Berkeley (CA)
U of California, Los Angeles (CA)
U of California, Santa Barbara (CA)
U of Central Arkansas (AR)
U of Cincinnati (OH)
U of Colorado Boulder (CO)
U of Colorado Colorado Springs (CO)
U of Colorado Denver (CO)
U of Denver (CO)
U of Hawaii at Manoa (HI)
U of Houston–Clear Lake (TX)
U of Idaho (ID)
The U of Iowa (IA)
The U of Kansas (KS)
U of Kentucky (KY)
U of Louisville (KY)
U of Mary Washington (VA)
U of Massachusetts Amherst (MA)
U of Memphis (TN)
U of Miami (FL)
U of Minnesota, Duluth (MN)
U of Minnesota, Twin Cities Campus (MN)
U of Montana (MT)
U of Nebraska at Kearney (NE)
U of Nebraska–Lincoln (NE)
U of Nevada, Reno (NV)
U of New Hampshire (NH)
U of New Mexico (NM)

The U of North Carolina at Chapel Hill (NC)
The U of North Carolina at Charlotte (NC)
The U of North Carolina at Greensboro (NC)
The U of North Carolina Wilmington (NC)
U of North Dakota (ND)
U of Northern Colorado (CO)
U of Northern Iowa (IA)
U of North Texas (TX)
U of Oregon (OR)
U of Richmond (VA)
U of South Alabama (AL)
U of South Carolina (SC)
U of Southern Mississippi (MS)
U of South Florida (FL)
U of South Florida, St. Petersburg (FL)
The U of Tennessee (TN)
The U of Texas at San Antonio (TX)
U of the Fraser Valley (BC, Canada)
The U of Toledo (OH)
U of Toronto (ON, Canada)
U of Vermont (VT)
U of Washington (WA)
U of Waterloo (ON, Canada)
The U of Western Ontario (ON, Canada)
U of West Georgia (GA)
U of Wisconsin–Eau Claire (WI)
U of Wisconsin–La Crosse (WI)
U of Wisconsin–Madison (WI)
U of Wisconsin–Milwaukee (WI)
U of Wisconsin–Parkside (WI)
U of Wisconsin–Platteville (WI)
U of Wyoming (WY)
Utah State U (UT)
Valparaiso U (IN)
Villanova U (PA)
Wayne State Coll (NE)
Weber State U (UT)
West Chester U of Pennsylvania (PA)
Western Carolina U (NC)
Western Michigan U (MI)
Western Oregon U (OR)
Western Washington U (WA)
West Virginia U (WV)
William Paterson U of New Jersey (NJ)
Worcester State U (MA)
Wright State U (OH)
Wright State U–Lake Campus (OH)
Youngstown State U (OH)

GEOGRAPHY RELATED
Arkansas Tech U (AR)
Bridgewater State U (MA)
Brigham Young U (UT)
Central Washington U (WA)
Emory & Henry Coll (VA)
Temple U (PA)
U of California, Los Angeles (CA)

GEOGRAPHY TEACHER EDUCATION
Aquinas Coll (MI)
Calvin Coll (MI)
Grand Valley State U (MI)
Mayville State U (ND)
Michigan State U (MI)
Rhode Island Coll (RI)
U of Nevada, Reno (NV)
Valparaiso U (IN)
Wayne State Coll (NE)
Weber State U (UT)

GEOLOGICAL AND EARTH SCIENCES/GEOSCIENCES RELATED
Allegheny Coll (PA)
Bridgewater State U (MA)
Brigham Young U (UT)
California State U, Dominguez Hills (CA)
California State U, Fullerton (CA)
Cedarville U (OH)
Central Washington U (WA)
The Coll of Wooster (OH)
Florida Gulf Coast U (FL)
Georgia Inst of Technology (GA)
Lehigh U (PA)
Missouri U of Science and Technology (MO)
Muskingum U (OH)
Old Dominion U (VA)
Penn State Abington (PA)
Penn State Altoona (PA)
Penn State Beaver (PA)
Penn State Berks (PA)
Penn State Brandywine (PA)
Penn State DuBois (PA)
Penn State Erie, The Behrend Coll (PA)
Penn State Fayette, The Eberly Campus (PA)
Penn State Greater Allegheny (PA)
Penn State Hazleton (PA)
Penn State Lehigh Valley (PA)
Penn State Mont Alto (PA)
Penn State New Kensington (PA)
Penn State Schuylkill (PA)
Penn State Shenango (PA)
Penn State U Park (PA)
Penn State Wilkes-Barre (PA)
Penn State York (PA)
Rocky Mountain Coll (MT)
Salisbury U (MD)
San Jose State U (CA)
Stanford U (CA)
Texas A&M U (TX)
Texas Christian U (TX)
Towson U (MD)
Union Coll (NY)
U at Buffalo, the State U of New York (NY)
U of Miami (FL)
U of Utah (UT)
U of Washington (WA)
U of Wyoming (WY)
Utica Coll (NY)
Worcester State U (MA)
Yale U (CT)

GEOLOGICAL/GEOPHYSICAL ENGINEERING
Colorado School of Mines (CO)
Michigan Technological U (MI)
Missouri U of Science and Technology (MO)
Montana Technological U (MT)
New Jersey Inst of Technology (NJ)
U of Alaska Fairbanks (AK)
U of California, Berkeley (CA)
U of California, Los Angeles (CA)
U of Michigan (MI)
U of Minnesota, Twin Cities Campus (MN)
U of Nevada, Reno (NV)
U of North Dakota (ND)
U of Toronto (ON, Canada)
U of Utah (UT)
U of Waterloo (ON, Canada)
U of Wisconsin–Madison (WI)

GEOLOGY/EARTH SCIENCE
Adams State U (CO)
Albion Coll (MI)
Alfred U (NY)
Allegheny Coll (PA)
Amherst Coll (MA)
Angelo State U (TX)
Appalachian State U (NC)
Arkansas Tech U (AR)
Auburn U (AL)
Augustana Coll (IL)
Austin Peay State U (TN)
Ball State U (IN)
Bates Coll (ME)
Baylor U (TX)
Beloit Coll (WI)
Bemidji State U (MN)
Bennington Coll (VT)
Binghamton U, State U of New York (NY)
Boise State U (ID)
Boston Coll (MA)
Bowdoin Coll (ME)
Bowling Green State U (OH)
Brandon U (MB, Canada)
Bridgewater State U (MA)
Brown U (RI)
Bucknell U (PA)
California Lutheran U (CA)
California Polytechnic State U, San Luis Obispo (CA)
California State Polytechnic U, Pomona (CA)
California State U, Bakersfield (CA)
California State U, Fresno (CA)
California State U, Fullerton (CA)
California State U, Long Beach (CA)
California State U, Los Angeles (CA)
California State U, Northridge (CA)
California State U, Sacramento (CA)
California State U, San Bernardino (CA)
California State U, Stanislaus (CA)
California U of Pennsylvania (PA)
Calvin Coll (MI)
Carleton Coll (MN)
Cedarville U (OH)
Central Connecticut State U (CT)
Central Michigan U (MI)
Central Washington U (WA)
City Coll of the City U of New York (NY)
Clarion U of Pennsylvania (PA)
Clark U (MA)
Clemson U (SC)
Colby Coll (ME)
Colgate U (NY)
Coll of Charleston (SC)
Coll of Staten Island of the City U of New York (NY)
The Coll of Wooster (OH)
The Colorado Coll (CO)
Colorado State U (CO)
Concordia U Chicago (IL)
Cornell Coll (IA)
Dartmouth Coll (NH)
DePauw U (IN)
Dickinson Coll (PA)
Drexel U (PA)
Earlham Coll (IN)
East Carolina U (NC)
Eastern Illinois U (IL)
Eastern Kentucky U (KY)
Eastern Michigan U (MI)
Eastern New Mexico U (NM)
Eastern Washington U (WA)
Edinboro U of Pennsylvania (PA)
Emporia State U (KS)
Fairleigh Dickinson U (NJ)
Florida Atlantic U (FL)
Florida State U (FL)
Framingham State U (MA)
George Mason U (VA)
The George Washington U (DC)
Georgia Southern U (GA)
Georgia State U (GA)
Guilford Coll (NC)
Gustavus Adolphus Coll (MN)
Hanover Coll (IN)
Harvard U (MA)
Hobart and William Smith Colls (NY)
Hofstra U (NY)
Hope Coll (MI)
Illinois State U (IL)
Indiana State U (IN)
Indiana U Bloomington (IN)
Indiana U Northwest (IN)
Indiana U of Pennsylvania (PA)
Indiana U-Purdue U Indianapolis (IN)
Iowa State U of Science and Technology (IA)
Jacksonville State U (AL)
James Madison U (VA)
Johns Hopkins U (MD)
Kansas State U (KS)
Kean U (NJ)
Kutztown U of Pennsylvania (PA)
Lafayette Coll (PA)
Lamar U (TX)
Lawrence U (WI)
Lehman Coll of the City U of New York (NY)
Lock Haven U of Pennsylvania (PA)
Louisiana State U and A&M Coll (LA)
Louisiana Tech U (LA)
Marietta Coll (OH)
Marshall U (WV)
Miami U (OH)
Miami U Hamilton (OH)
Miami U Middletown (OH)
Michigan State U (MI)
Michigan Technological U (MI)
Middlebury Coll (VT)
Middle Tennessee State U (TN)
Millersville U of Pennsylvania (PA)
Minnesota State U Mankato (MN)
Minot State U (ND)
Mississippi State U (MS)
Missouri State U (MO)
Missouri U of Science and Technology (MO)
Montana State U (MT)
Montclair State U (NJ)
Moravian Coll (PA)
Morehead State U (KY)
Mount Holyoke Coll (MA)
Murray State U (KY)
Muskingum U (OH)
New Mexico Highlands U (NM)
New Mexico Inst of Mining and Technology (NM)
Northeastern Illinois U (IL)
Northern Arizona U (AZ)
Northern Illinois U (IL)
Northern Kentucky U (KY)
Northwestern U (IL)
Northwest Missouri State U (MO)
Oberlin Coll (OH)
Occidental Coll (CA)
The Ohio State U (OH)
Ohio Wesleyan U (OH)
Oklahoma State U (OK)
Olivet Nazarene U (IL)
Penn State Abington (PA)
Penn State Altoona (PA)
Penn State Beaver (PA)
Penn State Berks (PA)
Penn State Brandywine (PA)
Penn State DuBois (PA)
Penn State Erie, The Behrend Coll (PA)
Penn State Fayette, The Eberly Campus (PA)
Penn State Greater Allegheny (PA)
Penn State Hazleton (PA)
Penn State Lehigh Valley (PA)
Penn State Mont Alto (PA)
Penn State New Kensington (PA)
Penn State Schuylkill (PA)
Penn State Shenango (PA)
Penn State U Park (PA)
Penn State Wilkes-Barre (PA)
Penn State York (PA)
Pomona Coll (CA)
Portland State U (OR)
Princeton U (NJ)
Purdue U Fort Wayne (IN)
Queens Coll of the City U of New York (NY)
Radford U (VA)
Rice U (TX)
Rocky Mountain Coll (MT)
Rowan U (NJ)
Saint Louis U (MO)
St. Norbert Coll (WI)
Salem State U (MA)
Sam Houston State U (TX)
San Diego State U (CA)
San Francisco State U (CA)
San Jose State U (CA)
Scripps Coll (CA)
Skidmore Coll (NY)
Slippery Rock U of Pennsylvania (PA)
Smith Coll (MA)
Southern Illinois U Carbondale (IL)
Southern Methodist U (TX)
Stanford U (CA)
State U of New York at Fredonia (NY)
State U of New York at New Paltz (NY)
State U of New York at Oswego (NY)
State U of New York Coll at Cortland (NY)
State U of New York Coll at Geneseo (NY)
State U of New York Coll at Oneonta (NY)
State U of New York Coll at Potsdam (NY)
Stockton U (NJ)
Stony Brook U, State U of New York (NY)
Susquehanna U (PA)
Tarleton State U (TX)
Texas A&M U (TX)
Texas A&M U–Corpus Christi (TX)
Texas A&M U–Kingsville (TX)
Texas Christian U (TX)
Texas Tech U (TX)
Towson U (MD)
Trinity U (TX)
Tulane U (LA)
Union Coll (NY)
U at Buffalo, the State U of New York (NY)
The U of Akron (OH)
The U of Alabama (AL)
U of Alaska Fairbanks (AK)
The U of Arizona (AZ)
U of Arkansas (AR)
U of Arkansas at Little Rock (AR)
U of California, Berkeley (CA)
U of California, Irvine (CA)
U of California, Los Angeles (CA)
U of California, Merced (CA)
U of California, Riverside (CA)
U of California, San Diego (CA)
U of California, Santa Barbara (CA)
U of California, Santa Cruz (CA)
U of Cincinnati (OH)
U of Colorado Boulder (CO)
U of Dayton (OH)
U of Hawaii at Manoa (HI)
U of Houston (TX)
U of Houston–Downtown (TX)
U of Idaho (ID)
U of Illinois at Chicago (IL)
The U of Iowa (IA)
The U of Kansas (KS)
U of Kentucky (KY)
U of Louisiana at Lafayette (LA)
U of Maine (ME)
U of Massachusetts Amherst (MA)
U of Memphis (TN)
U of Miami (FL)
U of Michigan (MI)
U of Michigan–Dearborn (MI)
U of Minnesota, Duluth (MN)
U of Minnesota, Morris (MN)
U of Minnesota, Twin Cities Campus (MN)
U of Montana (MT)
U of Nebraska–Lincoln (NE)
U of Nevada, Las Vegas (NV)
U of Nevada, Reno (NV)
U of New Hampshire (NH)
U of New Mexico (NM)
The U of North Carolina at Chapel Hill (NC)
The U of North Carolina at Charlotte (NC)
The U of North Carolina Wilmington (NC)
U of North Dakota (ND)
U of Northern Colorado (CO)
U of Northern Iowa (IA)
U of Oregon (OR)
U of Pennsylvania (PA)
U of Puget Sound (WA)
U of South Alabama (AL)
U of South Carolina (SC)
U of South Dakota (SD)
U of Southern Indiana (IN)
U of Southern Mississippi (MS)
U of South Florida (FL)
The U of Tennessee (TN)
The U of Tennessee at Chattanooga (TN)
The U of Tennessee at Martin (TN)
The U of Texas at Dallas (TX)
The U of Texas at El Paso (TX)
The U of Texas at San Antonio (TX)
The U of Texas of the Permian Basin (TX)
U of the Pacific (CA)
The U of the South (TN)
The U of Toledo (OH)
The U of Tulsa (OK)
U of Utah (UT)
U of Vermont (VT)
U of Washington (WA)
U of Waterloo (ON, Canada)
The U of Western Ontario (ON, Canada)
U of West Georgia (GA)
U of Wisconsin–Eau Claire (WI)
U of Wisconsin–Green Bay (WI)
U of Wisconsin–Madison (WI)
U of Wisconsin–Milwaukee (WI)
U of Wisconsin–Parkside (WI)
U of Wyoming (WY)
Utah State U (UT)
Utah Valley U (UT)
Valdosta State U (GA)
Vanderbilt U (TN)
Virginia Wesleyan U (VA)

Washington and Lee U (VA)
Washington State U (WA)
Washington State U–Tri-Cities (WA)
Washington State U–Vancouver (WA)
Washington U in St. Louis (MO)
Wayland Baptist U (TX)
Wayne State U (MI)
Weber State U (UT)
West Chester U of Pennsylvania (PA)
Western Carolina U (NC)
Western Colorado U (CO)
Western Connecticut State U (CT)
Western Kentucky U (KY)
Western Michigan U (MI)
Western Washington U (WA)
Westminster Coll (UT)
West Virginia U (WV)
Wheaton Coll (IL)
Wichita State U (KS)
Wilkes U (PA)
William & Mary (VA)
William Paterson U of New Jersey (NJ)
Williams Coll (MA)
Wittenberg U (OH)
Wright State U (OH)
Youngstown State U (OH)

GEOPHYSICS AND SEISMOLOGY
Baylor U (TX)
Boise State U (ID)
Boston Coll (MA)
Bowling Green State U (OH)
Brown U (RI)
Eastern Michigan U (MI)
Michigan Technological U (MI)
Missouri U of Science and Technology (MO)
Rice U (TX)
Saint Louis U (MO)
Southern Methodist U (TX)
Stanford U (CA)
State U of New York Coll at Geneseo (NY)
Texas A&M U (TX)
The U of Akron (OH)
U of California, Los Angeles (CA)
U of California, Riverside (CA)
U of California, San Diego (CA)
U of California, Santa Barbara (CA)
U of Houston (TX)
U of Nevada, Reno (NV)
U of South Carolina (SC)
The U of Texas at El Paso (TX)
The U of Tulsa (OK)
U of Utah (UT)
U of Washington (WA)
U of Waterloo (ON, Canada)
Washington U in St. Louis (MO)
Western Michigan U (MI)
Western Washington U (WA)

GERMAN
Agnes Scott Coll (GA)
Albion Coll (MI)
American U (DC)
Amherst Coll (MA)
Aquinas Coll (MI)
Arizona State U at the Tempe campus (AZ)
Auburn U (AL)
Augsburg U (MN)
Augustana Coll (IL)
Augustana U (SD)
Austin Coll (TX)
Baker U (KS)
Ball State U (IN)
Barnard Coll (NY)
Bates Coll (ME)
Baylor U (TX)
Belmont U (TN)
Beloit Coll (WI)
Berea Coll (KY)
Berry Coll (GA)
Binghamton U, State U of New York (NY)
Boise State U (ID)
Boston Coll (MA)
Bowdoin Coll (ME)
Bowling Green State U (OH)
Bucknell U (PA)
Butler U (IN)
California Lutheran U (CA)
California State U, Long Beach (CA)
Calvin Coll (MI)
Carleton Coll (MN)
Carnegie Mellon U (PA)
Carthage Coll (WI)
The Catholic U of America (DC)
Central Connecticut State U (CT)
Central Michigan U (MI)
Central Washington U (WA)
Centre Coll (KY)
Coe Coll (IA)
Colby Coll (ME)
Colgate U (NY)
Coll of Charleston (SC)
Coll of Saint Benedict (MN)
Coll of the Holy Cross (MA)
The Colorado Coll (CO)
Concordia Coll (MN)
Concordia U Wisconsin (WI)
Cornell Coll (IA)
Cornell U (NY)
Creighton U (NE)
Dartmouth Coll (NH)
Davidson Coll (NC)
DePaul U (IL)
DePauw U (IN)
Dickinson Coll (PA)
Doane U (NE)
Drew U (NJ)
Earlham Coll (IN)
Eastern Michigan U (MI)
Fairfield U (CT)
Florida State U (FL)
Fordham U (NY)
Furman U (SC)
Georgetown U (DC)
The George Washington U (DC)
Georgia State U (GA)
Grinnell Coll (IA)
Guilford Coll (NC)
Gustavus Adolphus Coll (MN)
Hamline U (MN)
Hampden-Sydney Coll (VA)
Harvard U (MA)
Hillsdale Coll (MI)
Hofstra U (NY)
Hope Coll (MI)
Howard U (DC)
Illinois Coll (IL)
Illinois State U (IL)
Indiana U-Purdue U Indianapolis (IN)
Indiana U South Bend (IN)
Indiana U Southeast (IN)
Ithaca Coll (NY)
Jacksonville State U (AL)
Johns Hopkins U (MD)
Kalamazoo Coll (MI)
Kenyon Coll (OH)
Knox Coll (IL)
Lafayette Coll (PA)
Lawrence U (WI)
Lehigh U (PA)
Lenoir-Rhyne U (NC)
Lewis & Clark Coll (OR)
Linfield Coll (OR)
Lipscomb U (TN)
Loyola U Chicago (IL)
Loyola U Maryland (MD)
Marquette U (WI)
McDaniel Coll (MD)
Mercer U, Macon (GA)
Messiah Coll (PA)
Miami U (OH)
Miami U Hamilton (OH)
Miami U Middletown (OH)
Michigan State U (MI)
Middlebury Coll (VT)
Minnesota State U Mankato (MN)
Minot State U (ND)
Missouri Southern State U (MO)
Missouri State U (MO)
Montclair State U (NJ)
Moravian Coll (PA)
Mount St. Mary's U (MD)
Muskingum U (OH)
Nebraska Wesleyan U (NE)
New Coll of Florida (FL)
New York U (NY)
Northern Kentucky U (KY)
Northern State U (SD)
Northwestern U (IL)
Oakland U (MI)
Oberlin Coll (OH)
The Ohio State U (OH)
Ohio Wesleyan U (OH)
Oklahoma State U (OK)
Pacific U (OR)
Penn State Abington (PA)
Penn State Altoona (PA)
Penn State Beaver (PA)
Penn State Berks (PA)
Penn State Brandywine (PA)
Penn State DuBois (PA)
Penn State Erie, The Behrend Coll (PA)
Penn State Fayette, The Eberly Campus (PA)
Penn State Greater Allegheny (PA)
Penn State Hazleton (PA)
Penn State Lehigh Valley (PA)
Penn State Mont Alto (PA)
Penn State New Kensington (PA)
Penn State Schuylkill (PA)
Penn State Shenango (PA)
Penn State U Park (PA)
Penn State Wilkes-Barre (PA)
Penn State York (PA)
Pepperdine U, Malibu (CA)
Pomona Coll (CA)
Portland State U (OR)
Princeton U (NJ)
Purdue U Fort Wayne (IN)
Queens Coll of the City U of New York (NY)
Randolph-Macon Coll (VA)
Rhodes Coll (TN)
Rice U (TX)
St. Cloud State U (MN)
Saint John's U (MN)
Saint Joseph's U (PA)
Saint Louis U (MO)
Saint Mary's Coll of California (CA)
St. Norbert Coll (WI)
St. Olaf Coll (MN)
Samford U (AL)
Sam Houston State U (TX)
San Diego State U (CA)
San Francisco State U (CA)
Sarah Lawrence Coll (NY)
Scripps Coll (CA)
Skidmore Coll (NY)
Smith Coll (MA)
South Dakota State U (SD)
Southern Methodist U (TX)
Southwestern U (TX)
State U of New York at Oswego (NY)
State U of New York Coll at Cortland (NY)
Stetson U (FL)
Stony Brook U, State U of New York (NY)
Susquehanna U (PA)
Temple U (PA)
Texas A&M U (TX)
Texas Christian U (TX)
Texas State U (TX)
Transylvania U (KY)
Trinity U (TX)
Tulane U (LA)
Union Coll (NY)
United States Military Acad (NY)
U at Buffalo, the State U of New York (NY)
The U of Arizona (AZ)
U of Arkansas (AR)
U of California, Berkeley (CA)
U of California, Los Angeles (CA)
U of California, San Diego (CA)
U of California, Santa Barbara (CA)
U of Cincinnati (OH)
U of Dallas (TX)
U of Dayton (OH)
U of Denver (CO)
U of Hawaii at Manoa (HI)
The U of Iowa (IA)
U of Jamestown (ND)
U of Kentucky (KY)
U of Miami (FL)
U of Michigan (MI)
U of Minnesota, Duluth (MN)
U of Montana (MT)
U of Nebraska at Kearney (NE)
U of Nebraska–Lincoln (NE)
U of Nevada, Las Vegas (NV)
U of New Hampshire (NH)
U of New Mexico (NM)
The U of North Carolina at Charlotte (NC)
The U of North Carolina Wilmington (NC)
U of North Dakota (ND)
U of North Texas (TX)
U of Notre Dame (IN)
U of Oregon (OR)
U of Pennsylvania (PA)
U of Puget Sound (WA)
The U of Scranton (PA)
U of South Carolina (SC)
U of South Dakota (SD)
U of Southern Indiana (IN)
U of South Florida (FL)
The U of Tennessee (TN)
U of the Pacific (CA)
The U of the South (TN)
The U of Toledo (OH)
U of Toronto (ON, Canada)
The U of Tulsa (OK)
U of Utah (UT)
U of Vermont (VT)
U of Virginia (VA)
U of Waterloo (ON, Canada)
The U of Western Ontario (ON, Canada)
U of Wisconsin–La Crosse (WI)
U of Wyoming (WY)
Utah State U (UT)
Valparaiso U (IN)
Vanderbilt U (TN)
Virginia Wesleyan U (VA)
Wabash Coll (IN)
Wake Forest U (NC)
Wartburg Coll (IA)
Washington & Jefferson Coll (PA)
Washington and Lee U (VA)
Washington Coll (MD)
Washington State U (WA)
Washington U in St. Louis (MO)
Wayne State U (MI)
Weber State U (UT)
Western Carolina U (NC)
Western Michigan U (MI)
Western Oregon U (OR)
Western Washington U (WA)
Wheaton Coll (IL)
Wheaton Coll (MA)
Willamette U (OR)
William & Mary (VA)
Williams Coll (MA)
Wittenberg U (OH)
Wofford Coll (SC)
Wright State U (OH)
Wright State U–Lake Campus (OH)
Xavier U (OH)
Yale U (CT)

GERMANIC LANGUAGES
Eastern Michigan U (MI)
Grand Valley State U (MI)
Indiana U Bloomington (IN)
U of Colorado Boulder (CO)
The U of Kansas (KS)
U of Washington (WA)
U of Wisconsin–Eau Claire (WI)
U of Wisconsin–Green Bay (WI)
U of Wisconsin–Madison (WI)
U of Wisconsin–Milwaukee (WI)
Washington U in St. Louis (MO)

GERMANIC LANGUAGES RELATED
Calvin Coll (MI)
U of Minnesota, Twin Cities Campus (MN)

GERMAN LANGUAGE TEACHER EDUCATION
Albion Coll (MI)
Auburn U (AL)
Augustana Coll (IL)
Ball State U (IN)
Boise State U (ID)
California Lutheran U (CA)
Calvin Coll (MI)
The Catholic U of America (DC)
Concordia U Wisconsin (WI)
Eastern Michigan U (MI)
Grand Valley State U (MI)
Hofstra U (NY)
Hope Coll (MI)
Indiana U South Bend (IN)
Ithaca Coll (NY)
Messiah Coll (PA)
Miami U (OH)
Miami U Hamilton (OH)
Miami U Middletown (OH)
Michigan State U (MI)
Minot State U (ND)
Missouri State U (MO)
New York U (NY)
Ohio Wesleyan U (OH)
Purdue U Fort Wayne (IN)
Queens Coll of the City U of New York (NY)
St. Cloud State U (MN)
Saint Joseph's U (PA)
U of Illinois at Chicago (IL)
The U of Iowa (IA)
U of Nebraska–Lincoln (NE)
U of South Dakota (SD)
U of Wisconsin–Milwaukee (WI)
Utah State U (UT)
Valparaiso U (IN)
Washington U in St. Louis (MO)
Weber State U (UT)
Western Michigan U (MI)
Western Washington U (WA)

GERMAN STUDIES
American U (DC)
Barnard Coll (NY)
Brandeis U (MA)
Brown U (RI)
Central Coll (IA)
Coe Coll (IA)
The Coll of Wooster (OH)
Cornell U (NY)
Emory U (GA)
Fordham U (NY)
Kutztown U of Pennsylvania (PA)
Linfield Coll (OR)
Moravian Coll (PA)
Mount Holyoke Coll (MA)
Pomona Coll (CA)
Scripps Coll (CA)
Smith Coll (MA)
Stanford U (CA)
U of California, Irvine (CA)
U of California, Riverside (CA)
U of California, San Diego (CA)
U of Illinois at Chicago (IL)
The U of Kansas (KS)
U of Massachusetts Amherst (MA)
U of Minnesota, Morris (MN)
U of Richmond (VA)
The U of Western Ontario (ON, Canada)
Wesleyan U (CT)
Wheaton Coll (MA)

GERONTOLOGY
Alfred U (NY)
Barton Coll (NC)
Bowling Green State U (OH)
California State U, Sacramento (CA)
California U of Pennsylvania (PA)
Gwynedd Mercy U (PA)
Ithaca Coll (NY)
Madonna U (MI)
Miami U (OH)
Miami U Hamilton (OH)
Miami U Middletown (OH)
Missouri State U (MO)
Mount Saint Mary's U (CA)
Niagara U (NY)
Regent U (VA)
St. Cloud State U (MN)
St. Thomas U - New Brunswick (NB, Canada)
San Diego State U (CA)
State U of New York Coll at Oneonta (NY)
U of Maryland Global Campus (MD)
U of Massachusetts Boston (MA)
U of Northern Iowa (IA)
U of North Texas (TX)
U of South Florida (FL)
Weber State U (UT)
Youngstown State U (OH)

GOLF COURSE OPERATION AND GROUNDS MANAGEMENT
Trine U (IN)
U of the Incarnate Word (TX)

GRAPHIC AND PRINTING EQUIPMENT OPERATION/ PRODUCTION
Lewis-Clark State Coll (ID)

GRAPHIC COMMUNICATIONS
Appalachian State U (NC)
Bradley U (IL)
California Polytechnic State U, San Luis Obispo (CA)

California State U, Los Angeles (CA)
Eastern Washington U (WA)
Illinois State U (IL)
Murray State U (KY)
New England Inst of Technology (RI)
Roger Williams U (RI)
Sam Houston State U (TX)
The U of Findlay (OH)
U of Maryland Global Campus (MD)
U of Northern Iowa (IA)
Walla Walla U (WA)

GRAPHIC COMMUNICATIONS RELATED
Bowling Green State U (OH)
Rasmussen Coll Aurora (IL)
Rasmussen Coll Blaine (MN)
Rasmussen Coll Bloomington (MN)
Rasmussen Coll Brooklyn Park (MN)
Rasmussen Coll Eagan (MN)
Rasmussen Coll Fargo (ND)
Rasmussen Coll Fort Myers (FL)
Rasmussen Coll Green Bay (WI)
Rasmussen Coll Lake Elmo/ Woodbury (MN)
Rasmussen Coll Land O' Lakes (FL)
Rasmussen Coll Mankato (MN)
Rasmussen Coll Mokena/Tinley Park (IL)
Rasmussen Coll New Port Richey (FL)
Rasmussen Coll Ocala (FL)
Rasmussen Coll Rockford (IL)
Rasmussen Coll Romeoville/Joliet (IL)
Rasmussen Coll St. Cloud (MN)
Rasmussen Coll Tampa/Brandon (FL)
Rasmussen Coll Wausau (WI)
U of Wisconsin–Stout (WI)

GRAPHIC DESIGN
Abilene Christian U (TX)
Academy of Art U (CA)
Adams State U (CO)
American Acad of Art (IL)
American U (DC)
American U of Beirut (Lebanon)
Anderson U (SC)
Andrews U (MI)
Appalachian State U (NC)
Arcadia U (PA)
Arizona State U at the Tempe campus (AZ)
Arkansas Tech U (AR)
Assumption Coll (MA)
Auburn U (AL)
Augsburg U (MN)
Augustana Coll (IL)
Aurora U (IL)
Becker Coll (MA)
Belhaven U (MS)
Benedictine U (IL)
Bethany Lutheran Coll (MN)
Bethel U (IN)
Bethel U (MN)
Bluffton U (OH)
Boise State U (ID)
Bradley U (IL)
Bridgewater State U (MA)
Brigham Young U (UT)
Caldwell U (NJ)
California State Polytechnic U, Pomona (CA)
California State U, Dominguez Hills (CA)
California State U, Fresno (CA)
California State U, Long Beach (CA)
California State U, Sacramento (CA)
California U of Pennsylvania (PA)
Calvin Coll (MI)
Carson-Newman U (TN)
Carthage Coll (WI)
Cazenovia Coll (NY)
Cedarville U (OH)
Central Michigan U (MI)
Central Washington U (WA)
Champlain Coll (VT)
Chatham U (PA)
City Coll of the City U of New York (NY)
Cleveland Inst of Art (OH)
Coastal Carolina U (SC)
Colby-Sawyer Coll (NH)
Coll of the Ozarks (MO)
Columbia Coll (MO)
Columbia Coll Chicago (IL)
Concordia U Wisconsin (WI)
Creative Center (NE)
Creighton U (NE)
Culver-Stockton Coll (MO)
Dallas Baptist U (TX)
DePaul U (IL)
Doane U (NE)
Dominican U of California (CA)
Drake U (IA)
Drexel U (PA)
East Central U (OK)
Eastern Washington U (WA)
Edgewood Coll (WI)
Edinboro U of Pennsylvania (PA)
Emmanuel Coll (MA)
Emory & Henry Coll (VA)
Endicott Coll (MA)
Eugene Lang Coll of Liberal Arts (NY)
Fairleigh Dickinson U (NJ)
Fashion Inst of Technology (NY)
Ferris State U (MI)
FIDM/Fashion Inst of Design & Merchandising, Los Angeles Campus (CA)
Fitchburg State U (MA)
Flagler Coll (FL)
Florida A&M U (FL)
Franklin Coll (IN)
Georgia Southern U (GA)
Harding U (AR)
Hardin-Simmons U (TX)
High Point U (NC)
Houston Baptist U (TX)
Inter American U of Puerto Rico, Aguadilla Campus (PR)
Inter American U of Puerto Rico, San Germán Campus (PR)
Iowa State U of Science and Technology (IA)
John Brown U (AR)
Kansas Wesleyan U (KS)
Lamar U (TX)
Lasell Coll (MA)
La Sierra U (CA)
Lebanese American U (Lebanon)
Lenoir-Rhyne U (NC)
Liberty U (VA)
Limestone Coll (SC)
Los Angeles Film School (CA)
Lynn U (FL)
Madonna U (MI)
Mansfield U of Pennsylvania (PA)
Marietta Coll (OH)
Marymount Manhattan Coll (NY)
Maryville U of Saint Louis (MO)
Marywood U (PA)
Mercer U, Macon (GA)
Mercy Coll (NY)
Meredith Coll (NC)
Messiah Coll (PA)
Miami U Hamilton (OH)
Miami U Middletown (OH)
Michigan State U (MI)
MidAmerica Nazarene U (KS)
Milligan Coll (TN)
Missouri Southern State U (MO)
Montclair State U (NJ)
Mount Mercy U (IA)
Mount Vernon Nazarene U (OH)
Northern State U (SD)
Northwestern Coll (IA)
Northwest Nazarene U (ID)
Nossi Coll of Art (TN)
Notre Dame Coll (OH)
Oakland U (MI)
Oklahoma Baptist U (OK)
Oral Roberts U (OK)
Otis Coll of Art and Design (CA)
Paier Coll of Art, Inc. (CT)
Palm Beach Atlantic U (FL)
Parsons School of Design (NY)
Penn State Abington (PA)
Penn State Altoona (PA)
Penn State Beaver (PA)
Penn State Berks (PA)
Penn State Brandywine (PA)
Penn State DuBois (PA)
Penn State Erie, The Behrend Coll (PA)
Penn State Fayette, The Eberly Campus (PA)
Penn State Greater Allegheny (PA)
Penn State Hazleton (PA)
Penn State Lehigh Valley (PA)
Penn State Mont Alto (PA)
Penn State New Kensington (PA)
Penn State Schuylkill (PA)
Penn State Shenango (PA)
Penn State U Park (PA)
Penn State Wilkes-Barre (PA)
Penn State York (PA)
Pensacola State Coll (FL)
Point Loma Nazarene U (CA)
Portland State U (OR)
Prairie View A&M U (TX)
Pratt Inst (NY)
Purdue U Fort Wayne (IN)
Queens Coll of the City U of New York (NY)
Queens U of Charlotte (NC)
Regent U (VA)
Rhode Island Coll (RI)
The Sage Colls (NY)
Saginaw Valley State U (MI)
St. Ambrose U (IA)
St. Cloud State U (MN)
Saint Mary's U of Minnesota (MN)
St. Norbert Coll (WI)
Saint Vincent Coll (PA)
Samford U (AL)
San Diego State U (CA)
San Jose State U (CA)
School of Visual Arts (NY)
Schreiner U (TX)
Siena Heights U (MI)
South Dakota State U (SD)
Southeastern U (FL)
Southwestern Oklahoma State U (OK)
Spring Arbor U (MI)
Spring Hill Coll (AL)
State U of New York at New Paltz (NY)
State U of New York Coll of Technology at Alfred (NY)
State U of New York Coll of Technology at Canton (NY)
Suffolk U (MA)
Susquehanna U (PA)
Tabor Coll (KS)
Taylor U (IN)
Temple U (PA)
Texas A&M U–Commerce (TX)
Texas A&M U–Corpus Christi (TX)
Texas Christian U (TX)
The U of Akron (OH)
U of Dayton (OH)
U of Denver (CO)
U of Hartford (CT)
U of Houston (TX)
U of Illinois at Chicago (IL)
U of Mary Hardin-Baylor (TX)
U of Massachusetts Dartmouth (MA)
U of Miami (FL)
U of Michigan (MI)
U of Minnesota, Twin Cities Campus (MN)
U of Nebraska–Lincoln (NE)
U of Nevada, Las Vegas (NV)
U of New Haven (CT)
U of North Dakota (ND)
U of Northern Iowa (IA)
U of Northwestern–St. Paul (MN)
U of South Florida, St. Petersburg (FL)
The U of Tampa (FL)
U of the Incarnate Word (TX)
U of Wisconsin–Parkside (WI)
U of Wisconsin–Stout (WI)
Virginia Commonwealth U (VA)
Walla Walla U (WA)
Washington U in St. Louis (MO)
Wayne State Coll (NE)
Weber State U (UT)
Western Michigan U (MI)
Whitworth U (WA)
Wichita State U (KS)
Xavier U (OH)
York Coll of Pennsylvania (PA)
Youngstown State U (OH)

HEALTH AND MEDICAL ADMINISTRATIVE SERVICES RELATED
Andrews U (MI)
Brenau U (GA)
Concordia U, St. Paul (MN)
Eastern Oregon U (OR)
Indiana U East (IN)
Indiana U Kokomo (IN)
Indiana U Northwest (IN)
Indiana U South Bend (IN)
Indiana U Southeast (IN)
Missouri Southern State U (MO)
Mount Mercy U (IA)
Southwest Baptist U (MO)
State U of New York Coll of Technology at Canton (NY)
U of Detroit Mercy (MI)
Western Michigan U (MI)

HEALTH AND PHYSICAL EDUCATION/FITNESS
Austin Peay State U (TN)
Averett U (VA)
Baker U (KS)
Barton Coll (NC)
Baylor U (TX)
Berea Coll (KY)
Bethel U (TN)
Biola U (CA)
Black Hills State U (SD)
Bluffton U (OH)
Boise State U (ID)
Bridgewater Coll (VA)
Bryan Coll (TN)
California Polytechnic State U, San Luis Obispo (CA)
California State Polytechnic U, Pomona (CA)
California State U, Dominguez Hills (CA)
California State U, Fullerton (CA)
California State U, Los Angeles (CA)
California State U, Monterey Bay (CA)
California State U, San Bernardino (CA)
California State U, San Marcos (CA)
California State U, Stanislaus (CA)
Cameron U (OK)
Capital U (OH)
Catawba Coll (NC)
Central Christian Coll of Kansas (KS)
Central Michigan U (MI)
Coll of the Ozarks (MO)
Concordia Coll (MN)
Concordia U, St. Paul (MN)
Concordia U Wisconsin (WI)
Doane U (NE)
East Central U (OK)
Eastern Michigan U (MI)
Eastern Oregon U (OR)
Eastern Washington U (WA)
East Texas Baptist U (TX)
Emory & Henry Coll (VA)
Emory U (GA)
Evangel U (MO)
Florida A&M U (FL)
Freed-Hardeman U (TN)
Friends U (KS)
George Fox U (OR)
Graceland U (IA)
Guilford Coll (NC)
Hanover Coll (IN)
Hillsdale Coll (MI)
Husson U (ME)
Indiana U Bloomington (IN)
Indiana U of Pennsylvania (PA)
Ithaca Coll (NY)
Jacksonville State U (AL)
Jacksonville U (FL)
James Madison U (VA)
Johnson U Florida (FL)
King U (TN)
La Sierra U (CA)
Lee U (TN)
Liberty U (VA)
Lincoln Memorial U (TN)
Lindenwood U (MO)
Louisiana Tech U (LA)
Marian U (IN)
Marywood U (PA)
Mayville State U (ND)
McDaniel Coll (MD)
Miami U Hamilton (OH)
Miami U Middletown (OH)
MidAmerica Nazarene U (KS)
Middle Tennessee State U (TN)
Milligan Coll (TN)
Muskingum U (OH)
Nebraska Wesleyan U (NE)
New England Coll (NH)
North Carolina Central U (NC)
Northern Illinois U (IL)
Northern State U (SD)
Northwestern State U of Louisiana (LA)
Northwest Nazarene U (ID)
Northwest U (WA)
Oakland City U (IN)
The Ohio State U (OH)
Oklahoma Baptist U (OK)
Oral Roberts U (OK)
Palm Beach Atlantic U (FL)
Point Loma Nazarene U (CA)
Randolph Coll (VA)
Rhode Island Coll (RI)
Rocky Mountain Coll (MT)
Rowan U (NJ)
St. Catherine U (MN)
St. Cloud State U (MN)
Salem State U (MA)
Sam Houston State U (TX)
San Diego State U (CA)
San Jose State U (CA)
Slippery Rock U of Pennsylvania (PA)
South Dakota State U (SD)
Southeast Missouri State U (MO)
Spring Arbor U (MI)
Sterling Coll (KS)
Tabor Coll (KS)
Tennessee Wesleyan U (TN)
Texas A&M U–Kingsville (TX)
Texas Christian U (TX)
Truman State U (MO)
U of Arkansas (AR)
The U of Findlay (OH)
U of Guam (GU)
U of Hawaii at Manoa (HI)
The U of Iowa (IA)
The U of Kansas (KS)
U of Louisville (KY)
U of Maine at Presque Isle (ME)
U of Massachusetts Boston (MA)
U of Michigan (MI)
U of Montevallo (AL)
The U of North Carolina at Chapel Hill (NC)
The U of North Carolina at Charlotte (NC)
The U of North Carolina at Pembroke (NC)
The U of North Carolina Wilmington (NC)
U of Northern Iowa (IA)
U of Providence (MT)
U of Science and Arts of Oklahoma (OK)
U of Southern Maine (ME)
U of Southern Mississippi (MS)
The U of Tampa (FL)
The U of Tennessee at Martin (TN)
U of Toronto (ON, Canada)
U of Utah (UT)
U of West Florida (FL)
U of Wisconsin–Superior (WI)
Utah Valley U (UT)
Valley City State U (ND)
Valparaiso U (IN)
Walla Walla U (WA)
Wayland Baptist U (TX)
Webber Intl U (FL)
Weber State U (UT)
West Chester U of Pennsylvania (PA)
Western New Mexico U (NM)
Westfield State U (MA)
West Virginia U (WV)
William & Mary (VA)
Wingate U (NC)
Youngstown State U (OH)

HEALTH AND PHYSICAL EDUCATION RELATED
Andrews U (MI)
Arizona State U at the Downtown Phoenix campus (AZ)
Averett U (VA)
Avila U (MO)
Benedictine Coll (KS)
Bowling Green State U (OH)
Bridgewater State U (MA)
California State U, Long Beach (CA)

Coe Coll (IA)
Concordia Coll (MN)
Concordia U Wisconsin (WI)
Cornell Coll (IA)
East Carolina U (NC)
Edinboro U of Pennsylvania (PA)
Gustavus Adolphus Coll (MN)
La Sierra U (CA)
Limestone Coll (SC)
Lock Haven U of Pennsylvania (PA)
Mayville State U (ND)
Missouri Southern State U (MO)
Mount Marty Coll (SD)
Mount Vernon Nazarene U (OH)
North Greenville U (SC)
Regis Coll (MA)
St. Ambrose U (IA)
Saint Mary's Coll of California (CA)
South Dakota State U (SD)
Texas Lutheran U (TX)
The U of Iowa (IA)
U of Utah (UT)
U of Wisconsin–Superior (WI)
Valdosta State U (GA)
Wayne State Coll (NE)
Weber State U (UT)
William Penn U (IA)

HEALTH AND WELLNESS

Arizona State U at the Downtown Phoenix campus (AZ)
Arizona State U at the West campus (AZ)
Bowling Green State U (OH)
Cedar Crest Coll (PA)
Chatham U (PA)
Creighton U (NE)
Culver-Stockton Coll (MO)
Dean Coll (MA)
DeSales U (PA)
Dominican U (IL)
Edinboro U of Pennsylvania (PA)
Farmingdale State Coll (NY)
Georgetown Coll (KY)
Granite State Coll (NH)
Hampton U (VA)
Indiana U Kokomo (IN)
Indiana U South Bend (IN)
Jacksonville State U (AL)
Keuka Coll (NY)
Lamar U (TX)
Lenoir-Rhyne U (NC)
Maryville U of Saint Louis (MO)
Millikin U (IL)
Montana Technological U (MT)
New York Inst of Technology (NY)
North Greenville U (SC)
Northwest Missouri State U (MO)
Northwest U (WA)
Oakland U (MI)
The Ohio State U (OH)
Point Loma Nazarene U (CA)
Portland State U (OR)
Prairie View A&M U (TX)
Rhode Island Coll (RI)
Rowan U (NJ)
Sam Houston State U (TX)
Slippery Rock U of Pennsylvania (PA)
State U of New York Coll at Potsdam (NY)
Texas A&M U (TX)
Texas Southern U (TX)
Texas Woman's U (TX)
Towson U (MD)
Tulane U (LA)
The U of Alabama at Birmingham (AL)
U of Houston (TX)
U of Nevada, Reno (NV)
U of New England (ME)
U of Saint Francis (IN)
The U of Texas at San Antonio (TX)
The U of Texas Rio Grande Valley (TX)
U of Vermont (VT)
U of West Georgia (GA)
U of Wisconsin–La Crosse (WI)
U of Wisconsin–Stout (WI)
U of Wisconsin–Superior (WI)
Wichita State U (KS)

ALTH COMMUNICATION

any Lutheran Coll (MN)
Coll (MI)
DeSales U (PA)
Dominican U (IL)
Eastern Illinois U (IL)
Grand Valley State U (MI)
Miami U (OH)
Miami U Hamilton (OH)
Miami U Middletown (OH)
Northern Kentucky U (KY)
San Diego State U (CA)
Southeast Missouri State U (MO)
U of Houston (TX)

HEALTH/HEALTH-CARE ADMINISTRATION

Adams State U (CO)
AdventHealth U (FL)
Alverno Coll (WI)
Appalachian State U (NC)
Arcadia U (PA)
Arizona State U at the Downtown Phoenix campus (AZ)
Arizona State U at the West campus (AZ)
Auburn U (AL)
Augustana U (SD)
Baptist Coll of Health Sciences (TN)
Barton Coll (NC)
Belhaven U (MS)
Benedictine U (IL)
Black Hills State U (SD)
Bluffton U (OH)
Bowling Green State U (OH)
Brenau U (GA)
Butler U (IN)
Caldwell U (NJ)
California Baptist U (CA)
California State U, Dominguez Hills (CA)
California State U, Long Beach (CA)
Carlow U (PA)
Central Michigan U (MI)
Charter Oak State Coll (CT)
Chestnut Hill Coll (PA)
Coastal Carolina U (SC)
Colby-Sawyer Coll (NH)
Coll of Saint Elizabeth (NJ)
The Coll of Westchester (NY)
Columbia Coll (MO)
Columbia Coll (SC)
Concordia U Chicago (IL)
Concordia U, St. Paul (MN)
Concordia U Wisconsin (WI)
Creighton U (NE)
Culver-Stockton Coll (MO)
Dallas Baptist U (TX)
Davenport U, Grand Rapids (MI)
Delta State U (MS)
DePaul U (IL)
DeSales U (PA)
Dillard U (LA)
Drexel U (PA)
East Carolina U (NC)
East Central U (OK)
Eastern Illinois U (IL)
Eastern Kentucky U (KY)
Eastern Michigan U (MI)
Eastern Washington U (WA)
ECPI U, Virginia Beach (VA)
Emmanuel Coll (MA)
Fayetteville State U (NC)
Felician U (NJ)
Ferris State U (MI)
Fisher Coll (MA)
Florida A&M U (FL)
Florida Atlantic U (FL)
Florida Southern Coll (FL)
Francis Marion U (SC)
Galveston Coll (TX)
Gannon U (PA)
Georgetown Coll (KY)
Granite State Coll (NH)
Harding U (AR)
Harris-Stowe State U (MO)
Immaculata U (PA)
Indiana U-Purdue U Indianapolis (IN)
Iona Coll (NY)
James Madison U (VA)
King U (TN)
La Sierra U (CA)
Lee U (TN)
Lehman Coll of the City U of New York (NY)
LeTourneau U (TX)
Lewis U (IL)
Liberty U (VA)
Limestone Coll (SC)
Lindenwood U (MO)
Loyola U Chicago (IL)
Lynn U (FL)
Madonna U (MI)
Maryville U of Saint Louis (MO)
Marywood U (PA)
Mercy Coll of Ohio (OH)
Mid-America Christian U (OK)
Midland Coll (TX)
Midway U (KY)
Misericordia U (PA)
Mississippi State U (MS)
Mount Mercy U (IA)
Muskingum U (OH)
National U (CA)
Nebraska Methodist Coll (NE)
New England Coll (NH)
New England Inst of Technology (RI)
Ottawa U (KS)
Peirce Coll (PA)
Penn State Abington (PA)
Penn State Altoona (PA)
Penn State Beaver (PA)
Penn State Berks (PA)
Penn State Brandywine (PA)
Penn State DuBois (PA)
Penn State Erie, The Behrend Coll (PA)
Penn State Fayette, The Eberly Campus (PA)
Penn State Greater Allegheny (PA)
Penn State Hazleton (PA)
Penn State Lehigh Valley (PA)
Penn State Mont Alto (PA)
Penn State New Kensington (PA)
Penn State Schuylkill (PA)
Penn State Shenango (PA)
Penn State U Park (PA)
Penn State Wilkes-Barre (PA)
Penn State York (PA)
Portland State U (OR)
Providence Coll (RI)
Purdue U Fort Wayne (IN)
Radford U (VA)
Rasmussen Coll Aurora (IL)
Rasmussen Coll Blaine (MN)
Rasmussen Coll Bloomington (MN)
Rasmussen Coll Brooklyn Park (MN)
Rasmussen Coll Eagan (MN)
Rasmussen Coll Fargo (ND)
Rasmussen Coll Fort Myers (FL)
Rasmussen Coll Green Bay (WI)
Rasmussen Coll Kansas City/Overland Park (KS)
Rasmussen Coll Lake Elmo/Woodbury (MN)
Rasmussen Coll Land O' Lakes (FL)
Rasmussen Coll Mankato (MN)
Rasmussen Coll Mokena/Tinley Park (IL)
Rasmussen Coll Moorhead (MN)
Rasmussen Coll New Port Richey (FL)
Rasmussen Coll Ocala (FL)
Rasmussen Coll Rockford (IL)
Rasmussen Coll Romeoville/Joliet (IL)
Rasmussen Coll St. Cloud (MN)
Rasmussen Coll Tampa/Brandon (FL)
Rasmussen Coll Topeka (KS)
Rasmussen Coll Wausau (WI)
Regent U (VA)
Rhode Island Coll (RI)
Roberts Wesleyan Coll (NY)
Roger Williams U (RI)
Saint Leo U (FL)
Saint Louis U (MO)
Saint Mary-of-the-Woods Coll (IN)
Saint Mary's Coll of California (CA)
Salve Regina U (RI)
Samford U (AL)
Sam Houston State U (TX)
San Jose State U (CA)
Southeast Missouri State U (MO)
Southern Illinois U Carbondale (IL)
Southwestern Coll (KS)
Southwestern Oklahoma State U (OK)
Spring Arbor U (MI)
Springfield Coll (MA)
State U of New York Coll of Technology at Alfred (NY)
State U of New York Coll of Technology at Canton (NY)
State U of New York Coll of Technology at Delhi (NY)
SUNY Brockport (NY)
Texas Southern U (TX)
Texas State U (TX)
Tiffin U (OH)
Towson U (MD)
Trevecca Nazarene U (TN)
Trine U (IN)
The U of Alabama at Birmingham (AL)
U of Central Florida (FL)
U of Cincinnati (OH)
U of Dubuque (IA)
U of Houston–Clear Lake (TX)
U of Kentucky (KY)
U of La Verne (CA)
U of Louisiana at Lafayette (LA)
U of Management and Technology (VA)
U of Maryland Global Campus (MD)
U of Massachusetts Dartmouth (MA)
U of Miami (FL)
U of Michigan–Flint (MI)
U of Minnesota, Duluth (MN)
U of Minnesota, Twin Cities Campus (MN)
U of Nevada, Las Vegas (NV)
U of New Hampshire (NH)
The U of North Carolina at Chapel Hill (NC)
The U of North Carolina at Charlotte (NC)
U of North Florida (FL)
U of Pennsylvania (PA)
U of Providence (MT)
U of St. Francis (IL)
U of Saint Francis (IN)
The U of Scranton (PA)
U of Southern Indiana (IN)
U of South Florida (FL)
The U of Texas at Dallas (TX)
U of Virginia (VA)
U of Wisconsin–Eau Claire (WI)
Upper Iowa U (IA)
Valdosta State U (GA)
Valparaiso U (IN)
Washington U in St. Louis (MO)
Waynesburg U (PA)
Weber State U (UT)
Western Carolina U (NC)
Western Kentucky U (KY)
Wichita State U (KS)

HEALTH INFORMATION/MEDICAL RECORDS ADMINISTRATION

American Public U System (WV)
Arkansas Tech U (AR)
Bowling Green State U (OH)
Charter Oak State Coll (CT)
The Coll of St. Scholastica (MN)
Dakota State U (SD)
Davenport U, Grand Rapids (MI)
East Carolina U (NC)
East Central U (OK)
Eastern Kentucky U (KY)
Eastern Washington U (WA)
Fairleigh Dickinson U (NJ)
Ferris State U (MI)
Fisher Coll (MA)
Florida A&M U (FL)
Georgian Court U (NJ)
Grand Valley State U (MI)
Granite State Coll (NH)
Gwynedd Mercy U (PA)
Illinois State U (IL)
Indiana U Northwest (IN)
Indiana U-Purdue U Indianapolis (IN)
Indiana U Southeast (IN)
Kean U (NJ)
Keiser U, Fort Lauderdale (FL)
Louisiana Tech U (LA)
The Ohio State U (OH)
Peirce Coll (PA)
Rasmussen Coll Aurora (IL)
Rasmussen Coll Blaine (MN)
Rasmussen Coll Bloomington (MN)
Rasmussen Coll Brooklyn Park (MN)
Rasmussen Coll Eagan (MN)
Rasmussen Coll Fargo (ND)
Rasmussen Coll Fort Myers (FL)
Rasmussen Coll Green Bay (WI)
Rasmussen Coll Kansas City/Overland Park (KS)
Rasmussen Coll Lake Elmo/Woodbury (MN)
Rasmussen Coll Land O' Lakes (FL)
Rasmussen Coll Mankato (MN)
Rasmussen Coll Mokena/Tinley Park (IL)
Rasmussen Coll Moorhead (MN)
Rasmussen Coll New Port Richey (FL)
Rasmussen Coll Ocala (FL)
Rasmussen Coll Rockford (IL)
Rasmussen Coll Romeoville/Joliet (IL)
Rasmussen Coll St. Cloud (MN)
Rasmussen Coll Tampa/Brandon (FL)
Rasmussen Coll Topeka (KS)
Rasmussen Coll Wausau (WI)
Saint Louis U (MO)
Samford U (AL)
Southwestern Oklahoma State U (OK)
Texas Southern U (TX)
Texas State U (TX)
Trevecca Nazarene U (TN)
U of Central Florida (FL)
U of Cincinnati (OH)
U of Detroit Mercy (MI)
U of Illinois at Chicago (IL)
The U of Kansas (KS)
U of Louisiana at Lafayette (LA)
U of Southern Indiana (IN)
The U of Toledo (OH)
U of Washington (WA)
U of Wisconsin–Green Bay (WI)
U of Wisconsin–La Crosse (WI)
U of Wisconsin–Parkside (WI)
Weber State U (UT)
Western Carolina U (NC)
Western Kentucky U (KY)

HEALTH INFORMATION/MEDICAL RECORDS TECHNOLOGY

East Central U (OK)
Fisher Coll (MA)
Keiser U, Fort Lauderdale (FL)
U of Saint Mary (KS)

HEALTH/MEDICAL PHYSICS

Belmont U (TN)
California State U, Dominguez Hills (CA)
California State U, Northridge (CA)
Creighton U (NE)
U of Nevada, Las Vegas (NV)

HEALTH/MEDICAL PREPARATORY PROGRAMS RELATED

Abilene Christian U (TX)
Aquinas Coll (MI)
Arizona State U at the Downtown Phoenix campus (AZ)
Arizona State U at the West campus (AZ)
Aurora U (IL)
Avila U (MO)
Baylor U (TX)
Benedictine U (IL)
Eastern Kentucky U (KY)
Edinboro U of Pennsylvania (PA)
Emory & Henry Coll (VA)
Gannon U (PA)
Georgian Court U (NJ)
Guilford Coll (NC)
Hofstra U (NY)
Indiana State U (IN)
Kansas Wesleyan U (KS)
Lee U (TN)
Le Moyne Coll (NY)
Lenoir-Rhyne U (NC)
Lipscomb U (TN)
Lock Haven U of Pennsylvania (PA)
Madonna U (MI)
Marshall U (WV)
Maryville U of Saint Louis (MO)
Mercer U, Macon (GA)
Meredith Coll (NC)
Mount Marty Coll (SD)

Northern Illinois U (IL)
Oakland U (MI)
Saginaw Valley State U (MI)
Seattle U (WA)
Southwestern Coll (KS)
The U of Findlay (OH)
U of South Alabama (AL)
U of Waterloo (ON, Canada)
U of Wisconsin–Parkside (WI)
Utica Coll (NY)
Valley City State U (ND)
Weber State U (UT)
Western Washington U (WA)

HEALTH/MEDICAL PSYCHOLOGY
Averett U (VA)
Bridgewater State U (MA)
U of Mary Hardin-Baylor (TX)
U of Northwestern–St. Paul (MN)

HEALTH OCCUPATIONS TEACHER EDUCATION
Northwest U (WA)

HEALTH POLICY ANALYSIS
Brandeis U (MA)
Mount Saint Mary's U (CA)
Siena Coll (NY)

HEALTH PROFESSIONS RELATED
American Public U System (WV)
Athens State U (AL)
Azusa Pacific U (CA)
Boise State U (ID)
Bowling Green State U (OH)
Bradley U (IL)
California State U, Fresno (CA)
California State U, Long Beach (CA)
California State U, Los Angeles (CA)
California State U, Sacramento (CA)
Clemson U (SC)
Cornell U (NY)
DeSales U (PA)
Ferris State U (MI)
Fisher Coll (MA)
Florida State U (FL)
Furman U (SC)
Gannon U (PA)
George Mason U (VA)
Georgetown U (DC)
Grand Valley State U (MI)
King's Coll (PA)
Lock Haven U of Pennsylvania (PA)
Maryville U of Saint Louis (MO)
Marywood U (PA)
Mercy Coll (NY)
Merrimack Coll (MA)
Minnesota State U Mankato (MN)
Missouri Southern State U (MO)
Molloy Coll (NY)
Mount St. Mary's U (MD)
Muskingum U (OH)
Newman U (KS)
New York Inst of Technology (NY)
New York U (NY)
Northeastern State U (OK)
Nova Southeastern U (FL)
Oakland U (MI)
Old Dominion U (VA)
Pacific U (OR)
Radford U (VA)
Rowan U (NJ)
The Sage Colls (NY)
Saint Joseph's U (PA)
Saint Mary-of-the-Woods Coll (IN)
Saint Mary's Coll of California (CA)
San Francisco State U (CA)
Southern Methodist U (TX)
Southwestern Oklahoma State U (OK)
State U of New York Coll at Cortland (NY)
Susquehanna U (PA)
Tennessee Wesleyan U (TN)
The U of Alabama at Birmingham (AL)
U of Arkansas at Little Rock (AR)
U of Central Arkansas (AR)
U of Charleston (WV)
U of Cincinnati (OH)
U of Hartford (CT)
U of Louisiana at Monroe (LA)
U of Maryland, Baltimore County (MD)
U of New England (ME)
U of New Hampshire (NH)
The U of North Carolina Wilmington (NC)
U of Northern Iowa (IA)
U of Pennsylvania (PA)
U of Utah (UT)
U of Waterloo (ON, Canada)
The U of Western Ontario (ON, Canada)
U of Wisconsin–Parkside (WI)
Walla Walla U (CA)
Washington U in St. Louis (MO)
Wayne State U (MI)
Weber State U (UT)
West Liberty U (WV)
Worcester State U (MA)
Youngstown State U (OH)

HEALTH SERVICES ADMINISTRATION
Alfred U (NY)
Anderson U (SC)
Arizona State U at the Downtown Phoenix campus (AZ)
Arizona State U at the West campus (AZ)
Bentley U (MA)
D'Youville Coll (NY)
Florida National U (FL)
Indiana U Northwest (IN)
Indiana U-Purdue U Indianapolis (IN)
Indiana U South Bend (IN)
Keiser U, Fort Lauderdale (FL)
McNeese State U (LA)
Northeastern State U (OK)
Purdue U Fort Wayne (IN)
St. Petersburg Coll (FL)
Southeastern Louisiana U (LA)
U of Detroit Mercy (MI)
U of San Francisco (CA)
U of Washington, Tacoma (WA)
Webber Intl U (FL)

HEALTH SERVICES/ALLIED HEALTH/HEALTH SCIENCES
AdventHealth U (FL)
Albion Coll (MI)
Angelo State U (TX)
Aquinas Coll (MI)
Assumption Coll (MA)
Biola U (CA)
Bradley U (IL)
Bryan Coll (TN)
Butler U (IN)
California Baptist U (CA)
California State U, Dominguez Hills (CA)
California State U, Fullerton (CA)
California State U, Los Angeles (CA)
California State U, Northridge (CA)
California State U, San Bernardino (CA)
California U of Pennsylvania (PA)
Cedar Crest Coll (PA)
Clarion U of Pennsylvania (PA)
Clayton State U (GA)
Colby-Sawyer Coll (NH)
The Coll of Idaho (ID)
The Coll of St. Scholastica (MN)
Coll of the Ozarks (MO)
DePaul U (IL)
Doane U (NE)
Dominican Coll (NY)
Eastern U (PA)
East Texas Baptist U (TX)
Edinboro U of Pennsylvania (PA)
Fairleigh Dickinson U (NJ)
Florida A&M U (FL)
Florida Gulf Coast U (FL)
Friends U (KS)
Georgian Court U (NJ)
Georgia Southern U (GA)
Graceland U (IA)
Granite State Coll (NH)
Hofstra U (NY)
Houston Baptist U (TX)
Howard U (DC)
Husson U (ME)
Ithaca Coll (NY)
Keiser U, Fort Lauderdale (FL)
Lasell Coll (MA)
Lee U (TN)
Lincoln U (PA)
Madonna U (MI)
Marian U (IN)
Marymount U (VA)
Marywood U (PA)
McKendree U (IL)
Mercy Coll (NY)
Mercy Coll of Ohio (OH)
Merrimack Coll (MA)
Messiah Coll (PA)
Miami Dade Coll (FL)
Milligan Coll (TN)
Misericordia U (PA)
Moravian Coll (PA)
National U (CA)
Nebraska Methodist Coll (NE)
New York Coll of Health Professions (NY)
Northern Kentucky U (KY)
Northwestern State U of Louisiana (LA)
Pace U, Pleasantville Campus (NY)
Portland State U (OR)
Purdue U Northwest (IN)
Queens U of Charlotte (NC)
Radford U (VA)
Regis Coll (MA)
Rhode Island Coll (RI)
Rochester U (MI)
The Sage Colls (NY)
Saginaw Valley State U (MI)
Saint Louis U (MO)
St. Luke's Coll (IA)
Samford U (AL)
Sam Houston State U (TX)
San Jose State U (CA)
Southeast Missouri State U (MO)
Southwestern Oklahoma State U (OK)
Spring Hill Coll (AL)
State U of New York Coll of Technology at Alfred (NY)
Stetson U (FL)
Stockton U (NJ)
Stony Brook U, State U of New York (NY)
SUNY Brockport (NY)
Taylor U (IN)
Texas A&M U–Corpus Christi (TX)
Texas Southern U (TX)
Texas State U (TX)
Texas Woman's U (TX)
Towson U (MD)
U of Central Florida (FL)
U of Colorado Colorado Springs (CO)
U of Hartford (CT)
U of Kentucky (KY)
U of Miami (FL)
U of Michigan–Flint (MI)
U of New Haven (CT)
U of Northern Colorado (CO)
U of North Florida (FL)
U of South Dakota (SD)
U of Southern Mississippi (MS)
U of South Florida (FL)
U of South Florida, St. Petersburg (FL)
The U of Tampa (FL)
The U of Texas at Dallas (TX)
The U of Texas Rio Grande Valley (TX)
U of the Incarnate Word (TX)
U of Utah (UT)
U of Washington, Bothell (WA)
The U of West Alabama (AL)
The U of Western Ontario (ON, Canada)
U of West Florida (FL)
Valparaiso U (IN)
Washington U in St. Louis (MO)
West Chester U of Pennsylvania (PA)
Western Kentucky U (KY)
Western New England U (MA)
Westfield State U (MA)
Westminster Coll (UT)
Wheaton Coll (IL)
Whitworth U (WA)
Widener U (PA)
William Paterson U of New Jersey (NJ)
Youngstown State U (OH)

HEALTH TEACHER EDUCATION
Alverno Coll (WI)
Auburn U (AL)
Augsburg U (MN)
Averett U (VA)
Ball State U (IN)
Bemidji State U (MN)
Bethel U (MN)
Bowling Green State U (OH)
Bridgewater State U (MA)
California State U, Stanislaus (CA)
Campbellsville U (KY)
Capital U (OH)
Central Christian Coll of Kansas (KS)
Central Michigan U (MI)
Central State U (OH)
Concordia Coll (MN)
Concordia U, St. Paul (MN)
Eastern Illinois U (IL)
Eastern Washington U (WA)
Elon U (NC)
George Mason U (VA)
Grand Valley State U (MI)
Gustavus Adolphus Coll (MN)
Hampton U (VA)
Harding U (AR)
Hofstra U (NY)
Illinois State U (IL)
Indiana U Bloomington (IN)
Inter American U of Puerto Rico, San Germán Campus (PR)
Ithaca Coll (NY)
Jacksonville State U (AL)
Kansas Wesleyan U (KS)
Lee U (TN)
Lehman Coll of the City U of New York (NY)
Lincoln Memorial U (TN)
Linfield Coll (OR)
Mayville State U (ND)
Michigan State U (MI)
Minnesota State U Mankato (MN)
Missouri Valley Coll (MO)
Montclair State U (NJ)
Morehead State U (KY)
Murray State U (KY)
National U (CA)
New Mexico Highlands U (NM)
New York U (NY)
North Carolina Central U (NC)
Northern Arizona U (AZ)
Northern Illinois U (IL)
Ohio Wesleyan U (OH)
Oral Roberts U (OK)
Portland State U (OR)
Rhode Island Coll (RI)
St. Cloud State U (MN)
Salisbury U (MD)
Sam Houston State U (TX)
Springfield Coll (MA)
State U of New York at Oswego (NY)
State U of New York Coll at Cortland (NY)
SUNY Brockport (NY)
Troy U (AL)
The U of Akron (OH)
U of Cincinnati (OH)
U of Dubuque (IA)
The U of Findlay (OH)
U of Kentucky (KY)
U of Nevada, Las Vegas (NV)
U of New Mexico (NM)
U of Northwestern–St. Paul (MN)
U of Providence (MT)
U of South Dakota (SD)
U of Toronto (ON, Canada)
U of Utah (UT)
Utah State U (UT)
Utah Valley U (UT)
Valley City State U (ND)
Virginia Commonwealth U (VA)
Washington State U (WA)
Wayne State U (MI)
Western Connecticut State U (CT)
Western Michigan U (MI)
West Liberty U (WV)
William Penn U (IA)
Wilmington Coll (OH)
Youngstown State U (OH)

HEATING, AIR CONDITIONING, VENTILATION AND REFRIGERATION MAINTENANCE TECHNOLOGY
Lewis-Clark State Coll (ID)

HEAVY EQUIPMENT MAINTENANCE TECHNOLOGY
Ferris State U (MI)

HEBREW
Baruch Coll of the City U of New York (NY)
Binghamton U, State U of New York (NY)
Brigham Young U (UT)
Concordia U Wisconsin (WI)
Hofstra U (NY)
Lehman Coll of the City U of New York (NY)
Multnomah U (OR)
New York U (NY)
The Ohio State U (OH)
Queens Coll of the City U of New York (NY)
U of Cincinnati (OH)
U of Utah (UT)
Washington U in St. Louis (MO)
Yeshiva U (NY)

HIGHER EDUCATION/HIGHER EDUCATION ADMINISTRATION
Geneva Coll (PA)
Tiffin U (OH)

HISPANIC-AMERICAN, PUERTO RICAN, AND MEXICAN-AMERICAN/ CHICANO STUDIES
Arizona State U at the Tempe campus (AZ)
Bennington Coll (VT)
Boston Coll (MA)
Bowling Green State U (OH)
Brown U (RI)
California State U, Dominguez Hills (CA)
California State U, Fresno (CA)
California State U, Fullerton (CA)
California State U, Long Beach (CA)
California State U, Los Angeles (CA)
California State U, Northridge (CA)
Claremont McKenna Coll (CA)
The Colorado Coll (CO)
Dartmouth Coll (NH)
Loyola Marymount U (CA)
Pepperdine U, Malibu (CA)
Pitzer Coll (CA)
Pomona Coll (CA)
San Diego State U (CA)
San Francisco State U (CA)
Scripps Coll (CA)
Southern Methodist U (TX)
Stanford U (CA)
State U of New York Coll at Oneonta (NY)
Tulane U (LA)
U at Albany, State U of New York (NY)
The U of Arizona (AZ)
U of California, Berkeley (CA)
U of California, Irvine (CA)
U of California, Riverside (CA)
U of California, Santa Barbara (CA)
U of California, Santa Cruz (CA)
U of Michigan (MI)
U of Minnesota, Twin Cities Campus (MN)
U of New Mexico (NM)
U of Northern Colorado (CO)
The U of Texas at El Paso (TX)
The U of Texas at San Antonio (TX)
The U of Texas Rio Grande Valley (TX)
Vanderbilt U (TN)
Wheaton Coll (MA)

HISPANIC AND LATIN AMERICAN LANGUAGES
Loyola U New Orleans (LA)
Molloy Coll (NY)
Roger Williams U (RI)
U of California, Merced (CA)
U of Washington, Tacoma (WA)

HISTOLOGIC TECHNICIAN
Tarleton State U (TX)

HISTOLOGIC TECHNOLOGY/ HISTOTECHNOLOGIST
Oakland U (MI)

HISTORIC PRESERVATION AND CONSERVATION
Coll of Charleston (SC)
Roger Williams U (RI)
Salve Regina U (RI)
Southeast Missouri State U (MO)
U of Mary Washington (VA)
U of Miami (FL)
Ursuline Coll (OH)

HISTORIC PRESERVATION AND CONSERVATION RELATED
Ursuline Coll (OH)

HISTORY
Abilene Christian U (TX)
Adams State U (CO)
Agnes Scott Coll (GA)
Albion Coll (MI)
Alfred U (NY)
Allegheny Coll (PA)
Alverno Coll (WI)
American Public U System (WV)
American U (DC)
American U of Beirut (Lebanon)
The American U of Paris (France)
Amherst Coll (MA)
Anderson U (IN)
Anderson U (SC)
Andrews U (MI)
Angelo State U (TX)
Appalachian State U (NC)
Aquinas Coll (MI)
Arcadia U (PA)
Arizona State U at the Polytechnic campus (AZ)
Arizona State U at the Tempe campus (AZ)
Arizona State U at the West campus (AZ)
Arkansas Tech U (AR)
Assumption Coll (MA)
Athens State U (AL)
Auburn U (AL)
Auburn U at Montgomery (AL)
Augsburg U (MN)
Augustana Coll (IL)
Augustana U (SD)
Aurora U (IL)
Austin Coll (TX)
Austin Peay State U (TN)
Averett U (VA)
Avila U (MO)
Azusa Pacific U (CA)
Baker U (KS)
Ball State U (IN)
The Baptist Coll of Florida (FL)
Barnard Coll (NY)
Barry U (FL)
Barton Coll (NC)
Baruch Coll of the City U of New York (NY)
Bates Coll (ME)
Baylor U (TX)
Belhaven U (MS)
Belmont Abbey Coll (NC)
Belmont U (TN)
Beloit Coll (WI)
Bemidji State U (MN)
Benedictine Coll (KS)
Benedictine U (IL)
Bennington Coll (VT)
Bentley U (MA)
Berea Coll (KY)
Berry Coll (GA)
Bethany Lutheran Coll (MN)
Bethel U (IN)
Bethel U (MN)
Bethel U (TN)
Binghamton U, State U of New York (NY)
Biola U (CA)
Birmingham-Southern Coll (AL)
Black Hills State U (SD)
Bluffton U (OH)
Boise State U (ID)
Boston Coll (MA)
Bowdoin Coll (ME)
Bowling Green State U (OH)
Bradley U (IL)
Brandeis U (MA)
Brandon U (MB, Canada)
Brenau U (GA)
Bridgewater Coll (VA)
Bridgewater State U (MA)
Brown U (RI)
Bryan Coll (TN)
Bryant U (RI)
Bucknell U (PA)
Butler U (IN)
Caldwell U (NJ)
California Baptist U (CA)
California Lutheran U (CA)
California Polytechnic State U, San Luis Obispo (CA)
California State Polytechnic U, Pomona (CA)
California State U, Bakersfield (CA)
California State U, Dominguez Hills (CA)
California State U, Fresno (CA)
California State U, Fullerton (CA)
California State U, Long Beach (CA)
California State U, Los Angeles (CA)
California State U, Northridge (CA)
California State U, Sacramento (CA)
California State U, San Bernardino (CA)
California State U, San Marcos (CA)
California State U, Stanislaus (CA)
California U of Pennsylvania (PA)
Calvin Coll (MI)
Cameron U (OK)
Campbellsville U (KY)
Capital U (OH)
Carleton Coll (MN)
Carlow U (PA)
Carnegie Mellon U (PA)
Carson-Newman U (TN)
Carthage Coll (WI)
Catawba Coll (NC)
The Catholic U of America (DC)
Cedar Crest Coll (PA)
Cedarville U (OH)
Central Christian Coll of Kansas (KS)
Central Coll (IA)
Central Connecticut State U (CT)
Central Methodist U (MO)
Central Michigan U (MI)
Central State U (OH)
Central Washington U (WA)
Centre Coll (KY)
Chatham U (PA)
Chestnut Hill Coll (PA)
The Citadel, The Military Coll of South Carolina (SC)
City Coll of the City U of New York (NY)
Claremont McKenna Coll (CA)
Clarion U of Pennsylvania (PA)
Clark Atlanta U (GA)
Clarkson U (NY)
Clark U (MA)
Clayton State U (GA)
Clemson U (SC)
Coastal Carolina U (SC)
Coe Coll (IA)
Colby Coll (ME)
Colgate U (NY)
Coll of Charleston (SC)
The Coll of Idaho (ID)
Coll of Saint Benedict (MN)
Coll of Saint Elizabeth (NJ)
The Coll of Saint Rose (NY)
The Coll of St. Scholastica (MN)
Coll of Staten Island of the City U of New York (NY)
Coll of the Holy Cross (MA)
Coll of the Ozarks (MO)
The Coll of Wooster (OH)
The Colorado Coll (CO)
Colorado State U (CO)
Columbia Coll (MO)
Concordia Coll (MN)
Concordia U Chicago (IL)
Concordia U, St. Paul (MN)
Concordia U Wisconsin (WI)
Cornell Coll (IA)
Cornell U (NY)
Covenant Coll (GA)
Creighton U (NE)
Culver-Stockton Coll (MO)
Dallas Baptist U (TX)
Dartmouth Coll (NH)
Davidson Coll (NC)
Dean Coll (MA)
Delta State U (MS)
DePaul U (IL)
DePauw U (IN)
DeSales U (PA)
Dickinson Coll (PA)
Dickinson State U (ND)
Dillard U (LA)
Doane U (NE)
Dominican Coll (NY)
Dominican U (IL)
Dominican U of California (CA)
Drake U (IA)
Drew U (NJ)
Drexel U (PA)
D'Youville Coll (NY)
Earlham Coll (IN)
East Carolina U (NC)
East Central U (OK)
Eastern Illinois U (IL)
Eastern Kentucky U (KY)
Eastern Mennonite U (VA)
Eastern Michigan U (MI)
Eastern New Mexico U (NM)
Eastern Oregon U (OR)
Eastern U (PA)
Eastern Washington U (WA)
East Texas Baptist U (TX)
Edgewood Coll (WI)
Edinboro U of Pennsylvania (PA)
Elms Coll (MA)
Elon U (NC)
Emmanuel Coll (MA)
Emory & Henry Coll (VA)
Emory U (GA)
Emporia State U (KS)
Endicott Coll (MA)
Eugene Lang Coll of Liberal Arts (NY)
Evangel U (MO)
Excelsior Coll (NY)
Fairfield U (CT)
Fairleigh Dickinson U (NJ)
Fayetteville State U (NC)
Felician U (NJ)
Ferris State U (MI)
Fitchburg State U (MA)
Flagler Coll (FL)
Florida A&M U (FL)
Florida Atlantic U (FL)
Florida Gulf Coast U (FL)
Florida Southern Coll (FL)
Florida State U (FL)
Fordham U (NY)
Fort Lewis Coll (CO)
Framingham State U (MA)
Francis Marion U (SC)
Franklin Coll (IN)
Freed-Hardeman U (TN)
Friends U (KS)
Furman U (SC)
Gannon U (PA)
Geneva Coll (PA)
George Fox U (OR)
George Mason U (VA)
Georgetown Coll (KY)
Georgetown U (DC)
The George Washington U (DC)
Georgia Coll & State U (GA)
Georgia Gwinnett Coll (GA)
Georgian Court U (NJ)
Georgia Southern U (GA)
Georgia State U (GA)
Glenville State Coll (WV)
Gonzaga U (WA)
Gordon Coll (MA)
Goshen Coll (IN)
Goucher Coll (MD)
Governors State U (IL)
Graceland U (IA)
Grambling State U (LA)
Grand Valley State U (MI)
Granite State Coll (NH)
Grinnell Coll (IA)
Guilford Coll (NC)
Gustavus Adolphus Coll (MN)
Gwynedd Mercy U (PA)
Hamline U (MN)
Hampden-Sydney Coll (VA)
Hampshire Coll (MA)
Hampton U (VA)
Hanover Coll (IN)
Harding U (AR)
Hardin-Simmons U (TX)
Harvard U (MA)
High Point U (NC)
Hillsdale Coll (MI)
Hobart and William Smith Colls (NY)
Hofstra U (NY)
Hollins U (VA)
Hope Coll (MI)
Houston Baptist U (TX)
Howard U (DC)
Illinois Coll (IL)
Illinois State U (IL)
Illinois Wesleyan U (IL)
Immaculata U (PA)
Indiana State U (IN)
Indiana U Bloomington (IN)
Indiana U East (IN)
Indiana U Kokomo (IN)
Indiana U Northwest (IN)
Indiana U of Pennsylvania (PA)
Indiana U-Purdue U Indianapolis (IN)
Indiana U South Bend (IN)
Indiana U Southeast (IN)
Inter American U of Puerto Rico, Metropolitan Campus (PR)
Inter American U of Puerto Rico, San Germán Campus (PR)
Iona Coll (NY)
Iowa State U of Science and Technology (IA)
Ithaca Coll (NY)
Jacksonville State U (AL)
Jacksonville U (FL)
James Madison U (VA)
John Brown U (AR)
John Cabot U (Italy)
John Carroll U (OH)
John Jay Coll of Criminal Justice of the City U of New York (NY)
Johns Hopkins U (MD)
Kalamazoo Coll (MI)
Kansas State U (KS)
Kansas Wesleyan U (KS)
Kean U (NJ)
Kennesaw State U (GA)
Kenyon Coll (OH)
Keuka Coll (NY)
King's Coll (PA)
The King's U (AB, Canada)
King U (TN)
Knox Coll (IL)
Kutztown U of Pennsylvania (PA)
Lafayette Coll (PA)
LaGrange Coll (GA)
Lake Forest Coll (IL)
Lamar U (TX)
La Roche U (PA)
Lasell Coll (MA)
La Sierra U (CA)
Lawrence U (WI)
Lebanese American U (Lebanon)
Lee U (TN)
Lehigh U (PA)
Lehman Coll of the City U of New York (NY)
Le Moyne Coll (NY)
Lenoir-Rhyne U (NC)
Lewis & Clark Coll (OR)
Lewis U (IL)
Liberty U (VA)
Limestone Coll (SC)
Lincoln Memorial U (TN)
Lincoln U (MO)
Lincoln U (PA)
Lindenwood U (MO)
Linfield Coll (OR)
Lipscomb U (TN)
Lock Haven U of Pennsylvania (PA)
Longwood U (VA)
Loras Coll (IA)
Louisiana State U and A&M Coll (LA)
Louisiana State U in Shreveport (LA)
Louisiana Tech U (LA)
Loyola Marymount U (CA)
Loyola U Chicago (IL)
Loyola U Maryland (MD)
Loyola U New Orleans (LA)
Madonna U (MI)
Malone U (OH)
Manhattan Coll (NY)
Manhattanville Coll (NY)
Mansfield U of Pennsylvania (PA)
Marian U (IN)
Marietta Coll (OH)
Marquette U (WI)
Marshall U (WV)
Marymount Manhattan Coll (NY)
Marymount U (VA)
Maryville U of Saint Louis (MO)
Marywood U (PA)
McDaniel Coll (MD)
McKendree U (IL)
McMurry U (TX)
McNeese State U (LA)
Mercer U, Macon (GA)
Mercy Coll (NY)
Meredith Coll (NC)
Merrimack Coll (MA)
Messiah Coll (PA)
Miami U (OH)
Miami U Hamilton (OH)
Miami U Middletown (OH)
Michigan State U (MI)
Michigan Technological U (MI)
Mid-America Christian U (OK)
MidAmerica Nazarene U (KS)
Middlebury Coll (VT)
Middle Tennessee State U (TN)
Millersville U of Pennsylvania (PA)
Milligan Coll (TN)
Millikin U (IL)
Minnesota State U Mankato (MN)
Minot State U (ND)
Misericordia U (PA)
Mississippi State U (MS)
Missouri Southern State U (MO)
Missouri State U (MO)
Missouri U of Science and Technology (MO)
Missouri Valley Coll (MO)
Molloy Coll (NY)
Montana State U (MT)
Montclair State U (NJ)
Moravian Coll (PA)
Morehead State U (KY)
Mount Holyoke Coll (MA)
Mount Marty Coll (SD)
Mount Mercy U (IA)
Mount Saint Mary Coll (NY)
Mount Saint Mary's U (CA)
Mount St. Mary's U (MD)
Mount Vernon Nazarene U (OH)
Muhlenberg Coll (PA)
Multnomah U (OR)
Murray State U (KY)
Muskingum U (OH)
National U (CA)
Nazareth Coll of Rochester (NY)
Nebraska Wesleyan U (NE)
New Coll of Florida (FL)
New England Coll (NH)
New Jersey Inst of Technology (NJ)
Newman U (KS)
New Mexico Highlands U (NM)
New York U (NY)
Niagara U (NY)
Nichols Coll (MA)
North Carolina Central U (NC)
Northeastern Illinois U (IL)
Northeastern State U (OK)
Northern Arizona U (AZ)
Northern Illinois U (IL)
Northern Kentucky U (KY)
Northern State U (SD)
North Greenville U (SC)
Northwest Christian U (OR)
Northwestern Coll (IA)
Northwestern State U of Louisiana (LA)
Northwestern U (IL)
Northwest Missouri State U (MO)
Northwest Nazarene U (ID)
Northwest U (WA)
Notre Dame Coll (OH)
Nova Southeastern U (FL)
Oakland City U (IN)
Oakland U (MI)
Oberlin Coll (OH)
Occidental Coll (CA)
Oglethorpe U (GA)
Ohio Christian U (OH)
Ohio Dominican U (OH)
The Ohio State U (OH)
The Ohio State U at Lima (OH)
The Ohio State U at Mansfield (OH)
The Ohio State U at Marion (OH)
The Ohio State U at Newark (OH)
Ohio Valley U (WV)
Ohio Wesleyan U (OH)
Oklahoma Baptist U (OK)
Oklahoma State U (OK)
Old Dominion U (VA)
Olivet Nazarene U (IL)
Oral Roberts U (OK)
Ottawa U (KS)
Pace U, Pleasantville Campus (NY)

Pacific U (OR)
Palm Beach Atlantic U (FL)
Patrick Henry Coll (VA)
Penn State Abington (PA)
Penn State Altoona (PA)
Penn State Beaver (PA)
Penn State Berks (PA)
Penn State Brandywine (PA)
Penn State DuBois (PA)
Penn State Erie, The Behrend Coll (PA)
Penn State Fayette, The Eberly Campus (PA)
Penn State Greater Allegheny (PA)
Penn State Hazleton (PA)
Penn State Lehigh Valley (PA)
Penn State Mont Alto (PA)
Penn State New Kensington (PA)
Penn State Schuylkill (PA)
Penn State Shenango (PA)
Penn State U Park (PA)
Penn State Wilkes-Barre (PA)
Penn State York (PA)
Pepperdine U, Malibu (CA)
Pittsburg State U (KS)
Pitzer Coll (CA)
Point Loma Nazarene U (CA)
Pomona Coll (CA)
Prairie View A&M U (TX)
Princeton U (NJ)
Providence Coll (RI)
Purchase Coll, State U of New York (NY)
Purdue U Fort Wayne (IN)
Purdue U Northwest (IN)
Queens Coll of the City U of New York (NY)
Queens U of Charlotte (NC)
Radford U (VA)
Ramapo Coll of New Jersey (NJ)
Randolph Coll (VA)
Randolph-Macon Coll (VA)
Regent U (VA)
Rhode Island Coll (RI)
Rhodes Coll (TN)
Rice U (TX)
Richmond, The American Intl U in London (United Kingdom)
Roanoke Coll (VA)
Roberts Wesleyan Coll (NY)
Rocky Mountain Coll (MT)
Rogers State U (OK)
Roger Williams U (RI)
Rollins Coll (FL)
Rosemont Coll (PA)
Rowan U (NJ)
Sacred Heart U (CT)
The Sage Colls (NY)
Saginaw Valley State U (MI)
St. Ambrose U (IA)
St. Bonaventure U (NY)
St. Catherine U (MN)
St. Cloud State U (MN)
Saint Francis U (PA)
St. John Fisher Coll (NY)
Saint John's U (MN)
Saint Joseph's U (PA)
Saint Leo U (FL)
Saint Louis U (MO)
Saint Mary's Coll (IN)
Saint Mary's Coll of California (CA)
St. Mary's Coll of Maryland (MD)
St. Mary's U (TX)
Saint Mary's U of Minnesota (MN)
St. Norbert Coll (WI)
St. Olaf Coll (MN)
St. Thomas Aquinas Coll (NY)
St. Thomas U - Florida (FL)
St. Thomas U - New Brunswick (NB, Canada)
Saint Vincent Coll (PA)
Salem State U (MA)
Salisbury U (MD)
Salve Regina U (RI)
Samford U (AL)
Sam Houston State U (TX)
San Diego State U (CA)
San Francisco State U (CA)
San Jose State U (CA)
Santa Clara U (CA)
Sarah Lawrence Coll (NY)
Schreiner U (TX)
Scripps Coll (CA)
Seattle U (WA)
Seton Hill U (PA)
Shenandoah U (VA)
Shepherd U (WV)
Siena Coll (NY)
Siena Heights U (MI)
Simmons U (MA)
Simon Fraser U (BC, Canada)
Skidmore Coll (NY)
Slippery Rock U of Pennsylvania (PA)
Smith Coll (MA)
South Dakota State U (SD)
Southeastern Louisiana U (LA)
Southeast Missouri State U (MO)
Southern Arkansas U–Magnolia (AR)
Southern Illinois U Carbondale (IL)
Southern Illinois U Edwardsville (IL)
Southern Methodist U (TX)
Southwest Baptist U (MO)
Southwestern Coll (KS)
Southwestern Oklahoma State U (OK)
Southwestern U (TX)
Spring Arbor U (MI)
Springfield Coll (MA)
Spring Hill Coll (AL)
Stanford U (CA)
State U of New York at Fredonia (NY)
State U of New York at New Paltz (NY)
State U of New York at Oswego (NY)
State U of New York Coll at Cortland (NY)
State U of New York Coll at Geneseo (NY)
State U of New York Coll at Old Westbury (NY)
State U of New York Coll at Oneonta (NY)
State U of New York Coll at Potsdam (NY)
State U of New York Empire State Coll (NY)
Sterling Coll (KS)
Stetson U (FL)
Stevens Inst of Technology (NJ)
Stevenson U (MD)
Stockton U (NJ)
Stony Brook U, State U of New York (NY)
Suffolk U (MA)
SUNY Brockport (NY)
Susquehanna U (PA)
Tabor Coll (KS)
Tarleton State U (TX)
Taylor U (IN)
Temple U (PA)
Tennessee Wesleyan U (TN)
Texas A&M Intl U (TX)
Texas A&M U (TX)
Texas A&M U–Central Texas (TX)
Texas A&M U–Commerce (TX)
Texas A&M U–Corpus Christi (TX)
Texas A&M U–Kingsville (TX)
Texas Christian U (TX)
Texas Lutheran U (TX)
Texas Southern U (TX)
Texas State U (TX)
Texas Tech U (TX)
Texas Woman's U (TX)
Tiffin U (OH)
Toccoa Falls Coll (GA)
Towson U (MD)
Transylvania U (KY)
Trevecca Nazarene U (TN)
Trinity U (TX)
Troy U (AL)
Truett McConnell U (GA)
Truman State U (MO)
Tulane U (LA)
Union Coll (NY)
Union U (TN)
Universidad Adventista de las Antillas (PR)
U at Albany, State U of New York (NY)
U at Buffalo, the State U of New York (NY)
The U of Akron (OH)
The U of Alabama (AL)
The U of Alabama at Birmingham (AL)
The U of Alabama in Huntsville (AL)
U of Alaska Fairbanks (AK)
U of Alaska Southeast (AK)
The U of Arizona (AZ)
U of Arkansas (AR)
U of Arkansas at Little Rock (AR)
U of California, Berkeley (CA)
U of California, Irvine (CA)
U of California, Los Angeles (CA)
U of California, Merced (CA)
U of California, Riverside (CA)
U of California, San Diego (CA)
U of California, Santa Barbara (CA)
U of California, Santa Cruz (CA)
U of Central Arkansas (AR)
U of Central Florida (FL)
U of Cincinnati (OH)
U of Colorado Boulder (CO)
U of Colorado Colorado Springs (CO)
U of Colorado Denver (CO)
U of Dallas (TX)
U of Dayton (OH)
U of Denver (CO)
U of Detroit Mercy (MI)
The U of Findlay (OH)
U of Guam (GU)
U of Hartford (CT)
U of Hawaii at Manoa (HI)
U of Houston (TX)
U of Houston–Clear Lake (TX)
U of Houston–Downtown (TX)
U of Idaho (ID)
U of Illinois at Chicago (IL)
U of Illinois at Springfield (IL)
The U of Iowa (IA)
U of Jamestown (ND)
The U of Kansas (KS)
U of Kentucky (KY)
U of La Verne (CA)
U of Louisiana at Lafayette (LA)
U of Louisiana at Monroe (LA)
U of Louisville (KY)
U of Maine (ME)
U of Maine at Presque Isle (ME)
U of Mary Hardin-Baylor (TX)
U of Maryland, Baltimore County (MD)
U of Maryland Global Campus (MD)
U of Mary Washington (VA)
U of Massachusetts Amherst (MA)
U of Massachusetts Boston (MA)
U of Massachusetts Dartmouth (MA)
U of Massachusetts Lowell (MA)
U of Memphis (TN)
U of Miami (FL)
U of Michigan (MI)
U of Michigan–Dearborn (MI)
U of Michigan–Flint (MI)
U of Minnesota, Duluth (MN)
U of Minnesota, Morris (MN)
U of Minnesota, Twin Cities Campus (MN)
U of Missouri–St. Louis (MO)
U of Montana (MT)
U of Montevallo (AL)
U of Nebraska at Kearney (NE)
U of Nebraska–Lincoln (NE)
U of Nevada, Las Vegas (NV)
U of Nevada, Reno (NV)
U of New England (ME)
U of New Hampshire (NH)
U of New Haven (CT)
U of New Mexico (NM)
The U of North Carolina at Chapel Hill (NC)
The U of North Carolina at Charlotte (NC)
The U of North Carolina at Greensboro (NC)
The U of North Carolina at Pembroke (NC)
The U of North Carolina Wilmington (NC)
U of North Dakota (ND)
U of Northern Colorado (CO)
U of Northern Iowa (IA)
U of North Florida (FL)
U of North Texas (TX)
U of Northwestern–St. Paul (MN)
U of Notre Dame (IN)
U of Oregon (OR)
U of Pennsylvania (PA)
U of Pikeville (KY)
U of Portland (OR)
U of Providence (MT)
U of Puget Sound (WA)
U of Richmond (VA)
U of St. Francis (IL)
U of Saint Francis (IN)
U of Saint Joseph (CT)
U of Saint Mary (KS)
U of St. Thomas (TX)
U of San Diego (CA)
U of San Francisco (CA)
U of Science and Arts of Oklahoma (OK)
The U of Scranton (PA)
U of South Alabama (AL)
U of South Carolina (SC)
U of South Carolina Aiken (SC)
U of South Carolina Beaufort (SC)
U of South Dakota (SD)
U of Southern Indiana (IN)
U of Southern Maine (ME)
U of Southern Mississippi (MS)
U of South Florida (FL)
U of South Florida, St. Petersburg (FL)
The U of Tampa (FL)
The U of Tennessee (TN)
The U of Tennessee at Chattanooga (TN)
The U of Tennessee at Martin (TN)
The U of Texas at Dallas (TX)
The U of Texas at El Paso (TX)
The U of Texas at San Antonio (TX)
The U of Texas of the Permian Basin (TX)
The U of Texas Rio Grande Valley (TX)
U of the Fraser Valley (BC, Canada)
U of the Incarnate Word (TX)
U of the Pacific (CA)
The U of the South (TN)
The U of Toledo (OH)
U of Toronto (ON, Canada)
The U of Tulsa (OK)
U of Utah (UT)
U of Vermont (VT)
U of Virginia (VA)
U of Washington (WA)
U of Washington, Tacoma (WA)
U of Waterloo (ON, Canada)
The U of West Alabama (AL)
The U of Western Ontario (ON, Canada)
U of West Florida (FL)
U of West Georgia (GA)
U of Wisconsin–Eau Claire (WI)
U of Wisconsin–Green Bay (WI)
U of Wisconsin–La Crosse (WI)
U of Wisconsin–Madison (WI)
U of Wisconsin–Milwaukee (WI)
U of Wisconsin–Parkside (WI)
U of Wisconsin–Platteville (WI)
U of Wisconsin–Superior (WI)
U of Wyoming (WY)
Utah State U (UT)
Utah Valley U (UT)
Utica Coll (NY)
Valdosta State U (GA)
Valley City State U (ND)
Valparaiso U (IN)
Vanderbilt U (TN)
Vanguard U of Southern California (CA)
Villanova U (PA)
Virginia Commonwealth U (VA)
Virginia Wesleyan U (VA)
Wabash Coll (IN)
Wake Forest U (NC)
Walla Walla U (WA)
Warren Wilson Coll (NC)
Wartburg Coll (IA)
Washington & Jefferson Coll (PA)
Washington and Lee U (VA)
Washington Coll (MD)
Washington State U (WA)
Washington State U–Tri-Cities (WA)
Washington State U–Vancouver (WA)
Washington U in St. Louis (MO)
Wayland Baptist U (TX)
Waynesburg U (PA)
Wayne State Coll (NE)
Wayne State U (MI)
Weber State U (UT)
Wesleyan Coll (GA)
Wesleyan U (CT)
West Chester U of Pennsylvania (PA)
Western Carolina U (NC)
Western Colorado U (CO)
Western Connecticut State U (CT)
Western Kentucky U (KY)
Western Michigan U (MI)
Western New England U (MA)
Western New Mexico U (NM)
Western Oregon U (OR)
Western Washington U (WA)
Westfield State U (MA)
West Liberty U (WV)
Westminster Coll (UT)
Westmont Coll (CA)
West Virginia U (WV)
Wheaton Coll (IL)
Wheaton Coll (MA)
Whitworth U (WA)
Wichita State U (KS)
Widener U (PA)
Wilkes U (PA)
Willamette U (OR)
William & Mary (VA)
William Jewell Coll (MO)
William Paterson U of New Jersey (NJ)
William Penn U (IA)
Williams Coll (MA)
Wilmington Coll (OH)
Wingate U (NC)
Winthrop U (SC)
Wittenberg U (OH)
Wofford Coll (SC)
Woodbury U (CA)
Worcester State U (MA)
Wright State U (OH)
Xavier U (OH)
Xavier U of Louisiana (LA)
Yale U (CT)
Yeshiva U (NY)
York Coll of Pennsylvania (PA)
Youngstown State U (OH)

HISTORY AND PHILOSOPHY OF SCIENCE AND TECHNOLOGY

Georgia Inst of Technology (GA)
Harvard U (MA)
Johns Hopkins U (MD)
Michigan State U (MI)
New York U (NY)
U of Pennsylvania (PA)
U of Toronto (ON, Canada)
U of Utah (UT)
U of Washington (WA)
U of Wisconsin–Madison (WI)

HISTORY RELATED

The American U of Paris (France)
Bridgewater Coll (VA)
Bridgewater State U (MA)
Bryn Athyn Coll of the New Church (PA)
Butler U (IN)
Carnegie Mellon U (PA)
Chaminade U of Honolulu (HI)
Harvard U (MA)
Indiana U Kokomo (IN)
LeTourneau U (TX)
Marquette U (WI)
The Ohio State U (OH)
Regent U (VA)
Saint Mary's U of Minnesota (MN)
Sarah Lawrence Coll (NY)
United States Military Acad (NY)
U at Albany, State U of New York (NY)
U of California, Riverside (CA)
U of California, Santa Barbara (CA)
U of Washington (WA)
U of Washington, Tacoma (WA)
Vanderbilt U (TN)
Virginia Wesleyan U (VA)
Worcester State U (MA)

HISTORY TEACHER EDUCATION

Abilene Christian U (TX)
Albion Coll (MI)
Appalachian State U (NC)
Aquinas Coll (MI)
Auburn U (AL)
Augustana Coll (IL)
Biola U (CA)
Boise State U (ID)
Bowling Green State U (OH)
Bradley U (IL)
Bryan Coll (TN)
California Lutheran U (CA)

Calvin Coll (MI)
Campbellsville U (KY)
The Catholic U of America (DC)
Central Christian Coll of Kansas (KS)
Central Michigan U (MI)
Central Washington U (WA)
Coll of Staten Island of the City U of New York (NY)
Coll of the Ozarks (MO)
Concordia U Chicago (IL)
Concordia U Wisconsin (WI)
Covenant Coll (GA)
Culver-Stockton Coll (MO)
Dickinson State U (ND)
Dominican Coll (NY)
East Central U (OK)
Eastern Kentucky U (KY)
Eastern Michigan U (MI)
East Texas Baptist U (TX)
Emory & Henry Coll (VA)
Evangel U (MO)
Ferris State U (MI)
Fitchburg State U (MA)
Florida Southern Coll (FL)
Friends U (KS)
Geneva Coll (PA)
Grand Valley State U (MI)
Gwynedd Mercy U (PA)
Hardin-Simmons U (TX)
Hope Coll (MI)
Houston Baptist U (TX)
Inter American U of Puerto Rico, Metropolitan Campus (PR)
Inter American U of Puerto Rico, San Germán Campus (PR)
Kansas Wesleyan U (KS)
Lee U (TN)
LeTourneau U (TX)
Lincoln Memorial U (TN)
Lipscomb U (TN)
Mayville State U (ND)
McKendree U (IL)
McMurry U (TX)
Merrimack Coll (MA)
Michigan State U (MI)
MidAmerica Nazarene U (KS)
Minot State U (ND)
Missouri State U (MO)
Mount Marty Coll (SD)
Mount Vernon Nazarene U (OH)
Nazareth Coll of Rochester (NY)
Northern Arizona U (AZ)
Northern State U (SD)
Northwest Nazarene U (ID)
Oakland City U (IN)
Ohio Wesleyan U (OH)
Ottawa U (KS)
Pittsburg State U (KS)
Providence Coll (RI)
Rhode Island Coll (RI)
Rocky Mountain Coll (MT)
Roger Williams U (RI)
Saginaw Valley State U (MI)
St. Ambrose U (IA)
Saint Francis U (PA)
St. John Fisher Coll (NY)
Saint Joseph's U (PA)
Salve Regina U (RI)
Schreiner U (TX)
Southwestern Oklahoma State U (OK)
Spring Arbor U (MI)
Spring Hill Coll (AL)
Sterling Coll (KS)
Texas Lutheran U (TX)
Tiffin U (OH)
Toccoa Falls Coll (GA)
Trevecca Nazarene U (TN)
Universidad Adventista de las Antillas (PR)
The U of Akron (OH)
U of Illinois at Chicago (IL)
The U of Iowa (IA)
U of Jamestown (ND)
U of Maine (ME)
U of Mary Hardin-Baylor (TX)
U of Nevada, Reno (NV)
U of Providence (MT)
U of South Dakota (SD)
U of Wisconsin–Superior (WI)
Utah Valley U (UT)
Utica Coll (NY)
Valley City State U (ND)
Valparaiso U (IN)
Wartburg Coll (IA)
Washington U in St. Louis (MO)
Wayne State Coll (NE)
Weber State U (UT)
Western Michigan U (MI)
Western Washington U (WA)
Widener U (PA)
Wingate U (NC)
Xavier U of Louisiana (LA)

HOME FURNISHINGS AND EQUIPMENT INSTALLATION
Brigham Young U (UT)

HOMELAND SECURITY
American Public U System (WV)
Anderson U (SC)
Angelo State U (TX)
DeSales U (PA)
Eastern Kentucky U (KY)
Excelsior Coll (NY)
Keiser U, Fort Lauderdale (FL)
Mercy Coll (NY)
National U (CA)
Northeastern State U (OK)
Oakland U (MI)
Regent U (VA)
Saint Leo U (FL)
Slippery Rock U of Pennsylvania (PA)
State U of New York Coll of Technology at Canton (NY)
Tulane U (LA)
U at Albany, State U of New York (NY)
The U of Arizona (AZ)
U of Management and Technology (VA)
U of New Hampshire (NH)
Wichita State U (KS)

HOMELAND SECURITY, LAW ENFORCEMENT, FIREFIGHTING AND PROTECTIVE SERVICES RELATED
Anderson U (SC)
Chestnut Hill Coll (PA)
Clayton State U (GA)
Eastern Michigan U (MI)
Florida Atlantic U (FL)
Florida SouthWestern State Coll (FL)
Madonna U (MI)
Massachusetts Maritime Acad (MA)
Miami Dade Coll (FL)
Penn State Altoona (PA)
Penn State Berks (PA)
Roberts Wesleyan Coll (NY)
St. Petersburg Coll (FL)
Tiffin U (OH)
The U of West Alabama (AL)
Virginia Commonwealth U (VA)

HORSE HUSBANDRY/EQUINE SCIENCE AND MANAGEMENT
Averett U (VA)
Becker Coll (MA)
Delaware Valley U (PA)
Feather River Coll (CA)
Saint Mary-of-the-Woods Coll (IN)
U of Kentucky (KY)
U of New Hampshire (NH)

HORTICULTURAL SCIENCE
Auburn U (AL)
California State U, Fresno (CA)
Clemson U (SC)
Coll of the Ozarks (MO)
Colorado State U (CO)
Delaware Valley U (PA)
Iowa State U of Science and Technology (IA)
Kansas State U (KS)
Michigan State U (MI)
Mississippi State U (MS)
Missouri State U (MO)
Montana State U (MT)
Northwest Missouri State U (MO)
Oklahoma State U (OK)
Penn State Abington (PA)
Penn State Altoona (PA)
Penn State Beaver (PA)
Penn State Berks (PA)
Penn State Brandywine (PA)
Penn State DuBois (PA)
Penn State Erie, The Behrend Coll (PA)
Penn State Fayette, The Eberly Campus (PA)
Penn State Greater Allegheny (PA)
Penn State Hazleton (PA)
Penn State Lehigh Valley (PA)
Penn State Mont Alto (PA)
Penn State New Kensington (PA)
Penn State Schuylkill (PA)
Penn State Shenango (PA)
Penn State Wilkes-Barre (PA)
Penn State York (PA)
Sam Houston State U (TX)
Temple U (PA)
U of Cincinnati (OH)
U of Idaho (ID)
U of Nebraska–Lincoln (NE)
U of Vermont (VT)
U of Wisconsin–Madison (WI)
U of Wisconsin–Platteville (WI)
Utah State U (UT)

HOSPITAL AND HEALTH-CARE FACILITIES ADMINISTRATION
Avila U (MO)
Black Hills State U (SD)
Champlain Coll (VT)
Clayton State U (GA)
Governors State U (IL)
Ithaca Coll (NY)
Newman U (KS)
New York City Coll of Technology of the City U of New York (NY)
Saint Joseph's U (PA)
Tiffin U (OH)
The U of Alabama (AL)
U of St. Francis (IL)
U of South Dakota (SD)
The U of Toledo (OH)
U of Wisconsin–Milwaukee (WI)
Youngstown State U (OH)

HOSPITALITY ADMINISTRATION
American Public U System (WV)
Appalachian State U (NC)
Arkansas Tech U (AR)
Auburn U (AL)
Ball State U (IN)
Beacon Coll (FL)
Belmont U (TN)
Bowling Green State U (OH)
California State Polytechnic U, Pomona (CA)
Central Connecticut State U (CT)
Central Michigan U (MI)
Coll of Charleston (SC)
Coll of the Ozarks (MO)
Columbia Coll (SC)
Concordia U, St. Paul (MN)
Dallas Baptist U (TX)
DePaul U (IL)
East Carolina U (NC)
Eastern Michigan U (MI)
ECPI U, Virginia Beach (VA)
Endicott Coll (MA)
Fairleigh Dickinson U (NJ)
Ferris State U (MI)
Fisher Coll (MA)
Flagler Coll (FL)
Florida Atlantic U (FL)
Framingham State U (MA)
Georgia State U (GA)
Grand Valley State U (MI)
Granite State Coll (NH)
Husson U (ME)
Indiana U Kokomo (IN)
Indiana U of Pennsylvania (PA)
Iowa State U of Science and Technology (IA)
James Madison U (VA)
Kansas State U (KS)
Lasell Coll (MA)
Lebanese American U (Lebanon)
Lewis-Clark State Coll (ID)
Lynn U (FL)
Madonna U (MI)
Marywood U (PA)
Michigan State U (MI)
Middle Tennessee State U (TN)
Missouri State U (MO)
Montclair State U (NJ)
New York City Coll of Technology of the City U of New York (NY)
Nichols Coll (MA)
North Carolina Central U (NC)
Northern Arizona U (AZ)
Northwestern State U of Louisiana (LA)
Oklahoma State U (OK)
Purdue U Northwest (IN)
Saint Leo U (FL)
St. Thomas Aquinas Coll (NY)
St. Thomas U - Florida (FL)
Salem State U (MA)
San Diego State U (CA)
San Francisco State U (CA)
San Jose State U (CA)
Seton Hill U (PA)
South Dakota State U (SD)
Southeastern U (FL)
State U of New York Coll of Technology at Delhi (NY)
Stockton U (NJ)
Sullivan U (KY)
Tiffin U (OH)
The U of Alabama (AL)
U of Central Florida (FL)
U of Cincinnati (OH)
U of Denver (CO)
The U of Findlay (OH)
U of Kentucky (KY)
U of Louisiana at Lafayette (LA)
U of Massachusetts Amherst (MA)
U of Memphis (TN)
U of Nebraska–Lincoln (NE)
U of Nevada, Las Vegas (NV)
U of New Hampshire (NH)
The U of North Carolina at Greensboro (NC)
U of North Texas (TX)
U of Pittsburgh at Bradford (PA)
U of San Francisco (CA)
U of South Alabama (AL)
U of South Carolina (SC)
U of South Carolina Beaufort (SC)
The U of Texas Rio Grande Valley (TX)
U of the Virgin Islands (VI)
U of West Florida (FL)
U of Wisconsin–Stout (WI)
Utah Valley U (UT)
Washington State U (WA)
Washington State U–Tri-Cities (WA)
Washington State U–Vancouver (WA)
Webber Intl U (FL)
Western Carolina U (NC)
Western Kentucky U (KY)
West Virginia U (WV)
Wilkes U (PA)
York Coll of Pennsylvania (PA)
Youngstown State U (OH)

HOSPITALITY ADMINISTRATION RELATED
Auburn U (AL)
California State U, Dominguez Hills (CA)
California State U, Fullerton (CA)
Florida State U (FL)
Mount Mercy U (IA)
Penn State Abington (PA)
Penn State Altoona (PA)
Penn State Beaver (PA)
Penn State Berks (PA)
Penn State Brandywine (PA)
Penn State DuBois (PA)
Penn State Erie, The Behrend Coll (PA)
Penn State Fayette, The Eberly Campus (PA)
Penn State Greater Allegheny (PA)
Penn State Hazleton (PA)
Penn State Lehigh Valley (PA)
Penn State Mont Alto (PA)
Penn State New Kensington (PA)
Penn State Schuylkill (PA)
Penn State Shenango (PA)
Penn State U Park (PA)
Penn State Wilkes-Barre (PA)
Penn State York (PA)
Southern Illinois U Carbondale (IL)
U of Central Florida (FL)
U of Nevada, Las Vegas (NV)
U of Southern Mississippi (MS)
Widener U (PA)

HOSPITALITY AND RECREATION MARKETING
Ferris State U (MI)
Husson U (ME)
Saint Joseph's U (PA)

HOTEL/MOTEL ADMINISTRATION
Auburn U (AL)
California State U, Long Beach (CA)
Cornell U (NY)
Drexel U (PA)
Ferris State U (MI)
Grand Valley State U (MI)
Hampton U (VA)
Howard U (DC)
Husson U (ME)
Inter American U of Puerto Rico, Aguadilla Campus (PR)
Kansas State U (KS)
New York U (NY)
The Ohio State U (OH)
Sacred Heart U (CT)
State U of New York Coll of Technology at Delhi (NY)
Texas Tech U (TX)
U of Denver (CO)
U of Houston (TX)
U of Memphis (TN)
U of New Haven (CT)
U of Southern Mississippi (MS)
The U of Tennessee (TN)
Washington State U (WA)
Widener U (PA)

HOTEL, MOTEL, AND RESTAURANT MANAGEMENT
Endicott Coll (MA)
New York Inst of Technology (NY)
Niagara U (NY)
State U of New York Coll of Technology at Delhi (NY)

HOUSING AND HUMAN ENVIRONMENTS
Harding U (AR)
Missouri State U (MO)
The U of Akron (OH)
U of Minnesota, Twin Cities Campus (MN)

HUMAN BIOLOGY
Baker U (KS)
Biola U (CA)
Hamline U (MN)
Indiana U-Purdue U Indianapolis (IN)
Johns Hopkins U (MD)
Pitzer Coll (CA)
St. Bonaventure U (NY)
Saint Leo U (FL)
Scripps Coll (CA)
U of California, Irvine (CA)
U of California, Los Angeles (CA)
U of California, San Diego (CA)
The U of Kansas (KS)
U of Saint Mary (KS)
U of Wisconsin–Green Bay (WI)

HUMAN COMPUTER INTERACTION
Hardin-Simmons U (TX)
Milwaukee School of Eng (WI)
Stony Brook U, State U of New York (NY)
Whitworth U (WA)
Woodbury U (CA)

HUMAN DEVELOPMENT AND FAMILY STUDIES
Abilene Christian U (TX)
Auburn U (AL)
Baylor U (TX)
Bowling Green State U (OH)
Brigham Young U (UT)
California State U, Long Beach (CA)
California State U, San Bernardino (CA)
California State U, San Marcos (CA)
Colorado State U (CO)
Columbia Coll (SC)
Concordia U, St. Paul (MN)
Cornell U (NY)
Eastern Kentucky U (KY)
Freed-Hardeman U (TN)
George Mason U (VA)
Georgia Southern U (GA)
Hope Intl U (CA)
Houston Baptist U (TX)
Illinois State U (IL)
Indiana State U (IN)
Indiana U of Pennsylvania (PA)
Kansas State U (KS)
Lamar U (TX)
Lesley U (MA)

Liberty U (VA)
Louisiana State U and A&M Coll (LA)
Miami U Hamilton (OH)
Miami U Middletown (OH)
Michigan State U (MI)
Mississippi State U (MS)
Missouri State U (MO)
Montclair State U (NJ)
Niagara U (NY)
Northern Illinois U (IL)
Nova Southeastern U (FL)
The Ohio State U (OH)
Oklahoma State U (OK)
Penn State Abington (PA)
Penn State Altoona (PA)
Penn State Beaver (PA)
Penn State Berks (PA)
Penn State Brandywine (PA)
Penn State DuBois (PA)
Penn State Erie, The Behrend Coll (PA)
Penn State Fayette, The Eberly Campus (PA)
Penn State Greater Allegheny (PA)
Penn State Harrisburg (PA)
Penn State Hazleton (PA)
Penn State Lehigh Valley (PA)
Penn State Mont Alto (PA)
Penn State New Kensington (PA)
Penn State Schuylkill (PA)
Penn State Shenango (PA)
Penn State U Park (PA)
Penn State Wilkes-Barre (PA)
Penn State York (PA)
Purdue U Northwest (IN)
Samford U (AL)
South Dakota State U (SD)
State U of New York at Oswego (NY)
Temple U (PA)
Texas A&M U–Kingsville (TX)
Texas State U (TX)
Texas Tech U (TX)
Texas Woman's U (TX)
U at Albany, State U of New York (NY)
The U of Alabama (AL)
The U of Arizona (AZ)
U of Arkansas (AR)
U of California, San Diego (CA)
U of Colorado Denver (CO)
U of Houston (TX)
U of Idaho (ID)
U of Louisiana at Lafayette (LA)
U of Maine (ME)
U of Memphis (TN)
U of Nevada, Reno (NV)
U of New Hampshire (NH)
U of New Mexico (NM)
The U of North Carolina at Greensboro (NC)
U of North Texas (TX)
The U of Tennessee (TN)
The U of Texas of the Permian Basin (TX)
U of Utah (UT)
U of Vermont (VT)
U of Waterloo (ON, Canada)
U of Wisconsin–Madison (WI)
Utah State U (UT)
Washington State U (WA)
Washington State U–Vancouver (WA)
Youngstown State U (OH)

HUMAN DEVELOPMENT AND FAMILY STUDIES RELATED
Auburn U (AL)
Binghamton U, State U of New York (NY)
Bowling Green State U (OH)
Clemson U (SC)
Harding U (AR)
Hope Intl U (CA)
Merrimack Coll (MA)
Portland State U (OR)
Rowan U (NJ)
The U of Alabama (AL)
Winthrop U (SC)

HUMANITIES
Athens State U (AL)
Baylor U (TX)
Beacon Coll (FL)
Belhaven U (MS)
Belmont Abbey Coll (NC)
Benedictine U (IL)
Bennington Coll (VT)
Bethel U (IN)
Biola U (CA)
Bucknell U (PA)
California State Polytechnic U, Pomona (CA)
California State U, Monterey Bay (CA)
California State U, Northridge (CA)
California State U, Sacramento (CA)
California State U, San Bernardino (CA)
Chaminade U of Honolulu (HI)
Clarkson U (NY)
Coastal Carolina U (SC)
Colgate U (NY)
Coll of Saint Mary (NE)
The Coll of St. Scholastica (MN)
Columbia Intl U (SC)
Concordia Coll (MN)
Concordia U Wisconsin (WI)
Dominican Coll (NY)
Dominican U of California (CA)
Drexel U (PA)
Eastern Kentucky U (KY)
Eastern Washington U (WA)
Emory U (GA)
Fairleigh Dickinson U (NJ)
Felician U (NJ)
Florida Inst of Technology (FL)
Florida Southern Coll (FL)
Florida State U (FL)
Fordham U (NY)
The George Washington U (DC)
Harding U (AR)
Holy Apostles Coll and Sem (CT)
Indiana U East (IN)
Indiana U Kokomo (IN)
Inter American U of Puerto Rico, Metropolitan Campus (PR)
Jacksonville U (FL)
John Cabot U (Italy)
John Carroll U (OH)
John Jay Coll of Criminal Justice of the City U of New York (NY)
Kansas State U (KS)
The King's Coll (NY)
Lasell Coll (MA)
Lawrence Technological U (MI)
Lee U (TN)
Lesley U (MA)
Lincoln Memorial U (TN)
Loyola Marymount U (CA)
Marshall U (WV)
Michigan State U (MI)
Milligan Coll (TN)
Minnesota State U Mankato (MN)
Montclair State U (NJ)
Muskingum U (OH)
New Coll of Florida (FL)
New York U (NY)
Northwestern Coll (IA)
Northwestern U (IL)
Northwest Nazarene U (ID)
Nova Southeastern U (FL)
Oakland City U (IN)
The Ohio State U (OH)
Ohio Wesleyan U (OH)
Oklahoma Baptist U (OK)
Pacific U (OR)
Penn State Harrisburg (PA)
Portland State U (OR)
Providence Coll (RI)
Purchase Coll, State U of New York (NY)
Roberts Wesleyan Coll (NY)
Roger Williams U (RI)
Rollins Coll (FL)
The Sage Colls (NY)
Saint Mary-of-the-Woods Coll (IN)
Saint Mary's Coll (IN)
St. Norbert Coll (WI)
Sam Houston State U (TX)
San Diego State U (CA)
San Francisco State U (CA)
San Jose State U (CA)
Scripps Coll (CA)
Seattle U (WA)
Siena Heights U (MI)
Sierra Nevada Coll (NV)
Simon Fraser U (BC, Canada)
State U of New York Coll at Old Westbury (NY)
Stevens Inst of Technology (NJ)
Tiffin U (OH)
Trinity U (TX)
Union Coll (NY)
The U of Akron (OH)
U of Alaska Southeast (AK)
The U of Arizona (AZ)
U of Arkansas at Little Rock (AR)
U of California, Irvine (CA)
U of Central Florida (FL)
U of Cincinnati (OH)
U of Colorado Boulder (CO)
U of Hawaii–West Oahu (HI)
U of Houston–Clear Lake (TX)
U of Houston–Downtown (TX)
The U of Kansas (KS)
U of Louisville (KY)
U of Massachusetts Amherst (MA)
U of Michigan (MI)
U of New Mexico (NM)
U of Northern Iowa (IA)
U of Oregon (OR)
U of Pennsylvania (PA)
U of Pittsburgh at Greensburg (PA)
U of Richmond (VA)
U of San Diego (CA)
U of Southern Maine (ME)
U of South Florida (FL)
The U of Tennessee at Chattanooga (TN)
The U of Texas at San Antonio (TX)
The U of Texas of the Permian Basin (TX)
U of the Virgin Islands (VI)
U of Toronto (ON, Canada)
U of Utah (UT)
U of Washington (WA)
U of Washington, Bothell (WA)
U of Washington, Tacoma (WA)
U of West Florida (FL)
U of Wisconsin–Green Bay (WI)
Ursuline Coll (OH)
Villanova U (PA)
Virginia Wesleyan U (VA)
Wabash Coll (IN)
Walla Walla U (WA)
Washington Coll (MD)
Washington State U (WA)
Washington State U–Tri-Cities (WA)
Washington State U–Vancouver (WA)
Washington U in St. Louis (MO)
Wesleyan U (CT)
Western Oregon U (OR)
Western Washington U (WA)
Widener U (PA)
Willamette U (OR)
Wofford Coll (SC)
Worcester Polytechnic Inst (MA)
Yale U (CT)
York Coll of Pennsylvania (PA)

HUMAN/MEDICAL GENETICS
U of Utah (UT)

HUMAN NUTRITION
Baylor U (TX)
Bridgewater Coll (VA)
Cedar Crest Coll (PA)
Central Washington U (WA)
Kansas State U (KS)
The Ohio State U (OH)
Penn State Abington (PA)
Penn State Altoona (PA)
Penn State Beaver (PA)
Penn State Berks (PA)
Penn State Brandywine (PA)
Penn State DuBois (PA)
Penn State Erie, The Behrend Coll (PA)
Penn State Fayette, The Eberly Campus (PA)
Penn State Greater Allegheny (PA)
Penn State Hazleton (PA)
Penn State Lehigh Valley (PA)
Penn State Mont Alto (PA)
Penn State New Kensington (PA)
Penn State Schuylkill (PA)
Penn State Shenango (PA)
Penn State Wilkes-Barre (PA)
Penn State York (PA)
The U of Alabama (AL)
U of Dayton (OH)
U of Houston (TX)
U of Kentucky (KY)
U of New England (ME)
U of North Dakota (ND)
Utah State U (UT)
Utica Coll (NY)
Weber State U (UT)

HUMAN RESOURCES DEVELOPMENT
Limestone Coll (SC)
Miami U Hamilton (OH)
Miami U Middletown (OH)
Oakland U (MI)
Southwestern Coll (KS)
Texas A&M U (TX)
U of Arkansas (AR)
U of Houston (TX)
U of Wisconsin–Milwaukee (WI)
Western Michigan U (MI)

HUMAN RESOURCES MANAGEMENT
Anderson U (SC)
Athens State U (AL)
Auburn U (AL)
Auburn U at Montgomery (AL)
Avila U (MO)
Ball State U (IN)
Baruch Coll of the City U of New York (NY)
Bayamón Central U (PR)
Baylor U (TX)
Belhaven U (MS)
Black Hills State U (SD)
Boston Coll (MA)
Bowling Green State U (OH)
Bradley U (IL)
Brenau U (GA)
Brigham Young U (UT)
Bryant U (RI)
California State U, Fresno (CA)
California State U, Long Beach (CA)
California U of Pennsylvania (PA)
Calvin Coll (MI)
The Catholic U of America (DC)
Central Christian Coll of Kansas (KS)
Central Michigan U (MI)
Central Washington U (WA)
Chestnut Hill Coll (PA)
The Coll of Saint Rose (NY)
Columbia Coll (MO)
Concordia U, St. Paul (MN)
Cornell Coll (IA)
Davenport U, Grand Rapids (MI)
DeSales U (PA)
Dickinson State U (ND)
East Central U (OK)
Eastern Washington U (WA)
Ferris State U (MI)
Fisher Coll (MA)
Florida State U (FL)
Friends U (KS)
The George Washington U (DC)
Granite State Coll (NH)
Gwynedd Mercy U (PA)
HEC Montreal (QC, Canada)
Immaculata U (PA)
Indiana State U (IN)
Indiana U of Pennsylvania (PA)
Inter American U of Puerto Rico, Aguadilla Campus (PR)
Inter American U of Puerto Rico, Barranquitas Campus (PR)
Inter American U of Puerto Rico, Bayamón Campus (PR)
Inter American U of Puerto Rico, Metropolitan Campus (PR)
Inter American U of Puerto Rico, San Germán Campus (PR)
John Carroll U (OH)
Keiser U, Fort Lauderdale (FL)
King's Coll (PA)
Lamar U (TX)
La Sierra U (CA)
Le Moyne Coll (NY)
LeTourneau U (TX)
Lewis U (IL)
Limestone Coll (SC)
Lindenwood U (MO)
Lipscomb U (TN)
Louisiana Tech U (LA)
Loyola U Chicago (IL)
Madonna U (MI)
Mansfield U of Pennsylvania (PA)
Marquette U (WI)
McKendree U (IL)
Mercer U, Macon (GA)
Merrimack Coll (MA)
Michigan State U (MI)
Mount Mercy U (IA)
New York Inst of Technology (NY)
Nichols Coll (MA)
Northeastern Illinois U (IL)
Notre Dame Coll (OH)
Oakland U (MI)
Oglethorpe U (GA)
The Ohio State U (OH)
Ohio Valley U (WV)
Ottawa U (KS)
Pace U, Pleasantville Campus (NY)
Peirce Coll (PA)
Purdue U Northwest (IN)
Rasmussen Coll Bloomington (MN)
Rasmussen Coll Brooklyn Park (MN)
Rasmussen Coll Eagan (MN)
Rasmussen Coll Fort Myers (FL)
Rasmussen Coll Kansas City/ Overland Park (KS)
Rasmussen Coll Lake Elmo/ Woodbury (MN)
Rasmussen Coll Land O' Lakes (FL)
Rasmussen Coll Mankato (MN)
Rasmussen Coll Moorhead (MN)
Rasmussen Coll New Port Richey (FL)
Rasmussen Coll Ocala (FL)
Rasmussen Coll Tampa/Brandon (FL)
Rasmussen Coll Topeka (KS)
Regent U (VA)
Rhode Island Coll (RI)
Roberts Wesleyan Coll (NY)
Rowan U (NJ)
Saint Francis U (PA)
Saint Joseph's U (PA)
Saint Mary's U of Minnesota (MN)
Salem State U (MA)
Sam Houston State U (TX)
San Diego State U (CA)
San Jose State U (CA)
Seton Hill U (PA)
Spring Arbor U (MI)
State U of New York at Oswego (NY)
State U of New York Coll of Technology at Alfred (NY)
State U of New York Coll of Technology at Delhi (NY)
Sullivan U (KY)
Tarleton State U (TX)
Temple U (PA)
Tennessee Wesleyan U (TN)
Texas A&M U–Central Texas (TX)
Texas Woman's U (TX)
Tiffin U (OH)
The U of Akron (OH)
The U of Alabama at Birmingham (AL)
The U of Arizona (AZ)
U of Cincinnati (OH)
U of Dubuque (IA)
The U of Findlay (OH)
U of Hawaii at Manoa (HI)
U of Idaho (ID)
The U of Iowa (IA)
U of Management and Technology (VA)
U of Maryland Global Campus (MD)
U of Miami (FL)
U of Michigan–Dearborn (MI)
U of Michigan–Flint (MI)
U of Minnesota, Duluth (MN)
U of Minnesota, Twin Cities Campus (MN)
The U of North Carolina at Chapel Hill (NC)
U of North Dakota (ND)
U of Pennsylvania (PA)
U of St. Francis (IL)
The U of Scranton (PA)
U of Southern Mississippi (MS)
The U of Tennessee (TN)
The U of Tennessee at Chattanooga (TN)
The U of Texas at Dallas (TX)
The U of Texas at San Antonio (TX)
U of the Incarnate Word (TX)
The U of Toledo (OH)
U of Washington (WA)
U of Waterloo (ON, Canada)
The U of Western Ontario (ON, Canada)
Upper Iowa U (IA)

Washington U in St. Louis (MO)
Weber State U (UT)
Western Michigan U (MI)
Wichita State U (KS)
William Penn U (IA)
Wright State U (OH)
Wright State U–Lake Campus (OH)
Xavier U (OH)
Youngstown State U (OH)

HUMAN RESOURCES MANAGEMENT AND SERVICES RELATED
Carlow U (PA)
Grand Valley State U (MI)
Immaculata U (PA)
Lynn U (FL)
Michigan State U (MI)
Oakland City U (IN)
Trine U (IN)
Widener U (PA)

HUMAN SERVICES
Anderson U (SC)
Beacon Coll (FL)
Bethel U (TN)
Black Hills State U (SD)
California State U, Dominguez Hills (CA)
California State U, Fullerton (CA)
California State U, Monterey Bay (CA)
California State U, San Bernardino (CA)
Calumet Coll of Saint Joseph (IN)
Carson-Newman U (TN)
Cazenovia Coll (NY)
Central Washington U (WA)
Chestnut Hill Coll (PA)
Columbia Coll (MO)
Dean Coll (MA)
Doane U (NE)
Dominican U (IL)
East Central U (OK)
Elon U (NC)
Emmanuel Coll (MA)
Excelsior Coll (NY)
Fisher Coll (MA)
Fitchburg State U (MA)
Geneva Coll (PA)
The George Washington U (DC)
Granite State Coll (NH)
Gwynedd Mercy U (PA)
Hardin-Simmons U (TX)
Kennesaw State U (GA)
Lackawanna Coll (PA)
Lasell Coll (MA)
Lenoir-Rhyne U (NC)
Lesley U (MA)
LeTourneau U (TX)
Liberty U (VA)
Lincoln U (PA)
Loyola U Chicago (IL)
Mercer U, Macon (GA)
Missouri Valley Coll (MO)
Mount Marty Coll (SD)
Mount Saint Mary Coll (NY)
New York City Coll of Technology of the City U of New York (NY)
Northern Illinois U (IL)
Nova Southeastern U (FL)
Ottawa U (KS)
Queens U of Charlotte (NC)
Saint Mary-of-the-Woods Coll (IN)
Saint Mary's U of Minnesota (MN)
Seton Hill U (PA)
Siena Heights U (MI)
Southeastern U (FL)
State U of New York Coll at Cortland (NY)
Tennessee Wesleyan U (TN)
Texas A&M U–Kingsville (TX)
Towson U (MD)
U of Colorado Colorado Springs (CO)
U of Massachusetts Boston (MA)
U of Minnesota, Morris (MN)
U of Nevada, Las Vegas (NV)
U of North Texas (TX)
U of Oregon (OR)
U of Providence (MT)
The U of Scranton (PA)
U of South Florida (FL)
Upper Iowa U (IA)
Valley City State U (ND)
Virginia Wesleyan U (VA)
Wayland Baptist U (TX)
Waynesburg U (PA)
Western Washington U (WA)
William Penn U (IA)
Wingate U (NC)

HYDROLOGY AND WATER RESOURCES SCIENCE
St. Cloud State U (MN)
State U of New York Coll at Oneonta (NY)
SUNY Brockport (NY)
Tarleton State U (TX)
The U of Arizona (AZ)
U of California, Santa Barbara (CA)
U of Idaho (ID)
U of Toronto (ON, Canada)
Western Michigan U (MI)

ILLUSTRATION
Academy of Art U (CA)
American Acad of Art (IL)
Arcadia U (PA)
Boise State U (ID)
Brigham Young U (UT)
California State U, Long Beach (CA)
Cleveland Inst of Art (OH)
Columbia Coll Chicago (IL)
Edinboro U of Pennsylvania (PA)
Eugene Lang Coll of Liberal Arts (NY)
Fashion Inst of Technology (NY)
Ferris State U (MI)
John Brown U (AR)
Marywood U (PA)
Minneapolis Coll of Art and Design (MN)
Nossi Coll of Art (TN)
Paier Coll of Art, Inc. (CT)
Paris Coll of Art (France)
Parsons School of Design (NY)
Pratt Inst (NY)
School of Visual Arts (NY)
U of Hartford (CT)
The U of Kansas (KS)
U of Massachusetts Dartmouth (MA)
U of Michigan (MI)
U of New Haven (CT)
Virginia Commonwealth U (VA)
Washington U in St. Louis (MO)

IMMUNOLOGY
The U of Alabama at Birmingham (AL)

INDUSTRIAL AND ORGANIZATIONAL PSYCHOLOGY
Avila U (MO)
Baruch Coll of the City U of New York (NY)
Bridgewater State U (MA)
Fitchburg State U (MA)
Ithaca Coll (NY)
Maryville U of Saint Louis (MO)
Marywood U (PA)
MidAmerica Nazarene U (KS)
Middle Tennessee State U (TN)
Multnomah U (OR)
Pepperdine U, Malibu (CA)
Saint Mary's Coll of California (CA)
United States Military Acad (NY)
U of St. Francis (IL)
Washington U in St. Louis (MO)

INDUSTRIAL AND PHYSICAL PHARMACY AND COSMETIC SCIENCES
The U of Toledo (OH)

INDUSTRIAL AND PRODUCT DESIGN
Academy of Art U (CA)
Appalachian State U (NC)
Arizona State U at the Tempe campus (AZ)
Auburn U (AL)
Bennington Coll (VT)
California State U, Long Beach (CA)
Carnegie Mellon U (PA)
Cedarville U (OH)
Clemson U (SC)
Cleveland Inst of Art (OH)
Drexel U (PA)
Eugene Lang Coll of Liberal Arts (NY)
Fashion Inst of Technology (NY)
Ferris State U (MI)
FIDM/Fashion Inst of Design & Merchandising, Los Angeles Campus (CA)
Georgia Inst of Technology (GA)
James Madison U (VA)
Kean U (NJ)
Lawrence Technological U (MI)
Massachusetts Coll of Art and Design (MA)
Montclair State U (NJ)
New Jersey Inst of Technology (NJ)
The Ohio State U (OH)
Otis Coll of Art and Design (CA)
Parsons School of Design (NY)
Pratt Inst (NY)
San Francisco State U (CA)
San Jose State U (CA)
Stanford U (CA)
U of Cincinnati (OH)
U of Houston (TX)
U of Illinois at Chicago (IL)
The U of Kansas (KS)
U of Louisiana at Lafayette (LA)
U of Michigan (MI)
U of Minnesota, Twin Cities Campus (MN)
U of Utah (UT)
U of Washington (WA)
U of Wisconsin–Stout (WI)
Walla Walla U (WA)
Wentworth Inst of Technology (MA)
Western Michigan U (MI)
Western Washington U (WA)

INDUSTRIAL ELECTRONICS TECHNOLOGY
Lewis-Clark State Coll (ID)

INDUSTRIAL ENGINEERING
American U of Beirut (Lebanon)
Aquinas Coll (MI)
Arizona State U at the Tempe campus (AZ)
Auburn U (AL)
Binghamton U, State U of New York (NY)
Bradley U (IL)
California Baptist U (CA)
California Polytechnic State U, San Luis Obispo (CA)
California State Polytechnic U, Pomona (CA)
California State U, Long Beach (CA)
Clemson U (SC)
Fairleigh Dickinson U (NJ)
Florida A&M U (FL)
Florida State U (FL)
Francis Marion U (SC)
Gannon U (PA)
Georgia Inst of Technology (GA)
Hofstra U (NY)
Inter American U of Puerto Rico, Bayamón Campus (PR)
Iowa State U of Science and Technology (IA)
Kansas State U (KS)
Kettering U (MI)
Lamar U (TX)
Lawrence Technological U (MI)
Lebanese American U (Lebanon)
Lehigh U (PA)
Liberty U (VA)
Louisiana State U and A&M Coll (LA)
Louisiana Tech U (LA)
Milwaukee School of Eng (WI)
Mississippi State U (MS)
Missouri U of Science and Technology (MO)
Montana State U (MT)
New Jersey Inst of Technology (NJ)
New York U (NY)
Northern Illinois U (IL)
Northwestern U (IL)
Oakland U (MI)
The Ohio State U (OH)
Oklahoma State U (OK)
Penn State Abington (PA)
Penn State Altoona (PA)
Penn State Beaver (PA)
Penn State Berks (PA)
Penn State Brandywine (PA)
Penn State DuBois (PA)
Penn State Erie, The Behrend Coll (PA)
Penn State Fayette, The Eberly Campus (PA)
Penn State Greater Allegheny (PA)
Penn State Hazleton (PA)
Penn State Lehigh Valley (PA)
Penn State Mont Alto (PA)
Penn State New Kensington (PA)
Penn State Schuylkill (PA)
Penn State Shenango (PA)
Penn State U Park (PA)
Penn State Wilkes-Barre (PA)
Penn State York (PA)
Polytechnic U of Puerto Rico (PR)
St. Ambrose U (IA)
St. Mary's U (TX)
San Jose State U (CA)
Slippery Rock U of Pennsylvania (PA)
Southern Illinois U Edwardsville (IL)
Stanford U (CA)
State U of New York Maritime Coll (NY)
Temple U (PA)
Texas A&M U (TX)
Texas A&M U–Commerce (TX)
Texas A&M U–Corpus Christi (TX)
Texas A&M U–Kingsville (TX)
Texas State U (TX)
Texas Tech U (TX)
U at Buffalo, the State U of New York (NY)
The U of Alabama in Huntsville (AL)
The U of Arizona (AZ)
U of Arkansas (AR)
U of Central Florida (FL)
U of Cincinnati (OH)
U of Dayton (OH)
U of Houston (TX)
U of Illinois at Chicago (IL)
The U of Iowa (IA)
U of Louisville (KY)
U of Massachusetts Amherst (MA)
U of Miami (FL)
U of Michigan (MI)
U of Michigan–Dearborn (MI)
U of Minnesota, Duluth (MN)
U of Minnesota, Twin Cities Campus (MN)
U of New Haven (CT)
U of San Diego (CA)
U of South Carolina Aiken (SC)
U of South Florida (FL)
The U of Tennessee (TN)
The U of Texas at El Paso (TX)
U of Toronto (ON, Canada)
U of Vermont (VT)
U of Washington (WA)
U of Wisconsin–Madison (WI)
U of Wisconsin–Milwaukee (WI)
U of Wisconsin–Platteville (WI)
Wayne State U (MI)
Western Michigan U (MI)
Western New England U (MA)
West Virginia U (WV)
Wichita State U (KS)
William Penn U (IA)
Worcester Polytechnic Inst (MA)
Youngstown State U (OH)

INDUSTRIAL PRODUCTION TECHNOLOGIES RELATED
Bowling Green State U (OH)
California U of Pennsylvania (PA)
Central Washington U (WA)
Ferris State U (MI)
Kennesaw State U (GA)
Millersville U of Pennsylvania (PA)
Mississippi State U (MS)
Missouri State U (MO)
Northwest Missouri State U (MO)
Saginaw Valley State U (MI)
Valdosta State U (GA)
Wayne State Coll (NE)

INDUSTRIAL RADIOLOGIC TECHNOLOGY
Concordia U Wisconsin (WI)
Howard U (DC)

INDUSTRIAL SAFETY TECHNOLOGY
Central Washington U (WA)
Eastern Kentucky U (KY)
Mansfield U of Pennsylvania (PA)
Northeastern State U (OK)
U of Houston–Downtown (TX)

INDUSTRIAL TECHNOLOGY
Ball State U (IN)
Bemidji State U (MN)
Black Hills State U (SD)
Bowling Green State U (OH)
California Polytechnic State U, San Luis Obispo (CA)
California State U, Fresno (CA)
California State U, Long Beach (CA)
California State U, Los Angeles (CA)
Central Connecticut State U (CT)
Central State U (OH)
Central Washington U (WA)
Clarion U of Pennsylvania (PA)
East Carolina U (NC)
Eastern Michigan U (MI)
Farmingdale State Coll (NY)
Ferris State U (MI)
Fitchburg State U (MA)
Illinois State U (IL)
Indiana State U (IN)
Iowa State U of Science and Technology (IA)
Jacksonville State U (AL)
Lamar U (TX)
Millersville U of Pennsylvania (PA)
Mississippi State U (MS)
Missouri Southern State U (MO)
Northwestern State U of Louisiana (LA)
Pittsburg State U (KS)
Roger Williams U (RI)
St. Cloud State U (MN)
Sam Houston State U (TX)
Southeastern Louisiana U (LA)
Southeast Missouri State U (MO)
Southern Arkansas U–Magnolia (AR)
Southern Illinois U Carbondale (IL)
Tarleton State U (TX)
Texas A&M U–Commerce (TX)
Texas A&M U–Kingsville (TX)
Texas Southern U (TX)
Texas State U (TX)
U of Dayton (OH)
U of Idaho (ID)
U of Louisiana at Lafayette (LA)
U of Massachusetts Lowell (MA)
U of North Dakota (ND)
U of Northern Iowa (IA)
U of Southern Maine (ME)
U of Southern Mississippi (MS)
The U of Texas of the Permian Basin (TX)
Vincennes U (IN)
Western Kentucky U (KY)
William Penn U (IA)

INFORMATICS
Allegheny Coll (PA)
American Coll of Thessaloniki (Greece)
Arizona State U at the Tempe campus (AZ)
Assumption Coll (MA)
Dominican U (IL)
Drexel U (PA)
Florida Gulf Coast U (FL)
Indiana U Bloomington (IN)
Indiana U East (IN)
Indiana U Kokomo (IN)
Indiana U Northwest (IN)
Indiana U-Purdue U Indianapolis (IN)
Indiana U South Bend (IN)
Indiana U Southeast (IN)
Liberty U (VA)
Northern Arizona U (AZ)
Texas Woman's U (TX)
Trine U (IN)
U at Buffalo, the State U of New York (NY)
U of California, Irvine (CA)
U of Louisiana at Lafayette (LA)
U of Massachusetts Amherst (MA)
U of Michigan (MI)
U of Washington (WA)

INFORMATION RESOURCES MANAGEMENT
Abilene Christian U (TX)
Athens State U (AL)
Chestnut Hill Coll (PA)
Lawrence Technological U (MI)
Lewis U (IL)
Lipscomb U (TN)

Michigan State U (MI)
Mount St. Mary's U (MD)
Rasmussen Coll Land O' Lakes (FL)
Rasmussen Coll New Port Richey (FL)
Rasmussen Coll Ocala (FL)
Rasmussen Coll Tampa/Brandon (FL)
U of California, Irvine (CA)
Western Michigan U (MI)

INFORMATION SCIENCE/ STUDIES
Averett U (VA)
Barry U (FL)
Baruch Coll of the City U of New York (NY)
Bemidji State U (MN)
Benedictine U (IL)
Boise State U (ID)
Bowling Green State U (OH)
Bradley U (IL)
California Lutheran U (CA)
California State U, Northridge (CA)
California State U, Stanislaus (CA)
Campbellsville U (KY)
Carson-Newman U (TN)
Central Coll (IA)
Clarion U of Pennsylvania (PA)
Clayton State U (GA)
Clemson U (SC)
Coastal Carolina U (SC)
Colegio Universitario de San Juan, San Juan (PR)
Coll of Charleston (SC)
Coll of Staten Island of the City U of New York (NY)
Colorado State U (CO)
Dakota State U (SD)
Davenport U, Grand Rapids (MI)
DePaul U (IL)
Dickinson State U (ND)
Doane U (NE)
Drexel U (PA)
East Carolina U (NC)
Emporia State U (KS)
Excelsior Coll (NY)
Fordham U (NY)
Friends U (KS)
Gallaudet U (DC)
George Fox U (OR)
Georgia Southern U (GA)
Glenville State Coll (WV)
Goshen Coll (IN)
Grambling State U (LA)
Grand Valley State U (MI)
Hampton U (VA)
Harris-Stowe State U (MO)
HEC Montreal (QC, Canada)
Howard U (DC)
Illinois Coll (IL)
Indiana U-Purdue U Indianapolis (IN)
Inter American U of Puerto Rico, San Germán Campus (PR)
Jacksonville U (FL)
James Madison U (VA)
Kansas State U (KS)
Kennesaw State U (GA)
La Sierra U (CA)
Lenoir-Rhyne U (NC)
LeTourneau U (TX)
Limestone Coll (SC)
Lincoln U (MO)
Lipscomb U (TN)
Mansfield U of Pennsylvania (PA)
Marietta Coll (OH)
McKendree U (IL)
Mercer U, Macon (GA)
Mercy Coll (NY)
Merrimack Coll (MA)
Minnesota State U Mankato (MN)
Missouri U of Science and Technology (MO)
Molloy Coll (NY)
Murray State U (KY)
New Jersey Inst of Technology (NJ)
Newman U (KS)
New Mexico Highlands U (NM)
New York City Coll of Technology of the City U of New York (NY)
Northern Kentucky U (KY)
Northwestern State U of Louisiana (LA)
Northwestern U (IL)
Oklahoma Baptist U (OK)
Olivet Nazarene U (IL)
Ottawa U (KS)
Penn State Abington (PA)
Penn State Altoona (PA)
Penn State Beaver (PA)
Penn State Berks (PA)
Penn State Brandywine (PA)
Penn State DuBois (PA)
Penn State Erie, The Behrend Coll (PA)
Penn State Fayette, The Eberly Campus (PA)
Penn State Greater Allegheny (PA)
Penn State Harrisburg (PA)
Penn State Lehigh Valley (PA)
Penn State Mont Alto (PA)
Penn State New Kensington (PA)
Penn State Schuylkill (PA)
Penn State Shenango (PA)
Penn State U Park (PA)
Penn State Wilkes-Barre (PA)
Penn State York (PA)
Portland State U (OR)
Radford U (VA)
Ramapo Coll of New Jersey (NJ)
Saint Joseph's U (PA)
St. Mary's U (TX)
Salisbury U (MD)
San Francisco State U (CA)
Simmons U (MA)
Slippery Rock U of Pennsylvania (PA)
Southern Illinois U Carbondale (IL)
State U of New York at Fredonia (NY)
State U of New York at Oswego (NY)
State U of New York Coll at Old Westbury (NY)
Stevenson U (MD)
Stockton U (NJ)
Stony Brook U, State U of New York (NY)
Suffolk U (MA)
SUNY Brockport (NY)
Susquehanna U (PA)
Texas A&M Intl U (TX)
Texas A&M U–Commerce (TX)
Texas Lutheran U (TX)
Texas Tech U (TX)
Towson U (MD)
Trine U (IN)
Tulane U (LA)
Union U (TN)
U at Albany, State U of New York (NY)
U of Arkansas at Little Rock (AR)
U of California, Riverside (CA)
U of Cincinnati (OH)
U of Colorado Boulder (CO)
U of Hartford (CT)
U of Illinois at Chicago (IL)
The U of Iowa (IA)
U of Kentucky (KY)
U of Management and Technology (VA)
U of Mary Hardin-Baylor (TX)
U of Maryland, Baltimore County (MD)
U of Maryland Global Campus (MD)
U of Massachusetts Lowell (MA)
U of Miami (FL)
U of Michigan (MI)
U of Michigan–Flint (MI)
U of Nevada, Las Vegas (NV)
The U of North Carolina at Chapel Hill (NC)
The U of North Carolina at Greensboro (NC)
U of North Texas (TX)
U of Northwestern–St. Paul (MN)
U of Providence (MT)
The U of Scranton (PA)
U of South Alabama (AL)
U of South Carolina (SC)
U of South Florida (FL)
The U of Texas of the Permian Basin (TX)
U of the Pacific (CA)
The U of Toledo (OH)
U of Utah (UT)
U of Washington, Bothell (WA)
The U of Western Ontario (ON, Canada)
U of Wisconsin–Green Bay (WI)
U of Wisconsin–Milwaukee (WI)
Utah State U (UT)
Utah Valley U (UT)
Valdosta State U (GA)
Virginia Commonwealth U (VA)
Wayne State Coll (NE)
Wayne State U (MI)
Weber State U (UT)
Wentworth Inst of Technology (MA)
Westfield State U (MA)
West Liberty U (WV)
Widener U (PA)
Wilkes U (PA)

INFORMATION TECHNOLOGY
Abilene Christian U (TX)
American Public U System (WV)
Anderson U (SC)
Arkansas Tech U (AR)
Auburn U at Montgomery (AL)
Austin Peay State U (TN)
Bay Atlantic U (DC)
Baylor U (TX)
Bethesda U (CA)
Bluffton U (OH)
Boise State U (ID)
Bradley U (IL)
Brigham Young U (UT)
Caldwell U (NJ)
California Baptist U (CA)
California State U, Dominguez Hills (CA)
California State U, Fullerton (CA)
California State U, Los Angeles (CA)
California State U, San Bernardino (CA)
California State U, Stanislaus (CA)
Cameron U (OK)
Central Michigan U (MI)
Central Washington U (WA)
Clayton State U (GA)
Coastal Carolina U (SC)
The Coll of Saint Rose (NY)
Coll of the Ozarks (MO)
The Coll of Westchester (NY)
Cornell U (NY)
Daytona State Coll (FL)
DePaul U (IL)
Donnelly Coll (KS)
East Carolina U (NC)
Fairleigh Dickinson U (NJ)
Ferris State U (MI)
Florida A&M U (FL)
Florida National U (FL)
Florida State U (FL)
Furman U (SC)
George Mason U (VA)
Georgia Gwinnett Coll (GA)
Georgia Southern U (GA)
Governors State U (IL)
Granite State Coll (NH)
Harding U (AR)
HEC Montreal (QC, Canada)
Illinois Inst of Technology (IL)
Illinois State U (IL)
Indiana State U (IN)
Indiana U-Purdue U Indianapolis (IN)
Inter American U of Puerto Rico, Bayamón Campus (PR)
Inter American U of Puerto Rico, Metropolitan Campus (PR)
Kansas Wesleyan U (KS)
Keiser U, Fort Lauderdale (FL)
Kennesaw State U (GA)
King U (TN)
La Roche U (PA)
Lasell Coll (MA)
La Sierra U (CA)
Lawrence Technological U (MI)
Lee U (TN)
Lehigh U (PA)
Liberty U (VA)
Life U (GA)
Limestone Coll (SC)
Lincoln U (PA)
Lindenwood U (MO)
Lipscomb U (TN)
Loyola U Chicago (IL)
Marquette U (WI)
Marymount U (VA)
McKendree U (IL)
McMurry U (TX)
Merrimack Coll (MA)
Miami Dade Coll (FL)
Miami U (OH)
Miami U Hamilton (OH)
Miami U Middletown (OH)
Misericordia U (PA)
Montclair State U (NJ)
Mount Aloysius Coll (PA)
Mount Saint Mary Coll (NY)
Murray State U (KY)
New England Inst of Technology (RI)
New Jersey Inst of Technology (NJ)
New Mexico Inst of Mining and Technology (NM)
New York Inst of Technology (NY)
New York U (NY)
Northern Kentucky U (KY)
Northwest U (WA)
Oakland U (MI)
Oklahoma State U (OK)
Ottawa U (KS)
Peirce Coll (PA)
Point Loma Nazarene U (CA)
Purdue U Northwest (IN)
Regent U (VA)
Sacred Heart U (CT)
San Diego State U (CA)
Simmons U (MA)
Slippery Rock U of Pennsylvania (PA)
Southeastern Louisiana U (LA)
State U of New York Coll of Agriculture and Technology at Cobleskill (NY)
State U of New York Coll of Technology at Canton (NY)
Stockton U (NJ)
Sullivan U (KY)
Tarleton State U (TX)
Temple U (PA)
Texas Christian U (TX)
Tiffin U (OH)
Towson U (MD)
Trevecca Nazarene U (TN)
United States Military Acad (NY)
U of California, Riverside (CA)
U of California, San Diego (CA)
U of Central Florida (FL)
U of Cincinnati (OH)
U of Denver (CO)
U of Houston–Clear Lake (TX)
U of Jamestown (ND)
The U of Kansas (KS)
U of La Verne (CA)
U of Management and Technology (VA)
U of Massachusetts Boston (MA)
U of New Hampshire (NH)
The U of North Carolina at Pembroke (NC)
The U of North Carolina Wilmington (NC)
U of North Texas (TX)
U of Providence (MT)
U of St. Francis (IL)
U of San Francisco (CA)
The U of Scranton (PA)
U of South Alabama (AL)
U of South Florida (FL)
The U of Texas at Dallas (TX)
The U of Texas at El Paso (TX)
The U of Toledo (OH)
The U of Tulsa (OK)
U of Washington (WA)
U of Washington, Tacoma (WA)
The U of Western Ontario (ON, Canada)
U of West Florida (FL)
Vermont Tech Coll (VT)
Washington & Jefferson Coll (PA)
Western Kentucky U (KY)
Western New England U (MA)
William Paterson U of New Jersey (NJ)
William Penn U (IA)
Youngstown State U (OH)

INFORMATION TECHNOLOGY PROJECT MANAGEMENT
American Public U System (WV)
Arizona State U at the Polytechnic campus (AZ)
Davenport U, Grand Rapids (MI)
Michigan State U (MI)
National U (CA)
Pace U, Pleasantville Campus (NY)
U of Miami (FL)

INORGANIC CHEMISTRY
The U of Western Ontario (ON, Canada)

INSTRUMENTATION TECHNOLOGY
Oklahoma State U Inst of Technology (OK)
U at Albany, State U of New York (NY)

INSURANCE
Appalachian State U (NC)
Ball State U (IN)
Baylor U (TX)
Bowling Green State U (OH)
Butler U (IN)
Eastern Kentucky U (KY)
Ferris State U (MI)
Florida State U (FL)
Gallaudet U (DC)
Gannon U (PA)
Georgia State U (GA)
Howard U (DC)
Illinois State U (IL)
Illinois Wesleyan U (IL)
Indiana State U (IN)
Middle Tennessee State U (TN)
Mississippi State U (MS)
Missouri State U (MO)
Ohio Dominican U (OH)
The Ohio State U (OH)
Saint Joseph's U (PA)
U of Central Arkansas (AR)
U of Cincinnati (OH)
U of Hartford (CT)
U of Houston–Downtown (TX)
U of Louisiana at Lafayette (LA)
U of Louisiana at Monroe (LA)
U of Minnesota, Twin Cities Campus (MN)
U of Nebraska–Lincoln (NE)
U of North Texas (TX)
U of Pennsylvania (PA)
U of Saint Francis (IN)
U of South Carolina (SC)
U of Wisconsin–Madison (WI)

INTELLIGENCE
The Citadel, The Military Coll of South Carolina (SC)
Coastal Carolina U (SC)
Excelsior Coll (NY)
Indiana State U (IN)

INTELLIGENCE, COMMAND CONTROL AND INFORMATION OPERATIONS RELATED
U of Utah (UT)

INTERCULTURAL/ MULTICULTURAL AND DIVERSITY STUDIES
Bethel U (IN)
Biola U (CA)
Columbia Intl U (SC)
Evangel U (MO)
Fort Lewis Coll (CO)
Ithaca Coll (NY)
MidAmerica Nazarene U (KS)
Missouri Valley Coll (MO)
North Central U (MN)
Northwest U (WA)
Nyack Coll (NY)
Pitzer Coll (CA)
St. Catherine U (MN)
Sarah Lawrence Coll (NY)
Southeastern U (FL)
Trevecca Nazarene U (TN)
U of the Incarnate Word (TX)
Villanova U (PA)
Western Oregon U (OR)
Wofford Coll (SC)
Wright State U (OH)
Wright State U–Lake Campus (OH)

INTERDISCIPLINARY STUDIES
Agnes Scott Coll (GA)
Alfred U (NY)
Amherst Coll (MA)
Arizona State U at the West campus (AZ)
Auburn U (AL)
Auburn U at Montgomery (AL)
Averett U (VA)
Azusa Pacific U (CA)
Barnard Coll (NY)
Beloit Coll (WI)
Berry Coll (GA)

Bethel U (IN)
Biola U (CA)
Birmingham-Southern Coll (AL)
Boston Coll (MA)
Bryn Athyn Coll of the New Church (PA)
Bucknell U (PA)
California Lutheran U (CA)
California State U, Bakersfield (CA)
California State U, Long Beach (CA)
Calvin Coll (MI)
Carleton Coll (MN)
Carson-Newman U (TN)
Central Methodist U (MO)
Clark U (MA)
Coe Coll (IA)
The Coll of Wooster (OH)
Cornell Coll (IA)
DePauw U (IN)
Doane U (NE)
Drexel U (PA)
Eastern Oregon U (OR)
Fairleigh Dickinson U (NJ)
FIDM/Fashion Inst of Design & Merchandising, Los Angeles Campus (CA)
Florida A&M U (FL)
Florida Gulf Coast U (FL)
Florida Inst of Technology (FL)
Geneva Coll (PA)
George Fox U (OR)
Georgetown U (DC)
The George Washington U (DC)
Georgian Court U (NJ)
Goshen Coll (IN)
Grinnell Coll (IA)
Gustavus Adolphus Coll (MN)
Harris-Stowe State U (MO)
Hollins U (VA)
Houston Baptist U (TX)
Illinois Coll (IL)
Indiana U Bloomington (IN)
Indiana U East (IN)
Indiana U Kokomo (IN)
Indiana U Northwest (IN)
Indiana U-Purdue U Indianapolis (IN)
Indiana U South Bend (IN)
Indiana U Southeast (IN)
Inter American U of Puerto Rico, Barranquitas Campus (PR)
Iowa State U of Science and Technology (IA)
Jacksonville U (FL)
John Carroll U (OH)
Johns Hopkins U (MD)
Keiser U, Fort Lauderdale (FL)
Keuka Coll (NY)
King U (TN)
Lehman Coll of the City U of New York (NY)
Lewis-Clark State Coll (ID)
Liberty U (VA)
Life U (GA)
Lipscomb U (TN)
Loyola U New Orleans (LA)
Marymount Manhattan Coll (NY)
Merrimack Coll (MA)
MidAmerica Nazarene U (KS)
Millersville U of Pennsylvania (PA)
Misericordia U (PA)
Mississippi State U (MS)
Mount Saint Mary Coll (NY)
Mount Saint Mary's U (CA)
National U (CA)
North Central U (MN)
Northern Arizona U (AZ)
North Greenville U (SC)
Northwestern U (IL)
Northwest U (WA)
Nyack Coll (NY)
Oberlin Coll (OH)
Occidental Coll (CA)
Oglethorpe U (GA)
Ohio Christian U (OH)
Ohio Dominican U (OH)
Oklahoma Baptist U (OK)
Purdue U Fort Wayne (IN)
Purdue U Northwest (IN)
Queens Coll of the City U of New York (NY)
Regis Coll (MA)
Rhode Island Coll (RI)
Rhodes Coll (TN)
Sacred Heart U (CT)
St. Thomas U - New Brunswick (NB, Canada)
Samford U (AL)
Siena Coll (NY)
Sierra Nevada Coll (NV)
Slippery Rock U of Pennsylvania (PA)
Smith Coll (MA)
Southern Illinois U Edwardsville (IL)
Southwestern Coll (KS)
Stanford U (CA)
State U of New York at Fredonia (NY)
State U of New York Coll at Oneonta (NY)
Sterling Coll (KS)
Stevenson U (MD)
Suffolk U (MA)
Tennessee Wesleyan U (TN)
Texas Christian U (TX)
Texas Southern U (TX)
Towson U (MD)
Trinity Coll of Florida (FL)
U at Albany, State U of New York (NY)
The U of Alabama (AL)
The U of Arizona (AZ)
U of Arkansas (AR)
U of California, San Diego (CA)
U of California, Santa Barbara (CA)
U of Central Florida (FL)
U of Colorado Colorado Springs (CO)
U of Dubuque (IA)
U of Hartford (CT)
The U of Iowa (IA)
U of Kentucky (KY)
U of Memphis (TN)
U of Michigan–Flint (MI)
U of Minnesota, Duluth (MN)
U of Montana (MT)
U of New Mexico (NM)
U of North Dakota (ND)
U of North Florida (FL)
U of Portland (OR)
U of Puget Sound (WA)
U of Saint Francis (IN)
U of Saint Mary (KS)
U of Science and Arts of Oklahoma (OK)
U of South Alabama (AL)
The U of Tennessee at Chattanooga (TN)
The U of Texas at Dallas (TX)
U of the Fraser Valley (BC, Canada)
U of the Pacific (CA)
The U of Toledo (OH)
U of Washington, Tacoma (WA)
U of Waterloo (ON, Canada)
The U of West Alabama (AL)
The U of Western Ontario (ON, Canada)
U of West Georgia (GA)
Virginia Wesleyan U (VA)
Warren Wilson Coll (NC)
Wayne State Coll (NE)
Wesleyan Coll (GA)
Western New Mexico U (NM)
Western Oregon U (OR)
Western Washington U (WA)
West Liberty U (WV)
Whitworth U (WA)
William & Mary (VA)
Wittenberg U (OH)
Yeshiva U (NY)

INTERIOR ARCHITECTURE

Auburn U (AL)
Boston Architectural Coll (MA)
Bowling Green State U (OH)
Chatham U (PA)
Colorado State U (CO)
Indiana State U (IN)
La Roche U (PA)
Lawrence Technological U (MI)
Lebanese American U (Lebanon)
Louisiana State U and A&M Coll (LA)
Louisiana Tech U (LA)
Marywood U (PA)
Miami U (OH)
Miami U Hamilton (OH)
Miami U Middletown (OH)
Mississippi State U (MS)
Paier Coll of Art, Inc. (CT)
Sam Houston State U (TX)
Texas Tech U (TX)
U of Houston (TX)
The U of Kansas (KS)
U of Louisiana at Lafayette (LA)
U of Nebraska–Lincoln (NE)
U of Nevada, Las Vegas (NV)
U of Oregon (OR)
U of Southern Mississippi (MS)
The U of Texas at San Antonio (TX)
Woodbury U (CA)

INTERIOR DESIGN

Abilene Christian U (TX)
Academy of Art U (CA)
Anderson U (SC)
Andrews U (MI)
Appalachian State U (NC)
Arizona State U at the Tempe campus (AZ)
Auburn U (AL)
Ball State U (IN)
Baylor U (TX)
Belmont U (TN)
California State U, Fresno (CA)
California State U, Long Beach (CA)
California State U, Sacramento (CA)
Carson-Newman U (TN)
Cazenovia Coll (NY)
Central Michigan U (MI)
Chaminade U of Honolulu (HI)
Cleveland Inst of Art (OH)
Colorado State U (CO)
Columbia Coll Chicago (IL)
Concordia U Wisconsin (WI)
Design Inst of San Diego (CA)
Drexel U (PA)
Dunwoody Coll of Technology (MN)
East Carolina U (NC)
Eastern Michigan U (MI)
Endicott Coll (MA)
Eugene Lang Coll of Liberal Arts (NY)
Fashion Inst of Technology (NY)
Ferris State U (MI)
FIDM/Fashion Inst of Design & Merchandising, Los Angeles Campus (CA)
Florida State U (FL)
Georgia Southern U (GA)
Hampton U (VA)
Harding U (AR)
High Point U (NC)
Howard U (DC)
Illinois State U (IL)
Indiana U Bloomington (IN)
Indiana U of Pennsylvania (PA)
Indiana U-Purdue U Indianapolis (IN)
Iowa State U of Science and Technology (IA)
Kansas State U (KS)
Kean U (NJ)
Lebanese American U (Lebanon)
Liberty U (VA)
Marymount U (VA)
Maryville U of Saint Louis (MO)
Marywood U (PA)
Meredith Coll (NC)
Michigan State U (MI)
Middle Tennessee State U (TN)
New England Inst of Technology (RI)
New Jersey Inst of Technology (NJ)
New York Inst of Technology (NY)
Northern Arizona U (AZ)
The Ohio State U (OH)
Oklahoma State U (OK)
Olivet Nazarene U (IL)
Otis Coll of Art and Design (CA)
Paier Coll of Art, Inc. (CT)
Paris Coll of Art (France)
Parsons School of Design (NY)
Polytechnic U of Puerto Rico (PR)
Pratt Inst (NY)
Queens U of Charlotte (NC)
The Sage Colls (NY)
Samford U (AL)
San Diego State U (CA)
San Francisco State U (CA)
San Jose State U (CA)
School of Visual Arts (NY)
South Dakota State U (SD)
Southern Illinois U Carbondale (IL)
Suffolk U (MA)
Sullivan U (KY)
Texas Christian U (TX)
Texas State U (TX)
The U of Alabama (AL)
U of Arkansas (AR)
U of Central Arkansas (AR)
U of Cincinnati (OH)
U of Idaho (ID)
U of Kentucky (KY)
U of Memphis (TN)
U of Minnesota, Twin Cities Campus (MN)
U of New Haven (CT)
The U of North Carolina at Greensboro (NC)
U of Northern Iowa (IA)
U of North Texas (TX)
The U of Tennessee (TN)
The U of Tennessee at Chattanooga (TN)
U of the Incarnate Word (TX)
U of Wisconsin–Madison (WI)
U of Wisconsin–Stout (WI)
Utah State U (UT)
Valdosta State U (GA)
Virginia Commonwealth U (VA)
Washington State U (WA)
Washington State U–Spokane (WA)
Weber State U (UT)
Wentworth Inst of Technology (MA)
Western Carolina U (NC)
Western Michigan U (MI)

INTERMEDIA/MULTIMEDIA

Bennington Coll (VT)
Biola U (CA)
Calumet Coll of Saint Joseph (IN)
City Coll of the City U of New York (NY)
Columbia Coll Chicago (IL)
Indiana U of Pennsylvania (PA)
Jacksonville U (FL)
Massachusetts Coll of Art and Design (MA)
Missouri State U (MO)
Platt Coll San Diego (CA)
Ramapo Coll of New Jersey (NJ)
State U of New York at Fredonia (NY)
State U of New York Coll of Technology at Alfred (NY)
U of Hartford (CT)
U of Oregon (OR)
U of the Incarnate Word (TX)
The U of Toledo (OH)
Weber State U (UT)

INTERNATIONAL AGRICULTURE

Coll of the Ozarks (MO)
Cornell U (NY)

INTERNATIONAL AND COMPARATIVE EDUCATION

Avila U (MO)

INTERNATIONAL AND INTERCULTURAL COMMUNICATION

The American U of Paris (France)
Becker Coll (MA)
DePaul U (IL)
Johnson U Florida (FL)
Linfield Coll (OR)
Michigan Technological U (MI)
Pepperdine U, Malibu (CA)
Suffolk U (MA)
The U of Western Ontario (ON, Canada)
Utah State U (UT)

INTERNATIONAL BUSINESS/TRADE/COMMERCE

Adams State U (CO)
Alverno Coll (WI)
The American U of Paris (France)
Anderson U (IN)
Anderson U (SC)
Andrews U (MI)
Angelo State U (TX)
Appalachian State U (NC)
Aquinas Coll (MI)
Arcadia U (PA)
Arizona State U at the West campus (AZ)
Assumption Coll (MA)
Auburn U (AL)
Auburn U at Montgomery (AL)
Augsburg U (MN)
Augustana Coll (IL)
Austin Coll (TX)
Avila U (MO)
Azusa Pacific U (CA)
Babson Coll (MA)
Baker U (KS)
Ball State U (IN)
Barry U (FL)
Baruch Coll of the City U of New York (NY)
Baylor U (TX)
Belmont U (TN)
Benedictine Coll (KS)
Benedictine U (IL)
Berry Coll (GA)
Binghamton U, State U of New York (NY)
Biola U (CA)
Birmingham-Southern Coll (AL)
Boise State U (ID)
Bowling Green State U (OH)
Bradley U (IL)
Bridgewater State U (MA)
Bryant U (RI)
Bucknell U (PA)
Butler U (IN)
Caldwell U (NJ)
California State U, Dominguez Hills (CA)
California State U, Fresno (CA)
California State U, Fullerton (CA)
California State U, Long Beach (CA)
California State U, San Marcos (CA)
Carnegie Mellon U (PA)
The Catholic U of America (DC)
Cedarville U (OH)
Central Coll (IA)
Central Michigan U (MI)
Chaminade U of Honolulu (HI)
Champlain Coll (VT)
Chatham U (PA)
Chestnut Hill Coll (PA)
Clarion U of Pennsylvania (PA)
Coll of Charleston (SC)
The Coll of Idaho (ID)
Columbia Coll (MO)
Columbia Coll (SC)
Concordia Coll (MN)
Concordia U, St. Paul (MN)
Concordia U Wisconsin (WI)
Cornell Coll (IA)
Creighton U (NE)
Davenport U, Grand Rapids (MI)
DeSales U (PA)
Dickinson Coll (PA)
Dickinson State U (ND)
Dillard U (LA)
Dominican U (IL)
Drake U (IA)
Drexel U (PA)
D'Youville Coll (NY)
East Central U (OK)
Eastern Mennonite U (VA)
Eastern Michigan U (MI)
Edinboro U of Pennsylvania (PA)
Elms Coll (MA)
Elon U (NC)
Emory & Henry Coll (VA)
Endicott Coll (MA)
Fairfield U (CT)
Farmingdale State Coll (NY)
Flagler Coll (FL)
Florida Atlantic U (FL)
Florida Inst of Technology (FL)
Fordham U (NY)
Fort Lewis Coll (CO)
Framingham State U (MA)
Friends U (KS)
Gannon U (PA)
George Fox U (OR)
Georgetown U (DC)
The George Washington U (DC)
Georgian Court U (NJ)
Georgia Southern U (GA)
Grand Valley State U (MI)
Gustavus Adolphus Coll (MN)
Hamline U (MN)
Harding U (AR)
HEC Montreal (QC, Canada)
High Point U (NC)
Hillsdale Coll (MI)
Hofstra U (NY)

Houston Baptist U (TX)
Howard U (DC)
Husson U (ME)
Illinois State U (IL)
Illinois Wesleyan U (IL)
Indiana U of Pennsylvania (PA)
Iona Coll (NY)
Jacksonville U (FL)
James Madison U (VA)
John Brown U (AR)
John Cabot U (Italy)
John Carroll U (OH)
Kean U (NJ)
Keiser U, Fort Lauderdale (FL)
Kennesaw State U (GA)
King's Coll (PA)
La Roche U (PA)
Lasell Coll (MA)
Lenoir-Rhyne U (NC)
Lewis U (IL)
Lindenwood U (MO)
Linfield Coll (OR)
Lipscomb U (TN)
Louisiana State U and A&M Coll (LA)
Loyola U Chicago (IL)
Loyola U New Orleans (LA)
Lynn U (FL)
Madonna U (MI)
Mansfield U of Pennsylvania (PA)
Marietta Coll (OH)
Marshall U (WV)
Marymount Manhattan Coll (NY)
Maryville U of Saint Louis (MO)
Marywood U (PA)
Massachusetts Maritime Acad (MA)
McMurry U (TX)
Mercer U, Macon (GA)
Merrimack Coll (MA)
Messiah Coll (PA)
Millikin U (IL)
Minnesota State U Mankato (MN)
Minot State U (ND)
Moravian Coll (PA)
Mount Mercy U (IA)
Mount Saint Mary's U (CA)
Mount Vernon Nazarene U (OH)
Muskingum U (OH)
Nebraska Wesleyan U (NE)
New Jersey Inst of Technology (NJ)
New York Inst of Technology (NY)
New York U (NY)
Nichols Coll (MA)
Northeastern State U (OK)
Northern State U (SD)
North Greenville U (SC)
Northwest Christian U (OR)
Northwest Missouri State U (MO)
Northwest Nazarene U (ID)
The Ohio State U (OH)
Ohio Wesleyan U (OH)
Oklahoma Baptist U (OK)
Oklahoma State U (OK)
Olivet Nazarene U (IL)
Oral Roberts U (OK)
Pace U, Pleasantville Campus (NY)
Palm Beach Atlantic U (FL)
Penn State DuBois (PA)
Penn State Erie, The Behrend Coll (PA)
Penn State Harrisburg (PA)
Penn State Lehigh Valley (PA)
Penn State Schuylkill (PA)
Pepperdine U, Malibu (CA)
Pittsburg State U (KS)
Queens Coll of the City U of New York (NY)
Ramapo Coll of New Jersey (NJ)
Rhode Island Coll (RI)
Rhodes Coll (TN)
Richmond, The American Intl U in London (United Kingdom)
Roger Williams U (RI)
Rollins Coll (FL)
Rosemont Coll (PA)
Saginaw Valley State U (MI)
St. Ambrose U (IA)
St. Catherine U (MN)
St. Cloud State U (MN)
Saint Joseph's U (PA)
Saint Louis U (MO)
St. Mary's U (TX)
Saint Mary's U of Minnesota (MN)
St. Norbert Coll (WI)
St. Petersburg Coll (FL)
St. Thomas U - Florida (FL)
Saint Vincent Coll (PA)
Salem State U (MA)
Salisbury U (MD)
Sam Houston State U (TX)
San Diego State U (CA)
San Francisco State U (CA)
San Jose State U (CA)
Seattle U (WA)
Seton Hill U (PA)
Sierra Nevada Coll (NV)
Southeastern U (FL)
Southeast Missouri State U (MO)
Southwest Baptist U (MO)
Spring Hill Coll (AL)
State U of New York at New Paltz (NY)
Stetson U (FL)
Suffolk U (MA)
SUNY Brockport (NY)
Susquehanna U (PA)
Tarleton State U (TX)
Taylor U (IN)
Temple U (PA)
Texas A&M U–Kingsville (TX)
Texas Tech U (TX)
Tiffin U (OH)
Trevecca Nazarene U (TN)
Trine U (IN)
Trinity U (TX)
U at Buffalo, the State U of New York (NY)
The U of Akron (OH)
U of Arkansas (AR)
U of Arkansas at Little Rock (AR)
U of California, San Diego (CA)
U of Cincinnati (OH)
U of Dayton (OH)
U of Denver (CO)
The U of Findlay (OH)
U of Hawaii at Manoa (HI)
U of Houston–Downtown (TX)
U of Jamestown (ND)
U of La Verne (CA)
U of Mary Hardin-Baylor (TX)
U of Memphis (TN)
U of Miami (FL)
U of Michigan–Flint (MI)
U of Minnesota, Twin Cities Campus (MN)
U of Montana (MT)
U of Nebraska–Lincoln (NE)
U of Nevada, Las Vegas (NV)
U of Nevada, Reno (NV)
U of New Haven (CT)
The U of North Carolina at Charlotte (NC)
The U of North Carolina at Greensboro (NC)
U of North Florida (FL)
U of Northwestern–St. Paul (MN)
U of Pennsylvania (PA)
U of Portland (OR)
U of Puget Sound (WA)
U of St. Francis (IL)
U of San Diego (CA)
U of San Francisco (CA)
The U of Scranton (PA)
U of South Alabama (AL)
U of South Carolina (SC)
U of Southern Mississippi (MS)
U of South Florida (FL)
U of South Florida, St. Petersburg (FL)
The U of Tampa (FL)
The U of Texas at Dallas (TX)
The U of Texas at El Paso (TX)
The U of Texas at San Antonio (TX)
The U of Texas Rio Grande Valley (TX)
U of the Incarnate Word (TX)
The U of Toledo (OH)
The U of Tulsa (OK)
U of Waterloo (ON, Canada)
The U of Western Ontario (ON, Canada)
U of Wisconsin–Eau Claire (WI)
U of Wisconsin–La Crosse (WI)
U of Wisconsin–Madison (WI)
U of Wisconsin–Superior (WI)
Utah State U (UT)
Utica Coll (NY)
Valdosta State U (GA)
Valparaiso U (IN)
Villanova U (PA)
Walla Walla U (WA)
Wartburg Coll (IA)
Washington & Jefferson Coll (PA)
Washington State U (WA)
Waynesburg U (PA)
Wayne State U (MI)
Wesleyan Coll (GA)
West Chester U of Pennsylvania (PA)
Western Kentucky U (KY)
Western Washington U (WA)
Westminster Coll (UT)
Wichita State U (KS)
Widener U (PA)
William Paterson U of New Jersey (NJ)
Worcester State U (MA)
Wright State U (OH)
Xavier U (OH)
Yeshiva U (NY)

INTERNATIONAL ECONOMICS
Albion Coll (MI)
The American U of Paris (France)
Austin Coll (TX)
Belmont U (TN)
Carthage Coll (WI)
The Coll of Idaho (ID)
The Colorado Coll (CO)
Elon U (NC)
Fitchburg State U (MA)
Georgetown U (DC)
Georgia State U (GA)
HEC Montreal (QC, Canada)
Howard U (DC)
Rhodes Coll (TN)
St. Catherine U (MN)
Salve Regina U (RI)
State U of New York at Oswego (NY)
Suffolk U (MA)
Susquehanna U (PA)
Texas Christian U (TX)
Texas Tech U (TX)
Trinity U (TX)
U of California, San Diego (CA)
U of California, Santa Cruz (CA)
U of New Haven (CT)
U of Puget Sound (WA)
U of Richmond (VA)
U of West Georgia (GA)
Valparaiso U (IN)
Washington U in St. Louis (MO)
Weber State U (UT)
Youngstown State U (OH)

INTERNATIONAL FINANCE
The American U of Paris (France)
Babson Coll (MA)
Brigham Young U (UT)
The Catholic U of America (DC)
HEC Montreal (QC, Canada)
Lenoir-Rhyne U (NC)
U of New Haven (CT)
Washington U in St. Louis (MO)

INTERNATIONAL/GLOBAL STUDIES
Abilene Christian U (TX)
Albion Coll (MI)
Alfred U (NY)
American Public U System (WV)
Andrews U (MI)
Appalachian State U (NC)
Arcadia U (PA)
Arizona State U at the Tempe campus (AZ)
Arkansas Tech U (AR)
Assumption Coll (MA)
Baker U (KS)
Belhaven U (MS)
Bemidji State U (MN)
Benedictine Coll (KS)
Benedictine U (IL)
Bennington Coll (VT)
Bentley U (MA)
Boston Coll (MA)
Bowling Green State U (OH)
Brandeis U (MA)
Bryant U (RI)
California Baptist U (CA)
California Lutheran U (CA)
California State U, San Marcos (CA)
Carnegie Mellon U (PA)
Cazenovia Coll (NY)
Cedar Crest Coll (PA)
Cedarville U (OH)
Central Coll (IA)
Central Connecticut State U (CT)
Centre Coll (KY)
Chatham U (PA)
Chestnut Hill Coll (PA)
City Coll of the City U of New York (NY)
Colby Coll (ME)
Coll of Charleston (SC)
Coll of Saint Elizabeth (NJ)
The Coll of St. Scholastica (MN)
Coll of Staten Island of the City U of New York (NY)
Coll of the Holy Cross (MA)
Colorado State U (CO)
Columbia Intl U (SC)
Concordia Coll (MN)
Culver-Stockton Coll (MO)
Dean Coll (MA)
Doane U (NE)
Dominican U of California (CA)
Drexel U (PA)
Eastern Kentucky U (KY)
Eastern Mennonite U (VA)
East Texas Baptist U (TX)
Emmanuel Coll (MA)
Emory & Henry Coll (VA)
Eugene Lang Coll of Liberal Arts (NY)
Flagler Coll (FL)
Framingham State U (MA)
Gannon U (PA)
George Fox U (OR)
Georgetown Coll (KY)
Georgia Inst of Technology (GA)
Graceland U (IA)
Grand Valley State U (MI)
Guilford Coll (NC)
Hamline U (MN)
Hampshire Coll (MA)
Hanover Coll (IN)
Harding U (AR)
Hofstra U (NY)
Hope Coll (MI)
Illinois Wesleyan U (IL)
Iowa State U of Science and Technology (IA)
John Brown U (AR)
Kean U (NJ)
Kenyon Coll (OH)
Knox Coll (IL)
Lasell Coll (MA)
La Sierra U (CA)
Lawrence U (WI)
Lee U (TN)
Lehigh U (PA)
Le Moyne Coll (NY)
Liberty U (VA)
Linfield Coll (OR)
Louisiana State U and A&M Coll (LA)
Malone U (OH)
Manhattanville Coll (NY)
Marymount Manhattan Coll (NY)
Maryville U of Saint Louis (MO)
McKendree U (IL)
Mercer U, Macon (GA)
Meredith Coll (NC)
Merrimack Coll (MA)
Miami U (OH)
Miami U Hamilton (OH)
Miami U Middletown (OH)
Michigan State U (MI)
Middle Tennessee State U (TN)
Milligan Coll (TN)
Missouri State U (MO)
Morehead State U (KY)
Multnomah U (OR)
National U (CA)
Nebraska Wesleyan U (NE)
New Coll of Florida (FL)
New York U (NY)
Northwest U (WA)
The Ohio State U (OH)
Oklahoma State U (OK)
Pace U, Pleasantville Campus (NY)
Pepperdine U, Malibu (CA)
Pitzer Coll (CA)
Point Loma Nazarene U (CA)
Portland State U (OR)
Providence Coll (RI)
Ramapo Coll of New Jersey (NJ)
Randolph Coll (VA)
Regent U (VA)
Rhode Island Coll (RI)
Roger Williams U (RI)
Rowan U (NJ)
Saginaw Valley State U (MI)
St. Bonaventure U (NY)
St. Cloud State U (MN)
Saint Leo U (FL)
Saint Mary's Coll (IN)
Saint Mary's Coll of California (CA)
Saint Mary's U of Minnesota (MN)
St. Norbert Coll (WI)
St. Thomas U - Florida (FL)
Salisbury U (MD)
Salve Regina U (RI)
Sarah Lawrence Coll (NY)
Seattle U (WA)
Sierra Nevada Coll (NV)
South Dakota State U (SD)
Southeast Missouri State U (MO)
Southern Illinois U Edwardsville (IL)
Southern Methodist U (TX)
Spring Arbor U (MI)
State U of New York Coll at Cortland (NY)
State U of New York Coll at Potsdam (NY)
Stony Brook U, State U of New York (NY)
Tabor Coll (KS)
Tarleton State U (TX)
Tennessee Wesleyan U (TN)
Texas A&M U (TX)
Texas State U (TX)
Texas Tech U (TX)
U at Albany, State U of New York (NY)
The U of Arizona (AZ)
U of California, Irvine (CA)
U of California, Los Angeles (CA)
U of California, Riverside (CA)
U of California, Santa Barbara (CA)
U of Central Arkansas (AR)
U of Central Florida (FL)
U of Colorado Boulder (CO)
U of Colorado Denver (CO)
U of Dayton (OH)
U of Illinois at Springfield (IL)
The U of Iowa (IA)
The U of Kansas (KS)
U of Kentucky (KY)
U of Maryland, Baltimore County (MD)
U of Michigan (MI)
U of Nebraska–Lincoln (NE)
U of New England (ME)
U of New Haven (CT)
U of New Mexico (NM)
The U of North Carolina at Charlotte (NC)
The U of North Carolina Wilmington (NC)
U of North Dakota (ND)
U of Northern Colorado (CO)
U of Northern Iowa (IA)
U of North Florida (FL)
U of North Texas (TX)
U of Notre Dame (IN)
U of Oregon (OR)
U of Pennsylvania (PA)
U of Saint Joseph (CT)
U of South Alabama (AL)
U of South Dakota (SD)
The U of Tampa (FL)
The U of the South (TN)
U of Utah (UT)
U of Vermont (VT)
U of Washington, Bothell (WA)
U of Washington, Tacoma (WA)
U of Waterloo (ON, Canada)
U of Wisconsin–Madison (WI)
U of Wisconsin–Milwaukee (WI)
U of Wisconsin–Platteville (WI)
U of Wyoming (WY)
Valparaiso U (IN)
Villanova U (PA)
Warren Wilson Coll (NC)
Washington & Jefferson Coll (PA)
Western Carolina U (NC)
Western Michigan U (MI)
Western New England U (MA)
Willamette U (OR)
William Peace U (NC)
Worcester State U (MA)
Wright State U (OH)
Wright State U–Lake Campus (OH)

INTERNATIONAL MARKETING
Fashion Inst of Technology (NY)
Husson U (ME)

Oklahoma Baptist U (OK)
Oral Roberts U (OK)
Pace U, Pleasantville Campus (NY)
U of New Haven (CT)
U of Northern Iowa (IA)

INTERNATIONAL POLICY ANALYSIS
Southern Methodist U (TX)
Waynesburg U (PA)

INTERNATIONAL PUBLIC HEALTH
Allegheny Coll (PA)
American U (DC)
Bethel U (IN)
California Baptist U (CA)
La Sierra U (CA)
Mercer U, Macon (GA)
U of California, San Diego (CA)
The U of Iowa (IA)

INTERNATIONAL RELATIONS AND AFFAIRS
Agnes Scott Coll (GA)
Allegheny Coll (PA)
Alverno Coll (WI)
American Coll of Thessaloniki (Greece)
American U (DC)
Anderson U (IN)
Aquinas Coll (MI)
Augsburg U (MN)
Augustana U (SD)
Austin Coll (TX)
Azusa Pacific U (CA)
Barry U (FL)
Baylor U (TX)
Belmont U (TN)
Beloit Coll (WI)
Benedictine U (IL)
Bennington Coll (VT)
Berry Coll (GA)
Bethel U (MN)
Binghamton U, State U of New York (NY)
Bowling Green State U (OH)
Bradley U (IL)
Bridgewater Coll (VA)
Bridgewater State U (MA)
Brown U (RI)
Bucknell U (PA)
Butler U (IN)
California Lutheran U (CA)
California State U, Long Beach (CA)
California State U, Monterey Bay (CA)
California State U, San Marcos (CA)
Calvin Coll (MI)
Capital U (OH)
Carleton Coll (MN)
Carnegie Mellon U (PA)
Central Michigan U (MI)
Chaminade U of Honolulu (HI)
Chatham U (PA)
City Coll of the City U of New York (NY)
Claremont McKenna Coll (CA)
Clark U (MA)
Colgate U (NY)
The Coll of Idaho (ID)
The Coll of Wooster (OH)
Cornell Coll (IA)
Creighton U (NE)
DePaul U (IL)
Dickinson Coll (PA)
Dominican U (IL)
Drake U (IA)
Drew U (NJ)
Earlham Coll (IN)
Eastern Michigan U (MI)
Eastern Washington U (WA)
Elon U (NC)
Emmanuel Coll (MA)
Emory U (GA)
Fairfield U (CT)
Fairleigh Dickinson U (NJ)
Fitchburg State U (MA)
Florida State U (FL)
Fordham U (NY)
George Mason U (VA)
Georgetown U (DC)
The George Washington U (DC)
Georgia Inst of Technology (GA)
Georgia Southern U (GA)
Gonzaga U (WA)
Gordon Coll (MA)
Goucher Coll (MD)
Grand Valley State U (MI)
Hampden-Sydney Coll (VA)
Hampshire Coll (MA)
High Point U (NC)
Hobart and William Smith Colls (NY)
Hollins U (VA)
Illinois Coll (IL)
Illinois Wesleyan U (IL)
Immaculata U (PA)
Indiana U Bloomington (IN)
Indiana U East (IN)
Indiana U of Pennsylvania (PA)
Indiana U-Purdue U Indianapolis (IN)
Indiana U Southeast (IN)
Intl U in Geneva (Switzerland)
Iona Coll (NY)
James Madison U (VA)
John Cabot U (Italy)
Johns Hopkins U (MD)
Kalamazoo Coll (MI)
Kennesaw State U (GA)
Knox Coll (IL)
Lafayette Coll (PA)
Lake Forest Coll (IL)
La Roche U (PA)
Lebanese American U (Lebanon)
Lehigh U (PA)
Lenoir-Rhyne U (NC)
Lewis & Clark Coll (OR)
Lewis U (IL)
Liberty U (VA)
Lindenwood U (MO)
Linfield Coll (OR)
Lock Haven U of Pennsylvania (PA)
Loras Coll (IA)
Loyola Marymount U (CA)
Loyola U Chicago (IL)
Manhattan Coll (NY)
Marquette U (WI)
Marshall U (WV)
McKendree U (IL)
Mercer U, Macon (GA)
Mercy Coll (NY)
Meredith Coll (NC)
Miami U (OH)
Miami U Hamilton (OH)
Miami U Middletown (OH)
Michigan State U (MI)
Middlebury Coll (VT)
Middle Tennessee State U (TN)
Minnesota State U Mankato (MN)
Missouri Southern State U (MO)
Mount Holyoke Coll (MA)
Mount Mercy U (IA)
Mount St. Mary's U (MD)
Muhlenberg Coll (PA)
Murray State U (KY)
Muskingum U (OH)
Nazareth Coll of Rochester (NY)
New York U (NY)
Niagara U (NY)
Northern Arizona U (AZ)
Northern Kentucky U (KY)
Northwestern U (IL)
Northwest Nazarene U (ID)
Nova Southeastern U (FL)
Oakland U (MI)
Occidental Coll (CA)
Oglethorpe U (GA)
The Ohio State U (OH)
Ohio Wesleyan U (OH)
Oklahoma Baptist U (OK)
Old Dominion U (VA)
Oral Roberts U (OK)
Pacific U (OR)
Penn State Abington (PA)
Penn State Altoona (PA)
Penn State Beaver (PA)
Penn State Berks (PA)
Penn State Brandywine (PA)
Penn State DuBois (PA)
Penn State Erie, The Behrend Coll (PA)
Penn State Fayette, The Eberly Campus (PA)
Penn State Greater Allegheny (PA)
Penn State Hazleton (PA)
Penn State Lehigh Valley (PA)
Penn State Mont Alto (PA)
Penn State New Kensington (PA)
Penn State Schuylkill (PA)
Penn State Shenango (PA)
Penn State U Park (PA)
Penn State Wilkes-Barre (PA)
Penn State York (PA)
Pomona Coll (CA)
Portland State U (OR)
Queens U of Charlotte (NC)
Randolph-Macon Coll (VA)
Richmond, The American Intl U in London (United Kingdom)
Roanoke Coll (VA)
Roger Williams U (RI)
Rollins Coll (FL)
Saginaw Valley State U (MI)
St. Catherine U (MN)
St. Cloud State U (MN)
St. John Fisher Coll (NY)
Saint Joseph's U (PA)
Saint Louis U (MO)
St. Mary's U (TX)
St. Norbert Coll (WI)
St. Thomas U - New Brunswick (NB, Canada)
Samford U (AL)
San Diego State U (CA)
San Francisco State U (CA)
Sarah Lawrence Coll (NY)
Seton Hill U (PA)
Simmons U (MA)
Skidmore Coll (NY)
Southwestern U (TX)
Spring Hill Coll (AL)
Stanford U (CA)
State U of New York at New Paltz (NY)
State U of New York at Oswego (NY)
State U of New York Coll at Cortland (NY)
State U of New York Coll at Geneseo (NY)
State U of New York Coll at Oneonta (NY)
State U of New York Coll at Potsdam (NY)
Stetson U (FL)
SUNY Brockport (NY)
Susquehanna U (PA)
Taylor U (IN)
Texas Christian U (TX)
Texas State U (TX)
Tiffin U (OH)
Towson U (MD)
Trinity U (TX)
Tulane U (LA)
United States Military Acad (NY)
The U of Alabama (AL)
U of Arkansas (AR)
U of California, Riverside (CA)
U of Cincinnati (OH)
U of Denver (CO)
U of Hartford (CT)
U of Idaho (ID)
U of La Verne (CA)
U of Maine (ME)
U of Mary Washington (VA)
U of Massachusetts Boston (MA)
U of Memphis (TN)
U of Miami (FL)
U of Minnesota, Duluth (MN)
U of Minnesota, Twin Cities Campus (MN)
U of Missouri–St. Louis (MO)
U of Nebraska at Kearney (NE)
U of Nebraska–Lincoln (NE)
U of Nevada, Reno (NV)
U of New Hampshire (NH)
U of New Haven (CT)
U of Pennsylvania (PA)
U of Pittsburgh at Bradford (PA)
U of Puget Sound (WA)
U of Richmond (VA)
U of St. Thomas (TX)
U of San Diego (CA)
U of San Francisco (CA)
The U of Scranton (PA)
U of South Carolina (SC)
U of Southern Indiana (IN)
U of Southern Mississippi (MS)
U of South Florida (FL)
The U of Tennessee at Martin (TN)
U of the Incarnate Word (TX)
U of the Pacific (CA)
The U of Toledo (OH)
U of Toronto (ON, Canada)
U of Virginia (VA)
U of Waterloo (ON, Canada)
The U of Western Ontario (ON, Canada)
U of West Florida (FL)
U of West Georgia (GA)
U of Wisconsin–Parkside (WI)
Utica Coll (NY)
Valparaiso U (IN)
Virginia Wesleyan U (VA)
Wartburg Coll (IA)
Washington Coll (MD)
Washington State U (WA)
Washington U in St. Louis (MO)
Western Kentucky U (KY)
Western Oregon U (OR)
Wheaton Coll (IL)
Wheaton Coll (MA)
Whitworth U (WA)
Widener U (PA)
Wilkes U (PA)
William & Mary (VA)
William Jewell Coll (MO)
Wittenberg U (OH)
Worcester Polytechnic Inst (MA)
Xavier U (OH)
Yale U (CT)
York Coll of Pennsylvania (PA)

INTERNATIONAL RELATIONS AND NATIONAL SECURITY RELATED
Fayetteville State U (NC)
Indiana U Bloomington (IN)
King U (TN)
Middlebury Coll (VT)
San Diego State U (CA)

INVESTMENTS AND SECURITIES
Babson Coll (MA)
Lynn U (FL)
Marymount Manhattan Coll (NY)
U of Nebraska–Lincoln (NE)
U of North Dakota (ND)
U of Northern Iowa (IA)

IRANIAN LANGUAGES
United States Military Acad (NY)
U of Utah (UT)

ISLAMIC STUDIES
Boston Coll (MA)
DePaul U (IL)
The Ohio State U (OH)
San Diego State U (CA)
Sarah Lawrence Coll (NY)
U of Washington (WA)
The U of Western Ontario (ON, Canada)
Villanova U (PA)
Washington U in St. Louis (MO)

ITALIAN
Arizona State U at the Tempe campus (AZ)
Barnard Coll (NY)
Bennington Coll (VT)
Binghamton U, State U of New York (NY)
Boston Coll (MA)
Bowdoin Coll (ME)
California State U, Long Beach (CA)
Central Connecticut State U (CT)
Coll of the Holy Cross (MA)
The Colorado Coll (CO)
Cornell U (NY)
Dartmouth Coll (NH)
DePaul U (IL)
Dominican U (IL)
Drew U (NJ)
Fairfield U (CT)
Florida State U (FL)
Fordham U (NY)
Georgetown U (DC)
Gonzaga U (WA)
Hofstra U (NY)
Indiana U Bloomington (IN)
Iona Coll (NY)
Ithaca Coll (NY)
Johns Hopkins U (MD)
Lehman Coll of the City U of New York (NY)
Loyola U Chicago (IL)
Middlebury Coll (VT)
Montclair State U (NJ)
Mount Holyoke Coll (MA)
Nazareth Coll of Rochester (NY)
New York U (NY)
Northwestern U (IL)
The Ohio State U (OH)
Penn State Abington (PA)
Penn State Altoona (PA)
Penn State Beaver (PA)
Penn State Berks (PA)
Penn State Brandywine (PA)
Penn State DuBois (PA)
Penn State Erie, The Behrend Coll (PA)
Penn State Fayette, The Eberly Campus (PA)
Penn State Greater Allegheny (PA)
Penn State Hazleton (PA)
Penn State Lehigh Valley (PA)
Penn State Mont Alto (PA)
Penn State New Kensington (PA)
Penn State Schuylkill (PA)
Penn State Shenango (PA)
Penn State U Park (PA)
Penn State Wilkes-Barre (PA)
Penn State York (PA)
Pepperdine U, Malibu (CA)
Providence Coll (RI)
Queens Coll of the City U of New York (NY)
Saint Joseph's U (PA)
Saint Louis U (MO)
Saint Mary's Coll of California (CA)
San Francisco State U (CA)
Santa Clara U (CA)
Sarah Lawrence Coll (NY)
Scripps Coll (CA)
Smith Coll (MA)
Stanford U (CA)
Stony Brook U, State U of New York (NY)
Temple U (PA)
Tulane U (LA)
U at Buffalo, the State U of New York (NY)
The U of Arizona (AZ)
U of California, Berkeley (CA)
U of California, Los Angeles (CA)
U of California, San Diego (CA)
U of Colorado Boulder (CO)
U of Dallas (TX)
U of Denver (CO)
U of Illinois at Chicago (IL)
The U of Iowa (IA)
U of Massachusetts Amherst (MA)
U of Massachusetts Boston (MA)
U of Michigan (MI)
U of Minnesota, Twin Cities Campus (MN)
U of New Hampshire (NH)
U of Notre Dame (IN)
U of Oregon (OR)
U of Pennsylvania (PA)
U of San Francisco (CA)
The U of Scranton (PA)
U of South Florida (FL)
The U of Tennessee (TN)
U of Toronto (ON, Canada)
U of Virginia (VA)
U of Washington (WA)
The U of Western Ontario (ON, Canada)
U of Wisconsin–Madison (WI)
U of Wisconsin–Milwaukee (WI)
Villanova U (PA)
Washington U in St. Louis (MO)
Yale U (CT)
Youngstown State U (OH)

ITALIAN STUDIES
Arcadia U (PA)
Bowdoin Coll (ME)
Brown U (RI)
The Colorado Coll (CO)
Dickinson Coll (PA)
Emory U (GA)
Fordham U (NY)
John Cabot U (Italy)
Merrimack Coll (MA)
Miami U (OH)
Miami U Hamilton (OH)
Miami U Middletown (OH)
The Ohio State U (OH)
Saint Joseph's U (PA)
Scripps Coll (CA)
Southern Methodist U (TX)
Tulane U (LA)
U of California, Santa Barbara (CA)
U of California, Santa Cruz (CA)
U of Richmond (VA)
U of San Diego (CA)
U of Vermont (VT)

The U of Western Ontario (ON, Canada)
Wesleyan U (CT)
Wheaton Coll (MA)

JAPANESE
Ball State U (IN)
Bates Coll (ME)
Beloit Coll (WI)
Bennington Coll (VT)
California State U, Fullerton (CA)
California State U, Long Beach (CA)
California State U, Los Angeles (CA)
California State U, Monterey Bay (CA)
Calvin Coll (MI)
Carnegie Mellon U (PA)
Carthage Coll (WI)
Central Washington U (WA)
Colgate U (NY)
Dartmouth Coll (NH)
Dickinson Coll (PA)
Earlham Coll (IN)
Eastern Michigan U (MI)
Emory U (GA)
Florida State U (FL)
Georgetown U (DC)
Gustavus Adolphus Coll (MN)
Hobart and William Smith Colls (NY)
Hofstra U (NY)
Lehigh U (PA)
Linfield Coll (OR)
Michigan State U (MI)
Middlebury Coll (VT)
Murray State U (KY)
Northern Kentucky U (KY)
Oakland U (MI)
Occidental Coll (CA)
The Ohio State U (OH)
Pacific U (OR)
Penn State Abington (PA)
Penn State Altoona (PA)
Penn State Beaver (PA)
Penn State Berks (PA)
Penn State Brandywine (PA)
Penn State DuBois (PA)
Penn State Erie, The Behrend Coll (PA)
Penn State Fayette, The Eberly Campus (PA)
Penn State Greater Allegheny (PA)
Penn State Hazleton (PA)
Penn State Lehigh Valley (PA)
Penn State Mont Alto (PA)
Penn State New Kensington (PA)
Penn State Schuylkill (PA)
Penn State Shenango (PA)
Penn State U Park (PA)
Penn State Wilkes-Barre (PA)
Penn State York (PA)
Pomona Coll (CA)
Portland State U (OR)
Saint Mary's Coll of California (CA)
St. Olaf Coll (MN)
San Diego State U (CA)
San Francisco State U (CA)
San Jose State U (CA)
Sarah Lawrence Coll (NY)
Scripps Coll (CA)
Stanford U (CA)
Temple U (PA)
U of Alaska Fairbanks (AK)
U of California, Berkeley (CA)
U of California, Irvine (CA)
U of California, Los Angeles (CA)
U of California, Riverside (CA)
U of California, San Diego (CA)
U of California, Santa Barbara (CA)
U of Colorado Boulder (CO)
The U of Findlay (OH)
U of Hawaii at Manoa (HI)
The U of Iowa (IA)
U of Kentucky (KY)
U of Massachusetts Amherst (MA)
U of Montana (MT)
The U of North Carolina at Charlotte (NC)
U of North Texas (TX)
U of Notre Dame (IN)
U of Oregon (OR)
U of Puget Sound (WA)
U of San Francisco (CA)
U of the Pacific (CA)
U of Utah (UT)
U of Vermont (VT)
U of Washington (WA)
The U of Western Ontario (ON, Canada)
U of Wisconsin–Madison (WI)
Wake Forest U (NC)
Washington State U (WA)
Washington U in St. Louis (MO)
Western Michigan U (MI)
Western Washington U (WA)
William & Mary (VA)
Williams Coll (MA)
Yale U (CT)

JAPANESE STUDIES
DePaul U (IL)
Earlham Coll (IN)
Gustavus Adolphus Coll (MN)
Hofstra U (NY)
Hope Coll (MI)
Linfield Coll (OR)
Oakland U (MI)
U at Albany, State U of New York (NY)
U of California, San Diego (CA)
U of Washington (WA)
Willamette U (OR)

JAZZ/JAZZ STUDIES
Berklee Coll of Music (MA)
Brigham Young U (UT)
Butler U (IN)
Capital U (OH)
Central State U (OH)
Central Washington U (WA)
City Coll of the City U of New York (NY)
DePaul U (IL)
Drake U (IA)
Eugene Lang Coll of Liberal Arts (NY)
Florida State U (FL)
Hampton U (VA)
Hofstra U (NY)
Hope Coll (MI)
Ithaca Coll (NY)
Jacksonville U (FL)
Limestone Coll (SC)
Loyola U New Orleans (LA)
Manhattan School of Music (NY)
Michigan State U (MI)
The New School Coll of Performing Arts (NY)
North Carolina Central U (NC)
Northwestern U (IL)
Oberlin Coll (OH)
The Ohio State U (OH)
Shenandoah U (VA)
Temple U (PA)
The U of Akron (OH)
The U of Arizona (AZ)
U of Hartford (CT)
The U of Iowa (IA)
U of Maryland, Baltimore County (MD)
U of Miami (FL)
U of Michigan (MI)
U of Northern Iowa (IA)
U of North Florida (FL)
U of North Texas (TX)
U of Oregon (OR)
U of Washington (WA)
U of Wyoming (WY)
Western Michigan U (MI)
Whitworth U (WA)
Youngstown State U (OH)

JEWISH/JUDAIC STUDIES
American U (DC)
Arizona State U at the Tempe campus (AZ)
Barnard Coll (NY)
Bennington Coll (VT)
Binghamton U, State U of New York (NY)
Brown U (RI)
California State U, Northridge (CA)
City Coll of the City U of New York (NY)
Clark U (MA)
Coll of Charleston (SC)
Dickinson Coll (PA)
Emory U (GA)
Florida Atlantic U (FL)
The George Washington U (DC)
Hofstra U (NY)
Indiana U Bloomington (IN)
Lehman Coll of the City U of New York (NY)
Muhlenberg Coll (PA)
Ner Israel Yeshiva Coll of Toronto (ON, Canada)
Oberlin Coll (OH)
The Ohio State U (OH)
Penn State Abington (PA)
Penn State Altoona (PA)
Penn State Beaver (PA)
Penn State Berks (PA)
Penn State Brandywine (PA)
Penn State DuBois (PA)
Penn State Erie, The Behrend Coll (PA)
Penn State Fayette, The Eberly Campus (PA)
Penn State Greater Allegheny (PA)
Penn State Hazleton (PA)
Penn State Lehigh Valley (PA)
Penn State Mont Alto (PA)
Penn State New Kensington (PA)
Penn State Schuylkill (PA)
Penn State Shenango (PA)
Penn State U Park (PA)
Penn State Wilkes-Barre (PA)
Penn State York (PA)
Portland State U (OR)
Queens Coll of the City U of New York (NY)
San Diego State U (CA)
San Francisco State U (CA)
Sarah Lawrence Coll (NY)
Scripps Coll (CA)
Temple U (PA)
Tulane U (LA)
U at Buffalo, the State U of New York (NY)
The U of Arizona (AZ)
U of California, Los Angeles (CA)
U of California, San Diego (CA)
U of California, Santa Cruz (CA)
U of Colorado Boulder (CO)
U of Hartford (CT)
The U of Kansas (KS)
U of Massachusetts Amherst (MA)
U of Miami (FL)
U of Michigan (MI)
U of Minnesota, Twin Cities Campus (MN)
U of Oregon (OR)
U of Pennsylvania (PA)
U of Washington (WA)
The U of Western Ontario (ON, Canada)
U of Wisconsin–Madison (WI)
U of Wisconsin–Milwaukee (WI)
Vanderbilt U (TN)
Washington U in St. Louis (MO)
Yale U (CT)
Yeshiva U (NY)

JOURNALISM
Academy of Art U (CA)
American U (DC)
The American U of Paris (France)
Andrews U (MI)
Angelo State U (TX)
Appalachian State U (NC)
Arkansas Tech U (AR)
Auburn U (AL)
Augustana U (SD)
Austin Peay State U (TN)
Averett U (VA)
Ball State U (IN)
Barry U (FL)
Baruch Coll of the City U of New York (NY)
Bayamón Central U (PR)
Baylor U (TX)
Belmont U (TN)
Benedictine Coll (KS)
Bennington Coll (VT)
Bethel U (MN)
Biola U (CA)
Bowling Green State U (OH)
Bradley U (IL)
Brigham Young U (UT)
Butler U (IN)
California Baptist U (CA)
California Lutheran U (CA)
California Polytechnic State U, San Luis Obispo (CA)
California State U, Dominguez Hills (CA)
California State U, Fresno (CA)
California State U, Fullerton (CA)
California State U, Long Beach (CA)
California State U, Northridge (CA)
California State U, Sacramento (CA)
Campbellsville U (KY)
Cedarville U (OH)
Central Connecticut State U (CT)
Central Michigan U (MI)
Central State U (OH)
Central Washington U (WA)
Chatham U (PA)
The Coll of St. Scholastica (MN)
Coll of the Ozarks (MO)
Colorado State U (CO)
Columbia Coll Chicago (IL)
Concordia U Chicago (IL)
Creighton U (NE)
DePaul U (IL)
Doane U (NE)
Dominican U (IL)
Drake U (IA)
Drury U (MO)
East Central U (OK)
Eastern Illinois U (IL)
Eastern Kentucky U (KY)
Eastern Michigan U (MI)
Eastern Washington U (WA)
Edinboro U of Pennsylvania (PA)
Elon U (NC)
Flagler Coll (FL)
Florida A&M U (FL)
Fordham U (NY)
Fort Lewis Coll (CO)
Franklin Coll (IN)
Freed-Hardeman U (TN)
Gannon U (PA)
George Fox U (OR)
The George Washington U (DC)
Georgia Coll & State U (GA)
Georgia Southern U (GA)
Georgia State U (GA)
Gonzaga U (WA)
Goshen Coll (IN)
Grand Valley State U (MI)
Hampton U (VA)
Harding U (AR)
High Point U (NC)
Hofstra U (NY)
Howard U (DC)
Illinois State U (IL)
Indiana U Bloomington (IN)
Indiana U of Pennsylvania (PA)
Indiana U-Purdue U Indianapolis (IN)
Indiana U Southeast (IN)
Iona Coll (NY)
Iowa State U of Science and Technology (IA)
Ithaca Coll (NY)
Kansas State U (KS)
Kennesaw State U (GA)
Lebanese American U (Lebanon)
Lehigh U (PA)
Lewis U (IL)
Liberty U (VA)
Lincoln U (MO)
Lindenwood U (MO)
Louisiana Tech U (LA)
Loyola Marymount U (CA)
Loyola U Chicago (IL)
Loyola U New Orleans (LA)
Madonna U (MI)
Marietta Coll (OH)
Marquette U (WI)
Marshall U (WV)
Marymount Manhattan Coll (NY)
Mercer U, Macon (GA)
Mercy Coll (NY)
Messiah Coll (PA)
Miami U (OH)
Miami U Hamilton (OH)
Miami U Middletown (OH)
Michigan State U (MI)
Middle Tennessee State U (TN)
Minnesota State U Mankato (MN)
Montclair State U (NJ)
Mount Mercy U (IA)
Mount Saint Mary Coll (NY)
Mount Saint Mary's U (CA)
Mount Vernon Nazarene U (OH)
Murray State U (KY)
Muskingum U (OH)
New England Coll (NH)
New York U (NY)
North Central U (MN)
Northeastern State U (OK)
Northern Arizona U (AZ)
Northern Illinois U (IL)
Northern Kentucky U (KY)
North Greenville U (SC)
Northwestern U (IL)
Oakland U (MI)
The Ohio State U (OH)
Ohio Wesleyan U (OH)
Oklahoma Baptist U (OK)
Pace U, Pleasantville Campus (NY)
Pacific U (OR)
Palm Beach Atlantic U (FL)
Patrick Henry Coll (VA)
Penn State Abington (PA)
Penn State Altoona (PA)
Penn State Beaver (PA)
Penn State Berks (PA)
Penn State Brandywine (PA)
Penn State DuBois (PA)
Penn State Erie, The Behrend Coll (PA)
Penn State Fayette, The Eberly Campus (PA)
Penn State Greater Allegheny (PA)
Penn State Hazleton (PA)
Penn State Lehigh Valley (PA)
Penn State Mont Alto (PA)
Penn State New Kensington (PA)
Penn State Schuylkill (PA)
Penn State Shenango (PA)
Penn State U Park (PA)
Penn State Wilkes-Barre (PA)
Penn State York (PA)
Pepperdine U, Malibu (CA)
Point Loma Nazarene U (CA)
Purchase Coll, State U of New York (NY)
Radford U (VA)
Rowan U (NJ)
St. Ambrose U (IA)
St. Bonaventure U (NY)
St. Catherine U (MN)
St. Thomas U - New Brunswick (NB, Canada)
Salem State U (MA)
Samford U (AL)
Sam Houston State U (TX)
San Diego State U (CA)
San Francisco State U (CA)
San Jose State U (CA)
Seattle U (WA)
Seton Hill U (PA)
South Dakota State U (SD)
Southeastern U (FL)
Southern Arkansas U–Magnolia (AR)
Southern Illinois U Carbondale (IL)
Southern Methodist U (TX)
Spring Hill Coll (AL)
State U of New York at New Paltz (NY)
State U of New York at Oswego (NY)
Stony Brook U, State U of New York (NY)
Suffolk U (MA)
Susquehanna U (PA)
Taylor U (IN)
Temple U (PA)
Texas Christian U (TX)
Texas Southern U (TX)
Texas State U (TX)
Texas Tech U (TX)
Tiffin U (OH)
Trevecca Nazarene U (TN)
Troy U (AL)
Union U (TN)
U at Albany, State U of New York (NY)
U of Alaska Fairbanks (AK)
The U of Arizona (AZ)
U of Arkansas (AR)
U of Arkansas at Little Rock (AR)
U of Central Arkansas (AR)
U of Central Florida (FL)
U of Cincinnati (OH)
U of Denver (CO)
The U of Findlay (OH)
U of Hawaii at Manoa (HI)
U of Houston (TX)
U of Idaho (ID)
The U of Iowa (IA)
The U of Kansas (KS)
U of Kentucky (KY)
U of La Verne (CA)
U of Maine (ME)
U of Massachusetts Amherst (MA)

U of Memphis (TN)
U of Miami (FL)
U of Minnesota, Duluth (MN)
U of Minnesota, Twin Cities Campus (MN)
U of Montana (MT)
U of Nebraska at Kearney (NE)
U of Nevada, Reno (NV)
U of New Mexico (NM)
The U of North Carolina at Chapel Hill (NC)
U of Northern Colorado (CO)
U of North Texas (TX)
U of Oregon (OR)
U of Pittsburgh at Greensburg (PA)
U of Richmond (VA)
U of South Carolina (SC)
U of Southern Indiana (IN)
U of Southern Mississippi (MS)
The U of Tennessee (TN)
U of the Incarnate Word (TX)
U of Washington (WA)
U of West Georgia (GA)
U of Wisconsin–Eau Claire (WI)
U of Wisconsin–Madison (WI)
U of Wyoming (WY)
Utah State U (UT)
Utica Coll (NY)
Walla Walla U (WA)
Wartburg Coll (IA)
Washington and Lee U (VA)
Washington State U (WA)
Washington U in St. Louis (MO)
Waynesburg U (PA)
Wayne State U (MI)
Weber State U (UT)
Western Kentucky U (KY)
Western Michigan U (MI)
Western Washington U (WA)
West Virginia U (WV)
Whitworth U (WA)
Youngstown State U (OH)

JOURNALISM RELATED
Abilene Christian U (TX)
Arizona State U at the Downtown Phoenix campus (AZ)
Benedictine U (IL)
Bowling Green State U (OH)
California State U, Long Beach (CA)
Columbia Coll (SC)
Concordia Coll (MN)
Fairfield U (CT)
Florida Inst of Technology (FL)
Marywood U (PA)
Oklahoma State U (OK)
Queens U of Charlotte (NC)
Richmond, The American Intl U in London (United Kingdom)
Taylor U (IN)
The U of Akron (OH)
U of California, Irvine (CA)
U of Colorado Boulder (CO)
U of Nebraska–Lincoln (NE)
Western Washington U (WA)
Worcester State U (MA)

JUVENILE CORRECTIONS
Harris-Stowe State U (MO)
Missouri Southern State U (MO)
Prairie View A&M U (TX)

KEYBOARD INSTRUMENTS
Anderson U (SC)
Barry U (FL)
Berklee Coll of Music (MA)
Birmingham-Southern Coll (AL)
Bowling Green State U (OH)
Brigham Young U (UT)
California Baptist U (CA)
Campbellsville U (KY)
Capital U (OH)
Carson-Newman U (TN)
The Catholic U of America (DC)
Central Washington U (WA)
Coll of the Ozarks (MO)
Dallas Baptist U (TX)
Drake U (IA)
East Central U (OK)
Hope Coll (MI)
Houston Baptist U (TX)
Illinois Wesleyan U (IL)
Jacksonville U (FL)
Liberty U (VA)
Lipscomb U (TN)
Madonna U (MI)
Manhattan School of Music (NY)
The New School Coll of Performing Arts (NY)
New York U (NY)
Northwestern U (IL)
Nyack Coll (NY)
Oakland U (MI)
Oberlin Coll (OH)
Oral Roberts U (OK)
Palm Beach Atlantic U (FL)
Point Loma Nazarene U (CA)
Roberts Wesleyan Coll (NY)
Samford U (AL)
Shenandoah U (VA)
Southeastern U (FL)
Southern Methodist U (TX)
Spring Arbor U (MI)
State U of New York at Fredonia (NY)
Stetson U (FL)
Texas Christian U (TX)
Union U (TN)
The U of Akron (OH)
The U of Arizona (AZ)
U of Cincinnati (OH)
The U of Iowa (IA)
The U of Kansas (KS)
U of Miami (FL)
U of the Pacific (CA)
U of Washington (WA)
The U of Western Ontario (ON, Canada)
Valparaiso U (IN)
Vanderbilt U (TN)
Walla Walla U (WA)
Weber State U (UT)
Western Michigan U (MI)
Wichita State U (KS)
Willamette U (OR)
Xavier U of Louisiana (LA)
Youngstown State U (OH)

KINDERGARTEN/PRESCHOOL EDUCATION
Arcadia U (PA)
Athens State U (AL)
Barry U (FL)
Bayamón Central U (PR)
Baylor U (TX)
Black Hills State U (SD)
Bowling Green State U (OH)
Brandon U (MB, Canada)
Bucknell U (PA)
California Polytechnic State U, San Luis Obispo (CA)
California U of Pennsylvania (PA)
Carson-Newman U (TN)
Catawba Coll (NC)
Central Christian Coll of Kansas (KS)
Central Connecticut State U (CT)
Central Methodist U (MO)
Concordia U Wisconsin (WI)
East Carolina U (NC)
Eastern Illinois U (IL)
Evangel U (MO)
Felician U (NJ)
Georgia State U (GA)
Glenville State Coll (WV)
Hampton U (VA)
Howard U (DC)
Illinois State U (IL)
Inter American U of Puerto Rico, Aguadilla Campus (PR)
Inter American U of Puerto Rico, Metropolitan Campus (PR)
Inter American U of Puerto Rico, San Germán Campus (PR)
Jacksonville State U (AL)
Kean U (NJ)
Lesley U (MA)
Lincoln Memorial U (TN)
Louisiana Tech U (LA)
Mansfield U of Pennsylvania (PA)
Marshall U (WV)
Michigan State U (MI)
Minnesota State U Mankato (MN)
New Mexico Highlands U (NM)
North Carolina Central U (NC)
Northern Kentucky U (KY)
Ohio Wesleyan U (OH)
Oklahoma Baptist U (OK)
Olivet Nazarene U (IL)
Pacific U (OR)
Purdue U Fort Wayne (IN)
St. Catherine U (MN)
Siena Heights U (MI)
State U of New York at Fredonia (NY)
State U of New York Coll at Cortland (NY)
State U of New York Coll at Oneonta (NY)
State U of New York Coll of Agriculture and Technology at Cobleskill (NY)
Union U (TN)
The U of Arizona (AZ)
U of Arkansas (AR)
U of Cincinnati (OH)
U of Minnesota, Duluth (MN)
U of Minnesota, Twin Cities Campus (MN)
The U of North Carolina at Charlotte (NC)
The U of North Carolina at Pembroke (NC)
The U of North Carolina Wilmington (NC)
U of Northern Iowa (IA)
U of Providence (MT)
The U of Toledo (OH)
Wartburg Coll (IA)
Western Carolina U (NC)
Western New Mexico U (NM)
Westfield State U (MA)
West Liberty U (WV)
Widener U (PA)

KINESIOLOGY AND EXERCISE SCIENCE
Adams State U (CO)
Albion Coll (MI)
Alverno Coll (WI)
Anderson U (IN)
Anderson U (SC)
Andrews U (MI)
Angelo State U (TX)
Appalachian State U (NC)
Aquinas Coll (MI)
Arizona State U at the Downtown Phoenix campus (AZ)
Auburn U at Montgomery (AL)
Augsburg U (MN)
Augustana U (SD)
Aurora U (IL)
Avila U (MO)
Azusa Pacific U (CA)
Baker U (KS)
Ball State U (IN)
Barry U (FL)
Barton Coll (NC)
Baylor U (TX)
Becker Coll (MA)
Belhaven U (MS)
Belmont U (TN)
Bemidji State U (MN)
Benedictine Coll (KS)
Berry Coll (GA)
Bethel U (IN)
Bethel U (MN)
Biola U (CA)
Boise State U (ID)
Brenau U (GA)
Bridgewater State U (MA)
Brigham Young U (UT)
California Baptist U (CA)
California Lutheran U (CA)
California State U, Long Beach (CA)
California State U, Los Angeles (CA)
California State U, Northridge (CA)
California State U, Sacramento (CA)
California State U, San Marcos (CA)
California U of Pennsylvania (PA)
Calvin Coll (MI)
Capital U (OH)
Carson-Newman U (TN)
Carthage Coll (WI)
Catawba Coll (NC)
Cedar Crest Coll (PA)
Cedarville U (OH)
Central Christian Coll of Kansas (KS)
Central Connecticut State U (CT)
Central Michigan U (MI)
Central State U (OH)
Central Washington U (WA)
Chatham U (PA)
Coastal Carolina U (SC)
Colby-Sawyer Coll (NH)
The Coll of Idaho (ID)
Coll of Saint Benedict (MN)
Coll of Saint Mary (NE)
Colorado State U (CO)
Columbia Coll (SC)
Concordia U Chicago (IL)
Concordia U, St. Paul (MN)
Cornell Coll (IA)
Dakota State U (SD)
Dean Coll (MA)
DePaul U (IL)
DePauw U (IN)
DeSales U (PA)
Dickinson State U (ND)
East Central U (OK)
Eastern Illinois U (IL)
Eastern Kentucky U (KY)
Eastern Michigan U (MI)
Eastern U (PA)
Eastern Washington U (WA)
East Texas Baptist U (TX)
Edinboro U of Pennsylvania (PA)
Elon U (NC)
Emmanuel Coll (GA)
Emory & Henry Coll (VA)
Endicott Coll (MA)
Felician U (NJ)
Fitchburg State U (MA)
Florida Atlantic U (FL)
Florida Gulf Coast U (FL)
Florida State U (FL)
Fort Lewis Coll (CO)
Franklin Coll (IN)
Freed-Hardeman U (TN)
Gannon U (PA)
George Mason U (VA)
Georgetown Coll (KY)
The George Washington U (DC)
Georgia Coll & State U (GA)
Georgia Gwinnett Coll (GA)
Georgian Court U (NJ)
Georgia Southern U (GA)
Goshen Coll (IN)
Grand Valley State U (MI)
Guilford Coll (NC)
Hamline U (MN)
Hampton U (VA)
Hanover Coll (IN)
Harding U (AR)
Hardin-Simmons U (TX)
High Point U (NC)
Hillsdale Coll (MI)
Hope Coll (MI)
Hope Intl U (CA)
Houston Baptist U (TX)
Husson U (ME)
Illinois State U (IL)
Immaculata U (PA)
Indiana State U (IN)
Indiana U Bloomington (IN)
Indiana U-Purdue U Indianapolis (IN)
Iowa State U of Science and Technology (IA)
Jacksonville State U (AL)
Jacksonville U (FL)
John Brown U (AR)
John Carroll U (OH)
Kansas State U (KS)
Kansas Wesleyan U (KS)
Keiser U, Fort Lauderdale (FL)
Kennesaw State U (GA)
King's Coll (PA)
King U (TN)
LaGrange Coll (GA)
Lamar U (TX)
La Roche U (PA)
Lasell Coll (MA)
La Sierra U (CA)
Lee U (TN)
Lenoir-Rhyne U (NC)
LeTourneau U (TX)
Lewis-Clark State Coll (ID)
Lewis U (IL)
Liberty U (VA)
Life U (GA)
Lincoln Memorial U (TN)
Lindenwood U (MO)
Linfield Coll (OR)
Lipscomb U (TN)
Longwood U (VA)
Loras Coll (IA)
Madonna U (MI)
Malone U (OH)
Marian U (IN)
Marshall U (WV)
Maryville U of Saint Louis (MO)
Marywood U (PA)
McDaniel Coll (MD)
McKendree U (IL)
McMurry U (TX)
McNeese State U (LA)
Mercy Coll (NY)
Meredith Coll (NC)
Miami U (OH)
Miami U Hamilton (OH)
Miami U Middletown (OH)
Michigan State U (MI)
Michigan Technological U (MI)
MidAmerica Nazarene U (KS)
Middle Tennessee State U (TN)
Millikin U (IL)
Mississippi State U (MS)
Missouri State U (MO)
Missouri Valley Coll (MO)
Montclair State U (NJ)
Morehead State U (KY)
Mount Marty Coll (SD)
Mount Mercy U (IA)
Mount Vernon Nazarene U (OH)
Murray State U (KY)
Nebraska Wesleyan U (NE)
Northeastern State U (OK)
Northern Arizona U (AZ)
Northwestern Coll (IA)
Northwest Nazarene U (ID)
Nova Southeastern U (FL)
Oakland U (MI)
Occidental Coll (CA)
Ohio Dominican U (OH)
The Ohio State U (OH)
Oklahoma Baptist U (OK)
Oklahoma State U (OK)
Olivet Nazarene U (IL)
Oral Roberts U (OK)
Ottawa U (KS)
Pacific U (OR)
Penn State Abington (PA)
Penn State Altoona (PA)
Penn State Beaver (PA)
Penn State Berks (PA)
Penn State Brandywine (PA)
Penn State DuBois (PA)
Penn State Erie, The Behrend Coll (PA)
Penn State Fayette, The Eberly Campus (PA)
Penn State Greater Allegheny (PA)
Penn State Hazleton (PA)
Penn State Lehigh Valley (PA)
Penn State Mont Alto (PA)
Penn State New Kensington (PA)
Penn State Schuylkill (PA)
Penn State Shenango (PA)
Penn State U Park (PA)
Penn State Wilkes-Barre (PA)
Penn State York (PA)
Pepperdine U, Malibu (CA)
Pittsburg State U (KS)
Prairie View A&M U (TX)
Queens Coll of the City U of New York (NY)
Regis Coll (MA)
Rice U (TX)
Roanoke Coll (VA)
Roberts Wesleyan Coll (NY)
Rocky Mountain Coll (MT)
Saginaw Valley State U (MI)
St. Ambrose U (IA)
Saint John's U (MN)
Saint Louis U (MO)
Saint Mary's Coll of California (CA)
St. Mary's U (TX)
St. Olaf Coll (MN)
St. Thomas Aquinas Coll (NY)
Salem State U (MA)
Salisbury U (MD)
Sam Houston State U (TX)
San Diego State U (CA)
San Francisco State U (CA)
Schreiner U (TX)
Seattle U (WA)
Seton Hill U (PA)
Simmons U (MA)
Simon Fraser U (BC, Canada)
Southeastern Louisiana U (LA)
Southeastern U (FL)
Southern Arkansas U–Magnolia (AR)
Southern Illinois U Carbondale (IL)
Southern Illinois U Edwardsville (IL)
Southwest Baptist U (MO)

Southwestern Oklahoma State U (OK)
Southwestern U (TX)
Spring Arbor U (MI)
Springfield Coll (MA)
State U of New York at Fredonia (NY)
State U of New York Coll at Cortland (NY)
State U of New York Coll at Potsdam (NY)
Stockton U (NJ)
Tabor Coll (KS)
Tarleton State U (TX)
Taylor U (IN)
Tennessee Wesleyan U (TN)
Texas A&M Intl U (TX)
Texas A&M U (TX)
Texas A&M U–Commerce (TX)
Texas A&M U–Corpus Christi (TX)
Texas A&M U–Kingsville (TX)
Texas Lutheran U (TX)
Texas State U (TX)
Texas Tech U (TX)
Texas Woman's U (TX)
Towson U (MD)
Transylvania U (KY)
Trine U (IN)
Troy U (AL)
Truett McConnell U (GA)
Truman State U (MO)
Union U (TN)
United States Military Acad (NY)
U of Arkansas (AR)
U of Central Arkansas (AR)
U of Charleston (WV)
U of Dayton (OH)
U of Dubuque (IA)
U of Hawaii at Manoa (HI)
U of Houston (TX)
U of Houston–Clear Lake (TX)
U of Idaho (ID)
U of Illinois at Chicago (IL)
U of Illinois at Springfield (IL)
The U of Iowa (IA)
U of Jamestown (ND)
The U of Kansas (KS)
U of La Verne (CA)
U of Louisiana at Monroe (LA)
U of Mary Hardin-Baylor (TX)
U of Memphis (TN)
U of Michigan (MI)
U of Minnesota, Duluth (MN)
U of Nevada, Las Vegas (NV)
U of New England (ME)
U of New Hampshire (NH)
U of New Haven (CT)
The U of North Carolina at Greensboro (NC)
The U of North Carolina Wilmington (NC)
U of North Dakota (ND)
U of Northern Colorado (CO)
U of North Texas (TX)
U of Northwestern–St. Paul (MN)
U of Pittsburgh at Bradford (PA)
U of Puget Sound (WA)
U of Saint Mary (KS)
U of San Francisco (CA)
The U of Scranton (PA)
U of South Carolina (SC)
U of South Carolina Aiken (SC)
U of Southern Indiana (IN)
The U of Tennessee (TN)
The U of Tennessee at Chattanooga (TN)
The U of Texas at El Paso (TX)
The U of Texas at San Antonio (TX)
The U of Texas of the Permian Basin (TX)
The U of Texas Rio Grande Valley (TX)
U of the Fraser Valley (BC, Canada)
U of the Incarnate Word (TX)
U of the Pacific (CA)
The U of Toledo (OH)
The U of Tulsa (OK)
U of Utah (UT)
U of Vermont (VT)
U of Virginia (VA)
U of Waterloo (ON, Canada)
The U of West Alabama (AL)
The U of Western Ontario (ON, Canada)
U of Wisconsin–Eau Claire (WI)
U of Wisconsin–La Crosse (WI)
U of Wisconsin–Madison (WI)
U of Wisconsin–Milwaukee (WI)
U of Wisconsin–Parkside (WI)
U of Wyoming (WY)
Upper Iowa U (IA)
Ursuline Coll (OH)
Valparaiso U (IN)
Vanguard U of Southern California (CA)
Wake Forest U (NC)
Walla Walla U (WA)
Wartburg Coll (IA)
Washington State U (WA)
Waynesburg U (PA)
Western Colorado U (CO)
Western Kentucky U (KY)
Western Michigan U (MI)
Western New Mexico U (NM)
Western Oregon U (OR)
Western Washington U (WA)
West Liberty U (WV)
Westmont Coll (CA)
Whitworth U (WA)
Wichita State U (KS)
Willamette U (OR)
William & Mary (VA)
William Paterson U of New Jersey (NJ)
William Peace U (NC)
William Penn U (IA)
Wingate U (NC)
Winthrop U (SC)
Wittenberg U (OH)
Wright State U (OH)
Wright State U–Lake Campus (OH)
Youngstown State U (OH)

KINESIOTHERAPY
Bridgewater State U (MA)
California State U, Long Beach (CA)

KNOWLEDGE MANAGEMENT
Framingham State U (MA)
Saint Joseph's U (PA)

KOREAN
Brigham Young U (UT)
The Ohio State U (OH)
U of California, Irvine (CA)
U of California, Los Angeles (CA)
U of Hawaii at Manoa (HI)
U of Washington (WA)

KOREAN STUDIES
U of Washington (WA)

LABOR AND INDUSTRIAL RELATIONS
Baruch Coll of the City U of New York (NY)
Bowling Green State U (OH)
Clarion U of Pennsylvania (PA)
Cornell U (NY)
Indiana U-Purdue U Indianapolis (IN)
New York U (NY)
Penn State Abington (PA)
Penn State Altoona (PA)
Penn State Beaver (PA)
Penn State Berks (PA)
Penn State Brandywine (PA)
Penn State DuBois (PA)
Penn State Erie, The Behrend Coll (PA)
Penn State Fayette, The Eberly Campus (PA)
Penn State Greater Allegheny (PA)
Penn State Hazleton (PA)
Penn State Lehigh Valley (PA)
Penn State Mont Alto (PA)
Penn State New Kensington (PA)
Penn State Schuylkill (PA)
Penn State Shenango (PA)
Penn State U Park (PA)
Penn State Wilkes-Barre (PA)
Penn State York (PA)
San Francisco State U (CA)
State U of New York at Fredonia (NY)
State U of New York Coll at Old Westbury (NY)
State U of New York Coll at Potsdam (NY)
State U of New York Empire State Coll (NY)
U of Cincinnati (OH)
The U of Iowa (IA)
U of Massachusetts Boston (MA)
U of Minnesota, Twin Cities Campus (MN)
U of Toronto (ON, Canada)
Wayne State U (MI)

LABOR STUDIES
California State U, Dominguez Hills (CA)
Eastern Michigan U (MI)
Hofstra U (NY)
Indiana U Bloomington (IN)
Indiana U Northwest (IN)
Indiana U-Purdue U Indianapolis (IN)
Indiana U South Bend (IN)
Queens Coll of the City U of New York (NY)

LANDSCAPE ARCHITECTURE
Academy of Art U (CA)
American U of Beirut (Lebanon)
Arizona State U at the Tempe campus (AZ)
Ball State U (IN)
Boston Architectural Coll (MA)
California Polytechnic State U, San Luis Obispo (CA)
California State Polytechnic U, Pomona (CA)
Clemson U (SC)
Colorado State U (CO)
Cornell U (NY)
Delaware Valley U (PA)
Iowa State U of Science and Technology (IA)
Louisiana State U and A&M Coll (LA)
Michigan State U (MI)
Mississippi State U (MS)
The Ohio State U (OH)
Oklahoma State U (OK)
Penn State Brandywine (PA)
Penn State Lehigh Valley (PA)
Penn State Schuylkill (PA)
Penn State U Park (PA)
Penn State Wilkes-Barre (PA)
South Dakota State U (SD)
Temple U (PA)
Texas A&M U (TX)
Texas Tech U (TX)
U of Arkansas (AR)
U of California, Berkeley (CA)
U of Idaho (ID)
U of Kentucky (KY)
U of Massachusetts Amherst (MA)
U of Nebraska–Lincoln (NE)
U of Nevada, Las Vegas (NV)
U of Oregon (OR)
U of Washington (WA)
U of Wisconsin–Madison (WI)
Utah State U (UT)
Washington State U (WA)
West Virginia U (WV)

LANDSCAPING AND GROUNDSKEEPING
Delaware Valley U (PA)
Mississippi State U (MS)
Oklahoma State U (OK)
Penn State Abington (PA)
Penn State Altoona (PA)
Penn State Beaver (PA)
Penn State Berks (PA)
Penn State Brandywine (PA)
Penn State DuBois (PA)
Penn State Erie, The Behrend Coll (PA)
Penn State Fayette, The Eberly Campus (PA)
Penn State Greater Allegheny (PA)
Penn State Hazleton (PA)
Penn State Lehigh Valley (PA)
Penn State Mont Alto (PA)
Penn State New Kensington (PA)
Penn State Schuylkill (PA)
Penn State Shenango (PA)
Penn State U Park (PA)
Penn State Wilkes-Barre (PA)
Penn State York (PA)
State U of New York Coll of Agriculture and Technology at Cobleskill (NY)
U of Nebraska–Lincoln (NE)
Washington State U (WA)

LAND USE PLANNING AND MANAGEMENT
California State U, Bakersfield (CA)
Central Michigan U (MI)
Marietta Coll (OH)
Montana State U (MT)
West Virginia U (WV)

LANGUAGE INTERPRETATION AND TRANSLATION
Aquinas Coll (MI)
Bennington Coll (VT)
Brigham Young U (UT)
Lebanese American U (Lebanon)
Northwestern Coll (IA)
The U of Texas Rio Grande Valley (TX)

LASER AND OPTICAL ENGINEERING
U of Central Florida (FL)

LATIN
Augustana Coll (IL)
Austin Coll (TX)
Barnard Coll (NY)
Baylor U (TX)
Binghamton U, State U of New York (NY)
Bowling Green State U (OH)
Carleton Coll (MN)
The Catholic U of America (DC)
Colgate U (NY)
Dartmouth Coll (NH)
DePauw U (IN)
Emory U (GA)
Florida State U (FL)
Furman U (SC)
Hampden-Sydney Coll (VA)
Hillsdale Coll (MI)
Hobart and William Smith Colls (NY)
Hofstra U (NY)
Houston Baptist U (TX)
Kenyon Coll (OH)
Lehman Coll of the City U of New York (NY)
Loyola U Chicago (IL)
Loyola U Maryland (MD)
Loyola U New Orleans (LA)
Mercer U, Macon (GA)
Montclair State U (NJ)
Mount Holyoke Coll (MA)
New York U (NY)
Oberlin Coll (OH)
Queens Coll of the City U of New York (NY)
Randolph-Macon Coll (VA)
Rice U (TX)
St. Olaf Coll (MN)
Samford U (AL)
Sarah Lawrence Coll (NY)
Smith Coll (MA)
Southwestern U (TX)
Trinity U (TX)
Tulane U (LA)
U of California, Berkeley (CA)
U of California, Los Angeles (CA)
U of Michigan (MI)
U of New Hampshire (NH)
U of Richmond (VA)
The U of Scranton (PA)
The U of the South (TN)
U of Toronto (ON, Canada)
U of Utah (UT)
U of Vermont (VT)
U of Washington (WA)
The U of Western Ontario (ON, Canada)
U of Wisconsin–Madison (WI)
Virginia Wesleyan U (VA)
Wabash Coll (IN)
Wake Forest U (NC)
Washington U in St. Louis (MO)
Western Michigan U (MI)
Wright State U (OH)
Wright State U–Lake Campus (OH)
Yale U (CT)

LATIN AMERICAN AND CARIBBEAN STUDIES
Coll of Charleston (SC)
Florida State U (FL)
Linfield Coll (OR)
Mount Holyoke Coll (MA)
Rollins Coll (FL)
Union Coll (NY)
The U of Kansas (KS)
U of Michigan (MI)
U of Vermont (VT)
U of Wisconsin–Madison (WI)
U of Wisconsin–Milwaukee (WI)

LATIN AMERICAN STUDIES
Albion Coll (MI)
Alverno Coll (WI)
American U (DC)
Arizona State U at the West campus (AZ)
Assumption Coll (MA)
Barnard Coll (NY)
Bates Coll (ME)
Baylor U (TX)
Bennington Coll (VT)
Binghamton U, State U of New York (NY)
Bowdoin Coll (ME)
Bowling Green State U (OH)
Brandeis U (MA)
Brown U (RI)
Bucknell U (PA)
California State U, Fullerton (CA)
California State U, Los Angeles (CA)
California State U, Northridge (CA)
Carleton Coll (MN)
City Coll of the City U of New York (NY)
Colby Coll (ME)
Colgate U (NY)
Coll of the Holy Cross (MA)
Cornell Coll (IA)
Dartmouth Coll (NH)
Davidson Coll (NC)
DePaul U (IL)
Dickinson Coll (PA)
Earlham Coll (IN)
Emory U (GA)
Fordham U (NY)
George Mason U (VA)
The George Washington U (DC)
Gonzaga U (WA)
Gustavus Adolphus Coll (MN)
Hampshire Coll (MA)
Hobart and William Smith Colls (NY)
Hofstra U (NY)
Illinois Wesleyan U (IL)
John Jay Coll of Criminal Justice of the City U of New York (NY)
Johns Hopkins U (MD)
Knox Coll (IL)
Lake Forest Coll (IL)
Lehigh U (PA)
Lehman Coll of the City U of New York (NY)
Marquette U (WI)
Miami U (OH)
Miami U Hamilton (OH)
Miami U Middletown (OH)
Middlebury Coll (VT)
New York U (NY)
Oakland U (MI)
Oberlin Coll (OH)
Occidental Coll (CA)
Ohio Wesleyan U (OH)
Penn State Abington (PA)
Penn State Altoona (PA)
Penn State Beaver (PA)
Penn State Berks (PA)
Penn State Brandywine (PA)
Penn State DuBois (PA)
Penn State Erie, The Behrend Coll (PA)
Penn State Fayette, The Eberly Campus (PA)
Penn State Greater Allegheny (PA)
Penn State Hazleton (PA)
Penn State Lehigh Valley (PA)
Penn State Mont Alto (PA)
Penn State New Kensington (PA)
Penn State Schuylkill (PA)
Penn State Shenango (PA)
Penn State U Park (PA)
Penn State Wilkes-Barre (PA)
Penn State York (PA)
Pepperdine U, Malibu (CA)
Pomona Coll (CA)
Portland State U (OR)
Purchase Coll, State U of New York (NY)
Queens Coll of the City U of New York (NY)
Rhode Island Coll (RI)
Rhodes Coll (TN)
Rice U (TX)

MAJORS LISTING

St. Cloud State U (MN)
Saint Louis U (MO)
Saint Mary's Coll of California (CA)
St. Olaf Coll (MN)
Samford U (AL)
San Diego State U (CA)
Sarah Lawrence Coll (NY)
Scripps Coll (CA)
Smith Coll (MA)
Southwestern U (TX)
Stanford U (CA)
State U of New York at New Paltz (NY)
Temple U (PA)
Texas Christian U (TX)
Trinity U (TX)
Tulane U (LA)
United States Military Acad (NY)
U at Albany, State U of New York (NY)
The U of Arizona (AZ)
U of California, Berkeley (CA)
U of California, Los Angeles (CA)
U of California, Riverside (CA)
U of California, San Diego (CA)
U of Central Florida (FL)
U of Cincinnati (OH)
U of Denver (CO)
U of Idaho (ID)
U of Illinois at Chicago (IL)
The U of Iowa (IA)
U of Kentucky (KY)
U of Louisville (KY)
U of Miami (FL)
U of Minnesota, Duluth (MN)
U of Minnesota, Morris (MN)
U of Nebraska–Lincoln (NE)
U of Nevada, Las Vegas (NV)
U of New Mexico (NM)
The U of North Carolina at Chapel Hill (NC)
The U of North Carolina at Charlotte (NC)
U of Oregon (OR)
U of Pennsylvania (PA)
U of Richmond (VA)
U of San Francisco (CA)
The U of Scranton (PA)
U of South Carolina (SC)
The U of Texas at Dallas (TX)
U of Toronto (ON, Canada)
U of Utah (UT)
U of Washington (WA)
U of Wisconsin–Eau Claire (WI)
Vanderbilt U (TN)
Villanova U (PA)
Washington Coll (MD)
Washington U in St. Louis (MO)
Wesleyan U (CT)
Western Washington U (WA)
Westminster Coll (UT)
Willamette U (OR)
William & Mary (VA)
William Paterson U of New Jersey (NJ)
Yale U (CT)

LATIN TEACHER EDUCATION
Ball State U (IN)
Brigham Young U (UT)
Miami U (OH)
Miami U Hamilton (OH)
Miami U Middletown (OH)
Missouri State U (MO)
Ohio Wesleyan U (OH)
Queens Coll of the City U of New York (NY)
Valparaiso U (IN)
Western Michigan U (MI)

LAW ENFORCEMENT INTELLIGENCE ANALYSIS
ECPI U, Virginia Beach (VA)

LAY MINISTRY
Arizona Christian U (AZ)
Bethel U (IN)
Bethel U (MN)
Liberty U (VA)
Northwest Christian U (OR)
Point Loma Nazarene U (CA)
Saint Mary's U of Minnesota (MN)
Trevecca Nazarene U (TN)
U of Saint Francis (IN)

LEARNING SCIENCES
The U of Alabama (AL)
The U of Arizona (AZ)

LEGAL ADMINISTRATIVE ASSISTANT/SECRETARY
Lewis-Clark State Coll (ID)

LEGAL ASSISTANT/ PARALEGAL
Champlain Coll (VT)
Clarion U of Pennsylvania (PA)
Clayton State U (GA)
Coll of Saint Mary (NE)
Concordia U Wisconsin (WI)
Davenport U, Grand Rapids (MI)
East Central U (OK)
Eastern Kentucky U (KY)
Eastern Michigan U (MI)
Elms Coll (MA)
Florida Gulf Coast U (FL)
Gannon U (PA)
Grand Valley State U (MI)
Hamline U (MN)
Hampton U (VA)
Husson U (ME)
Illinois State U (IL)
Indiana U-Purdue U Indianapolis (IN)
Lewis-Clark State Coll (ID)
Lewis U (IL)
Liberty U (VA)
Loyola U Chicago (IL)
Madonna U (MI)
Maryville U of Saint Louis (MO)
Mercy Coll (NY)
National U (CA)
New York City Coll of Technology of the City U of New York (NY)
Nova Southeastern U (FL)
Peirce Coll (PA)
Regent U (VA)
Roger Williams U (RI)
Saint Mary-of-the-Woods Coll (IN)
St. Petersburg Coll (FL)
Southern Illinois U Carbondale (IL)
State U of New York Coll of Technology at Canton (NY)
Stevenson U (MD)
Sullivan U (KY)
Texas A&M U–Commerce (TX)
Tiffin U (OH)
Tulane U (LA)
U of Houston–Clear Lake (TX)
U of La Verne (CA)
U of Providence (MT)
U of Southern Mississippi (MS)
U of West Florida (FL)
Ursuline Coll (OH)
Valdosta State U (GA)
Western Kentucky U (KY)

LEGAL PROFESSIONS AND STUDIES RELATED
Ball State U (IN)
Brenau U (GA)
California U of Pennsylvania (PA)
Drexel U (PA)
Georgia Southern U (GA)
John Jay Coll of Criminal Justice of the City U of New York (NY)
Loyola U Chicago (IL)
Maryville U of Saint Louis (MO)
Missouri Southern State U (MO)
Montclair State U (NJ)
New Jersey Inst of Technology (NJ)
Ramapo Coll of New Jersey (NJ)
Roger Williams U (RI)
Temple U (PA)
Tulane U (LA)
The U of Arizona (AZ)
U of Nebraska–Lincoln (NE)
U of Pennsylvania (PA)
The U of Tulsa (OK)
U of Wisconsin–Superior (WI)
Western Michigan U (MI)

LEGAL STUDIES
Adams State U (CO)
American Public U System (WV)
American U (DC)
Amherst Coll (MA)
Anderson U (SC)
Arizona State U at the Tempe campus (AZ)
Auburn U (AL)
Bethany Lutheran Coll (MN)
Bridgewater State U (MA)
Central Michigan U (MI)
Colby-Sawyer Coll (NH)
Culver-Stockton Coll (MO)
DeSales U (PA)
Dickinson Coll (PA)
Doane U (NE)
Dominican U (IL)
Elms Coll (MA)
Emory & Henry Coll (VA)
Florida National U (FL)
Hamline U (MN)
Hampshire Coll (MA)
Harding U (AR)
Houston Baptist U (TX)
Illinois State U (IL)
Ithaca Coll (NY)
John Jay Coll of Criminal Justice of the City U of New York (NY)
Keiser U, Fort Lauderdale (FL)
Lasell Coll (MA)
Lipscomb U (TN)
Mercy Coll (NY)
Morehead State U (KY)
Nazareth Coll of Rochester (NY)
New York U (NY)
Northeastern State U (OK)
Northern Kentucky U (KY)
Northwestern U (IL)
Northwest U (WA)
Oberlin Coll (OH)
Ramapo Coll of New Jersey (NJ)
St. John Fisher Coll (NY)
Saint Joseph's U (PA)
Samford U (AL)
Scripps Coll (CA)
Southeastern U (FL)
State U of New York at Fredonia (NY)
Stevenson U (MD)
Suffolk U (MA)
Susquehanna U (PA)
United States Military Acad (NY)
U of California, Berkeley (CA)
U of California, Santa Cruz (CA)
U of Central Florida (FL)
U of Denver (CO)
U of Detroit Mercy (MI)
U of Illinois at Springfield (IL)
The U of Kansas (KS)
U of La Verne (CA)
U of Maryland Global Campus (MD)
U of Massachusetts Amherst (MA)
U of Miami (FL)
U of Montana (MT)
U of New Haven (CT)
The U of Texas at San Antonio (TX)
U of Washington (WA)
U of Washington, Tacoma (WA)
U of Wisconsin–Madison (WI)
Western New England U (MA)
William Paterson U of New Jersey (NJ)

LEGAL SUPPORT SERVICES RELATED
U of Cincinnati (OH)

LIBERAL ARTS AND SCIENCES AND HUMANITIES RELATED
Anderson U (IN)
Anderson U (SC)
Auburn U (AL)
Augsburg U (MN)
Belhaven U (MS)
Brigham Young U (UT)
Bryan Coll (TN)
California Polytechnic State U, San Luis Obispo (CA)
California State U, Dominguez Hills (CA)
Carnegie Mellon U (PA)
Central Christian Coll of Kansas (KS)
Centre Coll (KY)
Coll of Charleston (SC)
Coll of Saint Mary (NE)
The Colorado Coll (CO)
Concordia Coll (MN)
Drexel U (PA)
Eastern U (PA)
Elms Coll (MA)
Fairfield U (CT)
Florida Atlantic U (FL)
George Mason U (VA)
Georgia Coll & State U (GA)
Graceland U (IA)
Hampshire Coll (MA)
Hofstra U (NY)
Illinois Inst of Technology (IL)
Indiana U Bloomington (IN)
Indiana U East (IN)
Indiana U Kokomo (IN)
Indiana U Northwest (IN)
Indiana U-Purdue U Indianapolis (IN)
Indiana U South Bend (IN)
Indiana U Southeast (IN)
Kansas Wesleyan U (KS)
Kent State U at Tuscarawas (OH)
The King's Coll (NY)
La Sierra U (CA)
Lewis & Clark Coll (OR)
Malone U (OH)
Marymount California U (CA)
Molloy Coll (NY)
Montclair State U (NJ)
Mount Aloysius Coll (PA)
New York U (NY)
Oakland U (MI)
Pepperdine U, Malibu (CA)
Purdue U Fort Wayne (IN)
Saint Mary's Coll of California (CA)
Salem State U (MA)
Seattle U (WA)
Southern Methodist U (TX)
Sterling Coll (KS)
Trine U (IN)
Truett McConnell U (GA)
Tulane U (LA)
The U of Akron (OH)
The U of Alabama at Birmingham (AL)
U of California, Los Angeles (CA)
U of California, Santa Barbara (CA)
U of Maryland Global Campus (MD)
U of Mary Washington (VA)
U of Massachusetts Amherst (MA)
U of Miami (FL)
U of Michigan–Dearborn (MI)
The U of Texas at San Antonio (TX)
U of Utah (UT)
U of Wisconsin–Milwaukee (WI)
U of Wisconsin–Platteville (WI)
Valdosta State U (GA)
Wayland Baptist U (TX)
Westminster Coll (UT)
Worcester Polytechnic Inst (MA)

LIBERAL ARTS AND SCIENCES/LIBERAL STUDIES
Abilene Christian U (TX)
Adams State U (CO)
Albion Coll (MI)
Alverno Coll (WI)
American U (DC)
Andrews U (MI)
Antioch U Santa Barbara (CA)
Appalachian State U (NC)
Aquinas Coll (MI)
Arcadia U (PA)
Arizona State U at the Polytechnic campus (AZ)
Athens State U (AL)
Augsburg U (MN)
Augustana Coll (IL)
Augustana U (SD)
Aurora U (IL)
Averett U (VA)
Azusa Pacific U (CA)
Ball State U (IN)
Barry U (FL)
Barton Coll (NC)
Baruch Coll of the City U of New York (NY)
Becker Coll (MA)
Belmont Abbey Coll (NC)
Belmont U (TN)
Bemidji State U (MN)
Benedictine Coll (KS)
Bennington Coll (VT)
Bentley U (MA)
Bethany Lutheran Coll (MN)
Bethel U (IN)
Biola U (CA)
Bowling Green State U (OH)
Bradley U (IL)
Brandon U (MB, Canada)
Brenau U (GA)
Bridgewater Coll (VA)
Brigham Young U (UT)
Bryan Coll (TN)
California Baptist U (CA)
California Lutheran U (CA)
California Polytechnic State U, San Luis Obispo (CA)
California State Polytechnic U, Pomona (CA)
California State U, Bakersfield (CA)
California State U, Dominguez Hills (CA)
California State U, Fresno (CA)
California State U, Fullerton (CA)
California State U, Long Beach (CA)
California State U, Los Angeles (CA)
California State U, Monterey Bay (CA)
California State U, Northridge (CA)
California State U, Sacramento (CA)
California State U, San Bernardino (CA)
California State U, San Marcos (CA)
California State U, Stanislaus (CA)
California U of Pennsylvania (PA)
Carlow U (PA)
Carnegie Mellon U (PA)
Carson-Newman U (TN)
The Catholic U of America (DC)
Cazenovia Coll (NY)
Cedarville U (OH)
Central Christian Coll of Kansas (KS)
Central Michigan U (MI)
Champlain Coll (VT)
Charter Oak State Coll (CT)
Chatham U (PA)
Chestnut Hill Coll (PA)
Clarkson U (NY)
Clayton State U (GA)
Coastal Carolina U (SC)
Coe Coll (IA)
The Coll of Saint Rose (NY)
The Coll of St. Scholastica (MN)
Colorado State U (CO)
Columbia Coll (SC)
Columbia Intl U (SC)
Concordia U Wisconsin (WI)
Cornell Coll (IA)
Culver-Stockton Coll (MO)
Dean Coll (MA)
DeSales U (PA)
Dominican U of California (CA)
Drexel U (PA)
East Carolina U (NC)
Eastern Illinois U (IL)
Eastern Mennonite U (VA)
Eastern New Mexico U (NM)
Elon U (NC)
Emmanuel Coll (MA)
Emory & Henry Coll (VA)
Endicott Coll (MA)
Eugene Lang Coll of Liberal Arts (NY)
Excelsior Coll (NY)
Fayetteville State U (NC)
Felician U (NJ)
Fisher Coll (MA)
Fitchburg State U (MA)
Flagler Coll (FL)
Florida Atlantic U (FL)
Florida Gulf Coast U (FL)
Florida National U (FL)
Framingham State U (MA)
Francis Marion U (SC)
Friends U (KS)
Gannon U (PA)
George Mason U (VA)
Georgetown U (DC)
The George Washington U (DC)
Governors State U (IL)
Grand Valley State U (MI)
Granite State Coll (NH)
Gutenberg Coll (OR)
Harris-Stowe State U (MO)
Harvard U (MA)
Hofstra U (NY)
Hope Intl U (CA)
Houston Baptist U (TX)
Husson U (ME)
Illinois Coll (IL)
Illinois Inst of Technology (IL)
Illinois State U (IL)
Illinois Wesleyan U (IL)
Immaculata U (PA)
Indiana State U (IN)
Indiana U Bloomington (IN)
Indiana U of Pennsylvania (PA)

Entrance Difficulty

This index groups colleges by their own assessment of their entrance difficulty level. The colleges were asked to select the level that most closely corresponds to their entrance difficulty, according to the guidelines below. Institutions for which high school class rank and/or standardized test scores do not apply as admission criteria were asked to select the level that best indicates their entrance difficulty as compared to other institutions.

MOST DIFFICULT

More than 75 percent of the freshmen were in the top 10 percent of their high school class and scored over 1310 on the SAT (critical reading and mathematical combined) or over 29 on the ACT (composite); about 30 percent or fewer of the applicants were accepted.

VERY DIFFICULT

More than 50 percent of the freshmen were in the top 10 percent of their high school class and scored over 1230 on the SAT or over 26 on the ACT; about 60 percent or fewer applicants were accepted.

MODERATELY DIFFICULT

More than 75 percent of the freshmen were in the top half of their high school class and scored over 1010 on the SAT or over 18 on the ACT; about 85 percent or fewer of the applicants were accepted.

Bryan Coll (TN)
Bryant U (RI)
Butler U (IN)
Caldwell U (NJ)
California Baptist U (CA)
California Lutheran U (CA)
California Polytechnic State U, San Luis Obispo (CA)
California State Polytechnic U, Pomona (CA)
California State U, Dominguez Hills (CA)
California State U, Fullerton (CA)
California State U, Long Beach (CA)
California State U, Los Angeles (CA)
California State U, Monterey Bay (CA)
California State U, Northridge (CA)
California State U, Sacramento (CA)
California State U, San Bernardino (CA)
California State U, San Marcos (CA)
California State U, Stanislaus (CA)
California U of Pennsylvania (PA)
Calvin Coll (MI)
Campbellsville U (KY)
Capital U (OH)
Carson-Newman U (TN)
Carthage Coll (WI)
Catawba Coll (NC)
The Catholic U of America (DC)
Cedar Crest Coll (PA)
Cedarville U (OH)
Central Coll (IA)
Central Connecticut State U (CT)
Central Methodist U (MO)
Central Michigan U (MI)
Central Washington U (WA)
Chaminade U of Honolulu (HI)
Champlain Coll (VT)
Charles R. Drew U of Medicine and Science (CA)
Chatham U (PA)
Chestnut Hill Coll (PA)
City Coll of the City U of New York (NY)
Clark Atlanta U (GA)
Clark U (MA)
Cleveland Inst of Art (OH)
Coastal Carolina U (SC)
Coe Coll (IA)
Cogswell Polytechnical Coll (CA)
Colby-Sawyer Coll (NH)
Coll of Charleston (SC)
The Coll of Idaho (ID)
Coll of Saint Benedict (MN)
The Coll of Saint Rose (NY)
The Coll of St. Scholastica (MN)
Coll of the Ozarks (MO)
The Coll of Wooster (OH)
Colorado State U (CO)
Colorado State U–Global Campus (CO)
Columbia Coll (SC)
Columbia Intl U (SC)
Concordia Coll (MN)
Concordia U Chicago (IL)
Concordia U Wisconsin (WI)
Covenant Coll (GA)
Creighton U (NE)
The Culinary Inst of America (NY)
Culver-Stockton Coll (MO)
Dakota State U (SD)
Dallas Baptist U (TX)
Dallas Christian Coll (TX)
Dean Coll (MA)
DePaul U (IL)
DePauw U (IN)
DeSales U (PA)
Dillard U (LA)
Dominican U (IL)
Dominican U of California (CA)
Drake U (IA)
Drew U (NJ)
Drexel U (PA)
Drury U (MO)
D'Youville Coll (NY)
East Carolina U (NC)
Eastern Illinois U (IL)
Eastern Mennonite U (VA)
Eastern Michigan U (MI)
East Texas Baptist U (TX)
ECPI U, Virginia Beach (VA)
Edgewood Coll (WI)
Elms Coll (MA)
Elon U (NC)
Emory & Henry Coll (VA)
Endicott Coll (MA)
Evangel U (MO)
Farmingdale State Coll (NY)
Fashion Inst of Technology (NY)
Felician U (NJ)
FIDM/Fashion Inst of Design & Merchandising, Los Angeles Campus (CA)
Florida A&M U (FL)
Florida Atlantic U (FL)
Florida Gulf Coast U (FL)
Florida Inst of Technology (FL)
Florida National U (FL)
Florida Polytechnic U (FL)
Florida Southern Coll (FL)
Fort Lewis Coll (CO)
Framingham State U (MA)
Francis Marion U (SC)
Franklin Coll (IN)
Freed-Hardeman U (TN)
Friends U (KS)
Furman U (SC)
Gallaudet U (DC)
Gannon U (PA)
Geneva Coll (PA)
George Fox U (OR)
George Mason U (VA)
Georgetown Coll (KY)
Georgia Coll & State U (GA)
Georgian Court U (NJ)
Georgia Southern U (GA)
Georgia State U (GA)
Gonzaga U (WA)
Gordon Coll (MA)
Goshen Coll (IN)
Goucher Coll (MD)
Governors State U (IL)
Graceland U (IA)
Grand Valley State U (MI)
Guilford Coll (NC)
Gutenberg Coll (OR)
Gwynedd Mercy U (PA)
Hamline U (MN)
Hampden-Sydney Coll (VA)
Hampshire Coll (MA)
Hampton U (VA)
Hanover Coll (IN)
Harding U (AR)
Hardin-Simmons U (TX)
HEC Montreal (QC, Canada)
High Point U (NC)
Hofstra U (NY)
Hollins U (VA)
Hope Coll (MI)
Hope Intl U (CA)
Houston Baptist U (TX)
Howard U (DC)
Husson U (ME)
Illinois Coll (IL)
Illinois Inst of Technology (IL)
Immaculata U (PA)
Indiana State U (IN)
Indiana U Bloomington (IN)
Indiana U East (IN)
Indiana U-Purdue U Indianapolis (IN)
Indiana U South Bend (IN)
Inter American U of Puerto Rico, Aguadilla Campus (PR)
Inter American U of Puerto Rico, Metropolitan Campus (PR)
Inter American U of Puerto Rico, San Germán Campus (PR)
Intl U in Geneva (Switzerland)
Iona Coll (NY)
Iowa State U of Science and Technology (IA)
Ithaca Coll (NY)
Jacksonville State U (AL)
Jacksonville U (FL)
John Brown U (AR)
John Carroll U (OH)
John Jay Coll of Criminal Justice of the City U of New York (NY)
Johnson U (TN)
Kansas Wesleyan U (KS)
Kean U (NJ)
Kennesaw State U (GA)
Keuka Coll (NY)
The King's Coll (NY)
King's Coll (PA)
King U (TN)
Kutztown U of Pennsylvania (PA)
LaGrange Coll (GA)
Lake Forest Coll (IL)
Lakeview Coll of Nursing (IL)
Lasell Coll (MA)
Lawrence Technological U (MI)
Lebanese American U (Lebanon)
Lee U (TN)
Lehman Coll of the City U of New York (NY)
Le Moyne Coll (NY)
Lenoir-Rhyne U (NC)
LeTourneau U (TX)
Lewis U (IL)
Lincoln Memorial U (TN)
Lindenwood U (MO)
Linfield Coll (OR)
Lipscomb U (TN)
Lock Haven U of Pennsylvania (PA)
Longwood U (VA)
Loras Coll (IA)
Louisiana State U and A&M Coll (LA)
Louisiana Tech U (LA)
Loyola U Chicago (IL)
Loyola U Maryland (MD)
Loyola U New Orleans (LA)
Lynn U (FL)
Madonna U (MI)
Malone U (OH)
Manhattan Coll (NY)
Mansfield U of Pennsylvania (PA)
Marian U (IN)
Marietta Coll (OH)
Marquette U (WI)
Marshall U (WV)
Martin Luther Coll (MN)
Marymount U (VA)
Maryville U of Saint Louis (MO)
Marywood U (PA)
Massachusetts Coll of Art and Design (MA)
Massachusetts Maritime Acad (MA)
McDaniel Coll (MD)
McKendree U (IL)
McMurry U (TX)
Mercy Coll (NY)
Mercy Coll of Ohio (OH)
Meredith Coll (NC)
Merrimack Coll (MA)
Messenger Coll (TX)
Messiah Coll (PA)
Miami U (OH)
Michigan State U (MI)
Michigan Technological U (MI)
Middle Tennessee State U (TN)
Millersville U of Pennsylvania (PA)
Milligan Coll (TN)
Millikin U (IL)
Milwaukee School of Eng (WI)
Minneapolis Coll of Art and Design (MN)
Minot State U (ND)
Misericordia U (PA)
Mississippi State U (MS)
Missouri Southern State U (MO)
Missouri State U (MO)
Molloy Coll (NY)
Montana State U (MT)
Montana Technological U (MT)
Montclair State U (NJ)
Moravian Coll (PA)
Mount Carmel Coll of Nursing (OH)
Mount Mercy U (IA)
Mount Saint Mary Coll (NY)
Mount St. Mary's U (MD)
Mount Vernon Nazarene U (OH)
Multnomah U (OR)
Murray State U (KY)
Muskingum U (OH)
Nebraska Methodist Coll (NE)
Nebraska Wesleyan U (NE)
New Jersey Inst of Technology (NJ)

Vermont Tech Coll (VT)
Virginia Wesleyan U (VA)
Wabash Coll (IN)
Walla Walla U (WA)
Warren Wilson Coll (NC)
Wartburg Coll (IA)
Washington Coll (MD)
Washington State U (WA)
Washington State U–Spokane (WA)
Washington State U–Tri-Cities (WA)
Washington State U–Vancouver (WA)
Waynesburg U (PA)
Wayne State U (MI)
Wentworth Inst of Technology (MA)
Wesleyan Coll (GA)
West Chester U of Pennsylvania (PA)
Western Carolina U (NC)
Western Colorado U (CO)
Western Connecticut State U (CT)
Western Michigan U (MI)
Western New England U (MA)
Western Oregon U (OR)
Western Washington U (WA)
Westfield State U (MA)
Westminster Coll (UT)
Westmont Coll (CA)
West Virginia U (WV)
Whitworth U (WA)
Widener U (PA)
Wilkes U (PA)
William Jewell Coll (MO)
William Paterson U of New Jersey (NJ)
William Peace U (NC)
Wilmington Coll (OH)
Wingate U (NC)
Winthrop U (SC)
Wittenberg U (OH)
Woodbury U (CA)
Worcester State U (MA)
Xavier U (OH)
Xavier U of Louisiana (LA)
Yeshiva U (NY)
York Coll of Pennsylvania (PA)

MINIMALLY DIFFICULT

Most freshmen were not in the top half of their high school class and scored somewhat below 1010 on the SAT or below 19 on the ACT; up to 95 percent of the applicants were accepted.

AdventHealth U (FL)
American Coll of Thessaloniki (Greece)
Anderson U (SC)
Avila U (MO)
Barton Coll (NC)
Benedictine Coll (KS)
Benjamin Franklin Inst of Technology (MA)
Bethel U (IN)
Bethel U (TN)
Bethesda U (CA)
Boise Bible Coll (ID)
Bryn Athyn Coll of the New Church (PA)
California Inst of Integral Studies (CA)
California State U, Fresno (CA)
Carlow U (PA)
Central Christian Coll of Kansas (KS)
Central State U (OH)
Clarion U of Pennsylvania (PA)
Clayton State U (GA)
Coll of Saint Elizabeth (NJ)
Coll of Saint Mary (NE)
The Coll of Westchester (NY)
Columbia Coll (MO)
Columbia Coll Chicago (IL)
Concordia U, St. Paul (MN)
Davenport U, Grand Rapids (MI)
Delaware Valley U (PA)
Dickinson State U (ND)
Dunwoody Coll of Technology (MN)
Eastern Kentucky U (KY)
Eastern Oregon U (OR)
Edinboro U of Pennsylvania (PA)
EDP U of Puerto Rico–San Sebastian (PR)
Emmanuel Coll (GA)
Eugene Lang Coll of Liberal Arts (NY)
Fayetteville State U (NC)
Ferris State U (MI)
Fitchburg State U (MA)
Georgia Gwinnett Coll (GA)
Illinois State U (IL)
Indiana U Kokomo (IN)
Indiana U Northwest (IN)
Indiana U of Pennsylvania (PA)
Indiana U Southeast (IN)
Johnson U Florida (FL)
Kansas State U (KS)
Kentucky Mountain Bible Coll (KY)
The King's U (AB, Canada)
Lamar U (TX)
Lancaster Bible Coll (PA)
La Roche U (PA)
La Sierra U (CA)
Lewis-Clark State Coll (ID)
Liberty U (VA)
Life U (GA)
Limestone Coll (SC)
Lincoln U (PA)
Manhattanville Coll (NY)
Marymount California U (CA)
MidAmerica Nazarene U (KS)
Midway U (KY)
Missouri Valley Coll (MO)
Morehead State U (KY)
Mount Aloysius Coll (PA)
Mount Marty Coll (SD)
New England Coll (NH)
New England Inst of Technology (RI)
Newman U (KS)
New Mexico Highlands U (NM)
Nichols Coll (MA)
North Carolina Central U (NC)
Northeastern Illinois U (IL)
Northern State U (SD)
North Greenville U (SC)
Northwest Christian U (OR)
Nyack Coll (NY)
Oakland City U (IN)
Ohio Christian U (OH)
Ohio Valley U (WV)
Pittsburg State U (KS)
Polytechnic U of Puerto Rico (PR)
Portland State U (OR)
Purdue U Fort Wayne (IN)
Radford U (VA)
Rasmussen Coll Brooklyn Park (MN)
Rasmussen Coll Ocala School of Nursing (FL)
Rasmussen Coll Romeoville/Joliet (IL)
Rasmussen Coll Topeka (KS)
Regent U (VA)
Rochester U (MI)
St. Luke's Coll (IA)
Saint Mary-of-the-Woods Coll (IN)
Salem State U (MA)
Southeastern U (FL)
Southwestern Coll (KS)
Southwestern Oklahoma State U (OK)
State U of New York Coll of Agriculture and Technology at Cobleskill (NY)
State U of New York Coll of Technology at Alfred (NY)
State U of New York Coll of Technology at Canton (NY)
Steinbach Bible Coll (MB, Canada)
Sterling Coll (KS)
Sullivan U (KY)
Tennessee Wesleyan U (TN)
Universidad Adventista de las Antillas (PR)
U of Alaska Fairbanks (AK)
U of Arkansas at Little Rock (AR)
U of Houston–Clear Lake (TX)
U of Jamestown (ND)
U of Maine at Presque Isle (ME)
U of North Dakota (ND)
U of Pittsburgh at Bradford (PA)
U of South Carolina Beaufort (SC)
The U of Texas at El Paso (TX)
U of the Incarnate Word (TX)
U of Washington, Bothell (WA)
The U of West Alabama (AL)
U of Wisconsin–Superior (WI)
Ursuline Coll (OH)
Wayland Baptist U (TX)
Webber Intl U (FL)
Western Kentucky U (KY)
West Liberty U (WV)
Wichita State U (KS)
William Penn U (IA)
Wright State U (OH)
Wright State U–Lake Campus (OH)
Youngstown State U (OH)

NONCOMPETITIVE

Virtually all applicants were accepted regardless of high school rank or test scores.

Academy of Art U (CA)
American Public U System (WV)
Arapahoe Comm Coll (CO)
Athens State U (AL)
Austin Comm Coll District (TX)
The Baptist Coll of Florida (FL)
Bay Atlantic U (DC)
Boston Architectural Coll (MA)
Brandon U (MB, Canada)
California Christian Coll (CA)
Calumet Coll of Saint Joseph (IN)
Cameron U (OK)
Carolina Christian Coll (NC)
Cascadia Coll (WA)
Charter Oak State Coll (CT)
Colegio Universitario de San Juan, San Juan (PR)
Coll of Staten Island of the City U of New York (NY)
Daytona State Coll (FL)
Dominican Coll (NY)
Eastern New Mexico U (NM)
Ecclesia Coll (AR)
Emmaus Bible Coll (IA)
Emporia State U (KS)
Feather River Coll (CA)
Florida SouthWestern State Coll (FL)
Front Range Comm Coll (CO)
Galveston Coll (TX)
Glenville State Coll (WV)
Grambling State U (LA)
Granite State Coll (NH)
Gulf Coast State Coll (FL)
Harris-Stowe State U (MO)
Hesston Coll (KS)
Holy Apostles Coll and Sem (CT)
Huntington U of Health Sciences (TN)
Kent State U at Tuscarawas (OH)
Lackawanna Coll (PA)
Lincoln U (MO)
Los Angeles Film School (CA)
Master's Coll and Sem (ON, Canada)
Mayville State U (ND)
Miami Dade Coll (FL)
Miami U Hamilton (OH)
Miami U Middletown (OH)
Mid-America Baptist Theological Sem (TN)
Mid-America Christian U (OK)
Midland Coll (TX)
MiraCosta Coll (CA)
National U (CA)
Nazarene Bible Coll (CO)
New Charter U (UT)
New York City Coll of Technology of the City U of New York (NY)
North Central U (MN)
The Ohio State U at Lima (OH)
The Ohio State U at Mansfield (OH)
The Ohio State U at Marion (OH)
The Ohio State U at Newark (OH)
Oklahoma State U Inst of Technology (OK)
Peirce Coll (PA)
Pensacola State Coll (FL)
Polk State Coll (FL)
Rogers State U (OK)
St. Petersburg Coll (FL)
Schoolcraft Coll (MI)
Southeastern Baptist Theological Sem (NC)
State U of New York Empire State Coll (NY)
Texas Southern U (TX)

Cost Ranges

LESS THAN $2000

Colleges with No Room and Board or with Room Only

Western Carolina U (NC)

$2000–$3999

Colleges with No Room and Board or with Room Only

Schoolcraft Coll (MI)

$4000–$5999

Colleges with No Room and Board or with Room Only

Georgia Coll & State U (GA)
Georgia Gwinnett Coll (GA)

Colleges with Room and Board

Galveston Coll (TX)

$6000–$7999

Colleges with No Room and Board or with Room Only

Clarion U of Pennsylvania (PA)
Granite State Coll (NH)
Indiana U East (IN)
Indiana U Kokomo (IN)
Indiana U Northwest (IN)
Inter American U of Puerto Rico, Barranquitas Campus (PR)
Lehman Coll of the City U of New York (NY)
Miami U Hamilton (OH)
Miami U Middletown (OH)
New Coll of Florida (FL)
New York City Coll of Technology of the City U of New York (NY)
State U of New York Empire State Coll (NY)
U of Alaska Anchorage, Kenai Peninsula Coll (AK)
U of Hawaii–West Oahu (HI)
U of Maryland Global Campus (MD)

$8000–$9999

Colleges with No Room and Board or with Room Only

American Coll of Thessaloniki (Greece)
California State U, Fullerton (CA)
Holy Apostles Coll and Sem (CT)
Huntington U of Health Sciences (TN)
State U of New York Coll at Oneonta (NY)
U of Houston–Downtown (TX)
U of Management and Technology (VA)

Colleges with Room and Board

Colegio Universitario de San Juan, San Juan (PR)
U of Guam (GU)

$10,000–$11,999

Colleges with No Room and Board or with Room Only

Charter Oak State Coll (CT)
Colorado State U–Global Campus (CO)
Nazarene Bible Coll (CO)

Colleges with Room and Board

Bayamón Central U (PR)
Carolina Christian Coll (NC)
Pensacola State Coll (FL)
Polk State Coll (FL)

$12,000–$13,999

Colleges with No Room and Board or with Room Only

Florida National U (FL)
Indiana U Southeast (IN) **(room only)**
Louisiana State U Health Sciences Center (LA) **(room only)**
Mid-America Baptist Theological Sem (TN) **(room only)**
Penn State DuBois (PA)
Penn State Fayette, The Eberly Campus (PA)
Penn State Shenango (PA)
Penn State Wilkes-Barre (PA)

Colleges with Room and Board

Bemidji State U (MN)
Brigham Young U (UT)
Collin County Comm Coll District (TX)
Southwestern Oklahoma State U (OK)
U of Houston–Clear Lake (TX)
The U of North Carolina at Pembroke (NC)
U of the Fraser Valley (BC, Canada)
Utah State U (UT)

$14,000–$15,999

Colleges with No Room and Board or with Room Only

Baptist Coll of Health Sciences (TN) **(room only)**
Indiana U South Bend (IN) **(room only)**
Penn State Lehigh Valley (PA)
Penn State York (PA)

Colleges with Room and Board

Brandon U (MB, Canada)
Dickinson State U (ND)
Eastern New Mexico U (NM)
Harris-Stowe State U (MO)
Inter American U of Puerto Rico, Bayamón Campus (PR)
Purdue U Northwest (IN)
State U of New York Coll of Agriculture and Technology at Cobleskill (NY)
Texas A&M U–Corpus Christi (TX)
U of the Virgin Islands (VI)
U of Wisconsin–Green Bay (WI)
U of Wisconsin–Platteville (WI)
Valdosta State U (GA)

$16,000–$17,999

Colleges with No Room and Board or with Room Only

Charles R. Drew U of Medicine and Science (CA)
ECPI U, Virginia Beach (VA)

Colleges with Room and Board

Auburn U at Montgomery (AL)
California Christian Coll (CA)
Central State U (OH)
Clayton State U (GA)
Columbia Intl U (SC)
Florida A&M U (FL)
Florida Polytechnic U (FL)
Lewis-Clark State Coll (ID)
Master's Coll and Sem (ON, Canada)
McNeese State U (LA)
Messenger Coll (TX)
Montana State U (MT)
Montana Technological U (MT)
North Carolina Central U (NC)
South Dakota State U (SD)
Southeast Missouri State U (MO)
Texas A&M U–Central Texas (TX)
Texas A&M U–Commerce (TX)
Texas A&M U–Kingsville (TX)
U of Alaska Southeast (AK)
U of Maine at Presque Isle (ME)
U of Michigan–Dearborn (MI)
U of South Alabama (AL)
U of South Dakota (SD)
U of South Florida, St. Petersburg (FL)
The U of Texas Rio Grande Valley (TX)
U of West Georgia (GA)
U of Wisconsin–Stout (WI)
U of Wyoming (WY)

$18,000–$19,999

Colleges with No Room and Board or with Room Only

Antioch U Santa Barbara (CA)
Mercy Coll of Ohio (OH)
Nossi Coll of Art (TN)
Texas State U (TX) **(room only)**

Colleges with Room and Board

Adams State U (CO)
Angelo State U (TX)
California State U, Long Beach (CA)
California State U, Stanislaus (CA)
Eastern Kentucky U (KY)
Florida Atlantic U (FL)
Gutenberg Coll (OR)
Indiana U-Purdue U Indianapolis (IN)
Jacksonville State U (AL)
Marshall U (WV)
Purdue U Fort Wayne (IN)
Shepherd U (WV)
Tarleton State U (TX)
Texas A&M Intl U (TX)
Texas Woman's U (TX)
U of Nevada, Las Vegas (NV)
U of Nevada, Reno (NV)
U of South Florida (FL)
The U of Texas of the Permian Basin (TX)
U of Utah (UT)
The U of West Alabama (AL)
Western Kentucky U (KY)
Western New Mexico U (NM)

$20,000–$24,999

Colleges with No Room and Board or with Room Only

AdventHealth U (FL) **(room only)**
Davenport U, Grand Rapids (MI)
Dunwoody Coll of Technology (MN) **(room only)**
Grambling State U (LA) **(room only)**
Johnson U (TN) **(room only)**
Johnson U Florida (FL) **(room only)**
Northeastern Illinois U (IL) **(room only)**
Penn State Abington (PA) **(room only)**
Platt Coll San Diego (CA)
St. Luke's Coll (IA)

Colleges with Room and Board

Ball State U (IN)
Bethany Global U (MN)
Bryan Coll (TN)
California State Polytechnic U, Pomona (CA)
California State U, Dominguez Hills (CA)
California State U, Los Angeles (CA)

California State U, Monterey Bay (CA)
California State U, Sacramento (CA)
California State U, San Bernardino (CA)
Central Washington U (WA)
The Citadel, The Military Coll of South Carolina (SC)
Ecclesia Coll (AR)
Framingham State U (MA)
Georgia State U (GA)
Governors State U (IL)
Illinois State U (IL)
Indiana State U (IN)
Indiana U Bloomington (IN)
The King's U (AB, Canada)
Mansfield U of Pennsylvania (PA)
Martin Luther Coll (MN)
Massachusetts Maritime Acad (MA)
Middle Tennessee State U (TN)
Northern Arizona U (AZ)
Northern Illinois U (IL)
Paier Coll of Art, Inc. (CT)
Penn State Schuylkill (PA)
Polytechnic U of Puerto Rico (PR)
Portland State U (OR)
San Jose State U (CA)
Southern Illinois U Edwardsville (IL)
State U of New York at Fredonia (NY)
State U of New York Coll of Technology at Delhi (NY)
SUNY Brockport (NY)
Trinity Coll of Florida (FL)
U at Albany, State U of New York (NY)
The U of Alabama in Huntsville (AL)
U of Alaska Fairbanks (AK)
U of Cincinnati (OH)
U of Colorado Denver (CO)
U of Montevallo (AL)
The U of North Carolina at Chapel Hill (NC)
U of Northern Colorado (CO)
U of Oregon (OR)
The U of Toledo (OH)
The U of Western Ontario (ON, Canada)
Virginia Wesleyan U (VA)
Western Colorado U (CO)

$25,000–$29,999

Colleges with No Room and Board or with Room Only

Boston Architectural Coll (MA)
Calumet Coll of Saint Joseph (IN) **(room only)**
City Coll of the City U of New York (NY) **(room only)**
Creative Center (NE)
Dillard U (LA) **(room only)**
Gallaudet U (DC) **(room only)**

Colleges with Room and Board

Allen Coll (IA)
Auburn U (AL)
Avila U (MO)
Belmont Abbey Coll (NC)
Binghamton U, State U of New York (NY)
Central Coll (IA)
Columbia Coll (SC)
Emmanuel Coll (GA)
Emmaus Bible Coll (IA)
Georgia Inst of Technology (GA)
Harding U (AR)
Keystone Coll (PA)
Lee U (TN)
Lindenwood U (MO)
Mid-America Christian U (OK)
Penn State Altoona (PA)
Penn State Beaver (PA)
Penn State Berks (PA)
Penn State Brandywine (PA)
Penn State Erie, The Behrend Coll (PA)
Penn State Greater Allegheny (PA)
Penn State Harrisburg (PA)
Penn State Hazleton (PA)
Penn State Mont Alto (PA)
Regent U (VA)
Toccoa Falls Coll (GA)
The U of Arizona (AZ)
U of California, San Diego (CA)
U of California, Santa Barbara (CA)
U of Hawaii at Manoa (HI)
Vermont Tech Coll (VT)
Western Connecticut State U (CT)

$30,000 AND OVER

Colleges with No Room and Board or with Room Only

Earlham Coll (IN) **(room only)**
The King's Coll (NY) **(room only)**
Marymount California U (CA)
Milwaukee School of Eng (WI) **(room only)**
Mount St. Mary's U (MD) **(room only)**
Palm Beach Atlantic U (FL) **(room only)**
School of Visual Arts (NY) **(room only)**
Sterling Coll (KS) **(room only)**
Trine U (IN) **(room only)**
Wake Forest U (NC) **(room only)**

Colleges with Room and Board

Abilene Christian U (TX)
Academy of Art U (CA)
Agnes Scott Coll (GA)
Albion Coll (MI)
Alfred U (NY)
Allegheny Coll (PA)
American U (DC)
The American U of Paris (France)
Amherst Coll (MA)
Anderson U (SC)
Andrews U (MI)
Aquinas Coll (MI)
Arizona Christian U (AZ)
Augsburg U (MN)
Augustana Coll (IL)
Augustana U (SD)
Aurora U (IL)
Azusa Pacific U (CA)
Babson Coll (MA)
Baylor U (TX)
Beacon Coll (FL)
Becker Coll (MA)
Belhaven U (MS)
Beloit Coll (WI)
Benedictine U (IL)
Bennington Coll (VT)
Berklee Coll of Music (MA)
Bethany Lutheran Coll (MN)
Bethel U (IN)
Bethel U (MN)
Biola U (CA)
Bluffton U (OH)
Bradley U (IL)
Brenau U (GA)
Bridgewater Coll (VA)
Brown U (RI)
Bryant U (RI)
Bucknell U (PA)
Butler U (IN)
Caldwell U (NJ)
California Baptist U (CA)
California Inst of the Arts (CA)
California Lutheran U (CA)
California State U, San Marcos (CA)
Calvin Coll (MI)
Campbellsville U (KY)
Capital U (OH)
Carnegie Mellon U (PA)
Carthage Coll (WI)
Catawba Coll (NC)
The Catholic U of America (DC)
Cazenovia Coll (NY)
Cedar Crest Coll (PA)
Cedarville U (OH)
Central Methodist U (MO)
Centre Coll (KY)
Chaminade U of Honolulu (HI)
Chatham U (PA)
Clark Atlanta U (GA)
Clarkson U (NY)
Cleveland Inst of Art (OH)
Coe Coll (IA)
Colby-Sawyer Coll (NH)
The Coll of Idaho (ID)
Coll of Saint Benedict (MN)
Coll of Saint Elizabeth (NJ)
The Coll of Saint Rose (NY)
The Coll of St. Scholastica (MN)
Coll of the Holy Cross (MA)
The Coll of Wooster (OH)
The Colorado Coll (CO)
Columbia Coll Chicago (IL)
Concordia Coll (MN)
Concordia U Chicago (IL)
Concordia U, St. Paul (MN)
Concordia U Wisconsin (WI)
Covenant Coll (GA)
Creighton U (NE)
Culver-Stockton Coll (MO)
Dallas Baptist U (TX)
Davidson Coll (NC)
Dean Coll (MA)
Delaware Valley U (PA)
DePauw U (IN)
Dickinson Coll (PA)
Dominican Coll (NY)
Dominican U (IL)
Dominican U of California (CA)
Drake U (IA)
Drury U (MO)
Eastern Mennonite U (VA)
Eastern U (PA)
Edgewood Coll (WI)
Elms Coll (MA)
Elon U (NC)
Emmanuel Coll (MA)
Emory & Henry Coll (VA)
Emory U (GA)
Endicott Coll (MA)
Fairfield U (CT)
Fairleigh Dickinson U (NJ)
Felician U (NJ)
Fisher Coll (MA)
Fordham U (NY)
Franklin Coll (IN)
Franklin W. Olin Coll of Eng (MA)
Freed-Hardeman U (TN)
Friends U (KS)
Furman U (SC)
Geneva Coll (PA)
Georgetown Coll (KY)
Georgian Court U (NJ)
Gonzaga U (WA)
Gordon Coll (MA)
Goshen Coll (IN)
Goucher Coll (MD)
Graceland U (IA)
Grinnell Coll (IA)
Guilford Coll (NC)
Gustavus Adolphus Coll (MN)
Gwynedd Mercy U (PA)
Hamline U (MN)
Hampden-Sydney Coll (VA)
Hampshire Coll (MA)
Hampton U (VA)
Hanover Coll (IN)
Hardin-Simmons U (TX)
Hesston Coll (KS)
Hillsdale Coll (MI)
Hobart and William Smith Colls (NY)
Hope Intl U (CA)
Houston Baptist U (TX)
Howard U (DC)
Husson U (ME)
Illinois Wesleyan U (IL)
Immaculata U (PA)
Iona Coll (NY)
Ithaca Coll (NY)
Jacksonville U (FL)
John Cabot U (Italy)
John Carroll U (OH)
Kalamazoo Coll (MI)
Kansas Wesleyan U (KS)
Keiser U, Fort Lauderdale (FL)
Kenyon Coll (OH)
Keuka Coll (NY)
King's Coll (PA)

King U (TN)
Knox Coll (IL)
Lafayette Coll (PA)
Lake Forest Coll (IL)
La Roche U (PA)
Lasell Coll (MA)
La Sierra U (CA)
Lawrence Technological U (MI)
Lehigh U (PA)
Le Moyne Coll (NY)
Lesley U (MA)
LeTourneau U (TX)
Lewis U (IL)
Liberty U (VA)
Limestone Coll (SC)
Lincoln Memorial U (TN)
Linfield Coll (OR)
Lipscomb U (TN)
Loras Coll (IA)
Loyola U Chicago (IL)
Loyola U New Orleans (LA)
Lynn U (FL)
Malone U (OH)
Manhattan School of Music (NY)
Manhattanville Coll (NY)
Marian U (IN)
Marietta Coll (OH)
Marquette U (WI)
Marymount Manhattan Coll (NY)
Marymount U (VA)
Maryville U of Saint Louis (MO)
Marywood U (PA)
McMurry U (TX)
Messiah Coll (PA)
MidAmerica Nazarene U (KS)
Midway U (KY)
Milligan Coll (TN)
Millikin U (IL)
Minneapolis Coll of Art and Design (MN)
Misericordia U (PA)
Moravian Coll (PA)
Mount Mercy U (IA)
Mount Saint Mary Coll (NY)
Mount Vernon Nazarene U (OH)
Multnomah U (OR)
Muskingum U (OH)
Nebraska Wesleyan U (NE)
New England Coll (NH)
New England Inst of Technology (RI)
New York Inst of Technology (NY)
Niagara U (NY)
Nichols Coll (MA)
North Central U (MN)
North Greenville U (SC)
Northwest Christian U (OR)
Northwest Nazarene U (ID)
Northwest U (WA)
Notre Dame Coll (OH)
Nova Southeastern U (FL)
Nyack Coll (NY)
Oakland City U (IN)
Oglethorpe U (GA)
Ohio Dominican U (OH)
Oklahoma Baptist U (OK)
Olivet Nazarene U (IL)
Oral Roberts U (OK)
Ottawa U (KS)
Pacific U (OR)
Patrick Henry Coll (VA)
Penn State U Park (PA)
Pratt Inst (NY)
Randolph Coll (VA)
Randolph-Macon Coll (VA)
Regis Coll (MA)
Roanoke Coll (VA)
Rochester U (MI)
Rocky Mountain Coll (MT)
Roger Williams U (RI)
Rollins Coll (FL)
St. Ambrose U (IA)
St. Bonaventure U (NY)
Saint Francis U (PA)
St. John Fisher Coll (NY)
St. John's Coll (NM)
Saint John's U (MN)
Saint Joseph's U (PA)
Saint Leo U (FL)
Saint Mary-of-the-Woods Coll (IN)
Saint Mary's Coll (IN)
Saint Mary's Coll of California (CA)
St. Mary's U (TX)
Saint Mary's U of Minnesota (MN)
St. Norbert Coll (WI)
St. Olaf Coll (MN)
St. Thomas U - Florida (FL)
Salve Regina U (RI)
San Francisco Art Inst (CA)
Santa Clara U (CA)
Schreiner U (TX)
Seattle U (WA)
Seton Hill U (PA)
Shenandoah U (VA)
Siena Coll (NY)
Siena Heights U (MI)
Sierra Nevada Coll (NV)
Simmons U (MA)
Smith Coll (MA)
Southern Methodist U (TX)
Southwest Baptist U (MO)
Southwestern Coll (KS)
Southwestern U (TX)
Springfield Coll (MA)
Stanford U (CA)
Stetson U (FL)
Stevens Inst of Technology (NJ)
Suffolk U (MA)
Susquehanna U (PA)
Tennessee Wesleyan U (TN)
Texas Christian U (TX)
Theatre of Arts (CA)
Tiffin U (OH)
Transylvania U (KY)
Trevecca Nazarene U (TN)
Trinity U (TX)
Truett McConnell U (GA)
Union Coll (NY)
Union U (TN)
U of California, Merced (CA)
U of Dallas (TX)
U of Denver (CO)
U of Detroit Mercy (MI)
U of Dubuque (IA)
U of Hartford (CT)
U of Jamestown (ND)
U of La Verne (CA)
U of Mary Hardin-Baylor (TX)
U of Miami (FL)
U of New Hampshire (NH)
U of Northwestern–St. Paul (MN)
U of Notre Dame (IN)
U of Pennsylvania (PA)
U of Pikeville (KY)
U of Providence (MT)
U of Puget Sound (WA)
U of Richmond (VA)
U of St. Francis (IL)
U of Saint Francis (IN)
U of St. Thomas (TX)
U of San Diego (CA)
U of San Francisco (CA)
The U of Tampa (FL)
U of the Incarnate Word (TX)
U of the Pacific (CA)
The U of the South (TN)
The U of Tulsa (OK)
U of Vermont (VT)
U of Virginia (VA)
Ursuline Coll (OH)
Valparaiso U (IN)
Vanderbilt U (TN)
Vanguard U of Southern California (CA)
Villanova U (PA)
Wabash Coll (IN)
Walla Walla U (WA)
Warren Wilson Coll (NC)
Wartburg Coll (IA)
Washington Coll (MD)
Washington U in St. Louis (MO)
Wayland Baptist U (TX)
Waynesburg U (PA)
Webber Intl U (FL)
Wentworth Inst of Technology (MA)
Wesleyan Coll (GA)
Western New England U (MA)
Westminster Coll (UT)
Wheaton Coll (IL)
Wheaton Coll (MA)
Whitworth U (WA)
Widener U (PA)
Willamette U (OR)
William Jewell Coll (MO)
William Peace U (NC)
William Penn U (IA)
Williams Coll (MA)
Wingate U (NC)
Wittenberg U (OH)
Wofford Coll (SC)
Woodbury U (CA)
Worcester Polytechnic Inst (MA)
Xavier U (OH)
Yale U (CT)
York Coll of Pennsylvania (PA)

Advertisers Index

Alphabetical Listing of Colleges and Universities

INDEXES

INDEXES

INDEXES

INDEXES

INDEXES

Geographic Listing of Close-Ups

NOTES

NOTES

NOTES

NOTES

NOTES

NOTES

NOTES

NOTES

NOTES

NOTES

NOTES

NOTES

NOTES

NOTES

NOTES

NOTES

NOTES